THE *Renovaré*

SPIRITUAL

FORMATION

BIBLE

NEW REVISED STANDARD VERSION

THE *Renovaré*

SPIRITUAL

FORMATION

BIBLE

New Revised Standard Version
with Deuterocanonical Books

Editor
Richard J. Foster

General Editors
Gayle Beebe, Lynda L. Graybeal,
Thomas C. Oden, Dallas Willard

Consulting Editors
Walter Brueggemann, Old Testament and Deuterocanonicals
Eugene H. Peterson, New Testament

HarperSanFrancisco
A Division of HarperCollinsPublishers

The Renovaré Spiritual Formation Bible
New Revised Standard Version with Deuterocanonical Books

📖®

HarperSanFrancisco
A Division of HarperCollins*Publishers*

Special thanks to:
    Lynda Graybeal and Julia Roller, who wrote the "Responding" exercises
    Ann Moru, who copyedited all of the original material
    Brenda Quinn, who wrote the character profiles
    Dallas Willard, who compiled the Spritual Disciplines Index

Design and typesetting by Blue Heron Bookcraft, Battle Ground, Washington.

FIRST EDITION

Library of Congress Cataloging-in-Publication Data is available.

ISBN 0-06-067108-4

05 06 07 08 09 / Courier / 10 9 8 7 6 5 4 3 2 1

Contents

Contents

The Deuterocanonical Books

The New Testament

Abbreviations

Genesis	Gen	2 Maccabees	2 Macc
Exodus	Exod	3 Maccabees	3 Macc
Leviticus	Lev	4 Maccabees	4 Macc
Numbers	Num	Psalm 151	Ps 151
Deuteronomy	Deut	Wisdom of Solomon	Wisd of Sol
Joshua	Josh	Wisdom of Jesus	
Judges	Judg	Son of Sirach	
Ruth	Ruth	(Ecclesiasticus)	Sir
1 Samuel	1 Sam	Baruch	Bar
2 Samuel	2 Sam	Letter of Jeremiah	Ltr of Jer
1 Kings	1 Kings	Prayer of Manasseh	Pr of Man
2 Kings	2 Kings	Tobit	Tob
1 Chronicles	1 Chron	Prayer of Azariah	
2 Chronicles	2 Chron	and the Song of	
Ezra	Ezra	the Three Jews	Pr of Azar
Nehemiah	Neh	Susanna	Sus
Esther	Esther	Bel and the Dragon	Bel and Dragon
Job	Job	Matthew	Matt
Psalms	Ps (pl. Pss)	Mark	Mark
Proverbs	Prov	Luke	Luke
Ecclesiastes	Eccl	John	John
Song of Solomon	Song of Sol	Acts	Acts
Isaiah	Isa	Romans	Rom
Jeremiah	Jer	1 Corinthians	1 Cor
Lamentations	Lam	2 Corinthians	2 Cor
Ezekiel	Ezek	Galatians	Gal
Daniel	Dan	Ephesians	Eph
Hosea	Hos	Philippians	Phil
Joel	Joel	Colossians	Col
Amos	Amos	1 Thessalonians	1 Thess
Obadiah	Obad	2 Thessalonians	2 Thess
Jonah	Jon	1 Timothy	1 Tim
Micah	Mic	2 Timothy	2 Tim
Nahum	Nah	Titus	Titus
Habakkuk	Hab	Philemon	Philem
Zephaniah	Zeph	Hebrews	Heb
Haggai	Hag	James	James
Zechariah	Zech	1 Peter	1 Pet
Malachi	Mal	2 Peter	2 Pet
Additions to Esther	Add to Esther	1 John	1 John
1 Esdras	1 Esd	2 John	2 John
2 Esdras	2 Esd	3 John	3 John
Judith	Jth	Jude	Jude
1 Maccabees	1 Macc	Revelation	Rev

Editors and Contributors

Richard J. Foster, Editor

General Editors
Gayle Beebe, Lynda L. Graybeal,
Thomas C. Oden, Dallas Willard

Project Editors
Stephen W. Hanselman, Michael G. Maudlin, Julia L. Roller

Consulting Editors
Walter Brueggemann, Old Testament and Deuterocanonicals
Eugene H. Peterson, New Testament

Contributing Editor
Brenda Quinn

Managing Editors
John R. Kohlenberger III and Terri Leonard

Editorial Assistant
Cynthia DiTiberio

Contributors

Howard Baker	William R. Long
Timothy K. Beal	Tremper Longman III
William H. Bellinger, Jr.	Howard R. Macy
Timothy Brown	James Earl Massey
Glandion Carney	J. Clinton McCann, Jr.
Ellen T. Charry	Trevor Miller
James L. Crenshaw	Rickie D. Moore
Marva J. Dawn	Barbara M. Musselman
Kerry Dearborn	Agnes W. Norfleet
Bruce Demarest	Virginia Stem Owens
David A. deSilva	Earl F. Palmer
James R. Edwards	Murray Andrew Pura
Peter Enns	Andrew Purves
Rebecca J. Kruger Gaudino	James M. Rand
Emilie Griffin	Kimberly Clayton Richter
Christopher A. Hall	Michael D. Riley
Andrew E. Hill	Edwin Searcy
Evan B. Howard	Roy Searle
Darlene Hyatt	Timothy F. Simpson
Walter C. Kaiser, Jr.	Felicia and Lyle SmithGraybeal
Joshua Choon Min Kang	Catherine Taylor
Ralph W. Klein	Bonnie Thurston
Nancy C. Lee	William H. Willimon
Rebekah Close LeMon	Ben Witherington III

Contributors

Howard Baker (*Galatians*) is an adjunct professor at Denver Seminary in Denver and at Fuller Theological Seminary in Colorado Springs, Colorado, teaching classes in spiritual formation and spiritual direction. He is the author of *Soul Keeping* and serves as spiritual director for the staff of Young Life in Colorado.

Timothy K. Beal (*Esther, Additions to Esther*) is Harkness Professor of Biblical Literature and director of the Baker-Nord Center for the Humanities at Case Western Reserve University in Cleveland, Ohio. He is co-editor of the Afterlives of the Bible series with University of Chicago Press and author of several books on biblical literature, including *The Book of Hiding, Religion and Its Monsters,* and a commentary on Esther in the Berit Olam series.

William H. Bellinger, Jr. (*Leviticus*), is the W. Marshall and Lulie Craig Professor of Bible and Director of Graduate Studies in the Religion department at Baylor University in Waco, Texas. He is the author of several works on the worship literature in the Old Testament, including works on Leviticus and the Psalms. He frequently preaches and leads Bible studies in churches.

Timothy Brown (*Ephesians*) is the Henry Bast Professor of Preaching at Western Theological Seminary. He has served on the Reformed Church in America's Board of Theological Education, the Hope College Board of Trustees, and the executive committee of Words of Hope, a worldwide radio ministry, and is currently a General Synod professor. He is also the author of *Witness Among Friends* and *Let's Preach Together.*

Walter Brueggemann (*Isaiah*) is professor emeritus at Columbia Theological Seminary, where he was the William Marcellus McPheeters Professor of Old Testament from 1992 to 2003. He is the author of many books, including *Theology of the Old Testament, Reverberations of Faith,* and *An Introduction to the Old Testament: The Canon and Christian Imagination.*

Glandion Carney (*Job, Baruch*) is the chaplain of the Christian Legal Society and the author of seven books, four of them with William R. Long. He serves on the RENOVARÉ Board of Trustees and lives with his wife, Marion Caples-Carney, in Helena, Alabama.

Ellen T. Charry (*2 Corinthians*) is the Margaret W. Harmon Associate Professor of Systematic Theology at Princeton Theological Seminary and editor of *Theology Today.* Her books include *By the Renewing of Your Minds* and *Inquiring After God.*

James L. Crenshaw (*Sirach*) is the Robert L. Flowers Professor of Old Testament at Duke University. He is the author of *Old Testament Wisdom, Education in Ancient Israel,* and *Defending God: Biblical Responses to the Problem of Evil* as well as commentaries on Joel, Ecclesiastes, and Sirach. A former editor of the SBL Monograph Series and chair of the section on wisdom literature, he currently edits Personalities of the Old Testament.

Marva J. Dawn (*John*) is a theologian, author, and educator with Christians Equipped for Ministry of Vancouver, Washington, and teaching Fellow in spiritual theology at Regent College in Vancouver, British Columbia. The author of almost twenty books and numerous articles, she has lectured and preached throughout North America, Europe, and Asia.

Kerry Dearborn (*1, 2, & 3 John*) is associate professor of theology at Seattle Pacific University. She is a board member of the Christian International Scholarship Foundation and a member of the advisory board of *Seven,* the journal of the Marion E. Wade Center in Wheaton, Illinois.

Bruce Demarest (*Micah, Malachi*) is professor of theology and spiritual formation and directs the Program in Evangelical Guidance at Denver Seminary in Denver, Colorado. He is the author of many books, including *Integrative Theology, The Cross and Salvation, Satisfy Your Soul: Restoring the Heart of Christian Spirituality,* and *Soul Guide: Following Jesus as Spiritual Director.*

David A. de Silva (*1, 2, 3, & 4 Maccabees; 1 & 2 Esdras*) is professor of New Testament and Greek at Ashland Theological Seminary. He is the author of many books, including *An Introduction to the New Testament; Introducing the Apocrypha; Honor, Patronage, Kinship and Purity: Unlocking New Testament Culture;* and *Perseverance in Gratitude: A Socio-Rhetorical Commentary on the Epistle "to the Hebrews."* In addition to his academic pursuits, he has been very active in music ministries throughout his life and is currently director of choirs at Christ United Methodist Church in Ashland, Ohio.

James R. Edwards (*Hebrews*) is professor of New Testament and chair of the Department of Religion and Philosophy at Whitworth College in Spokane, Washington. He is the author of several commentaries on New Testament books, including Romans and the Gospel of Mark. He is a contributing editor to *Christianity Today,* a conference speaker, and an essayist on theological subjects.

Peter Enns (*Additions to Daniel*) is associate professor of Old Testament at Westminster Theological Seminary. He is the author of the Exodus volume in the NIV Application Commentary.

Rebecca J. Kruger Gaudino (*1 & 2 Kings*) recently pastored Plymouth Congregational Church, United Church of Christ, in Tacoma, Washington, and has contributed to several worship and preaching resources. She has also taught courses in theology and literature, biblical studies, and world religion at Pacific Lutheran University and the University of Portland. She and her husband currently reside in Portland, Oregon.

Emilie Griffin (*Proverbs*) is a member of the Renovaré Board of Trustees. Educated in literature and classical and modern languages at Tulane University and the National University of Mexico, she did graduate studies in philosophy, systematic theology, and Scripture at Loyola University of the South (New Orleans) and Notre Dame Seminary (New Orleans). Author and editor of fifteen books and many articles, she serves as editor of the HarperCollins Spiritual Classics series.

Christopher A. Hall (*1 & 2 Peter, Jude*) is professor of biblical and theological Studies at Eastern University in St. Davids, Pennsylvania, where he teaches classes in theology and Christian spirituality. He is the author of a number of books, including *Reading Scripture with the Church Fathers* and *Learning Theology with the Church Fathers.*

Andrew E. Hill (*Ruth*) is professor of Old Testament studies at Wheaton College in Wheaton, Illinois, where he has served on the faculty since 1984. He earned his doctorate at the University of Michigan in the Department of Near Eastern Studies (1981). He is the author of numerous articles and several books, including *A Survey of the Old Testament* (with John H. Walton), *Enter His Courts with Praise: Malachi* (Anchor Bible 25D), and *1 & 2 Chronicles* (NIVAC). He and his wife, Teri, live in Wheaton and are members of Blanchard Road Alliance Church.

Evan B. Howard (*Philippians*) is a lecturer in philosophy and religion at Mesa State College in Grand Junction, Colorado, and is the director of Spirituality Shoppe: An Evangelical Center for the Study of Christian Spirituality. He is the author of *Praying the Scriptures: A Field Guide for Your Spiritual Journey* and other books and articles. He and his wife, Cheri, live in the foothills of the Rocky Mountains with two daughters, two cats, one dog, and a few goats and chickens.

Darlene Hyatt (*Matthew*) is a doctoral student at Asbury Theological Seminary's E. Stanley Jones School of Mission and World Evangelism and an adjunct professor at Asbury College, teaching in the area of spiritual formation. With Ben Witherington III, she is the co-author of *Paul's Letter to the Romans: A Socio-Rhetorical Commentary* and upcoming commentaries on Colossians, Ephesians, Philemon, and 1 & 2 Thessalonians.

Walter C. Kaiser, Jr. (*Joshua*) is president of Gordon-Conwell Theological Seminary in Hamilton, Massachusetts. He is also the author of over thirty books and numerous journal articles, including the commentary on Leviticus in the *New Interpreter's Commentary;* Exodus in *The Expositor's Bible Commentary;* and *Toward an Old Testament Theology, Toward Old Testament Ethics,* and *Toward an Exegetical Theology.*

Joshua Choon Min Kang (*Numbers*) is senior pastor of the Oriental Mission Church of Los Angeles and professor of spiritual formation and theology at World Mission University in Los Angeles. He is a well-known author (twenty published books) and speaker on spiritual formation to Korean Christians. He resides with his wife, Grace, and two daughters in Glendale, California.

Ralph W. Klein (*1 & 2 Chronicles*) is the Christ Seminary–Seminex Professor of Old Testament at the Lutheran School of Theology in Chicago. He is the editor of *Currents in Theology and Mission.*

Nancy C. Lee (*Amos*) is an associate professor at Elmhurst College near Chicago and director of the Niebuhr Center (Callings for the Common Good program). She is the author of *The Singers of Lamentations: Cities Under Siege, from Ur to Jerusalem to Sarajevo.* She edited the volume of Bosnian poetry by Borislav Arapović, *Between Despair and Lamentation,* and is the author of numerous articles on the Old Testament as well as on the intersection of religious and sociopolitical contexts.

Rebekah Close LeMon (*Haggai, Zechariah*) is a graduate of Columbia Theological Seminary. She lives in Atlanta, Georgia, where she works as a writer and editor.

William R. Long (*Job, Judith, Baruch, Letter of Jeremiah, Prayer of Manasseh, Tobit*) is adjunct professor of law at Willamette University College of Law in Salem, Oregon. He has been a trial attorney, pastor, professor of religion and humanities, professor of history and government, and a newspaper editorial writer; he is also the author of eight books, four of them with Glandion Carney.

Tremper Longman III (*Deuteronomy, Ecclesiastes, Song of Solomon*) is the Robert H. Gundry Professor of Biblical Studies at Westmont College in Santa Barbara, California. He has written a number of books, including full-length commentaries on Ecclesiastes and Song of Solomon as well as a book on interpreting the Bible for spiritual formation entitled *Reading the Bible with Heart and Mind.*

Howard R. Macy (*Psalms, Psalm 151*) is professor of religion and biblical studies at George Fox University in Newberg, Oregon. He is a recorded Friends minister, a frequent speaker in churches and at retreats, a regular contributor to religious magazines, and the author of *Rhythms of the Inner Life.*

James Earl Massey (*James*) is dean emeritus and Distinguished Professor-at-Large at Anderson University School of Theology in Anderson, Indiana. For forty years, he has served as a professor, pastor, preacher, campus minister, a speaker on the "Christian Brotherhood Hour" radio broadcast, and dean of the chapel of Tuskegee University.

J. Clinton McCann, Jr. (*Judges*) is the Evangelical Professor of Biblical Interpretation at Eden Theological Seminary in Webster Groves, Missouri. He is the author of several books and articles on the book of Psalms, including the Psalms commentary in *The New Interpreter's Bible,* as well as the author of *Judges* in the Interpretation Commentary Series.

Trevor Miller (*Obadiah*) is a Baptist minister and an overseer of the Northumbria Community based at the community's mother house at Hetton Hall in northern Northumberland, England.

Rickie D. Moore (*Hosea*) is professor of Old Testament at the Church of God Theological Seminary in Cleveland, Tennessee. He is a founding and current editor of the *Journal of Pentecostal Theology*. His numerous publications on the Old Testament prophets include *God Saves: Lessons from the Elisha Stories*. Most recently he has authored the introduction and Joel sections of *The Twelve Minor Prophets* in Sheffield's Pentecostal Commentary Series.

Barbara M. Musselman (*Joel, Jonah, Habakkuk*) is an Episcopal priest in Denver, Colorado. She is co-author of *A Prayerbook Home Companion*.

Agnes W. Norfleet (*Genesis*) is pastor of North Decatur Presbyterian Church in Decatur, Georgia. She has written for *The Abingdon Women's Preaching Annual, The Presbyterian Outlook,* and *Interpretation: A Journal for Bible and Theology* and is a regular contributor to *Journal for Preachers* and *Lectionary Homiletics*.

Virginia Stem Owens (*Revelation*) lives in Huntsville, Texas, with her husband, David, with whom she wrote *Living Next Door to the Death House*. On the editorial board of *Books & Culture,* she has written fifteen books, including *Looking for Jesus* and *Daughters of Eve*.

Earl F. Palmer (*1 & 2 Thessalonians*) is senior pastor of the University Presbyterian Church in Seattle, Washington. He is the author of many books, including *The Book That James Wrote, 24 Hour Christian,* and *The Humor of Jesus*. He serves on the Board of Trustees of Princeton Theological Seminary and the Board of Governors of Regent College in Vancouver, British Columbia.

Eugene H. Peterson (*Romans*), a Presbyterian pastor for thirty-five years, is professor emeritus of spiritual theology at Regent College, Vancouver, British Columbia. With his wife, Janice, he now lives and writes in Montana.

Murray Andrew Pura (*Exodus, Luke*) lives near Waterton-Glacier Peace Park in the foothills of the Canadian Rockies with his wife, Linda, and his children, Micah and Micaela. His books include *Mizzly Fitch, Mister Good Morning, The Poets of Windhover Marsh,* and *Vital Christianity: The Life and Spirituality of William Wilberforce*. He also works as a youth advocate in the area of family violence and pastors a church that meets in a hotel.

Andrew Purves (*Colossians, Philemon*) is the Hugh Thomson Kerr Professor of Pastoral Theology at Pittsburgh Theological Seminary. He has a deep concern for the renewal of the Church and speaks regularly around the country on matters of theological and spiritual renewal. Recent publications include *A Passion for the Gospel: Proclaiming Jesus Christ for the 21st Century* (with Mark Achtemeier) and *Pastoral Theology in the Classical Tradition*.

James M. Rand (*Daniel*) is a graduate of Lawrence University and Union Theological Seminary in Virginia. He is pastor of Wauwatosa Presbyterian Church in Milwaukee, Wisconsin. He previously served churches in Worcester, Massachusetts; Wilmington, Delaware; and the Bronx, New York.

Kimberly Clayton Richter (*Mark*) is the pastor of Grace Covenant Presbyterian Church in Asheville, North Carolina. She is a graduate of Columbia Theological Seminary in Decatur, Georgia. She is an author and editor of several denominational publications, including *Members Together: A Study for Adult New Members, Older Adult Ministry: A Guide for the Session and Congregation,* and *Rebuilding: Peacemaking in Nehemiah*.

Michael D. Riley (*Ezra, Nehemiah*) has served as pastor of Deermeadows Baptist Church in Jacksonville, Florida, since September 2001. He holds a PhD in Old Testament and Semitic Languages and an MDiv from Southwestern Baptist Theological Seminary. He received his undergraduate degree from Baylor University. Prior to moving to Jacksonville, he served churches in Texas and Oklahoma.

Edwin Searcy (*Ezekiel*) is pastor of University Hill Congregation of the United Church of Canada in Vancouver, British Columbia. He is the editor of *Awed to Heaven, Rooted in Earth: Prayers of Walter Brueggemann.*

Roy Searle (*Nahum, Zephaniah*) and his wife, Shirley, currently live in northern Northumberland, England. He is an overseer of the Northumbria Community and has recently been appointed part-time director of RENOVARÉ in Britain and Ireland. His first book on the spirituality of leadership will be published later this year, followed by a Lent book.

Timothy F. Simpson (*1 & 2 Samuel*) is adjunct professor of religious studies at the University of North Florida and editor of the journal *Political Theology.* He is an ordained minister in the Presbyterian Church USA.

Felicia SmithGraybeal (*Wisdom of Solomon*) is a priest in the Episcopal Church USA who enjoys pastoral care, preaching, and spiritual formation ministry. The daughter of an ordained minister, she earned an MDiv from the Protestant Episcopal Theological Seminary in Virginia. She is assistant priest at St. Mary Magdalene Episcopal Church in Boulder, Colorado, and is married to Lyle.

Lyle SmithGraybeal (*Wisdom of Solomon*) has been involved with RENOVARÉ for over a decade. He considers himself a Christian "mutt," as his background includes numerous evangelical and mainline Protestant denominations and a short time in the Roman Catholic Church. Lyle is the RENOVARÉ New Projects Director and lives with Felicia in Longmont, Colorado.

Catherine Taylor (*1 Corinthians*) is pastor of Church of the New Covenant, Presbyterian in the Atlanta suburb of Doraville, Georgia.

Bonnie Thurston (*Acts*), most recently William F. Orr Professor of New Testament at Pittsburgh Theological Seminary, lives as a solitary in West Virginia and continues her ministry of writing, spiritual direction, and holding retreats. Ordained in the Christian Church (Disciples of Christ), she has authored twelve books, including *Spiritual Life in the Early Church, Women in the New Testament, To Everything a Season: A Spirituality of Time, Preaching Mark,* and a volume of verse, *The Heart's Lands.*

William H. Willimon (*Jeremiah, Lamentations, 1 & 2 Timothy, Titus*) is dean of the chapel and professor of Christian ministry at Duke University, in Durham, North Carolina, as well as serving as bishop of the United Methodist Church for the Birmingham, Alabama, area. He is the author of over fifty books. His publications have sold over a million copies. In 1984, an international survey conducted by Baylor University named him one of the "Twelve Most Effective Preachers in the English-Speaking World."

Ben Witherington III (*Matthew*) is professor of New Testament at Asbury Theological Seminary and an ordained United Methodist minister. He has written twenty-seven books, including two that have won the *Christianity Today* book of the year award. Most recently he has published two best-sellers, *The Brother of Jesus* (with Hershel Shanks) and *The Gospel Code: Novel Ideas About Jesus, Mary Magdalene and Da Vinci.*

FOREWORD: HOW THIS BIBLE CAME TO BE

We are profoundly humbled and thankful to God that you have chosen to own a copy of the *Renovaré Spiritual Formation Bible*. It is a project that has been five years in the making and has involved over fifty scholars, theologians, pastors, and ordinary folk from all walks of life. In this Introduction we want to anticipate and respond to some of the questions—the "whys"—that may be in your mind regarding this study Bible.

- *Why another study Bible?* There is a desperate need today for a richer, fuller understanding of the relevance of Scripture for daily living. We need a study Bible that will help us experience Scripture as living and active, forming and transforming. We need a study Bible that will combine the highest possible biblical scholarship with the deepest possible heart devotion. We need a study Bible that will lead us step-by-step into the glorious and terrifying "with-God" life, which, like Ariadne's thread, weaves its way throughout Scripture. We need a study Bible that will be substantive *and* accessible, serious *and* inviting, rigorous *and* hopeful. We need a study Bible that will aid us in seeing the great panorama of divine interaction with the People of God throughout history and will invite us into this ongoing story. We need a study Bible that will draw us irresistibly into the biblical drama of love and terror and pity and pain and wonder, until the biblical witness becomes all over autobiographic of us.

- *Why this particular study Bible?* The *Renovaré Spiritual Formation Bible* is a multifaceted resource for approaching the Bible through the lens of Christian spiritual formation. It contains various unique features. An overarching essay describing the unifying theme in Scripture as the Immanuel Principle, or the "with-God" life, allows us to better recognize how God is with us and how we are with God, now, today. Fifteen progressive essays on the People of God are designed to help us see the flow of this "with-God" history—from individual to family to tribe to people to nation to all humanity. Character profiles highlight the struggle and journey of different biblical personages toward their own spiritual transformation. Carefully written introductions and notes for each book of the Bible accent the spiritual formation themes found in them. A Spiritual Disciplines Index guides us to the most critical biblical passages for teaching and practice of the Spiritual Disciplines. Pertinent exercises and questions help us reflect prayerfully upon the biblical text. And more, much more.

- *Why use the* NRSV *translation?* Three fundamental reasons make the NRSV our translation of choice. First, in our considered opinion it is simply the best English translation available today. Its scholarship is unsurpassed, and its accuracy and clarity of English are superior. Second, the translators' careful work on gender-accurate language when referring to human beings frees the text from linguistic sexism. Third, with its inclusion of the Deuterocanonical books the NRSV has gained the distinction of being officially authorized for use by all major Christian churches: Protestant, Anglican, Roman Catholic, and Eastern Orthodox.

- *Why include the Deuterocanonical books?* The word "Deuterocanonical" simply means "a second canon" and refers to those books written during the time between the Old and New Testaments. The *Renovaré Spiritual Formation Bible* includes the Deuterocanonical books for numerous reasons—let me give you five:

    1. The Deuterocanonical books were part of the ancient Greek Bible, the Septuagint, which was in circulation during the time of Christ. It was the Bible of the early Church. This Bible shaped the conscious awareness of God for the first Christians.

    2. The Deuterocanonical books help Christian readers understand the New Testament context—the context of Jesus' ministry as well as of the writers of the New Testament books. The people Jesus encountered and taught were in many ways spiritually formed by these writings.

    3. Most of the Church throughout most of its history has included the Deuterocanonical books as part of the Bible. The Eastern Orthodox Bible, the Greek Bible, the Slavonic Bible, the Anglican Bible, and the Roman Catholic Bible all include the Deuterocanonical books. Plus, while not viewing them as Scripture, early Protestant Bibles—Luther's translation, the Great Bible of 1539, the Geneva Bible of 1560 (supported by John Calvin and John Knox), the Bishops' Bible of 1568, and the King James Bible of 1611—included the Deuterocanonical books, or "Apocrypha," as something of an appendix.

    4. Throughout the ages, many questions have persisted about the value of the Deuterocanonical books. Even those groups in our time who include and use the Deuterocanonicals do not give them the same authority as the primary canon. And we, the general editors of the *Renovaré Spiritual Formation Bible,* would not want to accord these books the same authority as revealed Scripture. Still, their role in bridging the gap between Malachi and

Matthew is unquestioned, and they provide marvelous insight into the way in which the first Christians understood their relationship with God.

5. The Deuterocanonicals do not affect any central doctrine of the Christian faith, but they do contain many helpful insights for spiritual formation. For this reason alone they are worth reading and can function for us today in much the same way that good sermons and devotional writings do. Of them, Luther wrote, "Apocrypha—that is, books which are not regarded as equal to the holy Scriptures, and yet are profitable and good to read." For this purpose, we have organized the Deuterocanonical books into three categories: Law and History, Writings and Wisdom, and Prophets and Apocalyptic.

- *Why use the masculine pronoun when speaking of God?* We are wrestling here with the lack of a common-gender third-person singular pronoun in the English language. English simply does not have a singular personal pronoun that transcends our categories of gender, male and female. When speaking of God we simply cannot use plural pronouns, as we can when speaking of human beings, for biblical revelation is clear that God is one. The impersonal pronoun "it" is wholly unsuitable, for, above all, God is personal. Repeating the noun "God" when the sentence structure calls for a pronoun is simply an improper use of language and results in awkward and convoluted sentences. Hence, the only useful options we have in the English language are masculine or feminine pronouns. Therefore, when the sentence structure requires a pronoun, we have chosen to follow the pattern set by the NRSV Bible and use the masculine pronoun. In doing so we are confessing God's personhood. God, being wholly other than us, transcends the distinctions of human sexuality.

The *Renovaré Spiritual Formation Bible* is published in the hope that it will instill in its readers a deeper, fuller confidence in the Bible as a reliable resource for Christian spiritual formation. Our prayer is that God will use it to form in each of us his life, his will, and his way.

Richard J. Foster
For the General Editors

TO THE READER

This preface is addressed to you by the Committee of translators, who wish to explain, as briefly as possible, the origin and character of our work. The publication of our revision is yet another step in the long, continual process of making the Bible available in the form of the English language that is most widely current in our day. To summarize in a single sentence: the New Revised Standard Version of the Bible is an authorized revision of the Revised Standard Version, published in 1952, which was a revision of the American Standard Version, published in 1901, which, in turn, embodied earlier revisions of the King James Version, published in 1611.

In the course of time, the King James Version came to be regarded as "the Authorized Version." With good reason it has been termed "the noblest monument of English prose," and it has entered, as no other book has, into the making of the personal character and the public institutions of the English-speaking peoples. We owe to it an incalculable debt.

Yet the King James Version has serious defects. By the middle of the nineteenth century, the development of biblical studies and the discovery of many biblical manuscripts more ancient than those on which the King James Version was based made it apparent that these defects were so many as to call for revision. The task was begun, by authority of the Church of England, in 1870. The (British) Revised Version of the Bible was published in 1881–1885; and the American Standard Version, its variant embodying the preferences of the American scholars associated with the work, was published, as was mentioned above, in 1901. In 1928 the copyright of the latter was acquired by the International Council of Religious Education and thus passed into the ownership of the Churches of the United States and Canada that were associated in this Council through their boards of education and publication.

The Council appointed a committee of scholars to have charge of the text of the American Standard Version and to undertake inquiry concerning the need for further revision. After studying the questions whether or not revision should be undertaken, and if so, what its nature and extent should be, in 1937 the Council authorized a revision. The scholars who served as members of the Committee worked in two sections, one dealing with the Old Testament and one with the New Testament. In 1946 the Revised Standard Version of the New Testament was published.

The publication of the Revised Standard Version of the Bible, containing the Old and New Testaments, took place on September 30, 1952. A translation of the *Apocryphal/Deuterocanonical* Books of the Old Testament followed in 1957. In 1977 this collection was issued in an expanded edition, containing three additional texts received by Eastern Orthodox communions (3 & 4 Maccabees and Psalm 151). Thereafter the Revised Standard Version gained the distinction of being officially authorized for use by all major Christian churches: Protestant, Anglican, Roman Catholic, and Eastern Orthodox.

The Revised Standard Version Bible Committee is a continuing body, comprising about thirty members, both men and women. Ecumenical in representation, it includes scholars affiliated with various Protestant denominations, as well as several Roman Catholic members, an Eastern Orthodox member, and a Jewish member who serves in the Old Testament section. For a period of time the Committee included several members from Canada and from England.

Because no translation of the Bible is perfect or is acceptable to all groups of readers, and because discoveries of older manuscripts and further investigation of linguistic features of the text continue to become available, renderings of the Bible have proliferated. During the years following the publication of the Revised Standard Version, twenty-six other English translations and revisions of the Bible were produced by committees and by individual scholars—not to mention twenty-five other translations and revisions of the New Testament alone. One of the latter was the second edition of the RSV New Testament, issued in 1971, twenty-five years after its initial publication.

Following the publication of the RSV Old Testament in 1952, significant advances were made in the discovery and interpretation of documents in Semitic languages related to Hebrew. In addition to the information that had become available in the late 1940s from the Dead Sea texts of Isaiah and Habakkuk, subsequent acquisitions from the same area brought to light many other early copies of all the books of the Hebrew Scriptures (except Esther), though most of these copies are fragmentary. During the same period early Greek manuscript copies of books of the New Testament also became available.

In order to take these discoveries into account, along with recent studies of documents in Semitic languages related to Hebrew, in 1974 the Policies Committee of the Revised Standard Version, which is a standing committee of the National Council of the Churches of Christ in the U.S.A., authorized the preparation of a revision of the entire RSV Bible.

For the Old Testament the Committee has made use of the *Biblia Hebraica Stuttgartensia* (1977; ed. sec. emendata, 1983). This is an edition of the Hebrew and Aramaic text as current early in the Christian era and fixed by Jewish scholars (the "Masoretes") of the sixth to the ninth centuries. The vowel signs, which were added by the Masoretes, are accepted in the main, but where a more probable and convincing reading can be obtained by assuming different vowels, this has been done. No notes are given in such cases, because the vowel points are less ancient and reliable than the consonants. When an alternative reading given by the Masoretes is translated in a footnote, this is identified by the words "Another reading is."

Departures from the consonantal text of the best manuscripts have been made only where it seems clear that errors in copying had been made before the text was standardized. Most of the corrections adopted are based on the ancient versions (translations into Greek, Aramaic, Syriac, and Latin), which were made prior to the time of the work of the Masoretes and which therefore may reflect earlier forms of the Hebrew text. In such instances a footnote specifies the version or versions from which the correction has been derived and also gives a translation of the Masoretic Text. Where it was deemed appropriate to do so, information is supplied in footnotes from subsidiary Jewish traditions concerning other textual readings (the *Tiqqune Sopherim,* "emendations of the scribes"). These are identified in the footnotes as "Ancient Heb tradition."

Occasionally it is evident that the text has suffered in transmission and that none of the versions provides a satisfactory restoration. Here we can only follow the best judgment of competent scholars as to the most probable reconstruction of the original text. Such reconstructions are indicated in footnotes by the abbreviation Cn ("Correction"), and a translation of the Masoretic Text is added.

For the Apocryphal/Deuterocanonical Books of the Old Testament the Committee has made use of a number of texts. For most of these books the basic Greek text from which the present translation was made is the edition of the Septuagint prepared by Alfred Rahlfs and published by the Württemberg Bible Society (Stuttgart, 1935). For several of the books the more recently published individual volumes of the Göttingen Septuagint project were utilized. For the book of Tobit it was decided to follow the form of the Greek text found in codex Sinaiticus (supported as it is by evidence from Qumran); where this text is defective, it was supplemented and corrected by other Greek manuscripts. For the three Additions to Daniel (namely, the Prayer of Azariah and the Song of the Three Jews, Susanna, and Bel and the Dragon) the Committee continued to use the Greek version attributed to Theodotion (the so-called "Theodotion-Daniel"). In translating Ecclesiasticus (Sirach), while constant reference was made to the Hebrew fragments of a large portion of this book (those discovered at Qumran and Masada as well as those recovered from the Cairo Geniza), the Committee generally followed the Greek text (including verse numbers) published by Joseph Ziegler in the Göttingen Septuagint (1965). But in many places the Committee has translated the Hebrew text when this provides a reading that is clearly superior to the Greek; the Syriac and Latin versions were also consulted throughout and occasionally adopted. The basic text adopted in rendering 2 Esdras is the Latin version given in *Biblia Sacra,* edited by Robert Weber (Stuttgart, 1971). This was supplemented by consulting the Latin text as edited by R. L. Bensly (1895) and by Bruno Violet (1910), as well as by taking into account the several Oriental versions of 2 Esdras, namely, the Syriac, Ethiopic, Arabic (two forms, referred to as Arabic 1 and Arabic 2), Armenian, and Georgian versions. Finally, since the Additions to the Book of Esther are disjointed and quite unintelligible as they stand in most editions of the Apocrypha, we have provided them with their original context by translating the whole of the Greek version of Esther from Robert Hanhart's Göttingen edition (1983).

For the New Testament the Committee has based its work on the most recent edition of *The Greek New Testament,* prepared by an interconfessional and international committee and published by the United Bible Societies (1966; 3rd ed. corrected, 1983; information concerning changes to be introduced into the critical apparatus of the forthcoming 4th edition was available to the Committee). As in that edition, double brackets are used to enclose a few passages that are generally regarded to be later additions to the text, but which we have retained because of their evident antiquity and their importance in the textual tradition. Only in very rare instances have we replaced the text or the punctuation of the Bible Societies' edition by an alternative that seemed to us to be superior. Here and there in the footnotes the phrase "Other ancient authorities read" identifies alternative readings preserved by Greek manuscripts and early versions. In both Testaments, alternative renderings of the text are indicated by the word "Or."

As for the style of English adopted for the present revision, among the mandates given to the Committee in 1980 by the Division of Education and Ministry of the National Council of Churches of Christ (which now holds the copyright of the RSV Bible) was the directive to continue in the tradition of the King James Bible, but to introduce such changes as are warranted on the basis of accuracy, clarity, euphony, and current English usage. Within the constraints set by the original texts and by the mandates of the Division, the Committee has followed the maxim "As literal as possible, as free as necessary." As a consequence, the New Revised Standard Version (NRSV) remains essentially a literal translation. Paraphrastic renderings have been adopted only sparingly, and then chiefly to compensate for a deficiency in the English language—the lack of a common gender third person singular pronoun.

During the almost half century since the publication of the RSV, many in the churches have become sensitive to the danger of linguistic sexism arising from the inherent bias of the English language toward the masculine gender, a bias that in the case of the Bible has often restricted or obscured the meaning of the original text. The mandates from the Division specified that, in references to men and women, masculine-oriented language should be eliminated as far as this can be done without altering passages that reflect the historical situation of ancient patriarchal culture. As can be appreciated, more than once the Committee found that the several mandates stood in tension and even in conflict. The various concerns had to be balanced case by case in order to provide a faithful and acceptable rendering without using contrived English. Only very occasionally has the pronoun "he" or "him" been retained in passages where the reference may have been to a woman as well as to a man; for example, in several legal texts in Leviticus and Deuteronomy. In such instances of formal, legal language, the options of either putting the passage in the plural or of introducing additional nouns to avoid masculine pronouns in English seemed to the Committee to obscure the historic structure and literary character of the original. In the vast majority of cases, however, inclusiveness has been attained by simple rephrasing or by introducing plural forms when this does not distort the meaning of the passage. Of course, in narrative and in parable no attempt was made to generalize the sex of individual persons.

Another aspect of style will be detected by readers who compare the more state-ly English rendering of the Old Testament with the less formal rendering adopted for the New Testament. For example, the traditional distinction between *shall* and *will* in English has been retained in the Old Testament as appropriate in rendering a document that embodies what may be termed the classic form of Hebrew, while in the New Testament the abandonment of such distinctions in the usage of the future tense in English reflects the more colloquial nature of the koine Greek used by most New Testament authors except when they are quoting the Old Testament.

Careful readers will notice that here and there in the Old Testament the word LORD (or in certain cases GOD) is printed in capital letters. This represents the traditional manner in English versions of rendering the Divine Name, the "Tetragrammaton" (see the notes on Exodus 3:14, 15), following the precedent of the ancient Greek and Latin translators and the long established practice in the reading of the Hebrew Scriptures in the synagogue. While it is almost if not quite certain that the Name was originally pronounced "Yahweh," this pronunciation was not indicated when the Masoretes added vowel sounds to the consonantal Hebrew text. To the four consonants YHWH of the Name, which had come to be regarded as too sacred to be pronounced, they attached vowel signs indicating that in its place should be read the Hebrew word *Adonai*, meaning "Lord" (or *Elohim*, meaning "God"). Ancient Greek translators employed the word *Kyrios* ("Lord") for the Name. The Vulgate likewise used the Latin word *Dominus* ("Lord"). The form "Jehovah" is of late medieval origin; it is a combination of the consonants of the Divine Name and the vowels attached to it by the Masoretes but belonging to an entirely different word. Although the American Standard Version (1901) had used "Jehovah" to render the Tetragrammaton (the sound of Y being represented by J and the sound of W by V, as in Latin), for two reasons the Committees that produced the RSV and the NRSV returned to the more familiar usage of the King James Version. (1) The word "Jehovah" does not accurately represent any form of the Name ever used in Hebrew. (2) The use of any proper name for the one and only God, as though there were other gods from whom the true God had to be distinguished, began to be discontinued in Judaism before the Christian era and is inappropriate for the universal faith of the Christian Church.

It will be seen that in the Psalms and in other prayers addressed to God the archaic second person singular pronouns (*thee, thou, thine*) and verb forms (*art, hast, hadst*) are no longer used. Although some readers may regret this change, it should be pointed out that in the original languages neither the Old Testament nor the New makes any linguistic distinction between addressing a human being and addressing the Deity. Furthermore, in the tradition of the King James Version one will not expect to find the use of capital letters for pronouns that refer to the Deity—such capitalization is an unnecessary innovation that has only recently been introduced into a few English translations of the Bible. Finally, we have left to the discretion of the licensed publishers such matters as section headings, cross-references, and clues to the pronunciation of proper names.

This new version seeks to preserve all that is best in the English Bible as it has been known and used through the years. It is intended for use in public reading and congregational worship, as well as in private study, instruction, and meditation. We have resisted the temptation to introduce terms and phrases that merely reflect current moods, and have tried to put the message of the Scriptures in simple, enduring words and expressions that are worthy to stand in the great tradition of the King James Bible and its predecessors.

In traditional Judaism and Christianity, the Bible has been more than a historical document to be preserved or a classic of literature to be cherished and admired; it is recognized as the unique record of God's dealings with people over the ages. The Old Testament sets forth the call of a special people to enter into covenant relation with the God of justice and steadfast love and to bring God's law to the nations. The New Testament records the life and work of Jesus Christ, the one in whom "the Word became flesh," as well as describes the rise and spread of the early Christian Church. The Bible carries its full message, not to those who regard it simply as a noble literary heritage of the past or who wish to use it to enhance political purposes and advance otherwise desirable goals, but to all persons and communities who read it so that they may discern and understand what God is saying to them. That message must not be disguised in phrases that are no longer clear, or hidden under words that have changed or lost their meaning; it must be presented in language that is direct and plain and meaningful to people today. It is the hope and prayer of the translators that this version of the Bible may continue to hold a large place in congregational life and to speak to all readers, young and old alike, helping them to understand and believe and respond to its message.

For the Committee,
Bruce M. Metzger

THE WITH-GOD LIFE

A General Introduction to the
Renovaré Spiritual Formation Bible

CATCHING THE VISION

God, in sovereign grace and outrageous love, has given us a written revelation of who he is and what his purposes are for humanity. And God has chosen to accomplish this great work through his people on earth. This written revelation now resides as a massive fact at the heart of human history. There is, simply, no book that is remotely close to achieving the significance and influence of the Bible. It is truly "The Book" (*hay Biblos*).

But the intrinsic power and greatness of the Bible often make it difficult for us to receive the life it offers. The average "Bible consumer," publishing research tells us, owns nine Bibles and is looking for more. This is mute but powerful testimony to a deep and abiding sense of *lack*—a sense that we have not really achieved a grasp of the Bible that is adequate to our needs.

In point of fact, we can often use the Bible in ways that stifle spiritual life or even destroy the soul. This happened to any number of people who walked with Jesus, heard him teach, and saw him exercise the power of the kingdom of God. For many, their very study of the Scriptures prevented them from recognizing who he was and putting their confidence in him (John 5:39–47). And later, Peter speaks in very grim terms of how people can "twist" Scripture "to their own destruction" (2 Pet 3:16).

Is it possible that this still happens today? Sadly, we must admit that it does. Think of the millions of people who say, sincerely, that the Bible is *the* guide to life, but who still starve to death in the presence of its spiritual feast. This tragic situation is obvious from the usual effects (or lack of effects) that the study of the Bible has in the daily lives of people, even among those who speak most highly of it.

The source of the problem is rooted in the two most common objectives of Bible study. The first is the practice of studying the Bible for information or knowledge alone. This may include information about particular facts or historical events, knowledge of general truths or doctrines, or even knowledge of how others are mistaken in their religious views, beliefs, and practices.

We know from experience how knowledge can make people arrogant—even knowledge of the Bible and of God. It is not surprising, then, that study focusing on knowledge alone does not lead to the life transformation that is the real human need. No wonder we who love the Bible keep buying more editions of it, hoping to obtain what we know in our hearts is there for us.

The second common objective of Bible study is to find some formula that will solve the pressing need of the moment. Thus we seek out specific passages that speak to particular needs rather than seeking whole-life discipleship to Jesus. To be sure, these needs are important, desperately so when we are trapped in the harsh realities of life. These needs may involve comfort or forgiveness, physical healing, conformity to a particular denominational or political persuasion, special endowments or gifts of the Spirit, or works of social liberation. But in the end they always have to do with being "a good citizen," "a good spouse," or "a good something else"—perhaps even "a good Christian" by certain interpretations.

What we must face up to about these two common objectives for studying the Bible is that we or our human instructors are *in charge* of the process. They are, in fact, ways of trying to control what comes out of the Bible rather than a means of entering the process of transforming our whole person and our whole life into *Christlikeness*.

If we want to receive from the Bible the life "with God" that is portrayed *in* the Bible, we must be prepared to have our dearest and most fundamental assumptions about ourselves and our associations called into question. We must read humbly and in a constant attitude of repentance. Only in this way can we gain a thorough and practical grasp of the spiritual riches that God has made available to all humanity in his written Word. Only in this way can we keep from transforming The Book into a Catholic Bible, an Orthodox Bible, a Baptist, Methodist, Lutheran, or even a Renovaré Bible.

What will enable us to avoid this soul-crushing result?

The Supernatural Power of Love

Jesus founded on earth a new type of community, and in it and through him love—God-given *agape* love—came down to live with power on earth. Now, it is this God-given *agape* love that transforms our lives and gives us true spiritual substance as persons. Suppose, then, we simply agreed that the proper outcome of studying the Bible is growth in the supernatural power of love, the love of God and of all people.

We could call this the 1 Corinthians 13 Test: "If I . . . understand all mysteries and all knowledge, and if I have all faith, so as to remove mountains, but do not have love, I am nothing" (v 2). And so the test of whether we have really gotten the point of the Bible would then be the quality of love we show. Knowledge of the Bible and its teachings would, of course, continue to be of great value, but only insofar as it leads to greater love: to greater appropriation of God's love for us and to greater love on our part for God, others, and ourselves.

When we turn to Scripture in this way, our reason for "knowing" the Bible and everything it teaches would be that we might love more and know more of love. We would experience this love not as an abstraction, but as a practical reality by which we are possessed. And since all those who love through and through obey the law, we would become ever more obedient to Jesus Christ and his Abba.

Regarding the Bible, then, perhaps the most basic question is: Shall we try to control the Bible, that is, try to make it "come out right," or shall we simply seek to release its life into our lives and our world? Shall we try to "tilt" it this way or that, or shall we give it complete freedom to "tilt" us as it will?

Can we surrender freely to the life we see in the Bible, or must we remain in control of that life, only selectively endorsing it when we find it proper and safe from our "perspective"? Can we trust the living water that flows from Christ through the Bible, open ourselves to it and release it into the world as best we can, and then get out of its way? This, we believe, is the only worthy goal for a study of the Bible.

Life "With God": The Immanuel Principle

The Bible is all about human life "with God." It is about how God has made this "with-God" life possible and will bring it to pass. In fact, the name Immanuel, meaning in Hebrew "God is with us," is the title given to the one and only Redeemer, because it refers to God's everlasting intent for human life—namely, that we should be in every aspect a dwelling place of God. *Indeed, the unity of the Bible is discovered in the development of life "with God" as a reality on earth, centered in the person of Jesus.* We might call this the *Immanuel Principle* of life.

This dynamic, pulsating, with-God life is on nearly every page of the Bible. To the point of redundancy we hear that *God is with* his people: with Abraham and Moses, with Esther and David, with Isaiah, Jeremiah, Amos, Micah, Haggai, and Malachi, with Mary, Peter, James, and John, with Paul and Barnabas, with Priscilla and Aquila, with Lydia, Timothy, Epaphroditus, and Phoebe, and with a host of others too numerous to name.

Accordingly, the various introductions, essays, and notes that accompany the text in the *Renovaré Spiritual Formation Bible* all have as their primary aim enabling us to see and understand the Immanuel Principle. They serve to make clear how the "with-God" life works in all the circumstances of human existence, both for individuals and for groups, both in specific historical periods and through all times.

For example, what do the first eleven chapters of Genesis tell us about this with-God kind of life? And how are the particular stories about, for example, Cain or Noah relevant? Then we need to consider the Pentateuch as a whole, and the transition to Abraham, then to Moses, then to Joshua. What is really happening here in terms of the Immanuel Principle? Exactly how is *God with us* in these stories? What does Leviticus mean from the perspective of the Immanuel Principle? What are we to learn from the conquest of the Land of Promise and the manner in which it was carried out? Or from the period of the judges and the amazing persons and stories involved? What of Ruth and Esther, of Hosea and Nehemiah?

What was happening for the individual's life with God between Malachi and Matthew? What was happening in the People of God as a whole? What was happening with God's purposes in human history? Certainly the world into which Jesus was born was remarkably different from the one in which Malachi lived. What unique perspective does the intertestamental period bring to the Immanuel Principle? What did it do to prepare the world for Jesus' birth?

Then on to the New Testament documents, up to Revelation, which God gave to Jesus to show to his people (Rev 1:1). In these documents the biblical presentation of life with God comes to its fullness and completion. How, we may ask, do we read Luke or Romans or Revelation in the light of the Immanuel Principle?

The People of God—this all-inclusive community of loving persons—are seen in the New Testament as "God's household, built on the foundation of the apostles and prophets, with Christ Jesus himself as the chief cornerstone. In him the whole building is joined together and rises to become a holy temple in the Lord. And in him you too are being built together to become a dwelling in which God lives by his Spirit" (Eph 2:19–22, NIV). Even the fulfillment of God's purposes for humanity beyond human history is portrayed: " 'Now the dwelling of God is with human beings, and he will live with them. They will be his people, and God himself will be with them and be their God' " (Rev 21:3, NIVI).

And so we discover that the Immanuel Principle is, after all, a *cosmic* principle that God has used all along in creation and redemption. It alone serves to guide human life aright on earth now and even illuminates the future of the universe.

Of course, these brief examples hardly touch the surface of the river of life that flows through the Bible into the thirsty wastelands of the human soul. And any study Bible worthy of the name should help, and not hinder, the spreading of the waters of that river abroad. Now, once we decide to surrender freely to this river of life, we must learn how it is done. And we must learn how to help others see into the divine Life within the Bible and increasingly receive that Life as their own.

NURTURING THE INTENTION

God not only originated the Bible through human authorship; he remains with it always. It is God's book. No one owns it but God himself. It is the loving heart of God made visible and plain. And receiving this message of exquisite love is the great privilege of all who long for life with God. *Reading, studying, memorizing, and meditating upon Scripture have always been the foundation of the Christian disciplines.* All of the disciplines are built upon Scripture. Our practice of the Spiritual Disciplines is kept on course by our immersion in Scripture. And so it is, we come to see, that this reading, studying, memorizing, and meditating is totally in the service of "the life that really is life" (1 Tim 6:19). We long with all our heart to know *for ourselves* the with-God kind of life that Jesus brings in all its fullness.

And the Bible has been given to help us. God has so superintended the writing of Scripture that it serves as a most reliable guide for our own spiritual formation. But as in its authorship, so in its presentation to the world, God uses human action.

So we must consider how we can ourselves come to the Bible and also how we can present it to people in a way that does not destroy the soul, but inducts it into the eternal kind of life.

We begin by opening our lives in Christian community to the influx of God's life and by experientially finding, day-to-day, how to let Jesus Christ live in every dimension of our being. We can gather regularly in groups of two or more to encourage one another to discover the footprints of God in our daily existence and to venture out *with God* into areas where we have previously walked alone or not at all.

But the aim is not external conformity, whether to doctrine or deed, but the reformation of the inner self—of the spiritual core, the place of thought and feeling, of will and character. The psalmist cries, "You desire truth in the inward being; therefore teach me wisdom in my secret heart. . . . Create in me a clean heart, O God, and put a new and right spirit within me" (Ps 51:6, 10). It is "our inner nature" that is being "renewed (*renovare*) day by day" (2 Cor 4:16). (Renovare = to renew.)

Although the many Christian traditions differ over the details of spiritual formation, they all have the same objective: the transformation of the person into one of greater Christlikeness. "Spiritual formation" is the process of transforming the inner reality of the self (the "inward being" of the psalmist) in such a way that the overall with-God life seen in the Bible naturally and freely comes to pass in us. Our inner world (the "secret heart") becomes the home of Jesus by his initiative and our response. As a result, our interior world becomes increasingly like the inner self of Jesus and, therefore, the natural source of words and deeds that are characteristic of him. By his enabling presence we come to "let the same mind be in [us] that was in Christ Jesus" (Phil 2:5).

This, then, provides the orientation of the *Renovaré Spiritual Formation Bible*. And it provides the answer to our question about how we can present the Bible to people in a way that does not destroy the soul, but inducts it into the eternal kind of life. We simply do all we can to enable people to *see clearly* the Life that burns brightly on the pages of the Bible and to show, by practical steps, how they can *bring their entire life* into that Life. An intelligent, humble, careful, intensive, straightforward reading of the Bible will direct us into life in the kingdom of God.

Reading with the Mind

It is genuinely helpful as we read the Bible for spiritual formation to learn to identify the literary forms of Scripture. The first form we encounter are the books of the Law—Genesis, Exodus, Leviticus, Numbers, and Deuteronomy. In utter grace God stretched out his mighty hand to deliver the Israelites from bondage and, having delivered them, he made a covenant with them in which he would be their God and they were to be his people. The books of the Law then established the stipulations of the covenant God made with Israel. Composed of more than six hundred commandments, these laws defined the unique relationship between Israel and Yahweh. Carried across the pages of Scripture, these laws and the obedience they evoked provided Israel, now the People of God, with clear directions for living: keeping God's laws, exhibiting God's love, expressing God's righteousness.

2.   The second literary form is prophecy. In its original structure, Scripture distinguished between the former prophets (Joshua, Judges, Samuel, and Kings) and the latter prophets (Isaiah, Jeremiah, Ezekiel, and the twelve Minor Prophets). The primary purpose of prophecy is to speak for God in a particular situation. The prophets were viewed not so much as *fore-tellers* but as *forth-tellers,* constantly calling the People of God back to their covenant obligations of single-hearted obedience to God, mercy and compassion for the poor and dispossessed, and justice and *shalom* ("peace") toward all peoples.

3.   A third form of biblical literature (and a corollary to prophecy) is apocalyptic writing. In the Hebrew Scriptures, apocalyptic literature is found primarily in Ezekiel, Daniel, Zechariah, and parts of Isaiah. In this form of biblical writing, the prophets cried out against the people's disdain for the stipulations of the covenant and warned that the result of their disobedience would be divine wrath and destruction. Always, however, the apocalyptic writings held forth the vision of a coming day of hope and restoration, a day when "the wolf shall live with the lamb, the leopard shall lie down with the kid, the calf and the lion and the fatling together, and a little child shall lead them," a day when "the earth will be full of the knowledge of the LORD as the waters cover the sea" (Isa 11:6, 9).

4.   The final literary forms of the Hebrew Scriptures are found in the Writings. In the original arrangement, the Writings consisted of poetry (Psalms, Job, and Proverbs), festal writings (Ruth, Song of Solomon, Ecclesiastes, Lamentations, and Esther), and history (Ezra, Nehemiah, and Chronicles). This narrative literature outlines God's universal design for all creation. Scripture teaches that the forward movement of history is the dramatic unfolding of God's divine plans for life on earth, and these narratives demonstrate the way in which God creates and calls a people to experience life in the kingdom of God.

Next we encounter the Deuterocanonical literature, a body of writings covering the period between our Old and New Testaments. Most of the Church throughout much of history has accepted the Deuterocanonicals as Scripture, though Protestants do not give these writings the same authority. They deal with an important period in Israel's historical and spiritual development and contain many helpful insights into spiritual formation. The people Jesus encountered and taught were in many ways spiritually formed by these writings. In addition, the Deuterocanonical writings can function for us in much the same way that good sermons and devotional writings do. They contain histories (Judith, the Maccabees, 1 & 2 Esdras), wisdom writings (Wisdom of Solomon, Sirach), and works of theological reflection and moral instruction (Tobit, Baruch, the Letter of Jeremiah).

When we turn to the New Testament, we first encounter the majestic teachings of Jesus Christ in the Gospels. Here the brilliance of Jesus' words and actions catapult us into the life that is Life indeed, and that more abundantly (John 10:10). Through the dynamic use of parables, sermons, and proverbs we learn deeply and fully what it means to live *with God.* Even more, by himself coming as incarnate Lord, Jesus ushers us completely into the with-God life, a life that is in and through him who is "the way, and the truth, and the life" (John 14:6).

After the Gospels comes the book of Acts, which is a continuation of the acts and teachings of Jesus through the Holy Spirit (Acts 1:1). It displays in bold relief the great variety of Christian experience: from speaking in tongues and baptism by fire to logical analysis and philosophical debate (Acts 2:1–13; 17:16–34). We see the dramatic unfolding of life *with God,* the breathtaking works of healing, evangelism, and demonic encounter, the infinite variety of ways God calls his people to life with him, and much, much more. All of this, remember, is through the dynamic power of the Holy Spirit.

Following the historical drama of the book of Acts, the theological teaching of the New Testament is captured in the diverse Letters of Paul and others. Here we learn how the People of God, scattered in diverse local settings, live in the kingdom of God and, transformed by the power of God, obey the commands of God. These Letters provide the practical wisdom necessary for the with-God life.

The Bible concludes with the book of Revelation. This pulsating drama returns us to the dramatic style of apocalyptic prophecy. The cataclysmic clash between God and Satan, between good and evil, reaches feverish pitch when Satan's great scheme to destroy Christ is thwarted (Rev 12–18). As the drama moves toward its glorious conclusion, the new heaven and the new earth, God's ultimate intention of establishing an eternal relationship with us is fully revealed: "'See, the home of God is among mortals. He will dwell with them; they will be his peoples, and God himself will be with them;' . . . They will see his face, and his name will be on their foreheads. And there will be no more night; they need no light of lamp or sun, for the Lord God will be their light, and they will reign forever and ever" (Rev 21:3; 22:4–5).

Reading with Understanding

In seeking to discover the with-God life, it is helpful to read the Bible in four distinct ways. First, we read the Bible literally, from cover to cover, internalizing its life-giving message. By reading the whole of Scripture, we begin to capture the force and the power of the with-God life. We enter into the original dynamics and drama of Scripture: struggling with Abraham over the offering up of the son of promise; puzzling with Job at the tragedies of life; rejoicing with Moses at Israel's release from bondage; weeping with Jeremiah "for the slain of my poor people" (9:1); bowing in awe with Mary at the messianic promise.

Second, we read the Bible in context. This means allowing the way in which the author originally depicted life *with God* to establish the standard for understanding our life *with God* today. We read with a firm determination to discover the intent of the original author and then allow that intent to control our comprehension of the passage. This helps us grasp the way God continues to shape human life today.

Third, we read the Bible in conversation with itself. In other words, we seek to understand how the whole of Scripture gives structure and meaning to each of its parts. The unfolding drama of Scripture often raises puzzling questions, which are resolved only when more obscure and difficult passages are held under the light of clearer, more straightforward passages. In biblical interpretation systematic passages interpret incidental passages, universal passages interpret local ones, and didactic passages interpret symbolic ones. In this way the whole Bible guides us into a better understanding of its particular parts.

Fourth, Christians read the Bible in conversation with the historic witness of the People of God. The Church learned from the synagogue that it is the community that reads the Bible. This, in part, is what we mean when we speak of the "communion of saints." Christians throughout the centuries help us understand the nature of life *with God* and provide insight and discernment that enrich our own spiritual life. So we read the Bible in conversation with Origen and Jerome, Augustine of Hippo and Hildegard of Bingen, John Chrysostom and John Calvin, Martin Luther and Richard Baxter, Watchman Nee and Sundar Singh—and many others, including wise and mature interpreters of Scripture today. This corporate reading of the Bible illuminates for us the multifaceted ways the Immanuel Principle is experienced in ordinary life.

Reading with the Heart

Finally, as we approach the Bible it is helpful to slow down, breathe deeply, and read with the heart. Now, this "reading with the heart" way of approaching the sacred text has a very long and time-honored history among the People of God. It even has a name, *lectio divina,* divine or spiritual reading.

What does *lectio divina* mean? Well, it means *listening* to the text of Scripture—really listening, listening yielded and still. It means *submitting* to the text of Scripture, allowing its message to flow into us rather than attempting to master it. It means *reflecting* on the text of Scripture, permitting ourselves to become fully engaged—both mind and heart—by the drama of the passage. It means *praying* the text of Scripture, letting the biblical reality of the with-God life give rise to our heart cry of gratitude, confession, complaint, or petition. It means *applying* the text of Scripture, seeing how God's Holy Word provides a personal word for our life circumstances. And it means *obeying* the text of Scripture, turning, always turning, from our wicked way and into the way everlasting (Ps 139:23–24).

UNDERSTANDING THE MEANS

The with-God life that we see in the Bible is the very life to which we are called. It is, in fact, exactly the life Jesus is referring to when he declares, "I am come that they might have life, and that they might have it more abundantly" (John 10:10, KJV). It is a life of unhurried peace and power. It is solid, serene, simple, radiant. It takes no time, though it permeates all of our time.

But such a life does not simply fall into our hands. Frankly, it is no more automatic for us than it was for those luminaries who walk across the pages of our Bible. There is a God-ordained means to becoming the kind of persons and the kind of communities that can fully and joyfully enter into such abundant living. And these "means" involve us in a process of intentionally "train[ing] ... in godliness" (1 Tim 4:7). This is the purpose of the *disciplines* of the spiritual life. Indeed, the very purpose of this study Bible is to make Scripture itself a primary means for the discovery, instruction, and practice of the Spiritual Disciplines, which bring us all the more fully into the with-God life.

The Spiritual Disciplines, then, are the God-ordained means by which each of us is enabled to place the little, individualized power pack we all possess—the human body—before God as "a living sacrifice" (Rom 12:1). It is the way we go about training in the spiritual life. By means of this process we become, through time and experience, the kind of persons who naturally and freely express "love, joy, peace, patience, kindness, generosity, faithfulness, gentleness, and self-control" (Gal 5:22–23).

Many and Varied

What are the Spiritual Disciplines? They are many and varied: fasting and prayer, study and service, submission and solitude, confession and worship, meditation and silence, simplicity, frugality, secrecy, sacrifice, celebration, and the like. We see such Spiritual Disciplines cropping up repeatedly in the Bible as the way God's people trained toward godliness. And not only in the Bible; the saints down through history, even spilling over into our own time, have all practiced these ways of growing in grace (2 Pet 3:18).

Biblical examples abound of individual listings and common groupings of Spiritual Disciplines, which may be compared to athletes' basic regimen of training for particular sports. And this makes perfect sense, since biblical personages were (and we are) *athletae dei,* "athletes of God." As athletes of God they trained (and we train) to participate fully and freely in the with-God life. The Psalms virtually sing of the meditations of the People of God: "My eyes are awake before each watch of the night, that I may meditate on your promise" (Ps 119:148). The psalm that introduces the entire Psalter calls us to emulate those whose "delight is in the law of the Lord, and on his law they meditate day and night" (Ps 1:2). Daniel "turned to the Lord God" with prayer, supplication, fasting, and confession (9:3). Jesus, "in the morning, while it was still very dark, ... got up and went out to a deserted place" (Mark 1:35). The Christians at Antioch were "worshiping the Lord and fasting" when they received divine guidance to commission Paul and Barnabas for their missionary task (Acts 13:1–3).

We can see this process not only in the Bible, but also in the stories of God's people throughout the ages. Perhaps you have read or heard of *The Spiritual Exercises* of Ignatius of Loyola or Teresa of Avila's *Interior Castle* or Jeremy Taylor's *Holy Living and Holy Dying* or William Law's *A Serious Call to a Devout and Holy Life.* These writings, and many others like them, all discuss disciplines of the spiritual life for training in righteousness.

So groupings and patterns of Spiritual Disciplines abound. But we should never look for some exhaustive list of the Spiritual Disciplines or for any "formula for blessedness." No, this interactive life *with God* is far too dynamic for that.

Now, through all this we need not fear. We are not left to our own devices. God is with us. Christ is our ever-living Teacher. The Spirit will guide and direct. Wise Christian counsel abounds both in Scripture and among loving and mature friends. We will be taught which response is right and when, and which disciplines are needful and when. Our only tasks are to listen and obey.

The Principle of Indirection

When we engage in the Spiritual Disciplines we are seeking the righteousness of the kingdom of God through "indirection." You see, we cannot by direct effort make ourselves into the kind of people who can live fully alive to God. Only God can accomplish this in us. Only God can incline our heart toward him. Only God can reprogram the deeply ingrained habits and patterns of sin that constantly predispose us toward evil and transform them into even more deeply ingrained patterns of "righteousness and peace and joy in the Holy Spirit" (Rom 14:17). And God freely and graciously invites us to participate in this transforming process. But not on our own.

We do not, for example, become humble merely by trying to become humble. Action on our own would make us all the more proud of our humility. No, we instead train with Spiritual Disciplines appropriate to our need. In this particular example that would most surely involve learning numerous acts of service for others, which would incline us toward the good of all people. This indirect action will place us—body, mind, and spirit—before God as a living sacrifice. God then takes this little offering of ourselves and in his time and in his way produces in us things far greater than we could ever ask for or think of—in this case a life growing in and overflowing with the grace of humility. It is, to repeat, the righteousness of the kingdom of God by indirection.

What Is a Spiritual Discipline?

Now, to move forward in this life we must understand clearly what a Spiritual Discipline is. *A Spiritual Discipline is an intentionally directed action by which we do what we can do in order to receive from God the ability (or power) to do what we cannot do by direct effort.* It is not in us, for example, to love our enemies. If we go out and try very hard to love our enemies, we will fail miserably. Always. This strength, this power to love our enemies—that is, to genuinely and unconditionally love those who curse us and spitefully use us—is simply not within our natural abilities. We cannot do it by ourselves. Ever.

But this fact of life does not mean that we do nothing. Far from it! Instead, by an act of the will we choose to take up disciplines of the spiritual life that we can do. These disciplines are all actions of body, mind, and spirit that are within our power to do. Not always and not perfectly, to be sure, but they are things we can do—

by choice. For example, by choosing actions of *fasting* we can learn experientially that we do not live by bread alone, but by every word that proceeds from the mouth of God (Deut 8:3, Luke 4:4). By choosing actions of *study* we can learn how the mind takes on an order conforming to the order upon which it concentrates, which is precisely why we seek to turn our mind toward all things true, honorable, just, pure, pleasing, commendable, excellent, and worthy of praise (Phil 4:8). By choosing actions of *solitude* we can become intimately acquainted with the many things that control us, so that we can be set free from them by the power of God (Mark 6:31).

The Spiritual Disciplines in and of themselves have no merit whatsoever. They possess no righteousness, contain no rectitude. Their purpose—their only purpose—is to place us before God. After that they have come to the end of their usefulness. But it is enough. Then the grace of God steps in, takes this simple offering of ourselves, and creates out of it the kind of person who embodies the goodness of God—indeed, a person who can come to the place of truly loving even enemies.

Again, Spiritual Disciplines involve doing what we *can* to receive from God the power to do what we cannot. And God graciously uses this process to make us the kind of person who automatically will do what needs to be done when it needs to be done.

The ability to do what needs to be done when it needs to be done is the true freedom in life. Freedom comes not from the absence of restraint, but from the presence of discipline. Only the disciplined gymnast is free to score a perfect ten on the parallel bars. Only the disciplined violinist is free to play Paganini's Caprices. This, of course, is true in all of life, but it is never more true than in the spiritual life. When we are on the spot, when we find ourselves in the midst of a crisis, it is too late. Training in the Spiritual Disciplines is the God-ordained means for forming and transforming the human personality, so that when we are in the crisis we can be "response-able"—able to respond appropriately.

Grace, Grace, and More Grace

It is vitally important for us to see spiritual training in the context of the work and action of God's grace. As the apostle Paul reminds us, "It is God who is at work in you, enabling you both to will and to work for his good pleasure" (Phil 2:13). This is no "works righteousness," as it is sometimes called. Even our desiring the with-God life is an action of grace; it is "prevenient grace," say the theologians. You see, we are not just saved by grace, we live by grace. And we pray by grace and fast by grace and study by grace and serve by grace and worship by grace. *All the disciplines are permeated by the enabling grace of God.*

But do not misunderstand, there *are* things for us to do. Daily. Grace never means inaction or total passivity. In ordinary life we will encounter multiple moments of decision in which we must engage the will, saying yes to God's will and to God's way, as the People of God have been challenged throughout history.

The opposite of grace is works, but not effort. "Works" have to do with earning, and there simply is nothing any of us can do to earn God's love or acceptance. And, of course, we don't have to. God already loves us utterly and perfectly, and our complete acceptance is the free gift of God through Jesus Christ our Lord. In God's amazing grace "we live and move and have our being" (Acts 17:28). But if we ever hope to "grow in grace," we will find ourselves engaging in effort of the most strenuous kind. As Jesus says, we are to "*strive* to enter through the narrow door" (Luke 13:24, emphasis added). And Peter urges us to "make every *effort* to support [our] faith with goodness, and goodness with knowledge, and knowledge with self-control, and self-control with endurance, and endurance with godliness, and godliness with mutual affection, and mutual affection with love" (2 Pet 1:5–7, emphasis added).

GO AND DO LIKEWISE

So now, as you read the *Renovaré Spiritual Formation Bible,* be on the lookout for the formation—indeed, the transformation—of those who walk across its pages. Pay attention even to those who resist God's initiatives and are never really formed in Christlikeness: the Esaus and the Balaams, the Ahabs and the Manassehs, the Jezebels and the Judases. Note the struggles. Look for the intention, or the lack of intention. Observe the various and sundry Spiritual Disciplines used. Watch the movement back and forth: defiance and obedience, rebellion and submission, loyalty and unfaithfulness.

Pay special attention to those who do come through on the other side—albeit with many slips and falls. Note their joy, their peace, their strength, their love. They are the ones who are experiencing ever more fully the Immanuel Principle, the with-God life. Then, go and do likewise.

The General Editors
Gayle Beebe
Richard J. Foster
Lynda L. Graybeal
Thomas C. Oden
Dallas Willard

THE WITH-GOD LIFE

A Panoramic View of God's Purpose in History

In addition to understanding the Bible's overarching theme in the with-God life and its transformation of the People of God, it is also helpful to view the Bible panoramically across the expanse of time. From the beginning and into the unlimited future of God with humanity we can see the unity of the Bible in the interplay of two aspects of the with-God life: *human character transformation* and *divine mediation*—that is, God's ways of arranging to be *with us*. Every interaction in the biblical records shows this interplay.

Adam and Eve "fell" because, though innocent, they lacked character. Innocence is not virtue. Innocence, for all its beauty, is a form of ignorance and lack of character. God certainly could have stood over Adam and Eve ("been in their faces," as we sometimes say) and prevented them from succumbing to Satan's clever appeals. Instead, God arranged for them to be "on their own," and the result was then expressed in what they did. This allowing us to be "on our own" in order to develop character within us is an arrangement God still abides by and respects.

To develop Adam's and Eve's character—and ours too—God has to be "absent" as well as present in human life. Just as our parents care for us around the clock in infancy and early childhood and then gradually withdraw their presence from us as we physically mature, so God is intently present to us at our spiritual infancy and then allows us to be increasingly "on our own" as we spiritually mature. Through the ages God purposely works to establish a *balance* between his "manifest presence" and his "seeming absence," so that we will develop character: the character required of those who will not only "exercise dominion in life through the one man, Jesus Christ," but also will "reign forever and ever" with him, hence realizing his ultimate purpose for humanity (Rom 5:17; Rev 22:5).

As in the garden of Eden, God balances his manifest presence and seeming absence through divine mediation by providing appointed figures, forms of worship, social structures, cataclysmic events, Scripture, and other revelations. These forms of mediation change over time, always building on what has gone before. At the outset of human history—from Adam to Abraham—God works directly with individuals: speaking with them, appearing to them in angelic form, instructing them in dreams, and so forth. When God is "absent" to them, his presence is mediated only by the knowledge that he is "about" and "will be back."

Beginning with Abraham, by contrast, God begins working indirectly, mediating his presence through the social structure of the family unit: "In you," God says to Abraham—that is, through your family—"all the families of the earth shall be blessed" (Gen 12:3). This mediation develops over a long and painful history as Abraham's descendants become tribes, a people, and then, under the monarchy, a nation that rises to great power, dominating its neighbors. All the while, God's presence with the people of Israel is the central, unifying reality in its history.

From Abraham through the monarchy, God's presence—and absence—is mediated through Scripture, traditions, and rituals of the religion of Israel: the Torah, the judges, the levitical priests, the prophets, and more. These survive the collapse of the monarchy and the dispersion and continue to mediate God's presence not only to the exiled biological children of Abraham, but also to the Gentiles and their kings and leaders.

During the intertestamental period, the religious institutions of Israel continue to prosper in their own homeland, even under Greek and Roman rule, and throughout the Mediterranean world. During this time new possibilities of character development and relationship to God develop within the framework of the ethnic Israelite culture.

Then, into this Greco-Roman, Mediterranean world Jesus, the Incarnate Word, who personally mediates the presence of God, is born. By the means of his life, death, and resurrection, Jesus breaks open the ethnic vessel within which the treasure of God's presence had developed. The entire history of God-with-his-people now becomes, through Jesus Christ, the treasure of all peoples and fulfills the ancient promise to Abraham: "In you all the families of the earth shall be blessed." Now "there is also one mediator between God and humankind, Christ Jesus, himself human" (1 Tim 2:5).

After Jesus' ascension into the heavens we see God's all-inclusive people, the "light of the world" and "salt of the earth," being indwelt by the Holy Spirit, who also personally mediates God's presence for the formation of Christ's character in individuals and "all nations." This direct mediating of God's presence through the Holy Spirit continues to develop up to the present. Alongside this continues the indirect mediating work of Scripture (the Word of God written), preaching and prophetic utterance (the word of God spoken), and sacraments (the Word of God made visible).

Ahead lies an eternity beyond human history, when we will "know fully, even as [we] have been fully known" (1 Cor 13:12). There character formation and transformation will no longer require the mediation of God's presence and absence to us, for Christ will fully dwell in us and we in him. Then the fullness of Christ's character within us will eliminate any need for mediation, and we will be in direct and everlasting communion with God the Father, God the Son, and God the Holy Spirit. Omnipresence becomes manifest presence. No wonder Paul exclaims: "Now to him who by the power at work within us is able to accomplish abundantly far more than all we can ask or imagine, to him be glory in the church and in Christ Jesus to all generations, forever and ever. Amen" (Eph 3:20–21).

A Panoramic View of God's Purpose in History

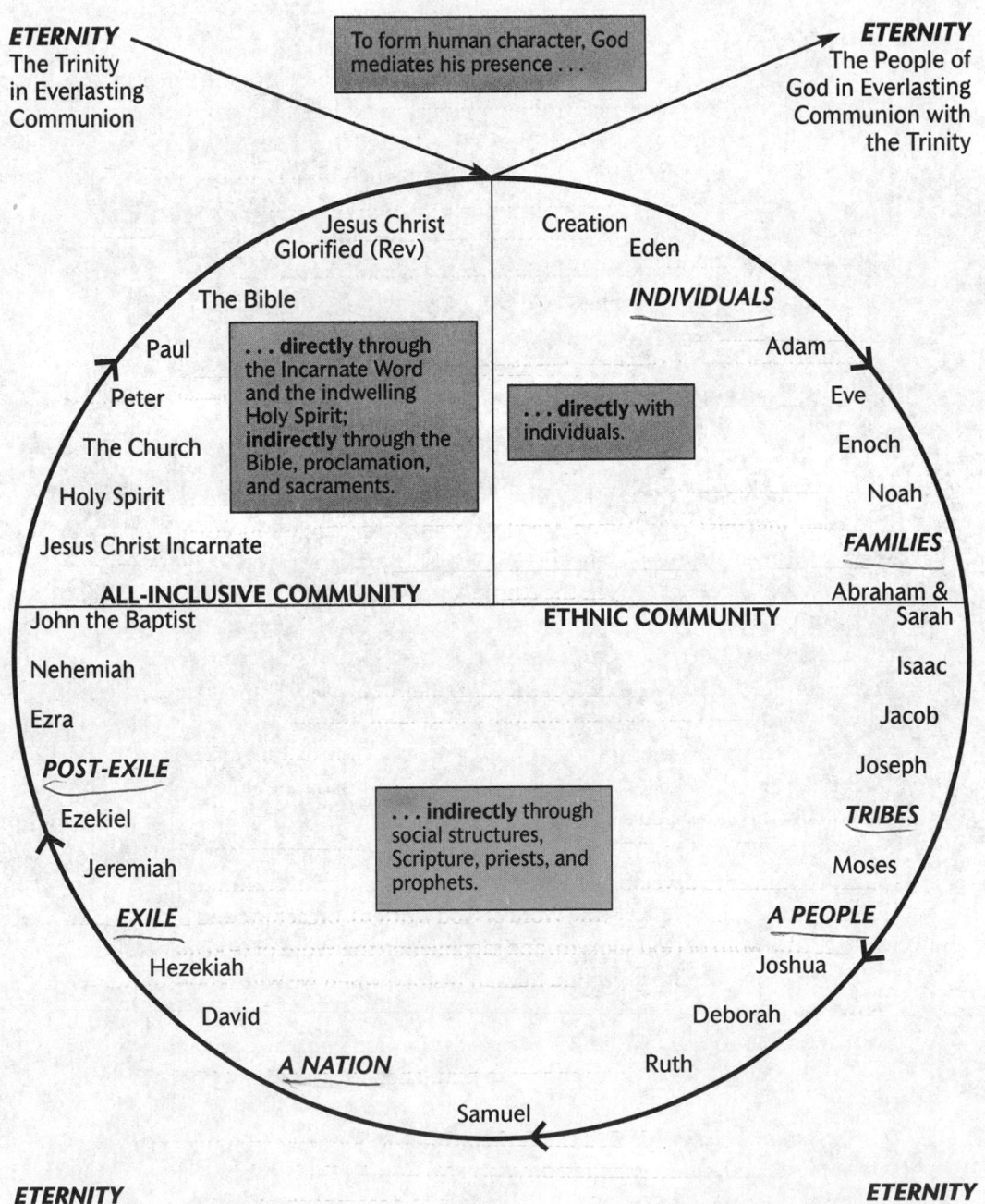

ETERNITY
The Trinity
in Everlasting
Communion

To form human character, God mediates his presence . . .

ETERNITY
The People of
God in Everlasting
Communion with
the Trinity

Jesus Christ
Glorified (Rev)

Creation
Eden

The Bible

INDIVIDUALS

Paul

Adam

. . . **directly** through
the Incarnate Word
and the indwelling
Holy Spirit;
indirectly through the
Bible, proclamation,
and sacraments.

Eve

Peter

Enoch

The Church

. . . **directly** with
individuals.

Holy Spirit

Noah

Jesus Christ Incarnate

FAMILIES

ALL-INCLUSIVE COMMUNITY

Abraham &

John the Baptist

ETHNIC COMMUNITY

Sarah

Nehemiah

Isaac

Ezra

Jacob

POST-EXILE

Joseph

Ezekiel

. . . **indirectly** through
social structures,
Scripture, priests, and
prophets.

TRIBES

Jeremiah

Moses

EXILE

A PEOPLE

Hezekiah

Joshua

David

Deborah

A NATION

Ruth

Samuel

ETERNITY

ETERNITY

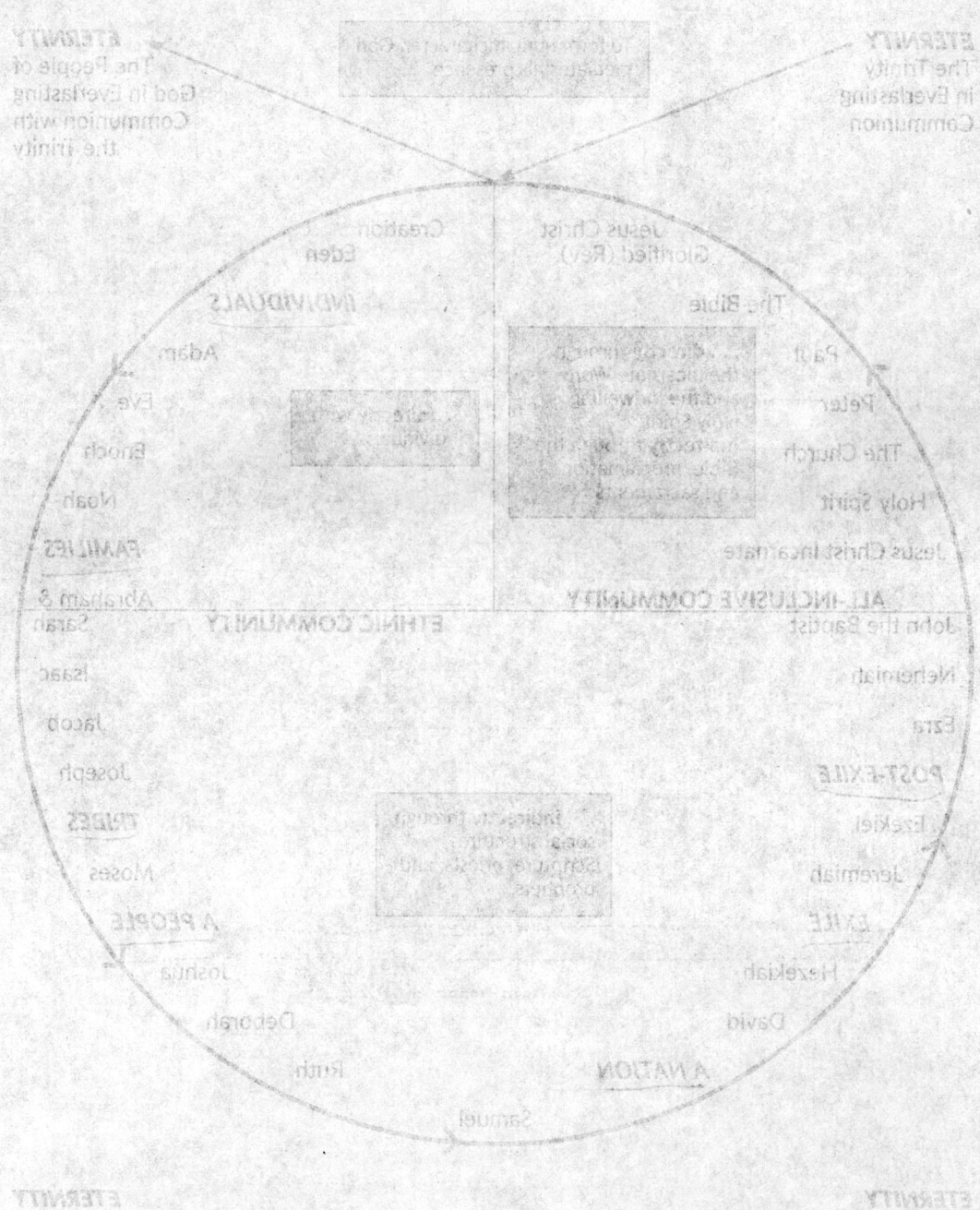

A Panoramic View of God's Purpose in History

THE WITH-GOD LIFE

A Brief Overview of the With-God Life

The panoramic view of biblical history helps us understand the progressive nature of how God has mediated his presence with individuals and groups over the ages to form an all-inclusive community of loving persons. In turn, a brief overview of biblical history helps us grasp how the divine drama took concrete forms in each age as people encountered God. These forms are determined by social context, the idiosyncrasies of individual characters, the specific purpose of divine action, and the limits of human response.

The People of God in Individual Communion. In the beginning God creates the world and places the first humans into the Garden of Eden to work and care for it. Here we see Adam and Eve in partnership encountering God face-to-face. "Then the LORD God made a woman from the rib he had taken out of the man, and he brought her to the man" (Gen 2:22, NIVI). But Adam and Eve disobey God's instructions, are banished from the garden (Gen 3:6–7), and suffer social and physical consequences: domination, alienation, travail, suffering, and mortality. For generations God's Spirit continues to strive with human beings during a downward spiral into immorality and political chaos. Finally, God destroys everyone except Noah and his family (Gen 6:1–7:23).

The People of God Become a Family. With God's appearance to Abram (Gen 12:7), God promises to work through a nomadic, ethnic, patriarchal family to bring blessing to all peoples on earth. But Abraham, Isaac, and Jacob all struggle with the promise: Abraham tries to force its fulfillment, Isaac lies about the identity of his wife, and Jacob tricks his brother out of his birthright. Joseph completes the next step in God's plan as he brings his family from Canaan to the land of Goshen, in the nation of Egypt, where they multiply and develop into tribes.

The People of God in Exodus. But eventually a new king who "did not know Joseph" comes to power in Egypt and enslaves the Israelites, whose "cry for help rose up to

God" (Exod 1:8; 2:23). God hears their groans and responds by sending a reluctant, tongue-tied Moses to lead Abraham's descendants into the Promised Land. During their journey, God gives the people the Mosaic law, the tabernacle, and the ark of the covenant to remind them of his presence.

The People of God in the Promised Land. When the Israelites arrive on the borders of Canaan, Joshua, Moses' successor, becomes their leader as they enter the Promised Land. Commanded by God to totally eliminate the Canaanites, the Israelites disobey, settling into Canaan and adopting many practices of their neighbors. They are obedient to Mosaic law throughout the lifetime of Joshua, but after his death its influence diminishes. When the Israelites begin to do "evil in the sight of the LORD" (e.g., Judg 2:11; 3:7), the surrounding tribes attack them. Because there is no political entity to unify and protect them, the people call out to God and he sends someone to rescue them. After the crisis they are faithful to God for a time, but then they fall into disobedience again. They cry out again, are rescued again, and the cycle repeats. The phrase "all the people did what was right in their own eyes" describes these times (Judg 21:25).

The People of God as a Nation. In spite of the Israelites' many failings, God remains faithful to them. When they ask to be ruled by a king, God tells them the consequences of their choice. Even though their request indicates that they do not want God as their king, in time Israel is transformed into a nation with a monarch. The second king, David, consolidates his power and brings the ark of the covenant to Jerusalem, the political capital. Under David's son Solomon, Israel becomes a center of commerce and trade, and the Temple is built. The people survive the division of the country into two parts—Israel and Judah—and a succession of corrupt rulers. Still they continue their pattern of alternately forsaking and returning to God. As a consequence, God allows Israel (the Northern Kingdom) and then Judah (the Southern Kingdom) to be conquered and their ruling class taken into captivity. God's presence (*shekinah*), which had been with the People of God since the exodus, departs.

The People of God in Travail. Job represents human suffering for all time. "The greatest of all the people of the east" lives a life of influence and luxury, but he loses everything, including the respect of his friends and of his wife, who advises him to "Curse God, and die" (Job 1:3; 2:9). But through his misfortune and grief, through his doubts and questions, through his pain and suffering, he perseveres and points us to the way of being faithful to God in spite of our circumstances.

Just as Job represents human suffering, so Israel becomes a type of the suffering servant. This, in time, evolves into a crucial part of the Jewish messianic expectation: "He was despised and rejected by others; a man of suffering. . . . He was wounded for our transgressions, crushed for our iniquities; . . . He was oppressed, and he was afflicted, yet he did not open his mouth; . . . The righteous one, my servant, shall make many righteous, and he shall bear their iniquities. . . . He poured out himself to death, and was numbered with the transgressors; yet he bore the sin of many, and made intercession for the transgressors" (Isa 53:3, 5, 7, 11–12).

The People of God in Prayer and Worship. Worship of God was formalized during the exodus with the ark of the covenant and the tabernacle. However, with the emergence of the monarchy the king establishes Jerusalem as the center of worship. The Psalms establish a liturgical framework for public worship with all the accoutrements—festivals, pilgrimages, a sacrificial system, a priestly class, and musicians.

The People of God in Daily Life. As the People of God are formed, God is able to transmit his wisdom for daily life. In such books as Proverbs, Ecclesiastes, Song of Solomon, Wisdom of Solomon, and Sirach, mothers and fathers, kings, and sages give counsel through wise sayings about situations faced by ordinary people every day—morality, romance, marriage, injustice, discouragement, laziness, and sexual purity, to name a few.

The People of God in Rebellion. Despite the people's often extreme unfaithfulness, God never passes judgment or takes disciplinary action before warning them about the consequences of their actions. God always sends messengers, emissaries, or prophets "rising early and speaking" (Jer 35:14, KJV) to warn the Israelites that their abandonment of the law, their "whoring" after other gods, and their neglect of the poor would bring disaster upon their heads. From Isaiah and Hosea, Joel and Amos, Obadiah and Micah, and Nahum and Zephaniah the people hear but still reject God's message—and as a result suffer occupation and domination by foreign powers.

The People of God in Exile. After Assyria overruns Israel, its leaders are deported and its political structure is dismantled. Babylon subsequently defeats Assyria and occupies Judah, taking its ruling class into bondage. Prophets are killed, and many of the people are deported. Those who remain work the land; Jerusalem and the Temple lie in ruins. The deported mourn and long to return to Jerusalem in hopes of rebuilding the Temple. Many begin meeting together in the embryonic synagogue. God teaches his people to pray and work for the peace of the cities in which they dwell and the people who oppress them (Jer 29:7). Despite their longing and loss, new avenues of seeking and finding God are found as the people learn to "sing the LORD's song in a strange land" (Ps 137:4, KJV).

The People of God in Restoration. After the Persians defeat the Babylonians, the emperor gives permission to the Jewish exiles to return to Israel and rebuild the Temple. Many of the exiles make the journey and eventually rebuild the Temple, which becomes the center of their identity.

During a series of foreign occupations, Jewish leaders are appointed to political office and the priests gain power as the trustees of religious traditions and practice.

Once the Roman Empire consolidates its power in the Mediterranean world, the governor of Judea, Herod, spearheads the building of yet another Temple. Now legions of priests, Pharisees, Sadducees, scribes, and a shadow government, the Sanhedrin, dictate the formal expression of Judaism, but the synagogue dominates village religious life.

The People of God with Immanuel. Into this maelstrom of political domination by other nations, which fueled age-old resentments and hostilities, Jesus is born in humble circumstances. His upbringing and day-to-day life as a resident of the Roman Empire are very conventional as he masters his father's trade, learns Greek, respects his mother, attends synagogue, keeps the Jewish festivals, and the like.

Jesus' ministry, however, breaks sharply with tradition. His proclamation that "the kingdom of God is among you" (Luke 17:21) breaks upon Jewish society like a tidal wave. People respond to their encounter with the Incarnate Word either by believing and following him or by resisting and rejecting his message. Jesus' execution as a common criminal followed by his bodily resurrection introduces a radical change in the way the People of God develop. The work of God now goes forward with a new intimacy under the direction of the Holy Spirit: "But the hour is coming, and is now here, when the true worshipers will worship the Father in spirit and truth, for the Father seeks such as these to worship him. God is spirit, and those who worship him must worship in spirit and truth" (John 4:23–24).

The People of God in Mission. Once unleashed on earth, the kingdom of God cannot stand still. It bursts the old wineskins of ethnicity and ritual. Jew and Greek, slave and free, male and female are all received freely. A common language, excellent roads, and an era of peace (the *Pax Romana*) open the doors for the growing community to take the message of the kingdom of God throughout the Roman Empire and beyond.

The People of God in Community. God creates us for community, but intimacy often leads to conflict. It was no different for the early Christian community, which brought together people from a multitude of backgrounds and ethnicities. So for Paul and other leaders, the task becomes not only proclaiming that the kingdom of God is here in the person of Jesus Christ, but actualizing it in the lives of individuals in the all-inclusive, loving community that this message creates. Because the leaders could not be with every community all of the time and God's purposes reach far beyond the contemporary problems, theological instruction, pastoral care, and training in discipleship are needed. Thus these first leaders instruct Christians by writing letters to the various groups, letters that continue to instruct us today.

The People of God into Eternity. The efforts of God to form an all-inclusive community of loving persons on earth comes to fulfillment beyond time in the formation of a new heaven and new earth. Old ways of oppression, alienation, travail, suffering, and mortality end, and life eternal takes their place. Worship of self gives way to worship of God. "And the leaves of the tree are for the healing of the nations. Nothing accursed will be found there any more. But the throne of God and of the Lamb will be in it, and his servants will worship him; they will see his face" (Rev 22:2–4). To everyone who longs to be part of this loving, nurturing, all-inclusive community: "The Spirit and the bride say, 'Come.' And let everyone who hears say, 'Come.' And let everyone who is thirsty come. Let anyone who wishes take the water of life as a gift" (Rev 22:17).

Stage of Formation	Scriptures	God's Action	Human Reaction
I. The People of God in Individual Communion	Genesis 1–11*	Creates, instructs, steward of a good creation, banishes, destroys, restores	Disobey, rebel, sacrifice, murder, repent, obey
II. The People of God Become a Family	Genesis 12–50	Gives promise and establishes Abrahamic covenant, makes a great people	Faith, wrestle with God, persevere
III. The People of God in Exodus	Exodus, Leviticus, Numbers, Deuteronomy	Extends mercy, grace, and deliverance from exile; delivers the Mosaic covenant/law	Obey and disobey, develop a distinctive form of ritual
IV. The People of God in the Promised Land	Joshua, Judges, Ruth, 1 Samuel 1–12	Establishes a theocracy, bequeaths the Promised Land	Inhabit the Promised Land, accept judges as mediators
V. The People of God as a Nation	1 Samuel 13–31 & 2 Samuel, 1 & 2 Kings, 1 & 2 Chronicles, 1 Esdras 1	Permits the monarchy, exalts good kings, uses secular nations for blessing	Embrace the monarchy
VI. The People of God in Travail	Job, Psalms of Lament, Ecclesiastes, Lamentations, Tobit	Permits tribulation, allows suffering to strengthen faith	Complain yet remain faithful
VII. The People of God in Prayer and Worship	Psalms, Psalm 151	Establishes liturgical worship	Praise, prayer
VIII. The People of God in Daily Life	Proverbs, Ecclesiastes, Song of Solomon, Wisdom of Solomon, The Wisdom of Jesus Son of Sirach (Ecclesiasticus)	Gives precepts for living in community	Teachable, learning, treasure beautiful words and artistic expression
IX. The People of God in Rebellion	1 Kings 12–2 Kings 25:10, 2 Chronicles 10–36:19, Isaiah, Jeremiah 1–36, Hosea, Joel, Amos, Jonah, Micah, Nahum, Habakkuk, Zephaniah, Judith, Prayer of Manasseh	Proclaims prophetic judgment and redemption, reveals his rule over all nations, promises Immanuel, uses secular nations to bring judgment	Disbelieve and reject, believe false prophets, a faithful remnant emerges
X. The People of God in Exile	2 Kings 25:11–30, 2 Chronicles 36:20–23, Jeremiah 37–52, Lamentations, Ezekiel, Daniel, Obadiah, Baruch, Letter of Jeremiah, Additions to Daniel	Judges, yet remains faithful to covenant promises	Mourn, survive, long for Jerusalem, stand for God without institutions
XI. The People of God in Restoration	Ezra, Nehemiah, Esther, Daniel, Haggai, Zechariah, Malachi, Additions to Esther, 1 Esdras 2–9, & 2 Esdras, 1, 2, 3, & 4 Maccabees, Tobit, Additions to Daniel	Regathers and redeems, restructures social life	Return, obey, rebuild, worship, pursue Messianic figure, compile Septuagint
XII. The People of God with Immanuel	Matthew, Mark, Luke, John	Sends the Son and acts with the Son	Hear and follow, resist and reject
XIII. The People of God in Mission	Acts	Sends the Holy Spirit and creates the Church	Believe and proclaim, disbelieve and persecute
XIV. The People of God in Community	Romans, 1 & 2 Corinthians, Galatians, Ephesians, Philippians, Colossians, 1 & 2 Thessalonians, 1 & 2 Timothy, Titus, Philemon, Hebrews, James, 1 & 2 Peter, 1, 2, & 3 John, Jude	Builds, nurtures, and mobilizes the Church	Become disciples of Jesus Christ and make disciples to the ends of the earth
XV. The People of God into Eternity	Revelation	Reveals infinite progress toward infinite good	Worship and praise, creativity that magnifies God

*Books are placed into categories by content, not by date of composition or type of literature.

Type of Mediation	Locus of Mediation	Social Context	Central Individual(s)	Key Spiritual Disciplines
Face-to-face	Garden, field, Noah's ark	Individuals	Adam, Eve, Enoch, Noah	Practicing the Presence, confession, sacrifice, obedience/submission
Through the family	Tent, desert, jail	Extended families and no-madic clans	Abraham and Sarah, Isaac, Jacob, Joseph	Pilgrimage, sacrifice, chastity
Through God's terrifying acts and the Law	Ark of the covenant, tabernacle	Nomadic tribes	Moses	Submission, silence, simplici-ty, worship
Through the conquest and learning to act with God	Shiloh, Bethel	An ethnic people with fluid leadership	Joshua, Deborah, Ruth, Samson, Gideon, Samuel	Guidance, radical obedience/submission, secrecy
Through the king, prophets, priests, and sacrifices	Altars, consecrated places, first (Solomonic) temple	Political nation on the world stage	Saul, David, Hezekiah, Elijah, Elisha	Worship, prayer
Through suffering and the disappointments of life	Ash heap, hard circum-stances of life	Individual	Job, Israel as the suffering servant	Fasting, solitude, silence, sub-mission, service, celebration
Through song, prayer, wor-ship	Jerusalem, flowering of indi-vidual experience	Nation	David	Prayer, worship, confession, celebration, meditation
Through wisdom	Temple, in the gate, home	Nation triumphant	Solomon	Study, guidance, celebration, meditation
Through the prophets and repression by the Gentiles	High places, Temple dese-crated and destroyed	Nation under siege and dis-persed	Isaiah, Hosea, Amos	Fasting, repentance, obedience/submission, solitude, silence, the law internalized
Through punishment, being a blessing to their captors	Babylon, anyplace, anytime	Ethnics abroad without a po-litical homeland	Ezekiel, Jeremiah	Detachment, fasting, simplic-ity, prayer, silence, service
Through repentance, ser-vice, synagogue study	Rebuilt Temple, synagogue	Remnant on the internation-al scene, ethnics in the lead-ership of other nations	Ezra, Cyrus the Persian, Nehemiah, Maccabees, Essenes, John the Baptist	Pilgrimage, confession, wor-ship, study, service
Through the Incarnate Word and the living presence of the kingdom	Temple and synagogue, boats and hillsides, gather-ings of disciples	Small groups, disciples, apostles, hostile critics	Jesus Christ Incarnate	Celebration, study, pilgrim-age, submission, prayer, sac-rifice, obedience, confession
Through the Holy Spirit, per-secution, and martyrdom	Temple, synagogue, schools, riversides, public square	Jew, Gentile, house churches, abandonment of social strata	Peter, Paul	Speaking and hearing the word, sacrifice, guidance, generosity/service, fasting, prayer
In one another, through Scripture, teaching, preach-ing, prophetic utterance, pastoral care, the Holy Spirit, the sacraments	Gathered community	Community redefined by the Body of Christ, decadent Greco-Roman culture	Peter, Paul, John	Prayer, study, accountability/submission, fellowship
Throughout the cosmos	Focused in the New Jerusalem and extending throughout the cosmos	The Trinity and its community	God the Father, Son, and Holy Spirit; apostles, prophets	Living beyond disciplines

THE OLD

TESTAMENT

I. The People of God in Individual Communion

Scriptures: *Genesis 1–11*

> *The aim of God in history is the creation of an all-inclusive community of loving persons with God himself at the very center of this community as its prime Sustainer and most glorious Inhabitant (Eph 2:19–22; 3:10). The Bible traces the formation of this community from the creation in the Garden of Eden all the way to the new heaven and the new earth. Come, join us as we explore the many dimensions of this with-God history—from individual to family to tribe to people to nation to all humanity—and apply what we learn to our own spiritual formation.*

The story of the Bible is best read by keeping in mind what is to come. We see in Genesis how God begins the process of forming an all-inclusive community with and through individuals.

God's Action

"Let us make humankind in our image, according to our likeness; and let them have dominion" (Gen 1:26). God not only creates; he infuses creativity into the dynamic universe he creates. Human beings reflect that same creativity even as they still need to develop ever more into the image of the Creator. The divine intent was that human beings should take responsibility for the earth ("have dominion") in union with God, and that together they would progressively bring about the condition on earth that God had envisioned.

In the early chapters of Genesis, how God interacts with humanity—the *with-God* life—is expressed in three characteristic ways: it is *conversational, direct,* and *intermittent.*

Conversational. Perhaps the most striking feature of this stage is the conversational tone of all that occurs: God speaks to human beings and they speak back to God. The content of this two-way communication is specific, practical, and propositional (Gen 2:15–16). Human beings respond to God as to Someone with whom they are working. They are constantly interacting with God: obeying, disobeying, questioning, objecting, and rationalizing. The "garden" is not merely a human enterprise they are running alone; rather, it is a cooperative enterprise human beings engage in *with God.*

Even at this early stage God gives the members of the human family substantial room to work out for themselves what they are to do and to be. In fact, God limits them only in the negative: they are not to eat of a certain tree. Everything else is for their choosing. Clearly human freedom is of fundamental importance in God's plan, though Adam and Eve are not set free from the consequences of their choices. They are responsible for their choices.

However, it soon becomes clear that responsibility requires *character,* and that such character will come only through a process of *formation.* Formation, or more specific to our topic, *spiritual formation,* occurs in the dynamic exercise of human choice in response to divine purposes. We are formed by our reactions and choices to what God puts before us, which leaves open the possibility of hazardous results, as we will see throughout the Bible and human history. God alerts human beings to the dangers and tells them what they must do. "Sin is lurking at the door," Cain is told, "but you must master it" (Gen 4:7; cf. 3:3).

Direct. Being conversational, the interaction between God and human beings is direct and not through intermediaries. In fact, in the early parts of the Genesis narrative there are suggestions that God is somehow *physically* present to the very senses of Adam and Eve: "They heard the sound of the LORD God walking in the garden at the time of the evening breeze, and the man and his wife hid themselves from the presence of the LORD God among the trees of the garden" (Gen 3:8). Scripture seems to imply they even see God's face (1:28–29; 2:15, 22), something that would later be forbidden to humanity on pain of death (Exod 33:20–23; Deut 5:24; Judg 13:22).

As the members of the human race choose to act independently and contrary to God's purposes, there is a gradual distancing of God from them; but God's *Spirit*—that is, his nonphysical presence—continues to strive with them (Gen 6:3, KJV). Now the people begin to call upon the name of the Lord in a way that implies One who is *absent* (4:26). Yet some, like Enoch and Noah, still "walked with" God, and God with them. Thus, although the direct interaction of individuals with God is becoming less frequent in general, it does continue with individuals of singularly developed character, whose example becomes a beacon for the whole human family.

Intermittent. It is important to note that God is not constantly present with Adam and Eve or their immediate descendants. He did not "stand over them," but instead made room for them to obey or disobey. And God even allowed them to hide from him in their shame, though he still spoke to them as they hid (Gen 3:8–13). This space allowed by God's "absence" is necessary. In order to move beyond unknowing innocence, we must develop a character and an identity that freely seek harmony with God. Of course, God's "absence" allows for the opposite to happen. Whenever we turn away from God, we take on an identity that focuses exclusively on ourselves, and we then try to master our life and our world on our own. This is exactly what happens in the Garden of Eden, and the dreadful decline catalogued in Paul's Letter to the Romans begins: "For though they knew God, they did not honor him as God or give thanks to him, but they became futile in their thinking, and their senseless minds were darkened" (1:21). The natural outcome is an earth "filled with violence," where "every inclination of the thoughts of their hearts [is] only evil continually" (Gen 6:11, 5).

In response to such an outcome, God judges. In the first general judgment of humanity after the fall of Adam and Eve, one person, Noah, is found worthy of escape and continued blessing. But after Noah, humankind continues on its path of independence from God (Gen 11:4). Hence, in the second general judgment at Babel, no individual is exempted. God sees that there is no limit to people's arrogance and depravity (11:6). To defeat their project of building "a tower with its top in the heavens," God permanently disrupts their communication with each other and scatters them over the face of the entire earth (11:1–9).

Human Reaction

So in the beginning God's presence to humankind was conversational, direct, and intermittent. And with the freedom granted human beings by God's "absenting" himself enough for humanity to make its choices, what did we do? Our responses were characterized by disobeying in God's absence (Adam and Eve) and pursuing human objectives without regard for God's gentle presence (Cain and Abel). Human beings go astray "like sheep"—*as* sheep do, following momentary interests, and the gentleness of God permits this to happen. Human self-will nurtures massive insensitivity and resistance to God's personal overtures and finally causes a hopeless immersion in evil (Gen 6:1–7, 11–13).

However, individuals of character, such as Enoch and Noah, still respond to God, are "selected," and in turn find "favor" with God (Gen 5:21–24; 6:8, 13–22). That is God's way, and it is always so. In this way God lays the foundation for the next form of God-with-us, in Abraham and his family. But early humanity as a whole rejects God and, as the population increases, asserts its power in unified activity against God at Babel.

Blessings and Benefits for Our Formation

The major formational advantage of this individual communion with God is the good effect of God's direct presence. Our lives find their direction when God *is* present with us, and we are directionless without him. Intimate, individual communication with God is something that cannot be done away with in spiritual formation. We must constantly seek out this intimate, individual communion. We need the full assurance of God's greatness and goodness that comes only from his direct presence. This, frankly, cannot be derived from any other source.

The eternal fact of our lives is that we are constantly being upheld by God's direct action upon us. This fact is not abolished by human withdrawal from God; rather, God preserves it and develops other ways to support it, as we shall see in later sections of the biblical record, starting with the stories of Abraham. But being aware of how God is upholding us must run through the texture of our entire life like a golden thread. And we can become aware of his constant work and presence only by experiencing individual communion with God.

The With-God Life

The With-God Life

Limits and Liabilities for Our Formation

But God-with-us in direct, conversational relationship cannot be our whole life. It gives us neither character nor identity. It promotes passivity instead of vigorous righteousness and self-identity with God, whether he is present *or* absent. When God is not actively present with us, there is nothing to pull us or sustain us in a direction toward God. We are left entirely on our own, facing bare choice. And our feelings, desires, and wayward thoughts will triumph—or become tools of God's great enemy, Satan.

The gentleness of God's presence can be resisted. We can even fail to recognize God's presence. Our heart can become hardened in self-will and thus incapable of recognizing when God is moving upon it. Or we may simply reject God's overtures even when we know it is God, failing to appreciate his gentleness. It is sobering to realize that we can grieve and resist the Spirit of God.

Within this conversational, direct, and intermittent form of God-with-us, humanity's progress and development under God is restricted to whatever occurs within individual lives. Humanity as a whole has no identifiable God center or God context within it or around it to draw it toward God. What is lacking in this early stage of human history is, in a word, *mediation*.

From this point onward, God will use mediation to be present with us even when he is "absent." Examples of this mediation are social structures such as the family, the tribe, the nation, and religious institutions such as the tabernacle, the Temple, and the Church. *Mediation* will now be the ongoing story of God-with-us, developing through various forms from Abraham, the friend of God, to the end of the Church age, reaching its fulfillment and perfection in *the* mediator between God and humankind, Christ Jesus (1 Tim 2:5), and in his continuing incarnation in his Body, the Church.   MEDIATOR

Insights and Instructions for Our Formation

What can we learn from this stage of God-with-us? First, we learn that God desires and intends cooperative efforts and direct, conversational relationship with us. Very simply, we are made for this. To use Augustine's famous words, "Thou has made us for thyself, and we are not at rest until we find our rest in thee."

God does not abandon this direct mode of his presence with us after the human failure witnessed in the first chapters of the Bible. God will not be defeated (Rom 8:3–4). Out of respect for the human condition, God establishes *indirect* means for working with us, for our own sake. This *fact* of indirection is plainly spelled out in biblical and human history. It is something we must understand and respect in our own day and in our own spiritual life.

A second thing we learn is why there must be a human, or *mediated,* side to God's relationship to us. Earthly institutions are needed to enable God to be present among us even when, from the merely human point of view, he appears absent. *God's presence on earth in mediated, outward forms is necessary because of the human condition.*

The human condition is such that earthly institutions serve as constant necessary points of reference to God without his being directly present to us.

We also learn from the biblical record that our finitude and limitation cannot be successfully overcome by the immediate presence of the infinite God. Adam and Eve fell despite directly being in God's presence. God has now shown us a different path. We need gradual and humble steps toward God, as can be seen, for example, in God's choice of an aged Bedouin and his barren wife. Or in a shaggy tabernacle built by escaped slaves. Or in a ruddy-cheeked boy smelling of sheep. Such are the humble steps God uses until the One comes who "humbled himself and became obedient to the point of death—even death on a cross" (Phil 2:7–8).

The biblical record of God using these "things on earth" to draw human beings closer to him can instruct us endlessly. And what about us? In the course of our own spiritual formation in Christlikeness, what physical things does God use as his instruments to bring us to the point where we will be able to "reign forever and ever" in a world where there will be no night and we will once again see his face (Rev 22:3–5)?

The With-God Life

[handwritten note: VERY GOOD O ARTICLE ON CHILDHOOD, & CHRISTIANS OF FAMILY]

II. The People of God Become a Family

Scriptures: *Genesis 12–50*

[handwritten note: THOUGHTS FOR MARINA & SARAH ABOUT THE SIGNIFICANCE OF FAMILY — POINT WITH FAMILY + GENEOLOGY]

> *The aim of God in history is the creation of an all-inclusive community of loving persons with God himself at the very center of this community as its prime Sustainer and most glorious Inhabitant (Eph 2:19–22; 3:10). The Bible traces the formation of this community from the creation in the Garden of Eden all the way to the new heaven and the new earth. Come, join us as we explore the many dimensions of this* with-God *history—from individual to family to tribe to people to nation to all humanity—and apply what we learn to our own spiritual formation.*

In Genesis 12–50 we will see the ways God begins to form an all-inclusive community—after the failures in the Garden of Eden and at the tower of Babel—by calling a special family into being.

God's Action

When we read in Genesis the accounts of Abraham lying about Sarah's identity or the selling of Joseph into slavery by his brothers, many of us may wonder how these stories fit into the ongoing history of God-with-us.

They "fit" or, more correctly, are important because this chosen family is the first beachhead of God's mediation, a divine process that will culminate in the incarnation of Jesus Christ, reversing humanity's alienation from God. Indeed, the key theme of Genesis 12–50 is the calling of a family whose impact stretches from its beginnings, throughout history, and into eternity.

Central to the biblical story line of the redemption of humans from their own waywardness is the narrative of a God-called family that gives birth to a nation and its relation to all other families and nations. Through this family all other human families are to be blessed: "This is my covenant with you: You shall be the ancestor of a multitude of nations. . . . I will indeed bless you . . . and by your offspring shall all the nations of the earth gain blessing for themselves, because you have obeyed my voice" (Gen 17:4; 22:17–18). This form of mediation reveals God's way of working in history: steady, grounded, and rooted. God desires to bring all humanity into the state of blessedness and happiness for which Adam and Eve were created, regardless of how long it takes.

With this family of Abraham, Sarah, and their descendants a new phase of God's way of being with us begins. We already have seen *individuals* with God—Adam and Eve in the garden, Noah's isolation in a faithless world, and the collapse of

The With-God Life

human language at Babel—but all of God's efforts to form a community of loving persons with these individuals partially fail. In each instance God does not coerce humans to trust and obey him. Despite the repeated faults and failures of humanity, God continues to find ways to show his grace. But after the massive failure at the tower of Babel, when humans decide to "build . . . a tower with its top in the heavens" and "make a name" for themselves (Gen 11:4), God starts anew and chooses Abraham, so "that he may charge his children and his household after him to keep the way of the LORD by doing righteousness and justice" and become a blessing to all humanity (18:19).

From the biblical record we know that Abraham's family is not the first, for the natural family came into existence with the creation of Eve. But from Adam and Eve to Abraham all families had existed in a state of hopeless sin and waywardness. Abraham's family is the first one called by God to be the means of redeeming all other families. However, for a family to be a blessing to many through the ages, it must be multigenerational, which mandates that it have a place of its own to live. In Abraham's time families could survive for a time without a permanent home, but to guarantee their survival for generations, they needed more secure roots than a Bedouin's tent provided. So with the promise to set apart this family comes also the promise to set apart a land: "And I will give to you, and to your offspring after you, the land where you are now an alien . . . for a perpetual holding" (Gen 17:8).

Each natural family has particularity; that is, it exists in a particular place and in a particular time, and membership is exclusive to those born or adopted into it. The physical descendants of Abraham and Sarah constitute a particular family that God sustains through successive generations. However, Abraham and Sarah's descendants are more than a particular, natural family; they form a unique family, a set-apart family, a family called by God to carry his blessing to all humanity. This family is not chosen because of any merit of its own, but only out of God's grace. It is brought into being not through its own initiative, but solely through the call of God, so that its physical descendants can provide the bloodline for the coming Messiah and so that its spiritual descendants can testify to the existence and love of God.

Human Reaction

Abram, the patriarch of the family, later renamed Abraham by God, responds to God's call in faith and utter trust after leaving his homeland, living in a strange land, and surviving a famine (Gen 15:6). Because of his trust in God's promise that he would have an heir, even heirs as numerous as the stars, Abraham is accounted righteous not by what he accomplishes, but solely because he believes God. Later, Abraham endures more trials—infertility, famine, discord, testing—and bumps up against his human limits as he wonders how the blessing works and, out of fear, tries to force its fulfillment when he fathers a child by the slave Hagar. In spite of his moral failures, Abraham is still counted righteous solely by his belief in God's promise.

How do Abraham's immediate descendants respond to the promise of God to make of them a mighty nation and give them a land of their own? In many different ways, but most show misplaced trust. Isaac shows a lack of trust in the promise when he leaves Canaan during a famine and lies about the identity of his wife, Rebekah. He later trusts his wife and children too much and is deceived into believing Jacob is Esau. Jacob, named "Supplanter," majors in deception and craftiness and is himself deceived by Laban, his father-in-law. In the midst of fleeing from Laban with his two wives and all their possessions, Jacob wrestles with God until he is blessed again. "'You shall no longer be called Jacob, but Israel, for you have striven with God and with humans, and have prevailed.' . . . And there he blessed him" (Gen 32:28–29). Jacob's elder sons sell their younger brother Joseph into slavery, who nevertheless remains a shining example of trust properly placed in God; he rises to a high position in Egypt through which he is able to save his entire family from starvation. In the stories of Abraham's descendants, trust emerges as one of the central signs of the transformation of human character according to God's purposes.

In this extended and often dysfunctional family God establishes and preserves his covenant even when, in the weakness of sinfulness and unformed character, the members of this family try to manipulate the blessing to their own advantage and purposes. Theirs is a nomadic existence until Jacob and his family settle in the region of Goshen in Egypt during a famine. There Jacob's sons become the ancestors of the twelve tribes of Israel, the heirs of the Abrahamic covenant to be fulfilled in Jesus Christ, and living examples of the grace of God.

Blessings and Benefits for Our Formation

When we look at our own nuclear family and all of its problems, we can only marvel that God chooses to be with not only individuals (Adam, Eve, Abel, Enoch, and Noah), but with Abraham and Sarah's entire extended family. By this one action, God embraces and amplifies the importance of a family's continuous history, a history that transcends any one person's life. In depositing his promise to bless all people with a family that has an ongoing history, God elevates that family to a unique position in human history. This family now becomes a repository for practicing and transmitting from generation to generation the teachings it has received from God. So it is today that we learn about our faith from our parents and pass that knowledge on to our children, just as Abraham and Sarah's children learned from them, as did their children in turn, and so on. Before there can be a global community of faith, God chooses to reveal his grace in a particular family that can be a witness to all families.

By choosing a family to carry his message of hope and redemption, God also puts his "stamp of approval" on natural reproductive processes and family relationships. It would have been easy for God to circumvent all human conventions and put in place a plan that would redeem humanity from its rebellion without any participation or cooperation from us. Instead, God reveals himself in the midst of the love and social cohesion of the family, where children are begotten through sexual intercourse and loyalty guarantees the family's survival. Through the nature of a family, God's love and grace is revealed.

The With-God Life

From the account of Abraham and Sarah and their descendants, we discover that God keeps his promises in spite of our faults and lack of trust. We may not be as wishy-washy as Abraham when he gave in to the demands of Sarah or as two-faced as Jacob, but we have our own failings that keep us from enjoying a full, intimate relationship with God. This does not keep him from loving us, providing refuge "under his wings," and delivering us (Ps 91:4). This is a blessing that cannot be calculated.

Another benefit of God-with-us in the family is that we have built-in support in all areas of our faith life. We have mothers and fathers who are praying for us as we take our first tentative steps toward faith. If we come from a large extended family, we can observe the faith of aunts and uncles in the everyday routine of life. They can also verify what our parents tell us about their faith and that of their parents.

Limits and Liabilities for Our Formation

As good as it is for God to mediate his presence through a family, such mediation is not complete. It is only the beginning of God's gradual revelation to a human race content to wallow in the pigpen of disobedience and indifference to the proper formation of individual character, despite God's continuing presence and intervening grace. It will take many more families and many more generations before we see the culmination of this revelation in Jesus Christ and the call of each person to Christ-likeness. Because God began the process of redemption in the context of a family, we are sometimes tempted to put our own family on a pedestal and place it above all other human institutions. The family is a wonderful place to learn our faith story and to advocate our belief in God, but this does not give us reason to worship the family. For the purposes of God's redemption of humanity, the family is not the end, but the means to the end.

The very nature of the family—its narrowness, self-centeredness, and small-mindedness—limits its ability to be the only carrier of the message of the kingdom of God. It is composed of blood relatives of one ethnicity who often fight and become bitter enemies. All of us know stories of siblings who will not speak to each other and of families so clannish that they fail to include anyone else in their circle of faith. These liabilities keep the good news of God's kingdom corked in an ethnic jug.

Just as it is in our own day, Abraham and his family had a limited awareness of what God was doing through them, an awareness that was at times further obscured by narrow family concerns. We can only imagine how Abraham explained to his parents that he was leaving home and going to, well, going to someplace where God promised to be with him. Or what Jacob told Rachel about his limp: "I wrestled with God all night!" She must have replied, "You've got to be joking!" Many of us learned the entire sweep of salvation history from the cradle on, but Abraham and his family did not have this advantage, not to mention the aid of the indwelling Holy Spirit or the fullness of biblical proclamation to help them understand what was happening.

Nor did Abraham's family have a broader faith community from which to derive inspiration. They had no priests, except for Melchezidek, who prefigured the future development of the priestly role. Although they built altars, they had no temple, no rituals, no ordered means of forgiveness manifested through a community of praise. In Abraham and his descendants God is with a family without a law, a priesthood, or a national identity. Small wonder that we might consider it a test to see if this family will be responsive to God's promise. For reasons beyond his control, Abraham's was a "Lone Ranger" faith.

Insights and Instructions for Our Formation

LESSON

In God's mediation through a chosen family we first of all learn that each person ① responds differently to the call of God. From Abraham we learn the primacy of trusting in the promise of God. From Sarah we learn the laughter that comes from ② unmerited grace and our inability to make sense of its workings. From Isaac we learn obedience as he goes with his father to Mt. Moriah to be offered as a sacrifice. From Esau we learn to refrain from self-indulgence. From Jacob we learn perseverance in times of adversity. From Joseph we learn to be persistent in hope and generous in victory. And on it goes.

Second, we learn to wait patiently, expectantly, for God's timing. "By faith ② Abraham obeyed when he was called to set out, . . . stayed for a time in the land he had been promised, . . . looked forward to the city that has foundations, . . . [and] received power of procreation, even though he was too old" (Heb 11:8–11). Today, how many of us would be as patient as Abraham and Sarah?

Third, in spite of our faith in God, we will inevitably fail. In Genesis we see the ③ awful effects of deception, murder, idolatry, distorted sensuality, and disobedience. Sin thwarts the divine purpose, even if temporarily. But amid the sin and disobedience, there is also a steady history of faith and obedience. Paul compares Christian believers to Isaac as "children of the promise," heirs to the blessing of God (Rom 9:7–8). In the midst of our failure, of our sin, of our testing, we trust that God will understand our weakness and provide a means of escape (1 Cor 10:13). We learn that our inevitable failures are opportunities for character formation, ways of overcoming our self-centeredness and moving our habits and actions closer to God's will for our daily lives.

Finally, we learn that we must establish our own family as a beachhead of faith ④ and promise in the midst of an unbelieving world. As grandparents, we interweave love and faith. As aunts and uncles, we make ourselves available to talk about life and its meaning to our nieces and nephews. As parents, we live our faith by example as well as tell about our faith. As siblings, we do all within our power to maintain peace and harmony within our family.

We all come into the world through a family as a result of human male-female relationships whose central purpose is to create families out of love. The focus in this stage of the with-God life is on the exploits and ironies and complications of Abraham and Sarah's family as they relate to each other and to all other families in the world. Join us as we look at the mysteries surrounding their selection and the beginning of God's plan of mediation that will, through this one family, bestow blessings upon all families.

The With-God Life

GENESIS

Spiritual formation begins in the Word of God. God spoke and all of creation came into being. Genesis means "beginning" and opens the Bible with the affirmation of faith that God alone is the source of creation. On the breathing wind of God's speech the earth was formed, night and day were ordered, and every kind of living thing emerged. Created in God's own image, human beings were blessed to become conversation partners with this great God. With a word and a promise God called Abraham and Sarah, and the first family of faith set off on a journey that continues through the community of faith. Through these stories of the creation, the garden of Eden, the flood, and the early ancestors of our faith, readers of Genesis are introduced to the with-God life in the grand scheme of God's creation.

A Narrative Passed Down

Genesis began as an oral tradition of narrative stories passed down from generation to generation in the early community of faith. As with all family history, the people of Israel grew to understand who they were and who they were in relationship to God by the stories that were told. As these stories were remembered and retold again and again, they preserved Israel's religious heritage and took on theological meaning and significance. Certain traditions associated with particular matriarchs and patriarchs centered at places of worship. The stories of Abraham and Sarah were remembered first at Hebron, Isaac and Rebekah at Beer-sheba, and Jacob and Rachel at Bethel. Gradually families gathered as clans and tribes for worship at festivals and covenant renewal ceremonies, and these sacred family narratives came to be shared in common. Over time what began as stories told of the founding families of the People of God were written down and collected together (Gen 12–50), and a prologue (Gen 1–11) was added to affirm the foundation of Israel's beginnings in the larger cosmic order of creation.

See also *"The With-God Life" essays for this section of the Bible, "The People of God in Individual Communion" (for Genesis 1–11), pp. 1–5, and "The People of God Become a Family" (for Genesis 12–50), pp. 7–11.*

From this rich oral tradition many different kinds of literary material came to make up this book of beginnings. There is eloquent hymnic poetry that may come from the early liturgy of ancient worshiping communities. Stories with parallels to ancient Near Eastern religious narrative and mythology were reshaped with monotheistic intent. Long sagas with rich detail narrate the founding characters of faith and formative events among the people of Israel. Cultic stories explain the foundation of particular places of worship, and etiologies describe the origins of customs, places, and names. Genealogies list generations of family members and frame large blocks of material into a coherent structure. These strands of varied materials were gathered and edited into the written text in order to ground all these beginnings in a theology of creation that proclaims that life itself is fashioned by the divine speech of the one sovereign God.

Our Story Within God's Story

The God of Genesis speaks, sees, listens, hears, acts, and is very much involved in the ordinary, everyday, familiar activities of human life. This ancient text is not only lively but relevant, for in the large characters of the Bible's beginnings we find reflections of ourselves; we too are created, ordered, blessed, and called by God. Their stories are our story, interwoven with complicated family sagas of blessing and suffering, sibling rivalry, complex social situations, political intrigue, seasons of abundance and economic hardship, alienation from loved ones, and joyous reunions. Genesis is a complex and richly woven narrative account of the beginnings of the universe, the earth, the human family, and the spiritual formation of the People of God.

Genesis 1–11

The opening chapters of Genesis stand at the beginning of the whole Bible as an affirmation of faith. Genesis 1–11 is Israel's theological narrative about God the Creator, who has a purpose for creation and who chooses to be intimately related to human creatures. The content of these first eleven chapters is sweeping: from the creation of the cosmos to the introduction of human sin and divine judgment, from the judgment of the flood and hope for a renewed creation to the scattering of Babel and the confusion of languages. However broad the dramatic scope, the theological intent is particular. The Creator God of all that is calls human creatures into close, conversational relationship.

The Genesis narrative of creation is prehistory. The individuals named in these early stories, such as Adam, Eve, Cain, Abel, and Noah, are larger-than-life archetypes representing the complex relationship between humankind and God. Similarly, specific events such as the Garden of Eden, Noah and the flood, and the tower of Babel are broadly representative of God's creative interaction with all of humankind.

The designation of these first eleven chapters as prehistory is not to say that the Genesis account of the world's beginnings is unconcerned with history. Indeed, it lays the theological foundation for all of history, showing how God, from the very beginning, is intimately involved in the daily affairs of human persons. The long genealogies serve as a bridge connecting the earliest beginnings of creation with the beginnings of Israel, joining God's intention for the whole created order with the community of the People of God. These genealogies, then, provide a narrative structure of transition from prehistory to historical narrative. The appellation of these opening chapters as prehistory also does not mean that these stories are simply myth. In literary form they parallel stories of creation, the garden, and the flood found in Near Eastern mythology. However, the authors and editors of Genesis were theologians whose clear intention was the proclamation of God. Borrowing from other creation accounts, these writers express the strong belief that the one God of Israel is the very same God of all creation.

Genesis 1–11 is prescientific insofar as it predates modern understandings of cosmology and anthropology. Again, this is not to say that ancient theologians were unconcerned with an explanation of how the world came into being, by what agency, and for what purpose. However, the bold intent of their proclamation was not primitive scientific explanation, but confession of faith. If the listening community were to ask of the account of creation in six days described in Gen 1:1–2:4, "Is it true?" the answer would be a resounding, "Yes, it is true!" God creates order out of chaos. God creates everything in goodness. God gives human creatures special responsibility as stewards of God's good earth. God delights in creation and invites Sabbath rest. These opening chapters of Genesis are an eloquent affirmation of faith for the people of Israel, whose spiritual identity as a worshiping community was rooted in and shaped by these creation stories. Similarly, our with-God story is founded and formed in these same stories.

Genesis 12–50

The call of Abraham moves the Genesis narrative from prehistory of the cosmos into the history of the patriarchs and matriarchs of the People of God. Genesis 1–11 begins with the vast realm of God's creation and ends with the wide scattering abroad of the human family throughout the earth. The whole world has been the stage of God's creative activity in the opening chapters as if seen through a wide-angle lens. In contrast, Genesis 12 zooms in to focus on the specific call of one person in a particular place, one family through whom all the families of the earth will be blessed. Abraham and Sarah send down roots for the family tree as historical individuals uniquely chosen to begin a family of heirs to the promises of God. These family stories are intended to show real people—husbands, wives, parents, and children—in real-life situations with experiences the listening community can identify with. Their with-God stories help interpret our own.

Although the narrative makes a dramatic shift at the beginning of Genesis 12, there is continuity in the role God plays. God's primary mode of communication continues to be divine speech. God, who spoke creation into being in the very beginning, initiates the relationship with the first family of faith with a word: "Now the LORD said to Abram, 'Go . . .'" (12:1). This personal imperative is followed by promises of blessing for this family and all of humankind and inaugurates the history of the People of God. Through the family stories of Abraham, Sarah, and their descendants, in all their rich complexity and ambiguity, the community of faith finds its life defined by the same theological categories of promise, blessing, judgment, redemption, and faithfulness that were implicit in the preceding creation narrative. Despite the wayward wanderings of human beings, God refused to abandon the creation. In sovereign love God's creative speech continues to call the human family into a close divine-human relationship. God continues to create by speaking.

The call of Abraham initiates a journey of faith, and God's intimate involvement with a people can be seen in the rich complexity of the human family. Through Abraham and Sarah, Isaac and Rebekah, Jacob and Rachel, and Joseph and his brothers, God's intimate, creative activity continues in their stories of birth and death and marriage and sibling rivalry and conflict and joy and despair and all the common aspects of human life. Through their hope and hopelessness, trust and mistrust, loyalty and treachery, we discover God's constant faithfulness. At times God is as close as a daily conversation partner, and at other times God's presence must be discerned as from far away. From generation to generation the words, promises, and actions of God work their way among this human family with divine, purposeful intention until the end, when Joseph says to his reunited brothers, "Even though you intended to do harm to me, God intended it for good, in order to preserve a numerous people, as he is doing today" (50:20).

When our contemporary listening community gathers around these ancient stories, what God is doing in our day is illumined by this rich Genesis narrative of beginnings. Even as God spoke creation into being and addressed Abraham with a particular word, so God speaks to individuals and whole communities, calling us into a journey of faith with God as our primary companion. For the Christian community, Genesis grounds our belief in Jesus Christ in the foundational creation narrative of the people of Israel. The promissory relationship God initiated at the beginning defines our life with God and invites us to profess God's good creative purpose through our own lives and in the world. To look back, receive, and embrace this ancient text as God's living word to us today is to look forward with hope. God continues to create order out of chaos. God engages individuals and human communities in conversation with a creative word. God intends that all the families of the earth will be blessed.

—*Agnes W. Norfleet*

Six Days of Creation and the Sabbath

1 In the beginning when God created *a* the heavens and the earth, ²the earth was a formless void and darkness covered the face of the deep, while a wind from God *b* swept over the face of the waters. ³Then God said, "Let there be light"; and there was light. ⁴And God saw that the light was good; and God separated the light from the darkness. ⁵God called the light Day, and the darkness he called Night. And there was evening and there was morning, the first day.

6 And God said, "Let there be a dome in the midst of the waters, and let it separate the waters from the waters." ⁷So God made the dome and separated the waters that were under the dome from the waters that were above the dome. And it was so. ⁸God called the dome Sky. And there was evening and there was morning, the second day.

9 And God said, "Let the waters under the sky be gathered together into one place, and let the dry land appear." And it was so. ¹⁰God called the dry land Earth, and the waters that were gathered together he called Seas. And

God saw that it was good. ¹¹Then God said, "Let the earth put forth vegetation: plants yielding seed, and fruit trees of every kind on earth that bear fruit with the seed in it." And it was so. ¹²The earth brought forth vegetation: plants yielding seed of every kind, and trees of every kind bearing fruit with the seed in it. And God saw that it was good. ¹³And there was evening and there was morning, the third day.

14 And God said, "Let there be lights in the dome of the sky to separate the day from the night; and let them be for signs and for seasons and for days and years, ¹⁵and let them be lights in the dome of the sky to give light upon the earth." And it was so. ¹⁶God made the two great lights—the greater light to rule the day and the lesser light to rule the night—and the stars. ¹⁷God set them in the dome of the sky to give light upon the earth, ¹⁸to rule over the day and over the night, and to separate the light from the darkness. And God

a Or *when God began to create* or *In the beginning God created*   *b* Or *while the spirit of God* or *while a mighty wind*

1:1–2 *In the beginning when God created.* The opening verse of the whole Bible affirms the unique power of God to create. God is the only subject of the verb "to create" in Scripture, and God is the primary subject of all that follows. Over a dark, watery void the Spirit of divine power hovers, preparing to breathe life and create order out of chaos. This exclusive work of God's creative power continues through the rest of Scripture and even extends to communion with humankind today.

1:3–4 *Then God said.* The mode of God's creative power is divine speech. All that is needed for the creation of light, even before the sun and stars have been created (1:16), is God's intrusive word. That word that creates also qualifies what it creates as "good." Before God spoke there had been only darkness and chaos, and now at the utterance of the divine word there is order and goodness.

1:5 *there was evening and there was morning.* The rhythm set by the first day of creation sounds like a solemn, majestic processional hymn of worship with a repeated pattern attesting to the beauty of God's good order. The

initial response to God's creation is praise. Each day begins with evening followed by morning, a reminder that God has been at work in the dark before the dawn's rays awaken a new creation. The generative activity of God precedes any new day.

1:6–8 *Let there be a dome.* God makes room for the life that is to come, separating the waters with a domelike sky and creating a space where there is air to breathe. A plan is under way for spiritual beings to have the breath of life.

1:9–13 *God called the dry land Earth.* A place is prepared with all that is needed to sustain life, and the earth itself is fashioned to produce life. In this one day of creation the word "seed" is used four times. A future is obviously being planted here for generations to come.

1:14–19 *for seasons and for days and years.* The future for which the seeds have been planted is given length of days. The light, which has already been separated from the darkness, is further ordered to distinguish seasons of time. So intensely focused is this Creator God on the earth's being prepared to sustain life that the mention of the stars sounds like an aside.

saw that it was good. ¹⁹And there was evening and there was morning, the fourth day.

20 And God said, "Let the waters bring forth swarms of living creatures, and let birds fly above the earth across the dome of the sky." ²¹So God created the great sea monsters and every living creature that moves, of every kind, with which the waters swarm, and every winged bird of every kind. And God saw that it was good. ²²God blessed them, saying, "Be fruitful and multiply and fill the waters in the seas, and let birds multiply on the earth." ²³And there was evening and there was morning, the fifth day.

24 And God said, "Let the earth bring forth living creatures of every kind: cattle and creeping things and wild animals of the earth of every kind." And it was so. ²⁵God made the wild animals of the earth of every kind, and the cattle of every kind, and everything that creeps upon the ground of every kind. And God saw that it was good.

26 Then God said, "Let us make humankind[a] in our image, according to our likeness; and let them have dominion over the fish of the sea, and over the birds of the air, and over the cattle, and over all the wild animals of the earth,[b] and over every creeping thing that creeps upon the earth."

27 So God created humankind[a] in his image,
    in the image of God he created them;[c]
    male and female he created them.
²⁸God blessed them, and God said to them, "Be fruitful and multiply, and fill the earth and subdue it; and have dominion over the fish of the sea and over the birds of the air and over every living thing that moves upon the earth." ²⁹God said, "See, I have given you every plant yielding seed that is upon the face of all the earth, and every tree with seed in its fruit; you shall have them for food. ³⁰And to every beast of the earth, and to every bird of the air, and to everything that creeps on the earth, everything that has the breath of life, I have given every green plant for food." And it was so. ³¹God saw everything that he had made, and indeed, it was very good. And there was evening and there was morning, the sixth day.

2 Thus the heavens and the earth were finished, and all their multitude. ²And on the seventh day God finished the work that he had done, and he rested on the seventh day from all the work that he had done. ³So God blessed the seventh day and hallowed it,

a Heb *adam*   b Syr: Heb *and over all the earth*
c Heb *him*

1:20–25 *living creatures of every kind.* As life appears to fill the seas and sky, we hear God's first blessing. The blessing to be fertile is the assurance of a future in God's good earth. The bringing forth of domestic as well as wild animals is moving us toward the culminating act of creation.

1:26–27 *Let us make humankind.* There is great scholarly debate as to why the plural "us" refers to God at this climactic moment of creation. Is the narrative referring to a heavenly council or the persons of the Trinity? Is it using a royal idiom? Or is the image of God in which humankind is created intentionally obscured? Apart from this textual mystery, what is absolutely clear is that within this vast creation God wants human company and conversation partners. The word for "humankind," *adam*, comes from the same root word as does "earth" and is a generic term for the human species;

humans, male and female, resemble the Creator.

1:26–30 **THE WITH-GOD LIFE**—*See* Spiritual Disciplines Index

1:28–31 *God blessed them.* Created to share a unique relationship with God, human beings are spoken to directly by the Creator, given capacities to be stewards of creation, and entrusted as caretakers of God's goodness. The story of creation is summarized for our special hearing. Upon the completion of all that God has created, culminating in his relationship with us human creatures, the order is proclaimed "very good."

2:1–3 *God rested.* Sabbath rest is the seventh day of creation. The cessation of work is part of the created order, not a fatigued response. This day looks back at what God has brought into being and is set apart as holy by the Creator, who rests in its goodness.

because on it God rested from all the work that he had done in creation.

4 These are the generations of the heavens and the earth when they were created.

Another Account of the Creation

In the day that the LORD[a] God made the earth and the heavens, [5]when no plant of the field was yet in the earth and no herb of the field had yet sprung up—for the LORD God had not caused it to rain upon the earth, and there was no one to till the ground; [6]but a stream would rise from the earth, and water the whole face of the ground—[7]then the LORD God formed man from the dust of the ground,[b] and breathed into his nostrils the breath of life; and the man became a living being. [8]And the LORD God planted a garden in Eden, in the east; and there he put the man whom he had formed. [9]Out of the ground the LORD God made to grow every tree that is pleasant to the sight and good for food, the tree of life also in the midst of the garden, and the tree of the knowledge of good and evil.

10 A river flows out of Eden to water the garden, and from there it divides and becomes four branches. [11]The name of the first is Pishon; it is the one that flows around the whole land of Havilah, where there is gold; [12]and the gold of that land is good; bdellium

and onyx stone are there. [13]The name of the second river is Gihon; it is the one that flows around the whole land of Cush. [14]The name of the third river is Tigris, which flows east of Assyria. And the fourth river is the Euphrates.

15 The LORD God took the man and put him in the garden of Eden to till it and keep it. [16]And the LORD God commanded the man, "You may freely eat of every tree of the garden; [17]but of the tree of the knowledge of good and evil you shall not eat, for in the day that you eat of it you shall die." *1st mention here*

18 Then the LORD God said, "It is not good that the man should be alone; I will make him a helper as his partner." [19]So out of the ground the LORD God formed every animal of the field and every bird of the air, and brought them to the man to see what he would call them; and whatever the man called every living creature, that was its name. [20]The man gave names to all cattle, and to the birds of the air, and to every animal of the field; but for the man[c] there was not found a helper as his partner. [21]So the LORD God caused a deep sleep to fall upon the man, and he slept; then he took one of his ribs and closed up its place with flesh. [22]And the rib

---

a Heb YHWH, as in other places where "LORD" is spelled with capital letters (see also Exod 3.14-15 with notes).   b Or *formed a man* (Heb *adam*) of *dust from the ground* (Heb *adamah*)   c Or *for Adam*

2:4–17 *the man became a living being.* The creation of man and woman is detailed in a second creation story (2:4–25). This account focuses more narrowly on the place of humankind within creation. God is pictured as a great artisan who forms man from the dust and breathes life into his nostrils, signifying a close and intimate relationship. The four rivers locate the Garden of Eden geographically as a fertile place prepared for human life to thrive. The occupant of the garden is given both freedom and limits, permission and prohibition. Death is mentioned for the first time; and although throughout the rest of the Bible it is understood as part of natural life, here death is related to obedience. Human choices made in freedom have consequences.

2:7–8 THE WITH-GOD LIFE—*See* Spiritual Disciplines Index.

2:18–25 *I will make him a helper.* Human beings are created to live in community. The garden with all of its living abundance is not enough. Even though human beings were created to be in relationship with God and given a vocation like that of God to use speech to name the animals, still they are not meant to be alone and need one another. The creation of woman begins in God's recognition of the human need for companionship. Only after man and woman are created, wholly connected as kin, are human words recorded and the goodness of creation spoken in human speech. It is important to note that the term translated "helper as his partner" (*ezer*) literally means "one corresponding to." It is a word bristling with implications for community. There is not the slightest hint of subordination in the term, and it is wrong and a tragedy that it has often been used in that way.

that the LORD God had taken from the man he made into a woman and brought her to the man. ²³Then the man said,

"This at last is bone of my bones
  and flesh of my flesh;
this one shall be called Woman, *a*
  for out of Man *b* this one was taken."

²⁴Therefore a man leaves his father and his mother and clings to his wife, and they become one flesh. ²⁵And the man and his wife were both naked, and were not ashamed.

The First Sin and Its Punishment

3 Now the serpent was more crafty than any other wild animal that the LORD God had made. He said to the woman, "Did God say, 'You shall not eat from any tree in the garden'?" ²The woman said to the serpent, "We may eat of the fruit of the trees in the garden; ³but God said, 'You shall not eat of the fruit of the tree that is in the middle of the garden, nor shall you touch it, or you shall die.' " ⁴But the serpent said to the woman, "You will not die; ⁵for God knows that when you eat of it your eyes will be opened, and you will be like God, *c* knowing good and evil." ⁶So

when the woman saw that the tree was good for food, and that it was a delight to the eyes, and that the tree was to be desired to make one wise, she took of its fruit and ate; and she also gave some to her husband, who was with her, and he ate. ⁷Then the eyes of both were opened, and they knew that they were naked; and they sewed fig leaves together and made loincloths for themselves.

8 They heard the sound of the LORD God walking in the garden at the time of the evening breeze, and the man and his wife hid themselves from the presence of the LORD God among the trees of the garden. ⁹But the LORD God called to the man, and said to him, "Where are you?" ¹⁰He said, "I heard the sound of you in the garden, and I was afraid, because I was naked; and I hid myself." ¹¹He said, "Who told you that you were naked? Have you eaten from the tree of which I commanded you not to eat?" ¹²The man said, "The woman whom you gave to be with me, she gave me fruit from the tree, and I ate." ¹³Then the LORD God said to the woman,

a Heb *ishshah*   *b* Heb *ish*   *c* Or *gods*

3:1–7 *be like God.* The story of the first temptation introduces us to the elemental conditions of human sin. Sin originates in the human desire to be like God. God, the Giver of enormous freedom, also establishes limits for humankind. When those boundaries are crossed, a break occurs in the divine-human relationship. The temptation provided by the crafty serpent indicates that sin is bound up in creation, perhaps residual chaos out of which God has established order. The wisdom that comes from eating the fruit is the recognition of nakedness, of self-consciousness. This introduction of human sin assures us that the creative work of God in partnership with humankind will be of necessity an ongoing process.

Responding
3:8 THE WITH-GOD LIFE. The phrase "walking in the garden" brings to mind C. Austin Miles's gospel hymn "In the Garden." In it he describes his vision of Mary's intimate, conversational relationship with the resurrected Jesus. Find the words to this song in a hymnal or download them from the Internet. Read them

and Gen 3:8a once a day for a week, lingering over the two selections until the words sink deep into your heart. How has the knowledge that God desires and welcomes human companionship affected your relationship with him? *See also* Spiritual Disciplines Index.

3:8–24 *hid themselves.* We are created with freedom to resist the will of God, and the resulting human sin leads rapidly to cover-up, embarrassment, fear, guilt, blame, and confrontation with the Creator. The man blames the woman, the woman blames the serpent, and God curses the serpent, but God never abandons the relationship with humankind. Indeed, as a gesture of reconciliation God himself fashions more appropriate clothing "of skins." Despite their disobedience man and woman never cease to be conversation partners with God. Although they are given a new vocation to till the land beyond the garden, they are never fully expelled from the presence of God. Even when sin removes us from close proximity with God, God is ever in pursuit of renewed relationship with us.

ADAM AND EVE

The Battle Against Temptation

Selected Scriptures: *Genesis 1–3; Romans 5:12–15; 7:14–25; 8:10*

Adam and Eve stand before us representing all that humanness entails. Their story reminds us that humans fall desperately short of living with God faithfully. Adam and Eve made the choice that any human would have made—they gave in to temptation and attached themselves to the deceiver, Satan, seeking to determine their own course. Adam and Eve broke relationship with God by choosing to eat fruit from the tree God had forbidden. In eating the fruit, they set a course for every human life to come—a course of battling sin and temptation.

In the fifteenth century, Thomas à Kempis wrote about the battle with temptation. Kempis, a monk, was part of a renewal movement in the Netherlands known as the Brothers and Sisters of the Common Life. In *The Imitation of Christ,* Kempis writes: "As long as we live in the world, we cannot escape temptations and tribulations. As it is written in Job, 'Our life on this earth is warfare.' For this reason we must be careful and concerned about our own temptations. We must be watchful in prayer, lest the devil be given an opportunity to deceive us.

"And yet," he continues, "temptations can be useful to us even though they seem to cause us nothing but pain. They are useful because they can make us humble, they can cleanse us, and they can teach us. All of the saints passed through times of temptation and tribulation, and they used them to make progress in the spiritual life. Those who did not deal with temptations successfully fell to the wayside."

"The key to victory," Kempis later explains, "is true humility and patience; in them we overcome the enemy."

Jesus became the holy parallel to Adam, taking for us the curse of sin. He took all that Adam and Eve brought upon themselves and, in humility and patience, endured death so that we could become right with God and have intimate relationship with God for all eternity.

Personal Reflection

- When you think about temptation, what is the first struggle that comes to mind in your life right now? What roles might humility and patience play in helping you overcome this temptation?
- Thomas à Kempis says, "Temptations reveal who we are." What do the temptations you face reveal about who you are? How would a deepened trust in God make these temptations less attractive?

"What is this that you have done?" The woman said, "The serpent tricked me, and I ate." [14]The LORD God said to the serpent,

"Because you have done this,
cursed are you among all animals
and among all wild creatures;
upon your belly you shall go,
and dust you shall eat
all the days of your life.
[15] I will put enmity between you and the woman,
and between your offspring and hers;
he will strike your head,
and you will strike his heel."

[16]To the woman he said,

"I will greatly increase your pangs in childbearing;
in pain you shall bring forth children,
yet your desire shall be for your husband,
and he shall rule over you."

[17]And to the man[a] he said,

"Because you have listened to the voice of your wife,
and have eaten of the tree
about which I commanded you,
'You shall not eat of it,'
cursed is the ground because of you;
in toil you shall eat of it all the days of your life;
[18] thorns and thistles it shall bring forth for you;
and you shall eat the plants of the field.
[19] By the sweat of your face
you shall eat bread
until you return to the ground,
for out of it you were taken;

you are dust,
and to dust you shall return."

20 The man named his wife Eve,[b] because she was the mother of all living. [21]And the LORD God made garments of skins for the man[c] and for his wife, and clothed them.

22 Then the LORD God said, "See, the man has become like one of us, knowing good and evil; and now, he might reach out his hand and take also from the tree of life, and eat, and live forever"— [23]therefore the LORD God sent him forth from the garden of Eden, to till the ground from which he was taken. [24]He drove out the man; and at the east of the garden of Eden he placed the cherubim, and a sword flaming and turning to guard the way to the tree of life.

Cain Murders Abel

4 Now the man knew his wife Eve, and she conceived and bore Cain, saying, "I have produced[d] a man with the help of the LORD." [2]Next she bore his brother Abel. Now Abel was a keeper of sheep, and Cain a tiller of the ground. [3]In the course of time Cain brought to the LORD an offering of the fruit of the ground, [4]and Abel for his part brought of the firstlings of his flock, their fat portions. And the LORD had regard for Abel and his offering, [5]but for Cain and his offering he had no regard. So Cain was very angry, and his countenance fell. [6]The LORD said to Cain, "Why are you angry, and why has your countenance fallen? [7]If you do well, will you not be accepted? And if you do not do well, sin is lurk-

a Or to Adam   b In Heb Eve resembles the word for living   c Or for Adam   d The verb in Heb resembles the word for Cain

---

4:1–16 *Cain . . . his brother Abel.* The story of Cain and Abel escalates the separation caused by sin, leading to competition, violence, and death. Paradoxically the alienation began in the attempt to please God with sacrifices. We are not told why God favored Abel's offering, because the focus of the narrative is on Cain's jealous rage, which follows. This ancient story of sibling rivalry sets the stage for many such stories to follow, including Jacob and Esau (Gen 25) and the prodigal son and the elder brother (Luke 15). In the context of the human family—

life in community with other persons—obedience to God comes hard. Cain's rhetorical question to God, "Am I my brother's keeper?" finds its positive response in God's punishment of Cain. When Cain argues that his judgment is harsh, God returns mercy, offering Cain protection. Though Cain is left to a life of wandering, further removed from the relationship God initially intended for humankind, he still bears the mark of God. God bridges chasms caused by our estrangements.

ing at the door; its desire is for you, but you must master it."

8 Cain said to his brother Abel, "Let us go out to the field."[a] And when they were in the field, Cain rose up against his brother Abel, and killed him. 9Then the LORD said to Cain, "Where is your brother Abel?" He said, "I do not know; am I my brother's keeper?" 10And the LORD said, "What have you done? Listen; your brother's blood is crying out to me from the ground! 11And now you are cursed from the ground, which has opened its mouth to receive your brother's blood from your hand. 12When you till the ground, it will no longer yield to you its strength; you will be a fugitive and a wanderer on the earth." 13Cain said to the LORD, "My punishment is greater than I can bear! 14Today you have driven me away from the soil, and I shall be hidden from your face; I shall be a fugitive and a wanderer on the earth, and anyone who meets me may kill me." 15Then the LORD said to him, "Not so![b] Whoever kills Cain will suffer a sevenfold vengeance." And the LORD put a mark on Cain, so that no one who came upon him would kill him. 16Then Cain went away from the presence of the LORD, and settled in the land of Nod,[c] east of Eden.

Beginnings of Civilization

17 Cain knew his wife, and she conceived and bore Enoch; and he built a city, and named it Enoch after his son Enoch. 18To Enoch was born Irad; and Irad was the father of Mehujael, and Mehujael the father of Methushael, and Methushael the father of Lamech. 19Lamech took two wives; the name of the one was Adah, and the name of the

other Zillah. 20Adah bore Jabal; he was the ancestor of those who live in tents and have livestock. 21His brother's name was Jubal; he was the ancestor of all those who play the lyre and pipe. 22Zillah bore Tubal-cain, who made all kinds of bronze and iron tools. The sister of Tubal-cain was Naamah.

23 Lamech said to his wives:

"Adah and Zillah, hear my voice;
   you wives of Lamech, listen to what I
      say:
 I have killed a man for wounding me,
   a young man for striking me.
24 If Cain is avenged sevenfold,
   truly Lamech seventy-sevenfold."

25 Adam knew his wife again, and she bore a son and named him Seth, for she said, "God has appointed[d] for me another child instead of Abel, because Cain killed him." 26To Seth also a son was born, and he named him Enosh. At that time people began to invoke the name of the LORD.

Adam's Descendants to Noah and His Sons

5 This is the list of the descendants of Adam. When God created humankind,[e] he made them[f] in the likeness of God. 2Male and female he created them, and he blessed them and named them "Humankind"[e] when they were created.

3 When Adam had lived one hundred thirty years, he became the father of a son in his likeness, according to his image, and named him Seth. 4The days of Adam after he became the father of Seth were eight

a Sam Gk Syr Compare Vg: MT lacks *Let us go out to the field*   b Gk Syr Vg: Heb *Therefore*   c That is *Wandering*   d The verb in Heb resembles the word for *Seth*   e Heb *adam*   f Heb *him*

4:14–16 THE WITH-GOD LIFE—*See* Spiritual Disciplines Index.

4:17–26 *people began to invoke the name of the LORD.* Chapter 4, which began with brothers offering individual sacrifices to God, ends in corporate worship. Fulfilling God's earlier blessings to multiply, daughters and sons are born, a city is founded, and a time arrives when people come together to worship God. Worship itself is rooted in the creation narrative of the People of God.

5:1–32 *the descendants of Adam.* This genealogy serves as a bridge connecting the earliest creation of humankind to the family of Noah. The vocation of Adam and Eve to be stewards of creation extends through time from generation to generation. Whatever happens next in the unfolding history of the People of God, we can always look back as far as the earliest beginnings and discover a divine-human relationship conjoined in a delicate and deliberate way.

CAIN

The Snare of Pride

Selected Scripture: *Genesis 4:1–26*

The world's first brotherly rivalry marked more than simply the beginning of family conflict. The story of Cain and his brother, Abel, illustrates from the start of time the continuing conflict between the presence of God and sin in every individual's life. Cain became a farmer, while Abel tended sheep. Both brought to the Lord an offering from their work, and yet God regarded only Abel's with favor. Cain became frustrated and angry. His response to God's displeasure revealed the condition of his heart. Rather than humbling himself before God and seeking how better to please God, he gave in to sin, walked away from God, and turned his anger on his brother. He brought Abel to a field and killed him.

As soon as God saw Cain's anger, God warned: "Sin is lurking at the door; its desire is for you, but you must master it" (Gen 4:7). Cain may not have understood the reason for God's displeasure. He may have viewed God as unjust in favoring Abel. But he had a choice about how to handle his human feelings toward a sovereign God. Through humbling himself and stepping away from his feelings, he could have entered into the Spiritual Discipline of confession, seeking to open himself to God and become right in God's eyes. Confession could have helped him master the sin "lurking at the door."

St. Alphonsus Liguori explains how confession works: "For a good confession three things are necessary: an examination of conscience, sorrow, and a determination to avoid sin." Cain needed, first, to look honestly inside himself. He needed to see his heart toward God for what it was. Upon seeing himself honestly, Cain needed to express sorrow. In *Celebration of Discipline,* Richard Foster describes this type of sorrow as "deep regret at having offended the heart of the Father." Foster warns that the sorrow involved in confession must reside deeper than at the merely emotional level. Rather, the needed sorrow must come as an intentional decision of the will.

Finally, Cain needed a determination to avoid sinning—he needed to yearn for holiness. If at this point in the process of confession he still did not want to avoid sin, he needed at least the desire to avoid sin. Just as Jesus taught about the mustard seed—the smallest bit of faith can move mountains (Matt 17:20)—so also with confession. God can work with even a fledgling effort at avoiding sin.

Personal Reflection

- What sin in your past has been most difficult to confess? Have you walked the path of true repentance, through examination of conscience, sorrow, and a determination to avoid sin? If not, how can you begin to walk it now?
- Have you made confession an ongoing Spiritual Discipline in your life? In what way might you need to involve another person to hear your confession and help you accept Christ's forgiveness? (Remember, "God has given us our brothers and sisters to stand in Christ's stead and make God's presence and forgiveness real to us"—Foster, *Celebration of Discipline.*)

hundred years; and he had other sons and daughters. [5]Thus all the days that Adam lived were nine hundred thirty years; and he died.

6 When Seth had lived one hundred five years, he became the father of Enosh. [7]Seth lived after the birth of Enosh eight hundred seven years, and had other sons and daughters. [8]Thus all the days of Seth were nine hundred twelve years; and he died.

9 When Enosh had lived ninety years, he became the father of Kenan. [10]Enosh lived after the birth of Kenan eight hundred fifteen years, and had other sons and daughters. [11]Thus all the days of Enosh were nine hundred five years; and he died.

12 When Kenan had lived seventy years, he became the father of Mahalalel. [13]Kenan lived after the birth of Mahalalel eight hundred and forty years, and had other sons and daughters. [14]Thus all the days of Kenan were nine hundred and ten years; and he died.

15 When Mahalalel had lived sixty-five years, he became the father of Jared. [16]Mahalalel lived after the birth of Jared eight hundred thirty years, and had other sons and daughters. [17]Thus all the days of Mahalalel were eight hundred ninety-five years; and he died.

18 When Jared had lived one hundred sixty-two years he became the father of Enoch. [19]Jared lived after the birth of Enoch eight hundred years, and had other sons and daughters. [20]Thus all the days of Jared were nine hundred sixty-two years; and he died.

21 When Enoch had lived sixty-five years, he became the father of Methuselah. [22]Enoch walked with God after the birth of Methuselah three hundred years, and had other sons and daughters. [23]Thus all the days of Enoch were three hundred sixty-five years. [24]Enoch walked with God; then he was no more, because God took him.

25 When Methuselah had lived one hundred eighty-seven years, he became the father of Lamech. [26]Methuselah lived after the birth of Lamech seven hundred eighty-two years, and had other sons and daughters. [27]Thus all the days of Methuselah were nine hundred sixty-nine years; and he died.

28 When Lamech had lived one hundred eighty-two years, he became the father of a son; [29]he named him Noah, saying, "Out of the ground that the LORD has cursed this one shall bring us relief from our work and from the toil of our hands." [30]Lamech lived after the birth of Noah five hundred ninety-five years, and had other sons and daughters. [31]Thus all the days of Lamech were seven hundred seventy-seven years; and he died.

32 After Noah was five hundred years old, Noah became the father of Shem, Ham, and Japheth.

The Wickedness of Humankind

6 When people began to multiply on the face of the ground, and daughters were born to them, [2]the sons of God saw that they were fair; and they took wives for themselves of all that they chose. [3]Then the LORD said, "My spirit shall not abide [a] in mortals forever, for they are flesh; their days shall be one hundred twenty years." [4]The Nephilim were on the earth in those days—and also afterward—when the sons of God went in to the daughters of humans, who bore children to them. These were the heroes that were of old, warriors of renown.

5 The LORD saw that the wickedness of humankind was great in the earth, and that

a Meaning of Heb uncertain

6:5–22 *the wickedness of humankind was great in the earth.* God prepares for the flood and makes a plan to save a family. The violence that began between the sibling children of Adam and Eve increases to the extent that God cannot bear to look upon it any longer. God surveys human life on earth with broad vision, reacts with divine anguish, and decides to destroy what has been created. Humanity is so mired in sin that the text reads as if God is considering the whole creation a mistake from the beginning. Yet God will not completely abandon creation. A righteous man is found to preserve a remnant of goodness. With precise instructions for building the ark and preparing for life upon it, God makes a covenant with Noah to preserve a future for all of humankind.

every inclination of the thoughts of their hearts was only evil continually. 6And the LORD was sorry that he had made humankind on the earth, and it grieved him to his heart. 7So the LORD said, "I will blot out from the earth the human beings I have created—people together with animals and creeping things and birds of the air, for I am sorry that I have made them." 8But Noah found favor in the sight of the LORD.

Noah Pleases God

9 These are the descendants of Noah. Noah was a righteous man, blameless in his generation; Noah walked with God. 10And Noah had three sons, Shem, Ham, and Japheth.

11 Now the earth was corrupt in God's sight, and the earth was filled with violence. 12And God saw that the earth was corrupt; for all flesh had corrupted its ways upon the earth. 13And God said to Noah, "I have determined to make an end of all flesh, for the earth is filled with violence because of them; now I am going to destroy them along with the earth. 14Make yourself an ark of cypress*a* wood; make rooms in the ark, and cover it inside and out with pitch. 15This is how you are to make it: the length of the ark three hundred cubits, its width fifty cubits, and its height thirty cubits. 16Make a roof*b* for the ark, and finish it to a cubit above; and put the door of the ark in its side; make it with lower, second, and third decks. 17For my part, I am going to bring a flood of waters on the earth, to destroy from under heaven all flesh in which is the breath of life; everything that is on the earth shall die. 18But I will establish my covenant with you; and you shall come into the ark, you, your sons, your wife, and your sons' wives with you. 19And of every living thing, of all flesh, you shall bring two of every kind into the ark, to keep them alive with you; they shall be male and female. 20Of the birds according to their kinds, and of the animals according to their kinds, of every creeping thing of the ground according to its kind, two of every kind shall come in to you, to keep them alive. 21Also take with you every kind of food that is eaten, and store it up; and it shall serve as food for you and for them." 22Noah did this; he did all that God commanded him.

The Great Flood

7 Then the LORD said to Noah, "Go into the ark, you and all your household, for I have seen that you alone are righteous before me in this generation. 2Take with you seven pairs of all clean animals, the male and its mate; and a pair of the animals that are not clean, the male and its mate; 3and seven pairs of the birds of the air also, male and female, to keep their kind alive on the face of all the earth. 4For in seven days I will send rain on the earth for forty days and forty nights; and every living thing that I have made I will blot out from the face of the ground." 5And Noah did all that the LORD had commanded him.

6 Noah was six hundred years old when the flood of waters came on the earth. 7And Noah with his sons and his wife and his sons' wives went into the ark to escape the waters of the flood. 8Of clean animals, and of animals that are not clean, and of birds, and of everything that creeps on the ground, 9two and two, male and female, went into the ark with Noah, as God had commanded Noah. 10And after seven days the waters of the flood came on the earth.

11 In the six hundredth year of Noah's life, in the second month, on the seventeenth day of the month, on that day all the fountains of the great deep burst forth, and the windows of the heavens were opened. 12The rain fell on the earth forty days and forty nights. 13On the very same day Noah with his sons, Shem and Ham and Japheth, and

a Meaning of Heb uncertain   *b* Or *window*

7:1–24 *the flood of waters came on the earth.* Only after careful preparation to preserve some life does God bring about the great flood. As a return to the primeval chaos of the opening verses of Genesis, waters once separated by the dome of the sky now burst forth from both below and above. All of creation is covered over unto death, save the ark with its hope for the future floating on the surface. The earth awaits a new creation.

Noah's wife and the three wives of his sons entered the ark, 14they and every wild animal of every kind, and all domestic animals of every kind, and every creeping thing that creeps on the earth, and every bird of every kind—every bird, every winged creature. 15They went into the ark with Noah, two and two of all flesh in which there was the breath of life. 16And those that entered, male and female of all flesh, went in as God had commanded him; and the LORD shut him in.

17 The flood continued forty days on the earth; and the waters increased, and bore up the ark, and it rose high above the earth. 18The waters swelled and increased greatly on the earth; and the ark floated on the face of the waters. 19The waters swelled so mightily on the earth that all the high mountains under the whole heaven were covered; 20the waters swelled above the mountains, covering them fifteen cubits deep. 21And all flesh died that moved on the earth, birds, domestic animals, wild animals, all swarming creatures that swarm on the earth, and all human beings; 22everything on dry land in whose nostrils was the breath of life died. 23He blotted out every living thing that was on the face of the ground, human beings and animals and creeping things and birds of the air; they were blotted out from the earth. Only Noah was left, and those that were with him in the ark. 24And the waters swelled on the earth for one hundred fifty days.

The Flood Subsides

8 But God remembered Noah and all the wild animals and all the domestic animals that were with him in the ark. And God made a wind blow over the earth, and the waters subsided; 2the fountains of the deep and the windows of the heavens were closed, the rain from the heavens was restrained, 3and the waters gradually receded from the earth. At the end of one hundred fifty days the waters had abated; 4and in the seventh month, on the seventeenth day of the month, the ark came to rest on the moun-

tains of Ararat. 5The waters continued to abate until the tenth month; in the tenth month, on the first day of the month, the tops of the mountains appeared.

6 At the end of forty days Noah opened the window of the ark that he had made 7and sent out the raven; and it went to and fro until the waters were dried up from the earth. 8Then he sent out the dove from him, to see if the waters had subsided from the face of the ground; 9but the dove found no place to set its foot, and it returned to him to the ark, for the waters were still on the face of the whole earth. So he put out his hand and took it and brought it into the ark with him. 10He waited another seven days, and again he sent out the dove from the ark; 11and the dove came back to him in the evening, and there in its beak was a freshly plucked olive leaf; so Noah knew that the waters had subsided from the earth. 12Then he waited another seven days, and sent out the dove; and it did not return to him any more.

13 In the six hundred first year, in the first month, on the first day of the month, the waters were dried up from the earth; and Noah removed the covering of the ark, and looked, and saw that the face of the ground was drying. 14In the second month, on the twenty-seventh day of the month, the earth was dry. 15Then God said to Noah, 16"Go out of the ark, you and your wife, and your sons and your sons' wives with you. 17Bring out with you every living thing that is with you of all flesh—birds and animals and every creeping thing that creeps on the earth—so that they may abound on the earth, and be fruitful and multiply on the earth." 18So Noah went out with his sons and his wife and his sons' wives. 19And every animal, every creeping thing, and every bird, everything that moves on the earth, went out of the ark by families.

God's Promise to Noah   WORSHIP

20 Then Noah built an altar to the LORD, and took of every clean animal and of every clean bird, and offered burnt offerings on

---

8:1–19 *God remembered* Noah. The covenant between God and Noah is dependent upon God's own memory. God remembers and again blesses creation and the human family through Noah. Our hope for all new beginnings emanates from God, who remembers.

NOAH

A Long Obedience

Selected Scriptures: *Genesis 6–9; Hebrews 11:7*

Imagine you live in an evil and corrupt world and God has selected *you* as the only righteous person. God tells you he plans to destroy all people except you and your family and that he wants you to begin a decades-long project in preparation for the destruction. The job will take all your time, involve your family, and cause you to appear senile or delusional to everyone around you. The scenario tends toward science fiction, yet it is Noah's story. Noah became obedient to a task perhaps more outrageous and more long-lasting than anything asked of anyone else in the Bible. He spent 120 years building a ship in a place where there was no great body of water for hundreds of miles. He did the unthinkable without objection or doubt, because he knew and loved God through many years of living in close union with him.

Obedience of Noah's kind appears laughable to many. Giving up one's entire life and reputation for a cause with no guaranteed outcome may seem absurd. Yet still God asks for unflagging, holy obedience. Whether he wants us to build a boat or befriend a neighbor, prepare for rain or prepare for life in another culture, shut our family in an ark or shut off the television, he asks that we obey for as long as he asks it.

In *A Long Obedience in the Same Direction* Eugene Peterson explains the challenge of such obedience in today's "instant society": "We assume that if something can be done at all, it can be done quickly and efficiently. Our attention spans have been conditioned by thirty-second commercials. . . . There is a great market for religious experience in our world; there is little inclination to sign up for a long apprenticeship in what earlier generations of Christians called holiness."

John Calvin said, "True knowledge of God is born out of obedience." At nearly five hundred years old when he began building the ark, Noah had already spent much time obeying God's voice in his life. He already knew God well. The years he spent building the ark only served to further deepen his knowledge of God, and this knowledge produced a great well of joy within. His long work of building was not a burdensome, doubt-ridden chore, but rather a joy-filled act of communion with the lover of his soul.

Personal Reflection

- When you consider the Spiritual Discipline of obedience, what comes to mind? Do you think of a prompting you have been receiving from God about a specific action you should take or a behavior you should change? What does this tell you about God and yourself?
- Have you had the experience, mentioned above, of obeying and finding later that through obedience you gained a deeper knowledge of God?

the altar. 21And when the LORD smelled the pleasing odor, the LORD said in his heart, "I will never again curse the ground because of humankind, for the inclination of the human heart is evil from youth; nor will I ever again destroy every living creature as I have done.

22 As long as the earth endures,
        seedtime and harvest, cold and heat,
    summer and winter, day and night,
        shall not cease."

The Covenant with Noah

9 God blessed Noah and his sons, and said to them, "Be fruitful and multiply, and fill the earth. 2The fear and dread of you shall rest on every animal of the earth, and on every bird of the air, on everything that creeps on the ground, and on all the fish of the sea; into your hand they are delivered. 3Every moving thing that lives shall be food for you; and just as I gave you the green plants, I give you everything. 4Only, you shall not eat flesh with its life, that is, its blood. 5For your own lifeblood I will surely require a reckoning: from every animal I will require it and from human beings, each one for the blood of another, I will require a reckoning for human life.

6   Whoever sheds the blood of a human,
        by a human shall that person's blood
            be shed;
    for in his own image
        God made humankind.

7And you, be fruitful and multiply, abound on the earth and multiply in it."

8   Then God said to Noah and to his sons with him, 9"As for me, I am establishing my covenant with you and your descendants after you, 10and with every living creature that is with you, the birds, the domestic animals, and every animal of the earth with you, as many as came out of the ark. a 11I establish my covenant with you, that never again shall all flesh be cut off by the waters of a flood, and never again shall there be a flood to destroy the earth." 12God said, "This is the sign of the covenant that I make between me and you and every living creature that is with you, for all future generations: 13I have set my bow in the clouds, and it shall be a sign of the covenant between me and the earth. 14When I bring clouds over the earth and the bow is seen in the clouds, 15I will remember my covenant that is between me and you and every living creature of all flesh; and the waters shall never again become a flood to destroy all flesh. 16When the bow is in the clouds, I will see it and remember the everlasting covenant between God and every living creature of all flesh that is on the earth." 17God said to Noah, "This is the sign of the covenant that I have established between me and all flesh that is on the earth."

Noah and His Sons

18   The sons of Noah who went out of the ark were Shem, Ham, and Japheth. Ham was

a Gk: Heb adds *every animal of the earth*

8:20–22 *Then Noah built an altar to the LORD.* The faithful response to God's saving activity is always worship. Worship is the focal point of this new relationship. At the pleasing smell of sacrifices God promises never to destroy the earth again because of the sin of humankind. God acknowledges the moral complexity of human creatures and concedes that even the waters of the flood cannot make amends. The future of this divine-human relationship must hold new possibilities. The Creator reestablishes the rhythm of creation, as orchestrated in the beginning, and commits to its future.

9:1–17 *God blessed Noah and his sons.* The drama of the flood gives way to a new

beginning, marked by the "sign of the covenant" (v 17). God takes the bow, an instrument of violence, and hangs it in the sky as a reminder *to God* that the peace of the covenant shall not be broken. God bends toward humankind beckoning a renewed contract, a covenantal relationship of mutual responsibility. God will never again destroy the earth with a flood; humans have renewed responsibility to care for one another. This covenant reminds us of the ever delicate balance in the divine-human relationship. God creates and blesses, judges and re-creates. We are invited to respond worshipfully and responsibly.

the father of Canaan. [19]These three were the sons of Noah; and from these the whole earth was peopled.

20 Noah, a man of the soil, was the first to plant a vineyard. [21]He drank some of the wine and became drunk, and he lay uncovered in his tent. [22]And Ham, the father of Canaan, saw the nakedness of his father, and told his two brothers outside. [23]Then Shem and Japheth took a garment, laid it on both their shoulders, and walked backward and covered the nakedness of their father; their faces were turned away, and they did not see their father's nakedness. [24]When Noah awoke from his wine and knew what his youngest son had done to him, [25]he said,

"Cursed be Canaan;
    lowest of slaves shall he be to his
        brothers."
[26]He also said,

"Blessed by the LORD my God be Shem;
    and let Canaan be his slave.
[27] May God make space for[a] Japheth,
    and let him live in the tents of Shem;
    and let Canaan be his slave."

28 After the flood Noah lived three hundred fifty years. [29]All the days of Noah were nine hundred fifty years; and he died.

Nations Descended from Noah

10 These are the descendants of Noah's sons, Shem, Ham, and Japheth; children were born to them after the flood.

2 The descendants of Japheth: Gomer, Magog, Madai, Javan, Tubal, Meshech, and Tiras. [3]The descendants of Gomer: Ashkenaz, Riphath, and Togarmah. [4]The descendants of Javan: Elishah, Tarshish, Kittim, and Rodanim.[b] [5]From these the coastland peoples spread. These are the descendants of Japheth[c] in their lands, with their own language, by their families, in their nations.

6 The descendants of Ham: Cush, Egypt, Put, and Canaan. [7]The descendants of Cush: Seba, Havilah, Sabtah, Raamah, and Sabteca. The descendants of Raamah: Sheba and Dedan. [8]Cush became the father of Nimrod; he was the first on earth to become a mighty warrior. [9]He was a mighty hunter before the LORD; therefore it is said, "Like Nimrod a mighty hunter before the LORD." [10]The beginning of his kingdom was Babel, Erech, and Accad, all of them in the land of Shinar. [11]From that land he went into Assyria, and built Nineveh, Rehoboth-ir, Calah, and [12]Resen between Nineveh and Calah; that is the great city. [13]Egypt became the father of Ludim, Anamim, Lehabim, Naphtuhim, [14]Pathrusim, Casluhim, and Caphtorim, from which the Philistines come.[d]

15 Canaan became the father of Sidon his firstborn, and Heth, [16]and the Jebusites, the Amorites, the Girgashites, [17]the Hivites, the Arkites, the Sinites, [18]the Arvadites, the Zemarites, and the Hamathites. Afterward the families of the Canaanites spread abroad. [19]And the territory of the Canaanites extended from Sidon, in the direction of Gerar, as far as Gaza, and in the direction of Sodom, Gomorrah, Admah, and Zeboiim, as far as Lasha. [20]These are the descendants of Ham, by their families, their languages, their lands, and their nations.

21 To Shem also, the father of all the children of Eber, the elder brother of Japheth, children were born. [22]The descendants of Shem: Elam, Asshur, Arpachshad, Lud, and Aram. [23]The descendants of Aram: Uz, Hul, Gether, and Mash. [24]Arpachshad became the father of Shelah; and Shelah became the father of Eber. [25]To Eber were born two sons: the name of the one was Peleg,[e] for in his days the earth was divided, and his broth-

---

a Heb yapht, a play on Japheth   b Heb Mss Sam Gk See 1 Chr 1.7: MT Dodanim   c Compare verses 20, 31. Heb lacks These are the descendants of Japheth d Cn: Heb Casluhim, from which the Philistines come, and Caphtorim   e That is Division

---

9:18–27 from these the whole earth was peopled. This wild story about Noah's latter career in agriculture and his drunken night is a narrative explanation for how the world became populated with varied and diverse peoples. As the first farmer, Noah fulfills the vocation of human beings as tillers of soil (3:23), and his sons are dispersed to multiply and fill the earth (1:28; 9:7). Varied peoples of neighboring lands find their origins in the story of creation, bridging the gap between prehistory and history.

er's name was Joktan. ²⁶Joktan became the father of Almodad, Sheleph, Hazarmaveth, Jerah, ²⁷Hadoram, Uzal, Diklah, ²⁸Obal, Abimael, Sheba, ²⁹Ophir, Havilah, and Jobab; all these were the descendants of Joktan. ³⁰The territory in which they lived extended from Mesha in the direction of Sephar, the hill country of the east. ³¹These are the descendants of Shem, by their families, their languages, their lands, and their nations.

32 These are the families of Noah's sons, according to their genealogies, in their nations; and from these the nations spread abroad on the earth after the flood.

The Tower of Babel

11 Now the whole earth had one language and the same words. ²And as they migrated from the east,ᵃ they came upon a plain in the land of Shinar and settled there. ³And they said to one another, "Come, let us make bricks, and burn them thoroughly." And they had brick for stone, and bitumen for mortar. ⁴Then they said, "Come, let us build ourselves a city, and a tower with its top in the heavens, and let us make a name for ourselves; otherwise we shall be scattered abroad upon the face of the whole earth." ⁵The LORD came down to see the city and the tower, which mortals had built. ⁶And the LORD said, "Look, they are one people, and they have all one language; and this is only

the beginning of what they will do; nothing that they propose to do will now be impossible for them. ⁷Come, let us go down, and confuse their language there, so that they will not understand one another's speech." ⁸So the LORD scattered them abroad from there over the face of all the earth, and they left off building the city. ⁹Therefore it was called Babel, because there the LORD confusedᵇ the language of all the earth; and from there the LORD scattered them abroad over the face of all the earth.

Descendants of Shem

10 These are the descendants of Shem. When Shem was one hundred years old, he became the father of Arpachshad two years after the flood; ¹¹and Shem lived after the birth of Arpachshad five hundred years, and had other sons and daughters.

12 When Arpachshad had lived thirty-five years, he became the father of Shelah; ¹³and Arpachshad lived after the birth of Shelah four hundred three years, and had other sons and daughters.

14 When Shelah had lived thirty years, he became the father of Eber; ¹⁵and Shelah lived after the birth of Eber four hundred three years, and had other sons and daughters.

16 When Eber had lived thirty-four years,

a Or *migrated eastward*   *b* Heb *balal*, meaning *to confuse*

11:1–9 *Now the whole earth had one language.* Different streams of the human family gather at Babel, and human aspirations grow. As in the Garden of Eden (3:5) they seek to overreach into the knowledge and realm of God. By their own accord they try to ascend to the heavens and seek to make a name for themselves. Individual disobedience had its own consequences resulting in expulsion from the garden (3:23), sibling rivalry gave way to a pervasive human wickedness (6:5), and now a collective maneuvering to become more like God results in the scattering of the people abroad. With a play on words, what happens at Babel foreshadows a future exile in Babylon. More significantly for Christian readers, what happens at Babel will be reversed at Pentecost (Acts 2), when those whose languages were once confused hear one another with miraculous understanding. The creation narrative, which began with God ordering chaos, ends with the chaotic scattering and confused tongues of the People of God. The prehistory ends awaiting yet another new intrusive and creative word.

11:10–32 *the descendants of Shem.* The narrative traces the genealogy from the son of Noah to Abraham. The wide-angle survey of creation in disarray turns to the narrow focus on a man named Abram, in a town called Ur, with a barren wife and no child. At this juncture the story appears to have reached a dead end, but, looking back, we know the creative power of God to bring life where there is seemingly no hope for the future.

he became the father of Peleg; 17and Eber lived after the birth of Peleg four hundred thirty years, and had other sons and daughters.

18 When Peleg had lived thirty years, he became the father of Reu; 19and Peleg lived after the birth of Reu two hundred nine years, and had other sons and daughters.

20 When Reu had lived thirty-two years, he became the father of Serug; 21and Reu lived after the birth of Serug two hundred seven years, and had other sons and daughters.

22 When Serug had lived thirty years, he became the father of Nahor; 23and Serug lived after the birth of Nahor two hundred years, and had other sons and daughters.

24 When Nahor had lived twenty-nine years, he became the father of Terah; 25and Nahor lived after the birth of Terah one hundred nineteen years, and had other sons and daughters.

26 When Terah had lived seventy years, he became the father of Abram, Nahor, and Haran.

Descendants of Terah

27 Now these are the descendants of Terah. Terah was the father of Abram, Nahor, and Haran; and Haran was the father of Lot. 28Haran died before his father Terah in the land of his birth, in Ur of the Chaldeans. 29Abram and Nahor took wives; the name of Abram's wife was Sarai, and the name of Nahor's wife was Milcah. She was the daughter of Haran the father of Milcah and Iscah. 30Now Sarai was barren; she had no child.

31 Terah took his son Abram and his grandson Lot son of Haran, and his daughter-in-law Sarai, his son Abram's wife, and they went out together from Ur of the Chaldeans to go into the land of Canaan; but when they came to Haran, they settled there. 32The days of Terah were two hundred five years; and Terah died in Haran.

The Call of Abram

12 Now the LORD said to Abram, "Go from your country and your kindred and your father's house to the land that I will show you. 2I will make of you a great nation, and I will bless you, and make your name great, so that you will be a blessing. 3I will bless those who bless you, and the one who curses you I will curse; and in you all the families of the earth shall be blessed."a

4 So Abram went, as the LORD had told him; and Lot went with him. Abram was seventy-five years old when he departed from Haran. 5Abram took his wife Sarai and his brother's son Lot, and all the possessions that they had gathered, and the persons whom they had acquired in Haran; and they set forth to go to the land of Canaan. When they

a Or by you all the families of the earth shall bless themselves

---

12:1–3 the LORD said to Abram, "Go." As in the beginning of creation, God's powerful word creates something new. Against a backdrop of barrenness (11:30), by dramatic summons, hope for the future is born by God's speaking. God calls Abram into relationship and life with God begins anew. The promise that follows assures Abram that when God makes such a radical command, he journeys forth not alone, but with God, who is leading him. The outline of God's promise is fivefold and provides the basis for all that follows: land, a great nation, blessing, blessing and curse, and other nations, which will be beneficiaries of blessing. The blessing includes what we still seek: a place to live and thrive, the security of community, prosperity, and prominence. The text reminds us that these are not acquired by our own doing, but are gifts from God—divine grace, divine blessing.

12:4–5 So Abram went. Without questioning God, Abram gets up and goes. This is a most remarkable commencement for the whole family of faith, including us. Faith begins in God's speaking the divine intrusive word that demands radical response. The life of faith is characterized as a journey. God calls, and we go forth in faith without a map, not quite sure where we are going, but with trust in God's promised presence. Abram's response is both individual and corporate. God speaks to him, and Abram takes his family along. Individual acts of obedience are never isolated from the family and community to which we are related.

had come to the land of Canaan, 6Abram passed through the land to the place at Shechem, to the oak*a* of Moreh. At that time the Canaanites were in the land. 7Then the LORD appeared to Abram, and said, "To your offspring*b* I will give this land." So he built there an altar to the LORD, who had appeared to him. 8From there he moved on to the hill country on the east of Bethel, and pitched his tent, with Bethel on the west and Ai on the east; and there he built an altar to the LORD and invoked the name of the LORD. 9And Abram journeyed on by stages toward the Negeb.

Abram and Sarai in Egypt

10 Now there was a famine in the land. So Abram went down to Egypt to reside there as an alien, for the famine was severe in the land. 11When he was about to enter Egypt, he said to his wife Sarai, "I know well that you are a woman beautiful in appearance; 12and when the Egyptians see you, they will say, 'This is his wife'; then they will kill me, but they will let you live. 13Say you are my sister, so that it may go well with me because of you, and that my life may be spared on your account." 14When Abram entered Egypt the Egyptians saw that the woman was very beautiful. 15When the officials of Pharaoh saw her, they praised her to Pharaoh. And the woman was taken into Pharaoh's house. 16And for her sake he dealt well with Abram; and he had sheep, oxen, male donkeys, male and female slaves, female donkeys, and camels.

17 But the LORD afflicted Pharaoh and his

house with great plagues because of Sarai, Abram's wife. 18So Pharaoh called Abram, and said, "What is this you have done to me? Why did you not tell me that she was your wife? 19Why did you say, 'She is my sister,' so that I took her for my wife? Now then, here is your wife, take her, and be gone." 20And Pharaoh gave his men orders concerning him; and they set him on the way, with his wife and all that he had.

Abram and Lot Separate

13 So Abram went up from Egypt, he and his wife, and all that he had, and Lot with him, into the Negeb.

2 Now Abram was very rich in livestock, in silver, and in gold. 3He journeyed on by stages from the Negeb as far as Bethel, to the place where his tent had been at the beginning, between Bethel and Ai, 4to the place where he had made an altar at the first; and there Abram called on the name of the LORD. 5Now Lot, who went with Abram, also had flocks and herds and tents, 6so that the land could not support both of them living together; for their possessions were so great that they could not live together, 7and there was strife between the herders of Abram's livestock and the herders of Lot's livestock. At that time the Canaanites and the Perizzites lived in the land.

8 Then Abram said to Lot, "Let there be no strife between you and me, and between your herders and my herders; for we are kindred. 9Is not the whole land before you? Separate

a Or *terebinth*   *b* Heb *seed*

12:6–9 *the Canaanites were in the land.* As soon as he obeys and follows God's word, Abram discovers that he will have to wait for the fulfillment of the promise. The land, the first part of the promise, upon which all other parts depend, is occupied. From the beginning of this narrative we discover there is no immediate gratification in God's plan. Nonetheless, Abram builds an altar and responds by worshiping the Promise Maker and calling the Lord by name.

12:10–20 *there was a famine in the land.* After this utterly faithful beginning, life circumstances call the promise into question,

and Abram tries to take matters into his own hands. Not only is the fulfillment of the promise in peril by famine, so is Abram's faith. As Abram maneuvers among the Egyptians, lying about his relations, this story foreshadows a future sojourn for this family in Egypt.

13:4, 18 *made an altar . . . built an altar.* The story of Abraham as the father of a nation among nations is bracketed by acts of worship. In the complex world of economics and national interests, worship is the appropriate posture of one seeking to be obedient to God in all things.

yourself from me. If you take the left hand, then I will go to the right; or if you take the right hand, then I will go to the left." 10Lot looked about him, and saw that the plain of the Jordan was well watered everywhere like the garden of the LORD, like the land of Egypt, in the direction of Zoar; this was before the LORD had destroyed Sodom and Gomorrah. 11So Lot chose for himself all the plain of the Jordan, and Lot journeyed eastward; thus they separated from each other. 12Abram settled in the land of Canaan, while Lot settled among the cities of the Plain and moved his tent as far as Sodom. 13Now the people of Sodom were wicked, great sinners against the LORD.

14 The LORD said to Abram, after Lot had separated from him, "Raise your eyes now, and look from the place where you are, northward and southward and eastward and westward; 15for all the land that you see I will give to you and to your offspring a forever. 16I will make your offspring like the dust of the earth; so that if one can count the dust of the earth, your offspring also can be counted. 17Rise up, walk through the length and the breadth of the land, for I will give it to you." 18So Abram moved his tent, and came and settled by the oaks b of Mamre, which are at Hebron; and there he built an altar to the LORD.

Lot's Captivity and Rescue

14 In the days of King Amraphel of Shinar, King Arioch of Ellasar, King Chedorlaomer of Elam, and King Tidal of Goiim, 2these kings made war with King Bera of Sodom, King Birsha of Gomorrah, King Shinab of Admah, King Shemeber of Zeboiim, and the king of Bela (that is, Zoar). 3All these joined forces in the Valley of Siddim (that is,

the Dead Sea). c 4Twelve years they had served Chedorlaomer, but in the thirteenth year they rebelled. 5In the fourteenth year Chedorlaomer and the kings who were with him came and subdued the Rephaim in Ashteroth-karnaim, the Zuzim in Ham, the Emim in Shaveh-kiriathaim, 6and the Horites in the hill country of Seir as far as El-paran on the edge of the wilderness; 7then they turned back and came to En-mishpat (that is, Kadesh), and subdued all the country of the Amalekites, and also the Amorites who lived in Hazazon-tamar. 8Then the king of Sodom, the king of Gomorrah, the king of Admah, the king of Zeboiim, and the king of Bela (that is, Zoar) went out, and they joined battle in the Valley of Siddim 9with King Chedorlaomer of Elam, King Tidal of Goiim, King Amraphel of Shinar, and King Arioch of Ellasar, four kings against five. 10Now the Valley of Siddim was full of bitumen pits; and as the kings of Sodom and Gomorrah fled, some fell into them, and the rest fled to the hill country. 11So the enemy took all the goods of Sodom and Gomorrah, and all their provisions, and went their way; 12they also took Lot, the son of Abram's brother, who lived in Sodom, and his goods, and departed.

13 Then one who had escaped came and told Abram the Hebrew, who was living by the oaks b of Mamre the Amorite, brother of Eshcol and of Aner; these were allies of Abram. 14When Abram heard that his nephew had been taken captive, he led forth his trained men, born in his house, three hundred eighteen of them, and went in pursuit as far as Dan. 15He divided his forces against them by night, he and his servants,

a Heb seed   b Or terebinths   c Heb Salt Sea

2707
Responding NOT APPLICABLE

13:8–18 SACRIFICE and SUBMISSION. Recall an instance when you had a disagreement with another member of your family over something you both wanted. How willing were you to let the other person have the item or have his or her own way? What growth needs to take place in your inner life to reach the spiritual maturity Abraham modeled

when he let Lot choose the best land? *See also* Spiritual Disciplines Index.

14:1–24 *In the days of King Amraphel.* Thrust into a conflict with nations and kings, Abram, every bit as powerful, remains loyal to his family, rescuing Lot and refusing to take advantage of the spoils of war. National conflicts always have local ramifications, and Abram's family loyalty brings him recognition as one identified with God.

New Hampton
Oct. 9. 2006 11½ Cent

and routed them and pursued them to Hobah, north of Damascus. ¹⁶Then he brought back all the goods, and also brought back his nephew Lot with his goods, and the women and the people.

Abram Blessed by Melchizedek

17 After his return from the defeat of Chedorlaomer and the kings who were with him, the king of Sodom went out to meet him at the Valley of Shaveh (that is, the King's Valley). ¹⁸And King Melchizedek of Salem brought out bread and wine; he was priest of God Most High.ᵃ ¹⁹He blessed him and said,

> "Blessed be Abram by God Most High,ᵃ
>   maker of heaven and earth;
> ²⁰ and blessed be God Most High,ᵃ
>   who has delivered your enemies into
>   your hand!"

And Abram gave him one-tenth of everything. ²¹Then the king of Sodom said to Abram, "Give me the persons, but take the goods for yourself." ²²But Abram said to the king of Sodom, "I have sworn to the LORD, God Most High,ᵃ maker of heaven and earth, ²³that I would not take a thread or a sandal-thong or anything that is yours, so that you might not say, 'I have made Abram rich.' ²⁴I will take nothing but what the young men have eaten, and the share of the men who went with me—Aner, Eshcol, and Mamre. Let them take their share."

God's Covenant with Abram

15 After these things the word of the LORD came to Abram in a vision, "Do not be afraid, Abram, I am your shield; your reward shall be very great." ²But Abram said, "O Lord GOD, what will you give me, for I continue childless, and the heir of my house is Eliezer of Damascus?"ᵇ ³And Abram said, "You have given me no offspring, and so a slave born in my house is to be my heir." ⁴But the word of the LORD came to him, "This man shall not be your heir; no one but your very own issue shall be your heir." ⁵He brought him outside and said, "Look toward heaven and count the stars, if you are able to count them." Then he said to him, "So shall your descendants be." And he believed the LORD; and the LORDᶜ reckoned it to him as righteousness.

7 Then he said to him, "I am the LORD who brought you from Ur of the Chaldeans, to give you this land to possess." ⁸But he said, "O Lord GOD, how am I to know that I shall possess it?" ⁹He said to him, "Bring me a heifer three years old, a female goat three years old, a ram three years old, a turtledove, and a young pigeon." ¹⁰He brought him all these and cut them in two, laying each half over against the other; but he did not cut the birds in two. ¹¹And when birds of prey came down on the carcasses, Abram drove them away.

ᵃ Heb *El Elyon*   ᵇ Meaning of Heb uncertain
ᶜ Heb *he*

15:1–6 *Do not be afraid.* The pivotal chapter 15 begins with the prophetic address frequently made by divine messengers: "Fear not." God allays the fear that naturally wells within us when we are in the direct presence of God. God reminds Abram of the promise. Abram, with no land and no heir, freely calls the promise of God into question with a bold statement of doubt. God reiterates the promise and points to the heavens, which prove nothing. With no proof, but only a word and a vision, Abram believes. Faith in the promise itself is also a gift of the Promise Maker. Abram has a radical trust in the power of God's speech to create some new reality. By his sheer belief Abram is named

righteous; he walks upright on the promises of God. Freedom from fear allows for faithful following.

15:7–21 *give you this land to possess.* The binding of a covenant (v 18) requires the participation of two parties who solemnly commit to one another. In a liturgical act of worship the covenant is prepared that graciously binds the promises of God to Abram's open-ended future. Abram does not know when they will be fulfilled, but consents to wait because he trusts his covenantal Partner.

15:9–14 SACRIFICE and SUBMISSION— *See* Spiritual Disciplines Index.

12 As the sun was going down, a deep sleep fell upon Abram, and a deep and terrifying darkness descended upon him. [13]Then the LORD[a] said to Abram, "Know this for certain, that your offspring shall be aliens in a land that is not theirs, and shall be slaves there, and they shall be oppressed for four hundred years; [14]but I will bring judgment on the nation that they serve, and afterward they shall come out with great possessions. [15]As for yourself, you shall go to your ancestors in peace; you shall be buried in a good old age. [16]And they shall come back here in the fourth generation; for the iniquity of the Amorites is not yet complete."

17 When the sun had gone down and it was dark, a smoking fire pot and a flaming torch passed between these pieces. [18]On that day the LORD made a covenant with Abram, saying, "To your descendants I give this land, from the river of Egypt to the great river, the river Euphrates, [19]the land of the Kenites, the Kenizzites, the Kadmonites, [20]the Hittites, the Perizzites, the Rephaim, [21]the Amorites, the Canaanites, the Girgashites, and the Jebusites."

The Birth of Ishmael

16 Now Sarai, Abram's wife, bore him no children. She had an Egyptian slave-girl whose name was Hagar, [2]and Sarai said to Abram, "You see that the LORD has prevented me from bearing children; go in to my slave-girl; it may be that I shall obtain children by her." And Abram listened to the voice of Sarai. [3]So, after Abram had lived ten years in the land of Canaan, Sarai, Abram's wife, took Hagar the Egyptian, her slave-girl, and gave her to her husband Abram as a wife. [4]He went in to Hagar, and she conceived; and when she saw that she had conceived, she looked with contempt on her mistress. [5]Then Sarai said to Abram, "May the wrong done to me be on you! I gave my slave-girl to your embrace, and when she saw that she had conceived, she looked on me with contempt. May the LORD judge between you and me!" [6]But Abram said to Sarai, "Your slave-girl is in your power; do to her as you please." Then Sarai dealt harshly with her, and she ran away from her.

7 The angel of the LORD found her by a spring of water in the wilderness, the spring on the way to Shur. [8]And he said, "Hagar, slave-girl of Sarai, where have you come from and where are you going?" She said, "I am running away from my mistress Sarai." [9]The angel of the LORD said to her, "Return to your mistress, and submit to her." [10]The angel of the LORD also said to her, "I will so greatly multiply your offspring that they cannot be counted for multitude." [11]And the angel of the LORD said to her,

"Now you have conceived and shall
        bear a son;
    you shall call him Ishmael,[b]
    for the LORD has given heed to your
        affliction.
[12] He shall be a wild ass of a man,
    with his hand against everyone,
        and everyone's hand against him;
    and he shall live at odds with all his
        kin."

[13]So she named the LORD who spoke to her,

a Heb he   b That is God hears

16:1–4 *Sarai . . . bore him no children.* How long can a person live on promises alone? The barrenness of Sarai and Abram persists, so they take the business of creating heirs into their own hands. It was customary for those of their stature to claim the children of their slaves as their own.

16:7–15 *The angel of the LORD found her.* Hagar, the cast-off slave woman and surrogate mother, a victim of a patriarchal subordination, still has a very special place in this story. She is the first person in all of Scripture to receive an angelic messenger from God. She is the first person to name God, calling him Elroi, which means "God sees." While Sarai and Abram are scheming to control their future, God takes a special interest in the one they cast away. In the promises made to Hagar and in the birth of Ishmael we begin to see glimpses that the promissory blessing ultimately includes "all the families of the earth" (12:3).

16:9 **SUBMISSION**—*See* Spiritual Disciplines Index.

ABRAHAM

Sacrificial Submission

Selected Scriptures: *Genesis 12–13; 15–16; 18; 21:1–7; 22:1–19; Galatians 3:6–14*

Abraham submitted to God, letting God move him to a new land and give him a child in old age. Abraham offered his beloved son on an altar in obedience to God. Abraham's descendants, the nation Israel, would not always imitate him, but they would use him repeatedly as a compass to find their way each time they strayed. All who look to Abraham as their father can learn from the pattern of submission and sacrifice that made his faith possible. His submission allowed God to make the decisions for his life. His willingness to sacrifice his belongings, his relationships, his security, and even his child allowed God the room to act in his life.

Abraham's story reminds us that faith must involve more than hoping for the best in times of uncertainty. Faith often *brings on* uncertainty through acts of submission to God. Faith often means taking a voluntary step from the known into the unknown in response to God's leading. And faith often requires a voluntary giving away of persons, positions, or possessions in response to God's nudging. It can involve acts of great, even heartrending, sacrifice. As Abraham's life portrays, true faith in God means a life lived *with God* in active response to his guiding Spirit.

At times Abraham did falter in his faith. He once lied about Sarah's identity, claiming she was his sister (Gen 20:2). And when Sarah and Abraham remained childless into their old age, Abraham fathered a child by Sarah's slave, Hagar (16:2). Yet the longer he lived with God, the more fully he submitted, until he obeyed even to the point of placing Isaac on the altar. Abraham left a legacy for all believers to imitate. He gave up his comfortable homeland to take on a role beyond his imagining. He submitted his own preferences to God's provision in allowing Lot to choose first between plots of land (13:9). And in Abraham's most complete act of submission and sacrifice, God showed himself trustworthy, more than able to take what was submitted to him and care for Abraham, providing all he had promised. Abraham didn't grow in submission only to see his life whittled away and left empty and powerless. Instead, each sacrifice Abraham made resulted in richer blessing. Through Abraham's release, God worked out a plan no one ever could have conceived.

Abraham embodied the prayer of Thomas à Kempis, who himself lived a commitment to the Spiritual Disciplines. In *The Imitation of Christ* Kempis puts into words the prayer Abraham lived by: "As thou wilt, what thou wilt; when thou wilt."

MOVE FROM (151)

Personal Reflection

- When has God asked you to submit to his direction and do something you would not have chosen for your life? How did you respond?
- In what way is God asking you to make a sacrifice now? How yielded is your spirit to the prayer of Abraham and Thomas à Kempis: "As thou wilt, what thou wilt, when thou wilt"?

PROFILE

"You are El-roi"; *a* for she said, "Have I really seen God and remained alive after seeing him?" *b* 14Therefore the well was called Beer-lahai-roi; *c* it lies between Kadesh and Bered.

15 Hagar bore Abram a son; and Abram named his son, whom Hagar bore, Ishmael. 16Abram was eighty-six years old when Hagar bore him *d* Ishmael.

The Sign of the Covenant

17 When Abram was ninety-nine years old, the LORD appeared to Abram, and said to him, "I am God Almighty; *e* walk before me, and be blameless. 2And I will make my covenant between me and you, and will make you exceedingly numerous." 3Then Abram fell on his face; and God said to him, 4"As for me, this is my covenant with you: You shall be the ancestor of a multitude of nations. 5No longer shall your name be Abram, *f* but your name shall be Abraham; *g* for I have made you the ancestor of a multitude of nations. 6I will make you exceedingly fruitful; and I will make nations of you, and kings shall come from you. 7I will establish my covenant between me and you, and your offspring after you throughout their generations, for an everlasting covenant, to be God to you and to your offspring *h* after you. 8And I will give to you, and to your offspring after you, the land where you are now an alien, all the land of Canaan, for a perpetual holding; and I will be their God."

9 God said to Abraham, "As for you, you shall keep my covenant, you and your offspring after you throughout their generations. 10This is my covenant, which you shall keep, between me and you and your offspring after you: Every male among you shall be circumcised. 11You shall circumcise the flesh of your foreskins, and it shall be a sign of the covenant between me and you. 12Throughout your generations every male among you shall be circumcised when he is eight days old, including the slave born in your house and the one bought with your money from any foreigner who is not of your offspring. 13Both the slave born in your house and the one bought with your money must be circumcised. So shall my covenant be in your flesh an everlasting covenant. 14Any uncircumcised male who is not circumcised in the flesh of his foreskin shall be cut off from his people; he has broken my covenant."

15 God said to Abraham, "As for Sarai your wife, you shall not call her Sarai, but Sarah shall be her name. 16I will bless her, and moreover I will give you a son by her. I will bless her, and she shall give rise to nations; kings of peoples shall come from her." 17Then Abraham fell on his face and laughed, and said to himself, "Can a child be born to a man who is a hundred years old? Can Sarah, who is ninety years old, bear a child?" 18And Abraham said to God, "O that Ishmael might live in your sight!" 19God said, "No, but your wife Sarah shall bear you a son, and you shall name him Isaac. *a* I will establish my covenant with him as an everlasting covenant for his offspring after him. 20As for Ishmael, I have heard you; I will bless him and make him fruitful and exceedingly numerous; he shall be the father of twelve princes, and I will make him a great nation. 21But my covenant I will establish with Isaac, whom Sarah shall bear to you at this season next year." 22And when he had finished talking with him, God went up from Abraham.

23 Then Abraham took his son Ishmael and all the slaves born in his house or bought with his money, every male among the men

a Perhaps *God of seeing* or *God who sees*
b Meaning of Heb uncertain   *c* That is *the Well of the Living One who sees me*   *d* Heb *Abram*
e Traditional rendering of Heb *El Shaddai*   *f* That is *exalted ancestor*   *g* Here taken to mean *ancestor of a multitude*   *h* Heb *seed*

17:1–2 THE WITH-GOD LIFE—*See* Spiritual Disciplines Index.
17:1–27 *my covenant between me and you.* The covenant is renewed and extended. Abram and Sarai are given new names, Abraham and Sarah, meaning "ancestor of a multitude" and "princess," and the people are given the sign of circumcision. Sarah's barrenness persists, but God adds to the lingering promise of an heir the name Isaac (v 21), and the narrative moves forward with this hint that fulfillment of promise draws closer.

of Abraham's house, and he circumcised the flesh of their foreskins that very day, as God had said to him. 24Abraham was ninety-nine years old when he was circumcised in the flesh of his foreskin. 25And his son Ishmael was thirteen years old when he was circumcised in the flesh of his foreskin. 26That very day Abraham and his son Ishmael were circumcised; 27and all the men of his house, slaves born in the house and those bought with money from a foreigner, were circumcised with him.

A Son Promised to Abraham and Sarah

18 The LORD appeared to Abraham[b] by the oaks[c] of Mamre, as he sat at the entrance of his tent in the heat of the day. 2He looked up and saw three men standing near him. When he saw them, he ran from the tent entrance to meet them, and bowed down to the ground. 3He said, "My lord, if I find favor with you, do not pass by your servant. 4Let a little water be brought, and wash your feet, and rest yourselves under the tree. 5Let me bring a little bread, that you may refresh yourselves, and after that you may pass on— since you have come to your servant." So they said, "Do as you have said." 6And Abraham hastened into the tent to Sarah, and said, "Make ready quickly three measures[d] of choice flour, knead it, and make cakes." 7Abraham ran to the herd, and took a calf, tender and good, and gave it to the servant, who hastened to prepare it. 8Then he took

curds and milk and the calf that he had prepared, and set it before them; and he stood by them under the tree while they ate.

9 They said to him, "Where is your wife Sarah?" And he said, "There, in the tent." 10Then one said, "I will surely return to you in due season, and your wife Sarah shall have a son." And Sarah was listening at the tent entrance behind him. 11Now Abraham and Sarah were old, advanced in age; it had ceased to be with Sarah after the manner of women. 12So Sarah laughed to herself, saying, "After I have grown old, and my husband is old, shall I have pleasure?" 13The LORD said to Abraham, "Why did Sarah laugh, and say, 'Shall I indeed bear a child, now that I am old?' 14Is anything too wonderful for the LORD? At the set time I will return to you, in due season, and Sarah shall have a son." 15But Sarah denied, saying, "I did not laugh"; for she was afraid. He said, "Oh yes, you did laugh."

Judgment Pronounced on Sodom

16 Then the men set out from there, and they looked toward Sodom; and Abraham went with them to set them on their way. 17The LORD said, "Shall I hide from Abraham what I am about to do, 18seeing that Abraham shall become a great and mighty nation, and all the nations of the earth shall be blessed in

a That is *he laughs*   b Heb *him*   c Or *terebinths*
d Heb *seahs*

18:1–15 *by the oaks of Mamre.* This visitation by God in the guise of three strangers is among the most obscure and intriguing tales in the Abrahamic cycle. Extending hospitality to his guests, Abraham prepares a feast. Overhearing their prediction of her giving birth to a son, Sarah falls over on the tent floor in laughter— still disbelieving the promise because, given her old age, pregnancy would be impossible. Sarah gives us permission to worship God with our laughter when ours is an uncertain future. In face of the incredulity of God's promises as we wait and wait, she offers comic relief. Up to this point the whole story of faith and obedience has been serious business. But here at a leisurely tent-side meal in the company of a

God we can barely recognize, we are invited to laugh. Sarah will in due time bear a son, and she will name him Isaac, which means "Laughter."

Responding
18:3–7 SERVICE. Many times we show hospitality only to those we know well or because we want to impress someone. This weekend invite an acquaintance to your home for a meal at which you prepare and serve the best food you can afford. Monitor your reactions as a person you barely know enjoys your hospitality. What did you learn? *See also* Spiritual Disciplines Index.

him?*a* 19No, for I have chosen*b* him, that he may charge his children and his household after him to keep the way of the LORD by doing righteousness and justice; so that the LORD may bring about for Abraham what he has promised him." 20Then the LORD said, "How great is the outcry against Sodom and Gomorrah and how very grave their sin! 21I must go down and see whether they have done altogether according to the outcry that has come to me; and if not, I will know."

22 So the men turned from there, and went toward Sodom, while Abraham remained standing before the LORD.*c* 23Then Abraham came near and said, "Will you indeed sweep away the righteous with the wicked? 24Suppose there are fifty righteous within the city; will you then sweep away the place and not forgive it for the fifty righteous who are in it? 25Far be it from you to do such a thing, to slay the righteous with the wicked, so that the righteous fare as the wicked! Far be that from you! Shall not the Judge of all the earth do what is just?" 26And the LORD said, "If I find at Sodom fifty righteous in the city, I will forgive the whole place for their sake." 27Abraham answered, "Let me take it upon myself to speak to the Lord, I who am but dust and ashes. 28Suppose five of the fifty righteous are lacking? Will you destroy the whole city for lack of five?" And he said, "I will not destroy it if I find forty-five there." 29Again he spoke to him, "Suppose forty are found there." He answered, "For the sake of forty I will not do it." 30Then he said, "Oh do not let the Lord be angry if I speak.

Suppose thirty are found there." He answered, "I will not do it, if I find thirty there." 31He said, "Let me take it upon myself to speak to the Lord. Suppose twenty are found there." He answered, "For the sake of twenty I will not destroy it." 32Then he said, "Oh do not let the Lord be angry if I speak just once more. Suppose ten are found there." He answered, "For the sake of ten I will not destroy it." 33And the LORD went his way, when he had finished speaking to Abraham; and Abraham returned to his place.

The Depravity of Sodom

19 The two angels came to Sodom in the evening, and Lot was sitting in the gateway of Sodom. When Lot saw them, he rose to meet them, and bowed down with his face to the ground. 2He said, "Please, my lords, turn aside to your servant's house and spend the night, and wash your feet; then you can rise early and go on your way." They said, "No; we will spend the night in the square." 3But he urged them strongly; so they turned aside to him and entered his house; and he made them a feast, and baked unleavened bread, and they ate. 4But before they lay down, the men of the city, the men of Sodom, both young and old, all the people to the last man, surrounded the house; 5and they called to Lot, "Where are the men who came to you tonight? Bring them out to us, so

a Or *and all the nations of the earth shall bless themselves by him* *b* Heb *known* *c* Another ancient tradition reads *while the LORD remained standing before Abraham*

18:16–33 *Sodom and Gomorrah.* In this fascinating text God reflects theologically, behind Abraham's back, about the future of Sodom and Gomorrah. Showing the wrath he exhibited before the flood, God is positioning to destroy the cities. However, God also considers what Abraham would think, given his influence in the world. Abraham intervenes, inquiring about the possibility of collateral damage, and God is ultimately swayed by Abraham's intercession and influenced by his righteousness. Here Abraham takes God to the mat in intense negotiation, reminding us that the One who calls us into relationship is a conversation

Partner in word and deed.

18:23–33 PRAYER—*See* Spiritual Disciplines Index.

19:1–29 *two angels came to Sodom.* Sodom and Gomorrah recall the condition of humankind before the flood, overcome with sin and destroyed by God. The text hints at the wickedness of sexual abuse, but considers more broadly how rejection of God's ordering governance creates such a violent, uninhabitable place. As Noah was saved from the flood, so Lot is saved from the destruction of the burning cities. God's severe judgment is always coupled with saving grace.

LOT

Divided Affections

Selected Scriptures: *Genesis 13; 19*

Abraham's nephew Lot shared the patriarch's moral conviction and his sorrow over the evil he saw around him. Yet Lot made choices that ushered him too close to evil—so close that Lot's life became entwined with that of the people of Sodom. And not only his life, but his affections as well.

Lot's first costly mistake was his choice of land. Abraham had graciously offered Lot his choice between two portions of land, so that each of them would have ample space for herds to graze and families to settle. Lot saw the fertile plain of the Jordan, home to the "wicked" cities of Sodom and Gomorrah, and chose to settle in this lush land. He even "moved his tent as far as Sodom" (Gen 13:12). Later, Lot moved into Sodom itself and arranged marriages for his daughters. Although he didn't participate in the evil behavior of the Sodomites, Lot gradually made compromises, allowing his affections to become more and more attached to this city.

When warned by angelic visitors that Sodom would be destroyed and Lot should take his family and flee, "he lingered," forcing the angels to escort him out of the city (19:16). Lot's wife had also become attached to Sodom. Against the command of God, she looked back as she fled and was turned into a pillar of salt (19:26).

Back when Lot lived in Sodom, he had become comfortable and came to enjoy the perks of a well-to-do life in a city with much energy and excitement. Although Lot did not approve of the morality of the people of Sodom, he considered living among them harmless, as long as he and his family remained moral. Yet even this became impossible when the men of the city sought out the angelic visitors in Lot's home. He found himself offering his virgin daughters in exchange for the safety of his visitors (19:8).

Why would a "righteous" and "godly" man, as Peter describes Lot (2 Pet 2:7–9), fall into such ties with sin and lead his family to do the same? God did save Lot from destruction; from that and Peter's words we must conclude that Lot was a true follower of God. Yet his affections were divided. It seems that Lot had no understanding of the power of *mammon* (Greek, "wealth") to draw even the godly into sinful affections and commitments. Lot's slide into compromise began when he chose material comfort over avoidance of evil. Lot reasoned just as many Christians through the ages have done: "Why not be joyful children of the world just as we are joyful children of God? Aren't the goods of the earth meant for our happiness?"

Richard Foster writes in *The Challenge of the Disciplined Life*:

"The thing that Jesus saw so clearly is the way in which mammon makes a bid for our hearts. . . . It seems that money is not willing to rest contented in its proper place alongside other things we value. No, it must have supremacy. It must crowd out all else. . . . Behind money are invisible spiritual powers, powers that are seductive and deceptive, powers that demand an all-embracing devotion. It is this fact that the apostle Paul saw when he observed that 'the love of money is the root of all evils' (1 Tim 6:10)."

As Martin Luther once stated, "There are three conversions necessary: the conversion of the heart, mind, and the purse." It seems Lot never reached this third stage of conversion.

Lot lost his wife, his home, all his possessions, and even his family's moral purity. Through his daughters he, unknowingly, fathered two groups of people, the Moabites and the Ammonites, who would struggle against Israel in future years. Lot's comfort was short-lived and the consequences of his compromise lasted for generations. Surely Lot ended his life feeling like anything but a joyful child of the world.

Personal Reflection

- Lot was a follower of God in a poisonous environment. Reflect on your environment. What in your neighborhood, work, and culture encourages you in your life with God and what draws you away from God? Whom in your life can you point to as positive examples of those staying close to God and his values while living in your world?

- What roles do money, wealth, and the lure of comfort play in your life? When do you feel fear, insecurity, guilt, or excitement in relationship to your wealth and comforts? Whom can you speak with honestly concerning these situations in your life? Pray now for God's guidance and protection as you seek to break the power of mammon.

- Richard Foster writes, "We are to be absolutely clear about the venomous nature of money. But rather than reject it we are to conquer it and use it for noneconomic purposes. . . . We are called to use money to advance the kingdom of God. What a tragedy it is if all we do is use money in the ordinary ways and not make any greater use of it" (*The Challenge of the Disciplined Life*). Have you ever been inclined to "reject" money or wealth because of the inherent dangers the Bible warns against? How are you, or could you be, using money now to advance God's kingdom?

that we may know them." 6Lot went out of the door to the men, shut the door after him, 7and said, "I beg you, my brothers, do not act so wickedly. 8Look, I have two daughters who have not known a man; let me bring them out to you, and do to them as you please; only do nothing to these men, for they have come under the shelter of my roof." 9But they replied, "Stand back!" And they said, "This fellow came here as an alien, and he would play the judge! Now we will deal worse with you than with them." Then they pressed hard against the man Lot, and came near the door to break it down. 10But the men inside reached out their hands and brought Lot into the house with them, and shut the door. 11And they struck with blindness the men who were at the door of the house, both small and great, so that they were unable to find the door.

Sodom and Gomorrah Destroyed

12 Then the men said to Lot, "Have you anyone else here? Sons-in-law, sons, daughters, or anyone you have in the city—bring them out of the place. 13For we are about to destroy this place, because the outcry against its people has become great before the LORD, and the LORD has sent us to destroy it." 14So Lot went out and said to his sons-in-law, who were to marry his daughters, "Up, get out of this place; for the LORD is about to destroy the city." But he seemed to his sons-in-law to be jesting.

15 When morning dawned, the angels urged Lot, saying, "Get up, take your wife and your two daughters who are here, or else you will be consumed in the punishment of the city." 16But he lingered; so the men seized him and his wife and his two daughters by the hand, the LORD being merciful to him, and they brought him out and left him outside the city. 17When they had brought them outside, they *a* said, "Flee for your life; do not look back or stop anywhere in the Plain; flee to the hills, or else you will be consumed." 18And Lot said to them, "Oh, no, my lords; 19your servant has found favor with you, and you have shown me great kindness in saving my life; but I cannot flee to the hills, for fear the disaster will overtake me and I die. 20Look, that city is near enough to flee to, and it is a little one. Let me escape there—is it not a little one?—and my life will be saved!" 21He said to him, "Very well, I grant you this favor too, and will not overthrow the city of which you have spoken. 22Hurry, escape there, for I can do nothing until you arrive there." Therefore the city was called Zoar. *b* 23The sun had risen on the earth when Lot came to Zoar.

24 Then the LORD rained on Sodom and Gomorrah sulfur and fire from the LORD out of heaven; 25and he overthrew those cities, and all the Plain, and all the inhabitants of the cities, and what grew on the ground. 26But Lot's wife, behind him, looked back, and she became a pillar of salt.

27 Abraham went early in the morning to the place where he had stood before the LORD; 28and he looked down toward Sodom and Gomorrah and toward all the land of the Plain and saw the smoke of the land going up like the smoke of a furnace.

29 So it was that, when God destroyed the cities of the Plain, God remembered Abraham, and sent Lot out of the midst of the overthrow, when he overthrew the cities in which Lot had settled.

The Shameful Origin of Moab and Ammon

30 Now Lot went up out of Zoar and settled in the hills with his two daughters, for he was afraid to stay in Zoar; so he lived in a cave with his two daughters. 31And the firstborn said to the younger, "Our father is old, and there is not a man on earth to come in to us after the manner of all the world. 32Come, let us make our father drink wine, and we will lie with him, so that we may preserve offspring through our father." 33So they made their father drink wine that night; and the firstborn went in, and lay with her father; he did not know when she lay down or when she rose. 34On the next day, the firstborn said to the younger, "Look, I lay last night with my father; let us make him drink wine tonight also; then you go in and lie with him, so that we may preserve offspring through our father." 35So they made their father drink wine that night also; and the younger rose, and lay with him; and he did not know when she lay

a Gk Syr Vg: Heb *he*   *b* That is *Little*

down or when she rose. 36Thus both the daughters of Lot became pregnant by their father. 37The firstborn bore a son, and named him Moab; he is the ancestor of the Moabites to this day. 38The younger also bore a son and named him Ben-ammi; he is the ancestor of the Ammonites to this day.

Abraham and Sarah at Gerar

20 From there Abraham journeyed toward the region of the Negeb, and settled between Kadesh and Shur. While residing in Gerar as an alien, 2Abraham said of his wife Sarah, "She is my sister." And King Abimelech of Gerar sent and took Sarah. 3But God came to Abimelech in a dream by night, and said to him, "You are about to die because of the woman whom you have taken; for she is a married woman." 4Now Abimelech had not approached her; so he said, "Lord, will you destroy an innocent people? 5Did he not himself say to me, 'She is my sister'? And she herself said, 'He is my brother.' I did this in the integrity of my heart and the innocence of my hands." 6Then God said to him in the dream, "Yes, I know that you did this in the integrity of your heart; furthermore it was I who kept you from sinning against me. Therefore I did not let you touch her. 7Now then, return the man's wife; for he is a prophet, and he will pray for you and you shall live. But if you do not restore her, know that you shall surely die, you and all that are yours."

8 So Abimelech rose early in the morning, and called all his servants and told them all these things; and the men were very much afraid. 9Then Abimelech called Abraham, and said to him, "What have you done to us? How have I sinned against you, that you have brought such great guilt on me and my kingdom? You have done things to me that ought not to be done." 10And Abimelech said to Abraham, "What were you thinking of, that you did this thing?" 11Abraham said, "I did it because I thought, There is no fear of God at all in this place, and they will kill me because of my wife. 12Besides, she is indeed my sister, the daughter of my father but not the daughter of my mother; and she became my wife. 13And when God caused me to wander from my father's house, I said to her, 'This is the kindness you must do me: at every place to which we come, say of me, He is my brother.' " 14Then Abimelech took sheep and oxen, and male and female slaves, and gave them to Abraham, and restored his wife Sarah to him. 15Abimelech said, "My land is before you; settle where it pleases you." 16To Sarah he said, "Look, I have given your brother a thousand pieces of silver; it is your exoneration before all who are with you; you are completely vindicated." 17Then Abraham prayed to God; and God healed Abimelech, and also healed his wife and female slaves so that they bore children. 18For the LORD had closed fast all the wombs of the house of Abimelech because of Sarah, Abraham's wife.

The Birth of Isaac

21 The LORD dealt with Sarah as he had said, and the LORD did for Sarah as he had promised. 2Sarah conceived and bore Abraham a son in his old age, at the time of which God had spoken to him. 3Abraham gave the name Isaac to his son whom Sarah bore him. 4And Abraham circumcised his

---

20:1–18 *She is my sister.* This story parallels 12:10–18 with a broader concern for the ethical issues related to Abraham's lying about Sarah's identity. Abraham calls Sarah his sister to save his own neck. He gets caught, offers excuses, and enjoys God's intervention in the end. Whenever Abraham tries to take control of his own life, it seems, he gets into trouble. Although Lot's faithfulness waxes and wanes, God continues to be faithful despite Abraham's doubt and disobedience.

Responding
20:7 PRAYER. Abimelech finds himself in a strange situation: God tells him that if he returns Sarah to Abraham, her spouse and the person who lied to him, Abraham will pray for him and he will live. Today recall someone you have lied to or about, write the name down on a piece of paper, and ask God to bless that person with well-being and health. *See also* Spiritual Disciplines Index.

son Isaac when he was eight days old, as God had commanded him. 5Abraham was a hundred years old when his son Isaac was born to him. 6Now Sarah said, "God has brought laughter for me; everyone who hears will laugh with me." 7And she said, "Who would ever have said to Abraham that Sarah would nurse children? Yet I have borne him a son in his old age."

Hagar and Ishmael Sent Away

8 The child grew, and was weaned; and Abraham made a great feast on the day that Isaac was weaned. 9But Sarah saw the son of Hagar the Egyptian, whom she had borne to Abraham, playing with her son Isaac.*a* 10So she said to Abraham, "Cast out this slave woman with her son; for the son of this slave woman shall not inherit along with my son Isaac." 11The matter was very distressing to Abraham on account of his son. 12But God said to Abraham, "Do not be distressed because of the boy and because of your slave woman; whatever Sarah says to you, do as she tells you, for it is through Isaac that offspring shall be named for you. 13As for the son of the slave woman, I will make a nation of him also, because he is your offspring." 14So Abraham rose early in the morning, and took bread and a skin of water, and gave it to Hagar, putting it on her shoulder, along with the child, and sent her away. And she departed, and wandered about in the wilderness of Beer-sheba.

15 When the water in the skin was gone,

she cast the child under one of the bushes. 16Then she went and sat down opposite him a good way off, about the distance of a bowshot; for she said, "Do not let me look on the death of the child." And as she sat opposite him, she lifted up her voice and wept. 17And God heard the voice of the boy; and the angel of God called to Hagar from heaven, and said to her, "What troubles you, Hagar? Do not be afraid; for God has heard the voice of the boy where he is. 18Come, lift up the boy and hold him fast with your hand, for I will make a great nation of him." 19Then God opened her eyes and she saw a well of water. She went, and filled the skin with water, and gave the boy a drink.

20 God was with the boy, and he grew up; he lived in the wilderness, and became an expert with the bow. 21He lived in the wilderness of Paran; and his mother got a wife for him from the land of Egypt.

Abraham and Abimelech Make a Covenant

22 At that time Abimelech, with Phicol the commander of his army, said to Abraham, "God is with you in all that you do; 23now therefore swear to me here by God that you will not deal falsely with me or with my offspring or with my posterity, but as I have dealt loyally with you, you will deal with me and with the land where you have resided as an alien." 24And Abraham said, "I swear it."

a Gk Vg: Heb lacks *with her son Isaac*

21:1–7 *Sarah conceived.* At last the promise is fulfilled. By the word of God old Sarah gives birth to Isaac (which means "Laughter"), recalling her laughter behind the flap of the tent (18:12) and in joyous celebration of a long-anticipated promise fulfilled. Faith looks at the ways of God that cannot be explained and rejoices with bold laughter.

21:8–21 *But Sarah saw the son of Hagar.* Sarah cannot rest content at the birth of Isaac, for having a son named "Laughter" turns into no laughing matter. Concerned that the older Ishmael may threaten Isaac's position as heir, she asks Abraham to cast out Hagar. In the wilderness, dying of thirst, with the welfare of

the child in peril, Hagar cries and God hears the cry of the child. God provides for the marginal characters of this larger family story and intervenes in human systems of exploitation. Although Hagar plays only a minor part, the narrative makes sure we see that she is not without importance. She recognizes that God sees (16:13); her son's name, Ishmael, means "God hears." Although God chose the particular family of Abraham and Sarah as heirs of blessing, Hagar attests to the universality of the promise that all the families of the earth will be blessed. Hagar and Ishmael represent the other families for whom God graciously provides a future too.

25 When Abraham complained to Abimelech about a well of water that Abimelech's servants had seized, 26Abimelech said, "I do not know who has done this; you did not tell me, and I have not heard of it until today." 27So Abraham took sheep and oxen and gave them to Abimelech, and the two men made a covenant. 28Abraham set apart seven ewe lambs of the flock. 29And Abimelech said to Abraham, "What is the meaning of these seven ewe lambs that you have set apart?" 30He said, "These seven ewe lambs you shall accept from my hand, in order that you may be a witness for me that I dug this well." 31Therefore that place was called Beer-sheba;*a* because there both of them swore an oath. 32When they had made a covenant at Beersheba, Abimelech, with Phicol the commander of his army, left and returned to the land of the Philistines. 33Abraham*b* planted a tamarisk tree in Beer-sheba, and called there on the name of the LORD, the Everlasting God.*c* 34And Abraham resided as an alien many days in the land of the Philistines.

The Command to Sacrifice Isaac

22 After these things God tested Abraham. He said to him, "Abraham!" And he said, "Here I am." 2He said, "Take your son, your only son Isaac, whom you love, and go to the land of Moriah, and offer him there as a burnt offering on one of the mountains that I shall show you." 3So Abraham rose early in the morning, saddled his donkey, and took two of his young men with him, and his son Isaac; he cut the wood for the burnt offering, and set out and went to the place in the distance that God had shown him. 4On the third day Abraham looked up and saw the place far away. 5Then Abraham said to his young men, "Stay here with the donkey; the boy and I will go over there; we will worship, and then we will come back to you." 6Abraham took the wood of the burnt offering and laid it on his son Isaac, and he himself carried the fire and the knife. So the two of them walked on together. 7Isaac said to his father Abraham, "Father!" And he said, "Here I am, my son." He said, "The fire and the wood are here, but where is the lamb for a burnt offering?" 8Abraham said, "God himself will provide the lamb for a burnt offering, my son." So the two of them walked on together.

9 When they came to the place that God had shown him, Abraham built an altar there and laid the wood in order. He bound his son Isaac, and laid him on the altar, on top of the wood. 10Then Abraham reached out his hand and took the knife to kill*d* his son. 11But

a That is *Well of seven* or *Well of the oath*
b Heb *He*   *c* Or *the* LORD, *El Olam*   *d* Or *to slaughter*

22:1–14 *God tested Abraham.* This is an important and theologically demanding text. Historically child sacrifice was common among the Canaanites and in surrounding cultures. The tradition of the people of Israel proclaims the Lord God is bent on saving the children of God and abolishing pagan child sacrifice. However, even though the tragedy is averted by God's intervention in the end, the mystery of God's initiating this dire test is unresolved. God not only creates the crisis for Abraham, God puts the fulfillment of his own promise at risk. No reason is given and Abraham doesn't ask for one; the sparse narration is unconcerned with human emotion. God calls, and trusting Abraham announces his readiness three times (vv 1, 7, 11), ever faithful to the inscrutable demand of God who both tests and provides. This child Isaac was pure gift, born beyond the time of human possibility. The unfolding of the future is gift as well. Abraham learns, and so must we, that life with God is an ongoing journey that demands both fearful and grateful response. Abraham's obedience here is born of a life of deep trust in the God who calls new futures into being. The ways of God may well be mysterious, yet God remains faithful. Ultimately the God who tests will be the same God who graciously provides.

Responding
22:5 WORSHIP. In the story of Abraham and Isaac we find obedience and worship intertwined: Abraham was obeying God's command to sacrifice Isaac as an act of worship. What do you think comes first, obedience or worship? Or are they inseparable? Explain. *See also* Spiritual Disciplines Index.

the angel of the LORD called to him from heaven, and said, "Abraham, Abraham!" And he said, "Here I am." 12He said, "Do not lay your hand on the boy or do anything to him; for now I know that you fear God, since you have not withheld your son, your only son, from me." 13And Abraham looked up and saw a ram, caught in a thicket by its horns. Abraham went and took the ram and offered it up as a burnt offering instead of his son. 14So Abraham called that place "The LORD will provide";*a* as it is said to this day, "On the mount of the LORD it shall be provided."*b*

15 The angel of the LORD called to Abraham a second time from heaven, 16and said, "By myself I have sworn, says the LORD: Because you have done this, and have not withheld your son, your only son, 17I will indeed bless you, and I will make your offspring as numerous as the stars of heaven and as the sand that is on the seashore. And your offspring shall possess the gate of their enemies, 18and by your offspring shall all the nations of the earth gain blessing for themselves, because you have obeyed my voice." 19So Abraham returned to his young men, and they arose and went together to Beer-sheba; and Abraham lived at Beer-sheba.

The Children of Nahor

20 Now after these things it was told Abraham, "Milcah also has borne children, to your brother Nahor: 21Uz the firstborn, Buz his brother, Kemuel the father of Aram, 22Chesed, Hazo, Pildash, Jidlaph, and Bethuel." 23Bethuel became the father of Rebekah. These eight Milcah bore to Nahor, Abraham's brother. 24Moreover, his concubine, whose name was Reumah, bore Tebah, Gaham, Tahash, and Maacah.

Sarah's Death and Burial

23 Sarah lived one hundred twenty-seven years; this was the length of Sarah's life. 2And Sarah died at Kiriath-arba (that is, Hebron) in the land of Canaan; and Abraham went in to mourn for Sarah and to weep for her. 3Abraham rose up from beside his dead, and said to the Hittites, 4"I am a stranger and an alien residing among you; give me property among you for a burying place, so that I may bury my dead out of my sight." 5The Hittites answered Abraham, 6"Hear us, my lord; you are a mighty prince among us. Bury your dead in the choicest of our burial places; none of us will withhold from you any burial ground for burying your dead." 7Abraham rose and bowed to the Hittites, the people of the land. 8He said to them, "If you are willing that I should bury my dead out of my sight, hear me, and entreat for me Ephron son of Zohar, 9so that he may give me the cave of Machpelah, which he owns; it is at the end of his field. For the full price let him give it to me in your presence as a possession for a burying place." 10Now Ephron was sitting among the Hittites; and Ephron the Hittite answered Abraham in the hearing of the Hittites, of all who went in at the gate of his city, 11"No, my lord, hear me; I give you the field, and I give you the cave that is in it; in the presence of my people I give it to you; bury your dead." 12Then Abraham bowed down before the people of the land.

---

a Or *will see*; Heb traditionally transliterated *Jehovah Jireh*   *b* Or *he shall be seen*

23:1–20 *the length of Sarah's life.* On the surface this looks like an overly detailed chapter to explain the purchase of a burial plot. Nowhere is God mentioned, but notice the location—in the land of Canaan. For the first time Abraham actually owns a piece of land. Like the text about the near sacrifice of Isaac before, this detailed text is about movement toward the fulfillment of promise. Although the key players in this patriarchal narrative are fathers and sons, through whom the blessing is passed to succeeding generations, the role of women is hardly peripheral. Burial practices are important matters for families and societies preserving local history. Rich detail of local custom and political negotiation pay tribute to Sarah, through whose lengthy barrenness God created an otherwise impossible future. Before Sarah's death, the text shows us that Rebekah (22:23) is waiting in the wings to take up the important role of mother in the ongoing story of the family of faith.

13He said to Ephron in the hearing of the people of the land, "If you only will listen to me! I will give the price of the field; accept it from me, so that I may bury my dead there." 14Ephron answered Abraham, 15"My lord, listen to me; a piece of land worth four hundred shekels of silver—what is that between you and me? Bury your dead." 16Abraham agreed with Ephron; and Abraham weighed out for Ephron the silver that he had named in the hearing of the Hittites, four hundred shekels of silver, according to the weights current among the merchants.

17 So the field of Ephron in Machpelah, which was to the east of Mamre, the field with the cave that was in it and all the trees that were in the field, throughout its whole area, passed 18to Abraham as a possession in the presence of the Hittites, in the presence of all who went in at the gate of his city. 19After this, Abraham buried Sarah his wife in the cave of the field of Machpelah facing Mamre (that is, Hebron) in the land of Canaan. 20The field and the cave that is in it passed from the Hittites into Abraham's possession as a burying place.

The Marriage of Isaac and Rebekah

24 Now Abraham was old, well advanced in years; and the LORD had blessed Abraham in all things. 2Abraham said to his servant, the oldest of his house, who had charge of all that he had, "Put your hand under my thigh 3and I will make you swear by the LORD, the God of heaven and earth, that you will not get a wife for my son from the daughters of the Canaanites, among whom I live, 4but will go to my country and to my kindred and get a wife for my son Isaac." 5The servant said to him, "Perhaps the woman may not be willing to follow me to this land; must I then take your son back to the land from which you came?" 6Abraham said to him, "See to it that you do not take my son back there. 7The LORD, the God of heaven, who took me from my father's house and from the land of my birth, and who spoke to me and swore to me, 'To your offspring I will give this land,' he will send his angel before you, and you shall take a wife for my son from there. 8But if the woman is not willing to follow you, then you will be free from this oath of mine; only you must not take my son back there." 9So the servant put his hand under the thigh of Abraham his master and swore to him concerning this matter.

10 Then the servant took ten of his master's camels and departed, taking all kinds of choice gifts from his master; and he set out and went to Aram-naharaim, to the city of Nahor. 11He made the camels kneel down outside the city by the well of water; it was toward evening, the time when women go out to draw water. 12And he said, "O LORD, God of my master Abraham, please grant me success today and show steadfast love to my master Abraham. 13I am standing here by the spring of water, and the daughters of the townspeople are coming out to draw water. 14Let the girl to whom I shall say, 'Please offer your jar that I may drink,' and who shall say, 'Drink, and I will water your camels'—let

---

24:1–67 *get a wife for my son.* With the death of Sarah, the promise of blessing needs a carrier into the future. The family plot moves to a new generation, and we are shown how betrothal and marriage customs are vitally important to individual families and whole communities. The son of Abraham will not marry a Canaanite, but only someone from among his own kinfolk. Canaan will be possessed only as blessing wrought by God, not married into. Although hidden in the dramatic plot, God is ever present as one who blesses and leads. Sometimes God's involvement in such human affairs as a courtship is not readily apparent; nor is the transmission of faith from one generation to the next. Often such discernment comes only in retrospect through the telling of a family tale. Here, Rebekah becomes Isaac's wife in Sarah's own tent, comforting him following his mother's death, a subtle indication of a much larger transition. By this delightful story we see that in his last days Abraham's faithful life has indeed been one of blessing, as life with God transitions to a new generation.

24:7, 27 **THE WITH-GOD LIFE**—*See* Spiritual Disciplines Index.

24:14 **SERVICE**—*See* Spiritual Disciplines Index.

her be the one whom you have appointed for your servant Isaac. By this I shall know that you have shown steadfast love to my master."

15 Before he had finished speaking, there was Rebekah, who was born to Bethuel son of Milcah, the wife of Nahor, Abraham's brother, coming out with her water jar on her shoulder. 16The girl was very fair to look upon, a virgin, whom no man had known. She went down to the spring, filled her jar, and came up. 17Then the servant ran to meet her and said, "Please let me sip a little water from your jar." 18"Drink, my lord," she said, and quickly lowered her jar upon her hand and gave him a drink. 19When she had finished giving him a drink, she said, "I will draw for your camels also, until they have finished drinking." 20So she quickly emptied her jar into the trough and ran again to the well to draw, and she drew for all his camels. 21The man gazed at her in silence to learn whether or not the LORD had made his journey successful.

22 When the camels had finished drinking, the man took a gold nose-ring weighing a half shekel, and two bracelets for her arms weighing ten gold shekels, 23and said, "Tell me whose daughter you are. Is there room in your father's house for us to spend the night?" 24She said to him, "I am the daughter of Bethuel son of Milcah, whom she bore to Nahor." 25She added, "We have plenty of straw and fodder and a place to spend the night." 26The man bowed his head and worshiped the LORD 27and said, "Blessed be the LORD, the God of my master Abraham, who has not forsaken his steadfast love and his faithfulness toward my master. As for me, the LORD has led me on the way to the house of my master's kin."

28 Then the girl ran and told her mother's household about these things. 29Rebekah had a brother whose name was Laban; and Laban ran out to the man, to the spring. 30As soon as he had seen the nose-ring, and the bracelets on his sister's arms, and when he heard the words of his sister Rebekah, "Thus the man

spoke to me," he went to the man; and there he was, standing by the camels at the spring. 31He said, "Come in, O blessed of the LORD. Why do you stand outside when I have prepared the house and a place for the camels?" 32So the man came into the house; and Laban unloaded the camels, and gave him straw and fodder for the camels, and water to wash his feet and the feet of the men who were with him. 33Then food was set before him to eat; but he said, "I will not eat until I have told my errand." He said, "Speak on."

34 So he said, "I am Abraham's servant. 35The LORD has greatly blessed my master, and he has become wealthy; he has given him flocks and herds, silver and gold, male and female slaves, camels and donkeys. 36And Sarah my master's wife bore a son to my master when she was old; and he has given him all that he has. 37My master made me swear, saying, 'You shall not take a wife for my son from the daughters of the Canaanites, in whose land I live; 38but you shall go to my father's house, to my kindred, and get a wife for my son.' 39I said to my master, 'Perhaps the woman will not follow me.' 40But he said to me, 'The LORD, before whom I walk, will send his angel with you and make your way successful. You shall get a wife for my son from my kindred, from my father's house. 41Then you will be free from my oath, when you come to my kindred; even if they will not give her to you, you will be free from my oath.'

42 "I came today to the spring, and said, 'O LORD, the God of my master Abraham, if now you will only make successful the way I am going! 43I am standing here by the spring of water; let the young woman who comes out to draw, to whom I shall say, "Please give me a little water from your jar to drink," 44and who will say to me, "Drink, and I will draw for your camels also"—let her be the woman whom the LORD has appointed for my master's son.'

45 "Before I had finished speaking in my heart, there was Rebekah coming out with her water jar on her shoulder; and she went

---

24:21 SILENCE—See Spiritual Disciplines Index.

down to the spring, and drew. I said to her, 'Please let me drink.' ⁴⁶She quickly let down her jar from her shoulder, and said, 'Drink, and I will also water your camels.' So I drank, and she also watered the camels. ⁴⁷Then I asked her, 'Whose daughter are you?' She said, 'The daughter of Bethuel, Nahor's son, whom Milcah bore to him.' So I put the ring on her nose, and the bracelets on her arms. ⁴⁸Then I bowed my head and worshiped the LORD, and blessed the LORD, the God of my master Abraham, who had led me by the right way to obtain the daughter of my master's kinsman for his son. ⁴⁹Now then, if you will deal loyally and truly with my master, tell me; and if not, tell me, so that I may turn either to the right hand or to the left."

⁵⁰ Then Laban and Bethuel answered, "The thing comes from the LORD; we cannot speak to you anything bad or good. ⁵¹Look, Rebekah is before you, take her and go, and let her be the wife of your master's son, as the LORD has spoken."

⁵² When Abraham's servant heard their words, he bowed himself to the ground before the LORD. ⁵³And the servant brought out jewelry of silver and of gold, and garments, and gave them to Rebekah; he also gave to her brother and to her mother costly ornaments. ⁵⁴Then he and the men who were with him ate and drank, and they spent the night there. When they rose in the morning, he said, "Send me back to my master." ⁵⁵Her brother and her mother said, "Let the girl remain with us a while, at least ten days; after that she may go." ⁵⁶But he said to them, "Do not delay me, since the LORD has made my journey successful; let me go that I may go to my master." ⁵⁷They said, "We will call the girl, and ask her." ⁵⁸And they called Rebekah, and said to her, "Will you go with this man?" She said, "I will." ⁵⁹So they sent away their sister Rebekah and her nurse along with Abraham's ser-

vant and his men. ⁶⁰And they blessed Rebekah and said to her,

"May you, our sister, become
   thousands of myriads;
may your offspring gain possession
   of the gates of their foes."

⁶¹Then Rebekah and her maids rose up, mounted the camels, and followed the man; thus the servant took Rebekah, and went his way.

62 Now Isaac had come from ᵃ Beer-lahai-roi, and was settled in the Negeb. ⁶³Isaac went out in the evening to walk ᵇ in the field; and looking up, he saw camels coming. ⁶⁴And Rebekah looked up, and when she saw Isaac, she slipped quickly from the camel, ⁶⁵and said to the servant, "Who is the man over there, walking in the field to meet us?" The servant said, "It is my master." So she took her veil and covered herself. ⁶⁶And the servant told Isaac all the things that he had done. ⁶⁷Then Isaac brought her into his mother Sarah's tent. He took Rebekah, and she became his wife; and he loved her. So Isaac was comforted after his mother's death.

Abraham Marries Keturah

25 Abraham took another wife, whose name was Keturah. ²She bore him Zimran, Jokshan, Medan, Midian, Ishbak, and Shuah. ³Jokshan was the father of Sheba and Dedan. The sons of Dedan were Asshurim, Letushim, and Leummim. ⁴The sons of Midian were Ephah, Epher, Hanoch, Abida, and Eldaah. All these were the children of Keturah. ⁵Abraham gave all he had to Isaac. ⁶But to the sons of his concubines Abraham gave gifts, while he was still living, and he sent them away from his son Isaac, eastward to the east country.

a Syr Tg: Heb *from coming to*   b Meaning of Heb word is uncertain

---

24:48 WORSHIP—*See* Spiritual Disciplines Index.

Responding
24:63 MEDITATION. The exact meaning of the Hebrew word translated "walk" in the NRSV is unclear, so it is often

translated "meditate." Why do open fields or spaces stimulate our desire to meditate? Set aside thirty minutes this week to go to a green-belt or open space. While walking, meditate on God's good creation: the beauty of the sky, the grass, the trees. *See also* Spiritual Disciplines Index.

The Death of Abraham

7 This is the length of Abraham's life, one hundred seventy-five years. 8Abraham breathed his last and died in a good old age, an old man and full of years, and was gathered to his people. 9His sons Isaac and Ishmael buried him in the cave of Machpelah, in the field of Ephron son of Zohar the Hittite, east of Mamre, 10the field that Abraham purchased from the Hittites. There Abraham was buried, with his wife Sarah. 11After the death of Abraham God blessed his son Isaac. And Isaac settled at Beer-lahai-roi.

Ishmael's Descendants

12 These are the descendants of Ishmael, Abraham's son, whom Hagar the Egyptian, Sarah's slave-girl, bore to Abraham. 13These are the names of the sons of Ishmael, named in the order of their birth: Nebaioth, the firstborn of Ishmael; and Kedar, Adbeel, Mibsam, 14Mishma, Dumah, Massa, 15Hadad, Tema, Jetur, Naphish, and Kedemah. 16These are the sons of Ishmael and these are their names, by their villages and by their encampments, twelve princes according to their tribes. 17(This is the length of the life of Ishmael, one hundred thirty-seven years; he breathed his last and died, and was gathered to his people.) 18They settled from Havilah to Shur, which is opposite Egypt in the direction of Assyria; he settled down a alongside of b all his people.

The Birth and Youth of Esau and Jacob

19 These are the descendants of Isaac, Abraham's son: Abraham was the father of Isaac, 20and Isaac was forty years old when he married Rebekah, daughter of Bethuel the Aramean of Paddan-aram, sister of Laban the Aramean. 21Isaac prayed to the LORD for his wife, because she was barren; and the LORD granted his prayer, and his wife Rebekah conceived. 22The children struggled together within her; and she said, "If it is to be this way, why do I live?" c So she went to inquire of the LORD. 23And the LORD said to her,

a Heb he fell   b Or down in opposition to
c Syr; Meaning of Heb uncertain

25:7–18 *Abraham breathed his last.* Together Isaac and Ishmael bury their father. The narrative lists their descendants, so that we know that Abraham died in the midst of God's kept promises, the gift of generations of heirs. God passes the blessing to Isaac, but Ishmael has a future too, a reminder that as the promise goes forth all families of the earth will be blessed. Although one family is chosen for special responsibility as heirs of promise, all families have a stake in God's blessing. God continues to create by speaking.

25:20–21 *she was barren.* The problem of barrenness persists in the next generation, again threatening the continuation of promise. Prayer figures prominently in the lives of these ancestors of faith as an essential component for a close relationship with God. Through prayer Rebekah and Isaac invoke the help of the Lord, who answers their prayers with the same intrusive divine speech present at creation.

25:21 PRAYER—*See* Spiritual Disciplines Index.

25:22–34 *The children struggled together within her.* Sibling rivalry begins in the womb! The oracle of 25:23 sets the stage for conflict to come. The children are different, representing two distinct nations, Israel and Edom, and two competing ways of life, hunters and shepherds; the prophecy Rebekah receives, that the elder shall serve the younger, begins an important theme that will continue through all of the Bible. We are not told why God chooses the younger brother to bear the blessing, but in so doing God disrupts the way human society is organized by categories of privilege given in birth order. God subverts long-held cultural traditions and laws establishing the priority of the eldest son, because the ways of God are never business as usual. The ready faith of Abraham gives way to a struggling Jacob, whose blessing is also a burden. The arena of God's involvement spans generations of a family marked by conflict, estrangement, and reconciliation. The whole Jacob narrative, which follows, will show how scandalous this God of Israel is as the promises work their way through the third generation's very earthy characters. They are a lot like us, a mixture of trust and distrust, hope and hopelessness, loyalty and treachery. The same God who works through them is present among us.

"Two nations are in your womb,
  and two peoples born of you shall be
    divided;
the one shall be stronger than the
    other,
  the elder shall serve the younger."
24When her time to give birth was at hand, there were twins in her womb. 25The first came out red, all his body like a hairy mantle; so they named him Esau. 26Afterward his brother came out, with his hand gripping Esau's heel; so he was named Jacob.*a* Isaac was sixty years old when she bore them.

27 When the boys grew up, Esau was a skillful hunter, a man of the field, while Jacob was a quiet man, living in tents. 28Isaac loved Esau, because he was fond of game; but Rebekah loved Jacob.

Esau Sells His Birthright

29 Once when Jacob was cooking a stew, Esau came in from the field, and he was famished. 30Esau said to Jacob, "Let me eat some of that red stuff, for I am famished!" (Therefore he was called Edom.*b*) 31Jacob said, "First sell me your birthright." 32Esau said, "I am about to die; of what use is a birthright to me?" 33Jacob said, "Swear to me first."*c* So he swore to him, and sold his birthright to Jacob. 34Then Jacob gave Esau bread and lentil stew, and he ate and drank, and rose and went his way. Thus Esau despised his birthright.

Isaac and Abimelech

26 Now there was a famine in the land, besides the former famine that had occurred in the days of Abraham. And Isaac went to Gerar, to King Abimelech of the Philistines. 2The LORD appeared to Isaac*d* and said, "Do not go down to Egypt; settle in the land that I shall show you. 3Reside in this land as an alien, and I will be with you, and will bless you; for to you and to your descendants I will give all these lands, and I will fulfill the oath that I swore to your father Abra-

ham. 4I will make your offspring as numerous as the stars of heaven, and will give to your offspring all these lands; and all the nations of the earth shall gain blessing for themselves through your offspring, 5because Abraham obeyed my voice and kept my charge, my commandments, my statutes, and my laws."

6 So Isaac settled in Gerar. 7When the men of the place asked him about his wife, he said, "She is my sister"; for he was afraid to say, "My wife," thinking, "or else the men of the place might kill me for the sake of Rebekah, because she is attractive in appearance." 8When Isaac had been there a long time, King Abimelech of the Philistines looked out of a window and saw him fondling his wife Rebekah. 9So Abimelech called for Isaac, and said, "So she is your wife! Why then did you say, 'She is my sister'?" Isaac said to him, "Because I thought I might die because of her." 10Abimelech said, "What is this you have done to us? One of the people might easily have lain with your wife, and you would have brought guilt upon us." 11So Abimelech warned all the people, saying, "Whoever touches this man or his wife shall be put to death."

12 Isaac sowed seed in that land, and in the same year reaped a hundredfold. The LORD blessed him, 13and the man became rich; he prospered more and more until he became very wealthy. 14He had possessions of flocks and herds, and a great household, so that the Philistines envied him. 15(Now the Philistines had stopped up and filled with earth all the wells that his father's servants had dug in the days of his father Abraham.) 16And Abimelech said to Isaac, "Go away from us; you have become too powerful for us."

17 So Isaac departed from there and camped in the valley of Gerar and settled

a That is *He takes by the heel* or *He supplants*
b That is *Red*   *c* Heb *today*   *d* Heb *him*

26:1–33 *as an alien.* These brief vignettes about Isaac show him as the bridge of God's blessings from one generation to the next. Despite numerous opportunities for conflicts, given Isaac's nomadic life, a precarious peace protects this carrier of God's promises. Isaac's resident alien status foreshadows the family's settling in the land. His material prosperity and increasing greatness are partial fulfillment of the blessing promised to his father, Abraham.

there. [18]Isaac dug again the wells of water that had been dug in the days of his father Abraham; for the Philistines had stopped them up after the death of Abraham; and he gave them the names that his father had given them. [19]But when Isaac's servants dug in the valley and found there a well of spring water, [20]the herders of Gerar quarreled with Isaac's herders, saying, "The water is ours." So he called the well Esek, [a] because they contended with him. [21]Then they dug another well, and they quarreled over that one also; so he called it Sitnah. [b] [22]He moved from there and dug another well, and they did not quarrel over it; so he called it Rehoboth, [c] saying, "Now the LORD has made room for us, and we shall be fruitful in the land."

23 From there he went up to Beer-sheba. [24]And that very night the LORD appeared to him and said, "I am the God of your father Abraham; do not be afraid, for I am with you and will bless you and make your offspring numerous for my servant Abraham's sake." [25]So he built an altar there, called on the name of the LORD, and pitched his tent there. And there Isaac's servants dug a well.

26 Then Abimelech went to him from Gerar, with Ahuzzath his adviser and Phicol the commander of his army. [27]Isaac said to them, "Why have you come to me, seeing that you hate me and have sent me away from you?" [28]They said, "We see plainly that the LORD has been with you; so we say, let there be an oath between you and us, and let us make a covenant with you [29]so that you will do us no harm, just as we have not touched you and have done to you nothing but good and have sent you away in peace. You are now the blessed of the LORD." [30]So he made them a feast, and they ate and drank. [31]In the morning they rose early and exchanged oaths; and Isaac set them on their way, and they departed from him in peace. [32]That same day Isaac's servants came and told him about the well that they had dug, and said to him, "We have found water!" [33]He called it Shibah; [d] therefore the name of the city is Beer-sheba [e] to this day.

Esau's Hittite Wives

34 When Esau was forty years old, he married Judith daughter of Beeri the Hittite, and Basemath daughter of Elon the Hittite; [35]and they made life bitter for Isaac and Rebekah.

Isaac Blesses Jacob

27 When Isaac was old and his eyes were dim so that he could not see, he called his elder son Esau and said to him, "My son"; and he answered, "Here I am." [2]He said, "See, I am old; I do not know the day of my death. [3]Now then, take your weapons, your quiver

a That is Contention   b That is Enmity   c That is Broad places or Room   d A word resembling the word for oath   e That is Well of the oath or Well of seven

---

26:24–28 THE WITH-GOD LIFE.—See Spiritual Disciplines Index.

27:1–45 When Isaac was old. The early, prenatal hints of conflict become full-blown as Jacob tricks Esau out of his blessing. The chosen one of God turns out to be a lying, duplicitous cheat of a brother. This is no easy morality tale, but rather a shadowy drama of family dysfunction brought on by divine election. The blessing is given in conjunction with a meal, showing the importance of ritual in religious life. The content of the blessing is material abundance from the good created earth, status among family and nations, and divine protection. The transmission of the blessing to a new generation happens amid a family devastated by deceit, grief, and hatred. Parents can take sides and scheme on behalf of children, but cannot repair broken dreams for the future. Spoken words and symbolic action matter, because once Isaac gives the blessing to Jacob, he cannot take it back. The blessed Jacob becomes a fugitive, showing how the blessing of God can bring with it a heavy burden. Esau is given a lesser blessing, indicating nonetheless that God's intentions extend beyond Israel. Through this tangled family soap opera God is making a holy people, set apart for his purposes. By choosing this younger brother, Jacob, God moves against the grain of customary practice. The story invites us to consider how God moves against the grain of our culture to call us, nurture us, compel us, and send us into a world to keep company with this strange and scandalous God.

and your bow, and go out to the field, and hunt game for me. ⁴Then prepare for me savory food, such as I like, and bring it to me to eat, so that I may bless you before I die."

5 Now Rebekah was listening when Isaac spoke to his son Esau. So when Esau went to the field to hunt for game and bring it, ⁶Rebekah said to her son Jacob, "I heard your father say to your brother Esau, ⁷'Bring me game, and prepare for me savory food to eat, that I may bless you before the LORD before I die.' ⁸Now therefore, my son, obey my word as I command you. ⁹Go to the flock, and get me two choice kids, so that I may prepare from them savory food for your father, such as he likes; ¹⁰and you shall take it to your father to eat, so that he may bless you before he dies." ¹¹But Jacob said to his mother Rebekah, "Look, my brother Esau is a hairy man, and I am a man of smooth skin. ¹²Perhaps my father will feel me, and I shall seem to be mocking him, and bring a curse on myself and not a blessing." ¹³His mother said to him, "Let your curse be on me, my son; only obey my word, and go, get them for me." ¹⁴So he went and got them and brought them to his mother; and his mother prepared savory food, such as his father loved. ¹⁵Then Rebekah took the best garments of her elder son Esau, which were with her in the house, and put them on her younger son Jacob; ¹⁶and she put the skins of the kids on his hands and on the smooth part of his neck. ¹⁷Then she handed the savory food, and the bread that she had prepared, to her son Jacob.

18 So he went in to his father, and said, "My father"; and he said, "Here I am; who are you, my son?" ¹⁹Jacob said to his father, "I am Esau your firstborn. I have done as you told me; now sit up and eat of my game, so that you may bless me." ²⁰But Isaac said to his son, "How is it that you have found it so quickly, my son?" He answered, "Because the LORD your God granted me success." ²¹Then Isaac said to Jacob, "Come near, that I may feel you, my son, to know whether you are really my son Esau or not." ²²So Jacob went up to his father Isaac, who felt him and said, "The voice is Jacob's voice, but the hands are the hands of Esau." ²³He did not recognize him, because his hands were hairy like his brother Esau's hands; so he blessed him. ²⁴He

said, "Are you really my son Esau?" He answered, "I am." ²⁵Then he said, "Bring it to me, that I may eat of my son's game and bless you." So he brought it to him, and he ate; and he brought him wine, and he drank. ²⁶Then his father Isaac said to him, "Come near and kiss me, my son." ²⁷So he came near and kissed him; and he smelled the smell of his garments, and blessed him, and said,

"Ah, the smell of my son
    is like the smell of a field that the
        LORD has blessed.
²⁸ May God give you of the dew of heaven,
    and of the fatness of the earth,
    and plenty of grain and wine.
²⁹ Let peoples serve you,
    and nations bow down to you.
Be lord over your brothers,
    and may your mother's sons bow
        down to you.
Cursed be everyone who curses you,
    and blessed be everyone who blesses
        you!"

Esau's Lost Blessing

30 As soon as Isaac had finished blessing Jacob, when Jacob had scarcely gone out from the presence of his father Isaac, his brother Esau came in from his hunting. ³¹He also prepared savory food, and brought it to his father. And he said to his father, "Let my father sit up and eat of his son's game, so that you may bless me." ³²His father Isaac said to him, "Who are you?" He answered, "I am your firstborn son, Esau." ³³Then Isaac trembled violently, and said, "Who was it then that hunted game and brought it to me, and I ate it all *a* before you came, and I have blessed him?— yes, and blessed he shall be!" ³⁴When Esau heard his father's words, he cried out with an exceedingly great and bitter cry, and said to his father, "Bless me, me also, father!" ³⁵But he said, "Your brother came deceitfully, and he has taken away your blessing." ³⁶Esau said, "Is he not rightly named Jacob? *a* For he has supplanted me these two times. He took away my birthright; and look, now he has taken away my blessing." Then he said, "Have you not reserved a blessing for me?" ³⁷Isaac answered Esau, "I have already made him your

a Cn: Heb *of all*

lord, and I have given him all his brothers as
servants, and with grain and wine I have sustained him. What then can I do for you, my
son?" 38Esau said to his father, "Have you only
one blessing, father? Bless me, me also, father!" And Esau lifted up his voice and wept.

39 Then his father Isaac answered him:

> "See, away from *b* the fatness of the
>   earth shall your home be,
>   and away from *c* the dew of heaven on
>   high.
> 40 By your sword you shall live,
>   and you shall serve your brother;
>   but when you break loose, *d*
>   you shall break his yoke from your
>   neck."

Jacob Escapes Esau's Fury

41 Now Esau hated Jacob because of the
blessing with which his father had blessed
him, and Esau said to himself, "The days of
mourning for my father are approaching;
then I will kill my brother Jacob." 42But the
words of her elder son Esau were told to Rebekah; so she sent and called her younger
son Jacob and said to him, "Your brother
Esau is consoling himself by planning to kill
you. 43Now therefore, my son, obey my voice;
flee at once to my brother Laban in Haran,
44and stay with him a while, until your brother's fury turns away— 45until your brother's
anger against you turns away, and he forgets
what you have done to him; then I will send,
and bring you back from there. Why should
I lose both of you in one day?"

46 Then Rebekah said to Isaac, "I am
weary of my life because of the Hittite
women. If Jacob marries one of the Hittite
women such as these, one of the women of
the land, what good will my life be to me?"

28 Then Isaac called Jacob and blessed
him, and charged him, "You shall

not marry one of the Canaanite women. 2Go
at once to Paddan-aram to the house of Bethuel, your mother's father; and take as wife
from there one of the daughters of Laban,
your mother's brother. 3May God Almighty *e*
bless you and make you fruitful and numerous, that you may become a company of peoples. 4May he give to you the blessing of Abraham, to you and to your offspring with you,
so that you may take possession of the land
where you now live as an alien—land that
God gave to Abraham." 5Thus Isaac sent Jacob
away; and he went to Paddan-aram, to Laban son of Bethuel the Aramean, the brother of Rebekah, Jacob's and Esau's mother.

Esau Marries Ishmael's Daughter

6 Now Esau saw that Isaac had blessed Jacob and sent him away to Paddan-aram to
take a wife from there, and that as he blessed
him he charged him, "You shall not marry
one of the Canaanite women," 7and that Jacob had obeyed his father and his mother
and gone to Paddan-aram. 8So when Esau
saw that the Canaanite women did not please
his father Isaac, 9Esau went to Ishmael and
took Mahalath daughter of Abraham's son
Ishmael, and sister of Nebaioth, to be his wife
in addition to the wives he had.

Jacob's Dream at Bethel

10 Jacob left Beer-sheba and went toward
Haran. 11He came to a certain place and stayed
there for the night, because the sun had set.
Taking one of the stones of the place, he put it
under his head and lay down in that place.
12And he dreamed that there was a ladder *f* set
up on the earth, the top of it reaching to heav-

a That is *He supplants* or *He takes by the heel*
b Or *See, of*   c Or *and of*   d Meaning of Heb
uncertain   e Traditional rendering of Heb *El
Shaddai*   f Or *stairway* or *ramp*

28:11–22 *he dreamed there was a ladder set
up.* Having duped his father, stolen the blessing,
and run from the rage of his brother, Jacob now
receives a glorious vision of God. He hardly
seems worthy. Although Jacob is alienated from
those closest to him, God appears and makes
the ancestral promise to Jacob directly. Dreams
are presented here and elsewhere as a special

medium for direct communication from God.
They come unbidden as gifts beyond any
control, and dreamers awake knowing they
have been visited and changed by God. In his
circumstances of estrangement, fear, and guilt,
Jacob unexpectedly encounters God and
discovers he is not alone. God is with Jacob
where he is, and the schemer becomes a

en; and the angels of God were ascending and descending on it. 13And the LORD stood beside him[a] and said, "I am the LORD, the God of Abraham your father and the God of Isaac; the land on which you lie I will give to you and to your offspring; 14and your offspring shall be like the dust of the earth, and you shall spread abroad to the west and to the east and to the north and to the south; and all the families of the earth shall be blessed[b] in you and in your offspring. 15Know that I am with you and will keep you wherever you go, and will bring you back to this land; for I will not leave you until I have done what I have promised you." 16Then Jacob woke from his sleep and said, "Surely the LORD is in this place—and I did not know it!" 17And he was afraid, and said, "How awesome is this place! This is none other than the house of God, and this is the gate of heaven."

18 So Jacob rose early in the morning, and he took the stone that he had put under his head and set it up for a pillar and poured oil on the top of it. 19He called that place Bethel;[c] but the name of the city was Luz at the first. 20Then Jacob made a vow, saying, "If God will be with me, and will keep me in this way that I go, and will give me bread to eat and clothing to wear, 21so that I come again to my father's house in peace, then the LORD shall be my God, 22and this stone, which I have set up for a pillar, shall be God's house; and of all that you give me I will surely give one-tenth to you."

Jacob Meets Rachel

29 Then Jacob went on his journey, and came to the land of the people of the east. 2As he looked, he saw a well in the field and three flocks of sheep lying there beside it; for out of that well the flocks were watered. The stone on the well's mouth was large, 3and when all the flocks were gathered there, the shepherds would roll the stone from the mouth of the well, and water the sheep, and put the stone back in its place on the mouth of the well.

4 Jacob said to them, "My brothers, where do you come from?" They said, "We are from Haran." 5He said to them, "Do you know Laban son of Nahor?" They said, "We do." 6He said to them, "Is it well with him?" "Yes," they replied, "and here is his daughter Rachel, coming with the sheep." 7He said, "Look, it is still broad daylight; it is not time for the animals to be gathered together. Water the sheep, and go, pasture them." 8But they said, "We cannot until all the flocks are gathered together, and the stone is rolled from the mouth of the well; then we water the sheep."

9 While he was still speaking with them, Rachel came with her father's sheep; for she kept them. 10Now when Jacob saw Rachel, the daughter of his mother's brother Laban, and the sheep of his mother's brother Laban, Jacob went up and rolled the stone from the well's mouth, and watered the flock of his mother's brother Laban. 11Then Jacob kissed Rachel, and wept aloud. 12And Jacob told Rachel that he was her father's kinsman, and that he was Rebekah's son; and she ran and told her father.

13 When Laban heard the news about his sister's son Jacob, he ran to meet him; he embraced him and kissed him, and brought him to his house. Jacob[d] told Laban all these things, 14and Laban said to him, "Surely you are my bone and my flesh!" And he stayed with him a month.

a Or *stood above it*   b Or *shall bless themselves*
c That is *House of God*   d Heb *He*

---

worshiper who marks the site as a sacred place. In naming the place Bethel, meaning "house of God," Jacob makes a deep commitment, reorienting his life toward worship of the One who journeys with him.

Responding
28:11–22 THE WITH-GOD LIFE. The children's song "We Are Climbing Jacob's Ladder" focuses on the ladder Jacob

saw in his dream, but fails to mention that the Lord stood beside Jacob and talked with him. Many centuries after Jacob, Peter quotes the prophet Joel, "Your old men shall dream dreams" (Acts 2:17). Have you or a person you know ever had a dream in which the Lord appeared and spoke? What emotions did the dream bring forth? How did it change you or your friend? See also Spiritual Disciplines Index.

Jacob Marries Laban's Daughters

15 Then Laban said to Jacob, "Because you are my kinsman, should you therefore serve me for nothing? Tell me, what shall your wages be?" ¹⁶Now Laban had two daughters; the name of the elder was Leah, and the name of the younger was Rachel. ¹⁷Leah's eyes were lovely,ᵃ and Rachel was graceful and beautiful. ¹⁸Jacob loved Rachel; so he said, "I will serve you seven years for your younger daughter Rachel." ¹⁹Laban said, "It is better that I give her to you than that I should give her to any other man; stay with me." ²⁰So Jacob served seven years for Rachel, and they seemed to him but a few days because of the love he had for her.

21 Then Jacob said to Laban, "Give me my wife that I may go in to her, for my time is completed." ²²So Laban gathered together all the people of the place, and made a feast. ²³But in the evening he took his daughter Leah and brought her to Jacob; and he went in to her. ²⁴(Laban gave his maid Zilpah to his daughter Leah to be her maid.) ²⁵When morning came, it was Leah! And Jacob said to Laban, "What is this you have done to me? Did I not serve with you for Rachel? Why then have you deceived me?" ²⁶Laban said, "This is not done in our country—giving the younger before the firstborn. ²⁷Complete the week of this one, and we will give you the other also in return for serving me another seven years." ²⁸Jacob did so, and completed her week; then Laban gave him his daughter Rachel as a wife. ²⁹(Laban gave his maid Bilhah to his daughter Rachel to be her maid.) ³⁰So Jacob went in to Rachel also, and he loved Rachel more than Leah. He served Labanᵇ for another seven years.

31 When the LORD saw that Leah was unloved, he opened her womb; but Rachel was barren. ³²Leah conceived and bore a son, and she named him Reuben;ᶜ for she said, "Because the LORD has looked on my affliction; surely now my husband will love me." ³³She conceived again and bore a son, and said, "Because the LORD has heardᵈ that I am hated, he has given me this son also"; and she named him Simeon. ³⁴Again she conceived and bore a son, and said, "Now this time my husband will be joinedᵉ to me, because I have borne him three sons"; therefore he was named Levi. ³⁵She conceived again and bore a son, and said, "This time I will praiseᶠ the LORD"; therefore she named him Judah; then she ceased bearing.

30 When Rachel saw that she bore Jacob no children, she envied her sister; and she said to Jacob, "Give me children, or I shall die!" ²Jacob became very angry with Rachel and said, "Am I in the place of God, who has withheld from you the fruit of the womb?" ³Then she said, "Here is my maid Bilhah; go in to her, that she may bear upon my knees and that I too may have children through her." ⁴So she gave him her maid Bilhah as a wife; and Jacob went in to her. ⁵And Bilhah conceived and bore Jacob a son. ⁶Then Rachel said, "God has judged me, and has also heard my voice and given me a son"; therefore she named him Dan.ᵍ ⁷Rachel's maid Bilhah conceived again and bore Jacob a second son. ⁸Then Rachel said, "With mighty wrestlings I have wrestledʰ with my sister, and have prevailed"; so she named him Naphtali.

9 When Leah saw that she had ceased

ᵃ Meaning of Heb uncertain   ᵇ Heb *him*
ᶜ That is *See, a son*   ᵈ Heb *shama*
ᵉ Heb *lawah*   ᶠ Heb *hodah*   ᵍ That is *He judged*
ʰ Heb *niphtal*

29:15–30 *Now Laban had two daughters.* The trickster is tricked! Jacob's troubled life continues with conflicts among family. This time Jacob is the one deceived. His uncle Laban tricks him into years of service and marriage to Leah before he can have Rachel. Again, barrenness persists for mothers in this family of promise. Leah and Rachel invoke the name of the Lord repeatedly in lament, hoping God will deliver the gift of children. However, they also try to take matters into their own hands, attempting to use the mandrake's presumed aphrodisiac powers to conceive. God is everywhere involved in this complex family drama of competing wives as the giver of children who will become the twelve tribes of Israel. The dream of innumerable heirs is coming to fruition.

29:20 SERVICE—*See* Spiritual Disciplines Index.

bearing children, she took her maid Zilpah and gave her to Jacob as a wife. ¹⁰Then Leah's maid Zilpah bore Jacob a son. ¹¹And Leah said, "Good fortune!" so she named him Gad.ᵃ ¹²Leah's maid Zilpah bore Jacob a second son. ¹³And Leah said, "Happy am I! For the women will call me happy"; so she named him Asher.ᵇ

14 In the days of wheat harvest Reuben went and found mandrakes in the field, and brought them to his mother Leah. Then Rachel said to Leah, "Please give me some of your son's mandrakes." ¹⁵But she said to her, "Is it a small matter that you have taken away my husband? Would you take away my son's mandrakes also?" Rachel said, "Then he may lie with you tonight for your son's mandrakes." ¹⁶When Jacob came from the field in the evening, Leah went out to meet him, and said, "You must come in to me; for I have hired you with my son's mandrakes." So he lay with her that night. ¹⁷And God heeded Leah, and she conceived and bore Jacob a fifth son. ¹⁸Leah said, "God has given me my hireᶜ because I gave my maid to my husband"; so she named him Issachar. ¹⁹And Leah conceived again, and she bore Jacob a sixth son. ²⁰Then Leah said, "God has endowed me with a good dowry; now my husband will honorᵈ me, because I have borne him six sons"; so she named him Zebulun. ²¹Afterwards she bore a daughter, and named her Dinah.

22 Then God remembered Rachel, and God heeded her and opened her womb. ²³She conceived and bore a son, and said, "God has taken away my reproach"; ²⁴and she named him Joseph,ᵉ saying, "May the LORD add to me another son!"

Jacob Prospers at Laban's Expense

25 When Rachel had borne Joseph, Jacob said to Laban, "Send me away, that I may go to my own home and country. ²⁶Give me my wives and my children for whom I have served you, and let me go; for you know very well the service I have given you." ²⁷But Laban said to him, "If you will allow me to say so, I have learned by divination that the LORD has blessed me because of you; ²⁸name your wages, and I will give it." ²⁹Jacob said to him, "You yourself know how I have served you, and how your cattle have fared with me. ³⁰For you had little before I came, and it has increased abundantly; and the LORD has blessed you wherever I turned. But now when shall I provide for my own household also?" ³¹He said, "What shall I give you?" Jacob said, "You shall not give me anything; if you will do this for me, I will again feed your flock and keep it: ³²let me pass through all your flock today, removing from it every speckled and spotted sheep and every black lamb, and the spotted and speckled among the goats; and such shall be my wages. ³³So my honesty will answer for me later, when you come to look into my wages with you. Every one that is not speckled and spotted among the goats and black among the lambs, if found with me, shall be counted stolen." ³⁴Laban said, "Good! Let it be as you have said." ³⁵But that day Laban removed the male goats that were striped and spotted, and all the female goats that were speckled and spotted, every one that had white on it, and every lamb that was black, and put them in charge of his sons; ³⁶and he set a distance of three days' journey between himself and Jacob, while Jacob was pasturing the rest of Laban's flock.

37 Then Jacob took fresh rods of poplar and almond and plane, and peeled white streaks in them, exposing the white of the rods. ³⁸He set the rods that he had peeled in front of the flocks in the troughs, that is, the watering places, where the flocks came to drink. And since they bred when they came

ᵃ That is *Fortune*   ᵇ That is *Happy*
ᶜ Heb *sakar*   ᵈ Heb *zabal*   ᵉ That is *He adds*

30:22–43 *God remembered Rachel.* The birth of Joseph is conceived in the memory of God. God hears Rachel's prayers, remembers, and responds, assuring a future for Jacob and his chosen wife, Rachel. With the birth of Joseph, Jacob is ready to settle in his own land. Conflict with Laban continues over the rightful earnings of his labor among his uncle's holdings. Bearing the blessing of God still requires hard work to see it come to fruition. Such is the struggle of faith on a journey with a God so entangled with human affairs.

to drink, ³⁹the flocks bred in front of the rods, and so the flocks produced young that were striped, speckled, and spotted. ⁴⁰Jacob separated the lambs, and set the faces of the flocks toward the striped and the completely black animals in the flock of Laban; and he put his own droves apart, and did not put them with Laban's flock. ⁴¹Whenever the stronger of the flock were breeding, Jacob laid the rods in the troughs before the eyes of the flock, that they might breed among the rods, ⁴²but for the feebler of the flock he did not lay them there; so the feebler were Laban's, and the stronger Jacob's. ⁴³Thus the man grew exceedingly rich, and had large flocks, and male and female slaves, and camels and donkeys.

Jacob Flees with Family and Flocks

31 Now Jacob heard that the sons of Laban were saying, "Jacob has taken all that was our father's; he has gained all this wealth from what belonged to our father." ²And Jacob saw that Laban did not regard him as favorably as he did before. ³Then the Lord said to Jacob, "Return to the land of your ancestors and to your kindred, and I will be with you." ⁴So Jacob sent and called Rachel and Leah into the field where his flock was, ⁵and said to them, "I see that your father does not regard me as favorably as he did before. But the God of my father has been with me. ⁶You know that I have served your father with all my strength; ⁷yet your father has cheated me and changed my wages ten times, but God did not permit him to harm me. ⁸If he said, 'The speckled shall be your wages,' then all the flock bore speckled; and if he said, 'The striped shall be your wages,' then all the flock bore striped. ⁹Thus God has taken away the livestock of your father, and given them to me.

10 "During the mating of the flock I once had a dream in which I looked up and saw that the male goats that leaped upon the flock were striped, speckled, and mottled. ¹¹Then the angel of God said to me in the dream, 'Jacob,' and I said, 'Here I am!' ¹²And he said, 'Look up and see that all the goats that leap on the flock are striped, speckled, and mottled; for I have seen all that Laban is doing to you. ¹³I am the God of Bethel, *a* where you anointed a pillar and made a vow to me. Now leave this land at once and return to the land of your birth.' " ¹⁴Then Rachel and Leah answered him, "Is there any portion or inheritance left to us in our father's house? ¹⁵Are we not regarded by him as foreigners? For he has sold us, and he has been using up the money given for us. ¹⁶All the property that God has taken away from our father belongs to us and to our children; now then, do whatever God has said to you."

17 So Jacob arose, and set his children and his wives on camels; ¹⁸and he drove away all his livestock, all the property that he had gained, the livestock in his possession that he had acquired in Paddan-aram, to go to his father Isaac in the land of Canaan.

19 Now Laban had gone to shear his sheep, and Rachel stole her father's household gods. ²⁰And Jacob deceived Laban the Aramean, in that he did not tell him that he intended to flee. ²¹So he fled with all that he had; starting out he crossed the Euphrates, *b* and set his face toward the hill country of Gilead.

Laban Overtakes Jacob

22 On the third day Laban was told that Jacob had fled. ²³So he took his kinsfolk with him and pursued him for seven days until he caught up with him in the hill country of Gilead. ²⁴But God came to Laban the

a Cn: Meaning of Heb uncertain   *b* Heb *the river*

31:3–54 *Return to the land of your ancestors.* Heeding the direct address of God and assured of God's promised presence, Jacob heads out on his own. Rich in flocks and with a large family in tow, Jacob departs the conflict-ridden relationship with Laban. A pillar marks the truce between them (vv 51–52). The conflict among in-laws in this family never dissipates, and yet God moves the family forward toward the realization of blessing. God never promises that family life will be harmoniously free of tension and competition. In the midst of dysfunction comes the goodness of the birth of children and bright hope for the future.

Aramean in a dream by night, and said to him, "Take heed that you say not a word to Jacob, either good or bad."

25 Laban overtook Jacob. Now Jacob had pitched his tent in the hill country, and Laban with his kinsfolk camped in the hill country of Gilead. 26Laban said to Jacob, "What have you done? You have deceived me, and carried away my daughters like captives of the sword. 27Why did you flee secretly and deceive me and not tell me? I would have sent you away with mirth and songs, with tambourine and lyre. 28And why did you not permit me to kiss my sons and my daughters farewell? What you have done is foolish. 29It is in my power to do you harm; but the God of your father spoke to me last night, saying, 'Take heed that you speak to Jacob neither good nor bad.' 30Even though you had to go because you longed greatly for your father's house, why did you steal my gods?" 31Jacob answered Laban, "Because I was afraid, for I thought that you would take your daughters from me by force. 32But anyone with whom you find your gods shall not live. In the presence of our kinsfolk, point out what I have that is yours, and take it." Now Jacob did not know that Rachel had stolen the gods.*a*

33 So Laban went into Jacob's tent, and into Leah's tent, and into the tent of the two maids, but he did not find them. And he went out of Leah's tent, and entered Rachel's. 34Now Rachel had taken the household gods and put them in the camel's saddle, and sat on them. Laban felt all about in the tent, but did not find them. 35And she said to her father, "Let not my lord be angry that I cannot rise before you, for the way of women is upon me." So he searched, but did not find the household gods.

36 Then Jacob became angry, and upbraided Laban. Jacob said to Laban, "What is my offense? What is my sin, that you have hotly pursued me? 37Although you have felt about through all my goods, what have you found of all your household goods? Set it here before my kinsfolk and your kinsfolk, so that they may decide between us two. 38These twenty years I have been with you; your ewes and your female goats have not

miscarried, and I have not eaten the rams of your flocks. 39That which was torn by wild beasts I did not bring to you; I bore the loss of it myself; of my hand you required it, whether stolen by day or stolen by night. 40It was like this with me: by day the heat consumed me, and the cold by night, and my sleep fled from my eyes. 41These twenty years I have been in your house; I served you fourteen years for your two daughters, and six years for your flock, and you have changed my wages ten times. 42If the God of my father, the God of Abraham and the Fear *b* of Isaac, had not been on my side, surely now you would have sent me away empty-handed. God saw my affliction and the labor of my hands, and rebuked you last night."

Laban and Jacob Make a Covenant

43 Then Laban answered and said to Jacob, "The daughters are my daughters, the children are my children, the flocks are my flocks, and all that you see is mine. But what can I do today about these daughters of mine, or about their children whom they have borne? 44Come now, let us make a covenant, you and I; and let it be a witness between you and me." 45So Jacob took a stone, and set it up as a pillar. 46And Jacob said to his kinsfolk, "Gather stones," and they took stones, and made a heap; and they ate there by the heap. 47Laban called it Jegar-sahadutha: *c* but Jacob called it Galeed. *d* 48Laban said, "This heap is a witness between you and me today." Therefore he called it Galeed, 49and the pillar *e* Mizpah, *f* for he said, "The LORD watch between you and me, when we are absent one from the other. 50If you ill-treat my daughters, or if you take wives in addition to my daughters, though no one else is with us, remember that God is witness between you and me."

51 Then Laban said to Jacob, "See this heap and see the pillar, which I have set between you and me. 52This heap is a witness, and the pillar is a witness, that I will not pass beyond this heap to you, and you will not

---

a Heb *them*   *b* Meaning of Heb uncertain
c In Aramaic *The heap of witness*   *d* In Hebrew
The heap of witness   *e* Compare Sam: MT lacks *the pillar*   *f* That is *Watchpost*

pass beyond this heap and this pillar to me, for harm. [53]May the God of Abraham and the God of Nahor"—the God of their father—"judge between us." So Jacob swore by the Fear[a] of his father Isaac, [54]and Jacob offered a sacrifice on the height and called his kinsfolk to eat bread; and they ate bread and tarried all night in the hill country.

[55][b] Early in the morning Laban rose up, and kissed his grandchildren and his daughters and blessed them; then he departed and returned home.

32 Jacob went on his way and the angels of God met him; [2]and when Jacob saw them he said, "This is God's camp!" So he called that place Mahanaim.[c]

Jacob Sends Presents to Appease Esau

[3] Jacob sent messengers before him to his brother Esau in the land of Seir, the country of Edom, [4]instructing them, "Thus you shall say to my lord Esau: Thus says your servant Jacob, 'I have lived with Laban as an alien, and stayed until now; [5]and I have oxen, donkeys, flocks, male and female slaves; and I have sent to tell my lord, in order that I may find favor in your sight.' "

[6] The messengers returned to Jacob, saying, "We came to your brother Esau, and he is coming to meet you, and four hundred men are with him." [7]Then Jacob was greatly afraid and distressed; and he divided the people that were with him, and the flocks and herds and camels, into two companies, [8]thinking, "If Esau comes to the one company and destroys it, then the company that is left will escape."

[9] And Jacob said, "O God of my father Abraham and God of my father Isaac, O LORD who said to me, 'Return to your country and to your kindred, and I will do you good,' [10]I am not worthy of the least of all the steadfast love and all the faithfulness that you have shown to your servant, for with only my staff I crossed this Jordan; and now I have become two companies. [11]Deliver me, please, from the hand of my brother, from the hand of Esau, for I am afraid of him; he may come and kill us all, the mothers with the children. [12]Yet you have said, 'I will surely do you good, and make your offspring as the sand of the sea, which cannot be counted because of their number.' "

[13] So he spent that night there, and from what he had with him he took a present for his brother Esau, [14]two hundred female goats and twenty male goats, two hundred ewes and twenty rams, [15]thirty milch camels and their colts, forty cows and ten bulls, twenty female donkeys and ten male donkeys. [16]These he delivered into the hand of his servants, every drove by itself, and said to his servants, "Pass on ahead of me, and put a space between drove and drove." [17]He instructed the foremost, "When Esau my brother meets you, and asks you, 'To whom do you belong? Where are you going? And whose are these ahead of you?' [18]then you shall say, 'They belong to your servant Jacob; they are a present sent to my lord Esau; and moreover he is behind us.' " [19]He likewise instructed the second and the third and all who followed the droves, "You shall say the same thing to Esau when you meet him, [20]and you shall say, 'Moreover your servant Jacob is behind us.' " For he thought, "I may appease him with the present that goes ahead of me, and afterwards I shall see his face; perhaps he will accept me." [21]So the present passed on ahead of him; and he himself spent that night in the camp.

a Meaning of Heb uncertain   b Ch 32.1 in Heb
c Here taken to mean *Two camps*

32:3–21 *Jacob sent messengers . . . to his brother Esau.* Jacob's hardships in the company of his uncle Laban coupled with the reassuring presence of God turn him toward reconciliation with his estranged brother, Esau. All of his children and his accumulated wealth cannot compensate for his old desire to be reunited with his twin. Jacob's preparation is practical, in his sending of messengers and provisions ahead, and spiritual, in his invocation of the God of his ancestors and confession of his fearful unworthiness. Jacob's perseverance through conflict seems to be maturing his faith.

32:10 SERVICE—See Spiritual Disciplines Index.

Jacob Wrestles at Peniel

22 The same night he got up and took his two wives, his two maids, and his eleven children, and crossed the ford of the Jabbok. 23He took them and sent them across the stream, and likewise everything that he had. 24Jacob was left alone, and a man wrestled with him until daybreak. 25When the man saw that he did not prevail against Jacob, he struck him on the hip socket; and Jacob's hip was put out of joint as he wrestled with him. 26Then he said, "Let me go, for the day is breaking." But Jacob said, "I will not let you go, unless you bless me." 27So he said to him, "What is your name?" And he said, "Jacob." 28Then the man*a* said, "You shall no longer be called Jacob, but Israel,*b* for you have striven with God and with humans,*c* and have prevailed." 29Then Jacob asked him, "Please tell me your name." But he said, "Why is it that you ask my name?" And there he blessed him. 30So Jacob called the place Peniel,*d* saying, "For I

have seen God face to face, and yet my life is preserved." 31The sun rose upon him as he passed Penuel, limping because of his hip. 32Therefore to this day the Israelites do not eat the thigh muscle that is on the hip socket, because he struck Jacob on the hip socket at the thigh muscle.

Jacob and Esau Meet

33 Now Jacob looked up and saw Esau coming, and four hundred men with him. So he divided the children among Leah and Rachel and the two maids. 2He put the maids with their children in front, then Leah with her children, and Rachel and Joseph last of all. 3He himself went on ahead of them, bowing himself to the ground seven times, until he came near his brother.

4 But Esau ran to meet him, and embraced

---

a Heb *he* *b* That is *The one who strives with God* or *God strives* *c* Or *with divine and human beings* *d* That is *The face of God*

32:22–32 *a man wrestled with him until daybreak.* Jacob's difficulties among his kin have been punctuated by appearances of God. Twenty years have passed since Jacob fled Esau's wrath with a stolen blessing. The anticipation of reunion is filled with anxiety, and before reconciliation with his brother occurs he must contend with God. The nighttime wrestling match with Someone divine is obscured in the shadows of mystery. It leaves room for interpretation of what such struggling with God entails. What is clear is that, although Jacob prevails, he also acquires a new name and a limp. Jacob's name, meaning "takes by the heel, overreacher, supplanter," connotes the struggle he has known. Insisting he be blessed by the midnight stranger, Jacob receives the new name Israel, indicating that "God rules," "God preserves," "God protects," "God strives." The faith community of Israel begins in an intense wrestling match with God, allaying any notion that communal life with God is easily maneuvered. Filled with mystery, this encounter with God is also characterized by remarkable intimacy. Notice that the wrestling stranger refuses to be named. God comes so close we cannot even see exactly who or what has gotten hold of us. However, after such an encounter we go

forward blessed—wounded perhaps, but always changed.

Responding
32:24 SOLITUDE. Why does the word "alone" often strike fear into the hearts of the bravest of us? Could one reason be an unhealthy reliance on other people instead of on God for our well-being and happiness? What are some other reasons? Pick the one reason that best describes why you fear being alone. During your lunch break this week find a place where you can be by yourself for a few minutes and quietly talk with God about that fear. *See also* Spiritual Disciplines Index.

33:1–16 *Jacob looked up and saw Esau coming.* Encounters with God affect how we deal with one another and make way for reconciliation. Even as Jacob prepares a line of defense to protect Rachel and Joseph, fully expecting Esau may seek to do harm, he meets instead his brother running toward him with arms outstretched for embracing. The graciousness of Esau, the narrator tells us, exemplifies the graciousness of God. Love for God and love for one another go hand in hand. Coming to terms with God allows for human reconciliation.

him, and fell on his neck and kissed him, and they wept. 5When Esau looked up and saw the women and children, he said, "Who are these with you?" Jacob said, "The children whom God has graciously given your servant." 6Then the maids drew near, they and their children, and bowed down; 7Leah likewise and her children drew near and bowed down; and finally Joseph and Rachel drew near, and they bowed down. 8Esau said, "What do you mean by all this company that I met?" Jacob answered, "To find favor with my lord." 9But Esau said, "I have enough, my brother; keep what you have for yourself." 10Jacob said, "No, please; if I find favor with you, then accept my present from my hand; for truly to see your face is like seeing the face of God—since you have received me with such favor. 11Please accept my gift that is brought to you, because God has dealt graciously with me, and because I have everything I want." So he urged him, and he took it.

12 Then Esau said, "Let us journey on our way, and I will go alongside you." 13But Jacob said to him, "My lord knows that the children are frail and that the flocks and herds, which are nursing, are a care to me; and if they are overdriven for one day, all the flocks will die. 14Let my lord pass on ahead of his servant, and I will lead on slowly, according to the pace of the cattle that are before me and according to the pace of the children, until I come to my lord in Seir."

15 So Esau said, "Let me leave with you some of the people who are with me." But he said, "Why should my lord be so kind to me?" 16So Esau returned that day on his way to Seir. 17But Jacob journeyed to Succoth, a and built himself a house, and made booths for his cattle; therefore the place is called Succoth.

Jacob Reaches Shechem

18 Jacob came safely to the city of Shechem, which is in the land of Canaan, on his way from Paddan-aram; and he camped before the city. 19And from the sons of Hamor, Shechem's father, he bought for one hundred pieces of money b the plot of land on which he had pitched his tent. 20There he erected an altar and called it El-Elohe-Israel. c

The Rape of Dinah

34 Now Dinah the daughter of Leah, whom she had borne to Jacob, went out to visit the women of the region. 2When Shechem son of Hamor the Hivite, prince of the region, saw her, he seized her and lay with her by force. 3And his soul was drawn to Dinah daughter of Jacob; he loved the girl, and spoke tenderly to her. 4So Shechem spoke to his father Hamor, saying, "Get me this girl to be my wife."

5 Now Jacob heard that Shechem d had defiled his daughter Dinah; but his sons were with his cattle in the field, so Jacob held his peace until they came. 6And Hamor the father of Shechem went out to Jacob to speak

a That is *Booths*   b Heb *one hundred qesitah*
c That is *God, the God of Israel*   d Heb *he*

33:18–20 *in the land of Canaan.* Finally, after Jacob and Esau are reconciled, the family settles in the land of Canaan. The promise-keeping companion of the scoundrel Jacob is worshiped as the God of Israel.

34:1–31 *Dinah the daughter of Leah.* The Promised Land is occupied, but the family's settlement doesn't come easily. No sooner is the land entered than the family's security is threatened by the violent rape of Dinah, Jacob's one named daughter. Shechem offers to marry Dinah, which is his right according to custom. He can pay her father for having raped the unbetrothed virgin daughter. If she is not allowed to marry Shechem, she will never

marry. The revenge of Jacob's sons then completely silences Dinah. The family of Israel is left to contend with intermingling and intermarrying among a people of pagan gods. This horrible story gives the listening community permission to discuss the oppression and violence against women and the cultural mores that support it. Although God is not explicitly mentioned, the inclusion of this story affirms that God is involved in the most painfully tragic of human affairs. Among a people of many gods, through the children of Israel, God is creating a different kind of faith community whose stories concern the status of all people.

with him, [7]just as the sons of Jacob came in from the field. When they heard of it, the men were indignant and very angry, because he had committed an outrage in Israel by lying with Jacob's daughter, for such a thing ought not to be done.

8 But Hamor spoke with them, saying, "The heart of my son Shechem longs for your daughter; please give her to him in marriage. [9]Make marriages with us; give your daughters to us, and take our daughters for yourselves. [10]You shall live with us; and the land shall be open to you; live and trade in it, and get property in it." [11]Shechem also said to her father and to her brothers, "Let me find favor with you, and whatever you say to me I will give. [12]Put the marriage present and gift as high as you like, and I will give whatever you ask me; only give me the girl to be my wife."

13 The sons of Jacob answered Shechem and his father Hamor deceitfully, because he had defiled their sister Dinah. [14]They said to them, "We cannot do this thing, to give our sister to one who is uncircumcised, for that would be a disgrace to us. [15]Only on this condition will we consent to you: that you will become as we are and every male among you be circumcised. [16]Then we will give our daughters to you, and we will take your daughters for ourselves, and we will live among you and become one people. [17]But if you will not listen to us and be circumcised, then we will take our daughter and be gone."

18 Their words pleased Hamor and Hamor's son Shechem. [19]And the young man did not delay to do the thing, because he was delighted with Jacob's daughter. Now he was the most honored of all his family. [20]So Hamor and his son Shechem came to the gate of their city and spoke to the men of their city, saying, [21]"These people are friendly with us; let them live in the land and trade in it, for the land is large enough for them; let us take their daughters in marriage, and let us give them our daughters. [22]Only on this condition will they agree to live among us, to become one people: that every male among us be circumcised as they are circumcised. [23]Will not their livestock, their property, and all their animals be ours? Only let us agree with them, and they will live among us." [24]And all who went out of the city gate heeded Hamor and his son Shechem; and every male was circumcised, all who went out of the gate of his city.

Dinah's Brothers Avenge Their Sister

25 On the third day, when they were still in pain, two of the sons of Jacob, Simeon and Levi, Dinah's brothers, took their swords and came against the city unawares, and killed all the males. [26]They killed Hamor and his son Shechem with the sword, and took Dinah out of Shechem's house, and went away. [27]And the other sons of Jacob came upon the slain, and plundered the city, because their sister had been defiled. [28]They took their flocks and their herds, their donkeys, and whatever was in the city and in the field. [29]All their wealth, all their little ones and their wives, all that was in the houses, they captured and made their prey. [30]Then Jacob said to Simeon and Levi, "You have brought trouble on me by making me odious to the inhabitants of the land, the Canaanites and the Perizzites; my numbers are few, and if they gather themselves against me and attack me, I shall be destroyed, both I and my household." [31]But they said, "Should our sister be treated like a whore?"

Jacob Returns to Bethel

35 God said to Jacob, "Arise, go up to Bethel, and settle there. Make an altar there to the God who appeared to you when you fled from your brother Esau." [2]So

---

35:1–20 *go up to Bethel.* On the move again because of his sons' violent revenge among the Canaanites, Israel returns to Bethel, a place of worship made sacred by God's appearance to him there. His youngest son, Benjamin, is born in the tragedy of his beloved Rachel's death, signifying again the passage of promise from one generation to the next. The pathos of a complex life follows this chosen one of God to the end. All of the natural rhythms of life, as we have seen them dramatically unfold in this story, including birth and death, joy and sorrow, estrangement and reunion, violence and prosperity, are the context for God's activity among us.

Jacob said to his household and to all who were with him, "Put away the foreign gods that are among you, and purify yourselves, and change your clothes; [3]then come, let us go up to Bethel, that I may make an altar there to the God who answered me in the day of my distress and has been with me wherever I have gone." [4]So they gave to Jacob all the foreign gods that they had, and the rings that were in their ears; and Jacob hid them under the oak that was near Shechem.

5 As they journeyed, a terror from God fell upon the cities all around them, so that no one pursued them. [6]Jacob came to Luz (that is, Bethel), which is in the land of Canaan, he and all the people who were with him, [7]and there he built an altar and called the place El-bethel,[a] because it was there that God had revealed himself to him when he fled from his brother. [8]And Deborah, Rebekah's nurse, died, and she was buried under an oak below Bethel. So it was called Allon-bacuth.[b]

9 God appeared to Jacob again when he came from Paddan-aram, and he blessed him. [10]God said to him, "Your name is Jacob; no longer shall you be called Jacob, but Israel shall be your name." So he was called Israel. [11]God said to him, "I am God Almighty:[c] be fruitful and multiply; a nation and a company of nations shall come from you, and kings shall spring from you. [12]The land that I gave to Abraham and Isaac I will give to you, and I will give the land to your offspring after you." [13]Then God went up from him at the place where he had spoken with him. [14]Jacob set up a pillar in the place where he had spoken with him, a pillar of stone; and he poured out a drink offering on it, and poured oil on it. [15]So Jacob called the place where God had spoken with him Bethel.

The Birth of Benjamin and the Death of Rachel

16 Then they journeyed from Bethel; and when they were still some distance from Eph-

rath, Rachel was in childbirth, and she had hard labor. [17]When she was in her hard labor, the midwife said to her, "Do not be afraid; for now you will have another son." [18]As her soul was departing (for she died), she named him Ben-oni;[d] but his father called him Benjamin.[e] [19]So Rachel died, and she was buried on the way to Ephrath (that is, Bethlehem), [20]and Jacob set up a pillar at her grave; it is the pillar of Rachel's tomb, which is there to this day. [21]Israel journeyed on, and pitched his tent beyond the tower of Eder.

22 While Israel lived in that land, Reuben went and lay with Bilhah his father's concubine; and Israel heard of it.

Now the sons of Jacob were twelve. [23]The sons of Leah: Reuben (Jacob's firstborn), Simeon, Levi, Judah, Issachar, and Zebulun. [24]The sons of Rachel: Joseph and Benjamin. [25]The sons of Bilhah, Rachel's maid: Dan and Naphtali. [26]The sons of Zilpah, Leah's maid: Gad and Asher. These were the sons of Jacob who were born to him in Paddan-aram.

The Death of Isaac

27 Jacob came to his father Isaac at Mamre, or Kiriath-arba (that is, Hebron), where Abraham and Isaac had resided as aliens. [28]Now the days of Isaac were one hundred eighty years. [29]And Isaac breathed his last; he died and was gathered to his people, old and full of days; and his sons Esau and Jacob buried him.

Esau's Descendants

36 These are the descendants of Esau (that is, Edom). [2]Esau took his wives from the Canaanites: Adah daughter of Elon the Hittite, Oholibamah daughter of Anah son[f] of Zibeon the Hivite, [3]and Basemath,

a That is *God of Bethel*   b That is *Oak of weeping*
c Traditional rendering of Heb *El Shaddai*
d That is *Son of my sorrow*   e That is *Son of the right hand* or *Son of the South*   f Sam Gk Syr: Heb *daughter*

36:1–43 *The descendants of Esau.* Just as the narrative included Ishmael along with Isaac at Abraham's death, so it is concerned here to communicate care for another one not chosen, Esau. In the end the text remembers Esau not merely as a fool for selling his birthright for a bowl of stew or as a victim of his brother's deception, but as the father of nations. It affirms the broad inclusivity of God's promise.

Ishmael's daughter, sister of Nebaioth. [4]Adah bore Eliphaz to Esau; Basemath bore Reuel; [5]and Oholibamah bore Jeush, Jalam, and Korah. These are the sons of Esau who were born to him in the land of Canaan.

6 Then Esau took his wives, his sons, his daughters, and all the members of his household, his cattle, all his livestock, and all the property he had acquired in the land of Canaan; and he moved to a land some distance from his brother Jacob. [7]For their possessions were too great for them to live together; the land where they were staying could not support them because of their livestock. [8]So Esau settled in the hill country of Seir; Esau is Edom.

9 These are the descendants of Esau, ancestor of the Edomites, in the hill country of Seir. [10]These are the names of Esau's sons: Eliphaz son of Adah the wife of Esau; Reuel, the son of Esau's wife Basemath. [11]The sons of Eliphaz were Teman, Omar, Zepho, Gatam, and Kenaz. [12](Timna was a concubine of Eliphaz, Esau's son; she bore Amalek to Eliphaz.) These were the sons of Adah, Esau's wife. [13]These were the sons of Reuel: Nahath, Zerah, Shammah, and Mizzah. These were the sons of Esau's wife, Basemath. [14]These were the sons of Esau's wife Oholibamah, daughter of Anah son[a] of Zibeon: she bore to Esau Jeush, Jalam, and Korah.

Clans and Kings of Edom

15 These are the clans[b] of the sons of Esau. The sons of Eliphaz the firstborn of Esau: the clans[b] Teman, Omar, Zepho, Kenaz, [16]Korah, Gatam, and Amalek; these are the clans[b] of Eliphaz in the land of Edom; they are the sons of Adah. [17]These are the sons of Esau's son Reuel: the clans[b] Nahath, Zerah, Shammah, and Mizzah; these are the clans[b] of Reuel in the land of Edom; they are the sons of Esau's wife Basemath. [18]These are the sons of Esau's wife Oholibamah: the clans[b] Jeush, Jalam, and Korah; these are the clans[b] born of Esau's wife Oholibamah, the daughter of Anah. [19]These are the sons of Esau (that is, Edom), and these are their clans.[b]

20 These are the sons of Seir the Horite, the inhabitants of the land: Lotan, Shobal, Zibeon, Anah, [21]Dishon, Ezer, and Dishan; these are the clans[c] of the Horites, the sons of Seir in the land of Edom. [22]The sons of Lotan were Hori and Heman; and Lotan's sister was Timna. [23]These are the sons of Shobal: Alvan, Manahath, Ebal, Shepho, and Onam. [24]These are the sons of Zibeon: Aiah and Anah; he is the Anah who found the springs[c] in the wilderness, as he pastured the donkeys of his father Zibeon. [25]These are the children of Anah: Dishon and Oholibamah daughter of Anah. [26]These are the sons of Dishon: Hemdan, Eshban, Ithran, and Cheran. [27]These are the sons of Ezer: Bilhan, Zaavan, and Akan. [28]These are the sons of Dishan: Uz and Aran. [29]These are the clans[b] of the Horites: the clans[b] Lotan, Shobal, Zibeon, Anah, [30]Dishon, Ezer, and Dishan; these are the clans[b] of the Horites, clan by clan[d] in the land of Seir.

31 These are the kings who reigned in the land of Edom, before any king reigned over the Israelites. [32]Bela son of Beor reigned in Edom, the name of his city being Dinhabah. [33]Bela died, and Jobab son of Zerah of Bozrah succeeded him as king. [34]Jobab died, and Husham of the land of the Temanites succeeded him as king. [35]Husham died, and Hadad son of Bedad, who defeated Midian in the country of Moab, succeeded him as king, the name of his city being Avith. [36]Hadad died, and Samlah of Masrekah succeeded him as king. [37]Samlah died, and Shaul of Rehoboth on the Euphrates succeeded him as king. [38]Shaul died, and Baal-hanan son of Achbor succeeded him as king. [39]Baal-hanan son of Achbor died, and Hadar succeeded him as king, the name of his city being Pau; his wife's name was Mehetabel, the daughter of Matred, daughter of Me-zahab.

40 These are the names of the clans[b] of Esau, according to their families and their localities by their names: the clans[b] Timna, Alvah, Jetheth, [41]Oholibamah, Elah, Pinon, [42]Kenaz, Teman, Mibzar, [43]Magdiel, and Iram; these are the clans[b] of Edom (that is, Esau, the father of Edom), according to their settlements in the land that they held.

a Gk Syr: Heb *daughter*   b Or *chiefs*
c Meaning of Heb uncertain   d Or *chief by chief*

Joseph Dreams of Greatness

37 Jacob settled in the land where his father had lived as an alien, the land of Canaan. [2]This is the story of the family of Jacob.

Joseph, being seventeen years old, was shepherding the flock with his brothers; he was a helper to the sons of Bilhah and Zilpah, his father's wives; and Joseph brought a bad report of them to their father. [3]Now Israel loved Joseph more than any other of his children, because he was the son of his old age; and he had made him a long robe with sleeves. [a] [4]But when his brothers saw that their father loved him more than all his brothers, they hated him, and could not speak peaceably to him.

[5] Once Joseph had a dream, and when he told it to his brothers, they hated him even more. [6]He said to them, "Listen to this dream that I dreamed. [7]There we were, binding sheaves in the field. Suddenly my sheaf rose and stood upright; then your sheaves gathered around it, and bowed down to my sheaf." [8]His brothers said to him, "Are you indeed to reign over us? Are you indeed to have dominion over us?" So they hated him even more because of his dreams and his words.

[9] He had another dream, and told it to his brothers, saying, "Look, I have had another dream: the sun, the moon, and eleven stars were bowing down to me." [10]But when he told it to his father and to his brothers, his father rebuked him, and said to him, "What kind of dream is this that you have had? Shall we indeed come, I and your mother and your brothers, and bow to the ground before you?" [11]So his brothers were jealous of him, but his father kept the matter in mind.

Joseph Is Sold by His Brothers

[12] Now his brothers went to pasture their father's flock near Shechem. [13]And Israel said to Joseph, "Are not your brothers pasturing the flock at Shechem? Come, I will send you to them." He answered, "Here I am." [14]So he said to him, "Go now, see if it is well with your brothers and with the flock; and bring word back to me." So he sent him from the valley of Hebron.

He came to Shechem, [15]and a man found him wandering in the fields; the man asked him, "What are you seeking?" [16]"I am seeking my brothers," he said; "tell me, please, where they are pasturing the flock." [17]The man said, "They have gone away, for I heard them say,

---

a Traditional rendering (compare Gk): *a coat of many colors*; meaning of Heb uncertain

---

37:1 *Jacob settled in the land.* The tale of the children of Jacob begins a continuous story, like a novella, with plot, character development, conflict, and resolution. It links the history of Israel's ancestors with the time of slavery in Egypt. Beginning with the great patriarch Jacob's settling in the land and ending with his death (37:1–49:33), this drama unfolds around Joseph and his brothers. God's presence in the narrative is often obscure. However, important spiritual formation themes are woven throughout. As with his father, Jacob, and counter to customary privileges extended to the eldest son, the younger Joseph is chosen to bear the divine promise. Created with freedom and burdened by sin, humans matter to God, who oversees the world with providential care. As in the stories of Abraham, Isaac, and Jacob, the listening community of the Joseph narrative is invited to trust the events of ordinary life to God. Joseph's story adds a dimension of God's

inexplicable, often hidden, presence. God moves in mysterious ways as protector and guide of human beings. Through the exploits of these children of Jacob a people, Israel, is emerging as a corporate community of faith, the People of God.

37:3–36 *Now Israel loved Joseph more.* Not unlike God's choosing Jacob over Esau is Jacob's blatant preference for Joseph. A father's favoritism of the younger son Joseph sets the stage for the jealous rage of his brothers. Joseph's prophetic dreams don't help matters, as they hold hope for him and yet increase hostility among his brothers. Their selling of Joseph into slavery suddenly puts the future of the landed family into jeopardy. Jacob, whose life began in deceit, is now deceived by his own sons. Readers cannot help but wonder how long human beings must suffer the consequences of broken relationships.

'Let us go to Dothan.' " So Joseph went after his brothers, and found them at Dothan. [18]They saw him from a distance, and before he came near to them, they conspired to kill him. [19]They said to one another, "Here comes this dreamer. [20]Come now, let us kill him and throw him into one of the pits; then we shall say that a wild animal has devoured him, and we shall see what will become of his dreams." [21]But when Reuben heard it, he delivered him out of their hands, saying, "Let us not take his life." [22]Reuben said to them, "Shed no blood; throw him into this pit here in the wilderness, but lay no hand on him"— that he might rescue him out of their hand and restore him to his father. [23]So when Joseph came to his brothers, they stripped him of his robe, the long robe with sleeves[a] that he wore; [24]and they took him and threw him into a pit. The pit was empty; there was no water in it.

[25] Then they sat down to eat; and looking up they saw a caravan of Ishmaelites coming from Gilead, with their camels carrying gum, balm, and resin, on their way to carry it down to Egypt. [26]Then Judah said to his brothers, "What profit is it if we kill our brother and conceal his blood? [27]Come, let us sell him to the Ishmaelites, and not lay our hands on him, for he is our brother, our own flesh." And his brothers agreed. [28]When some Midianite traders passed by, they drew Joseph up, lifting him out of the pit, and sold him to the Ishmaelites for twenty pieces of silver. And they took Joseph to Egypt.

[29] When Reuben returned to the pit and saw that Joseph was not in the pit, he tore his clothes. [30]He returned to his brothers, and said, "The boy is gone; and I, where can I turn?" [31]Then they took Joseph's robe, slaughtered a goat, and dipped the robe in the blood. [32]They had the long robe with sleeves[a] taken to their father, and they said, "This we

have found; see now whether it is your son's robe or not." [33]He recognized it, and said, "It is my son's robe! A wild animal has devoured him; Joseph is without doubt torn to pieces." [34]Then Jacob tore his garments, and put sackcloth on his loins, and mourned for his son many days. [35]All his sons and all his daughters sought to comfort him; but he refused to be comforted, and said, "No, I shall go down to Sheol to my son, mourning." Thus his father bewailed him. [36]Meanwhile the Midianites had sold him in Egypt to Potiphar, one of Pharaoh's officials, the captain of the guard.

Judah and Tamar

38 It happened at that time that Judah went down from his brothers and settled near a certain Adullamite whose name was Hirah. [2]There Judah saw the daughter of a certain Canaanite whose name was Shua; he married her and went in to her. [3]She conceived and bore a son; and he named him Er. [4]Again she conceived and bore a son whom she named Onan. [5]Yet again she bore a son, and she named him Shelah. She[b] was in Chezib when she bore him. [6]Judah took a wife for Er his firstborn; her name was Tamar. [7]But Er, Judah's firstborn, was wicked in the sight of the LORD, and the LORD put him to death. [8]Then Judah said to Onan, "Go in to your brother's wife and perform the duty of a brother-in-law to her; raise up offspring for your brother." [9]But since Onan knew that the offspring would not be his, he spilled his semen on the ground whenever he went in to his brother's wife, so that he would not give offspring to his brother. [10]What he did was displeasing in the sight of the LORD, and he put him to death also. [11]Then Judah said to his daughter-in-law Tamar, "Remain a widow

a See note on 37.3   b Gk: Heb *He*

38:1–30 *Judah went down from his brothers.* The inclusion of this tale explains the appearance of the house of Judah, which will figure prominently in relation to Israel in the future. From a story about an extended family emerges a national entity with a political history. The narrative broadens the scope of God's involvement and oversight of the world. Tamar is bold to act counter to customary practice, thus playing a significant role in moving the family toward fulfillment of the promises of God. In our life with God minor characters like Tamar matter.

in your father's house until my son Shelah grows up"—for he feared that he too would die, like his brothers. So Tamar went to live in her father's house.

12 In course of time the wife of Judah, Shua's daughter, died; when Judah's time of mourning was over, *a* he went up to Timnah to his sheepshearers, he and his friend Hirah the Adullamite. 13When Tamar was told, "Your father-in-law is going up to Timnah to shear his sheep," 14she put off her widow's garments, put on a veil, wrapped herself up, and sat down at the entrance to Enaim, which is on the road to Timnah. She saw that Shelah was grown up, yet she had not been given to him in marriage. 15When Judah saw her, he thought her to be a prostitute, for she had covered her face. 16He went over to her at the roadside, and said, "Come, let me come in to you," for he did not know that she was his daughter-in-law. She said, "What will you give me, that you may come in to me?" 17He answered, "I will send you a kid from the flock." And she said, "Only if you give me a pledge, until you send it." 18He said, "What pledge shall I give you?" She replied, "Your signet and your cord, and the staff that is in your hand." So he gave them to her, and went in to her, and she conceived by him. 19Then she got up and went away, and taking off her veil she put on the garments of her widowhood.

20 When Judah sent the kid by his friend the Adullamite, to recover the pledge from the woman, he could not find her. 21He asked the townspeople, "Where is the temple prostitute who was at Enaim by the wayside?" But they said, "No prostitute has been here." 22So he returned to Judah, and said, "I have not found her; moreover the townspeople said, 'No prostitute has been here.' " 23Judah

replied, "Let her keep the things as her own, otherwise we will be laughed at; you see, I sent this kid, and you could not find her."

24 About three months later Judah was told, "Your daughter-in-law Tamar has played the whore; moreover she is pregnant as a result of whoredom." And Judah said, "Bring her out, and let her be burned." 25As she was being brought out, she sent word to her father-in-law, "It was the owner of these who made me pregnant." And she said, "Take note, please, whose these are, the signet and the cord and the staff." 26Then Judah acknowledged them and said, "She is more in the right than I, since I did not give her to my son Shelah." And he did not lie with her again.

27 When the time of her delivery came, there were twins in her womb. 28While she was in labor, one put out a hand; and the midwife took and bound on his hand a crimson thread, saying, "This one came out first." 29But just then he drew back his hand, and out came his brother; and she said, "What a breach you have made for yourself!" Therefore he was named Perez. *b* 30Afterward his brother came out with the crimson thread on his hand; and he was named Zerah. *c*

Joseph and Potiphar's Wife

39 Now Joseph was taken down to Egypt, and Potiphar, an officer of Pharaoh, the captain of the guard, an Egyptian, bought him from the Ishmaelites who had brought him down there. 2The LORD was with Joseph, and he became a successful man; he was in the house of his Egyptian master.

a Heb *when Judah was comforted*   *b* That is *A breach*   *c* That is *Brightness*; perhaps alluding to the crimson thread

---

39:2–23 *The LORD was with Joseph.* The presence of God in Joseph's life is mentioned repeatedly. Joseph was destined for slavery, but by God's hand he outlasts the accusation of adultery. Even in prison he rises to a position of importance. Five times he is identified as a "Hebrew," a name normally reserved to designate Israel among other nations, foreshadowing the enslavement of the people of Israel in Egypt.

"Hebrew" is a derogatory term meaning "trashy outsider." Separated from the rest of his family in a foreign land and political system, Joseph enjoys the close companionship of God, who appears to be actively involved at every turn. God chooses intimacy with us in subtle ways and works with us through the complexities of difficult circumstances and complicated human relationships.

3His master saw that the LORD was with him, and that the LORD caused all that he did to prosper in his hands. 4So Joseph found favor in his sight and attended him; he made him overseer of his house and put him in charge of all that he had. 5From the time that he made him overseer in his house and over all that he had, the LORD blessed the Egyptian's house for Joseph's sake; the blessing of the LORD was on all that he had, in house and field. 6So he left all that he had in Joseph's charge; and, with him there, he had no concern for anything but the food that he ate.

Now Joseph was handsome and good-looking. 7And after a time his master's wife cast her eyes on Joseph and said, "Lie with me." 8But he refused and said to his master's wife, "Look, with me here, my master has no concern about anything in the house, and he has put everything that he has in my hand. 9He is not greater in this house than I am, nor has he kept back anything from me except yourself, because you are his wife. How then could I do this great wickedness, and sin against God?" 10And although she spoke to Joseph day after day, he would not consent to lie beside her or to be with her. 11One day, however, when he went into the house to do his work, and while no one else was in the house, 12she caught hold of his garment, saying, "Lie with me!" But he left his garment in her hand, and fled and ran outside. 13When she saw that he had left his garment in her hand and had fled outside, 14she called out to the members of her household and said to them, "See, my husband*a* has brought among us a Hebrew to insult us! He came in to me to lie with me, and I cried out with a loud voice; 15and when he heard me raise my voice and cry out, he left his garment beside me, and fled outside." 16Then she kept his garment by her until his master came home, 17and she told him the same story, saying, "The Hebrew servant,

whom you have brought among us, came in to me to insult me; 18but as soon as I raised my voice and cried out, he left his garment beside me, and fled outside."

19 When his master heard the words that his wife spoke to him, saying, "This is the way your servant treated me," he became enraged. 20And Joseph's master took him and put him into the prison, the place where the king's prisoners were confined; he remained there in prison. 21But the LORD was with Joseph and showed him steadfast love; he gave him favor in the sight of the chief jailer. 22The chief jailer committed to Joseph's care all the prisoners who were in the prison, and whatever was done there, he was the one who did it. 23The chief jailer paid no heed to anything that was in Joseph's care, because the LORD was with him; and whatever he did, the LORD made it prosper.

The Dreams of Two Prisoners

40 Some time after this, the cupbearer of the king of Egypt and his baker offended their lord the king of Egypt. 2Pharaoh was angry with his two officers, the chief cupbearer and the chief baker, 3and he put them in custody in the house of the captain of the guard, in the prison where Joseph was confined. 4The captain of the guard charged Joseph with them, and he waited on them; and they continued for some time in custody. 5One night they both dreamed—the cupbearer and the baker of the king of Egypt, who were confined in the prison—each his own dream, and each dream with its own meaning. 6When Joseph came to them in the morning, he saw that they were troubled. 7So he asked Pharaoh's officers, who were with him in custody in his master's house, "Why are your faces downcast today?" 8They said to him, "We have had dreams, and there

a Heb *he* TREASURY OUT SIDER

Responding
39:2–5, 21–23 THE WITH-GOD LIFE.
The Lord was with Joseph during circumstances that today seem especially extreme: sold into slavery, accused of rape and imprisoned, forgotten after giving wise counsel. But

in their midst he knew God was with him. What circumstances hinder your sense that God is with you? What helps you realize God's presence? How do you plan to "practice the presence of God" in the future? *See also* Spiritual Disciplines Index.

JOSEPH

A With-God Life

Selected Scriptures: Genesis 37–45; 47; 50

Joseph stands as a shining example of the Immanuel Principle—"God with us"—lived out in bewildering circumstances and real-life hardship. As a common thread weaving his story together, the Bible repeats, "The LORD was with Joseph" (Gen 39:2). At each new turn we're reminded that no trial befell him and no good occurred without God's intimate presence and involvement. Joseph walked with God, because he knew God walked with him.

From among twelve brothers, Joseph became Jacob's favorite son and God's chosen tool. From the beginning both father and son handled this favored status unwisely. Jacob made an unusual coat for teenage Joseph, arousing the jealousy of his brothers. Joseph, a dreamer who was perhaps the earliest charismatic, told his brothers of two dreams he'd had in which the family all bowed to honor him. The brothers conspired to kill Joseph, but relented and sold him, instead, into slavery.

Joseph ended up in Egypt and served so well he was promoted to chief steward in the household of Potiphar, a high-ranking official. "The LORD was with Joseph, and he became a successful man" (39:2). God likely used the trip to Egypt and into servitude to humble Joseph and draw him close for the job that was ahead.

When his master's wife propositioned him, Joseph refused to "sin against God" (39:9). Insulted, Potiphar's wife made Joseph look guilty of seducing her, causing him to be sent to prison. Still, "the LORD was with Joseph and showed him steadfast love" (39:21). Joseph was given care of all the other prisoners. When two of them had dreams, Joseph accurately interpreted the dreams. Later, Pharoah, who had heard rumors of Joseph's gift, called for Joseph to interpret his own dreams. Emphasizing God's role in providing the interpretation, Joseph explained that Pharoah's dreams foretold seven years of plenty in the land followed by seven years of famine. Upon hearing this, Pharoah appointed Joseph head governor over the land, in charge of preparing for the coming famine. When the years of plenty came to an end, Joseph had stored much food to provide for Egypt and other lands in need.

Joseph's family reentered his life when Jacob sent his sons to Egypt for grain. Joseph recognized them and, after a time, revealed himself. In answer to their guilt and dismay, he explained, "It was not you who sent me here, but God" (45:8). His forgiveness and faith are exemplary: "Even though you intended to do harm to me, God intended it for good, in order to preserve a numerous people" (50:20).

From a young age, Joseph understood the goodness of God that underlies all of our experiences. His faithfulness to certain Spiritual Disciplines helped him cling to that goodness even when he couldn't see it clearly or sense its outcome. Joseph persevered in submission, accepting his circumstances, even when unjust. He served his overseers and later the people of the land with excellence and loyalty, as if serving God. He was faithful in chastity when he could easily have indulged, and, after his first careless disclosure to his brothers, he was reverent and humble when he received guidance from God through dreams and visions. Joseph received the imposition of cruel events as disciplines rather than being embittered by them.

The fourteenth-century English mystic Julian of Norwich shared many of Joseph's disciplines and his trust in God's goodness. A Benedictine nun, she wrote at length about God's goodness in her book *Revelations of Divine Love*. Written in a time of social unrest and death by the Black Plague (Julian herself suffered a near-fatal illness at the age of thirty), Julian's message spoke to many: "Just as our flesh is covered by clothing, and our blood is covered by our flesh, so are we, soul and body, covered and enclosed by the goodness of God. Yet the clothing and the flesh will pass away, but the goodness of God will always remain and will remain closer to us than our own flesh."

This goodness of God inspired Julian's oft-quoted words—words that could also have become Joseph's message: "All shall be well and all shall be well, and all manner of things shall be well."

Personal Reflection

- Joseph's disciplined life allowed him to live with God through the ups and downs of his daily life. How much are you actively seeking discipline in the areas of submission, chastity, service, loyalty, and guidance? How
- Do you believe in the deepest recesses of your heart that God is good? Do you believe that God is always good *to you*? How do you reconcile God's goodness when bad things happen to you? Which of the above-mentioned Spiritual Disciplines might help you to experience God's goodness at a deeper level?
- This week consider making a prayer offered by Julian of Norwich a prayer of your own: "And lovingly I pray to thee O' God, by your goodness give me yourself, for you are enough for me."

PROFILE

is no one to interpret them." And Joseph said to them, "Do not interpretations belong to God? Please tell them to me."

9 So the chief cupbearer told his dream to Joseph, and said to him, "In my dream there was a vine before me, [10]and on the vine there were three branches. As soon as it budded, its blossoms came out and the clusters ripened into grapes. [11]Pharaoh's cup was in my hand; and I took the grapes and pressed them into Pharaoh's cup, and placed the cup in Pharaoh's hand." [12]Then Joseph said to him, "This is its interpretation: the three branches are three days; [13]within three days Pharaoh will lift up your head and restore you to your office; and you shall place Pharaoh's cup in his hand, just as you used to do when you were his cupbearer. [14]But remember me when it is well with you; please do me the kindness to make mention of me to Pharaoh, and so get me out of this place. [15]For in fact I was stolen out of the land of the Hebrews; and here also I have done nothing that they should have put me into the dungeon."

16 When the chief baker saw that the interpretation was favorable, he said to Joseph, "I also had a dream: there were three cake baskets on my head, [17]and in the uppermost basket there were all sorts of baked food for Pharaoh, but the birds were eating it out of the basket on my head." [18]And Joseph answered, "This is its interpretation: the three baskets are three days; [19]within three days Pharaoh will lift up your head—from you!— and hang you on a pole; and the birds will eat the flesh from you."

20 On the third day, which was Pharaoh's birthday, he made a feast for all his servants, and lifted up the head of the chief cupbearer and the head of the chief baker among his servants. [21]He restored the chief cupbearer to his cupbearing, and he placed the cup in Pharaoh's hand; [22]but the chief baker he hanged, just as Joseph had interpreted to them. [23]Yet the chief cupbearer did not remember Joseph, but forgot him.

Joseph Interprets Pharaoh's Dream

41 After two whole years, Pharaoh dreamed that he was standing by the Nile, [2]and there came up out of the Nile seven sleek and fat cows, and they grazed in the reed grass. [3]Then seven other cows, ugly and thin, came up out of the Nile after them, and stood by the other cows on the bank of the Nile. [4]The ugly and thin cows ate up the seven sleek and fat cows. And Pharaoh awoke. [5]Then he fell asleep and dreamed a second time; seven ears of grain, plump and good, were growing on one stalk. [6]Then seven ears, thin and blighted by the east wind, sprouted

---

40:5–23 *they both dreamed.* The dreamer becomes an interpreter of dreams. Dreams and their interpretation are a special medium for divine communication about the future. Joseph's ability to interpret is a gift from God (v 8), who alone has power to open the future. God is working in Joseph's life on many different levels as he prepares to ascend to power and privilege in Egypt. Joseph is blessed with discernment and is quick to credit God for inspiration. In a culture in which people attribute success to hard work, Joseph models dependence upon and trust in the providential care of God.

41:1–52 *Pharaoh dreamed.* Enjoying the gifts and protection of God in prison, Joseph still needed human help to get out. The cupbearer forgot him for two whole years. Joseph had to wait for his God-given gift of interpretation to lead him into Pharaoh's realm. God acts, but not according to our time lines and agendas. When the time is right, however, the "Hebrew" Joseph finds himself creating and executing national policy for Egypt as prime minister! The Spirit of God rests on Joseph, and even Pharaoh acknowledges the power of Joseph's God. In grateful response Joseph names his sons for the blessings of God. Manasseh means "making to forget," a letting go of a cruel past, and Ephraim means "to be fruitful," exhibiting a confident hope for the future. Once again, God has taken the younger and least likely and raised him to a position of enormous power and influence. The Spirit of God transcends all perceived barriers. As with the unlikely Joseph, God gives us the gifts we need to do the work we are called to do in many spheres of life—religious, political, economic, and social.

after them. 7The thin ears swallowed up the seven plump and full ears. Pharaoh awoke, and it was a dream. 8In the morning his spirit was troubled; so he sent and called for all the magicians of Egypt and all its wise men. Pharaoh told them his dreams, but there was no one who could interpret them to Pharaoh.

9 Then the chief cupbearer said to Pharaoh, "I remember my faults today. 10Once Pharaoh was angry with his servants, and put me and the chief baker in custody in the house of the captain of the guard. 11We dreamed on the same night, he and I, each having a dream with its own meaning. 12A young Hebrew was there with us, a servant of the captain of the guard. When we told him, he interpreted our dreams to us, giving an interpretation to each according to his dream. 13As he interpreted to us, so it turned out; I was restored to my office, and the baker was hanged."

14 Then Pharaoh sent for Joseph, and he was hurriedly brought out of the dungeon. When he had shaved himself and changed his clothes, he came in before Pharaoh. 15And Pharaoh said to Joseph, "I have had a dream, and there is no one who can interpret it. I have heard it said of you that when you hear a dream you can interpret it." 16Joseph answered Pharaoh, "It is not I; God will give Pharaoh a favorable answer." 17Then Pharaoh said to Joseph, "In my dream I was standing on the banks of the Nile; 18and seven cows, fat and sleek, came up out of the Nile and fed in the reed grass. 19Then seven other cows came up after them, poor, very ugly, and thin. Never had I seen such ugly ones in all the land of Egypt. 20The thin and ugly cows ate up the first seven fat cows, 21but when they had eaten them no one would have known that they had done so, for they were still as ugly as before. Then I awoke. 22I fell asleep a second time[a] and I saw in my dream seven ears of grain, full and good, growing on one stalk, 23and seven ears, withered, thin, and blighted by the east wind, sprouting after them; 24and the thin ears swallowed up the seven good ears. But when I told it to the magicians, there was no one who could explain it to me."

25 Then Joseph said to Pharaoh, "Pharaoh's dreams are one and the same; God has revealed to Pharaoh what he is about to do. 26The seven good cows are seven years, and the seven good ears are seven years; the dreams are one. 27The seven lean and ugly cows that came up after them are seven years, as are the seven empty ears blighted by the east wind. They are seven years of famine. 28It is as I told Pharaoh; God has shown to Pharaoh what he is about to do. 29There will come seven years of great plenty throughout all the land of Egypt. 30After them there will arise seven years of famine, and all the plenty will be forgotten in the land of Egypt; the famine will consume the land. 31The plenty will no longer be known in the land because of the famine that will follow, for it will be very grievous. 32And the doubling of Pharaoh's dream means that the thing is fixed by God, and God will shortly bring it about. 33Now therefore let Pharaoh select a man who is discerning and wise, and set him over the land of Egypt. 34Let Pharaoh proceed to appoint overseers over the land, and take one-fifth of the produce of the land of Egypt during the seven plenteous years. 35Let them gather all the food of these good years that are coming, and lay up grain under the authority of Pharaoh for food in the cities, and let them keep it. 36That food shall be a reserve for the land against the seven years of famine that are to befall the land of Egypt, so that the land may not perish through the famine."

Joseph's Rise to Power

37 The proposal pleased Pharaoh and all his servants. 38Pharaoh said to his servants, "Can we find anyone else like this—one in whom is the spirit of God?" 39So Pharaoh said to Joseph, "Since God has shown you all this, there is no one so discerning and wise as you. 40You shall be over my house, and all my people shall order themselves as you command; only with regard to the throne will I be greater than you." 41And Pharaoh said to Joseph, "See, I have set you over all the land of Egypt." 42Removing his signet ring from his hand, Pharaoh put it on Joseph's hand; he ar-

a Gk Syr Vg: Heb lacks *I fell asleep a second time*

rayed him in garments of fine linen, and put a gold chain around his neck. 43He had him ride in the chariot of his second-in-command; and they cried out in front of him, "Bow the knee!" *a* Thus he set him over all the land of Egypt. 44Moreover Pharaoh said to Joseph, "I am Pharaoh, and without your consent no one shall lift up hand or foot in all the land of Egypt." 45Pharaoh gave Joseph the name Zaphenath-paneah; and he gave him Asenath daughter of Potiphera, priest of On, as his wife. Thus Joseph gained authority over the land of Egypt.

46 Joseph was thirty years old when he entered the service of Pharaoh king of Egypt. And Joseph went out from the presence of Pharaoh, and went through all the land of Egypt. 47During the seven plenteous years the earth produced abundantly. 48He gathered up all the food of the seven years when there was plenty *b* in the land of Egypt, and stored up food in the cities; he stored up in every city the food from the fields around it. 49So Joseph stored up grain in such abundance—like the sand of the sea—that he stopped measuring it; it was beyond measure.

50 Before the years of famine came, Joseph had two sons, whom Asenath daughter of Potiphera, priest of On, bore to him. 51Joseph named the firstborn Manasseh, *c* "For," he said, "God has made me forget all my hardship and all my father's house." 52The second he named Ephraim, *d* "For God has made me fruitful in the land of my misfortunes."

53 The seven years of plenty that prevailed in the land of Egypt came to an end; 54and the seven years of famine began to come, just as Joseph had said. There was famine in every country, but throughout the land of Egypt there was bread. 55When all the land of Egypt was famished, the people cried to Pharaoh for bread. Pharaoh said to all the Egyptians, "Go to Joseph; what he says to you, do." 56And since the famine had spread over all the land, Joseph opened all the storehouses, *e* and sold to the Egyptians, for the famine was severe in the land of Egypt. 57Moreover, all the world came to Joseph in Egypt to buy grain, because the famine became severe throughout the world.

Joseph's Brothers Go to Egypt

42 When Jacob learned that there was grain in Egypt, he said to his sons, "Why do you keep looking at one another? 2I have heard," he said, "that there is grain in Egypt; go down and buy grain for us there, that we may live and not die." 3So ten of Joseph's brothers went down to buy grain in Egypt. 4But Jacob did not send Joseph's brother Benjamin with his brothers, for he feared that harm might come to him. 5Thus the sons of Israel were among the other people who came to buy grain, for the famine had reached the land of Canaan.

6 Now Joseph was governor over the land; it was he who sold to all the people of the land. And Joseph's brothers came and bowed themselves before him with their faces to the ground. 7When Joseph saw his brothers, he recognized them, but he treated them like strangers and spoke harshly to them. "Where do you come from?" he said. They said, "From the land of Canaan, to buy food." 8Although Joseph had recognized his brothers, they did not recognize him. 9Joseph also remembered the dreams that he had dreamed

a Abrek, apparently an Egyptian word similar in sound to the Hebrew word meaning *to kneel* *b* Sam Gk: MT *the seven years that were* *c* That is *Making to forget* *d* From a Hebrew word meaning *to be fruitful* *e* Gk Vg Compare Syr: Heb *opened all that was in* (or, *among*) *them*

42:1–38 *When Jacob learned that there was grain in Egypt.* Joseph keeps his identity hidden from his brothers, but the narrative shows his deep longing for reunion despite their cruel treatment of him. No reason is given for the test Joseph plots for them, but the brothers are aware of their guilt even without recognizing the one who imposes their penalty. Benjamin is absent; perhaps there can be no reunion unless every brother is present. Family life is filled with pain, and yet we are drawn to one another beyond our understanding. Sometimes it takes a long time to acknowledge our own complicity in broken relationships, but this tale reminds us how confession always precedes pardon.

about them. He said to them, "You are spies; you have come to see the nakedness of the land!" 10They said to him, "No, my lord; your servants have come to buy food. 11We are all sons of one man; we are honest men; your servants have never been spies." 12But he said to them, "No, you have come to see the nakedness of the land!" 13They said, "We, your servants, are twelve brothers, the sons of a certain man in the land of Canaan; the youngest, however, is now with our father, and one is no more." 14But Joseph said to them, "It is just as I have said to you; you are spies! 15Here is how you shall be tested: as Pharaoh lives, you shall not leave this place unless your youngest brother comes here! 16Let one of you go and bring your brother, while the rest of you remain in prison, in order that your words may be tested, whether there is truth in you; or else, as Pharaoh lives, surely you are spies." 17And he put them all together in prison for three days.

18 On the third day Joseph said to them, "Do this and you will live, for I fear God: 19if you are honest men, let one of your brothers stay here where you are imprisoned. The rest of you shall go and carry grain for the famine of your households, 20and bring your youngest brother to me. Thus your words will be verified, and you shall not die." And they agreed to do so. 21They said to one another, "Alas, we are paying the penalty for what we did to our brother; we saw his anguish when he pleaded with us, but we would not listen. That is why this anguish has come upon us." 22Then Reuben answered them, "Did I not tell you not to wrong the boy? But you would not listen. So now there comes a reckoning for his blood." 23They did not know that Joseph understood them, since he spoke with them through an interpreter. 24He turned away from them and wept; then he returned and spoke to them. And he picked out Simeon and had him bound before their eyes. 25Joseph then gave orders to fill their bags with grain, to return every man's money to his sack, and to give them provisions for their journey. This was done for them.

Joseph's Brothers Return to Canaan

26 They loaded their donkeys with their grain, and departed. 27When one of them opened his sack to give his donkey fodder at the lodging place, he saw his money at the top of the sack. 28He said to his brothers, "My money has been put back; here it is in my sack!" At this they lost heart and turned trembling to one another, saying, "What is this that God has done to us?"

29 When they came to their father Jacob in the land of Canaan, they told him all that had happened to them, saying, 30"The man, the lord of the land, spoke harshly to us, and charged us with spying on the land. 31But we said to him, 'We are honest men, we are not spies. 32We are twelve brothers, sons of our father; one is no more, and the youngest is now with our father in the land of Canaan.' 33Then the man, the lord of the land, said to us, 'By this I shall know that you are honest men: leave one of your brothers with me, take grain for the famine of your households, and go your way. 34Bring your youngest brother to me, and I shall know that you are not spies but honest men. Then I will release your brother to you, and you may trade in the land.' "

35 As they were emptying their sacks, there in each one's sack was his bag of money. When they and their father saw their bundles of money, they were dismayed. 36And their father Jacob said to them, "I am the one you have bereaved of children: Joseph is no more, and Simeon is no more, and now you would take Benjamin. All this has happened to me!" 37Then Reuben said to his father, "You may kill my two sons if I do not bring him back to you. Put him in my hands, and I will bring him back to you." 38But he said, "My son shall not go down with you, for his brother is dead, and he alone is left. If harm should come to him on the journey that you are to make, you would bring down my gray hairs with sorrow to Sheol."

The Brothers Come Again, Bringing Benjamin

43 Now the famine was severe in the land. 2And when they had eaten up the grain that they had brought from Egypt, their father said to them, "Go again, buy us a little more food." 3But Judah said to him,

"The man solemnly warned us, saying, 'You shall not see my face unless your brother is with you.' ⁴If you will send our brother with us, we will go down and buy you food; ⁵but if you will not send him, we will not go down, for the man said to us, 'You shall not see my face, unless your brother is with you.' " ⁶Israel said, "Why did you treat me so badly as to tell the man that you had another brother?" ⁷They replied, "The man questioned us carefully about ourselves and our kindred, saying, 'Is your father still alive? Have you another brother?' What we told him was in answer to these questions. Could we in any way know that he would say, 'Bring your brother down'?" ⁸Then Judah said to his father Israel, "Send the boy with me, and let us be on our way, so that we may live and not die—you and we and also our little ones. ⁹I myself will be surety for him; you can hold me accountable for him. If I do not bring him back to you and set him before you, then let me bear the blame forever. ¹⁰If we had not delayed, we would now have returned twice."

11 Then their father Israel said to them, "If it must be so, then do this: take some of the choice fruits of the land in your bags, and carry them down as a present to the man—a little balm and a little honey, gum, resin, pistachio nuts, and almonds. ¹²Take double the money with you. Carry back with you the money that was returned in the top of your sacks; perhaps it was an oversight. ¹³Take your brother also, and be on your way again to the man; ¹⁴may God Almighty*ᵃ* grant you mercy before the man, so that he may send back your other brother and Benjamin. As for me, if I am bereaved of my children, I am bereaved." ¹⁵So the men took the present, and they took double the money with them,

as well as Benjamin. Then they went on their way down to Egypt, and stood before Joseph.

16 When Joseph saw Benjamin with them, he said to the steward of his house, "Bring the men into the house, and slaughter an animal and make ready, for the men are to dine with me at noon." ¹⁷The man did as Joseph said, and brought the men to Joseph's house. ¹⁸Now the men were afraid because they were brought to Joseph's house, and they said, "It is because of the money, replaced in our sacks the first time, that we have been brought in, so that he may have an opportunity to fall upon us, to make slaves of us and take our donkeys." ¹⁹So they went up to the steward of Joseph's house and spoke with him at the entrance to the house. ²⁰They said, "Oh, my lord, we came down the first time to buy food; ²¹and when we came to the lodging place we opened our sacks, and there was each one's money in the top of his sack, our money in full weight. So we have brought it back with us. ²²Moreover we have brought down with us additional money to buy food. We do not know who put our money in our sacks." ²³He replied, "Rest assured, do not be afraid; your God and the God of your father must have put treasure in your sacks for you; I received your money." Then he brought Simeon out to them. ²⁴When the steward*ᵃ* had brought the men into Joseph's house, and given them water, and they had washed their feet, and when he had given their donkeys fodder, ²⁵they made the present ready for Joseph's coming at noon, for they had heard that they would dine there.

26 When Joseph came home, they

a Traditional rendering of Heb *El Shaddai*
b Heb *the man*

43:1–34 *the famine was severe.* The fact that Simeon is in prison seems to be forgotten. Only continued famine sends the brothers back to Egypt. Jacob's unwillingness to send Benjamin had suspended the movement, but the need to feed his family overrides his concern about losing his youngest son. The narration proceeds at an anguished pace for this deeply pained family. Jacob calls on Almighty God to protect them with mercy (v 14). Their need for unde-

served divine favor emphasizes the tension within this family system, so broken that only God can bring wholeness. By God's gracious presence the family is moving toward reunion (vv 23, 29). The meal is an important sign of hospitality even if it falls short of genuine community because Joseph eats apart from the others. Shared meals are filled with hope for full reunions in the future.

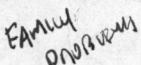

FAMILY PROBLEMS

brought him the present that they had carried into the house, and bowed to the ground before him. 27He inquired about their welfare, and said, "Is your father well, the old man of whom you spoke? Is he still alive?" 28They said, "Your servant our father is well; he is still alive." And they bowed their heads and did obeisance. 29Then he looked up and saw his brother Benjamin, his mother's son, and said, "Is this your youngest brother, of whom you spoke to me? God be gracious to you, my son!" 30With that, Joseph hurried out, because he was overcome with affection for his brother, and he was about to weep. So he went into a private room and wept there. 31Then he washed his face and came out; and controlling himself he said, "Serve the meal." 32They served him by himself, and them by themselves, and the Egyptians who ate with him by themselves, because the Egyptians could not eat with the Hebrews, for that is an abomination to the Egyptians. 33When they were seated before him, the firstborn according to his birthright and the youngest according to his youth, the men looked at one another in amazement. 34Portions were taken to them from Joseph's table, but Benjamin's portion was five times as much as any of theirs. So they drank and were merry with him.

Joseph Detains Benjamin

44 Then he commanded the steward of his house, "Fill the men's sacks with food, as much as they can carry, and put each man's money in the top of his sack. 2Put my cup, the silver cup, in the top of the sack of the youngest, with his money for the grain." And he did as Joseph told him. 3As soon as the morning was light, the men were sent away with their donkeys. 4When they had gone only a short distance from the city, Jo-

seph said to his steward, "Go, follow after the men; and when you overtake them, say to them, 'Why have you returned evil for good? Why have you stolen my silver cup?a 5Is it not from this that my lord drinks? Does he not indeed use it for divination? You have done wrong in doing this.' "

6 When he overtook them, he repeated these words to them. 7They said to him, "Why does my lord speak such words as these? Far be it from your servants that they should do such a thing! 8Look, the money that we found at the top of our sacks, we brought back to you from the land of Canaan; why then would we steal silver or gold from your lord's house? 9Should it be found with any one of your servants, let him die; moreover the rest of us will become my lord's slaves." 10He said, "Even so; in accordance with your words, let it be: he with whom it is found shall become my slave, but the rest of you shall go free." 11Then each one quickly lowered his sack to the ground, and each opened his sack. 12He searched, beginning with the eldest and ending with the youngest; and the cup was found in Benjamin's sack. 13At this they tore their clothes. Then each one loaded his donkey, and they returned to the city.

14 Judah and his brothers came to Joseph's house while he was still there; and they fell to the ground before him. 15Joseph said to them, "What deed is this that you have done? Do you not know that one such as I can practice divination?" 16And Judah said, "What can we say to my lord? What can we speak? How can we clear ourselves? God has found out the guilt of your servants; here we are then, my lord's slaves, both we and also the one in

a Gk Compare Vg: Heb lacks Why have you stolen my silver cup?

44:1–34 Fill the men's sacks with food. Joseph puts his brothers to a final test by hiding his silver cup in their grain, an incident that begins a conversation about returning evil for good. Each of these brothers, including Joseph, is complicit in creating a rift in this family. God is mentioned in this chapter once (v 16) as the one who discovers the brothers' guilt. As in this

broken family, God is present in the hidden contours of human relationships. God's presence is reflected in Judah's speech (vv 18–34) as he confesses his fault and sacrifices himself in order to protect his brother. It is this honest confession and demonstration of love that finally leads to reconciliation.

whose possession the cup has been found."
¹⁷But he said, "Far be it from me that I should
do so! Only the one in whose possession the
cup was found shall be my slave; but as for
you, go up in peace to your father."

Judah Pleads for Benjamin's Release

18 Then Judah stepped up to him and said,
"O my lord, let your servant please speak a
word in my lord's ears, and do not be angry
with your servant; for you are like Pharaoh
himself. ¹⁹My lord asked his servants, saying, 'Have you a father or a brother?' ²⁰And
we said to my lord, 'We have a father, an old
man, and a young brother, the child of his old
age. His brother is dead; he alone is left of
his mother's children, and his father loves
him.' ²¹Then you said to your servants, 'Bring
him down to me, so that I may set my eyes on
him.' ²²We said to my lord, 'The boy cannot
leave his father, for if he should leave his father, his father would die.' ²³Then you said to
your servants, 'Unless your youngest brother comes down with you, you shall see my
face no more.' ²⁴When we went back to your
servant my father we told him the words of
my lord. ²⁵And when our father said, 'Go
again, buy us a little food,' ²⁶we said, 'We
cannot go down. Only if our youngest brother goes with us, will we go down; for we cannot see the man's face unless our youngest
brother is with us.' ²⁷Then your servant my
father said to us, 'You know that my wife
bore me two sons; ²⁸one left me, and I said,
Surely he has been torn to pieces; and I have
never seen him since. ²⁹If you take this one
also from me, and harm comes to him, you
will bring down my gray hairs in sorrow to
Sheol.' ³⁰Now therefore, when I come to your
servant my father and the boy is not with us,
then, as his life is bound up in the boy's life,
³¹when he sees that the boy is not with us, he

will die; and your servants will bring down
the gray hairs of your servant our father with
sorrow to Sheol. ³²For your servant became
surety for the boy to my father, saying, 'If I do
not bring him back to you, then I will bear the
blame in the sight of my father all my life.'
³³Now therefore, please let your servant remain as a slave to my lord in place of the boy;
and let the boy go back with his brothers.
³⁴For how can I go back to my father if the
boy is not with me? I fear to see the suffering
that would come upon my father."

Joseph Reveals Himself to His Brothers

45 Then Joseph could no longer control
himself before all those who stood
by him, and he cried out, "Send everyone
away from me." So no one stayed with him
when Joseph made himself known to his
brothers. ²And he wept so loudly that the
Egyptians heard it, and the household of
Pharaoh heard it. ³Joseph said to his brothers,
"I am Joseph. Is my father still alive?" But his
brothers could not answer him, so dismayed
were they at his presence.

4 Then Joseph said to his brothers, "Come
closer to me." And they came closer. He said,
"I am your brother, Joseph, whom you sold
into Egypt. ⁵And now do not be distressed, or
angry with yourselves, because you sold me
here; for God sent me before you to preserve
life. ⁶For the famine has been in the land
these two years; and there are five more years
in which there will be neither plowing nor
harvest. ⁷God sent me before you to preserve
for you a remnant on earth, and to keep alive
for you many survivors. ⁸So it was not you
who sent me here, but God; he has made me
a father to Pharaoh, and lord of all his house
and ruler over all the land of Egypt. ⁹Hurry
and go up to my father and say to him, 'Thus
says your son Joseph, God has made me lord

45:1–15 *Joseph said to his brothers.* At last
the secrets are disclosed and reconciliation is
possible. Any yearning for revenge has given
way to reunion. Rather than wallowing in sorrow
and regret, Joseph reflects on his whole experience theologically. He proclaims that the hidden
will of God is to preserve life (v 5). Often only
in retrospect can we see how God has been

involved all along the way of our circuitous
journeys. Joseph articulates a creational
theology connecting this closing story to earlier
beginnings. The God who creates also saves.
Ironically the preservation of this family's life
moves the whole clan from the land of Canaan
into Egypt (v 10), and ultimately from prosperity
into slavery.

of all Egypt; come down to me, do not delay. [10]You shall settle in the land of Goshen, and you shall be near me, you and your children and your children's children, as well as your flocks, your herds, and all that you have. [11]I will provide for you there—since there are five more years of famine to come—so that you and your household, and all that you have, will not come to poverty.' [12]And now your eyes and the eyes of my brother Benjamin see that it is my own mouth that speaks to you. [13]You must tell my father how greatly I am honored in Egypt, and all that you have seen. Hurry and bring my father down here." [14]Then he fell upon his brother Benjamin's neck and wept, while Benjamin wept upon his neck. [15]And he kissed all his brothers and wept upon them; and after that his brothers talked with him.

[16] When the report was heard in Pharaoh's house, "Joseph's brothers have come," Pharaoh and his servants were pleased. [17]Pharaoh said to Joseph, "Say to your brothers, 'Do this: load your animals and go back to the land of Canaan. [18]Take your father and your households and come to me, so that I may give you the best of the land of Egypt, and you may enjoy the fat of the land.' [19]You are further charged to say, 'Do this: take wagons from the land of Egypt for your little ones and for your wives, and bring your father, and come. [20]Give no thought to your possessions, for the best of all the land of Egypt is yours.' "

[21] The sons of Israel did so. Joseph gave them wagons according to the instruction of Pharaoh, and he gave them provisions for the journey. [22]To each one of them he gave a set of garments; but to Benjamin he gave three hundred pieces of silver and five sets of garments. [23]To his father he sent the following: ten donkeys loaded with the good things of Egypt, and ten female donkeys loaded with grain, bread, and provision for his father on the journey. [24]Then he sent his brothers on their way, and as they were leaving he said to them, "Do not quarrel[a] along the way."

[25] So they went up out of Egypt and came to their father Jacob in the land of Canaan. [26]And they told him, "Joseph is still alive! He is even ruler over all the land of Egypt." He was stunned; he could not believe them. [27]But when they told him all the words of Joseph that he had said to them, and when he saw the wagons that Joseph had sent to carry him, the spirit of their father Jacob revived. [28]Israel said, "Enough! My son Joseph is still alive. I must go and see him before I die."

Jacob Brings His Whole Family to Egypt

46 When Israel set out on his journey with all that he had and came to Beersheba, he offered sacrifices to the God of his father Isaac. [2]God spoke to Israel in visions of the night, and said, "Jacob, Jacob." And he said, "Here I am." [3]Then he said, "I am God,[b] the God of your father; do not be afraid to go down to Egypt, for I will make of you a great nation there. [4]I myself will go down with you to Egypt, and I will also bring you up again; and Joseph's own hand shall close your eyes."

a Or be agitated   b Heb the God

Responding
45:25–28 CONFESSION. The Bible does not record if Joseph's brothers ever told their father, Jacob, that they were responsible for selling their brother into slavery. How do you think the relationship of the sons with their father would have been affected if they had openly confessed what they had done? Has there ever been a situation in your family that would have improved had family members been open and honest with each other? Describe. What can you do to restore those relationships? See also Spiritual Disciplines Index.

46:1–34 _Israel set out on his journey._ At the beginning of his journey toward Egypt Jacob worships. The narrative returns to earlier themes: God appears bearing promises and the future is laid out with a genealogy. It shows how from a person whose name was changed to Israel a people called Israel is emerging. Through intimate concern, protection, and the guiding of individuals, God is forging a people who know who they are by the stories of these ancestors. The divine attention given these individuals signifies divine intention for the world.

5 Then Jacob set out from Beer-sheba; and the sons of Israel carried their father Jacob, their little ones, and their wives, in the wagons that Pharaoh had sent to carry him. 6They also took their livestock and the goods that they had acquired in the land of Canaan, and they came into Egypt, Jacob and all his offspring with him, 7his sons, and his sons' sons with him, his daughters, and his sons' daughters; all his offspring he brought with him into Egypt.

8 Now these are the names of the Israelites, Jacob and his offspring, who came to Egypt. Reuben, Jacob's firstborn, 9and the children of Reuben: Hanoch, Pallu, Hezron, and Carmi. 10The children of Simeon: Jemuel, Jamin, Ohad, Jachin, Zohar, and Shaul,*a* the son of a Canaanite woman. 11The children of Levi: Gershon, Kohath, and Merari. 12The children of Judah: Er, Onan, Shelah, Perez, and Zerah (but Er and Onan died in the land of Canaan); and the children of Perez were Hezron and Hamul. 13The children of Issachar: Tola, Puvah, Jashub,*b* and Shimron. 14The children of Zebulun: Sered, Elon, and Jahleel 15(these are the sons of Leah, whom she bore to Jacob in Paddan-aram, together with his daughter Dinah; in all his sons and his daughters numbered thirty-three). 16The children of Gad: Ziphion, Haggi, Shuni, Ezbon, Eri, Arodi, and Areli. 17The children of Asher: Imnah, Ishvah, Ishvi, Beriah, and their sister Serah. The children of Beriah: Heber and Malchiel 18(these are the children of Zilpah, whom Laban gave to his daughter Leah; and these she bore to Jacob—sixteen persons). 19The children of Jacob's wife Rachel: Joseph and Benjamin. 20To Joseph in the land of Egypt were born Manasseh and Ephraim, whom Asenath daughter of Potiphera, priest of On, bore to him. 21The children of Benjamin: Bela, Becher, Ashbel, Gera, Naaman, Ehi, Rosh, Muppim, Huppim, and Ard 22(these are the children of Rachel, who were born to Jacob—fourteen persons in all). 23The children of Dan: Hashum.*c* 24The children of Naphtali: Jahzeel, Guni, Jezer, and Shillem 25(these are the children of Bilhah, whom Laban gave to his daughter Rachel, and these she bore to Jacob—seven persons in all). 26All the persons belonging to Jacob who came into Egypt, who were his own offspring, not including the wives of his sons, were sixty-six persons in all. 27The children of Joseph, who were born to him in Egypt, were two; all the persons of the house of Jacob who came into Egypt were seventy.

Jacob Settles in Goshen

28 Israel*d* sent Judah ahead to Joseph to lead the way before him into Goshen. When they came to the land of Goshen, 29Joseph made ready his chariot and went up to meet his father Israel in Goshen. He presented himself to him, fell on his neck, and wept on his neck a good while. 30Israel said to Joseph, "I can die now, having seen for myself that you are still alive." 31Joseph said to his brothers and to his father's household, "I will go up and tell Pharaoh, and will say to him, 'My brothers and my father's household, who were in the land of Canaan, have come to me. 32The men are shepherds, for they have been keepers of livestock; and they have brought their flocks, and their herds, and all that they have.' 33When Pharaoh calls you, and says, 'What is your occupation?' 34you shall say, 'Your servants have been keepers of livestock from our youth even until now, both we and our ancestors'—in order that you may settle in the land of Goshen, because all shepherds are abhorrent to the Egyptians."

47 So Joseph went and told Pharaoh, "My father and my brothers, with their flocks and herds and all that they possess, have come from the land of Canaan;

---

a Or *Saul*   *b* Compare Sam Gk Num 26.24; 1 Chr 7.1: MT *Iob*   *c* Gk: Heb *Hushim*
d Heb *He*

47:1–12 *So Joseph went and told Pharaoh.* Joseph, the bearer of divine blessing, meets Pharaoh, the ruler of the world's largest empire. The arena of God's activity is the whole world. Pharaoh's generosity toward Joseph foreshadows a day when another pharaoh will not know Joseph or care about his family. It may appear that all the promises made to Abraham have come to fruition; however, Jacob's insistence on being taken back to Canaan for burial (v 30) is a

they are now in the land of Goshen." 2From among his brothers he took five men and presented them to Pharaoh. 3Pharaoh said to his brothers, "What is your occupation?" And they said to Pharaoh, "Your servants are shepherds, as our ancestors were." 4They said to Pharaoh, "We have come to reside as aliens in the land; for there is no pasture for your servants' flocks because the famine is severe in the land of Canaan. Now, we ask you, let your servants settle in the land of Goshen." 5Then Pharaoh said to Joseph, "Your father and your brothers have come to you. 6The land of Egypt is before you; settle your father and your brothers in the best part of the land; let them live in the land of Goshen; and if you know that there are capable men among them, put them in charge of my livestock."

7 Then Joseph brought in his father Jacob, and presented him before Pharaoh, and Jacob blessed Pharaoh. 8Pharaoh said to Jacob, "How many are the years of your life?" 9Jacob said to Pharaoh, "The years of my earthly sojourn are one hundred thirty; few and hard have been the years of my life. They do not compare with the years of the life of my ancestors during their long sojourn." 10Then Jacob blessed Pharaoh, and went out from the presence of Pharaoh. 11Joseph settled his father and his brothers, and granted them a holding in the land of Egypt, in the best part of the land, in the land of Rameses, as Pharaoh had instructed. 12And Joseph provided his father, his brothers, and all his father's household with food, according to the number of their dependents.

The Famine in Egypt

13 Now there was no food in all the land, for the famine was very severe. The land of Egypt and the land of Canaan languished because of the famine. 14Joseph collected all the money to be found in the land of Egypt and in the land of Canaan, in exchange for the grain that they bought; and Joseph brought the money into Pharaoh's house.

15When the money from the land of Egypt and from the land of Canaan was spent, all the Egyptians came to Joseph, and said, "Give us food! Why should we die before your eyes? For our money is gone." 16And Joseph answered, "Give me your livestock, and I will give you food in exchange for your livestock, if your money is gone." 17So they brought their livestock to Joseph; and Joseph gave them food in exchange for the horses, the flocks, the herds, and the donkeys. That year he supplied them with food in exchange for all their livestock. 18When that year was ended, they came to him the following year, and said to him, "We can not hide from my lord that our money is all spent; and the herds of cattle are my lord's. There is nothing left in the sight of my lord but our bodies and our lands. 19Shall we die before your eyes, both we and our land? Buy us and our land in exchange for food. We with our land will become slaves to Pharaoh; just give us seed, so that we may live and not die, and that the land may not become desolate."

20 So Joseph bought all the land of Egypt for Pharaoh. All the Egyptians sold their fields, because the famine was severe upon them; and the land became Pharaoh's. 21As for the people, he made slaves of them a from one end of Egypt to the other. 22Only the land of the priests he did not buy; for the priests had a fixed allowance from Pharaoh, and lived on the allowance that Pharaoh gave them; therefore they did not sell their land. 23Then Joseph said to the people, "Now that I have this day bought you and your land for Pharaoh, here is seed for you; sow the land. 24And at the harvests you shall give one-fifth to Pharaoh, and four-fifths shall be your own, as seed for the field and as food for yourselves and your households, and as food for your little ones." 25They said, "You have saved our lives; may it please my lord, we will be slaves

a Sam Gk Compare Vg: MT *He removed them to the cities*

---

reminder that land in Egypt is not the Promised Land. Thus, resolution of conflict within the family doesn't bring an end to the complexity of God's movement through the human family.

47:13–26 *Now there was no food.* This story reminds us that even this great "Hebrew" gets caught up in worldly acquisitiveness and exploitation.

to Pharaoh." 26So Joseph made it a statute concerning the land of Egypt, and it stands to this day, that Pharaoh should have the fifth. The land of the priests alone did not become Pharaoh's.

The Last Days of Jacob

27 Thus Israel settled in the land of Egypt, in the region of Goshen; and they gained possessions in it, and were fruitful and multiplied exceedingly. 28Jacob lived in the land of Egypt seventeen years; so the days of Jacob, the years of his life, were one hundred forty-seven years.

29 When the time of Israel's death drew near, he called his son Joseph and said to him, "If I have found favor with you, put your hand under my thigh and promise to deal loyally and truly with me. Do not bury me in Egypt. 30When I lie down with my ancestors, carry me out of Egypt and bury me in their burial place." He answered, "I will do as you have said." 31And he said, "Swear to me"; and he swore to him. Then Israel bowed himself on the head of his bed.

Jacob Blesses Joseph's Sons

48 After this Joseph was told, "Your father is ill." So he took with him his two sons, Manasseh and Ephraim. 2When Jacob was told, "Your son Joseph has come to you," he*a* summoned his strength and sat up in bed. 3And Jacob said to Joseph, "God Almighty*b* appeared to me at Luz in the land of Canaan, and he blessed me, 4and said to me, 'I am going to make you fruitful and increase your numbers; I will make of you a company of peoples, and will give this land to your offspring after you for a perpetual holding.' 5Therefore your two sons, who were born to you in the land of Egypt before I came to you in Egypt, are now mine; Ephraim and Manasseh shall be mine, just as Reuben and Simeon are. 6As for the offspring born to you after them, they shall be yours. They shall be recorded under the names of their broth-

ers with regard to their inheritance. 7For when I came from Paddan, Rachel, alas, died in the land of Canaan on the way, while there was still some distance to go to Ephrath; and I buried her there on the way to Ephrath" (that is, Bethlehem).

8 When Israel saw Joseph's sons, he said, "Who are these?" 9Joseph said to his father, "They are my sons, whom God has given me here." And he said, "Bring them to me, please, that I may bless them." 10Now the eyes of Israel were dim with age, and he could not see well. So Joseph brought them near him; and he kissed them and embraced them. 11Israel said to Joseph, "I did not expect to see your face; and here God has let me see your children also." 12Then Joseph removed them from his father's knees,*c* and he bowed himself with his face to the earth. 13Joseph took them both, Ephraim in his right hand toward Israel's left, and Manasseh in his left hand toward Israel's right, and brought them near him. 14But Israel stretched out his right hand and laid it on the head of Ephraim, who was the younger, and his left hand on the head of Manasseh, crossing his hands, for Manasseh was the firstborn. 15He blessed Joseph, and said,

"The God before whom my ancestors
    Abraham and Isaac walked,
the God who has been my shepherd all
    my life to this day,
16 the angel who has redeemed me from
    all harm, bless the boys;
and in them let my name be
    perpetuated, and the name of my
    ancestors Abraham and Isaac;
and let them grow into a multitude on
    the earth."

17 When Joseph saw that his father laid his right hand on the head of Ephraim, it displeased him; so he took his father's hand, to remove it from Ephraim's head to Manasseh's head. 18Joseph said to his father, "Not

a Heb *Israel*   *b* Traditional rendering of Heb *El Shaddai*   *c* Heb *from his knees*

48:1–22 *Your father is ill.* With this long complex blessing (vv 8–22), again the text orchestrates a reversal. The younger will surpass the elder. Joseph's children are blessed by their grandfather to be two great tribes of this extended family.

so, my father! Since this one is the firstborn, put your right hand on his head." ¹⁹But his father refused, and said, "I know, my son, I know; he also shall become a people, and he also shall be great. Nevertheless his younger brother shall be greater than he, and his offspring shall become a multitude of nations." ²⁰So he blessed them that day, saying,

"By you ᵃ Israel will invoke blessings,
saying,
'God make you ᵃ like Ephraim and like
Manasseh.' "

So he put Ephraim ahead of Manasseh. ²¹Then Israel said to Joseph, "I am about to die, but God will be with you and will bring you again to the land of your ancestors. ²²I now give to you one portion ᵇ more than to your brothers, the portion ᵇ that I took from the hand of the Amorites with my sword and with my bow."

Jacob's Last Words to His Sons

49 Then Jacob called his sons, and said: "Gather around, that I may tell you what will happen to you in days to come.
2 Assemble and hear, O sons of Jacob;
listen to Israel your father.

3 Reuben, you are my firstborn,
my might and the first fruits of my
vigor,
excelling in rank and excelling in
power.
4 Unstable as water, you shall no longer
excel
because you went up onto your
father's bed;
then you defiled it—you ᶜ went up
onto my couch!

5 Simeon and Levi are brothers;
weapons of violence are their swords.
6 May I never come into their council;
may I not be joined to their
company—
for in their anger they killed men,
and at their whim they hamstrung
oxen.

7 Cursed be their anger, for it is fierce,
and their wrath, for it is cruel!
I will divide them in Jacob,
and scatter them in Israel.

8 Judah, your brothers shall praise you;
your hand shall be on the neck of
your enemies;
your father's sons shall bow down
before you.
9 Judah is a lion's whelp;
from the prey, my son, you have gone
up.
He crouches down, he stretches out like
a lion,
like a lioness—who dares rouse him
up?
10 The scepter shall not depart from Judah,
nor the ruler's staff from between his
feet,
until tribute comes to him; ᵈ
and the obedience of the peoples is
his.
11 Binding his foal to the vine
and his donkey's colt to the choice
vine,
he washes his garments in wine
and his robe in the blood of grapes;
12 his eyes are darker than wine,
and his teeth whiter than milk.

13 Zebulun shall settle at the shore of the
sea;
he shall be a haven for ships,
and his border shall be at Sidon.

14 Issachar is a strong donkey,
lying down between the sheepfolds;
15 he saw that a resting place was good,
and that the land was pleasant;
so he bowed his shoulder to the burden,
and became a slave at forced labor.

ᵃ you here is singular in Heb   ᵇ Or mountain slope (Heb shekem, a play on the name of the town and district of Shechem)   ᶜ Gk Syr Tg: Heb he   ᵈ Or until Shiloh comes or until he comes to Shiloh or (with Syr) until he comes to whom it belongs

---

49:2–28 O sons of Jacob. Jacob's poetic farewell to his sons, including judgment and blessing, establishes the twelve tribes of Israel.

16 Dan shall judge his people
    as one of the tribes of Israel.
17 Dan shall be a snake by the roadside,
    a viper along the path,
  that bites the horse's heels
    so that its rider falls backward.

18 I wait for your salvation, O LORD.

19 Gad shall be raided by raiders,
    but he shall raid at their heels.

20 Asher's *a* food shall be rich,
    and he shall provide royal delicacies.

21 Naphtali is a doe let loose
    that bears lovely fawns. *b*

22 Joseph is a fruitful bough,
    a fruitful bough by a spring;
  his branches run over the wall. *c*
23 The archers fiercely attacked him;
    they shot at him and pressed him
      hard.
24 Yet his bow remained taut,
    and his arms *d* were made agile
  by the hands of the Mighty One of
      Jacob,
    by the name of the Shepherd, the
      Rock of Israel,
25 by the God of your father, who will help
      you,
    by the Almighty *e* who will bless you
  with blessings of heaven above,
  blessings of the deep that lies beneath,
  blessings of the breasts and of the
      womb.
26 The blessings of your father
    are stronger than the blessings of the
      eternal mountains,

the bounties *f* of the everlasting hills;
  may they be on the head of Joseph,
    on the brow of him who was set apart
      from his brothers.

27 Benjamin is a ravenous wolf,
    in the morning devouring the prey,
    and at evening dividing the spoil."

28 All these are the twelve tribes of Israel,
and this is what their father said to them
when he blessed them, blessing each one of
them with a suitable blessing.

Jacob's Death and Burial

29 Then he charged them, saying to them,
"I am about to be gathered to my people.
Bury me with my ancestors—in the cave in
the field of Ephron the Hittite, 30in the cave
in the field at Machpelah, near Mamre, in
the land of Canaan, in the field that Abraham
bought from Ephron the Hittite as a burial
site. 31There Abraham and his wife Sarah were
buried; there Isaac and his wife Rebekah were
buried; and there I buried Leah— 32the field
and the cave that is in it were purchased from
the Hittites." 33When Jacob ended his charge
to his sons, he drew up his feet into the bed,
breathed his last, and was gathered to his
people.

50 Then Joseph threw himself on his father's face and wept over him and
kissed him. 2Joseph commanded the physicians in his service to embalm his father. So
the physicians embalmed Israel; 3they spent

a Gk Vg Syr: Heb *From Asher*   *b* Or *that gives
beautiful words*   *c* Meaning of Heb uncertain
d Heb *the arms of his hands*   *e* Traditional
rendering of Heb *Shaddai*   *f* Cn Compare Gk:
Heb *of my progenitors to the boundaries*

50:1–26 *Joseph threw himself on his father's
face and wept.* The death of Jacob (49:33)
coincides with the last days of Joseph as the
family narrative comes to a close. The solemn
burial of Jacob, with the whole clan and the
servants of Pharaoh in attendance, lays claim to
future possession of the land. Parents have a
way of holding a family of siblings together.
With the death of their father, the brothers
finally seek the forgiveness of Joseph (vv 15–18).

Joseph responds with a dramatic pronouncement in verse 20. There is no need for fear.
What humans may have intended as harm,
God intended for good. The will of God has
always been to preserve a people. The burial
of Joseph in Egypt (v 26) juxtaposes his father's
burial in Canaan. Now the Israelites are pre-
cariously bound to two nations—the last word
of Genesis is "Egypt."

forty days in doing this, for that is the time required for embalming. And the Egyptians wept for him seventy days.

4 When the days of weeping for him were past, Joseph addressed the household of Pharaoh, "If now I have found favor with you, please speak to Pharaoh as follows: 5My father made me swear an oath; he said, 'I am about to die. In the tomb that I hewed out for myself in the land of Canaan, there you shall bury me.' Now therefore let me go up, so that I may bury my father; then I will return." 6Pharaoh answered, "Go up, and bury your father, as he made you swear to do."

7 So Joseph went up to bury his father. With him went up all the servants of Pharaoh, the elders of his household, and all the elders of the land of Egypt, 8as well as all the household of Joseph, his brothers, and his father's household. Only their children, their flocks, and their herds were left in the land of Goshen. 9Both chariots and charioteers went up with him. It was a very great company. 10When they came to the threshing floor of Atad, which is beyond the Jordan, they held there a very great and sorrowful lamentation; and he observed a time of mourning for his father seven days. 11When the Canaanite inhabitants of the land saw the mourning on the threshing floor of Atad, they said, "This is a grievous mourning on the part of the Egyptians." Therefore the place was named Abel-mizraim;ª it is beyond the Jordan. 12Thus his sons did for him as he had instructed them. 13They carried him to the land of Canaan and buried him in the cave of the field at Machpelah, the field near Mamre, which Abraham bought as a burial site from Ephron the Hittite. 14After he had buried his father, Joseph returned to Egypt with his brothers and all who had gone up with him to bury his father.

Joseph Forgives His Brothers

15 Realizing that their father was dead, Joseph's brothers said, "What if Joseph still bears a grudge against us and pays us back in full for all the wrong that we did to him?" 16So they approached[b] Joseph, saying, "Your father gave this instruction before he died, 17'Say to Joseph: I beg you, forgive the crime of your brothers and the wrong they did in harming you.' Now therefore please forgive the crime of the servants of the God of your father." Joseph wept when they spoke to him. 18Then his brothers also wept,[c] fell down before him, and said, "We are here as your slaves." 19But Joseph said to them, "Do not be afraid! Am I in the place of God? 20Even though you intended to do harm to me, God intended it for good, in order to preserve a numerous people, as he is doing today. 21So have no fear; I myself will provide for you and your little ones." In this way he reassured them, speaking kindly to them.

Joseph's Last Days and Death

22 So Joseph remained in Egypt, he and his father's household; and Joseph lived one hundred ten years. 23Joseph saw Ephraim's children of the third generation; the children of Machir son of Manasseh were also born on Joseph's knees.

24 Then Joseph said to his brothers, "I am about to die; but God will surely come to you, and bring you up out of this land to the land that he swore to Abraham, to Isaac, and to Jacob." 25So Joseph made the Israelites swear, saying, "When God comes to you, you shall carry up my bones from here." 26And Joseph died, being one hundred ten years old; he was embalmed and placed in a coffin in Egypt.

a That is *mourning* (or *meadow*) *of Egypt*   b Gk Syr: Heb *they commanded*   c Cn: Heb *also came*

III. The People of God in Exodus

Scriptures: *Exodus, Leviticus, Numbers, Deuteronomy*

> *The aim of God in history is the creation of an all-inclusive community of loving persons with God himself at the very center of this community as its prime Sustainer and most glorious Inhabitant (Eph 2:19–22; 3:10). The Bible traces the formation of this community from the creation in the Garden of Eden all the way to the new heaven and the new earth. Come, join us as we explore the many dimensions of this with-God history—from individual to family to tribe to people to nation to all humanity—and apply what we learn to our own spiritual formation.*

In the second through fifth books of the Bible we will see the ways God continues the process of forming an all-inclusive community through the exodus of the children of Israel from Egypt; their journey to Sinai, where God gives them the law; and their forty years in the wilderness.

God's Action

The key theme of these Scriptures is God's deliverance of his people from bondage by working through the concrete social structures of a nation (Egypt) and the more abstract ethnicities of an emerging people (who become the Israelites). Working to make his presence known not exclusively with individuals, as we saw in Genesis 1–11, or within the simple confines of a family and its members, as described in Genesis 12–50, God now mediates his presence to a growing host in broader human history with the purpose of freeing his people from slavery in the face of defiance from human political structures. When God delivers Israel from Egyptian bondage, he makes a public display of his might and shows his power over worldly systems, however invulnerable they may seem. In this way the whole of history, and not simply individuals or a family, is brought under the sway of God's redemptive purposes for all to see.

For a time, after Jacob's family moved to Egypt, they "multiplied and grew exceedingly strong, so that the land was filled with them" (Exod 1:7). But "a new king arose over Egypt, who did not know Joseph. He said to his people, 'Look, the Israelite people are more numerous and more powerful than we. Come, let us deal shrewdly with them, or they will increase and, in the event of war, join our enemies and fight against us and escape from the land'" (1:8–10). From then on, the Egyptians feared the Israelites and enslaved them, forcing them to build cities, make mortar and bricks, and labor in the fields.

Into this furnace of slavery and oppression, Moses is born. Raised by royalty and exiled to Midian after murdering an Egyptian slave master, he reluctantly responds to the call of God and returns to Egypt as Israel's leader. When the rulers refuse to let the Israelites leave, God sends plagues designed to call them to repent of their harsh treatment of the people who would become the Israelites and to practice justice by letting them leave. The struggle culminates when Moses and the Israelites, under the direction of God, leave the land of Egypt, all of which prepares them for entry into a covenant, the Mosaic law, with God at Sinai (Lev 27:34).

The giving of the law by God puts in place a moral code (the Ten Commandments and accompanying instructions) and a religious practice (the tabernacle and its rituals) designed to keep God and his acts in history constantly in the hearts and minds of the people of Israel. Mosaic law provided a massive, steady discipline for the practice of the with-God life. In Egypt the Israelites were a loosely knit confederation of families without any common culture or religious life other than what had been handed down from their ancestors. Now, by being signatories to the covenant with Yahweh (see note in next paragraph), the law gives them a common heritage and religious faith and spells out God's expectations in the arenas of morality and worship. In their deliverance from Egypt and acceptance of the covenant obligations, the People of God now consist of all those who have Jacob as their ancestor. As a new people, they are brought into a lively relationship with the active presence of God as he appears to them in a "pillar of cloud" by day and a "pillar of fire" by night during the exodus and in the clouds as the "glory of the LORD" fills the tent of meeting, the tabernacle (Exod 13:21; 40:34–35).

(YHWH, usually pronounced Yahweh, is the most important name for God in the Old Testament. Used about sixty-eight hundred times in the Bible, the name most certainly comes from God's encounter with Moses at the burning bush when, in answer to Moses' question as to God's name [i.e., identity], God says, "I AM WHO I AM ['ehyeh 'asher 'ehyeh]. . . . Thus you shall say to the Israelites, 'I AM has sent me to you'" [Exod 3:13–14].)

Human Reaction

The reaction of this new, liberated people is predictable: when things are going well, they are obedient and happy. "All the Israelites did just as the LORD had commanded Moses and Aaron" (Exod 12:50). "At the end of four hundred thirty years, on that very day, all the companies of the LORD went out from the land of Egypt. . . . Then Moses and the Israelites sang this song to the LORD, 'I will sing to the LORD, for he has triumphed gloriously,' . . . and all the women went out after [Miriam] with tambourines and with dancing" (12:41; 15:1, 20). But as we have already seen in the lives of Abraham's immediate family, good times do not lend themselves to the formation of good character.

When things go badly, the Israelites are disobedient and grumble. They think God's plan is risky. They prefer to return to bondage in Egypt (Exod 14:11–12). They worship a golden calf (Exod 32), causing God to say, "You are a stiff-necked people"

The With-God Life

(33:5). They lack faith in the power of God to conquer the Promised Land and, as a result, wander in the wilderness for forty years until, with the exception of Joshua and Caleb, every person over the age of twenty dies (Num 13–14). Sadly—despite God's sending them a deliverer and making his presence with them known in physical forms they can see and experience each day—they fail to comprehend the overall divine purposes of God.

Despite these fluctuations, from the books of Exodus through Deuteronomy it becomes increasingly clear that God's purposes are based on a steadfast love, extending through Israel to all of humanity. God gives the law to the descendants of Abraham, Isaac, and Jacob not to elicit legalism, but love, a fact so preeminent that Jesus, the Messiah, quotes Deut 6:5 during his ministry: "You shall love the Lord your God with all your heart, and with all your soul, and with all your mind" (Matt 22:37). Clearly, love is at the center of the community that God is forming.

Blessings and Benefits for Our Formation

In the wilderness at the tent of meeting, God begins the long process of setting in place a standard way in which his presence is manifested to all humanity. At first, God works in spectacular ways. When he appears to Moses in the desert, it is in the form of a burning bush. During the trip from Egypt to Sinai, God is with the people as cloud and fire. On Sinai it is in thunder, lightning, trumpet blasts, a thick cloud, smoke, and fire. But with the completion of the tabernacle and the institution of the law and its rituals, God's presence becomes localized and a more routine part of everyday life: "Then the cloud covered the tent of meeting, and the glory of the LORD filled the tabernacle" (Exod 40:34). This is also how God appears to the people at the dedication of Solomon's Temple (1 Kings 8:10–11).

The decrease in the intensity of the supernatural ways by which God reveals himself is not because the people are bored. They were too much like you and me for that to be true. No, it is because now God can be with his people in a manner more suited to the requirements of a normalized daily life, through the disciplines of Mosaic law and religious ritual. In the law the people now find a resource for how they should act as the called-out People of God. Formed along with this law is a religious class of people, the priests (Levites), who preside at the rituals and liturgies held at the tent of meeting in the center of the community. These rituals and liturgies help to form the people's spirits in such a way that they worship the one true God. Idolatry, once rampant, gradually falls away. The priesthood provides an orderly, standard approach to God, just as do contemporary pastors, rabbis, and priests. They communicate God's blessings and requirements to us in the context of our own culture.

Through the Aaronic and levitical priesthoods, God makes himself available and accessible, so that grace meets the people concretely in daily life. The Israelites can now come daily to God—approach God, learn God's name, and call upon that name. At the heart of the place of worship, the tabernacle, is the ark of the covenant in the Holy of Holies. In the holy place are the altar of incense and the table of the

The With-God Life

bread of the Presence, which connect the heavenly (smoke and a sweet smell) with the physical (bread as the sustainer of life). On the altar in the outer court the priests preside over sacrifices for sins of commission and omission. Every action, every piece of furniture, every ritual makes the connection between heaven and earth and draws the People of God more deeply into the disciplines of spiritual formation: prayer, sacrifice, fasting, meditation, praise, celebration, and the like.

Another benefit is the establishment of a system to deal with misconduct and disagreements within the community. There is no standard way to handle such affairs until Jethro, Moses' father-in-law, advises Moses to appoint able people to "sit as judges for the people at all times; let them bring every important case to you, but decide every minor case themselves" (Exod 18:22). Moses, as the first judge, appoints officers "over thousands, hundreds, fifties, and tens. And they judged the people at all times" (18:25–26). The judge is the first level of an administrative or political structure that is also composed of priests and, ultimately, God. We call this kind of political system a "theocracy." The person of the judge becomes a primary way for God's presence to be mediated even in the everyday disputes between members of the community.

Limits and Liabilities for Our Formation

The law is limited in its ability to redeem us, because too many times it remains external to our will. It does not always reach the heart as intended. From reading the Old Testament we know that circumcision, an outward act, did not make people automatically love God from the heart, an inward condition. Today we can see in our own lives and the lives of others that baptism, the Christian equivalent of circumcision, is not a sure indicator of the inward condition of the heart. Likewise, merely obeying external laws is limited in its ability to make us compassionate, loving, and merciful. "Real circumcision is a matter of the heart—it is spiritual and not literal" (Rom 2:29, cf. Deut 10:16; 30:6).

It is often the case that, by focusing on the "letter of the law" and ignoring its spiritual intent, we lapse into idolatry, legalism, or priestly abuse, which hamper our spiritual formation. We may even end up worshiping the law rather than God. Such idolatry may unintentionally increase the power of religious leaders who are not exercising their responsibilities in keeping with the purposes of God. All of these examples have one constant: the desire to use the law to control our own destiny. The law is powerless to reach deep into this center of human willing, so, though good in itself, it is an incomplete expression of God-with-us.

Insights and Instructions for Our Formation

One of the first lessons we learn at this stage of God's mediating work for the transformation of human character is that, although we are part of a called-out people, each one of us stands before God as an individual with ultimate accountability to our Creator for our actions. This is a foundational assumption of God's law. God's public acts in history call for our total and radical response not simply in ritual, but in behavior and in life. The law provides clear moral guidelines that help us relate fittingly to the holy God and the needy neighbor. At the same time it provides a seasonal cycle of ritual events of praise, repentance, sacrifice, and glorification of God. The seasons of piety bring the community together to celebrate the seasons of God's presence, but these ritual events serve ultimately to foster a moral accountability that brings us increasingly to trust God and his unfolding aim in history to form an all-inclusive community of loving persons.

Second, we learn that at the heart of every community are leaders who have special responsibilities in God's kingdom. Abraham taught his family to have faith in God, a necessary part of life in God's community. Moses introduced a system of justice to deal with everyday conflict and misconduct, and Aaron oversaw the establishment of regular worship and ritual. Each played a vital role in preparing the Israelites to become a nation set apart for the worship of the true God and to attest to fallen, hurting humanity the reality of a future kingdom where God's Chosen Servant "will proclaim justice to the Gentiles" (Matt 12:18).

Third, though we may chafe under them, we see that every community has to have institutional structures. This is true regardless of the type of community—political, educational, social, or religious—but is particularly true in communities of faith. Without the structures that make possible adhering to a moral code, participating in regular rituals, reciting the historical acts of God, practicing acts of justice and love, and sharing in a community life, we would surely lose our sense of time and purpose. Religious rituals have a unique ability to keep us simultaneously grounded in the physical and in the spiritual.

At the end of Deuteronomy the Israelites stand poised to enter the Promised Land, having endured defeat, delay, and death in the wilderness. Their leader, Moses, is permitted to see the land from a distance, but not allowed to enter because of his own disobedience. His dual legacy—the law and the tabernacle—is an integral part of the Israelites' community experience as they reflect on God's fulfillment of his promise to Abraham to make of him a great people and look forward to a settled life in the Promised Land. They have come a long way from Egypt—a longer way from Eden—and have a long way to go. Join us as we learn the numerous ways God prepared Israel for the next stage in its with-God life.

The With-God Life

EXODUS

The ancient Egyptians called their nation Kemet. It means "Black Land," a name derived from the dark soil the Nile deposited each fall on its banks. The flooding began in July and receded in September, and the rich earth helped Egypt to prosper and become one of the great civilizations. According to Genesis it was Joseph, one of the twelve sons of Jacob (or Israel), who came to Egypt as a slave. Other ancient writings and archaeological evidence verify the biblical account's depiction of Egyptian life and customs. The account tells us that when Joseph rises to a prominent position in Pharaoh's court, he is able to save his family and his people in Canaan from a severe famine. Israel comes to settle in Egypt in the region of Goshen, and as the Egyptians have thrived close to the life-giving Nile, so too do the Israelites.

We know that during the eighteenth dynasty, 1570–1300 BC, Semitic peoples in vast numbers worked as slaves for the pharaoh in Thebes. We also know this continued on into the nineteenth dynasty in the northeast Delta, where Goshen is. The exodus probably occurs between 1300 and 1250. The pharaoh who did not know or care who Joseph had been, or that the Hebrews were his descendants, was most likely Seti I, who ruled from 1305 until 1290. It is during his reign, a reign of terror for the Hebrews, that Moses is placed in a basket on the waters of the Nile and rescued by one of the pharaoh's daughters. Moses is raised in Seti I's household, and it is during his upbringing that the enslavement of his people becomes more firmly entrenched. The pharaoh that Moses returns from exile to challenge is most likely Seti I's son, Rameses II (1290–1224), the pharaoh of the exodus. It is he who finally releases the slaves to begin their journey to Canaan by way of the Red Sea (a better translation is the Sea of Reeds). By the time this pivotal event occurs, the defining moment in the history of the people of Israel, the Hebrews have lived in Egypt for at least four hundred years.

Exodus is the account of a people discovering who they are, who their God is, and the kind of spirituality they must fashion their lives around if they wish to become the

See also *"The With-God Life"* essay for this section of the Bible,
"The People of God in Exodus," pp. 87–91.

93

nation they were called to be. Those who recorded the story of Moses and Israel at such a critical stage needed to be precise about the laws God had given their people to help shape who they were becoming. But they also wished to retain every scrap of information about what took place between Moses and God and between Israel and God, no matter how fantastic that information might seem. This was, after all, the story of their birth, and it was a time of great miracles. It is the inclusion of this material that gives the book of Exodus its unforgettable power and distinctive voice.

The Drama of the Exodus

Exodus is one of the great stories of the world. No other book in the Bible has been more dramatized and filmed except the life of Christ. God is not talked about. He is not theorized about. He is right there in the face of Moses. We see his anger, his fierce holiness, his power, his mercy. Nothing is at a distance. It is almost as if we could see the pores on the back of his hand as he stretches it out over Israel and Egypt.

The story is steeped in mud and blood and death. Lightning and thunder and darkness and fire spill out of it. God's radiance knifes into our eyes. One moment we watch in awe as water turns to blood. Another moment we see more blood being smeared on doorposts. One moment we gaze in horror as locusts make the land a crawling blackness. The next we see slaves running through the night to freedom. One day these slaves swear they will worship God. The next they are praying to a calf made out of the Egyptian gold they had stuffed in their pockets.

God is both obvious and unseen, both knowable and incomprehensible, both kindhearted and devastating. He appears all-powerful, yet there is nothing he does that does not require women and men and children for his wishes to be accomplished. Exodus is not so much Israel's story as it is God's story. At times enchanting, at times dazzling, at times bewildering, it is a story that never loses its appeal, a story we come back to again and again, a story that has inspired people around the earth.

Why does Exodus live forever while other Bible stories are unknown? Moses is part of it, the reluctant hero we can all identify with, the small figure who nevertheless stands up to both Pharaoh, the power of earth, and Yahweh, the power of heaven. God is part of it, the Lord of land and sky, hidden behind cloudbanks crackling with lightning, shimmering with firelight at night, blustery and intractable, yet still setting Israel free and forgiving its sins. The drama of the plagues is part of it, frogs and locusts and hail and the cruel shock of the death of the firstborn. The parting of the sea, manna in the desert, grim Mt. Sinai, Moses' arriving out of the ominous thunderhead with the Ten Commandments engraved in stone, the golden calf, the smashing of the stone tablets, the desperate prayer of Moses to save Israel, the gold and glitter and mystery of the tabernacle, God's settling within it in all his glory—these incredible images form part of the universal appeal of the story. Exodus is graphic, visual, and visceral, and one comes away from repeated readings or retellings with an imagination swirling with terror and wonder.

Yet possibly the greatest single aspect of Exodus's commanding the fascination of the world is that it is about freedom. The slaves are set free. Utterly free. Men like us, children like us, women like us. Their tormentors are vanquished and cannot hurt them any longer. God fights for them; Yahweh, the God of heaven and earth, fights for them in all his power and glory. Yahweh, the Lord of the universe, stands up for them and sets them free, and when he does that for them he does that for us. Exodus becomes not only a model for the liberation of those who are oppressed; it becomes a promise, a hope, that the God who has done it for one will do it for all. It must be God's nature, it must be, and that means Exodus can happen again, not just for a few, but for all peoples.

The Twelve Stages of the Exodus

Absence. When the story begins God is not there, conspicuous by his absence. The midwives act heroically because they fear God. We are told that God notices what is happening to the Hebrews. But still, for the majority of the time, God is not there. Moses is born, hidden, rescued, and raised and becomes a refugee, and still God is not there. Oppression turns into genocide and slavery and still God does not act. Or so it seems to the human eye.

Oppression. What began long before as a time of grace under Joseph, when living in Egypt in the land of Goshen was living in a sanctuary of peace and goodwill, becomes a horror under a new pharaoh. The Hebrews are forced to build cities and monuments and tombs. Their oppressors grow more and more ruthless. In time, the Hebrews are nothing more than slaves. Perpetually frightened by their numbers, Pharaoh enacts a policy of genocide—every Hebrew boy must be slain at birth. When this does not work due to the noncompliance of the midwives, he orders every Hebrew boy to be drowned in the Nile. It is out of this misery, with Moses long out of the picture and living a shepherd's life in Midian, that God is roused by the agony of the Hebrews in their slavery.

Vocation. At the very mountain where Moses will be given the Ten Commandments, deep in the wilderness, on an ordinary day when Moses is doing his normal work as a shepherd, he receives one of the great shocks of his life. God speaks to him out of a burning bush, reveals his holy name—YHWH, or Yahweh, "I AM WHO I AM"—and commands him to go to Egypt to free the Hebrews. They are Moses' people as well as God's, but Moses is reluctant. His excuses are swept aside; he has no choice. He has been called to lead God's people out of slavery and that is the end of the argument. His task will not be completed until he is dead.

Confrontation. Moses and his brother stand before the world power that is Egypt and declare that God, Yahweh, has sent them to lead the Hebrews out of Egypt. The Hebrews believe this, though later they have plenty of reasons to complain, but Pharaoh will not accept the loss of the Hebrew workforce. Plagues rain down upon his head and upon the backs of the Egyptians, but it is not until the death of the firstborn that Pharaoh agrees to release the Hebrews.

Liberation. The night Yahweh passes over the houses of the Hebrews, but strikes down the firstborn humans and animals in those of the Egyptians, is the very night Pharaoh rises from his bed and orders Moses to take the Hebrew people and leave.

In haste they depart and travel through the wilderness toward Canaan, the land God has promised to give them for their home. They are free.

Provision. Yahweh guides the Hebrews through the wilderness—he leads them by means of a pillar of cloud in the daylight and a pillar of fire by night. He rescues them from the pursuing Egyptians when Pharaoh decides to enslave them again. In the desert he provides them with food in the form of manna and quail, and he ensures they have ample water. As empty and dead as the wilderness appears, God is able to give them life here as well.

Creation. At Mt. Sinai, where Moses first spoke with Yahweh at the burning bush, God makes a covenant between himself and the Hebrew people he has rescued from slavery. The people are consecrated, God swears to be their God, and the relationship is established. No longer are they refugees or slaves. They are a nation. They are Israel.

Direction. God gives the Israelites the Ten Commandments as well as scores of other laws to guide them in their relationship with God, with each other, and with all the people of the earth.

Rebellion. Despite a promising start, the people are impatient when Moses stays on the mountain with God for forty days and forty nights. They demand Aaron make them a god they can see and comprehend, and Aaron takes their gold and creates a golden calf. When Moses returns to the camp and sees the worship of the calf and the revelry, he smashes the Ten Commandments on the ground. Nevertheless, he intercedes on their behalf before God, so that they are not utterly destroyed. There is punishment, there is death, but Israel lives because God has mercy and forgives.

Restoration. The covenant between Yahweh and Israel is renewed, Moses goes back up the mountain for another forty days and nights, and returns with a new set of the Ten Commandments engraved on stone by his own hand—the first set had been engraved by God. Moses' face is shining because he has been with Yahweh. It is a fresh start, and this time Moses finds no golden calf. "I hereby make a covenant," Yahweh declares. "It is an awesome thing that I will do with you."

Preparation. The tabernacle is built according to the meticulous directions of God. It will be the place within which he will dwell among his people—a place of beauty and of holiness. Once it is erected and anointed, once everything is in its proper place, there is nothing more for Moses or Israel to do but wait.

Presence. At the conclusion of Exodus the glory of God fills the tabernacle; Yahweh is among his people. A story that began with God's absence ends with God's presence. Of course, it is not an end. He continues to lead them toward the land that will be their home. But now he is the God who is seen, the God who is present, the God who is there for Israel. God is with Israel and it is with God. It is a new world.

The Way of the Exodus

The Way of Leaving. The spirituality of Exodus is a spirituality of leaving. That is what "exodus" means. Moses leaves Egypt to find a new life in Midian, only to leave Midian and return to Egypt, and then leave Egypt once again. The children of the patriarch Jacob, or Israel, had left Canaan and made homes in Egypt a long time before, but now the children of Israel must leave Egypt and make new homes in Canaan.

God had made sure that the Israelites came safely to Egypt and left them there, only to reappear and command Moses to lead them out of Egypt and back to Canaan. To leave one place is also to head toward someplace else. So the Way of Leaving is just as much the Way of Arriving. The Israelites leave slavery and come into freedom. Yet at no time in Exodus does anyone find a permanent place to live. They are sojourners. The closest anyone comes to this is God himself, who settles into the tabernacle at the end of the book. But even he will dwell in the tabernacle only when Israel makes various encampments during its long journey to the Promised Land. And goat-hair walls cannot provide a final home for the Lord of heaven and earth. So in a way it is a spirituality of journeying. In another way it is an invitation to the children of Israel to put their roots not into land or houses, but into God himself. In all their wanderings they have the opportunity of finding their identity and their purpose in God alone. (Christian preaching and piety have often viewed the life, death, and resurrection of Jesus as a "second exodus.")

The Way of Freedom. One of the strongest reasons for God's people to abolish slavery wherever they find it, and in whatever form, is that at the very beginning of the Bible, in only its second book, we have one of the most astonishing stories of liberation ever written. God detests the bondage of his people and goes to great lengths to extricate them from its horrors. But the release from physical slavery is only the first chapter of a long story, for it will be years before the ex-slaves can throw the shackles off their minds and spirits. In the end, and not in the book of Exodus, it will be the children of the people God first set free who will have the deeper freedom necessary to enter the Promised Land. The Way of Freedom is the spirituality of setting those in bondage at liberty—whether in body or soul.

The Way of Moses. Moses is a leader who is as human as any of us. It is by means of his humanity that God works his wonders. Moses' compassion for the Hebrew slaves and his passion—his anger and zeal to defend them—cause him to kill and make it necessary for him to flee Egypt, leaving behind the life of a prince. His compassion and passion cause him to fight for the priest of Midian's daughters, and he marries one of them and remains in Midian. His compassion for the Hebrews and his passion for their defense, once he has reluctantly returned to Egypt, give him the strength not only to stand up to Pharaoh in the name of God, but also to stand up to God himself. Having liberated the Israelites, God is ready to destroy them after their worship of the golden calf, but Moses recklessly places himself between heaven and earth, between God and the people, and demands that God obliterate his soul if he is going to obliterate the people they both rescued from slavery. The same temperament is well suited to dealing with the stubbornness and rebelliousness of the people themselves. Yet this fiery temper will block Moses' own entry into Canaan. Nevertheless, one day God will glorify him despite his flawed humanity. The Way of Moses is an anticipation of the Way of Grace. It is a way that limps due to our weaknesses, but it is also a way that makes them our strengths. Whether we choose to acknowledge it or not, it is the way of Everyman, of Everywoman, of Everychild.

The Way of the Desert. The desert or wilderness has always held a prominent place in Christian spirituality, and much of it can be traced to the journey of Israel between Egypt and Canaan. Other desert experiences are recorded in Scripture, but all of them seem to echo the forty years of Israel's struggle—Elijah's journey through the wilderness to Mt. Sinai takes forty days and forty nights; Jesus' period of temptation in the wilderness occurs over a period of forty days (1 Kings 19:8; Luke 4:2).

It is clear enough that the Way of the Desert is a Way of Testing for the human spirit. But it is too narrow to conceive of this way simply as one of warfare and temptation and self-denial. (Jesus did not eat for forty days, but God sent angels to make a suicidal Elijah both eat and drink.) Much prayer occurs in the desert, whether that desert is physical or metaphorical. Moses prayed some of the most intense prayers the Bible records. The people of Israel prayed. Elijah prayed. David prayed while he played cat and mouse with Saul. Jesus prayed. Paul prayed in Arabia. John on Patmos. The desert fathers and mothers in the land of Egypt. It is a place that makes prayer easy in the sense that there are precious few other resources to call upon. Yet the prayers cannot be shallow; they must go deep, as deep as a well for sweet water, for the presence of God is absolutely critical in the wilderness. We cannot take God for granted. Our spirituality must be single-minded and fierce.

The desert causes us to see more clearly our need for God. There are few distractions in the desert, little of human manufacture to blot God out, take his place, or hide our nakedness. The desert is a place where much spiritual work needs to be done, because the inadequacies of our faith in God and our commitment to God's love are all too obvious. The desert is blunt about who we are, as it was blunt to Moses and Aaron and Miriam and Israel.

Yet all who emerge from the Way of the Desert, all who have stubbornly clung to God and his goodness, emerge in great strength. Moses will die, but he will see the glory of Yahweh and be himself caught up and glorified in it. The Israelite parents at least know their children will inherit what they could not believe in. Joshua and Caleb will see the Promised Land, for they did not lose faith in the desert, but found more of it. Elijah will emerge with the strength to complete his vocation, pass the mantle to Elisha, and rise in a whirlwind to heaven. Jesus will burst out, filled with the power of the Holy Spirit, and begin his beginning in Galilee. John will see a Jesus unlike the one he knew, a Celestial Christ, one whose face is "like the sun shining with full force" (Rev 1:16). So the Way of the Desert is ultimately a way of empowerment, a way that makes the weak strong, that diminishes the pervasiveness of sin and unleashes vitality. The Way of the Desert is finally the Way of Truth.

But it takes time. The desert does not work on us quickly. There are days and nights, heat and cold, wind and sun and distance. There is much wondering. And much wandering. Yet, as J. R. R. Tolkien put it, "Not all who wander are lost."

—*Murray Andrew Pura*

1 These are the names of the sons of Israel who came to Egypt with Jacob, each with his household: [2]Reuben, Simeon, Levi, and Judah, [3]Issachar, Zebulun, and Benjamin, [4]Dan and Naphtali, Gad and Asher. [5]The total number of people born to Jacob was seventy. Joseph was already in Egypt. [6]Then Joseph died, and all his brothers, and that whole generation. [7]But the Israelites were fruitful and prolific; they multiplied and grew exceedingly strong, so that the land was filled with them.

The Israelites Are Oppressed

[8] Now a new king arose over Egypt, who did not know Joseph. [9]He said to his people, "Look, the Israelite people are more numerous and more powerful than we. [10]Come, let us deal shrewdly with them, or they will increase and, in the event of war, join our enemies and fight against us and escape from the land." [11]Therefore they set taskmasters over them to oppress them with forced labor. They built supply cities, Pithom and Rameses, for Pharaoh. [12]But the more they were oppressed, the more they multiplied and spread, so that the Egyptians came to dread the Israelites. [13]The Egyptians became ruthless in imposing tasks on the Israelites,

[14]and made their lives bitter with hard service in mortar and brick and in every kind of field labor. They were ruthless in all the tasks that they imposed on them.

[15] The king of Egypt said to the Hebrew midwives, one of whom was named Shiphrah and the other Puah, [16]"When you act as midwives to the Hebrew women, and see them on the birthstool, if it is a boy, kill him; but if it is a girl, she shall live." [17]But the midwives feared God; they did not do as the king of Egypt commanded them, but they let the boys live. [18]So the king of Egypt summoned the midwives and said to them, "Why have you done this, and allowed the boys to live?" [19]The midwives said to Pharaoh, "Because the Hebrew women are not like the Egyptian women; for they are vigorous and give birth before the midwife comes to them." [20]So God dealt well with the midwives; and the people multiplied and became very strong. [21]And because the midwives feared God, he gave them families. [22]Then Pharaoh commanded all his people, "Every boy that is born to the Hebrews [a] you shall throw into the Nile, but you shall let every girl live."

a Sam Gk Tg: Heb lacks *to the Hebrews*

1:11 *Therefore they set taskmasters over them to oppress them.* "Even though you intended to do harm to me," Joseph told his brothers who sold him into slavery, "God intended it for good" (Gen 50:20). When others do harm to us they unknowingly release God into our lives in ways we have never seen before. When life is life as usual God is at work, but slowly and quietly. When there is a crisis, a great deal happens all at once. If we are overwhelmed, if we are desperate and helpless, if our tormentors are crushing the life out of us, it is necessary for God to respond to our situation on a grand scale. This may not mean plagues or the parting of the Red Sea, but it always means liberation. What will stun us is that we go beyond what we ever were, because it is crucial for God to intervene in a way we never knew. The oppression of the slaves in Egypt will cause such movement on the part of God that it will change not only the history of the Hebrews, but the history of the earth.

1:15 *The king of Egypt said to the Hebrew midwives.* The story of Moses' birth (2:1–10) is a story that would be impossible without the strength and courage of women. There is the bravery of his own mother, who defies the law of the state to keep her son alive; Pharaoh's daughter, who takes the baby she knows is a Hebrew boy and, also in defiance of the state and her father, raises him as her own; his sister, Miriam, who guards Moses from a distance as he floats in his basket and eventually brings his own mother to Pharaoh's daughter to be his wet nurse. Yet the procession of heroines begins with the midwives Shiphrah and Puah. It is they who defy Pharaoh's edict and refuse to kill the Hebrew boys. This sets in motion a string of events that includes Pharaoh's command for ethnic cleansing—"Every boy that is born to the Hebrews you shall throw into the Nile" (1:22)—which is again countered by two other women, Moses' mother and his sister Miriam.

Birth and Youth of Moses

2 Now a man from the house of Levi went and married a Levite woman. ²The woman conceived and bore a son; and when she saw that he was a fine baby, she hid him three months. ³When she could hide him no longer she got a papyrus basket for him, and plastered it with bitumen and pitch; she put the child in it and placed it among the reeds on the bank of the river. ⁴His sister stood at a distance, to see what would happen to him.

5 The daughter of Pharaoh came down to bathe at the river, while her attendants walked beside the river. She saw the basket among the reeds and sent her maid to bring it. ⁶When she opened it, she saw the child. He was crying, and she took pity on him. "This must be one of the Hebrews' children," she said. ⁷Then his sister said to Pharaoh's daughter, "Shall I go and get you a nurse from the Hebrew women to nurse the child for you?" ⁸Pharaoh's daughter said to her, "Yes." So the girl went and called the child's mother. ⁹Pharaoh's daughter said to her, "Take this child and nurse it for me, and I will give you your wages." So the woman took the child and nursed it. ¹⁰When the child grew up, she brought him to Pharaoh's daughter, and she took him as her son. She named him Moses,ᵃ "because," she said, "I drew him outᵇ of the water."

Moses Flees to Midian

11 One day, after Moses had grown up, he went out to his people and saw their forced labor. He saw an Egyptian beating a Hebrew, one of his kinsfolk. ¹²He looked this way and that, and seeing no one he killed the Egyptian and hid him in the sand. ¹³When he went out the next day, he saw two Hebrews fighting; and he said to the one who was in the wrong, "Why do you strike your fellow Hebrew?" ¹⁴He answered, "Who made you a ruler and judge over us? Do you mean to kill me as you killed the Egyptian?" Then Moses was afraid and thought, "Surely the thing is known." ¹⁵When Pharaoh heard of it, he sought to kill Moses.

But Moses fled from Pharaoh. He settled in the land of Midian, and sat down by a well. ¹⁶The priest of Midian had seven daughters. They came to draw water, and filled the troughs to water their father's flock. ¹⁷But some shepherds came and drove them away. Moses got up and came to their defense and watered their flock. ¹⁸When they returned to their father Reuel, he said, "How is it that you have come back so soon today?" ¹⁹They said, "An Egyptian helped us against the shepherds; he even drew water for us and watered the flock." ²⁰He said to his daughters, "Where is he? Why did you leave the man? Invite him to break bread." ²¹Moses agreed to stay with the man, and he gave Moses his daughter Zipporah in marriage. ²²She bore a son, and he named him Gershom; for he said, "I have been an alienᶜ residing in a foreign land."

23 After a long time the king of Egypt died. The Israelites groaned under their slavery, and cried out. Out of the slavery their

a Heb Mosheh   b Heb mashah   c Heb ger

2:22 *I have been an alien residing in a foreign land.* God takes a convoluted path in raising up a leader to help save his people. Why did God not have Moses remain in Egypt and liberate the Hebrews directly from there? Why did he spirit him away for, as the Scriptures say, "a long time" (2:23)? Innocent people, then as today, were dying brutally while God seemed to be unconcerned. We may talk of God's timing, of how he sees the big picture that we do not, of how there is a season to everything, and we would be right to say all these things. Nevertheless, part of our humanness is to wonder and query and challenge, sometimes with the ferocity of Job or Jonah or the writers of the Psalms, even if we receive no answer that makes sense to us. Moses, the prince of a great kingdom, winds up in exile, walking through stones and brush of the wilderness, taking care of his father-in-law's livestock (vv 15–22), for decades before God acts to end the suffering of the Hebrew people. God chooses this convoluted path to shape the soul and destiny of Moses. We must not be surprised, then, if God chooses this indirect or convoluted path to shape our own souls and destinies as well.

cry for help rose up to God. 24God heard their groaning, and God remembered his covenant with Abraham, Isaac, and Jacob. 25God looked upon the Israelites, and God took notice of them.

Moses at the Burning Bush

3 Moses was keeping the flock of his father-in-law Jethro, the priest of Midian; he led his flock beyond the wilderness, and came to Horeb, the mountain of God. 2There the angel of the LORD appeared to him in a flame of fire out of a bush; he looked, and the bush was blazing, yet it was not consumed. 3Then Moses said, "I must turn aside and look at this great sight, and see why the bush is not burned up." 4When the LORD saw that he had turned aside to see, God called to him out of the bush, "Moses, Moses!" And he said, "Here I am." 5Then he said, "Come no closer! Remove the sandals from your feet, for the place on which you are standing is holy ground." 6He said further, "I am the God of your father, the God of Abraham, the God of Isaac, and the God of Jacob." And

Moses hid his face, for he was afraid to look at God.

7 Then the LORD said, "I have observed the misery of my people who are in Egypt; I have heard their cry on account of their taskmasters. Indeed, I know their sufferings, 8and I have come down to deliver them from the Egyptians, and to bring them up out of that land to a good and broad land, a land flowing with milk and honey, to the country of the Canaanites, the Hittites, the Amorites, the Perizzites, the Hivites, and the Jebusites. 9The cry of the Israelites has now come to me; I have also seen how the Egyptians oppress them. 10So come, I will send you to Pharaoh to bring my people, the Israelites, out of Egypt." 11But Moses said to God, "Who am I that I should go to Pharaoh, and bring the Israelites out of Egypt?" 12He said, "I will be with you; and this shall be the sign for you that it is I who sent you: when you have brought the people out of Egypt, you shall worship God on this mountain."

The Divine Name Revealed

13 But Moses said to God, "If I come to

2:24 *God heard their groaning, and God remembered.* This expression renders an image of a doddering old gentleman who means well, but is too busy being God of the universe to be expected to remember everything—unless somebody on earth does something to jar his memory. We need to keep in mind that a great deal of Scripture is written from a human point of view. Truths about God are often expressed in our own words exactly as it looks to us. There is nothing wrong with this. It happens from Genesis to Revelation. We lisp divinity by means of our humanity. So even though we read that God remembered as if he had forgotten, we need to remind ourselves this is not God's way of putting it, but ours; at the same time, we need to keep in mind that human vocabulary is a God-made instrument for telling us what is true. Our words are pottery that holds the substance of eternity. Our imperfections and disabilities and flaws, and sometimes our sublimities, were always meant to express the mysteries of holiness and always have done so.

3:1 *Moses was keeping the flock of his father-in-law Jethro.* More often than we know, God works in the uneventful routines of our lives. For decades Moses took care of his father-in-law's livestock. Day after day it was business as usual. An extreme challenge would one day occur at a burning bush, at an Egyptian throne, on a night of blood and death, on a mountain that thundered with God. Moses did not see these challenges coming. There was no time to prepare. There was only the cold sunrise, greeting his wife and children, doing his work, washing his face, eating his meals, saying his prayers, sleeping like a stone. Yet when the challenge came, as it came to the midwives Shiphrah and Puah in the middle of their careers, something had formed in Moses in the long years that enabled him, despite an initial reluctance, to stand before Pharaoh's throne and declare, "Thus says the LORD: 'Let my people go!'" (5:1; 8:1). God had been working in secret and in silence. The soul of Moses was being shaped by the Spirit of God long before Mt. Horeb and the burning bush. It is no different for us.

the Israelites and say to them, 'The God of your ancestors has sent me to you,' and they ask me, 'What is his name?' what shall I say to them?" [14]God said to Moses, "I AM WHO I AM." [a] He said further, "Thus you shall say to the Israelites, 'I AM has sent me to you.' " [15]God also said to Moses, "Thus you shall say to the Israelites, 'The LORD, [b] the God of your ancestors, the God of Abraham, the God of Isaac, and the God of Jacob, has sent me to you':

This is my name forever,
and this my title for all generations.

[16]Go and assemble the elders of Israel, and say to them, 'The LORD, the God of your ancestors, the God of Abraham, of Isaac, and of Jacob, has appeared to me, saying: I have given heed to you and to what has been done to you in Egypt. [17]I declare that I will bring you up out of the misery of Egypt, to the land of the Canaanites, the Hittites, the Amorites, the Perizzites, the Hivites, and the Jebusites, a land flowing with milk and honey.' [18]They will listen to your voice; and you and the elders of Israel shall go to the king of Egypt and say to him, 'The LORD, the God of the Hebrews, has met with us; let us now go a three days' journey into the wilderness, so that we may sacrifice to the LORD our God.' [19]I know, however, that the king of Egypt will not let you go unless compelled by a mighty hand. [c] [20]So I will stretch out my hand and strike Egypt with all my wonders that I will perform in it; after that he will let you go. [21]I will bring this people into such favor with the Egyptians that, when you go, you will not go empty-handed; [22]each woman shall ask her neighbor and any woman living in the neighbor's house for jewelry of silver and of gold, and clothing, and you shall put them on your sons and on your daughters; and so you shall plunder the Egyptians."

Moses' Miraculous Power

4 Then Moses answered, "But suppose they do not believe me or listen to me, but say, 'The LORD did not appear to you.' " [2]The LORD said to him, "What is that in your hand?" He said, "A staff." [3]And he said, "Throw it on the ground." So he threw the staff on the ground, and it became a snake;

a Or I AM WHAT I AM or I WILL BE WHAT I WILL BE
b The word "LORD" when spelled with capital letters stands for the divine name, YHWH, which is here connected with the verb hayah, "to be"
c Gk Vg: Heb no, not by a mighty hand

3:13–15 *God said to Moses, "I AM WHO I AM."* Part of the richness of the Bible is the variety of names it uses to address and speak of God. This story describes how Israel came to know the unique and most cherished name it had for God—Yahweh, Jehovah (traditional translation), or the LORD (NRSV, NIV, and others). Though the name occurs earlier in the biblical text, here it is both given to Moses and Israel for the first time and connected to the "God of your ancestors," whose presence and faithfulness Israel already knew. What kind of a name is this? "I AM WHO I AM" (*'ehyeh 'asher 'ehyeh*) and its related form Yahweh (v 15) both derive from the Hebrew verb "to be." Interpreters have suggested several meanings. Some treat "I AM" as meaning "I exist," but that seems to speak more to philosophers in Athens than Hebrews at Sinai. Another idea is that "I AM" tries to obscure meaning and to preserve mystery, so that people won't think they can use the name to manipulate God. A third option is that "I AM" points to God's presence, as in "I am with you," no doubt a welcome assurance. Yet another possibility builds on the connection between the names 'Ehyeh and Yahweh and interprets Yahweh as a causative verb, "He causes to be." This points to God as the One who creates and sustains the world and who acts powerfully in it with loving purpose, two powerful themes throughout the Old Testament. This is the God who is mover and shaker, the One who makes things happen. This suggestion works well in this context partly because the exodus pits Yahweh against Pharaoh, whom the Egyptians regard as a god. It also gives a stirring sense to the theme common in Exodus (and beyond) that God will act "so that you will know that I am Yahweh" (e.g., 7:5, 17; 10:2; 14:4, 18; 16:12; 29:46). The God who sends Moses is the God who acts. What better God to announce to Hebrew slaves who long for deliverance? What better God to rely on in our own longings?

and Moses drew back from it. ⁴Then the LORD said to Moses, "Reach out your hand, and seize it by the tail"—so he reached out his hand and grasped it, and it became a staff in his hand— ⁵"so that they may believe that the LORD, the God of their ancestors, the God of Abraham, the God of Isaac, and the God of Jacob, has appeared to you."

6 Again, the LORD said to him, "Put your hand inside your cloak." He put his hand into his cloak; and when he took it out, his hand was leprous,ᵃ as white as snow. ⁷Then God said, "Put your hand back into your cloak"—so he put his hand back into his cloak, and when he took it out, it was restored like the rest of his body— ⁸"If they will not believe you or heed the first sign, they may believe the second sign. ⁹If they will not believe even these two signs or heed you, you shall take some water from the Nile and pour it on the dry ground; and the water that you shall take from the Nile will become blood on the dry ground."

10 But Moses said to the LORD, "O my Lord, I have never been eloquent, neither in the past nor even now that you have spoken to your servant; but I am slow of speech and slow of tongue." ¹¹Then the LORD said to him, "Who gives speech to mortals? Who makes them mute or deaf, seeing or blind? Is it not I, the LORD? ¹²Now go, and I will be with your mouth and teach you what you are to speak." ¹³But he said, "O my Lord, please send someone else." ¹⁴Then the anger of the LORD was kindled against Moses and he said, "What of your brother Aaron the Levite? I know that he can speak fluently; even now he is coming out to meet you, and when he sees you his heart will be glad. ¹⁵You shall speak to him and put the words in his mouth; and I will be with your mouth and with his mouth, and

will teach you what you shall do. ¹⁶He indeed shall speak for you to the people; he shall serve as a mouth for you, and you shall serve as God for him. ¹⁷Take in your hand this staff, with which you shall perform the signs."

Moses Returns to Egypt

18 Moses went back to his father-in-law Jethro and said to him, "Please let me go back to my kindred in Egypt and see whether they are still living." And Jethro said to Moses, "Go in peace." ¹⁹The LORD said to Moses in Midian, "Go back to Egypt; for all those who were seeking your life are dead." ²⁰So Moses took his wife and his sons, put them on a donkey, and went back to the land of Egypt; and Moses carried the staff of God in his hand.

21 And the LORD said to Moses, "When you go back to Egypt, see that you perform before Pharaoh all the wonders that I have put in your power; but I will harden his heart, so that he will not let the people go. ²²Then you shall say to Pharaoh, 'Thus says the LORD: Israel is my firstborn son. ²³I said to you, "Let my son go that he may worship me." But you refused to let him go; now I will kill your firstborn son.' "

24 On the way, at a place where they spent the night, the LORD met him and tried to kill him. ²⁵But Zipporah took a flint and cut off her son's foreskin, and touched Moses'ᵇ feet with it, and said, "Truly you are a bridegroom of blood to me!" ²⁶So he let him alone. It was then she said, "A bridegroom of blood by circumcision."

27 The LORD said to Aaron, "Go into the

---

a A term for several skin diseases; precise meaning uncertain   *b* Heb *his*

4:12–16 THE WITH-GOD LIFE—*See* Spiritual Disciplines Index.

4:13 *O my Lord, please send someone else.* Moses' fivefold bid to wriggle out of God's will has its touch of humor, especially here when, all his excuses having been ably countered by God, Moses decides to just tell the truth—he simply doesn't want to do it. This is something we can understand. That's why this aspect of Moses'

character is so helpful to us. This is no "Man of Steel" that God has chosen. He has his weak spots just as we do. In fact, though Moses is indeed the one selected by God to lead the exodus of Israel out of Egypt, his human flaws can be only too glaring, and his flaming temper will eventually prevent his entry into the Promised Land (Deut 32:51).

wilderness to meet Moses." So he went; and he met him at the mountain of God and kissed him. 28Moses told Aaron all the words of the LORD with which he had sent him, and all the signs with which he had charged him. 29Then Moses and Aaron went and assembled all the elders of the Israelites. 30Aaron spoke all the words that the LORD had spoken to Moses, and performed the signs in the sight of the people. 31The people believed; and when they heard that the LORD had given heed to the Israelites and that he had seen their misery, they bowed down and worshiped.

Bricks without Straw

5 Afterward Moses and Aaron went to Pharaoh and said, "Thus says the LORD, the God of Israel, 'Let my people go, so that they may celebrate a festival to me in the wilderness.' " 2But Pharaoh said, "Who is the LORD, that I should heed him and let Israel go? I do not know the LORD, and I will not let Israel go." 3Then they said, "The God of the Hebrews has revealed himself to us; let us go a three days' journey into the wilderness to sacrifice to the LORD our God, or he will fall upon us with pestilence or sword." 4But the king of Egypt said to them, "Moses and Aaron, why are you taking the people away from their work? Get to your labors!" 5Pharaoh continued, "Now they are more numerous than the people of the land a and yet you want them to stop working!" 6That same day Pharaoh commanded the taskmasters of the people, as well as their supervisors, 7"You shall no longer give the people straw to

a Sam: Heb The people of the land are now many

4:31 *they bowed down and worshiped.* When Moses and Aaron first come to the Hebrews, the people believe and worship God. But it does not last. "They would not listen to Moses, because of their broken spirit and their cruel slavery" (6:9). Again and again, when they are still in Egypt, when they are in the desert, when they are at the foot of Mt. Sinai, they complain and rebel and refuse to trust God. We are no different. One month our faith is strong, another it is weak. One day we bask in spiritual peace and are a friend to all the earth, the next we are in turmoil and every man and woman is an enemy, including God. We have had a golden calf or two, often right after a period of profound spiritual blessing. Grace is essential for the follower of God. We can never make it on our best intentions. Yet even in our frailty, it is better if we seek worship that will last—worship that is wholly dependent on God himself and absolutely nothing else.

5:1 *Thus says the LORD, the God of Israel, "Let my people go."* Moses stands before the power of the earth despite all his personal weaknesses and flaws and speaks the words of God. It may be that God could do this without him, but if so, he does not do it. Moses, who seems so much less than galaxies and comets and the moons of Jupiter, is like God to Pharaoh (7:1). The God whose face cannot be seen is heard through the voice of a human. This dynamic did not end with the age of the Bible. It is the same today. The puny stand before the rulers of earth and cry, "Thus says the LORD, Let my people go!" They seem like nothing compared to towering buildings and massive armies and brutal war machines. But their spirit can never be extinguished in any generation, because their spirit is the Spirit of God. God will always press for an end to all forms of enslavement for the chaining of earth and its creatures. The earth is his and all that are within it. God will not be bound, and he will not permit the binding of what is part of him. We who live and stand now are not spectators of this phenomenon. Fragile as we may be, God continues to speak his word through our throats and tongues. As with Moses, God calls us to speak his words.

Responding
5:1 CELEBRATION. Worship precedes the first confrontation of Moses and Aaron with Pharaoh in which he is commanded by the Lord: "Let my people go, so that they may celebrate a festival to me in the wilderness." Recall a service you attended where celebration was intimately connected with worship. What did the leaders do to encourage the festive atmosphere? This Sunday note the elements of celebration in the worship service you attend and thank God for the joy they bring into your life. *See also* Spiritual Disciplines Index.

MOSES

Grounded in God

Selected Scriptures: *Exodus 1–19, 32; Numbers 9, 11–14, 20–21, 27;
Deuteronomy 8, 11, 31–34*

Moses didn't possess the strengths our world requires of a leader. He lacked charisma and confidence. He didn't covet leadership or aspire to greatness. Yet no prophet in the Bible received such commendation. "Never since has there arisen a prophet in Israel like Moses, whom the LORD knew face to face" (Deut 34:10). Moses was "very humble, more so than anyone else on the face of the earth" (Num 12:3) and proved "faithful in all [God's] house" (Num 12:7, NIV). Intimacy with God, humility, faithfulness—these traits exalted Moses in God's eyes and became his hallmark.

Moses' people, the Israelites, had been living in Egypt since the time of Joseph. But a new king grew bewildered by the many Hebrews living in his land and forced them into slavery. He vowed to have all male Hebrew infants killed. Moses should have died, but his mother placed him in a basket in the river. Pharoah's daughter was bathing and, discovering the basket, she had pity on the baby and took Moses as her own son. Moses went on to spend his first forty years as a member of the Egyptian royal family, receiving the elite training and education that accompanied his status. Still, he identified with his own people, the enslaved Israelites. One day Moses saw a Hebrew being beaten by an Egyptian. His anger flared, and he killed the Egyptian. When word got out, Moses was forced to flee (Exod 2:15).

Moses settled in Midian and spent the next forty years of his life as a shepherd. He married a Midianite woman and gained knowledge about the land and nomadic life that would prove invaluable in his final years as leader of the Israelite people.

Finally, God spoke to Moses (Exod 3:4). Through the fire of a burning bush, God announced he had heard the cry of the Israelites (3:7). Moses would lead them out of slavery to the Promised Land of Canaan (3:10). Humbled by this request from God, Moses asked: "Who am I that I should go?" (3:11). Answering each of his fears, God assured Moses he would go with him and give the miraculous signs necessary for belief. It was time for Moses to begin his mission.

Moses asked for the Israelites' release, but Pharoah refused (Exod 5:2). Finally, after ten oppressive plagues on the land and people, Pharoah begged the Israelites to leave (12:31). With Moses in the lead, the journey to the Promised Land began.

But the journey was far from easy. Forty years of wandering in the desert with a thankless and unfaithful multitude offered countless trials to test Moses' humility, faithfulness, and depth of intimacy with God. Yet Moses remained faithful and humble, meeting with God for the guidance he needed to lead the people. When they reached Mt. Sinai, amid thunder, lightening, cloud, and fire Moses received from God the Ten Commandments, which would form the foundation for life in Israel (Exod

20:1–17). He became an advocate for the Israelites before God. When they tired of manna, Moses asked for meat. When the people were unfaithful, crafting a golden calf to worship in Moses' absence, he grew enraged but later pled with God to forgive the people. Each time they complained, Moses turned to God for help.

However, late in their journey Moses let his frustration with the people erupt in disrespect toward God. Instead of speaking to a rock as God commanded, Moses struck it to bring forth water (Num 20:8–11). His disobedience, although seemingly minor in our eyes, demanded justice. Moses was excluded from at last entering Canaan (Deut 32:51). Not until Christ would one man be righteous enough to take God's people all the way from bondage to God's promise.

Yet even as he prepared to die on the threshold of the Promised Land, Moses expressed no anger, no sense of letdown at being unable to finish his long journey. Rather, he gave the people final words from God on establishing life as a nation. He taught them a song to comfort future generations prone to unfaithfulness (Deut 32). And he appointed Joshua to carry on the leadership of Israel. It is here that we see how much Moses' intimacy with God had meant. Rather than feeling entitled to enter the land, Moses knew he had been given something far better. He had known God. Daily he had experienced God's love. He had walked in friendship with God, and no reward could compare.

This ever-growing intimacy with God inspired a fourth-century bishop to write an entire work about Moses. In *The Life of Moses,* Gregory of Nyssa explains how we can see Moses' life as a model for our own soul's spiritual journey toward God:

"This is true perfection: not to avoid a wicked life because like slaves we servilely fear punishment, nor to do good because we hope for rewards, as if cashing in on the virtuous life by some business-like arrangement. On the contrary, disregarding all those things for which we hope and which have been reserved by promise, we regard falling from God's friendship as the only thing dreadful and we consider becoming God's friend the only thing worthy of honor and desire. This, as I have said, is the perfection of life."

Personal Reflection

- After Moses spent forty years living as royalty, his life changed. He went from palace to pasture, from high society to sheep. How might Moses have felt at such a change? When has God asked you to accept a great change in your life situation or status for reasons beyond your understanding?
- God called Moses to an enormous leadership role. Jesus said, "From everyone to whom much has been given, much will be required" (Luke 12:48). When we look at Moses' life, it seems clear that the opposite is also true—to those of whom much is required, much will be given. Moses' friendship with God sustained and empowered him for the work he was to do. Where is God calling you to lead? What kind of a difference will friendship with God make in your role as leader?

make bricks, as before; let them go and gather straw for themselves. [8]But you shall require of them the same quantity of bricks as they have made previously; do not diminish it, for they are lazy; that is why they cry, 'Let us go and offer sacrifice to our God.' [9]Let heavier work be laid on them; then they will labor at it and pay no attention to deceptive words."

10 So the taskmasters and the supervisors of the people went out and said to the people, "Thus says Pharaoh, 'I will not give you straw. [11]Go and get straw yourselves, wherever you can find it; but your work will not be lessened in the least.' " [12]So the people scattered throughout the land of Egypt, to gather stubble for straw. [13]The taskmasters were urgent, saying, "Complete your work, the same daily assignment as when you were given straw." [14]And the supervisors of the Israelites, whom Pharaoh's taskmasters had set over them, were beaten, and were asked, "Why did you not finish the required quantity of bricks yesterday and today, as you did before?"

15 Then the Israelite supervisors came to Pharaoh and cried, "Why do you treat your servants like this? [16]No straw is given to your servants, yet they say to us, 'Make bricks!' Look how your servants are beaten! You are unjust to your own people." [a] [17]He said, "You are lazy, lazy; that is why you say, 'Let us go and sacrifice to the LORD.' [18]Go now, and work; for no straw shall be given you, but you shall still deliver the same number of bricks." [19]The Israelite supervisors saw that they were in trouble when they were told, "You shall not lessen your daily number of bricks." [20]As they left Pharaoh, they came upon Moses and Aaron who were waiting to meet them. [21]They said to them, "The LORD look upon you and judge! You have brought us into bad odor with Pharaoh and his officials, and have put a sword in their hand to kill us."

22 Then Moses turned again to the LORD and said, "O LORD, why have you mistreated this people? Why did you ever send me? [23]Since I first came to Pharaoh to speak in your name, he has mistreated this people, and you have done nothing at all to deliver your people."

Israel's Deliverance Assured

6 Then the LORD said to Moses, "Now you shall see what I will do to Pharaoh: Indeed, by a mighty hand he will let them go; by a mighty hand he will drive them out of his land."

2 God also spoke to Moses and said to him: "I am the LORD. [3]I appeared to Abraham, Isaac, and Jacob as God Almighty, [b] but by my name 'The LORD' [c] I did not make myself known to them. [4]I also established my covenant with them, to give them the land of Canaan, the land in which they resided as aliens. [5]I have also heard the groaning of the Israelites whom the Egyptians are holding as slaves, and I have remembered my covenant. [6]Say therefore to the Israelites, 'I am the LORD, and I will free you from the burdens of the Egyptians and deliver you from slavery to them. I will redeem you with an outstretched arm and with mighty acts of judgment. [7]I will take you as my people, and I will be your God. You shall know that I am the LORD your God, who has freed you from the burdens of the Egyptians. [8]I will bring you into the land that I swore to give to Abraham, Isaac, and Jacob; I will give it to you for a possession. I am the LORD.' " [9]Moses told this to the Israelites; but they

a Gk Compare Syr Vg: Heb *beaten, and the sin of your people*   b Traditional rendering of Heb *El Shaddai*   c Heb *YHWH*; see note at 3.15

5:21 *You have brought us into bad odor with Pharaoh.* Following God does not guarantee a warm reception from those we try to help. Often enough God's mission and message rock too many boats and make things worse before they get better.

6:9 *they would not listen to Moses, because of their broken spirit.* An exhaustion comes upon people when they have had all they can take. For weeks or months or years they may have endured and hung on to every promise that came their way. But nothing changed, and finally they reached a point where they could no longer hope. It is at such junctures, when people can absolutely do no more, that a divine breakthrough often occurs. When we are most helpless, we are in a position to receive the most help. God does not chastise us when we become heartsick. He acts in ways we were too strong and self-reliant to experience before.

would not listen to Moses, because of their broken spirit and their cruel slavery.

10 Then the LORD spoke to Moses, 11 "Go and tell Pharaoh king of Egypt to let the Israelites go out of his land." 12But Moses spoke to the LORD, "The Israelites have not listened to me; how then shall Pharaoh listen to me, poor speaker that I am?"*a* 13Thus the LORD spoke to Moses and Aaron, and gave them orders regarding the Israelites and Pharaoh king of Egypt, charging them to free the Israelites from the land of Egypt.

The Genealogy of Moses and Aaron

14 The following are the heads of their ancestral houses: the sons of Reuben, the firstborn of Israel: Hanoch, Pallu, Hezron, and Carmi; these are the families of Reuben. 15The sons of Simeon: Jemuel, Jamin, Ohad, Jachin, Zohar, and Shaul,*b* the son of a Canaanite woman; these are the families of Simeon. 16The following are the names of the sons of Levi according to their genealogies: Gershon,*c* Kohath, and Merari, and the length of Levi's life was one hundred thirty-seven years. 17The sons of Gershon:*c* Libni and Shimei, by their families. 18The sons of Kohath: Amram, Izhar, Hebron, and Uzziel, and the length of Kohath's life was one hundred thirty-three years. 19The sons of Merari: Mahli and Mushi. These are the families of the Levites according to their genealogies. 20Amram married Jochebed his father's sister and she bore him Aaron and Moses, and the length of Amram's life was one hundred thirty-seven years. 21The sons of Izhar: Korah, Nepheg, and Zichri. 22The sons of Uzziel: Mishael, Elzaphan, and Sithri. 23Aaron married Elisheba, daughter of Amminadab and sister of Nahshon, and she bore him Nadab, Abihu, Eleazar, and Ithamar. 24The sons of Korah: Assir, Elkanah, and Abiasaph; these are the families of the Korahites. 25Aaron's son Eleazar married one of the daughters of Putiel, and she bore him Phinehas. These are the heads of the ancestral houses of the Levites by their families.

26 It was this same Aaron and Moses to whom the LORD said, "Bring the Israelites out of the land of Egypt, company by company." 27It was they who spoke to Pharaoh king of Egypt to bring the Israelites out of Egypt, the same Moses and Aaron.

Moses and Aaron Obey God's Commands

28 On the day when the LORD spoke to Moses in the land of Egypt, 29he said to him, "I am the LORD; tell Pharaoh king of Egypt all that I am speaking to you." 30But Moses said in the LORD's presence, "Since I am a poor speaker,*d* why would Pharaoh listen to me?"

7 The LORD said to Moses, "See, I have made you like God to Pharaoh, and your brother Aaron shall be your prophet. 2You shall speak all that I command you, and your brother Aaron shall tell Pharaoh to let the Israelites go out of his land. 3But I will harden Pharaoh's heart, and I will multiply my signs and wonders in the land of Egypt. 4When Pharaoh does not listen to you, I will lay my hand upon Egypt and bring my people the Israelites, company by company, out of the land of Egypt by great acts of judgment. 5The Egyptians shall know that I am the LORD, when I stretch out my hand against Egypt and bring the Israelites out from among them." 6Moses and Aaron did so; they did just as the LORD commanded them. 7Moses was eighty years old and Aaron eightythree when they spoke to Pharaoh.

Aaron's Miraculous Rod

8 The LORD said to Moses and Aaron,

a Heb *me? I am uncircumcised of lips*   b Or *Saul*
c Also spelled *Gershom*; see 2.22   d Heb *am uncircumcised of lips*; see 6.12

7:1 *I have made you like God to Pharaoh.* As weak as Moses feels he is, especially in leadership and eloquent speech, his obedience to God has put him in the position of deity. He has a strength and a substance and an authority he never possessed before, even if he doesn't see it. When we stumble after God in our humility and ignorance, we often have words and thoughts that were not available to us before. If we hang back, nothing changes. When we act upon the impossible obedience, we enter another world and become another person. That person may be known to others, but unknown to us.

9"When Pharaoh says to you, 'Perform a wonder,' then you shall say to Aaron, 'Take your staff and throw it down before Pharaoh, and it will become a snake.' " 10So Moses and Aaron went to Pharaoh and did as the LORD had commanded; Aaron threw down his staff before Pharaoh and his officials, and it became a snake. 11Then Pharaoh summoned the wise men and the sorcerers; and they also, the magicians of Egypt, did the same by their secret arts. 12Each one threw down his staff, and they became snakes; but Aaron's staff swallowed up theirs. 13Still Pharaoh's heart was hardened, and he would not listen to them, as the LORD had said.

The First Plague: Water Turned to Blood

14 Then the LORD said to Moses, "Pharaoh's heart is hardened; he refuses to let the people go. 15Go to Pharaoh in the morning, as he is going out to the water; stand by at the river bank to meet him, and take in your hand the staff that was turned into a snake. 16Say to him, 'The LORD, the God of the Hebrews, sent me to you to say, "Let my people go, so that they may worship me in the wilderness." But until now you have not listened. 17Thus says the LORD, "By this you shall know that I am the LORD." See, with the staff that is in my hand I will strike the water that is in the Nile, and it shall be turned to blood. 18The fish in the river shall die, the river itself shall stink, and the Egyptians shall be unable to drink water from the Nile.' " 19The LORD said to Moses, "Say to Aaron, 'Take your staff and stretch out your hand over the waters of Egypt—over its rivers, its canals, and its ponds, and all its pools of water—so that they may become blood; and there shall be blood throughout the whole land of Egypt, even in vessels of wood and in vessels of stone.' "

20 Moses and Aaron did just as the LORD commanded. In the sight of Pharaoh and of his officials he lifted up the staff and struck the water in the river, and all the water in the river was turned into blood, 21and the fish in the river died. The river stank so that the Egyptians could not drink its water, and there was blood throughout the whole land of Egypt. 22But the magicians of Egypt did the same by their secret arts; so Pharaoh's heart remained hardened, and he would not listen to them, as the LORD had said. 23Pharaoh turned and went into his house, and he did not take even this to heart. 24And all the Egyptians had to dig along the Nile for water to drink, for they could not drink the water of the river.

25 Seven days passed after the LORD had struck the Nile.

The Second Plague: Frogs

8ᵃ Then the LORD said to Moses, "Go to Pharaoh and say to him, 'Thus says the LORD: Let my people go, so that they may worship me. 2If you refuse to let them go, I will plague your whole country with frogs. 3The river shall swarm with frogs; they shall come up into your palace, into your bed-

a Ch 7.26 in Heb

7:20 *he lifted up the staff and struck the water in the river.* When Moses strikes the Nile, he strikes the first blow for the freedom of Israel. His action challenges Hapi, the god of the Nile. Before it is all over, Yahweh will confront and vanquish many of Egypt's most important deities: the goddess Nut, whose sky he will fill with thunder and hail; the god Shu whose air he will blacken with gnats and flies; the goddess and protector Amanuet, who will be able to provide no protection for the Egyptians against the boils that ravage their bodies; the god Geb, whose earth will crawl with frogs and locusts. The sun of Ra will be blotted out. Neither the warrior goddess Anta-Anat nor the savior god Anhur will be able to defeat Yahweh and prevent the death of the firstborn. Osiris, the god of death, will be helpless to reverse the passover, and the god of the pharaohs, Horus, will be as impotent as the king who worships him. In our own culture there are many gods and goddesses yet—sex, power, money, fame, violence, war, hate, racism—but their influence on us need not be the final word. God can still overturn the power of what is false and cruel in our lives and grant us a freedom that allows our spirits to thrive.

8:1 WORSHIP—See Spiritual Disciplines Index.

chamber and your bed, and into the houses of your officials and of your people, *a* and into your ovens and your kneading bowls. [4]The frogs shall come up on you and on your people and on all your officials.' " [5b] And the LORD said to Moses, "Say to Aaron, 'Stretch out your hand with your staff over the rivers, the canals, and the pools, and make frogs come up on the land of Egypt.' " [6]So Aaron stretched out his hand over the waters of Egypt; and the frogs came up and covered the land of Egypt. [7]But the magicians did the same by their secret arts, and brought frogs up on the land of Egypt.

[8] Then Pharaoh called Moses and Aaron, and said, "Pray to the LORD to take away the frogs from me and my people, and I will let the people go to sacrifice to the LORD." [9]Moses said to Pharaoh, "Kindly tell me when I am to pray for you and for your officials and for your people, that the frogs may be removed from you and your houses and be left only in the Nile." [10]And he said, "Tomorrow." Moses said, "As you say! So that you may know that there is no one like the LORD our God, [11]the frogs shall leave you and your houses and your officials and your people;

they shall be left only in the Nile." [12]Then Moses and Aaron went out from Pharaoh; and Moses cried out to the LORD concerning the frogs that he had brought upon Pharaoh. *c* [13]And the LORD did as Moses requested: the frogs died in the houses, the courtyards, and the fields. [14]And they gathered them together in heaps, and the land stank. [15]But when Pharaoh saw that there was a respite, he hardened his heart, and would not listen to them, just as the LORD had said.

The Third Plague: Gnats

[16] Then the LORD said to Moses, "Say to Aaron, 'Stretch out your staff and strike the dust of the earth, so that it may become gnats throughout the whole land of Egypt.' " [17]And they did so; Aaron stretched out his hand with his staff and struck the dust of the earth, and gnats came on humans and animals alike; all the dust of the earth turned into gnats throughout the whole land of Egypt. [18]The magicians tried to produce gnats by their secret arts, but they could not. There were gnats on both humans and animals.

a Gk: Heb *upon your people*   *b* Ch 8.1 in Heb
c Or *frogs, as he had agreed with Pharaoh*

8:7 *But the magicians did the same by their secret arts.* That the magicians could also produce frogs is a disconcerting event for Moses and Aaron and for us. Wasn't it the miracles themselves that proved who God was? How can they then be duplicated? We often encounter words and deeds that are the mirror image of the beautiful and powerful, strikingly similar to what we would expect of God. As we grasp on to them, we race along the path, and our fingers are stung; the forest closes in upon us. We begin to understand that our faith does not rest on miracles alone, but on the source of these miracles.

8:15 *he hardened his heart, and would not listen to them.* In a number of places in Exodus the emphasis is on Pharaoh's choosing to harden his heart and persist in refusing to release the Hebrew people from slavery. There are just as many places or more (e.g., 10:20; 10:27) where it says that God hardens Pharaoh's heart. What are we to make of this? Does God hold humans accountable for evil he forces

them to do, evil they have not willed or chosen? The only way to begin to come to grips with this enigma is to refuse the path of either/or. Yes, God says he will harden Pharaoh's heart. But the record also tells us Pharaoh does a pretty good job of hardening it on his own. We get the feeling that Pharaoh's inclination to say no is an inclination that is all his own, yet it is something God makes use of, and it gains a momentum God not only allows but eventually, since Pharaoh insists on it so fiercely, reinforces. God hardens Pharaoh's heart by giving Pharaoh the choice and ability to harden his own heart. The important thing for our own spiritual formation is to keep in mind that, whatever else is a mystery, this is still a route, the record tells us, that Pharaoh himself decided to take, regardless of what God did or did not do. We persist in a certain direction that we sense again and again is not wise, and sometimes we have no choice left at all. We are swallowed up in the way we have taken and no longer know how to want out of it. It consumes us.

19 And the magicians said to Pharaoh, "This is the finger of God!" But Pharaoh's heart was hardened, and he would not listen to them, just as the LORD had said.

The Fourth Plague: Flies

20 Then the LORD said to Moses, "Rise early in the morning and present yourself before Pharaoh, as he goes out to the water, and say to him, 'Thus says the LORD: Let my people go, so that they may worship me. 21 For if you will not let my people go, I will send swarms of flies on you, your officials, and your people, and into your houses; and the houses of the Egyptians shall be filled with swarms of flies; so also the land where they live. 22 But on that day I will set apart the land of Goshen, where my people live, so that no swarms of flies shall be there, that you may know that I the LORD am in this land. 23 Thus I will make a distinction[a] between my people and your people. This sign shall appear tomorrow.' " 24 The LORD did so, and great swarms of flies came into the house of Pharaoh and into his officials' houses; in all of Egypt the land was ruined because of the flies.

25 Then Pharaoh summoned Moses and Aaron, and said, "Go, sacrifice to your God within the land." 26 But Moses said, "It would not be right to do so; for the sacrifices that we offer to the LORD our God are offensive to the Egyptians. If we offer in the sight of the Egyptians sacrifices that are offensive to them, will they not stone us? 27 We must go a three days' journey into the wilderness and sacrifice to the LORD our God as he commands us." 28 So Pharaoh said, "I will let you go to sacrifice to the LORD your God in the wilderness, provided you do not go very far away.

Pray for me." 29 Then Moses said, "As soon as I leave you, I will pray to the LORD that the swarms of flies may depart tomorrow from Pharaoh, from his officials, and from his people; only do not let Pharaoh again deal falsely by not letting the people go to sacrifice to the LORD."

30 So Moses went out from Pharaoh and prayed to the LORD. 31 And the LORD did as Moses asked: he removed the swarms of flies from Pharaoh, from his officials, and from his people; not one remained. 32 But Pharaoh hardened his heart this time also, and would not let the people go.

The Fifth Plague: Livestock Diseased

9 Then the LORD said to Moses, "Go to Pharaoh, and say to him, 'Thus says the LORD, the God of the Hebrews: Let my people go, so that they may worship me. 2 For if you refuse to let them go and still hold them, 3 the hand of the LORD will strike with a deadly pestilence your livestock in the field: the horses, the donkeys, the camels, the herds, and the flocks. 4 But the LORD will make a distinction between the livestock of Israel and the livestock of Egypt, so that nothing shall die of all that belongs to the Israelites.' " 5 The LORD set a time, saying, "Tomorrow the LORD will do this thing in the land." 6 And on the next day the LORD did so; all the livestock of the Egyptians died, but of the livestock of the Israelites not one died. 7 Pharaoh inquired and found that not one of the livestock of the Israelites was dead. But the heart of Pharaoh was hardened, and he would not let the people go.

a Gk Vg: Heb *will set redemption*

8:19 *This is the finger of God!* This expression refers to something that is obviously marked as coming from God. An affirmation of our faith can come from the unlikeliest of sources. The magicians of Egypt are in fierce competition with Moses, yet when they fail, they are quick to acknowledge the source of Moses' power. We may hear it from enemies, atheists, or people of other faiths. Yet when they admit, grudgingly or otherwise, that God is up to something in our lives, the encouragement ought to mean so

much more to us. It is the last thing you would expect them to say.

Responding
8:19 THE WITH-GOD LIFE. It seems that with every new plague Pharaoh's heart grew harder. What circumstances harden our hearts to God's presence today? Take a moment to reflect on the hard spots in your heart, present them to God, and ask him to soften them. *See also* Spiritual Disciplines Index.

The Sixth Plague: Boils

8 Then the LORD said to Moses and Aaron, "Take handfuls of soot from the kiln, and let Moses throw it in the air in the sight of Pharaoh. 9It shall become fine dust all over the land of Egypt, and shall cause festering boils on humans and animals throughout the whole land of Egypt." 10So they took soot from the kiln, and stood before Pharaoh, and Moses threw it in the air, and it caused festering boils on humans and animals. 11The magicians could not stand before Moses because of the boils, for the boils afflicted the magicians as well as all the Egyptians. 12But the LORD hardened the heart of Pharaoh, and he would not listen to them, just as the LORD had spoken to Moses.

The Seventh Plague: Thunder and Hail

13 Then the LORD said to Moses, "Rise up early in the morning and present yourself before Pharaoh, and say to him, 'Thus says the LORD, the God of the Hebrews: Let my people go, so that they may worship me. 14For this time I will send all my plagues upon you yourself, and upon your officials, and upon your people, so that you may know that there is no one like me in all the earth. 15For by now I could have stretched out my hand and struck you and your people with pestilence, and you would have been cut off from the earth. 16But this is why I have let you live: to show you my power, and to make my name resound through all the earth. 17You are still exalting yourself against my people, and will not let them go. 18Tomorrow at this time I will cause the heaviest hail to fall that has ever fallen in Egypt from the day it was founded until now. 19Send, therefore, and have your livestock and everything that you have in the open field brought to a secure place; every human or animal that is in the open field and is not brought under shelter will die when the hail comes down upon them.' " 20Those officials of Pharaoh who feared the word of the LORD hurried their slaves and livestock off to a secure place. 21Those who did not regard the word of the LORD left their slaves and livestock in the open field.

22 The LORD said to Moses, "Stretch out your hand toward heaven so that hail may fall on the whole land of Egypt, on humans and animals and all the plants of the field in the land of Egypt." 23Then Moses stretched out his staff toward heaven, and the LORD sent thunder and hail, and fire came down on the earth. And the LORD rained hail on the land of Egypt; 24there was hail with fire flashing continually in the midst of it, such heavy hail as had never fallen in all the land of Egypt since it became a nation. 25The hail struck down everything that was in the open field throughout all the land of Egypt, both human and animal; the hail also struck down all the plants of the field, and shattered every tree in the field. 26Only in the land of Goshen, where the Israelites were, there was no hail.

27 Then Pharaoh summoned Moses and Aaron, and said to them, "This time I have sinned; the LORD is in the right, and I and my people are in the wrong. 28Pray to the LORD! Enough of God's thunder and hail! I will let you go; you need stay no longer." 29Moses said to him, "As soon as I have gone out of the city, I will stretch out my hands to the LORD; the thunder will cease, and there will be no more hail, so that you may know that the earth is the LORD's. 30But as for you and your officials, I know that you do not yet fear the LORD God." 31(Now the flax and the barley were ruined, for the barley was in the ear and the flax was in bud. 32But the wheat and the spelt were not ruined, for they are late in coming up.) 33So Moses left Pharaoh, went out of the city, and stretched out his hands to the LORD; then the thunder and the hail ceased, and the rain no longer poured down on the earth. 34But when Pharaoh saw that the rain and the hail and the thunder had ceased, he sinned once more and hardened his heart, he and his officials. 35So the heart of Pharaoh was hardened, and he would not let the Israelites go, just as the LORD had spoken through Moses.

9:13 WORSHIP—*See* Spiritual Disciplines Index.

The Eighth Plague: Locusts

10 Then the LORD said to Moses, "Go to Pharaoh; for I have hardened his heart and the heart of his officials, in order that I may show these signs of mine among them, 2and that you may tell your children and grandchildren how I have made fools of the Egyptians and what signs I have done among them—so that you may know that I am the LORD."

3 So Moses and Aaron went to Pharaoh, and said to him, "Thus says the LORD, the God of the Hebrews, 'How long will you refuse to humble yourself before me? Let my people go, so that they may worship me. 4For if you refuse to let my people go, tomorrow I will bring locusts into your country. 5They shall cover the surface of the land, so that no one will be able to see the land. They shall devour the last remnant left you after the hail, and they shall devour every tree of yours that grows in the field. 6They shall fill your houses, and the houses of all your officials and of all the Egyptians—something that neither your parents nor your grandparents have seen, from the day they came on earth to this day.' " Then he turned and went out from Pharaoh.

7 Pharaoh's officials said to him, "How long shall this fellow be a snare to us? Let the people go, so that they may worship the LORD their God; do you not yet understand that Egypt is ruined?" 8So Moses and Aaron were brought back to Pharaoh, and he said to them, "Go, worship the LORD your God! But which ones are to go?" 9Moses said, "We will go with our young and our old; we will go with our sons and daughters and with our flocks and herds, because we have the LORD's festival to celebrate." 10He said to them, "The LORD indeed will be with you, if ever I let your little ones go with you! Plainly, you have some evil purpose in mind. 11No, never! Your men may go and worship the LORD, for that is what you are asking." And they were driven out from Pharaoh's presence.

12 Then the LORD said to Moses, "Stretch out your hand over the land of Egypt, so that the locusts may come upon it and eat every plant in the land, all that the hail has left." 13So Moses stretched out his staff over the land of Egypt, and the LORD brought an east wind upon the land all that day and all that night; when morning came, the east wind had brought the locusts. 14The locusts came upon all the land of Egypt and settled on the whole country of Egypt, such a dense swarm of locusts as had never been before, nor ever shall be again. 15They covered the surface of the whole land, so that the land was black; and they ate all the plants in the land and all the fruit of the trees that the hail had left; nothing green was left, no tree, no plant in the field, in all the land of Egypt. 16Pharaoh hurriedly summoned Moses and Aaron and said, "I have sinned against the LORD your God, and against you. 17Do forgive my sin just this once, and pray to the LORD your God that at the least he remove this deadly thing from me." 18So he went out from Pharaoh and prayed to the LORD. 19The LORD changed the wind into a very strong west wind, which lifted the locusts and drove them into the Red Sea;a not a single locust was left in all the country of Egypt. 20But the LORD hardened Pharaoh's heart, and he would not let the Israelites go.

The Ninth Plague: Darkness

21 Then the LORD said to Moses, "Stretch out your hand toward heaven so that there may be darkness over the land of Egypt, a darkness that can be felt." 22So Moses stretched out his hand toward heaven, and there was dense darkness in all the land of Egypt for three days. 23People could not see one another, and for three days they could not move from where they were; but all the Israelites had light where they lived. 24Then Pharaoh summoned Moses, and said, "Go, worship the LORD. Only your flocks and your herds shall remain behind. Even your children may go with you." 25But Moses said, "You must also let us have sacrifices and burnt offerings to sacrifice to the LORD our God. 26Our livestock also must go with us; not a hoof shall be left behind, for we must choose some of them for the worship of the LORD our God, and we will not know what to use to worship the LORD until we arrive there." 27But the LORD hardened

a Or Sea of Reeds

Pharaoh's heart, and he was unwilling to let them go. 28Then Pharaoh said to him, "Get away from me! Take care that you do not see my face again, for on the day you see my face you shall die." 29Moses said, "Just as you say! I will never see your face again."

Warning of the Final Plague

11 The LORD said to Moses, "I will bring one more plague upon Pharaoh and upon Egypt; afterwards he will let you go from here; indeed, when he lets you go, he will drive you away. 2Tell the people that every man is to ask his neighbor and every woman is to ask her neighbor for objects of silver and gold." 3The LORD gave the people favor in the sight of the Egyptians. Moreover, Moses himself was a man of great importance in the land of Egypt, in the sight of Pharaoh's officials and in the sight of the people.

4 Moses said, "Thus says the LORD: About midnight I will go out through Egypt. 5Every firstborn in the land of Egypt shall die, from the firstborn of Pharaoh who sits on his throne to the firstborn of the female slave who is behind the handmill, and all the firstborn of the livestock. 6Then there will be a loud cry throughout the whole land of Egypt, such as has never been or will ever be again. 7But not a dog shall growl at any of the Israelites—not at people, not at animals—so that you may know that the LORD makes a distinction between Egypt and Israel. 8Then all these officials of yours shall come down to me, and bow low to me, saying, 'Leave us, you and all the people who follow you.' After that I will leave." And in hot anger he left Pharaoh.

9 The LORD said to Moses, "Pharaoh will not listen to you, in order that my wonders may be multiplied in the land of Egypt." 10Moses and Aaron performed all these wonders before Pharaoh; but the LORD hardened Pharaoh's heart, and he did not let the people of Israel go out of his land.

The First Passover Instituted

12 The LORD said to Moses and Aaron in the land of Egypt: 2This month shall mark for you the beginning of months; it shall be the first month of the year for you. 3Tell the whole congregation of Israel that on the tenth of this month they are to take a lamb for each family, a lamb for each household. 4If a household is too small for a whole lamb, it shall join its closest neighbor in obtaining one; the lamb shall be divided in proportion to the number of people who eat of it. 5Your lamb shall be without blemish, a year-old male; you may take it from the sheep or from the goats. 6You shall keep it until the fourteenth day of this month; then the whole assembled congregation of Israel shall slaughter it at twilight. 7They shall take some of the blood and put it on the two doorposts and the lintel of the houses in which they eat it. 8They shall eat the lamb that same night; they shall eat it roasted over the fire with unleavened bread and bitter herbs. 9Do not eat any of it raw or boiled in water, but roasted over the fire, with its head, legs, and inner organs. 10You shall let none of it remain until the morning; anything that remains until the morning you shall burn. 11This is how you shall eat it: your loins girded, your sandals on your feet, and your staff in your hand; and you shall eat it hurriedly. It is the passover of the LORD. 12For I will pass through the land of Egypt that night, and I will strike down

---

12:11 *It is the passover of the LORD.* Here we see that even in times of great danger and haste there is a place for ritual in the spiritual life. God is careful to give very specific instructions (vv 1–11) on how families should celebrate the first Passover. God is a God of symbols, who impregnates common objects with divine significance. The precision with which God creates the Passover meal will be a precision he brings to the law and to the construction of the tabernacle. Why is important, and what, but

also *how:* how we speak, how we pray, how we act, how we worship. This matters to God, and it ought to matter to us. It plays a role in what we retain and what kind of a person we become.

12:12 *I will strike down every firstborn in the land of Egypt.* The God of the exodus is a God with teeth. Who can dismiss blood on the doorposts or plagues of hail, locusts, and darkness and paint a portrait of divinity that is all sunshine and orchids? Who can read these

every firstborn in the land of Egypt, both human beings and animals; on all the gods of Egypt I will execute judgments: I am the LORD. 13The blood shall be a sign for you on the houses where you live: when I see the blood, I will pass over you, and no plague shall destroy you when I strike the land of Egypt.

14　This day shall be a day of remembrance for you. You shall celebrate it as a festival to the LORD; throughout your generations you shall observe it as a perpetual ordinance. 15Seven days you shall eat unleavened bread; on the first day you shall remove leaven from your houses, for whoever eats leavened bread from the first day until the seventh day shall be cut off from Israel. 16On the first day you shall hold a solemn assembly, and on the seventh day a solemn assembly; no work shall be done on those days; only what everyone must eat, that alone may be prepared by you. 17You shall observe the festival of unleavened bread, for on this very day I brought your companies out of the land of Egypt: you shall observe this day throughout your generations as a perpetual ordinance. 18In the first month, from the evening of the fourteenth day until the evening of the twenty-first day, you shall eat unleavened bread. 19For seven

days no leaven shall be found in your houses; for whoever eats what is leavened shall be cut off from the congregation of Israel, whether an alien or a native of the land. 20You shall eat nothing leavened; in all your settlements you shall eat unleavened bread.

21　Then Moses called all the elders of Israel and said to them, "Go, select lambs for your families, and slaughter the passover lamb. 22Take a bunch of hyssop, dip it in the blood that is in the basin, and touch the lintel and the two doorposts with the blood in the basin. None of you shall go outside the door of your house until morning. 23For the LORD will pass through to strike down the Egyptians; when he sees the blood on the lintel and on the two doorposts, the LORD will pass over that door and will not allow the destroyer to enter your houses to strike you down. 24You shall observe this rite as a perpetual ordinance for you and your children. 25When you come to the land that the LORD will give you, as he has promised, you shall keep this observance. 26And when your children ask you, 'What do you mean by this observance?' 27you shall say, 'It is the passover sacrifice to the LORD, for he passed over the houses of the Israelites in Egypt, when he

---

words—"Pharaoh arose in the night, he and all his officials and all the Egyptians; and there was a loud cry in Egypt, for there was not a house without someone dead" (v 30)—without stopping to wonder who this God really is and to what lengths he will go? This is not a comfortable or convenient God. This God is not the God of children's picture Bibles. He is not easily painted. He is wrapped in mystery. But neither did Moses understand everything that swirled about him, disaster after disaster wounding people and animals and the earth. His people certainly did not understand. Even as they rushed from slavery to freedom, clutching gold and silver and bread dough that had no yeast, there is no sense of comprehension, not then, and not later as they staggered through the wilderness, facing mountains of thunder, commandments, cloud by day, and fire by night. This God was inexhaustible in his ways to surprise and awe. He was known, but unknown. He could never be taken for granted.

We ought to ignore nothing, even what we do not like or what does not fit into our favorite theologies. The Christian faith is not a tidy faith. Not every i is dotted or every t crossed, at least not to our way of understanding. When we are in the presence of the Holy One, we are in control of nothing and we see only what we are permitted to see.

Responding

12:14 CELEBRATION. In this passage the Lord "passes over" the houses of the Israelites, thus sparing the lives of the firstborn in their households (vv 12–13). Recall one time in your life when death passed over you and your life was spared. If you didn't celebrate God's goodness and mercy for sparing your life at that time, do so this week. The celebration can be as simple as spending extra time with a loved one. See also Spiritual Disciplines Index.

struck down the Egyptians but spared our houses.' " And the people bowed down and worshiped.

28 The Israelites went and did just as the LORD had commanded Moses and Aaron.

The Tenth Plague: Death of the Firstborn

29 At midnight the LORD struck down all the firstborn in the land of Egypt, from the firstborn of Pharaoh who sat on his throne to the firstborn of the prisoner who was in the dungeon, and all the firstborn of the livestock. 30Pharaoh arose in the night, he and all his officials and all the Egyptians; and there was a loud cry in Egypt, for there was not a house without someone dead. 31Then he summoned Moses and Aaron in the night, and said, "Rise up, go away from my people, both you and the Israelites! Go, worship the LORD, as you said. 32Take your flocks and your herds, as you said, and be gone. And bring a blessing on me too!"

The Exodus: From Rameses to Succoth

33 The Egyptians urged the people to hasten their departure from the land, for they said, "We shall all be dead." 34So the people took their dough before it was leavened, with their kneading bowls wrapped up in their cloaks on their shoulders. 35The Israelites had done as Moses told them; they had asked the Egyptians for jewelry of silver and gold, and for clothing, 36and the LORD had given the people favor in the sight of the Egyptians, so that they let them have what they asked. And so they plundered the Egyptians.

37 The Israelites journeyed from Rameses to Succoth, about six hundred thousand men on foot, besides children. 38A mixed crowd also went up with them, and livestock in great numbers, both flocks and herds. 39They baked unleavened cakes of the dough that they had brought out of Egypt; it was not leavened, because they were driven out of Egypt and could not wait, nor had they prepared any provisions for themselves.

40 The time that the Israelites had lived in Egypt was four hundred thirty years. 41At the end of four hundred thirty years, on that very day, all the companies of the LORD went out from the land of Egypt. 42That was for

the LORD a night of vigil, to bring them out of the land of Egypt. That same night is a vigil to be kept for the LORD by all the Israelites throughout their generations.

Directions for the Passover

43 The LORD said to Moses and Aaron: This is the ordinance for the passover: no foreigner shall eat of it, 44but any slave who has been purchased may eat of it after he has been circumcised; 45no bound or hired servant may eat of it. 46It shall be eaten in one house; you shall not take any of the animal outside the house, and you shall not break any of its bones. 47The whole congregation of Israel shall celebrate it. 48If an alien who resides with you wants to celebrate the passover to the LORD, all his males shall be circumcised; then he may draw near to celebrate it; he shall be regarded as a native of the land. But no uncircumcised person shall eat of it; 49there shall be one law for the native and for the alien who resides among you.

50 All the Israelites did just as the LORD had commanded Moses and Aaron. 51That very day the LORD brought the Israelites out of the land of Egypt, company by company.

13 The LORD said to Moses: 2Consecrate to me all the firstborn; whatever is the first to open the womb among the Israelites, of human beings and animals, is mine.

The Festival of Unleavened Bread

3 Moses said to the people, "Remember this day on which you came out of Egypt, out of the house of slavery, because the LORD brought you out from there by strength of hand; no leavened bread shall be eaten. 4Today, in the month of Abib, you are going out. 5When the LORD brings you into the land of the Canaanites, the Hittites, the Amorites, the Hivites, and the Jebusites, which he swore to your ancestors to give you, a land flowing with milk and honey, you shall keep this observance in this month. 6Seven days you shall eat unleavened bread, and on the seventh day there shall be a festival to the LORD. 7Unleavened bread shall be eaten for seven days; no leavened bread shall be seen in your possession, and no leaven shall be seen among you in all your territory. 8You shall tell your

child on that day, 'It is because of what the LORD did for me when I came out of Egypt.' 9It shall serve for you as a sign on your hand and as a reminder on your forehead, so that the teaching of the LORD may be on your lips; for with a strong hand the LORD brought you out of Egypt. 10You shall keep this ordinance at its proper time from year to year.

The Consecration of the Firstborn

11 "When the LORD has brought you into the land of the Canaanites, as he swore to you and your ancestors, and has given it to you, 12you shall set apart to the LORD all that first opens the womb. All the firstborn of your livestock that are males shall be the LORD's. 13But every firstborn donkey you shall redeem with a sheep; if you do not redeem it, you must break its neck. Every firstborn male among your children you shall redeem. 14When in the future your child asks you, 'What does this mean?' you shall answer, 'By strength of hand the LORD brought us out of Egypt, from the house of slavery. 15When Pharaoh stubbornly refused to let us go, the LORD killed all the firstborn in the land of Egypt, from human firstborn to the firstborn of animals. Therefore I sacrifice to the LORD every male that first opens the womb, but every firstborn of my sons I redeem.' 16It shall serve as a sign on your hand and as an emblem*a* on your forehead that by strength of hand the LORD brought us out of Egypt."

The Pillars of Cloud and Fire

17 When Pharaoh let the people go, God did not lead them by way of the land of the Philistines, although that was nearer; for God thought, "If the people face war, they may change their minds and return to Egypt." 18So God led the people by the roundabout way of the wilderness toward the Red Sea.*b*

The Israelites went up out of the land of Egypt prepared for battle. 19And Moses took with him the bones of Joseph who had required a solemn oath of the Israelites, saying, "God will surely take notice of you, and then you must carry my bones with you from here." 20They set out from Succoth, and camped at Etham, on the edge of the wilderness. 21The LORD went in front of them in a pillar of cloud by day, to lead them along the way, and in a pillar of fire by night, to give them light, so that they might travel by day and by night. 22Neither the pillar of cloud by day nor the pillar of fire by night left its place in front of the people.

Crossing the Red Sea

14 Then the LORD said to Moses: 2Tell the Israelites to turn back and camp in front of Pi-hahiroth, between Migdol and the sea, in front of Baal-zephon; you shall camp opposite it, by the sea. 3Pharaoh will say of the Israelites, "They are wandering aimlessly in the land; the wilderness has closed in on them." 4I will harden Pharaoh's heart, and he will pursue them, so that I will gain glory for myself over Pharaoh and all his army; and the Egyptians shall know that I am the LORD. And they did so.

5 When the king of Egypt was told that the people had fled, the minds of Pharaoh and his officials were changed toward the people, and they said, "What have we done, letting Israel leave our service?" 6So he had his chariot made ready, and took his army with him; 7he took six hundred picked chariots and all the other chariots of Egypt with officers over all of them. 8The LORD hardened the heart of Pharaoh king of Egypt and he

a Or *as a frontlet*; meaning of Heb uncertain
b Or *Sea of Reeds*

13:22 *Neither the pillar of cloud by day nor the pillar of fire by night left its place.* Long before the tabernacle is built, long before the people are consecrated to God at Mt. Sinai, long before anyone has committed to anything, God is faithful and stays close to the people he has set free. We need to bear in mind that God is near even if we have not made momentous decisions to put our lives in his hands or follow him to the ends of the earth. Sometimes we recognize the pillars of cloud and fire, and sometimes we do not. But long before we are ready to establish any sort of permanent relationship with God, he is a constant throughout the days and nights of our life journey.

pursued the Israelites, who were going out boldly. 9 The Egyptians pursued them, all Pharaoh's horses and chariots, his chariot drivers and his army; they overtook them camped by the sea, by Pi-hahiroth, in front of Baal-zephon.

10 As Pharaoh drew near, the Israelites looked back, and there were the Egyptians advancing on them. In great fear the Israelites cried out to the LORD. 11 They said to Moses, "Was it because there were no graves in Egypt that you have taken us away to die in the wilderness? What have you done to us, bringing us out of Egypt? 12 Is this not the very thing we told you in Egypt, 'Let us alone and let us serve the Egyptians'? For it would have been better for us to serve the Egyptians than to die in the wilderness." 13 But Moses said to the people, "Do not be afraid, stand firm, and see the deliverance that the LORD will accomplish for you today; for the Egyptians whom you see today you shall never see again. 14 The LORD will fight for you, and you have only to keep still."

15 Then the LORD said to Moses, "Why do you cry out to me? Tell the Israelites to go forward. 16 But you lift up your staff, and stretch out your hand over the sea and divide it, that the Israelites may go into the sea on dry ground. 17 Then I will harden the hearts of the Egyptians so that they will go in after them; and so I will gain glory for myself

over Pharaoh and all his army, his chariots, and his chariot drivers. 18 And the Egyptians shall know that I am the LORD, when I have gained glory for myself over Pharaoh, his chariots, and his chariot drivers."

19 The angel of God who was going before the Israelite army moved and went behind them; and the pillar of cloud moved from in front of them and took its place behind them. 20 It came between the army of Egypt and the army of Israel. And so the cloud was there with the darkness, and it lit up the night; one did not come near the other all night.

21 Then Moses stretched out his hand over the sea. The LORD drove the sea back by a strong east wind all night, and turned the sea into dry land; and the waters were divided. 22 The Israelites went into the sea on dry ground, the waters forming a wall for them on their right and on their left. 23 The Egyptians pursued, and went into the sea after them, all of Pharaoh's horses, chariots, and chariot drivers. 24 At the morning watch the LORD in the pillar of fire and cloud looked down upon the Egyptian army, and threw the Egyptian army into panic. 25 He clogged *a* their chariot wheels so that they turned with difficulty. The Egyptians said, "Let us flee from the Israelites, for the LORD is fighting for them against Egypt."

a Sam Gk Syr: MT *removed*

14:13–16 THE WITH-GOD LIFE—*See* Spiritual Disciplines Index.

14:21 *the waters were divided.* It is in our nature to make plans. There is nothing wrong with that. Moses planned to lead Israel out of Egypt to Canaan. Paul planned to take the gospel to Spain. The only thing we must not do is make our plans our god. We must hold them lightly in our grasp, for we do not know if everything will work out as we expect. Our choice is either to trust our plans with all our heart or trust our God. Not only do the best laid plans of mice and men often fall to pieces, as Robert Burns knew, but often enough God prompts us to act without any plans in place and no guarantee that everything will come together as it should. Are we free enough to act without plans if the need arises? No one knew

what God was going to do to rescue the Hebrews from pursuit by the Egyptians. They could only trust that he was going to do something. Like us, they did not do very well when they saw that nothing had been prepared in advance—there was no bridge, there were no boats, only water in front and chariots and iron behind. Suppose they had known beforehand that God was planning to guide them toward an uncrossable body of water? Suppose they had insisted that, before they left Egypt, scouts sent in advance report back that the route was clear, the Red Sea parted and waiting? They would have remained slaves. The water was only parted once they had acted in faith and followed God. They could not count on any plans because God gave them none. He only gave them himself. God was the plan.

The Pursuers Drowned

26 Then the LORD said to Moses, "Stretch out your hand over the sea, so that the water may come back upon the Egyptians, upon their chariots and chariot drivers." 27So Moses stretched out his hand over the sea, and at dawn the sea returned to its normal depth. As the Egyptians fled before it, the LORD tossed the Egyptians into the sea. 28The waters returned and covered the chariots and the chariot drivers, the entire army of Pharaoh that had followed them into the sea; not one of them remained. 29But the Israelites walked on dry ground through the sea, the waters forming a wall for them on their right and on their left.

30 Thus the LORD saved Israel that day from the Egyptians; and Israel saw the Egyptians dead on the seashore. 31Israel saw the great work that the LORD did against the Egyptians. So the people feared the LORD and believed in the LORD and in his servant Moses.

The Song of Moses

15 Then Moses and the Israelites sang this song to the LORD:

"I will sing to the LORD, for he has
    triumphed gloriously;
horse and rider he has thrown into
    the sea.
2 The LORD is my strength and my
    might,[a]
and he has become my salvation;
this is my God, and I will praise him,
    my father's God, and I will exalt him.
3 The LORD is a warrior;
    the LORD is his name.

4 "Pharaoh's chariots and his army he
    cast into the sea;
his picked officers were sunk in the
    Red Sea.[b]
5 The floods covered them;

they went down into the depths like a
    stone.
6 Your right hand, O LORD, glorious in
    power—
    your right hand, O LORD, shattered
      the enemy.
7 In the greatness of your majesty you
    overthrew your adversaries;
you sent out your fury, it consumed
    them like stubble.
8 At the blast of your nostrils the waters
    piled up,
the floods stood up in a heap;
the deeps congealed in the heart of
    the sea.
9 The enemy said, 'I will pursue, I will
    overtake,
I will divide the spoil, my desire shall
    have its fill of them.
I will draw my sword, my hand shall
    destroy them.'
10 You blew with your wind, the sea
    covered them;
they sank like lead in the mighty
    waters.

11 "Who is like you, O LORD, among the
    gods?
Who is like you, majestic in holiness,
    awesome in splendor, doing wonders?
12 You stretched out your right hand,
    the earth swallowed them.

13 "In your steadfast love you led the
    people whom you redeemed;
you guided them by your strength to
    your holy abode.
14 The peoples heard, they trembled;
pangs seized the inhabitants of
    Philistia.
15 Then the chiefs of Edom were
    dismayed;

a Or *song*   *b* Or *Sea of Reeds*

Responding

15:13 GUIDANCE. In his book *Hearing God*, Dallas Willard names several ways we receive guidance from God—dreams, visions, circumstances, conversations—but this verse recounts that God guided the Israelites through his strength. What do you think this means? Does it have a sense of protection? Of looking after their needs? Of overcoming adversity? How can we be guided by God's strength? *See also* Spiritual Disciplines Index.

Handwritten margin notes: *Bitter Water / the Cross / Sufferings / Oil, Trials / to Branson / Cross*

trembling seized the leaders of Moab;
all the inhabitants of Canaan melted
away.
16 Terror and dread fell upon them;
by the might of your arm, they
became still as a stone
until your people, O LORD, passed by,
until the people whom you acquired
passed by.
17 You brought them in and planted them
on the mountain of your own
possession,
the place, O LORD, that you made your
abode,
the sanctuary, O LORD, that your
hands have established.
18 The LORD will reign forever and ever."

19 When the horses of Pharaoh with his
chariots and his chariot drivers went into the
sea, the LORD brought back the waters of the
sea upon them; but the Israelites walked
through the sea on dry ground.

The Song of Miriam

20 Then the prophet Miriam, Aaron's sister, took a tambourine in her hand; and all
the women went out after her with tambourines and with dancing. 21 And Miriam
sang to them:

"Sing to the LORD, for he has triumphed
gloriously;
horse and rider he has thrown into the
sea."

Bitter Water Made Sweet

22 Then Moses ordered Israel to set out
from the Red Sea,a and they went into the
wilderness of Shur. They went three days in

the wilderness and found no water. 23 When
they came to Marah, they could not drink
the water of Marah because it was bitter. That
is why it was called Marah.b 24 And the people complained against Moses, saying, "What
shall we drink?" 25 He cried out to the LORD;
and the LORD showed him a piece of wood;c
he threw it into the water, and the water became sweet.

There the LORDd made for them a statute
and an ordinance and there he put them to
the test. 26 He said, "If you will listen carefully to the voice of the LORD your God, and do
what is right in his sight, and give heed to his
commandments and keep all his statutes, I
will not bring upon you any of the diseases
that I brought upon the Egyptians; for I am
the LORD who heals you."

27 Then they came to Elim, where there
were twelve springs of water and seventy
palm trees; and they camped there by the
water.

Bread from Heaven

16 The whole congregation of the Israelites set out from Elim; and Israel
came to the wilderness of Sin, which is between Elim and Sinai, on the fifteenth day of
the second month after they had departed
from the land of Egypt. 2 The whole congregation of the Israelites complained against
Moses and Aaron in the wilderness. 3 The Israelites said to them, "If only we had died by
the hand of the LORD in the land of Egypt,
when we sat by the fleshpots and ate our fill

a Or *Sea of Reeds*   b That is *Bitterness*   c Or a
tree   d Heb *he*

15:25 *the water became sweet.* No doubt God
could have moved his people to another place
not far away where the water would have been
better. But he did not do that. He kept them
where they were and made the bitter water
good. Or perhaps there was nothing better at
hand, and it was critical that God transform
what was available. Often we want desperately
to change location. If we can just get somewhere else, everything will be all right. Unquestionably there are times God has to change our
geography. He did it with the Hebrews, after all.

But there are other times when he asks us to
trust him to alter what is sour and foul and
repugnant to us. Some things crucial to our
well-being must be pure and sweet or we will
die. If it is not time for a change of place, then it
must be time for God to change our experience,
a time for him to make nourishing what has
previously been deadly, a time for him to make
attainable what has been previously been
denied.

16:3 *we sat by the fleshpots and ate our fill of
bread.* Living as a free people means making

of bread; for you have brought us out into this wilderness to kill this whole assembly with hunger."

4 Then the LORD said to Moses, "I am going to rain bread from heaven for you, and each day the people shall go out and gather enough for that day. In that way I will test them, whether they will follow my instruction or not. 5On the sixth day, when they prepare what they bring in, it will be twice as much as they gather on other days." 6So Moses and Aaron said to all the Israelites, "In the evening you shall know that it was the LORD who brought you out of the land of Egypt, 7and in the morning you shall see the glory of the LORD, because he has heard your complaining against the LORD. For what are we, that you complain against us?" 8And Moses said, "When the LORD gives you meat to eat in the evening and your fill of bread in the morning, because the LORD has heard the complaining that you utter against him— what are we? Your complaining is not against us but against the LORD."

9 Then Moses said to Aaron, "Say to the whole congregation of the Israelites, 'Draw near to the LORD, for he has heard your complaining.' " 10And as Aaron spoke to the whole congregation of the Israelites, they looked toward the wilderness, and the glory of the LORD appeared in the cloud. 11The LORD spoke to Moses and said, 12"I have heard the complaining of the Israelites; say to them, 'At twilight you shall eat meat, and in the morning you shall have your fill of bread; then you shall know that I am the LORD your God.' "

13 In the evening quails came up and covered the camp; and in the morning there was a layer of dew around the camp. 14When the layer of dew lifted, there on the surface of the wilderness was a fine flaky substance, as fine as frost on the ground. 15When the Israelites saw it, they said to one another, "What is it?" a For they did not know what it was. Moses said to them, "It is the bread that the LORD has given you to eat. 16This is what the LORD has commanded: 'Gather as much of it as each of you needs, an omer to a person according to the number of persons, all providing for those in their own tents.' " 17The Israelites did so, some gathering more, some less. 18But when they measured it with an omer, those who gathered much had nothing over, and those who gathered little had no shortage; they gathered as much as each of them needed. 19And Moses said to them, "Let no one leave any of it over until morning." 20But they did not listen to Moses; some left part of it until morning, and it bred worms and became foul. And Moses was angry with them. 21Morning by morning they gathered it, as much as each needed; but when the sun grew hot, it melted.

22 On the sixth day they gathered twice as much food, two omers apiece. When all the

a Or "It is manna" (Heb man hu, see verse 31)

---

many decisions that previously were made for us. It means taking risks that there was never any need or possibility to take before. The new responsibilities can be unnerving. This is not just true for those who leave actual prisons or refugee camps. It is true for those who leave abusive and controlling relationships as well. It is true for children who finally leave a household that did everything for them. What must be resisted is the human quirk to romanticize the past, to goldplate what once entrapped and stifled us. One can enjoy a feast as a slave in chains or a loaf of bread as a free man or woman. Which is preferable?

16:4 *I am going to rain bread from heaven for you.* Much has been written about the manna that God provided for forty years in the wilderness. Many have commented on how manna is an example of God's provision for his people under difficult circumstances. All of this is true. But it is important to remember that the very word "manna" in Hebrew means "What is it?" How God chose to feed the people was unexpected. The way he worked to help them did not look like anything they had seen before. Yet they trusted it, ate it, and lived. We also must be prepared for God to work in unusual ways in our lives. We must be careful not to turn away from something because it appears odd and unfamiliar. Many times God does something and we say, "What is it?"—only to find out it is the very thing we need.

leaders of the congregation came and told Moses, 23he said to them, "This is what the LORD has commanded: 'Tomorrow is a day of solemn rest, a holy sabbath to the LORD; bake what you want to bake and boil what you want to boil, and all that is left over put aside to be kept until morning.' " 24So they put it aside until morning, as Moses commanded them; and it did not become foul, and there were no worms in it. 25Moses said, "Eat it today, for today is a sabbath to the LORD; today you will not find it in the field. 26Six days you shall gather it; but on the seventh day, which is a sabbath, there will be none."

27 On the seventh day some of the people went out to gather, and they found none. 28The LORD said to Moses, "How long will you refuse to keep my commandments and instructions? 29See! The LORD has given you the sabbath, therefore on the sixth day he gives you food for two days; each of you stay where you are; do not leave your place on the seventh day." 30So the people rested on the seventh day.

31 The house of Israel called it manna; it was like coriander seed, white, and the taste of it was like wafers made with honey. 32Moses said, "This is what the LORD has commanded: 'Let an omer of it be kept throughout your generations, in order that they may see the food with which I fed you in the wilderness, when I brought you out of the land of Egypt.' " 33And Moses said to Aaron, "Take a jar, and put an omer of manna in it, and place it before the LORD, to be kept throughout your generations." 34As the LORD commanded Moses, so Aaron placed it before the covenant,a for safekeeping. 35The Israelites ate manna forty years, until they came to a habitable land; they ate manna, until they came to the border of the land of Canaan. 36An omer is a tenth of an ephah.

Water from the Rock

17 From the wilderness of Sin the whole congregation of the Israelites journeyed by stages, as the LORD commanded. They camped at Rephidim, but there was no water for the people to drink. 2The people quarreled with Moses, and said, "Give us wa-

ter to drink." Moses said to them, "Why do you quarrel with me? Why do you test the LORD?" 3But the people thirsted there for water; and the people complained against Moses and said, "Why did you bring us out of Egypt, to kill us and our children and livestock with thirst?" 4So Moses cried out to the LORD, "What shall I do with this people? They are almost ready to stone me." 5The LORD said to Moses, "Go on ahead of the people, and take some of the elders of Israel with you; take in your hand the staff with which you struck the Nile, and go. 6I will be standing there in front of you on the rock at Horeb. Strike the rock, and water will come out of it, so that the people may drink." Moses did so, in the sight of the elders of Israel. 7He called the place Massahb and Meribah,c because the Israelites quarreled and tested the LORD, saying, "Is the LORD among us or not?"

Amalek Attacks Israel and Is Defeated

8 Then Amalek came and fought with Israel at Rephidim. 9Moses said to Joshua, "Choose some men for us and go out, fight with Amalek. Tomorrow I will stand on the top of the hill with the staff of God in my hand." 10So Joshua did as Moses told him, and fought with Amalek, while Moses, Aaron, and Hur went up to the top of the hill. 11Whenever Moses held up his hand, Israel prevailed; and whenever he lowered his hand, Amalek prevailed. 12But Moses' hands grew weary; so they took a stone and put it under him, and he sat on it. Aaron and Hur held up his hands, one on one side, and the other on the other side; so his hands were steady until the sun set. 13And Joshua defeated Amalek and his people with the sword.

14 Then the LORD said to Moses, "Write this as a reminder in a book and recite it in the hearing of Joshua: I will utterly blot out the remembrance of Amalek from under heaven." 15And Moses built an altar and called it, The LORD is my banner. 16He said, "A hand upon the banner of the LORD! d The LORD will have war with Amalek from generation to generation."

a Or treaty or testimony; Heb eduth   b That is Test
c That is Quarrel   d Cn: Meaning of Heb
uncertain

Jethro's Advice

18 Jethro, the priest of Midian, Moses' father-in-law, heard of all that God had done for Moses and for his people Israel, how the LORD had brought Israel out of Egypt. ²After Moses had sent away his wife Zipporah, his father-in-law Jethro took her back, ³along with her two sons. The name of the one was Gershom (for he said, "I have been an alien*a* in a foreign land"), ⁴and the name of the other, Eliezer*b* (for he said, "The God of my father was my help, and delivered me from the sword of Pharaoh"). ⁵Jethro, Moses' father-in-law, came into the wilderness where Moses was encamped at the mountain of God, bringing Moses' sons and wife to him. ⁶He sent word to Moses, "I, your father-in-law Jethro, am coming to you, with your wife and her two sons." ⁷Moses went out to meet his father-in-law; he bowed down and kissed him; each asked after the other's welfare, and they went into the tent. ⁸Then Moses told his father-in-law all that the LORD had done to Pharaoh and to the Egyptians for Israel's sake, all the hardship that had beset them on the way, and how the LORD had delivered them. ⁹Jethro rejoiced for all the good that the LORD had done to Israel, in delivering them from the Egyptians.

10 Jethro said, "Blessed be the LORD, who has delivered you from the Egyptians and from Pharaoh. ¹¹Now I know that the LORD is greater than all gods, because he delivered the people from the Egyptians,*c* when they dealt arrogantly with them." ¹²And Jethro, Moses' father-in-law, brought a burnt offering and sacrifices to God; and Aaron came with all the elders of Israel to eat bread with Moses' father-in-law in the presence of God.

13 The next day Moses sat as judge for the people, while the people stood around him from morning until evening. ¹⁴When Moses' father-in-law saw all that he was doing for the people, he said, "What is this that you are doing for the people? Why do you sit alone, while all the people stand around you from morning until evening?" ¹⁵Moses said to his father-in-law, "Because the people come to me to inquire of God. ¹⁶When they have a dispute, they come to me and I decide between one person and another, and I make known to them the statutes and instructions of God." ¹⁷Moses' father-in-law said to him, "What you are doing is not good. ¹⁸You will surely wear yourself out, both you and these people with you. For the task is too heavy for you; you cannot do it alone. ¹⁹Now listen to me. I will give you counsel, and God be with you! You should represent the people before God, and you should bring their cases before God; ²⁰teach them the statutes and instructions and make known to them the way they are to go and the things they are to do. ²¹You should also look for able men among all the people, men who fear God, are trustworthy, and hate dishonest gain; set such men over them as officers over thousands, hundreds, fifties, and tens. ²²Let them sit as judges for the people at all times; let them bring every important case to you, but decide every minor case themselves. So it will be easier for you, and they will bear the burden with you. ²³If you do this, and God so commands you, then you will be able to endure, and all these people will go to their home in peace."

24 So Moses listened to his father-in-law and did all that he had said. ²⁵Moses chose able men from all Israel and appointed them as heads over the people, as officers over thousands, hundreds, fifties, and tens. ²⁶And they judged the people at all times; hard cases they brought to Moses, but any minor case

a Heb *ger*   *b* Heb *Eli,* my God; *ezer,* help
c The clause *because . . . Egyptians* has been transposed from verse 10

18:18 *you cannot do it alone.* As important a leader as Moses has become, he is still one man. He needs help. Even if he is not the first to admit it. Aaron and Hur had to hold up his weary arms at the battle with Amalek (17:12). His father-in-law advises him to select judges to assist him in governing the people with justice and equity (18:22). Part of our spiritual journey consists of recognizing our limitations and seeking the support of significant others who can work alongside us to ensure the things that need to be done for the good of all are indeed done. The idea that a truly spiritual person is always more effective going it alone is a myth.

they decided themselves. 27Then Moses let his father-in-law depart, and he went off to his own country.

The Israelites Reach Mount Sinai

19 On the third new moon after the Israelites had gone out of the land of Egypt, on that very day, they came into the wilderness of Sinai. 2They had journeyed from Rephidim, entered the wilderness of Sinai, and camped in the wilderness; Israel camped there in front of the mountain. 3Then Moses went up to God; the LORD called to him from the mountain, saying, "Thus you shall say to the house of Jacob, and tell the Israelites: 4You have seen what I did to the Egyptians, and how I bore you on eagles' wings and brought you to myself. 5Now therefore, if you obey my voice and keep my covenant, you shall be my treasured possession out of all the peoples. Indeed, the whole earth is mine, 6but you shall be for me a priestly kingdom and a holy nation. These are the words that you shall speak to the Israelites."

7 So Moses came, summoned the elders of the people, and set before them all these words that the LORD had commanded him. 8The people all answered as one: "Everything that the LORD has spoken we will do." Moses reported the words of the people to the LORD. 9Then the LORD said to Moses, "I am going to come to you in a dense cloud, in order that the people may hear when I speak with you and so trust you ever after."

The People Consecrated

When Moses had told the words of the people to the LORD, 10the LORD said to Moses: "Go to the people and consecrate them today and tomorrow. Have them wash their clothes 11and prepare for the third day, because on the third day the LORD will come down upon Mount Sinai in the sight of all the people. 12You shall set limits for the people all around, saying, 'Be careful not to go up the mountain or to touch the edge of it. Any who touch the mountain shall be put to death. 13No hand shall touch them, but they shall be stoned or shot with arrows; *a* whether animal or human being, they shall not live.' When the trumpet sounds a long blast, they may go up on the mountain." 14So Moses went down from the mountain to the people. He consecrated the people, and they washed their clothes. 15And he said to the people, "Prepare for the third day; do not go near a woman."

16 On the morning of the third day there was thunder and lightning, as well as a thick cloud on the mountain, and a blast of a trumpet so loud that all the people who were in the camp trembled. 17Moses brought the people out of the camp to meet God. They took their stand at the foot of the mountain. 18Now Mount Sinai was wrapped in smoke, because the LORD had descended upon it in fire; the smoke went up like the smoke of a kiln, while the whole mountain shook violently. 19As the blast of the trumpet grew louder and louder, Moses would speak and God would answer him in thunder. 20When the LORD descended upon Mount Sinai, to the top of the mountain, the LORD summoned Moses to the top of the mountain, and Moses went up. 21Then the LORD said to Moses, "Go down and warn the people not to break through to the LORD to look; otherwise many of them will perish. 22Even the priests who approach the LORD must consecrate

a Heb lacks *with arrows*

19:3–6 THE WITH-GOD LIFE—*See* Spiritual Disciplines Index.

19:16 *all the people who were in the camp trembled.* God is indeed approachable and close to the human race. But we do not know what untainted light is like; we do not know how to categorize raw holiness; we do not have much experience with pure spirit, pure essence, pure being. What are these things? It is good to be reminded that when people in the Bible saw angels, they were frightened; when they saw God, they were overwhelmed. In our spirituality we can abuse God's intimacy and act as if we are his equal or even his master. God cannot be made to do our bidding and jump, like a genie, to appease our every whim. Not the God of the exodus or of the Bible.

themselves or the LORD will break out against them." 23Moses said to the LORD, "The people are not permitted to come up to Mount Sinai; for you yourself warned us, saying, 'Set limits around the mountain and keep it holy.' " 24The LORD said to him, "Go down, and come up bringing Aaron with you; but do not let either the priests or the people break through to come up to the LORD; otherwise he will break out against them." 25So Moses went down to the people and told them.

The Ten Commandments

20 Then God spoke all these words: 2 I am the LORD your God, who brought you out of the land of Egypt, out of the house of slavery; 3you shall have no other gods before a me.

4 You shall not make for yourself an idol, whether in the form of anything that is in heaven above, or that is on the earth beneath, or that is in the water under the earth. 5You shall not bow down to them or worship them; for I the LORD your God am a jealous God, punishing children for the iniquity of parents, to the third and the fourth genera-

tion of those who reject me, 6but showing steadfast love to the thousandth generation b of those who love me and keep my commandments.

7 You shall not make wrongful use of the name of the LORD your God, for the LORD will not acquit anyone who misuses his name.

8 Remember the sabbath day, and keep it holy. 9Six days you shall labor and do all your work. 10But the seventh day is a sabbath to the LORD your God; you shall not do any work—you, your son or your daughter, your male or female slave, your livestock, or the alien resident in your towns. 11For in six days the LORD made heaven and earth, the sea, and all that is in them, but rested the seventh day; therefore the LORD blessed the sabbath day and consecrated it.

12 Honor your father and your mother, so that your days may be long in the land that the LORD your God is giving you.

13 You shall not murder. c

14 You shall not commit adultery.

a Or besides   b Or to thousands   c Or kill

20:2–17 *I am the LORD your God.* The Decalogue, or "Ten Commandments" (literally, "ten utterances," see 34:28), follows the standard structure of the ancient suzerain-vassal treaties. The overlord (suzerain) makes a covenant with his servants (vassals) by first stating the numerous and gracious things he has done for the vassals. This is then followed by the stipulations of the covenant, that is, the things the vassals do in return, out of thanksgiving, for the great generosity of the suzerain. In this case Yahweh states in the most succinct way possible his great generosity to his people: deliverance from bondage. The stipulations of this covenant—what the people do in grateful response—are what we today commonly refer to as the Ten Commandments. The important thing for us to understand for our spiritual formation is the way in which grace precedes law. God first acts in grace and mercy by delivering the people, and then the people respond in gratitude and thanksgiving by obeying the commandments. Put succinctly: the crossing of the Red Sea comes before the giving of the Ten Commandments.

20:3 *you shall have no other gods before me.* Although Exodus emphasizes the mysteriousness of God, it also makes it clear that when God chooses to speak or otherwise reveal himself, the effect can be precise and obvious. The Ten Commandments is a strong example of this. Here are four declarations for keeping our relationship with God intact: no worship of other gods, no idolatry, no abuse of God's holy name, and no abuse of God's holy Sabbath; and six for keeping our relationships in the world in which we live intact: honoring parents, honoring others' lives, honoring marriage, honoring others' possessions, honoring the truth, and honoring what God gives others to live with and what he gives us to live with. Some dismiss these words as being part of the old covenant, something that is no longer valid for Christians under the new covenant. But Jesus himself on one occasion after another validated the words of the Ten Commandments. "If you wish to enter into life," he says, "keep the commandments," and then he proceeds to list five of the Ten Commandments and includes another from Leviticus (Matt 19:17–19). During the Sermon on

15 You shall not steal.

16 You shall not bear false witness against your neighbor.

17 You shall not covet your neighbor's house; you shall not covet your neighbor's wife, or male or female slave, or ox, or donkey, or anything that belongs to your neighbor.

18 When all the people witnessed the thunder and lightning, the sound of the trumpet, and the mountain smoking, they were afraid *a* and trembled and stood at a distance, [19]and said to Moses, "You speak to us, and we will listen; but do not let God speak to us, or we will die." [20]Moses said to the people, "Do not be afraid; for God has come only to test you and to put the fear of him upon you so that you do not sin." [21]Then the people stood at a distance, while Moses drew near to the thick darkness where God was.

The Law concerning the Altar

22 The LORD said to Moses: Thus you shall say to the Israelites: "You have seen for yourselves that I spoke with you from heaven. [23]You shall not make gods of silver alongside me, nor shall you make for yourselves gods of gold. [24]You need make for me only an altar of earth and sacrifice on it your burnt offerings and your offerings of well-being, your sheep and your oxen; in every place where I cause my name to be remembered I will come to you and bless you. [25]But if you make for me an altar of stone, do not build it of hewn stones; for if you use a chisel upon it you profane it. [26]You shall not go up by steps to my altar, so that your nakedness may not be exposed on it."

The Law concerning Slaves

21 These are the ordinances that you shall set before them:

2 When you buy a male Hebrew slave, he shall serve six years, but in the seventh he shall go out a free person, without debt. [3]If he comes in single, he shall go out single; if he comes in married, then his wife shall go out with him. [4]If his master gives him a wife and she bears him sons or daughters, the wife and her children shall be her master's and he shall go out alone. [5]But if the slave declares, "I love my master, my wife, and my children; I will not go out a free person," [6]then his master shall bring him before God. *b* He shall be brought to the door or the doorpost; and his master shall pierce his ear with an awl; and he shall serve him for life.

7 When a man sells his daughter as a slave, she shall not go out as the male slaves do. [8]If she does not please her master, who designated her for himself, then he shall let her be redeemed; he shall have no right to sell her to a foreign people, since he has dealt unfairly with her. [9]If he designates her for his son, he shall deal with her as with a daughter. [10]If he takes another wife to himself, he shall not diminish the food, clothing, or marital rights of the first wife. *c* [11]And if he does not do these three things for her, she shall go out without debt, without payment of money.

The Law concerning Violence

12 Whoever strikes a person mortally shall be put to death. [13]If it was not premeditated, but came about by an act of God, then I will

a Sam Gk Syr Vg: MT *they saw*   *b* Or *to the judges*
c Heb *of her*

---

the Mount he declares, "Until heaven and earth pass away, not one letter, not one stroke of a letter, will pass from the law until all is accomplished. Therefore, whoever breaks one of the least of these commandments, and teaches others to do the same, will be called least in the kingdom of heaven; but whoever does them and teaches them will be called great in the kingdom of heaven" (Matt 5:18–19). Paul points out that "whatever was written in former days was written for our instruction, so that by

steadfastness and by the encouragement of the scriptures we might have hope" (Rom 15:4). In our following after Jesus there is still a place for the Ten Commandments. One who ignores the Ten Commandments truncates the Christian life. We must view them, however, as Christ views them—as an invitation to a greater whole, not wooden rules locked into a legal document of the holy life.

20:5 WORSHIP—*See* Spiritual Disciplines Index.

appoint for you a place to which the killer may flee. [14]But if someone willfully attacks and kills another by treachery, you shall take the killer from my altar for execution.

15 Whoever strikes father or mother shall be put to death.

16 Whoever kidnaps a person, whether that person has been sold or is still held in possession, shall be put to death.

17 Whoever curses father or mother shall be put to death.

18 When individuals quarrel and one strikes the other with a stone or fist so that the injured party, though not dead, is confined to bed, [19]but recovers and walks around outside with the help of a staff, then the assailant shall be free of liability, except to pay for the loss of time, and to arrange for full recovery.

20 When a slaveowner strikes a male or female slave with a rod and the slave dies immediately, the owner shall be punished. [21]But if the slave survives a day or two, there is no punishment; for the slave is the owner's property.

22 When people who are fighting injure a pregnant woman so that there is a miscarriage, and yet no further harm follows, the one responsible shall be fined what the woman's husband demands, paying as much as the judges determine. [23]If any harm follows, then you shall give life for life, [24]eye for eye, tooth for tooth, hand for hand, foot for foot, [25]burn for burn, wound for wound, stripe for stripe.

26 When a slaveowner strikes the eye of a male or female slave, destroying it, the owner shall let the slave go, a free person, to compensate for the eye. [27]If the owner knocks out a tooth of a male or female slave, the slave shall be let go, a free person, to compensate for the tooth.

Laws concerning Property

28 When an ox gores a man or a woman to death, the ox shall be stoned, and its flesh shall not be eaten; but the owner of the ox shall not be liable. [29]If the ox has been accustomed to gore in the past, and its owner has been warned but has not restrained it, and it kills a man or a woman, the ox shall be stoned, and its owner also shall be put to death. [30]If a ransom is imposed on the owner, then the owner shall pay whatever is imposed for the redemption of the victim's life. [31]If it gores a boy or a girl, the owner shall be dealt with according to this same rule. [32]If the ox gores a male or female slave, the owner shall pay to the slaveowner thirty shekels of silver, and the ox shall be stoned.

33 If someone leaves a pit open, or digs a pit and does not cover it, and an ox or a donkey falls into it, [34]the owner of the pit shall make restitution, giving money to its owner, but keeping the dead animal.

35 If someone's ox hurts the ox of another, so that it dies, then they shall sell the live ox and divide the price of it; and the dead animal they shall also divide. [36]But if it was known that the ox was accustomed to gore in the past, and its owner has not restrained it, the owner shall restore ox for ox, but keep the dead animal.

Laws of Restitution

22 [a] When someone steals an ox or a sheep, and slaughters it or sells it, the thief shall pay five oxen for an ox, and four sheep for a sheep. [b] The thief shall make restitution, but if unable to do so, shall be sold for the theft. [4]When the animal, whether ox or donkey or sheep, is found alive in the thief's possession, the thief shall pay double.

2 [c]If a thief is found breaking in, and is beaten to death, no bloodguilt is incurred; [3]but if it happens after sunrise, bloodguilt is incurred.

5 When someone causes a field or vineyard to be grazed over, or lets livestock loose to graze in someone else's field, restitution shall be made from the best in the owner's field or vineyard.

6 When fire breaks out and catches in thorns so that the stacked grain or the standing grain or the field is consumed, the one who started the fire shall make full restitution.

7 When someone delivers to a neighbor money or goods for safekeeping, and they are stolen from the neighbor's house, then

a Ch 21.37 in Heb   b Verses 2, 3, and 4 rearranged thus: 3b, 4, 2, 3a   c Ch 22.1 in Heb the thief, if caught, shall pay double. 8If the thief is not caught, the owner of the house shall be brought before God, *a* to determine whether or not the owner had laid hands on the neighbor's goods.

9 In any case of disputed ownership involving ox, donkey, sheep, clothing, or any other loss, of which one party says, "This is mine," the case of both parties shall come before God; *a* the one whom God condemns *b* shall pay double to the other.

10 When someone delivers to another a donkey, ox, sheep, or any other animal for safekeeping, and it dies or is injured or is carried off, without anyone seeing it, 11an oath before the LORD shall decide between the two of them that the one has not laid hands on the property of the other; the owner shall accept the oath, and no restitution shall be made. 12But if it was stolen, restitution shall be made to its owner. 13If it was mangled by beasts, let it be brought as evidence; restitution shall not be made for the mangled remains.

14 When someone borrows an animal from another and it is injured or dies, the owner not being present, full restitution shall be made. 15If the owner was present, there shall be no restitution; if it was hired, only the hiring fee is due.

Social and Religious Laws

16 When a man seduces a virgin who is not engaged to be married, and lies with her, he shall give the bride-price for her and make her his wife. 17But if her father refuses to give her to him, he shall pay an amount equal to the bride-price for virgins.

18 You shall not permit a female sorcerer to live.

19 Whoever lies with an animal shall be put to death.

20 Whoever sacrifices to any god, other than the LORD alone, shall be devoted to destruction.

21 You shall not wrong or oppress a resident alien, for you were aliens in the land of Egypt. 22You shall not abuse any widow or orphan. 23If you do abuse them, when they cry out to me, I will surely heed their cry; 24my wrath will burn, and I will kill you with the sword, and your wives shall become widows and your children orphans.

25 If you lend money to my people, to the poor among you, you shall not deal with them as a creditor; you shall not exact interest from them. 26If you take your neighbor's cloak in pawn, you shall restore it before the sun goes down; 27for it may be your neighbor's only clothing to use as cover; in what else shall that person sleep? And if your neighbor cries out to me, I will listen, for I am compassionate.

28 You shall not revile God, or curse a leader of your people.

29 You shall not delay to make offerings from the fullness of your harvest and from the outflow of your presses. *c*

The firstborn of your sons you shall give to me. 30You shall do the same with your oxen and with your sheep: seven days it shall remain with its mother; on the eighth day you shall give it to me.

31 You shall be people consecrated to me; therefore you shall not eat any meat that is mangled by beasts in the field; you shall throw it to the dogs.

Justice for All

23 You shall not spread a false report. You shall not join hands with the wicked to act as a malicious witness. 2You shall not follow a majority in wrongdoing; when you bear witness in a lawsuit, you shall not side with the majority so as to pervert justice; 3nor shall you be partial to the poor in a lawsuit.

4 When you come upon your enemy's ox or donkey going astray, you shall bring it back.

5 When you see the donkey of one who hates you lying under its burden and you would hold back from setting it free, you must help to set it free. *c*

6 You shall not pervert the justice due to your poor in their lawsuits. 7Keep far from a false charge, and do not kill the innocent and those in the right, for I will not acquit the guilty. 8You shall take no bribe, for a bribe

a Or *before the judges*   *b* Or *the judges condemn*
c Meaning of Heb uncertain

blinds the officials, and subverts the cause of those who are in the right.

9 You shall not oppress a resident alien; you know the heart of an alien, for you were aliens in the land of Egypt.

Sabbatical Year and Sabbath

10 For six years you shall sow your land and gather in its yield; [11]but the seventh year you shall let it rest and lie fallow, so that the poor of your people may eat; and what they leave the wild animals may eat. You shall do the same with your vineyard, and with your olive orchard.

12 Six days you shall do your work, but on the seventh day you shall rest, so that your ox and your donkey may have relief, and your homeborn slave and the resident alien may be refreshed. [13]Be attentive to all that I have said to you. Do not invoke the names of other gods; do not let them be heard on your lips.

The Annual Festivals

14 Three times in the year you shall hold a festival for me. [15]You shall observe the festival of unleavened bread; as I commanded you, you shall eat unleavened bread for seven days at the appointed time in the month of Abib, for in it you came out of Egypt.

No one shall appear before me empty-handed.

16 You shall observe the festival of harvest, of the first fruits of your labor, of what you sow in the field. You shall observe the festival of ingathering at the end of the year, when you gather in from the field the fruit of your labor. [17]Three times in the year all your males shall appear before the Lord God.

18 You shall not offer the blood of my sacrifice with anything leavened, or let the fat of my festival remain until the morning.

19 The choicest of the first fruits of your

ground you shall bring into the house of the Lord your God.

You shall not boil a kid in its mother's milk.

The Conquest of Canaan Promised

20 I am going to send an angel in front of you, to guard you on the way and to bring you to the place that I have prepared. [21]Be attentive to him and listen to his voice; do not rebel against him, for he will not pardon your transgression; for my name is in him.

22 But if you listen attentively to his voice and do all that I say, then I will be an enemy to your enemies and a foe to your foes.

23 When my angel goes in front of you, and brings you to the Amorites, the Hittites, the Perizzites, the Canaanites, the Hivites, and the Jebusites, and I blot them out, [24]you shall not bow down to their gods, or worship them, or follow their practices, but you shall utterly demolish them and break their pillars in pieces. [25]You shall worship the Lord your God, and I[a] will bless your bread and your water; and I will take sickness away from among you. [26]No one shall miscarry or be barren in your land; I will fulfill the number of your days. [27]I will send my terror in front of you, and will throw into confusion all the people against whom you shall come, and I will make all your enemies turn their backs to you. [28]And I will send the pestilence[b] in front of you, which shall drive out the Hivites, the Canaanites, and the Hittites from before you. [29]I will not drive them out from before you in one year, or the land would become desolate and the wild animals would multiply against you. [30]Little by little I will drive them out from before you, until you have increased and possess the land. [31]I will set your borders from the Red Sea[c] to the sea of the Phi-

a Gk Vg: Heb *he*   b Or *hornets*: Meaning of Heb uncertain   c Or *Sea of Reeds*

Responding

23:25 WORSHIP. God promises to provide the Israelites with abundant food, pure water, and bodily health when they worship him, needs that are purely physical. But Jesus told the Samaritan woman that "God is spirit, and those who worship him must worship in spirit and truth" (John 4:24). Examine the reasons why you worship God and the spirit in which you worship. Are they at odds with each other? If so, what actions could you take to bring them into harmony? *See also* Spiritual Disciplines Index.

listines, and from the wilderness to the Euphrates; for I will hand over to you the inhabitants of the land, and you shall drive them out before you. 32You shall make no covenant with them and their gods. 33They shall not live in your land, or they will make you sin against me; for if you worship their gods, it will surely be a snare to you.

The Blood of the Covenant

24 Then he said to Moses, "Come up to the LORD, you and Aaron, Nadab, and Abihu, and seventy of the elders of Israel, and worship at a distance. 2Moses alone shall come near the LORD; but the others shall not come near, and the people shall not come up with him."

3 Moses came and told the people all the words of the LORD and all the ordinances; and all the people answered with one voice, and said, "All the words that the LORD has spoken we will do." 4And Moses wrote down all the words of the LORD. He rose early in the morning, and built an altar at the foot of the mountain, and set up twelve pillars, corresponding to the twelve tribes of Israel. 5He sent young men of the people of Israel, who offered burnt offerings and sacrificed oxen as offerings of well-being to the LORD. 6Moses took half of the blood and put it in basins, and half of the blood he dashed against the altar. 7Then he took the book of the covenant, and read it in the hearing of the people; and they said, "All that the LORD has spoken we will do, and we will be obedient." 8Moses took the blood and dashed it on the people, and said, "See the blood of the covenant that the LORD has made with you in accordance with all these words."

On the Mountain with God

9 Then Moses and Aaron, Nadab, and Abihu, and seventy of the elders of Israel went up, 10and they saw the God of Israel. Under his feet there was something like a pavement of sapphire stone, like the very heaven for clearness. 11God*a* did not lay his hand on the chief men of the people of Israel; also they beheld God, and they ate and drank.

12 The LORD said to Moses, "Come up to me on the mountain, and wait there; and I will give you the tablets of stone, with the law and the commandment, which I have written for their instruction." 13So Moses set out with his assistant Joshua, and Moses went up into the mountain of God. 14To the elders he had said, "Wait here for us, until we come to you again; for Aaron and Hur are with you; whoever has a dispute may go to them."

15 Then Moses went up on the mountain, and the cloud covered the mountain. 16The glory of the LORD settled on Mount Sinai, and the cloud covered it for six days; on the seventh day he called to Moses out of the cloud. 17Now the appearance of the glory of the LORD was like a devouring fire on the top of the mountain in the sight of the people of Israel. 18Moses entered the cloud, and went up on the mountain. Moses was on the mountain for forty days and forty nights.

Offerings for the Tabernacle

25 The LORD said to Moses: 2Tell the Israelites to take for me an offering; from all whose hearts prompt them to give you shall receive the offering for me. 3This is the offering that you shall receive from them: gold, silver, and bronze, 4blue, purple, and crimson yarns and fine linen, goats' hair, 5tanned rams' skins, fine leather, *b* acacia wood, 6oil for the lamps, spices for the anointing oil and for the fragrant incense, 7onyx stones and gems to be set in the ephod and for the breastpiece. 8And have them make me a sanctuary, so that I may dwell among them. 9In accordance with all that I show you concerning the pattern of the tabernacle and of all its furniture, so you shall make it.

The Ark of the Covenant

10 They shall make an ark of acacia wood; it shall be two and a half cubits long, a cubit and a half wide, and a cubit and a half high. 11You shall overlay it with pure gold, inside and outside you shall overlay it, and you shall make a molding of gold upon it all around. 12You shall cast four rings of gold for it and put them on its four feet, two rings on the one side of it, and two rings on the other side.

a Heb *He*   *b* Meaning of Heb uncertain

¹³You shall make poles of acacia wood, and overlay them with gold. ¹⁴And you shall put the poles into the rings on the sides of the ark, by which to carry the ark. ¹⁵The poles shall remain in the rings of the ark; they shall not be taken from it. ¹⁶You shall put into the ark the covenant*a* that I shall give you.

17 Then you shall make a mercy seat*b* of pure gold; two cubits and a half shall be its length, and a cubit and a half its width. ¹⁸You shall make two cherubim of gold; you shall make them of hammered work, at the two ends of the mercy seat.*c* ¹⁹Make one cherub at the one end, and one cherub at the other; of one piece with the mercy seat*c* you shall make the cherubim at its two ends. ²⁰The cherubim shall spread out their wings above, overshadowing the mercy seat*c* with their wings. They shall face one to another; the faces of the cherubim shall be turned toward the mercy seat.*c* ²¹You shall put the mercy seat*c* on the top of the ark; and in the ark you shall put the covenant*a* that I shall give you. ²²There I will meet with you, and from above the mercy seat,*c* from between the two cherubim that are on the ark of the covenant,*a* I will deliver to you all my commands for the Israelites.

The Table for the Bread of the Presence

23 You shall make a table of acacia wood, two cubits long, one cubit wide, and a cubit and a half high. ²⁴You shall overlay it with pure gold, and make a molding of gold around it. ²⁵You shall make around it a rim a handbreadth wide, and a molding of gold around the rim. ²⁶You shall make for it four rings of gold, and fasten the rings to the four corners at its four legs. ²⁷The rings that hold the poles used for carrying the table shall be close to the rim. ²⁸You shall make the poles of acacia wood, and overlay them with gold, and the table shall be carried with these. ²⁹You shall make its plates and dishes for incense, and its flagons and bowls with which to pour drink offerings; you shall make them of pure gold. ³⁰And you shall set the bread of the Presence on the table before me always.

The Lampstand

31 You shall make a lampstand of pure gold. The base and the shaft of the lamp-

stand shall be made of hammered work; its cups, its calyxes, and its petals shall be of one piece with it; ³²and there shall be six branches going out of its sides, three branches of the lampstand out of one side of it and three branches of the lampstand out of the other side of it; ³³three cups shaped like almond blossoms, each with calyx and petals, on one branch, and three cups shaped like almond blossoms, each with calyx and petals, on the other branch—so for the six branches going out of the lampstand. ³⁴On the lampstand itself there shall be four cups shaped like almond blossoms, each with its calyxes and petals. ³⁵There shall be a calyx of one piece with it under the first pair of branches, a calyx of one piece with it under the next pair of branches, and a calyx of one piece with it under the last pair of branches—so for the six branches that go out of the lampstand. ³⁶Their calyxes and their branches shall be of one piece with it, the whole of it one hammered piece of pure gold. ³⁷You shall make the seven lamps for it; and the lamps shall be set up so as to give light on the space in front of it. ³⁸Its snuffers and trays shall be of pure gold. ³⁹It, and all these utensils, shall be made from a talent of pure gold. ⁴⁰And see that you make them according to the pattern for them, which is being shown you on the mountain.

The Tabernacle

26 Moreover you shall make the tabernacle with ten curtains of fine twisted linen, and blue, purple, and crimson yarns; you shall make them with cherubim skillfully worked into them. ²The length of each curtain shall be twenty-eight cubits, and the width of each curtain four cubits; all the curtains shall be of the same size. ³Five curtains shall be joined to one another; and the other five curtains shall be joined to one another. ⁴You shall make loops of blue on the edge of the outermost curtain in the first set; and likewise you shall make loops on the edge of the outermost curtain in the second set. ⁵You shall make fifty loops on the one

a Or *treaty*, or *testimony*; Heb *eduth*   *b* Or *a cover*
c Or *the cover*

curtain, and you shall make fifty loops on the edge of the curtain that is in the second set; the loops shall be opposite one another. 6You shall make fifty clasps of gold, and join the curtains to one another with the clasps, so that the tabernacle may be one whole.

7 You shall also make curtains of goats' hair for a tent over the tabernacle; you shall make eleven curtains. 8The length of each curtain shall be thirty cubits, and the width of each curtain four cubits; the eleven curtains shall be of the same size. 9You shall join five curtains by themselves, and six curtains by themselves, and the sixth curtain you shall double over at the front of the tent. 10You shall make fifty loops on the edge of the curtain that is outermost in one set, and fifty loops on the edge of the curtain that is outermost in the second set.

11 You shall make fifty clasps of bronze, and put the clasps into the loops, and join the tent together, so that it may be one whole. 12The part that remains of the curtains of the tent, the half curtain that remains, shall hang over the back of the tabernacle. 13The cubit on the one side, and the cubit on the other side, of what remains in the length of the curtains of the tent, shall hang over the sides of the tabernacle, on this side and that side, to cover it. 14You shall make for the tent a covering of tanned rams' skins and an outer covering of fine leather.a

The Framework

15 You shall make upright frames of acacia wood for the tabernacle. 16Ten cubits shall be the length of a frame, and a cubit and a half the width of each frame. 17There shall be two pegs in each frame to fit the frames together; you shall make these for all the frames of the tabernacle. 18You shall make the frames for the tabernacle: twenty frames for the south side; 19and you shall make forty bases of silver under the twenty frames, two bases under the first frame for its two pegs, and two bases under the next frame for its two pegs; 20and for the second side of the tabernacle, on the north side twenty frames, 21and their forty bases of silver, two bases under the first frame, and two bases under the next frame; 22and for the rear of the tabernacle

westward you shall make six frames. 23You shall make two frames for corners of the tabernacle in the rear; 24they shall be separate beneath, but joined at the top, at the first ring; it shall be the same with both of them; they shall form the two corners. 25And so there shall be eight frames, with their bases of silver, sixteen bases; two bases under the first frame, and two bases under the next frame.

26 You shall make bars of acacia wood, five for the frames of the one side of the tabernacle, 27and five bars for the frames of the other side of the tabernacle, and five bars for the frames of the side of the tabernacle at the rear westward. 28The middle bar, halfway up the frames, shall pass through from end to end. 29You shall overlay the frames with gold, and shall make their rings of gold to hold the bars; and you shall overlay the bars with gold. 30Then you shall erect the tabernacle according to the plan for it that you were shown on the mountain.

The Curtain

31 You shall make a curtain of blue, purple, and crimson yarns, and of fine twisted linen; it shall be made with cherubim skillfully worked into it. 32You shall hang it on four pillars of acacia overlaid with gold, which have hooks of gold and rest on four bases of silver. 33You shall hang the curtain under the clasps, and bring the ark of the covenantb in there, within the curtain; and the curtain shall separate for you the holy place from the most holy. 34You shall put the mercy seatc on the ark of the covenantd in the most holy place. 35You shall set the table outside the curtain, and the lampstand on the south side of the tabernacle opposite the table; and you shall put the table on the north side.

36 You shall make a screen for the entrance of the tent, of blue, purple, and crimson yarns, and of fine twisted linen, embroidered with needlework. 37You shall make for the screen five pillars of acacia, and overlay them with gold; their hooks shall be of gold, and you shall cast five bases of bronze for them.

a Meaning of Heb uncertain   b Or treaty, or testimony; Heb eduth   c Or the cover
d Or treaty, or testimony; Heb eduth

The Altar of Burnt Offering

27 You shall make the altar of acacia wood, five cubits long and five cubits wide; the altar shall be square, and it shall be three cubits high. ²You shall make horns for it on its four corners; its horns shall be of one piece with it, and you shall overlay it with bronze. ³You shall make pots for it to receive its ashes, and shovels and basins and forks and firepans; you shall make all its utensils of bronze. ⁴You shall also make for it a grating, a network of bronze; and on the net you shall make four bronze rings at its four corners. ⁵You shall set it under the ledge of the altar so that the net shall extend halfway down the altar. ⁶You shall make poles for the altar, poles of acacia wood, and overlay them with bronze; ⁷the poles shall be put through the rings, so that the poles shall be on the two sides of the altar when it is carried. ⁸You shall make it hollow, with boards. They shall be made just as you were shown on the mountain.

The Court and Its Hangings

9 You shall make the court of the tabernacle. On the south side the court shall have hangings of fine twisted linen one hundred cubits long for that side; ¹⁰its twenty pillars and their twenty bases shall be of bronze, but the hooks of the pillars and their bands shall be of silver. ¹¹Likewise for its length on the north side there shall be hangings one hundred cubits long, their pillars twenty and their bases twenty, of bronze, but the hooks of the pillars and their bands shall be of silver. ¹²For the width of the court on the west side there shall be fifty cubits of hangings, with ten pillars and ten bases. ¹³The width of the court on the front to the east shall be fifty cubits. ¹⁴There shall be fifteen cubits of hangings on the one side, with three pillars and three bases. ¹⁵There shall be fifteen cubits of hangings on the other side, with three pillars and three bases. ¹⁶For the gate of the court there shall be a screen twenty cubits long, of blue, purple, and crimson yarns, and of fine twisted linen, embroidered with needlework; it shall have four pillars and with them four bases. ¹⁷All the pillars around the court shall be banded with silver; their hooks shall be of silver, and their bases of bronze. ¹⁸The length of the court shall be one hundred cubits, the width fifty, and the height five cubits, with hangings of fine twisted linen and bases of bronze. ¹⁹All the utensils of the tabernacle for every use, and all its pegs and all the pegs of the court, shall be of bronze.

The Oil for the Lamp

20 You shall further command the Israelites to bring you pure oil of beaten olives for the light, so that a lamp may be set up to burn regularly. ²¹In the tent of meeting, outside the curtain that is before the covenant,ᵃ Aaron and his sons shall tend it from evening to morning before the LORD. It shall be a perpetual ordinance to be observed throughout their generations by the Israelites.

Vestments for the Priesthood

28 Then bring near to you your brother Aaron, and his sons with him, from among the Israelites, to serve me as priests—Aaron and Aaron's sons, Nadab and Abihu, Eleazar and Ithamar. ²You shall make sacred vestments for the glorious adornment of your brother Aaron. ³And you shall speak to all who have ability, whom I have endowed with skill, that they make Aaron's vestments to consecrate him for my priesthood. ⁴These are the vestments that they shall make: a breastpiece, an ephod, a robe, a checkered tunic, a turban, and a sash. When they make these sacred vestments for your brother Aaron and his sons to serve me as priests, ⁵they shall use gold, blue, purple, and crimson yarns, and fine linen.

The Ephod

6 They shall make the ephod of gold, of blue, purple, and crimson yarns, and of fine twisted linen, skillfully worked. ⁷It shall have two shoulder-pieces attached to its two edges, so that it may be joined together. ⁸The decorated band on it shall be of the same workmanship and materials, of gold, of blue, purple, and crimson yarns, and of fine twisted linen. ⁹You shall take two onyx stones, and engrave on them the names of the sons of

---

a Or *treaty*, or *testimony*; Heb *eduth*

Israel, [10]six of their names on the one stone, and the names of the remaining six on the other stone, in the order of their birth. [11]As a gem-cutter engraves signets, so you shall engrave the two stones with the names of the sons of Israel; you shall mount them in settings of gold filigree. [12]You shall set the two stones on the shoulder-pieces of the ephod, as stones of remembrance for the sons of Israel; and Aaron shall bear their names before the LORD on his two shoulders for remembrance. [13]You shall make settings of gold filigree, [14]and two chains of pure gold, twisted like cords; and you shall attach the corded chains to the settings.

The Breastplate

15 You shall make a breastpiece of judgment, in skilled work; you shall make it in the style of the ephod; of gold, of blue and purple and crimson yarns, and of fine twisted linen you shall make it. [16]It shall be square and doubled, a span in length and a span in width. [17]You shall set in it four rows of stones. A row of carnelian,[a] chrysolite, and emerald shall be the first row; [18]and the second row a turquoise, a sapphire,[b] and a moonstone; [19]and the third row a jacinth, an agate, and an amethyst; [20]and the fourth row a beryl, an onyx, and a jasper; they shall be set in gold filigree. [21]There shall be twelve stones with names corresponding to the names of the sons of Israel; they shall be like signets, each engraved with its name, for the twelve tribes. [22]You shall make for the breastpiece chains of pure gold, twisted like cords; [23]and you shall make for the breastpiece two rings of gold, and put the two rings on the two edges of the breastpiece. [24]You shall put the two cords of gold in the two rings at the edges of the breastpiece; [25]the two ends of the two cords you shall attach to the two settings, and so attach it in front to the shoulder-pieces of the ephod. [26]You shall make two rings of gold, and put them at the two ends of the breastpiece, on its inside edge next to the ephod. [27]You shall make two rings of gold, and attach them in front to the lower part of the two shoulder-pieces of the ephod, at its joining above the decorated band of the ephod. [28]The breastpiece shall be bound by its rings to the rings of the ephod with a blue cord, so that it may lie on the decorated band of the ephod, and so that the breastpiece shall not come loose from the ephod. [29]So Aaron shall bear the names of the sons of Israel in the breastpiece of judgment on his heart when he goes into the holy place, for a continual remembrance before the LORD. [30]In the breastpiece of judgment you shall put the Urim and the Thummim, and they shall be on Aaron's heart when he goes in before the LORD; thus Aaron shall bear the judgment of the Israelites on his heart before the LORD continually.

Other Priestly Vestments

31 You shall make the robe of the ephod all of blue. [32]It shall have an opening for the head in the middle of it, with a woven binding around the opening, like the opening in a coat of mail,[c] so that it may not be torn. [33]On its lower hem you shall make pomegranates of blue, purple, and crimson yarns, all around the lower hem, with bells of gold between them all around— [34]a golden bell and a pomegranate alternating all around the lower hem of the robe. [35]Aaron shall wear it when he ministers, and its sound shall be heard when he goes into the holy place before the LORD, and when he comes out, so that he may not die.

36 You shall make a rosette of pure gold, and engrave on it, like the engraving of a signet, "Holy to the LORD." [37]You shall fasten it on the turban with a blue cord; it shall be on the front of the turban. [38]It shall be on Aaron's forehead, and Aaron shall take on himself any guilt incurred in the holy offering that the Israelites consecrate as their sacred donations; it shall always be on his forehead, in order that they may find favor before the LORD.

39 You shall make the checkered tunic of fine linen, and you shall make a turban of fine linen, and you shall make a sash embroidered with needlework.

40 For Aaron's sons you shall make tunics and sashes and headdresses; you shall make them for their glorious adornment. [41]You

a The identity of several of these stones is uncertain   b Or *lapis lazuli*   c Meaning of Heb uncertain

shall put them on your brother Aaron, and on his sons with him, and shall anoint them and ordain them and consecrate them, so that they may serve me as priests. 42You shall make for them linen undergarments to cover their naked flesh; they shall reach from the hips to the thighs; 43Aaron and his sons shall wear them when they go into the tent of meeting, or when they come near the altar to minister in the holy place; or they will bring guilt on themselves and die. This shall be a perpetual ordinance for him and for his descendants after him.

The Ordination of the Priests

29 Now this is what you shall do to them to consecrate them, so that they may serve me as priests. Take one young bull and two rams without blemish, 2and unleavened bread, unleavened cakes mixed with oil, and unleavened wafers spread with oil. You shall make them of choice wheat flour. 3You shall put them in one basket and bring them in the basket, and bring the bull and the two rams. 4You shall bring Aaron and his sons to the entrance of the tent of meeting, and wash them with water. 5Then you shall take the vestments, and put on Aaron the tunic and the robe of the ephod, and the ephod, and the breastpiece, and gird him with the decorated band of the ephod; 6and you shall set the turban on his head, and put the holy diadem on the turban. 7You shall take the anointing oil, and pour it on his head and anoint him. 8Then you shall bring his sons, and put tunics on them, 9and you shall gird them with sashes a and tie headdresses on them; and the priesthood shall be theirs by a perpetual ordinance. You shall then ordain Aaron and his sons.

10 You shall bring the bull in front of the tent of meeting. Aaron and his sons shall lay their hands on the head of the bull, 11and you shall slaughter the bull before the LORD, at the entrance of the tent of meeting, 12and shall take some of the blood of the bull and put it on the horns of the altar with your finger, and all the rest of the blood you shall pour out at the base of the altar. 13You shall take all the fat that covers the entrails, and the appendage of the liver, and the two kidneys

with the fat that is on them, and turn them into smoke on the altar. 14But the flesh of the bull, and its skin, and its dung, you shall burn with fire outside the camp; it is a sin offering.

15 Then you shall take one of the rams, and Aaron and his sons shall lay their hands on the head of the ram, 16and you shall slaughter the ram, and shall take its blood and dash it against all sides of the altar. 17Then you shall cut the ram into its parts, and wash its entrails and its legs, and put them with its parts and its head, 18and turn the whole ram into smoke on the altar; it is a burnt offering to the LORD; it is a pleasing odor, an offering by fire to the LORD.

19 You shall take the other ram; and Aaron and his sons shall lay their hands on the head of the ram, 20and you shall slaughter the ram, and take some of its blood and put it on the lobe of Aaron's right ear and on the lobes of the right ears of his sons, and on the thumbs of their right hands, and on the big toes of their right feet, and dash the rest of the blood against all sides of the altar. 21Then you shall take some of the blood that is on the altar, and some of the anointing oil, and sprinkle it on Aaron and his vestments and on his sons and his sons' vestments with him; then he and his vestments shall be holy, as well as his sons and his sons' vestments.

22 You shall also take the fat of the ram, the fat tail, the fat that covers the entrails, the appendage of the liver, the two kidneys with the fat that is on them, and the right thigh (for it is a ram of ordination), 23and one loaf of bread, one cake of bread made with oil, and one wafer, out of the basket of unleavened bread that is before the LORD; 24and you shall place all these on the palms of Aaron and on the palms of his sons, and raise them as an elevation offering before the LORD. 25Then you shall take them from their hands, and turn them into smoke on the altar on top of the burnt offering of pleasing odor before the LORD; it is an offering by fire to the LORD.

26 You shall take the breast of the ram of Aaron's ordination and raise it as an elevation

a Gk: Heb sashes, Aaron and his sons

offering before the Lord; and it shall be your portion. 27You shall consecrate the breast that was raised as an elevation offering and the thigh that was raised as an elevation offering from the ram of ordination, from that which belonged to Aaron and his sons. 28These things shall be a perpetual ordinance for Aaron and his sons from the Israelites, for this is an offering; and it shall be an offering by the Israelites from their sacrifice of offerings of well-being, their offering to the Lord.

29 The sacred vestments of Aaron shall be passed on to his sons after him; they shall be anointed in them and ordained in them. 30The son who is priest in his place shall wear them seven days, when he comes into the tent of meeting to minister in the holy place.

31 You shall take the ram of ordination, and boil its flesh in a holy place; 32and Aaron and his sons shall eat the flesh of the ram and the bread that is in the basket, at the entrance of the tent of meeting. 33They themselves shall eat the food by which atonement is made, to ordain and consecrate them, but no one else shall eat of them, because they are holy. 34If any of the flesh for the ordination, or of the bread, remains until the morning, then you shall burn the remainder with fire; it shall not be eaten, because it is holy.

35 Thus you shall do to Aaron and to his sons, just as I have commanded you; through seven days you shall ordain them. 36Also every day you shall offer a bull as a sin offering for atonement. Also you shall offer a sin offering for the altar, when you make atonement for it, and shall anoint it, to consecrate it. 37Seven days you shall make atonement for the altar, and consecrate it, and the altar shall be most holy; whatever touches the altar shall become holy.

The Daily Offerings

38 Now this is what you shall offer on the altar: two lambs a year old regularly each day. 39One lamb you shall offer in the morning, and the other lamb you shall offer in the evening; 40and with the first lamb one-tenth of a measure of choice flour mixed with one-fourth of a hin of beaten oil, and one-fourth of a hin of wine for a drink offering. 41And the other lamb you shall offer in the evening, and shall offer with it a grain offering and its drink offering, as in the morning, for a pleasing odor, an offering by fire to the Lord. 42It shall be a regular burnt offering throughout your generations at the entrance of the tent of meeting before the Lord, where I will meet with you, to speak to you there. 43I will meet with the Israelites there, and it shall be sanctified by my glory; 44I will consecrate the tent of meeting and the altar; Aaron also and his sons I will consecrate, to serve me as priests. 45I will dwell among the Israelites, and I will be their God. 46And they shall know that I am the Lord their God, who brought them out of the land of Egypt that I might dwell among them; I am the Lord their God.

The Altar of Incense

30 You shall make an altar on which to offer incense; you shall make it of acacia wood. 2It shall be one cubit long, and one cubit wide; it shall be square, and shall be two cubits high; its horns shall be of one piece with it. 3You shall overlay it with pure gold, its top, and its sides all around and its horns; and you shall make for it a molding of gold all around. 4And you shall make two golden rings for it; under its molding on two opposite sides of it you shall make them, and they shall hold the poles with which to carry it. 5You shall make the poles of acacia wood, and overlay them with gold. 6You shall place it in front of the curtain that is above

---

Responding
29:44—46 THE WITH-GOD LIFE. In these verses "dwell" has the sense of abiding, living among, taking up residence. How would you react if God's presence became visible in the building where you attend worship services? Next Sunday try a little experiment:

arrive at the worship service fifteen minutes early, sit quietly in the sanctuary, and pray for God's presence to be especially strong. What difference did this exercise make in your attitude during worship? See also Spiritual Disciplines Index.

the ark of the covenant, *a* in front of the mercy seat *b* that is over the covenant, *a* where I will meet with you. 7Aaron shall offer fragrant incense on it; every morning when he dresses the lamps he shall offer it, 8and when Aaron sets up the lamps in the evening, he shall offer it, a regular incense offering before the LORD throughout your generations. 9You shall not offer unholy incense on it, or a burnt offering, or a grain offering; and you shall not pour a drink offering on it. 10Once a year Aaron shall perform the rite of atonement on its horns. Throughout your generations he shall perform the atonement for it once a year with the blood of the atoning sin offering. It is most holy to the LORD.

The Half Shekel for the Sanctuary

11 The LORD spoke to Moses: 12When you take a census of the Israelites to register them, at registration all of them shall give a ransom for their lives to the LORD, so that no plague may come upon them for being registered. 13This is what each one who is registered shall give: half a shekel according to the shekel of the sanctuary (the shekel is twenty gerahs), half a shekel as an offering to the LORD. 14Each one who is registered, from twenty years old and upward, shall give the LORD's offering. 15The rich shall not give more, and the poor shall not give less, than the half shekel, when you bring this offering to the LORD to make atonement for your lives. 16You shall take the atonement money from the Israelites and shall designate it for the service of the tent of meeting; before the LORD it will be a reminder to the Israelites of the ransom given for your lives.

The Bronze Basin

17 The LORD spoke to Moses: 18You shall make a bronze basin with a bronze stand for washing. You shall put it between the tent of meeting and the altar, and you shall put water in it; 19with the water *c* Aaron and his sons shall wash their hands and their feet. 20When they go into the tent of meeting, or when they come near the altar to minister, to make an offering by fire to the LORD, they shall wash with water, so that they may not die. 21They shall wash their hands and their feet,

so that they may not die: it shall be a perpetual ordinance for them, for him and for his descendants throughout their generations.

The Anointing Oil and Incense

22 The LORD spoke to Moses: 23Take the finest spices: of liquid myrrh five hundred shekels, and of sweet-smelling cinnamon half as much, that is, two hundred fifty, and two hundred fifty of aromatic cane, 24and five hundred of cassia—measured by the sanctuary shekel—and a hin of olive oil; 25and you shall make of these a sacred anointing oil blended as by the perfumer; it shall be a holy anointing oil. 26With it you shall anoint the tent of meeting and the ark of the covenant, *b* 27and the table and all its utensils, and the lampstand and its utensils, and the altar of incense, 28and the altar of burnt offering with all its utensils, and the basin with its stand; 29you shall consecrate them, so that they may be most holy; whatever touches them will become holy. 30You shall anoint Aaron and his sons, and consecrate them, in order that they may serve me as priests. 31You shall say to the Israelites, "This shall be my holy anointing oil throughout your generations. 32It shall not be used in any ordinary anointing of the body, and you shall make no other like it in composition; it is holy, and it shall be holy to you. 33Whoever compounds any like it or whoever puts any of it on an unqualified person shall be cut off from the people."

34 The LORD said to Moses: Take sweet spices, stacte, and onycha, and galbanum, sweet spices with pure frankincense (an equal part of each), 35and make an incense blended as by the perfumer, seasoned with salt, pure and holy; 36and you shall beat some of it into powder, and put part of it before the covenant *b* in the tent of meeting where I shall meet with you; it shall be for you most holy. 37When you make incense according to this composition, you shall not make it for yourselves; it shall be regarded by you as holy to the LORD. 38Whoever makes any like it to use as perfume shall be cut off from the people.

---

a Or *treaty*, or *testimony*; Heb *eduth*   *b* Or *the cover*   *c* Heb *it*

Bezalel and Oholiab

31 The LORD spoke to Moses: [2]See, I have called by name Bezalel son of Uri son of Hur, of the tribe of Judah; [3]and I have filled him with divine spirit,[a] with ability, intelligence, and knowledge in every kind of craft, [4]to devise artistic designs, to work in gold, silver, and bronze, [5]in cutting stones for setting, and in carving wood, in every kind of craft. [6]Moreover, I have appointed with him Oholiab son of Ahisamach, of the tribe of Dan; and I have given skill to all the skillful, so that they may make all that I have commanded you: [7]the tent of meeting, and the ark of the covenant,[b] and the mercy seat[c] that is on it, and all the furnishings of the tent, [8]the table and its utensils, and the pure lampstand with all its utensils, and the altar of incense, [9]and the altar of burnt offering with all its utensils, and the basin with its stand, [10]and the finely worked vestments, the holy vestments for the priest Aaron and the vestments of his sons, for their service as priests, [11]and the anointing oil and the fra-grant incense for the holy place. They shall do just as I have commanded you.

The Sabbath Law

12 The LORD said to Moses: [13]You yourself are to speak to the Israelites: "You shall keep my sabbaths, for this is a sign between me and you throughout your generations, given in order that you may know that I, the LORD, sanctify you. [14]You shall keep the sabbath, because it is holy for you; everyone who profanes it shall be put to death; whoever does any work on it shall be cut off from among the people. [15]Six days shall work be done, but the seventh day is a sabbath of solemn rest, holy to the LORD; whoever does any work on the sabbath day shall be put to death. [16]Therefore the Israelites shall keep the sabbath, observing the sabbath throughout their generations, as a perpetual covenant. [17]It is a sign forever between me and the people of Israel that in six days the LORD made heaven

a Or *with the spirit of God*   b Or *treaty*, or *testimony*; Heb *eduth*   c Or *the cover*

31:3 *I have filled him with divine spirit, with ability, intelligence, and knowledge in every kind of craft, to devise artistic designs.* The first person the Bible mentions as being filled with the Spirit of God is an artist. Bezalel will help make the tabernacle, that forerunner of the Temple that Solomon will one day build in Jerusalem and also the first image of the coming Messiah: "The Word became flesh," John writes, "and lived [lit. tabernacled] among us" (John 1:14). Everything Bezalel and others fashion will spring from God's imagination. Only this time, humanity assists in creation, putting into three-dimensional form what is, at the beginning, only in God's mind. This is a tremendous honor and the fact that Bezalel is filled with the Spirit of God to do it immediately stresses the importance God places not only on the tabernacle, but the act of creation itself. It is a common thought that art is simply a fringe benefit of society, something that occurs when there is enough leisure time left over from the essentials to produce it. The Bible knows nothing of this sort of thinking. God's art is right in the middle of everything, not on the margins, and it is in fact what is essential to Israel's existence and identity. Without this art there is no tabernacle and therefore no presence of God among the people of Israel. Nor is the art characterized by a utilitarian drabness that might indicate that the art itself is not important. On page after page we hear about basins and altars and lampstands and tables—all of them beautiful as well as functional. There are also, as we might expect from this God, a few new wrinkles. Cherubim are made when no one knew what they looked like—which means an image is made of something in heaven. Isn't this forbidden? But how can it be if God commands the two cherubim to be created? The point is, they are not made to be worshiped. The priestly robe offers a twist as well. "On its lower hem," God stipulates, "you shall make pomegranates of blue, purple, and crimson yarns" (28:33). But there is no such thing as a blue pomegranate. So the art of the tabernacle is not only representational—the cherubim represent creatures that really exist—it is also abstract, and God has designed the place in which he will dwell to be composed of both types of art. These are not human ideas. They are divine.

and earth, and on the seventh day he rested, and was refreshed."

The Two Tablets of the Covenant

18 When God[a] finished speaking with Moses on Mount Sinai, he gave him the two tablets of the covenant,[b] tablets of stone, written with the finger of God.

The Golden Calf

32 When the people saw that Moses delayed to come down from the mountain, the people gathered around Aaron, and said to him, "Come, make gods for us, who shall go before us; as for this Moses, the man who brought us up out of the land of Egypt, we do not know what has become of him." 2Aaron said to them, "Take off the gold rings that are on the ears of your wives, your sons, and your daughters, and bring them to me." 3So all the people took off the gold rings from their ears, and brought them to Aaron. 4He took the gold from them, formed it in a mold,[c] and cast an image of a calf; and they said, "These are your gods, O Israel, who brought you up out of the land of Egypt!" 5When Aaron saw this, he built an altar before it; and Aaron made proclamation and said, "Tomorrow shall be a festival to the LORD." 6They rose early the next day, and offered burnt offerings and brought sacrifices of well-being; and the people sat down to eat and drink, and rose up to revel.

7 The LORD said to Moses, "Go down at once! Your people, whom you brought up out of the land of Egypt, have acted perversely; 8they have been quick to turn aside from the way that I commanded them; they have cast for themselves an image of a calf,

and have worshiped it and sacrificed to it, and said, 'These are your gods, O Israel, who brought you up out of the land of Egypt!' " 9The LORD said to Moses, "I have seen this people, how stiff-necked they are. 10Now let me alone, so that my wrath may burn hot against them and I may consume them; and of you I will make a great nation."

11 But Moses implored the LORD his God, and said, "O LORD, why does your wrath burn hot against your people, whom you brought out of the land of Egypt with great power and with a mighty hand? 12Why should the Egyptians say, 'It was with evil intent that he brought them out to kill them in the mountains, and to consume them from the face of the earth'? Turn from your fierce wrath; change your mind and do not bring disaster on your people. 13Remember Abraham, Isaac, and Israel, your servants, how you swore to them by your own self, saying to them, 'I will multiply your descendants like the stars of heaven, and all this land that I have promised I will give to your descendants, and they shall inherit it forever.' " 14And the LORD changed his mind about the disaster that he planned to bring on his people.

15 Then Moses turned and went down from the mountain, carrying the two tablets of the covenant[b] in his hands, tablets that were written on both sides, written on the front and on the back. 16The tablets were the work of God, and the writing was the writing of God, engraved upon the tablets. 17When Joshua heard the noise of the people as they

a Heb he   b Or treaty, or testimony; Heb eduth
c Or fashioned it with a graving tool; Meaning of Heb uncertain

---

32:11–14, 31–32 *change your mind and do not bring disaster on your people.* Yahweh seems intent on destroying the people he saved from slavery (v 10), and Moses prays desperately to Yahweh not to do so. Moses' prayer is an example of the bold and reckless praying that we also see Job, Abraham, and many of the prophets do. Indeed, we can find instances of it throughout the history of Israel and the Church. Moses goes further than anyone else, however, when he cries: "But now, if only you will forgive their sin—but if not, blot me out of the book that you have written" (v 32). Take my life for theirs, he seems to be saying, or else take me with them. The only biblical prayer that echoes the risk Moses takes is Paul's: "I could wish that I myself were accursed and cut off from Christ for the sake of my own people" (Rom 9:3). It is a powerful high-stakes prayer, an all-or-nothing fling of his own life between the wrath of God and the sin of the people.

shouted, he said to Moses, "There is a noise of war in the camp." [18]But he said,

"It is not the sound made by victors,
or the sound made by losers;
it is the sound of revelers that I hear."

[19]As soon as he came near the camp and saw the calf and the dancing, Moses' anger burned hot, and he threw the tablets from his hands and broke them at the foot of the mountain. [20]He took the calf that they had made, burned it with fire, ground it to powder, scattered it on the water, and made the Israelites drink it.

21 Moses said to Aaron, "What did this people do to you that you have brought so great a sin upon them?" [22]And Aaron said, "Do not let the anger of my lord burn hot; you know the people, that they are bent on evil. [23]They said to me, 'Make us gods, who shall go before us; as for this Moses, the man who brought us up out of the land of Egypt, we do not know what has become of him.' [24]So I said to them, 'Whoever has gold, take it off'; so they gave it to me, and I threw it into the fire, and out came this calf!"

25 When Moses saw that the people were running wild (for Aaron had let them run wild, to the derision of their enemies), [26]then Moses stood in the gate of the camp, and said, "Who is on the LORD's side? Come to me!" And all the sons of Levi gathered around him. [27]He said to them, "Thus says the LORD, the God of Israel, 'Put your sword on your side, each of you! Go back and forth from gate to gate throughout the camp, and each of you kill your brother, your friend, and your neighbor.' " [28]The sons of Levi did as Moses commanded, and about three thousand of the people fell on that day. [29]Moses said, "Today you have ordained yourselves[a] for the service of the LORD, each one at the cost of a son or a brother, and so have brought a blessing on yourselves this day."

30 On the next day Moses said to the peo-ple, "You have sinned a great sin. But now I will go up to the LORD; perhaps I can make atonement for your sin." [31]So Moses returned to the LORD and said, "Alas, this people has sinned a great sin; they have made for themselves gods of gold. [32]But now, if you will only forgive their sin—but if not, blot me out of the book that you have written." [33]But the LORD said to Moses, "Whoever has sinned against me I will blot out of my book. [34]But now go, lead the people to the place about which I have spoken to you; see, my angel shall go in front of you. Nevertheless, when the day comes for punishment, I will punish them for their sin."

35 Then the LORD sent a plague on the people, because they made the calf—the one that Aaron made.

The Command to Leave Sinai

33 The LORD said to Moses, "Go, leave this place, you and the people whom you have brought up out of the land of Egypt, and go to the land of which I swore to Abraham, Isaac, and Jacob, saying, 'To your descendants I will give it.' [2]I will send an angel before you, and I will drive out the Canaanites, the Amorites, the Hittites, the Perizzites, the Hivites, and the Jebusites. [3]Go up to a land flowing with milk and honey; but I will not go up among you, or I would consume you on the way, for you are a stiff-necked people."

4 When the people heard these harsh words, they mourned, and no one put on ornaments. [5]For the LORD had said to Moses, "Say to the Israelites, 'You are a stiff-necked people; if for a single moment I should go up among you, I would consume you. So now take off your ornaments, and I will decide what to do to you.' " [6]Therefore the Israelites

a Gk Vg Compare Tg: Heb Today ordain yourselves

32:24 *I threw it into the fire, and out came this calf!* The golden calf is what makes Moses' boldness in prayer crucial. We have just read about the Spirit of Yahweh filling Bezalel to create the tabernacle for the worship of the invisible God (31:2–11), and now we have Aaron

playing the artist as well, taking gold and creating a calf. The difference between Bezalel's art and Aaron's is that Bezalel's is meant to create a divine space in which God may be worshiped; Aaron's art is meant to be worshiped in and of itself and become a god in its own right.

stripped themselves of their ornaments, from Mount Horeb onward.

The Tent outside the Camp

7 Now Moses used to take the tent and pitch it outside the camp, far off from the camp; he called it the tent of meeting. And everyone who sought the LORD would go out to the tent of meeting, which was outside the camp. 8Whenever Moses went out to the tent, all the people would rise and stand, each of them, at the entrance of their tents and watch Moses until he had gone into the tent. 9When Moses entered the tent, the pillar of cloud would descend and stand at the entrance of the tent, and the LORD would speak with Moses. 10When all the people saw the pillar of cloud standing at the entrance of the tent, all the people would rise and bow down, all of them, at the entrance of their tent. 11Thus the LORD used to speak to Moses face to face, as one speaks to a friend. Then he would return to the camp; but his young assistant, Joshua son of Nun, would not leave the tent.

Moses' Intercession

12 Moses said to the LORD, "See, you have said to me, 'Bring up this people'; but you have not let me know whom you will send with me. Yet you have said, 'I know you by name, and you have also found favor in my sight.' 13Now if I have found favor in your sight, show me your ways, so that I may know you and find favor in your sight. Consider too that this nation is your people." 14He said, "My presence will go with you, and I will give you rest." 15And he said to him, "If your presence will not go, do not carry us up from here. 16For how shall it be known that I have found favor in your sight, I and your people, unless you go with us? In this way, we shall be distinct, I and your people, from every people on the face of the earth."

17 The LORD said to Moses, "I will do the very thing that you have asked; for you have found favor in my sight, and I know you by name." 18Moses said, "Show me your glory, I

pray." 19And he said, "I will make all my goodness pass before you, and will proclaim before you the name, 'The LORD'; a and I will be gracious to whom I will be gracious, and will show mercy on whom I will show mercy. 20But," he said, "you cannot see my face; for no one shall see me and live." 21And the LORD continued, "See, there is a place by me where you shall stand on the rock; 22and while my glory passes by I will put you in a cleft of the rock, and I will cover you with my hand until I have passed by; 23then I will take away my hand, and you shall see my back; but my face shall not be seen."

Moses Makes New Tablets

34 The LORD said to Moses, "Cut two tablets of stone like the former ones, and I will write on the tablets the words that were on the former tablets, which you broke. 2Be ready in the morning, and come up in the morning to Mount Sinai and present yourself there to me, on the top of the mountain. 3No one shall come up with you, and do not let anyone be seen throughout all the mountain; and do not let flocks or herds graze in front of that mountain." 4So Moses cut two tablets of stone like the former ones; and he rose early in the morning and went up on Mount Sinai, as the LORD had commanded him, and took in his hand the two tablets of stone. 5The LORD descended in the cloud and stood with him there, and proclaimed the name, "The LORD." a 6The LORD passed before him, and proclaimed,

"The LORD, the LORD,
a God merciful and gracious,
slow to anger,
and abounding in steadfast love and
        faithfulness,
7 keeping steadfast love for the
        thousandth generation, b
forgiving iniquity and transgression
        and sin,
yet by no means clearing the guilty,

a Heb YHWH; see note at 3.15   b Or for thousands

33:12–16 THE WITH-GOD LIFE—See Spiritual Disciplines Index.

Show me your glory

33:18 PRAYER—*See* Spiritual Disciplines Index.

but visiting the iniquity of the parents
upon the children
and the children's children,
to the third and the fourth generation."
[8]And Moses quickly bowed his head toward
the earth, and worshiped. [9]He said, "If now
I have found favor in your sight, O Lord, I
pray, let the Lord go with us. Although this is
a stiff-necked people, pardon our iniquity
and our sin, and take us for your inheritance."

The Covenant Renewed

10 He said: I hereby make a covenant. Before all your people I will perform marvels,
such as have not been performed in all the
earth or in any nation; and all the people
among whom you live shall see the work of
the LORD; for it is an awesome thing that I
will do with you.

11 Observe what I command you today.
See, I will drive out before you the Amorites,
the Canaanites, the Hittites, the Perizzites,
the Hivites, and the Jebusites. [12]Take care not
to make a covenant with the inhabitants of
the land to which you are going, or it will
become a snare among you. [13]You shall tear
down their altars, break their pillars, and cut
down their sacred poles[a] [14](for you shall worship no other god, because the LORD, whose
name is Jealous, is a jealous God). [15]You shall
not make a covenant with the inhabitants
of the land, for when they prostitute themselves to their gods and sacrifice to their gods,
someone among them will invite you, and

you will eat of the sacrifice. [16]And you will
take wives from among their daughters for
your sons, and their daughters who prostitute
themselves to their gods will make your sons
also prostitute themselves to their gods.

17 You shall not make cast idols.

18 You shall keep the festival of unleavened bread. Seven days you shall eat unleavened bread, as I commanded you, at the time
appointed in the month of Abib; for in the
month of Abib you came out from Egypt.

19 All that first opens the womb is mine,
all your male[b] livestock, the firstborn of cow
and sheep. [20]The firstborn of a donkey you
shall redeem with a lamb, or if you will not redeem it you shall break its neck. All the firstborn of your sons you shall redeem.

No one shall appear before me empty-
handed.

21 Six days you shall work, but on the seventh day you shall rest; even in plowing time
and in harvest time you shall rest. [22]You shall
observe the festival of weeks, the first fruits of
wheat harvest, and the festival of ingathering
at the turn of the year. [23]Three times in the
year all your males shall appear before the
LORD God, the God of Israel. [24]For I will cast
out nations before you, and enlarge your borders; no one shall covet your land when you
go up to appear before the LORD your God
three times in the year.

a Heb Asherim   b Gk Theodotion Vg Tg:
Meaning of Heb uncertain

34:9 *pardon our iniquity and our sin, and
take us for your inheritance.* It would be a
mistake to consider Exodus a book short on
mercy, grace, or the steadfast love of God;
there is more to Exodus than blood and
thunder and a deity wrapped in thick smoke.
A mercurial grace flashes from one end of the
great story to the other. How could Moses have
survived without the midwives' awe of God?
Who fought for the slaves and set them free?
Who stood by them at the Red Sea? Made
certain they had food and water in the desert?
Was it not God who gave them his name? His
law? His word? Whose Spirit filled their artist
Bezalel? Who filled the tabernacle with glory?
Guided them by day and by night through a

trackless wilderness? Was it not Yahweh who
forgave their sins, renewed his commitment
and covenant, and continued to lead them
despite the grotesque calf of gold? Was it not
God himself who chose to live among them,
so close he could be touched, the immortal
gracing mortality with its splendor? He chose
to be present and not distant, to show Moses
his glory, to get up close and personal as when
one speaks with a friend, to make the skin of
Moses' face blaze. Beyond all the trumpet
blasts and darkness and earthquakes and
roughness, Yahweh ultimately chose to love
and show compassion. That is Exodus.
    34:9-10, 29-35 THE WITH-GOD LIFE—*See*
Spiritual Disciplines Index.

25 You shall not offer the blood of my sacrifice with leaven, and the sacrifice of the festival of the passover shall not be left until the morning.

26 The best of the first fruits of your ground you shall bring to the house of the LORD your God.

You shall not boil a kid in its mother's milk.

27 The LORD said to Moses: Write these words; in accordance with these words I have made a covenant with you and with Israel. 28He was there with the LORD forty days and forty nights; he neither ate bread nor drank water. And he wrote on the tablets the words of the covenant, the ten commandments. a

The Shining Face of Moses

29 Moses came down from Mount Sinai. As he came down from the mountain with the two tablets of the covenant b in his hand, Moses did not know that the skin of his face shone because he had been talking with God. 30When Aaron and all the Israelites saw Moses, the skin of his face was shining, and they were afraid to come near him. 31But Moses called to them; and Aaron and all the leaders of the congregation returned to him, and Moses spoke with them. 32Afterward all the Israelites came near, and he gave them in commandment all that the LORD had spoken with him on Mount Sinai. 33When Moses had finished speaking with them, he put a veil on his face; 34but whenever Moses went in before the LORD to speak with him, he would take the veil off, until he came out; and when he came out, and told the Israelites what he had been commanded, 35the Israelites would see the face of Moses, that the skin of his face was shining; and Moses would put the veil on his face again, until he went in to speak with him.

Sabbath Regulations

35 Moses assembled all the congregation of the Israelites and said to them: These are the things that the LORD has commanded you to do:

2 Six days shall work be done, but on the seventh day you shall have a holy sabbath of solemn rest to the LORD; whoever does any work on it shall be put to death. 3You shall

kindle no fire in all your dwellings on the sabbath day.

Preparations for Making the Tabernacle

4 Moses said to all the congregation of the Israelites: This is the thing that the LORD has commanded: 5Take from among you an offering to the LORD; let whoever is of a generous heart bring the LORD's offering: gold, silver, and bronze; 6blue, purple, and crimson yarns, and fine linen; goats' hair, 7tanned rams' skins, and fine leather; c acacia wood, 8oil for the light, spices for the anointing oil and for the fragrant incense, 9and onyx stones and gems to be set in the ephod and the breastpiece.

10 All who are skillful among you shall come and make all that the LORD has commanded: the tabernacle, 11its tent and its covering, its clasps and its frames, its bars, its pillars, and its bases; 12the ark with its poles, the mercy seat, d and the curtain for the screen; 13the table with its poles and all its utensils, and the bread of the Presence; 14the lampstand also for the light, with its utensils and its lamps, and the oil for the light; 15and the altar of incense, with its poles, and the anointing oil and the fragrant incense, and the screen for the entrance, the entrance of the tabernacle; 16the altar of burnt offering, with its grating of bronze, its poles, and all its utensils, the basin with its stand; 17the hangings of the court, its pillars and its bases, and the screen for the gate of the court; 18the pegs of the tabernacle and the pegs of the court, and their cords; 19the finely worked vestments for ministering in the holy place, the holy vestments for the priest Aaron, and the vestments of his sons, for their service as priests.

Offerings for the Tabernacle

20 Then all the congregation of the Israelites withdrew from the presence of Moses. 21And they came, everyone whose heart was stirred, and everyone whose spirit was willing, and brought the LORD's offering to be used for the tent of meeting, and for all its service, and for the sacred vestments. 22So they

a Heb words   b Or treaty, or testimony; Heb eduth
c Meaning of Heb uncertain   d Or the cover

came, both men and women; all who were of a willing heart brought brooches and earrings and signet rings and pendants, all sorts of gold objects, everyone bringing an offering of gold to the LORD. 23And everyone who possessed blue or purple or crimson yarn or fine linen or goats' hair or tanned rams' skins or fine leather,*a* brought them. 24Everyone who could make an offering of silver or bronze brought it as the LORD's offering; and everyone who possessed acacia wood of any use in the work, brought it. 25All the skillful women spun with their hands, and brought what they had spun in blue and purple and crimson yarns and fine linen; 26all the women whose hearts moved them to use their skill spun the goats' hair. 27And the leaders brought onyx stones and gems to be set in the ephod and the breastpiece, 28and spices and oil for the light, and for the anointing oil, and for the fragrant incense. 29All the Israelite men and women whose hearts made them willing to bring anything for the work that the LORD had commanded by Moses to be done, brought it as a freewill offering to the LORD.

Bezalel and Oholiab

30 Then Moses said to the Israelites: See, the LORD has called by name Bezalel son of Uri son of Hur, of the tribe of Judah; 31he has filled him with divine spirit,*b* with skill, intelligence, and knowledge in every kind of craft, 32to devise artistic designs, to work in gold, silver, and bronze, 33in cutting stones for setting, and in carving wood, in every kind of craft. 34And he has inspired him to teach, both him and Oholiab son of Ahisamach, of the tribe of Dan. 35He has filled them with skill to do every kind of work done by an artisan or by a designer or by an embroiderer in blue, purple, and crimson yarns, and in fine linen, or by a weaver—by any sort of artisan or skilled designer.

36 Bezalel and Oholiab and every skillful one to whom the LORD has given skill and understanding to know how to do any work in the construction of the sanctuary shall work in accordance with all that the LORD has commanded.

2 Moses then called Bezalel and Oholiab and every skillful one to whom the LORD had given skill, everyone whose heart was stirred to come to do the work; 3and they received from Moses all the freewill offerings that the Israelites had brought for doing the work on the sanctuary. They still kept bringing him freewill offerings every morning, 4so that all the artisans who were doing every sort of task on the sanctuary came, each from the task being performed, 5and said to Moses, "The people are bringing much more than enough for doing the work that the LORD has commanded us to do." 6So Moses gave command, and word was proclaimed throughout the camp: "No man or woman is to make anything else as an offering for the sanctuary." So the people were restrained from

a Meaning of Heb uncertain   *b* Or *the spirit of God*

Responding
35:21, 29 SERVICE. Would your heart be "stirred" and your spirit "willing" to give your gold jewelry and silver flatware to your place of worship to be melted down to make a Communion set or altar pieces? When you were considering this possibility, how much resistance did you feel: none, a little, some, a lot? Bring whatever feeling of resistance you have before the Lord and humbly ask him to show you ways to overcome it. Be prepared for surprises! *See also* Spiritual Disciplines Index.

35:29 *All the Israelite men and women whose hearts made them willing.* Bezalel is filled with the Holy Spirit to work on the tabernacle. The people who contribute to its construction do it of their own free will. "And they came, everyone whose heart was stirred, and everyone whose spirit was willing" (v 21). "All who were of a willing heart brought brooches and earrings" (v 22). "All the women whose hearts moved them to use their skill spun the goats' hair" (v 26). A community builds the tabernacle, not an elite handful; a community creates a house for God. All the people contribute, not just the leaders. Everyone who has a heart for it is part of it. It is a spirituality of the many, not the few, that makes it possible for God to have a home among his people.

bringing; 7for what they had already brought was more than enough to do all the work.

Construction of the Tabernacle

8 All those with skill among the workers made the tabernacle with ten curtains; they were made of fine twisted linen, and blue, purple, and crimson yarns, with cherubim skillfully worked into them. 9The length of each curtain was twenty-eight cubits, and the width of each curtain four cubits; all the curtains were of the same size.

10 He joined five curtains to one another, and the other five curtains he joined to one another. 11He made loops of blue on the edge of the outermost curtain of the first set; likewise he made them on the edge of the outermost curtain of the second set; 12he made fifty loops on the one curtain, and he made fifty loops on the edge of the curtain that was in the second set; the loops were opposite one another. 13And he made fifty clasps of gold, and joined the curtains one to the other with clasps; so the tabernacle was one whole.

14 He also made curtains of goats' hair for a tent over the tabernacle; he made eleven curtains. 15The length of each curtain was thirty cubits, and the width of each curtain four cubits; the eleven curtains were of the same size. 16He joined five curtains by themselves, and six curtains by themselves. 17He made fifty loops on the edge of the outermost curtain of the one set, and fifty loops on the edge of the other connecting curtain. 18He made fifty clasps of bronze to join the tent together so that it might be one whole. 19And he made for the tent a covering of tanned rams' skins and an outer covering of fine leather. *a*

20 Then he made the upright frames for the tabernacle of acacia wood. 21Ten cubits was the length of a frame, and a cubit and a half the width of each frame. 22Each frame had two pegs for fitting together; he did this for all the frames of the tabernacle. 23The frames for the tabernacle he made in this way: twenty frames for the south side; 24and he made forty bases of silver under the twenty frames, two bases under the first frame for its two pegs, and two bases under the next

frame for its two pegs. 25For the second side of the tabernacle, on the north side, he made twenty frames 26and their forty bases of silver, two bases under the first frame and two bases under the next frame. 27For the rear of the tabernacle westward he made six frames. 28He made two frames for corners of the tabernacle in the rear. 29They were separate beneath, but joined at the top, at the first ring; he made two of them in this way, for the two corners. 30There were eight frames with their bases of silver: sixteen bases, under every frame two bases.

31 He made bars of acacia wood, five for the frames of the one side of the tabernacle, 32and five bars for the frames of the other side of the tabernacle, and five bars for the frames of the tabernacle at the rear westward. 33He made the middle bar to pass through from end to end halfway up the frames. 34And he overlaid the frames with gold, and made rings of gold for them to hold the bars, and overlaid the bars with gold.

35 He made the curtain of blue, purple, and crimson yarns, and fine twisted linen, with cherubim skillfully worked into it. 36For it he made four pillars of acacia, and overlaid them with gold; their hooks were of gold, and he cast for them four bases of silver. 37He also made a screen for the entrance to the tent, of blue, purple, and crimson yarns, and fine twisted linen, embroidered with needlework; 38and its five pillars with their hooks. He overlaid their capitals and their bases with gold, but their five bases were of bronze.

Making the Ark of the Covenant

37 Bezalel made the ark of acacia wood; it was two and a half cubits long, a cubit and a half wide, and a cubit and a half high. 2He overlaid it with pure gold inside and outside, and made a molding of gold around it. 3He cast for it four rings of gold for its four feet, two rings on its one side and two rings on its other side. 4He made poles of acacia wood, and overlaid them with gold, 5and put the poles into the rings on the sides of the ark, to carry the ark. 6He made a mercy

a Meaning of Heb uncertain

seat[a] of pure gold; two cubits and a half was its length, and a cubit and a half its width. [7]He made two cherubim of hammered gold; at the two ends of the mercy seat[b] he made them, [8]one cherub at the one end, and one cherub at the other end; of one piece with the mercy seat[b] he made the cherubim at its two ends. [9]The cherubim spread out their wings above, overshadowing the mercy seat[b] with their wings. They faced one another; the faces of the cherubim were turned toward the mercy seat.[b]

Making the Table for the Bread of the Presence

10 He also made the table of acacia wood, two cubits long, one cubit wide, and a cubit and a half high. [11]He overlaid it with pure gold, and made a molding of gold around it. [12]He made around it a rim a handbreadth wide, and made a molding of gold around the rim. [13]He cast for it four rings of gold, and fastened the rings to the four corners at its four legs. [14]The rings that held the poles used for carrying the table were close to the rim. [15]He made the poles of acacia wood to carry the table, and overlaid them with gold. [16]And he made the vessels of pure gold that were to be on the table, its plates and dishes for incense, and its bowls and flagons with which to pour drink offerings.

Making the Lampstand

17 He also made the lampstand of pure gold. The base and the shaft of the lampstand were made of hammered work; its cups, its calyxes, and its petals were of one piece with it. [18]There were six branches going out of its sides, three branches of the lampstand out of one side of it and three branches of the lampstand out of the other side of it; [19]three cups shaped like almond blossoms, each with calyx and petals, on one branch, and three cups shaped like almond blossoms, each with calyx and petals, on the other branch—so for the six branches going out of the lampstand. [20]On the lampstand itself there were four cups shaped like almond blossoms, each with its calyxes and petals. [21]There was a calyx of one piece with it under the first pair of branches, a calyx of one piece with it under

the next pair of branches, and a calyx of one piece with it under the last pair of branches. [22]Their calyxes and their branches were of one piece with it, the whole of it one hammered piece of pure gold. [23]He made its seven lamps and its snuffers and its trays of pure gold. [24]He made it and all its utensils of a talent of pure gold.

Making the Altar of Incense

25 He made the altar of incense of acacia wood, one cubit long, and one cubit wide; it was square, and was two cubits high; its horns were of one piece with it. [26]He overlaid it with pure gold, its top, and its sides all around, and its horns; and he made for it a molding of gold all around, [27]and made two golden rings for it under its molding, on two opposite sides of it, to hold the poles with which to carry it. [28]And he made the poles of acacia wood, and overlaid them with gold.

Making the Anointing Oil and the Incense

29 He made the holy anointing oil also, and the pure fragrant incense, blended as by the perfumer.

Making the Altar of Burnt Offering

38 He made the altar of burnt offering also of acacia wood; it was five cubits long, and five cubits wide; it was square, and three cubits high. [2]He made horns for it on its four corners; its horns were of one piece with it, and he overlaid it with bronze. [3]He made all the utensils of the altar, the pots, the shovels, the basins, the forks, and the firepans: all its utensils he made of bronze. [4]He made for the altar a grating, a network of bronze, under its ledge, extending halfway down. [5]He cast four rings on the four corners of the bronze grating to hold the poles; [6]he made the poles of acacia wood, and overlaid them with bronze. [7]And he put the poles through the rings on the sides of the altar, to carry it with them; he made it hollow, with boards.

8 He made the basin of bronze with its stand of bronze, from the mirrors of the women who served at the entrance to the tent of meeting.

a Or *a cover*   b Or *the cover*

Making the Court of the Tabernacle

9 He made the court; for the south side the hangings of the court were of fine twisted linen, one hundred cubits long; 10its twenty pillars and their twenty bases were of bronze, but the hooks of the pillars and their bands were of silver. 11For the north side there were hangings one hundred cubits long; its twenty pillars and their twenty bases were of bronze, but the hooks of the pillars and their bands were of silver. 12For the west side there were hangings fifty cubits long, with ten pillars and ten bases; the hooks of the pillars and their bands were of silver. 13And for the front to the east, fifty cubits. 14The hangings for one side of the gate were fifteen cubits, with three pillars and three bases. 15And so for the other side; on each side of the gate of the court were hangings of fifteen cubits, with three pillars and three bases. 16All the hangings around the court were of fine twisted linen. 17The bases for the pillars were of bronze, but the hooks of the pillars and their bands were of silver; the overlaying of their capitals was also of silver, and all the pillars of the court were banded with silver. 18The screen for the entrance to the court was embroidered with needlework in blue, purple, and crimson yarns and fine twisted linen. It was twenty cubits long and, along the width of it, five cubits high, corresponding to the hangings of the court. 19There were four pillars; their four bases were of bronze, their hooks of silver, and the overlaying of their capitals and their bands of silver. 20All the pegs for the tabernacle and for the court all around were of bronze.

Materials of the Tabernacle

21 These are the records of the tabernacle, the tabernacle of the covenant, *a* which were drawn up at the commandment of Moses, the work of the Levites being under the direction of Ithamar son of the priest Aaron. 22Bezalel son of Uri son of Hur, of the tribe of Judah, made all that the LORD commanded Moses; 23and with him was Oholiab son of Ahisamach, of the tribe of Dan, engraver, designer, and embroiderer in blue, purple, and crimson yarns, and in fine linen.

24 All the gold that was used for the work, in all the construction of the sanctuary, the gold from the offering, was twenty-nine talents and seven hundred thirty shekels, measured by the sanctuary shekel. 25The silver from those of the congregation who were counted was one hundred talents and one thousand seven hundred seventy-five shekels, measured by the sanctuary shekel; 26a beka a head (that is, half a shekel, measured by the sanctuary shekel), for everyone who was counted in the census, from twenty years old and upward, for six hundred three thousand, five hundred fifty men. 27The hundred talents of silver were for casting the bases of the sanctuary, and the bases of the curtain; one hundred bases for the hundred talents, a talent for a base. 28Of the thousand seven hundred seventy-five shekels he made hooks for the pillars, and overlaid their capitals and made bands for them. 29The bronze that was contributed was seventy talents, and two thousand four hundred shekels; 30with it he made the bases for the entrance of the tent of meeting, the bronze altar and the bronze grating for it and all the utensils of the altar, 31the bases all around the court, and the bases of the gate of the court, all the pegs of the tabernacle, and all the pegs around the court.

Making the Vestments for the Priesthood

39 Of the blue, purple, and crimson yarns they made finely worked vestments, for ministering in the holy place; they made the sacred vestments for Aaron; as the LORD had commanded Moses.

2 He made the ephod of gold, of blue, purple, and crimson yarns, and of fine twisted linen. 3Gold leaf was hammered out and cut into threads to work into the blue, purple, and crimson yarns and into the fine twisted linen, in skilled design. 4They made for the ephod shoulder-pieces, joined to it at its two edges. 5The decorated band on it was of the same materials and workmanship, of gold, of blue, purple, and crimson yarns, and of fine twisted linen; as the LORD had commanded Moses.

a Or *treaty*, or *testimony*; Heb *eduth*

6 The onyx stones were prepared, enclosed in settings of gold filigree and engraved like the engravings of a signet, according to the names of the sons of Israel. 7He set them on the shoulder-pieces of the ephod, to be stones of remembrance for the sons of Israel; as the LORD had commanded Moses.

8 He made the breastpiece, in skilled work, like the work of the ephod, of gold, of blue, purple, and crimson yarns, and of fine twisted linen. 9It was square; the breastpiece was made double, a span in length and a span in width when doubled. 10They set in it four rows of stones. A row of carnelian, *a* chrysolite, and emerald was the first row; 11and the second row, a turquoise, a sapphire, *b* and a moonstone; 12and the third row, a jacinth, an agate, and an amethyst; 13and the fourth row, a beryl, an onyx, and a jasper; they were enclosed in settings of gold filigree. 14There were twelve stones with names corresponding to the names of the sons of Israel; they were like signets, each engraved with its name, for the twelve tribes. 15They made on the breastpiece chains of pure gold, twisted like cords; 16and they made two settings of gold filigree and two gold rings, and put the two rings on the two edges of the breastpiece; 17and they put the two cords of gold in the two rings at the edges of the breastpiece. 18Two ends of the two cords they had attached to the two settings of filigree; in this way they attached it in front to the shoulder-pieces of the ephod. 19Then they made two rings of gold, and put them at the two ends of the breastpiece, on its inside edge next to the ephod. 20They made two rings of gold, and attached them in front to the lower part of the two shoulder-pieces of the ephod, at its joining above the decorated band of the ephod. 21They bound the breastpiece by its rings to the rings of the ephod with a blue cord, so that it should lie on the decorated band of the ephod, and that the breastpiece should not come loose from the ephod; as the LORD had commanded Moses.

22 He also made the robe of the ephod woven all of blue yarn; 23and the opening of the robe in the middle of it was like the opening in a coat of mail, *c* with a binding around the opening, so that it might not be torn. 24On the lower hem of the robe they made pomegranates of blue, purple, and crimson yarns, and of fine twisted linen. 25They also made bells of pure gold, and put the bells between the pomegranates on the lower hem of the robe all around, between the pomegranates; 26a bell and a pomegranate, a bell and a pomegranate all around on the lower hem of the robe for ministering; as the LORD had commanded Moses.

27 They also made the tunics, woven of fine linen, for Aaron and his sons, 28and the turban of fine linen, and the headdresses of fine linen, and the linen undergarments of fine twisted linen, 29and the sash of fine twisted linen, and of blue, purple, and crimson yarns, embroidered with needlework; as the LORD had commanded Moses.

30 They made the rosette of the holy diadem of pure gold, and wrote on it an inscription, like the engraving of a signet, "Holy to the LORD." 31They tied to it a blue cord, to fasten it on the turban above; as the LORD had commanded Moses.

The Work Completed

32 In this way all the work of the tabernacle of the tent of meeting was finished; the Israelites had done everything just as the LORD had commanded Moses. 33Then they brought the tabernacle to Moses, the tent and all its utensils, its hooks, its frames, its bars, its pillars, and its bases; 34the covering of tanned rams' skins and the covering of

a The identification of several of these stones is uncertain   *b* Or *lapis lazuli*   *c* Meaning of Heb uncertain

---

39:33 *Then they brought the tabernacle to Moses, the tent and all its utensils.* For thousands of years believers have puzzled about what each part of the tabernacle means in spiritual terms. The lampstand (v 37), some say, stands for the light of God; others say for the words of God, which are a lamp to our feet. The fragrant incense (v 38) stands for prayer or for God's Spirit, the crimson yarn (v 29) for the blood of the Messiah. No doubt some of the

fine leather, *a* and the curtain for the screen; [35]the ark of the covenant *b* with its poles and the mercy seat; *c* [36]the table with all its utensils, and the bread of the Presence; [37]the pure lampstand with its lamps set on it and all its utensils, and the oil for the light; [38]the golden altar, the anointing oil and the fragrant incense, and the screen for the entrance of the tent; [39]the bronze altar, and its grating of bronze, its poles, and all its utensils; the basin with its stand; [40]the hangings of the court, its pillars, and its bases, and the screen for the gate of the court, its cords, and its pegs; and all the utensils for the service of the tabernacle, for the tent of meeting; [41]the finely worked vestments for ministering in the holy place, the sacred vestments for the priest Aaron, and the vestments of his sons to serve as priests. [42]The Israelites had done all of the work just as the LORD had commanded Moses. [43]When Moses saw that they had done all the work just as the LORD had commanded, he blessed them.

The Tabernacle Erected and Its Equipment Installed

40 The LORD spoke to Moses: [2]On the first day of the first month you shall set up the tabernacle of the tent of meeting. [3]You shall put in it the ark of the covenant, *b* and you shall screen the ark with the curtain. [4]You shall bring in the table, and arrange its setting; and you shall bring in the lampstand, and set up its lamps. [5]You shall put the golden altar for incense before the ark of the covenant, *b* and set up the screen for the entrance of the tabernacle. [6]You shall set the altar of burnt offering before the entrance of the tabernacle of the tent of meeting, [7]and place the basin between the tent of meeting and the altar, and put water in it. [8]You shall set up the court all around, and hang up the screen for the gate of the court. [9]Then you shall take the anointing oil, and anoint the tabernacle and all that is in it, and consecrate it and all its furniture, so that it shall become holy. [10]You shall also anoint the altar of burnt offering and all its utensils, and consecrate the altar, so that the altar shall be most holy. [11]You shall also anoint the basin with its stand, and consecrate it. [12]Then you shall bring Aaron and his sons to the entrance of the tent of meeting, and shall wash them with water, [13]and put on Aaron the sacred vestments, and you shall anoint him and consecrate him, so that he may serve me as priest. [14]You shall bring his sons also and put tunics on them, [15]and anoint them, as you anointed their father, that they may serve me as priests: and their anointing shall admit them to a perpetual priesthood throughout all generations to come.

16 Moses did everything just as the LORD had commanded him. [17]In the first month in the second year, on the first day of the month, the tabernacle was set up. [18]Moses set up the tabernacle; he laid its bases, and set up its frames, and put in its poles, and raised up its pillars; [19]and he spread the tent over the tabernacle, and put the covering of the tent over it; as the LORD had commanded Moses. [20]He took the covenant *b* and put it into the ark, and put the poles on the ark, and set the mercy seat *c* above the ark; [21]and he brought the ark into the tabernacle, and set up the curtain for screening, and screened the ark of

---

a Meaning of Heb uncertain   *b* Or *treaty*, or *testimony*; Heb *eduth*   *c* Or *the cover*

---

interpretations have been fanciful. Yet the exercise is not without its spiritual value. You get the sense from Scripture that God does nothing on a whim. Everything has a purpose. There is significance to what he chooses. We are right to suspect the furniture of his house is more than just functional decor. After all, Paul tells us that every aspect of creation—every rock, every feather, every ocean, every lion—is a window to God. Everything he has made says something about him. "His eternal power and divine nature . . . have been understood and seen through the things he has made" (Rom 1:20). If this is the case, then acacia wood says something about him. And gold. And the metals that form bronze. And yarn spun from the hair of goats. God, because he is invisible, must be a God of symbols and representations and sacraments if he is going to communicate himself to the human race.

the covenant; *a* as the LORD had commanded Moses. 22He put the table in the tent of meeting, on the north side of the tabernacle, outside the curtain, 23and set the bread in order on it before the LORD; as the LORD had commanded Moses. 24He put the lampstand in the tent of meeting, opposite the table on the south side of the tabernacle, 25and set up the lamps before the LORD; as the LORD had commanded Moses. 26He put the golden altar in the tent of meeting before the curtain, 27and offered fragrant incense on it; as the LORD had commanded Moses. 28He also put in place the screen for the entrance of the tabernacle. 29He set the altar of burnt offering at the entrance of the tabernacle of the tent of meeting, and offered on it the burnt offering and the grain offering as the LORD had commanded Moses. 30He set the basin between the tent of meeting and the altar, and put water in it for washing, 31with which Moses and Aaron and his sons washed their hands and their feet. 32When they went into the tent of meeting, and when they approached the altar, they washed; as the LORD had commanded Moses. 33He set up the court around the tabernacle and the altar, and put up the screen at the gate of the court. So Moses finished the work.

The Cloud and the Glory

34 Then the cloud covered the tent of meeting, and the glory of the LORD filled the tabernacle. 35Moses was not able to enter the tent of meeting because the cloud settled upon it, and the glory of the LORD filled the tabernacle. 36Whenever the cloud was taken up from the tabernacle, the Israelites would set out on each stage of their journey; 37but if the cloud was not taken up, then they did not set out until the day that it was taken up. 38For the cloud of the LORD was on the tabernacle by day, and fire was in the cloud *b* by night, before the eyes of all the house of Israel at each stage of their journey.

a Or *treaty*, or *testimony*; Heb *eduth*   *b* Heb *it*

40:33 *So Moses finished the work.* Not only in the creation of the tabernacle, but in all God's interactions with Israel in Exodus human involvement has been essential. Who stands before Pharaoh in God's name but two humans named Moses and Aaron? Who climbs Mt. Sinai to receive the Ten Commandments from God? Who conveys Yahweh's messages to his people? Who wears the priest's robe? Who inspects the tabernacle to make sure it has been made precisely according to the Lord's plan? The holiest actions of God are embedded in human toes and fingers and tongues. We play a considerable role in bringing God's beauty and justice to earth.

40:34 *Then the cloud covered the tent of meeting, and the glory of the LORD filled the tabernacle.* When humans can do no more, then God acts. In the truest sense all those who have had a hand in building the tabernacle have prepared the way for the Lord (Isa 40:3). Now it is their job to respond appropriately to God's leading. When the cloud lifts, the children of Israel "set out on each stage of their journey" (Exod 40:36). When it does not move, they do not move. When it is night, they know God is still with them because the light of fire glows in the cloud. This is the presence of God among his people, and all the Israelites can do is make themselves ready for it. They cannot force God to come. Yet when God does come, it is no longer a time of preparing or waiting, but of moving. In the same way, on each stage of our journey, God is with us in the brightest light of our lives and also when we step through the greatest darkness. There is a fire of God that is not seen unless all that is spiritual appears opaque. Little is known about the journey except the promise of a destination. Our eyes are therefore fixed upon God because he is the one constant.

Responding
40:34–38 THE WITH-GOD LIFE. We often think that if we could only see God, believing in him would be much easier. But would it be? Why or why not? *See also* Spiritual Disciplines Index.

LEVITICUS

R eading Leviticus can be overwhelming. The key for hearing the book's message is to see it in its context. The immediate setting comes from the book of Exodus. Ancient Israel's God has delivered the people from slavery in Egypt. At Sinai, God and the people forge a relationship, a covenant. God proceeds through the mediator Moses to instruct the people in how to live as the covenant People of God, and a significant component of that instruction relates to worship. Such instruction is in a block of material that begins in Exodus 25 and continues through Leviticus and the first part of Numbers.

Leviticus consists of four major sections:

1. Manual of Sacrifice (chapters 1–7)
2. Worship at the Tabernacle (chapters 8–10)
3. Manual of Purity (chapters 11–16)
4. Code of Holiness (chapters 17–27)

Worship at the tabernacle is covered in chapters 8–10. The opening chapters in Leviticus offer instruction in the sacrifices to be offered in that worship. The remainder of the book concerns preparation for worship. Within a framework of instruction on worship, Leviticus reveals several recurring themes.

Present and Holy

The first theme is *God's presence*. The primary reality pervading Leviticus is that God is truly present with the people. The beginning of the book suggests that its words are divine revelation, and the sanctuary with Yahweh's presence in it is at the heart of the text. The reality of God's presence is always just beneath the surface of the book. God is truly *with* his people. This presence is holy, awesome, life-giving, and dangerous. Such a view of God's presence reflects a holistic view of life.

See also *"The With-God Life" essay for this section of the Bible,*
"The People of God in Exodus," pp. 87–91.

That the God present with ancient Israel is a *holy* God is a second theme. God is set apart; there is no other like God. As God is different, so ancient Israel is to be different because it is the People of God. In Leviticus "holiness" is used less as a separatist term than as a positive term in relationship to God. Ancient Israel is to reflect God's holiness, to be distinct as God's people. That is Israel's witness to the nations. Leviticus applies this view to various lifestyle issues. Instructions in holiness then sustain life and faith. The people are called to holiness; on this premise the holy God will continue to be present with them and give them life.

Though contemporary readers may be puzzled by the dangers here associated with the holiness of the divine presence, Leviticus reminds us of how awesome God is and that worship can be dangerous indeed. Worshipers might realize that the God of all creation is present and be shaken by that reality. Prayers might lead us to realize that certain behavior is wrong and should stop. Scripture readings could lead to the painful decision that our life has been invested in the wrong things. Worship could affect us in unplanned ways. Worship could transform a whole life. Though the encounter with the living God in worship should not alienate or be inaccessible, Leviticus makes it abundantly clear that being confronted by the living God is not always comfortable or easily understandable. The journey of faith is not a cozy one. Churches and individuals could benefit from this perspective.

Purity and Sacrifice

A third theme in Leviticus is *purity.* In Leviticus, the world is divided between those things that are holy and those that are common. The holy is dedicated to God (tabernacle, priests, furniture, vessels, etc.). Common things are divided into two additional categories, clean and unclean, or pure and impure. What is clean can become holy, but the unclean and the holy are to be kept separate. Mixing these brings danger, so the clean is tolerated and the unclean is prohibited. Further, impurity is contagious. Leviticus seeks to help the people avoid impurity, because it disqualifies them from worship; the explosive mixing of the holy and the unclean must be avoided.

The important element in dealing with impurity, *sacrifice,* constitutes a fourth theme. The following suggestions can help readers understand the sacrifices described in Leviticus. First, sacrifice can be seen as a gift. With one type of gift, the giver recognizes what comes from God and gives part of it back to God; with another kind of gift a giver seeks favor from God. The grain offering in Leviticus 2 is a gift. The notion of communion also underlies sacrifice. Communion and relationship with God and the other members of the community are enriched in the sacrificial meal. Such a meal would have been tied to the offering of well-being in Leviticus 3. Other sacrifices in Leviticus relate to atonement (Lev 1; 4; 5). Their purpose is to restore a relationship that has been fractured. Sacrifice restores the covenant relationship and so functions to keep chaos and social disruption at bay. Those who move into the realm of chaos can return to the realm of the clean by way of rituals of incorporation, including sacrifice.

The writers of Leviticus assume that sin and impurity will come into play and interrupt relationship with God, and thus they provide a means to repair that relationship. So sacrifice is central in the relation between God and congregation. One brings a sacrifice, and the crucial event is the death of the sacrificial animal and the passing of the animal's very life from the human to the divine world. The benefit accrues to the donor, who has identified with the sacrifice. When the animal is killed, the blood is shed, and the life is in the blood. Thus the donor is giving the life to God, a risky act since the life belongs to God and should only be taken by God. Yahweh mysteriously honors this act and cleanses, and the relationship is back at one. Leviticus describes the ritual of the sacrifices, though the text is not only about external acts. It assumes an internal motivation for atonement effected by this costly sacrifice of an animal. Thus, sacrifice is a critical way that God is with his people throughout Leviticus.

Covenant and Creation

These central themes of presence, holiness, purity, and sacrifice are put in a literary context in Leviticus. One may recall how the book relates to what comes before in Exodus. Leviticus is part of the Sinaitic covenant instruction. The book is a gift from God instructing in the structuring of this covenant community. It is not legalistic in the sense that it provides the people with a means of earning God's favor; rather, it is a multifaceted response of the people to God. Leviticus is a piece of covenant theology.

The book also relates to a broader context. Some commentators have noted parallels between the creation of the world in Genesis 1 and the building of the tabernacle in Exodus. The tabernacle contains a number of creation symbols. No sooner is sacrifice inaugurated at the tabernacle than a problem arises in Leviticus 10, when Aaron's sons offer "unholy fire" before the LORD. Chapters 11–16 of the book then instruct in how to restore the created order in the tabernacle. We might thus see worship in the tabernacle with its sacrifice and purification as a means of righting the creation's order when it is fractured by the effects of sin and uncleanness. Both covenant and creation underlie Leviticus.

Reading Leviticus Today

Leviticus is tough sledding for contemporary readers. It requires us to dive into a document far removed from our culture. Thus it is important to attend to the cultural structures that generated the book, its literary shape, and its theological perspectives. It seems clear that a primary purpose of Leviticus is to articulate the priestly view of life for ancient Israel. It presents instruction for that community as "a priestly kingdom and a holy nation" (Exod 19:6). The writers passing on the tradition of Leviticus were laying their grid on the world and commending that order to their community. That grid offers us much:

- A world with worship of an awesome God at the center.

- A world shaped by our identity as the People of God.

- A world offering hope for recourse when the community's structures go awry.

- A world with a healthy respect for life and creation.

We can benefit from dialogue with such a view of life and the world. We live in a world in which the center has faded, if not disintegrated. Ecology and community suffer, and people search for identity and hope. Leviticus still speaks a word to contemporary readers. The book also presents a portrait of faith that can shape subsequent generations. It calls the community to love God in holiness and to love one's neighbor as oneself, a theme we will return to often in the Scriptures.

— William H. Bellinger, Jr.

The Burnt Offering

1 The LORD summoned Moses and spoke to him from the tent of meeting, saying: ²Speak to the people of Israel and say to them: When any of you bring an offering of livestock to the LORD, you shall bring your offering from the herd or from the flock.

3 If the offering is a burnt offering from the herd, you shall offer a male without blemish; you shall bring it to the entrance of the tent of meeting, for acceptance in your behalf before the LORD. ⁴You shall lay your hand on the head of the burnt offering, and it shall be acceptable in your behalf as atonement for you. ⁵The bull shall be slaughtered before the LORD; and Aaron's sons the priests shall offer the blood, dashing the blood against all sides of the altar that is at the entrance of the tent of meeting. ⁶The burnt offering shall be flayed and cut up into its parts. ⁷The sons of the priest Aaron shall put fire on the altar and arrange wood on the fire. ⁸Aaron's sons the priests shall arrange the parts, with the head and the suet, on the wood that is on the fire on the altar; ⁹but its entrails and its legs shall be washed with water. Then the priest shall turn the whole into smoke on the altar as a burnt offering, an offering by fire of pleasing odor to the LORD.

10 If your gift for a burnt offering is from

1:1 *The LORD summoned Moses and spoke to him from the tent of meeting.* The opening verse casts the book of Leviticus as divinely inspired instruction. The tent is where the faith community of ancient Israel met in the hope of encountering the life-giving God. Chapters 1–7 constitute a Manual of Sacrifice.

1:2 *you shall bring your offering from the herd or from the flock.* The opening chapters of Leviticus are addressed to the whole faith community, the whole people of ancient Israel. The word used to describe the animals usually refers to domestic rather than wild animals. Those from the herd would be cattle, those from the flock sheep or goats. The sacrifice of these animals was costly for ancient Israelites. Meat was a rare luxury in that world; the offering was to be genuinely sacrificial. The ancient Israelite practice of animal sacrifice illustrates the sacrificial nature of a life of faith. Genuine faith is in a real sense a commitment, a giving of one's life to God—it is costly.

1:3 *without blemish.* The animal, a young bull, is to be whole, without defect. The unblemished quality of the animal demonstrates the seriousness of sacrifice. The best is to be offered to God.

1:9 *a burnt offering, an offering by fire of pleasing odor to the LORD.* The whole burnt offering (vv 2–17), in which the whole animal was consumed on the altar, was the most common of the Old Testament sacrifices. It symbolized the commitment of one's whole life to God and was an atoning sacrifice. Leviticus assumes that God and ancient Israel are in a covenant relationship, and that the relationship will be broken by the effects of sin and uncleanness. This sacrifice provides a possibility for restoring the relationship between people and God. The goal of the ritual is to give the

the flock, from the sheep or goats, your offering shall be a male without blemish. 11It shall be slaughtered on the north side of the altar before the LORD, and Aaron's sons the priests shall dash its blood against all sides of the altar. 12It shall be cut up into its parts, with its head and its suet, and the priest shall arrange them on the wood that is on the fire on the altar; 13but the entrails and the legs shall be washed with water. Then the priest shall offer the whole and turn it into smoke on the altar; it is a burnt offering, an offering by fire of pleasing odor to the LORD.

14 If your offering to the LORD is a burnt offering of birds, you shall choose your offering from turtledoves or pigeons. 15The priest shall bring it to the altar and wring off its head, and turn it into smoke on the altar; and its blood shall be drained out against the side of the altar. 16He shall remove its crop with its contents a and throw it at the east side of the altar, in the place for ashes. 17He shall tear it open by its wings without severing it. Then the priest shall turn it into smoke on the altar, on the wood that is on the fire; it is a burnt offering, an offering by fire of pleasing odor to the LORD.

Grain Offerings

2 When anyone presents a grain offering to the LORD, the offering shall be of choice flour; the worshiper shall pour oil on it, and put frankincense on it, 2and bring it to Aaron's sons the priests. After taking from it a handful of the choice flour and oil, with all its frankincense, the priest shall turn this to-

ken portion into smoke on the altar, an offering by fire of pleasing odor to the LORD. 3And what is left of the grain offering shall be for Aaron and his sons, a most holy part of the offerings by fire to the LORD.

4 When you present a grain offering baked in the oven, it shall be of choice flour: unleavened cakes mixed with oil, or unleavened wafers spread with oil. 5If your offering is grain prepared on a griddle, it shall be of choice flour mixed with oil, unleavened; 6break it in pieces, and pour oil on it; it is a grain offering. 7If your offering is grain prepared in a pan, it shall be made of choice flour in oil. 8You shall bring to the LORD the grain offering that is prepared in any of these ways; and when it is presented to the priest, he shall take it to the altar. 9The priest shall remove from the grain offering its token portion and turn this into smoke on the altar, an offering by fire of pleasing odor to the LORD. 10And what is left of the grain offering shall be for Aaron and his sons; it is a most holy part of the offerings by fire to the LORD.

11 No grain offering that you bring to the LORD shall be made with leaven, for you must not turn any leaven or honey into smoke as an offering by fire to the LORD. 12You may bring them to the LORD as an offering of choice products, but they shall not be offered on the altar for a pleasing odor. 13You shall not omit from your grain offerings the salt of the covenant with your God; with all your offerings you shall offer salt.

a Meaning of Heb uncertain

---

offering, the pleasing aroma, to God in the hope of God's granting atonement. The concern of the text is to regulate the ritual so that it can be acceptable to God. The themes of Leviticus 1 also appear in the New Testament: forgiveness (1 John 1:5–10) and total commitment (Matt 10:34–39; Heb 13:15–16). Also of central importance is the crucifixion as the ultimate sacrifice effecting atonement (Mark 10:45; Eph 5:2; 1 Pet 1:18–19). Spiritual formation is about the deepening and maturation of one's relationship with God. Sin is the great hindrance to this relationship. As a result, repentance and forgiveness are important parts of our journey toward spiritual maturity.

1:14 *a burnt offering of birds.* The sacrifice of birds makes provision for those who could not afford a sacrifice from herd or flock.

2:1 *When anyone presents a grain offering to the LORD.* The term translated "grain offering" suggests that the sacrifice is a gift recognizing that the everyday diet of grain is a gift from God.

2:13 *the salt of the covenant with your God.* Salt was the primary preservative in the ancient Near East. The reference to salt emphasizes the abiding nature of God's covenant with ancient Israel. Salt seasoned and preserved the grain offering; the preservative quality leads to the association with a preserved or irrevocable covenant relationship.

14 If you bring a grain offering of first fruits to the LORD, you shall bring as the grain offering of your first fruits coarse new grain from fresh ears, parched with fire. 15You shall add oil to it and lay frankincense on it; it is a grain offering. 16And the priest shall turn a token portion of it into smoke—some of the coarse grain and oil with all its frankincense; it is an offering by fire to the LORD.

Offerings of Well-Being

3 If the offering is a sacrifice of well-being, if you offer an animal of the herd, whether male or female, you shall offer one without blemish before the LORD. 2You shall lay your hand on the head of the offering and slaughter it at the entrance of the tent of meeting; and Aaron's sons the priests shall dash the blood against all sides of the altar. 3You shall offer from the sacrifice of well-being, as an offering by fire to the LORD, the fat that covers the entrails and all the fat that is around the entrails; 4the two kidneys with the fat that is on them at the loins, and the appendage of the liver, which he shall remove with the kidneys. 5Then Aaron's sons shall turn these into smoke on the altar, with the burnt offering that is on the wood on the fire, as an offering by fire of pleasing odor to the LORD.

6 If your offering for a sacrifice of well-being to the LORD is from the flock, male or female, you shall offer one without blemish. 7If you present a sheep as your offering, you shall bring it before the LORD 8and lay your hand on the head of the offering. It shall be slaughtered before the tent of meeting, and Aaron's sons shall dash its blood against all sides of the altar. 9You shall present its fat from the sacrifice of well-being, as an offering by fire to the LORD: the whole broad tail, which shall be removed close to the backbone, the fat that covers the entrails, and all the fat that is around the entrails; 10the two kidneys with the fat that is on them at the loins, and the appendage of the liver, which you shall remove with the kidneys. 11Then the priest shall turn these into smoke on the altar as a food offering by fire to the LORD.

12 If your offering is a goat, you shall bring it before the LORD 13and lay your hand on its head; it shall be slaughtered before the tent of meeting; and the sons of Aaron shall dash its blood against all sides of the altar. 14You shall present as your offering from it, as an offering by fire to the LORD, the fat that covers the entrails, and all the fat that is around the entrails; 15the two kidneys with the fat that is on them at the loins, and the appendage of the liver, which you shall remove with the kidneys. 16Then the priest shall turn these into smoke on the altar as a food offering by fire for a pleasing odor.

All fat is the LORD's. 17It shall be a perpetual statute throughout your generations, in all your settlements: you must not eat any fat or any blood.

Sin Offerings

4 The LORD spoke to Moses, saying, 2Speak to the people of Israel, saying: When anyone sins unintentionally in any of the LORD's commandments about things not to be done, and does any one of them:

3 If it is the anointed priest who sins, thus bringing guilt on the people, he shall offer for the sin that he has committed a bull of the herd without blemish as a sin offering to the LORD. 4He shall bring the bull to the entrance of the tent of meeting before the LORD and lay

---

3:1 *If the offering is a sacrifice of well-being.* The sacrifice of well-being (vv 1–17), also translated "fellowship offering," concludes with worship and family or friends joining in a sacred meal of the meat not burned on the altar. The meal was a reenactment of the covenant. God was present in this communion meal, and so the relationship between God and the community is deepened. Christians often speak of joyful communal meals such as those associated with the fellowship offering, though the specific name of the sacrifice is not used in the New Testament. At the Last Supper, Jesus refers to the blood of the new covenant, a reference to the levitical sacrificial system. The new covenant brings rejoicing in communion. Though to a great extent our spiritual lives are experienced as individuals, spiritual growth takes place in a community of believers. Community is essential to spiritual formation.

his hand on the head of the bull; the bull shall be slaughtered before the LORD. 5The anointed priest shall take some of the blood of the bull and bring it into the tent of meeting. 6The priest shall dip his finger in the blood and sprinkle some of the blood seven times before the LORD in front of the curtain of the sanctuary. 7The priest shall put some of the blood on the horns of the altar of fragrant incense that is in the tent of meeting before the LORD; and the rest of the blood of the bull he shall pour out at the base of the altar of burnt offering, which is at the entrance of the tent of meeting. 8He shall remove all the fat from the bull of sin offering: the fat that covers the entrails and all the fat that is around the entrails; 9the two kidneys with the fat that is on them at the loins; and the appendage of the liver, which he shall remove with the kidneys, 10just as these are removed from the ox of the sacrifice of well-being. The priest shall turn them into smoke upon the altar of burnt offering. 11But the skin of the bull and all its flesh, as well as its head, its legs, its entrails, and its dung— 12all the rest of the bull—he shall carry out to a clean place outside the camp, to the ash heap, and shall burn it on a wood fire; at the ash heap it shall be burned.

13 If the whole congregation of Israel errs unintentionally and the matter escapes the notice of the assembly, and they do any one of the things that by the LORD's commandments ought not to be done and incur guilt; 14when the sin that they have committed becomes known, the assembly shall offer a bull of the herd for a sin offering and bring it before the tent of meeting. 15The elders of the congregation shall lay their hands on the head of the bull before the LORD, and the bull shall be slaughtered before the LORD. 16The anointed priest shall bring some of the blood of the bull into the tent of meeting, 17and the priest shall dip his finger in the blood and sprinkle it seven times before the LORD, in front of the curtain. 18He shall put some of the blood on the horns of the altar that is before the LORD in the tent of meeting; and the rest of the blood he shall pour out at the base of the altar of burnt offering that is at the entrance of the tent of meeting. 19He shall remove all its fat and turn it into smoke on the altar. 20He shall do with the bull just as is done with the bull of sin offering; he shall do the same with this. The priest shall make atonement for them, and they shall be forgiven. 21He shall carry the bull outside the camp, and burn it as he burned the first bull; it is the sin offering for the assembly.

22 When a ruler sins, doing unintentionally any one of all the things that by commandments of the LORD his God ought not to be done and incurs guilt, 23once the sin that he has committed is made known to him, he shall bring as his offering a male goat without blemish. 24He shall lay his hand on the head of the goat; it shall be slaughtered at the spot where the burnt offering is slaughtered before the LORD; it is a sin offering. 25The priest shall take some of the blood of the sin offering with his finger and put it on the horns of the altar of burnt offering, and pour out the rest of its blood at the base of the altar of burnt offering. 26All its fat he shall turn into smoke on

---

4:5–7 *take some of the blood.* The use of the blood distinguishes the sin, or purification, offering. The blood here is a purifying agent, a kind of "holy detergent." Modern readers must make the leap to a text from a very different culture. The use of blood might conjure disgusting images for us, but in ancient Israel sacrificial blood had a sacred cleansing effect. This cleansing effect is central to the ritual because it enacts the restoration of wholeness for the people. The purification offering illustrates that dealing with sin is a significant part of spiritual formation.

4:20 *The priest shall make atonement for them, and they shall be forgiven.* God forgives the worshipers and puts the divine-human relationship back together. God wipes the slate clean for the congregation. Accordingly, God remains present to give life to the community and stability to the created order.

4:22–26 *When a ruler sins.* It is understood that community leaders will err and sin, but provision is made for the restoration of the leader's relationship with God and the community.

the altar, like the fat of the sacrifice of well-being. Thus the priest shall make atonement on his behalf for his sin, and he shall be forgiven.

27 If anyone of the ordinary people among you sins unintentionally in doing any one of the things that by the LORD's commandments ought not to be done and incurs guilt, 28when the sin that you have committed is made known to you, you shall bring a female goat without blemish as your offering, for the sin that you have committed. 29You shall lay your hand on the head of the sin offering; and the sin offering shall be slaughtered at the place of the burnt offering. 30The priest shall take some of its blood with his finger and put it on the horns of the altar of burnt offering, and he shall pour out the rest of its blood at the base of the altar. 31He shall remove all its fat, as the fat is removed from the offering of well-being, and the priest shall turn it into smoke on the altar for a pleasing odor to the LORD. Thus the priest shall make atonement on your behalf, and you shall be forgiven.

32 If the offering you bring as a sin offering is a sheep, you shall bring a female without blemish. 33You shall lay your hand on the head of the sin offering; and it shall be slaughtered as a sin offering at the spot where the burnt offering is slaughtered. 34The priest shall take some of the blood of the sin offering with his finger and put it on the horns of the altar of burnt offering, and pour out the rest of its blood at the base of the altar. 35You shall remove all its fat, as the fat of the sheep is removed from the sacrifice of well-being, and the priest shall turn it into smoke on the altar, with the offerings by fire to the LORD. Thus the priest shall make atonement on your behalf for the sin that you have committed, and you shall be forgiven.

5 When any of you sin in that you have heard a public adjuration to testify and—though able to testify as one who has seen or learned of the matter—do not speak up, you are subject to punishment. 2Or when any of you touch any unclean thing—whether the carcass of an unclean beast or the carcass of unclean livestock or the carcass of an unclean swarming thing—and are unaware of it, you have become unclean, and are guilty. 3Or when you touch human uncleanness—any uncleanness by which one can become unclean—and are unaware of it, when you come to know it, you shall be guilty. 4Or when any of you utter aloud a rash oath for a bad or a good purpose, whatever people utter in an oath, and are unaware of it, when you come to know it, you shall in any of these be guilty. 5When you realize your guilt in any of these, you shall confess the sin that you have committed. 6And you shall bring to the LORD, as your penalty for the sin that you have committed, a female from the flock, a sheep or a goat, as a sin offering; and the priest shall make atonement on your behalf for your sin.

7 But if you cannot afford a sheep, you shall bring to the LORD, as your penalty for the sin that you have committed, two turtledoves or two pigeons, one for a sin offering and the

Responding

5:5 CONFESSION. In verses 1–4 the Israelites were commanded to confess their sin when they were guilty of refusing to testify when they could have, touching unclean things, touching an unclean human, or uttering a rash oath even though they were unaware of doing anything wrong. Recall a time when you did something and only later became aware that it was wrong. Take a moment now to confess it to God. *See also* Spiritual Disciplines Index.

5:6–13 *as a sin [purification] offering.* The underlying perspective is that God is holy and

cannot stand to dwell in the midst of the effects of sin and uncleanness and yet seeks to be present with the community to give life. The Manual of Sacrifice understands that the community will fracture the relationship with God through sin and uncleanness, but this rite of purification provides a way for the community to cleanse the sanctuary as a divine dwelling place. God could thus continue to be present and bless the covenant community. The danger is the loss of the divine presence and thus the loss of full life, but the act of purification makes possible a return to wholeness of life in relationship with God.

other for a burnt offering. [8]You shall bring them to the priest, who shall offer first the one for the sin offering, wringing its head at the nape without severing it. [9]He shall sprinkle some of the blood of the sin offering on the side of the altar, while the rest of the blood shall be drained out at the base of the altar; it is a sin offering. [10]And the second he shall offer for a burnt offering according to the regulation. Thus the priest shall make atonement on your behalf for the sin that you have committed, and you shall be forgiven.

11 But if you cannot afford two turtledoves or two pigeons, you shall bring as your offering for the sin that you have committed one-tenth of an ephah of choice flour for a sin offering; you shall not put oil on it or lay frankincense on it, for it is a sin offering. [12]You shall bring it to the priest, and the priest shall scoop up a handful of it as its memorial portion, and turn this into smoke on the altar, with the offerings by fire to the LORD; it is a sin offering. [13]Thus the priest shall make atonement on your behalf for whichever of these sins you have committed, and you shall be forgiven. Like the grain offering, the rest shall be for the priest.

Offerings with Restitution

14 The LORD spoke to Moses, saying: [15]When any of you commit a trespass and sin unintentionally in any of the holy things of the LORD, you shall bring, as your guilt offering to the LORD, a ram without blemish from the flock, convertible into silver by the sanctuary shekel; it is a guilt offering. [16]And you shall make restitution for the holy thing in which you were remiss, and shall add one-fifth to it and give it to the priest. The priest shall make atonement on your behalf with the ram of the guilt offering, and you shall be forgiven.

17 If any of you sin without knowing it, doing any of the things that by the LORD's commandments ought not to be done, you have incurred guilt, and are subject to punishment. [18]You shall bring to the priest a ram without blemish from the flock, or the equivalent, as a guilt offering; and the priest shall make atonement on your behalf for the error that you committed unintentionally, and you shall be forgiven. [19]It is a guilt offering; you have incurred guilt before the LORD.

6 [a]The LORD spoke to Moses, saying: [2]When any of you sin and commit a trespass against the LORD by deceiving a neighbor in a matter of a deposit or a pledge, or by robbery, or if you have defrauded a neighbor, [3]or have found something lost and lied about it—if you swear falsely regarding any of the various things that one may do and sin thereby— [4]when you have sinned and realize your guilt, and would restore what you took by

a Ch 5.20 in Heb

How sin effects the whole community

The purification offering seems odd to contemporary Western believers, but it is actually a gracious provision for the faith community. The New Testament uses images of the purification rite, especially the cleansing significance of blood, to interpret the crucifixion in Hebrews 9–10; 13; and 1 John 1:7. The Christ event completes the life-giving efficacy of sacrifice.

5:19 *a guilt offering*. Guilt is a cause of psychological dysfunction today. Many people seem to think that if they feel guilty, they have fulfilled their religious responsibilities. These texts (5:14–6:7), on the other hand, deal not so much with emotion as with breaches of relationship with God and with fellow members of the covenant community, neighbors (6:2).

Violating the covenant relationship, human or divine, brings responsibility and calls for acts of repentance and reconciliation. Ignoring the violations jeopardizes the community in relationship with God, for the effects of sin have an impact on God's presence with the people. The text connects worship and ethics in the call for restitution (20 percent) to the neighbor who has been wronged. The reparation provides the guilty person a means of acting upon the need for reconciliation and is thus a helpful and healthy dimension of the ritual. In Leviticus, spiritual living is not only a matter of one's relationship with God, but also involves one's relationship with others. This too is vital to spiritual formation.

E. Burns

robbery or by fraud or the deposit that was committed to you, or the lost thing that you found, 5or anything else about which you have sworn falsely, you shall repay the principal amount and shall add one-fifth to it. You shall pay it to its owner when you realize your guilt. 6And you shall bring to the priest, as your guilt offering to the LORD, a ram without blemish from the flock, or its equivalent, for a guilt offering. 7The priest shall make atonement on your behalf before the LORD, and you shall be forgiven for any of the things that one may do and incur guilt thereby.

Instructions concerning Sacrifices

8*a* The LORD spoke to Moses, saying: 9Command Aaron and his sons, saying: This is the ritual of the burnt offering. The burnt offering itself shall remain on the hearth upon the altar all night until the morning, while the fire on the altar shall be kept burning. 10The priest shall put on his linen vestments after putting on his linen undergarments next to his body; and he shall take up the ashes to which the fire has reduced the burnt offering on the altar, and place them beside the altar. 11Then he shall take off his vestments and put on other garments, and carry the ashes out to a clean place outside the camp. 12The fire on the altar shall be kept burning; it shall not go out. Every morning the priest shall add wood to it, lay out the burnt offering on it, and turn into smoke the fat pieces of the offerings of well-being. 13A perpetual fire shall be kept burning on the altar; it shall not go out.

14 This is the ritual of the grain offering: The sons of Aaron shall offer it before the LORD, in front of the altar. 15They shall take from it a handful of the choice flour and oil of the grain offering, with all the frankincense that is on the offering, and they shall turn its memorial portion into smoke on the

altar as a pleasing odor to the LORD. 16Aaron and his sons shall eat what is left of it; it shall be eaten as unleavened cakes in a holy place; in the court of the tent of meeting they shall eat it. 17It shall not be baked with leaven. I have given it as their portion of my offerings by fire; it is most holy, like the sin offering and the guilt offering. 18Every male among the descendants of Aaron shall eat of it, as their perpetual due throughout your generations, from the LORD's offerings by fire; anything that touches them shall become holy.

19 The LORD spoke to Moses, saying: 20This is the offering that Aaron and his sons shall offer to the LORD on the day when he is anointed: one-tenth of an ephah of choice flour as a regular offering, half of it in the morning and half in the evening. 21It shall be made with oil on a griddle; you shall bring it well soaked, as a grain offering of baked*b* pieces, and you shall present it as a pleasing odor to the LORD. 22And so the priest, anointed from among Aaron's descendants as a successor, shall prepare it; it is the LORD's—a perpetual due—to be turned entirely into smoke. 23Every grain offering of a priest shall be wholly burned; it shall not be eaten.

24 The LORD spoke to Moses, saying: 25Speak to Aaron and his sons, saying: This is the ritual of the sin offering. The sin offering shall be slaughtered before the LORD at the spot where the burnt offering is slaughtered; it is most holy. 26The priest who offers it as a sin offering shall eat of it; it shall be eaten in a holy place, in the court of the tent of meeting. 27Whatever touches its flesh shall become holy; and when any of its blood is spattered on a garment, you shall wash the bespattered part in a holy place. 28An earthen vessel in which it was boiled shall be broken; but if it is boiled in a bronze vessel, that

a Ch 6.1 in Heb   *b* Meaning of Heb uncertain

6:9–7:37 *Command Aaron and his sons.* These passages are instructions to the priests about the administration of the various sacrifices. The priests are essential leaders for this worshiping community.

6:12 *it shall not go out.* The priests are instructed to keep the fire on top of the altar

overnight and to ensure that the fire does not go out. The continuity of the fire illustrates the divine presence continuing with the community. Thus the continuing flame is an important reminder that God is present. Realizing that God is actually present and seeking to bless is one of the first steps toward a life of spiritual growth.

shall be scoured and rinsed in water. 29Every male among the priests shall eat of it; it is most holy. 30But no sin offering shall be eaten from which any blood is brought into the tent of meeting for atonement in the holy place; it shall be burned with fire.

7 This is the ritual of the guilt offering. It is most holy; 2at the spot where the burnt offering is slaughtered, they shall slaughter the guilt offering, and its blood shall be dashed against all sides of the altar. 3All its fat shall be offered: the broad tail, the fat that covers the entrails, 4the two kidneys with the fat that is on them at the loins, and the appendage of the liver, which shall be removed with the kidneys. 5The priest shall turn them into smoke on the altar as an offering by fire to the LORD; it is a guilt offering. 6Every male among the priests shall eat of it; it shall be eaten in a holy place; it is most holy.

7 The guilt offering is like the sin offering, there is the same ritual for them; the priest who makes atonement with it shall have it. 8So, too, the priest who offers anyone's burnt offering shall keep the skin of the burnt offering that he has offered. 9And every grain offering baked in the oven, and all that is prepared in a pan or on a griddle, shall belong to the priest who offers it. 10But every other grain offering, mixed with oil or dry, shall belong to all the sons of Aaron equally.

Further Instructions

11 This is the ritual of the sacrifice of the offering of well-being that one may offer to the LORD. 12If you offer it for thanksgiving, you shall offer with the thank offering unleavened cakes mixed with oil, unleavened wafers spread with oil, and cakes of choice flour well soaked in oil. 13With your thanksgiving sacrifice of well-being you shall bring your offering with cakes of leavened bread. 14From this you shall offer one cake from

each offering, as a gift to the LORD; it shall belong to the priest who dashes the blood of the offering of well-being. 15And the flesh of your thanksgiving sacrifice of well-being shall be eaten on the day it is offered; you shall not leave any of it until morning. 16But if the sacrifice you offer is a votive offering or a freewill offering, it shall be eaten on the day that you offer your sacrifice, and what is left of it shall be eaten the next day; 17but what is left of the flesh of the sacrifice shall be burned up on the third day. 18If any of the flesh of your sacrifice of well-being is eaten on the third day, it shall not be acceptable, nor shall it be credited to the one who offers it; it shall be an abomination, and the one who eats of it shall incur guilt.

19 Flesh that touches any unclean thing shall not be eaten; it shall be burned up. As for other flesh, all who are clean may eat such flesh. 20But those who eat flesh from the LORD's sacrifice of well-being while in a state of uncleanness shall be cut off from their kin. 21When any one of you touches any unclean thing—human uncleanness or an unclean animal or any unclean creature—and then eats flesh from the LORD's sacrifice of well-being, you shall be cut off from your kin.

22 The LORD spoke to Moses, saying: 23Speak to the people of Israel, saying: You shall eat no fat of ox or sheep or goat. 24The fat of an animal that died or was torn by wild animals may be put to any other use, but you must not eat it. 25If any one of you eats the fat from an animal of which an offering by fire may be made to the LORD, you who eat it shall be cut off from your kin. 26You must not eat any blood whatever, either of bird or of animal, in any of your settlements. 27Any one of you who eats any blood shall be cut off from your kin.

28 The LORD spoke to Moses, saying: 29Speak to the people of Israel, saying: Any

---

7:11–15 *the offering of well-being.* The Hebrew notion of thanksgiving is closely tied to praise. The worshiper recounts the story of how God has delivered or blessed and as a part of the rejoicing brings a fellowship offering along with cereal products similar to those used in the grain offering. This ancient notion may serve well in

the spiritual formation of believers today. In real life, spiritual development is not a matter of unbroken and constant growth; it takes place in stages over time and includes periods of flatness and stagnation. In times of spiritual drought, it is an important discipline to remember and recount how God has acted in one's own past.

one of you who would offer to the LORD your sacrifice of well-being must yourself bring to the LORD your offering from your sacrifice of well-being. 30Your own hands shall bring the LORD's offering by fire; you shall bring the fat with the breast, so that the breast may be raised as an elevation offering before the LORD. 31The priest shall turn the fat into smoke on the altar, but the breast shall belong to Aaron and his sons. 32And the right thigh from your sacrifices of well-being you shall give to the priest as an offering; 33the one among the sons of Aaron who offers the blood and fat of the offering of well-being shall have the right thigh for a portion. 34For I have taken the breast of the elevation offering, and the thigh that is offered, from the people of Israel, from their sacrifices of well-being, and have given them to Aaron the priest and to his sons, as a perpetual due from the people of Israel. 35This is the portion allotted to Aaron and to his sons from the offerings made by fire to the LORD, once they have been brought forward to serve the LORD as priests; 36these the LORD commanded to be given them, when he anointed them, as a perpetual due from the people of Israel throughout their generations.

37 This is the ritual of the burnt offering, the grain offering, the sin offering, the guilt offering, the offering of ordination, and the sacrifice of well-being, 38which the LORD commanded Moses on Mount Sinai, when he commanded the people of Israel to bring their offerings to the LORD, in the wilderness of Sinai.

The Rites of Ordination

8 The LORD spoke to Moses, saying: 2Take Aaron and his sons with him, the vestments, the anointing oil, the bull of sin offering, the two rams, and the basket of unleavened bread; 3and assemble the whole congregation at the entrance of the tent of meeting. 4And Moses did as the LORD commanded him. When the congregation was assembled at the entrance of the tent of meeting, 5Moses said to the congregation, "This is what the LORD has commanded to be done."

6 Then Moses brought Aaron and his sons forward, and washed them with water. 7He put the tunic on him, fastened the sash around him, clothed him with the robe, and put the ephod on him. He then put the decorated band of the ephod around him, tying the ephod to him with it. 8He placed the breastpiece on him, and in the breastpiece he put the Urim and the Thummim. 9And he set the turban on his head, and on the turban, in front, he set the golden ornament, the holy crown, as the LORD commanded Moses.

10 Then Moses took the anointing oil and

7:37–38 burnt . . . grain . . . sin . . . guilt . . . well-being. These last two verses conclude the Manual of Sacrifice (chaps 1–7), which treats five types of sacrifice. (The treatment of ordination is ahead, in chapter 8.) It is easy for contemporary readers to dismiss these texts as an unending mix of curious relics the significance of which has been lost in the mists of time. It is also easy to read these instructions as legalistic requirements from an obsessively hostile god. But their dramatic and intense nature suggests that these texts were instructions for people who fervently believed in their effective power. The acts are set rituals, but fallible humans tend to follow reliable conventions in all their relationships, including the divine-human relationship. As Scripture, Leviticus challenges our notions of God, worship, and atonement. These texts show that care and attention to detail, rather than casual sloppiness, are inherent to powerful worship. We might think of the image of the actor or musician who practices unceasingly and attends to minute details to give great and lively concerts. So too the careful preparation of congregation and worship leaders, as is witnessed in Leviticus 1–7, helps to facilitate the genuine worship of God, the empowering divine-human encounter.

8:1–36 Take Aaron and his sons. Chapters 8–10 describe the beginning of worship and sacrifice at the tabernacle. The priests are, in a sense, set apart from the rest of the community. Their life will become a vocation, wholly given to service of the living God in worship. Their leadership in the community is central to the worship of the whole congregation. In a similar way, spiritual growth requires a life that is set apart, wholly dedicated to God.

anointed the tabernacle and all that was in it, and consecrated them. [11]He sprinkled some of it on the altar seven times, and anointed the altar and all its utensils, and the basin and its base, to consecrate them. [12]He poured some of the anointing oil on Aaron's head and anointed him, to consecrate him. [13]And Moses brought forward Aaron's sons, and clothed them with tunics, and fastened sashes around them, and tied headdresses on them, as the LORD commanded Moses.

14 He led forward the bull of sin offering; and Aaron and his sons laid their hands upon the head of the bull of sin offering, [15]and it was slaughtered. Moses took the blood and with his finger put some on each of the horns of the altar, purifying the altar; then he poured out the blood at the base of the altar. Thus he consecrated it, to make atonement for it. [16]Moses took all the fat that was around the entrails, and the appendage of the liver, and the two kidneys with their fat, and turned them into smoke on the altar. [17]But the bull itself, its skin and flesh and its dung, he burned with fire outside the camp, as the LORD commanded Moses.

18 Then he brought forward the ram of burnt offering. Aaron and his sons laid their hands on the head of the ram, [19]and it was slaughtered. Moses dashed the blood against all sides of the altar. [20]The ram was cut into its parts, and Moses turned into smoke the head and the parts and the suet. [21]And after the entrails and the legs were washed with water, Moses turned into smoke the whole ram on the altar; it was a burnt offering for a pleasing odor, an offering by fire to the LORD, as the LORD commanded Moses.

22 Then he brought forward the second ram, the ram of ordination. Aaron and his sons laid their hands on the head of the ram, [23]and it was slaughtered. Moses took some of its blood and put it on the lobe of Aaron's right ear and on the thumb of his right hand and on the big toe of his right foot. [24]After Aaron's sons were brought forward, Moses put some of the blood on the lobes of their right ears and on the thumbs of their right hands and on the big toes of their right feet; and Moses dashed the rest of the blood

against all sides of the altar. [25]He took the fat—the broad tail, all the fat that was around the entrails, the appendage of the liver, and the two kidneys with their fat—and the right thigh. [26]From the basket of unleavened bread that was before the LORD, he took one cake of unleavened bread, one cake of bread with oil, and one wafer, and placed them on the fat and on the right thigh. [27]He placed all these on the palms of Aaron and on the palms of his sons, and raised them as an elevation offering before the LORD. [28]Then Moses took them from their hands and turned them into smoke on the altar with the burnt offering. This was an ordination offering for a pleasing odor, an offering by fire to the LORD. [29]Moses took the breast and raised it as an elevation offering before the LORD; it was Moses' portion of the ram of ordination, as the LORD commanded Moses.

30 Then Moses took some of the anointing oil and some of the blood that was on the altar and sprinkled them on Aaron and his vestments, and also on his sons and their vestments. Thus he consecrated Aaron and his vestments, and also his sons and their vestments.

31 And Moses said to Aaron and his sons, "Boil the flesh at the entrance of the tent of meeting, and eat it there with the bread that is in the basket of ordination offerings, as I was commanded, 'Aaron and his sons shall eat it'; [32]and what remains of the flesh and the bread you shall burn with fire. [33]You shall not go outside the entrance of the tent of meeting for seven days, until the day when your period of ordination is completed. For it will take seven days to ordain you; [34]as has been done today, the LORD has commanded to be done to make atonement for you. [35]You shall remain at the entrance of the tent of meeting day and night for seven days, keeping the LORD's charge so that you do not die; for so I am commanded." [36]Aaron and his sons did all the things that the LORD commanded through Moses.

Aaron's Priesthood Inaugurated

9 On the eighth day Moses summoned Aaron and his sons and the elders of Israel. [2]He said to Aaron, "Take a bull calf for a

sin offering and a ram for a burnt offering, without blemish, and offer them before the LORD. ³And say to the people of Israel, 'Take a male goat for a sin offering; a calf and a lamb, yearlings without blemish, for a burnt offering; ⁴and an ox and a ram for an offering of well-being to sacrifice before the LORD; and a grain offering mixed with oil. For today the LORD will appear to you.' " ⁵They brought what Moses commanded to the front of the tent of meeting; and the whole congregation drew near and stood before the LORD. ⁶And Moses said, "This is the thing that the LORD commanded you to do, so that the glory of the LORD may appear to you." ⁷Then Moses said to Aaron, "Draw near to the altar and sacrifice your sin offering and your burnt offering, and make atonement for yourself and for the people; and sacrifice the offering of the people, and make atonement for them; as the LORD has commanded."

8 Aaron drew near to the altar, and slaughtered the calf of the sin offering, which was for himself. ⁹The sons of Aaron presented the blood to him, and he dipped his finger in the blood and put it on the horns of the altar; and the rest of the blood he poured out at the base of the altar. ¹⁰But the fat, the kidneys, and the appendage of the liver from the sin offering he turned into smoke on the altar, as the LORD commanded Moses; ¹¹and the flesh

and the skin he burned with fire outside the camp.

12 Then he slaughtered the burnt offering. Aaron's sons brought him the blood, and he dashed it against all sides of the altar. ¹³And they brought him the burnt offering piece by piece, and the head, which he turned into smoke on the altar. ¹⁴He washed the entrails and the legs and, with the burnt offering, turned them into smoke on the altar.

15 Next he presented the people's offering. He took the goat of the sin offering that was for the people, and slaughtered it, and presented it as a sin offering like the first one. ¹⁶He presented the burnt offering, and sacrificed it according to regulation. ¹⁷He presented the grain offering, and, taking a handful of it, he turned it into smoke on the altar, in addition to the burnt offering of the morning.

18 He slaughtered the ox and the ram as a sacrifice of well-being for the people. Aaron's sons brought him the blood, which he dashed against all sides of the altar, ¹⁹and the fat of the ox and of the ram—the broad tail, the fat that covers the entrails, the two kidneys and the fat on them,ᵃ and the appendage of the liver. ²⁰They first laid the fat on the breasts, and the fat was turned into

ᵃ Gk: Heb *the broad tail, and that which covers, and the kidneys*

9:1–10:20 *On the eighth day*. This eighth day (following the week of consecration) was a significant one. It was full of triumph and tragedy. The divine presence brought great reverence and joy when the sacrifices were consumed by fire at the end of chapter 9. It brought great tragedy and grief with the sin of Nadab and Abihu at the beginning of chapter 10. These incidents of holy fire demonstrate in startling ways the power of God's presence and the need for people and priest to observe the divine instruction. These chapters portray the ancient Israelites as a people who understood the seriousness, significance, and potency of God's presence. This understanding could be of great benefit to our seeking a relationship with God today.

9:1–7 *Take a bull calf for a sin offering. . . . For today the LORD will appear to you.* All of this

preparation, it is important to see, is in the context of the hope of a "theophany," an appearance of God to the community. Central to theophany in the Old Testament is proper preparation to encounter the divine presence. In this sense, encountering God as a way of life is not an "off the cuff" matter. Instead, it is something that requires preparation and practice. In other words, encountering God is a lifelong discipline.

Responding
9:7 SACRIFICE. The note for 1:2 says, "The sacrifice of these animals was costly for ancient Israelites. . . . The practice of animal sacrifice illustrates the sacrificial nature of a life of faith." What sacrifices have you made to be true to your faith in Jesus Christ? *See also* Spiritual Disciplines Index.

smoke on the altar; 21and the breasts and the right thigh Aaron raised as an elevation offering before the LORD, as Moses had commanded.

22 Aaron lifted his hands toward the people and blessed them; and he came down after sacrificing the sin offering, the burnt offering, and the offering of well-being. 23Moses and Aaron entered the tent of meeting, and then came out and blessed the people; and the glory of the LORD appeared to all the people. 24Fire came out from the LORD and consumed the burnt offering and the fat on the altar; and when all the people saw it, they shouted and fell on their faces.

Nadab and Abihu

10 Now Aaron's sons, Nadab and Abihu, each took his censer, put fire in it, and laid incense on it; and they offered unholy fire before the LORD, such as he had not commanded them. 2And fire came out from the presence of the LORD and consumed them, and they died before the LORD. 3Then Moses said to Aaron, "This is what the LORD meant when he said,

'Through those who are near me
    I will show myself holy,
    and before all the people
    I will be glorified.' "
And Aaron was silent.

4 Moses summoned Mishael and Elzaphan, sons of Uzziel the uncle of Aaron, and said to them, "Come forward, and carry your kinsmen away from the front of the sanctuary to a place outside the camp." 5They came forward and carried them by their tunics out of the camp, as Moses had ordered. 6And Moses said to Aaron and to his sons Eleazar and Ithamar, "Do not dishevel your hair, and do not tear your vestments, or you will die and wrath will strike all the congregation; but your kindred, the whole house of Israel, may mourn the burning that the LORD has sent. 7You shall not go outside the entrance of the tent of meeting, or you will die; for the anointing oil of the LORD is on you." And they did as Moses had ordered.

8 And the LORD spoke to Aaron: 9Drink no wine or strong drink, neither you nor your sons, when you enter the tent of meeting, that you may not die; it is a statute forever throughout your generations. 10You are to distinguish between the holy and the common, and between the unclean and the clean; 11and you are to teach the people of Israel all

---

10:1–3 *and they offered unholy fire before the LORD, such as he had not commanded them.* The Hebrew word translated "unholy" here could mean "alien" and so refer to fire from other cults. The warning may be against any idolatrous practice. Readers today need to remember that the idolatrous practices were the established, culturally accepted ones in the world surrounding ancient Israel. This incident puzzles and disturbs many contemporary readers. Death through divine punishment seems out of place with the grace of the Christian God and the gospel. The difficulty is not limited to Leviticus or to the Old Testament, where a number of texts raise the issue. Certain New Testament texts also do, such as the beginning of Acts 5 with the deaths of Ananias and Sapphira. In the case of Leviticus 10, it is important to remember that the text assumes the danger inherent in the holy presence of God. The divine presence gives life and is powerful, so much so that, when encountered in

an unprepared or improper way, it can bring death. The text serves as a reminder that believers encounter an all-powerful God, and that our spiritual formation should be undertaken with utmost seriousness.

10:8–11 *distinguish between the holy and the common, and between the unclean and the clean.* The categories the priests distinguish are significant in Leviticus. The holy is what is exclusively divine, while the common can be used by humans. The clean and the unclean are both within the common category. The clean is available for use, while the unclean breaches the proper boundaries, as a result is dangerous, and should be avoided. People today tend to think of the unclean as something "dirty" that needs to be washed. In Leviticus "unclean" suggests something that is unacceptable for worship. The priests are to instruct the people so that they may avoid the unclean. Contact with the unclean makes people unclean and thus unable to worship.

the statutes that the LORD has spoken to them through Moses.

12 Moses spoke to Aaron and to his remaining sons, Eleazar and Ithamar: Take the grain offering that is left from the LORD's offerings by fire, and eat it unleavened beside the altar, for it is most holy; [13]you shall eat it in a holy place, because it is your due and your sons' due, from the offerings by fire to the LORD; for so I am commanded. [14]But the breast that is elevated and the thigh that is raised, you and your sons and daughters as well may eat in any clean place; for they have been assigned to you and your children from the sacrifices of the offerings of well-being of the people of Israel. [15]The thigh that is raised and the breast that is elevated they shall bring, together with the offerings by fire of the fat, to raise for an elevation offering before the LORD; they are to be your due and that of your children forever, as the LORD has commanded.

16 Then Moses made inquiry about the goat of the sin offering, and—it had already been burned! He was angry with Eleazar and Ithamar, Aaron's remaining sons, and said, [17]"Why did you not eat the sin offering in the sacred area? For it is most holy, and God[a] has given it to you that you may remove the guilt of the congregation, to make atonement on their behalf before the LORD. [18]Its blood was not brought into the inner part of the sanctuary. You should certainly have eaten it in the sanctuary, as I commanded." [19]And Aaron spoke to Moses, "See, today they offered their sin offering and their burnt offering before the LORD; and yet such things as these have befallen me! If I had eaten the sin offering today, would it have been agreeable to the LORD?" [20]And when Moses heard that, he agreed.

Clean and Unclean Foods

11 The LORD spoke to Moses and Aaron, saying to them: [2]Speak to the people of Israel, saying:

From among all the land animals, these are the creatures that you may eat. [3]Any animal that has divided hoofs and is cleft-footed and chews the cud—such you may eat. [4]But among those that chew the cud or have divided hoofs, you shall not eat the following: the camel, for even though it chews the cud, it does not have divided hoofs; it is unclean for you. [5]The rock badger, for even though it chews the cud, it does not have divided hoofs; it is unclean for you. [6]The hare, for even though it chews the cud, it does not have divided hoofs; it is unclean for you. [7]The pig, for even though it has divided hoofs and is cleft-footed, it does not chew the cud; it is unclean for you. [8]Of their flesh you shall not eat, and their carcasses you shall not touch; they are unclean for you.

9 These you may eat, of all that are in the waters. Everything in the waters that has fins and scales, whether in the seas or in the streams—such you may eat. [10]But anything in the seas or the streams that does not have fins and scales, of the swarming creatures in

a Heb he

11:1–47 *these . . . you may eat.* Chapters 11–15 are a Manual of Purity followed closely by the description of the Day of Atonement (chap 16). Although no one explanation will do, the dietary laws in chapter 11 may be a system of boundaries. The unclean animals exhibit some kind of physical characteristic or quality that is an anomaly for their environment, whereas the clean animals do not. For example, in verses 9–12 the animals with fins and scales follow a normal means of moving around and thus symbolize normality, wholeness, or purity, whereas the "swarming creatures" follow a chaotic movement pattern and are disqualified

as detestable. The idea is that this purity system organizes life into a whole and provides a means of seeking wholeness for the faith community. The purpose of this instruction is to inform members of the community how to avoid impurity so they can worship. The concluding verses of the chapter remind readers of the covenantal context and the call to holiness. Avoiding impurity is part of that call (see 1 Pet 2:9). The New Testament call is the same, though it does seek to move beyond the boundaries of clean and unclean to wholeness determined by faith.

the waters and among all the other living creatures that are in the waters—they are detestable to you [11] and detestable they shall remain. Of their flesh you shall not eat, and their carcasses you shall regard as detestable. [12] Everything in the waters that does not have fins and scales is detestable to you.

13 These you shall regard as detestable among the birds. They shall not be eaten; they are an abomination: the eagle, the vulture, the osprey, [14] the buzzard, the kite of any kind; [15] every raven of any kind; [16] the ostrich, the nighthawk, the sea gull, the hawk of any kind; [17] the little owl, the cormorant, the great owl, [18] the water hen, the desert owl, [a] the carrion vulture, [19] the stork, the heron of any kind, the hoopoe, and the bat. [b]

20 All winged insects that walk upon all fours are detestable to you. [21] But among the winged insects that walk on all fours you may eat those that have jointed legs above their feet, with which to leap on the ground. [22] Of them you may eat: the locust according to its kind, the bald locust according to its kind, the cricket according to its kind, and the grasshopper according to its kind. [23] But all other winged insects that have four feet are detestable to you.

Unclean Animals

24 By these you shall become unclean; whoever touches the carcass of any of them shall be unclean until the evening, [25] and whoever carries any part of the carcass of any of them shall wash his clothes and be unclean until the evening. [26] Every animal that has divided hoofs but is not cleft-footed or does not chew the cud is unclean for you; everyone who touches one of them shall be unclean. [27] All that walk on their paws, among the animals that walk on all fours, are unclean for you; whoever touches the carcass of any of them shall be unclean until the evening, [28] and the one who carries the carcass shall wash his clothes and be unclean until the evening; they are unclean for you.

29 These are unclean for you among the creatures that swarm upon the earth: the weasel, the mouse, the great lizard according to its kind, [30] the gecko, the land crocodile, the lizard, the sand lizard, and the chameleon. [31] These are unclean for you among all that swarm; whoever touches one of them when they are dead shall be unclean until the evening. [32] And anything upon which any of them falls when they are dead shall be unclean, whether an article of wood or cloth or skin or sacking, any article that is used for any purpose; it shall be dipped into water, and it shall be unclean until the evening, and then it shall be clean. [33] And if any of them falls into any earthen vessel, all that is in it shall be unclean, and you shall break the vessel. [34] Any food that could be eaten shall be unclean if water from any such vessel comes upon it; and any liquid that could be drunk shall be unclean if it was in any such vessel. [35] Everything on which any part of the carcass falls shall be unclean; whether an oven or stove, it shall be broken in pieces; they are unclean, and shall remain unclean for you. [36] But a spring or a cistern holding water shall be clean, while whatever touches the carcass in it shall be unclean. [37] If any part of their carcass falls upon any seed set aside for sowing, it is clean; [38] but if water is put on the seed and any part of their carcass falls on it, it is unclean for you.

39 If an animal of which you may eat dies, anyone who touches its carcass shall be unclean until the evening. [40] Those who eat of its carcass shall wash their clothes and be unclean until the evening; and those who carry the carcass shall wash their clothes and be unclean until the evening.

41 All creatures that swarm upon the earth are detestable; they shall not be eaten. [42] Whatever moves on its belly, and whatever moves on all fours, or whatever has many feet, all the creatures that swarm upon the earth, you shall not eat; for they are detestable. [43] You shall not make yourselves detestable with any creature that swarms; you shall not defile yourselves with them, and so become unclean. [44] For I am the LORD your God; sanctify yourselves therefore, and be holy, for I am holy. You shall not defile yourselves with any swarming creature that moves on the earth. [45] For I am the LORD who

a Or pelican   b Identification of several of the birds in verses 13-19 is uncertain

brought you up from the land of Egypt, to be your God; you shall be holy, for I am holy.

46 This is the law pertaining to land animal and bird and every living creature that moves through the waters and every creature that swarms upon the earth, [47]to make a distinction between the unclean and the clean, and between the living creature that may be eaten and the living creature that may not be eaten.

Purification of Women after Childbirth

12 The LORD spoke to Moses, saying: [2]Speak to the people of Israel, saying:

If a woman conceives and bears a male child, she shall be ceremonially unclean seven days; as at the time of her menstruation, she shall be unclean. [3]On the eighth day the flesh of his foreskin shall be circumcised. [4]Her time of blood purification shall be thirty-three days; she shall not touch any holy thing, or come into the sanctuary, until the days of her purification are completed. [5]If she bears a female child, she shall be unclean two weeks, as in her menstruation; her time of blood purification shall be sixty-six days.

6 When the days of her purification are completed, whether for a son or for a daughter, she shall bring to the priest at the entrance of the tent of meeting a lamb in its first year for a burnt offering, and a pigeon or a turtledove for a sin offering. [7]He shall offer it before the LORD, and make atonement on her behalf; then she shall be clean from her flow of blood. This is the law for her who bears a child, male or female. [8]If she cannot afford a sheep, she shall take two turtledoves

or two pigeons, one for a burnt offering and the other for a sin offering; and the priest shall make atonement on her behalf, and she shall be clean.

Leprosy, Varieties and Symptoms

13 The LORD spoke to Moses and Aaron, saying:

2 When a person has on the skin of his body a swelling or an eruption or a spot, and it turns into a leprous[a] disease on the skin of his body, he shall be brought to Aaron the priest or to one of his sons the priests. [3]The priest shall examine the disease on the skin of his body, and if the hair in the diseased area has turned white and the disease appears to be deeper than the skin of his body, it is a leprous[a] disease; after the priest has examined him he shall pronounce him ceremonially unclean. [4]But if the spot is white in the skin of his body, and appears no deeper than the skin and the hair in it has not turned white, the priest shall confine the diseased person for seven days. [5]The priest shall examine him on the seventh day, and if he sees that the disease is checked and the disease has not spread in the skin, then the priest shall confine him seven days more. [6]The priest shall examine him again on the seventh day, and if the disease has abated and the disease has not spread in the skin, the priest shall pronounce him clean; it is only an eruption; and he shall wash his clothes, and be clean. [7]But if the eruption spreads in the

a A term for several skin diseases; precise meaning uncertain

---

12:1–8 *she shall be ceremonially unclean.* This chapter does not suggest that reproduction and birth are disgusting or evil. Rather, the offerings for cultic purification speak of the sacredness of life and concern for it. The event of childbirth is risky, and this chapter expresses an understanding that life is beyond human control. This text does reflect a social preference for males, which is not abnormal for the ancient priestly way of thinking. At the same time, the text provides hope as it celebrates the move from the dangers of childbirth back to full community in faith. Readers will also do well to remember

that the concern about blood reflects an ancient understanding of the mystery of life. Blood was tied to forgiveness and thus held sacred qualities. Leviticus 12 is a reminder that human life is sacred, mysterious, and fragile. Understanding the value of life—indeed, one's own life—is critical to spiritual development.

13:2 *a leprous disease.* The term used does not refer to what contemporary readers know as leprosy, Hansen's disease; rather, it refers to a variety of skin diseases from heavy dandruff to malignancies. Priests served also as public-health officers. Faith pervades every dimension of life.

skin after he has shown himself to the priest for his cleansing, he shall appear again before the priest. 8The priest shall make an examination, and if the eruption has spread in the skin, the priest shall pronounce him unclean; it is a leprous*a* disease.

9 When a person contracts a leprous*a* disease, he shall be brought to the priest. 10The priest shall make an examination, and if there is a white swelling in the skin that has turned the hair white, and there is quick raw flesh in the swelling, 11it is a chronic leprous*a* disease in the skin of his body. The priest shall pronounce him unclean; he shall not confine him, for he is unclean. 12But if the disease breaks out in the skin, so that it covers all the skin of the diseased person from head to foot, so far as the priest can see, 13then the priest shall make an examination, and if the disease has covered all his body, he shall pronounce him clean of the disease; since it has all turned white, he is clean. 14But if raw flesh ever appears on him, he shall be unclean; 15the priest shall examine the raw flesh and pronounce him unclean. Raw flesh is unclean, for it is a leprous*a* disease. 16But if the raw flesh again turns white, he shall come to the priest; 17the priest shall examine him, and if the disease has turned white, the priest shall pronounce the diseased person clean. He is clean.

18 When there is on the skin of one's body a boil that has healed, 19and in the place of the boil there appears a white swelling or a reddish-white spot, it shall be shown to the priest. 20The priest shall make an examination, and if it appears deeper than the skin and its hair has turned white, the priest shall pronounce him unclean; this is a leprous*a* disease, broken out in the boil. 21But if the priest examines it and the hair on it is not white, nor is it deeper than the skin but has abated, the priest shall confine him seven days. 22If it spreads in the skin, the priest shall pronounce him unclean; it is diseased. 23But if the spot remains in one place and does not spread, it is the scar of the boil; the priest shall pronounce him clean.

24 Or, when the body has a burn on the skin and the raw flesh of the burn becomes a spot, reddish-white or white, 25the priest shall examine it. If the hair in the spot has turned white and it appears deeper than the skin, it is a leprous*a* disease; it has broken out in the burn, and the priest shall pronounce him unclean. This is a leprous*a* disease. 26But if the priest examines it and the hair in the spot is not white, and it is no deeper than the skin but has abated, the priest shall confine him seven days. 27The priest shall examine him the seventh day; if it is spreading in the skin, the priest shall pronounce him unclean. This is a leprous*a* disease. 28But if the spot remains in one place and does not spread in the skin but has abated, it is a swelling from the burn, and the priest shall pronounce him clean; for it is the scar of the burn.

29 When a man or woman has a disease on the head or in the beard, 30the priest shall examine the disease. If it appears deeper than the skin and the hair in it is yellow and thin, the priest shall pronounce him unclean; it is an itch, a leprous*a* disease of the head or the beard. 31If the priest examines the itching disease, and it appears no deeper than the skin and there is no black hair in it, the priest shall confine the person with the itching disease for seven days. 32On the seventh day the priest shall examine the itch; if the itch has not spread, and there is no yellow hair in it, and the itch appears to be no deeper than the skin, 33he shall shave, but the itch he shall not shave. The priest shall confine the person with the itch for seven days more. 34On the seventh day the priest shall examine the itch; if the itch has not spread in the skin and it appears to be no deeper than the skin, the priest shall pronounce him clean. He shall wash his clothes and be clean. 35But if the itch spreads in the skin after he was pronounced clean, 36the priest shall examine him. If the itch has spread in the skin, the priest need not seek for the yellow hair; he is unclean. 37But if in his eyes the itch is checked, and black hair has grown in it, the itch is healed, he is clean; and the priest shall pronounce him clean.

38 When a man or a woman has spots on the skin of the body, white spots, 39the priest shall make an examination, and if the spots

a A term for several skin diseases; precise meaning uncertain

on the skin of the body are of a dull white, it is a rash that has broken out on the skin; he is clean.

40 If anyone loses the hair from his head, he is bald but he is clean. ⁴¹If he loses the hair from his forehead and temples, he has baldness of the forehead but he is clean. ⁴²But if there is on the bald head or the bald forehead a reddish-white diseased spot, it is a leprous*a* disease breaking out on his bald head or his bald forehead. ⁴³The priest shall examine him; if the diseased swelling is reddish-white on his bald head or on his bald forehead, which resembles a leprous*a* disease in the skin of the body, ⁴⁴he is leprous, *a* he is unclean. The priest shall pronounce him unclean; the disease is on his head.

45 The person who has the leprous*a* disease shall wear torn clothes and let the hair of his head be disheveled; and he shall cover his upper lip and cry out, "Unclean, unclean." ⁴⁶He shall remain unclean as long as he has the disease; he is unclean. He shall live alone; his dwelling shall be outside the camp.

47 Concerning clothing: when a leprous*a* disease appears in it, in woolen or linen cloth, ⁴⁸in warp or woof of linen or wool, or in a skin or in anything made of skin, ⁴⁹if the disease shows greenish or reddish in the garment, whether in warp or woof or in skin or in anything made of skin, it is a leprous*a* disease and shall be shown to the priest. ⁵⁰The priest shall examine the disease, and put the diseased article aside for seven days. ⁵¹He shall examine the disease on the seventh day. If the disease has spread in the cloth, in warp or woof, or in the skin, whatever be the use of the skin, this is a spreading leprous*a* disease; it is unclean. ⁵²He shall burn the clothing, whether diseased in warp or woof, woolen or linen, or anything of skin, for it is a spreading leprous*a* disease; it shall be burned in fire.

53 If the priest makes an examination, and the disease has not spread in the clothing, in warp or woof or in anything of skin, ⁵⁴the priest shall command them to wash the article in which the disease appears, and he shall put it aside seven days more. ⁵⁵The priest shall examine the diseased article after it has been washed. If the diseased spot has not changed color, though the disease has not spread, it is unclean; you shall burn it in fire, whether the leprous*t* spot is on the inside or on the outside.

56 If the priest makes an examination, and the disease has abated after it is washed, he shall tear the spot out of the cloth, in warp or woof, or out of skin. ⁵⁷If it appears again in the garment, in warp or woof, or in anything of skin, it is spreading; you shall burn with fire that in which the disease appears. ⁵⁸But the cloth, warp or woof, or anything of skin from which the disease disappears when you have washed it, shall then be washed a second time, and it shall be clean.

59 This is the ritual for a leprous*a* disease in a cloth of wool or linen, either in warp or woof, or in anything of skin, to decide whether it is clean or unclean.

Purification of Lepers and Leprous Houses

14 The LORD spoke to Moses, saying: ²This shall be the ritual for the leprous*a* person at the time of his cleansing:

He shall be brought to the priest; ³the priest shall go out of the camp, and the priest shall make an examination. If the disease is healed in the leprous*a* person, ⁴the priest shall command that two living clean birds and cedarwood and crimson yarn and hyssop be brought for the one who is to be cleansed. ⁵The priest shall command that one of the birds be slaughtered over fresh water in an earthen vessel. ⁶He shall take the living bird with the cedarwood and the crimson yarn and the hyssop, and dip them and the living bird in the blood of the bird that was slaughtered over the fresh water. ⁷He shall sprinkle it seven times upon the one who is to be cleansed of the leprous*a* disease; then he shall pronounce him clean, and he shall let the living bird go into the open field. ⁸The one who is to be cleansed shall wash his clothes, and shave off all his hair, and bathe himself in water, and he shall be clean. After that he shall come into the camp, but shall live outside his tent seven days. ⁹On the seventh day he shall shave all his hair: of head, beard, eyebrows; he shall shave all his hair. Then he

a A term for several skin diseases; precise meaning uncertain shall wash his clothes, and bathe his body in water, and he shall be clean.

10 On the eighth day he shall take two male lambs without blemish, and one ewe lamb in its first year without blemish, and a grain offering of three-tenths of an ephah of choice flour mixed with oil, and one log[a] of oil. 11The priest who cleanses shall set the person to be cleansed, along with these things, before the LORD, at the entrance of the tent of meeting. 12The priest shall take one of the lambs, and offer it as a guilt offering, along with the log[a] of oil, and raise them as an elevation offering before the LORD. 13He shall slaughter the lamb in the place where the sin offering and the burnt offering are slaughtered in the holy place; for the guilt offering, like the sin offering, belongs to the priest: it is most holy. 14The priest shall take some of the blood of the guilt offering and put it on the lobe of the right ear of the one to be cleansed, and on the thumb of the right hand, and on the big toe of the right foot. 15The priest shall take some of the log[a] of oil and pour it into the palm of his own left hand, 16and dip his right finger in the oil that is in his left hand and sprinkle some oil with his finger seven times before the LORD. 17Some of the oil that remains in his hand the priest shall put on the lobe of the right ear of the one to be cleansed, and on the thumb of the right hand, and on the big toe of the right foot, on top of the blood of the guilt offering. 18The rest of the oil that is in the priest's hand he shall put on the head of the one to be cleansed. Then the priest shall make atonement on his behalf before the LORD: 19the priest shall offer the sin offering, to make atonement for the one to be cleansed from his uncleanness. Afterward he shall slaughter the burnt offering; 20and the priest shall offer the burnt offering and the grain offering on the altar. Thus the priest shall make atonement on his behalf and he shall be clean.

21 But if he is poor and cannot afford so much, he shall take one male lamb for a guilt offering to be elevated, to make atonement on his behalf, and one-tenth of an ephah of choice flour mixed with oil for a grain offering and a log[a] of oil; 22also two turtledoves or two pigeons, such as he can afford, one for a sin offering and the other for a burnt offering. 23On the eighth day he shall bring them for his cleansing to the priest, to the entrance of the tent of meeting, before the LORD; 24and the priest shall take the lamb of the guilt offering and the log[a] of oil, and the priest shall raise them as an elevation offering before the LORD. 25The priest shall slaughter the lamb of the guilt offering and shall take some of the blood of the guilt offering, and put it on the lobe of the right ear of the one to be cleansed, and on the thumb of the right hand, and on the big toe of the right foot. 26The priest shall pour some of the oil into the palm of his own left hand, 27and shall sprinkle with his right finger some of the oil that is in his left hand seven times before the LORD. 28The priest shall put some of the oil that is in his hand on the lobe of the right ear of the one to be cleansed, and on the thumb of the right hand, and the big toe of the right foot, where the blood of the guilt offering was placed. 29The rest of the oil that is in the priest's hand he shall put on the head of the one to be cleansed, to make atonement on his behalf before the LORD. 30And he shall offer, of the turtledoves or pigeons such as he can afford, 31one[b] for a sin offering and the other for a burnt offering, along with a grain offering; and the priest shall make atonement before the LORD on behalf of the one being cleansed. 32This is the ritual for the one who has a leprous[c] disease, who cannot afford the offerings for his cleansing.

33 The LORD spoke to Moses and Aaron, saying:

34 When you come into the land of Canaan, which I give you for a possession, and I put a leprous[c] disease in a house in the land of your possession, 35the owner of the house shall come and tell the priest, saying, "There seems to me to be some sort of disease in my house." 36The priest shall command that they empty the house before the priest goes to examine the disease, or all that is in the house will become unclean; and afterward the priest shall go in to inspect the house.

a A liquid measure   b Gk Syr: Heb afford, 31such as he can afford, one   c A term for several skin diseases; precise meaning uncertain

37He shall examine the disease; if the disease is in the walls of the house with greenish or reddish spots, and if it appears to be deeper than the surface, 38the priest shall go outside to the door of the house and shut up the house seven days. 39The priest shall come again on the seventh day and make an inspection; if the disease has spread in the walls of the house, 40the priest shall command that the stones in which the disease appears be taken out and thrown into an unclean place outside the city. 41He shall have the inside of the house scraped thoroughly, and the plaster that is scraped off shall be dumped in an unclean place outside the city. 42They shall take other stones and put them in the place of those stones, and take other plaster and plaster the house.

43 If the disease breaks out again in the house, after he has taken out the stones and scraped the house and plastered it, 44the priest shall go and make inspection; if the disease has spread in the house, it is a spreading leprousa disease in the house; it is unclean. 45He shall have the house torn down, its stones and timber and all the plaster of the house, and taken outside the city to an unclean place. 46All who enter the house while it is shut up shall be unclean until the evening; 47and all who sleep in the house shall wash their clothes; and all who eat in the house shall wash their clothes.

48 If the priest comes and makes an inspection, and the disease has not spread in the house after the house was plastered, the priest shall pronounce the house clean; the disease is healed. 49For the cleansing of the house he shall take two birds, with cedarwood and crimson yarn and hyssop, 50and shall slaughter one of the birds over fresh water in an earthen vessel, 51and shall take the cedarwood and the hyssop and the crimson yarn, along with the living bird, and dip them in the blood of the slaughtered bird and the fresh water, and sprinkle the house seven times. 52Thus he shall cleanse the house with the blood of the bird, and with the fresh water, and with the living bird, and with the cedarwood and hyssop and crimson yarn; 53and he shall let the living bird go out of the city into the open field; so he shall make atonement for the house, and it shall be clean.

54 This is the ritual for any leprousa disease: for an itch, 55for leprousa diseases in clothing and houses, 56and for a swelling or an eruption or a spot, 57to determine when it is unclean and when it is clean. This is the ritual for leprousa diseases.

Concerning Bodily Discharges

15 The LORD spoke to Moses and Aaron, saying: 2Speak to the people of Israel and say to them:

When any man has a discharge from his member,b his discharge makes him ceremonially unclean. 3The uncleanness of his discharge is this: whether his memberb flows with his discharge, or his memberb is stopped

---

a A term for several skin diseases; precise meaning uncertain b Heb flesh

---

14:48–53 *so he shall make atonement for the house.* The instructions on atonement for a house are not related to the magical or demonic. The house is ceremonially unclean. Atonement here puts the building back into a whole state, into cleanness, and into a state in which it can be used by people without their becoming unclean. The text assumes that cleanness is fundamentally connected to wholeness, and its acute concern for cleanness demonstrates the importance of wholeness. This notion of wholeness (applied here even to a building) seems to permeate the ancient priestly way of thinking. Wholeness—a way of

being in right relationship to the community of faith—is necessary in Leviticus for encountering God and maintaining one's connection to God. If people in the community became unclean by contact with an unclean building, they would be unable to worship.

15:1–33 *uncleanness.* As in the preceding chapters, the priests are here establishing the boundaries of clean and unclean. These boundaries protect normality or wholeness for the people and in that sense protect the holy and enable God to continue to dwell with the faith community of ancient Israel and to bless them with fullness of life. God's presence is the

from discharging, it is uncleanness for him. [4]Every bed on which the one with the discharge lies shall be unclean; and everything on which he sits shall be unclean. [5]Anyone who touches his bed shall wash his clothes, and bathe in water, and be unclean until the evening. [6]All who sit on anything on which the one with the discharge has sat shall wash their clothes, and bathe in water, and be unclean until the evening. [7]All who touch the body of the one with the discharge shall wash their clothes, and bathe in water, and be unclean until the evening. [8]If the one with the discharge spits on persons who are clean, then they shall wash their clothes, and bathe in water, and be unclean until the evening. [9]Any saddle on which the one with the discharge rides shall be unclean. [10]All who touch anything that was under him shall be unclean until the evening, and all who carry such a thing shall wash their clothes, and bathe in water, and be unclean until the evening. [11]All those whom the one with the discharge touches without his having rinsed his hands in water shall wash their clothes, and bathe in water, and be unclean until the evening. [12]Any earthen vessel that the one with the discharge touches shall be broken; and every vessel of wood shall be rinsed in water.

13 When the one with a discharge is cleansed of his discharge, he shall count seven days for his cleansing; he shall wash his clothes and bathe his body in fresh water, and he shall be clean. [14]On the eighth day he shall take two turtledoves or two pigeons and come before the LORD to the entrance of the tent of meeting and give them to the priest. [15]The priest shall offer them, one for a sin offering and the other for a burnt offering;

and the priest shall make atonement on his behalf before the LORD for his discharge.

16 If a man has an emission of semen, he shall bathe his whole body in water, and be unclean until the evening. [17]Everything made of cloth or of skin on which the semen falls shall be washed with water, and be unclean until the evening. [18]If a man lies with a woman and has an emission of semen, both of them shall bathe in water, and be unclean until the evening.

19 When a woman has a discharge of blood that is her regular discharge from her body, she shall be in her impurity for seven days, and whoever touches her shall be unclean until the evening. [20]Everything upon which she lies during her impurity shall be unclean; everything also upon which she sits shall be unclean. [21]Whoever touches her bed shall wash his clothes, and bathe in water, and be unclean until the evening. [22]Whoever touches anything upon which she sits shall wash his clothes, and bathe in water, and be unclean until the evening; [23]whether it is the bed or anything upon which she sits, when he touches it he shall be unclean until the evening. [24]If any man lies with her, and her impurity falls on him, he shall be unclean seven days; and every bed on which he lies shall be unclean.

25 If a woman has a discharge of blood for many days, not at the time of her impurity, or if she has a discharge beyond the time of her impurity, all the days of the discharge she shall continue in uncleanness; as in the days of her impurity, she shall be unclean. [26]Every bed on which she lies during all the days of her discharge shall be treated as the bed of her impurity; and everything on which she sits shall be unclean, as in the un-

---

key to vitality for the community. These ideas show up in the New Testament also. In Mark 5:25–34, Jesus heals a woman who is suffering from an abnormal discharge like that described in Lev 15:25–30. Since Jesus touches the woman, according to these instructions he would have become unclean. Instead, she is healed. In Matt 15:10–20, Jesus redefines the notion of uncleanness in terms of faith. Uncleanness comes from what is inside one and has an effect

on one's relationship with God. A number of the instructions in Leviticus appear to relate to the tedious parts of everyday life. The book explores the profound spiritual dimensions of the mundane—diet, illness, the condition of buildings, and so forth. There is an important physical part to the spirituality in Leviticus. Our physical health has a direct impact upon our spiritual health.

cleanness of her impurity. 27Whoever touches these things shall be unclean, and shall wash his clothes, and bathe in water, and be unclean until the evening. 28If she is cleansed of her discharge, she shall count seven days, and after that she shall be clean. 29On the eighth day she shall take two turtledoves or two pigeons and bring them to the priest at the entrance of the tent of meeting. 30The priest shall offer one for a sin offering and the other for a burnt offering; and the priest shall make atonement on her behalf before the LORD for her unclean discharge.

31 Thus you shall keep the people of Israel separate from their uncleanness, so that they do not die in their uncleanness by defiling my tabernacle that is in their midst.

32 This is the ritual for those who have a discharge: for him who has an emission of semen, becoming unclean thereby, 33for her who is in the infirmity of her period, for anyone, male or female, who has a discharge, and for the man who lies with a woman who is unclean.

The Day of Atonement

16 The LORD spoke to Moses after the death of the two sons of Aaron, when they drew near before the LORD and died. 2The LORD said to Moses:

Tell your brother Aaron not to come just at any time into the sanctuary inside the curtain before the mercy seat *a* that is upon the ark, or he will die; for I appear in the cloud upon the mercy seat. *a* 3Thus shall Aaron come into the holy place: with a young bull for a sin offering and a ram for a burnt offering. 4He shall put on the holy linen tunic, and shall have the linen undergarments next to his body, fasten the linen sash, and wear the linen turban; these are the holy vestments. He shall bathe his body in water, and then put them on. 5He shall take from the congregation of the people of Israel two male goats for a sin offering, and one ram for a burnt offering.

6 Aaron shall offer the bull as a sin offering for himself, and shall make atonement for himself and for his house. 7He shall take the two goats and set them before the LORD at the entrance of the tent of meeting; 8and Aaron shall cast lots on the two goats, one lot for the LORD and the other lot for Azazel. *b* 9Aaron shall present the goat on which the lot fell for the LORD, and offer it as a sin offering; 10but the goat on which the lot fell for Azazel *b* shall be presented alive before the

a Or *the cover*   *b* Traditionally rendered *a scapegoat*

Responding
16:1–2 THE WITH-GOD LIFE. Aaron's two sons died because they "drew near before the LORD" (see 10:1–3), and Aaron is cautioned about going before the mercy seat in an untimely manner. Why would God take such radical measures? *See also* Spiritual Disciplines Index.

16:1–34 *Thus shall Aaron come into the holy place.* The Day of Atonement is central in Leviticus. The actions are ritual and clearly have significance for the community and its members. The same kind of actions are described in Ps 35:13. Hebrews 9 speaks of the tabernacle, and of Christ as both high priest and ultimate sacrifice for the Church. Heb 10:1–25 speaks of the impermanence of these sacrifices and the permanence of Christ's sacrifice (see also 2 Cor 5:21). It is important to note that this

chapter follows the instructions on clean and unclean. The Day of Atonement ritual provides for purification from any uncleanness; it provides a rite of passage back to cleanness. This ritual is a gracious provision for the people. Aaron makes atonement for himself and for the congregation. He places the sins of the people on the "scapegoat," which is removed far from the community (v 10). For the Church the events of Holy Week approximate the function of the Day of Atonement. The holy God acts for humanity in Christ's crucifixion and resurrection, which make atonement possible. It is certainly appropriate to find a similar emphasis at a central point in Leviticus. Experiencing God's grace can be one of the most formative events of our spiritual life. Finding "at-one-ment" with God reconciles and reconnects us to the very source and goal of our spiritual lives. It is central to the with-God life.

LORD to make atonement over it, that it may be sent away into the wilderness to Azazel. *a*

11 Aaron shall present the bull as a sin offering for himself, and shall make atonement for himself and for his house; he shall slaughter the bull as a sin offering for himself. 12He shall take a censer full of coals of fire from the altar before the LORD, and two handfuls of crushed sweet incense, and he shall bring it inside the curtain 13and put the incense on the fire before the LORD, that the cloud of the incense may cover the mercy seat *b* that is upon the covenant, *c* or he will die. 14He shall take some of the blood of the bull, and sprinkle it with his finger on the front of the mercy seat, *b* and before the mercy seat *b* he shall sprinkle the blood with his finger seven times.

15 He shall slaughter the goat of the sin offering that is for the people and bring its blood inside the curtain, and do with its blood as he did with the blood of the bull, sprinkling it upon the mercy seat *b* and before the mercy seat. *b* 16Thus he shall make atonement for the sanctuary, because of the uncleannesses of the people of Israel, and because of their transgressions, all their sins; and so he shall do for the tent of meeting, which remains with them in the midst of their uncleannesses. 17No one shall be in the tent of meeting from the time he enters to make atonement in the sanctuary until he comes out and has made atonement for himself and for his house and for all the assembly of Israel. 18Then he shall go out to the altar that is before the LORD and make atonement on its behalf, and shall take some of the blood of the bull and of the blood of the goat, and put it on each of the horns of the altar. 19He shall sprinkle some of the blood on it with his finger seven times, and cleanse it and hallow it from the uncleannesses of the people of Israel.

20 When he has finished atoning for the holy place and the tent of meeting and the altar, he shall present the live goat. 21Then Aaron shall lay both his hands on the head of the live goat, and confess over it all the iniquities of the people of Israel, and all their transgressions, all their sins, putting them on the head of the goat, and sending it away into the wilderness by means of someone designated for the task. *d* 22The goat shall bear on itself all their iniquities to a barren region; and the goat shall be set free in the wilderness.

23 Then Aaron shall enter the tent of meeting, and shall take off the linen vestments that he put on when he went into the holy place, and shall leave them there. 24He shall bathe his body in water in a holy place, and put on his vestments; then he shall come out and offer his burnt offering and the burnt offering of the people, making atonement for himself and for the people. 25The fat of the sin offering he shall turn into smoke on the altar. 26The one who sets the goat free for Azazel *a* shall wash his clothes and bathe his body in water, and afterward may come into the camp. 27The bull of the sin offering and the goat of the sin offering, whose blood was brought in to make atonement in the holy place, shall be taken outside the camp; their skin and their flesh and their dung shall be consumed in fire. 28The one who burns them shall wash his clothes and bathe his body in water, and afterward may come into the camp.

29 This shall be a statute to you forever: In the seventh month, on the tenth day of the month, you shall deny yourselves, *e* and shall do no work, neither the citizen nor the alien who resides among you. 30For on this day atonement shall be made for you, to cleanse you; from all your sins you shall be clean before the LORD. 31It is a sabbath of complete rest to you, and you shall deny yourselves; *e* it is a statute forever. 32The priest who is anointed and consecrated as priest in his father's place shall make atonement, wearing the linen vestments, the holy vestments. 33He shall make atonement for the sanctuary, and he shall make atonement for the tent of meeting and for the altar, and he shall make atonement for the priests and for all the people of the assembly. 34This shall be an everlasting statute for you, to make atonement for the people of Israel once in the year for all their sins. And Moses did as the LORD had commanded him.

a Traditionally rendered *a scapegoat*   *b* Or *the cover*   *c* Or *treaty*, or *testament*; Heb *eduth*   *d* Meaning of Heb uncertain   *e* Or *shall fast*

The Slaughtering of Animals

17 The LORD spoke to Moses: 2 Speak to Aaron and his sons and to all the people of Israel and say to them: This is what the LORD has commanded. ³If anyone of the house of Israel slaughters an ox or a lamb or a goat in the camp, or slaughters it outside the camp, ⁴and does not bring it to the entrance of the tent of meeting, to present it as an offering to the LORD before the tabernacle of the LORD, he shall be held guilty of bloodshed; he has shed blood, and he shall be cut off from the people. ⁵This is in order that the people of Israel may bring their sacrifices that they offer in the open field, that they may bring them to the LORD, to the priest at the entrance of the tent of meeting, and offer them as sacrifices of well-being to the LORD. ⁶The priest shall dash the blood against the altar of the LORD at the entrance of the tent of meeting, and turn the fat into smoke as a pleasing odor to the LORD, ⁷so that they may no longer offer their sacrifices for goat-demons, to whom they prostitute themselves. This shall be a statute forever to them throughout their generations.

8 And say to them further: Anyone of the house of Israel or of the aliens who reside among them who offers a burnt offering or sacrifice, ⁹and does not bring it to the entrance of the tent of meeting, to sacrifice it to the LORD, shall be cut off from the people.

Eating Blood Prohibited

10 If anyone of the house of Israel or of the aliens who reside among them eats any blood, I will set my face against that person who eats blood, and will cut that person off from the people. ¹¹For the life of the flesh is in the blood; and I have given it to you for making atonement for your lives on the altar; for, as life, it is the blood that makes atonement. ¹²Therefore I have said to the people of Israel: No person among you shall eat blood, nor shall any alien who resides among you eat blood. ¹³And anyone of the people of Israel, or of the aliens who reside among them, who hunts down an animal or bird that may be eaten shall pour out its blood and cover it with earth.

14 For the life of every creature—its blood is its life; therefore I have said to the people of Israel: You shall not eat the blood of any creature, for the life of every creature is its blood; whoever eats it shall be cut off. ¹⁵All persons, citizens or aliens, who eat what dies of itself or what has been torn by wild animals, shall wash their clothes, and bathe themselves in water, and be unclean until the evening; then they shall be clean. ¹⁶But if they do not wash themselves or bathe their body, they shall bear their guilt.

Sexual Relations

18 The LORD spoke to Moses, saying: 2 Speak to the people of Israel and say to them: I am the LORD your God. ³You shall not do as they do in the land of Egypt, where you lived, and you shall not do as they do in the land of Canaan, to which I am bringing you. You shall not follow their statutes. ⁴My ordinances you shall observe and

---

17:2–7 *so that they may no longer offer their sacrifices for goat-demons, to whom they prostitute themselves.* The regulation of sacrifice is to discourage worship of idols. Idolatry brings only death-giving ways to the spirit. Chapters 17–27 constitute the Holiness Code and include instruction in worship and ethics.

17:11–14 *No person among you shall eat blood.* These verses reflect the centrality of blood for life and atonement and offer insight into the atoning sacrifices described in chapters 1–7.

18:1–30 *You shall not follow their statutes. My ordinances you shall observe.* The introductory verses (vv 1–5) put the instruction in context.

The faith community is to be characterized by allegiance to neither the Egyptian nor Canaanite lifestyle, but by practices formed in its relationship with God. The concluding verses (vv 24–30) reiterate the view of the chapter based on divine revelation: maintain holiness. In Leviticus, holiness means being distinctive as the People of God. The issue this text raises for contemporary communities of faith is how to demonstrate distinctiveness of faith today. The concern pervades all of life—family life and sexual conduct are certainly included. Prophetic calls for justice are also relevant to the task of forming life as a holy community.

my statutes you shall keep, following them: I am the LORD your God. ⁵You shall keep my statutes and my ordinances; by doing so one shall live: I am the LORD.

6 None of you shall approach anyone near of kin to uncover nakedness: I am the LORD. ⁷You shall not uncover the nakedness of your father, which is the nakedness of your mother; she is your mother, you shall not uncover her nakedness. ⁸You shall not uncover the nakedness of your father's wife; it is the nakedness of your father. ⁹You shall not uncover the nakedness of your sister, your father's daughter or your mother's daughter, whether born at home or born abroad. ¹⁰You shall not uncover the nakedness of your son's daughter or of your daughter's daughter, for their nakedness is your own nakedness. ¹¹You shall not uncover the nakedness of your father's wife's daughter, begotten by your father, since she is your sister. ¹²You shall not uncover the nakedness of your father's sister; she is your father's flesh. ¹³You shall not uncover the nakedness of your mother's sister, for she is your mother's flesh. ¹⁴You shall not uncover the nakedness of your father's brother, that is, you shall not approach his wife; she is your aunt. ¹⁵You shall not uncover the nakedness of your daughter-in-law: she is your son's wife; you shall not uncover her nakedness. ¹⁶You shall not uncover the nakedness of your brother's wife; it is your brother's nakedness. ¹⁷You shall not uncover the nakedness of a woman and her daughter, and you shall not take*ᵃ* her son's daughter or her daughter's daughter to uncover her nakedness; they are your*ᵇ* flesh; it is depravity. ¹⁸And you shall not take*ᵃ* a woman as a rival to her sister, uncovering her nakedness while her sister is still alive.

19 You shall not approach a woman to uncover her nakedness while she is in her menstrual uncleanness. ²⁰You shall not have sexual relations with your kinsman's wife, and defile yourself with her. ²¹You shall not give any of your offspring to sacrifice them*ᶜ* to Molech, and so profane the name of your God: I am the LORD. ²²You shall not lie with a male as with a woman; it is an abomination. ²³You shall not have sexual relations with any animal and defile yourself with it, nor shall any woman give herself to an animal to have sexual relations with it: it is perversion.

24 Do not defile yourselves in any of these ways, for by all these practices the nations I am casting out before you have defiled themselves. ²⁵Thus the land became defiled; and I punished it for its iniquity, and the land vomited out its inhabitants. ²⁶But you shall keep my statutes and my ordinances and commit none of these abominations, either the citizen or the alien who resides among you ²⁷(for the inhabitants of the land, who were before you, committed all of these abominations, and the land became defiled); ²⁸otherwise the land will vomit you out for defiling it, as it vomited out the nation that was before you. ²⁹For whoever commits any of these abominations shall be cut off from their people. ³⁰So keep my charge not to commit any of these abominations that were done before you, and not to defile yourselves by them: I am the LORD your God.

Ritual and Moral Holiness

19 The LORD spoke to Moses, saying: 2 Speak to all the congregation of the people of Israel and say to them: You shall be holy, for I the LORD your God am holy. ³You shall each revere your mother and father, and you shall keep my sabbaths: I am the

a Or marry   b Gk: Heb lacks your   c Heb to pass them over

19:2 *be holy, for † the LORD your God am holy.* The chapter opens with a classic statement from the Holiness Code. The living God is different and so Israel as God's people is called to be different. This kind of holiness includes orderliness and justice. The point is that a consequence of spiritual formation is change: we change the way we conduct ourselves as well as the way we treat others. It is an outward, observable expression of an inner, spiritual reality.

19:3 *and you shall keep my sabbaths.* The Sabbath was a day of rest for humans and animals as well as a time of worship. Sabbath observance is important in Old Testament faith and was a special distinctive for the Israelites

LORD your God. ⁴Do not turn to idols or make cast images for yourselves: I am the LORD your God.

5 When you offer a sacrifice of well-being to the LORD, offer it in such a way that it is acceptable in your behalf. ⁶It shall be eaten on the same day you offer it, or on the next day; and anything left over until the third day shall be consumed in fire. ⁷If it is eaten at all on the third day, it is an abomination; it will not be acceptable. ⁸All who eat it shall be subject to punishment, because they have profaned what is holy to the LORD; and any such person shall be cut off from the people.

9 When you reap the harvest of your land, you shall not reap to the very edges of your field, or gather the gleanings of your harvest. ¹⁰You shall not strip your vineyard bare, or gather the fallen grapes of your vineyard; you shall leave them for the poor and the alien: I am the LORD your God.

11 You shall not steal; you shall not deal falsely; and you shall not lie to one another. ¹²And you shall not swear falsely by my name,

profaning the name of your God: I am the LORD.

13 You shall not defraud your neighbor; you shall not steal; and you shall not keep for yourself the wages of a laborer until morning. ¹⁴You shall not revile the deaf or put a stumbling block before the blind; you shall fear your God: I am the LORD.

15 You shall not render an unjust judgment; you shall not be partial to the poor or defer to the great: with justice you shall judge your neighbor. ¹⁶You shall not go around as a slanderer*a* among your people, and you shall not profit by the blood*b* of your neighbor: I am the LORD.

17 You shall not hate in your heart anyone of your kin; you shall reprove your neighbor, or you will incur guilt yourself. ¹⁸You shall not take vengeance or bear a grudge against any of your people, but you shall love your neighbor as yourself: I am the LORD.

19 You shall keep my statutes. You shall

---

a Meaning of Heb uncertain   *b* Heb *stand against the blood*

---

during the Babylonian captivity. A habit of rest is as important as respect for one's parents and avoiding the worship of idols (vv 3–4). The ancient Israelites understood the need for regular times of pause, of peaceful reflection on God. The frenzied pace that characterizes much of contemporary life can hamper spiritual growth. Times of "sabbath" are no less important today.

19:11–16 *You shall not steal.* These verses relate to social justice. In verses 11–12, stealing, lying, deception, and swearing falsely are prohibited. Verses 15–16 move to the setting of the court or assembly where judicial proceedings occur. The plea is for impartiality in legal proceedings. The responsibility of the witness is to tell the truth and not engage in gossip. The reference may well be to serious defamation of character or malicious libel. This malicious slander could endanger the life of another (v 16). The business of living as holy People of God has to do with more than individual piety; it has profound social ramifications.

19:17–18 *you shall love your neighbor as yourself.* The love of neighbor consists of a commitment to the welfare and best interests of

another person, citizen or sojourner (vv 11–16). These two verses are built on contrasting hate and vengeance with honest relationships and love. The climax of verses 11–18, then, is the call to love one's neighbor, companion, or friend. This call is part of Jesus' text in Matt 22:34–39 in speaking of the two great commandments. Many readers of the Gospels are unaware that this text comes from the Old Testament and especially from Leviticus. The concerns for holiness relate to much of life and so contain a strong ethical dimension. This emphasis is not in conflict with the concerns about proper ritual that dominate the first parts of Leviticus, but is consistent with them. The chapters of the Holiness Code are more explicit in combining the cultic and the ethical dimensions of life. The whole of the book of Leviticus reflects awareness of the community as the basis for life as God's people, and this call to love the neighbor fits that theme. In Leviticus, the way one worships and the way one lives are tied to one's relationship with God. Our spiritual formation is shaped not only by the reverence we show toward God, but also by the justice we extend toward others.

not let your animals breed with a different kind; you shall not sow your field with two kinds of seed; nor shall you put on a garment made of two different materials.

20 If a man has sexual relations with a woman who is a slave, designated for another man but not ransomed or given her freedom, an inquiry shall be held. They shall not be put to death, since she has not been freed; 21but he shall bring a guilt offering for himself to the LORD, at the entrance of the tent of meeting, a ram as guilt offering. 22And the priest shall make atonement for him with the ram of guilt offering before the LORD for his sin that he committed; and the sin he committed shall be forgiven him.

23 When you come into the land and plant all kinds of trees for food, then you shall regard their fruit as forbidden;a three years it shall be forbiddenb to you, it must not be eaten. 24In the fourth year all their fruit shall be set apart for rejoicing in the LORD. 25But in the fifth year you may eat of their fruit, that their yield may be increased for you: I am the LORD your God.

26 You shall not eat anything with its blood. You shall not practice augury or witchcraft. 27You shall not round off the hair on your temples or mar the edges of your beard. 28You shall not make any gashes in your flesh for the dead or tattoo any marks upon you: I am the LORD.

29 Do not profane your daughter by making her a prostitute, that the land not become prostituted and full of depravity. 30You shall keep my sabbaths and reverence my sanctuary: I am the LORD.

31 Do not turn to mediums or wizards; do not seek them out, to be defiled by them: I am the LORD your God.

32 You shall rise before the aged, and defer to the old; and you shall fear your God: I am the LORD.

33 When an alien resides with you in your land, you shall not oppress the alien. 34The alien who resides with you shall be to you as the citizen among you; you shall love the alien as yourself, for you were aliens in the land of Egypt: I am the LORD your God.

35 You shall not cheat in measuring length, weight, or quantity. 36You shall have honest balances, honest weights, an honest ephah, and an honest hin: I am the LORD your God, who brought you out of the land of Egypt. 37You shall keep all my statutes and all my ordinances, and observe them: I am the LORD.

Penalties for Violations of Holiness

20 The LORD spoke to Moses, saying: 2Say further to the people of Israel:

Any of the people of Israel, or of the aliens who reside in Israel, who give any of their offspring to Molech shall be put to death; the people of the land shall stone them to death. 3I myself will set my face against them, and will cut them off from the people, because they have given of their offspring to Molech, defiling my sanctuary and profaning my holy name. 4And if the people of the land should ever close their eyes to them, when they give of their offspring to Molech, and do not put them to death, 5I myself will set my face against them and against their family, and will cut them off from among their people, them and all who follow them in prostituting themselves to Molech.

6 If any turn to mediums and wizards, prostituting themselves to them, I will set my face against them, and will cut them off

a Heb as their uncircumcision
b Heb uncircumcision

19:33–34 *love the alien as yourself.* The motivation here is that the Israelites should remember the oppression they had experienced as aliens in Egypt and seek to overcome it in their relationships. The concern is that the holy people of God are to live in justice, and the ethical demands flowing from that concern include care for the powerless, such as resident aliens. Once again, Leviticus connects holiness (being distinctive as the People of God) with justice and ethical living.

20:1–27 *for I am the LORD your God.* A number of topics in this chapter have been covered earlier. The concern is loyalty to the one true God in worship and family life.

from the people. 7Consecrate yourselves therefore, and be holy; for I am the LORD your God. 8Keep my statutes, and observe them; I am the LORD; I sanctify you. 9All who curse father or mother shall be put to death; having cursed father or mother, their blood is upon them.

10 If a man commits adultery with the wife of*a* his neighbor, both the adulterer and the adulteress shall be put to death. 11The man who lies with his father's wife has uncovered his father's nakedness; both of them shall be put to death; their blood is upon them. 12If a man lies with his daughter-in-law, both of them shall be put to death; they have committed perversion, their blood is upon them. 13If a man lies with a male as with a woman, both of them have committed an abomination; they shall be put to death; their blood is upon them. 14If a man takes a wife and her mother also, it is depravity; they shall be burned to death, both he and they, that there may be no depravity among you. 15If a man has sexual relations with an animal, he shall be put to death; and you shall kill the animal. 16If a woman approaches any animal and has sexual relations with it, you shall kill the woman and the animal; they shall be put to death, their blood is upon them.

17 If a man takes his sister, a daughter of his father or a daughter of his mother, and sees her nakedness, and she sees his nakedness, it is a disgrace, and they shall be cut off in the sight of their people; he has uncovered his sister's nakedness, he shall be subject to punishment. 18If a man lies with a woman having her sickness and uncovers her nakedness, he has laid bare her flow and she has laid bare her flow of blood; both of them shall be cut off from their people. 19You shall not uncover the nakedness of your mother's sister or of your father's sister, for that is to lay bare one's own flesh; they shall be subject to punishment. 20If a man lies with his uncle's wife, he has uncovered his uncle's nakedness; they shall be subject to punishment; they shall

die childless. 21If a man takes his brother's wife, it is impurity; he has uncovered his brother's nakedness; they shall be childless.

22 You shall keep all my statutes and all my ordinances, and observe them, so that the land to which I bring you to settle in may not vomit you out. 23You shall not follow the practices of the nation that I am driving out before you. Because they did all these things, I abhorred them. 24But I have said to you: You shall inherit their land, and I will give it to you to possess, a land flowing with milk and honey. I am the LORD your God; I have separated you from the peoples. 25You shall therefore make a distinction between the clean animal and the unclean, and between the unclean bird and the clean; you shall not bring abomination on yourselves by animal or by bird or by anything with which the ground teems, which I have set apart for you to hold unclean. 26You shall be holy to me; for I the LORD am holy, and I have separated you from the other peoples to be mine.

27 A man or a woman who is a medium or a wizard shall be put to death; they shall be stoned to death, their blood is upon them.

The Holiness of Priests

21 The LORD said to Moses: Speak to the priests, the sons of Aaron, and say to them:

No one shall defile himself for a dead person among his relatives, 2except for his nearest kin: his mother, his father, his son, his daughter, his brother; 3likewise, for a virgin sister, close to him because she has had no husband, he may defile himself for her. 4But he shall not defile himself as a husband among his people and so profane himself. 5They shall not make bald spots upon their heads, or shave off the edges of their beards, or make any gashes in their flesh. 6They shall be holy to their God, and not profane the name of their God; for they offer the LORD's

a Heb repeats *if a man commits adultery with the wife of*

21:1–24 *Speak to the priests.* The priests are divinely chosen leaders in ancient Israel, so they are to exemplify the community's wholeness

and to avoid death as an enemy of God as well as any practices raising questions about loyalty to the one true God.

offerings by fire, the food of their God; therefore they shall be holy. ⁷They shall not marry a prostitute or a woman who has been defiled; neither shall they marry a woman divorced from her husband. For they are holy to their God, ⁸and you shall treat them as holy, since they offer the food of your God; they shall be holy to you, for I the LORD, I who sanctify you, am holy. ⁹When the daughter of a priest profanes herself through prostitution, she profanes her father; she shall be burned to death.

10 The priest who is exalted above his fellows, on whose head the anointing oil has been poured and who has been consecrated to wear the vestments, shall not dishevel his hair, nor tear his vestments. ¹¹He shall not go where there is a dead body; he shall not defile himself even for his father or mother. ¹²He shall not go outside the sanctuary and thus profane the sanctuary of his God; for the consecration of the anointing oil of his God is upon him: I am the LORD. ¹³He shall marry only a woman who is a virgin. ¹⁴A widow, or a divorced woman, or a woman who has been defiled, a prostitute, these he shall not marry. He shall marry a virgin of his own kin, ¹⁵that he may not profane his offspring among his kin; for I am the LORD; I sanctify him.

16 The LORD spoke to Moses, saying: ¹⁷Speak to Aaron and say: No one of your offspring throughout their generations who has a blemish may approach to offer the food of his God. ¹⁸For no one who has a blemish shall draw near, one who is blind or lame, or one who has a mutilated face or a limb too long, ¹⁹or one who has a broken foot or a broken hand, ²⁰or a hunchback, or a dwarf, or a man with a blemish in his eyes or an itching disease or scabs or crushed testicles. ²¹No descendant of Aaron the priest who has a blemish shall come near to offer the LORD's offerings by fire; since he has a blemish, he shall not come near to offer the food of his God. ²²He may eat the food of his God, of the most holy as well as of the holy. ²³But he shall not come near the curtain or approach the altar, because he has a blemish, that he may not profane my sanctuaries; for I am the LORD; I sanctify them. ²⁴Thus Moses spoke to Aaron and to his sons and to all the people of Israel.

The Use of Holy Offerings

22 The LORD spoke to Moses, saying: ²Direct Aaron and his sons to deal carefully with the sacred donations of the people of Israel, which they dedicate to me, so that they may not profane my holy name; I am the LORD. ³Say to them: If anyone among all your offspring throughout your generations comes near the sacred donations, which the people of Israel dedicate to the LORD, while he is in a state of uncleanness, that person shall be cut off from my presence: I am the LORD. ⁴No one of Aaron's offspring who has a leprous*ᵃ* disease or suffers a discharge may eat of the sacred donations until he is clean. Whoever touches anything made unclean by a corpse or a man who has had an emission of semen, ⁵and whoever touches any swarming thing by which he may be made unclean or any human being by whom he may be made unclean—whatever his uncleanness may be— ⁶the person who touches any such shall be unclean until evening and shall not eat of the sacred donations unless he has washed his body in water. ⁷When the sun sets he shall be clean; and afterward he may eat of the sacred donations, for they are his

a A term for several skin diseases; precise meaning uncertain

---

22:1–33 *deal carefully with the sacred donations of the people of Israel.* The chapter is addressed to Aaron and his sons through Moses and begins with a warning to treat the sacred offerings with respect. These instructions also operate from the notion that sacrifice should not be a casual thing. The best is to be given to God. Sacrifice is not an opportunity to get rid of cast-off animals. What is given to God is to be without blemish. With all the demands in life, it is often difficult to keep our relationship with God as the priority. Moses' instruction to Aaron and his sons is a reminder to us as well: giving our best to God is a sacrificial commitment that creates spiritual growth; giving God the leftovers of our life leads to spiritual stagnation.

food. [8]That which died or was torn by wild animals he shall not eat, becoming unclean by it: I am the LORD. [9]They shall keep my charge, so that they may not incur guilt and die in the sanctuary[a] for having profaned it: I am the LORD; I sanctify them.

10 No lay person shall eat of the sacred donations. No bound or hired servant of the priest shall eat of the sacred donations; [11]but if a priest acquires anyone by purchase, the person may eat of them; and those that are born in his house may eat of his food. [12]If a priest's daughter marries a layman, she shall not eat of the offering of the sacred donations; [13]but if a priest's daughter is widowed or divorced, without offspring, and returns to her father's house, as in her youth, she may eat of her father's food. No lay person shall eat of it. [14]If a man eats of the sacred donation unintentionally, he shall add one-fifth of its value to it, and give the sacred donation to the priest. [15]No one shall profane the sacred donations of the people of Israel, which they offer to the LORD, [16]causing them to bear guilt requiring a guilt offering, by eating their sacred donations: for I am the LORD; I sanctify them.

Acceptable Offerings

17 The LORD spoke to Moses, saying: [18]Speak to Aaron and his sons and all the people of Israel and say to them: When anyone of the house of Israel or of the aliens residing in Israel presents an offering, whether in payment of a vow or as a freewill offering that is offered to the LORD as a burnt offering, [19]to be acceptable in your behalf it shall be a male without blemish, of the cattle or the sheep or the goats. [20]You shall not offer anything that has a blemish, for it will not be acceptable in your behalf.

21 When anyone offers a sacrifice of well-being to the LORD, in fulfillment of a vow or as a freewill offering, from the herd or from the flock, to be acceptable it must be perfect; there shall be no blemish in it. [22]Anything blind, or injured, or maimed, or having a discharge or an itch or scabs—these you shall not offer to the LORD or put any of them on the altar as offerings by fire to the LORD. [23]An ox or a lamb that has a limb too long or too short you may present for a freewill offering; but it will not be accepted for a vow. [24]Any animal that has its testicles bruised or crushed or torn or cut, you shall not offer to the LORD; such you shall not do within your land, [25]nor shall you accept any such animals from a foreigner to offer as food to your God; since they are mutilated, with a blemish in them, they shall not be accepted in your behalf.

26 The LORD spoke to Moses, saying: [27]When an ox or a sheep or a goat is born, it shall remain seven days with its mother, and from the eighth day on it shall be acceptable as the LORD's offering by fire. [28]But you shall not slaughter, from the herd or the flock, an animal with its young on the same day. [29]When you sacrifice a thanksgiving offering to the LORD, you shall sacrifice it so that it may be acceptable in your behalf. [30]It shall be eaten on the same day; you shall not leave any of it until morning: I am the LORD.

31 Thus you shall keep my commandments and observe them: I am the LORD. [32]You shall not profane my holy name, that I may be sanctified among the people of Israel: I am the LORD; I sanctify you, [33]I who brought you out of the land of Egypt to be your God: I am the LORD.

a Vg: Heb incur guilt for it and die in it

22:31–33 *Thus you shall keep my commandments.* The chapter's concluding verses exhort the people to follow God's commands. "Commandments" is a general term that indicates the instructions in the Holiness Code. These verses are typical of the instruction found in the Holiness Code and reveal its theology. In the deliverance from oppression in Egypt, God created a people in relationship with this holy God. Israel's holiness is to be a reflection of God's holiness and as such is a gift. The people are called to maintain that relationship by way of these instructions in living a life as God's holy people. In so doing Israel acknowledges God as holy.

Appointed Festivals

23 The LORD spoke to Moses, saying: ²Speak to the people of Israel and say to them: These are the appointed festivals of the LORD that you shall proclaim as holy convocations, my appointed festivals.

The Sabbath, Passover, and Unleavened Bread

3 Six days shall work be done; but the seventh day is a sabbath of complete rest, a holy convocation; you shall do no work: it is a sabbath to the LORD throughout your settlements.

4 These are the appointed festivals of the LORD, the holy convocations, which you shall celebrate at the time appointed for them. ⁵In the first month, on the fourteenth day of the month, at twilight,ᵃ there shall be a passover offering to the LORD, ⁶and on the fifteenth day of the same month is the festival of unleavened bread to the LORD; seven days you shall eat unleavened bread. ⁷On the first day you shall have a holy convocation; you shall not work at your occupations. ⁸For seven days you shall present the LORD's offerings by fire; on the seventh day there shall be a holy convocation: you shall not work at your occupations.

The Offering of First Fruits

9 The LORD spoke to Moses: ¹⁰Speak to the people of Israel and say to them: When you enter the land that I am giving you and you reap its harvest, you shall bring the sheaf of the first fruits of your harvest to the priest. ¹¹He shall raise the sheaf before the LORD, that you may find acceptance; on the day after the sabbath the priest shall raise it. ¹²On the day when you raise the sheaf, you shall offer a lamb a year old, without blemish, as a burnt offering to the LORD. ¹³And the grain offering with it shall be two-tenths of an ephah of choice flour mixed with oil, an offering by fire of pleasing odor to the LORD; and the drink offering with it shall be of wine, one-fourth of a hin. ¹⁴You shall eat no bread or parched grain or fresh ears until that very day, until you have brought the offering of your God: it is a statute forever throughout your generations in all your settlements.

The Festival of Weeks

15 And from the day after the sabbath, from the day on which you bring the sheaf of the elevation offering, you shall count off seven weeks; they shall be complete. ¹⁶You shall count until the day after the seventh sabbath, fifty days; then you shall present an offering of new grain to the LORD. ¹⁷You shall bring from your settlements two loaves of bread as an elevation offering, each made of two-tenths of an ephah; they shall be of choice flour, baked with leaven, as first fruits

_a_ Heb _between the two evenings_

23:3 _but the seventh day is a sabbath._ The Sabbath principle is well established in ancient Israel: six days of work and a day of stopping and resting. Its two elements are humanitarian and theological. The Sabbath brings rest for humans and animals and is a time reserved for the worship of God. The injunction against work on the Sabbath is strong in this verse, as is the emphasis on the pervasiveness of Sabbath observance. The Sabbath principle is basic to much of the remainder of the Holiness Code. The connection Leviticus makes between rest and worship is an important one, considering the pace of contemporary life. A chaotic and overextended daily life can be hazardous to spiritual development.

23:4–38 _These are the appointed festivals of_ the LORD. The great festivals in spring, summer, and fall provide special opportunities to focus on the relationship with God in the various seasons of the year.

Responding
23:4, 37 CELEBRATION. The church year, like the ancient Israelite year, is governed by numerous celebrations—Advent, Christmas, Lent, Easter, and so forth. This year make a special effort to observe the numerous church festivals and holidays in ways that are distinctly Christian; for example, at Christmas do things that celebrate the gift of God in Jesus Christ in lieu of giving expensive presents to many people. _See also_ Spiritual Disciplines Index..

to the LORD. [18]You shall present with the bread seven lambs a year old without blemish, one young bull, and two rams; they shall be a burnt offering to the LORD, along with their grain offering and their drink offerings, an offering by fire of pleasing odor to the LORD. [19]You shall also offer one male goat for a sin offering, and two male lambs a year old as a sacrifice of well-being. [20]The priest shall raise them with the bread of the first fruits as an elevation offering before the LORD, together with the two lambs; they shall be holy to the LORD for the priest. [21]On that same day you shall make proclamation; you shall hold a holy convocation; you shall not work at your occupations. This is a statute forever in all your settlements throughout your generations.

22 When you reap the harvest of your land, you shall not reap to the very edges of your field, or gather the gleanings of your harvest; you shall leave them for the poor and for the alien: I am the LORD your God.

The Festival of Trumpets

23 The LORD spoke to Moses, saying: [24]Speak to the people of Israel, saying: In the seventh month, on the first day of the month, you shall observe a day of complete rest, a holy convocation commemorated with trumpet blasts. [25]You shall not work at your occupations; and you shall present the LORD's offering by fire.

The Day of Atonement

26 The LORD spoke to Moses, saying: [27]Now, the tenth day of this seventh month is the day of atonement; it shall be a holy convocation for you: you shall deny yourselves[a] and present the LORD's offering by fire; [28]and you shall do no work during that entire day; for it is a day of atonement, to make atonement on your behalf before the LORD your God. [29]For anyone who does not practice self-denial[b] during that entire day shall be cut off from the people. [30]And anyone who does any work during that entire day, such a one I will destroy from the midst

of the people. [31]You shall do no work: it is a statute forever throughout your generations in all your settlements. [32]It shall be to you a sabbath of complete rest, and you shall deny yourselves;[a] on the ninth day of the month at evening, from evening to evening you shall keep your sabbath.

The Festival of Booths

33 The LORD spoke to Moses, saying: [34]Speak to the people of Israel, saying: On the fifteenth day of this seventh month, and lasting seven days, there shall be the festival of booths[c] to the LORD. [35]The first day shall be a holy convocation; you shall not work at your occupations. [36]Seven days you shall present the LORD's offerings by fire; on the eighth day you shall observe a holy convocation and present the LORD's offerings by fire; it is a solemn assembly; you shall not work at your occupations.

37 These are the appointed festivals of the LORD, which you shall celebrate as times of holy convocation, for presenting to the LORD offerings by fire—burnt offerings and grain offerings, sacrifices and drink offerings, each on its proper day— [38]apart from the sabbaths of the LORD, and apart from your gifts, and apart from all your votive offerings, and apart from all your freewill offerings, which you give to the LORD.

39 Now, the fifteenth day of the seventh month, when you have gathered in the produce of the land, you shall keep the festival of the LORD, lasting seven days; a complete rest on the first day, and a complete rest on the eighth day. [40]On the first day you shall take the fruit of majestic[d] trees, branches of palm trees, boughs of leafy trees, and willows of the brook; and you shall rejoice before the LORD your God for seven days. [41]You shall keep it as a festival to the LORD seven days in the year; you shall keep it in the seventh month as a statute forever throughout your generations. [42]You shall live in booths for

a Or *shall fast*   b Or *does not fast*
c Or *tabernacles*: Heb *succoth*   d Meaning of Heb uncertain

---

23:37 SACRIFICE—*See* Spiritual Disciplines Index.

seven days; all that are citizens in Israel shall live in booths, [43]so that your generations may know that I made the people of Israel live in booths when I brought them out of the land of Egypt: I am the LORD your God.

44 Thus Moses declared to the people of Israel the appointed festivals of the LORD.

The Lamp

24 The LORD spoke to Moses, saying: [2]Command the people of Israel to bring you pure oil of beaten olives for the lamp, that a light may be kept burning regularly. [3]Aaron shall set it up in the tent of meeting, outside the curtain of the covenant, *a* to burn from evening to morning before the LORD regularly; it shall be a statute forever throughout your generations. [4]He shall set up the lamps on the lampstand of pure gold *b* before the LORD regularly.

The Bread for the Tabernacle

5 You shall take choice flour, and bake twelve loaves of it; two-tenths of an ephah shall be in each loaf. [6]You shall place them in two rows, six in a row, on the table of pure gold. *c* [7]You shall put pure frankincense with each row, to be a token offering for the bread, as an offering by fire to the LORD. [8]Every sabbath day Aaron shall set them in order before the LORD regularly as a commitment of the people of Israel, as a covenant forever. [9]They shall be for Aaron and his descendants, who shall eat them in a holy place, for they are most holy portions for him from the offerings by fire to the LORD, a perpetual due.

Blasphemy and Its Punishment

10 A man whose mother was an Israelite and whose father was an Egyptian came out among the people of Israel; and the Israelite woman's son and a certain Israelite began fighting in the camp. [11]The Israelite woman's son blasphemed the Name in a curse. And they brought him to Moses—now his mother's name was Shelomith, daughter of Dibri, of the tribe of Dan— [12]and they put him in custody, until the decision of the LORD should be made clear to them.

13 The LORD said to Moses, saying: [14]Take the blasphemer outside the camp; and let all who were within hearing lay their hands on his head, and let the whole congregation stone him. [15]And speak to the people of Israel, saying: Anyone who curses God shall bear the sin. [16]One who blasphemes the name of the LORD shall be put to death; the whole congregation shall stone the blasphemer. Aliens as well as citizens, when they blaspheme the Name, shall be put to death. [17]Anyone who kills a human being shall be put to death. [18]Anyone who kills an animal shall make restitution for it, life for life. [19]Anyone who maims another shall suffer the same injury in return: [20]fracture for fracture, eye for eye, tooth for tooth; the injury inflicted is the injury to be

a Or *treaty*, or *testament*; Heb *eduth*   *b* Heb *pure lampstand*   *c* Heb *pure table*

23:39–44 *so that your generations may know*. These last verses of the chapter give a more explicit indication of the importance of the festivals in ancient Israel's worship experience. That worship experience emphasized memory, in this case memory of the exodus experience. That experience was one of deliverance and guidance, as God brought the people out of bondage and preserved them through the wilderness as God's people and eventually brought them into the land of Canaan. The purpose of worship is to remember that experience, to live it, rehearse and reenact it, and so to bring it into the present. The people then can see that God is still the one who delivers and guides and can remember to structure their lives on that basis and move into the future with hope. This kind of memory is extremely important to our spiritual life. As we might expect, the spiritual journey includes high points and low points—it is not a steady rate of growth. Remembering God's work in the past has a sustaining and renewing effect during times of spiritual drought. Memory and worship are thus keys to a long life of spiritual formation.

24:1–9 *that a light may be kept burning regularly*. These verses provide for regular worship at the sanctuary as a complement to activities tied to the great festivals (chap 23).

24:20–21 *eye for eye*. Contemporary readers often think of this injunction as harsh or even

suffered. [21]One who kills an animal shall make restitution for it; but one who kills a human being shall be put to death. [22]You shall have one law for the alien and for the citizen: for I am the LORD your God. [23]Moses spoke thus to the people of Israel; and they took the blasphemer outside the camp, and stoned him to death. The people of Israel did as the LORD had commanded Moses.

The Sabbatical Year

25 The LORD spoke to Moses on Mount Sinai, saying: [2]Speak to the people of Israel and say to them: When you enter the land that I am giving you, the land shall observe a sabbath for the LORD. [3]Six years you shall sow your field, and six years you shall prune your vineyard, and gather in their yield; [4]but in the seventh year there shall be a sabbath of complete rest for the land, a sabbath for the LORD: you shall not sow your field or prune your vineyard. [5]You shall not reap the aftergrowth of your harvest or gather the grapes of your unpruned vine: it shall be a year of complete rest for the land. [6]You may eat what the land yields during its sabbath— you, your male and female slaves, your hired and your bound laborers who live with you; [7]for your livestock also, and for the wild animals in your land all its yield shall be for food.

The Year of Jubilee

8 You shall count off seven weeks[a] of years, seven times seven years, so that the period of seven weeks of years gives forty-nine years. [9]Then you shall have the trumpet sounded

loud; on the tenth day of the seventh month— on the day of atonement—you shall have the trumpet sounded throughout all your land. [10]And you shall hallow the fiftieth year and you shall proclaim liberty throughout the land to all its inhabitants. It shall be a jubilee for you: you shall return, every one of you, to your property and every one of you to your family. [11]That fiftieth year shall be a jubilee for you: you shall not sow, or reap the aftergrowth, or harvest the unpruned vines. [12]For it is a jubilee; it shall be holy to you: you shall eat only what the field itself produces.

13 In this year of jubilee you shall return, every one of you, to your property. [14]When you make a sale to your neighbor or buy from your neighbor, you shall not cheat one another. [15]When you buy from your neighbor, you shall pay only for the number of years since the jubilee; the seller shall charge you only for the remaining crop years. [16]If the years are more, you shall increase the price, and if the years are fewer, you shall diminish the price; for it is a certain number of harvests that are being sold to you. [17]You shall not cheat one another, but you shall fear your God; for I am the LORD your God.

18 You shall observe my statutes and faithfully keep my ordinances, so that you may live on the land securely. [19]The land will yield its fruit, and you will eat your fill and live on it securely. [20]Should you ask, "What shall we eat in the seventh year, if we may not sow or gather in our crop?" [21]I will order my blessing

a Or sabbaths

---

barbaric, but it must be set in the ancient Near Eastern context. Hebrew law was not as severe as Assyrian and Babylonian law. In those traditions, a life would have been required for injury. Here the principle is equal compensation. The Hebrew view is more "humanitarian," reflecting a respect for human life based on the theological perspective that God is the creator and lord of human life. When we look at the chapter as a whole, we can see the connection between worship in the first section (vv 1–9) and order in the second (vv 10–23). There is also a connection between worship in the first section

and ethics in the second.

25:8–17 *It shall be a jubilee for you.* The jubilee is associated with the sound of trumpets announcing liberty throughout the land. All people get a new start. This practice is a remarkable witness to hope and God's justice.

Responding
25:18–22 THE WITH-GOD LIFE. What would our culture look like if people viewed God as the owner of the land (v 23)? Would this change be good or bad? Explain. *See also* Spiritual Disciplines Index.

for you in the sixth year, so that it will yield a crop for three years. 22When you sow in the eighth year, you will be eating from the old crop; until the ninth year, when its produce comes in, you shall eat the old. 23The land shall not be sold in perpetuity, for the land is mine; with me you are but aliens and tenants. 24Throughout the land that you hold, you shall provide for the redemption of the land.

25 If anyone of your kin falls into difficulty and sells a piece of property, then the next of kin shall come and redeem what the relative has sold. 26If the person has no one to redeem it, but then prospers and finds sufficient means to do so, 27the years since its sale shall be computed and the difference shall be refunded to the person to whom it was sold, and the property shall be returned. 28But if there are not sufficient means to recover it, what was sold shall remain with the purchaser until the year of jubilee; in the jubilee it shall be released, and the property shall be returned.

29 If anyone sells a dwelling house in a walled city, it may be redeemed until a year has elapsed since its sale; the right of redemption shall be one year. 30If it is not redeemed before a full year has elapsed, a house that is in a walled city shall pass in perpetuity to the purchaser, throughout the generations; it shall not be released in the jubilee. 31But houses in villages that have no walls around them shall be classed as open country; they may be redeemed, and they shall be released in the jubilee. 32As for the cities of the Levites, the Levites shall forever have the right of redemption of the houses in the cities belonging to them. 33Such property as may be redeemed from the Levites—houses sold in a city belonging to them—shall be released in the jubilee; because the houses in the cities of the Levites are their possession among the people of Israel. 34But the open land around their cities may not be sold; for that is their possession for all time.

35 If any of your kin fall into difficulty and become dependent on you,*a* you shall support them; they shall live with you as though resident aliens. 36Do not take interest in advance or otherwise make a profit from them, but fear your God; let them live with you. 37You shall not lend them your money at interest taken in advance, or provide them food at a profit. 38I am the LORD your God, who brought you out of the land of Egypt, to give you the land of Canaan, to be your God.

39 If any who are dependent on you become so impoverished that they sell themselves to you, you shall not make them serve as slaves. 40They shall remain with you as hired or bound laborers. They shall serve with you until the year of the jubilee. 41Then they and their children with them shall be free from your authority; they shall go back to their own family and return to their ancestral property. 42For they are my servants, whom I brought out of the land of Egypt; they shall not be sold as slaves are sold. 43You shall not rule over them with harshness, but shall fear your God. 44As for the male and female slaves whom you may have, it is from the nations around you that you may acquire male and female slaves. 45You may also acquire them from among the aliens residing with you, and from their families that are with you, who have been born in your land; and they may be your property. 46You may keep them as a possession for your children after you, for them to inherit as property. These you may treat as slaves, but as for your fellow Israelites, no one shall rule over the other with harshness.

a Meaning of Heb uncertain

25:18–24 *for the land is mine.* Redemption (v 24) is the buying back of land by the next of kin. The key theological basis for the practice is in verse 23. God is the owner of the land and so it is not to be sold permanently; that is, it is not to be sold completely or finally so that it is beyond reclamation. God's ownership of the land is the theological affirmation that shapes this whole chapter. The people then are characterized as God's aliens and tenants. The sense of the first term is those who are not citizens of the community, but still reside with the people. Israel had this experience in Egypt, as the text of Leviticus has already pointed out. In a deeper sense, one always lives in such a graced status.

47 If resident aliens among you prosper, and if any of your kin fall into difficulty with one of them and sell themselves to an alien, or to a branch of the alien's family, 48after they have sold themselves they shall have the right of redemption; one of their brothers may redeem them, 49or their uncle or their uncle's son may redeem them, or anyone of their family who is of their own flesh may redeem them; or if they prosper they may redeem themselves. 50They shall compute with the purchaser the total from the year when they sold themselves to the alien until the jubilee year; the price of the sale shall be applied to the number of years: the time they were with the owner shall be rated as the time of a hired laborer. 51If many years remain, they shall pay for their redemption in proportion to the purchase price; 52and if few years remain until the jubilee year, they shall compute thus: according to the years involved they shall make payment for their redemption. 53As a laborer hired by the year they shall be under the alien's authority, who shall not, however, rule with harshness over them in your sight. 54And if they have not been redeemed in any of these ways, they and their children with them shall go free in the jubilee year. 55For to me the people of Israel are servants; they are my servants whom I brought out from the land of Egypt: I am the LORD your God.

Rewards for Obedience

26 You shall make for yourselves no idols and erect no carved images or pillars, and you shall not place figured stones in your land, to worship at them; for I am the LORD your God. 2You shall keep my sabbaths and reverence my sanctuary: I am the LORD.

3 If you follow my statutes and keep my commandments and observe them faithfully, 4I will give you your rains in their season, and the land shall yield its produce, and the trees of the field shall yield their fruit. 5Your threshing shall overtake the vintage, and the vintage shall overtake the sowing; you shall eat your bread to the full, and live securely in your land. 6And I will grant peace in the land, and you shall lie down, and no one shall make you afraid; I will remove dangerous animals from the land, and no sword shall go through your land. 7You shall give chase to your enemies, and they shall fall before you by the sword. 8Five of you shall give chase to a hundred, and a hundred of you shall give chase to ten thousand; your enemies shall fall before you by the sword. 9I will look with favor upon you and make you fruitful and multiply you; and I will maintain my covenant with you. 10You shall eat old grain long stored, and you shall have to clear out the old to make way for the new. 11I will place my dwelling in your midst, and I shall not abhor you. 12And I will walk among you, and will be your God, and you shall be my people. 13I am the LORD your God who brought you out of the land of Egypt, to be their slaves no more; I have broken the bars of your yoke and made you walk erect.

Penalties for Disobedience

14 But if you will not obey me, and do not observe all these commandments, 15if you spurn my statutes, and abhor my ordinances, so that you will not observe all my commandments, and you break my covenant, 16I in turn will do this to you: I will bring terror on you; consumption and fever that waste the eyes and cause life to pine away. You shall sow your seed in vain, for your enemies shall eat it. 17I will set my face against you, and you shall be struck down by your enemies; your foes shall rule over you, and you shall flee though no one pursues you. 18And if in spite of this you will not obey me, I will continue to punish you sevenfold for your sins. 19I will break your proud glory, and I will make your sky like iron and your earth like copper. 20Your strength shall be spent to no purpose: your land shall not yield its produce, and the trees of the land shall not yield their fruit.

21 If you continue hostile to me, and will not obey me, I will continue to plague you sevenfold for your sins. 22I will let loose wild animals against you, and they shall bereave you of your children and destroy your livestock; they shall make you few in number, and your roads shall be deserted.

23 If in spite of these punishments you have not turned back to me, but continue

hostile to me, 24then I too will continue hostile to you: I myself will strike you sevenfold for your sins. 25I will bring the sword against you, executing vengeance for the covenant; and if you withdraw within your cities, I will send pestilence among you, and you shall be delivered into enemy hands. 26When I break your staff of bread, ten women shall bake your bread in a single oven, and they shall dole out your bread by weight; and though you eat, you shall not be satisfied.

27 But if, despite this, you disobey me, and continue hostile to me, 28I will continue hostile to you in fury; I in turn will punish you myself sevenfold for your sins. 29You shall eat the flesh of your sons, and you shall eat the flesh of your daughters. 30I will destroy your high places and cut down your incense altars; I will heap your carcasses on the carcasses of your idols. I will abhor you. 31I will lay your cities waste, will make your sanctuaries desolate, and I will not smell your pleasing odors. 32I will devastate the land, so that your enemies who come to settle in it shall be appalled at it. 33And you I will scatter among the nations, and I will unsheathe the sword against you; your land shall be a desolation, and your cities a waste.

34 Then the land shall enjoy*a* its sabbath years as long as it lies desolate, while you are in the land of your enemies; then the land shall rest, and enjoy*a* its sabbath years. 35As long as it lies desolate, it shall have the rest it did not have on your sabbaths when you were living on it. 36And as for those of you who survive, I will send faintness into their hearts in the lands of their enemies; the sound of a driven leaf shall put them to flight, and they shall flee as one flees from the sword, and they shall fall though no one pursues. 37They shall stumble over one another, as if to es-

cape a sword, though no one pursues; and you shall have no power to stand against your enemies. 38You shall perish among the nations, and the land of your enemies shall devour you. 39And those of you who survive shall languish in the land of your enemies because of their iniquities; also they shall languish because of the iniquities of their ancestors.

40 But if they confess their iniquity and the iniquity of their ancestors, in that they committed treachery against me and, moreover, that they continued hostile to me— 41so that I, in turn, continued hostile to them and brought them into the land of their enemies; if then their uncircumcised heart is humbled and they make amends for their iniquity, 42then will I remember my covenant with Jacob; I will remember also my covenant with Isaac and also my covenant with Abraham, and I will remember the land. 43For the land shall be deserted by them, and enjoy*a* its sabbath years by lying desolate without them, while they shall make amends for their iniquity, because they dared to spurn my ordinances, and they abhorred my statutes. 44Yet for all that, when they are in the land of their enemies, I will not spurn them, or abhor them so as to destroy them utterly and break my covenant with them; for I am the LORD their God; 45but I will remember in their favor the covenant with their ancestors whom I brought out of the land of Egypt in the sight of the nations, to be their God: I am the LORD.

46 These are the statutes and ordinances and laws that the LORD established between himself and the people of Israel on Mount Sinai through Moses.

---

a Or *make up for*

26:46 *These are the statutes . . . that the LORD established.* Chapter 26 concludes the Holiness Code. Holiness is distinctiveness. God is holy or set apart, different from any other. Ancient Israel is called to be holy, to reflect that divine holiness. In following divine instruction, Israel will demonstrate holiness or difference or distinctness as people of the holy God. All of this instruction is part of the covenant material in the Pentateuch. Covenant is a way of speaking of the divine-human relationship in which God initiates relationship with Israel and Israel responds. God first says, "I will be your God" and Israel responds, "We will be your people." In living out that covenant relationship persons and communities find wholeness or blessing. In rejecting that relationship they find trouble.

Votive Offerings

27 The LORD spoke to Moses, saying: ²Speak to the people of Israel and say to them: When a person makes an explicit vow to the LORD concerning the equivalent for a human being, ³the equivalent for a male shall be: from twenty to sixty years of age the equivalent shall be fifty shekels of silver by the sanctuary shekel. ⁴If the person is a female, the equivalent is thirty shekels. ⁵If the age is from five to twenty years of age, the equivalent is twenty shekels for a male and ten shekels for a female. ⁶If the age is from one month to five years, the equivalent for a male is five shekels of silver, and for a female the equivalent is three shekels of silver. ⁷And if the person is sixty years old or over, then the equivalent for a male is fifteen shekels, and for a female ten shekels. ⁸If any cannot afford the equivalent, they shall be brought before the priest and the priest shall assess them; the priest shall assess them according to what each one making a vow can afford.

9 If it concerns an animal that may be brought as an offering to the LORD, any such that may be given to the LORD shall be holy. ¹⁰Another shall not be exchanged or substituted for it, either good for bad or bad for good; and if one animal is substituted for another, both that one and its substitute shall be holy. ¹¹If it concerns any unclean animal that may not be brought as an offering to the LORD, the animal shall be presented before the priest. ¹²The priest shall assess it: whether good or bad, according to the assessment of the priest, so it shall be. ¹³But if it is to be redeemed, one-fifth must be added to the assessment.

14 If a person consecrates a house to the LORD, the priest shall assess it: whether good or bad, as the priest assesses it, so it shall stand. ¹⁵And if the one who consecrates the house wishes to redeem it, one-fifth shall be added to its assessed value, and it shall revert to the original owner.

16 If a person consecrates to the LORD any inherited landholding, its assessment shall be in accordance with its seed requirements: fifty shekels of silver to a homer of barley seed. ¹⁷If the person consecrates the field as of the year of jubilee, that assessment shall stand; ¹⁸but if the field is consecrated after the jubilee, the priest shall compute the price for it according to the years that remain until the year of jubilee, and the assessment shall be reduced. ¹⁹And if the one who consecrates the field wishes to redeem it, then one-fifth shall be added to its assessed value, and it shall revert to the original owner; ²⁰but if the field is not redeemed, or if it has been sold to someone else, it shall no longer be redeemable. ²¹But when the field is released in the jubilee, it shall be holy to the LORD as a devoted field; it becomes the priest's holding. ²²If someone consecrates to the LORD a field that has been purchased, which is not a part of the inherited landholding, ²³the priest shall compute for it the proportionate assessment up to the year of jubilee, and the assessment shall be paid as of that day, a sacred donation to the LORD. ²⁴In the year of jubilee the field shall return to the one from whom it was bought, whose holding the land is. ²⁵All assessments shall be by the sanctuary shekel: twenty gerahs shall make a shekel.

26 A firstling of animals, however, which as a firstling belongs to the LORD, cannot be consecrated by anyone; whether ox or sheep, it is the LORD's. ²⁷If it is an unclean animal, it shall be ransomed at its assessment, with one-fifth added; if it is not redeemed, it shall be sold at its assessment.

28 Nothing that a person owns that has been devoted to destruction for the LORD, be it human or animal, or inherited landholding, may be sold or redeemed; every devoted thing is most holy to the LORD. ²⁹No human beings who have been devoted to destruction can be ransomed; they shall be put to death.

30 All tithes from the land, whether the seed from the ground or the fruit from the tree, are the LORD's; they are holy to the LORD. ³¹If persons wish to redeem any of their tithes, they must add one-fifth to them. ³²All

---

27:1–34 *The LORD spoke to Moses.* Chapter 27 constitutes an appendix to the book of Leviticus dealing with vows or pledges made to the sanctuary.

tithes of herd and flock, every tenth one that passes under the shepherd's staff, shall be holy to the LORD. 33Let no one inquire whether it is good or bad, or make substitution for it; if one makes substitution for it, then both it and the substitute shall be holy and cannot be redeemed.

34 These are the commandments that the LORD gave to Moses for the people of Israel on Mount Sinai.

27:34 *These are the commandments that the LORD gave . . . for the people of Israel.* The book's theology begins with divine presence and urges the people to avoid the effects of sin and uncleanness, so that God will continue to be present among them and give them life—hence all the instruction on purity and holiness. The book also provides means of restoring that relationship. All of this instruction is to make wholeness of life a real hope for the faith community of ancient Israel, and in that sense the instruction is a sign of divine grace. The instruction educates for living.

NUMBERS

[handwritten notes in margin: "moving / IN THE WILDERNESS / going from RESPONSIVENESS / TO RESPONSIBILITY / from Freedom / TO RESPONSIBILITY"]

"Numbers," the English and Greek title of the fourth book of the Pentateuch (the Five Books of Moses), emphasizes the two censuses recorded in its text. However, the censuses do not constitute the whole of the book. The more accurate Hebrew title for the book is "In the Wilderness" (*b'midbar*). Indeed, the entire story of Numbers takes place in the wilderness. The main subject of the book might seem to be the thirty-eight years the tribes of Israel wandered there, but the story of Numbers goes much deeper. From the standpoint of a loving, sovereign God for whom nothing is ever wasted, the forty years God's people spent wandering between Egypt and Canaan were a time of spiritual transformation.

The Journey to Freedom

God is always at work. During the Israelites' years as slaves in Egypt, God was fulfilling part of his promise to Abraham. Israel—a nation begun with Abraham's promised seed, Isaac—grew from a mere seventy people to over six hundred thousand men, not to mention women and children. Now was the time for God's people to enter and possess the Promised Land (Exod 1:5; Num 2:32).

But while they sojourned in Egypt, passivity had become a way of life for the Israelites. In their 430 years of slavery, generation upon generation of God's people had learned from their parents and taught their children to survive by acting as the Egyptians instructed them. They learned to live passive lives.

The exodus brought the Israelites freedom, which at first they embraced wholeheartedly. Like many new believers, the newly freed slaves met everything God did with approval and compliance. But freedom brings responsibility. When they began to encounter difficulties in their wilderness journey, the Israelites discovered that they preferred the relative "comforts" of obeying the Egyptians in slavery to the hardships of following God in freedom (11:1, 5–13). They began to rebel.

[handwritten note in margin: "LIKE IRAQ NEW GOVT"]

See also *"The With-God Life" essay for this section of the Bible, "The People of God in Exodus," pp. 87–91.*

193

God's holy people are always formed through training; they are not born that way. For the seed to form a nation and grow into the People of God, the Israelites needed times of testing and struggle. Spiritual formation is a transformation process that takes believers from a responsive lifestyle to a more responsible/creative style of life. Within such a journey we are brought into a deeper faith in and knowledge of God. Numbers tells the story of how God prepared a people who had been slaves for more than four hundred years for the freedom he had always intended for them. The book's truest, deepest story is that of the transformation, through a journey into the wilderness by the hand of God, of a passive people of small vision and little faith into a powerful, faithful visionary people ready to claim the Promised Land.

The spiritual formation process necessarily requires the presence of God. When the Israelites were rescued from Egypt, they did not know God personally. The journey to freedom would challenge them. Their deepening awareness of God's presence was key. However, for any but the most holy to see God's glory would bring death (Exod 19:21–24). For this reason, God led them in the desert by means of a pillar of cloud by day and a pillar of fire by night (Exod 13:21–22), until the Israelites could build a tabernacle for God's dwelling place. Now God could dwell among his people and yet protect them from the overwhelming sight of his glory (Exod 25–27). The tabernacle (and later Temple) remained God's means for dwelling among his people until God came in the form of Jesus and later by means of the Holy Spirit. God continues to live among his people today. God is, after all, Immanuel—"God with us" (John 1:14).

Prerequisites for Spiritual Formation

God is concerned that each believer experience personal transformation and maturity. Spiritual formation begins with the willingness on the part of each individual to submit to God as master and progresses as he or she develops a personal relationship with God alone. In Numbers, God's conversations with Moses, Aaron, and Miriam demonstrate his special concern for relationship as a vital part of spiritual formation.

Spiritual formation is both an individual and a group process. There is a reciprocal need in the spiritual formation process for community. Here believers receive support for their spiritual growth and also are held accountable. Moreover, as each person within a community becomes mature, a healthier community becomes possible. In Numbers, God took the entire community of his people through a time of spiritual formation.

The spiritual formation process requires time spent in the wilderness. The wilderness is a dangerous and difficult place. It is in the wilderness that we are most aware of our need for God's provision and protection. When we are open to God, then we can best hear his voice. The wilderness is also quiet, desolate, and lonely. We can hear God more easily there. Thus, the wilderness is God's special meeting and training place for his people (Deut 32:10). The story of Numbers takes place entirely in the wilderness.

A successful time of spiritual formation requires mature spiritual guides to lead us through the obstacles. God himself is the perfect spiritual guide, yet God prepares and provides us with visible guides to show us the way. A good spiritual guide is a person of deep faith and integrity who already has gone down the path and knows it well. Moses was God's choice as spiritual guide for the Israelites.

Moses was trained in the secular world for forty years and then disciplined for another forty years in the wilderness. He entered the wilderness with a sense of entitlement. Once Moses was there, his character was transformed as he realized how truly small he was. Moses became "very humble, more so than anyone else on the face of the earth" (12:3). When Moses was finally commissioned by the Lord to lead his people out of bondage, his leadership was no longer dependent on the power of his flesh or the knowledge of the world, but upon the guidance and power of God. He would serve as a leader in the wilderness for another forty years.

The spiritual formation process requires structure and order. In addition, the spiritual formation process requires discipline, which is learned in large part through external structure and order. Exodus tells how God began creating order for his newly freed people as soon as they entered the wilderness. In Leviticus and Numbers God provided additional directions for organizing the people. The military censuses recorded in Numbers were part of God's ordering of the people. The new nation needed warriors to defend it. But the army would also provide training and discipline for the warriors. Moreover, God directed that the censuses be taken tribe by tribe. In this way God established a representative structure to govern the new nation. So important was order for the formation of his people that God himself dealt with those who challenged the leadership of Moses and Aaron. God did this to maintain the community order.

The structural elements of spiritual formation include the presence of God, a willingness on the part of individuals to bind themselves to God as master, a community within which to receive support and be held accountable, time in the wilderness, training and discipleship by mature spiritual guides, and sources of external structure and order. God provided each of these. As Numbers begins, the stage is set for the spiritual transformation of the Israelites.

The Disciplines of Freedom

The goal of spiritual formation is the development of an inward character that does naturally (and supernaturally) the works of the law. It produces an inward personality that will spontaneously react to the demands of life with "love, joy, peace, patience, kindness, generosity, faithfulness, gentleness, and self-control" (Gal 5:22). This, again, is the goal of spiritual formation.

The means to realizing this goal involve Spiritual Disciplines, which must be learned through practice and repetition until we make them our own. These include disciplines of silence; seeking guidance and seeking heavenly things; learning to hear the voice of God; knowing God; depending on God; obedience to God; and holiness in our thoughts and words. Each of these is a "Spiritual Discipline." The Spiritual Disciplines transform those who are enslaved by their ingrained habits through new, holy habits. This is the process we see in Numbers.

God wanted the Israelites to leave their habits of slavery behind and attain holy habits with which to enter their new lives. As you read the book of Numbers you may wish to read with an eye to discovering how God worked to develop each of these habits in his people. You will see how many of those Israelites who were brought out from slavery into the desert failed to receive what God wanted to give and teach them—and how richly God rewarded and blessed those who were open to being made new.

The story Numbers tells is powerful and highly relevant for Christians today. Scripture reveals that God longs for each of his followers to live powerful, joy-filled lives. Our acceptance of Christ—our agreement to become "his people"—is only the beginning of a wilderness journey each of us will take in order that God may transform us from unwitting slaves to comfort into followers given over to God, followers ready to embrace the freedom and rewards such obedience brings. When we read Numbers from the perspective of spiritual formation, it is no longer an ancient history, but the living Word of God presented to God's people throughout the ages.

—*Joshua Choon Min Kang*

The First Census of Israel

1 The LORD spoke to Moses in the wilderness of Sinai, in the tent of meeting, on the first day of the second month, in the second year after they had come out of the land of Egypt, saying: 2Take a census of the whole congregation of Israelites, in their clans, by ancestral houses, according to the number of names, every male individually; 3from twenty years old and upward, everyone in Israel able to go to war. You and Aaron shall enroll them, company by company. 4A man from each tribe shall be with you, each man the head of his ancestral house. 5These are the names of the men who shall assist you:

From Reuben, Elizur son of Shedeur.
6 From Simeon, Shelumiel son of Zurishaddai.

7 From Judah, Nahshon son of Amminadab.
8 From Issachar, Nethanel son of Zuar.
9 From Zebulun, Eliab son of Helon.
10 From the sons of Joseph:
from Ephraim, Elishama son of Ammihud;
from Manasseh, Gamaliel son of Pedahzur.
11 From Benjamin, Abidan son of Gideoni.
12 From Dan, Ahiezer son of Ammishaddai.
13 From Asher, Pagiel son of Ochran.
14 From Gad, Eliasaph son of Deuel.
15 From Naphtali, Ahira son of Enan.
16These were the ones chosen from the congregation, the leaders of their ancestral tribes, the heads of the divisions of Israel.
17 Moses and Aaron took these men who

1:1 *The LORD spoke to Moses.* God spoke, Moses listened. The spiritual life actually begins with Yahweh speaking to us and our listening to his voice. Our spirits grow when we listen to the voice of God. There is nothing more important than being still within and attending to him. As we mature, we will grow more sensitive to God's voice. Too often today the tables are turned. We speak, and God listens. We never stop to listen to what God wants to say. As a result we wonder if God has heard our voice. But the better question is, Have we heard his voice?

had been designated by name, [18]and on the first day of the second month they assembled the whole congregation together. They registered themselves in their clans, by their ancestral houses, according to the number of names from twenty years old and upward, individually, [19]as the LORD commanded Moses. So he enrolled them in the wilderness of Sinai.

20 The descendants of Reuben, Israel's firstborn, their lineage, in their clans, by their ancestral houses, according to the number of names, individually, every male from twenty years old and upward, everyone able to go to war: [21]those enrolled of the tribe of Reuben were forty-six thousand five hundred.

22 The descendants of Simeon, their lineage, in their clans, by their ancestral houses, those of them that were numbered, according to the number of names, individually, every male from twenty years old and upward, everyone able to go to war: [23]those enrolled of the tribe of Simeon were fifty-nine thousand three hundred.

24 The descendants of Gad, their lineage, in their clans, by their ancestral houses, according to the number of the names, from twenty years old and upward, everyone able to go to war: [25]those enrolled of the tribe of Gad were forty-five thousand six hundred fifty.

26 The descendants of Judah, their lineage, in their clans, by their ancestral houses, according to the number of names, from twenty years old and upward, everyone able to go to war: [27]those enrolled of the tribe of Judah were seventy-four thousand six hundred.

28 The descendants of Issachar, their lineage, in their clans, by their ancestral houses, according to the number of names, from twenty years old and upward, everyone able to go to war: [29]those enrolled of the tribe of Issachar were fifty-four thousand four hundred.

30 The descendants of Zebulun, their lineage, in their clans, by their ancestral houses, according to the number of names, from twenty years old and upward, everyone able to go to war: [31]those enrolled of the tribe of Zebulun were fifty-seven thousand four hundred.

32 The descendants of Joseph, namely, the descendants of Ephraim, their lineage, in their clans, by their ancestral houses, according to the number of names, from twenty years old and upward, everyone able to go to war: [33]those enrolled of the tribe of Ephraim were forty thousand five hundred.

34 The descendants of Manasseh, their lineage, in their clans, by their ancestral houses, according to the number of names, from twenty years old and upward, everyone able to go to war: [35]those enrolled of the tribe of Manasseh were thirty-two thousand two hundred.

36 The descendants of Benjamin, their lineage, in their clans, by their ancestral houses, according to the number of names, from twenty years old and upward, everyone able to go to war: [37]those enrolled of the tribe of Benjamin were thirty-five thousand four hundred.

38 The descendants of Dan, their lineage, in their clans, by their ancestral houses, according to the number of names, from twenty years old and upward, everyone able to go to war: [39]those enrolled of the tribe of Dan were sixty-two thousand seven hundred.

40 The descendants of Asher, their lineage, in their clans, by their ancestral houses, according to the number of names, from twenty years old and upward, everyone able to go to war: [41]those enrolled of the tribe of Asher were forty-one thousand five hundred.

42 The descendants of Naphtali, their lineage, in their clans, by their ancestral houses, according to the number of names, from twenty years old and upward, everyone able to go to war: [43]those enrolled of the tribe of Naphtali were fifty-three thousand four hundred.

44 These are those who were enrolled, whom Moses and Aaron enrolled with the help of the leaders of Israel, twelve men, each representing his ancestral house. [45]So the whole number of the Israelites, by their ancestral houses, from twenty years old and upward, everyone able to go to war in Israel— [46]their whole number was six hundred three thousand five hundred fifty. [47]The Levites,

however, were not numbered by their ancestral tribe along with them.

48 The LORD had said to Moses: 49Only the tribe of Levi you shall not enroll, and you shall not take a census of them with the other Israelites. 50Rather you shall appoint the Levites over the tabernacle of the covenant, *a* and over all its equipment, and over all that belongs to it; they are to carry the tabernacle and all its equipment, and they shall tend it, and shall camp around the tabernacle. 51When the tabernacle is to set out, the Levites shall take it down; and when the tabernacle is to be pitched, the Levites shall set it up. And any outsider who comes near shall be put to death. 52The other Israelites shall camp in their respective regimental camps, by companies; 53but the Levites shall camp around the tabernacle of the covenant, *a* that there may be no wrath on the congregation of the Israelites; and the Levites shall perform the guard duty of the tabernacle of the covenant. *a* 54The Israelites did so; they did just as the LORD commanded Moses.

The Order of Encampment and Marching

2 The LORD spoke to Moses and Aaron, saying: 2The Israelites shall camp each in their respective regiments, under ensigns by their ancestral houses; they shall camp facing the tent of meeting on every side. 3Those to camp on the east side toward the sunrise shall be of the regimental encampment of Judah by companies. The leader of the people of Judah shall be Nahshon son of Amminadab,

4with a company as enrolled of seventy-four thousand six hundred. 5Those to camp next to him shall be the tribe of Issachar. The leader of the Issacharites shall be Nethanel son of Zuar, 6with a company as enrolled of fifty-four thousand four hundred. 7Then the tribe of Zebulun: The leader of the Zebulunites shall be Eliab son of Helon, 8with a company as enrolled of fifty-seven thousand four hundred. 9The total enrollment of the camp of Judah, by companies, is one hundred eighty-six thousand four hundred. They shall set out first on the march.

10 On the south side shall be the regimental encampment of Reuben by companies. The leader of the Reubenites shall be Elizur son of Shedeur, 11with a company as enrolled of forty-six thousand five hundred. 12And those to camp next to him shall be the tribe of Simeon. The leader of the Simeonites shall be Shelumiel son of Zurishaddai, 13with a company as enrolled of fifty-nine thousand three hundred. 14Then the tribe of Gad: The leader of the Gadites shall be Eliasaph son of Reuel, 15with a company as enrolled of forty-five thousand six hundred fifty. 16The total enrollment of the camp of Reuben, by companies, is one hundred fifty-one thousand four hundred fifty. They shall set out second.

17 The tent of meeting, with the camp of the Levites, shall set out in the center of the camps; they shall set out just as they camp, each in position, by their regiments.

a Or *treaty*, or *testimony*; Heb *eduth*

2:2 *they shall camp facing the tent [tabernacle] of meeting on every side.* God wanted to be near his people, and God wanted his people to be near him. So God commanded the Israelites to camp around the "tent of meeting." The tent of meeting (tabernacle) was the dwelling place for God among his people. Moses met with the Lord there. The people also experienced God's presence as they camped around the tabernacle. Likewise, in the New Testament, Jesus dwelt among his disciples and so revealed God's glory to them in ways they could only comprehend through his human form (John 1:14). Just as God dwelt among the Israelites to reassure them in the wilderness, God wants

us to experience his presence now. In the spiritual life, we are called to "camp" in God's presence—to go deeper into our own hearts, where Christ dwells, as we learn to be loved by and to worship him.

2:17 *they shall set out just as they camp, each in position, by their regiments.* After the Passover the Israelites escaped from Egypt, leaving hurriedly and not without disorder. Now, as they began their lives in the wilderness, they needed structure and organization. Counting the numbers of men who could fight, establishing structured camps, and setting up the tent of meeting in a specific and precise manner were some of the ways God brought

18 On the west side shall be the regimental encampment of Ephraim by companies. The leader of the people of Ephraim shall be Elishama son of Ammihud, ¹⁹with a company as enrolled of forty thousand five hundred. ²⁰Next to him shall be the tribe of Manasseh. The leader of the people of Manasseh shall be Gamaliel son of Pedahzur, ²¹with a company as enrolled of thirty-two thousand two hundred. ²²Then the tribe of Benjamin: The leader of the Benjaminites shall be Abidan son of Gideoni, ²³with a company as enrolled of thirty-five thousand four hundred. ²⁴The total enrollment of the camp of Ephraim, by companies, is one hundred eight thousand one hundred. They shall set out third on the march.

25 On the north side shall be the regimental encampment of Dan by companies. The leader of the Danites shall be Ahiezer son of Ammishaddai, ²⁶with a company as enrolled of sixty-two thousand seven hundred. ²⁷Those to camp next to him shall be the tribe of Asher. The leader of the Asherites shall be Pagiel son of Ochran, ²⁸with a company as enrolled of forty-one thousand five hundred. ²⁹Then the tribe of Naphtali: The leader of the Naphtalites shall be Ahira son of Enan, ³⁰with a company as enrolled of fifty-three thousand four hundred. ³¹The total enrollment of the camp of Dan is one hundred fifty-seven thousand six hundred. They shall set out last, by companies. *a*

32 This was the enrollment of the Israelites by their ancestral houses; the total enrollment in the camps by their companies was six hundred three thousand five hundred fifty. ³³Just as the LORD had commanded Moses, the Levites were not enrolled among the other Israelites.

34 The Israelites did just as the LORD had commanded Moses: They camped by regiments, and they set out the same way, everyone by clans, according to ancestral houses.

The Sons of Aaron

3 This is the lineage of Aaron and Moses at the time when the LORD spoke with Moses on Mount Sinai. ²These are the names of the sons of Aaron: Nadab the firstborn, and Abihu, Eleazar, and Ithamar; ³these are the names of the sons of Aaron, the anointed priests, whom he ordained to minister as priests. ⁴Nadab and Abihu died before the LORD when they offered unholy fire before the LORD in the wilderness of Sinai, and they had no children. Eleazar and Ithamar served as priests in the lifetime of their father Aaron.

The Duties of the Levites

5 Then the LORD spoke to Moses, saying: ⁶Bring the tribe of Levi near, and set them before Aaron the priest, so that they may assist him. ⁷They shall perform duties for him and for the whole congregation in front of the tent of meeting, doing service at the tabernacle; ⁸they shall be in charge of all the furnishings of the tent of meeting, and attend to the duties for the Israelites as they do service at the tabernacle. ⁹You shall give the Levites to Aaron and his descendants; they are unreservedly given to him from among the Israelites. ¹⁰But you shall make a register of Aaron and his descendants; it is they who shall attend to the priesthood, and any outsider who comes near shall be put to death.

11 Then the LORD spoke to Moses, saying: ¹²I hereby accept the Levites from among the Israelites as substitutes for all the firstborn that open the womb among the Israelites. The Levites shall be mine, ¹³for all the firstborn are mine; when I killed all the firstborn in the land of Egypt, I consecrated for my own all the firstborn in Israel, both human and animal; they shall be mine. I am the LORD.

a Compare verses 9, 16, 24: Heb *by their regiments*

---

order to the people. Organization was needed for God's people even with the presence of God by means of the tabernacle and Moses' visible spiritual leadership. The spiritual life involves learning to live with discipline—learning to live lives of order. In the spiritual life discipline and order are closely associated with freedom. Freedom rarely means chaos. Freedom means peace. Order and responsibility are essential to true freedom.

A Census of the Levites

14 Then the LORD spoke to Moses in the wilderness of Sinai, saying: 15Enroll the Levites by ancestral houses and by clans. You shall enroll every male from a month old and upward. 16So Moses enrolled them according to the word of the LORD, as he was commanded. 17The following were the sons of Levi, by their names: Gershon, Kohath, and Merari. 18These are the names of the sons of Gershon by their clans: Libni and Shimei. 19The sons of Kohath by their clans: Amram, Izhar, Hebron, and Uzziel. 20The sons of Merari by their clans: Mahli and Mushi. These are the clans of the Levites, by their ancestral houses.

21 To Gershon belonged the clan of the Libnites and the clan of the Shimeites; these were the clans of the Gershonites. 22Their enrollment, counting all the males from a month old and upward, was seven thousand five hundred. 23The clans of the Gershonites were to camp behind the tabernacle on the west, 24with Eliasaph son of Lael as head of the ancestral house of the Gershonites. 25The responsibility of the sons of Gershon in the tent of meeting was to be the tabernacle, the tent with its covering, the screen for the entrance of the tent of meeting, 26the hangings of the court, the screen for the entrance of the court that is around the tabernacle and the altar, and its cords—all the service pertaining to these.

27 To Kohath belonged the clan of the Amramites, the clan of the Izharites, the clan of the Hebronites, and the clan of the Uzzielites; these are the clans of the Kohathites. 28Counting all the males, from a month old and upward, there were eight thousand six hundred, attending to the duties of the sanctuary. 29The clans of the Kohathites were to camp on the south side of the tabernacle, 30with Elizaphan son of Uzziel as head of the ancestral house of the clans of the Kohathites. 31Their responsibility was to be the ark, the table, the lampstand, the altars, the vessels of the sanctuary with which the priests minister, and the screen—all the service pertaining to these. 32Eleazar son of Aaron the priest was to be chief over the leaders of the Levites, and to have oversight of those who had charge of the sanctuary.

33 To Merari belonged the clan of the Mahlites and the clan of the Mushites: these are the clans of Merari. 34Their enrollment, counting all the males from a month old and upward, was six thousand two hundred. 35The head of the ancestral house of the clans of Merari was Zuriel son of Abihail; they were to camp on the north side of the tabernacle. 36The responsibility assigned to the sons of Merari was to be the frames of the tabernacle, the bars, the pillars, the bases, and all their accessories—all the service pertaining to these; 37also the pillars of the court all around, with their bases and pegs and cords.

38 Those who were to camp in front of the tabernacle on the east—in front of the tent of meeting toward the east—were Moses and Aaron and Aaron's sons, having charge of the rites within the sanctuary, whatever had to be done for the Israelites; and any outsider who came near was to be put to death. 39The total enrollment of the Levites whom Moses and Aaron enrolled at the commandment of the LORD, by their clans, all the males from a month old and upward, was twenty-two thousand.

The Redemption of the Firstborn

40 Then the LORD said to Moses: Enroll all the firstborn males of the Israelites, from a month old and upward, and count their names. 41But you shall accept the Levites for me—I am the LORD—as substitutes for all the firstborn among the Israelites, and the livestock of the Levites as substitutes for all the firstborn among the livestock of the Israelites. 42So Moses enrolled all the firstborn among the Israelites, as the LORD commanded him. 43The total enrollment, all the firstborn males from a month old and upward, counting the number of names, was twenty-two thousand two hundred seventy-three.

44 Then the LORD spoke to Moses, saying: 45Accept the Levites as substitutes for all the firstborn among the Israelites, and the livestock of the Levites as substitutes for their livestock; and the Levites shall be mine. I am the LORD. 46As the price of redemption of the two hundred seventy-three of the firstborn of

the Israelites, over and above the number of the Levites, 47you shall accept five shekels apiece, reckoning by the shekel of the sanctuary, a shekel of twenty gerahs. 48Give to Aaron and his sons the money by which the excess number of them is redeemed. 49So Moses took the redemption money from those who were over and above those redeemed by the Levites; 50from the firstborn of the Israelites he took the money, one thousand three hundred sixty-five shekels, reckoned by the shekel of the sanctuary; 51and Moses gave the redemption money to Aaron and his sons, according to the word of the LORD, as the LORD had commanded Moses.

The Kohathites

4 The LORD spoke to Moses and Aaron, saying: 2Take a census of the Kohathites separate from the other Levites, by their clans and their ancestral houses, 3from thirty years old up to fifty years old, all who qualify to do work relating to the tent of meeting. 4The service of the Kohathites relating to the tent of meeting concerns the most holy things.

5 When the camp is to set out, Aaron and his sons shall go in and take down the screening curtain, and cover the ark of the covenant*a* with it; 6then they shall put on it a covering of fine leather,*b* and spread over that a cloth all of blue, and shall put its poles in place. 7Over the table of the bread of the Presence they shall spread a blue cloth, and put on it the plates, the dishes for incense, the bowls, and the flagons for the drink offering; the regular bread also shall be on it; 8then they shall spread over them a crimson cloth, and cover it with a covering of fine leather,*b* and shall put its poles in place. 9They shall take a blue cloth, and cover the lampstand for the light, with its lamps, its snuffers, its trays, and all the vessels for oil with which it is supplied; 10and they shall put it with all its utensils in a covering of fine leather,*b* and put it on the carrying frame. 11Over the golden altar they shall

spread a blue cloth, and cover it with a covering of fine leather,*b* and shall put its poles in place; 12and they shall take all the utensils of the service that are used in the sanctuary, and put them in a blue cloth, and cover them with a covering of fine leather,*b* and put them on the carrying frame. 13They shall take away the ashes from the altar, and spread a purple cloth over it; 14and they shall put on it all the utensils of the altar, which are used for the service there, the firepans, the forks, the shovels, and the basins, all the utensils of the altar; and they shall spread on it a covering of fine leather,*b* and shall put its poles in place. 15When Aaron and his sons have finished covering the sanctuary and all the furnishings of the sanctuary, as the camp sets out, after that the Kohathites shall come to carry these, but they must not touch the holy things, or they will die. These are the things of the tent of meeting that the Kohathites are to carry.

16 Eleazar son of Aaron the priest shall have charge of the oil for the light, the fragrant incense, the regular grain offering, and the anointing oil, the oversight of all the tabernacle and all that is in it, in the sanctuary and in its utensils.

17 Then the LORD spoke to Moses and Aaron, saying: 18You must not let the tribe of the clans of the Kohathites be destroyed from among the Levites. 19This is how you must deal with them in order that they may live and not die when they come near to the most holy things: Aaron and his sons shall go in and assign each to a particular task or burden. 20But the Kohathites*c* must not go in to look on the holy things even for a moment; otherwise they will die.

The Gershonites and Merarites

21 Then the LORD spoke to Moses, saying: 22Take a census of the Gershonites also, by

a Or *treaty*, or *testimony*; Heb *eduth*   *b* Meaning of Heb uncertain   *c* Heb *they*

3:45 *and the Levites shall be mine.* God set the Levites apart as his own and claimed them for his service. God provides for, protects, and nurtures his own, especially, as we see with Moses and the Levites, those whom God has called to serve him. Unlike those who lived in Moses' day, today each believer is called to be part of the "holy priesthood" (1 Pet 2:5). We can be sure that God is personally concerned with each of our lives.

their ancestral houses and by their clans; [23]from thirty years old up to fifty years old you shall enroll them, all who qualify to do work in the tent of meeting. [24]This is the service of the clans of the Gershonites, in serving and bearing burdens: [25]They shall carry the curtains of the tabernacle, and the tent of meeting with its covering, and the outer covering of fine leather[a] that is on top of it, and the screen for the entrance of the tent of meeting, [26]and the hangings of the court, and the screen for the entrance of the gate of the court that is around the tabernacle and the altar, and their cords, and all the equipment for their service; and they shall do all that needs to be done with regard to them. [27]All the service of the Gershonites shall be at the command of Aaron and his sons, in all that they are to carry, and in all that they have to do; and you shall assign to their charge all that they are to carry. [28]This is the service of the clans of the Gershonites relating to the tent of meeting, and their responsibilities are to be under the oversight of Ithamar son of Aaron the priest.

29 As for the Merarites, you shall enroll them by their clans and their ancestral houses; [30]from thirty years old up to fifty years old you shall enroll them, everyone who qualifies to do the work of the tent of meeting. [31]This is what they are charged to carry, as the whole of their service in the tent of meeting: the frames of the tabernacle, with its bars, pillars, and bases, [32]and the pillars of the court all around with their bases, pegs, and cords, with all their equipment and all their related service; and you shall assign by name the objects that they are required to carry. [33]This is the service of the clans of the Merarites, the whole of their service relating to the tent of meeting, under the hand of Ithamar son of Aaron the priest.

Census of the Levites

34 So Moses and Aaron and the leaders of the congregation enrolled the Kohathites, by their clans and their ancestral houses, [35]from thirty years old up to fifty years old, everyone who qualified for work relating to the tent of meeting; [36]and their enrollment by clans was two thousand seven hundred fifty. [37]This was the enrollment of the clans of the Kohathites, all who served at the tent of meeting, whom Moses and Aaron enrolled according to the commandment of the LORD by Moses.

38 The enrollment of the Gershonites, by their clans and their ancestral houses, [39]from thirty years old up to fifty years old, everyone who qualified for work relating to the tent of meeting— [40]their enrollment by their clans and their ancestral houses was two thousand six hundred thirty. [41]This was the enrollment of the clans of the Gershonites, all who served at the tent of meeting, whom Moses and Aaron enrolled according to the commandment of the LORD.

42 The enrollment of the clans of the Merarites, by their clans and their ancestral houses, [43]from thirty years old up to fifty years old, everyone who qualified for work relating to the tent of meeting— [44]their enrollment by their clans was three thousand two hundred. [45]This is the enrollment of the clans of the Merarites, whom Moses and Aaron enrolled according to the commandment of the LORD by Moses.

46 All those who were enrolled of the Levites, whom Moses and Aaron and the leaders of Israel enrolled, by their clans and their ancestral houses, [47]from thirty years old up to fifty years old, everyone who qualified to do the work of service and the work of bearing burdens relating to the tent of meeting, [48]their enrollment was eight thousand five

a Meaning of Heb uncertain

Responding

4:24, 27 SERVICE. As the Israelites were moving from place to place in the wilderness, specific levitical clans were enrolled to break down the tabernacle, carry it to the new site, and reassemble it. Scripture refers to these tasks as "serving" or "carrying." This week make an effort to help those people in your life whose duties include serving and carrying; for example, help serve coffee to business associates, help carry a heavy piece of furniture. See also Spiritual Disciplines Index.

hundred eighty. [49]According to the commandment of the LORD through Moses they were appointed to their several tasks of serving or carrying; thus they were enrolled by him, as the LORD commanded Moses.

Unclean Persons

5 The LORD spoke to Moses, saying: [2]Command the Israelites to put out of the camp everyone who is leprous, *a* or has a discharge, and everyone who is unclean through contact with a corpse; [3]you shall put out both male and female, putting them outside the camp; they must not defile their camp, where I dwell among them. [4]The Israelites did so, putting them outside the camp; as the LORD had spoken to Moses, so the Israelites did.

Confession and Restitution

5 The LORD spoke to Moses, saying: [6]Speak to the Israelites: When a man or a woman wrongs another, breaking faith with the LORD, that person incurs guilt [7]and shall confess the sin that has been committed. The person shall make full restitution for the wrong, adding one-fifth to it, and giving it to the one who was wronged. [8]If the injured

party has no next of kin to whom restitution may be made for the wrong, the restitution for wrong shall go to the LORD for the priest, in addition to the ram of atonement with which atonement is made for the guilty party. [9]Among all the sacred donations of the Israelites, every gift that they bring to the priest shall be his. [10]The sacred donations of all are their own; whatever anyone gives to the priest shall be his.

Concerning an Unfaithful Wife

11 The LORD spoke to Moses, saying: [12]Speak to the Israelites and say to them: If any man's wife goes astray and is unfaithful to him, [13]if a man has had intercourse with her but it is hidden from her husband, so that she is undetected though she has defiled herself, and there is no witness against her since she was not caught in the act; [14]if a spirit of jealousy comes on him, and he is jealous of his wife who has defiled herself; or if a spirit of jealousy comes on him, and he is jealous of his wife, though she has not defiled herself; [15]then the man shall bring his

a A term for several skin diseases; precise meaning uncertain

HEALTHY COMMUNITY

4:49 *they were appointed to their several tasks.* God calls us to be part of his community. To contribute to one's community is to participate in it. God assigns his tasks in accordance with each individual's talents and gifts. God gave the Israelites work to do, because he was interested in the spiritual transformation and maturity of each individual. Just as God appointed the duties of the priests, he assigns work to each of us. And God actually desires that we do our best work for him. Balance is essential to the spiritual life. It is important to balance character (who we are) and ministry (what we do). Emphasizing ministry at the cost of personal character formation will hinder our spiritual growth. On the other hand, offering service to God is an important aspect of our continued growth in character. A spiritual act of balancing of our worship, doing our best to serve in our God-given ministries, and constantly pursuing spiritual maturity is pleasing to God.   *BALANCE*

5:3 *they must not defile their camp.* God was concerned with building a healthy community.

God wanted to keep his people pure and sanctified for their own sakes. Their purity, or holiness, was important, both for their own edification and so they would not defile the holiness of God. All the laws regarding uncleanness or defilement mentioned in Numbers are concerned with the purification of the community. It was to this end that God told the Israelites to expel any who were unclean, so as to protect the purity and welfare of the community. Even today, the purity of any community member helps determine the purity of the community as a whole. Our purity as Christians, however, is guided less by laws and customs than by our call to live our lives in ways that honor and glorify God. We become pure as we allow God to sanctify our thoughts and behavior. Our personal spiritual growth and the holiness it brings are an integral part of communal spiritual formation.

5:7 **CONFESSION**—*See* Spiritual Disciplines Index.

wife to the priest. And he shall bring the offering required for her, one-tenth of an ephah of barley flour. He shall pour no oil on it and put no frankincense on it, for it is a grain offering of jealousy, a grain offering of remembrance, bringing iniquity to remembrance.

16 Then the priest shall bring her near, and set her before the LORD; 17the priest shall take holy water in an earthen vessel, and take some of the dust that is on the floor of the tabernacle and put it into the water. 18The priest shall set the woman before the LORD, dishevel the woman's hair, and place in her hands the grain offering of remembrance, which is the grain offering of jealousy. In his own hand the priest shall have the water of bitterness that brings the curse. 19Then the priest shall make her take an oath, saying, "If no man has lain with you, if you have not turned aside to uncleanness while under your husband's authority, be immune to this water of bitterness that brings the curse. 20But if you have gone astray while under your husband's authority, if you have defiled yourself and some man other than your husband has had intercourse with you," 21—let the priest make the woman take the oath of the curse and say to the woman—"the LORD make you an execration and an oath among your people, when the LORD makes your uterus drop, your womb discharge; 22now may this water that brings the curse enter your bowels and make your womb discharge, your uterus drop!" And the woman shall say, "Amen. Amen."

23 Then the priest shall put these curses in writing, and wash them off into the water of bitterness. 24He shall make the woman drink the water of bitterness that brings the curse, and the water that brings the curse shall enter her and cause bitter pain. 25The priest shall take the grain offering of jealousy out of the woman's hand, and shall elevate the grain offering before the LORD and bring it to the altar; 26and the priest shall take a handful of the grain offering, as its memorial portion, and turn it into smoke on the altar, and afterward shall make the woman drink the water. 27When he has made her drink the water, then, if she has defiled herself and has

been unfaithful to her husband, the water that brings the curse shall enter into her and cause bitter pain, and her womb shall discharge, her uterus drop, and the woman shall become an execration among her people. 28But if the woman has not defiled herself and is clean, then she shall be immune and be able to conceive children.

29 This is the law in cases of jealousy, when a wife, while under her husband's authority, goes astray and defiles herself, 30or when a spirit of jealousy comes on a man and he is jealous of his wife; then he shall set the woman before the LORD, and the priest shall apply this entire law to her. 31The man shall be free from iniquity, but the woman shall bear her iniquity.

The Nazirites

6 The LORD spoke to Moses, saying: 2Speak to the Israelites and say to them: When either men or women make a special vow, the vow of a nazirite,*a* to separate themselves to the LORD, 3they shall separate themselves from wine and strong drink; they shall drink no wine vinegar or other vinegar, and shall not drink any grape juice or eat grapes, fresh or dried. 4All their days as nazirites*b* they shall eat nothing that is produced by the grapevine, not even the seeds or the skins.

5 All the days of their nazirite vow no razor shall come upon the head; until the time is completed for which they separate themselves to the LORD, they shall be holy; they shall let the locks of the head grow long.

6 All the days that they separate themselves to the LORD they shall not go near a corpse. 7Even if their father or mother, brother or sister, should die, they may not defile themselves; because their consecration to God is upon the head. 8All their days as nazirites*b* they are holy to the LORD.

9 If someone dies very suddenly nearby, defiling the consecrated head, then they shall shave the head on the day of their cleansing; on the seventh day they shall shave it. 10On the eighth day they shall bring two turtledoves or two young pigeons to the priest at

a That is *one separated* or *one consecrated*   *b* That is *those separated* or *those consecrated*

the entrance of the tent of meeting, [11]and the priest shall offer one as a sin offering and the other as a burnt offering, and make atonement for them, because they incurred guilt by reason of the corpse. They shall sanctify the head that same day, [12]and separate themselves to the LORD for their days as nazirites,[a] and bring a male lamb a year old as a guilt offering. The former time shall be void, because the consecrated head was defiled.

13 This is the law for the nazirites[a] when the time of their consecration has been completed: they shall be brought to the entrance of the tent of meeting, [14]and they shall offer their gift to the LORD, one male lamb a year old without blemish as a burnt offering, one ewe lamb a year old without blemish as a sin offering, one ram without blemish as an offering of well-being, [15]and a basket of unleavened bread, cakes of choice flour mixed with oil and unleavened wafers spread with oil, with their grain offering and their drink offerings. [16]The priest shall present them before the LORD and offer their sin offering and burnt offering, [17]and shall offer the ram as a sacrifice of well-being to the LORD, with the basket of unleavened bread; the priest also shall make the accompanying grain offering and drink offering. [18]Then the nazirites[a] shall shave the consecrated head at the entrance of the tent of meeting, and shall take the hair from the consecrated head and put it on the fire under the sacrifice of well-being. [19]The priest shall take the shoulder of the ram, when it is boiled, and one unleavened cake out of the basket, and one unleavened wafer, and shall put them in the palms of the

nazirites,[a] after they have shaved the consecrated head. [20]Then the priest shall elevate them as an elevation offering before the LORD; they are a holy portion for the priest, together with the breast that is elevated and the thigh that is offered. After that the nazirites[a] may drink wine.

21 This is the law for the nazirites[a] who take a vow. Their offering to the LORD must be in accordance with the nazirite[b] vow, apart from what else they can afford. In accordance with whatever vow they take, so they shall do, following the law for their consecration.

The Priestly Benediction

22 The LORD spoke to Moses, saying: [23]Speak to Aaron and his sons, saying, Thus you shall bless the Israelites: You shall say to them,
  24 The LORD bless you and keep you;
  25 the LORD make his face to shine upon
      you, and be gracious to you;
  26 the LORD lift up his countenance upon
      you, and give you peace.
  27 So they shall put my name on the Israelites, and I will bless them.

Offerings of the Leaders

7 On the day when Moses had finished setting up the tabernacle, and had anointed and consecrated it with all its furnishings, and had anointed and consecrated the altar with all its utensils, [2]the leaders of Israel, heads of their ancestral houses, the

---

a That is those separated or those consecrated
b That is one separated or one consecrated

6:23 *Thus you shall bless the Israelites.* God purposes and desires to bless his people. Our God is a God who blesses. Thus, the community of God is a blessed community. As his representatives, God directed the priests to bless the people. As part of the priesthood of all believers, we are all now God's representatives. We are all called to bless others. We are spiritually mature when we can overcome our emotions and pray for, even ask God to bless, our enemies. We are called today, not to repay evil for evil or to return abuse for abuse, but to repay evil with blessings (1 Pet 3:9).

6:24—26 THE WITH-GOD LIFE—*See* Spiritual Disciplines Index.

7:1 *when Moses . . . had anointed and consecrated it.* God called his people to be holy. He anoints not only his priests, but also all the things used in worship and service, in order to make them holy. To be holy is to be set apart for God. The spiritual life is a pursuit of holiness. We must be holy, for our God, who has set us apart for himself, is holy. Today we are sanctified through our faith in Jesus Christ. We can increasingly reflect God's holiness in our lives through our own spiritual discipline and growth.

leaders of the tribes, who were over those who were enrolled, made offerings. 3They brought their offerings before the LORD, six covered wagons and twelve oxen, a wagon for every two of the leaders, and for each one an ox; they presented them before the tabernacle. 4Then the LORD said to Moses: 5Accept these from them, that they may be used in doing the service of the tent of meeting, and give them to the Levites, to each according to his service. 6So Moses took the wagons and the oxen, and gave them to the Levites. 7Two wagons and four oxen he gave to the Gershonites, according to their service; 8and four wagons and eight oxen he gave to the Merarites, according to their service, under the direction of Ithamar son of Aaron the priest. 9But to the Kohathites he gave none, because they were charged with the care of the holy things that had to be carried on the shoulders.

10 The leaders also presented offerings for the dedication of the altar at the time when it was anointed; the leaders presented their offering before the altar. 11The LORD said to Moses: They shall present their offerings, one leader each day, for the dedication of the altar.

12 The one who presented his offering the first day was Nahshon son of Amminadab, of the tribe of Judah; 13his offering was one silver plate weighing one hundred thirty shekels, one silver basin weighing seventy shekels, according to the shekel of the sanctuary, both of them full of choice flour mixed with oil for a grain offering; 14one golden dish weighing ten shekels, full of incense; 15one young bull, one ram, one male lamb a year old, for a burnt offering; 16one male goat for a sin offering; 17and for the sacrifice of well-being, two oxen, five rams, five male goats, and five male lambs a year old. This was the offering of Nahshon son of Amminadab.

18 On the second day Nethanel son of Zuar, the leader of Issachar, presented an offering; 19he presented for his offering one silver plate weighing one hundred thirty shekels, one silver basin weighing seventy shekels, according to the shekel of the sanctuary, both of them full of choice flour mixed with oil for a grain offering; 20one golden dish weighing ten shekels, full of incense; 21one young bull, one ram, one male lamb a year old, as a burnt offering; 22one male goat as a sin offering; 23and for the sacrifice of well-being, two oxen, five rams, five male goats, and five male lambs a year old. This was the offering of Nethanel son of Zuar.

24 On the third day Eliab son of Helon, the leader of the Zebulunites: 25his offering was one silver plate weighing one hundred thirty shekels, one silver basin weighing seventy shekels, according to the shekel of the sanctuary, both of them full of choice flour mixed with oil for a grain offering; 26one golden dish weighing ten shekels, full of incense; 27one young bull, one ram, one male lamb a year old, for a burnt offering; 28one male goat for a sin offering; 29and for the sacrifice of well-being, two oxen, five rams, five male goats, and five male lambs a year old. This was the offering of Eliab son of Helon.

30 On the fourth day Elizur son of Shedeur, the leader of the Reubenites: 31his offering was one silver plate weighing one hundred thirty shekels, one silver basin weighing seventy shekels, according to the shekel of the sanctuary, both of them full of choice flour mixed with oil for a grain offering; 32one golden dish weighing ten shekels, full of incense; 33one young bull, one ram, one male lamb a year old, for a burnt offering; 34one male goat for a sin offering; 35and for the sacrifice of well-being, two oxen, five rams, five male goats, and five male lambs a year old. This was the offering of Elizur son of Shedeur.

36 On the fifth day Shelumiel son of Zurishaddai, the leader of the Simeonites: 37his offering was one silver plate weighing one hundred thirty shekels, one silver basin weighing seventy shekels, according to the shekel of the sanctuary, both of them full of choice flour mixed with oil for a grain offering; 38one golden dish weighing ten shekels, full of incense; 39one young bull, one ram, one male lamb a year old, for a burnt offering; 40one male goat for a sin offering; 41and for the sacrifice of well-being, two oxen, five rams, five male goats, and five male lambs a year old. This was the offering of Shelumiel son of Zurishaddai.

42 On the sixth day Eliasaph son of Deuel, the leader of the Gadites: 43his offering was one silver plate weighing one hundred thirty shekels, one silver basin weighing seventy shekels, according to the shekel of the sanctuary, both of them full of choice flour mixed with oil for a grain offering; 44one golden dish weighing ten shekels, full of incense; 45one young bull, one ram, one male lamb a year old, for a burnt offering; 46one male goat for a sin offering; 47and for the sacrifice of well-being, two oxen, five rams, five male goats, and five male lambs a year old. This was the offering of Eliasaph son of Deuel.

48 On the seventh day Elishama son of Ammihud, the leader of the Ephraimites: 49his offering was one silver plate weighing one hundred thirty shekels, one silver basin weighing seventy shekels, according to the shekel of the sanctuary, both of them full of choice flour mixed with oil for a grain offering; 50one golden dish weighing ten shekels, full of incense; 51one young bull, one ram, one male lamb a year old, for a burnt offering; 52one male goat for a sin offering; 53and for the sacrifice of well-being, two oxen, five rams, five male goats, and five male lambs a year old. This was the offering of Elishama son of Ammihud.

54 On the eighth day Gamaliel son of Pedahzur, the leader of the Manassites: 55his offering was one silver plate weighing one hundred thirty shekels, one silver basin weighing seventy shekels, according to the shekel of the sanctuary, both of them full of choice flour mixed with oil for a grain offering; 56one golden dish weighing ten shekels, full of incense; 57one young bull, one ram, one male lamb a year old, for a burnt offering; 58one male goat for a sin offering; 59and for the sacrifice of well-being, two oxen, five rams, five male goats, and five male lambs a year old. This was the offering of Gamaliel son of Pedahzur.

60 On the ninth day Abidan son of Gideoni, the leader of the Benjaminites: 61his offering was one silver plate weighing one hundred thirty shekels, one silver basin weighing seventy shekels, according to the shekel of the sanctuary, both of them full of choice flour mixed with oil for a grain offering; 62one golden dish weighing ten shekels, full of incense; 63one young bull, one ram, one male lamb a year old, for a burnt offering; 64one male goat for a sin offering; 65and for the sacrifice of well-being, two oxen, five rams, five male goats, and five male lambs a year old. This was the offering of Abidan son of Gideoni.

66 On the tenth day Ahiezer son of Ammishaddai, the leader of the Danites: 67his offering was one silver plate weighing one hundred thirty shekels, one silver basin weighing seventy shekels, according to the shekel of the sanctuary, both of them full of choice flour mixed with oil for a grain offering; 68one golden dish weighing ten shekels, full of incense; 69one young bull, one ram, one male lamb a year old, for a burnt offering; 70one male goat for a sin offering; 71and for the sacrifice of well-being, two oxen, five rams, five male goats, and five male lambs a year old. This was the offering of Ahiezer son of Ammishaddai.

72 On the eleventh day Pagiel son of Ochran, the leader of the Asherites: 73his offering was one silver plate weighing one hundred thirty shekels, one silver basin weighing seventy shekels, according to the shekel of the sanctuary, both of them full of choice flour mixed with oil for a grain offering; 74one golden dish weighing ten shekels, full of incense; 75one young bull, one ram, one male lamb a year old, for a burnt offering; 76one male goat for a sin offering; 77and for the sacrifice of well-being, two oxen, five rams, five male goats, and five male lambs a year old. This was the offering of Pagiel son of Ochran.

78 On the twelfth day Ahira son of Enan, the leader of the Naphtalites: 79his offering was one silver plate weighing one hundred thirty shekels, one silver basin weighing seventy shekels, according to the shekel of the sanctuary, both of them full of choice flour mixed with oil for a grain offering; 80one golden dish weighing ten shekels, full of incense; 81one young bull, one ram, one male lamb a year old, for a burnt offering; 82one male goat for a sin offering; 83and for the sacrifice of well-being, two oxen, five rams, five male goats, and five male lambs a year old. This was the offering of Ahira son of Enan.

84 This was the dedication offering for the altar, at the time when it was anointed, from the leaders of Israel: twelve silver plates, twelve silver basins, twelve golden dishes, [85]each silver plate weighing one hundred thirty shekels and each basin seventy, all the silver of the vessels two thousand four hundred shekels according to the shekel of the sanctuary, [86]the twelve golden dishes, full of incense, weighing ten shekels apiece according to the shekel of the sanctuary, all the gold of the dishes being one hundred twenty shekels; [87]all the livestock for the burnt offering twelve bulls, twelve rams, twelve male lambs a year old, with their grain offering; and twelve male goats for a sin offering; [88]and all the livestock for the sacrifice of well-being twenty-four bulls, the rams sixty, the male goats sixty, the male lambs a year old sixty. This was the dedication offering for the altar, after it was anointed.

89 When Moses went into the tent of meeting to speak with the LORD,*a* he would hear the voice speaking to him from above the mercy seat*b* that was on the ark of the covenant*c* from between the two cherubim; thus it spoke to him.

The Seven Lamps

8 The LORD spoke to Moses, saying: [2]Speak to Aaron and say to him: When you set up the lamps, the seven lamps shall give light in front of the lampstand. [3]Aaron did so; he set up its lamps to give light in front of the lampstand, as the LORD had commanded Moses. [4]Now this was how the lampstand was made, out of hammered work of gold. From its base to its flowers, it was hammered work; according to the pattern that the LORD had shown Moses, so he made the lampstand.

Consecration and Service of the Levites

5 The LORD spoke to Moses, saying: [6]Take the Levites from among the Israelites and cleanse them. [7]Thus you shall do to them, to cleanse them: sprinkle the water of purification on them, have them shave their whole body with a razor and wash their clothes, and so cleanse themselves. [8]Then let them take a young bull and its grain offering of choice flour mixed with oil, and you shall take another young bull for a sin offering. [9]You shall bring the Levites before the tent of meeting, and assemble the whole congregation of the Israelites. [10]When you bring the Levites before the LORD, the Israelites shall lay their hands on the Levites, [11]and Aaron shall present the Levites before the LORD as an elevation offering from the Israelites, that they may do the service of the LORD. [12]The Levites shall lay their hands on the heads of the bulls, and he shall offer the one for a sin offering and the other for a burnt offering to the LORD, to make atonement for the Levites. [13]Then you shall have

a Heb *him*   *b* Or *the cover*   *c* Or *treaty*, or *testimony*; Heb *eduth*

7:89 *he would hear the voice speaking to him.* Moses heard the voice of God in the tabernacle in the Holy of Holies. Moses obeyed, thus living his life in accordance with God's will. The foundation of spiritual growth is our obedience to God. To hear and obey the voice of the Lord is essential if we are to receive his best. Spiritual growth takes place as we hear the voice of God speaking to us, whether through his word or other means, and grow in our willingness to obey.

Responding
7:89 **THE WITH-GOD LIFE.** Do you agree that our willingness to obey the voice of God affects our spiritual growth? What can we do to become more sensitive to God's voice? *See also* Spiritual Disciplines Index.

8:11 **SERVICE**—*See* Spiritual Disciplines Index.

8:11 *present the Levites before the LORD.* The priests needed to be consecrated for God's service. Consecrated means "declared or set apart as sacred, dedicated to God." Today we are set apart for God when we are baptized, but many of us forget to live our lives that way. We must be concerned to first present ourselves before the Lord, not before people. As we learn to live our lives knowing we are standing before the living God, we will grow in simplicity and transparency.

the Levites stand before Aaron and his sons, and you shall present them as an elevation offering to the LORD.

14 Thus you shall separate the Levites from among the other Israelites, and the Levites shall be mine. ¹⁵Thereafter the Levites may go in to do service at the tent of meeting, once you have cleansed them and presented them as an elevation offering. ¹⁶For they are unreservedly given to me from among the Israelites; I have taken them for myself, in place of all that open the womb, the firstborn of all the Israelites. ¹⁷For all the firstborn among the Israelites are mine, both human and animal. On the day that I struck down all the firstborn in the land of Egypt I consecrated them for myself, ¹⁸but I have taken the Levites in place of all the firstborn among the Israelites. ¹⁹Moreover, I have given the Levites as a gift to Aaron and his sons from among the Israelites, to do the service for the Israelites at the tent of meeting, and to make atonement for the Israelites, in order that there may be no plague among the Israelites for coming too close to the sanctuary.

20 Moses and Aaron and the whole congregation of the Israelites did with the Levites accordingly; the Israelites did with the Levites just as the LORD had commanded Moses concerning them. ²¹The Levites purified themselves from sin and washed their clothes; then Aaron presented them as an elevation offering before the LORD, and Aaron made atonement for them to cleanse them. ²²Thereafter the Levites went in to do their service in the tent of meeting in attendance on Aaron and his sons. As the LORD had commanded Moses concerning the Levites, so they did with them.

23 The LORD spoke to Moses, saying: ²⁴This applies to the Levites: from twenty-five years old and upward they shall begin to do duty in the service of the tent of meeting; ²⁵and from the age of fifty years they shall retire from the duty of the service and serve no more. ²⁶They may assist their brothers in the tent of meeting in carrying out their duties, but they shall perform no service. Thus you shall do with the Levites in assigning their duties.

The Passover at Sinai

9 The LORD spoke to Moses in the wilderness of Sinai, in the first month of the second year after they had come out of the land of Egypt, saying: ²Let the Israelites keep the passover at its appointed time. ³On the fourteenth day of this month, at twilight,ᵃ you shall keep it at its appointed time; according to all its statutes and all its regulations you shall keep it. ⁴So Moses told the Israelites that they should keep the passover. ⁵They kept the passover in the first month, on the fourteenth day of the month, at twilight,ᵃ in the wilderness of Sinai. Just as the LORD had commanded Moses, so the Israelites did. ⁶Now there were certain people who were unclean through touching a corpse, so that they could not keep the passover on that day. They came before Moses and Aaron on that day, ⁷and said to him, "Although we are unclean through touching a corpse, why must we be kept from presenting the LORD's offering at its appointed time among the Israelites?" ⁸Moses spoke to them, "Wait, so that I may hear what the LORD will command concerning you."

9 The LORD spoke to Moses, saying: ¹⁰Speak to the Israelites, saying: Anyone of you or your descendants who is unclean through touching a corpse, or is away on a journey, shall still keep the passover to the LORD. ¹¹In the second month on the fourteenth day, at twilight,ᵃ they shall keep it; they shall eat it with unleavened bread and bitter herbs. ¹²They shall leave none of it until morning, nor break a bone of it; according to all the statute for the passover they shall keep it. ¹³But anyone who is clean and is not on a journey, and yet refrains from keeping the passover, shall be cut off from the people for not presenting the LORD's offering at its appointed time; such a one shall bear the consequences for the sin. ¹⁴Any alien residing among you who wishes to keep the passover to the LORD shall do so according to the statute of the passover and according to its regulation; you shall have one statute for both the resident alien and the native.

---

a Heb *between the two evenings*

The Cloud and the Fire

15 On the day the tabernacle was set up, the cloud covered the tabernacle, the tent of the covenant;[a] and from evening until morning it was over the tabernacle, having the appearance of fire. 16It was always so: the cloud covered it by day[b] and the appearance of fire by night. 17Whenever the cloud lifted from over the tent, then the Israelites would set out; and in the place where the cloud settled down, there the Israelites would camp. 18At the command of the LORD the Israelites would set out, and at the command of the LORD they would camp. As long as the cloud rested over the tabernacle, they would remain in camp. 19Even when the cloud continued over the tabernacle many days, the Israelites would keep the charge of the LORD, and would not set out. 20Sometimes the cloud would remain a few days over the tabernacle, and according to the command of the LORD they would remain in camp; then according to the command of the LORD they would set out. 21Sometimes the cloud would remain from evening until morning; and when the cloud lifted in the morning, they would set out, or if it continued for a day and a night, when the cloud lifted they would set out. 22Whether it was two days, or a month, or a longer time, that the cloud continued over the tabernacle, resting upon it, the Israelites would remain in camp and would not set out; but when it lifted they would set out. 23At the command of the LORD they would camp, and at the command of the LORD they would set out. They kept the charge of the LORD, at the command of the LORD by Moses.

The Silver Trumpets

10 The LORD spoke to Moses, saying: 2Make two silver trumpets; you shall make them of hammered work; and you shall use them for summoning the congregation, and for breaking camp. 3When both are blown, the whole congregation shall assemble before you at the entrance of the tent of meeting. 4But if only one is blown, then the leaders, the heads of the tribes of Israel, shall assemble before you. 5When you blow an alarm, the camps on the east side shall set out; 6when you blow a second alarm, the camps on the south side shall set out. An alarm is to be blown whenever they are to set out. 7But when the assembly is to be gathered, you shall blow, but you shall not sound an alarm. 8The sons of Aaron, the priests, shall blow the trumpets; this shall be a perpetual institution for you throughout your generations. 9When you go to war in your land against the adversary who oppresses you, you shall sound an alarm with the trumpets, so that you may be remembered before the LORD your God and be saved from your enemies. 10Also on your days of rejoicing,

a Or treaty, or testimony; Heb eduth   b Gk Syr Vg: Heb lacks by day

---

9:18 *At the command of the LORD the Israelites would set out, and at the command of the LORD they would camp.* The people of Israel followed the movements of the cloud that represented the divine presence. They traveled when the cloud moved, and they camped wherever it stopped. Thus, the Israelites did not move of their own accord, but only when they were following God's guidance. Learning to look for and rely on direction by God is one of the key elements in the spiritual life. Like the Israelites, we must learn to be guided not only individually, but also as a community.

10:2 *Make two silver trumpets.* God used trumpets to coordinate the movements of the people. They were God's instruments for bringing about order and discipline. The whole community was directed by their sound.

Numbers describes God's work in teaching and organizing the Israelites and in shaping them, once slaves in Egypt, into a great nation. That he would make for them beautiful-sounding silver trumpets shows God's attention to detail, his loving care and concern for directing the Israelites in their wilderness journey.

Responding
10:10 CELEBRATION. In most churches a procession, prelude, or special music summons people to gather for worship. Many times, however, people linger in the foyer or narthex and wait until the last minute to enter the sanctuary. What can you do to help break this cycle? Pick one of your answers, and do it this Sunday. *See also* Spiritual Disciplines Index.

at your appointed festivals, and at the beginnings of your months, you shall blow the trumpets over your burnt offerings and over your sacrifices of well-being; they shall serve as a reminder on your behalf before the LORD your God: I am the LORD your God.

Departure from Sinai

11 In the second year, in the second month, on the twentieth day of the month, the cloud lifted from over the tabernacle of the covenant. *a* 12Then the Israelites set out by stages from the wilderness of Sinai, and the cloud settled down in the wilderness of Paran. 13They set out for the first time at the command of the LORD by Moses. 14The standard of the camp of Judah set out first, company by company, and over the whole company was Nahshon son of Amminadab. 15Over the company of the tribe of Issachar was Nethanel son of Zuar; 16and over the company of the tribe of Zebulun was Eliab son of Helon.

17 Then the tabernacle was taken down, and the Gershonites and the Merarites, who carried the tabernacle, set out. 18Next the standard of the camp of Reuben set out, company by company; and over the whole company was Elizur son of Shedeur. 19Over the company of the tribe of Simeon was Shelumiel son of Zurishaddai, 20and over the company of the tribe of Gad was Eliasaph son of Deuel.

21 Then the Kohathites, who carried the holy things, set out; and the tabernacle was set up before their arrival. 22Next the standard of the Ephraimite camp set out, company by company, and over the whole company was Elishama son of Ammihud. 23Over the company of the tribe of Manasseh was Gamaliel son of Pedahzur, 24and over the company of the tribe of Benjamin was Abidan son of Gideoni.

25 Then the standard of the camp of Dan, acting as the rear guard of all the camps, set out, company by company, and over the whole company was Ahiezer son of Ammishaddai. 26Over the company of the tribe

of Asher was Pagiel son of Ochran, 27and over the company of the tribe of Naphtali was Ahira son of Enan. 28This was the order of march of the Israelites, company by company, when they set out.

29 Moses said to Hobab son of Reuel the Midianite, Moses' father-in-law, "We are setting out for the place of which the LORD said, 'I will give it to you'; come with us, and we will treat you well; for the LORD has promised good to Israel." 30But he said to him, "I will not go, but I will go back to my own land and to my kindred." 31He said, "Do not leave us, for you know where we should camp in the wilderness, and you will serve as eyes for us. 32Moreover, if you go with us, whatever good the LORD does for us, the same we will do for you."

33 So they set out from the mount of the LORD three days' journey with the ark of the covenant of the LORD going before them three days' journey, to seek out a resting place for them, 34the cloud of the LORD being over them by day when they set out from the camp.

35 Whenever the ark set out, Moses would say,

"Arise, O LORD, let your enemies be scattered,
and your foes flee before you."
36And whenever it came to rest, he would say,
"Return, O LORD of the ten thousand thousands of Israel." *b*

Complaining in the Desert

11 Now when the people complained in the hearing of the LORD about their misfortunes, the LORD heard it and his anger was kindled. Then the fire of the LORD burned against them, and consumed some outlying parts of the camp. 2But the people cried out to Moses; and Moses prayed to the LORD, and the fire abated. 3So that place was called Taberah, *c* because the fire of the LORD burned against them.

a Or *treaty*, or *testimony*; Heb *eduth*   *b* Meaning of Heb uncertain   *c* That is *Burning*

10:10 SACRIFICE—*See* Spiritual Disciplines Index.

4 The rabble among them had a strong craving; and the Israelites also wept again, and said, "If only we had meat to eat! 5We remember the fish we used to eat in Egypt for nothing, the cucumbers, the melons, the leeks, the onions, and the garlic; 6but now our strength is dried up, and there is nothing at all but this manna to look at."

7 Now the manna was like coriander seed, and its color was like the color of gum resin. 8The people went around and gathered it, ground it in mills or beat it in mortars, then boiled it in pots and made cakes of it; and the taste of it was like the taste of cakes baked with oil. 9When the dew fell on the camp in the night, the manna would fall with it.

10 Moses heard the people weeping throughout their families, all at the entrances of their tents. Then the LORD became very angry, and Moses was displeased. 11So Moses said to the LORD, "Why have you treated your servant so badly? Why have I not found favor in your sight, that you lay the burden of all this people on me? 12Did I conceive all this people? Did I give birth to them, that you should say to me, 'Carry them in your bosom, as a nurse carries a sucking child, to the land that you promised on oath to their ancestors'? 13Where am I to get meat to give to all this people? For they come weeping to me and say, 'Give us meat to eat!' 14I am not able to carry all this people alone, for they are too heavy for me. 15If this is the way you are going to treat me, put me to death at once—if I have found favor in your sight—and do not let me see my misery."

The Seventy Elders

16 So the LORD said to Moses, "Gather for me seventy of the elders of Israel, whom you know to be the elders of the people and officers over them; bring them to the tent of meeting, and have them take their place there with you. 17I will come down and talk with you there; and I will take some of the spirit that is on you and put it on them; and they shall bear the burden of the people along with you so that you will not bear it all by yourself. 18And say to the people: Consecrate yourselves for tomorrow, and you shall eat meat; for you have wailed in the hearing of the LORD, saying, 'If only we had meat to eat! Surely it was better for us in Egypt.' Therefore the LORD will give you meat, and you shall eat. 19You shall eat not only one day, or two days, or five days, or ten days, or twenty days, 20but for a whole month—until it comes out of your nostrils and becomes loathsome to you—because you have rejected the LORD who is among you, and have wailed before him, saying, 'Why did we ever leave Egypt?' " 21But Moses said, "The people I am with number six hundred thousand on foot; and you say, 'I will give them meat, that they may eat for a whole month'! 22Are there enough flocks and herds to slaughter for them? Are there enough fish in the sea to catch for them?" 23The LORD said to Moses, "Is the LORD's power limited? a Now you shall see whether my word will come true for you or not."

24 So Moses went out and told the people the words of the LORD; and he gathered seventy elders of the people, and placed them all around the tent. 25Then the LORD came down in the cloud and spoke to him, and took some

a Heb LORD's hand too short?

11:4 *The rabble among them had a strong craving.* The "rabble"—that is, the lowest and coarsest among the people—began to complain about the food and to remind the others of the seemingly better life they had had as slaves in Egypt. They caused almost all of God's people to long for Egypt and grumble against God. From the wilderness perspective, the food in Egypt seemed exciting, desirable, and physically satisfying. By contrast, the manna God provided seemed mundane and simple, even though it was nourishing and good. Those who pursue spiritual growth must pay careful attention to the people with whom they interact. We are all influenced by the people around us. What God offers as food for our spiritual health may not be as exciting or exotic as what the world offers. Spiritual food may seem unsubstantial and simple. Indeed, Jesus Christ, who is the "bread of life" (John 6:35), might to some seem simple, yet he satisfies our deepest hunger and can make us whole. AMEN!!

of the spirit that was on him and put it on the seventy elders; and when the spirit rested upon them, they prophesied. But they did not do so again.

26 Two men remained in the camp, one named Eldad, and the other named Medad, and the spirit rested on them; they were among those registered, but they had not gone out to the tent, and so they prophesied in the camp. 27 And a young man ran and told Moses, "Eldad and Medad are prophesying in the camp." 28 And Joshua son of Nun, the assistant of Moses, one of his chosen men,*a* said, "My lord Moses, stop them!" 29 But Moses said to him, "Are you jealous for my sake? Would that all the LORD's people were prophets, and that the LORD would put his spirit on them!" 30 And Moses and the elders of Israel returned to the camp.

The Quails

31 Then a wind went out from the LORD, and it brought quails from the sea and let them fall beside the camp, about a day's journey on this side and a day's journey on the other side, all around the camp, about two cubits deep on the ground. 32 So the people worked all that day and night and all the next day, gathering the quails; the least anyone gathered was ten homers; and they spread them out for themselves all around the camp. 33 But while the meat was still between their teeth, before it was consumed, the anger of the LORD was kindled against the people, and the LORD struck the people with a very great plague. 34 So that place was called Kibroth-hattaavah,*b* because there they buried the people who had the craving. 35 From Kibroth-hattaavah the people journeyed to Hazeroth.

Aaron and Miriam Jealous of Moses

12 While they were at Hazeroth, Miriam and Aaron spoke against Moses because of the Cushite woman whom he had married (for he had indeed married a Cushite woman); 2 and they said, "Has the LORD spoken only through Moses? Has he not spoken through us also?" And the LORD heard it. 3 Now the man Moses was very humble,*c* more so than anyone else on the face of the earth. 4 Suddenly the LORD said to Moses, Aaron, and Miriam, "Come out, you three, to the tent of meeting." So the three of them came out. 5 Then the LORD came down in a pillar of cloud, and stood at the entrance of the tent, and called Aaron and Miriam; and they both came forward. 6 And he said, "Hear my words:

When there are prophets among you,
  I the LORD make myself known to
    them in visions;
  I speak to them in dreams.
7 Not so with my servant Moses;
  he is entrusted with all my house.
8 With him I speak face to face—clearly,
    not in riddles;
  and he beholds the form of the LORD.
Why then were you not afraid to speak

a Or *of Moses from his youth*   *b* That is *Graves of craving* *c* Or *devout*

11:24–29 *Are you jealous for my sake?* Moses was open to sharing his authority and power. When God anointed the seventy elders with the Spirit, Moses was not resentful of their recognition, but was glad for them. God's anointing of the seventy was so strong that it even fell on two men who had disobeyed Moses and had not gone to the tent of meeting as Moses had instructed them to do. Joshua, knowing the two continued to prophesy, asked Moses to restrain them. Instead, Moses welcomed their anointing. He desired that God's gifts be shared among all of the people in the community rather than reserved for only the elders. The absence of jealousy in ministry is a mark of spiritual maturity.

12:1–13 *Now the man Moses was very humble.* God punished Miriam and Aaron when they criticized and challenged Moses' authority. But when Miriam became a leper, Moses did not rejoice in her fate. Rather, he felt compassion toward her and cried out to God on her behalf. He was humble, tender, and very loyal. And he was a man of prayer, a faithful leader for God's people.

12:7–8 SERVICE—*See* Spiritual Disciplines Index.

against my servant Moses?" 9And the anger of the LORD was kindled against them, and he departed.

10 When the cloud went away from over the tent, Miriam had become leprous,*a* as white as snow. And Aaron turned towards Miriam and saw that she was leprous. 11Then Aaron said to Moses, "Oh, my lord, do not punish us*b* for a sin that we have so foolishly committed. 12Do not let her be like one stillborn, whose flesh is half consumed when it comes out of its mother's womb." 13And Moses cried to the LORD, "O God, please heal her." 14But the LORD said to Moses, "If her father had but spit in her face, would she not bear her shame for seven days? Let her be shut out of the camp for seven days, and after that she may be brought in again." 15So Miriam was shut out of the camp for seven days; and the people did not set out on the march until Miriam had been brought in again. 16After that the people set out from Hazeroth, and camped in the wilderness of Paran.

Spies Sent into Canaan

13 The LORD said to Moses, 2"Send men to spy out the land of Canaan, which I am giving to the Israelites; from each of their ancestral tribes you shall send a man, every one a leader among them." 3So Moses sent them from the wilderness of Paran, according to the command of the LORD, all of them leading men among the Israelites. 4These were their names: From the tribe of Reuben, Shammua son of Zaccur; 5from the tribe of Simeon, Shaphat son of Hori; 6from the tribe of Judah, Caleb son of Jephunneh; 7from the tribe of Issachar, Igal son of Joseph; 8from the tribe of Ephraim, Hoshea son of Nun; 9from the tribe of Benjamin, Palti son of Raphu; 10from the tribe of Zebulun, Gaddiel son of Sodi; 11from the tribe of Joseph (that is, from the tribe of Manasseh), Gaddi

son of Susi; 12from the tribe of Dan, Ammiel son of Gemalli; 13from the tribe of Asher, Sethur son of Michael; 14from the tribe of Naphtali, Nahbi son of Vophsi; 15from the tribe of Gad, Geuel son of Machi. 16These were the names of the men whom Moses sent to spy out the land. And Moses changed the name of Hoshea son of Nun to Joshua.

17 Moses sent them to spy out the land of Canaan, and said to them, "Go up there into the Negeb, and go up into the hill country, 18and see what the land is like, and whether the people who live in it are strong or weak, whether they are few or many, 19and whether the land they live in is good or bad, and whether the towns that they live in are unwalled or fortified, 20and whether the land is rich or poor, and whether there are trees in it or not. Be bold, and bring some of the fruit of the land." Now it was the season of the first ripe grapes.

21 So they went up and spied out the land from the wilderness of Zin to Rehob, near Lebo-hamath. 22They went up into the Negeb, and came to Hebron; and Ahiman, Sheshai, and Talmai, the Anakites, were there. (Hebron was built seven years before Zoan in Egypt.) 23And they came to the Wadi Eshcol, and cut down from there a branch with a single cluster of grapes, and they carried it on a pole between two of them. They also brought some pomegranates and figs. 24That place was called the Wadi Eshcol,*c* because of the cluster that the Israelites cut down from there.

The Report of the Spies

25 At the end of forty days they returned from spying out the land. 26And they came to Moses and Aaron and to all the congrega-

a A term for several skin diseases; precise meaning uncertain   *b* Heb *do not lay sin upon us*   *c* That is *Cluster*

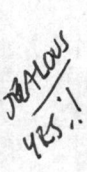

Responding
12:8 GUIDANCE. God's statement that he speaks to Moses face-to-face is evoked by the jealousy of Miriam and Aaron over Moses' special relationship with God. Have you ever been jealous of a person who has

received clear, unmistakable guidance from God? What was this a symptom of? Read Num 12:1–8 several times this week while asking the Lord for guidance in this area of your life. *See also* Spiritual Disciplines Index.

tion of the Israelites in the wilderness of Paran, at Kadesh; they brought back word to them and to all the congregation, and showed them the fruit of the land. 27And they told him, "We came to the land to which you sent us; it flows with milk and honey, and this is its fruit. 28Yet the people who live in the land are strong, and the towns are fortified and very large; and besides, we saw the descendants of Anak there. 29The Amalekites live in the land of the Negeb; the Hittites, the Jebusites, and the Amorites live in the hill country; and the Canaanites live by the sea, and along the Jordan."

30 But Caleb quieted the people before Moses, and said, "Let us go up at once and occupy it, for we are well able to overcome it." 31Then the men who had gone up with him said, "We are not able to go up against this people, for they are stronger than we." 32So they brought to the Israelites an unfavorable report of the land that they had spied out, saying, "The land that we have gone through as spies is a land that devours its inhabitants; and all the people that we saw in it are of great size. 33There we saw the Nephilim (the Anakites come from the Nephilim); and to ourselves we seemed like grasshoppers, and so we seemed to them."

The People Rebel

14 Then all the congregation raised a loud cry, and the people wept that night. 2And all the Israelites complained against Moses and Aaron; the whole congregation said to them, "Would that we had died in the land of Egypt! Or would that we had died in this wilderness! 3Why is the LORD bringing us into this land to fall by the sword? Our wives and our little ones will become booty; would it not be better for us to go back to Egypt?" 4So they said to one another, "Let us choose a captain, and go back to Egypt."

5 Then Moses and Aaron fell on their faces before all the assembly of the congregation of the Israelites. 6And Joshua son of Nun and Caleb son of Jephunneh, who were among those who had spied out the land, tore their clothes 7and said to all the congregation of the Israelites, "The land that we went through as spies is an exceedingly good land. 8If the LORD is pleased with us, he will bring us into this land and give it to us, a land that flows with milk and honey. 9Only, do not rebel against the LORD; and do not fear the people of the land, for they are no more than bread for us; their protection is removed from them, and the LORD is with us; do not fear them." 10But the whole congregation threatened to stone them.

Then the glory of the LORD appeared at the tent of meeting to all the Israelites. 11And the LORD said to Moses, "How long will this people despise me? And how long will they refuse to believe in me, in spite of all the signs that I have done among them? 12I will strike them with pestilence and disinherit them, and I will make of you a nation greater and mightier than they."

Moses Intercedes for the People

13 But Moses said to the LORD, "Then the Egyptians will hear of it, for in your might you brought up this people from among them,

---

13:33 *to ourselves we seemed like grasshoppers.* The Israelites seemed to have a problematic self-image, so much so that they saw themselves as "grasshoppers." They underestimated themselves and overestimated the people of Canaan. Their inability to see the truth was certainly rooted in distorted images they held of themselves and of God. A healthy self-image is the result of our spiritual growth. God desires that we learn to replace our distorted view of ourselves with the sight of ourselves in God's eyes—our true identities as the children of God.

14:6–9 *If the LORD is pleased with us.* Joshua and Caleb were a unique minority: they had a clear idea of who God was and who they were. Their perspective was different from that of the other ten spies. They were aware that God was with them, and they realized that the Anakites were no threat to them. Joshua and Caleb saw themselves and their enemies as God saw them. The spiritual life requires that we learn to see things as God does. As we grow in this Spiritual Discipline, we will find healing for ourselves and transformation in our understanding of God.

¹⁴and they will tell the inhabitants of this land. They have heard that you, O LORD, are in the midst of this people; for you, O LORD, are seen face to face, and your cloud stands over them and you go in front of them, in a pillar of cloud by day and in a pillar of fire by night. ¹⁵Now if you kill this people all at one time, then the nations who have heard about you will say, ¹⁶'It is because the LORD was not able to bring this people into the land he swore to give them that he has slaughtered them in the wilderness.' ¹⁷And now, therefore, let the power of the LORD be great in the way that you promised when you spoke, saying,

¹⁸ 'The LORD is slow to anger,
and abounding in steadfast love,
forgiving iniquity and transgression,
but by no means clearing the guilty,
visiting the iniquity of the parents
upon the children
to the third and the fourth generation.'
¹⁹Forgive the iniquity of this people according to the greatness of your steadfast love, just as you have pardoned this people, from Egypt even until now."

20 Then the LORD said, "I do forgive, just as you have asked; ²¹nevertheless—as I live, and as all the earth shall be filled with the glory of the LORD— ²²none of the people who have seen my glory and the signs that I did in Egypt and in the wilderness, and yet have tested me these ten times and have not obeyed my voice, ²³shall see the land that I swore to give to their ancestors; none of those who despised me shall see it. ²⁴But my servant Caleb, because he has a different spirit and has followed me wholeheartedly, I will bring

into the land into which he went, and his descendants shall possess it. ²⁵Now, since the Amalekites and the Canaanites live in the valleys, turn tomorrow and set out for the wilderness by the way to the Red Sea."*a*

An Attempted Invasion is Repulsed

26 And the LORD spoke to Moses and to Aaron, saying: ²⁷How long shall this wicked congregation complain against me? I have heard the complaints of the Israelites, which they complain against me. ²⁸Say to them, "As I live," says the LORD, "I will do to you the very things I heard you say: ²⁹your dead bodies shall fall in this very wilderness; and of all your number, included in the census, from twenty years old and upward, who have complained against me, ³⁰not one of you shall come into the land in which I swore to settle you, except Caleb son of Jephunneh and Joshua son of Nun. ³¹But your little ones, who you said would become booty, I will bring in, and they shall know the land that you have despised. ³²But as for you, your dead bodies shall fall in this wilderness. ³³And your children shall be shepherds in the wilderness for forty years, and shall suffer for your faithlessness, until the last of your dead bodies lies in the wilderness. ³⁴According to the number of the days in which you spied out the land, forty days, for every day a year, you shall bear your iniquity, forty years, and you shall know my displeasure." ³⁵I the LORD have spoken; surely I will do thus to all this wicked congregation gathered together

a Or *Sea of Reeds*

Responding

14:24 SERVICE. God calls Caleb his "servant" and describes him as having a "different spirit." What qualities of spirit do servants have? Write one of these qualities on a three-by-five card and post it in a place where you will see it several times a day. Each time you see it, ask God for the grace to receive that quality into your life. *See also* Spiritual Disciplines Index.

14:27 *I have heard the complaints of the Israelites.* God was deeply displeased with his

people when they constantly spoke against him. Their problem was their negative use of language. This kind of problem is rooted in the mind and heart. The hearts and minds of the Israelites were full of pride, rebellion, and ingratitude. Those who have immature souls tend to grumble, but a mature soul gives thanks to God constantly and learns how and when to be silent. One of the Spiritual Disciplines is learning to reform the bad habits of the tongue through a change in the habits of the mind and heart.

CALEB

Wholehearted Devotion

Selected Scriptures: *Numbers 13–14*

"None of the people who have seen my glory and the signs that I did in Egypt and in the wilderness, and yet have tested me . . . and have not obeyed my voice, shall see the land that I swore to give to their ancestors. . . . But my servant Caleb, because he has a different spirit and has followed me wholeheartedly, I will bring into the land into which he went, and his descendants shall possess it" (Num 14:22–24).

When the Israelites began to near Canaan, their supposed Promised Land, they sent out twelve spies to scope out the land and learn about the people, the crops, and the towns, as God commanded them. Reporting back, ten of the spies spoke fear: the land was lush with fruit, but the people were big and strong and the towns were well fortified. Only Caleb and Joshua remained confident. "We are well able to overcome it," Caleb assured the Hebrew people (13:30).

It is this faithful and trusting spirit that set Caleb apart from the rest of the Israelites and became his trademark. After all, God had afflicted the Egyptians and moved them to release thousands upon thousands of Israelite slaves. He had parted the sea. He had provided daily manna in the desert to feed the people and meat to give them variety. He had displayed his glory at Mt. Sinai. Now, how could they express doubt at God's ability to hand over the land he had promised? However, the other spies and the people clung to a spirit of fear. Their stubbornness and lack of trust led God to leave this generation of Isrealites behind. Only Caleb and Joshua, who pled with the Israelites to believe in God's provision, would forty years later make it into the Promised Land.

In *Mere Christianity* the contemporary writer C. S. Lewis examines what it means for a Christian to follow wholeheartedly:

"The Christian way is different: harder, and easier. Christ says, 'Give me All. I don't want so much of your time and so much of your money and so much of your work: I want You. I have not come to torment your natural self, but to kill it. No half-measures are any good. I don't want to cut off a branch here and a branch there, I want to have the whole tree down. Hand over the whole natural self, all the desires which you think innocent as well the ones you think wicked—the whole outfit. I will give you a new self instead. In fact, I will give you Myself: my own will shall become yours.'"

A spirit to follow wholeheartedly, a will united with God's—they are the crux of devotion. May we, like Caleb, bury our fears once and for all and step into a spirit of wholehearted devotion.

Personal Reflection

- When in your life have you approached a great risk with a spirit of confidence and joy, as Caleb did? Forgive
- Consider Lewis's analogy between the natural self and a tree. Has God taken down your whole tree, or have you offered only select branches for his pruning? What needs to happen if you are to hand over your whole self to be replaced with Christ?

PROFILE

against me: in this wilderness they shall come to a full end, and there they shall die.

36 And the men whom Moses sent to spy out the land, who returned and made all the congregation complain against him by bringing a bad report about the land— 37the men who brought an unfavorable report about the land died by a plague before the LORD. 38But Joshua son of Nun and Caleb son of Jephunneh alone remained alive, of those men who went to spy out the land.

39 When Moses told these words to all the Israelites, the people mourned greatly. 40They rose early in the morning and went up to the heights of the hill country, saying, "Here we are. We will go up to the place that the LORD has promised, for we have sinned." 41But Moses said, "Why do you continue to transgress the command of the LORD? That will not succeed. 42Do not go up, for the LORD is not with you; do not let yourselves be struck down before your enemies. 43For the Amalekites and the Canaanites will confront you there, and you shall fall by the sword; because you have turned back from following the LORD, the LORD will not be with you." 44But they presumed to go up to the heights of the hill country, even though the ark of the covenant of the LORD, and Moses, had not left the camp. 45Then the Amalekites and the Canaanites who lived in that hill country came down and defeated them, pursuing them as far as Hormah.

Various Offerings

15 The LORD spoke to Moses, saying: 2Speak to the Israelites and say to them: When you come into the land you are to inhabit, which I am giving you, 3and you make an offering by fire to the LORD from the herd or from the flock—whether a burnt offering or a sacrifice, to fulfill a vow or as a freewill offering or at your appointed festivals—to make a pleasing odor for the LORD, 4then whoever presents such an offering to the LORD shall present also a grain offering, one-tenth of an ephah of choice flour, mixed with one-fourth of a hin of oil. 5Moreover, you shall offer one-fourth of a hin of wine as a drink offering with the burnt offering or the sacrifice, for each lamb. 6For a ram, you shall

offer a grain offering, two-tenths of an ephah of choice flour mixed with one-third of a hin of oil; 7and as a drink offering you shall offer one-third of a hin of wine, a pleasing odor to the LORD. 8When you offer a bull as a burnt offering or a sacrifice, to fulfill a vow or as an offering of well-being to the LORD, 9then you shall present with the bull a grain offering, three-tenths of an ephah of choice flour, mixed with half a hin of oil, 10and you shall present as a drink offering half a hin of wine, as an offering by fire, a pleasing odor to the LORD.

11 Thus it shall be done for each ox or ram, or for each of the male lambs or the kids. 12According to the number that you offer, so you shall do with each and every one. 13Every native Israelite shall do these things in this way, in presenting an offering by fire, a pleasing odor to the LORD. 14An alien who lives with you, or who takes up permanent residence among you, and wishes to offer an offering by fire, a pleasing odor to the LORD, shall do as you do. 15As for the assembly, there shall be for both you and the resident alien a single statute, a perpetual statute throughout your generations; you and the alien shall be alike before the LORD. 16You and the alien who resides with you shall have the same law and the same ordinance.

17 The LORD spoke to Moses, saying: 18Speak to the Israelites and say to them: After you come into the land to which I am bringing you, 19whenever you eat of the bread of the land, you shall present a donation to the LORD. 20From your first batch of dough you shall present a loaf as a donation; you shall present it just as you present a donation from the threshing floor. 21Throughout your generations you shall give to the LORD a donation from the first of your batch of dough.

22 But if you unintentionally fail to observe all these commandments that the LORD has spoken to Moses— 23everything that the LORD has commanded you by Moses, from the day the LORD gave commandment and thereafter, throughout your generations— 24then if it was done unintentionally without the knowledge of the congregation, the whole congregation shall offer one young

bull for a burnt offering, a pleasing odor to the LORD, together with its grain offering and its drink offering, according to the ordinance, and one male goat for a sin offering. 25The priest shall make atonement for all the congregation of the Israelites, and they shall be forgiven; it was unintentional, and they have brought their offering, an offering by fire to the LORD, and their sin offering before the LORD, for their error. 26All the congregation of the Israelites shall be forgiven, as well as the aliens residing among them, because the whole people was involved in the error.

27 An individual who sins unintentionally shall present a female goat a year old for a sin offering. 28And the priest shall make atonement before the LORD for the one who commits an error, when it is unintentional, to make atonement for the person, who then shall be forgiven. 29For both the native among the Israelites and the alien residing among them—you shall have the same law for anyone who acts in error. 30But whoever acts high-handedly, whether a native or an alien, affronts the LORD, and shall be cut off from among the people. 31Because of having despised the word of the LORD and broken his commandment, such a person shall be utterly cut off and bear the guilt.

Penalty for Violating the Sabbath

32 When the Israelites were in the wilderness, they found a man gathering sticks on the sabbath day. 33Those who found him gathering sticks brought him to Moses, Aaron, and to the whole congregation. 34They put him in custody, because it was not clear what should be done to him. 35Then the LORD said to Moses, "The man shall be put to death; all the congregation shall stone him outside the camp." 36The whole congregation brought him outside the camp and stoned him to death, just as the LORD had commanded Moses.

Fringes on Garments

37 The LORD said to Moses: 38Speak to the Israelites, and tell them to make fringes on the corners of their garments throughout their generations and to put a blue cord on the fringe at each corner. 39You have the fringe so that, when you see it, you will remember all the commandments of the LORD and do them, and not follow the lust of your own heart and your own eyes. 40So you shall remember and do all my commandments, and you shall be holy to your God. 41I am the LORD your God, who brought you out of the land of Egypt, to be your God: I am the LORD your God.

Revolt of Korah, Dathan, and Abiram

16 Now Korah son of Izhar son of Kohath son of Levi, along with Dathan and Abiram sons of Eliab, and On son of Peleth—descendants of Reuben—took 2two hundred fifty Israelite men, leaders of the congregation, chosen from the assembly, well-known men, a and they confronted Moses. 3They assembled against Moses and against Aaron and said to them, "You have gone too far! All the congregation are holy, every one of them, and the LORD is among

a Cn: Heb and they confronted Moses, and two hundred fifty men . . . well-known men

---

15:38 to make fringes on the corners of their garments. God told the Israelites to add "fringes" to their garments, so they would remember and obey his laws whenever they saw the fringe. By remembering and following God's laws they would have the strength to avoid following their fleshly desires and greed. Because they were his set-apart children, God desired holiness in the Israelites. He wants the same in us. God exhorts us to meditate on his word constantly and to obey.

16:3 They assembled against Moses. Moses led the people on their journey out of Egypt into the land of Canaan. However, the people did not always value Moses' spiritual leadership and guidance. They often spoke against Moses, and they rebelled, time and again, against his authority. The role of a good spiritual leader or director in spiritual formation is critical. Every person on the journey of spiritual formation needs good guidance. Through judgment upon their behavior, God taught the Israelites the importance of spiritual guidance and authority.

them. So why then do you exalt yourselves above the assembly of the LORD?" 4When Moses heard it, he fell on his face. 5Then he said to Korah and all his company, "In the morning the LORD will make known who is his, and who is holy, and who will be allowed to approach him; the one whom he will choose he will allow to approach him. 6Do this: take censers, Korah and all your[a] company, 7and tomorrow put fire in them, and lay incense on them before the LORD; and the man whom the LORD chooses shall be the holy one. You Levites have gone too far!" 8Then Moses said to Korah, "Hear now, you Levites! 9Is it too little for you that the God of Israel has separated you from the congregation of Israel, to allow you to approach him in order to perform the duties of the LORD's tabernacle, and to stand before the congregation and serve them? 10He has allowed you to approach him, and all your brother Levites with you; yet you seek the priesthood as well! 11Therefore you and all your company have gathered together against the LORD. What is Aaron that you rail against him?"

12 Moses sent for Dathan and Abiram sons of Eliab; but they said, "We will not come! 13Is it too little that you have brought us up out of a land flowing with milk and honey to kill us in the wilderness, that you must also lord it over us? 14It is clear you have not brought us into a land flowing with milk and honey, or given us an inheritance of fields and vineyards. Would you put out the eyes of these men? We will not come!"

15 Moses was very angry and said to the LORD, "Pay no attention to their offering. I have not taken one donkey from them, and I have not harmed any one of them." 16And Moses said to Korah, "As for you and all your company, be present tomorrow before the LORD, you and they and Aaron; 17and let each one of you take his censer, and put incense on it, and each one of you present his censer before the LORD, two hundred fifty censers; you also, and Aaron, each his censer." 18So each man took his censer, and they put fire in the censers and laid incense on them, and they stood at the entrance of the tent of meeting with Moses and Aaron. 19Then Korah assembled the whole congregation against

them at the entrance of the tent of meeting. And the glory of the LORD appeared to the whole congregation.

20 Then the LORD spoke to Moses and to Aaron, saying: 21Separate yourselves from this congregation, so that I may consume them in a moment. 22They fell on their faces, and said, "O God, the God of the spirits of all flesh, shall one person sin and you become angry with the whole congregation?"

23 And the LORD spoke to Moses, saying: 24Say to the congregation: Get away from the dwellings of Korah, Dathan, and Abiram. 25So Moses got up and went to Dathan and Abiram; the elders of Israel followed him. 26He said to the congregation, "Turn away from the tents of these wicked men, and touch nothing of theirs, or you will be swept away for all their sins." 27So they got away from the dwellings of Korah, Dathan, and Abiram; and Dathan and Abiram came out and stood at the entrance of their tents, together with their wives, their children, and their little ones. 28And Moses said, "This is how you shall know that the LORD has sent me to do all these works; it has not been of my own accord: 29If these people die a natural death, or if a natural fate comes on them, then the LORD has not sent me. 30But if the LORD creates something new, and the ground opens its mouth and swallows them up, with all that belongs to them, and they go down alive into Sheol, then you shall know that these men have despised the LORD."

31 As soon as he finished speaking all these words, the ground under them was split apart. 32The earth opened its mouth and swallowed them up, along with their households—everyone who belonged to Korah and all their goods. 33So they with all that belonged to them went down alive into Sheol; the earth closed over them, and they perished from the midst of the assembly. 34All Israel around them fled at their outcry, for they said, "The earth will swallow us too!" 35And fire came out from the LORD and consumed the two hundred fifty men offering the incense.

36[b] Then the LORD spoke to Moses, say-

a Heb his   b Ch 17.1 in Heb

ing: [37]Tell Eleazar son of Aaron the priest to take the censers out of the blaze; then scatter the fire far and wide. [38]For the censers of these sinners have become holy at the cost of their lives. Make them into hammered plates as a covering for the altar, for they presented them before the LORD and they became holy. Thus they shall be a sign to the Israelites. [39]So Eleazar the priest took the bronze censers that had been presented by those who were burned; and they were hammered out as a covering for the altar— [40]a reminder to the Israelites that no outsider, who is not of the descendants of Aaron, shall approach to offer incense before the LORD, so as not to become like Korah and his company—just as the LORD had said to him through Moses.

41 On the next day, however, the whole congregation of the Israelites rebelled against Moses and against Aaron, saying, "You have killed the people of the LORD." [42]And when the congregation had assembled against them, Moses and Aaron turned toward the tent of meeting; the cloud had covered it and the glory of the LORD appeared. [43]Then Moses and Aaron came to the front of the tent of meeting, [44]and the LORD spoke to Moses, saying, [45]"Get away from this congregation, so that I may consume them in a moment." And they fell on their faces. [46]Moses said to Aaron, "Take your censer, put fire on it from the altar and lay incense on it, and carry it quickly to the congregation and make atonement for them. For wrath has gone out from the LORD; the plague has begun." [47]So Aaron took it as Moses had ordered, and ran into the middle of the assembly, where the plague had already begun among the people. He put on the incense, and made atonement for the people. [48]He stood between the dead and the living; and the plague was stopped. [49]Those who died by the plague were fourteen thousand seven hundred, besides those who died in the affair of Korah. [50]When the plague was stopped, Aaron returned to Moses at the entrance of the tent of meeting.

The Budding of Aaron's Rod

17[a] The LORD spoke to Moses, saying: [2]Speak to the Israelites, and get twelve staffs from them, one for each ancestral house, from all the leaders of their ancestral houses. Write each man's name on his staff, [3]and write Aaron's name on the staff of Levi. For there shall be one staff for the head of each ancestral house. [4]Place them in the tent of meeting before the covenant,[b] where I meet with you. [5]And the staff of the man whom I choose shall sprout; thus I will put a stop to the complaints of the Israelites that they continually make against you. [6]Moses spoke to the Israelites; and all their leaders gave him staffs, one for each leader, according to their ancestral houses, twelve staffs; and the staff of Aaron was among theirs. [7]So Moses placed the staffs before the LORD in the tent of the covenant.[b]

8 When Moses went into the tent of the covenant[b] on the next day, the staff of Aaron for the house of Levi had sprouted. It put forth buds, produced blossoms, and bore ripe almonds. [9]Then Moses brought out all the staffs from before the LORD to all the Israelites; and they looked, and each man took his staff. [10]And the LORD said to Moses, "Put back the staff of Aaron before the covenant,[b] to be kept as a warning to rebels, so that you may make an end of their complaints against me, or else they will die." [11]Moses did so; just as the LORD commanded him, so he did.

12 The Israelites said to Moses, "We are perishing; we are lost, all of us are lost! [13]Everyone who approaches the tabernacle of the LORD will die. Are we all to perish?"

Responsibility of Priests and Levites

18 The LORD said to Aaron: You and your sons and your ancestral house with you shall bear responsibility for offenses connected with the sanctuary, while you and your sons alone shall bear responsibility for offenses connected with the priesthood. [2]So bring with you also your brothers of the tribe

a Ch 17.16 in Heb   b Or treaty, or testimony; Heb eduth

RESPONSIVENESS TO RESPONSIBILITY IN THE DESERT WILDERNESS

of Levi, your ancestral tribe, in order that they may be joined to you, and serve you while you and your sons with you are in front of the tent of the covenant. *a* 3They shall perform duties for you and for the whole tent. But they must not approach either the utensils of the sanctuary or the altar, otherwise both they and you will die. 4They are attached to you in order to perform the duties of the tent of meeting, for all the service of the tent; no outsider shall approach you. 5You yourselves shall perform the duties of the sanctuary and the duties of the altar, so that wrath may never again come upon the Israelites. 6It is I who now take your brother Levites from among the Israelites; they are now yours as a gift, dedicated to the LORD, to perform the service of the tent of meeting. 7But you and your sons with you shall diligently perform your priestly duties in all that concerns the altar and the area behind the curtain. I give your priesthood as a gift; *b* any outsider who approaches shall be put to death.

The Priests' Portion

8 The LORD spoke to Aaron: I have given you charge of the offerings made to me, all the holy gifts of the Israelites; I have given them to you and your sons as a priestly portion due you in perpetuity. 9This shall be yours from the most holy things, reserved from the fire: every offering of theirs that they render to me as a most holy thing, whether grain offering, sin offering, or guilt offering, shall belong to you and your sons. 10As a most holy thing you shall eat it; every male may eat it; it shall be holy to you. 11This also is yours: I have given to you, together with your sons and daughters, as a perpetual due, whatever is set aside from the gifts of all the elevation offerings of the Israelites; everyone who is clean in your house may eat them. 12All the best of the oil and all the best of the wine and of the grain, the choice produce that they give to the LORD, I have given

to you. 13The first fruits of all that is in their land, which they bring to the LORD, shall be yours; everyone who is clean in your house may eat of it. 14Every devoted thing in Israel shall be yours. 15The first issue of the womb of all creatures, human and animal, which is offered to the LORD, shall be yours; but the firstborn of human beings you shall redeem, and the firstborn of unclean animals you shall redeem. 16Their redemption price, reckoned from one month of age, you shall fix at five shekels of silver, according to the shekel of the sanctuary (that is, twenty gerahs). 17But the firstborn of a cow, or the firstborn of a sheep, or the firstborn of a goat, you shall not redeem; they are holy. You shall dash their blood on the altar, and shall turn their fat into smoke as an offering by fire for a pleasing odor to the LORD; 18but their flesh shall be yours, just as the breast that is elevated and as the right thigh are yours. 19All the holy offerings that the Israelites present to the LORD I have given to you, together with your sons and daughters, as a perpetual due; it is a covenant of salt forever before the LORD for you and your descendants as well. 20Then the LORD said to Aaron: You shall have no allotment in their land, nor shall you have any share among them; I am your share and your possession among the Israelites.

21 To the Levites I have given every tithe in Israel for a possession in return for the service that they perform, the service in the tent of meeting. 22From now on the Israelites shall no longer approach the tent of meeting, or else they will incur guilt and die. 23But the Levites shall perform the service of the tent of meeting, and they shall bear responsibility for their own offenses; it shall be a perpetual statute throughout your generations. But among the Israelites they shall have no allotment, 24because I have given to the Levites as their portion the tithe of the Israelites, which

a Or *treaty,* or *testimony;* Heb *eduth*   *b* Heb *as a service of gift*

18:20 *I am your share and your possession.* God did not give a share of goods to the Levites, because *he* was to be their portion. The ultimate goal of God's people must be God himself. The

climax of the spiritual life is the realization that there is no greater joy than what comes from partaking of the fullness of God.

they set apart as an offering to the LORD. Therefore I have said of them that they shall have no allotment among the Israelites.

25 Then the LORD spoke to Moses, saying: 26You shall speak to the Levites, saying: When you receive from the Israelites the tithe that I have given you from them for your portion, you shall set apart an offering from it to the LORD, a tithe of the tithe. 27It shall be reckoned to you as your gift, the same as the grain of the threshing floor and the fullness of the wine press. 28Thus you also shall set apart an offering to the LORD from all the tithes that you receive from the Israelites; and from them you shall give the LORD's offering to the priest Aaron. 29Out of all the gifts to you, you shall set apart every offering due to the LORD; the best of all of them is the part to be consecrated. 30Say also to them: When you have set apart the best of it, then the rest shall be reckoned to the Levites as produce of the threshing floor, and as produce of the wine press. 31You may eat it in any place, you and your households; for it is your payment for your service in the tent of meeting. 32You shall incur no guilt by reason of it, when you have offered the best of it. But you shall not profane the holy gifts of the Israelites, on pain of death.

Ceremony of the Red Heifer

19 The LORD spoke to Moses and Aaron, saying: 2This is a statute of the law that the LORD has commanded: Tell the Israelites to bring you a red heifer without defect, in which there is no blemish and on which no yoke has been laid. 3You shall give it to the priest Eleazar, and it shall be taken outside the camp and slaughtered in his presence. 4The priest Eleazar shall take some of its blood with his finger and sprinkle it seven times towards the front of the tent of meeting. 5Then the heifer shall be burned in his sight;

its skin, its flesh, and its blood, with its dung, shall be burned. 6The priest shall take cedarwood, hyssop, and crimson material, and throw them into the fire in which the heifer is burning. 7Then the priest shall wash his clothes and bathe his body in water, and afterwards he may come into the camp; but the priest shall remain unclean until evening. 8The one who burns the heifer[a] shall wash his clothes in water and bathe his body in water; he shall remain unclean until evening. 9Then someone who is clean shall gather up the ashes of the heifer, and deposit them outside the camp in a clean place; and they shall be kept for the congregation of the Israelites for the water for cleansing. It is a purification offering. 10The one who gathers the ashes of the heifer shall wash his clothes and be unclean until evening.

This shall be a perpetual statute for the Israelites and for the alien residing among them. 11Those who touch the dead body of any human being shall be unclean seven days. 12They shall purify themselves with the water on the third day and on the seventh day, and so be clean; but if they do not purify themselves on the third day and on the seventh day, they will not become clean. 13All who touch a corpse, the body of a human being who has died, and do not purify themselves, defile the tabernacle of the LORD; such persons shall be cut off from Israel. Since water for cleansing was not dashed on them, they remain unclean; their uncleanness is still on them.

14 This is the law when someone dies in a tent: everyone who comes into the tent, and everyone who is in the tent, shall be unclean seven days. 15And every open vessel with no cover fastened on it is unclean. 16Whoever in the open field touches one who has been killed by a sword, or who has died naturally,[b]

a Heb it   b Heb lacks naturally

18:26 *you shall set apart an offering from it to the LORD.* God commanded all the people, even the Levites, to tithe and make offerings to him. How we use our resources is important for the spiritual life. Those committed to God must be able to give their best to him. In order to grow spiritually, we must treat our possessions in a manner that is honoring and pleasing to God. Jesus warns us in the parable of the sower (Matt 13:22) that the lure of wealth will cause unfruitfulness. Only those who overcome the temptation of riches can grow in their spiritual life.

or a human bone, or a grave, shall be unclean seven days. [17] For the unclean they shall take some ashes of the burnt purification offering, and running water shall be added in a vessel; [18] then a clean person shall take hyssop, dip it in the water, and sprinkle it on the tent, on all the furnishings, on the persons who were there, and on whoever touched the bone, the slain, the corpse, or the grave. [19] The clean person shall sprinkle the unclean ones on the third day and on the seventh day, thus purifying them on the seventh day. Then they shall wash their clothes and bathe themselves in water, and at evening they shall be clean. [20] Any who are unclean but do not purify themselves, those persons shall be cut off from the assembly, for they have defiled the sanctuary of the LORD. Since the water for cleansing has not been dashed on them, they are unclean.

21 It shall be a perpetual statute for them. The one who sprinkles the water for cleansing shall wash his clothes, and whoever touches the water for cleansing shall be unclean until evening. [22] Whatever the unclean person touches shall be unclean, and anyone who touches it shall be unclean until evening.

The Waters of Meribah

20 The Israelites, the whole congregation, came into the wilderness of Zin in the first month, and the people stayed in Kadesh. Miriam died there, and was buried there.

2 Now there was no water for the congregation; so they gathered together against Moses and against Aaron. [3] The people quarreled with Moses and said, "Would that we had died when our kindred died before the LORD! [4] Why have you brought the assembly of the LORD into this wilderness for us and our livestock to die here? [5] Why have you brought us up out of Egypt, to bring us to this wretched place? It is no place for grain, or figs, or vines, or pomegranates; and there is no water to drink." [6] Then Moses and Aaron went away from the assembly to the entrance of the tent of meeting; they fell on their faces, and the glory of the LORD appeared to them. [7] The LORD spoke to Moses, saying: [8] Take the staff, and assemble the congregation, you and your brother Aaron, and command the rock before their eyes to yield its water. Thus you shall bring water out of the rock for them; thus you shall provide drink for the congregation and their livestock.

9 So Moses took the staff from before the LORD, as he had commanded him. [10] Moses and Aaron gathered the assembly together before the rock, and he said to them, "Listen, you rebels, shall we bring water for you out of this rock?" [11] Then Moses lifted up his hand and struck the rock twice with his staff; water came out abundantly, and the congregation and their livestock drank. [12] But the LORD said to Moses and Aaron, "Because you did not trust in me, to show my holiness before the eyes of the Israelites, therefore you shall not bring this assembly into the land that I have given them." [13] These are the waters of Meribah, *a* where the people of Israel quarreled with the LORD, and by which he showed his holiness.

Passage through Edom Refused

14 Moses sent messengers from Kadesh to the king of Edom, "Thus says your brother Israel: You know all the adversity that has befallen us: [15] how our ancestors went down to

a That is *Quarrel*

20:12 *Because you did not trust in me, to show my holiness.* When God told Moses to command the rock to yield water, Moses instead struck the rock twice with his staff (vv 8, 11). For this disobedience Moses was not allowed to bring the people into the Promised Land. Moses' punishment might seem harsh to us, but in the economy of God, the crime was significant. Moses' failure to obey God to the letter meant he missed an opportunity to demonstrate God's power in a new way to the Israelites and to validate his own God-given leadership. What's more, this great leader who had been hand-picked by God showed that he didn't fully trust God. We must be diligent in obeying God in the details, no matter how well we are doing spiritually. This is as important at the beginning as it is at the end of our spiritual journey.

Egypt, and we lived in Egypt a long time; and the Egyptians oppressed us and our ancestors; 16and when we cried to the LORD, he heard our voice, and sent an angel and brought us out of Egypt; and here we are in Kadesh, a town on the edge of your territory. 17Now let us pass through your land. We will not pass through field or vineyard, or drink water from any well; we will go along the King's Highway, not turning aside to the right hand or to the left until we have passed through your territory."

18 But Edom said to him, "You shall not pass through, or we will come out with the sword against you." 19The Israelites said to him, "We will stay on the highway; and if we drink of your water, we and our livestock, then we will pay for it. It is only a small matter; just let us pass through on foot." 20But he said, "You shall not pass through." And Edom came out against them with a large force, heavily armed. 21Thus Edom refused to give Israel passage through their territory; so Israel turned away from them.

The Death of Aaron

22 They set out from Kadesh, and the Israelites, the whole congregation, came to Mount Hor. 23Then the LORD said to Moses and Aaron at Mount Hor, on the border of the land of Edom, 24"Let Aaron be gathered to his people. For he shall not enter the land that I have given to the Israelites, because you rebelled against my command at the waters of Meribah. 25Take Aaron and his son Eleazar, and bring them up Mount Hor; 26strip Aaron of his vestments, and put them on his son Eleazar. But Aaron shall be gathered to his people, a and shall die there." 27Moses did as the LORD had commanded; they went up Mount Hor in the sight of the whole congregation. 28Moses stripped Aaron of his vestments, and put them on his son Eleazar; and Aaron died

there on the top of the mountain. Moses and Eleazar came down from the mountain. 29When all the congregation saw that Aaron had died, all the house of Israel mourned for Aaron thirty days.

The Bronze Serpent

21 When the Canaanite, the king of Arad, who lived in the Negeb, heard that Israel was coming by the way of Atharim, he fought against Israel and took some of them captive. 2Then Israel made a vow to the LORD and said, "If you will indeed give this people into our hands, then we will utterly destroy their towns." 3The LORD listened to the voice of Israel, and handed over the Canaanites; and they utterly destroyed them and their towns; so the place was called Hormah. b

4 From Mount Hor they set out by the way to the Red Sea, c to go around the land of Edom; but the people became impatient on the way. 5The people spoke against God and against Moses, "Why have you brought us up out of Egypt to die in the wilderness? For there is no food and no water, and we detest this miserable food." 6Then the LORD sent poisonous d serpents among the people, and they bit the people, so that many Israelites died. 7The people came to Moses and said, "We have sinned by speaking against the LORD and against you; pray to the LORD to take away the serpents from us." So Moses prayed for the people. 8And the LORD said to Moses, "Make a poisonous e serpent, and set it on a pole; and everyone who is bitten shall look at it and live." 9So Moses made a serpent of bronze, and put it upon a pole; and whenever a ser-

a Heb lacks to his people   b Heb Destruction
c Or Sea of Reeds   d Or fiery; Heb seraphim
e Or fiery; Heb seraph

21:6–9 that person would look at the serpent of bronze and live. When God sent fiery serpents among the people, Moses pleaded to God to save those who were mortally bitten. God instructed him to make a bronze serpent and set it upon a pole, so the people could look upon it and be healed. It was an odd prescription. If the people stared at the lifeless bronze image of the

same creature that had almost killed them, they would be set free from the effects of the poison. God sent the serpents to bring death to the rebellious Israelites and then put a symbolic serpent on a pole to heal them. When the bronze serpent was lifted up and the people gazed upon it, they received healing, life. The serpent of bronze foreshadowed the cross of

pent bit someone, that person would look at the serpent of bronze and live.

The Journey to Moab

10 The Israelites set out, and camped in Oboth. [11]They set out from Oboth, and camped at Iye-abarim, in the wilderness bordering Moab toward the sunrise. [12]From there they set out, and camped in the Wadi Zered. [13]From there they set out, and camped on the other side of the Arnon, in[a] the wilderness that extends from the boundary of the Amorites; for the Arnon is the boundary of Moab, between Moab and the Amorites. [14]Wherefore it is said in the Book of the Wars of the LORD,

> "Waheb in Suphah and the wadis.
> The Arnon [15]and the slopes of the wadis
> that extend to the seat of Ar,
> and lie along the border of Moab."[b]

16 From there they continued to Beer;[c] that is the well of which the LORD said to Moses, "Gather the people together, and I will give them water." [17]Then Israel sang this song:

> "Spring up, O well!—Sing to it!—
> [18] the well that the leaders sank,
> that the nobles of the people dug,
> with the scepter, with the staff."

From the wilderness to Mattanah, [19]from Mattanah to Nahaliel, from Nahaliel to Bamoth, [20]and from Bamoth to the valley lying in the region of Moab by the top of Pisgah that overlooks the wasteland.[d]

King Sihon Defeated

21 Then Israel sent messengers to King Sihon of the Amorites, saying, [22]"Let me pass through your land; we will not turn aside into field or vineyard; we will not drink the water of any well; we will go by the King's Highway until we have passed through your territory." [23]But Sihon would not allow Israel to pass through his territory. Sihon gathered all his people together, and went out against Israel to the wilderness; he came to Jahaz, and fought against Israel. [24]Israel put him to the sword, and took possession of his land from the Arnon to the Jabbok, as far as to the Ammonites; for the boundary of the Ammonites was strong. [25]Israel took all these towns, and Israel settled in all the towns of the Amorites, in Heshbon, and in all its villages. [26]For Heshbon was the city of King Sihon of the Amorites, who had fought against the former king of Moab and captured all his land as far as the Arnon. [27]Therefore the ballad singers say,

> "Come to Heshbon, let it be built;
> let the city of Sihon be established.
> [28] For fire came out from Heshbon,
> flame from the city of Sihon.
> It devoured Ar of Moab,
> and swallowed up[e] the heights of the Arnon.
> [29] Woe to you, O Moab!
> You are undone, O people of Chemosh!
> He has made his sons fugitives,
> and his daughters captives,
> to an Amorite king, Sihon.
> [30] So their posterity perished
> from Heshbon[f] to Dibon,
> and we laid waste until fire spread to Medeba."[g]

31 Thus Israel settled in the land of the Amorites. [32]Moses sent to spy out Jazer; and they captured its villages, and dispossessed the Amorites who were there.

a Gk: Heb *which is in*   b Meaning of Heb uncertain   c That is *Well*   d Or *Jeshimon*   e Gk: Heb *and the lords of*   f Gk: Heb *we have shot at them; Heshbon has perished*   g Compare Sam Gk: Meaning of MT uncertain

---

Jesus Christ. Jesus himself said, "Just as Moses lifted up the serpent in the wilderness, so must the Son of Man be lifted up" (John 3:14). God sent Jesus to bring us life that would never end. When Jesus was lifted upon the cross and the people gazed upon the sight, they were distressed. It seemed Satan had won the victory. But then God raised Christ from the dead, conquering death once and for all. The cross upon which we gaze is empty—for Christ has risen. But just as staring upon the serpent on the pole healed the Israelites, gazing at the empty cross and believing Jesus died for our sins brings us eternal life. The spiritual life is based on our remembrance and belief that Christ died for our salvation.

King Og Defeated

33 Then they turned and went up the road to Bashan; and King Og of Bashan came out against them, he and all his people, to battle at Edrei. 34But the LORD said to Moses, "Do not be afraid of him; for I have given him into your hand, with all his people, and all his land. You shall do to him as you did to King Sihon of the Amorites, who ruled in Heshbon." 35So they killed him, his sons, and all his people, until there was no survivor left; and they took possession of his land.

Balak Summons Balaam to Curse Israel

22 The Israelites set out, and camped in the plains of Moab across the Jordan from Jericho. 2Now Balak son of Zippor saw all that Israel had done to the Amorites. 3Moab was in great dread of the people, because they were so numerous; Moab was overcome with fear of the people of Israel. 4And Moab said to the elders of Midian, "This horde will now lick up all that is around us, as an ox licks up the grass of the field." Now Balak son of Zippor was king of Moab at that time. 5He sent messengers to Balaam son of Beor at Pethor, which is on the Euphrates, in the land of Amaw, *a* to summon him, saying, "A people has come out of Egypt; they have spread over the face of the earth, and they have settled next to me. 6Come now, curse this people for me, since they are stronger than I; perhaps I shall be able to defeat them and drive them from the land; for I know that whomever you bless is blessed, and whomever you curse is cursed."

7 So the elders of Moab and the elders of Midian departed with the fees for divination in their hand; and they came to Balaam, and gave him Balak's message. 8He said to them, "Stay here tonight, and I will bring back word to you, just as the LORD speaks to me"; so the officials of Moab stayed with Balaam. 9God came to Balaam and said, "Who are these

men with you?" 10Balaam said to God, "King Balak son of Zippor of Moab, has sent me this message: 11'A people has come out of Egypt and has spread over the face of the earth; now come, curse them for me; perhaps I shall be able to fight against them and drive them out.' " 12God said to Balaam, "You shall not go with them; you shall not curse the people, for they are blessed." 13So Balaam rose in the morning, and said to the officials of Balak, "Go to your own land, for the LORD has refused to let me go with you." 14So the officials of Moab rose and went to Balak, and said, "Balaam refuses to come with us."

15 Once again Balak sent officials, more numerous and more distinguished than these. 16They came to Balaam and said to him, "Thus says Balak son of Zippor: 'Do not let anything hinder you from coming to me; 17for I will surely do you great honor, and whatever you say to me I will do; come, curse this people for me.' " 18But Balaam replied to the servants of Balak, "Although Balak were to give me his house full of silver and gold, I could not go beyond the command of the LORD my God, to do less or more. 19You remain here, as the others did, so that I may learn what more the LORD may say to me." 20That night God came to Balaam and said to him, "If the men have come to summon you, get up and go with them; but do only what I tell you to do." 21So Balaam got up in the morning, saddled his donkey, and went with the officials of Moab.

Balaam, the Donkey, and the Angel

22 God's anger was kindled because he was going, and the angel of the LORD took his stand in the road as his adversary. Now he was riding on the donkey, and his two servants were with him. 23The donkey saw the angel of the LORD standing in the road, with a drawn sword in his hand; so the donkey

a Or land of his kinsfolk

Responding
22:18–35 GUIDANCE. We most generally remember Balaam because his donkey talked to him, not because he was a non-Israelite who received guidance from God. Have you ever known anyone who did not profess to be a Christian yet seemed to receive guidance that could have come only from God? What does this reveal about God? *See also* Spiritual Disciplines Index.

turned off the road, and went into the field; and Balaam struck the donkey, to turn it back onto the road. 24Then the angel of the LORD stood in a narrow path between the vineyards, with a wall on either side. 25When the donkey saw the angel of the LORD, it scraped against the wall, and scraped Balaam's foot against the wall; so he struck it again. 26Then the angel of the LORD went ahead, and stood in a narrow place, where there was no way to turn either to the right or to the left. 27When the donkey saw the angel of the LORD, it lay down under Balaam; and Balaam's anger was kindled, and he struck the donkey with his staff. 28Then the LORD opened the mouth of the donkey, and it said to Balaam, "What have I done to you, that you have struck me these three times?" 29Balaam said to the donkey, "Because you have made a fool of me! I wish I had a sword in my hand! I would kill you right now!" 30But the donkey said to Balaam, "Am I not your donkey, which you have ridden all your life to this day? Have I been in the habit of treating you this way?" And he said, "No."

31 Then the LORD opened the eyes of Balaam, and he saw the angel of the LORD standing in the road, with his drawn sword in his hand; and he bowed down, falling on his face. 32The angel of the LORD said to him, "Why have you struck your donkey these three times? I have come out as an adversary, because your way is perverse*a* before me. 33The donkey saw me, and turned away from me these three times. If it had not turned away from me, surely just now I would have killed you and let it live." 34Then Balaam said to the angel of the LORD, "I have sinned, for I did not know that you were standing in the road to oppose me. Now therefore, if it is displeasing to you, I will return home." 35The angel of the LORD said to Balaam, "Go with the men; but speak only what I tell you to

speak." So Balaam went on with the officials of Balak.

36 When Balak heard that Balaam had come, he went out to meet him at Ir-moab, on the boundary formed by the Arnon, at the farthest point of the boundary. 37Balak said to Balaam, "Did I not send to summon you? Why did you not come to me? Am I not able to honor you?" 38Balaam said to Balak, "I have come to you now, but do I have power to say just anything? The word God puts in my mouth, that is what I must say." 39Then Balaam went with Balak, and they came to Kiriath-huzoth. 40Balak sacrificed oxen and sheep, and sent them to Balaam and to the officials who were with him.

Balaam's First Oracle

41 On the next day Balak took Balaam and brought him up to Bamoth-baal; and from there he could see part of the people of Israel.*b*

23 1Then Balaam said to Balak, "Build me seven altars here, and prepare seven bulls and seven rams for me." 2Balak did as Balaam had said; and Balak and Balaam offered a bull and a ram on each altar. 3Then Balaam said to Balak, "Stay here beside your burnt offerings while I go aside. Perhaps the LORD will come to meet me. Whatever he shows me I will tell you." And he went to a bare height.

4 Then God met Balaam; and Balaam said to him, "I have arranged the seven altars, and have offered a bull and a ram on each altar." 5The LORD put a word in Balaam's mouth, and said, "Return to Balak, and this is what you must say." 6So he returned to Balak,*c* who was standing beside his burnt offerings with all the officials of Moab. 7Then Balaam*d* uttered his oracle, saying:

a Meaning of Heb uncertain   b Heb lacks of Israel   c Heb him   d Heb he

---

22:28 *Then the LORD opened the mouth of the donkey.* God can speak even through the mouths of animals. God used the donkey to get Balaam's attention. And Peter repented after he heard the rooster's crow (Matt 26:34). Sometimes we fail to hear the voice of God not because he is silent, but because we are not listening. In the spiritual

life, we learn to be attentive to the Lord's voice whenever and however he may speak. Here not only speaks through a donkey, but to a prophet of the Moabites. We cannot predict how or through whom God will speak. We will hear his voice when we have ears to hear. Developing listening ears is essential to spiritual growth.

"Balak has brought me from Aram,
  the king of Moab from the eastern
  mountains:
'Come, curse Jacob for me;
  Come, denounce Israel!'
8 How can I curse whom God has not
  cursed?
  How can I denounce those whom the
  LORD has not denounced?
9 For from the top of the crags I see him,
  from the hills I behold him.
  Here is a people living alone,
  and not reckoning itself among the
  nations!
10 Who can count the dust of Jacob,
  or number the dust-cloud*a* of Israel?
  Let me die the death of the upright,
  and let my end be like his!"

11 Then Balak said to Balaam, "What have you done to me? I brought you to curse my enemies, but now you have done nothing but bless them." 12He answered, "Must I not take care to say what the LORD puts into my mouth?"

Balaam's Second Oracle

13 So Balak said to him, "Come with me to another place from which you may see them; you shall see only part of them, and shall not see them all; then curse them for me from there." 14So he took him to the field of Zophim, to the top of Pisgah. He built seven altars, and offered a bull and a ram on each altar. 15Balaam said to Balak, "Stand here beside your burnt offerings, while I meet the LORD over there." 16The LORD met Balaam, put a word into his mouth, and said, "Return to Balak, and this is what you shall say." 17When he came to him, he was standing beside his burnt offerings with the officials of Moab. Balak said to him, "What has the LORD said?" 18Then Balaam uttered his oracle, saying:

"Rise, Balak, and hear;
  listen to me, O son of Zippor:

19 God is not a human being, that he
  should lie,
  or a mortal, that he should change
  his mind.
  Has he promised, and will he not do it?
  Has he spoken, and will he not fulfill it?
20 See, I received a command to bless;
  he has blessed, and I cannot revoke it.
21 He has not beheld misfortune in Jacob;
  nor has he seen trouble in Israel.
  The LORD their God is with them,
  acclaimed as a king among them.
22 God, who brings them out of Egypt,
  is like the horns of a wild ox for them.
23 Surely there is no enchantment against
  Jacob,
  no divination against Israel;
  now it shall be said of Jacob and Israel,
  'See what God has done!'
24 Look, a people rising up like a lioness,
  and rousing itself like a lion!
  It does not lie down until it has eaten
  the prey
  and drunk the blood of the slain."

25 Then Balak said to Balaam, "Do not curse them at all, and do not bless them at all." 26But Balaam answered Balak, "Did I not tell you, 'Whatever the LORD says, that is what I must do'?"

27 So Balak said to Balaam, "Come now, I will take you to another place; perhaps it will please God that you may curse them for me from there." 28So Balak took Balaam to the top of Peor, which overlooks the wasteland.*b* 29Balaam said to Balak, "Build me seven altars here, and prepare seven bulls and seven rams for me." 30So Balak did as Balaam had said, and offered a bull and a ram on each altar.

Balaam's Third Oracle

24 Now Balaam saw that it pleased the LORD to bless Israel, so he did not go, as at other times, to look for omens, but set

a Or *fourth part*   *b* Or *overlooks Jeshimon*

23:9 SOLITUDE—*See* Spiritual Disciplines Index.

23:19 *God is not a human being, that he should lie.* The goal of the spiritual life is to take on, or bear, the image of God. God never lies.

God acts upon what he says, and God keeps his promises. To resemble God means to resemble his character, including his faithfulness. We grow in godliness when we learn to be faithful to God in word and deed.

his face toward the wilderness. ²Balaam looked up and saw Israel camping tribe by tribe. Then the spirit of God came upon him, ³and he uttered his oracle, saying:

"The oracle of Balaam son of Beor,
    the oracle of the man whose eye is
        clear, *a*
⁴ the oracle of one who hears the words
    of God,
    who sees the vision of the Almighty, *b*
    who falls down, but with eyes
        uncovered:
⁵ how fair are your tents, O Jacob,
    your encampments, O Israel!
⁶ Like palm groves that stretch far away,
    like gardens beside a river,
like aloes that the LORD has planted,
    like cedar trees beside the waters.
⁷ Water shall flow from his buckets,
    and his seed shall have abundant
        water,
his king shall be higher than Agag,
    and his kingdom shall be exalted.
⁸ God who brings him out of Egypt,
    is like the horns of a wild ox for him;
he shall devour the nations that are his
        foes
    and break their bones.
    He shall strike with his arrows. *c*
⁹ He crouched, he lay down like a lion,
    and like a lioness; who will rouse him
        up?
    Blessed is everyone who blesses you,
    and cursed is everyone who curses
        you."

10 Then Balak's anger was kindled against Balaam, and he struck his hands together. Balak said to Balaam, "I summoned you to curse my enemies, but instead you have blessed them these three times. ¹¹Now be off with you! Go home! I said, 'I will reward you richly,' but the LORD has denied you any reward." ¹²And Balaam said to Balak, "Did I not tell your messengers whom you sent to me, ¹³'If Balak should give me his house full of silver and gold, I would not be able to go beyond the word of the LORD, to do either good or bad of my own will; what the LORD says, that is what I will say'? ¹⁴So now, I am going to my people; let me advise you what this people will do to your people in days to come."

Balaam's Fourth Oracle

15 So he uttered his oracle, saying:
"The oracle of Balaam son of Beor,
    the oracle of the man whose eye is
        clear, *a*
¹⁶ the oracle of one who hears the words
    of God,
    and knows the knowledge of the Most
        High, *d*
who sees the vision of the Almighty, *b*
    who falls down, but with his eyes
        uncovered:
¹⁷ I see him, but not now;
    I behold him, but not near—
a star shall come out of Jacob,
    and a scepter shall rise out of Israel;
it shall crush the borderlands *e* of Moab,
    and the territory *f* of all the Shethites.
¹⁸ Edom will become a possession,
    Seir a possession of its enemies, *g*
    while Israel does valiantly.
¹⁹ One out of Jacob shall rule,
    and destroy the survivors of Ir."

20 Then he looked on Amalek, and uttered his oracle, saying:
"First among the nations was Amalek,
    but its end is to perish forever."
21 Then he looked on the Kenite, and uttered his oracle, saying:
"Enduring is your dwelling place,
    and your nest is set in the rock;
²² yet Kain is destined for burning.
    How long shall Asshur take you away
        captive?"
23 Again he uttered his oracle, saying:

a Or *closed* or *open*   *b* Traditional rendering of Heb *Shaddai*   *c* Meaning of Heb uncertain *d* Or *of Elyon*   *e* Or *forehead*   *f* Some Mss read *skull*   *g* Heb *Seir, its enemies, a possession*

24:13 *I would not be able to go beyond the word of the LORD.* Balaam did not go beyond God's words. Even knowing he would incur Balak's wrath, he was obedient and spoke exactly as he was told. Such obedience requires keeping the *debar Yahweh,* the word of God, in our hearts and following it.

"Alas, who shall live when God does this?
24   But ships shall come from Kittim
       and shall afflict Asshur and Eber;
       and he also shall perish forever."

25 Then Balaam got up and went back to his place, and Balak also went his way.

Worship of Baal of Peor

25 While Israel was staying at Shittim, the people began to have sexual relations with the women of Moab. ²These invited the people to the sacrifices of their gods, and the people ate and bowed down to their gods. ³Thus Israel yoked itself to the Baal of Peor, and the LORD's anger was kindled against Israel. ⁴The LORD said to Moses, "Take all the chiefs of the people, and impale them in the sun before the LORD, in order that the fierce anger of the LORD may turn away from Israel." ⁵And Moses said to the judges of Israel, "Each of you shall kill any of your people who have yoked themselves to the Baal of Peor."

6 Just then one of the Israelites came and brought a Midianite woman into his family, in the sight of Moses and in the sight of the whole congregation of the Israelites, while they were weeping at the entrance of the tent of meeting. ⁷When Phinehas son of Eleazar, son of Aaron the priest, saw it, he got up and left the congregation. Taking a spear in his hand, ⁸he went after the Israelite man into the tent, and pierced the two of them, the Israelite and the woman, through the belly. So the plague was stopped among the people of Israel. ⁹Nevertheless those that died by the plague were twenty-four thousand.

10 The LORD spoke to Moses, saying: ¹¹"Phinehas son of Eleazar, son of Aaron the priest, has turned back my wrath from the Israelites by manifesting such zeal among them on my behalf that in my jealousy I did not consume the Israelites. ¹²Therefore say, 'I hereby grant him my covenant of peace. ¹³It shall be for him and for his descendants after him a covenant of perpetual priesthood, because he was zealous for his God, and made atonement for the Israelites.' "

14 The name of the slain Israelite man, who was killed with the Midianite woman, was Zimri son of Salu, head of an ancestral house belonging to the Simeonites. ¹⁵The name of the Midianite woman who was killed was Cozbi daughter of Zur, who was the head of a clan, an ancestral house in Midian.

16 The LORD said to Moses, ¹⁷"Harass the Midianites, and defeat them; ¹⁸for they have harassed you by the trickery with which they deceived you in the affair of Peor, and in the affair of Cozbi, the daughter of a leader of Midian, their sister; she was killed on the day of the plague that resulted from Peor."

A Census of the New Generation

26 After the plague the LORD said to Moses and to Eleazar son of Aaron the priest, ²"Take a census of the whole congregation of the Israelites, from twenty years old and upward, by their ancestral houses, everyone in Israel able to go to war." ³Moses and Eleazar the priest spoke with them in the plains of Moab by the Jordan opposite Jericho, saying, ⁴"Take a census of the

---

25:1–3 *the people began to have sexual relations with the women of Moab.* God wants his people to be pure and holy in all aspects of life, including the arena of sexual morality. God's anger was kindled against the Israelites when they engaged in the fertility rites of Baal with the Moabites. Sexual immorality and the worship of other gods (idolatry) go hand in hand. Nor is this an accident. Human sexuality was given by God as the highest form of intimacy between a man and a woman. The human sexual act is a spiritual act. Hence, sexual immorality has not only physical ramifications, but spiritual ones as well. With regard to our sexual thoughts and

behavior, we must be alert at all times so that we may be pure before the Lord. Beware of these vices: the worship of other gods and sexual immorality, for our "body is a temple of the Holy Spirit" (1 Cor 6:19).

26:2 *everyone in Israel able to go to war.* When Moses counted the people, God instructed him to identify the able-bodied men fit for the battlefield. The Israelites had not needed an army when they were slaves to the Egyptians. Now they needed to prepare for the conquest of Canaan. God was preparing his people to be strong soldiers. The military is an excellent place to learn discipline; likewise, the discipline gained

people,[a] from twenty years old and upward," as the LORD commanded Moses.

The Israelites, who came out of the land of Egypt, were:

5 Reuben, the firstborn of Israel. The descendants of Reuben: of Hanoch, the clan of the Hanochites; of Pallu, the clan of the Palluites; [6]of Hezron, the clan of the Hezronites; of Carmi, the clan of the Carmites. [7]These are the clans of the Reubenites; the number of those enrolled was forty-three thousand seven hundred thirty. [8]And the descendants of Pallu: Eliab. [9]The descendants of Eliab: Nemuel, Dathan, and Abiram. These are the same Dathan and Abiram, chosen from the congregation, who rebelled against Moses and Aaron in the company of Korah, when they rebelled against the LORD, [10]and the earth opened its mouth and swallowed them up along with Korah, when that company died, when the fire devoured two hundred fifty men; and they became a warning. [11]Notwithstanding, the sons of Korah did not die.

12 The descendants of Simeon by their clans: of Nemuel, the clan of the Nemuelites; of Jamin, the clan of the Jaminites; of Jachin, the clan of the Jachinites; [13]of Zerah, the clan of the Zerahites; of Shaul, the clan of the Shaulites.[b] [14]These are the clans of the Simeonites, twenty-two thousand two hundred.

15 The children of Gad by their clans: of Zephon, the clan of the Zephonites; of Haggi, the clan of the Haggites; of Shuni, the clan of the Shunites; [16]of Ozni, the clan of the Oznites; of Eri, the clan of the Erites; [17]of Arod, the clan of the Arodites; of Areli, the clan of the Arelites. [18]These are the clans of the Gadites: the number of those enrolled was forty thousand five hundred.

19 The sons of Judah: Er and Onan; Er and Onan died in the land of Canaan. [20]The descendants of Judah by their clans were: of Shelah, the clan of the Shelanites; of Perez, the clan of the Perezites; of Zerah, the clan of the Zerahites. [21]The descendants of Perez were:

of Hezron, the clan of the Hezronites; of Hamul, the clan of the Hamulites. [22]These are the clans of Judah: the number of those enrolled was seventy-six thousand five hundred.

23 The descendants of Issachar by their clans: of Tola, the clan of the Tolaites; of Puvah, the clan of the Punites; [24]of Jashub, the clan of the Jashubites; of Shimron, the clan of the Shimronites. [25]These are the clans of Issachar: sixty-four thousand three hundred enrolled.

26 The descendants of Zebulun by their clans: of Sered, the clan of the Seredites; of Elon, the clan of the Elonites; of Jahleel, the clan of the Jahleelites. [27]These are the clans of the Zebulunites; the number of those enrolled was sixty thousand five hundred.

28 The sons of Joseph by their clans: Manasseh and Ephraim. [29]The descendants of Manasseh: of Machir, the clan of the Machirites; and Machir was the father of Gilead; of Gilead, the clan of the Gileadites. [30]These are the descendants of Gilead: of Iezer, the clan of the Iezerites; of Helek, the clan of the Helekites; [31]and of Asriel, the clan of the Asrielites; and of Shechem, the clan of the Shechemites; [32]and of Shemida, the clan of the Shemidaites; and of Hepher, the clan of the Hepherites. [33]Now Zelophehad son of Hepher had no sons, but daughters: and the names of the daughters of Zelophehad were Mahlah, Noah, Hoglah, Milcah, and Tirzah. [34]These are the clans of Manasseh; the number of those enrolled was fifty-two thousand seven hundred.

35 These are the descendants of Ephraim according to their clans: of Shuthelah, the clan of the Shuthelahites; of Becher, the clan of the Becherites; of Tahan, the clan of the Tahanites. [36]And these are the descendants of Shuthelah: of Eran, the clan of the Eranites. [37]These are the clans of the Ephraimites: the number of those enrolled was thirty-two thousand five hundred. These are the descendants of Joseph by their clans.

a Heb lacks take a census of the people: Compare verse 2   b Or Saul . . . Saulites

---

in pursuit of the spiritual life is essential for training spiritual warriors. We must grow, mature, and be armed for spiritual warfare. As Ephesians

admonishes, we must "put on the whole armor of God" and take the "sword of the Spirit" to stand against the "wiles of the devil" (6:11, 17).

38 The descendants of Benjamin by their clans: of Bela, the clan of the Belaites; of Ashbel, the clan of the Ashbelites; of Ahiram, the clan of the Ahiramites; 39of Shephupham, the clan of the Shuphamites; of Hupham, the clan of the Huphamites. 40And the sons of Bela were Ard and Naaman: of Ard, the clan of the Ardites; of Naaman, the clan of the Naamites. 41These are the descendants of Benjamin by their clans; the number of those enrolled was forty-five thousand six hundred.

42 These are the descendants of Dan by their clans: of Shuham, the clan of the Shuhamites. These are the clans of Dan by their clans. 43All the clans of the Shuhamites: sixty-four thousand four hundred enrolled.

44 The descendants of Asher by their families: of Imnah, the clan of the Imnites; of Ishvi, the clan of the Ishvites; of Beriah, the clan of the Beriites. 45Of the descendants of Beriah: of Heber, the clan of the Heberites; of Malchiel, the clan of the Malchielites. 46And the name of the daughter of Asher was Serah. 47These are the clans of the Asherites: the number of those enrolled was fifty-three thousand four hundred.

48 The descendants of Naphtali by their clans: of Jahzeel, the clan of the Jahzeelites; of Guni, the clan of the Gunites; 49of Jezer, the clan of the Jezerites; of Shillem, the clan of the Shillemites. 50These are the Naphtalites a by their clans: the number of those enrolled was forty-five thousand four hundred.

51 This was the number of the Israelites enrolled: six hundred and one thousand seven hundred thirty.

52 The LORD spoke to Moses, saying: 53To these the land shall be apportioned for inheritance according to the number of names. 54To a large tribe you shall give a large inheritance, and to a small tribe you shall give a small inheritance; every tribe shall be given its inheritance according to its enrollment. 55But the land shall be apportioned by lot; according to the names of their ancestral tribes they shall inherit. 56Their inheritance shall be apportioned according to lot between the larger and the smaller.

57 This is the enrollment of the Levites by their clans: of Gershon, the clan of the Gershonites; of Kohath, the clan of the Kohathites; of Merari, the clan of the Merarites. 58These are the clans of Levi: the clan of the Libnites, the clan of the Hebronites, the clan of the Mahlites, the clan of the Mushites, the clan of the Korahites. Now Kohath was the father of Amram. 59The name of Amram's wife was Jochebed daughter of Levi, who was born to Levi in Egypt; and she bore to Amram: Aaron, Moses, and their sister Miriam. 60To Aaron were born Nadab, Abihu, Eleazar, and Ithamar. 61But Nadab and Abihu died when they offered unholy fire before the LORD. 62The number of those enrolled was twenty-three thousand, every male one month old and upward; for they were not enrolled among the Israelites because there was no allotment given to them among the Israelites.

63 These were those enrolled by Moses and Eleazar the priest, who enrolled the Israelites in the plains of Moab by the Jordan opposite Jericho. 64Among these there was not one of those enrolled by Moses and Aaron the priest, who had enrolled the Israelites in the wilderness of Sinai. 65For the LORD had said of them, "They shall die in the wilderness." Not one of them was left, except Caleb son of Jephunneh and Joshua son of Nun.

The Daughters of Zelophehad

27 Then the daughters of Zelophehad came forward. Zelophehad was son of Hepher son of Gilead son of Machir son of Manasseh son of Joseph, a member of the Manassite clans. The names of his daughters were: Mahlah, Noah, Hoglah, Milcah, and Tirzah. 2They stood before Moses, Eleazar the priest, the leaders, and all the congregation, at the entrance of the tent of meeting, and they said, 3"Our father died in the wilderness; he was not among the company of those who gathered themselves together against the LORD in the company of Korah, but died for his own sin; and he had no sons. 4Why should the name of our father be taken away from his clan because he had no son? Give to us a possession among our father's brothers."

a Heb *clans of Naphtali*

5 Moses brought their case before the LORD, 6And the LORD spoke to Moses, saying: 7The daughters of Zelophehad are right in what they are saying; you shall indeed let them possess an inheritance among their father's brothers and pass the inheritance of their father on to them. 8You shall also say to the Israelites, "If a man dies, and has no son, then you shall pass his inheritance on to his daughter. 9If he has no daughter, then you shall give his inheritance to his brothers. 10If he has no brothers, then you shall give his inheritance to his father's brothers. 11And if his father has no brothers, then you shall give his inheritance to the nearest kinsman of his clan, and he shall possess it. It shall be for the Israelites a statute and ordinance, as the LORD commanded Moses."

Joshua Appointed Moses' Successor

12 The LORD said to Moses, "Go up this mountain of the Abarim range, and see the land that I have given to the Israelites. 13When you have seen it, you also shall be gathered to your people, as your brother Aaron was, 14because you rebelled against my word in the wilderness of Zin when the congregation quarreled with me.ᵃ You did not show my holiness before their eyes at the waters." (These are the waters of Meribath-kadesh in the wilderness of Zin.) 15Moses spoke to the LORD, saying, 16"Let the LORD, the God of the spirits of all flesh, appoint someone over the congregation 17who shall go out be-

fore them and come in before them, who shall lead them out and bring them in, so that the congregation of the LORD may not be like sheep without a shepherd." 18So the LORD said to Moses, "Take Joshua son of Nun, a man in whom is the spirit, and lay your hand upon him; 19have him stand before Eleazar the priest and all the congregation, and commission him in their sight. 20You shall give him some of your authority, so that all the congregation of the Israelites may obey. 21But he shall stand before Eleazar the priest, who shall inquire for him by the decision of the Urim before the LORD; at his word they shall go out, and at his word they shall come in, both he and all the Israelites with him, the whole congregation." 22So Moses did as the LORD commanded him. He took Joshua and had him stand before Eleazar the priest and the whole congregation; 23he laid his hands on him and commissioned him—as the LORD had directed through Moses.

Daily Offerings

28 The LORD spoke to Moses, saying: 2Command the Israelites, and say to them: My offering, the food for my offerings by fire, my pleasing odor, you shall take care to offer to me at its appointed time. 3And you shall say to them, This is the offering by fire that you shall offer to the LORD: two male lambs a year old without blemish, daily, as a

ᵃ Heb lacks with me

27:5 *Moses brought their case before the LORD.* Good spiritual directors must be able to listen to the voice of God and to those of their people at the same time. Leaders are listeners. They hear not only God, but also their people. What the people needed in this episode (vv 1–11) was a clear rule for inheritance. After Moses heard the daughters of Zelophehad, he brought their case before the Lord. Spiritually mature leaders love and are concerned for their people. They will care for them in even the smallest matters. Loving people enough to carefully lead them on the right path is the most central task of a spiritual director.

27:18 *Take Joshua son of Nun, a man in whom is the spirit.* One's spiritual leadership

may be measured by how many leaders one has helped develop. Because he was looking ahead, Moses developed Joshua as a spiritual leader. However, before Moses identified Joshua as his spiritual successor, he asked for God's guidance (vv 16–17). God picked Joshua, explaining that he was "a man in whom is the spirit." God's standards for the appointment of spiritual leaders are different from those of the world. God often chooses as leaders those who are especially sensitive and obedient to the voice of the Spirit.

28:3 *two male lambs a year old without blemish, daily, as a regular offering.* God commanded the people of Israel to provide daily burnt offerings. The people followed God's

regular offering. 4One lamb you shall offer in the morning, and the other lamb you shall offer at twilight;*a* 5also one-tenth of an ephah of choice flour for a grain offering, mixed with one-fourth of a hin of beaten oil. 6It is a regular burnt offering, ordained at Mount Sinai for a pleasing odor, an offering by fire to the LORD. 7Its drink offering shall be one-fourth of a hin for each lamb; in the sanctuary you shall pour out a drink offering of strong drink to the LORD. 8The other lamb you shall offer at twilight*a* with a grain offering and a drink offering like the one in the morning; you shall offer it as an offering by fire, a pleasing odor to the LORD.

Sabbath Offerings

9 On the sabbath day: two male lambs a year old without blemish, and two-tenths of an ephah of choice flour for a grain offering, mixed with oil, and its drink offering— 10this is the burnt offering for every sabbath, in addition to the regular burnt offering and its drink offering.

Monthly Offerings

11 At the beginnings of your months you shall offer a burnt offering to the LORD: two young bulls, one ram, seven male lambs a year old without blemish; 12also three-tenths of an ephah of choice flour for a grain offering, mixed with oil, for each bull; and two-tenths of choice flour for a grain offering, mixed with oil, for the one ram; 13and one-tenth of choice flour mixed with oil as a grain offering for every lamb—a burnt offering of pleasing odor, an offering by fire to the LORD. 14Their drink offerings shall be half a hin of wine for a bull, one-third of a hin for a ram, and one-fourth of a hin for a lamb. This is the burnt offering of every month throughout the months of the year. 15And there shall be one male goat for a sin offering to the LORD; it shall be offered in addition to the regular burnt offering and its drink offering.

Offerings at Passover

16 On the fourteenth day of the first month there shall be a passover offering to the LORD. 17And on the fifteenth day of this month is a festival; seven days shall unleavened bread be eaten. 18On the first day there shall be a holy convocation. You shall not work at your occupations. 19You shall offer an offering by fire, a burnt offering to the LORD: two young bulls, one ram, and seven male lambs a year old; see that they are without blemish. 20Their grain offering shall be of choice flour mixed with oil: three-tenths of an ephah shall you offer for a bull, and two-tenths for a ram; 21one-tenth shall you offer for each of the seven lambs; 22also one male goat for a sin offering, to make atonement for you. 23You shall offer these in addition to the burnt offering of the morning, which belongs to the regular burnt offering. 24In the same way you shall offer daily, for seven days, the food of an offering by fire, a pleasing odor to the LORD; it shall be offered in addition to the regular burnt offering and its drink offering. 25And on the seventh day you shall have a holy convocation; you shall not work at your occupations.

Offerings at the Festival of Weeks

26 On the day of the first fruits, when you offer a grain offering of new grain to the LORD at your festival of weeks, you shall have a holy convocation; you shall not work at your occupations. 27You shall offer a burnt offering, a pleasing odor to the LORD: two young bulls, one ram, seven male lambs a year old. 28Their grain offering shall be of choice flour mixed with oil, three-tenths of an ephah for each bull, two-tenths for one ram, 29one-tenth for each of the seven lambs; 30with one male goat, to make atonement for you. 31In addition to the regular burnt offering with its grain offering, you shall offer them and their drink offering. They shall be without blemish.

a Heb *between the two evenings*

---

specific instructions concerning every detail of preparing the offerings for God and conducting services of worship. We must not be absentminded or careless when we worship God, either in our preparations for or our manner of service. Nor should we worship only as we choose. We must be prepared day or night to offer to worship according to God's direction. Constancy and repetition are keys to success in spiritual growth.

Offerings at the Festival of Trumpets

29 On the first day of the seventh month you shall have a holy convocation; you shall not work at your occupations. It is a day for you to blow the trumpets, [2]and you shall offer a burnt offering, a pleasing odor to the LORD: one young bull, one ram, seven male lambs a year old without blemish. [3]Their grain offering shall be of choice flour mixed with oil, three-tenths of one ephah for the bull, two-tenths for the ram, [4]and one-tenth for each of the seven lambs; [5]with one male goat for a sin offering, to make atonement for you. [6]These are in addition to the burnt offering of the new moon and its grain offering, and the regular burnt offering and its grain offering, and their drink offerings, according to the ordinance for them, a pleasing odor, an offering by fire to the LORD.

Offerings on the Day of Atonement

[7]On the tenth day of this seventh month you shall have a holy convocation, and deny yourselves; [a] you shall do no work. [8]You shall offer a burnt offering to the LORD, a pleasing odor: one young bull, one ram, seven male lambs a year old. They shall be without blemish. [9]Their grain offering shall be of choice flour mixed with oil, three-tenths of an ephah for the bull, two-tenths for the one ram, [10]one-tenth for each of the seven lambs; [11]with one male goat for a sin offering, in addition to the sin offering of atonement, and

the regular burnt offering and its grain offering, and their drink offerings.

Offerings at the Festival of Booths

[12]On the fifteenth day of the seventh month you shall have a holy convocation; you shall not work at your occupations. You shall celebrate a festival to the LORD seven days. [13]You shall offer a burnt offering, an offering by fire, a pleasing odor to the LORD: thirteen young bulls, two rams, fourteen male lambs a year old. They shall be without blemish. [14]Their grain offering shall be of choice flour mixed with oil, three-tenths of an ephah for each of the thirteen bulls, two-tenths for each of the two rams, [15]and one-tenth for each of the fourteen lambs; [16]also one male goat for a sin offering, in addition to the regular burnt offering, its grain offering and its drink offering.

17 On the second day: twelve young bulls, two rams, fourteen male lambs a year old without blemish, [18]with the grain offering and the drink offerings for the bulls, for the rams, and for the lambs, as prescribed in accordance with their number; [19]also one male goat for a sin offering, in addition to the regular burnt offering and its grain offering, and their drink offerings.

20 On the third day: eleven bulls, two rams, fourteen male lambs a year old without blemish, [21]with the grain offering and the drink offerings for the bulls, for the rams,

a Or and fast

29:1 *On the first day . . . you shall not work at your occupations.* Taking time to rest is also important in the spiritual life. Rest is not merely the state of doing no work. Rest is a time for refreshment. It may be a time to reflect on the past or plan for the future. It is also a time for worshiping God. The Sabbath is an intentional time set apart for worship. Our souls receive true peace and strength when we worship God. Rest is a Spiritual Discipline that requires and also restores our trust in God. Our trust grows as we see how God fulfills our needs even when we are working. We realize we don't need to earn God's provision. Rest

helps us reside in the unconditional, unfailing, and forgiving love of God.

Responding
29:12 CELEBRATION. Verses 12–39 describe the Festival of Booths, when the Israelites remembered and celebrated what many considered a hardship—living in tents during their wilderness wanderings. Describe the times in your life or that of your family when you suffered great hardship, but can now look back with fondness on them. The next time you are with those with whom you shared these experiences, make a special effort to recall and celebrate them. *See also* Spiritual Disciplines Index.

and for the lambs, as prescribed in accordance with their number; ²²also one male goat for a sin offering, in addition to the regular burnt offering and its grain offering and its drink offering.

23 On the fourth day: ten bulls, two rams, fourteen male lambs a year old without blemish, ²⁴with the grain offering and the drink offerings for the bulls, for the rams, and for the lambs, as prescribed in accordance with their number; ²⁵also one male goat for a sin offering, in addition to the regular burnt offering, its grain offering and its drink offering.

26 On the fifth day: nine bulls, two rams, fourteen male lambs a year old without blemish, ²⁷with the grain offering and the drink offerings for the bulls, for the rams, and for the lambs, as prescribed in accordance with their number; ²⁸also one male goat for a sin offering, in addition to the regular burnt offering and its grain offering and its drink offering.

29 On the sixth day: eight bulls, two rams, fourteen male lambs a year old without blemish, ³⁰with the grain offering and the drink offerings for the bulls, for the rams, and for the lambs, as prescribed in accordance with their number; ³¹also one male goat for a sin offering, in addition to the regular burnt offering, its grain offering, and its drink offerings.

32 On the seventh day: seven bulls, two rams, fourteen male lambs a year old without blemish, ³³with the grain offering and the drink offerings for the bulls, for the rams, and for the lambs, as prescribed in accordance with their number; ³⁴also one male goat for a sin offering, besides the regular burnt offering, its grain offering, and its drink offering.

35 On the eighth day you shall have a solemn assembly; you shall not work at your occupations. ³⁶You shall offer a burnt offering, an offering by fire, a pleasing odor to the LORD: one bull, one ram, seven male lambs a year old without blemish, ³⁷and the grain offering and the drink offerings for the bull, for the ram, and for the lambs, as prescribed in accordance with their number; ³⁸also one male goat for a sin offering, in addition to the regular burnt offering and its grain offering and its drink offering.

39 These you shall offer to the LORD at your appointed festivals, in addition to your votive offerings and your freewill offerings, as your burnt offerings, your grain offerings, your drink offerings, and your offerings of well-being.

40ᵃ So Moses told the Israelites everything just as the LORD had commanded Moses.

Vows Made by Women

30 Then Moses said to the heads of the tribes of the Israelites: This is what the LORD has commanded. ²When a man makes a vow to the LORD, or swears an oath to bind himself by a pledge, he shall not break his word; he shall do according to all that proceeds out of his mouth.

3 When a woman makes a vow to the LORD, or binds herself by a pledge, while within her father's house, in her youth, ⁴and her father hears of her vow or her pledge by which she has bound herself, and says nothing to her; then all her vows shall stand, and any pledge by which she has bound herself shall stand. ⁵But if her father expresses disapproval to her at the time that he hears of it, no vow of hers, and no pledge by which she has bound herself, shall stand; and the LORD will forgive her, because her father had expressed to her his disapproval.

6 If she marries, while obligated by her vows or any thoughtless utterance of her lips by which she has bound herself, ⁷and her husband hears of it and says nothing to her at

a Ch 30.1 in Heb

30:2 *he shall not break his word.* God values the family. He taught the Israelites to value their family promises. Spiritually mature persons fulfill the promises they make to God concerning the family and do not enter such promises rashly. The degree of agreement between our words and our behavior creates or destroys our integrity. We are responsible for the words we say, and we should keep our promises even when doing so proves personally disadvantageous. We must not break our promises.

the time that he hears, then her vows shall stand, and her pledges by which she has bound herself shall stand. 8But if, at the time that her husband hears of it, he expresses disapproval to her, then he shall nullify the vow by which she was obligated, or the thoughtless utterance of her lips, by which she bound herself; and the LORD will forgive her. 9(But every vow of a widow or of a divorced woman, by which she has bound herself, shall be binding upon her.) 10And if she made a vow in her husband's house, or bound herself by a pledge with an oath, 11and her husband heard it and said nothing to her, and did not express disapproval to her, then all her vows shall stand, and any pledge by which she bound herself shall stand. 12But if her husband nullifies them at the time that he hears them, then whatever proceeds out of her lips concerning her vows, or concerning her pledge of herself, shall not stand. Her husband has nullified them, and the LORD will forgive her. 13Any vow or any binding oath to deny herself,a her husband may allow to stand, or her husband may nullify. 14But if her husband says nothing to her from day to day,b then he validates all her vows, or all her pledges, by which she is obligated; he has validated them, because he said nothing to her at the time that he heard of them. 15But if he nullifies them some time after he has heard of them, then he shall bear her guilt.

16 These are the statutes that the LORD commanded Moses concerning a husband and his wife, and a father and his daughter while she is still young and in her father's house.

War against Midian

31 The LORD spoke to Moses, saying, 2"Avenge the Israelites on the Midianites; afterward you shall be gathered to your people." 3So Moses said to the people,

"Arm some of your number for the war, so that they may go against Midian, to execute the LORD's vengeance on Midian. 4You shall send a thousand from each of the tribes of Israel to the war." 5So out of the thousands of Israel, a thousand from each tribe were conscripted, twelve thousand armed for battle. 6Moses sent them to the war, a thousand from each tribe, along with Phinehas son of Eleazar the priest,c with the vessels of the sanctuary and the trumpets for sounding the alarm in his hand. 7They did battle against Midian, as the LORD had commanded Moses, and killed every male. 8They killed the kings of Midian: Evi, Rekem, Zur, Hur, and Reba, the five kings of Midian, in addition to others who were slain by them; and they also killed Balaam son of Beor with the sword. 9The Israelites took the women of Midian and their little ones captive; and they took all their cattle, their flocks, and all their goods as booty. 10All their towns where they had settled, and all their encampments, they burned, 11but they took all the spoil and all the booty, both people and animals. 12Then they brought the captives and the booty and the spoil to Moses, to Eleazar the priest, and to the congregation of the Israelites, at the camp on the plains of Moab by the Jordan at Jericho.

Return from the War

13 Moses, Eleazar the priest, and all the leaders of the congregation went to meet them outside the camp. 14Moses became angry with the officers of the army, the commanders of thousands and the commanders of hundreds, who had come from service in the war. 15Moses said to them, "Have you allowed all the women to live? 16These women

a Or to fast   b Or from that day to the next
c Gk: Heb adds to the war

31:3 *Arm some of your number for the war.* Before sending them off to battle, God commanded Moses to arm the men for war. The spiritual journey is not an easy path. It is an endless series of spiritual battles. The battles are often invisible and yet crucial. Good preparation is necessary to ensure victory. We have to be properly armed in order to endure rigorous training and difficulties and become strong spiritually. The Spiritual Disciplines help equip us for spiritual warfare. The undisciplined warrior is ineffective and weak. We must embrace the Spiritual Disciplines daily to become strong spiritual warriors.

here, on Balaam's advice, made the Israelites act treacherously against the LORD in the affair of Peor, so that the plague came among the congregation of the LORD. 17Now therefore, kill every male among the little ones, and kill every woman who has known a man by sleeping with him. 18But all the young girls who have not known a man by sleeping with him, keep alive for yourselves. 19Camp outside the camp seven days; whoever of you has killed any person or touched a corpse, purify yourselves and your captives on the third and on the seventh day. 20You shall purify every garment, every article of skin, everything made of goats' hair, and every article of wood."

21 Eleazar the priest said to the troops who had gone to battle: "This is the statute of the law that the LORD has commanded Moses: 22gold, silver, bronze, iron, tin, and lead— 23everything that can withstand fire, shall be passed through fire, and it shall be clean. Nevertheless it shall also be purified with the water for purification; and whatever cannot withstand fire, shall be passed through the water. 24You must wash your clothes on the seventh day, and you shall be clean; afterward you may come into the camp."

Disposition of Captives and Booty

25 The LORD spoke to Moses, saying, 26"You and Eleazar the priest and the heads of the ancestral houses of the congregation make an inventory of the booty captured, both human and animal. 27Divide the booty into two parts, between the warriors who went out to battle and all the congregation. 28From the share of the warriors who went out to battle, set aside as tribute for the LORD, one item out of every five hundred, whether persons, oxen, donkeys, sheep, or goats. 29Take it from their half and give it to Eleazar the priest as an offering to the LORD. 30But from the Israelites' half you shall take one out of every fifty, whether persons, oxen, donkeys, sheep, or goats—all the animals— and give them to the Levites who have charge of the tabernacle of the LORD."

31 Then Moses and Eleazar the priest did as the LORD had commanded Moses:

32 The booty remaining from the spoil that the troops had taken totaled six hundred seventy-five thousand sheep, 33seventy-two thousand oxen, 34sixty-one thousand donkeys, 35and thirty-two thousand persons in all, women who had not known a man by sleeping with him.

36 The half-share, the portion of those who had gone out to war, was in number three hundred thirty-seven thousand five hundred sheep and goats, 37and the LORD's tribute of sheep and goats was six hundred seventy-five. 38The oxen were thirty-six thousand, of which the LORD's tribute was seventy-two. 39The donkeys were thirty thousand five hundred, of which the LORD's tribute was sixty-one. 40The persons were sixteen thousand, of which the LORD's tribute was thirty-two persons. 41Moses gave the tribute, the offering for the LORD, to Eleazar the priest, as the LORD had commanded Moses.

42 As for the Israelites' half, which Moses separated from that of the troops, 43the congregation's half was three hundred thirty-seven thousand five hundred sheep and goats, 44thirty-six thousand oxen, 45thirty thousand five hundred donkeys, 46and sixteen thousand persons. 47From the Israelites' half Moses took one of every fifty, both of persons and of animals, and gave them to the Levites who had charge of the tabernacle of the LORD; as the LORD had commanded Moses.

48 Then the officers who were over the thousands of the army, the commanders of thousands and the commanders of hundreds, approached Moses, 49and said to Moses, "Your servants have counted the warriors who are under our command, and not one of us is missing. 50And we have brought the LORD's offering, what each of us found, articles of gold, armlets and bracelets, signet rings, earrings, and pendants, to make atonement for ourselves before the LORD." 51Moses and Eleazar the priest received the gold from them, all in the form of crafted articles. 52And all the gold of the offering that they offered to the LORD, from the commanders of thousands and the commanders of hundreds, was sixteen thousand seven hundred fifty shekels. 53(The troops had all taken plunder for themselves.) 54So Moses and

Eleazar the priest received the gold from the commanders of thousands and of hundreds, and brought it into the tent of meeting as a memorial for the Israelites before the LORD.

Conquest and Division of Transjordan

32 Now the Reubenites and the Gadites owned a very great number of cattle. When they saw that the land of Jazer and the land of Gilead was a good place for cattle, [2]the Gadites and the Reubenites came and spoke to Moses, to Eleazar the priest, and to the leaders of the congregation, saying, [3]"Ataroth, Dibon, Jazer, Nimrah, Heshbon, Elealeh, Sebam, Nebo, and Beon— [4]the land that the LORD subdued before the congregation of Israel—is a land for cattle; and your servants have cattle." [5]They continued, "If we have found favor in your sight, let this land be given to your servants for a possession; do not make us cross the Jordan."

6 But Moses said to the Gadites and to the Reubenites, "Shall your brothers go to war while you sit here? [7]Why will you discourage the hearts of the Israelites from going over into the land that the LORD has given them? [8]Your fathers did this, when I sent them from Kadesh-barnea to see the land. [9]When they went up to the Wadi Eshcol and saw the land, they discouraged the hearts of the Israelites from going into the land that the LORD had given them. [10]The LORD's anger was kindled on that day and he swore, saying, [11]'Surely none of the people who came up out of Egypt, from twenty years old and upward, shall see the land that I swore to give to Abraham, to Isaac, and to Jacob, because they have not unreservedly followed me— [12]none except Caleb son of Jephunneh the Kenizzite and Joshua son of Nun, for they have unreservedly followed the LORD.' [13]And the LORD's anger was kindled against Israel, and he made them wander in the wilderness for forty years, until all the generation that had done evil in the sight of the LORD had disappeared. [14]And now you, a brood of sinners, have risen in place of your fathers, to increase the LORD's fierce anger against Israel! [15]If you turn away from following him, he will again abandon them in the wilderness; and you will destroy all this people."

16 Then they came up to him and said, "We will build sheepfolds here for our flocks, and towns for our little ones, [17]but we will take up arms as a vanguard[a] before the Israelites, until we have brought them to their place. Meanwhile our little ones will stay in the fortified towns because of the inhabitants of the land. [18]We will not return to our homes until all the Israelites have obtained their inheritance. [19]We will not inherit with them on the other side of the Jordan and beyond, because our inheritance has come to us on this side of the Jordan to the east."

20 So Moses said to them, "If you do this— if you take up arms to go before the LORD for the war, [21]and all those of you who bear arms cross the Jordan before the LORD, until he has driven out his enemies from before him [22]and the land is subdued before the LORD—then after that you may return and be free of obligation to the LORD and to Israel, and this land shall be your possession before the LORD. [23]But if you do not do this, you have sinned against the LORD; and be sure your sin will find you out. [24]Build towns for your little ones, and folds for your flocks; but do what you have promised."

25 Then the Gadites and the Reubenites said to Moses, "Your servants will do as my lord commands. [26]Our little ones, our wives, our flocks, and all our livestock shall remain there in the towns of Gilead; [27]but your servants will cross over, everyone armed for war,

a Cn: Heb hurrying

32:11–12 *for they have unreservedly followed the LORD.* God waited for the older generation of the Israelites to pass away in the wilderness before he led the Israelites into the land of Canaan. The older generation, with the exception of Joshua and Caleb, did not see the Promised Land, because they had been disobedient. Both Joshua and Caleb had "unreservedly followed the LORD," and so they were allowed to lead the Israelite people into the land of Canaan. Unreserved obedience is crucial in the spiritual life. God works through the faithful few who are able to serve the Lord with undivided hearts.

to do battle for the LORD, just as my lord orders."

28 So Moses gave command concerning them to Eleazar the priest, to Joshua son of Nun, and to the heads of the ancestral houses of the Israelite tribes. 29 And Moses said to them, "If the Gadites and the Reubenites, everyone armed for battle before the LORD, will cross over the Jordan with you and the land shall be subdued before you, then you shall give them the land of Gilead for a possession; 30 but if they will not cross over with you armed, they shall have possessions among you in the land of Canaan." 31 The Gadites and the Reubenites answered, "As the LORD has spoken to your servants, so we will do. 32 We will cross over armed before the LORD into the land of Canaan, but the possession of our inheritance shall remain with us on this side of a the Jordan."

33 Moses gave to them—to the Gadites and to the Reubenites and to the half-tribe of Manasseh son of Joseph—the kingdom of King Sihon of the Amorites and the kingdom of King Og of Bashan, the land and its towns, with the territories of the surrounding towns. 34 And the Gadites rebuilt Dibon, Ataroth, Aroer, 35 Atroth-shophan, Jazer, Jogbehah, 36 Beth-nimrah, and Beth-haran, fortified cities, and folds for sheep. 37 And the Reubenites rebuilt Heshbon, Elealeh, Kiriathaim, 38 Nebo, and Baal-meon (some names being changed), and Sibmah; and they gave names to the towns that they rebuilt. 39 The descendants of Machir son of Manasseh went to Gilead, captured it, and dispossessed the Amorites who were there; 40 so Moses gave Gilead to Machir son of Manasseh, and he settled there. 41 Jair son of Manasseh went and captured their villages, and renamed them Havvoth-jair. b 42 And Nobah went and captured Kenath and its villages, and renamed it Nobah after himself.

The Stages of Israel's Journey from Egypt

33 These are the stages by which the Israelites went out of the land of Egypt in military formation under the leadership of Moses and Aaron. 2 Moses wrote down their starting points, stage by stage, by command of the LORD; and these are their stages according to their starting places. 3 They set out from Rameses in the first month, on the fifteenth day of the first month; on the day after the passover the Israelites went out boldly in the sight of all the Egyptians, 4 while the Egyptians were burying all their firstborn, whom the LORD had struck down among them. The LORD executed judgments even against their gods.

5 So the Israelites set out from Rameses, and camped at Succoth. 6 They set out from Succoth, and camped at Etham, which is on the edge of the wilderness. 7 They set out from Etham, and turned back to Pi-hahiroth, which faces Baal-zephon; and they camped before Migdol. 8 They set out from Pi-hahiroth, passed through the sea into the wilderness, went a three days' journey in the wilderness of Etham, and camped at Marah. 9 They set out from Marah and came to Elim; at Elim there were twelve springs of water and seventy palm trees, and they camped there. 10 They set out from Elim and camped by the Red Sea. c 11 They set out from the Red Sea c and camped in the wilderness of Sin. 12 They set out from the wilderness of Sin and camped at Dophkah. 13 They set out from Dophkah and camped at Alush. 14 They set out from Alush and camped at Rephidim, where there was no water for the people to drink. 15 They set out from Rephidim and camped in the wilderness of Sinai. 16 They set out from the wilderness of Sinai and camped at Kibroth-hattaavah. 17 They set out from Kibroth-hattaavah and camped at Hazeroth. 18 They set out from Hazeroth and camped at Rithmah. 19 They set out from Rithmah and camped at Rimmon-perez. 20 They set out from Rimmon-perez and camped at Libnah. 21 They set out from Libnah and camped at Rissah. 22 They set out from Rissah and camped at Kehelathah. 23 They set out from Kehelathah and camped at Mount Shepher. 24 They set out from Mount Shepher and camped at Haradah. 25 They set out from Haradah and camped at Makheloth. 26 They set out from Makheloth and camped at Tahath. 27 They set out from Tahath and camped at Terah. 28 They set out from Terah and camped at

a Heb *beyond*   b That is *the villages of Jair*
c Or *Sea of Reeds*

Mithkah. 29They set out from Mithkah and camped at Hashmonah. 30They set out from Hashmonah and camped at Moseroth. 31They set out from Moseroth and camped at Bene-jaakan. 32They set out from Bene-jaakan and camped at Hor-haggidgad. 33They set out from Hor-haggidgad and camped at Jotbathah. 34They set out from Jotbathah and camped at Abronah. 35They set out from Abronah and camped at Ezion-geber. 36They set out from Ezion-geber and camped in the wilderness of Zin (that is, Kadesh). 37They set out from Kadesh and camped at Mount Hor, on the edge of the land of Edom.

38 Aaron the priest went up Mount Hor at the command of the LORD and died there in the fortieth year after the Israelites had come out of the land of Egypt, on the first day of the fifth month. 39Aaron was one hundred twenty-three years old when he died on Mount Hor.

40 The Canaanite, the king of Arad, who lived in the Negeb in the land of Canaan, heard of the coming of the Israelites.

41 They set out from Mount Hor and camped at Zalmonah. 42They set out from Zalmonah and camped at Punon. 43They set out from Punon and camped at Oboth. 44They set out from Oboth and camped at Iye-abarim, in the territory of Moab. 45They set out from Iyim and camped at Dibon-gad. 46They set out from Dibon-gad and camped at Almon-diblathaim. 47They set out from Almon-diblathaim and camped in the mountains of Abarim, before Nebo. 48They set out from the mountains of Abarim and camped in the plains of Moab by the Jordan at Jericho; 49they camped by the Jordan from Beth-jeshi-

moth as far as Abel-shittim in the plains of Moab.

Directions for the Conquest of Canaan

50 In the plains of Moab by the Jordan at Jericho, the LORD spoke to Moses, saying: 51Speak to the Israelites, and say to them: When you cross over the Jordan into the land of Canaan, 52you shall drive out all the inhabitants of the land from before you, destroy all their figured stones, destroy all their cast images, and demolish all their high places. 53You shall take possession of the land and settle in it, for I have given you the land to possess. 54You shall apportion the land by lot according to your clans; to a large one you shall give a large inheritance, and to a small one you shall give a small inheritance; the inheritance shall belong to the person on whom the lot falls; according to your ancestral tribes you shall inherit. 55But if you do not drive out the inhabitants of the land from before you, then those whom you let remain shall be as barbs in your eyes and thorns in your sides; they shall trouble you in the land where you are settling. 56And I will do to you as I thought to do to them.

The Boundaries of the Land

34 The LORD spoke to Moses, saying: 2Command the Israelites, and say to them: When you enter the land of Canaan (this is the land that shall fall to you for an inheritance, the land of Canaan, defined by its boundaries), 3your south sector shall extend from the wilderness of Zin along the side of Edom. Your southern boundary shall

---

33:52 *you shall drive out all the inhabitants of the land from before you.* God commanded Israel to drive out all the inhabitants of Canaan, so that they would not continue to trouble God's people or cause them to stumble in the future. True freedom follows total commitment. Partial obedience may snare us.

34:2 *When you enter the land of Canaan.* When God brought Israel out of Egypt he promised his people a land "that flows with milk and honey" (14:8). He commanded the twelve spies to investigate the land promised to them. But ten of the men doubted God (13:25–33).

Only Joshua and Caleb believed God's word and courageously embraced his promise (14:7–9). Because of their open minds and hearts to see what God wanted them to see, both men interpreted their experiences of the punishing journey in the wilderness in the light of that vision. Their time in the wilderness, which they could have seen as a curse, became a blessing to them. The wilderness became their training ground for future challenges and the place where they experienced God's presence in a deeper way.

begin from the end of the Dead Sea*a* on the east; ⁴your boundary shall turn south of the ascent of Akrabbim, and cross to Zin, and its outer limit shall be south of Kadesh-barnea; then it shall go on to Hazar-addar, and cross to Azmon; ⁵the boundary shall turn from Azmon to the Wadi of Egypt, and its termination shall be at the Sea.

6 For the western boundary, you shall have the Great Sea and its*b* coast; this shall be your western boundary.

7 This shall be your northern boundary: from the Great Sea you shall mark out your line to Mount Hor; ⁸from Mount Hor you shall mark it out to Lebo-hamath, and the outer limit of the boundary shall be at Zedad; ⁹then the boundary shall extend to Ziphron, and its end shall be at Hazar-enan; this shall be your northern boundary.

10 You shall mark out your eastern boundary from Hazar-enan to Shepham; ¹¹and the boundary shall continue down from Shepham to Riblah on the east side of Ain; and the boundary shall go down, and reach the eastern slope of the sea of Chinnereth; ¹²and the boundary shall go down to the Jordan, and its end shall be at the Dead Sea.*a* This shall be your land with its boundaries all around.

13 Moses commanded the Israelites, saying: This is the land that you shall inherit by lot, which the LORD has commanded to give to the nine tribes and to the half-tribe; ¹⁴for the tribe of the Reubenites by their ancestral houses and the tribe of the Gadites by their ancestral houses have taken their inheritance, and also the half-tribe of Manasseh; ¹⁵the two tribes and the half-tribe have taken their inheritance beyond the Jordan at Jericho eastward, toward the sunrise.

Tribal Leaders

16 The LORD spoke to Moses, saying: ¹⁷These are the names of the men who shall apportion the land to you for inheritance: the priest Eleazar and Joshua son of Nun. ¹⁸You shall take one leader of every tribe to apportion the land for inheritance. ¹⁹These are the names of the men: Of the tribe of Judah, Caleb son of Jephunneh. ²⁰Of the tribe of the Simeonites, Shemuel son of Ammi-

hud. ²¹Of the tribe of Benjamin, Elidad son of Chislon. ²²Of the tribe of the Danites a leader, Bukki son of Jogli. ²³Of the Josephites: of the tribe of the Manassites a leader, Hanniel son of Ephod, ²⁴and of the tribe of the Ephraimites a leader, Kemuel son of Shiphtan. ²⁵Of the tribe of the Zebulunites a leader, Elizaphan son of Parnach. ²⁶Of the tribe of the Issacharites a leader, Paltiel son of Azzan. ²⁷And of the tribe of the Asherites a leader, Ahihud son of Shelomi. ²⁸Of the tribe of the Naphtalites a leader, Pedahel son of Ammihud. ²⁹These were the ones whom the LORD commanded to apportion the inheritance for the Israelites in the land of Canaan.

Cities for the Levites

35 In the plains of Moab by the Jordan at Jericho, the LORD spoke to Moses, saying: ²Command the Israelites to give, from the inheritance that they possess, towns for the Levites to live in; you shall also give to the Levites pasture lands surrounding the towns. ³The towns shall be theirs to live in, and their pasture lands shall be for their cattle, for their livestock, and for all their animals. ⁴The pasture lands of the towns, which you shall give to the Levites, shall reach from the wall of the town outward a thousand cubits all around. ⁵You shall measure, outside the town, for the east side two thousand cubits, for the south side two thousand cubits, for the west side two thousand cubits, and for the north side two thousand cubits, with the town in the middle; this shall belong to them as pasture land for their towns.

6 The towns that you give to the Levites shall include the six cities of refuge, where you shall permit a slayer to flee, and in addition to them you shall give forty-two towns. ⁷The towns that you give to the Levites shall total forty-eight, with their pasture lands. ⁸And as for the towns that you shall give from the possession of the Israelites, from the larger tribes you shall take many, and from the smaller tribes you shall take few; each, in proportion to the inheritance that it obtains, shall give of its towns to the Levites.

a Heb *Salt Sea*   *b* Syr: Heb lacks *its*

Cities of Refuge

9 The LORD spoke to Moses, saying: [10]Speak to the Israelites, and say to them: When you cross the Jordan into the land of Canaan, [11]then you shall select cities to be cities of refuge for you, so that a slayer who kills a person without intent may flee there. [12]The cities shall be for you a refuge from the avenger, so that the slayer may not die until there is a trial before the congregation.

13 The cities that you designate shall be six cities of refuge for you: [14]you shall designate three cities beyond the Jordan, and three cities in the land of Canaan, to be cities of refuge. [15]These six cities shall serve as refuge for the Israelites, for the resident or transient alien among them, so that anyone who kills a person without intent may flee there.

Concerning Murder and Blood Revenge

16 But anyone who strikes another with an iron object, and death ensues, is a murderer; the murderer shall be put to death. [17]Or anyone who strikes another with a stone in hand that could cause death, and death ensues, is a murderer; the murderer shall be put to death. [18]Or anyone who strikes another with a weapon of wood in hand that could cause death, and death ensues, is a murderer; the murderer shall be put to death. [19]The avenger of blood is the one who shall put the murderer to death; when they meet, the avenger of blood shall execute the sentence. [20]Likewise, if someone pushes another from hatred, or hurls something at another, lying in wait, and death ensues, [21]or in enmity strikes another with the hand, and death ensues, then the one who struck the blow shall be put to death; that person is a murderer; the avenger of blood shall put the murderer to death, when they meet.

22 But if someone pushes another suddenly without enmity, or hurls any object without lying in wait, [23]or, while handling any stone that could cause death, unintentionally[a] drops it on another and death ensues, though they were not enemies, and no harm was intended, [24]then the congregation shall judge between the slayer and the avenger of blood, in accordance with these ordinances; [25]and the congregation shall rescue the slayer from the avenger of blood. Then the congregation shall send the slayer back to the original city of refuge. The slayer shall live in it until the death of the high priest who was anointed with the holy oil. [26]But if the slayer shall at any time go outside the bounds of the original city of refuge, [27]and is found by the avenger of blood outside the bounds of the city of refuge, and is killed by the avenger, no bloodguilt shall be incurred. [28]For the slayer must remain in the city of refuge until the death of the high priest; but after the death of the high priest the slayer may return home.

29 These things shall be a statute and ordinance for you throughout your generations wherever you live.

30 If anyone kills another, the murderer shall be put to death on the evidence of witnesses; but no one shall be put to death on the testimony of a single witness. [31]Moreover you shall accept no ransom for the life of a murderer who is subject to the death penalty; a murderer must be put to death. [32]Nor shall you accept ransom for one who has fled to a city of refuge, enabling the fugitive to return to live in the land before the death of the high priest. [33]You shall not pollute the land in which you live; for blood pollutes the land, and no expiation can be made for the land, for the blood that is shed in it, except by the blood of the one who shed it. [34]You shall not defile the land in which you live, in which I

a Heb *without seeing*

35:9–15 *cities of refuge.* Moses was told to designate six cities as "cities of refuge." Representing God's grace to sinners, these were places where God dwelt among the outcast. God knows our limitations and weaknesses, and he prepares a "refuge," or safe place, for us. Just as the cities of refuge sheltered the sinners who would otherwise have been banned from society, Jesus Christ is a city of refuge for sinners like us—for we all fall short of God's holiness. Jesus protects us, and we take rest in him. Jesus brings God's grace to us as we pursue the spiritual life. We flourish in the light of God's grace.

also dwell; for I the LORD dwell among the Israelites.

Marriage of Female Heirs

36 The heads of the ancestral houses of the clans of the descendants of Gilead son of Machir son of Manasseh, of the Josephite clans, came forward and spoke in the presence of Moses and the leaders, the heads of the ancestral houses of the Israelites; ²they said, "The LORD commanded my lord to give the land for inheritance by lot to the Israelites; and my lord was commanded by the LORD to give the inheritance of our brother Zelophehad to his daughters. ³But if they are married into another Israelite tribe, then their inheritance will be taken from the inheritance of our ancestors and added to the inheritance of the tribe into which they marry; so it will be taken away from the allotted portion of our inheritance. ⁴And when the jubilee of the Israelites comes, then their inheritance will be added to the inheritance of the tribe into which they have married; and their inheritance will be taken from the inheritance of our ancestral tribe."

5 Then Moses commanded the Israelites according to the word of the LORD, saying, "The descendants of the tribe of Joseph are right in what they are saying. ⁶This is what the LORD commands concerning the daughters of Zelophehad, 'Let them marry whom they think best; only it must be into a clan of their father's tribe that they are married, ⁷so that no inheritance of the Israelites shall be transferred from one tribe to another; for all Israelites shall retain the inheritance of their ancestral tribes. ⁸Every daughter who possesses an inheritance in any tribe of the Israelites shall marry one from the clan of her father's tribe, so that all Israelites may continue to possess their ancestral inheritance. ⁹No inheritance shall be transferred from one tribe to another; for each of the tribes of the Israelites shall retain its own inheritance.' "

10 The daughters of Zelophehad did as the LORD had commanded Moses. ¹¹Mahlah, Tirzah, Hoglah, Milcah, and Noah, the daughters of Zelophehad, married sons of their father's brothers. ¹²They were married into the clans of the descendants of Manasseh son of Joseph, and their inheritance remained in the tribe of their father's clan.

13 These are the commandments and the ordinances that the LORD commanded through Moses to the Israelites in the plains of Moab by the Jordan at Jericho.

with God

35:34 *for I the LORD dwell among the Israelites.* God gave the Israelites the tabernacle to remind them of his constant presence. He was with his people wherever they were, as Immanuel ("God with us"). God dwelt among his people in their bondage in Egypt, during the wanderings in the wilderness, and as they entered the land of Canaan. He made his presence evident to the Israelites. We can't see God in the same ways today, but he still dwells among his people and goes wherever we go. He dwells with us now through the Holy Spirit. The spiritual life is a life lived in God's presence. God is with us and within us.

36:13 *These are the commandments and the ordinances.* Through Moses, God gave commandments and ordinances to Israel to help his people become a great nation. These laws were necessary to help the Israelites claim their freedom, for they had been enslaved to Egypt for a long time. As slaves, the Israelites had lived under laws of bondage. Since they were now free, they needed to learn to live under God's laws. God, the King of kings, uses commandments and instructions to mold us into the People of God. Life based on the word of God helps us grow in the likeness of God. This transformation is true spiritual formation.

DEUTERONOMY

Deuteronomy presents the final sermons of Moses, delivered at the climax of the forty years of Israel's wilderness wandering and on the eve of its entrance into the Promised Land. One cannot overestimate the enormity of the moment. The Israelites had spent four decades in the wilderness because of their rebellion against God. The book of Numbers tells the story of the death of the first generation, who had left Egypt, and the rise of the second generation, who would soon enter the land. With the exception of Joshua and Caleb, two spies who demonstrated trust in God at a crucial moment and were thus permitted to enter the land (Num 13), Moses' audience in Deuteronomy is the second generation, the generation of hope. Accordingly, Moses' message is heavy with law, expressions of God's will for how Israel should live its life in the land it is about to possess. In essence, Moses is saying, "Don't behave like your parents did in the wilderness. Obey God and live well in the land."

Moses thus reiterates, expands, and reapplies the law already recorded in Exodus 19–24, Leviticus, and Numbers. It is in recognition of this that the book commonly goes by the name Deuteronomy, Greek for "second law" or "second giving of the law."

Another fact makes these sermons particularly significant. Moses led the Israelites through the wilderness. For the most part, he was a pillar of strength and leadership for them. He guided them like a shepherd and even on one occasion convinced God not to destroy them in spite of their sin (Exod 32:30–35). But Moses himself wasn't perfect; he disobeyed God in the wilderness, and for his sin he was not permitted to enter the land either. Because of this, Deuteronomy represents his last words to the Israelites, who will enter a dangerous period of transition to new leadership under Joshua.

Covenant Theology

We may think of Deuteronomy as a series of sermons whose purpose is to elicit obedience from God's people. Moreover, these sermons, interestingly, take the form of

---

See also *"The With-God Life" essay for this section of the Bible,*
"The People of God in Exodus," pp. 87–91.

a covenant agreement, showing a structure roughly similar to that of an ancient Near Eastern treaty. It is important to realize that Deuteronomy itself is not a covenant treaty, but it does have many elements that are characteristic of a treaty. These include:

1. Introduction of the parties entering into covenant (1:1–5)
2. Historical prologue recounting the relationship between the two parties (1:9–3:27)
3. Law (4:1–26:19)
4. Blessings and curses (27:1–28:68)
5. Witnesses (30:19–20)
6. Review and succession (31:9–13)

As we look at this treatylike structure, we see just how important law is to the book—it comprises twenty-three of the chapters. However, it is significant that the law is preceded by historical prologue. The historical prologue serves the purpose of showing how God has already cared for Israel. In other words, the demand of the law is preceded by relationship with God established by grace (see note on 5:6).

Nonetheless, law is important to the maintenance of that relationship. The blessings and curses flow from the law and signal the fact that obedience brings reward and disobedience results in punishment. As we will soon see, at the heart of blessing and curse is the maintenance of the Israelites' happy life in the Promised Land, which they are about to possess.

The legal nature of the book is highlighted by the need for witnesses. These witnesses watch whether the two parties of the covenant keep their end of the agreement. If either party does not, the witnesses may be called to condemn the transgressing party and affirm the justice of their punishment.

Looking Ahead

Thus, Deuteronomy expresses a decided theology of retribution. Obedience brings reward, and disobedience results in punishment. Here we see the rationale for later prophets, such as Jeremiah, who announce Israel's punishment and removal from the Promised Land. Why? Because the people have broken the covenant and deserve the full force of the covenant curses. We also see in Deuteronomy the theology that undergirds the historical project we know as Samuel–Kings. This work seems to have been edited during the exile and responds to the burning question of that time period ("Why are we in exile?") by cataloging the history of covenant transgression, particularly as the covenant has been articulated in Deuteronomy.

Deuteronomy thus occupies a pivotal place in the canon. It provides a culmination of the Pentateuch (ending with a "second giving of the law") and it casts its long shadow of influence over much of the rest of the canon. But how and when did this important work come into existence? The questions of authorship and date of the book have been a vigorously debated issue.

Setting

The setting of Deuteronomy is the time of Moses at the end of the forty years of wilderness wandering. Though the book is anonymous, traditionally it has been ascribed to Moses. However, even the most vehement defenders of Mosaic authorship have admitted that the final form of the book comes from after the time of Moses. After all, the book concludes with a report of Moses' death and an assessment of his ministry (Deut 34). Although many limit the post-Mosaic contributions to the book to that one chapter, attentive readers will note a narrative strand running throughout the book that clearly comes from after the time of Moses. This narrator occasionally talks about events that take place "across the [Jordan] river" in reference to the Transjordan. But such a perspective implies that the speaker is in the Promised Land, a place that Moses never entered.

Many scholars suggest an even more distant relationship to Moses by connecting its origins to the story in 2 Kings 22. During the eighteenth year of the reign of King Hezekiah (623 BC), a "book of the law" is discovered during the purification of the Temple, apparently suppressed by the apostate kings who had preceded him. Upon its discovery Josiah and his officials respond to its contents by tearing down local altars in favor of the central altar at the Temple in Jerusalem, a clear indication that what they found included Deuteronomy 12, so the found "book of law" was either Deuteronomy or a portion of Deuteronomy that included that chapter. This story leads some scholars to suggest that the book was produced, rather than found, at this time. Its authors, seeing it as an extension of Moses' theology, associated it with him in order to give it authority. The advocates of this view suggest that such a move did not carry the same negative ethical implications that it might today.

Thus, opinions differ on the origins of the book, but all agree that the book's contents are set in the last days of Moses, and it will be from that perspective that we will interpret and apply its message to us.

Reading Deuteronomy from a New Testament Perspective

In Deuteronomy Moses warns the second wilderness generation that they must obey God's will as expressed in the law. If they do obey, blessings will abound, but judgment will be the consequence of disobedience (Deut 27–29). Reading the book from our historical perspective, we know the results. Samuel and Kings catalog the many ways in which the leaders and people of Israel and Judah failed God. As a result, they experienced exile and oppression at the hands of powerful foreign enemies. Indeed, by the end of the Old Testament period, voices were heard anticipating that something greater was coming. The People of God had repeatedly broken the old covenant, represented in part by Deuteronomy, but God promises to make a new covenant with the people of Israel and Judah (Jer 31:31–35).

The New Testament tells us that Jesus came to establish the new covenant with his followers (Luke 22:20). This new covenant does not so much replace the old covenant as fulfill it. As a matter of fact, Jesus tells us that he did not come to abolish the law, but to fulfill it (Matt 5:17–20).

The question of the relationship of God's people to Old Testament law today is a complicated one and one on which people differ. It is clear that some laws are no longer relevant (sacrifices, distinctions between clean and unclean food, etc.), while others still are to be observed (the injunction against murder). It is best to reflect on individual laws on a case-by-case basis to know their significance for today. What is obvious, however, is that people today are no more able to perfectly keep God's law than they were during the period of the Old Testament. Indeed, according to the New Testament, there is only one person who has fully heeded Moses' call to obedience, and that is Jesus Christ.

We learn this in the story of the wilderness temptations. In Matt 4:1–11, we see that after his baptism Jesus went into the wilderness for forty days and nights. The setting and time are intentionally reminiscent of Israel's forty years in the wilderness. This impression is heightened when we read that Jesus faced three temptations at the hand of the devil. These temptations are the same as those faced by the wilderness generation: hunger, testing God, and worshiping false gods to gain power. In all three cases, Jesus proves himself obedient. Strikingly, in resisting these temptations Jesus quotes Deuteronomy (8:3; 6:16; 6:13). In this way he shows, as the only obedient son of God, precisely where the Israelites were disobedient and brought on themselves the curses of the covenant.

In conclusion, Christians read Deuteronomy in part to see how God worked among his people in antiquity, but also to hear an expression of God's will for behavior today. The latter is not an easy procedure, since the law does not apply to Christians in precisely the same way it applied to Israelites at the time it was written. Perhaps most important, though, the book shows us how we all fall short and deserve God's judgment. All but one, that is. Jesus shows himself to be God-with-us—the one who hears and obeys the book of Deuteronomy.

—*Tremper Longman III*

Events at Horeb Recalled

1 These are the words that Moses spoke to all Israel beyond the Jordan—in the wilderness, on the plain opposite Suph, between Paran and Tophel, Laban, Hazeroth, and Di-zahab. [2](By the way of Mount Seir it takes eleven days to reach Kadesh-barnea from Horeb.) [3]In the fortieth year, on the first day of the eleventh month, Moses spoke to the Israelites just as the LORD had commanded him to speak to them. [4]This was after he had defeated King Sihon of the Amorites, who reigned in Heshbon, and King Og of Bashan, who reigned in Ashtaroth and[a] in Edrei. [5]Beyond the Jordan in the land of Moab, Moses undertook to expound this law as follows:

6 The LORD our God spoke to us at Horeb, saying, "You have stayed long enough at this mountain. [7]Resume your journey, and go into the hill country of the Amorites as well as into the neighboring regions—the Arabah, the hill country, the Shephelah, the Negeb, and the seacoast—the land of the Canaanites and the Lebanon, as far as the great river, the river Euphrates. [8]See, I have set the land before you; go in and take possession of the land that I[b] swore to your ancestors, to Abraham, to Isaac, and to Jacob, to give to them and to their descendants after them."

a Gk Syr Vg Compare Josh 12.4: Heb lacks *and*
b Sam Gk: MT *the* LORD

Appointment of Tribal Leaders

9 At that time I said to you, "I am unable by myself to bear you. ¹⁰The LORD your God has multiplied you, so that today you are as numerous as the stars of heaven. ¹¹May the LORD, the God of your ancestors, increase you a thousand times more and bless you, as he has promised you! ¹²But how can I bear the heavy burden of your disputes all by myself? ¹³Choose for each of your tribes individuals who are wise, discerning, and reputable to be your leaders." ¹⁴You answered me, "The plan you have proposed is a good one." ¹⁵So I took the leaders of your tribes, wise and reputable individuals, and installed them as leaders over you, commanders of thousands, commanders of hundreds, commanders of fifties, commanders of tens, and officials, throughout your tribes. ¹⁶I charged your judges at that time: "Give the members of your community a fair hearing, and judge rightly between one person and another, whether citizen or resident alien. ¹⁷You must not be partial in judging: hear out the small and the great alike; you shall not be intimidated by anyone, for the judgment is God's. Any case that is too hard for you, bring to me, and I will hear it." ¹⁸So I charged you at that time with all the things that you should do.

Israel's Refusal to Enter the Land

19 Then, just as the LORD our God had ordered us, we set out from Horeb and went through all that great and terrible wilderness that you saw, on the way to the hill country of the Amorites, until we reached Kadesh-barnea. ²⁰I said to you, "You have reached the hill country of the Amorites, which the LORD our God is giving us. ²¹See, the LORD your God has given the land to you; go up, take possession, as the LORD, the God of your ancestors, has promised you; do not fear or be dismayed."

22 All of you came to me and said, "Let us send men ahead of us to explore the land for us and bring back a report to us regarding the route by which we should go up and the cities we will come to." ²³The plan seemed good to me, and I selected twelve of you, one from each tribe. ²⁴They set out and went up into the hill country, and when they reached the Valley of Eshcol they spied it out ²⁵and gathered some of the land's produce, which they brought down to us. They brought back a report to us, and said, "It is a good land that the LORD our God is giving us."

26 But you were unwilling to go up. You rebelled against the command of the LORD your God; ²⁷you grumbled in your tents and said, "It is because the LORD hates us that he has brought us out of the land of Egypt, to hand us over to the Amorites to destroy us. ²⁸Where are we headed? Our kindred have made our hearts melt by reporting, 'The people are stronger and taller than we; the cities are large and fortified up to heaven! We ac-

---

1:8 *I swore . . . to Abraham.* Centuries ago God promised Abraham that his descendants would become a great nation (Gen 12:1–3). This promise entails the possession of land, the land to which God sent Abraham. But Abraham never actually took possession of the land, at least no more of it than a grave site (Gen 23). But the moment of the fulfillment of the promise has come. Imagine the excitement of the people. As members of the new covenant we too have been given divine promises that we will enter the fullness of God's kingdom. Reading about the fulfillment of God's centuries-old promise to Abraham encourages us in the time between promise and fulfillment.

1:17 *You must not be partial in judging.* Here and throughout the book, Deuteronomy emphasizes fairness and justice in dealings between people. In a day when it often seems like the wealthy can manipulate the law to their own advantage, this theme is a healthy reminder to us and to our leaders that it is justice that must determine our attitudes and behavior.

1:27 *you grumbled in your tents.* God had promised the people that he would take care of them and bring them into the Promised Land. However, faced with threats, they immediately lost faith and turned against God. Life today is also full of obstacles to faith. Often it doesn't seem as if God takes good care of us or is in control of our lives. These are the moments that we too are tempted to grumble against the Lord rather than respond in confidence.

tually saw there the offspring of the Anakim!' " [29]I said to you, "Have no dread or fear of them. [30]The LORD your God, who goes before you, is the one who will fight for you, just as he did for you in Egypt before your very eyes, [31]and in the wilderness, where you saw how the LORD your God carried you, just as one carries a child, all the way that you traveled until you reached this place. [32]But in spite of this, you have no trust in the LORD your God, [33]who goes before you on the way to seek out a place for you to camp, in fire by night, and in the cloud by day, to show you the route you should take."

The Penalty for Israel's Rebellion

[34] When the LORD heard your words, he was wrathful and swore: [35]"Not one of these—not one of this evil generation—shall see the good land that I swore to give to your ancestors, [36]except Caleb son of Jephunneh. He shall see it, and to him and to his descendants I will give the land on which he set foot, because of his complete fidelity to the LORD." [37]Even with me the LORD was angry on your account, saying, "You also shall not enter there. [38]Joshua son of Nun, your assistant, shall enter there; encourage him, for he is the one who will secure Israel's possession of it. [39]And as for your little ones, who you thought would become booty, your children, who today do not yet know right from wrong, they shall enter there; to them I will give it, and they shall take possession of it. [40]But as for you, journey back into the wilderness, in the direction of the Red Sea." [a]

[41] You answered me, "We have sinned against the LORD! We are ready to go up and fight, just as the LORD our God commanded us." So all of you strapped on your battle gear, and thought it easy to go up into the hill country. [42]The LORD said to me, "Say to them, 'Do not go up and do not fight, for I am not in the midst of you; otherwise you will be defeated by your enemies.' " [43]Although I told you, you would not listen. You rebelled against the command of the LORD and presumptuously went up into the hill country. [44]The Amorites who lived in that hill country then came out against you and chased you as bees do. They beat you down in Seir as far as Hormah. [45]When you returned and wept before the LORD, the LORD would neither heed your voice nor pay you any attention.

The Desert Years

[46] After you had stayed at Kadesh as many days as you did, [1]we journeyed back into the wilderness, in the direction of the Red Sea, [a] as the LORD had told me and skirted Mount Seir for many days. [2]Then the LORD said to me: [3]"You have been skirting this hill country long enough. Head north, [4]and charge the people as follows: You are about to pass through the territory of your kindred, the descendants of Esau, who live in Seir. They will be afraid of you, so, be very careful [5]not to engage in battle with them, for I will not give you even so much as a foot's length of their land, since I have given Mount Seir to Esau as a possession. [6]You shall purchase food from them for money, so that you may eat; and you shall also buy water from them for money, so that you may drink. [7]Surely the LORD your God has blessed you in all your undertakings; he knows your going through this great wilderness. These forty years the LORD your God has been with you; you have lacked nothing." [8]So we passed by our kin, the descendants of Esau who live in Seir, leaving behind the route of the Arabah, and leaving behind Elath and Ezion-geber.

When we had headed out along the route of the wilderness of Moab, [9]the LORD said to me: "Do not harass Moab or engage them in

a Or *Sea of Reeds*

2:5 *I have given Mount Seir to Esau.* A surface reading of the Old Testament makes one think that God was for Israel and against all the other nations. We forget that God chose Abraham so he could be a blessing to the nations (Gen 12:1–3). Although Esau and his descendants were not the conduit through which God would effect his work of redemption, Genesis is careful to inform readers that God cared and made provision for Esau (Gen 36), Ishmael (Gen 21:8–20), and their descendants.

battle, for I will not give you any of its land as a possession, since I have given Ar as a possession to the descendants of Lot." 10(The Emim—a large and numerous people, as tall as the Anakim—had formerly inhabited it. 11Like the Anakim, they are usually reckoned as Rephaim, though the Moabites call them Emim. 12Moreover, the Horim had formerly inhabited Seir, but the descendants of Esau dispossessed them, destroying them and settling in their place, as Israel has done in the land that the LORD gave them as a possession.) 13"Now then, proceed to cross over the Wadi Zered."

So we crossed over the Wadi Zered. 14And the length of time we had traveled from Kadesh-barnea until we crossed the Wadi Zered was thirty-eight years, until the entire generation of warriors had perished from the camp, as the LORD had sworn concerning them. 15Indeed, the LORD's own hand was against them, to root them out from the camp, until all had perished.

16 Just as soon as all the warriors had died off from among the people, 17the LORD spoke to me, saying, 18"Today you are going to cross the boundary of Moab at Ar. 19When you approach the frontier of the Ammonites, do not harass them or engage them in battle, for I will not give the land of the Ammonites to you as a possession, because I have given it to the descendants of Lot." 20(It also is usually reckoned as a land of Rephaim. Rephaim formerly inhabited it, though the Ammonites call them Zamzummim, 21a strong and numerous people, as tall as the Anakim. But the LORD destroyed them from before the Ammonites so that they could dispossess them and settle in their place. 22He did the same for the descendants of Esau, who live in Seir, by destroying the Horim before them so that they could dispossess them and settle in their place even to this day. 23As for the Avvim, who had lived in settlements in the vicinity

of Gaza, the Caphtorim, who came from Caphtor, destroyed them and settled in their place.) 24"Proceed on your journey and cross the Wadi Arnon. See, I have handed over to you King Sihon the Amorite of Heshbon, and his land. Begin to take possession by engaging him in battle. 25This day I will begin to put the dread and fear of you upon the peoples everywhere under heaven; when they hear report of you, they will tremble and be in anguish because of you."

Defeat of King Sihon

26 So I sent messengers from the wilderness of Kedemoth to King Sihon of Heshbon with the following terms of peace: 27"If you let me pass through your land, I will travel only along the road; I will turn aside neither to the right nor to the left. 28You shall sell me food for money, so that I may eat, and supply me water for money, so that I may drink. Only allow me to pass through on foot— 29just as the descendants of Esau who live in Seir have done for me and likewise the Moabites who live in Ar—until I cross the Jordan into the land that the LORD our God is giving us." 30But King Sihon of Heshbon was not willing to let us pass through, for the LORD your God had hardened his spirit and made his heart defiant in order to hand him over to you, as he has now done.

31 The LORD said to me, "See, I have begun to give Sihon and his land over to you. Begin now to take possession of his land." 32So when Sihon came out against us, he and all his people for battle at Jahaz, 33the LORD our God gave him over to us; and we struck him down, along with his offspring and all his people. 34At that time we captured all his towns, and in each town we utterly destroyed men, women, and children. We left not a single survivor. 35Only the livestock we kept as spoil for ourselves, as well as the plunder of the towns that we had captured. 36From

---

2:33 the LORD our God gave [Sihon] over to us. Victory comes from the Lord. In this case, he not only gave the Israelites military success, but the text also suggests that the Lord hardened Sihon's disposition to fight against them in the first place (v 30). God's people today do not engage in military conquests to advance the cause of the Church; such an idea is repugnant. However, the New Testament understands that we are in the midst of conflict, a spiritual battle, and God still is in the business of giving his people the resources to withstand the onslaught (Eph 6:10–20).

Aroer on the edge of the Wadi Arnon (including the town that is in the wadi itself) as far as Gilead, there was no citadel too high for us. The LORD our God gave everything to us. 37You did not encroach, however, on the land of the Ammonites, avoiding the whole upper region of the Wadi Jabbok as well as the towns of the hill country, just as*a* the LORD our God had charged.

Defeat of King Og

3 When we headed up the road to Bashan, King Og of Bashan came out against us, he and all his people, for battle at Edrei. 2The LORD said to me, "Do not fear him, for I have handed him over to you, along with his people and his land. Do to him as you did to King Sihon of the Amorites, who reigned in Heshbon." 3So the LORD our God also handed over to us King Og of Bashan and all his people. We struck him down until not a single survivor was left. 4At that time we captured all his towns; there was no citadel that we did not take from them—sixty towns, the whole region of Argob, the kingdom of Og in Bashan. 5All these were fortress towns with high walls, double gates, and bars, besides a great many villages. 6And we utterly destroyed them, as we had done to King Sihon of Heshbon, in each city utterly destroying men, women, and children. 7But all the livestock and the plunder of the towns we kept as spoil for ourselves.

8 So at that time we took from the two kings of the Amorites the land beyond the Jordan, from the Wadi Arnon to Mount Hermon 9(the Sidonians call Hermon Sirion, while the Amorites call it Senir), 10all the towns of the tableland, the whole of Gilead, and all of Bashan, as far as Salecah and Edrei, towns of Og's kingdom in Bashan. 11(Now only King Og of Bashan was left of the remnant of the Rephaim. In fact his bed, an iron bed, can still be seen in Rabbah of the Ammonites. By the common cubit it is nine cu-

bits long and four cubits wide.) 12As for the land that we took possession of at that time, I gave to the Reubenites and Gadites the territory north of Aroer,*b* that is on the edge of the Wadi Arnon, as well as half the hill country of Gilead with its towns, 13and I gave to the half-tribe of Manasseh the rest of Gilead and all of Bashan, Og's kingdom. (The whole region of Argob: all that portion of Bashan used to be called a land of Rephaim; 14Jair the Manassite acquired the whole region of Argob as far as the border of the Geshurites and the Maacathites, and he named them—that is, Bashan—after himself, Havvoth-jair,*c* as it is to this day.) 15To Machir I gave Gilead. 16And to the Reubenites and the Gadites I gave the territory from Gilead as far as the Wadi Arnon, with the middle of the wadi as a boundary, and up to the Jabbok, the wadi being boundary of the Ammonites; 17the Arabah also, with the Jordan and its banks, from Chinnereth down to the sea of the Arabah, the Dead Sea,*d* with the lower slopes of Pisgah on the east.

18 At that time, I charged you as follows: "Although the LORD your God has given you this land to occupy, all your troops shall cross over armed as the vanguard of your Israelite kin. 19Only your wives, your children, and your livestock—I know that you have much livestock—shall stay behind in the towns that I have given to you. 20When the LORD gives rest to your kindred, as to you, and they too have occupied the land that the LORD your God is giving them beyond the Jordan, then each of you may return to the property that I have given to you." 21And I charged Joshua as well at that time, saying: "Your own eyes have seen everything that the LORD your God has done to these two kings; so the LORD will do to all the kingdoms into which you are

a Gk Tg: Heb *and all*   *b* Heb *territory from Aroer*
c That is *Settlement of Jair*   *d* Heb *Salt Sea*

3:18 *all your troops shall cross over armed as the vanguard.* The Reubenites, Gadites, and half-tribe of Manasseh benefited from the victories over the kings Sihon and Og in the Transjordan. They received their tribal allotment even before Israel crossed the Jordan River (vv 8–17). However, they were not relieved of their duty to help the community as a whole (vv 18–20). God's people stand together in their struggle against the forces of evil.

about to cross. 22Do not fear them, for it is the LORD your God who fights for you."

Moses Views Canaan from Pisgah

23 At that time, too, I entreated the LORD, saying: 24"O Lord GOD, you have only begun to show your servant your greatness and your might; what god in heaven or on earth can perform deeds and mighty acts like yours! 25Let me cross over to see the good land beyond the Jordan, that good hill country and the Lebanon." 26But the LORD was angry with me on your account and would not heed me. The LORD said to me, "Enough from you! Never speak to me of this matter again! 27Go up to the top of Pisgah and look around you to the west, to the north, to the south, and to the east. Look well, for you shall not cross over this Jordan. 28But charge Joshua, and encourage and strengthen him, because it is he who shall cross over at the head of this people and who shall secure their possession of the land that you will see." 29So we remained in the valley opposite Beth-peor.

Moses Commands Obedience

4 So now, Israel, give heed to the statutes and ordinances that I am teaching you to observe, so that you may live to enter and occupy the land that the LORD, the God of your ancestors, is giving you. 2You must neither add anything to what I command you nor take away anything from it, but keep the commandments of the LORD your God with which I am charging you. 3You have seen for yourselves what the LORD did with regard to

the Baal of Peor—how the LORD your God destroyed from among you everyone who followed the Baal of Peor, 4while those of you who held fast to the LORD your God are all alive today.

5 See, just as the LORD my God has charged me, I now teach you statutes and ordinances for you to observe in the land that you are about to enter and occupy. 6You must observe them diligently, for this will show your wisdom and discernment to the peoples, who, when they hear all these statutes, will say, "Surely this great nation is a wise and discerning people!" 7For what other great nation has a god so near to it as the LORD our God is whenever we call to him? 8And what other great nation has statutes and ordinances as just as this entire law that I am setting before you today?

9 But take care and watch yourselves closely, so as neither to forget the things that your eyes have seen nor to let them slip from your mind all the days of your life; make them known to your children and your children's children— 10how you once stood before the LORD your God at Horeb, when the LORD said to me, "Assemble the people for me, and I will let them hear my words, so that they may learn to fear me as long as they live on the earth, and may teach their children so"; 11you approached and stood at the foot of the mountain while the mountain was blazing up to the very heavens, shrouded in dark clouds. 12Then the LORD spoke to you out of the fire. You heard the sound of words but saw no form; there was only a voice. 13He de-

---

Responding
3:24 SERVICE. Moses describes himself as a servant of God. In what ways did Moses serve God? In what ways can we serve God? Name as many as you can. *See also* Spiritual Disciplines Index.

4:2 *neither add anything . . . nor take away anything.* The vast bulk of Deuteronomy records God's will for his people in the form of the law. Before the law is given, Moses warns Israel not to add or take away from the law. The latter we do by simply disobeying the law, while the former is a more subtle problem because we can

do it with the best intentions. We don't want to offend God by having premarital sex, so we prohibit dancing. We don't want to transgress by getting drunk, so we ban drinking. We don't want to take God's name in vain, so we never speak God's name. Such fencing of the law with legalism is as offensive to God as breaking it.

4:6 *this will show your wisdom.* Wisdom is the ability to navigate life well, that is, to live in conformity with the rhythms of creation. God is the author of creation, and he also expressed his will for our lives in the law. Following the law is best for us in the long run and will demonstrate to others our discernment.

clared to you his covenant, which he charged you to observe, that is, the ten commandments;*a* and he wrote them on two stone tablets. [14]And the LORD charged me at that time to teach you statutes and ordinances for you to observe in the land that you are about to cross into and occupy.

15 Since you saw no form when the LORD spoke to you at Horeb out of the fire, take care and watch yourselves closely, [16]so that you do not act corruptly by making an idol for yourselves, in the form of any figure— the likeness of male or female, [17]the likeness of any animal that is on the earth, the likeness of any winged bird that flies in the air, [18]the likeness of anything that creeps on the ground, the likeness of any fish that is in the water under the earth. [19]And when you look up to the heavens and see the sun, the moon, and the stars, all the host of heaven, do not be led astray and bow down to them and serve them, things that the LORD your God has allotted to all the peoples everywhere under heaven. [20]But the LORD has taken you and brought you out of the iron-smelter, out of Egypt, to become a people of his very own possession, as you are now.

21 The LORD was angry with me because of you, and he vowed that I should not cross the Jordan and that I should not enter the good land that the LORD your God is giving for your possession. [22]For I am going to die in this land without crossing over the Jordan, but you are going to cross over to take possession of that good land. [23]So be careful not to forget the covenant that the LORD your God made with you, and not to make for yourselves an idol in the form of anything that the LORD your God has forbidden you. [24]For the LORD your God is a devouring fire, a jealous God.

25 When you have had children and children's children, and become complacent in the land, if you act corruptly by making an idol in the form of anything, thus doing what is evil in the sight of the LORD your God, and provoking him to anger, [26]I call heaven and earth to witness against you today that you will soon utterly perish from the land that you are crossing the Jordan to occupy; you will not live long on it, but will be utterly destroyed. [27]The LORD will scatter you among the peoples; only a few of you will be left among the nations where the LORD will lead you. [28]There you will serve other gods made by human hands, objects of wood and stone that neither see, nor hear, nor eat, nor smell. [29]From there you will seek the LORD your God, and you will find him if you search after him with all your heart and soul. [30]In your distress, when all these things have happened to you in time to come, you will return to the LORD your God and heed him. [31]Because the LORD your God is a merciful God, he will neither abandon you nor destroy you; he will not forget the covenant with your ancestors that he swore to them.

32 For ask now about former ages, long before your own, ever since the day that God created human beings on the earth; ask from one end of heaven to the other: has anything so great as this ever happened or has its like ever been heard of? [33]Has any people ever heard the voice of a god speaking out of a fire, as you have heard, and lived? [34]Or has any god ever attempted to go and take a nation for himself from the midst of another nation, by trials, by signs and wonders, by war, by a mighty hand and an outstretched arm, and by terrifying displays of power, as the LORD your God did for you in Egypt before your very eyes? [35]To you it was shown so that you would acknowledge that the LORD is God; there is no other besides him. [36]From heaven he made you hear his voice to discipline you.

a Heb *the ten words*

4:16 *by making an idol.* The Lord is not visible, nor is he a part of the creation. Thus, it is a perversion to create an image of God in the form of a creature and then worship that image. Such behavior is nothing more than trying to control God. The prohibition against idolatry keeps us from false worship. Today idolatry may be much more subtle. Instead of making an image in the form of an animal, we may worship an abstraction such as power or wealth by making it the most important thing in our lives. Treating an idol as a god will always let us down and lead to frustration.

On earth he showed you his great fire, while you heard his words coming out of the fire. [37]And because he loved your ancestors, he chose their descendants after them. He brought you out of Egypt with his own presence, by his great power, [38]driving out before you nations greater and mightier than yourselves, to bring you in, giving you their land for a possession, as it is still today. [39]So acknowledge today and take to heart that the LORD is God in heaven above and on the earth beneath; there is no other. [40]Keep his statutes and his commandments, which I am commanding you today for your own well-being and that of your descendants after you, so that you may long remain in the land that the LORD your God is giving you for all time.

Cities of Refuge East of the Jordan

41 Then Moses set apart on the east side of the Jordan three cities [42]to which a homicide could flee, someone who unintentionally kills another person, the two not having been at enmity before; the homicide could flee to one of these cities and live: [43]Bezer in the wilderness on the tableland belonging to the Reubenites, Ramoth in Gilead belonging to the Gadites, and Golan in Bashan belonging to the Manassites.

Transition to the Second Address

44 This is the law that Moses set before the Israelites. [45]These are the decrees and the statutes and ordinances that Moses spoke to the Israelites when they had come out of Egypt,

[46]beyond the Jordan in the valley opposite Beth-peor, in the land of King Sihon of the Amorites, who reigned at Heshbon, whom Moses and the Israelites defeated when they came out of Egypt. [47]They occupied his land and the land of King Og of Bashan, the two kings of the Amorites on the eastern side of the Jordan: [48]from Aroer, which is on the edge of the Wadi Arnon, as far as Mount Sirion[a] (that is, Hermon), [49]together with all the Arabah on the east side of the Jordan as far as the Sea of the Arabah, under the slopes of Pisgah.

The Ten Commandments

5 Moses convened all Israel, and said to them:

Hear, O Israel, the statutes and ordinances that I am addressing to you today; you shall learn them and observe them diligently. [2]The LORD our God made a covenant with us at Horeb. [3]Not with our ancestors did the LORD make this covenant, but with us, who are all of us here alive today. [4]The LORD spoke with you face to face at the mountain, out of the fire. [5](At that time I was standing between the LORD and you to declare to you the words[b] of the LORD; for you were afraid because of the fire and did not go up the mountain.) And he said:

6 I am the LORD your God, who brought you out of the land of Egypt, out of the house of slavery; [7]you shall have no other gods before[c] me.

a Syr: Heb *Sion*   b Q Mss Sam Gk Syr Vg Tg: MT *word*   c Or *besides*

5:3 *Not with our ancestors . . . but with us.* The covenant at Horeb (v 2) refers to the covenant established at Mt. Sinai (the more common name of Horeb) recorded in Exodus 19–24. The people assembled before Moses on the plains of Moab are the second generation of those who wandered in the wilderness, some of whom may have been young at the time of Sinai, but many of whom were not yet born. There is thus a connection between the Mosaic covenant given at Horeb and this "second law" (Deuteronomy). As we read on, we see that this is no mere repetition of the law, but a reshaping of it to conform to the new social conditions of the people once they settle in the land.

5:6 *who brought you out of the land of Egypt.* Grace precedes the law in Deuteronomy. Israel does not establish its relationship with God by keeping the Ten Commandments; rather, keeping the commandments is an expression of gratitude for the things that God has already done and a means for maintaining a healthy relationship with God. The principle that it is grace and not our own good behavior that is the basis of our relationship with God runs throughout the biblical text (see Rom 4).

5:7 *no other gods before me.* The foundation of the Ten Commandments is a commitment to worship only the Lord. The expression of the command does not even definitively rule out

8 You shall not make for yourself an idol, whether in the form of anything that is in heaven above, or that is on the earth beneath, or that is in the water under the earth. 9You shall not bow down to them or worship them; for I the LORD your God am a jealous God, punishing children for the iniquity of parents, to the third and fourth generation of those who reject me, 10but showing steadfast love to the thousandth generation*a* of those who love me and keep my commandments.

11 You shall not make wrongful use of the name of the LORD your God, for the LORD will not acquit anyone who misuses his name.

12 Observe the sabbath day and keep it holy, as the LORD your God commanded you. 13Six days you shall labor and do all your work. 14But the seventh day is a sabbath to the LORD your God; you shall not do any work—you, or your son or your daughter, or your male or female slave, or your ox or your donkey, or any of your livestock, or the resident alien in your towns, so that your male and female slave may rest as well as you. 15Remember that you were a slave in the land of Egypt, and the LORD your God brought you out from there with a mighty hand and an outstretched arm; therefore the LORD your

God commanded you to keep the sabbath day.

16 Honor your father and your mother, as the LORD your God commanded you, so that your days may be long and that it may go well with you in the land that the LORD your God is giving you.

17 You shall not murder.*b*

18 Neither shall you commit adultery.

19 Neither shall you steal.

20 Neither shall you bear false witness against your neighbor.

21 Neither shall you covet your neighbor's wife.

Neither shall you desire your neighbor's house, or field, or male or female slave, or ox, or donkey, or anything that belongs to your neighbor.

Moses the Mediator of God's Will

22 These words the LORD spoke with a loud voice to your whole assembly at the mountain, out of the fire, the cloud, and the thick darkness, and he added no more. He wrote them on two stone tablets, and gave them to me. 23When you heard the voice out of the darkness, while the mountain was burning with fire, you approached me, all the

a Or *to thousands*   *b* Or *kill*

the existence of other gods, but the important thing for Israel to note is that there is only one God that matters and that is the Lord, and it is only to him that worship should be directed.

5:8 *You shall not make . . . an idol.* See note on 4:16.

5:12 *observe the sabbath day.* In the Old Testament, Sabbath means "cessation" and refers to stopping regular work on the last day of the week. Most Christians observe the Sabbath on the first day of the week in what appears to be conformity with early church practice (Acts 20:7; 1 Cor 16:2) and in recognition that Christ's work of redemption on the cross has been accomplished. How the Sabbath is observed today is the subject of debate among Christians, but ceasing from work one day a week puts us in touch with the pattern of God's creation (Exod 20:11) and recollection of our redemption (Deut 5:15).

5:16 *Honor your father and your mother.* Thus begins the second part of the Ten Words, the final six commandments (vv 16–21). The first four commandments (vv 6–15) regulate our relationship with God; these six concern our relationship to other human beings.

5:21 *Neither shall you covet.* The tenth commandment renders the others internal and leads to the teaching of Jesus in the Sermon on the Mount (Matt 5–7). The commandments not to murder, commit adultery, and steal focus on external behavior, not attitude, but mention of coveting internalizes all of these requirements. Not only are we not to murder, but we shouldn't even want to take another person's life (we shouldn't hate). Not only are we not to steal or commit adultery, but we shouldn't desire another person's possessions or spouse (we shouldn't lust).

heads of your tribes and your elders; 24and you said, "Look, the LORD our God has shown us his glory and greatness, and we have heard his voice out of the fire. Today we have seen that God may speak to someone and the person may still live. 25So now why should we die? For this great fire will consume us; if we hear the voice of the LORD our God any longer, we shall die. 26For who is there of all flesh that has heard the voice of the living God speaking out of fire, as we have, and remained alive? 27Go near, you yourself, and hear all that the LORD our God will say. Then tell us everything that the LORD our God tells you, and we will listen and do it."

28 The LORD heard your words when you spoke to me, and the LORD said to me: "I have heard the words of this people, which they have spoken to you; they are right in all that they have spoken. 29If only they had such a mind as this, to fear me and to keep all my commandments always, so that it might go well with them and with their children forever! 30Go say to them, 'Return to your tents.' 31But you, stand here by me, and I will tell you all the commandments, the statutes and the ordinances, that you shall teach them, so that they may do them in the land that I am giving them to possess." 32You must therefore be careful to do as the LORD your God has commanded you; you shall not turn to the right or to the left. 33You must follow exactly the path that the LORD your God has commanded you, so that you may live, and that it may go well with you, and that you may live long in the land that you are to possess.

The Great Commandment

6 Now this is the commandment—the statutes and the ordinances—that the LORD your God charged me to teach you to observe in the land that you are about to cross into and occupy, 2so that you and your children and your children's children may fear the LORD your God all the days of your life, and keep all his decrees and his commandments that I am commanding you, so that your days may be long. 3Hear therefore, O Israel, and observe them diligently, so that it may go well with you, and so that you may multiply greatly in a land flowing with milk and honey, as the LORD, the God of your ancestors, has promised you.

4 Hear, O Israel: The LORD is our God, the LORD alone. *a* 5You shall love the LORD your God with all your heart, and with all your soul, and with all your might. 6Keep these words that I am commanding you today in your heart. 7Recite them to your children and talk about them when you are at home and when you are away, when you lie down and when you rise. 8Bind them as a sign on your hand, fix them as an emblem *b* on your forehead, 9and write them on the doorposts of your house and on your gates.

Caution against Disobedience

10 When the LORD your God has brought you into the land that he swore to your ancestors, to Abraham, to Isaac, and to Jacob, to give you—a land with fine, large cities that you did not build, 11houses filled with all sorts of goods that you did not fill, hewn cisterns that you did not hew, vineyards and olive groves that you did not plant—and when you have eaten your fill, 12take care that you do not forget the LORD, who brought you out of the land of Egypt, out of the house of slavery. 13The LORD your God you shall fear; him you shall serve, and by his name alone you shall swear. 14Do not follow other gods, any of the gods of the peoples who are all around you, 15because the LORD your God, who is present with you, is a jealous God. The anger of the LORD your God would be

a Or *The* LORD *our God is one* LORD, or *The* LORD *our God, the* LORD *is one,* or *The* LORD *is our God, the* LORD *is one*   *b* Or *as a frontlet*

6:4 *Hear, O Israel.* Thus begins the Shema, an assertion of passionate and exclusive commitment to believe and obey the Lord. The Shema is a confession of the heart of Israelite faith and is repeated by Jesus, who calls this "the greatest and first commandment," to be followed by the second, "You shall love your neighbor as yourself" (see Matt 22:34–40). Our faith today begins with our response to the love of God, which elicits our love of others.

kindled against you and he would destroy you from the face of the earth.

16 Do not put the LORD your God to the test, as you tested him at Massah. [17]You must diligently keep the commandments of the LORD your God, and his decrees, and his statutes that he has commanded you. [18]Do what is right and good in the sight of the LORD, so that it may go well with you, and so that you may go in and occupy the good land that the LORD swore to your ancestors to give you, [19]thrusting out all your enemies from before you, as the LORD has promised.

20 When your children ask you in time to come, "What is the meaning of the decrees and the statutes and the ordinances that the LORD our God has commanded you?" [21]then you shall say to your children, "We were Pharaoh's slaves in Egypt, but the LORD brought us out of Egypt with a mighty hand. [22]The LORD displayed before our eyes great and awesome signs and wonders against Egypt, against Pharaoh and all his household. [23]He brought us out from there in order to bring us in, to give us the land that he promised on oath to our ancestors. [24]Then the LORD commanded us to observe all these statutes, to fear the LORD our God, for our lasting good, so as to keep us alive, as is now the case. [25]If we diligently observe this entire commandment before the LORD our God, as he has commanded us, we will be in the right."

A Chosen People

7 When the LORD your God brings you into the land that you are about to enter and occupy, and he clears away many nations before you—the Hittites, the Girgashites, the Amorites, the Canaanites, the Perizzites, the Hivites, and the Jebusites, seven nations mightier and more numerous than you— [2]and when the LORD your God gives them over to you and you defeat them, then you must utterly destroy them. Make no covenant with them and show them no mercy. [3]Do not intermarry with them, giving your daughters to their sons or taking their daughters for your sons, [4]for that would turn away your children from following me, to serve other gods. Then the anger of the LORD would be kindled against you, and he would destroy you quickly. [5]But this is how you must deal with them: break down their altars, smash their pillars, hew down their sacred poles,[a] and burn their idols with fire. [6]For you are a people holy to the LORD your God; the LORD your God has chosen you out of all the peoples on earth to be his people, his treasured possession.

7 It was not because you were more numerous than any other people that the LORD set his heart on you and chose you—for you were the fewest of all peoples. [8]It was because the LORD loved you and kept the oath that he swore to your ancestors, that the LORD has brought you out with a mighty hand, and redeemed you from the house of slavery, from the hand of Pharaoh king of Egypt. [9]Know therefore that the LORD your God is God, the faithful God who maintains covenant loyalty with those who love him and keep his commandments, to a thousand generations, [10]and who repays in their own person those

a Heb Asherim

6:16 *Do not put the LORD your God to the test.* Our doubts tempt us to test God. We want to know he is there, and so we ask for him to do certain things to show us he cares. But Moses warns us all against the kind of skepticism that led to the situation at Massah, where the people insisted that God miraculously provide them with water (Exod 17:1–13). Moses warns the next generation not to test God in this way, and through them us. Jesus illustrates the proper attitude of faith that refuses to test God (Matt 4:1–11). Paul warns Christians not to test Jesus, because it shows a fundamental lack of faith in his saving action toward us (1 Cor 10:9).

7:7 *you were the fewest of all peoples.* God does not love Israel because it is strong, wise, numerous, or even more devout. Love does not have its reasons. Israel's special position and responsibility during the Old Testament period is a result of God's love, not Israel's character or ability. Realizing this should have led to humility. God's people today are called to this type of humility as well.

who reject him. He does not delay but repays in their own person those who reject him. [11]Therefore, observe diligently the commandment—the statutes and the ordinances—that I am commanding you today.

Blessings for Obedience

12 If you heed these ordinances, by diligently observing them, the LORD your God will maintain with you the covenant loyalty that he swore to your ancestors; [13]he will love you, bless you, and multiply you; he will bless the fruit of your womb and the fruit of your ground, your grain and your wine and your oil, the increase of your cattle and the issue of your flock, in the land that he swore to your ancestors to give you. [14]You shall be the most blessed of peoples, with neither sterility nor barrenness among you or your livestock. [15]The LORD will turn away from you every illness; all the dread diseases of Egypt that you experienced, he will not inflict on you, but he will lay them on all who hate you. [16]You shall devour all the peoples that the LORD your God is giving over to you, showing them no pity; you shall not serve their gods, for that would be a snare to you.

17 If you say to yourself, "These nations are more numerous than I; how can I dispossess them?" [18]do not be afraid of them. Just remember what the LORD your God did to Pharaoh and to all Egypt, [19]the great trials that your eyes saw, the signs and wonders, the mighty hand and the outstretched arm by which the LORD your God brought you out. The LORD your God will do the same to all the peoples of whom you are afraid. [20]Moreover, the LORD your God will send the pestilence[a] against them, until even the survivors and the fugitives are destroyed. [21]Have no dread of them, for the LORD your God, who is present with you, is a great and awesome God. [22]The LORD your God will clear away these nations before you little by little; you will not be able to make a quick end of them, otherwise the wild animals would become too numerous for you. [23]But the LORD your God will give them over to you, and throw them into great panic, until they are destroyed. [24]He will hand their kings over to you and you shall blot out their name from under heaven; no one will be able to stand against you, until you have destroyed them. [25]The images of their gods you shall burn with fire. Do not covet the silver or the gold that is on them and take it for yourself, because you could be ensnared by it; for it is abhorrent to the LORD your God. [26]Do not bring an abhorrent thing into your house, or you will be set apart for destruction like it. You must utterly detest and abhor it, for it is set apart for destruction.

A Warning Not to Forget God in Prosperity

8 This entire commandment that I command you today you must diligently observe, so that you may live and increase, and go in and occupy the land that the LORD promised on oath to your ancestors. [2]Remember the long way that the LORD your God has led you these forty years in the wilderness, in order to humble you, testing you to know what was in your heart, whether or not you would keep his commandments. [3]He humbled you by letting you hunger, then by feeding you with manna, with which nei-

a Or hornets: Meaning of Heb uncertain

7:23 *your God will give them over to you.* The people of Israel are about to enter the land and go to war against its inhabitants. They will win great battles, but when they do, they must realize that the victory is won not by their power, but because God goes before them. They need to respond by worshiping the Lord alone and not idols. Today we have the tendency to think that things such as money and political power are the key to success, but the Bible requires us to think otherwise.

Whatever successes the idols of money and power bring are short-lived and unimportant.
   8:2–5 THE WITH-GOD LIFE—*See* Spiritual Disciplines Index.

Responding
   8:3 FASTING. In this verse we learn that God imposed fasting on the Israelites. He then provided them with manna, a food they did not recognize, in order to teach them that life consisted of more than satisfying

ther you nor your ancestors were acquainted, in order to make you understand that one does not live by bread alone, but by every word that comes from the mouth of the LORD.*a* 4The clothes on your back did not wear out and your feet did not swell these forty years. 5Know then in your heart that as a parent disciplines a child so the LORD your God disciplines you. 6Therefore keep the commandments of the LORD your God, by walking in his ways and by fearing him. 7For the LORD your God is bringing you into a good land, a land with flowing streams, with springs and underground waters welling up in valleys and hills, 8a land of wheat and barley, of vines and fig trees and pomegranates, a land of olive trees and honey, 9a land where you may eat bread without scarcity, where you will lack nothing, a land whose stones are iron and from whose hills you may mine copper. 10You shall eat your fill and bless the LORD your God for the good land that he has given you.

11 Take care that you do not forget the LORD your God, by failing to keep his commandments, his ordinances, and his statutes, which I am commanding you today. 12When you have eaten your fill and have built fine houses and live in them, 13and when your herds and flocks have multiplied, and your silver and gold is multiplied, and all that you have is multiplied, 14then do not exalt yourself, forgetting the LORD your God, who brought you out of the land of Egypt, out of the house of slavery, 15who led you through the great and terrible wilderness, an arid wasteland with poisonous*b* snakes

and scorpions. He made water flow for you from flint rock, 16and fed you in the wilderness with manna that your ancestors did not know, to humble you and to test you, and in the end to do you good. 17Do not say to yourself, "My power and the might of my own hand have gotten me this wealth." 18But remember the LORD your God, for it is he who gives you power to get wealth, so that he may confirm his covenant that he swore to your ancestors, as he is doing today. 19If you do forget the LORD your God and follow other gods to serve and worship them, I solemnly warn you today that you shall surely perish. 20Like the nations that the LORD is destroying before you, so shall you perish, because you would not obey the voice of the LORD your God.

The Consequences of Rebelling against God

9 Hear, O Israel! You are about to cross the Jordan today, to go in and dispossess nations larger and mightier than you, great cities, fortified to the heavens, 2a strong and tall people, the offspring of the Anakim, whom you know. You have heard it said of them, "Who can stand up to the Anakim?" 3Know then today that the LORD your God is the one who crosses over before you as a devouring fire; he will defeat them and subdue them before you, so that you may dispossess and destroy them quickly, as the LORD has promised you.

a Or *by anything that the LORD decrees*   *b* Or *fiery;* Heb *seraph*

---

physical appetites, that they also had a spiritual hunger that only God could satisfy. Set aside one day this week and fast from solid food. During the time you would normally spend eating, feast on 1 Corinthians 13. *See also* Spiritual Disciplines Index.

8:12–18 *When you have eaten your fill.* Deuteronomy astutely warns its readers to beware of the complacency of success. God blesses us and we stop praying or caring about our relationship with God. We become self-sufficient. When life goes well, we forget God

because we think we don't need him. However, life is such that it isn't too long before our complacency lands us in trouble and we desperately seek God again (see also Ps 30).

8:14–18 **THE WITH-GOD LIFE**—*See* Spiritual Disciplines Index.

8:17 *My power and the might of my own hand have gotten me this wealth.* So speaks the doomed arrogance of those who mistake their own resources for the blessing of God. In the West today self-reliance is considered a virtue. Not so in the Bible, where the emphasis is on community in dependence upon God.

4 When the LORD your God thrusts them out before you, do not say to yourself, "It is because of my righteousness that the LORD has brought me in to occupy this land"; it is rather because of the wickedness of these nations that the LORD is dispossessing them before you. 5It is not because of your righteousness or the uprightness of your heart that you are going in to occupy their land; but because of the wickedness of these nations the LORD your God is dispossessing them before you, in order to fulfill the promise that the LORD made on oath to your ancestors, to Abraham, to Isaac, and to Jacob.

6 Know, then, that the LORD your God is not giving you this good land to occupy because of your righteousness; for you are a stubborn people. 7Remember and do not forget how you provoked the LORD your God to wrath in the wilderness; you have been rebellious against the LORD from the day you came out of the land of Egypt until you came to this place.

8 Even at Horeb you provoked the LORD to wrath, and the LORD was so angry with you that he was ready to destroy you. 9When I went up the mountain to receive the stone tablets, the tablets of the covenant that the LORD made with you, I remained on the mountain forty days and forty nights; I neither ate bread nor drank water. 10And the LORD gave me the two stone tablets written with the finger of God; on them were all the words that the LORD had spoken to you at the mountain out of the fire on the day of the assembly. 11At the end of forty days and forty nights the LORD gave me the two stone tablets, the tablets of the covenant. 12Then the LORD said to me, "Get up, go down quickly from here, for your people whom you have brought from Egypt have acted corruptly. They have

been quick to turn from the way that I commanded them; they have cast an image for themselves." 13Furthermore the LORD said to me, "I have seen that this people is indeed a stubborn people. 14Let me alone that I may destroy them and blot out their name from under heaven; and I will make of you a nation mightier and more numerous than they."

15 So I turned and went down from the mountain, while the mountain was ablaze; the two tablets of the covenant were in my two hands. 16Then I saw that you had indeed sinned against the LORD your God, by casting for yourselves an image of a calf; you had been quick to turn from the way that the LORD had commanded you. 17So I took hold of the two tablets and flung them from my two hands, smashing them before your eyes. 18Then I lay prostrate before the LORD as before, forty days and forty nights; I neither ate bread nor drank water, because of all the sin you had committed, provoking the LORD by doing what was evil in his sight. 19For I was afraid that the anger that the LORD bore against you was so fierce that he would destroy you. But the LORD listened to me that time also. 20The LORD was so angry with Aaron that he was ready to destroy him, but I interceded also on behalf of Aaron at that same time. 21Then I took the sinful thing you had made, the calf, and burned it with fire and crushed it, grinding it thoroughly, until it was reduced to dust; and I threw the dust of it into the stream that runs down the mountain.

22 At Taberah also, and at Massah, and at Kibroth-hattaavah, you provoked the LORD to wrath. 23And when the LORD sent you from Kadesh-barnea, saying, "Go up and occupy the land that I have given you," you rebelled against the command of the LORD your God,

---

9:10 *stone tablets written with the finger of God.* Although this expression is certainly a metaphor, it does not diminish the bold assertion of divine authority given to the content of the stone tablets. God is intimately tied to the Mosaic covenant and in particular the Ten Commandments.

9:19 *But the LORD listened to me.* God is sovereign and does not change his mind (Num 23:19; 1 Sam 15:29; Mal 3:6), but he is responsive

to our prayers. How are these two biblical truths reconciled? No more easily than we can harmonize the teaching on the divine and human natures of Christ or the three-in-one Trinity. The important thing to note in the present passage is that God hears prayer and responds to it. Moses interceded in prayer with the Lord, and Aaron was saved from destruction (v 20). That God listens to our prayers should be all the motivation we need to constantly speak with him.

neither trusting him nor obeying him. 24You have been rebellious against the LORD as long as he has*a* known you.

25 Throughout the forty days and forty nights that I lay prostrate before the LORD when the LORD intended to destroy you, 26I prayed to the LORD and said, "Lord GOD, do not destroy the people who are your very own possession, whom you redeemed in your greatness, whom you brought out of Egypt with a mighty hand. 27Remember your servants, Abraham, Isaac, and Jacob; pay no attention to the stubbornness of this people, their wickedness and their sin, 28otherwise the land from which you have brought us might say, 'Because the LORD was not able to bring them into the land that he promised them, and because he hated them, he has brought them out to let them die in the wilderness.' 29For they are the people of your very own possession, whom you brought out by your great power and by your outstretched arm."

The Second Pair of Tablets

10 At that time the LORD said to me, "Carve out two tablets of stone like the former ones, and come up to me on the mountain, and make an ark of wood. 2I will write on the tablets the words that were on the former tablets, which you smashed, and you shall put them in the ark." 3So I made an ark of acacia wood, cut two tablets of stone like the former ones, and went up the mountain with the two tablets in my hand. 4Then he wrote on the tablets the same words as before, the ten commandments*b* that the LORD had spoken to you on the mountain out of the fire on the day of the assembly; and the LORD gave them to me. 5So I turned and came down from the mountain, and put the tablets in the ark that I had made; and there they are, as the LORD commanded me.

6 (The Israelites journeyed from Beeroth-bene-jaakan*c* to Moserah. There Aaron died, and there he was buried; his son Eleazar succeeded him as priest. 7From there they journeyed to Gudgodah, and from Gudgodah to Jotbathah, a land with flowing streams. 8At that time the LORD set apart the tribe of Levi to carry the ark of the covenant of the LORD, to stand before the LORD to minister to him, and to bless in his name, to this day. 9Therefore Levi has no allotment or inheritance with his kindred; the LORD is his inheritance, as the LORD your God promised him.)

10 I stayed on the mountain forty days and forty nights, as I had done the first time. And once again the LORD listened to me. The LORD was unwilling to destroy you. 11The LORD said to me, "Get up, go on your journey at the head of the people, that they may go in and occupy the land that I swore to their ancestors to give them."

The Essence of the Law

12 So now, O Israel, what does the LORD your God require of you? Only to fear the

a Sam Gk: MT *I have* — *b* Heb *the ten words*
c Or *the wells of the Bene-jaakan*

10:9 *Levi has no allotment.* The story of Levi goes back to Genesis 34, when he and his brother Simeon used treachery to avenge the rape of their sister. In Gen 49:5–7, their father, Jacob, cursed them and announced that their descendants would have no land. However, because of their role in helping Moses deal with those who worshiped the golden calf, they were set apart for special service to the Lord (Exod 32:29). God turned the curse of being scattered into the blessing of distinctive service to him.

10:12 *what does the LORD your God require of you?* Israel now learns what covenant relationship entails. First is fear of the Lord. Fear here means neither abject terror nor simple respect. It involves recognition that God is our creator and we are totally dependent on him for our very life. We are to walk in all his ways. His way is a metaphor for his will for our lives. That will is largely expressed in terms of the law that will follow. We are to love him. Like fear, love is an emotion, but in a covenant context it certainly refers to the feeling of gratitude and a commitment to stay in relationship. Also, in the covenant God proclaims himself king and his people are his servants. Thus we are not surprised to learn that we are to serve him. On the basis of that relationship we are to obey his commandments.

LORD your God, to walk in all his ways, to love him, to serve the LORD your God with all your heart and with all your soul, 13and to keep the commandments of the LORD your God[a] and his decrees that I am commanding you today, for your own well-being. 14Although heaven and the heaven of heavens belong to the LORD your God, the earth with all that is in it, 15yet the LORD set his heart in love on your ancestors alone and chose you, their descendants after them, out of all the peoples, as it is today. 16Circumcise, then, the foreskin of your heart, and do not be stubborn any longer. 17For the LORD your God is God of gods and Lord of lords, the great God, mighty and awesome, who is not partial and takes no bribe, 18who executes justice for the orphan and the widow, and who loves the strangers, providing them food and clothing. 19You shall also love the stranger, for you were strangers in the land of Egypt. 20You shall fear the LORD your God; him alone you shall worship; to him you shall hold fast, and by his name you shall swear. 21He is your praise; he is your God, who has done for you these great and awesome things that your own eyes have seen. 22Your ancestors went down to Egypt seventy persons; and now the LORD your God has made you as numerous as the stars in heaven.

Rewards for Obedience

11 You shall love the LORD your God, therefore, and keep his charge, his decrees, his ordinances, and his commandments always. 2Remember today that it was not your children (who have not known or seen the discipline of the LORD your God), but it is you who must acknowledge his greatness, his mighty hand and his outstretched arm, 3his signs and his deeds that he did in Egypt to Pharaoh, the king of Egypt, and to all his land; 4what he did to the Egyptian army, to their horses and chariots, how he made the water of the Red Sea[b] flow over them as they pursued you, so that the LORD has destroyed them to this day; 5what he did to you in the wilderness, until you came to this place; 6and what he did to Dathan and Abiram, sons of Eliab son of Reuben, how in the midst of all Israel the earth opened its mouth and swallowed them up, along with their households, their tents, and every living being in their company; 7for it is your own eyes that have seen every great deed that the LORD did.

8 Keep, then, this entire commandment that I am commanding you today, so that you may have strength to go in and occupy the land that you are crossing over to occupy, 9and so that you may live long in the land that the LORD swore to your ancestors to give them and to their descendants, a land flowing with milk and honey. 10For the land that you are about to enter to occupy is not like the land of Egypt, from which you have come, where you sow your seed and irrigate by foot like a vegetable garden. 11But the land that you are crossing over to occupy is a land of hills and valleys, watered by rain from the sky, 12a land that the LORD your God looks after. The eyes of the LORD your God are always on it, from the beginning of the year to the end of the year.

13 If you will only heed his every commandment[c] that I am commanding you today—loving the LORD your God, and serving

---

a Q Ms Gk Syr: MT lacks *your God*　　*b* Or *Sea of Reeds*　　*c* Compare Gk: Heb *my commandments*

10:16 *Circumcise, then, the foreskin of your heart.* Our relationship with God is not something that is simply external, as might be implied by the ritual of circumcision. To circumcise the heart is to have the proper attitude toward God, one that desires to obey him out of love and proper fear rather than simple duty (see Rom 2:25–29).

11:13 *If you will only heed his every commandment.* In Deuteronomy prosperity depends on obedience, and disobedience leads to trouble. In this way keeping the law is "for your own well-being" (10:13). Although we can affirm as true the principle that obeying God is a healthier lifestyle than disobedience, we must be careful not to make the mistake of Job's friends and turn this into a mechanistic and absolute principle of living. It simply is not true that obedience always leads to a good life here on earth.

him with all your heart and with all your soul— [14]then he[a] will give the rain for your land in its season, the early rain and the later rain, and you will gather in your grain, your wine, and your oil; [15]and he[b] will give grass in your fields for your livestock, and you will eat your fill. [16]Take care, or you will be seduced into turning away, serving other gods and worshiping them, [17]for then the anger of the LORD will be kindled against you and he will shut up the heavens, so that there will be no rain and the land will yield no fruit; then you will perish quickly off the good land that the LORD is giving you.

18 You shall put these words of mine in your heart and soul, and you shall bind them as a sign on your hand, and fix them as an emblem[c] on your forehead. [19]Teach them to your children, talking about them when you are at home and when you are away, when you lie down and when you rise. [20]Write them on the doorposts of your house and on your gates, [21]so that your days and the days of your children may be multiplied in the land that the LORD swore to your ancestors to give them, as long as the heavens are above the earth.

22 If you will diligently observe this entire commandment that I am commanding you, loving the LORD your God, walking in all his ways, and holding fast to him, [23]then the LORD will drive out all these nations before you, and you will dispossess nations larger and mightier than yourselves. [24]Every place on which you set foot shall be yours; your territory shall extend from the wilderness to the Lebanon and from the River, the river Euphrates, to the Western Sea. [25]No one will be able to stand against you; the LORD your God will put the fear and dread of you on all

the land on which you set foot, as he promised you.

26 See, I am setting before you today a blessing and a curse: [27]the blessing, if you obey the commandments of the LORD your God that I am commanding you today; [28]and the curse, if you do not obey the commandments of the LORD your God, but turn from the way that I am commanding you today, to follow other gods that you have not known.

29 When the LORD your God has brought you into the land that you are entering to occupy, you shall set the blessing on Mount Gerizim and the curse on Mount Ebal. [30]As you know, they are beyond the Jordan, some distance to the west, in the land of the Canaanites who live in the Arabah, opposite Gilgal, beside the oak[d] of Moreh.

31 When you cross the Jordan to go in to occupy the land that the LORD your God is giving you, and when you occupy it and live in it, [32]you must diligently observe all the statutes and ordinances that I am setting before you today.

Pagan Shrines to Be Destroyed

12 These are the statutes and ordinances that you must diligently observe in the land that the LORD, the God of your ancestors, has given you to occupy all the days that you live on the earth.

2 You must demolish completely all the places where the nations whom you are about to dispossess served their gods, on the mountain heights, on the hills, and under every leafy tree. [3]Break down their altars, smash their pillars, burn their sacred poles[e] with

a Sam Gk Vg: MT V   b Sam Gk Vg: MT I
c Or as a frontlet   d Gk Syr: Compare Gen 12.6;
Heb oaks or terebinths   e Heb Asherim

11:18 *you shall bind them as a sign on your hand, and . . . on your forehead.* Although some interpret this verse literally and wear boxes containing Scripture strapped to their wrists and forehead (phylacteries) on special religious occasions, the phrase may be understood metaphorically as indicating that the faithful must reflect on the law (forehead) and act on its contents (hand).

12:3 *Break down their altars.* This law recognizes that places of false worship are dangerous, since they might tempt the Israelites to serve the wrong god. They are to destroy them. Although few of us today would be tempted to worship a false god as such, we have many things that tempt our hearts to put them first and God second. We must root out the desire to worship these things and focus on the true God.

fire, and hew down the idols of their gods, and thus blot out their name from their places. 4You shall not worship the LORD your God in such ways. 5But you shall seek the place that the LORD your God will choose out of all your tribes as his habitation to put his name there. You shall go there, 6bringing there your burnt offerings and your sacrifices, your tithes and your donations, your votive gifts, your freewill offerings, and the firstlings of your herds and flocks. 7And you shall eat there in the presence of the LORD your God, you and your households together, rejoicing in all the undertakings in which the LORD your God has blessed you.

8 You shall not act as we are acting here today, all of us according to our own desires, 9for you have not yet come into the rest and the possession that the LORD your God is giving you. 10When you cross over the Jordan and live in the land that the LORD your God is allotting to you, and when he gives you rest from your enemies all around so that you live in safety, 11then you shall bring everything that I command you to the place that the LORD your God will choose as a dwelling for his name: your burnt offerings and your sacrifices, your tithes and your donations, and all your choice votive gifts that you vow to the LORD. 12And you shall rejoice before the LORD your God, you together with your sons and your daughters, your male and female slaves, and the Levites who reside in your towns (since they have no allotment or inheritance with you).

A Prescribed Place of Worship

13 Take care that you do not offer your burnt offerings at any place you happen to see. 14But only at the place that the LORD will choose in one of your tribes—there you shall offer your burnt offerings and there you shall do everything I command you.

15 Yet whenever you desire you may slaughter and eat meat within any of your towns, according to the blessing that the LORD your God has given you; the unclean and the clean may eat of it, as they would of gazelle or deer. 16The blood, however, you must not eat; you shall pour it out on the ground like water. 17Nor may you eat within your towns the tithe of your grain, your wine, and your oil, the firstlings of your herds and your flocks, any of your votive gifts that you vow, your freewill offerings, or your donations; 18these you shall eat in the presence of the LORD your God at the place that the LORD your God will choose, you together with your son and your daughter, your male and female slaves, and the Levites resident in your towns, rejoicing in the presence of the LORD your God in all your undertakings. 19Take care that you do not neglect the Levite as long as you live in your land.

20 When the LORD your God enlarges your territory, as he has promised you, and you say, "I am going to eat some meat," because you wish to eat meat, you may eat meat whenever you have the desire. 21If the place where the LORD your God will choose to put his name is too far from you, and you slaughter as I have commanded you any of your herd or flock that the LORD has given you,

---

WHY WOULD PEOPLE CHOOSE WORSHIP THERE?

Responding

12:4 WORSHIP. God tells the Israelites that they are not to "worship the LORD" in the ways of the Canaanites. Instead, they are to seek the place that God chooses. What are the advantages in our choosing where we want to worship? What are the dangers? Explain why the church you attend should be God's choice, not yours. *See also* Spiritual Disciplines Index.

12:5 *the place that the LORD your God will choose.* This famous law is often referred to as the law of centralization when it is interpreted

to mean that God will sanction only one central place of worship once the people are settled in the land. This reference is often taken to refer to the future building of the Temple after God has given rest from Israel's enemies (cf. Deut 12:10–11; 2 Sam 7:1–13). Others take this law to mean that, though there may be multiple altars, the only legitimate ones are those that God has authorized. Whichever interpretation is correct, the principle, which should still be honored today, is that God defines the conditions of our worship of him.

then you may eat within your towns whenever you desire. 22Indeed, just as gazelle or deer is eaten, so you may eat it; the unclean and the clean alike may eat it. 23Only be sure that you do not eat the blood; for the blood is the life, and you shall not eat the life with the meat. 24Do not eat it; you shall pour it out on the ground like water. 25Do not eat it, so that all may go well with you and your children after you, because you do what is right in the sight of the LORD. 26But the sacred donations that are due from you, and your votive gifts, you shall bring to the place that the LORD will choose. 27You shall present your burnt offerings, both the meat and the blood, on the altar of the LORD your God; the blood of your other sacrifices shall be poured out beside *a* the altar of the LORD your God, but the meat you may eat.

28 Be careful to obey all these words that I command you today, *b* so that it may go well with you and with your children after you forever, because you will be doing what is good and right in the sight of the LORD your God.

Warning against Idolatry

29 When the LORD your God has cut off before you the nations whom you are about to enter to dispossess them, when you have dispossessed them and live in their land, 30take care that you are not snared into imitating them, after they have been destroyed before you: do not inquire concerning their gods, saying, "How did these nations worship their gods? I also want to do the same." 31You must not do the same for the LORD your God, because every abhorrent thing that the LORD hates they have done for their gods. They would even burn their sons and their daughters in the fire to their gods. 32 *c* You must diligently observe everything that I command you; do not add to it or take anything from it.

13 *d* If prophets or those who divine by dreams appear among you and promise you omens or portents, 2and the omens or the portents declared by them take place, and they say, "Let us follow other gods" (whom you have not known) "and let us serve them," 3you must not heed the words of those prophets or those who divine by dreams; for the LORD your God is testing you, to know whether you indeed love the LORD your God with all your heart and soul. 4The LORD your God you shall follow, him alone you shall fear, his commandments you shall keep, his voice you shall obey, him you shall serve, and to him you shall hold fast. 5But those prophets or those who divine by dreams shall be put to death for having spoken treason against the LORD your God—who brought you out of the land of Egypt and redeemed you from the house of slavery—to turn you from the way in which the LORD your God commanded you to walk. So you shall purge the evil from your midst.

6 If anyone secretly entices you—even if it is your brother, your father's son or *e* your mother's son, or your own son or daughter, or the wife you embrace, or your most intimate friend—saying, "Let us go worship other gods," whom neither you nor your ancestors have known, 7any of the gods of the peoples that are around you, whether near you or far away from you, from one end of the earth to the other, 8you must not yield to or heed any such persons. Show them no pity or compassion and do not shield them. 9But you shall surely kill them; your own hand shall be first against them to execute them, and afterwards the hand of all the people. 10Stone them to death for trying to turn you away from the LORD your God, who brought you out of the

a Or *on*   *b* Gk Sam Syr: MT lacks *today*   *c* Ch 13.1 in Heb   *d* Ch 13.2 in Heb   *e* Sam Gk Compare Tg: MT lacks *your father's son or*

13:1–5 *you must not heed the words of those prophets.* In this passage, we have the first of two (see 18:15–22) provisions concerning prophets. Here we learn that, though certain prophets' words turn out to be true, if they lure Israel to false gods, then they are by definition false prophets and should be put to death. This text alerts us to the fact that false prophets may actually utter true prophecies, and we are thus warned not to be deceived into following their advice. Indeed, we should "test the prophets."

land of Egypt, out of the house of slavery. [11]Then all Israel shall hear and be afraid, and never again do any such wickedness.

12 If you hear it said about one of the towns that the LORD your God is giving you to live in, [13]that scoundrels from among you have gone out and led the inhabitants of the town astray, saying, "Let us go and worship other gods," whom you have not known, [14]then you shall inquire and make a thorough investigation. If the charge is established that such an abhorrent thing has been done among you, [15]you shall put the inhabitants of that town to the sword, utterly destroying it and everything in it—even putting its livestock to the sword. [16]All of its spoil you shall gather into its public square; then burn the town and all its spoil with fire, as a whole burnt offering to the LORD your God. It shall remain a perpetual ruin, never to be rebuilt. [17]Do not let anything devoted to destruction stick to your hand, so that the LORD may turn from his fierce anger and show you compassion, and in his compassion multiply you, as he swore to your ancestors, [18]if you obey the voice of the LORD your God by keeping all his commandments that I am commanding you today, doing what is right in the sight of the LORD your God.

Pagan Practices Forbidden

14 You are children of the LORD your God. You must not lacerate yourselves or shave your forelocks for the dead. [2]For you are a people holy to the LORD your God; it is you the LORD has chosen out of all the peoples on earth to be his people, his treasured possession.

Clean and Unclean Foods

3 You shall not eat any abhorrent thing. [4]These are the animals you may eat: the ox, the sheep, the goat, [5]the deer, the gazelle, the roebuck, the wild goat, the ibex, the antelope, and the mountain-sheep. [6]Any animal that divides the hoof and has the hoof cleft in two, and chews the cud, among the animals, you may eat. [7]Yet of those that chew the cud or have the hoof cleft you shall not eat these: the camel, the hare, and the rock badger, because they chew the cud but do not divide the hoof; they are unclean for you. [8]And the pig, because it divides the hoof but does not chew the cud, is unclean for you. You shall not eat their meat, and you shall not touch their carcasses.

9 Of all that live in water you may eat these: whatever has fins and scales you may eat. [10]And whatever does not have fins and scales you shall not eat; it is unclean for you.

11 You may eat any clean birds. [12]But these are the ones that you shall not eat: the eagle, the vulture, the osprey, [13]the buzzard, the kite of any kind; [14]every raven of any kind; [15]the ostrich, the nighthawk, the sea gull, the hawk of any kind; [16]the little owl and the great owl, the water hen [17]and the desert owl,[a] the carrion vulture and the cormorant,

a Or *pelican*

14:1 *You are children of the LORD your God.* The motivation for obeying many of the laws that follow has to do with Israel's special relationship to God. The Israelites are God's children; therefore, they should not act like those who worship other gods. For this reason, we assume that a number of the prohibitions in verses 1–21 are ceremonies associated with the worship of other gods. For instance, it was wrong to shave one's forelocks during the Old Testament period not because there was anything inherently evil about doing this, but because it indicated service to non-Israelite gods.

14:3–21 *You shall not eat any abhorrent thing.* The rationale for the distinction between clean and unclean food is difficult to understand. Perhaps certain animals were thought to conform to the norms of creation, while others were thought to blur the boundaries. For instance, fish that have "fins and scales" are true fish, while other animals in the deep that do not have them (lobsters) somehow do not seem to fit the category. Whatever the rationale, it is clear that the food laws were a way to distinguish Israel from other nations, a way to preserve the distinction between Israelites and Gentiles. Once this distinction passes away, God's people no longer have to keep these laws (Acts 10).

18the stork, the heron of any kind; the hoopoe and the bat.[a] 19And all winged insects are unclean for you; they shall not be eaten. 20You may eat any clean winged creature.

21 You shall not eat anything that dies of itself; you may give it to aliens residing in your towns for them to eat, or you may sell it to a foreigner. For you are a people holy to the LORD your God.

You shall not boil a kid in its mother's milk.

Regulations concerning Tithes

22 Set apart a tithe of all the yield of your seed that is brought in yearly from the field. 23In the presence of the LORD your God, in the place that he will choose as a dwelling for his name, you shall eat the tithe of your grain, your wine, and your oil, as well as the firstlings of your herd and flock, so that you may learn to fear the LORD your God always. 24But if, when the LORD your God has blessed you, the distance is so great that you are unable to transport it, because the place where the LORD your God will choose to set his name is too far away from you, 25then you may turn it into money. With the money secure in hand, go to the place that the LORD your God will choose; 26spend the money for whatever you wish—oxen, sheep, wine, strong drink, or whatever you desire. And you shall eat there in the presence of the LORD your God, you and your household rejoicing together. 27As for the Levites resident in your towns, do not neglect them, because they have no allotment or inheritance with you.

28 Every third year you shall bring out the full tithe of your produce for that year, and store it within your towns; 29the Levites, because they have no allotment or inheritance with you, as well as the resident aliens, the orphans, and the widows in your towns, may come and eat their fill so that the LORD your God may bless you in all the work that you undertake.

Laws concerning the Sabbatical Year

15 Every seventh year you shall grant a remission of debts. 2And this is the manner of the remission: every creditor shall remit the claim that is held against a neighbor, not exacting it of a neighbor who is a member of the community, because the LORD's remission has been proclaimed. 3Of a foreigner you may exact it, but you must remit your claim on whatever any member of your community owes you. 4There will, however, be no one in need among you, because the LORD is sure to bless you in the land that the LORD your God is giving you as a possession to occupy, 5if only you will obey the LORD your God by diligently observing this entire commandment that I command you today. 6When the LORD your God has blessed you, as he promised you, you will lend to many nations, but you will not borrow; you will rule over many nations, but they will not rule over you.

7 If there is among you anyone in need, a member of your community in any of your

a Identification of several of the birds in verses 12-18 is uncertain

---

14:22–29 CELEBRATION—See Spiritual Disciplines Index.

14:22–29 *Set apart a tithe*. As we have already described, Deuteronomy is a covenant renewal, reaffirming the relationship between the Great King, Yahweh, and his servant people, Israel. Here we see that the people are to bring tribute to their King. This tithe, or a tenth of the yield (or its monetary equivalent), was to be used in the worship of God, and every third year the tithe was to be used for the support of those who were not able to work the fields themselves (Levites, whom God set apart for special service to him, widows, orphans, and resident aliens).

15:1–3 *a remission of debts*. As part of the sabbatical system in ancient Israel, God commanded that every debt be canceled every seventh year. In this way a people would not be under permanent onerous debt obligation to creditors. Although this law certainly was not put in place for debtors to abuse, it prohibits creditors from exploiting those who owe them money. Interestingly, such problems never should have arisen, however, since the land in which the Israelites would live had enough resources to adequately support everyone (vv 4–6).

towns <u>within the land that the</u> L<small>ORD</small> your God is giving you, do not be hard-hearted or tight-fisted toward your needy neighbor. 8You should rather <u>open your hand</u>, willingly lending enough <u>to meet the need</u>, whatever it may be. 9Be careful that you do not entertain a mean thought, thinking, "The seventh year, the year of remission, is near," and therefore view your needy neighbor with hostility and give nothing; your neighbor might cry to the L<small>ORD</small> against you, and you would incur guilt. 10Give liberally and be ungrudging wh<u>en you do so</u>, for on this account the L<small>ORD</small> your God will bless you in all your work and in all that you undertake. 11Since there will never <u>cease</u> to be some in need on the earth, I therefore command you, "Open your hand to the poor and needy neighbor in your land."

12 If a <u>member of your community</u>, whether a Hebrew man or a Hebrew woman, is sold a to you and works for you six years, in the seventh year you shall set that person free. 13And when you send a male slave b out from you a <u>free person</u>, you shall not send him out empty-<u>handed. 14Provide liberally out of your flock, your threshing floor, and your wine</u> press, thus giving to him some of the bounty with which the L<small>ORD</small> your God has blessed you. 15<u>Remember that you were a</u> slave in the land of Egypt, and the L<small>ORD</small> your God redeemed you; for this reason I lay this command upon you today. 16But if he says to

you, "I will not go out from you," because he loves you and your household, since he is well off with you, 17then you shall take an awl and thrust it through his earlobe into the door, and he shall be your slave c forever.

You shall do the same with regard to your female slave. d

18 Do not consider it a hardship when you send them out from you free persons, because for six years they have given you services worth the wages of hired laborers; and the L<small>ORD</small> your God will bless you in all that you do.

The Firstborn of Livestock

19 Every firstling male born of your herd and <u>flock you shall consecrate to the</u> L<small>ORD</small> your God; you shall not do work with your firstling ox nor shear the firstling of your flock. 20You shall eat it, you together with your <u>household, in the presence of the</u> L<small>ORD</small> your God year by year at the place that the L<small>ORD</small> will choose. 21But if it has any defect— any serious defect, such as lameness or blindness—you shall not sacrifice it to the L<small>ORD</small> your God; 22within your towns you may eat it, the unclean and the clean alike, as you would a gazelle or deer. 23Its blood, however, you must not eat; you shall pour it out on the ground like water.

a Or *sells himself or herself*   b Heb *him*
c Or *bondman*   d Or *bondwoman*

15:15 *you were a slave in the land of Egypt.* This phrase reverberates throughout Deuteronomy (see also 5:15; 16:12; 24:18, 22) and provides a foundation for Israel's social conscience. The Israelites should not exploit others, here Hebrew slaves, since they themselves know what it is like to be exploited. Today, we should also treat others in ways that we would want to be treated if we were in a similar situation. Social injustice should not become a reason to exploit others; rather, it should become motivation to treat others with dignity.

15:19–21 *Every firstling male born of your herd and flock.* The principle here is that the best belongs to God, not what is left over. In this

way we show how we love God with all our heart, mind, and body.

Responding
15:21 SACRIFICE. Every firstborn animal sacrificed to the Lord was to be free of serious defects. Today many of us think we are being generous when we give second-hand equipment and furnishings to our churches. As you attend services this week, look around. Is the ministry of your church being hampered by its dependence on substandard accoutrements? If so, note an item that needs to be replaced or updated. Buy another in a quality better than you would purchase for your own home and give it to your church. How did you feel? *See also* Spiritual Disciplines Index.

The Passover Reviewed

16 Observe the month *a* of Abib by keeping the passover to the LORD your God, for in the month of Abib the LORD your God brought you out of Egypt by night. ²You shall offer the passover sacrifice to the LORD your God, from the flock and the herd, at the place that the LORD will choose as a dwelling for his name. ³You must not eat with it anything leavened. For seven days you shall eat unleavened bread with it—the bread of affliction—because you came out of the land of Egypt in great haste, so that all the days of your life you may remember the day of your departure from the land of Egypt. ⁴No leaven shall be seen with you in all your territory for seven days; and none of the meat of what you slaughter on the evening of the first day shall remain until morning. ⁵You are not permitted to offer the passover sacrifice within any of your towns that the LORD your God is giving you. ⁶But at the place that the LORD your God will choose as a dwelling for his name, only there shall you offer the passover sacrifice, in the evening at sunset, the time of day when you departed from Egypt. ⁷You shall cook it and eat it at the place that the LORD your God will choose; the next morning you may go back to your tents. ⁸For six days you shall continue to eat unleavened bread, and on the seventh day there shall be a solemn assembly for the LORD your God, when you shall do no work.

The Festival of Weeks Reviewed

9 You shall count seven weeks; begin to count the seven weeks from the time the sickle is first put to the standing grain. ¹⁰Then you shall keep the festival of weeks to the LORD your God, contributing a freewill offering in proportion to the blessing that you have received from the LORD your God. ¹¹Rejoice before the LORD your God—you and your sons and your daughters, your male and female slaves, the Levites resident in your towns, as well as the strangers, the orphans, and the widows who are among you—at the place that the LORD your God will choose as a dwelling for his name. ¹²Remember that you were a slave in Egypt, and diligently observe these statutes.

The Festival of Booths Reviewed

13 You shall keep the festival of booths *b* for seven days, when you have gathered in the produce from your threshing floor and your wine press. ¹⁴Rejoice during your festival, you and your sons and your daughters, your male and female slaves, as well as the Levites, the strangers, the orphans, and the widows resident in your towns. ¹⁵Seven days you shall keep the festival to the LORD your God at the place that the LORD will choose; for the LORD your God will bless you in all your produce and in all your undertakings, and you shall surely celebrate.

16 Three times a year all your males shall appear before the LORD your God at the place that he will choose: at the festival of unleavened bread, at the festival of weeks, and at the festival of booths. *b* They shall not appear before the LORD empty-handed; ¹⁷all shall give as they are able, according to the blessing of the LORD your God that he has given you.

Municipal Judges and Officers

18 You shall appoint judges and officials throughout your tribes, in all your towns that the LORD your God is giving you, and they shall render just decisions for the people. ¹⁹You must not distort justice; you must not

a Or *new moon*   *b* Or *tabernacles*; Heb *succoth*

16:15 CELEBRATION—*See Spiritual Disciplines Index.*

16:16 *Three times a year all your males shall appear before the LORD your God.* Three times a year Israelites were to appear before the Lord to offer him thanks for agricultural bounty and, in some cases, for historical deliverance. He saved them from Egypt and now provides the crops that

sustain them. Today, we should look back in the past to thank God for Jesus, the Passover Lamb who saves us (1 Cor 5:6–8) and provides for us.

16:19 *You must not distort justice.* God hates those who treat the guilty as if innocent and the innocent as if guilty. Favoritism in justice is an abomination. People should treat other people as they deserve.

show partiality; and you must not accept bribes, for a bribe blinds the eyes of the wise and subverts the cause of those who are in the right. 20Justice, and only justice, you shall pursue, so that you may live and occupy the land that the LORD your God is giving you.

Forbidden Forms of Worship

21 You shall not plant any tree as a sacred pole*a* beside the altar that you make for the LORD your God; 22nor shall you set up a stone pillar—things that the LORD your God hates.

17 You must not sacrifice to the LORD your God an ox or a sheep that has a defect, anything seriously wrong; for that is abhorrent to the LORD your God.

2 If there is found among you, in one of your towns that the LORD your God is giving you, a man or woman who does what is evil in the sight of the LORD your God, and transgresses his covenant 3by going to serve other gods and worshiping them—whether the sun or the moon or any of the host of heaven, which I have forbidden— 4and if it is reported to you or you hear of it, and you make a thorough inquiry, and the charge is proved true that such an abhorrent thing has occurred in Israel, 5then you shall bring out to your gates that man or that woman who has committed this crime and you shall stone the man or woman to death. 6On the evidence of two or three witnesses the death sentence shall be executed; a person must not be put to death on the evidence of only one witness. 7The hands of the witnesses shall be the first raised against the person to execute the death penalty, and afterward the hands of all the people. So you shall purge the evil from your midst.

Legal Decisions by Priests and Judges

8 If a judicial decision is too difficult for you to make between one kind of bloodshed and another, one kind of legal right and another, or one kind of assault and another—any such matters of dispute in your towns—then you shall immediately go up to the place that the LORD your God will choose, 9where you shall consult with the levitical priests and the judge who is in office in those days; they shall announce to you the decision in the case. 10Carry out exactly the decision that they announce to you from the place that the LORD will choose, diligently observing everything they instruct you. 11You must carry out fully the law that they interpret for you or the ruling that they announce to you; do not turn aside from the decision that they announce to you, either to the right or to the left. 12As for anyone who presumes to disobey the priest appointed to minister there to the LORD your God, or the judge, that person shall die. So you shall purge the evil from Israel. 13All the people will hear and be afraid, and will not act presumptuously again.

Limitations of Royal Authority

14 When you have come into the land that the LORD your God is giving you, and have taken possession of it and settled in it, and you say, "I will set a king over me, like all the nations that are around me," 15you may indeed set over you a king whom the LORD your God will choose. One of your own community you may set as king over you; you are not permitted to put a foreigner over you, who is not of your own community. 16Even so, he must not acquire many horses for him-

a Heb *Asherah*

17:16–17 *he must not acquire.* Israel is permitted to have a king, but the king has certain restrictions. After all, he is not the ultimate king, and he must know his place. The Israelite kingship is not a place for personal aggrandizement. Leadership of the covenant people is not to be done for one's own benefit, but out of service for God and for those led. Israelite history is peppered with kings who fall far short of this divine prescription for proper

rule (especially Solomon) and so, unfortunately, is the modern Church.

Responding
17:16–17 SIMPLICITY/FRUGALITY.
This passage records God's warning to future kings of Israel against acquiring the trappings associated with wealth. This warning, however, did not deter David and later Solomon from acquiring great wealth. Today we all know stories of contemporary leaders who take office

self, or return the people to Egypt in order to acquire more horses, since the LORD has said to you, "You must never return that way again." 17And he must not acquire many wives for himself, or else his heart will turn away; also silver and gold he must not acquire in great quantity for himself. 18When he has taken the throne of his kingdom, he shall have a copy of this law written for him in the presence of the levitical priests. 19It shall remain with him and he shall read in it all the days of his life, so that he may learn to fear the LORD his God, diligently observing all the words of this law and these statutes, 20neither exalting himself above other members of the community nor turning aside from the commandment, either to the right or to the left, so that he and his descendants may reign long over his kingdom in Israel.

Privileges of Priests and Levites

18 The levitical priests, the whole tribe of Levi, shall have no allotment or inheritance within Israel. They may eat the sacrifices that are the LORD's portion a 2but they shall have no inheritance among the other members of the community; the LORD is their inheritance, as he promised them.

3 This shall be the priests' due from the people, from those offering a sacrifice, whether an ox or a sheep: they shall give to the priest the shoulder, the two jowls, and the stomach. 4The first fruits of your grain, your wine, and your oil, as well as the first of the fleece of your sheep, you shall give him. 5For

the LORD your God has chosen Levi b out of all your tribes, to stand and minister in the name of the LORD, him and his sons for all time.

6 If a Levite leaves any of your towns, from wherever he has been residing in Israel, and comes to the place that the LORD will choose (and he may come whenever he wishes), 7then he may minister in the name of the LORD his God, like all his fellow-Levites who stand to minister there before the LORD. 8They shall have equal portions to eat, even though they have income from the sale of family possessions. a

Child-Sacrifice, Divination, and Magic Prohibited

9 When you come into the land that the LORD your God is giving you, you must not learn to imitate the abhorrent practices of those nations. 10No one shall be found among you who makes a son or daughter pass through fire, or who practices divination, or is a soothsayer, or an augur, or a sorcerer, 11or one who casts spells, or who consults ghosts or spirits, or who seeks oracles from the dead. 12For whoever does these things is abhorrent to the LORD; it is because of such abhorrent practices that the LORD your God is driving them out before you. 13You must remain completely loyal to the LORD your God. 14Although these nations that you are about to dispossess do give heed

a Meaning of Heb uncertain   b Heb him

---

with good intentions, but whose service is later compromised by money. What is so seductive about money and what it can buy? How do they keep us from living a life of simplicity? See also Spiritual Disciplines Index.

17:19 so that he may learn to fear the LORD his God. The king must know his proper place before God. He must fear the Lord, demonstrating that he knows he is a creature and has power only at God's discretion. Such a king will not exploit his people.
17:19–20 STUDY—See Spiritual Disciplines Index.

18:1–2 SACRIFICE—See Spiritual Disciplines Index.
18:14 the LORD your God does not permit you to do so. God does not permit his people to consult those who try to discern and control the future by mechanistic means. The prohibited practices (vv 10–11) are those that try to control the future by forcing information out of Yahweh. In the Bible God does freely reveal to his prophets what he wants his people to know about the future. At times he even allows for what appears to be divination (Urim and Thummim). However even in the case of the latter, God is never forced to tell the future. The Urim and Thummim may come up blank (1 Sam 28:4–7).

to soothsayers and diviners, as for you, the LORD your God does not permit you to do so.

A New Prophet Like Moses

15 The LORD your God will raise up for you a prophet *a* like me from among your own people; you shall heed such a prophet. *b* 16This is what you requested of the LORD your God at Horeb on the day of the assembly when you said: "If I hear the voice of the LORD my God any more, or ever again see this great fire, I will die." 17Then the LORD replied to me: "They are right in what they have said. 18I will raise up for them a prophet *a* like you from among their own people; I will put my words in the mouth of the prophet, *c* who shall speak to them everything that I command. 19Anyone who does not heed the words that the prophet *d* shall speak in my name, I myself will hold accountable. 20But any prophet who speaks in the name of other gods, or who presumes to speak in my name a word that I have not commanded the prophet to speak—that prophet shall die." 21You may say to yourself, "How can we recognize a word that the LORD has not spoken?" 22If a prophet speaks in the name of the LORD but the thing does not take place or prove true, it is a word that the LORD has not spoken. The prophet has spoken it presumptuously; do not be frightened by it.

Laws concerning the Cities of Refuge

19 When the LORD your God has cut off the nations whose land the LORD your God is giving you, and you have dispossessed them and settled in their towns and in their houses, 2you shall set apart three cities in the land that the LORD your God is giving you to possess. 3You shall calculate the distances *e* and divide into three regions the land that the LORD your God gives you as a possession, so that any homicide can flee to one of them.

4 Now this is the case of a homicide who might flee there and live, that is, someone who has killed another person unintentionally when the two had not been at enmity before: 5Suppose someone goes into the forest with another to cut wood, and when one of them swings the ax to cut down a tree, the head slips from the handle and strikes the other person who then dies; the killer may flee to one of these cities and live. 6But if the distance is too great, the avenger of blood in hot anger might pursue and overtake and put the killer to death, although a death sentence was not deserved, since the two had not been at enmity before. 7Therefore I command you: You shall set apart three cities.

8 If the LORD your God enlarges your territory, as he swore to your ancestors—and he will give you all the land that he promised your ancestors to give you, 9provided you diligently observe this entire commandment that I command you today, by loving the LORD your God and walking always in his ways—then you shall add three more cities to these three, 10so that the blood of an innocent person may not be shed in the land that the LORD your God is giving you as an inheritance, thereby bringing bloodguilt upon you.

11 But if someone at enmity with another lies in wait and attacks and takes the life of

a Or *prophets*   *b* Or *such prophets*
c Or *mouths of the prophets*   *d* Heb *he*
e Or *prepare roads to them*

18:15 *a prophet like me.* God promises to provide a prophet like Moses for the people, someone who will teach the people himself. Although the collective singular "prophet" points to the long line of Old Testament prophets whom God used to speak to Israel (e.g., Isaiah, Jeremiah, Ezekiel), the New Testament takes the singular literally and points to Jesus as that prophet (Acts 3:22–23). Through Jesus God speaks to us in a way that surpasses the Old Testament prophets (Heb 1:1–2), even Moses (Heb 3).

19:1–10 *you shall set apart three cities.* This section mandates the establishment of cities of refuge, places where people who commit an unintentional homicide may flee in order to avoid death at the hands of an avenging relative of the deceased. This law shows God's concern to protect from harm those who do not deserve death even though their actions, perhaps even negligence, led to the death of another. This text shows that God's people should be slow to send individuals to their death, being very careful that the accused get proper justice.

that person, and flees into one of these cities, [12]then the elders of the killer's city shall send to have the culprit taken from there and handed over to the avenger of blood to be put to death. [13]Show no pity; you shall purge the guilt of innocent blood from Israel, so that it may go well with you.

Property Boundaries

14 You must not move your neighbor's boundary marker, set up by former generations, on the property that will be allotted to you in the land that the LORD your God is giving you to possess.

Law concerning Witnesses

15 A single witness shall not suffice to convict a person of any crime or wrongdoing in connection with any offense that may be committed. Only on the evidence of two or three witnesses shall a charge be sustained. [16]If a malicious witness comes forward to accuse someone of wrongdoing, [17]then both parties to the dispute shall appear before the LORD, before the priests and the judges who are in office in those days, [18]and the judges shall make a thorough inquiry. If the witness is a false witness, having testified falsely against another, [19]then you shall do to the false witness just as the false witness had meant to do to the other. So you shall purge

the evil from your midst. [20]The rest shall hear and be afraid, and a crime such as this shall never again be committed among you. [21]Show no pity: life for life, eye for eye, tooth for tooth, hand for hand, foot for foot.

Rules of Warfare

20 When you go out to war against your enemies, and see horses and chariots, an army larger than your own, you shall not be afraid of them; for the LORD your God is with you, who brought you up from the land of Egypt. [2]Before you engage in battle, the priest shall come forward and speak to the troops, [3]and shall say to them: "Hear, O Israel! Today you are drawing near to do battle against your enemies. Do not lose heart, or be afraid, or panic, or be in dread of them; [4]for it is the LORD your God who goes with you, to fight for you against your enemies, to give you victory." [5]Then the officials shall address the troops, saying, "Has anyone built a new house but not dedicated it? He should go back to his house, or he might die in the battle and another dedicate it. [6]Has anyone planted a vineyard but not yet enjoyed its fruit? He should go back to his house, or he might die in the battle and another be first to enjoy its fruit. [7]Has anyone become engaged to a woman but not yet married her? He should go back to his house, or he might die

19:11–13 *Show no pity.* Although the law is careful to protect people from an illegitimate application of capital punishment, it also requires the severest penalty for those who intentionally kill another human being (see also Gen 9:5). Both are a part of true justice according to Deuteronomy.

19:14 *You must not move your neighbor's boundary marker.* In ancient times property lines were indicated by stones. Archaeologists have unearthed ancient Mesopotamian boundary stones, which were distinctive in shape and often inscribed (*kudurru*). To move a boundary stone was to steal land from a neighbor and thus break the eighth commandment. Such laws demonstrate the book's concern with economic dealings.

19:18–21 *you shall do to the false witness just as the false witness had meant to do.* The law is

severe. If a witness lies in a capital trial, then the witness should receive capital punishment. The situation and the penalty show just how evil false witness can be (the ninth commandment prohibits it). It can lead to the death of an innocent person, and this present law discourages someone from uttering a lie.

20:1 *for the LORD your God is with you.* When the Israelites were specifically commanded by God to go to war, they could be assured that God would go with them and secure the victory. They did not need superior weapons or vast numbers of troops. Today, God does not command specific nations to go to battle in his name, but this principle still applies in the context of our battle against evil. We are charged to use the armor and weapons, spiritual weapons such as prayer, love, and faith, that God himself provides to us (Eph 6:10–20).

in the battle and another marry her." [8]The officials shall continue to address the troops, saying, "Is anyone afraid or disheartened? He should go back to his house, or he might cause the heart of his comrades to melt like his own." [9]When the officials have finished addressing the troops, then the commanders shall take charge of them.

10 When you draw near to a town to fight against it, offer it terms of peace. [11]If it accepts your terms of peace and surrenders to you, then all the people in it shall serve you at forced labor. [12]If it does not submit to you peacefully, but makes war against you, then you shall besiege it; [13]and when the LORD your God gives it into your hand, you shall put all its males to the sword. [14]You may, however, take as your booty the women, the children, livestock, and everything else in the town, all its spoil. You may enjoy the spoil of your enemies, which the LORD your God has given you. [15]Thus you shall treat all the towns that are very far from you, which are not towns of the nations here. [16]But as for the towns of these peoples that the LORD your God is giving you as an inheritance, you must not let anything that breathes remain alive. [17]You shall annihilate them—the Hittites and the Amorites, the Canaanites and the Perizzites, the Hivites and the Jebusites—just as the LORD your God has commanded, [18]so that they may not teach you to do all the abhorrent things that they do for their gods, and you thus sin against the LORD your God.

19 If you besiege a town for a long time, making war against it in order to take it, you must not destroy its trees by wielding an ax against them. Although you may take food from them, you must not cut them down. Are trees in the field human beings that they should come under siege from you? [20]You may destroy only the trees that you know do not produce food; you may cut them down for use in building siegeworks against the town that makes war with you, until it falls.

Law concerning Murder by Persons Unknown

21 If, in the land that the LORD your God is giving you to possess, a body is found lying in open country, and it is not known who struck the person down, [2]then your elders and your judges shall come out to measure the distances to the towns that are near the body. [3]The elders of the town nearest the body shall take a heifer that has never been worked, one that has not pulled in the yoke; [4]the elders of that town shall bring the heifer down to a wadi with running water, which is neither plowed nor sown, and shall break the heifer's neck there in the wadi. [5]Then the priests, the sons of Levi, shall come forward, for the LORD your God has chosen them to minister to him and to pronounce blessings in the name of the LORD, and by their decision all cases of dispute and assault shall be settled. [6]All the elders of that town nearest the body shall wash their hands over the heifer whose neck was broken in the wadi, [7]and they shall declare: "Our hands did not shed this blood, nor were we witnesses to it. [8]Absolve, O LORD, your people Israel, whom you redeemed; do not let the guilt of innocent blood remain in the midst of your people Israel." Then they will be absolved of bloodguilt. [9]So you shall purge the guilt of innocent blood from your midst, because you must do what is right in the sight of the LORD.

Female Captives

10 When you go out to war against your enemies, and the LORD your God hands them over to you and you take them captive, [11]suppose you see among the captives a beautiful

---

21:1–9 *it is not known who struck the person down.* It takes witnesses to convict a murderer (19:15–21), and in this case no one saw who committed the crime. It is a testimony to the importance of human life, created in the image of God, that even in such cases a ritual must be performed to declare the innocence of those who live nearby.

21:10–14 *among the captives a . . . woman whom you . . . want to marry.* These laws may seem strange, even primitive to us. However, we should not miss the fact that they served to protect defenseless women (captives and multiple wives) against exploitation within the context of the culture. Some may chafe that the book does not speak against the practices

woman whom you desire and want to marry, [12]and so you bring her home to your house: she shall shave her head, pare her nails, [13]discard her captive's garb, and shall remain in your house a full month, mourning for her father and mother; after that you may go in to her and be her husband, and she shall be your wife. [14]But if you are not satisfied with her, you shall let her go free and not sell her for money. You must not treat her as a slave, since you have dishonored her.

The Right of the Firstborn

15 If a man has two wives, one of them loved and the other disliked, and if both the loved and the disliked have borne him sons, the firstborn being the son of the one who is disliked, [16]then on the day when he wills his possessions to his sons, he is not permitted to treat the son of the loved as the firstborn in preference to the son of the disliked, who is the firstborn. [17]He must acknowledge as firstborn the son of the one who is disliked, giving him a double portion[a] of all that he has; since he is the first issue of his virility, the right of the firstborn is his.

Rebellious Children

18 If someone has a stubborn and rebellious son who will not obey his father and mother, who does not heed them when they discipline him, [19]then his father and his mother shall take hold of him and bring him out to the elders of his town at the gate of that place. [20]They shall say to the elders of his town, "This son of ours is stubborn and rebellious. He will not obey us. He is a glutton and a drunkard." [21]Then all the men of the

town shall stone him to death. So you shall purge the evil from your midst; and all Israel will hear, and be afraid.

Miscellaneous Laws

22 When someone is convicted of a crime punishable by death and is executed, and you hang him on a tree, [23]his corpse must not remain all night upon the tree; you shall bury him that same day, for anyone hung on a tree is under God's curse. You must not defile the land that the LORD your God is giving you for possession.

22 You shall not watch your neighbor's ox or sheep straying away and ignore them; you shall take them back to their owner. [2]If the owner does not reside near you or you do not know who the owner is, you shall bring it to your own house, and it shall remain with you until the owner claims it; then you shall return it. [3]You shall do the same with a neighbor's donkey; you shall do the same with a neighbor's garment; and you shall do the same with anything else that your neighbor loses and you find. You may not withhold your help.

4 You shall not see your neighbor's donkey or ox fallen on the road and ignore it; you shall help to lift it up.

5 A woman shall not wear a man's apparel, nor shall a man put on a woman's garment; for whoever does such things is abhorrent to the LORD your God.

6 If you come on a bird's nest, in any tree or on the ground, with fledglings or eggs, with the mother sitting on the fledglings or

---

a Heb *two-thirds*

described here in the first place, and indeed the institution of marriage as described in Genesis 2 serves to undermine them in favor of an equal partnership of husband and wife. However, we should not be so culturally blind as to not realize that there are exploitative practices in our own marriages that need correction.

21:22–23 *his corpse must not remain all night upon the tree.* The temptation would be to display the body of a criminal for a long period of time to serve as a warning to others. However, the law provides some measure of dignity even

for the corpse of a criminal whom the law considered worthy of death. Christians know this passage from its quotation in Gal 3:13 in reference to Christ's crucifixion. Jesus became a curse by hanging on the cross in order to free us from God's original curse at the fall.

22:3 *You may not withhold your help.* Deuteronomy mandates a community ethic. We do not need to be the Lone Ranger riding in to save the day in every situation, but we must be concerned about the welfare of our neighbors. We must help them out in any way we can.

on the eggs, you shall not take the mother with the young. 7Let the mother go, taking only the young for yourself, in order that it may go well with you and you may live long.

8 When you build a new house, you shall make a parapet for your roof; otherwise you might have bloodguilt on your house, if anyone should fall from it.

9 You shall not sow your vineyard with a second kind of seed, or the whole yield will have to be forfeited, both the crop that you have sown and the yield of the vineyard itself.

10 You shall not plow with an ox and a donkey yoked together.

11 You shall not wear clothes made of wool and linen woven together.

12 You shall make tassels on the four corners of the cloak with which you cover yourself.

Laws concerning Sexual Relations

13 Suppose a man marries a woman, but after going in to her, he dislikes her 14and makes up charges against her, slandering her by saying, "I married this woman; but when I lay with her, I did not find evidence of her virginity." 15The father of the young woman and her mother shall then submit the evidence of the young woman's virginity to the elders of the city at the gate. 16The father of the young woman shall say to the elders: "I gave my daughter in marriage to this man but he dislikes her; 17now he has made up charges against her, saying, 'I did not find evidence of your daughter's virginity.' But here is the evidence of my daughter's virginity." Then they shall spread out the cloth before the elders of the town. 18The elders of that town shall take the man and punish him; 19they shall fine him one hundred shekels of silver (which they shall give to the young woman's father) because he has slan-

dered a virgin of Israel. She shall remain his wife; he shall not be permitted to divorce her as long as he lives.

20 If, however, this charge is true, that evidence of the young woman's virginity was not found, 21then they shall bring the young woman out to the entrance of her father's house and the men of her town shall stone her to death, because she committed a disgraceful act in Israel by prostituting herself in her father's house. So you shall purge the evil from your midst.

22 If a man is caught lying with the wife of another man, both of them shall die, the man who lay with the woman as well as the woman. So you shall purge the evil from Israel.

23 If there is a young woman, a virgin already engaged to be married, and a man meets her in the town and lies with her, 24you shall bring both of them to the gate of that town and stone them to death, the young woman because she did not cry for help in the town and the man because he violated his neighbor's wife. So you shall purge the evil from your midst.

25 But if the man meets the engaged woman in the open country, and the man seizes her and lies with her, then only the man who lay with her shall die. 26You shall do nothing to the young woman; the young woman has not committed an offense punishable by death, because this case is like that of someone who attacks and murders a neighbor. 27Since he found her in the open country, the engaged woman may have cried for help, but there was no one to rescue her.

28 If a man meets a virgin who is not engaged, and seizes her and lies with her, and they are caught in the act, 29the man who lay with her shall give fifty shekels of silver to the young woman's father, and she shall be-

---

22:7 *Let the mother go.* The law to take the young birds, presumably for food, but not the mother is not an indication of early animal rights. Rather, it recognizes the fact that the mother will produce more young that will serve as food.

22:8 *you shall make a parapet for your roof.* The law to build a parapet, or fence, around a

roof makes little sense in the world of modern Western architecture. However, in ancient Israel, people used the roofs of houses as living space, and the lack of a fence may well have led to death. Thus this law is an extension of the sixth commandment, which not only has a negative side (do not murder), but implies the positive (create conditions for the preservation of life).

come his wife. Because he violated her he shall not be permitted to divorce her as long as he lives.

30 [a] A man shall not marry his father's wife, thereby violating his father's rights. [b]

Those Excluded from the Assembly

23 No one whose testicles are crushed or whose penis is cut off shall be admitted to the assembly of the LORD.

2 Those born of an illicit union shall not be admitted to the assembly of the LORD. Even to the tenth generation, none of their descendants shall be admitted to the assembly of the LORD.

3 No Ammonite or Moabite shall be admitted to the assembly of the LORD. Even to the tenth generation, none of their descendants shall be admitted to the assembly of the LORD, 4because they did not meet you with food and water on your journey out of Egypt, and because they hired against you Balaam son of Beor, from Pethor of Mesopotamia, to curse you. 5(Yet the LORD your God refused to heed Balaam; the LORD your God turned the curse into a blessing for you, because the LORD your God loved you.) 6You shall never promote their welfare or their prosperity as long as you live.

7 You shall not abhor any of the Edomites, for they are your kin. You shall not abhor any of the Egyptians, because you were an alien residing in their land. 8The children of the third generation that are born to them may be admitted to the assembly of the LORD.

Sanitary, Ritual, and Humanitarian Precepts

9 When you are encamped against your enemies you shall guard against any impropriety.

10 If one of you becomes unclean because of a nocturnal emission, then he shall go outside the camp; he must not come within the camp. 11When evening comes, he shall wash himself with water, and when the sun has set, he may come back into the camp.

12 You shall have a designated area outside the camp to which you shall go. 13With your utensils you shall have a trowel; when you relieve yourself outside, you shall dig a hole with it and then cover up your excrement. 14Because the LORD your God travels along with your camp, to save you and to hand over your enemies to you, therefore your camp must be holy, so that he may not see anything indecent among you and turn away from you.

15 Slaves who have escaped to you from their owners shall not be given back to them. 16They shall reside with you, in your midst, in any place they choose in any one of your towns, wherever they please; you shall not oppress them.

17 None of the daughters of Israel shall be a temple prostitute; none of the sons of Israel shall be a temple prostitute. 18You shall not bring the fee of a prostitute or the wages of a male prostitute[c] into the house of the LORD your God in payment for any vow, for both of these are abhorrent to the LORD your God.

a Ch 23.1 in Heb   *b* Heb *uncovering his father's skirt*   *c* Heb *a dog*

23:3 *No Ammonite or Moabite shall be admitted to the assembly.* Ammonites and Moabites are specifically prohibited from the assembly of the Lord due to their treatment of Israelites when the Israelites passed through their territory on the way to the Promised Land (see esp. Num 21:10–25:18). However, this prohibition is difficult to reconcile with the treatment of Ruth, the Moabite woman who clearly aligns herself with the Lord and is treated positively as an ancestor of none other than David himself. We should also note Isa 56:3–8, in which both foreigners and eunuchs (see Deut 23:1) are allowed to enter the assembly if they observe the covenant.

23:10–11 *unclean because of a nocturnal emission.* This law does not condemn masturbation. Indeed, this verse is a ceremonial rather than a moral law. As a matter of fact, an emission of semen even in the context of marital intercourse makes one temporarily unclean (Lev 15:16–17). The point of the law has to do with the sanctity of life—life-bearing substances such as semen and blood (in the context of a woman's menstrual cycle; Lev 15:19–33) are surrounded by taboo.

19 You shall not charge interest on loans to another Israelite, interest on money, interest on provisions, interest on anything that is lent. 20On loans to a foreigner you may charge interest, but on loans to another Israelite you may not charge interest, so that the LORD your God may bless you in all your undertakings in the land that you are about to enter and possess.

21 If you make a vow to the LORD your God, do not postpone fulfilling it; for the LORD your God will surely require it of you, and you would incur guilt. 22But if you refrain from vowing, you will not incur guilt. 23Whatever your lips utter you must diligently perform, just as you have freely vowed to the LORD your God with your own mouth.

24 If you go into your neighbor's vineyard, you may eat your fill of grapes, as many as you wish, but you shall not put any in a container.

25 If you go into your neighbor's standing grain, you may pluck the ears with your hand, but you shall not put a sickle to your neighbor's standing grain.

Laws concerning Marriage and Divorce

24 Suppose a man enters into marriage with a woman, but she does not please him because he finds something objectionable about her, and so he writes her a certificate of divorce, puts it in her hand, and sends her out of his house; she then leaves his house 2and goes off to become another man's wife. 3Then suppose the second man dislikes her, writes her a bill of divorce, puts it in her hand, and sends her out of his house (or the second man who married her dies); 4her first husband, who sent her away, is not permitted to take her again to be his wife after she has been defiled; for that would be abhorrent to the LORD, and you shall not bring guilt on the land that the LORD your God is giving you as a possession.

Miscellaneous Laws

5 When a man is newly married, he shall not go out with the army or be charged with any related duty. He shall be free at home one year, to be happy with the wife whom he has married.

6 No one shall take a mill or an upper millstone in pledge, for that would be taking a life in pledge.

7 If someone is caught kidnaping another Israelite, enslaving or selling the Israelite, then that kidnaper shall die. So you shall purge the evil from your midst.

8 Guard against an outbreak of a leprous*a* skin disease by being very careful; you shall carefully observe whatever the levitical priests instruct you, just as I have commanded them. 9Remember what the LORD your God did to Miriam on your journey out of Egypt.

10 When you make your neighbor a loan of any kind, you shall not go into the house

a A term for several skin diseases; precise meaning uncertain

---

23:21–23 *If you make a vow.* A vow was a voluntary gift sometimes contingent on God's answering a prayer for help. The point of the passage is that, since it is voluntary, one must follow through with paying the vow. Eccles 5:2 discourages rash vows, as does the story of Jephthah, which serves as an object lesson warning against quick vows (Judg 11:29–40). In the Sermon on the Mount Jesus teaches against the taking of vows, arguing that our yes or no should stand on its own (Matt 5:33–37).

23:24 *you may eat your fill of grapes.* As is typical of many of the property laws in Deuteronomy, this law walks a fine line between respecting the ownership of property and making sure that such ownership does not override concern for those who are less well off. Those who are hungry may satisfy their appetite in a vineyard, but they cannot take any produce with them to sell or even preserve for their own use later. They can presumably come back, but since it is not their vineyard, they must make the effort to come back.

24:5 *When a man is newly married.* Marriage involves the creation of a new relationship that takes time to deepen. After leaving their parents, it is necessary for a couple to weave their lives together (Gen 2:24). For this reason, military service may not be imposed on a man for one year after marriage. In any case, the Israelites knew their military success depended on the Lord rather than on the size of their army.

to take the pledge. 11You shall wait outside, while the person to whom you are making the loan brings the pledge out to you. 12If the person is poor, you shall not sleep in the garment given you as*a* the pledge. 13You shall give the pledge back by sunset, so that your neighbor may sleep in the cloak and bless you; and it will be to your credit before the LORD your God.

14 You shall not withhold the wages of poor and needy laborers, whether other Israelites or aliens who reside in your land in one of your towns. 15You shall pay them their wages daily before sunset, because they are poor and their livelihood depends on them; otherwise they might cry to the LORD against you, and you would incur guilt.

16 Parents shall not be put to death for their children, nor shall children be put to death for their parents; only for their own crimes may persons be put to death.

17 You shall not deprive a resident alien or an orphan of justice; you shall not take a widow's garment in pledge. 18Remember that you were a slave in Egypt and the LORD your God redeemed you from there; therefore I command you to do this.

19 When you reap your harvest in your field and forget a sheaf in the field, you shall not go back to get it; it shall be left for the alien, the orphan, and the widow, so that the LORD your God may bless you in all your undertakings. 20When you beat your olive trees, do not strip what is left; it shall be for the alien, the orphan, and the widow.

21 When you gather the grapes of your vineyard, do not glean what is left; it shall be for the alien, the orphan, and the widow. 22Remember that you were a slave in the land of Egypt; therefore I am commanding you to do this.

25 Suppose two persons have a dispute and enter into litigation, and the judges decide between them, declaring one to be in the right and the other to be in the wrong. 2If the one in the wrong deserves to be flogged, the judge shall make that person lie down and be beaten in his presence with the number of lashes proportionate to the offense. 3Forty lashes may be given but not more; if more lashes than these are given, your neighbor will be degraded in your sight.

4 You shall not muzzle an ox while it is treading out the grain.

Levirate Marriage

5 When brothers reside together, and one of them dies and has no son, the wife of the deceased shall not be married outside the family to a stranger. Her husband's brother shall go in to her, taking her in marriage, and performing the duty of a husband's brother to her, 6and the firstborn whom she bears shall succeed to the name of the deceased brother, so that his name may not be blotted out of Israel. 7But if the man has no desire to marry his brother's widow, then his brother's widow shall go up to the elders at the gate and say, "My husband's brother refuses to perpetuate his brother's name in Israel; he will

---

a Heb lacks *the garment given you as*

24:13 *You shall give the pledge back by sunset.* The law of Deuteronomy here and elsewhere protects those in need from being exploited in harmful ways. The garment taken in pledge must be returned by sunset so the person won't freeze during the night. Modern business has much to learn from this ancient law, which prohibits financial gain from the exploitation of people's basic needs.

24:17 *a resident alien . . . an orphan . . . . a widow.* Resident aliens, orphans, and widows were considered the most socially vulnerable in Israelite society. However, God's law and God himself provides them with the protection they lack. Again, modern readers should identify the most vulnerable members of the society they live in and show concern for their well-being.

25:5–6 *performing the duty of a husband's brother to her.* This law, strange to our modern sensibilities, makes sense against the background of ancient Near Eastern social and inheritance laws. Without a husband or a son, a woman was in a particularly weakened position, and the inheritance of ancestral land would be in question. Thus the brother, at some personal sacrifice, would be called upon to father a child who would be considered the son of his deceased brother and the woman.

not perform the duty of a husband's brother to me." 8Then the elders of his town shall summon him and speak to him. If he persists, saying, "I have no desire to marry her," 9then his brother's wife shall go up to him in the presence of the elders, pull his sandal off his foot, spit in his face, and declare, "This is what is done to the man who does not build up his brother's house." 10Throughout Israel his family shall be known as "the house of him whose sandal was pulled off."

Various Commands

11 If men get into a fight with one another, and the wife of one intervenes to rescue her husband from the grip of his opponent by reaching out and seizing his genitals, 12you shall cut off her hand; show no pity.

13 You shall not have in your bag two kinds of weights, large and small. 14You shall not have in your house two kinds of measures, large and small. 15You shall have only a full and honest weight; you shall have only a full and honest measure, so that your days may be long in the land that the LORD your God is giving you. 16For all who do such things, all who act dishonestly, are abhorrent to the LORD your God.

17 Remember what Amalek did to you on your journey out of Egypt, 18how he attacked you on the way, when you were faint and weary, and struck down all who lagged behind you; he did not fear God. 19Therefore when the LORD your God has given you rest from all your enemies on every hand, in the land that the LORD your God is giving you as an inheritance to possess, you shall blot out the remembrance of Amalek from under heaven; do not forget.

First Fruits and Tithes

26 When you have come into the land that the LORD your God is giving you as an inheritance to possess, and you possess it, and settle in it, 2you shall take some of the first of all the fruit of the ground, which you harvest from the land that the LORD your God is giving you, and you shall put it in a basket and go to the place that the LORD your God will choose as a dwelling for his name. 3You shall go to the priest who is in office at that time, and say to him, "Today I declare to the LORD your God that I have come into the land that the LORD swore to our ancestors to give us." 4When the priest takes the basket from your hand and sets it down before the altar of the LORD your God, 5you shall make this response before the LORD your God: "A wandering Aramean was my ancestor; he went down into Egypt and lived there as an alien, few in number, and there he became a great nation, mighty and populous. 6When the Egyptians treated us harshly and afflicted us, by imposing hard labor on us, 7we cried to the LORD, the God of our ancestors; the LORD heard our voice and saw our affliction, our toil, and our oppression. 8The LORD brought us out of Egypt with a mighty hand and an outstretched arm, with a terrifying display of power, and with signs and wonders; 9and he brought us into this place and gave us this land, a land flowing with milk and honey. 10So now I bring the first of the fruit of the ground that you, O LORD, have given me." You shall set it down before the LORD your God and bow down

---

25:15 *You shall have only a full and honest weight.* Again, the law protects against economic injustice. Cheating in business is considered an offense not only against one's customer, but against God himself.

26:1–11 *you shall take some of the first of all the fruit of the ground.* Moses anticipates that the people will soon enter and settle in the land. When they do, they will work the land, which will produce crops. Moses instructs them to take the first of the produce of the land and offer it to the Lord as an acknowledgment that their presence in the land and their agricultural bounty are gifts from the sovereign Lord. With this they are to rehearse the great narrative of their deliverance from Egypt and entry into the land. God's people today can look back in history to the cross and tell the story of their deliverance. Although Deuteronomy 26 commands that this ritual take place on the occasion of the first harvest, Israel does establish an annual festival (Festival of Weeks; Num 28:26–31) in which the first of the crops are offered in the context of a holy assembly. We too should be moved to offer the best of our efforts to the God, who saved us and provides for us.

before the LORD your God. ¹¹Then you, together with the Levites and the aliens who reside among you, shall celebrate with all the bounty that the LORD your God has given to you and to your house.

12 When you have finished paying all the tithe of your produce in the third year (which is the year of the tithe), giving it to the Levites, the aliens, the orphans, and the widows, so that they may eat their fill within your towns, ¹³then you shall say before the LORD your God: "I have removed the sacred portion from the house, and I have given it to the Levites, the resident aliens, the orphans, and the widows, in accordance with your entire commandment that you commanded me; I have neither transgressed nor forgotten any of your commandments: ¹⁴I have not eaten of it while in mourning; I have not removed any of it while I was unclean; and I have not offered any of it to the dead. I have obeyed the LORD my God, doing just as you commanded me. ¹⁵Look down from your holy habitation, from heaven, and bless your people Israel and the ground that you have given us, as you swore to our ancestors— a land flowing with milk and honey."

Concluding Exhortation

16 This very day the LORD your God is commanding you to observe these statutes and ordinances; so observe them diligently with all your heart and with all your soul. ¹⁷Today you have obtained the LORD's agreement: to be your God; and for you to walk in his ways, to keep his statutes, his commandments, and his ordinances, and to obey him. ¹⁸Today the LORD has obtained your agreement: to be his treasured people, as he promised you, and to keep his commandments; ¹⁹for him to set you high above all nations that he has made, in praise and in fame and in honor; and for you to be a people holy to the LORD your God, as he promised.

The Inscribed Stones and Altar on Mount Ebal

27 Then Moses and the elders of Israel charged all the people as follows: Keep the entire commandment that I am commanding you today. ²On the day that you cross over the Jordan into the land that the LORD your God is giving you, you shall set up large stones and cover them with plaster. ³You shall write on them all the words of this law when you have crossed over, to enter the land that the LORD your God is giving you, a land flowing with milk and honey, as the LORD, the God of your ancestors, promised you. ⁴So when you have crossed over the Jordan, you shall set up these stones, about which I am commanding you today, on Mount Ebal, and you shall cover them with plaster. ⁵And you shall build an altar there to the LORD your God, an altar of stones on which you have not used an iron tool. ⁶You must build the altar of the LORD your God of unhewn ᵃ stones. Then offer up burnt offerings on it to the LORD your God, ⁷make sacrifices of well-being, and eat them there, rejoicing before the LORD your God. ⁸You shall write on the stones all the words of this law very clearly.

9 Then Moses and the levitical priests spoke to all Israel, saying: Keep silence and hear, O Israel! This very day you have become an inheritance to possess, as you shall plot out

a Heb whole

26:12 *paying all the tithe . . . in the third year.* Moses instructs Israel to observe the first of the triennial tithes in support of those who do not maintain their own lands (see 14:28–29).

26:17 *Today you have obtained the LORD's agreement.* Deuteronomy is a reaffirmation of the covenant (agreement) made between God and Israel at Mt. Sinai (Exod 19–24). The significance of the moment is that the people are about to enter the Promised Land and also they are about to lose their long-term leader, Moses. Moses has exposited the law in a fashion that will be relevant for their entry into the land.

27:9 *This very day you have become the people of the LORD your God.* By virtue of their reaffirmation of their commitment to the Lord on the eve of entering a new situation, the Israelites constitute themselves as the People of God. It is not as if they were not God's people before that moment, but new circumstances require renewed commitment. Christians too undertake sacred acts (particularly Communion) through which we renew our relationship with Christ.

the people of the LORD your God. ¹⁰There-
fore obey the LORD your God, observing his
commandments and his statutes that I am
commanding you today.

Twelve Curses

11 The same day Moses charged the people as follows: ¹²When you have crossed over
the Jordan, these shall stand on Mount Gerizim for the blessing of the people: Simeon,
Levi, Judah, Issachar, Joseph, and Benjamin.
¹³And these shall stand on Mount Ebal for
the curse: Reuben, Gad, Asher, Zebulun, Dan,
and Naphtali. ¹⁴Then the Levites shall declare in a loud voice to all the Israelites:

15 "Cursed be anyone who makes an idol
or casts an image, anything abhorrent to the
LORD, the work of an artisan, and sets it up in
secret." All the people shall respond, saying,
"Amen!"

16 "Cursed be anyone who dishonors father or mother." All the people shall say,
"Amen!"

17 "Cursed be anyone who moves a neighbor's boundary marker." All the people shall
say, "Amen!"

18 "Cursed be anyone who misleads a
blind person on the road." All the people
shall say, "Amen!"

19 "Cursed be anyone who deprives the
alien, the orphan, and the widow of justice."
All the people shall say, "Amen!"

20 "Cursed be anyone who lies with his father's wife, because he has violated his father's rights."ᵃ All the people shall say,
"Amen!"

21 "Cursed be anyone who lies with any
animal." All the people shall say, "Amen!"

22 "Cursed be anyone who lies with his
sister, whether the daughter of his father or
the daughter of his mother." All the people
shall say, "Amen!"

23 "Cursed be anyone who lies with his
mother-in-law." All the people shall say,
"Amen!"

24 "Cursed be anyone who strikes down a
neighbor in secret." All the people shall say,
"Amen!"

25 "Cursed be anyone who takes a bribe to
shed innocent blood." All the people shall
say, "Amen!"

26 "Cursed be anyone who does not uphold the words of this law by observing
them." All the people shall say, "Amen!"

Blessings for Obedience

28 If you will only obey the LORD your
God, by diligently observing all his
commandments that I am commanding you
today, the LORD your God will set you high
above all the nations of the earth; ²all these
blessings shall come upon you and overtake
you, if you obey the LORD your God:

3 Blessed shall you be in the city, and
blessed shall you be in the field.

4 Blessed shall be the fruit of your womb,
the fruit of your ground, and the fruit of your
livestock, both the increase of your cattle and
the issue of your flock.

5 Blessed shall be your basket and your
kneading bowl.

6 Blessed shall you be when you come in,
and blessed shall you be when you go out.

7 The LORD will cause your enemies who

---

a Heb *uncovered his father's skirt*

27:15–26 *Cursed be.* Infractions of God's law
bring painful consequences. Twelve specific
requirements are spelled out, all flowing from
the Ten Commandments. The people affirm
their commitment to abide by them by
declaring, "Amen!"

28:1–14 *all these blessings shall come upon
you.* Obedience brings blessings. These verses
elaborate on the nature of those blessings, and
they are extensive, having to do with military
success, material well-being, agricultural bounty,
and reproductive fertility. Such a listing of the

potential blessings encourages covenant
obedience. Indeed, Deuteronomy invites the
hope that obedience leads to a better life. Other
books of the Old Testament grapple with the
obvious questions that arise from such a
perspective (Job and Ecclesiastes), questions
such as "Why do bad things happen to good
people?" In the New Testament Paul encourages
obedience ("Live your life in a manner worthy of
the gospel of Christ," v 27) in the context of his
teaching about joy experienced in the midst of
suffering (Phil 1:12–30).

rise against you to be defeated before you; they shall come out against you one way, and flee before you seven ways. 8The LORD will command the blessing upon you in your barns, and in all that you undertake; he will bless you in the land that the LORD your God is giving you. 9The LORD will establish you as his holy people, as he has sworn to you, if you keep the commandments of the LORD your God and walk in his ways. 10All the peoples of the earth shall see that you are called by the name of the LORD, and they shall be afraid of you. 11The LORD will make you abound in prosperity, in the fruit of your womb, in the fruit of your livestock, and in the fruit of your ground in the land that the LORD swore to your ancestors to give you. 12The LORD will open for you his rich storehouse, the heavens, to give the rain of your land in its season and to bless all your undertakings. You will lend to many nations, but you will not borrow. 13The LORD will make you the head, and not the tail; you shall be only at the top, and not at the bottom—if you obey the commandments of the LORD your God, which I am commanding you today, by diligently observing them, 14and if you do not turn aside from any of the words that I am commanding you today, either to the right or to the left, following other gods to serve them.

Warnings against Disobedience

15 But if you will not obey the LORD your God by diligently observing all his commandments and decrees, which I am commanding you today, then all these curses shall come upon you and overtake you:

16 Cursed shall you be in the city, and cursed shall you be in the field.

17 Cursed shall be your basket and your kneading bowl.

18 Cursed shall be the fruit of your womb, the fruit of your ground, the increase of your cattle and the issue of your flock.

19 Cursed shall you be when you come in, and cursed shall you be when you go out.

20 The LORD will send upon you disaster, panic, and frustration in everything you attempt to do, until you are destroyed and perish quickly, on account of the evil of your deeds, because you have forsaken me. 21The LORD will make the pestilence cling to you until it has consumed you off the land that you are entering to possess. 22The LORD will afflict you with consumption, fever, inflammation, with fiery heat and drought, and with blight and mildew; they shall pursue you until you perish. 23The sky over your head shall be bronze, and the earth under you iron. 24The LORD will change the rain of your land into powder, and only dust shall come down upon you from the sky until you are destroyed.

25 The LORD will cause you to be defeated before your enemies; you shall go out against them one way and flee before them seven ways. You shall become an object of horror to all the kingdoms of the earth. 26Your corpses shall be food for every bird of the air and animal of the earth, and there shall be no one to frighten them away. 27The LORD will afflict you with the boils of Egypt, with ulcers, scurvy, and itch, of which you cannot be healed. 28The LORD will afflict you with madness, blindness, and confusion of mind; 29you shall grope about at noon as blind peo-

---

Responding
28:1–14 THE WITH-GOD LIFE. God promises to be with the Israelites, blessing every aspect of their lives with only one condition: "If you keep the commandments of the LORD your God and walk in his ways" (v 9). Recall a time when God's presence was especially evident in your life. Did it coincide with a time when you were making every effort to "to walk humbly with your God" (Mic 6:8)? What does this suggest? *See also* Spiritual Disciplines Index.

28:15–68 *then all these curses shall come upon you.* As a contrast to the list of blessings Deuteronomy also offers a much longer list of curses attendant on disobedience. As the history of God's people will prove, the curses will be more relevant than the blessings. Samuel–Kings will explain the exile by looking at their behavior in the light of Deuteronomy, and the prophets will bring a case against later Israel with these curses in mind.

ple grope in darkness, but you shall be unable to find your way; and you shall be continually abused and robbed, without anyone to help. ³⁰You shall become engaged to a woman, but another man shall lie with her. You shall build a house, but not live in it. You shall plant a vineyard, but not enjoy its fruit. ³¹Your ox shall be butchered before your eyes, but you shall not eat of it. Your donkey shall be stolen in front of you, and shall not be restored to you. Your sheep shall be given to your enemies, without anyone to help you. ³²Your sons and daughters shall be given to another people, while you look on; you will strain your eyes looking for them all day but be powerless to do anything. ³³A people whom you do not know shall eat up the fruit of your ground and of all your labors; you shall be continually abused and crushed, ³⁴and driven mad by the sight that your eyes shall see. ³⁵The Lord will strike you on the knees and on the legs with grievous boils of which you cannot be healed, from the sole of your foot to the crown of your head. ³⁶The Lord will bring you, and the king whom you set over you, to a nation that neither you nor your ancestors have known, where you shall serve other gods, of wood and stone. ³⁷You shall become an object of horror, a proverb, and a byword among all the peoples where the Lord will lead you.

38 You shall carry much seed into the field but shall gather little in, for the locust shall consume it. ³⁹You shall plant vineyards and dress them, but you shall neither drink the wine nor gather the grapes, for the worm shall eat them. ⁴⁰You shall have olive trees throughout all your territory, but you shall not anoint yourself with the oil, for your olives shall drop off. ⁴¹You shall have sons and daughters, but they shall not remain yours, for they shall go into captivity. ⁴²All your trees and the fruit of your ground the cicada shall take over. ⁴³Aliens residing among you shall ascend above you higher and higher, while you shall descend lower and lower. ⁴⁴They shall lend to you but you shall not lend to them; they shall be the head and you shall be the tail.

45 All these curses shall come upon you, pursuing and overtaking you until you are destroyed, because you did not obey the Lord your God, by observing the commandments and the decrees that he commanded you. ⁴⁶They shall be among you and your descendants as a sign and a portent forever.

47 Because you did not serve the Lord your God joyfully and with gladness of heart for the abundance of everything, ⁴⁸therefore you shall serve your enemies whom the Lord will send against you, in hunger and thirst, in nakedness and lack of everything. He will put an iron yoke on your neck until he has destroyed you. ⁴⁹The Lord will bring a nation from far away, from the end of the earth, to swoop down on you like an eagle, a nation whose language you do not understand, ⁵⁰a grim-faced nation showing no respect to the old or favor to the young. ⁵¹It shall consume the fruit of your livestock and the fruit of your ground until you are destroyed, leaving you neither grain, wine, and oil, nor the increase of your cattle and the issue of your flock, until it has made you perish. ⁵²It shall besiege you in all your towns until your high and fortified walls, in which you trusted, come down throughout your land; it shall besiege you in all your towns throughout the land that the Lord your God has given you. ⁵³In the desperate straits to which the enemy siege reduces you, you will eat the fruit of your womb, the flesh of your own sons and daughters whom the Lord your God has given you. ⁵⁴Even the most refined and gentle of men among you will begrudge food to his own brother, to the wife whom he embraces, and to the last of his remaining children, ⁵⁵giving to none of them any of the flesh of his children whom he is eating, because nothing else remains to him, in the desperate straits to which the enemy siege will reduce you in all your towns. ⁵⁶She who is the most refined and gentle among you, so gentle and refined that she does not venture to set the sole of her foot on the ground, will begrudge food to the husband whom she embraces, to her own son, and to her own daughter, ⁵⁷begrudging even the afterbirth that comes out from between her thighs, and the children that she bears, because she is eating them in secret for lack of anything else, in the des-

perate straits to which the enemy siege will reduce you in your towns.

58 If you do not diligently observe all the words of this law that are written in this book, fearing this glorious and awesome name, the LORD your God, 59then the LORD will overwhelm both you and your offspring with severe and lasting afflictions and grievous and lasting maladies. 60He will bring back upon you all the diseases of Egypt, of which you were in dread, and they shall cling to you. 61Every other malady and affliction, even though not recorded in the book of this law, the LORD will inflict on you until you are destroyed. 62Although once you were as numerous as the stars in heaven, you shall be left few in number, because you did not obey the LORD your God. 63And just as the LORD took delight in making you prosperous and numerous, so the LORD will take delight in bringing you to ruin and destruction; you shall be plucked off the land that you are entering to possess. 64The LORD will scatter you among all peoples, from one end of the earth to the other; and there you shall serve other gods, of wood and stone, which neither you nor your ancestors have known. 65Among those nations you shall find no ease, no resting place for the sole of your foot. There the LORD will give you a trembling heart, failing eyes, and a languishing spirit. 66Your life shall hang in doubt before you; night and day you shall be in dread, with no assurance of your life. 67In the morning you shall say, "If only it were evening!" and at evening you shall say, "If only it were morning!"—because of the dread that your heart shall feel and the sights that your eyes shall see. 68The LORD will bring you back in ships to Egypt, by a route that I promised you would never see again; and there you shall offer yourselves for sale to your enemies as male and female slaves, but there will be no buyer.

29 *a* These are the words of the covenant that the LORD commanded Moses to make with the Israelites in the land of Moab, in addition to the covenant that he had made with them at Horeb.

The Covenant Renewed in Moab

2 *b* Moses summoned all Israel and said to them: You have seen all that the LORD did

before your eyes in the land of Egypt, to Pharaoh and to all his servants and to all his land, 3the great trials that your eyes saw, the signs, and those great wonders. 4But to this day the LORD has not given you a mind to understand, or eyes to see, or ears to hear. 5I have led you forty years in the wilderness. The clothes on your back have not worn out, and the sandals on your feet have not worn out; 6you have not eaten bread, and you have not drunk wine or strong drink—so that you may know that I am the LORD your God. 7When you came to this place, King Sihon of Heshbon and King Og of Bashan came out against us for battle, but we defeated them. 8We took their land and gave it as an inheritance to the Reubenites, the Gadites, and the half-tribe of Manasseh. 9Therefore diligently observe the words of this covenant, in order that you may succeed *c* in everything that you do.

10 You stand assembled today, all of you, before the LORD your God—the leaders of your tribes, *d* your elders, and your officials, all the men of Israel, 11your children, your women, and the aliens who are in your camp, both those who cut your wood and those who draw your water— 12to enter into the covenant of the LORD your God, sworn by an oath, which the LORD your God is making with you today; 13in order that he may establish you today as his people, and that he may be your God, as he promised you and as he swore to your ancestors, to Abraham, to Isaac, and to Jacob. 14I am making this covenant, sworn by an oath, not only with you who stand here with us today before the LORD our God, 15but also with those who are not here with us today. 16You know how we lived in the land of Egypt, and how we came through the midst of the nations through which you passed. 17You have seen their detestable things, the filthy idols of wood and stone, of silver and gold, that were among them. 18It may be that there is among you a man or woman, or a family or tribe, whose heart is already turning away from the LORD our God to serve the gods of those nations. It

---

a Ch 28.69 in Heb   *b* Ch 29.1 in Heb
c Or *deal wisely*   *d* Gk Syr: Heb *your leaders, your tribes*

may be that there is among you a root sprouting poisonous and bitter growth. ¹⁹All who hear the words of this oath and bless themselves, thinking in their hearts, "We are safe even though we go our own stubborn ways" (thus bringing disaster on moist and dry alike)ᵃ— ²⁰the Lᴏʀᴅ will be unwilling to pardon them, for the Lᴏʀᴅ's anger and passion will smoke against them. All the curses written in this book will descend on them, and the Lᴏʀᴅ will blot out their names from under heaven. ²¹The Lᴏʀᴅ will single them out from all the tribes of Israel for calamity, in accordance with all the curses of the covenant written in this book of the law. ²²The next generation, your children who rise up after you, as well as the foreigner who comes from a distant country, will see the devastation of that land and the afflictions with which the Lᴏʀᴅ has afflicted it— ²³all its soil burned out by sulfur and salt, nothing planted, nothing sprouting, unable to support any vegetation, like the destruction of Sodom and Gomorrah, Admah and Zeboiim, which the Lᴏʀᴅ destroyed in his fierce anger— ²⁴they and indeed all the nations will wonder, "Why has the Lᴏʀᴅ done thus to this land? What caused this great display of anger?" ²⁵They will conclude, "It is because they abandoned the covenant of the Lᴏʀᴅ, the God of their ancestors, which he made with them when he brought them out of the land of Egypt. ²⁶They turned and served other gods, worshiping them, gods whom they had not known and whom he had not allotted to them; ²⁷so the anger of the Lᴏʀᴅ was kindled against that land, bringing on it every curse written in this book. ²⁸The Lᴏʀᴅ uprooted them from their land in anger, fury, and great wrath, and cast them into another land, as is now the case." ²⁹The secret things belong to the Lᴏʀᴅ our God, but the revealed things belong to us and to our children forever, to observe all the words of this law.

God's Fidelity Assured

30 When all these things have happened to you, the blessings and the curses that I have set before you, if you call them to mind among all the nations where the Lᴏʀᴅ your God has driven you, ²and return to the Lᴏʀᴅ your God, and you and your children obey him with all your heart and with all your soul, just as I am commanding you today, ³then the Lᴏʀᴅ your God will restore your fortunes and have compassion on you, gathering you again from all the peoples among whom the Lᴏʀᴅ your God has scattered you. ⁴Even if you are exiled to the ends of the world,ᵇ from there the Lᴏʀᴅ your God will gather you, and from there he will bring you back. ⁵The Lᴏʀᴅ your God will bring you into the land that your ancestors possessed, and you will possess it; he will make you more prosperous and numerous than your ancestors.

6 Moreover, the Lᴏʀᴅ your God will circumcise your heart and the heart of your descendants, so that you will love the Lᴏʀᴅ your God with all your heart and with all your soul, in order that you may live. ⁷The Lᴏʀᴅ your God will put all these curses on your enemies and on the adversaries who took advantage of you. ⁸Then you shall again obey the Lᴏʀᴅ, observing all his commandments that I am commanding you today, ⁹and the Lᴏʀᴅ your God will make you abundantly prosperous in all your undertakings, in the fruit of your body, in the fruit of your livestock, and in the fruit of your soil. For the Lᴏʀᴅ will again take delight in prospering you, just as he delighted in pros-

ᵃ Meaning of Heb uncertain   ᵇ Heb of heaven

29:24 *Why has the Lᴏʀᴅ done thus to this land?* Chapter 29 ends envisioning a time when Israel's disobedience will cause the covenant curses to go into effect, so that the land is devastated. The question is that of the nations; they ask why Israel's God allows his people's land to be destroyed. The answer is an appeal to the covenant curses that served as a warning against disobedience.

30:3 *the Lᴏʀᴅ your God will restore your fortunes and have compassion on you.* Although Deuteronomy warns of judgment for disobedience, it also reminds God's people that grace is available contingent on repentance. Exile and separation from God can end if God's people acknowledge their sin and turn back to God. In this way, despair can give way to hope.

pering your ancestors, [10]when you obey the LORD your God by observing his commandments and decrees that are written in this book of the law, because you turn to the LORD your God with all your heart and with all your soul.

Exhortation to Choose Life

11 Surely, this commandment that I am commanding you today is not too hard for you, nor is it too far away. [12]It is not in heaven, that you should say, "Who will go up to heaven for us, and get it for us so that we may hear it and observe it?" [13]Neither is it beyond the sea, that you should say, "Who will cross to the other side of the sea for us, and get it for us so that we may hear it and observe it?" [14]No, the word is very near to you; it is in your mouth and in your heart for you to observe.

15 See, I have set before you today life and prosperity, death and adversity. [16]If you obey the commandments of the LORD your God[a] that I am commanding you today, by loving the LORD your God, walking in his ways, and observing his commandments, decrees, and ordinances, then you shall live and become numerous, and the LORD your God will bless you in the land that you are entering to possess. [17]But if your heart turns away and you do not hear, but are led astray to bow down to other gods and serve them, [18]I declare to you today that you shall perish; you shall not live long in the land that you are crossing the Jordan to enter and possess. [19]I call heaven and earth to witness against you today that I have set before you life and death, blessings and curses. Choose life so that you and your descendants may live, [20]loving the LORD your God, obeying him, and holding fast to him; for that means life to you and length of days, so that you may live in the land that the LORD swore to give to your ancestors, to Abraham, to Isaac, and to Jacob.

Joshua Becomes Moses' Successor

31 When Moses had finished speaking all[b] these words to all Israel, [2]he said to them: "I am now one hundred twenty years old. I am no longer able to get about, and the LORD has told me, 'You shall not cross over this Jordan.' [3]The LORD your God himself will cross over before you. He will destroy these nations before you, and you shall dispossess them. Joshua also will cross over before you, as the LORD promised. [4]The LORD will do to them as he did to Sihon and Og, the kings of the Amorites, and to their land, when he destroyed them. [5]The LORD will give them over to you and you shall deal with them in full accord with the command that I have given to you. [6]Be strong and bold; have no fear or dread of them, because it is the LORD your God who goes with you; he will not fail you or forsake you."

7 Then Moses summoned Joshua and said to him in the sight of all Israel: "Be strong and bold, for you are the one who will go with this people into the land that the LORD has sworn to their ancestors to give them; and you will put them in possession of it. [8]It is the LORD who goes before you. He will be with you; he will not fail you or forsake you. Do not fear or be dismayed."

The Law to Be Read Every Seventh Year

9 Then Moses wrote down this law, and gave it to the priests, the sons of Levi, who carried the ark of the covenant of the LORD, and to all the elders of Israel. [10]Moses commanded them: "Every seventh year, in the scheduled year of remission, during the festival of

a Gk: Heb lacks *If you obey the commandments of the LORD your God* — b Q Ms Gk: MT *Moses went and spoke*

30:19 *Choose life.* Moses now places before the Israelites the fundamental question: Will they choose life by obeying their God or will they opt for the path of death by rejecting him? Although this choice is a discrete moment in Israel's history, it also is something that constantly confronts God's people.

31:6 THE WITH-GOD LIFE—*See* Spiritual Disciplines Index.

31:6 *Be strong and bold.* Moses will not accompany the people into the land. But before he departs, he encourages them, and particularly Joshua (v 7), to remain confident. The source of their confidence is based on God's presence with them as they face their enemies (cf. Matt 28:20; Eph 6:10).

31:10–13 *Every seventh year.* One's commitment to follow God is not a single

booths,[a] [11]when all Israel comes to appear before the LORD your God at the place that he will choose, you shall read this law before all Israel in their hearing. [12]Assemble the people—men, women, and children, as well as the aliens residing in your towns—so that they may hear and learn to fear the LORD your God and to observe diligently all the words of this law, [13]and so that their children, who have not known it, may hear and learn to fear the LORD your God, as long as you live in the land that you are crossing over the Jordan to possess."

Moses and Joshua Receive God's Charge

14 The LORD said to Moses, "Your time to die is near; call Joshua and present yourselves in the tent of meeting, so that I may commission him." So Moses and Joshua went and presented themselves in the tent of meeting, [15]and the LORD appeared at the tent in a pillar of cloud; the pillar of cloud stood at the entrance to the tent.

16 The LORD said to Moses, "Soon you will lie down with your ancestors. Then this people will begin to prostitute themselves to the foreign gods in their midst, the gods of the land into which they are going; they will forsake me, breaking my covenant that I have made with them. [17]My anger will be kindled against them in that day. I will forsake them and hide my face from them; they will become easy prey, and many terrible troubles will come upon them. In that day they will say, 'Have not these troubles come upon us because our God is not in our midst?' [18]On that day I will surely hide my face on account of all the evil they have done by turning to other gods. [19]Now therefore write this song, and teach it to the Israelites; put it in their mouths, in order that this song may be a wit-

ness for me against the Israelites. [20]For when I have brought them into the land flowing with milk and honey, which I promised on oath to their ancestors, and they have eaten their fill and grown fat, they will turn to other gods and serve them, despising me and breaking my covenant. [21]And when many terrible troubles come upon them, this song will confront them as a witness, because it will not be lost from the mouths of their descendants. For I know what they are inclined to do even now, before I have brought them into the land that I promised them on oath." [22]That very day Moses wrote this song and taught it to the Israelites.

23 Then the LORD commissioned Joshua son of Nun and said, "Be strong and bold, for you shall bring the Israelites into the land that I promised them; I will be with you."

24 When Moses had finished writing down in a book the words of this law to the very end, [25]Moses commanded the Levites who carried the ark of the covenant of the LORD, saying, [26]"Take this book of the law and put it beside the ark of the covenant of the LORD your God; let it remain there as a witness against you. [27]For I know well how rebellious and stubborn you are. If you already have been so rebellious toward the LORD while I am still alive among you, how much more after my death! [28]Assemble to me all the elders of your tribes and your officials, so that I may recite these words in their hearing and call heaven and earth to witness against them. [29]For I know that after my death you will surely act corruptly, turning aside from the way that I have commanded you. In time to come trouble will befall you, because you will do what is evil in the sight of the LORD,

a Or tabernacles; Heb succoth

---

decision at a single moment. Here Israel's leaders are instructed to periodically gather the people to renew their allegiance to their God.

Responding

31:10–13 STUDY. The reading of the law to Israel during the Festival of Booths reminds us of our reading of the Bible to the congregation during worship services. The

most systematic way of reading the Scriptures is according to lectionaries designed to present the whole Bible over a span of three or more years. As you are able, learn which churches in your town use lectionaries and attend worship in one, noticing the central place that the reading of Scripture plays in the service. *See also* Spiritual Disciplines Index.

provoking him to anger through the work of your hands."

The Song of Moses

30 Then Moses recited the words of this song, to the very end, in the hearing of the whole assembly of Israel:

32 Give ear, O heavens, and I will speak;
    let the earth hear the words of my mouth.
2 May my teaching drop like the rain,
    my speech condense like the dew;
  like gentle rain on grass,
    like showers on new growth.
3 For I will proclaim the name of the LORD;
    ascribe greatness to our God!

4 The Rock, his work is perfect,
    and all his ways are just.
  A faithful God, without deceit,
    just and upright is he;
5 yet his degenerate children have dealt falsely with him, *a*
  a perverse and crooked generation.
6 Do you thus repay the LORD,
    O foolish and senseless people?
  Is not he your father, who created you,
    who made you and established you?
7 Remember the days of old,
    consider the years long past;
  ask your father, and he will inform you;
    your elders, and they will tell you.
8 When the Most High *b* apportioned the nations,
    when he divided humankind,
  he fixed the boundaries of the peoples
    according to the number of the gods; *c*
9 the LORD's own portion was his people,
    Jacob his allotted share.

10 He sustained *d* him in a desert land,
  in a howling wilderness waste;
  he shielded him, cared for him,
    guarded him as the apple of his eye.
11 As an eagle stirs up its nest,
    and hovers over its young;
  as it spreads its wings, takes them up,
    and bears them aloft on its pinions,
12 the LORD alone guided him;
    no foreign god was with him.
13 He set him atop the heights of the land,
    and fed him with *e* produce of the field;
  he nursed him with honey from the crags,
    with oil from flinty rock;
14 curds from the herd, and milk from the flock,
    with fat of lambs and rams;
  Bashan bulls and goats,
    together with the choicest wheat—
  you drank fine wine from the blood of grapes.
15 Jacob ate his fill; *f*
    Jeshurun grew fat, and kicked.
  You grew fat, bloated, and gorged!
  He abandoned God who made him,
    and scoffed at the Rock of his salvation.
16 They made him jealous with strange gods,
    with abhorrent things they provoked him.
17 They sacrificed to demons, not God,
    to deities they had never known,
  to new ones recently arrived,
    whom your ancestors had not feared.
18 You were unmindful of the Rock that bore you; *g*
    you forgot the God who gave you birth.

a Meaning of Heb uncertain   *b* Traditional rendering of Heb *Elyon*   *c* Q Ms Compare Gk Tg: MT *the Israelites*   *d* Sam Gk Compare Tg: MT *found*   *e* Sam Gk Syr Tg: MT *he ate*   *f* Q Mss Sam Gk: MT lacks *Jacob ate his fill*   *g* Or *that begot you*

32:9 *the LORD's own portion was his people.* God has a special relationship with Israel. Earlier Moses describes him as its father (v 6). Now he points out that when the Lord divided humankind into different nations, he reserved Israel for himself, while the other nations were permitted to continue choosing idolatry. The status of these gods is debated, but one thing is clear: they are subordinate to and under the command of the Lord. It is Israel's special relationship with God that makes its betrayal and rebellion all the worse (vv 5, 15–18). When the people God has been intimately involved with turn their back on him, the offense is all the worse.

19 The LORD saw it, and was jealous;[a]
   he spurned[b] his sons and daughters.
20 He said: I will hide my face from them,
   I will see what their end will be;
for they are a perverse generation,
   children in whom there is no
      faithfulness.
21 They made me jealous with what is no
      god,
   provoked me with their idols.
So I will make them jealous with what is
      no people,
   provoke them with a foolish nation.
22 For a fire is kindled by my anger,
   and burns to the depths of Sheol;
it devours the earth and its increase,
   and sets on fire the foundations of the
      mountains.
23 I will heap disasters upon them,
   spend my arrows against them:
24 wasting hunger,
   burning consumption,
   bitter pestilence.
The teeth of beasts I will send against
      them,
   with venom of things crawling in the
      dust.
25 In the street the sword shall bereave,
   and in the chambers terror,
for young man and woman alike,
   nursing child and old gray head.
26 I thought to scatter them[c]
   and blot out the memory of them
      from humankind;
27 but I feared provocation by the enemy,
   for their adversaries might
      misunderstand
and say, "Our hand is triumphant;
   it was not the LORD who did all this."

28 They are a nation void of sense;
   there is no understanding in them.
29 If they were wise, they would
      understand this;
   they would discern what the end
      would be.
30 How could one have routed a
      thousand,
   and two put a myriad to flight,
unless their Rock had sold them,
   the LORD had given them up?

31 Indeed their rock is not like our Rock;
   our enemies are fools.[c]
32 Their vine comes from the vinestock of
      Sodom,
   from the vineyards of Gomorrah;
their grapes are grapes of poison,
   their clusters are bitter;
33 their wine is the poison of serpents,
   the cruel venom of asps.

34 Is not this laid up in store with me,
   sealed up in my treasuries?
35 Vengeance is mine, and recompense,
   for the time when their foot shall slip;
because the day of their calamity is at
      hand,
   their doom comes swiftly.

36 Indeed the LORD will vindicate his
      people,
   have compassion on his servants,
when he sees that their power is gone,
   neither bond nor free remaining.
37 Then he will say: Where are their gods,
   the rock in which they took refuge,
38 who ate the fat of their sacrifices,
   and drank the wine of their
      libations?
Let them rise up and help you,
   let them be your protection!

39 See now that I, even I, am he;
   there is no god besides me.
I kill and I make alive;
   I wound and I heal;
   and no one can deliver from my
      hand.
40 For I lift up my hand to heaven,
   and swear: As I live forever,
41 when I whet my flashing sword,
   and my hand takes hold on
      judgment;
I will take vengeance on my adversaries,
   and will repay those who hate me.
42 I will make my arrows drunk with
      blood,
   and my sword shall devour flesh—

a Q Mss Gk: MT lacks was jealous   b Cn: Heb he
spurned because of provocation   c Gk: Meaning of
Heb uncertain

with the blood of the slain and the
captives,
  from the long-haired enemy.

43 Praise, O heavens, *a* his people,
  worship him, all you gods! *b*
For he will avenge the blood of his
    children, *c*
and take vengeance on his
    adversaries;
  he will repay those who hate him, *b*
  and cleanse the land for his people. *d*

44 Moses came and recited all the words of
this song in the hearing of the people, he
and Joshua *e* son of Nun. 45 When Moses had
finished reciting all these words to all Israel,
46 he said to them: "Take to heart all the words
that I am giving in witness against you today; give them as a command to your children, so that they may diligently observe all
the words of this law. 47 This is no trifling
matter for you, but rather your very life;
through it you may live long in the land that
you are crossing over the Jordan to possess."

Moses' Death Foretold

48 On that very day the LORD addressed
Moses as follows: 49 "Ascend this mountain
of the Abarim, Mount Nebo, which is in the
land of Moab, across from Jericho, and view
the land of Canaan, which I am giving to the
Israelites for a possession; 50 you shall die there
on the mountain that you ascend and shall be
gathered to your kin, as your brother Aaron
died on Mount Hor and was gathered to his
kin; 51 because both of you broke faith with me
among the Israelites at the waters of Meribath-kadesh in the wilderness of Zin, by failing to maintain my holiness among the Israelites. 52 Although you may view the land from
a distance, you shall not enter it—the land
that I am giving to the Israelites."

Moses' Final Blessing on Israel

33 This is the blessing with which Moses, the man of God, blessed the Israelites before his death. 2 He said:
  The LORD came from Sinai,
    and dawned from Seir upon us; *f*
  he shone forth from Mount Paran.
  With him were myriads of holy ones; *g*
    at his right, a host of his own. *h*
3 Indeed, O favorite among *i* peoples,
    all his holy ones were in your charge;
  they marched at your heels,
    accepted direction from you.
4 Moses charged us with the law,
    as a possession for the assembly of
      Jacob.
5 There arose a king in Jeshurun,
    when the leaders of the people
      assembled—
    the united tribes of Israel.

6 May Reuben live, and not die out,
    even though his numbers are few.

7 And this he said of Judah:
  O LORD, give heed to Judah,
    and bring him to his people;
  strengthen his hands for him, *j*
    and be a help against his adversaries.

8 And of Levi he said:
  Give to Levi *k* your Thummim,
    and your Urim to your loyal one,

a Q Ms Gk: MT *nations*   *b* Q Ms Gk: MT lacks
this line   *c* Q Ms Gk: MT *his servants*   *d* Q Ms
Sam Gk Vg: MT *his land his people*   *e* Sam Gk Syr
Vg: MT *Hoshea*   *f* Gk Syr Vg Compare Tg: Heb
upon them   *g* Cn Compare Gk Sam Syr Vg: MT *He
came from Ribeboth-kodesh,*   *h* Cn Compare Gk:
meaning of Heb uncertain   *i* Or *O lover of the*
j Cn: Heb *with his hands he contended*   *k* Q Ms
Gk: MT lacks *Give to Levi*

32:40–42 *I will make my arrows drunk with
blood.* Christians often shrink from hearing this
kind of bloody language associated with God.
They ignore the Old Testament depictions of
God, thinking that the New Testament has a
higher conception. However, to maintain this
kind of separation between Old and New
Testaments, one has to carefully omit large

portions of the New Testament, particularly
texts such as Revelation. The truth of the matter
is that both Testaments bear witness to a loving
and holy God who saves and judges. Although
the Gospels present a nonviolent Jesus, who
dies on the cross to defeat evil, Revelation looks
forward to a warring Messiah who will win the
final battle against evil.

whom you tested at Massah,
　　with whom you contended at the
　　　waters of Meribah;
9　who said of his father and mother,
　　"I regard them not";
　he ignored his kin,
　　and did not acknowledge his
　　　children.
　For they observed your word,
　　and kept your covenant.
10 They teach Jacob your ordinances,
　　and Israel your law;
　they place incense before you,
　　and whole burnt offerings on your
　　　altar.
11 Bless, O LORD, his substance,
　　and accept the work of his hands;
　crush the loins of his adversaries,
　　of those that hate him, so that they
　　　do not rise again.

12 Of Benjamin he said:
　The beloved of the LORD rests in safety—
　the High God*a* surrounds him all day
　　long—
　　the beloved*b* rests between his
　　　shoulders.

13 And of Joseph he said:
　Blessed by the LORD be his land,
　　with the choice gifts of heaven above,
　　and of the deep that lies beneath;
14 with the choice fruits of the sun,
　　and the rich yield of the months;
15 with the finest produce of the ancient
　　　mountains,
　　and the abundance of the everlasting
　　　hills;

16 with the choice gifts of the earth and its
　　　fullness,
　　and the favor of the one who dwells
　　　on Sinai.*c*
　Let these come on the head of Joseph,
　　on the brow of the prince among his
　　　brothers.
17 A firstborn*d* bull—majesty is his!
　His horns are the horns of a wild ox;
　with them he gores the peoples,
　　driving them to*e* the ends of the earth;
　such are the myriads of Ephraim,
　　such the thousands of Manasseh.

18 And of Zebulun he said:
　Rejoice, Zebulun, in your going out;
　　and Issachar, in your tents.
19 They call peoples to the mountain;
　　there they offer the right sacrifices;
　for they suck the affluence of the seas
　　and the hidden treasures of the sand.

20 And of Gad he said:
　Blessed be the enlargement of Gad!
　　Gad lives like a lion;
　　he tears at arm and scalp.
21 He chose the best for himself,
　　for there a commander's allotment
　　　was reserved;
　he came at the head of the people,
　　he executed the justice of the LORD,
　　and his ordinances for Israel.

22 And of Dan he said:
　Dan is a lion's whelp
　　that leaps forth from Bashan.

a Heb *above him*　　b Heb *he*　　c Cn: Heb *in the bush*　　d Q Ms Gk Syr Vg: MT *His firstborn*
e Cn: Heb *the peoples, together*

33:9 *he ignored his kin.* Typically to ignore one's kin is a vice not a virtue. However, the blessing has reference to a special circumstance, namely, the role of the Levites during the incident of the golden calf. The story of the Levites as a whole is the story of God bringing a blessing out of a curse. In Genesis 34 Levi and Simeon anger their father, Jacob, when they deceptively slaughter the inhabitants of Shechem in revenge for what they consider the violation of their

sister. Thus, at the end of his life Jacob curses the brothers by saying that their descendants will not receive an allotment of land (Gen 49:5–7). However, because they came to Moses' aid and slaughtered those of their kin who worshiped the golden calf, Moses set them apart for special service to God (Exod 32:25–29). So instead of being lost through assimilation to another tribe (as happened to Simeon), the Levites actually are commissioned to teach Israel God's law.

23 And of Naphtali he said:
O Naphtali, sated with favor,
    full of the blessing of the LORD,
    possess the west and the south.

24 And of Asher he said:
Most blessed of sons be Asher;
    may he be the favorite of his brothers,
    and may he dip his foot in oil.
25 Your bars are iron and bronze;
    and as your days, so is your strength.

26 There is none like God, O Jeshurun,
    who rides through the heavens to
        your help,
    majestic through the skies.
27 He subdues the ancient gods,a
    shattersb the forces of old;c
he drove out the enemy before you,
    and said, "Destroy!"
28 So Israel lives in safety,
    untroubled is Jacob's abode d
in a land of grain and wine,
    where the heavens drop down dew.
29 Happy are you, O Israel! Who is like
        you,
    a people saved by the LORD,
the shield of your help,
    and the sword of your triumph!
Your enemies shall come fawning to
        you,
    and you shall tread on their backs.

Moses Dies and Is Buried in the Land of Moab

34 Then Moses went up from the plains of Moab to Mount Nebo, to the top of Pisgah, which is opposite Jericho, and the LORD showed him the whole land: Gilead as far as Dan, 2all Naphtali, the land of Ephraim and Manasseh, all the land of Judah as far as the Western Sea, 3the Negeb, and the Plain—that is, the valley of Jericho, the city of palm trees—as far as Zoar. 4The LORD said to him, "This is the land of which I swore to Abraham, to Isaac, and to Jacob, saying, 'I will give it to your descendants'; I have let you see it with your eyes, but you shall not cross over there." 5Then Moses, the servant of the LORD, died there in the land of Moab, at the LORD's command. 6He was buried in a valley in the land of Moab, opposite Beth-peor, but no one knows his burial place to this day. 7Moses was one hundred twenty years old when he died; his sight was unimpaired and his vigor had not abated. 8The Israelites wept for Moses in the plains of Moab thirty days; then the period of mourning for Moses was ended.

9 Joshua son of Nun was full of the spirit of wisdom, because Moses had laid his hands on him; and the Israelites obeyed him, doing as the LORD had commanded Moses.

10 Never since has there arisen a prophet in Israel like Moses, whom the LORD knew face to face. 11He was unequaled for all the signs and wonders that the LORD sent him to perform in the land of Egypt, against Pharaoh and all his servants and his entire land, 12and for all the mighty deeds and all the terrifying displays of power that Moses performed in the sight of all Israel.

a Or The eternal God is a dwelling place
b Cn: Heb from underneath   c Or the everlasting
arms   d Or fountain

33:26–29 THE WITH-GOD LIFE—See Spiritual Disciplines Index.
34:10 *Never since has there arisen a prophet in Israel like Moses.* The tradition of the Pentateuch is that Moses had an especially close relationship with Yahweh. God used him in extraordinary ways at a crucial moment in Israel's redemption. Although there will be prophets like Moses in the future (18:15), they will not have the same intimate relationship with the Lord, since God spoke to Moses "face to face" (Num 12:8). That is, no prophets until Jesus. Jesus is "worthy of more glory than Moses" (Heb 3:3). Jesus is the ultimate prophet; we "must listen to whatever he tells" us (Acts 3:22).

IV. The People of God in the Promised Land

Scriptures: [Joshua, Judges, Ruth, 1 Samuel 1–12]

> The aim of God in history is the creation of an all-inclusive community of loving persons with God himself at the very center of this community as its prime Sustainer and most glorious Inhabitant (Eph 2:19–22; 3:10). The Bible traces the formation of this community from the creation in the Garden of Eden all the way to the new heaven and the new earth. Come, join us as we explore the many dimensions of this with-God history—from individual to family to tribe to people to nation to all humanity—and apply what we learn to our own spiritual formation.

In the Scriptures listed above we will see the ways God continues the process of forming an all-inclusive community through the conquest and occupation of the Promised Land. This occupation lays the foundation for the formation of the twelve tribes of Israel into a holy nation set apart for the worship of Yahweh.

God's Action

Following the biblical creation account, we find God mediating his presence to individuals; then to a family, which became a people liberated from bondage; and now to an emerging tribal confederation, the twelve tribes of Israel. As God leads them to the borders of Canaan, the Promised Land, he reveals himself through the administrative leadership of Moses, the first "superior court" judge; the religious instruction of Eleazar, who is the son of Aaron, the first high priest; and a visible divine presence in the tent of meeting, in the Holy of Holies. By obeying the law, keeping the Sabbath, and celebrating seasonal cycles, the children of Abraham bring into being a community that keeps alive God's historical, public acts and nurtures and protects their destiny to become a blessing to all nations.

Administrative leadership shifts from Moses to Joshua as God leads the Israelites across the Jordan into Canaan, the land first promised to Abraham. Joshua mobilizes the people and calls them to remember the words of Moses (Josh 1:10–12), as he conscripts an army from among their number and prepares them for a difficult entrance into a strange land. God miraculously holds back the waters of the Jordan to let the Israelites pass into Canaan when the priests enter the water with the ark of the covenant. Once everyone crosses safely, representatives from each tribe set up a permanent twelve-stone memorial in the middle of the Jordan. When they are done, the priests walk to the Canaanite side of the river, and water floods the crossing place.

The Jordan crossing marks the beginning of a political and military campaign in which God performs miracles to help the children of Israel conquer and inhabit the towns and cities of Canaan, making them their own. It is God who is fighting for the people to give them a land of rest, a land scarred by the idolatry of its current inhabitants, a land "flowing with milk and honey" (Deut 8:8; 11:9; 26:9).

The people are in awe of Joshua as he leads the military campaign in the power of God. After Jericho and Ai fall, the Israelites defeat the armies of numerous other kings; time passes and Joshua ages, although there is much of the land yet to be conquered. Still, God commands Joshua to assign particular geographic areas to the tribes, promising to drive out the present inhabitants "before the Israelites" (Josh 13:6). Joshua dies before he sees all of the tribes occupy the territory given them, but he witnesses Israel serving and worshiping the Lord all of his days (Josh 24:31; Judg 2:7).

At the death of Joshua, the Lord appoints the tribe of Judah to lead the fight against the Canaanites. This begins a period when God is with the people through anointed judges whose duties include administering justice, destroying centers of idolatry, and leading military campaigns. The emergence of judges sets in place a theocracy, a society solely under God's direction without a human government, and their anointed leadership gives birth to the messianic theme that we find throughout Jewish life. The legal and religious institutions brought to life under Moses are now being adapted to the conditions of a more settled life under the charismatic leadership of these judges. The progressive mediating work of God is present vividly in the experience and social structures of the Israelites as they face the life and death challenges of securing a promised homeland and increasingly move toward becoming a people with a national identity.

Human Reaction

After wandering for forty years in the desert, the Israelites are ready to enter into their promise. It takes great courage for the People of God to trust God sufficiently to fulfill the promise made to Abraham and cross over the Jordan into the well-defended Promised Land. All objective indicators point to probable defeat, but leaders who respond to God's call arise from within their ranks and, by God's grace, they claim the land of promise. As did Abraham long ago, they trust God to give them wisdom and courage in all things.

When in the land, the Israelites embrace God's initiatives by responding positively to the leaders and judges responsible for their judicial, military, and religious well-being. The same awe and high regard accorded to Joshua by the people continues after he dies, as they actively seek and heed the advice and counsel of their new leaders, the judges. The power of this accepted form of leadership can be seen in many examples: when the people come up to Deborah for judgment (Judg 4:5); when a Canaanite ruler oppresses the children of Israel and Deborah recruits Barak and men from the tribes of Naphtali and Zebulun to fight the king's army (4:4–23); or when Gideon personally destroys an altar of Baal and builds an altar to the Lord (6:25–27). These leaders deal with the immediate, pressing issues of friction and disagree-

The With~God Life

ments between individuals and tribes now scattered across the land and in the process of developing their own identities. The judges also deal with the reality of living in a land still inhabited by people of different ethnicities and religions who resent their very presence and constantly try to evict them.

In response to God's constant presence with them during the exodus, the Israelites made the tent of meeting; now they set it up at Shiloh, where the Spiritual Disciplines of prayer, celebration, worship, and sacrifice develop to help preserve and extend through time the memory of this deliverance. Without the visible reminder of God's presence, centered on the ark of the covenant in the tabernacle, the people would have more easily forgotten who they were—slaves rescued by the hand of God from the furnace of Egypt—and neglected the law and its instructions. However, the distance to this new center of religious life and a growing and widely dispersed population make it difficult for many to visit more than occasionally, placing limits upon the memory and celebration of God's faithfulness and upon the daily seeking of his living presence.

In spite of God's clear guidance and support for the Israelites, their faith in his provisions wavers. They respond inconsistently and ambiguously to the incomparable gifts of occupation and possession of the land. Abraham's descendants intermarry with the people they are trying to conquer and worship their gods. Their resolve to occupy all of the land, giving no quarter to any of its inhabitants, softens. Disputes between tribes become a recurring problem. After the triumphant entry into the Promised Land and the military victories recorded in Joshua, and despite the people's faith in their charismatic leaders, the book of Judges tells a sad story of disobedience, disunity, and dysfunction. The period of Joshua and the judges ends in anarchy: "In those days there was no king in Israel; all the people did what was right in their own eyes" (Judg 21:25).

Blessings and Benefits for Our Formation

There are blessings and benefits in this form of God-with-us, not the least of which is rest. After all of their wanderings, the Israelites enter the land, where they settle down with the possibility of becoming a united People of God. They at last have a place in the world where they can live out their faithfulness to God. The divisions that had existed since Joseph's brothers sold him into slavery can be put behind them, because they are now one people in a permanent home where sibling jealousy and tribal rivalries can be set aside as they worship the holy God. We too need such a place where we are free to worship God and become the people that God desires us to be. The author of Hebrews confirms this by writing, "Let us therefore make every effort to enter . . . rest" (4:11).

The bustling period of the judges, when charismatic leaders like Gideon and Samson were active, is wonderful. During this time of settlement, all have the freedom to seek God as they are led. People are free from the restrictions imposed by a central government. Individuals can develop their own talents or farm their own land without interference from any outside authority. However great a blessing, such freedom is unsustainable. All of us may long for this kind of freedom, but could we handle it? Would we continue to worship God regularly without the accountability of our community of faith? How often would we make the trip to Shiloh? Would we obey voluntary laws not established and enforced by a central government? Could we really become the kind of people who can glorify God in all areas of our life on our own? Probably not.

The benefits and blessings of this period in God's work to form human character illustrate the continued importance of individual accountability in divine history. Yes, God's presence is visible to all in the tent of meeting at Shiloh, but individuals like Joshua and the judges find ways to bring God into everyday life through their obedience and wisdom. God is "with them" in the midst of military campaigns and insurrections, rededications and pilgrimages. Their example affirms that we as individuals can be used by God to bring his grace, love, and justice to our family and neighbors.

Limits and Liabilities for Our Formation

For the theocracy to have worked during the period of the judges, Mosaic law had to be obeyed, the rituals practiced, and the leaders followed without question. However, there is no indication that this happened. In fact, Joshua warns the people to be "careful to act in accordance with all the law that my servant Moses commanded you" right after he is chosen their leader (Josh 1:7); and later he reminds the tribes of Reuben, Gad, and Manasseh to "be very careful to observe the commandment and the law which Moses the servant of the LORD commanded you" (Josh 22:5, NASB). Interestingly, Mosaic law is never directly mentioned in Judges. We can only speculate that because the average Israelite did not have a written record, the requirements of the law were very quickly forgotten in daily life, as they would be for us in a similar situation. The disciplines of study and meditation upon God's precepts were missing in this time of rapid transition. By comparison, this should make us very thankful for the written Word of God, which is useful "for teaching, for reproof, for correction, and for training in righteousness, so that everyone who belongs to God may be proficient, equipped for every good work" (2 Tim 3:16–17).

Because there is no central authority, the judges lack a support group to back them up or an independent rule to refer to in their decisions and activities. In truth, they do not have the power over life and death that can force compliance to God's law. The strongest judges wield this power on the strength of their own charismatic leadership, but that is sporadic, and for the most part they are unable to force the people to obey the law and practice the rituals. This is further complicated by the fact that the people are scattered throughout the land, and the judges' influence is confined to a local region.

The story of Samson is a clear depiction of the limits and ambiguities of leadership during this period. Although Samson is unique among the judges as one who acts decisively to exercise the superhuman strength God gave him, he is yet an ambivalent figure, prone to succumb to sexual temptation though bound by a Nazirite vow (Judg 13–16). His example argues strongly for the need for mutual spiritual support and individual accountability, both for our leaders and for ourselves.

The With-God Life

Since the participation of the People of God in the rituals and seasonal celebrations is sporadic during this time, alternative local shrines and altars to idols are built upon the hills in order to satisfy their yearnings for religious rituals as well as those of their "foreign" spouses. In such an environment, many people forsake God and worship pagan idols.

Insights and Instructions for Our Formation

One of the clearest lessons for our formation is that often charisma outruns character, as it did with Samson. The danger is that our gifts will take us to places where our character cannot keep us. We see numerous instances of this in our own time: in politicians, religious leaders, educational figures, and entertainers. A single issue of any newspaper contains articles about notable people lying, deceiving, murdering, and robbing, while their winsome, charismatic personalities seem to isolate them from the consequences of their actions. Often the "sizzle" of charisma will ruin the "steak" of character formation—a reminder that if God has given us natural or even supernatural charisma, then we need to align it with the kingdom God and not with our own self-interest.

Second, the example of infighting between the twelve tribes should motivate us to work to overcome the modern example of tribalism in the Christian faith: denominationalism. We may laugh about the number of factions within the Church (the number has ballooned from 1,900 to over 35,500 during the twentieth century) and the reasons behind those splits, but in the overall scheme of God's kingdom they are a disaster. Although it almost always starts out with good intentions, in the end sectarianism alienates sincere, faith-filled brothers and sisters from one another and brings universal disrepute upon the Body of Christ. Divisions in the Church are not to be greeted by our laughter, but overcome through our prayers.

Third, we must make a special effort to handle power rightly. Power without God is abusive and destructive. "So Abimelech son of Jerubbaal . . . killed his brothers . . . and they went and made Abimelech king" (Judg 9:1–6). Authentic kingdom power blesses, heals, enlightens, and creates.

Fourth, we will reap what we sow. If we insist on replacing God with the idols of wealth or pleasure or fame, then, like the Israelites at the end of the period of the judges, the hand of the Lord will be against us. We can expect to experience discontent in our spiritual life, dysfunction in our family life, and disharmony in our public life. The only wise course is to put God first, loving him with all of our heart, all of our soul, all of our mind, and all of our strength (Deut 6:5; Mark 12:30).

Finally, the book of Ruth presents a beautiful account of personal faithfulness. When Ruth, a hated Moabite, and her mother-in-law, Naomi, a devout Israelite, become widows, Ruth elects to remain with Naomi and to be faithful to her God. Ruth's faithfulness to Naomi preserves the family line through which, "in the fullness of time," the incarnate Messianic Servant Lord is born. In Ruth we see a breathtaking picture of God's faithfulness despite Israel's frequent unfaithfulness and a glimpse of the grace that will later extend to all humanity.

The With-God Life

JOSHUA

The book of Joshua is at once a story of the nation of Israel and a study of the life of Joshua, who spent the first eighty years of his days in training to be a leader marked by the life and skills of his mentor, Moses. The themes of the book of Joshua and those for the formation of the nation Israel are deeply intertwined: both bear witness to the promise-keeping God who was ever present for the nation and for its new leader.

The story of the nation is told in an action-packed first half of the book, chapters 1–12. Never are the ancient promises made to the fathers of Israel (Abraham, Isaac, and Jacob) far from the mind of the writer. More than fifty times in Joshua we are reminded that God's "gift" to Israel is the land of Canaan. It does not belong to the nation; instead, the land is owned uniquely by God (as also noted in Lev 25:2–7; Deut 9:4–5). The military victories at Jericho, Ai, Gibeon, Hazor, and other cities depict a dramatic picture, to say the least. But what appears to be a swashbuckling record is neither the full story nor the main point of the writer. The possession of the land means the accomplishment of the "rest" that God wanted to give to his people. This "rest" is more than relief from Israel's enemies and conquest; it is the gift of the land itself (Josh 1:13).

The second half of the book, chapters 13–21, settles down to a more staid and what for the moment appears to be a less interesting part of the narrative after all the excitement and dramatic activity of the first part of the book. However, the thrust remains the same: the land has been secured in principle, if not completely in reality. God's promised blessings have been inaugurated, and the ancient divine promises are on the road to being fulfilled. The fact that the land is now mapped out and divided up among the tribes is tantamount to a reality check: "See, God has kept his promise."

See also *"The With-God Life" essay for this section of the Bible,*
"The People of God in the Promised Land," pp. 297–301.

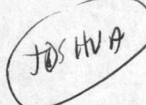

Groomed for Leadership

But what shall we say of Joshua the leader? To be sure, he certainly did not emerge out of the blue, for he underwent eighty years of training for the task he was to undertake. Joshua's life can be divided into three segments: forty years in Egypt, forty years in the wilderness with Israel, and twenty-five years as leader over the nation.

Interestingly enough, we are told nothing about Joshua in Egypt, or about him during Moses' contest with Pharaoh, or even about Joshua's role when Israel crossed the Red Sea. He is first mentioned when the Amalekites attack Israel (Exod 17:8–9). Here, for the first time, Joshua takes charge of the army, while Moses raises his hands (apparently in prayer) on the mountain overlooking the battle. The lesson Joshua recalls and writes down (Exod 17:14) for recounting in later years is that real power does not rest in the sword, but in unceasing prayer to God.

Surprisingly, Joshua came from a family that had some skeletons in its closet. Although he was a member of a prominent family of Ephraim, Joshua's early ancestors were killed by the men of Gath for cattle rustling (1 Chron 7:20–27). Nine generations later, however, Joshua was able to rise above such an ignominious heritage.

At Mt. Sinai Moses chose Joshua to go part way up the mountain, leaving even the seventy elders farther down the mount. There, for six days, a cloud of God's glory covered Moses and Joshua (Exod 24:13–17). Six days in the presence of God and then another thirty-four days in solitary meditation on the living God were enough to mark this man for a whole lifetime. A vision of the glory of God forever formed Joshua and supplied the basis for effective leadership.

An additional insight into Joshua's preparation for leadership came in Exod 33:11. Joshua would customarily accompany Moses when he went to the tent to meet with God. However, Joshua was apparently so overcome by the presence of God that he would not depart from the tent when Moses left. His personal devotion to God is given special notice in this text, perhaps to explain in part why he became such a great leader. Nevertheless, Joshua still had to learn that jealousy of his mentor's honor would make him a small, petty person unfit for leadership. When Joshua asked Moses to stop the elders Eldad and Medad from prophesying in the camp long after the other sixty-eight elders had stopped, Moses had to rebuke him (Num 11:24–30). Rather than promoting himself or Moses, he had to learn how to support those around him. Understanding service was a vital prerequisite to genuine spiritual leadership.

Finally, Joshua was also chosen to be one of the twelve spies to investigate the land of Canaan in Numbers 13–14. He and Caleb brought the minority report, despite the majority vote by the ten, who said that Israel should not go up into the land. This is not altogether surprising, for Caleb had a different attitude and spirit about himself (Num 14:24) and Joshua was "a man in whom [was] the spirit" (27:18). Both of these men had a proper confidence in God (14:8), a disregard for the obstacles (14:9), a proper fear of God (14:9), and a proper trust in the promise of God (14:7).

The God of Joshua

The book of Joshua, then, is more about the God of Joshua than it is about the man whose name we now use to signal that portion of the Scriptures relating his call by God to lead the nation. Given the fact of God's presence made the difference in all that happened in the forward movement of Joshua's people, it is small wonder that the idea of Israel's call to be separate from the seven nations that were in Canaan should lead us to the concept of God's holiness. That is why Israel was called to be holy as well, for God was holy (Lev 19). Simply put: the Israelites were to be separate from evil and to draw a line between the sacred and the mundane; yet they were to be set apart for the good, for what was sacred and all that was directly given over to God.

We need here to address what appears to modern sensibilities as the excessive violence of the conquest of Canaan. This is especially so with the *herem,* the ban, in which the spoils of war are devoted to God and God commands that they all be wiped out: men, women, children, cattle, sheep, goats, houses, possessions—everything (see Deut 7:2; 13:15; Josh 9:24). Indeed, the text indicates that at Jericho the sin of Achan in failing to destroy some of the "devoted things" resulted in Israel's defeat at the city of Ai (Josh 7; see also 1 Sam 15 in regard to Saul). What do we make of this?

No answer is fully satisfying, but a few observations might be helpful. Note, first of all, that the text's express reason for the *herem* is to secure holiness for Israel by protecting it from the idolatry and multiple wicked practices of the Canaanites: "For you are a people holy to the LORD your God; the LORD your God has chosen you out of all the peoples on earth to be his people, his treasured possession" (Deut 7:6). Then too, theologically the emphasis upon complete sacrificial offering to God was a way of stressing that Yahweh's army, not Israel's, won the battle. All the booty of war belongs to God alone, and burning it up was a way of offering it all to God by making it useless to human beings.

Also, it can be said that God at times accommodates himself to human context and need, and that through time and history the progressive revelation of God shows his people a more excellent way. Finally, it is instructive to see the tension in the Old Testament text itself. This is not simply a matter of an Old Testament God of wrath versus a New Testament God of love. The main thrust of the Old Testament teaching is to show that Yahweh's steadfast love endures forever and that his love is for all kinds of people, including foreigners. And so the text of Scripture itself refuses to resolve the problem we feel over the *herem.* Rather, it teaches us to live with the tension inherent within mystery and paradox.

Joshua 5 records three separate incidents that show the importance of ritual and practical purity. First is the ceremony of circumcision (vv 12–13). Then the Passover is observed (vv 10–12). And finally Joshua himself is confronted by the captain of the Lord's host (vv 13–15) and commanded to remove his sandals, much as Moses had been instructed in a similar scene in Exod 3:5–6. Later, in chapter 22, an altar for commemoration is built that again signals the uniqueness and separateness of God over against all competing rivals.

Another prominent theme is faithfulness to the covenant (Josh 1:7–8; 22:5;

23:6, 16; 24:15). Twice in this book Joshua leads the people in services dedicated to renewing the covenant: one at Mt. Ebal (8:30–35) and a second one at Shechem (chap 24). The call is for the nation to follow God alone and to keep all his instructions given in the book of the law.

But it is the theme of the land that features centrally in Joshua. Here is the fulfillment of what had been promised to Abraham (Gen 12:7; 13:14–15, 17; 15:18–21; 17:8; 22:17) and Isaac (26:3–4), and repeated also to Jacob (28:4, 13; 35:12) as well as to succeeding generations (48:4; 50:24). This "good and broad land" "flowing with milk and honey" (Exod 3:8, 17) was God's gift. It was God's to give, for he owned it (a nuance often lost in the politicization of this issue in subsequent history). Hence, the use of the lot to divide the land was not a chance operation, but another sign of God's intervention in even the parceling up of the turf. Israel's possession of the land and the wiping out of the inhabitants found in the land was in direct obedience to God's command (Josh 10:40; 11:20, 23; 23:9–13).

The concluding three chapters of the book of Joshua record a leader's farewell to the tribes east of the Jordan (22:1–34), his first farewell to all the nation (23:1–16), his second farewell to Israel (24:1–28), and an apparent addition of his burial notice (24:29–33).

Some may be tempted to conclude: what a magnificent man! But this book would call for another conclusion: what an awesome God!

—*Walter C. Kaiser, Jr.*

God's Commission to Joshua

1 After the death of Moses the servant of the LORD, the LORD spoke to Joshua son of Nun, Moses' assistant, saying, ²"My servant Moses is dead. Now proceed to cross the Jordan, you and all this people, into the land that I am giving to them, to the Israelites. ³Every place that the sole of your foot will tread upon I have given to you, as I promised to Moses. ⁴From the wilderness and the Lebanon as far as the great river, the river Euphrates, all the land of the Hittites, to the Great Sea in the west shall be your territory. ⁵No one shall be able to stand against you all the days of your life. As I was with Moses, so I will be with you; I will not fail you or forsake

1:1 *After the death of Moses . . . the LORD spoke to Joshua.* Joshua son of Nun was "Moses' assistant." Moses had served as his mentor for more than forty years, even though Joshua possessed obvious gifts of his own. Deut 34:9 commends this "assistant" as one who "was full of the spirit of wisdom, because Moses had laid his hands on him; and the Israelites obeyed him, doing as the LORD had commanded Moses."

1:2 *Now proceed to cross the Jordan . . . into the land that I am giving.* The land was a gift promised centuries ago to Abraham, Isaac, and Jacob (Gen 12:7; 13:14–15, 17; 15:7, 18–21; 17:8; 22:17; 24:7; 26:3–4; 28:13–14; 35:12). The Israelites would go into slavery in a foreign land,

but God would bring them back to their own land (Gen 15:13, 16). This promise continued to be repeated numerous times over (Exod 6:4, 8; Deut 1:6–8; 4:38, 40; 5:31; 7:13; 8:1-10; 9:4–6; 11:8–12; 26:1, 9; 32:49; 34:4).

1:5 *As I was with Moses, so I will be with you.* The greatest promise of all was "I will be with you," which was a repetition of the same promise God had given to Moses (Exod 3:12). This Immanuel principle is stressed again in Josh 1:9; 3:7. Joshua had seen what God's presence meant to his predecessor; therefore he was greatly encouraged, as all God's people should be by the promise of the presence of God in their lives. It appears again in 1:17.

you. [6]Be strong and courageous; for you shall put this people in possession of the land that I swore to their ancestors to give them. [7]Only be strong and very courageous, being careful to act in accordance with all the law that my servant Moses commanded you; do not turn from it to the right hand or to the left, so that you may be successful wherever you go. [8]This book of the law shall not depart out of your mouth; you shall meditate on it day and night, so that you may be careful to act in accordance with all that is written in it. For then you shall make your way prosperous, and then you shall be successful. [9]I hereby command you: Be strong and courageous; do not be frightened or dismayed, for the LORD your God is with you wherever you go."

Preparations for the Invasion

10 Then Joshua commanded the officers of the people, [11]"Pass through the camp, and command the people: 'Prepare your provisions; for in three days you are to cross over the Jordan, to go in to take possession of the land that the LORD your God gives you to possess.' "

12 To the Reubenites, the Gadites, and the half-tribe of Manasseh Joshua said, [13]"Remember the word that Moses the servant of

---

Responding
1:5 THE WITH-GOD LIFE. Joshua's faith that God would help the Israelites conquer Canaan results in God promising to be with him (see Num 14:6–9). Almost as an aside, God also promises Joshua not to fail or forsake him. Why do you think God approached his promise to Joshua from two directions? Could it have been because God foresaw the tough challenges Joshua would face in the future? Name one difficult time in your life when you needed special reassurance that God was with you. See also Spiritual Disciplines Index.

1:6 Be strong and courageous. Four times the command to "be strong and courageous" (vv 6, 7, 9, 18) is repeated in words very similar to Deut 3:28; 31:7, 23. Strength and courage were needed to face the opposition, to live personally by the teaching of the word of God, and to walk in fellowship with the living God.

1:7–8 do not turn from it . . . meditate on it day and night. Effective leadership called for concentrated meditation and musing on the law of God. This word was not to "depart" from his "mouth," for mortals do not live by bread alone, but by every word that proceeds from the mouth of God (Deut 8:3). Like Joshua, we are to talk about the word, think about the word, and obey the word (Ps 1:2–3).

Responding
1:8 MEDITATION and STUDY. We often perceive study as reading or concentrating on one subject until we know it with our mind, while the common view of meditation is that it disengages our mind.

In this passage, study and meditation are inseparable; Joshua had to know the law before he could meditate on it. Read Exod 20:1–17 and commentaries that explain it several times during the next few days, making a special effort to understand it with your mind. Then, for the next seventeen days meditate on each verse in turn. Did your mind begin to conform to the teachings of the law? See also Spiritual Disciplines Index.

1:11 Prepare . . . for in three days. All impurities had to be removed if Israel was to get ready for God to act. The "three days" seem to be a reenactment of the three days of purification at the foot of Mt. Sinai (Exod 19:10–11). The people were to take possession of the land. The archaic meaning of "to possess" here seems to be from the same root as the identical term "to tread on," as in to tread on grapes (as in Mic 6:15). Hence, it meant to tread on the land as owner and conqueror. Ultimately, Israel's "seed shall possess [tread on] the nations" (Isa 54:3).

1:12–18 To the Reubenites, the Gadites, and the half-tribe of Manasseh. Unity among the People of God is not a luxury, but a necessity. This section must be read against the background of Numbers, where Moses at first blasted the Reubenites and Gadites' request as coming from "a brood of sinners" (32:14), for he thought they were opting out of the conquest of the land west of the Jordan, thereby disheartening and discouraging the other tribes. Fortunately this was not what the two tribes meant. So Joshua quotes Moses' response to this new finding with words that are

the LORD commanded you, saying, 'The LORD your God is providing you a place of rest, and will give you this land.' [14]Your wives, your little ones, and your livestock shall remain in the land that Moses gave you beyond the Jordan. But all the warriors among you shall cross over armed before your kindred and shall help them, [15]until the LORD gives rest to your kindred as well as to you, and they too take possession of the land that the LORD your God is giving them. Then you shall return to your own land and take possession of it, the land that Moses the servant of the LORD gave you beyond the Jordan to the east."

16 They answered Joshua: "All that you have commanded us we will do, and wherever you send us we will go. [17]Just as we obeyed Moses in all things, so we will obey you. Only may the LORD your God be with you, as he was with Moses! [18]Whoever rebels against your orders and disobeys your words, whatever you command, shall be put to death. Only be strong and courageous."

Spies Sent to Jericho

2 Then Joshua son of Nun sent two men secretly from Shittim as spies, saying, "Go, view the land, especially Jericho." So they went, and entered the house of a prostitute whose name was Rahab, and spent the night there. [2]The king of Jericho was told, "Some Israelites have come here tonight to search out the land." [3]Then the king of Jericho sent orders to Rahab, "Bring out the men who have come to you, who entered your house, for they have come only to search out the whole land." [4]But the woman took the two men and hid them. Then she said, "True, the men came to me, but I did not know where they came from. [5]And when it was time to close the gate at dark, the men went out. Where the men went I do not know. Pursue them quickly, for you can overtake them." [6]She had, however, brought them up to the roof and hidden them with the stalks of flax that she had laid out on the roof. [7]So the men pursued them on the way to the Jordan as far as the fords. As soon as the pursuers had gone out, the gate was shut.

8 Before they went to sleep, she came up to them on the roof [9]and said to the men: "I know that the LORD has given you the land, and that dread of you has fallen on us, and that all the inhabitants of the land melt in fear before you. [10]For we have heard how the LORD dried up the water of the Red Sea [a] before you when you came out of Egypt, and what you did to the two kings of the Amorites that were beyond the Jordan, to Sihon and Og, whom you utterly destroyed. [11]As soon as we heard it, our hearts melted, and there was no courage left in any of us because of you. The LORD your God is indeed God in heaven above

_a_ Or _Sea of Reeds_

---

almost verbatim to Moses' original instructions (see also vv 13–15; Deut 3:18–20).

1:13, 15 _God is providing you a place of rest._ "Rest" for the people of God was a sign of God's presence and security. It echoed the promise made in Exod 33:14; Num 32:20–22; and Deut 3:18–20; 12:9–10. It signaled spiritual as well as physical rest (Heb 3:1–4:3, 11). By faith we are to cast on the Lord all our labors and all that weighs us down (Matt 11:28). This also is a picture of the Sabbath rest that is to come for the people of God (Heb 4:9).

2:1 _So they went, and entered the house of a prostitute whose name was Rahab._ Some ask if it is fitting to include Rahab, a prostitute, as a main character in the story of the conquest. Even more unsettling to some is the fact that she later became the wife of a prince in Judah (see Ruth 4:18–22; Matt 1:4–6). Of course it is fitting and altogether appropriate to the gospel! There but for the grace of God goes every sinner from Rahab's day to our own! Rahab, therefore, is in the chapter of those who are heroes of faith, where she is praised for her trust in God (Heb 11:31). We would do well to imitate rather than be offended by her.

2:9–11 _I know that the LORD has given you the land._ Rahab confidently asserted her faith as she said, "The LORD your God is indeed God in heaven above and on earth below." Her use of the personal name Yahweh, translated here as LORD, indicates that her faith was in the living Lord. The sovereignty of God is taught in similar terms in Deut 4:39; 1 Kings 8:60; 2 Kings 19:19; Ps 100:3. Here Rahab acts as a representative of "all the peoples of the earth."

and on earth below. 12Now then, since I have dealt kindly with you, swear to me by the LORD that you in turn will deal kindly with my family. Give me a sign of good faith 13that you will spare my father and mother, my brothers and sisters, and all who belong to them, and deliver our lives from death." 14The men said to her, "Our life for yours! If you do not tell this business of ours, then we will deal kindly and faithfully with you when the LORD gives us the land."

15 Then she let them down by a rope through the window, for her house was on the outer side of the city wall and she resided within the wall itself. 16She said to them, "Go toward the hill country, so that the pursuers may not come upon you. Hide yourselves there three days, until the pursuers have returned; then afterward you may go your way." 17The men said to her, "We will be released from this oath that you have made us swear to you 18if we invade the land and you do not tie this crimson cord in the window through which you let us down, and you do not gather into your house your father and mother, your brothers, and all your family. 19If any of you go out of the doors of your house into the street, they shall be responsible for their own death, and we shall be innocent; but if a hand is laid upon any who are with you in the house, we shall bear the re-

sponsibility for their death. 20But if you tell this business of ours, then we shall be released from this oath that you made us swear to you." 21She said, "According to your words, so be it." She sent them away and they departed. Then she tied the crimson cord in the window.

22 They departed and went into the hill country and stayed there three days, until the pursuers returned. The pursuers had searched all along the way and found nothing. 23Then the two men came down again from the hill country. They crossed over, came to Joshua son of Nun, and told him all that had happened to them. 24They said to Joshua, "Truly the LORD has given all the land into our hands; moreover all the inhabitants of the land melt in fear before us."

Israel Crosses the Jordan

3 Early in the morning Joshua rose and set out from Shittim with all the Israelites, and they came to the Jordan. They camped there before crossing over. 2At the end of three days the officers went through the camp 3and commanded the people, "When you see the ark of the covenant of the LORD your God being carried by the levitical priests, then you shall set out from your place. Follow it, 4so that you may know the way you should go, for you have not passed

---

2:11 *As soon as we heard it, our hearts melted.* When potential opponents in Jericho got word of the Red Sea crossing and Israel's victories over the kings Sihon and Og on the other side of the Jordan River, their hearts melted and their courage faded.

2:21 *she tied the crimson cord in the window.* The "crimson cord" has been used from the days of Clement of Rome until the present to represent Christ's blood of the atonement, but Scripture does not make that point here. However, it was, nonetheless, a marker that put Rahab's house under as much protection as did the blood of the paschal lamb shed at the first Passover in Egypt.

3:3 *When you see the ark of the covenant.* The ark of the covenant is mentioned eleven times in chapter 3. It represented the mighty presence of God. In later passages, it is referred

to as a portable throne of the invisible God, who was seated, as it were, between the cherubim above the ark (Ps 80:1; 99:1). The ark contained a jar of manna (Exod 16:33–34), which was a reminder of the grace of God in the wilderness; it also functioned as a teaching device that "one does not live by bread alone, but by every word that comes from the mouth of the LORD" (Deut 8:3). There is also a cosmic dimension to God's rule and reign: "the ark of the LORD, the Lord of all the earth" (3:13).

3:4 *Yet there shall be a space.* Because of the holiness of God's character, the people were to stay back six-tenths of a mile from the ark to demonstrate that God is separate and different in his being and his holiness. Too often we treat God casually. This is a reminder that a more common biblical response is fear, awe, and respect.

this way before. Yet there shall be a space between you and it, a distance of about two thousand cubits; do not come any nearer to it." [5]Then Joshua said to the people, "Sanctify yourselves; for tomorrow the LORD will do wonders among you." [6]To the priests Joshua said, "Take up the ark of the covenant, and pass on in front of the people." So they took up the ark of the covenant and went in front of the people.

[7] The LORD said to Joshua, "This day I will begin to exalt you in the sight of all Israel, so that they may know that I will be with you as I was with Moses. [8]You are the one who shall command the priests who bear the ark of the covenant, 'When you come to the edge of the waters of the Jordan, you shall stand still in the Jordan.'" [9]Joshua then said to the Israelites, "Draw near and hear the words of the LORD your God." [10]Joshua said, "By this you shall know that among you is the living God who without fail will drive out from before you the Canaanites, Hittites, Hivites, Perizzites, Girgashites, Amorites, and Jebusites: [11]the ark of the covenant of the Lord of all the earth is going to pass before you into the Jordan. [12]So now select twelve men from the tribes of Israel, one from each tribe. [13]When the soles of the feet of the priests who bear the ark of the LORD, the Lord of all the earth, rest in the waters of the Jordan,

the waters of the Jordan flowing from above shall be cut off; they shall stand in a single heap."

14 When the people set out from their tents to cross over the Jordan, the priests bearing the ark of the covenant were in front of the people. [15]Now the Jordan overflows all its banks throughout the time of harvest. So when those who bore the ark had come to the Jordan, and the feet of the priests bearing the ark were dipped in the edge of the water, [16]the waters flowing from above stood still, rising up in a single heap far off at Adam, the city that is beside Zarethan, while those flowing toward the sea of the Arabah, the Dead Sea,[a] were wholly cut off. Then the people crossed over opposite Jericho. [17]While all Israel were crossing over on dry ground, the priests who bore the ark of the covenant of the LORD stood on dry ground in the middle of the Jordan, until the entire nation finished crossing over the Jordan.

Twelve Stones Set Up at Gilgal

4 When the entire nation had finished crossing over the Jordan, the LORD said to Joshua: [2]"Select twelve men from the people, one from each tribe, [3]and command them, 'Take twelve stones from here out of the middle of the Jordan, from the place

a Heb Salt Sea

3:5 *for tomorrow the LORD will do wonders.* "Sanctify yourselves," urged Joshua, for if God was going to enter the camp to do his "wonders" (i.e., miracles), all must be separated from whatever was common or unclean. Special preparation is demanded whenever God is to reveal himself in a special way.

3:7 *I will begin to exalt you.* God will "exalt" Joshua in the sight of all Israel, not in order to "puff him up" the way the media or politicians puff up certain candidates for honor. On the contrary, God will honor Joshua so that others will "know that I will be with [him] as I was with Moses."

3:10 *among you is the living God.* "Living God" is found fourteen times in the Old Testament and fourteen times in the New Testament. It means that God is not an idea, a force, a doctrine, or a philosophy; no, God is a

real person. And what's more, he is alive and active in the affairs of human beings even today.

3:10–13 *By this you shall know.* The logic here is simple: if God can tame a raging river overflowing its banks in a spring flood, then he can repel and subdue the Canaanites, Hittites, Hivites, Perizzites, Girgashites, Amorites, and Jebusites! To do the one is to set the stage for confidence that he can do the other as well. We should not underestimate God.

3:16 *the waters flowing from above stood still.* The flood waters were cut off at Adam, near Zarethan, about eighteen miles north of Jericho, where the walls of the cliffs are periodically undercut by the strong spring current, causing parts of the cliffs to fall in and temporarily dam up the river. The "wonder" is in both the act and the timing of God.

JOSHUA

Strength Grounded in God's Word

Selected Scripture: *Joshua*

God's early words to Joshua reverberate throughout his years of leadership and military conquest for Israel: "Be strong and very courageous; . . . do not be frightened or dismayed, for the LORD your God is with you wherever you go" (Josh 1:7, 9). As Joshua's story unfolds we see a man who finds his courage day by day, battle by battle, in the strength God provides him. True to his name, which means "Yahweh is salvation," Joshua becomes a living testimony to God's provision for those who spend their lives "with God."

On the surface, he lived against an often grisly backdrop of battle, bloodshed, and conquest, yet the enduring message Joshua delivered is one of God's holiness prevailing and God's promises fulfilled. "Tomorrow the LORD will do wonders among you," Joshua declared to the people before they crossed the Jordan River on dry ground (3:5). He could have used the same words all his days to follow, for again and again God performed wonders as he worked with Joshua to bring the Israelites into the long-awaited Promised Land and remove its former inhabitants, who were consumed by idol worship and immorality.

God sent a heavenly "commander" to assure Joshua before the march on Jericho. Seven days later the walls of this invincible city fell at the blast of a trumpet (6:20). God directed Joshua to ambush the city of Ai, and with thirty thousand warriors he defeated the city and set it aflame (chap 8). Later, God responded to Joshua's command of the sun and the moon. As he asked, time stood still for a day, with no darkness falling, to give Joshua and his army more hours to defeat five Amorite kings joined against Israel (10:12–14). On and on the victories went, with Joshua repeating to the commanders under him, "Do not be afraid or dismayed; be strong and courageous; for thus the LORD will do to all the enemies against whom you fight" (10:25).

Joshua "left nothing undone of all that the LORD had commanded Moses" (11:15), and in return, "not one of all the good promises that the LORD had made to the house of Israel had failed; all came to pass" (21:45). If any life in the Bible provides a clear recipe for success, it is Joshua's. He spent his life "with God," and he spent it in obedience to God's word. His early commission from God had included more than a command to strength and courage; it had made clear that Joshua was to center his life on the law of God given to Moses: "This book of the law shall not depart out of your mouth; you shall meditate on it day and night, so that you may be careful to act in accordance with all that is written in it. For then you shall make your way prosperous, and then you shall be successful" (1:8).

He was to *speak* it, *meditate* on it, and *act* according to it. Then he would prosper, then he would find success. The story of Joshua displays a reality that lives on. God's Word shows us the way to uninterrupted fellowship with God. Those who live this way will prosper, as God defines prosperity.

PROFILE

PROFILE: JOSHUA

Such was the teaching of another leader not so long ago. Her outward life differed greatly from Joshua's, yet her life and her message were a Christ-illuminated version of his. Lilias Trotter, born to a wealthy family in London, opened a hostel for women in her twenties and began a ministry to the poor in North Africa in her thirties. Rather than fighting a mortal enemy, she fought sickness, poverty, and physical and spiritual repression. Through God-given strength and courage Lilias built a thriving ministry and gained the trust and respect of the Arab people, even providing spiritual leadership to elite groups of men. As Joshua did, Lilias understood the importance of living by God's Word:

"You must look up with the vision of the heart to the Person of Christ, and listen for the impress of His will on your will through His words, that is, through the Book of the Gospel that was written to be the means of communication with the souls of His people. As you become familiar with them He will by His Spirit bring them to your memory as you need them, to be your defense in the dangers of the way, even as David said in the Psalms: 'Thy word have I hid in my heart that I might not sin against Thee' (Ps 119:11, KJV)" (*The Way of the Sevenfold Secret*).

God's law gave Joshua guidance and kept him from sin. It did the same for Lilias Trotter. Both knew an Immanuel—"God with us"—relationship with their Savior, sustained through daily commitment to his Word. They were able to be strong and courageous when facing the "dangers of the way," because God, truly, was with them.

Personal Reflection

- In what situation of your life does God say to you, "Be strong and courageous, for the Lord your God is with you"?
- How can you make meditation upon God's Word a more regular part of your life? How can this practice help you to walk more closely with God?

where the priests' feet stood, carry them over with you, and lay them down in the place where you camp tonight.' " ⁴Then Joshua summoned the twelve men from the Israelites, whom he had appointed, one from each tribe. ⁵Joshua said to them, "Pass on before the ark of the LORD your God into the middle of the Jordan, and each of you take up a stone on his shoulder, one for each of the tribes of the Israelites, ⁶so that this may be a sign among you. When your children ask in time to come, 'What do those stones mean to you?' ⁷then you shall tell them that the waters of the Jordan were cut off in front of the ark of the covenant of the LORD. When it crossed over the Jordan, the waters of the Jordan were cut off. So these stones shall be to the Israelites a memorial forever."

8 The Israelites did as Joshua commanded. They took up twelve stones out of the middle of the Jordan, according to the number of the tribes of the Israelites, as the LORD told Joshua, carried them over with them to the place where they camped, and laid them down there. ⁹(Joshua set up twelve stones in the middle of the Jordan, in the place where the feet of the priests bearing the ark of the covenant had stood; and they are there to this day.)

10 The priests who bore the ark remained standing in the middle of the Jordan, until everything was finished that the LORD commanded Joshua to tell the people, according to all that Moses had commanded Joshua. The people crossed over in haste. ¹¹As soon as all the people had finished crossing over, the

---

4:6 *so that this may be a sign among you.* Twelve stones, representing the twelve tribes, were to be taken from the Jordan River bed and placed on the west bank as a memorial. In later days when the children asked what these things meant, the parents were to: (1) recite the works of God, (2) give glory to God, and (3) remind future generations that such "remembering" called for appropriate actions of love and obedience to such a great living God. The word "sign" in verse 6 can also be rendered "miracle" or "memorial," in this passage and in Exod 12:13–14 for celebrating the Passover and Feast of Unleavened Bread.

ark of the LORD, and the priests, crossed over in front of the people. 12The Reubenites, the Gadites, and the half-tribe of Manasseh crossed over armed before the Israelites, as Moses had ordered them. 13About forty thousand armed for war crossed over before the LORD to the plains of Jericho for battle.

14 On that day the LORD exalted Joshua in the sight of all Israel; and they stood in awe of him, as they had stood in awe of Moses, all the days of his life.

15 The LORD said to Joshua, 16"Command the priests who bear the ark of the covenant,[a] to come up out of the Jordan." 17Joshua therefore commanded the priests, "Come up out of the Jordan." 18When the priests bearing the ark of the covenant of the LORD came up from the middle of the Jordan, and the soles of the priests' feet touched dry ground, the waters of the Jordan returned to their place and overflowed all its banks, as before.

19 The people came up out of the Jordan on the tenth day of the first month, and they camped in Gilgal on the east border of Jericho. 20Those twelve stones, which they had taken out of the Jordan, Joshua set up in Gilgal, 21saying to the Israelites, "When your children ask their parents in time to come, 'What do these stones mean?' 22then you shall let your children know, 'Israel crossed over the Jordan here on dry ground.' 23For the LORD your God dried up the waters of the Jordan for you until you crossed over, as the LORD your God did to the Red Sea,[b]

which he dried up for us until we crossed over, 24so that all the peoples of the earth may know that the hand of the LORD is mighty, and so that you may fear the LORD your God forever."

The New Generation Circumcised

5 When all the kings of the Amorites beyond the Jordan to the west, and all the kings of the Canaanites by the sea, heard that the LORD had dried up the waters of the Jordan for the Israelites until they had crossed over, their hearts melted, and there was no longer any spirit in them, because of the Israelites.

2 At that time the LORD said to Joshua, "Make flint knives and circumcise the Israelites a second time." 3So Joshua made flint knives, and circumcised the Israelites at Gibeath-haaraloth.[c] 4This is the reason why Joshua circumcised them: all the males of the people who came out of Egypt, all the warriors, had died during the journey through the wilderness after they had come out of Egypt. 5Although all the people who came out had been circumcised, yet all the people born on the journey through the wilderness after they had come out of Egypt had not been circumcised. 6For the Israelites traveled forty years in the wilderness, until all the nation, the warriors who came out of Egypt, perished, not having listened to the voice of

a Or treaty, or testimony; Heb eduth   b Or Sea of Reeds   c That is the Hill of the Foreskins

---

4:14 the LORD exalted Joshua in the sight of all Israel. Once again Yahweh ("exalted Joshua," with the result that the people stood in awe of their leader all his days, just as they had honored Moses.

4:15 the ark of the covenant. Here the ark of the covenant is also called "the ark of the testimony" (see NRSV note). It was thereby a witness to God's person and presence.

4:19 The people came up out of the Jordan on the tenth day of the first month. The tenth day of the first month was the same day forty years earlier when the Israelites set out for Canaan by setting aside the paschal lamb (Exod 12:2–3). This day was the anniversary of the beginning of the march through the wilderness; it also

marked the day when their redemption had been completed.

4:23–24 so that all the peoples of the earth may know. God dried up the Jordan River as he did the Red Sea. Just as the Gentiles of Jericho had heard about the deeds of Israel's God (2:10–11), so here at the Jordan divine acts are done so that mortals all over the earth might come to realize that God is powerful and is to be feared and reverenced by all.

5:1 When all the kings . . . heard, . . . there was no longer any spirit in them. The special providential work of God is to be recognized in the panic that came over all these nations in Canaan.

the LORD. To them the LORD swore that he would not let them see the land that he had sworn to their ancestors to give us, a land flowing with milk and honey. 7So it was their children, whom he raised up in their place, that Joshua circumcised; for they were uncircumcised, because they had not been circumcised on the way.

8 When the circumcising of all the nation was done, they remained in their places in the camp until they were healed. 9The LORD said to Joshua, "Today I have rolled away from you the disgrace of Egypt." And so that place is called Gilgal*a* to this day.

The Passover at Gilgal

10 While the Israelites were camped in Gilgal they kept the passover in the evening on the fourteenth day of the month in the plains of Jericho. 11On the day after the passover, on that very day, they ate the produce of the land, unleavened cakes and parched grain. 12The manna ceased on the day they ate the produce of the land, and the Israelites no longer had manna; they ate the crops of the land of Canaan that year.

Joshua's Vision

13 Once when Joshua was by Jericho, he looked up and saw a man standing before him with a drawn sword in his hand. Joshua went to him and said to him, "Are you one of us, or one of our adversaries?" 14He replied, "Neither; but as commander of the army of the LORD I have now come." And Joshua fell on his face to the earth and worshiped, and he said to him, "What do you command your servant, my lord?" 15The commander of the army of the LORD said to Joshua, "Remove the sandals from your feet, for the place where you stand is holy." And Joshua did so.

a Related to Heb *galal* to roll

5:9 *Today I have rolled away from you the disgrace.* The "disgrace" or "reproach" resulting from the Egyptian bondage left a mark or stigma on Israel. God will stop the insults and taunts that had come because of the humiliation of slavery in Egypt.

5:11–12 *The manna ceased.* In celebrating the Passover, the nation began a significant turning around to obey the Lord and to live for him from that point on. Then it was that the manna stopped. There was no need to expect an extraordinary or miraculous supply of food when it could now be sought from the land itself. When we come to depend on God's extraordinary intervention as a matter of everyday occurrence, our Lord teaches us to get up and serve ourselves instead.

5:13 *saw a man standing before him with a drawn sword.* Joshua "saw a man," or at least one who had the appearance of a man. But this turned out to be a supernatural being, the "commander of the army of the LORD" (v 15), implying he was ruler of the armies of heaven and earth. Also the fact that this "man" received worship from Joshua pointed to his supernatural origins. Moreover, the place where he stood was holy, requiring, as it did in Exod 3:5, the removal of sandals. And if 6:2 is the continuation of the same narrative, then he is designated as Yahweh himself. All of this is not surprising, for the same Lord is addressed as "a warrior" in Exod 15:3. If God was for Joshua, who could be against him? Although God the Father cannot be seen (John 6:46), John 1:18 seems to allow for earlier appearances of the Word who became incarnate in Jesus. It is important to note here that "the army of the LORD" is not the same as "the army of Israel."

Responding
5:14 WORSHIP. Read verses 13–15 several times. What struck you? The commander's presence and communication with Joshua or Joshua's humble response, falling on his face in worship and calling himself a servant? On a three-by-five card list as many different postures of worship recorded in the Bible as you can recall. What posture is the most common today? Most uncommon? Sometime this week in a place where you won't be disturbed, choose the posture that is most unfamiliar to you and worship God in this way until you feel the time is over. *See also* Spiritual Disciplines Index.

5:15 *for the place where you stand is holy.* "Remove the sandals" is almost identical to the command given to Moses at the burning bush

Jericho Taken and Destroyed

6 Now Jericho was shut up inside and out because of the Israelites; no one came out and no one went in. ²The LORD said to Joshua, "See, I have handed Jericho over to you, along with its king and soldiers. ³You shall march around the city, all the warriors circling the city once. Thus you shall do for six days, ⁴with seven priests bearing seven trumpets of rams' horns before the ark. On the seventh day you shall march around the city seven times, the priests blowing the trumpets. ⁵When they make a long blast with the ram's horn, as soon as you hear the sound of the trumpet, then all the people shall shout with a great shout; and the wall of the city will fall down flat, and all the people shall charge straight ahead." ⁶So Joshua son of Nun summoned the priests and said to them, "Take up the ark of the covenant, and have seven priests carry seven trumpets of rams' horns in front of the ark of the LORD." ⁷To the people he said, "Go forward and march around the city; have the armed men pass on before the ark of the LORD."

8 As Joshua had commanded the people, the seven priests carrying the seven trumpets of rams' horns before the LORD went forward, blowing the trumpets, with the ark of the covenant of the LORD following them.

⁹And the armed men went before the priests who blew the trumpets; the rear guard came after the ark, while the trumpets blew continually. ¹⁰To the people Joshua gave this command: "You shall not shout or let your voice be heard, nor shall you utter a word, until the day I tell you to shout. Then you shall shout." ¹¹So the ark of the LORD went around the city, circling it once; and they came into the camp, and spent the night in the camp.

12 Then Joshua rose early in the morning, and the priests took up the ark of the LORD. ¹³The seven priests carrying the seven trumpets of rams' horns before the ark of the LORD passed on, blowing the trumpets continually. The armed men went before them, and the rear guard came after the ark of the LORD, while the trumpets blew continually. ¹⁴On the second day they marched around the city once and then returned to the camp. They did this for six days.

15 On the seventh day they rose early, at dawn, and marched around the city in the same manner seven times. It was only on that day that they marched around the city seven times. ¹⁶And at the seventh time, when the priests had blown the trumpets, Joshua said to the people, "Shout! For the LORD has given you the city. ¹⁷The city and all that is in it shall be devoted to the LORD for destruction.

(Exod 3:5). Thus, Joshua was confronted with the living God, as Moses had been (Exod 33:9–11).

6:2 *I have handed Jericho over to you.* God's role in this conquest was not to be minimized or confused with what the nation accomplished.

6:5 *when they make a long blast with the ram's horn.* The "long blast" appears to be the same "long blast" that precedes the theophany (appearance of God) on Mt. Sinai (Exod 19:13). It only occurs in these two passages.

6:6–14 *the ark of the LORD.* The ark of God still holds center stage, as it is mentioned ten times in this chapter, but nine times in these verses. As a symbol of the real presence of God its lesson is that mortals are well advised not to go forth in the service of God on their own strength and wits, but with the Immanuel Principle ("God with us") operating fully.

6:10 *You shall not shout.* The silence of the

people as they marched around the city of Jericho brings to mind that often the work of God goes on quietly and mostly unseen.

6:15 *On the seventh day they rose early.* Was the seventh day the Sabbath? Did God command Israel to break Mosaic law about the Sabbath? Some urge that the solemn procession of the ark was an act of worship and thus the labor on the Sabbath was justified. But regardless of where the Sabbath day fell in the series of seven days, it had to hit on one of them. If this was an exception to the Sabbath principle, it was one authorized by God, and it was a resting and waiting until God should arise from his place and grant Israel its own "rest." With this Ps 44:3 agrees.

6:17–18 *shall be devoted to the LORD for destruction.* "Things devoted to destruction" is a technical term (in Hebrew, *herem;* Deut 13:12–15). The things that could not be burned in the destruction of the city were to be both

Only Rahab the prostitute and all who are with her in her house shall live because she hid the messengers we sent. [18] As for you, keep away from the things devoted to destruction, so as not to covet[a] and take any of the devoted things and make the camp of Israel an object for destruction, bringing trouble upon it. [19] But all silver and gold, and vessels of bronze and iron, are sacred to the LORD; they shall go into the treasury of the LORD." [20] So the people shouted, and the trumpets were blown. As soon as the people heard the sound of the trumpets, they raised a great shout, and the wall fell down flat; so the people charged straight ahead into the city and captured it. [21] Then they devoted to destruction by the edge of the sword all in the city, both men and women, young and old, oxen, sheep, and donkeys.

22 Joshua said to the two men who had spied out the land, "Go into the prostitute's house, and bring the woman out of it and all who belong to her, as you swore to her." [23] So the young men who had been spies went in and brought Rahab out, along with her father, her mother, her brothers, and all who belonged to her—they brought all her kindred out—and set them outside the camp of Israel. [24] They burned down the city, and everything in it; only the silver and gold, and the vessels of bronze and iron, they put into the treasury of the house of the LORD. [25] But Rahab the prostitute, with her family and all

who belonged to her, Joshua spared. Her family[b] has lived in Israel ever since. For she hid the messengers whom Joshua sent to spy out Jericho.

26 Joshua then pronounced this oath, saying,

"Cursed before the LORD be anyone who tries
to build this city—this Jericho!
At the cost of his firstborn he shall lay its foundation,
and at the cost of his youngest he shall set up its gates!"

27 So the LORD was with Joshua; and his fame was in all the land.

The Sin of Achan and Its Punishment

7 But the Israelites broke faith in regard to the devoted things: Achan son of Carmi son of Zabdi son of Zerah, of the tribe of Judah, took some of the devoted things; and the anger of the LORD burned against the Israelites.

2 Joshua sent men from Jericho to Ai, which is near Beth-aven, east of Bethel, and said to them, "Go up and spy out the land." And the men went up and spied out Ai. [3] Then they returned to Joshua and said to him, "Not all the people need go up; about two or three thousand men should go up and attack Ai. Since they are so few, do not make the whole

a Gk: Heb devote to destruction Compare 7.21
b Heb She

---

banned and devoted to God as an involuntary offering. All who took any of these banned goods would themselves become infected and thus come under the same ban as the objects themselves (Deut 7:26). This ban and involuntary dedication is the flip side of the voluntary offering of Rom 12:1–2. Since the whole earth and all that is in it belongs to the Lord (Ps 24:1), God has the right to reclaim it at any time. Here the people's day of judgment comes after repeated invitations to repent are finally and absolutely refused. (See discussion of *herem* in the Introduction.)

6:19 *treasury of the LORD.* Articles of silver, gold, bronze, or iron taken from the destruction were "sacred" to the Lord and therefore were to be put in the sanctuary, since they were already

dedicated as an involuntary offering to God.

6:20 *they raised a great shout, and the wall fell.* The "wall [of Jericho] fell down flat" or "under itself." The victory was an act of God!

6:26 *Cursed . . . be anyone who tries to build this city.* Jericho, meaning "moon city" (as Beth-shemesh was the "house of the sun"), was never to be rebuilt. A curse was put on any who did rebuild it or its gates. Later, the predicted tragedy happened to Hiel, who rebuilt Jericho and laid his oldest son in the foundation of the city and his youngest son in the gate foundation (1 Kings 16:34).

7:1 *Achan son of Carmi.* Achan came from a prominent family in Judah (1 Chron 2:4–7), so it was not poverty that drove him to take the banned and devoted things.

RAHAB

A Risk Worth Taking

Selected Scriptures: *Joshua 2; 6; Matthew 1:5; Hebrews 11:31*

When Joshua and the Israelites had safely crossed the Jordan, their possession of the Promised Land, Canaan, still had to be secured. Many nations held territory in Canaan, and their kings controlled cities home to thousands of people. Positioned just west of the Israelites' camp at Gilgal, Jericho stood as perhaps the most impregnable of all the walled cities of the land. And Israel's only weapons—slings, arrows, and spears—were practically useless against a walled city prepared for a siege.

What Joshua did not know was that the reputation of the Israelites and their God had preceded them. The inhabitants of Jericho had heard about the crossing of the Red Sea and the Israelites' defeat of the kingdoms east of the Jordan. When two spies went into Jericho to survey their coming task, they were welcomed into the house of Rahab, a local prostitute, who told them that all the people in the land were melting in fear of Israel (Josh 2:9). Rahab assured the spies that circumstances were right for taking Canaan.

Rahab didn't simply assure the spies of Israel's certain success; she also risked her life by protecting them. When the king of Jericho demanded that she deliver the foreign spies over to him, Rahab creatively thought to hide them on the roof, sent the authorities away on a false tip, and made a plan for their safe escape.

Something had happened to Rahab as she heard the stories of God's deliverance. She had come to knowledge of God, and she was willing to risk her life to live in obedience to him: "The LORD your God is indeed God in heaven above and on earth below" (2:11).

Rahab's story is a merciful reminder of God's love for all people—Jews, Gentiles, and sinners of all kinds. Rahab's soul was restless and lonely. Although not an Israelite, she had traveled a wilderness of her own. Now, as Thomas Kelly, a twentieth-century Quaker, describes, she had met the Lover of her soul:

"It is an overwhelming experience to fall into the hands of the living God, to be invaded to the depths of one's being by His presence, to be, without warning, wholly uprooted from all earth-born securities and assurances, and to be blown by a tempest of unbelievable power which leaves one's old proud self utterly, utterly defenseless, until one cries, 'All Thy waves and Thy billows are gone over me' (Ps 42:7)" (*A Testament of Devotion*).

Turning from loyalty to her townspeople, who were mired in idolatry and immorality, Rahab cared only that she obey God and, with her family, join in life with his people. Kelly continues: "One knows ever after that the Eternal Lover of the world, the Hound of Heaven, is utterly, utterly real, and that life must henceforth

PROFILE: RAHAB

be forever determined by that Real. . . . In glad, amazed humility we cast on Him our little lives in trusting obedience."

Because of her faith in God and his protection of his people, when the city of Jericho was destroyed, Rahab and her family were spared, and Rahab had the great honor of becoming an ancestor of Christ. As he has done many times, God demonstrated that a person's past has no bearing on what that person can do for God, once surrendered. Rahab had given herself to many mortals. Now she gave herself to the Immortal One and, even as she watched her city burn before her, she knew peace.

Personal Reflection

- *Obedience.* Rahab obeyed immediately. Yet, Thomas Kelly says, "Most people . . . must struggle and, like Jacob of old, wrestle with the angel until the morning dawns, the active way wherein the will must be subjected bit by bit, piecemeal and progressively, to the divine Will." What piece of your will is God currently shaping?
- *Peace.* Thank God now for an area of your life in which you are experiencing God-given peace.

people toil up there." 4So about three thousand of the people went up there; and they fled before the men of Ai. 5The men of Ai killed about thirty-six of them, chasing them from outside the gate as far as Shebarim and killing them on the slope. The hearts of the people melted and turned to water.

6 Then Joshua tore his clothes, and fell to the ground on his face before the ark of the LORD until the evening, he and the elders of Israel; and they put dust on their heads. 7Joshua said, "Ah, Lord GOD! Why have you brought this people across the Jordan at all, to hand us over to the Amorites so as to destroy us? Would that we had been content to settle beyond the Jordan! 8O Lord, what can I say, now that Israel has turned their backs to their enemies! 9The Canaanites and all the inhabitants of the land will hear of it, and surround us, and cut off our name from the earth. Then what will you do for your great name?"

10 The LORD said to Joshua, "Stand up! Why have you fallen upon your face? 11Israel has sinned; they have transgressed my covenant that I imposed on them. They have taken some of the devoted things; they have stolen, they have acted deceitfully, and they have put them among their own belongings. 12Therefore the Israelites are unable to stand before their enemies; they turn their backs to their enemies, because they have become a thing devoted for destruction themselves. I will be with you no more, unless you destroy

---

7:9 *all the inhabitants of the land will hear of it.* When thirty-six men were killed as three thousand men tried to take Ai, forcing the Israelites to retreat (vv 4–5), Joshua fell on his face and cried out to God, "What will you do for your great name?" The honor and reputation of God was his primary concern, as it should always be ours as well.

7:11 *Israel has sinned.* Just as one traitor can put a whole army at risk, so the sin of an individual can place a whole community under the discipline of God. Joshua must get up off the ground (v 10) and deal with the secret sin in their midst. The whole community of Israel had "become a thing devoted for destruction themselves" (v 12; see note on 6:17–18).

the devoted things from among you. 13Proceed to sanctify the people, and say, 'Sanctify yourselves for tomorrow; for thus says the LORD, the God of Israel, "There are devoted things among you, O Israel; you will be unable to stand before your enemies until you take away the devoted things from among you." 14In the morning therefore you shall come forward tribe by tribe. The tribe that the LORD takes shall come near by clans, the clan that the LORD takes shall come near by households, and the household that the LORD takes shall come near one by one. 15And the one who is taken as having the devoted things shall be burned with fire, together with all that he has, for having transgressed the covenant of the LORD, and for having done an outrageous thing in Israel.' "

16 So Joshua rose early in the morning, and brought Israel near tribe by tribe, and the tribe of Judah was taken. 17He brought near the clans of Judah, and the clan of the Zerahites was taken; and he brought near the clan of the Zerahites, family by family, *a* and Zabdi was taken. 18And he brought near his household one by one, and Achan son of Carmi son of Zabdi son of Zerah, of the tribe of Judah, was taken. 19Then Joshua said to Achan, "My son, give glory to the LORD God of Israel and make confession to him. Tell me now what you have done; do not hide it from me." 20And Achan answered Joshua, "It is true; I am the one who sinned against the LORD God of Israel. This is what I did: 21when I saw among the spoil a beautiful mantle from Shinar, and two hundred shekels of silver, and a bar of gold weighing fifty shekels, then I coveted them and took them.

They now lie hidden in the ground inside my tent, with the silver underneath."

22 So Joshua sent messengers, and they ran to the tent; and there it was, hidden in his tent with the silver underneath. 23They took them out of the tent and brought them to Joshua and all the Israelites; and they spread them out before the LORD. 24Then Joshua and all Israel with him took Achan son of Zerah, with the silver, the mantle, and the bar of gold, with his sons and daughters, with his oxen, donkeys, and sheep, and his tent and all that he had; and they brought them up to the Valley of Achor. 25Joshua said, "Why did you bring trouble on us? The LORD is bringing trouble on you today." And all Israel stoned him to death; they burned them with fire, cast stones on them, 26and raised over him a great heap of stones that remains to this day. Then the LORD turned from his burning anger. Therefore that place to this day is called the Valley of Achor. *b*

Ai Captured by a Stratagem and Destroyed

8 Then the LORD said to Joshua, "Do not fear or be dismayed; take all the fighting men with you, and go up now to Ai. See, I have handed over to you the king of Ai with his people, his city, and his land. 2You shall do to Ai and its king as you did to Jericho and its king; only its spoil and its livestock you may take as booty for yourselves. Set an ambush against the city, behind it."

3 So Joshua and all the fighting men set out to go up against Ai. Joshua chose thirty thousand warriors and sent them out by

a Mss Syr: MT *man by man*   *b* That is *Trouble*

7:19 *give glory to the LORD . . . and make confession to him.* Joshua urges Achan to confess. God is honored when we refuse to hide our sin, but instead confess that sin to him.

7:21 *when I saw . . . I coveted them and took them.* Achan's confession of seeing, coveting, and taking is a pattern as old as Gen 3:6, where the same three stages are given for Eve's temptation. 1 John 2:16 warns against the same three: the lust of the eyes, the coveting or cravings of the flesh, and the boasting about what one has.

7:24 *they brought them up to the Valley of Achor.* The Valley of Achor, or "valley of trouble," where Achan and his family were stoned, would in the grace of God become a "door of hope" (Hos 2:15) in a future day as God turned trouble into hope and deliverance.

8:1 *take all the fighting men.* The "fighting men" represents the unusual term "people of war," who are elsewhere called the "warriors" (5:4, 6). The term implies that the whole nation was involved in the battles even though only the men did the fighting.

night [4]with the command, "You shall lie in ambush against the city, behind it; do not go very far from the city, but all of you stay alert. [5]I and all the people who are with me will approach the city. When they come out against us, as before, we shall flee from them. [6]They will come out after us until we have drawn them away from the city; for they will say, 'They are fleeing from us, as before.' While we flee from them, [7]you shall rise up from the ambush and seize the city; for the LORD your God will give it into your hand. [8]And when you have taken the city, you shall set the city on fire, doing as the LORD has ordered; see, I have commanded you." [9]So Joshua sent them out; and they went to the place of ambush, and lay between Bethel and Ai, to the west of Ai; but Joshua spent that night in the camp.[a]

10 In the morning Joshua rose early and mustered the people, and went up, with the elders of Israel, before the people to Ai. [11]All the fighting men who were with him went up, and drew near before the city, and camped on the north side of Ai, with a ravine between them and Ai. [12]Taking about five thousand men, he set them in ambush between Bethel and Ai, to the west of the city. [13]So they stationed the forces, the main encampment that was north of the city and its rear guard west of the city. But Joshua spent that night in the valley. [14]When the king of Ai saw this, he and all his people, the inhabitants of the city, hurried out early in the morning to the meeting place facing the Arabah to meet Israel in battle; but he did not know that there was an ambush against him behind the city. [15]And Joshua and all Israel made a pretense of being beaten before them, and fled in the direction of the wilderness. [16]So all the people who were in the city were called together to pursue them, and as they pursued Joshua they were drawn away from

the city. [17]There was not a man left in Ai or Bethel who did not go out after Israel; they left the city open, and pursued Israel.

18 Then the LORD said to Joshua, "Stretch out the sword that is in your hand toward Ai; for I will give it into your hand." And Joshua stretched out the sword that was in his hand toward the city. [19]As soon as he stretched out his hand, the troops in ambush rose quickly out of their place and rushed forward. They entered the city, took it, and at once set the city on fire. [20]So when the men of Ai looked back, the smoke of the city was rising to the sky. They had no power to flee this way or that, for the people who fled to the wilderness turned back against the pursuers. [21]When Joshua and all Israel saw that the ambush had taken the city and that the smoke of the city was rising, then they turned back and struck down the men of Ai. [22]And the others came out from the city against them; so they were surrounded by Israelites, some on one side, and some on the other; and Israel struck them down until no one was left who survived or escaped. [23]But the king of Ai was taken alive and brought to Joshua.

24 When Israel had finished slaughtering all the inhabitants of Ai in the open wilderness where they pursued them, and when all of them to the very last had fallen by the edge of the sword, all Israel returned to Ai, and attacked it with the edge of the sword. [25]The total of those who fell that day, both men and women, was twelve thousand—all the people of Ai. [26]For Joshua did not draw back his hand, with which he stretched out the sword, until he had utterly destroyed all the inhabitants of Ai. [27]Only the livestock and the spoil of that city Israel took as their booty, according to the word of the LORD that he had issued to Joshua. [28]So Joshua burned

a Heb among the people

8:26 *Joshua did not draw back his hand.* Joshua held out his hand, with his sword extended (also v 18), in an act that seems to mirror how Moses held up his hands for Joshua in his battle with the Amalekites in Exod 17:8–16. The presence of God was the only hope for victory.

8:26–29 *Joshua burned Ai, . . . hanged the king.* Was God being fair and just in these actions? Yes, he had waited some four hundred years (Gen 15:16) until the Canaanites either repented or added so much iniquity that the measure of their just deserts was finally filled up; there was no chance of turning back.

Ai, and made it forever a heap of ruins, as it is to this day. 29And he hanged the king of Ai on a tree until evening; and at sunset Joshua commanded, and they took his body down from the tree, threw it down at the entrance of the gate of the city, and raised over it a great heap of stones, which stands there to this day.

Joshua Renews the Covenant

30 Then Joshua built on Mount Ebal an altar to the LORD, the God of Israel, 31just as Moses the servant of the LORD had commanded the Israelites, as it is written in the book of the law of Moses, "an altar of unhewn*a* stones, on which no iron tool has been used"; and they offered on it burnt offerings to the LORD, and sacrificed offerings of well-being. 32And there, in the presence of the Israelites, Joshua*b* wrote on the stones a copy of the law of Moses, which he had written. 33All Israel, alien as well as citizen, with their elders and officers and their judges, stood on opposite sides of the ark in front of the levitical priests who carried the ark of the covenant of the LORD, half of them in front of Mount Gerizim and half of them in front of Mount Ebal, as Moses the servant of the LORD had commanded at the first, that they should bless the people of Israel. 34And afterward he read all the words of the law, blessings and curses, according to all that is written in the book of the law. 35There was not a word of all that Moses commanded that Joshua did not read before all the assembly of Israel, and the women, and the little ones, and the aliens who resided among them.

The Gibeonites Save Themselves by Trickery

9 Now when all the kings who were beyond the Jordan in the hill country and in the lowland all along the coast of the Great Sea toward Lebanon—the Hittites, the Amorites, the Canaanites, the Perizzites, the Hivites, and the Jebusites—heard of this, 2they gathered together with one accord to fight Joshua and Israel.

3 But when the inhabitants of Gibeon heard what Joshua had done to Jericho and to Ai, 4they on their part acted with cunning: they went and prepared provisions,*c* and took worn-out sacks for their donkeys, and wineskins, worn-out and torn and mended, 5with worn-out, patched sandals on their feet, and worn-out clothes; and all their provisions were dry and moldy. 6They went to Joshua in the camp at Gilgal, and said to him and to the Israelites, "We have come from a far country; so now make a treaty with us." 7But the Israelites said to the Hivites, "Perhaps you live among us; then how can we make a treaty with you?" 8They said to Joshua, "We are your servants." And Joshua said to them, "Who are you? And where do you come from?" 9They said to him, "Your servants have come from a very far country, because of the name of the LORD your God; for we have heard a report of him, of all that he did in Egypt, 10and of all that he did to the two kings of the Amorites who were beyond the Jordan, King Sihon of Heshbon, and King Og of Bashan who lived in Ashtaroth. 11So our elders and all the inhabitants of our country said to us, 'Take provisions in your hand for the journey; go to

a Heb *whole*   b Heb *he*   c Cn: Meaning of Heb uncertain

Responding

8:31 SACRIFICE. Having watched news clips of the great celebrations that engulfed the United States and other countries when World War II ended, we can understand how the Israelites felt when Ai fell. There is one difference: after Ai fell the Israelites gave the best of their possessions as burnt and well-being offerings to the Lord. What should their reaction teach us? *See also* Spiritual Disciplines Index.

9:6–13 *we have heard a report of him.* The Gibeonites, a four-city confederation about five miles north of Jerusalem, put on an Oscar-worthy performance for Joshua at Gilgal that not only consisted of lies, but reflected the same knowledge of what God had previously done for Israel in his victory over the two kings east of the Jordan River as that testified by Rahab in 2:10–13.

meet them, and say to them, "We are your servants; come now, make a treaty with us." ' [12]Here is our bread; it was still warm when we took it from our houses as our food for the journey, on the day we set out to come to you, but now, see, it is dry and moldy; [13]these wineskins were new when we filled them, and see, they are burst; and these garments and sandals of ours are worn out from the very long journey." [14]So the leaders[a] partook of their provisions, and did not ask direction from the LORD. [15]And Joshua made peace with them, guaranteeing their lives by a treaty; and the leaders of the congregation swore an oath to them.

16 But when three days had passed after they had made a treaty with them, they heard that they were their neighbors and were living among them. [17]So the Israelites set out and reached their cities on the third day. Now their cities were Gibeon, Chephirah, Beeroth, and Kiriath-jearim. [18]But the Israelites did not attack them, because the leaders of the congregation had sworn to them by the LORD, the God of Israel. Then all the congregation murmured against the leaders. [19]But all the leaders said to all the congregation, "We have sworn to them by the LORD, the God of Israel, and now we must not touch them. [20]This is what we will do to them: We will let them live, so that wrath may not come upon us, because of the oath that we swore to them." [21]The leaders said to them, "Let them live." So they became hewers of wood and drawers of water for all the congregation, as the leaders had decided concerning them.

22 Joshua summoned them, and said to them, "Why did you deceive us, saying, 'We are very far from you,' while in fact you are living among us? [23]Now therefore you are cursed, and some of you shall always be slaves, hewers of wood and drawers of water for the house of my God." [24]They answered Joshua, "Because it was told to your servants for a certainty that the LORD your God had commanded his servant Moses to give you all the land, and to destroy all the inhabitants of the land before you; so we were in great fear for our lives because of you, and did this thing. [25]And now we are in your hand: do as it seems good and right in your sight to do to us." [26]This is what he did for them: he saved them from the Israelites; and they did not kill them. [27]But on that day Joshua made them hewers of wood and drawers of water for the congregation and for the altar of the LORD, to continue to this day, in the place that he should choose.

The Sun Stands Still

10 When King Adoni-zedek of Jerusalem heard how Joshua had taken Ai, and had utterly destroyed it, doing to Ai and its king as he had done to Jericho and its king, and how the inhabitants of Gibeon had made peace with Israel and were among them, [2]he[b] became greatly frightened, because Gibeon was a large city, like one of the royal cities, and was larger than Ai, and all its men were warriors. [3]So King Adoni-zedek of Jerusalem sent a message to King Hoham of Hebron, to King Piram of Jarmuth, to King Japhia of Lachish, and to King Debir of Eglon, saying, [4]"Come up and help me, and let us attack Gibeon; for it has made peace with Joshua and with the Israelites." [5]Then the five kings of the Amorites—the king of Jerusalem, the king of Hebron, the king of Jarmuth, the king of Lachish, and the king of Eglon—gathered their forces, and went up with all their armies and camped against Gibeon, and made war against it.

a Gk: Heb *men*   b Heb *they*

9:14 *the leaders . . . did not ask direction from the LORD.* Because the leaders did not go to God in prayer (as Prov 3:5–6 will later advise and as Moses had illustrated in the Amalekite battle in Exodus 17), three days later they learned that the Gibeonites were near neighbors, not distant foreigners. Again and again in Joshua we are reminded that God is the actual leader of his people and cannot be treated as a distant figure to whom we pay occasional homage.

9:27 *Joshua made them hewers of wood and drawers of water.* Never again did the Gibeonites side with their blood relatives, the Hivites; they became, instead, workers in perpetuity for Israel. Thus, despite their heritage of deception, the Gibeonites become part of the People of God. We worship a God who provides second chances.

6 And the Gibeonites sent to Joshua at the camp in Gilgal, saying, "Do not abandon your servants; come up to us quickly, and save us, and help us; for all the kings of the Amorites who live in the hill country are gathered against us." 7So Joshua went up from Gilgal, he and all the fighting force with him, all the mighty warriors. 8The LORD said to Joshua, "Do not fear them, for I have handed them over to you; not one of them shall stand before you." 9So Joshua came upon them suddenly, having marched up all night from Gilgal. 10And the LORD threw them into a panic before Israel, who inflicted a great slaughter on them at Gibeon, chased them by the way of the ascent of Beth-horon, and struck them down as far as Azekah and Makkedah. 11As they fled before Israel, while they were going down the slope of Beth-horon, the LORD threw down huge stones from heaven on them as far as Azekah, and they died; there were more who died because of the hailstones than the Israelites killed with the sword.

12 On the day when the LORD gave the Amorites over to the Israelites, Joshua spoke to the LORD; and he said in the sight of Israel,
"Sun, stand still at Gibeon,
    and Moon, in the valley of Aijalon."
13 And the sun stood still, and the moon stopped,
    until the nation took vengeance on
    their enemies.
Is this not written in the Book of Jashar? The sun stopped in midheaven, and did not hurry to set for about a whole day. 14There has been no day like it before or since, when the LORD heeded a human voice; for the LORD fought for Israel.

15 Then Joshua returned, and all Israel with him, to the camp at Gilgal.

Five Kings Defeated

16 Meanwhile, these five kings fled and hid themselves in the cave at Makkedah. 17And it was told Joshua, "The five kings have been found, hidden in the cave at Makkedah." 18Joshua said, "Roll large stones against the mouth of the cave, and set men by it to guard them; 19but do not stay there yourselves; pursue your enemies, and attack them from the rear. Do not let them enter their towns, for the LORD your God has given them into your hand." 20When Joshua and the Israelites had finished inflicting a very great slaughter on them, until they were wiped out, and when the survivors had entered into the fortified towns, 21all the people returned safe to Joshua in the camp at Makkedah; no one dared to speak a against any of the Israelites.

22 Then Joshua said, "Open the mouth of the cave, and bring those five kings out to me from the cave." 23They did so, and brought the five kings out to him from the cave, the king of Jerusalem, the king of Hebron, the king of Jarmuth, the king of Lachish, and the king of Eglon. 24When they brought the kings out to Joshua, Joshua summoned all the Israelites, and said to the chiefs of the warriors who had gone with him, "Come near, put your feet on the necks of these kings." Then they came near and put their feet on their necks. 25And Joshua said to them, "Do not be afraid or dismayed; be strong and courageous; for thus the LORD will do to all the enemies against whom you fight." 26Afterward

a Heb moved his tongue

10:8 *not one of them shall stand before you.* Joshua must fight a coalition (of five city-state kings) for the first time. Nevertheless, God's word is still the same: "Do not fear them, for I have handed them over to you." Like Joshua, we cannot settle for earthly perspectives when God wants something accomplished. If God is present, we need to set aside our natural phobias and hesitancies.

10:10 *the LORD threw them into a panic.* As at the Red Sea, "The LORD will fight for you" (Exod

14:14), so here God throws in thunder and a hailstorm to defeat the coalition.

10:14 *the LORD heeded a human voice.* In answer to Joshua's prayer, God used the forces of nature to effect his own victory. Whether Joshua was asking for the sun to stop moving or to cease shining is hotly debated. Regardless of which answer is adopted, what we are sure of is that God intervened in the course of events at the precise moment help was needed.

Joshua struck them down and put them to death, and he hung them on five trees. And they hung on the trees until evening. 27 At sunset Joshua commanded, and they took them down from the trees and threw them into the cave where they had hidden themselves; they set large stones against the mouth of the cave, which remain to this very day.

28 Joshua took Makkedah on that day, and struck it and its king with the edge of the sword; he utterly destroyed every person in it; he left no one remaining. And he did to the king of Makkedah as he had done to the king of Jericho.

29 Then Joshua passed on from Makkedah, and all Israel with him, to Libnah, and fought against Libnah. 30 The LORD gave it also and its king into the hand of Israel; and he struck it with the edge of the sword, and every person in it; he left no one remaining in it; and he did to its king as he had done to the king of Jericho.

31 Next Joshua passed on from Libnah, and all Israel with him, to Lachish, and laid siege to it, and assaulted it. 32 The LORD gave Lachish into the hand of Israel, and he took it on the second day, and struck it with the edge of the sword, and every person in it, as he had done to Libnah.

33 Then King Horam of Gezer came up to help Lachish; and Joshua struck him and his people, leaving him no survivors.

34 From Lachish Joshua passed on with all Israel to Eglon; and they laid siege to it, and assaulted it; 35 and they took it that day, and struck it with the edge of the sword; and every person in it he utterly destroyed that day, as he had done to Lachish.

36 Then Joshua went up with all Israel from Eglon to Hebron; they assaulted it, 37 and took it, and struck it with the edge of the sword, and its king and its towns, and every person in it; he left no one remaining, just as

he had done to Eglon, and utterly destroyed it with every person in it.

38 Then Joshua, with all Israel, turned back to Debir and assaulted it, 39 and he took it with its king and all its towns; they struck them with the edge of the sword, and utterly destroyed every person in it; he left no one remaining; just as he had done to Hebron, and, as he had done to Libnah and its king, so he did to Debir and its king.

40 So Joshua defeated the whole land, the hill country and the Negeb and the lowland and the slopes, and all their kings; he left no one remaining, but utterly destroyed all that breathed, as the LORD God of Israel commanded. 41 And Joshua defeated them from Kadesh-barnea to Gaza, and all the country of Goshen, as far as Gibeon. 42 Joshua took all these kings and their land at one time, because the LORD God of Israel fought for Israel. 43 Then Joshua returned, and all Israel with him, to the camp at Gilgal.

The United Kings of Northern Canaan Defeated

11 When King Jabin of Hazor heard of this, he sent to King Jobab of Madon, to the king of Shimron, to the king of Achshaph, 2 and to the kings who were in the northern hill country, and in the Arabah south of Chinneroth, and in the lowland, and in Naphoth-dor on the west, 3 to the Canaanites in the east and the west, the Amorites, the Hittites, the Perizzites, and the Jebusites in the hill country, and the Hivites under Hermon in the land of Mizpah. 4 They came out, with all their troops, a great army, in number like the sand on the seashore, with very many horses and chariots. 5 All these kings joined their forces, and came and camped together at the waters of Merom, to fight with Israel.

6 And the LORD said to Joshua, "Do not be afraid of them, for tomorrow at this time I

10:25 *Do not be afraid or dismayed.* Once again Joshua exhorts the people to "be strong and courageous," as he had been encouraged in 1:6, 9.

11:6 *I will hand over all of them.* After completing the central and southern campaigns, Joshua turned to the north to face Hazor, the

"head of all those kingdoms" (v 10). Despite the overwhelming numbers arraying against Israel, God announced that he would deliver victory. Once again God's presence made the difference; this time even the time when the deliverance would be accomplished was noted.

will hand over all of them, slain, to Israel; you shall hamstring their horses, and burn their chariots with fire." 7So Joshua came suddenly upon them with all his fighting force, by the waters of Merom, and fell upon them. 8And the LORD handed them over to Israel, who attacked them and chased them as far as Great Sidon and Misrephoth-maim, and eastward as far as the valley of Mizpeh. They struck them down, until they had left no one remaining. 9And Joshua did to them as the LORD commanded him; he hamstrung their horses, and burned their chariots with fire.

10 Joshua turned back at that time, and took Hazor, and struck its king down with the sword. Before that time Hazor was the head of all those kingdoms. 11And they put to the sword all who were in it, utterly destroying them; there was no one left who breathed, and he burned Hazor with fire. 12And all the towns of those kings, and all their kings, Joshua took, and struck them with the edge of the sword, utterly destroying them, as Moses the servant of the LORD had commanded. 13But Israel burned none of the towns that stood on mounds except Hazor, which Joshua did burn. 14All the spoil of these towns, and the livestock, the Israelites took for their booty; but all the people they struck down with the edge of the sword, until they had destroyed them, and they did not leave any who breathed. 15As the LORD had commanded his servant Moses, so Moses commanded Joshua, and so Joshua did; he left nothing undone of all that the LORD had commanded Moses.

Summary of Joshua's Conquests

16 So Joshua took all that land: the hill country and all the Negeb and all the land of Goshen and the lowland and the Arabah and the hill country of Israel and its lowland, 17from Mount Halak, which rises toward Seir, as far as Baal-gad in the valley of Lebanon

below Mount Hermon. He took all their kings, struck them down, and put them to death. 18Joshua made war a long time with all those kings. 19There was not a town that made peace with the Israelites, except the Hivites, the inhabitants of Gibeon; all were taken in battle. 20For it was the LORD's doing to harden their hearts so that they would come against Israel in battle, in order that they might be utterly destroyed, and might receive no mercy, but be exterminated, just as the LORD had commanded Moses.

21 At that time Joshua came and wiped out the Anakim from the hill country, from Hebron, from Debir, from Anab, and from all the hill country of Judah, and from all the hill country of Israel; Joshua utterly destroyed them with their towns. 22None of the Anakim was left in the land of the Israelites; some remained only in Gaza, in Gath, and in Ashdod. 23So Joshua took the whole land, according to all that the LORD had spoken to Moses; and Joshua gave it for an inheritance to Israel according to their tribal allotments. And the land had rest from war.

The Kings Conquered by Moses

12 Now these are the kings of the land, whom the Israelites defeated, whose land they occupied beyond the Jordan toward the east, from the Wadi Arnon to Mount Hermon, with all the Arabah eastward: 2King Sihon of the Amorites who lived at Heshbon, and ruled from Aroer, which is on the edge of the Wadi Arnon, and from the middle of the valley as far as the river Jabbok, the boundary of the Ammonites, that is, half of Gilead, 3and the Arabah to the Sea of Chinneroth eastward, and in the direction of Beth-jeshimoth, to the sea of the Arabah, the Dead Sea,[a] southward to the foot of the slopes of

a Heb Salt Sea

11:20 *it was the LORD's doing.* The Lord hardens the hearts of all who are already committed irreconcilably to doing evil and refusing to turn to God, just as he hardened Pharaoh's heart for the same reason.

11:23 *Joshua took the whole land . . . and gave it for an inheritance to Israel.* This verse

brings the first section of the book to a close. Joshua took the whole land—at least in principle; but that did not mean that there was not a lot of mopping up to do. All this happened just as the Lord had indicated to Moses. Here also were some early fulfillments of the predicted word of God.

Pisgah; 4and King Og*a* of Bashan, one of the last of the Rephaim, who lived at Ashtaroth and at Edrei 5and ruled over Mount Hermon and Salecah and all Bashan to the boundary of the Geshurites and the Maacathites, and over half of Gilead to the boundary of King Sihon of Heshbon. 6Moses, the servant of the LORD, and the Israelites defeated them; and Moses the servant of the LORD gave their land for a possession to the Reubenites and the Gadites and the half-tribe of Manasseh.

The Kings Conquered by Joshua

7 The following are the kings of the land whom Joshua and the Israelites defeated on the west side of the Jordan, from Baal-gad in the valley of Lebanon to Mount Halak, that rises toward Seir (and Joshua gave their land to the tribes of Israel as a possession according to their allotments, 8in the hill country, in the lowland, in the Arabah, in the slopes, in the wilderness, and in the Negeb, the land of the Hittites, Amorites, Canaanites, Perizzites, Hivites, and Jebusites):

9 the king of Jericho	one
the king of Ai, which is next to Bethel	one
10 the king of Jerusalem	one
the king of Hebron	one
11 the king of Jarmuth	one
the king of Lachish	one
12 the king of Eglon	one
the king of Gezer	one
13 the king of Debir	one
the king of Geder	one
14 the king of Hormah	one
the king of Arad	one
15 the king of Libnah	one
the king of Adullam	one
16 the king of Makkedah	one
the king of Bethel	one
17 the king of Tappuah	one
the king of Hepher	one
18 the king of Aphek	one
the king of Lasharon	one
19 the king of Madon	one
the king of Hazor	one
20 the king of Shimron-meron	one
the king of Achshaph	one
21 the king of Taanach	one
the king of Megiddo	one
22 the king of Kedesh	one
the king of Jokneam in Carmel	one
23 the king of Dor in Naphath-dor	one
the king of Goiim in Galilee,*b*	one
24 the king of Tirzah	one

thirty-one kings in all.

The Parts of Canaan Still Unconquered

13 Now Joshua was old and advanced in years; and the LORD said to him, "You are old and advanced in years, and very much of the land still remains to be possessed. 2This is the land that still remains: all the regions of the Philistines, and all those of the Geshurites 3(from the Shihor, which is east of Egypt, northward to the boundary of Ekron, it is reckoned as Canaanite; there are five rulers of the Philistines, those of Gaza, Ashdod, Ashkelon, Gath, and Ekron), and those of the Avvim 4in the south; all the land of the Canaanites, and Mearah that belongs to the Sidonians, to Aphek, to the boundary of the Amorites, 5and the land of the Gebalites, and all Lebanon, toward the east, from Baal-gad below Mount Hermon to Lebo-hamath, 6all the inhabitants of the hill country from Lebanon to Misrephoth-maim, even all the Sidonians. I will myself drive them out from before the Israel-

a Gk: Heb *the boundary of King Og*   *b* Gk: Heb *Gilgal*

12:6–7 *Moses . . . defeated them. . . . Joshua . . . defeated on the west side.* Moses and the Israelites had won the land east of the Jordan, and Joshua and the Israelites had won the land west of the Jordan. The two men are described in parallel terms, as both conquerors of the land and possessors of it, to show their equality in honor and significance.

13:1 *very much of the land still remains to be possessed.* After all the victories, the land still to be possessed included the territory of the Philistines, the Phoenician coastlands, and the mountains of Lebanon plus numerous spots in the central and coastal plain of Canaan. God himself would take care of that (v 6); Joshua, now advanced in age, needed only to apportion the land to the remaining nine and a half tribes.

ites; only allot the land to Israel for an inheritance, as I have commanded you. 7Now therefore divide this land for an inheritance to the nine tribes and the half-tribe of Manasseh."

The Territory East of the Jordan

8 With the other half-tribe of Manasseh*a* the Reubenites and the Gadites received their inheritance, which Moses gave them, beyond the Jordan eastward, as Moses the servant of the LORD gave them: 9from Aroer, which is on the edge of the Wadi Arnon, and the town that is in the middle of the valley, and all the tableland from*b* Medeba as far as Dibon; 10and all the cities of King Sihon of the Amorites, who reigned in Heshbon, as far as the boundary of the Ammonites; 11and Gilead, and the region of the Geshurites and Maacathites, and all Mount Hermon, and all Bashan to Salecah; 12all the kingdom of Og in Bashan, who reigned in Ashtaroth and in Edrei (he alone was left of the survivors of the Rephaim); these Moses had defeated and driven out. 13Yet the Israelites did not drive out the Geshurites or the Maacathites; but Geshur and Maacath live within Israel to this day.

14 To the tribe of Levi alone Moses gave no inheritance; the offerings by fire to the LORD God of Israel are their inheritance, as he said to them.

The Territory of Reuben

15 Moses gave an inheritance to the tribe of the Reubenites according to their clans. 16Their territory was from Aroer, which is on the edge of the Wadi Arnon, and the town that is in the middle of the valley, and all the tableland by Medeba; 17with Heshbon, and all its towns that are in the tableland; Dibon, and Bamoth-baal, and Beth-baal-meon, 18and Jahaz, and Kedemoth, and Mephaath, 19and Kiriathaim, and Sibmah, and Zereth-shahar on the hill of the valley, 20and Beth-peor, and the slopes of

Pisgah, and Beth-jeshimoth, 21that is, all the towns of the tableland, and all the kingdom of King Sihon of the Amorites, who reigned in Heshbon, whom Moses defeated with the leaders of Midian, Evi and Rekem and Zur and Hur and Reba, as princes of Sihon, who lived in the land. 22Along with the rest of those they put to death, the Israelites also put to the sword Balaam son of Beor, who practiced divination. 23And the border of the Reubenites was the Jordan and its banks. This was the inheritance of the Reubenites according to their families with their towns and villages.

The Territory of Gad

24 Moses gave an inheritance also to the tribe of the Gadites, according to their families. 25Their territory was Jazer, and all the towns of Gilead, and half the land of the Ammonites, to Aroer, which is east of Rabbah, 26and from Heshbon to Ramath-mizpeh and Betonim, and from Mahanaim to the territory of Debir,*c* 27and in the valley Beth-haram, Beth-nimrah, Succoth, and Zaphon, the rest of the kingdom of King Sihon of Heshbon, the Jordan and its banks, as far as the lower end of the Sea of Chinnereth, eastward beyond the Jordan. 28This is the inheritance of the Gadites according to their clans, with their towns and villages.

The Territory of the Half-Tribe of Manasseh (East)

29 Moses gave an inheritance to the half-tribe of Manasseh; it was allotted to the half-tribe of the Manassites according to their families. 30Their territory extended from Mahanaim, through all Bashan, the whole kingdom of King Og of Bashan, and all the settlements of Jair, which are in Bashan, sixty

a Cn: Heb *With it*   *b* Compare Gk: Heb lacks *from*   *c* Gk Syr Vg: Heb *Lidebir*

13:14 *To the tribe of Levi alone Moses gave no inheritance.* The Levites received no territory; instead, God promised that he himself would be their "inheritance." (This is repeated again in v 33; see Gen 49:5–7; Exod 32:25–28; Deut 33:8–11.)

13:22 *also put to the sword Balaam . . . who practiced divination.* The prophet Balaam's death, noted in Num 31:8, is still recalled here with its stern warning against divination. God's people were to gain all supernatural revelation from God and his word rather than from occult sources originating in the netherworld.

towns, 31and half of Gilead, and Ashtaroth, and Edrei, the towns of the kingdom of Og in Bashan; these were allotted to the people of Machir son of Manasseh according to their clans—for half the Machirites.

32 These are the inheritances that Moses distributed in the plains of Moab, beyond the Jordan east of Jericho. 33But to the tribe of Levi Moses gave no inheritance; the LORD God of Israel is their inheritance, as he said to them.

The Distribution of Territory West of the Jordan

14 These are the inheritances that the Israelites received in the land of Canaan, which the priest Eleazar, and Joshua son of Nun, and the heads of the families of the tribes of the Israelites distributed to them. 2Their inheritance was by lot, as the LORD had commanded Moses for the nine and one-half tribes. 3For Moses had given an inheritance to the two and one-half tribes beyond the Jordan; but to the Levites he gave no inheritance among them. 4For the people of Joseph were two tribes, Manasseh and Ephraim; and no portion was given to the Levites in the land, but only towns to live in, with their pasture lands for their flocks and herds. 5The Israelites did as the LORD commanded Moses; they allotted the land.

Hebron Allotted to Caleb

6 Then the people of Judah came to Joshua at Gilgal; and Caleb son of Jephunneh the Kenizzite said to him, "You know what the LORD said to Moses the man of God in Kadesh-barnea concerning you and me. 7I was

forty years old when Moses the servant of the LORD sent me from Kadesh-barnea to spy out the land; and I brought him an honest report. 8But my companions who went up with me made the heart of the people melt; yet I wholeheartedly followed the LORD my God. 9And Moses swore on that day, saying, 'Surely the land on which your foot has trodden shall be an inheritance for you and your children forever, because you have wholeheartedly followed the LORD my God.' 10And now, as you see, the LORD has kept me alive, as he said, these forty-five years since the time that the LORD spoke this word to Moses, while Israel was journeying through the wilderness; and here I am today, eighty-five years old. 11I am still as strong today as I was on the day that Moses sent me; my strength now is as my strength was then, for war, and for going and coming. 12So now give me this hill country of which the LORD spoke on that day; for you heard on that day how the Anakim were there, with great fortified cities; it may be that the LORD will be with me, and I shall drive them out, as the LORD said."

13 Then Joshua blessed him, and gave Hebron to Caleb son of Jephunneh for an inheritance. 14So Hebron became the inheritance of Caleb son of Jephunneh the Kenizzite to this day, because he wholeheartedly followed the LORD, the God of Israel. 15Now the name of Hebron formerly was Kiriatharba;[a] this Arba was[b] the greatest man among the Anakim. And the land had rest from war.

a That is *the city of Arba*   b Heb lacks *this Arba was*

14:2 *Their inheritance was by lot.* The land was to be divided by the casting of lots. The use of lots here does not advocate the concept of chance, because the lot was determined by God himself (also 18:8, 10). Prov 16:1, 33 teaches that even what looks like happenstance or chance is the providential work of God.

14:13 *Then Joshua blessed . . . Caleb.* By blessing Caleb, Joshua was calling on God to grant to him power, resources, children, and all that he would need for a good life. This was not merely wishful thinking or a formula that was said automatically; no, the blessing was offered

in the name of God, who alone is the source of every good.

14:14 *he wholeheartedly followed the LORD.* Caleb is a model for all of us. Not all of a believer's gifts from the Heavenly Father are only in the life to come; some are given in the here and now, and so it was with Caleb. This is still short of the health, wealth, and prosperity gospel taught by some in which we demand immediate rewards from God and receive them without ever experiencing any sorrow, sickness, or the effects of an evil world. This teaching is not found in Scripture.

The Territory of Judah

15 The lot for the tribe of the people of Judah according to their families reached southward to the boundary of Edom, to the wilderness of Zin at the farthest south. ²And their south boundary ran from the end of the Dead Sea, *a* from the bay that faces southward; ³it goes out southward of the ascent of Akrabbim, passes along to Zin, and goes up south of Kadesh-barnea, along by Hezron, up to Addar, makes a turn to Karka, ⁴passes along to Azmon, goes out by the Wadi of Egypt, and comes to its end at the sea. This shall be your south boundary. ⁵And the east boundary is the Dead Sea, *a* to the mouth of the Jordan. And the boundary on the north side runs from the bay of the sea at the mouth of the Jordan; ⁶and the boundary goes up to Beth-hoglah, and passes along north of Beth-arabah; and the boundary goes up to the Stone of Bohan, Reuben's son; ⁷and the boundary goes up to Debir from the Valley of Achor, and so northward, turning toward Gilgal, which is opposite the ascent of Adummim, which is on the south side of the valley; and the boundary passes along to the waters of En-shemesh, and ends at En-rogel; ⁸then the boundary goes up by the valley of the son of Hinnom at the southern slope of the Jebusites (that is, Jerusalem); and the boundary goes up to the top of the mountain that lies over against the valley of Hinnom, on the west, at the northern end of the valley of Rephaim; ⁹then the boundary extends from the top of the mountain to the spring of the Waters of Nephtoah, and from there to the towns of Mount Ephron; then the boundary bends around to Baalah (that is, Kiriath-jearim); ¹⁰and the boundary circles west of Baalah to Mount Seir, passes along to the northern slope of Mount Jearim (that is, Chesalon), and goes down to Beth-shemesh, and passes along by Timnah; ¹¹the boundary goes out to the slope of the hill north of Ekron, then the boundary bends around to Shikkeron, and passes along to Mount Baalah, and goes out to Jabneel; then the boundary comes to an end at the sea. ¹²And the west boundary was the Mediterranean with its coast. This is the boundary surrounding the people of Judah according to their families.

Caleb Occupies His Portion

13 According to the commandment of the Lord to Joshua, he gave to Caleb son of Jephunneh a portion among the people of Judah, Kiriath-arba, *b* that is, Hebron (Arba was the father of Anak). ¹⁴And Caleb drove out from there the three sons of Anak: Sheshai, Ahiman, and Talmai, the descendants of Anak. ¹⁵From there he went up against the inhabitants of Debir; now the name of Debir formerly was Kiriath-sepher. ¹⁶And Caleb said, "Whoever attacks Kiriath-sepher and takes it, to him I will give my daughter Achsah as wife." ¹⁷Othniel son of Kenaz, the brother of Caleb, took it; and he gave him his daughter Achsah as wife. ¹⁸When she came to him, she urged him to ask her father for a field. As she dismounted from her donkey, Caleb said to her, "What do you wish?" ¹⁹She said to him, "Give me a present; since you have set me in the land of the Negeb, give me springs of water as well." So Caleb gave her the upper springs and the lower springs.

The Towns of Judah

20 This is the inheritance of the tribe of the people of Judah according to their families. ²¹The towns belonging to the tribe of the people of Judah in the extreme south, toward the boundary of Edom, were Kabzeel, Eder, Jagur, ²²Kinah, Dimonah, Adadah, ²³Kedesh, Hazor, Ithnan, ²⁴Ziph, Telem, Bealoth, ²⁵Hazor-hadattah, Kerioth-hezron (that is, Hazor), ²⁶Amam, Shema, Moladah, ²⁷Hazar-gaddah, Heshmon, Beth-pelet, ²⁸Hazar-shual, Beer-sheba, Biziothiah, ²⁹Baalah, Iim, Ezem, ³⁰Eltolad, Chesil, Hormah, ³¹Ziklag, Madmannah, Sansannah, ³²Lebaoth, Shilhim, Ain, and Rimmon: in all, twenty-nine towns, with their villages.

33 And in the lowland, Eshtaol, Zorah, Ashnah, ³⁴Zanoah, En-gannim, Tappuah, Enam, ³⁵Jarmuth, Adullam, Socoh, Azekah, ³⁶Shaaraim, Adithaim, Gederah, Gederothaim: fourteen towns with their villages.

37 Zenan, Hadashah, Migdal-gad, ³⁸Dilan, Mizpeh, Jokthe-el, ³⁹Lachish, Bozkath, Eglon, ⁴⁰Cabbon, Lahmam, Chitlish, ⁴¹Ge-

---

a Heb *Salt Sea*   *b* That is *the city of Arba*

deroth, Beth-dagon, Naamah, and Makke-dah: sixteen towns with their villages.

42 Libnah, Ether, Ashan, 43Iphtah, Ash-nah, Nezib, 44Keilah, Achzib, and Mareshah: nine towns with their villages.

45 Ekron, with its dependencies and its villages; 46from Ekron to the sea, all that were near Ashdod, with their villages.

47 Ashdod, its towns and its villages; Gaza, its towns and its villages; to the Wadi of Egypt, and the Great Sea with its coast.

48 And in the hill country, Shamir, Jattir, Socoh, 49Dannah, Kiriath-sannah (that is, Debir), 50Anab, Eshtemoh, Anim, 51Goshen, Holon, and Giloh: eleven towns with their villages.

52 Arab, Dumah, Eshan, 53Janim, Beth-tappuah, Aphekah, 54Humtah, Kiriath-arba (that is, Hebron), and Zior: nine towns with their villages.

55 Maon, Carmel, Ziph, Juttah, 56Jezreel, Jokdeam, Zanoah, 57Kain, Gibeah, and Tim-nah: ten towns with their villages.

58 Halhul, Beth-zur, Gedor, 59Maarath, Beth-anoth, and Eltekon: six towns with their villages.

60 Kiriath-baal (that is, Kiriath-jearim) and Rabbah: two towns with their villages.

61 In the wilderness, Beth-arabah, Mid-din, Secacah, 62Nibshan, the City of Salt, and En-gedi: six towns with their villages.

63 But the people of Judah could not drive out the Jebusites, the inhabitants of Jerusa-lem; so the Jebusites live with the people of Judah in Jerusalem to this day.

The Territory of Ephraim

16 The allotment of the Josephites went from the Jordan by Jericho, east of the waters of Jericho, into the wilderness, going up from Jericho into the hill country to Bethel; 2then going from Bethel to Luz, it passes along to Ataroth, the territory of the Archites; 3then it goes down westward to the territory of the Japhletites, as far as the terri-tory of Lower Beth-horon, then to Gezer, and it ends at the sea.

4 The Josephites—Manasseh and Ephra-im—received their inheritance.

5 The territory of the Ephraimites by their families was as follows: the boundary of their inheritance on the east was Ataroth-addar as far as Upper Beth-horon, 6and the bound-ary goes from there to the sea; on the north is Michmethath; then on the east the bound-ary makes a turn toward Taanath-shiloh, and passes along beyond it on the east to Janoah, 7then it goes down from Janoah to Ataroth and to Naarah, and touches Jericho, ending at the Jordan. 8From Tappuah the boundary goes westward to the Wadi Kanah, and ends at the sea. Such is the inheritance of the tribe of the Ephraimites by their families, 9together with the towns that were set apart for the Ephraimites within the inheritance of the Manassites, all those towns with their villages. 10They did not, however, drive out the Canaanites who lived in Gezer: so the Canaanites have lived within Ephraim to this day but have been made to do forced labor.

The Other Half-Tribe of Manasseh (West)

17 Then allotment was made to the tribe of Manasseh, for he was the firstborn of Joseph. To Machir the firstborn of Manas-seh, the father of Gilead, were allotted Gile-ad and Bashan, because he was a warrior. 2And allotments were made to the rest of the tribe of Manasseh, by their families, Abiezer, Helek, Asriel, Shechem, Hepher, and Shemi-da; these were the male descendants of Ma-nasseh son of Joseph, by their families.

3 Now Zelophehad son of Hepher son of Gilead son of Machir son of Manasseh had no sons, but only daughters; and these are the names of his daughters: Mahlah, Noah, Hog-lah, Milcah, and Tirzah. 4They came before the priest Eleazar and Joshua son of Nun and the leaders, and said, "The LORD commanded Moses to give us an inheritance along with our male kin." So according to the command-

---

17:3–6 *give us an inheritance along with our male kin.* Joshua made sure that the daughters of Zelophehad, who had no sons, received the inheritance they had been promised by Moses in Num 26:33; 27:1–11. Not only does God keep his promises, but so should leaders and all of God's people.

ment of the LORD he gave them an inheritance among the kinsmen of their father. 5Thus there fell to Manasseh ten portions, besides the land of Gilead and Bashan, which is on the other side of the Jordan, 6because the daughters of Manasseh received an inheritance along with his sons. The land of Gilead was allotted to the rest of the Manassites.

7 The territory of Manasseh reached from Asher to Michmethath, which is east of Shechem; then the boundary goes along southward to the inhabitants of En-tappuah. 8The land of Tappuah belonged to Manasseh, but the town of Tappuah on the boundary of Manasseh belonged to the Ephraimites. 9Then the boundary went down to the Wadi Kanah. The towns here, to the south of the wadi, among the towns of Manasseh, belong to Ephraim. Then the boundary of Manasseh goes along the north side of the wadi and ends at the sea. 10The land to the south is Ephraim's and that to the north is Manasseh's, with the sea forming its boundary; on the north Asher is reached, and on the east Issachar. 11Within Issachar and Asher, Manasseh had Beth-shean and its villages, Ibleam and its villages, the inhabitants of Dor and its villages, the inhabitants of En-dor and its villages, the inhabitants of Taanach and its villages, and the inhabitants of Megiddo and its villages (the third is Naphath).a 12Yet the Manassites could not take possession of those towns; but the Canaanites continued to live in that land. 13But when the Israelites grew strong, they put the Canaanites to forced labor, but did not utterly drive them out.

The Tribe of Joseph Protests

14 The tribe of Joseph spoke to Joshua, saying, "Why have you given me but one lot

and one portion as an inheritance, since we are a numerous people, whom all along the LORD has blessed?" 15And Joshua said to them, "If you are a numerous people, go up to the forest, and clear ground there for yourselves in the land of the Perizzites and the Rephaim, since the hill country of Ephraim is too narrow for you." 16The tribe of Joseph said, "The hill country is not enough for us; yet all the Canaanites who live in the plain have chariots of iron, both those in Bethshean and its villages and those in the Valley of Jezreel." 17Then Joshua said to the house of Joseph, to Ephraim and Manasseh, "You are indeed a numerous people, and have great power; you shall not have one lot only, 18but the hill country shall be yours, for though it is a forest, you shall clear it and possess it to its farthest borders; for you shall drive out the Canaanites, though they have chariots of iron, and though they are strong."

The Territories of the Remaining Tribes

18 Then the whole congregation of the Israelites assembled at Shiloh, and set up the tent of meeting there. The land lay subdued before them.

2 There remained among the Israelites seven tribes whose inheritance had not yet been apportioned. 3So Joshua said to the Israelites, "How long will you be slack about going in and taking possession of the land that the LORD, the God of your ancestors, has given you? 4Provide three men from each tribe, and I will send them out that they may begin to go throughout the land, writing a description of it with a view to their inheritances. Then come back to me. 5They shall di-

a Meaning of Heb uncertain

17:14–18 *The tribe of Joseph spoke to Joshua.* In contrast to Caleb's taking the initiative to possess his land (14:6–15), the two cantankerous half-tribes of Joseph are better at complaining about their one lot than rising up to take possession of what had been given to them. Their laziness and preference for griping rather than changing the situation match a lot of human experience.

18:1 *the Israelites assembled at Shiloh.* At this point the Israelites move from their encampment at Gilgal to Shiloh, some fifteen miles northwest of Jericho. There they set up the tent of meeting, which will be the focal point of worship until it is captured by the Philistines during the days of Eli (1 Sam 4:10,11).

18:3–7 *slack about going in and taking possession of the land.* The Israelites were lazy; Joshua had to rebuke them for their failure to act as they had been instructed in 13:1.

vide it into seven portions, Judah continuing in its territory on the south, and the house of Joseph in their territory on the north. 6You shall describe the land in seven divisions and bring the description here to me; and I will cast lots for you here before the LORD our God. 7The Levites have no portion among you, for the priesthood of the LORD is their heritage; and Gad and Reuben and the half-tribe of Manasseh have received their inheritance beyond the Jordan eastward, which Moses the servant of the LORD gave them."

8 So the men started on their way; and Joshua charged those who went to write the description of the land, saying, "Go throughout the land and write a description of it, and come back to me; and I will cast lots for you here before the LORD in Shiloh." 9So the men went and traversed the land and set down in a book a description of it by towns in seven divisions; then they came back to Joshua in the camp at Shiloh, 10and Joshua cast lots for them in Shiloh before the LORD; and there Joshua apportioned the land to the Israelites, to each a portion.

The Territory of Benjamin

11 The lot of the tribe of Benjamin according to its families came up, and the territory allotted to it fell between the tribe of Judah and the tribe of Joseph. 12On the north side their boundary began at the Jordan; then the boundary goes up to the slope of Jericho on the north, then up through the hill country westward; and it ends at the wilderness of Beth-aven. 13From there the boundary passes along southward in the direction of Luz, to the slope of Luz (that is, Bethel), then the boundary goes down to Ataroth-addar, on the mountain that lies south of Lower Beth-horon. 14Then the boundary goes in another direction, turning on the western side southward from the mountain that lies to the south, opposite Beth-horon, and it ends at Kiriath-baal (that is, Kiriath-jearim), a town belonging to the tribe of Judah. This forms the western side. 15The southern side begins at the outskirts of Kiriath-jearim; and the boundary goes from there to Ephron,ª to the spring of the Waters of Nephtoah; 16then the boundary goes down to the border of the mountain that overlooks the valley of the son of Hinnom, which is at the north end of the valley of Rephaim; and it then goes down the valley of Hinnom, south of the slope of the Jebusites, and downward to En-rogel; 17then it bends in a northerly direction going on to En-shemesh, and from there goes to Geliloth, which is opposite the ascent of Adummim; then it goes down to the Stone of Bohan, Reuben's son; 18and passing on to the north of the slope of Beth-arabahᵇ it goes down to the Arabah; 19then the boundary passes on to the north of the slope of Beth-hoglah; and the boundary ends at the northern bay of the Dead Sea,ᶜ at the south end of the Jordan: this is the southern border. 20The Jordan forms its boundary on the eastern side. This is the inheritance of the tribe of Benjamin, according to its families, boundary by boundary all around.

21 Now the towns of the tribe of Benjamin according to their families were Jericho, Beth-hoglah, Emek-keziz, 22Beth-arabah, Zemaraim, Bethel, 23Avvim, Parah, Ophrah, 24Chephar-ammoni, Ophni, and Geba—twelve towns with their villages: 25Gibeon, Ramah, Beeroth, 26Mizpeh, Chephirah, Mozah, 27Rekem, Irpeel, Taralah, 28Zela, Haeleph, Jebusᵈ (that is, Jerusalem), Gibeahᵉ and Kiriath-jearimᶠ—fourteen towns with their villages. This is the inheritance of the tribe of Benjamin according to its families.

The Territory of Simeon

19 The second lot came out for Simeon, for the tribe of Simeon, according to its families; its inheritance lay within the inheritance of the tribe of Judah. 2It had for its inheritance Beer-sheba, Sheba, Moladah, 3Hazar-shual, Balah, Ezem, 4Eltolad, Bethul, Hormah, 5Ziklag, Beth-marcaboth, Hazar-susah, 6Beth-lebaoth, and Sharuhen—thirteen towns with their villages; 7Ain, Rimmon, Ether, and Ashan—four towns with their villages; 8together with all the villages all around these towns as far as Baalath-beer, Ramah of the Negeb. This was the inheri-

a Cn See 15.9. Heb *westward*   b Gk: Heb *to the slope over against the Arabah*   c Heb *Salt Sea*   d Gk Syr Vg: Heb *the Jebusite*   e Heb *Gibeath*   f Gk: Heb *Kiriath*

tance of the tribe of Simeon according to its families. [9]The inheritance of the tribe of Simeon formed part of the territory of Judah; because the portion of the tribe of Judah was too large for them, the tribe of Simeon obtained an inheritance within their inheritance.

The Territory of Zebulun

10 The third lot came up for the tribe of Zebulun, according to its families. The boundary of its inheritance reached as far as Sarid; [11]then its boundary goes up westward, and on to Maralah, and touches Dabbesheth, then the wadi that is east of Jokneam; [12]from Sarid it goes in the other direction eastward toward the sunrise to the boundary of Chisloth-tabor; from there it goes to Daberath, then up to Japhia; [13]from there it passes along on the east toward the sunrise to Gath-hepher, to Eth-kazin, and going on to Rimmon it bends toward Neah; [14]then on the north the boundary makes a turn to Hannathon, and it ends at the valley of Iphtah-el; [15]and Kattath, Nahalal, Shimron, Idalah, and Bethlehem—twelve towns with their villages. [16]This is the inheritance of the tribe of Zebulun, according to its families—these towns with their villages.

The Territory of Issachar

17 The fourth lot came out for Issachar, for the tribe of Issachar, according to its families. [18]Its territory included Jezreel, Chesulloth, Shunem, [19]Hapharaim, Shion, Anaharath, [20]Rabbith, Kishion, Ebez, [21]Remeth, En-gannim, En-haddah, Beth-pazzez; [22]the boundary also touches Tabor, Shahazumah, and Beth-shemesh, and its boundary ends at the Jordan—sixteen towns with their villages. [23]This is the inheritance of the tribe of Issachar, according to its families—the towns with their villages.

The Territory of Asher

24 The fifth lot came out for the tribe of Asher according to its families. [25]Its boundary included Helkath, Hali, Beten, Achshaph, [26]Allammelech, Amad, and Mishal; on the west it touches Carmel and Shihor-libnath, [27]then it turns eastward, goes to Beth-dagon, and touches Zebulun and the valley of Iphtah-el northward to Beth-emek and Neiel; then it continues in the north to Cabul, [28]Ebron, Rehob, Hammon, Kanah, as far as Great Sidon; [29]then the boundary turns to Ramah, reaching to the fortified city of Tyre; then the boundary turns to Hosah, and it ends at the sea; Mahalab,[a] Achzib, [30]Ummah, Aphek, and Rehob—twenty-two towns with their villages. [31]This is the inheritance of the tribe of Asher according to its families—these towns with their villages.

The Territory of Naphtali

32 The sixth lot came out for the tribe of Naphtali, for the tribe of Naphtali, according to its families. [33]And its boundary ran from Heleph, from the oak in Zaanannim, and Adami-nekeb, and Jabneel, as far as Lakkum; and it ended at the Jordan; [34]then the boundary turns westward to Aznoth-tabor, and goes from there to Hukkok, touching Zebulun at the south, and Asher on the west, and Judah on the east at the Jordan. [35]The fortified towns are Ziddim, Zer, Hammath, Rakkath, Chinnereth, [36]Adamah, Ramah, Hazor, [37]Kedesh, Edrei, En-hazor, [38]Iron, Migdal-el, Horem, Beth-anath, and Beth-shemesh—nineteen towns with their villages. [39]This is the inheritance of the tribe of Naphtali according to its families—the towns with their villages.

The Territory of Dan

40 The seventh lot came out for the tribe of Dan, according to its families. [41]The territory of its inheritance included Zorah, Eshtaol, Ir-shemesh, [42]Shaalabbin, Aijalon, Ithlah, [43]Elon, Timnah, Ekron, [44]Eltekeh, Gibbethon, Baalath, [45]Jehud, Bene-berak, Gath-rimmon, [46]Me-jarkon, and Rakkon at the border opposite Joppa. [47]When the territory of the Danites was lost to them, the Danites went up and fought against Leshem, and after capturing it and putting it to the sword, they took possession of it and settled in it, calling Leshem, Dan, after their ancestor Dan. [48]This is the inheritance of the tribe of Dan, according to their families—these towns with their villages.

a Cn Compare Gk: Heb *Mehebel*

Joshua's Inheritance

49 When they had finished distributing the several territories of the land as inheritances, the Israelites gave an inheritance among them to Joshua son of Nun. 50By command of the LORD they gave him the town that he asked for, Timnath-serah in the hill country of Ephraim; he rebuilt the town, and settled in it.

51 These are the inheritances that the priest Eleazar and Joshua son of Nun and the heads of the families of the tribes of the Israelites distributed by lot at Shiloh before the LORD, at the entrance of the tent of meeting. So they finished dividing the land.

The Cities of Refuge

20 Then the LORD spoke to Joshua, saying, 2"Say to the Israelites, 'Appoint the cities of refuge, of which I spoke to you through Moses, 3so that anyone who kills a person without intent or by mistake may flee there; they shall be for you a refuge from the avenger of blood. 4The slayer shall flee to one of these cities and shall stand at the entrance of the gate of the city, and explain the case to the elders of that city; then the fugitive shall be taken into the city, and given a place, and shall remain with them. 5And if the avenger of blood is in pursuit, they shall not give up the slayer, because the neighbor was killed by mistake, there having been no enmity between them before. 6The slayer shall remain in that city until there is a trial before the congregation, until the death of the one who is high priest at the time: then the slayer may return home, to the town in which the deed was done.' "

7 So they set apart Kedesh in Galilee in the hill country of Naphtali, and Shechem in the hill country of Ephraim, and Kiriath-arba (that is, Hebron) in the hill country of Judah. 8And beyond the Jordan east of Jericho, they appointed Bezer in the wilderness on the tableland, from the tribe of Reuben, and Ramoth in Gilead, from the tribe of Gad, and Golan in Bashan, from the tribe of Manasseh. 9These were the cities designated for all the Israelites, and for the aliens residing among them, that anyone who killed a person without intent could flee there, so as not to die by the hand of the avenger of blood, until there was a trial before the congregation.

Cities Allotted to the Levites

21 Then the heads of the families of the Levites came to the priest Eleazar and to Joshua son of Nun and to the heads of the families of the tribes of the Israelites; 2they said to them at Shiloh in the land of Canaan, "The LORD commanded through Moses that we be given towns to live in, along with their pasture lands for our livestock." 3So by command of the LORD the Israelites gave to the Levites the following towns and pasture lands out of their inheritance.

4 The lot came out for the families of the Kohathites. So those Levites who were descendants of Aaron the priest received by lot thirteen towns from the tribes of Judah, Simeon, and Benjamin.

5 The rest of the Kohathites received by lot ten towns from the families of the tribe of Ephraim, from the tribe of Dan, and the half-tribe of Manasseh.

6 The Gershonites received by lot thirteen

19:49–51 *the Israelites gave . . . to Joshua.* Though Caleb and Joshua were both promised an inheritance in Num 14:30, the precise divine command about Joshua's portion was not recorded earlier. But he finally received here what had been promised "by the command of the LORD."

20:2–6 *anyone who kills a person without intent or by mistake.* Mosaic law provided allowances for motive and intent, which is where our modern law gets its distinctions on the various degrees of murder. After

unintentional murders, perpetrators could flee for refuge to one of the six cities of refuge. Curiously, they were to remain there for life unless the death of the high priest occurred, in which case they were free to leave the city of refuge and no one was to avenge the previous death under any circumstances. The life of the high priest was another pointer to the theme of a vicarious substitution that was to be offered on behalf of the guilty person. Reconciliation could come only with payment of the debt owed.

towns from the families of the tribe of Issachar, from the tribe of Asher, from the tribe of Naphtali, and from the half-tribe of Manasseh in Bashan.

7 The Merarites according to their families received twelve towns from the tribe of Reuben, the tribe of Gad, and the tribe of Zebulun.

8 These towns and their pasture lands the Israelites gave by lot to the Levites, as the LORD had commanded through Moses.

9 Out of the tribe of Judah and the tribe of Simeon they gave the following towns mentioned by name, 10which went to the descendants of Aaron, one of the families of the Kohathites who belonged to the Levites, since the lot fell to them first. 11They gave them Kiriath-arba (Arba being the father of Anak), that is Hebron, in the hill country of Judah, along with the pasture lands around it. 12But the fields of the town and its villages had been given to Caleb son of Jephunneh as his holding.

13 To the descendants of Aaron the priest they gave Hebron, the city of refuge for the slayer, with its pasture lands, Libnah with its pasture lands, 14Jattir with its pasture lands, Eshtemoa with its pasture lands, 15Holon with its pasture lands, Debir with its pasture lands, 16Ain with its pasture lands, Juttah with its pasture lands, and Beth-shemesh with its pasture lands—nine towns out of these two tribes. 17Out of the tribe of Benjamin: Gibeon with its pasture lands, Geba with its pasture lands, 18Anathoth with its pasture lands, and Almon with its pasture lands—four towns. 19The towns of the descendants of Aaron—the priests—were thirteen in all, with their pasture lands.

20 As to the rest of the Kohathites belonging to the Kohathite families of the Levites, the towns allotted to them were out of the tribe of Ephraim. 21To them were given Shechem, the city of refuge for the slayer, with its pasture lands in the hill country of Ephraim, Gezer with its pasture lands, 22Kibzaim with its pasture lands, and Beth-horon with its pasture lands—four towns. 23Out of the tribe of Dan: Elteke with its pasture lands, Gibbethon with its pasture lands, 24Aijalon with its pasture lands, Gath-rimmon with

its pasture lands—four towns. 25Out of the half-tribe of Manasseh: Taanach with its pasture lands, and Gath-rimmon with its pasture lands—two towns. 26The towns of the families of the rest of the Kohathites were ten in all, with their pasture lands.

27 To the Gershonites, one of the families of the Levites, were given out of the half-tribe of Manasseh, Golan in Bashan with its pasture lands, the city of refuge for the slayer, and Beeshterah with its pasture lands—two towns. 28Out of the tribe of Issachar: Kishion with its pasture lands, Daberath with its pasture lands, 29Jarmuth with its pasture lands, En-gannim with its pasture lands—four towns. 30Out of the tribe of Asher: Mishal with its pasture lands, Abdon with its pasture lands, 31Helkath with its pasture lands, and Rehob with its pasture lands—four towns. 32Out of the tribe of Naphtali: Kedesh in Galilee with its pasture lands, the city of refuge for the slayer, Hammoth-dor with its pasture lands, and Kartan with its pasture lands—three towns. 33The towns of the several families of the Gershonites were in all thirteen, with their pasture lands.

34 To the rest of the Levites—the Merarite families—were given out of the tribe of Zebulun: Jokneam with its pasture lands, Kartah with its pasture lands, 35Dimnah with its pasture lands, Nahalal with its pasture lands—four towns. 36Out of the tribe of Reuben: Bezer with its pasture lands, Jahzah with its pasture lands, 37Kedemoth with its pasture lands, and Mephaath with its pasture lands—four towns. 38Out of the tribe of Gad: Ramoth in Gilead with its pasture lands, the city of refuge for the slayer, Mahanaim with its pasture lands, 39Heshbon with its pasture lands, Jazer with its pasture lands—four towns in all. 40As for the towns of the several Merarite families, that is, the remainder of the families of the Levites, those allotted to them were twelve in all.

41 The towns of the Levites within the holdings of the Israelites were in all forty-eight towns with their pasture lands. 42Each of these towns had its pasture lands around it; so it was with all these towns.

43 Thus the LORD gave to Israel all the land that he swore to their ancestors that he would

give them; and having taken possession of it, they settled there. 44And the LORD gave them rest on every side just as he had sworn to their ancestors; not one of all their enemies had withstood them, for the LORD had given all their enemies into their hands. 45Not one of all the good promises that the LORD had made to the house of Israel had failed; all came to pass.

The Eastern Tribes Return to Their Territory

22 Then Joshua summoned the Reubenites, the Gadites, and the half-tribe of Manasseh, 2and said to them, "You have observed all that Moses the servant of the LORD commanded you, and have obeyed me in all that I have commanded you; 3you have not forsaken your kindred these many days, down to this day, but have been careful to keep the charge of the LORD your God. 4And now the LORD your God has given rest to your kindred, as he promised them; therefore turn and go to your tents in the land where your possession lies, which Moses the servant of the LORD gave you on the other side of the Jordan. 5Take good care to observe the commandment and instruction that Moses the servant of the LORD commanded you, to love the LORD your God, to walk in all his ways, to keep his commandments, and to hold fast to him, and to serve him with all your heart and with all your soul." 6So Joshua blessed them and sent them away, and they went to their tents.

7 Now to the one half of the tribe of Manasseh Moses had given a possession in Bashan; but to the other half Joshua had given a possession beside their fellow Israelites in the land west of the Jordan. And when Joshua sent them away to their tents and blessed them, 8he said to them, "Go back to your tents with much wealth, and with very much livestock, with silver, gold, bronze, and iron, and with a great quantity of clothing; divide the spoil of your enemies with your kindred." 9So the Reubenites and the Gadites and the half-tribe of Manasseh returned home, parting from the Israelites at Shiloh, which is in the land of Canaan, to go to the land of Gilead, their own land of which they had taken possession by command of the LORD through Moses.

A Memorial Altar East of the Jordan

10 When they came to the region[a] near the Jordan that lies in the land of Canaan, the Reubenites and the Gadites and the half-tribe of Manasseh built there an altar by the Jordan, an altar of great size. 11The Israelites heard that the Reubenites and the Gadites and the half-tribe of Manasseh had built an altar at the frontier of the land of Canaan, in the region[a] near the Jordan, on the side that belongs to the Israelites. 12And when the people of Israel heard of it, the whole assembly of the Israelites gathered at Shiloh, to make war against them.

13 Then the Israelites sent the priest Phinehas son of Eleazar to the Reubenites and the Gadites and the half-tribe of Manasseh, in the land of Gilead, 14and with him ten chiefs, one from each of the tribal families of Israel, every one of them the head of a family among the clans of Israel. 15They came to the Reubenites, the Gadites, and the half-

a Or to Geliloth

21:43–45 all came to pass. This passage concludes the first two main sections of the book, the conquest and the division of the land. God had proven himself the faithful God who had not forgotten any of the promises made to the patriarchs or Moses. Moreover, God had also given the people "rest on every side." In principle, everything promised had come to pass.

22:2–5 You have observed. Joshua's final speech to the Transjordanian tribes is a veritable summary of Deuteronomy. They were to "take good care" to "observe" the law, to "love" the Lord, to "walk" in all his ways, to "keep" his commandments, to "hold fast" by clinging to him, and to "serve" the Lord "with all [their] heart[s] . . . and soul[s]."

22:13–14 one from each. Procedure was carefully followed in selecting a representative from each tribe of Israel, under the direction of the priest Phinehas.

tribe of Manasseh, in the land of Gilead, and they said to them, 16"Thus says the whole congregation of the Lord, 'What is this treachery that you have committed against the God of Israel in turning away today from following the Lord, by building yourselves an altar today in rebellion against the Lord? 17Have we not had enough of the sin at Peor from which even yet we have not cleansed ourselves, and for which a plague came upon the congregation of the Lord, 18that you must turn away today from following the Lord! If you rebel against the Lord today, he will be angry with the whole congregation of Israel tomorrow. 19But now, if your land is unclean, cross over into the Lord's land where the Lord's tabernacle now stands, and take for yourselves a possession among us; only do not rebel against the Lord, or rebel against us*a* by building yourselves an altar other than the altar of the Lord our God. 20Did not Achan son of Zerah break faith in the matter of the devoted things, and wrath fell upon all the congregation of Israel? And he did not perish alone for his iniquity!' "

21 Then the Reubenites, the Gadites, and the half-tribe of Manasseh said in answer to the heads of the families of Israel, 22"The Lord, God of gods! The Lord, God of gods! He knows; and let Israel itself know! If it was in rebellion or in breach of faith toward the Lord, do not spare us today 23for building an altar to turn away from following the Lord; or if we did so to offer burnt offerings or grain offerings or offerings of well-being on it, may the Lord himself take vengeance. 24No! We did it from fear that in time to come your children might say to our children, 'What have you to do with the Lord, the God of Is-

rael? 25For the Lord has made the Jordan a boundary between us and you, you Reubenites and Gadites; you have no portion in the Lord.' So your children might make our children cease to worship the Lord. 26Therefore we said, 'Let us now build an altar, not for burnt offering, nor for sacrifice, 27but to be a witness between us and you, and between the generations after us, that we do perform the service of the Lord in his presence with our burnt offerings and sacrifices and offerings of well-being; so that your children may never say to our children in time to come, "You have no portion in the Lord." ' 28And we thought, If this should be said to us or to our descendants in time to come, we could say, 'Look at this copy of the altar of the Lord, which our ancestors made, not for burnt offerings, nor for sacrifice, but to be a witness between us and you.' 29Far be it from us that we should rebel against the Lord, and turn away this day from following the Lord by building an altar for burnt offering, grain offering, or sacrifice, other than the altar of the Lord our God that stands before his tabernacle!"

30 When the priest Phinehas and the chiefs of the congregation, the heads of the families of Israel who were with him, heard the words that the Reubenites and the Gadites and the Manassites spoke, they were satisfied. 31The priest Phinehas son of Eleazar said to the Reubenites and the Gadites and the Manassites, "Today we know that the Lord is among us, because you have not committed this treachery against the Lord; now

a Or make rebels of us

22:17 *Have we not had enough of the sin at Peor.* The sin at Baal Peor (Num 25) was very much on Israel's mind as it tried to ascertain if the Transjordanian altar was evidence of a rebel movement. Apparently the nation still had "not cleansed [itself]" of that sin, with its association of prostitution in connection with the worship of the Moabite god. The attraction of this idolatry and immorality can be seen in the fact that Israel still flirted with it, even though that event had occurred a number of years ago.

22:26–27 SERVICE—*See* Spiritual Disciplines Index.

22:28 *this copy of the altar . . . to be a witness.* The altar erected on the eastern side of the Jordan River was only meant to be a copy or a replica of the true altar in the tabernacle. The word translated "copy" here is the same one used in Exod 25:9, 40 ("pattern") for Moses' making the tabernacle as a copy or imitation of the archetype that was shown to him on Mt. Sinai.

you have saved the Israelites from the hand of the LORD."

32 Then the priest Phinehas son of Eleazar and the chiefs returned from the Reubenites and the Gadites in the land of Gilead to the land of Canaan, to the Israelites, and brought back word to them. 33 The report pleased the Israelites; and the Israelites blessed God and spoke no more of making war against them, to destroy the land where the Reubenites and the Gadites were settled. 34 The Reubenites and the Gadites called the altar Witness;a "For," said they, "it is a witness between us that the LORD is God."

Joshua Exhorts the People

23 A long time afterward, when the LORD had given rest to Israel from all their enemies all around, and Joshua was old and well advanced in years, 2 Joshua summoned all Israel, their elders and heads, their judges and officers, and said to them, "I am now old and well advanced in years; 3 and you have seen all that the LORD your God has done to all these nations for your sake, for it is the LORD your God who has fought for you. 4 I have allotted to you as an inheritance for your tribes those nations that remain, along with all the nations that I have already cut off, from the Jordan to the Great Sea in the west. 5 The LORD your God will push them back before you, and drive them out of your sight; and you shall possess their land, as the LORD your God promised you. 6 Therefore be very steadfast to observe and do all that is written in the book of the law of Moses, turning aside from it neither to the right nor to the left, 7 so that you may not be mixed with these nations left here among you, or make mention of the names of their gods, or swear by them, or serve them, or bow yourselves down to them, 8 but hold fast to the LORD your God, as you have done to this day.

9 For the LORD has driven out before you great and strong nations; and as for you, no one has been able to withstand you to this day. 10 One of you puts to flight a thousand, since it is the LORD your God who fights for you, as he promised you. 11 Be very careful, therefore, to love the LORD your God. 12 For if you turn back, and join the survivors of these nations left here among you, and intermarry with them, so that you marry their women and they yours, 13 know assuredly that the LORD your God will not continue to drive out these nations before you; but they shall be a snare and a trap for you, a scourge on your sides, and thorns in your eyes, until you perish from this good land that the LORD your God has given you.

14 "And now I am about to go the way of all the earth, and you know in your hearts and souls, all of you, that not one thing has failed of all the good things that the LORD your God promised concerning you; all have come to pass for you, not one of them has failed. 15 But just as all the good things that the LORD your God promised concerning you have been fulfilled for you, so the LORD will bring upon you all the bad things, until he has destroyed you from this good land that the LORD your God has given you. 16 If you transgress the covenant of the LORD your God, which he enjoined on you, and go and serve other gods and bow down to them, then the anger of the LORD will be kindled against you, and you shall perish quickly from the good land that he has given to you."

The Tribes Renew the Covenant

24 Then Joshua gathered all the tribes of Israel to Shechem, and summoned the elders, the heads, the judges, and the officers of Israel; and they presented them-

a Cn Compare Syr: Heb lacks *Witness*

23:6 *be very steadfast to observe and do all that is written.* Once more Joshua calls the nation in his farewell speech to keep the law, just as he too was challenged in his commissioning service in 1:7-9.

23:9-10 *For the LORD has driven out before you great and strong nations.* As God had

promised in 1:5, "No one shall be able to stand against you all days of your life." Indeed, as Lev 26:7-8 had promised, Joshua says, "One of you puts to flight a thousand" (v 10). The presence of God had made such a powerful difference that even the weakest of the Israelites seemed to be an unmatched hero.

selves before God. ²And Joshua said to all the people, "Thus says the LORD, the God of Israel: Long ago your ancestors—Terah and his sons Abraham and Nahor—lived beyond the Euphrates and served other gods. ³Then I took your father Abraham from beyond the River and led him through all the land of Canaan and made his offspring many. I gave him Isaac; ⁴and to Isaac I gave Jacob and Esau. I gave Esau the hill country of Seir to possess, but Jacob and his children went down to Egypt. ⁵Then I sent Moses and Aaron, and I plagued Egypt with what I did in its midst; and afterwards I brought you out. ⁶When I brought your ancestors out of Egypt, you came to the sea; and the Egyptians pursued your ancestors with chariots and horsemen to the Red Sea.ᵃ ⁷When they cried out to the LORD, he put darkness between you and the Egyptians, and made the sea come upon them and cover them; and your eyes saw what I did to Egypt. Afterwards you lived in the wilderness a long time. ⁸Then I brought you to the land of the Amorites, who lived on the other side of the Jordan; they fought with you, and I handed them over to you, and you took possession of their land, and I destroyed them before you. ⁹Then King Balak son of Zippor of Moab, set out to fight against Israel. He sent and invited Balaam son of Beor to curse you, ¹⁰but I would not listen to Balaam; therefore he blessed you; so I rescued you out of his hand. ¹¹When you went over the Jordan and came to Jericho, the citizens of Jericho fought against you, and also the Amorites, the Perizzites,

the Canaanites, the Hittites, the Girgashites, the Hivites, and the Jebusites; and I handed them over to you. ¹²I sent the hornetᵇ ahead of you, which drove out before you the two kings of the Amorites; it was not by your sword or by your bow. ¹³I gave you a land on which you had not labored, and towns that you had not built, and you live in them; you eat the fruit of vineyards and oliveyards that you did not plant.

14 "Now therefore revere the LORD, and serve him in sincerity and in faithfulness; put away the gods that your ancestors served beyond the River and in Egypt, and serve the LORD. ¹⁵Now if you are unwilling to serve the LORD, choose this day whom you will serve, whether the gods your ancestors served in the region beyond the River or the gods of the Amorites in whose land you are living; but as for me and my household, we will serve the LORD."

16 Then the people answered, "Far be it from us that we should forsake the LORD to serve other gods; ¹⁷for it is the LORD our God who brought us and our ancestors up from the land of Egypt, out of the house of slavery, and who did those great signs in our sight. He protected us along all the way that we went, and among all the peoples through whom we passed; ¹⁸and the LORD drove out before us all the peoples, the Amorites who lived in the land. Therefore we also will serve the LORD, for he is our God."

ᵃ Or *Sea of Reeds*   ᵇ Meaning of Heb uncertain

24:2–13 *Long ago.* These words are used at Passover celebrations by Jewish people all over the world to this day. God's choice of Abraham and his line had very little to do with their faithfulness; it really was a demonstration of the grace of God.

24:14–15 *choose this day whom you will serve.* Joshua left his people with the choice to serve the God who had chosen, liberated, and provided for them (vv 2–13) or to lapse back into worship of the false gods of their ancestors on the other side of the Euphrates before God called Abraham. This choice is the one left for us as well; we must "choose this day

whom we will serve." If we choose false gods, such lapses today are a reversion to what we too had once been but for the grace of God.

Responding
24:15 SERVICE. In this often quoted verse Joshua declares his intention to serve the Lord and tells the people to choose whom they will serve. Meditate on the phrase, "As for me and my household, we will serve the LORD." What does it mean for a family to "serve the Lord"? Is it more difficult today than it was in Joshua's time? Why or why not? *See also* Spiritual Disciplines Index.

19 But Joshua said to the people, "You cannot serve the LORD, for he is a holy God. He is a jealous God; he will not forgive your transgressions or your sins. 20If you forsake the LORD and serve foreign gods, then he will turn and do you harm, and consume you, after having done you good." 21And the people said to Joshua, "No, we will serve the LORD!" 22Then Joshua said to the people, "You are witnesses against yourselves that you have chosen the LORD, to serve him." And they said, "We are witnesses." 23He said, "Then put away the foreign gods that are among you, and incline your hearts to the LORD, the God of Israel." 24The people said to Joshua, "The LORD our God we will serve, and him we will obey." 25So Joshua made a covenant with the people that day, and made statutes and ordinances for them at Shechem. 26Joshua wrote these words in the book of the law of God; and he took a large stone, and set it up there under the oak in the sanctuary of the LORD. 27Joshua said to all the people, "See, this stone shall be a witness against us; for it has heard all the words of the LORD that he spoke to us; therefore it shall be a witness against you, if you deal falsely with your God." 28So Joshua sent the people away to their inheritances.

Death of Joshua and Eleazar

29 After these things Joshua son of Nun, the servant of the LORD, died, being one hundred ten years old. 30They buried him in his own inheritance at Timnath-serah, which is in the hill country of Ephraim, north of Mount Gaash.

31 Israel served the LORD all the days of Joshua, and all the days of the elders who outlived Joshua and had known all the work that the LORD did for Israel.

32 The bones of Joseph, which the Israelites had brought up from Egypt, were buried at Shechem, in the portion of ground that Jacob had bought from the children of Hamor, the father of Shechem, for one hundred pieces of money;a it became an inheritance of the descendants of Joseph.

33 Eleazar son of Aaron died; and they buried him at Gibeah, the town of his son Phinehas, which had been given him in the hill country of Ephraim.

a Heb one hundred qesitah

24:16–18 *we also will serve the LORD, for he is our God.* The people's response is exemplary, but unfortunately it was short-lived.

24:19 *He is a jealous God.* Nominal, superficial faith is deadly in light of the fact that God is holy and altogether separate and different from our way of thinking, living, and acting.

24:22–24 *We are witnesses.* This covenant was sealed at Shechem under an oak tree, where a large stone was erected as a witness;

the people were also witnesses. A large standing stone dating to the Late Bronze Age has been found at Shechem and may well be the very stone mentioned here.

24:29 *Joshua . . . the servant of the LORD.* Joshua is called "the servant of the LORD" for the first time in this book. This humble, but later distinguished title will be the one also assigned to the messianic figure in Isaiah 42–53.

JUDGES

T he book of Judges is not a source to which the People of God have readily turned for guidance in spiritual formation or instruction in the Spiritual Disciplines. Rather, Judges has been largely ignored due to what many consider to be its excessively violent content and its portrayal of a partisan God who unfairly favors Israelites at the expense of Canaanites, Midianites, Ammonites, and Philistines. Given the slaughter of so many people at the hands of the Israelites, it has been difficult to discern God's work toward the formation of an all-inclusive community that is a blessing to the nations (Gen 12:3). It is precisely this difficulty that suggests the critical importance of hearing Judges as the continuation of a story that begins in Genesis and will not be over until God's covenant people have become "a light to the nations" (Isa 42:6; 49:6), participating with God in effecting "the healing of the nations" (Rev 22:2).

That Scripture begins with creation in Genesis 1–2 is extraordinarily important, because it affirms from the beginning God's love for the whole creation, as well as God's will for life for all humanity. Everything that follows in the Bible, including Judges, must be heard in light of these initial affirmations. Even when the story seems to narrow its focus from humankind to Abraham, Sarah, and their descendants, it still affirms God's ultimate intent to effect through a particular people a blessing for "all the families of the earth" (Gen 12:3).

In Exodus, when Pharaoh's death-dealing policies aim at thwarting God's will for life, God acts to deliver those threatened with death. Thus, the exodus articulates again God's will for life. The people whose lives are saved are then instructed by God at Sinai on how to live as God intends. They promise to obey God (see Exod 24:3, 7); but even when they prove to be immediately disobedient (see 32:1–14), God does not withdraw the divine presence (33:14). Rather, God reveals the divine self to be "merciful and gracious, slow to anger, and abounding in steadfast love and faithfulness" (34:6). To be sure, there will always be destructive and hurtful consequences

See also *"The With-God Life"* essay for this section of the Bible,
"The People of God in the Promised Land," pp. 297–301.

of disobedience. In this sense, the guilty are by no means cleared (34:7); but neither are the guilty abandoned by the God of grace.

The book of Joshua represents a replaying of the exodus and the covenant established at Sinai. The crossing of the Jordan in Joshua 3 recalls the crossing of the sea to escape death in Exodus 14; the gift of the land and its promise of life parallel the rescue from death at the hands of Pharaoh and his forces; and the people promise again in Joshua 24 to serve and obey God alone, as they had promised in Exodus 24. In short, as Judges begins, the People of God have another chance to respond to God faithfully and obediently. Will the people whom God has entrusted with effecting a blessing for all nations fulfill their vocation by worshiping and serving God alone?

As Judges demonstrates repeatedly, the answer to this question is no. The people's unfaithfulness and disobedience raise another question: How will God respond to the people's failure? As Judges also demonstrates repeatedly, despite the people's disobedience, God remains present and graciously raises up another judge to deliver and lead the people. To be sure, as always, there are the hurtful and destructive consequences of disobedience; but God simply will not abandon the people whom he loves.

In this respect, Judges anticipates subsequent books in the prophetic canon (Joshua through 2 Kings constitute the Former Prophets; and Isaiah, Jeremiah, Ezekiel, and the Book of the Twelve constitute the Latter Prophets). For instance, after the people's and kings' disobedience that results in the exile, the book of Isaiah also proclaims that God has not abandoned the people, who will be reconstituted as "a light to the nations" (Isa 42:6; 49:6). When Judges is interpreted in the context of what precedes and follows it, then it will not be heard merely as the violent story of a God who capriciously favors Israelites over other nations. Rather, it will be heard as an episode in the ongoing story of a God who is preparing a particular people to fulfill their mission of effecting a blessing for all nations. Like the other prophetic books and like Scripture as a whole, Judges simultaneously articulates God's demand for faithful obedience, illustrates the destructive consequences of disobedience, and portrays a faithful, gracious God who will not abandon a faithless, ungrateful people. In a word, the crucial Spiritual Disciplines in view in Judges are worship of God alone and obedience to God's will, which is often summed up in the Old Testament by the word "justice."

Submission to the Will of God

The crucial word "justice," often paired in Scripture with the word "righteousness," is a sort of one-word summary of the will of God (see Deut 16:19–20; Pss 72:1–7; 82:1–4; Isa 1:17; 32:16–17; Amos 5:24; Mic 6:8). Thus, it is very important to realize that the persons called by God to lead the people in Judges are named by a form of the same Hebrew root that serves as the foundation for the word "justice." The traditional translation is "judges," but a better translation would be something like "establishers of justice." As Isa 32:16–17 makes clear, the enactment of justice and righteousness produces "peace" (Hebrew *shalom*), "quietness," and "trust:"

Then justice will dwell in the wilderness,
> and righteousness abide in the fruitful field.

The effect of righteousness will be peace,
> and the result of righteousness, quietness and trust forever.

Not coincidentally, the Hebrew word translated "quietness" in Isa 32:17 plays a major role in Judges, in which it is translated "rest."

The phrase "the land had rest" (3:11, 30; 5:31; 8:28) describes the results of the faithful, obedient work of Othniel, Ehud, Deborah, and Gideon after God had raised them up in response to the people's cry for help (see 2:18; 3:9, 15; 4:3; 6:6; 10:10). The cry for help was necessitated by the oppression of enemies that had resulted from God's anger (see 2:14–15; 3:8, 12–14; 4:2; 6:1–5; 10:7–10; 13:1) at the people for the "evil" they had done by worshiping Baal and other gods (see 2:11–13; 3:7, 12; 4:1; 6:1; 10:6; 13:1). What God wills and what Othniel, Ehud, Deborah, and Gideon effect is "rest," the peace that derives from worshiping God alone and pursuing God's will for the ordering of the world. The pattern that characterizes Judges thus highlights the Spiritual Disciplines of faithful worship of God alone and submission to God's will.

Reaping What Is Sown

At the same time, the pattern in Judges also demonstrates the truth that disobedience always has hurtful and destructive consequences—that is, disobedience angers God, and it inevitably results in oppression. Furthermore, the breakdown of the pattern as Judges proceeds serves to emphasize this truth. After 8:28, which occurs near the end of the material devoted to Gideon, there is no further announcement that "the land had rest." Gideon's story, in fact, represents a turning point in Judges—in particular, a turn for the worse. Unlike previous announcements of "rest," 8:28 does not conclude Gideon's story. Instead, Gideon, who had already reintroduced idolatrous practices among the Israelites (see 8:27), leaves a violent legacy that is described in Judges 9.

Indeed, as Judges proceeds beyond Gideon, the pattern that dominated the first half of the book continues to break down. Not only is there no further "rest" for the land, but also the people do not cry for help in the stories of Jephthah (10:6–12:7) and Samson (13:1–16:31). And in the story of Samson, no deliverance is effected. Rather, Samson only "begin[s] to deliver Israel from the hand of the Philistines" (13:5). Plus, a different pattern emerges following Gideon—namely, the careers of Gideon and the two subsequent major judges, Jephthah and Samson, are followed by internal, Israelite-on-Israelite violence. Just as Abimelech's violent coup follows Gideon's judgeship (chap 9), so a bloody civil war follows Jephthah's rule (12:1–6). And after Samson, total chaos reigns (17:1–21:25). As "all the people did what was right in their own eyes" (17:6; 21:25; see 18:1; 19:1), the order of the day is theft, idolatry, rape, and murder; and the tribe of Benjamin in nearly wiped out.

The progressive deterioration that leads to the chaotic ending of the book serves to illustrate that persistent idolatry and disobedience inevitably yield violence, chaos, and destruction. The people reap what they sow. But just as in Judges God repeatedly delivers the people, so beyond Judges God continues to try. God never fails to be with his people, and God continues to will for them and for all humanity a with-God life. Hence, by demonstrating the destructive consequences of disobedience, Judges calls the People of God in all times and places to the worship and submission that promise life.

—J. Clinton McCann, Jr.

Israel's Failure to Complete the Conquest of Canaan

1 After the death of Joshua, the Israelites inquired of the LORD, "Who shall go up first for us against the Canaanites, to fight against them?" ²The LORD said, "Judah shall go up. I hereby give the land into his hand." ³Judah said to his brother Simeon, "Come up with me into the territory allotted to me, that we may fight against the Canaanites; then I too will go with you into the territory allotted to you." So Simeon went with him. ⁴Then Judah went up and the LORD gave the Canaanites and the Perizzites into their hand; and they defeated ten thousand of them at Bezek. ⁵They came upon Adoni-bezek at Bezek, and fought against him, and defeated the Canaanites and the Perizzites. ⁶Adoni-bezek fled; but they pursued him, and caught him, and cut off his thumbs and big toes. ⁷Adoni-bezek said, "Seventy kings with their thumbs and big toes cut off used to pick up scraps under my table; as I have done, so God has paid me back." They brought him to Jerusalem, and he died there.

8 Then the people of Judah fought against Jerusalem and took it. They put it to the sword and set the city on fire. ⁹Afterward the people of Judah went down to fight against the Canaanites who lived in the hill country, in the Negeb, and in the lowland. ¹⁰Judah went against the Canaanites who lived in Hebron (the name of Hebron was formerly Kiriath-arba); and they defeated Sheshai and Ahiman and Talmai.

11 From there they went against the inhabitants of Debir (the name of Debir was formerly Kiriath-sepher). ¹²Then Caleb said, "Whoever attacks Kiriath-sepher and takes it, I will give him my daughter Achsah as wife." ¹³And Othniel son of Kenaz, Caleb's younger brother, took it; and he gave him his daughter Achsah as wife. ¹⁴When she came to him, she urged him to ask her father for a field. As she dismounted from her donkey, Caleb said to her, "What do you wish?" ¹⁵She said to him, "Give me a present; since you have set me in the land of the Negeb, give me also Gulloth-mayim." *ᵃ* So Caleb gave her Upper Gulloth and Lower Gulloth.

16 The descendants of Hobab *ᵇ* the Kenite,

a That is *Basins of Water*   *b* Gk: Heb lacks *Hobab*

1:1 *Who shall go up first for us against the Canaanites?* In the context of a story that begins with creation and includes God's commission to Abraham, Sarah, and their descendants to effect a blessing for all nations (Gen 12:3), the repeated references to the "Canaanites" must be understood symbolically. The point is not that God hates Canaanites, but rather that the Canaanites represent an oppressive, death-dealing way of life that God opposes, just as God had earlier opposed Pharaoh and his oppressive, death-dealing policies. Like the book of Exodus, Judges offers testimony to a God who opposes and

hence must "fight" (vv 1, 3) oppressors. Submission to God's will thus impels the People of God to oppose what the Canaanites represent. The Israelites are called to serve only one master, and there can be no collaboration with the systemic oppression found in the land (2:2; Exod 23:23–33).

1:15 *"Give me a present".... So Caleb gave her.* That Achsah asks for a "blessing" ("present," NRSV) and receives it is significant. In the opening chapters of Judges, women are respected; they even occupy positions of authority and leadership (chaps 4–5). As the book proceeds,

Moses' father-in-law, went up with the people of Judah from the city of palms into the wilderness of Judah, which lies in the Negeb near Arad. Then they went and settled with the Amalekites. *a* 17Judah went with his brother Simeon, and they defeated the Canaanites who inhabited Zephath, and devoted it to destruction. So the city was called Hormah. 18Judah took Gaza with its territory, Ashkelon with its territory, and Ekron with its territory. 19The LORD was with Judah, and he took possession of the hill country, but could not drive out the inhabitants of the plain, because they had chariots of iron. 20Hebron was given to Caleb, as Moses had said; and he drove out from it the three sons of Anak. 21But the Benjaminites did not drive out the Jebusites who lived in Jerusalem; so the Jebusites have lived in Jerusalem among the Benjaminites to this day.

22 The house of Joseph also went up against Bethel; and the LORD was with them. 23The house of Joseph sent out spies to Bethel (the name of the city was formerly Luz). 24When the spies saw a man coming out of the city, they said to him, "Show us the way into the city, and we will deal kindly with you." 25So he showed them the way into the city; and they put the city to the sword, but they let the man and all his family go. 26So the man went to the land of the Hittites and built a city, and named it Luz; that is its name to this day.

27 Manasseh did not drive out the inhabitants of Beth-shean and its villages, or Taanach and its villages, or the inhabitants of Dor and its villages, or the inhabitants of Ibleam and its villages, or the inhabitants of Megiddo and its villages; but the Canaanites continued to live in that land. 28When Isra-

el grew strong, they put the Canaanites to forced labor, but did not in fact drive them out.

29 And Ephraim did not drive out the Canaanites who lived in Gezer; but the Canaanites lived among them in Gezer.

30 Zebulun did not drive out the inhabitants of Kitron, or the inhabitants of Nahalol; but the Canaanites lived among them, and became subject to forced labor.

31 Asher did not drive out the inhabitants of Acco, or the inhabitants of Sidon, or of Ahlab, or of Achzib, or of Helbah, or of Aphik, or of Rehob; 32but the Asherites lived among the Canaanites, the inhabitants of the land; for they did not drive them out.

33 Naphtali did not drive out the inhabitants of Beth-shemesh, or the inhabitants of Beth-anath, but lived among the Canaanites, the inhabitants of the land; nevertheless the inhabitants of Beth-shemesh and of Beth-anath became subject to forced labor for them.

34 The Amorites pressed the Danites back into the hill country; they did not allow them to come down to the plain. 35The Amorites continued to live in Har-heres, in Aijalon, and in Shaalbim, but the hand of the house of Joseph rested heavily on them, and they became subject to forced labor. 36The border of the Amorites ran from the ascent of Akrabbim, from Sela and upward.

Israel's Disobedience

2 Now the angel of the LORD went up from Gilgal to Bochim, and said, "I brought you up from Egypt, and brought you into the land that I had promised to your ancestors. I

a See 1 Sam 15.6: Heb *people*

---

however, the deteriorating conditions caused by the people's disobedience increasingly lead to the victimization of women (see notes on 11:34–40; 19:1–30; 21:1–25). Then, as now, the equitable treatment of women and all those without power is a major indicator of a people's adherence to the justice and righteousness that God wills.

1:17 *they defeated the Canaanites who inhabited Zephath.* The total destruction of

Canaanite cities symbolizes total devotion to God and God's purposes (Deut 20:17–18). Failure to observe this requirement represents collaboration with injustice and oppression (see note on 1:1). For instance, putting "the Canaanites to forced labor" (1:28), rather than destroying them, represents the people's failure, which is marked by the repeated notice that the tribes "did not drive out the inhabitants" of particular places (1:27–33).

said, 'I will never break my covenant with you. ²For your part, do not make a covenant with the inhabitants of this land; tear down their altars.' But you have not obeyed my command. See what you have done! ³So now I say, I will not drive them out before you; but they shall become adversaries*a* to you, and their gods shall be a snare to you." ⁴When the angel of the LORD spoke these words to all the Israelites, the people lifted up their voices and wept. ⁵So they named that place Bochim,*b* and there they sacrificed to the LORD.

Death of Joshua

6 When Joshua dismissed the people, the Israelites all went to their own inheritances to take possession of the land. ⁷The people worshiped the LORD all the days of Joshua, and all the days of the elders who outlived Joshua, who had seen all the great work that the LORD had done for Israel. ⁸Joshua son of Nun, the servant of the LORD, died at the age of one hundred ten years. ⁹So they buried him within the bounds of his inheritance in Timnath-heres, in the hill country of Ephraim, north of Mount Gaash. ¹⁰Moreover, that whole generation was gathered to their ancestors, and another generation grew up after them, who did not know the LORD or the work that he had done for Israel.

Israel's Unfaithfulness

11 Then the Israelites did what was evil in the sight of the LORD and worshiped the Baals; ¹²and they abandoned the LORD, the God of their ancestors, who had brought them out of the land of Egypt; they followed oth-

er gods, from among the gods of the peoples who were all around them, and bowed down to them; and they provoked the LORD to anger. ¹³They abandoned the LORD, and worshiped Baal and the Astartes. ¹⁴So the anger of the LORD was kindled against Israel, and he gave them over to plunderers who plundered them, and he sold them into the power of their enemies all around, so that they could no longer withstand their enemies. ¹⁵Whenever they marched out, the hand of the LORD was against them to bring misfortune, as the LORD had warned them and sworn to them; and they were in great distress.

16 Then the LORD raised up judges, who delivered them out of the power of those who plundered them. ¹⁷Yet they did not listen even to their judges; for they lusted after other gods and bowed down to them. They soon turned aside from the way in which their ancestors had walked, who had obeyed the commandments of the LORD; they did not follow their example. ¹⁸Whenever the LORD raised up judges for them, the LORD was with the judge, and he delivered them from the hand of their enemies all the days of the judge; for the LORD would be moved to pity by their groaning because of those who persecuted and oppressed them. ¹⁹But whenever the judge died, they would relapse and behave worse than their ancestors, following other gods, worshiping them and bowing down to them. They would not drop any of their practices or their stubborn ways. ²⁰So the anger of the LORD was kindled against Israel; and he

a OL Vg Compare Gk: Heb *sides*   *b* That is *Weepers*

2:1–5 *you have not obeyed my command.* The people's disobedience, implied in chapter 1, is explicit here. Collaboration with the Canaanites amounts to idolatry and injustice. The hurtful and destructive consequences of disobedience are indicated by the people's weeping (vv 4–5). This weeping does not bode well; and indeed, the people are still weeping as Judges draws to a close (20:23, 26; 21:2).

2:11–19 *they abandoned the LORD, . . . they followed other gods.* These verses highlight the Spiritual Disciplines of worship and submission

to God's will (see "worshiped" or "worshiping" in 2:11, 13, 19; the verb could also be translated "serve" or "serving," indicating submission to God's will), and they also introduce the pattern that recurs throughout the book. Disobedience inevitably has destructive consequences, but it also proclaims the good news that a gracious God simply will not abandon the faithless people (2:18). In what amounts to a series of new exoduses, the people will be delivered repeatedly by the judges that God raises up.

said, "Because this people have transgressed my covenant that I commanded their ancestors, and have not obeyed my voice, 21 I will no longer drive out before them any of the nations that Joshua left when he died." 22 In order to test Israel, whether or not they would take care to walk in the way of the LORD as their ancestors did, 23 the LORD had left those nations, not driving them out at once, and had not handed them over to Joshua.

Nations Remaining in the Land

3 Now these are the nations that the LORD left to test all those in Israel who had no experience of any war in Canaan 2 (it was only that successive generations of Israelites might know war, to teach those who had no experience of it before): 3 the five lords of the Philistines, and all the Canaanites, and the Sidonians, and the Hivites who lived on Mount Lebanon, from Mount Baal-hermon as far as Lebo-hamath. 4 They were for the testing of Israel, to know whether Israel would obey the commandments of the LORD, which he commanded their ancestors by Moses. 5 So the Israelites lived among the Canaanites, the Hittites, the Amorites, the Perizzites, the Hivites, and the Jebusites; 6 and they took their daughters as wives for themselves, and their own daughters they gave to their sons; and they worshiped their gods.

Othniel

7 The Israelites did what was evil in the sight of the LORD, forgetting the LORD their God, and worshiping the Baals and the Asherahs. 8 Therefore the anger of the LORD was kindled against Israel, and he sold them into the hand of King Cushan-rishathaim of Aram-naharaim; and the Israelites served Cushan-rishathaim eight years. 9 But when the Israelites cried out to the LORD, the LORD raised up a deliverer for the Israelites, who delivered them, Othniel son of Kenaz, Caleb's younger brother. 10 The spirit of the LORD came upon him, and he judged Israel; he went out to war, and the LORD gave King Cushan-rishathaim of Aram into his hand; and his hand prevailed over Cushan-rishathaim. 11 So the land had rest forty years. Then Othniel son of Kenaz died.

Ehud

12 The Israelites again did what was evil in the sight of the LORD; and the LORD strengthened King Eglon of Moab against Israel, because they had done what was evil in the sight of the LORD. 13 In alliance with the Ammonites and the Amalekites, he went and defeated Israel; and they took possession of the city of palms. 14 So the Israelites served King Eglon of Moab eighteen years.

15 But when the Israelites cried out to the

3:2 *it was only that successive generations of Israelites might know war.* As the book unfolds, the irony of 3:2 becomes apparent. The people *do* learn war, but they end up using their military skills against each other, nearly decimating the tribe of Benjamin (chaps 20–21). Such are the results of disobedience. After failed military pursuits that led to the exile, the book of Isaiah suggests that God wills that Israel and the nations *not* "learn war any more" (Isa 2:4).

3:7–11 *the LORD raised up a deliverer.* Othniel, the first judge, leads the land to "rest" (v 11), the condition of peace with justice that God wills. The "spirit of the LORD" (v 10) will later come upon Gideon (6:34), Jephthah (11:29), and Samson (13:25; 14:6, 19; 15:14), but it will not have the salutary effects that it has here, especially in the cases of Jephthah and Samson. The Spirit represents giftedness and power from

God; but for the Spirit to effect God's purposes, there must be a cooperative and faithful response by the person who receives the gift. Obedience is paramount.

3:12–30 *the LORD raised up . . . Ehud.* The bawdy and violent story of Ehud is another reminder that God opposes and fights oppression and oppressors like King Eglon (see note on 1:1). This is not a matter of playing favorites, since later, when Israelite and Judean kings prove to be oppressors, God opposes them too, resulting in the exile. Because the Moabite oppression here is, in a sense, the fault of the people's own "evil" (v 12), their deliverance is grounded in God's gracious willingness to forgive and stay with a faithless people until they have "rest" (v 30; see note on 3:7–11). Thus, Judges invites loyalty and obedience, grounded in gratitude.

LORD, the LORD raised up for them a deliverer, Ehud son of Gera, the Benjaminite, a left-handed man. The Israelites sent tribute by him to King Eglon of Moab. 16Ehud made for himself a sword with two edges, a cubit in length; and he fastened it on his right thigh under his clothes. 17Then he presented the tribute to King Eglon of Moab. Now Eglon was a very fat man. 18When Ehud had finished presenting the tribute, he sent the people who carried the tribute on their way. 19But he himself turned back at the sculptured stones near Gilgal, and said, "I have a secret message for you, O king." So the king said,*a* "Silence!" and all his attendants went out from his presence. 20Ehud came to him, while he was sitting alone in his cool roof chamber, and said, "I have a message from God for you." So he rose from his seat. 21Then Ehud reached with his left hand, took the sword from his right thigh, and thrust it into Eglon's*b* belly; 22the hilt also went in after the blade, and the fat closed over the blade, for he did not draw the sword out of his belly; and the dirt came out.*c* 23Then Ehud went out into the vestibule,*d* and closed the doors of the roof chamber on him, and locked them.

24 After he had gone, the servants came. When they saw that the doors of the roof chamber were locked, they thought, "He must be relieving himself*e* in the cool chamber." 25So they waited until they were embarrassed. When he still did not open the doors of the roof chamber, they took the key and opened them. There was their lord lying dead on the floor.

26 Ehud escaped while they delayed, and passed beyond the sculptured stones, and escaped to Seirah. 27When he arrived, he sounded the trumpet in the hill country of Ephraim; and the Israelites went down with him from the hill country, having him at their head. 28He said to them, "Follow after me; for the LORD has given your enemies the Moabites into your hand." So they went down after him, and seized the fords of the Jordan against the Moabites, and allowed no one to cross over. 29At that time they killed about ten thousand of the Moabites, all strong, able-bodied men; no one escaped. 30So Moab was subdued that day under the hand of Israel. And the land had rest eighty years.

Shamgar

31 After him came Shamgar son of Anath, who killed six hundred of the Philistines with an oxgoad. He too delivered Israel.

Deborah and Barak

4 The Israelites again did what was evil in the sight of the LORD, after Ehud died. 2So the LORD sold them into the hand of King Jabin of Canaan, who reigned in Hazor; the commander of his army was Sisera, who lived in Harosheth-ha-goiim. 3Then the Israelites cried out to the LORD for help; for he had nine hundred chariots of iron, and had oppressed the Israelites cruelly twenty years.

a Heb *he said*   *b* Heb *his*   *c* With Tg Vg: Meaning of Heb uncertain   *d* Meaning of Heb uncertain   *e* Heb *covering his feet*

3:31 *After him came Shamgar.* Many commentators suggest that Shamgar's name is not Israelite. Furthermore, he is called "son of Anath," a Canaanite goddess. The strong possibility that Shamgar is a Canaanite among Israel's judges reinforces the conclusion stated above (see note on 1:1)—namely, that the "Canaanites" in Judges refer not to a particular people that God opposes, but rather symbolize an oppressive, death-dealing system. Obedience to God, then and now, invites faithful opposition to injustice.

4:1–16 *Deborah, a prophetess,. . . was judging Israel.* Deborah's authority—she is both judge

and prophet (v 4)—and her effectiveness in leading the land to "rest" (5:31; see note on 3:7–11) cohere with the respect accorded to women in the opening chapters of Judges (see note on 1:15). Like Othniel, Ehud, and Shamgar, Deborah is faithful to God and obedient to her calling. In the poetic celebration of Deborah's leadership in chapter 5, she receives a designation of the highest honor, "mother in Israel" (5:7), indicating her leadership of the people out of oppression (4:3) toward life as God intends it. As if to signify that Deborah is a sort of embodiment of the divine presence, Barak refuses to enter battle without her (4:8).

4 At that time Deborah, a prophetess, wife of Lappidoth, was judging Israel. [5]She used to sit under the palm of Deborah between Ramah and Bethel in the hill country of Ephraim; and the Israelites came up to her for judgment. [6]She sent and summoned Barak son of Abinoam from Kedesh in Naphtali, and said to him, "The LORD, the God of Israel, commands you, 'Go, take position at Mount Tabor, bringing ten thousand from the tribe of Naphtali and the tribe of Zebulun. [7]I will draw out Sisera, the general of Jabin's army, to meet you by the Wadi Kishon with his chariots and his troops; and I will give him into your hand.' " [8]Barak said to her, "If you will go with me, I will go; but if you will not go with me, I will not go." [9]And she said, "I will surely go with you; nevertheless, the road on which you are going will not lead to your glory, for the LORD will sell Sisera into the hand of a woman." Then Deborah got up and went with Barak to Kedesh. [10]Barak summoned Zebulun and Naphtali to Kedesh; and ten thousand warriors went up behind him; and Deborah went up with him.

11 Now Heber the Kenite had separated from the other Kenites, [a] that is, the descendants of Hobab the father-in-law of Moses, and had encamped as far away as Elon-bezaanannim, which is near Kedesh.

12 When Sisera was told that Barak son of Abinoam had gone up to Mount Tabor, [13]Sisera called out all his chariots, nine hundred chariots of iron, and all the troops who were with him, from Harosheth-ha-goiim to the Wadi Kishon. [14]Then Deborah said to Barak, "Up! For this is the day on which the LORD has given Sisera into your hand. The LORD is indeed going out before you." So Barak went down from Mount Tabor with ten thousand warriors following him. [15]And the LORD threw Sisera and all his chariots and all his army into a panic[b] before Barak; Sisera got down from his chariot and fled away on foot, [16]while Barak pursued the chariots and the army to Harosheth-ha-goiim. All the army of Sisera fell by the sword; no one was left.

17 Now Sisera had fled away on foot to the tent of Jael wife of Heber the Kenite; for there was peace between King Jabin of Hazor and the clan of Heber the Kenite. [18]Jael came out to meet Sisera, and said to him, "Turn aside, my lord, turn aside to me; have no fear." So he turned aside to her into the tent, and she covered him with a rug. [19]Then he said to her, "Please give me a little water to drink; for I am thirsty." So she opened a skin of milk and gave him a drink and covered him. [20]He said to her, "Stand at the entrance of the tent, and if anybody comes and asks you, 'Is anyone here?' say, 'No.' " [21]But Jael wife of Heber took a tent peg, and took a hammer in her hand, and went softly to him and drove the peg into his temple, until it went down into the ground—he was lying fast asleep from weariness—and he died. [22]Then, as Barak came in pursuit of Sisera, Jael went out to meet him, and said to him, "Come, and I will show you the man whom you are seeking." So he went into her tent; and there was Sisera lying dead, with the tent peg in his temple.

23 So on that day God subdued King Jabin of Canaan before the Israelites. [24]Then the hand of the Israelites bore harder and harder on King Jabin of Canaan, until they destroyed King Jabin of Canaan.

a Heb *from the Kain*   b Heb adds *to the sword*; compare verse 16

4:17–23 *Jael came out to meet Sisera.* Jael, another woman, also plays a key role. Like Deborah, the text honors her in the most exalted of terms, "most blessed of women" (5:24; cf. Luke 1:42; see notes on 1:15; 4:1–16). Unfortunately, commentators have often accused Jael of violating the Spiritual Discipline of hospitality in her dealings with Sisera, but this is entirely unfair. It is actually Sisera who violates the code of hospitality by making demands upon Jael, his host, and by requesting her to lie, alerting Jael to his evil intent, in particular the possibility that Sisera would rape her (see note on 5:28–31). Accordingly, the narrator clearly indicates that Jael's killing of Sisera is self-defense; and indeed, it is nothing short of God's own work (4:23). Like Deborah, Jael is God's agent in battling an oppressor.

The Song of Deborah

5 Then Deborah and Barak son of Abinoam sang on that day, saying:
2 "When locks are long in Israel,
    when the people offer themselves
      willingly—
    bless *a* the LORD!

3 "Hear, O kings; give ear, O princes;
    to the LORD I will sing,
    I will make melody to the LORD, the
      God of Israel.

4 "LORD, when you went out from Seir,
    when you marched from the region
      of Edom,
  the earth trembled,
    and the heavens poured,
    the clouds indeed poured water.
5 The mountains quaked before the LORD,
    the One of Sinai,
    before the LORD, the God of Israel.

6 "In the days of Shamgar son of Anath,
    in the days of Jael, caravans ceased
    and travelers kept to the byways.
7 The peasantry prospered in Israel,
    they grew fat on plunder,
  because you arose, Deborah,
    arose as a mother in Israel.
8 When new gods were chosen,
    then war was in the gates.
  Was shield or spear to be seen
    among forty thousand in Israel?
9 My heart goes out to the commanders
      of Israel
    who offered themselves willingly
      among the people.
    Bless the LORD.

10 "Tell of it, you who ride on white
      donkeys,
    you who sit on rich carpets *b*
    and you who walk by the way.

11 To the sound of musicians *b* at the
      watering places,
    there they repeat the triumphs of the
      LORD,
    the triumphs of his peasantry in
      Israel.

  "Then down to the gates marched the
      people of the LORD.

12 "Awake, awake, Deborah!
    Awake, awake, utter a song!
  Arise, Barak, lead away your captives,
    O son of Abinoam.
13 Then down marched the remnant of
      the noble;
    the people of the LORD marched down
      for him *c* against the mighty.
14 From Ephraim they set out *d* into the
      valley, *e*
    following you, Benjamin, with your
      kin;
  from Machir marched down the
      commanders,
    and from Zebulun those who bear the
      marshal's staff;
15 the chiefs of Issachar came with
      Deborah,
    and Issachar faithful to Barak;
    into the valley they rushed out at his
      heels.
  Among the clans of Reuben
    there were great searchings of heart.
16 Why did you tarry among the
      sheepfolds,
    to hear the piping for the flocks?
  Among the clans of Reuben
    there were great searchings of heart.
17 Gilead stayed beyond the Jordan;
    and Dan, why did he abide with the
      ships?

a Or *You who offer yourselves willingly among the
people, bless*   b Meaning of Heb uncertain
c Gk: Heb *me*   d Cn: Heb *From Ephraim their root*
e Gk: Heb *in Amalek*

5:11 *there they repeat the triumphs of the
LORD.* The Hebrew word translated "triumphs" is
more literally "righteousnesses." It is frequently
parallel to the word "justice," suggesting again

that by their opposition to oppression, Deborah,
Barak, and Jael are modeling the Spiritual
Discipline of obedience to God's will.

DEBORAH

The Fight for Fidelity

Selected Scriptures: *Judges 4–5*

Deborah served Israel as judge, prophet, spiritual leader, and guide during a period some two hundred years after the Israelites left Egypt for the Promised Land. After their entry into Canaan, God appointed judges to provide military and civil leadership to Israel. Many times the people had fallen into idolatry and through the leadership of a judge had returned to God. Deborah again drew the Israelites back to God as they cried out under Canaanite oppression, their punishment for idolatry.

Deborah heard the cries of her people and, as God's judge for her people, knew that action lay in her hands. She summoned Barak, Israel's military commander, and ordered him to take men and get into position to overtake Sisera, the general of the Canaanite army (Judg 4:6). Barak agreed, on the condition that Deborah accompany him. She assured him that she would go with him, but warned Barak that this victory would not lead to his glory, but instead would exalt a woman (4:9).

Indeed, "the army of Sisera fell by the sword" and only the general himself escaped on foot (4:16). Finding refuge in what seemed a friendly tent, Sisera fell asleep, never expecting that Jael, his female host, would drive a tent peg through his head. The Song of Deborah follows, in which she praises this brave woman: "Most blessed of women be Jael" (5:24). Considered by many a beautiful literary work, this song praises God for his deliverance and for the people's cooperation with God. "When the people offer themselves willingly—bless the LORD!" (5:2). Deborah's prayer of praise holds as much gratitude for the turning of the people's hearts toward God as for the turning of the battle to Israel's favor. Deborah rejoices to see the Israelites once again worshiping God and placing themselves in his hands.

As we see again and again through the Old Testament, this devotion and cooperation never remained constant. The people cycled from living "with God" to living "with gods" that enticed them. Only by God's continued leading and the people's ongoing cooperation would they see God's good promise worked out.

Deborah herself modeled willing cooperation with God. In a patriarchal society, she took on the role of highest leadership, offering her gifts and her passion to God for his use. Arising "as a mother in Israel" (5:7), she became one more living reminder of God's whole love for his people—God guides not just as father but as mother as well.

Another woman, much later, became just such a leader, modeling for the people of her day a person who offered all of herself for God's use. Phoebe Palmer was one of the first women of the nineteenth century to make a great impact in the public arena, working as an evangelist, social reformer, humanitarian, and poet. A small weekly meeting in her home, where people of many denominations gathered to seek

PROFILE: DEBORAH

growth in holiness, grew to accommodate four hundred at its height. Phoebe's personal spiritual journey involved an ardent quest for holiness. Although writing in the third person, she wrote personally about how finally her "heart was emptied of self, and cleansed of all idols":

"Over and over again . . . had she endeavored to give herself away in covenant to God. But she had never, till this hour, deliberately resolved on counting the cost, with the solemn intention to 'reckon herself dead *indeed* unto sin, but alive unto God through Jesus Christ our Lord'; to account herself permanently the Lord's, and in verity no more at *her own* disposal, but *irrevocably the Lord's property,* for time and eternity" (*The Way of Holiness*).

Both Deborah and Phoebe realized the beautiful power of fidelity to God. Their deep devotion and commitment to guiding others back into the with-God life led them to become models of discipleship for all generations.

Personal Reflection

- In your life right now, are you more in the position of Deborah, guiding and encouraging people to offer themselves wholly to God, or in the position of the Israelite people, needing this encouragement?
- What will it take to keep you from cycling, as the Israelites did, between offering yourself to God and offering yourself to idolatry? How can you reach a place, as Phoebe Palmer did, where you are "irrevocably the Lord's property"?

Asher sat still at the coast of the sea,
   settling down by his landings.
18 Zebulun is a people that scorned death;
   Naphtali too, on the heights of the
      field.

19 "The kings came, they fought;
   then fought the kings of Canaan,
at Taanach, by the waters of Megiddo;
   they got no spoils of silver.
20 The stars fought from heaven,
   from their courses they fought against
      Sisera.
21 The torrent Kishon swept them away,
   the onrushing torrent, the torrent
      Kishon.
   March on, my soul, with might!

22 "Then loud beat the horses' hoofs
   with the galloping, galloping of his
      steeds.

23 "Curse Meroz, says the angel of the
      LORD,
   curse bitterly its inhabitants,
because they did not come to the help
      of the LORD,
   to the help of the LORD against the
      mighty.

24 "Most blessed of women be Jael,
   the wife of Heber the Kenite,
   of tent-dwelling women most blessed.
25 He asked water and she gave him milk,
   she brought him curds in a lordly
      bowl.
26 She put her hand to the tent peg
   and her right hand to the workmen's
      mallet;
she struck Sisera a blow,
   she crushed his head,
   she shattered and pierced his temple.
27 He sank, he fell,
   he lay still at her feet;
at her feet he sank, he fell;
   where he sank, there he fell dead.

28 "Out of the window she peered,
   the mother of Sisera gazed[a] through
      the lattice:

a Gk Compare Tg: Heb *exclaimed*

'Why is his chariot so long in coming?
  Why tarry the hoofbeats of his
    chariots?'
29 Her wisest ladies make answer,
  indeed, she answers the question
    herself:
30 'Are they not finding and dividing the
    spoil?—
  A girl or two for every man;
spoil of dyed stuffs for Sisera,
  spoil of dyed stuffs embroidered,
  two pieces of dyed work embroidered
    for my neck as spoil?'

31 "So perish all your enemies, O LORD!
  But may your friends be like the sun
    as it rises in its might."

And the land had rest forty years.

The Midianite Oppression

6 The Israelites did what was evil in the sight of the LORD, and the LORD gave them into the hand of Midian seven years. 2The hand of Midian prevailed over Israel; and because of Midian the Israelites provided for themselves hiding places in the mountains, caves and strongholds. 3For whenever the Israelites put in seed, the Midianites and the Amalekites and the people of the east would come up against them. 4They would encamp against them and destroy the produce of the land, as far as the neighborhood of Gaza, and leave no sustenance in Israel, and no sheep or ox or donkey. 5For they and their livestock would come up, and they would even bring their tents, as thick as locusts; neither they nor their camels could be counted; so they wasted the land as they came in. 6Thus Israel was greatly impoverished because of Midian; and the Israelites cried out to the LORD for help.

7 When the Israelites cried to the LORD on account of the Midianites, 8the LORD sent a prophet to the Israelites; and he said to them, "Thus says the LORD, the God of Israel: I led you up from Egypt, and brought you out of the house of slavery; 9and I delivered you from the hand of the Egyptians, and from the hand of all who oppressed you, and drove them out before you, and gave you their land; 10and I said to you, 'I am the LORD your God; you shall not pay reverence to the gods of the Amorites, in whose land you live.' But you have not given heed to my voice."

The Call of Gideon

11 Now the angel of the LORD came and sat under the oak at Ophrah, which belonged to Joash the Abiezrite, as his son Gideon was beating out wheat in the wine press, to hide it from the Midianites. 12The angel of the LORD appeared to him and said to him, "The LORD is with you, you mighty warrior." 13Gideon answered him, "But sir, if the LORD is with us, why then has all this happened to us? And where are all his wonderful deeds that our ancestors recounted to us, saying, 'Did not the LORD bring us up from Egypt?' But now the LORD has cast us off, and given us into the hand of Midian." 14Then the LORD turned to him and said, "Go in this might of

---

5:28–31 *dyed work embroidered for my neck as spoil.* The portrayal of Sisera's mother and her attendants realistically depicts what drives an oppressive system—namely, greed and lust. The phrase "a girl or two for every man" (v 30) is more literally "a womb or two for every man," graphically communicating the unbridled brutality of the oppressive enemies that God opposes. God's "friends" include not only Deborah, Barak, and Jael, but also faithful persons in every place and time who join God in his work of establishing justice, righteousness, and peace in the world.

6:11–32 *The angel of the Lord appeared to*

[Gideon]. Gideon's career starts out well. Timid and hesitant at first, like Moses in Exodus, Gideon receives the same promise Moses had received, "But I will be with you" (v 16; Exod 3:12). The altar Gideon builds is named, "The LORD is peace" (v 24). The name both captures the essence of God's will and anticipates the "rest" that will result from Gideon's leadership (8:28). Gideon displays the Spiritual Discipline of obedience as he destroys the altar of Baal (vv 25–27) in accordance with God's desire for exclusive loyalty and obedience (2:2). Even so, as Gideon's career unfolds, his leadership grows increasingly problematic.

yours and deliver Israel from the hand of Midian; I hereby commission you." 15He responded, "But sir, how can I deliver Israel? My clan is the weakest in Manasseh, and I am the least in my family." 16The LORD said to him, "But I will be with you, and you shall strike down the Midianites, every one of them." 17Then he said to him, "If now I have found favor with you, then show me a sign that it is you who speak with me. 18Do not depart from here until I come to you, and bring out my present, and set it before you." And he said, "I will stay until you return."

19 So Gideon went into his house and prepared a kid, and unleavened cakes from an ephah of flour; the meat he put in a basket, and the broth he put in a pot, and brought them to him under the oak and presented them. 20The angel of God said to him, "Take the meat and the unleavened cakes, and put them on this rock, and pour out the broth." And he did so. 21Then the angel of the LORD reached out the tip of the staff that was in his hand, and touched the meat and the unleavened cakes; and fire sprang up from the rock and consumed the meat and the unleavened cakes; and the angel of the LORD vanished from his sight. 22Then Gideon perceived that it was the angel of the LORD; and Gideon said, "Help me, Lord GOD! For I have seen the angel of the LORD face to face." 23But the LORD said to him, "Peace be to you; do not fear, you shall not die." 24Then Gideon built an altar there to the LORD, and called it, The LORD is peace. To this day it still stands at Ophrah, which belongs to the Abiezrites.

25 That night the LORD said to him, "Take your father's bull, the second bull seven years old, and pull down the altar of Baal that belongs to your father, and cut down the sacred pole[a] that is beside it; 26and build an altar to the LORD your God on the top of the stronghold here, in proper order; then take the second bull, and offer it as a burnt offering with the wood of the sacred pole[a] that you shall cut down." 27So Gideon took ten of his servants, and did as the LORD had told him; but because he was too afraid of his family and the townspeople to do it by day, he did it by night.

Gideon Destroys the Altar of Baal

28 When the townspeople rose early in the morning, the altar of Baal was broken down, and the sacred pole[a] beside it was cut down, and the second bull was offered on the altar that had been built. 29So they said to one another, "Who has done this?" After searching and inquiring, they were told, "Gideon son of Joash did it." 30Then the townspeople said to Joash, "Bring out your son, so that he may die, for he has pulled down the altar of Baal and cut down the sacred pole[a] beside it." 31But Joash said to all who were arrayed against him, "Will you contend for Baal? Or will you defend his cause? Whoever contends for him shall be put to death by morning. If he is a god, let him contend for himself, because his altar has been pulled down." 32Therefore on that day Gideon[b] was called Jerubbaal, that is to say, "Let Baal contend against him," because he pulled down his altar.

33 Then all the Midianites and the Amalekites and the people of the east came together, and crossing the Jordan they encamped in the Valley of Jezreel. 34But the spirit of the LORD took possession of Gideon; and he sounded the trumpet, and the Abiezrites were called out to follow him. 35He sent messengers throughout all Manasseh, and they too were called out to follow him. He also sent messengers to Asher, Zebulun, and Naphtali, and they went up to meet them.

a Heb Asherah   b Heb he

Responding
6:16 THE WITH-GOD LIFE. Gideon, a farmer's son, initially responds with skepticism and excuses when the Lord appears to him and commissions him to "deliver Israel from the hand of Midian" (v 14). Even after the Lord tells him "I will be with you," Gideon asks for a sign that it is the Lord speaking. Have you ever asked for a sign from God? What conditions prompted the request? What were the results? See also Spiritual Disciplines Index.

The Sign of the Fleece

36 Then Gideon said to God, "In order to see whether you will deliver Israel by my hand, as you have said, 37I am going to lay a fleece of wool on the threshing floor; if there is dew on the fleece alone, and it is dry on all the ground, then I shall know that you will deliver Israel by my hand, as you have said." 38And it was so. When he rose early next morning and squeezed the fleece, he wrung enough dew from the fleece to fill a bowl with water. 39Then Gideon said to God, "Do not let your anger burn against me, let me speak one more time; let me, please, make trial with the fleece just once more; let it be dry only on the fleece, and on all the ground let there be dew." 40And God did so that night. It was dry on the fleece only, and on all the ground there was dew.

Gideon Surprises and Routs the Midianites

7 Then Jerubbaal (that is, Gideon) and all the troops that were with him rose early and encamped beside the spring of Harod; and the camp of Midian was north of them, below*a* the hill of Moreh, in the valley.

2 The LORD said to Gideon, "The troops with you are too many for me to give the Midianites into their hand. Israel would only take the credit away from me, saying, 'My own hand has delivered me.' 3Now therefore proclaim this in the hearing of the troops, 'Whoever is fearful and trembling, let him return home.' " Thus Gideon sifted them out;*b* twenty-two thousand returned, and ten thousand remained.

4 Then the LORD said to Gideon, "The troops are still too many; take them down to the water and I will sift them out for you there. When I say, 'This one shall go with you,' he shall go with you; and when I say, 'This one shall not go with you,' he shall not go." 5So he brought the troops down to the water; and the LORD said to Gideon, "All those who lap the water with their tongues, as a dog laps, you shall put to one side; all those who kneel down to drink, putting their hands to their mouths,*c* you shall put to the other side." 6The number of those that lapped was three hundred; but all the rest of the troops knelt down to drink water. 7Then the LORD said to Gideon, "With the three hundred that lapped I will deliver you, and give the Midianites into your hand. Let all the others go to their homes." 8So he took the jars of the troops from their hands,*d* and their trumpets; and he sent all the rest of Israel back to their own tents, but retained the three hundred. The camp of Midian was below him in the valley.

9 That same night the LORD said to him, "Get up, attack the camp; for I have given it into your hand. 10But if you fear to attack,

a Heb from   *b* Cn: Heb home, and depart from Mount Gilead' "   *c* Heb places the words putting their hands to their mouths after the word lapped in verse 6   *d* Cn: Heb So the people took provisions in their hands

---

6:36–40 In order to see whether you will deliver. The responses to the gift of the Spirit in Judges are revealing. Whereas the Spirit immediately impelled Othniel to effective leadership (see note on 3:7–11), the Spirit's effect on Gideon is more ambiguous. To be sure, Gideon swings into action (vv 34–35); but he still has doubts about God's help, and so he devises a test for God (two tests, in fact). When the Spirit later falls upon Samson, it does not lead him to deliver the people. This pattern of growing ineffectiveness emphasizes the necessity of obedient human response to God's gift. As for Gideon, his ambivalent response to the Spirit anticipates what will become grievous disobedience by the end of Gideon's career (see note on 8:22–35).

7:1–8:3 The troops with you are too many. . . . Israel would only take the credit away from me. The theological point of the reduction of Gideon's fighting force is expressed in 7:2. It involves the issue of the "credit" for Israel's victory, and the strategy is meant to ensure that only God gets the "credit" (Deut 20:1–9). It is precisely this issue that is clouded in Gideon's battle cry in v 18, "For the LORD and for Gideon!" It appears that Gideon is willing to take at least some of the credit for the victory (v 20). This indicates Gideon's growing propensity for disobedience, which will clearly characterize the conclusion of his career.

go down to the camp with your servant Purah; [11]and you shall hear what they say, and afterward your hands shall be strengthened to attack the camp." Then he went down with his servant Purah to the outposts of the armed men that were in the camp. [12]The Midianites and the Amalekites and all the people of the east lay along the valley as thick as locusts; and their camels were without number, countless as the sand on the seashore. [13]When Gideon arrived, there was a man telling a dream to his comrade; and he said, "I had a dream, and in it a cake of barley bread tumbled into the camp of Midian, and came to the tent, and struck it so that it fell; it turned upside down, and the tent collapsed." [14]And his comrade answered, "This is no other than the sword of Gideon son of Joash, a man of Israel; into his hand God has given Midian and all the army."

15 When Gideon heard the telling of the dream and its interpretation, he worshiped; and he returned to the camp of Israel, and said, "Get up; for the LORD has given the army of Midian into your hand." [16]After he divided the three hundred men into three companies, and put trumpets into the hands of all of them, and empty jars, with torches inside the jars, [17]he said to them, "Look at me, and do the same; when I come to the outskirts of the camp, do as I do. [18]When I blow the trumpet, I and all who are with me, then you also blow the trumpets around the whole camp, and shout, 'For the LORD and for Gideon!' "

19 So Gideon and the hundred who were with him came to the outskirts of the camp at the beginning of the middle watch, when they had just set the watch; and they blew the trumpets and smashed the jars that were in their hands. [20]So the three companies blew the trumpets and broke the jars, holding in their left hands the torches, and in their right hands the trumpets to blow; and they cried, "A sword for the LORD and for Gideon!" [21]Every man stood in his place all around the camp, and all the men in camp ran; they cried out and fled. [22]When they blew the three hundred trumpets, the LORD set every man's sword against his fellow and against all the army; and the army fled as far as Beth-shittah toward Zererah, [a] as far as the border of Abel-meholah, by Tabbath. [23]And the men of Israel were called out from Naphtali and from Asher and from all Manasseh, and they pursued after the Midianites.

24 Then Gideon sent messengers throughout all the hill country of Ephraim, saying, "Come down against the Midianites and seize the waters against them, as far as Beth-barah, and also the Jordan." So all the men of Ephraim were called out, and they seized the waters as far as Beth-barah, and also the Jordan. [25]They captured the two captains of Midian, Oreb and Zeeb; they killed Oreb at the rock of Oreb, and Zeeb they killed at the wine press of Zeeb, as they pursued the Midianites. They brought the heads of Oreb and Zeeb to Gideon beyond the Jordan.

Gideon's Triumph and Vengeance

8 Then the Ephraimites said to him, "What have you done to us, not to call us when you went to fight against the Midianites?" And they upbraided him violently. [2]So he said to them, "What have I done now in comparison with you? Is not the gleaning of the grapes of Ephraim better than the vintage of Abiezer? [3]God has given into your hands the captains of Midian, Oreb and Zeeb; what have I been able to do in comparison with

a Another reading is Zeredah

Responding

7:15 WORSHIP. God has to continually prod and encourage the hesitant, timid Gideon in a variety of ways. Immediately before this verse Gideon eavesdrops on a Midianite soldier who has had a dream. It is interpreted by the soldier's companion that Midian and all its army would be given into

the hand of God. Instantly Gideon worships. Try to imagine Gideon silently worshiping God in an attitude of thanksgiving and praise while standing on the perimeter of the enemy's camp. Like Gideon, go to a site you consider hostile toward God and silently worship; then write about the experience in your journal. *See also* Spiritual Disciplines Index.

GIDEON

Serving God Despite Fear

Selected Scriptures: *Judges 6–8; Hebrews 11:32*

Gideon saw no reason why God should choose him to deliver the Israelites from Midian and had no difficulty admitting his weakness and insecurity. Coming from the weakest clan in his tribe, he was also the least among his family. When the Lord commissioned him—"Go in this might of yours and deliver Israel"—he replied politely and honestly, "But sir, how can I deliver Israel?" (Judg 6:15). After hearing God's promise "I will be with you," Gideon wanted proof that this presence was in fact real and was in fact God. God provided evidence and miraculously burned Gideon's offering.

This was not the only time that Gideon's faith wavered and he required more tangible proof of God's presence. His second test involved a fleece; if overnight the fleece became wet with dew but everything around it was dry, he would believe. God passed the test. But Gideon needed a bit more. This time, if everything around the fleece was wet with dew but the fleece was dry, then he would believe in God's deliverance. Again, God provided (6:36–40). Even later, God was sympathetic to Gideon's need for tangible promises and provided Gideon with assurance before he even asked for it: Gideon overhead his enemies telling of his coming victory (7:15). The acts God required of Gideon took great courage. He tore down his father's altar to Baal, which the entire community worshiped (6:25–27). He pared down his army to a mere three hundred soldiers, because God didn't want the Israelites taking credit for the victory themselves (7:2–7). But God showed patience with Gideon's fear and in turn Gideon obeyed despite his insecurity.

Perhaps no other area of the spiritual life elicits more interest and attention than that of hearing God's voice. Many have said, "If God would just sit down with me and tell me what to do, I'd do it." God did tell Gideon what to do, yet Gideon still needed to be sure it was, indeed, God who was speaking. How can we listen and be sure it is God who speaks?

In *Hearing God,* Dallas Willard tells of three lights we can consult in determining what God wants us to do: circumstances, impressions of the Spirit, and passages from the Bible. "When these three things point in the same direction . . . we [can] be sure the direction they point is the one God intends for us."

Although Gideon did not understand why God had allowed the Midianite oppression, he trusted in God's voice after seeing God act with the offering, the fleece, and the enemy's words. He also listened to the impressions of God's Spirit. After his initial visit with the angel of the Lord, God then spoke to Gideon each time through his Spirit, and when the time came to gather the army we're told, "the spirit of the Lord took possession of Gideon" (6:34). After God had Gideon pare back the troops, Gideon followed the Spirit's direction and led them to victory.

PROFILE: GIDEON

As we hold Willard's instruction about the three lights up to Gideon's story, we see that the final light, the place of the Bible in relating God's voice, is tragically absent in Gideon's later experience. When Israel broke free of Midian, Gideon's ego, rather than God's law, became his guide. He made an ephod, or vest, of gold and allowed the people to worship it. This was the beginning of the Israelites' return to idolatry.

Gideon refused to be crowned king over Israel, stating, "The LORD will rule over you" (8:23). Nevertheless, Gideon viewed himself as the rightful ruler of the people. He took many wives and named the son of a concubine Abimelech, meaning "My father is king." This son later murdered his brothers and tried to establish himself as king over Israel.

Perhaps Gideon had never been trained in God's law due to Israel's idolatry in his youth. Whatever the reason, this absence of the use of God's Word in discerning God's will crippled Gideon's final years of leadership and had a great impact on the role his sons would take on in Israel. Never again in the time of the judges would Israel enjoy peace.

Personal Reflection

- Hebrews 11:32 includes Gideon among the heroes of faith. He trusted God's voice and acted. When have you done the same? What did God accomplish?
- How does the Bible remain central in your growth in the with-God life? How do you allow circumstances and impressions of the Spirit to be means by which you hear God's voice? In what ways can Scripture play a greater part as you seek to listen to God?

you?" When he said this, their anger against him subsided.

4 Then Gideon came to the Jordan and crossed over, he and the three hundred who were with him, exhausted and famished. [a] 5So he said to the people of Succoth, "Please give some loaves of bread to my followers, for they are exhausted, and I am pursuing Zebah and Zalmunna, the kings of Midian." 6But the officials of Succoth said, "Do you already have in your possession the hands of Zebah and Zalmunna, that we should give bread to your army?" 7Gideon replied, "Well then, when the LORD has given Zebah and Zalmunna into my hand, I will trample your flesh on the thorns of the wilderness and on briers." 8From there he went up to Penuel, and made the same request of them; and the people of Penuel answered him as the people of Succoth had answered. 9So he said to the people of Penuel, "When I come back victorious, I will break down this tower."

10 Now Zebah and Zalmunna were in Karkor with their army, about fifteen thousand men, all who were left of all the army of the people of the east; for one hundred twenty thousand men bearing arms had fallen. 11So Gideon went up by the caravan route east of Nobah and Jogbehah, and attacked the army; for the army was off its guard. 12Zebah and Zalmunna fled; and he pursued them and took the two kings of Midian, Zebah

a Gk: Heb pursuing

8:4–21 *I will trample your flesh.* These verses do not portray Gideon in a very flattering light. Rather, the once timid Gideon, who should have understood the hesitancy of the people of Succoth (v 6), is now a brash, self-assertive, vengeful bully. His violent cruelty to the people of Succoth amounts to nothing more than personal revenge; it contributes nothing to the deliverance of the Israelites. The self-assertiveness intimated in 7:18, 21 is now full-blown, indicating that Gideon's exclusive loyalty and obedience to God have waned. Gideon's disobedience becomes even clearer in the final episode of his story (see note on 8:22–35); and the destructive consequences of this disobedience are evident in Gideon's violent legacy (see note on 9:1–56).

and Zalmunna, and threw all the army into a panic.

13 When Gideon son of Joash returned from the battle by the ascent of Heres, [14]he caught a young man, one of the people of Succoth, and questioned him; and he listed for him the officials and elders of Succoth, seventy-seven people. [15]Then he came to the people of Succoth, and said, "Here are Zebah and Zalmunna, about whom you taunted me, saying, 'Do you already have in your possession the hands of Zebah and Zalmunna, that we should give bread to your troops who are exhausted?' " [16]So he took the elders of the city and he took thorns of the wilderness and briers and with them he trampled[a] the people of Succoth. [17]He also broke down the tower of Penuel, and killed the men of the city.

18 Then he said to Zebah and Zalmunna, "What about the men whom you killed at Tabor?" They answered, "As you are, so were they, every one of them; they resembled the sons of a king." [19]And he replied, "They were my brothers, the sons of my mother; as the LORD lives, if you had saved them alive, I would not kill you." [20]So he said to Jether his firstborn, "Go kill them!" But the boy did not draw his sword, for he was afraid, because he was still a boy. [21]Then Zebah and Zalmunna said, "You come and kill us; for as the man is, so is his strength." So Gideon proceeded to kill Zebah and Zalmunna; and he took the crescents that were on the necks of their camels.

Gideon's Idolatry

22 Then the Israelites said to Gideon, "Rule over us, you and your son and your grandson also; for you have delivered us out of the hand of Midian." [23]Gideon said to them, "I will not rule over you, and my son will not rule over you; the LORD will rule over you." [24]Then Gideon said to them, "Let me make a request of you; each of you give me an earring he has taken as booty." (For the enemy[b] had golden earrings, because they were Ishmaelites.) [25]"We will willingly give them," they answered. So they spread a garment, and each threw into it an earring he had taken as booty. [26]The weight of the golden earrings that he requested was one thousand seven hundred shekels of gold (apart from the crescents and the pendants and the purple garments worn by the kings of Midian, and the collars that were on the necks of their camels). [27]Gideon made an ephod of it and put it in his town, in Ophrah; and all Israel prostituted themselves to it there, and it became a snare to Gideon and to his family. [28]So Midian was subdued before the Israelites, and they lifted up their heads no more. So the land had rest forty years in the days of Gideon.

Death of Gideon

29 Jerubbaal son of Joash went to live in his own house. [30]Now Gideon had seventy sons,

a With verse 7, Compare Gk: Heb he taught
b Heb they

8:22–35 *Rule over us.* Given Gideon's violent treatment of the people of Succoth (vv 16–17) and his disposal of Zebah and Zalmunna (v 21), it seems that fear of Gideon may have motivated the people's request to Gideon in verse 22. To Gideon's credit, he refuses, citing God's exclusive claim on the people (v 23). Unfortunately, however, Gideon does not practice what he preaches. In an episode reminiscent of the golden calf debacle in Exod 32:1–14, Gideon collects golden jewelry from the people and makes an ephod that leads the people astray (vv 24–27). The word "prostituted" (vv 27, 33) indicates idolatry, and the whole episode represents "a snare to Gideon" (v 27; 2:3). In short, Gideon, who started his career by opposing idolatry, ends his career by leading the people back into idolatry. Gideon has not handled well the temptations of power. Even though it is reported that "the land had rest" (v 28), it is clear that something has gone very wrong. Unlike previous reports of "rest" for the land (3:11, 30; 5:31), this one does not conclude Gideon's story; and it is the last time that "rest" is mentioned in the book. The terribly destructive consequences of Gideon's disobedience are evident in the people's renewed idolatry (vv 27, 33) and in the violent legacy Gideon leaves (see note on 9:1–56).

his own offspring, for he had many wives. 31His concubine who was in Shechem also bore him a son, and he named him Abimelech. 32Then Gideon son of Joash died at a good old age, and was buried in the tomb of his father Joash at Ophrah of the Abiezrites.

33 As soon as Gideon died, the Israelites relapsed and prostituted themselves with the Baals, making Baal-berith their god. 34The Israelites did not remember the LORD their God, who had rescued them from the hand of all their enemies on every side; 35and they did not exhibit loyalty to the house of Jerubbaal (that is, Gideon) in return for all the good that he had done to Israel.

Abimelech Attempts to Establish a Monarchy

9 Now Abimelech son of Jerubbaal went to Shechem to his mother's kinsfolk and said to them and to the whole clan of his mother's family, 2"Say in the hearing of all the lords of Shechem, 'Which is better for you, that all seventy of the sons of Jerubbaal rule over you, or that one rule over you?' Remember also that I am your bone and your flesh." 3So his mother's kinsfolk spoke all these words on his behalf in the hearing of all the lords of Shechem; and their hearts inclined to follow Abimelech, for they said, "He is our brother." 4They gave him seventy pieces of silver out of the temple of Baal-berith with which Abimelech hired worthless and reckless fellows, who followed him. 5He went to his father's house at Ophrah, and killed his brothers the sons of Jerubbaal, seventy men, on one stone; but Jotham, the youngest son of Jerubbaal, survived, for he hid himself. 6Then all the lords of Shechem and all Beth-millo came together, and they went and made Abimelech king, by the oak of the pillar[a] at Shechem.

The Parable of the Trees

7 When it was told to Jotham, he went and stood on the top of Mount Gerizim, and cried aloud and said to them, "Listen to me, you lords of Shechem, so that God may listen to you.

8 The trees once went out
    to anoint a king over themselves.
So they said to the olive tree,
    'Reign over us.'
9 The olive tree answered them,
    'Shall I stop producing my rich oil
        by which gods and mortals are
            honored,
        and go to sway over the trees?'
10 Then the trees said to the fig tree,
    'You come and reign over us.'
11 But the fig tree answered them,
    'Shall I stop producing my sweetness
        and my delicious fruit,
        and go to sway over the trees?'
12 Then the trees said to the vine,
    'You come and reign over us.'
13 But the vine said to them,
    'Shall I stop producing my wine
        that cheers gods and mortals,
        and go to sway over the trees?'
14 So all the trees said to the bramble,
    'You come and reign over us.'
15 And the bramble said to the trees,
    'If in good faith you are anointing me
        king over you,
        then come and take refuge in my
            shade;
    but if not, let fire come out of the
        bramble
    and devour the cedars of Lebanon.'

16 "Now therefore, if you acted in good faith and honor when you made Abimelech king, and if you have dealt well with Jerubbaal and his house, and have done to him as his actions deserved— 17for my father fought for you, and risked his life, and rescued you from the hand of Midian; 18but you have risen up against my father's house this day, and have killed his sons, seventy men on one stone, and have made Abimelech, the son of

a Cn: Meaning of Heb uncertain

9:1–56 *killed his brothers . . . seventy men.* The name Abimelech, which means "my father (is) king," casts further suspicion upon Gideon (see note on 8:22–35). In any case, this sordid story of out-of-control violence must be seen as Gideon's legacy. It is a graphic reminder that sowing seeds of idolatry and self-assertion yields a bitter harvest of violent chaos.

his slave woman, king over the lords of She-chem, because he is your kinsman— [19]if, I say, you have acted in good faith and honor with Jerubbaal and with his house this day, then rejoice in Abimelech, and let him also rejoice in you; [20]but if not, let fire come out from Abimelech, and devour the lords of She-chem, and Beth-millo; and let fire come out from the lords of Shechem, and from Beth-millo, and devour Abimelech." [21]Then Jo-tham ran away and fled, going to Beer, where he remained for fear of his brother Abim-elech.

The Downfall of Abimelech

22 Abimelech ruled over Israel three years. [23]But God sent an evil spirit between Abim-elech and the lords of Shechem; and the lords of Shechem dealt treacherously with Abim-elech. [24]This happened so that the violence done to the seventy sons of Jerubbaal might be avenged[a] and their blood be laid on their brother Abimelech, who killed them, and on the lords of Shechem, who strengthened his hands to kill his brothers. [25]So, out of hostil-ity to him, the lords of Shechem set ambushes on the mountain tops. They robbed all who passed by them along that way; and it was re-ported to Abimelech.

26 When Gaal son of Ebed moved into Shechem with his kinsfolk, the lords of She-chem put confidence in him. [27]They went out into the field and gathered the grapes from their vineyards, trod them, and cele-brated. Then they went into the temple of their god, ate and drank, and ridiculed Abim-elech. [28]Gaal son of Ebed said, "Who is Abim-elech, and who are we of Shechem, that we should serve him? Did not the son of Jerub-baal and Zebul his officer serve the men of Hamor father of Shechem? Why then should we serve him? [29]If only this people were un-der my command! Then I would remove Abimelech; I would say[b] to him, 'Increase your army, and come out.' "

30 When Zebul the ruler of the city heard the words of Gaal son of Ebed, his anger was kindled. [31]He sent messengers to Abimelech at Arumah,[c] saying, "Look, Gaal son of Ebed and his kinsfolk have come to Shechem, and they are stirring up[d] the city against you.

[32]Now therefore, go by night, you and the troops that are with you, and lie in wait in the fields. [33]Then early in the morning, as soon as the sun rises, get up and rush on the city; and when he and the troops that are with him come out against you, you may deal with them as best you can."

34 So Abimelech and all the troops with him got up by night and lay in wait against Shechem in four companies. [35]When Gaal son of Ebed went out and stood in the en-trance of the gate of the city, Abimelech and the troops with him rose from the ambush. [36]And when Gaal saw them, he said to Zebul, "Look, people are coming down from the mountain tops!" And Zebul said to him, "The shadows on the mountains look like people to you." [37]Gaal spoke again and said, "Look, people are coming down from Tabbur-erez, and one company is coming from the direc-tion of Elon-meonenim."[e] [38]Then Zebul said to him, "Where is your boast[f] now, you who said, 'Who is Abimelech, that we should serve him?' Are not these the troops you made light of? Go out now and fight with them." [39]So Gaal went out at the head of the lords of Shechem, and fought with Abimelech. [40]Abimelech chased him, and he fled before him. Many fell wounded, up to the entrance of the gate. [41]So Abimelech resided at Aru-mah; and Zebul drove out Gaal and his kins-folk, so that they could not live on at She-chem.

42 On the following day the people went out into the fields. When Abimelech was told, [43]he took his troops and divided them into three companies, and lay in wait in the fields. When he looked and saw the people coming out of the city, he rose against them and killed them. [44]Abimelech and the com-pany that was[g] with him rushed forward and stood at the entrance of the gate of the city, while the two companies rushed on all who were in the fields and killed them. [45]Abim-elech fought against the city all that day; he took the city, and killed the people that were

a Heb *might come*　b Gk: Heb *and he said*
c Cn See 9.41. Heb *Tormah*　d Cn: Heb *are besieging*　e That is *Diviners' Oak*　f Heb *mouth*
g Vg and some Gk Mss: Heb *companies that were*

in it; and he razed the city and sowed it with salt.

46 When all the lords of the Tower of Shechem heard of it, they entered the stronghold of the temple of El-berith. 47 Abimelech was told that all the lords of the Tower of Shechem were gathered together. 48 So Abimelech went up to Mount Zalmon, he and all the troops that were with him. Abimelech took an ax in his hand, cut down a bundle of brushwood, and took it up and laid it on his shoulder. Then he said to the troops with him, "What you have seen me do, do quickly, as I have done." 49 So every one of the troops cut down a bundle and following Abimelech put it against the stronghold, and they set the stronghold on fire over them, so that all the people of the Tower of Shechem also died, about a thousand men and women.

50 Then Abimelech went to Thebez, and encamped against Thebez, and took it. 51 But there was a strong tower within the city, and all the men and women and all the lords of the city fled to it and shut themselves in; and they went to the roof of the tower. 52 Abimelech came to the tower, and fought against it, and came near to the entrance of the tower to burn it with fire. 53 But a certain woman threw an upper millstone on Abimelech's head, and crushed his skull. 54 Immediately he called to the young man who carried his armor and said to him, "Draw your sword and kill me, so people will not say about me, 'A woman killed him.' " So the young man thrust him through, and he died. 55 When the Israelites saw that Abimelech was dead, they all went home. 56 Thus God repaid Abimelech for the crime he committed against his father in killing his seventy brothers; 57 and God also made all the wickedness of the people of Shechem fall back on their heads, and on them came the curse of Jotham son of Jerubbaal.

Tola and Jair

10 After Abimelech, Tola son of Puah son of Dodo, a man of Issachar, who lived at Shamir in the hill country of Ephraim, rose to deliver Israel. 2 He judged Israel twenty-three years. Then he died, and was buried at Shamir.

3 After him came Jair the Gileadite, who judged Israel twenty-two years. 4 He had thirty sons who rode on thirty donkeys; and they had thirty towns, which are in the land of Gilead, and are called Havvoth-jair to this day. 5 Jair died, and was buried in Kamon.

Oppression by the Ammonites

6 The Israelites again did what was evil in the sight of the LORD, worshiping the Baals and the Astartes, the gods of Aram, the gods of Sidon, the gods of Moab, the gods of the Ammonites, and the gods of the Philistines. Thus they abandoned the LORD, and did not worship him. 7 So the anger of the LORD was kindled against Israel, and he sold them into the hand of the Philistines and into the hand of the Ammonites, 8 and they crushed and oppressed the Israelites that year. For eighteen years they oppressed all the Israelites that were beyond the Jordan in the land of the Amorites, which is in Gilead. 9 The Ammonites also crossed the Jordan to fight against Judah and against Benjamin and

---

10:1–5 *Tola . . . judged Israel. . . . Jair . . . judged Israel.* Coming as it does between the violent episode of Abimelech and Jephthah's tragic career, the routine notice about Tola and Jair provides welcome relief. The theological function of these verses may be to suggest that even amid the growing unfaithfulness of the people and their leaders, evidenced by Gideon's idolatry and Jephthah's unfaithful vow (see notes on 11:29–33; 11:34–40), God is still with the people (see note on 12:8–15).

10:6–16 *The Israelites again did . . . . evil.* Instead of crying out to God for help, the people here offer a confession of sin (v 10), which God seems to reject (v 13). However, God simply cannot abandon the people; and as God does throughout Judges, he raises up another deliverer for the sinful people because he "could no longer bear to see Israel suffer" (v 16). The seeming inconsistency between what God says and what God does serves to communicate his essentially gracious character (note how 10:16 recalls 2:18).

against the house of Ephraim; so that Israel was greatly distressed.

10　So the Israelites cried to the LORD, saying, "We have sinned against you, because we have abandoned our God and have worshiped the Baals." 11And the LORD said to the Israelites, "Did I not deliver you*a* from the Egyptians and from the Amorites, from the Ammonites and from the Philistines? 12The Sidonians also, and the Amalekites, and the Maonites, oppressed you; and you cried to me, and I delivered you out of their hand. 13Yet you have abandoned me and worshiped other gods; therefore I will deliver you no more. 14Go and cry to the gods whom you have chosen; let them deliver you in the time of your distress." 15And the Israelites said to the LORD, "We have sinned; do to us whatever seems good to you; but deliver us this day!" 16So they put away the foreign gods from among them and worshiped the LORD; and he could no longer bear to see Israel suffer.

17　Then the Ammonites were called to arms, and they encamped in Gilead; and the Israelites came together, and they encamped at Mizpah. 18The commanders of the people of Gilead said to one another, "Who will begin the fight against the Ammonites? He shall be head over all the inhabitants of Gilead."

Jephthah

11 Now Jephthah the Gileadite, the son of a prostitute, was a mighty warrior. Gilead was the father of Jephthah. 2Gilead's wife also bore him sons; and when his wife's sons grew up, they drove Jephthah away, saying to him, "You shall not inherit anything in our father's house; for you are the son of another woman." 3Then Jephthah fled from his brothers and lived in the land of Tob. Outlaws collected around Jephthah and went raiding with him.

4　After a time the Ammonites made war against Israel. 5And when the Ammonites made war against Israel, the elders of Gilead

went to bring Jephthah from the land of Tob. 6They said to Jephthah, "Come and be our commander, so that we may fight with the Ammonites." 7But Jephthah said to the elders of Gilead, "Are you not the very ones who rejected me and drove me out of my father's house? So why do you come to me now when you are in trouble?" 8The elders of Gilead said to Jephthah, "Nevertheless, we have now turned back to you, so that you may go with us and fight with the Ammonites, and become head over us, over all the inhabitants of Gilead." 9Jephthah said to the elders of Gilead, "If you bring me home again to fight with the Ammonites, and the LORD gives them over to me, I will be your head." 10And the elders of Gilead said to Jephthah, "The LORD will be witness between us; we will surely do as you say." 11So Jephthah went with the elders of Gilead, and the people made him head and commander over them; and Jephthah spoke all his words before the LORD at Mizpah.

12　Then Jephthah sent messengers to the king of the Ammonites and said, "What is there between you and me, that you have come to me to fight against my land?" 13The king of the Ammonites answered the messengers of Jephthah, "Because Israel, on coming from Egypt, took away my land from the Arnon to the Jabbok and to the Jordan; now therefore restore it peaceably." 14Once again Jephthah sent messengers to the king of the Ammonites 15and said to him: "Thus says Jephthah: Israel did not take away the land of Moab or the land of the Ammonites, 16but when they came up from Egypt, Israel went through the wilderness to the Red Sea*b* and came to Kadesh. 17Israel then sent messengers to the king of Edom, saying, 'Let us pass through your land'; but the king of Edom would not listen. They also sent to the king of Moab, but he would not consent. So Israel

a Heb lacks *Did I not deliver you*　　*b* Or *Sea of Reeds*

---

remained at Kadesh. ¹⁸Then they journeyed through the wilderness, went around the land of Edom and the land of Moab, arrived on the east side of the land of Moab, and camped on the other side of the Arnon. They did not enter the territory of Moab, for the Arnon was the boundary of Moab. ¹⁹Israel then sent messengers to King Sihon of the Amorites, king of Heshbon; and Israel said to him, 'Let us pass through your land to our country.' ²⁰But Sihon did not trust Israel to pass through his territory; so Sihon gathered all his people together, and encamped at Jahaz, and fought with Israel. ²¹Then the LORD, the God of Israel, gave Sihon and all his people into the hand of Israel, and they defeated them; so Israel occupied all the land of the Amorites, who inhabited that country. ²²They occupied all the territory of the Amorites from the Arnon to the Jabbok and from the wilderness to the Jordan. ²³So now the LORD, the God of Israel, has conquered the Amorites for the benefit of his people Israel. Do you intend to take their place? ²⁴Should you not possess what your god Chemosh gives you to possess? And should we not be the ones to possess everything that the LORD our God has conquered for our benefit? ²⁵Now are you any better than King Balak son of Zippor of Moab? Did he ever enter into conflict with Israel, or did he ever go to war with them? ²⁶While Israel lived in Heshbon and its villages, and in Aroer and its villages, and in all the towns that are along the Arnon, three hundred years, why did you not recover them within that time? ²⁷It is not I who have sinned against you, but you are the one who does me wrong by making war on me. Let the LORD, who is judge, decide today for the Israelites or for the Ammonites." ²⁸But the king of the Ammonites did not heed the message that Jephthah sent him.

Jephthah's Vow

29 Then the spirit of the LORD came upon Jephthah, and he passed through Gilead and Manasseh. He passed on to Mizpah of Gilead, and from Mizpah of Gilead he passed on to the Ammonites. ³⁰And Jephthah made a vow to the LORD, and said, "If you will give the Ammonites into my hand, ³¹then whoever comes out of the doors of my house to meet me, when I return victorious from the Ammonites, shall be the LORD's, to be offered up by me as a burnt offering." ³²So Jephthah crossed over to the Ammonites to fight against them; and the LORD gave them into his hand. ³³He inflicted a massive defeat on them from Aroer to the neighborhood of Minnith, twenty towns, and as far as Abel-keramim. So the Ammonites were subdued before the people of Israel.

Jephthah's Daughter

34 Then Jephthah came to his home at Mizpah; and there was his daughter coming out to meet him with timbrels and with dancing. She was his only child; he had no son or daughter except her. ³⁵When he saw her, he tore his clothes, and said, "Alas, my daughter! You have brought me very low; you have become the cause of great trouble to me. For I have opened my mouth to the LORD, and I cannot take back my vow." ³⁶She said to him, "My father, if you have opened your mouth to the LORD, do to me according to what has gone out of your mouth, now that the LORD has given you vengeance against your enemies, the Ammonites." ³⁷And she said to her father, "Let this thing be done for me: Grant me two months, so that I may go and wander[a] on the moun-

a Cn: Heb go down

11:29–33 *If you will give . . . then.* The gift of God's Spirit seems to sound an auspicious note, but the record of the Spirit's effectiveness in Judges is revealing. Whereas Othniel responds to the Spirit with immediately effective action (see note on 3:7–11), Gideon hesitates and proposes a test for God when he is possessed by the Spirit (see note on 6:36–40). And although Samson is gifted by the Spirit several times (13:25; 14:6, 19; 15:14), he fails to deliver Israel. This pattern of growing ineffectiveness reveals the necessity of a faithful human response, which Jephthah here does not demonstrate. Instead, he displays a lack of faith by making an unnecessary vow that turns out to have tragically violent consequences, the death of his only child.

tains, and bewail my virginity, my companions and I." [38]"Go," he said and sent her away for two months. So she departed, she and her companions, and bewailed her virginity on the mountains. [39]At the end of two months, she returned to her father, who did with her according to the vow he had made. She had never slept with a man. So there arose an Israelite custom that [40]for four days every year the daughters of Israel would go out to lament the daughter of Jephthah the Gileadite.

Intertribal Dissension

12 The men of Ephraim were called to arms, and they crossed to Zaphon and said to Jephthah, "Why did you cross over to fight against the Ammonites, and did not call us to go with you? We will burn your house down over you!" [2]Jephthah said to them, "My people and I were engaged in conflict with the Ammonites who oppressed us [a] severely. But when I called you, you did not deliver me from their hand. [3]When I saw that you would not deliver me, I took my life in my hand, and crossed over against the Ammonites, and the LORD gave them into my hand. Why then have you come up to me this day, to fight against me?" [4]Then Jephthah gathered all the men of Gilead and fought with Ephraim; and the men of Gilead defeated Ephraim, because they said, "You are fugitives from Ephraim, you Gileadites—in the heart of Ephraim and Manasseh." [b]

[5]Then the Gileadites took the fords of the Jordan against the Ephraimites. Whenever one of the fugitives of Ephraim said, "Let me go over," the men of Gilead would say to him, "Are you an Ephraimite?" When he said, "No," [6]they said to him, "Then say Shibboleth," and he said, "Sibboleth," for he could not pronounce it right. Then they seized him and killed him at the fords of the Jordan. Forty-two thousand of the Ephraimites fell at that time.

7 Jephthah judged Israel six years. Then Jephthah the Gileadite died, and was buried in his town in Gilead. [c]

Ibzan, Elon, and Abdon

8 After him Ibzan of Bethlehem judged Israel. [9]He had thirty sons. He gave his thirty daughters in marriage outside his clan and brought in thirty young women from outside for his sons. He judged Israel seven years. [10]Then Ibzan died, and was buried at Bethlehem.

11 After him Elon the Zebulunite judged Israel; and he judged Israel ten years. [12]Then Elon the Zebulunite died, and was buried at Aijalon in the land of Zebulun.

13 After him Abdon son of Hillel the Pirathonite judged Israel. [14]He had forty sons and thirty grandsons, who rode on seventy donkeys; he judged Israel eight years. [15]Then

a Gk OL, Syr H: Heb lacks *who oppressed us*
b Meaning of Heb uncertain: Gk omits *because . . . Manasseh*   c Gk: Heb *in the towns of Gilead*

11:34–40 *I cannot take back my vow.* Commentators have often misguidedly commended Jephthah for keeping his word, but there is no virtue in keeping a vow that was both unnecessary and unfaithful. Rather, the tragic death of Jephthah's daughter demonstrates the terribly destructive consequences of unfaithfulness. Her weeping and that of her friends (vv 37–38; notice "bewail" and "bewailed") recall the weeping near the beginning and end of Judges (2:4–5; 20:23, 26; 21:2). The death of Jephthah's daughter reveals the sad state of affairs that inevitably results from unfaithfulness and disobedience. This truth, in conjunction with the increasing victimization of women in Judges, invites contemporary people of faith to join the ancient companions of Jephthah's daughter in keeping her memory alive. To remember Jephthah's daughter partakes of the Spiritual Discipline of obedience, which contributes to the just and equitable treatment of women.

12:1–7 *The men of Ephraim were called to arms.* Jephthah's unfaithfulness results in a legacy of violence, within both his own family and the larger Israelite family, as a bloody civil war claims the lives of forty-two thousand Ephraimites. Consequently, there is no "rest" for the land. Persistent unfaithfulness and disobedience yield increasingly violent and chaotic results as Judges proceeds.

Abdon son of Hillel the Pirathonite died, and was buried at Pirathon in the land of Ephraim, in the hill country of the Amalekites.

The Birth of Samson

13 The Israelites again did what was evil in the sight of the LORD, and the LORD gave them into the hand of the Philistines forty years.

2 There was a certain man of Zorah, of the tribe of the Danites, whose name was Manoah. His wife was barren, having borne no children. ³And the angel of the LORD appeared to the woman and said to her, "Although you are barren, having borne no children, you shall conceive and bear a son. ⁴Now be careful not to drink wine or strong drink, or to eat anything unclean, ⁵for you shall conceive and bear a son. No razor is to come on his head, for the boy shall be a nazirite ᵃ to God from birth. It is he who shall begin to deliver Israel from the hand of the Philistines." ⁶Then the woman came and told her husband, "A man of God came to me, and his appearance was like that of an angel ᵇ of God, most awe-inspiring; I did not ask him where

he came from, and he did not tell me his name; ⁷but he said to me, 'You shall conceive and bear a son. So then drink no wine or strong drink, and eat nothing unclean, for the boy shall be a nazirite ᵃ to God from birth to the day of his death.' "

8 Then Manoah entreated the LORD, and said, "O LORD, I pray, let the man of God whom you sent come to us again and teach us what we are to do concerning the boy who will be born." ⁹God listened to Manoah, and the angel of God came again to the woman as she sat in the field; but her husband Manoah was not with her. ¹⁰So the woman ran quickly and told her husband, "The man who came to me the other day has appeared to me." ¹¹Manoah got up and followed his wife, and came to the man and said to him, "Are you the man who spoke to this woman?" And he said, "I am." ¹²Then Manoah said, "Now when your words come true, what is to be the boy's rule of life; what is he to do?" ¹³The angel of the LORD said to Manoah, "Let the woman give heed to all that I said to her.

a That is *one separated* or *one consecrated*
b Or *the angel*

12:8–15 *Ibzan, . . . Elon, . . . Abdon . . . judged.* Like the similar notice in 10:1–5, these verses may indicate that even amid the unfaithfulness of leaders like Gideon and Jephthah, relatively normal life is still possible. Abdon, for instance, has forty sons and thirty grandsons (vv 13–14; 10:3–4). Since children are viewed elsewhere in Scripture as evidence of God's blessing (Ps 128), Abdon's large family may suggest that, although the Israelites and their leaders are increasingly abandoning God, God is not abandoning them.

13:1–25 *Although you are barren . . . you shall conceive.* The details of this chapter create high expectations for Samson's leadership. Like the births of Isaac, Jacob, and Joseph, Samson's birth is announced by an angel to a barren woman. Furthermore, Samson is to be set apart from birth as a Nazirite (v 5; Num 6:1–21); and God "blessed him" (v 24), including with the presence of God's Spirit (v 25). But there are also hints that Samson will not live up to these expectations. First, the angel tells Samson's mother that Samson "shall begin to deliver Israel from the hand of the Philistines" (v 5). In

short, as impressive as are Samson's feats, he effects no deliverance. Then too, the pattern of the Spirit's increasing ineffectiveness in Judges is a bad sign (see notes on 3:7–11; 6:36–40; 11:29–33). The Spirit is *most* present in Samson's story, but with the *least* effect in terms of the accomplishment of God's purposes. Without human receptiveness and faithfulness, God's gifts are wasted; and there is no better biblical example of this than Samson. His abundant energy is spent chasing Philistine women, and his extraordinary strength is dedicated primarily to exacting personal revenge against the Philistines. Along the way, Samson violates every aspect of his Nazirite status; and he fails to deliver Israel from the Philistines. So, although Samson is often viewed as a hero and even interpreted as a type of Christ, he is actually the least successful of all the judges, thus illustrating the detrimental and destructive results of unfaithfulness and disobedience. Against all expectations, if there is a hero in Samson's story, it is Samson's wise and faithful mother, whose name we do not even know!

14 She may not eat of anything that comes from the vine. She is not to drink wine or strong drink, or eat any unclean thing. She is to observe everything that I commanded her."

15 Manoah said to the angel of the LORD, "Allow us to detain you, and prepare a kid for you." 16 The angel of the LORD said to Manoah, "If you detain me, I will not eat your food; but if you want to prepare a burnt offering, then offer it to the LORD." (For Manoah did not know that he was the angel of the LORD.) 17 Then Manoah said to the angel of the LORD, "What is your name, so that we may honor you when your words come true?" 18 But the angel of the LORD said to him, "Why do you ask my name? It is too wonderful."

19 So Manoah took the kid with the grain offering, and offered it on the rock to the LORD, to him who works a wonders. b 20 When the flame went up toward heaven from the altar, the angel of the LORD ascended in the flame of the altar while Manoah and his wife looked on; and they fell on their faces to the ground. 21 The angel of the LORD did not appear again to Manoah and his wife. Then Manoah realized that it was the angel of the LORD. 22 And Manoah said to his wife, "We shall surely die, for we have seen God." 23 But his wife said to him, "If the LORD had meant to kill us, he would not have accepted a burnt offering and a grain offering at our hands, or shown us all these things, or now announced to us such things as these."

24 The woman bore a son, and named him Samson. The boy grew, and the LORD blessed him. 25 The spirit of the LORD began to stir him in Mahaneh-dan, between Zorah and Eshtaol.

Samson's Marriage

14 Once Samson went down to Timnah, and at Timnah he saw a Philistine woman. 2 Then he came up, and told his father and mother, "I saw a Philistine woman at Timnah; now get her for me as my wife." 3 But his father and mother said to him, "Is there not a woman among your kin, or among all our c people, that you must go to take a wife from the uncircumcised Philistines?" But Samson said to his father, "Get her for me, because she pleases me." 4 His father and mother did not know that this was from the LORD; for he was seeking a pretext to act against the Philistines. At that time the Philistines had dominion over Israel.

5 Then Samson went down with his father and mother to Timnah. When he came to the vineyards of Timnah, suddenly a young lion roared at him. 6 The spirit of the LORD rushed on him, and he tore the lion apart barehanded as one might tear apart a kid. But he did not tell his father or his mother what he had done. 7 Then he went down and talked with the woman, and she pleased Samson. 8 After a while he returned to marry her, and he turned aside to see the carcass of the lion, and there was a swarm of bees in the body of the lion, and honey. 9 He scraped it out into his hands, and went on, eating as he went. When he came to his father and mother, he gave some to them, and they ate it. But he did not tell them that he had taken the honey from the carcass of the lion.

a Gk Vg: Heb and working   b Heb wonders, while Manoah and his wife looked on   c Cn: Heb my

---

14:1–15:20 *Samson . . . saw a Philistine woman.* As Samson's parents suggest, it is a problem that Samson wants a Philistine wife. His desire probably violated his Nazirite status, which obligated him to keep separate from uncleanness, and clearly violated God's stated intent that the Israelites not collaborate with the peoples of the land (2:2; 3:6). Samson's rationale, "she pleases me" (14:3), is more literally "she (is) right in my eyes," thus anticipating the unbridled self-assertion of the people in chapters 17–21 (see esp. 17:6; 21:25). Apparently, God sees Samson's desire as an "opportunity" (14:4; "pretext") to oppose oppression; but Samson proves ineffective in this regard. His gifts, represented by God's Spirit (14:6, 19; 15:14), are squandered on impressive deeds that have nothing to do with deliverance. Given Samson's unfaithfulness and ineffectiveness, God's granting of Samson's request for water (15:18–19) represents a remarkable display of divine patience and grace.

10 His father went down to the woman, and Samson made a feast there as the young men were accustomed to do. 11When the people saw him, they brought thirty companions to be with him. 12Samson said to them, "Let me now put a riddle to you. If you can explain it to me within the seven days of the feast, and find it out, then I will give you thirty linen garments and thirty festal garments. 13But if you cannot explain it to me, then you shall give me thirty linen garments and thirty festal garments." So they said to him, "Ask your riddle; let us hear it." 14He said to them,

> "Out of the eater came something to
>   eat.
> Out of the strong came something
>   sweet."

But for three days they could not explain the riddle.

15 On the fourth *a* day they said to Samson's wife, "Coax your husband to explain the riddle to us, or we will burn you and your father's house with fire. Have you invited us here to impoverish us?" 16So Samson's wife wept before him, saying, "You hate me; you do not really love me. You have asked a riddle of my people, but you have not explained it to me." He said to her, "Look, I have not told my father or my mother. Why should I tell you?" 17She wept before him the seven days that their feast lasted; and because she nagged him, on the seventh day he told her. Then she explained the riddle to her people. 18The men of the town said to him on the seventh day before the sun went down,

> "What is sweeter than honey?
> What is stronger than a lion?"

And he said to them,

> "If you had not plowed with my heifer,
>   you would not have found out my
>   riddle."

19Then the spirit of the LORD rushed on him, and he went down to Ashkelon. He killed thirty men of the town, took their spoil, and gave the festal garments to those who had explained the riddle. In hot anger he went back to his father's house. 20And Samson's wife was given to his companion, who had been his best man.

Samson Defeats the Philistines

15 After a while, at the time of the wheat harvest, Samson went to visit his wife, bringing along a kid. He said, "I want to go into my wife's room." But her father would not allow him to go in. 2Her father said, "I was sure that you had rejected her; so I gave her to your companion. Is not her younger sister prettier than she? Why not take her instead?" 3Samson said to them, "This time, when I do mischief to the Philistines, I will be without blame." 4So Samson went and caught three hundred foxes, and took some torches; and he turned the foxes *b* tail to tail, and put a torch between each pair of tails. 5When he had set fire to the torches, he let the foxes go into the standing grain of the Philistines, and burned up the shocks and the standing grain, as well as the vineyards and *c* olive groves. 6Then the Philistines asked, "Who has done this?" And they said, "Samson, the son-in-law of the Timnite, because he has taken Samson's wife and given her to his companion." So the Philistines came up, and burned her and her father. 7Samson said to them, "If this is what you do, I swear I will not stop until I have taken revenge on you." 8He struck them down hip and thigh with great slaughter; and he went down and stayed in the cleft of the rock of Etam.

9 Then the Philistines came up and encamped in Judah, and made a raid on Lehi. 10The men of Judah said, "Why have you come up against us?" They said, "We have come up to bind Samson, to do to him as he did to us." 11Then three thousand men of Judah went down to the cleft of the rock of Etam, and they said to Samson, "Do you not know that the Philistines are rulers over us? What then have you done to us?" He replied, "As they did to me, so I have done to them." 12They said to him, "We have come down to bind you, so that we may give you into the hands of the Philistines." Samson answered them, "Swear to me that you yourselves will not attack me." 13They said to him, "No, we will only bind you and give you into their hands; we will not kill you." So they bound

a Gk Syr: Heb *seventh*   *b* Heb *them*   *c* Gk Tg Vg: Heb lacks *and*

SAMSON

Undermining God's Gifts

Selected Scriptures: *Judges 13–16*

Samson is lauded for his extraordinary physical strength. Like no one else in the Bible, Samson received the strength from God to tear a lion apart bare-handed, catch and tie together three hundred foxes, kill a thousand Philistines with the jawbone of a donkey, break new ropes bound around him, remove a city gate and carry it up a hill, and bring down the pillars of a great house. His feats resembled those of a mythical hero, yet with these acts his heroism ended. Considered a judge in Israel because of his God-given strength, Samson had the opportunity to lead the Israelites out of bondage to the Philistines. He could have led them spiritually as well. He did neither.

As strong as Samson was physically, he was weak morally and spiritually. Despite his upbringing by godly parents and his knowledge that God had specially chosen and gifted him, Samson allowed his sensual appetites to control his actions again and again. Against Mosaic law, Samson demanded a pagan woman for a wife, visited a prostitute, and allowed his passion for Delilah to put him into the hands of the Philistines. His appetites moved him to violate each of the three conditions of his Nazirite vow: he touched the dead carcass of a lion to get honey, joined in a feast with much wine before his wedding, and let his hair be cut. Samson did not possess the inner strength to accompany his outer strength, and this void became his downfall.

Samson's life story offers a sobering reminder of the limitations of God-given talents and gifts. The temptation to rely on these gifts and ignore a commitment to personal growth in holiness can make us fall short of all God intends us to be. One commentary states: "Though Samson had received great gifts from the Spirit of God, he fell far short of holiness. . . . *Often the very area in which a person is most gifted proves to be his or her weakness*" (italics added).

For Samson, it was strength. Great strength masked great weakness. Without personal discipline his bodily power was not enough to equip him to serve well. We face similar challenges. For some of us, a gift of teaching might mask hypocrisy. A gift of speaking might mask an inability to relate intimately to others. A gift of the ability to create or build might mask a hollow family life. A gift of the ability to bring beauty might mask inattention to the beautifying of the spirit. A gift of compassion might mask cynicism.

The list could go on. Yet as we recognize our own forms of strength and weakness, let us not grow discouraged. The God who has created us stands with us, ready to keep forming us in response to our obedience. In pondering Samson's story, let's ask God for insight and help as we seek the discipline needed to live out in fullness all God has created us to be.

PROFILE

PROFILE: SAMSON

Personal Reflection

- Samson had strong arms and strong appetites. Which Spiritual Disciplines in particular might have helped him receive from God the inner strength to match his physical strength?
- God gifts every person in some way. What gifts has God given you?
- In what areas related to your gifts might you be weak? What have been the consequences of this weakness in your life? Which Spiritual Disciplines could be especially helpful in seeking growth in holiness? Consider now how you can begin practicing these disciplines and placing your weakness before God for his transformation. Pray now for his help.

him with two new ropes, and brought him up from the rock.

14 When he came to Lehi, the Philistines came shouting to meet him; and the spirit of the LORD rushed on him, and the ropes that were on his arms became like flax that has caught fire, and his bonds melted off his hands. 15 Then he found a fresh jawbone of a donkey, reached down and took it, and with it he killed a thousand men. 16 And Samson said,

"With the jawbone of a donkey,
    heaps upon heaps,
with the jawbone of a donkey
    I have slain a thousand men."

17 When he had finished speaking, he threw away the jawbone; and that place was called Ramath-lehi. *a*

18 By then he was very thirsty, and he called on the LORD, saying, "You have granted this great victory by the hand of your servant. Am I now to die of thirst, and fall into the hands of the uncircumcised?" 19 So God split open the hollow place that is at Lehi, and water came from it. When he drank, his spirit returned, and he revived. Therefore it was named En-hakkore, *b* which is at Lehi to this day. 20 And he judged Israel in the days of the Philistines twenty years.

Samson and Delilah

16 Once Samson went to Gaza, where he saw a prostitute and went in to her. 2 The Gazites were told, *c* "Samson has come here." So they circled around and lay in wait for him all night at the city gate. They kept quiet all night, thinking, "Let us wait until the light of the morning; then we will kill

---

a That is *The Hill of the Jawbone*   *b* That is *The Spring of the One who Called*   *c* Gk: Heb lacks *were told*

16:1–3 *he saw a prostitute and went in to her.* As in chapters 14–15, Samson is in pursuit of another Philistine woman. Despite another impressive feat—carrying away the city gate (v 3; Gen 22:17; 24:60)—Samson does nothing to contribute to the deliverance of Israel. What might have been an impetus to rally resistance against the Philistines amounts to nothing except another waste of Samson's gifts.

him." [3]But Samson lay only until midnight. Then at midnight he rose up, took hold of the doors of the city gate and the two posts, pulled them up, bar and all, put them on his shoulders, and carried them to the top of the hill that is in front of Hebron.

4 After this he fell in love with a woman in the valley of Sorek, whose name was Delilah. [5]The lords of the Philistines came to her and said to her, "Coax him, and find out what makes his strength so great, and how we may overpower him, so that we may bind him in order to subdue him; and we will each give you eleven hundred pieces of silver." [6]So Delilah said to Samson, "Please tell me what makes your strength so great, and how you could be bound, so that one could subdue you." [7]Samson said to her, "If they bind me with seven fresh bowstrings that are not dried out, then I shall become weak, and be like anyone else." [8]Then the lords of the Philistines brought her seven fresh bowstrings that had not dried out, and she bound him with them. [9]While men were lying in wait in an inner chamber, she said to him, "The Philistines are upon you, Samson!" But he snapped the bowstrings, as a strand of fiber snaps when it touches the fire. So the secret of his strength was not known.

10 Then Delilah said to Samson, "You have mocked me and told me lies; please tell me how you could be bound." [11]He said to her, "If they bind me with new ropes that have not been used, then I shall become weak, and be like anyone else." [12]So Delilah took new ropes and bound him with them, and said to him, "The Philistines are upon you, Samson!" (The men lying in wait were in an inner chamber.) But he snapped the ropes off his arms like a thread.

13 Then Delilah said to Samson, "Until now you have mocked me and told me lies; tell me how you could be bound." He said to her, "If you weave the seven locks of my head with the web and make it tight with the pin, then I shall become weak, and be like anyone else." [14]So while he slept, Delilah took the seven locks of his head and wove them into the web,[a] and made them tight with the pin. Then she said to him, "The Philistines are upon you, Samson!" But he awoke from his sleep, and pulled away the pin, the loom, and the web.

15 Then she said to him, "How can you say, 'I love you,' when your heart is not with me? You have mocked me three times now and have not told me what makes your strength so great." [16]Finally, after she had nagged him with her words day after day, and pestered him, he was tired to death. [17]So he told her his whole secret, and said to her, "A razor has never come upon my head; for I have been a nazirite[b] to God from my mother's womb. If my head were shaved, then my strength would leave me; I would become weak, and be like anyone else."

18 When Delilah realized that he had told her his whole secret, she sent and called the lords of the Philistines, saying, "This time come up, for he has told his whole secret to me." Then the lords of the Philistines came up to her, and brought the money in their hands. [19]She let him fall asleep on her lap; and she called a man, and had him shave off the seven locks of his head. He began to weaken,[c] and his strength left him. [20]Then she

a Compare Gk: in verses 13-14, Heb lacks *and make it tight . . . into the web*   b That is *one separated* or *one consecrated*   c Gk: Heb *She began to torment him*

16:4–22 *he fell in love with . . . Delilah.* Samson's relationship with Delilah, another Philistine woman, portrays Samson at his worst—incredibly foolish as well as faithless. Collaboration with the Philistines violates God's purposes (2:2; 3:6); and by revealing the secret that leads to the cutting of his hair, Samson violates his Nazirite status (v 17). Samson's capture and humiliation demonstrate dramatically the destructive consequences of

disobedience. To be sure, Samson turns to God one final time (v 28), but his destruction of the temple of Dagon is a hollow victory. Samson dies, and his final impressive feat still does not lead to the deliverance of Israel. As was the case following the deaths of Gideon and Jephthah, violence and chaos reign following the death of Samson. Indeed, as chapters 17–21 suggest, things are worse than ever in Israel.

said, "The Philistines are upon you, Samson!" When he awoke from his sleep, he thought, "I will go out as at other times, and shake myself free." But he did not know that the Lord had left him. 21So the Philistines seized him and gouged out his eyes. They brought him down to Gaza and bound him with bronze shackles; and he ground at the mill in the prison. 22But the hair of his head began to grow again after it had been shaved.

Samson's Death

23 Now the lords of the Philistines gathered to offer a great sacrifice to their god Dagon, and to rejoice; for they said, "Our god has given Samson our enemy into our hand." 24When the people saw him, they praised their god; for they said, "Our god has given our enemy into our hand, the ravager of our country, who has killed many of us." 25And when their hearts were merry, they said, "Call Samson, and let him entertain us." So they called Samson out of the prison, and he performed for them. They made him stand between the pillars; 26and Samson said to the attendant who held him by the hand, "Let me feel the pillars on which the house rests, so that I may lean against them." 27Now the house was full of men and women; all the lords of the Philistines were there, and on the roof there were about three thousand men and women, who looked on while Samson performed.

28 Then Samson called to the Lord and said, "Lord God, remember me and strengthen me only this once, O God, so that with this one act of revenge I may pay back the Philistines for my two eyes." a 29And Samson grasped the two middle pillars on which the house rested, and he leaned his weight against them, his right hand on the one and his left hand on the other. 30Then Samson said, "Let me die with the Philistines." He strained with all his might; and the house fell on the lords and all the people who were in it. So those he killed at his death were more than those he had killed during his life. 31Then his brothers and all his family came down and took him and brought him up and buried him between Zorah and Eshtaol in the tomb of his father Manoah. He had judged Israel twenty years.

Micah and the Levite

17 There was a man in the hill country of Ephraim whose name was Micah. 2He said to his mother, "The eleven hundred pieces of silver that were taken from you, about which you uttered a curse, and even spoke it in my hearing,—that silver is in my possession; I took it; but now I will return it to you." b And his mother said, "May my son be blessed by the Lord!" 3Then he returned the eleven hundred pieces of silver to his mother; and his mother said, "I consecrate the silver to the Lord from my hand for my son, to make an idol of cast metal." 4So when he returned the money to his mother, his mother took two hundred pieces of silver, and gave it to the silversmith, who made it into an idol of cast metal; and it was in the house of Micah. 5This man Micah had a shrine, and he made an ephod and teraphim, and installed one of his sons, who became his priest. 6In those days there was no king in Israel; all the people did what was right in their own eyes.

a Or so that I may be avenged upon the Philistines for one of my two eyes   b The words but now I will return it to you are transposed from the end of verse 3 in Heb

---

Responding
16:20 THE WITH-GOD LIFE. This timeless story about Samson highlights the dangers of taking God's spiritual gifts for granted and being careless about his presence. Samson's casual attitude results in the Lord's leaving him without his knowledge. When in your life did you feel the Lord's presence had left you? Did his presence leave you or did your attitude leave him? What promise did you hold to that helped you during this time? See also Spiritual Disciplines Index.

17:1–13 all the people did what was right in their own eyes. This notice (v 6) is repeated in 21:25, the final verse of the book, suggesting that everything that takes place in the final chapters of the book is evidence of idolatrous self-assertion. These chapters are full of disobedience; and they illustrate climactically

7 Now there was a young man of Bethlehem in Judah, of the clan of Judah. He was a Levite residing there. 8This man left the town of Bethlehem in Judah, to live wherever he could find a place. He came to the house of Micah in the hill country of Ephraim to carry on his work.ᵃ 9Micah said to him, "From where do you come?" He replied, "I am a Levite of Bethlehem in Judah, and I am going to live wherever I can find a place." 10Then Micah said to him, "Stay with me, and be to me a father and a priest, and I will give you ten pieces of silver a year, a set of clothes, and your living."ᵇ 11The Levite agreed to stay with the man; and the young man became to him like one of his sons. 12So Micah installed the Levite, and the young man became his priest, and was in the house of Micah. 13Then Micah said, "Now I know that the LORD will prosper me, because the Levite has become my priest."

The Migration of Dan

18 In those days there was no king in Israel. And in those days the tribe of the Danites was seeking for itself a territory to live in; for until then no territory among the tribes of Israel had been allotted to them. 2So the Danites sent five valiant men from the whole number of their clan, from Zorah and from Eshtaol, to spy out the land and to explore it; and they said to them, "Go, explore the land." When they came to the hill country of Ephraim, to the house of Micah, they stayed there. 3While they were at Micah's house, they recognized the voice of the young Levite; so they went over and asked him, "Who brought you here? What are you doing in this place? What is your business here?" 4He said to them, "Micah did such and such for me, and he hired me, and I have become his priest." 5Then they said to him, "Inquire of God that we may know whether the mission we are undertaking will succeed." 6The priest replied, "Go in peace. The mission you are on is under the eye of the LORD."

7 The five men went on, and when they came to Laish, they observed the people who were there living securely, after the manner of the Sidonians, quiet and unsuspecting, lackingᶜ nothing on earth, and possessing

a Or Ephraim, continuing his journey　　b Heb living, and the Levite went　　c Cn Compare 18.10: Meaning of Heb uncertain

---

the violent, chaotic consequences of idolatrous self-assertion that flaunts God and God's purposes. For starters, Micah steals from his mother. Although he returns the silver, it is used to make an idol, which apparently becomes the focal point of Micah's private shrine (v 4). Micah also presumes to appoint his son as priest until an unemployed Levite comes along, whom Micah hires and in whom he seems to place unwarranted trust (v 13). In view of the legal material found in the books of Exodus through Deuteronomy, including the Ten Commandments, the whole situation is simply ludicrous. But this is precisely the point. The final chapters of Judges intend to point out that prolonged unfaithfulness and disobedience lead to absurd behavior.

18:1–31 *the tribe of the Danites was seeking for itself a territory.* The ridiculous behavior seen in chapter 17 continues here. Although the Danites appear to have divine sanction for their quest (v 6), the blessing comes from a bogus priest, who later reveals his true character by abandoning Micah when he receives a better offer (vv 18–20). The Danites proceed to steal Micah's idol, using it to perpetuate the idolatrous worship that Micah had started. Their worship is presided over by the descendants of Moses (vv 30–31). It is hard to imagine anything more ludicrous than the descendants of Moses officiating at the worship of an idolatrous shrine! But again (see note on 17:1–13), this is precisely the point. Furthermore, the utterly repulsive behavior of the Danites includes the slaughter of the people of Laish, who are identified as "quiet" (vv 7, 27). The word "quiet" comes from the same Hebrew root that is translated as "rest" in 3:11, 30; 5:31; and 8:28, where it indicates a situation in which God's will for justice, righteousness, and peace is being observed. In short, the Danites, motivated only by what is "right in their own eyes" (17:6; 21:25), wipe out those who model God's ways. It is another powerful lesson in the tragically destructive consequences of idolatry and disobedience.

wealth. *a* Furthermore, they were far from the Sidonians and had no dealings with Aram. *b* 8When they came to their kinsfolk at Zorah and Eshtaol, they said to them, "What do you report?" 9They said, "Come, let us go up against them; for we have seen the land, and it is very good. Will you do nothing? Do not be slow to go, but enter in and possess the land. 10When you go, you will come to an unsuspecting people. The land is broad— God has indeed given it into your hands—a place where there is no lack of anything on earth."

11 Six hundred men of the Danite clan, armed with weapons of war, set out from Zorah and Eshtaol, 12and went up and encamped at Kiriath-jearim in Judah. On this account that place is called Mahaneh-dan *c* to this day; it is west of Kiriath-jearim. 13From there they passed on to the hill country of Ephraim, and came to the house of Micah.

14 Then the five men who had gone to spy out the land (that is, Laish) said to their comrades, "Do you know that in these buildings there are an ephod, teraphim, and an idol of cast metal? Now therefore consider what you will do." 15So they turned in that direction and came to the house of the young Levite, at the home of Micah, and greeted him. 16While the six hundred men of the Danites, armed with their weapons of war, stood by the entrance of the gate, 17the five men who had gone to spy out the land proceeded to enter and take the idol of cast metal, the ephod, and the teraphim. *d* The priest was standing by the entrance of the gate with the six hundred men armed with weapons of war. 18When the men went into Micah's house and took the idol of cast metal, the ephod, and the teraphim, the priest said to them, "What are you doing?" 19They said to him, "Keep quiet! Put your hand over your mouth, and come with us, and be to us a father and a priest. Is it better for you to be priest to the house of one person, or to be priest to a tribe and clan in Israel?" 20Then the priest accepted the offer. He took the ephod, the teraphim, and the idol, and went along with the people.

21 So they resumed their journey, putting the little ones, the livestock, and the goods in front of them. 22When they were some distance from the home of Micah, the men who were in the houses near Micah's house were called out, and they overtook the Danites. 23They shouted to the Danites, who turned around and said to Micah, "What is the matter that you come with such a company?" 24He replied, "You take my gods that I made, and the priest, and go away, and what have I left? How then can you ask me, 'What is the matter?' " 25And the Danites said to him, "You had better not let your voice be heard among us or else hot-tempered fellows will attack you, and you will lose your life and the lives of your household." 26Then the Danites went their way. When Micah saw that they were too strong for him, he turned and went back to his home.

The Danites Settle in Laish

27 The Danites, having taken what Micah had made, and the priest who belonged to him, came to Laish, to a people quiet and unsuspecting, put them to the sword, and burned down the city. 28There was no deliverer, because it was far from Sidon and they had no dealings with Aram. *e* It was in the valley that belongs to Beth-rehob. They rebuilt the city, and lived in it. 29They named the city Dan, after their ancestor Dan, who was born to Israel; but the name of the city was formerly Laish. 30Then the Danites set up the idol for themselves. Jonathan son of Gershom, son of Moses, *f* and his sons were priests to the tribe of the Danites until the time the land went into captivity. 31So they maintained as their own Micah's idol that he had made, as long as the house of God was at Shiloh.

The Levite's Concubine

19 In those days, when there was no king in Israel, a certain Levite, residing in the remote parts of the hill country of Ephraim, took to himself a concubine from Bethlehem in Judah. 2But his concubine became

a Meaning of Heb uncertain   *b* Symmachus: Heb *with anyone*   *c* That is *Camp of Dan*
d Compare 17.4, 5; 18.14: Heb *teraphim and the cast metal*   *e* Cn Compare verse 7: Heb *with anyone*
f Another reading is *son of Manasseh*

angry with[a] him, and she went away from him to her father's house at Bethlehem in Judah, and was there some four months. [3]Then her husband set out after her, to speak tenderly to her and bring her back. He had with him his servant and a couple of donkeys. When he reached[b] her father's house, the girl's father saw him and came with joy to meet him. [4]His father-in-law, the girl's father, made him stay, and he remained with him three days; so they ate and drank, and he[c] stayed there. [5]On the fourth day they got up early in the morning, and he prepared to go; but the girl's father said to his son-in-law, "Fortify yourself with a bit of food, and after that you may go." [6]So the two men sat and ate and drank together; and the girl's father said to the man, "Why not spend the night and enjoy yourself?" [7]When the man got up to go, his father-in-law kept urging him until he spent the night there again. [8]On the fifth day he got up early in the morning to leave; and the girl's father said, "Fortify yourself." So they lingered[d] until the day declined, and the two of them ate and drank. [e] [9]When the man with his concubine and his servant got up to leave, his father-in-law, the girl's father, said to him, "Look, the day has worn on until it is almost evening. Spend the night. See, the day has drawn to a close. Spend the night here and enjoy yourself. Tomorrow you can get up early in the morning for your journey, and go home."

[10] But the man would not spend the night; he got up and departed, and arrived opposite Jebus (that is, Jerusalem). He had with him a couple of saddled donkeys, and his concubine was with him. [11]When they were near Jebus, the day was far spent, and the servant said to his master, "Come now, let us turn aside to this city of the Jebusites, and spend the night in it." [12]But his master said to him, "We will not turn aside into a city of foreigners, who do not belong to the people of Israel; but we will continue on to Gibeah." [13]Then he said to his servant, "Come, let us try to reach one of these places, and spend the night at Gibeah or at Ramah." [14]So they passed on and went their way; and the sun went down on them near Gibeah, which belongs to Benjamin. [15]They turned aside there, to go in and spend the night at Gibeah. He went in and sat down in the open square of the city, but no one took them in to spend the night.

[16] Then at evening there was an old man coming from his work in the field. The man was from the hill country of Ephraim, and he was residing in Gibeah. (The people of the place were Benjaminites.) [17]When the old man looked up and saw the wayfarer in the open square of the city, he said, "Where are

a Gk OL: Heb *prostituted herself against*
b Gk: Heb *she brought him to*   c Compare verse 7
and Gk: Heb *they*   d Cn: Heb *Linger*
e Gk: Heb lacks *and drank*

19:1–30 *In those days, when there was no king in Israel.* It is a bad sign that 19:1 begins like 18:1, and the foolish behavior of chapters 17–18 continues unabated in chapters 19–21. Verse 15 signals trouble. That no one took in the Levite and his concubine means that the covenant obligation, or Spiritual Discipline of hospitality, was not being practiced in Israel (Exod 22:21; 23:9; Lev 19:33–34; Deut 16:14; 26:12). The inhospitality of the men of Gibeah is obvious, but the behavior of the Levite, a person entrusted with teaching God's ways, is no better. He puts his concubine out to be raped (v 25); and the next morning, he shows no concern for her whatsoever (vv 27–28). That the dead concubine rides upon a donkey recalls 1:14, where Achsah rode a donkey. But whereas

Achsah was honored, the Levite's concubine is utterly victimized, signaling how wrong everything is when people do "what is right in their own eyes" (17:6; 21:25) rather than what God wills. In short, everybody looks bad here, and everything is desperately wrong, illustrating again that violence and chaos are the inevitable results of idolatrous self-assertion and disobedience. This lesson calls the People of God in all times and places to pure worship and to obedient pursuit of God's justice, righteousness, and peace. Chapter 19, especially when heard in conjunction with chapter 1, is a timely reminder that the equitable treatment of women is a litmus test of whether God's justice, righteousness, and peace are being faithfully embodied.

you going and where do you come from?" [18]He answered him, "We are passing from Bethlehem in Judah to the remote parts of the hill country of Ephraim, from which I come. I went to Bethlehem in Judah; and I am going to my home. [a] Nobody has offered to take me in. [19]We your servants have straw and fodder for our donkeys, with bread and wine for me and the woman and the young man along with us. We need nothing more." [20]The old man said, "Peace be to you. I will care for all your wants; only do not spend the night in the square." [21]So he brought him into his house, and fed the donkeys; they washed their feet, and ate and drank.

Gibeah's Crime

22 While they were enjoying themselves, the men of the city, a perverse lot, surrounded the house, and started pounding on the door. They said to the old man, the master of the house, "Bring out the man who came into your house, so that we may have intercourse with him." [23]And the man, the master of the house, went out to them and said to them, "No, my brothers, do not act so wickedly. Since this man is my guest, do not do this vile thing. [24]Here are my virgin daughter and his concubine; let me bring them out now. Ravish them and do whatever you want to them; but against this man do not do such a vile thing." [25]But the men would not listen to him. So the man seized his concubine, and put her out to them. They wantonly raped her, and abused her all through the night

until the morning. And as the dawn began to break, they let her go. [26]As morning appeared, the woman came and fell down at the door of the man's house where her master was, until it was light.

27 In the morning her master got up, opened the doors of the house, and when he went out to go on his way, there was his concubine lying at the door of the house, with her hands on the threshold. [28]"Get up," he said to her, "we are going." But there was no answer. Then he put her on the donkey; and the man set out for his home. [29]When he had entered his house, he took a knife, and grasping his concubine he cut her into twelve pieces, limb by limb, and sent her throughout all the territory of Israel. [30]Then he commanded the men whom he sent, saying, "Thus shall you say to all the Israelites, 'Has such a thing ever happened [b] since the day that the Israelites came up from the land of Egypt until this day? Consider it, take counsel, and speak out.' "

The Other Tribes Attack Benjamin

20 Then all the Israelites came out, from Dan to Beer-sheba, including the land of Gilead, and the congregation assembled in one body before the LORD at Mizpah. [2]The chiefs of all the people, of all the tribes of Israel, presented themselves in the assembly of the people of God, four hundred thou-

a Gk Compare 19.29. Heb *to the house of the LORD*
b Compare Gk: Heb [30]*And all who saw it said, "Such a thing has not happened or been seen*

20:1–48 *Then all the Israelites came out.* To put the best possible light on the Levite's behavior, he makes the crime committed by the men of Gibeah into a communal matter (vv 1–7). His motives, however, are suspect. For instance, his testimony (vv 4–7) omits any mention of his own complicity in his concubine's death, and readers know that the Levite showed no compassion for her at all. Furthermore, the dismemberment of her body is excessively brutal (cf. 1 Sam 11:6–11), leading readers to conclude that the Levite is more upset about being personally insulted than he is about the death of his concubine. The community's response is equally preposterous. Although the

Torah permits retribution, it suggests that the punishment should fit the crime—that is, no more than an eye for an eye or a tooth for a tooth (Exod 21:24). But here, the punishment is all out of proportion. Not only is Gibeah destroyed, but also the whole tribe of Benjamin is nearly wiped out. Everything is wrong, and the terrible lack of proportion belies the narrator's report that God "defeated Benjamin before Israel" (v 35). Rather, the excessively violent chaos is further evidence that everyone was doing "what was right in their own eyes" (17:6; 21:25); and it illustrates again the tragic results of disobedience.

sand foot-soldiers bearing arms. ³(Now the Benjaminites heard that the people of Israel had gone up to Mizpah.) And the Israelites said, "Tell us, how did this criminal act come about?" ⁴The Levite, the husband of the woman who was murdered, answered, "I came to Gibeah that belongs to Benjamin, I and my concubine, to spend the night. ⁵The lords of Gibeah rose up against me, and surrounded the house at night. They intended to kill me, and they raped my concubine until she died. ⁶Then I took my concubine and cut her into pieces, and sent her throughout the whole extent of Israel's territory; for they have committed a vile outrage in Israel. ⁷So now, you Israelites, all of you, give your advice and counsel here."

8 All the people got up as one, saying, "We will not any of us go to our tents, nor will any of us return to our houses. ⁹But now this is what we will do to Gibeah: we will go up*a* against it by lot. ¹⁰We will take ten men of a hundred throughout all the tribes of Israel, and a hundred of a thousand, and a thousand of ten thousand, to bring provisions for the troops, who are going to repay*b* Gibeah of Benjamin for all the disgrace that they have done in Israel." ¹¹So all the men of Israel gathered against the city, united as one.

12 The tribes of Israel sent men through all the tribe of Benjamin, saying, "What crime is this that has been committed among you? ¹³Now then, hand over those scoundrels in Gibeah, so that we may put them to death, and purge the evil from Israel." But the Benjaminites would not listen to their kinsfolk, the Israelites. ¹⁴The Benjaminites came together out of the towns to Gibeah, to go out to battle against the Israelites. ¹⁵On that day the Benjaminites mustered twenty-six thousand armed men from their towns, besides the inhabitants of Gibeah. ¹⁶Of all this force, there were seven hundred picked men who were left-handed; every one could sling a stone at a hair, and not miss. ¹⁷And the Israelites, apart from Benjamin, mustered four hundred thousand armed men, all of them warriors.

18 The Israelites proceeded to go up to Bethel, where they inquired of God, "Which of us shall go up first to battle against the Benjaminites?" And the LORD answered, "Judah shall go up first."

19 Then the Israelites got up in the morning, and encamped against Gibeah. ²⁰The Israelites went out to battle against Benjamin; and the Israelites drew up the battle line against them at Gibeah. ²¹The Benjaminites came out of Gibeah, and struck down on that day twenty-two thousand of the Israelites. ²³*c* The Israelites went up and wept before the LORD until the evening; and they inquired of the LORD, "Shall we again draw near to battle against our kinsfolk the Benjaminites?" And the LORD said, "Go up against them." ²²The Israelites took courage, and again formed the battle line in the same place where they had formed it on the first day.

24 So the Israelites advanced against the Benjaminites the second day. ²⁵Benjamin moved out against them from Gibeah the second day, and struck down eighteen thousand of the Israelites, all of them armed men. ²⁶Then all the Israelites, the whole army, went back to Bethel and wept, sitting there before the LORD; they fasted that day until evening. Then they offered burnt offerings and sacrifices of well-being before the LORD. ²⁷And the Israelites inquired of the LORD (for the ark of the covenant of God was there in those days, ²⁸and Phinehas son of Eleazar, son of Aaron, ministered before it in those days), saying, "Shall we go out once more to battle against our kinsfolk the Benjaminites, or shall we desist?" The LORD answered, "Go up, for tomorrow I will give them into your hand."

29 So Israel stationed men in ambush around Gibeah. ³⁰Then the Israelites went up against the Benjaminites on the third day, and set themselves in array against Gibeah, as before. ³¹When the Benjaminites went out against the army, they were drawn away from the city. As before they began to inflict casualties on the troops, along the main roads, one of which goes up to Bethel and the other to Gibeah, as well as in the open country, killing about thirty men of Israel. ³²The Benjaminites thought, "They are being routed

a Gk: Heb lacks *we will go up*   *b* Compare Gk: Meaning of Heb uncertain   *c* Verses 22 and 23 are transposed

before us, as previously." But the Israelites said, "Let us retreat and draw them away from the city toward the roads." 33The main body of the Israelites drew back its battle line to Baal-tamar, while those Israelites who were in ambush rushed out of their place west*a* of Geba. 34There came against Gibeah ten thousand picked men out of all Israel, and the battle was fierce. But the Benjaminites did not realize that disaster was close upon them.

35 The LORD defeated Benjamin before Israel; and the Israelites destroyed twenty-five thousand one hundred men of Benjamin that day, all of them armed.

36 Then the Benjaminites saw that they were defeated.*b*

The Israelites gave ground to Benjamin, because they trusted to the troops in ambush that they had stationed against Gibeah. 37The troops in ambush rushed quickly upon Gibeah. Then they put the whole city to the sword. 38Now the agreement between the main body of Israel and the men in ambush was that when they sent up a cloud of smoke out of the city 39the main body of Israel should turn in battle. But Benjamin had begun to inflict casualties on the Israelites, killing about thirty of them; so they thought, "Surely they are defeated before us, as in the first battle." 40But when the cloud, a column of smoke, began to rise out of the city, the Benjaminites looked behind them—and there was the whole city going up in smoke toward the sky! 41Then the main body of Israel turned, and the Benjaminites were dismayed, for they saw that disaster was close upon them. 42Therefore they turned away from the Israelites in the direction of the wilderness; but the battle overtook them, and those who came out of the city*c* were slaughtering them in between.*d* 43Cutting down*e* the Benjaminites, they pursued them from Nohah*f* and trod them down as far as a place east of Gibeah. 44Eighteen thousand Benjaminites fell, all of them courageous fighters. 45When they turned and fled toward the wilderness to the rock of Rimmon, five thousand of them were cut down on the main roads, and they were pursued as far as Gidom, and two thousand of them were slain. 46So all who fell that day of Benjamin were twenty-five thousand arms-bearing men, all of them courageous fighters. 47But six hundred turned and fled toward the wilderness to the rock of Rimmon, and remained at the rock of Rimmon for four months. 48Meanwhile, the Israelites turned back against the Benjaminites, and put them to the sword—the city, the people, the animals, and all that remained. Also the remaining towns they set on fire.

The Benjaminites Saved from Extinction

21 Now the Israelites had sworn at Mizpah, "No one of us shall give his daughter in marriage to Benjamin." 2And the people came to Bethel, and sat there until evening before God, and they lifted up their voices and wept bitterly. 3They said, "O LORD, the God of Israel, why has it come to pass that today there should be one tribe

a Gk Vg: Heb *in the plain*   b This sentence is continued by verse 45.   c Compare Vg and some Gk Mss: Heb *cities*   d Compare Syr: Meaning of Heb uncertain   e Gk: Heb *Surrounding*   f Gk: Heb *pursued them at their resting place*

21:1–25 *the people came . . . and sat there until evening before God.* Given the absurd series of events in chapters 17–20, it is no wonder the people are weeping (v 2; see note on 2:1–5). This seems to be a good sign, but the ridiculous question that follows in verse 3 suggests that the people still have no clue about what they have done or are doing. The people's compassion for the few surviving Benjaminites also seems to be a good sign (vv 5, 15); but rather than admit the foolishness of their own oath (v 1), the Israelites attempt to solve the current problem by adding even more violence to the excessive violence already perpetrated in chapter 20. The entire population of Jabesh-gilead is murdered, except for four hundred virgins, who are kidnapped as wives for the Benjaminites (vv 8–12). Again, ludicrous behavior is the order of the day. And to top it off, the people then sanction the abduction of innocent young women in order to avoid taking personal responsibility for their own foolishness (vv 15–24). All in all, things could hardly be more ludicrous, aptly demonstrating the

lacking in Israel?" 4On the next day, the people got up early, and built an altar there, and offered burnt offerings and sacrifices of well-being. 5Then the Israelites said, "Which of all the tribes of Israel did not come up in the assembly to the LORD?" For a solemn oath had been taken concerning whoever did not come up to the LORD to Mizpah, saying, "That one shall be put to death." 6But the Israelites had compassion for Benjamin their kin, and said, "One tribe is cut off from Israel this day. 7What shall we do for wives for those who are left, since we have sworn by the LORD that we will not give them any of our daughters as wives?"

8 Then they said, "Is there anyone from the tribes of Israel who did not come up to the LORD to Mizpah?" It turned out that no one from Jabesh-gilead had come to the camp, to the assembly. 9For when the roll was called among the people, not one of the inhabitants of Jabesh-gilead was there. 10So the congregation sent twelve thousand soldiers there and commanded them, "Go, put the inhabitants of Jabesh-gilead to the sword, including the women and the little ones. 11This is what you shall do; every male and every woman that has lain with a male you shall devote to destruction." 12And they found among the inhabitants of Jabesh-gilead four hundred young virgins who had never slept with a man and brought them to the camp at Shiloh, which is in the land of Canaan.

13 Then the whole congregation sent word to the Benjaminites who were at the rock of Rimmon, and proclaimed peace to them. 14Benjamin returned at that time; and they gave them the women whom they had saved alive of the women of Jabesh-gilead; but they did not suffice for them.

15 The people had compassion on Benjamin because the LORD had made a breach in the tribes of Israel. 16So the elders of the congregation said, "What shall we do for wives for those who are left, since there are no women left in Benjamin?" 17And they said, "There must be heirs for the survivors of Benjamin, in order that a tribe may not be blotted out from Israel. 18Yet we cannot give any of our daughters to them as wives." For the Israelites had sworn, "Cursed be anyone who gives a wife to Benjamin." 19So they said, "Look, the yearly festival of the LORD is taking place at Shiloh, which is north of Bethel, on the east of the highway that goes up from Bethel to Shechem, and south of Lebonah." 20And they instructed the Benjaminites, saying, "Go and lie in wait in the vineyards, 21and watch; when the young women of Shiloh come out to dance in the dances, then come out of the vineyards and each of you carry off a wife for himself from the young women of Shiloh, and go to the land of Benjamin. 22Then if their fathers or their brothers come to complain to us, we will say to them, 'Be generous and allow us to have them; because we did not capture in battle a wife for each man. But neither did you incur guilt by giving your daughters to them.' " 23The Benjaminites did so; they took wives for each of them from the dancers whom they abducted. Then they went and returned to their territory, and rebuilt the towns, and lived in them. 24So the Israelites departed from there at that time by tribes and families, and they went out from there to their own territories.

25 In those days there was no king in Israel; all the people did what was right in their own eyes. LED TO IDOLATRY & DISOBEDIENCE

MUST LIVE UNDER AUTHORITY

concluding assessment that everyone was doing "what was right in their own eyes" (v 25), as well as illustrating one final time the tragic consequences of idolatry and disobedience. By graphically portraying the violent and chaotic consequences of disobedience driven by self-centeredness, the final chapters of Judges serve as a timely and prophetic warning to a contemporary world in which self-centeredness reigns supreme.

Thus, Judges invites covenant loyalty in the form of the Spiritual Disciplines of worshiping and obeying God alone. Such worship and obedience are grounded in the amazing grace and unfailing love of a God who simply will not abandon people as incessantly idolatrous and frustratingly faithless as the Israelites prove to be in Judges. Despite the abysmal conclusion to Judges, the story will continue!

RUTH

The book of Ruth is one of two books of the Bible named after women; the other is Esther. The backdrop for the story of Ruth is the period of the Hebrew judges, an era marked by apostasy (such as when Israel worshiped the Baals, Judg 2:12), lawlessness (such as the fratricide of Gideon's household, Judg 9:5), and savagery (such as the gang rape and dismemberment of the Levite's concubine, Judg 19). By contrast, there are no murders and no villains in Ruth. Rather, the story portrays life in a peaceable village setting among hardworking agrarian peasants. Neither are there supranormal events in the story. The Spirit of God descends upon no one (compared to Judg 3:10; 6:34) and the angel of the Lord visits no one (Judg 6:11; 13:3). Instead, we see God working behind the scenes—a God of "coincidences" (see 2:1–3), accomplishing his purposes through ordinary people who overcome adversity by means of personal initiative, ingenuity, and acts of selfless devotion.

The story of Ruth the Moabite is another example of God making good on earlier promises to bless all the nations through the progeny of Abraham and Sarah (Gen 12:1–3). In keeping with God's flair for inverting conventions, the story of Ruth is also an illustration of the nations blessing Israel, as the Moabite widow is an ancestor of the great King David (Ruth 4:17) and ultimately Jesus, the Messiah (Matt 1:5).

The book of Ruth opens with the ominous words "there was a famine in the land" (1:1). Readers of the Bible are familiar with such reports of "natural disaster," because it was famine that drove Abraham into Egypt (Gen 12:10), forced Isaac to seek aid from the Philistines (Gen 26:1), and eventually compelled Jacob's entire clan to seek relief in Egypt (Gen 43:1; 47:4). The struggle for sheer physical survival during food shortages is one of the universal conflicts humanity faces in relationship to the natural environment, whether in biblical times or the modern era. The storyteller adds an element of suspense to the story by immediately introducing this type of plot conflict and, in so doing, sets the stage for the interplay between the work of God and the human response in the face of such natural disasters. As a result we encounter unlikely examples

---

See also *"The With-God Life" essay for this section of the Bible,*
"The People of God in the Promised Land," pp. 297–301.

of heroic faith in the lives of two peasant women, Naomi and Ruth. These women belong to that great "cloud of witnesses" who serve to encourage personal faith and instruct each new generation in "running the race" God has marked out (Heb 12:1–2).

Ruth in the Hebrew Bible

The story of Ruth's faithfulness serves as a foil to the faithlessness of the Hebrew people during the days of the judges. But the book offers an ironic twist, since it is a Moabite woman who pledges loyalty to Yahweh! In Jewish tradition the book of Ruth is included among the Five Megillah, or Festival Scrolls. Fittingly, the story of Ruth was read as a part of the ritual observed during the feast of Pentecost in later Judaism. This feast celebrated the spring wheat and barley harvests and was one of the three annual pilgrimage festivals in the Hebrew calendar established by Mosaic law (cf. Exod 23:14–17; Lev 23:15–22; Num 28:26–31; Deut 16:9–12). The book of Ruth follows Proverbs in the canonical order of the Hebrew Bible, so that the story provides an illustration of the noble woman commended in Prov 31:10–31.

The storyteller also assumes the audience is familiar with earlier Hebrew traditions. Three biblical texts are especially important to the background of the story of Ruth, namely, the account of Lot's incestuous relationship with his daughters (Gen 19:30–38), the seduction of Israelite men by Moabite women and the consequent lapse into idolatry at Baal-peor after the Hebrew exodus from Egypt (Num 25:1–3), and the exclusion of the Moabites from the assembly of Hebrew worship stipulated by Mosaic law (Deut 23:3–6).

The Story of Ruth

The genre or literary type of the book of Ruth is usually identified as a Hebrew "short story." The book contains all the ingredients of an engaging narrative. The plot is lively and suspenseful, utilizing both the test motif and various types of conflict. The development of the story line moves from a pathetic plot in which a character undergoes adversity through no particular personal fault to a comedic plot in which a character undergoes a change of fortune resulting in happiness. The exchange of extensive dialogue between believable characters as well as the use of symbolism and irony in the names of people and places further enhances the story. Even the setting of the action in a remote time and unfamiliar culture piques the imagination. For these reasons, "story" is a good vehicle for spiritual formation, because it invites listeners or readers to share some universal life experience with the characters portrayed in the narrative.

Ruth and Spiritual Formation

The book of Ruth introduces us to an "earthy spirituality"—earthy in that it deals with ordinary people coping with everyday life, and spirituality in that the characters of the story are alive to God. Life is messy, making theology untidy at times. This is especially true when it seems as if the Almighty has dealt bitterly with us (1:20–21). Recall the words of Jesus: "In this world you will have trouble. But take heart! I have overcome the world" (John 16:33, NIV). The story of Ruth shows us that God is able to undertake and make the necessary provisions to help those in "trouble" overcome their circumstances. In fact, the story of Ruth is one of a series of biblical sequels to the lesson Abraham and Isaac learned on Mt. Moriah—God is Jehovah Jireh, "the LORD will provide" (Gen 22:14). This is why Jesus is able to assure his followers that the heavenly Father is ever ready to provide for us in our daily troubles as we seek his kingdom and his righteousness (Matt 6:32–34).

At the same time, we learn that spiritual formation is our work too, as symbolized in Ruth's diligent daily gleaning of grain in the fields of Boaz (2:7). Ruth made a decision to stay with her mother-in-law, Naomi, and by an act of her will she chose to identify with Naomi's God, Yahweh, rather than the gods of her own people (1:16–17). The pattern of obedience seen in Ruth's life is embodied in the statement, "All that you tell me I will do" (3:5). Ruth's example of unswerving obedience is a model for the community of faith.

The plot of the story of Ruth turns on a number of unexpected reversals or twists of divine providence. The literary device of "reversal" is testimony to the reality that no work of divine restoration or spiritual formation is too difficult for God. God delights in showing mercy (Mic 7:18) and his "hand is not too short to save" (Isa 59:1). In the story of Ruth we are encouraged to learn that there are no "hopeless cases," because "for God all things are possible" (Matt 19:26). A childless widow, and moreover a foreigner, not only becomes a part of the Hebrew community of faith, but she finds her place in biblical history as one of the women listed in the genealogy of Jesus, the Messiah (Matt 1:5). Lest we forget, all this reveals that the Bible is not a record about "great people," but a record of people with a great God!

One tangible outcome of spiritual formation leading to maturity is reconciliation. Ruth belonged to a "cursed" people group (Deut 23:3–6), yet Boaz extends remarkable hospitality to this "foreign" woman (2:8–9). Ruth's surprise that a Hebrew would show such compassionate interest in a Moabite stems from the long-standing conflict between the two groups during the era of the judges (2:10; see also Judg 3:12–14, 30; 11:17). The transparency of her response to Boaz is refreshing and calls to mind the more self-serving query Jesus fielded from the lawyer seeking to justify himself, "And who is my neighbor?" (Luke 10:29). Part of our journey in Christian formation is identifying our "neighbors" and finding ways to respond to them with Christlike compassion. The common denominator of people as human beings made in God's image erases all the societal fences like gender, race, or social class that we sometimes erect to define our "neighbor." God shows no partiality (Rom 2:11; Eph 6:9); neither should we (James 2:1).

Finally, the story of Ruth exhorts us not to underestimate the value of simple acts of kindness or the profound impact that an individual faithful to God may have on the course of human events. Zechariah still beckons us not to despise the day of small things (Zech 4:10). Paul informs us that God still chooses to work through the lowly and despised things of this world so that he may receive the glory (1 Cor 1:28–29). When we attend to the hungry, the thirsty, the strangers, the naked, the sick, and those in prison, we serve Jesus as we minister to the needs of the "least" of his brothers and sisters (Matt 25:40–45).

—*Andrew E. Hill*

Elimelech's Family Goes to Moab

1 In the days when the judges ruled, there was a famine in the land, and a certain man of Bethlehem in Judah went to live in the country of Moab, he and his wife and two sons. ²The name of the man was Elimelech and the name of his wife Naomi, and the names of his two sons were Mahlon and Chilion; they were Ephrathites from Bethlehem in Judah. They went into the country of Moab and remained there. ³But Elimelech, the husband of Naomi, died, and she was left with her two sons. ⁴These took Moabite wives; the name of the one was Orpah and the name of the other Ruth. When they had lived there about ten years, ⁵both Mahlon and Chilion also died, so that the woman was left without her two sons and her husband.

Naomi and Her Moabite Daughters-in-Law

6 Then she started to return with her daughters-in-law from the country of Moab, for she had heard in the country of Moab that the LORD had considered his people and given them food. ⁷So she set out from the place where she had been living, she and her two daughters-in-law, and they went on their way to go back to the land of Judah. ⁸But Naomi said to her two daughters-in-law, "Go back each of you to your mother's house. May the LORD deal kindly with you, as you have dealt with the dead and with me. ⁹The LORD grant that you may find security, each of you in the house of your husband." Then she kissed them, and they wept aloud. ¹⁰They said to her, "No, we will return with you to your people." ¹¹But Naomi said, "Turn back, my daughters, why will you go with me? Do I still have sons in my womb that they may become your husbands? ¹²Turn back, my daughters, go your way, for I am too old to have a husband. Even if I thought there was hope for me, even if I should have a husband tonight and bear sons, ¹³would you then wait until they were grown? Would you then refrain from marrying? No, my daughters, it has been far more bitter for me than for you, because the hand of the LORD has turned against me." ¹⁴Then they wept aloud again. Orpah kissed her mother-in-law, but Ruth clung to her.

15 So she said, "See, your sister-in-law has gone back to her people and to her gods; return after your sister-in-law." ¹⁶But Ruth said,

---

1:1 *there was a famine in the land.* "Natural disasters" are often a means of testing to strengthen the faith of the People of God. After the exodus from Egypt the wilderness journey was a similar type of experience for the Hebrews, as God tested his people in order to discern what was in their hearts (Deut 8:2). The test was intended to expose the hearts of the Israelites—not for God's sake, but to show them their need for utter dependence upon the Lord. Naomi and Ruth passed their test! With the help of each other and the community of faithful relatives and friends surrounding them, they demonstrated unswerving loyalty to God in the midst of desperate, even tragic circumstances.

1:6 *the LORD had considered his people.* God is faithful to respond to his people when they are in need—"a very present help in trouble" (Ps 46:1). This divine aid to those in distress is rooted in God's goodness (Pss 68:10; 86:5). God's flawless record of showing goodness to his people instills confidence and motivates prayer for his help (Pss 69:16; 109:21; cf. Matt 6:32–33; 7:11).

1:8 *May the LORD deal kindly with you.* Naomi is formally releasing her daughters-in-law from any future responsibility toward her. She entrusts these women to God's care through her prayer, since she is unable to provide for them. Naomi understood that the Almighty is a God who does *hesed,* or shows merciful kindness, to all people (Exod 34:6–7; Ps 25:10). Despite her own distress, Naomi also recognized the need to look to the welfare of others (Phil 2:4). Her example reminds us that our hope is not misplaced when it is rooted in the kindness of God (Ps 145:17). She also models biblical humility in esteeming others more than herself (Phil 2:3).

1:13 *the hand of the LORD has turned against me.* God our Father has compassion on us because he knows we are dust (Ps 103:13–14). Although there may be times when God disciplines the children he loves (Ps 94:12; Prov 3:11; cf. Heb 12:6), like the psalmist we can rejoice that his anger lasts only for a moment, but his favor lasts for a lifetime (Ps 30:5).

RUTH

Losing One's Life

Selected Scriptures: *Ruth*

A Moabite, Ruth had married an Israelite living in her homeland. When he died, Ruth walked away from her Moabite heritage, her own mother and father, and the religious system she had learned from childhood. She gave up all she had known. Yet she never turned back or wavered in her decision: "Where you go, I will go; . . . your people shall be my people, and your God my God" (Ruth 1:16).

Ruth faced an unpromising future, which makes her resolve all the more remarkable. Still, Ruth joined Naomi in journeying to Bethlehem and, upon arriving, followed all of Naomi's instructions as the two sought their survival. Ruth didn't demand things go her way, but allowed God to guide her life through Naomi.

Ruth married Boaz, and their son, Obed, became the grandfather of King David and ancestor of Christ. *We* know the genealogy; Ruth did not. She knew only that God had called her to himself, and she pledged to follow his lead. Ruth followed in the steps of another relative by marriage: Rahab. A few hundred years earlier Rahab also had broken from her people to join the Israelites and give herself to God. Boaz descended from Rahab and perhaps because of his lineage possessed a greater measure of acceptance for a foreigner such as Ruth. Now Ruth, an outsider, would also share in God's plan to save all people.

Ruth lived out one of Jesus' essential teachings: that we must be willing to renounce family for the sake of Christ. Others have renounced portions of their own lives—their plans, rights, comfort, safety, heritage, or status—to follow God's lead without, perhaps, ever seeing the fruit of their sacrifice.

One Indian follower of Christ has left such a story. Sundar Singh was raised a Sikh and as a child studied the Sikh and Hindu sacred books intently. His mother died when he was a teenager, and he grieved to the point of suicide. Desperate to hear from God or end his life, he waited one night for a revelation. Christ came in a cloud of light, showing himself and saying, "I am the Way." After this conversion experience Sundar went on to travel the villages of India proclaiming the news of Christ.

Sundar had no home and no possessions. He chose to share in the suffering of his people. Yet he knew a joy that runs deeper than any outward condition of life: "I saw that in this world of sorrow and suffering there is a hidden and inexhaustible mine of great joy of which the world knows nothing" (*With and Without Christ*).

Ruth must have known this same joy. She gave up much, yet experienced Christ's truth that "those who lose their life for my sake will find it" (Matt 10:39).

Personal Reflection

- In what ways are you an outsider? How has God called you to stand apart from your heritage to follow him?
- Where might you struggle in releasing control to God? Your comfort? Safety? Finances? Your standing in your family or community?

PROFILE

"Do not press me to leave you
  or to turn back from following you!
Where you go, I will go;
  where you lodge, I will lodge;
your people shall be my people,
  and your God my God.
17 Where you die, I will die—
  there will I be buried.
May the Lord do thus and so to me,
  and more as well,
if even death parts me from you!"
18 When Naomi saw that she was determined
to go with her, she said no more to her.

19 So the two of them went on until they
came to Bethlehem. When they came to
Bethlehem, the whole town was stirred because of them; and the women said, "Is this
Naomi?" 20 She said to them,

"Call me no longer Naomi, *a*
  call me Mara, *b*
  for the Almighty *c* has dealt bitterly
    with me.
21 I went away full,
  but the Lord has brought me back
    empty;
why call me Naomi
  when the Lord has dealt harshly
    with *d* me,

and the Almighty *c* has brought
  calamity upon me?"

22 So Naomi returned together with Ruth
the Moabite, her daughter-in-law, who came
back with her from the country of Moab.
They came to Bethlehem at the beginning
of the barley harvest.

Ruth Meets Boaz

2 Now Naomi had a kinsman on her husband's side, a prominent rich man, of
the family of Elimelech, whose name was
Boaz. 2 And Ruth the Moabite said to Naomi,
"Let me go to the field and glean among the
ears of grain, behind someone in whose sight
I may find favor." She said to her, "Go, my
daughter." 3 So she went. She came and
gleaned in the field behind the reapers. As it
happened, she came to the part of the field belonging to Boaz, who was of the family of
Elimelech. 4 Just then Boaz came from Bethlehem. He said to the reapers, "The Lord be
with you." They answered, "The Lord bless
you." 5 Then Boaz said to his servant who was
in charge of the reapers, "To whom does this

---

a That is *Pleasant*   *b* That is *Bitter*
c Traditional rendering of Heb *Shaddai*
d Or *has testified against*

1:16 *your God [shall be] my God.* Ruth's vow
of loyalty to Naomi and the Hebrew God is
certainly a countercultural decision by this
Moabite widow. She willingly exchanges her
ethnic and religious heritage for the people,
culture, and religion of Naomi. What an ironic
twist of sentiments, after Naomi just lamented
the impact of God's cruel hand in her life (v 13).
Our oath of allegiance to God runs counter to
our culture of narcissism. Part of the mystery of
the gospel is the fact that only by losing our life
are we able to find it (Matt 10:39; Mark 8:35;
Luke 17:33).

1:21 *the Almighty has brought calamity upon
me.* One should not be quick to judge another's
adverse circumstances as evidence of divine
punishment (Job 11:13–15; cf. Luke 13:4; John
9:3). The world is "crooked" according to
Hebrew wisdom tradition, and the ill effects of
collective human behavior produce ripples,
even shock waves, in human societies, so that
occasionally events of "time and chance"

happen to all those living life "under the sun"
(Eccl 1:15; 9:11). Like Joseph, the People of God
know that in his providence God overcomes
such events and overturns evil for good in the
lives of the faithful (Gen 50:20). So too Naomi's
bitterness is later turned into joy (4:15).

2:4 *the Lord be with you.* Boaz's statement to
the workers in the field goes beyond the simple
shalom ("peace [to you]") normally used by the
Israelites as their common greeting (e.g., Judg
6:23; 1 Sam 25:6). The formulaic expression is
both a greeting and a blessing, perhaps a special
form of salutation associated with agricultural
seasons like the harvest. The greeting is a
reminder that "death and life are in the power of
the tongue" (Prov 18:21). Our speech is crucial
to the spiritual formation of others as well,
because the words of the wise have the capacity
to both cheer and heal (Prov 12:18, 25). All this
makes the Spiritual Discipline of managing the
tongue vital to spiritual formation; otherwise our
"religion is worthless" (James 1:26).

young woman belong?" 6The servant who was in charge of the reapers answered, "She is the Moabite who came back with Naomi from the country of Moab. 7She said, 'Please, let me glean and gather among the sheaves behind the reapers.' So she came, and she has been on her feet from early this morning until now, without resting even for a moment." a

8 Then Boaz said to Ruth, "Now listen, my daughter, do not go to glean in another field or leave this one, but keep close to my young women. 9Keep your eyes on the field that is being reaped, and follow behind them. I have ordered the young men not to bother you. If you get thirsty, go to the vessels and drink from what the young men have drawn." 10Then she fell prostrate, with her face to the ground, and said to him, "Why have I found favor in your sight, that you should take notice of me, when I am a foreigner?" 11But Boaz answered her, "All that you have done for your mother-in-law since the death of your husband has been fully told me, and how you left your father and mother and your native land and came to a people that you did not know before. 12May the LORD reward you for your deeds, and may you have a full reward from the LORD, the God of Israel, under whose wings you have come for refuge!" 13Then she said, "May I continue to find favor in your sight, my lord, for you have comforted me and spoken kindly to your servant, even though I am not one of your servants."

14 At mealtime Boaz said to her, "Come here, and eat some of this bread, and dip your morsel in the sour wine." So she sat beside the reapers, and he heaped up for her some parched grain. She ate until she was satisfied, and she had some left over. 15When she got up to glean, Boaz instructed his young men, "Let her glean even among the standing sheaves, and do not reproach her. 16You must also pull out some handfuls for her from the bundles, and leave them for her to glean, and do not rebuke her."

17 So she gleaned in the field until evening. Then she beat out what she had gleaned, and it was about an ephah of barley. 18She picked it up and came into the town, and her mother-in-law saw how much she had gleaned. Then she took out and gave her what was left over after she herself had been satisfied. 19Her mother-in-law said to her, "Where did you glean today? And where have you worked? Blessed be the man who took notice of you." So she told her mother-in-law with whom she had worked, and said, "The name of the man with whom I worked today is Boaz." 20Then Naomi said to her daughter-in-law, "Blessed be he by the LORD, whose kindness has not forsaken the living or the dead!" Naomi also said to her, "The man is a relative of ours, one of our nearest kin." b 21Then Ruth the Moabite said, "He even said to me, 'Stay close by my servants, until they

a Compare Gk Vg: Meaning of Heb uncertain
b Or one with the right to redeem

2:10 *that you should take notice of me, when I am a foreigner.* Ruth's words and posture ("face to the ground") in response to the generosity of Boaz are indicators of the social distance between the Israelite man and the Moabite woman. Ruth identifies herself as a "foreigner" (*nokri*), a person of lesser status than that of the "sojourner" or "resident alien" (*ger*) in Hebrew social structure. The "foreigner" was an outsider to Israelite culture and religion and was denied covenant privileges extended to the other socially disadvantaged classes like widows, orphans, and aliens (e.g., Deut 14:21; 15:3; cf. Exod 22:22; Deut 10:18). The kindness of Boaz, like God's justice, shows no partiality (2 Chron 19:7; cf. James 2:1). Boaz helps us understand the "second great commandment": loving our neighbor as we love ourselves (Matt 22:39).

Responding
2:11–16 SERVICE. Boaz praises Ruth for her service to her mother-in-law and rewards that service with food and the privilege to harvest uncut grain. Why should we serve other people? Examine your motivations for serving. Are you helping people because you love them or because you expect praise or a reward? During the next month make a special effort to concentrate on doing works of service as an expression of your love for the people you are serving, not because you expect something in return. *See also* Spiritual Disciplines Index.

have finished all my harvest.' " 22Naomi said to Ruth, her daughter-in-law, "It is better, my daughter, that you go out with his young women, otherwise you might be bothered in another field." 23So she stayed close to the young women of Boaz, gleaning until the end of the barley and wheat harvests; and she lived with her mother-in-law.

Ruth and Boaz at the Threshing Floor

3 Naomi her mother-in-law said to her, "My daughter, I need to seek some security for you, so that it may be well with you. 2Now here is our kinsman Boaz, with whose young women you have been working. See, he is winnowing barley tonight at the threshing floor. 3Now wash and anoint yourself, and put on your best clothes and go down to the threshing floor; but do not make yourself known to the man until he has finished eating and drinking. 4When he lies down, observe the place where he lies; then,

go and uncover his feet and lie down; and he will tell you what to do." 5She said to her, "All that you tell me I will do."

6 So she went down to the threshing floor and did just as her mother-in-law had instructed her. 7When Boaz had eaten and drunk, and he was in a contented mood, he went to lie down at the end of the heap of grain. Then she came stealthily and uncovered his feet, and lay down. 8At midnight the man was startled, and turned over, and there, lying at his feet, was a woman! 9He said, "Who are you?" And she answered, "I am Ruth, your servant; spread your cloak over your servant, for you are next-of-kin." a 10He said, "May you be blessed by the LORD, my daughter; this last instance of your loyalty is better than the first; you have not gone after young men, whether poor or rich. 11And now, my daughter, do not be afraid, I will do for

a Or one with the right to redeem

2:20 whose kindness has not forsaken the living or the dead As "kinsman-redeemer" to Naomi and Ruth, Boaz modeled the "true fasting" that the prophet Isaiah called Israel to observe—sharing food with hungry and helping relatives in their time of need (Isa 58:7). There is a need today for "kinsman-redeemers" to come to the aid of their relatives, whether they are neglected children, the sick and infirm, or the forgotten elderly.

2:23 gleaning until the end of the barley and wheat harvests. Ruth industriously gleaned in the fields each day through the harvest season to provide "daily bread" for herself and Naomi. Naturally, such a work ethic encourages us to avoid idleness and to earn a living by working quietly as unto the Lord in all things (1 Thess 2:9,12; cf. Col 3:23). The work of spiritual formation is no less demanding, though, fortunately, we are not alone on this journey, but aided and accompanied by the Holy Spirit and the community of faith.

3:5 All that you tell me I will do. The provocative threshing floor scene is another illustration of the storyteller's skill in piquing audience interest in the everyday lives of ordinary characters (3:1–4). Naomi's counsel to her daughter-in-law to "uncover his feet" after Boaz had retired for the night has overtones of

sexual intimacy, since "feet" can also be a sexual euphemism (3:4; cf. Exod 4:25; Isa 7:20). The larger context of the encounter suggests that the relationship between the two was honorable according to the customs of the time. The scene is an important reminder that spiritual formation takes place within a cultural setting—faith in God and life in the world are not meant to be mutually exclusive concepts. Quite apart from the issues of culture and sexuality, Ruth's submission to the advice of Naomi teaches us that our spiritual formation is rooted in a posture of obedience. This response of obedience to the commands of God is one of the injunctions that bridges the Old and New Testaments (Deut 30:2, 8, 11, 16, 20; 1 John 2:3, 5; 3:24; 5:2).

3:10 May you be blessed by the Lord. Boaz responds with praise to Ruth's example of self-sacrificing loyalty to Naomi, Naomi's people, and the God of the Hebrews. Boaz also rightly recognizes God as the source of blessing, a truth established at creation (Gen 1:22). The new covenant affirms the practice of recognizing Christian virtues in others with a blessing (cf. Matt 5:3–11). Jesus calls his disciples to extend the word of divine blessing even to those who may persecute and curse Christians (Luke 6:28; cf. Rom 12:14).

you all that you ask, for all the assembly of my people know that you are a worthy woman. 12But now, though it is true that I am a near kinsman, there is another kinsman more closely related than I. 13Remain this night, and in the morning, if he will act as next-of-kin*a* for you, good; let him do it. If he is not willing to act as next-of-kin*a* for you, then, as the LORD lives, I will act as next-of-kin*a* for you. Lie down until the morning."

14 So she lay at his feet until morning, but got up before one person could recognize another; for he said, "It must not be known that the woman came to the threshing floor." 15Then he said, "Bring the cloak you are wearing and hold it out." So she held it, and he measured out six measures of barley, and put it on her back; then he went into the city. 16She came to her mother-in-law, who said, "How did things go with you,*b* my daughter?" Then she told her all that the man had done for her, 17saying, "He gave me these six measures of barley, for he said, 'Do not go back to your mother-in-law empty-handed.' " 18She replied, "Wait, my daughter, until you learn how the matter turns out, for the man will not rest, but will settle the matter today."

The Marriage of Boaz and Ruth

4 No sooner had Boaz gone up to the gate and sat down there than the next-of-kin,*a* of whom Boaz had spoken, came passing by. So Boaz said, "Come over, friend; sit down here." And he went over and sat down. 2Then Boaz took ten men of the elders of the city, and said, "Sit down here"; so they sat down. 3He then said to the next-of-kin,*a* "Naomi, who has come back from the country of Moab, is selling the parcel of land that belonged to our kinsman Elimelech. 4So I thought I would tell you of it, and say: Buy it in the presence of those sitting here, and in the presence of the elders of my people. If you will redeem it, redeem it; but if you will not, tell me, so that I may know; for there is no one prior to you to redeem it, and I come after you." So he said, "I will redeem it." 5Then Boaz said, "The day you acquire the field from the hand of Naomi, you are also acquiring Ruth*c* the Moabite, the widow of the dead man, to maintain the dead man's name on his inheritance." 6At this, the next-

a Or *one with the right to redeem*   *b* Or *"Who are you,*   *c* OL Vg: Heb *from the hand of Naomi and from Ruth*

3:11 *you are a worthy woman.* Ruth is deemed a worthy woman because of her faith in the Hebrew God and because of her loyalty to her mother-in-law, Naomi. This loyalty was demonstrated in her daily labor in the fields and her acts of kindness, those "good works" that Jesus said brings praise to our Father in heaven (Matt 5:16).

3:13 *as the LORD lives.* This expression is associated with the oath formula in the Old Testament (e.g., Judg 8:19; 1 Kings 18:15). Oath taking and vow making were important in the biblical world as means of strengthening one's intention to keep a promise. Only a living God can hold us accountable to our vows—only by the divine surveillance of a living God will people be liable at the day of judgment for the words they have spoken (Matt 12:37). This is why Jesus instructs his disciples to let a simple yes or no be enough said (Matt 5:37).

4:5 *Ruth the Moabite, the widow.* The Hebrew community of faith was obligated by the stipulations of the Mosaic covenant to practice justice toward the disadvantaged in society—the poor, widows, orphans, resident aliens (Exod 22:22; Deut 24:14–22). The Christian community of faith shoulders a similar responsibility, since the "royal law" of the new covenant in Christ calls us to love our neighbors as ourselves (James 2:8; cf. 1 Tim 5:3–8). Such care for the socially disadvantaged is "religion that is pure and undefiled before God" (James 1:27).

Responding
4:5 SACRIFICE. Connect, for the moment, the Mosaic law in which a male next-of-kin marries a widow to secure an inheritance for the dead husband (Deut 25:5–10) to that of the command of Christ to "love your neighbor as yourself" (Matt 22:39). What sacrifices would the brother of a dead man have to make to marry his widow? What sacrifices do we have to make to love our neighbor? How similar are they? *See also* Spiritual Disciplines Index.

of-kin [a] said, "I cannot redeem it for myself without damaging my own inheritance. Take my right of redemption yourself, for I cannot redeem it."

7 Now this was the custom in former times in Israel concerning redeeming and exchanging: to confirm a transaction, the one took off a sandal and gave it to the other; this was the manner of attesting in Israel. [8]So when the next-of-kin [a] said to Boaz, "Acquire it for yourself," he took off his sandal. [9]Then Boaz said to the elders and all the people, "Today you are witnesses that I have acquired from the hand of Naomi all that belonged to Elimelech and all that belonged to Chilion and Mahlon. [10]I have also acquired Ruth the Moabite, the wife of Mahlon, to be my wife, to maintain the dead man's name on his inheritance, in order that the name of the dead may not be cut off from his kindred and from the gate of his native place; today you are witnesses." [11]Then all the people who were at the gate, along with the elders, said, "We are witnesses. May the LORD make the woman who is coming into your house like Rachel and Leah, who together built up the house of Israel. May you produce children in Ephrathah and bestow a name in Bethlehem; [12]and, through the children that the LORD

will give you by this young woman, may your house be like the house of Perez, whom Tamar bore to Judah."

The Genealogy of David

13 So Boaz took Ruth and she became his wife. When they came together, the LORD made her conceive, and she bore a son. [14]Then the women said to Naomi, "Blessed be the LORD, who has not left you this day without next-of-kin; [a] and may his name be renowned in Israel! [15]He shall be to you a restorer of life and a nourisher of your old age; for your daughter-in-law who loves you, who is more to you than seven sons, has borne him." [16]Then Naomi took the child and laid him in her bosom, and became his nurse. [17]The women of the neighborhood gave him a name, saying, "A son has been born to Naomi." They named him Obed; he became the father of Jesse, the father of David.

18 Now these are the descendants of Perez: Perez became the father of Hezron, [19]Hezron of Ram, Ram of Amminadab, [20]Amminadab of Nahshon, Nahshon of Salmon, [21]Salmon of Boaz, Boaz of Obed, [22]Obed of Jesse, and Jesse of David.

a Or one with the right to redeem

4:11 _bestow a name._ A name tells an individual's "story," just like the name "Ruth" relates a marvelous biblical story of faith in God. An important dimension of the fellowship that characterizes the People of God is the sharing of personal stories, testimonies of God's goodness and faithfulness in the lives of his people. This is why John the Elder encourages us to greet friends "each by name"—and in so doing discover their "story" (3 John 15).

4:12 _the children that the LORD will give you._ The Psalms celebrate children as a heritage from the Lord (Pss 127:4; 128:3). God's first

promise to rebellious humanity also concerned a child, the offspring of the woman who would set all things right (Gen 3:15). The wise reflection of Margaret Rauch, a godly Christian woman, is worthy of repeating: "Some trees produce fruit and others provide shade." God's people need both of these types of "trees." Godly mothers who raise their children in the nurture and admonition of the Lord (e.g., 2 Tim 1:5) and godly women who provide all manner of "shade" for people, young and old, both inside and outside of the community of faith, are vital to spiritual formation.

V. The People of God as a Nation

Scriptures: *1 Samuel 13–31 & 2 Samuel, 1 & 2 Kings, 1 & 2 Chronicles*

Deuterocanonical Books: *1 Esdras 1*

> *The aim of God in history is the creation of an all-inclusive community of loving persons with God himself at the very center of this community as its prime Sustainer and most glorious Inhabitant (Eph 2:19–22; 3:10). The Bible traces the formation of this community from the creation in the Garden of Eden all the way to the new heaven and the new earth. Come, join us as we explore the many dimensions of this with-God history—from individual to family to tribe to people to nation to all humanity—and apply what we learn to our own spiritual formation.*

In the Scriptures listed above we will see the ways God continues to form an all-inclusive community through the formation of the People of God as a nation with the central locus of worship in the Temple at Jerusalem.

God's Action

After the tumultuous period of the judges, God acts to create new institutions and new ways of being with his people. The Israelites are increasingly determined to have a monarchy, with a king, like the nations surrounding them. What seems a clear solution to the people is itself a rejection of the kingship of God. Rejecting the theocracy mediated through the judges, the people are determined to become a nation with a king, even if the odds are against its success. Divine permission thus allows a loose tribal federation to become a nation.

Here we see God working to nurture his people toward maturity amid vying conditions of human freedom. It is not beneath God's dignity to get involved in ordinary history and national politics. God is willing to work concretely through the entangled political, military, and social structures of primitive nation building. He permits the monarchy on the condition that the covenant promise is reaffirmed: Israel is called to be a holy people. This covenant renewal is made more explicit when God permits the construction of a central holy place, the Temple, where the people come into the active presence of God when they make sacrifices and gather during seasonal celebrations.

The decisive transitional figure during the shift from a tribal confederacy to a monarchy is Samuel. Promised to the service of God before his birth, Samuel is called to prophetic leadership by the Lord, who speaks to him directly while he serves as an intern under the judge and priest Eli at Shiloh. As we have seen, during the time of the judges, the twelve tribes form a loose confederation with separate tribal identities and minimal unity or cohesion. When the people ask for a king to govern them so that they can be like the nations around them, Samuel is displeased by their request, because he still views God as king of Israel over them (1 Sam 8:5, 19–20). He subsequently prays to the Lord, who responds to him, "Listen to the voice of the people in all that they say to you; for they have not rejected you, but they have rejected me from being king over them" (8:7). He then instructs Samuel to warn the people about what to expect under the rule of a king. Samuel obeys, but the people refuse to listen and repeat their demand. Going back before God, Samuel repeats the people's demand, to which God replies, "Listen to their voice and set a king over them" (8:22). When Samuel anoints Saul as king, Israel makes the transition from a theocracy to a monarchy.

In choosing Saul, God is working through an unknown young man from the smallest and most marginalized of the twelve tribes (Benjamin, the youngest son of Jacob). Saul has no political or military qualifications, but is merely a tall and handsome innocent in search of his wealthy father's lost donkeys. Not particularly blessed with the charisma of the judges or the prophetic insight of Samuel, he nevertheless proves to be an effective military leader in a time of increasing Philistine incursions. But without the charisma and insight marking the character of previous leaders, Saul seems destined for disobedience, resulting in waning popularity, declining power, and his family's ultimate loss of the throne.

The central figure in the period of the monarchy is without question David. Anointed by Samuel into the service of Saul, David is blessed by God with amazing military successes, beginning with his youthful victory over the giant Goliath. As David's influence grows, the people trust him, but Saul becomes angry and jealous. Yet David remains faithful to Saul until his death, despite Saul's paranoid misperceptions. After many often-bloody skirmishes with Saul's heirs, David finally ascends to the throne of Israel. Throughout his forty-year reign, David shows a strong sense of God's aim in establishing the monarchy, never losing the understanding that the kingdom ultimately belongs only to God (1 Chron 29:10–20). Although David is never perfect, plagued by his own character flaws and tragic losses, his clear sense of God's aim still allows him to usher in what will always after be seen as a golden age for Israel.

David's son Solomon brings the glory of this golden age to fruition. Describing himself as "only a little child" when he becomes king (1 Kings 3:7), Solomon presides over the true unification of the tribes into one nation, bringing prosperity to the people, defending them against enemies, and ensuring the promise of an eternal future for David's heirs. During Solomon's reign God at last gives Israel a national identity and raises it into its full glory, with Jerusalem as the center of government, the site of Solomon's majestic Temple, and the location of the king's residence.

Human Reaction

Against Samuel's prophetic counsel, the Israelites demand a king—and get one. In the period of the judges, when the Israelites were new to the land, they had been content to be led by people with special anointing from God. But as time passed and their neighbors who had kings oppressed them, the prospect of a leader who could muster a standing army to protect their borders became more appealing. Now they become like their neighbors and install a king who not only leads their armies, but declares to them his rights and duties as set forth by Samuel with God's direction (1 Sam 10:25). The old freedom from rules and regulations emanating from a central bureaucratic authority is past. They trade tribal independence for national security.

The Israelites love this time of relative peace, security, and prosperity and as a result come to idolize the monarchy. They live in a time when it is common for rulers to declare themselves gods and erect huge monuments testifying to their own greatness. In fact, these very practices were part of the Egyptian culture in which they had been enslaved. Once unthinkable, it is now natural for them to place themselves under a monarch's authority without a quibble. The king maintains treasuries to support the royal household established by David. Solomon conscripts forced labor from among the citizenry to build the Temple. In the royal household he supports scores of wives and concubines with monies collected from the populace. Much of the wealth of the nation flows into Jerusalem to support the monarchy and to build and decorate the Temple. And there is no record that the people object to any of the actions of the king.

Along with willingly placing themselves under the authority of a monarchy, the Israelites give the kings unlimited and uncontrolled power. And the kings constantly abuse it: "Solomon gathered together chariots and horses; . . . decided to build a temple for the name of the LORD, and a royal palace for himself. Solomon conscripted seventy thousand laborers and eighty thousand stonecutters" (2 Chron 1:14–2:2). And then later, Jeroboam "took counsel, and made two calves of gold" (1 Kings 12:28). And Ahab "took as his wife Jezebel daughter of King Ethbaal of the Sidonians, and went and served Baal, and worshiped him" (1 Kings 16:31). The Israelites truly learn what it means to be ruled by a human king.

Blessings and Benefits for Our Formation

Under the monarchy the narrowness and belligerency of defensive tribalism is gradually curbed and transcended. Once a king is installed, the infighting between the twelve tribes decreases as they unite to fight common enemies: the Philistines, Ammonites, and Amalekites. But the blessings of God upon the kings were not as great as they might have been. There is still infighting, this time between different groups who are in positions of power within the monarchy or who want to overthrow the king. Remnants of tribal discord from the time of the judges often disrupt the monarchy as these elements vie for political favor, disrupting the peace and security of the people.

Nevertheless, because God was willing to modify his theocratic rule by allowing the concentration of power in the office of an earthly king, new benefits for the formation of the People of God emerge. The foremost of these blessings is the establishment of enduring institutions, such as the great Temple, where the religious life

The With-God Life

and spiritual practices of the people will reach new depths of meaning and impact in daily life. This state-supported and permanent place of worship in Jerusalem protects the vulnerable ark of the covenant, which had previously been housed in the temporary tent of meeting. Before the installation of Saul as king, the Philistines had captured the ark of the covenant from the tent of meeting (1 Sam 4:17), and this is the last mention of the tabernacle in the biblical record. We know that the ark is returned by the Philistines and is shifted from site to site over the years. In fact, it is used much like a good-luck charm when it precedes the Israelites as they go into battle. Once the internal dissension between factions within the monarchy is settled during David's reign, he brings the ark to Jerusalem and pitches a tent for it (2 Sam 6:12). Then he makes preparations for building the Temple, but is not himself authorized by God to build it. Rather, he charges his son Solomon to build a house for the Lord (1 Chron 22:2–16).

Upon David's death Solomon ascends to the throne. Blessed with extraordinary wisdom, he overcomes opposition to his reign and makes alliances with foreign adversaries. A resplendent Temple, unsurpassed in beauty, is erected under his direction. At the dedication of the Temple, Solomon reminds the people of their covenant relationship with God and prays for God's blessing. Solomon's Temple, now the center of worship and celebration for the people of Israel, provides a visible anchor for their faith and an enduring physical space for the disciplines of spiritual formation that had developed since the establishment of the tent of meeting at Shiloh.

With the development of this grand physical space for the spiritual formation of a people comes the flowering of the ancient levitical institutions—priests, musicians, gatekeepers, treasurers, officers, and judges. After the completion of the Temple, the Levites preside over the sacrificial rituals and seasonal celebrations. The permanent building provides the continuity needed to develop songs and liturgies that enhance the Israelites' worship experience. Imagine walking up several flights of steps to bring sacrifices to the priests, who then kill the animals and place them upon the huge altar while trumpets blare and choirs sing. The rituals we participate in while worshiping in the great cathedrals throughout the world might be comparable. There is something in this type of worship that lifts our spirit and gives us a glimpse into what our worship of God can and should be.

Limits and Liabilities for Our Formation

Pride, shortsightedness, and lack of gratitude limit the spiritual formation of the People of God during the monarchy, but the worship of other gods is still their most consistent failure. In spite of the warning that the Israelites would be cut off from the land and cast from God's sight if they served and worshiped other gods, there is still evidence that the people and even Solomon ignore the warning (1 Sam 19:13–16; 1 Kings 11:4–8). In the abundance and relative peace of this golden age of national unity, the human capacity for idolatry and neglect of the source of all blessings stubbornly shines through. We struggle with the very same problems in our own day. We may not worship statues of gold shaped like animals or ourselves,

The With-God Life

but we most certainly find many other things besides God to rely upon—our 401(k), our profession, education, marriage, physical appearance, and the like. For the sake of our spirit, we need to bring them all to God as a sacrifice of praise, much as the faithful did in Solomon's great Temple.

The monarchy itself, like all good things, becomes a new source of temptation to idolatry, pride, and sensuality without consistent responsibility to God. In spite of being a magnificent leader, memorable musician, and brilliant songwriter, David commits adultery and arranges the death of a loyal soldier. When the prophet Nathan confronts David with his sin, he repents, but the effects ripple throughout his entire household and dynasty. David's humility in belatedly accepting responsibility before God for his actions fulfills Samuel's prophecy that he was "a man after [God's] own heart" (1 Sam 13:14). However, most of the kings who follow in David's footsteps and the people of Israel themselves take the easy way out and fail to take responsibility for their own actions before God, thus manifesting their lack of character.

During the monarchy, the priesthood attains elevated status in the Temple, but at the same time becomes subservient to the whims of the king. It is the king who designs the Temple, assigns duties to the families within the Levites, composes the songs, and determines the liturgies. This illustrates the dangers inherent in human government dictating matters of faith.

Insights and Instructions for Our Formation

First, although we can see clearly that a strong national presence is needed to maintain peace and promote justice, it is not an answer in itself to the fundamental human problem of character development. Today we see many examples of this insight all around us. Like Israel during the monarchy, in our day the United States is rich and powerful, but its citizenry is mired in a moral crisis. Prosperity and political might do not build character. In fact, they often militate against it. Power also tends to work against the development of character, because it may make us feel we can solve anything through the use of coercion or force. Trusting God alone and his provision, by contrast, develops character. This was something the young David exemplified but later lost to the temptations of his God-given office.

Second, we see that a unified and well-defined system of law and religion does not guarantee that people will be faithful to God. The Israelites had access to Mosaic law and ordered worship for hundreds of years, but with the passage of time their memories faded and their affections were drawn toward other gods, guaranteeing suffering and social disorder. We observe similar situations today in the West, where Christianity is so ingrained that people forget that their culture is built upon biblical teaching and principles. In western Europe a mere 2–5 percent of the population attend church, and social problems such as drug abuse and crime abound. Only spiritual sensitivity to the desires of God guarantees faithfulness to his ways.

Third, we learn again that obedience to God is a key component in the spiritual life, as we have seen in the lives of Abraham, Isaac, Jacob, Joseph, Moses, Joshua,

The With-God Life

Ruth, and Samuel. In this new era of the monarch and centralized political power, King Saul broke this pattern of following the guidance of God by offering unlawful sacrifice, making a rash oath, sparing the lives of enemies, and consulting with mediums—all in direct contradiction to what he was supposed to do. Solomon loved and married many foreign women in defiance of the Lord's instructions: "You shall not enter into marriage with them, neither shall they with you; for they will surely incline your heart to follow their gods" (1 Kings 11:1–2). As a result, God tears the kingdom from his descendants and divides the Israelites into two nations—Israel and Judah—and the divine kingship established by God through Saul, David, and Solomon turns into reigns by rulers who are on a level playing field with the kings of the nations surrounding them.

Since monarchies are so foreign to our modern way of thinking, we may struggle to understand how such a political system was used by God to continue the ongoing formation of his people. But we must recall that God's intention is to be present on the world stage through his people and their governments, however flawed. As we persevere in our study, we will see how these Scriptures are central to God's eternal plan to form an all-inclusive community.

The With-God Life

1 SAMUEL

Composed by an unknown author or authors sometime in or around the exile (ca. 600–500 BC), 1 & 2 Samuel narrate the transitional period between the tribal confederation and the monarchy in the life of the People of God. Although Samuel is divided in English Bibles into two separate works, this is an artificial distinction that may have more to do with scroll length than anything else. This is indicated by the oldest manuscript of Samuel that we currently have, found at Qumran in the collection known as the Dead Sea Scrolls, as well as by the Masoretic text of the Hebrew, which marks 1 Sam 28:24 as the midpoint of the book of Samuel.

The books of 1 & 2 Samuel, along with Joshua, Judges, and 1 & 2 Kings, are part of a larger section of the Old Testament that scholars call the Deuteronomistic History. The name derives from the relation of these "historical books" to Deuteronomy, the last of the five "books of Moses," in which Moses preaches his last sermon to the Israelites right before he dies and before they cross the Jordan River into the Land of Promise. Deuteronomy is an expanded reworking of the Sinai covenant made by God with Israel immediately upon leaving Egypt (Exod 20–23). In that first giving of the covenant, there were no conditions (such as "Do not steal," "Do not covet"), simply directives Israel was to follow. The Deuteronomistic legislation, however, is much different in this regard. Here there are clear conditions placed on the community's observance of God's Torah (law). If the Israelites followed the Torah and heeded all of God's decrees, commandments, and statutes, they were promised fertility, safety, and comfort (cf., e.g., Deut 28:1–14; 29:11–16). By contrast, if they failed to do what God had enjoined and disobeyed what God had directed, then severe judgment would be rendered upon them, which would result in death, destruction, and displacement in exile (Deut 28:15–68). Even the ground beneath Israel's feet would refuse to yield if Israel lived outside the boundaries of covenant.

As it turned out, Israel did not do what Deuteronomy commanded, and thus the

---

See also *"The With-God Life" essays for this section of the Bible, "The People of God in the Promised Land," pp. 297–301, and "The People of God as a Nation," pp. 391–96.*

Deuteronomistic History presents the flowering and then the unraveling of Israel's status as an independent nation. The book of 1 Samuel thus becomes part of this larger tale of success and failure.

Hannah's Faith

The book begins with a poignant account of a barren woman, a story line that has a long history in the biblical narrative (Gen 18; Judg 13). Hannah does not give in to either the circumstances of her childlessness or her fertile rival, Peninnah, who mocks her condition (1:6). Hannah makes a vow to give any child born back to God for service in the local shrine, and so the Lord opens her womb. Here the story line of the barren woman intersects with another literary staple from antiquity, namely, the miraculous birth of a mighty figure (cf., e.g., the birth of Moses or of the great Assyrian military leader Sargon), for the child that is born to Hannah and delivered dutifully to the shrine does not wander off into an obscure life of religious obligation, but instead develops into the last and greatest of the judges of Israel, Samuel.

Hannah's prayer in chapter 2 is one of the great biblical texts pointing to the reversal of fortunes for those whose lives have been lived on the margin. Those who have been left out will have a place at the table, while those who have long feasted will be sent away. This sort of rhetoric will later become an essential feature of the biblical prophets, who speak of God's siding with those most in socioeconomic and political distress (Amos 9:11–15; Isa 61:1–4; 62:1–5; Mic 4:6–13), as well as find a place in the teachings of Jesus (e.g., the Sermon on the Mount in Matt 5).

The Last Judge

The story of Samuel is artfully woven around the story of the ark of the covenant. When the ark is lost to the Philistines, Israel is faced with an unprecedented theological, political, and military crisis. Samuel's "call story" in chapter 3 accomplishes several purposes. First, it shows the faith of the boy, who, like his godly mother, seeks for and listens to God and is willing to do what such listening requires. He will grow to be a man of deep faith and steady leadership in Israel. Second, the calling of Samuel demonstrates that the leadership of the house of Eli, the current high priest, is at an end and will be displaced, ironically by this little boy who hears what the old priest and his offspring cannot. Third, the placement of the early calling of Samuel prior to the loss of the ark signals readers that, though the divine presence is absent from Israel, God is not yet finished with Israel and has left the people in the capable hands of a new leader. Thus Samuel's calling foreshadows God's later dealings with Israel through him, though there will be a very long interlude in which the divine presence will remain outside Israel's territorial boundaries.

The so-called ark narrative of chapters 4–6 presents a free, sovereign God who, though seemingly captured by the Philistines, needs no help from Israel in maintaining his sovereign freedom. This illustrates a powerful lesson to Israel that God neither can be nor desires to be controlled in any fashion, either inside Israel or out of it. The presence of God was not to be taken for granted, as if the Israelites could trot out the ark for whatever purpose suited them and make its divine inhabitant "perform" on cue. On the surface, at the beginning of the calamity, one might have suspected that God's power had been overcome by the power of the Philistine gods, thus explaining how the ark was captured. But the alacrity with which the Philistine deity Dagan is dispatched in chapter 5 and the humorous manner in which the Philistines first desire and then loathe the ark as a trophy of war clearly show the power of God exerting itself in enemy territory.

On the other side of the ark narrative the story of Samuel continues as the last judge becomes the transitional figure to the kingship that will be inaugurated with Saul. Samuel defends the previous covenantal arrangement, originating at Sinai, which had directly linked the people with God, as being the best way for the people to proceed (chap 8). But the people drown out his protests with their demand to be "like the nations," which will mean more than just the creation of a monarchy, an army, and the bureaucracy to manage them. Not only will the unique ethos of the Hebrew community be sacrificed in favor of the more common international norm of a stratified society, this novel move in Israel's theology and politics will result in a distancing of the relationship between Yahweh and the people. Instead of living in deep connection with his people and turning to judges primarily only in times of crisis, Yahweh will now deal with Israel through its kings.

The First King

Two stories are told of the inauguration of King Saul, one flattering him as a military leader (11:1–14), the other poignantly portraying his reluctance to serve (9:1–21). Scholars have long debated the historicity of both narratives as well as their relationship, if any. Read as a literary unit, however, the two stories highlight the two sides of Saul's character that will be manifested throughout his story. He will at times be strong and decisive, while at other times weak and doubt-ridden. From Israel's perspective, Saul had been made king for one reason only: to deal with the Philistine menace. This issue of national security dominates the political agenda as the militarily and technologically outmatched Israelites are continually harassed by the Philistines, who in their quest for expansion repeatedly encroach on Israelite territory.

Saul looks the part, standing a head taller than the next largest Israelite and being possessed of the good looks that so often people imagine denote other skills, virtues, and abilities. But Saul was hollow on the inside. There was no such virtue in him, and above all, this lack of character made his a "one-term" dynasty.

Specifically, we are given two stories (again) of the wresting of Saul's kingship from him, both of which present vexing issues. In the first, Saul offers a sacrifice without Samuel's presence after having waited for the old prophet longer than the seven days that Samuel said it would take to arrive to be with Saul. Samuel arrives outraged and says that the kingship has been taken from Saul and given to another (13:8–15). In the next story, Saul achieves a great military victory in defeating Israel's ancient enemy the Amalekites, but is viciously chastised by the prophet for not executing the Amalekite king and for saving some of the Amalekite animals for sacrifice to

Yahweh. Again the threat to take the kingship from Saul is made by Samuel, who hacks the Amalekite king, Agag, to death, an event that symbolizes the reign of Saul was also falling to pieces (chap 15).

Theological problems arise from the fact that, in the first story, the punishment of Saul does not seem to fit the crime and, in the second story, David will later be guilty of the same offense and yet will get off scot-free. The most telling illustration of the favor of Yahweh, withheld from Saul but given with abundance to David, is in the oft-repeated phrase that each king "inquired of the LORD." Every time David turns to Yahweh, divine guidance seems to be freely given, even before David becomes king (1 Sam 22:10; 23:2; 30:8; 2 Sam 2:1; 5:23; 21:1). When Saul asks for such direction, however, God does not answer (1 Sam 14:37; 28:6). In the end, readers are left with a bewildering sense that there is no discerning the reasons for what Yahweh is doing. God bestows his blessing on whomever he chooses, and we are not privy to his counsels. Living with this puzzling paradox is an important growth point in the spiritual formation of the People of God.

The Great King

David will grow to dominate the theological and political horizon in Israel's worldview. The success achieved by him and his son Solomon will be the "golden age" to which later generations will look for inspiration, the benchmark for international influence and financial stability to which all other administrations will aspire. Even the setting of the account of Jesus' birth in Bethlehem, David's hometown, in Luke 2 links the king with the new Messiah.

But in 1 Samuel, David appears as but a boy, still living in his father's house. From this inauspicious beginning readers follow David to the military camp where his brothers are serving in a protracted standoff with the Philistines. Here David makes his mark by slaying the giant Goliath, an event that will foreshadow his total defeat of the Philistines in years to come. Thus even as a child David demonstrates that he is blessed by God and will not be intimidated by Philistine might because he is faithful to the Lord of Hosts. From here we follow David into the king's household, where he ironically becomes a figure beloved by the very family he will one day supplant. Indeed, the whole of Israel will come to love and honor David far more than King Saul, who will grow to despise him. When Saul tries to assassinate him, David takes refuge, again with heavy irony, under the protection of the Philistine king, whom David beguiles even as he wreaks havoc in guerrilla raids on the Philistines and their allies. David does not seek vengeance from Saul, but spares his life twice, thus manifesting the qualities of forgiveness and restraint, leaving vengeance to Yahweh.

1 Samuel and Spiritual Formation

Numerous examples of spiritual formation are found in 1 Samuel. Some of them have a public dimension, such as when David repeatedly seeks Yahweh's guidance (22:10; 23:2; 30:8) or when he shows deference to Saul's anointed status by not taking his life (24:6; 26:10). There is also an instance of public worship as Saul makes sacrifice after a military victory (14:35) as well as the public acknowledgment of Samuel's honest leadership of the people (12:5). There is even one example of the people's discerning God's will and publicly averting the death of Jonathan after Saul had made a rash public vow to Yahweh (chap 14). We also see the monument-raising ceremony of the Ebenezer stone to Yahweh that celebrates Yahweh's favor in subduing the Philistines (7:12–14). Mostly, however, incidents of spiritual formation in 1 Samuel are personal in nature, for example, the detailed worship, prayers, and rejoicings of Hannah (chaps 1–2) and the abiding friendship sealed by covenant between David and Jonathan (chaps 18–20).

Equally significant are the negative examples of spiritual formation, wherein the characters manifest precisely what not to do in relationship to God and neighbor. In three instances the failings of one character make it possible for the advancement of another person in the drama. First, the rise of Samuel comes as a result of the deficient parenting of Eli (2:12–17, 27–36). Then the rise of Saul seems to come as a result of the people's failing to look beyond the surface in their quest for leadership (9:2). Finally, the rise of David comes from the failings of Saul, first in neglecting the demands of holy war (chap 15), then in succumbing to petty jealousy over David's popularity (18:10–11), and finally in devolving into butchery (22:6–19).

—Timothy F. Simpson

Samuel's Birth and Dedication

1 There was a certain man of Ramathaim, a Zuphite[a] from the hill country of Ephraim, whose name was Elkanah son of Jeroham son of Elihu son of Tohu son of Zuph, an Ephraimite. [2]He had two wives; the name of the one was Hannah, and the name of the other Peninnah. Peninnah had children, but Hannah had no children.

3 Now this man used to go up year by year from his town to worship and to sacrifice to the LORD of hosts at Shiloh, where the two sons of Eli, Hophni and Phinehas, were priests of the LORD. [4]On the day when Elkanah sacrificed, he would give portions to his wife Peninnah and to all her sons and daughters; [5]but to Hannah he gave a double portion,[b] because he loved her, though the LORD had closed her womb. [6]Her rival used to provoke her severely, to irritate her, because the LORD had closed her womb. [7]So it went on year by year; as often as she went up to the house of the LORD, she used

a Compare Gk and 1 Chr 6.35-36: Heb *Ramathaim-zophim*   b Syr: Meaning of Heb uncertain

1:3–5 *On the day when Elkanah sacrificed.* The portrait here is of an entire family engaged in the regular worship of God. Elkanah's piety is marked both by his consistency in worship and by the extra measure of grace he extends to his barren wife in giving her a double portion. When she does have a child, Hannah will have already formed the spiritual character of her own life through worship, and that will then provide her with a reserve to form his.

1:5 *the LORD had closed her womb.* The barren woman motif is a familiar one in the Old Testament, having been characteristic of two of the matriarchs in Genesis, Sarah and Rachel, as well as the unnamed wife of Manoah in Judges. Because it has been at such critical junctures of infertility that God's glory has been made so magnificently manifest, through the births of Isaac, Joseph, and Samson, readers are primed for another awesome display of God's life-giving power. It is difficult to imagine in our own society the social significance of barrenness, but in a society in which social status was gained or lost by means of accruing honor or shame rather than wealth, the lack of children was an agonizing social stigma.

to provoke her. Therefore Hannah wept and would not eat. [8]Her husband Elkanah said to her, "Hannah, why do you weep? Why do you not eat? Why is your heart sad? Am I not more to you than ten sons?"

9 After they had eaten and drunk at Shiloh, Hannah rose and presented herself before the LORD.[a] Now Eli the priest was sitting on the seat beside the doorpost of the temple of the LORD. [10]She was deeply distressed and prayed to the LORD, and wept bitterly. [11]She made this vow, "O LORD of hosts, if only you will look on the misery of your servant, and remember me, and not forget your servant, but will give to your servant a male child, then I will set him before you as a nazirite[b] until the day of his death. He shall drink neither wine nor intoxicants,[c] and no razor shall touch his head."

12 As she continued praying before the LORD, Eli observed her mouth. [13]Hannah was praying silently; only her lips moved, but her voice was not heard; therefore Eli thought

she was drunk. [14]So Eli said to her, "How long will you make a drunken spectacle of yourself? Put away your wine." [15]But Hannah answered, "No, my lord, I am a woman deeply troubled; I have drunk neither wine nor strong drink, but I have been pouring out my soul before the LORD. [16]Do not regard your servant as a worthless woman, for I have been speaking out of my great anxiety and vexation all this time." [17]Then Eli answered, "Go in peace; the God of Israel grant the petition you have made to him." [18]And she said, "Let your servant find favor in your sight." Then the woman went to her quarters,[d] ate and drank with her husband,[e] and her countenance was sad no longer.[f]

a Gk: Heb lacks *and presented herself before the LORD*
b That is *one separated* or *one consecrated*
c Cn Compare Gk Q Ms 1.22: MT *then I will give him to the LORD all the days of his life*   d Gk: Heb *went her way*   e Gk: Heb lacks *and drank with her husband*   f Gk: Meaning of Heb uncertain

---

1:10 *She was deeply distressed and prayed.* Hannah's piety is first displayed by her refusal to turn against the gloating Peninnah. Hannah maintains her own spirituality by turning her distress not toward her neighbor in anger and revenge, but by directing it instead, like the psalmist, toward God (see Ps 22).

Responding
1:9–20 PRAYER. Some might call Hannah's prayer selfish because she prayed to become pregnant. But when Hannah gave Samuel to the service of the Lord in the tabernacle, she easily refuted that charge. What is the difference between a selfish prayer and a prayer that complies with God's way? Write on a piece of paper all of the things you have asked God for today. Now rank them on a "selfish" scale with 1 being very selfish and 10 complying with God's will. How did you do? *See also* Spiritual Disciplines Index.

1:11 **SERVICE**—*See* Spiritual Disciplines Index.
1:11 *She made this vow.* Hannah's piety is next displayed by the making of a vow to God. The Old Testament is replete with comments on making vows to the Lord, although they are virtually absent in the New Testament. Such vows were a sign of the deep relationship

that existed between God and the people and were undertaken with great seriousness (see Gen 28:20; Judg 11:29–39; Pss 56:12; 66:13). In Israelite practice, a Nazirite was someone who was particularly holy and separate from others, even within the people of Israel, who were called to be holy themselves (Num 6). Here Hannah promises that if God removes from her the social stain of childlessness, she will give the child back to God for service.

1:13 **SILENCE**—*See* Spiritual Disciplines Index.
1:15 *I have been pouring out my soul before the LORD.* In her prayers, Hannah loses all restraint, and her fervency leads an observer to imagine she is intoxicated. Such a model of prayer is in stark contrast to the ways in which most believers regularly approach God, with tentativeness and formality that often manifest themselves in lapses into King James English.
1:18 *her countenance was sad no longer.* The experience of worship, prayer, and the unburdening transaction that occurred in the making of her vow to the Lord left Hannah a new person. This transformation is the reason the community regularly enacts each week the old ways in the face of contemporary challenges that threaten our life of faith, just as Hannah's social world threatened her.

19 They rose early in the morning and worshiped before the LORD; then they went back to their house at Ramah. Elkanah knew his wife Hannah, and the LORD remembered her. 20In due time Hannah conceived and bore a son. She named him Samuel, for she said, "I have asked him of the LORD."

21 The man Elkanah and all his household went up to offer to the LORD the yearly sacrifice, and to pay his vow. 22But Hannah did not go up, for she said to her husband, "As soon as the child is weaned, I will bring him, that he may appear in the presence of the LORD, and remain there forever; I will offer him as a nazirite*a* for all time."*b* 23Her husband Elkanah said to her, "Do what seems best to you, wait until you have weaned him; only—may the LORD establish his word."*c* So the woman remained and nursed her son, until she weaned him. 24When she had weaned him, she took him up with her, along with a three-year-old bull,*d* an ephah of flour, and a skin of wine. She brought him to the house of the LORD at Shiloh; and the child was young. 25Then they slaughtered the bull, and they brought the child to Eli. 26And she said, "Oh, my lord! As you live, my lord, I am the woman who was standing here in your presence, praying to the LORD. 27For this child I prayed; and the LORD has granted me the petition that I made to him. 28Therefore I have lent him to the LORD; as long as he lives, he is given to the LORD."

She left him there for*e* the LORD.

Hannah's Prayer

2 Hannah prayed and said,
  "My heart exults in the LORD;
    my strength is exalted in my God.*f*
  My mouth derides my enemies,
    because I rejoice in my*g* victory.

2 "There is no Holy One like the LORD,
    no one besides you;
    there is no Rock like our God.
3 Talk no more so very proudly,

let not arrogance come from your
    mouth;
  for the LORD is a God of knowledge,
    and by him actions are weighed.
4 The bows of the mighty are broken,
    but the feeble gird on strength.
5 Those who were full have hired
    themselves out for bread,
    but those who were hungry are fat
      with spoil.
  The barren has borne seven,
    but she who has many children is
      forlorn.
6 The LORD kills and brings to life;
    he brings down to Sheol and raises
      up.
7 The LORD makes poor and makes rich;
    he brings low, he also exalts.
8 He raises up the poor from the dust;
    he lifts the needy from the ash heap,
  to make them sit with princes
    and inherit a seat of honor.*h*
  For the pillars of the earth are the
    LORD'S,
    and on them he has set the world.

9 "He will guard the feet of his faithful
    ones,
  but the wicked shall be cut off in
    darkness;
  for not by might does one prevail.
10 The LORD! His adversaries shall be
    shattered;
  the Most High*i* will thunder in
    heaven.

a That is one separated or one consecrated
b Cn Compare Q Ms: MT lacks I will offer him as a nazirite for all time   *c* MT: Q Ms Gk Compare Syr that which goes out of your mouth   *d* Q Ms Gk Syr: MT three bulls   *e* Gk (Compare Q Ms) and Gk at 2.11: MT And he (that is, Elkanah) worshiped there before   *f* Gk: Heb the LORD   *g* Q Ms: MT your *h* Gk (Compare Q Ms) adds He grants the vow of the one who vows, and blesses the years of the just *i* Cn Heb against him he

---

2:1–10 *My heart exults in the LORD.* Hannah's prayer is an enormously powerful theological statement that sings a song of triumph in the midst of travail and paints a picture of the coming day of the Lord, when all that is wrong with the world will be turned on its head. Ostensibly about Hannah's victory over her social tormentors, the subject of the prayer opens up to include the marginalized in every time and place.

> The LORD will judge the ends of the earth;
> he will give strength to his king,
> and exalt the power of his anointed."

Eli's Wicked Sons

11 Then Elkanah went home to Ramah, while the boy remained to minister to the LORD, in the presence of the priest Eli.

12 Now the sons of Eli were scoundrels; they had no regard for the LORD 13or for the duties of the priests to the people. When anyone offered sacrifice, the priest's servant would come, while the meat was boiling, with a three-pronged fork in his hand, 14and he would thrust it into the pan, or kettle, or caldron, or pot; all that the fork brought up the priest would take for himself.a This is what they did at Shiloh to all the Israelites who came there. 15Moreover, before the fat was burned, the priest's servant would come and say to the one who was sacrificing, "Give meat for the priest to roast; for he will not accept boiled meat from you, but only raw." 16And if the man said to him, "Let them burn the fat first, and then take whatever you wish," he would say, "No, you must give it now; if not, I will take it by force." 17Thus the sin of the young men was very great in the sight of the LORD; for they treated the offerings of the LORD with contempt.

The Child Samuel at Shiloh

18 Samuel was ministering before the LORD, a boy wearing a linen ephod. 19His mother used to make for him a little robe and take it to him each year, when she went up with her husband to offer the yearly sacrifice. 20Then Eli would bless Elkanah and his wife, and say, "May the LORD repayb you with children by this woman for the gift that she made toc the LORD"; and then they would return to their home.

21 Andd the LORD took note of Hannah; she conceived and bore three sons and two daughters. And the boy Samuel grew up in the presence of the LORD.

Prophecy against Eli's Household

22 Now Eli was very old. He heard all that his sons were doing to all Israel, and how they lay with the women who served at the entrance to the tent of meeting. 23He said to them, "Why do you do such things? For I hear of your evil dealings from all these people. 24No, my sons; it is not a good report that I hear the people of the LORD spreading abroad. 25If one person sins against another, someone can intercede for the sinner with the LORD;e but if someone sins against the LORD, who can make intercession?" But they would not listen to the voice of their father; for it was the will of the LORD to kill them.

26 Now the boy Samuel continued to grow both in stature and in favor with the LORD and with the people.

27 A man of God came to Eli and said to him, "Thus the LORD has said, 'I revealedf

a Gk Syr Vg: Heb *with it* ~ b Q Ms Gk: MT *give*
c Q Ms Gk: MT *for the petition that she asked of*
d Q Ms Gk: MT *When* ~ e Gk Compare Q Ms: MT *another, God will mediate for him* ~ f Gk Tg Syr: Heb *Did I reveal*

2:11–26 SERVICE—*See* Spiritual Disciplines Index.

2:12 *the sons of Eli were scoundrels.* The godly parenting by the woman who sends her child to minister before the Lord in the holy shrine is in stark contrast to the parenting results of the man who lives in the shrine and whose children should have grown up knowing better. Hannah is no longer in the narrative, but her value continues to rise in the estimation of readers when compared to the miserable failure that Eli's sons represent, into whose hands the spiritual leadership of Israel has fallen. The man of God, Eli, has attended to the things of God, while failing to tend to the spiritual practices of his own household, much like the proverbial plumber whose own pipes leak.

2:26 *the boy Samuel continued to grow.* Samuel was only three when he was left with the old priest, but he had already imbibed enough of the things of God from his pious mother that he remained spiritually unscathed by his close contact with his wicked housemates. The narrative strongly implies that such a righteous upbringing by godly parents will provide some immunity against contact with those whose values are at variance with the faith.

myself to the family of your ancestor in Egypt when they were slaves*a* to the house of Pharaoh. 28I chose him out of all the tribes of Israel to be my priest, to go up to my altar, to offer incense, to wear an ephod before me; and I gave to the family of your ancestor all my offerings by fire from the people of Israel. 29Why then look with greedy eye*b* at my sacrifices and my offerings that I commanded, and honor your sons more than me by fattening yourselves on the choicest parts of every offering of my people Israel?' 30Therefore the LORD the God of Israel declares: 'I promised that your family and the family of your ancestor should go in and out before me forever'; but now the LORD declares: 'Far be it from me; for those who honor me I will honor, and those who despise me shall be treated with contempt. 31See, a time is coming when I will cut off your strength and the strength of your ancestor's family, so that no one in your family will live to old age. 32Then in distress you will look with greedy eye*c* on all the prosperity that shall be bestowed upon Israel; and no one in your family shall ever live to old age. 33The only one of you whom I shall not cut off from my altar shall be spared to weep out his*d* eyes and grieve his*e* heart; all the members of your household shall die by the sword.*f* 34The fate of your two sons, Hophni and Phinehas, shall be the sign to you—both of them shall die on the same day. 35I will raise up for myself a faithful priest, who shall do according to what is in my heart and in my mind. I will build him a sure house, and he shall go in and out before my anointed one forever. 36Everyone who is left in your family shall come to implore him for a piece of silver or a loaf of bread, and shall say, Please put me in one of the priest's places, that I may eat a morsel of bread.' "

Samuel's Calling and Prophetic Activity

3 Now the boy Samuel was ministering to the LORD under Eli. The word of the LORD was rare in those days; visions were not widespread.

2 At that time Eli, whose eyesight had begun to grow dim so that he could not see, was lying down in his room; 3the lamp of God had not yet gone out, and Samuel was lying down in the temple of the LORD, where the ark of God was. 4Then the LORD called, "Samuel! Samuel!"*g* and he said, "Here I am!" 5and ran to Eli, and said, "Here I am, for you called me." But he said, "I did not call; lie down again." So he went and lay down. 6The LORD called again, "Samuel!" Samuel got up and went to Eli, and said, "Here I am, for you called me." But he said, "I did not call, my son; lie down again." 7Now Samuel did not yet know the LORD, and the word of the LORD had not yet been revealed to him. 8The LORD called Samuel again, a third time. And he got up and went to Eli, and said, "Here I am, for you called me." Then Eli perceived that the LORD was calling the boy. 9Therefore Eli said to Samuel, "Go, lie down; and if he calls you, you shall say, 'Speak, LORD, for your servant is listening.' " So Samuel went and lay down in his place.

10 Now the LORD came and stood there, calling as before, "Samuel! Samuel!" And Samuel said, "Speak, for your servant is listening." 11Then the LORD said to Samuel, "See, I am about to do something in Israel that will make both ears of anyone who hears of it tin-

a Q Ms Gk: MT lacks *slaves*   *b* Q Ms Gk: MT *then kick*   *c* Q Ms Gk: MT *will kick*   *d* Q Ms Gk: MT *your*   *e* Q Ms Gk: Heb *your*   *f* Q Ms See Gk: MT *die like mortals*   *g* Q Ms Gk See 3.10: MT *the LORD called Samuel*

🕊 **Responding**
3:9 SERVICE. Samuel obeyed Eli, returned to his bed, lay down, and waited for the Lord to speak. Why did God choose Samuel, a child, to carry on his work rather than someone more experienced and educated? Read Matt 19:13–15 for additional insight. *See also* Spiritual Disciplines Index.

3:10 *Speak, for your servant is listening.* Though but a child, Samuel is nonetheless called by God. That God has not called Eli or his sons, the more obviously qualified adult candidates, but rather a child, is both ironic and startling, for it calls into question the deeply cherished assumption that the experienced, the educated, and the privileged are the vessels through which God works. In Israel's case, all of

gle. [12]On that day I will fulfill against Eli all that I have spoken concerning his house, from beginning to end. [13]For I have told him that I am about to punish his house forever, for the iniquity that he knew, because his sons were blaspheming God,[a] and he did not restrain them. [14]Therefore I swear to the house of Eli that the iniquity of Eli's house shall not be expiated by sacrifice or offering forever."

15 Samuel lay there until morning; then he opened the doors of the house of the LORD. Samuel was afraid to tell the vision to Eli. [16]But Eli called Samuel and said, "Samuel, my son." He said, "Here I am." [17]Eli said, "What was it that he told you? Do not hide it from me. May God do so to you and more also, if you hide anything from me of all that he told you." [18]So Samuel told him everything and hid nothing from him. Then he said, "It is the LORD; let him do what seems good to him."

19 As Samuel grew up, the LORD was with him, and let none of his words fall to the ground. [20]And all Israel from Dan to Beersheba knew that Samuel was a trustworthy prophet of the LORD. [21]The LORD continued to appear at Shiloh, for the LORD revealed himself to Samuel at Shiloh by the word of the 4 LORD. [1]And the word of Samuel came to all Israel.

The Ark of God Captured

In those days the Philistines mustered for war against Israel,[b] and Israel went out to battle against them;[c] they encamped at Ebenezer, and the Philistines encamped at Aphek. [2]The Philistines drew up in line against Israel, and when the battle was joined,[d] Israel was defeated by the Philistines, who killed about four thousand men on the field of battle. [3]When the troops came to the camp, the elders of Israel said, "Why has the LORD put us to rout today before the Philistines? Let us bring the ark of the covenant of the LORD here from Shiloh, so that he may come among us and save us from the power of our enemies." [4]So the people sent to Shiloh, and brought from there the ark of the covenant of the LORD of hosts, who is enthroned on the cherubim. The two sons of Eli, Hophni and Phinehas, were there with the ark of the covenant of God.

5 When the ark of the covenant of the LORD came into the camp, all Israel gave a mighty shout, so that the earth resounded. [6]When the Philistines heard the noise of the shouting, they said, "What does this great shouting in the camp of the Hebrews mean?" When they learned that the ark of the LORD had come to the camp, [7]the Philistines were afraid; for they said, "Gods have[e] come into the camp." They also said, "Woe to us! For nothing like this has happened before. [8]Woe to us! Who can deliver us from the power of these mighty gods? These are the gods who struck the Egyptians with every sort of plague in the wilderness. [9]Take courage, and be men, O Philistines, in order not to become slaves to

---

a Another reading is *for themselves*   *b* Gk: Heb lacks *In those days the Philistines mustered for war against Israel*   *c* Gk: Heb *against the Philistines*   *d* Meaning of Heb uncertain   *e* Or *A god has*

---

those types have wandered from the ways of Yahweh, and thus God chooses an almost laughable vessel, a child, through whom the word of the Lord will be delivered (cf. 4:1). It is a characteristic of this God, who chooses the second-born Jacob rather than the firstborn Esau and the politically and economically weak Israel rather than the rich and powerful Egypt, to align himself with such figures—a fact that should compel us to reach out to the marginalized as well.

3:18 *It is the LORD.* In a surprising burst of insight, Eli's blindness lifts for a brief moment as he discerns that the judgment of Yahweh is against him. A similar statement will be made by David, who realizes the same thing in 2 Sam 16:14. Both Eli and David bear witness that no matter how far from the path one has strayed, it is never too late to return. Situated within the Deuteronomistic History (Joshua–2 Kings; see the Introduction), which is the larger tale of Israel's wandering, Eli is representative of the theological drift that has occurred, as well as a model of the possible awakening of the sort of insight that might draw the community back to its proper path.

the Hebrews as they have been to you; be men and fight."

10 So the Philistines fought; Israel was defeated, and they fled, everyone to his home. There was a very great slaughter, for there fell of Israel thirty thousand foot soldiers. ¹¹The ark of God was captured; and the two sons of Eli, Hophni and Phinehas, died.

Death of Eli

12 A man of Benjamin ran from the battle line, and came to Shiloh the same day, with his clothes torn and with earth upon his head. ¹³When he arrived, Eli was sitting upon his seat by the road watching, for his heart trembled for the ark of God. When the man came into the city and told the news, all the city cried out. ¹⁴When Eli heard the sound of the outcry, he said, "What is this uproar?" Then the man came quickly and told Eli. ¹⁵Now Eli was ninety-eight years old and his eyes were set, so that he could not see. ¹⁶The man said to Eli, "I have just come from the battle; I fled from the battle today." He said, "How did it go, my son?" ¹⁷The messenger replied, "Israel has fled before the Philistines, and there has also been a great slaughter among the troops; your two sons also, Hophni and Phinehas, are dead, and the ark of God has been captured." ¹⁸When he mentioned the ark of God, Eli[a] fell over backward from his seat by the side of the gate; and his neck was broken and he died, for he was an old man, and heavy. He had judged Israel forty years.

19 Now his daughter-in-law, the wife of Phinehas, was pregnant, about to give birth. When she heard the news that the ark of God was captured, and that her father-in-law and her husband were dead, she bowed and gave birth; for her labor pains overwhelmed her.

²⁰As she was about to die, the women attending her said to her, "Do not be afraid, for you have borne a son." But she did not answer or give heed. ²¹She named the child Ichabod, meaning, "The glory has departed from Israel," because the ark of God had been captured and because of her father-in-law and her husband. ²²She said, "The glory has departed from Israel, for the ark of God has been captured."

The Philistines and the Ark

5 When the Philistines captured the ark of God, they brought it from Ebenezer to Ashdod; ²then the Philistines took the ark of God and brought it into the house of Dagon and placed it beside Dagon. ³When the people of Ashdod rose early the next day, there was Dagon, fallen on his face to the ground before the ark of the LORD. So they took Dagon and put him back in his place. ⁴But when they rose early on the next morning, Dagon had fallen on his face to the ground before the ark of the LORD, and the head of Dagon and both his hands were lying cut off upon the threshold; only the trunk of[b] Dagon was left to him. ⁵This is why the priests of Dagon and all who enter the house of Dagon do not step on the threshold of Dagon in Ashdod to this day.

6 The hand of the LORD was heavy upon the people of Ashdod, and he terrified and struck them with tumors, both in Ashdod and in its territory. ⁷And when the inhabitants of Ashdod saw how things were, they said, "The ark of the God of Israel must not remain with us; for his hand is heavy on us and on our god Dagon." ⁸So they sent and gathered together all the lords of the Philis-

a Heb *he*   b Heb lacks *the trunk of*

4:11 *The ark of God was captured.* Outmatched militarily by the Philistines, Israel imagines that it can trot out the ark of the covenant, the symbol of Yahweh's dwelling with Israel, and thereby solve the problem at its borders (v 4). But this God, sovereign and unrestrained, will not be so domesticated. Israel's bungling attempt to manage God ends in the triple disaster of defeat in battle, the toppling of the high priest's dynasty, and the loss of the ark to the Philistines.

5:4 *both his hands were lying cut off.* Despite their prowess against the Israelites, the Philistines are no more successful at co-opting the power of Yahweh than were the Israelites. The hand is the symbol of power in the literature of antiquity, and the defeat of Dagon could not be more plainly manifest than by his double amputation.

tines, and said, "What shall we do with the ark of the God of Israel?" The inhabitants of Gath replied, "Let the ark of God be moved on to us."[a] So they moved the ark of the God of Israel to Gath.[b] [9]But after they had brought it to Gath,[c] the hand of the LORD was against the city, causing a very great panic; he struck the inhabitants of the city, both young and old, so that tumors broke out on them. [10]So they sent the ark of the God of Israel[d] to Ekron. But when the ark of God came to Ekron, the people of Ekron cried out, "Why[e] have they brought around to us[f] the ark of the God of Israel to kill us[f] and our[g] people?" [11]They sent therefore and gathered together all the lords of the Philistines, and said, "Send away the ark of the God of Israel, and let it return to its own place, that it may not kill us and our people." For there was a deathly panic[h] throughout the whole city. The hand of God was very heavy there; [12]those who did not die were stricken with tumors, and the cry of the city went up to heaven.

The Ark Returned to Israel

6 The ark of the LORD was in the country of the Philistines seven months. [2]Then the Philistines called for the priests and the diviners and said, "What shall we do with the ark of the LORD? Tell us what we should send with it to its place." [3]They said, "If you send away the ark of the God of Israel, do not send it empty, but by all means return him a guilt offering. Then you will be healed and will be ransomed;[i] will not his hand then turn from you?" [4]And they said, "What is the guilt offering that we shall return to him?" They answered, "Five gold tumors and five gold mice, according to the number of the lords of the Philistines; for the same plague was upon all of you and upon your lords. [5]So you must make images of your tumors and images of your mice that ravage the land, and give glory to the God of Israel; perhaps he will lighten his hand on you and your gods and your land. [6]Why should you harden your hearts as the Egyptians and Pharaoh hardened their hearts? After he had made fools of them, did they not let the people go, and they departed? [7]Now then, get ready a new cart and two milch cows that have never borne a yoke,

and yoke the cows to the cart, but take their calves home, away from them. [8]Take the ark of the LORD and place it on the cart, and put in a box at its side the figures of gold, which you are returning to him as a guilt offering. Then send it off, and let it go its way. [9]And watch; if it goes up on the way to its own land, to Beth-shemesh, then it is he who has done us this great harm; but if not, then we shall know that it is not his hand that struck us; it happened to us by chance."

10 The men did so; they took two milch cows and yoked them to the cart, and shut up their calves at home. [11]They put the ark of the LORD on the cart, and the box with the gold mice and the images of their tumors. [12]The cows went straight in the direction of Beth-shemesh along one highway, lowing as they went; they turned neither to the right nor to the left, and the lords of the Philistines went after them as far as the border of Beth-shemesh.

13 Now the people of Beth-shemesh were reaping their wheat harvest in the valley. When they looked up and saw the ark, they went with rejoicing to meet it.[j] [14]The cart came into the field of Joshua of Beth-shemesh, and stopped there. A large stone was there; so they split up the wood of the cart and offered the cows as a burnt offering to the LORD. [15]The Levites took down the ark of the LORD and the box that was beside it, in which were the gold objects, and set them upon the large stone. Then the people of Beth-shemesh offered burnt offerings and presented sacrifices on that day to the LORD. [16]When the five lords of the Philistines saw it, they returned that day to Ekron.

17 These are the gold tumors, which the Philistines returned as a guilt offering to the LORD: one for Ashdod, one for Gaza, one for Ashkelon, one for Gath, one for Ekron; [18]also the gold mice, according to the number of all the cities of the Philistines belonging to the

a Gk Compare Q Ms: MT *They answered, "Let the ark of the God of Israel be brought around to Gath."* b Gk: Heb lacks *to Gath*   c Q Ms: MT lacks *to Gath*   d Q Ms Gk: MT lacks *of Israel*   e Q Ms Gk: MT lacks *Why*   f Heb *me*   g Heb *my*   h Q Ms reads *a panic from the LORD*   i Q Ms Gk: MT *and it will be known to you*   j Gk: Heb *rejoiced to see it*

SAMUEL

The Prayer Warrior

Selected Scriptures: *1 Samuel 1–3; 7–12; 15–16; 25:1; 28*

Prayer stood at the center of Samuel's entire life. Before Samuel was even conceived, his mother, Hannah, dedicated him to God: "O LORD of hosts, if only you will . . . give to your servant a male child, then I will set him before you as a nazirite [one designated to the service of God] until the day of his death" (1 Sam 1:11). She had long been barren and endured the taunts of her husband's other, fertile wife. God granted Hannah a son, and she kept her promise. From the time he was weaned, Samuel lived with Eli in the Temple and there, as a boy, responded to God's call: "Speak, for your servant is listening" (3:10). Samuel was to become an important prophetic voice of God in this period of Israel's life.

Early in Samuel's adult life the Philistines overtook Israel and for more than twenty years posed a continual threat. Finally, Samuel, who had become a judge of Israel, directed the Israelites to serve God wholeheartedly and rid themselves of all foreign gods: "If you are returning to the LORD with all your heart, then put away the foreign gods. . . . Direct your heart to the LORD, and serve him only, and he will deliver you out of the hand of the Philistines" (7:3). When Samuel cried out to the Lord on behalf of his people, "the LORD answered him," and for the remainder of Samuel's life, God restrained the Philistines, and the Israelites lived at peace with them (7:12–14).

When Samuel was old, he made his sons judges over Israel, yet they did not follow in his God-honoring ways. The people recognized their unfaithfulness and demanded, instead, that Samuel appoint a king to rule over them. Although he was not pleased with their request, "Samuel prayed to the LORD, and the LORD said to Samuel, 'Listen to the voice of the people in all that they say to you; for they have not rejected you, but they have rejected me from being king over them'" (8:6–7). After warning the people of the consequences to come, Samuel obeyed God and anointed Saul as Israel's first king (11:15).

In Samuel's farewell speech, before Saul's reign began, Samuel spoke with the people about Israel's history of unfaithfulness and their need now for fearing God and serving him. To emphasize God's anger at their unfaithfulness, Samuel called on God to bring thunder and rain on an early summer day when such rain was unusual. The rain came. As the Israelites begged for mercy, Samuel said, "Far be it from me that I should sin against the LORD by ceasing to pray for you; and I will instruct you in the good and the right way" (12:23).

Even after Saul became king, Samuel played a large role in the lives of the Israelites. When Saul defeated the Amalekites yet disobeyed God, setting up a monument to himself, "Samuel was angry; and he cried out to the LORD all night"

PROFILE: SAMUEL

(15:11), feeling cut to the heart because of Saul's distance and offense to the goodness of God. Samuel grieved until God told him to stop. He would anoint a new king, a son of Jesse. King David would serve as a forerunner to Christ, the resurrected and eternal King. In anointing David (16:13), Samuel performed a fitting duty to end his service to Israel. David would walk in Samuel's footsteps, living a life of prayer and intimacy with God.

In *Celebration of Discipline* Richard Foster explained, "Of all the Spiritual Disciplines prayer is the most central because it ushers us into perpetual communion with the Father." For Samuel, prayer nurtured an Immanuel relationship, "God with us." God *was* with Samuel, and he started right and finished right largely because he viewed this Immanuel relationship, kept alive through prayer, as the main business of his life.

Personal Reflection

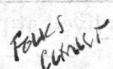

- Has anyone prayed for you since your childhood or even before your birth? What was the substance of these prayers?
- When God first called to Samuel in the night, Samuel listened and faithfully served as God asked. How attentive are you to God's voice in your life? What has God recently asked you to do?
- How much do you use prayer as a way of staying "with God" through your days?

five lords, both fortified cities and unwalled villages. The great stone, beside which they set down the ark of the LORD, is a witness to this day in the field of Joshua of Beth-shemesh.

The Ark at Kiriath-jearim

19 The descendants of Jeconiah did not rejoice with the people of Beth-shemesh when they greeted *a* the ark of the LORD; and he killed seventy men of them. *b* The people mourned because the LORD had made a great slaughter among the people. ²⁰Then the people of Beth-shemesh said, "Who is able to stand before the LORD, this holy God? To whom shall he go so that we may be rid of him?" ²¹So they sent messengers to the inhabitants of Kiriath-jearim, saying, "The Philistines have returned the ark of the LORD. 7 Come down and take it up to you." ¹And the people of Kiriath-jearim came and took up the ark of the LORD, and brought it to the house of Abinadab on the hill. They consecrated his son, Eleazar, to have charge of the ark of the LORD.

2 From the day that the ark was lodged at Kiriath-jearim, a long time passed, some twenty years, and all the house of Israel lamented *c* after the LORD.

Samuel as Judge

3 Then Samuel said to all the house of Israel, "If you are returning to the LORD with all your heart, then put away the foreign gods

a Gk: Heb *And he killed some of the people of Beth-shemesh, because they looked into* *b* Heb *killed seventy men, fifty thousand men* *c* Meaning of Heb uncertain

6:19 *and he killed seventy men of them.* The ark is back home, but it is still not manageable by Israel. The community, whose spiritual understanding appears to be at low ebb, must still reckon with the inscrutability of Yahweh, whose holiness has lethal force even against the People of God. It will be many years before the community is able to develop the kind of ethos that will produce leaders capable of properly approaching the ark again.

7:3 *put away the foreign gods.* Samuel, of course, had never heard of a separation between church and state and thus does not

and the Astartes from among you. Direct your heart to the LORD, and serve him only, and he will deliver you out of the hand of the Philistines." 4So Israel put away the Baals and the Astartes, and they served the LORD only.

5 Then Samuel said, "Gather all Israel at Mizpah, and I will pray to the LORD for you." 6So they gathered at Mizpah, and drew water and poured it out before the LORD. They fasted that day, and said, "We have sinned against the LORD." And Samuel judged the people of Israel at Mizpah.

7 When the Philistines heard that the people of Israel had gathered at Mizpah, the lords of the Philistines went up against Israel. And when the people of Israel heard of it they were afraid of the Philistines. 8The people of Israel said to Samuel, "Do not cease to cry out to the LORD our God for us, and pray that he may save us from the hand of the Philistines." 9So Samuel took a sucking lamb and offered it as a whole burnt offering to the LORD; Samuel cried out to the LORD for Israel, and the LORD answered him. 10As Samuel was offering up the burnt offering, the Philistines drew near to attack Israel; but the LORD thundered with a mighty voice that day against the Philistines and threw them into confusion; and they were routed before Israel. 11And the men of Israel went out of Mizpah and pursued the Philistines, and struck them down as far as beyond Beth-car.

12 Then Samuel took a stone and set it up between Mizpah and Jeshanah,*a* and named it Ebenezer;*b* for he said, "Thus far the LORD has helped us." 13So the Philistines were subdued and did not again enter the territory of Israel; the hand of the LORD was against the Philistines all the days of Samuel. 14The towns that the Philistines had taken from Israel were restored to Israel, from Ekron to Gath; and Israel recovered their territory from the hand of the Philistines. There was peace also between Israel and the Amorites.

15 Samuel judged Israel all the days of his life. 16He went on a circuit year by year to Bethel, Gilgal, and Mizpah; and he judged Israel in all these places. 17Then he would

a Gk Syr: Heb *Shen*   *b* That is *Stone of Help*

---

shrink from connecting the community's spirituality with foreign policy. The chaos occasioned by the Philistine incursions into Israelite territory was merely a symptom of an even more fundamental spiritual disorder that could be remedied only by detaching from non-Yahwistic allegiances and returning to covenant life. He seems to have had no support from any other quarter for such a claim, but makes it nonetheless, even if standing by himself.

7:6 *They fasted . . . and said, "We have sinned."* The Spiritual Discipline of fasting as preparation for an encounter with the holy is an ancient one, as this text illustrates. By turning from the needs of the body toward the needs of the soul, the community is able to see in much sharper relief its need for repentance and restoration. In our own society, overfed yet spiritually malnourished as we have become, the recovery of such a practice may well be necessary for the community once again to come to this point.

Responding
7:6 FASTING. Do you agree that denying our body food and focusing on the needs of our soul help us "see in much sharper relief" our need for repentance and restoration? What other things surface when we fast from food? If you haven't tried it already, abstain from solid food for twenty-four hours starting and ending with breakfast while constantly monitoring your soul's reaction to being physically hungry. What did you learn? See *also* Spiritual Disciplines Index.

7:8 PRAYER—See Spiritual Disciplines Index.
7:12 *the LORD has helped us.* The raising of the stone named Ebenezer (which literally means "the stone of help") denotes the community's awareness that it is not self-made. Whenever it imagines itself to be so, it need simply turn to the monument as a reminder of its contingent status. Thus the marker has the dual function of being thanksgiving for Yahweh's assistance and a prompt to maintain a faithful posture before the one whose faithfulness knows no bounds. The problem will be, as the Deuteronomistic History demonstrates in painful detail, that the marker ends up not being enough to remind Israel of its need to remain vigilant in relying on Yahweh.

come back to Ramah, for his home was there; he administered justice there to Israel, and built there an altar to the LORD.

Israel Demands a King

8 When Samuel became old, he made his sons judges over Israel. [2]The name of his firstborn son was Joel, and the name of his second, Abijah; they were judges in Beer-she-ba. [3]Yet his sons did not follow in his ways, but turned aside after gain; they took bribes and perverted justice.

4 Then all the elders of Israel gathered together and came to Samuel at Ramah, [5]and said to him, "You are old and your sons do not follow in your ways; appoint for us, then, a king to govern us, like other nations." [6]But the thing displeased Samuel when they said, "Give us a king to govern us." Samuel prayed to the LORD, [7]and the LORD said to Samuel, "Listen to the voice of the people in all that they say to you; for they have not rejected you, but they have rejected me from being king over them. [8]Just as they have done to me, [a] from the day I brought them up out of Egypt to this day, forsaking me and serving other gods, so also they are doing to you. [9]Now then, listen to their voice; only—you shall solemnly warn them, and show them the ways of the king who shall reign over them."

10 So Samuel reported all the words of the LORD to the people who were asking him for a king. [11]He said, "These will be the ways of the king who will reign over you: he will take your sons and appoint them to his chariots and to be his horsemen, and to run before his chariots; [12]and he will appoint for himself commanders of thousands and commanders of fifties, and some to plow his ground and to reap his harvest, and to make his imple-

ments of war and the equipment of his chariots. [13]He will take your daughters to be perfumers and cooks and bakers. [14]He will take the best of your fields and vineyards and olive orchards and give them to his courtiers. [15]He will take one-tenth of your grain and of your vineyards and give it to his officers and his courtiers. [16]He will take your male and female slaves, and the best of your cattle [b] and donkeys, and put them to his work. [17]He will take one-tenth of your flocks, and you shall be his slaves. [18]And in that day you will cry out because of your king, whom you have chosen for yourselves; but the LORD will not answer you in that day."

Israel's Request for a King Granted

19 But the people refused to listen to the voice of Samuel; they said, "No! but we are determined to have a king over us, [20]so that we also may be like other nations, and that our king may govern us and go out before us and fight our battles." [21]When Samuel had heard all the words of the people, he repeated them in the ears of the LORD. [22]The LORD said to Samuel, "Listen to their voice and set a king over them." Samuel then said to the people of Israel, "Each of you return home."

Saul Chosen to Be King

9 There was a man of Benjamin whose name was Kish son of Abiel son of Zeror son of Becorath son of Aphiah, a Benjaminite, a man of wealth. [2]He had a son whose name was Saul, a handsome young man. There was not a man among the people of Israel more handsome than he; he stood head and shoulders above everyone else.

3 Now the donkeys of Kish, Saul's father,

a Gk: Heb lacks to me   b Gk: Heb young men

8:10 *Samuel reported all the words of the* LORD *to the people.* Here Samuel faithfully does what he does not want to do and even what is against his own best interests, thus demonstrating loyalty to Yahweh and fulfilling the fundamental responsibility of his office. Good leadership does not seek its own benefit, but rather the welfare of the people served. Clearly, Samuel believes that a monarchy will not promote the commu-

nity's goals, but does what Yahweh bids him do anyway, trusting that the divine plan can discern aspects of reality unseen by him.

9:2 *handsome . . . head and shoulders above everyone else.* The shallowness of the people's response to Samuel's warnings (8:19–20) is mirrored by the narrator's comments on the outward characteristics of the one who will become the first king, suggesting that they may

had strayed. So Kish said to his son Saul, "Take one of the boys with you; go and look for the donkeys." [4]He passed through the hill country of Ephraim and passed through the land of Shalishah, but they did not find them. And they passed through the land of Shaalim, but they were not there. Then he passed through the land of Benjamin, but they did not find them.

5 When they came to the land of Zuph, Saul said to the boy who was with him, "Let us turn back, or my father will stop worrying about the donkeys and worry about us." [6]But he said to him, "There is a man of God in this town; he is a man held in honor. Whatever he says always comes true. Let us go there now; perhaps he will tell us about the journey on which we have set out." [7]Then Saul replied to the boy, "But if we go, what can we bring the man? For the bread in our sacks is gone, and there is no present to bring to the man of God. What have we?" [8]The boy answered Saul again, "Here, I have with me a quarter shekel of silver; I will give it to the man of God, to tell us our way." [9](Formerly in Israel, anyone who went to inquire of God would say, "Come, let us go to the seer"; for the one who is now called a prophet was formerly called a seer.) [10]Saul said to the boy, "Good; come, let us go." So they went to the town where the man of God was.

11 As they went up the hill to the town, they met some girls coming out to draw water, and said to them, "Is the seer here?" [12]They answered, "Yes, there he is just ahead of you. Hurry; he has come just now to the town, because the people have a sacrifice today at the shrine. [13]As soon as you enter the town, you will find him, before he goes up to the shrine to eat. For the people will not eat until he comes, since he must bless the sacrifice; afterward those eat who are invited. Now go up, for you will meet him immediately." [14]So they went up to the town. As they were entering the town, they saw Samuel coming out toward them on his way up to the shrine.

15 Now the day before Saul came, the LORD had revealed to Samuel: [16]"Tomorrow about this time I will send to you a man from the land of Benjamin, and you shall anoint him to be ruler over my people Israel. He shall save my people from the hand of the Philistines; for I have seen the suffering of[a] my people, because their outcry has come to me." [17]When Samuel saw Saul, the LORD told him, "Here is the man of whom I spoke to you. He it is who shall rule over my people." [18]Then Saul approached Samuel inside the gate, and said, "Tell me, please, where is the house of the seer?" [19]Samuel answered Saul, "I am the seer; go up before me to the shrine, for today you shall eat with me, and in the morning I will let you go and will tell you all that is on your mind. [20]As for your donkeys that were lost three days ago, give no further thought to them, for they have been found. And on whom is all Israel's desire fixed, if not on you and on all your ancestral house?" [21]Saul answered, "I am only a Benjaminite, from the least of the tribes of Israel, and my family is the humblest of all the families of the tribe of Benjamin. Why then have you spoken to me in this way?"

22 Then Samuel took Saul and his servant-boy and brought them into the hall, and gave them a place at the head of those who had been invited, of whom there were about thirty. [23]And Samuel said to the cook, "Bring the portion I gave you, the one I asked you to put aside." [24]The cook took up the thigh and what went with it[b] and set them before Saul. Samuel said, "See, what was kept is set before you. Eat; for it is set[c] before you at the appointed time, so that you might eat with the guests."[d]

a Gk: Heb lacks *the suffering of*   b Meaning of Heb uncertain   c Q Ms Gk: MT *it was kept*   d Cn: Heb *it was kept for you, saying, I have invited the people*

---

be looking for the wrong sort of person. In our own time the cult of beauty and youth holds even the Church in its thrall.

9:21 *Why then have you spoken to me?* Saul responds to the call to leadership in the manner

appropriate throughout the tradition (and remaining so to this day) by professing his unworthiness. The humility does not appear to be feigned in any way.

So Saul ate with Samuel that day. 25 When they came down from the shrine into the town, a bed was spread for Saul *a* on the roof, and he lay down to sleep. *b* 26 Then at the break of dawn *c* Samuel called to Saul upon the roof, "Get up, so that I may send you on your way." Saul got up, and both he and Samuel went out into the street.

Samuel Anoints Saul

27 As they were going down to the outskirts of the town, Samuel said to Saul, "Tell the boy to go on before us, and when he has passed on, stop here yourself for a while, that I may make known to you the word of God."

10 1 Samuel took a vial of oil and poured it on his head, and kissed him; he said, "The LORD has anointed you ruler over his people Israel. You shall reign over the people of the LORD and you will save them from the hand of their enemies all around. Now this shall be the sign to you that the LORD has anointed you ruler *d* over his heritage: 2 When you depart from me today you will meet two men by Rachel's tomb in the territory of Benjamin at Zelzah; they will say to you, 'The donkeys that you went to seek are found, and now your father has stopped worrying about them and is worrying about you, saying: What shall I do about my son?' 3 Then you shall go on from there further and come to the oak of Tabor; three men going up to God at Bethel will meet you there, one carrying three kids, another carrying three loaves of bread, and another carrying a skin of wine. 4 They will greet you and give you two loaves of bread, which you shall accept from them. 5 After that you shall come to Gibeath-elohim, *e* at the place where the Philistine garrison is; there, as you come to the town, you will meet a band of prophets coming down from the shrine with harp, tambourine, flute, and lyre playing in front of them; they will be in a prophetic frenzy.

6 Then the spirit of the LORD will possess you, and you will be in a prophetic frenzy along with them and be turned into a different person. 7 Now when these signs meet you, do whatever you see fit to do, for God is with you. 8 And you shall go down to Gilgal ahead of me; then I will come down to you to present burnt offerings and offer sacrifices of well-being. Seven days you shall wait, until I come to you and show you what you shall do."

Saul Prophesies

9 As he turned away to leave Samuel, God gave him another heart; and all these signs were fulfilled that day. 10 When they were going from there *f* to Gibeah, *g* a band of prophets met him; and the spirit of God possessed him, and he fell into a prophetic frenzy along with them. 11 When all who knew him before saw how he prophesied with the prophets, the people said to one another, "What has come over the son of Kish? Is Saul also among the prophets?" 12 A man of the place answered, "And who is their father?" Therefore it became a proverb, "Is Saul also among the prophets?" 13 When his prophetic frenzy had ended, he went home. *h*

14 Saul's uncle said to him and to the boy, "Where did you go?" And he replied, "To seek the donkeys; and when we saw they were not to be found, we went to Samuel." 15 Saul's uncle said, "Tell me what Samuel said to you." 16 Saul said to his uncle, "He told us that the donkeys had been found." But about the matter of the kingship, of which Samuel had spoken, he did not tell him anything.

a Gk: Heb *and he spoke with Saul*   *b* Gk: Heb lacks *and he lay down to sleep*   *c* Gk: Heb *and they arose early and at break of dawn*   *d* Gk: Heb lacks *over his people Israel. You shall . . . anointed you ruler*   *e* Or *the Hill of God*   *f* Gk: Heb *they came there*   *g* Or *the hill*   *h* Cn: Heb *he came to the shrine*

10:10–13 *he fell into a prophetic frenzy.* In the only instance of any of Israel's (or Judah's) kings engaging in ecstatic utterance, Saul, under the influence of the Spirit, manifests the behavior of the prophets (see the same behavior by Saul in 19:23–24). Although often feared by the religious establishment because of the difficulty of controlling them, such practices nonetheless have a long history in Israel and the Church. They can clearly be the work of the Spirit and hence a faithful Spiritual Discipline and grace for the community.

SAUL
Unwilling to Wait

Selected Scriptures: *1 Samuel 9–31*

John Calvin said, "The surest source of destruction to men is to obey themselves." His words make a fitting summary of the life of Israel's first king, Saul. The Israelites showed their lack of faith in God by asking for a king, and in turn they got a ruler who himself chose repeatedly to obey his own inclinations rather than God.

Not long after becoming king, Saul grew fearful when the Philistines were pressing in and the judge and prophet Samuel didn't show up as promised to offer a sacrifice (1 Sam 13:8). Instead of waiting and trusting in God's provision, Saul watched his army slowly deserting him and grew impatient. Against God's law, Saul offered the sacrifice himself (13:9). As soon as Saul finished, Samuel arrived and rebuked him for his sin. Now Saul's kingdom was doomed to failure (13:14).

Next, Saul led his army in victory over the Amalekites, but refrained from destroying them completely as God had commanded. He spared the king and the choicest herds (15:9) and then built a monument to himself. Trying to rationalize his disobedience, Saul claimed he wanted to sacrifice the animals to God. Yet Samuel was angry: "To obey is better than sacrifice" (15:22). Samuel announced that Saul's rule was over: "The LORD has torn the kingdom of Israel from you this very day, and has given it to a neighbor of yours, who is better than you" (15:28).

Saul's sin ended his future as king not because he was unforgivable, but because he wouldn't realize his desperate need for forgiveness. In *Renovation of the Heart*, Dallas Willard explains: "Without [the] realization of our utter ruin and without the genuine revisioning and redirecting of our lives . . . no clear path to inner transformation can be found. It is psychologically and spiritually impossible." Saul needed to see his great sin and grieve this sin before God.

Calvin went on to explain: "For as the surest source of destruction to men is to obey themselves, so the only haven of safety is to have no other will, no other wisdom, than to follow the Lord wherever he leads. Let this, then, be the first step, to abandon ourselves, and devote the whole energy of our minds to the service of God."

Saul doubted God up to his last day. As the Philistines lay waiting to attack the Israelites, Saul cried out to God, but heard no response. Desperate to hear from God, he again took his needs into his own hands and went in disguise to a medium, seeking the deceased Samuel for guidance: "I have summoned you to tell me what I should do" (28:15). Samuel reacted with anger and frustration that Saul was still stubbornly disobedient. Now, Samuel pronounced, not only Saul, but Israel's army, would fall into the hands of the Philistines (28:19). In the end, Saul's lack of trust in God brought about his own destruction as well as the death of those in his care.

PROFILE: SAUL

Saul's actions force us to wonder: When we choose to obey ourselves, who else are we leading into destruction?

Personal Reflection

- Most of us in today's modern culture are accustomed to looking out for ourselves and meeting our own needs. When Saul offered the sacrifice himself at Gilgal, he didn't consider God's command to wait or God's power to deliver. When has God called you to wait for his deliverance without seeking your own solutions?
- Saul disobeyed when he spared the Amalekite king and herds. Then he rationalized his disobedience before God. He went on to suffer depression, jealousy, and fits of anger. When has your disobedience and rationalization released a flood of destructive emotions within you?

Saul Proclaimed King

17 Samuel summoned the people to the LORD at Mizpah 18and said to them, *a* "Thus says the LORD, the God of Israel, 'I brought up Israel out of Egypt, and I rescued you from the hand of the Egyptians and from the hand of all the kingdoms that were oppressing you.' 19But today you have rejected your God, who saves you from all your calamities and your distresses; and you have said, 'No! but set a king over us.' Now therefore present yourselves before the LORD by your tribes and by your clans."

20 Then Samuel brought all the tribes of Israel near, and the tribe of Benjamin was taken by lot. 21He brought the tribe of Benjamin near by its families, and the family of the Matrites was taken by lot. Finally he brought the family of the Matrites near man by man, *b* and Saul the son of Kish was taken by lot. But when they sought him, he could not be found. 22So they inquired again of the LORD, "Did the man come here?" *c* and the LORD said, "See, he has hidden himself among the baggage." 23Then they ran and brought him from there. When he took his stand among the people, he was head and shoulders taller than any of them. 24Samuel said to all the people, "Do you see the one whom the LORD has chosen? There is no one like him among all the people." And all the people shouted, "Long live the king!"

25 Samuel told the people the rights and duties of the kingship; and he wrote them in a book and laid it up before the LORD. Then Samuel sent all the people back to their homes. 26Saul also went to his home at Gibeah, and with him went warriors whose hearts God had touched. 27But some worthless fellows said, "How can this man save us?" They despised him and brought him no present. But he held his peace.

Now Nahash, king of the Ammonites, had been grievously oppressing the Gadites and the Reubenites. He would gouge out the right eye of each of them and would not grant Israel a deliverer. No one was left of the

---

a Heb *to the people of Israel*   *b* Gk: Heb lacks
Finally . . . man by man   *c* Gk: Heb *Is there yet a man to come here?*

Israelites across the Jordan whose right eye Nahash, king of the Ammonites, had not gouged out. But there were seven thousand men who had escaped from the Ammonites and had entered Jabesh-gilead.*a*

Saul Defeats the Ammonites

11 About a month later,*b* Nahash the Ammonite went up and besieged Jabesh-gilead; and all the men of Jabesh said to Nahash, "Make a treaty with us, and we will serve you." 2But Nahash the Ammonite said to them, "On this condition I will make a treaty with you, namely that I gouge out everyone's right eye, and thus put disgrace upon all Israel." 3The elders of Jabesh said to him, "Give us seven days' respite that we may send messengers through all the territory of Israel. Then, if there is no one to save us, we will give ourselves up to you." 4When the messengers came to Gibeah of Saul, they reported the matter in the hearing of the people; and all the people wept aloud.

5 Now Saul was coming from the field behind the oxen; and Saul said, "What is the matter with the people, that they are weeping?" So they told him the message from the inhabitants of Jabesh. 6And the spirit of God came upon Saul in power when he heard these words, and his anger was greatly kindled. 7He took a yoke of oxen, and cut them in pieces and sent them throughout all the territory of Israel by messengers, saying, "Whoever does not come out after Saul and Samuel, so shall it be done to his oxen!" Then the dread of the LORD fell upon the people, and they came out as one. 8When he mustered them at Bezek, those from Israel were three hundred thousand, and those from Judah seventy*c* thousand. 9They said to the messengers who had come, "Thus shall you say to the inhabitants of Jabesh-gilead: 'Tomorrow, by the time the sun is hot, you shall have deliverance.' " When the messengers

came and told the inhabitants of Jabesh, they rejoiced. 10So the inhabitants of Jabesh said, "Tomorrow we will give ourselves up to you, and you may do to us whatever seems good to you." 11The next day Saul put the people in three companies. At the morning watch they came into the camp and cut down the Ammonites until the heat of the day; and those who survived were scattered, so that no two of them were left together.

12 The people said to Samuel, "Who is it that said, 'Shall Saul reign over us?' Give them to us so that we may put them to death." 13But Saul said, "No one shall be put to death this day, for today the LORD has brought deliverance to Israel."

14 Samuel said to the people, "Come, let us go to Gilgal and there renew the kingship." 15So all the people went to Gilgal, and there they made Saul king before the LORD in Gilgal. There they sacrificed offerings of well-being before the LORD, and there Saul and all the Israelites rejoiced greatly.

Samuel's Farewell Address

12 Samuel said to all Israel, "I have listened to you in all that you have said to me, and have set a king over you. 2See, it is the king who leads you now; I am old and gray, but my sons are with you. I have led you from my youth until this day. 3Here I am; testify against me before the LORD and before his anointed. Whose ox have I taken? Or whose donkey have I taken? Or whom have I defrauded? Whom have I oppressed? Or from whose hand have I taken a bribe to blind my eyes with it? Testify against me*d* and I will restore it to you." 4They said, "You

---

a Q Ms Compare Josephus, *Antiquities* VI.v.1 (68-71): MT lacks *Now Nahash . . . entered Jabesh-gilead.*
b Q Ms Gk: MT lacks *About a month later*
c Q Ms Gk: MT *thirty*   *d* Gk: Heb lacks *Testify against me*

11:13 *No one shall be put to death this day.* Strength is often equated with the use of force, but here strength manifests itself in the capacity for forgiveness and reconciliation. A wise leader recognizes that always using a coercive approach will harden into patterns of abuse that will end

up undermining the goals of the community. Saul's development of self-assured behavior demonstrates growth; he is no longer the young man who had once hidden among the baggage in order to demur from the responsibilities of the kingship (10:22).

have not defrauded us or oppressed us or taken anything from the hand of anyone." [5]He said to them, "The LORD is witness against you, and his anointed is witness this day, that you have not found anything in my hand." And they said, "He is witness."

6 Samuel said to the people, "The LORD is witness, who[a] appointed Moses and Aaron and brought your ancestors up out of the land of Egypt. [7]Now therefore take your stand, so that I may enter into judgment with you before the LORD, and I will declare to you[b] all the saving deeds of the LORD that he performed for you and for your ancestors. [8]When Jacob went into Egypt and the Egyptians oppressed them,[c] then your ancestors cried to the LORD and the LORD sent Moses and Aaron, who brought forth your ancestors out of Egypt, and settled them in this place. [9]But they forgot the LORD their God; and he sold them into the hand of Sisera, commander of the army of King Jabin of[d] Hazor, and into the hand of the Philistines, and into the hand of the king of Moab; and they fought against them. [10]Then they cried to the LORD, and said, 'We have sinned, because we have forsaken the LORD, and have served the Baals and the Astartes; but now rescue us out of the hand of our enemies, and we will serve you.' [11]And the LORD sent Jerubbaal and Barak,[e] and Jephthah, and Samson,[f] and rescued you out of the hand of your enemies on every side; and you lived in safety. [12]But when you saw that King Nahash of the Ammonites came against you, you said to me, 'No, but a king shall reign over us,' though the LORD your God was your king. [13]See, here is the king whom you have chosen, for whom you have asked; see, the LORD has set a king over you. [14]If you will fear the LORD and serve

him and heed his voice and not rebel against the commandment of the LORD, and if both you and the king who reigns over you will follow the LORD your God, it will be well; [15]but if you will not heed the voice of the LORD, but rebel against the commandment of the LORD, then the hand of the LORD will be against you and your king.[g] [16]Now therefore take your stand and see this great thing that the LORD will do before your eyes. [17]Is it not the wheat harvest today? I will call upon the LORD, that he may send thunder and rain; and you shall know and see that the wickedness that you have done in the sight of the LORD is great in demanding a king for yourselves." [18]So Samuel called upon the LORD, and the LORD sent thunder and rain that day; and all the people greatly feared the LORD and Samuel.

19 All the people said to Samuel, "Pray to the LORD your God for your servants, so that we may not die; for we have added to all our sins the evil of demanding a king for ourselves." [20]And Samuel said to the people, "Do not be afraid; you have done all this evil, yet do not turn aside from following the LORD, but serve the LORD with all your heart; [21]and do not turn aside after useless things that cannot profit or save, for they are useless. [22]For the LORD will not cast away his people, for his great name's sake, because it has pleased the LORD to make you a people for himself. [23]Moreover as for me, far be it from me that I should sin against the LORD by ceasing to pray for you; and I will instruct you in

a Gk: Heb lacks is witness, who   b Gk: Heb lacks and I will declare to you   c Gk: Heb lacks and the Egyptians oppressed them   d Gk: Heb lacks King Jabin of   e Gk Syr: Heb Bedan   f Gk: Heb Samuel   g Gk: Heb and your ancestors

---

12:5 *you have not found anything in my hand.* The tangible sign that Samuel offers of his moral leadership (to which the people agree) is the fact that he has not enriched himself through his office. There is nothing wrong with making one's living from the gifts received for ministry, but the lifestyle of the one who ministers should reflect that of the community within which she or he is situated. That the community agrees with Samuel is the sign that he has mastered

the balance between having his needs met and not evoking resentment among the people.

Responding
12:23 PRAYER. Today we would call Samuel a "prayer warrior." What gifts and qualities does a person who prays continuously for other people possess? *See also* Spiritual Disciplines Index.

the good and the right way. 24Only fear the
LORD, and serve him faithfully with all your
heart; for consider what great things he has
done for you. 25But if you still do wickedly,
you shall be swept away, both you and your
king."

Saul's Unlawful Sacrifice

13 Saul was . . .*a* years old when he began
to reign; and he reigned . . . and two*b*
years over Israel.

2 Saul chose three thousand out of Israel;
two thousand were with Saul in Michmash
and the hill country of Bethel, and a thousand were with Jonathan in Gibeah of Benjamin; the rest of the people he sent home to
their tents. 3Jonathan defeated the garrison
of the Philistines that was at Geba; and the
Philistines heard of it. And Saul blew the
trumpet throughout all the land, saying, "Let
the Hebrews hear!" 4When all Israel heard
that Saul had defeated the garrison of the
Philistines, and also that Israel had become
odious to the Philistines, the people were
called out to join Saul at Gilgal.

5 The Philistines mustered to fight with Israel, thirty thousand chariots, and six thousand horsemen, and troops like the sand on
the seashore in multitude; they came up and
encamped at Michmash, to the east of Beth-
aven. 6When the Israelites saw that they were
in distress (for the troops were hard pressed),
the people hid themselves in caves and in
holes and in rocks and in tombs and in cisterns. 7Some Hebrews crossed the Jordan to
the land of Gad and Gilead. Saul was still at
Gilgal, and all the people followed him trembling.

8 He waited seven days, the time appointed by Samuel; but Samuel did not come
to Gilgal, and the people began to slip away
from Saul.*c* 9So Saul said, "Bring the burnt offering here to me, and the offerings of well-

being." And he offered the burnt offering.
10As soon as he had finished offering the
burnt offering, Samuel arrived; and Saul went
out to meet him and salute him. 11Samuel
said, "What have you done?" Saul replied,
"When I saw that the people were slipping
away from me, and that you did not come
within the days appointed, and that the Philistines were mustering at Michmash, 12I said,
'Now the Philistines will come down upon
me at Gilgal, and I have not entreated the favor of the LORD'; so I forced myself, and offered the burnt offering." 13Samuel said to
Saul, "You have done foolishly; you have not
kept the commandment of the LORD your
God, which he commanded you. The LORD
would have established your kingdom over Israel forever, 14but now your kingdom will not
continue; the LORD has sought out a man after his own heart; and the LORD has appointed him to be ruler over his people, because
you have not kept what the LORD commanded you." 15And Samuel left and went on his
way from Gilgal.*d* The rest of the people followed Saul to join the army; they went up
from Gilgal toward Gibeah of Benjamin.*e*

Preparations for Battle

Saul counted the people who were present with him, about six hundred men. 16Saul,
his son Jonathan, and the people who were
present with them stayed in Geba of Benjamin; but the Philistines encamped at Michmash. 17And raiders came out of the camp
of the Philistines in three companies; one
company turned toward Ophrah, to the land
of Shual, 18another company turned toward

a The number is lacking in the Heb text (the verse
is lacking in the Septuagint).   *b* *Two* is not the
entire number; something has dropped out.
c Heb *him*   *d* Gk: Heb *went up from Gilgal to
Gibeah of Benjamin*   *e* Gk: Heb lacks *The rest . . .
of Benjamin*

12:24 SERVICE—*See* Spiritual Disciplines
Index.

13:8–14 *And he offered the burnt offering.*
This is a difficult section of the narrative to
grasp, because readers can sympathize with
Saul's dilemma when Samuel does not follow
through with his promise to appear. But the text

insists that Saul should have waited, nonetheless, and not taken upon himself what God
had called Samuel to perform. His seemingly
reasonable impatience leads him to a rash act
that will ultimately undo his kingship. Once
again, "to obey is better than sacrifice" (15:22).

Beth-horon, and another company turned toward the mountain*a* that looks down upon the valley of Zeboim toward the wilderness.

19 Now there was no smith to be found throughout all the land of Israel; for the Philistines said, "The Hebrews must not make swords or spears for themselves"; 20so all the Israelites went down to the Philistines to sharpen their plowshares, mattocks, axes, or sickles;*b* 21The charge was two-thirds of a shekel*c* for the plowshares and for the mattocks, and one-third of a shekel for sharpening the axes and for setting the goads.*d* 22So on the day of the battle neither sword nor spear was to be found in the possession of any of the people with Saul and Jonathan; but Saul and his son Jonathan had them.

Jonathan Surprises and Routs the Philistines

23 Now a garrison of the Philistines had gone out to the pass of Michmash. 14 1One day Jonathan son of Saul said to the young man who carried his armor, "Come, let us go over to the Philistine garrison on the other side." But he did not tell his father. 2Saul was staying in the outskirts of Gibeah under the pomegranate tree that is at Migron; the troops that were with him were about six hundred men, 3along with Ahijah son of Ahitub, Ichabod's brother, son of Phinehas son of Eli, the priest of the LORD in Shiloh, carrying an ephod. Now the people did not know that Jonathan had gone. 4In the pass,*e* by which Jonathan tried to go over to the Philistine garrison, there was a rocky crag on one side and a rocky crag on the other; the name of the one was Bozez, and the name of the other Seneh. 5One crag rose on the north in front of Michmash, and the other on the south in front of Geba.

6 Jonathan said to the young man who carried his armor, "Come, let us go over to the garrison of these uncircumcised; it may be that the LORD will act for us; for nothing can hinder the LORD from saving by many or

by few." 7His armor-bearer said to him, "Do all that your mind inclines to.*f* I am with you; as your mind is, so is mine."*g* 8Then Jonathan said, "Now we will cross over to those men and will show ourselves to them. 9If they say to us, 'Wait until we come to you,' then we will stand still in our place, and we will not go up to them. 10But if they say, 'Come up to us,' then we will go up; for the LORD has given them into our hand. That will be the sign for us." 11So both of them showed themselves to the garrison of the Philistines; and the Philistines said, "Look, Hebrews are coming out of the holes where they have hidden themselves." 12The men of the garrison hailed Jonathan and his armor-bearer, saying, "Come up to us, and we will show you something." Jonathan said to his armor-bearer, "Come up after me; for the LORD has given them into the hand of Israel." 13Then Jonathan climbed up on his hands and feet, with his armor-bearer following after him. The Philistines*h* fell before Jonathan, and his armor-bearer, coming after him, killed them. 14In that first slaughter Jonathan and his armor-bearer killed about twenty men within an area about half a furrow long in an acre of land. 15There was a panic in the camp, in the field, and among all the people; the garrison and even the raiders trembled; the earth quaked; and it became a very great panic.

16 Saul's lookouts in Gibeah of Benjamin were watching as the multitude was surging back and forth.*i* 17Then Saul said to the troops that were with him, "Call the roll and see who has gone from us." When they had called the roll, Jonathan and his armor-bearer were not there. 18Saul said to Ahijah, "Bring

---

a Cn Compare Gk: Heb *toward the border*
b Gk: Heb *plowshare*   *c* Heb *was a pim*
d Cn: Meaning of Heb uncertain   *e* Heb *Between the passes*   *f* Gk: Heb *Do all that is in your mind. Turn*   *g* Gk: Heb lacks *so is mine*   *h* Heb *They*
i Heb *yoke*   *j* Gk: Heb *they went and there*

13:22 *neither sword nor spear.* The lack of technology points to both the disparity between Israel and its neighbors and the enormous faith that Israel possesses to trust God even in the face

of such massive odds. The community will often despair that it lacks the accoutrements possessed by its neighbors, but it is in its lack that God is made most abundantly manifest in its life.

the ark*a* of God here." For at that time the ark*a* of God went with the Israelites. 19While Saul was talking to the priest, the tumult in the camp of the Philistines increased more and more; and Saul said to the priest, "Withdraw your hand." 20Then Saul and all the people who were with him rallied and went into the battle; and every sword was against the other, so that there was very great confusion. 21Now the Hebrews who previously had been with the Philistines and had gone up with them into the camp turned and joined the Israelites who were with Saul and Jonathan. 22Likewise, when all the Israelites who had gone into hiding in the hill country of Ephraim heard that the Philistines were fleeing, they too followed closely after them in the battle. 23So the LORD gave Israel the victory that day.

The battle passed beyond Beth-aven, and the troops with Saul numbered altogether about ten thousand men. The battle spread out over the hill country of Ephraim.

Saul's Rash Oath

24 Now Saul committed a very rash act on that day.*b* He had laid an oath on the troops, saying, "Cursed be anyone who eats food before it is evening and I have been avenged on my enemies." So none of the troops tasted food. 25All the troops*c* came upon a honeycomb; and there was honey on the ground. 26When the troops came upon the honeycomb, the honey was dripping out; but they did not put their hands to their mouths, for they feared the oath. 27But Jonathan had not heard his father charge the troops with the oath; so he extended the staff that was in his hand, and dipped the tip of it in the honeycomb, and put his hand to his mouth; and his eyes brightened. 28Then one of the soldiers said, "Your father strictly charged the troops with an oath, saying, 'Cursed be anyone who eats food this day.' And so the troops are faint." 29Then Jonathan said, "My father has troubled the land; see how my eyes have brightened because I tasted a little of this honey. 30How much better if today the troops had eaten freely of the spoil taken from their enemies; for now the slaughter among the Philistines has not been great."

31 After they had struck down the Philistines that day from Michmash to Aijalon, the troops were very faint; 32so the troops flew upon the spoil, and took sheep and oxen and calves, and slaughtered them on the ground; and the troops ate them with the blood. 33Then it was reported to Saul, "Look, the troops are sinning against the LORD by eating with the blood." And he said, "You have dealt treacherously; roll a large stone before me here."*d* 34Saul said, "Disperse yourselves among the troops, and say to them, 'Let all bring their oxen or their sheep, and slaughter them here, and eat; and do not sin against the LORD by eating with the blood.' " So all of the troops brought their oxen with them that night, and slaughtered them there. 35And Saul built an altar to the LORD; it was the first altar that he built to the LORD.

Jonathan in Danger of Death

36 Then Saul said, "Let us go down after the Philistines by night and despoil them until the morning light; let us not leave one of them." They said, "Do whatever seems good to you." But the priest said, "Let us draw near to God here." 37So Saul inquired of God, "Shall I go down after the Philistines? Will you give them into the hand of Israel?" But he did not answer him that day. 38Saul said, "Come here, all you leaders of the people; and let us find out how this sin has arisen today. 39For as the LORD lives who saves Israel, even if it is in my son Jonathan, he shall surely die!" But there was no one among all the people who answered him. 40He said to all Israel, "You shall be on one side, and I and my son Jonathan will be on the other side." The people said to Saul, "Do what seems good to you." 41Then Saul said, "O LORD God of Israel, why have you not answered your servant today? If this guilt is in me or in my son Jonathan, O LORD God of Israel, give Urim; but if this guilt is in your people Israel,*e* give Thummim." And Jonathan and Saul were indicat-

a Gk *the ephod*   *b* Gk: Heb *The Israelites were distressed that day*   *c* Heb *land*   *d* Gk: Heb *me this day*   *e* Vg Compare Gk: Heb 41*Saul said to the* LORD, *the God of Israel*

ed by the lot, but the people were cleared. 42Then Saul said, "Cast the lot between me and my son Jonathan." And Jonathan was taken.

43 Then Saul said to Jonathan, "Tell me what you have done." Jonathan told him, "I tasted a little honey with the tip of the staff that was in my hand; here I am, I will die." 44Saul said, "God do so to me and more also; you shall surely die, Jonathan!" 45Then the people said to Saul, "Shall Jonathan die, who has accomplished this great victory in Israel? Far from it! As the LORD lives, not one hair of his head shall fall to the ground; for he has worked with God today." So the people ransomed Jonathan, and he did not die. 46Then Saul withdrew from pursuing the Philistines; and the Philistines went to their own place.

Saul's Continuing Wars

47 When Saul had taken the kingship over Israel, he fought against all his enemies on every side—against Moab, against the Ammonites, against Edom, against the kings of Zobah, and against the Philistines; wherever he turned he routed them. 48He did valiantly, and struck down the Amalekites, and rescued Israel out of the hands of those who plundered them.

49 Now the sons of Saul were Jonathan, Ishvi, and Malchishua; and the names of his two daughters were these: the name of the firstborn was Merab, and the name of the younger, Michal. 50The name of Saul's wife was Ahinoam daughter of Ahimaaz. And the name of the commander of his army was Abner son of Ner, Saul's uncle; 51Kish was the father of Saul, and Ner the father of Abner was the son of Abiel.

52 There was hard fighting against the Philistines all the days of Saul; and when Saul saw any strong or valiant warrior, he took him into his service.

Saul Defeats the Amalekites but Spares Their King

15 Samuel said to Saul, "The LORD sent me to anoint you king over his people Israel; now therefore listen to the words of the LORD. 2Thus says the LORD of hosts, 'I will punish the Amalekites for what they did in opposing the Israelites when they came up out of Egypt. 3Now go and attack Amalek, and utterly destroy all that they have; do not spare them, but kill both man and woman, child and infant, ox and sheep, camel and donkey.' "

4 So Saul summoned the people, and numbered them in Telaim, two hundred thousand foot soldiers, and ten thousand soldiers of Judah. 5Saul came to the city of the Amalekites and lay in wait in the valley. 6Saul said to the Kenites, "Go! Leave! Withdraw from among the Amalekites, or I will destroy you with them; for you showed kindness to all the people of Israel when they came up out of Egypt." So the Kenites withdrew from the Amalekites. 7Saul defeated the Amalekites, from Havilah as far as Shur, which is east of Egypt. 8He took King Agag of the Amalekites alive, but utterly destroyed all the people with the edge of the sword. 9Saul and the people spared Agag, and the best of the sheep and of the cattle and of the fatlings, and the lambs, and all that was valuable, and would not utterly destroy them; all that was despised and worthless they utterly destroyed.

Saul Rejected as King

10 The word of the LORD came to Samuel: 11"I regret that I made Saul king, for he has turned back from following me, and has not carried out my commands." Samuel was angry; and he cried out to the LORD all night. 12Samuel rose early in the morning to meet Saul, and Samuel was told, "Saul went to Carmel, where he set up a monument for

---

14:45 *Shall Jonathan die? . . . Far from it!* A basic practice of spiritual formation is carrying out God's standard for justice. The people rise up and overturn the regrettable oath made by Saul in verse 24. The making of promises to God, as we saw with Hannah in chapter 1, is a

time-honored practice in Israel, but the essential unjustness of this one rightly causes the faithful community, which sees in Jonathan's actions that day the handiwork of Yahweh, to dissuade Saul from following through with it.

himself, and on returning he passed on down to Gilgal." [13]When Samuel came to Saul, Saul said to him, "May you be blessed by the LORD; I have carried out the command of the LORD." [14]But Samuel said, "What then is this bleating of sheep in my ears, and the lowing of cattle that I hear?" [15]Saul said, "They have brought them from the Amalekites; for the people spared the best of the sheep and the cattle, to sacrifice to the LORD your God; but the rest we have utterly destroyed." [16]Then Samuel said to Saul, "Stop! I will tell you what the LORD said to me last night." He replied, "Speak."

17 Samuel said, "Though you are little in your own eyes, are you not the head of the tribes of Israel? The LORD anointed you king over Israel. [18]And the LORD sent you on a mission, and said, 'Go, utterly destroy the sinners, the Amalekites, and fight against them until they are consumed.' [19]Why then did you not obey the voice of the LORD? Why did you swoop down on the spoil, and do what was evil in the sight of the LORD?" [20]Saul said to Samuel, "I have obeyed the voice of the LORD, I have gone on the mission on which the LORD sent me, I have brought Agag the king of Amalek, and I have utterly destroyed the Amalekites. [21]But from the spoil the people took sheep and cattle, the best of the things devoted to destruction, to sacrifice to the LORD your God in Gilgal." [22]And Samuel said,

"Has the LORD as great delight in burnt offerings and sacrifices,
as in obedience to the voice of the LORD?
Surely, to obey is better than sacrifice,
and to heed than the fat of rams.
[23] For rebellion is no less a sin than divination,
and stubbornness is like iniquity and idolatry.
Because you have rejected the word of the LORD,
he has also rejected you from being king."

24 Saul said to Samuel, "I have sinned; for I have transgressed the commandment of the LORD and your words, because I feared the people and obeyed their voice. [25]Now therefore, I pray, pardon my sin, and return with me, so that I may worship the LORD." [26]Samuel said to Saul, "I will not return with you; for you have rejected the word of the LORD, and the LORD has rejected you from being king over Israel." [27]As Samuel turned to go away, Saul caught hold of the hem of his robe,

---

15:22 SACRIFICE—*See* Spiritual Disciplines Index.

15:22–23 *Has the LORD as great delight in . . . sacrifices, as in obedience?* This stylized, poetic statement, we might guess, has been placed on the lips of Samuel by the narrator, as it is hard to imagine the old judge composing poetry while in a fit of anger. Its origin aside, the poem is a clear presentation of what covenant fidelity entails, which is more than just adherence to the ritual life of the community. The poet does not denigrate ritual life, as has been the tendency of much of later Christianity, as if ritual were something extraneous that could be jettisoned, but rather prioritizes obedience above ritual in the proper development of spirituality.

15:24 *I have sinned.* Saul adopts the only response available to him in the face of the withering criticism of Samuel. The Amalekites are under the "ban," which is to say they were to be utterly wiped out (15:2; cf. Exod 17:8–14; Deut 25:17–19). Saul does not utterly destroy them as Deuteronomy demands (v 9), so he is technically guilty. Saul weakens his apology, as many of us often do, by offering up reasons, in this case other people, for why he did what he did ("I feared the people"). Not only does this make Saul look weak, it also does not fit the circumstances—there doesn't seem to be any reason why the people would have gone against Saul, had he killed Agag and all the animals. Even when there are reasons for a misdeed, an admission of guilt should never be qualified or rationalized, because it conveys the sense that the individual is more sorry for having been caught than thoroughly repentant for the actual offense. So Saul sinned by overstepping his role as king by editing God's command and then fell short again by not taking responsibility for his decisions as king and blaming his people for his failure.

and it tore. 28And Samuel said to him, "The LORD has torn the kingdom of Israel from you this very day, and has given it to a neighbor of yours, who is better than you. 29Moreover the Glory of Israel will not recant[a] or change his mind; for he is not a mortal, that he should change his mind." 30Then Saul[b] said, "I have sinned; yet honor me now before the elders of my people and before Israel, and return with me, so that I may worship the LORD your God." 31So Samuel turned back after Saul; and Saul worshiped the LORD.

32 Then Samuel said, "Bring Agag king of the Amalekites here to me." And Agag came to him haltingly.[c] Agag said, "Surely this is the bitterness of death."[d] 33But Samuel said,

> "As your sword has made women
> childless,
> so your mother shall be childless
> among women."

And Samuel hewed Agag in pieces before the LORD in Gilgal.

34 Then Samuel went to Ramah; and Saul went up to his house in Gibeah of Saul. 35Samuel did not see Saul again until the day of his death, but Samuel grieved over Saul. And the LORD was sorry that he had made Saul king over Israel.

David Anointed as King

16 The LORD said to Samuel, "How long will you grieve over Saul? I have rejected him from being king over Israel. Fill your horn with oil and set out; I will send you to Jesse the Bethlehemite, for I have provided for myself a king among his sons." 2Samuel said, "How can I go? If Saul hears of it, he will kill me." And the LORD said, "Take a heifer with you, and say, 'I have come to sacrifice to the LORD.' 3Invite Jesse to the sacrifice, and I will show you what you shall do; and you shall anoint for me the one whom I

name to you." 4Samuel did what the LORD commanded, and came to Bethlehem. The elders of the city came to meet him trembling, and said, "Do you come peaceably?" 5He said, "Peaceably; I have come to sacrifice to the LORD; sanctify yourselves and come with me to the sacrifice." And he sanctified Jesse and his sons and invited them to the sacrifice.

6 When they came, he looked on Eliab and thought, "Surely the LORD's anointed is now before the LORD."[e] 7But the LORD said to Samuel, "Do not look on his appearance or on the height of his stature, because I have rejected him; for the LORD does not see as mortals see; they look on the outward appearance, but the LORD looks on the heart." 8Then Jesse called Abinadab, and made him pass before Samuel. He said, "Neither has the LORD chosen this one." 9Then Jesse made Shammah pass by. And he said, "Neither has the LORD chosen this one." 10Jesse made seven of his sons pass before Samuel, and Samuel said to Jesse, "The LORD has not chosen any of these." 11Samuel said to Jesse, "Are all your sons here?" And he said, "There remains yet the youngest, but he is keeping the sheep." And Samuel said to Jesse, "Send and bring him; for we will not sit down until he comes here." 12He sent and brought him in. Now he was ruddy, and had beautiful eyes, and was handsome. The LORD said, "Rise and anoint him; for this is the one." 13Then Samuel took the horn of oil, and anointed him in the presence of his brothers; and the spirit of the LORD came mightily upon David from that day forward. Samuel then set out and went to Ramah.

a Q Ms Gk: MT *deceive*   b Heb *he*
c Cn Compare Gk: Meaning of Heb uncertain
d Q Ms Gk: MT *Surely the bitterness of death is past*
e Heb *him*

16:7 *Do not look on his appearance.* The same mistake will not be made twice in Israel, which is imagining that the outward strength and beauty of the potential monarch necessarily indicate a person of character on the inside (cf. Israel's first impression of Saul in 9:2). Nor will the criterion of primogeniture (the firstborn inherits) prevail in the selection, as that is not

the way of this God (see the stories of Isaac, Jacob, and Joseph in Genesis). Samuel is pressed to search further for the one who has caught Yahweh's eye, the emphasis being that those whose minds are spiritually attuned to the same values as Yahweh's will be drawn to a different set of qualities than those valued by the larger society.

David Plays the Lyre for Saul

14 Now the spirit of the LORD departed from Saul, and an evil spirit from the LORD tormented him. 15 And Saul's servants said to him, "See now, an evil spirit from God is tormenting you. 16 Let our lord now command the servants who attend you to look for someone who is skillful in playing the lyre; and when the evil spirit from God is upon you, he will play it, and you will feel better." 17 So Saul said to his servants, "Provide for me someone who can play well, and bring him to me." 18 One of the young men answered, "I have seen a son of Jesse the Bethlehemite who is skillful in playing, a man of valor, a warrior, prudent in speech, and a man of good presence; and the LORD is with him." 19 So Saul sent messengers to Jesse, and said, "Send me your son David who is with the sheep." 20 Jesse took a donkey loaded with bread, a skin of wine, and a kid, and sent them by his son David to Saul. 21 And David came to Saul, and entered his service. Saul loved him greatly, and he became his armor-bearer. 22 Saul sent to Jesse, saying, "Let David remain in my service, for he has found favor in my sight." 23 And whenever the evil spirit from God came upon Saul, David took the lyre and played it with his hand, and Saul would be relieved and feel better, and the evil spirit would depart from him.

David and Goliath

17 Now the Philistines gathered their armies for battle; they were gathered at Socoh, which belongs to Judah, and encamped between Socoh and Azekah, in Ephes-dammim. 2 Saul and the Israelites gathered and encamped in the valley of Elah, and formed ranks against the Philistines. 3 The Philistines stood on the mountain on the one side, and Israel stood on the mountain on the other side, with a valley between them. 4 And there came out from the camp of the Philistines a champion named Goliath, of Gath, whose height was six *a* cubits and a span. 5 He had a helmet of bronze on his head, and he was armed with a coat of mail; the weight of the coat was five thousand shekels of bronze. 6 He had greaves of bronze on his legs and a javelin of bronze slung between his shoulders. 7 The shaft of his spear was like a weaver's beam, and his spear's head weighed six hundred shekels of iron; and his shield-bearer went before him. 8 He stood and shouted to the ranks of Israel, "Why have you come out to draw up for battle? Am I not a Philistine, and are you not servants of Saul? Choose a man for yourselves, and let him come down to me. 9 If he is able to fight with me and kill me, then we will be your servants; but if I prevail against him and kill him, then you shall be our servants and serve us." 10 And the Philistine said, "Today I defy the ranks of Israel! Give me a man, that we may fight together." 11 When Saul and all Israel heard these words of the Philistine, they were dismayed and greatly afraid.

12 Now David was the son of an Ephrathite of Bethlehem in Judah, named Jesse, who had eight sons. In the days of Saul the man was already old and advanced in years. *b* 13 The three eldest sons of Jesse had followed Saul to the battle; the names of his three sons who went to the battle were Eliab the firstborn, and next to him Abinadab, and

a MT: Q Ms Gk *four*   *b* Gk Syr: Heb *among men*

Responding

16:16–22 SERVICE. Many of us recoil from this story because we can't imagine a father sending his teenage child away from home to be an "involuntary servant" to a king. In Rom 13:1 the apostle Paul writes, "Let every person be subject to the governing authorities." In what voluntary ways can we serve and be subject to the leaders of our country? Choose one and do it this week. *See also* Spiritual Disciplines Index.

16:23 *the evil spirit would depart from him.* The capacity of art, whether music or some other form, has long been known, even from antiquity, as this text demonstrates, to have a soothing effect on the troubled soul. Saul's servants (v 15) wisely make the suggestion that Saul apply this remedy to his own mental illness, a remedy that ironically ends up being transmitted through the skills of David, whose anointing as king will come to trouble Saul far more than he can yet know.

the third Shammah. ¹⁴David was the youngest; the three eldest followed Saul, ¹⁵but David went back and forth from Saul to feed his father's sheep at Bethlehem. ¹⁶For forty days the Philistine came forward and took his stand, morning and evening.

17 Jesse said to his son David, "Take for your brothers an ephah of this parched grain and these ten loaves, and carry them quickly to the camp to your brothers; ¹⁸also take these ten cheeses to the commander of their thousand. See how your brothers fare, and bring some token from them."

19 Now Saul, and they, and all the men of Israel, were in the valley of Elah, fighting with the Philistines. ²⁰David rose early in the morning, left the sheep with a keeper, took the provisions, and went as Jesse had commanded him. He came to the encampment as the army was going forth to the battle line, shouting the war cry. ²¹Israel and the Philistines drew up for battle, army against army. ²²David left the things in charge of the keeper of the baggage, ran to the ranks, and went and greeted his brothers. ²³As he talked with them, the champion, the Philistine of Gath, Goliath by name, came up out of the ranks of the Philistines, and spoke the same words as before. And David heard him.

24 All the Israelites, when they saw the man, fled from him and were very much afraid. ²⁵The Israelites said, "Have you seen this man who has come up? Surely he has come up to defy Israel. The king will greatly enrich the man who kills him, and will give him his daughter and make his family free in Israel." ²⁶David said to the men who stood by him, "What shall be done for the man who kills this Philistine, and takes away the reproach from Israel? For who is this uncircumcised Philistine that he should defy the armies of the living God?" ²⁷The people answered him in the same way, "So shall it be done for the man who kills him."

28 His eldest brother Eliab heard him talking to the men; and Eliab's anger was kindled against David. He said, "Why have you come down? With whom have you left those few sheep in the wilderness? I know your presumption and the evil of your heart; for you have come down just to see the battle." ²⁹David said, "What have I done now? It was only a question." ³⁰He turned away from him toward another and spoke in the same way; and the people answered him again as before.

31 When the words that David spoke were heard, they repeated them before Saul; and he sent for him. ³²David said to Saul, "Let no one's heart fail because of him; your servant will go and fight with this Philistine." ³³Saul said to David, "You are not able to go against this Philistine to fight with him; for you are just a boy, and he has been a warrior from his youth." ³⁴But David said to Saul, "Your servant used to keep sheep for his father; and whenever a lion or a bear came, and took a lamb from the flock, ³⁵I went after it and struck it down, rescuing the lamb from its mouth; and if it turned against me, I would catch it by the jaw, strike it down, and kill it. ³⁶Your servant has killed both lions and bears; and this uncircumcised Philistine shall be like one of them, since he has defied the armies of the living God." ³⁷David said, "The LORD, who saved me from the paw of the lion and from the paw of the bear, will save me from the hand of this Philistine." So Saul said to David, "Go, and may the LORD be with you!"

38 Saul clothed David with his armor; he put a bronze helmet on his head and clothed him with a coat of mail. ³⁹David strapped Saul's sword over the armor, and he tried in vain to walk, for he was not used to them. Then David said to Saul, "I cannot walk with these; for I am not used to them." So David removed them. ⁴⁰Then he took his staff in his hand, and chose five smooth stones from the wadi, and put them in his shepherd's bag, in the pouch; his sling was in his hand, and he drew near to the Philistine.

17:32 *your servant will go and fight with this Philistine.* Young David is willing to take a stand against the mocker of Yahweh even if no one else is. Although the narrative clearly shows that the victor will gain many rewards (vv 25–27), the text does not linger there, but instead focuses on David's enormous courage and his faith in Yahweh to deliver him.

41 The Philistine came on and drew near to David, with his shield-bearer in front of him. 42When the Philistine looked and saw David, he disdained him, for he was only a youth, ruddy and handsome in appearance. 43The Philistine said to David, "Am I a dog, that you come to me with sticks?" And the Philistine cursed David by his gods. 44The Philistine said to David, "Come to me, and I will give your flesh to the birds of the air and to the wild animals of the field." 45But David said to the Philistine, "You come to me with sword and spear and javelin; but I come to you in the name of the LORD of hosts, the God of the armies of Israel, whom you have defied. 46This very day the LORD will deliver you into my hand, and I will strike you down and cut off your head; and I will give the dead bodies of the Philistine army this very day to the birds of the air and to the wild animals of the earth, so that all the earth may know that there is a God in Israel, 47and that all this assembly may know that the LORD does not save by sword and spear; for the battle is the LORD's and he will give you into our hand."

48 When the Philistine drew nearer to meet David, David ran quickly toward the battle line to meet the Philistine. 49David put his hand in his bag, took out a stone, slung it, and struck the Philistine on his forehead; the stone sank into his forehead, and he fell face down on the ground.

50 So David prevailed over the Philistine with a sling and a stone, striking down the Philistine and killing him; there was no sword in David's hand. 51Then David ran and stood over the Philistine; he grasped his sword, drew it out of its sheath, and killed him; then he cut off his head with it.

When the Philistines saw that their champion was dead, they fled. 52The troops of Israel and Judah rose up with a shout and pursued the Philistines as far as Gath*a* and the gates of Ekron, so that the wounded Philistines fell on the way from Shaaraim as far as Gath and Ekron. 53The Israelites came back from chasing the Philistines, and they plundered their camp. 54David took the head of the Philistine and brought it to Jerusalem; but he put his armor in his tent.

55 When Saul saw David go out against the Philistine, he said to Abner, the commander of the army, "Abner, whose son is this young man?" Abner said, "As your soul lives, O king, I do not know." 56The king said, "Inquire whose son the stripling is." 57On David's return from killing the Philistine, Abner took him and brought him before Saul, with the head of the Philistine in his hand. 58Saul said to him, "Whose son are you, young man?" And David answered, "I am the son of your servant Jesse the Bethlehemite."

Jonathan's Covenant with David

18 When David*b* had finished speaking to Saul, the soul of Jonathan was bound to the soul of David, and Jonathan loved him as his own soul. 2Saul took him that day and would not let him return to his father's house. 3Then Jonathan made a covenant with David, because he loved him as his own soul. 4Jonathan stripped himself of the robe that he was wearing, and gave it to David, and his armor, and even his sword and his bow and his belt. 5David went out and was successful wherever Saul sent him; as

a Gk Syr: Heb *Gai*   *b* Heb *he*

17:46–47 THE WITH-GOD LIFE—*See* Spiritual Disciplines Index.

18:3 *Jonathan . . . loved him as his own soul.* Jonathan makes a decision to place his friendship for David above his loyalty to his father as well as above his own claims to the throne, even to the point of lying to his father about David's activities (20:28–29). He does not utterly forsake his father in following what is to him an unjust scheme (cf. 19:4; 20:32), but avoids becoming

entangled in his father's anger and opposition. Michal will follow a similar path in opposing her father (19:8–17). Covenant life, as especially the Gospel traditions around Jesus will later make clear, may require putting aside "family loyalties" when they are opposed to God's work in the world.

18:5 SERVICE—*See* Spiritual Disciplines Index.

a result, Saul set him over the army. And all the people, even the servants of Saul, approved.

6 As they were coming home, when David returned from killing the Philistine, the women came out of all the towns of Israel, singing and dancing, to meet King Saul, with tambourines, with songs of joy, and with musical instruments. *a* 7 And the women sang to one another as they made merry,

"Saul has killed his thousands,
   and David his ten thousands."

8 Saul was very angry, for this saying displeased him. He said, "They have ascribed to David ten thousands, and to me they have ascribed thousands; what more can he have but the kingdom?" 9 So Saul eyed David from that day on.

Saul Tries to Kill David

10 The next day an evil spirit from God rushed upon Saul, and he raved within his house, while David was playing the lyre, as he did day by day. Saul had his spear in his hand; 11 and Saul threw the spear, for he thought, "I will pin David to the wall." But David eluded him twice.

12 Saul was afraid of David, because the LORD was with him but had departed from Saul. 13 So Saul removed him from his presence, and made him a commander of a thousand; and David marched out and came in, leading the army. 14 David had success in all his undertakings; for the LORD was with him. 15 When Saul saw that he had great success, he stood in awe of him. 16 But all Israel and Judah loved David; for it was he who marched out and came in leading them.

David Marries Michal

17 Then Saul said to David, "Here is my elder daughter Merab; I will give her to you as a wife; only be valiant for me and fight the LORD's battles." For Saul thought, "I will not raise a hand against him; let the Philistines deal with him." 18 David said to Saul, "Who am I and who are my kinsfolk, my father's family in Israel, that I should be son-in-law to the king?" 19 But at the time when Saul's daughter Merab should have been given to David, she was given to Adriel the Meholathite as a wife.

20 Now Saul's daughter Michal loved David. Saul was told, and the thing pleased him. 21 Saul thought, "Let me give her to him that she may be a snare for him and that the hand of the Philistines may be against him." Therefore Saul said to David a second time, *b* "You shall now be my son-in-law." 22 Saul commanded his servants, "Speak to David in private and say, 'See, the king is delighted with you, and all his servants love you; now then, become the king's son-in-law.' " 23 So Saul's servants reported these words to David in private. And David said, "Does it seem to you a little thing to become the king's son-in-law, seeing that I am a poor man and of no repute?" 24 The servants of Saul told him, "This is what David said." 25 Then Saul said, "Thus shall you say to David, 'The king desires no marriage present except a hundred foreskins of the Philistines, that he may be avenged on the king's enemies.' " Now Saul planned to make David fall by the hand of the Philistines. 26 When his servants told David these words, David was well pleased to be the king's son-in-law. Before the time had expired, 27 David rose and went, along with his men, and killed one hundred *c* of the Philistines; and David brought their foreskins, which were given in full number to the king, that he might become the king's son-in-law. Saul gave him his daughter Michal as a wife. 28 But when Saul realized that the LORD was with

a Or triangles, or three-stringed instruments
b Heb by two   *c* Gk Compare 2 Sam 3.14: Heb two hundred

Responding

18:12–15 THE WITH-GOD LIFE. Saul now becomes like Samson—the Lord has departed from him. But unlike Samson, Saul knows a person whom the Lord is with—David—and becomes jealous of him. Using only their first names, list those you have known who "glowed" from the presence of the Lord. Were you jealous of their experience? If so, hold this tenderly before the Lord and ask for forgiveness and a heart big enough to accept the Lord's way with them. See also Spiritual Disciplines Index.

David, and that Saul's daughter Michal loved him, 29Saul was still more afraid of David. So Saul was David's enemy from that time forward.

30 Then the commanders of the Philistines came out to battle; and as often as they came out, David had more success than all the servants of Saul, so that his fame became very great.

Jonathan Intercedes for David

19 Saul spoke with his son Jonathan and with all his servants about killing David. But Saul's son Jonathan took great delight in David. 2Jonathan told David, "My father Saul is trying to kill you; therefore be on guard tomorrow morning; stay in a secret place and hide yourself. 3I will go out and stand beside my father in the field where you are, and I will speak to my father about you; if I learn anything I will tell you." 4Jonathan spoke well of David to his father Saul, saying to him, "The king should not sin against his servant David, because he has not sinned against you, and because his deeds have been of good service to you; 5for he took his life in his hand when he attacked the Philistine, and the LORD brought about a great victory for all Israel. You saw it, and rejoiced; why then will you sin against an innocent person by killing David without cause?" 6Saul heeded the voice of Jonathan; Saul swore, "As the LORD lives, he shall not be put to death." 7So Jonathan called David and related all these things to him. Jonathan then brought David to Saul, and he was in his presence as before.

Michal Helps David Escape from Saul

8 Again there was war, and David went out to fight the Philistines. He launched a heavy attack on them, so that they fled before him. 9Then an evil spirit from the LORD came upon Saul, as he sat in his house with his spear in his hand, while David was playing music. 10Saul sought to pin David to the wall with the spear; but he eluded Saul, so that he struck the spear into the wall. David fled and escaped that night.

11 Saul sent messengers to David's house to keep watch over him, planning to kill him in the morning. David's wife Michal told him, "If you do not save your life tonight, tomorrow you will be killed." 12So Michal let David down through the window; he fled away and escaped. 13Michal took an idol*a* and laid it on the bed; she put a net*b* of goats' hair on its head, and covered it with the clothes. 14When Saul sent messengers to take David, she said, "He is sick." 15Then Saul sent the messengers to see David for themselves. He said, "Bring him up to me in the bed, that I may kill him." 16When the messengers came in, the idol*c* was in the bed, with the covering*b* of goats' hair on its head. 17Saul said to Michal, "Why have you deceived me like this, and let my enemy go, so that he has escaped?" Michal answered Saul, "He said to me, 'Let me go; why should I kill you?'"

David Joins Samuel in Ramah

18 Now David fled and escaped; he came to Samuel at Ramah, and told him all that Saul had done to him. He and Samuel went and settled at Naioth. 19Saul was told, "David is at Naioth in Ramah." 20Then Saul sent messengers to take David. When they saw the company of the prophets in a frenzy, with Samuel standing in charge of*b* them, the spirit of God came upon the messengers of Saul, and they also fell into a prophetic frenzy. 21When Saul was told, he sent other messengers, and they also fell into a frenzy. Saul sent messengers again the third time, and they also fell into a frenzy. 22Then he himself went to Ramah. He came to the great well that is in Secu;*d* he asked, "Where are Samuel and David?" And someone said, "They are at Naioth in Ramah." 23He went there, toward Naioth in Ramah; and the spirit of God came upon him. As he was going, he fell into a prophetic frenzy, until he came to Naioth in Ramah. 24He too stripped off his clothes, and he too fell into a frenzy before Samuel. He lay naked all that day and all that night. Therefore it is said, "Is Saul also among the prophets?"

a Heb *took the teraphim*   *b* Meaning of Heb uncertain   *c* Heb *the teraphim*   *d* Gk reads *to the well of the threshing floor on the bare height*

The Friendship of David and Jonathan

20 David fled from Naioth in Ramah. He came before Jonathan and said, "What have I done? What is my guilt? And what is my sin against your father that he is trying to take my life?" ²He said to him, "Far from it! You shall not die. My father does nothing either great or small without disclosing it to me; and why should my father hide this from me? Never!" ³But David also swore, "Your father knows well that you like me; and he thinks, 'Do not let Jonathan know this, or he will be grieved.' But truly, as the LORD lives and as you yourself live, there is but a step between me and death." ⁴Then Jonathan said to David, "Whatever you say, I will do for you." ⁵David said to Jonathan, "Tomorrow is the new moon, and I should not fail to sit with the king at the meal; but let me go, so that I may hide in the field until the third evening. ⁶If your father misses me at all, then say, 'David earnestly asked leave of me to run to Bethlehem his city; for there is a yearly sacrifice there for all the family.' ⁷If he says, 'Good!' it will be well with your servant; but if he is angry, then know that evil has been determined by him. ⁸Therefore deal kindly with your servant, for you have brought your servant into a sacred covenant*a* with you. But if there is guilt in me, kill me yourself; why should you bring me to your father?" ⁹Jonathan said, "Far be it from you! If I knew that it was decided by my father that evil should come upon you, would I not tell you?" ¹⁰Then David said to Jonathan, "Who will tell me if your father answers you harshly?" ¹¹Jonathan replied to David, "Come, let us go out into the field." So they both went out into the field.

12 Jonathan said to David, "By the LORD, the God of Israel! When I have sounded out my father, about this time tomorrow, or on the third day, if he is well disposed toward David, shall I not then send and disclose it to you? ¹³But if my father intends to do you harm, the LORD do so to Jonathan, and more also, if I do not disclose it to you, and send you away, so that you may go in safety. May the LORD be with you, as he has been with my father. ¹⁴If I am still alive, show me the faithful love of the LORD; but if I die, *b* ¹⁵never cut off your faithful love from my house, even if the LORD were to cut off every one of the enemies of David from the face of the earth." ¹⁶Thus Jonathan made a covenant with the house of David, saying, "May the LORD seek out the enemies of David." ¹⁷Jonathan made David swear again by his love for him; for he loved him as he loved his own life.

18 Jonathan said to him, "Tomorrow is the new moon; you will be missed, because your place will be empty. ¹⁹On the day after tomorrow, you shall go a long way down; go to the place where you hid yourself earlier, and remain beside the stone there. *b* ²⁰I will shoot three arrows to the side of it, as though I shot at a mark. ²¹Then I will send the boy, saying, 'Go, find the arrows.' If I say to the boy, 'Look, the arrows are on this side of you, collect them,' then you are to come, for, as the LORD lives, it is safe for you and there is no danger. ²²But if I say to the young man, 'Look, the arrows are beyond you,' then go; for the LORD has sent you away. ²³As for the matter about which you and I have spoken, the LORD is witness*c* between you and me forever."

24 So David hid himself in the field. When the new moon came, the king sat at the feast to eat. ²⁵The king sat upon his seat, as at other times, upon the seat by the wall. Jonathan stood, while Abner sat by Saul's side; but David's place was empty.

26 Saul did not say anything that day; for he thought, "Something has befallen him; he is not clean, surely he is not clean." ²⁷But on the second day, the day after the new moon, David's place was empty. And Saul said to his son Jonathan, "Why has the son of Jesse not come to the feast, either yesterday or today?" ²⁸Jonathan answered Saul, "David earnestly asked leave of me to go to Bethlehem; ²⁹he said, 'Let me go; for our family is holding a sacrifice in the city, and my brother has commanded me to be there. So now, if I have found favor in your sight, let me get away, and see my brothers.' For this reason he has not come to the king's table."

30 Then Saul's anger was kindled against Jonathan. He said to him, "You son of a per-

---

a Heb *a covenant of the LORD*   *b* Meaning of Heb uncertain   *c* Gk: Heb lacks *witness* verse, rebellious woman! Do I not know that you have chosen the son of Jesse to your own shame, and to the shame of your mother's nakedness? 31For as long as the son of Jesse lives upon the earth, neither you nor your kingdom shall be established. Now send and bring him to me, for he shall surely die." 32Then Jonathan answered his father Saul, "Why should he be put to death? What has he done?" 33But Saul threw his spear at him to strike him; so Jonathan knew that it was the decision of his father to put David to death. 34Jonathan rose from the table in fierce anger and ate no food on the second day of the month, for he was grieved for David, and because his father had disgraced him.

35 In the morning Jonathan went out into the field to the appointment with David, and with him was a little boy. 36He said to the boy, "Run and find the arrows that I shoot." As the boy ran, he shot an arrow beyond him. 37When the boy came to the place where Jonathan's arrow had fallen, Jonathan called after the boy and said, "Is the arrow not beyond you?" 38Jonathan called after the boy, "Hurry, be quick, do not linger." So Jonathan's boy gathered up the arrows and came to his master. 39But the boy knew nothing; only Jonathan and David knew the arrangement. 40Jonathan gave his weapons to the boy and said to him, "Go and carry them to the city." 41As soon as the boy had gone, David rose from beside the stone heap*a* and prostrated himself with his face to the ground. He bowed three times, and they kissed each other, and wept with each other; David wept the more. *b* 42Then Jonathan said to David, "Go in peace, since both of us have sworn in the name of the LORD, saying, 'The LORD shall be between me and you, and between my descendants and your descendants, forever.' " He got up and left; and Jonathan went into the city. *c*

David and the Holy Bread

21 *d* David came to Nob to the priest Ahimelech. Ahimelech came trembling to meet David, and said to him, "Why are you alone, and no one with you?" 2David said to the priest Ahimelech, "The king has charged me with a matter, and said to me, 'No one must know anything of the matter about which I send you, and with which I have charged you.' I have made an appointment*e* with the young men for such and such a place. 3Now then, what have you at hand? Give me five loaves of bread, or whatever is here." 4The priest answered David, "I have no ordinary bread at hand, only holy bread—provided that the young men have kept themselves from women." 5David answered the priest, "Indeed women have been kept from us as always when I go on an expedition; the vessels of the young men are holy even when it is a common journey; how much more today will their vessels be holy?" 6So the priest gave him the holy bread; for there was no bread there except the bread of the Presence, which is removed from before the LORD, to be replaced by hot bread on the day it is taken away.

7 Now a certain man of the servants of Saul was there that day, detained before the LORD; his name was Doeg the Edomite, the chief of Saul's shepherds.

8 David said to Ahimelech, "Is there no spear or sword here with you? I did not bring my sword or my weapons with me, because the king's business required haste." 9The priest said, "The sword of Goliath the Philistine, whom you killed in the valley of Elah, is here wrapped in a cloth behind the ephod; if you will take that, take it, for there is none

a Gk: Heb *from beside the south*   b Vg: Meaning of Heb uncertain   c This sentence is 21.1 in Heb   d Ch 21.2 in Heb   e Q Ms Vg Compare Gk: Meaning of MT uncertain

---

21:1–6 *Give me five loaves of bread.* David's extraordinary faith leads him to solutions that others would not seek, in this case using the holy bread from the local shrine as provision. This story will be central in the Gospel accounts of Jesus and his disciples plucking grain on the Sabbath (Matt 12:1–8; Mark 2:23–28; Luke 6:1–5), in which the law is placed in a position subordinate to the human need for sustenance. Note that the men have remained sexually chaste in preparation for holy war (v 5).

here except that one." David said, "There is none like it; give it to me."

David Flees to Gath

10 David rose and fled that day from Saul; he went to King Achish of Gath. 11The servants of Achish said to him, "Is this not David the king of the land? Did they not sing to one another of him in dances,

'Saul has killed his thousands,
and David his ten thousands'?"

12David took these words to heart and was very much afraid of King Achish of Gath. 13So he changed his behavior before them; he pretended to be mad when in their presence.*a* He scratched marks on the doors of the gate, and let his spittle run down his beard. 14Achish said to his servants, "Look, you see the man is mad; why then have you brought him to me? 15Do I lack madmen, that you have brought this fellow to play the madman in my presence? Shall this fellow come into my house?"

David and His Followers at Adullam

22 David left there and escaped to the cave of Adullam; when his brothers and all his father's house heard of it, they went down there to him. 2Everyone who was in distress, and everyone who was in debt, and everyone who was discontented gathered to him; and he became captain over them. Those who were with him numbered about four hundred.

3 David went from there to Mizpeh of Moab. He said to the king of Moab, "Please let my father and mother come*b* to you, until I know what God will do for me." 4He left them with the king of Moab, and they stayed with him all the time that David was in the stronghold. 5Then the prophet Gad said to David, "Do not remain in the stronghold; leave, and go into the land of Judah." So David left, and went into the forest of Hereth.

Saul Slaughters the Priests at Nob

6 Saul heard that David and those who were with him had been located. Saul was sitting at Gibeah, under the tamarisk tree on the height, with his spear in his hand, and all his servants were standing around him. 7Saul said to his servants who stood around him, "Hear now, you Benjaminites; will the son of Jesse give every one of you fields and vineyards, will he make you all commanders of thousands and commanders of hundreds? 8Is that why all of you have conspired against me? No one discloses to me when my son makes a league with the son of Jesse, none of you is sorry for me or discloses to me that my son has stirred up my servant against me, to lie in wait, as he is doing today." 9Doeg the Edomite, who was in charge of Saul's servants, answered, "I saw the son of Jesse coming to Nob, to Ahimelech son of Ahitub; 10he inquired of the LORD for him, gave him provisions, and gave him the sword of Goliath the Philistine."

11 The king sent for the priest Ahimelech son of Ahitub and for all his father's house, the priests who were at Nob; and all of them came to the king. 12Saul said, "Listen now, son of Ahitub." He answered, "Here I am, my lord." 13Saul said to him, "Why have you conspired against me, you and the son of Jesse, by giving him bread and a sword, and by inquiring of God for him, so that he has risen against me, to lie in wait, as he is doing today?"

14 Then Ahimelech answered the king, "Who among all your servants is so faithful as David? He is the king's son-in-law, and is quick*d* to do your bidding, and is honored in your house. 15Is today the first time that I have inquired of God for him? By no means! Do not let the king impute anything to his servant or to any member of my father's house; for your servant has known nothing of all this, much or little." 16The king said, "You shall surely die, Ahimelech, you and all your father's house." 17The king said to the guard who stood around him, "Turn and kill the priests of the LORD, because their hand

a Heb *in their hands*   *b* Syr Vg: Heb *come out*
c Heb *and turns aside*   *d* Gk Vg: Meaning of Heb uncertain

---

22:14 SERVICE—*See* Spiritual Disciplines Index.

also is with David; they knew that he fled, and did not disclose it to me." But the servants of the king would not raise their hand to attack the priests of the LORD. 18Then the king said to Doeg, "You, Doeg, turn and attack the priests." Doeg the Edomite turned and attacked the priests; on that day he killed eighty-five who wore the linen ephod. 19Nob, the city of the priests, he put to the sword; men and women, children and infants, oxen, donkeys, and sheep, he put to the sword.

20 But one of the sons of Ahimelech son of Ahitub, named Abiathar, escaped and fled after David. 21Abiathar told David that Saul had killed the priests of the LORD. 22David said to Abiathar, "I knew on that day, when Doeg the Edomite was there, that he would surely tell Saul. I am responsible*c* for the lives of all your father's house. 23Stay with me, and do not be afraid; for the one who seeks my life seeks your life; you will be safe with me."

David Saves the City of Keilah

23 Now they told David, "The Philistines are fighting against Keilah, and are robbing the threshing floors." 2David inquired of the LORD, "Shall I go and attack these Philistines?" The LORD said to David, "Go and attack the Philistines and save Keilah." 3But David's men said to him, "Look, we are afraid here in Judah; how much more then if we go to Keilah against the armies of the Philistines?" 4Then David inquired of the LORD again. The LORD answered him, "Yes, go down to Keilah; for I will give the Philistines into your hand." 5So David and his men went to Keilah, fought with the Philistines, brought away their livestock, and dealt them a heavy defeat. Thus David rescued the inhabitants of Keilah.

6 When Abiathar son of Ahimelech fled to David at Keilah, he came down with an ephod in his hand. 7Now it was told Saul that David had come to Keilah. And Saul said, "God has given*a* him into my hand; for he has shut himself in by entering a town that has gates and bars." 8Saul summoned all the people to war, to go down to Keilah, to besiege David and his men. 9When David learned that Saul was plotting evil against

him, he said to the priest Abiathar, "Bring the ephod here." 10David said, "O LORD, the God of Israel, your servant has heard that Saul seeks to come to Keilah, to destroy the city on my account. 11And now, will*b* Saul come down as your servant has heard? O LORD, the God of Israel, I beseech you, tell your servant." The LORD said, "He will come down." 12Then David said, "Will the men of Keilah surrender me and my men into the hand of Saul?" The LORD said, "They will surrender you." 13Then David and his men, who were about six hundred, set out and left Keilah; they wandered wherever they could go. When Saul was told that David had escaped from Keilah, he gave up the expedition. 14David remained in the strongholds in the wilderness, in the hill country of the Wilderness of Ziph. Saul sought him every day, but the LORD*c* did not give him into his hand.

David Eludes Saul in the Wilderness

15 David was in the Wilderness of Ziph at Horesh when he learned that*d* Saul had come out to seek his life. 16Saul's son Jonathan set out and came to David at Horesh; there he strengthened his hand through the LORD.*e* 17He said to him, "Do not be afraid; for the hand of my father Saul shall not find you; you shall be king over Israel, and I shall be second to you; my father Saul also knows that this is so." 18Then the two of them made a covenant before the LORD; David remained at Horesh, and Jonathan went home.

19 Then some Ziphites went up to Saul at Gibeah and said, "David is hiding among us in the strongholds of Horesh, on the hill of Hachilah, which is south of Jeshimon. 20Now, O king, whenever you wish to come down, do so; and our part will be to surrender him into the king's hand." 21Saul said, "May you be blessed by the LORD for showing me compassion! 22Go and make sure once more; find out exactly where he is, and who has seen him there; for I am told that he is very cunning. 23Look around and learn all the hiding places where he lurks, and come back

---

a Gk Tg: Heb *made a stranger of*   *b* Q Ms Compare Gk: MT *Will the men of Keilah surrender me into his hand? Will*   *c* Q Ms Gk: MT *God*   *d* Or *saw that*   *e* Compare Q Ms Gk: MT *God*

to me with sure information. Then I will go with you; and if he is in the land, I will search him out among all the thousands of Judah." 24So they set out and went to Ziph ahead of Saul.

David and his men were in the wilderness of Maon, in the Arabah to the south of Jeshimon. 25Saul and his men went to search for him. When David was told, he went down to the rock and stayed in the wilderness of Maon. When Saul heard that, he pursued David into the wilderness of Maon. 26Saul went on one side of the mountain, and David and his men on the other side of the mountain. David was hurrying to get away from Saul, while Saul and his men were closing in on David and his men to capture them. 27Then a messenger came to Saul, saying, "Hurry and come; for the Philistines have made a raid on the land." 28So Saul stopped pursuing David, and went against the Philistines; therefore that place was called the Rock of Escape.a 29b David then went up from there, and lived in the strongholds of Engedi.

David Spares Saul's Life

24 When Saul returned from following the Philistines, he was told, "David is in the wilderness of En-gedi." 2Then Saul took three thousand chosen men out of all Israel, and went to look for David and his men in the direction of the Rocks of the Wild Goats. 3He came to the sheepfolds beside the road, where there was a cave; and Saul went in to relieve himself.c Now David and his men were sitting in the innermost parts of the cave. 4The men of David said to him, "Here is the day of which the LORD said to you, 'I will give your enemy into your hand, and you shall do to him as it seems good to you.' " Then David went and stealthily cut off a corner of Saul's cloak. 5Afterward David was stricken to the heart because he had cut off a

corner of Saul's cloak. 6He said to his men, "The LORD forbid that I should do this thing to my lord, the LORD's anointed, to raise my hand against him; for he is the LORD's anointed." 7So David scolded his men severely and did not permit them to attack Saul. Then Saul got up and left the cave, and went on his way.

8 Afterwards David also rose up and went out of the cave and called after Saul, "My lord the king!" When Saul looked behind him, David bowed with his face to the ground, and did obeisance. 9David said to Saul, "Why do you listen to the words of those who say, 'David seeks to do you harm'? 10This very day your eyes have seen how the LORD gave you into my hand in the cave; and some urged me to kill you, but I sparedd you. I said, 'I will not raise my hand against my lord; for he is the LORD's anointed.' 11See, my father, see the corner of your cloak in my hand; for by the fact that I cut off the corner of your cloak, and did not kill you, you may know for certain that there is no wrong or treason in my hands. I have not sinned against you, though you are hunting me to take my life. 12May the LORD judge between me and you! May the LORD avenge me on you; but my hand shall not be against you. 13As the ancient proverb says, 'Out of the wicked comes forth wickedness'; but my hand shall not be against you. 14Against whom has the king of Israel come out? Whom do you pursue? A dead dog? A single flea? 15May the LORD therefore be judge, and give sentence between me and you. May he see to it, and plead my cause, and vindicate me against you."

16 When David had finished speaking these words to Saul, Saul said, "Is this your

---

a Or *Rock of Division*; meaning of Heb uncertain
b Ch 24.1 in Heb   c Heb *to cover his feet*
d Gk Syr Tg Vg: Heb *it* (my eye) *spared*

24:6 *he is the LORD's anointed.* David clearly has grounds to take Saul's life but does not do so, instead following the high road of forgiveness and reconciliation. Although he too is the Lord's anointed (16:13), David refuses to accept the old king as anything other than what he has always

been to him, which is his sovereign. Such a text is a counterweight to the impulses of our own culture, as eager as we are to assert and to protect our rights, particularly to use force against those who have wronged us.

voice, my son David?" Saul lifted up his voice and wept. [17]He said to David, "You are more righteous than I; for you have repaid me good, whereas I have repaid you evil. [18]Today you have explained how you have dealt well with me, in that you did not kill me when the LORD put me into your hands. [19]For who has ever found an enemy, and sent the enemy safely away? So may the LORD reward you with good for what you have done to me this day. [20]Now I know that you shall surely be king, and that the kingdom of Israel shall be established in your hand. [21]Swear to me therefore by the LORD that you will not cut off my descendants after me, and that you will not wipe out my name from my father's house." [22]So David swore this to Saul. Then Saul went home; but David and his men went up to the stronghold.

Death of Samuel

25 Now Samuel died; and all Israel assembled and mourned for him. They buried him at his home in Ramah.

Then David got up and went down to the wilderness of Paran.

David and the Wife of Nabal

2 There was a man in Maon, whose property was in Carmel. The man was very rich; he had three thousand sheep and a thousand goats. He was shearing his sheep in Carmel. [3]Now the name of the man was Nabal, and the name of his wife Abigail. The woman was clever and beautiful, but the man was surly and mean; he was a Calebite. [4]David heard in the wilderness that Nabal was shearing his sheep. [5]So David sent ten young men; and David said to the young men, "Go up to Carmel, and go to Nabal, and greet him in my name. [6]Thus you shall salute him: 'Peace be to you, and peace be to your house, and peace be to all that you have. [7]I hear that you have shearers; now your shepherds have been with us, and we did them no harm, and they missed nothing, all the time they were in Carmel. [8]Ask your young men, and they will tell you. Therefore let my young men find favor in your sight; for we have come on a feast day. Please give whatever you have at

hand to your servants and to your son David.' "

9 When David's young men came, they said all this to Nabal in the name of David; and then they waited. [10]But Nabal answered David's servants, "Who is David? Who is the son of Jesse? There are many servants today who are breaking away from their masters. [11]Shall I take my bread and my water and the meat that I have butchered for my shearers, and give it to men who come from I do not know where?" [12]So David's young men turned away, and came back and told him all this. [13]David said to his men, "Every man strap on his sword!" And every one of them strapped on his sword; David also strapped on his sword; and about four hundred men went up after David, while two hundred remained with the baggage.

14 But one of the young men told Abigail, Nabal's wife, "David sent messengers out of the wilderness to salute our master; and he shouted insults at them. [15]Yet the men were very good to us, and we suffered no harm, and we never missed anything when we were in the fields, as long as we were with them; [16]they were a wall to us both by night and by day, all the while we were with them keeping the sheep. [17]Now therefore know this and consider what you should do; for evil has been decided against our master and against all his house; he is so ill-natured that no one can speak to him."

18 Then Abigail hurried and took two hundred loaves, two skins of wine, five sheep ready dressed, five measures of parched grain, one hundred clusters of raisins, and two hundred cakes of figs. She loaded them on donkeys [19]and said to her young men, "Go on ahead of me; I am coming after you." But she did not tell her husband Nabal. [20]As she rode on the donkey and came down under cover of the mountain, David and his men came down toward her; and she met them. [21]Now David had said, "Surely it was in vain that I protected all that this fellow has in the wilderness, so that nothing was missed of all that belonged to him; but he has returned me evil for good. [22]God do so to David[a] and

a Gk Compare Syr: Heb the enemies of David

[handwritten margin note at top: A SOFT ANSWER TURNS AWAY WRATH. RESCUES THE DYING ONE (X DEATH ON CROSS WAS A SOFT ANSWER)]

more also, if by morning I leave so much as one male of all who belong to him."

23 When Abigail saw David, she hurried and alighted from the donkey, and fell before David on her face, bowing to the ground. 24She fell at his feet and said, "Upon me alone, my lord, be the guilt; please let your servant speak in your ears, and hear the words of your servant. 25My lord, do not take seriously this ill-natured fellow, Nabal; for as his name is, so is he; Nabal*a* is his name, and folly is with him; but I, your servant, did not see the young men of my lord, whom you sent.

26 "Now then, my lord, as the LORD lives, and as you yourself live, since the LORD has restrained you from bloodguilt and from taking vengeance with your own hand, now let your enemies and those who seek to do evil to my lord be like Nabal. 27And now let this present that your servant has brought to my lord be given to the young men who follow my lord. 28Please forgive the trespass of your servant; for the LORD will certainly make my lord a sure house, because my lord is fighting the battles of the LORD; and evil shall not be found in you so long as you live. 29If anyone should rise up to pursue you and to seek your life, the life of my lord shall be bound in the bundle of the living under the care of the LORD your God; but the lives of your enemies he shall sling out as from the hollow of a sling. 30When the LORD has done to my lord according to all the good that he has spoken concerning you, and has appointed you prince over Israel, 31my lord shall have no cause of grief, or pangs of conscience, for having shed blood without cause or for having saved himself. And when the LORD has

[handwritten margin note: INEXCUSABLE]

dealt well with my lord, then remember your servant."

32 David said to Abigail, "Blessed be the LORD, the God of Israel, who sent you to meet me today! 33Blessed be your good sense, and blessed be you, who have kept me today from bloodguilt and from avenging myself by my own hand! 34For as surely as the LORD the God of Israel lives, who has restrained me from hurting you, unless you had hurried and come to meet me, truly by morning there would not have been left to Nabal so much as one male." 35Then David received from her hand what she had brought him; he said to her, "Go up to your house in peace; see, I have heeded your voice, and I have granted your petition."

36 Abigail came to Nabal; he was holding a feast in his house, like the feast of a king. Nabal's heart was merry within him, for he was very drunk; so she told him nothing at all until the morning light. 37In the morning, when the wine had gone out of Nabal, his wife told him these things, and his heart died within him; he became like a stone. 38About ten days later the LORD struck Nabal, and he died.

39 When David heard that Nabal was dead, he said, "Blessed be the LORD who has judged the case of Nabal's insult to me, and has kept back his servant from evil; the LORD has returned the evildoing of Nabal upon his own head." Then David sent and wooed Abigail, to make her his wife. 40When David's servants came to Abigail at Carmel, they said to her, "David has sent us to you to take you to him as his wife." 41She rose and bowed

a That is *Fool*

25:39 *and has kept back his servant from evil.* In a most unflattering passage, the tender, forgiving David of the previous chapter now appears as a snarling, vindictive marauder who, even he himself claims, is spared from evil only by the staying hand of Yahweh. Not only is David overly prone to violence; there is clearly something in the air between him and Abigail, whose fawning comments demonstrate an unusual interest in the future king even before her spouse is dead. This tendency will be

brought into full relief in 2 Samuel 11 in the episode with Bathsheba, the wife of Uriah. Martin Luther's dictum that the believer is *simul iustus et peccator* ("both saint and sinner") is illustrative here. David, who forgives the murderous Saul just verses before, now rages at the pitiful Nabal (whose name means "fool") and appears to have designs on his wife, which are soon fulfilled. No matter how mature in the faith one is, one is always vulnerable to the flaws of human passion.

down, with her face to the ground, and said, "Your servant is a slave to wash the feet of the servants of my lord." 42Abigail got up hurriedly and rode away on a donkey; her five maids attended her. She went after the messengers of David and became his wife.

43 David also married Ahinoam of Jezreel; both of them became his wives. 44Saul had given his daughter Michal, David's wife, to Palti son of Laish, who was from Gallim.

David Spares Saul's Life a Second Time

26 Then the Ziphites came to Saul at Gibeah, saying, "David is in hiding on the hill of Hachilah, which is opposite Jeshimon."*a* 2So Saul rose and went down to the Wilderness of Ziph, with three thousand chosen men of Israel, to seek David in the Wilderness of Ziph. 3Saul encamped on the hill of Hachilah, which is opposite Jeshimon*b* beside the road. But David remained in the wilderness. When he learned that Saul had come after him into the wilderness, 4David sent out spies, and learned that Saul had indeed arrived. 5Then David set out and came to the place where Saul had encamped; and David saw the place where Saul lay, with Abner son of Ner, the commander of his army. Saul was lying within the encampment, while the army was encamped around him.

6 Then David said to Ahimelech the Hittite, and to Joab's brother Abishai son of Zeruiah, "Who will go down with me into the camp to Saul?" Abishai said, "I will go down with you." 7So David and Abishai went to the army by night; there Saul lay sleeping within the encampment, with his spear stuck in the ground at his head; and Abner and the army lay around him. 8Abishai said to David, "God has given your enemy into your hand today; now therefore let me pin him to the ground with one stroke of the spear; I will not strike him twice." 9But David said to Abishai, "Do not destroy him; for who can

raise his hand against the LORD's anointed, and be guiltless?" 10David said, "As the LORD lives, the LORD will strike him down; or his day will come to die; or he will go down into battle and perish. 11The LORD forbid that I should raise my hand against the LORD's anointed; but now take the spear that is at his head, and the water jar, and let us go." 12So David took the spear that was at Saul's head and the water jar, and they went away. No one saw it, or knew it, nor did anyone awake; for they were all asleep, because a deep sleep from the LORD had fallen upon them.

13 Then David went over to the other side, and stood on top of a hill far away, with a great distance between them. 14David called to the army and to Abner son of Ner, saying, "Abner! Will you not answer?" Then Abner replied, "Who are you that calls to the king?" 15David said to Abner, "Are you not a man? Who is like you in Israel? Why then have you not kept watch over your lord the king? For one of the people came in to destroy your lord the king. 16This thing that you have done is not good. As the LORD lives, you deserve to die, because you have not kept watch over your lord, the LORD's anointed. See now, where is the king's spear, or the water jar that was at his head?"

17 Saul recognized David's voice, and said, "Is this your voice, my son David?" David said, "It is my voice, my lord, O king." 18And he added, "Why does my lord pursue his servant? For what have I done? What guilt is on my hands? 19Now therefore let my lord the king hear the words of his servant. If it is the LORD who has stirred you up against me, may he accept an offering; but if it is mortals, may they be cursed before the LORD, for they have driven me out today from my share in the heritage of the LORD, saying, 'Go, serve other

a Or *opposite the wasteland*   *b* Or *opposite the wasteland*

Responding
25:41 SERVICE. What are some modern equivalents of washing the feet of guests? How do we cultivate a servant's heart? List the ways. *See also* Spiritual Disciplines Index.

26:10 *the LORD will.* The second time David spares Saul's life (see 24:6 for the first), he makes the theological assertion that Saul's fate would be decided by Yahweh and not by himself.

gods.' [20]Now therefore, do not let my blood fall to the ground, away from the presence of the LORD; for the king of Israel has come out to seek a single flea, like one who hunts a partridge in the mountains."

21 Then Saul said, "I have done wrong; come back, my son David, for I will never harm you again, because my life was precious in your sight today; I have been a fool, and have made a great mistake." [22]David replied, "Here is the spear, O king! Let one of the young men come over and get it. [23]The LORD rewards everyone for his righteousness and his faithfulness; for the LORD gave you into my hand today, but I would not raise my hand against the LORD's anointed. [24]As your life was precious today in my sight, so may my life be precious in the sight of the LORD, and may he rescue me from all tribulation." [25]Then Saul said to David, "Blessed be you, my son David! You will do many things and will succeed in them." So David went his way, and Saul returned to his place.

David Serves King Achish of Gath

27 David said in his heart, "I shall now perish one day by the hand of Saul; there is nothing better for me than to escape to the land of the Philistines; then Saul will despair of seeking me any longer within the borders of Israel, and I shall escape out of his hand." [2]So David set out and went over, he and the six hundred men who were with him, to King Achish son of Maoch of Gath. [3]David stayed with Achish at Gath, he and his troops, every man with his household, and David with his two wives, Ahinoam of Jezreel, and Abigail of Carmel, Nabal's widow. [4]When Saul was told that David had fled to Gath, he no longer sought for him.

5 Then David said to Achish, "If I have found favor in your sight, let a place be given me in one of the country towns, so that I may live there; for why should your servant live in the royal city with you?" [6]So that day Achish gave him Ziklag; therefore Ziklag has belonged to the kings of Judah to this day. [7]The length of time that David lived in the country of the Philistines was one year and four months.

8 Now David and his men went up and made raids on the Geshurites, the Girzites, and the Amalekites; for these were the landed settlements from Telam[a] on the way to Shur and on to the land of Egypt. [9]David struck the land, leaving neither man nor woman alive, but took away the sheep, the oxen, the donkeys, the camels, and the clothing, and came back to Achish. [10]When Achish asked, "Against whom[b] have you made a raid today?" David would say, "Against the Negeb of Judah," or "Against the Negeb of the Jerahmeelites," or, "Against the Negeb of the Kenites." [11]David left neither man nor woman alive to be brought back to Gath, thinking, "They might tell about us, and say, 'David has done so and so.'" Such was his practice all the time he lived in the country of the Philistines. [12]Achish trusted David, thinking, "He has made himself utterly abhorrent to his people Israel; therefore he shall always be my servant."

28 In those days the Philistines gathered their forces for war, to fight against Israel. Achish said to David, "You know, of course, that you and your men are to go out with me in the army." [2]David said to Achish, "Very well, then you shall know what your servant can do." Achish said to David, "Very well, I will make you my bodyguard for life."

Saul Consults a Medium

3 Now Samuel had died, and all Israel had mourned for him and buried him in Ramah, his own city. Saul had expelled the mediums and the wizards from the land. [4]The Philistines assembled, and came and encamped at Shunem. Saul gathered all Israel, and they encamped at Gilboa. [5]When Saul saw the army of the Philistines, he was afraid, and his heart trembled greatly. [6]When Saul inquired of the LORD, the LORD did not answer him, not by dreams, or by Urim, or by prophets. [7]Then Saul said to his servants, "Seek out for me a woman who is a medium, so that I may go to her and inquire of her." His servants said to him, "There is a medium at Endor."

a Compare Gk 15.4: Heb *from of old*   b Q Ms Gk Vg: MT lacks *whom*

8 So Saul disguised himself and put on other clothes and went there, he and two men with him. They came to the woman by night. And he said, "Consult a spirit for me, and bring up for me the one whom I name to you." 9The woman said to him, "Surely you know what Saul has done, how he has cut off the mediums and the wizards from the land. Why then are you laying a snare for my life to bring about my death?" 10But Saul swore to her by the LORD, "As the LORD lives, no punishment shall come upon you for this thing." 11Then the woman said, "Whom shall I bring up for you?" He answered, "Bring up Samuel for me." 12When the woman saw Samuel, she cried out with a loud voice; and the woman said to Saul, "Why have you deceived me? You are Saul!" 13The king said to her, "Have no fear; what do you see?" The woman said to Saul, "I see a divine being*a* coming up out of the ground." 14He said to her, "What is his appearance?" She said, "An old man is coming up; he is wrapped in a robe." So Saul knew that it was Samuel, and he bowed with his face to the ground, and did obeisance.

15 Then Samuel said to Saul, "Why have you disturbed me by bringing me up?" Saul answered, "I am in great distress, for the Philistines are warring against me, and God has turned away from me and answers me no more, either by prophets or by dreams; so I have summoned you to tell me what I should do." 16Samuel said, "Why then do you ask me, since the LORD has turned from you and become your enemy? 17The LORD has done to you just as he spoke by me; for the LORD has torn the kingdom out of your hand, and given it to your neighbor, David. 18Because you did not obey the voice of the LORD, and did

not carry out his fierce wrath against **Amalek**, therefore the LORD has done this thing to you today. 19Moreover the LORD will give **Israel** along with you into the hands of the Philistines; and tomorrow you and your sons shall be with me; the LORD will also give the army of Israel into the hands of the Philistines."

20 Immediately Saul fell full length on the ground, filled with fear because of the words of Samuel; and there was no strength in him, for he had eaten nothing all day and all night. 21The woman came to Saul, and when she saw that he was terrified, she said to him, "Your servant has listened to you; I have taken my life in my hand, and have listened to what you have said to me. 22Now therefore, you also listen to your servant; let me set a morsel of bread before you. Eat, that you may have strength when you go on your way." 23He refused, and said, "I will not eat." But his servants, together with the woman, urged him; and he listened to their words. So he got up from the ground and sat on the bed. 24Now the woman had a fatted calf in the house. She quickly slaughtered it, and she took flour, kneaded it, and baked unleavened cakes. 25She put them before Saul and his servants, and they ate. Then they rose and went away that night.

The Philistines Reject David

29 Now the Philistines gathered all their forces at Aphek, while the **Israelites** were encamped by the fountain that is in Jezreel. 2As the lords of the Philistines were passing on by hundreds and by thousands, and David and his men were passing on in the rear with Achish, 3the commanders of the

a Or *a god*; or *gods*

28:3–25 *Seek out for me . . . a medium.* Again readers are faced with a complex text. The consultation of a medium is an offense punishable by death (Deut 18:10–12). Yet the medium surprisingly produces the dead prophet, who repeats the word of the Lord to the king. The medium knows that what she has heard has placed her life in jeopardy, given that this king is about to be replaced by Yahweh, but she aids him nonetheless. His political weakness has not

diminished his basic humanness, nor has the medium's questionable vocation rendered her utterly without virtue. In an act of tenderness she unexpectedly ministers to the physical needs of the pitiable king. Ironically, the medium, who engages in nefarious and heretical practices, nevertheless embodies mercy (*hesed*) to the king of Israel, who himself is to be the embodiment of righteousness, but who has fallen into the depths of spiritual infidelity.

Philistines said, "What are these Hebrews doing here?" Achish said to the commanders of the Philistines, "Is this not David, the servant of King Saul of Israel, who has been with me now for days and years? Since he deserted to me I have found no fault in him to this day." 4But the commanders of the Philistines were angry with him; and the commanders of the Philistines said to him, "Send the man back, so that he may return to the place that you have assigned to him; he shall not go down with us to battle, or else he may become an adversary to us in the battle. For how could this fellow reconcile himself to his lord? Would it not be with the heads of the men here? 5Is this not David, of whom they sing to one another in dances,

'Saul has killed his thousands,
and David his ten thousands'?"

6 Then Achish called David and said to him, "As the LORD lives, you have been honest, and to me it seems right that you should march out and in with me in the campaign; for I have found nothing wrong in you from the day of your coming to me until today. Nevertheless the lords do not approve of you. 7So go back now; and go peaceably; do nothing to displease the lords of the Philistines." 8David said to Achish, "But what have I done? What have you found in your servant from the day I entered your service until now, that I should not go and fight against the enemies of my lord the king?" 9Achish replied to David, "I know that you are as blameless in my sight as an angel of God; nevertheless, the commanders of the Philistines have said, 'He shall not go up with us to the battle.' 10Now then rise early in the morning, you and the servants of your lord who came with you, and go to the place that I appointed for you. As for the evil report, do not take it to heart, for you have done well before me.a Start early in the morning, and leave as soon as you have light." 11So David set out with his men early in the morning, to return to the land of the Philistines. But the Philistines went up to Jezreel.

David Avenges the Destruction of Ziklag

30 Now when David and his men came to Ziklag on the third day, the Amalekites had made a raid on the Negeb and on Ziklag. They had attacked Ziklag, burned it down, 2and taken captive the women and allb who were in it, both small and great; they killed none of them, but carried them off, and went their way. 3When David and his men came to the city, they found it burned down, and their wives and sons and daughters taken captive. 4Then David and the people who were with him raised their voices and wept, until they had no more strength to weep. 5David's two wives also had been taken captive, Ahinoam of Jezreel, and Abigail the widow of Nabal of Carmel. 6David was in great danger; for the people spoke of stoning him, because all the people were bitter in spirit for their sons and daughters. But David strengthened himself in the LORD his God.

7 David said to the priest Abiathar son of Ahimelech, "Bring me the ephod." So Abiathar brought the ephod to David. 8David inquired of the LORD, "Shall I pursue this band? Shall I overtake them?" He answered him, "Pursue; for you shall surely overtake and shall surely rescue." 9So David set out, he and the six hundred men who were with him. They came to the Wadi Besor, where those stayed who were left behind. 10But David went on with the pursuit, he and four hundred men; two hundred stayed behind, too exhausted to cross the Wadi Besor.

11 In the open country they found an Egyptian, and brought him to David. They gave him bread and he ate; they gave him water to drink; 12they also gave him a piece of

a Gk: Heb lacks and go to the place . . . done well before me   b Gk: Heb lacks and all

---

30:8 *inquired of the LORD.* The contrast between Saul, who seeks out a medium in chapter 28, and David, who seeks out Yahweh for wisdom, could not be plainer. When faced with important decisions, David characteristically makes the right choice by turning to wisdom's ultimate source, a move that the larger narrative will make plain is the cause of his political and military success (1 Sam 22:10; 23:2; 2 Sam 2:1; 5:23; 21:1).

fig cake and two clusters of raisins. When he had eaten, his spirit revived; for he had not eaten bread or drunk water for three days and three nights. [13]Then David said to him, "To whom do you belong? Where are you from?" He said, "I am a young man of Egypt, servant to an Amalekite. My master left me behind because I fell sick three days ago. [14]We had made a raid on the Negeb of the Cherethites and on that which belongs to Judah and on the Negeb of Caleb; and we burned Ziklag down." [15]David said to him, "Will you take me down to this raiding party?" He said, "Swear to me by God that you will not kill me, or hand me over to my master, and I will take you down to them."

16 When he had taken him down, they were spread out all over the ground, eating and drinking and dancing, because of the great amount of spoil they had taken from the land of the Philistines and from the land of Judah. [17]David attacked them from twilight until the evening of the next day. Not one of them escaped, except four hundred young men, who mounted camels and fled. [18]David recovered all that the Amalekites had taken; and David rescued his two wives. [19]Nothing was missing, whether small or great, sons or daughters, spoil or anything that had been taken; David brought back everything. [20]David also captured all the flocks and herds, which were driven ahead of the other cattle; people said, "This is David's spoil."

21 Then David came to the two hundred men who had been too exhausted to follow David, and who had been left at the Wadi Besor. They went out to meet David and to meet the people who were with him. When David drew near to the people he saluted them. [22]Then all the corrupt and worthless fellows among the men who had gone with David said, "Because they did not go with us, we will not give them any of the spoil that we have recovered, except that each man may take his wife and children, and leave." [23]But David said, "You shall not do so, my brothers, with what the LORD has given us; he has preserved us and handed over to us the raiding party that attacked us. [24]Who would listen to you in this matter? For the share of the one who goes down into the battle shall be the same as the share of the one who stays by the baggage; they shall share alike." [25]From that day forward he made it a statute and an ordinance for Israel; it continues to the present day.

26 When David came to Ziklag, he sent part of the spoil to his friends, the elders of Judah, saying, "Here is a present for you from the spoil of the enemies of the LORD"; [27]it was for those in Bethel, in Ramoth of the Negeb, in Jattir, [28]in Aroer, in Siphmoth, in Eshtemoa, [29]in Racal, in the towns of the Jerahmeelites, in the towns of the Kenites, [30]in Hormah, in Bor-ashan, in Athach, [31]in Hebron, all the places where David and his men had roamed.

The Death of Saul and His Sons

31 Now the Philistines fought against Israel; and the men of Israel fled before the Philistines, and many fell[a] on Mount Gil-

a/Heb and they fell slain

30:20 *This is David's spoil.* Having "inquired of the LORD" in making his military move (v 8), David gets a free pass from the condemnation leveled at Saul, who had simply spared the Amalekite king (15:1–9). David spares all the war booty, which Saul had destroyed per God's command, and yet gets nothing but praise! The point of the narrative seems to be that the closeness that David cultivates with Yahweh relativizes the regular ethical norms of the community, a point that will later be made about Jesus in the Gospel of Mark (2:23–28).

30:22–25 *they shall share alike.* David's closeness to Yahweh continues to have positive consequences in the political realm. David perceives that an inequitable disposition of the spoils of war is about to occur and moves to rectify it. The narrative recounts no resistance to David's logic, and this practice is said to have persisted into times contemporary to the author. It is never enough in the community of faith to assert closeness to God. Such a relationship, if it is actual rather than rhetorical, will always issue forth in concrete acts of justice and righteousness, which David's balanced partition of the plunder manifests.

boa. [2]The Philistines overtook Saul and his sons; and the Philistines killed Jonathan and Abinadab and Malchishua, the sons of Saul. [3]The battle pressed hard upon Saul; the archers found him, and he was badly wounded by them. [4]Then Saul said to his armor-bearer, "Draw your sword and thrust me through with it, so that these uncircumcised may not come and thrust me through, and make sport of me." But his armor-bearer was unwilling; for he was terrified. So Saul took his own sword and fell upon it. [5]When his armor-bearer saw that Saul was dead, he also fell upon his sword and died with him. [6]So Saul and his three sons and his armor-bearer and all his men died together on the same day. [7]When the men of Israel who were on the other side of the valley and those beyond the Jordan saw that the men of Israel had fled and that Saul and his sons were dead, they forsook their towns and fled; and the Philistines came and occupied them.

[8]The next day, when the Philistines came to strip the dead, they found Saul and his three sons fallen on Mount Gilboa. [9]They cut off his head, stripped off his armor, and sent messengers throughout the land of the Philistines to carry the good news to the houses of their idols and to the people. [10]They put his armor in the temple of Astarte;[a] and they fastened his body to the wall of Beth-shan. [11]But when the inhabitants of Jabesh-gilead heard what the Philistines had done to Saul, [12]all the valiant men set out, traveled all night long, and took the body of Saul and the bodies of his sons from the wall of Beth-shan. They came to Jabesh and burned them there. [13]Then they took their bones and buried them under the tamarisk tree in Jabesh, and fasted seven days.

a Heb plural

31:4 *thrust me through with it.* The mortally wounded king realistically appraises his condition, sees that the end is near, and takes steps to keep his death from giving advantage to the enemy. By laying down his life, Saul thwarts the enemies of Israel who will turn his execution into a political victory by means of public humiliation, which will only result in the demoralization of Israel, thus making it more vulnerable to future assaults. This is not a suicide in the conventional sense, but rather surrender to the impending inevitably of death. As theologian Karl Barth has taught us, the duty of members of this community is not to resist death absolutely, but rather to acknowledge with humility the God who is sovereign over life and death.

Responding
31:13 FASTING. About the only contemporary parallel to the fast that the inhabitants of Jabesh-gilead undertook after the burial of Saul and his sons are the times of mourning that nations experience following the death or assassination of their leaders. However, the customs vary widely—military funerals, wakes, public demonstrations, religious services. Do you think fasting from food would help citizens deal with their grief? Why or why not? *See also* Spiritual Disciplines Index.

2 SAMUEL

A s we noted in the Introduction to 1 Samuel, 1 & 2 Samuel were originally one book, arbitrarily split in two, probably due to the length of scrolls at the time. Chapters 1–8 of 2 Samuel narrate the growth and development of David's empire. Now that Saul and his heir Jonathan are dead, David's rise is impeded only momentarily by Ishbaal, another son of Saul who appears to be a puppet choreographed by the general Abner and who will soon be out of the way. The narrator is careful to protect David from any responsibility for the events surrounding the downfall of the Saulides. First, David makes a great show at the funerals of the two great men (1:11–27). Second, David takes bloody revenge on the killer of Saul (1:15–16). Third, following a long conflict with the House of Saul, David shows himself to be an adroit politician, maneuvering Israel into submission via the defection of Abner, which prevents further bloodshed (3:12–21). Fourth, when Ishbaal is killed, David manifests the same outrage that he has demonstrated against the killers of Saul and Jonathan (4:9–12). All of these actions reflect positively on David's character and lead casual observers to think well of the man who will soon unite the two kingdoms under one dynastic house.

Yet there are certain aspects of David's behavior that point in another direction. For one thing, David's alliance with Abner seems to betray his obligations to David's own family. Abner had killed David's nephew Asahel, so David should have been bound to avenge this loss (2:24–27). Likewise, he seems to have forgotten his previous vicious condemnation of Abner for failing to have adequately protected Saul, choosing instead the road of political compromise with someone he had previously regarded with contempt, perhaps in the name of political expediency (1 Sam 26:15–17). Another troubling matter can be seen in the conquest of Jerusalem, which is conquered not in the name of Judah, but in David's own name (5:6–12). Finally there is the brash, uninvited proposal to build Yahweh a "house" in chapter 7, a proposal that Yahweh deftly rebukes but also turns into an extravagant gift

---

See also *"The With-God Life" essay for this section of the Bible,*
"The People of God as a Nation," pp. 391–96.

---

in David's favor, thus saving him from what could have been a deeply embarrassing moment.

So which David is the authentic one? We will discover David to be a complicated, shrewd, fallible character whose main attribute is the one that shines the brightest: a heart for God.

The Succession Narrative

Chapters 9–20 (along with 1 Kings 1–2) comprise a textual unit with a broad theme of sifting through the various heirs of David in search of a successor. Interspersed with the account of who will be the next ruler is the sordid tale of the current king's moral implosion. The precipitating incident is the adulterous affair with Bathsheba (11:1–6) and the murder of her loyal but ultimately uncooperative husband, Uriah, who refuses a home visit when David finds himself with a pregnant but already wed mistress (11:14–21). The tragic death of the newlyweds' infant son will be but the first of David's family woes (12:15–19), although the breakdown of his family was already foreshadowed by the tense relationship and disobedience of his nephew Joab (cf. 3:22–39; 11:6–24).

That David's sons have learned his ways is evident in the stories of Amnon and Absalom, both of whom looked as if they would be the ones to be the next king. Amnon, who as the heir apparent could have undoubtedly had any number of women, instead turns his licentious longings in the direction of his sister, Tamar (13:1–19). Tamar's other brother, Absalom, briefly becomes a sympathetic character in the narrative as he, in sympathy with his grievously wronged sister, lays and springs a murderous trap for Amnon (13:23–29). After returning from exile for murdering his brother, Absalom then leads a coup d'etat against his father (15:1–18:15) that will parallel all the grief that David gave the House of Saul (although that will not be made completely clear until chapter 21). In the episode and aftermath of Tamar's rape, David's lustful and murderous impulses will manifest themselves in grossly magnified form in the actions of his sons. Likewise in the episode of Absalom's revolution one can clearly see David receiving payback for all of the grief he caused the House of Saul when the situations were reversed. In this regard even the House of Saul makes a short-lived stab at retaking the throne, in the forms of Mephibosheth, Jonathan's son (16:1–4), and Shimei, another Saulide of undetermined relation to the king (16:5–13).

After overcoming the attempted coup, David begins to recover from his own destructive behavior and its consequences. With Absalom dead, David returns to Jerusalem a changed and chastened man. In rapid sequence, he extends the olive branch to the elders of Israel and Judah (19:8b–15), forgives Shimei (19:18b–23), recalls the covenant with Jonathan by overlooking the possible disloyalty of Mephibosheth (19:24–30), and repays the kindness of Barzillai (19:31–40). He then shows that the moral shift in his character has its analog in the regaining of his political and military savviness as he puts down the rebellion of Sheba (20:1–22). The question of who will be Israel's next king ultimately gets resolved with the story of the rise of Solomon in 1 Kings 1–2.

An Appendix

The story then takes a surprising turn that seems to be out of sequence from the events of the previous chapters. Chapters 21–24 seem to be a kind of appendix tacked on to the body of 2 Samuel that contains some very revealing and significant information about David, not much of it flattering. The first story is indicative of much of what the appendix will contain. In response to the crisis of a national famine, David "inquired of the LORD" (see also 1 Sam 22:10; 23:2; 30:8; 2 Sam 2:1; 5:23; 21:1), only to find out that there was unaddressed bloodguilt from the previous administration that was the cause of the calamity. Apparently Saul had attempted to suppress the Gibeonites, a tribe of the previous Canaanite inhabitants of the land with whom Israel had entered into a treaty. The Gibeonites demand that David turn over to them seven sons of Saul for execution, which he promptly does. This event presents several elements that paint David in an unfavorable light. For one thing, as mentioned above, when David should have been avenging the bloodguilt of his nephew Asahel, he was instead making a deal with Asahel's killer. Moreover, the killing of the sons of Saul belies David's public displays of pain and anger when Saul, Jonathan, and Ishbaal were all killed (1:17–27; 4:9–12). It also makes clear the previously indecipherable anger of Shimei in 16:5–13, who had accused David of such bloodshed against the House of Saul even though readers had not yet been given the details of the violence.

In addition to the execution of Saul's sons, at least two other negative stories are told about David in this section. In the first, the narrator makes the startling disclosure that it was not David, but Elhanan, one of the king's mighty men from his hometown, who killed the giant Goliath (21:19), information that the later tradition will attempt to explain (1 Chron 20:5). In the second, we are given a detailed account of David's great sin of conducting a census of the people (24:1–17), perhaps a misguided attempt to raise taxes in order to build his government's bureaucratic infrastructure. The narrator does not give us the details of why this numbering of the people is such a grave moral lapse, but it is nonetheless clear that the narrator and his or her community understand it to be so.

Finally, tucked in between the "dirt" of David's administration, however, is a psalm attributed to the king (22:2–51; see also 1:19–27 for another such composition). The appearance of such a composition in the midst of all the unfavorable material highlights the ambiguity that characterizes the career of David as a whole, who displays extremes in piety, mercy, and generosity as well in political manipulation, lust, and violence. Again we meet a complicated, flawed human being who nevertheless has a heart open to God and poignantly sings his Lord's praises.

2 Samuel and Spiritual Formation

In virtue of its position in the Deuteronomistic History (Joshua–2 Kings), 2 Samuel has an inordinate number of negative examples of spiritual formation. This is consistent with the canonical intention to present the downward spiral of Israel into gross sin as the explanation for how the community that formerly had been secure in the land devoid of harmful influences or compromised theological commitments (as was the case in Josh 24) wound up at the mercy of the idolatrous Babylonians (2 Kings 25).

The centerpiece of the unseemly behavior is the episode of David's affair with Bathsheba in chapter 11. But spreading out from that incident is an enveloping cloud of spiritual darkness that enshrouds virtually everyone in David's family. The narrator does not "connect the dots" for readers, but the impression is unmistakable that the downward spiral can be traced to a particular moment in the family's life. The incident turns Amnon into a sexual predator, makes Tamar into a victim of incestuous rape, and transforms Absalom into a practitioner of fratricide and a usurper of his father's throne, only to die belatedly at the hand of cousin Joab. Readers may recoil at the text's bald declaration that Yahweh struck down the infant child of David and Bathsheba (12:15), but in light of the violence that befalls the rest of the family, the death of the child looks almost merciful.

In 2 Samuel, then, we witness the golden era of Israel in David's reign, but we also see the seeds of what was to come. God would not and will not tolerate the casual disregard of the covenant, even by his most favored servant David, and if there was an abandonment of righteousness in the land, the whole enterprise would ultimately collapse. There was ample opportunity for a painful lesson to be learned at the very outset of the monarchical period, but this was ignored.

The unspoken contemporary notion that the demands of the covenant are for others, and not for us, or that taking a brief holiday from it will be without consequence is demonstrated in this text to be an error and an illusion. Nevertheless, in the face of infidelity, God stays with the people, albeit as a corrective presence. Even when the people have no interest in covenant, God clearly has a "one-track mind" about it. There will be no abandonment of David or his family; nor will the divine plan to bless the first family be thwarted, as God uses even the most horrible of David's actions and their consequences to bring him back into leadership and, more important, to ensure the orderly succession of his throne to his son. In much the same way, God stays with us even in the midst of our unfaithful entanglements, using even our worst moments to shape us into the kind of partners to the covenant of which God imagines us to be capable.

—*Timothy F. Simpson*

David Mourns for Saul and Jonathan

1 After the death of Saul, when David had returned from defeating the Amalekites, David remained two days in Ziklag. 2On the third day, a man came from Saul's camp, with his clothes torn and dirt on his head. When he came to David, he fell to the ground and did obeisance. 3David said to him, "Where have you come from?" He said to him, "I have escaped from the camp of Israel." 4David said to him, "How did things go? Tell me!" He answered, "The army fled from the battle, but also many of the army fell and died; and Saul and his son Jonathan also died." 5Then David asked the young man who was reporting to him, "How do you know that Saul and his son Jonathan died?" 6The young man reporting to him said, "I happened to be on Mount Gilboa; and there was Saul leaning on his spear, while the chariots and the horsemen drew close to him. 7When he looked behind him, he saw me, and called to me. I answered, 'Here sir.' 8And he said to me, 'Who are you?' I answered him, 'I am an Amalekite.' 9He said to me, 'Come, stand over me and kill me; for convulsions have seized me, and yet my life still lingers.' 10So I stood over him, and killed him, for I knew that he could not live after he had fallen. I took the crown that was on his head and the armlet that was on his arm, and I have brought them here to my lord."

11 Then David took hold of his clothes and tore them; and all the men who were with him did the same. 12They mourned and wept, and fasted until evening for Saul and for his son Jonathan, and for the army of the LORD and for the house of Israel, because they had fallen by the sword. 13David said to the young man who had reported to him, "Where do you come from?" He answered, "I

am the son of a resident alien, an Amalekite." 14David said to him, "Were you not afraid to lift your hand to destroy the LORD's anointed?" 15Then David called one of the young men and said, "Come here and strike him down." So he struck him down and he died. 16David said to him, "Your blood be on your head; for your own mouth has testified against you, saying, 'I have killed the LORD's anointed.' "

17 David intoned this lamentation over Saul and his son Jonathan. 18(He ordered that The Song of the Bow*a* be taught to the people of Judah; it is written in the Book of Jashar.) He said:

19 Your glory, O Israel, lies slain upon your
        high places!
    How the mighty have fallen!
20 Tell it not in Gath,
        proclaim it not in the streets of
        Ashkelon;
    or the daughters of the Philistines will
        rejoice,
    the daughters of the uncircumcised
        will exult.

21 You mountains of Gilboa,
        let there be no dew or rain upon you,
        nor bounteous fields!*b*
    For there the shield of the mighty was
        defiled,
    the shield of Saul, anointed with oil
        no more.

22 From the blood of the slain,
        from the fat of the mighty,
    the bow of Jonathan did not turn back,
        nor the sword of Saul return empty.

a Heb *that The Bow*   b Meaning of Heb uncertain

1:19–27 *Your glory, O Israel.* It is an essential practice of the community to mourn as well as to celebrate. Laments such as this one are to be found characteristically in the Psalms, Israel's hymnbook, where some scholars have argued it is the primary genre around which the rest of the Psalter coalesced. In contemporary times, especially with the advent of certain kinds of "praise music," the capacity for lament and its attendant public expressions of grief have been eroded, as all that is sad, painful, and in any way distressing is left at the door like a coat or hat when people come into worship. Doing so is alien to biblical faith, which recognizes that all of life—good as well as bad—is within the zone of Yahweh's influence and thus is forever being processed not outside of or beyond worship, but rather within it.

23 Saul and Jonathan, beloved and lovely!
   In life and in death they were not
      divided;
   they were swifter than eagles,
   they were stronger than lions.

24 O daughters of Israel, weep over Saul,
   who clothed you with crimson, in
      luxury,
   who put ornaments of gold on your
      apparel.

25 How the mighty have fallen
   in the midst of the battle!

   Jonathan lies slain upon your high
      places.
26 I am distressed for you, my brother
      Jonathan;
   greatly beloved were you to me;
   your love to me was wonderful,
   passing the love of women.

27 How the mighty have fallen,
   and the weapons of war perished!

David Anointed King of Judah

2 After this David inquired of the LORD,
   "Shall I go up into any of the cities of
Judah?" The LORD said to him, "Go up." David said, "To which shall I go up?" He said,
"To Hebron." 2So David went up there, along
with his two wives, Ahinoam of Jezreel, and
Abigail the widow of Nabal of Carmel. 3David
brought up the men who were with him,
every one with his household; and they settled in the towns of Hebron. 4Then the people of Judah came, and there they anointed
David king over the house of Judah.

When they told David, "It was the people
of Jabesh-gilead who buried Saul," 5David
sent messengers to the people of Jabesh-gilead, and said to them, "May you be blessed by
the LORD, because you showed this loyalty to
Saul your lord, and buried him! 6Now may
the LORD show steadfast love and faithfulness to you! And I too will reward you because you have done this thing. 7Therefore let
your hands be strong, and be valiant; for Saul
your lord is dead, and the house of Judah has
anointed me king over them."

Ishbaal King of Israel

8 But Abner son of Ner, commander of
Saul's army, had taken Ishbaal[a] son of Saul,
and brought him over to Mahanaim. 9He
made him king over Gilead, the Ashurites,
Jezreel, Ephraim, Benjamin, and over all Israel. 10Ishbaal,[a] Saul's son, was forty years
old when he began to reign over Israel, and he
reigned two years. But the house of Judah
followed David. 11The time that David was
king in Hebron over the house of Judah was
seven years and six months.

The Battle of Gibeon

12 Abner son of Ner, and the servants of
Ishbaal[a] son of Saul, went out from Mahanaim to Gibeon. 13Joab son of Zeruiah, and
the servants of David, went out and met them
at the pool of Gibeon. One group sat on one
side of the pool, while the other sat on the
other side of the pool. 14Abner said to Joab,
"Let the young men come forward and have
a contest before us." Joab said, "Let them

a Gk Compare 1 Chr 8.33; 9.39: Heb Ish-bosheth,
"man of shame"

1:27 *the weapons of war perished!* The poet
ends with a stinging critique of the conventional
wisdom that military strength and the force of
arms are the sufficient means for the preservation of life. This critique will echo throughout
Israel's history until the time of Jesus, who
refuses to take up arms against the Romans to
establish God's reign. Nonetheless, this remains
a profound statement on the limits of warfare,
which has claimed the life of Israel's first king
and his heir.

2:5–7 *May you be blessed.* David continues
his long-standing practice of honoring Saul
(1 Sam 24; 26). The citizens of Jabesh-gilead
do their duty to the slain king, despite the fact
that he was unable to end the foreign menace
at Israel's borders. The honor given here to
this leader of Israel, even when he has failed,
contrasts with our own society's habit of
vilifying those leaders whose politics we do
not share.

come forward." [15]So they came forward and were counted as they passed by, twelve for Benjamin and Ishbaal[a] son of Saul, and twelve of the servants of David. [16]Each grasped his opponent by the head, and thrust his sword in his opponent's side; so they fell down together. Therefore that place was called Helkath-hazzurim,[b] which is at Gibeon. [17]The battle was very fierce that day; and Abner and the men of Israel were beaten by the servants of David.

18 The three sons of Zeruiah were there, Joab, Abishai, and Asahel. Now Asahel was as swift of foot as a wild gazelle. [19]Asahel pursued Abner, turning neither to the right nor to the left as he followed him. [20]Then Abner looked back and said, "Is it you, Asahel?" He answered, "Yes, it is." [21]Abner said to him, "Turn to your right or to your left, and seize one of the young men, and take his spoil." But Asahel would not turn away from following him. [22]Abner said again to Asahel, "Turn away from following me; why should I strike you to the ground? How then could I show my face to your brother Joab?" [23]But he refused to turn away. So Abner struck him in the stomach with the butt of his spear, so that the spear came out at his back. He fell there, and died where he lay. And all those who came to the place where Asahel had fallen and died, stood still.

24 But Joab and Abishai pursued Abner. As the sun was going down they came to the hill of Ammah, which lies before Giah on the way to the wilderness of Gibeon. [25]The Benjaminites rallied around Abner and formed a single band; they took their stand on the top of a hill. [26]Then Abner called to Joab, "Is the sword to keep devouring forever? Do you not know that the end will be bitter? How long will it be before you order your people to turn from the pursuit of their kinsmen?" [27]Joab said, "As God lives, if you had

not spoken, the people would have continued to pursue their kinsmen, not stopping until morning." [28]Joab sounded the trumpet and all the people stopped; they no longer pursued Israel or engaged in battle any further.

29 Abner and his men traveled all that night through the Arabah; they crossed the Jordan, and, marching the whole forenoon,[c] they came to Mahanaim. [30]Joab returned from the pursuit of Abner; and when he had gathered all the people together, there were missing of David's servants nineteen men besides Asahel. [31]But the servants of David had killed of Benjamin three hundred sixty of Abner's men. [32]They took up Asahel and buried him in the tomb of his father, which was at Bethlehem. Joab and his men marched all night, and the day broke upon them at Hebron.

Abner Defects to David

3 There was a long war between the house of Saul and the house of David; David grew stronger and stronger, while the house of Saul became weaker and weaker.

2 Sons were born to David at Hebron: his firstborn was Amnon, of Ahinoam of Jezreel; [3]his second, Chileab, of Abigail the widow of Nabal of Carmel; the third, Absalom son of Maacah, daughter of King Talmai of Geshur; [4]the fourth, Adonijah son of Haggith; the fifth, Shephatiah son of Abital; [5]and the sixth, Ithream, of David's wife Eglah. These were born to David in Hebron.

6 While there was war between the house of Saul and the house of David, Abner was making himself strong in the house of Saul. [7]Now Saul had a concubine whose name was Rizpah daughter of Aiah. And Ishbaal[d] said to

a Gk Compare 1 Chr 8.33; 9.39: Heb *Ish-bosheth*, "man of shame"   b That is *Field of Sword-edges*
c Meaning of Heb uncertain   d Heb *And he*

2:23 *He fell there.* Asahel and his two very high-strung brothers, Joab and Abishai, are a bloodthirsty lot. Asahel imagines that his speed will overcome Abner's skill as a fighter and pays for his mistake with his life. Asahel thus provides a negative example of the fate of those whose hotheadedness causes them to lose self-control

or who fail to first seek wise counsel before acting. The fact that these "sons of Zeruiah" (v 18) are the nephews of David means that their lack of restraint will have enormous consequences for David's kingship (e.g., ch 14; 18:14).

Abner, "Why have you gone in to my father's concubine?" [8]The words of Ishbaal[a] made Abner very angry; he said, "Am I a dog's head for Judah? Today I keep showing loyalty to the house of your father Saul, to his brothers, and to his friends, and have not given you into the hand of David; and yet you charge me now with a crime concerning this woman. [9]So may God do to Abner and so may he add to it! For just what the LORD has sworn to David, that will I accomplish for him, [10]to transfer the kingdom from the house of Saul, and set up the throne of David over Israel and over Judah, from Dan to Beer-sheba." [11]And Ishbaal[b] could not answer Abner another word, because he feared him.

[12] Abner sent messengers to David at He-bron,[c] saying, "To whom does the land belong? Make your covenant with me, and I will give you my support to bring all Israel over to you." [13]He said, "Good; I will make a covenant with you. But one thing I require of you: you shall never appear in my presence unless you bring Saul's daughter Michal when you come to see me." [14]Then David sent messengers to Saul's son Ishbaal,[d] saying, "Give me my wife Michal, to whom I became engaged at the price of one hundred foreskins of the Philistines." [15]Ishbaal[d] sent and took her from her husband Paltiel the son of Laish. [16]But her husband went with her, weeping as he walked behind her all the way to Bahurim. Then Abner said to him, "Go back home!" So he went back.

[17] Abner sent word to the elders of Israel, saying, "For some time past you have been seeking David as king over you. [18]Now then bring it about; for the LORD has promised David: Through my servant David I will save my people Israel from the hand of the Philistines, and from all their enemies." [19]Abner also spoke directly to the Benjaminites; then Abner went to tell David at Hebron all that Israel and the whole house of Benjamin were ready to do.

[20] When Abner came with twenty men to David at Hebron, David made a feast for Abner and the men who were with him. [21]Abner said to David, "Let me go and rally all Israel to my lord the king, in order that they may make a covenant with you, and that you may reign over all that your heart desires." So David dismissed Abner, and he went away in peace.

Abner Is Killed by Joab

[22] Just then the servants of David arrived with Joab from a raid, bringing much spoil with them. But Abner was not with David at Hebron, for David[e] had dismissed him, and he had gone away in peace. [23]When Joab and

---

a Gk Compare 1 Chr 8.33; 9.39: Heb *Ish-bosheth*, "man of shame"   b Heb *And he*   c Gk: Heb *where he was*   d Heb *Ish-bosheth*   e Heb *he*

3:13 *I will make a covenant with you.* Covenant making is a basic faith practice of the community, sometimes between God and the people (Gen 9; 17) or between individuals (Gen 25:28; 31:44). A covenant is different from the contemporary notion of "contract" in that it is imbued with a sacred significance that mitigates against either party failing to follow through with its stipulations. David himself has already made an often mentioned covenant with Saul's now deceased son Jonathan (1 Sam 18:3; 20:8; 23:18) to take care of any offspring that Jonathan might leave behind in the event of his untimely death. The covenant here functions to cement an alliance between Abner, the real power behind the Northern throne, and David, the Southern king. This is a surprising development, given David's harsh words to Abner when the

latter was inattentive to guarding King Saul (1 Sam 26:15–16) and because Abner killed one of David's nephews, Asahel (2:23).

3:14–16 *her husband went with her, weeping.* Once again we see David's weakness for women insinuate itself into the narrative (1 Sam 25). It is not clear whether David cares for Michal, to whom he refers as the woman whose hand he won by conquest, or whether this is just a political ploy to demonstrate his power and virility by taking possession of her as a spoil of war, in this case won by deftly maneuvering Abner into an alliance. Whether he cares for her or not, David's silence regarding his feelings for Michal, when contrasted with the heartrending cries of Paltiel, does not portray the new king in a favorable light.

all the army that was with him came, it was told Joab, "Abner son of Ner came to the king, and he has dismissed him, and he has gone away in peace." 24Then Joab went to the king and said, "What have you done? Abner came to you; why did you dismiss him, so that he got away? 25You know that Abner son of Ner came to deceive you, and to learn your comings and goings and to learn all that you are doing."

26 When Joab came out from David's presence, he sent messengers after Abner, and they brought him back from the cistern of Sirah; but David did not know about it. 27When Abner returned to Hebron, Joab took him aside in the gateway to speak with him privately, and there he stabbed him in the stomach. So he died for shedding*a* the blood of Asahel, Joab's*b* brother. 28Afterward, when David heard of it, he said, "I and my kingdom are forever guiltless before the LORD for the blood of Abner son of Ner. 29May the guilt*c* fall on the head of Joab, and on all his father's house; and may the house of Joab never be without one who has a discharge, or who is leprous,*d* or who holds a spindle, or who falls by the sword, or who lacks food!" 30So Joab and his brother Abishai murdered Abner because he had killed their brother Asahel in the battle at Gibeon.

31 Then David said to Joab and to all the people who were with him, "Tear your clothes, and put on sackcloth, and mourn over Abner." And King David followed the bier. 32They buried Abner at Hebron. The king lifted up his voice and wept at the grave of Abner, and all the people wept. 33The king lamented for Abner, saying,

"Should Abner die as a fool dies?
34 Your hands were not bound,
     your feet were not fettered;
as one falls before the wicked
     you have fallen."
And all the people wept over him again.

35Then all the people came to persuade David to eat something while it was still day; but David swore, saying, "So may God do to me, and more, if I taste bread or anything else before the sun goes down!" 36All the people took notice of it, and it pleased them; just as everything the king did pleased all the people. 37So all the people and all Israel understood that day that the king had no part in the killing of Abner son of Ner. 38And the king said to his servants, "Do you not know that a prince and a great man has fallen this day in Israel? 39Today I am powerless, even though anointed king; these men, the sons of Zeruiah, are too violent for me. The LORD pay back the one who does wickedly in accordance with his wickedness!"

Ishbaal Assassinated

4 When Saul's son Ishbaal*e* heard that Abner had died at Hebron, his courage failed, and all Israel was dismayed. 2Saul's son had two captains of raiding bands; the name of the one was Baanah, and the name of the other Rechab. They were sons of Rimmon a Benjaminite from Beeroth—for Beeroth is considered to belong to Benjamin. 3(Now the people of Beeroth had fled to Gittaim and are there as resident aliens to this day).

4 Saul's son Jonathan had a son who was crippled in his feet. He was five years old when the news about Saul and Jonathan came from Jezreel. His nurse picked him up and fled; and, in her haste to flee, it happened that he fell and became lame. His name was Mephibosheth.*f*

5 Now the sons of Rimmon the Beerothite, Rechab and Baanah, set out, and about

a Heb lacks *shedding*   b Heb *his*   c Heb *May it*
d A term for several skin diseases; precise meaning uncertain   e Heb lacks *Ishbaal*   f In 1 Chr 8.34 and 9.40, *Merib-baal*

3:27 *he died for shedding the blood of Asahel.* Here it is difficult to discern who is in the right. David has made a covenant with Abner, a sacred obligation, which means that Joab is bound to honor his king's commitment and give protection to Abner. But Joab's deed reminds us that there

was a prior obligation that David had to avenge the death of his nephew, a duty David seems to ignore. We can read Joab as either a vengeful, bloodthirsty murderer or as someone holding fast to family and to the *lex talionis, the law of* retribution (i.e., an eye for an eye, Lev 24:20).

the heat of the day they came to the house of Ishbaal, *a* while he was taking his noonday rest. 6They came inside the house as though to take wheat, and they struck him in the stomach; then Rechab and his brother Baanah escaped. *b* 7Now they had come into the house while he was lying on his couch in his bedchamber; they attacked him, killed him, and beheaded him. Then they took his head and traveled by way of the Arabah all night long. 8They brought the head of Ishbaal*a* to David at Hebron and said to the king, "Here is the head of Ishbaal, *a* son of Saul, your enemy, who sought your life; the LORD has avenged my lord the king this day on Saul and on his offspring."

9 David answered Rechab and his brother Baanah, the sons of Rimmon the Beerothite, "As the LORD lives, who has redeemed my life out of every adversity, 10when the one who told me, 'See, Saul is dead,' thought he was bringing good news, I seized him and killed him at Ziklag—this was the reward I gave him for his news. 11How much more then, when wicked men have killed a righteous man on his bed in his own house! And now shall I not require his blood at your hand, and destroy you from the earth?" 12So David commanded the young men, and they killed them; they cut off their hands and feet, and hung their bodies beside the pool at Hebron. But the head of Ishbaal*a* they took and buried in the tomb of Abner at Hebron.

David Anointed King of All Israel

5 Then all the tribes of Israel came to David at Hebron, and said, "Look, we are your bone and flesh. 2For some time, while Saul was king over us, it was you who led out Israel and brought it in. The LORD said to you: It is you who shall be shepherd of my people Israel, you who shall be ruler over Israel." 3So all the elders of Israel came to the king at Hebron; and King David made a covenant with them at Hebron before the LORD, and they

anointed David king over Israel. 4David was thirty years old when he began to reign, and he reigned forty years. 5At Hebron he reigned over Judah seven years and six months; and at Jerusalem he reigned over all Israel and Judah thirty-three years.

Jerusalem Made Capital of the United Kingdom

6 The king and his men marched to Jerusalem against the Jebusites, the inhabitants of the land, who said to David, "You will not come in here, even the blind and the lame will turn you back"—thinking, "David cannot come in here." 7Nevertheless David took the stronghold of Zion, which is now the city of David. 8David had said on that day, "Whoever would strike down the Jebusites, let him get up the water shaft to attack the lame and the blind, those whom David hates."*c* Therefore it is said, "The blind and the lame shall not come into the house." 9David occupied the stronghold, and named it the city of David. David built the city all around from the Millo inward. 10And David became greater and greater, for the LORD, the God of hosts, was with him.

11 King Hiram of Tyre sent messengers to David, along with cedar trees, and carpenters and masons who built David a house. 12David then perceived that the LORD had established him king over Israel, and that he had exalted his kingdom for the sake of his people Israel.

13 In Jerusalem, after he came from Hebron, David took more concubines and wives; and more sons and daughters were born to David. 14These are the names of those who were born to him in Jerusalem: Shammua, Shobab, Nathan, Solomon, 15Ibhar, Elishua,

a Heb *Ish-bosheth*   *b* Meaning of Heb of verse 6 uncertain   *c* Another reading is *those who hate David*

5:9–10 *the LORD, the God of hosts, was with him.* Aside from the setback with the death of Abner in chapter 3, the narrative is replete with David's successes. Here he has established the city that to this day is known as being *his* city,

Jerusalem. But the narrator insists that David is no self-made man; he owes everything to the God of hosts, that is, the God of heavenly armies, who has made all of this possible.

Nepheg, Japhia, [16]Elishama, Eliada, and Eliphelet.

Philistine Attack Repulsed

17 When the Philistines heard that David had been anointed king over Israel, all the Philistines went up in search of David; but David heard about it and went down to the stronghold. [18]Now the Philistines had come and spread out in the valley of Rephaim. [19]David inquired of the LORD, "Shall I go up against the Philistines? Will you give them into my hand?" The LORD said to David, "Go up; for I will certainly give the Philistines into your hand." [20]So David came to Baal-perazim, and David defeated them there. He said, "The LORD has burst forth against[a] my enemies before me, like a bursting flood." Therefore that place is called Baal-perazim.[b] [21]The Philistines abandoned their idols there, and David and his men carried them away.

22 Once again the Philistines came up, and were spread out in the valley of Rephaim. [23]When David inquired of the LORD, he said, "You shall not go up; go around to their rear, and come upon them opposite the balsam trees. [24]When you hear the sound of marching in the tops of the balsam trees, then be on the alert; for then the LORD has gone out be-

fore you to strike down the army of the Philistines." [25]David did just as the LORD had commanded him; and he struck down the Philistines from Geba all the way to Gezer.

David Brings the Ark to Jerusalem

6 David again gathered all the chosen men of Israel, thirty thousand. [2]David and all the people with him set out and went from Baale-judah, to bring up from there the ark of God, which is called by the name of the LORD of hosts who is enthroned on the cherubim. [3]They carried the ark of God on a new cart, and brought it out of the house of Abinadab, which was on the hill. Uzzah and Ahio,[c] the sons of Abinadab, were driving the new cart [4]with the ark of God;[d] and Ahio[c] went in front of the ark. [5]David and all the house of Israel were dancing before the LORD with all their might, with songs[e] and lyres and harps and tambourines and castanets and cymbals.

6 When they came to the threshing floor of Nacon, Uzzah reached out his hand to the

---

a Heb paraz   b That is Lord of Bursting Forth
c Or and his brother   d Compare Gk: Heb and brought it out of the house of Abinadab, which was on the hill with the ark of God   e Q Ms Gk 1 Chr 13.8: Heb fir trees

---

Responding

5:19 GUIDANCE. David asked the Lord if he should attack the Philistines, and if he did, whether he would be victorious. The practice of waiting for guidance from the Lord is common among charismatic Christians, but is largely ignored in other groups. How do you feel about the Lord's giving direct guidance to us today? As you are considering this issue, read Isa 30:19–21, God's promise to Zion, and Acts 2:17–18, God's promise to us. What are the advantages in waiting for the Lord to speak before we act? The dangers? *See also* Spiritual Disciplines Index.

5:24 THE WITH-GOD LIFE—*See* Spiritual Disciplines Index.

5:25 *David did just as the LORD had commanded him.* David's military success is rooted not in his great skill as a tactician or as a motivator of the troops, but rather in the fact that

he submits his plans to Yahweh for approval first (v 19). This contrasts with the practice of the dead king, Saul, who instead consorted with a medium (1 Sam 28:3–20). So long as David continues in this faithful practice, he will live in a zone protected by the favor of Yahweh, the result of which will be prosperity for both himself and his people.

6:6–7 *God struck him.* The ark has been in the same spot it was left in in 1 Sam 6–7:2. David, having been so successful elsewhere, both militarily and diplomatically, takes steps to begin to move the ark. But the "era of good feeling" that has resulted from David's string of successes comes to a screeching halt with the death of Uzzah, who tries to manage the ark. Once again, the awesome holiness of Yahweh manifests itself, as it did in 1 Samuel 4–6, against any attempts, even well-meaning ones, to exert any control whatsoever over Yahweh.

[handwritten margin notes: "Celebration to regain the joy / example (mood swings)", "Can't control / manage the Ark of God", "How does one move the Ark of God?"]

ark of God and took hold of it, for the oxen shook it. 7The anger of the LORD was kindled against Uzzah; and God struck him there because he reached out his hand to the ark; a and he died there beside the ark of God. 8David was angry because the LORD had burst forth with an outburst upon Uzzah; so that place is called Perez-uzzah, b to this day. 9David was afraid of the LORD that day; he said, "How can the ark of the LORD come into my care?" 10So David was unwilling to take the ark of the LORD into his care in the city of David; instead David took it to the house of Obed-edom the Gittite. 11The ark of the LORD remained in the house of Obed-edom the Gittite three months; and the LORD blessed Obed-edom and all his household.

12 It was told King David, "The LORD has blessed the household of Obed-edom and all that belongs to him, because of the ark of God." So David went and brought up the ark of God from the house of Obed-edom to the city of David with rejoicing; 13and when those who bore the ark of the LORD had gone six paces, he sacrificed an ox and a fatling.

14David danced before the LORD with all his might; David was girded with a linen ephod. 15So David and all the house of Israel brought up the ark of the LORD with shouting, and with the sound of the trumpet.

16 As the ark of the LORD came into the city of David, Michal daughter of Saul looked out of the window, and saw King David leaping and dancing before the LORD; and she despised him in her heart.

17 They brought in the ark of the LORD, and set it in its place, inside the tent that David had pitched for it; and David offered burnt offerings and offerings of well-being before the LORD. 18When David had finished offering the burnt offerings and the offerings of well-being, he blessed the people in the name of the LORD of hosts, 19and distributed food among all the people, the whole multitude of Israel, both men and women, to each a cake of bread, a portion of meat, c and

a 1 Chr 13.10 Compare Q Ms: Meaning of Heb uncertain   b That is *Bursting Out Against Uzzah*   c Vg: Meaning of Heb uncertain

---

6:10–12 *the LORD blessed Obed-edom.* In contrast to what happened to Uzzah in verse 6, Obed-edom and his family are blessed by Yahweh—not because of anything they have done, but precisely because they did nothing; that is, they made no attempt to try to manage Yahweh, who resists all efforts at manipulation. Uzzah's death may appear to modern readers as an unduly harsh penalty for such a minor infraction, but the story is included as a cautionary tale against any similar acts that would presume to control Yahweh.

6:12–13 *sacrificed an ox and a fatling.* Although God cannot be managed, God's holiness can be acknowledged through appropriate humility, in this case through acts of sacrifice, which create the conditions under which the ark may be moved. The narrative makes the point that approaching Yahweh cannot be a matter of indifference or curiosity or be motivated by selfishness. Scholars debate whether the sacrifice was made after the first six steps only or every six steps throughout the journey to the ark's resting place, but the text is not clear on that point. What is evident, though, is that the ancient practice of sacrifice, the

taking of life, makes ready the environment for moving the divine presence. Once David and his companions recognize the seriousness of what they are doing, which they acknowledge now by the sacrifice, then it becomes possible to move the ark.

Responding
6:14 CELEBRATION. As the ark was being taken from the house of Obed-edom to the tent erected for it in Jerusalem, David leaped and "danced before the LORD." We normally think of dancing in terms of type—ballroom, ballet, tap, salsa, hip-hop—but David spontaneously danced as a way to celebrate. Has there ever been a time in your life when your heart was so full of divine joy that you felt like dancing? Did you? Explain. *See also* Spiritual Disciplines Index.

6:17–19 *and a cake of raisins.* Moving away from the tragic and serious, the story now concentrates on the celebratory. As was the case for the journey in verse 13, the settling of the ark is accompanied by sacrifice, and then also blessing and a feast, all of which will be

a cake of raisins. Then all the people went back to their homes.

20 David returned to bless his household. But Michal the daughter of Saul came out to meet David, and said, "How the king of Israel honored himself today, uncovering himself today before the eyes of his servants' maids, as any vulgar fellow might shamelessly uncover himself!" 21David said to Michal, "It was before the LORD, who chose me in place of your father and all his household, to appoint me as prince over Israel, the people of the LORD, that I have danced before the LORD. 22I will make myself yet more contemptible than this, and I will be abased in my own eyes; but by the maids of whom you have spoken, by them I shall be held in honor." 23And Michal the daughter of Saul had no child to the day of her death.

God's Covenant with David

7 Now when the king was settled in his house, and the LORD had given him rest from all his enemies around him, 2the king said to the prophet Nathan, "See now, I am living in a house of cedar, but the ark of God stays in a tent." 3Nathan said to the king, "Go, do all that you have in mind; for the LORD is with you."

4 But that same night the word of the LORD came to Nathan: 5Go and tell my servant David: Thus says the LORD: Are you the one to build me a house to live in? 6I have not lived

in a house since the day I brought up the people of Israel from Egypt to this day, but I have been moving about in a tent and a tabernacle. 7Wherever I have moved about among all the people of Israel, did I ever speak a word with any of the tribal leaders[a] of Israel, whom I commanded to shepherd my people Israel, saying, "Why have you not built me a house of cedar?" 8Now therefore thus you shall say to my servant David: Thus says the LORD of hosts: I took you from the pasture, from following the sheep to be prince over my people Israel; 9and I have been with you wherever you went, and have cut off all your enemies from before you; and I will make for you a great name, like the name of the great ones of the earth. 10And I will appoint a place for my people Israel and will plant them, so that they may live in their own place, and be disturbed no more; and evildoers shall afflict them no more, as formerly, 11from the time that I appointed judges over my people Israel; and I will give you rest from all your enemies. Moreover the LORD declares to you that the LORD will make you a house. 12When your days are fulfilled and you lie down with your ancestors, I will raise up your offspring after you, who shall come forth from your body, and I will establish his kingdom. 13He shall build a house for my name, and I will establish the throne of his kingdom forever. 14I

a Or any of the tribes

---

echoed later in the eucharistic meal celebrated in Christian worship after the resurrection of Jesus. In the dangerous presence of Yahweh there is, for those whose hearts are clean and whose motives are pure, great joy and happiness—a reason to rejoice. Undoubtedly this is why David desires to have the ark nearby.

6:20–23 *But Michal . . . said.* Michal is deeply offended by David's unbridled reveling, during which he exposes himself publicly (vv 14–16). Nothing is said about her reaction at having been taken from her husband, Paltiel, in chapter 3, but here she is clearly seething at David's display. Unapologetic, David promises even more of the same kind of behavior, perhaps unintentionally foreshadowing his own impending moral collapse in chapter 11. Michal

makes her point, but will live her life under the social stain of childlessness, whether by her own choice to cease marital relations with David, or by David's choice to cease them with her, or even by the hand of God, who disciplines Michal for opposing his favorite.

7:2 *the ark of God stays in a tent.* Unlike his practice earlier in the story, in which he consults Yahweh on his every move, David, intoxicated with success, begins to operate independently; he decides he will build a house for the Lord. Nathan the prophet, whose job it is to head off schemes that are contrary to the divine will, is likewise bowled over by the aura of David's triumphs and provides sanction for the project before properly consulting Yahweh's wishes.

7:8 **SERVICE**—See Spiritual Disciplines Index.

will be a father to him, and he shall be a son to me. When he commits iniquity, I will punish him with a rod such as mortals use, with blows inflicted by human beings. 15But I will not take[a] my steadfast love from him, as I took it from Saul, whom I put away from before you. 16Your house and your kingdom shall be made sure forever before me;[b] your throne shall be established forever. 17In accordance with all these words and with all this vision, Nathan spoke to David.

David's Prayer

18 Then King David went in and sat before the LORD, and said, "Who am I, O Lord GOD, and what is my house, that you have brought me thus far? 19And yet this was a small thing in your eyes, O Lord GOD; you have spoken also of your servant's house for a great while to come. May this be instruction for the people,[c] O Lord GOD! 20And what more can David say to you? For you know your servant, O Lord GOD! 21Because of your promise, and according to your own heart, you have wrought all this greatness, so that your servant may know it. 22Therefore you are great, O LORD God; for there is no one like you, and there is no God besides you, according to all that we have heard with our ears. 23Who is like your people, like Israel? Is there another[d] nation on earth whose God went to redeem it as a people, and to make a name for himself, doing great and awesome things for them,[e] by driving out[f] before his people nations and their gods?[g] 24And you established your people Israel for yourself to be your people forever; and you, O LORD, became their God. 25And now, O LORD God, as for the word that you have spoken concerning your servant and concerning his house, confirm it forever; do as you have promised. 26Thus your name will be magnified forever in the saying, 'The LORD of hosts is God over Israel'; and the house of your servant David will be established before you. 27For you, O LORD of hosts, the God of Israel, have made this revelation to your servant, saying, 'I will build you a house'; therefore your servant has found courage to pray this prayer to you. 28And now, O Lord GOD, you are God, and your words are true, and you have promised this good thing to your servant; 29now therefore may it please you to bless the house of your servant, so that it may continue forever before you; for you, O Lord GOD, have spoken, and with your blessing shall the house of your servant be blessed forever."

David's Wars

8 Some time afterward, David attacked the Philistines and subdued them; David took Metheg-ammah out of the hand of the Philistines.

2 He also defeated the Moabites and, making them lie down on the ground, measured them off with a cord; he measured two

a Gk Syr Vg 1 Chr 17.13: Heb *shall not depart*
b Gk Heb Mss: MT *before you*; Compare 2 Sam 7.26, 29 c Meaning of Heb uncertain d Gk: Heb *one* e Heb *you* f Gk 1 Chr 17.21: Heb *for your land* g Cn: Heb *before your people, whom you redeemed for yourself from Egypt, nations and its gods*

7:18–29 *David . . . sat before the LORD and said.* David offers a model prayer of thanksgiving to God after the astonishing promise that his offspring will be the bearers of a royal dynasty down through the ages. One can imagine that David is thankful not just for the incredible beneficence of God's gift, but also for the fact that he has been saved from his untimely suggestion of building God a house (v 2).

Responding
7:21 SERVICE. Through the prophet Nathan David learns that he would not get the privilege of building the Lord a house.

But instead of pouting or becoming angry, David humbly presents himself to God as a servant and praises God for his promise and everything he had done in the life of Israel. Describe one thing in your life that you have been unable to do—earning a college degree, working at your favorite vocation, becoming a parent—and in the spirit of David, praise God for what he *has* done in your life—giving you a loving spouse, guiding you into a caring congregation, directing your steps during difficult times. *See also* Spiritual Disciplines Index.

lengths of cord for those who were to be put to death, and one length *a* for those who were to be spared. And the Moabites became servants to David and brought tribute.

3 David also struck down King Hadadezer son of Rehob of Zobah, as he went to restore his monument *b* at the river Euphrates. 4David took from him one thousand seven hundred horsemen, and twenty thousand foot soldiers. David hamstrung all the chariot horses, but left enough for a hundred chariots. 5When the Arameans of Damascus came to help King Hadadezer of Zobah, David killed twenty-two thousand men of the Arameans. 6Then David put garrisons among the Arameans of Damascus; and the Arameans became servants to David and brought tribute. The LORD gave victory to David wherever he went. 7David took the gold shields that were carried by the servants of Hadadezer, and brought them to Jerusalem. 8From Betah and from Berothai, towns of Hadadezer, King David took a great amount of bronze.

9 When King Toi of Hamath heard that David had defeated the whole army of Hadadezer, 10Toi sent his son Joram to King David, to greet him and to congratulate him because he had fought against Hadadezer and defeated him. Now Hadadezer had often been at war with Toi. Joram brought with him articles of silver, gold, and bronze; 11these also King David dedicated to the LORD, together with the silver and gold that he dedicated from all the nations he subdued, 12from

Edom, Moab, the Ammonites, the Philistines, Amalek, and from the spoil of King Hadadezer son of Rehob of Zobah.

13 David won a name for himself. When he returned, he killed eighteen thousand Edomites *c* in the Valley of Salt. 14He put garrisons in Edom; throughout all Edom he put garrisons, and all the Edomites became David's servants. And the LORD gave victory to David wherever he went.

David's Officers

15 So David reigned over all Israel; and David administered justice and equity to all his people. 16Joab son of Zeruiah was over the army; Jehoshaphat son of Ahilud was recorder; 17Zadok son of Ahitub and Ahimelech son of Abiathar were priests; Seraiah was secretary; 18Benaiah son of Jehoiada was over *d* the Cherethites and the Pelethites; and David's sons were priests.

David's Kindness to Mephibosheth

9 David asked, "Is there still anyone left of the house of Saul to whom I may show kindness for Jonathan's sake?" 2Now there was a servant of the house of Saul whose name was Ziba, and he was summoned to David. The king said to him, "Are you Ziba?" And he said, "At your service!" 3The king

---

a Heb *one full length*   *b* Compare 1 Sam 15.12 and 2 Sam 18.18   *c* Gk: Heb *returned from striking down eighteen thousand Arameans*   *d* Syr Tg Vg 20.23; 1 Chr 18.17: Heb lacks *was over*

8:11 *dedicated to the LORD.* Demonstrating that his prayer at the end of chapter 7 was not just hollow words, David dedicates the spoils of his victory to Yahweh. Genuine spirituality will always manifest itself in an attitude of generosity toward possessions. The spoils of war were never David's to begin with; hence it is not difficult for him to give back what was never truly his. The text's perspective on wealth is counter to that prevailing in our own society, which has valorized the acquisition and maintenance of private property as the ends toward which human existence should be directed.

8:15 *David administered justice and equity.* As every leader of a nation knows, success in

foreign policy does not necessarily solve domestic difficulties. Clearly David's primary obstacle at the beginning of his reign, as it was Saul's before him, was to deal with the Philistine menace. This he did with astonishing swiftness. Had his reign gone no further than this, he would have been remembered as an extraordinary success. Yet the text asserts that David's kingship is not only strong, but it is also good, which even more than military success is the sine qua non of the ideal leader. In the West, where most leaders at the local and national level want to be identified as members of the faith community, the proof of this affiliation is to be found not in the labels worn, but in the justice and equity administered.

said, "Is there anyone remaining of the house of Saul to whom I may show the kindness of God?" Ziba said to the king, "There remains a son of Jonathan; he is crippled in his feet." 4The king said to him, "Where is he?" Ziba said to the king, "He is in the house of Machir son of Ammiel, at Lo-debar." 5Then King David sent and brought him from the house of Machir son of Ammiel, at Lo-debar. 6Mephibosheth*a* son of Jonathan son of Saul came to David, and fell on his face and did obeisance. David said, "Mephibosheth!"*a* He answered, "I am your servant." 7David said to him, "Do not be afraid, for I will show you kindness for the sake of your father Jonathan; I will restore to you all the land of your grandfather Saul, and you yourself shall eat at my table always." 8He did obeisance and said, "What is your servant, that you should look upon a dead dog such as I?"

9 Then the king summoned Saul's servant Ziba, and said to him, "All that belonged to Saul and to all his house I have given to your master's grandson. 10You and your sons and your servants shall till the land for him, and shall bring in the produce, so that your master's grandson may have food to eat; but your master's grandson Mephibosheth*a* shall always eat at my table." Now Ziba had fifteen sons and twenty servants. 11Then Ziba said to the king, "According to all that my lord the king commands his servant, so your servant will do." Mephibosheth*a* ate at David's*b* table, like one of the king's sons. 12Mephibosheth*a* had a young son whose name was Mica. And all who lived in Ziba's house became Mephibosheth's*c* servants. 13Mephibosheth*a* lived in Jerusalem, for he always ate at the king's table. Now he was lame in both his feet.

The Ammonites and Arameans Are Defeated

10 Some time afterward, the king of the Ammonites died, and his son Hanun succeeded him. 2David said, "I will deal loyally with Hanun son of Nahash, just as his father dealt loyally with me." So David sent envoys to console him concerning his father. When David's envoys came into the land of the Ammonites, 3the princes of the Ammonites said to their lord Hanun, "Do you really think that David is honoring your father just because he has sent messengers with condolences to you? Has not David sent his envoys to you to search the city, to spy it out, and to overthrow it?" 4So Hanun seized David's envoys, shaved off half the beard of each, cut off their garments in the middle at their hips, and sent them away. 5When David was told, he sent to meet them, for the men were greatly ashamed. The king said, "Remain at Jericho until your beards have grown, and then return."

6 When the Ammonites saw that they had become odious to David, the Ammonites sent and hired the Arameans of Beth-rehob and the Arameans of Zobah, twenty thousand foot soldiers, as well as the king of Maacah, one thousand men, and the men of Tob, twelve thousand men. 7When David heard of it, he sent Joab and all the army with the warriors. 8The Ammonites came out and

a Or *Merib-baal*: See 4.4 note   b Gk: Heb *my*
c Or *Merib-baal's*: See 4.4 note

9:1–13 *show kindness for Jonathan's sake.* Although David has reached the pinnacle of his military and political career, he has not yet become so high and mighty that he has forgotten his obligations to those who made his unprecedented rise possible. Specifically, Jonathan, the son and heir apparent of the former king, had loved David (1 Sam 18:3) and recognized that God's hand was upon David. Jonathan had thus kept his father from taking David's life (1 Sam 20:12–42). For this favor, all Jonathan asked was that David look after

Jonathan's family if anything happened to him (1 Sam 20:15). It may seem a bit late for David to be remembering that promise, but the narrator has actually placed this remembrance of duty at the highest point in David's career, when he would have been most likely to forget the obligation and certainly when he was least likely to need the help of anyone else. The effect of the head of state and commander in chief taking time and energy to keep his vow has the effect of enhancing David's image as deeply pious and spiritual, ideal attributes for any leader.

drew up in battle array at the entrance of the gate; but the Arameans of Zobah and of Rehob, and the men of Tob and Maacah, were by themselves in the open country.

9 When Joab saw that the battle was set against him both in front and in the rear, he chose some of the picked men of Israel, and arrayed them against the Arameans; 10the rest of his men he put in the charge of his brother Abishai, and he arrayed them against the Ammonites. 11He said, "If the Arameans are too strong for me, then you shall help me; but if the Ammonites are too strong for you, then I will come and help you. 12Be strong, and let us be courageous for the sake of our people, and for the cities of our God; and may the LORD do what seems good to him." 13So Joab and the people who were with him moved forward into battle against the Arameans; and they fled before him. 14When the Ammonites saw that the Arameans fled, they likewise fled before Abishai, and entered the city. Then Joab returned from fighting against the Ammonites, and came to Jerusalem.

15 But when the Arameans saw that they had been defeated by Israel, they gathered themselves together. 16Hadadezer sent and brought out the Arameans who were beyond the Euphrates; and they came to Helam, with Shobach the commander of the army of Hadadezer at their head. 17When it was told David, he gathered all Israel together, and crossed the Jordan, and came to Helam. The Arameans arrayed themselves against David and fought with him. 18The Arameans fled before Israel; and David killed of the Arameans seven hundred chariot teams, and forty thousand horsemen,*a* and wounded Shobach the commander of their army, so that he died there. 19When all the kings who were servants of Hadadezer saw that they had been defeated by Israel, they made peace with Israel, and became subject to them. So the Arameans were afraid to help the Ammonites any more.

David Commits Adultery with Bathsheba

11 In the spring of the year, the time when kings go out to battle, David sent Joab with his officers and all Israel with him; they ravaged the Ammonites, and besieged Rabbah. But David remained at Jerusalem.

2 It happened, late one afternoon, when David rose from his couch and was walking about on the roof of the king's house, that he saw from the roof a woman bathing; the woman was very beautiful. 3David sent someone to inquire about the woman. It was reported, "This is Bathsheba daughter of Eliam, the wife of Uriah the Hittite." 4So David sent messengers to get her, and she came to him, and he lay with her. (Now she was purifying herself after her period.) Then she returned to her house. 5The woman conceived; and she sent and told David, "I am pregnant."

6 So David sent word to Joab, "Send me Uriah the Hittite." And Joab sent Uriah to David. 7When Uriah came to him, David asked how Joab and the people fared, and how the war was going. 8Then David said to Uriah, "Go down to your house, and wash your feet." Uriah went out of the king's house, and there followed him a present from the king. 9But Uriah slept at the entrance of the king's house with all the servants of his lord, and did not go down to his house. 10When they told David, "Uriah did not go down to his house," David said to Uriah, "You have just come from a journey. Why did you not go down to your house?" 11Uriah said to David,

---

a 1 Chr 19.18 and some Gk Mss read *foot soldiers*

11:1 *David remained at Jerusalem.* The narrator signals up front that David's not being in the right place is going to be his undoing. Sometime between the end of chapter 10 and the beginning of chapter 11 David seems to have decided that he does not need to be in his customary place at the head of his army, but can turn that over to underlings. This decision will have enormous consequences for both himself and all those around him. A good leader learns the importance of delegating authority to others, but some things leaders must do themselves. In this case, David's failure at leadership precipitates a flood of bad judgments.

"The ark and Israel and Judah remain in booths;[a] and my lord Joab and the servants of my lord are camping in the open field; shall I then go to my house, to eat and to drink, and to lie with my wife? As you live, and as your soul lives, I will not do such a thing." [12]Then David said to Uriah, "Remain here today also, and tomorrow I will send you back." So Uriah remained in Jerusalem that day. On the next day, [13]David invited him to eat and drink in his presence and made him drunk; and in the evening he went out to lie on his couch with the servants of his lord, but he did not go down to his house.

David Has Uriah Killed

14 In the morning David wrote a letter to Joab, and sent it by the hand of Uriah. [15]In the letter he wrote, "Set Uriah in the forefront of the hardest fighting, and then draw back from him, so that he may be struck down and die." [16]As Joab was besieging the city, he assigned Uriah to the place where he knew there were valiant warriors. [17]The men of the city came out and fought with Joab; and some of the servants of David among the people fell. Uriah the Hittite was killed as well. [18]Then Joab sent and told David all the news about the fighting; [19]and he instructed the messenger, "When you have finished telling the king all the news about the fighting, [20]then, if the king's anger rises, and if he says to you, 'Why did you go so near the city to fight? Did you not know that they would shoot from the wall? [21]Who killed Abimelech son of Jerubbaal?[b] Did not a woman throw an upper millstone on him from the wall, so that he died at Thebez? Why did you go so near the wall?' then you shall say, 'Your servant Uriah the Hittite is dead too.' "

22 So the messenger went, and came and told David all that Joab had sent him to tell. [23]The messenger said to David, "The men gained an advantage over us, and came out against us in the field; but we drove them back to the entrance of the gate. [24]Then the archers shot at your servants from the wall; some of the king's servants are dead; and your servant Uriah the Hittite is dead also." [25]David said to the messenger, "Thus you shall say to Joab, 'Do not let this matter trouble you, for the sword devours now one and now another; press your attack on the city, and overthrow it.' And encourage him."

26 When the wife of Uriah heard that her husband was dead, she made lamentation for him. [27]When the mourning was over, David sent and brought her to his house, and she became his wife, and bore him a son.

Nathan Condemns David

But the thing that David had done displeased the LORD, [1]and the LORD sent **12** Nathan to David. He came to him, and said to him, "There were two men in a certain city, the one rich and the other poor. [2]The rich man had very many flocks and

a Or at Succoth   b Gk Syr Judg 7.1: Heb Jerubbesheth

Responding
11:11 SERVICE. When given the opportunity to "go to [his own] house"—shorthand for being reunited with his wife and having conjugal relations—Uriah chose instead to stay with David's other servants. In Uriah's response to David, we get a peek into a heart that makes Uriah intent on fulfilling his duties as a soldier and a servant of the king regardless of the cost. Whom do you know who has a heart like Uriah's? As the opportunity arises, thank those persons for their service. See also Spiritual Disciplines Index.

11:12–13 *but he did not go down to his house.* In ironic contrast to the king who refuses to go where he is supposed to (to battle), and instead goes where he wants (to Bathsheba), Uriah refuses to go where he wants (to Bathsheba) as a silent demand to be allowed by the king to return to the place where both he and the king should be (in battle). It is a double irony because Uriah is a Hittite (v 6), a foreigner, and thus not one born into covenant life. It is a sign of how far the king has fallen that he has to be schooled in faithfulness by such a person, but also a clear sign that those outside the family by birth can embrace and embody the core values of the People of God.

herds; 3but the poor man had nothing but one little ewe lamb, which he had bought. He brought it up, and it grew up with him and with his children; it used to eat of his meager fare, and drink from his cup, and lie in his bosom, and it was like a daughter to him. 4Now there came a traveler to the rich man, and he was loath to take one of his own flock or herd to prepare for the wayfarer who had come to him, but he took the poor man's lamb, and prepared that for the guest who had come to him." 5Then David's anger was greatly kindled against the man. He said to Nathan, "As the LORD lives, the man who has done this deserves to die; 6he shall restore the lamb fourfold, because he did this thing, and because he had no pity."

7 Nathan said to David, "You are the man! Thus says the LORD, the God of Israel: I anointed you king over Israel, and I rescued you from the hand of Saul; 8I gave you your master's house, and your master's wives into your bosom, and gave you the house of Israel and of Judah; and if that had been too little, I would have added as much more. 9Why have you despised the word of the LORD, to do what is evil in his sight? You have struck down Uriah the Hittite with the sword, and have taken his wife to be your wife, and have killed him with the sword of the Ammonites. 10Now therefore the sword shall never depart from your house, for you have despised me, and have taken the wife of Uriah the Hittite to be your wife. 11Thus says the LORD: I will raise up trouble against you from within your own house; and I will take your wives before your eyes, and give them to your neighbor, and he shall lie with your wives in the sight of this very sun. 12For you did it secretly; but I will do this thing before all Israel, and before the sun." 13David said to Nathan, "I have sinned against the LORD." Nathan said to David, "Now the LORD has put away your sin; you shall not die. 14Nevertheless, because by this deed you have utterly scorned the LORD,a the child that is born to you shall die." 15Then Nathan went to his house.

Bathsheba's Child Dies

The LORD struck the child that Uriah's wife bore to David, and it became very ill. 16David therefore pleaded with God for the child;

a Ancient scribal tradition: Compare 1 Sam 25.22 note: Heb *scorned the enemies of the LORD*

12:7–12 *You are the man!* This scene repeats a similar episode between Samuel and Saul in 1 Samuel 15 in which a prophet speaks truth to power. Nathan appears to be what scholars call a "court prophet," that is, one who functions as an insider within the government (e.g., Isaiah) rather than as an outside critic (e.g., Amos). What is therefore remarkable about this unmistakably firm statement of moral condemnation is that it is uttered by someone who, we may imagine, stands to lose everything because of his strong words. The direct confrontation of sin in the life of a person we know or work with, especially someone in a position of authority over us, is one of the most difficult and potentially hazardous social situations to negotiate. Yet, as the example of Nathan demonstrates, authentic spirituality will nevertheless issue forth in such situations when we say what needs to be said in spite of the discomfort or the consequences.

12:13 *I have sinned against the LORD.* David responds with almost the same words as did Saul when he was confronted by the prophet (1 Sam 15:24), although the offense in this case is far clearer for readers to grasp. Unlike Saul, however, who went on in his admission of guilt to mention all of the contributing factors in his misdeeds, David has the grace and good sense to avoid attributing his mistakes to any contributing factors. Bathsheba, for example, is not cast as the seductress who tempted him. Instead, David takes full responsibility for what he has done, which is the first step to genuine repentance and restoration into right relation with God and the community.

12:16 *David fasted.* Intercessory prayer on behalf of the neighbor is characteristic of biblical faith at least since the time of Abraham (Gen 18:23–33) and Moses (Exod 32:30–32), who both prayed to stay the judging hand of the Lord. In this case the prayer is accompanied by fasting. As a Spiritual Discipline, fasting has several settings in Israel's faith. It can accompany mourning practices (Judg 20:26; 1 Sam 31:13), it can signify repentance (1 Sam 7:6) or preparation for further

David fasted, and went in and lay all night on the ground. [17]The elders of his house stood beside him, urging him to rise from the ground; but he would not, nor did he eat food with them. [18]On the seventh day the child died. And the servants of David were afraid to tell him that the child was dead; for they said, "While the child was still alive, we spoke to him, and he did not listen to us; how then can we tell him the child is dead? He may do himself some harm." [19]But when David saw that his servants were whispering together, he perceived that the child was dead; and David said to his servants, "Is the child dead?" They said, "He is dead."

20 Then David rose from the ground, washed, anointed himself, and changed his clothes. He went into the house of the LORD, and worshiped; he then went to his own house; and when he asked, they set food before him and he ate. [21]Then his servants said to him, "What is this thing that you have done? You fasted and wept for the child while it was alive; but when the child died, you rose and ate food." [22]He said, "While the child was still alive, I fasted and wept; for I said, 'Who knows? The LORD may be gracious to me, and the child may live.' [23]But now he is dead; why should I fast? Can I bring him back again? I shall go to him, but he will not return to me."

Solomon Is Born

24 Then David consoled his wife Bathsheba, and went to her, and lay with her; and she bore a son, and he named him Solomon. The LORD loved him, [25]and sent a message by the prophet Nathan; so he named him Jedidiah,[a] because of the LORD.

The Ammonites Crushed

26 Now Joab fought against Rabbah of the Ammonites, and took the royal city. [27]Joab sent messengers to David, and said, "I have fought against Rabbah; moreover, I have taken the water city. [28]Now, then, gather the rest of the people together, and encamp against the city, and take it; or I myself will take the city, and it will be called by my name." [29]So David gathered all the people together and went to Rabbah, and fought against it and took it. [30]He took the crown of Milcom[b] from his head; the weight of it was a talent of gold, and in it was a precious stone; and it was placed on David's head. He also brought forth the spoil of the city, a very great amount. [31]He brought out the people who were in it, and set them to work with saws and iron picks and iron axes, or sent them to the brickworks. Thus he did to all the cities of the Ammonites. Then David and all the people returned to Jerusalem.

Amnon and Tamar

13 Some time passed. David's son Absalom had a beautiful sister whose name was Tamar; and David's son Amnon fell in love with her. [2]Amnon was so tormented that he made himself ill because of his sister Tamar, for she was a virgin and it seemed impossible to Amnon to do anything to her. [3]But Amnon had a friend whose name was Jonadab, the son of David's brother Shimeah; and Jonadab was a very crafty man. [4]He said to him, "O son of the king, why are you so haggard morning after morning? Will you not tell me?" Amnon said to him, "I love

a That is *Beloved of the LORD*   *b* Gk See 1 Kings 11.5, 33: Heb *their kings*

---

service (Matt 4:2), or, as it is used in this case, it can accompany intercessory prayer (Ezra 8:23; 2 Chron 20:3). The theological significance in each case seems to be that the denial of bodily needs for specified periods of time focuses the soul for greater attentiveness to God. In this instance, David's actions will not be effective, as the child dies. But note the faithfulness in David's response, "He went into the house of the LORD, and worshiped" (v 20).

Responding
12:16, 21–23 FASTING. David's actions were exactly the opposite of what people expected of him: he fasted from food while the child was sick and ate after he died. According to the Bible, why does fasting increase the power of our prayers (see Matt 4:1–11; NRSV note to 17:21)? *See also* Spiritual Disciplines Index.

Tamar, my brother Absalom's sister." ⁵Jona-dab said to him, "Lie down on your bed, and pretend to be ill; and when your father comes to see you, say to him, 'Let my sister Tamar come and give me something to eat, and pre-pare the food in my sight, so that I may see it and eat it from her hand.' " ⁶So Amnon lay down, and pretended to be ill; and when the king came to see him, Amnon said to the king, "Please let my sister Tamar come and make a couple of cakes in my sight, so that I may eat from her hand."

7 Then David sent home to Tamar, say-ing, "Go to your brother Amnon's house, and prepare food for him." ⁸So Tamar went to her brother Amnon's house, where he was lying down. She took dough, kneaded it, made cakes in his sight, and baked the cakes. ⁹Then she took the pan and set them ª out before him, but he refused to eat. Amnon said, "Send out everyone from me." So everyone went out from him. ¹⁰Then Amnon said to Tamar, "Bring the food into the chamber, so that I may eat from your hand." So Tamar took the cakes she had made, and brought them into the chamber to Amnon her brother. ¹¹But when she brought them near him to eat, he took hold of her, and said to her, "Come, lie with me, my sister." ¹²She answered him, "No, my brother, do not force me; for such a thing is not done in Israel; do not do any-thing so vile! ¹³As for me, where could I car-

ry my shame? And as for you, you would be as one of the scoundrels in Israel. Now there-fore, I beg you, speak to the king; for he will not withhold me from you." ¹⁴But he would not listen to her; and being stronger than she, he forced her and lay with her.

15 Then Amnon was seized with a very great loathing for her; indeed, his loathing was even greater than the lust he had felt for her. Amnon said to her, "Get out!" ¹⁶But she said to him, "No, my brother; ᵇ for this wrong in sending me away is greater than the oth-er that you did to me." But he would not lis-ten to her. ¹⁷He called the young man who served him and said, "Put this woman out of my presence, and bolt the door after her." ¹⁸(Now she was wearing a long robe with sleeves; for this is how the virgin daughters of the king were clothed in earlier times. ᶜ) So his servant put her out, and bolted the door af-ter her. ¹⁹But Tamar put ashes on her head, and tore the long robe that she was wearing; she put her hand on her head, and went away, crying aloud as she went.

20 Her brother Absalom said to her, "Has Amnon your brother been with you? Be qui-et for now, my sister; he is your brother; do not take this to heart." So Tamar remained, a desolate woman, in her brother Absalom's

a Heb and poured   b Cn Compare Gk Vg: Meaning of Heb uncertain   c Cn: Heb were clothed in robes

---

13:19 *put ashes on her head, and tore the long robe, . . . and went away, crying aloud.* Putting ashes on the head, tearing the clothes, and crying aloud were the traditional mourning rituals of the ancient Near East (Gen 37:34; Josh 7:6; Esther 4:1; Jer 25:34; Dan 9:3). As a woman in antiquity, Tamar has good reason to weep. She has been incestuously raped by her brother, who is now lost to her. She has lost her virginity and hence her worth on the "market," thus diminishing her value to her father and his administration, which could have used her as a means to cement relations with rival kingdoms. This being the script handed to her by her time and place, she lacks the options of modern Western women and hence mourns as if she were dead, which in social terms she truly is.

13:20 *do not take this to heart.* To his credit,

Tamar's other sibling, Absalom, refuses to accept the social stain that Tamar now bears and sees her, rather, as the sister he always loved. Significant in this regard is the contrast with David's silence regarding his son's foul deed and the pain wrought in the life of his daughter. Would not a Spirit-led king and father minister to his daughter's anguish and take steps to bring her to wholeness? Would he not also take steps to discipline the offender, even if he is son and heir? Instead, as in chapter 11 when someone else does what David should have done himself, Absalom comforts his sister; such aid should have come from her father. Had David intervened in this instance and banished Amnon, he might have avoided Amnon's later murder by Absalom (v 29) and Absalom's later rebellion against him (chaps 15–16).

house. 21When King David heard of all these things, he became very angry, but he would not punish his son Amnon, because he loved him, for he was his firstborn.*a* 22But Absalom spoke to Amnon neither good nor bad; for Absalom hated Amnon, because he had raped his sister Tamar.

Absalom Avenges the Violation of His Sister

23 After two full years Absalom had sheepshearers at Baal-hazor, which is near Ephraim, and Absalom invited all the king's sons. 24Absalom came to the king, and said, "Your servant has sheepshearers; will the king and his servants please go with your servant?" 25But the king said to Absalom, "No, my son, let us not all go, or else we will be burdensome to you." He pressed him, but he would not go but gave him his blessing. 26Then Absalom said, "If not, please let my brother Amnon go with us." The king said to him, "Why should he go with you?" 27But Absalom pressed him until he let Amnon and all the king's sons go with him. Absalom made a feast like a king's feast.*b* 28Then Absalom commanded his servants, "Watch when Amnon's heart is merry with wine, and when I say to you, 'Strike Amnon,' then kill him. Do not be afraid; have I not myself commanded you? Be courageous and valiant." 29So the servants of Absalom did to Amnon as Absalom had commanded. Then all the king's sons rose, and each mounted his mule and fled.

30 While they were on the way, the report came to David that Absalom had killed all the king's sons, and not one of them was left. 31The king rose, tore his garments, and lay on the ground; and all his servants who were standing by tore their garments. 32But Jonadab, the son of David's brother Shimeah, said, "Let not my lord suppose that they have killed all the young men the king's sons; Amnon alone is dead. This has been determined by Absalom from the day Amnon*c* raped his sister Tamar. 33Now therefore, do not let my lord the king take it to heart, as if all the king's sons were dead; for Amnon alone is dead."

34 But Absalom fled. When the young man who kept watch looked up, he saw many people coming from the Horonaim road*d* by the side of the mountain. 35Jonadab said to the king, "See, the king's sons have come; as your servant said, so it has come about." 36As soon as he had finished speaking, the king's sons arrived, and raised their voices and wept; and the king and all his servants also wept very bitterly.

37 But Absalom fled, and went to Talmai son of Ammihud, king of Geshur. David mourned for his son day after day. 38Absalom, having fled to Geshur, stayed there three years. 39And the heart of*e* the king went out, yearning for Absalom; for he was now consoled over the death of Amnon.

Absalom Returns to Jerusalem

14 Now Joab son of Zeruiah perceived that the king's mind was on Absalom. 2Joab sent to Tekoa and brought from there a wise woman. He said to her, "Pretend to be a mourner; put on mourning garments, do not anoint yourself with oil, but behave like a woman who has been mourning many days for the dead. 3Go to the king and speak to him as follows." And Joab put the words into her mouth.

4 When the woman of Tekoa came to the king, she fell on her face to the ground and did obeisance, and said, "Help, O king!" 5The

a Q Ms Gk: MT lacks *but he would not punish . . . firstborn*   *b* Gk Compare Q Ms: MT lacks *Absalom made a feast like a king's feast*   *c* Heb *he*   *d* Cn Compare Gk: Heb *the road behind him*   *e* Q Ms Gk: MT *And David*

14:4–20 *When the woman of Tekoa came to the king.* The exchange between the woman and David, which parallels the discussion between Nathan and David in chapter 11, is one of the most subtle in all of Scripture, as the woman carefully maneuvers David into seeing clearly the consequences and meaning of his actions by offering him a fable of her own life constructed by Joab. This is a completely different tack than the one that might have been taken by someone more rigid and less emotionally secure and hence wedded to one particular confrontational style. Joab could have simply marched up to the king and demanded that he "snap out of it" and

king asked her, "What is your trouble?" She answered, "Alas, I am a widow; my husband is dead. 6Your servant had two sons, and they fought with one another in the field; there was no one to part them, and one struck the other and killed him. 7Now the whole family has risen against your servant. They say, 'Give up the man who struck his brother, so that we may kill him for the life of his brother whom he murdered, even if we destroy the heir as well.' Thus they would quench my one remaining ember, and leave to my husband neither name nor remnant on the face of the earth."

8 Then the king said to the woman, "Go to your house, and I will give orders concerning you." 9The woman of Tekoa said to the king, "On me be the guilt, my lord the king, and on my father's house; let the king and his throne be guiltless." 10The king said, "If anyone says anything to you, bring him to me, and he shall never touch you again." 11Then she said, "Please, may the king keep the LORD your God in mind, so that the avenger of blood may kill no more, and my son not be destroyed." He said, "As the LORD lives, not one hair of your son shall fall to the ground."

12 Then the woman said, "Please let your servant speak a word to my lord the king." He said, "Speak." 13The woman said, "Why then have you planned such a thing against the people of God? For in giving this decision the king convicts himself, inasmuch as the king does not bring his banished one home again. 14We must all die; we are like water spilled on the ground, which cannot be gathered up. But God will not take away a life; he will devise plans so as not to keep an outcast banished forever from his presence. *a* 15Now I have come to say this to my lord the king because the people have made me afraid; your servant thought, 'I will speak to the king; it may be that the king will perform the request of his servant. 16For the king will hear, and deliver his servant from the hand of the man who would cut both me and my son off from the heritage of God.' 17Your servant thought,

'The word of my lord the king will set me at rest'; for my lord the king is like the angel of God, discerning good and evil. The LORD your God be with you!"

18 Then the king answered the woman, "Do not withhold from me anything I ask you." The woman said, "Let my lord the king speak." 19The king said, "Is the hand of Joab with you in all this?" The woman answered and said, "As surely as you live, my lord the king, one cannot turn right or left from anything that my lord the king has said. For it was your servant Joab who commanded me; it was he who put all these words into the mouth of your servant. 20In order to change the course of affairs your servant Joab did this. But my lord has wisdom like the wisdom of the angel of God to know all things that are on the earth."

21 Then the king said to Joab, "Very well, I grant this; go, bring back the young man Absalom." 22Joab prostrated himself with his face to the ground and did obeisance, and blessed the king; and Joab said, "Today your servant knows that I have found favor in your sight, my lord the king, in that the king has granted the request of his servant." 23So Joab set off, went to Geshur, and brought Absalom to Jerusalem. 24The king said, "Let him go to his own house; he is not to come into my presence." So Absalom went to his own house, and did not come into the king's presence.

David Forgives Absalom

25 Now in all Israel there was no one to be praised so much for his beauty as Absalom; from the sole of his foot to the crown of his head there was no blemish in him. 26When he cut the hair of his head (for at the end of every year he used to cut it; when it was heavy on him, he cut it), he weighed the hair of his head, two hundred shekels by the king's weight. 27There were born to Absalom three

---

a Meaning of Heb uncertain

---

do what needed to be done. But since Joab allowed David to come to his conclusion by means of clever suggestions, David, rather than simply complying after having been bullied, fully owns the decision as his, making its possibility for success all the greater.

sons, and one daughter whose name was Tamar; she was a beautiful woman.

28 So Absalom lived two full years in Jerusalem, without coming into the king's presence. 29Then Absalom sent for Joab to send him to the king; but Joab would not come to him. He sent a second time, but Joab would not come. 30Then he said to his servants, "Look, Joab's field is next to mine, and he has barley there; go and set it on fire." So Absalom's servants set the field on fire. 31Then Joab rose and went to Absalom at his house, and said to him, "Why have your servants set my field on fire?" 32Absalom answered Joab, "Look, I sent word to you: Come here, that I may send you to the king with the question, 'Why have I come from Geshur? It would be better for me to be there still.' Now let me go into the king's presence; if there is guilt in me, let him kill me!" 33Then Joab went to the king and told him; and he summoned Absalom. So he came to the king and prostrated himself with his face to the ground before the king; and the king kissed Absalom.

Absalom Usurps the Throne

15 After this Absalom got himself a chariot and horses, and fifty men to run ahead of him. 2Absalom used to rise early and stand beside the road into the gate; and when anyone brought a suit before the king for judgment, Absalom would call out and say, "From what city are you?" When the person said, "Your servant is of such and such a tribe in Israel," 3Absalom would say, "See, your claims are good and right; but there is no one deputed by the king to hear you." 4Absalom said moreover, "If only I were judge in the land! Then all who had a suit or cause might come to me, and I would give them justice." 5Whenever people came near to do obeisance to him, he would put out his hand and take hold of them, and kiss them. 6Thus Absalom did to every Israelite who came to the king for judgment; so Absalom stole the hearts of the people of Israel.

7 At the end of four*a* years Absalom said to the king, "Please let me go to Hebron and pay the vow that I have made to the LORD. 8For your servant made a vow while I lived at Geshur in Aram: If the LORD will indeed bring me back to Jerusalem, then I will worship the LORD in Hebron." *b* 9The king said to him, "Go in peace." So he got up, and went to Hebron. 10But Absalom sent secret messengers throughout all the tribes of Israel, saying, "As soon as you hear the sound of the trumpet, then shout: Absalom has become king at Hebron!" 11Two hundred men from Jerusalem went with Absalom; they were invited guests, and they went in their innocence, knowing nothing of the matter. 12While Absalom was offering the sacrifices, he sent for*c* Ahithophel the Gilonite, David's counselor, from his city Giloh. The conspiracy grew in strength, and the people with Absalom kept increasing.

David Flees from Jerusalem

13 A messenger came to David, saying, "The hearts of the Israelites have gone after Absalom." 14Then David said to all his officials who were with him at Jerusalem, "Get up! Let us flee, or there will be no escape for us from Absalom. Hurry, or he will soon overtake us, and bring disaster down upon us, and attack the city with the edge of the sword." 15The king's officials said to the king, "Your servants are ready to do whatever our lord the king decides." 16So the king left, followed by all his household, except ten concubines whom he left behind to look after the house. 17The king left, followed by all the people; and they stopped at the last house. 18All his officials passed by him; and all the Cherethites, and all the Pelethites, and all the six hundred Gittites who had followed him from Gath, passed on before the king.

19 Then the king said to Ittai the Gittite, "Why are you also coming with us? Go back, and stay with the king; for you are a foreigner, and also an exile from your home. 20You came only yesterday, and shall I today make you wander about with us, while I go wherever I can? Go back, and take your kinsfolk with you; and may the LORD show*d* steadfast love and faithfulness to you." 21But Ittai answered the king, "As the LORD lives, and as my

a Gk Syr: Heb *forty*   *b* Gk Mss: Heb lacks *in Hebron*   *c* Or *he sent*   *d* Gk Compare 2.6: Heb lacks *may the LORD show* lord the king lives, wherever my lord the king may be, whether for death or for life, there also your servant will be." [22]David said to Ittai, "Go then, march on." So Ittai the Gittite marched on, with all his men and all the little ones who were with him. [23]The whole country wept aloud as all the people passed by; the king crossed the Wadi Kidron, and all the people moved on toward the wilderness.

24 Abiathar came up, and Zadok also, with all the Levites, carrying the ark of the covenant of God. They set down the ark of God, until the people had all passed out of the city. [25]Then the king said to Zadok, "Carry the ark of God back into the city. If I find favor in the eyes of the LORD, he will bring me back and let me see both it and the place where it stays. [26]But if he says, 'I take no pleasure in you,' here I am, let him do to me what seems good to him.'" [27]The king also said to the priest Zadok, "Look,[a] go back to the city in peace, you and Abiathar,[b] with your two sons, Ahimaaz your son, and Jonathan son of Abiathar. [28]See, I will wait at the fords of the wilderness until word comes from you to inform me." [29]So Zadok and Abiathar carried the ark of God back to Jerusalem, and they remained there.

30 But David went up the ascent of the Mount of Olives, weeping as he went, with his head covered and walking barefoot; and all the people who were with him covered their heads and went up, weeping as they went. [31]David was told that Ahithophel was among the conspirators with Absalom. And

David said, "O LORD, I pray you, turn the counsel of Ahithophel into foolishness."

Hushai Becomes David's Spy

32 When David came to the summit, where God was worshiped, Hushai the Archite came to meet him with his coat torn and earth on his head. [33]David said to him, "If you go on with me, you will be a burden to me. [34]But if you return to the city and say to Absalom, 'I will be your servant, O king; as I have been your father's servant in time past, so now I will be your servant,' then you will defeat for me the counsel of Ahithophel. [35]The priests Zadok and Abiathar will be with you there. So whatever you hear from the king's house, tell it to the priests Zadok and Abiathar. [36]Their two sons are with them there, Zadok's son Ahimaaz and Abiathar's son Jonathan; and by them you shall report to me everything you hear." [37]So Hushai, David's friend, came into the city, just as Absalom was entering Jerusalem.

David's Adversaries

16 When David had passed a little beyond the summit, Ziba the servant of Mephibosheth[c] met him, with a couple of donkeys saddled, carrying two hundred loaves of bread, one hundred bunches of raisins, one hundred of summer fruits, and one skin of wine. [2]The king said to Ziba,

a Gk: Heb *Are you a seer* or *Do you see?*
b Cn: Heb lacks *and Abiathar*   c Or *Merib-baal*: See 4.4 note

---

15:21 *there also your servant will be.* Chapters 15 and 16 are dominated by questions of loyalty as each character has to take sides in the developing civil war. Ittai, who is from Gath (the same city as Goliath the giant) and thus a Philistine, shows surprising resilience in holding fast his allegiance to David after so many others have abandoned him. He is a positive example of devotion to friendship in contrast to David's "fair-weather friends" who have abandoned him in favor of Absalom. It takes great character to stand against the rising consensus in favor of Absalom, and because Ittai does not take a poll to determine his values, he is able both to stand

with David himself and to provide leadership to his men who look to him for guidance to do the same thing.

Responding
16:1 SERVICE. In spite of being in danger, many of David's subjects remain loyal to him as he is fleeing from Absalom. This is a hard concept for us to wrap our minds around as we observe employees and confidants of leaders write "tell-all" books that make the bestseller lists. On one sheet write out what you feel a servant's loyalty to his or her leader should look like. *See also* Spiritual Disciplines Index.

"Why have you brought these?" Ziba answered, "The donkeys are for the king's household to ride, the bread and summer fruit for the young men to eat, and the wine is for those to drink who faint in the wilderness." 3The king said, "And where is your master's son?" Ziba said to the king, "He remains in Jerusalem; for he said, 'Today the house of Israel will give me back my grandfather's kingdom.' " 4Then the king said to Ziba, "All that belonged to Mephibosheth*a* is now yours." Ziba said, "I do obeisance; let me find favor in your sight, my lord the king."

Shimei Curses David

5 When King David came to Bahurim, a man of the family of the house of Saul came out whose name was Shimei son of Gera; he came out cursing. 6He threw stones at David and at all the servants of King David; now all the people and all the warriors were on his right and on his left. 7Shimei shouted while he cursed, "Out! Out! Murderer! Scoundrel! 8The LORD has avenged on all of you the blood of the house of Saul, in whose place you have reigned; and the LORD has given the kingdom into the hand of your son Absalom. See, disaster has overtaken you; for you are a man of blood."

9 Then Abishai son of Zeruiah said to the king, "Why should this dead dog curse my lord the king? Let me go over and take off his head." 10But the king said, "What have I to do with you, you sons of Zeruiah? If he is cursing because the LORD has said to him, 'Curse David,' who then shall say, 'Why have you done so?' " 11David said to Abishai and to all his servants, "My own son seeks my life; how much more now may this Benjaminite! Let him alone, and let him curse; for the LORD has bidden him. 12It may be that the LORD will look on my distress,*b* and the LORD will repay me with good for this cursing of me today."

13So David and his men went on the road, while Shimei went along on the hillside opposite him and cursed as he went, throwing stones and flinging dust at him. 14The king and all the people who were with him arrived weary at the Jordan;*c* and there he refreshed himself.

The Counsel of Ahithophel

15 Now Absalom and all the Israelites*d* came to Jerusalem; Ahithophel was with him. 16When Hushai the Archite, David's friend, came to Absalom, Hushai said to Absalom, "Long live the king! Long live the king!" 17Absalom said to Hushai, "Is this your loyalty to your friend? Why did you not go with your friend?" 18Hushai said to Absalom, "No; but the one whom the LORD and this people and all the Israelites have chosen, his I will be, and with him I will remain. 19Moreover, whom should I serve? Should it not be his son? Just as I have served your father, so I will serve you."

20 Then Absalom said to Ahithophel, "Give us your counsel; what shall we do?" 21Ahithophel said to Absalom, "Go in to your father's concubines, the ones he has left to look after the house; and all Israel will hear that you have made yourself odious to your father, and the hands of all who are with you will be strengthened." 22So they pitched a tent for Absalom upon the roof; and Absalom went in to his father's concubines in the sight of all Israel. 23Now in those days the counsel that Ahithophel gave was as if one consulted the oracle*e* of God; so all the counsel of Ahithophel was esteemed, both by David and by Absalom.

a Or *Merib-baal:* See 4.4 note   *b* Gk Vg: Heb *iniquity*   *c* Gk: Heb lacks *at the Jordan*
d Gk: Heb *all the people, the men of Israel*
e Heb *word*

16:5–12 *Shimei . . . came out cursing.* This is an extraordinary passage in which all three of the participants claim to speak for God. Shimei, a relative of the dead King Saul, invokes divine judgment for the death of the House of Saul, for which he blames David (the information that David was in fact responsible for this will not be disclosed to readers until 21:1–14). Abishai invokes the Torah's injunctions against cursing the leader, which Shimei has violated. But David makes the most surprising statement of all when he essentially sides with Shimei in speculating that perhaps this judgment has indeed been at the hand of God.

17

Moreover Ahithophel said to Absalom, "Let me choose twelve thousand men, and I will set out and pursue David tonight. [2]I will come upon him while he is weary and discouraged, and throw him into a panic; and all the people who are with him will flee. I will strike down only the king, [3]and I will bring all the people back to you as a bride comes home to her husband. You seek the life of only one man, [a] and all the people will be at peace." [4]The advice pleased Absalom and all the elders of Israel.

The Counsel of Hushai

5 Then Absalom said, "Call Hushai the Archite also, and let us hear too what he has to say." [6]When Hushai came to Absalom, Absalom said to him, "This is what Ahithophel has said; shall we do as he advises? If not, you tell us." [7]Then Hushai said to Absalom, "This time the counsel that Ahithophel has given is not good." [8]Hushai continued, "You know that your father and his men are warriors, and that they are enraged, like a bear robbed of her cubs in the field. Besides, your father is expert in war; he will not spend the night with the troops. [9]Even now he has hidden himself in one of the pits, or in some other place. And when some of our troops [b] fall at the first attack, whoever hears it will say, 'There has been a slaughter among the troops who follow Absalom.' [10]Then even the valiant warrior, whose heart is like the heart of a lion, will utterly melt with fear; for all Israel knows that your father is a warrior, and that those who are with him are valiant warriors. [11]But my counsel is that all Israel be gathered to you, from Dan to Beer-sheba, like the sand by the sea for multitude, and that you go to battle in person. [12]So we shall come upon him in whatever place he may be found, and we shall light on him as the dew falls on the ground; and he will not survive, nor will any of those with him. [13]If he withdraws into a city, then all Israel will bring ropes to that city, and we shall drag it into the valley, until not even a pebble is to be found there." [14]Absalom and all the men of Israel said, "The counsel of Hushai the Archite is better than the counsel of Ahithophel." For the LORD had ordained to defeat the good

counsel of Ahithophel, so that the LORD might bring ruin on Absalom.

Hushai Warns David to Escape

15 Then Hushai said to the priests Zadok and Abiathar, "Thus and so did Ahithophel counsel Absalom and the elders of Israel; and thus and so I have counseled. [16]Therefore send quickly and tell David, 'Do not lodge tonight at the fords of the wilderness, but by all means cross over; otherwise the king and all the people who are with him will be swallowed up.' " [17]Jonathan and Ahimaaz were waiting at En-rogel; a servant-girl used to go and tell them, and they would go and tell King David; for they could not risk being seen entering the city. [18]But a boy saw them, and told Absalom; so both of them went away quickly, and came to the house of a man at Bahurim, who had a well in his courtyard; and they went down into it. [19]The man's wife took a covering, stretched it over the well's mouth, and spread out grain on it; and nothing was known of it. [20]When Absalom's servants came to the woman at the house, they said, "Where are Ahimaaz and Jonathan?" The woman said to them, "They have crossed over the brook [c] of water." And when they had searched and could not find them, they returned to Jerusalem.

21 After they had gone, the men came up out of the well, and went and told King David. They said to David, "Go and cross the water quickly; for thus and so has Ahithophel counseled against you." [22]So David and all the people who were with him set out and crossed the Jordan; by daybreak not one was left who had not crossed the Jordan.

23 When Ahithophel saw that his counsel was not followed, he saddled his donkey and went off home to his own city. He set his house in order, and hanged himself; he died and was buried in the tomb of his father.

24 Then David came to Mahanaim, while Absalom crossed the Jordan with all the men of Israel. [25]Now Absalom had set Amasa over the army in the place of Joab. Amasa was the son of a man named Ithra the Ishmaelite, [d]

---

a Gk: Heb like the return of the whole (is) the man whom you seek   b Gk Mss: Heb some of them
c Meaning of Heb uncertain   d 1 Chr 2.17: Heb Israelite

who had married Abigal daughter of Nahash, sister of Zeruiah, Joab's mother. 26The Israelites and Absalom encamped in the land of Gilead.

27 When David came to Mahanaim, Shobi son of Nahash from Rabbah of the Ammonites, and Machir son of Ammiel from Lo-debar, and Barzillai the Gileadite from Rogelim, 28brought beds, basins, and earthen vessels, wheat, barley, meal, parched grain, beans and lentils, *a* 29honey and curds, sheep, and cheese from the herd, for David and the people with him to eat; for they said, "The troops are hungry and weary and thirsty in the wilderness."

The Defeat and Death of Absalom

18 Then David mustered the men who were with him, and set over them commanders of thousands and commanders of hundreds. 2And David divided the army into three groups: *b* one third under the command of Joab, one third under the command of Abishai son of Zeruiah, Joab's brother, and one third under the command of Ittai the Gittite. The king said to the men, "I myself will also go out with you." 3But the men said, "You shall not go out. For if we flee, they will not care about us. If half of us die, they will not care about us. But you are worth ten thousand of us; *c* therefore it is better that you send us help from the city." 4The king said to them, "Whatever seems best to you I will do." So the king stood at the side of the gate, while all the army marched out by hundreds and by thousands. 5The king ordered Joab and Abishai and Ittai, saying, "Deal gently for my sake with the young man Absalom." And all the people heard when the king gave orders to all the commanders concerning Absalom.

6 So the army went out into the field against Israel; and the battle was fought in the forest of Ephraim. 7The men of Israel were defeated there by the servants of David, and the slaughter there was great on that day, twenty thousand men. 8The battle spread over the face of all the country; and the forest claimed more victims that day than the sword.

9 Absalom happened to meet the servants of David. Absalom was riding on his mule, and the mule went under the thick branches of a great oak. His head caught fast in the oak, and he was left hanging *d* between heaven and earth, while the mule that was under him went on. 10A man saw it, and told Joab, "I saw Absalom hanging in an oak." 11Joab said to the man who told him, "What, you saw him! Why then did you not strike him there to the ground? I would have been glad to give you ten pieces of silver and a belt." 12But the man said to Joab, "Even if I felt in my hand the weight of a thousand pieces of silver, I would not raise my hand against the king's son; for in our hearing the king commanded you and Abishai and Ittai, saying: For my sake protect the young man Absalom! 13On the other hand, if I had dealt treacherously against his life *e* (and there is nothing hidden from the king), then you yourself would have stood aloof." 14Joab said, "I will not waste time like this with you." He took three spears in his hand, and thrust them into the heart of Absalom, while he was still alive in the oak. 15And ten young men, Joab's armor-bearers, surrounded Absalom and struck him, and killed him.

16 Then Joab sounded the trumpet, and the troops came back from pursuing Israel, for Joab restrained the troops. 17They took Absalom, threw him into a great pit in the forest, and raised over him a very great heap of stones. Meanwhile all the Israelites fled to their homes. 18Now Absalom in his lifetime had taken and set up for himself a pillar that is in the King's Valley, for he said, "I have no son to keep my name in remembrance"; he called the pillar by his own name. It is called Absalom's Monument to this day.

David Hears of Absalom's Death

19 Then Ahimaaz son of Zadok said, "Let me run, and carry tidings to the king that the LORD has delivered him from the power of his enemies." 20Joab said to him, "You are not to carry tidings today; you may carry tidings another day, but today you shall not do

a Heb *and lentils and parched grain*   *b* Gk: Heb *sent forth the army*   *c* Gk Vg Symmachus: Heb *for now there are ten thousand such as we*   *d* Gk Syr Tg: Heb *was put*   *e* Another reading is *at the risk of my life*

so, because the king's son is dead." 21Then Joab said to a Cushite, "Go, tell the king what you have seen." The Cushite bowed before Joab, and ran. 22Then Ahimaaz son of Zadok said again to Joab, "Come what may, let me also run after the Cushite." And Joab said, "Why will you run, my son, seeing that you have no reward*a* for the tidings?" 23"Come what may," he said, "I will run." So he said to him, "Run." Then Ahimaaz ran by the way of the Plain, and outran the Cushite.

24 Now David was sitting between the two gates. The sentinel went up to the roof of the gate by the wall, and when he looked up, he saw a man running alone. 25The sentinel shouted and told the king. The king said, "If he is alone, there are tidings in his mouth." He kept coming, and drew near. 26Then the sentinel saw another man running; and the sentinel called to the gatekeeper and said, "See, another man running alone!" The king said, "He also is bringing tidings." 27The sentinel said, "I think the running of the first one is like the running of Ahimaaz son of Zadok." The king said, "He is a good man, and comes with good tidings."

28 Then Ahimaaz cried out to the king, "All is well!" He prostrated himself before the king with his face to the ground, and said, "Blessed be the LORD your God, who has delivered up the men who raised their hand against my lord the king." 29The king said, "Is it well with the young man Absalom?" Ahimaaz answered, "When Joab sent your servant,*b* I saw a great tumult, but I do not know what it was." 30The king said, "Turn aside, and stand here." So he turned aside, and stood still.

31 Then the Cushite came; and the Cushite said, "Good tidings for my lord the king! For the LORD has vindicated you this day, delivering you from the power of all who rose up against you." 32The king said to the Cushite, "Is it well with the young man Absalom?" The Cushite answered, "May the enemies of my lord the king, and all who rise up to do you harm, be like that young man."

David Mourns for Absalom

33*c* The king was deeply moved, and went up to the chamber over the gate, and wept;

and as he went, he said, "O my son Absalom, my son, my son Absalom! Would I had died instead of you, O Absalom, my son, my son!"

19 It was told Joab, "The king is weeping and mourning for Absalom." 2So the victory that day was turned into mourning for all the troops; for the troops heard that day, "The king is grieving for his son." 3The troops stole into the city that day as soldiers steal in who are ashamed when they flee in battle. 4The king covered his face, and the king cried with a loud voice, "O my son Absalom, O Absalom, my son, my son!" 5Then Joab came into the house to the king, and said, "Today you have covered with shame the faces of all your officers who have saved your life today, and the lives of your sons and your daughters, and the lives of your wives and your concubines, 6for love of those who hate you and for hatred of those who love you. You have made it clear today that commanders and officers are nothing to you; for I perceive that if Absalom were alive and all of us were dead today, then you would be pleased. 7So go out at once and speak kindly to your servants; for I swear by the LORD, if you do not go, not a man will stay with you this night; and this will be worse for you than any disaster that has come upon you from your youth until now." 8Then the king got up and took his seat in the gate. The troops were all told, "See, the king is sitting in the gate"; and all the troops came before the king.

David Recalled to Jerusalem

Meanwhile, all the Israelites had fled to their homes. 9All the people were disputing throughout all the tribes of Israel, saying, "The king delivered us from the hand of our enemies, and saved us from the hand of the Philistines; and now he has fled out of the land because of Absalom. 10But Absalom, whom we anointed over us, is dead in battle. Now therefore why do you say nothing about bringing the king back?"

11 King David sent this message to the priests Zadok and Abiathar, "Say to the elders of Judah, 'Why should you be the last to bring

a Meaning of Heb uncertain   *b* Heb *the king's servant, your servant*   *c* Ch 19.1 in Heb the king back to his house? The talk of all Israel has come to the king.ᵃ ¹²You are my kin, you are my bone and my flesh; why then should you be the last to bring back the king?' ¹³And say to Amasa, 'Are you not my bone and my flesh? So may God do to me, and more, if you are not the commander of my army from now on, in place of Joab.' " ¹⁴Amasaᵇ swayed the hearts of all the people of Judah as one, and they sent word to the king, "Return, both you and all your servants." ¹⁵So the king came back to the Jordan; and Judah came to Gilgal to meet the king and to bring him over the Jordan.

16 Shimei son of Gera, the Benjaminite, from Bahurim, hurried to come down with the people of Judah to meet King David; ¹⁷with him were a thousand people from Benjamin. And Ziba, the servant of the house of Saul, with his fifteen sons and his twenty servants, rushed down to the Jordan ahead of the king, ¹⁸while the crossing was taking place,ᶜ to bring over the king's household, and to do his pleasure.

David's Mercy to Shimei

Shimei son of Gera fell down before the king, as he was about to cross the Jordan, ¹⁹and said to the king, "May my lord not hold me guilty or remember how your servant did wrong on the day my lord the king left Jerusalem; may the king not bear it in mind. ²⁰For your servant knows that I have sinned; therefore, see, I have come this day, the first of all the house of Joseph to come down to meet my lord the king." ²¹Abishai son of Zeruiah answered, "Shall not Shimei be put to death for this, because he cursed the LORD's anointed?" ²²But David said, "What have I to do with you, you sons of Zeruiah, that you should today become an adversary to me? Shall anyone be put to death in Israel this day? For do I not know that I am this day king over Israel?" ²³The king said to Shimei, "You shall not die." And the king gave him his oath.

David and Mephibosheth Meet

24 Mephiboshethᵈ grandson of Saul came down to meet the king; he had not taken care of his feet, or trimmed his beard, or washed his clothes, from the day the king left until the day he came back in safety. ²⁵When he came from Jerusalem to meet the king, the king said to him, "Why did you not go with me, Mephibosheth?"ᵈ ²⁶He answered, "My lord, O king, my servant deceived me; for your servant said to him, 'Saddle a donkey for me,ᵉ so that I may ride on it and go with the king.' For your servant is lame. ²⁷He has slandered your servant to my lord the king. But my lord the king is like the angel of God; do therefore what seems good to you. ²⁸For all my father's house were doomed to death before my lord the king; but you set your servant among those who eat at your table. What further right have I, then, to appeal to the king?" ²⁹The king said to him, "Why speak any more of your affairs? I have decided: you and Ziba shall divide the land." ³⁰Mephiboshethᵈ said to the king, "Let him take it all, since my lord the king has arrived home safely."

David's Kindness to Barzillai

31 Now Barzillai the Gileadite had come down from Rogelim; he went on with the king to the Jordan, to escort him over the

ᵃ Gk: Heb to the king, to his house   ᵇ Heb He
ᶜ Cn: Heb the ford crossed   ᵈ Or Merib-baal: See
4.4 note   ᵉ Gk Syr Vg: Heb said, 'I will saddle a
donkey for myself

19:16–23 *May my lord not hold me guilty.*
David may have been extending his covenant with Jonathan to protect the latter man's family to also include Shimei, a member of the House of Saul of undetermined origin. But he need not have done this, for the covenant would not have allowed for treason against the king. By all rights David could have put Shimei to death, after the humiliating spectacle to which he had subjected the king while David was on the run from Absalom (16:5–14). But David's magnanimity in showing mercy rather than vengeance allows for healing instead of a continuation of the bloodletting. Such mercy is characteristic of Yahweh's covenantal relationship with Israel; Yahweh is renowned for offering mercy and extending forgiveness despite the continuing recalcitrance of the people (Exod 34:6–7).

Jordan. ³²Barzillai was a very aged man, eighty years old. He had provided the king with food while he stayed at Mahanaim, for he was a very wealthy man. ³³The king said to Barzillai, "Come over with me, and I will provide for you in Jerusalem at my side." ³⁴But Barzillai said to the king, "How many years have I still to live, that I should go up with the king to Jerusalem? ³⁵Today I am eighty years old; can I discern what is pleasant and what is not? Can your servant taste what he eats or what he drinks? Can I still listen to the voice of singing men and singing women? Why then should your servant be an added burden to my lord the king? ³⁶Your servant will go a little way over the Jordan with the king. Why should the king recompense me with such a reward? ³⁷Please let your servant return, so that I may die in my own town, near the graves of my father and my mother. But here is your servant Chimham; let him go over with my lord the king; and do for him whatever seems good to you." ³⁸The king answered, "Chimham shall go over with me, and I will do for him whatever seems good to you; and all that you desire of me I will do for you." ³⁹Then all the people crossed over the Jordan, and the king crossed over; the king kissed Barzillai and blessed him, and he returned to his own home. ⁴⁰The king went on to Gilgal, and Chimham went on with him; all the people of Judah, and also half the people of Israel, brought the king on his way.

41 Then all the people of Israel came to the king, and said to him, "Why have our kindred the people of Judah stolen you away, and brought the king and his household over the Jordan, and all David's men with him?" ⁴²All the people of Judah answered the people of Israel, "Because the king is near of kin to us. Why then are you angry over this matter? Have we eaten at all at the king's expense? Or has he given us any gift?" ⁴³But the people of Israel answered the people of Judah, "We have ten shares in the king, and in David also we have more than you. Why then did you despise us? Were we not the first to speak of bringing back our king?" But the words of the people of Judah were fiercer than the words of the people of Israel.

The Rebellion of Sheba

20 Now a scoundrel named Sheba son of Bichri, a Benjaminite, happened to be there. He sounded the trumpet and cried out,

"We have no portion in David,
no share in the son of Jesse!
Everyone to your tents, O Israel!"

²So all the people of Israel withdrew from David and followed Sheba son of Bichri; but the people of Judah followed their king steadfastly from the Jordan to Jerusalem.

3 David came to his house at Jerusalem; and the king took the ten concubines whom he had left to look after the house, and put them in a house under guard, and provided for them, but did not go in to them. So they were shut up until the day of their death, living as if in widowhood.

4 Then the king said to Amasa, "Call the men of Judah together to me within three days, and be here yourself." ⁵So Amasa went to summon Judah; but he delayed beyond the set time that had been appointed him. ⁶David said to Abishai, "Now Sheba son of Bichri will do us more harm than Absalom; take your lord's servants and pursue him, or he will find fortified cities for himself, and escape from us." ⁷Joab's men went out after him, along with the Cherethites, the Pelethites, and all the warriors; they went out from Jerusalem to pursue Sheba son of Bichri. ⁸When they were at the large stone that is in Gibeon, Amasa came to meet them. Now Joab was wearing a soldier's garment and over it was a belt with a sword in its sheath fastened at his waist; as he went forward it fell out. ⁹Joab said to Amasa, "Is it well with you, my brother?" And Joab took Amasa by the beard with his right hand to kiss him. ¹⁰But Amasa did not notice the sword in Joab's hand; Joab struck him in the belly so that his entrails poured out on the ground, and he died. He did not strike a second blow.

Then Joab and his brother Abishai pursued Sheba son of Bichri. ¹¹And one of Joab's men took his stand by Amasa, and said, "Whoever favors Joab, and whoever is for David, let him follow Joab." ¹²Amasa lay wallowing in his blood on the highway, and the man saw that all the people were stopping. Since he saw that all who came by him were stopping, he carried Amasa from the highway into a field, and threw a garment over him. [13]Once he was removed from the highway, all the people went on after Joab to pursue Sheba son of Bichri.

[14] Sheba[a] passed through all the tribes of Israel to Abel of Beth-maacah;[b] and all the Bichrites[c] assembled, and followed him inside. [15]Joab's forces[d] came and besieged him in Abel of Beth-maacah; they threw up a siege ramp against the city, and it stood against the rampart. Joab's forces were battering the wall to break it down. [16]Then a wise woman called from the city, "Listen! Listen! Tell Joab, 'Come here, I want to speak to you.'" [17]He came near her; and the woman said, "Are you Joab?" He answered, "I am." Then she said to him, "Listen to the words of your servant." He answered, "I am listening." [18]Then she said, "They used to say in the old days, 'Let them inquire at Abel'; and so they would settle a matter. [19]I am one of those who are peaceable and faithful in Israel; you seek to destroy a city that is a mother in Israel; why will you swallow up the heritage of the LORD?" [20]Joab answered, "Far be it from me, far be it, that I should swallow up or destroy! [21]That is not the case! But a man of the hill country of Ephraim, called Sheba son of

Bichri, has lifted up his hand against King David; give him up alone, and I will withdraw from the city." The woman said to Joab, "His head shall be thrown over the wall to you." [22]Then the woman went to all the people with her wise plan. And they cut off the head of Sheba son of Bichri, and threw it out to Joab. So he blew the trumpet, and they dispersed from the city, and all went to their homes, while Joab returned to Jerusalem to the king.

[23] Now Joab was in command of all the army of Israel;[e] Benaiah son of Jehoiada was in command of the Cherethites and the Pelethites; [24]Adoram was in charge of the forced labor; Jehoshaphat son of Ahilud was the recorder; [25]Sheva was secretary; Zadok and Abiathar were priests; [26]and Ira the Jairite was also David's priest.

David Avenges the Gibeonites

21 Now there was a famine in the days of David for three years, year after year; and David inquired of the LORD. The LORD said, "There is bloodguilt on Saul and on his house, because he put the Gibeonites to death." [2]So the king called the Gibeonites and spoke to them. (Now the Gibeonites were not of the

a Heb *He*   b Compare 20.15: Heb *and Beth-maacah*   c Compare Gk Vg: Heb *Berites*
d Heb *They*   e Cn: Heb *Joab to all the army, Israel*

20:16–22 *Then a wise woman called from the city.* This is the second time in a relatively short section of the narrative that a woman is presented as saving the country from calamity (cf. 14:1–20). Most of the other women who appear in the book are the sexual pawns of the men of the story (e.g., Michal, Tamar, the concubines shared by David and then Absalom); but even these two women do not rate high enough in the patriarchal society in which the narrative is situated to have their names mentioned. Nevertheless, their deeds are too significant for the narrator to ignore. One of the clear marks of the People of God is the recognition that women are meant by God to be full partners in guiding the community's faith and life. Communities sensitive to the direction of the Spirit will learn to receive leadership from whatever quarter it is presented.

21:1–9 *There is bloodguilt on Saul and on his house.* The matter of "bloodguilt," which requires vengeance, is a largely alien concept to modern readers. It is more than just "evening the score"; it is, instead, a mending of the tear in the social fabric of a community that has been devastated by violence. David's actions here, which may well be out of sequence with the larger story, seemingly explain the anger of Shimei in 16:5–13. The portrait of David in this passage is deeply complex. On the surface, David looks like a faithful protector of the commonweal, removing as he does this spiritual impediment to the community. Yet there is also a subtle rebuke here as well, for David ignored his responsibility for avenging bloodguilt in his own family in the matter of Abner's killing of David's nephew Asahel (2:18–23). Moreover, throughout the story he

people of Israel, but of the remnant of the Amorites; although the people of Israel had sworn to spare them, Saul had tried to wipe them out in his zeal for the people of Israel and Judah.) ³David said to the Gibeonites, "What shall I do for you? How shall I make expiation, that you may bless the heritage of the LORD?" ⁴The Gibeonites said to him, "It is not a matter of silver or gold between us and Saul or his house; neither is it for us to put anyone to death in Israel." He said, "What do you say that I should do for you?" ⁵They said to the king, "The man who consumed us and planned to destroy us, so that we should have no place in all the territory of Israel— ⁶let seven of his sons be handed over to us, and we will impale them before the LORD at Gibeon on the mountain of the LORD." ᵃ The king said, "I will hand them over."

7 But the king spared Mephibosheth, ᵇ the son of Saul's son Jonathan, because of the oath of the LORD that was between them, between David and Jonathan son of Saul. ⁸The king took the two sons of Rizpah daughter of Aiah, whom she bore to Saul, Armoni and Mephibosheth; ᵇ and the five sons of Merab ᶜ daughter of Saul, whom she bore to Adriel son of Barzillai the Meholathite; ⁹he gave them into the hands of the Gibeonites, and they impaled them on the mountain before the LORD. The seven of them perished together. They were put to death in the first days of harvest, at the beginning of barley harvest.

10 Then Rizpah the daughter of Aiah took sackcloth, and spread it on a rock for herself, from the beginning of harvest until rain fell on them from the heavens; she did not allow the birds of the air to come on the bodies ᵈ by day, or the wild animals by night. ¹¹When David was told what Rizpah daughter of Aiah, the concubine of Saul, had done, ¹²David went and took the bones of Saul and the bones of his son Jonathan from the people of Jabesh-gilead, who had stolen them from the public square of Beth-shan, where the Philistines had hung them up, on the day the Philistines killed Saul on Gilboa. ¹³He brought up from there the bones of Saul and the bones of his son Jonathan; and they gathered the bones of those who had been impaled. ¹⁴They buried the bones of Saul and of his son Jonathan in the land of Benjamin in Zela, in the tomb of his father Kish; they did all that the king commanded. After that, God heeded supplications for the land.

Exploits of David's Men

15 The Philistines went to war again with Israel, and David went down together with his servants. They fought against the Philistines, and David grew weary. ¹⁶Ishbi-benob, one of the descendants of the giants, whose spear weighed three hundred shekels of bronze, and who was fitted out with new weapons, ᵉ said he would kill David. ¹⁷But Abishai son of Zeruiah came to his aid, and attacked the Philistine and killed him. Then David's men swore to him, "You shall not go out with us to battle any longer, so that you do not quench the lamp of Israel."

18 After this a battle took place with the Philistines, at Gob; then Sibbecai the Hushathite killed Saph, who was one of the descendants of the giants. ¹⁹Then there was another battle with the Philistines at Gob; and Elhanan son of Jaare-oregim, the Bethlehemite, killed Goliath the Gittite, the shaft of whose spear was like a weaver's beam. ²⁰There was again war at Gath, where there was a man of great size, who had six fingers on each hand, and six toes on each foot, twenty-four in number; he too was descended from the giants. ²¹When he taunted Israel, Jonathan son of David's brother Shimei, killed him. ²²These four were descended from the giants in Gath; they fell by the hands of David and his servants.

---

a Cn Compare Gk and 21.9: Heb *at Gibeah of Saul, the chosen of the LORD*   *b* Or *Merib-baal*: See 4.4 note   *c* Two Heb Mss Syr Compare Gk: MT *Michal*   *d* Heb *them*   *e* Heb *was belted anew*

---

has continually protested his innocence concerning the destruction of the Saulides, carefully cultivating an attitude of regretful inevitability regarding the shift in power from the House of Saul to himself, yet all the while having ordered the execution of seven of the chief claimants to the throne on which he now sits (21:6).

David's Song of Thanksgiving

22 David spoke to the LORD the words of this song on the day when the LORD delivered him from the hand of all his enemies, and from the hand of Saul. ²He said:
The LORD is my rock, my fortress, and
    my deliverer,
3   my God, my rock, in whom I take
        refuge,
    my shield and the horn of my
        salvation,
    my stronghold and my refuge,
    my savior; you save me from violence.
4 I call upon the LORD, who is worthy to
        be praised,
    and I am saved from my enemies.

5 For the waves of death encompassed
        me,
    the torrents of perdition assailed me;
6 the cords of Sheol entangled me,
    the snares of death confronted me.

7 In my distress I called upon the LORD;
    to my God I called.
    From his temple he heard my voice,
    and my cry came to his ears.

8 Then the earth reeled and rocked;
    the foundations of the heavens
        trembled
    and quaked, because he was angry.
9 Smoke went up from his nostrils,
    and devouring fire from his mouth;
    glowing coals flamed forth from him.
10 He bowed the heavens, and came down;
    thick darkness was under his feet.
11 He rode on a cherub, and flew;
    he was seen upon the wings of the
        wind.

12 He made darkness around him a
        canopy,
    thick clouds, a gathering of water.
13 Out of the brightness before him
    coals of fire flamed forth.
14 The LORD thundered from heaven;
    the Most High uttered his voice.
15 He sent out arrows, and scattered them
    —lightning, and routed them.
16 Then the channels of the sea were seen,
    the foundations of the world were
        laid bare
    at the rebuke of the LORD,
    at the blast of the breath of his
        nostrils.

17 He reached from on high, he took me,
    he drew me out of mighty waters.
18 He delivered me from my strong enemy,
    from those who hated me;
    for they were too mighty for me.
19 They came upon me in the day of my
        calamity,
    but the LORD was my stay.
20 He brought me out into a broad place;
    he delivered me, because he delighted
        in me.

21 The LORD rewarded me according to my
        righteousness;
    according to the cleanness of my
        hands he recompensed me.
22 For I have kept the ways of the LORD,
    and have not wickedly departed from
        my God.
23 For all his ordinances were before me,
    and from his statutes I did not turn
        aside.
24 I was blameless before him,
    and I kept myself from guilt.

22:2–51 *The LORD is my rock.* This text, which is also recorded in Psalm 18, may be the basis for the tradition that David composed the Psalter. Though scholars are skeptical of the claim historically, this should not detract from the enormous theological power of this composition. A moving song of praise and thanksgiving, it comes at the end of a string of events that, for the poet, must have seemed like the end of the world.

Responding
22:17–51. THE WITH-GOD LIFE.
David's song of thanksgiving is replete with images of David's pleading for God's help, of God's answering, and of David's response of praise. Difficult as it may be to stomach the images of war and crushing enemies, read this song once a day for two weeks. What did you learn about the with-God life? *See also* Spiritual Disciplines Index.

25 Therefore the LORD has recompensed
  me according to my
  righteousness,
    according to my cleanness in his
    sight.

26 With the loyal you show yourself
    loyal;
  with the blameless you show yourself
    blameless;
27 with the pure you show yourself pure,
    and with the crooked you show
    yourself perverse.
28 You deliver a humble people,
    but your eyes are upon the haughty to
    bring them down.
29 Indeed, you are my lamp, O LORD,
    the LORD lightens my darkness.
30 By you I can crush a troop,
    and by my God I can leap over a wall.
31 This God—his way is perfect;
    the promise of the LORD proves true;
  he is a shield for all who take refuge in
    him.

32 For who is God, but the LORD?
    And who is a rock, except our God?
33 The God who has girded me with
    strength*a*
  has opened wide my path. *b*
34 He made my *c* feet like the feet of deer,
    and set me secure on the heights.
35 He trains my hands for war,
    so that my arms can bend a bow of
    bronze.
36 You have given me the shield of your
    salvation,
    and your help *d* has made me great.
37 You have made me stride freely,
    and my feet do not slip;
38 I pursued my enemies and destroyed
    them,
  and did not turn back until they were
    consumed.
39 I consumed them; I struck them down,
    so that they did not rise;
  they fell under my feet.
40 For you girded me with strength for the
    battle;
  you made my assailants sink under
    me.

41 You made my enemies turn their backs
    to me,
  those who hated me, and I destroyed
    them.
42 They looked, but there was no one to
    save them;
  they cried to the LORD, but he did not
    answer them.
43 I beat them fine like the dust of the
    earth,
  I crushed them and stamped them
    down like the mire of the streets.

44 You delivered me from strife with the
    peoples; *e*
  you kept me as the head of the
    nations;
  people whom I had not known served
    me.
45 Foreigners came cringing to me;
    as soon as they heard of me, they
    obeyed me.
46 Foreigners lost heart,
    and came trembling out of their
    strongholds.

47 The LORD lives! Blessed be my rock,
    and exalted be my God, the rock of
    my salvation,
48 the God who gave me vengeance
    and brought down peoples under me,
49 who brought me out from my enemies;
    you exalted me above my adversaries,
    you delivered me from the violent.

50 For this I will extol you, O LORD, among
    the nations,
    and sing praises to your name.
51 He is a tower of salvation for his king,
    and shows steadfast love to his
    anointed,
  to David and his descendants forever.

The Last Words of David

23 Now these are the last words of David:
  The oracle of David, son of Jesse,

a Q Ms Gk Syr Vg Compare Ps 18.32: MT *God is my
strong refuge*   *b* Meaning of Heb uncertain
c Another reading is *his*   *d* Q Ms: MT *your
answering*   *e* Gk: Heb *from strife with my people*

the oracle of the man whom God
   exalted,ᵃ
the anointed of the God of Jacob,
   the favorite of the Strong One of
      Israel:

2 The spirit of the LORD speaks through
      me,
   his word is upon my tongue.
3 The God of Israel has spoken,
   the Rock of Israel has said to me:
One who rules over people justly,
   ruling in the fear of God,
4 is like the light of morning,
   like the sun rising on a cloudless
      morning,
   gleaming from the rain on the grassy
      land.

5 Is not my house like this with God?
   For he has made with me an
      everlasting covenant,
   ordered in all things and secure.
Will he not cause to prosper
   all my help and my desire?
6 But the godless areᵇ all like thorns that
      are thrown away;
   for they cannot be picked up with the
      hand;
7 to touch them one uses an iron bar
   or the shaft of a spear.
   And they are entirely consumed in
      fire on the spot.ᶜ

David's Mighty Men

8 These are the names of the warriors
whom David had: Josheb-basshebeth a
Tahchemonite; he was chief of the Three;ᵈ he
wielded his spearᵉ against eight hundred
whom he killed at one time.
9 Next to him among the three warriors
was Eleazar son of Dodo son of Ahohi. He
was with David when they defied the Philis-

tines who were gathered there for battle. The
Israelites withdrew, 10but he stood his
ground. He struck down the Philistines until
his arm grew weary, though his hand clung
to the sword. The LORD brought about a great
victory that day. Then the people came back
to him—but only to strip the dead.
11 Next to him was Shammah son of Agee,
the Hararite. The Philistines gathered together at Lehi, where there was a plot of
ground full of lentils; and the army fled from
the Philistines. 12But he took his stand in the
middle of the plot, defended it, and killed
the Philistines; and the LORD brought about
a great victory.
13 Towards the beginning of harvest three
of the thirtyᶠ chiefs went down to join David
at the cave of Adullam, while a band of Philistines was encamped in the valley of Rephaim. 14David was then in the stronghold; and
the garrison of the Philistines was then at
Bethlehem. 15David said longingly, "O that
someone would give me water to drink from
the well of Bethlehem that is by the gate!"
16Then the three warriors broke through the
camp of the Philistines, drew water from the
well of Bethlehem that was by the gate, and
brought it to David. But he would not drink
of it; he poured it out to the LORD, 17for he
said, "The LORD forbid that I should do this.
Can I drink the blood of the men who went
at the risk of their lives?" Therefore he would
not drink it. The three warriors did these
things.
18 Now Abishai son of Zeruiah, the brother of Joab, was chief of the Thirty.ᵍ With his
spear he fought against three hundred men

ᵃ Q Ms: MT *who was raised on high*   ᵇ Heb *But
worthlessness*   ᶜ Heb *in sitting*   ᵈ Gk Vg
Compare 1 Chr 11.11: Meaning of Heb uncertain
ᵉ 1 Chr 11.11: Meaning of Heb uncertain
ᶠ Heb adds *head*   ᵍ Two Heb Mss Syr: MT *Three*

23:1–7 *last words of David.* Today many
people hope to die quickly, without any pain or
suffering, but historically this has not always
been the case. For many in the West, a quick
death was the worst possible outcome, particularly under the influence of the ancient
Christian tradition in which one always wanted
to die in a "state of grace," having had last rites.
David's final words manifest the kind of piety
that one would like to hear from the lips of the
great king as well what we wish we might say at
our own death. The text may be read as a
model for such individual preparation.

and killed them, and won a name beside the Three. [19]He was the most renowned of the Thirty,[a] and became their commander; but he did not attain to the Three.

20 Benaiah son of Jehoiada was a valiant warrior[b] from Kabzeel, a doer of great deeds; he struck down two sons of Ariel[c] of Moab. He also went down and killed a lion in a pit on a day when snow had fallen. [21]And he killed an Egyptian, a handsome man. The Egyptian had a spear in his hand; but Benaiah went against him with a staff, snatched the spear out of the Egyptian's hand, and killed him with his own spear. [22]Such were the things Benaiah son of Jehoiada did, and won a name beside the three warriors. [23]He was renowned among the Thirty, but he did not attain to the Three. And David put him in charge of his bodyguard.

24 Among the Thirty were Asahel brother of Joab; Elhanan son of Dodo of Bethlehem; [25]Shammah of Harod; Elika of Harod; [26]Helez the Paltite; Ira son of Ikkesh of Tekoa; [27]Abiezer of Anathoth; Mebunnai the Hushathite; [28]Zalmon the Ahohite; Maharai of Netophah; [29]Heleb son of Baanah of Netophah; Ittai son of Ribai of Gibeah of the Benjaminites; [30]Benaiah of Pirathon; Hiddai of the torrents of Gaash; [31]Abi-albon the Arbathite; Azmaveth of Bahurim; [32]Eliahba of Shaalbon; the sons of Jashen: Jonathan [33]son of[d] Shammah the Hararite; Ahiam son of Sharar the Hararite; [34]Eliphelet son of Ahasbai of Maacah; Eliam son of Ahithophel the Gilonite; [35]Hezro[e] of Carmel; Paarai the Arbite; [36]Igal son of Nathan of Zobah; Bani the Gadite; [37]Zelek the Ammonite; Naharai of Beeroth, the armor-bearer of Joab son of Zeruiah; [38]Ira the Ithrite; Gareb the Ithrite; [39]Uriah the Hittite—thirty-seven in all.

David's Census of Israel and Judah

24 Again the anger of the LORD was kindled against Israel, and he incited David against them, saying, "Go, count the people of Israel and Judah." [2]So the king said to Joab and the commanders of the army,[f] who were with him, "Go through all the tribes of Israel, from Dan to Beer-sheba, and take a census of the people, so that I may know how many there are." [3]But Joab said to the king,

"May the LORD your God increase the number of the people a hundredfold, while the eyes of my lord the king can still see it! But why does my lord the king want to do this?" [4]But the king's word prevailed against Joab and the commanders of the army. So Joab and the commanders of the army went out from the presence of the king to take a census of the people of Israel. [5]They crossed the Jordan, and began from[g] Aroer and from the city that is in the middle of the valley, toward Gad and on to Jazer. [6]Then they came to Gilead, and to Kadesh in the land of the Hittites;[h] and they came to Dan, and from Dan[i] they went around to Sidon, [7]and came to the fortress of Tyre and to all the cities of the Hivites and Canaanites; and they went out to the Negeb of Judah at Beer-sheba. [8]So when they had gone through all the land, they came back to Jerusalem at the end of nine months and twenty days. [9]Joab reported to the king the number of those who had been recorded: in Israel there were eight hundred thousand soldiers able to draw the sword, and those of Judah were five hundred thousand.

Judgment on David's Sin

10 But afterward, David was stricken to the heart because he had numbered the people. David said to the LORD, "I have sinned greatly in what I have done. But now, O LORD, I pray you, take away the guilt of your servant; for I have done very foolishly." [11]When David rose in the morning, the word of the LORD came to the prophet Gad, David's seer, saying, [12]"Go and say to David: Thus says the LORD: Three things I offer[j] you; choose one of them, and I will do it to you." [13]So Gad came to David and told him; he asked him, "Shall three[k] years of famine come to you on your land? Or will you flee three months before

a Syr Compare 1 Chr 11.25: Heb Was he the most renowned of the Three?   b Another reading is the son of Ish-hai   c Gk: Heb lacks sons of d Gk: Heb lacks son of   e Another reading is Hezrai   f 1 Chr 21.2 Gk: Heb to Joab the commander of the army   g Gk Mss: Heb encamped in Aroer south of   h Gk: Heb to the land of Tahtim-hodshi   i Cn Compare Gk: Heb they came to Dan-jaan and   j Or hold over   k 1 Chr 21.12 Gk: Heb seven

your foes while they pursue you? Or shall there be three days' pestilence in your land? Now consider, and decide what answer I shall return to the one who sent me." [14]Then David said to Gad, "I am in great distress; let us fall into the hand of the LORD, for his mercy is great; but let me not fall into human hands."

15 So the LORD sent a pestilence on Israel from that morning until the appointed time; and seventy thousand of the people died, from Dan to Beer-sheba. [16]But when the angel stretched out his hand toward Jerusalem to destroy it, the LORD relented concerning the evil, and said to the angel who was bringing destruction among the people, "It is enough; now stay your hand." The angel of the LORD was then by the threshing floor of Araunah the Jebusite. [17]When David saw the angel who was destroying the people, he said to the LORD, "I alone have sinned, and I alone have done wickedly; but these sheep, what have they done? Let your hand, I pray, be against me and against my father's house."

David's Altar on the Threshing Floor

18 That day Gad came to David and said to him, "Go up and erect an altar to the LORD on the threshing floor of Araunah the Jebusite."

[19]Following Gad's instructions, David went up, as the LORD had commanded. [20]When Araunah looked down, he saw the king and his servants coming toward him; and Araunah went out and prostrated himself before the king with his face to the ground. [21]Araunah said, "Why has my lord the king come to his servant?" David said, "To buy the threshing floor from you in order to build an altar to the LORD, so that the plague may be averted from the people." [22]Then Araunah said to David, "Let my lord the king take and offer up what seems good to him; here are the oxen for the burnt offering, and the threshing sledges and the yokes of the oxen for the wood. [23]All this, O king, Araunah gives to the king." And Araunah said to the king, "May the LORD your God respond favorably to you."

24 But the king said to Araunah, "No, but I will buy them from you for a price; I will not offer burnt offerings to the LORD my God that cost me nothing." So David bought the threshing floor and the oxen for fifty shekels of silver. [25]David built there an altar to the LORD, and offered burnt offerings and offerings of well-being. So the LORD answered his supplication for the land, and the plague was averted from Israel.

24:24 *that cost me nothing.* David understands that although there is nothing that God needs from him, there is nonetheless an inescapable relationship between his spirituality and the level of his giving. There is no benefit in giving back to God what does not press David to sacrifice something of his own cherished possessions. In our own age of unprecedented economic growth and prosperity, such sacrificial giving would be a healthy corrective to the Church.

Responding
24:24 SACRIFICE. In spite of the fact that Araunah offers to give David the

threshing floor and animals to sacrifice on it, David insists on paying for them. Now, we may not think that this was a great feat for a king, but it is the principle of sacrificing for the sake of another that this passage highlights. If David had accepted Araunah's offer, Araunah would not only have been bereft of a livelihood, but would have had no money to start anew. David's sacrifice to God would have cost him nothing, but it would have been cheapened. Try to recall another biblical story that reinforces this teaching. How can these examples be applied to our lives? *See also* Spiritual Disciplines Index.

1 KINGS

1 & 2 Kings are a theological reflection on the story of Israel's public life. They are an answer to the haunting question: <u>How did this once</u> united nation, recipient of the <u>great gifts of freedom and land, end up in captivity</u> and exile? Listening to this story and reflections on it long ago were the exiles themselves, who wept "by the rivers of Babylon" (Ps 137:1) and longed for Jerusalem and the Temple, which was utterly destroyed.

Speaking to them long ago were their godly leaders, also in captivity, but not wholly bereft. They had carried with them their deep knowledge of Israel's covenants, especially the covenant of Moses, forged at Mt. Sinai, and the covenant of David. These believers-in-exile <u>were certain that the story of Israel</u> had everything to do with their covenants.

To read 1 & 2 Kings today is to be invited into an unsettling reflection on Israel's public life—and on *our* public life. The theologians of 1 & 2 Kings insist that public life can and must be aligned with the law of God, and they mourn and rage that public life is, instead, the very place of routine compromise. To read 1 & 2 Kings is to see that all areas of public life—political, religious, economic, judicial, and military—and the lives of individuals caught up in this public life are open to God's review and resolve. It is also to see that understanding God's resolve for public life is an absolutely essential, and yet regularly perplexing, task.

The Settings

The chief setting of 1 & 2 Kings is the royal court. The text plays on our usual assumption that the history of public life is the story of the powerful, especially kings, queens, queen mothers, heirs apparent (and not so apparent), courtiers, and foreign rulers. From the start, with the story of Solomon's ascension to the throne, we find ourselves in the midst of palace intrigue, bloody plots, and lavish consumption

---

See also *"The With-God Life" essays for this section of the Bible, "The People of God as a Nation,"*
pp. 391–96, and "The People of God in Rebellion," pp. 975–79.

(1 Kings 1–4). And we quickly discover that places of royal power are often places of ill-gotten and ill-used power—counterfeit power, as far as God sees it.

One measure of the legitimacy of a king's power is the building that soon shares royal space: the Temple. In 1 & 2 Kings, the Temple is *the* great sign that God is the true ruler of Israel, symbolically enthroned in the Temple, faithfully present with Israel (1 Kings 8:6–13; 9:3). This is how God is with God's people. In turn, the Temple and its use become one sign of the degree to which Israel's kings and people are faithful to God, their Sovereign. Over and over, 1 & 2 Kings let us know that the interests of those in the royal court eclipse this Temple and what it represents. Royal settings quickly become places of increasing failure as kings choose not to found their rule in the life-giving power of God.

Places of Vulnerability and Protest

Interrupting the almost seamless attention to royal stories in royal settings are surprising stories in improbable places. 1 & 2 Kings toss out on its ear the assumption that history is about courts and kings, the rich and the famous! We travel to unlikely places: a road outside Jerusalem, a vineyard in Jezreel, a settlement near the Jordan River. In all these places, we meet what appear to be nobodies, as most kings would see it: widows and orphans, bands of odd prophets, and peasants.

The fact is that these are the very people affected by the royal court. When a famine strikes because of a king's folly, these are the people who starve (1 Kings 17:8–12; 2 Kings 4:38–40). When the king eyes their property, they had better agree to sell (1 Kings 21:1–16). When the king conscripts and enslaves them, they work for the king, like it or not (1 Kings 5:13–18; 15:22). 1 & 2 Kings take us to often out-of-the-way places where we encounter these vulnerable people and suggest that these people are a key measure of a nation's public life and the success of its governance. God's eye is on these sparrows, God's ear is alert to their cries. And God's life-giving power moves freely and mercifully in these out-of-the-way places. God is with the people of Israel here too.

Royal Power and Prophets

It makes sense, then, that figures of immense, God-given power—the prophets—step out of these improbable places and from the ranks of these "no-account" people to speak the truth about the kingdom. God mobilizes the prophets to invade royal space and stand nose to nose with the king. Backed by the authority of the true Sovereign of Israel, the prophets look kings up and down and pronounce God's word, in often searing language.

As the prophets of 1 & 2 Kings speak, we discover that their imaginations are saturated with covenantal thinking, as is all of 1 & 2 Kings. The covenant of David plays a key role in their thought. The prophets are familiar with God's unconditional promise of an everlasting dynasty to David (2 Sam 7:12–16; 1 Kings 11:36). This promise holds out the hope that God's people will never be abandoned. A descendant of David will always rule in Jerusalem.

But the covenant that ignites the prophets' speech—and the thinking of 1 & 2 Kings as a whole—is the covenant of Moses, a conditional covenant involving judgment. The way this covenant is presented in 1 & 2 Kings seems to draw heavily on Deuteronomy, a book that reinterprets Moses' teachings for a settled, no longer nomadic people. God's once wandering people now own land and must consider its faithful ownership and use. They must also decide whom they will worship, for they now have neighbors who worship fertility gods to ensure good crops.

Deuteronomy reminds these settlers that a loving God brought their ancestors out of slavery and gave their descendants—the settlers themselves—this land on which they live. Now these descendants are called to heed the covenant of Moses by loving God alone and obeying the law of God. The theologians of Deuteronomy lay out the exacting conditions of this covenant: the statutes and commandments of God (Deut 12–26). They also lay out the consequences of covenant loyalty and disloyalty: obedience to God will bring blessing, life, and land; disobedience will bring curse, death, and exile (Deut 30:15–20; cf. 2 Kings 17:7–20).

The Word of God

The call to heed the covenant of Moses burns through the pages of 1 & 2 Kings. Two major concerns of this covenant stand out, the first of which is the worship of other gods. Bedrock to Israel's faith is the assertion that "The LORD is our God, the LORD alone" (Deut 6:4). And yet the kings and people of 1 & 2 Kings worship the gods of their neighbors. They also practice idolatry in other ways, placing their trust in the "gods" of treasuries, armies, and alliances.

Injustice is the second concern. The law teaches that all must receive equal justice (e.g., Deut 16:18–20) and that the weak and undefended must be protected (15:1–18; 24:10–22). Reflecting the old ways of Israel before the kings, when tribal life was more egalitarian, the law also teaches that kings must not elevate themselves above others (17:14–20). And yet the kings of 1 & 2 Kings amass great power and wealth, enslave their own people, steal their land, and spill innocent blood.

Although the prophets and theologians of these biblical texts wrestle with the tension between the unconditional Davidic covenant and the conditional Mosaic covenant, they come down time and time again on the side of God's judgment. But even here they have no simple equations. They testify, thank goodness, that divine judgment is never rigid. God sees signs of human repentance and human suffering and responds with compassion, second chances, and delayed judgment. They also testify to the difficulty of discerning and implementing God's desires and will in a nation's public life. In this story, political policy, self-interest, and moral certainty shape and reshape one another in ways that are sometimes ugly and morally ambiguous.

Nonetheless, 1 & 2 Kings as a whole announce that loyalty to God and obedience to the law must not be compromised. Standing in Babylon, remembering a history of compromise, the theologians of 1 & 2 Kings point to the exile as the inescapable testimony to God's judgment on Israel.

Reading 1 & 2 Kings Today

Reading 1 & 2 Kings as Christians today is an unsettling experience. These biblical texts vehemently assert that there is a moral order in God's creation, that God has a tenacious resolve about this world's life—and that we resist this resolve at our peril.

In particular, 1 & 2 Kings are deeply insistent that God is invested in the public life of our churches, nations, and world. And this investment involves each of us as members of the various communities that make up our public life. 1 & 2 Kings contain fierce, uncompromising speech spoken into the very places of our daily accommodation. To read these texts is to invite the prophets to leap off the page and stand nose to nose with *us* and the various systems of power we participate in and represent. This is a dangerous invitation, indeed, for these prophets do not mince words and are not fond of the status quo!

Instead, their words flame out in the cause of God. They call for true worship and justice. Jesus stands shoulder to shoulder with the prophets of 1 & 2 Kings when he quotes the two commandments that encapsulate all other commandments: " 'Hear, O Israel: the Lord our God, the Lord is one; you shall love the Lord your God with all your heart, and with all your soul, and with all your mind, and with all your strength.' . . . 'You shall love your neighbor as yourself' " (Mark 12:29–31; Deut 6:4–5; Lev 19:18).

Today, as followers of Jesus, we Christians are called to heed the prophets of 1 & 2 Kings. They summon us to see the gods we and all our institutions and governments worship, often the very gods of 1 & 2 Kings: might, influence, wealth. And they summon us to recognize the injustice and lack of compassion that pervade our dealings. Their words of judgment sound over us and all our systems of power, calling us to repent and to choose the path of life.

Even as 1 & 2 Kings are deeply insistent that God is invested in our public life, they are also deeply suspicious of power, for bad *and* for good. They recognize how immensely tempting power is, so tempting that moral compromise becomes the easy choice—for those who have the power *and* for those who hope to reform this power. 1 & 2 Kings offer no easy manual for translating God's word into policy. At the same time, these texts never relent in asserting that God has boundless claims on our public life. This refusal to both simplify life and reduce God's claims suggests that we in the Church must be diligent and faithful in dialogue and discernment about public life—and ever wary about our own certainties and schemes.

May we hear the fiery oracles of 1 & 2 Kings without dismissing them because of their stridency or despairing over them because of their severity. They are one language in Scripture that discloses the passionate yearning of God for people who seek after the Holy One with all their being, for a world that reflects this seeking in its splendid transformation.

—*Rebecca J. Kruger Gaudino*

The Struggle for the Succession

1 King David was old and advanced in years; and although they covered him with clothes, he could not get warm. 2So his servants said to him, "Let a young virgin be sought for my lord the king, and let her wait on the king, and be his attendant; let her lie in your bosom, so that my lord the king may be warm." 3So they searched for a beautiful girl throughout all the territory of Israel, and found Abishag the Shunammite, and brought her to the king. 4The girl was very beautiful. She became the king's attendant and served him, but the king did not know her sexually.

5 Now Adonijah son of Haggith exalted himself, saying, "I will be king"; he prepared for himself chariots and horsemen, and fifty men to run before him. 6His father had never at any time displeased him by asking, "Why have you done thus and so?" He was also a very handsome man, and he was born next after Absalom. 7He conferred with Joab son of Zeruiah and with the priest Abiathar, and they supported Adonijah. 8But the priest Zadok, and Benaiah son of Jehoiada, and the prophet Nathan, and Shimei, and Rei, and David's own warriors did not side with Adonijah.

9 Adonijah sacrificed sheep, oxen, and fatted cattle by the stone Zoheleth, which is beside En-rogel, and he invited all his brothers, the king's sons, and all the royal officials of Judah, 10but he did not invite the prophet Nathan or Benaiah or the warriors or his brother Solomon.

11 Then Nathan said to Bathsheba, Solomon's mother, "Have you not heard that Adonijah son of Haggith has become king and our lord David does not know it? 12Now therefore come, let me give you advice, so that you may save your own life and the life of your son Solomon. 13Go in at once to King David, and say to him, 'Did you not, my lord the king, swear to your servant, saying: Your son Solomon shall succeed me as king, and he shall sit on my throne? Why then is Adonijah king?' 14Then while you are still there speaking with the king, I will come in after you and confirm your words."

15 So Bathsheba went to the king in his room. The king was very old; Abishag the Shunammite was attending the king. 16Bathsheba bowed and did obeisance to the king, and the king said, "What do you wish?" 17She said to him, "My lord, you swore to your servant by the LORD your God, saying: Your son Solomon shall succeed me as king, and he shall sit on my throne. 18But now suddenly Adonijah has become king, though you, my lord the king, do not know it. 19He has sacrificed oxen, fatted cattle, and sheep in abundance, and has invited all the children of the king, the priest Abiathar, and Joab the commander of the army; but your servant Solomon he has not invited. 20But you, my lord the king—the eyes of all Israel are on you to tell them who shall sit on the throne of my lord the king after him. 21Otherwise it will come to pass, when my lord the king sleeps with his ancestors, that my son Solomon and I will be counted offenders."

22 While she was still speaking with the king, the prophet Nathan came in. 23The king was told, "Here is the prophet Nathan."

1:5 *I will be king.* Concern about David's age and virility (1:1–4) leads to concern about succession. Adonijah makes his bid for the throne, but who will follow David has not been clarified. God's broad-brush desire for the dynasty of David to rule may be apparent (2 Sam 7:12–16), but humans are left to discern and work out the details without a clear script from the Lord. Still, God works his will even when the players are not aware of his plan.

1:7 *and they supported Adonijah.* Adonijah uses the institutions of the state—the priesthood and the military—to sacralize and legitimize his power. Seizing power is dangerous business, and the presence of the priest Abiathar and the five-star general Joab proclaims that both divine and human might are on Adonijah's side. (See also 1:38–40.)

1:13 *Did you not . . . swear . . . Solomon shall succeed?* This vow of David's is not recorded. The palace intrigue of Nathan and Bathsheba makes this gap all the more troubling. God does not appear in the first two chapters of 1 Kings, although much is claimed in God's name, a fact that enlivens and troubles our public life too. What *is* God's will?

When he came in before the king, he did obeisance to the king, with his face to the ground. 24Nathan said, "My lord the king, have you said, 'Adonijah shall succeed me as king, and he shall sit on my throne'? 25For to-day he has gone down and has sacrificed oxen, fatted cattle, and sheep in abundance, and has invited all the king's children, Joab the commander a of the army, and the priest Abiathar, who are now eating and drinking before him, and saying, 'Long live King Adonijah!' 26But he did not invite me, your servant, and the priest Zadok, and Benaiah son of Jehoiada, and your servant Solomon. 27Has this thing been brought about by my lord the king and you have not let your servants know who should sit on the throne of my lord the king after him?"

The Accession of Solomon

28 King David answered, "Summon Bathsheba to me." So she came into the king's presence, and stood before the king. 29The king swore, saying, "As the LORD lives, who has saved my life from every adversity, 30as I swore to you by the LORD, the God of Israel, 'Your son Solomon shall succeed me as king, and he shall sit on my throne in my place,' so will I do this day." 31Then Bathsheba bowed with her face to the ground, and did obeisance to the king, and said, "May my lord King David live forever!"

32 King David said, "Summon to me the priest Zadok, the prophet Nathan, and Benaiah son of Jehoiada." When they came before the king, 33the king said to them, "Take with you the servants of your lord, and have my son Solomon ride on my own mule, and bring him down to Gihon. 34There let the priest Zadok and the prophet Nathan anoint him king over Israel; then blow the trumpet, and say, 'Long live King Solomon!' 35You shall go up following him. Let him enter and sit on my throne; he shall be king in my place; for I have appointed him to be ruler over Israel

and over Judah." 36Benaiah son of Jehoiada answered the king, "Amen! May the LORD, the God of my lord the king, so ordain. 37As the LORD has been with my lord the king, so may he be with Solomon, and make his throne greater than the throne of my lord King David."

38 So the priest Zadok, the prophet Nathan, and Benaiah son of Jehoiada, and the Cherethites and the Pelethites, went down and had Solomon ride on King David's mule, and led him to Gihon. 39There the priest Zadok took the horn of oil from the tent and anointed Solomon. Then they blew the trumpet, and all the people said, "Long live King Solomon!" 40And all the people went up following him, playing on pipes and rejoicing with great joy, so that the earth quaked at their noise.

41 Adonijah and all the guests who were with him heard it as they finished feasting. When Joab heard the sound of the trumpet, he said, "Why is the city in an uproar?" 42While he was still speaking, Jonathan son of the priest Abiathar arrived. Adonijah said, "Come in, for you are a worthy man and surely you bring good news." 43Jonathan answered Adonijah, "No, for our lord King David has made Solomon king; 44the king has sent with him the priest Zadok, the prophet Nathan, and Benaiah son of Jehoiada, and the Cherethites and the Pelethites; and they had him ride on the king's mule; 45the priest Zadok and the prophet Nathan have anointed him king at Gihon; and they have gone up from there rejoicing, so that the city is in an uproar. This is the noise that you heard. 46Solomon now sits on the royal throne. 47Moreover the king's servants came to congratulate our lord King David, saying, 'May God make the name of Solomon more famous than yours, and make his throne greater than your throne.' The king bowed in worship on

a Gk: Heb the commanders

---

the bed [48]and went on to pray thus, 'Blessed be the LORD, the God of Israel, who today has granted one of my offspring[a] to sit on my throne and permitted me to witness it.' "

49 Then all the guests of Adonijah got up trembling and went their own ways. [50]Adonijah, fearing Solomon, got up and went to grasp the horns of the altar. [51]Solomon was informed, "Adonijah is afraid of King Solomon; see, he has laid hold of the horns of the altar, saying, 'Let King Solomon swear to me first that he will not kill his servant with the sword.' " [52]So Solomon responded, "If he proves to be a worthy man, not one of his hairs shall fall to the ground; but if wickedness is found in him, he shall die." [53]Then King Solomon sent to have him brought down from the altar. He came to do obeisance to King Solomon; and Solomon said to him, "Go home."

David's Instruction to Solomon

2 When David's time to die drew near, he charged his son Solomon, saying: [2]"I am about to go the way of all the earth. Be strong, be courageous, [3]and keep the charge of the LORD your God, walking in his ways and keeping his statutes, his commandments, his ordinances, and his testimonies, as it is written in the law of Moses, so that you may prosper in all that you do and wherever you turn. [4]Then the LORD will establish his word that he spoke concerning me: 'If your heirs take heed to their way, to walk before me in faithfulness with all their heart and with all their soul,

there shall not fail you a successor on the throne of Israel.'

5 "Moreover you know also what Joab son of Zeruiah did to me, how he dealt with the two commanders of the armies of Israel, Abner son of Ner, and Amasa son of Jether, whom he murdered, retaliating in time of peace for blood that had been shed in war, and putting the blood of war on the belt around his waist, and on the sandals on his feet. [6]Act therefore according to your wisdom, but do not let his gray head go down to Sheol in peace. [7]Deal loyally, however, with the sons of Barzillai the Gileadite, and let them be among those who eat at your table; for with such loyalty they met me when I fled from your brother Absalom. [8]There is also with you Shimei son of Gera, the Benjaminite from Bahurim, who cursed me with a terrible curse on the day when I went to Mahanaim; but when he came down to meet me at the Jordan, I swore to him by the LORD, 'I will not put you to death with the sword.' [9]Therefore do not hold him guiltless, for you are a wise man; you will know what you ought to do to him, and you must bring his gray head down with blood to Sheol."

Death of David

10 Then David slept with his ancestors, and was buried in the city of David. [11]The time that David reigned over Israel was forty years; he reigned seven years in Hebron, and

a Gk: Heb *one*

2:1–9 *he charged his son Solomon.* David's parting words to his son move from the faithful to the ruthless. He stresses the importance of remembering the covenant of Moses, a covenant with conditions—the statutes and commandments, or law (vv 3–4). The "law of Moses" most likely refers to Deuteronomy (cf. Deut 4:40, 45; 30:16). In 2 Sam 7:12–16, God promised to establish David's throne forever— no matter what. But here David remembers this second covenant differently: God requires obedience to the law of Moses in order to sustain David's dynasty. Then David abruptly shifts gears when he gets down to the grim business of settling old scores (v 5; for the

stories of Joab's murder of Abner and Amasa, see 2 Sam 3:12–30; 19:11–14; 20:4–10). Both Abner and Amasa had been enemies on whom David vowed no vengeance. David also gave an oath not to kill another of his enemies, Shimei (2 Sam 19:22–23; 16:5–14). Now David tells his son that carrying out the executions of Joab and Shimei will demonstrate wisdom (vv 6, 9). This story suggests how easily we humans guard some of who we are and what we do from the claims of God. David's faithfulness to the law stops at the point where this faithfulness gets in the way of carrying out political and personal vendettas through his son. Here self-interest outweighs the law.

thirty-three years in Jerusalem. 12So Solomon sat on the throne of his father David; and his kingdom was firmly established.

Solomon Consolidates His Reign

13 Then Adonijah son of Haggith came to Bathsheba, Solomon's mother. She asked, "Do you come peaceably?" He said, "Peaceably." 14Then he said, "May I have a word with you?" She said, "Go on." 15He said, "You know that the kingdom was mine, and that all Israel expected me to reign; however, the kingdom has turned about and become my brother's, for it was his from the LORD. 16And now I have one request to make of you; do not refuse me." She said to him, "Go on." 17He said, "Please ask King Solomon—he will not refuse you—to give me Abishag the Shunammite as my wife." 18Bathsheba said, "Very well; I will speak to the king on your behalf."

19 So Bathsheba went to King Solomon, to speak to him on behalf of Adonijah. The king rose to meet her, and bowed down to her; then he sat on his throne, and had a throne brought for the king's mother, and she sat on his right. 20Then she said, "I have one small request to make of you; do not refuse me." And the king said to her, "Make your request, my mother; for I will not refuse you." 21She said, "Let Abishag the Shunammite be given to your brother Adonijah as his wife." 22King Solomon answered his mother, "And why do you ask Abishag the Shunammite for Adonijah? Ask for him the kingdom as well! For he is my elder brother; ask not only for him but also for the priest Abiathar and for Joab son of Zeruiah!" 23Then King Solomon swore by the LORD, "So may God do to me, and more also, for Adonijah has devised this scheme at the risk of his life! 24Now therefore as the LORD lives, who has established me and placed me on the throne of my father David, and who has made me a house as he promised, today Adonijah shall be put to death." 25So King Solomon sent Benaiah son of Jehoiada; he struck him down, and he died.

26 The king said to the priest Abiathar, "Go to Anathoth, to your estate; for you deserve death. But I will not at this time put you to death, because you carried the ark of the Lord GOD before my father David, and because you shared in all the hardships my father endured." 27So Solomon banished Abiathar from being priest to the LORD, thus fulfilling the word of the LORD that he had spoken concerning the house of Eli in Shiloh.

28 When the news came to Joab—for Joab had supported Adonijah though he had not supported Absalom—Joab fled to the tent of the LORD and grasped the horns of the altar. 29When it was told King Solomon, "Joab has fled to the tent of the LORD and now is beside the altar," Solomon sent Benaiah son of Jehoiada, saying, "Go, strike him down." 30So Benaiah came to the tent of the LORD and said to him, "The king commands, 'Come out.' " But he said, "No, I will die here." Then Benaiah brought the king word again, saying, "Thus said Joab, and thus he answered me." 31The king replied to him, "Do as he has said, strike him down and bury him; and thus take away from me and from my father's house the guilt for the blood that Joab shed without cause. 32The LORD will bring back his bloody deeds on his own head, because, without the knowledge of my father David, he attacked and killed with the sword two men more righteous and better than himself, Abner son of Ner, commander of the army of Israel, and Amasa son of Jether, commander of the army of Judah. 33So shall their blood come back on the head of Joab and on the head of his descendants forever; but to David, and to his descendants, and to his house, and to his throne, there shall be peace from the LORD forevermore." 34Then Benaiah son of Jehoiada went up and struck him down and killed him; and he was buried at his own house near the wilderness. 35The king put Benaiah son of Jehoiada over the army in his place, and the king put the priest Zadok in the place of Abiathar.

36 Then the king sent and summoned Shimei, and said to him, "Build yourself a house in Jerusalem, and live there, and do not go out from there to any place whatever. 37For on the day you go out, and cross the Wadi Kidron, know for certain that you shall die; your blood shall be on your own head." 38And Shimei said to the king, "The sentence is fair; as my lord the king has said, so will your servant do." So Shimei lived in Jerusalem many days.

39 But it happened at the end of three years that two of Shimei's slaves ran away to King Achish son of Maacah of Gath. When it was told Shimei, "Your slaves are in Gath," [40]Shimei arose and saddled a donkey, and went to Achish in Gath, to search for his slaves; Shimei went and brought his slaves from Gath. [41]When Solomon was told that Shimei had gone from Jerusalem to Gath and returned, [42]the king sent and summoned Shimei, and said to him, "Did I not make you swear by the LORD, and solemnly adjure you, saying, 'Know for certain that on the day you go out and go to any place whatever, you shall die'? And you said to me, 'The sentence is fair; I accept.' [43]Why then have you not kept your oath to the LORD and the commandment with which I charged you?" [44]The king also said to Shimei, "You know in your own heart all the evil that you did to my father David; so the LORD will bring back your evil on your own head. [45]But King Solomon shall be blessed, and the throne of David shall be established before the LORD forever." [46]Then the king commanded Benaiah son of Jehoiada; and he went out and struck him down, and he died.

So the kingdom was established in the hand of Solomon.

Solomon's Prayer for Wisdom

3 Solomon made a marriage alliance with Pharaoh king of Egypt; he took Pharaoh's daughter and brought her into the city of David, until he had finished building his own house and the house of the LORD and the wall around Jerusalem. [2]The people were sacrificing at the high places, however, because no house had yet been built for the name of the LORD.

3 Solomon loved the LORD, walking in the statutes of his father David; only, he sacrificed and offered incense at the high places. [4]The king went to Gibeon to sacrifice there, for that was the principal high place; Solomon used to offer a thousand burnt offerings on that altar. [5]At Gibeon the LORD appeared to Solomon in a dream by night; and God said, "Ask what I should give you." [6]And Solomon said, "You have shown great and steadfast love to your servant my father David, because he walked before you in faithfulness, in righteousness, and in uprightness of heart toward you; and you have kept for him this great and steadfast love, and have given him a son to sit on his throne today. [7]And now, O LORD my God, you have made your servant king in place of my father David, although I am only a little child; I do not know how to go out or come in. [8]And your servant is in the midst of the people whom you have chosen, a great people, so numerous they cannot be numbered or counted. [9]Give your servant therefore an understanding mind to govern your people, able to discern between good and evil; for who can govern this your great people?"

10 It pleased the Lord that Solomon had asked this. [11]God said to him, "Because you

---

2:35 *and the king put the priest Zadok in the place of Abiathar.* Solomon has added two more names to the hit list: Adonijah and Abiathar. Adonijah has already shown his colors, vying with Solomon for power. Note that in 1:5–8 both Abiathar and Joab have thrown their lot in with Adonijah. Not only old disputes with David but also new power struggles between Solomon and his rivals explain the swiftness with which the young king moves to destroy both Adonijah and Joab and to banish Abiathar. Solomom uses his father's "wisdom" to consolidate power.

3:3 *sacrificed . . . at the high places.* The place of worship for Israel has not yet been centralized. Local shrines, often elevated ("high places"), are also used. However, 1 & 2 Kings will later denounce these shrines for two reasons: first, after the construction of the Temple and the attempt to centralize worship in Jerusalem, outlying sanctuaries will be seen as places of illegitimate worship; and, second, they are identified with Canaanite religious beliefs and practices (Deut 12:2–7; 1 Kings 11:7; 13:33).

3:6–14 *for who can govern this your great people?* Solomon presents himself to God in all humility and asks for an "understanding mind" (v 9). In God's answer, as in David's last words (2:6, 9), wisdom is the focus. For David, wisdom was often political savvy. For God, wisdom is having "understanding to discern what is right" (v 11). It is reverence for God and knowledge of the law that lead the wise to "walk in my ways,

have asked this, and have not asked for yourself long life or riches, or for the life of your enemies, but have asked for yourself understanding to discern what is right, 12I now do according to your word. Indeed I give you a wise and discerning mind; no one like you has been before you and no one like you shall arise after you. 13I give you also what you have not asked, both riches and honor all your life; no other king shall compare with you. 14If you will walk in my ways, keeping my statutes and my commandments, as your father David walked, then I will lengthen your life."

15 Then Solomon awoke; it had been a dream. He came to Jerusalem where he stood before the ark of the covenant of the LORD. He offered up burnt offerings and offerings of well-being, and provided a feast for all his servants.

Solomon's Wisdom in Judgment

16 Later, two women who were prostitutes came to the king and stood before him. 17The one woman said, "Please, my lord, this woman and I live in the same house; and I gave birth while she was in the house. 18Then on the third day after I gave birth, this woman also gave birth. We were together; there was no one else with us in the house, only the two of us were in the house. 19Then this woman's son died in the night, because she lay on him. 20She got up in the middle of the night and took my son from beside me while your servant slept. She laid him at her breast, and laid her dead son at my breast. 21When I rose in the morning to nurse my son, I saw that he was dead; but when I looked at him closely in the morning, clearly it was not the son I had borne." 22But the other woman said, "No, the living son is mine, and the dead son is yours." The first said, "No, the dead son is yours, and the living son is mine." So they argued before the king.

23 Then the king said, "The one says, 'This is my son that is alive, and your son is dead'; while the other says, 'Not so! Your son is dead, and my son is the living one.' " 24So the king said, "Bring me a sword," and they brought a sword before the king. 25The king said, "Divide the living boy in two; then give half to the one, and half to the other." 26But the woman whose son was alive said to the king—because compassion for her son burned within her—"Please, my lord, give her the living boy; certainly do not kill him!" The other said, "It shall be neither mine nor yours; divide it." 27Then the king responded: "Give the first woman the living boy; do not kill him. She is his mother." 28All Israel heard of the judgment that the king had rendered; and they stood in awe of the king, because they perceived that the wisdom of God was in him, to execute justice.

Solomon's Administrative Officers

4 King Solomon was king over all Israel, 2and these were his high officials: Azariah son of Zadok was the priest; 3Elihoreph and Ahijah sons of Shisha were secretaries; Jehoshaphat son of Ahilud was recorder; 4Benaiah son of Jehoiada was in command of the army; Zadok and Abiathar were priests; 5Azariah son of Nathan was over the officials; Zabud son of Nathan was priest and king's friend; 6Ahishar was in charge of the palace; and Adoniram son of Abda was in charge of the forced labor.

---

keeping my statutes and my commandments," as God counsels Solomon (v 14; see Prov 2). The text places the Solomon of chapter 2, the shrewd political realist, next to the Solomon of chapter 3, the humble seeker of wisdom, making no attempt to harmonize these views. This placement suggests that the complexities within Solomon are within all of us as we struggle with the obligations and seductions of power.

3:9 SERVICE—See Spiritual Disciplines Index.

4:6 _forced labor._ Solomon undertakes a massive building program, using forced labor to accomplish his aims (9:15–19). This labor seems to involve both Israelites and non-Israelites ("all Israel," 5:13–18), although 9:20–22 claims that only non-Israelites are enslaved. However, the brutal murder of taskmaster Ado(ni)ram by "all Israel" in 12:18 suggests that the claims of 9:22 are court propaganda. Also, 11:28 refers to the "forced labor of the house of Joseph"—clearly Israelite labor. The example of Israel shows how easily the political process can set aside communal memories and values—for the Israelites, the memories and values that flowed from the exodus from Egypt—all for economic and political gain and glory.

SOLOMON

Wisdom That Waned

Selected Scriptures: *1 Kings 1–11; Proverbs 1–3, 10–11; Song of Solomon 1–8*

The son of Israel's beloved King David and his wife Bathsheba, Solomon was chosen by God to succeed David as king (1 Kings 1:39). Although he was only twenty when he took the throne, his prayer for wisdom early in his reign set him apart. Instead of asking for riches, success, and power, Solomon asked for understanding: "Give your servant therefore an understanding mind to govern your people, able to discern between good and evil; for who can govern this your great people?" (3:9). God was pleased, and from that time on Solomon became the wisest king Israel would ever know, as well as the richest and most productive king in the nation's history.

Israel already held much territory as a result of David's rule, and Solomon maintained strong armies while forming diplomatic ties with many nations surrounding him, gaining control of major trade routes, and increasing his wealth, all of which made him the most revered ruler in that part of the world. He built the Temple, a lavish palace for himself, and the wall of Jerusalem, and he reinforced key cities. With seemingly unending talent, Solomon also excelled intellectually, even spending time cataloging plant and animal life. He was the author of hundreds of proverbs and songs (4:32).

Solomon's single-minded focus on God and his spiritual leadership of the nation began to wane as he became increasingly engaged with his various building projects, his wealth, his notoriety, and his relationships with hundreds of foreign wives. His success became too much for him, and Solomon's passions overwhelmed his commitment to the one true God. Any love he first had for God was nearly smothered by all of his competing earthly loves.

Despite being known for his wisdom, Solomon made choices about wealth, productivity, and companionship that put him in a position in which he could no longer love God with all his heart, soul, mind, and strength. For Solomon, money became too great a pursuit. To accomplish his elaborate building projects he raised taxes and consigned thousands of Israelites to forced labor. Solomon found it necessary to build cities simply to house his chariots and cavalry, yet God had commanded kings not to multiply gold or to amass horses and chariots (Deut 17:16–17). His passion for sex led him to marry hundreds of pagan women, violating God's law: "You shall not enter into marriage with them, neither shall they with you; for they will surely incline your heart to follow their gods" (1 Kings 11:2). Solomon's sense of power likely made him feel entitled to break God's law, as if he were impervious to the consequences of his sin. But God observed as Solomon fell away and promised to punish his son (11:12). Solomon's life ended without any of the sense of glory and gusto with which it had begun. He had grown glum, a man who understood, finally, that we should fear God and keep his commandments and that, in truth, joy can be found only in God (Eccles 2:26; 12:13).

Solomon's story is all too common. He wasn't the first or the last to let his passions eclipse his love for God. Early church leaders understood these passions and for centuries have sought ways to restrict the hold they can have on us. Richard Foster writes: "I have always been intrigued by the vows of poverty, chastity, and obedience. . . . Why these particular three vows? . . . Then one day it dawned on me that these were designed to respond to the three great ethical issues of human life: money, sex, and power. These are the crucial themes all of us struggle with throughout our lives." Perhaps poverty may be more than God is asking; chastity is not an option for those who are married; and obedience is often only a vague commitment for we who live in self-driven societies. Foster writes: "My own answer, in brief, is this: in response to the issue of money we learn to live in simplicity; in response to the issue of sex we learn to live in fidelity; in response to the issue of power we learn to live in service."

Certainly Solomon, born to David at the height of his reign, never knew simplicity. David had erred once in fidelity, resulting in marriage to Solomon's mother; Solomon erred many times over by marrying hundreds of pagan wives. And any service Solomon did perform for his people was more self-centered than other-centered. Living in these three key areas so far outside of God's protective ideals resulted in a growing love for self, rather than for God. Solomon differed greatly from David, even early on, in his seeming lack of the passionate love for God that David possessed. His choices did nothing to kindle a growing love for the God he honored.

Can we avoid, for a lifetime, taking the paths that Solomon took and that our culture assumes we will take? Daily we choose. These choices determine the depth of our relationship with our Lord. "The vows of simplicity, fidelity, and service are for all Christians at all times. They are categorical imperatives for obedient followers of the obedient Christ. They are the beginning point from which we explore the depths of the spiritual life and discover our mission in the world" (Foster, *The Challenge of the Disciplined Life*).

Personal Reflection

- What is, or has been, your view of success? For you, which of these three areas—money, sex, or power—most defines success? Which of these areas poses the most temptation for you?
- Richard Foster describes the yen for power: "For us, it is never enough to enjoy good work. No, we must obtain supremacy; we must possess; we must hoard; we must conquer. The sin of power is the yearning to be more than we are created to be. We want to be gods." Where in your life does the yen for power most take hold?
- God gave Solomon wisdom, riches, honor. Yet Solomon focused his life on the gifts rather than the Giver. In all his wisdom, he made wrong choices. What gifts has God given you? Where does your focus lie? Spend some moments now focusing on the Giver, according him glory, honor, and adoration.

7 Solomon had twelve officials over all Israel, who provided food for the king and his household; each one had to make provision for one month in the year. [8]These were their names: Ben-hur, in the hill country of Ephraim; [9]Ben-deker, in Makaz, Shaalbim, Beth-shemesh, and Elon-beth-hanan; [10]Ben-hesed, in Arubboth (to him belonged Socoh and all the land of Hepher); [11]Ben-abinadab, in all Naphath-dor (he had Taphath, Solomon's daughter, as his wife); [12]Baana son of Ahilud, in Taanach, Megiddo, and all Beth-shean, which is beside Zarethan below Jezreel, and from Beth-shean to Abel-meholah, as far as the other side of Jokmeam; [13]Ben-geber, in Ramoth-gilead (he had the villages of Jair son of Manasseh, which are in Gilead, and he had the region of Argob, which is in Bashan, sixty great cities with walls and bronze bars); [14]Ahinadab son of Iddo, in Mahanaim; [15]Ahimaaz, in Naphtali (he had taken Basemath, Solomon's daughter, as his wife); [16]Baana son of Hushai, in Asher and Bealoth; [17]Jehoshaphat son of Paruah, in Issachar; [18]Shimei son of Ela, in Benjamin; [19]Geber son of Uri, in the land of Gilead, the country of King Sihon of the Amorites and of King Og of Bashan. And there was one official in the land of Judah.

Magnificence of Solomon's Rule

20 Judah and Israel were as numerous as the sand by the sea; they ate and drank and were happy. [21] [a] Solomon was sovereign over all the kingdoms from the Euphrates to the land of the Philistines, even to the border of Egypt; they brought tribute and served Solomon all the days of his life.

22 Solomon's provision for one day was thirty cors of choice flour, and sixty cors of meal, [23]ten fat oxen, and twenty pasture-fed cattle, one hundred sheep, besides deer, gazelles, roebucks, and fatted fowl. [24]For he had dominion over all the region west of the Euphrates from Tiphsah to Gaza, over all the kings west of the Euphrates; and he had peace on all sides. [25]During Solomon's lifetime Judah and Israel lived in safety, from Dan even to Beer-sheba, all of them under their vines and fig trees. [26]Solomon also had forty thou-

a Ch 5.1 in Heb

4:7–19 *Solomon had twelve officials over all Israel.* Although we are told, "Judah and Israel . . . ate and drank and were happy" (v 20), the list of taxation districts suggests the opposite. This list informs us that Solomon bucked tradition and divided the kingdom into twelve districts rather than tribes. The list names twelve officials, including two of Solomon's sons-in-law, who are responsible for taxing those living within their districts. Although the list purportedly represents "all Israel," these twelve officials represent areas outside of Judah. The tribe of the Davidic house, Judah, seems to be exempt from paying taxes. We will soon read the complaints of the people to Solomon's son: "Your father made our yoke heavy. Now therefore lighten the hard service of your father" (12:4–5). 1 & 2 Kings show us how governance goes beyond careful stewardship (Deut 17:14–20) to become favoritism and acquisition.

4:20–28 *Solomon was sovereign.* We could take the description of Solomon's rule at face value and exclaim at the might and luxury of this empire, but the warning of God, spoken by Samuel, sounds ominously through this chapter and beyond (1 Sam 8:10–22). Samuel warned Israel of the king who would take the best of Israel for his court and army. With memories of Egypt still lingering, Samuel was reminding the people of the Mosaic covenant, which allowed the tribes considerable freedom. The people owed full allegiance to God alone. Standing with Samuel is the writer of Deuteronomy, who warns any king against "exalting himself above other members of the community" (17:18–20). Allegiance to a ruler with all the trappings— splendid palaces, groaning tables, standing armies, imposing edifices—involves many tradeoffs. The theologians of 1 & 2 Kings assert that God cares deeply how humans shape their societies and governments.

4:25 *all of them under their vines and fig trees.* The metaphor of dwelling under one's own vines and fig trees refers to Israel's vision of the "good life," which differs from life under Solomon's rule. First, this vision gets at each household's ability to own land and have enough resources for its daily needs. Israel envisions an economy that is distributed among

sand stalls of horses for his chariots, and twelve thousand horsemen. 27Those officials supplied provisions for King Solomon and for all who came to King Solomon's table, each one in his month; they let nothing be lacking. 28They also brought to the required place barley and straw for the horses and swift steeds, each according to his charge.

Fame of Solomon's Wisdom

29 God gave Solomon very great wisdom, discernment, and breadth of understanding as vast as the sand on the seashore, 30so that Solomon's wisdom surpassed the wisdom of all the people of the east, and all the wisdom of Egypt. 31He was wiser than anyone else, wiser than Ethan the Ezrahite, and Heman, Calcol, and Darda, children of Mahol; his fame spread throughout all the surrounding nations. 32He composed three thousand proverbs, and his songs numbered a thousand and five. 33He would speak of trees, from the cedar that is in the Lebanon to the hyssop that grows in the wall; he would speak of animals, and birds, and reptiles, and fish. 34People came from all the nations to hear the wisdom of Solomon; they came from all the kings of the earth who had heard of his wisdom.

Preparations and Materials for the Temple

5 [a] Now King Hiram of Tyre sent his servants to Solomon, when he heard that they had anointed him king in place of his father; for Hiram had always been a friend to David. 2Solomon sent word to Hiram, saying, 3"You know that my father David could not build a house for the name of the LORD his God because of the warfare with which his enemies surrounded him, until the LORD put them under the soles of his feet.[b] 4But now the LORD my God has given me rest on every side; there is neither adversary nor misfortune. 5So I intend to build a house for the name of the LORD my God, as the LORD said to my father David, 'Your son, whom I will set on your throne in your place, shall build the house for my name.' 6Therefore command that cedars from the Lebanon be cut for me. My servants will join your servants, and I will give you whatever wages you set for your servants; for you know that there is no one among us who knows how to cut timber like the Sidonians."

7 When Hiram heard the words of Solomon, he rejoiced greatly, and said, "Blessed be the LORD today, who has given to David a wise son to be over this great people." 8Hiram sent word to Solomon, "I have heard the message that you have sent to me; I will fulfill all your needs in the matter of cedar and cypress timber. 9My servants shall bring it down to the sea from the Lebanon; I will make it into rafts to go by sea to the place you indicate. I will have them broken up there for you to take away. And you shall meet my needs by providing food for my household."

a Ch 5.15 in Heb   *b* Gk Tg Vg: Heb *my feet* or *his feet*

the people, with property and goods belonging to each household. In contrast, Solomon concentrates extravagant wealth around the court and its functions. Second, this vision understands true peace and security to be founded on God, not military might (see Mic 4:1–4). The psalmist puts it this way: "A king is not saved by his great army. . . . Our soul waits for the LORD . . . our help and shield" (33:16, 20). In contrast, Solomon creates a massive army, a temptation to trust in human power. Appearing as it does in a description of Solomon's empire building, the metaphor of the vine and fig tree (e.g., Zech 3:10; 2 Kings 18:31; Isa 36:16; Ps 105:33; Hos 2:12) seems to criticize this government of costly rule.

4:30 *and all the wisdom of Egypt.* The study of wisdom was revered in the Fertile Crescent; early wisdom literature dates to the Sumerians in Mesopotamia and to the Old Kingdom of Egypt. This regional interest in wisdom influenced Israel. As David is *the* poet and singer of Israel (much of Psalms is ascribed to him), so his son is identified as *the* sage of Israel. Proverbs (1:1), Ecclesiastes (1:1), and the Wisdom of Solomon, among other texts, are ascribed to him. Naming and categorizing nature was one form of this wisdom tradition (v 33). Another form involved advice for living life well. Israel linked this latter form to the covenant of Moses: to live wisely is to know God and obey the law.

10So Hiram supplied Solomon's every need for timber of cedar and cypress. 11Solomon in turn gave Hiram twenty thousand cors of wheat as food for his household, and twenty cors of fine oil. Solomon gave this to Hiram year by year. 12So the LORD gave Solomon wisdom, as he promised him. There was peace between Hiram and Solomon; and the two of them made a treaty.

13 King Solomon conscripted forced labor out of all Israel; the levy numbered thirty thousand men. 14He sent them to the Lebanon, ten thousand a month in shifts; they would be a month in the Lebanon and two months at home; Adoniram was in charge of the forced labor. 15Solomon also had seventy thousand laborers and eighty thousand stonecutters in the hill country, 16besides Solomon's three thousand three hundred supervisors who were over the work, having charge of the people who did the work. 17At the king's command, they quarried out great, costly stones in order to lay the foundation of the house with dressed stones. 18So Solomon's builders and Hiram's builders and the Gebalites did the stonecutting and prepared the timber and the stone to build the house.

Solomon Builds the Temple

6 In the four hundred eightieth year after the Israelites came out of the land of Egypt, in the fourth year of Solomon's reign over Israel, in the month of Ziv, which is the second month, he began to build the house of the LORD. 2The house that King Solomon built for the LORD was sixty cubits long, twenty cubits wide, and thirty cubits high. 3The vestibule in front of the nave of the house was twenty cubits wide, across the width of the house. Its depth was ten cubits in front of the house. 4For the house he made windows with recessed frames. a 5He also built a structure against the wall of the house, running around the walls of the house, both the nave and the inner sanctuary; and he made side chambers all around. 6The lowest story b was five cubits wide, the middle one was six cubits wide, and the third was seven cubits wide; for around the outside of the house he made offsets on the wall in order that the supporting beams should not be inserted into the walls of the house.

7 The house was built with stone finished at the quarry, so that neither hammer nor ax nor any tool of iron was heard in the temple while it was being built.

8 The entrance for the middle story was on the south side of the house: one went up by winding stairs to the middle story, and from the middle story to the third. 9So he built the house, and finished it; he roofed the house with beams and planks of cedar. 10He built the structure against the whole house, each story c five cubits high, and it was joined to the house with timbers of cedar.

a Gk: Meaning of Heb uncertain   b Gk: Heb structure   c Heb lacks each story

---

5:13 the levy numbered thirty thousand men. See note on 4:6.

6:1 he began to build the house of the LORD. Once enslaved in Egypt, God's people are now a wealthy nation with a much-praised king (4:34; 10:6–7, 23–24). The Temple will be the apex of Israel's journey: the place symbolizing the presence of Yahweh, Israel's God, and the place of worship for Israel, the place of its praises and petitions. But the description of forced labor in 5:13–18 suggests another reading. The irony of the fact that conscripted laborers now build a temple to the God who freed Israel from slavery hints at the possibility that Solomon's governance will be a return to Egypt. The Temple of Jerusalem is any place of worship

that comes to represent both divine presence in all its holy power and majesty and human presence in its aspiration to power and majesty.

Responding
6:1 WORSHIP. Solomon carefully planned the Temple to be a grand house of worship, but the ritual of building it was also an act of worship. Consider creating something to use in your own worship—a prayer or special Bible verse written in calligraphy, a stepping stone, a prayer bench, a story—and treat each step of your labor as an act of worship. See also Spiritual Disciplines Index.

11 Now the word of the LORD came to Solomon, 12"Concerning this house that you are building, if you will walk in my statutes, obey my ordinances, and keep all my commandments by walking in them, then I will establish my promise with you, which I made to your father David. 13I will dwell among the children of Israel, and will not forsake my people Israel."

14 So Solomon built the house, and finished it. 15He lined the walls of the house on the inside with boards of cedar; from the floor of the house to the rafters of the ceiling, he covered them on the inside with wood; and he covered the floor of the house with boards of cypress. 16He built twenty cubits of the rear of the house with boards of cedar from the floor to the rafters, and he built this within as an inner sanctuary, as the most holy place. 17The house, that is, the nave in front of the inner sanctuary, was forty cubits long. 18The cedar within the house had carvings of gourds and open flowers; all was cedar, no stone was seen. 19The inner sanctuary he prepared in the innermost part of the house, to set there the ark of the covenant of the LORD. 20The interior of the inner sanctuary was twenty cubits long, twenty cubits wide, and twenty cubits high; he overlaid it with pure gold. He also overlaid the altar with cedar.*a* 21Solomon overlaid the inside of the house with pure gold, then he drew chains of gold across, in front of the inner sanctuary, and overlaid it with gold. 22Next he overlaid the whole house with gold, in order that the whole house might be perfect; even the whole altar that belonged to the inner sanctuary he overlaid with gold.

The Furnishings of the Temple

23 In the inner sanctuary he made two cherubim of olivewood, each ten cubits high. 24Five cubits was the length of one wing of the cherub, and five cubits the length of the other wing of the cherub; it was ten cubits from the tip of one wing to the tip of the other. 25The other cherub also measured ten cubits; both cherubim had the same measure and the same form. 26The height of one cherub was ten cubits, and so was that of the other cherub. 27He put the cherubim in the innermost part of the house; the wings of the cherubim were spread out so that a wing of

a Meaning of Heb uncertain

6:11–13 *Concerning this house that you are building.* Although the Temple represents God's dwelling with Israel, God prefers not to be confined. God imagines obedience to the law as walking in paths created by God. Only if Solomon lives in a manner that involves this faithful "walking with God" can God consider a narrower way of expressing divine presence, the Temple. These two metaphors of God's presence—the first dynamic and open, and the second static and confining—are related to two long-standing traditions of understanding divine presence. The first understands God to be wholly free and sovereign, interacting with humans in surprising and even dangerous ways (see the meeting of Jacob and God, Gen 32:22–32, and the description of the tent of meeting, Exod 33:7–11). The second holds that God is fixed, enthroned in the worship space and life of the community, predictably present. In this passage, God holds out for a flexible, dynamic, and mutual relationship, which will come to be the primary way of understanding God's presence as we see how the with-God life unfolds in Scripture.

6:14 *and finished it.* The upcoming description of the Temple indicates that it was similar to other temples in the region in architecture and ornamentation. Scholars have wondered if and how non-Israelite forms and symbols influenced the Israelite faith. Their speculation raises the question of how culture shapes faith, particularly since cultural forms and symbols are part of the inescapable "container" within which we live and worship and through which God works when accommodating his communication to something we can hear.

6:27 *the wings of the cherubim.* Phoenician examples of winged cherubim show them supporting the king's throne. These examples parallel the biblical concept of cherubim supporting God's throne (e.g., 2 Kings 19:15). In this case, the ark of the covenant is God's footstool (1 Chron 28:2). The Temple as a whole symbolizes the enthronement of God within Israel.

one was touching the one wall, and a wing of the other cherub was touching the other wall; their other wings toward the center of the house were touching wing to wing. 28 He also overlaid the cherubim with gold.

29 He carved the walls of the house all around about with carved engravings of cherubim, palm trees, and open flowers, in the inner and outer rooms. 30 The floor of the house he overlaid with gold, in the inner and outer rooms.

31 For the entrance to the inner sanctuary he made doors of olivewood; the lintel and the doorposts were five-sided. *a* 32 He covered the two doors of olivewood with carvings of cherubim, palm trees, and open flowers; he overlaid them with gold, and spread gold on the cherubim and on the palm trees.

33 So also he made for the entrance to the nave doorposts of olivewood, four-sided each, 34 and two doors of cypress wood; the two leaves of the one door were folding, and the two leaves of the other door were folding. 35 He carved cherubim, palm trees, and open flowers, overlaying them with gold evenly applied upon the carved work. 36 He built the inner court with three courses of dressed stone to one course of cedar beams.

37 In the fourth year the foundation of the house of the LORD was laid, in the month of Ziv. 38 In the eleventh year, in the month of Bul, which is the eighth month, the house was finished in all its parts, and according to all its specifications. He was seven years in building it.

Solomon's Palace and Other Buildings

7 Solomon was building his own house thirteen years, and he finished his entire house.

2 He built the House of the Forest of the Lebanon one hundred cubits long, fifty cubits wide, and thirty cubits high, built on four rows of cedar pillars, with cedar beams on the pillars. 3 It was roofed with cedar on the forty-five rafters, fifteen in each row, which were on the pillars. 4 There were window frames in the three rows, facing each other in the three rows. 5 All the doorways and doorposts had four-sided frames, opposite, facing each other in the three rows.

6 He made the Hall of Pillars fifty cubits long and thirty cubits wide. There was a porch in front with pillars, and a canopy in front of them.

7 He made the Hall of the Throne where he was to pronounce judgment, the Hall of Justice, covered with cedar from floor to floor.

8 His own house where he would reside, in the other court back of the hall, was of the same construction. Solomon also made a house like this hall for Pharaoh's daughter, whom he had taken in marriage.

9 All these were made of costly stones, cut according to measure, sawed with saws, back and front, from the foundation to the coping, and from outside to the great court. 10 The foundation was of costly stones, huge stones, stones of eight and ten cubits. 11 There were costly stones above, cut to measure, and cedarwood. 12 The great court had three courses of dressed stone to one layer of cedar beams all around; so had the inner court of the house of the LORD, and the vestibule of the house.

Products of Hiram the Bronzeworker

13 Now King Solomon invited and received Hiram from Tyre. 14 He was the son of a widow of the tribe of Naphtali, whose father, a man of Tyre, had been an artisan in bronze; he was full of skill, intelligence, and knowledge in working bronze. He came to King Solomon, and did all his work.

15 He cast two pillars of bronze. Eighteen cubits was the height of the one, and a cord of twelve cubits would encircle it; the second pillar was the same. *b* 16 He also made two capitals of molten bronze, to set on the tops of the pillars; the height of the one capital was five cubits, and the height of the other capital was five cubits. 17 There were nets of checker work with wreaths of chain work for the capitals on the tops of the pillars; seven *c* for the one capital, and seven *c* for the other capital. 18 He made the columns with two rows around each latticework to cover the capitals that were above the pomegranates; he did the same with the other capital. 19 Now

a Meaning of Heb uncertain   b Cn: Heb *and a cord of twelve cubits encircled the second pillar;* Compare Jer 52.21   c Heb: Gk *a net*

the capitals that were on the tops of the pillars in the vestibule were of lily-work, four cubits high. 20The capitals were on the two pillars and also above the rounded projection that was beside the latticework; there were two hundred pomegranates in rows all around; and so with the other capital. 21He set up the pillars at the vestibule of the temple; he set up the pillar on the south and called it Jachin; and he set up the pillar on the north and called it Boaz. 22On the tops of the pillars was lily-work. Thus the work of the pillars was finished.

23 Then he made the molten sea; it was round, ten cubits from brim to brim, and five cubits high. A line of thirty cubits would encircle it completely. 24Under its brim were panels all around it, each of ten cubits, surrounding the sea; there were two rows of panels, cast when it was cast. 25It stood on twelve oxen, three facing north, three facing west, three facing south, and three facing east; the sea was set on them. The hindquarters of each were toward the inside. 26Its thickness was a handbreadth; its brim was made like the brim of a cup, like the flower of a lily; it held two thousand baths. a

27 He also made the ten stands of bronze; each stand was four cubits long, four cubits wide, and three cubits high. 28This was the construction of the stands: they had borders; the borders were within the frames; 29on the borders that were set in the frames were lions, oxen, and cherubim. On the frames, both above and below the lions and oxen, there were wreaths of beveled work. 30Each stand had four bronze wheels and axles of bronze; at the four corners were supports for a basin. The supports were cast with wreaths at the side of each. 31Its opening was within the crown whose height was one cubit; its opening was round, as a pedestal is made; it was a cubit and a half wide. At its opening there were carvings; its borders were four-sided, not round. 32The four wheels were underneath the borders; the axles of the wheels were in the stands; and the height of a wheel was a cubit and a half. 33The wheels were made like a chariot wheel; their axles, their rims, their spokes, and their hubs were all cast. 34There were four supports at the four

corners of each stand; the supports were of one piece with the stands. 35On the top of the stand there was a round band half a cubit high; on the top of the stand, its stays and its borders were of one piece with it. 36On the surfaces of its stays and on its borders he carved cherubim, lions, and palm trees, where each had space, with wreaths all around. 37In this way he made the ten stands; all of them were cast alike, with the same size and the same form.

38 He made ten basins of bronze; each basin held forty baths, a each basin measured four cubits; there was a basin for each of the ten stands. 39He set five of the stands on the south side of the house, and five on the north side of the house; he set the sea on the southeast corner of the house.

40 Hiram also made the pots, the shovels, and the basins. So Hiram finished all the work that he did for King Solomon on the house of the LORD: 41the two pillars, the two bowls of the capitals that were on the tops of the pillars, the two latticeworks to cover the two bowls of the capitals that were on the tops of the pillars; 42the four hundred pomegranates for the two latticeworks, two rows of pomegranates for each latticework, to cover the two bowls of the capitals that were on the pillars; 43the ten stands, the ten basins on the stands; 44the one sea, and the twelve oxen underneath the sea.

45 The pots, the shovels, and the basins, all these vessels that Hiram made for King Solomon for the house of the LORD were of burnished bronze. 46In the plain of the Jordan the king cast them, in the clay ground between Succoth and Zarethan. 47Solomon left all the vessels unweighed, because there were so many of them; the weight of the bronze was not determined.

48 So Solomon made all the vessels that were in the house of the LORD: the golden altar, the golden table for the bread of the Presence, 49the lampstands of pure gold, five on the south side and five on the north, in front of the inner sanctuary; the flowers, the lamps, and the tongs, of gold; 50the cups, snuffers, basins, dishes for incense, and firepans, of

a A Heb measure of volume

pure gold; the sockets for the doors of the innermost part of the house, the most holy place, and for the doors of the nave of the temple, of gold.

51 Thus all the work that King Solomon did on the house of the LORD was finished. Solomon brought in the things that his father David had dedicated, the silver, the gold, and the vessels, and stored them in the treasuries of the house of the LORD.

Dedication of the Temple

8 Then Solomon assembled the elders of Israel and all the heads of the tribes, the leaders of the ancestral houses of the Israelites, before King Solomon in Jerusalem, to bring up the ark of the covenant of the LORD out of the city of David, which is Zion. ²All the people of Israel assembled to King Solomon at the festival in the month Ethanim, which is the seventh month. ³And all the elders of Israel came, and the priests carried the ark. ⁴So they brought up the ark of the LORD, the tent of meeting, and all the holy vessels that were in the tent; the priests and

the Levites brought them up. ⁵King Solomon and all the congregation of Israel, who had assembled before him, were with him before the ark, sacrificing so many sheep and oxen that they could not be counted or numbered. ⁶Then the priests brought the ark of the covenant of the LORD to its place, in the inner sanctuary of the house, in the most holy place, underneath the wings of the cherubim. ⁷For the cherubim spread out their wings over the place of the ark, so that the cherubim made a covering above the ark and its poles. ⁸The poles were so long that the ends of the poles were seen from the holy place in front of the inner sanctuary; but they could not be seen from outside; they are there to this day. ⁹There was nothing in the ark except the two tablets of stone that Moses had placed there at Horeb, where the LORD made a covenant with the Israelites, when they came out of the land of Egypt. ¹⁰And when the priests came out of the holy place, a cloud filled the house of the LORD, ¹¹so that the priests could not stand to min-

---

8:2 *All the people of Israel assembled . . . in . . . the seventh month.* Solomon brings together the leaders and people of Israel to dedicate the Temple as the only house of God in the land. The dedication of the Temple has been delayed to coincide with the Festival of Booths, a harvest celebration in which the people remember their journey from Egypt and the gift that God gave them on this journey: the law of Moses. This festival is a time of renewing the covenant of Moses (Deut 16:13–15; 31:9–13).

8:3–6 *the priests carried the ark.* Straining to express the mystery of divine presence, chapter 8 presents a number of Israel's understandings and representations of God's presence and invites us to meditate on this mystery too. The ancient tradition of the ark resonates with the sense that divine presence is mighty, unfathomable, and beyond control. The ark is handled with the greatest reverence and fear. The captured ark of God wreaked havoc on the Philistine house of Dagon (1 Sam 5:1–5). When an unfortunate Israelite touched the ark to steady it on its journey to Jerusalem, God killed this man (2 Sam 6:6–7). Now the priests carry the ark, and sacrifices accompany the

procession of this potent object and mysterious presence.

8:9 *nothing in the ark except the two tablets of stone.* Here we encounter another understanding of the ark, one stripped of the mystery alluded to in verses 3–6. What is important about the ark is the inscribed law inside, the gift and mediating presence of God. Mt. Sinai is also called Horeb, especially in the tradition of Deuteronomy.

8:10 *a cloud filled the house of the LORD.* The cloud is another ancient sign of God's presence, appearing throughout Exodus. There the cloud is the sign of a dynamic and mysterious presence, always on the move, deigning to "meet" Israel in its tent of meeting. But Solomon voices his hopes for a God who will settle into the Temple and stay (vv 12–13). The king envisions God fixed in the Temple, no longer the dynamic God of the ark and the cloud, an understanding that serves Solomon's desire to have a sure future for himself and his dynasty. The various understandings of divine presence in this chapter permit us to ponder how we understand God and why. Do we see God as a presence comfortably within reach, as

ister because of the cloud; for the glory of the LORD filled the house of the LORD.

12 Then Solomon said,

"The LORD has said that he would dwell
  in thick darkness.
13 I have built you an exalted house,
  a place for you to dwell in forever."

Solomon's Speech

14 Then the king turned around and blessed all the assembly of Israel, while all the assembly of Israel stood. 15He said, "Blessed be the LORD, the God of Israel, who with his hand has fulfilled what he promised with his mouth to my father David, saying, 16'Since the day that I brought my people Israel out of Egypt, I have not chosen a city from any of the tribes of Israel in which to build a house, that my name might be there; but I chose David to be over my people Israel.' 17My father David had it in mind to build a house for the name of the LORD, the God of Israel. 18But the LORD said to my father David, 'You did well to consider building a house for my name; 19nevertheless you shall not build the house, but your son who shall be born to you shall build the house for my name.' 20Now the LORD has upheld the promise that he made; for I have risen in the place of my father David; I sit on the throne of Israel, as the LORD promised, and have built the house for the name of the LORD, the God

of Israel. 21There I have provided a place for the ark, in which is the covenant of the LORD that he made with our ancestors when he brought them out of the land of Egypt."

Solomon's Prayer of Dedication

22 Then Solomon stood before the altar of the LORD in the presence of all the assembly of Israel, and spread out his hands to heaven. 23He said, "O LORD, God of Israel, there is no God like you in heaven above or on earth beneath, keeping covenant and steadfast love for your servants who walk before you with all their heart, 24the covenant that you kept for your servant my father David as you declared to him; you promised with your mouth and have this day fulfilled with your hand. 25Therefore, O LORD, God of Israel, keep for your servant my father David that which you promised him, saying, 'There shall never fail you a successor before me to sit on the throne of Israel, if only your children look to their way, to walk before me as you have walked before me.' 26Therefore, O God of Israel, let your word be confirmed, which you promised to your servant my father David.

27 "But will God indeed dwell on the earth? Even heaven and the highest heaven cannot contain you, much less this house that I have built! 28Regard your servant's prayer and his plea, O LORD my God, heeding the cry and the prayer that your servant prays

---

a mysterious presence whose power is fearful, or as a presence we know through our study of what is right and wrong? This chapter invites us to reflect on all these understandings. Exactly how is God "with us"?

Responding
8:10–11 THE WITH-GOD LIFE. A cloud is one of the classic biblical signs of God's presence, but every time two or more gather in Christ's name, he is there—cloud or no (Matt 18:20). The next time you're in church or small group, look around. What are the visible and invisible signs of God's presence among you? See also Spiritual Disciplines Index.

8:25 *if only your children . . . walk before me.* Although Solomon may prefer no conditions to

God's promise of accompaniment (vv 12–13), he cannot escape the covenant of Moses, which requires obedience. More than this, he melds the Mosaic and Davidic covenants. Faithfulness to the Mosaic covenant becomes God's condition for fulfilling the Davidic covenant. The people must obey the stipulations of the Mosaic covenant—these *are* the expressions of the Spiritual Disciplines for the people.

Responding
8:28–53 PRAYER. In anticipating the sins of the people and asking God to honor their repentance, Solomon's prayer of dedication is as much for the gathered people as for God. Are your prayers ultimately more for God or for you? What effect does prayer have on you? See also Spiritual Disciplines Index.

to you today; [29]that your eyes may be open night and day toward this house, the place of which you said, 'My name shall be there,' that you may heed the prayer that your servant prays toward this place. [30]Hear the plea of your servant and of your people Israel when they pray toward this place; O hear in heaven your dwelling place; heed and forgive.

31 "If someone sins against a neighbor and is given an oath to swear, and comes and swears before your altar in this house, [32]then hear in heaven, and act, and judge your servants, condemning the guilty by bringing their conduct on their own head, and vindicating the righteous by rewarding them according to their righteousness.

33 "When your people Israel, having sinned against you, are defeated before an enemy but turn again to you, confess your name, pray and plead with you in this house, [34]then hear in heaven, forgive the sin of your people Israel, and bring them again to the land that you gave to their ancestors.

35 "When heaven is shut up and there is no rain because they have sinned against you, and then they pray toward this place, confess your name, and turn from their sin, because you punish[a] them, [36]then hear in heaven, and forgive the sin of your servants, your people Israel, when you teach them the good way in which they should walk; and grant rain on your land, which you have given to your people as an inheritance.

37 "If there is famine in the land, if there

is p... lar; ... their ci... ness there... plea there is ..st, or caterpillar... your people Israe...m in any[b] of of their own hearts, whatever sicktheir hands toward th...r from all heaven your dwelling pla...fflictions render to all whose hearts hear in cording to all their ways, for o...t, and what is in every human heart—[40]s...how may fear you all the days that the...ey the land that you gave to our ancestors.

41 "Likewise when a foreigner, who is n... of your people Israel, comes from a distant land because of your name [42]—for they shall hear of your great name, your mighty hand, and your outstretched arm—when a foreigner comes and prays toward this house, [43]then hear in heaven your dwelling place, and do according to all that the foreigner calls to you, so that all the peoples of the earth may know your name and fear you, as do your people Israel, and so that they may know that your name has been invoked on this house that I have built.

44 "If your people go out to battle against their enemy, by whatever way you shall send them, and they pray to the LORD toward the city that you have chosen and the house that I have built for your name, [45]then hear in

a Or when you answer   b Gk Syr: Heb in the land

8:29 *My name shall be there.* The theologians of 1 & 2 Kings include yet another way of understanding how God is "with us." A name is a symbolic extension of personal authority and presence, even in the absence of the person named. This manner of understanding divine presence communicates the freedom of God and also points to God's faithful presence with Israel.

8:30 *O hear in heaven your dwelling place; heed and forgive.* In this chapter, the final note on how God is with us comes down on the side of freedom: God cannot be contained in any building or by any ritual action. Even Solomon in his prayers cannot command, but only beseech, God. Solomon then waits for God's response.

Nonetheless, the king trusts in God's remarkable connectedness to Israel. Solomon speaks to a God with a long history of hearing petitioners, especially the groans of slaves (Exod 2:24). In fact, Solomon reminds God of the exodus, *the defining act of compassion and liberation in the Old Testament* (vv 51–53). In 1 and 2 Kings, prayer is an act of intimate and profound trust that links all petitioners through the ages to the exodus experience of a people whose God listened, an act of compassion that made all the difference. This is the God we trust to listen again.

8:33 CONFESSION—*See* Spiritual Disciplines Index.

...eir plea, and main-
...hea...nst you—for there is
...tain sin—and you are angry
...e them to an enemy, so
no...ed away captive to the land
...ar off or near; [47]yet if they
th...senses in the land to which
of ...een taken captive, and repent,
c...with you in the land of their cap-
...ang, 'We have sinned, and have done
...we have acted wickedly'; [48]if they re-
with all their heart and soul in the land
...their enemies, who took them captive,
...d pray to you toward their land, which you
...ve to their ancestors, the city that you have
...hosen, and the house that I have built for
your name; [49]then hear in heaven your
dwelling place their prayer and their plea,
maintain their cause [50]and forgive your people who have sinned against you, and all their
transgressions that they have committed
against you; and grant them compassion in
the sight of their captors, so that they may
have compassion on them [51](for they are your
people and heritage, which you brought out
of Egypt, from the midst of the iron-smelter).
[52]Let your eyes be open to the plea of your servant, and to the plea of your people Israel, listening to them whenever they call to you.
[53]For you have separated them from among
all the peoples of the earth, to be your heritage, just as you promised through Moses,
your servant, when you brought our ancestors out of Egypt, O Lord GOD."

Solomon Blesses the Assembly

54 Now when Solomon finished offering
all this prayer and this plea to the LORD, he
arose from facing the altar of the LORD, where
he had knelt with hands outstretched toward
heaven; [55]he stood and blessed all the assembly of Israel with a loud voice:

56 "Blessed be the LORD, who has given
rest to his people Israel according to all that
he promised; not one word has failed of all his
good promise, which he spoke through his
servant Moses. [57]The LORD our God be with
us, as he was with our ancestors; may he not
leave us or abandon us, [58]but incline our
hearts to him, to walk in all his ways, and to
keep his commandments, his statutes, and
his ordinances, which he commanded our
ancestors. [59]Let these words of mine, with
which I pleaded before the LORD, be near to
the LORD our God day and night, and may he
maintain the cause of his servant and the
cause of his people Israel, as each day requires;
[60]so that all the peoples of the earth may
know that the LORD is God; there is no other.
[61]Therefore devote yourselves completely to
the LORD our God, walking in his statutes and
keeping his commandments, as at this day."

Solomon Offers Sacrifices

62 Then the king, and all Israel with him,
offered sacrifice before the LORD. [63]Solomon
offered as sacrifices of well-being to the LORD
twenty-two thousand oxen and one hundred
twenty thousand sheep. So the king and all
the people of Israel dedicated the house of the
LORD. [64]The same day the king consecrated
the middle of the court that was in front of
the house of the LORD; for there he offered the
burnt offerings and the grain offerings and
the fat pieces of the sacrifices of well-being,
because the bronze altar that was before the
LORD was too small to receive the burnt offerings and the grain offerings and the fat
pieces of the sacrifices of well-being.

65 So Solomon held the festival at that
time, and all Israel with him—a great assembly, people from Lebo-hamath to the Wadi of
Egypt—before the LORD our God, seven days.[a]
[66]On the eighth day he sent the people away;
and they blessed the king, and went to their
tents, joyful and in good spirits because of all
the goodness that the LORD had shown to his
servant David and to his people Israel.

God Appears Again to Solomon

9 When Solomon had finished building
the house of the LORD and the king's
house and all that Solomon desired to build,
[2]the LORD appeared to Solomon a second
time, as he had appeared to him at Gibeon.
[3]The LORD said to him, "I have heard your
prayer and your plea, which you made before me; I have consecrated this house that
you have built, and put my name there for-

a Compare Gk: Heb *seven days and seven days,
fourteen days*

ever; my eyes and my heart will be there for all time. [4]As for you, if you will walk before me, as David your father walked, with integrity of heart and uprightness, doing according to all that I have commanded you, and keeping my statutes and my ordinances, [5]then I will establish your royal throne over Israel forever, as I promised your father David, saying, 'There shall not fail you a successor on the throne of Israel.'

6 "If you turn aside from following me, you or your children, and do not keep my commandments and my statutes that I have set before you, but go and serve other gods and worship them, [7]then I will cut Israel off from the land that I have given them; and the house that I have consecrated for my name I will cast out of my sight; and Israel will become a proverb and a taunt among all peoples. [8]This house will become a heap of ruins;[a] everyone passing by it will be astonished, and will hiss; and they will say, 'Why has the LORD done such a thing to this land and to this house?' [9]Then they will say, 'Because they have forsaken the LORD their God, who brought their ancestors out of the land of Egypt, and embraced other gods, worshiping them and serving them; therefore the LORD has brought this disaster upon them.'"

10 At the end of twenty years, in which Solomon had built the two houses, the house of the LORD and the king's house, [11]King Hiram of Tyre having supplied Solomon with cedar and cypress timber and gold, as much as he desired, King Solomon gave to Hiram twenty cities in the land of Galilee. [12]But when Hiram came from Tyre to see the cities that Solomon had given him, they did not please him. [13]Therefore he said, "What kind of cities are these that you have given me, my brother?" So they are called the land of Cabul[b] to this day. [14]But Hiram had sent to the king one hundred twenty talents of gold.

Other Acts of Solomon

15 This is the account of the forced labor that King Solomon conscripted to build the house of the LORD and his own house, the Millo and the wall of Jerusalem, Hazor, Megiddo, Gezer [16](Pharaoh king of Egypt had gone up and captured Gezer and burned it down, had killed the Canaanites who lived in the city, and had given it as dowry to his daughter, Solomon's wife; [17]so Solomon rebuilt Gezer), Lower Beth-horon, [18]Baalath, Tamar in the wilderness, within the land, [19]as well as all of Solomon's storage cities, the cities for his chariots, the cities for his cavalry, and whatever Solomon desired to build, in Jerusalem, in Lebanon, and in all the land of his dominion. [20]All the people who were left of the Amorites, the Hittites, the Perizzites, the Hivites, and the Jebusites, who were not of the people of Israel— [21]their descendants who were still left in the land, whom the Israelites were unable to destroy

a Syr Old Latin: Heb will become high   b Perhaps meaning a land good for nothing

---

9:1–9 the LORD appeared to Solomon. This second dream epiphany communicates little of the hope of the first (3:5–14). God accepts the Temple as the residence of God's name forever (v 3), yet lays out conditions for this presence (vv 6–9). Once again there is tension between the unconditional and conditional nature of God's promises. Verses 6–9 underline the mutuality of God's relationship with humankind: in liberating Israel, God has already acted in love; now God's people must respond in love to God.

9:3 PRAYER—See Spiritual Disciplines Index.

9:20–21 not of the people of Israel . . . conscripted for slave labor. See note on 4:6. That Solomon would enslave all non-Israelites violates the Deuteronomic code, which calls for justice to aliens, as the conquered Canaanites are called (Deut 1:16; 10:17–19; 24:17; 27:19). Why? "Remember that you were a slave in Egypt and the LORD your God redeemed you from there; therefore I command you to do this" (Deut 24:18). At the same time, the writer of Deuteronomy, fearing the influence of these very "aliens" on Israel, calls for their annihilation (20:17–18). This ambivalence runs throughout the Old Testament, as various texts address a question that the Church continues to wrestle with: whether openness to outsiders is a gift or danger to the community of faith.

completely—these Solomon conscripted for slave labor, and so they are to this day. 22But of the Israelites Solomon made no slaves; they were the soldiers, they were his officials, his commanders, his captains, and the commanders of his chariotry and cavalry.

23 These were the chief officers who were over Solomon's work: five hundred fifty, who had charge of the people who carried on the work.

24 But Pharaoh's daughter went up from the city of David to her own house that Solomon had built for her; then he built the Millo.

25 Three times a year Solomon used to offer up burnt offerings and sacrifices of well-being on the altar that he built for the LORD, offering incense*a* before the LORD. So he completed the house.

Solomon's Commercial Activity

26 King Solomon built a fleet of ships at Ezion-geber, which is near Eloth on the shore of the Red Sea, *b* in the land of Edom. 27Hiram sent his servants with the fleet, sailors who were familiar with the sea, together with the servants of Solomon. 28They went to Ophir, and imported from there four hundred twenty talents of gold, which they delivered to King Solomon.

Visit of the Queen of Sheba

10 When the queen of Sheba heard of the fame of Solomon (fame due to*c* the name of the LORD), she came to test him with hard questions. 2She came to Jerusalem

with a very great retinue, with camels bearing spices, and very much gold, and precious stones; and when she came to Solomon, she told him all that was on her mind. 3Solomon answered all her questions; there was nothing hidden from the king that he could not explain to her. 4When the queen of Sheba had observed all the wisdom of Solomon, the house that he had built, 5the food of his table, the seating of his officials, and the attendance of his servants, their clothing, his valets, and his burnt offerings that he offered at the house of the LORD, there was no more spirit in her.

6 So she said to the king, "The report was true that I heard in my own land of your accomplishments and of your wisdom, 7but I did not believe the reports until I came and my own eyes had seen it. Not even half had been told me; your wisdom and prosperity far surpass the report that I had heard. 8Happy are your wives!*d* Happy are these your servants, who continually attend you and hear your wisdom! 9Blessed be the LORD your God, who has delighted in you and set you on the throne of Israel! Because the LORD loved Israel forever, he has made you king to execute justice and righteousness." 10Then she gave the king one hundred twenty talents of gold, a great quantity of spices, and precious stones; never again did spices come in such quantity as that which the queen of Sheba gave to King Solomon.

a Gk: Heb *offering incense with it that was*
b Or *Sea of Reeds*   c Meaning of Heb uncertain
d Gk Syr: Heb *men*

10:1–10 *the queen of Sheba had observed all the wisdom of Solomon.* These verses focus on the wisdom of Solomon once again. The queen of Sheba believes that she sees Solomon's wisdom in his answers to her questions (v 3) as well as in his imperial arrangements: his architecture, household administration, sophisticated etiquette, and perhaps showy worship (vv 4–5), all aimed, it seems, at winning acclaim. Ironically, the queen's reference to Solomon's "justice and righteousness" (v 9) brings up entirely different "wisdom matters." For the theologians of 1 & 2 Kings, wisdom and keeping the Mosaic covenant are interrelated.

And a community founded on this covenant is a community that practices mutual care and respect—justice and righteousness. These constitute Spiritual Disciplines for the people. To exploit or abandon members of the community is to violate this covenant. Soon we will hear the voices of those who live under Solomon's thumb and disagree with the queen's praise of Solomon (12:1–19). The call for justice and righteousness among God's people is at the heart of the message of Israel's prophets in 1 & 2 Kings and elsewhere (1 Kings 21; Isa 5:7; 32:1–8; Jer 22:1–5; Amos 5:11–24; Mal 3:3–5).

11 Moreover, the fleet of Hiram, which carried gold from Ophir, brought from Ophir a great quantity of almug wood and precious stones. 12From the almug wood the king made supports for the house of the LORD, and for the king's house, lyres also and harps for the singers; no such almug wood has come or been seen to this day.

13 Meanwhile King Solomon gave to the queen of Sheba every desire that she expressed, as well as what he gave her out of Solomon's royal bounty. Then she returned to her own land, with her servants.

14 The weight of gold that came to Solomon in one year was six hundred sixty-six talents of gold, 15besides that which came from the traders and from the business of the merchants, and from all the kings of Arabia and the governors of the land. 16King Solomon made two hundred large shields of beaten gold; six hundred shekels of gold went into each large shield. 17He made three hundred shields of beaten gold; three minas of gold went into each shield; and the king put them in the House of the Forest of Lebanon. 18The king also made a great ivory throne, and overlaid it with the finest gold. 19The throne had six steps. The top of the throne was rounded in the back, and on each side of the seat were arm rests and two lions standing beside the arm rests, 20while twelve lions were standing, one on each end of a step on the six steps. Nothing like it was ever made in any kingdom. 21All King Solomon's drinking vessels were of gold, and all the vessels of the House of the Forest of Lebanon were of pure gold; none were of silver—it was not considered as anything in the days of Solomon. 22For the king had a fleet of ships of Tarshish at sea with the fleet of Hiram. Once every three years the fleet of ships of Tarshish used to come bringing gold, silver, ivory, apes, and peacocks. a

23 Thus King Solomon excelled all the kings of the earth in riches and in wisdom. 24The whole earth sought the presence of Solomon to hear his wisdom, which God had put into his mind. 25Every one of them brought a present, objects of silver and gold, garments, weaponry, spices, horses, and mules, so much year by year.

26 Solomon gathered together chariots and horses; he had fourteen hundred chariots and twelve thousand horses, which he stationed in the chariot cities and with the king in Jerusalem. 27The king made silver as common in Jerusalem as stones, and he made cedars as numerous as the sycamores of the Shephelah. 28Solomon's import of horses was from Egypt and Kue, and the king's traders received them from Kue at a price. 29A chariot could be imported from Egypt for six hundred shekels of silver, and a horse for one hundred fifty; so through the king's traders they were exported to all the kings of the Hittites and the kings of Aram.

a Or baboons

10:22 *bringing gold, silver, ivory, apes, and peacocks.* The words of Deuteronomy echo in this description, particularly the word "gold": "Also silver and gold [a king] must not acquire in great quantity for himself" (17:17). Note that Solomon's gold is used to ornament buildings on display to courtiers and visiting dignitaries. The remainder of chapter 10, like sections of previous chapters (e.g., 9:10–14), shows Solomon amassing his wealth. Deuteronomy warns against those who exalt themselves, believing that their own efforts have brought them wealth. This self-aggrandizement will come, Deuteronomy warns, "when you have eaten your fill and have built fine houses and live in them . . . and your silver and gold is multiplied"; then the self-impressed will be tempted to forget God (8:12–17).

10:28 *Solomon's import of horses was from Egypt and Kue.* See Deut 17:16, where God warns Israel against acquiring many horses, especially from Egypt. To buy many horses is to build a massive army, a temptation for humans to forget God. To buy horses "from Egypt" is to return to and participate in upholding a place of tyranny and enslavement. 1 & 2 Kings point out the ease with which those who have known exploitation gain power and begin supporting the very patterns of misrule from which God rescued them.

Solomon's Errors

11 King Solomon loved many foreign women along with the daughter of Pharaoh: Moabite, Ammonite, Edomite, Sidonian, and Hittite women, ²from the nations concerning which the LORD had said to the Israelites, "You shall not enter into marriage with them, neither shall they with you; for they will surely incline your heart to follow their gods"; Solomon clung to these in love. ³Among his wives were seven hundred princesses and three hundred concubines; and his wives turned away his heart. ⁴For when Solomon was old, his wives turned away his heart after other gods; and his heart was not true to the LORD his God, as was the heart of his father David. ⁵For Solomon followed Astarte the goddess of the Sidonians, and Milcom the abomination of the Ammonites. ⁶So Solomon did what was evil in the sight of the LORD, and did not completely follow the LORD, as his father David had done. ⁷Then Solomon built a high place for Chemosh the abomination of Moab, and for Molech the abomination of the Ammonites, on the mountain east of Jerusalem. ⁸He did the same for all his foreign wives, who offered incense and sacrificed to their gods.

9 Then the LORD was angry with Solomon, because his heart had turned away from the LORD, the God of Israel, who had appeared to him twice, ¹⁰and had commanded him concerning this matter, that he should not follow other gods; but he did not observe what the LORD commanded. ¹¹Therefore the LORD said to Solomon, "Since this has been your mind and you have not kept my covenant and my statutes that I have commanded you, I will surely tear the kingdom from you and give it

to your servant. ¹²Yet for the sake of your father David I will not do it in your lifetime; I will tear it out of the hand of your son. ¹³I will not, however, tear away the entire kingdom; I will give one tribe to your son, for the sake of my servant David and for the sake of Jerusalem, which I have chosen."

Adversaries of Solomon

14 Then the LORD raised up an adversary against Solomon, Hadad the Edomite; he was of the royal house in Edom. ¹⁵For when David was in Edom, and Joab the commander of the army went up to bury the dead, he killed every male in Edom ¹⁶(for Joab and all Israel remained there six months, until he had eliminated every male in Edom); ¹⁷but Hadad fled to Egypt with some Edomites who were servants of his father. He was a young boy at that time. ¹⁸They set out from Midian and came to Paran; they took people with them from Paran and came to Egypt, to Pharaoh king of Egypt, who gave him a house, assigned him an allowance of food, and gave him land. ¹⁹Hadad found great favor in the sight of Pharaoh, so that he gave him his sister-in-law for a wife, the sister of Queen Tahpenes. ²⁰The sister of Tahpenes gave birth by him to his son Genubath, whom Tahpenes weaned in Pharaoh's house; Genubath was in Pharaoh's house among the children of Pharaoh. ²¹When Hadad heard in Egypt that David slept with his ancestors and that Joab the commander of the army was dead, Hadad said to Pharaoh, "Let me depart, that I may go to my own country." ²²But Pharaoh said to him, "What do you lack with me that you now seek to go to your own country?" And he said, "No, do let me go."

11:2 *Solomon clung to these in love.* The Hebrew words for "cling" and "love" are the words Moses uses in Deuteronomy to describe what should be the devotion of God's people toward God alone (e.g., "love": 6:5; 10:12; "cling" or "hold fast": 13:4; see also Deut 7:3–4; 17:17).

11:7 *Solomon built a high place for Chemosh the abomination of Moab.* For "high place," see note on 3:3. 1 Kings no longer delays open judgment, denouncing Solomon for failing on

the central point of Israel's faith: "Hear, O Israel: the LORD is our God, the LORD alone. You shall love the LORD your God with all your heart, and with all your soul, and with all your might" (Deut 6:4–5).

11:14–22 *Hadad the Edomite.* There are echoes of the story of Moses in the details of Hadad's life. Perhaps Hadad is the Moses of his people, oppressed by Solomon. The story hints that God hears the groans of other peoples and plans their liberation and nationhood too.

23 God raised up another adversary against Solomon,[a] Rezon son of Eliada, who had fled from his master, King Hadadezer of Zobah. 24He gathered followers around him and became leader of a marauding band, after the slaughter by David; they went to Damascus, settled there, and made him king in Damascus. 25He was an adversary of Israel all the days of Solomon, making trouble as Hadad did; he despised Israel and reigned over Aram.

Jeroboam's Rebellion

26 Jeroboam son of Nebat, an Ephraimite of Zeredah, a servant of Solomon, whose mother's name was Zeruah, a widow, rebelled against the king. 27The following was the reason he rebelled against the king. Solomon built the Millo, and closed up the gap in the wall[b] of the city of his father David. 28The man Jeroboam was very able, and when Solomon saw that the young man was industrious he gave him charge over all the forced labor of the house of Joseph. 29About that time, when Jeroboam was leaving Jerusalem, the prophet Ahijah the Shilonite found him on the road. Ahijah had clothed himself with a new garment. The two of them were alone in the open country 30when Ahijah laid hold of the new garment he was wearing and tore it into twelve pieces. 31He then said to Jeroboam: Take for yourself ten pieces; for thus says the LORD, the God of Israel, "See, I am about to tear the kingdom from the hand of Solomon, and will give you ten tribes. 32One tribe will remain his, for the sake of my servant David and for the sake of Jerusalem, the city that I have chosen out of all the tribes of Israel. 33This is

because he has[c] forsaken me, worshiped Astarte the goddess of the Sidonians, Chemosh the god of Moab, and Milcom the god of the Ammonites, and has[c] not walked in my ways, doing what is right in my sight and keeping my statutes and my ordinances, as his father David did. 34Nevertheless I will not take the whole kingdom away from him but will make him ruler all the days of his life, for the sake of my servant David whom I chose and who did keep my commandments and my statutes; 35but I will take the kingdom away from his son and give it to you—that is, the ten tribes. 36Yet to his son I will give one tribe, so that my servant David may always have a lamp before me in Jerusalem, the city where I have chosen to put my name. 37I will take you, and you shall reign over all that your soul desires; you shall be king over Israel. 38If you will listen to all that I command you, walk in my ways, and do what is right in my sight by keeping my statutes and my commandments, as David my servant did, I will be with you, and will build you an enduring house, as I built for David, and I will give Israel to you. 39For this reason I will punish the descendants of David, but not forever." 40Solomon sought therefore to kill Jeroboam; but Jeroboam promptly fled to Egypt, to King Shishak of Egypt, and remained in Egypt until the death of Solomon.

Death of Solomon

41 Now the rest of the acts of Solomon, all that he did as well as his wisdom, are they not

---

a Heb *him*   *b* Heb lacks *in the wall*   *c* Gk Syr Vg: Heb *they have*

11:31 *I am about to tear the kingdom from . . . Solomon.* God now mobilizes Israel's community of resistance (see also 12:1–19). It is telling that Ahijah is from Shiloh, the worship center of the former tribal confederacy where Samuel ministered and where, no doubt, believers in "the old way"—faithfulness to Yahweh alone—still reside. Ahijah is a new Samuel, a king-maker and -breaker whose God tears the kingdom from Solomon's grasp, as happened with Saul (1 Sam 15:27–28). For the first time in 1 Kings, the action moves outside Jerusalem.

11:36 *a lamp . . . where I have chosen to put*

my name. The lamp is a symbol of God's presence and direction (1 Sam 3:3; 2 Sam 22:29; Ps 119:105) as well as of the Davidic dynasty kept alive by God (2 Sam 21:17). Just as these two meanings overlay one another in this symbol, the Davidic dynasty comes to represent God's presence with Israel. God's presence shines through this human presence. Shifting the language ever so slightly, the New Testament extends this symbol to Jesus, the light of the world (John 1:4–5; 8:12), as the descendant of David and divine representative. It then applies this symbol to the Church itself (Matt 5:14–16).

written in the Book of the Acts of Solomon? [42]The time that Solomon reigned in Jerusalem over all Israel was forty years. [43]Solomon slept with his ancestors and was buried in the city of his father David; and his son Rehoboam succeeded him.

The Northern Tribes Secede

12 Rehoboam went to Shechem, for all Israel had come to Shechem to make him king. [2]When Jeroboam son of Nebat heard of it (for he was still in Egypt, where he had fled from King Solomon), then Jeroboam returned from[a] Egypt. [3]And they sent and called him; and Jeroboam and all the assembly of Israel came and said to Rehoboam, [4]"Your father made our yoke heavy. Now therefore lighten the hard service of your father and his heavy yoke that he placed on us, and we will serve you." [5]He said to them, "Go away for three days, then come again to me." So the people went away.

[6] Then King Rehoboam took counsel with the older men who had attended his father Solomon while he was still alive, saying, "How do you advise me to answer this people?" [7]They answered him, "If you will be a servant to this people today and serve them, and speak good words to them when you answer them, then they will be your servants forever." [8]But he disregarded the advice that the older men gave him, and consulted with the young men who had grown up with him and now attended him. [9]He said to them, "What do you advise that we answer this people who have said to me, 'Lighten the yoke that your father put on us'?" [10]The young men who had grown up with him said to him, "Thus you should say to this people who spoke to you, 'Your father made our yoke heavy, but you must lighten it for us'; thus you should say to them, 'My little finger is thicker than my father's loins. [11]Now, where-

as my father laid on you a heavy yoke, I will add to your yoke. My father disciplined you with whips, but I will discipline you with scorpions.'"

[12] So Jeroboam and all the people came to Rehoboam the third day, as the king had said, "Come to me again the third day." [13]The king answered the people harshly. He disregarded the advice that the older men had given him [14]and spoke to them according to the advice of the young men, "My father made your yoke heavy, but I will add to your yoke; my father disciplined you with whips, but I will discipline you with scorpions." [15]So the king did not listen to the people, because it was a turn of affairs brought about by the LORD that he might fulfill his word, which the LORD had spoken by Ahijah the Shilonite to Jeroboam son of Nebat.

[16] When all Israel saw that the king would not listen to them, the people answered the king,

"What share do we have in David?
    We have no inheritance in the son of Jesse.
To your tents, O Israel!
    Look now to your own house,
    O David."

So Israel went away to their tents. [17]But Rehoboam reigned over the Israelites who were living in the towns of Judah. [18]When King Rehoboam sent Adoram, who was taskmaster over the forced labor, all Israel stoned him to death. King Rehoboam then hurriedly mounted his chariot to flee to Jerusalem. [19]So Israel has been in rebellion against the house of David to this day.

First Dynasty: Jeroboam Reigns over Israel

[20] When all Israel heard that Jeroboam had returned, they sent and called him to

a Gk Vg Compare 2 Chr 10.2: Heb lived in

12:1 to Shechem to make him king. Shechem was the first meeting place of the tribal confederacy. Joshua called all Israel to convene at Shechem to hear a reading of the Mosaic covenant and to renew vows to God (Josh 24). Like Shiloh, it is a place that represents old, diehard convictions about tribal freedom

constrained only by this covenant with God (Josh 24:15–16).

12:11 I will add to your yoke. Compare Pharaoh's response to Moses and Aaron (Exod 5:9).

12:18 stoned him to death. See note on 4:6.

the assembly and made him king over all Israel. There was no one who followed the house of David, except the tribe of Judah alone.

21 When Rehoboam came to Jerusalem, he assembled all the house of Judah and the tribe of Benjamin, one hundred eighty thousand chosen troops to fight against the house of Israel, to restore the kingdom to Rehoboam son of Solomon. 22But the word of God came to Shemaiah the man of God: 23Say to King Rehoboam of Judah, son of Solomon, and to all the house of Judah and Benjamin, and to the rest of the people, 24"Thus says the LORD, You shall not go up or fight against your kindred the people of Israel. Let everyone go home, for this thing is from me." So they heeded the word of the LORD and went home again, according to the word of the LORD.

Jeroboam's Golden Calves

25 Then Jeroboam built Shechem in the hill country of Ephraim, and resided there; he went out from there and built Penuel. 26Then Jeroboam said to himself, "Now the kingdom may well revert to the house of David. 27If this people continues to go up to offer sacrifices in the house of the LORD at Jerusalem, the heart of this people will turn again to their master, King Rehoboam of Judah; they will kill me and return to King Rehoboam of Judah." 28So the king took counsel, and made two calves of gold. He said to the people, a "You have gone up to Jerusalem long enough. Here are your gods, O Israel, who brought you up out of the land of Egypt." 29He set one in Bethel, and the other he put in Dan. 30And this thing became a sin, for the people went to worship before the one at Bethel and before the other as far as Dan. b 31He also made houses c on high places, and appointed priests from among all the people, who were not Levites. 32Jeroboam appointed a festival on the fifteenth day of the eighth month like the festival that was in Judah, and he offered sacrifices on the altar; so he did in Bethel, sacrificing to the calves that he had made.

a Gk: Heb to them   b Compare Gk: Heb went to the one as far as Dan   c Gk Vg Compare 13.32: Heb a house

12:19 *So Israel has been in rebellion against the house of David to this day.* The name Israel is now applied to the Northern Kingdom, which will be ruled by Jeroboam. The Southern Kingdom is called Judah.

12:28 *gods . . . who brought you up out of the land of Egypt.* Jeroboam's words resemble the people's words when Aaron presents them with the golden calf (Exod 32:4).

12:32 *high places that he had made.* For "high places," see note on 3:3. The theologians of 1 & 2 Kings condemn Jeroboam for creating a new religious infrastructure. At this point, 1 & 2 Kings hold that faithful worship is carried out in Jerusalem (8:14–21), where God has placed the divine name forever (9:3). Jeroboam's new religious program competes with the Jerusalem Temple. The calves of gold that Jeroboam installs at Bethel call to mind the golden calf in Exod 32:1–4 and the worship of the local god Baal. But many scholars believe that these calves, like the cherubim in the Jerusalem Temple, serve solely as symbolic supports of God's throne. Rivalry between Northern worship sites and the Jerusalem Temple continues throughout 1 & 2 Kings. It adds to the complexity of understanding the text's judgment of worship in the Northern Kingdom. Is this worship wrong because it occurs outside the control of the Jerusalem priesthood or because it involves other divinities? The impetus for the Northern religious institution, Jeroboam's political fears and ambitions (vv 26–27), can lead us to consider the uneasy partnership between faithfulness and ambition in the religious institution.

Responding
12:32 WORSHIP. Jeroboam is portrayed as the ultimate idolater, mimicking the worship of the Lord but offering his sacrifices and his prayers to golden calves. What is one thing you worship with your time, thoughts, and attention—television, sex, food, Web surfing, sports—in place of God? Abstain from your golden calf for one week. Give the time to God instead. At the end of the week, reevaluate your golden calf. Have your thoughts about it changed? *See also* Spiritual Disciplines Index.

And he placed in Bethel the priests of the high places that he had made. 33He went up to the altar that he had made in Bethel on the fifteenth day in the eighth month, in the month that he alone had devised; he appointed a festival for the people of Israel, and he went up to the altar to offer incense.

A Man of God from Judah

13 While Jeroboam was standing by the altar to offer incense, a man of God came out of Judah by the word of the LORD to Bethel 2and proclaimed against the altar by the word of the LORD, and said, "O altar, altar, thus says the LORD: 'A son shall be born to the house of David, Josiah by name; and he shall sacrifice on you the priests of the high places who offer incense on you, and human bones shall be burned on you.' " 3He gave a sign the same day, saying, "This is the sign that the LORD has spoken: 'The altar shall be torn down, and the ashes that are on it shall be poured out.' " 4When the king heard what the man of God cried out against the altar at Bethel, Jeroboam stretched out his hand from the altar, saying, "Seize him!" But the hand that he stretched out against him withered so that he could not draw it back to himself. 5The altar also was torn down, and the ashes poured out from the altar, according to the sign that the man of God had given by the word of the LORD. 6The king said to the man of God, "Entreat now the favor of the LORD your God, and pray for me, so that my hand may be restored to me." So the man of God entreated the LORD; and the king's hand was restored to him, and became as it was before. 7Then the king said to the man of God, "Come home with me and dine, and I will give you a gift." 8But the man of God said to the king, "If you give me half your kingdom, I will not go in with you; nor will I eat food or drink water in this place. 9For thus I was commanded by the word of the LORD: You shall not eat food, or drink water, or return by the way that you came." 10So he went another

way, and did not return by the way that he had come to Bethel.

11 Now there lived an old prophet in Bethel. One of his sons came and told him all that the man of God had done that day in Bethel; the words also that he had spoken to the king, they told to their father. 12Their father said to them, "Which way did he go?" And his sons showed him the way that the man of God who came from Judah had gone. 13Then he said to his sons, "Saddle a donkey for me." So they saddled a donkey for him, and he mounted it. 14He went after the man of God, and found him sitting under an oak tree. He said to him, "Are you the man of God who came from Judah?" He answered, "I am." 15Then he said to him, "Come home with me and eat some food." 16But he said, "I cannot return with you, or go in with you; nor will I eat food or drink water with you in this place; 17for it was said to me by the word of the LORD: You shall not eat food or drink water there, or return by the way that you came." 18Then the other[a] said to him, "I also am a prophet as you are, and an angel spoke to me by the word of the LORD: Bring him back with you into your house so that he may eat food and drink water." But he was deceiving him. 19Then the man of God[a] went back with him, and ate food and drank water in his house.

20 As they were sitting at the table, the word of the LORD came to the prophet who had brought him back; 21and he proclaimed to the man of God who came from Judah, "Thus says the LORD: Because you have disobeyed the word of the LORD, and have not kept the commandment that the LORD your God commanded you, 22but have come back and have eaten food and drunk water in the place of which he said to you, 'Eat no food, and drink no water,' your body shall not come to your ancestral tomb." 23After the man of God[a] had eaten food and had drunk,

a Heb he

13:9 *For thus I was commanded by . . . the LORD.* 1 & 2 Kings contend that power has a way of leeching out integrity. The man of God is not to compromise the message from God by

accepting the king's favor. As Proverbs puts it: "Do not desire the ruler's delicacies, for they are deceptive food" (23:3; see also Dan 1:8–12).

they saddled for him a donkey belonging to the prophet who had brought him back. 24Then as he went away, a lion met him on the road and killed him. His body was thrown in the road, and the donkey stood beside it; the lion also stood beside the body. 25People passed by and saw the body thrown in the road, with the lion standing by the body. And they came and told it in the town where the old prophet lived.

26 When the prophet who had brought him back from the way heard of it, he said, "It is the man of God who disobeyed the word of the LORD; therefore the LORD has given him to the lion, which has torn him and killed him according to the word that the LORD spoke to him." 27Then he said to his sons, "Saddle a donkey for me." So they saddled one, 28and he went and found the body thrown in the road, with the donkey and the lion standing beside the body. The lion had not eaten the body or attacked the donkey. 29The prophet took up the body of the man of God, laid it on the donkey, and brought it back to the city, *a* to mourn and to bury him. 30He laid the body in his own grave; and they mourned over him, saying, "Alas, my brother!" 31After he had buried him, he said to his sons, "When I die, bury me in the grave in which the man of God is buried; lay my bones beside his bones. 32For the saying that he proclaimed by the word of the LORD against the altar in Bethel, and against all the houses of the high

places that are in the cities of Samaria, shall surely come to pass."

33 Even after this event Jeroboam did not turn from his evil way, but made priests for the high places again from among all the people; any who wanted to be priests he consecrated for the high places. 34This matter became sin to the house of Jeroboam, so as to cut it off and to destroy it from the face of the earth.

Judgment on the House of Jeroboam

14 At that time Abijah son of Jeroboam fell sick. 2Jeroboam said to his wife, "Go, disguise yourself, so that it will not be known that you are the wife of Jeroboam, and go to Shiloh; for the prophet Ahijah is there, who said of me that I should be king over this people. 3Take with you ten loaves, some cakes, and a jar of honey, and go to him; he will tell you what shall happen to the child."

4 Jeroboam's wife did so; she set out and went to Shiloh, and came to the house of Ahijah. Now Ahijah could not see, for his eyes were dim because of his age. 5But the LORD said to Ahijah, "The wife of Jeroboam is coming to inquire of you concerning her son; for he is sick. Thus and thus you shall say to her."

When she came, she pretended to be another woman. 6But when Ahijah heard the

a Gk: Heb *he came to the town of the old prophet*

13:24 *a lion met him on the road and killed him.* The story of the man of God's death is enigmatic. Perhaps it is a story of the necessity of living out the divine calling and not being led astray. God's word compels, even as we humans step away from it, particularly when other voices promise us comfort. Perhaps it is a story of God's word, which, when tested, as it seems to be by the old prophet, proves itself authoritative and awe-full—even when this proof means its bearer's death. The fate of Bethel is unmistakably and urgently defined in this death.

13:32 *the saying that he proclaimed . . . shall surely come to pass.* The old prophet and his sons finally recognize in the dead man a brother: one called to speak for God, even at

great cost. Perhaps the old prophet has compromised himself in this place of new royalty and power. But God has now seized even him, and he too prophesies the fall of the North. *high places.* See note on 3:3.

14:1–3 *Abijah son of Jeroboam fell sick.* 1 Kings 13:34, which speaks of the destruction of the house of Jeroboam, is followed immediately by the story of the illness of Jeroboam's son, heir to the throne. The text implies God's behind-the-scenes workings to shape political life. Clearly, the new royal order is not working. The king cannot send for help from his own priests. He sends his wife to Ahijah of Shiloh, but in asking her to disguise herself and take a gift, he seeks a word from God in a manner that is deceitful and manipulative.

sound of her feet, as she came in at the door, he said, "Come in, wife of Jeroboam; why do you pretend to be another? For I am charged with heavy tidings for you. 7Go, tell Jeroboam, 'Thus says the LORD, the God of Israel: Because I exalted you from among the people, made you leader over my people Israel, 8and tore the kingdom away from the house of David to give it to you; yet you have not been like my servant David, who kept my commandments and followed me with all his heart, doing only that which was right in my sight, 9but you have done evil above all those who were before you and have gone and made for yourself other gods, and cast images, provoking me to anger, and have thrust me behind your back; 10therefore, I will bring evil upon the house of Jeroboam. I will cut off from Jeroboam every male, both bond and free in Israel, and will consume the house of Jeroboam, just as one burns up dung until it is all gone. 11Anyone belonging to Jeroboam who dies in the city, the dogs shall eat; and anyone who dies in the open country, the birds of the air shall eat; for the LORD has spoken.' 12Therefore set out, go to your house. When your feet enter the city, the child shall die. 13All Israel shall mourn for him and bury him; for he alone of Jeroboam's family shall come to the grave, because in him there is found something pleasing to the LORD, the God of Israel, in the house of Jeroboam. 14Moreover the LORD will raise up for himself a king over Israel, who shall cut off the house of Jeroboam today, even right now!a 15 "The LORD will strike Israel, as a reed is shaken in the water; he will root up Israel out of this good land that he gave to their ancestors, and scatter them beyond the Euphrates, because they have made their sacred poles,b provoking the LORD to anger. 16He will give Israel up because of the sins of Jeroboam, which he sinned and which he caused Israel to commit."

17 Then Jeroboam's wife got up and went away, and she came to Tirzah. As she came to the threshold of the house, the child died. 18All Israel buried him and mourned for him, according to the word of the LORD, which he spoke by his servant the prophet Ahijah.

Death of Jeroboam

19 Now the rest of the acts of Jeroboam, how he warred and how he reigned, are written in the Book of the Annals of the Kings of Israel. 20The time that Jeroboam reigned was twenty-two years; then he slept with his ancestors, and his son Nadab succeeded him.

Rehoboam Reigns over Judah

21 Now Rehoboam son of Solomon reigned in Judah. Rehoboam was forty-one years old when he began to reign, and he reigned seventeen years in Jerusalem, the city that the LORD had chosen out of all the tribes of Israel, to put his name there. His mother's name was Naamah the Ammonite. 22Judah did what was evil in the sight of the LORD; they provoked him to jealousy with their sins that they committed, more than all that their

a Meaning of Heb uncertain   b Heb Asherim

14:15 *The LORD will . . . scatter them beyond the Euphrates, because they have made their sacred poles.* The phrase "beyond the Euphrates" refers to the deportation of the people of Northern Kingdom, Israel, by Assyria in 722/721 BC. "Sacred poles" (*asherim*) were objects used in worshiping the goddess Asherah, consort to Baal. In Canaanite mythology, divinities of death/barrenness and of life/growth engaged in cosmic battles that explained and brought about the seasons. Rituals, including cultic prostitution, were intended to influence these battles and ensure the return of the rains under the aegis of Baal, god of rain and fertility.

Although these ancient beliefs and practices are long gone today, they invite us to consider what, within our own culture, we lift up as our source of well-being and prosperity.

14:22 *they provoked him to jealousy with their sins.* The idea of God's jealousy goes back to the core assertion of the Mosaic covenant: "I am the LORD your God . . . you shall have no other gods before me" (Deut 5:6–7). Deuteronomy explains: "So be careful not to forget the covenant that the LORD your God made with you, and not to make for yourselves an idol. . . . For the LORD your God is a devouring fire, a jealous God" (4:23–24).

ancestors had done. 23For they also built for themselves high places, pillars, and sacred poles*a* on every high hill and under every green tree; 24there were also male temple prostitutes in the land. They committed all the abominations of the nations that the LORD drove out before the people of Israel.

25 In the fifth year of King Rehoboam, King Shishak of Egypt came up against Jerusalem; 26he took away the treasures of the house of the LORD and the treasures of the king's house; he took everything. He also took away all the shields of gold that Solomon had made; 27so King Rehoboam made shields of bronze instead, and committed them to the hands of the officers of the guard, who kept the door of the king's house. 28As often as the king went into the house of the LORD, the guard carried them and brought them back to the guardroom.

29 Now the rest of the acts of Rehoboam, and all that he did, are they not written in the Book of the Annals of the Kings of Judah? 30There was war between Rehoboam and Jeroboam continually. 31Rehoboam slept with his ancestors and was buried with his ancestors in the city of David. His mother's name was Naamah the Ammonite. His son Abijam succeeded him.

Abijam Reigns over Judah: Idolatry and War

15 Now in the eighteenth year of King Jeroboam son of Nebat, Abijam began to reign over Judah. 2He reigned for three years in Jerusalem. His mother's name was Maacah daughter of Abishalom. 3He committed all the sins that his father did before him; his heart was not true to the LORD his God, like the heart of his father David. 4Nevertheless for David's sake the LORD his God gave him a lamp in Jerusalem, setting up his son after him, and establishing Jerusalem; 5because David did what was right in the sight of the LORD, and did not turn aside from anything that he commanded him all the days of his life, except in the matter of Uriah the Hittite. 6The war begun between Rehoboam and Jeroboam continued all the days of his life. 7The rest of the acts of Abijam, and all that he did, are they not written in the Book of the Annals of the Kings of Judah? There was war between Abijam and Jeroboam. 8Abijam slept with his ancestors, and they buried him in the city of David. Then his son Asa succeeded him.

Asa Reigns over Judah

9 In the twentieth year of King Jeroboam of Israel, Asa began to reign over Judah; 10he reigned forty-one years in Jerusalem. His mother's name was Maacah daughter of Abishalom. 11Asa did what was right in the sight of the LORD, as his father David had done. 12He put away the male temple prostitutes out of the land, and removed all the idols that his ancestors had made. 13He also removed his mother Maacah from being queen mother, because she had made an abominable image for Asherah; Asa cut down her image and burned it at the Wadi Kidron. 14But the

a Heb *Asherim*

14:25 *King Shishak . . . came up against Jerusalem.* Shishak I of Egypt invaded and plundered both Israel and Judah around 918 BC. Although God is not mentioned in verses 25–28, the preceding indictment of Judah (vv 21–24) permits us to infer God's hidden hand in the invasion of Shishak.

15:4 *God gave him a lamp in Jerusalem.* According to the text, the Davidic throne continues (see note on 11:36) only because God remembers David and, by implication, God's promise to David.

15:9–24 *Asa began to reign.* At first we are told that Asa rules rightly (although he neglects

some details), consolidating worship in Jerusalem (he leaves the "high places"). But then we learn that he uses Temple treasures to pay Damascus for an "alliance" (same Hebrew word also translated "covenant") and security (v 19). He also conscripts laborers from all Judah in the name of security (v 22). The odd detail about Asa's diseased feet (v 23) suggests a king who cannot quite walk rightly in the paths of God. This report on Asa suggests the difficulty of sorting out right from wrong in the political realm, especially in morally uncertain circumstances. Nonetheless, the text also asserts God's right to make this assessment.

high places were not taken away. Nevertheless the heart of Asa was true to the LORD all his days. ¹⁵He brought into the house of the LORD the votive gifts of his father and his own votive gifts—silver, gold, and utensils.

Alliance with Aram against Israel

16 There was war between Asa and King Baasha of Israel all their days. ¹⁷King Baasha of Israel went up against Judah, and built Ramah, to prevent anyone from going out or coming in to King Asa of Judah. ¹⁸Then Asa took all the silver and the gold that were left in the treasures of the house of the LORD and the treasures of the king's house, and gave them into the hands of his servants. King Asa sent them to King Ben-hadad son of Tabrimmon son of Hezion of Aram, who resided in Damascus, saying, ¹⁹"Let there be an alliance between me and you, like that between my father and your father: I am sending you a present of silver and gold; go, break your alliance with King Baasha of Israel, so that he may withdraw from me." ²⁰Ben-hadad listened to King Asa, and sent the commanders of his armies against the cities of Israel. He conquered Ijon, Dan, Abel-beth-maacah, and all Chinneroth, with all the land of Naphtali. ²¹When Baasha heard of it, he stopped building Ramah and lived in Tirzah. ²²Then King Asa made a proclamation to all Judah, none was exempt: they carried away the stones of Ramah and its timber, with which Baasha had been building; with them King Asa built Geba of Benjamin and Mizpah. ²³Now the rest of all the acts of Asa, all his power, all that he did, and the cities that he built, are they not written in the Book of the Annals of the Kings of Judah? But in his old age he was diseased in his feet. ²⁴Then Asa slept with his ancestors, and was buried with his ancestors in the city of his father David; his son Jehoshaphat succeeded him.

Nadab Reigns over Israel

25 Nadab son of Jeroboam began to reign over Israel in the second year of King Asa of Judah; he reigned over Israel two years. ²⁶He did what was evil in the sight of the LORD, walking in the way of his ancestor and in the sin that he caused Israel to commit.

27 Baasha son of Ahijah, of the house of Issachar, conspired against him; and Baasha struck him down at Gibbethon, which belonged to the Philistines; for Nadab and all Israel were laying siege to Gibbethon. ²⁸So Baasha killed Nadab*ᵃ* in the third year of King Asa of Judah, and succeeded him. ²⁹As soon as he was king, he killed all the house of Jeroboam; he left to the house of Jeroboam not one that breathed, until he had destroyed it, according to the word of the LORD that he spoke by his servant Ahijah the Shilonite—³⁰because of the sins of Jeroboam that he committed and that he caused Israel to commit, and because of the anger to which he provoked the LORD, the God of Israel.

31 Now the rest of the acts of Nadab, and all that he did, are they not written in the Book of the Annals of the Kings of Israel? ³²There was war between Asa and King Baasha of Israel all their days.

Second Dynasty: Baasha Reigns over Israel

33 In the third year of King Asa of Judah, Baasha son of Ahijah began to reign over all Israel at Tirzah; he reigned twenty-four years. ³⁴He did what was evil in the sight of the LORD, walking in the way of Jeroboam and in the sin that he caused Israel to commit.

16 The word of the LORD came to Jehu son of Hanani against Baasha, saying, ²"Since I exalted you out of the dust and made you leader over my people Israel, and you have walked in the way of Jeroboam, and have caused my people Israel to sin, provoking me to anger with their sins, ³therefore, I will consume Baasha and his house, and I will make your house like the house of Jeroboam son of Nebat. ⁴Anyone belonging to Baasha who dies in the city the dogs shall eat; and anyone of his who dies in the field the birds of the air shall eat."

5 Now the rest of the acts of Baasha, what he did, and his power, are they not written in

a Heb *him*

15:13–14 *image for Asherah . . . the high places.* See notes on 14:15; 3:3.

the Book of the Annals of the Kings of Israel? 6Baasha slept with his ancestors, and was buried at Tirzah; and his son Elah succeeded him. 7Moreover the word of the LORD came by the prophet Jehu son of Hanani against Baasha and his house, both because of all the evil that he did in the sight of the LORD, provoking him to anger with the work of his hands, in being like the house of Jeroboam, and also because he destroyed it.

Elah Reigns over Israel

8 In the twenty-sixth year of King Asa of Judah, Elah son of Baasha began to reign over Israel in Tirzah; he reigned two years. 9But his servant Zimri, commander of half his chariots, conspired against him. When he was at Tirzah, drinking himself drunk in the house of Arza, who was in charge of the palace at Tirzah, 10Zimri came in and struck him down and killed him, in the twenty-seventh year of King Asa of Judah, and succeeded him.

11 When he began to reign, as soon as he had seated himself on his throne, he killed all the house of Baasha; he did not leave him a single male of his kindred or his friends. 12Thus Zimri destroyed all the house of Baasha, according to the word of the LORD, which he spoke against Baasha by the prophet Jehu— 13because of all the sins of Baasha and the sins of his son Elah that they committed, and that they caused Israel to commit, provoking the LORD God of Israel to anger with their idols. 14Now the rest of the acts of Elah, and all that he did, are they not written in the Book of the Annals of the Kings of Israel?

Third Dynasty: Zimri Reigns over Israel

15 In the twenty-seventh year of King Asa of Judah, Zimri reigned seven days in Tirzah. Now the troops were encamped against Gibbethon, which belonged to the Philistines, 16and the troops who were encamped heard

it said, "Zimri has conspired, and he has killed the king"; therefore all Israel made Omri, the commander of the army, king over Israel that day in the camp. 17So Omri went up from Gibbethon, and all Israel with him, and they besieged Tirzah. 18When Zimri saw that the city was taken, he went into the citadel of the king's house; he burned down the king's house over himself with fire, and died— 19because of the sins that he committed, doing evil in the sight of the LORD, walking in the way of Jeroboam, and for the sin that he committed, causing Israel to sin. 20Now the rest of the acts of Zimri, and the conspiracy that he made, are they not written in the Book of the Annals of the Kings of Israel?

Fourth Dynasty: Omri Reigns over Israel

21 Then the people of Israel were divided into two parts; half of the people followed Tibni son of Ginath, to make him king, and half followed Omri. 22But the people who followed Omri overcame the people who followed Tibni son of Ginath; so Tibni died, and Omri became king. 23In the thirty-first year of King Asa of Judah, Omri began to reign over Israel; he reigned for twelve years, six of them in Tirzah.

Samaria the New Capital

24 He bought the hill of Samaria from Shemer for two talents of silver; he fortified the hill, and called the city that he built, Samaria, after the name of Shemer, the owner of the hill.

25 Omri did what was evil in the sight of the LORD; he did more evil than all who were before him. 26For he walked in all the way of Jeroboam son of Nebat, and in the sins that he caused Israel to commit, provoking the LORD, the God of Israel, to anger by their idols. 27Now the rest of the acts of Omri that he did, and the power that he showed, are

---

16:21–28 *Omri began to reign.* Omri is dismissed in only eight verses as having done more evil than his predecessors (v 25). Historical records indicate, however, that Omri ruled successfully, forming important alliances, extending the Northern Kingdom's rule, and building the strategically located capital city of Samaria, excavation of which demonstrates its wealth. Long after Omri and his brief dynasty were gone, Assyrian rulers continued to describe the Northern Kingdom as "the land of the house of Omri." But the usual measures of success do not matter to the theologians of 1 & 2 Kings.

they not written in the Book of the Annals of the Kings of Israel? 28 Omri slept with his ancestors, and was buried in Samaria; his son Ahab succeeded him.

Ahab Reigns over Israel

29 In the thirty-eighth year of King Asa of Judah, Ahab son of Omri began to reign over Israel; Ahab son of Omri reigned over Israel in Samaria twenty-two years. 30 Ahab son of Omri did evil in the sight of the LORD more than all who were before him.

Ahab Marries Jezebel and Worships Baal

31 And as if it had been a light thing for him to walk in the sins of Jeroboam son of Nebat, he took as his wife Jezebel daughter of King Ethbaal of the Sidonians, and went and served Baal, and worshiped him. 32 He erected an altar for Baal in the house of Baal, which he built in Samaria. 33 Ahab also made a sacred pole.*a* Ahab did more to provoke the anger of the LORD, the God of Israel, than had all the kings of Israel who were before him. 34 In his days Hiel of Bethel built Jericho; he laid its foundation at the cost of Abiram his firstborn, and set up its gates at the cost of his youngest son Segub, according to the

word of the LORD, which he spoke by Joshua son of Nun.

Elijah Predicts a Drought

17 Now Elijah the Tishbite, of Tishbe*b* in Gilead, said to Ahab, "As the LORD the God of Israel lives, before whom I stand, there shall be neither dew nor rain these years, except by my word." 2 The word of the LORD came to him, saying, 3 "Go from here and turn eastward, and hide yourself by the Wadi Cherith, which is east of the Jordan. 4 You shall drink from the wadi, and I have commanded the ravens to feed you there." 5 So he went and did according to the word of the LORD; he went and lived by the Wadi Cherith, which is east of the Jordan. 6 The ravens brought him bread and meat in the morning, and bread and meat in the evening; and he drank from the wadi. 7 But after a while the wadi dried up, because there was no rain in the land.

The Widow of Zarephath

8 Then the word of the LORD came to him, saying, 9 "Go now to Zarephath, which belongs to Sidon, and live there; for I have commanded a widow there to feed you."

a Heb *Asherah*   *b* Gk: Heb *of the settlers*

16:34 *by Joshua son of Nun.* See Josh 6:26.

17:1 *neither dew nor rain . . . except by my word.* The previous chapters have focused on the death and disorder of kings and royal settings. Now the text breaks open with renewed vitality. A powerful new presence, Elijah the prophet of God, comes to upset the status quo. Elijah (meaning "Yahweh is God") stands in the royal city of Samaria with its temple to the rain god Baal and announces that Yahweh, the God of Israel, alone sends and stays rain. According to 1 & 2 Kings, the earth's vigor mirrors the faithfulness of the nation and its leaders (see also Deut 11:13–17; 28:15–24).

17:4 *drink from the wadi . . . the ravens [will] feed you there.* As with the man of God in chapter 13, Elijah must be careful about his food and drink. He is sent away from places of royal power and provision to places that seem to promise little: a brook with ravens and a Phoenician town with a widow (v 9). God's system of provision is effective, if contrary to

what we would expect, because it falls outside the geographic and cultural centers we have been dealing with in the narrative.

Responding
17:4 SOLITUDE. Can you even imagine a place so remote that only the ravens are available to feed you? Yet that was God's hiding place for Elijah. Think of the most remote place in your town or office building, somewhere you can't imagine running into any other people. Go there with your Bible. Use the Spiritual Disciplines Index to find other verses about solitude and spend half an hour studying and reflecting about the role of solitude in the human soul. *See also* Spiritual Disciplines Index.

17:9 *a widow there to feed you.* God sends Elijah into the heart of the land of Baal, where the God of Israel—not Baal—rules the earth and sends drought. See also Luke 4:24–26.

ELIJAH

Open to God's Care

Selected Scriptures: *1 Kings 17–21*

Two extraordinary periods in the Old Testament were marked by multiple miracles—the time of Moses and the exodus and the years of the prophets Elijah and Elisha. Just as Moses spent forty years tending sheep before leading the Israelites from Egypt and then spent time alone with God throughout the trek in the desert, Elijah also spent important time in solitude before and during his role as messenger of God.

His story opens with his prophecy to Israel's King Ahab, a worshiper of the idol Baal: "As the LORD the God of Israel lives, before whom I stand, there shall be neither dew nor rain these years, except by my word" (1 Kings 17:1). He then gets a personal instruction from God: "Go . . . and hide yourself by the Wadi Cherith" (17:3). And so God withheld both dew and rain, yet he cared for Elijah by bringing him to a stream and providing ravens to feed him with bread and meat, morning and evening.

When the wadi dried up, God told Elijah to seek out a certain widow who would feed him (17:9). God kept filling her jar of meal and her jug of oil so that she, her son, and Elijah could eat. When her son died of illness, she regretted her kindness to Elijah and blamed him for her son's death. Through prayer, Elijah brought him back to life (17:20–22).

After many days, God again called Elijah to go to the king. Elijah announced a contest between God and the false god of Ahab, Baal. After the prophets of Baal failed to bring fire to an altar sacrifice, Elijah prayed and God rained down fire, consuming the burnt offering, wood, stones, and even the water surrounding the altar. God's power had been displayed, and the drought ended (chap 18).

Elijah then learned that Ahab's wife, Jezebel, was seeking to take his life. Once more, he went into the wilderness for refuge. He was afraid. God met him there with food and water and an angel who encouraged him: "Get up and eat, otherwise the journey will be too much for you" (19:7). Elijah traveled forty days until he came to a cave, where God again met him. Elijah confessed that he was feeling afraid and alone: "I alone am left, and they are seeking my life, to take it away" (19:10). To show his presence, after a great wind, earthquake, and fire, God came in silence, instructing Elijah to anoint two new kings, and Elisha as his own successor. Elisha became his disciple and was present when Elijah was taken by divine horse and chariot into heaven (2 Kings 2:11).

Elijah lived a fantastic life, seeing God's might firsthand as few others have. Yet even Elijah needed times of solitude, where God could meet him alone, giving refreshment and guidance. The fifteenth-century Dutch theologian Thomas à

PROFILE

PROFILE: ELIJAH

Kempis lived out such a commitment to solitude, and he encouraged followers of Christ to imitate Jesus by doing the same. In his devotional classic *The Imitation of Christ*, he writes: "The person who wants to arrive at interiority and spirituality has to leave the crowd behind and spend some time with Jesus. Nobody's comfortable in public unless he's spent a good deal of time in the quiet of his home." Kempis goes on to warn against losing balance in our service to God: "Better to lie still in one's cubicle and worry about one's spiritual welfare. Worse, to roam the streets a wonder-worker for others to the neglect of one's own spiritual life."

God instructs us, as he did Elijah, "Go and hide yourself by the stream." He is there to give us food and drink and rest. He will guide us in the way we should go.

Personal Reflection

- Can you recall a time when you saw God's power at work in your life? Since that time have you ever doubted God's care for you? What place do, or could, times of solitude have in steadying you in your journey with God?
- What things keep you from making solitude a more regular part of your life?
- Does your busyness fulfill you? How can you invite God to remove your loneliness and give you, instead, fulfillment through solitude?

[10]So he set out and went to Zarephath. When he came to the gate of the town, a widow was there gathering sticks; he called to her and said, "Bring me a little water in a vessel, so that I may drink." [11]As she was going to bring it, he called to her and said, "Bring me a morsel of bread in your hand." [12]But she said, "As the LORD your God lives, I have nothing baked, only a handful of meal in a jar, and a little oil in a jug; I am now gathering a couple of sticks, so that I may go home and prepare it for myself and my son, that we may eat it, and die." [13]Elijah said to her, "Do not be afraid; go and do as you have said; but first make me a little cake of it and bring it to me, and afterwards make something for yourself and your son. [14]For thus says the LORD the God of Israel: The jar of meal will not be emptied and the jug of oil will not fail until the day that the LORD sends rain on the earth." [15]She went and did as Elijah said, so that she as well as he and her household ate for many days. [16]The jar of meal was not emptied, neither did the jug of oil fail, according to the word of the LORD that he spoke by Elijah.

Elijah Revives the Widow's Son

17 After this the son of the woman, the mistress of the house, became ill; his illness was so severe that there was no breath left in him. [18]She then said to Elijah, "What have you against me, O man of God? You have come to me to bring my sin to remembrance, and to cause the death of my son!" [19]But he said to her, "Give me your son." He took him from her bosom, carried him up into the upper chamber where he was lodging, and laid him on his own bed. [20]He cried out to the LORD, "O LORD my God, have you brought

17:12 *that we may eat it, and die.* In the midst of this miracle story, we get an intimate look at life outside the palace. While kings vie for power and wealth, a widow and her son struggle for their daily bread, like most of the people of the land, no matter what their country. They subsist on baked cakes, not the vast repasts of kings (4:22–23). When the king chooses wrongly, the humble live with and die by the consequences.

calamity even upon the widow with whom I am staying, by killing her son?" 21Then he stretched himself upon the child three times, and cried out to the LORD, "O LORD my God, let this child's life come into him again." 22The LORD listened to the voice of Elijah; the life of the child came into him again, and he revived. 23Elijah took the child, brought him down from the upper chamber into the house, and gave him to his mother; then Elijah said, "See, your son is alive." 24So the woman said to Elijah, "Now I know that you are a man of God, and that the word of the LORD in your mouth is truth."

Elijah's Message to Ahab

18 After many days the word of the LORD came to Elijah, in the third year of the drought,*a* saying, "Go, present yourself to Ahab; I will send rain on the earth." 2So Elijah went to present himself to Ahab. The famine was severe in Samaria. 3Ahab summoned Obadiah, who was in charge of the palace. (Now Obadiah revered the LORD greatly; 4when Jezebel was killing off the prophets of the LORD, Obadiah took a hundred prophets, hid them fifty to a cave, and provided them with bread and water.) 5Then Ahab said to Obadiah, "Go through the land to all the springs of water and to all the wadis; perhaps we may find grass to keep the horses and mules alive, and not lose some of the animals." 6So they divided the land between them to pass through it; Ahab went in one direction by himself, and Obadiah went in another direction by himself.

7 As Obadiah was on the way, Elijah met him; Obadiah recognized him, fell on his face, and said, "Is it you, my lord Elijah?" 8He answered him, "It is I. Go, tell your lord that Elijah is here." 9And he said, "How have I sinned, that you would hand your servant over to Ahab, to kill me? 10As the LORD your God lives, there is no nation or kingdom to which my lord has not sent to seek you; and when they would say, 'He is not here,' he would require an oath of the kingdom or nation, that they had not found you. 11But now you say, 'Go, tell your lord that Elijah is here.' 12As soon as I have gone from you, the spirit of the LORD will carry you I know not where; so, when I come and tell Ahab and he cannot find you, he will kill me, although I your servant have revered the LORD from my youth. 13Has it not been told my lord what I did when Jezebel killed the prophets of the LORD, how I hid a hundred of the LORD's prophets fifty to a cave, and provided them with bread and water? 14Yet now you say, 'Go, tell your lord that Elijah is here'; he will surely kill me." 15Elijah said, "As the LORD of hosts lives,

a Heb lacks *of the drought*

17:17–24 *See, your son is alive.* Into a hopeless situation, God brings new life. As in the psalms of Israel, the lament of the faithful— honest, pained, and urgent—moves God to action (Pss 13; 22; 28). This transformation of death to life is also a foretaste of the good news of the Church: that the Easter of Jesus Christ is the Easter of all who fall into deathly situations and rise to new life through God's power (cf. Mark 7:24–30).

18:4 *Obadiah . . . provided them with bread and water.* Obadiah is an example of a covenant keeper who survives under the noses of the powerful while subverting their policies. As we will see with Elijah, power seeks to destroy those who disrupt the status quo. Like the ravens and the widow of Zarephath, Obadiah feeds God's prophets (the Hebrew term translated "feed" in 17:4, 9 is the same as that translated "provided" in 18:4, 13).

18:5 *perhaps we may . . . not lose some of the animals.* Ahab is not concerned about the well-being of his people, who are suffering from severe famine (v 2), but worries about his army's horses and mules. While the queen kills (Hebrew, "cuts off") God's prophets (v 4), Ahab ensures that the livestock do not die (Hebrew, "be cut off"). The North is an example of a kingdom whose policies are horribly askew, protecting the military while sacrificing the citizenry.

18:10 *there is no . . . kingdom to which my lord has not sent to seek you.* Ahab has looked in all the wrong places: royal courts. The locus of true power has been the home of one whom the court considers a nobody, a widow. Ahab simply cannot fathom the ways of God.

before whom I stand, I will surely show myself to him today." 16So Obadiah went to meet Ahab, and told him; and Ahab went to meet Elijah.

17 When Ahab saw Elijah, Ahab said to him, "Is it you, you troubler of Israel?" 18He answered, "I have not troubled Israel; but you have, and your father's house, because you have forsaken the commandments of the LORD and followed the Baals. 19Now therefore have all Israel assemble for me at Mount Carmel, with the four hundred fifty prophets of Baal and the four hundred prophets of Asherah, who eat at Jezebel's table."

Elijah's Triumph over the Priests of Baal

20 So Ahab sent to all the Israelites, and assembled the prophets at Mount Carmel. 21Elijah then came near to all the people, and said, "How long will you go limping with two different opinions? If the LORD is God, follow him; but if Baal, then follow him." The people did not answer him a word. 22Then Elijah said to the people, "I, even I only, am left a prophet of the LORD; but Baal's prophets number four hundred fifty. 23Let two bulls be given to us; let them choose one bull for themselves, cut it in pieces, and lay it on the wood, but put no fire to it; I will prepare the other bull and lay it on the wood, but put no fire to it. 24Then you call on the name of your god and I will call on the name of the LORD; the god who answers by fire is indeed God." All the people answered, "Well spoken!" 25Then Elijah said to the prophets of Baal, "Choose for yourselves one bull and prepare it first, for you are many; then call on the name of your god, but put no fire to it." 26So they took the bull that was given them, pre-

pared it, and called on the name of Baal from morning until noon, crying, "O Baal, answer us!" But there was no voice, and no answer. They limped about the altar that they had made. 27At noon Elijah mocked them, saying, "Cry aloud! Surely he is a god; either he is meditating, or he has wandered away, or he is on a journey, or perhaps he is asleep and must be awakened." 28Then they cried aloud and, as was their custom, they cut themselves with swords and lances until the blood gushed out over them. 29As midday passed, they raved on until the time of the offering of the oblation, but there was no voice, no answer, and no response.

30 Then Elijah said to all the people, "Come closer to me"; and all the people came closer to him. First he repaired the altar of the LORD that had been thrown down; 31Elijah took twelve stones, according to the number of the tribes of the sons of Jacob, to whom the word of the LORD came, saying, "Israel shall be your name"; 32with the stones he built an altar in the name of the LORD. Then he made a trench around the altar, large enough to contain two measures of seed. 33Next he put the wood in order, cut the bull in pieces, and laid it on the wood. He said, "Fill four jars with water and pour it on the burnt offering and on the wood." 34Then he said, "Do it a second time"; and they did it a second time. Again he said, "Do it a third time"; and they did it a third time, 35so that the water ran all around the altar, and filled the trench also with water.

36 At the time of the offering of the oblation, the prophet Elijah came near and said, "O LORD, God of Abraham, Isaac, and Israel, let it be known this day that you are God in

---

18:19 *prophets of Baal and . . . Asherah, who eat at Jezebel's table.* While the prophet has eaten at the Phoenician widow's table, these prophets eat at a Phoenician queen's table (see notes on 13:9; 17:4). The attention to tables and food in 1 & 2 Kings raises the question of where we find our (literal and figurative) sources of nourishment and how these sources influence our faith and action. The New Testament picks up this theme in various "food stories," including that of the Last Supper. As in 1 &

2 Kings, to eat at the table of the Bread of Life (John 6:51) is an act of subversion when the status quo does not support the God of Israel. Many voices beckon us to tables of death in hopes that God's message can be sedated and the powers that be left unchanged. (For Baal and Asherah, see note on 14:15.)

18:31 *Israel shall be your name.* Elijah alludes to the story of Jacob's return to Bethel (Gen 35:1–15).

AHAB

Addicted to Sin

Selected Scriptures: *1 Kings 16:29–22:40*

Scripture's account of Ahab begins: "Ahab son of Omri did evil in the sight of the LORD more than all who were before him" (1 Kings 16:30). In many ways, Ahab's story is familiar: a powerful ruler continues the evil practices instituted before him, marries one who encourages further evil, and has significant opportunity to repent and turn to God, but continues in disobedience, bringing much suffering to his nation and his own untimely death.

The story is all too common, yet the specifics are anything but common. Despite all he saw God doing, Ahab remained bent toward sin. Ahab witnessed one of God's most awesome displays of power. During a drought the prophet Elijah and the prophets of Baal both prepared altars. The prophets of Baal called on their god—a fertility god believed to send both rain and fire—to answer with fire on the altar. A day of dancing, shrieking, and drawing their own blood produced nothing (18:29). At the time of evening sacrifice, Elijah readied his altar to God and instructed the people three times to pour large jars of water on the offering and the wood. Then he prayed to God, "Answer me, so that this people may know that you, O LORD, are God, and that you have turned their hearts back" (18:37). Fire fell and consumed the offering, the altar, and even the surrounding stones and water. The people fell on their faces before God (18:39), yet Ahab seems to have remained unmoved, and the event only invoked the anger of his wife, Jezebel, who was zealously committed to Baal.

Later God gave Ahab two great victories in war against the Arameans. Again, God wanted Ahab to "know that [he was] the LORD" (20:13). In all he witnessed, Ahab softened only once in repentance. Hearing Elijah's prophecy of disaster to come, Ahab humbled himself before God, fasting and tearing his clothes. God responded by reserving much of the disaster for Ahab's sons (21:29). Yet Ahab's character did not change. He didn't rid Israel of the idolatry he had embraced. He continued to consult false prophets and to spurn the prophets of God. He died an ignoble death, and all God foretold came to pass.

As Ahab's life demonstrates, sin can gain an increasing hold on our soul. Especially when we are allied with another drawn to evil, sin acts to numb our spirit to the truths of God. The church father John Chrysostom wrote and preached passionately in the fourth century about such dangers of sin. Troubled by the apathy he saw in the clergy, he exhorted believers in Christ to resist the return to sinful lives. "Tears come into my eyes," he said, "when I think of . . . how little we have changed after our baptism, yielding ourselves to sin, going back to the oldness we had before. . . . But we must see that it is not for a few days that we are required to change, but

PROFILE: AHAB

rather for a whole lifetime. The youth of grace must not lead to the old age of sin. The love of money, the slavery to wrong desires, or any sin whatsoever, makes us grow old in soul and body. Our souls become rheumatic, distorted, decayed, and tottering with many sins. . . . The sinful lose their ability to see, to hear, and to speak, for they spew forth words that are foul."

Yet just as sin becomes habitual, so holy living can become habitual. Chrysostom encouraged Christians to turn away from sin for one day, then two, "then twenty, then a hundred, then your whole life." And just as sin numbs the spirit to the things of God, so obedience opens the spirit to God's transforming power. No sinner is beyond change. Even Ahab could have turned from evil and given his life over to God to realize restoration. We too can turn from the habits of sin, building instead habits of holiness. As we work to instill these habits, we'll find God instilling in us a nature bent toward him.

Personal Reflection

- Do you have a relationship similar to that of Ahab and Jezebel, in which a person close to you encourages you toward sin? Do you sense God guiding you to make a change in this relationship?
- What kind of idolatry is alive in your life? Money? Reputation? Career? Appearance? Comfort? In what ways does this idolatry cause you to turn your back on God or his people?

Israel, that I am your servant, and that I have done all these things at your bidding. [37] Answer me, O LORD, answer me, so that this people may know that you, O LORD, are God, and that you have turned their hearts back." [38] Then the fire of the LORD fell and consumed the burnt offering, the wood, the stones, and the dust, and even licked up the water that was in the trench. [39] When all the people saw it, they fell on their faces and said, "The LORD indeed is God; the LORD indeed is God." [40] Elijah said to them, "Seize the prophets of Baal; do not let one of them escape." Then they seized them; and Elijah brought them down to the Wadi Kishon, and killed them there.

The Drought Ends

41 Elijah said to Ahab, "Go up, eat and drink; for there is a sound of rushing rain." [42] So Ahab went up to eat and to drink. Elijah went up to the top of Carmel; there he bowed himself down upon the earth and put his face between his knees. [43] He said to his servant, "Go up now, look toward the sea." He went up and looked, and said, "There is nothing." Then he said, "Go again seven times." [44] At the seventh time he said, "Look, a little cloud no bigger than a person's hand is rising out of the sea." Then he said, "Go say to Ahab, 'Harness your chariot and go down before the rain stops you.' " [45] In a little while the heavens grew black with clouds and wind; there was a heavy rain. Ahab rode off and went to Jezreel. [46] But the hand of the LORD was on Elijah; he girded up his loins and ran in front of Ahab to the entrance of Jezreel.

Elijah Flees from Jezebel

19 Ahab told Jezebel all that Elijah had done, and how he had killed all the prophets with the sword. [2] Then Jezebel sent a messenger to Elijah, saying, "So may the gods do to me, and more also, if I do not make your life like the life of one of them by this time tomorrow." [3] Then he was afraid; he got up and fled for his life, and came to Beer-sheba, which belongs to Judah; he left his servant there.

4 But he himself went a day's journey into the wilderness, and came and sat down under

a solitary broom tree. He asked that he might die: "It is enough; now, O LORD, take away my life, for I am no better than my ancestors." 5Then he lay down under the broom tree and fell asleep. Suddenly an angel touched him and said to him, "Get up and eat." 6He looked, and there at his head was a cake baked on hot stones, and a jar of water. He ate and drank, and lay down again. 7The angel of the LORD came a second time, touched him, and said, "Get up and eat, otherwise the journey will be too much for you." 8He got up, and ate and drank; then he went in the strength of that food forty days and forty nights to Horeb the mount of God. 9At that place he came to a cave, and spent the night there.

Then the word of the LORD came to him, saying, "What are you doing here, Elijah?"

10He answered, "I have been very zealous for the LORD, the God of hosts; for the Israelites have forsaken your covenant, thrown down your altars, and killed your prophets with the sword. I alone am left, and they are seeking my life, to take it away."

Elijah Meets God at Horeb

11 He said, "Go out and stand on the mountain before the LORD, for the LORD is about to pass by." Now there was a great wind, so strong that it was splitting mountains and breaking rocks in pieces before the LORD, but the LORD was not in the wind; and after the wind an earthquake, but the LORD was not in the earthquake; 12and after the earthquake a fire, but the LORD was not in the fire; and after the fire a sound of sheer silence. 13When Elijah heard it, he wrapped

---

19:4 for I am no better than my ancestors. Fear is power's propagandist, teaching that security comes only in relinquishing truth or in giving up the struggle and fleeing. Elijah's humanity is revealed as we witness his deep discouragement after so great a demonstration of God's power. His example shows that we can confess our weaknesses, discouragements, and fears to the Lord, who can both hear them and minister to us regarding them (and work through us despite them).

19:8 to Horeb the mount of God. Elijah travels to the mountain where Moses saw God and where God revealed the covenant and law to Moses (Exod 33:17–34:28). Horeb is Sinai in other biblical traditions.

19:10 I alone am left. Elijah lays out his issues before God. His lament is honest, even if out of touch with reality. Obadiah has mentioned one hundred prophets saved (18:13). The experience on Mt. Carmel has caused many to seek God (18:39). Yet Elijah feels alone and beleaguered. His deep discouragement suggests the strength that comes in remaining connected to the community of faith, especially in the dangerous and uncompromising service of taking on worldly power. It also suggests the temptation of self-aggrandizement in this service.

Responding
19:10 FELLOWSHIP. Elijah obeyed the Lord's commands, even when they

required solitude and other kinds of sacrifice. But the loneliness of his life as a prophet is beginning to wear on him. What kind of benefits do you receive each day from the people you work or interact with? Consider this week taking at least two or three of them aside and thanking them for their gift of fellowship. See also Spiritual Disciplines Index.

19:11–12 and after the fire a sound of sheer silence. Elijah found that Yahweh was not in the earthquake, wind, or fire, but in the silence. This stunning event stands in direct contrast to the experience of Moses on Sinai. Moses experienced divine fireworks and Elijah experienced "sheer silence," but both experienced God. This is a vital teaching for us about the with-God life. God may come to us in the dramatic and the spectacular or in the hidden and the ordinary. However and whenever and wherever God comes, we are to hear and obey.

Responding
19:12 SILENCE. Dallas Willard writes, "Silence is frightening because it strips us as nothing else does, throwing us upon the stark realities of our life." When's the last time you sat in utter silence? What do you learn about yourself by turning off all the background noise of your everyday life? See also Spiritual Disciplines Index.

his face in his mantle and went out and stood at the entrance of the cave. Then there came a voice to him that said, "What are you doing here, Elijah?" 14He answered, "I have been very zealous for the LORD, the God of hosts; for the Israelites have forsaken your covenant, thrown down your altars, and killed your prophets with the sword. I alone am left, and they are seeking my life, to take it away." 15Then the LORD said to him, "Go, return on your way to the wilderness of Damascus; when you arrive, you shall anoint Hazael as king over Aram. 16Also you shall anoint Jehu son of Nimshi as king over Israel; and you shall anoint Elisha son of Shaphat of Abel-meholah as prophet in your place. 17Whoever escapes from the sword of Hazael, Jehu shall kill; and whoever escapes from the sword of Jehu, Elisha shall kill. 18Yet I will leave seven thousand in Israel, all the knees that have not bowed to Baal, and every mouth that has not kissed him."

Elisha Becomes Elijah's Disciple

19 So he set out from there, and found Elisha son of Shaphat, who was plowing. There were twelve yoke of oxen ahead of him, and he was with the twelfth. Elijah passed by him and threw his mantle over him. 20He left the oxen, ran after Elijah, and said, "Let me kiss my father and my mother, and then I will follow you." Then Elijah*a* said to him, "Go back again; for what have I done to you?" 21He returned from following him, took the yoke of oxen, and slaughtered them; using the equipment from the oxen, he boiled their flesh, and gave it to the people, and they ate. Then he set out and followed Elijah, and became his servant.

Ahab's Wars with the Arameans

20 King Ben-hadad of Aram gathered all his army together; thirty-two kings were with him, along with horses and chariots. He marched against Samaria, laid siege to it, and attacked it. 2Then he sent messengers into the city to King Ahab of Israel, and said to him: "Thus says Ben-hadad: 3Your silver and gold are mine; your fairest wives and children also are mine." 4The king of Israel answered, "As you say, my lord, O king, I am yours, and all that I have." 5The messengers came again and said: "Thus says Ben-hadad: I sent to you, saying, 'Deliver to me your silver and gold, your wives and children'; 6nevertheless I will send my servants to you tomorrow about this time, and they shall search your house and the houses of your servants, and lay hands on whatever pleases them,*b* and take it away."

7 Then the king of Israel called all the elders of the land, and said, "Look now! See how this man is seeking trouble; for he sent to me for my wives, my children, my silver, and my gold; and I did not refuse him." 8Then all the elders and all the people said to him, "Do not listen or consent." 9So he said to the messengers of Ben-hadad, "Tell my lord the king: All that you first demanded of your servant I will do; but this thing I cannot do." The messengers left and brought him word again. 10Ben-hadad sent to him and said, "The gods do so to me, and more also, if the dust of Samaria will provide a handful for each of the people who follow me." 11The king of Israel answered, "Tell him: One who puts on armor should not brag like one who takes it off." 12When Ben-hadad heard this message—now he had been drinking with the kings in the booths—he said to his men,

a Heb *he*   *b* Gk Syr Vg: Heb *you*

19:15–18 *Then the LORD said to him.* God does not remonstrate with Elijah, but addresses the prophet's weariness and sense of isolation. God tenderly meets his needs. Elijah learns that he will soon have an apprentice to replace him and that seven thousand in Israel remain faithful to God. He also learns that God has more work for him. Like Moses, Elijah moves forward under

the impelling force of God and the covenant.

19:19–21 *Elisha . . . became his servant.* Here we see the call of God in action, one servant of God bringing another into service. The slaughter of the oxen represents Elisha's break with his old life. See Jesus' even more urgent call to discipleship in Matt 8:19–22.

"Take your positions!" And they took their positions against the city.

Prophetic Opposition to Ahab

13 Then a certain prophet came up to King Ahab of Israel and said, "Thus says the LORD, Have you seen all this great multitude? Look, I will give it into your hand today; and you shall know that I am the LORD." 14Ahab said, "By whom?" He said, "Thus says the LORD, By the young men who serve the district governors." Then he said, "Who shall begin the battle?" He answered, "You." 15Then he mustered the young men who served the district governors, two hundred thirty-two; after them he mustered all the people of Israel, seven thousand.

16 They went out at noon, while Ben-hadad was drinking himself drunk in the booths, he and the thirty-two kings allied with him. 17The young men who served the district governors went out first. Ben-hadad had sent out scouts,*a* and they reported to him, "Men have come out from Samaria." 18He said, "If they have come out for peace, take them alive; if they have come out for war, take them alive."

19 But these had already come out of the city: the young men who served the district governors, and the army that followed them. 20Each killed his man; the Arameans fled and Israel pursued them, but King Ben-hadad of Aram escaped on a horse with the cavalry. 21The king of Israel went out, attacked the horses and chariots, and defeated the Arameans with a great slaughter.

22 Then the prophet approached the king of Israel and said to him, "Come, strengthen yourself, and consider well what you have to do; for in the spring the king of Aram will come up against you."

The Arameans Are Defeated

23 The servants of the king of Aram said to him, "Their gods are gods of the hills, and so they were stronger than we; but let us fight against them in the plain, and surely we shall be stronger than they. 24Also do this: remove the kings, each from his post, and put commanders in place of them; 25and muster an army like the army that you have lost, horse for horse, and chariot for chariot; then we will fight against them in the plain, and surely we shall be stronger than they." He heeded their voice, and did so.

26 In the spring Ben-hadad mustered the Arameans and went up to Aphek to fight against Israel. 27After the Israelites had been mustered and provisioned, they went out to engage them; the people of Israel encamped opposite them like two little flocks of goats, while the Arameans filled the country. 28A man of God approached and said to the king of Israel, "Thus says the LORD: Because the Arameans have said, 'The LORD is a god of the hills but he is not a god of the valleys,' therefore I will give all this great multitude into your hand, and you shall know that I am the LORD." 29They encamped opposite one another seven days. Then on the seventh day the battle began; the Israelites killed one hundred thousand Aramean foot soldiers in one day. 30The rest fled into the city of Aphek; and the wall fell on twenty-seven thousand men that were left.

Ben-hadad also fled, and entered the city to hide. 31His servants said to him, "Look, we have heard that the kings of the house of Israel are merciful kings; let us put sackcloth around our waists and ropes on our heads, and go out to the king of Israel; perhaps he will spare your life." 32So they tied sackcloth around their waists, put ropes on their heads, went to the king of Israel, and said, "Your servant Ben-hadad says, 'Please let me live.'" And he said, "Is he still alive? He is my brother." 33Now the men were watching for an omen; they quickly took it up from him and said, "Yes, Ben-hadad is your brother." Then he said, "Go and bring him." So Ben-

a Heb lacks *scouts*

20:13 *you shall know that I am the LORD.* The phrase "I am the LORD" hearkens back to the exodus experience (Exod 7:17; 10:2; 14:4). It clearly conveys the message that God is at the heart of this military venture, bringing about the divine will in this matter. The political landscape will shift because of divine intention.

hadad came out to him; and he had him come up into the chariot. 34 Ben-hadad*a* said to him, "I will restore the towns that my father took from your father; and you may establish bazaars for yourself in Damascus, as my father did in Samaria." The king of Israel responded,*b* "I will let you go on those terms." So he made a treaty with him and let him go.

A Prophet Condemns Ahab

35 At the command of the LORD a certain member of a company of prophets*c* said to another, "Strike me!" But the man refused to strike him. 36 Then he said to him, "Because you have not obeyed the voice of the LORD, as soon as you have left me, a lion will kill you." And when he had left him, a lion met him and killed him. 37 Then he found another man and said, "Strike me!" So the man hit him, striking and wounding him. 38 Then the prophet departed, and waited for the king along the road, disguising himself with a bandage over his eyes. 39 As the king passed by, he cried to the king and said, "Your servant went out into the thick of the battle; then a soldier turned and brought a man to me, and said, 'Guard this man; if he is missing, your life shall be given for his life, or else

you shall pay a talent of silver.' 40 While your servant was busy here and there, he was gone." The king of Israel said to him, "So shall your judgment be; you yourself have decided it." 41 Then he quickly took the bandage away from his eyes. The king of Israel recognized him as one of the prophets. 42 Then he said to him, "Thus says the LORD, 'Because you have let the man go whom I had devoted to destruction, therefore your life shall be for his life, and your people for his people.' " 43 The king of Israel set out toward home, resentful and sullen, and came to Samaria.

Naboth's Vineyard

21 Later the following events took place: Naboth the Jezreelite had a vineyard in Jezreel, beside the palace of King Ahab of Samaria. 2 And Ahab said to Naboth, "Give me your vineyard, so that I may have it for a vegetable garden, because it is near my house; I will give you a better vineyard for it; or, if it seems good to you, I will give you its value in money." 3 But Naboth said to Ahab, "The LORD forbid that I should give you my ancestral inheritance." 4 Ahab went home resentful and sullen because of what Naboth the

---

a Heb *He*   *b* Heb lacks *The king of Israel*
responded   *c* Heb *of the sons of the prophets*

20:35 *a company of prophets.* The Hebrew reads "sons of the prophets," a phrase understood to mean one of the schools of prophets. The first mention of these bands is in 1 Sam 10:5–13. These prophets lived in community, often with an elder prophet ("master," 2 Kings 2:3; "father," 2:12), some traveling (1 Sam 10:5–13), others associated with particular cities (2 Kings 2:3–5), still others affiliated with court and Temple (1 Kings 22:5–6).

20:42 *your life shall be for his life.* The largesse of Ahab's letting Ben-hadad go (v 34) is radically reinterpreted. The prophet's desire for Ben-hadad's destruction comes from the rules of engagement for holy war, understood as war ultimately fought by God (Deut 20). In a holy war, gains of war belong exclusively to God as sacrifice. One purpose of this rule is to maintain the purity of God's people by destroying other influences. The pragmatic ploy of turning one day's mortal enemies into the next day's

bedfellows has no place. In verse 31, the Hebrew root word for "merciful" is the same word used to describe the "steadfast love" that God has for Israel and that God desires from Israel (8:23). Ahab has practiced this loyal love with his enemy, forgetting love for God (see also 1 Sam 15:10–33).

21:3 *my ancestral inheritance.* In Joshua, as the descendants of freed Israelite slaves enter Canaan, God, true owner of the land, grants them an inheritance of land (Josh 13–14), and they become essentially stewards of this land. Thus, a plot of land should remain within a family entrusted with it, and this ancestral land should not be stolen (Deut 19:14; 27:17; Lev 25:10, 13–14, 23–25). The royal concept of land as a resource that can be acquired and used at will (e.g., Solomon's districts in 1 Kings 4) undercuts the ancient tribal understanding of land ownership.

Jezreelite had said to him; for he had said, "I will not give you my ancestral inheritance." He lay down on his bed, turned away his face, and would not eat.

5 His wife Jezebel came to him and said, "Why are you so depressed that you will not eat?" [6]He said to her, "Because I spoke to Naboth the Jezreelite and said to him, 'Give me your vineyard for money; or else, if you prefer, I will give you another vineyard for it'; but he answered, 'I will not give you my vineyard.' " [7]His wife Jezebel said to him, "Do you now govern Israel? Get up, eat some food, and be cheerful; I will give you the vineyard of Naboth the Jezreelite."

8 So she wrote letters in Ahab's name and sealed them with his seal; she sent the letters to the elders and the nobles who lived with Naboth in his city. [9]She wrote in the letters, "Proclaim a fast, and seat Naboth at the head of the assembly; [10]seat two scoundrels opposite him, and have them bring a charge against him, saying, 'You have cursed God and the king.' Then take him out, and stone him to death." [11]The men of his city, the elders and the nobles who lived in his city, did as Jezebel had sent word to them. Just as it was written in the letters that she had sent to them, [12]they proclaimed a fast and seated Naboth at the head of the assembly. [13]The two scoundrels came in and sat opposite him; and the scoundrels brought a charge against Naboth, in the presence of the people, saying, "Naboth cursed God and the king." So they took him outside the city, and stoned him to death. [14]Then they sent to Jezebel, saying, "Naboth has been stoned; he is dead."

15 As soon as Jezebel heard that Naboth had been stoned and was dead, Jezebel said to Ahab, "Go, take possession of the vineyard of Naboth the Jezreelite, which he refused to give you for money; for Naboth is not alive, but dead." [16]As soon as Ahab heard that Naboth was dead, Ahab set out to go down to the vineyard of Naboth the Jezreelite, to take possession of it.

Elijah Pronounces God's Sentence

17 Then the word of the LORD came to Elijah the Tishbite, saying: [18]Go down to meet King Ahab of Israel, who rules[a] in Samaria; he is now in the vineyard of Naboth, where he has gone to take possession. [19]You shall say to him, "Thus says the LORD: Have you killed, and also taken possession?" You shall say to him, "Thus says the LORD: In the place where dogs licked up the blood of Naboth, dogs will also lick up your blood."

20 Ahab said to Elijah, "Have you found me, O my enemy?" He answered, "I have found you. Because you have sold yourself to do what is evil in the sight of the LORD, [21]I will bring disaster on you; I will consume you, and will cut off from Ahab every male, bond or free, in Israel; [22]and I will make your house like the house of Jeroboam son of Nebat, and like the house of Baasha son of Ahijah, because you have provoked me to anger and have caused Israel to sin. [23]Also concerning Jezebel the LORD said, 'The dogs shall eat Jezebel within the bounds of Jezreel.' [24]Anyone belonging to Ahab who dies in the city the dogs shall eat; and anyone of his who dies in the open country the birds of the air shall eat."

25 (Indeed, there was no one like Ahab, who sold himself to do what was evil in the sight of the LORD, urged on by his wife Jezebel. [26]He acted most abominably in going after idols, as the Amorites had done, whom the LORD drove out before the Israelites.)

27 When Ahab heard those words, he tore his clothes and put sackcloth over his bare flesh; he fasted, lay in the sackcloth, and went about dejectedly. [28]Then the word of the LORD came to Elijah the Tishbite: [29]"Have you seen how Ahab has humbled himself

a Heb who is

21:8–14 *Proclaim a fast . . . and stone him to death.* A fast, used to indicate repentance (1 Sam 7:6), becomes a means of committing evil. The elders and nobles of Jezreel offer no wisdom to the assembly (Deut 19:11–12), only complicity in a murder and cover-up. Two witnesses, required to secure justice (Deut 19:15), secure the execution of an innocent man. Power can make a mockery of the religious, political, and judicial systems of a nation.

before me? Because he has humbled himself before me, I will not bring the disaster in his days; but in his son's days I will bring the disaster on his house."

Joint Campaign with Judah against Aram

22 For three years Aram and Israel continued without war. ²But in the third year King Jehoshaphat of Judah came down to the king of Israel. ³The king of Israel said to his servants, "Do you know that Ramoth-gilead belongs to us, yet we are doing nothing to take it out of the hand of the king of Aram?" ⁴He said to Jehoshaphat, "Will you go with me to battle at Ramoth-gilead?" Jehoshaphat replied to the king of Israel, "I am as you are; my people are your people, my horses are your horses."

5 But Jehoshaphat also said to the king of Israel, "Inquire first for the word of the LORD." ⁶Then the king of Israel gathered the prophets together, about four hundred of them, and said to them, "Shall I go to battle against Ramoth-gilead, or shall I refrain?" They said, "Go up; for the LORD will give it into the hand of the king." ⁷But Jehoshaphat said, "Is there no other prophet of the LORD here of whom we may inquire?" ⁸The king of Israel said to Jehoshaphat, "There is still one other by whom we may inquire of the LORD, Micaiah son of Imlah; but I hate him, for he never prophesies anything favorable about me, but only disaster." Jehoshaphat said, "Let the king not say such a thing." ⁹Then the king of Israel summoned an officer and said, "Bring

quickly Micaiah son of Imlah." ¹⁰Now the king of Israel and King Jehoshaphat of Judah were sitting on their thrones, arrayed in their robes, at the threshing floor at the entrance of the gate of Samaria; and all the prophets were prophesying before them. ¹¹Zedekiah son of Chenaanah made for himself horns of iron, and he said, "Thus says the LORD: With these you shall gore the Arameans until they are destroyed." ¹²All the prophets were prophesying the same and saying, "Go up to Ramoth-gilead and triumph; the LORD will give it into the hand of the king."

Micaiah Predicts Failure

13 The messenger who had gone to summon Micaiah said to him, "Look, the words of the prophets with one accord are favorable to the king; let your word be like the word of one of them, and speak favorably." ¹⁴But Micaiah said, "As the LORD lives, whatever the LORD says to me, that I will speak."

15 When he had come to the king, the king said to him, "Micaiah, shall we go to Ramoth-gilead to battle, or shall we refrain?" He answered him, "Go up and triumph; the LORD will give it into the hand of the king." ¹⁶But the king said to him, "How many times must I make you swear to tell me nothing but the truth in the name of the LORD?" ¹⁷Then Micaiah ᵃ said, "I saw all Israel scattered on the mountains, like sheep that have no shepherd; and the LORD said, 'These have

a Heb *he*

Responding
21:27–29 FASTING. Ahab's humbling himself before the Lord through fasting was enough to make God postpone his judgment. Surely this is a lesson to us about how God views such discipline. This week consider fasting from one meal with a specific thought—a prayer request or an issue on which you need guidance—in mind. *See also* Spiritual Disciplines Index.

21:29 *but in his son's days I will bring the disaster on his house.* 1 & 2 Kings do not hold an inflexible understanding of the Mosaic covenant. God has mercy even for Ahab.

Nonetheless, the text will not let go of the idea that evil will have its recompense.

22:7 *Is there no other prophet of the LORD here?* Jehoshaphat has heard the prophets on the court payroll. Now he asks for a "prophet of the LORD"—someone who lives free and clear of the royal dole and diet. See note on 18:19.

22:14 *whatever the LORD says . . . that I will speak.* Here Micaiah gives a good definition of what it means to be a prophet. Although many are willing to speak what people want to hear, Micaiah shows that deep down people notice an authentic voice for God. The authenticity of God's message can break through our barriers so that we hear the word of the Lord.

no master; let each one go home in peace.' "
¹⁸The king of Israel said to Jehoshaphat, "Did I not tell you that he would not prophesy anything favorable about me, but only disaster?"

19 Then Micaiah *a* said, "Therefore hear the word of the Lord: I saw the Lord sitting on his throne, with all the host of heaven standing beside him to the right and to the left of him. ²⁰And the Lord said, 'Who will entice Ahab, so that he may go up and fall at Ramoth-gilead?' Then one said one thing, and another said another, ²¹until a spirit came forward and stood before the Lord, saying, 'I will entice him.' ²²'How?' the Lord asked him. He replied, 'I will go out and be a lying spirit in the mouth of all his prophets.' Then the Lord *a* said, 'You are to entice him, and you shall succeed; go out and do it.' ²³So you see, the Lord has put a lying spirit in the mouth of all these your prophets; the Lord has decreed disaster for you."

24 Then Zedekiah son of Chenaanah came up to Micaiah, slapped him on the cheek, and said, "Which way did the spirit of the Lord pass from me to speak to you?" ²⁵Micaiah replied, "You will find out on that day when you go in to hide in an inner chamber." ²⁶The king of Israel then ordered, "Take Micaiah, and return him to Amon the governor of the city and to Joash the king's son, ²⁷and say, 'Thus says the king: Put this fellow in prison, and feed him on reduced rations of bread and water until I come in peace.' " ²⁸Micaiah said, "If you return in peace, the Lord has not spoken by me." And he said, "Hear, you peoples, all of you!"

Defeat and Death of Ahab

29 So the king of Israel and King Jehoshaphat of Judah went up to Ramoth-gilead. ³⁰The king of Israel said to Jehoshaphat, "I will disguise myself and go into battle, but you wear your robes." So the king of Israel disguised himself and went into battle. ³¹Now the king of Aram had commanded the thirty-two captains of his chariots, "Fight with no one small or great, but only with the king of Israel." ³²When the captains of the chariots saw Jehoshaphat, they said, "It is surely the king of Israel." So they turned to fight against him; and Jehoshaphat cried out. ³³When the captains of the chariots saw that it was not the king of Israel, they turned back from pursuing him. ³⁴But a certain man drew his bow and unknowingly struck the king of Israel between the scale armor and the breastplate; so he said to the driver of his chariot, "Turn around, and carry me out of the battle, for I am wounded." ³⁵The battle grew hot that day, and the king was propped up in his chariot facing the Arameans, until at evening he died; the blood from the wound had flowed into the bottom of the chariot. ³⁶Then about sunset a shout went through the army, "Every man to his city, and every man to his country!"

37 So the king died, and was brought to Samaria; they buried the king in Samaria. ³⁸They washed the chariot by the pool of Samaria; the dogs licked up his blood, and the prostitutes washed themselves in it, *b* according to the word of the Lord that he had spoken. ³⁹Now the rest of the acts of Ahab, and all that he did, and the ivory house that he built, and all the cities that he built, are they not written in the Book of the Annals of the Kings of Israel? ⁴⁰So Ahab slept with his ancestors; and his son Ahaziah succeeded him.

Jehoshaphat Reigns over Judah

41 Jehoshaphat son of Asa began to reign over Judah in the fourth year of King Ahab of

a Heb *he*   *b* Heb lacks *in it*

22:19 *with all the host of heaven standing beside him.* The throne room of Samaria is populated by the obsequious, but God's throne room is populated by the creative who come up with an idea that is clearly "out of the box." God will use all parties to point to and bring about Ahab's fall: those who think they know what is happening (vv 11–12), those who know nothing (v 34), and those who truly know (v 17). The resolve of God bends all to its course.

22:38 *according to the word of the Lord.* Once again, the narrators of 1 & 2 Kings assert the immense sway of God on the public life of the kingdom. The word of God has been spoken—and Ahab lies dead.

Israel. 42Jehoshaphat was thirty-five years old when he began to reign, and he reigned twenty-five years in Jerusalem. His mother's name was Azubah daughter of Shilhi. 43He walked in all the way of his father Asa; he did not turn aside from it, doing what was right in the sight of the LORD; yet the high places were not taken away, and the people still sacrificed and offered incense on the high places. 44Jehoshaphat also made peace with the king of Israel.

45 Now the rest of the acts of Jehoshaphat, and his power that he showed, and how he waged war, are they not written in the Book of the Annals of the Kings of Judah? 46The remnant of the male temple prostitutes who were still in the land in the days of his father Asa, he exterminated.

47 There was no king in Edom; a deputy was king. 48Jehoshaphat made ships of the Tarshish type to go to Ophir for gold; but they did not go, for the ships were wrecked at Ezion-geber. 49Then Ahaziah son of Ahab said to Jehoshaphat, "Let my servants go with your servants in the ships," but Jehoshaphat was not willing. 50Jehoshaphat slept with his ancestors and was buried with his ancestors in the city of his father David; his son Jehoram succeeded him.

Ahaziah Reigns over Israel

51 Ahaziah son of Ahab began to reign over Israel in Samaria in the seventeenth year of King Jehoshaphat of Judah; he reigned two years over Israel. 52He did what was evil in the sight of the LORD, and walked in the way of his father and mother, and in the way of Jeroboam son of Nebat, who caused Israel to sin. 53He served Baal and worshiped him; he provoked the LORD, the God of Israel, to anger, just as his father had done.

2 KINGS

Because 1 & 2 Kings were, originally, an undivided work, the concerns of 1 Kings continue through 2 Kings. Like 1 Kings, 2 Kings is interested in the accustomed places of power—courts, palaces, and royal sanctuaries—and in the usual powerful people—kings, queens, and courtiers. But it also continues to recognize that *true* power is found in out-of-the-way places and unexpected people. (See the introduction to 1 Kings.)

Looming Threats

In 2 Kings, the theme of security plays an increasingly important role. For good reason. Both the Northern Kingdom, Israel, and the Southern Kingdom, Judah, face mounting threats as the chapters unfold. There are internal threats, particularly for the Northern Kingdom, whose succession history is bloody. There are external threats from neighbors like Aram (Syria) and from distant empires. Egypt sends its armies north again and again, trying to regain control over the region. Around 745 BC, the Assyrian Empire mobilizes its immense army and begins a stranglehold on the Fertile Crescent that includes the destruction of the Northern Kingdom (722/721 BC). Waiting in the wings is the Neo-Babylonian Empire, which decimates the Assyrians (605 BC)—and Judah (597, 587 BC).

The Security of Kings

In facing these considerable threats, the kings of 1 & 2 Kings labor to shore up their lines of defense. They build massive armies, form alliances, and pay enormous bribes. But military might does not win the battles of 1 & 2 Kings. With the power of God, one man alone, Elisha, triumphs over the army of Aram (2 Kings 6:8–23). And the Assyrian army disappears in the night without the deployment of a single Judean soldier (1 Kings 19:35). Nor are alliances and treaties always helpful. At

---

*See also "The With-God Life" essays for this section of the Bible, "The People of God as a Nation,"
pp. 391–96, "The People of God in Rebellion," pp. 975–79, and
"The People of God in Exile," pp. 1171–74.)*

---

times they put God's people into the very hands of those who ultimately destroy them (2 Kings 16:5–9). Bribes do not buy compassion or fidelity either. When Hezekiah strips the Temple to pay off Sennacherib, he finds the Assyrian army at his doorstep just the same (2 Kings 18:13–17). The stories of 2 Kings suggest these attempts at security are, at best, arrogant. Truly, there is "no hidin' place down here."

The Security of God

Throughout 1 & 2 Kings are reminders that God alone is the security of Israel. At the dedication of the Temple, Solomon reminds the people that it was God who delivered Israel from slavery in Egypt (1 Kings 8:16) and keeps "covenant and steadfast love" with God's servants (8:23). God is the mighty deliverer of Israel and the mighty cause of its continued existence—God alone.

When an Assyrian official arrogantly proclaims that Sennacherib is more powerful than all the conquered nations and their conquered gods, God retorts to this king: "By your messengers you have mocked the Lord, and you have said, 'With *my* many chariots *I* have gone up the heights of the mountains, to the far recesses of Lebanon, *I* felled its tallest cedars, . . *I* entered its farthest retreat, . . *I* dug wells and drank foreign waters, *I* dried up with the sole of my foot all the streams of Egypt.' Have you not heard that *I* determined it long ago?" (2 Kings 19:23–25, emphasis added). Unknowingly, Sennacherib serves God.

Human arrogance, Israelite or Assyrian, flies in the face of a central profession of 1 & 2 Kings: that God plays the decisive role in human history. To believe or behave otherwise is to mock God and to inflate humankind. The kings of the Northern and Southern Kingdoms trust in their own schemes and reject God, who has secured Israel all along. The theologians of 1 & 2 Kings announce that, in response, God has set in motion the very threats that these mighty kings, in all their (puny) power, have been unable to defeat.

Interestingly, those who recognize God's weighty role in history are the vulnerable—widows and orphans, hungry prophets, a king on his deathbed—who realize that they have no power to save their own lives. They have nowhere else to turn but to God. The close of 2 Kings suggests that this humble band now includes the exiles—powerless, with nowhere else to turn, waiting for their Deliverer.

Reading 1 & 2 Kings Today

To read 1 & 2 Kings today is to recognize our own anxious world—a threatening place, where amassing might and wealth to shore up lines of defense is the order of the day. The sober message of this ancient text is hard to hear: all our configurations of power, tended with such care and at such cost, cannot save us. Human power is a brittle illusion: Solomon's Israel, Omri's Northern Kingdom, Azariah's Judah, Sennacherib's Assyria—all gone.

Instead, these ancient and severe texts call the People of God, as individuals and as communities, to daring belief and life. In a world that finds no place for the divine, 1 & 2 Kings proclaim God's presence, not easily explained, but certain. They call on the People of God to trust in this mysterious but resolute God, not in human power in all its expressions—political, economic, judicial, and so forth. At the same time, they assert that God's purposes are worked out in these very arenas of human power.

With this complex treatment of God's ways in the world, 1 & 2 Kings give no road maps for how to live out trust in the face of threat. But they suggest that a life that recognizes and confesses vulnerability is a life of well-being and power through God. This is a life that sends the People of God *to God* for wisdom and for security—and that is the main message of these books. It is a life that has room for such seemingly weak and trusting acts as prayer and prophecy. And perhaps the most dangerous suggestion, it is a life that involves releasing our tight grip on all our arrangements for power so that God may inaugurate hopeful newness.

For the Church, this is a familiar message. It is the witness of the cross, ever challenging, ever compelling.

—*Rebecca J. Kruger Gaudino*

Elijah Denounces Ahaziah

1 After the death of Ahab, Moab rebelled against Israel.

2 Ahaziah had fallen through the lattice in his upper chamber in Samaria, and lay injured; so he sent messengers, telling them, "Go, inquire of Baal-zebub, the god of Ekron, whether I shall recover from this injury." 3But the angel of the LORD said to Elijah the Tishbite, "Get up, go to meet the messengers of the king of Samaria, and say to them, 'Is it because there is no God in Israel that you are going to inquire of Baal-zebub, the god of Ekron?' 4Now therefore thus says the LORD, 'You shall not leave the bed to which you have gone, but you shall surely die.' " So Elijah went.

5 The messengers returned to the king, who said to them, "Why have you returned?" 6They answered him, "There came a man to meet us, who said to us, 'Go back to the king who sent you, and say to him: Thus says the LORD: Is it because there is no God in Israel that you are sending to inquire of Baal-zebub, the god of Ekron? Therefore you shall not leave the bed to which you have gone, but

you shall surely die.' " 7He said to them, "What sort of man was he who came to meet you and told you these things?" 8They answered him, "A hairy man, with a leather belt around his waist." He said, "It is Elijah the Tishbite."

9 Then the king sent to him a captain of fifty with his fifty men. He went up to Elijah, who was sitting on the top of a hill, and said to him, "O man of God, the king says, 'Come down.' " 10But Elijah answered the captain of fifty, "If I am a man of God, let fire come down from heaven and consume you and your fifty." Then fire came down from heaven, and consumed him and his fifty.

11 Again the king sent to him another captain of fifty with his fifty. He went up[a] and said to him, "O man of God, this is the king's order: Come down quickly!" 12But Elijah answered them, "If I am a man of God, let fire come down from heaven and consume you and your fifty." Then the fire of God came down from heaven and consumed him and his fifty.

13 Again the king sent the captain of a third fifty with his fifty. So the third captain

a Gk Compare verses 9, 13: Heb *He answered*

1:2 *Go, inquire of Baal-zebub.* Baal-zebub means "lord of the flies" and may be a reworking of Baal-zebul ("exalted lord" or "lord

of the heavens"). In the New Testament, this deity's name becomes one of the names for Satan (Mark 3:22–23).

of fifty went up, and came and fell on his knees before Elijah, and entreated him, "O man of God, please let my life, and the life of these fifty servants of yours, be precious in your sight. 14Look, fire came down from heaven and consumed the two former captains of fifty men with their fifties; but now let my life be precious in your sight." 15Then the angel of the LORD said to Elijah, "Go down with him; do not be afraid of him." So he set out and went down with him to the king, 16and said to him, "Thus says the LORD: Because you have sent messengers to inquire of Baal-zebub, the god of Ekron,—is it because there is no God in Israel to inquire of his word?—therefore you shall not leave the bed to which you have gone, but you shall surely die."

Death of Ahaziah

17 So he died according to the word of the LORD that Elijah had spoken. His brother,[a] Jehoram succeeded him as king in the second year of King Jehoram son of Jehoshaphat of Judah, because Ahaziah had no son. 18Now the rest of the acts of Ahaziah that he did, are they not written in the Book of the Annals of the Kings of Israel?

Elijah Ascends to Heaven

2 Now when the LORD was about to take Elijah up to heaven by a whirlwind, Elijah and Elisha were on their way from Gilgal. 2Elijah said to Elisha, "Stay here; for the LORD has sent me as far as Bethel." But Elisha said, "As the LORD lives, and as you yourself live, I will not leave you." So they went down to Bethel. 3The company of prophets[b] who were in Bethel came out to Elisha, and said to him, "Do you know that today the LORD will take your master away from you?" And he said, "Yes, I know; keep silent."

4 Elijah said to him, "Elisha, stay here; for the LORD has sent me to Jericho." But he said, "As the LORD lives, and as you yourself live, I will not leave you." So they came to Jericho. 5The company of prophets[b] who were at Jericho drew near to Elisha, and said to him, "Do you know that today the LORD will take your master away from you?" And he answered, "Yes, I know; be silent."

6 Then Elijah said to him, "Stay here; for the LORD has sent me to the Jordan." But he said, "As the LORD lives, and as you yourself live, I will not leave you." So the two of them went on. 7Fifty men of the company of prophets[b] also went, and stood at some distance from them, as they both were standing by the Jordan. 8Then Elijah took his mantle and rolled it up, and struck the water; the water was parted to the one side and to the other, until the two of them crossed on dry ground.

9 When they had crossed, Elijah said to Elisha, "Tell me what I may do for you, before

a Gk Syr: Heb lacks *His brother*   b Heb *sons of the prophets*

1:17 *the word of the LORD that Elijah had spoken.* The long arm of the king has been unable to control Elijah as it did the two captains and their dutiful soldiers, who believed in "the king's order" (v 11). In the end, the king takes orders from the prophet. "You shall surely die" (v 16) is promptly followed by "So he died according to the word of the LORD." God is sovereign, beyond royal decrees.

2:1–14 *Elijah and Elisha were on their way from Gilgal.* 2 Kings drops the report of royal succession to pick up another succession story: that of Elijah's departure and Elisha's receiving of Elijah's mantle. Once again, the text leaves the scene of royal failure and disaster to take us to a scene alive with the news of a new divine

initiative. The text suggests that God continues to put into play initiatives that can break open patterns of defeat and disappointment. God's interests include how an important ministry will continue after the departure of its leader.

2:3 *The company of prophets.* See note on 1 Kings 20:35. Elisha represents the teachings of those who, like his mentor Elijah, value the old religious traditions of Israel (the worship of Yahweh, God of Israel, alone) and the old political traditions (the egalitarian vision of old Israel). The text gets at the importance of communities that can discern faithfulness in public life and policy. From these communities, God calls forth prophets. God forms communities that sustain and sharpen those faithful to their Lord.

I am taken from you." Elisha said, "Please let me inherit a double share of your spirit." 10He responded, "You have asked a hard thing; yet, if you see me as I am being taken from you, it will be granted you; if not, it will not." 11As they continued walking and talking, a chariot of fire and horses of fire separated the two of them, and Elijah ascended in a whirlwind into heaven. 12Elisha kept watching and crying out, "Father, father! The chariots of Israel and its horsemen!" But when he could no longer see him, he grasped his own clothes and tore them in two pieces.

Elisha Succeeds Elijah

13 He picked up the mantle of Elijah that had fallen from him, and went back and stood on the bank of the Jordan. 14He took the mantle of Elijah that had fallen from him, and struck the water, saying, "Where is the LORD, the God of Elijah?" When he had struck the water, the water was parted to the one side and to the other, and Elisha went over. 15 When the company of prophets a who were at Jericho saw him at a distance, they declared, "The spirit of Elijah rests on Elisha." They came to meet him and bowed to the

ground before him. 16They said to him, "See now, we have fifty strong men among your servants; please let them go and seek your master; it may be that the spirit of the LORD has caught him up and thrown him down on some mountain or into some valley." He responded, "No, do not send them." 17But when they urged him until he was ashamed, he said, "Send them." So they sent fifty men who searched for three days but did not find him. 18When they came back to him (he had remained at Jericho), he said to them, "Did I not say to you, Do not go?"

Elisha Performs Miracles

19 Now the people of the city said to Elisha, "The location of this city is good, as my lord sees; but the water is bad, and the land is unfruitful." 20He said, "Bring me a new bowl, and put salt in it." So they brought it to him. 21Then he went to the spring of water and threw the salt into it, and said, "Thus says the LORD, I have made this water wholesome; from now on neither death nor miscarriage shall come from it." 22So the water has been whole-

a Heb sons of the prophets

2:8 *crossed on dry ground.* Like Moses and Joshua, both of whom parted waters to lead God's people to new life (Exod 14:21–31; Josh 3:7–17), Elijah and Elisha (v 14) have come to lead Israel out of bondage and into new life under the covenant. God uses past divine acts to inform God's present work, allowing people to grasp more readily the divine purposes for the present.

2:9 *a double share of your spirit.* Elisha asks for the spirit (Hebrew, *ruah*) of Elijah! In Old Testament terms, the *ruah* is not an individual soul or spirit. Rather, it is the creative energy of God: the creative "wind" that broods over the waters of chaos (Gen 1:1–2) and the breath of life from God (Ps 104:29–30). It is the vital element of life, a dynamic, uncontained expression of God's power, often called the "spirit of the LORD" (Judg 3:10; 1 Sam 10:6; 1 Kings 18:12). Elisha recognizes in Elijah a unique and mighty gift of this divine vitality and asks for this same gift, only twofold. The early Church would come to speak of the Spirit not just as divine power but as God's own

self, present to God's people in all the power and mystery of wind (John 3:8), fire (Acts 2:2–4), and water (John 3:5). God as Spirit/Wind hovers over the chaotic waters of our lives, granting Elisha's request and more to all who believe. The power of Elisha invites us to ponder how much and how well we in the Church recognize and live out the power and Presence given us.

2:12 *The chariots of Israel and its horsemen!* Perhaps Elisha likens Elijah, in his bold power, to all the chariots and troops of Israel. Because Elijah does not die, his presence and the radical hope it represents continue to linger in Israel's imagination (Mal 4:5–6). This wild power and hope will be recognized again in John the Baptist (Luke 1:17) and Jesus (Mark 8:27–28; 9:2–8), whose counterestablishment words win them the ire of the Ahabs of their day.

2:22 *according to the word that Elisha spoke.* To Jericho, a city under a curse (1 Kings 16:34), Elisha, new bearer of God's power, brings blessing. God delights in bestowing forgiveness and grace.

some to this day, according to the word that Elisha spoke.

23 He went up from there to Bethel; and while he was going up on the way, some small boys came out of the city and jeered at him, saying, "Go away, baldhead! Go away, baldhead!" 24When he turned around and saw them, he cursed them in the name of the LORD. Then two she-bears came out of the woods and mauled forty-two of the boys. 25From there he went on to Mount Carmel, and then returned to Samaria.

Jehoram Reigns over Israel

3 In the eighteenth year of King Jehoshaphat of Judah, Jehoram son of Ahab became king over Israel in Samaria; he reigned twelve years. 2He did what was evil in the sight of the LORD, though not like his father and mother, for he removed the pillar of Baal that his father had made. 3Nevertheless he clung to the sin of Jeroboam son of Nebat, which he caused Israel to commit; he did not depart from it.

War with Moab

4 Now King Mesha of Moab was a sheep breeder, who used to deliver to the king of Israel one hundred thousand lambs, and the wool of one hundred thousand rams. 5But when Ahab died, the king of Moab rebelled against the king of Israel. 6So King Jehoram marched out of Samaria at that time and mustered all Israel. 7As he went he sent word to King Jehoshaphat of Judah, "The king of Moab has rebelled against me; will you go with me to battle against Moab?" He answered, "I will; I am with you, my people are your people, my horses are your horses." 8Then he asked, "By which way shall we march?" Jehoram answered, "By the way of the wilderness of Edom."

9 So the king of Israel, the king of Judah, and the king of Edom set out; and when they had made a roundabout march of seven days, there was no water for the army or for the animals that were with them. 10Then the king of Israel said, "Alas! The LORD has summoned us, three kings, only to be handed over to Moab." 11But Jehoshaphat said, "Is there no prophet of the LORD here, through whom we may inquire of the LORD?" Then one of the servants of the king of Israel answered, "Elisha son of Shaphat, who used to pour water on the hands of Elijah, is here." 12Jehoshaphat said, "The word of the LORD is with him." So the king of Israel and Jehoshaphat and the king of Edom went down to him.

13 Elisha said to the king of Israel, "What have I to do with you? Go to your father's prophets or to your mother's." But the king of Israel said to him, "No; it is the LORD who has summoned us, three kings, only to be handed over to Moab." 14Elisha said, "As the LORD of hosts lives, whom I serve, were it not that I have regard for King Jehoshaphat of Judah, I would give you neither a look nor a glance. 15But get me a musician." And then, while the musician was playing, the power of the LORD came on him. 16And he said, "Thus says the LORD, 'I will make this wadi full of pools.' 17For thus says the LORD, 'You shall see neither wind nor rain, but the wadi shall be filled with water, so that you shall drink, you, your cattle, and your animals.' 18This is only a trifle in the sight of the LORD, for he will also hand Moab over to you. 19You shall conquer every fortified city and every choice city; every good tree you shall fell, all springs of water you shall stop up, and every good piece of land you shall ruin with stones." 20The next day, about the time of the morning offering, suddenly water began to flow from the direction of Edom, until the country was filled with water.

21 When all the Moabites heard that the kings had come up to fight against them, all

---

2:23–25 *some small boys . . . jeered.* Two points seem to underlie this difficult story. First, Elisha is jeered by those who do not recognize his authority. To mock a prophet is to mock God. This story reinforces to the community Elisha's new authority as God's prophet. Second, that mother bears come to the aid of Elisha as they would to a bear cub suggests the wildness of Elisha—he is fathered by Elijah and mothered by two bears. What a formidable lineage! The dynamic and unpredictable force of Elijah's spirit—the *ruah*—is indeed with him (see note on 2:9).

who were able to put on armor, from the youngest to the oldest, were called out and were drawn up at the frontier. 22When they rose early in the morning, and the sun shone upon the water, the Moabites saw the water opposite them as red as blood. 23They said, "This is blood; the kings must have fought together, and killed one another. Now then, Moab, to the spoil!" 24But when they came to the camp of Israel, the Israelites rose up and attacked the Moabites, who fled before them; as they entered Moab they continued the attack. *a* 25The cities they overturned, and on every good piece of land everyone threw a stone, until it was covered; every spring of water they stopped up, and every good tree they felled. Only at Kir-hareseth did the stone walls remain, until the slingers surrounded and attacked it. 26When the king of Moab saw that the battle was going against him, he took with him seven hundred swordsmen to break through, opposite the king of Edom; but they could not. 27Then he took his firstborn son who was to succeed him, and offered him as a burnt offering on the wall. And great wrath came upon Israel, so they withdrew from him and returned to their own land.

Elisha and the Widow's Oil

4 Now the wife of a member of the company of prophets*b* cried to Elisha, "Your servant my husband is dead; and you know that your servant feared the LORD, but a creditor has come to take my two children as slaves." 2Elisha said to her, "What shall I do for you? Tell me, what do you have in the house?" She answered, "Your servant has nothing in the house, except a jar of oil." 3He said, "Go outside, borrow vessels from all your neighbors, empty vessels and not just a few. 4Then go in, and shut the door behind you and your children, and start pouring into all these vessels; when each is full, set it aside." 5So she left him and shut the door behind her and her children; they kept bringing vessels to her, and she kept pouring. 6When the vessels were full, she said to her son, "Bring me another vessel." But he said to her, "There are no more." Then the oil stopped flowing. 7She came and told the man of God, and he said, "Go sell the oil and pay your debts, and you and your children can live on the rest."

Elisha Raises the Shunammite's Son

8 One day Elisha was passing through Shunem, where a wealthy woman lived, who urged him to have a meal. So whenever he passed that way, he would stop there for a meal. 9She said to her husband, "Look, I am sure that this man who regularly passes our way is a holy

a Compare Gk Syr: Meaning of Heb uncertain
b Heb *the sons of the prophets*

3:27 *great wrath came upon Israel.* This phrase is elusive. The Hebrew word for "wrath" usually refers to God's wrath (e.g., Deut 29:27; Josh 9:18–20). If this wrath is God's, then God has acted against Israel and Judah, as in 1 Kings 22, though it is hard to fathom God condoning child sacrifice. If this wrath is that of Chemosh, god of Moab, 2 Kings undercuts this understanding in 5:15 and 19:19, which deny there is more than one God, the God of Israel. More likely, this wrath may be a general assertion that acts of great evil can unleash chaos and panic that test even God's intentions. Evil is no trifling matter.

4:1–7 *a creditor has come to take my two children as slaves.* See 1 Kings 17:8–16. This story is the first of four in this chapter that give us some insight into Elisha's community, which

knows poverty and death and lives with the consequences of royal choices (famine). Into these places of need, Elisha conveys God's power to do what seems impossible. Unfortunately, the kings of 2 Kings are not aware of their true vulnerability, surrounded as they are by their wealth and might, and they usually resist divine power to transform the dire conditions of the people under their rule.

4:8–37 *One day Elisha was passing through Shunem.* See 1 Kings 17:17–24. Elisha encounters a woman who, like the widow of 4:1–7, refuses to accept loss as the final answer (vv 24–25, 30). The two women of 2 Kings 4 are powerful examples of those who bring their lament and protest to God's attention. They live out the bold hope that God hears the brokenhearted and acts in mercy and power.

man of God. [10]Let us make a small roof chamber with walls, and put there for him a bed, a table, a chair, and a lamp, so that he can stay there whenever he comes to us."

11 One day when he came there, he went up to the chamber and lay down there. [12]He said to his servant Gehazi, "Call the Shunammite woman." When he had called her, she stood before him. [13]He said to him, "Say to her, Since you have taken all this trouble for us, what may be done for you? Would you have a word spoken on your behalf to the king or to the commander of the army?" She answered, "I live among my own people." [14]He said, "What then may be done for her?" Gehazi answered, "Well, she has no son, and her husband is old." [15]He said, "Call her." When he had called her, she stood at the door. [16]He said, "At this season, in due time, you shall embrace a son." She replied, "No, my lord, O man of God; do not deceive your servant."

17 The woman conceived and bore a son at that season, in due time, as Elisha had declared to her.

18 When the child was older, he went out one day to his father among the reapers. [19]He complained to his father, "Oh, my head, my head!" The father said to his servant, "Carry him to his mother." [20]He carried him and brought him to his mother; the child sat on her lap until noon, and he died. [21]She went up and laid him on the bed of the man of God, closed the door on him, and left. [22]Then she called to her husband, and said, "Send me one of the servants and one of the donkeys, so that I may quickly go to the man of God and come back again." [23]He said, "Why go to him today? It is neither new moon nor sabbath." She said, "It will be all right." [24]Then she saddled the donkey and said to her servant, "Urge the animal on; do not hold back for me unless I tell you." [25]So she set out, and came to the man of God at Mount Carmel.

When the man of God saw her coming, he said to Gehazi his servant, "Look, there is the Shunammite woman; [26]run at once to meet her, and say to her, Are you all right? Is your husband all right? Is the child all right?" She answered, "It is all right." [27]When she came to the man of God at the mountain, she caught hold of his feet. Gehazi approached to push her away. But the man of God said, "Let her alone, for she is in bitter distress; the LORD has hidden it from me and has not told me." [28]Then she said, "Did I ask my lord for a son? Did I not say, Do not mislead me?" [29]He said to Gehazi, "Gird up your loins, and take my staff in your hand, and go. If you meet anyone, give no greeting, and if anyone greets you, do not answer; and lay my staff on the face of the child." [30]Then the mother of the child said, "As the LORD lives, and as you yourself live, I will not leave without you." So he rose up and followed her. [31]Gehazi went on ahead and laid the staff on the face of the child, but there was no sound or sign of life. He came back to meet him and told him, "The child has not awakened."

32 When Elisha came into the house, he saw the child lying dead on his bed. [33]So he went in and closed the door on the two of them, and prayed to the LORD. [34]Then he got up on the bed[a] and lay upon the child, putting his mouth upon his mouth, his eyes upon his eyes, and his hands upon his hands; and while he lay bent over him, the flesh of the child became warm. [35]He got down, walked once to and fro in the room, then got up again and bent over him; the child sneezed seven times, and the child opened his eyes. [36]Elisha[b] summoned Gehazi and said, "Call the Shunammite woman." So he called her. When she came to him, he said, "Take your son." [37]She came and fell at his feet, bowing to the ground; then she took her son and left.

Elisha Purifies the Pot of Stew

38 When Elisha returned to Gilgal, there was a famine in the land. As the company of prophets was[c] sitting before him, he said to his servant, "Put the large pot on, and make some stew for the company of prophets."[d] [39]One of them went out into the field to gather herbs; he found a wild vine and gathered from it a lapful of wild gourds, and came and cut them up into the pot of stew, not knowing what they were. [40]They served some for the men to eat. But while they were eating the

a Heb lacks *on the bed*   b Heb *he*   c Heb *sons of the prophets were*   d Heb *sons of the prophets*

stew, they cried out, "O man of God, there is death in the pot!" They could not eat it. [41]He said, "Then bring some flour." He threw it into the pot, and said, "Serve the people and let them eat." And there was nothing harmful in the pot.

Elisha Feeds One Hundred Men

42 A man came from Baal-shalishah, bringing food from the first fruits to the man of God: twenty loaves of barley and fresh ears of grain in his sack. Elisha said, "Give it to the people and let them eat." [43]But his servant said, "How can I set this before a hundred people?" So he repeated, "Give it to the people and let them eat, for thus says the LORD, 'They shall eat and have some left.'" [44]He set it before them, they ate, and had some left, according to the word of the LORD.

The Healing of Naaman

5 Naaman, commander of the army of the king of Aram, was a great man and in high favor with his master, because by him the LORD had given victory to Aram. The man, though a mighty warrior, suffered from leprosy. [a] [2]Now the Arameans on one of their raids had taken a young girl captive from the land of Israel, and she served Naaman's wife. [3]She said to her mistress, "If only my lord were with the prophet who is in Samaria! He would cure him of his leprosy." [a] [4]So Naaman [b] went in and told his lord just what the girl from the land of Israel had said. [5]And the king of Aram said, "Go then, and I will send along a letter to the king of Israel."

He went, taking with him ten talents of silver, six thousand shekels of gold, and ten sets of garments. [6]He brought the letter to the king of Israel, which read, "When this letter reaches you, know that I have sent to you my servant Naaman, that you may cure him of his leprosy." [a] [7]When the king of Israel read the letter, he tore his clothes and said, "Am I God, to give death or life, that this man sends word to me to cure a man of his leprosy? [a] Just look and see how he is trying to pick a quarrel with me."

8 But when Elisha the man of God heard that the king of Israel had torn his clothes, he sent a message to the king, "Why have you torn your clothes? Let him come to me, that he may learn that there is a prophet in Israel." [9]So Naaman came with his horses and chariots, and halted at the entrance of Elisha's house. [10]Elisha sent a messenger to him, saying, "Go, wash in the Jordan seven times, and your flesh shall be restored and you shall be clean." [11]But Naaman became angry and went away, saying, "I thought that for me he would surely come out, and stand and call on the name of the LORD his God, and would wave his hand over the spot, and cure the leprosy! [a] [12]Are not Abana [c] and Pharpar, the rivers of Damascus, better than all the waters of Israel? Could I not wash in them, and be clean?" He turned and went away in a rage. [13]But his servants approached and said to him, "Father, if the prophet had commanded you to do something difficult, would you not have done it? How much more, when

---

[a] A term for several skin diseases; precise meaning uncertain   [b] Heb *he*   [c] Another reading is *Amana*

5:1 *the LORD had given victory to Aram.* The story returns to the royal court—of enemy Aram! Once controlled by Israel (2 Sam 8:3–6), Aram now poses an increasing threat to the Northern Kingdom. Indeed, the writers of 1 & 2 Kings make the surprising claim that God has thrown in with Aram, making possible this nation's victories.

5:1–14 *Naaman . . . suffered from leprosy.* Naaman's journey for healing took him first to the king of Israel. His search has now brought him to Elisha, whose backwater etiquette offends Naaman. But the commander's

servants—those who know what it means to have no resources and power and, therefore, to have to trust others—are now instrumental in this healing, as was the Israelite slave girl (v 4). They are the unexpected voice of God, wisely pointing out the need to trust and obey. This story of healing and new life, brought about through the power of God and the gift of water, is a progenitor of the New Testament stories of new life through baptism. This healing "baptism" ferries Naaman to a new identity and community of faith. Often the first step to healing and redemption is practicing humility.

all he said to you was, 'Wash, and be clean'?" [14]So he went down and immersed himself seven times in the Jordan, according to the word of the man of God; his flesh was restored like the flesh of a young boy, and he was clean.

15 Then he returned to the man of God, he and all his company; he came and stood before him and said, "Now I know that there is no God in all the earth except in Israel; please accept a present from your servant." [16]But he said, "As the LORD lives, whom I serve, I will accept nothing!" He urged him to accept, but he refused. [17]Then Naaman said, "If not, please let two mule-loads of earth be given to your servant; for your servant will no longer offer burnt offering or sacrifice to any god except the LORD. [18]But may the LORD pardon your servant on one count: when my master goes into the house of Rimmon to worship there, leaning on my arm, and I bow down in the house of Rimmon, when I do bow down in the house of Rimmon, may the LORD pardon your servant on this one count." [19]He said to him, "Go in peace."

Gehazi's Greed

But when Naaman had gone from him a short distance, [20]Gehazi, the servant of Elisha the man of God, thought, "My master has let that Aramean Naaman off too lightly by not accepting from him what he offered. As the LORD lives, I will run after him and get some-

thing out of him." [21]So Gehazi went after Naaman. When Naaman saw someone running after him, he jumped down from the chariot to meet him and said, "Is everything all right?" [22]He replied, "Yes, but my master has sent me to say, 'Two members of a company of prophets[a] have just come to me from the hill country of Ephraim; please give them a talent of silver and two changes of clothing.' " [23]Naaman said, "Please accept two talents." He urged him, and tied up two talents of silver in two bags, with two changes of clothing, and gave them to two of his servants, who carried them in front of Gehazi. [b] [24]When he came to the citadel, he took the bags[c] from them, and stored them inside; he dismissed the men, and they left.

25 He went in and stood before his master; and Elisha said to him, "Where have you been, Gehazi?" He answered, "Your servant has not gone anywhere at all." [26]But he said to him, "Did I not go with you in spirit when someone left his chariot to meet you? Is this a time to accept money and to accept clothing, olive orchards and vineyards, sheep and oxen, and male and female slaves? [27]Therefore the leprosy[d] of Naaman shall cling to you, and to your descendants forever." So he left his presence leprous,[d] as white as snow.

a Heb *sons of the prophets*   b Heb *him*
c Heb lacks *the bags*   d A term for several skin diseases; precise meaning uncertain

---

5:15–19 *Go in peace.* Naaman confesses that the God of Israel alone is God, a remarkable confession for one outside God's people. Naaman takes some of Israel's soil home with him, probably under the impression that the God of Israel cannot be worshiped outside Israel. However, Naaman's conversion poses problems. Is it acceptable for him to make compromises in his new faith in order to continue his public life in Aram? Perhaps Elisha extends a blessing of peace knowing that this military man, well acquainted with the need for a clear line of authority, will wrestle with the claims of two masters. Naaman's dilemma and Elisha's blessing raise the question about which compromises we may safely make and which finally unravel our faith.

Responding
5:18–19 WORSHIP. Naaman accepts the God of Israel, but with one small exception—that he be permitted to still go into the temple of Rimmon with his king. What is the part of your life that you are holding back from the revealing light of God? What is your "except for"? Give it to God today. *See also* Spiritual Disciplines Index.

5:20–27 *leprosy . . . shall cling to you.* The Israelite is afflicted, while the non-Israelite is healed. Gehazi violates God's and Elisha's trust, exploiting the power and gifts of God as well as the generosity of Naaman.

The Miracle of the Ax Head

6 Now the company of prophets[a] said to Elisha, "As you see, the place where we live under your charge is too small for us. [2]Let us go to the Jordan, and let us collect logs there, one for each of us, and build a place there for us to live." He answered, "Do so." [3]Then one of them said, "Please come with your servants." And he answered, "I will." [4]So he went with them. When they came to the Jordan, they cut down trees. [5]But as one was felling a log, his ax head fell into the water; he cried out, "Alas, master! It was borrowed." [6]Then the man of God said, "Where did it fall?" When he showed him the place, he cut off a stick, and threw it in there, and made the iron float. [7]He said, "Pick it up." So he reached out his hand and took it.

The Aramean Attack Is Thwarted

8 Once when the king of Aram was at war with Israel, he took counsel with his officers. He said, "At such and such a place shall be my camp." [9]But the man of God sent word to the king of Israel, "Take care not to pass this place, because the Arameans are going down there." [10]The king of Israel sent word to the place of which the man of God spoke. More than once or twice he warned such a place[b] so that it was on the alert.

11 The mind of the king of Aram was greatly perturbed because of this; he called his officers and said to them, "Now tell me who among us sides with the king of Israel?" [12]Then one of his officers said, "No one, my lord king. It is Elisha, the prophet in Israel,

who tells the king of Israel the words that you speak in your bedchamber." [13]He said, "Go and find where he is; I will send and seize him." He was told, "He is in Dothan." [14]So he sent horses and chariots there and a great army; they came by night, and surrounded the city.

15 When an attendant of the man of God rose early in the morning and went out, an army with horses and chariots was all around the city. His servant said, "Alas, master! What shall we do?" [16]He replied, "Do not be afraid, for there are more with us than there are with them." [17]Then Elisha prayed: "O Lord, please open his eyes that he may see." So the Lord opened the eyes of the servant, and he saw; the mountain was full of horses and chariots of fire all around Elisha. [18]When the Arameans[c] came down against him, Elisha prayed to the Lord, and said, "Strike this people, please, with blindness." So he struck them with blindness as Elisha had asked. [19]Elisha said to them, "This is not the way, and this is not the city; follow me, and I will bring you to the man whom you seek." And he led them to Samaria.

20 As soon as they entered Samaria, Elisha said, "O Lord, open the eyes of these men so that they may see." The Lord opened their eyes, and they saw that they were inside Samaria. [21]When the king of Israel saw them he said to Elisha, "Father, shall I kill them? Shall I kill them?" [22]He answered, "No! Did

---

a Heb *sons of the prophets*   b Heb *warned it*
c Heb *they*

6:8–23 *But the man of God sent word to the king of Israel.* The king, his intelligence experts, and military have proven themselves unable to detect and deflect threats. National security rests with Elisha. Without God and God's prophet, the Northern Kingdom would be utterly vulnerable. The outcome of Elisha's rout contrasts with another battle, in 1 Kings 20:26–43, where a prophet imagined bloodshed as the appropriate conclusion. Here Elisha imagines and brings about an entirely different outcome: a feast that hints at the end-time feast of Isaiah's visions (Isa 25:6–10). This feast is one of those still points in history, a foretaste of a

world thoroughly transformed by God. For the Church, this foretaste is also the Eucharist, a meal that allows us to stock our experience and imagination with powerful images of hospitality and peace.

Responding
6:16–17 THE WITH-GOD LIFE. What would we see around us if we would ask the Lord to open our eyes? *See also* Spiritual Disciplines Index.

6:17 PRAYER—*See* Spiritual Disciplines Index.

you capture with your sword and your bow those whom you want to kill? Set food and water before them so that they may eat and drink; and let them go to their master." 23So he prepared for them a great feast; after they ate and drank, he sent them on their way, and they went to their master. And the Arameans no longer came raiding into the land of Israel.

Ben-hadad's Siege of Samaria

24 Some time later King Ben-hadad of Aram mustered his entire army; he marched against Samaria and laid siege to it. 25As the siege continued, famine in Samaria became so great that a donkey's head was sold for eighty shekels of silver, and one-fourth of a kab of dove's dung for five shekels of silver. 26Now as the king of Israel was walking on the city wall, a woman cried out to him, "Help, my lord king!" 27He said, "No! Let the LORD help you. How can I help you? From the threshing floor or from the wine press?" 28But then the king asked her, "What is your complaint?" She answered, "This woman said to me, 'Give up your son; we will eat him today, and we will eat my son tomorrow.' 29So we cooked my son and ate him. The next day I said to her, 'Give up your son and we will eat him.' But she has hidden her son." 30When the king heard the words of the woman he tore his clothes—now since he was walking on the city wall, the people could see that he had sackcloth on his body underneath—31and he said, "So may God do to me, and more, if the head of Elisha son of Shaphat stays on his shoulders today." 32So he dispatched a man from his presence.

Now Elisha was sitting in his house, and the elders were sitting with him. Before the messenger arrived, Elisha said to the elders, "Are you aware that this murderer has sent someone to take off my head? When the mes-

senger comes, see that you shut the door and hold it closed against him. Is not the sound of his master's feet behind him?" 33While he was still speaking with them, the king[a] came down to him and said, "This trouble is from the LORD! Why should I hope in the LORD any longer?" 7 1But Elisha said, "Hear the word of the LORD: thus says the LORD, Tomorrow about this time a measure of choice meal shall be sold for a shekel, and two measures of barley for a shekel, at the gate of Samaria." 2Then the captain on whose hand the king leaned said to the man of God, "Even if the LORD were to make windows in the sky, could such a thing happen?" But he said, "You shall see it with your own eyes, but you shall not eat from it."

The Arameans Flee

3 Now there were four leprous[b] men outside the city gate, who said to one another, "Why should we sit here until we die? 4If we say, 'Let us enter the city,' the famine is in the city, and we shall die there; but if we sit here, we shall also die. Therefore, let us desert to the Aramean camp; if they spare our lives, we shall live; and if they kill us, we shall but die." 5So they arose at twilight to go to the Aramean camp; but when they came to the edge of the Aramean camp, there was no one there at all. 6For the Lord had caused the Aramean army to hear the sound of chariots, and of horses, the sound of a great army, so that they said to one another, "The king of Israel has hired the kings of the Hittites and the kings of Egypt to fight against us." 7So they fled away in the twilight and abandoned their tents, their horses, and their donkeys leaving the camp just as it was, and fled for their lives. 8When these

a See 7:2: Heb messenger   b A term for several skin diseases; precise meaning uncertain

---

6:30 *sackcloth on his body.* For the two women who fight over a child (vv 28–29), this king is no Solomon (1 Kings 3:16–28). Royal policies have led to intense suffering for the populace and, for these women, desperate action. Wearing sackcloth is usually accompanied by fasting (1 Kings 21:27), but we hear

no mention of fasting, only hostility toward God's prophet Elisha. Pursuing the outward requirements of the Spiritual Disciplines without the corresponding inner commitment to humble oneself before the Lord is of no spiritual benefit.

leprous[a] men had come to the edge of the camp, they went into a tent, ate and drank, carried off silver, gold, and clothing, and went and hid them. Then they came back, entered another tent, carried off things from it, and went and hid them.

9 Then they said to one another, "What we are doing is wrong. This is a day of good news; if we are silent and wait until the morning light, we will be found guilty; therefore let us go and tell the king's household." 10So they came and called to the gatekeepers of the city, and told them, "We went to the Aramean camp, but there was no one to be seen or heard there, nothing but the horses tied, the donkeys tied, and the tents as they were." 11Then the gatekeepers called out and proclaimed it to the king's household. 12The king got up in the night, and said to his servants, "I will tell you what the Arameans have prepared against us. They know that we are starving; so they have left the camp to hide themselves in the open country, thinking, 'When they come out of the city, we shall take them alive and get into the city.' " 13One of his servants said, "Let some men take five of the remaining horses, since those left here will suffer the fate of the whole multitude of Israel that have perished already;[b] let us send and find out." 14So they took two mounted men, and the king sent them after the Aramean army, saying, "Go and find out." 15So they went after them as far as the Jordan; the whole way was littered with garments and equipment that the Arameans had thrown away in their haste. So the messengers returned, and told the king.

16 Then the people went out, and plundered the camp of the Arameans. So a measure of choice meal was sold for a shekel, and two measures of barley for a shekel, according to the word of the LORD. 17Now the king had appointed the captain on whose hand he leaned to have charge of the gate; the people trampled him to death in the gate, just as the man of God had said when the king came down to him. 18For when the man of God had said to the king, "Two measures of barley shall be sold for a shekel, and a measure of choice meal for a shekel, about this time tomorrow in the gate of Samaria," 19the captain had answered the man of God, "Even if the LORD were to make windows in the sky, could such a thing happen?" And he had answered, "You shall see it with your own eyes, but you shall not eat from it." 20It did indeed happen to him; the people trampled him to death in the gate.

The Shunammite Woman's Land Restored

8 Now Elisha had said to the woman whose son he had restored to life, "Get up and go with your household, and settle wherever you can; for the LORD has called for a famine, and it will come on the land for seven years." 2So the woman got up and did according to the word of the man of God; she went with her household and settled in the land of the Philistines seven years. 3At the end of the seven years, when the woman returned from the land of the Philistines, she set out to appeal to the king for her house and her land. 4Now the king was talking with Gehazi the servant of the man of God, saying, "Tell me all the great things that Elisha has done." 5While he was telling the king how Elisha had restored a dead person to life, the woman whose son he had restored to life appealed to the king for her house and her land. Gehazi said, "My lord king, here is the woman, and here is her son whom Elisha restored to life." 6When the king questioned the woman, she told him. So the king appointed an official for her, saying, "Restore all

a A term for several skin diseases; precise meaning uncertain   b Compare Gk Syr Vg: Meaning of Heb uncertain

---

7:6–10 *good news . . . let us go and tell the king's household.* Outcasts of their own society, deserters to the enemy (v 4), the four lepers become the unexpected aides of God, the one responsible for delivering unexpected good news. These lepers announce "good news," which is very different from their typical public cries of "Unclean, unclean!" (Lev 13:45–46). The compassion God has shown the community of Elisha now erupts within the capital.

8:3, 6 *she set out to appeal . . . for . . . her land.* See notes on 1 Kings 21:3; 2 Kings 4:8–37.

that was hers, together with all the revenue of the fields from the day that she left the land until now."

Death of Ben-hadad

7 Elisha went to Damascus while King Ben-hadad of Aram was ill. When it was told him, "The man of God has come here," 8the king said to Hazael, "Take a present with you and go to meet the man of God. Inquire of the LORD through him, whether I shall recover from this illness." 9So Hazael went to meet him, taking a present with him, all kinds of goods of Damascus, forty camel loads. When he entered and stood before him, he said, "Your son King Ben-hadad of Aram has sent me to you, saying, 'Shall I recover from this illness?' " 10Elisha said to him, "Go, say to him, 'You shall certainly recover'; but the LORD has shown me that he shall certainly die." 11He fixed his gaze and stared at him, until he was ashamed. Then the man of God wept. 12Hazael asked, "Why does my lord weep?" He answered, "Because I know the evil that you will do to the people of Israel; you will set their fortresses on fire, you will kill their young men with the sword, dash in pieces their little ones, and rip up their pregnant women." 13Hazael said, "What is your servant, who is a mere dog, that he should do this great thing?" Elisha answered, "The LORD has shown me that you are to be king over Aram." 14Then he left Elisha, and went to his master Ben-hadad,*a* who said to him, "What did Elisha say to you?" And he answered, "He told me that you would certainly recover." 15But the next day he took the bed-cover and dipped it in water and spread it over the king's face, until he died. And Hazael succeeded him.

Jehoram Reigns over Judah

16 In the fifth year of King Joram son of Ahab of Israel,*b* Jehoram son of King Jehoshaphat of Judah began to reign. 17He was thirty-two years old when he became king, and he reigned eight years in Jerusalem. 18He walked in the way of the kings of Israel, as the house of Ahab had done, for the daughter of Ahab was his wife. He did what was evil in the sight of the LORD. 19Yet the LORD would not destroy Judah, for the sake of his servant David, since he had promised to give a lamp to him and to his descendants forever.

20 In his days Edom revolted against the rule of Judah, and set up a king of their own. 21Then Joram crossed over to Zair with all his chariots. He set out by night and attacked the Edomites and their chariot commanders who had surrounded him;*c* but his army fled home. 22So Edom has been in revolt

a Heb lacks *Ben-hadad*   *b* Gk Syr: Heb adds *Jehoshaphat being king of Judah,*   *c* Meaning of Heb uncertain

---

8:10 *say to him, "You shall certainly recover"; but . . . he shall certainly die.* See note on 1 Kings 22:19.

8:11–13 *you are to be king over Aram.* Elisha fulfills the first of God's commissions to Elijah (1 Kings 19:15–17), but weeps at the suffering it will bring. Destruction will fall on the military (young men and fortresses) as well as the citizenry, including the most vulnerable, children and pregnant women. His prophecy raises many questions. Significant traditions within Scripture, including 1 & 2 Kings, describe God as one who at times advocates violence. What do we make of such a God? Scripture is clear about two matters that help us here. First, Scripture in general and 1 & 2 Kings in particular show that God's decrees need to be followed explicitly and in detail. God takes full responsi-

bility for divine decrees. We cannot always fathom the reasons for God's will; our responsibility is to obey. Second, when God's will is not immediately and absolutely clear, then we know we are responsible and will be judged by God's measure of justice and the plight of the most vulnerable. God is our Creator, Judge, and Savior. We are none of these. We are God's creatures who are called to love, mercy, justice, good works, and obedience. The commonplace role of violence in public policy and action, often in the name of God, summons the Church to discernment.

8:19 *a lamp to him and to his descendants forever.* For the Davidic lamp, see note on 1 Kings 11:36. God honors old commitments to David despite the encroaching influence of Ahab's family on Judah.

against the rule of Judah to this day. Libnah also revolted at the same time. 23Now the rest of the acts of Joram, and all that he did, are they not written in the Book of the Annals of the Kings of Judah? 24So Joram slept with his ancestors, and was buried with them in the city of David; his son Ahaziah succeeded him.

Ahaziah Reigns over Judah

25 In the twelfth year of King Joram son of Ahab of Israel, Ahaziah son of King Jehoram of Judah began to reign. 26Ahaziah was twenty-two years old when he began to reign; he reigned one year in Jerusalem. His mother's name was Athaliah, a granddaughter of King Omri of Israel. 27He also walked in the way of the house of Ahab, doing what was evil in the sight of the LORD, as the house of Ahab had done, for he was son-in-law to the house of Ahab.

28 He went with Joram son of Ahab to wage war against King Hazael of Aram at Ramoth-gilead, where the Arameans wounded Joram. 29King Joram returned to be healed in Jezreel of the wounds that the Arameans had inflicted on him at Ramah, when he fought against King Hazael of Aram. King Ahaziah son of Jehoram of Judah went down to see Joram son of Ahab in Jezreel, because he was wounded.

Anointing of Jehu

9 Then the prophet Elisha called a member of the company of prophets*a* and said to him, "Gird up your loins; take this flask of oil in your hand, and go to Ramoth-gilead. 2When you arrive, look there for Jehu son of Jehoshaphat, son of Nimshi; go in and get him to leave his companions, and take him

into an inner chamber. 3Then take the flask of oil, pour it on his head, and say, 'Thus says the LORD: I anoint you king over Israel.' Then open the door and flee; do not linger."

4 So the young man, the young prophet, went to Ramoth-gilead. 5He arrived while the commanders of the army were in council, and he announced, "I have a message for you, commander." "For which one of us?" asked Jehu. "For you, commander." 6So Jehu*b* got up and went inside; the young man poured the oil on his head, saying to him, "Thus says the LORD the God of Israel: I anoint you king over the people of the LORD, over Israel. 7You shall strike down the house of your master Ahab, so that I may avenge on Jezebel the blood of my servants the prophets, and the blood of all the servants of the LORD. 8For the whole house of Ahab shall perish; I will cut off from Ahab every male, bond or free, in Israel. 9I will make the house of Ahab like the house of Jeroboam son of Nebat, and like the house of Baasha son of Ahijah. 10The dogs shall eat Jezebel in the territory of Jezreel, and no one shall bury her." Then he opened the door and fled.

11 When Jehu came back to his master's officers, they said to him, "Is everything all right? Why did that madman come to you?" He answered them, "You know the sort and how they babble." 12They said, "Liar! Come on, tell us!" So he said, "This is just what he said to me: 'Thus says the LORD, I anoint you king over Israel.' " 13Then hurriedly they all took their cloaks and spread them for him on the bare*c* steps; and they blew the trumpet, and proclaimed, "Jehu is king."

a Heb sons of the prophets   b Heb he
c Meaning of Heb uncertain

9:3 *I anoint you king over Israel.* Elisha fulfills the second of God's assignments to Elijah by having Jehu anointed (1 Kings 19:15–17). Anointing is the act of setting apart a person for divine purposes. See 1 Sam 16:1–13.

9:10 *no one shall bury her.* The prophet links Jehu's action to Elijah's prophecy (1 Kings 21:20–24).

9:13 *Jehu is king.* Although Jehu's fellow officers believe the prophet is a "madman"

(v 11), they also acknowledge his authority to inaugurate a new king. The reference to the prophet's madness perhaps involves the ecstatic practices of some prophets (1 Sam 10:5–6). It also reveals that God's followers are heard and recognized even when the wider society seems merely to mock them. That is why we cannot always measure the effectiveness of our faithfulness; nor are we called to.

Joram of Israel Killed

14 Thus Jehu son of Jehoshaphat son of Nimshi conspired against Joram. Joram with all Israel had been on guard at Ramoth-gilead against King Hazael of Aram; 15but King Joram had returned to be healed in Jezreel of the wounds that the Arameans had inflicted on him, when he fought against King Hazael of Aram. So Jehu said, "If this is your wish, then let no one slip out of the city to go and tell the news in Jezreel." 16Then Jehu mounted his chariot and went to Jezreel, where Joram was lying ill. King Ahaziah of Judah had come down to visit Joram.

17 In Jezreel, the sentinel standing on the tower spied the company of Jehu arriving, and said, "I see a company." Joram said, "Take a horseman; send him to meet them, and let him say, 'Is it peace?' " 18So the horseman went to meet him; he said, "Thus says the king, 'Is it peace?' " Jehu responded, "What have you to do with peace? Fall in behind me." The sentinel reported, saying, "The messenger reached them, but he is not coming back." 19Then he sent out a second horseman, who came to them and said, "Thus says the king, 'Is it peace?' " Jehu answered, "What have you to do with peace? Fall in behind me." 20Again the sentinel reported, "He reached them, but he is not coming back. It looks like the driving of Jehu son of Nimshi; for he drives like a maniac."

21 Joram said, "Get ready." And they got his chariot ready. Then King Joram of Israel and King Ahaziah of Judah set out, each in his chariot, and went to meet Jehu; they met him at the property of Naboth the Jezreelite. 22When Joram saw Jehu, he said, "Is it peace, Jehu?" He answered, "What peace can there be, so long as the many whoredoms and sorceries of your mother Jezebel continue?" 23Then Joram reined about and fled, saying to Ahaziah, "Treason, Ahaziah!" 24Jehu drew his bow with all his strength, and shot Joram between the shoulders, so that the arrow pierced his heart; and he sank in his chariot. 25Jehu said to his aide Bidkar, "Lift him out, and throw him on the plot of ground belonging to Naboth the Jezreelite; for remember, when you and I rode side by side behind his father Ahab how the LORD uttered this oracle against him: 26'For the blood of Naboth and for the blood of his children that I saw yesterday, says the LORD, I swear I will repay you on this very plot of ground.' Now therefore lift him out and throw him on the plot of ground, in accordance with the word of the LORD."

Ahaziah of Judah Killed

27 When King Ahaziah of Judah saw this, he fled in the direction of Beth-haggan. Jehu pursued him, saying, "Shoot him also!" And they shot him[a] in the chariot at the ascent to Gur, which is by Ibleam. Then he fled to Megiddo, and died there. 28His officers carried him in a chariot to Jerusalem, and buried him in his tomb with his ancestors in the city of David.

29 In the eleventh year of Joram son of Ahab, Ahaziah began to reign over Judah.

Jezebel's Violent Death

30 When Jehu came to Jezreel, Jezebel heard of it; she painted her eyes, and adorned her head, and looked out of the window. 31As Jehu entered the gate, she said, "Is it peace, Zimri, murderer of your master?" 32He looked up to the window and said, "Who is on my side? Who?" Two or three eunuchs looked out at him. 33He said, "Throw her down." So they threw her down; some of her blood spat-

a Syr Vg Compare Gk: Heb lacks *and they shot him*

9:21–22 *What peace can there be?* These verses lay out God's issues with the Northern Kingdom: injustice and worship of other gods. For the story of Naboth, see 1 Kings 21. "Whoredoms and sorceries" refers to the worship of the fertility gods Baal and Asherah (see note on 1 Kings 14:15). Jehu's actions serve as warning that there can be no true peace (*shalom*) where there is injustice and wrong worship (Jer 6:13–15).

9:27 *Shoot him also!* Elijah's prophecy does not mention destruction of the house of David (1 Kings 21:20–24). Jehu quotes this prophecy to justify killing Joram (vv 24–26), but he gives no justification for killing Ahaziah.

tered on the wall and on the horses, which trampled on her. 34Then he went in and ate and drank; he said, "See to that cursed woman and bury her; for she is a king's daughter." 35But when they went to bury her, they found no more of her than the skull and the feet and the palms of her hands. 36When they came back and told him, he said, "This is the word of the LORD, which he spoke by his servant Elijah the Tishbite, 'In the territory of Jezreel the dogs shall eat the flesh of Jezebel; 37the corpse of Jezebel shall be like dung on the field in the territory of Jezreel, so that no one can say, This is Jezebel.' "

Massacre of Ahab's Descendants

10 Now Ahab had seventy sons in Samaria. So Jehu wrote letters and sent them to Samaria, to the rulers of Jezreel,[a] to the elders, and to the guardians of the sons of[b] Ahab, saying, 2"Since your master's sons are with you and you have at your disposal chariots and horses, a fortified city, and weapons, 3select the son of your master who is the best qualified, set him on his father's throne, and fight for your master's house." 4But they were utterly terrified and said, "Look, two kings could not withstand him; how then can we stand?" 5So the steward of the palace, and the governor of the city, along with the elders and the guardians, sent word to Jehu: "We are your servants; we will do anything you say. We will not make anyone king; do whatever you think right." 6Then he wrote them a second letter, saying, "If you are on my side, and if you are ready to obey me, take the heads of your master's sons and come to me at Jezreel tomorrow at this time." Now the king's sons, seventy persons, were with the leaders of the city, who were charged with their upbringing. 7When the letter reached them, they took the

king's sons and killed them, seventy persons; they put their heads in baskets and sent them to him at Jezreel. 8When the messenger came and told him, "They have brought the heads of the king's sons," he said, "Lay them in two heaps at the entrance of the gate until the morning." 9Then in the morning when he went out, he stood and said to all the people, "You are innocent. It was I who conspired against my master and killed him; but who struck down all these? 10Know then that there shall fall to the earth nothing of the word of the LORD, which the LORD spoke concerning the house of Ahab; for the LORD has done what he said through his servant Elijah." 11So Jehu killed all who were left of the house of Ahab in Jezreel, all his leaders, close friends, and priests, until he left him no survivor.

12 Then he set out and went to Samaria. On the way, when he was at Beth-eked of the Shepherds, 13Jehu met relatives of King Ahaziah of Judah and said, "Who are you?" They answered, "We are kin of Ahaziah; we have come down to visit the royal princes and the sons of the queen mother." 14He said, "Take them alive." They took them alive, and slaughtered them at the pit of Beth-eked, forty-two in all; he spared none of them.

15 When he left there, he met Jehonadab son of Rechab coming to meet him; he greeted him, and said to him, "Is your heart as true to mine as mine is to yours?"[c] Jehonadab answered, "It is." Jehu said,[d] "If it is, give me your hand." So he gave him his hand. Jehu took him up with him into the chariot. 16He said, "Come with me, and see my zeal for the

a Or of the city; Vg Compare Gk   b Gk: Heb lacks of the sons of   c Gk: Heb Is it right with your heart, as my heart is with your heart?   d Gk: Heb lacks Jehu said

---

10:7–11 *but who struck down all these?* Jehu takes responsibility for the coup against Joram, but sidesteps responsibility for executing Ahab's seventy descendants. Instead, he implicates the royal officials—and then claims God's will in these beheadings. Jehu proves himself adroit in managing the fallout from his coup.

10:14 *he spared none of them.* Once again, Jehu provides no warrant from God for

executing members of the Davidic house, although he is at pains to do so for purging the house of Ahab (see 9:26; 10:10; cf. 1 Kings 21:20–24).

10:15 *Jehonadab son of Rechab.* Jehonadab son of Rechab appears to have been a leader of a purist community that hearkened back to the desert life and faith of early Israel. See Jeremiah 35.

LORD." So he[a] had him ride in his chariot. [17]When he came to Samaria, he killed all who were left to Ahab in Samaria, until he had wiped them out, according to the word of the LORD that he spoke to Elijah.

Slaughter of Worshipers of Baal

18 Then Jehu assembled all the people and said to them, "Ahab offered Baal small service; but Jehu will offer much more. [19]Now therefore summon to me all the prophets of Baal, all his worshipers, and all his priests; let none be missing, for I have a great sacrifice to offer to Baal; whoever is missing shall not live." But Jehu was acting with cunning in order to destroy the worshipers of Baal. [20]Jehu decreed, "Sanctify a solemn assembly for Baal." So they proclaimed it. [21]Jehu sent word throughout all Israel; all the worshipers of Baal came, so that there was no one left who did not come. They entered the temple of Baal, until the temple of Baal was filled from wall to wall. [22]He said to the keeper of the wardrobe, "Bring out the vestments for all the worshipers of Baal." So he brought out the vestments for them. [23]Then Jehu entered the temple of Baal with Jehonadab son of Rechab; he said to the worshipers of Baal, "Search and see that there is no worshiper of the LORD here among you, but only worshipers of Baal." [24]Then they proceeded to offer sacrifices and burnt offerings.

Now Jehu had stationed eighty men outside, saying, "Whoever allows any of those to escape whom I deliver into your hands shall forfeit his life." [25]As soon as he had finished presenting the burnt offering, Jehu said to the guards and to the officers, "Come in and kill them; let no one escape." So they put them to the sword. The guards and the officers threw them out, and then went into the citadel of the temple of Baal. [26]They brought out the pillar[b] that was in the temple of Baal, and burned it. [27]Then they demolished the pillar of Baal, and destroyed the temple of Baal, and made it a latrine to this day.

28 Thus Jehu wiped out Baal from Israel. [29]But Jehu did not turn aside from the sins of Jeroboam son of Nebat, which he caused Israel to commit—the golden calves that were in Bethel and in Dan. [30]The LORD said to Jehu, "Because you have done well in carrying out what I consider right, and in accordance with all that was in my heart have dealt with the house of Ahab, your sons of the fourth generation shall sit on the throne of Israel." [31]But Jehu was not careful to follow the law of the LORD the God of Israel with all his heart; he did not turn from the sins of Jeroboam, which he caused Israel to commit.

Death of Jehu

32 In those days the LORD began to trim off parts of Israel. Hazael defeated them throughout the territory of Israel: [33]from the Jordan eastward, all the land of Gilead, the Gadites, the Reubenites, and the Manassites, from Aroer, which is by the Wadi Arnon, that is, Gilead and Bashan. [34]Now the rest of the acts of Jehu, all that he did, and all his power, are they not written in the Book of the Annals of the Kings of Israel? [35]So Jehu slept with his ancestors, and they buried him in Samaria. His son Jehoahaz succeeded him. [36]The time that Jehu reigned over Israel in Samaria was twenty-eight years.

Athaliah Reigns over Judah

11 Now when Athaliah, Ahaziah's mother, saw that her son was dead, she set

a Gk Syr Tg: Heb *they*   *b* Gk Vg Syr Tg: Heb *pillars*

10:29–30 *Because you have done well.* Jehu wins approval from God. The severe program of the Mosaic covenant seems to have been implemented: Baal worship has been dealt a blow, and the patrons of this worship and of injustice, the house of Ahab, are gone. But the bloody purge leaves questions, especially given Jehu's violation of the law of Moses. Prophecy played out on the political landscape holds the possibility of renewal in Israel, but the move from prophetic word to action is incredibly vulnerable to self-interest, savagery, and the replication of failed configurations. 1 & 2 Kings call the People of God to the endless task of scrutinizing the policies and actions of those who speak and act for God. See note on 8:11–13. Compare the assessment of Jehu in Hos 1:4–5.

about to destroy all the royal family. ²But Jehosheba, King Joram's daughter, Ahaziah's sister, took Joash son of Ahaziah, and stole him away from among the king's children who were about to be killed; she put*a* him and his nurse in a bedroom. Thus she*b* hid him from Athaliah, so that he was not killed; ³he remained with her six years, hidden in the house of the LORD, while Athaliah reigned over the land.

Jehoiada Anoints the Child Joash

4 But in the seventh year Jehoiada summoned the captains of the Carites and of the guards and had them come to him in the house of the LORD. He made a covenant with them and put them under oath in the house of the LORD; then he showed them the king's son. ⁵He commanded them, "This is what you are to do: one-third of you, those who go off duty on the sabbath and guard the king's house ⁶(another third being at the gate Sur and a third at the gate behind the guards), shall guard the palace; ⁷and your two divisions that come on duty in force on the sabbath and guard the house of the LORD*c* ⁸shall surround the king, each with weapons in hand; and whoever approaches the ranks is to be killed. Be with the king in his comings and goings."

9 The captains did according to all that the priest Jehoiada commanded; each brought his men who were to go off duty on the sabbath, with those who were to come on duty on the sabbath, and came to the priest Jehoiada. ¹⁰The priest delivered to the captains the spears and shields that had been King David's, which were in the house of the LORD; ¹¹the guards stood, every man with his weapons in his hand, from the south side of the house to the north side of the house, around the altar and the house, to guard the king on every side. ¹²Then he brought out the king's son, put the crown on him, and gave him the covenant;*d* they proclaimed him king, and anointed him; they clapped their hands and shouted, "Long live the king!"

Death of Athaliah

13 When Athaliah heard the noise of the guard and of the people, she went into the house of the LORD to the people; ¹⁴when she looked, there was the king standing by the pillar, according to custom, with the captains and the trumpeters beside the king, and all the people of the land rejoicing and blowing trumpets. Athaliah tore her clothes and cried, "Treason! Treason!" ¹⁵Then the priest Jehoiada commanded the captains who were set over the army, "Bring her out between the ranks, and kill with the sword anyone who follows her." For the priest said, "Let her not be killed in the house of the LORD." ¹⁶So they laid hands on her; she went through the horses' entrance to the king's house, and there she was put to death.

17 Jehoiada made a covenant between the LORD and the king and people, that they should be the LORD's people; also between the king and the people. ¹⁸Then all the people of the land went to the house of Baal, and tore it down; his altars and his images they broke in pieces, and they killed Mattan, the priest of Baal, before the altars. The priest posted guards

a With 2 Chr 22.11: Heb lacks *she put*   *b* Gk Syr Vg Compare 2 Chr 22.11: Heb *they*   *c* Heb *the* LORD *to the king*   *d* Or *treaty* or *testimony*; Heb *eduth*

11:1 *she set about to destroy all the royal family.* Athaliah is the Jezebel of the Southern Kingdom, a granddaughter of Omri (8:26) and most likely a worshiper of Baal (11:18). God's promise to David rests with an endangered infant. See Exod 2:1–10; Matt 2:1–18.

11:14 *all the people of the land rejoicing and blowing trumpets.* Scholars speculate that "people of the land" refers to people from rural Judah who supported the old covenantal faith rather than the new, syncretistic faith of urban Jerusalem with its temple of Baal (v 18).

11:17 *Jehoiada made a covenant.* Jehoiada the priest initiates reform in the South. He reintroduces the covenant of Moses, reminding the people that they are "the LORD's people" (see Deut 27:9–10). Jehoiada also renews the covenant between king and people, perhaps highlighting obligations between ruler and ruled (Deut 17:14–20; 2 Sam 5:3).

over the house of the LORD. [19]He took the captains, the Carites, the guards, and all the people of the land; then they brought the king down from the house of the LORD, marching through the gate of the guards to the king's house. He took his seat on the throne of the kings. [20]So all the people of the land rejoiced; and the city was quiet after Athaliah had been killed with the sword at the king's house.

[21][a]Jehoash[b] was seven years old when he began to reign.

The Temple Repaired

12 In the seventh year of Jehu, Jehoash began to reign; he reigned forty years in Jerusalem. His mother's name was Zibiah of Beer-sheba. [2]Jehoash did what was right in the sight of the LORD all his days, because the priest Jehoiada instructed him. [3]Nevertheless the high places were not taken away; the people continued to sacrifice and make offerings on the high places.

[4] Jehoash said to the priests, "All the money offered as sacred donations that is brought into the house of the LORD, the money for which each person is assessed—the money from the assessment of persons—and the money from the voluntary offerings brought into the house of the LORD, [5]let the priests receive from each of the donors; and let them repair the house wherever any need of repairs is discovered." [6]But by the twenty-third year of King Jehoash the priests had made no repairs on the house. [7]Therefore King Jehoash summoned the priest Jehoiada with the other priests and said to them, "Why are you not repairing the house? Now therefore do not accept any more money from your donors but hand it over for the repair of the house." [8]So the priests agreed that they would neither accept more money from the people nor repair the house.

[9] Then the priest Jehoiada took a chest, made a hole in its lid, and set it beside the altar on the right side as one entered the house of the LORD; the priests who guarded the threshold put in it all the money that was brought into the house of the LORD. [10]Whenever they saw that there was a great deal of money in the chest, the king's secretary and the high priest went up, counted the money that was found in the house of the LORD, and tied it up in bags. [11]They would give the money that was weighed out into the hands of the workers who had the oversight of the house of the LORD; then they paid it out to the carpenters and the builders who worked on the house of the LORD, [12]to the masons and the stonecutters, as well as to buy timber and quarried stone for making repairs on the house of the LORD, as well as for any outlay for repairs of the house. [13]But for the house of the LORD no basins of silver, snuffers, bowls, trumpets, or any vessels of gold, or of silver, were made from the money that was brought into the house of the LORD, [14]for that was given to the workers who were repairing the house of the LORD with it. [15]They did not ask an accounting from those into whose hand they delivered the money to pay out to the workers, for they dealt honestly. [16]The money from the guilt offerings and the money from the sin offerings was not brought into the house of the LORD; it belonged to the priests.

Hazael Threatens Jerusalem

[17] At that time King Hazael of Aram went up, fought against Gath, and took it. But when Hazael set his face to go up against Jerusalem, [18]King Jehoash of Judah took all the votive gifts that Jehoshaphat, Jehoram, and

[a] Ch 12.1 in Heb   [b] Another spelling is *Joash*; see verse 19

12:3 *high places.* See note on 1 Kings 3:3.
12:18 *all the gold . . . in the treasuries.* Repairing the Temple (vv 11–12) seems at first to symbolize renewal of this nation's faith (11:17), but soon this renewal becomes suspect. Reports of fiscal irregularities at the Temple suggest activities out of step with the law. A holy place of worship, this Temple is also a

human institution, vulnerable to self-interest. Now the Temple's appointment has gone downhill (v 13), and Temple treasuries have become payment to Hazael. Two dire developments suggest divine judgment on what has proved a superficial renewal movement: the new Aramean threat and Joash's assassination (v 20).

Ahaziah, his ancestors, the kings of Judah, had dedicated, as well as his own votive gifts, all the gold that was found in the treasuries of the house of the LORD and of the king's house, and sent these to King Hazael of Aram. Then Hazael withdrew from Jerusalem.

Death of Joash

19 Now the rest of the acts of Joash, and all that he did, are they not written in the Book of the Annals of the Kings of Judah? 20His servants arose, devised a conspiracy, and killed Joash in the house of Millo, on the way that goes down to Silla. 21It was Jozacar son of Shimeath and Jehozabad son of Shomer, his servants, who struck him down, so that he died. He was buried with his ancestors in the city of David; then his son Amaziah succeeded him.

Jehoahaz Reigns over Israel

13 In the twenty-third year of King Joash son of Ahaziah of Judah, Jehoahaz son of Jehu began to reign over Israel in Samaria; he reigned seventeen years. 2He did what was evil in the sight of the LORD, and followed the sins of Jeroboam son of Nebat, which he caused Israel to sin; he did not depart from them. 3The anger of the LORD was kindled against Israel, so that he gave them repeatedly into the hand of King Hazael of Aram, then into the hand of Ben-hadad son of Hazael. 4But Jehoahaz entreated the LORD, and the LORD heeded him; for he saw the oppression of Israel, how the king of Aram oppressed them. 5Therefore the LORD gave Israel a savior, so that they escaped from the hand of the Arameans; and the people of Israel lived in their homes as formerly. 6Nevertheless they did not depart from the sins of the house of Jeroboam, which he caused Israel to sin, but walked*a* in them; the sacred pole*b* also remained in Samaria. 7So Jehoahaz was left with an army of not more than fifty

horsemen, ten chariots and ten thousand footmen; for the king of Aram had destroyed them and made them like the dust at threshing. 8Now the rest of the acts of Jehoahaz and all that he did, including his might, are they not written in the Book of the Annals of the Kings of Israel? 9So Jehoahaz slept with his ancestors, and they buried him in Samaria; then his son Joash succeeded him.

Jehoash Reigns over Israel

10 In the thirty-seventh year of King Joash of Judah, Jehoash son of Jehoahaz began to reign over Israel in Samaria; he reigned sixteen years. 11He also did what was evil in the sight of the LORD; he did not depart from all the sins of Jeroboam son of Nebat, which he caused Israel to sin, but he walked in them. 12Now the rest of the acts of Joash, and all that he did, as well as the might with which he fought against King Amaziah of Judah, are they not written in the Book of the Annals of the Kings of Israel? 13So Joash slept with his ancestors, and Jeroboam sat upon his throne; Joash was buried in Samaria with the kings of Israel.

Death of Elisha

14 Now when Elisha had fallen sick with the illness of which he was to die, King Joash of Israel went down to him, and wept before him, crying, "My father, my father! The chariots of Israel and its horsemen!" 15Elisha said to him, "Take a bow and arrows"; so he took a bow and arrows. 16Then he said to the king of Israel, "Draw the bow"; and he drew it. Elisha laid his hands on the king's hands. 17Then he said, "Open the window eastward"; and he opened it. Elisha said, "Shoot"; and he shot. Then he said, "The LORD's arrow of victory, the arrow of victory over Aram! For you shall fight the Arameans in Aphek until you

---

a Gk Syr Tg Vg: Heb *he walked*   *b* Heb *Asherah*

13:2–5 *He did what was evil.* The fourfold movement in these verses (evil, oppression, entreaty, salvation) repeats a pattern that recurs throughout Judges (e.g., 2:11–23). The term "savior" refers to the person whom God calls

and equips to deliver God's people from danger and oppression (Judg 3:9, 15; Neh 9:27).

13:6 *sacred pole.* See note on 1 Kings 14:15.

13:14 *The chariots of Israel and its horsemen!* See note on 2:12.

have made an end of them." 18He continued, "Take the arrows"; and he took them. He said to the king of Israel, "Strike the ground with them"; he struck three times, and stopped. 19Then the man of God was angry with him, and said, "You should have struck five or six times; then you would have struck down Aram until you had made an end of it, but now you will strike down Aram only three times."

20 So Elisha died, and they buried him. Now bands of Moabites used to invade the land in the spring of the year. 21As a man was being buried, a marauding band was seen and the man was thrown into the grave of Elisha; as soon as the man touched the bones of Elisha, he came to life and stood on his feet.

Israel Recaptures Cities from Aram

22 Now King Hazael of Aram oppressed Israel all the days of Jehoahaz. 23But the LORD was gracious to them and had compassion on them; he turned toward them, because of his covenant with Abraham, Isaac, and Jacob, and would not destroy them; nor has he banished them from his presence until now.

24 When King Hazael of Aram died, his son Ben-hadad succeeded him. 25Then Jehoash son of Jehoahaz took again from Ben-hadad son of Hazael the towns that he had taken from his father Jehoahaz in war. Three times Joash defeated him and recovered the towns of Israel.

Amaziah Reigns over Judah

14 In the second year of King Joash son of Joahaz of Israel, King Amaziah son of Joash of Judah, began to reign. 2He was twenty-five years old when he began to reign, and he reigned twenty-nine years in Jerusalem. His mother's name was Jehoaddin of Je-

rusalem. 3He did what was right in the sight of the LORD, yet not like his ancestor David; in all things he did as his father Joash had done. 4But the high places were not removed; the people still sacrificed and made offerings on the high places. 5As soon as the royal power was firmly in his hand he killed his servants who had murdered his father the king. 6But he did not put to death the children of the murderers; according to what is written in the book of the law of Moses, where the LORD commanded, "The parents shall not be put to death for the children, or the children be put to death for the parents; but all shall be put to death for their own sins."

7 He killed ten thousand Edomites in the Valley of Salt and took Sela by storm; he called it Joktheel, which is its name to this day.

8 Then Amaziah sent messengers to King Jehoash son of Jehoahaz, son of Jehu, of Israel, saying, "Come, let us look one another in the face." 9King Jehoash of Israel sent word to King Amaziah of Judah, "A thornbush on Lebanon sent to a cedar on Lebanon, saying, 'Give your daughter to my son for a wife'; but a wild animal of Lebanon passed by and trampled down the thornbush. 10You have indeed defeated Edom, and your heart has lifted you up. Be content with your glory, and stay at home; for why should you provoke trouble so that you fall, you and Judah with you?"

11 But Amaziah would not listen. So King Jehoash of Israel went up; he and King Amaziah of Judah faced one another in battle at Beth-shemesh, which belongs to Judah. 12Judah was defeated by Israel; everyone fled home. 13King Jehoash of Israel captured King Amaziah of Judah son of Jehoash, son of Ahaziah, at Beth-shemesh; he came to Jerusalem, and broke down the wall of Jerusalem

---

13:23 *because of his covenant with Abraham, Isaac, and Jacob.* 1 & 2 Kings' primary touchstones have been the Mosaic and Davidic covenants. Here the text refers to the covenant with Abraham, Isaac, and Jacob (Gen 12:1–3; 17:1–14; Deut 9:25–29). The foundational promise of Israel commits God to the faltering Northern Kingdom.

14:9–10 *A thornbush . . . sent to a cedar.* Jehoash scoffs at Amaziah's hand-on-hilt strutting, reminding the king that Judah is a thornbush compared to the regal cedar of the North. In this parable, the wild beast is any expected threat a nation faces (for wild beasts are forest denizens), but a threat that is greater to a nation weakened by unsound ventures like Amaziah's.

from the Ephraim Gate to the Corner Gate, a distance of four hundred cubits. [14]He seized all the gold and silver, and all the vessels that were found in the house of the LORD and in the treasuries of the king's house, as well as hostages; then he returned to Samaria.

15 Now the rest of the acts that Jehoash did, his might, and how he fought with King Amaziah of Judah, are they not written in the Book of the Annals of the Kings of Israel? [16]Jehoash slept with his ancestors, and was buried in Samaria with the kings of Israel; then his son Jeroboam succeeded him.

17 King Amaziah son of Joash of Judah lived fifteen years after the death of King Jehoash son of Jehoahaz of Israel. [18]Now the rest of the deeds of Amaziah, are they not written in the Book of the Annals of the Kings of Judah? [19]They made a conspiracy against him in Jerusalem, and he fled to Lachish. But they sent after him to Lachish, and killed him there. [20]They brought him on horses; he was buried in Jerusalem with his ancestors in the city of David. [21]All the people of Judah took Azariah, who was sixteen years old, and made him king to succeed his father Amaziah. [22]He rebuilt Elath and restored it to Judah, after King Amaziah[a] slept with his ancestors.

Jeroboam II Reigns over Israel

23 In the fifteenth year of King Amaziah son of Joash of Judah, King Jeroboam son of Joash of Israel began to reign in Samaria; he reigned forty-one years. [24]He did what was evil in the sight of the LORD; he did not depart from all the sins of Jeroboam son of Nebat, which he caused Israel to sin. [25]He restored the border of Israel from Lebo-hamath as far as the Sea of the Arabah, according to the word of the LORD, the God of Israel, which he spoke by his servant Jonah son of Amittai, the prophet, who was from Gath-hepher. [26]For the LORD saw that the distress of Israel was very bitter; there was no one left, bond or free, and no one to help Israel. [27]But the LORD had not said that he would blot out the name of Israel from under heaven, so he saved them by the hand of Jeroboam son of Joash.

28 Now the rest of the acts of Jeroboam, and all that he did, and his might, how he fought, and how he recovered for Israel Damascus and Hamath, which had belonged to Judah, are they not written in the Book of the Annals of the Kings of Israel? [29]Jeroboam slept with his ancestors, the kings of Israel; his son Zechariah succeeded him.

Azariah Reigns over Judah

15 In the twenty-seventh year of King Jeroboam of Israel King Azariah son of Amaziah of Judah began to reign. [2]He was sixteen years old when he began to reign, and he reigned fifty-two years in Jerusalem. His mother's name was Jecoliah of Jerusalem. [3]He did what was right in the sight of the LORD, just as his father Amaziah had done. [4]Nevertheless the high places were not taken away; the people still sacrificed and made offerings on the high places. [5]The LORD struck the king, so that he was leprous[b] to the day of his death, and lived in a separate house.

---

a Heb the king   b A term for several skin diseases; precise meaning uncertain

---

14:25 *the word of the LORD, . . . which he spoke by his servant Jonah.* Once again a prophet speaks, this time Jonah, who speaks words of blessing for the Northern Kingdom concerning its territorial holdings. Under Jeroboam II, Israel entered a period of great prosperity, territorial expansion, and building. Both Amos and Hosea began to prophesy during the reign of Jeroboam II, indicting this king for the worship of other gods and for injustice in the land, despite its wealth.

14:27 *he saved them.* The strict formula that evil is followed by punishment is not the whole story, because of God's great mercy and commitment to divine promises (see 13:23; Deut 26:6–7). The instrument of God's response to suffering is, surprisingly, Jeroboam II, through whom God saves the Northern Kingdom. God's choice of agents defies easy logic.

15:5 *The LORD struck the king, so that he was leprous.* Azariah is also called Uzziah (see vv 13, 30). Although Azariah rules successfully for over fifty years (2 Chron 26), the text does not find his accomplishments noteworthy. Azariah does good (mostly; vv 3–4), and God strikes him with a feared disease, while Jeroboam II does evil

Jotham the king's son was in charge of the palace, governing the people of the land. [6]Now the rest of the acts of Azariah, and all that he did, are they not written in the Book of the Annals of the Kings of Judah? [7]Azariah slept with his ancestors; they buried him with his ancestors in the city of David; his son Jotham succeeded him.

Zechariah Reigns over Israel

8 In the thirty-eighth year of King Azariah of Judah, Zechariah son of Jeroboam reigned over Israel in Samaria six months. [9]He did what was evil in the sight of the LORD, as his ancestors had done. He did not depart from the sins of Jeroboam son of Nebat, which he caused Israel to sin. [10]Shallum son of Jabesh conspired against him, and struck him down in public and killed him, and reigned in place of him. [11]Now the rest of the deeds of Zechariah are written in the Book of the Annals of the Kings of Israel. [12]This was the promise of the LORD that he gave to Jehu, "Your sons shall sit on the throne of Israel to the fourth generation." And so it happened.

Shallum Reigns over Israel

13 Shallum son of Jabesh began to reign in the thirty-ninth year of King Uzziah of Judah; he reigned one month in Samaria. [14]Then Menahem son of Gadi came up from Tirzah and came to Samaria; he struck down Shallum son of Jabesh in Samaria and killed him; he reigned in place of him. [15]Now the rest of the deeds of Shallum, including the conspiracy that he made, are written in the Book of the Annals of the Kings of Israel. [16]At that time Menahem sacked Tiphsah, all who were in it and its territory from Tirzah on; because

they did not open it to him, he sacked it. He ripped open all the pregnant women in it.

Menahem Reigns over Israel

17 In the thirty-ninth year of King Azariah of Judah, Menahem son of Gadi began to reign over Israel; he reigned ten years in Samaria. [18]He did what was evil in the sight of the LORD; he did not depart all his days from any of the sins of Jeroboam son of Nebat, which he caused Israel to sin. [19]King Pul of Assyria came against the land; Menahem gave Pul a thousand talents of silver, so that he might help him confirm his hold on the royal power. [20]Menahem exacted the money from Israel, that is, from all the wealthy, fifty shekels of silver from each one, to give to the king of Assyria. So the king of Assyria turned back, and did not stay there in the land. [21]Now the rest of the deeds of Menahem, and all that he did, are they not written in the Book of the Annals of the Kings of Israel? [22]Menahem slept with his ancestors, and his son Pekahiah succeeded him.

Pekahiah Reigns over Israel

23 In the fiftieth year of King Azariah of Judah, Pekahiah son of Menahem began to reign over Israel in Samaria; he reigned two years. [24]He did what was evil in the sight of the LORD; he did not turn away from the sins of Jeroboam son of Nebat, which he caused Israel to sin. [25]Pekah son of Remaliah, his captain, conspired against him with fifty of the Gileadites, and attacked him in Samaria, in the citadel of the palace along with Argob and Arieh; he killed him, and reigned in place of him. [26]Now the rest of the deeds of Peka-

---

and, because of God, succeeds in his ventures (14:27). There is no hard-and-fast formula of blessing and curse. In attempting to explain the history of Israel and Judah, 1 & 2 Kings time and time again run up against the mystery of God's dealings. The text contends that God is intimately involved in public life, but provides no easy rules concerning this involvement. God refuses to be put into neat, clear-cut categories. Isaiah's call as prophet dates to the year of Azariah's death (Isa 6:1).

15:19 *Menahem gave Pul a thousand talents.* While the Northern Kingdom endures paroxysms of violence, a new menace appears, Assyrian king Pul, or Tiglath-pileser III. To amass wealth and power, this king conquered territories that would secure trade routes to the Mediterranean Sea and Egypt. Menahem paid dearly to protect his position: around 745 BC, the Northern Kingdom became a vassal state and remained so until its destruction.

hiah, and all that he did, are written in the Book of the Annals of the Kings of Israel.

Pekah Reigns over Israel

27 In the fifty-second year of King Azariah of Judah, Pekah son of Remaliah began to reign over Israel in Samaria; he reigned twenty years. 28He did what was evil in the sight of the LORD; he did not depart from the sins of Jeroboam son of Nebat, which he caused Israel to sin.

29 In the days of King Pekah of Israel, King Tiglath-pileser of Assyria came and captured Ijon, Abel-beth-maacah, Janoah, Kedesh, Hazor, Gilead, and Galilee, all the land of Naphtali; and he carried the people captive to Assyria. 30Then Hoshea son of Elah made a conspiracy against Pekah son of Remaliah, attacked him, and killed him; he reigned in place of him, in the twentieth year of Jotham son of Uzziah. 31Now the rest of the acts of Pekah, and all that he did, are written in the Book of the Annals of the Kings of Israel.

Jotham Reigns over Judah

32 In the second year of King Pekah son of Remaliah of Israel, King Jotham son of Uzziah of Judah began to reign. 33He was twenty-five years old when he began to reign and reigned sixteen years in Jerusalem. His mother's name was Jerusha daughter of Zadok. 34He did what was right in the sight of the LORD, just as his father Uzziah had done. 35Nevertheless the high places were not removed; the people still sacrificed and made offerings on the high places. He built the upper gate of the house of the LORD. 36Now the rest of the acts of Jotham, and all that he did,

are they not written in the Book of the Annals of the Kings of Judah? 37In those days the LORD began to send King Rezin of Aram and Pekah son of Remaliah against Judah. 38Jotham slept with his ancestors, and was buried with his ancestors in the city of David, his ancestor; his son Ahaz succeeded him.

Ahaz Reigns over Judah

16 In the seventeenth year of Pekah son of Remaliah, King Ahaz son of Jotham of Judah began to reign. 2Ahaz was twenty years old when he began to reign; he reigned sixteen years in Jerusalem. He did not do what was right in the sight of the LORD his God, as his ancestor David had done, 3but he walked in the way of the kings of Israel. He even made his son pass through fire, according to the abominable practices of the nations whom the LORD drove out before the people of Israel. 4He sacrificed and made offerings on the high places, on the hills, and under every green tree.

5 Then King Rezin of Aram and King Pekah son of Remaliah of Israel came up to wage war on Jerusalem; they besieged Ahaz but could not conquer him. 6At that time the king of Edom*a* recovered Elath for Edom,*b* and drove the Judeans from Elath; and the Edomites came to Elath, where they live to this day. 7Ahaz sent messengers to King Tiglath-pileser of Assyria, saying, "I am your servant and your son. Come up, and rescue me from the hand of the king of Aram and from the hand of the king of Israel, who are attacking me." 8Ahaz also took the silver and

a Cn: Heb *King Rezin of Aram*   *b* Cn: Heb *Aram*

16:3 *made his son pass through fire.* Human sacrifice played a role in some Canaanite religions (see Deut 12:31; 18:10). Notice that the king of Judah is now walking in the "way of the kings of Israel"—not in the way of God. *high places.* See note on 1 Kings 3:3.

16:7–9 *Come up, and rescue me.* Ahaz turns to Assyria for help, even though Aram and Israel "could not conquer" Judah (v 5). Ahaz's plea to Tiglath-pileser is telling. Those who worship God are God's servants (5:16; 1 Kings 8:24, 53), but Ahaz describes himself as the servant of

Tiglath-pileser. God speaks of David's ruling descendants as God's own sons (2 Sam 7:14), but Ahaz describes himself to the Assyrian as "your son." Ahaz presents silver and gold from God's own Temple to Tiglath-pileser, who replaces God as Ahaz's source of security and well-being. The text informs us that the Assyrian king "listened to" Ahaz. Here the Hebrew verb translated "listen to" is the very verb used to describe how God "hears" the pleas of the slaves in Egypt (Exod 2:24). God's hearing leads to liberation. The Assyrian king's

gold found in the house of the LORD and in the treasures of the king's house, and sent a present to the king of Assyria. [9]The king of Assyria listened to him; the king of Assyria marched up against Damascus, and took it, carrying its people captive to Kir; then he killed Rezin.

10 When King Ahaz went to Damascus to meet King Tiglath-pileser of Assyria, he saw the altar that was at Damascus. King Ahaz sent to the priest Uriah a model of the altar, and its pattern, exact in all its details. [11]The priest Uriah built the altar; in accordance with all that King Ahaz had sent from Damascus, just so did the priest Uriah build it, before King Ahaz arrived from Damascus. [12]When the king came from Damascus, the king viewed the altar. Then the king drew near to the altar, went up on it, [13]and offered his burnt offering and his grain offering, poured his drink offering, and dashed the blood of his offerings of well-being against the altar. [14]The bronze altar that was before the LORD he removed from the front of the house, from the place between his altar and the house of the LORD, and put it on the north side of his altar. [15]King Ahaz commanded the priest Uriah, saying, "Upon the great altar offer the morning burnt offering, and the evening grain offering, and the king's burnt offering, and his grain offering, with the burnt offering of all the people of the land, their grain offering, and their drink offering; then dash against it all the blood of the burnt offering, and all the blood of the sacrifice; but the bronze altar shall be for me to inquire by." [16]The priest Uriah did everything that King Ahaz commanded.

17 Then King Ahaz cut off the frames of the stands, and removed the laver from them; he removed the sea from the bronze oxen that were under it, and put it on a pediment of stone. [18]The covered portal for use on the sabbath that had been built inside the palace, and the outer entrance for the king he removed from[a] the house of the LORD. He did this because of the king of Assyria. [19]Now the rest of the acts of Ahaz that he did, are they not written in the Book of the Annals of the Kings of Judah? [20]Ahaz slept with his ancestors, and was buried with his ancestors in the city of David; his son Hezekiah succeeded him.

Hoshea Reigns over Israel

17 In the twelfth year of King Ahaz of Judah, Hoshea son of Elah began to reign in Samaria over Israel; he reigned nine years. [2]He did what was evil in the sight of the LORD, yet not like the kings of Israel who were before him. [3]King Shalmaneser of Assyria came up against him; Hoshea became his vassal, and paid him tribute. [4]But the king of Assyria found treachery in Hoshea; for he had sent messengers to King So of Egypt, and offered no tribute to the king of Assyria, as he had done year by year; therefore the king of Assyria confined him and imprisoned him.

Israel Carried Captive to Assyria

5 Then the king of Assyria invaded all the land and came to Samaria; for three years he besieged it. [6]In the ninth year of Hoshea the king of Assyria captured Samaria; he carried the Israelites away to Assyria. He placed them

a Cn: Heb lacks *from*

---

hearing leads to subjugation. This passage is a knowing explanation of the ways in which God's people reidentify themselves and realign their lives and resources in relationship to human powers that promise well-being. As this passage implies, this realignment is idolatry. (Cf. chap 16; Isa 7–8.)

16:10–16 *The priest Uriah built the altar.* This new altar was inspired by one in Damascus, perhaps where Ahaz worshiped with Tiglath-pileser III. If so, this altar is Ahaz's bow to the new order and a sign of spiritual compromise. The presence of this Damascene altar in the Jerusalem Temple reminds us how our politics shapes our worship (and vice versa). Where we find our security is always tied to who we worship.

17:4 *he had sent messengers to King So of Egypt.* Like Ahaz, Hoshea seeks safety from another nation. God is not mentioned in either one's decision—not a good sign.

in Halah, on the Habor, the river of Gozan, and in the cities of the Medes.

7 This occurred because the people of Israel had sinned against the LORD their God, who had brought them up out of the land of Egypt from under the hand of Pharaoh king of Egypt. They had worshiped other gods 8and walked in the customs of the nations whom the LORD drove out before the people of Israel, and in the customs that the kings of Israel had introduced. *a* 9The people of Israel secretly did things that were not right against the LORD their God. They built for themselves high places at all their towns, from watchtower to fortified city; 10they set up for themselves pillars and sacred poles *b* on every high hill and under every green tree; 11there they made offerings on all the high places, as the nations did whom the LORD carried away before them. They did wicked things, provoking the LORD to anger; 12they served idols, of which the LORD had said to them, "You shall not do this." 13Yet the LORD warned Israel and Judah by every prophet and every seer, saying, "Turn from your evil ways and keep my commandments and my statutes, in accordance with all the law that I commanded your ancestors and that I sent to you by my servants the prophets." 14They would not lis-

ten but were stubborn, as their ancestors had been, who did not believe in the LORD their God. 15They despised his statutes, and his covenant that he made with their ancestors, and the warnings that he gave them. They went after false idols and became false; they followed the nations that were around them, concerning whom the LORD had commanded them that they should not do as they did. 16They rejected all the commandments of the LORD their God and made for themselves cast images of two calves; they made a sacred pole, *c* worshiped all the host of heaven, and served Baal. 17They made their sons and their daughters pass through fire; they used divination and augury; and they sold themselves to do evil in the sight of the LORD, provoking him to anger. 18Therefore the LORD was very angry with Israel and removed them out of his sight; none was left but the tribe of Judah alone.

19 Judah also did not keep the commandments of the LORD their God but walked in the customs that Israel had introduced. 20The LORD rejected all the descendants of Israel; he punished them and gave them into

a Meaning of Heb uncertain   *b* Heb *Asherim*
c Heb *Asherah*

17:6 *the king . . . carried the Israelites away to Assyria.* Sargon II (see Isa 20:1) completed the campaign against the Northern Kingdom in 722/721 BC. The Assyrians practiced an especially cruel form of deportation, breaking up families and communities and scattering them to all reaches of the empire. Sargon's records indicate he removed 27,290 inhabitants.

17:7–18, 21–23 *because the people of Israel had sinned against the LORD.* This passage is a lengthy theological reflection on the destruction of the Northern Kingdom. Why did this nation fall? The answer to this question is much influenced by the theology and language of Deuteronomy. The narrator charges the people of Israel with failing to keep God's commandments, turning their backs on God. The narrator alludes again and again to the foundational truth of the covenant of Moses: that God alone is God and alone must be worshiped. But the people, following the

example of their kings (v 8), chose to worship other gods. They pursued "evil ways" (v 13)— all wrongdoing proceeds from the failure to worship and obey God alone.

17:9, 11 *high places.* See note on 1 Kings 3:3.

17:10 *sacred poles.* See note on 1 Kings 14:15.

17:15 *They went after false idols and became false.* The Hebrew for "false idols" and "false" (*hebel*) means "vapor" or "breath." It is the word in Ecclesiastes that is translated "vanity" (e.g., 1:2). *Hebel* is not the breath that gives life and that inspires Elijah and Elisha (*ruah;* see note on 2:9). It is what is insubstantial and momentary. 1 & 2 Kings assert that those who worship what is insubstantial become insubstantial.

17:16 *worshiped all the host of heaven.* The worship of sun, moon, and stars, an Assyrian cult, is a new charge.

17:17 *pass through fire.* See note on 16:3.

the hand of plunderers, until he had banished them from his presence.

21 When he had torn Israel from the house of David, they made Jeroboam son of Nebat king. Jeroboam drove Israel from following the LORD and made them commit great sin. 22The people of Israel continued in all the sins that Jeroboam committed; they did not depart from them 23until the LORD removed Israel out of his sight, as he had foretold through all his servants the prophets. So Israel was exiled from their own land to Assyria until this day.

Assyria Resettles Samaria

24 The king of Assyria brought people from Babylon, Cuthah, Avva, Hamath, and Sepharvaim, and placed them in the cities of Samaria in place of the people of Israel; they took possession of Samaria, and settled in its cities. 25When they first settled there, they did not worship the LORD; therefore the LORD sent lions among them, which killed some of them. 26So the king of Assyria was told, "The nations that you have carried away and placed in the cities of Samaria do not know the law of the god of the land; therefore he has sent lions among them; they are killing them, because they do not know the law of the god of the land." 27Then the king of Assyria commanded, "Send there one of the priests whom you carried away from there; let him a go and live there, and teach them the law of the god of the land." 28So one

of the priests whom they had carried away from Samaria came and lived in Bethel; he taught them how they should worship the LORD.

29 But every nation still made gods of its own and put them in the shrines of the high places that the people of Samaria had made, every nation in the cities in which they lived; 30the people of Babylon made Succoth-benoth, the people of Cuth made Nergal, the people of Hamath made Ashima; 31the Avites made Nibhaz and Tartak; the Sepharvites burned their children in the fire to Adrammelech and Anammelech, the gods of Sepharvaim. 32They also worshiped the LORD and appointed from among themselves all sorts of people as priests of the high places, who sacrificed for them in the shrines of the high places. 33So they worshiped the LORD but also served their own gods, after the manner of the nations from among whom they had been carried away. 34To this day they continue to practice their former customs.

They do not worship the LORD and they do not follow the statutes or the ordinances or the law or the commandment that the LORD commanded the children of Jacob, whom he named Israel. 35The LORD had made a covenant with them and commanded them, "You shall not worship other gods or bow yourselves to them or serve them or sacrifice to them, 36but you shall worship the

a Syr Vg: Heb them

17:24 *settled in its cities.* The Assyrians settled other conquered peoples in the area that was once the Northern Kingdom and called it Samaria.

Responding
17:24–41 WORSHIP. The people from other nations relocated in Samaria by the Assyrians worshiped God out of fear of death by lions, but they continued to worship their own idols with their hearts. It is a common state among Christians as well. As the demon Uncle Screwtape writes in C. S. Lewis's *The Screwtape Letters:* "Hundreds of these adult converts have been reclaimed after a brief sojourn in the enemy's camp and are now with

us. All the *habits* of the patient, both mental and bodily, are still in our favour." What mental or bodily habits in your life incline you away from God? *See also* Spiritual Disciplines Index.

17:35–39 *The LORD had made a covenant with them.* Although 1 & 2 Kings denounce Israel for failing to destroy all former occupants of Canaan (1 Kings 9:20–21), these verses imply that the promises of God to Israel are now open to non-Israelites. Like the Israelites escaping Egypt, these newcomers have suffered at the hands of an empire and may now find both home and God. What a remarkable vision of the embrace of God's covenant!

LORD, who brought you out of the land of Egypt with great power and with an outstretched arm; you shall bow yourselves to him, and to him you shall sacrifice. 37The statutes and the ordinances and the law and the commandment that he wrote for you, you shall always be careful to observe. You shall not worship other gods; 38you shall not forget the covenant that I have made with you. You shall not worship other gods, 39but you shall worship the LORD your God; he will deliver you out of the hand of all your enemies." 40They would not listen, however, but they continued to practice their former custom.

41 So these nations worshiped the LORD, but also served their carved images; to this day their children and their children's children continue to do as their ancestors did.

Hezekiah's Reign over Judah

18 In the third year of King Hoshea son of Elah of Israel, Hezekiah son of King Ahaz of Judah began to reign. 2He was twenty-five years old when he began to reign; he reigned twenty-nine years in Jerusalem. His mother's name was Abi daughter of Zechariah. 3He did what was right in the sight of the LORD just as his ancestor David had done. 4He removed the high places, broke down the pillars, and cut down the sacred pole.a He broke in pieces the bronze serpent that Moses had made, for until those days the people of Israel had made offerings to it; it was called Nehushtan. 5He trusted in the LORD the God of Israel; so that there was no one like him among all the kings of Judah after him, or among those who were before him. 6For he held fast to the LORD; he did not depart from

following him but kept the commandments that the LORD commanded Moses. 7The LORD was with him; wherever he went, he prospered. He rebelled against the king of Assyria and would not serve him. 8He attacked the Philistines as far as Gaza and its territory, from watchtower to fortified city.

9 In the fourth year of King Hezekiah, which was the seventh year of King Hoshea son of Elah of Israel, King Shalmaneser of Assyria came up against Samaria, besieged it, 10and at the end of three years, took it. In the sixth year of Hezekiah, which was the ninth year of King Hoshea of Israel, Samaria was taken. 11The king of Assyria carried the Israelites away to Assyria, settled them in Halah, on the Habor, the river of Gozan, and in the cities of the Medes, 12because they did not obey the voice of the LORD their God but transgressed his covenant—all that Moses the servant of the LORD had commanded; they neither listened nor obeyed.

Sennacherib Invades Judah

13 In the fourteenth year of King Hezekiah, King Sennacherib of Assyria came up against all the fortified cities of Judah and captured them. 14King Hezekiah of Judah sent to the king of Assyria at Lachish, saying, "I have done wrong; withdraw from me; whatever you impose on me I will bear." The king of Assyria demanded of King Hezekiah of Judah three hundred talents of silver and thirty talents of gold. 15Hezekiah gave him all the silver that was found in the house of the LORD and in the treasuries of the king's house. 16At that time Hezekiah stripped the gold

a Heb Asherah

18:1–8 just as his ancestor David had done. Hezekiah is described as a new David. He trusts in God and holds fast to God, obeying the commandments and reforming worship. His goodness is rewarded with success: independence from Assyria and expanded territory.
18:4 high places. See note on 1 Kings 3:3. sacred pole. See note on 1 Kings 14:15. bronze serpent. That the people made offerings to the bronze serpent of Num 21:6–9 seems to indicate

that it became a cultic symbol in its own right.
18:13–17 Sennacherib . . . captured them. Although historical records are incomplete, Sennacherib invaded Judah in 701 BC, capturing many fortified cities and receiving an enormous tribute payment from Hezekiah. Sennacherib's often inflated annals also claim that the Assyrians took captive over two hundred thousand of Judah's inhabitants, a number scholars tend to doubt. Tartan, Rabsaris, and Rabshakeh (v 17) are titles of Assyrian officials.

from the doors of the temple of the LORD, and from the doorposts that King Hezekiah of Judah had overlaid and gave it to the king of Assyria. [17]The king of Assyria sent the Tartan, the Rabsaris, and the Rabshakeh with a great army from Lachish to King Hezekiah at Jerusalem. They went up and came to Jerusalem. When they arrived, they came and stood by the conduit of the upper pool, which is on the highway to the Fuller's Field. [18]When they called for the king, there came out to them Eliakim son of Hilkiah, who was in charge of the palace, and Shebnah the secretary, and Joah son of Asaph, the recorder.

19 The Rabshakeh said to them, "Say to Hezekiah: Thus says the great king, the king of Assyria: On what do you base this confidence of yours? [20]Do you think that mere words are strategy and power for war? On whom do you now rely, that you have rebelled against me? [21]See, you are relying now on Egypt, that broken reed of a staff, which will pierce the hand of anyone who leans on it. Such is Pharaoh king of Egypt to all who rely on him. [22]But if you say to me, 'We rely on the LORD our God,' is it not he whose high places and altars Hezekiah has removed, saying to Judah and to Jerusalem, 'You shall worship before this altar in Jerusalem'? [23]Come now, make a wager with my master the king of Assyria: I will give you two thousand horses, if you are able on your part to set riders on them. [24]How then can you repulse a single captain among the least of my master's servants, when you rely on Egypt for chariots and for horsemen? [25]Moreover, is it

without the LORD that I have come up against this place to destroy it? The LORD said to me, Go up against this land, and destroy it."

26 Then Eliakim son of Hilkiah, and Shebnah, and Joah said to the Rabshakeh, "Please speak to your servants in the Aramaic language, for we understand it; do not speak to us in the language of Judah within the hearing of the people who are on the wall." [27]But the Rabshakeh said to them, "Has my master sent me to speak these words to your master and to you, and not to the people sitting on the wall, who are doomed with you to eat their own dung and to drink their own urine?"

28 Then the Rabshakeh stood and called out in a loud voice in the language of Judah, "Hear the word of the great king, the king of Assyria! [29]Thus says the king: 'Do not let Hezekiah deceive you, for he will not be able to deliver you out of my hand. [30]Do not let Hezekiah make you rely on the LORD by saying, The LORD will surely deliver us, and this city will not be given into the hand of the king of Assyria.' [31]Do not listen to Hezekiah; for thus says the king of Assyria: 'Make your peace with me and come out to me; then every one of you will eat from your own vine and your own fig tree, and drink water from your own cistern, [32]until I come and take you away to a land like your own land, a land of grain and wine, a land of bread and vineyards, a land of olive oil and honey, that you may live and not die. Do not listen to Hezekiah when he misleads you by saying, The LORD will deliver us. [33]Has any of the gods of the nations ever de-

---

18:19–25 *The Rabshakeh said to them.* The Rabshakeh interprets history in ways that at first seem remarkably God-oriented! In what or in whom do the citizens of Judah put their confidence? The theme of trust has been at the heart of 2 Kings with all the crises that have emerged to threaten the North and the South. But this Assyrian theologian stumbles when he asserts that God has sent the Assyrians to conquer Judah (v 25)! We will soon hear God's mind on this matter.

18:28 *called out . . . in the language of Judah.* Judah's leaders ask the Rabshakeh to use Aramaic, the language of diplomacy (v 26), but

he chooses Hebrew, so that all the citizens of Jerusalem will understand his threats.

18:31–32 *Make your peace with me.* The Rabshakeh uses powerful imagery familiar to the Israelites to entice them to surrender and accept exile. They will eat from their own vines and fig trees (Mic 4:4; see note on 1 Kings 4:25). Fertile land will spread before them (Deut 8:7–9). Speaking for Sennacherib, this official mimics God, offering life for obedience, death for disobedience (Deut 30:15–20). Once again human power poses as God, stealing the language of security and well-being to entice humans to displace God and trust in lesser powers.

livered its land out of the hand of the king of Assyria? [34]Where are the gods of Hamath and Arpad? Where are the gods of Sepharvaim, Hena, and Ivvah? Have they delivered Samaria out of my hand? [35]Who among all the gods of the countries have delivered their countries out of my hand, that the LORD should deliver Jerusalem out of my hand?' "

36 But the people were silent and answered him not a word, for the king's command was, "Do not answer him." [37]Then Eliakim son of Hilkiah, who was in charge of the palace, and Shebna the secretary, and Joah son of Asaph, the recorder, came to Hezekiah with their clothes torn and told him the words of the Rabshakeh.

Hezekiah Consults Isaiah

19 When King Hezekiah heard it, he tore his clothes, covered himself with sackcloth, and went into the house of the LORD. [2]And he sent Eliakim, who was in charge of the palace, and Shebna the secretary, and the senior priests, covered with sackcloth, to the prophet Isaiah son of Amoz. [3]They said to him, "Thus says Hezekiah, This day is a day of distress, of rebuke, and of disgrace; children have come to the birth, and there is no strength to bring them forth. [4]It may be that the LORD your God heard all the words of the Rabshakeh, whom his master the king of Assyria has sent to mock the living God, and will rebuke the words that the LORD your God has heard; therefore lift up your prayer for the remnant that is left." [5]When the servants of King Hezekiah came to Isaiah, [6]Isaiah said to them, "Say to your master, 'Thus says the LORD: Do not be afraid because of the words that you have heard,

with which the servants of the king of Assyria have reviled me. [7]I myself will put a spirit in him, so that he shall hear a rumor and return to his own land; I will cause him to fall by the sword in his own land.' "

Sennacherib's Threat

8 The Rabshakeh returned, and found the king of Assyria fighting against Libnah; for he had heard that the king had left Lachish. [9]When the king[a] heard concerning King Tirhakah of Ethiopia,[b] "See, he has set out to fight against you," he sent messengers again to Hezekiah, saying, [10]"Thus shall you speak to King Hezekiah of Judah: Do not let your God on whom you rely deceive you by promising that Jerusalem will not be given into the hand of the king of Assyria. [11]See, you have heard what the kings of Assyria have done to all lands, destroying them utterly. Shall you be delivered? [12]Have the gods of the nations delivered them, the nations that my predecessors destroyed, Gozan, Haran, Rezeph, and the people of Eden who were in Telassar? [13]Where is the king of Hamath, the king of Arpad, the king of the city of Sepharvaim, the king of Hena, or the king of Ivvah?"

Hezekiah's Prayer

14 Hezekiah received the letter from the hand of the messengers and read it; then Hezekiah went up to the house of the LORD and spread it before the LORD. [15]And Hezekiah prayed before the LORD, and said: "O LORD the God of Israel, who are enthroned above the cherubim, you are God, you alone, of all

a Heb he   b Or Nubia; Heb Cush

19:4 *lift up your prayer for the remnant that is left.* Hezekiah seeks help from God and appeals to the prophet (vv 1–2). The reference to the remnant is to those who have survived Sennacherib's destructive campaign against Judah (see note on 18:13–17).

19:14 *spread it before the LORD.* Hezekiah is described as a king who trusts in God (18:5). Now in great distress, he seeks God (19:1), bringing matters of the state into the Temple before God. The situation is dangerous and

the kingdoms of the earth; you have made heaven and earth. [16]Incline your ear, O LORD, and hear; open your eyes, O LORD, and see; hear the words of Sennacherib, which he has sent to mock the living God. [17]Truly, O LORD, the kings of Assyria have laid waste the nations and their lands, [18]and have hurled their gods into the fire, though they were no gods but the work of human hands—wood and stone—and so they were destroyed. [19]So now, O LORD our God, save us, I pray you, from his hand, so that all the kingdoms of the earth may know that you, O LORD, are God alone."

20 Then Isaiah son of Amoz sent to Hezekiah, saying, "Thus says the LORD, the God of Israel: I have heard your prayer to me about King Sennacherib of Assyria. [21]This is the word that the LORD has spoken concerning him:

She despises you, she scorns you—
    virgin daughter Zion;
she tosses her head—behind your back,
    daughter Jerusalem.

[22] "Whom have you mocked and reviled?
    Against whom have you raised your
        voice
and haughtily lifted your eyes?
    Against the Holy One of Israel!
[23] By your messengers you have mocked
        the Lord,
    and you have said, 'With my many
        chariots
I have gone up the heights of the
        mountains,
    to the far recesses of Lebanon;
I felled its tallest cedars,
    its choicest cypresses;
I entered its farthest retreat,
    its densest forest.

[24] I dug wells
    and drank foreign waters,
I dried up with the sole of my foot
    all the streams of Egypt.'

[25] "Have you not heard
    that I determined it long ago?
I planned from days of old
    what now I bring to pass,
that you should make fortified cities
    crash into heaps of ruins,
[26] while their inhabitants, shorn of
        strength,
    are dismayed and confounded;
they have become like plants of the
        field
    and like tender grass,
like grass on the housetops,
    blighted before it is grown.

[27] "But I know your rising[a] and your
        sitting,
    your going out and coming in,
    and your raging against me.
[28] Because you have raged against me
    and your arrogance has come to my
        ears,
I will put my hook in your nose
    and my bit in your mouth;
I will turn you back on the way
    by which you came.

29 "And this shall be the sign for you: This year you shall eat what grows of itself, and in the second year what springs from that; then in the third year sow, reap, plant vineyards, and eat their fruit. [30]The surviving remnant

a Gk Compare Isa 37.27 Q Ms: MT lacks rising

---

potentially explosive: the Assyrians are poised for attack, and the citizens of Jerusalem have heard, in their own language, a potent appeal to their dreams and a potent attack on their king. Into this highly charged situation, Hezekiah introduces prayer, an act of ultimate trust and vulnerability. 1 & 2 Kings claim the power of prayer because it invites the full expression of God's loyalty and power into human circumstances. Prayer is the Spiritual Discipline for the hour.

Responding
19:15–19 PRAYER. In the note on 19:14, prayer is described as "an act of ultimate trust and vulnerability." Do you agree? How can you be more vulnerable in your prayer? More trusting? See also Spiritual Disciplines Index.

19:22–28 Whom have you mocked? God's response is a mighty indictment of Sennacherib. Believing that he alone has

of the house of Judah shall again take root downward, and bear fruit upward; ³¹for from Jerusalem a remnant shall go out, and from Mount Zion a band of survivors. The zeal of the Lord of hosts will do this.

32 "Therefore thus says the Lord concerning the king of Assyria: He shall not come into this city, shoot an arrow there, come before it with a shield, or cast up a siege ramp against it. ³³By the way that he came, by the same he shall return; he shall not come into this city, says the Lord. ³⁴For I will defend this city to save it, for my own sake and for the sake of my servant David."

Sennacherib's Defeat and Death

35 That very night the angel of the Lord set out and struck down one hundred eighty-five thousand in the camp of the Assyrians; when morning dawned, they were all dead bodies. ³⁶Then King Sennacherib of Assyria left, went home, and lived at Nineveh. ³⁷As he was worshiping in the house of his god Nisroch, his sons Adrammelech and Sharezer killed him with the sword, and they escaped into the land of Ararat. His son Esar-haddon succeeded him.

Hezekiah's Illness

20 In those days Hezekiah became sick and was at the point of death. The prophet Isaiah son of Amoz came to him, and said to him, "Thus says the Lord: Set

your house in order, for you shall die; you shall not recover." ²Then Hezekiah turned his face to the wall and prayed to the Lord: ³"Remember now, O Lord, I implore you, how I have walked before you in faithfulness with a whole heart, and have done what is good in your sight." Hezekiah wept bitterly. ⁴Before Isaiah had gone out of the middle court, the word of the Lord came to him: ⁵"Turn back, and say to Hezekiah prince of my people, Thus says the Lord, the God of your ancestor David: I have heard your prayer, I have seen your tears; indeed, I will heal you; on the third day you shall go up to the house of the Lord. ⁶I will add fifteen years to your life. I will deliver you and this city out of the hand of the king of Assyria; I will defend this city for my own sake and for my servant David's sake." ⁷Then Isaiah said, "Bring a lump of figs. Let them take it and apply it to the boil, so that he may recover."

8 Hezekiah said to Isaiah, "What shall be the sign that the Lord will heal me, and that I shall go up to the house of the Lord on the third day?" ⁹Isaiah said, "This is the sign to you from the Lord, that the Lord will do the thing that he has promised: the shadow has now advanced ten intervals; shall it retreat ten intervals?" ¹⁰Hezekiah answered, "It is normal for the shadow to lengthen ten intervals; rather let the shadow retreat ten intervals." ¹¹The prophet Isaiah cried to the Lord; and he brought the shadow back the

---

achieved his power (note the use of "I" in vv 23–24), Sennacherib now hears that he is mighty only because of the God of Israel (vv 25–27). For 1 & 2 Kings, the arrogant "I" of Sennacherib is replaced by the mighty "I" of God, *the* decisive agent in history.

19:29–31 *This year you shall eat.* These verses promise the healing of the land after war and the return of agricultural yields for those remaining in Judah (see note on 18:13–17).

19:34 *for my own sake and for . . . David.* God will save Jerusalem "for my own sake," unlike the wooden or metal gods who can do nothing (v 18). The city is also saved in remembrance of the Davidic covenant.

19:35–37 *the angel of the Lord . . . struck down.* Hezekiah's trust in God and God's

prophet is answered with the news of Sennacherib's defeat: 185,000 Assyrians are killed in the night, and the mighty Sennacherib heads home in the morning, only to be murdered by his own sons in the temple of a god who cannot protect him—even on that god's turf. The theologians of 1 & 2 Kings leave no question about who is responsible for this mysterious victory: the God of Israel.

20:6 *I will deliver you and this city.* Hezekiah's prayer is again powerful in moving God to mercy for both Jerusalem and himself. God remembers the Davidic promise in heeding this prayer: Hezekiah is called "prince" (v 5), as was David (1 Sam 25:30). Prayer stands as the Spiritual Discipline that moves the heart and hand of God.

ten intervals, by which the sun[a] had declined on the dial of Ahaz.

Envoys from Babylon

12 At that time King Merodach-baladan son of Baladan of Babylon sent envoys with letters and a present to Hezekiah, for he had heard that Hezekiah had been sick. [13]Hezekiah welcomed them;[b] he showed them all his treasure house, the silver, the gold, the spices, the precious oil, his armory, all that was found in his storehouses; there was nothing in his house or in all his realm that Hezekiah did not show them. [14]Then the prophet Isaiah came to King Hezekiah, and said to him, "What did these men say? From where did they come to you?" Hezekiah answered, "They have come from a far country, from Babylon." [15]He said, "What have they seen in your house?" Hezekiah answered, "They have seen all that is in my house; there is nothing in my storehouses that I did not show them."

16 Then Isaiah said to Hezekiah, "Hear the word of the LORD: [17]Days are coming when all that is in your house, and that which your ancestors have stored up until this day, shall be carried to Babylon; nothing shall be left, says the LORD. [18]Some of your own sons who are born to you shall be taken away; they shall be eunuchs in the palace of the king of Babylon." [19]Then Hezekiah said to Isaiah, "The word of the LORD that you have spoken is good." For he thought, "Why not, if there will be peace and security in my days?"

Death of Hezekiah

20 The rest of the deeds of Hezekiah, all his power, how he made the pool and the conduit and brought water into the city, are they not written in the Book of the Annals of the Kings of Judah? [21]Hezekiah slept with his an-

cestors; and his son Manasseh succeeded him.

Manasseh Reigns over Judah

21 Manasseh was twelve years old when he began to reign; he reigned fifty-five years in Jerusalem. His mother's name was Hephzibah. [2]He did what was evil in the sight of the LORD, following the abominable practices of the nations that the LORD drove out before the people of Israel. [3]For he rebuilt the high places that his father Hezekiah had destroyed; he erected altars for Baal, made a sacred pole,[c] as King Ahab of Israel had done, worshiped all the host of heaven, and served them. [4]He built altars in the house of the LORD, of which the LORD had said, "In Jerusalem I will put my name." [5]He built altars for all the host of heaven in the two courts of the house of the LORD. [6]He made his son pass through fire; he practiced soothsaying and augury, and dealt with mediums and with wizards. He did much evil in the sight of the LORD, provoking him to anger. [7]The carved image of Asherah that he had made he set in the house of which the LORD said to David and to his son Solomon, "In this house, and in Jerusalem, which I have chosen out of all the tribes of Israel, I will put my name forever; [8]I will not cause the feet of Israel to wander any more out of the land that I gave to their ancestors, if only they will be careful to do according to all that I have commanded them, and according to all the law that my servant Moses commanded them." [9]But they did not listen; Manasseh misled them to do more evil than the

---

a Syr See Isa 38.8 and Tg: Heb *it*   b Gk Vg Syr: Heb *When Hezekiah heard about them*   c Heb *Asherah*

20:12–19 *Merodach-baladan . . . sent envoys.* As king of Babylon, Merodach-baladan sought to free his province from Assyrian rule, fomenting revolution in the region. Hezekiah may think that Babylon is just a "far country" (v 14) and that display of Judah's wealth is a sign of alliance, but the prophet Isaiah seems to imply that Hezekiah has been unwise. Hezekiah has played the political game, hoping to win an ally

rather than first seeking wisdom from God. When Isaiah predicts eventual destruction by Babylon (vv 16–18), we see Hezekiah's narrow perspective again (v 19).

21:3 *high places.* See note on 1 Kings 3:3. *sacred pole.* See note on 1 Kings 14:15. *host of heaven.* See note on 17:16.

21:6 *pass through fire.* See note on 16:3.

nations had done that the LORD destroyed before the people of Israel.

10 The LORD said by his servants the prophets, 11"Because King Manasseh of Judah has committed these abominations, has done things more wicked than all that the Amorites did, who were before him, and has caused Judah also to sin with his idols; 12therefore thus says the LORD, the God of Israel, I am bringing upon Jerusalem and Judah such evil that the ears of everyone who hears of it will tingle. 13I will stretch over Jerusalem the measuring line for Samaria, and the plummet for the house of Ahab; I will wipe Jerusalem as one wipes a dish, wiping it and turning it upside down. 14I will cast off the remnant of my heritage, and give them into the hand of their enemies; they shall become a prey and a spoil to all their enemies, 15because they have done what is evil in my sight and have provoked me to anger, since the day their ancestors came out of Egypt, even to this day."

16 Moreover Manasseh shed very much innocent blood, until he had filled Jerusalem from one end to another, besides the sin that he caused Judah to sin so that they did what was evil in the sight of the LORD.

17 Now the rest of the acts of Manasseh, all that he did, and the sin that he committed, are they not written in the Book of the Annals of the Kings of Judah? 18Manasseh slept with his ancestors, and was buried in the garden of his house, in the garden of Uzza. His son Amon succeeded him.

Amon Reigns over Judah

19 Amon was twenty-two years old when he began to reign; he reigned two years in Jerusalem. His mother's name was Meshullemeth daughter of Haruz of Jotbah. 20He did what was evil in the sight of the LORD, as his father Manasseh had done. 21He walked in all the way in which his father walked, served the idols that his father served, and worshiped them; 22he abandoned the LORD, the God of his ancestors, and did not walk in the way of the LORD. 23The servants of Amon conspired against him, and killed the king in his house. 24But the people of the land killed all those who had conspired against King Amon, and the people of the land made his son Josiah king in place of him. 25Now the rest of the acts of Amon that he did, are they not written in the Book of the Annals of the Kings of Judah? 26He was buried in his tomb in the garden of Uzza; then his son Josiah succeeded him.

Josiah Reigns over Judah

22 Josiah was eight years old when he began to reign; he reigned thirty-one years in Jerusalem. His mother's name was Jedidah daughter of Adaiah of Bozkath. 2He did what was right in the sight of the LORD, and walked in all the way of his father David; he did not turn aside to the right or to the left.

21:10–15 *by his servants the prophets.* God mobilizes the prophets once again, this time to speak words of dreadful judgment. More than all other kings, the text contends, Manasseh has breached the law and caused the people of Judah to sin. Where God has put the divine name, Manasseh "sets" (same Hebrew word as "put") a "carved image of Asherah," consort of Baal (v 7). In this wordplay, 1 & 2 Kings lay bare the chasm between these two acts: the first is an act of covenant loyalty; the second, an act of blatant disloyalty. The upcoming judgment points to Manasseh's "abominations," the final breaking point for God. But Manasseh is not solely responsible for God's judgment. The history of the people's disobedience is traced back to the days of the exodus from Egypt (v 15).

21:16 *shed very much innocent blood.* This phrase can be read both literally and metaphorically. Perhaps Manasseh persecutes the faithful who speak against his faithless rule. Perhaps he exploits the poor and helpless for his own gain (e.g., Jer 7:6; 22:3). Again, justice becomes a central consideration in God's judgment of this king and nation.

21:24 *made . . . Josiah king.* The "people of the land" rise up and install the faithful Josiah as king (see note on 11:14). Judah begins to resemble Israel, with its history of violent succession.

22:2 *did not turn aside.* Josiah is described in terms reserved for the ruler after Moses' and

Hilkiah Finds the Book of the Law

3 In the eighteenth year of King Josiah, the king sent Shaphan son of Azaliah, son of Meshullam, the secretary, to the house of the LORD, saying, 4 "Go up to the high priest Hilkiah, and have him count the entire sum of the money that has been brought into the house of the LORD, which the keepers of the threshold have collected from the people; 5 let it be given into the hand of the workers who have the oversight of the house of the LORD; let them give it to the workers who are at the house of the LORD, repairing the house, 6 that is, to the carpenters, to the builders, to the masons; and let them use it to buy timber and quarried stone to repair the house. 7 But no accounting shall be asked from them for the money that is delivered into their hand, for they deal honestly."

8 The high priest Hilkiah said to Shaphan the secretary, "I have found the book of the law in the house of the LORD." When Hilkiah gave the book to Shaphan, he read it. 9 Then Shaphan the secretary came to the king, and reported to the king, "Your servants have emptied out the money that was found in the house, and have delivered it into the hand of the workers who have oversight of the house of the LORD." 10 Shaphan the secretary informed the king, "The priest Hilkiah has given me a book." Shaphan then read it aloud to the king.

11 When the king heard the words of the book of the law, he tore his clothes. 12 Then the king commanded the priest Hilkiah, Ahikam son of Shaphan, Achbor son of Micaiah, Shaphan the secretary, and the king's servant Asaiah, saying, 13 "Go, inquire of the LORD for me, for the people, and for all Judah, concerning the words of this book that has been found; for great is the wrath of the LORD that is kindled against us, because our ancestors did not obey the words of this book, to do according to all that is written concerning us."

14 So the priest Hilkiah, Ahikam, Achbor, Shaphan, and Asaiah went to the prophetess Huldah the wife of Shallum son of Tikvah, son of Harhas, keeper of the wardrobe; she resided in Jerusalem in the Second Quarter, where they consulted her. 15 She declared to them, "Thus says the LORD, the God of Israel: Tell the man who sent you to me, 16 Thus says the LORD, I will indeed bring disaster on this place and on its inhabitants—all the words of the book that the king of Judah has read. 17 Because they have abandoned me and have made offerings to other gods, so that they have provoked me to anger with all the work of their hands, therefore my wrath will be kindled against this place, and it will not be quenched. 18 But as to the king of Judah, who sent you to inquire of the LORD, thus shall you say to him, Thus says the LORD, the

---

God's heart: one who is not "turning aside . . . to the right or to the left" (Deut 17:20). This phrase refers to walking without being distracted or enticed from a path (Num 20:17; 1 Sam 6:12–13). It is related to the metaphor of walking in the paths of God, a metaphor at the heart of divine desires for God's people (Deut 5:32–33; 1 Kings 6:11–12).

22:8 *book of the law.* This probably refers to an earlier form of Deuteronomy (see Deut 28:61; 31:26 for the use of this phrase). Given the particulars of Josiah's upcoming reforms (chap 23), scholars have suggested portions of Deuteronomy (probably chaps 12–26) as this earlier document.

22:14 *went to the prophetess Huldah.* A prophet is needed to interpret the law for the here and now of Josiah and Judah. Note that

court officials must go outside the court to find the prophet who will speak the upcoming words. Other prophets active at this time are Jeremiah (1:2) and Zephaniah (1:1)—no milquetoasts either.

Responding

22:14 GUIDANCE. Part of being "a royal priesthood, a holy nation, God's own people" means that we must all look to each other for help discerning God's will (1 Pet 2:9). An ancient practice gaining modern popularity is that of spiritual direction. Is there someone in your church or small group who could serve as your spiritual director? Pray about whether this is an appropriate step for you to take. *See also* Spiritual Disciplines Index.

DKANDA

God of Israel: Regarding the words that you have heard, [19]because your heart was penitent, and you humbled yourself before the LORD, when you heard how I spoke against this place, and against its inhabitants, that they should become a desolation and a curse, and because you have torn your clothes and wept before me, I also have heard you, says the LORD. [20]Therefore, I will gather you to your ancestors, and you shall be gathered to your grave in peace; your eyes shall not see all the disaster that I will bring on this place." They took the message back to the king.

Josiah's Reformation

23 Then the king directed that all the elders of Judah and Jerusalem should be gathered to him. [2]The king went up to the house of the LORD, and with him went all the people of Judah, all the inhabitants of Jerusalem, the priests, the prophets, and all the people, both small and great; he read in their hearing all the words of the book of the covenant that had been found in the house of the LORD. [3]The king stood by the pillar and made a covenant before the LORD, to follow the LORD, keeping his commandments, his decrees, and his statutes, with all his heart and all his soul, to perform the words of this covenant that were written in this book. All the people joined in the covenant.

4 The king commanded the high priest Hilkiah, the priests of the second order, and the guardians of the threshold, to bring out of the temple of the LORD all the vessels made for Baal, for Asherah, and for all the host of heaven; he burned them outside Jerusalem in the fields of the Kidron, and carried their ashes to Bethel. [5]He deposed the idolatrous priests whom the kings of Judah had ordained to make offerings in the high places at the cities of Judah and around Jerusalem; those also who made offerings to Baal, to the sun, the moon, the constellations, and all the host of the heavens. [6]He brought out the image of[a] Asherah from the house of the LORD, outside Jerusalem, to the Wadi Kidron, burned it at the Wadi Kidron, beat it to dust and threw the dust of it upon the graves of the common people. [7]He broke down the houses of the male temple prostitutes that were in the house of the LORD, where the women did weaving for Asherah. [8]He brought all the priests out of the towns of Judah, and defiled the high places where the priests had made offerings, from Geba to Beer-sheba; he broke down the high places of the gates that were at the entrance of the gate of Joshua the governor of the city, which were on the left at the gate of the city. [9]The priests of the high places, however, did not come up to the altar of the LORD in Jerusalem, but ate unleavened bread among their kindred. [10]He defiled Topheth, which is in the valley of Ben-hinnom, so that no one would make a son or a daughter pass through fire as an offering to Molech. [11]He removed the horses that the kings of Judah had dedicated to the sun, at the entrance to the house of the LORD, by the chamber of the eunuch Nathan-melech, which

a Heb lacks image of

23:2–3 *All the people joined in the covenant.* The Temple book, now called the "book of the covenant" (v 2), becomes the impetus for a recovenanting ceremony. Anticipating this renewal are the Sinai ceremony (Exod 24:1–11) and the ceremonies in Moab (Deut 29) and at Shechem (Josh 24). These ceremonies, as well as the ones in 1 Kings 8 and 2 Kings 11:17, suggest how necessary it is for the community of faith to identify itself again and again as the People of God and to learn again and again what this identity means for individual and communal life. In many ways, this lesson is what worship and Christian education are all about.

But the special nature of these biblical ceremonies suggests that, at transitional points in a community's story, a ceremony may anchor new generations in their faith while summoning divine wind in their sails for meeting new challenges.

23:4 *Baal . . . Asherah.* See note on 1 Kings 14:15. *host of heaven.* See note on 17:16.

23:4–25 *The king commanded.* The word of the law comes alive, reshaping the worship of the people through the dramatic reforms of Temple and shrines throughout the land.

23:5 *high places.* See note on 1 Kings 3:3.

23:10 *pass through fire.* See note on 16:3.

was in the precincts;*a* then he burned the chariots of the sun with fire. 12The altars on the roof of the upper chamber of Ahaz, which the kings of Judah had made, and the altars that Manasseh had made in the two courts of the house of the LORD, he pulled down from there and broke in pieces, and threw the rubble into the Wadi Kidron. 13The king defiled the high places that were east of Jerusalem, to the south of the Mount of Destruction, which King Solomon of Israel had built for Astarte the abomination of the Sidonians, for Chemosh the abomination of Moab, and for Milcom the abomination of the Ammonites. 14He broke the pillars in pieces, cut down the sacred poles,*b* and covered the sites with human bones.

15 Moreover, the altar at Bethel, the high place erected by Jeroboam son of Nebat, who caused Israel to sin—he pulled down that altar along with the high place. He burned the high place, crushing it to dust; he also burned the sacred pole.*c* 16As Josiah turned, he saw the tombs there on the mount; and he sent and took the bones out of the tombs, and burned them on the altar, and defiled it, according to the word of the LORD that the man of God proclaimed,*d* when Jeroboam stood by the altar at the festival; he turned and looked up at the tomb of the man of God who had predicted these things. 17Then he said, "What is that monument that I see?" The people of the city told him, "It is the tomb of the man of God who came from Judah and predicted these things that you have done against the altar at Bethel." 18He said, "Let him rest; let no one move his bones." So they let his bones alone, with the bones of the prophet who came out of Samaria. 19Moreover, Josiah removed all the shrines of the high places that were in the towns of Samaria,

which kings of Israel had made, provoking the LORD to anger; he did to them just as he had done at Bethel. 20He slaughtered on the altars all the priests of the high places who were there, and burned human bones on them. Then he returned to Jerusalem.

The Passover Celebrated

21 The king commanded all the people, "Keep the passover to the LORD your God as prescribed in this book of the covenant." 22No such passover had been kept since the days of the judges who judged Israel, even during all the days of the kings of Israel and of the kings of Judah; 23but in the eighteenth year of King Josiah this passover was kept to the LORD in Jerusalem.

24 Moreover Josiah put away the mediums, wizards, teraphim,*e* idols, and all the abominations that were seen in the land of Judah and in Jerusalem, so that he established the words of the law that were written in the book that the priest Hilkiah had found in the house of the LORD. 25Before him there was no king like him, who turned to the LORD with all his heart, with all his soul, and with all his might, according to all the law of Moses; nor did any like him arise after him.

26 Still the LORD did not turn from the fierceness of his great wrath, by which his anger was kindled against Judah, because of all the provocations with which Manasseh had provoked him. 27The LORD said, "I will remove Judah also out of my sight, as I have removed Israel; and I will reject this city that I have chosen, Jerusalem, and the house of which I said, My name shall be there."

a Meaning of Heb uncertain   *b* Heb *Asherim*
c Heb *Asherah*   *d* Gk: Heb *proclaimed, who had predicted these things*   *e* Or *household gods*

23:15 *the altar at Bethel . . . he pulled down.* See 1 Kings 12:25–33 for the story of Jeroboam's erection of this sanctuary. *sacred pole.* See note on 1 Kings 14:15.

23:16–18 *the man of God who had predicted these things.* For the story of the man of God and his prophecy, see 1 Kings 13.

23:21 *Keep the passover.* Observing the Passover, last mentioned in Josh 5:10–12, is one

of the commandments of God (Deut 16:1–8) and a reminder of God's great liberation of Israel from slavery in Egypt.

23:24 *teraphim.* Teraphim are household gods.

23:26–27 *I will reject this city.* Josiah's reforms are laudable but cannot turn aside God's wrath. God has set aside old promises ("My name shall be there"). The consequences of covenantal disobedience have been set in motion. The

Josiah Dies in Battle

28 Now the rest of the acts of Josiah, and all that he did, are they not written in the Book of the Annals of the Kings of Judah? 29In his days Pharaoh Neco king of Egypt went up to the king of Assyria to the river Euphrates. King Josiah went to meet him; but when Pharaoh Neco met him at Megiddo, he killed him. 30His servants carried him dead in a chariot from Megiddo, brought him to Jerusalem, and buried him in his own tomb. The people of the land took Jehoahaz son of Josiah, anointed him, and made him king in place of his father.

Reign and Captivity of Jehoahaz

31 Jehoahaz was twenty-three years old when he began to reign; he reigned three months in Jerusalem. His mother's name was Hamutal daughter of Jeremiah of Libnah. 32He did what was evil in the sight of the LORD, just as his ancestors had done. 33Pharaoh Neco confined him at Riblah in the land of Hamath, so that he might not reign in Jerusalem, and imposed tribute on the land of one hundred talents of silver and a talent of gold. 34Pharaoh Neco made Eliakim son of Josiah king in place of his father Josiah, and changed his name to Jehoiakim. But he took Jehoahaz away; he came to Egypt, and died there. 35Jehoiakim gave the silver and the gold to Pharaoh, but he taxed the land in order to meet Pharaoh's demand for money. He exacted the silver and the gold from the people of the land, from all according to their assessment, to give it to Pharaoh Neco.

Jehoiakim Reigns over Judah

36 Jehoiakim was twenty-five years old when he began to reign; he reigned eleven years in Jerusalem. His mother's name was Zebidah daughter of Pedaiah of Rumah. 37He did what was evil in the sight of the LORD, just as all his ancestors had done.

Judah Overrun by Enemies

24 In his days King Nebuchadnezzar of Babylon came up; Jehoiakim became his servant for three years; then he turned and rebelled against him. 2The LORD sent against him bands of the Chaldeans, bands of the Arameans, bands of the Moabites, and bands of the Ammonites; he sent them against Judah to destroy it, according to the word of the LORD that he spoke by his servants the prophets. 3Surely this came upon Judah at the command of the LORD, to remove them out of his sight, for the sins of Manasseh, for all that he had committed, 4and also for the innocent blood that he had shed; for he filled Jerusalem with innocent blood, and the LORD was not willing to pardon. 5Now the rest of the deeds of Jehoiakim, and all that he did, are they not written in the Book of the Annals of the Kings of Judah? 6So Jehoiakim slept with his ancestors; then his son Jehoiachin succeeded him. 7The king of Egypt did not come again out of his land, for the king of Babylon had taken over all that belonged to the king of Egypt from the Wadi of Egypt to the River Euphrates.

Reign and Captivity of Jehoiachin

8 Jehoiachin was eighteen years old when he began to reign; he reigned three months

---

theologians of 1 & 2 Kings are certain that God cannot abide further disloyalty to the covenant.

23:29 *he killed him.* Together, Assyria and Egypt attempted to eclipse Babylonia's rise to power. Historians believe Josiah may have thrown his hand in with Babylonia, intercepting the Egyptian army at Megiddo, only to lose his life (ca. 609 BC; cf. 22:20). Judah became a vassal state of Egypt (vv 31–35).

24:2 *he sent them against Judah to destroy it.* The Babylonians (also Chaldeans or neo-Babylonians) are now on the scene (20:16–18). The harrowing news is that they come at God's behest, as the prophets have spoken (20:17–18; 21:10–16; 22:15–17). Although God is little mentioned in the following report, 1 & 2 Kings hold that God has chosen Babylonia to accomplish divine purposes. (See Jer 22; 26.)

24:4 *for the innocent blood that he had shed.* See note on 21:16.

24:7 *the king of Babylon had taken over.* The Egyptian and Assyrian armies met crown prince Nebuchadnezzar II's army in 605 BC at Carchemish, where the Babylonian army defeated the other armies and established control over the entire region. (See Jer 46:2.)

in Jerusalem. His mother's name was Ne-hushta daughter of Elnathan of Jerusalem. [9]He did what was evil in the sight of the LORD, just as his father had done.

10　At that time the servants of King Neb-uchadnezzar of Babylon came up to Jerusa-lem, and the city was besieged. [11]King Nebu-chadnezzar of Babylon came to the city, while his servants were besieging it; [12]King Je-hoiachin of Judah gave himself up to the king of Babylon, himself, his mother, his ser-vants, his officers, and his palace officials. The king of Babylon took him prisoner in the eighth year of his reign.

Capture of Jerusalem

13　He carried off all the treasures of the house of the LORD, and the treasures of the king's house; he cut in pieces all the vessels of gold in the temple of the LORD, which King Solomon of Israel had made, all this as the LORD had foretold. [14]He carried away all Jeru-salem, all the officials, all the warriors, ten thousand captives, all the artisans and the smiths; no one remained, except the poorest people of the land. [15]He carried away Je-hoiachin to Babylon; the king's mother, the king's wives, his officials, and the elite of the land, he took into captivity from Jerusalem to Babylon. [16]The king of Babylon brought cap-tive to Babylon all the men of valor, seven thousand, the artisans and the smiths, one thousand, all of them strong and fit for war. [17]The king of Babylon made Mattaniah, Je-hoiachin's uncle, king in his place, and changed his name to Zedekiah.

Zedekiah Reigns over Judah

18　Zedekiah was twenty-one years old

when he began to reign; he reigned eleven years in Jerusalem. His mother's name was Hamutal daughter of Jeremiah of Libnah. [19]He did what was evil in the sight of the LORD, just as Jehoiakim had done. [20]Indeed, Jerusalem and Judah so angered the LORD that he expelled them from his presence.

The Fall and Captivity of Judah

Zedekiah rebelled against the king of Bab-ylon. [1]And in the ninth year of his reign, in the tenth month, on the tenth day of the month, King Nebuchad-nezzar of Babylon came with all his army against Jerusalem, and laid siege to it; they built siegeworks against it all around. [2]So the city was besieged until the eleventh year of King Zedekiah. [3]On the ninth day of the fourth month the famine became so severe in the city that there was no food for the people of the land. [4]Then a breach was made in the city wall; [a] the king with all the soldiers fled [b] by night by the way of the gate between the two walls, by the king's garden, though the Chaldeans were all around the city. They went in the direction of the Arabah. [5]But the army of the Chaldeans pursued the king, and overtook him in the plains of Jericho; all his army was scattered, deserting him. [6]Then they captured the king and brought him up to the king of Babylon at Riblah, who passed sentence on him. [7]They slaughtered the sons of Zedekiah before his eyes, then put out the eyes of Zedekiah; they bound him in fetters and took him to Babylon.

8　In the fifth month, on the seventh day of the month—which was the nineteenth

a Heb lacks *wall*　　*b* Gk Compare Jer 39.4; 52.7: Heb lacks *the king* and lacks *fled*

24:12–20 *King Jehoiachin . . . gave himself up.* Jehoiachin capitulates to Nebuchadnezzar II (697 BC). The first of the deportations, which includes the prophet Ezekiel, takes place at this time (vv 14, 16; Ezek 1:1–3). 2 Kings asserts that these deportations are effected by God, who "expelled [Jerusalem and Judah] from his presence" (v 20). With this assertion, God's voice is not heard from again in 2 Kings—a frightening prospect for a people going through truly apocalyptic changes.

25:1 *Nebuchadnezzar . . . came with all his army against Jerusalem.* In 588 BC, Nebuchad-nezzar's army returned to Jerusalem to put down rebellion once and for all. The Babylonian Empire moves in and does what invading empires do. See Jeremiah 39 and 52 for parallel passages.

25:7 *took him to Babylon.* The suffering of this time is immense. See Lamentations. The Davidic "lamp" seems about to be extinguished: the sons of Zedekiah are dead; the king is in utmost defeat (Jer 52:11).

year of King Nebuchadnezzar, king of Babylon—Nebuzaradan, the captain of the bodyguard, a servant of the king of Babylon, came to Jerusalem. 9He burned the house of the LORD, the king's house, and all the houses of Jerusalem; every great house he burned down. 10All the army of the Chaldeans who were with the captain of the guard broke down the walls around Jerusalem. 11Nebuzaradan the captain of the guard carried into exile the rest of the people who were left in the city and the deserters who had defected to the king of Babylon—all the rest of the population. 12But the captain of the guard left some of the poorest people of the land to be vinedressers and tillers of the soil.

13 The bronze pillars that were in the house of the LORD, as well as the stands and the bronze sea that were in the house of the LORD, the Chaldeans broke in pieces, and carried the bronze to Babylon. 14They took away the pots, the shovels, the snuffers, the dishes for incense, and all the bronze vessels used in the temple service, 15as well as the firepans and the basins. What was made of gold the captain of the guard took away for the gold, and what was made of silver, for the silver. 16As for the two pillars, the one sea, and the stands, which Solomon had made for the house of the LORD, the bronze of all these vessels was beyond weighing. 17The height of the one pillar was eighteen cubits, and on it was a bronze capital; the height of the capital was three cubits; latticework and pomegranates, all of bronze, were on the capital all around. The second pillar had the same, with the latticework.

18 The captain of the guard took the chief priest Seraiah, the second priest Zephaniah, and the three guardians of the threshold; 19from the city he took an officer who had been in command of the soldiers, and five men of the king's council who were found in the city; the secretary who was the commander of the army who mustered the people of the land; and sixty men of the people of the land who were found in the city. 20Nebuzaradan the captain of the guard took them, and brought them to the king of Babylon at Riblah. 21The king of Babylon struck them down and put them to death at Riblah in the land of Hamath. So Judah went into exile out of its land.

Gedaliah Made Governor of Judah

22 He appointed Gedaliah son of Ahikam son of Shaphan as governor over the people who remained in the land of Judah, whom King Nebuchadnezzar of Babylon had left. 23Now when all the captains of the forces and their men heard that the king of Babylon had appointed Gedaliah as governor, they came with their men to Gedaliah at Mizpah, namely, Ishmael son of Nethaniah, Johanan son of Kareah, Seraiah son of Tanhumeth the Netophathite, and Jaazaniah son of the Maacathite. 24Gedaliah swore to them and their men, saying, "Do not be afraid because of the Chaldean officials; live in the land, serve the king of Babylon, and it shall be well with you." 25But in the seventh month, Ishmael son of Nethaniah son of Elishama, of the royal family, came with ten men; they struck down Gedaliah so that he

---

25:11 the rest of the population. A second wave of deportations occurred in 587 BC. The narrator informs us that just the poor and powerless are left in the land (24:14; 25:12), once again forgotten, but, if the claims of 1 & 2 Kings still hold, secured by God—perhaps through their powerlessness (see Matt 5:5).

25:13 carried the bronze to Babylon. The symbol of God's presence in Judah and with the Davidic king is now decimated. The dismantling of the Temple echoes the description of its construction (1 Kings 7:15–45) as the story seems to reverse itself in time. God's promise to

withdraw is symbolically made complete.

25:22 He appointed Gedaliah. Gedaliah's grandfather Shaphan had served as Josiah's secretary, his father as Josiah's adviser (22:3, 14). Gedaliah seems to have won the respect of some Judeans (Jer 26:24; 40:6).

25:25–26 they struck down Gedaliah. Perhaps Gedaliah is seen as a collaborator (v 24). Ishmael, in the royal line of David, and his followers assassinate him. Fearing Babylonian punishment, they flee the land and reenter Egypt. The great story of the exodus is fully reversed. Read Jeremiah 38–44.

died, along with the Judeans and Chaldeans who were with him at Mizpah. 26Then all the people, high and low, *a* and the captains of the forces set out and went to Egypt; for they were afraid of the Chaldeans.

Jehoiachin Released from Prison

27 In the thirty-seventh year of the exile of King Jehoiachin of Judah, in the twelfth month, on the twenty-seventh day of the month, King Evil-merodach of Babylon, in the year that he began to reign, released King Jehoiachin of Judah from prison; 28he spoke kindly to him, and gave him a seat above the other seats of the kings who were with him in Babylon. 29So Jehoiachin put aside his prison clothes. Every day of his life he dined regularly in the king's presence. 30For his allowance, a regular allowance was given him by the king, a portion every day, as long as he lived.

a Or *young and old*

25:27–30 *released King Jehoiachin . . . from prison.* Much ink has flowed in discussion of these verses. Does 2 Kings end on a note of hope or despair? One king in the line of David remains, but no king's sons are mentioned (24:15). God's promise to David appears to end here, with this captive king living out his days

sumptuously at the Babylonian court. 2 Kings closes without closure. If we listen closely enough, we may hear the voices of the bereft: "O God, why do you cast us off forever? Why does your anger smoke against the sheep of your pasture? Remember your congregation" (Ps 74:1–2).

PEOPLE WORSHI

1 CHRONICLES

The books of 1 & 2 Chronicles begin with a long genealogical section in 1 Chronicles 1–9 and then tell a history of the monarchy from the death of Saul, the first king, to the fall of the kingdom of Judah to the Babylonians in 586 BC (1 Chron 10–2 Chron 36). A short coda at the end of 2 Chronicles 36 announces the decree of Cyrus, the Persian king, authorizing the return of the exiled Israelites to Palestine and the rebuilding of the Temple.

The genealogical prologue to 1 Chronicles begins in 1:1–2:2 with Adam and follows his descendants down through the immediate sons of the patriarch Israel (Jacob). All of this material is drawn from genealogies scattered throughout the book of Genesis. What follows in 1 Chron 2:3–8:40 are genealogies of the tribes of Israel: (1) the genealogy of Judah, from which came David and his royal heirs (2:3–4:43); (2) the genealogies of the tribes belonging to Israel, the Northern Kingdom, that lived east of the Jordan River (5:1–26); (3) several genealogies of the tribe of Levi (6:1–81); (4) the genealogies of the tribes belonging to the Northern Kingdom that lived west of the Jordan (7:1–40); and (5) the genealogy of Benjamin, from which came Saul, the first king (8:1–40). Chapter 9 lists the inhabitants of Jerusalem after the exile, but concludes with a repetition of the genealogy of Saul (9:35–44) that repeats 1 Chron 8:29–38.

To understand the significance of this genealogical prologue we need to note the time and circumstances under which the author of 1 & 2 Chronicles, the Chronicler, wrote. He lived in the postexilic period, probably in the middle of the fourth century BC. A number of priests and lay leaders had returned from the Babylonian exile about a century and a half before his time, and they, together with those who had never left the land, rebuilt the Temple in Jerusalem in 516 BC. Ezra and Nehemiah had returned in the middle of the fifth century, under Persian auspices. Ezra convinced the people to follow the provisions of the law (presumably some form of the Pentateuch), and Nehemiah oversaw the rebuilding of the walls of Jerusalem and served as governor of the province. The Persian Empire incorporated most of the

---

See also "The With-God Life" essay for this section of the Bible,
"The People of God as a Nation," pp. 391–96.

ancient Near East in its control, including Egypt. The small community in Palestine, whose territory was called Judah, lived in relative security within that empire, but with no hope for political independence.

worship

The religious center of Judah was the Temple in Jerusalem, its priesthood, and its worship life. The books of Chronicles argue passionately for the authority and validity of the Temple and its worship, and they extend an invitation to Israelites who are not part of Judah to recognize the Temple and to participate in its worship. Although the community of the Chronicler was small in number, the Chronicler understood it to be, at least potentially, all Israel. Hence his enumeration of the genealogies of the twelve tribes is both a reminder of Israel's past and a vision of what it might become. The first and last tribes, Judah and Benjamin, were the mainstays of the postexilic population and also the tribes from which Israel's greatest king, David, and its first king, Saul, came. At the middle of the tribal genealogies stand the genealogies of the Levites, who are a special favorite of the Chronicler. In addition to the high priests, the regular priests, and generic Levites, the Chronicler speaks of special orders of Levites called singers and gatekeepers and of forty-eight levitical cities spread out through the entire land called Israel.

By prefacing the tribal genealogies in 1 Chronicles 2–8 with the genealogies drawn from Genesis, the Chronicler establishes a chronological continuity for Israel that goes back to creation and a lateral perspective that understands Israel in relation to those nations whose genealogical ancestry is given in broad outline. Hence the first chapter implies the election of Israel without actually mentioning it. It emphasizes the diversity and the unity of the world. Israel, like the elect People of God in any age, is a witness to all of humanity.

A Ceremonial David

After reporting the death of Saul and a negative judgment on his reign, the rest of 1 Chronicles narrates the story of the kingship of David. Here the Chronicler retells part of the story reported two centuries before his time in Joshua, Judges, 1 & 2 Samuel, and 1 & 2 Kings, but with his own theological interpretation and application. He omits the stories from Joshua and Judges, all but the final chapter of 1 Samuel, and the whole history of the Northern Kingdom from 1 & 2 Kings, except where it is necessary for the telling of the story of Judah. He also omits from the story King David's adultery with Bathsheba and the murder of her husband, Uriah, David's son Amnon's rape of his half sister Tamar, Absalom's execution of Amnon, the revolt and death of Absalom, the dismemberment of Saul's descendants, the account of the exploits of David's warriors, and two poems attributed to David—or almost all of 2 Sam 11:1–23:7. In part, this is an idealized picture of David and an attempt to maintain his prestige and authority, but it also results from the Chronicler's single-minded focus on what he thought was David's principal contribution to Israel's religious legacy—his plans for building the Temple and his appointment of the various categories of priests that served in Jerusalem at the time of the Chronicler.

The Chronicler also added a number of major passages: chapter 12, a list of the leaders and soldiers who rallied to David at Hebron; most of chapters 15–16, which report the ceremonies connected with the arrival of the ark in Jerusalem; chapters 22 and 28–29, the farewell discourses of David; and chapters 23–27, David's appointment of various kinds of Levites and other officials.

A Focus on Worship

Chronicles reminds us that all history, including biblical history, is told from a particular point of view and that the message that one generation draws from the past may be irrelevant to the concerns of a later generation. The earlier history of Israel in Joshua through Kings justified the destruction of Jerusalem because of the sins of the people. Three centuries later the fate of Jerusalem at the hands of the Babylonians no longer needed justification.

Instead, the worship of God in sacrifice and song was central to the Chronicler's faith. He understood how central worship was to the spiritual formation of the People of God. It was in this way that God was building hearts and minds that would turn to him. This the Chronicler knew and this he emphasized. He judged that such worship would best take place in the Temple of his day, which claimed the heritage of David and Solomon, and with a priesthood and a sacrificial system endorsed by Moses and the two kings of the United Monarchy, individuals who were but agents of God. The king of Persia played a role in making this worship possible, and the Chronicler apparently came to the conclusion that such worship was the first priority and the central mission of his age, even as he accepted the status quo of colonial life within the empire. His many welcoming gestures to those outside the province of Judah, especially the residents of the old Northern Kingdom, put him in sharp contrast with many separatist aspects of the books of Ezra and Nehemiah. All Israel was involved in the coronation of David and Solomon, in the capture of Jerusalem, in the transfer of the ark to that city, and in the building of the Temple.

At the conclusion of a sermon that is sharply critical of the North, Abijah still calls these Northerners "Israelites" (2 Chron 13:12). Great numbers of people from the North deserted to Asa, because they perceived that Yahweh was with him. Hezekiah invited all Israel and Judah, including especially the Northern tribes of Ephraim and Manasseh, to his Passover, and Josiah's reforms extended to the towns of Manasseh, Ephraim, and Naphtali. None of these Northern territories were a part of Judah in the Chronicler's day. The hospitable attitude toward the North by kings in the past surely expressed what the Chronicler hoped would be the attitude of the Israel of his day. Openness to others through ecumenism and mission, then and now, is a central virtue of the People of God.

Although the nature and validity of worship in the Jerusalem Temple is his central theme, the Chronicler also emphasizes a number of other significant points in his telling of Israel's history. David's kingship is identified in Chronicles with the kingdom of Yahweh, and this divine commitment to the Davidic dynasty decreases the attention given to the events of the exodus and Sinai. The gospel is always the good news of God addressed to the challenges or bad situations of a particular time, place, and culture.

Throughout the Bible it is expected that faithfulness is followed by reward and unfaithfulness by punishment, but in Chronicles these rewards and punishments are more immediate and individual, normally taking place within a person's lifetime. The consequences of sin or the rewards for righteous behavior are not accumulated over generations. In one of his farewell speeches, David remarks: "If you seek him, he will be found by you; but if you forsake him, he will abandon you forever" (1 Chron 28:9). Such retribution theology is not a principle of absolute divine justice, but must be assessed against the backdrop of Yahweh's irrevocable covenantal mercy (1 Chron 17:13). The stories of kings Asa, Jehoram, Joash, Amaziah, and Uzziah are divided into periods of faithfulness followed by reward and periods of unfaithfulness followed by punishment. For Manasseh the reverse is true: there is great unfaithfulness and yet prosperity. The Chronicler gives all this interactive cause-and-effect relationship between God and king as spiritual formation instruction for the People of God.

A Joyful, Inclusive Faith

The focus on the worship in the Temple and the rights of the priesthood might tempt us to think that the Chronicler had a very wooden idea of piety and the religious life. But we need to note how much the word "joy" is used in his history and how warmly he speaks of faith: "Believe in Yahweh your God, and you will be established; believe his prophets and you will succeed" (2 Chron 20:20, author's translation). Worship must be performed with the whole heart (1 Chron 28:9), and with exuberant music. Humbling ourselves is always viewed as appropriate action (2 Chron 7:14; 12:6–12; 30:6–11, 32:26; 33:12–14). Prayer too is effective (2 Chron 32:20, 24; 33:13).

While joyfully affirming the worshiping community as he knew it, the Chronicler also hoped for a different, better future. The geographical notes in the opening genealogies are programmatic, outlining a land of Israel that is modeled on the past and still expected for the future. In 2 Chron 30:6–9, it is promised that repentance by those who are in the land will lead to the return of the exiles in Mesopotamia. Placed in the mouths of the singers, a psalm reads: "Save us, O God of our salvation, and gather and rescue us from among the nations" (1 Chron 16:35). It is unclear, however, whether the Chronicler himself hoped for an eventual restoration of the monarchy.

The Chronicler offers one example of how to envisage the purpose and freedom of the People of God in a specific historical context. He is an example of how the theology of one generation needs to "change" in order to address the life of another generation at a later time. His quest to include the whole People of God, as he knew it from tradition, rejects the opinion of those who settle for the narrow parameters of their own community, let alone the divisions that still plague the People of God. For all of his stress on the merits of David and Solomon in building the Temple and inaugurating worship, he also knew that the plan for the Temple was given by Yahweh (1 Chron 18:19) and that fire from heaven at the first sacrifice in Solomon's Temple gave the first confirmation of that plan (2 Chron 7:1).

—*Ralph W. Klein*

From Adam to Abraham

1 Adam, Seth, Enosh; [2]Kenan, Mahalalel, Jared; [3]Enoch, Methuselah, Lamech; [4]Noah, Shem, Ham, and Japheth.

5 The descendants of Japheth: Gomer, Magog, Madai, Javan, Tubal, Meshech, and Tiras. [6]The descendants of Gomer: Ashkenaz, Diphath, [a] and Togarmah. [7]The descendants of Javan: Elishah, Tarshish, Kittim, and Rodanim.[b]

8 The descendants of Ham: Cush, Egypt, Put, and Canaan. [9]The descendants of Cush: Seba, Havilah, Sabta, Raama, and Sabteca. The descendants of Raamah: Sheba and Dedan. [10]Cush became the father of Nimrod; he was the first to be a mighty one on the earth.

11 Egypt became the father of Ludim, Anamim, Lehabim, Naphtuhim, [12]Pathrusim, Casluhim, and Caphtorim, from whom the Philistines come.[c]

13 Canaan became the father of Sidon his firstborn, and Heth, [14]and the Jebusites, the Amorites, the Girgashites, [15]the Hivites, the Arkites, the Sinites, [16]the Arvadites, the Zemarites, and the Hamathites.

17 The descendants of Shem: Elam, Asshur, Arpachshad, Lud, Aram, Uz, Hul, Gether, and Meshech. [d] [18]Arpachshad became the father of Shelah; and Shelah became the father of Eber. [19]To Eber were born two sons: the name of the one was Peleg (for in his days the earth was divided), and the name of his brother Joktan. [20]Joktan became the father of Almodad, Sheleph, Hazarmaveth, Jerah, [21]Hadoram, Uzal, Diklah, [22]Ebal, Abimael,

Sheba, [23]Ophir, Havilah, and Jobab; all these were the descendants of Joktan.

24 Shem, Arpachshad, Shelah; [25]Eber, Peleg, Reu; [26]Serug, Nahor, Terah; [27]Abram, that is, Abraham.

From Abraham to Jacob

28 The sons of Abraham: Isaac and Ishmael. [29]These are their genealogies: the firstborn of Ishmael, Nebaioth; and Kedar, Adbeel, Mibsam, [30]Mishma, Dumah, Massa, Hadad, Tema, [31]Jetur, Naphish, and Kedemah. These are the sons of Ishmael. [32]The sons of Keturah, Abraham's concubine: she bore Zimran, Jokshan, Medan, Midian, Ishbak, and Shuah. The sons of Jokshan: Sheba and Dedan. [33]The sons of Midian: Ephah, Epher, Hanoch, Abida, and Eldaah. All these were the descendants of Keturah.

34 Abraham became the father of Isaac. The sons of Isaac: Esau and Israel. [35]The sons of Esau: Eliphaz, Reuel, Jeush, Jalam, and Korah. [36]The sons of Eliphaz: Teman, Omar, Zephi, Gatam, Kenaz, Timna, and Amalek. [37]The sons of Reuel: Nahath, Zerah, Shammah, and Mizzah.

38 The sons of Seir: Lotan, Shobal, Zibeon, Anah, Dishon, Ezer, and Dishan. [39]The sons of Lotan: Hori and Homam; and Lotan's sister was Timna. [40]The sons of Shobal: Alian, Manahath, Ebal, Shephi, and Onam. The sons of Zibeon: Aiah and Anah. [41]The sons of

---

a Gen 10.3 *Ripath*; See Gk Vg   *b* Gen 10.4 *Dodanim*; See Syr Vg   *c* Heb *Casluhim, from which the Philistines come, Caphtorim*; See Am 9.7, Jer 47.4   *d* *Mash* in Gen 10.23

1:1–4 *Adam . . . Japheth.* The first thirteen names in this genealogy are presented in the form of a list. The Chronicler assumes that readers can fill in the genealogical connections from their knowledge of Genesis.

1:5–23 *The descendants of Japheth.* The genealogical materials in these verses are drawn from the Table of Nations in Genesis 10, but the listing of the sons of Noah is in reverse order to that in 1:4. The sons of Shem, the ancestors of Abraham, are listed last to indicate their elect status.

1:28–2:2 *The sons of Abraham.* The descendants of the three mothers of Abraham's

children are listed in the order Hagar (vv 29–31), Keturah (vv 32–33), and Sarah (1:34–2:2), although only Keturah is mentioned by name.

1:34 *The sons of Isaac: Esau and Israel.* Throughout the books of Chronicles (except for 1 Chron 16:13, 17, a citation from Psalms) the patriarch known as Jacob is called Israel.

1:35–54 *The sons of Esau.* Although the fact that Esau is listed before Israel (2:1–2) shows the elect status of the latter, the kinship of Esau is acknowledged even at a time when the province of Judah was experiencing considerable territorial pressure from Esau's descendants, the Edomites.

Anah: Dishon. The sons of Dishon: Hamran, Eshban, Ithran, and Cheran. 42The sons of Ezer: Bilhan, Zaavan, and Jaakan. *a* The sons of Dishan: *b* Uz and Aran.

43 These are the kings who reigned in the land of Edom before any king reigned over the Israelites: Bela son of Beor, whose city was called Dinhabah. 44When Bela died, Jobab son of Zerah of Bozrah succeeded him. 45When Jobab died, Husham of the land of the Temanites succeeded him. 46When Husham died, Hadad son of Bedad, who defeated Midian in the country of Moab, succeeded him; and the name of his city was Avith. 47When Hadad died, Samlah of Masrekah succeeded him. 48When Samlah died, Shaul *c* of Rehoboth on the Euphrates succeeded him. 49When Shaul *c* died, Baal-hanan son of Achbor succeeded him. 50When Baal-hanan died, Hadad succeeded him; the name of his city was Pai, and his wife's name Mehetabel daughter of Matred, daughter of Me-zahab. 51And Hadad died.

The clans *d* of Edom were: clans *d* Timna, Aliah, *e* Jetheth, 52Oholibamah, Elah, Pinon, 53Kenaz, Teman, Mibzar, 54Magdiel, and Iram; these are the clans *d* of Edom.

The Sons of Israel and the Descendants of Judah

2 These are the sons of Israel: Reuben, Simeon, Levi, Judah, Issachar, Zebulun, 2Dan, Joseph, Benjamin, Naphtali, Gad, and Asher. 3The sons of Judah: Er, Onan, and Shelah; these three the Canaanite woman Bath-shua bore to him. Now Er, Judah's firstborn, was wicked in the sight of the LORD, and he put him to death. 4His daughter-in-law Tamar also bore him Perez and Zerah. Judah had five sons in all.

5 The sons of Perez: Hezron and Hamul. 6The sons of Zerah: Zimri, Ethan, Heman, Calcol, and Dara, *f* five in all. 7The sons of Carmi: Achar, the troubler of Israel, who transgressed in the matter of the devoted thing; 8and Ethan's son was Azariah.

9 The sons of Hezron, who were born to him: Jerahmeel, Ram, and Chelubai. 10Ram became the father of Amminadab, and Amminadab became the father of Nahshon, prince of the sons of Judah. 11Nahshon became the father of Salma, Salma of Boaz, 12Boaz of Obed, Obed of Jesse. 13Jesse became the father of Eliab his firstborn, Abinadab the second, Shimea the third, 14Nethanel the fourth, Raddai the fifth, 15Ozem the sixth, David the seventh; 16and their sisters were Zeruiah and Abigail. The sons of Zeruiah: Abishai, Joab, and Asahel, three. 17Abigail

a Or *and Akan*; See Gen 36.27   *b* See 1.38: Heb *Dishon*   *c* Or *Saul*   *d* Or *chiefs*   *e* Or *Alvah*; See Gen 36.40   *f* Or *Darda*; Compare Syr Tg some Gk Mss; See 1 Kings 4.31

2:1–2 *These are the sons of Israel.* This list of the descendants of Israel is very similar to the one in Gen 36:22–26, except for Dan, who appears after Benjamin in that list. His position at the head of the sons of Rachel here may result from his being the first son legally attributable to Rachel, though actually born to her handmaid.

2:3–4 *The sons of Judah.* The immediate descendants of the patriarch Judah are known from Genesis 38 and include the three sons born to his wife Bath-shua and the two born to his daughter-in-law Tamar. The Chronicler makes no criticism of Judah's marriage to Bath-shua, a Canaanite woman. There are five additional references to intermarriage with foreigners in the genealogy of Judah—all recorded without criticism: Jether the Ishmaelite was married to

Abigail, the sister of David (2:17); an unnamed daughter of Sheshan was married to an Egyptian slave (2:34–35); David himself was married to Maacah, the daughter of Talmai, king of Geshur (3:2); Mered, a Judahite, married Bithiah, the daughter of Pharaoh (4:17); and some of the descendants of Shelah married into Moab (4:22).

2:10 *Ram.* Ram is the first member in a linear genealogy leading to Jesse in the tenth generation after Judah. Jesse is the father of King David.

2:15 *David the seventh.* The Chronicler had access to an alternate list of David's brothers, since he identifies David as the seventh son, whereas in 1 Samuel he is the eighth son (1 Sam 16:10–11; 17:12). David is also in the seventh generation after Ram.

bore Amasa, and the father of Amasa was Jether the Ishmaelite.

18 Caleb son of Hezron had children by his wife Azubah, and by Jerioth; these were her sons: Jesher, Shobab, and Ardon. ¹⁹When Azubah died, Caleb married Ephrath, who bore him Hur. ²⁰Hur became the father of Uri, and Uri became the father of Bezalel.

21 Afterward Hezron went in to the daughter of Machir father of Gilead, whom he married when he was sixty years old; and she bore him Segub; ²²and Segub became the father of Jair, who had twenty-three towns in the land of Gilead. ²³But Geshur and Aram took from them Havvoth-jair, Kenath and its villages, sixty towns. All these were descendants of Machir, father of Gilead. ²⁴After the death of Hezron, in Caleb-ephrathah, Abijah wife of Hezron bore him Ashhur, father of Tekoa.

25 The sons of Jerahmeel, the firstborn of Hezron: Ram his firstborn, Bunah, Oren, Ozem, and Ahijah. ²⁶Jerahmeel also had another wife, whose name was Atarah; she was the mother of Onam. ²⁷The sons of Ram, the firstborn of Jerahmeel: Maaz, Jamin, and Eker. ²⁸The sons of Onam: Shammai and Jada. The sons of Shammai: Nadab and Abishur. ²⁹The name of Abishur's wife was Abihail, and she bore him Ahban and Molid. ³⁰The sons of Nadab: Seled and Appaim; and Seled died childless. ³¹The son*ᵃ* of Appaim: Ishi. The son*ᵃ* of Ishi: Sheshan. The son*ᵃ* of Sheshan: Ahlai. ³²The sons of Jada, Shammai's brother: Jether and Jonathan; and Jether died childless. ³³The sons of Jonathan: Peleth and Zaza. These were the descendants of Jerahmeel. ³⁴Now Sheshan had no sons, only daughters; but Sheshan had an Egyptian slave, whose name was Jarha. ³⁵So Sheshan gave his daughter in marriage to his slave Jar-

ha; and she bore him Attai. ³⁶Attai became the father of Nathan, and Nathan of Zabad. ³⁷Zabad became the father of Ephlal, and Ephlal of Obed. ³⁸Obed became the father of Jehu, and Jehu of Azariah. ³⁹Azariah became the father of Helez, and Helez of Eleasah. ⁴⁰Eleasah became the father of Sismai, and Sismai of Shallum. ⁴¹Shallum became the father of Jekamiah, and Jekamiah of Elishama.

42 The sons of Caleb brother of Jerahmeel: Mesha *ᵇ* his firstborn, who was father of Ziph. The sons of Mareshah father of Hebron. ⁴³The sons of Hebron: Korah, Tappuah, Rekem, and Shema. ⁴⁴Shema became father of Raham, father of Jorkeam; and Rekem became the father of Shammai. ⁴⁵The son of Shammai: Maon; and Maon was the father of Beth-zur. ⁴⁶Ephah also, Caleb's concubine, bore Haran, Moza, and Gazez; and Haran became the father of Gazez. ⁴⁷The sons of Jahdai: Regem, Jotham, Geshan, Pelet, Ephah, and Shaaph. ⁴⁸Maacah, Caleb's concubine, bore Sheber and Tirhanah. ⁴⁹She also bore Shaaph father of Madmannah, Sheva father of Machbenah and father of Gibea; and the daughter of Caleb was Achsah. ⁵⁰These were the descendants of Caleb.

The sons*ᶜ* of Hur the firstborn of Ephrathah: Shobal father of Kiriath-jearim, ⁵¹Salma father of Bethlehem, and Hareph father of Bethgader. ⁵²Shobal father of Kiriath-jearim had other sons: Haroeh, half of the Menuhoth. ⁵³And the families of Kiriath-jearim: the Ithrites, the Puthites, the Shumathites, and the Mishraites; from these came the Zorathites and the Eshtaolites. ⁵⁴The sons of Salma: Bethlehem, the Netophathites, Atroth-beth-joab,

a Heb *sons*   *b* Gk reads *Mareshah*   *c* Gk Vg: Heb *son*

2:16 *their sisters were Zeruiah and Abigail.* This is the first and only time these women are identified as sisters of David in the Bible. *Abishai, Joab, and Asahel.* These three military leaders are often identified as sons of Zeruiah in 1 & 2 Samuel, but Zeruiah's relationship to David in those books is not clear.

2:35 *marriage to his slave Jarha.* The marriage of Sheshan's daughter to an Egyptian

slave would not have meant loss of family property, since in such a case the children would have belonged to Sheshan and not to the Egyptian slave according to Israelite law. The text shows no disapproval of such a mixed marriage, in sharp distinction to Deut 7:3–4; 1 Kings 11:1–13; Ezra 9–10; Neh 10:30; 13:23–27.

and half of the Manahathites, the Zorites. [55]The families also of the scribes that lived at Jabez: the Tirathites, the Shimeathites, and the Sucathites. These are the Kenites who came from Hammath, father of the house of Rechab.

Descendants of David and Solomon

3 These are the sons of David who were born to him in Hebron: the firstborn Amnon, by Ahinoam the Jezreelite; the second Daniel, by Abigail the Carmelite; [2]the third Absalom, son of Maacah, daughter of King Talmai of Geshur; the fourth Adonijah, son of Haggith; [3]the fifth Shephatiah, by Abital; the sixth Ithream, by his wife Eglah; [4]six were born to him in Hebron, where he reigned for seven years and six months. And he reigned thirty-three years in Jerusalem. [5]These were born to him in Jerusalem: Shimea, Shobab, Nathan, and Solomon, four by Bath-shua, daughter of Ammiel; [6]then Ibhar, Elishama, Eliphelet, [7]Nogah, Nepheg, Japhia, [8]Elishama, Eliada, and Eliphelet, nine. [9]All these were David's sons, besides the sons of the concubines; and Tamar was their sister.

10 The descendants of Solomon: Rehoboam, Abijah his son, Asa his son, Jehoshaphat his son, [11]Joram his son, Ahaziah his son, Joash his son, [12]Amaziah his son, Azariah his son, Jotham his son, [13]Ahaz his son, Hezekiah his son, Manasseh his son, [14]Amon his son, Josiah his son. [15]The sons of Josiah: Johanan the firstborn, the second Jehoiakim, the third Zedekiah, the fourth Shallum. [16]The descendants of Jehoiakim: Jeconiah his son, Zedekiah his son; [17]and the sons of Jeconiah, the captive: Shealtiel his son, [18]Malchiram, Pedaiah, Shenazzar, Jekamiah, Hoshama, and Nedabiah; [19]The sons of Pedaiah: Zerubbabel and Shimei; and the sons of Zerubbabel: Meshullam and Hananiah, and Shelomith was their sister; [20]and Hashubah, Ohel, Berechiah, Hasadiah, and Jushab-hesed, five. [21]The sons of Hananiah: Pelatiah and Jeshaiah, his son[a] Rephaiah, his son[a] Arnan, his son[a] Obadiah, his son[a] Shecaniah. [22]The son[b] of Shecaniah: Shemaiah. And the sons of Shemaiah: Hattush, Igal, Bariah, Neariah, and Shaphat, six. [23]The sons of Neariah: Elioenai, Hizkiah, and Azrikam, three. [24]The sons of Elioenai: Hodaviah, Eliashib, Pelaiah, Akkub, Johanan, Delaiah, and Anani, seven.

Descendants of Judah

4 The sons of Judah: Perez, Hezron, Carmi, Hur, and Shobal. [2]Reaiah son of Shobal became the father of Jahath, and Jahath became the father of Ahumai and Lahad. These were the families of the Zorathites. [3]These were the sons[c] of Etam: Jezreel, Ishma, and Idbash; and the name of their sister was Hazzelelponi, [4]and Penuel was the father of

---

a Gk Compare Syr Vg: Heb *sons of*　　b Heb *sons*
c Gk Compare Vg: Heb *the father*

3:1–4 *born to him in Hebron.* David resided at Hebron for the first seven and a half years of his reign. In 2 Samuel, Amnon, Absalom, and Adonijah, who were born in Hebron, are involved in a series of unsuccessful struggles to succeed their father. None of these events, however, are reported in Chronicles.

3:5 *Shimea, Shobab, Nathan, and Solomon.* Solomon is the most important of David's sons. Surprisingly (2 Sam 12:24 indicates that he is their first son who lived beyond infancy), he is listed as the fourth son of David and Bath-shua. As with David, the three older brothers are disqualified and the youngest is chosen.

3:17 *the sons of Jeconiah, the captive.* Jeconiah, or Jehoiachin, had seven sons. Jeconiah and Zerubbabel (v 19) were fulfilling the command to have sons and daughters in exile, to multiply there and not decrease (Jer 29:6).

3:19 *Zerubbabel . . . Shelomith.* Zerubbabel here is identified as the son of Pedaiah, but elsewhere (Ezra 3:2, 8; 5:2; Neh 12:1; Haggai) Zerubbabel is the son of Shealtiel (cf. v 17). Zerubbabel may have been the product of a levirate marriage, in which Pedaiah married the widow of Shealtiel. Shelomith's name has appeared in an inscription as the wife of the postexilic governor Elnathan.

3:24 *Anani.* Anani may be identified with a person of the same name in the Elephantine Papyri, dated to 407 BC. Since the Chronicler was writing in the mid-fourth century, this genealogy ends in a period virtually contemporaneous with him.

Gedor, and Ezer the father of Hushah. These were the sons of Hur, the firstborn of Ephrathah, the father of Bethlehem. 5Ashhur father of Tekoa had two wives, Helah and Naarah; 6Naarah bore him Ahuzzam, Hepher, Temeni, and Haahashtari. *a* These were the sons of Naarah. 7The sons of Helah: Zereth, Izhar, *b* and Ethnan. 8Koz became the father of Anub, Zobebah, and the families of Aharhel son of Harum. 9Jabez was honored more than his brothers; and his mother named him Jabez, saying, "Because I bore him in pain." 10Jabez called on the God of Israel, saying, "Oh that you would bless me and enlarge my border, and that your hand might be with me, and that you would keep me from hurt and harm!" And God granted what he asked. 11Chelub the brother of Shuhah became the father of Mehir, who was the father of Eshton. 12Eshton became the father of Beth-rapha, Paseah, and Tehinnah the father of Ir-nahash. These are the men of Recah. 13The sons of Kenaz: Othniel and Seraiah; and the sons of Othniel: Hathath and Meonothai. *c* 14Meonothai became the father of Ophrah; and Seraiah became the father of Joab father of Ge-harashim, *d* so-called because they were artisans. 15The sons of Caleb son of Jephunneh: Iru, Elah, and Naam; and the son *e* of Elah: Kenaz. 16The sons of Jehallelel: Ziph, Ziphah, Tiria, and Asarel. 17The sons of Ezrah: Jether, Mered, Epher, and Jalon. These are the sons of Bithiah, daughter of Pharaoh, whom Mered married; *f* and she conceived and bore *g* Miriam, Shammai, and Ishbah father of Eshtemoa. 18And his Judean wife bore Jered father of Gedor, Heber father of Soco, and Jekuthiel father of Zanoah. 19The sons of the wife of Hodiah, the sister of Naham, were the fathers of Keilah the Garmite and Eshtemoa the Maacathite. 20The sons of Shimon: Amnon, Rinnah, Ben-hanan, and Tilon. The sons of Ishi: Zoheth and Ben-zoheth. 21The sons of Shelah son of Judah: Er father of Lecah, Laadah father of Mareshah, and the families of the guild of linen workers at Beth-ashbea; 22and Jokim, and the men of Cozeba, and Joash, and Saraph, who married into Moab but returned to Lehem *h* (now the records *i* are ancient). 23These were the potters and inhabitants of Netaim and Gederah; they lived there with the king in his service.

Descendants of Simeon

24 The sons of Simeon: Nemuel, Jamin, Jarib, Zerah, Shaul; *j* 25Shallum was his son, Mibsam his son, Mishma his son. 26The sons of Mishma: Hammuel his son, Zaccur his son, Shimei his son. 27Shimei had sixteen sons and six daughters; but his brothers did not have many children, nor did all their family multiply like the Judeans. 28They lived in Beer-sheba, Moladah, Hazar-shual, 29Bilhah, Ezem, Tolad, 30Bethuel, Hormah, Ziklag, 31Beth-marcaboth, Hazar-susim, Beth-biri, and Shaaraim. These were their towns until David became king. 32And their villages were Etam, Ain, Rimmon, Tochen, and Ashan, five towns, 33along with all their villages that were around these towns as far as Baal. These were their settlements. And they kept a genealogical record.

34 Meshobab, Jamlech, Joshah son of Amaziah, 35Joel, Jehu son of Joshibiah son of Seraiah son of Asiel, 36Elioenai, Jaakobah,

a Or *Ahashtari*   *b* Another reading is *Zohar*
c Gk Vg: Heb lacks *and Meonothai*   *d* That is
Valley of artisans   *e* Heb *sons*   *f* The clause:
These are . . . married is transposed from verse 18
g Heb lacks *and bore*   *h* Vg Compare Gk: Heb
and Jashubi-lahem   *i* Or *matters*   *j* Or *Saul*

4:10 *bless me and enlarge my border.* Jabez wanted the expansion of his territory and liberation from the consequences of his birth and name (which is a pun on the word "pain" in Hebrew). A recent book touting this verse as the basis for a prayer for material prosperity misunderstands the nature of this genealogy and advocates a spirituality contrary to biblical models.

4:24-43 *The sons of Simeon.* The tribe of Simeon had largely disappeared by the time of the Chronicler. Simeon was the second of Israel's sons and Judah was the fourth. This genealogy is taken in part from Num 26:12-14; Gen 46:10; Exod 6:15. The place-names in this chapter, in so far as they are known, are beyond the boundaries of Judah.

Jeshohaiah, Asaiah, Adiel, Jesimiel, Benaiah, 37Ziza son of Shiphi son of Allon son of Jedaiah son of Shimri son of Shemaiah— 38these mentioned by name were leaders in their families, and their clans increased greatly. 39They journeyed to the entrance of Gedor, to the east side of the valley, to seek pasture for their flocks, 40where they found rich, good pasture, and the land was very broad, quiet, and peaceful; for the former inhabitants there belonged to Ham. 41These, registered by name, came in the days of King Hezekiah of Judah, and attacked their tents and the Meunim who were found there, and exterminated them to this day, and settled in their place, because there was pasture there for their flocks. 42And some of them, five hundred men of the Simeonites, went to Mount Seir, having as their leaders Pelatiah, Neariah, Rephaiah, and Uzziel, sons of Ishi; 43they destroyed the remnant of the Amalekites that had escaped, and they have lived there to this day.

Descendants of Reuben

5 The sons of Reuben the firstborn of Israel. (He was the firstborn, but because he defiled his father's bed his birthright was given to the sons of Joseph son of Israel, so that he is not enrolled in the genealogy according to the birthright; 2though Judah became prominent among his brothers and a ruler came from him, yet the birthright belonged to Joseph.) 3The sons of Reuben, the firstborn of Israel: Hanoch, Pallu, Hezron, and Carmi. 4The sons of Joel: Shemaiah his son, Gog his son, Shimei his son, 5Micah his son, Reaiah his son, Baal his son, 6Beerah his son, whom King Tilgath-pilneser of Assyria carried away into exile; he was a chieftain of the Reubenites. 7And his kindred by their families, when the genealogy of their generations was reckoned: the chief, Jeiel, and Zechariah, 8and Bela son of Azaz, son of Shema, son of Joel, who lived in Aroer, as far as Nebo and Baal-meon. 9He also lived to the east as far as the beginning of the desert this side of the Euphrates, because their cattle had multiplied in the land of Gilead. 10And in the days of Saul they made war on the Hagrites, who fell by their hand; and they lived in their tents throughout all the region east of Gilead.

Descendants of Gad

11 The sons of Gad lived beside them in the land of Bashan as far as Salecah: 12Joel the chief, Shapham the second, Janai, and Shaphat in Bashan. 13And their kindred according to their clans: Michael, Meshullam, Sheba, Jorai, Jacan, Zia, and Eber, seven. 14These were the sons of Abihail son of Huri, son of Jaroah, son of Gilead, son of Michael, son of Jeshishai, son of Jahdo, son of Buz; 15Ahi son of Abdiel, son of Guni, was chief in their clan; 16and they lived in Gilead, in Bashan and in its towns, and in all the pasture lands of Sharon to their limits. 17All of these were enrolled by genealogies in the days of King Jotham of Judah, and in the days of King Jeroboam of Israel.

18 The Reubenites, the Gadites, and the half-tribe of Manasseh had valiant warriors, who carried shield and sword, and drew the bow, expert in war, forty-four thousand seven hundred sixty, ready for service. 19They

---

5:1 *he defiled his father's bed.* Although Reuben was the firstborn of Israel/Jacob, he lost the advantages of this position because of his incestuous relationship with his father's concubine (Gen 35:22; 49:3–4). The Chronicler uses this incident to explain why Judah and not Reuben is the first in the tribal genealogies and why the right of the firstborn passed from Reuben to the sons of Joseph. The honored position of Ephraim and Manasseh in the genealogies shows the Chronicler's open attitude toward the North.

5:6 *Tilgath-pilneser.* The Assyrian king Tiglath-pileser III, who ruled 745–727 BC, captured the city of Gaza in 734 and defeated the coalition of Rezin, king of Damascus, and Pekah, king of the Northern Kingdom in 732. The cities attacked by Tiglath-pileser according to 2 Kings 15:29 are far to the north of the tribe of Reuben.

5:10 *in the days of Saul.* This is the first reference to Saul in Chronicles (cf. 1 Chron 8:29–40; 9:35–44). *Hagrites.* The relationship of the Hagrites to Hagar, the concubine of Abraham, is unclear.

made war on the Hagrites, Jetur, Naphish, and Nodab; 20and when they received help against them, the Hagrites and all who were with them were given into their hands, for they cried to God in the battle, and he granted their entreaty because they trusted in him. 21They captured their livestock: fifty thousand of their camels, two hundred fifty thousand sheep, two thousand donkeys, and one hundred thousand captives. 22Many fell slain, because the war was of God. And they lived in their territory until the exile.

The Half-Tribe of Manasseh

23 The members of the half-tribe of Manasseh lived in the land; they were very numerous from Bashan to Baal-hermon, Senir, and Mount Hermon. 24These were the heads of their clans: Epher,ᵃ Ishi, Eliel, Azriel, Jeremiah, Hodaviah, and Jahdiel, mighty warriors, famous men, heads of their clans. 25But they transgressed against the God of their ancestors, and prostituted themselves to the gods of the peoples of the land, whom God had destroyed before them. 26So the God of Israel stirred up the spirit of King Pul of Assyria, the spirit of King Tilgath-pilneser of Assyria, and he carried them away, namely, the Reubenites, the Gadites, and the half-tribe of

Manasseh, and brought them to Halah, Habor, Hara, and the river Gozan, to this day.

Descendants of Levi

6ᵇ The sons of Levi: Gershom,ᶜ Kohath, and Merari. 2The sons of Kohath: Amram, Izhar, Hebron, and Uzziel. 3The children of Amram: Aaron, Moses, and Miriam. The sons of Aaron: Nadab, Abihu, Eleazar, and Ithamar. 4Eleazar became the father of Phinehas, Phinehas of Abishua, 5Abishua of Bukki, Bukki of Uzzi, 6Uzzi of Zerahiah, Zerahiah of Meraioth, 7Meraioth of Amariah, Amariah of Ahitub, 8Ahitub of Zadok, Zadok of Ahimaaz, 9Ahimaaz of Azariah, Azariah of Johanan, 10and Johanan of Azariah (it was he who served as priest in the house that Solomon built in Jerusalem). 11Azariah became the father of Amariah, Amariah of Ahitub, 12Ahitub of Zadok, Zadok of Shallum, 13Shallum of Hilkiah, Hilkiah of Azariah, 14Azariah of Seraiah, Seraiah of Jehozadak; 15and Jehozadak went into exile when the LORD sent Judah and Jerusalem into exile by the hand of Nebuchadnezzar.

16ᵈ The sons of Levi: Gershom, Kohath,

a Gk Vg: Heb and Epher   b Ch 5.27 in Heb
c Heb Gershon, variant of Gershom; See 6.16
d Ch 6.1 in Heb

5:17 *Jotham . . . Jeroboam.* Jotham of Judah and Jeroboam II of Israel reigned as contemporaries for seven or eight years, but it is unlikely that both of these kings would have engaged in a common census of Transjordan, since this territory was never controlled by Judah.

5:20 *because they trusted in him.* This is the only use of the verb "trust" in Chronicles except for its use by Sennacherib in 2 Chron 32:10.

5:21 *fifty thousand of their camels.* The unusually large number of camels seems to be designed to contrast what happens when people trust Yahweh with what happens when they act faithlessly (cf. v 25).

5:25–26 *they transgressed against the God of their ancestors.* In the final verses of this chapter the Chronicler presents the negative alternative in the theory of retribution, following the positive presentation of this notion (vv 18–22). The exile of the two and a half Transjordanian tribes is seen as retribution for their infidelity.

5:26 *stirred up the spirit.* God's stirring up the spirit of Tiglath-Pileser (Tilgath-pilneser) is balanced at the end of 2 Chronicles by God's stirring up the spirit of Cyrus to send the exiles home and to authorize the rebuilding of the Temple.

6:3–15 *The sons of Aaron.* This genealogy of the high priests begins with Aaron and ends with Jehozadak, who was exiled by the Babylonian king Nebuchadnezzar. This is the master list of high priests, but there are shorter versions of it in 1 Chron 6:50–53; Ezra 7:1–5; 2 Esd 1:1–3; Neh 11:10–11; 1 Chron 9:10–11. This list claims that all high priests are descendants of Aaron, the brother of Moses, and of Zadok, the high priest under David.

6:15 *by the hand of Nebuchadnezzar.* This is the first reference to Nebuchadnezzar and the fall of the Southern Kingdom after three previous references to the exile of the Northern Kingdom in 5:6, 22, 26.

and Merari. [17]These are the names of the sons of Gershom: Libni and Shimei. [18]The sons of Kohath: Amram, Izhar, Hebron, and Uzziel. [19]The sons of Merari: Mahli and Mushi. These are the clans of the Levites according to their ancestry. [20]Of Gershom: Libni his son, Jahath his son, Zimmah his son, [21]Joah his son, Iddo his son, Zerah his son, Jeatherai his son. [22]The sons of Kohath: Amminadab his son, Korah his son, Assir his son, [23]Elkanah his son, Ebiasaph his son, Assir his son, [24]Tahath his son, Uriel his son, Uzziah his son, and Shaul his son. [25]The sons of Elkanah: Amasai and Ahimoth, [26]Elkanah his son, Zophai his son, Nahath his son, [27]Eliab his son, Jeroham his son, Elkanah his son. [28]The sons of Samuel: Joel[a] his firstborn, the second Abijah.[b] [29]The sons of Merari: Mahli, Libni his son, Shimei his son, Uzzah his son, [30]Shimea his son, Haggiah his son, and Asaiah his son.

Musicians Appointed by David

[31] These are the men whom David put in charge of the service of song in the house of the LORD, after the ark came to rest there. [32]They ministered with song before the tabernacle of the tent of meeting, until Solomon had built the house of the LORD in Jerusalem; and they performed their service in due order. [33]These are the men who served, and their sons were: Of the Kohathites: Heman, the singer, son of Joel, son of Samuel, [34]son of Elkanah, son of Jeroham, son of Eli-el, son of Toah, [35]son of Zuph, son of Elkanah, son of Mahath, son of Amasai, [36]son of Elkanah, son of Joel, son of Azariah, son of Zephaniah, [37]son of Tahath, son of Assir, son of Ebiasaph, son of Korah, [38]son of Izhar, son of Kohath, son of Levi, son of Israel; [39]and his brother Asaph, who stood on his right, namely, Asaph son of Berechiah, son of Shimea, [40]son of Michael, son of Baaseiah, son of Malchijah, [41]son of Ethni, son of Zerah, son of Adaiah, [42]son of Ethan, son of Zimmah, son of Shimei, [43]son of Jahath, son of Gershom, son of Levi. [44]On the left were their kindred the sons of Merari: Ethan son of Kishi, son of Abdi, son of Malluch, [45]son of Hashabiah, son of Amaziah, son of Hilkiah, [46]son of Amzi, son of Bani, son of Shemer, [47]son of Mahli, son of Mushi, son of Merari, son of Levi; [48]and their kindred the Levites were appointed for all the service of the tabernacle of the house of God.

[49] But Aaron and his sons made offerings on the altar of burnt offering and on the altar of incense, doing all the work of the most holy place, to make atonement for Israel, according to all that Moses the servant of God had commanded. [50]These are the sons of Aaron: Eleazar his son, Phinehas his son, Abishua his son, [51]Bukki his son, Uzzi his son, Zerahiah his son, [52]Meraioth his son,

a Gk Syr Compare verse 33 and 1 Sam 8.2: Heb lacks *Joel*   *b* Heb reads *Vashni, and Abijah* for *the second Abijah*, taking *the second* as a proper name

---

6:20–30 *Of Gershom.* These verses provide linear genealogies for Levi's sons Gershom, Kohath, and Merari through their oldest sons, ending with the heads of these three families, who are named Jeatherai, Shaul, and Asaiah.

6:28 *The sons of Samuel.* Inserted into the genealogy of Kohath is a linear genealogy leading to Samuel and his two sons. In 1 Sam 1:1 Samuel is identified as an Ephraimite. Later tradition apparently found it offensive that Samuel, an Ephraimite, had ministered at the sanctuary of Shiloh.

Responding
6:31–32 WORSHIP. David found great joy in worshiping God through song and promoted music as a ministry, a practice that continues today through traditional hymns and modern praise bands. Why is singing such an enduring form of worship? What does it do for the mind? The emotions? The soul? *See also* Spiritual Disciplines Index.

6:31–48 *the service of song.* The singers play a very important role in the worship described by the Chronicler, and they are here given a levitical pedigree (but cf. Ezra 2:41 and Neh 7:44, where they have not yet attained that rank). The heads of the singer guilds are Heman (v 33), Asaph (v 39), and Ethan (v 44), who served in this role at the time of David.

Amariah his son, Ahitub his son, [53]Zadok his son, Ahimaaz his son.

Settlements of the Levites

54 These are their dwelling places according to their settlements within their borders: to the sons of Aaron of the families of Kohathites—for the lot fell to them first— [55]to them they gave Hebron in the land of Judah and its surrounding pasture lands, [56]but the fields of the city and its villages they gave to Caleb son of Jephunneh. [57]To the sons of Aaron they gave the cities of refuge: Hebron, Libnah with its pasture lands, Jattir, Eshtemoa with its pasture lands, [58]Hilen[a] with its pasture lands, Debir with its pasture lands, [59]Ashan with its pasture lands, and Beth-shemesh with its pasture lands. [60]From the tribe of Benjamin, Geba with its pasture lands, Alemeth with its pasture lands, and Anathoth with its pasture lands. All their towns throughout their families were thirteen.

61 To the rest of the Kohathites were given by lot out of the family of the tribe, out of the half-tribe, the half of Manasseh, ten towns. [62]To the Gershomites according to their families were allotted thirteen towns out of the tribes of Issachar, Asher, Naphtali, and Manasseh in Bashan. [63]To the Merarites according to their families were allotted twelve towns out of the tribes of Reuben, Gad, and Zebulun. [64]So the people of Israel gave the Levites the towns with their pasture lands. [65]They also gave them by lot out of the tribes of Judah, Simeon, and Benjamin these towns that are mentioned by name.

66 And some of the families of the sons of Kohath had towns of their territory out of the tribe of Ephraim. [67]They were given the cities of refuge: Shechem with its pasture lands in the hill country of Ephraim, Gezer with its pasture lands, [68]Jokmeam with its pasture lands, Beth-horon with its pasture lands, [69]Aijalon with its pasture lands, Gath-

rimmon with its pasture lands; [70]and out of the half-tribe of Manasseh, Aner with its pasture lands, and Bileam with its pasture lands, for the rest of the families of the Kohathites.

71 To the Gershomites: out of the half-tribe of Manasseh: Golan in Bashan with its pasture lands and Ashtaroth with its pasture lands; [72]and out of the tribe of Issachar: Kedesh with its pasture lands, Daberath[b] with its pasture lands, [73]Ramoth with its pasture lands, and Anem with its pasture lands; [74]out of the tribe of Asher: Mashal with its pasture lands, Abdon with its pasture lands, [75]Hukok with its pasture lands, and Rehob with its pasture lands; [76]and out of the tribe of Naphtali: Kedesh in Galilee with its pasture lands, Hammon with its pasture lands, and Kiriathaim with its pasture lands. [77]To the rest of the Merarites out of the tribe of Zebulun: Rimmono with its pasture lands, Tabor with its pasture lands, [78]and across the Jordan from Jericho, on the east side of the Jordan, out of the tribe of Reuben: Bezer in the steppe with its pasture lands, Jahzah with its pasture lands, [79]Kedemoth with its pasture lands, and Mephaath with its pasture lands; [80]and out of the tribe of Gad: Ramoth in Gilead with its pasture lands, Mahanaim with its pasture lands, [81]Heshbon with its pasture lands, and Jazer with its pasture lands.

Descendants of Issachar

7 The sons[c] of Issachar: Tola, Puah, Jashub, and Shimron, four. [2]The sons of Tola: Uzzi, Rephaiah, Jeriel, Jahmai, Ibsam, and Shemuel, heads of their ancestral houses, namely of Tola, mighty warriors of their generations, their number in the days of David being twenty-two thousand six hundred. [3]The son[d] of Uzzi: Izrahiah. And the sons of

a Other readings *Hilez, Holon*; See Josh 21.15
b Or *Dobrath*   c Syr Compare Vg: Heb *And to the sons*   d Heb *sons*

6:54–81 *These are their dwelling places.* This list of the levitical cities was taken with slight modifications from Josh 21:1–40. The list functions in Chronicles to identify forty-eight sites throughout the entire land where the Levites lived at the time of David. The "all

Israel" theme is pervasive in Chronicles.
7:1–40 *the sons of Issachar.* The Chronicler provides genealogies in this chapter for Northern tribes that lived on the west side of the Jordan. The absence of Dan and Zebulun is unexplained.

Izrahiah: Michael, Obadiah, Joel, and Isshiah, five, all of them chiefs; [4]and along with them, by their generations, according to their ancestral houses, were units of the fighting force, thirty-six thousand, for they had many wives and sons. [5]Their kindred belonging to all the families of Issachar were in all eighty-seven thousand mighty warriors, enrolled by genealogy.

Descendants of Benjamin

6 The sons of Benjamin: Bela, Becher, and Jediael, three. [7]The sons of Bela: Ezbon, Uzzi, Uzziel, Jerimoth, and Iri, five, heads of ancestral houses, mighty warriors; and their enrollment by genealogies was twenty-two thousand thirty-four. [8]The sons of Becher: Zemirah, Joash, Eliezer, Elioenai, Omri, Jeremoth, Abijah, Anathoth, and Alemeth. All these were the sons of Becher; [9]and their enrollment by genealogies, according to their generations, as heads of their ancestral houses, mighty warriors, was twenty thousand two hundred. [10]The sons of Jediael: Bilhan. And the sons of Bilhan: Jeush, Benjamin, Ehud, Chenaanah, Zethan, Tarshish, and Ahishahar. [11]All these were the sons of Jediael according to the heads of their ancestral houses, mighty warriors, seventeen thousand two hundred, ready for service in war. [12]And Shuppim and Huppim were the sons of Ir, Hushim the son[a] of Aher.

Descendants of Naphtali

13 The descendants of Naphtali: Jahziel, Guni, Jezer, and Shallum, the descendants of Bilhah.

Descendants of Manasseh

14 The sons of Manasseh: Asriel, whom his Aramean concubine bore; she bore Machir the father of Gilead. [15]And Machir took a wife for Huppim and for Shuppim. The name of his sister was Maacah. And the name of the second was Zelophehad; and Zelophehad had daughters. [16]Maacah the wife of Machir bore a son, and she named him Peresh; the name of his brother was Sheresh; and his sons were Ulam and Rekem. [17]The son[a] of Ulam: Bedan. These were the sons of Gilead son of Machir, son of Manasseh. [18]And his sister Hammolecheth bore Ishhod, Abiezer, and Mahlah. [19]The sons of Shemida were Ahian, Shechem, Likhi, and Aniam.

Descendants of Ephraim

20 The sons of Ephraim: Shuthelah, and Bered his son, Tahath his son, Eleadah his son, Tahath his son, [21]Zabad his son, Shuthelah his son, and Ezer and Elead. Now the people of Gath, who were born in the land, killed them, because they came down to raid their cattle. [22]And their father Ephraim mourned many days, and his brothers came to comfort him. [23]Ephraim[b] went in to his wife, and she conceived and bore a son; and he named him Beriah, because disaster[c] had befallen his house. [24]His daughter was Sheerah, who built both Lower and Upper Beth-horon, and Uzzen-sheerah. [25]Rephah was his son, Resheph his son, Telah his son, Tahan his son, [26]Ladan his son, Ammihud his son, Elishama his son, [27]Nun[d] his son, Joshua his son. [28]Their possessions and settlements were Bethel and its towns, and eastward Naaran, and westward Gezer and its towns, Shechem and its towns, as far as Ayyah and its towns; [29]also along the borders of the Manassites, Beth-shean and its towns, Taanach and its towns, Megiddo and its towns, Dor and its towns. In these lived the sons of Joseph son of Israel.

Descendants of Asher

30 The sons of Asher: Imnah, Ishvah, Ishvi, Beriah, and their sister Serah. [31]The sons of Beriah: Heber and Malchiel, who was the father of Birzaith. [32]Heber became the father of Japhlet, Shomer, Hotham, and their sister Shua. [33]The sons of Japhlet: Pasach, Bimhal, and Ashvath. These are the sons of Japhlet. [34]The sons of Shemer: Ahi, Rohgah, Hubbah, and Aram. [35]The sons of Helem[e] his brother:

a Heb sons   b Heb He   c Heb beraah
d Here spelled Non; see Ex 33.11   e Or Hotham; see 7.32

7:27 *Joshua his son.* A seven-member, linear genealogy culminates in Joshua, the leader of the conquest of the land.

Zophah, Imna, Shelesh, and Amal. 36The sons of Zophah: Suah, Harnepher, Shual, Beri, Imrah, 37Bezer, Hod, Shamma, Shilshah, Ithran, and Beera. 38The sons of Jether: Jephunneh, Pispa, and Ara. 39The sons of Ulla: Arah, Hanniel, and Rizia. 40All of these were men of Asher, heads of ancestral houses, select mighty warriors, chief of the princes. Their number enrolled by genealogies, for service in war, was twenty-six thousand men.

Descendants of Benjamin

8 Benjamin became the father of Bela his firstborn, Ashbel the second, Aharah the third, 2Nohah the fourth, and Rapha the fifth. 3And Bela had sons: Addar, Gera, Abihud,*a* 4Abishua, Naaman, Ahoah, 5Gera, Shephuphan, and Huram. 6These are the sons of Ehud (they were heads of ancestral houses of the inhabitants of Geba, and they were carried into exile to Manahath): 7Naaman,*b* Ahijah, and Gera, that is, Heglam,*c* who became the father of Uzza and Ahihud. 8And Shaharaim had sons in the country of Moab after he had sent away his wives Hushim and Baara. 9He had sons by his wife Hodesh: Jobab, Zibia, Mesha, Malcam, 10Jeuz, Sachia, and Mirmah. These were his sons, heads of ancestral houses. 11He also had sons by Hushim: Abitub and Elpaal. 12The sons of Elpaal: Eber, Misham, and Shemed, who built Ono and Lod with its towns, 13and Beriah and Shema (they were heads of ancestral houses of the inhabitants of Aijalon, who put to flight the inhabitants of Gath); 14and Ahio, Shashak, and Jeremoth. 15Zebadiah, Arad, Eder, 16Michael, Ishpah, and Joha were sons of Beriah. 17Zebadiah, Meshullam, Hizki, Heber, 18Ishmerai, Izliah, and Jobab were

the sons of Elpaal. 19Jakim, Zichri, Zabdi, 20Elienai, Zillethai, Eliel, 21Adaiah, Beraiah, and Shimrath were the sons of Shimei. 22Ishpan, Eber, Eliel, 23Abdon, Zichri, Hanan, 24Hananiah, Elam, Anthothijah, 25Iphdeiah, and Penuel were the sons of Shashak. 26Shamsherai, Shehariah, Athaliah, 27Jaareshiah, Elijah, and Zichri were the sons of Jeroham. 28These were the heads of ancestral houses, according to their generations, chiefs. These lived in Jerusalem.

29 Jeiel*d* the father of Gibeon lived in Gibeon, and the name of his wife was Maacah. 30His firstborn son: Abdon, then Zur, Kish, Baal,*e* Nadab, 31Gedor, Ahio, Zecher, 32and Mikloth, who became the father of Shimeah. Now these also lived opposite their kindred in Jerusalem, with their kindred. 33Ner became the father of Kish, Kish of Saul,*f* Saul*f* of Jonathan, Malchishua, Abinadab, and Eshbaal; 34and the son of Jonathan was Meribbaal; and Merib-baal became the father of Micah. 35The sons of Micah: Pithon, Melech, Tarea, and Ahaz. 36Ahaz became the father of Jehoaddah; and Jehoaddah became the father of Alemeth, Azmaveth, and Zimri; Zimri became the father of Moza. 37Moza became the father of Binea; Raphah was his son, Eleasah his son, Azel his son. 38Azel had six sons, and these are their names: Azrikam, Bocheru, Ishmael, Sheariah, Obadiah, and Hanan; all these were the sons of Azel. 39The sons of his brother Eshek: Ulam his firstborn, Jeush the second, and Eliphelet the third. 40The sons of Ulam were mighty warriors, archers, having

a Or *father of Ehud*; see 8.6   *b* Heb *and Naaman*
c Or *he carried them into exile*   *d* Compare 9.35:
Heb lacks *Jeiel*   *e* Gk Ms adds *Ner*; Compare 8.33
and 9.36   *f* Or *Shaul*

8:1–40 *Benjamin.* The lengthy genealogy for Benjamin in this chapter forms an *inclusio* (narrative unit bracketed by two similar details) with the genealogy of Judah in 1 Chron 2:3–4:23. The Chronicler gives Judah and Benjamin prominence because of their past loyalty to David and because they are the two main tribes that returned from the exile.
8:29–32 *Jeiel the father of Gibeon.* All of the Gibeonites mentioned were now living in

Jerusalem. This information is repeated in 1 Chron 9:35–38.
8:33–40 *Ner became the father of Kish.* These verses, most of which are repeated in 9:39–44, provide a genealogy beginning with Ner, the grandfather of King Saul, and continuing for twelve or thirteen generations after Saul. In its present form the genealogy traces the ancestry of a military group called the "sons of Ulam" back to Saul. In this chapter it functions to flesh out the genealogy of the Benjaminites.

many children and grandchildren, one hundred fifty. All these were Benjaminites.

9 So all Israel was enrolled by genealogies; and these are written in the Book of the Kings of Israel. And Judah was taken into exile in Babylon because of their unfaithfulness. 2Now the first to live again in their possessions in their towns were Israelites, priests, Levites, and temple servants.

Inhabitants of Jerusalem after the Exile

3 And some of the people of Judah, Benjamin, Ephraim, and Manasseh lived in Jerusalem: 4Uthai son of Ammihud, son of Omri, son of Imri, son of Bani, from the sons of Perez son of Judah. 5And of the Shilonites: Asaiah the firstborn, and his sons. 6Of the sons of Zerah: Jeuel and their kin, six hundred ninety. 7Of the Benjaminites: Sallu son of Meshullam, son of Hodaviah, son of Hassenuah, 8Ibneiah son of Jeroham, Elah son of Uzzi, son of Michri, and Meshullam son of Shephatiah, son of Reuel, son of Ibnijah; 9and their kindred according to their generations, nine hundred fifty-six. All these were heads of families according to their ancestral houses.

Priestly Families

10 Of the priests: Jedaiah, Jehoiarib, Jachin, 11and Azariah son of Hilkiah, son of Meshullam, son of Zadok, son of Meraioth, son of Ahitub, the chief officer of the house of God; 12and Adaiah son of Jeroham, son of Pashhur, son of Malchijah, and Maasai son of Adiel, son of Jahzerah, son of Meshullam, son of Meshillemith, son of Immer; 13besides their kindred, heads of their ancestral houses, one thousand seven hundred sixty, qualified for the work of the service of the house of God.

Levitical Families

14 Of the Levites: Shemaiah son of Hasshub, son of Azrikam, son of Hashabiah, of the sons of Merari; 15and Bakbakkar, Heresh, Galal, and Mattaniah son of Mica, son of Zichri, son of Asaph; 16and Obadiah son of Shemaiah, son of Galal, son of Jeduthun, and Berechiah son of Asa, son of Elkanah, who lived in the villages of the Netophathites.

17 The gatekeepers were: Shallum, Akkub, Talmon, Ahiman; and their kindred Shallum was the chief, 18stationed previously in the king's gate on the east side. These were the gatekeepers of the camp of the Levites. 19Shallum son of Kore, son of Ebiasaph, son of Korah, and his kindred of his ancestral house, the Korahites, were in charge of the work of the service, guardians of the thresholds of the tent, as their ancestors had been in charge of the camp of the LORD, guardians of the entrance. 20And Phinehas son of Eleazar was chief over them in former times; the LORD was with him. 21Zechariah son of Meshelemiah was gatekeeper at the entrance of the tent of meeting. 22All these, who were chosen as gatekeepers at the thresholds, were two hundred twelve. They were enrolled by genealogies in their villages. David and the seer Samuel established them in their office of trust. 23So they and their descendants were in charge of the gates of the house of the LORD, that is, the house of the tent, as guards. 24The gatekeepers were on the four sides, east, west, north, and south; 25and their kindred who were in their villages were obliged to come in every seven days, in turn, to be with them; 26for the four chief gatekeepers, who were Levites, were in charge of the chambers and the treasures of the house of God. 27And they would spend the night near the house of God; for on them lay the duty of watching, and they had charge of opening it every morning.

28 Some of them had charge of the utensils of service, for they were required to count them when they were brought in and taken out. 29Others of them were appointed over the furniture, and over all the holy utensils,

---

9:2–17 *the first to live again in their possessions.* Those who lived in the land and in Jerusalem after the exile were Israelites (laypeople), priests, Levites (generic Levites, levitical gatekeepers, and levitical singers), and Temple servants. The laypeople hailed from at least the tribes of Judah, Benjamin, Ephraim, and Manasseh. These verses are taken from Neh 11:3–19.

also over the choice flour, the wine, the oil, the incense, and the spices. 30Others, of the sons of the priests, prepared the mixing of the spices, 31and Mattithiah, one of the Levites, the firstborn of Shallum the Korahite, was in charge of making the flat cakes. 32Also some of their kindred of the Kohathites had charge of the rows of bread, to prepare them for each sabbath.

33 Now these are the singers, the heads of ancestral houses of the Levites, living in the chambers of the temple free from other service, for they were on duty day and night. 34These were heads of ancestral houses of the Levites, according to their generations; these leaders lived in Jerusalem.

The Family of King Saul

35 In Gibeon lived the father of Gibeon, Jeiel, and the name of his wife was Maacah. 36His firstborn son was Abdon, then Zur, Kish, Baal, Ner, Nadab, 37Gedor, Ahio, Zechariah, and Mikloth; 38and Mikloth became the father of Shimeam; and these also lived opposite their kindred in Jerusalem, with their kindred. 39Ner became the father of Kish, Kish of Saul, Saul of Jonathan, Malchishua, Abinadab, and Esh-baal; 40and the son of Jonathan was Merib-baal; and Merib-baal became the father of Micah. 41The sons of Micah: Pithon, Melech, Tahrea, and Ahaz; a 42and Ahaz became the father of Jarah, and Jarah of Alemeth, Azmaveth, and Zimri; and Zimri became the father of Moza. 43Moza became the father of Binea; and Rephaiah was his son, Eleasah his son, Azel his son. 44Azel had six sons, and these are their names: Azrikam, Bocheru, Ishmael, Sheariah, Obadiah, and Hanan; these were the sons of Azel.

Death of Saul and His Sons

10 Now the Philistines fought against Israel; and the men of Israel fled before the Philistines, and fell slain on Mount Gilboa. 2The Philistines overtook Saul and his sons; and the Philistines killed Jonathan and Abinadab and Malchishua, sons of Saul. 3The battle pressed hard on Saul; and the archers found him, and he was wounded by the archers. 4Then Saul said to his armor-bearer, "Draw your sword, and thrust me through with it, so that these uncircumcised may not come and make sport of me." But his armor-bearer was unwilling, for he was terrified. So Saul took his own sword and fell on it. 5When his armor-bearer saw that Saul was dead, he also fell on his sword and died. 6Thus Saul died; he and his three sons and all his house died together. 7When all the men of Israel who were in the valley saw that the army b had fled and that Saul and his sons were dead, they abandoned their towns and fled; and the Philistines came and occupied them.

8 The next day when the Philistines came to strip the dead, they found Saul and his sons fallen on Mount Gilboa. 9They stripped him and took his head and his armor, and sent messengers throughout the land of the Philistines to carry the good news to their idols and to the people. 10They put his armor in the temple of their gods, and fastened

a Compare 8.35: Heb lacks *and Ahaz*   b Heb *they*

9:39–44 *Ner became the father of Kish.* The genealogical material on Saul in this chapter prepares readers for the narrative about the death of Saul. It also indicates that although Saul's family suffered a severe blow at Gilboa, the whole family was not wiped out, least of all by David. By not repeating 8:39–40, the Chronicler does not end his genealogical prologue with the ringing words, "All these were Benjaminites." However unfaithful the Benjaminite Saul had proven to be, the indictment against him did not make all of the members of his tribe guilty.

10:1–12 *Now the Philistines fought against Israel.* This passage is based on 1 Sam 31:1–13. The Chronicler begins his story of Saul with Saul's death, making no mention of Saul's early kingship (1 Sam 9–15) or other material from 1 Sam 16:14–30:31, where Saul and David contest with one another.

10:4 *Saul took his own sword and fell on it.* The Chronicler includes the account of Saul's suicide from 1 Samuel 31 rather than the alternate account in 2 Sam 1:1–10, where Saul is killed by one of his own warriors, according to an Amalekite who carries this news to David.

his head in the temple of Dagon. ¹¹But when all Jabesh-gilead heard everything that the Philistines had done to Saul, ¹²all the valiant warriors got up and took away the body of Saul and the bodies of his sons, and brought them to Jabesh. Then they buried their bones under the oak in Jabesh, and fasted seven days.

13 So Saul died for his unfaithfulness; he was unfaithful to the LORD in that he did not keep the command of the LORD; moreover, he had consulted a medium, seeking guidance, ¹⁴and did not seek guidance from the LORD. Therefore the LORD*a* put him to death and turned the kingdom over to David son of Jesse.

David Anointed King of All Israel

11 Then all Israel gathered together to David at Hebron and said, "See, we are your bone and flesh. ²For some time now,

even while Saul was king, it was you who commanded the army of Israel. The LORD your God said to you: It is you who shall be shepherd of my people Israel, you who shall be ruler over my people Israel." ³So all the elders of Israel came to the king at Hebron, and David made a covenant with them at Hebron before the LORD. And they anointed David king over Israel, according to the word of the LORD by Samuel.

Jerusalem Captured

4 David and all Israel marched to Jerusalem, that is Jebus, where the Jebusites were, the inhabitants of the land. ⁵The inhabitants of Jebus said to David, "You will not come in here." Nevertheless David took the stronghold of Zion, now the city of David. ⁶David had said, "Whoever attacks the Jebusites first

a Heb *he*

10:13–14 *So Saul died for his unfaithfulness.* Saul's unfaithfulness anticipates the unfaithfulness of a number of kings, which resulted in the Babylonian exile (9:1; 2 Chron 36:14). Unfaithfulness by the Transjordanian tribes had also led to their exile (1 Chron 5:25). Saul did not keep the word of Yahweh and he consulted a medium. The latter is a reference to the incident with the medium at Endor (1 Sam 28). Inquiring of a medium at a time of military danger seems to be comparable in the Chronicler's judgment to reliance on military alliances, which the Chronicler uniformly rejects. Above all it demonstrated distrust in Yahweh and disobedience to him.

Responding
10:13–14 GUIDANCE. Saul's sin was a lack of trust in God. When God doesn't give us clear answers, it's tempting to look elsewhere for reassurance that we're on the right path. Galatians tells us that we are on the right path if we show the fruit of the Spirit: love, joy, peace, patience, kindness, generosity, faithfulness, gentleness, and self-control (Gal 5:22–23). Write these qualities on an index card and put it in a place where you will come across it often. When making a difficult decision, prayerfully consider whether your choice will

lead you closer to manifesting these qualities. See also Spiritual Disciplines Index.

10:14 *turned the kingdom over to David.* This is the first mention of David within the narrative of Chronicles, and the story of David's reign occupies the rest of 1 Chronicles. The Chronicler is silent about the struggle between David and Ishbaal in 2 Samuel 1–4. The change from the kingship of Saul to that of David is as momentous for the Chronicler as the change from the United Monarchy to the Divided Monarchy. Both of them were "turn[s] of affairs" brought about by God, who is in charge of the affairs of human beings (2 Chron 10:15).

11:1–3, 4–9 *all Israel gathered together to David at Hebron.* These verses are based on 2 Sam 5:1–3 and 6–10. The unanimous participation of Israel in the coronation of David at Hebron in the Chronicler's version is quite different from that in 2 Sam 5:1. There all the Northern tribes of Israel gave David a second anointing, after the people of Judah had already anointed him as their king in 2 Sam 2:4. In Chronicles, a united Israel backs David from the very beginning.

11:4 *all Israel marched to Jerusalem.* The capture of Jerusalem by all Israel lends prestige to the city and its Temple. In 2 Sam 5:7, David's private army captured the city.

shall be chief and commander." And Joab son of Zeruiah went up first, so he became chief. [7]David resided in the stronghold; therefore it was called the city of David. [8]He built the city all around, from the Millo in complete circuit; and Joab repaired the rest of the city. [9]And David became greater and greater, for the LORD of hosts was with him.

David's Mighty Men and Their Exploits

10 Now these are the chiefs of David's warriors, who gave him strong support in his kingdom, together with all Israel, to make him king, according to the word of the LORD concerning Israel. [11]This is an account of David's mighty warriors: Jashobeam, son of Hachmoni,[a] was chief of the Three;[b] he wielded his spear against three hundred whom he killed at one time.

12 And next to him among the three warriors was Eleazar son of Dodo, the Ahohite. [13]He was with David at Pas-dammim when the Philistines were gathered there for battle. There was a plot of ground full of barley. Now the people had fled from the Philistines, [14]but he and David took their stand in the middle of the plot, defended it, and killed the Philistines; and the LORD saved them by a great victory.

15 Three of the thirty chiefs went down to the rock to David at the cave of Adullam, while the army of Philistines was encamped in the valley of Rephaim. [16]David was then in the stronghold; and the garrison of the Philistines was then at Bethlehem. [17]David said longingly, "O that someone would give me water to drink from the well of Bethlehem that is by the gate!" [18]Then the Three broke through the camp of the Philistines, and drew water from the well of Bethlehem that was by the gate, and they brought it to David. But David would not drink of it; he poured it out

to the LORD, [19]and said, "My God forbid that I should do this. Can I drink the blood of these men? For at the risk of their lives they brought it." Therefore he would not drink it. The three warriors did these things.

20 Now Abishai,[c] the brother of Joab, was chief of the Thirty. [d] With his spear he fought against three hundred and killed them, and won a name beside the Three. [21]He was the most renowned[e] of the Thirty,[d] and became their commander; but he did not attain to the Three.

22 Benaiah son of Jehoiada was a valiant man[f] of Kabzeel, a doer of great deeds; he struck down two sons of[g] Ariel of Moab. He also went down and killed a lion in a pit on a day when snow had fallen. [23]And he killed an Egyptian, a man of great stature, five cubits tall. The Egyptian had in his hand a spear like a weaver's beam; but Benaiah went against him with a staff, snatched the spear out of the Egyptian's hand, and killed him with his own spear. [24]Such were the things Benaiah son of Jehoiada did, and he won a name beside the three warriors. [25]He was renowned among the Thirty, but he did not attain to the Three. And David put him in charge of his bodyguard.

26 The warriors of the armies were Asahel brother of Joab, Elhanan son of Dodo of Bethlehem, [27]Shammoth of Harod,[h] Helez the Pelonite, [28]Ira son of Ikkesh of Tekoa, Abiezer of Anathoth, [29]Sibbecai the Hushathite, Ilai the Ahohite, [30]Maharai of Netophah, Heled son of Baanah of Netophah,

a Or a Hachmonite   b Compare 2 Sam 23.8: Heb Thirty or captains   c Gk Vg Tg Compare 2 Sam 23.18: Heb Abshai   d Syr: Heb Three   e Compare 2 Sam 23.19: Heb more renowned among the two   f Syr: Heb the son of a valiant man   g See 2 Sam 23.20: Heb lacks sons of   h Compare 2 Sam 23.25: Heb the Harorite

---

11:8 *He built the city all around.* This is the first building project by an Israelite king. Only pious kings in Chronicles engage in building programs, and their productivity is seen as an appropriate reward for their good behavior.

11:10–47 *strong support in his kingdom.* In this passage, based on a list of mighty men from 2 Sam 23:8–39 and supplemented by sixteen

names taken from another source, the Chronicler indicates the support given David's rule by the warrior heads, who are joined by all Israel.

11:10 *according to the word of the LORD concerning Israel.* In addition to the unanimous support of the people and the military personnel, the promise of Yahweh brought the kingship of David to pass (10:14; 11:3).

31Ithai son of Ribai of Gibeah of the Benjaminites, Benaiah of Pirathon, 32Hurai of the wadis of Gaash, Abiel the Arbathite, 33Azmaveth of Baharum, Eliahba of Shaalbon, 34Hashem[a] the Gizonite, Jonathan son of Shagee the Hararite, 35Ahiam son of Sachar the Hararite, Eliphal son of Ur, 36Hepher the Mecherathite, Ahijah the Pelonite, 37Hezro of Carmel, Naarai son of Ezbai, 38Joel the brother of Nathan, Mibhar son of Hagri, 39Zelek the Ammonite, Naharai of Beeroth, the armorbearer of Joab son of Zeruiah, 40Ira the Ithrite, Gareb the Ithrite, 41Uriah the Hittite, Zabad son of Ahlai, 42Adina son of Shiza the Reubenite, a leader of the Reubenites, and thirty with him, 43Hanan son of Maacah, and Joshaphat the Mithnite, 44Uzzia the Ashterathite, Shama and Jeiel sons of Hotham the Aroerite, 45Jediael son of Shimri, and his brother Joha the Tizite, 46Eliel the Mahavite, and Jeribai and Joshaviah sons of Elnaam, and Ithmah the Moabite, 47Eliel, and Obed, and Jaasiel the Mezobaite.

David's Followers in the Wilderness

12 The following are those who came to David at Ziklag, while he could not move about freely because of Saul son of Kish; they were among the mighty warriors who helped him in war. 2They were archers, and could shoot arrows and sling stones with either the right hand or the left; they were Benjaminites, Saul's kindred. 3The chief was Ahiezer, then Joash, both sons of Shemaah of Gibeah; also Jeziel and Pelet sons of Azmaveth; Beracah, Jehu of Anathoth, 4Ishmaiah of Gibeon, a warrior among the Thirty and a leader over the Thirty; Jeremiah,[b] Jahaziel, Johanan, Jozabad of Gederah, 5Eluzai,[c] Jerimoth, Bealiah, Shemariah, Shephatiah the Haruphite; 6Elkanah, Isshiah, Azarel, Joezer, and Jashobeam, the Korahites; 7and Joelah and Zebadiah, sons of Jeroham of Gedor.

8 From the Gadites there went over to David at the stronghold in the wilderness mighty and experienced warriors, expert with shield and spear, whose faces were like the faces of lions, and who were swift as gazelles on the mountains: 9Ezer the chief, Obadiah second, Eliab third, 10Mishmannah fourth, Jeremiah fifth, 11Attai sixth, Eliel seventh, 12Johanan eighth, Elzabad ninth, 13Jeremiah tenth, Machbannai eleventh. 14These Gadites were officers of the army, the least equal to a hundred and the greatest to a thousand. 15These are the men who crossed the Jordan in the first month, when it was overflowing all its banks, and put to flight all those in the valleys, to the east and to the west.

16 Some Benjaminites and Judahites came to the stronghold to David. 17David went out to meet them and said to them, "If you have come to me in friendship, to help me, then my heart will be knit to you; but if you have come to betray me to my adversaries, though my hands have done no wrong, then may the God of our ancestors see and give judgment." 18Then the spirit came upon Amasai, chief of the Thirty, and he said,

"We are yours, O David;
    and with you, O son of Jesse!
Peace, peace to you,
    and peace to the one who helps you!
For your God is the one who helps
        you."

Then David received them, and made them officers of his troops.

19 Some of the Manassites deserted to David when he came with the Philistines for the battle against Saul. (Yet he did not help them, for the rulers of the Philistines took counsel and sent him away, saying, "He will desert to his master Saul at the cost of our heads.") 20As he went to Ziklag these Manassites deserted to him: Adnah, Jozabad, Jediael, Michael, Jozabad, Elihu, and Zillethai, chiefs of the thousands in Manasseh. 21They helped David against the band of raiders,[d] for they were all warriors and commanders in the army. 22Indeed from day to day people

a Compare Gk and 2 Sam 23.32: Heb the sons of Hashem   b Heb verse 5   c Heb verse 6   d Or as officers of his troops

---

12:1 *those who came to David at Ziklag.* Soldiers rallied to David already during the days of Saul.

kept coming to David to help him, until there was a great army, like an army of God.

David's Army at Hebron

23 These are the numbers of the divisions of the armed troops who came to David in Hebron to turn the kingdom of Saul over to him, according to the word of the LORD. 24The people of Judah bearing shield and spear numbered six thousand eight hundred armed troops. 25Of the Simeonites, mighty warriors, seven thousand one hundred. 26Of the Levites four thousand six hundred. 27Jehoiada, leader of the house of Aaron, and with him three thousand seven hundred. 28Zadok, a young warrior, and twenty-two commanders from his own ancestral house. 29Of the Benjaminites, the kindred of Saul, three thousand, of whom the majority had continued to keep their allegiance to the house of Saul. 30Of the Ephraimites, twenty thousand eight hundred, mighty warriors, notables in their ancestral houses. 31Of the half-tribe of Manasseh, eighteen thousand, who were expressly named to come and make David king. 32Of Issachar, those who had understanding of the times, to know what Israel ought to do, two hundred chiefs, and all their kindred under their command. 33Of Zebulun, fifty thousand seasoned troops, equipped for battle with all the weapons of war, to help David[a] with singleness of purpose. 34Of Naphtali, a thousand commanders, with whom there were thirty-seven thousand armed with shield and spear. 35Of the Danites, twenty-eight thousand six hundred equipped for battle. 36Of Asher, forty thousand seasoned troops ready for battle. 37Of the Reubenites and Gadites and the half-tribe of Manasseh from beyond the Jordan, one hundred twenty thousand armed with all the weapons of war.

38 All these, warriors arrayed in battle order, came to Hebron with full intent to make David king over all Israel; likewise all the rest of Israel were of a single mind to make David king. 39They were there with David for three days, eating and drinking, for their kindred had provided for them. 40And also their neighbors, from as far away as Issachar and Zebulun and Naphtali, came bringing food on donkeys, camels, mules, and oxen—abundant provisions of meal, cakes of figs, clusters of raisins, wine, oil, oxen, and sheep, for there was joy in Israel.

The Ark Brought from Kiriath-jearim

13 David consulted with the commanders of the thousands and of the hundreds, with every leader. 2David said to the whole assembly of Israel, "If it seems good to you, and if it is the will of the LORD our God, let us send abroad to our kindred who remain in all the land of Israel, including the priests and Levites in the cities that have pasture lands, that they may come together to us. 3Then let us bring again the ark of our God to us; for we did not turn to it in the days of Saul." 4The whole assembly agreed to do so, for the thing pleased all the people.

5 So David assembled all Israel from the Shihor of Egypt to Lebo-hamath, to bring the ark of God from Kiriath-jearim. 6And David and all Israel went up to Baalah, that is, to Kiriath-jearim, which belongs to Judah, to bring up from there the ark of God, the LORD, who is enthroned on the cherubim, which is called by his[b] name. 7They carried the ark of God on a new cart, from the house of Abinadab, and Uzzah and Ahio[c] were driving the cart. 8David and all Israel were dancing before God with all their might, with song and lyres and harps and tambourines and cymbals and trumpets.

9 When they came to the threshing floor

a Gk: Heb lacks *David*   b Heb lacks *his*
c Or *and his brother*

12:23–37 *who came to David in Hebron.* Twelve tribal groups rallied to David at Hebron to make him king. The more remote the tribe, the larger its delegation at David's coronation.

12:38 *all the rest of Israel.* The soldiers' commitment to David is matched by that of the civilian population.

13:1–16:43 *the ark of our God.* The ark narrative includes material from 2 Samuel (6:1–11; 5:11–25; 6:12–23), the Psalter, and the Chronicler himself. The transfer of the ark to Jerusalem is David's first act as king after his conquest of Jerusalem itself.

of Chidon, Uzzah put out his hand to hold the ark, for the oxen shook it. [10]The anger of the LORD was kindled against Uzzah; he struck him down because he put out his hand to the ark; and he died there before God. [11]David was angry because the LORD had burst out against Uzzah; so that place is called Perez-uzzah[a] to this day. [12]David was afraid of God that day; he said, "How can I bring the ark of God into my care?" [13]So David did not take the ark into his care into the city of David; he took it instead to the house of Obed-edom the Gittite. [14]The ark of God remained with the household of Obed-edom in his house three months, and the LORD blessed the household of Obed-edom and all that he had.

David Established at Jerusalem

14 King Hiram of Tyre sent messengers to David, along with cedar logs, and masons and carpenters to build a house for him. [2]David then perceived that the LORD had established him as king over Israel, and that his kingdom was highly exalted for the sake of his people Israel.

3 David took more wives in Jerusalem, and David became the father of more sons and daughters. [4]These are the names of the children whom he had in Jerusalem: Shammua, Shobab, and Nathan; Solomon, [5]Ibhar, Elishua, and Elpelet; [6]Nogah, Nepheg, and Japhia; [7]Elishama, Beeliada, and Eliphelet.

Defeat of the Philistines

8 When the Philistines heard that David had been anointed king over all Israel, all the Philistines went up in search of David; and David heard of it and went out against them. [9]Now the Philistines had come and made a raid in the valley of Rephaim. [10]David inquired of God, "Shall I go up against the Philistines? Will you give them into my hand?" The LORD said to him, "Go up, and I will give them into your hand." [11]So he went up to Baal-perazim, and David defeated them there. David said, "God has burst out[b] against my enemies by my hand, like a bursting flood." Therefore that place is called Baal-perazim.[c] [12]They abandoned their gods there, and at David's command they were burned.

13 Once again the Philistines made a raid in the valley. [14]When David again inquired of God, God said to him, "You shall not go up after them; go around and come on them opposite the balsam trees. [15]When you hear the sound of marching in the tops of the balsam trees, then go out to battle; for God has gone out before you to strike down the army of the Philistines." [16]David did as God had commanded him, and they struck down the Philistine army from Gibeon to Gezer. [17]The fame of David went out into all lands, and the LORD brought the fear of him on all nations.

The Ark Brought to Jerusalem

15 David[d] built houses for himself in the city of David, and he prepared a place for the ark of God and pitched a tent for it. [2]Then David commanded that no one but the Levites were to carry the ark of God, for the LORD had chosen them to carry the ark of the LORD and to minister to him forever. [3]David assembled all Israel in Jerusalem to bring up the ark of the LORD to its place, which he had prepared for it. [4]Then David gathered together

a That is *Bursting Out Against Uzzah*   *b* Heb *paraz*
c That is *Lord of Bursting Out*   *d* Heb *He*

13:10 *he struck him down.* The death of Uzzah for touching the ark is a typical example of immediate retribution.

14:1–17 *Hiram of Tyre sent messengers to David.* All but the last verse of this chapter is taken from 2 Sam 5:11–25, but this section has been moved to a position after the failure of the first attempt to bring the ark to Jerusalem instead of before it. Yahweh blessed David for attempting to bring the ark to Jerusalem, and David had the strength and organizational ability to complete the transfer of the ark on his second try. The notice of David's international renown (v 17) demonstrates that Yahweh is in full support of him.

15:2 *the Levites were to carry the ark.* David's decree that the Levites alone carry the ark follows pentateuchal legislation and is a correction to the procedure in the first, failed effort to bring the ark to Jerusalem. When the ark was carried by non-Levites, it did not receive proper care (v 13).

the descendants of Aaron and the Levites: 5of the sons of Kohath, Uriel the chief, with one hundred twenty of his kindred; 6of the sons of Merari, Asaiah the chief, with two hundred twenty of his kindred; 7of the sons of Gershom, Joel the chief, with one hundred thirty of his kindred; 8of the sons of Elizaphan, Shemaiah the chief, with two hundred of his kindred; 9of the sons of Hebron, Eliel the chief, with eighty of his kindred; 10of the sons of Uzziel, Amminadab the chief, with one hundred twelve of his kindred.

11 David summoned the priests Zadok and Abiathar, and the Levites Uriel, Asaiah, Joel, Shemaiah, Eliel, and Amminadab. 12He said to them, "You are the heads of families of the Levites; sanctify yourselves, you and your kindred, so that you may bring up the ark of the Lord, the God of Israel, to the place that I have prepared for it. 13Because you did not carry it the first time, a the Lord our God burst out against us, because we did not give it proper care." 14So the priests and the Levites sanctified themselves to bring up the ark of the Lord, the God of Israel. 15And the Levites carried the ark of God on their shoulders with the poles, as Moses had commanded according to the word of the Lord.

16 David also commanded the chiefs of the Levites to appoint their kindred as the singers to play on musical instruments, on harps and lyres and cymbals, to raise loud sounds of joy. 17So the Levites appointed Heman son of Joel; and of his kindred Asaph son of Berechiah; and of the sons of Merari, their kindred, Ethan son of Kushaiah; 18and with them their kindred of the second order, Zechariah, Jaaziel, Shemiramoth, Jehiel, Unni, Eliab, Benaiah, Maaseiah, Mattithiah, Eliphelehu, and Mikneiah, and the gatekeepers Obed-edom and Jeiel. 19The singers Heman, Asaph, and Ethan were to sound bronze cymbals; 20Zechariah, Aziel, Shemiramoth, Jehiel, Unni, Eliab, Maaseiah,

and Benaiah were to play harps according to Alamoth; 21but Mattithiah, Eliphelehu, Mikneiah, Obed-edom, Jeiel, and Azaziah were to lead with lyres according to the Sheminith. 22Chenaniah, leader of the Levites in music, was to direct the music, for he understood it. 23Berechiah and Elkanah were to be gatekeepers for the ark. 24Shebaniah, Joshaphat, Nethanel, Amasai, Zechariah, Benaiah, and Eliezer, the priests, were to blow the trumpets before the ark of God. Obed-edom and Jehiah also were to be gatekeepers for the ark.

25 So David and the elders of Israel, and the commanders of the thousands, went to bring up the ark of the covenant of the Lord from the house of Obed-edom with rejoicing. 26And because God helped the Levites who were carrying the ark of the covenant of the Lord, they sacrificed seven bulls and seven rams. 27David was clothed with a robe of fine linen, as also were all the Levites who were carrying the ark, and the singers, and Chenaniah the leader of the music of the singers; and David wore a linen ephod. 28So all Israel brought up the ark of the covenant of the Lord with shouting, to the sound of the horn, trumpets, and cymbals, and made loud music on harps and lyres.

29 As the ark of the covenant of the Lord came to the city of David, Michal daughter of Saul looked out of the window, and saw King David leaping and dancing; and she despised him in her heart.

The Ark Placed in the Tent

16 They brought in the ark of God, and set it inside the tent that David had pitched for it; and they offered burnt offerings and offerings of well-being before God. 2When David had finished offering the burnt offerings and the offerings of well-being, he blessed

a Meaning of Heb uncertain

15:15 *as Moses had commanded.* Moses is referred to for the first time.

15:16 *the singers.* The additional duties of the Levites in the service of song are instituted and authorized by the first and greatest king of the Davidic dynasty.

16:2 *he blessed the people.* David's blessing of

the people echoes Yahweh's own blessing of the house of Obed-edom (13:14), and it anticipates David's blessing of his own household at the end of the ceremony (v 43). David, who pitched a tent for the ark (v 1) and blessed the people, is a second Moses, who also pitched a tent (Exod 33:7) and blessed the people (Deut 33:1).

the people in the name of the LORD; ³and he distributed to every person in Israel—man and woman alike—to each a loaf of bread, a portion of meat,ᵃ and a cake of raisins.

4 He appointed certain of the Levites as ministers before the ark of the LORD, to invoke, to thank, and to praise the LORD, the God of Israel. ⁵Asaph was the chief, and second to him Zechariah, Jeiel, Shemiramoth, Jehiel, Mattithiah, Eliab, Benaiah, Obededom, and Jeiel, with harps and lyres; Asaph was to sound the cymbals, ⁶and the priests Benaiah and Jahaziel were to blow trumpets regularly, before the ark of the covenant of God.

David's Psalm of Thanksgiving

7 Then on that day David first appointed the singing of praises to the LORD by Asaph and his kindred.

worship

8 O give thanks to the LORD, call on his
    name,
    make known his deeds among the
    peoples.
9 Sing to him, sing praises to him,
    tell of all his wonderful works.
10 Glory in his holy name;
    let the hearts of those who seek the
    LORD rejoice.
11 Seek the LORD and his strength,
    seek his presence continually.
12 Remember the wonderful works he has
    done,
    his miracles, and the judgments he
    uttered,
13 O offspring of his servant Israel,ᵇ
    children of Jacob, his chosen ones.

14 He is the LORD our God;
    his judgments are in all the earth.
15 Remember his covenant forever,
    the word that he commanded, for a
    thousand generations,

16 the covenant that he made with
    Abraham,
    his sworn promise to Isaac,
17 which he confirmed to Jacob as a
    statute,
    to Israel as an everlasting covenant,
18 saying, "To you I will give the land of
    Canaan
    as your portion for an inheritance."

19 When they were few in number,
    of little account, and strangers in the
    land,ᶜ
20 wandering from nation to nation,
    from one kingdom to another people,
21 he allowed no one to oppress them;
    he rebuked kings on their account,
22 saying, "Do not touch my anointed
    ones;
    do my prophets no harm."

23 Sing to the LORD, all the earth.
    Tell of his salvation from day to day.
24 Declare his glory among the nations,
    his marvelous works among all the
    peoples.
25 For great is the LORD, and greatly to be
    praised;
    he is to be revered above all gods.
26 For all the gods of the peoples are idols,
    but the LORD made the heavens.
27 Honor and majesty are before him;
    strength and joy are in his place.

28 Ascribe to the LORD, O families of the
    peoples,
    ascribe to the LORD glory and
    strength.
29 Ascribe to the LORD the glory due his
    name;

a Compare Gk Syr Vg: Meaning of Heb uncertain
b Another reading is *Abraham* (compare Ps 105.6)
c Heb *in it*

16:7–36 *the singing of praises to the LORD.* The song of the Levites in this chapter is a medley of Pss 105:1–15; 96:1–10; 106:1, 47–48. It expresses Israel's praise (vv 9–22), international praise (vv 23–30), and cosmic praise (vv 31–33). Indeed, praise constitutes a central Spiritual Discipline in the worship life of the People of God. The Levites' participation in the Temple worship of the Chronicler's day is justified by their appointment by David to regular duty before the ark (v 37).

bring an offering, and come before
him.
Worship the LORD in holy splendor;
30 tremble before him, all the earth.
The world is firmly established; it
shall never be moved.
31 Let the heavens be glad, and let the
earth rejoice,
and let them say among the nations,
"The LORD is king!"
32 Let the sea roar, and all that fills it;
let the field exult, and everything in it.
33 Then shall the trees of the forest sing for
joy
before the LORD, for he comes to judge
the earth.
34 O give thanks to the LORD, for he is
good;
for his steadfast love endures forever.

35 Say also:
"Save us, O God of our salvation,
and gather and rescue us from among
the nations,
that we may give thanks to your holy
name,
and glory in your praise.
36 Blessed be the LORD, the God of Israel,
from everlasting to everlasting."
Then all the people said "Amen!" and praised
the LORD.

Regular Worship Maintained

37 David left Asaph and his kinsfolk there
before the ark of the covenant of the LORD to
minister regularly before the ark as each day
required, 38 and also Obed-edom and his*a* sixty-eight kinsfolk; while Obed-edom son of
Jeduthun and Hosah were to be gatekeepers.
39 And he left the priest Zadok and his kindred
the priests before the tabernacle of the LORD

in the high place that was at Gibeon, 40 to offer burnt offerings to the LORD on the altar of
burnt offering regularly, morning and
evening, according to all that is written in
the law of the LORD that he commanded Israel. 41 With them were Heman and Jeduthun, and the rest of those chosen and expressly named to render thanks to the LORD,
for his steadfast love endures forever. 42 Heman and Jeduthun had with them trumpets
and cymbals for the music, and instruments
for sacred song. The sons of Jeduthun were
appointed to the gate.
43 Then all the people departed to their
homes, and David went home to bless his
household.

God's Covenant with David

17 Now when David settled in his house,
David said to the prophet Nathan, "I
am living in a house of cedar, but the ark of
the covenant of the LORD is under a tent."
2 Nathan said to David, "Do all that you have
in mind, for God is with you."
3 But that same night the word of the LORD
came to Nathan, saying: 4 Go and tell my servant David: Thus says the LORD: You shall
not build me a house to live in. 5 For I have not
lived in a house since the day I brought out Israel to this very day, but I have lived in a tent
and a tabernacle.*b* 6 Wherever I have moved
about among all Israel, did I ever speak a word
with any of the judges of Israel, whom I commanded to shepherd my people, saying, Why
have you not built me a house of cedar? 7 Now
therefore thus you shall say to my servant
David: Thus says the LORD of hosts: I took
you from the pasture, from following the

---

a Gk Syr Vg: Heb *their*   *b* Gk 2 Sam 7.6: Heb *but I
have been from tent to tent and from tabernacle*

16:39 *before the tabernacle . . . at Gibeon.*
The Chronicler locates the tabernacle at
Gibeon, without biblical precedent, in an
attempt to justify Solomon's pilgrimage to
the high place at that site (2 Chron 1:3–7;
1 Kings 3:4–5).

17:1 *the ark . . . is under a tent.* After his
anointing (11:1–3), capture of Jerusalem
(11:4–9), and bringing the ark of the covenant of

Yahweh to Jerusalem (chaps 13–16), the first
thing that David mentions is his desire to build a
temple there. The Chronicler used 2 Samuel 7 in
writing this chapter.

17:4 *You shall not build me a house.* David is
rejected as a temple builder because he was a
man of blood (22:8; 28:3) and because Yahweh
had not found such permanent accommodations
necessary in the past.

sheep, to be ruler over my people Israel; 8and I have been with you wherever you went, and have cut off all your enemies before you; and I will make for you a name, like the name of the great ones of the earth. 9I will appoint a place for my people Israel, and will plant them, so that they may live in their own place, and be disturbed no more; and evil-doers shall wear them down no more, as they did formerly, 10from the time that I appoint-ed judges over my people Israel; and I will subdue all your enemies.

Moreover I declare to you that the LORD will build you a house. 11When your days are fulfilled to go to be with your ancestors, I will raise up your offspring after you, one of your own sons, and I will establish his kingdom. 12He shall build a house for me, and I will es-tablish his throne forever. 13I will be a father to him, and he shall be a son to me. I will not take my steadfast love from him, as I took it from him who was before you, 14but I will confirm him in my house and in my king-dom forever, and his throne shall be estab-lished forever. 15In accordance with all these words and all this vision, Nathan spoke to David.

David's Prayer

16 Then King David went in and sat before the LORD, and said, "Who am I, O LORD God, and what is my house, that you have brought me thus far? 17And even this was a small thing in your sight, O God; you have also spoken of your servant's house for a great while to come. You regard me as someone of high rank,[a] O LORD God! 18And what more can David say to you for honoring your ser-vant? You know your servant. 19For your ser-vant's sake, O LORD, and according to your own heart, you have done all these great deeds, making known all these great things. 20There is no one like you, O LORD, and there is no God besides you, according to all that we have heard with our ears. 21Who is like your people Israel, one nation on the earth whom God went to redeem to be his people, making for yourself a name for great and terrible things, in driving out nations before your people whom you redeemed from Egypt? 22And you made your people Israel to be your people forever; and you, O LORD, became their God.

23 "And now, O LORD, as for the word that you have spoken concerning your servant and concerning his house, let it be estab-lished forever, and do as you have promised. 24Thus your name will be established and magnified forever in the saying, 'The LORD of hosts, the God of Israel, is Israel's God'; and the house of your servant David will be established in your presence. 25For you, my God, have revealed to your servant that you will build a house for him; therefore your ser-vant has found it possible to pray before you. 26And now, O LORD, you are God, and you

a Meaning of Heb uncertain

17:10 *the LORD will build you a house.* Building a house here refers to Yahweh establishing the dynasty of David.

17:12 *He shall build a house for me.* The promise to David about descendants has been narrowed down to one person, still unnamed, and it is he, not David, who will be empowered to build the Temple.

17:13 *I will be a father to him.* The Chronicler omits a sentence from 2 Sam 7:14 that made all subsequent Davidic kings subject to divine retribution. The focus in this chapter is primarily on Solomon rather than his successors, and the Chronicler's Solomon commits no such iniquity (1 Kings 11 is not included in his narrative).

17:16–27 *David . . . sat before the LORD, and*

said. David's prayer deals exclusively with the dynastic promise and does not even mention the Temple. David emphasizes his own insig-nificance and Yahweh's beneficence toward him.

Responding

17:16–27 PRAYER. David responds to the disappointing news that he will not build the Temple with a prayer expressing humility, certainly an atypical quality in a king, even one who came from the humblest of beginnings. Why does prayer often involve reminding God of his greatness and our small-ness? What does that recognition teach us? *See also* Spiritual Disciplines Index.

have promised this good thing to your servant; 27therefore may it please you to bless the house of your servant, that it may continue forever before you. For you, O LORD, have blessed and are blessed*a* forever."

David's Kingdom Established and Extended

18 Some time afterward, David attacked the Philistines and subdued them; he took Gath and its villages from the Philistines.

2 He defeated Moab, and the Moabites became subject to David and brought tribute.

3 David also struck down King Hadadezer of Zobah, toward Hamath,*b* as he went to set up a monument at the river Euphrates. 4David took from him one thousand chariots, seven thousand cavalry, and twenty thousand foot soldiers. David hamstrung all the chariot horses, but left one hundred of them. 5When the Arameans of Damascus came to help King Hadadezer of Zobah, David killed twenty-two thousand Arameans. 6Then David put garrisons*c* in Aram of Damascus; and the Arameans became subject to David, and brought tribute. The LORD gave victory to David wherever he went. 7David took the gold shields that were carried by the servants of Hadadezer, and brought them to Jerusalem. 8From Tibhath and from Cun, cities of Hadadezer, David took a vast quantity of bronze; with it Solomon made the bronze sea and the pillars and the vessels of bronze.

9 When King Tou of Hamath heard that David had defeated the whole army of King Hadadezer of Zobah, 10he sent his son Hadoram to King David, to greet him and to congratulate him, because he had fought against Hadadezer and defeated him. Now Hadadezer had often been at war with Tou. He sent all sorts of articles of gold, of silver, and of bronze; 11these also King David dedicated to the LORD, together with the silver and gold that he had carried off from all the nations, from Edom, Moab, the Ammonites, the Philistines, and Amalek.

12 Abishai son of Zeruiah killed eighteen thousand Edomites in the Valley of Salt. 13He put garrisons in Edom; and all the Edomites became subject to David. And the LORD gave victory to David wherever he went.

David's Administration

14 So David reigned over all Israel; and he administered justice and equity to all his people. 15Joab son of Zeruiah was over the army; Jehoshaphat son of Ahilud was recorder; 16Zadok son of Ahitub and Ahimelech son of Abiathar were priests; Shavsha was secretary; 17Benaiah son of Jehoiada was over the Cherethites and the Pelethites; and David's sons were the chief officials in the service of the king.

Defeat of the Ammonites and Arameans

19 Some time afterward, King Nahash of the Ammonites died, and his son succeeded him. 2David said, "I will deal loyally with Hanun son of Nahash, for his father dealt loyally with me." So David sent messengers to console him concerning his father. When David's servants came to

a Or *and it is blessed*   *b* Meaning of Heb uncertain   *c* Gk Vg 2 Sam 8.6 Compare Syr: Heb lacks *garrisons*

18:1–17 *David attacked the Philistines.* The material in this chapter is drawn from 2 Sam 8:1–18. David's victories extend to all points of the compass: the Philistines in the west, Moab in the east, Hadadezer and the Arameans of Damascus in the north and northeast, and Edom in the southeast. The point of these war stories is that God is rewarding David for his faithfulness, especially in bringing the ark to Jerusalem, and is keeping his promise to subdue all of David's enemies (17:10).

18:8 *the bronze sea and the pillars and the*

vessels of bronze. The bronze booty taken by David in war was used by Solomon to manufacture a number of furnishings for the Temple.

18:16 *Ahimelech son of Abiathar.* In fact, Abiathar, David's priest, was the son of Ahimelech. This mistaken genealogy is repeated in 24:3, 6.

19:1–19 *his son succeeded him.* In materials taken from 2 Sam 10:1–19, the Chronicler describes David's victory over an Aramean-Ammonite coalition.

Hanun in the land of the Ammonites, to console him, ³the officials of the Ammonites said to Hanun, "Do you think, because David has sent consolers to you, that he is honoring your father? Have not his servants come to you to search and to overthrow and to spy out the land?" ⁴So Hanun seized David's servants, shaved them, cut off their garments in the middle at their hips, and sent them away; ⁵and they departed. When David was told about the men, he sent messengers to them, for they felt greatly humiliated. The king said, "Remain at Jericho until your beards have grown, and then return."

6 When the Ammonites saw that they had made themselves odious to David, Hanun and the Ammonites sent a thousand talents of silver to hire chariots and cavalry from Mesopotamia, from Aram-maacah and from Zobah. ⁷They hired thirty-two thousand chariots and the king of Maacah with his army, who came and camped before Medeba. And the Ammonites were mustered from their cities and came to battle. ⁸When David heard of it, he sent Joab and all the army of the warriors. ⁹The Ammonites came out and drew up in battle array at the entrance of the city, and the kings who had come were by themselves in the open country.

10 When Joab saw that the line of battle was set against him both in front and in the rear, he chose some of the picked men of Israel and arrayed them against the Arameans; ¹¹the rest of his troops he put in the charge of his brother Abishai, and they were arrayed against the Ammonites. ¹²He said, "If the Arameans are too strong for me, then you shall help me; but if the Ammonites are too strong for you, then I will help you. ¹³Be strong, and let us be courageous for our people and for the cities of our God; and may the LORD do what seems good to him." ¹⁴So Joab and the troops who were with him advanced toward the Arameans for battle; and they fled before him. ¹⁵When the Ammonites saw that the Arameans fled, they likewise fled before Abishai,

Joab's brother, and entered the city. Then Joab came to Jerusalem.

16 But when the Arameans saw that they had been defeated by Israel, they sent messengers and brought out the Arameans who were beyond the Euphrates, with Shophach the commander of the army of Hadadezer at their head. ¹⁷When David was informed, he gathered all Israel together, crossed the Jordan, came to them, and drew up his forces against them. When David set the battle in array against the Arameans, they fought with him. ¹⁸The Arameans fled before Israel; and David killed seven thousand Aramean charioteers and forty thousand foot soldiers, and also killed Shophach the commander of their army. ¹⁹When the servants of Hadadezer saw that they had been defeated by Israel, they made peace with David, and became subject to him. So the Arameans were not willing to help the Ammonites any more.

Siege and Capture of Rabbah

20 In the spring of the year, the time when kings go out to battle, Joab led out the army, ravaged the country of the Ammonites, and came and besieged Rabbah. But David remained at Jerusalem. Joab attacked Rabbah, and overthrew it. ²David took the crown of Milcom*ᵃ* from his head; he found that it weighed a talent of gold, and in it was a precious stone; and it was placed on David's head. He also brought out the booty of the city, a very great amount. ³He brought out the people who were in it, and set them to work*ᵇ* with saws and iron picks and axes.*ᶜ* Thus David did to all the cities of the Ammonites. Then David and all the people returned to Jerusalem.

Exploits against the Philistines

4 After this, war broke out with the Philistines at Gezer; then Sibbecai the Hushathite

a Gk Vg See 1 Kings 11.5, 33: MT *of their king*
b Compare 2 Sam 12.31: Heb *and he sawed*
c Compare 2 Sam 12.31: Heb *saws*

20:1–3 *besieged Rabbah.* David and Joab defeat the Ammonites and capture the city of Rabbah. These verses are taken from 2 Sam

11:1; 12:26, 30–31. In 2 Samuel they are the setting for David's adultery with Bathsheba.

killed Sippai, who was one of the descendants of the giants; and the Philistines were subdued. 5Again there was war with the Philistines; and Elhanan son of Jair killed Lahmi the brother of Goliath the Gittite, the shaft of whose spear was like a weaver's beam. 6Again there was war at Gath, where there was a man of great size, who had six fingers on each hand, and six toes on each foot, twenty-four in number; he also was descended from the giants. 7When he taunted Israel, Jonathan son of Shimea, David's brother, killed him. 8These were descended from the giants in Gath; they fell by the hand of David and his servants.

The Census and Plague

21 Satan stood up against Israel, and incited David to count the people of Israel. 2So David said to Joab and the commanders of the army, "Go, number Israel, from Beer-sheba to Dan, and bring me a report, so that I may know their number." 3But Joab said, "May the LORD increase the number of his people a hundredfold! Are they not, my lord the king, all of them my lord's servants? Why then should my lord require this? Why should he bring guilt on Israel?" 4But the king's word prevailed against Joab. So Joab departed and went throughout all Israel, and came back to Jerusalem. 5Joab gave the total count of the people to David. In all

Israel there were one million one hundred thousand men who drew the sword, and in Judah four hundred seventy thousand who drew the sword. 6But he did not include Levi and Benjamin in the numbering, for the king's command was abhorrent to Joab.

7 But God was displeased with this thing, and he struck Israel. 8David said to God, "I have sinned greatly in that I have done this thing. But now, I pray you, take away the guilt of your servant; for I have done very foolishly." 9The LORD spoke to Gad, David's seer, saying, 10"Go and say to David, 'Thus says the LORD: Three things I offer you; choose one of them, so that I may do it to you.' " 11So Gad came to David and said to him, "Thus says the LORD, 'Take your choice: 12either three years of famine; or three months of devastation by your foes, while the sword of your enemies overtakes you; or three days of the sword of the LORD, pestilence on the land, and the angel of the LORD destroying throughout all the territory of Israel.' Now decide what answer I shall return to the one who sent me." 13Then David said to Gad, "I am in great distress; let me fall into the hand of the LORD, for his mercy is very great; but let me not fall into human hands."

14 So the LORD sent a pestilence on Israel; and seventy thousand persons fell in Israel. 15And God sent an angel to Jerusalem to destroy it; but when he was about to destroy it,

---

20:4–8 *Elhanan . . . killed Lahmi.* The anecdotes in these verses are drawn from 2 Sam 21:18–22. An alternate tradition recorded in 2 Sam 21:19 asserts that Elhanan, an obscure hero from Bethlehem, killed Goliath. To harmonize this tradition with the story of David and Goliath, the Chronicler asserts that Elhanan killed Lahmi, the brother of Goliath.

21:1 *Satan . . . incited David.* The Chronicler ascribes the reason for David's military census to Satan rather than to the anger of Yahweh as in 2 Sam 24:1. Taking a census was an indication of a lack of trust in God's role in bringing about victory.

21:5 *one million one hundred thousand.* On the basis of 2 Sam 24:9, the Chronicler calculated that there were one million three hundred thousand in Israel, but reduced this by

two hundred thousand, since Levi and Benjamin were excluded from the census. The number ascribed to Judah later in the verse is a secondary addition.

21:7 *God was displeased with this thing.* The king's decision to number the people is abhorrent to Joab and evil in the eyes of Yahweh.

21:13 *let me fall into the hand of the LORD.* Given a choice between three punishments, David decides on pestilence sent by God. David counts on the fact that the one delivering these blows is the same one whose mercies are exceedingly manifold. The pestilence killed seventy thousand persons (v 14); David's culpability in the shedding of their blood may be the reason he is not allowed to build the Temple (22:8; 28:3).

the LORD took note and relented concerning the calamity; he said to the destroying angel, "Enough! Stay your hand." The angel of the LORD was then standing by the threshing floor of Ornan the Jebusite. 16David looked up and saw the angel of the LORD standing between earth and heaven, and in his hand a drawn sword stretched out over Jerusalem. Then David and the elders, clothed in sackcloth, fell on their faces. 17And David said to God, "Was it not I who gave the command to count the people? It is I who have sinned and done very wickedly. But these sheep, what have they done? Let your hand, I pray, O LORD my God, be against me and against my father's house; but do not let your people be plagued!"

David's Altar and Sacrifice

18 Then the angel of the LORD commanded Gad to tell David that he should go up and erect an altar to the LORD on the threshing floor of Ornan the Jebusite. 19So David went up following Gad's instructions, which he had spoken in the name of the LORD. 20Ornan turned and saw the angel; and while his four sons who were with him hid themselves, Ornan continued to thresh wheat. 21As David came to Ornan, Ornan looked and saw David; he went out from the threshing floor, and did obeisance to David with his face to the ground. 22David said to Ornan, "Give me the site of the threshing floor that I may build on

it an altar to the LORD—give it to me at its full price—so that the plague may be averted from the people." 23Then Ornan said to David, "Take it; and let my lord the king do what seems good to him; see, I present the oxen for burnt offerings, and the threshing sledges for the wood, and the wheat for a grain offering. I give it all." 24But King David said to Ornan, "No; I will buy them for the full price. I will not take for the LORD what is yours, nor offer burnt offerings that cost me nothing." 25So David paid Ornan six hundred shekels of gold by weight for the site. 26David built there an altar to the LORD and presented burnt offerings and offerings of well-being. He called upon the LORD, and he answered him with fire from heaven on the altar of burnt offering. 27Then the LORD commanded the angel, and he put his sword back into its sheath.

The Place Chosen for the Temple

28 At that time, when David saw that the LORD had answered him at the threshing floor of Ornan the Jebusite, he made his sacrifices there. 29For the tabernacle of the LORD, which Moses had made in the wilderness, and the altar of burnt offering were at that time in the high place at Gibeon; 30but David could not go before it to inquire of God, for he was afraid of the sword of the angel of the LORD. 22 1Then David said, "Here shall be the house of the LORD God and here the altar of burnt offering for Israel."

21:17 *I who have sinned.* David acknowledges his fault and intercedes with God not to punish the people any further.

Responding
21:17 PRAYER. Putting his people before himself, David accepted responsibility for his sin and asked God to punish him alone. This week keep a prayer journal with a list of people for whom to offer prayers. In prayer, focus on those on your list before any personal concerns. What do you learn? *See also* Spiritual Disciplines Index.

21:18–27 *the threshing floor of Ornan.* David's purchase of the threshing floor of Ornan has many parallels with Abraham's purchase of

a burial spot for Sarah in Genesis 23. See especially the reference to "full price" (vv 22, 24; Gen 23:9, 13).

21:26 *fire from heaven.* This fire indicates divine approval for David's sacrifice, and it also indicates that this altar will replace the altar at the tabernacle, which received similar divine approval when sacrifice was first offered at it (Lev 9:24). Fire from heaven also kindled the first sacrifice in Solomon's Temple (2 Chron 7:1).

22:1 *Here shall be the house of the LORD.* David states that the altar on Ornan's threshing floor will be the site for the temple Solomon will build (cf. 2 Chron 3:1). The forgiveness David received will be replicated in the Temple (2 Chron 6:24–31, 36–40).

David Prepares to Build the Temple

2 David gave orders to gather together the aliens who were residing in the land of Israel, and he set stonecutters to prepare dressed stones for building the house of God. [3]David also provided great stores of iron for nails for the doors of the gates and for clamps, as well as bronze in quantities beyond weighing, [4]and cedar logs without number—for the Sidonians and Tyrians brought great quantities of cedar to David. [5]For David said, "My son Solomon is young and inexperienced, and the house that is to be built for the LORD must be exceedingly magnificent, famous and glorified throughout all lands; I will therefore make preparation for it." So David provided materials in great quantity before his death.

David's Charge to Solomon and the Leaders

6 Then he called for his son Solomon and charged him to build a house for the LORD, the God of Israel. [7]David said to Solomon, "My son, I had planned to build a house to the name of the LORD my God. [8]But the word of the LORD came to me, saying, 'You have shed much blood and have waged great wars; you shall not build a house to my name, because you have shed so much blood in my sight on the earth. [9]See, a son shall be born to you; he shall be a man of peace. I will give him peace from all his enemies on every side; for his name shall be Solomon,[a] and I will give peace[b] and quiet to Israel in his days. [10]He shall build a house for my name. He shall be a son to me, and I will be a father to him, and I will establish his royal throne in Israel forever.' [11]Now, my son, the LORD be with you, so that you may succeed in building the house of the LORD your God, as he has spoken concerning you. [12]Only, may the LORD grant you discretion and understanding, so that when he gives you charge over Israel you may keep the law of the LORD your God. [13]Then you will prosper if you are careful to observe the statutes and the ordinances that the LORD commanded Moses for Israel. Be strong and of good courage. Do not be afraid or dismayed. [14]With great pains I have provided for the house of the LORD one hundred thousand talents of gold, one million talents of silver, and bronze and iron beyond weighing, for there is so much of it; timber and stone too I have provided. To these you must add more. [15]You have an abundance of workers: stonecutters, masons, carpenters, and all kinds of artisans without number, skilled in working [16]gold, silver, bronze, and iron. Now begin the work, and the LORD be with you."

17 David also commanded all the leaders of Israel to help his son Solomon, saying, [18]"Is not the LORD your God with you? Has he not given you peace on every side? For he has delivered the inhabitants of the land into my hand; and the land is subdued before the LORD and his people. [19]Now set your mind and heart to seek the LORD your God. Go and build the sanctuary of the LORD God so that

a Heb *Shelomoh*   *b* Heb *shalom*

22:2 *David gave orders.* From here to the end of 1 Chronicles, the Chronicler supplies his own material or cites noncanonical sources.

22:6–16 *he called for his son Solomon.* David's private speech to Solomon, modeled on the transition from Moses to Joshua, is the first of his farewell discourses. David designates Solomon as the one to build the Temple, since he himself was disqualified because of his wars (1 Kings 5:3–5) and his shedding of blood.

22:9 *a man of peace.* Solomon will be a person of peace (*shalom*), of "rest." David himself achieved rest from all his enemies according to 2 Sam 7:1, 11, but in 1 Chronicles he is called a "warrior" (28:3).

22:12 *discretion and understanding.* Keeping the law will result from Solomon's God-given discretion and understanding.

22:14 *I have provided for the house of the LORD.* David contributed more than three thousand tons of gold and thirty-three thousand tons of silver to the Temple! This stresses David's generosity and the grandeur of the Temple. Solomon is to add to these contributions. The generosity of Israel's first kings is an example to the Chronicler's audience.

22:17 *the leaders of Israel.* David urges the leaders to provide support to Solomon in general and for his building of the Temple.

the ark of the covenant of the LORD and the holy vessels of God may be brought into a house built for the name of the LORD."

Families of the Levites and Their Functions

23 When David was old and full of days, he made his son Solomon king over Israel.

2 David assembled all the leaders of Israel and the priests and the Levites. ³The Levites, thirty years old and upward, were counted, and the total was thirty-eight thousand. ⁴"Twenty-four thousand of these," David said, "shall have charge of the work in the house of the LORD, six thousand shall be officers and judges, ⁵four thousand gatekeepers, and four thousand shall offer praises to the LORD with the instruments that I have made for praise." ⁶And David organized them in divisions corresponding to the sons of Levi: Gershon,ᵃ Kohath, and Merari.

7 The sons of Gershonᵇ were Ladan and Shimei. ⁸The sons of Ladan: Jehiel the chief, Zetham, and Joel, three. ⁹The sons of Shimei: Shelomoth, Haziel, and Haran, three. These were the heads of families of Ladan. ¹⁰And the sons of Shimei: Jahath, Zina, Jeush, and Beriah. These four were the sons of Shimei. ¹¹Jahath was the chief, and Zizah the second; but Jeush and Beriah did not have many sons, so they were enrolled as a single family.

12 The sons of Kohath: Amram, Izhar, Hebron, and Uzziel, four. ¹³The sons of Amram: Aaron and Moses. Aaron was set apart to consecrate the most holy things, so that he and his sons forever should make offerings before the LORD, and minister to him and pronounce blessings in his name forever; ¹⁴but as for Moses the man of God, his sons were to be reckoned among the tribe of Levi. ¹⁵The sons of Moses: Gershom and Eliezer. ¹⁶The sons of Gershom: Shebuel the chief. ¹⁷The sons of Eliezer: Rehabiah the chief; Eliezer had no other sons, but the sons of Rehabiah were very numerous. ¹⁸The sons of Izhar: Shelo-

mith the chief. ¹⁹The sons of Hebron: Jeriah the chief, Amariah the second, Jahaziel the third, and Jekameam the fourth. ²⁰The sons of Uzziel: Micah the chief and Isshiah the second.

21 The sons of Merari: Mahli and Mushi. The sons of Mahli: Eleazar and Kish. ²²Eleazar died having no sons, but only daughters; their kindred, the sons of Kish, married them. ²³The sons of Mushi: Mahli, Eder, and Jeremoth, three.

24 These were the sons of Levi by their ancestral houses, the heads of families as they were enrolled according to the number of the names of the individuals from twenty years old and upward who were to do the work for the service of the house of the LORD. ²⁵For David said, "The LORD, the God of Israel, has given rest to his people; and he resides in Jerusalem forever. ²⁶And so the Levites no longer need to carry the tabernacle or any of the things for its service"—²⁷for according to the last words of David these were the number of the Levites from twenty years old and upward—²⁸"but their duty shall be to assist the descendants of Aaron for the service of the house of the LORD, having the care of the courts and the chambers, the cleansing of all that is holy, and any work for the service of the house of God; ²⁹to assist also with the rows of bread, the choice flour for the grain offering, the wafers of unleavened bread, the baked offering, the offering mixed with oil, and all measures of quantity or size. ³⁰And they shall stand every morning, thanking and praising the LORD, and likewise at evening, ³¹and whenever burnt offerings are offered to the LORD on sabbaths, new moons, and appointed festivals, according to the number required of them, regularly before the LORD. ³²Thus they shall keep charge of the tent of meeting and the sanctuary, and

---

a Or *Gershom*; See 1 Chr 6.1, note, and 23.15
b Vg Compare Gk Syr: Heb *to the Gershonite*

23:1 *David . . . made . . . Solomon king.* Long before his death David installed Solomon as his successor on the throne of Israel.

23:6–32 *the sons of Levi.* The remainder of the chapter contains a list of the Levites and a

description of their duties. These Levites could trace themselves back genealogically to Gershon, Kohath, and Merari, the sons of the patriarch Levi. Their duties in the Temple took the place of their former task of carrying the ark.

shall attend the descendants of Aaron, their kindred, for the service of the house of the LORD."

Divisions of the Priests

24 The divisions of the descendants of Aaron were these. The sons of Aaron: Nadab, Abihu, Eleazar, and Ithamar. ²But Nadab and Abihu died before their father, and had no sons; so Eleazar and Ithamar became the priests. ³Along with Zadok of the sons of Eleazar, and Ahimelech of the sons of Ithamar, David organized them according to the appointed duties in their service. ⁴Since more chief men were found among the sons of Eleazar than among the sons of Ithamar, they organized them under sixteen heads of ancestral houses of the sons of Eleazar, and eight of the sons of Ithamar. ⁵They organized them by lot, all alike, for there were officers of the sanctuary and officers of God among both the sons of Eleazar and the sons of Ithamar. ⁶The scribe Shemaiah son of Nethanel, a Levite, recorded them in the presence of the king, and the officers, and Zadok the priest, and Ahimelech son of Abiathar, and the heads of ancestral houses of the priests and of the Levites; one ancestral house being chosen for Eleazar and one chosen for Ithamar.

7 The first lot fell to Jehoiarib, the second to Jedaiah, ⁸the third to Harim, the fourth to Seorim, ⁹the fifth to Malchijah, the sixth to Mijamin, ¹⁰the seventh to Hakkoz, the eighth to Abijah, ¹¹the ninth to Jeshua, the tenth to Shecaniah, ¹²the eleventh to Eliashib, the twelfth to Jakim, ¹³the thirteenth to Huppah, the fourteenth to Jeshebeab, ¹⁴the fifteenth to Bilgah, the sixteenth to Immer, ¹⁵the seventeenth to Hezir, the eighteenth to Happizzez, ¹⁶the nineteenth to Pethahiah, the twentieth to Jehezkel, ¹⁷the twenty-first to Jachin, the twenty-second to Gamul, ¹⁸the twenty-third to Delaiah, the twenty-fourth to Maaziah. ¹⁹These had as their appointed duty in their service to enter the house of the LORD according to the procedure established for them by their ancestor Aaron, as the LORD God of Israel had commanded him.

Other Levites

20 And of the rest of the sons of Levi: of the sons of Amram, Shubael; of the sons of Shubael, Jehdeiah. ²¹Of Rehabiah: of the sons of Rehabiah, Isshiah the chief. ²²Of the Izharites, Shelomoth; of the sons of Shelomoth, Jahath. ²³The sons of Hebron: ᵃ Jeriah the chief, ᵇ Amariah the second, Jahaziel the third, Jekameam the fourth. ²⁴The sons of Uzziel, Micah; of the sons of Micah, Shamir. ²⁵The brother of Micah, Isshiah; of the sons of Isshiah, Zechariah. ²⁶The sons of Merari: Mahli and Mushi. The sons of Jaaziah: Beno. ᶜ ²⁷The sons of Merari: of Jaaziah, Beno, ᶜ Shoham, Zaccur, and Ibri. ²⁸Of Mahli: Eleazar, who had no sons. ²⁹Of Kish, the sons of Kish: Jerahmeel. ³⁰The sons of Mushi: Mahli, Eder, and Jerimoth. These were the sons of the Levites according to their ancestral houses. ³¹These also cast lots corresponding to their kindred, the descendants of Aaron, in the presence of King David, Zadok, Ahimelech, and the heads of ancestral houses of the priests and of the Levites, the chief as well as the youngest brother.

The Temple Musicians

25 David and the officers of the army also set apart for the service the sons

---

ᵃ See 23.19: Heb lacks *Hebron*   ᵇ See 23.19: Heb lacks *the chief*   ᶜ Or *his son*: Meaning of Heb uncertain

---

24:1–19 *the descendants of Aaron.* The priests are divided into twenty-four courses by David. The obligations of the priests are attributed to Aaron. The names and order of these priestly courses persist throughout the rest of the Second Temple period (515 BC to 70 AD).
24:20–31 *the rest of the sons of Levi.* A secondary genealogy extends five families of Kohath and one family of Merari by another generation.
25:1–6 *the sons of Asaph, and of Heman, and of Jeduthun.* The Chronicler supplies a list of the twenty-four families of singers. The singers achieve levitical status in Chronicles, and their music is considered a kind of prophesying.

of Asaph, and of Heman, and of Jeduthun, who should prophesy with lyres, harps, and cymbals. The list of those who did the work and of their duties was: 2Of the sons of Asaph: Zaccur, Joseph, Nethaniah, and Asarelah, sons of Asaph, under the direction of Asaph, who prophesied under the direction of the king. 3Of Jeduthun, the sons of Jeduthun: Gedaliah, Zeri, Jeshaiah, Shimei,*a* Hashabiah, and Mattithiah, six, under the direction of their father Jeduthun, who prophesied with the lyre in thanksgiving and praise to the LORD. 4Of Heman, the sons of Heman: Bukkiah, Mattaniah, Uzziel, Shebuel, and Jerimoth, Hananiah, Hanani, Eliathah, Giddalti, and Romamti-ezer, Joshbekashah, Mallothi, Hothir, Mahazioth. 5All these were the sons of Heman the king's seer, according to the promise of God to exalt him; for God had given Heman fourteen sons and three daughters. 6They were all under the direction of their father for the music in the house of the LORD with cymbals, harps, and lyres for the service of the house of God. Asaph, Jeduthun, and Heman were under the order of the king. 7They and their kindred, who were trained in singing to the LORD, all of whom were skillful, numbered two hundred eighty-eight. 8And they cast lots for their duties, small and great, teacher and pupil alike.

9 The first lot fell for Asaph to Joseph; the second to Gedaliah, to him and his brothers and his sons, twelve; 10the third to Zaccur, his sons and his brothers, twelve; 11the fourth to Izri, his sons and his brothers, twelve; 12the fifth to Nethaniah, his sons and his brothers, twelve; 13the sixth to Bukkiah, his sons and his brothers, twelve; 14the seventh to Jesarelah,*b* his sons and his brothers, twelve; 15the eighth to Jeshaiah, his sons and his brothers, twelve; 16the ninth to Mattaniah, his sons and his brothers, twelve; 17the tenth to Shimei, his sons and his brothers, twelve; 18the eleventh to Azarel, his sons and his brothers, twelve; 19the twelfth to Hashabiah, his sons and his brothers, twelve; 20to the thir-

teenth, Shubael, his sons and his brothers, twelve; 21to the fourteenth, Mattithiah, his sons and his brothers, twelve; 22to the fifteenth, to Jeremoth, his sons and his brothers, twelve; 23to the sixteenth, to Hananiah, his sons and his brothers, twelve; 24to the seventeenth, to Joshbekashah, his sons and his brothers, twelve; 25to the eighteenth, to Hanani, his sons and his brothers, twelve; 26to the nineteenth, to Mallothi, his sons and his brothers, twelve; 27to the twentieth, to Eliathah, his sons and his brothers, twelve; 28to the twenty-first, to Hothir, his sons and his brothers, twelve; 29to the twenty-second, to Giddalti, his sons and his brothers, twelve; 30to the twenty-third, to Mahazioth, his sons and his brothers, twelve; 31to the twenty-fourth, to Romamti-ezer, his sons and his brothers, twelve.

The Gatekeepers

26 As for the divisions of the gatekeepers: of the Korahites, Meshelemiah son of Kore, of the sons of Asaph. 2Meshelemiah had sons: Zechariah the firstborn, Jediael the second, Zebadiah the third, Jathniel the fourth, 3Elam the fifth, Jehohanan the sixth, Eliehoenai the seventh. 4Obededom had sons: Shemaiah the firstborn, Jehozabad the second, Joah the third, Sachar the fourth, Nethanel the fifth, 5Ammiel the sixth, Issachar the seventh, Peullethai the eighth; for God blessed him. 6Also to his son Shemaiah sons were born who exercised authority in their ancestral houses, for they were men of great ability. 7The sons of Shemaiah: Othni, Rephael, Obed, and Elzabad, whose brothers were able men, Elihu and Semachiah. 8All these, sons of Obed-edom with their sons and brothers, were able men qualified for the service; sixty-two of Obed-edom. 9Meshelemiah had sons and brothers, able men, eighteen. 10Hosah, of the sons

a One Ms: Gk: MT lacks *Shimei*   *b* Or *Asarelah*; see 25.2

25:7–31 *two hundred eighty-eight*. A lot-casting ceremony distributes the levitical singers into twenty-four teams consisting of the leader and eleven other musicians.

26:1–19 *the gatekeepers*. Chronicles lists the gatekeepers at the time of David and describes their duties.

of Merari, had sons: Shimri the chief (for though he was not the firstborn, his father made him chief), [11]Hilkiah the second, Tebaliah the third, Zechariah the fourth: all the sons and brothers of Hosah totaled thirteen.

[12] These divisions of the gatekeepers, corresponding to their leaders, had duties, just as their kindred did, ministering in the house of the LORD; [13]and they cast lots by ancestral houses, small and great alike, for their gates. [14]The lot for the east fell to Shelemiah. They cast lots also for his son Zechariah, a prudent counselor, and his lot came out for the north. [15]Obed-edom's came out for the south, and to his sons was allotted the storehouse. [16]For Shuppim and Hosah it came out for the west, at the gate of Shallecheth on the ascending road. Guard corresponded to guard. [17]On the east there were six Levites each day,[a] on the north four each day, on the south four each day, as well as two and two at the storehouse; [18]and for the colonnade[b] on the west there were four at the road and two at the colonnade.[b] [19]These were the divisions of the gatekeepers among the Korahites and the sons of Merari.

The Treasurers, Officers, and Judges

[20] And of the Levites, Ahijah had charge of the treasuries of the house of God and the treasuries of the dedicated gifts. [21]The sons of Ladan, the sons of the Gershonites belonging to Ladan, the heads of families belonging to Ladan the Gershonite: Jehieli.[c] [22] The sons of Jehieli, Zetham and his brother Joel, were in charge of the treasuries of the house of the LORD. [23]Of the Amramites, the Izharites, the Hebronites, and the Uzzielites: [24]Shebuel son of Gershom, son of Moses, was chief officer in charge of the treasuries. [25]His brothers: from Eliezer were his son Rehabiah, his son Jeshaiah, his son Jo-

ram, his son Zichri, and his son Shelomoth. [26]This Shelomoth and his brothers were in charge of all the treasuries of the dedicated gifts that King David, and the heads of families, and the officers of the thousands and the hundreds, and the commanders of the army, had dedicated. [27]From booty won in battles they dedicated gifts for the maintenance of the house of the LORD. [28]Also all that Samuel the seer, and Saul son of Kish, and Abner son of Ner, and Joab son of Zeruiah had dedicated—all dedicated gifts were in the care of Shelomoth[d] and his brothers.

[29] Of the Izharites, Chenaniah and his sons were appointed to outside duties for Israel, as officers and judges. [30]Of the Hebronites, Hashabiah and his brothers, one thousand seven hundred men of ability, had the oversight of Israel west of the Jordan for all the work of the LORD and for the service of the king. [31]Of the Hebronites, Jerijah was chief of the Hebronites. (In the fortieth year of David's reign search was made, of whatever genealogy or family, and men of great ability among them were found at Jazer in Gilead.) [32]King David appointed him and his brothers, two thousand seven hundred men of ability, heads of families, to have the oversight of the Reubenites, the Gadites, and the half-tribe of the Manassites for everything pertaining to God and for the affairs of the king.

The Military Divisions

27 This is the list of the people of Israel, the heads of families, the commanders of the thousands and the hundreds, and their officers who served the king in all matters con-

a Gk: Heb lacks *each day*   b Heb *parbar*: meaning uncertain   c The Hebrew text of verse 21 is confused   d Gk Compare 26.28: Heb *Shelomith*

26:20–32 *And of the Levites.* The Chronicler appends a list of levitical treasurers, officers, and judges.

27:1–34 *the people of Israel.* The Chronicler rounds out the appointments of David by describing his secular administration: twelve divisions of twenty-four thousand men who

served on a monthly basis, under the leadership of one of the military heroes associated with David (vv 1–15); chief officers of the tribes of Israel (vv 16–24); supervisors over the king's property (vv 25–31); and advisers to David (vv 32–34).

cerning the divisions that came and went, month after month throughout the year, each division numbering twenty-four thousand:

2 Jashobeam son of Zabdiel was in charge of the first division in the first month; in his division were twenty-four thousand. [3]He was a descendant of Perez, and was chief of all the commanders of the army for the first month. [4]Dodai the Ahohite was in charge of the division of the second month; Mikloth was the chief officer of his division. In his division were twenty-four thousand. [5]The third commander, for the third month, was Benaiah son of the priest Jehoiada, as chief; in his division were twenty-four thousand. [6]This is the Benaiah who was a mighty man of the Thirty and in command of the Thirty; his son Ammizabad was in charge of his division.[a] [7]Asahel brother of Joab was fourth, for the fourth month, and his son Zebadiah after him; in his division were twenty-four thousand. [8]The fifth commander, for the fifth month, was Shamhuth, the Izrahite; in his division were twenty-four thousand. [9]Sixth, for the sixth month, was Ira son of Ikkesh the Tekoite; in his division were twenty-four thousand. [10]Seventh, for the seventh month, was Helez the Pelonite, of the Ephraimites; in his division were twenty-four thousand. [11]Eighth, for the eighth month, was Sibbecai the Hushathite, of the Zerahites; in his division were twenty-four thousand. [12]Ninth, for the ninth month, was Abiezer of Anathoth, a Benjaminite; in his division were twenty-four thousand. [13]Tenth, for the tenth month, was Maharai of Netophah, of the Zerahites; in his division were twenty-four thousand. [14]Eleventh, for the eleventh month, was Benaiah of Pirathon, of the Ephraimites; in his division were twenty-four thousand. [15]Twelfth, for the twelfth month, was Heldai the Netophathite, of Othniel; in his division were twenty-four thousand.

Leaders of Tribes

16 Over the tribes of Israel, for the Reubenites, Eliezer son of Zichri was chief officer; for the Simeonites, Shephatiah son of Maacah; [17]for Levi, Hashabiah son of Kemuel; for Aaron, Zadok; [18]for Judah, Elihu, one of David's brothers; for Issachar, Omri son of Michael; [19]for Zebulun, Ishmaiah son of Obadiah; for Naphtali, Jerimoth son of Azriel; [20]for the Ephraimites, Hoshea son of Azaziah; for the half-tribe of Manasseh, Joel son of Pedaiah; [21]for the half-tribe of Manasseh in Gilead, Iddo son of Zechariah; for Benjamin, Jaasiel son of Abner; [22]for Dan, Azarel son of Jeroham. These were the leaders of the tribes of Israel. [23]David did not count those below twenty years of age, for the LORD had promised to make Israel as numerous as the stars of heaven. [24]Joab son of Zeruiah began to count them, but did not finish; yet wrath came upon Israel for this, and the number was not entered into the account of the Annals of King David.

Other Civic Officials

25 Over the king's treasuries was Azmaveth son of Adiel. Over the treasuries in the country, in the cities, in the villages and in the towers, was Jonathan son of Uzziah. [26]Over those who did the work of the field, tilling the soil, was Ezri son of Chelub. [27]Over the vineyards was Shimei the Ramathite. Over the produce of the vineyards for the wine cellars was Zabdi the Shiphmite. [28]Over the olive and sycamore trees in the Shephelah was Baal-hanan the Gederite. Over the stores of oil was Joash. [29]Over the herds that pastured in Sharon was Shitrai the Sharonite. Over the herds in the valleys was Shaphat son of Adlai. [30]Over the camels was Obil the Ishmaelite. Over the donkeys was Jehdeiah the Meronothite. Over the flocks was Jaziz the Hagrite. [31]All these were stewards of King David's property.

32 Jonathan, David's uncle, was a counselor, being a man of understanding and a scribe; Jehiel son of Hachmoni attended the king's sons. [33]Ahithophel was the king's counselor, and Hushai the Archite was the king's friend. [34]After Ahithophel came Jehoiada son of Benaiah, and Abiathar. Joab was commander of the king's army.

Solomon Instructed to Build the Temple

28 David assembled at Jerusalem all the officials of Israel, the officials of the

---

a Gk Vg: Heb *Ammizabad was his division*

tribes, the officers of the divisions that served the king, the commanders of the thousands, the commanders of the hundreds, the stewards of all the property and cattle of the king and his sons, together with the palace officials, the mighty warriors, and all the warriors. 2Then King David rose to his feet and said: "Hear me, my brothers and my people. I had planned to build a house of rest for the ark of the covenant of the LORD, for the footstool of our God; and I made preparations for building. 3But God said to me, 'You shall not build a house for my name, for you are a warrior and have shed blood.' 4Yet the LORD God of Israel chose me from all my ancestral house to be king over Israel forever; for he chose Judah as leader, and in the house of Judah my father's house, and among my father's sons he took delight in making me king over all Israel. 5And of all my sons, for the LORD has given me many, he has chosen my son Solomon to sit upon the throne of the kingdom of the LORD over Israel. 6He said to me, 'It is your son Solomon who shall build my house and my courts, for I have chosen him to be a son to me, and I will be a father to him. 7I will establish his kingdom forever if he continues resolute in keeping my commandments and my ordinances, as he is today.' 8Now therefore in the sight of all Israel, the assembly of the LORD, and in the hearing of our God, observe and search out all the commandments of the LORD your God; that you may possess this good land, and leave it for an inheritance to your children after you forever.

9 "And you, my son Solomon, know the God of your father, and serve him with single mind and willing heart; for the LORD searches every mind, and understands every plan and thought. If you seek him, he will be found by you; but if you forsake him, he will abandon you forever. 10Take heed now, for the LORD has chosen you to build a house as the sanctuary; be strong, and act."

11 Then David gave his son Solomon the plan of the vestibule of the temple, and of its houses, its treasuries, its upper rooms, and its inner chambers, and of the room for the mercy seat;a 12and the plan of all that he had in mind: for the courts of the house of the LORD, all the surrounding chambers, the treasuries of the house of God, and the treasuries for dedicated gifts; 13for the divisions of the priests and of the Levites, and all the work of the service in the house of the LORD; for all the vessels for the service in the house of the LORD, 14the weight of gold for all golden vessels for each service, the weight of silver vessels for each service, 15the weight of the golden lampstands and their lamps, the weight of gold for each lampstand and its lamps, the weight of silver for a lampstand and its lamps, according to the use of each in the service, 16the weight of gold for each table for the rows of bread, the silver for the silver tables, 17and pure gold for the forks, the basins, and the cups; for the golden bowls and the weight of each; for the silver bowls and the weight of each; 18for the altar of incense made of refined gold, and its weight; also his plan for the golden chariot of the cherubim that spread their wings and covered the ark of the covenant of the LORD.

19 "All this, in writing at the LORD's direction, he made clear to me—the plan of all the works."

20 David said further to his son Solomon,

a Or the cover

28:2–10 *Hear me, my brothers and my people.* David addresses the officials of the people, citing a divine oracle (vv 3, 6–7) and giving a special exhortation to Solomon (vv 9–10). David was barred from building the Temple even though he had made extensive preparations for its construction. The divine oracles forbid David to build the Temple and identify Solomon as the Temple builder. David promises Solomon blessing for obedience and

threatens divine abandonment should he disobey.

28:11–18 *the plan.* David provides the plan for the future Temple and contributes gold and silver for furnishing it. In handing over a written plan, David is repeating an action of Moses at the time of the construction of the tabernacle (Exod 25:9, 40). In carrying out the plan Solomon will play the role of Bezalel, who constructed the tabernacle (Exod 31:2–38:22).

"Be strong and of good courage, and act. Do not be afraid or dismayed; for the LORD God, my God, is with you. He will not fail you or forsake you, until all the work for the service of the house of the LORD is finished. [21] Here are the divisions of the priests and the Levites for all the service of the house of God; and with you in all the work will be every volunteer who has skill for any kind of service; also the officers and all the people will be wholly at your command."

Offerings for Building the Temple

29 King David said to the whole assembly, "My son Solomon, whom alone God has chosen, is young and inexperienced, and the work is great; for the temple[a] will not be for mortals but for the LORD God. [2] So I have provided for the house of my God, so far as I was able, the gold for the things of gold, the silver for the things of silver, and the bronze for the things of bronze, the iron for the things of iron, and wood for the things of wood, besides great quantities of onyx and stones for setting, antimony, colored stones, all sorts of precious stones, and marble in abundance. [3] Moreover, in addition to all that I have provided for the holy house, I have a treasure of my own of gold and silver, and because of my devotion to the house of my God I give it to the house of my God: [4] three thousand talents of gold, of the gold of Ophir, and seven thousand talents of refined silver, for overlaying the walls of the house, [5] and for all the work to be done by artisans, gold for the things of gold and silver for the things of silver. Who then will offer willingly, consecrating themselves today to the LORD?"

6 Then the leaders of ancestral houses made their freewill offerings, as did also the leaders of the tribes, the commanders of the thousands and of the hundreds, and the officers over the king's work. [7] They gave for the service of the house of God five thousand talents and ten thousand darics of gold, ten thousand talents of silver, eighteen thousand talents of bronze, and one hundred thousand talents of iron. [8] Whoever had precious stones gave them to the treasury of the house of the LORD, into the care of Jehiel the Gershonite. [9] Then the people rejoiced because these had given willingly, for with single mind they had offered freely to the LORD; King David also rejoiced greatly.

David's Praise to God

10 Then David blessed the LORD in the presence of all the assembly; David said: "Blessed are you, O LORD, the God of our ancestor Israel, forever and ever. [11] Yours, O LORD, are the greatness, the power, the glory, the victory, and the majesty; for all that is in the heavens and on the earth is yours; yours is

a Heb fortress

28:20–21 *David said further to . . . Solomon.* David assures Solomon that he will have the wholehearted support of the people in the Temple project. Yahweh himself will be "with" Solomon.

29:1–9 *David said to the whole assembly.* David invites the people to give generously to the Temple, the people respond enthusiastically, and all rejoice. Giving is a joyous discipline of the People of God in all ages.

29:10–19 *David blessed the LORD.* David praises the people's generosity and asks God to give the people and Solomon an obedient heart and to sustain Solomon in his building project. David's admonitions to generosity are directed as much to the Chronicler's audience as to the people assembled before him.

Responding
29:10–19 THE WITH-GOD LIFE. David was a master of public prayer, but for many of us praying aloud—particularly in public—is difficult or embarrassing. But as Dallas Willard writes, "The disciplines we need to practice are precisely the ones we are not 'good at.'" If praying aloud is a challenge for you, volunteer to lead your family or friends in a mealtime prayer this week. Maybe even challenge yourself to lead a prayer in your small group or at church. How does praying aloud with the community differ from your private prayer practice? *See also* Spiritual Disciplines Index.

29:11 *the power, the glory, . . . the kingdom.* The doxology in Matt 6:13 (see NRSV note) is dependent on this verse.

the kingdom, O LORD, and you are exalted as head above all. [12]Riches and honor come from you, and you rule over all. In your hand are power and might; and it is in your hand to make great and to give strength to all. [13]And now, our God, we give thanks to you and praise your glorious name.

[14] "But who am I, and what is my people, that we should be able to make this freewill offering? For all things come from you, and of your own have we given you. [15]For we are aliens and transients before you, as were all our ancestors; our days on the earth are like a shadow, and there is no hope. [16]O LORD our God, all this abundance that we have provided for building you a house for your holy name comes from your hand and is all your own. [17]I know, my God, that you search the heart, and take pleasure in uprightness; in the uprightness of my heart I have freely offered all these things, and now I have seen your people, who are present here, offering freely and joyously to you. [18]O LORD, the God of Abraham, Isaac, and Israel, our ancestors, keep forever such purposes and thoughts in the hearts of your people, and direct their hearts toward you. [19]Grant to my son Solomon that with single mind he may keep your commandments, your decrees, and your statutes, performing all of them, and that he may build the temple[a] for which I have made provision."

[20] Then David said to the whole assembly, "Bless the LORD your God." And all the assembly blessed the LORD, the God of their ancestors, and bowed their heads and prostrated themselves before the LORD and the king. [21]On the next day they offered sacrifices and burnt offerings to the LORD, a thousand bulls, a thousand rams, and a thousand lambs, with their libations, and sacrifices in abundance for all Israel; [22]and they ate and drank before the LORD on that day with great joy.

Solomon Anointed King

They made David's son Solomon king a second time; they anointed him as the LORD's prince, and Zadok as priest. [23]Then Solomon sat on the throne of the LORD, succeeding his father David as king; he prospered, and all Israel obeyed him. [24]All the leaders and the mighty warriors, and also all the sons of King David, pledged their allegiance to King Solomon. [25]The LORD highly exalted Solomon in the sight of all Israel, and bestowed upon him such royal majesty as had not been on any king before him in Israel.

Summary of David's Reign

[26] Thus David son of Jesse reigned over all Israel. [27]The period that he reigned over Israel was forty years; he reigned seven years in Hebron, and thirty-three years in Jerusalem. [28]He died in a good old age, full of days, riches, and honor; and his son Solomon succeeded him. [29]Now the acts of King David, from first to last, are written in the records of the seer Samuel, and in the records of the prophet Nathan, and in the records of the seer Gad, [30]with accounts of all his rule and his might and of the events that befell him and Israel and all the kingdoms of the earth.

a Heb fortress

29:22 *Solomon . . . they anointed . . . and Zadok.* Solomon and Zadok the priest are anointed. These actions ratify David's own initiative in making Solomon king in 23:1.

29:26–28 *David . . . reigned over all Israel.* The Chronicler recounts David's death and summarizes his reign in an expanded and revised version of 1 Kings 2:10–12.

29:29 *the records of the seer Samuel, . . . Nathan, . . . Gad.* The Chronicler cites prophetic sources that could be consulted. It is unlikely that he is referring to noncanonical sources. Rather, he is attributing prophetic authorship to 1 & 2 Samuel, which are considered among the Former Prophets in the Jewish canon.

TRIP TO MEXICO
FEB 18, 2006

MAY JESUS CHRIST BE HONORED

MAY I LISTEN, LEARN, CONTINUOUSE

MAY I BE FAITHFUL TO JESUS

MAY I HELP FOR TUREANCE.
ENCOUNTERING TO DIVE + THE EMBERS
LOVING WITH ALL
BY THE POWER OF THE HOLY SPIRIT

Len Meetty

FEB 25,
THANKS
FROM SAFF
JAPAN

600 BLESS LAVERNE, CHRISTIE + KEVIN
JOHN + SARAH, JOKE + MARIKA
+ ALL 7 GRANDCHILDREN
I COMMITT THEM ALL
FOR AN ETERNITY
INTO CHRIST'S HANDS
LEN HONDA
FEB 18, 2006

MY ENERGY IS DRAINED
I HAVE ABSORBED SOME PAIN
I FEEL WITH ST DOMINILA + HER 3 CHILDREN
I APPRECIATE ESTHER SARAH POLITICA KIKO JOY

 *TEMPLE & WORSHIP*

2 CHRONICLES

In 2 Chronicles the Chronicler provides a history of Solomon and Judah, the Southern Kingdom, based on the books of Kings, but seen through the Chronicler's own theological perspectives and supplemented by additional stories about a number of the kings. In retelling the story of Solomon and the subsequent history of Judah until its destruction, the Chronicler is advocating support for the post-exilic Jerusalem Temple and its worship practices, whose origins and validity he traces to the work of David and Solomon, the idealized kings of the United Monarchy.

Solomon and the Kingdom of Judah

The Chronicler gives extensive treatment to the reign of Solomon, who, with David, is credited with the construction of the First Temple and the inauguration of the types of Temple personnel operative in the Chronicler's day. The Chronicler seems to have had only the information about Solomon contained in the book of Kings, although he rearranges part of the account and omits several incidents, including especially the critique of Solomon's mixed marriages recorded in 1 Kings 11.

For the history of the Divided Kingdom, the Chronicler focuses primarily on the kingdom of Judah, though he records items from the Northern Kingdom, Israel, when they are necessary to understand the history of Judah. He considered the Northern Kingdom to be illegitimate, as seen particularly in Abijah's sermon in 2 Chron 13:4–12, but he also records a number of invitations by kings of Jerusalem to their Northern comrades, reflecting his own desire for residents in the former Northern Kingdom to participate in the worship of the postexilic Temple at Jerusalem.

Sources

One of the primary sources used in the composition of 2 Chronicles is the account of Israel's history in 1 & 2 Kings, composed about two centuries before the writing

---

See also "The With-God Life" essays for this section of the Bible, "The People of God as a Nation," pp. 391–96, "The People of God in Rebellion," pp. 975–79, and "The People of God in Exile," pp. 1171–74.)

of Chronicles in the mid-fourth century BC. The Chronicler reinterprets the history of the Southern Kingdom, sometimes strictly on theological grounds, but also on the basis of additional information he supplies. Students of Chronicles remain sharply divided on how much of this additional information stems from authentic historical sources and how much is merely part of the rhetorical effort of the Chronicler to drive home his theological points.

Chronicles refers frequently to source documents, usually at the exact place where Kings had appealed to such documents, but the Chronicler often gives these source documents new or revised names. Instead of the "Book of the Acts of Solomon" in 1 Kings 11:41, for example, the Chronicler refers to the "history of the prophet Nathan," the "prophecy of Ahijah the Shilonite," and the "visions of the seer Iddo concerning Jeroboam son of Nebat" in 2 Chron 9:29. The Chronicler had, it seems, access to other oral or written sources for the additional information he provides, even though he does not specify where this information comes from. The genealogical materials in 1 Chronicles 2–8, for example, he took from genealogical collections or even in some cases from living tribal memories. The fact that the Chronicler had much more information for some tribes than for others strongly suggests that he was dependent on whatever genealogical sources were available to him and that he did not manufacture these data.

The Chronicler's use of specific names and geographic locations has led many students to propose that he often did have authentic, alternative information about the Southern Kingdom that had not been included in the books of Kings. He attributed building projects, military might, and riches to kings he considered faithful, some of which may represent specific historical information and other parts of which may merely reflect the Chronicler's judgment on a given reign. Although the Chronicler incorporated with some changes five prophetic speeches from the books of Samuel and Kings, he also included speeches for the following prophetic figures whose words and ideas often reflect those of the Chronicler himself: Shemaiah (2 Chron 12:5–8), Azariah (15:1–7), Hanani (16:7–9), Jehu son of Hanani (19:2–3), Eliezer (20:37), Elijah (21:12–15), Zechariah (24:20–22), a man of God (25:7–9), an anonymous prophet (25:15–16), and Oded (28:9–11). These ten speeches all support the doctrine of retribution, which is central to the Chronicler's message, and they all appear in the period of the Divided Monarchy, from Rehoboam to Ahaz.

Structure

2 Chronicles can be divided into two major units: the reign of Solomon (chaps 1–9) and the reigns of the kings of Judah from Rehoboam to Zedekiah (10–36). The latter section can be further subdivided into the Divided Kingdom from Rehoboam to Ahaz (10–28) and the Reunited Kingdom from Hezekiah to Zedekiah (29–36). Hezekiah is portrayed as a second Solomon who restored and purified the Temple in the first month of his reign. He is the first king of Judah to reign after the defeat and exile of the Northern Kingdom.

2 Chronicles ends on an expectant note: the Persian king Cyrus authorizes a re-

turn to Jerusalem and a rebuilding of the Temple. By the time of the Chronicler that Temple had been built, and he is the greatest advocate for the widest possible support for worship at that place and for the various ranks of those who serve there. The Chronicler understands that once again God is using institutional ritual means for the formation of his people. A special place, a specific liturgy, a particular music— all are used to draw the People of God into the presence of the Holy.

—Ralph W. Klein

Solomon Requests Wisdom

1 Solomon son of David established himself in his kingdom; the LORD his God was with him and made him exceedingly great.

2 Solomon summoned all Israel, the commanders of the thousands and of the hundreds, the judges, and all the leaders of all Israel, the heads of families. 3Then Solomon, and the whole assembly with him, went to the high place that was at Gibeon; for God's tent of meeting, which Moses the servant of the LORD had made in the wilderness, was there. 4(But David had brought the ark of God up from Kiriath-jearim to the place that David had prepared for it; for he had pitched a tent for it in Jerusalem.) 5Moreover the bronze altar that Bezalel son of Uri, son of Hur, had made, was there in front of the tabernacle of the LORD. And Solomon and the assembly inquired at it. 6Solomon went up there to the bronze altar before the LORD, which was at the tent of meeting, and offered a thousand burnt offerings on it.

7 That night God appeared to Solomon, and said to him, "Ask what I should give you." 8Solomon said to God, "You have shown great and steadfast love to my father David, and have made me succeed him as king. 9O LORD God, let your promise to my father David now be fulfilled, for you have made me king over a people as numerous as the dust of the earth. 10Give me now wisdom and knowledge to go out and come in before this people, for who can rule this great people of yours?" 11God answered Solomon, "Because this was in your heart, and you have not asked for possessions, wealth, honor, or the life of those who hate you, and have not even asked for long life, but have asked for wisdom and knowledge for yourself that you may rule my people over whom I have made you king, 12wisdom and knowledge are granted to you. I will also give you riches, possessions, and honor, such as none of the kings had who were before you, and none after you shall have the like." 13So Solomon came from*a* the high place at Gibeon, from the tent of meeting, to Jerusalem. And he reigned over Israel.

Solomon's Military and Commercial Activity

14 Solomon gathered together chariots and horses; he had fourteen hundred chariots and twelve thousand horses, which he stationed in the chariot cities and with the

a Gk Vg: Heb *to*

1:3 *the high place that was at Gibeon.* Solomon and all Israel make a pilgrimage to Gibeon, whose legitimacy is certified by the presence there of the tent of meeting and the bronze altar, both made during Israel's journey through the wilderness.

1:10, 12 *Give me now wisdom and knowledge.* Solomon's request for wisdom is granted, but God shows his approval of Solomon also by giving him unparalleled riches.

1:14–17 *chariots and horses.* The wealth represented by Solomon's numerous chariots and horses fulfills God's promise (v 12). The Chronicler transferred this paragraph here from a position later in Solomon's reign in 1 Kings 10:26–29, but he also repeats it at that later point in 2 Chron 9:25, 27–28.

king in Jerusalem. 15The king made silver and gold as common in Jerusalem as stone, and he made cedar as plentiful as the sycamore of the Shephelah. 16Solomon's horses were imported from Egypt and Kue; the king's traders received them from Kue at the prevailing price. 17They imported from Egypt, and then exported, a chariot for six hundred shekels of silver, and a horse for one hundred fifty; so through them these were exported to all the kings of the Hittites and the kings of Aram.

Preparations for Building the Temple

2 a Solomon decided to build a temple for the name of the LORD, and a royal palace for himself. 2 b Solomon conscripted seventy thousand laborers and eighty thousand stonecutters in the hill country, with three thousand six hundred to oversee them.

Alliance with Huram of Tyre

3 Solomon sent word to King Huram of Tyre: "Once you dealt with my father David and sent him cedar to build himself a house to live in. 4I am now about to build a house for the name of the LORD my God and dedicate it to him for offering fragrant incense before him, and for the regular offering of the rows of bread, and for burnt offerings morning and evening, on the sabbaths and the new moons and the appointed festivals of the LORD our God, as ordained forever for Israel. 5The house that I am about to build will be great, for our God is greater than other gods. 6But who is able to build him a house, since heaven, even highest heaven, cannot contain him? Who am I to build a house for him, except as a place to make offerings before him? 7So now send me an artisan skilled to work in gold, silver, bronze, and iron, and in purple, crimson, and blue fabrics, trained also in engraving, to join the skilled workers who are with me in Judah and Jerusalem, whom my father David provided. 8Send me

also cedar, cypress, and algum timber from Lebanon, for I know that your servants are skilled in cutting Lebanon timber. My servants will work with your servants 9to prepare timber for me in abundance, for the house I am about to build will be great and wonderful. 10I will provide for your servants, those who cut the timber, twenty thousand cors of crushed wheat, twenty thousand cors of barley, twenty thousand baths c of wine, and twenty thousand baths of oil."

11 Then King Huram of Tyre answered in a letter that he sent to Solomon, "Because the LORD loves his people he has made you king over them." 12Huram also said, "Blessed be the LORD God of Israel, who made heaven and earth, who has given King David a wise son, endowed with discretion and understanding, who will build a temple for the LORD, and a royal palace for himself.

13 "I have dispatched Huram-abi, a skilled artisan, endowed with understanding, 14the son of one of the Danite women, his father a Tyrian. He is trained to work in gold, silver, bronze, iron, stone, and wood, and in purple, blue, and crimson fabrics and fine linen, and to do all sorts of engraving and execute any design that may be assigned him, with your artisans, the artisans of my lord, your father David. 15Now, as for the wheat, barley, oil, and wine, of which my lord has spoken, let him send them to his servants. 16We will cut whatever timber you need from Lebanon, and bring it to you as rafts by sea to Joppa; you will take it up to Jerusalem."

17 Then Solomon took a census of all the aliens who were residing in the land of Israel, after the census that his father David had taken; and there were found to be one hundred fifty-three thousand six hundred. 18Seventy thousand of them he assigned as labor-

a Ch 1.18 in Heb   b Ch 2.1 in Heb
c A Hebrew measure of volume

2:13 *Huram-abi, a skilled artisan.* King Huram sent an artisan by the name of Huram-abi to work on the Temple. His mother was Danite, which is the same ancestry as that of Oholiab, one of the artisans who worked on the tabernacle (Exod 31:6; 35:34; 38:23).

2:17 *a census of all the aliens.* According to the Chronicler, the workers referred to in verse 2 were recruited from resident aliens rather than from Israelite citizens. 1 Kings 5:13–14 reports that Solomon had in fact conscripted thirty thousand Israelites for forced labor.

ers, eighty thousand as stonecutters in the hill country, and three thousand six hundred as overseers to make the people work.

Solomon Builds the Temple

3 Solomon began to build the house of the LORD in Jerusalem on Mount Moriah, where the LORD had appeared to his father David, at the place that David had designated, on the threshing floor of Ornan the Jebusite. ²He began to build on the second day of the second month of the fourth year of his reign. ³These are Solomon's measurements[a] for building the house of God: the length, in cubits of the old standard, was sixty cubits, and the width twenty cubits. ⁴The vestibule in front of the nave of the house was twenty cubits long, across the width of the house;[b] and its height was one hundred twenty cubits. He overlaid it on the inside with pure gold. ⁵The nave he lined with cypress, covered it with fine gold, and made palms and chains on it. ⁶He adorned the house with settings of precious stones. The gold was gold from Parvaim. ⁷So he lined the house with gold—its beams, its thresholds, its walls, and its doors; and he carved cherubim on the walls.

8 He made the most holy place; its length, corresponding to the width of the house, was twenty cubits, and its width was twenty cubits; he overlaid it with six hundred talents of fine gold. ⁹The weight of the nails was fifty shekels of gold. He overlaid the upper chambers with gold.

10 In the most holy place he made two carved cherubim and overlaid[c] them with gold. ¹¹The wings of the cherubim together extended twenty cubits: one wing of the one, five cubits long, touched the wall of the house, and its other wing, five cubits long, touched the wing of the other cherub; ¹²and

of this cherub, one wing, five cubits long, touched the wall of the house, and the other wing, also five cubits long, was joined to the wing of the first cherub. ¹³The wings of these cherubim extended twenty cubits; the cherubim[d] stood on their feet, facing the nave. ¹⁴And Solomon[e] made the curtain of blue and purple and crimson fabrics and fine linen, and worked cherubim into it.

15 In front of the house he made two pillars thirty-five cubits high, with a capital of five cubits on the top of each. ¹⁶He made encircling[f] chains and put them on the tops of the pillars; and he made one hundred pomegranates, and put them on the chains. ¹⁷He set up the pillars in front of the temple, one on the right, the other on the left; the one on the right he called Jachin, and the one on the left, Boaz.

Furnishings of the Temple

4 He made an altar of bronze, twenty cubits long, twenty cubits wide, and ten cubits high. ²Then he made the molten sea; it was round, ten cubits from rim to rim, and five cubits high. A line of thirty cubits would encircle it completely. ³Under it were panels all around, each of ten cubits, surrounding the sea; there were two rows of panels, cast when it was cast. ⁴It stood on twelve oxen, three facing north, three facing west, three facing south, and three facing east; the sea was set on them. The hindquarters of each were toward the inside. ⁵Its thickness was a handbreadth; its rim was made like the rim of a cup, like the flower of a lily; it held three thousand baths.[g] ⁶He also made ten basins in

a Syr: Heb *foundations*   b Compare 1 Kings 6.3: Meaning of Heb uncertain   c Heb *they overlaid* d Heb *they*   e Heb *he*   f Cn: Heb *in the inner sanctuary*   g A Hebrew measure of volume

---

3:1 *Mount Moriah.* Solomon locates the Temple at the threshing floor where David built an altar in 1 Chronicles 21 and at the site of Abraham's near sacrifice of Isaac (Gen 22:2, 14). Chronicles omits much of 1 Kings 6 and 1 Kings 7:1–12, which describe Solomon's palace, which took thirteen years to build, and the house Solomon built for his unnamed

wife, who was Pharaoh's daughter.

3:14 *made the curtain of blue and purple.* According to the Chronicler a curtain closed off the most holy place, as in the Second Temple. In Solomon's actual Temple, two olivewood doors closed off the inner shrine (1 Kings 6:31–32).

4:1 *altar of bronze.* The account of this altar has been omitted in the present text of 1 Kings 7.

which to wash, and set five on the right side, and five on the left. In these they were to rinse what was used for the burnt offering. The sea was for the priests to wash in.

7 He made ten golden lampstands as prescribed, and set them in the temple, five on the south side and five on the north. 8He also made ten tables and placed them in the temple, five on the right side and five on the left. And he made one hundred basins of gold. 9He made the court of the priests, and the great court, and doors for the court; he overlaid their doors with bronze. 10He set the sea at the southeast corner of the house.

11 And Huram made the pots, the shovels, and the basins. Thus Huram finished the work that he did for King Solomon on the house of God: 12the two pillars, the bowls, and the two capitals on the top of the pillars; and the two latticeworks to cover the two bowls of the capitals that were on the top of the pillars; 13the four hundred pomegranates for the two latticeworks, two rows of pomegranates for each latticework, to cover the two bowls of the capitals that were on the pillars. 14He made the stands, the basins on the stands, 15the one sea, and the twelve oxen underneath it. 16The pots, the shovels, the forks, and all the equipment for these Huram-abi made of burnished bronze for King Solomon for the house of the LORD. 17In the plain of the Jordan the king cast them, in the clay ground between Succoth and Zeredah. 18Solomon made all these things in great quantities, so that the weight of the bronze was not determined.

19 So Solomon made all the things that were in the house of God: the golden altar, the tables for the bread of the Presence, 20the lampstands and their lamps of pure gold to burn before the inner sanctuary, as prescribed; 21the flowers, the lamps, and the tongs, of purest gold; 22the snuffers, basins, ladles, and firepans, of pure gold. As for the entrance to the temple: the inner doors to the most holy place and the doors of the nave of the temple were of gold.

5 Thus all the work that Solomon did for the house of the LORD was finished. Solomon brought in the things that his father David had dedicated, and stored the silver, the gold, and all the vessels in the treasuries of the house of God.

The Ark Brought into the Temple

2 Then Solomon assembled the elders of Israel and all the heads of the tribes, the leaders of the ancestral houses of the people of Israel, in Jerusalem, to bring up the ark of the covenant of the LORD out of the city of David, which is Zion. 3And all the Israelites assembled before the king at the festival that is in the seventh month. 4And all the elders of Israel came, and the Levites carried the ark. 5So they brought up the ark, the tent of meeting, and all the holy vessels that were in the tent; the priests and the Levites brought them up. 6King Solomon and all the congregation of Israel, who had assembled before him, were before the ark, sacrificing so many sheep and oxen that they could not be numbered or counted. 7Then the priests brought the ark of the covenant of the LORD to its place, in the inner sanctuary of the house, in the most holy place, underneath the wings of the cherubim. 8For the cherubim spread out their wings over the place of the ark, so that the cherubim made a covering above the ark and its poles. 9The poles were so long that the ends of the poles were seen from the holy place in front of the inner sanctuary; but they could not be seen from outside; they

---

4:10–22 *He set the sea.* This passage was secondarily imported into 2 Chronicles from 1 Kings 7:39–50. That the shrine had inner doors (v 22) is in contrast to the notion that a veil closed off that shrine (see note on 3:14).

5:4 *the Levites carried the ark.* The Levites carried the ark into the sanctuary in accordance with pentateuchal law (cf. 1 Chron 15:2; Deut

10:8). In 1 Kings 8:3 the priests carried the ark into the Temple.

5:5 *the tent of meeting.* The ark had already been brought to Jerusalem by David (1 Chron 13–16), but the tent of meeting had to be brought up from Gibeon, where, according to the Chronicler, it was stationed before the construction of the Temple (1 Chron 16:39; 21:29; 2 Chron 1:3, 5).

are there to this day. [10]There was nothing in the ark except the two tablets that Moses put there at Horeb, where the LORD made a covenant[a] with the people of Israel after they came out of Egypt.

11 Now when the priests came out of the holy place (for all the priests who were present had sanctified themselves, without regard to their divisions), [12]all the levitical singers, Asaph, Heman, and Jeduthun, their sons and kindred, arrayed in fine linen, with cymbals, harps, and lyres, stood east of the altar with one hundred twenty priests who were trumpeters. [13]It was the duty of the trumpeters and singers to make themselves heard in unison in praise and thanksgiving to the LORD, and when the song was raised, with trumpets and cymbals and other musical instruments, in praise to the LORD,

"For he is good,
    for his steadfast love endures forever,"
the house, the house of the LORD, was filled with a cloud, [14]so that the priests could not stand to minister because of the cloud; for the glory of the LORD filled the house of God.

Dedication of the Temple

6 Then Solomon said, "The LORD has said that he would reside in thick darkness. [2]I have built you an exalted house, a place for you to reside in forever."

3 Then the king turned around and blessed all the assembly of Israel, while all the assembly of Israel stood. [4]And he said, "Blessed be the LORD, the God of Israel, who with his hand has fulfilled what he prom-

ised with his mouth to my father David, saying, [5]'Since the day that I brought my people out of the land of Egypt, I have not chosen a city from any of the tribes of Israel in which to build a house, so that my name might be there, and I chose no one as ruler over my people Israel; [6]but I have chosen Jerusalem in order that my name may be there, and I have chosen David to be over my people Israel.' [7]My father David had it in mind to build a house for the name of the LORD, the God of Israel. [8]But the LORD said to my father David, 'You did well to consider building a house for my name; [9]nevertheless you shall not build the house, but your son who shall be born to you shall build the house for my name.' [10]Now the LORD has fulfilled his promise that he made; for I have succeeded my father David, and sit on the throne of Israel, as the LORD promised, and have built the house for the name of the LORD, the God of Israel. [11]There I have set the ark, in which is the covenant of the LORD that he made with the people of Israel."

Solomon's Prayer of Dedication

12 Then Solomon[b] stood before the altar of the LORD in the presence of the whole assembly of Israel, and spread out his hands. [13]Solomon had made a bronze platform five cubits long, five cubits wide, and three cubits high, and had set it in the court; and he stood on it. Then he knelt on his knees in the presence of the whole assembly of Israel, and

a Heb lacks a covenant   b Heb he

5:12 *levitical singers.* The Chronicler adds this reference to the levitical singers and their leaders Asaph, Heman, and Jeduthun (cf. 1 Chron 16:37–42). As usual, the priests played the trumpets (cf. 1 Chron 16:6; 2 Chron 7:6).

5:13 *for his steadfast love endures forever.* This refrain from Psalm 136 is frequently used in Chronicles (1 Chron 16:34, 41; 2 Chron 7:3, 6; 20:21). It is a warm reminder of the genuine substance that informs the worship of the People of God. *filled with a cloud.* At its dedication the Temple was filled with the cloud of the glory of Yahweh, just as the tabernacle had been at its dedication (Exod 40:34–38). It is a

vivid demonstration that, even as Yahweh stoops to our human need for incarnational expression of the divine life, he is still in charge of the entire enterprise. Only the priests are mentioned at this theophany, but a second theophany, in 7:1–3, is visible to all the people.

6:6 *I have chosen Jerusalem . . . and I have chosen David.* Solomon refers to the complementary elections of Jerusalem and David. This double election gives validity to Jerusalem and its Temple in the Chronicler's day.

6:10 *fulfilled his promise.* Solomon doubly fulfills God's promise: he succeeds his father as king and he builds the Temple.

spread out his hands toward heaven. ¹⁴He said, "O LORD, God of Israel, there is no God like you, in heaven or on earth, keeping covenant in steadfast love with your servants who walk before you with all their heart— ¹⁵you who have kept for your servant, my father David, what you promised to him. Indeed, you promised with your mouth and this day have fulfilled with your hand. ¹⁶Therefore, O LORD, God of Israel, keep for your servant, my father David, that which you promised him, saying, 'There shall never fail you a successor before me to sit on the throne of Israel, if only your children keep to their way, to walk in my law as you have walked before me.' ¹⁷Therefore, O LORD, God of Israel, let your word be confirmed, which you promised to your servant David.

18 "But will God indeed reside with mortals on earth? Even heaven and the highest heaven cannot contain you, how much less this house that I have built! ¹⁹Regard your servant's prayer and his plea, O LORD my God, heeding the cry and the prayer that your servant prays to you. ²⁰May your eyes be open day and night toward this house, the place where you promised to set your name, and may you heed the prayer that your servant prays toward this place. ²¹And hear the plea of your servant and of your people Israel, when they pray toward this place; may you hear from heaven your dwelling place; hear and forgive.

22 "If someone sins against another and is required to take an oath and comes and swears before your altar in this house, ²³may you hear from heaven, and act, and judge your servants, repaying the guilty by bringing their conduct on their own head, and vindicating those who are in the right by reward-

ing them in accordance with their righteousness.

24 "When your people Israel, having sinned against you, are defeated before an enemy but turn again to you, confess your name, pray and plead with you in this house, ²⁵may you hear from heaven, and forgive the sin of your people Israel, and bring them again to the land that you gave to them and to their ancestors.

26 "When heaven is shut up and there is no rain because they have sinned against you, and then they pray toward this place, confess your name, and turn from their sin, because you punish them, ²⁷may you hear in heaven, forgive the sin of your servants, your people Israel, when you teach them the good way in which they should walk; and send down rain upon your land, which you have given to your people as an inheritance.

28 "If there is famine in the land, if there is plague, blight, mildew, locust, or caterpillar; if their enemies besiege them in any of the settlements of the lands; whatever suffering, whatever sickness there is; ²⁹whatever prayer, whatever plea from any individual or from all your people Israel, all knowing their own suffering and their own sorrows so that they stretch out their hands toward this house; ³⁰may you hear from heaven, your dwelling place, forgive, and render to all whose heart you know, according to all their ways, for only you know the human heart. ³¹Thus may they fear you and walk in your ways all the days that they live in the land that you gave to our ancestors.

32 "Likewise when foreigners, who are not of your people Israel, come from a distant land because of your great name, and your mighty hand, and your outstretched arm, when they come and pray toward this house,

---

6:16 *walk in my law.* Solomon makes the continuation of the dynasty conditional upon keeping Yahweh's law. In 1 Kings 8:25 its continuation is conditional on "walk[ing] before me."

6:19 PRAYER—*See* Spiritual Disciplines Index.

Responding

6:26–27 CONFESSION. Too often it is only in times of trouble, when there is no rain, no money, no health, that we are driven to the confession of our sins. Try an experiment this week. When you catch yourself in a sin, take a moment and confess it to God immediately. What does regular confession teach you? *See also* Spiritual Disciplines Index.

33may you hear from heaven your dwelling place, and do whatever the foreigners ask of you, in order that all the peoples of the earth may know your name and fear you, as do your people Israel, and that they may know that your name has been invoked on this house that I have built.

34 "If your people go out to battle against their enemies, by whatever way you shall send them, and they pray to you toward this city that you have chosen and the house that I have built for your name, 35then hear from heaven their prayer and their plea, and maintain their cause.

36 "If they sin against you—for there is no one who does not sin—and you are angry with them and give them to an enemy, so that they are carried away captive to a land far or near; 37then if they come to their senses in the land to which they have been taken captive, and repent, and plead with you in the land of their captivity, saying, 'We have sinned, and have done wrong; we have acted wickedly'; 38if they repent with all their heart and soul in the land of their captivity, to which they were taken captive, and pray toward their land, which you gave to their ancestors, the city that you have chosen, and the house that I have built for your name, 39then hear from heaven your dwelling place

their prayer and their pleas, maintain their cause and forgive your people who have sinned against you. 40Now, O my God, let your eyes be open and your ears attentive to prayer from this place.

41 "Now rise up, O LORD God, and go to
    your resting place,
  you and the ark of your might.
Let your priests, O LORD God, be clothed
    with salvation,
  and let your faithful rejoice in your
    goodness.
42 O LORD God, do not reject your
    anointed one.
  Remember your steadfast love for
    your servant David."

Solomon Dedicates the Temple

7 When Solomon had ended his prayer, fire came down from heaven and consumed the burnt offering and the sacrifices; and the glory of the LORD filled the temple. 2The priests could not enter the house of the LORD, because the glory of the LORD filled the LORD's house. 3When all the people of Israel saw the fire come down and the glory of the LORD on the temple, they bowed down on the pavement with their faces to the ground, and worshiped and gave thanks to the LORD, saying,

---

6:40 *prayer from this place.* Solomon asks God to recognize prayers that come from this sanctuary, perhaps referring to the postexilic Temple. In 1 Kings 8:52 Solomon asks God to pay attention to his own and the people's prayer.

6:41–42 *Now rise up.* The conclusion to Solomon's prayer in Chronicles has been expanded by a citation from Ps 132:8–10, 1. Hope for the future is based on Yahweh's loyalty to David. The psalmist had asked God to remember in David's favor all the hardships he had endured (Ps 132:1). (Note that some interpreters alternatively translate this passage as referring to the loyalties of David toward Yahweh.)

7:1 *fire came down from heaven.* Fire sent from heaven kindled the first burnt offering and gave divine approval to the Temple and its worship life (cf. Lev 9:23–24; 1 Chron 21:26).

Responding

7:1 SACRIFICE. In the Old Testament, God often appears as fire, but this image is particularly striking because the fire of God consumes the sin offerings of the people. What is the significance of the burning of the sacrifices? What does the image of God as fire suggest to you? *See also* Spiritual Disciplines Index.

7:2 *priests could not enter.* The priests are overcome by the appearance of the glory of Yahweh (Exod 40:35).

7:3 WORSHIP—*See* Spiritual Disciplines Index.

7:3 *for his steadfast love endures forever.* All the people bow to the ground and raise the refrain sung by the musicians in 5:11–13. The living presence of God makes this the only appropriate response.

"For he is good,
    for his steadfast love endures forever."

4 Then the king and all the people offered sacrifice before the LORD. 5King Solomon offered as a sacrifice twenty-two thousand oxen and one hundred twenty thousand sheep. So the king and all the people dedicated the house of God. 6The priests stood at their posts; the Levites also, with the instruments for music to the LORD that King David had made for giving thanks to the LORD—for his steadfast love endures forever—whenever David offered praises by their ministry. Opposite them the priests sounded trumpets; and all Israel stood.

7 Solomon consecrated the middle of the court that was in front of the house of the LORD; for there he offered the burnt offerings and the fat of the offerings of well-being because the bronze altar Solomon had made could not hold the burnt offering and the grain offering and the fat parts.

8 At that time Solomon held the festival for seven days, and all Israel with him, a very great congregation, from Lebo-hamath to the Wadi of Egypt. 9On the eighth day they held a solemn assembly; for they had observed the dedication of the altar seven days and the festival seven days. 10On the twenty-third day of the seventh month he sent the people away to their homes, joyful and in good spirits because of the goodness that the LORD had shown to David and to Solomon and to his people Israel.

11 Thus Solomon finished the house of the LORD and the king's house; all that Solomon had planned to do in the house of the LORD and in his own house he successfully accomplished.

God's Second Appearance to Solomon

12 Then the LORD appeared to Solomon in the night and said to him: "I have heard your prayer, and have chosen this place for myself as a house of sacrifice. 13When I shut up the heavens so that there is no rain, or command the locust to devour the land, or send pestilence among my people, 14if my people who are called by my name humble themselves, pray, seek my face, and turn from their wicked ways, then I will hear from heaven, and will forgive their sin and heal their land. 15Now my eyes will be open and my ears attentive to the prayer that is made in this place. 16For now I have chosen and consecrated this house so that my name may be there forever; my eyes and my heart will be there for all time. 17As for you, if you walk before me, as your father David walked, doing according to all that I have commanded you and keeping my statutes and my ordinances, 18then I will establish your royal throne, as I made covenant with your father David saying, 'You shall never lack a successor to rule over Israel.'

19 'But if you a turn aside and forsake my statutes and my commandments that I have set before you, and go and serve other gods

a The word you in this verse is plural

7:5 *oxen . . . sheep.* The enormous number of sacrifices was found already in 1 Kings 8:62–63 (cf. Hezekiah [2 Chron 29:32–36] and Josiah [2 Chron 35:7–9]).

7:8 *from Lebo-hamath to the Wadi of Egypt.* The dedication is attended by "all Israel," from the traditional northern to the traditional southern border of the country. There was also participation by "all Israel" when David brought the ark to Jerusalem (1 Chron 13:5).

7:9 *the altar seven days and the festival seven days.* The festivities lasted for a total of fourteen days. Hezekiah, considered by the Chronicler a second Solomon, held his Passover for two weeks (30:23).

7:10 *to David and to Solomon.* 1 Kings 8:66 speaks only of God's goodness to David. The Chronicler puts David and Solomon on the same plane.

7:12–15 *if my people . . . humble themselves.* According to this positive assertion of the doctrine of retribution, self-abnegation will cause God to hear and forgive.

7:14 **PRAYER**—*See* Spiritual Disciplines Index.

7:18 *as I made covenant.* The Chronicler strengthens Yahweh's commitment to David by calling it a covenant. In 1 Kings 9:5 Yahweh only makes promises to David.

and worship them, [20]then I will pluck you[a] up from the land that I have given you;[a] and this house, which I have consecrated for my name, I will cast out of my sight, and will make it a proverb and a byword among all peoples. [21]And regarding this house, now exalted, everyone passing by will be astonished, and say, 'Why has the LORD done such a thing to this land and to this house?' [22]Then they will say, 'Because they abandoned the LORD the God of their ancestors who brought them out of the land of Egypt, and they adopted other gods, and worshiped them and served them; therefore he has brought all this calamity upon them.' "

Various Activities of Solomon

8 At the end of twenty years, during which Solomon had built the house of the LORD and his own house, [2]Solomon rebuilt the cities that Huram had given to him, and settled the people of Israel in them.

[3] Solomon went to Hamath-zobah, and captured it. [4]He built Tadmor in the wilderness and all the storage towns that he built in Hamath. [5]He also built Upper Beth-horon and Lower Beth-horon, fortified cities, with walls, gates, and bars, [6]and Baalath, as well as all Solomon's storage towns, and all the towns for his chariots, the towns for his cavalry, and whatever Solomon desired to build, in Jerusalem, in Lebanon, and in all the land of his dominion. [7]All the people who were left of the Hittites, the Amorites, the Perizzites, the Hivites, and the Jebusites, who were not of Israel, [8]from their descendants who were still left in the land, whom the

people of Israel had not destroyed—these Solomon conscripted for forced labor, as is still the case today. [9]But of the people of Israel Solomon made no slaves for his work; they were soldiers, and his officers, the commanders of his chariotry and cavalry. [10]These were the chief officers of King Solomon, two hundred fifty of them, who exercised authority over the people.

[11] Solomon brought Pharaoh's daughter from the city of David to the house that he had built for her, for he said, "My wife shall not live in the house of King David of Israel, for the places to which the ark of the LORD has come are holy."

[12] Then Solomon offered up burnt offerings to the LORD on the altar of the LORD that he had built in front of the vestibule, [13]as the duty of each day required, offering according to the commandment of Moses for the sabbaths, the new moons, and the three annual festivals—the festival of unleavened bread, the festival of weeks, and the festival of booths. [14]According to the ordinance of his father David, he appointed the divisions of the priests for their service, and the Levites for their offices of praise and ministry alongside the priests as the duty of each day required, and the gatekeepers in their divisions for the several gates; for so David the man of God had commanded. [15]They did not turn away from what the king had commanded the priests and Levites regarding anything at all, or regarding the treasuries.

[16] Thus all the work of Solomon was ac-

---

a Heb them

8:2 *cities that Huram had given to him.* In 1 Kings 9:10–13, Solomon gives Hiram twenty cities in exchange for lumber and gold. The Chronicler reverses the transaction so that Solomon receives Israelite cities rather than giving them away.

8:4 *Tadmor in the wilderness.* Tadmor is a city 140 miles northeast of Damascus. Solomon's building of the Temple thus is rewarded by enormous territorial expansion. 1 Kings 9:18 refers to Tamar, a small site in southern Judah.

8:9 *of the people of Israel Solomon made no slaves.* Solomon conscripted forced labor from

the pre-Israelite inhabitants of the land, but not from the Israelites themselves, according to the Chronicler.

8:11 *the places to which the ark . . . has come are holy.* Solomon moves Pharaoh's daughter from the city of David to her own house in the new part of Jerusalem added by Solomon since David's city had been sanctified by the ark's presence in it.

8:13 *according to the commandment of Moses.* The sacrifices are made in accordance with pentateuchal legislation (Num 28–29).

complished from *a* the day the foundation of the house of the LORD was laid until the house of the LORD was finished completely.

17 Then Solomon went to Ezion-geber and Eloth on the shore of the sea, in the land of Edom. 18Huram sent him, in the care of his servants, ships and servants familiar with the sea. They went to Ophir, together with the servants of Solomon, and imported from there four hundred fifty talents of gold and brought it to King Solomon.

Visit of the Queen of Sheba

9 When the queen of Sheba heard of the fame of Solomon, she came to Jerusalem to test him with hard questions, having a very great retinue and camels bearing spices and very much gold and precious stones. When she came to Solomon, she discussed with him all that was on her mind. 2Solomon answered all her questions; there was nothing hidden from Solomon that he could not explain to her. 3When the queen of Sheba had observed the wisdom of Solomon, the house that he had built, 4the food of his table, the seating of his officials, and the attendance of his servants, and their clothing, his valets, and their clothing, and his burnt offerings *b* that he offered at the house of the LORD, there was no more spirit left in her.

5 So she said to the king, "The report was true that I heard in my own land of your accomplishments and of your wisdom, 6but I did not believe the *c* reports until I came and my own eyes saw it. Not even half of the greatness of your wisdom had been told to me; you far surpass the report that I had heard. 7Happy are your people! Happy are these your servants, who continually attend you and hear your wisdom! 8Blessed be the LORD your God, who has delighted in you and set you on his throne as king for the LORD your God. Because your God loved Israel and would establish them forever, he has made you king over them, that you may execute justice and righteousness." 9Then she gave the king one

hundred twenty talents of gold, a very great quantity of spices, and precious stones: there were no spices such as those that the queen of Sheba gave to King Solomon.

10 Moreover the servants of Huram and the servants of Solomon who brought gold from Ophir brought algum wood and precious stones. 11From the algum wood, the king made steps *d* for the house of the LORD and for the king's house, lyres also and harps for the singers; there never was seen the like of them before in the land of Judah.

12 Meanwhile King Solomon granted the queen of Sheba every desire that she expressed, well beyond what she had brought to the king. Then she returned to her own land, with her servants.

Solomon's Great Wealth

13 The weight of gold that came to Solomon in one year was six hundred sixty-six talents of gold, 14besides that which the traders and merchants brought; and all the kings of Arabia and the governors of the land brought gold and silver to Solomon. 15King Solomon made two hundred large shields of beaten gold; six hundred shekels of beaten gold went into each large shield. 16He made three hundred shields of beaten gold; three hundred shekels of gold went into each shield; and the king put them in the House of the Forest of Lebanon. 17The king also made a great ivory throne, and overlaid it with pure gold. 18The throne had six steps and a footstool of gold, which were attached to the throne, and on each side of the seat were arm rests and two lions standing beside the arm rests, 19while twelve lions were standing, one on each end of a step on the six steps. The like of it was never made in any kingdom. 20All King Solomon's drinking vessels were of gold, and all the vessels of the House of the Forest

a Gk Syr Vg: Heb *to*   *b* Gk Syr Vg 1 Kings 10.5: Heb *ascent*   *c* Heb *their*   *d* Gk Vg: Meaning of Heb uncertain

---

9:1 *queen of Sheba.* This unnamed queen, from a distant land, acknowledges the wisdom of Solomon and that Yahweh loves Israel. Hence foreign nations—Phoenicia (via Huram) and

Sheba—recognize the stature of Solomon.

9:12 *beyond what she had brought.* Solomon outdoes the queen of Sheba in showing generosity.

of Lebanon were of pure gold; silver was not considered as anything in the days of Solomon. 21For the king's ships went to Tarshish with the servants of Huram; once every three years the ships of Tarshish used to come bringing gold, silver, ivory, apes, and peacocks.*a*

22 Thus King Solomon excelled all the kings of the earth in riches and in wisdom. 23All the kings of the earth sought the presence of Solomon to hear his wisdom, which God had put into his mind. 24Every one of them brought a present, objects of silver and gold, garments, weaponry, spices, horses, and mules, so much year by year. 25Solomon had four thousand stalls for horses and chariots, and twelve thousand horses, which he stationed in the chariot cities and with the king in Jerusalem. 26He ruled over all the kings from the Euphrates to the land of the Philistines, and to the border of Egypt. 27The king made silver as common in Jerusalem as stone, and cedar as plentiful as the sycamore of the Shephelah. 28Horses were imported for Solomon from Egypt and from all lands.

Death of Solomon

29 Now the rest of the acts of Solomon, from first to last, are they not written in the history of the prophet Nathan, and in the prophecy of Ahijah the Shilonite, and in the visions of the seer Iddo concerning Jeroboam son of Nebat? 30Solomon reigned in Jerusalem over all Israel forty years. 31Solomon slept with his ancestors and was buried in the city of his father David; and his son Rehoboam succeeded him.

The Revolt against Rehoboam

10 Rehoboam went to Shechem, for all Israel had come to Shechem to make him king. 2When Jeroboam son of Nebat heard of it (for he was in Egypt, where he had fled from King Solomon), then Jeroboam returned from Egypt. 3They sent and called him; and Jeroboam and all Israel came and said to Rehoboam, 4"Your father made our yoke heavy. Now therefore lighten the hard service of your father and his heavy yoke that he placed on us, and we will serve you." 5He said to them, "Come to me again in three days." So the people went away.

6 Then King Rehoboam took counsel with the older men who had attended his father Solomon while he was still alive, saying, "How do you advise me to answer this people?" 7They answered him, "If you will be kind to this people and please them, and speak good words to them, then they will be your servants forever." 8But he rejected the advice that the older men gave him, and consulted the young men who had grown up with him and now attended him. 9He said to them, "What do you advise that we answer this people who have said to me, 'Lighten the yoke that your father put on us'?" 10The young men who had grown up with him said to him, "Thus should you speak to the people who said to you, 'Your father made our yoke heavy, but you must lighten it for us'; tell them, 'My little finger is thicker than my father's loins. 11Now, whereas my father laid on you a heavy yoke, I will add to your yoke. My father disciplined you with whips, but I will discipline you with scorpions.' "

a Or *baboons*

9:26 *from the Euphrates . . . to the border of Egypt.* This passage showing the extent of Solomon's empire is also found in 1 Kings 4:21. The Chronicler omits the denunciation of Solomon's marriages in 1 Kings 11:1–43.

9:29 *the prophet Nathan . . . Ahijah . . . Iddo.* The Chronicler gives prophetic authority to the sources dealing with Solomon's reign.

10:4 *lighten the hard service.* The Israelites demand that Rehoboam lighten the burden that his father, Solomon, imposed on them.

According to the Chronicler in 8:9, of course, Solomon had not conscripted forced labor from the Israelites themselves.

10:7 *your servants forever.* Rehoboam's senior advisers urge him to accede to the people's request.

10:11 *discipline you with scorpions.* Rehoboam foolishly listens to his younger advisers, who urged him to be even tougher than his father.

12 So Jeroboam and all the people came to Rehoboam the third day, as the king had said, "Come to me again the third day." 13The king answered them harshly. King Rehoboam rejected the advice of the older men; 14he spoke to them in accordance with the advice of the young men, "My father made your yoke heavy, but I will add to it; my father disciplined you with whips, but I will discipline you with scorpions." 15So the king did not listen to the people, because it was a turn of affairs brought about by God so that the LORD might fulfill his word, which he had spoken by Ahijah the Shilonite to Jeroboam son of Nebat.

16 When all Israel saw that the king would not listen to them, the people answered the king,

"What share do we have in David?
    We have no inheritance in the son of
        Jesse.
Each of you to your tents, O Israel!
Look now to your own house,
    O David."

So all Israel departed to their tents. 17But Rehoboam reigned over the people of Israel who were living in the cities of Judah. 18When King Rehoboam sent Hadoram, who was taskmaster over the forced labor, the people of Israel stoned him to death. King Rehoboam hurriedly mounted his chariot to flee to Jerusalem. 19So Israel has been in rebellion against the house of David to this day.

Judah and Benjamin Fortified

11 When Rehoboam came to Jerusalem, he assembled one hundred eighty thousand chosen troops of the house of Judah and Benjamin to fight against Israel, to restore the kingdom to Rehoboam. 2But the word of the LORD came to Shemaiah the man of God: 3Say to King Rehoboam of Judah, son of Solomon, and to all Israel in Judah and Benjamin, 4"Thus says the LORD: You shall not go up or fight against your kindred. Let everyone return home, for this thing is from me." So they heeded the word of the LORD and turned back from the expedition against Jeroboam.

5 Rehoboam resided in Jerusalem, and he built cities for defense in Judah. 6He built up Bethlehem, Etam, Tekoa, 7Beth-zur, Soco, Adullam, 8Gath, Mareshah, Ziph, 9Adoraim, Lachish, Azekah, 10Zorah, Aijalon, and Hebron, fortified cities that are in Judah and in Benjamin. 11He made the fortresses strong, and put commanders in them, and stores of food, oil, and wine. 12He also put large shields and spears in all the cities, and made them very strong. So he held Judah and Benjamin.

Priests and Levites Support Rehoboam

13 The priests and the Levites who were in all Israel presented themselves to him from all their territories. 14The Levites had left their common lands and their holdings and had come to Judah and Jerusalem, because Jeroboam and his sons had prevented them from

---

10:15 *which he had spoken by Ahijah the Shilonite.* The king's harsh answer to the people's request is interpreted as a "turn of affairs" (cf. the transition from Saul to David in 1 Chron 10:14) brought about by God in fulfillment of the word of the prophet Ahijah. This prophecy is recorded only in 1 Kings 11:29–39, a passage the Chronicler does not include in his account.

10:16–17 *the cities of Judah.* The people rebel against Rehoboam, and he is left as king over only the rump state of Judah.

10:18 *stoned him to death.* The people from the Northern tribes stone Hadoram, the supervisor of the king's forced labor gangs. The Chronicler omits 1 Kings 12:20, which reports Jeroboam's installation as king of the Northern

Kingdom. Subsequently he will report only the history of Judah, except where the North's interaction with the South requires attention.

11:1 *one hundred eighty thousand . . . troops.* The number of troops would appear quite large for antiquity, but the Chronicler reports even larger figures later (14:8; 26:13).

11:2–4 *Shemaiah the man of God.* Rehoboam heeds a word from the prophet Shemaiah not to fight against the North. *this thing is from me.* The division of the kingdoms is God's will.

11:5 *cities for defense.* The Chronicler lists fifteen fortresses designed to protect Rehoboam from the west, south, and east. Rehoboam's aggressive building project indicates that he is under God's favor.

serving as priests of the LORD, [15]and had appointed his own priests for the high places, and for the goat-demons, and for the calves that he had made. [16]Those who had set their hearts to seek the LORD God of Israel came after them from all the tribes of Israel to Jerusalem to sacrifice to the LORD, the God of their ancestors. [17]They strengthened the kingdom of Judah, and for three years they made Rehoboam son of Solomon secure, for they walked for three years in the way of David and Solomon.

Rehoboam's Marriages

18 Rehoboam took as his wife Mahalath daughter of Jerimoth son of David, and of Abihail daughter of Eliab son of Jesse. [19]She bore him sons: Jeush, Shemariah, and Zaham. [20]After her he took Maacah daughter of Absalom, who bore him Abijah, Attai, Ziza, and Shelomith. [21]Rehoboam loved Maacah daughter of Absalom more than all his other wives and concubines (he took eighteen wives and sixty concubines, and became the father of twenty-eight sons and sixty daughters). [22]Rehoboam appointed Abijah son of Maacah as chief prince among his brothers, for he intended to make him king. [23]He dealt wisely, and distributed some of his sons through all the districts of Judah and Benjamin, in all the fortified cities; he gave them abundant provisions, and found many wives for them.

Egypt Attacks Judah

12 When the rule of Rehoboam was established and he grew strong, he abandoned the law of the LORD, he and all Israel with him. [2]In the fifth year of King Rehoboam, because they had been unfaithful to the LORD, King Shishak of Egypt came up against Jerusalem [3]with twelve hundred chariots and sixty thousand cavalry. A countless army came with him from Egypt—Libyans, Sukkiim, and Ethiopians. [a] [4]He took the fortified cities of Judah and came as far as Jerusalem. [5]Then the prophet Shemaiah came to Rehoboam and to the officers of Judah, who had gathered at Jerusalem because of Shishak, and said to them, "Thus says the LORD: You abandoned me, so I have abandoned you to the hand of Shishak." [6]Then the officers of Israel and the king humbled themselves and said, "The LORD is in the right." [7]When the LORD saw that they humbled themselves, the word of the LORD came to Shemaiah, saying: "They have humbled themselves; I will not destroy them, but I will grant them some deliverance, and my wrath shall not be poured out on Jerusalem by the hand of Shishak. [8]Nevertheless they shall be his servants, so

a Or *Nubians*; Heb *Cushites*

11:13–15 *presented themselves to him.* The priests and the Levites rally to Rehoboam, since they were not allowed to serve in the North. Jeroboam had, instead, instituted worship of goat-demons and (golden) calves. Similar theological charges against the North are made by Abijah (13:8–9).

11:16 *Those who . . . seek the LORD God.* Many lay Northerners also fled to Rehoboam in the South. Their piety is indicated by their "seeking" Yahweh, a favorite term of the Chronicler.

11:17 *walked for three years in the way.* The population of the South followed Yahweh faithfully for three years during Rehoboam's period of fidelity.

11:21 *eighteen wives . . . sixty daughters.* Rehoboam's wives and children are considered signs of his prospering under Yahweh's blessing.

Rehoboam designates Abijah as his heir apparent.

12:1–4 *he abandoned the law of the LORD.* Rehoboam rebels against the Torah, which initiates a period of decline that begins with the invasion of Shishak. The charge of infidelity (v 2) is the same charge leveled against Saul in 1 Chron 10:13.

12:6–8 *humbled themselves.* After the Judahites humble themselves, Shemaiah issues another oracle granting them partial deliverance and sparing Jerusalem itself from Shishak. Service to Shishak would teach them the difference between serving Yahweh and serving other kingdoms. Humility has a way of forming the soul like little else in life, and, in this case at least, it transformed the situation the people were facing.

that they may know the difference between serving me and serving the kingdoms of other lands."

9 So King Shishak of Egypt came up against Jerusalem; he took away the treasures of the house of the LORD and the treasures of the king's house; he took everything. He also took away the shields of gold that Solomon had made; [10]but King Rehoboam made in place of them shields of bronze, and committed them to the hands of the officers of the guard, who kept the door of the king's house. [11]Whenever the king went into the house of the LORD, the guard would come along bearing them, and would then bring them back to the guardroom. [12]Because he humbled himself the wrath of the LORD turned from him, so as not to destroy them completely; moreover, conditions were good in Judah.

Death of Rehoboam

13 So King Rehoboam established himself in Jerusalem and reigned. Rehoboam was forty-one years old when he began to reign; he reigned seventeen years in Jerusalem, the city that the LORD had chosen out of all the tribes of Israel to put his name there. His mother's name was Naamah the Ammonite. [14]He did evil, for he did not set his heart to seek the LORD.

15 Now the acts of Rehoboam, from first to last, are they not written in the records of the prophet Shemaiah and of the seer Iddo, recorded by genealogy? There were continual wars between Rehoboam and Jeroboam. [16]Rehoboam slept with his ancestors and was buried in the city of David; and his son Abijah succeeded him.

Abijah Reigns over Judah

13 In the eighteenth year of King Jeroboam, Abijah began to reign over Judah. [2]He reigned for three years in Jerusalem. His mother's name was Micaiah daughter of Uriel of Gibeah.

Now there was war between Abijah and Jeroboam. [3]Abijah engaged in battle, having an army of valiant warriors, four hundred thousand picked men; and Jeroboam drew up his line of battle against him with eight hundred thousand picked mighty warriors. [4]Then Abijah stood on the slope of Mount Zemaraim that is in the hill country of Ephraim, and said, "Listen to me, Jeroboam and all Israel! [5]Do you not know that the LORD God of Israel gave the kingship over Israel forever to David and his sons by a covenant of salt? [6]Yet Jeroboam son of Nebat, a servant of Solomon son of David, rose up and rebelled against his lord; [7]and certain worthless scoundrels gathered around him and defied Rehoboam son of Solomon, when Rehoboam was young and irresolute and could not withstand them.

8 "And now you think that you can withstand the kingdom of the LORD in the hand of the sons of David, because you are a great multitude and have with you the golden

---

12:9–10 *came up against Jerusalem.* Shishak's attack on Jerusalem results in serious losses for the Temple and the palace. Rehoboam has to replace the shields of gold Solomon had made (9:15–16) with shields of bronze.

12:14 *he did not . . . seek the LORD.* Rehoboam's evil is defined as not seeking Yahweh. In the corresponding text in 1 Kings 14:22 Judah is accused of doing evil in the eyes of Yahweh.

12:15 *the records of the prophet Shemaiah and of the seer Iddo.* The Chronicler again ascribes prophetic authority to the records of a king's reign. The prophet Iddo is mentioned also in the summaries of Solomon's (9:29) and Abijah's reigns (13:22).

13:1 *Abijah.* The Chronicler has replaced the name Abijam ("the god Yam is my divine father") with the name Abijah ("Yahweh is my divine father"), perhaps because of his positive evaluation of Abijah (cf. 1 Kings 15:3–5).

13:3 *valiant warriors . . . mighty warriors.* Abijah's troops are outnumbered two to one, but they will win a victory through Yahweh's help (vv 15–16).

13:5 *covenant of salt.* The dynastic promise to David is affirmed as an everlasting covenant (cf. Lev 2:13; Num 18:19).

13:7 *certain worthless scoundrels.* The Chronicler excuses the failures of Rehoboam because he was young and irresolute.

13:8 *kingdom of the LORD.* The kingdom of Yahweh belongs to the sons of David.

calves that Jeroboam made as gods for you. [9]Have you not driven out the priests of the LORD, the descendants of Aaron, and the Levites, and made priests for yourselves like the peoples of other lands? Whoever comes to be consecrated with a young bull or seven rams becomes a priest of what are no gods. [10]But as for us, the LORD is our God, and we have not abandoned him. We have priests ministering to the LORD who are descendants of Aaron, and Levites for their service. [11]They offer to the LORD every morning and every evening burnt offerings and fragrant incense, set out the rows of bread on the table of pure gold, and care for the golden lampstand so that its lamps may burn every evening; for we keep the charge of the LORD our God, but you have abandoned him. [12]See, God is with us at our head, and his priests have their battle trumpets to sound the call to battle against you. O Israelites, do not fight against the LORD, the God of your ancestors; for you cannot succeed."

13 Jeroboam had sent an ambush around to come on them from behind; thus his troops[a] were in front of Judah, and the ambush was behind them. [14]When Judah turned, the battle was in front of them and behind them. They cried out to the LORD, and the priests blew the trumpets. [15]Then the people of Judah raised the battle shout. And when the people of Judah shouted, God defeated Jeroboam and all Israel before Abijah and Judah. [16]The Israelites fled before Judah, and God gave them into their hands. [17]Abijah and his army defeated them with great slaughter; five hundred thousand picked men of Israel fell slain. [18]Thus the Israelites were subdued at that time, and the people of Judah prevailed, because they relied on the LORD, the God of their ancestors. [19]Abijah pursued Jeroboam, and took cities from him: Bethel with its villages and Jeshanah with its villages and Ephron[b] with its villages. [20]Jeroboam did not recover his power in the days of Abijah; the LORD struck him down, and he died. [21]But Abijah grew strong. He took fourteen wives, and became the father of twenty-two sons and sixteen daughters. [22]The rest of the acts of Abijah, his behavior and his deeds, are written in the story of the prophet Iddo.

Asa Reigns

14 [c]So Abijah slept with his ancestors, and they buried him in the city of David. His son Asa succeeded him. In his days the land had rest for ten years. [2][d]Asa did what was good and right in the sight of the LORD his God. [3]He took away the foreign altars and the high places, broke down the pil-

a Heb they   b Another reading is *Ephrain*
c Ch 13.23 in Heb   d Ch 14.1 in Heb

13:8–9 *calves . . . made as gods for you.* Abijah accuses the North of apostasy from Yahweh and of using priests without genealogical connection to Aaron or Levi.

13:10–11 *we have not abandoned him . . . but you have.* Abijah claims that Judah has not abandoned Yahweh, but the Northern tribes have.

13:12 *O Israelites.* Despite his severe charges against the Northerners, Abijah still addresses the people of the North as Israelites and urges them not to fight against Yahweh.

13:18 *they relied on the LORD.* Judah's victory over the North is attributed to its reliance on Yahweh (cf. 14:12; 16:7–8). The battle is described as a holy war: Judahites cried to Yahweh; the priests blew the trumpets; Judahites raised the battle cry; God defeated

Jeroboam (vv 14–15; cf. 14:8–14; 20:1–30; 26:6–8; 27:5–6).

13:19 *Bethel with its villages.* Abijah pushed the border of Judah more than ten miles into Northern territory.

13:21 *Abijah grew strong.* As a faithful king Abijah prospers, with fourteen wives and thirty-eight children. The first four kings of Judah—Rehoboam, Abijah, Asa, and Jehoshaphat—are judged positively, giving a sense of legitimacy to their state and its postexilic counterpart in the province of Yehud (the Persian name for the territory occupied by the Jews at this time).

14:1–4 *rest for ten years.* Asa's piety leads to peace for his first ten years in office. He commanded Judah to seek Yahweh and get rid of the high places.

lars, hewed down the sacred poles,[a] [4]and commanded Judah to seek the LORD, the God of their ancestors, and to keep the law and the commandment. [5]He also removed from all the cities of Judah the high places and the incense altars. And the kingdom had rest under him. [6]He built fortified cities in Judah while the land had rest. He had no war in those years, for the LORD gave him peace. [7]He said to Judah, "Let us build these cities, and surround them with walls and towers, gates and bars; the land is still ours because we have sought the LORD our God; we have sought him, and he has given us peace on every side." So they built and prospered. [8]Asa had an army of three hundred thousand from Judah, armed with large shields and spears, and two hundred eighty thousand troops from Benjamin who carried shields and drew bows; all these were mighty warriors.

Ethiopian Invasion Repulsed

[9] Zerah the Ethiopian[b] came out against them with an army of a million men and three hundred chariots, and came as far as Mareshah. [10]Asa went out to meet him, and they drew up their lines of battle in the valley of Zephathah at Mareshah. [11]Asa cried to the LORD his God, "O LORD, there is no difference for you between helping the mighty and the weak. Help us, O LORD our God, for we rely on you, and in your name we have come against this multitude. O LORD, you are our God; let no mortal prevail against you." [12]So the LORD defeated the Ethiopians[c] before Asa and before Judah, and the Ethiopians[c] fled. [13]Asa and the army with him pursued them as far as Gerar, and the Ethiopians[c] fell until no one remained alive; for they were broken before the LORD and his army. The people of Judah[d] carried away a great quan-

tity of booty. [14]They defeated all the cities around Gerar, for the fear of the LORD was on them. They plundered all the cities; for there was much plunder in them. [15]They also attacked the tents of those who had livestock,[e] and carried away sheep and goats in abundance, and camels. Then they returned to Jerusalem.

15 The spirit of God came upon Azariah son of Oded. [2]He went out to meet Asa and said to him, "Hear me, Asa, and all Judah and Benjamin: The LORD is with you, while you are with him. If you seek him, he will be found by you, but if you abandon him, he will abandon you. [3]For a long time Israel was without the true God, and without a teaching priest, and without law; [4]but when in their distress they turned to the LORD, the God of Israel, and sought him, he was found by them. [5]In those times it was not safe for anyone to go or come, for great disturbances afflicted all the inhabitants of the lands. [6]They were broken in pieces, nation against nation and city against city, for God troubled them with every sort of distress. [7]But you, take courage! Do not let your hands be weak, for your work shall be rewarded."

[8] When Asa heard these words, the prophecy of Azariah son of Oded,[f] he took courage, and put away the abominable idols from all the land of Judah and Benjamin and from the towns that he had taken in the hill country of Ephraim. He repaired the altar of the LORD that was in front of the vestibule of the house of the LORD.[g] [9]He gathered all Judah and Benjamin, and those from Ephraim,

a Heb *Asherim*   b Or *Nubian*; Heb *Cushite*
c Or *Nubians*; Heb *Cushites*   d Heb *They*
e Meaning of Heb uncertain   f Compare Syr Vg: Heb *the prophecy, the prophet Obed*   g Heb *the vestibule of the LORD*

14:9–15 *Zerah the Ethiopian.* When Zerah invaded with a million-man army, he was defeated because Judah relied on Yahweh. None of the Cushites (Ethiopians) survived. The numbers ascribed to Zerah seem quite high for that time, and Zerah may have been a Midianite rather than an Ethiopian.

15:1–7 *The spirit of God came upon Azariah son of Oded.* Azariah affirms the theology of

retribution and urges Judah to show courage. The spirit also came upon Amasai (1 Chron 12:18), Jahaziel (2 Chron 20:14), and Zechariah (2 Chron 24:20).

15:8 *When Asa heard these words.* In obedience to prophetic instruction, Asa initiates religious reform in Judah and in the territory that had been captured from the North. The result is a heartfelt spiritual renewal among the people.

Manasseh, and Simeon who were residing as aliens with them, for great numbers had deserted to him from Israel when they saw that the LORD his God was with him. 10They were gathered at Jerusalem in the third month of the fifteenth year of the reign of Asa. 11They sacrificed to the LORD on that day, from the booty that they had brought, seven hundred oxen and seven thousand sheep. 12They entered into a covenant to seek the LORD, the God of their ancestors, with all their heart and with all their soul. 13Whoever would not seek the LORD, the God of Israel, should be put to death, whether young or old, man or woman. 14They took an oath to the LORD with a loud voice, and with shouting, and with trumpets, and with horns. 15All Judah rejoiced over the oath; for they had sworn with all their heart, and had sought him with their whole desire, and he was found by them, and the LORD gave them rest all around.

16 King Asa even removed his mother Maacah from being queen mother because she had made an abominable image for Asherah. Asa cut down her image, crushed it, and burned it at the Wadi Kidron. 17But the high places were not taken out of Israel. Nevertheless the heart of Asa was true all his days. 18He brought into the house of God the votive gifts of his father and his own votive gifts—silver, gold, and utensils. 19And there was no more war until the thirty-fifth year of the reign of Asa.

Alliance with Aram Condemned

16 In the thirty-sixth year of the reign of Asa, King Baasha of Israel went up against Judah, and built Ramah, to prevent anyone from going out or coming into the territory of[a] King Asa of Judah. 2Then Asa took silver and gold from the treasures of the house of the LORD and the king's house, and sent them to King Ben-hadad of Aram, who resided in Damascus, saying, 3"Let there be an alliance between me and you, like that between my father and your father; I am sending to you silver and gold; go, break your alliance with King Baasha of Israel, so that he may withdraw from me." 4Ben-hadad listened to King Asa, and sent the commanders of his armies against the cities of Israel. They conquered Ijon, Dan, Abel-maim, and all the store-cities of Naphtali. 5When Baasha heard of it, he stopped building Ramah, and let his work cease. 6Then King Asa brought all Judah, and they carried away the stones of Ramah and its timber, with which Baasha had been building, and with them he built up Geba and Mizpah.

7 At that time the seer Hanani came to King Asa of Judah, and said to him, "Because you relied on the king of Aram, and did not rely on the LORD your God, the army of the king of Aram has escaped you. 8Were not the Ethiopians[b] and the Libyans a huge army with exceedingly many chariots and cavalry? Yet because you relied on the LORD, he gave

a Heb lacks *the territory of*   *b* Or *Nubians*; Heb *Cushites*

15:9 *Ephraim, Manasseh.* Representatives of two Northern tribes participate in Asa's celebration.

15:9 THE WITH-GOD LIFE—*See* Spiritual Disciplines Index.

15:15 *he was found by them.* Faithful seeking is rewarded with finding Yahweh and with divine rest (cf. vv 2, 4).

15:16–19 *an abominable image for Asherah.* Asa deposed his own mother from office because of her worship of Asherah. His fidelity gains him freedom from war until his thirty-fifth year.

16:1 *built Ramah.* King Baasha rolled back the southern border of Israel, reversing the gains of Abijah.

16:2–6 *Ben-hadad of Aram.* Asa raids the Temple and palace treasuries to bribe the king of Damascus to put pressure on Baasha. Ben-hadad complies and captures several cities on Israel's northern border, forcing Baasha to desert Ramah. Asa used materials from Ramah to rebuild Geba and Mizpah.

16:7–9 *the seer Hanani.* Hanani castigates Asa for relying on the king of Aram instead of relying on Yahweh. When Zerah invaded, Asa had relied on Yahweh and he had been delivered. *the entire earth.* Hanani seems to cite the postexilic prophet Zechariah (4:10).

them into your hand. 9For the eyes of the LORD range throughout the entire earth, to strengthen those whose heart is true to him. You have done foolishly in this; for from now on you will have wars." 10Then Asa was angry with the seer, and put him in the stocks, in prison, for he was in a rage with him because of this. And Asa inflicted cruelties on some of the people at the same time.

Asa's Disease and Death

11 The acts of Asa, from first to last, are written in the Book of the Kings of Judah and Israel. 12In the thirty-ninth year of his reign Asa was diseased in his feet, and his disease became severe; yet even in his disease he did not seek the LORD, but sought help from physicians. 13Then Asa slept with his ancestors, dying in the forty-first year of his reign. 14They buried him in the tomb that he had hewn out for himself in the city of David. They laid him on a bier that had been filled with various kinds of spices prepared by the perfumer's art; and they made a very great fire in his honor.

Jehoshaphat's Reign

17 His son Jehoshaphat succeeded him, and strengthened himself against Is-

rael. 2He placed forces in all the fortified cities of Judah, and set garrisons in the land of Judah, and in the cities of Ephraim that his father Asa had taken. 3The LORD was with Jehoshaphat, because he walked in the earlier ways of his father; a he did not seek the Baals, 4but sought the God of his father and walked in his commandments, and not according to the ways of Israel. 5Therefore the LORD established the kingdom in his hand. All Judah brought tribute to Jehoshaphat, and he had great riches and honor. 6His heart was courageous in the ways of the LORD; and furthermore he removed the high places and the sacred poles b from Judah.

7 In the third year of his reign he sent his officials, Ben-hail, Obadiah, Zechariah, Nethanel, and Micaiah, to teach in the cities of Judah. 8With them were the Levites, Shemaiah, Nethaniah, Zebadiah, Asahel, Shemiramoth, Jehonathan, Adonijah, Tobijah, and Tob-adonijah; and with these Levites, the priests Elishama and Jehoram. 9They taught in Judah, having the book of the law of the LORD with them; they went around through all the cities of Judah and taught among the people.

a Another reading is *his father David*
b Heb *Asherim*

Responding

16:9 THE WITH-GOD LIFE. In J. R. R. Tolkien's *The Lord of the Rings*, the flaming disembodied eye of the dark lord Sauron sees all and terrifies even the strongest. But here the eyes of the Lord see all toward a very different end: to give strength to those who love him. How does the idea of God's eyes always watching you make you feel? *See also* Spiritual Disciplines Index.

16:10 *put him in the stocks.* Instead of listening to Hanani, Asa puts him in the stocks (cf. Jer 20:2–3) and inflicts violence on the people.

16:12 *diseased in his feet.* The Chronicler's emphasis on Asa's sins explains the reason for the king's foot problem (cf. 1 Kings 15:23–24). The disease may refer to gangrene or to a venereal disease. Asa still did not seek Yahweh, instead committing another sin by seeking physicians.

17:1–10 THE WITH-GOD LIFE—*See* Spiritual Disciplines Index.

17:3–6 *the earlier ways of his father.* Jehoshaphat prospers because he sought the God of his father and not the Baals. The Septuagint interprets "his father" as Asa, while the Hebrew text considers David as his (ultimate) father. Jehoshaphat carried out religious reforms by removing the high places (but see 20:33) and the sacred poles, or Asherahs, from Judah. Most important of all for our understanding of the with-God life, "The LORD was with Jehoshaphat."

17:9–12 *the book of the law.* In his third year Jehoshaphat sends a delegation to teach the law in Judah. In the Chronicler's day, this book of the law would have been the Pentateuch. As a result of Jehoshaphat's piety, the surrounding nations do not fight against him, but send him tribute instead. He also initiated building projects.

10 The fear of the LORD fell on all the kingdoms of the lands around Judah, and they did not make war against Jehoshaphat. 11Some of the Philistines brought Jehoshaphat presents, and silver for tribute; and the Arabs also brought him seven thousand seven hundred rams and seven thousand seven hundred male goats. 12Jehoshaphat grew steadily greater. He built fortresses and storage cities in Judah. 13He carried out great works in the cities of Judah. He had soldiers, mighty warriors, in Jerusalem. 14This was the muster of them by ancestral houses: Of Judah, the commanders of the thousands: Adnah the commander, with three hundred thousand mighty warriors, 15and next to him Jehohanan the commander, with two hundred eighty thousand, 16and next to him Amasiah son of Zichri, a volunteer for the service of the LORD, with two hundred thousand mighty warriors. 17Of Benjamin: Eliada, a mighty warrior, with two hundred thousand armed with bow and shield, 18and next to him Jehozabad with one hundred eighty thousand armed for war. 19These were in the service of the king, besides those whom the king had placed in the fortified cities throughout all Judah.

Micaiah Predicts Failure

18 Now Jehoshaphat had great riches and honor; and he made a marriage alliance with Ahab. 2After some years he went down to Ahab in Samaria. Ahab slaughtered an abundance of sheep and oxen for him and for the people who were with him, and induced him to go up against Ramoth-gilead. 3King Ahab of Israel said to King Jehoshaphat of Judah, "Will you go with me to Ramoth-gilead?" He answered him, "I am with

you, my people are your people. We will be with you in the war."

4 But Jehoshaphat also said to the king of Israel, "Inquire first for the word of the LORD." 5Then the king of Israel gathered the prophets together, four hundred of them, and said to them, "Shall we go to battle against Ramoth-gilead, or shall I refrain?" They said, "Go up; for God will give it into the hand of the king." 6But Jehoshaphat said, "Is there no other prophet of the LORD here of whom we may inquire?" 7The king of Israel said to Jehoshaphat, "There is still one other by whom we may inquire of the LORD, Micaiah son of Imlah; but I hate him, for he never prophesies anything favorable about me, but only disaster." Jehoshaphat said, "Let the king not say such a thing." 8Then the king of Israel summoned an officer and said, "Bring quickly Micaiah son of Imlah." 9Now the king of Israel and King Jehoshaphat of Judah were sitting on their thrones, arrayed in their robes; and they were sitting at the threshing floor at the entrance of the gate of Samaria; and all the prophets were prophesying before them. 10Zedekiah son of Chenaanah made for himself horns of iron, and he said, "Thus says the LORD: With these you shall gore the Arameans until they are destroyed." 11All the prophets were prophesying the same and saying, "Go up to Ramoth-gilead and triumph; the LORD will give it into the hand of the king."

12 The messenger who had gone to summon Micaiah said to him, "Look, the words of the prophets with one accord are favorable to the king; let your word be like the word of one of them, and speak favorably." 13But Micaiah said, "As the LORD lives, whatever my God says, that I will speak."

17:13–19 *He had soldiers.* Jehoshaphat had more than a million troops in Jerusalem and stationed other troops throughout Judah. Wealth, building projects, and military prowess are typical characteristics of pious kings.

18:1 *marriage alliance.* Jehoshaphat errs in making an alliance with Ahab through the marriage of his son Jehoram to Athaliah, the daughter of Ahab (2 Kings 8:18) or Omri (2 Kings 8:26). Opposition to alliances is also

found in 16:1–4; 20:35–37; 25:6–8; 28:16–23.

18:3–34 *Ramoth-gilead.* This account is the only extended text about the Northern Kingdom in Chronicles. It is taken from 1 Kings 22:4–35.

18:10 *Zedekiah son of Chenaanah . . . said.* Zedekiah urges the two kings to go to war in the name of Yahweh. He reinforces a message previously given by four hundred other false prophets (v 5).

14 When he had come to the king, the king said to him, "Micaiah, shall we go to Ramoth-gilead to battle, or shall I refrain?" He answered, "Go up and triumph; they will be given into your hand." 15But the king said to him, "How many times must I make you swear to tell me nothing but the truth in the name of the LORD?" 16Then Micaiah*a* said, "I saw all Israel scattered on the mountains, like sheep without a shepherd; and the LORD said, 'These have no master; let each one go home in peace.' " 17The king of Israel said to Jehoshaphat, "Did I not tell you that he would not prophesy anything favorable about me, but only disaster?"

18 Then Micaiah*a* said, "Therefore hear the word of the LORD: I saw the LORD sitting on his throne, with all the host of heaven standing to the right and to the left of him. 19And the LORD said, 'Who will entice King Ahab of Israel, so that he may go up and fall at Ramoth-gilead?' Then one said one thing, and another said another, 20until a spirit came forward and stood before the LORD, saying, 'I will entice him.' The LORD asked him, 'How?' 21He replied, 'I will go out and be a lying spirit in the mouth of all his prophets.' Then the LORD*a* said, 'You are to entice him, and you shall succeed; go out and do it.' 22So you see, the LORD has put a lying spirit in the mouth of these your prophets; the LORD has decreed disaster for you."

23 Then Zedekiah son of Chenaanah came up to Micaiah, slapped him on the cheek, and said, "Which way did the spirit of the LORD pass from me to speak to you?" 24Mi-

caiah replied, "You will find out on that day when you go in to hide in an inner chamber." 25The king of Israel then ordered, "Take Micaiah, and return him to Amon the governor of the city and to Joash the king's son; 26and say, 'Thus says the king: Put this fellow in prison, and feed him on reduced rations of bread and water until I return in peace.' " 27Micaiah said, "If you return in peace, the LORD has not spoken by me." And he said, "Hear, you peoples, all of you!"

Defeat and Death of Ahab

28 So the king of Israel and King Jehoshaphat of Judah went up to Ramoth-gilead. 29The king of Israel said to Jehoshaphat, "I will disguise myself and go into battle, but you wear your robes." So the king of Israel disguised himself, and they went into battle. 30Now the king of Aram had commanded the captains of his chariots, "Fight with no one small or great, but only with the king of Israel." 31When the captains of the chariots saw Jehoshaphat, they said, "It is the king of Israel." So they turned to fight against him; and Jehoshaphat cried out, and the LORD helped him. God drew them away from him, 32for when the captains of the chariots saw that it was not the king of Israel, they turned back from pursuing him. 33But a certain man drew his bow and unknowingly struck the king of Israel between the scale armor and the breastplate; so he said to the driver of his chariot, "Turn around, and carry me out of the battle,

a Heb *he*

18:12 *speak favorably.* A messenger sent to fetch another prophet, Micaiah, whom Ahab hates, urges him to give the kings a positive message. But Micaiah insists he will say only what God tells him.

18:14–22 *I saw all Israel scattered on the mountains.* After initially delivering a positive message, Micaiah tells Ahab the truth: all Israel will be defeated. Micaiah goes on to explain the source of his oracle. He "saw" a meeting of the divine council, at which a lying spirit had agreed to motivate the false prophets to give the kings a deceptive message. But Micaiah's determination stands in counterdistinction to all the other

prophets and is a word of formation instruction to us: "As the LORD lives, whatever my God says, that I will speak" (v 13).

18:27 *the LORD has not spoken by me.* Micaiah says that if Ahab does return in peace, his own word would be proven untrue (cf. Deut 18:22). The history of the subsequent battle, however, proved the veracity of Micaiah.

18:31 *cried out.* When Jehoshaphat cries out (in prayer?), Yahweh helps him (cf. 14:10; 25:8; 26:7) and lures the enemy away from Judah's king (cf. v 2).

18:33 *struck the king of Israel.* An archer unwittingly shoots the king of Israel with an

for I am wounded." [34]The battle grew hot that day, and the king of Israel propped himself up in his chariot facing the Arameans until evening; then at sunset he died.

19 King Jehoshaphat of Judah returned in safety to his house in Jerusalem. [2]Jehu son of Hanani the seer went out to meet him and said to King Jehoshaphat, "Should you help the wicked and love those who hate the LORD? Because of this, wrath has gone out against you from the LORD. [3]Nevertheless, some good is found in you, for you destroyed the sacred poles[a] out of the land, and have set your heart to seek God."

The Reforms of Jehoshaphat

4 Jehoshaphat resided at Jerusalem; then he went out again among the people, from Beer-sheba to the hill country of Ephraim, and brought them back to the LORD, the God of their ancestors. [5]He appointed judges in the land in all the fortified cities of Judah, city by city, [6]and said to the judges, "Consider what you are doing, for you judge not on behalf of human beings but on the LORD's behalf; he is with you in giving judgment. [7]Now, let the fear of the LORD be upon you; take care what you do, for there is no perversion of justice with the LORD our God, or partiality, or taking of bribes."

8 Moreover in Jerusalem Jehoshaphat appointed certain Levites and priests and heads of families of Israel, to give judgment for the LORD and to decide disputed cases. They had their seat at Jerusalem. [9]He charged them: "This is how you shall act: in the fear of the LORD, in faithfulness, and with your whole heart; [10]whenever a case comes to you from your kindred who live in their cities, concerning bloodshed, law or commandment, statutes or ordinances, then you shall instruct them, so that they may not incur guilt before the LORD and wrath may not come on you and your kindred. Do so, and you will not incur guilt. [11]See, Amariah the chief priest is over you in all matters of the LORD; and Zebadiah son of Ishmael, the governor of the house of Judah, in all the king's matters; and the Levites will serve you as officers. Deal courageously, and may the LORD be with the good!"

Invasion from the East

20 After this the Moabites and Ammonites, and with them some of the Meunites,[b] came against Jehoshaphat for battle. [2]Messengers[c] came and told Jehoshaphat, "A great multitude is coming against you from Edom,[d] from beyond the sea; already they are at Hazazon-tamar" (that is, En-gedi). [3]Jehoshaphat was afraid; he set himself to

a Heb *Asheroth*   b Compare 26.7; Heb *Ammonites*   c Heb *They*   d One Ms: MT *Aram*

---

arrow and he dies at the end of the day. Ahab had disguised himself in a vain attempt to save his life (v 29).

19:2–3 *Jehu son of Hanani the seer.* Jehu rebukes Jehoshaphat for helping Ahab and predicts that Yahweh's wrath will be against him. Jehoshaphat is spared further punishment because of his religious reforms and his seeking God. His judicial reform in 19:4–11 and his war against Edom in chapter 20 demonstrate his goodness.

19:4 *the hill country of Ephraim.* Jehoshaphat's call for repentance extends into the Northern Kingdom.

19:5, 8 *appointed judges in the land.* Jehoshaphat stationed judges in the cities of Judah and created a court of appeals or supreme court in Jerusalem.

19:11 *Amariah . . . Zebadiah.* Jehoshaphat assigns sacral cases to Amariah and civil cases to Zebadiah.

20:1–4 *came against Jehoshaphat for battle.* Attacked by a coalition of eastern neighbors, Jehoshaphat seeks Yahweh and proclaims a fast.

Responding
20:3 FASTING. Jehoshaphat understands that his victory will come from God, not from his military. Instead of preparing for a potential invasion with battle plans and arms, he proclaims a fast throughout his entire kingdom. Think of something coming up that frightens you—a doctor's appointment, a plane trip, an exam or presentation. Prepare for it with a fast of some sort (fasting need not always be from food), remembering that your strength lies in God. *See also* Spiritual Disciplines Index.

seek the LORD, and proclaimed a fast throughout all Judah. 4Judah assembled to seek help from the LORD; from all the towns of Judah they came to seek the LORD.

Jehoshaphat's Prayer and Victory

5 Jehoshaphat stood in the assembly of Judah and Jerusalem, in the house of the LORD, before the new court, 6and said, "O LORD, God of our ancestors, are you not God in heaven? Do you not rule over all the kingdoms of the nations? In your hand are power and might, so that no one is able to withstand you. 7Did you not, O our God, drive out the inhabitants of this land before your people Israel, and give it forever to the descendants of your friend Abraham? 8They have lived in it, and in it have built you a sanctuary for your name, saying, 9'If disaster comes upon us, the sword, judgment,a or pestilence, or famine, we will stand before this house, and before you, for your name is in this house, and cry to you in our distress, and you will hear and save.' 10See now, the people of Ammon, Moab, and Mount Seir, whom you would not let Israel invade when they came from the land of Egypt, and whom they avoided and did not destroy— 11they reward us by coming to drive us out of your possession that you have given us to inherit. 12O our God, will you not execute judgment upon them? For we are powerless against this great multitude that is coming against us.

We do not know what to do, but our eyes are on you."

13 Meanwhile all Judah stood before the LORD, with their little ones, their wives, and their children. 14Then the spirit of the LORD came upon Jahaziel son of Zechariah, son of Benaiah, son of Jeiel, son of Mattaniah, a Levite of the sons of Asaph, in the middle of the assembly. 15He said, "Listen, all Judah and inhabitants of Jerusalem, and King Jehoshaphat: Thus says the LORD to you: 'Do not fear or be dismayed at this great multitude; for the battle is not yours but God's. 16Tomorrow go down against them; they will come up by the ascent of Ziz; you will find them at the end of the valley, before the wilderness of Jeruel. 17This battle is not for you to fight; take your position, stand still, and see the victory of the LORD on your behalf, O Judah and Jerusalem.' Do not fear or be dismayed; tomorrow go out against them, and the LORD will be with you."

18 Then Jehoshaphat bowed down with his face to the ground, and all Judah and the inhabitants of Jerusalem fell down before the LORD, worshiping the LORD. 19And the Levites, of the Kohathites and the Korahites, stood up to praise the LORD, the God of Israel, with a very loud voice.

20 They rose early in the morning and went out into the wilderness of Tekoa; and as they went out, Jehoshaphat stood and said,

a Or the sword of judgment

20:6–12 *O LORD, God of our ancestors.* Jehoshaphat's prayer, in which he rehearses Yahweh's help in the conquest of the land and the people's faithfulness in building the Temple, is one of the finest model prayers in all of Scripture for the formation of the People of God. Its conclusion strikes exactly the right posture: "We do not know what to do, but our eyes are on you."

20:10–11 *whom they . . . did not destroy.* Ironically, the nations spared at the time of the conquest are attacking Judah now.

20:14–17 *the spirit of the LORD came upon Jahaziel.* Jahaziel, a spirit-endowed Levite, predicts that Yahweh will win a victory over the enemies. Despite the large army available from

Judah and Benjamin (17:14–19), the people were not to fight at all.

Responding
20:15–22, 29–30 THE WITH-GOD LIFE. Jehoshaphat's piety delivers a victory that has nothing to do with his military might. Meditate on these words and those of Exod 14:14, "The LORD will fight for you, and you have only to keep still." What is preventing you from keeping still? *See also* Spiritual Disciplines Index.

20:18–19 *with a very loud voice.* Jehoshaphat and the citizens of Judah and Jerusalem believe the word of Jahaziel and worship the Lord, and the levitical singers add their praises to Yahweh.

"Listen to me, O Judah and inhabitants of Jerusalem! Believe in the LORD your God and you will be established; believe his prophets." [21] When he had taken counsel with the people, he appointed those who were to sing to the LORD and praise him in holy splendor, as they went before the army, saying,

"Give thanks to the LORD,
for his steadfast love endures forever."
[22] As they began to sing and praise, the LORD set an ambush against the Ammonites, Moab, and Mount Seir, who had come against Judah, so that they were routed. [23] For the Ammonites and Moab attacked the inhabitants of Mount Seir, destroying them utterly; and when they had made an end of the inhabitants of Seir, they all helped to destroy one another.

24 When Judah came to the watchtower of the wilderness, they looked toward the multitude; they were corpses lying on the ground; no one had escaped. [25] When Jehoshaphat and his people came to take the booty from them, they found livestock[a] in great numbers, goods, clothing, and precious things, which they took for themselves until they could carry no more. They spent three days taking the booty, because of its abundance. [26] On the fourth day they assembled in the Valley of Beracah, for there they blessed the LORD; therefore that place has been called the Valley of Beracah[b] to this day. [27] Then all the people of Judah and Jerusalem, with Jehoshaphat at their head, re-turned to Jerusalem with joy, for the LORD had enabled them to rejoice over their enemies. [28] They came to Jerusalem, with harps and lyres and trumpets, to the house of the LORD. [29] The fear of God came on all the kingdoms of the countries when they heard that the LORD had fought against the enemies of Israel. [30] And the realm of Jehoshaphat was quiet, for his God gave him rest all around.

The End of Jehoshaphat's Reign

31 So Jehoshaphat reigned over Judah. He was thirty-five years old when he began to reign; he reigned twenty-five years in Jerusalem. His mother's name was Azubah daughter of Shilhi. [32] He walked in the way of his father Asa and did not turn aside from it, doing what was right in the sight of the LORD. [33] Yet the high places were not removed; the people had not yet set their hearts upon the God of their ancestors.

34 Now the rest of the acts of Jehoshaphat, from first to last, are written in the Annals of Jehu son of Hanani, which are recorded in the Book of the Kings of Israel.

35 After this King Jehoshaphat of Judah joined with King Ahaziah of Israel, who did wickedly. [36] He joined him in building ships to go to Tarshish; they built the ships in Ezion-geber. [37] Then Eliezer son of Dodavahu of Mareshah prophesied against Jehoshaphat, saying, "Because you have joined with

a Gk: Heb *among them*   b That is *Blessing*

20:20 *believe his prophets.* Jehoshaphat urges belief in Yahweh and his prophets. Compare Isaiah's admonition to Ahaz in Isa 7:9. The singers repeat the refrain about Yahweh's loyalty (cf. 1 Chron 16:34, 41; 2 Chron 5:13; 7:3, 6).

20:23–30 *they all helped to destroy one another.* The enemy nations began to attack one another and no one escaped alive. It took three days to collect all the booty. The fear of God came on the surrounding nations (cf 17:10), and God gave peace to Jehoshaphat's realm.

20:33 *the high places were not removed.* In contradiction to 17:6, this verse taken from 1 Kings 22:43 states that the high places were *not* removed during Jehoshaphat's reign. Overall, however, Jehoshaphat did what was right in the eyes of Yahweh.

20:34 *Annals of Jehu.* The sources for Jehoshaphat's reign are given prophetic authority.

20:35 *joined with King Ahaziah.* The Chronicler criticizes Jehoshaphat's alliance with Ahaziah of the Northern Kingdom. At the beginning of his reign, Jehoshaphat had strengthened himself *against* Israel (17:1).

20:37 *Eliezer son of Dodavahu . . . prophesied.* Eliezer denounces Jehoshaphat's alliance with the Northern king and predicts that their naval venture will come to ruin. This prophetic word proved to be true. The alliance with one "who did wickedly" (v 35) undermined all the reforms of Jehoshaphat.

Ahaziah, the LORD will destroy what you have made." And the ships were wrecked and were not able to go to Tarshish.

Jehoram's Reign

21 Jehoshaphat slept with his ancestors and was buried with his ancestors in the city of David; his son Jehoram succeeded him. ²He had brothers, the sons of Jehoshaphat: Azariah, Jehiel, Zechariah, Azariah, Michael, and Shephatiah; all these were the sons of King Jehoshaphat of Judah.*a* ³Their father gave them many gifts, of silver, gold, and valuable possessions, together with fortified cities in Judah; but he gave the kingdom to Jehoram, because he was the firstborn. ⁴When Jehoram had ascended the throne of his father and was established, he put all his brothers to the sword, and also some of the officials of Israel. ⁵Jehoram was thirty-two years old when he began to reign; he reigned eight years in Jerusalem. ⁶He walked in the way of the kings of Israel, as the house of Ahab had done; for the daughter of Ahab was his wife. He did what was evil in the sight of the LORD. ⁷Yet the LORD would not destroy the house of David because of the covenant that he had made with David, and since he had promised to give a lamp to him and to his descendants forever.

Revolt of Edom

8 In his days Edom revolted against the rule of Judah and set up a king of their own. ⁹Then Jehoram crossed over with his commanders and all his chariots. He set out by night and attacked the Edomites, who had surrounded him and his chariot commanders. ¹⁰So Edom has been in revolt against the rule of Judah to this day. At that time Libnah also revolted against his rule, because he

Elijah's Letter

11 Moreover he made high places in the hill country of Judah, and led the inhabitants of Jerusalem into unfaithfulness, and made Judah go astray. ¹²A letter came to him from the prophet Elijah, saying: "Thus says the LORD, the God of your father David: Because you have not walked in the ways of your father Jehoshaphat or in the ways of King Asa of Judah, ¹³but have walked in the way of the kings of Israel, and have led Judah and the inhabitants of Jerusalem into unfaithfulness, as the house of Ahab led Israel into unfaithfulness, and because you also have killed your brothers, members of your father's house, who were better than yourself, ¹⁴see, the LORD will bring a great plague on your people, your children, your wives, and all your possessions, ¹⁵and you yourself will have a severe sickness with a disease of your bowels, until your bowels come out, day after day, because of the disease."

16 The LORD aroused against Jehoram the anger of the Philistines and of the Arabs who are near the Ethiopians.*b* ¹⁷They came up against Judah, invaded it, and carried away all the possessions they found that belonged to the king's house, along with his sons and his wives, so that no son was left to him except Jehoahaz, his youngest son.

Disease and Death of Jehoram

18 After all this the LORD struck him in his bowels with an incurable disease. ¹⁹In course of time, at the end of two years, his bowels came out because of the disease, and

a Gk Syr: Heb *Israel*   *b* Or *Nubians*; Heb *Cushites*

21:7 *covenant that he had made with David.* Jehoram is judged harshly by the Chronicler, but the dynasty was spared because of Yahweh's loyalty to the covenant he had made with David. Jehoram was married to Athaliah, the daughter of Ahab, and was unable to quell a revolt by the Edomites. The Chronicler explains the revolt of Edom and Libnah by saying that Jehoram had abandoned Yahweh, built high

places, and made Jerusalem and Judah go astray.

21:12–15 *A letter . . . from the prophet Elijah.* The Chronicler cites a letter from Elijah, the prophet to the Northern Kingdom, criticizing Jehoram for following the practices of the Northern kings and for murdering his brothers. He threatens the people with a plague and Jehoram himself with a bowel disease.

he died in great agony. His people made no fire in his honor, like the fires made for his ancestors. [20]He was thirty-two years old when he began to reign; he reigned eight years in Jerusalem. He departed with no one's regret. They buried him in the city of David, but not in the tombs of the kings.

Ahaziah's Reign

22 The inhabitants of Jerusalem made his youngest son Ahaziah king as his successor; for the troops who came with the Arabs to the camp had killed all the older sons. So Ahaziah son of Jehoram reigned as king of Judah. [2]Ahaziah was forty-two years old when he began to reign; he reigned one year in Jerusalem. His mother's name was Athaliah, a granddaughter of Omri. [3]He also walked in the ways of the house of Ahab, for his mother was his counselor in doing wickedly. [4]He did what was evil in the sight of the LORD, as the house of Ahab had done; for after the death of his father they were his counselors, to his ruin. [5]He even followed their advice, and went with Jehoram son of King Ahab of Israel to make war against King Hazael of Aram at Ramoth-gilead. The Arameans wounded Joram, [6]and he returned to be healed in Jezreel of the wounds that he had received at Ramah, when he fought King Hazael of Aram. And Ahaziah son of King Jehoram of Judah went down to see Joram son of Ahab in Jezreel, because he was sick.

7 But it was ordained by God that the downfall of Ahaziah should come about through his going to visit Joram. For when he came there he went out with Jehoram to meet Jehu son of Nimshi, whom the LORD had anointed to destroy the house of Ahab. [8]When Jehu was executing judgment on the house of Ahab, he met the officials of Judah and the sons of Ahaziah's brothers, who attended Ahaziah, and he killed them. [9]He searched for Ahaziah, who was captured while hiding in Samaria and was brought to Jehu, and put to death. They buried him, for they said, "He is the grandson of Jehoshaphat, who sought the LORD with all his heart." And the house of Ahaziah had no one able to rule the kingdom.

Athaliah Seizes the Throne

10 Now when Athaliah, Ahaziah's mother, saw that her son was dead, she set about to destroy all the royal family of the house of Judah. [11]But Jehoshabeath, the king's daughter, took Joash son of Ahaziah, and stole him away from among the king's children who were about to be killed; she put him and his nurse in a bedroom. Thus Jehoshabeath, daughter of King Jehoram and wife of the priest Jehoiada—because she was a sister of Ahaziah—hid him from Athaliah, so that she did not kill him; [12]he remained with them six years, hidden in the house of God, while Athaliah reigned over the land.

23 But in the seventh year Jehoiada took courage, and entered into a compact with the commanders of the hundreds,

---

21:20 *with no one's regret.* Jehoram's reign was unpopular. No fires were kindled at his funeral (cf. 16:14), and he was not buried in the royal tombs.

22:1–6 *his youngest son Ahaziah.* Ahaziah succeeded his father; he is to be identified with Jehoahaz mentioned in 21:17 (the names are quite similar in Hebrew). The text says Ahaziah was forty-two at his coronation, even though his father was only forty when he died! 2 Kings 8:26 makes him twenty-two at his accession. He followed his mother's advice and participated in the sins of the Northern kings. He made an alliance with Jehoram of the Northern Kingdom (Ahab's son), who was wounded in a battle against the Arameans.

22:7–9 *ordained by God.* Ahaziah visits his wounded ally in Jezreel, but the two kings run into Jehu, who was leading a revolt in the North at Yahweh's direction. Jehu kills Ahaziah's nephews and Ahaziah himself. The Chronicler views this as divine retribution for Ahaziah's wicked conduct.

22:10–12 *Athaliah, Ahaziah's mother.* Athaliah seizes the throne and wipes out the rest of the royal family except for the infant Joash, who is rescued by Jehoshabeath, the sister of Ahaziah and the aunt of Joash. Jehoshabeath is the wife of the priest Jehoiada. This explains why Joash could be hidden in the Temple.

Azariah son of Jeroham, Ishmael son of Je-hohanan, Azariah son of Obed, Maaseiah son of Adaiah, and Elishaphat son of Zichri. ²They went around through Judah and gathered the Levites from all the towns of Judah, and the heads of families of Israel, and they came to Jerusalem. ³Then the whole assembly made a covenant with the king in the house of God. Jehoiada*a* said to them, "Here is the king's son! Let him reign, as the LORD promised concerning the sons of David. ⁴This is what you are to do: one-third of you, priests and Levites, who come on duty on the sabbath, shall be gatekeepers, ⁵one-third shall be at the king's house, and one-third at the Gate of the Foundation; and all the people shall be in the courts of the house of the LORD. ⁶Do not let anyone enter the house of the LORD except the priests and ministering Levites; they may enter, for they are holy, but all the other*b* people shall observe the instructions of the LORD. ⁷The Levites shall surround the king, each with his weapons in his hand; and whoever enters the house shall be killed. Stay with the king in his comings and goings."

Joash Crowned King

8 The Levites and all Judah did according to all that the priest Jehoiada commanded; each brought his men, who were to come on duty on the sabbath, with those who were to go off duty on the sabbath; for the priest Jehoiada did not dismiss the divisions. ⁹The priest Jehoiada delivered to the captains the spears and the large and small shields that had been King David's, which were in the house of God; ¹⁰and he set all the people as a guard for the king, everyone with weapon in hand, from the south side of the house to the north side of the house, around the altar and the house. ¹¹Then he brought out the king's son, put the crown on him, and gave him the covenant;*c* they proclaimed him king, and Jehoiada and his sons anointed him; and they shouted, "Long live the king!"

Athaliah Murdered

12 When Athaliah heard the noise of the people running and praising the king, she went into the house of the LORD to the people; ¹³and when she looked, there was the king standing by his pillar at the entrance, and the captains and the trumpeters beside the king, and all the people of the land rejoicing and blowing trumpets, and the singers with their musical instruments leading in the celebration. Athaliah tore her clothes, and cried, "Treason! Treason!" ¹⁴Then the priest Jehoiada brought out the captains who were set over the army, saying to them, "Bring her out between the ranks; anyone who follows her is to be put to the sword." For the priest said, "Do not put her to death in the house of the LORD." ¹⁵So they laid hands on her; she went into the entrance of the Horse Gate of the king's house, and there they put her to death.

16 Jehoiada made a covenant between himself and all the people and the king that they should be the LORD's people. ¹⁷Then all the people went to the house of Baal, and tore it down; his altars and his images they broke in pieces, and they killed Mattan, the priest of Baal, in front of the altars. ¹⁸Jehoiada assigned the care of the house of the LORD to the levitical priests whom David had organized to be in charge of the house of the LORD, to offer burnt offerings to the LORD, as it is written in the law of Moses, with rejoicing and with singing, according to the order of David. ¹⁹He stationed the gatekeepers at the gates of the house of the LORD so that no one should en-

---

a Heb *He*   *b* Heb lacks *other*   *c* Or *treaty*, or *testimony*; Heb *eduth*

23:1–3 *made a covenant with the king.* Seven years later Jehoiada arranges a revolt and gets the whole assembly to make a covenant with the young prince Joash.

23:11 *gave him the covenant.* Jehoiada puts the crown on Joash and gives him the "covenant," a reference to a document certifying his kingship and spelling out his rights and duties. Jehoiada and his sons anoint Joash.

23:12–15 *Treason!* Athaliah discovers the plot and brands it treason. At Jehoiada's direction she is removed from the Temple and taken to the royal palace, where she is executed. Killing her in the Temple would have been inappropriate (but see 24:21).

ter who was in any way unclean. ²⁰And he took the captains, the nobles, the governors of the people, and all the people of the land, and they brought the king down from the house of the Lord, marching through the upper gate to the king's house. They set the king on the royal throne. ²¹So all the people of the land rejoiced, and the city was quiet after Athaliah had been killed with the sword.

Joash Repairs the Temple

24 Joash was seven years old when he began to reign; he reigned forty years in Jerusalem; his mother's name was Zibiah of Beer-sheba. ²Joash did what was right in the sight of the Lord all the days of the priest Jehoiada. ³Jehoiada got two wives for him, and he became the father of sons and daughters.

4 Some time afterward Joash decided to restore the house of the Lord. ⁵He assembled the priests and the Levites and said to them, "Go out to the cities of Judah and gather money from all Israel to repair the house of your God, year by year; and see that you act quickly." But the Levites did not act quickly. ⁶So the king summoned Jehoiada the chief, and said to him, "Why have you not required the Levites to bring in from Judah and Jerusalem the tax levied by Moses, the servant of the Lord, on ᵃ the congregation of Israel for the tent of the covenant?" ᵇ ⁷For the children of Athaliah, that wicked woman, had broken into the house of God, and had even used all the dedicated things of the house of the Lord for the Baals.

8 So the king gave command, and they made a chest, and set it outside the gate of the house of the Lord. ⁹A proclamation was made throughout Judah and Jerusalem to bring in for the Lord the tax that Moses the servant of God laid on Israel in the wilderness. ¹⁰All the leaders and all the people rejoiced and brought their tax and dropped it into the chest until it was full. ¹¹Whenever the chest was brought to the king's officers by the Levites, when they saw that there was a large amount of money in it, the king's secretary and the officer of the chief priest would come and empty the chest and take it and return it to its place. So they did day after day, and collected money in abundance. ¹²The king and Jehoiada gave it to those who had charge of the work of the house of the Lord, and they hired masons and carpenters to restore the house of the Lord, and also workers in iron and bronze to repair the house of the Lord. ¹³So those who were engaged in the work labored, and the repairing went forward at their hands, and they restored the house of God to its proper condition and strengthened it. ¹⁴When they had finished, they brought the rest of the money to the king and Jehoiada, and with it were made utensils for the house of the Lord, utensils for the service and for the burnt offerings, and ladles, and vessels of gold and silver. They offered burnt offerings in the house of the Lord regularly all the days of Jehoiada.

Apostasy of Joash

15 But Jehoiada grew old and full of days, and died; he was one hundred thirty years old

---

ᵃ Compare Vg: Heb *and*   ᵇ Or *treaty*, or *testimony*; Heb *eduth*

24:2 *all the days of the priest Jehoiada.* Joash remained faithful to Yahweh only during the first part of his reign when Jehoiada was still alive.

24:4, 8–14 *to restore the house of the Lord.* Joash carries out a renovation of the Temple and collects a tax to support this work. The tax was prescribed by Moses (Exod 30:11–16; 38:25–26) and was not mentioned in the Kings account. The people joyfully pay this tax, thus setting an example for the Chronicler's audience. They repair the Temple and manufacture new vessels for it (cf. Exod 25; 31:1–10, describing contributions for the

paraphernalia of the tabernacle).

24:15–22 *Jehoiada grew old and . . . died.* Jehoiada's long life testifies to his piety, and he is given a royal burial. The king's counselors lead Joash into apostasy, and the people do not listen to prophets who call them to repent. Jehoiada's son Zechariah, endowed with the spirit, rebukes the people and reminds them that forsaking Yahweh will lead to Yahweh forsaking them. A conspiracy in which Joash plays a part leads to the execution of Zechariah in the Temple. Zechariah calls on Yahweh to avenge this evil.

at his death. ¹⁶And they buried him in the city of David among the kings, because he had done good in Israel, and for God and his house.

17 Now after the death of Jehoiada the officials of Judah came and did obeisance to the king; then the king listened to them. ¹⁸They abandoned the house of the LORD, the God of their ancestors, and served the sacred poles*a* and the idols. And wrath came upon Judah and Jerusalem for this guilt of theirs. ¹⁹Yet he sent prophets among them to bring them back to the LORD; they testified against them, but they would not listen.

20 Then the spirit of God took possession of*b* Zechariah son of the priest Jehoiada; he stood above the people and said to them, "Thus says God: Why do you transgress the commandments of the LORD, so that you cannot prosper? Because you have forsaken the LORD, he has also forsaken you." ²¹But they conspired against him, and by command of the king they stoned him to death in the court of the house of the LORD. ²²King Joash did not remember the kindness that Jehoiada, Zechariah's father, had shown him, but killed his son. As he was dying, he said, "May the LORD see and avenge!"

Death of Joash

23 At the end of the year the army of Aram came up against Joash. They came to Judah and Jerusalem, and destroyed all the officials of the people from among them, and sent all the booty they took to the king of Damascus. ²⁴Although the army of Aram had come with few men, the LORD delivered into their hand a very great army, because they had abandoned the LORD, the God of their ancestors. Thus they executed judgment on Joash.

25 When they had withdrawn, leaving him severely wounded, his servants conspired

against him because of the blood of the son*c* of the priest Jehoiada, and they killed him on his bed. So he died; and they buried him in the city of David, but they did not bury him in the tombs of the kings. ²⁶Those who conspired against him were Zabad son of Shimeath the Ammonite, and Jehozabad son of Shimrith the Moabite. ²⁷Accounts of his sons, and of the many oracles against him, and of the rebuilding*d* of the house of God are written in the Commentary on the Book of the Kings. And his son Amaziah succeeded him.

Reign of Amaziah

25 Amaziah was twenty-five years old when he began to reign, and he reigned twenty-nine years in Jerusalem. His mother's name was Jehoaddan of Jerusalem. ²He did what was right in the sight of the LORD, yet not with a true heart. ³As soon as the royal power was firmly in his hand he killed his servants who had murdered his father the king. ⁴But he did not put their children to death, according to what is written in the law, in the book of Moses, where the LORD commanded, "The parents shall not be put to death for the children, or the children be put to death for the parents; but all shall be put to death for their own sins."

Slaughter of the Edomites

5 Amaziah assembled the people of Judah, and set them by ancestral houses under commanders of the thousands and of the hundreds for all Judah and Benjamin. He mustered those twenty years old and upward, and found that they were three hundred thousand picked troops fit for war, able to handle spear and shield. ⁶He also hired one hundred thousand mighty warriors from Is-

a Heb *Asherim*   b Heb *clothed itself with*
c Gk Vg: Heb *sons*   d Heb *founding*

24:23–25 *the army of Aram came up against Joash.* This invasion had significant results because it was supported by Yahweh in response to the people's abandoning him (v 24; cf. vv 18, 20). Joash's servants assassinated the king because of his bloodguilt for Zechariah. Joash was buried in Jerusalem, but not in the royal tombs.

25:1–4 *Amaziah was twenty-five years old.* Amaziah succeeds his father and executes his father's assassins. He does not kill the children of the assassins, however, in accordance with the law of Moses (Deut 24:16).

25:6–13 *warriors from Israel.* A prophet chastises Amaziah for allying himself with the

rael for one hundred talents of silver. 7But a man of God came to him and said, "O king, do not let the army of Israel go with you, for the LORD is not with Israel—all these Ephraimites. 8Rather, go by yourself and act; be strong in battle, or God will fling you down before the enemy; for God has power to help or to overthrow." 9Amaziah said to the man of God, "But what shall we do about the hundred talents that I have given to the army of Israel?" The man of God answered, "The LORD is able to give you much more than this." 10Then Amaziah discharged the army that had come to him from Ephraim, letting them go home again. But they became very angry with Judah, and returned home in fierce anger.

11 Amaziah took courage, and led out his people; he went to the Valley of Salt, and struck down ten thousand men of Seir. 12The people of Judah captured another ten thousand alive, took them to the top of Sela, and threw them down from the top of Sela, so that all of them were dashed to pieces. 13But the men of the army whom Amaziah sent back, not letting them go with him to battle, fell on the cities of Judah from Samaria to Beth-horon; they killed three thousand people in them, and took much booty.

14 Now after Amaziah came from the slaughter of the Edomites, he brought the gods of the people of Seir, set them up as his gods, and worshiped them, making offerings to them. 15The LORD was angry with Amaziah and sent to him a prophet, who said to him, "Why have you resorted to a people's gods who could not deliver their own people from your hand?" 16But as he was speaking the king*a* said to him, "Have we made you a royal counselor? Stop! Why should you be put to death?" So the prophet stopped, but said, "I know that God has determined to destroy you, because you have done this and have not listened to my advice."

Israel Defeats Judah

17 Then King Amaziah of Judah took counsel and sent to King Joash son of Jehoahaz son of Jehu of Israel, saying, "Come, let us look one another in the face." 18King Joash of Israel sent word to King Amaziah of Judah, "A thornbush on Lebanon sent to a cedar on Lebanon, saying, 'Give your daughter to my son for a wife'; but a wild animal of Lebanon passed by and trampled down the thornbush. 19You say, 'See, I have defeated Edom,' and your heart has lifted you up in boastfulness. Now stay at home; why should you provoke trouble so that you fall, you and Judah with you?"

20 But Amaziah would not listen—it was God's doing, in order to hand them over, because they had sought the gods of Edom. 21So King Joash of Israel went up; he and King Amaziah of Judah faced one another in battle at Beth-shemesh, which belongs to Judah. 22Judah was defeated by Israel; everyone fled home. 23King Joash of Israel captured King Amaziah of Judah, son of Joash, son of Ahaziah, at Beth-shemesh; he brought him to Jerusalem, and broke down the wall of Jerusalem from the Ephraim Gate to the Corner Gate, a distance of four hundred cubits. 24He seized all the gold and silver, and all the vessels that were found in the house of God, and Obed-edom with them; he seized also the treasuries of the king's house, also hostages; then he returned to Samaria.

Death of Amaziah

25 King Amaziah son of Joash of Judah, lived fifteen years after the death of King Joash son of Jehoahaz of Israel. 26Now the rest of the deeds of Amaziah, from first to last, are they not written in the Book of the Kings of Judah and Israel? 27From the time that Amaziah turned away from the LORD they made a conspiracy against him in Jerusalem,

a Heb *he*

North (cf. 19:1–3). Amaziah dismissed the Israelite mercenaries he had hired, but on their way home they sacked numerous cities, killed three thousand people, and took much booty.

Meanwhile Amaziah killed ten thousand Edomites directly and threw another ten thousand off a cliff.

and he fled to Lachish. But they sent after him to Lachish, and killed him there. [28]They brought him back on horses; he was buried with his ancestors in the city of David.

Reign of Uzziah

26 Then all the people of Judah took Uzziah, who was sixteen years old, and made him king to succeed his father Amaziah. [2]He rebuilt Eloth and restored it to Judah, after the king slept with his ancestors. [3]Uzziah was sixteen years old when he began to reign, and he reigned fifty-two years in Jerusalem. His mother's name was Jecoliah of Jerusalem. [4]He did what was right in the sight of the Lord, just as his father Amaziah had done. [5]He set himself to seek God in the days of Zechariah, who instructed him in the fear of God; and as long as he sought the Lord, God made him prosper.

[6] He went out and made war against the Philistines, and broke down the wall of Gath and the wall of Jabneh and the wall of Ashdod; he built cities in the territory of Ashdod and elsewhere among the Philistines. [7]God helped him against the Philistines, against the Arabs who lived in Gur-baal, and against the Meunites. [8]The Ammonites paid tribute to Uzziah, and his fame spread even to the border of Egypt, for he became very strong. [9]Moreover Uzziah built towers in Jerusalem at the Corner Gate, at the Valley Gate, and at the Angle, and fortified them. [10]He built towers in the wilderness and hewed out many cisterns, for he had large herds, both in the Shephelah and in the plain, and he had farmers and vinedressers in the hills and in the fertile lands, for he loved the soil. [11]Moreover Uzziah had an army of soldiers, fit for war, in divisions according to the numbers in the muster made by the secretary Jeiel and the officer Maaseiah, under the direction of Hananiah, one of the king's commanders. [12]The whole number of the heads of ancestral houses of mighty warriors was two thousand six hundred. [13]Under their command was an army of three hundred seven thousand five hundred, who could make war with mighty power, to help the king against the enemy. [14]Uzziah provided for all the army the shields, spears, helmets, coats of mail, bows, and stones for slinging. [15]In Jerusalem he set up machines, invented by skilled workers, on the towers and the corners for shooting arrows and large stones. And his fame spread far, for he was marvelously helped until he became strong.

Pride and Apostasy

[16] But when he had become strong he grew proud, to his destruction. For he was false to the Lord his God, and entered the temple of the Lord to make offering on the altar of incense. [17]But the priest Azariah went in after him, with eighty priests of the Lord who were men of valor; [18]they withstood King Uzziah, and said to him, "It is not for you, Uzziah, to make offering to the Lord, but for the priests the descendants of Aaron, who are consecrated to make offering. Go out of the sanctuary; for you have done wrong, and it will bring you no honor from the Lord God." [19]Then Uzziah was angry. Now he had a censer in his hand to make offering, and when he became angry with the priests a leprous[a] disease broke out on his forehead, in the presence of the priests in the house of the Lord, by the altar of incense. [20]When the chief priest Azariah, and all the

a A term for several skin diseases; precise meaning uncertain

---

26:4 *just as his father Amaziah had done.* Both Amaziah and Uzziah followed Yahweh during the first part of their reigns, but the second parts of their reigns were marked by sin and tragic consequences. Uzziah is called Azariah in the book of Kings.

26:5–15 *God made him prosper.* Seeking God leads Uzziah to great prosperity. He fights successful battles, begins building projects, and assembles a vast army

26:16–21 *grew proud.* Pride becomes a problem for Uzziah as it had been for his father (25:19). He enters the Temple to offer incense, for which he is chastised by the priest Azariah and eighty of his supporters. Yahweh strikes Uzziah with leprosy. Uzziah lives in a separate house, and his son Jotham becomes his coregent.

priests, looked at him, he was leprous*a* in his forehead. They hurried him out, and he himself hurried to get out, because the LORD had struck him. 21King Uzziah was leprous*a* to the day of his death, and being leprous*a* lived in a separate house, for he was excluded from the house of the LORD. His son Jotham was in charge of the palace of the king, governing the people of the land.

22 Now the rest of the acts of Uzziah, from first to last, the prophet Isaiah son of Amoz wrote. 23Uzziah slept with his ancestors; they buried him near his ancestors in the burial field that belonged to the kings, for they said, "He is leprous." *a* His son Jotham succeeded him.

Reign of Jotham

27 Jotham was twenty-five years old when he began to reign; he reigned sixteen years in Jerusalem. His mother's name was Jerushah daughter of Zadok. 2He did what was right in the sight of the LORD just as his father Uzziah had done—only he did not invade the temple of the LORD. But the people still followed corrupt practices. 3He built the upper gate of the house of the LORD, and did extensive building on the wall of Ophel. 4Moreover he built cities in the hill country of Judah, and forts and towers on the wooded hills. 5He fought with the king of the Ammonites and prevailed against them. The Ammonites gave him that year one hundred talents of silver, ten thousand cors of wheat and ten thousand of barley. The Ammonites paid him the same amount in the second and the third years. 6So Jotham became strong because he ordered his ways before the LORD his God. 7Now the rest of the acts of Jotham, and all his wars and his ways, are written in the Book of the Kings of Israel and Judah. 8He was twenty-five years old when he began to reign; he reigned sixteen years in Jerusalem. 9Jotham slept with his ancestors,

and they buried him in the city of David; and his son Ahaz succeeded him.

Reign of Ahaz

28 Ahaz was twenty years old when he began to reign; he reigned sixteen years in Jerusalem. He did not do what was right in the sight of the LORD, as his ancestor David had done, 2but he walked in the ways of the kings of Israel. He even made cast images for the Baals; 3and he made offerings in the valley of the son of Hinnom, and made his sons pass through fire, according to the abominable practices of the nations whom the LORD drove out before the people of Israel. 4He sacrificed and made offerings on the high places, on the hills, and under every green tree.

Aram and Israel Defeat Judah

5 Therefore the LORD his God gave him into the hand of the king of Aram, who defeated him and took captive a great number of his people and brought them to Damascus. He was also given into the hand of the king of Israel, who defeated him with great slaughter. 6Pekah son of Remaliah killed one hundred twenty thousand in Judah in one day, all of them valiant warriors, because they had abandoned the LORD, the God of their ancestors. 7And Zichri, a mighty warrior of Ephraim, killed the king's son Maaseiah, Azrikam the commander of the palace, and Elkanah the next in authority to the king.

Intervention of Oded

8 The people of Israel took captive two hundred thousand of their kin, women, sons, and daughters; they also took much booty from them and brought the booty to Samaria. 9But a prophet of the LORD was there, whose name was Oded; he went out to meet the

---

a A term for several skin diseases; precise meaning uncertain

---

26:22 *Isaiah.* The sources on Uzziah's reign are attributed to the prophet Isaiah (cf. Isa 6:1).
27:2–6 *He built.* The Chronicler ascribes building projects to Jotham and a military victory over the Ammonites. His strength resulted from

his following the ways of Yahweh. He did not invade the Temple like his father, but the people still followed corrupt practices (cf. 2 Kings 15:35).

army that came to Samaria, and said to them, "Because the LORD, the God of your ancestors, was angry with Judah, he gave them into your hand, but you have killed them in a rage that has reached up to heaven. 10Now you intend to subjugate the people of Judah and Jerusalem, male and female, as your slaves. But what have you except sins against the LORD your God? 11Now hear me, and send back the captives whom you have taken from your kindred, for the fierce wrath of the LORD is upon you." 12Moreover, certain chiefs of the Ephraimites, Azariah son of Johanan, Berechiah son of Meshillemoth, Jehizkiah son of Shallum, and Amasa son of Hadlai, stood up against those who were coming from the war, 13and said to them, "You shall not bring the captives in here, for you propose to bring on us guilt against the LORD in addition to our present sins and guilt. For our guilt is already great, and there is fierce wrath against Israel." 14So the warriors left the captives and the booty before the officials and all the assembly. 15Then those who were mentioned by name got up and took the captives, and with the booty they clothed all that were naked among them; they clothed them, gave them sandals, provided them with food and drink, and anointed them; and carrying all the feeble among them on donkeys, they brought them to their kindred at Jericho, the city of palm trees. Then they returned to Samaria.

Assyria Refuses to Help Judah

16 At that time King Ahaz sent to the king[a] of Assyria for help. 17For the Edomites had

again invaded and defeated Judah, and carried away captives. 18And the Philistines had made raids on the cities in the Shephelah and the Negeb of Judah, and had taken Beth-shemesh, Aijalon, Gederoth, Soco with its villages, Timnah with its villages, and Gimzo with its villages; and they settled there. 19For the LORD brought Judah low because of King Ahaz of Israel, for he had behaved without restraint in Judah and had been faithless to the LORD. 20So King Tilgath-pilneser of Assyria came against him, and oppressed him instead of strengthening him. 21For Ahaz plundered the house of the LORD and the houses of the king and of the officials, and gave tribute to the king of Assyria; but it did not help him.

Apostasy and Death of Ahaz

22 In the time of his distress he became yet more faithless to the LORD—this same King Ahaz. 23For he sacrificed to the gods of Damascus, which had defeated him, and said, "Because the gods of the kings of Aram helped them, I will sacrifice to them so that they may help me." But they were the ruin of him, and of all Israel. 24Ahaz gathered together the utensils of the house of God, and cut in pieces the utensils of the house of God. He shut up the doors of the house of the LORD and made himself altars in every corner of Jerusalem. 25In every city of Judah he made high places to make offerings to other gods, provoking to anger the LORD, the God of his ancestors. 26Now the rest of his acts and all his

a Gk Syr Vg Compare 2 Kings 16.7: Heb kings

28:9–11 *send back the captives.* Oded concedes the guilt of the Judahites, but accuses the Israelite army of excesses and orders them to return the captive Judahites.

28:12 *Ephraimites.* Several Ephraimites rebuke their fellow Northerners and accuse them of adding to the guilt of the Israelites by bringing Judahite captives to Samaria (13:4–12).

28:15 *Jericho.* The army heeds these admonitions, gives clothes, food, and drink to the captives, and returns them to Jericho. They had become good Samaritans.

28:16–21 *sent . . . for help.* In response to invasions by the Edomites and Philistines, Ahaz errs by seeking an alliance with the king of Assyria. He had become faithless (cf. 1 Chron 10:13). Tiglath-pileser responds to Ahaz's request by oppressing him instead of helping him. Ahaz in vain pays Tiglath-pileser bribes from the Temple treasuries.

28:22–25 *more faithless.* Ahaz sacrifices to the gods of Aram, which had defeated him (v 5). He cuts up the Temple's utensils, closes the Temple, erects altars throughout Jerusalem, and makes sacrifices to other gods.

ways, from first to last, are written in the Book of the Kings of Judah and Israel. ²⁷Ahaz slept with his ancestors, and they buried him in the city, in Jerusalem; but they did not bring him into the tombs of the kings of Israel. His son Hezekiah succeeded him.

Reign of Hezekiah

29 Hezekiah began to reign when he was twenty-five years old; he reigned twenty-nine years in Jerusalem. His mother's name was Abijah daughter of Zechariah. ²He did what was right in the sight of the LORD, just as his ancestor David had done.

The Temple Cleansed

3 In the first year of his reign, in the first month, he opened the doors of the house of the LORD and repaired them. ⁴He brought in the priests and the Levites and assembled them in the square on the east. ⁵He said to them, "Listen to me, Levites! Sanctify yourselves, and sanctify the house of the LORD, the God of your ancestors, and carry out the filth from the holy place. ⁶For our ancestors have been unfaithful and have done what was evil in the sight of the LORD our God; they have forsaken him, and have turned away their faces from the dwelling of the LORD, and turned their backs. ⁷They also shut the doors of the vestibule and put out the lamps, and have not offered incense or made burnt offerings in the holy place to the God of Israel. ⁸Therefore the wrath of the LORD came upon Judah and Jerusalem, and he has made them an object of horror, of astonishment, and of hissing, as you see with your own eyes. ⁹Our fathers have fallen by the sword and our sons and our daughters and our wives are in captivity for this. ¹⁰Now it is in my heart to make a covenant with the LORD, the God of Israel, so that his fierce anger may turn away from us.

¹¹My sons, do not now be negligent, for the LORD has chosen you to stand in his presence to minister to him, and to be his ministers and make offerings to him."

12 Then the Levites arose, Mahath son of Amasai, and Joel son of Azariah, of the sons of the Kohathites; and of the sons of Merari, Kish son of Abdi, and Azariah son of Jehallelel; and of the Gershonites, Joah son of Zimmah, and Eden son of Joah; ¹³and of the sons of Elizaphan, Shimri and Jeuel; and of the sons of Asaph, Zechariah and Mattaniah; ¹⁴and of the sons of Heman, Jehuel and Shimei; and of the sons of Jeduthun, Shemaiah and Uzziel. ¹⁵They gathered their brothers, sanctified themselves, and went in as the king had commanded, by the words of the LORD, to cleanse the house of the LORD. ¹⁶The priests went into the inner part of the house of the LORD to cleanse it, and they brought out all the unclean things that they found in the temple of the LORD into the court of the house of the LORD; and the Levites took them and carried them out to the Wadi Kidron. ¹⁷They began to sanctify on the first day of the first month, and on the eighth day of the month they came to the vestibule of the LORD; then for eight days they sanctified the house of the LORD, and on the sixteenth day of the first month they finished. ¹⁸Then they went inside to King Hezekiah and said, "We have cleansed all the house of the LORD, the altar of burnt offering and all its utensils, and the table for the rows of bread and all its utensils. ¹⁹All the utensils that King Ahaz repudiated during his reign when he was faithless, we have made ready and sanctified; see, they are in front of the altar of the LORD."

Temple Worship Restored

20 Then King Hezekiah rose early, assembled the officials of the city, and went up to

---

28:27 *buried him in the city.* Ahaz was not interred in the royal tombs either.

29:2 *just as his ancestor David had done.* Hezekiah is highly praised by the Chronicler as a second Solomon. He is the first king to serve without a counterpart in the Northern Kingdom.

29:3 *he opened the doors of the house of the*

LORD. On the very first day of his reign Hezekiah begins a renovation of the Temple and a reform movement.

29:16–17 *carried them out to the Wadi Kidron.* The Levites cleanse the house of Yahweh and deposit the unclean things from the Temple in the Wadi Kidron. The reform was finished within a sixteen-day period.

the house of the LORD. 21They brought seven bulls, seven rams, seven lambs, and seven male goats for a sin offering for the kingdom and for the sanctuary and for Judah. He commanded the priests the descendants of Aaron to offer them on the altar of the LORD. 22So they slaughtered the bulls, and the priests received the blood and dashed it against the altar; they slaughtered the rams and their blood was dashed against the altar; they also slaughtered the lambs and their blood was dashed against the altar. 23Then the male goats for the sin offering were brought to the king and the assembly; they laid their hands on them, 24and the priests slaughtered them and made a sin offering with their blood at the altar, to make atonement for all Israel. For the king commanded that the burnt offering and the sin offering should be made for all Israel.

25 He stationed the Levites in the house of the LORD with cymbals, harps, and lyres, according to the commandment of David and of Gad the king's seer and of the prophet Nathan, for the commandment was from the LORD through his prophets. 26The Levites stood with the instruments of David, and the priests with the trumpets. 27Then Hezekiah commanded that the burnt offering be offered on the altar. When the burnt offering began, the song to the LORD began also, and the trumpets, accompanied by the instruments of King David of Israel. 28The whole assembly worshiped, the singers sang, and the trumpeters sounded; all this continued until the burnt offering was finished. 29When the offering was finished, the king and all who were present with him bowed down and worshiped. 30King Hezekiah and the officials commanded the Levites to sing praises to the LORD with the words of David and of the seer Asaph. They sang praises with gladness, and they bowed down and worshiped.

31 Then Hezekiah said, "You have now consecrated yourselves to the LORD; come near, bring sacrifices and thank offerings to the house of the LORD." The assembly brought sacrifices and thank offerings; and all who were of a willing heart brought burnt offerings. 32The number of the burnt offerings that the assembly brought was seventy bulls, one hundred rams, and two hundred lambs; all these were for a burnt offering to the LORD. 33The consecrated offerings were six hundred bulls and three thousand sheep. 34But the priests were too few and could not skin all the burnt offerings, so, until other priests had sanctified themselves, their kindred, the Levites, helped them until the work was finished—for the Levites were more conscientious*a* than the priests in sanctifying themselves. 35Besides the great number of burnt offerings there was the fat of the offerings of well-being, and there were the drink offerings for the burnt offerings. Thus the service of the house of the LORD was restored. 36And Hezekiah and all the people rejoiced because of what God had done for the people; for the thing had come about suddenly.

The Great Passover

30 Hezekiah sent word to all Israel and Judah, and wrote letters also to Ephraim and Manasseh, that they should come to the house of the LORD at Jerusalem, to keep the passover to the LORD the God of Israel. 2For the king and his officials and all the assembly in Jerusalem had taken counsel to keep the passover in the second month 3(for they could not keep it at its proper time because the priests had not sanctified themselves in sufficient number, nor had the people assembled in Jerusalem). 4The plan seemed right to the king and all the assembly.

a Heb *upright in heart*

29:24 *to make atonement for all Israel.* Hezekiah commands the priests to make a sin offering for all Israel—the only time this sacrifice is mentioned in Chronicles.

29:25 *stationed the Levites in the house of the LORD.* Hezekiah stations the singers in accord with the commands of David, Gad, and Nathan.

Their lyrics were composed by David and Asaph (v 30).

29:34 *the Levites were more conscientious.* The Levites assist the priests, who had not sanctified themselves in sufficient numbers. The Chronicler notes that the Levites were more conscientious than the priests.

⁵So they decreed to make a proclamation throughout all Israel, from Beer-sheba to Dan, that the people should come and keep the passover to the LORD the God of Israel, at Jerusalem; for they had not kept it in great numbers as prescribed. ⁶So couriers went throughout all Israel and Judah with letters from the king and his officials, as the king had commanded, saying, "O people of Israel, return to the LORD, the God of Abraham, Isaac, and Israel, so that he may turn again to the remnant of you who have escaped from the hand of the kings of Assyria. ⁷Do not be like your ancestors and your kindred, who were faithless to the LORD God of their ancestors, so that he made them a desolation, as you see. ⁸Do not now be stiff-necked as your ancestors were, but yield yourselves to the LORD and come to his sanctuary, which he has sanctified forever, and serve the LORD your God, so that his fierce anger may turn away from you. ⁹For as you return to the LORD, your kindred and your children will find compassion with their captors, and return to this land. For the LORD your God is gracious and merciful, and will not turn away his face from you, if you return to him."

10 So the couriers went from city to city through the country of Ephraim and Manasseh, and as far as Zebulun; but they laughed them to scorn, and mocked them.

¹¹Only a few from Asher, Manasseh, and Zebulun humbled themselves and came to Jerusalem. ¹²The hand of God was also on Judah to give them one heart to do what the king and the officials commanded by the word of the LORD.

13 Many people came together in Jerusalem to keep the festival of unleavened bread in the second month, a very large assembly. ¹⁴They set to work and removed the altars that were in Jerusalem, and all the altars for offering incense they took away and threw into the Wadi Kidron. ¹⁵They slaughtered the passover lamb on the fourteenth day of the second month. The priests and the Levites were ashamed, and they sanctified themselves and brought burnt offerings into the house of the LORD. ¹⁶They took their accustomed posts according to the law of Moses the man of God; the priests dashed the blood that they received*a* from the hands of the Levites. ¹⁷For there were many in the assembly who had not sanctified themselves; therefore the Levites had to slaughter the passover lamb for everyone who was not clean, to make it holy to the LORD. ¹⁸For a multitude of the people, many of them from Ephraim, Manasseh, Issachar, and Zebulun, had not cleansed themselves, yet they ate

a Heb lacks *that they received*

30:1 *to keep the passover.* Hezekiah sends out invitations to a centralized Passover celebration (Deut 16; 2 Kings 23:21–23), including invitations to Ephraim and Manasseh. Hezekiah calls for repentance, so that Yahweh might return to the remnant who had escaped the king of Assyria. Israelite repentance would cause a change of mind in those who had taken Israelites captive, leading them to return the captives to the land.

30:11 *came to Jerusalem.* Although many rejected Hezekiah's invitation, a few from the tribes of Asher, Manasseh, and Zebulun humbled themselves and came to Jerusalem.

30:13 *second month.* Normally Passover was held on the fourteenth day of the first month, but since Hezekiah's reforms were not completed by then, it was postponed until the second month (cf. Num 9:9–11).

Responding

30:18–19 PRAYER. Hezekiah's prayer demonstrates his understanding that the law is a tool to help us to seek God, not God himself. In the same way, following Jesus is about training our souls to become more like his, not thoughtlessly trying to follow his every command. As Scottish minister Oswald Chambers writes: "The Sermon on the Mount is not a set of principles to be obeyed apart from identification with Jesus Christ. The Sermon on the Mount is a statement of the life we will live when the Holy Spirit is getting his way with us." Think of a time when you've hidden behind the letter of the law and not followed the way of the Holy Spirit—perhaps in criticizing the action of a friend or fellow church member or perhaps in your own actions—and ask God for forgiveness. *See also* Spiritual Disciplines Index.

the passover otherwise than as prescribed. But Hezekiah prayed for them, saying, "The good LORD pardon all ¹⁹who set their hearts to seek God, the LORD the God of their ancestors, even though not in accordance with the sanctuary's rules of cleanness." ²⁰The LORD heard Hezekiah, and healed the people. ²¹The people of Israel who were present at Jerusalem kept the festival of unleavened bread seven days with great gladness; and the Levites and the priests praised the LORD day by day, accompanied by loud instruments for the LORD. ²²Hezekiah spoke encouragingly to all the Levites who showed good skill in the service of the LORD. So the people ate the food of the festival for seven days, sacrificing offerings of well-being and giving thanks to the LORD the God of their ancestors.

23 Then the whole assembly agreed together to keep the festival for another seven days; so they kept it for another seven days with gladness. ²⁴For King Hezekiah of Judah gave the assembly a thousand bulls and seven thousand sheep for offerings, and the officials gave the assembly a thousand bulls and ten thousand sheep. The priests sanctified themselves in great numbers. ²⁵The whole assembly of Judah, the priests and the Levites, and the whole assembly that came out of Israel, and the resident aliens who came out of the land of Israel, and the resident aliens who lived in Judah, rejoiced. ²⁶There was great joy in Jerusalem, for since the time of Solomon son of King David of Israel there had been nothing like this in Jerusalem. ²⁷Then the priests and the Levites stood up and blessed the people, and their voice was heard; their prayer came to his holy dwelling in heaven.

Pagan Shrines Destroyed

31 Now when all this was finished, all Israel who were present went out to the cities of Judah and broke down the pillars, hewed down the sacred poles, *a* and pulled down the high places and the altars throughout all Judah and Benjamin, and in Ephraim and Manasseh, until they had destroyed them all. Then all the people of Israel returned to their cities, all to their individual properties.

2 Hezekiah appointed the divisions of the priests and of the Levites, division by division, everyone according to his service, the priests and the Levites, for burnt offerings and offerings of well-being, to minister in the gates of the camp of the LORD and to give thanks and praise. ³The contribution of the king from his own possessions was for the burnt offerings: the burnt offerings of morning and evening, and the burnt offerings for the sabbaths, the new moons, and the appointed festivals, as it is written in the law of the LORD. ⁴He commanded the people who lived in Jerusalem to give the portion due to the priests and the Levites, so that they might devote themselves to the law of the LORD. ⁵As soon as the word spread, the people of Israel gave in abundance the first fruits of grain, wine, oil, honey, and of all the produce of the field; and they brought in abundantly the tithe of everything. ⁶The people of Israel and Judah who lived in the cities of Judah also brought in the tithe of cattle and sheep, and the tithe of the dedicated things that had been consecrated to the LORD their God, and laid them in heaps. ⁷In the third month they began to pile up the heaps, and finished them in the seventh month. ⁸When Hezekiah and the officials came and saw the heaps, they blessed the LORD and his people Israel.

a Heb *Asherim*

30:23 *another seven days.* The fourteen days of Hezekiah's festival have a precedent in Solomon's dedication of the Temple (7:8–9).

30:26 *since the time of Solomon.* This was the first centralized celebration of Passover since the time of the United Kingdom.

31:1 *destroyed them all.* The celebration of

Passover was followed by vigorous acts of reform that destroyed various unorthodox worship sites. This included incursions into the territories of Ephraim and Manasseh.

31:3 *contribution of the king.* Hezekiah contributes animals for sacrifice just like later Persian kings (Ezra 6:9; 7:21–23).

9Hezekiah questioned the priests and the Levites about the heaps. 10The chief priest Azariah, who was of the house of Zadok, answered him, "Since they began to bring the contributions into the house of the LORD, we have had enough to eat and have plenty to spare; for the LORD has blessed his people, so that we have this great supply left over."

Reorganization of Priests and Levites

11 Then Hezekiah commanded them to prepare store-chambers in the house of the LORD; and they prepared them. 12Faithfully they brought in the contributions, the tithes and the dedicated things. The chief officer in charge of them was Conaniah the Levite, with his brother Shimei as second; 13while Jehiel, Azaziah, Nahath, Asahel, Jerimoth, Jozabad, Eliel, Ismachiah, Mahath, and Benaiah were overseers assisting Conaniah and his brother Shimei, by the appointment of King Hezekiah and of Azariah the chief officer of the house of God. 14Kore son of Imnah the Levite, keeper of the east gate, was in charge of the freewill offerings to God, to apportion the contribution reserved for the LORD and the most holy offerings. 15Eden, Miniamin, Jeshua, Shemaiah, Amariah, and Shecaniah were faithfully assisting him in the cities of the priests, to distribute the portions to their kindred, old and young alike, by divisions, 16except those enrolled by genealogy, males from three years old and upwards, all who entered the house of the LORD as the duty of each day required, for their service according to their offices, by their divisions. 17The enrollment of the priests was according to their ancestral houses; that of the Levites from twenty years old and upwards was according to their offices, by their divisions. 18The priests were enrolled with all their little children, their wives, their sons, and their daughters, the whole multitude; for they were faithful in keeping themselves holy. 19And for the descendants of Aaron, the priests, who were in the fields of common land belonging to their towns, town by town, the people designated by name were to distribute portions to every male among the priests and to everyone among the Levites who was enrolled.

20 Hezekiah did this throughout all Judah; he did what was good and right and faithful before the LORD his God. 21And every work that he undertook in the service of the house of God, and in accordance with the law and the commandments, to seek his God, he did with all his heart; and he prospered.

Sennacherib's Invasion

32 After these things and these acts of faithfulness, King Sennacherib of Assyria came and invaded Judah and encamped against the fortified cities, thinking to win them for himself. 2When Hezekiah saw that Sennacherib had come and intended to fight against Jerusalem, 3he planned with his officers and his warriors to stop the flow of the springs that were outside the city; and they helped him. 4A great many people were gathered, and they stopped all the springs and the wadi that flowed through the land, saying, "Why should the Assyrian kings come and find water in abundance?" 5Hezekiah[a] set to work resolutely and built up the entire wall that was broken down, and raised towers on it,[b] and outside it he built another wall; he also strengthened the Millo in the city of David, and made weapons and shields in abundance. 6He appointed combat commanders over the people, and gathered them together to him in the square at the gate of the city and spoke encouragingly to them, saying, 7"Be strong and of good courage. Do

---

a Heb *He*   *b* Vg: Heb *and raised on the towers*

31:10 *plenty to spare.* Azariah assures Hezekiah that the priests have plenty of food because of the people's generosity (cf. generosity for the tabernacle in Exod 36:2–7 and for the Temple in 1 Chron 29:6–9).

32:1–23 *Sennacherib of Assyria came and invaded Judah.* The Chronicler has extensively rearranged the materials on the invasion of Sennacherib from 2 Kings 18–19.

32:3–4 *to stop the flow of the springs.* Hezekiah hides the sources for Jerusalem's water supply and digs what is known today as the Siloam tunnel (cf. v 30).

not be afraid or dismayed before the king of Assyria and all the horde that is with him; for there is one greater with us than with him. [8]With him is an arm of flesh; but with us is the LORD our God, to help us and to fight our battles." The people were encouraged by the words of King Hezekiah of Judah.

9 After this, while King Sennacherib of Assyria was at Lachish with all his forces, he sent his servants to Jerusalem to King Hezekiah of Judah and to all the people of Judah that were in Jerusalem, saying, [10]"Thus says King Sennacherib of Assyria: On what are you relying, that you undergo the siege of Jerusalem? [11]Is not Hezekiah misleading you, handing you over to die by famine and by thirst, when he tells you, 'The LORD our God will save us from the hand of the king of Assyria'? [12]Was it not this same Hezekiah who took away his high places and his altars and commanded Judah and Jerusalem, saying, 'Before one altar you shall worship, and upon it you shall make your offerings'? [13]Do you not know what I and my ancestors have done to all the peoples of other lands? Were the gods of the nations of those lands at all able to save their lands out of my hand? [14]Who among all the gods of those nations that my ancestors utterly destroyed was able to save his people from my hand, that your God should be able to save you from my hand? [15]Now therefore do not let Hezekiah deceive you or mislead you in this fashion, and do not believe him, for no god of any nation or kingdom has been able to save his people from my hand or from the hand of my ancestors. How much less will your God save you out of my hand!"

16 His servants said still more against the Lord GOD and against his servant Hezekiah. [17]He also wrote letters to throw contempt on the LORD the God of Israel and to speak against him, saying, "Just as the gods of the nations in other lands did not rescue their people from my hands, so the God of Hezekiah will not rescue his people from my hand." [18]They shouted it with a loud voice in the language of Judah to the people of Jerusalem who were on the wall, to frighten and terrify them, in order that they might take the city. [19]They spoke of the God of Jerusalem as if he were like the gods of the peoples of the earth, which are the work of human hands.

Sennacherib's Defeat and Death

20 Then King Hezekiah and the prophet Isaiah son of Amoz prayed because of this and cried to heaven. [21]And the LORD sent an angel who cut off all the mighty warriors and commanders and officers in the camp of the king of Assyria. So he returned in disgrace to his own land. When he came into the house of his god, some of his own sons struck him down there with the sword. [22]So the LORD saved Hezekiah and the inhabitants of Jerusalem from the hand of King Sennacherib of Assyria and from the hand of all his enemies; he gave them rest[a] on every side. [23]Many brought gifts to the LORD in Jerusalem and precious things to King Hezekiah of Judah, so that he was exalted in the sight of all nations from that time onward.

Hezekiah's Sickness

24 In those days Hezekiah became sick and was at the point of death. He prayed to

a Gk Vg: Heb *guided them*

32:7–8 THE WITH-GOD LIFE—*See* Spiritual Disciplines Index.

32:11–12 *Is not Hezekiah misleading you?* The servants of Sennacherib charge that Hezekiah was wrong in saying that Yahweh would deliver Judah, since Hezekiah had torn down Yahweh's high places and altars. Hezekiah's strength is interpreted by the Assyrians as duplicity.

32:15 *no god . . . has been able to save his people from my hand.* The Assyrians claim that no god has been able to resist them and therefore Yahweh could also not save Judah. They mock the God of Jerusalem as if he were a product of human hands.

32:20–23 *Hezekiah and . . . Isaiah . . . prayed.* Yahweh answers Hezekiah and Isaiah by sending an angel to cut off the warriors. When Sennacherib returned to his own land, his own sons killed him. Historically, this happened twenty years later. Hezekiah is honored among the nations, thus making him parallel to Solomon.

the LORD, and he answered him and gave him a sign. 25But Hezekiah did not respond according to the benefit done to him, for his heart was proud. Therefore wrath came upon him and upon Judah and Jerusalem. 26Then Hezekiah humbled himself for the pride of his heart, both he and the inhabitants of Jerusalem, so that the wrath of the LORD did not come upon them in the days of Hezekiah.

Hezekiah's Prosperity and Achievements

27 Hezekiah had very great riches and honor; and he made for himself treasuries for silver, for gold, for precious stones, for spices, for shields, and for all kinds of costly objects; 28storehouses also for the yield of grain, wine, and oil; and stalls for all kinds of cattle, and sheepfolds. a 29He likewise provided cities for himself, and flocks and herds in abundance; for God had given him very great possessions. 30This same Hezekiah closed the upper outlet of the waters of Gihon and directed them down to the west side of the city of David. Hezekiah prospered in all his works. 31So also in the matter of the envoys of the officials of Babylon, who had been sent to him to inquire about the sign that had been done in the land, God left him to himself, in order to test him and to know all that was in his heart.

32 Now the rest of the acts of Hezekiah, and his good deeds, are written in the vision of the prophet Isaiah son of Amoz in the Book of the Kings of Judah and Israel. 33Hezekiah slept with his ancestors, and they buried him on the ascent to the tombs of the descendants of David; and all Judah and the inhabitants of Jerusalem did him honor at his death. His son Manasseh succeeded him.

Reign of Manasseh

33 Manasseh was twelve years old when he began to reign; he reigned fifty-five years in Jerusalem. 2He did what was evil in the sight of the LORD, according to the abominable practices of the nations whom the LORD drove out before the people of Israel. 3For he rebuilt the high places that his father Hezekiah had pulled down, and erected altars to the Baals, made sacred poles, b worshiped all the host of heaven, and served them. 4He built altars in the house of the LORD, of which the LORD had said, "In Jerusalem shall my name be forever." 5He built altars for all the host of heaven in the two courts of the house of the LORD. 6He made his son pass through fire in the valley of the son of Hinnom, practiced soothsaying and augury and sorcery, and dealt with mediums and with wizards. He did much evil in the sight of the LORD, provoking him to anger. 7The carved image of the idol that he had made he set in the house of God, of which God said to David and to his son Solomon, "In this house, and in Jerusalem, which I have chosen out of all the tribes of Israel, I will put my name forever; 8I will never again remove the feet of Israel from the land that I appointed for your ancestors, if only they will be careful to do all that I have commanded them, all the law, the statutes, and the ordinances given through Moses." 9Manasseh misled Judah and the inhabitants of Jerusalem, so that they did more evil than the nations whom the LORD had destroyed before the people of Israel.

Manasseh Restored after Repentance

10 The LORD spoke to Manasseh and to his people, but they gave no heed. 11Therefore

a Gk Vg: Heb *flocks for folds*   b Heb *Asheroth*

32:24–26 *Hezekiah became sick and . . . prayed.* Hezekiah recovers from a serious illness because of his prayer, but pride keeps him from responding appropriately to God for this benefit. Exposed to God's wrath, Hezekiah and the inhabitants of Jerusalem humble themselves (cf. 7:14; 12:1–12; 30:11), so that they are spared the effects of God's wrath.

32:27–33 *riches and honor.* Hezekiah's faithfulness led to great prosperity. All Judah

and Jerusalem honored him at his death.

33:1–9 *he reigned fifty-five years.* Manasseh rules for a very long time and for the first part of his reign is a very wicked king. This contradicts the doctrine of retribution. Manasseh reverses the religious policies of his father Hezekiah, institutes child sacrifice, and sets up an idol in the Temple. Manasseh misleads the inhabitants of Judah and Jerusalem to do more evil than the pre-Israelite inhabitants of the land.

the LORD brought against them the commanders of the army of the king of Assyria, who took Manasseh captive in manacles, bound him with fetters, and brought him to Babylon. 12While he was in distress he entreated the favor of the LORD his God and humbled himself greatly before the God of his ancestors. 13He prayed to him, and God received his entreaty, heard his plea, and restored him again to Jerusalem and to his kingdom. Then Manasseh knew that the LORD indeed was God.

14 Afterward he built an outer wall for the city of David west of Gihon, in the valley, reaching the entrance at the Fish Gate; he carried it around Ophel, and raised it to a very great height. He also put commanders of the army in all the fortified cities in Judah. 15He took away the foreign gods and the idol from the house of the LORD, and all the altars that he had built on the mountain of the house of the LORD and in Jerusalem, and he threw them out of the city. 16He also restored the altar of the LORD and offered on it sacrifices of well-being and of thanksgiving; and he commanded Judah to serve the LORD the God of Israel. 17The people, however, still sacrificed at the high places, but only to the LORD their God.

Death of Manasseh

18 Now the rest of the acts of Manasseh, his prayer to his God, and the words of the seers who spoke to him in the name of the LORD God of Israel, these are in the Annals of the Kings of Israel. 19His prayer, and how God received his entreaty, all his sin and his faithlessness, the sites on which he built high places and set up the sacred poles[a] and the images, before he humbled himself, these are written in the records of the seers.[b] 20So Manasseh slept with his ancestors, and they buried him in his house. His son Amon succeeded him.

Amon's Reign and Death

21 Amon was twenty-two years old when he began to reign; he reigned two years in Jerusalem. 22He did what was evil in the sight of the LORD, as his father Manasseh had done. Amon sacrificed to all the images that his father Manasseh had made, and served them. 23He did not humble himself before the LORD, as his father Manasseh had humbled himself, but this Amon incurred more and more guilt. 24His servants conspired against him and killed him in his house. 25But the people of the land killed all those who had conspired against King Amon; and the people of the land made his son Josiah king to succeed him.

Reign of Josiah

34 Josiah was eight years old when he began to reign; he reigned thirty-one years in Jerusalem. 2He did what was right in the sight of the LORD, and walked in the ways of his ancestor David; he did not turn aside to the right or to the left. 3For in the eighth year of his reign, while he was still a boy, he began to seek the God of his ancestor David, and in the twelfth year he began to purge

a Heb Asherim   b One Ms Gk: MT of Hozai

33:11–13 *brought him to Babylon.* Manasseh is taken captive by the king of Assyria and put in a Babylonian prison. While there, he comes to his senses, humbles himself (7:14), and prays. God hears his prayer and restores him to the land. Hence Manasseh recognizes that Yahweh is the true God. For the People of God there is no more welcome word than that "God received his entreaty, heard his plea, and restored him" (v 13).

33:13 PRAYER—*See* Spiritual Disciplines Index.

33:14–17 *he built an outer wall.* The second half of Manasseh's reign is marked by piety and prosperity. He initiates building programs, expands military operations, and carries out religious reforms. Although people still worshiped at the high places, this worship was dedicated solely to Yahweh.

34:3–7 *eighth year of his reign.* The Chronicler asserts that Josiah began his reforms already in his eighth and twelfth years and did not wait until his eighteenth year as in 2 Kings 22:3. His reforms extended into Manasseh, Ephraim, Simeon, and Naphtali. Josiah demolished incense altars throughout the land.

MANASSEH

A Change of Heart

Selected Scriptures: *2 Kings 21:1–18; 2 Chronicles 33; Prayer of Manasseh*

Manasseh probably did more evil than any other king of Israel. Scripture's accounts of him read simply as a factual record of his reign, listing his many offenses against God and his people. We're given little detail about God's dealings with Manasseh or God's distress over his "abominable" behavior (2 Chron 33:2). Yet we can imagine easily the grief this man must have caused God when we take a moment to consider what Manasseh did.

He had watched his father, Hezekiah, tear down the high places and altars that his grandfather, Ahaz, had erected to other gods. Manasseh rebuilt these high places and even put some altars inside the Temple (2 Chron 33:4). Within the very house Solomon had built for the worship of God, Manasseh bowed to other gods. Rather than seeking the prophets of God for direction, he employed wizards and mediums, turning to the occult to see the future (33:6). He sacrificed his own son in fire, a common cultic practice of the day, and he shed so much blood in the city that "he had filled Jerusalem from one end to another" (2 Kings 21:16). Moreover, his evil didn't stop with him. Manasseh caused many others in Judah to sin as he did.

His deeds resemble those of others throughout history who performed atrocities against people and dishonored God in horrifying ways. Many of them remained mired in evil all their days, never turning from their wickedness. Not so with Manasseh. He had a change of heart and became truly repentant. After his capture by the king of Assyria, Manasseh recognized his sin and prayed for forgiveness and help (2 Chron 33:11–12). God heard and delivered him, restoring Manasseh to Jerusalem and his kingdom (33:13). Manasseh proved that his repentance was sincere by removing the altars he had raised and commanding the people to worship Yahweh only.

Manasseh was punished for his disobedience by being captured by his enemies. It's not surprising that he finally called on God. More surprising is God's quick and total forgiveness and Manasseh's restoration to his throne. "How could God do that?" we may ask. Philip Yancey, in his book *What's So Amazing About Grace?* writes: "Most ethicists would agree . . . with the philosopher Immanuel Kant, who argued that a person should be forgiven only if he deserves it. But the very word *forgive* contains the word 'give' (just as the word *pardon* contains *donum,* or 'gift'). Like grace, forgiveness has about it the maddening quality of being undeserved, unmerited, unfair."

Manasseh's prayer of repentance appears in the apocryphal Prayer of Manasseh. Although it is thought to have been written several hundred years after Manasseh lived, the prayer offers a beautiful model of confession of sin and recognition of God's core character of mercy and forgiveness.

PROFILE

PROFILE: MANASSEH

Manasseh didn't deserve God's forgiveness, but he knew God's character well enough to believe that God would give it. Although he had chosen to live without God for much of his life, he held inside a knowledge of the unfailing love and mercy of the One who truly reigned. Abominable as he had been, not even Manasseh was beyond God's grace.

Yet as sincere as his return to God was, Manasseh could reach only so far to undo the evil that had infiltrated Judah as a result of his leadership. After Manasseh's death, his son Amon and the people he ruled soon turned back to idolatry. Manasseh served God for the remainder of his life, but he was powerless to undo the consequences of his earlier actions.

Most certainly, the with-God life changes us and those around us. In the same way, life without God forms us and all who come in contact with us. God's grace is always available, yet, as Dallas Willard writes in *Renovation of the Heart,* "On the path of self-will people eventually come to the place where they cannot choose what God wants and cannot want God. They can only want—themselves!" Our choices matter. The life we live with God, or without God, matters now for our own souls and for the souls of those around us.

Personal Reflection

- Have you ever wondered whether God could ever forgive you for something you did? Do you still wonder? How does Manasseh's story speak to you about God's attitude toward your sin?
- Consider Dallas Willard's words above. How can we pray for ourselves and for those in our lives who seem bent on the path of self-will? Talk with God now about his forgiveness in your life and your struggles with self-will. Thank him for his grace to help you each time you need it.

Judah and Jerusalem of the high places, the sacred poles,*a* and the carved and the cast images. ⁴In his presence they pulled down the altars of the Baals; he demolished the incense altars that stood above them. He broke down the sacred poles *a* and the carved and the cast images; he made dust of them and scattered it over the graves of those who had sacrificed to them. ⁵He also burned the bones of the priests on their altars, and purged Judah and Jerusalem. ⁶In the towns of Manasseh, Ephraim, and Simeon, and as far as Naphtali, in their ruins *b* all around, ⁷he broke down the altars, beat the sacred poles *a* and the images into powder, and demolished all the incense altars throughout all the land of Israel. Then he returned to Jerusalem.

Discovery of the Book of the Law

8 In the eighteenth year of his reign, when he had purged the land and the house, he sent Shaphan son of Azaliah, Maaseiah the governor of the city, and Joah son of Joahaz, the recorder, to repair the house of the LORD his God. ⁹They came to the high priest Hilkiah and delivered the money that had been brought into the house of God, which the Levites, the keepers of the threshold, had collected from Manasseh and Ephraim and from all the remnant of Israel and from all Judah and Benjamin and from the inhabitants of Jerusalem. ¹⁰They delivered it to the workers who had the oversight of the house of the LORD, and the workers who were working in the house of the LORD gave it for repairing and restoring the house. ¹¹They gave it to the carpenters and the builders to buy quarried stone, and timber for binders, and beams for the buildings that the kings of Judah had let go to ruin. ¹²The people did the work faithfully. Over them were appointed the Levites Jahath and Obadiah, of the sons of Merari, along with Zechariah and Meshullam, of the

---

a Heb *Asherim*   *b* Meaning of Heb uncertain

34:8–18 *to repair the house of the LORD.* Josiah reforms the Temple and, in the course of making repairs, finds the book of the law given by Moses. Money was collected from Ephraim, Manasseh, and the remnant of Israel.

sons of the Kohathites, to have oversight. Other Levites, all skillful with instruments of music, 13 were over the burden bearers and directed all who did work in every kind of service; and some of the Levites were scribes, and officials, and gatekeepers.

14 While they were bringing out the money that had been brought into the house of the LORD, the priest Hilkiah found the book of the law of the LORD given through Moses. 15 Hilkiah said to the secretary Shaphan, "I have found the book of the law in the house of the LORD"; and Hilkiah gave the book to Shaphan. 16 Shaphan brought the book to the king, and further reported to the king, "All that was committed to your servants they are doing. 17 They have emptied out the money that was found in the house of the LORD and have delivered it into the hand of the overseers and the workers." 18 The secretary Shaphan informed the king, "The priest Hilkiah has given me a book." Shaphan then read it aloud to the king.

19 When the king heard the words of the law he tore his clothes. 20 Then the king commanded Hilkiah, Ahikam son of Shaphan, Abdon son of Micah, the secretary Shaphan, and the king's servant Asaiah: 21 "Go, inquire of the LORD for me and for those who are left in Israel and in Judah, concerning the words of the book that has been found; for the wrath of the LORD that is poured out on us is great, because our ancestors did not keep the word of the LORD, to act in accordance with all that is written in this book."

The Prophet Huldah Consulted

22 So Hilkiah and those whom the king had sent went to the prophet Huldah, the wife of Shallum son of Tokhath son of Hasrah, keeper of the wardrobe (who lived in Jerusalem in the Second Quarter) and spoke

to her to that effect. 23 She declared to them, "Thus says the LORD, the God of Israel: Tell the man who sent you to me, 24 Thus says the LORD: I will indeed bring disaster upon this place and upon its inhabitants, all the curses that are written in the book that was read before the king of Judah. 25 Because they have forsaken me and have made offerings to other gods, so that they have provoked me to anger with all the works of their hands, my wrath will be poured out on this place and will not be quenched. 26 But as to the king of Judah, who sent you to inquire of the LORD, thus shall you say to him: Thus says the LORD, the God of Israel: Regarding the words that you have heard, 27 because your heart was penitent and you humbled yourself before God when you heard his words against this place and its inhabitants, and you have humbled yourself before me, and have torn your clothes and wept before me, I also have heard you, says the LORD. 28 I will gather you to your ancestors and you shall be gathered to your grave in peace; your eyes shall not see all the disaster that I will bring on this place and its inhabitants." They took the message back to the king.

The Covenant Renewed

29 Then the king sent word and gathered together all the elders of Judah and Jerusalem. 30 The king went up to the house of the LORD, with all the people of Judah, the inhabitants of Jerusalem, the priests and the Levites, all the people both great and small; he read in their hearing all the words of the book of the covenant that had been found in the house of the LORD. 31 The king stood in his place and made a covenant before the LORD, to follow the LORD, keeping his commandments, his decrees, and his statutes, with all his heart and all his soul, to perform the words of the

---

34:21 *inquire of the LORD.* Josiah has his priests and officials inquire about the meaning of the book for him and for those who were left in Israel and in Judah.

34:22–28 *the prophet Huldah.* Huldah promises that the curses written in the book (Deut 27:9–26; 28:15–68) will come upon the land. In a second oracle she congratulates

Josiah for being penitent and humbling himself. Josiah will die in peace and not live to see the disasters that were coming.

34:31–33 *made a covenant before the LORD.* Josiah makes a covenant to follow God's commands, decrees, and statutes. Josiah removes the abominations from the lands of the Israelites and makes all in Israel worship Yahweh.

covenant that were written in this book. ³²Then he made all who were present in Jerusalem and in Benjamin pledge themselves to it. And the inhabitants of Jerusalem acted according to the covenant of God, the God of their ancestors. ³³Josiah took away all the abominations from all the territory that belonged to the people of Israel, and made all who were in Israel worship the LORD their God. All his days they did not turn away from following the LORD the God of their ancestors.

Celebration of the Passover

35 Josiah kept a passover to the LORD in Jerusalem; they slaughtered the passover lamb on the fourteenth day of the first month. ²He appointed the priests to their offices and encouraged them in the service of the house of the LORD. ³He said to the Levites who taught all Israel and who were holy to the LORD, "Put the holy ark in the house that Solomon son of David, king of Israel, built; you need no longer carry it on your shoulders. Now serve the LORD your God and his people Israel. ⁴Make preparations by your ancestral houses by your divisions, following the written directions of King David of Israel and the written directions of his son Solomon. ⁵Take position in the holy place according to the groupings of the ancestral houses of your kindred the people, and let there be Levites for each division of an ancestral house.ᵃ ⁶Slaughter the passover lamb, sanctify yourselves, and on behalf of your kindred make preparations, acting according to the word of the LORD by Moses."

7 Then Josiah contributed to the people, as passover offerings for all that were present, lambs and kids from the flock to the number of thirty thousand, and three thousand bulls; these were from the king's possessions. ⁸His officials contributed willingly to the people, to the priests, and to the Levites. Hilkiah, Zechariah, and Jehiel, the chief officers of the house of God, gave to the priests for the passover offerings two thousand six hundred lambs and kids and three

hundred bulls. ⁹Conaniah also, and his brothers Shemaiah and Nethanel, and Hashabiah and Jeiel and Jozabad, the chiefs of the Levites, gave to the Levites for the passover offerings five thousand lambs and kids and five hundred bulls.

10 When the service had been prepared for, the priests stood in their place, and the Levites in their divisions according to the king's command. ¹¹They slaughtered the passover lamb, and the priests dashed the blood that they receivedᵇ from them, while the Levites did the skinning. ¹²They set aside the burnt offerings so that they might distribute them according to the groupings of the ancestral houses of the people, to offer to the LORD, as it is written in the book of Moses. And they did the same with the bulls. ¹³They roasted the passover lamb with fire according to the ordinance; and they boiled the holy offerings in pots, in caldrons, and in pans, and carried them quickly to all the people. ¹⁴Afterward they made preparations for themselves and for the priests, because the priests the descendants of Aaron were occupied in offering the burnt offerings and the fat parts until night; so the Levites made preparations for themselves and for the priests, the descendants of Aaron. ¹⁵The singers, the descendants of Asaph, were in their place according to the command of David, and Asaph, and Heman, and the king's seer Jeduthun. The gatekeepers were at each gate; they did not need to interrupt their service, for their kindred the Levites made preparations for them.

16 So all the service of the LORD was prepared that day, to keep the passover and to offer burnt offerings on the altar of the LORD, according to the command of King Josiah. ¹⁷The people of Israel who were present kept the passover at that time, and the festival of unleavened bread seven days. ¹⁸No passover like it had been kept in Israel since the days of the prophet Samuel; none of the kings of Israel

a Meaning of Heb uncertain   *b* Heb lacks *that they received*

35:1–19 *kept a passover.* Josiah's Passover was held on the date prescribed in the Pentateuch (Exod 12:1–6). David and Solomon had

established the duties of the Levites, and the slaughter of the animals followed the instructions of Moses.

had kept such a passover as was kept by Josiah, by the priests and the Levites, by all Judah and Israel who were present, and by the inhabitants of Jerusalem. ¹⁹In the eighteenth year of the reign of Josiah this passover was kept.

Defeat by Pharaoh Neco and Death of Josiah

20 After all this, when Josiah had set the temple in order, King Neco of Egypt went up to fight at Carchemish on the Euphrates, and Josiah went out against him. ²¹But Neco*ᵃ* sent envoys to him, saying, "What have I to do with you, king of Judah? I am not coming against you today, but against the house with which I am at war; and God has commanded me to hurry. Cease opposing God, who is with me, so that he will not destroy you." ²²But Josiah would not turn away from him, but disguised himself in order to fight with him. He did not listen to the words of Neco from the mouth of God, but joined battle in the plain of Megiddo. ²³The archers shot King Josiah; and the king said to his servants, "Take me away, for I am badly wounded." ²⁴So his servants took him out of the chariot and carried him in his second chariot*ᵇ* and brought him to Jerusalem. There he died, and was buried in the tombs of his ancestors. All Judah and Jerusalem mourned for Josiah. ²⁵Jeremiah also uttered a lament for Josiah, and all the singing men and singing women have spoken of Josiah in their laments to this day. They made these a custom in Israel; they are recorded in the Laments. ²⁶Now the rest of the acts of Josiah and his faithful deeds in accordance with what is written in the law of the LORD, ²⁷and his acts, first and last, are written in the Book of the Kings of Israel and Judah.

Reign of Jehoahaz

36 The people of the land took Jehoahaz son of Josiah and made him king to succeed his father in Jerusalem. ²Jehoahaz was twenty-three years old when he began to reign; he reigned three months in Jerusalem. ³Then the king of Egypt deposed him in Jerusalem and laid on the land a tribute of one hundred talents of silver and one talent of gold. ⁴The king of Egypt made his brother Eliakim king over Judah and Jerusalem, and changed his name to Jehoiakim; but Neco took his brother Jehoahaz and carried him to Egypt.

Reign and Captivity of Jehoiakim

5 Jehoiakim was twenty-five years old when he began to reign; he reigned eleven years in Jerusalem. He did what was evil in the sight of the LORD his God. ⁶Against him King Nebuchadnezzar of Babylon came up, and bound him with fetters to take him to Babylon. ⁷Nebuchadnezzar also carried some of the vessels of the house of the LORD to Babylon and put them in his palace in Babylon. ⁸Now the rest of the acts of Jehoiakim, and the abominations that he did, and what was found against him, are written in the Book of the Kings of Israel and Judah; and his son Jehoiachin succeeded him.

Reign and Captivity of Jehoiachin

9 Jehoiachin was eight years old when he began to reign; he reigned three months and ten days in Jerusalem. He did what was evil in the sight of the LORD. ¹⁰In the spring of the

a Heb *he*   *b* Or *the chariot of his deputy*

35:18 *the days of the prophet Samuel.* This is the most unique Passover since the time of Samuel, perhaps because of the leading role the Levites play in it.

35:20–24 *King Neco of Egypt.* Neco tried to prop up the remains of the Assyrian Empire as a buffer against the Neo-Babylonian Empire (but cf. 2 Kings 23:29). The Chronicler criticizes Josiah for not listening to the word of God transmitted by Neco. The archers shot Josiah at Megiddo, but he died in Jerusalem. In 2 Kings 23:29–30 Josiah dies at Megiddo.

36:1–4 *Jehoahaz son of Josiah.* Neco deposes Jehoahaz, takes him to Egypt, and makes his brother Eliakim king under the name Jehoiakim.

36:5–7 *did what was evil.* Jehoiakim's reign is condemned by the Chronicler. Nebuchadnezzar takes him in fetters to Babylon, where he also deposits vessels from the Temple.

36:9–21 *Jehoiachin was eight years old.* Jehoiachin rules three months and then he too is taken to Babylon. He is replaced by Zedekiah, his brother. According to 2 Kings 24:17, Zedekiah was the uncle of Jehoiachin. Zedekiah does not

year King Nebuchadnezzar sent and brought him to Babylon, along with the precious vessels of the house of the LORD, and made his brother Zedekiah king over Judah and Jerusalem.

Reign of Zedekiah

11 Zedekiah was twenty-one years old when he began to reign; he reigned eleven years in Jerusalem. 12He did what was evil in the sight of the LORD his God. He did not humble himself before the prophet Jeremiah who spoke from the mouth of the LORD. 13He also rebelled against King Nebuchadnezzar, who had made him swear by God; he stiffened his neck and hardened his heart against turning to the LORD, the God of Israel. 14All the leading priests and the people also were exceedingly unfaithful, following all the abominations of the nations; and they polluted the house of the LORD that he had consecrated in Jerusalem.

The Fall of Jerusalem

15 The LORD, the God of their ancestors, sent persistently to them by his messengers, because he had compassion on his people and on his dwelling place; 16but they kept mocking the messengers of God, despising his words, and scoffing at his prophets, until the wrath of the LORD against his people became so great that there was no remedy.

17 Therefore he brought up against them the king of the Chaldeans, who killed their youths with the sword in the house of their sanctuary, and had no compassion on young man or young woman, the aged or the feeble; he gave them all into his hand. 18All the vessels of the house of God, large and small, and the treasures of the house of the LORD, and the treasures of the king and of his officials, all these he brought to Babylon. 19They burned the house of God, broke down the wall of Jerusalem, burned all its palaces with fire, and destroyed all its precious vessels. 20He took into exile in Babylon those who had escaped from the sword, and they became servants to him and to his sons until the establishment of the kingdom of Persia, 21to fulfill the word of the LORD by the mouth of Jeremiah, until the land had made up for its sabbaths. All the days that it lay desolate it kept sabbath, to fulfill seventy years.

Cyrus Proclaims Liberty for the Exiles

22 In the first year of King Cyrus of Persia, in fulfillment of the word of the LORD spoken by Jeremiah, the LORD stirred up the spirit of King Cyrus of Persia so that he sent a herald throughout all his kingdom and also declared in a written edict: 23"Thus says King Cyrus of Persia: The LORD, the God of heaven, has given me all the kingdoms of the earth, and he has charged me to build him a house at Jerusalem, which is in Judah. Whoever is among you of all his people, may the LORD his God be with him! Let him go up."

---

humble himself before Jeremiah. The priests and the people are exceedingly unfaithful and reject God's numerous prophetic messengers. Hence there is no remedy for the wrath of God. The Temple vessels are brought to Babylon, and the Temple itself is burned down.

36:21 *to fulfill the word of the LORD.* The exile lasted seventy years to fulfill the word of Yahweh spoken by Jeremiah (25:11–12; 29:10). During the exile the land kept its Sabbaths.

36:22–23 *King Cyrus of Persia.* In his first year, the Persian king, stirred up by the spirit of Yahweh, authorizes the return of the exiles and the rebuilding of the Temple.

EZRA

In the Hebrew Bible the books of Ezra and Nehemiah were originally one volume. Although the authorship of these books is uncertain, talmudic tradition credits Ezra as the primary writer for not only Ezra and Nehemiah, but also for Chronicles as well. Overall, the works provide detailed and significant information concerning the return of the Hebrew people to Jerusalem from Babylonian captivity and the reformation of the religion of the returned captives during the Persian period.

Traditionally, Ezra and Nehemiah have not created much of a stir within the Christian community. There are few if any memorable passages in these books. What sermons are preached from this material usually center around Nehemiah's "construction of the walls campaign" with the hope that his model of sacrifice and determination will inspire congregations to be more generous with their building-fund contributions. Compared to the teachings of Jesus or the writings of Paul, Ezra and Nehemiah appear rather provincial and sometimes primitive in their understanding of God. The books contain no overt miracles, little if any groundbreaking theology, and, with the exception of the walls being completed in fifty-two days, no bulletin-board material for church libraries.

Yet Ezra and Nehemiah play an important role in spiritual formation for the Church, especially in today's narcissistic and schizophrenic culture. The problems that the priest Ezra and the governor Nehemiah face are not unlike the issues the Church faces today. Identity as the People of God and living a life of faithful obedience continue to be challenges, as in the times of Ezra and Nehemiah. Church life today too often reflects the materialism, greed, and self-centeredness of the popular culture. Jesus said the Church is to be the "salt of the earth" (Matt 5:13). It does not take much salt to make a difference, but somehow the Church has managed to be rather bland in today's culture. A close reading of Ezra and Nehemiah may help remind the Church of the importance of being a faithful people.

The work of Ezra and Nehemiah centers on two critical problems. First, are the

See also *"The With-God Life"* essay for this section of the Bible,
"The People of God in Restoration," pp. 1355–59.

Jews returning from captivity the true People of God or mere impostors? And second, could the exilic community that had lived in a pagan culture for several generations recover its spiritual edge? How could the Jews who returned to Jerusalem be reformed as God's holy people? From a superficial vantage point, one might consider the small population of Jerusalem and the lack of a defensive barricade to be the more immediate problems for the returned community of faith. Although these difficulties were addressed, Ezra and Nehemiah considered the first priority to be the reestablishment of Israel's identity as the People of God. Thus the books of Ezra and Nehemiah focus on spiritual formation.

Identity as the People of God

It was imperative to Ezra and Nehemiah to validate the returned Jews as the true Israel. Both books intend to show that the Israel of Ezra and Nehemiah is none other than the Israel of Moses and David. From the first verse in the book of Ezra, the restoration of the people to Jerusalem is viewed as a fulfillment of the prophetic oracle of Jeremiah. Furthermore, the Temple vessels, plundered by Nebuchadnezzar in 587/586 BC, are returned to the newly constructed Temple in Jerusalem as a symbol that Yahweh has indeed set his stamp of approval on this second exodus. Even the names of the returned captives are related to earlier generations of Israelites in an attempt to connect present with past.

By establishing linkage with the traditions of the past, the Church develops a clearer picture of its identity as a community of faith. Much like scanning the pages of the family album of our grandparents gives us a sense of who we are, becoming acquainted with the traditions of previous generations of faith reminds us of who we are in the Church. The Church has family members like Abraham and Moses, Peter and Paul, but also those like Augustine and Luther—what a family! And each generation of faith contributes a unique and special perspective. The music and liturgy of past generations continue to bless and nurture the Church today, because they have been tried and tested in the crucible of life again and again. Cultural relevance does not mean severing ties with our faith history.

It was not enough, however, for the returning Jews to be linked to the Israel of old; the books of Ezra and Nehemiah had to challenge the people to recommit themselves to what it meant to be a people of faith in their own day. It was important to be related to the Israel of old through sacred traditions, but now the new community had to make its own spiritual legacy. The people had to learn again the disciplines of faith if they were going to be a "holy people."

Spiritual Formation

Worship. The story of Ezra begins with Cyrus issuing a decree that the captive Jews are free "to go up to Jerusalem . . . and rebuild the house of the LORD" (Ezra 1:3). It is not Israel as a nation with which the author is primarily preoccupied, but Israel as a worshiping community. Worship is the intrinsic reason-to-be for God's people. Not long after the arrival of Zerubbabel and his people in Jerusalem during the first return, the altar of the Lord is rebuilt and sacrifices initiated (Ezra 3). With the completion of the Temple, the people meet in celebration and worship (Ezra 6). After the reading of the law, the people once again erupt into worship "with their faces to the ground" (Neh 8:6). In Ezra and Nehemiah prayer, confession of sin, and fasting are all incorporated into the worship experience. Worship would provide the mold that would forge these returned Jews into the People of God. Sometimes worship was joyful and celebratory, and sometimes the people could not stop crying. The Church has many things to do—evangelism, pastoral ministry, teaching, and preaching—but the most important is worship. The house of God is first and foremost a "house of prayer."

The Word. The spiritual reforms of Ezra and Nehemiah embrace Scripture as essential to the life of spiritual formation. Many scholars believe, in fact, that it was during this time that Israel became a "People of the Book." From this point forward in the life of Israel, Scripture would play an indispensable role. The books of Moses guide the reforms of Ezra and Nehemiah by reminding the people of the obligations of covenant. But not only does God's Word remind Israel of the duties of faith; the sacred text also demands obedience. Thus Scripture is not just a book to be used for information; the written word is, rather, an agent of transformation. The Bible does not serve merely as an interesting book in the pew, but rather as a powerful story that shapes and transforms life. Watching home movies of someone else's family is rather boring, but watching movies of one's own family—now *that* is a different story. The story of faith is a story of our family. And it has the power to change lives.

Justice. The prophets Amos, Hosea, Isaiah, and Micah, more than a hundred years before the Babylonian captivity, vigorously voiced their concern that Israel was ignoring the plight of the poor and the marginalized of society. God's own compassion for the poor was highlighted by his concern for the Israelites when they were captives in Egypt, and he would not now in Ezra's day tolerate his people's abuse of the impoverished. Ezra and Nehemiah are quick to point out that the returned Jews are once again mistreating the "powerless" members of the community (Neh 5:5). Reforms are immediately instituted to protect these weaker members and to restore to them the means to live with dignity. Compassion for the less fortunate is one of the marks of a child of God (Matt 25:31–46). No true spiritual formation can take place without concern for people on the margins of life.

Spirit. Sensitivity and reliance on the Spirit of God are not uncommon events in the record of Ezra and Nehemiah. Such expressions as the "hand of God" or the "help of God" signify this Spirit dynamic. It is a subtle yet strong element in the reformation of the new community. The "hand of God" determines the fate of Israel's destiny throughout Ezra and Nehemiah. Both leaders reveal hearts and minds receptive to the working of the Spirit. The Spirit of God is a powerful yet gentle presence. The Spirit does not enter where the door is closed and the lock bolted. God's Holy Spirit enters only where there is a welcome sign.

Holiness. Critics have reserved harsh judgment for the reforms that led to family separation in Ezra and Nehemiah. The sending away of foreign wives (Ezra 9–10) and of anyone outside the community of faith (Neh 9; 13) has been viewed as an

MIGRANTS

attempt to build an exclusive community (see notes on Ezra 9). The context of these reforms weighs heavily in these radical decisions. The very faith of Israel was in a life-or-death struggle, and the reforms served to strengthen Israel's understanding of the cost of obedience. Nehemiah's instructions for the sons and daughters of Israel not to take foreign spouses somewhat mitigate the harshness of the reforms (Neh 10; 13). On the other hand, the emphasis on keeping the Sabbath and obeying the covenant requirements provided a needed corrective to Israel's religious permissiveness. Living a life of holiness separates believers from the world, yet Jesus also bids us to be "in" the world. In many ways the early Church modeled how to live in a worldly culture without submitting to the spirit of the age.

Spiritual Formation: Only a Beginning

Ezra and Nehemiah recognized that the community of faith was in danger of spiritually imploding. In order to reclaim their identity as the People of God, they reinstituted disciplines of the spiritual life learned by previous generations of faith—worship, prayer, fasting, social justice, sensitivity to the Spirit, and many others. Ezra and Nehemiah believed they could develop an ideal spiritual community by closely observing the ways and traditions of the past. Unfortunately, even after all the reforms, the postexilic community was far less than ideal. Soon its spiritual conduct became a source of pride and arrogance. By the time of Jesus, Israel had once again plunged into spiritual barrenness. First-century Judaism had deteriorated into an endless series of disputes on the Torah. There is always a danger for the person or community who takes the way of God seriously to make the Spiritual Disciplines an end in themselves. They merely allow our hearts to be compliant to the only One who can truly transform us. Faith is all about God. The prayer of one who lived long ago continues to guide, for the beginning of all true spiritual formation is the confession, "You are the Lord, you alone" (Neh 9:6).

—Michael D. Riley

End of the Babylonian Captivity

1 In the first year of King Cyrus of Persia, in order that the word of the Lord by the mouth of Jeremiah might be accomplished, the Lord stirred up the spirit of King Cyrus of Persia so that he sent a herald throughout all his kingdom, and also in a written edict declared:

2 "Thus says King Cyrus of Persia: The Lord, the God of heaven, has given me all the kingdoms of the earth, and he has charged me to build him a house at Jerusalem in Judah. ³Any of those among you who are of his people—may their God be with them!—are now permitted to go up to Jerusalem in Judah, and rebuild the house of the

---

1:1–4 *The Lord stirred up the spirit of King Cyrus.* To most casual observers, the rich and powerful leaders and rulers of the world determine the course of history. But there are those who view life through the lenses of faith and see the hand of God in history. For people with such vision, history is being guided and pushed along by an unseen hand. From this perspective a powerful king does not arbitrarily make a decision to free captive Jews, but rather is unwittingly an instrument of "the God of heaven."

LORD, the God of Israel—he is the God who is in Jerusalem; [4]and let all survivors, in whatever place they reside, be assisted by the people of their place with silver and gold, with goods and with animals, besides freewill offerings for the house of God in Jerusalem."

5 The heads of the families of Judah and Benjamin, and the priests and the Levites—everyone whose spirit God had stirred—got ready to go up and rebuild the house of the LORD in Jerusalem. [6]All their neighbors aided them with silver vessels, with gold, with goods, with animals, and with valuable gifts, besides all that was freely offered. [7]King Cyrus himself brought out the vessels of the house of the LORD that Nebuchadnezzar had carried away from Jerusalem and placed in the house of his gods. [8]King Cyrus of Persia had them released into the charge of Mithredath the treasurer, who counted them out to Sheshbazzar the prince of Judah. [9]And this was the inventory: gold basins, thirty; silver basins, one thousand; knives,[a] twenty-nine; [10]gold bowls, thirty; other silver bowls, four hundred ten; other vessels, one thousand; [11]the total of the gold and silver vessels was

five thousand four hundred. All these Sheshbazzar brought up, when the exiles were brought up from Babylonia to Jerusalem.

List of the Returned Exiles

2 Now these were the people of the province who came from those captive exiles whom King Nebuchadnezzar of Babylon had carried captive to Babylonia; they returned to Jerusalem and Judah, all to their own towns. [2]They came with Zerubbabel, Jeshua, Nehemiah, Seraiah, Reelaiah, Mordecai, Bilshan, Mispar, Bigvai, Rehum, and Baanah.

The number of the Israelite people: [3]the descendants of Parosh, two thousand one hundred seventy-two. [4]Of Shephatiah, three hundred seventy-two. [5]Of Arah, seven hundred seventy-five. [6]Of Pahath-moab, namely the descendants of Jeshua and Joab, two thousand eight hundred twelve. [7]Of Elam, one thousand two hundred fifty-four. [8]Of Zattu, nine hundred forty-five. [9]Of Zaccai, seven hundred sixty. [10]Of Bani, six hundred

a Vg: Meaning of Heb uncertain

1:3 *rebuild the house of the LORD.* Worship has always been at the center of our relationship with God. The rebuilding of the Temple would serve as a visible reminder that worship is the highest priority of God's children. A church's life consists of many wonderful and good works, but the most important of these is worship.

1:5–6 *everyone whose spirit God had stirred.* The People of God often find the comfort of this world difficult to abandon for the more demanding and disciplined life of faith. There is evidence that the Jews in captivity had more than made themselves at home in Babylon. A story such as Daniel's, about faithfulness, only serves to underscore that all too many exiled Jews compromised their religious convictions. Consequently, God had to stir the hearts of his own children as well as the heart of Cyrus. The Church must continually be attentive to the stirrings of God; otherwise, the Church nods off into spiritual slumber, sedated by the "culture of Babylon."

1:7–11 *brought out the vessels . . . that Nebuchadnezzar had carried away.* King Cyrus gave the vessels of the Temple of Solomon back

to the returning Jews. These Temple utensils would link the present community of believers with the traditions and faith of past generations. Biblical faith is multilayered, with each generation of faith contributing to the growth of God's people. Ancient traditions and symbols provide deep biblical roots that are necessary in order to guide contemporary expressions of worship and practice, lest they become mere fads of popular culture.

2:1–63 *Now these were the people.* All too frequently readers of the Bible brush past these lists of names in Scripture, thinking they are of little importance. The often strange and obscure names, however, deserve pause and reflection. These names represent families who abandoned a secure life in Babylon in exchange for an uncertain future in desolate Jerusalem. But the names also trigger memories of indebtedness for future generations of faith. Without the legacy of our spiritual ancestors, the faith of the present would be greatly impoverished. The "great . . . cloud of witnesses" (Heb 12:1) has illuminated well the path to God.

forty-two. [11]Of Bebai, six hundred twenty-three. [12]Of Azgad, one thousand two hundred twenty-two. [13]Of Adonikam, six hundred sixty-six. [14]Of Bigvai, two thousand fifty-six. [15]Of Adin, four hundred fifty-four. [16]Of Ater, namely of Hezekiah, ninety-eight. [17]Of Bezai, three hundred twenty-three. [18]Of Jorah, one hundred twelve. [19]Of Hashum, two hundred twenty-three. [20]Of Gibbar, ninety-five. [21]Of Bethlehem, one hundred twenty-three. [22]The people of Netophah, fifty-six. [23]Of Anathoth, one hundred twenty-eight. [24]The descendants of Azmaveth, forty-two. [25]Of Kiriatharim, Chephirah, and Beeroth, seven hundred forty-three. [26]Of Ramah and Geba, six hundred twenty-one. [27]The people of Michmas, one hundred twenty-two. [28]Of Bethel and Ai, two hundred twenty-three. [29]The descendants of Nebo, fifty-two. [30]Of Magbish, one hundred fifty-six. [31]Of the other Elam, one thousand two hundred fifty-four. [32]Of Harim, three hundred twenty. [33]Of Lod, Hadid, and Ono, seven hundred twenty-five. [34]Of Jericho, three hundred forty-five. [35]Of Senaah, three thousand six hundred thirty.

[36] The priests: the descendants of Jedaiah, of the house of Jeshua, nine hundred seventy-three. [37]Of Immer, one thousand fifty-two. [38]Of Pashhur, one thousand two hundred forty-seven. [39]Of Harim, one thousand seventeen.

[40] The Levites: the descendants of Jeshua and Kadmiel, of the descendants of Hodaviah, seventy-four. [41]The singers: the descendants of Asaph, one hundred twenty-eight. [42]The descendants of the gatekeepers: of Shallum, of Ater, of Talmon, of Akkub, of Hatita, and of Shobai, in all one hundred thirty-nine.

[43] The temple servants: the descendants of Ziha, Hasupha, Tabbaoth, [44]Keros, Siaha, Padon, [45]Lebanah, Hagabah, Akkub, [46]Hagab, Shamlai, Hanan, [47]Giddel, Gahar, Rea-iah, [48]Rezin, Nekoda, Gazzam, [49]Uzza, Paseah, Besai, [50]Asnah, Meunim, Nephisim, [51]Bakbuk, Hakupha, Harhur, [52]Bazluth, Mehida, Harsha, [53]Barkos, Sisera, Temah, [54]Neziah, and Hatipha.

[55] The descendants of Solomon's servants: Sotai, Hassophereth, Peruda, [56]Jaalah, Darkon, Giddel, [57]Shephatiah, Hattil, Pochereth-hazzebaim, and Ami.

[58] All the temple servants and the descendants of Solomon's servants were three hundred ninety-two.

[59] The following were those who came up from Tel-melah, Tel-harsha, Cherub, Addan, and Immer, though they could not prove their families or their descent, whether they belonged to Israel: [60]the descendants of Delaiah, Tobiah, and Nekoda, six hundred fifty-two. [61]Also, of the descendants of the priests: the descendants of Habaiah, Hakkoz, and Barzillai (who had married one of the daughters of Barzillai the Gileadite, and was called by their name). [62]These looked for their entries in the genealogical records, but they were not found there, and so they were excluded from the priesthood as unclean; [63]the governor told them that they were not to partake of the most holy food, until there should be a priest to consult Urim and Thummim.

[64] The whole assembly together was forty-two thousand three hundred sixty, [65]besides their male and female servants, of whom there were seven thousand three hundred thirty-seven; and they had two hundred male and female singers. [66]They had seven hundred thirty-six horses, two hundred forty-five mules, [67]four hundred thirty-five camels, and six thousand seven hundred twenty donkeys.

[68] As soon as they came to the house of the LORD in Jerusalem, some of the heads of families made freewill offerings for the house of God, to erect it on its site. [69]According to

---

2:68–69 *families made freewill offerings for the house of God.* The families who arrived in Jerusalem found a city in ruins. The walls of the city had been leveled, the houses lay in piles of rubble, and even the population had dwindled to only a few thousand. Yet the first priority for the returning exiles was to tend to the "house of God." In the modern church scene the "house of God" often seems the last priority. On any given Sunday in America, according to denominational reports, less than half of church members attend services.

their resources they gave to the building fund sixty-one thousand darics of gold, five thousand minas of silver, and one hundred priestly robes.

70 The priests, the Levites, and some of the people lived in Jerusalem and its vicinity;[a] and the singers, the gatekeepers, and the temple servants lived in their towns, and all Israel in their towns.

Worship Restored at Jerusalem

3 When the seventh month came, and the Israelites were in the towns, the people gathered together in Jerusalem. [2]Then Jeshua son of Jozadak, with his fellow priests, and Zerubbabel son of Shealtiel with his kin set out to build the altar of the God of Israel, to offer burnt offerings on it, as prescribed in the law of Moses the man of God. [3]They set up the altar on its foundation, because they were in dread of the neighboring peoples, and they offered burnt offerings upon it to the Lord, morning and evening. [4]And they kept the festival of booths,[a] as prescribed, and offered the daily burnt offerings by number according to the ordinance, as required for each day, [5]and after that the regular burnt offerings, the offerings at the new moon and at all the sacred festivals of the Lord, and the offerings of everyone who made a freewill offering to the Lord. [6]From the first day of the seventh month they began to offer burnt offerings to the Lord. But the foundation of the temple of the Lord was not yet laid. [7]So they gave money to the masons and the carpenters, and food, drink, and oil to the Sidonians and the Tyrians to bring cedar trees from Lebanon to the sea, to Joppa, according to the grant that they had from King Cyrus of Persia.

Foundation Laid for the Temple

8 In the second year after their arrival at the house of God at Jerusalem, in the second month, Zerubbabel son of Shealtiel and Jeshua son of Jozadak made a beginning, together with the rest of their people, the priests and the Levites and all who had come to Jerusalem from the captivity. They appointed the Levites, from twenty years old and upward, to have the oversight of the work on the house of the Lord. [9]And Jeshua with his sons and his kin, and Kadmiel and his sons, Binnui and Hodaviah[b] along with the sons of Henadad, the Levites, their sons and kin, together took charge of the workers in the house of God.

10 When the builders laid the foundation of the temple of the Lord, the priests in their vestments were stationed to praise the Lord with trumpets, and the Levites, the sons of

a 1 Esdras 5:46: Heb lacks *lived in Jerusalem and its vicinity*   b Or *tabernacles*; Heb *succoth*
c Compare 2:40; Neh 7:43; 1 Esdras 5:58: Heb *sons of Judah*

3:1–3 *his kin set out to build the altar of the God of Israel.* Authentic response to God must never be manipulated or coerced, but should issue from heartfelt gratitude for the work of God in our lives. How refreshing that in these verses there is no summons or official call for the people to come together to build the altar. The Church should never have to beg people to do the work of God. Cross bearing is a voluntary act of love, not a burden for the unlucky.

3:4–6 *as prescribed . . . according to the ordinance.* The construction of the altar and the observance of the sacrifices followed strictly the ancient traditions of Moses. The resettled community recognized time and again the importance of continuity with the Mosaic tradition. "Tradition" need not be a bad word in the life of the Church. In challenging and confusing times, tradition can give guidance and direction.

3:8–13 *When the builders laid the foundation.* Worship began in the Temple even before construction was completed, just as true worship begins long before people enter the sanctuary.

Responding
3:10–13 WORSHIP. Worship experiences vary. Some worshipers shout for joy, others laugh, while still others weep. Each of us comes to worship with a different history, and God mysteriously touches our hearts at their point of greatest need. How does God meet you in worship? *See also* Spiritual Disciplines Index.

Asaph, with cymbals, according to the directions of King David of Israel; [11]and they sang responsively, praising and giving thanks to the LORD,

"For he is good,
for his steadfast love endures forever
toward Israel."

And all the people responded with a great shout when they praised the LORD, because the foundation of the house of the LORD was laid. [12]But many of the priests and Levites and heads of families, old people who had seen the first house on its foundations, wept with a loud voice when they saw this house, though many shouted aloud for joy, [13]so that the people could not distinguish the sound of the joyful shout from the sound of the people's weeping, for the people shouted so loudly that the sound was heard far away.

Resistance to Rebuilding the Temple

4 When the adversaries of Judah and Benjamin heard that the returned exiles were building a temple to the LORD, the God of Israel, [2]they approached Zerubbabel and the heads of families and said to them, "Let us build with you, for we worship your God as you do, and we have been sacrificing to him ever since the days of King Esar-haddon of Assyria who brought us here." [3]But Zerubbabel, Jeshua, and the rest of the heads of families in Israel said to them, "You shall have no part with us in building a house to our God; but we alone will build to the LORD, the God of Israel, as King Cyrus of Persia has commanded us."

[4]Then the people of the land discour-

4:1–4 *the people of the land discouraged the people of Judah.* It should be no surprise that there was opposition to the rebuilding of the Temple. Seldom is the work of the kingdom accomplished without conflict. In this case the opposition came in the guise of support. The "adversaries" offered to help in the construction of the Temple, but Zerubbabel and the other leaders quickly declined their offer of assistance. Although it was true that the "adversaries" worshiped Yahweh, they also paid homage to a number of other gods as well. The returned exiles were well aware that their captivity was a

aged the people of Judah, and made them afraid to build, [5]and they bribed officials to frustrate their plan throughout the reign of King Cyrus of Persia and until the reign of King Darius of Persia.

Rebuilding of Jerusalem Opposed

[6] In the reign of Ahasuerus, in his accession year, they wrote an accusation against the inhabitants of Judah and Jerusalem.

[7] And in the days of Artaxerxes, Bishlam and Mithredath and Tabeel and the rest of their associates wrote to King Artaxerxes of Persia; the letter was written in Aramaic and translated. *a* [8]Rehum the royal deputy and Shimshai the scribe wrote a letter against Jerusalem to King Artaxerxes as follows [9](then Rehum the royal deputy, Shimshai the scribe, and the rest of their associates, the judges, the envoys, the officials, the Persians, the people of Erech, the Babylonians, the people of Susa, that is, the Elamites, [10]and the rest of the nations whom the great and noble Osnappar deported and settled in the cities of Samaria and in the rest of the province Beyond the River wrote—and now [11]this is a copy of the letter that they sent):

"To King Artaxerxes: Your servants, the people of the province Beyond the River, send greeting. And now [12]may it be known to the king that the Jews who came up from you to us have gone to Jerusalem. They are rebuilding that rebellious and wicked city; they are

---

a Heb adds *in Aramaic,* indicating that 4.8-6.18 is in Aramaic. Another interpretation is *The letter was written in the Aramaic script and set forth in the Aramaic language*

---

result of religious syncretism. In the centuries leading up to Israel's destruction, Israel had never completely abandoned God; it had just added a few other gods to its religious shopping cart (see 2 Kings 17:24–41). Today many sensitive people struggle with intolerant religions. Hatred that all too often leads to bloodshed between competing religions is certainly still a bane of modern civilization. The incarnational life of being "in" the world without being "of" the world continues to be one of faith's greatest challenges.

finishing the walls and repairing the foundations. [13]Now may it be known to the king that, if this city is rebuilt and the walls finished, they will not pay tribute, custom, or toll, and the royal revenue will be reduced. [14]Now because we share the salt of the palace and it is not fitting for us to witness the king's dishonor, therefore we send and inform the king, [15]so that a search may be made in the annals of your ancestors. You will discover in the annals that this is a rebellious city, hurtful to kings and provinces, and that sedition was stirred up in it from long ago. On that account this city was laid waste. [16]We make known to the king that, if this city is rebuilt and its walls finished, you will then have no possession in the province Beyond the River."

17 The king sent an answer: "To Rehum the royal deputy and Shimshai the scribe and the rest of their associates who live in Samaria and in the rest of the province Beyond the River, greeting. And now [18]the letter that you sent to us has been read in translation before me. [19]So I made a decree, and someone searched and discovered that this city has risen against kings from long ago, and that rebellion and sedition have been made in it. [20]Jerusalem has had mighty kings who ruled over the whole province Beyond the River, to whom tribute, custom, and toll were paid. [21]Therefore issue an order that these people be made to cease, and that this city not be rebuilt, until I make a decree. [22]Moreover, take care not to be slack in this matter; why should damage grow to the hurt of the king?"

23 Then when the copy of King Artaxerxes' letter was read before Rehum and the scribe Shimshai and their associates, they hurried to the Jews in Jerusalem and by force and power made them cease. [24]At that time the work on the house of God in Jerusalem stopped and was discontinued until the second year of the reign of King Darius of Persia.

Restoration of the Temple Resumed

5 Now the prophets, Haggai[a] and Zechariah son of Iddo, prophesied to the Jews who were in Judah and Jerusalem, in the name of the God of Israel who was over them. [2]Then Zerubbabel son of Shealtiel and Jeshua son of Jozadak set out to rebuild the house of God in Jerusalem; and with them were the prophets of God, helping them.

3 At the same time Tattenai the governor of the province Beyond the River and Shethar-bozenai and their associates came to them and spoke to them thus, "Who gave you a decree to build this house and to finish this structure?" [4]They[b] also asked them this, "What are the names of the men who are building this building?" [5]But the eye of their God was upon the elders of the Jews, and they did not stop them until a report reached Darius and then answer was returned by letter in reply to it.

6 The copy of the letter that Tattenai the governor of the province Beyond the River and Shethar-bozenai and his associates the envoys who were in the province Beyond the River sent to King Darius; [7]they sent him a report, in which was written as follows: "To Darius the king, all peace! [8]May it be known to the king that we went to the province of Judah, to the house of the great God. It is being built of hewn stone, and timber is laid in the walls; this work is being done diligently and prospers in their hands. [9]Then we spoke to those elders and asked them, 'Who gave you a decree to build this house and to finish this structure?' [10]We also asked them their names, for your information, so that we might write down the names of the men at their head. [11]This was their reply to us: 'We are the servants of the God of heaven and earth, and we are rebuilding the house that was built many

a Aram adds *the prophet*   b Gk Syr: Aram *We*

5:5 *the eye of their God was upon the elders.* God's watchful care over his children is one of the recurring themes of the Bible. Without question there are periods in life when God's presence seems distant, but in retrospect faith sees how God works "good" out of the most evil circumstances of life.

5:11–16 *We are the servants of the God of heaven and earth.* So responded the Jews, when asked to identify themselves. Christians publicly identify with God when they are baptized in the name of the Father, Son, and Holy Spirit. But one's recognition as a child of God is also borne out in service. Jesus said that his disciples would

years ago, which a great king of Israel built and finished. ¹²But because our ancestors had angered the God of heaven, he gave them into the hand of King Nebuchadnezzar of Babylon, the Chaldean, who destroyed this house and carried away the people to Babylonia. ¹³However, King Cyrus of Babylon, in the first year of his reign, made a decree that this house of God should be rebuilt. ¹⁴Moreover, the gold and silver vessels of the house of God, which Nebuchadnezzar had taken out of the temple in Jerusalem and had brought into the temple of Babylon, these King Cyrus took out of the temple of Babylon, and they were delivered to a man named Sheshbazzar, whom he had made governor. ¹⁵He said to him, "Take these vessels; go and put them in the temple in Jerusalem, and let the house of God be rebuilt on its site." ¹⁶Then this Sheshbazzar came and laid the foundations of the house of God in Jerusalem; and from that time until now it has been under construction, and it is not yet finished.' ¹⁷And now, if it seems good to the king, have a search made in the royal archives there in Babylon, to see whether a decree was issued by King Cyrus for the rebuilding of this house of God in Jerusalem. Let the king send us his pleasure in this matter."

The Decree of Darius

6 Then King Darius made a decree, and they searched the archives where the documents were stored in Babylon. ²But it was in Ecbatana, the capital in the province

of Media, that a scroll was found on which this was written: "A record. ³In the first year of his reign, King Cyrus issued a decree: Concerning the house of God at Jerusalem, let the house be rebuilt, the place where sacrifices are offered and burnt offerings are brought;ᵃ its height shall be sixty cubits and its width sixty cubits, ⁴with three courses of hewn stones and one course of timber; let the cost be paid from the royal treasury. ⁵Moreover, let the gold and silver vessels of the house of God, which Nebuchadnezzar took out of the temple in Jerusalem and brought to Babylon, be restored and brought back to the temple in Jerusalem, each to its place; you shall put them in the house of God."

6 "Now you, Tattenai, governor of the province Beyond the River, Shethar-bozenai, and you, their associates, the envoys in the province Beyond the River, keep away; ⁷let the work on this house of God alone; let the governor of the Jews and the elders of the Jews rebuild this house of God on its site. ⁸Moreover I make a decree regarding what you shall do for these elders of the Jews for the rebuilding of this house of God: the cost is to be paid to these people, in full and without delay, from the royal revenue, the tribute of the province Beyond the River. ⁹Whatever is needed—young bulls, rams, or sheep for burnt offerings to the God of heaven, wheat, salt, wine, or oil, as the priests in Jerusalem re-

ᵃ Meaning of Aram uncertain

be known by their love for one another (John 13:35). To be a servant of God puts us squarely in the service of others.

5:12 *because our ancestors had angered the God of heaven.* Jerusalem fell to the Babylonians in 587/586 BC not because the walls of the city were not strong enough or because its armies were not powerful enough. The city of David was defeated because the nation broke covenant with its Creator. Following the path of God does not guarantee that life will be free from pain and hardship, but rejecting his way is a sure recipe for ruin. Life is lived best when it is lived in faithful obedience to "the God of heaven."

6:5 *each to its place.* Meticulous care was taken to ensure that the "house of God" was properly built and furnished. Every vessel was placed in its former position. As the returned Jews reinstituted worship practice in Jerusalem, there was a great concern to do things right. God's work is not haphazard, a kind of fly-by-the-seat-of-your-pants effort. The planning and coordinating of worship services, hours of sermon study by the pastor, and thoughtful prayers by the worshipers do not quench the stirrings of the Spirit. On the contrary, deliberate and intentional preparation for entering into God's presence rids the mind and heart of trivial and worldly distractions.

EZRA

The Devoted Student

Selected Scriptures: *Ezra 1; 7–10; Nehemiah 8–10*

Some eighty years after the first Israelite captives in Babylon were allowed to return to Jerusalem, Ezra too made his way back. In fact, the Persian king Artaxerxes commissioned Ezra to return to Jerusalem and to take with him priests and other Temple servants to help lead the people in the worship of God.

Captivity had acted to purify the Jews in a spiritual sense. After cycling in and out of idolatry and unfaithfulness during the years in the wilderness and the Promised Land, finally, during the captivity in Babylon, the Jews took on the daily discipline of worship and the study of Scripture. From this period forward, God's law became a regular focus of Jewish life, and leaders, like the scribe Ezra, who immersed themselves in God's law held great sway over the people.

God had chosen Ezra to be the spiritual leader of the Jewish people. They needed God's law more than ever as they began to reestablish life in Jerusalem as God's community. Ezra had "set his heart to study the law of the LORD, and to do it, and to teach the statutes and ordinances in Israel" (Ezra 7:10). His whole-life commitment to Scripture had knit Ezra's life closely with God, so that many times throughout the books of Ezra and Nehemiah Ezra acknowledged that "the gracious hand of his God was upon him" (7:9).

Indeed, God gave Ezra favor with the pagan king, supplied the needed priests and Levites to journey back to Jerusalem, and protected Ezra and his party of a few thousand as they traveled. Upon their arrival in Jerusalem, God's hand was once more upon Ezra, this time moving him to lead the people in holiness. He learned that many priests and Levites, the leaders of the people already settled in Jerusalem, had ignored God's laws about marriage and taken foreign wives. God's grief at this early act of disobedience came upon Ezra at once, and he tore at his clothes and hair (Ezra 9:3). With fasting and contrition, Ezra fell before God, voicing his sorrow.

Ezra's study of God's law and his commitment to the law in his own life had formed his heart like God's. Israel's past sin and God's mercy ("You, our God, have punished us less than our iniquities deserved," Ezra 9:13) caused him such torment that his body spoke the grief of his spirit. So true and full was Ezra's grief that a "very great assembly" of men, women, and children gathered around him and "wept bitterly" (10:1). Ezra's love for God and God's ways was catching. The Israelites repented. They obeyed by forfeiting their foreign wives and children.

As we see in Ezra's life, committed study of Scripture can bring about much more than merely head knowledge. It can bring God himself into all the recesses of our being, for "the word of God is living and active" (Heb 4:12). John describes this presence of God in his Word, writing of Jesus, "the Word was with God, and the Word was God" (John 1:1). Ezra's desire not only to *study* God's law but also to *obey* it allowed the Immanuel presence of God to transform his heart and make him a leader who could powerfully move his people.

One fourth-century bishop experienced a similar transformation. After many early years of secular philosophical studies and an undying propensity for sexual pursuits, Aurelius Augustine was drawn to God through the writings of the apostle Paul. His final moments of struggle with God occurred in a garden, where he wept and then heard the voice of a child nearby chanting, "Take it and read, take it and read." Opening his book of Paul's Letters, he first saw Rom 13:13–14: "Let us live . . . not in reveling and drunkenness, not in debauchery and licentiousness, not in quarreling and jealousy. Instead, put on the Lord Jesus Christ, and make no provision for the flesh, to gratify its desires."

At that moment, "the light of confidence flooded into my heart and all the darkness of doubt was dispelled." Augustine went on to seclude himself for many months, along with friends, to study and reflect on the Scriptures. He became a bishop and served out of a monastic community in Hippo for the remainder of his life; he wrote many books, spoke prodigiously, and influenced Christian theology for every generation to follow. Like Ezra, Augustine was so filled with God and his Word that hardly a person could sit in his presence without being moved. And Augustine, like Ezra, not only knew Scripture, but lived it. Serving the poor, living simply, and showing hospitality, Augustine revealed the truth of his words: "One loving heart sets another on fire."

Augustine and Ezra grew loving hearts largely through their disciplined study of God's Word. In studying Scripture they took on the heart and mind of God. From them, the fire of God spread to countless generations.

Personal Reflection

- To what extent is study a regular discipline in your life? Does the study of Scripture have a prominent place?
- Richard Foster's *Celebration of Discipline* suggests that study involves four steps: repetition, concentration, comprehension, and reflection. Are any of these steps missing in your usual practice of study?
- Richard Foster also warns that "a vast difference exists between the study of Scripture and the devotional reading of Scripture. In the study of Scripture a high priority is placed upon interpretation: what it means. In the devotional reading of Scripture a high priority is placed upon application: what it means for me. All too often people rush to the application stage and bypass the interpretation stage: they want to know what it means for them before they know what it means!" How do Foster's words speak to your life? Pray now about how God wants to teach and transform you through the Spiritual Discipline of study.

PROFILE

quire—let that be given to them day by day without fail, ¹⁰so that they may offer pleasing sacrifices to the God of heaven, and pray for the life of the king and his children. ¹¹Furthermore I decree that if anyone alters this edict, a beam shall be pulled out of the house of the perpetrator, who then shall be impaled on it. The house shall be made a dunghill. ¹²May the God who has established his name there overthrow any king or people that shall put forth a hand to alter this, or to destroy this house of God in Jerusalem. I, Darius, make a decree; let it be done with all diligence."

Completion and Dedication of the Temple

13 Then, according to the word sent by King Darius, Tattenai, the governor of the province Beyond the River, Shethar-bozenai, and their associates did with all diligence what King Darius had ordered. ¹⁴So the elders of the Jews built and prospered, through the prophesying of the prophet Haggai and Zechariah son of Iddo. They finished their building by command of the God of Israel and by decree of Cyrus, Darius, and King Artaxerxes of Persia; ¹⁵and this house was finished on the third day of the month of Adar, in the sixth year of the reign of King Darius.

16 The people of Israel, the priests and the

Levites, and the rest of the returned exiles, celebrated the dedication of this house of God with joy. ¹⁷They offered at the dedication of this house of God one hundred bulls, two hundred rams, four hundred lambs, and as a sin offering for all Israel, twelve male goats, according to the number of the tribes of Israel. ¹⁸Then they set the priests in their divisions and the Levites in their courses for the service of God at Jerusalem, as it is written in the book of Moses.

The Passover Celebrated

19 On the fourteenth day of the first month the returned exiles kept the passover. ²⁰For both the priests and the Levites had purified themselves; all of them were clean. So they killed the passover lamb for all the returned exiles, for their fellow priests, and for themselves. ²¹It was eaten by the people of Israel who had returned from exile, and also by all who had joined them and separated themselves from the pollutions of the nations of the land to worship the LORD, the God of Israel. ²²With joy they celebrated the festival of unleavened bread seven days; for the LORD had made them joyful, and had turned the heart of the king of Assyria to them, so that he aided them in the work on the house of God, the God of Israel.

6:14 *They finished their building.* The Second Temple was finished in just under five years, thereby fulfilling the prophecy of Jeremiah (Jer 25:11–12; 29:10; also Zech 1:12–17). The people overcame many obstacles and difficulties to complete the project. The books of Ezra and Nehemiah show that God's work is accomplished in partnership with his people. When one teaches a Sunday school class of eighth-grade boys, serves in a soup kitchen in an inner city, or participates in any of a number of other ministries of the Church, one labors side by side with God.

6:21 *all who had joined them and separated themselves from the pollutions of the nations.* "Pollutions" were generally associated with the worship of foreign gods. Thus everyone who had declared allegiance to the God of Israel was welcomed to the Passover celebration. True worship invites the whole world to the sanctuary.

The faith of Israel and the Church is not an exclusive activity reserved for a few. The majority view in Scripture is that everyone receives an invitation to worship the living God.

Responding

6:22 CELEBRATION. It is hard to overestimate the joy the People of God must have felt to be celebrating in the newly completed Temple in Jerusalem after so many years in exile. It must have been especially meaningful that the festival was Passover, that traditional celebration of freedom and deliverance. Is there a particular event in your past or present for which you owe God continued praise? Select a day to remember and celebrate your own deliverance with a special meal shared with a close friend or family member. You could even make this an annual event. *See also* Spiritual Disciplines Index.

The Coming and Work of Ezra

7 After this, in the reign of King Artaxerxes of Persia, Ezra son of Seraiah, son of Azariah, son of Hilkiah, ²son of Shallum, son of Zadok, son of Ahitub, ³son of Amariah, son of Azariah, son of Meraioth, ⁴son of Zerahiah, son of Uzzi, son of Bukki, ⁵son of Abishua, son of Phinehas, son of Eleazar, son of the chief priest Aaron— ⁶this Ezra went up from Babylonia. He was a scribe skilled in the law of Moses that the LORD the God of Israel had given; and the king granted him all that he asked, for the hand of the LORD his God was upon him.

7 Some of the people of Israel, and some of the priests and Levites, the singers and gatekeepers, and the temple servants also went up to Jerusalem, in the seventh year of King Artaxerxes. ⁸They came to Jerusalem in the fifth month, which was in the seventh year of the king. ⁹On the first day of the first month the journey up from Babylon was begun, and on the first day of the fifth month he came to Jerusalem, for the gracious hand of his God was upon him. ¹⁰For Ezra had set his heart to study the law of the LORD, and to do it, and to teach the statutes and ordinances in Israel.

The Letter of Artaxerxes to Ezra

11 This is a copy of the letter that King Artaxerxes gave to the priest Ezra, the scribe, a scholar of the text of the commandments of the LORD and his statutes for Israel: ¹²"Artaxerxes, king of kings, to the priest Ezra, the scribe of the law of the God of heaven: Peace. *a* And now ¹³I decree that any of the people of Israel or their priests or Levites in my kingdom who freely offers to go to Jerusalem may go with you. ¹⁴For you are sent by the king and his seven counselors to make inquiries about Judah and Jerusalem according to the

a Syr Vg 1 Esdras 8.9: Aram *Perfect*

7:1–6 *Ezra.* Over fifty years had elapsed between the events of chapter 6 and the beginning of the ministry of Ezra in chapter 7. One would think that the dedication of the Temple would have caused a spiritual renewal among the returned Jews. If there were such a revival, it was short-lived. The prophets Isaiah (chaps 55–66) and Malachi indicate that the years following the Temple's completion were for the most part spiritually bankrupt. Great houses of worship and even large gatherings of people do not necessarily translate into spiritual vitality. Regardless of how magnificent the building, if the hearts of the people are not right toward God and others, the Church becomes a "den of thieves."

7:7 *also went up to Jerusalem.* In both Old and New Testament the journey to Jerusalem is usually understood as going "up." Although the city is indeed on a hill, the reference is theological as well as geographical. One goes "up" to the place of God and worship. There is nothing more significant in a person's life than going "up" to meet with God, whether in worship or in the ordinary routines of life.

7:10 *to study the law . . . to do it, and to teach.* Ezra arrived in Jerusalem determined to accomplish three things. First, Ezra desired to study the law. We do not master the Word of God and then move on to something else. Scripture continues to bring new insights and challenges throughout life. Rabbinical teachings suggest that among the duties of prayer, good works, and study, the most important of these is study. Study forms the basis of the other two. Second, Ezra committed himself to practice what he had learned. A teacher who models the lessons is a powerful influence on students. Third, Ezra was called to teach others what he had learned. The word "scribe" implies both the knowing as well as the teaching of Scripture. The word "witness," found in the New Testament (for example, Acts 1:8), aptly describes Ezra's life. The word expresses much more than just the "telling" of the good news; it suggests "doing" and "being" the good news as well.

Responding

7:10 STUDY. Ezra knew the importance of learning, for each of us must know God's law before we can put it into practice. If consistently finding the time to study God's Word is a challenge for you, try setting a small, manageable goal of taking a five- to ten-minute study break every day for a week to focus on a particular passage that is meaningful to you. See what you learn. *See also* Spiritual Disciplines Index.

law of your God, which is in your hand, 15and also to convey the silver and gold that the king and his counselors have freely offered to the God of Israel, whose dwelling is in Jerusalem, 16with all the silver and gold that you shall find in the whole province of Babylonia, and with the freewill offerings of the people and the priests, given willingly for the house of their God in Jerusalem. 17With this money, then, you shall with all diligence buy bulls, rams, and lambs, and their grain offerings and their drink offerings, and you shall offer them on the altar of the house of your God in Jerusalem. 18Whatever seems good to you and your colleagues to do with the rest of the silver and gold, you may do, according to the will of your God. 19The vessels that have been given you for the service of the house of your God, you shall deliver before the God of Jerusalem. 20And whatever else is required for the house of your God, which you are responsible for providing, you may provide out of the king's treasury.

21 "I, King Artaxerxes, decree to all the treasurers in the province Beyond the River: Whatever the priest Ezra, the scribe of the law of the God of heaven, requires of you, let it be done with all diligence, 22up to one hundred talents of silver, one hundred cors of wheat, one hundred baths*a* of wine, one hundred baths*a* of oil, and unlimited salt. 23Whatever is commanded by the God of heaven, let it be done with zeal for the house of the God of heaven, or wrath will come upon the realm of the king and his heirs. 24We also notify you that it shall not be lawful to impose tribute, custom, or toll on any of the priests, the Levites, the singers, the doorkeepers, the temple servants, or other servants of this house of God.

25 "And you, Ezra, according to the God-given wisdom you possess, appoint magistrates and judges who may judge all the people in the province Beyond the River who know the laws of your God; and you shall teach those who do not know them. 26All who will not obey the law of your God and the law of the king, let judgment be strictly executed on them, whether for death or for banishment or for confiscation of their goods or for imprisonment."

27 Blessed be the LORD, the God of our ancestors, who put such a thing as this into the heart of the king to glorify the house of the LORD in Jerusalem, 28and who extended to me steadfast love before the king and his counselors, and before all the king's mighty officers. I took courage, for the hand of the LORD my God was upon me, and I gathered leaders from Israel to go up with me.

Heads of Families Who Returned with Ezra

8 These are their family heads, and this is the genealogy of those who went up with me from Babylonia, in the reign of King Artaxerxes: 2Of the descendants of Phinehas, Gershom. Of Ithamar, Daniel. Of David, Hattush, 3of the descendants of Shecaniah. Of Parosh, Zechariah, with whom were registered one hundred fifty males. 4Of the descendants of Pahath-moab, Eliehoenai son of Zerahiah, and with him two hundred males. 5Of the descendants of Zattu,*b* Shecaniah son of Jahaziel, and with him three hundred males. 6Of the descendants of Adin, Ebed son of Jonathan, and with him fifty males. 7Of the descendants of Elam, Jeshaiah son of Athaliah, and with him seventy males. 8Of the descendants of Shephatiah, Zebadiah son of Michael, and with him eighty males. 9Of the descendants of Joab, Obadiah son of Jehiel, and with him two hundred eighteen males. 10Of the descendants of Bani,*c* Shelomith son of Josiphiah, and with

---

a A Heb measure of volume   *b* Gk 1 Esdras 8.32: Heb lacks *of Zattu*   *c* Gk 1 Esdras 8.36: Heb lacks *Bani*

7:27–28 *Blessed be the* LORD . . . *who put such a thing as this into the heart of the king.* To see God working in the world is in itself an act of faith. To disinterested observers the king's response may have appeared like "good strategy." But spiritually alert Ezra saw the "hand of God" in the king's actions. The attentive recognize the presence of God in the ordinary experiences of life—such as a baby born in a manger or a cup of water given to a thirsty person.

him one hundred sixty males. [11]Of the descendants of Bebai, Zechariah son of Bebai, and with him twenty-eight males. [12]Of the descendants of Azgad, Johanan son of Hakkatan, and with him one hundred ten males. [13]Of the descendants of Adonikam, those who came later, their names being Eliphelet, Jeuel, and Shemaiah, and with them sixty males. [14]Of the descendants of Bigvai, Uthai and Zaccur, and with them seventy males.

Servants for the Temple

15 I gathered them by the river that runs to Ahava, and there we camped three days. As I reviewed the people and the priests, I found there none of the descendants of Levi. [16]Then I sent for Eliezer, Ariel, Shemaiah, Elnathan, Jarib, Elnathan, Nathan, Zechariah, and Meshullam, who were leaders, and for Joiarib and Elnathan, who were wise, [17]and sent them to Iddo, the leader at the place called Casiphia, telling them what to say to Iddo and his colleagues the temple servants at Casiphia, namely, to send us ministers for the house of our God. [18]Since the gracious hand of our God was upon us, they brought us a man of discretion, of the descendants of Mahli son of Levi son of Israel, namely Sherebiah, with his sons and kin, eighteen; [19]also Hashabiah and with him Jeshaiah of the descendants of Merari, with his kin and their sons, twenty; [20]besides two hundred twenty of the temple servants, whom David and his officials had set apart to attend the Levites. These were all mentioned by name.

Fasting and Prayer for Protection

21 Then I proclaimed a fast there, at the river Ahava, that we might deny ourselves[a] before our God, to seek from him a safe journey for ourselves, our children, and all our possessions. [22]For I was ashamed to ask the king for a band of soldiers and cavalry to protect us against the enemy on our way, since we had told the king that the hand of our God is gracious to all who seek him, but his power and his wrath are against all who forsake him. [23]So we fasted and petitioned our God for this, and he listened to our entreaty.

Gifts for the Temple

24 Then I set apart twelve of the leading priests: Sherebiah, Hashabiah, and ten of their kin with them. [25]And I weighed out to them the silver and the gold and the vessels, the offering for the house of our God that the king, his counselors, his lords, and all Israel there present had offered; [26]I weighed out into their hand six hundred fifty talents of silver, and one hundred silver vessels worth . . . talents,[b] and one hundred talents of gold, [27]twenty gold bowls worth a thousand darics, and two vessels of fine polished bronze as precious as gold. [28]And I said to them, "You are holy to the LORD, and the vessels are holy; and the silver and the gold are a freewill offering to the LORD, the God of your ancestors. [29]Guard them and keep them

a Or might fast   b The number of talents is lacking

8:15–23 *I gathered them by the river.* When it came to living out faithful obedience, Ezra "walked the talk." Preparing for his journey to Jerusalem, Ezra uncovered several critical issues. His party of returning exiles had no Levites to help the people understand the law. In addition Ezra and his entourage were defenseless in their trek across hostile territory. Some scholars have theorized that the Jews were carrying enough silver and gold to equal the yearly income of between a hundred and five hundred thousand people. In response to these problems Ezra trusted the "hand of God" and called his people to a time of fasting and prayer. The Church can learn much from the life of Ezra. Spending time being attentive to the Spirit of God through fasting and prayer is a far more effective way to solve Church problems than endless hours in debate and confrontation.

Responding
8:21–23 FASTING. Passages like this one make it clear that "deny[ing] ourselves before our God," deliberately turning away from the needs of our bodies, is an effective and powerful way to focus our prayers. What demands of your body are you most attuned to? What would your prayer life be like if you could focus on God with the same level of intensity? *See also* Spiritual Disciplines Index.

until you weigh them before the chief priests and the Levites and the heads of families in Israel at Jerusalem, within the chambers of the house of the LORD." [30]So the priests and the Levites took over the silver, the gold, and the vessels as they were weighed out, to bring them to Jerusalem, to the house of our God.

The Return to Jerusalem

31 Then we left the river Ahava on the twelfth day of the first month, to go to Jerusalem; the hand of our God was upon us, and he delivered us from the hand of the enemy and from ambushes along the way. [32]We came to Jerusalem and remained there three days. [33]On the fourth day, within the house of our God, the silver, the gold, and the vessels were weighed into the hands of the priest Meremoth son of Uriah, and with him was Eleazar son of Phinehas, and with them were the Levites, Jozabad son of Jeshua and Noadiah son of Binnui. [34]The total was counted and weighed, and the weight of everything was recorded.

35 At that time those who had come from captivity, the returned exiles, offered burnt offerings to the God of Israel, twelve bulls for all Israel, ninety-six rams, seventy-seven lambs, and as a sin offering twelve male goats; all this was a burnt offering to the LORD. [36]They also delivered the king's commissions to the king's satraps and to the governors of the province Beyond the River; and they supported the people and the house of God.

Denunciation of Mixed Marriages

9 After these things had been done, the officials approached me and said, "The people of Israel, the priests, and the Levites have not separated themselves from the peoples of the lands with their abominations, from the Canaanites, the Hittites, the Perizzites, the Jebusites, the Ammonites, the Moabites, the Egyptians, and the Amorites. [2]For they have taken some of their daughters as wives for themselves and for their sons. Thus the holy seed has mixed itself with the peoples of the lands, and in this faithlessness the officials and leaders have led the way." [3]When I heard this, I tore my garment and my mantle, and pulled hair from my head and beard, and sat appalled. [4]Then all who trembled at the words of the God of Israel, because of the faithlessness of the returned exiles, gathered around me while I sat appalled until the evening sacrifice.

Ezra's Prayer

5 At the evening sacrifice I got up from my fasting, with my garments and my mantle torn, and fell on my knees, spread out my hands to the LORD my God, [6]and said,

"O my God, I am too ashamed and embarrassed to lift my face to you, my God, for our iniquities have risen higher than our heads, and our guilt has mounted up to the heavens. [7]From the days of our ancestors to this day we have been deep in guilt, and for our iniquities we, our kings, and our priests have been handed over to the kings of the

---

9:1–2 *have not separated themselves from the peoples of the lands.* Not long after Ezra and his group had arrived in Jerusalem, reports informed him that the Israelites looked and acted more like Canaanites and Hittites than they did the People of God. The community of returned Jews was to be "holy seed" bearing witness to God's presence in the world, yet their behavior and lifestyle did not distinguish them from the immoral people of the land. Tragically, even the morals of religious leaders had deteriorated. How unfortunate that the Church often blends in with the culture of consumerism and hedonism! Instead of a people "set apart," the

Church often behaves as a people comfortably settled in the world.

9:5–15 *spread out my hands to the LORD . . . and said.* Ezra's prayer models authentic spiritual leadership. He did not point his finger at those who had broken faith with God, but rather identified with them in acknowledging that "our iniquities" and "our guilt" have created our dire circumstances (v 6). But Ezra does not leave the people without hope. His prayer rejoices that even in their present condition of slavery, God is steadfast in his love for Israel. The phrase "given us a stake" (v 8) indicates that God still has a future and a promise for Israel in spite of its repeated failures.

lands, to the sword, to captivity, to plundering, and to utter shame, as is now the case. [8]But now for a brief moment favor has been shown by the LORD our God, who has left us a remnant, and given us a stake in his holy place, in order that he[a] may brighten our eyes and grant us a little sustenance in our slavery. [9]For we are slaves; yet our God has not forsaken us in our slavery, but has extended to us his steadfast love before the kings of Persia, to give us new life to set up the house of our God, to repair its ruins, and to give us a wall in Judea and Jerusalem.

10 "And now, our God, what shall we say after this? For we have forsaken your commandments, [11]which you commanded by your servants the prophets, saying, 'The land that you are entering to possess is a land unclean with the pollutions of the peoples of the lands, with their abominations. They have filled it from end to end with their uncleanness. [12]Therefore do not give your daughters to their sons, neither take their daughters for your sons, and never seek their peace or prosperity, so that you may be strong and eat the good of the land and leave it for an inheritance to your children forever.' [13]After all that has come upon us for our evil

deeds and for our great guilt, seeing that you, our God, have punished us less than our iniquities deserved and have given us such a remnant as this, [14]shall we break your commandments again and intermarry with the peoples who practice these abominations? Would you not be angry with us until you destroy us without remnant or survivor? [15]O LORD, God of Israel, you are just, but we have escaped as a remnant, as is now the case. Here we are before you in our guilt, though no one can face you because of this."

The People's Response

10 While Ezra prayed and made confession, weeping and throwing himself down before the house of God, a very great assembly of men, women, and children gathered to him out of Israel; the people also wept bitterly. [2]Shecaniah son of Jehiel, of the descendants of Elam, addressed Ezra, saying, "We have broken faith with our God and have married foreign women from the peoples of the land, but even now there is hope for Israel in spite of this. [3]So now let us make a covenant with our God to send away all these wives and their children, according to

a Heb our God

10:1 PRAYER—See Spiritual Disciplines Index.

Responding
10:1 CONFESSION. Ezra's confession here is notable in that he is confessing the sins of the entire community, rather than just his own personal iniquities. Although many liturgical churches recite a communal confession of sin as a congregation, most of us don't confess the sins of our community in our private prayers. Today take some time to list the sins of your community, your city, or your nation. Consider your own complicity in these sins and ask God for forgiveness. *See also* Spiritual Disciplines Index.

10:1–15 *let us make a covenant with our God to send away all these wives and their children.* The sending away of foreign wives and children has troubled many thoughtful Christians. The expulsion of these unbelievers from Israel's

community surely caused hardship for them, perhaps even death. There are no easy answers in regard to this passage. There are, however, a few thoughts to consider. First, the returned Jews were in danger of losing their identity as the People of God. Clearly, they had not separated themselves from pagan influences and practices. As harsh as the judgment appears to be, the alternative was for Israel to cease to exist as a people. Second, the Bible must always be read with the big picture in mind. It is not a flat book with only one perspective of faith. The book of Ruth, for instance, celebrates the role of a foreign woman in Israel's history. Malachi, who wrote shortly after Ezra, strongly objects to divorce (Mal 2:16). In Exod 22:21 the Israelites are instructed to be kind to aliens because they were once outsiders in Egypt. Moreover, Ezra 1–6 has an inclusive theme regarding the foreigner. In listening to the Word of God in Scripture, one must consider all the voices of faith.

the counsel of my lord and of those who tremble at the commandment of our God; and let it be done according to the law. 4Take action, for it is your duty, and we are with you; be strong, and do it." 5Then Ezra stood up and made the leading priests, the Levites, and all Israel swear that they would do as had been said. So they swore.

Foreign Wives and Their Children Rejected

6 Then Ezra withdrew from before the house of God, and went to the chamber of Je-hohanan son of Eliashib, where he spent the night. *a* He did not eat bread or drink water, for he was mourning over the faithlessness of the exiles. 7They made a proclamation throughout Judah and Jerusalem to all the re-turned exiles that they should assemble at Jerusalem, 8and that if any did not come within three days, by order of the officials and the elders all their property should be for-feited, and they themselves banned from the congregation of the exiles.

9 Then all the people of Judah and Benja-min assembled at Jerusalem within the three days; it was the ninth month, on the twen-tieth day of the month. All the people sat in the open square before the house of God, trembling because of this matter and because of the heavy rain. 10Then Ezra the priest stood up and said to them, "You have trespassed and married foreign women, and so increased the guilt of Israel. 11Now make confession to the LORD the God of your ancestors, and do his will; separate yourselves from the peo-ples of the land and from the foreign wives." 12Then all the assembly answered with a loud voice, "It is so; we must do as you have said. 13But the people are many, and it is a time of heavy rain; we cannot stand in the open. Nor is this a task for one day or for two, for many of us have transgressed in this matter. 14Let our officials represent the whole assembly, and let all in our towns who have taken for-eign wives come at appointed times, and with

them the elders and judges of every town, until the fierce wrath of our God on this ac-count is averted from us." 15Only Jonathan son of Asahel and Jahzeiah son of Tikvah op-posed this, and Meshullam and Shabbethai the Levites supported them.

16 Then the returned exiles did so. Ezra the priest selected men, *b* heads of families, ac-cording to their families, each of them des-ignated by name. On the first day of the tenth month they sat down to examine the matter. 17By the first day of the first month they had come to the end of all the men who had mar-ried foreign women.

18 There were found of the descendants of the priests who had married foreign women, of the descendants of Jeshua son of Jozadak and his brothers: Maaseiah, Eliezer, Jarib, and Gedaliah. 19They pledged themselves to send away their wives, and their guilt offering was a ram of the flock for their guilt. 20Of the de-scendants of Immer: Hanani and Zebadiah. 21Of the descendants of Harim: Maaseiah, Elijah, Shemaiah, Jehiel, and Uzziah. 22Of the descendants of Pashhur: Elioenai, Maa-seiah, Ishmael, Nethanel, Jozabad, and Ela-sah.

23 Of the Levites: Jozabad, Shimei, Kelaiah (that is, Kelita), Pethahiah, Judah, and Eliezer. 24Of the singers: Eliashib. Of the gatekeepers: Shallum, Telem, and Uri.

25 And of Israel: of the descendants of Pa-rosh: Ramiah, Izziah, Malchijah, Mijamin, Eleazar, Hashabiah, *c* and Benaiah. 26Of the descendants of Elam: Mattaniah, Zechariah, Jehiel, Abdi, Jeremoth, and Elijah. 27Of the descendants of Zattu: Elioenai, Eliashib, Mat-taniah, Jeremoth, Zabad, and Aziza. 28Of the descendants of Bebai: Jehohanan, Hanani-ah, Zabbai, and Athlai. 29Of the descendants of Bani: Meshullam, Malluch, Adaiah,

a 1 Esdras 9.2: Heb *where he went*   *b* 1 Esdras 9.16: Syr: Heb *And there were selected Ezra,*
c 1 Esdras 9.26 Gk: Heb *Malchijah*

10:10–12 *make confession . . . separate your-selves.* It is not enough merely to acknowledge that one has disobeyed God. Israel promised to act to correct its lifestyle and behavior. True repentance is always linked with a changed life.

The word for repentance in both Testaments implies the idea of a "return" to God or to the ways of God. Repentance results in a commit-ment to put one's entire life under the authority of "the God of heaven."

Jashub, Sheal, and Jeremoth. 30Of the descendants of Pahath-moab: Adna, Chelal, Benaiah, Maaseiah, Mattaniah, Bezalel, Binnui, and Manasseh. 31Of the descendants of Harim: Eliezer, Isshijah, Malchijah, Shemaiah, Shimeon, 32Benjamin, Malluch, and Shemariah. 33Of the descendants of Hashum: Mattenai, Mattattah, Zabad, Eliphelet, Jeremai, Manasseh, and Shimei. 34Of the descendants of Bani: Maadai, Amram, Uel, 35Benaiah, Bedeiah, Cheluhi, 36Vaniah, Meremoth, Eliashib, 37Mattaniah, Mattenai, and

Jaasu. 38Of the descendants of Binnui: a Shimei, 39Shelemiah, Nathan, Adaiah, 40Machnadebai, Shashai, Sharai, 41Azarel, Shelemiah, Shemariah, 42Shallum, Amariah, and Joseph. 43Of the descendants of Nebo: Jeiel, Mattithiah, Zabad, Zebina, Jaddai, Joel, and Benaiah. 44All these had married foreign women, and they sent them away with their children. b

a Gk: Heb *Bani, Binnui*   b 1 Esdras 9.36; meaning of Heb uncertain

NEHEMIAH

Four and a half centuries before Jesus (445 BC) the people living in Jerusalem were crushed and broken. The former glorious Temple, built by Solomon and destroyed by Nebuchadnezzar, had been rebuilt, but the inferior construction only served to remind the Israelites of how far they had fallen. If Jerusalem appeared to outsiders as a defeated and ruined city, it was only because Jerusalem was a defeated and ruined city. Quite simply the people living in the once proud metropolis of David and Solomon were "in great trouble and shame" (1:3). The population had dwindled to only a few thousand people, and the walls and the gates of the city were piles of ash and broken stones. Even the Hebrew language was in danger of extinction, as the Israelite children were learning the foreign tongues of surrounding nations (13:23–24). The inability of Hebrew children to read the law of Moses in their native language was the final humiliation for a people who once had pledged themselves to be "a priestly kingdom and a holy nation" (Exod 19:6).

The Cupbearer from Judah

Nehemiah became aware of the desperate situation in Jerusalem while serving as cupbearer for Artaxerxes I. The book opens with Nehemiah's prayer that God would act favorably toward Israel and restore its identity as the People of God. Nehemiah's prayer and concern for the struggling Jews living in Jerusalem moved him to put a risky plan into action. As the wine taster for the king, Nehemiah had privileged access to Artaxerxes I. Nehemiah's heart was heavy for the people in Jerusalem, and he allowed the king to observe his depression while serving him wine. Such a show of negative emotion in the presence of the king could very well have cost Nehemiah his life. The king immediately noticed the sad behavior and demanded to know the reason Nehemiah was downcast. Nehemiah breathed a quick prayer and then tactfully explained that "the city, the place of my ancestors' graves, lies waste" (2:3). Touched by Nehemiah's explanation, the king granted his request to return to

---

See also "The With-God Life" essay for this section of the Bible,
"The People of God in Restoration," pp. 1355–59.

681

Judah to rebuild the city of his ancestors' graves. The remainder of the book records the events following Nehemiah's return to Jerusalem.

Most scholars believe that Ezra and Nehemiah were originally one book in the Hebrew Bible (see Introduction to Ezra). Ezra was a scribe and priest who led the people back to the Scripture; Nehemiah was a "man of action" who led the people forward in rebuilding not only the walls of Jerusalem, but also the spiritual lives of the people. There is general agreement that the cupbearer of Artaxerxes I arrived in Jerusalem in 445 BC. Immediately upon arrival Nehemiah faced serious opposition to his efforts, but was resolute in his determination to restore the city's walls and spiritually renovate the people's lives.

Although this book may very well have been written by Ezra, the book preserves many of Nehemiah's actual recollections or memoirs. Chapters 1–7 and 13 are thought to be the personal notes of Nehemiah's work in Jerusalem and are regarded by many scholars as providing accurate historical details of that time period.

"God Comforts"

Nehemiah was not part of the priestly guild. He was a layman committed to doing the work of the Lord wherever he found a need, and he used his influential appointment as a governor to further God's work. His name means "God comforts." In Isa 40:1 the prophet announces "comfort" to the captives returning to Jerusalem from Babylon. With perhaps little awareness that he would be God's instrument, Nehemiah brought "comfort" to the returning exiles, as well as to those Jews who had escaped captivity, by working to restore dignity and spiritual discipline to the postexilic community.

Although Nehemiah lived his life as a man of action, he was also a man of prayer. The rebuilding of the walls, the ethical reforms, and the repopulation of Jerusalem are obviously the accomplishments of a man who had great organizational and leadership skills. Nehemiah, however, was also a man of pious faith and strong religious convictions. Some of the most studied prayers in the Hebrew Bible are found in the book of Nehemiah. Nehemiah's prayers are simple and direct petitions, usually with heavy allusions to earlier writings of the Old Testament. Time and again Nehemiah's actions are preceded by prayer. Prayer, for Nehemiah, was not merely an exercise in piety, but a means for the strengthening and reshaping of his own heart. Nehemiah's prayers sometimes appear rather crude and spiritually primitive (see 4:4–5), but these prayers represent the honest feelings and thoughts of a man still growing in his relationship with God. It is reassuring to know that God listens to the prayers of his children even when they are marred by human weakness.

Nehemiah's life reflects those of millions of ordinary people who struggle daily with living lives "acceptable to God" (Rom 12:1). People like Nehemiah seldom craft perfect prayers; they pray while driving to work or weeping over a confused and rebellious teen or sitting in a courtroom, brokenhearted over a divorce. They simply pray as they can.

Contrasting Examples of Faith

Ezra and Nehemiah present a contrast not only between the religious professional and the layperson, but also between people who have different understandings of faith. When Ezra journeyed to Jerusalem, he went without an armed guard; Nehemiah, on the other hand, was accompanied to Jerusalem by a military escort. Both men were examples of faith and yet each man applied faith in a unique way. Too often followers of God spend too much time debating what constitutes faith and not enough time living from faith. In truth, the living out of faith is determined by the Spirit of God in each individual's life.

Ezra led the people back to their religious roots, and Nehemiah showed the people of Jerusalem how to live what they had learned from Scripture. Both men played pivotal roles in the spiritual reformation of Israel during a critical time. Throughout Israel's history God consistently called men and women to lead his people to spiritual renewal. Even today God's Spirit beckons for a new Ezra or Nehemiah to guide his people by both word and deed, but hearing God's whisper requires an attentive ear and an open heart.

Nehemiah's life and work represent the laypeople of the Church who labor and pray daily for the "professional staff." These people make visits to nursing homes and organize volunteers to clean church bathrooms and mow church lawns and prepare dinner on Wednesday nights. Their work is often a thankless act of love. Like Nehemiah they simply want to be remembered as good people who did what was right.

—Michael D. Riley

Nehemiah Prays for His People

1 The words of Nehemiah son of Hacaliah.
In the month of Chislev, in the twentieth year, while I was in Susa the capital, ²one of my brothers, Hanani, came with certain men from Judah; and I asked them about the Jews that survived, those who had escaped the captivity, and about Jerusalem. ³They replied, "The survivors there in the province who escaped captivity are in great trouble and shame; the wall of Jerusalem is broken down, and its gates have been destroyed by fire."

4 When I heard these words I sat down and wept, and mourned for days, fasting and pray-

1:1 *The words of Nehemiah.* In Hebrew this phrase can be translated "The acts of Nehemiah." Nehemiah was a "man of action" as much as he was a man of words. Without question words are important in the life of faith, but faith is essentially a life of action. Believing in God is not a mental exercise, but a life committed to following his will.

1:2 *I asked them about the Jews.* Nehemiah took the initiative by asking about the welfare of the Jews living in Jerusalem. For lesser people, the situation in Judah would have been someone else's problem, but for Nehemiah, even in a distant land, the condition of those who had "survived" was a cause of intense concern.

1:4 FASTING—*See* Spiritual Disciplines Index.

Responding
1:4–11 PRAYER. Almost every phrase in Nehemiah's eloquent prayer is derived from other parts of Scripture, which Nehemiah had internalized after much study. Nehemiah repeated this prayer "day and night." Copy out this prayer, study it, and pray it for a week. See if its words become a part of you. *See also* Spiritual Disciplines Index.

ing before the God of heaven. [5]I said, "O LORD God of heaven, the great and awesome God who keeps covenant and steadfast love with those who love him and keep his commandments; [6]let your ear be attentive and your eyes open to hear the prayer of your servant that I now pray before you day and night for your servants, the people of Israel, confessing the sins of the people of Israel, which we have sinned against you. Both I and my family have sinned. [7]We have offended you deeply, failing to keep the commandments, the statutes, and the ordinances that you commanded your servant Moses. [8]Remember the word that you commanded your servant Moses, 'If you are unfaithful, I will scatter you among the peoples; [9]but if you return to me and keep my commandments and do them, though your outcasts are under the farthest skies, I will gather them from there and bring them to the place at which I have chosen to establish my name.' [10]They are your servants and your people, whom you redeemed by your great power and your strong hand. [11]O Lord, let your ear be attentive to the prayer of your servant, and to the prayer of your servants who delight in revering your name. Give success to your servant today, and grant him mercy in the sight of this man!"

At the time, I was cupbearer to the king.

Nehemiah Sent to Judah

2 In the month of Nisan, in the twentieth year of King Artaxerxes, when wine was served him, I carried the wine and gave it to the king. Now, I had never been sad in his presence before. [2]So the king said to me, "Why is your face sad, since you are not sick? This can only be sadness of the heart." Then I was very much afraid. [3]I said to the king, "May the king live forever! Why should my face not be sad, when the city, the place of my ancestors' graves, lies waste, and its gates have been destroyed by fire?" [4]Then the king said to me, "What do you request?" So I prayed to the God of heaven. [5]Then I said to the king, "If it pleases the king, and if your servant has found favor with you, I ask that you send me to Judah, to the city of my ancestors' graves, so that I may rebuild it." [6]The king said to me (the queen also was sitting beside him), "How long will you be gone, and when will you return?" So it pleased the king to send me, and

---

1:5–11 *the great and awesome God who keeps covenant.* Nehemiah's prayer reflects a thorough knowledge of Scripture. Almost every phrase in the prayer is derived from the sacred text (see Deut 7:9, 21; 10:17; 1 Kings 8:52; Ps 130:2; Deut 34:5; 4:27; 30:1–4; 9:29). The prayer reflects Nehemiah's saturation with Scripture. The text was so firmly embedded in his memory that the words of Scripture had become the thoughts of Nehemiah. In the prayer life of Jesus, as well as the Church, the Bible has often served as a resource for addressing God. Nehemiah's prayer contrasts the faithfulness of God with the unfaithfulness of Israel. It was not necessary for Nehemiah to remind God of his obligations to Israel, but the prayer serves to alert Nehemiah and Israel that God was the brooding Father waiting for his children to return to him that he might once again enter into relationship with them.

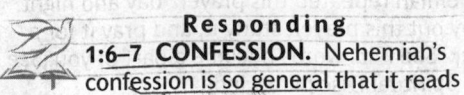

Responding
1:6–7 CONFESSION. Nehemiah's confession is so general that it reads like an admission that we always have and always will sin. Recognizing this can lead to despair and an inability to let go of past sins for which we have already repented. The philosopher Søren Kierkegaard wrote this prayer: "Hold not our sins up against us, but hold us up against our sins, so that the thought of You when it wakens in our soul . . . should not remind us of what we have committed, but of what You did forgive, not of how we went astray, but of how You did save us." The next time you feel haunted by a past sin, pray Kierkegaard's prayer and think of your sin not just as a failing, but as a reminder of God's saving grace. *See also* Spiritual Disciplines Index.

2:1–2 *sadness of the heart.* Nehemiah prayed for the "success" (1:11) of his mission, but here he stands before the king "very much afraid." Even the knees of those who possess a vibrant faith in God knock together from time to time. Fear can be an important emotion that forces us to trust in God. Nehemiah's conversation with the king is bathed in prayer from beginning to end (see v 4).

I set him a date. 7Then I said to the king, "If it pleases the king, let letters be given me to the governors of the province Beyond the River, that they may grant me passage until I arrive in Judah; 8and a letter to Asaph, the keeper of the king's forest, directing him to give me timber to make beams for the gates of the temple fortress, and for the wall of the city, and for the house that I shall occupy." And the king granted me what I asked, for the gracious hand of my God was upon me.

9 Then I came to the governors of the province Beyond the River, and gave them the king's letters. Now the king had sent officers of the army and cavalry with me. 10When Sanballat the Horonite and Tobiah the Ammonite official heard this, it displeased them greatly that someone had come to seek the welfare of the people of Israel.

Nehemiah's Inspection of the Walls

11 So I came to Jerusalem and was there for three days. 12Then I got up during the night, I and a few men with me; I told no one what my God had put into my heart to do for Jerusalem. The only animal I took was the animal I rode. 13I went out by night by the Valley Gate past the Dragon's Spring and to the Dung Gate, and I inspected the walls of Jerusalem that had been broken down and its gates that had been destroyed by fire. 14Then I went on to the Fountain Gate and to the King's Pool; but there was no place for the animal I was riding to continue. 15So I went up by way of the valley by night and inspected the wall. Then I turned back and entered by the Valley Gate, and so returned. 16The officials did not know where I had gone or what I was doing; I had not yet told the Jews, the priests, the nobles, the officials, and the rest that were to do the work.

Decision to Restore the Walls

17 Then I said to them, "You see the trouble we are in, how Jerusalem lies in ruins with its gates burned. Come, let us rebuild the wall of Jerusalem, so that we may no longer suffer disgrace." 18I told them that the hand of my God had been gracious upon me, and also the words that the king had spoken to me. Then they said, "Let us start building!" So they committed themselves to the common good. 19But when Sanballat the Horonite and Tobiah the Ammonite official, and Geshem

---

Responding
2:4–5 PRAYER. After the king's question, Nehemiah quickly prayed before responding, as was his habit. How many times do we speak without thinking, act without praying? Keeping Nehemiah's example in mind, try to be more conscious this week of praying briefly before speaking or acting. The prayer can be as simple as "Help me" or "Thank you," or it can be a line of Scripture, such as "For God all things are possible" (Mark 10:27). See also Spiritual Disciplines Index.

2:6 *How long will you be gone, and when will you return?* The king's attachment to Nehemiah sounds almost parental. Nehemiah had spent much time in the service of the king, and Artaxerxes I had developed a fondness for Nehemiah. Knowing Nehemiah to be a good man, the king trusted him enough to send him into service in Judah. The world will more readily take the People of God seriously when the Church seriously enters into service of the world.

Responding
2:8, 18 THE WITH-GOD LIFE. Nehemiah knew with utter confidence that "the gracious hand" of God was upon him. Was there ever a time when you knew God's gracious hand rested on your shoulder? If so, how did you feel his presence? As you look back, were there times when God's hand was with you even though you didn't realize it at the time? See also Spiritual Disciplines Index.

2:9 *the army and cavalry with me.* Nehemiah journeyed to Jerusalem with a military escort. Ezra, on the other hand, refused armed security, trusting in God alone to protect him. Both men exhibited remarkable confidence in God, but each man chose to express his confidence in different ways. Faith does not come in only one flavor; it is as varied as the people who embrace it.

the Arab heard of it, they mocked and ridiculed us, saying, "What is this that you are doing? Are you rebelling against the king?" [20]Then I replied to them, "The God of heaven is the one who will give us success, and we his servants are going to start building; but you have no share or claim or historic right in Jerusalem."

Organization of the Work

3 Then the high priest Eliashib set to work with his fellow priests and rebuilt the Sheep Gate. They consecrated it and set up its doors; they consecrated it as far as the Tower of the Hundred and as far as the Tower of Hananel. [2]And the men of Jericho built next to him. And next to them[a] Zaccur son of Imri built.

3 The sons of Hassenaah built the Fish Gate; they laid its beams and set up its doors, its bolts, and its bars. [4]Next to them Meremoth son of Uriah son of Hakkoz made repairs. Next to them Meshullam son of Berechiah son of Meshezabel made repairs. Next to them Zadok son of Baana made repairs. [5]Next to them the Tekoites made repairs; but their nobles would not put their shoulders to the work of their Lord.[b]

6 Joiada son of Paseah and Meshullam son of Besodeiah repaired the Old Gate; they laid its beams and set up its doors, its bolts, and its bars. [7]Next to them repairs were made by Melatiah the Gibeonite and Jadon the Meronothite—the men of Gibeon and of Mizpah—who were under the jurisdiction of[c] the governor of the province Beyond the River. [8]Next to them Uzziel son of Harhaiah, one of the goldsmiths, made repairs. Next to him Hananiah, one of the perfumers, made repairs; and they restored Jerusalem as far as the Broad Wall. [9]Next to them Rephaiah son of Hur, ruler of half the district of[d] Jerusalem, made repairs. [10]Next to them Jedaiah son of Harumaph made repairs opposite his house; and next to him Hattush son of Hashabneiah made repairs. [11]Malchijah son of Harim and Hasshub son of Pahath-moab repaired another section and the Tower of the Ovens. [12]Next to him Shallum son of Hallohesh, ruler of half the district of[d] Jerusalem, made repairs, he and his daughters.

13 Hanun and the inhabitants of Zanoah repaired the Valley Gate; they rebuilt it and set up its doors, its bolts, and its bars, and repaired a thousand cubits of the wall, as far as the Dung Gate.

14 Malchijah son of Rechab, ruler of the district of[e] Beth-haccherem, repaired the Dung Gate; he rebuilt it and set up its doors, its bolts, and its bars.

---

a Heb *him*   b Or *lords*   c Meaning of Heb uncertain   d Or *supervisor of half the portion assigned to*   e Or *supervisor of the portion assigned to*

2:19 *they mocked and ridiculed us.* Opposition is to be expected in doing the work of God. Unfortunately, the idea has developed that if the hand of God is with us, then all will be well. The idea is based more on superstition than biblical faith. Those who labor in the service of the Lord seldom go through life unscathed. In the job description of every Christian the cross is not a footnote; the cross is a major heading that marks clearly the road to God.

3:1–32 *They consecrated . . . set up . . . built . . . made repairs.* The construction on the walls would make an interesting sociological study. From the names listed there are priests and Levites, administrative heads and merchants, and entire families, including daughters. There were laborers from neighboring cities and communities, craftsmen and artists, and of course common, ordinary people. There is even listed a group of people who refused to have any part in the building project (v 5)! The work of the Church is carried out by an assortment of people—the preacher and the plumber, the professional and the day laborer, the young and the old. There are also those in the pews who stand idly by, refusing to participate in the common good. Overall, the rather mundane and pedestrian construction details in this chapter may not appear to provide a great deal of spiritual food. Yet much of the work of the Church falls into this category. There are meetings to attend, carpets to clean, and grass to mow—all seemingly spiritually insignificant. But the routine tasks of life are in themselves incarnational acts, even the giving of a cup of water.

15 And Shallum son of Col-hozeh, ruler of the district of *a* Mizpah, repaired the Fountain Gate; he rebuilt it and covered it and set up its doors, its bolts, and its bars; and he built the wall of the Pool of Shelah of the king's garden, as far as the stairs that go down from the City of David. 16 After him Nehemiah son of Azbuk, ruler of half the district of *b* Beth-zur, repaired from a point opposite the graves of David, as far as the artificial pool and the house of the warriors. 17 After him the Levites made repairs: Rehum son of Bani; next to him Hashabiah, ruler of half the district of *b* Keilah, made repairs for his district. 18 After him their kin made repairs: Binnui, *c* son of Henadad, ruler of half the district of *b* Keilah; 19 next to him Ezer son of Jeshua, ruler *d* of Mizpah, repaired another section opposite the ascent to the armory at the Angle. 20 After him Baruch son of Zabbai repaired another section from the Angle to the door of the house of the high priest Eliashib. 21 After him Meremoth son of Uriah son of Hakkoz repaired another section from the door of the house of Eliashib to the end of the house of Eliashib. 22 After him the priests, the men of the surrounding area, made repairs. 23 After them Benjamin and Hasshub made repairs opposite their house. After them Azariah son of Maaseiah son of Ananiah made repairs beside his own house. 24 After him Binnui son of Henadad repaired another section, from the house of Azariah to the Angle and to the corner. 25 Palal son of Uzai repaired opposite the Angle and the tower projecting from the upper house of the king at the court of the guard. After him Pedaiah son of Parosh 26 and the temple servants living *e* on Ophel made repairs up to a point opposite the Water Gate on the east

and the projecting tower. 27 After him the Tekoites repaired another section opposite the great projecting tower as far as the wall of Ophel.

28 Above the Horse Gate the priests made repairs, each one opposite his own house. 29 After them Zadok son of Immer made repairs opposite his own house. After him Shemaiah son of Shecaniah, the keeper of the East Gate, made repairs. 30 After him Hananiah son of Shelemiah and Hanun sixth son of Zalaph repaired another section. After him Meshullam son of Berechiah made repairs opposite his living quarters. 31 After him Malchijah, one of the goldsmiths, made repairs as far as the house of the temple servants and of the merchants, opposite the Muster Gate, *f* and to the upper room of the corner. 32 And between the upper room of the corner and the Sheep Gate the goldsmiths and the merchants made repairs.

Hostile Plots Thwarted

4 *g* Now when Sanballat heard that we were building the wall, he was angry and greatly enraged, and he mocked the Jews. 2 He said in the presence of his associates and of the army of Samaria, "What are these feeble Jews doing? Will they restore things? Will they sacrifice? Will they finish it in a day? Will they revive the stones out of the heaps of rubbish—and burned ones at that?" 3 Tobiah the Ammonite was beside him, and he said, "That stone wall they are building—any fox going up on it would break it down!"

a Or *supervisor of the portion assigned to*
b Or *supervisor of half the portion assigned to*
c Gk Syr Compare verse 24, 10.9: Heb *Bavvai*
d Or *supervisor*   *e* Cn: Heb *were living*
f Or *Hammiphkad Gate*   *g* Ch 3.33 in Heb

4:3 *any fox going up on it would break it down!* The reconstructed walls must have been judged as shoddy work. The critics of the project were more than happy to ridicule the amateur builders. Archaeological evidence confirms that the walls were indeed of inferior construction. The community assembled to do the building was not, after all, made up of professionals skilled in brick and mortar. By and large the work of God in the world is not done by experts. Skeptics throw insults at those foolish enough to follow the way of God, such as "Who do you think you are anyway? Do you really think you can change the world?" From all appearances the Church barely makes a ripple. But God's work cannot often be measured by external observation. A baby born in a manger to peasant parents hardly impresses a world enamored with power and wealth.

[4]Hear, O our God, for we are despised; turn their taunt back on their own heads, and give them over as plunder in a land of captivity. [5]Do not cover their guilt, and do not let their sin be blotted out from your sight; for they have hurled insults in the face of the builders.

6 So we rebuilt the wall, and all the wall was joined together to half its height; for the people had a mind to work.

7[a] But when Sanballat and Tobiah and the Arabs and the Ammonites and the Ashdodites heard that the repairing of the walls of Jerusalem was going forward and the gaps were beginning to be closed, they were very angry, [8]and all plotted together to come and fight against Jerusalem and to cause confusion in it. [9]So we prayed to our God, and set a guard as a protection against them day and night.

10 But Judah said, "The strength of the burden bearers is failing, and there is too much rubbish so that we are unable to work on the wall." [11]And our enemies said, "They will not know or see anything before we come upon them and kill them and stop the work." [12]When the Jews who lived near them came, they said to us ten times, "From all the places where they live[b] they will come up against us."[c] [13]So in the lowest parts of the space behind the wall, in open places, I stationed the people according to their families,[d] with their swords, their spears, and their bows. [14]After I looked these things over, I stood up and said to the nobles and the officials and the rest of the people, "Do not be afraid of them. Remember the LORD, who is great and awe-some, and fight for your kin, your sons, your daughters, your wives, and your homes."

15 When our enemies heard that their plot was known to us, and that God had frustrated it, we all returned to the wall, each to his work. [16]From that day on, half of my servants worked on construction, and half held the spears, shields, bows, and body-armor; and the leaders posted themselves behind the whole house of Judah, [17]who were building the wall. The burden bearers carried their loads in such a way that each labored on the work with one hand and with the other held a weapon. [18]And each of the builders had his sword strapped at his side while he built. The man who sounded the trumpet was beside me. [19]And I said to the nobles, the officials, and the rest of the people, "The work is great and widely spread out, and we are separated far from one another on the wall. [20]Rally to us wherever you hear the sound of the trumpet. Our God will fight for us."

21 So we labored at the work, and half of them held the spears from break of dawn until the stars came out. [22]I also said to the people at that time, "Let every man and his servant pass the night inside Jerusalem, so that they may be a guard for us by night and may labor by day." [23]So neither I nor my brothers nor my servants nor the men of the guard who followed me ever took off our clothes; each kept his weapon in his right hand.[e]

a Ch 4.1 in Heb   *b* Cn: Heb *you return*
c Compare Gk Syr: Meaning of Heb uncertain
d Meaning of Heb uncertain   *e* Cn: Heb *each his weapon the water*

4:4–5 *Hear, O our God, for we are despised.* The man of action did not trade taunts with his opponents. Nehemiah simply prayed. The Church often finds itself besieged with criticism. Too often, unfortunately, the Church spends valuable resources and time arguing with adversaries instead of making opposition a matter of prayer and then getting on with the work. Still, the prayer of Nehemiah may be questioned. Clearly it was not a prayer of Jesus, who instructed his disciples to love their enemies (Matt 5:44). But all authentic prayer is a scraping of the heart whereby the dregs of the soul are offered up to God. Nehemiah's prayer reveals his heart, which God welcomes even if God does not always approve of its sentiments.

4:9 PRAYER—*See* Spiritual Disciplines Index.

4:10–12, 20 *too much rubbish.* How often workers in the Church voice the same problem: "There is just too much to do. We will never be able to finish." Sometimes the complaint is registered by sincere servants and sometimes by naysayers, but in truth the work of ministry is at times overwhelming. John Wesley once said, "I often tire *in* my work but I never tire *of* my work." Ultimately, when all is said and done there will still be many uncompleted tasks. God alone will bear responsibility for any unfinished business.

Nehemiah Deals with Oppression

5 Now there was a great outcry of the people and of their wives against their Jewish kin. ²For there were those who said, "With our sons and our daughters, we are many; we must get grain, so that we may eat and stay alive." ³There were also those who said, "We are having to pledge our fields, our vineyards, and our houses in order to get grain during the famine." ⁴And there were those who said, "We are having to borrow money on our fields and vineyards to pay the king's tax. ⁵Now our flesh is the same as that of our kindred; our children are the same as their children; and yet we are forcing our sons and daughters to be slaves, and some of our daughters have been ravished; we are powerless, and our fields and vineyards now belong to others."

6 I was very angry when I heard their outcry and these complaints. ⁷After thinking it over, I brought charges against the nobles and the officials; I said to them, "You are all taking interest from your own people." And I called a great assembly to deal with them, ⁸and said to them, "As far as we were able, we have bought back our Jewish kindred who had been sold to other nations; but now you are selling your own kin, who must then be bought back by us!" They were silent, and could not find a word to say. ⁹So I said, "The thing that you are doing is not good. Should you not walk in the fear of our God, to prevent the taunts of the nations our enemies? ¹⁰Moreover I and my brothers and my servants are lending them money and grain. Let us stop this taking of interest. ¹¹Restore to them, this very day, their fields, their vineyards, their olive orchards, and their houses, and the interest on money, grain, wine, and oil that you have been exacting from them." ¹²Then they said, "We will restore everything and demand nothing more from them. We will do as you say." And I called the priests, and made them take an oath to do as they had promised. ¹³I also shook out the fold of my garment and said, "So may God shake out everyone from house and from property who does not perform this promise. Thus may they be shaken out and emptied." And all the assembly said, "Amen," and praised the LORD. And the people did as they had promised.

The Generosity of Nehemiah

14 Moreover from the time that I was appointed to be their governor in the land of Judah, from the twentieth year to the thirty-second year of King Artaxerxes, twelve years, neither I nor my brothers ate the food allowance of the governor. ¹⁵The former governors who were before me laid heavy burdens on the people, and took food and wine from them, besides forty shekels of silver. Even their servants lorded it over the people. But I did not do so, because of the fear

---

5:2 *we must get grain.* Physical needs must be met even in the midst of doing God's work. The poor and the marginalized of society are too often overlooked by those who are doing "the really important work of the kingdom"— things like building walls or building a church. But Nehemiah knew, versed in Scripture as he was, that the God of Israel cared especially for the "powerless" (v 5).

5:8–11 *Let us stop this taking of interest.* Those who live with awe and reverence for God should also live with compassion and love for their neighbors. Affluent believers are not free to do with their wealth as they please; they are free to do with their wealth as God pleases.

5:14–19 *neither I nor my brothers ate the food allowance.* Nehemiah's sense of justice was derived from both his relationship with God and his concern for his fellow humans. Nehemiah, the man of action, practiced what he preached. He refused to profit at the expense of the less fortunate. In the New Testament the picture is clear that Jesus too was both radically obedient to God and selfless in his love for others. The lives of Nehemiah and Jesus demonstrate that theology and ethics are inseparable.

Responding
5:15–16 SERVICE. Rejecting the examples of his predecessors, Nehemiah devotes himself to the building of the wall rather than the building of his earthly wealth and influence, knowing that was the best way to serve his people. Today take a few minutes to

of God. 16Indeed, I devoted myself to the work on this wall, and acquired no land; and all my servants were gathered there for the work. 17Moreover there were at my table one hundred fifty people, Jews and officials, besides those who came to us from the nations around us. 18Now that which was prepared for one day was one ox and six choice sheep; also fowls were prepared for me, and every ten days skins of wine in abundance; yet with all this I did not demand the food allowance of the governor, because of the heavy burden of labor on the people. 19Remember for my good, O my God, all that I have done for this people.

Intrigues of Enemies Foiled

6 Now when it was reported to Sanballat and Tobiah and to Geshem the Arab and to the rest of our enemies that I had built the wall and that there was no gap left in it (though up to that time I had not set up the doors in the gates), 2Sanballat and Geshem sent to me, saying, "Come and let us meet together in one of the villages in the plain of Ono." But they intended to do me harm. 3So I sent messengers to them, saying, "I am doing a great work and I cannot come down. Why should the work stop while I leave it to come down to you?" 4They sent to me four times in this way, and I answered them in the same manner. 5In the same way Sanballat for the fifth time sent his servant to me with an open letter in his hand. 6In it was written, "It is reported among the nations— and Geshem a also says it—that you and the Jews intend to rebel; that is why you are building the wall; and according to this report you wish to become their king. 7You have also set up prophets to proclaim in Jerusalem concerning you, 'There is a king in Judah!' And now it will be reported to the king according to these words. So come, therefore, and let us

confer together." 8Then I sent to him, saying, "No such things as you say have been done; you are inventing them out of your own mind" 9—for they all wanted to frighten us, thinking, "Their hands will drop from the work, and it will not be done." But now, O God, strengthen my hands.

10 One day when I went into the house of Shemaiah son of Delaiah son of Mehetabel, who was confined to his house, he said, "Let us meet together in the house of God, within the temple, and let us close the doors of the temple, for they are coming to kill you; indeed, tonight they are coming to kill you." 11But I said, "Should a man like me run away? Would a man like me go into the temple to save his life? I will not go in!" 12Then I perceived and saw that God had not sent him at all, but he had pronounced the prophecy against me because Tobiah and Sanballat had hired him. 13He was hired for this purpose, to intimidate me and make me sin by acting in this way, and so they could give me a bad name, in order to taunt me. 14Remember Tobiah and Sanballat, O my God, according to these things that they did, and also the prophetess Noadiah and the rest of the prophets who wanted to make me afraid.

The Wall Completed

15 So the wall was finished on the twenty-fifth day of the month Elul, in fifty-two days. 16And when all our enemies heard of it, all the nations around us were afraid b and fell greatly in their own esteem; for they perceived that this work had been accomplished with the help of our God. 17Moreover in those days the nobles of Judah sent many letters to Tobiah, and Tobiah's letters came to them. 18For many in Judah were bound by oath to him, because he was the son-in-law of Shecaniah son of

a Heb *Gashmu*   b Another reading is *saw*

---

meditate with a pencil in your hand. Focus on asking God the ways he would like you to serve and write down everything that comes to mind. Afterwards look over your written meditation and select one or two ideas to pursue now, saving the others for another time. *See also* Spiritual Disciplines Index.

6:3 *I am doing a great work and I cannot come down.* Nehemiah's response might better be expressed: "This work is too important for me to leave." The important work for Christians is living for Jesus. Distractions abound in the life of faith, but staying focused on following Jesus is the priority.

Arah: and his son Jehohanan had married the daughter of Meshullam son of Berechiah. [19]Also they spoke of his good deeds in my presence, and reported my words to him. And Tobiah sent letters to intimidate me.

7 Now when the wall had been built and I had set up the doors, and the gatekeepers, the singers, and the Levites had been appointed, [2]I gave my brother Hanani charge over Jerusalem, along with Hananiah the commander of the citadel—for he was a faithful man and feared God more than many. [3]And I said to them, "The gates of Jerusalem are not to be opened until the sun is hot; while the gatekeepers[a] are still standing guard, let them shut and bar the doors. Appoint guards from among the inhabitants of Jerusalem, some at their watch posts, and others before their own houses." [4]The city was wide and large, but the people within it were few and no houses had been built.

Lists of the Returned Exiles

5 Then my God put it into my mind to assemble the nobles and the officials and the people to be enrolled by genealogy. And I found the book of the genealogy of those who were the first to come back, and I found the following written in it:

6 These are the people of the province who came up out of the captivity of those exiles whom King Nebuchadnezzar of Babylon had carried into exile; they returned to Jerusalem and Judah, each to his town. [7]They came with Zerubbabel, Jeshua, Nehemiah, Azariah, Raamiah, Nahamani, Mordecai, Bilshan, Mispereth, Bigvai, Nehum, Baanah.

The number of the Israelite people: [8]the descendants of Parosh, two thousand one hundred seventy-two. [9]Of Shephatiah, three hundred seventy-two. [10]Of Arah, six hundred fifty-two. [11]Of Pahath-moab, namely the descendants of Jeshua and Joab, two thousand eight hundred eighteen. [12]Of Elam, one thousand two hundred fifty-four. [13]Of Zattu, eight hundred forty-five. [14]Of Zaccai, seven hundred sixty. [15]Of Binnui, six hundred forty-eight. [16]Of Bebai, six hundred twenty-eight. [17]Of Azgad, two thousand three hundred twenty-two. [18]Of Adonikam, six hundred sixty-seven. [19]Of Bigvai, two thousand sixty-seven. [20]Of Adin, six hundred fifty-five. [21]Of Ater, namely of Hezekiah, ninety-eight. [22]Of Hashum, three hundred twenty-eight. [23]Of Bezai, three hundred twenty-four. [24]Of Hariph, one hundred twelve. [25]Of Gibeon, ninety-five. [26]The people of Bethlehem and Netophah, one hundred eighty-eight. [27]Of Anathoth, one hundred twenty-eight. [28]Of Beth-azmaveth, forty-two. [29]Of Kiriath-jearim, Chephirah, and Beeroth, seven hundred forty-three. [30]Of Ramah and Geba, six hundred twenty-one. [31]Of Michmas, one hundred twenty-two. [32]Of Bethel and Ai, one hundred twenty-three. [33]Of the other Nebo, fifty-two. [34]The descendants of the other Elam, one thousand two hundred fifty-four. [35]Of Harim, three hundred twenty. [36]Of Jericho, three hundred forty-five. [37]Of Lod, Hadid, and Ono, seven hundred twenty-one. [38]Of Senaah, three thousand nine hundred thirty.

39 The priests: the descendants of Jedaiah, namely the house of Jeshua, nine hundred seventy-three. [40]Of Immer, one thousand fifty-two. [41]Of Pashhur, one thousand two hundred forty-seven. [42]Of Harim, one thousand seventeen.

43 The Levites: the descendants of Jeshua, namely of Kadmiel of the descendants of Hodevah, seventy-four. [44]The singers: the descendants of Asaph, one hundred forty-eight. [45]The gatekeepers: the descendants of Shallum, of Ater, of Talmon, of Akkub, of Hatita, of Shobai, one hundred thirty-eight.

46 The temple servants: the descendants

_a_ Heb _while they_

6:16 _all the nations around us were afraid._ The Hebrew of this verse is uncertain, but from the context the sense is that the nations were "bowled over" by what the Jews had accomplished in fifty-two days. The neighboring communities thought that only the power of God could have made such achievement possible. When we as the People of God prioritize the living out of faith, the world will more clearly recognize the truth of our claims.

7:1–73 _Now when the wall had been built._ See note on Ezra 2:1–63.

of Ziha, of Hasupha, of Tabbaoth, [47]of Keros, of Sia, of Padon, [48]of Lebana, of Hagaba, of Shalmai, [49]of Hanan, of Giddel, of Gahar, [50]of Reaiah, of Rezin, of Nekoda, [51]of Gazzam, of Uzza, of Paseah, [52]of Besai, of Meunim, of Nephushesim, [53]of Bakbuk, of Hakupha, of Harhur, [54]of Bazlith, of Mehida, of Harsha, [55]of Barkos, of Sisera, of Temah, [56]of Neziah, of Hatipha.

57 The descendants of Solomon's servants: of Sotai, of Sophereth, of Perida, [58]of Jaala, of Darkon, of Giddel, [59]of Shephatiah, of Hattil, of Pochereth-hazzebaim, of Amon.

60 All the temple servants and the descendants of Solomon's servants were three hundred ninety-two.

61 The following were those who came up from Tel-melah, Tel-harsha, Cherub, Addon, and Immer, but they could not prove their ancestral houses or their descent, whether they belonged to Israel: [62]the descendants of Delaiah, of Tobiah, of Nekoda, six hundred forty-two. [63]Also, of the priests: the descendants of Hobaiah, of Hakkoz, of Barzillai (who had married one of the daughters of Barzillai the Gileadite and was called by their name). [64]These sought their registration among those enrolled in the genealogies, but it was not found there, so they were excluded from the priesthood as unclean; [65]the governor told them that they were not to partake of the most holy food, until a priest with Urim and Thummim should come.

66 The whole assembly together was forty-two thousand three hundred sixty, [67]besides their male and female slaves, of whom there were seven thousand three hundred thirty-seven; and they had two hundred forty-five singers, male and female. [68]They had seven hundred thirty-six horses, two hundred forty-five mules,[a] [69]four hundred thirty-five camels, and six thousand seven hundred twenty donkeys.

70 Now some of the heads of ancestral houses contributed to the work. The governor gave to the treasury one thousand darics of gold, fifty basins, and five hundred thirty priestly robes. [71]And some of the heads of ancestral houses gave into the building fund twenty thousand darics of gold and two thousand two hundred minas of silver. [72]And what the rest of the people gave was twenty thousand darics of gold, two thousand minas of silver, and sixty-seven priestly robes.

73 So the priests, the Levites, the gatekeepers, the singers, some of the people, the temple servants, and all Israel settled in their towns.

Ezra Summons the People to Obey the Law

When the seventh month came—the people of Israel being settled in their towns—

8 [1]all the people gathered together into the square before the Water Gate. They told the scribe Ezra to bring the book of the law of Moses, which the LORD had given to Israel. [2]Accordingly, the priest Ezra brought the law before the assembly, both men and women and all who could hear with understanding. This was on the first day of the seventh month. [3]He read from it facing the square before the Water Gate from early morning until midday, in the presence of the men and the women and those who could understand; and the ears of all the people were attentive to the book of the law. [4]The scribe Ezra stood on a wooden platform that had been made for the purpose; and beside him stood Mattithiah, Shema, Anaiah, Uriah, Hilkiah, and Maaseiah on his right hand; and Pedaiah, Mishael, Malchijah, Hashum, Hash-baddanah, Zechariah, and Meshullam on his left hand. [5]And Ezra opened the book in the sight of all the people, for he was stand-

a Ezra 2.66 and the margins of some Hebrew Mss: MT lacks They had . . . forty-five mules

---

8:3 *the ears of all the people were attentive.* Hearing is one of the most demanding of the Spiritual Disciplines. Listening to God's Word is not merely an auditory function, but involves a painful process of opening our lives to the judgment of the Holy One. Luther once observed, "If we hear the Word of God, and it doesn't offend us, then we have not heard it." To be sure there are times when Scripture comforts us, but if the Bible becomes merely the book that confirms our biases and prejudices, then we have misused it.

ing above all the people; and when he opened it, all the people stood up. 6 Then Ezra blessed the LORD, the great God, and all the people answered, "Amen, Amen," lifting up their hands. Then they bowed their heads and worshiped the LORD with their faces to the ground. 7 Also Jeshua, Bani, Sherebiah, Jamin, Akkub, Shabbethai, Hodiah, Maaseiah, Kelita, Azariah, Jozabad, Hanan, Pelaiah, the Levites, *a* helped the people to understand the law, while the people remained in their places. 8 So they read from the book, from the law of God, with interpretation. They gave the sense, so that the people understood the reading.

9 And Nehemiah, who was the governor, and Ezra the priest and scribe, and the Levites who taught the people said to all the people, "This day is holy to the LORD your God; do not mourn or weep." For all the people wept when they heard the words of the law. 10 Then he said to them, "Go your way, eat the fat and drink sweet wine and send portions of them to those for whom nothing is prepared, for this day is holy to our LORD; and do not be grieved, for the joy of the LORD is your strength." 11 So the Levites stilled all the people, saying, "Be quiet, for this day is holy; do not be grieved." 12 And all the people went their way to eat and drink and to send portions and to make great rejoicing, because they had understood the words that were declared to them.

The Festival of Booths Celebrated

13 On the second day the heads of ancestral houses of all the people, with the priests and the Levites, came together to the scribe Ezra in order to study the words of the law. 14 And they found it written in the law, which the LORD had commanded by Moses, that the people of Israel should live in booths *b* during the festival of the seventh month, 15 and that they should publish and proclaim in all their towns and in Jerusalem as follows, "Go out to the hills and bring branches of olive, wild olive, myrtle, palm, and other leafy trees to make booths, *b* as it is written." 16 So the people went out and brought them, and made booths *b* for themselves, each on the roofs of their houses, and in their courts and in the courts of the house of God, and in the square at the Water Gate and in the square at the Gate of Ephraim. 17 And all the assembly of those who had returned from the captivity made booths *b* and lived in them; for from the days of Jeshua son of Nun to that day the people of Israel had not done so. And there was very great rejoicing. 18 And day by day, from the first day to the last day, he read from the book of the law of God. They kept the festival seven days; and on the eighth day there was a solemn assembly, according to the ordinance.

a 1 Esdras 9.48 Vg: Heb *and the Levites*
b Or *tabernacles*; Heb *succoth*

Responding
8:6 WORSHIP. Two postures of worship are demonstrated here— raising our hands to God and bowing down to him. Try an experiment during your private prayer time. Begin standing with your hands raised as high as you like. Then, when you feel ready, kneel and bow your head to the ground as you are able. What feelings are evoked by each position? Did one or the other feel more natural? Why? *See also* Spiritual Disciplines Index.

8:7–8 *So they read from the book.* From this point forward Israel would be known as the "People of the Book." The community would revolve around the study of Torah and the interpretation and application of its laws. There is nothing simplistic about Scripture. The understanding of God's Word demands our whole attention, and even then there is ongoing need for the traditions of the Church, and the Holy Spirit.

8:10–12 *all the people went their way to eat and drink . . . and make great rejoicing.* Although the hearing of Scripture can be a disturbing event, the ultimate result for obedient and careful listeners is joy. Joy is not to be equated with momentary happiness; rather, biblical joy is a deep sense of peace that all is well with one's soul. The psalmist knew this deep peace when he wrote, "May those who sow in tears, reap with shouts of joy" (Ps 126:5).

National Confession

9 Now on the twenty-fourth day of this month the people of Israel were assembled with fasting and in sackcloth, and with earth on their heads. *a* 2Then those of Israelite descent separated themselves from all foreigners, and stood and confessed their sins and the iniquities of their ancestors. 3They stood up in their place and read from the book of the law of the LORD their God for a fourth part of the day, and for another fourth they made confession and worshiped the LORD their God. 4Then Jeshua, Bani, Kadmiel, Shebaniah, Bunni, Sherebiah, Bani, and Chenani stood on the stairs of the Levites and cried out with a loud voice to the LORD their God. 5Then the Levites, Jeshua, Kadmiel, Bani, Hashabneiah, Sherebiah, Hodiah, Shebaniah, and Pethahiah, said, "Stand up and bless the LORD your God from everlasting to everlasting. Blessed be your glorious name, which is exalted above all blessing and praise."

6 And Ezra said: *b* "You are the LORD, you alone; you have made heaven, the heaven of heavens, with all their host, the earth and all that is on it, the seas and all that is in them. To all of them you give life, and the host of heaven worships you. 7You are the LORD, the God who chose Abram and brought him out of Ur of the Chaldeans and gave him the name Abraham; 8and you found his heart faithful before you, and made with him a covenant to give to his descendants the land of the Canaanite, the Hittite, the Amorite, the Perizzite, the Jebusite, and the Girgashite; and you have fulfilled your promise, for you are righteous.

9 "And you saw the distress of our ancestors in Egypt and heard their cry at the Red Sea. *c* 10You performed signs and wonders against Pharaoh and all his servants and all the people of his land, for you knew that they acted insolently against our ancestors. You made a name for yourself, which remains to this day. 11And you divided the sea before them, so that they passed through the sea on dry land, but you threw their pursuers into the depths, like a stone into mighty waters. 12Moreover, you led them by day with a pillar of cloud, and by night with a pillar of fire, to give them light on the way in which they should go. 13You came down also upon Mount Sinai, and spoke with them from heaven, and gave them right ordinances and true laws, good statutes and commandments, 14and you made known your holy sabbath to them and gave them commandments and statutes and a law through your servant Moses. 15For their hunger you gave them bread from heaven, and for their thirst you brought water for them out of the rock, and you told them to go in to possess the land that you swore to give them.

16 "But they and our ancestors acted presumptuously and stiffened their necks and did not obey your commandments; 17they refused to obey, and were not mindful of the wonders that you performed among them; but they stiffened their necks and determined to return to their slavery in Egypt. But you are a God ready to forgive, gracious and merciful, slow to anger and abounding in steadfast love, and you did not forsake them. 18Even when they had cast an image of a calf for themselves and said, 'This is your God who brought you up out of Egypt,' and had committed great blasphemies, 19you in your great mercies did not forsake them in the wilderness; the pillar of cloud that led them in the way did not leave them by day, nor the pillar of fire by night that gave them light on the way by which they should go. 20You gave your good spirit to instruct them, and did not with-

a Heb *on them*   *b* Gk: Heb lacks *And Ezra said*
c Or *Sea of Reeds*

Responding

9:1 FASTING. The actions described here—refraining from eating, wearing sackcloth (from which funeral shrouds were made), and covering the head with dirt—all symbolize death. What is the connection between repenting and dying? What does reflecting on death teach us about life? *See also* Spiritual Disciplines Index.

9:6 WORSHIP—*See* Spiritual Disciplines Index.

hold your manna from their mouths, and gave them water for their thirst. 21 Forty years you sustained them in the wilderness so that they lacked nothing; their clothes did not wear out and their feet did not swell. 22 And you gave them kingdoms and peoples, and allotted to them every corner,*a* so they took possession of the land of King Sihon of Heshbon and the land of King Og of Bashan. 23 You multiplied their descendants like the stars of heaven, and brought them into the land that you had told their ancestors to enter and possess. 24 So the descendants went in and possessed the land, and you subdued before them the inhabitants of the land, the Canaanites, and gave them into their hands, with their kings and the peoples of the land, to do with them as they pleased. 25 And they captured fortress cities and a rich land, and took possession of houses filled with all sorts of goods, hewn cisterns, vineyards, olive orchards, and fruit trees in abundance; so they ate, and were filled and became fat, and delighted themselves in your great goodness.

26 "Nevertheless they were disobedient and rebelled against you and cast your law behind their backs and killed your prophets, who had warned them in order to turn them back to you, and they committed great blasphemies. 27 Therefore you gave them into the hands of their enemies, who made them suffer. Then in the time of their suffering they cried out to you and you heard them from heaven, and according to your great mercies you gave them saviors who saved them from the hands of their enemies. 28 But after they had rest, they again did evil before you, and you abandoned them to the hands of their enemies, so that they had dominion over them; yet when they turned and cried to you, you heard from heaven, and many times you rescued them according to your mercies. 29 And you warned them in order to turn them back

to your law. Yet they acted presumptuously and did not obey your commandments, but sinned against your ordinances, by the observance of which a person shall live. They turned a stubborn shoulder and stiffened their neck and would not obey. 30 Many years you were patient with them, and warned them by your spirit through your prophets; yet they would not listen. Therefore you handed them over to the peoples of the lands. 31 Nevertheless, in your great mercies you did not make an end of them or forsake them, for you are a gracious and merciful God.

32 "Now therefore, our God—the great and mighty and awesome God, keeping covenant and steadfast love—do not treat lightly all the hardship that has come upon us, upon our kings, our officials, our priests, our prophets, our ancestors, and all your people, since the time of the kings of Assyria until today. 33 You have been just in all that has come upon us, for you have dealt faithfully and we have acted wickedly; 34 our kings, our officials, our priests, and our ancestors have not kept your law or heeded the commandments and the warnings that you gave them. 35 Even in their own kingdom, and in the great goodness you bestowed on them, and in the large and rich land that you set before them, they did not serve you and did not turn from their wicked works. 36 Here we are, slaves to this day—slaves in the land that you gave to our ancestors to enjoy its fruit and its good gifts. 37 Its rich yield goes to the kings whom you have set over us because of our sins; they have power also over our bodies and over our livestock at their pleasure, and we are in great distress."

Those Who Signed the Covenant

38 *b* Because of all this we make a firm agreement in writing, and on that sealed doc-

a Meaning of Heb uncertain   *b* Ch 10.1 in Heb

9:37 *they have power . . . we are in great distress.* In Hebrew, Ezra's prayer ends with the phrase "in great distress we are." The words are an obvious cry for help to the God whose character has been extolled in the early part of the prayer. Given Israel's miserable record of failing God time and again, Ezra recognized the

Jews were hardly deserving of God's favor. Yet once again the Israelites plead for God to have mercy on them. The Israelites' history with God gave them hope that once again he would intervene on their behalf. The good news of Jesus Christ is God's gracious reply not only to the failures of Israel, but to the sin of the world.

ument are inscribed the names of our officials, our Levites, and our priests.

10 *a* Upon the sealed document are the names of Nehemiah the governor, son of Hacaliah, and Zedekiah; 2Seraiah, Azariah, Jeremiah, 3Pashhur, Amariah, Malchijah, 4Hattush, Shebaniah, Malluch, 5Harim, Meremoth, Obadiah, 6Daniel, Ginnethon, Baruch, 7Meshullam, Abijah, Mijamin, 8Maaziah, Bilgai, Shemaiah; these are the priests. 9And the Levites: Jeshua son of Azaniah, Binnui of the sons of Henadad, Kadmiel; 10and their associates, Shebaniah, Hodiah, Kelita, Pelaiah, Hanan, 11Mica, Rehob, Hashabiah, 12Zaccur, Sherebiah, Shebaniah, 13Hodiah, Bani, Beninu. 14The leaders of the people: Parosh, Pahath-moab, Elam, Zattu, Bani, 15Bunni, Azgad, Bebai, 16Adonijah, Bigvai, Adin, 17Ater, Hezekiah, Azzur, 18Hodiah, Hashum, Bezai, 19Hariph, Anathoth, Nebai, 20Magpiash, Meshullam, Hezir, 21Meshezabel, Zadok, Jaddua, 22Pelatiah, Hanan, Anaiah, 23Hoshea, Hananiah, Hasshub, 24Hallohesh, Pilha, Shobek, 25Rehum, Hashabnah, Maaseiah, 26Ahiah, Hanan, Anan, 27Malluch, Harim, and Baanah.

Summary of the Covenant

28 The rest of the people, the priests, the Levites, the gatekeepers, the singers, the temple servants, and all who have separated themselves from the peoples of the lands to adhere to the law of God, their wives, their sons, their daughters, all who have knowledge and understanding, 29join with their kin, their nobles, and enter into a curse and an oath to walk in God's law, which was given by Moses the servant of God, and to observe and do all the commandments of the LORD our Lord and his ordinances and his statutes. 30We will not give our daughters to the peoples of the land or take their daughters for our sons; 31and if the peoples of the land bring in merchandise or any grain on the sabbath day to sell, we will not buy it from them on the sabbath or on a holy day; and we will forego the crops of the seventh year and the exaction of every debt.

32 We also lay on ourselves the obligation to charge ourselves yearly one-third of a shekel for the service of the house of our God: 33for the rows of bread, the regular grain offering, the regular burnt offering, the sabbaths, the new moons, the appointed festivals, the sacred donations, and the sin offerings to make atonement for Israel, and for all the work of the house of our God. 34We have also cast lots among the priests, the Levites, and the people, for the wood offering, to bring it into the house of our God, by ancestral houses, at appointed times, year by year, to burn on the altar of the LORD our God, as it is written in the law. 35We obligate ourselves to bring the first fruits of our soil and the first fruits of all fruit of every tree, year by year, to the house of the LORD; 36also to bring to the house of our God, to the priests who minister in the house of our God, the firstborn of our sons and of our livestock, as it is written in the law, and the firstlings of our herds and of our flocks; 37and to bring the first of our dough, and our contributions, the fruit of every tree, the wine and the oil, to the priests, to the chambers of the house of our God; and to bring to the Levites the tithes from our soil, for it is the Levites who collect

a Ch 10.2 in Heb

10:28–29 *enter into a curse and an oath to walk in God's law.* The prayer in chapter 9 ends rather abruptly without even so much as an "Amen." But the "Amen" was supplied by the people, who put their very lives on the line. They vowed to "observe and do all the commandments of the LORD." Yes, God's forgiveness is an act of grace, but it takes effort on our part to live out the disciplines of faith. The "doing" of the commandments is our signature of faith, our "Amen" to God's grace.

10:39 *We will not neglect the house of our God.* The maintenance of the building is certainly in view in this verse. But paying attention to the house of God also implies participating in worship and entering into fellowship with the people. Being attentive to the house of God involves one's entire way of life. "Strive first for the kingdom of God and his righteousness" (Matt 6:33) catches the intent of this verse.

the tithes in all our rural towns. 38And the priest, the descendant of Aaron, shall be with the Levites when the Levites receive the tithes; and the Levites shall bring up a tithe of the tithes to the house of our God, to the chambers of the storehouse. 39For the people of Israel and the sons of Levi shall bring the contribution of grain, wine, and oil to the storerooms where the vessels of the sanctuary are, and where the priests that minister, and the gatekeepers and the singers are. We will not neglect the house of our God.

Population of the City Increased

11 Now the leaders of the people lived in Jerusalem; and the rest of the people cast lots to bring one out of ten to live in the holy city Jerusalem, while nine-tenths remained in the other towns. 2And the people blessed all those who willingly offered to live in Jerusalem.

3 These are the leaders of the province who lived in Jerusalem; but in the towns of Judah all lived on their property in their towns: Israel, the priests, the Levites, the temple servants, and the descendants of Solomon's servants. 4And in Jerusalem lived some of the Judahites and of the Benjaminites. Of the Judahites: Athaiah son of Uzziah son of Zechariah son of Amariah son of Shephatiah son of Mahalalel, of the descendants of Perez; 5and Maaseiah son of Baruch son of Col-hozeh son of Hazaiah son of Adaiah son of Joiarib son of Zechariah son of the Shilonite. 6All the descendants of Perez who lived in Jerusalem were four hundred sixty-eight valiant warriors.

7 And these are the Benjaminites: Sallu son of Meshullam son of Joed son of Pedaiah son of Kolaiah son of Maaseiah son of Ithiel son of Jeshaiah. 8And his brothers*a* Gabbai, Sallai: nine hundred twenty-eight. 9Joel son

of Zichri was their overseer; and Judah son of Hassenuah was second in charge of the city.

10 Of the priests: Jedaiah son of Joiarib, Jachin, 11Seraiah son of Hilkiah son of Meshullam son of Zadok son of Meraioth son of Ahitub, officer of the house of God, 12and their associates who did the work of the house, eight hundred twenty-two; and Adaiah son of Jeroham son of Pelaliah son of Amzi son of Zechariah son of Pashhur son of Malchijah, 13and his associates, heads of ancestral houses, two hundred forty-two; and Amashsai son of Azarel son of Ahzai son of Meshillemoth son of Immer, 14and their associates, valiant warriors, one hundred twenty-eight; their overseer was Zabdiel son of Haggedolim.

15 And of the Levites: Shemaiah son of Hasshub son of Azrikam son of Hashabiah son of Bunni; 16and Shabbethai and Jozabad, of the leaders of the Levites, who were over the outside work of the house of God; 17and Mattaniah son of Mica son of Zabdi son of Asaph, who was the leader to begin the thanksgiving in prayer, and Bakbukiah, the second among his associates; and Abda son of Shammua son of Galal son of Jeduthun. 18All the Levites in the holy city were two hundred eighty-four.

19 The gatekeepers, Akkub, Talmon and their associates, who kept watch at the gates, were one hundred seventy-two. 20And the rest of Israel, and of the priests and the Levites, were in all the towns of Judah, all of them in their inheritance. 21But the temple servants lived on Ophel; and Ziha and Gishpa were over the temple servants.

22 The overseer of the Levites in Jerusalem was Uzzi son of Bani son of Hashabiah son of Mattaniah son of Mica, of the descendants of Asaph, the singers, in charge of the work of

a Gk Mss: Heb *And after him*

11:1–2 *one out of ten to live in the holy city.* The holy city of Jerusalem had walls and a Temple but few people. Yes, there were priests and Levites, but ordinary folks were needed as well. Every congregation has its leaders, but the Church moves forward on the shoulders of working people—the single mom who teaches a

Sunday school class or the teen who works in the kitchen on Wednesday nights. A simple blessing is still appreciated by those who willingly offer their lives in service.

11:17 PRAYER—*See* Spiritual Disciplines Index.

the house of God. 23For there was a command from the king concerning them, and a settled provision for the singers, as was required every day. 24And Pethahiah son of Meshezabel, of the descendants of Zerah son of Judah, was at the king's hand in all matters concerning the people.

Villages outside Jerusalem

25 And as for the villages, with their fields, some of the people of Judah lived in Kiriath-arba and its villages, and in Dibon and its villages, and in Jekabzeel and its villages, 26and in Jeshua and in Moladah and Beth-pelet, 27in Hazar-shual, in Beer-sheba and its villages, 28in Ziklag, in Meconah and its villages, 29in En-rimmon, in Zorah, in Jarmuth, 30Zanoah, Adullam, and their villages, Lachish and its fields, and Azekah and its villages. So they camped from Beer-sheba to the valley of Hinnom. 31The people of Benjamin also lived from Geba onward, at Michmash, Aija, Bethel and its villages, 32Anathoth, Nob, Ananiah, 33Hazor, Ramah, Gittaim, 34Hadid, Zeboim, Neballat, 35Lod, and Ono, the valley of artisans. 36And certain divisions of the Levites in Judah were joined to Benjamin.

A List of Priests and Levites

12 These are the priests and the Levites who came up with Zerubbabel son of Shealtiel, and Jeshua: Seraiah, Jeremiah, Ezra, 2Amariah, Malluch, Hattush, 3Shecaniah, Rehum, Meremoth, 4Iddo, Ginnethoi, Abijah, 5Mijamin, Maadiah, Bilgah, 6Shemaiah, Joiarib, Jedaiah, 7Sallu, Amok, Hilkiah, Jedaiah. These were the leaders of the priests and of their associates in the days of Jeshua.

8 And the Levites: Jeshua, Binnui, Kadmiel, Sherebiah, Judah, and Mattaniah, who with his associates was in charge of the songs of thanksgiving. 9And Bakbukiah and Unno their associates stood opposite them in the service. 10Jeshua was the father of Joiakim, Joiakim the father of Eliashib, Eliashib the father of Joiada, 11Joiada the father of Jonathan, and Jonathan the father of Jaddua.

12 In the days of Joiakim the priests, heads of ancestral houses, were: of Seraiah, Meraiah; of Jeremiah, Hananiah; 13of Ezra, Meshullam; of Amariah, Jehohanan; 14of Malluchi, Jonathan; of Shebaniah, Joseph; 15of Harim, Adna; of Meraioth, Helkai; 16of Iddo, Zechariah; of Ginnethon, Meshullam; 17of Abijah, Zichri; of Miniamin, of Moadiah, Piltai; 18of Bilgah, Shammua; of Shemaiah, Jehonathan; 19of Joiarib, Mattenai; of Jedaiah, Uzzi; 20of Sallai, Kallai; of Amok, Eber; 21of Hilkiah, Hashabiah; of Jedaiah, Nethanel.

22 As for the Levites, in the days of Eliashib, Joiada, Johanan, and Jaddua, there were recorded the heads of ancestral houses; also the priests until the reign of Darius the Persian. 23The Levites, heads of ancestral houses, were recorded in the Book of the Annals until the days of Johanan son of Eliashib. 24And the leaders of the Levites: Hashabiah, Sherebiah, and Jeshua son of Kadmiel, with their associates over against them, to praise and to give thanks, according to the commandment of David the man of God, section opposite to section. 25Mattaniah, Bakbukiah, Obadiah, Meshullam, Talmon, and Akkub were gatekeepers standing guard at the storehouses of the gates. 26These were in the days of Joiakim son of Jeshua son of Jozadak, and in the days of the governor Nehemiah and of the priest Ezra, the scribe.

Dedication of the City Wall

27 Now at the dedication of the wall of Jerusalem they sought out the Levites in all their places, to bring them to Jerusalem to celebrate the dedication with rejoicing, with thanksgivings and with singing, with cymbals, harps, and lyres. 28The companies of the

---

12:1–26 *the priests and the Levites.* Western culture tends to dismiss the significance of priests and leaders of worship. Guides who help us find our way to "still waters" and "paths of righteousness" have been replaced by marketing experts, economic gurus, and motivational speakers. But the thinness of our lives calls out for priests and pastors and leaders, called of God, to lead us to green pastures. And the names of those who have helped us hear the Word or experience God's presence are remembered.

12:27 CELEBRATION—*See* Spiritual Disciplines Index.

singers gathered together from the circuit around Jerusalem and from the villages of the Netophathites; [29]also from Beth-gilgal and from the region of Geba and Azmaveth; for the singers had built for themselves villages around Jerusalem. [30]And the priests and the Levites purified themselves; and they purified the people and the gates and the wall.

31 Then I brought the leaders of Judah up onto the wall, and appointed two great companies that gave thanks and went in procession. One went to the right on the wall to the Dung Gate; [32]and after them went Hoshaiah and half the officials of Judah, [33]and Azariah, Ezra, Meshullam, [34]Judah, Benjamin, Shemaiah, and Jeremiah, [35]and some of the young priests with trumpets: Zechariah son of Jonathan son of Shemaiah son of Mattaniah son of Micaiah son of Zaccur son of Asaph; [36]and his kindred, Shemaiah, Azarel, Milalai, Gilalai, Maai, Nethanel, Judah, and Hanani, with the musical instruments of David the man of God; and the scribe Ezra went in front of them. [37]At the Fountain Gate, in front of them, they went straight up by the stairs of the city of David, at the ascent of the wall, above the house of David, to the Water Gate on the east.

38 The other company of those who gave thanks went to the left, [a] and I followed them with half of the people on the wall, above the Tower of the Ovens, to the Broad Wall, [39]and above the Gate of Ephraim, and by the Old Gate, and by the Fish Gate and the Tower of Hananel and the Tower of the Hundred, to the Sheep Gate; and they came to a halt at the Gate of the Guard. [40]So both companies of those who gave thanks stood in the house of God, and I and half of the officials with me; [41]and the priests Eliakim, Maaseiah, Miniamin, Micaiah, Elioenai, Zechariah, and Hananiah, with trumpets; [42]and Maaseiah, Shemaiah, Eleazar, Uzzi, Jehohanan, Malchijah, Elam, and Ezer. And the singers sang with Jezrahiah as their leader. [43]They offered great

sacrifices that day and rejoiced, for God had made them rejoice with great joy; the women and children also rejoiced. The joy of Jerusalem was heard far away.

Temple Responsibilities

44 On that day men were appointed over the chambers for the stores, the contributions, the first fruits, and the tithes, to gather into them the portions required by the law for the priests and for the Levites from the fields belonging to the towns; for Judah rejoiced over the priests and the Levites who ministered. [45]They performed the service of their God and the service of purification, as did the singers and the gatekeepers, according to the command of David and his son Solomon. [46]For in the days of David and Asaph long ago there was a leader of the singers, and there were songs of praise and thanksgiving to God. [47]In the days of Zerubbabel and in the days of Nehemiah all Israel gave the daily portions for the singers and the gatekeepers. They set apart that which was for the Levites; and the Levites set apart that which was for the descendants of Aaron.

Foreigners Separated from Israel

13 On that day they read from the book of Moses in the hearing of the people; and in it was found written that no Ammonite or Moabite should ever enter the assembly of God, [2]because they did not meet the Israelites with bread and water, but hired Balaam against them to curse them—yet our God turned the curse into a blessing. [3]When the people heard the law, they separated from Israel all those of foreign descent.

The Reforms of Nehemiah

4 Now before this, the priest Eliashib, who was appointed over the chambers of the

a Cn: Heb *opposite*

12:27–43 *to celebrate the dedication with rejoicing, with thanksgivings and with singing.* Can you hear the music and dancing, the laughter and singing? Pious Ezra, priest and scribe, with a grin from ear to ear, dances a jig on the wall overlooking the Temple. The

reserved Nehemiah lifts his hands and voice in praise as he nears the sacred area. The people, after long days and nights of toil and labor, are delirious with joy. God is in their midst. Time for celebration, time for singing. The joy can be heard for miles. Can you hear it?

house of our God, and who was related to Tobiah, 5prepared for Tobiah a large room where they had previously put the grain offering, the frankincense, the vessels, and the tithes of grain, wine, and oil, which were given by commandment to the Levites, singers, and gatekeepers, and the contributions for the priests. 6While this was taking place I was not in Jerusalem, for in the thirty-second year of King Artaxerxes of Babylon I went to the king. After some time I asked leave of the king 7and returned to Jerusalem. I then discovered the wrong that Eliashib had done on behalf of Tobiah, preparing a room for him in the courts of the house of God. 8And I was very angry, and I threw all the household furniture of Tobiah out of the room. 9Then I gave orders and they cleansed the chambers, and I brought back the vessels of the house of God, with the grain offering and the frankincense.

10 I also found out that the portions of the Levites had not been given to them; so that the Levites and the singers, who had conducted the service, had gone back to their fields. 11So I remonstrated with the officials and said, "Why is the house of God forsaken?" And I gathered them together and set them in their stations. 12Then all Judah brought the tithe of the grain, wine, and oil into the storehouses. 13And I appointed as treasurers over the storehouses the priest Shelemiah, the scribe Zadok, and Pedaiah of the Levites, and as their assistant Hanan son of Zaccur son of Mattaniah, for they were considered faithful; and their duty was to distribute to their associates. 14Remember me, O my God, concerning this, and do not wipe out my good deeds that I have done for the house of my God and for his service.

Sabbath Reforms Begun

15 In those days I saw in Judah people treading wine presses on the sabbath, and bringing in heaps of grain and loading them on donkeys; and also wine, grapes, figs, and all kinds of burdens, which they brought into Jerusalem on the sabbath day; and I warned them at that time against selling food. 16Tyrians also, who lived in the city, brought in fish and all kinds of merchandise and sold them on the sabbath to the people of Judah, and in Jerusalem. 17Then I remonstrated with the nobles of Judah and said to them, "What is this evil thing that you are doing, profaning the sabbath day? 18Did not your ancestors act in this way, and did not our God bring all this disaster on us and on this city? Yet you bring more wrath on Israel by profaning the sabbath."

19 When it began to be dark at the gates of Jerusalem before the sabbath, I commanded that the doors should be shut and gave orders that they should not be opened until after the sabbath. And I set some of my servants over the gates, to prevent any burden from being brought in on the sabbath day. 20Then the merchants and sellers of all kinds of merchandise spent the night outside Jerusalem once or twice. 21But I warned them and said to them, "Why do you spend the night in front of the wall? If you do so again, I will lay hands on you." From that time on they did not come on the sabbath. 22And I commanded the Levites that they should purify themselves and come and guard the gates, to keep the sabbath day holy. Remember this also in my favor, O my God, and spare me according to the greatness of your steadfast love.

Mixed Marriages Condemned

23 In those days also I saw Jews who had married women of Ashdod, Ammon, and Moab; 24and half of their children spoke the language of Ashdod, and they could not speak the language of Judah, but spoke the language of various peoples. 25And I contended with them and cursed them and beat

---

13:15–22 *sabbath day.* Keeping the Sabbath Day (the Lord's Day for Christians) is a reflection of faithfulness to God. By setting aside one day of the week for worship, prayer, and rest and turning our backs on the world, believers are empowered to live "in" yet not "of" the world during the remainder of the week. Too often the Lord's Day becomes a day of frantic worldly activity that destroys not only one's witness of God in the world, but wears down believers for the ensuing week.

some of them and pulled out their hair; and I made them take an oath in the name of God, saying, "You shall not give your daughters to their sons, or take their daughters for your sons or for yourselves. 26Did not King Solomon of Israel sin on account of such women? Among the many nations there was no king like him, and he was beloved by his God, and God made him king over all Israel; nevertheless, foreign women made even him to sin. 27Shall we then listen to you and do all this great evil and act treacherously against our God by marrying foreign women?"

28 And one of the sons of Jehoiada, son of the high priest Eliashib, was the son-in-law of Sanballat the Horonite; I chased him away from me. 29Remember them, O my God, because they have defiled the priesthood, the covenant of the priests and the Levites.

30 Thus I cleansed them from everything foreign, and I established the duties of the priests and Levites, each in his work; 31and I provided for the wood offering, at appointed times, and for the first fruits. Remember me, O my God, for good.

13:24 *spoke the language of various peoples.* Because of mixing with other cultures, some of the Israelite children lost the ability to speak Hebrew. Without being able to speak the language of faith, the children would not be able to read the Word of God or to follow the teachings of Scripture. Every generation of faith has to reeducate its children in the culture of faith or risk losing them to the culture of the world.

13:31 *Remember me, O my God.* Nehemiah's final prayer is that God would remember him. It was the prayer of the thief on the cross; it is the hope and prayer of all those who face eternity—"God, remember my good." And by the grace of our Lord, he will.

ESTHER

The book of Esther is a work of subtle complexity and insight. On first reading, it appears straightforward and simple. But the more time we spend with it and the closer we attend to it, the more fascinating it becomes. In the end, it leaves at least as much left unsaid as it says and raises at least as many questions as it answers.

In many ways Esther is a strange book, like none other in the Bible. For one, the story it tells is of a world largely unfamiliar to the rest of the Bible, namely, that of the Jewish diaspora in ancient Persia after the Babylonian exile. When Persia conquered Babylon, many Jews returned to Judea to resettle and rebuild Jerusalem. But many others did not, choosing instead to remain in the land of exile, which had become home. The book of Esther is the only biblical story about them. It is like a little window onto a world of ancient Jewish life that is otherwise lost to us.

In other ways, the book of Esther is only too familiar. We have a jealous king, a campaign to scapegoat innocent immigrants, and a government run by self-promoters who are out of touch with their own population. All of this confronts a young woman who finds herself caught in an impossible situation she had no part in creating. It is a world much like our own, in which the politics of "us against them" are driven by sexism, ethnocentrism, and nationalism.

Indeed, the world of Esther is a world of chance and insecurity in which nothing seems certain. And in this world, as in our own, the question that keeps pressing in is, "Where is God in all this?"

Living with Ambiguity

In the story Esther's world is one of ambiguity, even and especially *theological* ambiguity. In fact, God is never mentioned in the Hebrew book of Esther (in contrast to the Greek version of the story; see the Additions to Esther). God does not intervene on behalf of the Jewish people. God speaks to no one, and no one speaks to God. God is literally absent from the story.

See also *"The With-God Life"* essay for this section of the Bible,
"The People of God in Restoration," pp. 1355–59.

This absence is not accidental, a matter of oversight on the part of the narrator. The tale of Esther is told in a way that puts it in dialogue with many other biblical narratives, including the Joseph cycle in Genesis, the story of Saul in 1 Samuel, and the Passover story in Exodus. In those biblical narratives, God is very much present and active. Given the connections between Esther and these other Scriptures, the absence of any reference to God in Esther is all the more remarkable. Indeed, it would require a concerted effort to avoid God talk while remaining in conversation with these other biblical stories.

What do we make of this remarkable absence? Some interpret it as a sign of divine judgment. In rabbinic tradition, for example, Esther's name, which can be read as a first-person form of the Hebrew verb "hide" (*satar*), is taken as a message from God: "I will hide." Where is God in Esther? The Talmud finds an answer in Deut 31:17, where God declares that, on account of the Israelites' disobedience, "I will . . . hide my face [from them]." Of course, this answer is not exactly comforting, for it means that God is hiding from the Jews in the story as punishment for their disobedience. There is no blessed assurance in this rabbinic interpretation of God-forsakenness.

On the other hand, some find the hiddenness of God in Esther to be, paradoxically, a clear and undeniable reference to God's veiled presence in this story world. That is, for those who have eyes to see and ears to hear, the lack of any explicit mention of God is taken to be a clear affirmation that God is at work between the lines throughout the story. The silence cries out divine presence.

The amazing thing about the book of Esther is that it allows for so many answers to this question without letting us settle confidently on any one of them. Although it is certainly possible to see God at work between the lines and beneath the surface of the human motives and actions in the story, the book leaves at least as much room for us to read the story as one of chance, good luck, bad luck, and human ingenuity without recourse to divine intervention of any kind. In the end, the book of Esther seems to insist that there really is no knowing for sure. Indeed, what is most remarkable about this strange biblical book is its insistence on the *question* of God's presence over every possible answer.

For those of us who seek lessons in spiritual formation, the challenge here will be to stay with the question, to let ourselves remain restless and unsettled a while. Often darkness and uncertainty provide the environment most conducive to the growth of the soul. In the spiritual library of the Bible, we should consider cataloging Esther alongside Job and Ecclesiastes as one of those books that opens space in our lives to entertain questions—real questions, the kind that survive all the answers given to them. Like Job and Ecclesiastes, the book of Esther challenges us to live in the faith that our spiritual lives deepen and widen as we stay with these questions, resisting the temptation to settle them too quickly. Spiritual formation is not about finding security behind an arsenal of answers. It is about embracing a world infused with mystery and ambiguity, a world in which living by faith is anything but safe and secure.

Celebration and Laughter in an Uncertain World

Not only does the book of Esther encourage us to acknowledge the theological ambiguities and uncertainties of life in this world, it has fun with them, celebrates them, and invites us to go and do likewise. In this we have much to learn from our Jewish sisters and brothers.

In Jewish tradition, Esther is called Megillah, "the scroll," and has its very own holiday, named Purim, or "lots," after the fateful lottery cast by the king and Haman in Esther 3. Purim is the wildest, most playful, and most subversive celebration in the Jewish calendar. Like the Christian festival of Mardi Gras, which precedes Lent, Purim is a carnival time, a time when people are encouraged to undermine the laws and authority structures that are revered on every other day of the year. The centerpiece of Purim is a raucous public reading of the Esther scroll. Children and adults gather together in the evening to hear the scroll read aloud. But this is not a passive hearing. Many come in costume, dressed as characters from the story (Esther, Vashti, Mordecai, Haman, a eunuch) or something more outlandish (a Martian, a movie star, a fallen political leader). In any case, audience participation is a must. Some congregation members act out the story in a Purimspiel ("Purim play"); others use noisemakers and their loud voices to cheer for Esther and Mordecai, jeer at Haman, and laugh at the king.

Purim is a live-action, communal celebration of the story of Esther. It is a highly appropriate way to acknowledge both the wonderful strangeness and the troubling familiarity of this ancient text. It is a time when the familiar becomes strange and the strange becomes familiar, a time when distinctions between "us" and "them" can blur. It is a time when the rules of social hierarchy that normally guarantee those distinctions lose their holding power. Yet this wild carnival time, like the story of Esther itself, is also haunted by the many times throughout history when the Jews did not escape the deadly grasp of their enemies. The carnival celebration of Purim is haunted by countless pogroms, numerous attempted genocides, and above all, the Holocaust, in which Haman's order "to destroy, to kill, and to annihilate all Jews, young and old, women and children" (3:13) came dreadfully close to fulfillment.

Writer and Holocaust survivor Elie Wiesel captures the story's strange mix of carnival and dread horror in his play *The Trial of God,* which is set on Purim eve in a small town whose Jewish population was all but destroyed in a pogrom the night before. In the play, the minstrel Avrémel muses, "I imagine Purim without the miracle of Purim. And I know everything."

Still, every year, amid the haunting memories of many Purims without the miracle of Purim, Jewish congregations around the world embrace the story of Esther in this wildly playful way. Purim is not a denial of those haunting realities. Nor is it a denial of the profoundly real and pressing question, "Where is God in all this?" Without denying the harsh historical realities and the hard theological questions, Jews on Purim persist in celebrating, playing, and having laugh-out-loud fun with Esther.

As a living celebration of the story of Esther, Purim reminds us that spirituality is not all solemnity and austerity. Nor is spirituality all solitude and silent prayer. Our

WAKING!!
LAUGHTER

spiritual lives take form within community, as we join with other people to share food and drink, memories and hopes, faiths and doubts. Indeed, the deepest and hardest questions need not be depressing when we share them with others. They can bring us together and even, most astonishingly, bring us to laughter.

—Timothy K. Beal

King Ahasuerus Deposes Queen Vashti

1 This happened in the days of Ahasuerus, the same Ahasuerus who ruled over one hundred twenty-seven provinces from India to Ethiopia. *a* 2In those days when King Ahasuerus sat on his royal throne in the citadel of Susa, 3in the third year of his reign, he gave a banquet for all his officials and ministers. The army of Persia and Media and the nobles and governors of the provinces were present, 4while he displayed the great wealth of his kingdom and the splendor and pomp of his majesty for many days, one hundred eighty days in all.

5 When these days were completed, the king gave for all the people present in the citadel of Susa, both great and small, a banquet lasting for seven days, in the court of the garden of the king's palace. 6There were white cotton curtains and blue hangings tied with cords of fine linen and purple to silver rings *b* and marble pillars. There were couches of gold and silver on a mosaic pavement of porphyry, marble, mother-of-pearl, and colored stones. 7Drinks were served in golden goblets, goblets of different kinds, and the royal wine was lavished according to the bounty of the king. 8Drinking was by flagons, without restraint; for the king had given orders to all the officials of his palace to do as each one desired. 9Furthermore, Queen Vashti gave a banquet for the women in the palace of King Ahasuerus.

10 On the seventh day, when the king was merry with wine, he commanded Mehuman, Biztha, Harbona, Bigtha and Abagtha, Zethar and Carkas, the seven eunuchs who attended him, 11to bring Queen Vashti before the king, wearing the royal crown, in order to show the peoples and the officials her beauty; for she was fair to behold. 12But Queen Vashti refused to come at the king's command conveyed by the eunuchs. At this the king was enraged, and his anger burned within him.

13 Then the king consulted the sages who knew the laws *c* (for this was the king's procedure toward all who were versed in law and custom, 14and those next to him were Carshena, Shethar, Admatha, Tarshish, Meres, Marsena, and Memucan, the seven officials of Persia and Media, who had access to the king,

a Or *Nubia*; Heb *Cush*   *b* Or *rods*
c Cn: Heb *times*

1:1 *This happened in the days of.* These opening words (lit., "And it was in the days of . . .") are identical to those of Ruth. In Hebrew, they give both stories a "once upon a time" quality, introducing them as stories from the distant past. Indeed, historical record is not the primary interest of this story. The brief sketch of the historical context (vv 1–2) serves as a quick lead-in to the primary royal subject, namely, King Ahasuerus, which is the Hebrew name for Xerxes I, son of Darius, who ruled the empire of Persia from 485 to 465 BC. In this opening chapter and throughout the book, Ahasuerus is presented as insecure, impulsive, and prone to fits of rage. This characterization is consistent with depictions of him in other historical sources.

1:3 *he gave a banquet.* The Hebrew word translated "banquet" here and throughout the book is a noun form of the verb "drink." These banquets are, quite literally, "drinking parties." In this first chapter, there are three of them, two hosted by the king (lasting just over half a year all together) and one private party hosted by Queen Vashti for the women of the palace. The king's aim in throwing his parties is explicit: public demonstration of his wealth and power.

and sat first in the kingdom): [15] "According to the law, what is to be done to Queen Vashti because she has not performed the command of King Ahasuerus conveyed by the eunuchs?" [16] Then Memucan said in the presence of the king and the officials, "Not only has Queen Vashti done wrong to the king, but also to all the officials and all the peoples who are in all the provinces of King Ahasuerus. [17] For this deed of the queen will be made known to all women, causing them to look with contempt on their husbands, since they will say, 'King Ahasuerus commanded Queen Vashti to be brought before him, and she did not come.' [18] This very day the noble ladies of Persia and Media who have heard of the queen's behavior will rebel against[a] the king's officials, and there will be no end of contempt and wrath! [19] If it pleases the king, let a royal order go out from him, and let it be written among the laws of the Persians and the Medes so that it may not be altered, that Vashti is never again to come before King Ahasuerus; and let the king give her royal position to another who is better than she. [20] So when the decree made by the king is proclaimed throughout all his kingdom, vast as it is, all women will give honor to their husbands, high and low alike."

21 This advice pleased the king and the officials, and the king did as Memucan proposed; [22] he sent letters to all the royal provinces, to every province in its own script and to every people in its own language, declaring that every man should be master in his own house.[b]

Esther Becomes Queen

2 After these things, when the anger of King Ahasuerus had abated, he remembered Vashti and what she had done and what had been decreed against her. [2] Then the king's servants who attended him said, "Let beautiful young virgins be sought out for the king. [3] And let the king appoint commissioners in all the provinces of his kingdom to gather all the beautiful young virgins to the harem in the citadel of Susa under custody of Hegai, the king's eunuch, who is in charge of the women; let their cosmetic treatments be given them. [4] And let the girl who pleases the king be queen instead of Vashti." This pleased the king, and he did so.

5 Now there was a Jew in the citadel of Susa whose name was Mordecai son of Jair son of Shimei son of Kish, a Benjaminite. [6] Kish[c] had been carried away from Jerusalem among the captives carried away with King Jeconiah of Judah, whom King Nebuchadnezzar of Babylon had carried away. [7] Mordecai[d] had brought up Hadassah, that is Esther, his cousin, for she had neither father nor mother; the girl was fair and beautiful, and when her father and her mother died, Mordecai adopted her as his own daughter. [8] So when the king's order and his edict were proclaimed, and when many young women were gathered in the citadel of Susa in custody of Hegai, Esther also was taken into the king's palace and put in custody of Hegai, who had

a Cn: Heb *will tell*   *b* Heb adds *and speak according to the language of his people*   *c* Heb *a Benjaminite* [6] *who*   *d* Heb *He*

1:12 *At this the king was enraged.* The king, by now drunk, has in mind to bring Vashti before his fellows as the climactic display of his greatness. Her refusal is a refusal to be put on display, a refusal to be objectified by him. Such a refusal, of course, does not reflect well on him, sending him into a hot rage and his officers into a panic. (What if their wives hear about this and start undermining them as well?) The solution—not only to dethrone and banish Vashti, but also to make her an object lesson for all the women of Persia—is extreme to the point of ridiculous.

It leaves readers with little respect for anyone in chapter 1 except Vashti.

Responding
1:12 SUBMISSION. Queen Vashti certainly was justified in refusing to submit to her husband's request. How can we determine when it is right to submit to the authority of others in the Christian fellowship? Study some of the passages listed under "Submission" in the Spiritual Disciplines Index with this question in mind. What do you learn? *See also* Spiritual Disciplines Index.

charge of the women. [9]The girl pleased him and won his favor, and he quickly provided her with her cosmetic treatments and her portion of food, and with seven chosen maids from the king's palace, and advanced her and her maids to the best place in the harem. [10]Esther did not reveal her people or kindred, for Mordecai had charged her not to tell. [11]Every day Mordecai would walk around in front of the court of the harem, to learn how Esther was and how she fared.

12 The turn came for each girl to go in to King Ahasuerus, after being twelve months under the regulations for the women, since this was the regular period of their cosmetic treatment, six months with oil of myrrh and six months with perfumes and cosmetics for women. [13]When the girl went in to the king she was given whatever she asked for to take with her from the harem to the king's palace. [14]In the evening she went in; then in the morning she came back to the second harem in custody of Shaashgaz, the king's eunuch, who was in charge of the concubines; she did not go in to the king again, unless the king delighted in her and she was summoned by name.

15 When the turn came for Esther daughter of Abihail the uncle of Mordecai, who had adopted her as his own daughter, to go in to the king, she asked for nothing except what Hegai the king's eunuch, who had charge of the women, advised. Now Esther was admired by all who saw her. [16]When Esther was taken to King Ahasuerus in his royal palace in the tenth month, which is the month of Tebeth, in the seventh year of his reign, [17]the king loved Esther more than all the other women; of all the virgins she won his favor and devotion, so that he set the royal crown on her head and made her queen instead of Vashti. [18]Then the king gave a great banquet to all his officials and ministers—"Esther's banquet." He also granted a holiday[a] to the provinces, and gave gifts with royal liberality.

Mordecai Discovers a Plot

19 When the virgins were being gathered together,[b] Mordecai was sitting at the king's gate. [20]Now Esther had not revealed her kindred or her people, as Mordecai had charged her; for Esther obeyed Mordecai just as when she was brought up by him. [21]In those days, while Mordecai was sitting at the king's gate, Bigthan and Teresh, two of the king's eunuchs, who guarded the threshold, became angry and conspired to assassinate[c] King Ahasuerus. [22]But the matter came to the knowledge of Mordecai, and he told it to Queen Esther, and Esther told the king in the name of Mordecai. [23]When the affair was investigated and found to be so, both the men were hanged on the gallows. It was recorded in the book of the annals in the presence of the king.

Haman Undertakes to Destroy the Jews

3 After these things King Ahasuerus promoted Haman son of Hammedatha the

---

a Or *an amnesty*   b Heb adds *a second time*
c Heb *to lay hands on*

2:17 *and made her queen instead of Vashti.* The king sees Esther as an antidote for the harm Vashti did to his royal male ego. From our perspective, however, we might see Vashti and Esther as spiritual sisters. Both must live and move in a world dominated by insecure men who treat them as objects to bolster their own power and status. Yet the two women relate differently to the social system in which they find themselves. On the one hand, Vashti says no to it, and so it says no to her. She refuses the king's command, refuses to be objectified by him, and is banished from power. On the other hand, Esther will find her power by working within the system to bring about change. Do we not face similar dilemmas in our own lives? When are we called to work within imperfect and even unjust institutions and social structures in order to bring about positive changes, and when are we called to abandon them? Every day we must seek discernment for "such a time as this."

2:20 *Now Esther had not revealed her kindred or her people.* Note that the text does not say that Esther hid her Jewish identity, only that she did not reveal it. Here and elsewhere, it appears that Jewish identity is by no means obvious in appearance, speech, or behavior. Unless it is explicitly revealed, it goes unnoticed.

ESTHER

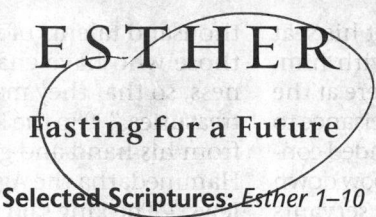

Fasting for a Future

Selected Scriptures: *Esther 1–10*

Although Queen Esther lived long before Paul wrote his words of Eph 6:11–13, she understood the reality of spiritual warfare. Esther understood as well that in periods of heightened danger, God's people need to seek his help in a committed, undivided way. They need to humble themselves and break from routine, seeking the deliverance only he can accomplish.

Esther lived in Persia, along with many Jews whose families had been taken captive in Judah a hundred years earlier. An orphan, Esther grew up in the home of her cousin Mordecai until she won the favor of the king and became queen (Esther 2:17).

When Mordecai brought news of a plot to kill the Jews, she knew the stakes. She would risk her life in approaching the king, or the Jews would almost certainly lose theirs. Esther instructed Mordecai and the Jews to hold a fast of the most serious kind—three days without food or water. Esther and her maids would do the same, and then she would go to the king (4:16). After three days of fasting and, no doubt, accompanying prayer, Esther found favor with the king (8:8). The Jewish people were spared.

Living in a land not their own, the Jews could rely only on God for their safety and provision. When the "spiritual forces of evil" pressed in, Esther knew that only God's unseen forces could prevail. The crisis called for God's people to place themselves before him in a corporate fast, confident that, whether they lived or died, God's purpose would prevail.

Surely in response to their fast, God moved the king to welcome Esther and then prompted him to lie restless and call for the royal records, thereby learning that he was indebted to Mordecai for his life. When God's people submitted themselves to him in true humility through fasting, God set in motion his infinite power to bring about his will.

Personal Reflection

- The three-day fast that Esther and the Jews undertook, abstaining from not only food but also water, is an "absolute fast" not recommended without a very clear command from God. Regular fasts from food only, however, are beneficial for most healthy Christians. Richard Foster explains in *Celebration of Discipline:* "It is obvious that [Jesus] proceeded on the principle that the children of the kingdom of God would fast." How could you benefit from incorporating this discipline into your life?
- "Fasting must forever center on God. It must be God-initiated and God-ordained.... Physical benefits, success in prayer, the enduing with power, spiritual insights—these must never replace God as the center of our fasting," Foster writes. Esther communicated this same conviction in her submission to life or death after the fast. How can you seek to keep God as the center?

Agagite, and advanced him and set his seat above all the officials who were with him. ²And all the king's servants who were at the king's gate bowed down and did obeisance to Haman; for the king had so commanded concerning him. But Mordecai did not bow down or do obeisance. ³Then the king's servants who were at the king's gate said to Mordecai, "Why do you disobey the king's command?" ⁴When they spoke to him day after day and he would not listen to them, they told Haman, in order to see whether Mordecai's words would avail; for he had told them that he was a Jew. ⁵When Haman saw that Mordecai did not bow down or do obeisance to him, Haman was infuriated. ⁶But he thought it beneath him to lay hands on Mordecai alone. So, having been told who Mordecai's people were, Haman plotted to destroy all the Jews, the people of Mordecai, throughout the whole kingdom of Ahasuerus.

7 In the first month, which is the month of Nisan, in the twelfth year of King Ahasuerus, they cast Pur—which means "the lot"—before Haman for the day and for the month, and the lot fell on the thirteenth day*a* of the twelfth month, which is the month of Adar. ⁸Then Haman said to King Ahasuerus, "There is a certain people scattered and separated among the peoples in all the provinces of your kingdom; their laws are different from those of every other people, and they do not keep the king's laws, so that it is not appropriate for the king to tolerate them. ⁹If it pleases the king, let a decree be issued for their destruction, and I will pay ten

thousand talents of silver into the hands of those who have charge of the king's business, so that they may put it into the king's treasuries." ¹⁰So the king took his signet ring from his hand and gave it to Haman son of Hammedatha the Agagite, the enemy of the Jews. ¹¹The king said to Haman, "The money is given to you, and the people as well, to do with them as it seems good to you."

12 Then the king's secretaries were summoned on the thirteenth day of the first month, and an edict, according to all that Haman commanded, was written to the king's satraps and to the governors over all the provinces and to the officials of all the peoples, to every province in its own script and every people in its own language; it was written in the name of King Ahasuerus and sealed with the king's ring. ¹³Letters were sent by couriers to all the king's provinces, giving orders to destroy, to kill, and to annihilate all Jews, young and old, women and children, in one day, the thirteenth day of the twelfth month, which is the month of Adar, and to plunder their goods. ¹⁴A copy of the document was to be issued as a decree in every province by proclamation, calling on all the peoples to be ready for that day. ¹⁵The couriers went quickly by order of the king, and the decree was issued in the citadel of Susa. The king and Haman sat down to drink; but the city of Susa was thrown into confusion.

a Cn Compare Gk and verse 13 below: Heb *the twelfth month*

3:2 *But Mordecai did not bow down.* Why does Mordecai refuse to bow down? Is it in obedience to the first commandment? Or is it because he is indignant about Haman's promotion, since it took place immediately after Mordecai had helped save the king from the assassination plot (2:21–22)? Or is it because Haman is an Agagite and therefore a descendant of King Agag, who was the cause of the downfall of Mordecai's Benjaminite ancestor Saul? The text leaves open all these possibilities.

3:8 *There is a certain people.* Haman alleges that the Jewish people of Persia are uniquely threatening to the king and his kingdom (an

ironic allegation to be sure, since we have already seen that Jewish identity is far from obvious within Persian society). They are a threat to the nation, and they must be annihilated. Remember, moreover, what prompted Haman to make this proposal: not some long-standing prejudice against Jews, but the fact that Mordecai, self-described as Jewish, humiliated him by refusing to bow before him. Just as Vashti's individual refusal to reflect well on the king led to a nationwide assertion of male dominance and wifely submission, so Mordecai's individual refusal to reflect well on Haman leads to a national plan for Jewish genocide.

Esther Agrees to Help the Jews

4 When Mordecai learned all that had been done, Mordecai tore his clothes and put on sackcloth and ashes, and went through the city, wailing with a loud and bitter cry; 2he went up to the entrance of the king's gate, for no one might enter the king's gate clothed with sackcloth. 3In every province, wherever the king's command and his decree came, there was great mourning among the Jews, with fasting and weeping and lamenting, and most of them lay in sackcloth and ashes.

4 When Esther's maids and her eunuchs came and told her, the queen was deeply distressed; she sent garments to clothe Mordecai, so that he might take off his sackcloth; but he would not accept them. 5Then Esther called for Hathach, one of the king's eunuchs, who had been appointed to attend her, and ordered him to go to Mordecai to learn what was happening and why. 6Hathach went out to Mordecai in the open square of the city in front of the king's gate, 7and Mordecai told him all that had happened to him, and the exact sum of money that Haman had promised to pay into the king's treasuries for the destruction of the Jews. 8Mordecai also gave him a copy of the written decree issued in Susa for their destruction, that he might show it to Esther, explain it to her, and charge her to go to the king to make supplication to him and entreat him for her people.

9 Hathach went and told Esther what Mordecai had said. 10Then Esther spoke to Hathach and gave him a message for Mordecai, saying, 11"All the king's servants and the people of the king's provinces know that if any man or woman goes to the king inside the inner court without being called, there is but one law—all alike are to be put to death. Only if the king holds out the golden scepter to someone, may that person live. I myself have not been called to come in to the king for thirty days." 12When they told Mordecai what Esther had said, 13Mordecai told them to reply to Esther, "Do not think that in the king's palace you will escape any more than all the other Jews. 14For if you keep silence at such a time as this, relief and deliverance will rise for the Jews from another quarter, but you and your father's family will perish. Who knows? Perhaps you have come to royal dignity for just such a time as this." 15Then Esther said in reply to Mordecai, 16"Go, gather all the Jews to be found in Susa, and hold a fast

---

Responding

4:3 FASTING. Like Esther's people, we too often abstain from food during times of crisis or mourning, because we lose our appetites or because we view eating, particularly sharing a meal, as a way of celebrating. At your next meal, take time to consider your attitude toward food. Does it represent fuel to make your body healthy? Is it a symbol of shared time with family or friends? Does eating bring feelings of guilt about your appearance? Is it too important in your life or is it not appreciated enough? *See also* Spiritual Disciplines Index.

4:14 *if you keep silence . . . relief and deliverance will rise . . . from another quarter.* Mordecai's declaration that deliverance will come from "another quarter" is often interpreted as an allusion to divine deliverance; that is, "another quarter" is taken to refer to God. In fact, rabbinic tradition, inspired by this passage, sometimes uses the Hebrew word for "quarter" or "place" (*maqom*) as an epithet for God. Whether or not we read "another quarter" as a reference to God, we must remember that Mordecai is making a conditional statement: *if* Esther keeps silent, *then* deliverance will rise from another quarter. As we will soon see, Esther will not keep silence, so the condition will not be met. Mordecai's "other" source of deliverance will not be needed. Esther will deliver.

4:16 *Go, gather all the Jews.* Up to this point, Esther has been altogether obedient to Mordecai and deferential to the king. Now her commands to Mordecai, and Mordecai's unquestioning obedience, reveal her in a very different light. From here on, Esther will be the one in the power seat, the one with the plan. Mordecai will have only to do what she says. Esther commands a three-day fast by all the Jews of Susa and says that she and her maids will do likewise. The discipline of fasting can be a means of creating

on my behalf, and neither eat nor drink for three days, night or day. I and my maids will also fast as you do. After that I will go to the king, though it is against the law; and if I perish, I perish." [17]Mordecai then went away and did everything as Esther had ordered him.

Esther's Banquet

5 On the third day Esther put on her royal robes and stood in the inner court of the king's palace, opposite the king's hall. The king was sitting on his royal throne inside the palace opposite the entrance to the palace. [2]As soon as the king saw Queen Esther standing in the court, she won his favor and he held out to her the golden scepter that was in his hand. Then Esther approached and touched the top of the scepter. [3]The king said to her, "What is it, Queen Esther? What is your request? It shall be given you, even to the half of my kingdom." [4]Then Esther said, "If it pleases the king, let the king and Haman come today to a banquet that I have prepared for the king." [5]Then the king said, "Bring Haman quickly, so that we may do as Esther desires." So the king and Haman came to the banquet that Esther had prepared. [6]While they were drinking wine, the king said to Esther, "What is your petition? It shall be granted you. And what is your request? Even to the half of my kingdom, it shall be fulfilled." [7]Then Esther said, "This is my petition and request: [8]If I have won the king's favor, and if it pleases the king to grant my petition and fulfill my request, let the king and Haman come tomorrow to the banquet that I will prepare for them, and then I will do as the king has said."

Haman Plans to Have Mordecai Hanged

9 Haman went out that day happy and in good spirits. But when Haman saw Mordecai in the king's gate, and observed that he neither rose nor trembled before him, he was infuriated with Mordecai; [10]nevertheless Haman restrained himself and went home. Then he sent and called for his friends and his wife Zeresh, [11]and Haman recounted to them the splendor of his riches, the number of his sons, all the promotions with which the king had honored him, and how he had advanced him above the officials and the ministers of the king. [12]Haman added, "Even Queen Esther let no one but myself come with the king to the banquet that she prepared. Tomorrow also I am invited by her, together with the king. [13]Yet all this does me no good so long as I see the Jew Mordecai sitting at the king's gate." [14]Then his wife Zeresh and all his friends said to him, "Let a gallows fifty cubits high be made, and in the morning tell the king to have Mordecai hanged on it; then go with the king to the banquet in good spirits." This advice pleased Haman, and he had the gallows made.

The King Honors Mordecai

6 On that night the king could not sleep, and he gave orders to bring the book of records, the annals, and they were read to the king. [2]It was found written how Mordecai had told about Bigthana and Teresh, two of the king's eunuchs, who guarded the

---

solidarity among people who are separated from one another. Fasting, moreover, reminds us that spirituality cannot be divorced from physical, embodied experience. As she prepares to confront the king, she knows that her community is with her in spirit *and* in body.

Responding
4:16 FASTING. When Esther asks her community to join with her in a three-day fast, she is asking them to support her with their bodies as well as their hearts. Consider engaging in a daylong fast to join in solidarity with those who fast not out of choice, but

because they do not have enough food. *See also* Spiritual Disciplines Index.

6:1 *that night the king could not sleep.* More literally, "That night sleep deserted the king." As sleep deserts him, he is left in restless wakefulness. His insomnia opens his mind to the memory of Mordecai, unacknowledged for his good deed (2:22). Sleeplessness often has a way of opening us to those we are not normally open to and to those we have forgotten in the light of day. Insomnia can be an opportunity to open new possibilities of relationship with forgotten others.

threshold, and who had conspired to assassinate[a] King Ahasuerus. ³Then the king said, "What honor or distinction has been bestowed on Mordecai for this?" The king's servants who attended him said, "Nothing has been done for him." ⁴The king said, "Who is in the court?" Now Haman had just entered the outer court of the king's palace to speak to the king about having Mordecai hanged on the gallows that he had prepared for him. ⁵So the king's servants told him, "Haman is there, standing in the court." The king said, "Let him come in." ⁶So Haman came in, and the king said to him, "What shall be done for the man whom the king wishes to honor?" Haman said to himself, "Whom would the king wish to honor more than me?" ⁷So Haman said to the king, "For the man whom the king wishes to honor, ⁸let royal robes be brought, which the king has worn, and a horse that the king has ridden, with a royal crown on its head. ⁹Let the robes and the horse be handed over to one of the king's most noble officials; let him[b] robe the man whom the king wishes to honor, and let him[c] conduct the man on horseback through the open square of the city, proclaiming before him: 'Thus shall it be done for the man whom the king wishes to honor.' " ¹⁰Then the king said to Haman, "Quickly, take the robes and the horse, as you have said, and do so to the Jew Mordecai who sits at the king's gate. Leave out nothing that you have mentioned." ¹¹So Haman took the robes and the horse and robed Mordecai and led him riding through the open square of the city, proclaiming, "Thus shall it be done for the man whom the king wishes to honor."

12 Then Mordecai returned to the king's gate, but Haman hurried to his house, mourning and with his head covered. ¹³When Haman told his wife Zeresh and all his friends everything that had happened to him, his advisers and his wife Zeresh said to him, "If Mordecai, before whom your downfall has begun, is of the Jewish people, you will not prevail against him, but will surely fall before him."

Haman's Downfall and Mordecai's Advancement

14 While they were still talking with him, the king's eunuchs arrived and hurried Haman off to the banquet that Esther had prepared. ¹So the king and Haman went in to feast with Queen Esther. ²On the second day, as they were drinking wine, the king again said to Esther, "What is your petition, Queen Esther? It shall be granted you. And what is your request? Even to the half of my kingdom, it shall be fulfilled." ³Then Queen Esther answered, "If I have won your favor, O king, and if it pleases the king, let my life be given me—that is my petition—and the lives of my people—that is my request. ⁴For we have been sold, I and my people, to be destroyed, to be killed, and to be annihilated. If we had been sold merely as slaves, men and women, I would have held my peace; but no enemy can compensate for this damage to the king."[d] ⁵Then King Ahasuerus said to Queen Esther, "Who is he, and where is he, who has presumed to do this?" ⁶Esther said, "A foe and enemy, this wicked Haman!" Then Haman was terrified before the king and the queen. ⁷The king rose from the feast in wrath and went into the palace garden,

a Heb *to lay hands on*   b Heb *them*
c Heb *them*   d Meaning of Heb uncertain

7:4 *For we have been sold, I and my people, to be destroyed.* With this declaration, Esther "comes out" as Jewish—an extremely risky thing to do at this point. Since Haman's edict in chapter 3, Esther has had two mutually incompatible social identities. On the one hand, she is the queen of Persia, the quintessential royal subject. On the other hand, she is a Jew, a member of the kingdom's despised minority, marked for annihilation by the royal law with which she is, as queen, closely identified. Now she reveals herself as a convergence of these two mutually incompatible identities, leading to a crisis in the cozy set of relationships between herself, the king, and Haman. Either she or Haman will not survive. For Esther to succeed, moreover, she must give the king an out; that is, she must make it appear as though he had no direct responsibility for the edict against the Jews (even though we as readers know that he did).

but Haman stayed to beg his life from Queen Esther, for he saw that the king had determined to destroy him. 8When the king returned from the palace garden to the banquet hall, Haman had thrown himself on the couch where Esther was reclining; and the king said, "Will he even assault the queen in my presence, in my own house?" As the words left the mouth of the king, they covered Haman's face. 9Then Harbona, one of the eunuchs in attendance on the king, said, "Look, the very gallows that Haman has prepared for Mordecai, whose word saved the king, stands at Haman's house, fifty cubits high." And the king said, "Hang him on that." 10So they hanged Haman on the gallows that he had prepared for Mordecai. Then the anger of the king abated.

Esther Saves the Jews

8 On that day King Ahasuerus gave to Queen Esther the house of Haman, the enemy of the Jews; and Mordecai came before the king, for Esther had told what he was to her. 2Then the king took off his signet ring, which he had taken from Haman, and gave it to Mordecai. So Esther set Mordecai over the house of Haman.

3 Then Esther spoke again to the king; she fell at his feet, weeping and pleading with him to avert the evil design of Haman the Agagite and the plot that he had devised against the Jews. 4The king held out the golden scepter to Esther, 5and Esther rose and stood before the king. She said, "If it pleases the king, and if I have won his favor, and if the thing seems right before the king, and I have his approval, let an order be written to revoke the letters devised by Haman son of Hammedatha the Agagite, which he wrote giving orders to destroy the Jews who are in all the provinces of the king. 6For how can I bear to see the calamity that is coming on my people? Or how can I bear to see the destruction of my kindred?" 7Then King Ahasuerus said to Queen Esther and to the Jew Mordecai, "See, I have given Esther the house of Haman, and they have hanged him on the gallows, because he plotted to lay hands on the Jews. 8You may write as you please with regard to the Jews, in the name of the king,

and seal it with the king's ring; for an edict written in the name of the king and sealed with the king's ring cannot be revoked."

9 The king's secretaries were summoned at that time, in the third month, which is the month of Sivan, on the twenty-third day; and an edict was written, according to all that Mordecai commanded, to the Jews and to the satraps and the governors and the officials of the provinces from India to Ethiopia,*a* one hundred twenty-seven provinces, to every province in its own script and to every people in its own language, and also to the Jews in their script and their language. 10He wrote letters in the name of King Ahasuerus, sealed them with the king's ring, and sent them by mounted couriers riding on fast steeds bred from the royal herd.*b* 11By these letters the king allowed the Jews who were in every city to assemble and defend their lives, to destroy, to kill, and to annihilate any armed force of any people or province that might attack them, with their children and women, and to plunder their goods 12on a single day throughout all the provinces of King Ahasuerus, on the thirteenth day of the twelfth month, which is the month of Adar. 13A copy of the writ was to be issued as a decree in every province and published to all peoples, and the Jews were to be ready on that day to take revenge on their enemies. 14So the couriers, mounted on their swift royal steeds, hurried out, urged by the king's command. The decree was issued in the citadel of Susa.

15 Then Mordecai went out from the presence of the king, wearing royal robes of blue and white, with a great golden crown and a mantle of fine linen and purple, while the city of Susa shouted and rejoiced. 16For the Jews there was light and gladness, joy and honor. 17In every province and in every city, wherever the king's command and his edict came, there was gladness and joy among the Jews, a festival and a holiday. Furthermore, many of the peoples of the country professed to be Jews, because the fear of the Jews had fallen upon them.

a Or *Nubia;* Heb *Cush*   *b* Meaning of Heb uncertain

Destruction of the Enemies of the Jews

9 Now in the twelfth month, which is the month of Adar, on the thirteenth day, when the king's command and edict were about to be executed, on the very day when the enemies of the Jews hoped to gain power over them, but which had been changed to a day when the Jews would gain power over their foes, [2]the Jews gathered in their cities throughout all the provinces of King Ahasuerus to lay hands on those who had sought their ruin; and no one could withstand them, because the fear of them had fallen upon all peoples. [3]All the officials of the provinces, the satraps and the governors, and the royal officials were supporting the Jews, because the fear of Mordecai had fallen upon them. [4]For Mordecai was powerful in the king's house, and his fame spread throughout all the provinces as the man Mordecai grew more and more powerful. [5]So the Jews struck down all their enemies with the sword, slaughtering, and destroying them, and did as they pleased to those who hated them. [6]In the citadel of Susa the Jews killed and destroyed five hundred people. [7]They killed Parshandatha, Dalphon, Aspatha, [8]Poratha, Adalia, Aridatha, [9]Parmashta, Arisai, Aridai, Vaizatha, [10]the ten sons of Haman son of Hammedatha, the enemy of the Jews; but they did not touch the plunder.

11 That very day the number of those killed in the citadel of Susa was reported to the king. [12]The king said to Queen Esther, "In the citadel of Susa the Jews have killed five hundred people and also the ten sons of Haman. What have they done in the rest of the king's provinces? Now what is your petition? It shall be granted you. And what further is your request? It shall be fulfilled." [13]Esther said, "If it pleases the king, let the Jews who are in Susa be allowed tomorrow also to do according to this day's edict, and let the ten

sons of Haman be hanged on the gallows." [14]So the king commanded this to be done; a decree was issued in Susa, and the ten sons of Haman were hanged. [15]The Jews who were in Susa gathered also on the fourteenth day of the month of Adar and they killed three hundred persons in Susa; but they did not touch the plunder.

16 Now the other Jews who were in the king's provinces also gathered to defend their lives, and gained relief from their enemies, and killed seventy-five thousand of those who hated them; but they laid no hands on the plunder. [17]This was on the thirteenth day of the month of Adar, and on the fourteenth day they rested and made that a day of feasting and gladness.

The Feast of Purim Inaugurated

18 But the Jews who were in Susa gathered on the thirteenth day and on the fourteenth, and rested on the fifteenth day, making that a day of feasting and gladness. [19]Therefore the Jews of the villages, who live in the open towns, hold the fourteenth day of the month of Adar as a day for gladness and feasting, a holiday on which they send gifts of food to one another.

20 Mordecai recorded these things, and sent letters to all the Jews who were in all the provinces of King Ahasuerus, both near and far, [21]enjoining them that they should keep the fourteenth day of the month Adar and also the fifteenth day of the same month, year by year, [22]as the days on which the Jews gained relief from their enemies, and as the month that had been turned for them from sorrow into gladness and from mourning into a holiday; that they should make them days of feasting and gladness, days for sending gifts of food to one another and presents to the poor. [23]So the Jews adopted as a custom

---

8:17 *professed to be Jews.* More literally, "were Jewing" or "were being Jewish." The Hebrew translated here as "professed to be Jews" is a verb form of the word for "Jew." As things get turned inside out and upside down, being Jewish has suddenly become all the rage. But what does it mean to "be Jewish" or to

"Jew" in a story in which Jewish identity has been far from obvious?

9:20–32 *days of feasting and gladness, days for sending gifts of food to one another and presents to the poor.* With the letters sent by Mordecai and Esther, the institution of Purim as an annual holiday becomes part of the story

what they had begun to do, as Mordecai had written to them.

24 Haman son of Hammedatha the Agagite, the enemy of all the Jews, had plotted against the Jews to destroy them, and had cast Pur—that is "the lot"—to crush and destroy them; 25 but when Esther came before the king, he gave orders in writing that the wicked plot that he had devised against the Jews should come upon his own head, and that he and his sons should be hanged on the gallows. 26 Therefore these days are called Purim, from the word Pur. Thus because of all that was written in this letter, and of what they had faced in this matter, and of what had happened to them, 27 the Jews established and accepted as a custom for themselves and their descendants and all who joined them, that without fail they would continue to observe these two days every year, as it was written and at the time appointed. 28 These days should be remembered and kept throughout every generation, in every family, province, and city; and these days of Purim should never fall into disuse among the Jews, nor should the commemoration of these days cease among their descendants.

29 Queen Esther daughter of Abihail, along with the Jew Mordecai, gave full written authority, confirming this second letter about Purim. 30 Letters were sent wishing peace and security to all the Jews, to the one hundred twenty-seven provinces of the kingdom of Ahasuerus, 31 and giving orders that these days of Purim should be observed at their appointed seasons, as the Jew Mordecai and Queen Esther enjoined on the Jews, just as they had laid down for themselves and for their descendants regulations concerning their fasts and their lamentations. 32 The command of Queen Esther fixed these practices of Purim, and it was recorded in writing.

10 King Ahasuerus laid tribute on the land and on the islands of the sea. 2 All the acts of his power and might, and the full account of the high honor of Mordecai, to which the king advanced him, are they not written in the annals of the kings of Media and Persia? 3 For Mordecai the Jew was next in rank to King Ahasuerus, and he was powerful among the Jews and popular with his many kindred, for he sought the good of his people and interceded for the welfare of all his descendants.

---

itself. As a direct response to the experience of deliverance "from sorrow into gladness and from mourning into a holiday" (v 22), Purim focuses not on the dread and sorrow of the ordeal but the joyful astonishment of the reversal of fortune. It is a celebration of a deliverance that almost did not happen. Haunted as it is by so many true stories in which the Hamans of the world succeed, Purim is nonetheless commanded to be joyous and festive. As a response to this deliverance, Purim is not only a time of feasting, but also a time of giving to one another and to the poor. Community celebrations need not turn us inward. As with Purim, they may open us up to the larger society of which we are a part.

Responding
9:22 CELEBRATION. Purim is a unique holiday in that it includes the element of giving to the poor alongside the more usual feasting. The next time you host a celebration—a birthday party, dinner party, even a wedding—consider following the example of Purim and sharing your celebration with those less fortunate by making or buying an extra cake or main course to donate to your local shelter. Many shelters will also accept leftovers from large events, a gracious alternative to throwing away extra food. *See also* Spiritual Disciplines Index.

9:31 FASTING—*See* Spiritual Disciplines Index.

VI. The People of God in Travail

Scriptures: *Job, Psalms of Lament (3–7, 10, 12–14, 17, 22, 25–26, 28, 31, 35, 38–44, 51–61, 64, 69–71, 74, 77, 79–80, 83, 85–86, 88–90, 94, 102, 109, 120, 123, 126, 129–130, 137, 139–143), Ecclesiastes, Lamentations*

Deuterocanonical Book: *Tobit*

> *The aim of God in history is the creation of an all-inclusive community of loving persons with God himself at the very center of this community as its prime Sustainer and most glorious Inhabitant (Eph 2:19–22; 3:10). The Bible traces the formation of this community from the creation in the Garden of Eden all the way to the new heaven and the new earth. Come, join us as we explore the many dimensions of this with-God history—from individual to family to tribe to people to nation to all humanity—and apply what we learn to our own spiritual formation.*

Previously, we explored the "with-God" life as it took shape in the glory of an established nation. In these Scriptures we will see the continued formation of the People of God into an all-inclusive community through the deep mystery of suffering.

God's Action

At the heart of Scripture is the reality of a loving God who is present to us even in the midst of our deepest setbacks and sufferings. But why does God allow suffering? This question perplexes people in every age and is especially relevant to building our life with God. Consider just a few passages of Scripture. The psalmist cries out, "Deliver me from my enemies, O my God; . . . Deliver me from those who work evil [against me]" (Ps 59:1–2). And elsewhere, "I am weary with my crying; my throat is parched. My eyes grow dim with waiting for my God" (Ps 69:3). Or consider the book of Job, in which Job and his friends struggle to explain the possible causes of suffering—it can be a result of human evil, or of individual sin, or even of corporate unrighteousness.

Ultimately, though, Scripture teaches that many times suffering just "is." Its mystery extends beyond human comprehension. Suffering is a reality whose existence eludes any ultimate explanation. It defies our human understanding. As much as we try, the limits of the human mind simply fail to make sense of it. Although we struggle to understand why God has chosen to place us in a world where suffering exists, God always makes provision for the deepening of our character.

Human Reaction

The quest to understand and explain suffering has led to some of the most magnificent breakthroughs in our knowledge of God. As different biblical writers have pondered its reality, they in turn have challenged some of the most fundamental teachings in the Old Testament. Job, in reaction to his own suffering, demonstrates that there simply is no easy relationship between good fortune and righteousness or between misfortune and wrath. He finds that life is a mystery that can be faced only by trust in and reliance upon God. And this mystery eludes the easy answers of his companions and even his own best explanations. It defies Job's reason and shatters the boundaries of his understanding—as it does our own. In the end, suffering challenges us to trust in a God, who, in ways beyond our knowing, controls the ultimate destinies of humans and nations. In one of the most dramatic exchanges in all Scripture, God states, "Shall a faultfinder contend with the Almighty? . . . Will you condemn me that you may be justified?" (40:1–8).

In the lament Psalms we find kings and ordinary people who react to suffering with anger in their hearts, revenge on their minds, or even despair in their emotions, all the while knowing that God is in control of their destiny. In their anguish they call out to God for deliverance from their enemies, rail at him when they are wronged, plead their case to a brass heaven, and sigh into their pillows. Many times their cause seems hopeless and God seems heartless. But the psalmist acknowledges that, constant like the needle of a compass, "the LORD sits enthroned forever, he has established his throne for judgment" (9:7).

The writer of Ecclesiastes, called the Teacher, considers the utter futility of human life without any reference to God. "Vanity of vanities," he begins. "All is vanity" (1:1–2). His questions are troubling even to us today. When the distinctions between virtue and wickedness appear to be ignored by God, why should we even try to be good? Why should we pursue righteousness if there is no apparent reward in this life and no awareness of a life to come? His conclusion feels far from a complete answer to these perplexing questions: "Fear God, and keep his commandments; for that is the whole duty of everyone" (12:13).

Lamentations returns to and reinforces the teaching of the Torah by suggesting that the terrible suffering befalling the Israelites is a result of their sin. And certainly in this case it is. "How lonely sits the city that once was full of people! . . . she that was great among the nations! . . . Jerusalem sinned grievously, . . . her downfall was appalling" (1:1–9).

The dissolution of society is indeed often a consequence of sin. At the very beginning of Genesis we learn that when human beings are alienated from God, they quickly become alienated from one another (Gen 3–4). In Lamentations, this truth is revealed in stark terms with dire consequences. The nation of Israel ceased to exist as a consequence of its sin. Tragedy does happen, and the awful consequences of turning away from God are real and troublesome. In the midst of such tragedy the Israelites (and we, like them) cry out, "Where is God?"

In Tobit and in his young relative Sarah we see many parallels with Job. They learn, as does Job, that being righteous and pious does not protect them from suffering. They struggle to come to terms with suffering in the context of a teaching that assures health and wealth to those who follow the precepts of the law. Finally, in the end, Tobit is able to declare, "As for me, I exalt my God, and my soul rejoices in the King of heaven," and he dies in peace (13:7).

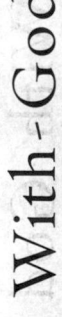

The With-God Life

Blessings and Benefits for Our Formation

Although suffering can genuinely disrupt our life with God, Scripture also points to the many ways suffering helps us find God and increase our understanding of his nature and ways. Up to this point in the history of the People of God, we have seen how divine purpose has provided for spiritual formation through rigorous adherence to ritual codes, purity laws, and observance of God's commands. The Torah establishes a measuring stick to evaluate the people's righteousness before God, and, if they keep its precepts, they will have health and wealth. Then comes Job.

Many of the basic tenets of the religious life of Israel are inverted in Job. Although Old Testament law establishes an objective standard that distinguishes the righteous from the wicked, suffering yet befalls the righteous and the wicked alike, leading Job to see this standard as too limited an understanding of our relationship to God. Job's insight lays bare another dimension of idolatry that prevents us from knowing God fully: we can't make idols of physical blessings or curses as if they were unfailing indicators of God's approval or disapproval. Through this insight we come to see with Job that suffering helps us know God in bad times as well as good. Only in this way do we gain a clearer vision of God and know that he is with us even when we cannot hear or see him. In suffering we learn the ways God is truly present even when he seems far, far away.

Suffering also teaches us that our desire to be happy can be satisfied only in a life with God. Often we miss this happiness by giving our love to the things of this world. Giving our love to God requires that we refuse to give our ultimate love to anything of this earth. Through suffering, a deeper dimension of our life with God is unveiled. Suffering clarifies the precarious nature of our life and our purpose in the world. It establishes clear boundaries within which we can find God.

Finally, suffering instructs us in the limitations of our life, our finitude, our inevitable death, and our need to prepare for our eternal destiny. Ultimately, all suffering reminds us that our days are "like a shadow" and we "fade like the grass," and that there is an eternal reality beyond this life (Eccl 8:13; Ps 37:2).

Limits and Liabilities for Our Formation

Still, while showing us the limited and precarious nature of our own existence, the harshness and randomness of suffering can radically challenge our belief in the goodness of God and the deep satisfaction we seek in him. Why do friends who are fine people fall prey to cancer? Why do leaders of a community die in an accident? Why do loving parents have children with horrible and debilitating birth defects? What of tornadoes, hurricanes, fires, and earthquakes and the massive destruction and loss of life they cause? And what of "man's inhumanity to man"? There are no easy answers to these thorny questions.

These sufferings, and many more like them, remind us that this life is not all there is and that there is a reality beyond this life that is the source of our lasting joy and enduring happiness. We come to see that suffering is only one side of the human experience with God, and we come to depend on him more and more to carry us through it.

But there is no celebration in suffering. We live with the stark awareness that even if we could do everything right, life still may not turn out the way we hope or intend. Suffering is not only beyond our control; it is beyond our understanding. It literally eludes our grasp. Indeed, at times it feels as though all of life is suffering. Like Job we cry out, "O that I had one to hear me!" (31:35). Yet even in the midst of the perplexity of suffering, we can gradually learn to live in a posture of humility and submission before God's purposes and ways.

Insights and Instructions for Our Formation

What can we learn from the vexing reality of suffering? First of all, we can learn that suffering will challenge our deepest convictions and strongest beliefs. Our quest to reconcile suffering with the love of God can lead to despair. Or it can lead to a deeper knowledge of the love of God. When the end was near for John, he wrote, "Beloved, let us love one another, because love is from God; everyone who loves is born of God and knows God" (1 John 4:7). Faced in faith and with grace, our suffering can bring us to the same place as John.

Second, suffering can teach us patience and endurance. We no longer demand a "quick fix" to heal our broken heart and cure our pain. The formation of our soul takes a lifetime, indeed an eternity. The developing patience and endurance within us are central qualities of character in the person being transformed according to divine purpose. Suffering is a crucial component of that transformation.

Third, suffering can lead us to trust in God so as to avoid despair. Although we wish God would bring relief, we eventually discover that God is not simply an extension of our will, and we come to accept his role as greater than the quick satisfaction of our personal desires.

Fourth, as we persevere through suffering we can see that God's reality is beyond the scope of our individual wishes and desires. We discover God's graciousness has nothing to do with our wish that he serve us as a celestial "butler." We learn that God "makes his sun rise on the evil and on the good, and sends rain on the righteous and on the unrighteous" (Matt 5:45). In this new awareness we discover the abiding presence of the love of God for all peoples.

In summary, all suffering is redeemable. All things do "work together for good for those who love God, who are called according to his purpose" (Rom 8:28). Suffering endured in faith helps us realize that God allows it because it inculcates great good into our lives through the transforming effect it has on our character. We become more compassionate, tolerant, and humble. We come to the place where we can see life realistically and hopefully at the same time. We discover that our ultimate destiny lies not in suffering, but beyond suffering in a life where God "will wipe every tear. . . . Death will be no more; mourning and crying and pain will be no more, for the first things have passed away" (Rev 21:4). We discover the abiding, caring presence of the God who holds each and every one of us in the hollow of his hand during our own experiences of suffering.

The With-God Life

JOB

The cast of characters in this drama is small, but they have profoundly shaped the religious imagination of generations: Job, a wealthy and righteous man from the land of Uz; God, the Ruler of the universe; Satan, otherwise known as the Accuser, the Adversary, or the Advocate of Evil (see note for 1:6); Job's wife; Job's three friends, Eliphaz, Bildad, and Zophar; and finally Elihu, a young man who gives advice to Job.

The book of Job is replete with themes that run through the Scriptures, but the one it explores more deeply than any other biblical book is the mystery of God and suffering. Suffering, especially suffering out of proportion to legitimate expectation, is a problem for all who believe in a loving and merciful God. Echoes of the problem of suffering appear in the Psalms of lament, prophetic books such as Jeremiah and Ezekiel, and the words of Jesus, but in no other place is the experience of the one who suffers disclosed in such detail as in Job.

Suffering is a problem for Job primarily *because* he believes in the living and loving God. His integrity in suffering arises because he refuses to accept the comforting or judgmental clichés and nostrums of the tradition—that life must be simplistically fair and so God must be punishing Job either for his sin or as a means of divine discipline. Job is searching for the true reasons for his distress. Every speech or dramatic soliloquy in Job is carefully crafted to explore the sensations of pain, grief, anger, and hope and the possible meaning that may lie behind the distress that has come upon Job.

The book of Job also explores a series of interlocking mysteries about life, the world, and God. For Job it is a deep mystery of the human heart to endure suffering while keeping faith alive, despite God's silence and seeming punishment. We also encounter the mystery of "the Satan" or "the Adversary," a force opposing God who desires to test Job's fidelity.

See also *"The With-God Life"* essay for this section of the Bible,
"The People of God in Travail," pp. 717–20.

The Drama

The book of Job can profitably be read as a drama with character development, speeches, action, tension, and resolution. It eludes easy placement in classical categories of tragedy, history, or comedy, but partakes of all. Just as elusive as the specific type of drama present is its date of composition. Some scholars argue that it is the oldest book in the Bible, while others point to it as a work of the exilic period in Israel's history because its language seems indebted to other biblical traditions.

Job's beautiful monologues reflect the profound drama of the heart's spiritual formation; his speeches explore shades of despair, bitterness, anger, grief, resignation, false hope, and genuine hope. His struggle to understand the contours of his pain inspires us to delve into the mysteries of God and our own heart and understanding. Our struggle with suffering mirrors and is fueled by Job's earlier struggle.

The drama opens with a description of Job, an upright and wealthy man. Soon, however, the Adversary approaches God and, under the guise of testing Job's fidelity, urges God to allow all manner of disaster to fall upon Job. God consents to Satan's request. In chapter 1, Job's children are killed and his wealth destroyed. In chapter 2 he breaks out in loathsome and painful sores. Despite his wife's urging to curse God and die, Job blesses God. Three friends travel a long distance to console Job. They keep silent for seven days because they see his great grief.

The balance of the drama (chaps 3–42) explores Job's loss, anger, grief, hope, and, finally, his restoration. In chapters 3–31 are three cycles of speeches (the third of which is incomplete) by Job and the friends who came to console him (2:11–13). Chapters 32–41 present two very long speeches, the former by a young man named Elihu and the latter by God. Elihu's often ignored speech is crucial in preparing Job to hear and respond to the words of God in chapters 38–41. Chapter 42 is the conclusion of the drama but, as in the resolution of any good drama, it leaves several potential loose ends unresolved for careful readers.

Suffering and Spiritual Formation

Because suffering is such a chaos-inducing experience, the lessons of suffering resist easy categorization. In the narrative we witness several different phases of the experience of suffering. At first we witness the torrent of emotions surrounding a sudden tragedy. Next we see Job's struggle to find some meaning for the evil. Those who suffer learn to discern various kinds of pain—from the feeling of being trapped in a net, to being abandoned in a pit, to being flooded by waters, to being torn by arrows. Job's reality is the agonizing tearing of his flesh by God's arrows (chap 6).

Job is also clearly angry. Anger boils to the surface of Job's complaint. It is manifest in bitterness, cutting sarcasm, flagrant overreaction against the friends, and cynicism toward God. Job's grief immobilizes him, distorts his view of time, gives him sleepless nights and painful days, and saps all his energy. By searching Job's grief we understand the world and our lives as never before.

In this context, we watch Job battle despair while also fighting off false explanations. In the midst of confusion, wisdom is available. It comes through a most unexpected source, Elihu, who is the model of a spiritual director, listening to Job and giving sage interpretation of his distress (chaps 28, 32–37).

One of the deep lessons Job learns is that the God he thought he knew is different from the God who had been watching over him all along. Pain limited Job's reality, but gave him the tools to deepen it also. A new knowledge of God is the blessed result.

The Mysteries

A mystery is something not discernible to human understanding. Biblically speaking, a mystery is something that only God can clarify through various means of disclosure. Even as the book of Job explores suffering in exquisite and lucid detail, it does so in the context of swirling mysteries that arrest our attention and invite our consideration.

For Job it is the mystery of the human heart. When we meet Job he seems as transparent and balanced as the clear and rhythmic language of the first few verses of the book. He has family, wealth, and honor. He is scrupulously religious. Life seemingly could not get any better. But it is what we are *not* told about Job that fascinates us. We know he serves God faithfully, but what kind of service is it? Is it motivated by fear or by genuine gratitude? We know he is a respected member of the community, but does Job feel that he deserves this position he enjoys? Does Job feel that the blessed life he has is an entitlement for him and that God has become bound to a sort of contract with him to continue the blessedness as long as Job keeps dispensing sage advice and caring for his family and religious duties? These are the questions Satan decides to test.

The mystery of Satan is the mystery of darkness. We do not really know who this creature is. All we are told is that it travels to and fro over the earth and that it seeks to test Job's faith. But its methods are so slick. All of us entertain doubts sometimes whether others love us for ourselves or only for some pleasure or benefit we provide them. The Adversary plays on this and preys on this before God. "Maybe Job's faithfulness is really the faithfulness of the one who has been paid off big-time, God," Satan intones. Only a test will determine the purity of Job's faith.

Even if smart readers can easily see through this "test," there is something more insidious in Satan. It loves knowledge. It says that faithfulness is to be discovered through tests, through experiments, through data collection, through increased information. How many of us today are knowledge-driven people living in an information-driven culture? The mystery of the Adversary arrests those who love knowledge, for it makes us wonder to what extent we seek knowledge to undermine rather than edify.

Finally, the mystery of God is the mystery of silence and wisdom. How can it be compatible with the wisdom of God even to listen to the blandishments and accusations of Satan, much less to go along with them? Surely we have no story if God does not permit Job's suffering, but the fact that God permits it raises the urgency of the question. Doesn't God know Job's heart? What kind of God is in view here, anyway? Are we mere pawns in a game God is playing?

The central problem for Job is that God will not talk to him, will not explain to him why this disproportionate suffering has been visited upon him. The long silence of God is a theological problem in the book of Job. The silence of God was also arguably the largest theological question of the last century. How could God be so distant, so seemingly unconcerned, as millions of Jews, among others, were brutally, systematically, and unmercifully cut down? Faithful readers sometimes rush in to defend God's ways. God will not enter and defend the divine ways until the end of the book. We honor the mysteries of God in Job by allowing our confusion, anger, hopelessness, and grief to mount as the book develops.

The nature of a mystery is that it escapes from our hands the moment we try to squeeze it. When we think we have come up with good reasons to explain how God is fully consistent in his actions throughout the book of Job, the text throws us a verse that boggles the mind. Job uses words of unparalleled vitriol in the book. He curses his birth, rails against God, calls his friends traitors, and accuses God of destroying his life. Finally, Job says he is sorry. But, at the end of the book (42:7–8), God implies that Job was right all along. We should not expect all the mysteries to be solved by this enigmatic book.

—Glandion Carney and William R. Long

Job and His Family

1 There was once a man in the land of Uz whose name was Job. That man was blameless and upright, one who feared God and turned away from evil. 2There were born to him seven sons and three daughters. 3He had seven thousand sheep, three thousand camels, five hundred yoke of oxen, five hundred donkeys, and very many servants; so that this man was the greatest of all the people of the east. 4His sons used to go and hold feasts in one another's houses in turn; and they would send and invite their three sisters to eat and drink with them. 5And when the feast days had run their course, Job would send and sanctify them, and he would rise early in the morning and offer burnt offerings according to the number of them all; for Job said, "It may be that my children have sinned, and cursed God in their hearts." This is what Job always did.

Attack on Job's Character

6 One day the heavenly beings[a] came to present themselves before the LORD, and Satan[b] also came among them. 7The LORD said

a Heb *sons of God*   b Or *the Accuser*; Heb *ha-satan*

1:1 *blameless and upright.* The balanced cadences of the opening verse reflect the orderliness of Job's life before God. He possessed goods, family, and faithfulness, the triad of biblical blessings that attend the blessed life. Job is also a respected member of the community and freely and compassionately dispenses wisdom and aid to all comers.

1:5 *It may be that my children have sinned.* Job's religious life was characterized by scrupulous fidelity on his own and his family's behalf. Job's concept of loyalty is thus a familial or communal one—it is not enough just to care for one's own spiritual life. That he rose early in the morning to sacrifice for his children indicates the priority that faithful service assumed in his life. Morning time was God's time.

1:6 *Satan also came.* Satan enters as a jarring presence in the otherwise idyllic world of Job. The text describes Satan as one who travels upon the earth with authority to appear before God. This being is really "the Satan," best translated as "the Accuser" or "the Adversary."

to Satan,[a] "Where have you come from?" Satan[a] answered the LORD, "From going to and fro on the earth, and from walking up and down on it." [8]The LORD said to Satan,[a] "Have you considered my servant Job? There is no one like him on the earth, a blameless and upright man who fears God and turns away from evil." [9]Then Satan[a] answered the LORD, "Does Job fear God for nothing? [10]Have you not put a fence around him and his house and all that he has, on every side? You have blessed the work of his hands, and his possessions have increased in the land. [11]But stretch out your hand now, and touch all that he has, and he will curse you to your face." [12]The LORD said to Satan,[a] "Very well, all that he has is in your power; only do not stretch out your hand against him!" So Satan[a] went out from the presence of the LORD.

Job Loses Property and Children

13 One day when his sons and daughters were eating and drinking wine in the eldest brother's house, [14]a messenger came to Job and said, "The oxen were plowing and the donkeys were feeding beside them, [15]and the Sabeans fell on them and carried them off, and killed the servants with the edge of the sword; I alone have escaped to tell you." [16]While he was still speaking, another came and said, "The fire of God fell from heaven and burned up the sheep and the servants, and consumed them; I alone have escaped to tell you." [17]While he was still speaking, another came and said, "The Chaldeans formed three columns, made a raid on the camels and carried them off, and killed the servants with the edge of the sword; I alone have escaped to tell you." [18]While he was still speaking, another came and said, "Your sons and daughters were eating and drinking wine in their eldest brother's house, [19]and suddenly a great wind came across the desert, struck the four corners of the house, and it fell on the young people, and they are dead; I alone have escaped to tell you."

20 Then Job arose, tore his robe, shaved his head, and fell on the ground and worshiped. [21]He said, "Naked I came from my mother's womb, and naked shall I return there; the LORD gave, and the LORD has taken away; blessed be the name of the LORD."

a Or the Accuser; Heb ha-satan

Its presence brings an element of mystery, drama, and uncertainty to the story.

1:8 *Have you considered my servant Job?* As a parent might feel justly proud of a child, God happily points out to the Adversary Job's fidelity. God takes delight in Job. Faithful service to God brings satisfaction not only to the person performing the service, but also to God.

1:9–11 *Does Job fear God for nothing?* The true colors of the Adversary begin to emerge in this challenge to God. Under the guise of searching for deep knowledge about Job's faithfulness, the Adversary wants to undermine the network of blessings and associations in Job's life. There is enough truth in what the Adversary says, however, to give pause. Isn't devotion to God supposed to be irrespective of physical condition? In the same way, we are tempted to think our understanding of God and how the world works is undermined when we experience personal tragedy. This is Satan's challenge.

1:20 *Then Job arose.* Job's reaction to his great pain is in actions and words (v 21). His actions show just how deeply rooted his piety is.

There is a solemnity in his actions, and we can see him in the mind's eye shaving his head, tearing his robe, falling on his face, and quietly worshiping God. The power of good ritual bears us through many a time of distress.

Responding

1:20 WORSHIP. Other than his wife, Job has just lost everything dear to him—children, servants, property. Yet he "fell on the ground and worshiped." Is this a romanticized notion or is it truly possible to worship God in the midst of great grief? What does Job's ability to worship God at this time reveal about his life with God? *See also* Spiritual Disciplines Index.

1:21 *blessed be the name of the LORD.* The first word we hear from Job ("Naked") reflects inner vulnerability as his external world collapses. The noble rhythm of the verse is Job's attempt to retain psychic and spiritual order. We get no window into his soul and we do not hear the tone of his voice, but his faith seems to hold firm.

22 In all this Job did not sin or charge God with wrongdoing.

Attack on Job's Health

2 One day the heavenly beings*a* came to present themselves before the LORD, and Satan*b* also came among them to present himself before the LORD. 2The LORD said to Satan,*b* "Where have you come from?" Satan*b* answered the LORD, "From going to and fro on the earth, and from walking up and down on it." 3The LORD said to Satan,*b* "Have you considered my servant Job? There is no one like him on the earth, a blameless and upright man who fears God and turns away from evil. He still persists in his integrity, although you incited me against him, to destroy him for no reason." 4Then Satan*b* answered the LORD, "Skin for skin! All that people have they will give to save their lives.*c* 5But stretch out your hand now and touch his bone and his flesh, and he will curse you to your face." 6The LORD said to Satan,*b* "Very well, he is in your power; only spare his life."

7 So Satan*b* went out from the presence of the LORD, and inflicted loathsome sores on Job from the sole of his foot to the crown of his head. 8Job*d* took a potsherd with which to scrape himself, and sat among the ashes.

9 Then his wife said to him, "Do you still persist in your integrity? Curse*e* God, and die." 10But he said to her, "You speak as any foolish woman would speak. Shall we receive the good at the hand of God, and not receive the bad?" In all this Job did not sin with his lips.

Job's Three Friends

11 Now when Job's three friends heard of all these troubles that had come upon him, each of them set out from his home—Eliphaz the Temanite, Bildad the Shuhite, and Zophar the Naamathite. They met together to go and console and comfort him. 12When they saw him from a distance, they did not recognize him, and they raised their voices and wept aloud; they tore their robes and threw dust in the air upon their heads. 13They sat with him on the ground seven days and seven nights, and no one spoke a word to him, for they saw that his suffering was very great.

Job Curses the Day He Was Born

3 After this Job opened his mouth and cursed the day of his birth. 2Job said:
3 "Let the day perish in which I was born,
    and the night that said,
    'A man-child is conceived.'
4 Let that day be darkness!
    May God above not seek it,
    or light shine on it.

a Heb *sons of God*   *b* Or *the Accuser*; Heb *ha-satan*   *c* Or *All that the man has he will give for his life*   *d* Heb *He*   *e* Heb *Bless*

2:1–6 *Satan also came.* The Adversary persists. "Maybe the screws haven't been tightened enough," he observes to God. "As long as you don't touch people's bodies, they remain faithful. Give me a little more play." God accedes to the Adversary's request. Mysteries abound here. The story might end here without further torment, but there is no easy answer to why God acquiesces in the Adversary's challenges and blandishments.

2:9–10 *Curse God, and die.* This verse contains Job's wife's only words in the book. The Hebrew text can also be translated, "Bless God, and die"—which shows the playful richness of the language of the book of Job. How are these words spoken? From sarcasm, exasperation? Certainly from great pain. Perhaps she speaks them because she knows Job better than anyone else and knows his current struggle. She too has lost home and family for no apparent reason. She invites despair, but Job rebukes her for basing their faithfulness on their circumstances.

2:11 *console and comfort him.* The friends come to Job in his need. They weep with him and sit quietly with him. Their quiet ministry of presence speaks loudly to those who think that only words heal.

3:3 *Let the day perish.* Job's tone changes completely. When pain first comes, we sometimes deny its full scope. But it is a jealous and insistent guest. It often exacts much more of us than originally thought. Job's ritual, friends, and words are now exposed as paper-thin defenses against the rushing onslaught of unimaginable pain.

5 Let gloom and deep darkness claim it.
  Let clouds settle upon it;
  let the blackness of the day terrify it.
6 That night—let thick darkness seize it!
  let it not rejoice among the days of
    the year;
  let it not come into the number of the
    months.
7 Yes, let that night be barren;
  let no joyful cry be heard *a* in it.
8 Let those curse it who curse the Sea, *b*
  those who are skilled to rouse up
    Leviathan.
9 Let the stars of its dawn be dark;
  let it hope for light, but have none;
  may it not see the eyelids of the
    morning—
10 because it did not shut the doors of my
    mother's womb,
  and hide trouble from my eyes.

11 "Why did I not die at birth,
  come forth from the womb and
    expire?
12 Why were there knees to receive me,
  or breasts for me to suck?
13 Now I would be lying down and quiet;
  I would be asleep; then I would be at
    rest
14 with kings and counselors of the earth
  who rebuild ruins for themselves,
15 or with princes who have gold,
  who fill their houses with silver.
16 Or why was I not buried like a stillborn
    child,
  like an infant that never sees the
    light?
17 There the wicked cease from troubling,
  and there the weary are at rest.

18 There the prisoners are at ease together;
  they do not hear the voice of the
    taskmaster.
19 The small and the great are there,
  and the slaves are free from their
    masters.

20 "Why is light given to one in misery,
  and life to the bitter in soul,
21 who long for death, but it does not
    come,
  and dig for it more than for hidden
    treasures;
22 who rejoice exceedingly,
  and are glad when they find the
    grave?
23 Why is light given to one who cannot
    see the way,
  whom God has fenced in?
24 For my sighing comes like *c* my bread,
  and my groanings are poured out like
    water.
25 Truly the thing that I fear comes upon
    me,
  and what I dread befalls me.
26 I am not at ease, nor am I quiet;
  I have no rest; but trouble comes."

Eliphaz Speaks: Job Has Sinned

4 Then Eliphaz the Temanite answered:
2 "If one ventures a word with you, will
    you be offended?
  But who can keep from speaking?
3 See, you have instructed many;
  you have strengthened the weak
    hands.

a Heb *come*   *b* Cn: Heb *day*   *c* Heb *before*

3:13–19 *I would be at rest.* In the midst of Job's cry of enormous pain comes an unexpected reverie of imagined peace. Death would not be so bad. He would join all kinds of distinguished people in the democratic realm of death. Even great pain is not unrelenting; there are mental breaks, lest the pain break us completely.

3:26 *but trouble comes.* Job's searing pain returns. As chapter 3 concludes, the sentences and phrases get shorter and shorter. The shortened sentences speak of the shrinking of Job's psychic space. He now feels the full weight of inner oppression. When he says "but trouble comes," he not only feels the pain anew, but he probably notices his fidgeting friends, who now want to get into the action by speaking.

4:3–4 *you have instructed many.* Eliphaz, presumably the oldest, is Job's first friend to speak. He is not judgmental and tries to build rapport with Job by reminding him of his words to others when they were in need. "Take your own advice, Job," he gently intones.

4 Your words have supported those who
        were stumbling,
    and you have made firm the feeble
        knees.
5 But now it has come to you, and you are
        impatient;
    it touches you, and you are dismayed.
6 Is not your fear of God your confidence,
    and the integrity of your ways your
        hope?

7 "Think now, who that was innocent
        ever perished?
    Or where were the upright cut off?
8 As I have seen, those who plow iniquity
    and sow trouble reap the same.
9 By the breath of God they perish,
    and by the blast of his anger they are
        consumed.
10 The roar of the lion, the voice of the
        fierce lion,
    and the teeth of the young lions are
        broken.
11 The strong lion perishes for lack of prey,
    and the whelps of the lioness are
        scattered.

12 "Now a word came stealing to me,
    my ear received the whisper of it.
13 Amid thoughts from visions of the
        night,
    when deep sleep falls on mortals,
14 dread came upon me, and trembling,
    which made all my bones shake.
15 A spirit glided past my face;
    the hair of my flesh bristled.
16 It stood still,
    but I could not discern its appearance.
    A form was before my eyes;
        there was silence, then I heard a
        voice:
17 'Can mortals be righteous before*a* God?
    Can human beings be pure before*a*
        their Maker?
18 Even in his servants he puts no trust,
    and his angels he charges with error;

19 how much more those who live in
        houses of clay,
    whose foundation is in the dust,
    who are crushed like a moth.
20 Between morning and evening they are
        destroyed;
    they perish forever without any
        regarding it.
21 Their tent-cord is plucked up within
        them,
    and they die devoid of wisdom.'

Job Is Corrected by God

5 "Call now; is there anyone who will
        answer you?
    To which of the holy ones will you
        turn?
2 Surely vexation kills the fool,
    and jealousy slays the simple.
3 I have seen fools taking root,
    but suddenly I cursed their dwelling.
4 Their children are far from safety,
        they are crushed in the gate,
    and there is no one to deliver them.
5 The hungry eat their harvest,
    and they take it even out of the
        thorns;*b*
    and the thirsty*c* pant after their
        wealth.
6 For misery does not come from the
        earth,
    nor does trouble sprout from the
        ground;
7 but human beings are born to trouble
    just as sparks*d* fly upward.

8 "As for me, I would seek God,
    and to God I would commit my cause.
9 He does great things and unsearchable,
    marvelous things without number.
10 He gives rain on the earth
    and sends waters on the fields;

a Or *more than*   *b* Meaning of Heb uncertain
c Aquila Symmachus Syr Vg: Heb *snare*
d Or *birds*; Heb *sons of Resheph*

5:8–27 *I would seek God.* Eliphaz's theology is
clear and well-stated. Commit your way to God.
God brings trials, but that is a sign of God's care
for us. God disciplines those God loves. God

wounds only to bind up. Happiness will yet
be your lot. Eliphaz provides a neatly tied
theological package of how God works, which
mirrors many of our working assumptions.

11 he sets on high those who are lowly,
    and those who mourn are lifted to
        safety.
12 He frustrates the devices of the crafty,
    so that their hands achieve no
        success.
13 He takes the wise in their own
        craftiness;
    and the schemes of the wily are
        brought to a quick end.
14 They meet with darkness in the
        daytime,
    and grope at noonday as in the night.
15 But he saves the needy from the sword
        of their mouth,
    from the hand of the mighty.
16 So the poor have hope,
    and injustice shuts its mouth.

17 "How happy is the one whom God
        reproves;
    therefore do not despise the
        discipline of the Almighty. *a*
18 For he wounds, but he binds up;
    he strikes, but his hands heal.
19 He will deliver you from six troubles;
    in seven no harm shall touch you.
20 In famine he will redeem you from
        death,
    and in war from the power of the
        sword.
21 You shall be hidden from the scourge of
        the tongue,
    and shall not fear destruction when it
        comes.
22 At destruction and famine you shall
        laugh,
    and shall not fear the wild animals of
        the earth.
23 For you shall be in league with the
        stones of the field,
    and the wild animals shall be at peace
        with you.
24 You shall know that your tent is safe,

    you shall inspect your fold and miss
        nothing.
25 You shall know that your descendants
        will be many,
    and your offspring like the grass of
        the earth.
26 You shall come to your grave in ripe old
        age,
    as a shock of grain comes up to the
        threshing floor in its season.
27 See, we have searched this out; it is true.
    Hear, and know it for yourself."

Job Replies: My Complaint Is Just

6 Then Job answered:
    2 "O that my vexation were weighed,
        and all my calamity laid in the
            balances!
3   For then it would be heavier than the
            sand of the sea;
        therefore my words have been rash.
4   For the arrows of the Almighty *a* are in
            me;
        my spirit drinks their poison;
        the terrors of God are arrayed against
            me.
5   Does the wild ass bray over its grass,
        or the ox low over its fodder?
6   Can that which is tasteless be eaten
            without salt,
        or is there any flavor in the juice of
            mallows? *b*
7   My appetite refuses to touch them;
        they are like food that is loathsome to
            me. *b*

8   "O that I might have my request,
        and that God would grant my desire;
9   that it would please God to crush me,
        that he would let loose his hand and
            cut me off!
10 This would be my consolation;

a Traditional rendering of Heb *Shaddai*
b Meaning of Heb uncertain

6:4 *the arrows of the Almighty.* The Bible provides several pictures or images of pain. It is like waters (Ps 66:12; Lam 3:54), like the pit (Lam 3:55), like the net (Ps 66:11), like the arrows. Waters flood or slowly seep in, the pit surrounds, the net enmeshes, the arrows tear. Here Job's pain is not a dull ache, but a burning, ripping wound. God has even poisoned the arrows. Job here first realizes that his great spiritual and emotional battle is with God.

I would even exult[a] in unrelenting
    pain;
for I have not denied the words of the
    Holy One.
11 What is my strength, that I should
    wait?
    And what is my end, that I should be
        patient?
12 Is my strength the strength of stones,
    or is my flesh bronze?
13 In truth I have no help in me,
    and any resource is driven from me.

14 "Those who withhold[b] kindness from a
    friend
    forsake the fear of the Almighty.[c]
15 My companions are treacherous like a
        torrent-bed,
    like freshets that pass away,
16 that run dark with ice,
    turbid with melting snow.
17 In time of heat they disappear;
    when it is hot, they vanish from their
        place.
18 The caravans turn aside from their
        course;
    they go up into the waste, and perish.
19 The caravans of Tema look,
    the travelers of Sheba hope.
20 They are disappointed because they
        were confident;
    they come there and are confounded.
21 Such you have now become to me;[d]
    you see my calamity, and are afraid.
22 Have I said, 'Make me a gift'?

Or, 'From your wealth offer a bribe for
    me'?
23 Or, 'Save me from an opponent's hand'?
    Or, 'Ransom me from the hand of
        oppressors'?

24 "Teach me, and I will be silent;
    make me understand how I have gone
        wrong.
25 How forceful are honest words!
    But your reproof, what does it
        reprove?
26 Do you think that you can reprove
        words,
    as if the speech of the desperate were
        wind?
27 You would even cast lots over the
        orphan,
    and bargain over your friend.

28 "But now, be pleased to look at me;
    for I will not lie to your face.
29 Turn, I pray, let no wrong be done.
    Turn now, my vindication is at stake.
30 Is there any wrong on my tongue?
    Cannot my taste discern calamity?

Job: My Suffering Is without End

7 "Do not human beings have a hard
        service on earth,
    and are not their days like the days of
        a laborer?

a Meaning of Heb uncertain   b Syr Vg Compare
Tg: Meaning of Heb uncertain   c Traditional
rendering of Heb *Shaddai*   d Cn Compare Gk
Syr: Meaning of Heb uncertain

6:15 *treacherous like a torrent-bed.* Isn't Job
overreacting? The friends have wept with him,
sat with him, felt with him. Eliphaz gently
consoled him. Extreme pain has the capacity to
distort vision, to confuse, to elicit wild and
untested accusations from our lips. Job is
entering a long, dark tunnel.

6:21 *you . . . are afraid.* One of the most painful things about great loss is that it affects dearly
held relationships. Some are deepened, but many
are lost. Why? Perhaps, as here, it is because
people see pain and are afraid. Maybe the pain
is contagious. Maybe it reminds them of their
mortality. Maybe it just confuses them too much.

Responding
6:24 SILENCE. "Teach me, and I will
be silent." Job's statement reveals a
heart willing to listen as he is being taught and
a willingness to be proven wrong. How willing
are we to receive teaching that points out our
mistakes and misconceptions? Are we more
prone to make excuses than to accept the
teaching in silence? If during the next month
someone points out a mistake you have made or
an idea of yours that might be wrong, make a
concerted effort to remain silent and not offer
excuses. *See also* Spiritual Disciplines Index.

2 Like a slave who longs for the shadow,
      and like laborers who look for their
         wages,
3 so I am allotted months of emptiness,
      and nights of misery are apportioned
         to me.
4 When I lie down I say, 'When shall I
         rise?'
      But the night is long,
      and I am full of tossing until dawn.
5 My flesh is clothed with worms and
         dirt;
      my skin hardens, then breaks out
         again.
6 My days are swifter than a weaver's
         shuttle,
      and come to their end without hope. *a*

7 "Remember that my life is a breath;
      my eye will never again see good.
8 The eye that beholds me will see me no
         more;
      while your eyes are upon me, I shall
         be gone.
9 As the cloud fades and vanishes,
      so those who go down to Sheol do not
         come up;
10 they return no more to their houses,
      nor do their places know them any
         more.

11 "Therefore I will not restrain my mouth;
      I will speak in the anguish of my spirit;
      I will complain in the bitterness of my
         soul.
12 Am I the Sea, or the Dragon,
      that you set a guard over me?
13 When I say, 'My bed will comfort me,
      my couch will ease my complaint,'

14 then you scare me with dreams
      and terrify me with visions,
15 so that I would choose strangling
      and death rather than this body.
16 I loathe my life; I would not live
         forever.
      Let me alone, for my days are a
         breath.
17 What are human beings, that you make
         so much of them,
      that you set your mind on them,
18 visit them every morning,
      test them every moment?
19 Will you not look away from me for a
         while,
      let me alone until I swallow my
         spittle?
20 If I sin, what do I do to you, you watcher
         of humanity?
      Why have you made me your target?
      Why have I become a burden to
         you?
21 Why do you not pardon my
         transgression
      and take away my iniquity?
   For now I shall lie in the earth;
      you will seek me, but I shall not be."

Bildad Speaks: Job Should Repent

8 Then Bildad the Shuhite answered:
   2 "How long will you say these things,
      and the words of your mouth be a
         great wind?
3 Does God pervert justice?
      Or does the Almighty *b* pervert the
         right?

a Or *as the thread runs out*   *b* Traditional
rendering of Heb *Shaddai*

7:4–6 *the night is long . . . My days are swifter.*
Job's pain brings with it a distortion in his perception of time. Usually the days are long and
nights short. Here it is the opposite for Job.
Suffering brings an unsettling of all predictable
things. We don't realize how much we love our
routine until our rhythms of time are taken
from us.

7:12 *Am I the Sea?* This is an example of Job's
biting sarcasm, directed at God. The Sea is the
great and dangerous mythological sea monster

whom God tamed in primeval times. Job is
asking, "Am I so dangerous that you have to
keep a watch on me like you did on Yamm or
Tiamat or Leviathan?"

7:17 *What are human beings?* In Psalm 8
David is lost in wonder when he says, "What are
human beings that you are mindful of them?"
(v 4). Here Job expresses the cynical opposite.
"Why are we so special that you sharpen your
arrows at us?" One has to know the Bible very
well to turn it on its head so skillfully.

4 If your children sinned against him,
    he delivered them into the power of
        their transgression.
5 If you will seek God
    and make supplication to the
        Almighty, *a*
6 if you are pure and upright,
    surely then he will rouse himself for
        you
    and restore to you your rightful place.
7 Though your beginning was small,
    your latter days will be very great.

8 "For inquire now of bygone generations,
    and consider what their ancestors
        have found;
9 for we are but of yesterday, and we know
        nothing,
    for our days on earth are but a shadow.
10 Will they not teach you and tell you
    and utter words out of their
        understanding?

11 "Can papyrus grow where there is no
        marsh?
    Can reeds flourish where there is no
        water?
12 While yet in flower and not cut down,
    they wither before any other plant.
13 Such are the paths of all who forget
        God;
    the hope of the godless shall perish.
14 Their confidence is gossamer,
    a spider's house their trust.
15 If one leans against its house, it will not
        stand;
    if one lays hold of it, it will not
        endure.
16 The wicked thrive *b* before the sun,
    and their shoots spread over the
        garden.

17 Their roots twine around the
        stoneheap;
    they live among the rocks. *c*
18 If they are destroyed from their place,
    then it will deny them, saying, 'I have
        never seen you.'
19 See, these are their happy ways, *d*
    and out of the earth still others will
        spring.

20 "See, God will not reject a blameless
        person,
    nor take the hand of evildoers.
21 He will yet fill your mouth with laughter,
    and your lips with shouts of joy.
22 Those who hate you will be clothed
        with shame,
    and the tent of the wicked will be no
        more."

Job Replies: There Is No Mediator

9 Then Job answered:
  2 "Indeed I know that this is so;
    but how can a mortal be just before
        God?
  3 If one wished to contend with him,
    one could not answer him once in a
        thousand.
  4 He is wise in heart, and mighty in
        strength
    —who has resisted him, and
        succeeded?—
  5 he who removes mountains, and they
        do not know it,
    when he overturns them in his anger;
  6 who shakes the earth out of its place,
    and its pillars tremble;

a Traditional rendering of Heb *Shaddai*
b Heb *He thrives*   *c* Gk Vg: Meaning of Heb
uncertain   *d* Meaning of Heb uncertain

8:4 *If your children sinned.* Bildad, the second
friend, weighs in. He expresses a viewpoint,
prevalent in Job's day, that would explain
suffering. In short, it is that the children were
punished for their own sin. The diplomacy of
Eliphaz is abandoned in favor of this shockingly
confrontational tactic. But note that Bildad keeps
it in the conditional mood—"If your children
sinned." "Only a suggestion, Job." Right.

9:3–12 *If one wished to contend with him.*
Legal language pervades the book of Job. The
fight that Job envisions with God is one of
words, but he is afraid that God might appear
and just overwhelm him with power. This is
Job's dilemma. He wants an audience with
God, but is afraid that he will be obliterated
by God.

7 who commands the sun, and it does not
     rise;
   who seals up the stars;
8 who alone stretched out the heavens
     and trampled the waves of the Sea;[a]
9 who made the Bear and Orion,
     the Pleiades and the chambers of the
     south;
10 who does great things beyond
     understanding,
   and marvelous things without
     number.
11 Look, he passes by me, and I do not see
     him;
   he moves on, but I do not perceive
     him.
12 He snatches away; who can stop him?
   Who will say to him, 'What are you
     doing?'

13 "God will not turn back his anger;
   the helpers of Rahab bowed beneath
     him.
14 How then can I answer him,
   choosing my words with him?
15 Though I am innocent, I cannot answer
     him;
   I must appeal for mercy to my
     accuser.[b]
16 If I summoned him and he answered
     me,
   I do not believe that he would listen
     to my voice.
17 For he crushes me with a tempest,
   and multiplies my wounds without
     cause;
18 he will not let me get my breath,
   but fills me with bitterness.
19 If it is a contest of strength, he is the
     strong one!
   If it is a matter of justice, who can
     summon him?[c]

20 Though I am innocent, my own mouth
     would condemn me;
   though I am blameless, he would
     prove me perverse.
21 I am blameless; I do not know myself;
   I loathe my life.
22 It is all one; therefore I say,
   he destroys both the blameless and
     the wicked.
23 When disaster brings sudden death,
   he mocks at the calamity[d] of the
     innocent.
24 The earth is given into the hand of the
     wicked;
   he covers the eyes of its judges—
   if it is not he, who then is it?

25 "My days are swifter than a runner;
   they flee away, they see no good.
26 They go by like skiffs of reed,
   like an eagle swooping on the prey.
27 If I say, 'I will forget my complaint;
   I will put off my sad countenance and
     be of good cheer,'
28 I become afraid of all my suffering,
   for I know you will not hold me
     innocent.
29 I shall be condemned;
   why then do I labor in vain?
30 If I wash myself with soap
   and cleanse my hands with lye,
31 yet you will plunge me into filth,
   and my own clothes will abhor me.
32 For he is not a mortal, as I am, that I
     might answer him,
   that we should come to trial together.
33 There is no umpire[e] between us,
   who might lay his hand on us both.

a Or trampled the back of the sea dragon   b Or for
my right   c Compare Gk: Heb me   d Meaning
of Heb uncertain   e Another reading is Would
that there were an umpire

9:18 *fills me with bitterness.* Job is on an
emotional roller coaster. Bitterness is an
emotion he mentions elsewhere (7:11; 10:1).
Provoking the bitterness is Job's inability to
figure out why he suffers such monstrous pain
when he was living an upright life.

9:33 *There is no umpire.* This is the first of
Job's breakthrough thoughts. For the first time

he is letting his heart imagine someone other
than God who might be able to mediate
between the two of them. But the thought
disappears as quickly as it comes. "There is no
umpire" has an air of finality to it. Yet he has
opened the mental door to a new thought, a
thought that will eventually transform his life.

34 If he would take his rod away from me,
    and not let dread of him terrify me,
35 then I would speak without fear of him,
    for I know I am not what I am
        thought to be. *a*

Job: I Loathe My Life

10 "I loathe my life;
    I will give free utterance to my
        complaint;
    I will speak in the bitterness of my
        soul.
2 I will say to God, Do not condemn me;
    let me know why you contend against
        me.
3 Does it seem good to you to oppress,
    to despise the work of your hands
    and favor the schemes of the wicked?
4 Do you have eyes of flesh?
    Do you see as humans see?
5 Are your days like the days of mortals,
    or your years like human years,
6 that you seek out my iniquity
    and search for my sin,
7 although you know that I am not guilty,
    and there is no one to deliver out of
        your hand?
8 Your hands fashioned and made me;
    and now you turn and destroy me. *b*
9 Remember that you fashioned me like
        clay;
    and will you turn me to dust again?
10 Did you not pour me out like milk
    and curdle me like cheese?
11 You clothed me with skin and flesh,
    and knit me together with bones and
        sinews.
12 You have granted me life and steadfast
        love,
    and your care has preserved my spirit.
13 Yet these things you hid in your heart;
    I know that this was your purpose.

14 If I sin, you watch me,
    and do not acquit me of my iniquity.
15 If I am wicked, woe to me!
    If I am righteous, I cannot lift up my
        head,
    for I am filled with disgrace
    and look upon my affliction.
16 Bold as a lion you hunt me;
    you repeat your exploits against me.
17 You renew your witnesses against me,
    and increase your vexation toward
        me;
    you bring fresh troops against me. *c*

18 "Why did you bring me forth from the
        womb?
    Would that I had died before any eye
        had seen me,
19 and were as though I had not been,
    carried from the womb to the grave.
20 Are not the days of my life few? *d*
    Let me alone, that I may find a little
        comfort *e*
21 before I go, never to return,
    to the land of gloom and deep
        darkness,
22 the land of gloom *f* and chaos,
    where light is like darkness."

Zophar Speaks: Job's Guilt Deserves Punishment

11 Then Zophar the Naamathite an-
    swered:
2 "Should a multitude of words go
        unanswered,

a Cn: Heb *for I am not so in myself*
b Cn Compare Gk Syr: Heb *made me together all around, and you destroy me*   *c* Cn Compare Gk: Heb *toward me; changes and a troop are with me*
d Cn Compare Gk Syr: Heb *Are not my days few? Let him cease!*   *e* Heb *that I may brighten up a little*
f Heb *gloom as darkness, deep darkness*

10:8–12 *Your hands fashioned . . . me; and now you . . . destroy me.* A thought of immense intensity and pain. God's tenderness toward Job is reflected in the careful divine fashioning of Job. Sinews were knit. Skin was stretched out. God's very hands did it. Steadfast love accompanied it all. Now God destroys. It just doesn't make any sense at all to Job.

10:20 *Let me alone.* The psalmist wants to "dwell in the house of the LORD [his] whole life long" (23:6), but Job will have none of it. As a sign of how his thought pattern has become completely reversed, Job now longs for separation from God. He seeks the comfort of solitude.

and should one full of talk be
  vindicated?
3 Should your babble put others to
    silence,
  and when you mock, shall no one
    shame you?
4 For you say, 'My conduct*a* is pure,
  and I am clean in God's*b* sight.'
5 But O that God would speak,
  and open his lips to you,
6 and that he would tell you the secrets of
    wisdom!
  For wisdom is many-sided.*c*
  Know then that God exacts of you less
    than your guilt deserves.

7 "Can you find out the deep things of
    God?
  Can you find out the limit of the
    Almighty?*d*
8 It is higher than heaven*e*—what can
    you do?
  Deeper than Sheol—what can you
    know?
9 Its measure is longer than the earth,
  and broader than the sea.
10 If he passes through, and imprisons,
  and assembles for judgment, who can
    hinder him?
11 For he knows those who are worthless;
  when he sees iniquity, will he not
    consider it?
12 But a stupid person will get
    understanding,
  when a wild ass is born human.*c*

13 "If you direct your heart rightly,
  you will stretch out your hands
    toward him.
14 If iniquity is in your hand, put it far
    away,
  and do not let wickedness reside in
    your tents.

15 Surely then you will lift up your face
    without blemish;
  you will be secure, and will not fear.
16 You will forget your misery;
  you will remember it as waters that
    have passed away.
17 And your life will be brighter than the
    noonday;
  its darkness will be like the morning.
18 And you will have confidence, because
    there is hope;
  you will be protected*f* and take your
    rest in safety.
19 You will lie down, and no one will make
    you afraid;
  many will entreat your favor.
20 But the eyes of the wicked will fail;
  all way of escape will be lost to them,
  and their hope is to breathe their
    last."

Job Replies: I Am a Laughingstock

12 Then Job answered:
2 "No doubt you are the people,
  and wisdom will die with you.
3 But I have understanding as well as you;
  I am not inferior to you.
  Who does not know such things as
    these?
4 I am a laughingstock to my friends;
  I, who called upon God and he
    answered me,
  a just and blameless man, I am a
    laughingstock.
5 Those at ease have contempt for
    misfortune,*c*
  but it is ready for those whose feet are
    unstable.

a Gk: Heb *teaching*   *b* Heb *your*   *c* Meaning of
Heb uncertain   *d* Traditional rendering of Heb
Shaddai   *e* Heb *The heights of heaven*   *f* Or *you
will look around*

11:6 *less than your guilt deserves.* If Eliphaz
was diplomatic and Bildad potentially ambiguous, Zophar is downright cruel. Job
defended his purity, but Zophar thinks Job
could not have been blameless, since he has
been so obviously punished. If anything, Job
should see God's judgment as merciful, as less
than he deserves.

12:4 *I am a laughingstock.* The cultures of the
ancient Near East and the present Middle East
are honor-based cultures. Personal slights cut
deeper than knives. That Job is a laughingstock
to others now completes his humiliation.

6 The tents of robbers are at peace,
    and those who provoke God are
        secure,
    who bring their god in their hands. *a*

7 "But ask the animals, and they will
        teach you;
    the birds of the air, and they will tell
        you;
8 ask the plants of the earth, *b* and they
        will teach you;
    and the fish of the sea will declare to
        you.
9 Who among all these does not know
    that the hand of the LORD has done
        this?
10 In his hand is the life of every living
        thing
    and the breath of every human being.
11 Does not the ear test words
    as the palate tastes food?
12 Is wisdom with the aged,
    and understanding in length of days?

13 "With God *c* are wisdom and strength;
    he has counsel and understanding.
14 If he tears down, no one can rebuild;
    if he shuts someone in, no one can
        open up.
15 If he withholds the waters, they dry up;
    if he sends them out, they overwhelm
        the land.
16 With him are strength and wisdom;
    the deceived and the deceiver are his.
17 He leads counselors away stripped,
    and makes fools of judges.
18 He looses the sash of kings,
    and binds a waistcloth on their loins.
19 He leads priests away stripped,
    and overthrows the mighty.
20 He deprives of speech those who are
        trusted,

and takes away the discernment of
    the elders.
21 He pours contempt on princes,
    and looses the belt of the strong.
22 He uncovers the deeps out of darkness,
    and brings deep darkness to light.
23 He makes nations great, then destroys
        them;
    he enlarges nations, then leads them
        away.
24 He strips understanding from the
        leaders *d* of the earth,
    and makes them wander in a pathless
        waste.
25 They grope in the dark without light;
    he makes them stagger like a
        drunkard.

13 "Look, my eye has seen all this,
    my ear has heard and understood it.
2 What you know, I also know;
    I am not inferior to you.
3 But I would speak to the Almighty, *e*
    and I desire to argue my case with
        God.
4 As for you, you whitewash with lies;
    all of you are worthless physicians.
5 If you would only keep silent,
    that would be your wisdom!
6 Hear now my reasoning,
    and listen to the pleadings of my lips.
7 Will you speak falsely for God,
    and speak deceitfully for him?
8 Will you show partiality toward him,
    will you plead the case for God?
9 Will it be well with you when he
        searches you out?

a Or *whom God brought forth by his hand*; Meaning
of Heb uncertain   *b* Or *speak to the earth*
c Heb *him*   *d* Heb adds *of the people*
e Traditional rendering of Heb *Shaddai*

13:3 *argue my case.* Legal language returns.
Job's "case" is based on God's violation of the
unspoken agreement they had that blessedness
would continue as long as fidelity remained.
God, therefore, has breached his contract with
Job. Job will later sign the complaint (31:35)
and desire to appear before God for oral
argument (23:4).

Responding
13:5 SILENCE. Here Job chastises
Eliphaz, Bildad, and Zophar for not
listening. But we get the sense that Job is not
listening fully to the words of his three companions either. Try going about your normal
activities this week while making every effort to
talk as little as possible. When you do talk, make

Or can you deceive him, as one
    person deceives another?
10 He will surely rebuke you
    if in secret you show partiality.
11 Will not his majesty terrify you,
    and the dread of him fall upon you?
12 Your maxims are proverbs of ashes,
    your defenses are defenses of clay.

13 "Let me have silence, and I will speak,
    and let come on me what may.
14 I will take my flesh in my teeth,
    and put my life in my hand. *a*
15 See, he will kill me; I have no hope; *b*
    but I will defend my ways to his face.
16 This will be my salvation,
    that the godless shall not come before
        him.
17 Listen carefully to my words,
    and let my declaration be in your ears.
18 I have indeed prepared my case;
    I know that I shall be vindicated.
19 Who is there that will contend with me?
    For then I would be silent and die.

Job's Despondent Prayer

20 Only grant two things to me,
    then I will not hide myself from your
        face:
21 withdraw your hand far from me,
    and do not let dread of you terrify me.
22 Then call, and I will answer;
    or let me speak, and you reply to me.

23 How many are my iniquities and my
        sins?
    Make me know my transgression and
        my sin.
24 Why do you hide your face,
    and count me as your enemy?
25 Will you frighten a windblown leaf
    and pursue dry chaff?
26 For you write bitter things against me,
    and make me reap *c* the iniquities of
        my youth.
27 You put my feet in the stocks,
    and watch all my paths;
    you set a bound to the soles of my feet.
28 One wastes away like a rotten thing,
    like a garment that is moth-eaten.

14 "A mortal, born of woman, few of
        days and full of trouble,
2   comes up like a flower and withers,
    flees like a shadow and does not last.
3 Do you fix your eyes on such a one?
    Do you bring me into judgment with
        you?
4 Who can bring a clean thing out of an
        unclean?
    No one can.
5 Since their days are determined,
    and the number of their months is
        known to you,

a Gk: Heb *Why should I take . . . in my hand?*
b Or *Though he kill me, yet I will trust in him*
c Heb *inherit*

every word count. How did your silence affect your relationships with family, friends, and co-workers (see also 13:17)? *See also* Spiritual Disciplines Index.

13:17 *Listen carefully.* Job and his friends are not listening to one another, but each has so much to say. One of the reasons God may be silent so long in the book is that, since they are not listening to one another, why intervene? Something about pain requires it to be fully expressed and fully heard before healing occurs. We say in English that a person needs to be "all talked out," but where are the listeners?

14:1–22 *A mortal, born of woman.* This chapter contains one of the most powerful poems of the Bible, on the pain of false hope. In the depths of despair we sometimes think we see an escape. We follow it, and it is a mirage. The pain returns with brutal intensity. When the pain returns, many of us vow never to hope again, since the possible pain of another rejection is so daunting that we would rather live with the distress that slowly erodes life. The poem explores these emotions.

14:2 *like a flower.* Throughout this great poem nature is used to both teach and destroy hope. It is not just the building block of grace or the first step in grace; it also seems to work against it, giving lessons of great destruction and impermanence. The flower is beautiful while it briefly lasts, but then it withers. We long for permanence, for eternity, but nature teaches us that this hope is elusive.

and you have appointed the bounds
    that they cannot pass,
6 look away from them, and desist,*a*
    that they may enjoy, like laborers,
        their days.

7 "For there is hope for a tree,
    if it is cut down, that it will sprout
        again,
    and that its shoots will not cease.
8 Though its root grows old in the earth,
    and its stump dies in the ground,
9 yet at the scent of water it will bud
    and put forth branches like a young
        plant.
10 But mortals die, and are laid low;
    humans expire, and where are they?
11 As waters fail from a lake,
    and a river wastes away and dries up,
12 so mortals lie down and do not rise
        again;
    until the heavens are no more, they
        will not awake
    or be roused out of their sleep.
13 O that you would hide me in Sheol,
    that you would conceal me until your
        wrath is past,
    that you would appoint me a set time,
        and remember me!
14 If mortals die, will they live again?
    All the days of my service I would
        wait
    until my release should come.
15 You would call, and I would answer you;
    you would long for the work of your
        hands.
16 For then you would not*b* number my
        steps,

you would not keep watch over my
        sin;
17 my transgression would be sealed up in
        a bag,
    and you would cover over my
        iniquity.

18 "But the mountain falls and crumbles
        away,
    and the rock is removed from its
        place;
19 the waters wear away the stones;
    the torrents wash away the soil of the
        earth;
    so you destroy the hope of mortals.
20 You prevail forever against them, and
        they pass away;
    you change their countenance, and
        send them away.
21 Their children come to honor, and they
        do not know it;
    they are brought low, and it goes
        unnoticed.
22 They feel only the pain of their own
        bodies,
    and mourn only for themselves."

Eliphaz Speaks: Job Undermines Religion

15 Then Eliphaz the Temanite answered:
2 "Should the wise answer with windy
        knowledge,
    and fill themselves with the east
        wind?
3 Should they argue in unprofitable talk,
    or in words with which they can do
        no good?

a Cn: Heb *that they may desist*   *b* Syr: Heb lacks
not

14:7–9 *hope for a tree.* Yet the realm of
nature gives hope. The tree or bush is cut down,
but springs back to life at the slightest whiff of
water. Nature is always on the brink of rebirth.
Why shouldn't this be the case for mortals too
(v 10)? Job will not let go of his questions until
insights break forth.

14:14 *If mortals die, will they live again?* This
is the question to which Job's pain ultimately
leads him. Though his complaint is worded in
legal language, Job longs for intimacy with God.

Instead of the legal forum, where Job demands
an appearance of God, Job longs for God to call
and he would answer (v 15).

14:19 *destroy the hope of mortals.* Just as
nature gives hope, nature takes away hope. A
whiff of water brings trees back to life, but
waters also wear away stones. There is almost a
palpable sense, as the poem concludes, that the
possibility of hope for a blessed future life for
humans is utterly foreclosed.

4 But you are doing away with the fear of
    God,
   and hindering meditation before
    God.
5 For your iniquity teaches your mouth,
   and you choose the tongue of the
    crafty.
6 Your own mouth condemns you, and
    not I;
   your own lips testify against you.

7 "Are you the firstborn of the human
    race?
   Were you brought forth before the
    hills?
8 Have you listened in the council of
    God?
   And do you limit wisdom to yourself?
9 What do you know that we do not
    know?
   What do you understand that is not
    clear to us?
10 The gray-haired and the aged are on our
    side,
   those older than your father.
11 Are the consolations of God too small
    for you,
   or the word that deals gently with
    you?
12 Why does your heart carry you away,
   and why do your eyes flash, a
13 so that you turn your spirit against God,
   and let such words go out of your
    mouth?
14 What are mortals, that they can be
    clean?
   Or those born of woman, that they
    can be righteous?
15 God puts no trust even in his holy ones,
   and the heavens are not clean in his
    sight;
16 how much less one who is abominable
    and corrupt,
   one who drinks iniquity like water!

17 "I will show you; listen to me;
   what I have seen I will declare—
18 what sages have told,
   and their ancestors have not hidden,
19 to whom alone the land was given,
   and no stranger passed among them.
20 The wicked writhe in pain all their days,
   through all the years that are laid up
    for the ruthless.
21 Terrifying sounds are in their ears;
   in prosperity the destroyer will come
    upon them.
22 They despair of returning from
    darkness,
   and they are destined for the sword.
23 They wander abroad for bread, saying,
    'Where is it?'
   They know that a day of darkness is
    ready at hand;
24 distress and anguish terrify them;
   they prevail against them, like a king
    prepared for battle.
25 Because they stretched out their hands
    against God,
   and bid defiance to the Almighty, b
26 running stubbornly against him
   with a thick-bossed shield;
27 because they have covered their faces
    with their fat,
   and gathered fat upon their loins,
28 they will live in desolate cities,
   in houses that no one should inhabit,
   houses destined to become heaps of
    ruins;
29 they will not be rich, and their wealth
    will not endure,
   nor will they strike root in the earth; c
30 they will not escape from darkness;
   the flame will dry up their shoots,
   and their blossom d will be swept
    away e by the wind.

a Meaning of Heb uncertain   b Traditional
rendering of Heb *Shaddai*   c Vg: Meaning of Heb
uncertain   d Gk: Heb *mouth*   e Cn: Heb *will
depart*

Responding
15:4 MEDITATION. In this verse
Eliphaz accuses Job of "hindering meditation before God." Has there ever been a time
in your life when what one person said or did
seemed to hamper your ability to meditate
on the things of God or talk with God? What
happened to solve the problem? *See also*
Spiritual Disciplines Index.

31 Let them not trust in emptiness,
      deceiving themselves;
   for emptiness will be their
      recompense.
32 It will be paid in full before their time,
   and their branch will not be green.
33 They will shake off their unripe grape,
      like the vine,
   and cast off their blossoms, like the
      olive tree.
34 For the company of the godless is
      barren,
   and fire consumes the tents of
      bribery.
35 They conceive mischief and bring forth
      evil
   and their heart prepares deceit."

Job Reaffirms His Innocence

16 Then Job answered:
   2 "I have heard many such things;
   miserable comforters are you all.
3 Have windy words no limit?
      Or what provokes you that you keep
         on talking?
4 I also could talk as you do,
      if you were in my place;
   I could join words together against you,
      and shake my head at you.
5 I could encourage you with my mouth,
      and the solace of my lips would
         assuage your pain.

6 "If I speak, my pain is not assuaged,
      and if I forbear, how much of it leaves
         me?
7 Surely now God has worn me out;
      he has[a] made desolate all my
         company.
8 And he has[a] shriveled me up,
      which is a witness against me;
   my leanness has risen up against me,
      and it testifies to my face.

9 He has torn me in his wrath, and hated
      me;
   he has gnashed his teeth at me;
   my adversary sharpens his eyes
      against me.
10 They have gaped at me with their
      mouths;
   they have struck me insolently on the
      cheek;
   they mass themselves together
      against me.
11 God gives me up to the ungodly,
   and casts me into the hands of the
      wicked.
12 I was at ease, and he broke me in two;
      he seized me by the neck and dashed
         me to pieces;
   he set me up as his target;
13   his archers surround me.
   He slashes open my kidneys, and shows
      no mercy;
   he pours out my gall on the ground.
14 He bursts upon me again and again;
      he rushes at me like a warrior.
15 I have sewed sackcloth upon my skin,
      and have laid my strength in the dust.
16 My face is red with weeping,
      and deep darkness is on my eyelids,
17 though there is no violence in my
      hands,
      and my prayer is pure.

18 "O earth, do not cover my blood;
      let my outcry find no resting place.
19 Even now, in fact, my witness is in
      heaven,
      and he that vouches for me is on
         high.
20 My friends scorn me;
      my eye pours out tears to God,

a Heb *you have*

16:12–14 *he broke me in two.* Images of
violence flow from Job's mouth. In these words
of almost unparalleled intensity, Job continues
the theme of God the destroyer of his life.

16:19–21 *my witness is in heaven.* In the time
of bleakest dark, a hopeful thought erupts. Here
Job develops the thought first mentioned in 9:33.

The umpire who did not exist is transformed
into the witness in heaven. As Job's pain and
anguish intensify, his hope solidifies. It is now
taking on human form. A witness speaks on his
behalf. Job may weep, but now he imagines
someone speaks for him on high.

21 that he would maintain the right of a
    mortal with God,
    as^a one does for a neighbor.
22 For when a few years have come,
    I shall go the way from which I shall
    not return.

Job Prays for Relief

17 My spirit is broken, my days are
    extinct,
    the grave is ready for me.
2 Surely there are mockers around me,
    and my eye dwells on their
    provocation.

3 "Lay down a pledge for me with
    yourself;
    who is there that will give surety for
    me?
4 Since you have closed their minds to
    understanding,
    therefore you will not let them
    triumph.
5 Those who denounce friends for
    reward—
    the eyes of their children will fail.

6 "He has made me a byword of the
    peoples,
    and I am one before whom people
    spit.
7 My eye has grown dim from grief,
    and all my members are like a
    shadow.
8 The upright are appalled at this,
    and the innocent stir themselves up
    against the godless.
9 Yet the righteous hold to their way,
    and they that have clean hands grow
    stronger and stronger.
10 But you, come back now, all of you,
    and I shall not find a sensible person
    among you.
11 My days are past, my plans are broken
    off,
    the desires of my heart.

12 They make night into day;
    'The light,' they say, 'is near to the
    darkness.'^b
13 If I look for Sheol as my house,
    if I spread my couch in darkness,
14 if I say to the Pit, 'You are my father,'
    and to the worm, 'My mother,' or 'My
    sister,'
15 where then is my hope?
    Who will see my hope?
16 Will it go down to the bars of Sheol?
    Shall we descend together into the
    dust?"

Bildad Speaks: God Punishes the Wicked

18 Then Bildad the Shuhite answered:
2 "How long will you hunt for
    words?
    Consider, and then we shall speak.
3 Why are we counted as cattle?
    Why are we stupid in your sight?
4 You who tear yourself in your anger—
    shall the earth be forsaken because of
    you,
    or the rock be removed out of its
    place?

5 "Surely the light of the wicked is put
    out,
    and the flame of their fire does not
    shine.
6 The light is dark in their tent,
    and the lamp above them is put out.
7 Their strong steps are shortened,
    and their own schemes throw them
    down.
8 For they are thrust into a net by their
    own feet,
    and they walk into a pitfall.
9 A trap seizes them by the heel;
    a snare lays hold of them.
10 A rope is hid for them in the ground,
    a trap for them in the path.

a Syr Vg Tg: Heb *and*   b Meaning of Heb
uncertain

17:11 *my plans are broken off.* Job's energy is at its lowest ebb. He is overcome by unmastered grief. Anger can give one energy that results in productive activity, but cloying grief enervates and immobilizes. His heart is broken. All life's desires are gone. The perceived finality of his condition squeezes all hope from him.

11 Terrors frighten them on every side,
      and chase them at their heels.
12 Their strength is consumed by hunger, *a*
      and calamity is ready for their
         stumbling.
13 By disease their skin is consumed, *b*
      the firstborn of Death consumes their
         limbs.
14 They are torn from the tent in which
         they trusted,
      and are brought to the king of terrors.
15 In their tents nothing remains;
      sulfur is scattered upon their
         habitations.
16 Their roots dry up beneath,
      and their branches wither above.
17 Their memory perishes from the earth,
      and they have no name in the street.
18 They are thrust from light into
         darkness,
      and driven out of the world.
19 They have no offspring or descendant
         among their people,
      and no survivor where they used to
         live.
20 They of the west are appalled at their
         fate,
      and horror seizes those of the east.
21 Surely such are the dwellings of the
         ungodly,
      such is the place of those who do not
         know God."

Job Replies: I Know That My Redeemer Lives

19 Then Job answered:
   2 "How long will you torment me,
      and break me in pieces with words?
3 These ten times you have cast reproach
         upon me;
      are you not ashamed to wrong me?
4 And even if it is true that I have erred,
      my error remains with me.
5 If indeed you magnify yourselves
         against me,
      and make my humiliation an
         argument against me,
6 know then that God has put me in the
         wrong,
      and closed his net around me.

7 Even when I cry out, 'Violence!' I am
         not answered;
      I call aloud, but there is no justice.
8 He has walled up my way so that I
         cannot pass,
      and he has set darkness upon my
         paths.
9 He has stripped my glory from me,
      and taken the crown from my head.
10 He breaks me down on every side, and I
         am gone,
      he has uprooted my hope like a tree.
11 He has kindled his wrath against me,
      and counts me as his adversary.
12 His troops come on together;
      they have thrown up siegeworks *c*
         against me,
      and encamp around my tent.

13 "He has put my family far from me,
      and my acquaintances are wholly
         estranged from me.
14 My relatives and my close friends have
         failed me;
15   the guests in my house have forgotten
         me;
      my serving girls count me as a
         stranger;
      I have become an alien in their eyes.
16 I call to my servant, but he gives me no
         answer;
      I must myself plead with him.
17 My breath is repulsive to my wife;
      I am loathsome to my own family.
18 Even young children despise me;
      when I rise, they talk against me.
19 All my intimate friends abhor me,
      and those whom I loved have turned
         against me.
20 My bones cling to my skin and to my
         flesh,
      and I have escaped by the skin of my
         teeth.
21 Have pity on me, have pity on me,
         O you my friends,
      for the hand of God has touched me!
22 Why do you, like God, pursue me,
      never satisfied with my flesh?

a Or *Disaster is hungry for them*   *b* Cn: Heb *It consumes the limbs of his skin*   *c* Cn: Heb *their way*

23 "O that my words were written down!
    O that they were inscribed in a book!
24 O that with an iron pen and with lead
    they were engraved on a rock forever!
25 For I know that my Redeemer*a* lives,
    and that at the last he*b* will stand
        upon the earth;*c*
26 and after my skin has been thus
        destroyed,
    then in*d* my flesh I shall see God,*e*
27 whom I shall see on my side,*f*
    and my eyes shall behold, and not
        another.
    My heart faints within me!
28 If you say, 'How we will persecute him!'
    and, 'The root of the matter is found
        in him';
29 be afraid of the sword,
    for wrath brings the punishment of
        the sword,
    so that you may know there is a
        judgment."

Zophar Speaks: Wickedness Receives Just Retribution

20 Then Zophar the Naamathite an-
        swered:
2 "Pay attention! My thoughts urge me to
        answer,
    because of the agitation within me.
3 I hear censure that insults me,
    and a spirit beyond my
        understanding answers me.
4 Do you not know this from of old,
    ever since mortals were placed on
        earth,
5 that the exulting of the wicked is short,

and the joy of the godless is but for a
    moment?
6 Even though they mount up high as the
    heavens,
    and their head reaches to the clouds,
7 they will perish forever like their own
        dung;
    those who have seen them will say,
        'Where are they?'
8 They will fly away like a dream, and not
        be found;
    they will be chased away like a vision
        of the night.
9 The eye that saw them will see them no
        more,
    nor will their place behold them any
        longer.
10 Their children will seek the favor of the
        poor,
    and their hands will give back their
        wealth.
11 Their bodies, once full of youth,
    will lie down in the dust with them.

12 "Though wickedness is sweet in their
        mouth,
    though they hide it under their
        tongues,
13 though they are loath to let it go,
    and hold it in their mouths,
14 yet their food is turned in their
        stomachs;
    it is the venom of asps within them.

a Or *Vindicator*   *b* Or *that he the Last*
c Heb *dust*   *d* Or *without*   *e* Meaning of Heb
of this verse uncertain   *f* Or *for myself*

Responding
19:25 WORSHIP. In the midst of his
companions' accusations and his own
physical, mental, and spiritual suffering, Job
proclaims, "I know that my Redeemer liveth,
and that he shall stand in the latter day upon
the earth" (KJV). Describe one time in your life
when you were going through deep suffering.
What were the results? With Job, did you cling
more tightly to God's promises? Or did you
reject them as hopelessly outdated? *See also*
Spiritual Disciplines Index.

19:25–27 *I know that my Redeemer lives*.
Immobilizing grief vies with gleaming hope.
Now the witness has become a Redeemer who
will save his life. The Redeemer is a heavenly
figure who will come to earth. Somehow
through the Redeemer Job will see God. The
Christian Church has always seen this longing as
fulfilled in Jesus Christ. Job's heart now takes
wing, and he is completely overcome with
longing.

15 They swallow down riches and vomit
   them up again;
   God casts them out of their bellies.
16 They will suck the poison of asps;
   the tongue of a viper will kill them.
17 They will not look on the rivers,
   the streams flowing with honey and
   curds.
18 They will give back the fruit of their
   toil,
   and will not swallow it down;
   from the profit of their trading
   they will get no enjoyment.
19 For they have crushed and abandoned
   the poor,
   they have seized a house that they did
   not build.

20 "They knew no quiet in their bellies;
   in their greed they let nothing escape.
21 There was nothing left after they had
   eaten;
   therefore their prosperity will not
   endure.
22 In full sufficiency they will be in
   distress;
   all the force of misery will come upon
   them.
23 To fill their belly to the full
   God*a* will send his fierce anger into
   them,
   and rain it upon them as their food.*b*
24 They will flee from an iron weapon;
   a bronze arrow will strike them
   through.
25 It is drawn forth and comes out of their
   body,
   and the glittering point comes out of
   their gall;
   terrors come upon them.
26 Utter darkness is laid up for their
   treasures;
   a fire fanned by no one will devour
   them;
   what is left in their tent will be
   consumed.
27 The heavens will reveal their iniquity,
   and the earth will rise up against
   them.
28 The possessions of their house will be
   carried away,

dragged off in the day of God's*c*
   wrath.
29 This is the portion of the wicked from
   God,
   the heritage decreed for them by
   God."

Job Replies: The Wicked Often Go Unpunished

21 Then Job answered:
2 "Listen carefully to my words,
   and let this be your consolation.
3 Bear with me, and I will speak;
   then after I have spoken, mock on.
4 As for me, is my complaint addressed to
   mortals?
   Why should I not be impatient?
5 Look at me, and be appalled,
   and lay your hand upon your mouth.
6 When I think of it I am dismayed,
   and shuddering seizes my flesh.
7 Why do the wicked live on,
   reach old age, and grow mighty in
   power?
8 Their children are established in their
   presence,
   and their offspring before their eyes.
9 Their houses are safe from fear,
   and no rod of God is upon them.
10 Their bull breeds without fail;
   their cow calves and never miscarries.
11 They send out their little ones like a
   flock,
   and their children dance around.
12 They sing to the tambourine and the
   lyre,
   and rejoice to the sound of the pipe.
13 They spend their days in prosperity,
   and in peace they go down to Sheol.
14 They say to God, 'Leave us alone!
   We do not desire to know your ways.
15 What is the Almighty,*d* that we should
   serve him?
   And what profit do we get if we pray
   to him?'
16 Is not their prosperity indeed their own
   achievement?*e*

a Heb *he* *b* Cn: Meaning of Heb uncertain
c Heb *his* *d* Traditional rendering of Heb
Shaddai *e* Heb *in their hand*

The plans of the wicked are
repugnant to me.

17 "How often is the lamp of the wicked
      put out?
    How often does calamity come upon
      them?
    How often does God[a] distribute pains
      in his anger?
18 How often are they like straw before the
      wind,
    and like chaff that the storm carries
      away?
19 You say, 'God stores up their iniquity for
      their children.'
    Let it be paid back to them, so that
      they may know it.
20 Let their own eyes see their destruction,
    and let them drink of the wrath of the
      Almighty.[b]
21 For what do they care for their
      household after them,
    when the number of their months is
      cut off?
22 Will any teach God knowledge,
    seeing that he judges those that are
      on high?
23 One dies in full prosperity,
    being wholly at ease and secure,
24 his loins full of milk
    and the marrow of his bones moist.
25 Another dies in bitterness of soul,
    never having tasted of good.
26 They lie down alike in the dust,
    and the worms cover them.

27 "Oh, I know your thoughts,
    and your schemes to wrong me.
28 For you say, 'Where is the house of the
      prince?
    Where is the tent in which the wicked
      lived?'
29 Have you not asked those who travel
      the roads,
    and do you not accept their
      testimony,

30 that the wicked are spared in the day of
      calamity,
    and are rescued in the day of wrath?
31 Who declares their way to their face,
    and who repays them for what they
      have done?
32 When they are carried to the grave,
    a watch is kept over their tomb.
33 The clods of the valley are sweet to
      them;
    everyone will follow after,
    and those who went before are
      innumerable.
34 How then will you comfort me with
      empty nothings?
    There is nothing left of your answers
      but falsehood."

Eliphaz Speaks: Job's Wickedness Is Great

22 Then Eliphaz the Temanite answered:
   2 "Can a mortal be of use to God?
    Can even the wisest be of service to
      him?
3 Is it any pleasure to the Almighty[b] if
      you are righteous,
    or is it gain to him if you make your
      ways blameless?
4 Is it for your piety that he reproves you,
    and enters into judgment with you?
5 Is not your wickedness great?
    There is no end to your iniquities.
6 For you have exacted pledges from your
      family for no reason,
    and stripped the naked of their
      clothing.
7 You have given no water to the weary to
      drink,
    and you have withheld bread from
      the hungry.
8 The powerful possess the land,
    and the favored live in it.
9 You have sent widows away empty-
      handed,

a Heb he   b Traditional rendering of Heb
Shaddai

21:17–20 *the lamp of the wicked.* Job's
criticism of God continues. God, as he sees it,
runs a morally flawed universe. The wicked
remain unpunished. The defenders of God say

that God is storing up judgment for the children
of the wicked. "Show it now," Job says. "Let the
wicked pay now." But they don't.

and the arms of the orphans you have
  crushed. *a*

10 Therefore snares are around you,
  and sudden terror overwhelms you,

11 or darkness so that you cannot see;
  a flood of water covers you.

12 "Is not God high in the heavens?
  See the highest stars, how lofty they
    are!

13 Therefore you say, 'What does God
    know?
  Can he judge through the deep
    darkness?

14 Thick clouds enwrap him, so that he
    does not see,
  and he walks on the dome of heaven.'

15 Will you keep to the old way
  that the wicked have trod?

16 They were snatched away before their
    time;
  their foundation was washed away by
    a flood.

17 They said to God, 'Leave us alone,'
  and 'What can the Almighty *b* do to
    us?' *c*

18 Yet he filled their houses with good
    things—
  but the plans of the wicked are
    repugnant to me.

19 The righteous see it and are glad;
  the innocent laugh them to scorn,

20 saying, 'Surely our adversaries are cut
    off,
  and what they left, the fire has
    consumed.'

21 "Agree with God, *d* and be at peace;
  in this way good will come to you.

22 Receive instruction from his mouth,
  and lay up his words in your heart.

23 If you return to the Almighty, *b* you will
    be restored,
  if you remove unrighteousness from
    your tents,

24 if you treat gold like dust,

and gold of Ophir like the stones of
  the torrent-bed,

25 and if the Almighty *b* is your gold
  and your precious silver,

26 then you will delight yourself in the
    Almighty, *b*
  and lift up your face to God.

27 You will pray to him, and he will hear
    you,
  and you will pay your vows.

28 You will decide on a matter, and it will
    be established for you,
  and light will shine on your ways.

29 When others are humiliated, you say it
    is pride;
  for he saves the humble.

30 He will deliver even those who are
    guilty;
  they will escape because of the
    cleanness of your hands." *e*

Job Replies: My Complaint Is Bitter

23 Then Job answered:

2 "Today also my complaint is
    bitter; *f*
  his *g* hand is heavy despite my
    groaning.

3 Oh, that I knew where I might find him,
  that I might come even to his
    dwelling!

4 I would lay my case before him,
  and fill my mouth with arguments.

5 I would learn what he would answer
    me,
  and understand what he would say to
    me.

6 Would he contend with me in the
    greatness of his power?
  No; but he would give heed to me.

7 There an upright person could reason
    with him,

a Gk Syr Tg Vg: Heb *were crushed*   b Traditional
rendering of Heb *Shaddai*   c Gk Syr: Heb *them*
d Heb *him*   e Meaning of Heb uncertain
f Syr Vg Tg: Heb *rebellious*   g Gk Syr: Heb *my*

23:4 *lay my case.* Job has been carefully
gathering data for his case against God. He may
have lost all his children and wealth, but he still
has his case. It is an airtight case against God,
Job thinks. He can hardly wait to "fill [his]
mouth with arguments."

and I should be acquitted forever by
   my judge.

8 "If I go forward, he is not there;
      or backward, I cannot perceive him;
9 on the left he hides, and I cannot
         behold him;
   I turn*a* to the right, but I cannot see
      him.
10 But he knows the way that I take;
      when he has tested me, I shall come
         out like gold.
11 My foot has held fast to his steps;
      I have kept his way and have not
         turned aside.
12 I have not departed from the
         commandment of his lips;
   I have treasured in*b* my bosom the
      words of his mouth.
13 But he stands alone and who can
      dissuade him?
   What he desires, that he does.
14 For he will complete what he appoints
      for me;
   and many such things are in his mind.
15 Therefore I am terrified at his presence;
      when I consider, I am in dread of him.
16 God has made my heart faint;
      the Almighty*c* has terrified me;
17 If only I could vanish in darkness,
      and thick darkness would cover my
         face!*d*

Job Complains of Violence on the Earth

24 "Why are times not kept by the
      Almighty,*c*
   and why do those who know him
      never see his days?
2 The wicked*e* remove landmarks;
      they seize flocks and pasture them.
3 They drive away the donkey of the
      orphan;
   they take the widow's ox for a pledge.
4 They thrust the needy off the road;
      the poor of the earth all hide
         themselves.
5 Like wild asses in the desert

   they go out to their toil,
   scavenging in the wasteland
      food for their young.
6 They reap in a field not their own
      and they glean in the vineyard of the
         wicked.
7 They lie all night naked, without
         clothing,
   and have no covering in the cold.
8 They are wet with the rain of the
         mountains,
   and cling to the rock for want of
      shelter.

9 "There are those who snatch the
         orphan child from the breast,
   and take as a pledge the infant of the
      poor.
10 They go about naked, without clothing;
      though hungry, they carry the
         sheaves;
11 between their terraces*f* they press out oil;
      they tread the wine presses, but suffer
         thirst.
12 From the city the dying groan,
      and the throat of the wounded cries
         for help;
   yet God pays no attention to their
      prayer.

13 "There are those who rebel against the
         light,
   who are not acquainted with its ways,
      and do not stay in its paths.
14 The murderer rises at dusk
      to kill the poor and needy,
   and in the night is like a thief.
15 The eye of the adulterer also waits for
         the twilight,
   saying, 'No eye will see me';
      and he disguises his face.

a Syr Vg: Heb *he turns*   *b* Gk Vg: Heb *from*
c Traditional rendering of Heb *Shaddai*   *d* Or *But*
I am not destroyed by the darkness; he has concealed the
thick darkness from me   *e* Gk: Heb *they*
f Meaning of Heb uncertain

24:1–27:23 *Why are times?* Chapters 24–27
are textually confusing. It is not always clear
who is speaking. The literary puzzle reflects the

reality of a complete communication
breakdown.

16 In the dark they dig through houses;
  by day they shut themselves up;
  they do not know the light.
17 For deep darkness is morning to all of
    them;
  for they are friends with the terrors of
    deep darkness.

18 "Swift are they on the face of the waters;
  their portion in the land is cursed;
  no treader turns toward their
    vineyards.
19 Drought and heat snatch away the
    snow waters;
  so does Sheol those who have sinned.
20 The womb forgets them;
  the worm finds them sweet;
  they are no longer remembered;
  so wickedness is broken like a tree.

21 "They harm *a* the childless woman,
  and do no good to the widow.
22 Yet God *b* prolongs the life of the
    mighty by his power;
  they rise up when they despair of life.
23 He gives them security, and they are
    supported;
  his eyes are upon their ways.
24 They are exalted a little while, and then
    are gone;
  they wither and fade like the mallow; *c*
  they are cut off like the heads of grain.
25 If it is not so, who will prove me a liar,
  and show that there is nothing in
    what I say?"

Bildad Speaks: How Can a Mortal Be Righteous Before God?

25 Then Bildad the Shuhite answered:
  2 "Dominion and fear are with God; *d*
  he makes peace in his high heaven.
3 Is there any number to his armies?
  Upon whom does his light not arise?
4 How then can a mortal be righteous
    before God?
  How can one born of woman be pure?
5 If even the moon is not bright
  and the stars are not pure in his sight,
6 how much less a mortal, who is a
    maggot,
  and a human being, who is a worm!"

Job Replies: God's Majesty Is Unsearchable

26 Then Job answered:
  2 "How you have helped one who
    has no power!
  How you have assisted the arm that
    has no strength!
3 How you have counseled one who has
    no wisdom,
  and given much good advice!
4 With whose help have you uttered
    words,
  and whose spirit has come forth from
    you?
5 The shades below tremble,
  the waters and their inhabitants.
6 Sheol is naked before God,
  and Abaddon has no covering.
7 He stretches out Zaphon *e* over the void,
  and hangs the earth upon nothing.
8 He binds up the waters in his thick
    clouds,
  and the cloud is not torn open by
    them.
9 He covers the face of the full moon,
  and spreads over it his cloud.
10 He has described a circle on the face of
    the waters,
  at the boundary between light and
    darkness.
11 The pillars of heaven tremble,
  and are astounded at his rebuke.
12 By his power he stilled the Sea;
  by his understanding he struck down
    Rahab.
13 By his wind the heavens were made fair;
  his hand pierced the fleeing serpent.
14 These are indeed but the outskirts of his
    ways;
  and how small a whisper do we hear
    of him!
  But the thunder of his power who can
    understand?"

Job Maintains His Integrity

27 Job again took up his discourse and
    said:
  2 "As God lives, who has taken away my
    right,

---

a Gk Tg: Heb *feed on* or *associate with*   *b* Heb *he*
c Gk: Heb *like all others*   *d* Heb *him*   *e* Or *the North*

and the Almighty,[a] who has made my
    soul bitter,
3 as long as my breath is in me
    and the spirit of God is in my nostrils,
4 my lips will not speak falsehood,
    and my tongue will not utter deceit.
5 Far be it from me to say that you are
    right;
  until I die I will not put away my
    integrity from me.
6 I hold fast my righteousness, and will
    not let it go;
  my heart does not reproach me for
    any of my days.

7 "May my enemy be like the wicked,
    and may my opponent be like the
    unrighteous.
8 For what is the hope of the godless
    when God cuts them off,
  when God takes away their lives?
9 Will God hear their cry
    when trouble comes upon them?
10 Will they take delight in the
    Almighty?[a]
  Will they call upon God at all times?
11 I will teach you concerning the hand of
    God;
  that which is with the Almighty[a] I
    will not conceal.
12 All of you have seen it yourselves;
    why then have you become
    altogether vain?

13 "This is the portion of the wicked with
    God,
  and the heritage that oppressors
    receive from the Almighty:[a]
14 If their children are multiplied, it is for
    the sword;
  and their offspring have not enough
    to eat.
15 Those who survive them the pestilence
    buries,
  and their widows make no
    lamentation.

16 Though they heap up silver like dust,
    and pile up clothing like clay—
17 they may pile it up, but the just will
    wear it,
  and the innocent will divide the
    silver.
18 They build their houses like nests,
    like booths made by sentinels of the
    vineyard.
19 They go to bed with wealth, but will do
    so no more;
  they open their eyes, and it is gone.
20 Terrors overtake them like a flood;
    in the night a whirlwind carries them
    off.
21 The east wind lifts them up and they are
    gone;
  it sweeps them out of their place.
22 It[b] hurls at them without pity;
  they flee from its[c] power in headlong
    flight.
23 It[b] claps its[c] hands at them,
  and hisses at them from its[c] place.

Interlude: Where Wisdom Is Found

28   "Surely there is a mine for silver,
    and a place for gold to be refined.
2 Iron is taken out of the earth,
    and copper is smelted from ore.
3 Miners put[d] an end to darkness,
    and search out to the farthest bound
    the ore in gloom and deep darkness.
4 They open shafts in a valley away from
    human habitation;
  they are forgotten by travelers,
  they sway suspended, remote from
    people.
5 As for the earth, out of it comes bread;
    but underneath it is turned up as by
    fire.
6 Its stones are the place of sapphires,[e]
    and its dust contains gold.

a Traditional rendering of Heb *Shaddai*   b Or *He*
(that is God)   c Or *his*   d Heb *He puts*
e Or *lapis lazuli*

28:1–28 *Surely there is a mine for silver.*
Chapter 28 is a beautiful hymn celebrating both
the elusiveness and the accessibility of wisdom.
Wisdom is needed to solve the huge tangle
between Job and the friends. Only God
understands the way (v 23). Now readers, as
well as the participants in the drama, long for
God's intervention.

7 "That path no bird of prey knows,
 and the falcon's eye has not seen it.
8 The proud wild animals have not
   trodden it;
 the lion has not passed over it.

9 "They put their hand to the flinty rock,
 and overturn mountains by the roots.
10 They cut out channels in the rocks,
 and their eyes see every precious
   thing.
11 The sources of the rivers they probe;[a]
 hidden things they bring to light.

12 "But where shall wisdom be found?
 And where is the place of
   understanding?
13 Mortals do not know the way to it,[b]
 and it is not found in the land of the
   living.
14 The deep says, 'It is not in me,'
 and the sea says, 'It is not with me.'
15 It cannot be gotten for gold,
 and silver cannot be weighed out as
   its price.
16 It cannot be valued in the gold of
   Ophir,
 in precious onyx or sapphire.[c]
17 Gold and glass cannot equal it,
 nor can it be exchanged for jewels of
   fine gold.
18 No mention shall be made of coral or of
   crystal;
 the price of wisdom is above pearls.
19 The chrysolite of Ethiopia[d] cannot
   compare with it,
 nor can it be valued in pure gold.

20 "Where then does wisdom come from?
 And where is the place of
   understanding?
21 It is hidden from the eyes of all living,
 and concealed from the birds of the air.

22 Abaddon and Death say,
 'We have heard a rumor of it with our
   ears.'

23 "God understands the way to it,
 and he knows its place.
24 For he looks to the ends of the earth,
 and sees everything under the
   heavens.
25 When he gave to the wind its weight,
 and apportioned out the waters by
   measure;
26 when he made a decree for the rain,
 and a way for the thunderbolt;
27 then he saw it and declared it;
 he established it, and searched it out.
28 And he said to humankind,
 'Truly, the fear of the Lord, that is
   wisdom;
 and to depart from evil is
   understanding.' "

Job Finishes His Defense

29 Job again took up his discourse and
   said:
2 "O that I were as in the months of old,
 as in the days when God watched
   over me;
3 when his lamp shone over my head,
 and by his light I walked through
   darkness;
4 when I was in my prime,
 when the friendship of God was upon
   my tent;
5 when the Almighty[e] was still with me,
 when my children were around me;
6 when my steps were washed with milk,
 and the rock poured out for me
   streams of oil!

a Gk Vg: Heb bind   b Gk: Heb its price
c Or lapis lazuli   d Or Nubia; Heb Cush
e Traditional rendering of Heb Shaddai

29:1–31:40 *Job again took up his discourse.* In chapters 29–31, Job's last words, he reviews his past and his present before signing the complaint (31:35). Great dignity, defiance, and persistence, great eloquence, emotion, and yearning characterize this man. He is not the patient sufferer or hopeless victim. When it says, "The words of Job are ended" (31:40), it is almost as if a symphonic orchestra has just finished playing the last note of Beethoven's *Ninth.*

29:6 *when my steps were washed with milk.* The power of the book of Job resides partly in its vivid visual language. Job's pain is intensified when he recalls the abundance of earlier days.

7 When I went out to the gate of the city,
  when I took my seat in the square,
8 the young men saw me and withdrew,
  and the aged rose up and stood;
9 the nobles refrained from talking,
  and laid their hands on their mouths;
10 the voices of princes were hushed,
  and their tongues stuck to the roof of
    their mouths.
11 When the ear heard, it commended me,
  and when the eye saw, it approved;
12 because I delivered the poor who cried,
  and the orphan who had no helper.
13 The blessing of the wretched came
    upon me,
  and I caused the widow's heart to sing
    for joy.
14 I put on righteousness, and it clothed
    me;
  my justice was like a robe and a
    turban.
15 I was eyes to the blind,
  and feet to the lame.
16 I was a father to the needy,
  and I championed the cause of the
    stranger.
17 I broke the fangs of the unrighteous,
  and made them drop their prey from
    their teeth.
18 Then I thought, 'I shall die in my nest,
  and I shall multiply my days like the
    phoenix; *a*
19 my roots spread out to the waters,
  with the dew all night on my
    branches;
20 my glory was fresh with me,
  and my bow ever new in my hand.'
21 "They listened to me, and waited,
  and kept silence for my counsel.
22 After I spoke they did not speak again,
  and my word dropped upon them like
    dew. *b*

23 They waited for me as for the rain;
  they opened their mouths as for the
    spring rain.
24 I smiled on them when they had no
    confidence;
  and the light of my countenance they
    did not extinguish. *c*
25 I chose their way, and sat as chief,
  and I lived like a king among his
    troops,
  like one who comforts mourners.

30 "But now they make sport of me,
    those who are younger than I,
  whose fathers I would have disdained
    to set with the dogs of my flock.
2 What could I gain from the strength of
    their hands?
  All their vigor is gone.
3 Through want and hard hunger
  they gnaw the dry and desolate
    ground,
4 they pick mallow and the leaves of
    bushes,
  and to warm themselves the roots of
    broom.
5 They are driven out from society;
  people shout after them as after a
    thief.
6 In the gullies of wadis they must live,
  in holes in the ground, and in the
    rocks.
7 Among the bushes they bray;
  under the nettles they huddle together.
8 A senseless, disreputable brood,
  they have been whipped out of the
    land.
9 "And now they mock me in song;
  I am a byword to them.

a Or *like sand*   *b* Heb lacks *like dew*
c Meaning of Heb uncertain

So plentiful was the milk from his herd that it
overflowed on his steps. Rather than seeing this
as an example of waste, Job recognizes it as a
sign of incredible divine benevolence toward
him in the past. Now, in chapter 29, he is
overwhelmed by how much he has lost.

30:1 *But now.* There are no more wrenching
words than "But now" (see also "and now" in
30:9, 16). Job's anguish results partly from the
belief that God and the blessings of his past
were inseparable. When blessings disappeared,
God's goodness, mercy, and presence also
became suspect.

10 They abhor me, they keep aloof from
  me;
  they do not hesitate to spit at the
  sight of me.
11 Because God has loosed my bowstring
  and humbled me,
  they have cast off restraint in my
  presence.
12 On my right hand the rabble rise up;
  they send me sprawling,
  and build roads for my ruin.
13 They break up my path,
  they promote my calamity;
  no one restrains[a] them.
14 As through a wide breach they come;
  amid the crash they roll on.
15 Terrors are turned upon me;
  my honor is pursued as by the wind,
  and my prosperity has passed away
  like a cloud.

16 "And now my soul is poured out within
  me;
  days of affliction have taken hold of
  me.
17 The night racks my bones,
  and the pain that gnaws me takes no
  rest.
18 With violence he seizes my garment;[b]
  he grasps me by[c] the collar of my
  tunic.
19 He has cast me into the mire,
  and I have become like dust and
  ashes.
20 I cry to you and you do not answer me;
  I stand, and you merely look at me.
21 You have turned cruel to me;
  with the might of your hand you
  persecute me.
22 You lift me up on the wind, you make
  me ride on it,

and you toss me about in the roar of
  the storm.
23 I know that you will bring me to death,
  and to the house appointed for all
  living.

24 "Surely one does not turn against the
  needy,[d]
  when in disaster they cry for help.[e]
25 Did I not weep for those whose day was
  hard?
  Was not my soul grieved for the poor?
26 But when I looked for good, evil came;
  and when I waited for light, darkness
  came.
27 My inward parts are in turmoil, and are
  never still;
  days of affliction come to meet me.
28 I go about in sunless gloom;
  I stand up in the assembly and cry for
  help.
29 I am a brother of jackals,
  and a companion of ostriches.
30 My skin turns black and falls from me,
  and my bones burn with heat.
31 My lyre is turned to mourning,
  and my pipe to the voice of those
  who weep.

31 "I have made a covenant with my
  eyes;
  how then could I look upon a virgin?
2 What would be my portion from God
  above,
  and my heritage from the Almighty[f]
  on high?
3 Does not calamity befall the unrighteous,
  and disaster the workers of iniquity?

a Cn: Heb *helps*   b Gk: Heb *my garment is
disfigured*   c Heb *like*   d Heb *ruin*
e Cn: Meaning of Heb uncertain   f Traditional
rendering of Heb *Shaddai*

30:9 *They mock me in song.* One of the things
Job cannot abide is the dishonor his distress has
brought him. Formerly, when people met him,
their voices were hushed because of his great
dignity (29:7–9). Now when people speak his
name, they compose tunes of derision to
humiliate him.
  31:1–40 *I have made a covenant.* This chapter

is Job's long oath of innocence or defense of his
earlier conduct. Convinced that God is still in
the wrong, Job hopes that God will recognize
his integrity (v 6) and moral uprightness. Job
was not insensible to the needs of the poor
(v 16). His trust was not in gold (v 24). His
moral life was always pure (v 9). Now the ball
is in God's court.

4 Does he not see my ways,
    and number all my steps?

5 "If I have walked with falsehood,
    and my foot has hurried to deceit—
6 let me be weighed in a just balance,
    and let God know my integrity!—
7 if my step has turned aside from the
        way,
    and my heart has followed my eyes,
    and if any spot has clung to my
        hands;
8 then let me sow, and another eat;
    and let what grows for me be rooted
        out.

9 "If my heart has been enticed by a
        woman,
    and I have lain in wait at my
        neighbor's door;
10 then let my wife grind for another,
    and let other men kneel over her.
11 For that would be a heinous crime;
    that would be a criminal offense;
12 for that would be a fire consuming
        down to Abaddon,
    and it would burn to the root all my
        harvest.

13 "If I have rejected the cause of my male
        or female slaves,
    when they brought a complaint
        against me;
14 what then shall I do when God rises up?
    When he makes inquiry, what shall I
        answer him?
15 Did not he who made me in the womb
        make them?
    And did not one fashion us in the
        womb?

16 "If I have withheld anything that the
        poor desired,

or have caused the eyes of the widow
        to fail,
17 or have eaten my morsel alone,
    and the orphan has not eaten from
        it—
18 for from my youth I reared the orphan*a*
        like a father,
    and from my mother's womb I guided
        the widow*b*—
19 if I have seen anyone perish for lack of
        clothing,
    or a poor person without covering,
20 whose loins have not blessed me,
    and who was not warmed with the
        fleece of my sheep;
21 if I have raised my hand against the
        orphan,
    because I saw I had supporters at the
        gate;
22 then let my shoulder blade fall from my
        shoulder,
    and let my arm be broken from its
        socket.
23 For I was in terror of calamity from God,
    and I could not have faced his
        majesty.

24 "If I have made gold my trust,
    or called fine gold my confidence;
25 if I have rejoiced because my wealth was
        great,
    or because my hand had gotten
        much;
26 if I have looked at the sun*c* when it
        shone,
    or the moon moving in splendor,
27 and my heart has been secretly enticed,
    and my mouth has kissed my hand;
28 this also would be an iniquity to be
        punished by the judges,
    for I should have been false to God
        above.

a Heb *him*   *b* Heb *her*   *c* Heb *the light*

Responding
31:7–10 CHASTITY. In his challenge to God Job names adultery as an action he should be punished for if he were guilty of committing it. Job names two actions in his culture—heart following eyes and being enticed by a woman—that lead to adultery. How does adultery damage the relationship between husband and wife? At the first opportunity make a list of the ways that we can avoid the temptation of being unfaithful to our spouse. *See also* Spiritual Disciplines Index.

29 "If I have rejoiced at the ruin of those
    who hated me,
  or exulted when evil overtook them—
30 I have not let my mouth sin
  by asking for their lives with a curse—
31 if those of my tent ever said,
  'O that we might be sated with his
    flesh!' *a*—
32 the stranger has not lodged in the street;
  I have opened my doors to the
    traveler—
33 if I have concealed my transgressions as
    others do, *b*
  by hiding my iniquity in my bosom,
34 because I stood in great fear of the
    multitude,
  and the contempt of families terrified
    me,
  so that I kept silence, and did not go
    out of doors—
35 O that I had one to hear me!
  (Here is my signature! Let the
    Almighty *c* answer me!)
  O that I had the indictment written
    by my adversary!
36 Surely I would carry it on my shoulder;
  I would bind it on me like a crown;
37 I would give him an account of all my
    steps;
  like a prince I would approach him.

38 "If my land has cried out against me,
  and its furrows have wept together;
39 if I have eaten its yield without payment,
  and caused the death of its owners;

40 let thorns grow instead of wheat,
  and foul weeds instead of barley."

The words of Job are ended.

Elihu Rebukes Job's Friends

32 So these three men ceased to answer Job, because he was righteous in his own eyes. 2Then Elihu son of Barachel the Buzite, of the family of Ram, became angry. He was angry at Job because he justified himself rather than God; 3he was angry also at Job's three friends because they had found no answer, though they had declared Job to be in the wrong. *d* 4Now Elihu had waited to speak to Job, because they were older than he. 5But when Elihu saw that there was no answer in the mouths of these three men, he became angry.

6 Elihu son of Barachel the Buzite answered:

  "I am young in years,
    and you are aged;
  therefore I was timid and afraid
    to declare my opinion to you.
7 I said, 'Let days speak,
    and many years teach wisdom.'
8 But truly it is the spirit in a mortal,
    the breath of the Almighty, *c* that
      makes for understanding.
9 It is not the old *e* that are wise,

a Meaning of Heb uncertain   b Or *as Adam did*
c Traditional rendering of Heb *Shaddai*
d Another ancient tradition reads *answer, and had put God in the wrong*   e Gk Syr Vg: Heb *many*

32:5 *he became angry.* A new friend appears, Elihu, a younger man. Elihu has patiently waited while others spoke. He was angry at the proceedings, but held his tongue. Now he will enter the fray. Though his debilities are obvious—youth, wordiness, and anger—he will enable Job to understand his distress in a new way.

32:8–9 *the spirit in a mortal.* Elihu breaks the mold of wisdom teacher by claiming it is the divine spirit, rather than the gray beard or hair, that makes for understanding. As Elihu speaks, we recognize in him a model spiritual director. He listens carefully, gives alternative explanations, suggests a reason for the current distress, and directs Job to God.

Responding
32:8–9 GUIDANCE. The young, wise Elihu timidly approaches Job and declares that it is God who gives understanding and wisdom, not advanced age. David pleads to the Lord, "Teach me your paths" (Ps 25:4), and Jesus explains to the Twelve, "The Holy Spirit, whom the Father will send in my name, will teach you everything" (John 14:26). When you are alone with God this week, examine how open you have been to God's guidance. How could you be more open? *See also* Spiritual Disciplines Index.

nor the aged that understand what is
  right.
10 Therefore I say, 'Listen to me;
  let me also declare my opinion.'

11 "See, I waited for your words,
  I listened for your wise sayings,
  while you searched out what to say.
12 I gave you my attention,
    but there was in fact no one that
      confuted Job,
    no one among you that answered his
      words.
13 Yet do not say, 'We have found wisdom;
  God may vanquish him, not a
    human.'
14 He has not directed his words against
    me,
  and I will not answer him with your
    speeches.

15 "They are dismayed, they answer no
    more;
  they have not a word to say.
16 And am I to wait, because they do not
    speak,
  because they stand there, and answer
    no more?
17 I also will give my answer;
  I also will declare my opinion.
18 For I am full of words;
  the spirit within me constrains me.
19 My heart is indeed like wine that has no
    vent;
  like new wineskins, it is ready to
    burst.
20 I must speak, so that I may find relief;
  I must open my lips and answer.
21 I will not show partiality to any person
  or use flattery toward anyone.
22 For I do not know how to flatter—
  or my Maker would soon put an end
    to me!

Elihu Rebukes Job

33 "But now, hear my speech, O Job,
      and listen to all my words.
2 See, I open my mouth;
  the tongue in my mouth speaks.
3 My words declare the uprightness of my
    heart,
  and what my lips know they speak
    sincerely.
4 The spirit of God has made me,
  and the breath of the Almighty[a] gives
    me life.
5 Answer me, if you can;
  set your words in order before me;
  take your stand.
6 See, before God I am as you are;
  I too was formed from a piece of clay.
7 No fear of me need terrify you;
  my pressure will not be heavy on you.

8 "Surely, you have spoken in my hearing,
  and I have heard the sound of your
    words.
9 You say, 'I am clean, without
    transgression;
  I am pure, and there is no iniquity in
    me.
10 Look, he finds occasions against me,
  he counts me as his enemy;
11 he puts my feet in the stocks,
  and watches all my paths.'

12 "But in this you are not right. I will
    answer you:
  God is greater than any mortal.
13 Why do you contend against him,
  saying, 'He will answer none of my[b]
    words'?
14 For God speaks in one way,
  and in two, though people do not
    perceive it.
15 In a dream, in a vision of the night,

a Traditional rendering of Heb *Shaddai*
b Compare Gk: Heb *his*

33:6 *I am as you are.* The starting point for
sage spiritual advice is a recognition of shared
humanity. We cannot imagine the mystical
Eliphaz or judgmental Bildad or puritanical
Zophar helping Job scrape his sores with a
potsherd (2:8). People are full of advice when
we are suffering. But the question is, do they
truly believe they too were "formed from a
piece of clay"?

when deep sleep falls on mortals,
  while they slumber on their beds,
16 then he opens their ears,
  and terrifies them with warnings,
17 that he may turn them aside from their
      deeds,
  and keep them from pride,
18 to spare their souls from the Pit,
  their lives from traversing the River.
19 They are also chastened with pain upon
      their beds,
  and with continual strife in their
      bones,
20 so that their lives loathe bread,
  and their appetites dainty food.
21 Their flesh is so wasted away that it
      cannot be seen;
  and their bones, once invisible, now
      stick out.
22 Their souls draw near the Pit,
  and their lives to those who bring
      death.
23 Then, if there should be for one of them
      an angel,
  a mediator, one of a thousand,
  one who declares a person upright,
24 and he is gracious to that person, and
      says,
  'Deliver him from going down into
      the Pit;
  I have found a ransom;
25 let his flesh become fresh with youth;
  let him return to the days of his
      youthful vigor';
26 then he prays to God, and is accepted
      by him,
  he comes into his presence with joy,
  and God*a* repays him for his
      righteousness.
27   That person sings to others and says,
  'I sinned, and perverted what was right,
  and it was not paid back to me.
28 He has redeemed my soul from going
      down to the Pit,
  and my life shall see the light.'

29 "God indeed does all these things,
  twice, three times, with mortals,
30 to bring back their souls from the Pit,
  so that they may see the light of life.*b*
31 Pay heed, Job, listen to me;
  be silent, and I will speak.
32 If you have anything to say, answer me;
  speak, for I desire to justify you.
33 If not, listen to me;
  be silent, and I will teach you
      wisdom."

Elihu Proclaims God's Justice

34 Then Elihu continued and said:
  2 "Hear my words, you wise men,
  and give ear to me, you who know;
3 for the ear tests words
  as the palate tastes food.
4 Let us choose what is right;
  let us determine among ourselves
      what is good.
5 For Job has said, 'I am innocent,
  and God has taken away my right;
6 in spite of being right I am counted a
      liar;
  my wound is incurable, though I am
      without transgression.'
7 Who is there like Job,
  who drinks up scoffing like water,
8 who goes in company with evildoers
  and walks with the wicked?
9 For he has said, 'It profits one nothing
  to take delight in God.'

10 "Therefore, hear me, you who have
      sense,
  far be it from God that he should do
      wickedness,
  and from the Almighty*c* that he
      should do wrong.
11 For according to their deeds he will
      repay them,

a Heb *he*   b Syr: Heb *to be lighted with the light of
life*   c Traditional rendering of Heb *Shaddai*

34:4 *Let us choose.* Once a common
humanity is established, a common task is
joined. Seeking wisdom is a communal venture.
  34:5–6 *For Job has said.* The remarkable
thing about these unremarkable words is that
they show Elihu has been listening to Job. He
cares enough to quote Job's precise words.
Listening humbles us because it requires us to
put aside our prejudices and truly see how
another understands the world.

and according to their ways he will
    make it befall them.
12 Of a truth, God will not do wickedly,
    and the Almighty *a* will not pervert
    justice.
13 Who gave him charge over the earth
    and who laid on him *b* the whole
    world?
14 If he should take back his spirit *c* to
    himself,
    and gather to himself his breath,
15 all flesh would perish together,
    and all mortals return to dust.

16 "If you have understanding, hear this;
    listen to what I say.
17 Shall one who hates justice govern?
    Will you condemn one who is
    righteous and mighty,
18 who says to a king, 'You scoundrel!'
    and to princes, 'You wicked men!';
19 who shows no partiality to nobles,
    nor regards the rich more than the
    poor,
    for they are all the work of his hands?
20 In a moment they die;
    at midnight the people are shaken
      and pass away,
    and the mighty are taken away by no
    human hand.

21 "For his eyes are upon the ways of
    mortals,
    and he sees all their steps.
22 There is no gloom or deep darkness
    where evildoers may hide themselves.
23 For he has not appointed a time *d* for
    anyone
    to go before God in judgment.
24 He shatters the mighty without
    investigation,
    and sets others in their place.
25 Thus, knowing their works,
    he overturns them in the night, and
      they are crushed.
26 He strikes them for their wickedness
    while others look on,
27 because they turned aside from
    following him,
    and had no regard for any of his ways,

28 so that they caused the cry of the poor
    to come to him,
    and he heard the cry of the afflicted—
29 When he is quiet, who can condemn?
    When he hides his face, who can
    behold him,
    whether it be a nation or an
    individual?—
30 so that the godless should not reign,
    or those who ensnare the people.

31 "For has anyone said to God,
    'I have endured punishment; I will
      not offend any more;
32 teach me what I do not see;
    if I have done iniquity, I will do it no
    more'?
33 Will he then pay back to suit you,
    because you reject it?
    For you must choose, and not I;
    therefore declare what you know. *e*
34 Those who have sense will say to me,
    and the wise who hear me will say,
35 'Job speaks without knowledge,
    his words are without insight.'
36 Would that Job were tried to the limit,
    because his answers are those of the
    wicked.
37 For he adds rebellion to his sin;
    he claps his hands among us,
    and multiplies his words against
    God."

Elihu Condemns Self-Righteousness

35 Elihu continued and said:
2 "Do you think this to be just?
    You say, 'I am in the right before
    God.'
3 If you ask, 'What advantage have I?
    How am I better off than if I had
    sinned?'
4 I will answer you
    and your friends with you.
5 Look at the heavens and see;
    observe the clouds, which are higher
    than you.

---

a Traditional rendering of Heb *Shaddai*
b Heb lacks *on him*   *c* Heb *his heart his spirit*
d Cn: Heb *yet*   *e* Meaning of Heb of verses 29-33
uncertain

6 If you have sinned, what do you
  accomplish against him?
  And if your transgressions are
  multiplied, what do you do to
  him?
7 If you are righteous, what do you give to
  him;
  or what does he receive from your
  hand?
8 Your wickedness affects others like you,
  and your righteousness, other human
  beings.

9 "Because of the multitude of
  oppressions people cry out;
  they call for help because of the arm
  of the mighty.
10 But no one says, 'Where is God my
  Maker,
  who gives strength in the night,
11 who teaches us more than the animals
  of the earth,
  and makes us wiser than the birds of
  the air?'
12 There they cry out, but he does not
  answer,
  because of the pride of evildoers.
13 Surely God does not hear an empty cry,
  nor does the Almighty *a* regard it.
14 How much less when you say that you
  do not see him,
  that the case is before him, and you
  are waiting for him!
15 And now, because his anger does not
  punish,
  and he does not greatly heed
  transgression, *b*
16 Job opens his mouth in empty talk,
  he multiplies words without
  knowledge."

Elihu Exalts God's Goodness

36 Elihu continued and said:
2 "Bear with me a little, and I will
  show you,
  for I have yet something to say on
  God's behalf.

3 I will bring my knowledge from far away,
  and ascribe righteousness to my
  Maker.
4 For truly my words are not false;
  one who is perfect in knowledge is
  with you.

5 "Surely God is mighty and does not
  despise any;
  he is mighty in strength of
  understanding.
6 He does not keep the wicked alive,
  but gives the afflicted their right.
7 He does not withdraw his eyes from the
  righteous,
  but with kings on the throne
  he sets them forever, and they are
  exalted.
8 And if they are bound in fetters
  and caught in the cords of affliction,
9 then he declares to them their work
  and their transgressions, that they are
  behaving arrogantly.
10 He opens their ears to instruction,
  and commands that they return from
  iniquity.
11 If they listen, and serve him,
  they complete their days in
  prosperity,
  and their years in pleasantness.
12 But if they do not listen, they shall
  perish by the sword,
  and die without knowledge.

13 "The godless in heart cherish anger;
  they do not cry for help when he
  binds them.
14 They die in their youth,
  and their life ends in shame. *c*
15 He delivers the afflicted by their
  affliction,
  and opens their ear by adversity.

a Traditional rendering of Heb *Shaddai*
b Theodotion Symmachus Compare Vg: Meaning
of Heb uncertain   c Heb *ends among the temple
prostitutes*

36:15 *He delivers the afflicted by their
affliction.* Elihu argues that God speaks through
Job's distress. Job thought that God was silent.

God opens the ear through adversity. Maybe
there are messages we simply have not heard.
Can we hear God in adversity?

16 He also allured you out of distress
    into a broad place where there was no
        constraint,
    and what was set on your table was
        full of fatness.

17 "But you are obsessed with the case of
        the wicked;
    judgment and justice seize you.
18 Beware that wrath does not entice you
        into scoffing,
    and do not let the greatness of the
        ransom turn you aside.
19 Will your cry avail to keep you from
        distress,
    or will all the force of your strength?
20 Do not long for the night,
    when peoples are cut off in their
        place.
21 Beware! Do not turn to iniquity;
    because of that you have been tried by
        affliction.
22 See, God is exalted in his power;
    who is a teacher like him?
23 Who has prescribed for him his way,
    or who can say, 'You have done
        wrong'?

Elihu Proclaims God's Majesty

24 "Remember to extol his work,
    of which mortals have sung.
25 All people have looked on it;
    everyone watches it from far away.
26 Surely God is great, and we do not know
        him;
    the number of his years is
        unsearchable.

27 For he draws up the drops of water;
    he distills[a] his mist in rain,
28 which the skies pour down
    and drop upon mortals abundantly.
29 Can anyone understand the spreading
        of the clouds,
    the thunderings of his pavilion?
30 See, he scatters his lightning around
        him
    and covers the roots of the sea.
31 For by these he governs peoples;
    he gives food in abundance.
32 He covers his hands with the lightning,
    and commands it to strike the mark.
33 Its crashing[b] tells about him;
    he is jealous[b] with anger against
        iniquity.

37 "At this also my heart trembles,
    and leaps out of its place.
2 Listen, listen to the thunder of his voice
    and the rumbling that comes from
        his mouth.
3 Under the whole heaven he lets it loose,
    and his lightning to the corners of the
        earth.
4 After it his voice roars;
    he thunders with his majestic voice
    and he does not restrain the
        lightnings[c] when his voice is
        heard.
5 God thunders wondrously with his
        voice;

a Cn: Heb *they distill*   b Meaning of Heb
uncertain   c Heb *them*

36:16 *allured you out of distress into a broad place.* Elihu interprets Job's distress as God's wooing Job from his former life to a new life characterized by freedom and abundance. A most remarkable verse, this challenges Job to see his pain as the avenue to freedom, the birth pangs of a new life. Elihu does not deny the great pain and dislocation Job experienced, but he sees this evil in the greater context of a developing relationship to God. Elihu's understanding takes the quarrel between Job and God out of the legal arena and puts it in the context of covenantal intimacy.

36:17 *judgment and justice seize you.* Job is so caught up in the legal niceties of his case, in his need to be right, that he has lost the ability to perceive that God is speaking to him in his suffering. Job is under the impression that law will solve his problem, while, in fact, law perpetuates his inability to see his life differently.

37:2 *Listen, listen.* Elihu still speaks. He who has listened to Job now exhorts Job to listen to the deep thunder, which betokens the coming of God. Elihu has modeled good listening. Now Job, for the first time, will truly be able to listen. God's word is not far off (chap 38).

he does great things that we cannot
  comprehend.
6 For to the snow he says, 'Fall on the
    earth';
  and the shower of rain, his heavy
    shower of rain,
7 serves as a sign on everyone's hand,
  so that all whom he has made may
    know it. *a*
8 Then the animals go into their lairs
  and remain in their dens.
9 From its chamber comes the whirlwind,
  and cold from the scattering winds.
10 By the breath of God ice is given,
  and the broad waters are frozen fast.
11 He loads the thick cloud with moisture;
  the clouds scatter his lightning.
12 They turn round and round by his
    guidance,
  to accomplish all that he commands
    them
  on the face of the habitable world.
13 Whether for correction, or for his land,
  or for love, he causes it to happen.

14 "Hear this, O Job;
  stop and consider the wondrous
    works of God.
15 Do you know how God lays his
    command upon them,
  and causes the lightning of his cloud
    to shine?
16 Do you know the balancings of the
    clouds,
  the wondrous works of the one whose
    knowledge is perfect,
17 you whose garments are hot

when the earth is still because of the
    south wind?
18 Can you, like him, spread out the skies,
  hard as a molten mirror?
19 Teach us what we shall say to him;
  we cannot draw up our case because
    of darkness.
20 Should he be told that I want to speak?
  Did anyone ever wish to be swallowed
    up?
21 Now, no one can look on the light
  when it is bright in the skies,
  when the wind has passed and
    cleared them.
22 Out of the north comes golden
    splendor;
  around God is awesome majesty.
23 The Almighty *b*—we cannot find him;
  he is great in power and justice,
  and abundant righteousness he will
    not violate.
24 Therefore mortals fear him;
  he does not regard any who are wise
    in their own conceit."

The LORD Answers Job

38 Then the LORD answered Job out of
  the whirlwind:
2 "Who is this that darkens counsel by
    words without knowledge?
3 Gird up your loins like a man,
  I will question you, and you shall
    declare to me.

a Meaning of Heb of verse 7 uncertain
b Traditional rendering of Heb *Shaddai*

37:14–24 *Hear this, O Job.* Again, Elihu urges Job to listen for the word of God. Elihu will then ask Job a series of questions that are almost identical to those God poses. It is as if he has "foreheard" God. Those who listen well can hear the very groanings of the universe.

38:1–41 *the LORD answered Job.* Central to our approach to the book of Job is that Elihu's words softened Job and prepared him to hear the voice of God. God speaks in majesty. Just as Job feared, God does not come alongside Job gently to comfort him. God's words are pugilistic; they strike out at Job the way Job's words had earlier

attacked God. The language of God's speech is rhythmic and visual. In these words we see the bounding and pounding surf abruptly halt at the command of God (v 11). The language reveals God's grandeur as well as Job's ignorance. God knows light and darkness (vv 12–21), snow and rain (vv 22–30), the heavens and the earth (vv 31–41). God's answer to Job is not direct; a mystery remains. God's tour of the natural realm in this chapter shows that we human beings do not have the knowledge or perspective to even imagine the answers to the riddles we pose. God alone knows how the world works.

4 "Where were you when I laid the
        foundation of the earth?
    Tell me, if you have understanding.
5 Who determined its measurements—
        surely you know!
    Or who stretched the line upon it?
6 On what were its bases sunk,
        or who laid its cornerstone
7 when the morning stars sang together
        and all the heavenly beings[a] shouted
        for joy?

8 "Or who shut in the sea with doors
        when it burst out from the womb?—
9 when I made the clouds its garment,
        and thick darkness its swaddling
        band,
10 and prescribed bounds for it,
        and set bars and doors,
11 and said, 'Thus far shall you come, and
        no farther,
    and here shall your proud waves be
        stopped'?

12 "Have you commanded the morning
        since your days began,
    and caused the dawn to know its
        place,
13 so that it might take hold of the skirts of
        the earth,
    and the wicked be shaken out of it?
14 It is changed like clay under the seal,
    and it is dyed[b] like a garment.
15 Light is withheld from the wicked,
    and their uplifted arm is broken.

16 "Have you entered into the springs of
        the sea,
    or walked in the recesses of the deep?
17 Have the gates of death been revealed to
        you,
    or have you seen the gates of deep
        darkness?
18 Have you comprehended the expanse of
        the earth?
    Declare, if you know all this.

19 "Where is the way to the dwelling of
        light,
    and where is the place of darkness,
20 that you may take it to its territory
    and that you may discern the paths to
        its home?
21 Surely you know, for you were born
        then,
    and the number of your days is great!

22 "Have you entered the storehouses of
        the snow,
    or have you seen the storehouses of
        the hail,
23 which I have reserved for the time of
        trouble,
    for the day of battle and war?
24 What is the way to the place where the
        light is distributed,
    or where the east wind is scattered
        upon the earth?

25 "Who has cut a channel for the torrents
        of rain,
    and a way for the thunderbolt,
26 to bring rain on a land where no one
        lives,
    on the desert, which is empty of
        human life,
27 to satisfy the waste and desolate land,
    and to make the ground put forth
        grass?

28 "Has the rain a father,
    or who has begotten the drops of
        dew?
29 From whose womb did the ice come
        forth,
    and who has given birth to the
        hoarfrost of heaven?
30 The waters become hard like stone,
    and the face of the deep is frozen.

a Heb sons of God   b Cn: Heb and they stand
forth

38:21 *Surely you know*. God adds to the
mockery of Job that we saw in 30:1, 9. God's
relentless questioning exposes the limitations of
Job's knowledge. God is toying with Job, much
like an adult with a headstrong child. Is this
really necessary or helpful?

31 "Can you bind the chains of the
Pleiades,
or loose the cords of Orion?
32 Can you lead forth the Mazzaroth in
their season,
or can you guide the Bear with its
children?
33 Do you know the ordinances of the
heavens?
Can you establish their rule on the
earth?

34 "Can you lift up your voice to the
clouds,
so that a flood of waters may cover
you?
35 Can you send forth lightnings, so that
they may go
and say to you, 'Here we are'?
36 Who has put wisdom in the inward
parts,[a]
or given understanding to the mind?[a]
37 Who has the wisdom to number the
clouds?
Or who can tilt the waterskins of the
heavens,
38 when the dust runs into a mass
and the clods cling together?

39 "Can you hunt the prey for the lion,
or satisfy the appetite of the young
lions,
40 when they crouch in their dens,
or lie in wait in their covert?
41 Who provides for the raven its prey,
when its young ones cry to God,
and wander about for lack of food?

39 "Do you know when the mountain
goats give birth?
Do you observe the calving of the
deer?
2 Can you number the months that they
fulfill,

and do you know the time when they
give birth,
3 when they crouch to give birth to their
offspring,
and are delivered of their young?
4 Their young ones become strong, they
grow up in the open;
they go forth, and do not return to
them.

5 "Who has let the wild ass go free?
Who has loosed the bonds of the
swift ass,
6 to which I have given the steppe for its
home,
the salt land for its dwelling place?
7 It scorns the tumult of the city;
it does not hear the shouts of the
driver.
8 It ranges the mountains as its pasture,
and it searches after every green thing.

9 "Is the wild ox willing to serve you?
Will it spend the night at your crib?
10 Can you tie it in the furrow with ropes,
or will it harrow the valleys after you?
11 Will you depend on it because its
strength is great,
and will you hand over your labor to it?
12 Do you have faith in it that it will
return,
and bring your grain to your
threshing floor?[b]

13 "The ostrich's wings flap wildly,
though its pinions lack plumage.[a]
14 For it leaves its eggs to the earth,
and lets them be warmed on the
ground,
15 forgetting that a foot may crush them,
and that a wild animal may trample
them.

a Meaning of Heb uncertain   b Heb your grain
and your threshing floor

39:1–30 *Do you know?* God turns from
catechizing Job on the wonders of the physical
universe to the mysteries of the animal kingdom.
Job is remarkably ignorant of the birthing
patterns of the goats and deer (vv 1–3), the

habits of wild asses and oxen (vv 5, 9), the
forgetfulness of the ostrich (v 15), the mighti-
ness of the horse (v 19), and the instinct of
the hawk (v 26).

16 It deals cruelly with its young, as if they
    were not its own;
  though its labor should be in vain, yet
    it has no fear;
17 because God has made it forget wisdom,
    and given it no share in
    understanding.
18 When it spreads its plumes aloft, *a*
  it laughs at the horse and its rider.

19 "Do you give the horse its might?
  Do you clothe its neck with mane?
20 Do you make it leap like the locust?
  Its majestic snorting is terrible.
21 It paws *b* violently, exults mightily;
  it goes out to meet the weapons.
22 It laughs at fear, and is not dismayed;
  it does not turn back from the sword.
23 Upon it rattle the quiver,
  the flashing spear, and the javelin.
24 With fierceness and rage it swallows the
    ground;
  it cannot stand still at the sound of
    the trumpet.
25 When the trumpet sounds, it says 'Aha!'
  From a distance it smells the battle,
  the thunder of the captains, and the
    shouting.

26 "Is it by your wisdom that the hawk
    soars,
  and spreads its wings toward the
    south?
27 Is it at your command that the eagle
    mounts up
  and makes its nest on high?
28 It lives on the rock and makes its home
  in the fastness of the rocky crag.
29 From there it spies the prey;
  its eyes see it from far away.
30 Its young ones suck up blood;
  and where the slain are, there it is."

40 And the LORD said to Job:
  2 "Shall a faultfinder contend with
    the Almighty? *c*
  Anyone who argues with God must
    respond."

Job's Response to God

3 Then Job answered the LORD:
4 "See, I am of small account; what shall I
    answer you?
  I lay my hand on my mouth.
5 I have spoken once, and I will not
    answer;
  twice, but will proceed no further."

God's Challenge to Job

6 Then the LORD answered Job out of the
whirlwind:
7 "Gird up your loins like a man;
  I will question you, and you declare to
    me.
8 Will you even put me in the wrong?
  Will you condemn me that you may
    be justified?
9 Have you an arm like God,
  and can you thunder with a voice like
    his?

10 "Deck yourself with majesty and
    dignity;
  clothe yourself with glory and
    splendor.
11 Pour out the overflowings of your anger,
  and look on all who are proud, and
    abase them.
12 Look on all who are proud, and bring
    them low;
  tread down the wicked where they
    stand.

a Meaning of Heb uncertain   *b* Gk Syr Vg: Heb
they dig   *c* Traditional rendering of Heb *Shaddai*

40:3–5 *I am of small account.* When God
takes a breath and asks Job to speak, Job is
speechless and overcome with emotion. He is
meeting a God he never really knew. Job so
much wanted God to respond. Now God is
giving a full answer to Job. Job's airtight
case is melting under the heat of the divine
presence.

40:9 *Have you an arm like God?* Job's deepest
worry was that if his encounter with God was a
contest of strength, God would easily prevail
(9:19). Thus he hoped that God would not
contend with him in the "greatness of his
power," but rather "give heed to me" (23:6).
Now it appears that God is making it a strength
contest between him and Job after all.

13 Hide them all in the dust together;
   bind their faces in the world below. *a*
14 Then I will also acknowledge to you
   that your own right hand can give
   you victory.

15 "Look at Behemoth,
   which I made just as I made you;
   it eats grass like an ox.
16 Its strength is in its loins,
   and its power in the muscles of its belly.
17 It makes its tail stiff like a cedar;
   the sinews of its thighs are knit
   together.
18 Its bones are tubes of bronze,
   its limbs like bars of iron.

19 "It is the first of the great acts of God—
   only its Maker can approach it with
   the sword.
20 For the mountains yield food for it
   where all the wild animals play.
21 Under the lotus plants it lies,
   in the covert of the reeds and in the
   marsh.
22 The lotus trees cover it for shade;
   the willows of the wadi surround it.
23 Even if the river is turbulent, it is not
   frightened;
   it is confident though Jordan rushes
   against its mouth.
24 Can one take it with hooks *b*
   or pierce its nose with a snare?

41 *c* "Can you draw out Leviathan *d* with
   a fishhook,
   or press down its tongue with a cord?
2 Can you put a rope in its nose,
   or pierce its jaw with a hook?
3 Will it make many supplications to you?
   Will it speak soft words to you?

4 Will it make a covenant with you
   to be taken as your servant forever?
5 Will you play with it as with a bird,
   or will you put it on leash for your
   girls?
6 Will traders bargain over it?
   Will they divide it up among the
   merchants?
7 Can you fill its skin with harpoons,
   or its head with fishing spears?
8 Lay hands on it;
   think of the battle; you will not do it
   again!
9 *e* Any hope of capturing it *f* will be
   disappointed;
   were not even the gods *g* overwhelmed
   at the sight of it?
10 No one is so fierce as to dare to stir
   it up.
   Who can stand before it? *h*
11 Who can confront it *h* and be safe? *i*
   —under the whole heaven, who? *j*

12 "I will not keep silence concerning its
   limbs,
   or its mighty strength, or its splendid
   frame.
13 Who can strip off its outer garment?
   Who can penetrate its double coat of
   mail? *k*
14 Who can open the doors of its face?
   There is terror all around its teeth.
15 Its back *l* is made of shields in rows,
   shut up closely as with a seal.

a Heb *the hidden place*   b Cn: Heb *in his eyes*
c Ch 40.25 in Heb   d Or *the crocodile*   e Ch
41.1 in Heb   f Heb *of it*   g Cn Compare
Symmachus Syr: Heb *one is*   h Heb *me*
i Gk: Heb *that I shall repay*   j Heb *to me*
k Gk: Heb *bridle*   l Cn Compare Gk Vg: Heb
pride

41:1–11 *Can you draw out Leviathan?* Job
thought he scored a point against God when he
sarcastically asked God if Job was the great sea
monster that God was trying to control (7:12).
Instead, God has subdued all those monsters,
Leviathan included. "Want to go fishing for
Leviathan, Job?" God asks. Sarcasm cuts both
ways.

41:12–34 *I will not keep silence concerning its
limbs.* God spends more time describing
Leviathan than any other creature. The minute
description shows that God has seen this
creature "up close." Leviathan was, as it were,
God's biggest challenge in bringing order to
the world. God therefore brought Job into the
divine theater not simply to behold the wonder
of the divine activity, but also to see the danger.

JOB

Steadfast Through Suffering

Selected Scriptures: *Job; James 5:7–11*

Job was a man who was "blameless and upright, one who feared God and turned away from evil" (Job 1:1). He had a large family and numerous animals and servants; he was "the greatest of all the people of the east" (1:3). Yet suddenly, in the midst of his prosperity and wealth, Job was stripped of all that had once defined him. Job first lost his herds, his servants, and his grown children (1:13–19). Then he lost his health (2:7). The next thirty-six chapters record Job's response to this tragedy, his grappling with his intense suffering, and his three friends' winded explanations of the probable causes of his suffering.

Job feels disoriented, deserted by God, and defensive toward his friends, who move from grieving with him to concluding that this suffering must be punishment for some sin in his life. Job is surprisingly honest in his discontent and anger toward God: "He breaks me down on every side, and I am gone, he has uprooted my hope like a tree" (19:10). Yet for most of the book, Job clings to his conviction of God's sovereignty. He feels God has left him; yet he can't give up his belief in God's ultimate goodness. Job declares, "I know that my Redeemer lives, and that at the last he will stand upon the earth; and after my skin has been thus destroyed, then in my flesh I shall see God, whom I shall see on my side, and my eyes shall behold, and not another" (19:25–27). Although Job grapples with God's justice, he remains unable to accuse him of being unjust. In the end, God addresses Job's questions and complaints with his own strain of questions and a strong argument for his ultimate sovereignty: "Can you lift up your voice to the clouds, so that a flood of waters may cover you? Can you send forth lightnings, so that they may go and say to you, 'Here we are'?" (38:34–35).

We know that Job's suffering came as the result of a wager between God and Satan. What appeared cruel and unusual punishment had at its root the purpose of defining for all time the parameters of faith in God. Is God worthy of praise because we receive just reward for our actions, or is he praiseworthy regardless of the circumstances we face?

One man wrote at length about experiences such as Job's, and through his wisdom we can come to better understand many of the truths first revealed in the book of Job. John of the Cross's *The Dark Night of the Soul* describes God's process of maturing souls through allowing times of suffering and darkness in their lives. A sixteenth-century Carmelite monk, John faced such a dark night himself while under arrest and in confinement for his work of reform within the Church.

"God must take [spiritual consolation] away in order to purify the soul," John writes. He describes how God worked in Job's life and how he works in the lives of

PROFILE: JOB

those who know him today: "Because of his love for us, [God] urges us to grow up. His love is not content to leave us in our weakness, and for this reason he takes us into a dark night. He weans us from all of the pleasures by giving us dry times and inward darkness. . . . Through the dark night pride becomes humility, greed becomes simplicity, wrath becomes contentment, luxury becomes peace, gluttony becomes moderation, envy becomes joy, and sloth becomes strength. No soul will ever grow deep in the spiritual life unless God works passively in that soul by means of the dark night."

Personal Reflection

- Have you experienced a dark night of the soul? What were the circumstances of your suffering?
- What can you learn from Job about how to care for a friend who is experiencing a dark night of the soul?
- How has God used suffering to develop any of these or other virtues in your life: humility, simplicity, contentment, peace, moderation, joy, strength?

16 One is so near to another
   that no air can come between them.
17 They are joined one to another;
   they clasp each other and cannot be separated.
18 Its sneezes flash forth light,
   and its eyes are like the eyelids of the dawn.
19 From its mouth go flaming torches;
   sparks of fire leap out.
20 Out of its nostrils comes smoke,
   as from a boiling pot and burning rushes.
21 Its breath kindles coals,
   and a flame comes out of its mouth.
22 In its neck abides strength,
   and terror dances before it.
23 The folds of its flesh cling together;
   it is firmly cast and immovable.
24 Its heart is as hard as stone,
   as hard as the lower millstone.
25 When it raises itself up the gods are afraid;
   at the crashing they are beside themselves.
26 Though the sword reaches it, it does not avail,
   nor does the spear, the dart, or the javelin.
27 It counts iron as straw,
   and bronze as rotten wood.
28 The arrow cannot make it flee;
   slingstones, for it, are turned to chaff.
29 Clubs are counted as chaff;
   it laughs at the rattle of javelins.
30 Its underparts are like sharp potsherds;
   it spreads itself like a threshing sledge on the mire.
31 It makes the deep boil like a pot;
   it makes the sea like a pot of ointment.
32 It leaves a shining wake behind it;
   one would think the deep to be white-haired.
33 On earth it has no equal,
   a creature without fear.
34 It surveys everything that is lofty;
   it is king over all that are proud."

Job Is Humbled and Satisfied

42 Then Job answered the LORD:
² "I know that you can do all things,
and that no purpose of yours can be
thwarted.
³ 'Who is this that hides counsel without
knowledge?'
Therefore I have uttered what I did not
understand,
things too wonderful for me, which I
did not know.
⁴ 'Hear, and I will speak;
I will question you, and you declare to
me.'
⁵ I had heard of you by the hearing of the
ear,
but now my eye sees you;
⁶ therefore I despise myself,
and repent in dust and ashes."

Job's Friends Are Humiliated

7 After the LORD had spoken these words
to Job, the LORD said to Eliphaz the Temanite:

"My wrath is kindled against you and against
your two friends; for you have not spoken of
me what is right, as my servant Job has. ⁸Now
therefore take seven bulls and seven rams,
and go to my servant Job, and offer up for
yourselves a burnt offering; and my servant
Job shall pray for you, for I will accept his
prayer not to deal with you according to your
folly; for you have not spoken of me what is
right, as my servant Job has done." ⁹So Eliphaz the Temanite and Bildad the Shuhite
and Zophar the Naamathite went and did
what the LORD had told them; and the LORD
accepted Job's prayer.

Job's Fortunes Are Restored Twofold

10 And the LORD restored the fortunes of
Job when he had prayed for his friends; and
the LORD gave Job twice as much as he had
before. ¹¹Then there came to him all his
brothers and sisters and all who had known
him before, and they ate bread with him in
his house; they showed him sympathy and

42:2 *I know that you can do all things.* A
breathtaking verse—previously Job had confessed God's omnipotence (chap 9), but here he
does so in a new way. The one who knows that
God can do all things is the one who knows that
his Redeemer lives. His knowledge of God is now
stitched to his soul. The pleasantries of wisdom
theology are now discarded, along with his
judicial papers.

42:5 *now my eye sees you.* The intensity of
Job's words does not let up. Now he "sees" God.
Language is not supple enough to capture the
intimacy and power of Job's feeling. He has
realized, in the depths of his being, that the goal
of his entire life is to be in God's presence and
have the reality of God's awesome power
accompany him always. He is overwhelmed by
gratitude, by his rashness, by his limitations, by
God's grandeur.

42:6 *therefore I despise myself.* The overwhelming vision of God leads Job to repentance
and self-rejection. The one who was absolutely
sure he was right is now utterly sure he was
wrong, willfully, arrogantly, shamefully wrong.
Such a contrast between experience and
understanding leads him to this extreme
expression of self-abasement.

42:7 *as my servant Job has.* Just when Job
has given up any need to be found in the right,
God seems to tell him, in a subordinate clause
of a sentence, that he has been right all along.
This verse packs explosions in it. Were all Job's
questionings and laments "right" or just his
closing humble admissions? But Job's friends
are rebuked. The thought is repeated (v 8), but
never explained. Mysteries continue as Job is
restored.

42:8 *take seven bulls.* God wants friends to
reconcile. Things were said among the friends
that would strain any relationship. Each now has
to do something that exposes his vulnerability
to the others. The friends sacrifice, admitting
their errors. Job prays for them, thus opening
himself up to them again.

Responding
42:10 PRAYER. This verse can only be
described as ironic. After defending
himself against the accusations of his friends,
Job prays for them. How hard do we find it to
pray for someone who has made numerous false
accusations against us or spread false rumors
about us? When we do pray for them, how does
it affect our soul? *See also* Spiritual Disciplines
Index.

comforted him for all the evil that the LORD had brought upon him; and each of them gave him a piece of money*a* and a gold ring. [12]The LORD blessed the latter days of Job more than his beginning; and he had fourteen thousand sheep, six thousand camels, a thousand yoke of oxen, and a thousand donkeys. [13]He also had seven sons and three daughters. [14]He named the first Jemimah, the second Keziah, and the third Keren-happuch. [15]In all the land there were no women so beautiful as Job's daughters; and their father gave them an inheritance along with their brothers. [16]After this Job lived one hundred and forty years, and saw his children, and his children's children, four generations. [17]And Job died, old and full of days.

a Heb *a qesitah*

42:14–15 *He named.* Only the girls' names are given here. They inherit equal portions with their living brothers. This is a development of biblical thought (see Num 27). Job is breaking new social ground in Israel. Once you have seen God, you can never look at the world in the same way.

42:17 *old and full of days.* Job receives double not just of material possessions, but of the expected biblical lifetime. He dies full of days. The abundance that Elihu had said was the lesson of Job's suffering is now experienced by Job in his long life. The book of Job does not tie up all loose ends of the problem of suffering, but it gives us Job the man, a most alluring man.

VII. The People of God in Prayer and Worship

Scriptures: Psalms

 *PRAISE & PRAYER*

Deuterocanonical Book: Psalm 151

> *The aim of God in history is the creation of an all-inclusive community of loving persons with God himself at the very center of this community as its prime Sustainer and most glorious Inhabitant (Eph 2:19–22; 3:10). The Bible traces the formation of this community from the creation in the Garden of Eden all the way to the new heaven and the new earth. Come, join us as we explore the many dimensions of this with-God history—from individual to family to tribe to people to nation to all humanity—and apply what we learn to our own spiritual formation.*

In the Psalms we see and hear the ways God nurtures the nation of Israel and continues to form an all-inclusive community through the development of liturgical praise and prayer.

God's Action

Psalms is a book of praise and prayer. The psalmist sings to us that God is "enthroned on the praises of Israel" and addresses God as "you who answer prayer" (22:3; 65:2). Praise and prayer—these two spiritual practices articulate our most fundamental relationship to God. The Psalter expresses, with more immediacy and completeness than any other part of the Bible, how the People of God are formed spiritually. This is because it gathers up the historical and corporate experiences of the Israelites—as well as very intimate, personal experiences of individuals—and then expresses those experiences in the full depth and richness of poetry, classically understood as public reading and remembrance.

Ideally, the Psalms were performed in suitable architectural and liturgical settings, beginning with the tabernacle in the wilderness and continuing up through the glorious Temple of Jesus' day. Undoubtedly they were simply read or chanted without any accompaniment, but indications are that their performance was at times replete with musical instruments, choir, and dance. The Psalms are works of art that skillfully and vigorously embody what cannot simply be stated or said. No doubt their primary use was in public worship, but individuals also utilized them frequently, and both of these practices continue in our own day. The language and images conveyed by the Psalms are unsurpassed for powerfully forming our spiritual life.

The With-God Life

The Psalms are primary instruments for forming the inner life of the faithful, but much of their effectiveness derives from the fact that they are also about how this formation occurs. They speak forth, in suitable poetic tones, of how God and human beings interact to shape the inner and outer life of individuals and groups. Though the Psalms do teach, most of their power for forming our inner life and character lies in their beauty and capacity to penetrate our emotions, our body, our social relations—indeed, our entire life.

Praise and prayer are the pulse beat of the Psalms. The praise or adulation often looks like proclamation (Pss 1; 23; the Song of Moses and Miriam in Exod 15), but poetic proclamation is our natural response when we have entered into surpassing magnificence—the Person and the Creation of the Lord God, the Almighty. We simply *must* bear witness to it, proclaim it, shout it from the rooftops as an essential part of engaging, enjoying, and being faithful to it.

With regard to content, the Psalms move between two poles; on one side is the desperate condition of human beings when left to stand on their own and, on the other, the unlimited greatness and goodness of God. From those two poles there emerges, strangely but beautifully, the greatness of humanity under God and within God's life and cosmic plan. This is the result of God's salvation or deliverance, which in psalm after psalm is remembered, praised, and anticipated. "God-with-us" is the essence of deliverance regardless of the specific circumstance.

The book of Psalms graphically depicts the desperate human condition: our natural weakness, transience, insignificance, isolation, foolishness, inner wickedness, outer wickedness, oppression of others, oppression by others—indeed, our overall hopelessness. Now, this is raw realism about human existence wherever it may be. Who can deny it?

Yet, at the same time, the goodness and greatness of God are seen and celebrated: in God's covenant with Israel, in the lives of Israel's great ones, in the beauty and strength of Torah, in the great historical acts of national and individual deliverance, in magnificent Jerusalem and the glorious Temple, in the unsurpassed works of nature, in righteous judgment, in the searching of the inmost heart, and in God's majestic rule over all—including all the nations of the earth. All this, and more, is held before the faithful in poetic performance to impress upon them what life with God is like and to lead them ever more deeply into that life. And finally, the practices and the character of godly persons are described, illustrated, and glorified.

Human Reaction

The attraction of the Psalter is great and obvious. It is a "natural" form for expressing the drama of life: our precarious human condition and God's gracious offer of life-giving relationship with himself. The combination of poetic form, historical narrative, and profound insight makes the Psalms attractive even to unbelievers. Their sweeping vision and accurate reflection of the common experiences of human life provide a framework for the interpretation of human existence that has few, if any, rivals.

In the individual and corporate enactment of the Psalms a public form of life takes shape. In reality, the Psalter is a prayer book—or, better, a soul book—that correctly represents God and the life that we can have in him. This explains the huge role that the book of Psalms actually played in the Jewish religion and, later, in the life of the Church. In the Christian era the apostle Paul's emphasis upon singing is genuinely remarkable: "Be filled with the Spirit, as you sing psalms and hymns and spiritual songs among yourselves, singing and making melody to the Lord in your hearts" (Eph 5:18–19). And more recently, from the Protestant Reformation on, great advances and renewals in Christendom have often been times of great singing. Beyond all doubt, singing is a most powerful force in our spiritual formation.

Blessings and Benefits for Our Formation

In the Psalter the language of praise, adoration, thanksgiving, intercession, petition, complaint, disappointment, remembrance, anger, relinquishment, and repentance is beautifully and memorably available. Ordinary persons like ourselves simply cannot come up with such language on our own, but we can enter into it if it is presented in a suitable context. And these inspired poetic expressions can, under God, be the locus of great joy and character transformation as we allow them to sink deep into our heart.

If we enter into the Psalms honestly and faithfully, they can induce experiences and actions within us that truly reflect the words expressed. This, in turn, will reshape our inner being and character into the state God would have it. And maintain it! The testimony of the People of God throughout the ages, even up to our day, confirms this. Nothing on earth matches the Psalter as a public exercise for cultivating a right heart in relation to God.

Limits and Liabilities for Our Formation

But for all the glory and power of the Psalms, our response to them can have serious limitations. Any activity can become mere performance. As we have seen with the law, the limitation of liturgical language and ritual is that it can remain external and not touch the heart. This is true even though the content of the Psalms themselves flatly opposes it. We can sing, "Search me, O God, and know my heart" (139:23), and even enjoy the thought expressed, but avoid the reality like the plague. Merely singing about God's searching our heart can also leave us with the mistaken impression that by virtue of the singing we have participated in its reality. The same is true for all the great expressions of the Psalter.

When the practices of praise and worship remain external, they can also bind our devotion to God to specific times and places ("church work"), to legalism, or to culture (ethnicity). When this happens, our religion becomes a performance—or worse yet, turns us into being merely spectators of a performance. Worship of God can be replaced by worship of beauty or merely "propriety" and even become simply entertainment.

The With-God Life

Worship without heart is what the prophetic witness had to combat during the heyday of religious practices in the First Temple and in Samaria: "I hate, I despise your festivals, and I take no delight in your solemn assemblies" (Amos 5:21). "I cannot endure solemn assemblies with iniquity. Your new moons and your appointed festivals my soul hates; . . . Even though you make many prayers, I will not listen; your hands are full of blood" (Isa 1:13–15).

In addition, merely external worship leaves us incapable of devotion when the "props" are taken away. We then are at a loss about how we can "sing the LORD's song in a foreign land" (Ps 137:4). By contrast, Paul and Silas in a Philippian jail pray and sing hymns at midnight and bring God's life to their fellow prisoners, indeed, to the jail keeper himself (Acts 16:25–34).

Externalization is *not* inevitable. By being aware of it and guarding against it we can appropriate the richness of the Psalms for great benefit to our inner life. Moving from the surface experience into the depths of our mind, will, and heart, we reach the place of true formation and begin the transformation of character that God intends.

The danger of substituting ritual behavior for heartfelt devotion to God, for moral integrity, and for justice is always close at hand in those public practices that foster group solidarity and depend upon social approval. This is why the prophetic witness, reaffirmed by Jesus, always emphasizes mercy over sacrifice (Matt 9:13; 12:7). Mercy, you see, is of the heart, while sacrifice may or may not be. Sadly, there seems no limit to the perversion of heart that can exist alongside the reciting of creeds and the singing of hymns in sacred settings. What the great prophets relentlessly condemned—pious ritual without inward and outward transformation—was perhaps even worse in the days of Jesus, and it remains a terrible problem today. Just think how different our life would be if we actually lived the words we mouth in religious services. What a tremendous step forward in spiritual formation that would be!

Insights and Instructions for Our Formation

Liturgical and ritual performance can be a source of great strength and direction in our spiritual formation, but it must be used and used well. Frankly, there is no such thing as purely inward religion. That would defy the reality of our embodied selves and the significance of the body and behavior in our godly formation. The contribution of poetry and ritual to the formation of the heart and life in corporate as well as individual worship is indispensable to all robust formation in Christlikeness. The Psalms and the forms of life they represent are a great gift to the People of God—really, to all humanity. We are to read and sing them *from the heart*. And the Psalms themselves show us in exquisite detail just how we can do exactly that—how we can "with gratitude in [our] hearts sing psalms, hymns, and spiritual songs to God" (Col 3:16).

The With-God Life

PSALMS

"**O** sing to the LORD a new song," the old song says (Ps 96:1), and we do, but the old songs, the Psalms, still stand at the heart of Christian life and worship. The Psalms are the oldest, most universally accepted texts of faith, constantly in use for millennia. To us they are old; most of the psalms we have were probably written between 1000 and 400 BC. Yet the People of God have sung them in Israel's Temple, in synagogues, at Qumran, in the houses and catacombs of early Christianity, in cathedrals and monasteries, in prisons and jungles, on street corners and in simple buildings, wherever they met to worship. They are Israel's and the Church's first prayer book and first hymnbook. Other wonderful texts and tunes have come to us, of course, from Bernard of Clairvaux, Martin Luther, Isaac Watts, Charles Wesley, Fanny Crosby, Brian Wren, and a host of others. But the Psalms are still the deep well from which we draw gladly to worship.

It is moving to know that anytime we sing or pray a psalm, we are never alone. We are always joining others somewhere around the world who are reciting it at the same time. Though we grow greatly in using them privately, we profit even more when we embrace the Psalms as the songs of God's people. God's people shaped the Psalms—composing, gathering, and preserving them—and the Psalms in turn continue to shape the people. As we enter into these songs, they teach us and give us words to pray. They teach us about the world we live in with all its glory and brokenness. They teach us about the human condition, sometimes by mirroring our own condition, sometimes by sharing the prayers of others as we sing with them or even on their behalf. They teach us the language of prayer with its words and cadences, its gladness and mystery. They give us words when we don't have words. And, of course, they teach us to see, even when we're befuddled, how God is with us.

The Psalms embrace the wide experience and insight of the community of faith. So we have great variety: hymns of praise, lament, and thanksgiving; songs recalling God's active presence in Israel's history; songs rooted in prophetic and wisdom

---

See also "The With-God Life" essays for this section of the Bible, "The People of God in Prayer and Worship," pp. 769–72, and "The People of God in Travail," pp. 717–20.

teaching; songs of repentance and trust; songs about the king's and God's rule; and songs of longing and hope and irrepressible joy. No single psalm captures all that needs to be said, of course, but taken together the Psalms offer a very full witness. No wonder Martin Luther called the Psalms "the Bible in miniature." That's why he insists, as do many others, that we should pray them all.

The Shape of the Psalms

Over the centuries, Israelite worshipers wrote many "new" songs to the Lord, of which the 150 most enduring are gathered in the book of Psalms. This makes the Psalter, in effect, an "all-time favorites" collection. Most interpreters agree that the Psalms are now divided into five books, each ending with words of praise. But they also see signs of earlier collections that precede the one we have. The songs have varied themes, as noted above, but the superscriptions, or descriptive headings, that stand at the beginning of many psalms also suggest they have varied musical settings and come from different times and different authors.

Often we would like to know more about the Psalms than we can. Even with the names of David, Asaph, and others in the headings, it's hard to tell who wrote a particular psalm. And when the singers complain bitterly about their enemies, we seldom can tell precisely who these enemies were and why they were so awful. That frustrates those of us who like to use such details in interpreting the Bible. But not knowing these things helps make the Psalms more timeless and accessible to us all. Certainly this ambiguity sustains their power in the worshiping community. We can more easily let their language of joy and thanksgiving or complaint and desperation speak for us in the nitty-gritty of our own lives.

The "Cursing" Psalms

For many readers the "cursing" or "imprecatory" psalms bring a challenge, even a hindrance, to embracing and praying the Psalms. Their language seems harsh, cruel, and contrary to the teaching and example of Jesus. The challenge is even greater because these songs are not isolated or fleeting. Many made it into the ancient hymnbook to be sung again and again over the centuries.

It helps to know that these sometimes shrill songs explore the mystery of God's justice and God's inexhaustible love. For the psalmists, seeking God's "vengeance" and "wrath" had far more to do with establishing justice than with the expression of negative emotions. So the bombastic hyperbole of these psalms shouts that evil is real, is awful, and is undercutting God's loving purposes for the world. It urges God to act to overturn it, to even things up, to bring justice or "vengeance." God is the only one who can overcome evil, and the singers believe that God will not ignore it. The psalmists plead for justice and leave it to God to act.

The enemies are also real. Spiritualizing this language to talk of inner struggle may sometimes give us words we need, but the psalmists are talking about flesh-and-blood enemies. Some of them are personal, like those who sweet-talk you only to stab you in the back. Some are social, like those who buy off judges, profit as slum landlords, entrap people in debt, misuse immigrant workers, and rule to reward the rich at the expense of the poor. (See the Prophets.) Some enemies are peoples and nations, like a very real army that is trying to kill you. All of them act contrary to how God dearly wants the world to work. The psalmists know this and plead for God to fix it.

So "cursing" songs are not merely angry, personal songs. In reading the imprecatory psalms, modern readers need to guard against arrogance and self-righteousness. First of all, the Israelites weren't ignorant, not having heard Jesus. Though Jesus pushes God's teachings to new heights in both word and example, God's people already knew to love neighbors, be kind to enemies, and leave "vengeance" to God (see Lev 19:17–18; Deut 32:35; Prov 24:17; 25:21–22).

Second, these psalms may serve as a mirror for our own struggles with resentment, anger, and despair in our encounters with real evil and real enemies. After all, knowing we should love and pray for our enemies is different from doing it. For some of us, at least, such songs may challenge us to test whether we are indeed innocent victims (see 7:3–4) or whether we might even be among the arrogant "enemies" who lie and cheat and prey on the poor.

Finally, we may use these songs to ponder how God's love mysteriously satisfies God's justice without the mathematics of payback (see 103:8–10) and how that love will ultimately prevail to mend the world and bring God's purposes to full fruit.

Shaped by the Psalms

Christian writers throughout history have insisted that the only way we can come to understand the Psalms is by praying them and by using them in ways that allow them to shape us. This involves a conscious choice that contradicts common habits. It means that, instead of working on the text, we let the text work on us. It means reading formationally rather than informationally, which is the habit we bring to reports, newspapers, textbooks, and most of the reading we do. It means embracing the text rather than holding it at arm's length. It means being vulnerable to hear how God might address us through the text rather than managing the text to serve our curiosity and need to control.

This is a study Bible, and study does help us to understand and be shaped by Scripture. But even in study we can stiff-arm texts rather than engage them. The study that transforms us moves with patient, focused attention and listens deeply, ready to respond. For example, in studying psalms that are hymns we can list all of the reasons why people are called to praise or the variety of ways people are invited to praise. Study that shapes us, however, is willing to join in praise and to ponder the reasons why. Or in exploring the form of the lament song, we can patiently reflect on why confessions of trust are typically sandwiched between complaints and pleas for help.

Freely entering into the poetry of the Psalms also helps them shape us. Typically we use music and poetry to try to speak about what is dearest to us or, more precisely, to point toward what is so precious or disturbing or powerful that ordinary words fail us. So we pack poetic lines full of vivid words, intense imagery, and high exaggeration that try to tell the truth that bursts the boundaries of telling. Reading that shapes us lets such poetry capture our imaginations and grab our hearts.

Happily, what we've learned about how Hebrew poetry works can help. Its most important feature is parallelism, in which two or three poetic lines together try to convey a single idea. It's the feature that best survives translation and that very often corresponds to the verse numberings in a psalm. Sometimes successive lines will say the same thing in a similar way using synonyms. Sometimes they will present the same idea in opposite ways. At still other times successive lines will build on what's gone before and complete an idea. What is important in reading is to keep the families of lines together.

Understanding poetic device and structure, however, has a double edge. It can help us enter the poetry or, if we depend on mechanics alone, it can slam the door. Ultimately we have to slow down enough to really hear, really see. To gaze on the bountiful tree planted by steady streams. Walk in the valley's dark shadows. Thirst with the parched ground crying out in desperation. Enjoy being a doorkeeper in the lovely courts of the Lord. Break into applause with the wild waters and join the sea monsters' praise-filled chorus. When we can give ourselves to the poetry of the Psalms, refusing to drag it down to prosaic literalism or formula, the Psalms can shape us.

Lectio divina, the classic spiritual exercise of "holy reading," offers still another way to let the Psalms shape us. It shares the patient listening and receptivity already mentioned, since those reading this way are in no hurry to get through the text. After all, it's not so much a question of how much we read as it is how well we read. Usually it helps to begin "holy reading" with silence, partly to quiet ourselves to listen and partly to consciously choose to read in a way much different from the other reading we do. Then we can read, proceeding prayerfully, ready to stop, to soak in a word or a verse as God opens it to us, to brood gently over it, to take it in slowly like a mint melting in the mouth. This kind of listening to the text invites God to teach us in direct and transforming ways. We respond by pondering such teaching and acting on it.

Often *lectio divina* moves into praying the psalm, not simply knowing it as another's prayer, but coming to know it as our own. The Psalms use the language of intimacy and relationship, and they are our words toward God more than they are God's words to us. Understanding this change in direction opens the Psalms for many people. Though God's Spirit certainly helped to raise up these words of prayer and to preserve them for us, these texts are not words of instruction like those we find in the Prophets, the Gospels, or the Letters. Instead, they are words we bring to God, words of confession, confusion, desperation, hope, trust, thanks, and praise. As we pray them, we learn, of course, especially as we learn to pray them all. But we also draw nearer to God to be present, to listen, and to be changed.

(*Lectio Divina*)

Singing the Psalms also shapes us. Since we so often encounter the Psalms only as printed text, it is easy to forget that they are songs. Because they are songs, the Psalms draw on the power music has to affect us, and the People of God have relied on this powerful effect in all ages. Starting with the Psalms themselves, which refer to some tunes, instruments, and musical directions, these songs have been sung in almost every imaginable style—chant, chorale, hymns, country, bluegrass, gospel, oratorio, rock, and many more, not to mention the world of instruments that have supported the singers. In studying, using, and praying the Psalms, finding ways to share in them as songs can be very powerful. Perhaps it can be in listening to or singing a song based on a Psalm text. Maybe it could include learning to chant or improvising a simple tune of our own. And it is always wonderful to join in singing the Psalms together with others.

Responding to the Psalms creatively in still other ways also helps us enter a dialogue with them that can change us. It might include doodling or creative movement, thoughtful paraphrase or craft, photography or pottery, painting or calligraphy, or myriad other ways that lead us to listen deeply and respond to the Psalms. These varied channels into our minds and hearts again invite God to shape us through the words of the Psalms.

By whatever means, the Psalms teach and shape us most powerfully as we immerse ourselves in them day-to-day over time. In subtle and even surprising ways they show us the "real world," they draw us ever steadily toward authentic wholeness, and they bring us to see and delight in the God who is with us.

One final note, beyond the 150 psalms that all Christians are familiar with in the Bible, we know of some additional psalms that are included in ancient versions of the Old Testament or in the Psalms manuscript from Qumran, the community of the Dead Sea Scrolls. We have included in this study Bible one such psalm (in the Deuterocanonical selections), Psalm 151, which is part of the Bible of the Orthodox Christian community.

—*Howard R. Macy*

BOOK I

(Psalms 1–41)

Psalm 1

The Two Ways

1 Happy are those
who do not follow the advice of the
wicked,
or take the path that sinners tread,
or sit in the seat of scoffers;
2 but their delight is in the law of the
LORD,
and on his law they meditate day and
night.
3 They are like trees
planted by streams of water,
which yield their fruit in its season,
and their leaves do not wither.
In all that they do, they prosper.

4 The wicked are not so,
but are like chaff that the wind drives
away.
5 Therefore the wicked will not stand in
the judgment,
nor sinners in the congregation of the
righteous;
6 for the LORD watches over the way of
the righteous,
but the way of the wicked will
perish.

Psalm 2

God's Promise to His Anointed

1 Why do the nations conspire,
and the peoples plot in vain?
2 The kings of the earth set themselves,

1:1–2:11 *Happy are those.* Psalms 1 and 2 offer an introduction to the Psalter as a whole, emphasizing God's goodness and power and inviting us to walk gladly in God's ways.

1:1–6 *Happy are those.* Psalm 1 challenges readers to make a choice between two ways, the way of the righteous and the way of the wicked. The choice is boldly stated in both habit and result, pointing to sharp, not subtle, differences in intention and outcome.

Responding

1:1–6 STUDY. This psalm, along with Psalm 2, introduces the Psalter and exalts in the instruction offered by God's law. Many people memorize it because the progression is easy to remember: "follow, take, sit . . . delight, meditate . . . tree, fruit, prosper," and so on. In *Celebration of Discipline* Richard Foster writes that repetition is the first step of study. Even if you have trouble memorizing, try committing Psalm 1 to memory. A hint to make it easier: post the psalm in various places throughout your house and work space. *See also* Spiritual Disciplines Index.

1:1–2 *Happy are those.* The opening verses point directly to a central issue in spiritual formation: What do you give your attention to? What do you immerse yourself in? What do you take pleasure in? Where do you take your life

cues from? The verbs suggest habits: following, walking, sitting, meditating. Do we loiter with and turn our ears to rebels and scoffers, or do we go beyond mere duty and eagerly attend to God's guidance and teaching?

1:2 MEDITATION—*See* Spiritual Disciplines Index.

1:3–6 *like trees planted by streams of water.* God is engaged in the events of our lives in the real world, generously caring for the righteous (well-fed trees bearing their proper fruit) and shriveling the wicked to be driven before the wind.

2:1–12 *Why do the nations conspire?* This song was originally a royal song, supporting the Davidic monarchy centered in Jerusalem ("I have set my king on Zion," v 6). It assumes that God's purposes will find fulfillment through the collaboration of the earthly king. The Church came to use it often as a song about God's rule through Jesus Christ, the ultimate "anointed one" who rules even now over the kingdom of God.

2:1 *the peoples plot in vain.* The word translated "meditate" in 1:2 is here translated "plot," establishing a sharp contrast in people's habits. The righteous think about how to follow God's ways while, in contrast, others think about how to rebel against God's authority and purposes. The verse continues the theme of two "ways" or "paths," again inviting us to make a wise choice.

and the rulers take counsel
  together,
against the LORD and his anointed,
  saying,
3 "Let us burst their bonds asunder,
  and cast their cords from us."

4 He who sits in the heavens laughs;
  the LORD has them in derision.
5 Then he will speak to them in his
    wrath,
  and terrify them in his fury,
    saying,
6 "I have set my king on Zion, my holy
    hill."

7 I will tell of the decree of the LORD:
He said to me, "You are my son;
  today I have begotten you.
8 Ask of me, and I will make the nations
    your heritage,
  and the ends of the earth your
    possession.
9 You shall break them with a rod of
    iron,
  and dash them in pieces like a potter's
    vessel."

10 Now therefore, O kings, be wise;
  be warned, O rulers of the earth.
11 Serve the LORD with fear,
  with trembling 12kiss his feet,[a]
or he will be angry, and you will perish
    in the way;
  for his wrath is quickly kindled.

Happy are all who take refuge in him.

Psalm 3

Trust in God under Adversity

A Psalm of David, when he fled from his son
Absalom.

1 O LORD, how many are my foes!
  Many are rising against me;
2 many are saying to me,
  "There is no help for you[b] in God."
                                     Selah

3 But you, O LORD, are a shield around
    me,
  my glory, and the one who lifts up my
    head.
4 I cry aloud to the LORD,
  and he answers me from his holy hill.
                                     Selah
5 I lie down and sleep;
  I wake again, for the LORD sustains
    me.
6 I am not afraid of ten thousands of
    people
  who have set themselves against me
    all around.

7 Rise up, O LORD!
  Deliver me, O my God!
For you strike all my enemies on the
    cheek;
  you break the teeth of the wicked.

8 Deliverance belongs to the LORD;
  may your blessing be on your people!
                                     Selah

a Cn: Meaning of Heb of verses 11b and 12a is
uncertain   b Syr: Heb *him*

2:4 *He who sits in the heavens laughs.* We
often laugh at the absurd, and what could be
more absurd than waving our little fists and
plotting against God, whose purposes are
wonderful and whose authority is unrivaled?
How silly can we get?

2:10–11 *Serve the LORD with fear.* True
wisdom and happiness come to those who
reject rebellion to serve and rely on God.

3:1–8 *the LORD sustains me.* Despite the
attackers' claim that God can't help him, the
singer doesn't lose sleep. He rests easily,
knowing God's power is adequate to shield him
even in the face of "many." Not all lament songs
seeking God's help show such serenity, but this
one reminds us that focusing on God more than
on our "many" human enemies can quiet our
hearts.

3:2 *Selah.* This term, which appears at the
end of stanzas throughout the book of Psalms, is
of unknown origin; it is possibly a musical
notation or liturgical direction.

Psalm 4

Confident Plea for Deliverance from Enemies

To the leader: with stringed instruments.
A Psalm of David.

1 Answer me when I call, O God of my
right!
You gave me room when I was in
distress.
Be gracious to me, and hear my
prayer.

2 How long, you people, shall my honor
suffer shame?
How long will you love vain words,
and seek after lies?   *Selah*

3 But know that the LORD has set apart
the faithful for himself;
the LORD hears when I call to him.

4 When you are disturbed,*a* do not sin;
ponder it on your beds, and be silent.
Selah

5 Offer right sacrifices,
and put your trust in the LORD.

6 There are many who say, "O that we
might see some good!
Let the light of your face shine on us,
O LORD!"

7 You have put gladness in my heart
more than when their grain and wine
abound.

8 I will both lie down and sleep in peace;
for you alone, O LORD, make me lie
down in safety.

Psalm 5

Trust in God for Deliverance from Enemies

To the leader: for the flutes. A Psalm of
David.

1 Give ear to my words, O LORD;
give heed to my sighing.

2 Listen to the sound of my cry,
my King and my God,
for to you I pray.

3 O LORD, in the morning you hear my
voice;
in the morning I plead my case to
you, and watch.

4 For you are not a God who delights in
wickedness;
evil will not sojourn with you.

5 The boastful will not stand before your
eyes;
you hate all evildoers.

6 You destroy those who speak lies;
the LORD abhors the bloodthirsty and
deceitful.

7 But I, through the abundance of your
steadfast love,
will enter your house,
I will bow down toward your holy temple
in awe of you.

8 Lead me, O LORD, in your righteousness
because of my enemies;
make your way straight before me.

9 For there is no truth in their mouths;
their hearts are destruction;
their throats are open graves;
they flatter with their tongues.

a Or *are angry*

4:1, 3 *the LORD hears when I call to him.*
Though the singer calls for help, doing so shows
a settled confidence based on experience.

4:4 SILENCE—*See* Spiritual Disciplines Index.

4:5 SACRIFICE—*See* Spiritual Disciplines
Index.

4:7–8 *sleep in peace.* Letting go joyfully at the
end of each day, resting in God's abundant and
protective care, is a choice. Letting these verses
soak in can help us choose this rest.

5:3 *in the morning I plead my case to you, and
watch.* Notice the order. The singer begins the
day first pleading his case to God and then
watching God at work. That is faith—praying
and expecting God to answer.

5:8 *make your way straight before me.* God
will guard and guide the righteous. The singer
asks God to lay out a safe path through his
enemies. Asking for guidance through life's
booby traps still makes sense.

10 Make them bear their guilt, O God;
   let them fall by their own counsels;
because of their many transgressions
   cast them out,
   for they have rebelled against you.

11 But let all who take refuge in you rejoice;
   let them ever sing for joy.
Spread your protection over them,
   so that those who love your name
   may exult in you.
12 For you bless the righteous, O LORD;
   you cover them with favor as with a
   shield.

Psalm 6

Prayer for Recovery from Grave Illness

To the leader: with stringed instruments;
according to The Sheminith. A Psalm of
David.

1 O LORD, do not rebuke me in your anger,
   or discipline me in your wrath.
2 Be gracious to me, O LORD, for I am
   languishing;
   O LORD, heal me, for my bones are
   shaking with terror.
3 My soul also is struck with terror,
   while you, O LORD—how long?

4 Turn, O LORD, save my life;
   deliver me for the sake of your
   steadfast love.

5 For in death there is no remembrance of
   you;
   in Sheol who can give you praise?

6 I am weary with my moaning;
   every night I flood my bed with tears;
   I drench my couch with my weeping.
7 My eyes waste away because of grief;
   they grow weak because of all my
   foes.

8 Depart from me, all you workers of evil,
   for the LORD has heard the sound of
   my weeping.
9 The LORD has heard my supplication;
   the LORD accepts my prayer.
10 All my enemies shall be ashamed and
   struck with terror;
   they shall turn back, and in a
   moment be put to shame.

Psalm 7

Plea for Help against Persecutors

A Shiggaion of David, which he sang to the
LORD concerning Cush, a Benjaminite.

1 O LORD my God, in you I take refuge;
   save me from all my pursuers, and
   deliver me,
2 or like a lion they will tear me apart;
   they will drag me away, with no one
   to rescue.

6:1–10 *O LORD, do not rebuke me in your anger.* The form and spirit of songs of repentance overlap with those of lament songs. This is one of seven such "penitential psalms" (see also Pss 32; 38; 51; 102; 130; 143).

6:2–3, 10 *struck with terror.* Threatening enemies are typical in laments, as is the prayer that God will return to these enemies the evil they intend, among them here "terrors." But this is God's business, not the psalmist's, or ours.

6:4 *deliver me for the sake of your steadfast love.* Afflicted by illness (real or metaphorical) and terror, apparently the discipline of God's wrath, the psalmist appeals to God's never-give-up-on-you love, which outlasts and overrides wrath. Like all true repentance, it is not self-justifying, but hopes wholly in God's love.

6:5 *Sheol.* The Psalms often use "Sheol" or "the Pit" to refer to the realm of the dead, a dusty, shadowy place for all who die. Sometimes Sheol is seen as creeping into and nibbling on life itself, a foreshadow and threat. The psalmists, and we with them, plead with God for deliverance from the shadows of death that would draw down a joyous, praise-filled life (see also 16:9–10; 30:2–3).

7:1–17 *O LORD my God, in you I take refuge.* The psalmist appeals to God to find him innocent of false charges made against him. He is confident both of his own innocence (vv 3–5, 8) and of God as a truly righteous judge (vv 9–11). In this judgment, strategies, appearances, and clever words will not mislead the one "who test[s] the minds and hearts" (v 9).

3 O LORD my God, if I have done this,
    if there is wrong in my hands,
4 if I have repaid my ally with harm
    or plundered my foe without cause,
5 then let the enemy pursue and overtake
        me,
    trample my life to the ground,
    and lay my soul in the dust.   *Selah*

6 Rise up, O LORD, in your anger;
    lift yourself up against the fury of my
        enemies;
    awake, O my God;[a] you have
        appointed a judgment.
7 Let the assembly of the peoples be
        gathered around you,
    and over it take your seat[b] on high.
8 The LORD judges the peoples;
    judge me, O LORD, according to my
        righteousness
    and according to the integrity that is
        in me.

9 O let the evil of the wicked come to an
        end,
    but establish the righteous,
    you who test the minds and hearts,
        O righteous God.
10 God is my shield,
    who saves the upright in heart.
11 God is a righteous judge,
    and a God who has indignation every
        day.

12 If one does not repent, God[c] will whet
        his sword;
    he has bent and strung his bow;
13 he has prepared his deadly weapons,
    making his arrows fiery shafts.
14 See how they conceive evil,
    and are pregnant with mischief,

and bring forth lies.
15 They make a pit, digging it out,
    and fall into the hole that they have
        made.
16 Their mischief returns upon their own
        heads,
    and on their own heads their violence
        descends.

17 I will give to the LORD the thanks due to
        his righteousness,
    and sing praise to the name of the
        LORD, the Most High.

Psalm 8

Divine Majesty and Human Dignity

To the leader: according to The Gittith.
A Psalm of David.

1 O LORD, our Sovereign,
    how majestic is your name in all the
        earth!

You have set your glory above the
        heavens.
2   Out of the mouths of babes and
            infants
you have founded a bulwark because of
        your foes,
    to silence the enemy and the avenger.

3 When I look at your heavens, the work
        of your fingers,
    the moon and the stars that you have
        established;
4 what are human beings that you are
        mindful of them,
    mortals[d] that you care for them?

a Or *awake for me*   *b* Cn: Heb *return*   *c* Heb *he*
d Heb *ben adam*, lit. *son of man*

8:1, 9 *how majestic is your name.* The
opening verse also concludes the psalm,
celebrating the splendor of God's "name,"
which represents his presence and power.

8:1–2 *heavens . . . mouths of babes.* The
fortress built on God's glory is both "above the
heavens" and proclaimed "out of the mouths of
babes." This is flashing, crashing power beyond
imagination.

8:3–4 *When I look at your heavens.* At this
writing, the spacecraft *Voyager 1* is leaving our
solar system after 26 years and 8.4 billion miles.
It must travel 40,000 years to encounter another
star. Even for those of us here on the earth, just
looking upward at the stars on a clear night can
make us share the awe of Israel's singers. Who,
indeed, are mere mortals that God even gives
them a thought?

5 Yet you have made them a little lower
        than God, *a*
    and crowned them with glory and
        honor.
6 You have given them dominion over
        the works of your hands;
    you have put all things under their
        feet,
7 all sheep and oxen,
    and also the beasts of the field,
8 the birds of the air, and the fish of the
        sea,
    whatever passes along the paths of
        the seas.

9 O LORD, our Sovereign,
    how majestic is your name in all the
        earth!

Psalm 9

God's Power and Justice

To the leader: according to Muth-labben.
        A Psalm of David.

1 I will give thanks to the LORD with my
        whole heart;
    I will tell of all your wonderful deeds.
2 I will be glad and exult in you;
    I will sing praise to your name,
        O Most High.

3 When my enemies turned back,
    they stumbled and perished before
        you.
4 For you have maintained my just cause;
    you have sat on the throne giving
        righteous judgment.

5 You have rebuked the nations, you have
        destroyed the wicked;
    you have blotted out their name
        forever and ever.
6 The enemies have vanished in
        everlasting ruins;
    their cities you have rooted out;
    the very memory of them has
        perished.

7 But the LORD sits enthroned forever,
    he has established his throne for
        judgment.
8 He judges the world with righteousness;
    he judges the peoples with equity.
9 The LORD is a stronghold for the
        oppressed,
    a stronghold in times of trouble.
10 And those who know your name put
        their trust in you,

a Or *than the divine beings* or *angels*: Heb *elohim*

8:5 *a little lower than God.* To make the point absolutely clear, this verse stands dead center in the psalm. It echoes Gen 1:26–27, which teaches that mere mortals though we are, we are made "in the image of God," full of power and dignity that we can scarcely comprehend.

8:6–8 *You have given them dominion.* God has given us a remarkable responsibility and partnership. God wants us to collaborate in the care of the world. The world is not so much for us as we are for the world (cf. Gen 1:26–28; 2:5). God's love for each of us calls us to join in God's purposes and loving action for all of creation.

Responding
8:6–8 SERVICE. Sadly, these verses and Gen 1:28 have been used to justify wreaking havoc on God's creation rather than encouraging responsible stewardship of its resources. In what ways can we encourage being good stewards of God's wonderful and marvelous creation simply because creation consists of "the works of [his] hands"? *See also* Spiritual Disciplines Index.

9:1–10:18 *I will give thanks to the LORD.* Psalms 9 and 10 may well be read together. The early Greek translation of the Old Testament, the Septuagint, actually treats them as a single psalm, and an alphabetic acrostic device bridges the two to draw them together.

9:7–8 *he has established his throne for judgment.* The confidence in God as righteous ruler anchors both the preceding verses of thanksgiving and the appeals for God's deliverance that follow. The Psalms often declare that God's effective rule is not remote, though the wicked in Psalm 10 think it is.

for you, O LORD, have not forsaken
those who seek you.

11 Sing praises to the LORD, who dwells in
Zion.
Declare his deeds among the peoples.
12 For he who avenges blood is mindful of
them;
he does not forget the cry of the
afflicted.

13 Be gracious to me, O LORD.
See what I suffer from those who hate
me;
you are the one who lifts me up from
the gates of death,
14 so that I may recount all your praises,
and, in the gates of daughter Zion,
rejoice in your deliverance.

15 The nations have sunk in the pit that
they made;
in the net that they hid has their own
foot been caught.
16 The LORD has made himself known, he
has executed judgment;
the wicked are snared in the work of
their own hands. *Higgaion. Selah*

17 The wicked shall depart to Sheol,
all the nations that forget God.

18 For the needy shall not always be
forgotten,
nor the hope of the poor perish
forever.

19 Rise up, O LORD! Do not let mortals
prevail;
let the nations be judged before you.
20 Put them in fear, O LORD;
let the nations know that they are
only human. *Selah*

Psalm 10

Prayer for Deliverance from Enemies

1 Why, O LORD, do you stand far off?
Why do you hide yourself in times of
trouble?
2 In arrogance the wicked persecute the
poor—
let them be caught in the schemes
they have devised.

3 For the wicked boast of the desires of
their heart,
those greedy for gain curse and
renounce the LORD.
4 In the pride of their countenance the
wicked say, "God will not seek it
out";
all their thoughts are, "There is no
God."

5 Their ways prosper at all times;
your judgments are on high, out of
their sight;
as for their foes, they scoff at them.
6 They think in their heart, "We shall not
be moved;
throughout all generations we shall
not meet adversity."
7 Their mouths are filled with cursing
and deceit and oppression;
under their tongues are mischief and
iniquity.
8 They sit in ambush in the villages;
in hiding places they murder the
innocent.

Their eyes stealthily watch for the
helpless;
9   they lurk in secret like a lion in its
covert;
they lurk that they may seize the poor;
they seize the poor and drag them off
in their net.

10:1–18 *Why do you hide yourself in times of trouble?* See note on 9:1–10:18. Here the singer accuses God of being hidden, of letting the wicked prevail. The wicked themselves think God is no threat. Their statement "There is no God" is not real atheism, but a swaggering sense that God won't notice or do anything (vv 4, 11–13).

10 They stoop, they crouch,
　　and the helpless fall by their
　　　might.
11 They think in their heart, "God has
　　forgotten,
　　he has hidden his face, he will never
　　　see it."

12 Rise up, O LORD; O God, lift up your
　　hand;
　　do not forget the oppressed.
13 Why do the wicked renounce God,
　　and say in their hearts, "You will not
　　　call us to account"?

14 But you do see! Indeed you note trouble
　　and grief,
　　that you may take it into your
　　hands;
　　the helpless commit themselves to
　　　you;
　　you have been the helper of the
　　　orphan.

15 Break the arm of the wicked and
　　evildoers;
　　seek out their wickedness until you
　　　find none.
16 The LORD is king forever and ever;
　　the nations shall perish from his
　　　land.

17 O LORD, you will hear the desire of the
　　meek;
　　you will strengthen their heart, you
　　　will incline your ear
18 to do justice for the orphan and the
　　oppressed,
　　so that those from earth may strike
　　　terror no more. a

Psalm 11

Song of Trust in God

To the leader. Of David.

1 In the LORD I take refuge; how can you
　　say to me,
　　"Flee like a bird to the mountains; b
2 for look, the wicked bend the bow,
　　they have fitted their arrow to the
　　　string,
　　to shoot in the dark at the upright in
　　　heart.
3 If the foundations are destroyed,
　　what can the righteous do?"

4 The LORD is in his holy temple;
　　the LORD's throne is in heaven.
　　His eyes behold, his gaze examines
　　　humankind.
5 The LORD tests the righteous and the
　　wicked,
　　and his soul hates the lover of violence.
6 On the wicked he will rain coals of fire
　　and sulfur;
　　a scorching wind shall be the portion
　　　of their cup.
7 For the LORD is righteous;
　　he loves righteous deeds;
　　the upright shall behold his face.

Psalm 12

Plea for Help in Evil Times

To the leader: according to The Sheminith.
A Psalm of David.

1 Help, O LORD, for there is no longer
　　anyone who is godly;

a Meaning of Heb uncertain   b Gk Syr Jerome
Tg: Heb *flee to your mountain, O bird*

10:14–18 *But you do see!* God not only sees,
but notices and helps the people who are invisible to most folk—the helpless, the orphaned,
the oppressed. People of faith learn to see
through God's eyes and act in God's ways (cf.
Matt 25:31–46).

11:1–7 *In the LORD I take refuge.* Running
to God is safer than running away. You can
no more flee your enemies than they can

escape God's justice.

12:1–8 *Help, O LORD.* The entire community
has gone awry. Every last person lies, flatters,
betrays, boasts, plunders the poor—and they're
proud of it, because they believe God has no
power to stop them. But God's ironclad
guarantee says the lying braggarts are wrong.
The lies won't last, but God's promises and
protection will.

the faithful have disappeared from
   humankind.
2 They utter lies to each other;
   with flattering lips and a double heart
      they speak.

3 May the LORD cut off all flattering lips,
   the tongue that makes great boasts,
4 those who say, "With our tongues we
      will prevail;
   our lips are our own—who is our
      master?"

5 "Because the poor are despoiled,
      because the needy groan,
   I will now rise up," says the LORD;
   "I will place them in the safety for
      which they long."
6 The promises of the LORD are promises
      that are pure,
   silver refined in a furnace on the
      ground,
   purified seven times.

7 You, O LORD, will protect us;
   you will guard us from this
      generation forever.
8 On every side the wicked prowl,
   as vileness is exalted among
      humankind.

Psalm 13

Prayer for Deliverance from Enemies

To the leader. A Psalm of David.

1 How long, O LORD? Will you forget me
      forever?

How long will you hide your face
   from me?
2 How long must I bear pain[a] in my soul,
   and have sorrow in my heart all day
      long?
   How long shall my enemy be exalted
      over me?

3 Consider and answer me, O LORD my
      God!
   Give light to my eyes, or I will sleep
      the sleep of death,
4 and my enemy will say, "I have
      prevailed";
   my foes will rejoice because I am
      shaken.

5 But I trusted in your steadfast love;
   my heart shall rejoice in your
      salvation.
6 I will sing to the LORD,
   because he has dealt bountifully with
      me.

Psalm 14

Denunciation of Godlessness

To the leader. Of David.

1 Fools say in their hearts, "There is no
      God."
   They are corrupt, they do abominable
      deeds;
   there is no one who does good.

a Syr: Heb hold counsels

13:1–4 *How long, O LORD? Will you forget me forever?* The lament (or complaint) songs often feature questions about God's apparent hiddenness or inattention and how long it will continue. Feeling forgotten does not mean that we are forgotten, but these phrases are honest reflections of how we feel when we're impatient and desperate.

13:5–6 *But I trusted.* Here we find an unexpected turn from lament and hoping for deliverance to thanksgiving after having been delivered. It's good to recount how God deals

"bountifully" with us. Often it will hold us firm when we're desperate.

14:1–4 *Fools say in their hearts.* Here Hebrew hyperbole goes all out. There's not a single person who does good, "no, not one" (vv 1, 3). Things are awful, though if we read the whole psalm we see that there still exists "the company of the righteous" (v 5), which God protects from this crowd of thugs. Even when things seem hopelessly bad, God is there for his faithful people.

2 The LORD looks down from heaven on
        humankind
    to see if there are any who are wise,
    who seek after God.

3 They have all gone astray, they are all
        alike perverse;
    there is no one who does good,
    no, not one.

4 Have they no knowledge, all the
        evildoers
    who eat up my people as they eat
        bread,
    and do not call upon the LORD?

5 There they shall be in great terror,
    for God is with the company of the
        righteous.
6 You would confound the plans of the
        poor,
    but the LORD is their refuge.

7 O that deliverance for Israel would
        come from Zion!
    When the LORD restores the fortunes
        of his people,
    Jacob will rejoice; Israel will be glad.

Psalm 15

Who Shall Abide in God's Sanctuary?

A Psalm of David.

1 O LORD, who may abide in your tent?
    Who may dwell on your holy hill?

2 Those who walk blamelessly, and do
        what is right,
    and speak the truth from their heart;
3 who do not slander with their tongue,
    and do no evil to their friends,

nor take up a reproach against their
        neighbors;
4 in whose eyes the wicked are despised,
    but who honor those who fear the
        LORD;
    who stand by their oath even to their
        hurt;
5 who do not lend money at interest,
    and do not take a bribe against the
        innocent.

Those who do these things shall never
    be moved.

Psalm 16

Song of Trust and Security in God

A Miktam of David.

1 Protect me, O God, for in you I take
        refuge.
2 I say to the LORD, "You are my Lord;
    I have no good apart from you." [a]

3 As for the holy ones in the land, they
        are the noble,
    in whom is all my delight.

4 Those who choose another god
        multiply their sorrows; [b]
    their drink offerings of blood I will
        not pour out
    or take their names upon my lips.

5 The LORD is my chosen portion and my
        cup;
    you hold my lot.
6 The boundary lines have fallen for me
        in pleasant places;
    I have a goodly heritage.

a Jerome Tg: Meaning of Heb uncertain
b Cn: Meaning of Heb uncertain

15:1–5 *O LORD, who may abide in your tent?*
A song for entering the sanctuary (cf. Ps 24).
The question of who belongs there is addressed
to God.

15:2–5 *Those who walk blamelessly.* The
overview answer that it's those who "walk
straight, act right, tell the truth" (*The Message*)

is not left vague. Coming before God has a lot to
do with practical things such as how we talk
about our neighbors and use our money, even
when it costs us. (On helping rather than bilking
people in a tight spot, see Exod 22:25; Lev
25:35–36; Deut 23:19.) A growing faith seeks
nitty-gritty integration into our ordinary life.

7 I bless the LORD who gives me counsel;
    in the night also my heart instructs
      me.
8 I keep the LORD always before me;
    because he is at my right hand, I shall
      not be moved.

9 Therefore my heart is glad, and my soul
      rejoices;
    my body also rests secure.
10 For you do not give me up to Sheol,
    or let your faithful one see the Pit.

11 You show me the path of life.
    In your presence there is fullness of
      joy;
    in your right hand are pleasures
      forevermore.

Psalm 17

Prayer for Deliverance from Persecutors

A Prayer of David.

1 Hear a just cause, O LORD; attend to my
      cry;
    give ear to my prayer from lips free of
      deceit.
2 From you let my vindication come;
    let your eyes see the right.

3 If you try my heart, if you visit me by
      night,
    if you test me, you will find no
      wickedness in me;
    my mouth does not transgress.
4 As for what others do, by the word of
      your lips

    I have avoided the ways of the
      violent.
5 My steps have held fast to your paths;
    my feet have not slipped.

6 I call upon you, for you will answer me,
      O God;
    incline your ear to me, hear my
      words.
7 Wondrously show your steadfast love,
    O savior of those who seek refuge
    from their adversaries at your right
      hand.

8 Guard me as the apple of the eye;
    hide me in the shadow of your wings,
9 from the wicked who despoil me,
    my deadly enemies who surround
      me.
10 They close their hearts to pity;
    with their mouths they speak
      arrogantly.
11 They track me down;[a] now they
      surround me;
    they set their eyes to cast me to the
      ground.
12 They are like a lion eager to tear,
    like a young lion lurking in ambush.

13 Rise up, O LORD, confront them,
    overthrow them!
    By your sword deliver my life from the
      wicked,
14 from mortals—by your hand, O LORD—
    from mortals whose portion in life is
      in this world.

a One Ms Compare Syr: MT *Our steps*

Responding

16:8–11 THE WITH-GOD LIFE. The phrase "I keep the LORD always before me" suggests that the psalmist used his imagination to make the presence of the Lord more real and God's security more tangible. As a spiritual exercise, each night for a week imagine that Jesus is sitting on the edge of your bed as you talk with him about the events of the day. Did God's presence seem closer? Did you feel more secure? *See also* Spiritual Disciplines Index.

16:10 *you do not give me up to Sheol.* See note on 6:5.

16:11 *In your presence is fullness of joy.* This verse distills the reasons the psalmist relies on and is loyal to God. It's no burden.

17:1 PRAYER—*See* Spiritual Disciplines Index.

17:1–12 *From you let my vindication come.* The singer boldly claims innocence, a claim to be honored, and asks God's vindication and protection in the face of enemies who want to destroy him.

May their bellies be filled with what you
 have stored up for them;
may their children have more than
 enough;
may they leave something over to
 their little ones.

15 As for me, I shall behold your face in
 righteousness;
when I awake I shall be satisfied,
 beholding your likeness.

Psalm 18

Royal Thanksgiving for Victory

To the leader. A Psalm of David the servant of
the LORD, who addressed the words of this
song to the LORD on the day when the LORD
delivered him from the hand of all his
enemies, and from the hand of Saul. He said:

1 I love you, O LORD, my strength.
2 The LORD is my rock, my fortress, and
 my deliverer,
 my God, my rock in whom I take
  refuge,
 my shield, and the horn of my
  salvation, my stronghold.
3 I call upon the LORD, who is worthy to
 be praised,
 so I shall be saved from my enemies.

4 The cords of death encompassed me;
 the torrents of perdition assailed me;
5 the cords of Sheol entangled me;
 the snares of death confronted me.

6 In my distress I called upon the LORD;
 to my God I cried for help.
From his temple he heard my voice,

and my cry to him reached his ears.

7 Then the earth reeled and rocked;
 the foundations also of the
  mountains trembled
 and quaked, because he was angry.
8 Smoke went up from his nostrils,
 and devouring fire from his mouth;
 glowing coals flamed forth from him.
9 He bowed the heavens, and came down;
 thick darkness was under his feet.
10 He rode on a cherub, and flew;
 he came swiftly upon the wings of the
  wind.
11 He made darkness his covering around
 him,
 his canopy thick clouds dark with
  water.
12 Out of the brightness before him
 there broke through his clouds
 hailstones and coals of fire.
13 The LORD also thundered in the heavens,
 and the Most High uttered his voice. a
14 And he sent out his arrows, and
  scattered them;
 he flashed forth lightnings, and
  routed them.
15 Then the channels of the sea were seen,
 and the foundations of the world
  were laid bare
 at your rebuke, O LORD,
 at the blast of the breath of your
  nostrils.

16 He reached down from on high, he took
 me;
 he drew me out of mighty waters.

a Gk See 2 Sam 22.14: Heb adds hailstones and coals
of fire

17:13–15 *May their bellies be filled with what
you have stored up for them.* Interpretations vary
here. One suggests that God should give the
wicked a belly full of judgment. Another is that
even generous, "this-worldly" provision scarcely
matches up to the delights of face-to-face
fellowship with God.

18:1–50 *I love you, O LORD, my strength.* A
royal song of thanksgiving that celebrates God's
action, both received and anticipated, for David

and his descendants (vv 1–6, 49–50).

18:7–19 *He bowed the heavens, and came
down.* The Old Testament often uses dramatic
imagery of God's coming to deliver, often of God
on the march in ways that make nature itself
quake, melt, flee in fear. The picture here of
God's coming in a frightening storm is a good
example (cf. Exod 15:1–12; Mic 1:3–4; Hab
3:1–15). Such powerful pictures help us to avoid
taming God or making God small.

17 He delivered me from my strong enemy,
  and from those who hated me;
  for they were too mighty for me.
18 They confronted me in the day of my
    calamity;
  but the LORD was my support.
19 He brought me out into a broad place;
  he delivered me, because he delighted
    in me.

20 The LORD rewarded me according to my
    righteousness;
  according to the cleanness of my
    hands he recompensed me.
21 For I have kept the ways of the LORD,
  and have not wickedly departed from
    my God.
22 For all his ordinances were before me,
  and his statutes I did not put away
    from me.
23 I was blameless before him,
  and I kept myself from guilt.
24 Therefore the LORD has recompensed me
    according to my righteousness,
  according to the cleanness of my
    hands in his sight.

25 With the loyal you show yourself loyal;
  with the blameless you show yourself
    blameless;
26 with the pure you show yourself pure;
  and with the crooked you show
    yourself perverse.
27 For you deliver a humble people,
  but the haughty eyes you bring down.
28 It is you who light my lamp;
  the LORD, my God, lights up my
    darkness.
29 By you I can crush a troop,
  and by my God I can leap over a wall.
30 This God—his way is perfect;
  the promise of the LORD proves true;
  he is a shield for all who take refuge in
    him.

31 For who is God except the LORD?
  And who is a rock besides our God?—

32 the God who girded me with strength,
  and made my way safe.
33 He made my feet like the feet of a deer,
  and set me secure on the heights.
34 He trains my hands for war,
  so that my arms can bend a bow of
    bronze.
35 You have given me the shield of your
    salvation,
  and your right hand has supported
    me;
  your help[a] has made me great.
36 You gave me a wide place for my steps
    under me,
  and my feet did not slip.
37 I pursued my enemies and overtook
    them;
  and did not turn back until they were
    consumed.
38 I struck them down, so that they were
    not able to rise;
  they fell under my feet.
39 For you girded me with strength for the
    battle;
  you made my assailants sink under
    me.
40 You made my enemies turn their backs
    to me,
  and those who hated me I destroyed.
41 They cried for help, but there was no
    one to save them;
  they cried to the LORD, but he did not
    answer them.
42 I beat them fine, like dust before the
    wind;
  I cast them out like the mire of the
    streets.

43 You delivered me from strife with the
    peoples;[b]
  you made me head of the nations;
  people whom I had not known served
    me.
44 As soon as they heard of me they
    obeyed me;
  foreigners came cringing to me.

a Or *gentleness* b Gk Tg: Heb *people*

18:20–30 *rewarded me according to my
righteousness*. Note the psalmist's confidence
that God will respond in kind to human
faithfulness.

45 Foreigners lost heart,
   and came trembling out of their
      strongholds.

46 The LORD lives! Blessed be my rock,
   and exalted be the God of my
      salvation,
47 the God who gave me vengeance
   and subdued peoples under me;
48 who delivered me from my enemies;
   indeed, you exalted me above my
      adversaries;
   you delivered me from the violent.

49 For this I will extol you, O LORD, among
      the nations,
   and sing praises to your name.
50 Great triumphs he gives to his king,
   and shows steadfast love to his
      anointed,
      to David and his descendants forever.

Psalm 19

God's Glory in Creation and the Law

To the leader. A Psalm of David.

1 The heavens are telling the glory of
      God;
   and the firmament*a* proclaims his
      handiwork.
2 Day to day pours forth speech,
   and night to night declares
      knowledge.
3 There is no speech, nor are there words;
   their voice is not heard;
4 yet their voice*b* goes out through all the
      earth,
   and their words to the end of the
      world.

In the heavens*c* he has set a tent for the
      sun,

5 which comes out like a bridegroom
      from his wedding canopy,
   and like a strong man runs its course
      with joy.
6 Its rising is from the end of the
      heavens,
   and its circuit to the end of them;
   and nothing is hid from its heat.

7 The law of the LORD is perfect,
   reviving the soul;
   the decrees of the LORD are sure,
   making wise the simple;
8 the precepts of the LORD are right,
   rejoicing the heart;
   the commandment of the LORD is clear,
   enlightening the eyes;
9 the fear of the LORD is pure,
   enduring forever;
   the ordinances of the LORD are true
   and righteous altogether.
10 More to be desired are they than gold,
   even much fine gold;
   sweeter also than honey,
   and drippings of the honeycomb.

11 Moreover by them is your servant
      warned;
   in keeping them there is great reward.
12 But who can detect their errors?
   Clear me from hidden faults.
13 Keep back your servant also from the
      insolent;*d*
   do not let them have dominion over
      me.
   Then I shall be blameless,
   and innocent of great transgression.

14 Let the words of my mouth and the
   meditation of my heart

a Or *dome*   *b* Gk Jerome Compare Syr: Heb *line*
c Heb *In them*   *d* Or *from proud thoughts*

19:1–14 STUDY—*See* Spiritual Disciplines Index.

19:1–4a *The heavens are telling the glory of God.* The terms "natural revelation" or "general revelation" aptly point to how the world itself pours out on us wordless speech about God. In our wordy, busy lives we can learn a lot by

listening more closely to creation's voices.

19:7–11 *The law of the LORD is perfect.* God's guidance and teaching through the law is a gift, not a burden (see notes on 119:1–176; 119:26–27; 119:59; 119:70).

19:14 *Let . . . the meditation of my heart be acceptable.* This familiar verse invites God's

be acceptable to you,
O LORD, my rock and my redeemer.

Psalm 20

Prayer for Victory

To the leader. A Psalm of David.

1 The LORD answer you in the day of
     trouble!
   The name of the God of Jacob protect
     you!
2 May he send you help from the
     sanctuary,
   and give you support from Zion.
3 May he remember all your offerings,
   and regard with favor your burnt
     sacrifices.   *Selah*

4 May he grant you your heart's desire,
   and fulfill all your plans.
5 May we shout for joy over your victory,
   and in the name of our God set up
     our banners.
   May the LORD fulfill all your petitions.

6 Now I know that the LORD will help his
     anointed;
   he will answer him from his holy
     heaven
   with mighty victories by his right
     hand.
7 Some take pride in chariots, and some
     in horses,

but our pride is in the name of the
     LORD our God.
8 They will collapse and fall,
   but we shall rise and stand upright.

9 Give victory to the king, O LORD;
   answer us when we call. *a*

Psalm 21

Thanksgiving for Victory

To the leader. A Psalm of David.

1 In your strength the king rejoices,
     O LORD,
   and in your help how greatly he
     exults!
2 You have given him his heart's desire,
   and have not withheld the request of
     his lips.   *Selah*
3 For you meet him with rich blessings;
   you set a crown of fine gold on his
     head.
4 He asked you for life; you gave it to
     him—
   length of days forever and ever.
5 His glory is great through your help;
   splendor and majesty you bestow on
     him.
6 You bestow on him blessings forever;
   you make him glad with the joy of
     your presence.

a Gk: Heb *give victory, O LORD; let the King answer us
when we call*

---

scrutiny and correction (see 139:23–24). The
word translated "meditation" here would be
better rendered as "whisperings" or "mur-
murings." Welcoming God's knowing and
shaping of our inner talk deepens our vulnerability. It is a huge step in our formation.

Responding
19:14 MEDITATION. In this verse the
psalmist prays that his speech and
"heart thoughts" be acceptable to the Lord,
but in Matt 12:34 Jesus says, "For out of the
abundance of the heart the mouth speaks."
What is the connection between praying that
our speech and meditation be acceptable to

God and Jesus' statement about the heart? *See
also* Spiritual Disciplines Index.

   20:1–9 *The LORD answer you in the day of
trouble!* A prayer on behalf of the king, perhaps
as he anticipates going to battle. The people
bring requests on behalf of the king (vv 1–5),
and a worship leader responds with assurance
that God will indeed answer (vv 6–8).
   20:8–9 *we shall rise and stand upright.*
Defensive schemes and tools aside, only God
gives victory. Only God merits our trust.
   21:1–7 *His glory is great through your help.*
This passage recounts God's blessing, making it
clear that the king prospers because he trusts in
what God can do.

7 For the king trusts in the Lord,
   and through the steadfast love of the
      Most High he shall not be moved.

8 Your hand will find out all your enemies;
   your right hand will find out those
      who hate you.
9 You will make them like a fiery furnace
   when you appear.
   The Lord will swallow them up in his
      wrath,
   and fire will consume them.
10 You will destroy their offspring from
      the earth,
   and their children from among
      humankind.
11 If they plan evil against you,
   if they devise mischief, they will not
      succeed.
12 For you will put them to flight;
   you will aim at their faces with your
      bows.

13 Be exalted, O Lord, in your strength!
   We will sing and praise your power.

Psalm 22

Plea for Deliverance from Suffering and Hostility

To the leader: according to The Deer of the
      Dawn. A Psalm of David.

1 My God, my God, why have you
      forsaken me?
   Why are you so far from helping me,
      from the words of my groaning?

2 O my God, I cry by day, but you do not
      answer;
   and by night, but find no rest.

3 Yet you are holy,
   enthroned on the praises of Israel.
4 In you our ancestors trusted;
   they trusted, and you delivered
      them.
5 To you they cried, and were saved;
   in you they trusted, and were not put
      to shame.

6 But I am a worm, and not human;
   scorned by others, and despised by
      the people.
7 All who see me mock at me;
   they make mouths at me, they shake
      their heads;
8 "Commit your cause to the Lord; let
      him deliver—
   let him rescue the one in whom he
      delights!"

9 Yet it was you who took me from the
      womb;
   you kept me safe on my mother's
      breast.
10 On you I was cast from my birth,
   and since my mother bore me you
      have been my God.
11 Do not be far from me,
   for trouble is near
   and there is no one to help.

12 Many bulls encircle me,
   strong bulls of Bashan surround me;

21:8–12 *Your hand will find out all your enemies.* This declares to the king that in God's power he will overcome his enemies. Throughout the psalm it's clear that there is no room for the king to brag. We can easily let success go to our heads and forget the Source. Rather than forget, "we will sing and praise your power" (v 13).

22:1–2 *My God, my God, why have you forsaken me?* Jesus used these anguished words of lament on the cross, sharing the singer's despair at apparent abandonment. To feel abandoned doesn't mean we are abandoned, but even in such darkness we can pray honestly.

"Dark night" experiences in our journey are a definite part of the work of spiritual formation.

22:3–5, 9–11 *Yet it was you who took me from the womb.* Typical of the lament, the singer appeals to God's faithfulness as a confession of trust, a reason to hope; abandonment is not the last word.

22:6–8, 12–18 *But I am a worm.* The exaggerated language of distress is faithful to the heart—enemies like brawny bulls and roaring lions, a heart like wax, counting "all" of one's bones, piercing taunts about faith in a dark hour.

¹³ they open wide their mouths at me,
  like a ravening and roaring lion.

¹⁴ I am poured out like water,
    and all my bones are out of joint;
  my heart is like wax;
    it is melted within my breast;
¹⁵ my mouth *a* is dried up like a
        potsherd,
    and my tongue sticks to my jaws;
  you lay me in the dust of death.

¹⁶ For dogs are all around me;
    a company of evildoers encircles
        me.
  My hands and feet have shriveled; *b*
¹⁷ I can count all my bones.
  They stare and gloat over me;
¹⁸ they divide my clothes among
        themselves,
    and for my clothing they cast lots.

¹⁹ But you, O LORD, do not be far away!
    O my help, come quickly to my aid!
²⁰ Deliver my soul from the sword,
    my life *c* from the power of the dog!
²¹   Save me from the mouth of the
        lion!

  From the horns of the wild oxen you
        have rescued *d* me.
²² I will tell of your name to my brothers
        and sisters; *e*
    in the midst of the congregation I will
        praise you:
²³ You who fear the LORD, praise him!
    All you offspring of Jacob, glorify
        him;
    stand in awe of him, all you offspring
        of Israel!
²⁴ For he did not despise or abhor

the affliction of the afflicted;
  he did not hide his face from me, *f*
    but heard when I *g* cried to him.

²⁵ From you comes my praise in the great
        congregation;
    my vows I will pay before those who
        fear him.
²⁶ The poor *h* shall eat and be satisfied;
    those who seek him shall praise the
        LORD.
  May your hearts live forever!

²⁷ All the ends of the earth shall
        remember
    and turn to the LORD;
  and all the families of the nations
    shall worship before him. *i*
²⁸ For dominion belongs to the LORD,
    and he rules over the nations.

²⁹ To him, *j* indeed, shall all who sleep in *k*
        the earth bow down;
  before him shall bow all who go down
        to the dust,
    and I shall live for him. *l*
³⁰ Posterity will serve him;
    future generations will be told about
        the Lord,
³¹ and *m* proclaim his deliverance to a
        people yet unborn,
    saying that he has done it.

---

a Cn: Heb *strength*   *b* Meaning of Heb uncertain
c Heb *my only one*   *d* Heb *answered*
e Or *kindred*   *f* Heb *him*   *g* Heb *he*
h Or *afflicted*   *i* Gk Syr Jerome: Heb *you*
j Cn: Heb *They have eaten and*   *k* Cn: Heb *all the
fat ones*   *l* Compare Gk Syr Vg: Heb *and he who
cannot keep himself alive*   *m* Compare Gk: Heb *it
will be told about the Lord to the generation,* ³¹*they will
come and*

22:21b–31 *stand in awe of him!* A call to
praise, perhaps even a thanksgiving song, for
God's deliverance.

23:1–4 *The LORD is my shepherd.* Throughout
the Old Testament the metaphors of shepherd
and king often overlap (see, e.g., Ps 95), a
common combination in ancient Israel's world.
Here the wise Shepherd knows where the good
pastures are season to season and leads us right

to them. He provides what we need. It is not
only adequate, but also generous.

Responding
23:1–6 THE WITH-GOD LIFE. How
does one comment on this most famous
of Psalms? Countless songs have been composed, pictures painted, and sermons preached
on the shepherd image, but most of us who live

Psalm 23

The Divine Shepherd

A Psalm of David.

1 The LORD is my shepherd, I shall not
     want.
2 He makes me lie down in green
     pastures;
he leads me beside still waters; *a*
3 he restores my soul. *b*
He leads me in right paths *c*
     for his name's sake.

4 Even though I walk through the darkest
     valley, *d*
     I fear no evil;
for you are with me;
     your rod and your staff—
     they comfort me.

5 You prepare a table before me
     in the presence of my enemies;
you anoint my head with oil;
     my cup overflows.
6 Surely *e* goodness and mercy *f* shall
     follow me
all the days of my life,
and I shall dwell in the house of the
     LORD
     my whole life long. *g*

Psalm 24

Entrance into the Temple

Of David. A Psalm.

1 The earth is the LORD's and all that is in
     it,
     the world, and those who live in it;
2 for he has founded it on the seas,
     and established it on the rivers.

3 Who shall ascend the hill of the LORD?
     And who shall stand in his holy
     place?
4 Those who have clean hands and pure
     hearts,
     who do not lift up their souls to what
     is false,
     and do not swear deceitfully.
5 They will receive blessing from the
     LORD,
     and vindication from the God of their
     salvation.
6 Such is the company of those who seek
     him,
     who seek the face of the God of
     Jacob. *h*   *Selah*

7 Lift up your heads, O gates!
     and be lifted up, O ancient doors!
     that the King of glory may come in.

a Heb *waters of rest*   *b* Or *life*   *c* Or *paths of righteousness*   *d* Or *the valley of the shadow of death*   *e* Or *Only*   *f* Or *kindness*   *g* Heb *for length of days*   *h* Gk Syr: Heb *your face, O Jacob*

in urban settings today cannot imagine the Lord watching over us as a shepherd watches over his sheep. What would be a good metaphor that we could understand? As you are thinking about a good substitute for the shepherd image, try rewriting the psalm to reflect contemporary urban life. *See also* Spiritual Disciplines Index.

23:6 *goodness and mercy shall follow me.* "Mercy" here is God's *hesed*, the love that never quits. It is a love that doesn't just follow, but always pursues us. To perceive God's love as pursuing rather than begrudged deepens our ability to trust.

24:1–10 *Who is the King of glory? The LORD, strong and mighty.* Generally understood as a processional song, this psalm perhaps initially accompanied the ark of the covenant into the sanctuary. The questions and answers suggest antiphonal singing.

24:1–2, 7–10 *The earth is the LORD's.* These verses identify God as transcendent, a God not to be trifled with—the Creator and Master of the world, Glorious King, Commander.

24:3–6 *who shall stand in his holy place?* Who is welcome before such a God? People of integrity and genuine devotion, single-minded and not double-dealing. Pure hearts lead to clean hands (cf. Ps 15).

8 Who is the King of glory?
   The LORD, strong and mighty,
   the LORD, mighty in battle.
9 Lift up your heads, O gates!
   and be lifted up, O ancient doors!
   that the King of glory may come in.
10 Who is this King of glory?
   The LORD of hosts,
   he is the King of glory.   *Selah*

Psalm 25

Prayer for Guidance and for Deliverance

Of David.

1 To you, O LORD, I lift up my soul.
2 O my God, in you I trust;
   do not let me be put to shame;
   do not let my enemies exult over me.
3 Do not let those who wait for you be put
     to shame;
   let them be ashamed who are
     wantonly treacherous.

4 Make me to know your ways, O LORD;
   teach me your paths.
5 Lead me in your truth, and teach me,
   for you are the God of my salvation;
   for you I wait all day long.

6 Be mindful of your mercy, O LORD, and
     of your steadfast love,
   for they have been from of old.
7 Do not remember the sins of my youth
     or my transgressions;
   according to your steadfast love
     remember me,
   for your goodness' sake, O LORD!

8 Good and upright is the LORD;
   therefore he instructs sinners in the
     way.
9 He leads the humble in what is right,
   and teaches the humble his way.

10 All the paths of the LORD are steadfast
     love and faithfulness,
   for those who keep his covenant and
     his decrees.

11 For your name's sake, O LORD,
   pardon my guilt, for it is great.
12 Who are they that fear the LORD?
   He will teach them the way that they
     should choose.

13 They will abide in prosperity,
   and their children shall possess the
     land.
14 The friendship of the LORD is for those
     who fear him,
   and he makes his covenant known to
     them.
15 My eyes are ever toward the LORD,
   for he will pluck my feet out of the
     net.

16 Turn to me and be gracious to me,
   for I am lonely and afflicted.
17 Relieve the troubles of my heart,
   and bring me *a* out of my distress.
18 Consider my affliction and my trouble,
   and forgive all my sins.
19 Consider how many are my foes,
   and with what violent hatred they
     hate me.
20 O guard my life, and deliver me;
   do not let me be put to shame, for I
     take refuge in you.
21 May integrity and uprightness preserve
     me,
   for I wait for you.

22 Redeem Israel, O God,
   out of all its troubles.

a Or *The troubles of my heart are enlarged; bring me*

25:1–22 *teach me your paths.* In Hebrew this is an alphabetic acrostic poem, which may help account for some abrupt shifts in theme. Throughout, however, the singer seeks God's guidance ("paths"), forgiveness, and watchful care. The poet paints a striking picture of the character of the God he trusts. This God shows goodness, steadfast love, faithfulness, compassion, and more. Surely this invites us to want "the friendship of the LORD" (v 14).

DAVID

Shaped in Solitude

Selected Scriptures: *1 Samuel 17—19:17; 20; 24; 2 Samuel 5; 6; 11; 12; Psalms 23; 139*

From the early days as a young shepherd boy to the later years as a sorrowful parent and beloved king of Israel, David's life centered on God and his daily, sustaining relationship with him. Showing what it means to love God in complete humanness, David turned to God in all his passion and pain. He loved through his creative life, writing psalms, playing the harp, dancing before God, and making plans for the building of the Temple. He loved God through his service to others, honoring King Saul, God's anointed, when even God had forsaken Saul. He served the Israelite people, killing the enemy giant Goliath with just a sling and stones and later governing them as king and commanding their army. And he loved God even when caught in sin. After committing adultery with Bathsheba, David confessed his sin against God, recognizing the affront he had brought to his with-God relationship.

David became a "man after [God's] own heart" (1 Sam 13:14) in great measure through his times of solitude and silence. Shaped early by days and nights with God in lonely places herding sheep, David understood from his youth the reality of God as shepherd of his own life. Later, when on the run from Saul, David again experienced God as companion and protector (19:10). "My times are in your hand," he sings (Ps 31:15).

David's rootedness in God continued through all the seasons of his life. When he became king and won victories in war, when he established Jerusalem as the political and spiritual hub of the nation, and as he planned for the construction of the Temple, David held God central. Through all his successes and popularity, David kept the focus on God, not himself, and continued in his inner worship of God.

"If we possess inward solitude we do not fear being alone, for we know that we are not alone. Neither do we fear being with others, for they do not control us," Richard Foster explains. "In the midst of noise and confusion we are settled into a deep inner silence. Whether alone or among people, we always carry with us a portable sanctuary of the heart" (*Celebration of Discipline*).

David's sanctuary of the heart moved him to make music, dance, and write in worship of God. His psalms were, in essence, prayers to God. "The solitary life is above all a life of prayer," writes twentieth-century Trappist monk Thomas Merton in his *Thoughts in Solitude*. David and Merton, both well acquainted with the solitary life, knew that the inner conversations with God that grow out of solitude and silence foster an ongoing life of prayer.

PROFILE

This life of prayer is filled with both worship and need. "The solitary, more than anyone else, is always aware of his poverty and of his needs before God," continues Merton. David's psalms record the many times he cried out to God in need. Because David was a faithful follower of God, but also one who failed, his prayers are steeped in the kinds of raw emotions all humans experience—grief, joy, sadness, anger, exaltation.

And in prayer, "the solitary . . . will come to know God by knowing that his prayer is always answered," explains Merton. "Gratitude is therefore the heart of the solitary life, as it is the heart of the Christian life."

Above all, David's psalms and his with-God life communicate his love and gratitude toward God. "I will give thanks to the LORD with my whole heart; I will tell of all your wonderful deeds" (Ps 9:1), David proclaimed. "At night his song is with me, a prayer to the God of my life" (Ps 42:8).

Day and night, David lived with God, filled and surrounded by God's love and care. We too live such a God-filled existence, yet we may not sense it the way David did. His time in solitude tuned him to know and see God everywhere. It moved David so powerfully that he couldn't help but sing and dance and write and worship. David understood God's heart, and in David's living with God his heart took on the very shape of God's.

Personal Reflection

- Have you experienced a time when, like David herding sheep, you were required to spend a significant amount of time alone? Did you face solitude in the quiet or amid crowds? Did you come to know God in a deeper way? Why or why not?

- How do you respond to silence? Is it unnerving, or soothing? Have you persevered in silence long enough to hear and see God in new ways? Dallas Willard writes, "Only silence will allow us life-transforming concentration upon God" (*The Spirit of the Disciplines*). How might God be guiding you to enter into the disciplines of solitude and silence in intentional ways? As Thomas Merton stresses, prayer and gratitude are the natural outgrowth of time spent with God in solitude and silence. How often do your mind and heart turn to God in prayer? How much is gratitude to God a part of your outlook? Pray now for times of solitude and silence with God, where God will shape your heart to be like his.

Psalm 26

Plea for Justice and Declaration of Righteousness

Of David.

1 Vindicate me, O LORD,
  for I have walked in my integrity,
  and I have trusted in the LORD
    without wavering.
2 Prove me, O LORD, and try me;
  test my heart and mind.
3 For your steadfast love is before my eyes,
  and I walk in faithfulness to you. *a*

4 I do not sit with the worthless,
  nor do I consort with hypocrites;
5 I hate the company of evildoers,
  and will not sit with the wicked.

6 I wash my hands in innocence,
  and go around your altar, O LORD,
7 singing aloud a song of thanksgiving,
  and telling all your wondrous deeds.

8 O LORD, I love the house in which you
    dwell,
  and the place where your glory
    abides.
9 Do not sweep me away with sinners,
  nor my life with the bloodthirsty,
10 those in whose hands are evil devices,
  and whose right hands are full of
    bribes.

11 But as for me, I walk in my integrity;
  redeem me, and be gracious to me.
12 My foot stands on level ground;
  in the great congregation I will bless
    the LORD.

Psalm 27

Triumphant Song of Confidence

Of David.

1 The LORD is my light and my salvation;
    whom shall I fear?
  The LORD is the stronghold *b* of my life;
    of whom shall I be afraid?

2 When evildoers assail me
    to devour my flesh—
  my adversaries and foes—
    they shall stumble and fall.

3 Though an army encamp against me,
    my heart shall not fear;
  though war rise up against me,
    yet I will be confident.

4 One thing I asked of the LORD,
    that will I seek after:
  to live in the house of the LORD
    all the days of my life,
  to behold the beauty of the LORD,
    and to inquire in his temple.

5 For he will hide me in his shelter
    in the day of trouble;
  he will conceal me under the cover of
    his tent;
  he will set me high on a rock.

6 Now my head is lifted up
    above my enemies all around me,
  and I will offer in his tent
    sacrifices with shouts of joy;
  I will sing and make melody to the
    LORD.

7 Hear, O LORD, when I cry aloud,
    be gracious to me and answer me!

a Or *in your faithfulness*   *b* Or *refuge*

26:1–12 *I have trusted in the LORD without wavering.* This song asks God to render a verdict ("judge") that the worshiper is innocent and wholly devoted to God. Perhaps it lays claim to the right to be in the sanctuary (cf. Pss 15; 24). The innocence is rooted in habits of faithfulness (v 3–5, 11; cf. Ps 1) rather than momentary piety.

27:1–6 *whom shall I fear?* The utmost confidence here is stirring. The singer doesn't just put on a brave face, but lets this confidence break out in glad worship, singing, and shouts of joy (v 6).

8 "Come," my heart says, "seek his face!"
   Your face, LORD, do I seek.
9   Do not hide your face from me.

Do not turn your servant away in anger,
   you who have been my help.
Do not cast me off, do not forsake me,
   O God of my salvation!
10 If my father and mother forsake me,
   the LORD will take me up.

11 Teach me your way, O LORD,
   and lead me on a level path
   because of my enemies.
12 Do not give me up to the will of my
      adversaries,
   for false witnesses have risen
      against me,
   and they are breathing out violence.

13 I believe that I shall see the goodness of
      the LORD
   in the land of the living.
14 Wait for the LORD;
   be strong, and let your heart take
      courage;
   wait for the LORD!

Psalm 28

Prayer for Help and Thanksgiving for It

Of David.

1 To you, O LORD, I call;
   my rock, do not refuse to hear me,
for if you are silent to me,
   I shall be like those who go down to
      the Pit.
2 Hear the voice of my supplication,
   as I cry to you for help,
as I lift up my hands

toward your most holy sanctuary. *a*

3 Do not drag me away with the wicked,
   with those who are workers of evil,
who speak peace with their neighbors,
   while mischief is in their hearts.
4 Repay them according to their work,
   and according to the evil of their deeds;
repay them according to the work of
      their hands;
   render them their due reward.
5 Because they do not regard the works of
      the LORD,
   or the work of his hands,
he will break them down and build
   them up no more.

6 Blessed be the LORD,
   for he has heard the sound of my
      pleadings.
7 The LORD is my strength and my shield;
   in him my heart trusts;
so I am helped, and my heart exults,
   and with my song I give thanks to him.

8 The LORD is the strength of his people;
   he is the saving refuge of his anointed.
9 O save your people, and bless your
      heritage;
   be their shepherd, and carry them
      forever.

Psalm 29

The Voice of God in a Great Storm

A Psalm of David.

1 Ascribe to the LORD, O heavenly
      beings, *b*

a Heb *your innermost sanctuary*   *b* Heb *sons of
gods*

27:13–14 *I believe that I shall see.* The
psalmist expects deliverance and urges others to
"wait for" (the same Hebrew word could also be
translated "hope in") the Lord, the stronghold
who can face down whole armies on our behalf.
28:1–5 *Do not drag me away with the wicked.*
Perhaps the singer fears he'll get swept away in
the judgment that people around him so richly
deserve. Sometimes the innocent do suffer the

judgment brought on the wicked, just as they
suffer at their hands.
29:1–11 *Ascribe to the LORD.* This powerful
song declares Yahweh's unrivaled authority and
power. Its use of an archaic poetic style of
repetitive parallelism ("The voice of the LORD")
and place-names in Lebanon and Syria may
enhance its intended effect—to make clear that
the Canaanite god Baal is no rival.

ascribe to the LORD glory and
  strength.
2 Ascribe to the LORD the glory of his
  name;
  worship the LORD in holy splendor.

3 The voice of the LORD is over the waters;
  the God of glory thunders,
  the LORD, over mighty waters.
4 The voice of the LORD is powerful;
  the voice of the LORD is full of
    majesty.

5 The voice of the LORD breaks the cedars;
  the LORD breaks the cedars of
    Lebanon.
6 He makes Lebanon skip like a calf,
  and Sirion like a young wild ox.

7 The voice of the LORD flashes forth
    flames of fire.
8 The voice of the LORD shakes the
    wilderness;
  the LORD shakes the wilderness of
    Kadesh.

9 The voice of the LORD causes the oaks to
    whirl,ᵃ
  and strips the forest bare;
  and in his temple all say, "Glory!"

10 The LORD sits enthroned over the flood;
   the LORD sits enthroned as king
     forever.
11 May the LORD give strength to his
     people!
   May the LORD bless his people with
     peace!

Psalm 30

Thanksgiving for Recovery from Grave Illness

A Psalm. A Song at the dedication of the
temple. Of David.

1 I will extol you, O LORD, for you have
    drawn me up,
  and did not let my foes rejoice over
    me.
2 O LORD my God, I cried to you for help,
  and you have healed me.
3 O LORD, you brought up my soul from
    Sheol,
  restored me to life from among those
    gone down to the Pit.ᵇ

4 Sing praises to the LORD, O you his
    faithful ones,
  and give thanks to his holy name.
5 For his anger is but for a moment;
    his favor is for a lifetime.
  Weeping may linger for the night,
    but joy comes with the morning.

6 As for me, I said in my prosperity,
  "I shall never be moved."
7 By your favor, O LORD,
  you had established me as a strong
    mountain;
  you hid your face;
    I was dismayed.

8 To you, O LORD, I cried,
  and to the LORD I made supplication:
9 "What profit is there in my death,
  if I go down to the Pit?

a Or *causes the deer to calve*   b Or *that I should not go down to the Pit*

29:1 *O heavenly beings.* This refers to those in Yahweh's court, all of whom are to worship him and honor his strength.

29:10–11 *The LORD sits enthroned.* It is recognizing and relying on the unrivaled God that gives us strength to live and brings genuine peace.

30:1–12 *I will extol you, O LORD.* As is typical in thanksgiving songs, the singer recalls how he cried out to God in distress and how in faithfulness God rescued him.

30:3, 9 *What profit is there in my death?* See note on 6:5. In this imagery, the singer, nearly dead, reminds God that he's not much good in the choir once he has returned to dust.

30:5 *his anger is but for a moment.* Much to their harm, some people see God as perpetually angry. But God controls, rather than is controlled by, anger, and anger is fleeting, especially when compared to God's lifelong love.

Will the dust praise you?
Will it tell of your faithfulness?
10 Hear, O LORD, and be gracious to me!
O LORD, be my helper!"

11 You have turned my mourning into
dancing;
you have taken off my sackcloth
and clothed me with joy,
12 so that my soul[a] may praise you and not
be silent.
O LORD my God, I will give thanks to
you forever.

Psalm 31

Prayer and Praise for Deliverance from Enemies

To the leader. A Psalm of David.

1 In you, O LORD, I seek refuge;
do not let me ever be put to shame;
in your righteousness deliver me.
2 Incline your ear to me;
rescue me speedily.
Be a rock of refuge for me,
a strong fortress to save me.

3 You are indeed my rock and my fortress;
for your name's sake lead me and
guide me,
4 take me out of the net that is hidden for
me,
for you are my refuge.
5 Into your hand I commit my spirit;
you have redeemed me, O LORD,
faithful God.

6 You hate[b] those who pay regard to
worthless idols,
but I trust in the LORD.
7 I will exult and rejoice in your steadfast
love,
because you have seen my affliction;
you have taken heed of my
adversities,
8 and have not delivered me into the
hand of the enemy;
you have set my feet in a broad place.

9 Be gracious to me, O LORD, for I am in
distress;
my eye wastes away from grief,
my soul and body also.
10 For my life is spent with sorrow,
and my years with sighing;
my strength fails because of my misery,[c]
and my bones waste away.

11 I am the scorn of all my adversaries,
a horror[d] to my neighbors,
an object of dread to my acquaintances;
those who see me in the street flee
from me.
12 I have passed out of mind like one who
is dead;
I have become like a broken vessel.
13 For I hear the whispering of many—
terror all around!—
as they scheme together against me,
as they plot to take my life.

a Heb *that glory*   b One Heb Ms Gk Syr Jerome:
MT *I hate*   c Gk Syr: Heb *my iniquity*
d Cn: Heb *exceedingly*

30:11–12 *You have turned my mourning into dancing.* Beyond thankful words, or even grateful silence, we can celebrate God's mercy with exuberance, even with joyful dancing. Celebration is the kind of "Amen!" that God deserves and that we need.

31:1, 17 *do not let me ever be put to shame.* Sometimes it looks and feels precarious to trust God, and people around us may taunt and scorn (see also 22:6–8). In such difficult times we can become anxious for God to deliver us and to discredit our detractors.

Responding
31:3 GUIDANCE. Embedded in a psalm asking to be delivered from enemies is a plea for God to lead and guide the psalmist. What circumstances have you faced that prompted you to pray for God's guidance? How did the guidance come? *See also* Spiritual Disciplines Index.

31:5 *Into your hand I commit my spirit.* Luke 23:46 reports that these are Jesus' last words on the cross. Fittingly, in the psalm the words stand in the tension between trust and affliction.

14 But I trust in you, O LORD;
    I say, "You are my God."
15 My times are in your hand;
    deliver me from the hand of my
        enemies and persecutors.
16 Let your face shine upon your servant;
    save me in your steadfast love.
17 Do not let me be put to shame, O LORD,
    for I call on you;
    let the wicked be put to shame;
    let them go dumbfounded to Sheol.
18 Let the lying lips be stilled
    that speak insolently against the
        righteous
    with pride and contempt.

19 O how abundant is your goodness
    that you have laid up for those who
        fear you,
    and accomplished for those who take
        refuge in you,
    in the sight of everyone!
20 In the shelter of your presence you hide
        them
    from human plots;
    you hold them safe under your shelter
        from contentious tongues.

21 Blessed be the LORD,
    for he has wondrously shown his
        steadfast love to me
    when I was beset as a city under siege.
22 I had said in my alarm,
    "I am driven far *a* from your sight."
    But you heard my supplications
    when I cried out to you for help.

23 Love the LORD, all you his saints.
    The LORD preserves the faithful,
    but abundantly repays the one who
        acts haughtily.

24 Be strong, and let your heart take
        courage,
    all you who wait for the LORD.

Psalm 32

The Joy of Forgiveness

Of David. A Maskil.

1 Happy are those whose transgression is
        forgiven,
    whose sin is covered.
2 Happy are those to whom the LORD
        imputes no iniquity,
    and in whose spirit there is no deceit.

3 While I kept silence, my body wasted
        away
    through my groaning all day long.
4 For day and night your hand was heavy
        upon me;
    my strength was dried up *b* as by the
        heat of summer.   *Selah*

5 Then I acknowledged my sin to you,
        and I did not hide my iniquity;
    I said, "I will confess my transgressions
        to the LORD,"
    and you forgave the guilt of my sin.
                                     Selah

6 Therefore let all who are faithful
        offer prayer to you;
    at a time of distress, *c* the rush of mighty
        waters
    shall not reach them.
7 You are a hiding place for me;
    you preserve me from trouble;
    you surround me with glad cries of
        deliverance.   *Selah*

a Another reading is *cut off*   b Meaning of Heb
uncertain   c Cn: Heb *at a time of finding* only

32:1–11 *Happy are those.* Another song of
repentance (see Ps 6), but this one is in the
spirit of thanksgiving, and the singer basks in
the delight of having been forgiven.
32:2–5 *While I kept silence.* The ill effects of
living in the silence of denial and deceit stand in
sharp contrast to the joy of forgiveness for those
who can honestly confess their sin. The steady
use of the Spiritual Discipline of confession
helps us overcome the many and subtle ways
we are tempted to fool ourselves and others.
32:5 CONFESSION—*See* Spiritual Disciplines
Index.
32:6 PRAYER—*See* Spiritual Disciplines
Index.

8 I will instruct you and teach you the
  way you should go;
  I will counsel you with my eye upon
  you.
9 Do not be like a horse or a mule,
  without understanding,
  whose temper must be curbed with
  bit and bridle,
  else it will not stay near you.

10 Many are the torments of the wicked,
   but steadfast love surrounds those
   who trust in the LORD.
11 Be glad in the LORD and rejoice,
   O righteous,
   and shout for joy, all you upright in
   heart.

Psalm 33

The Greatness and Goodness of God

1 Rejoice in the LORD, O you righteous.
  Praise befits the upright.
2 Praise the LORD with the lyre;
  make melody to him with the harp of
  ten strings.
3 Sing to him a new song;
  play skillfully on the strings, with
  loud shouts.

4 For the word of the LORD is upright,
  and all his work is done in
  faithfulness.
5 He loves righteousness and justice;
  the earth is full of the steadfast love of
  the LORD.

6 By the word of the LORD the heavens
  were made,
  and all their host by the breath of his
  mouth.
7 He gathered the waters of the sea as in a
  bottle;
  he put the deeps in storehouses.

8 Let all the earth fear the LORD;
  let all the inhabitants of the world
  stand in awe of him.
9 For he spoke, and it came to be;
  he commanded, and it stood firm.

10 The LORD brings the counsel of the
   nations to nothing;
   he frustrates the plans of the peoples.
11 The counsel of the LORD stands forever,
   the thoughts of his heart to all
   generations.
12 Happy is the nation whose God is the
   LORD,
   the people whom he has chosen as
   his heritage.

13 The LORD looks down from heaven;
   he sees all humankind.
14 From where he sits enthroned he
   watches
   all the inhabitants of the earth—
15 he who fashions the hearts of them all,
   and observes all their deeds.
16 A king is not saved by his great army;
   a warrior is not delivered by his great
   strength.
17 The war horse is a vain hope for victory,
   and by its great might it cannot save.
18 Truly the eye of the LORD is on those
   who fear him,
   on those who hope in his steadfast
   love,
19 to deliver their soul from death,
   and to keep them alive in famine.

20 Our soul waits for the LORD;
   he is our help and shield.
21 Our heart is glad in him,
   because we trust in his holy name.
22 Let your steadfast love, O LORD, be
   upon us,
   even as we hope in you.

32:8–9 *Do not be like a horse or a mule, without understanding.* Probably a word of God to worshipers, offering ready guidance to those who won't resist like stubborn mules.

33:1–22 *Rejoice in the LORD.* This joyous song celebrates God's gracious action in creation and in the life of the world. We can rely gladly on God, who is watching over "those who fear him" (v 18).

33:13–22 THE WITH-GOD LIFE—*See* Spiritual Disciplines Index.

Psalm 34

Praise for Deliverance from Trouble

*Of David, when he feigned madness before
Abimelech, so that he drove him out, and he
went away.*

1 I will bless the LORD at all times;
   his praise shall continually be in my
     mouth.
2 My soul makes its boast in the LORD;
   let the humble hear and be glad.
3 O magnify the LORD with me,
   and let us exalt his name together.

4 I sought the LORD, and he answered me,
   and delivered me from all my fears.
5 Look to him, and be radiant;
   so your[a] faces shall never be ashamed.
6 This poor soul cried, and was heard by
     the LORD,
   and was saved from every trouble.
7 The angel of the LORD encamps
   around those who fear him, and
     delivers them.
8 O taste and see that the LORD is good;
   happy are those who take refuge in
     him.
9 O fear the LORD, you his holy ones,
   for those who fear him have no want.
10 The young lions suffer want and
     hunger,
   but those who seek the LORD lack no
     good thing.

11 Come, O children, listen to me;
   I will teach you the fear of the LORD.
12 Which of you desires life,
   and covets many days to enjoy good?
13 Keep your tongue from evil,
   and your lips from speaking deceit.
14 Depart from evil, and do good;
   seek peace, and pursue it.

15 The eyes of the LORD are on the
     righteous,
   and his ears are open to their cry.
16 The face of the LORD is against evildoers,
   to cut off the remembrance of them
     from the earth.
17 When the righteous cry for help, the
     LORD hears,
   and rescues them from all their
     troubles.
18 The LORD is near to the brokenhearted,
   and saves the crushed in spirit.

19 Many are the afflictions of the
     righteous,
   but the LORD rescues them from them
     all.
20 He keeps all their bones;
   not one of them will be broken.
21 Evil brings death to the wicked,
   and those who hate the righteous will
     be condemned.
22 The LORD redeems the life of his
     servants;
   none of those who take refuge in him
     will be condemned.

Psalm 35

Prayer for Deliverance from Enemies

Of David.

1 Contend, O LORD, with those who
     contend with me;
   fight against those who fight against
     me!
2 Take hold of shield and buckler,
   and rise up to help me!
3 Draw the spear and javelin
   against my pursuers;
   say to my soul,
   "I am your salvation."

a Gk Syr Jerome: Heb *their*

34:11–14 *Keep your tongue from evil.* This
passage gives some practical instruction about
living in "the fear of the LORD." This psalm
reflects the wisdom tradition, but also overlaps
prophetic instruction. The charge to do good
and to seek and pursue peace sounds a lot like
Isa 1:16–17; Amos 5:14–15; Mic 6:8. We are to
take the initiative for justice and compassion.
   34:15–19 THE WITH-GOD LIFE—See
Spiritual Disciplines Index.
   34:15–22 *the righteous . . . evildoers.* See note
on 1:1–6.

4 Let them be put to shame and dishonor
      who seek after my life.
   Let them be turned back and
      confounded
   who devise evil against me.
5 Let them be like chaff before the wind,
      with the angel of the LORD driving
      them on.
6 Let their way be dark and slippery,
      with the angel of the LORD pursuing
      them.

7 For without cause they hid their net[a]
      for me;
   without cause they dug a pit[b] for my
      life.
8 Let ruin come on them unawares.
   And let the net that they hid ensnare
      them;
   let them fall in it—to their ruin.

9 Then my soul shall rejoice in the LORD,
      exulting in his deliverance.
10 All my bones shall say,
      "O LORD, who is like you?
   You deliver the weak
      from those too strong for them,
      the weak and needy from those who
      despoil them."

11 Malicious witnesses rise up;
      they ask me about things I do not
      know.
12 They repay me evil for good;
      my soul is forlorn.
13 But as for me, when they were sick,
      I wore sackcloth;
   I afflicted myself with fasting.

   I prayed with head bowed[c] on my
      bosom,
14   as though I grieved for a friend or a
      brother;
   I went about as one who laments for a
      mother,
      bowed down and in mourning.

15 But at my stumbling they gathered in
      glee,
      they gathered together against me;
   ruffians whom I did not know
      tore at me without ceasing;
16 they impiously mocked more and more,[d]
      gnashing at me with their teeth.

17 How long, O LORD, will you look on?
      Rescue me from their ravages,
      my life from the lions!
18 Then I will thank you in the great
      congregation;
      in the mighty throng I will praise you.

19 Do not let my treacherous enemies
      rejoice over me,
      or those who hate me without cause
      wink the eye.
20 For they do not speak peace,
      but they conceive deceitful words
      against those who are quiet in the
      land.
21 They open wide their mouths against
      me;
      they say, "Aha, Aha,
      our eyes have seen it."

_a_ Heb _a pit, their net_   _b_ The word _pit_ is
transposed from the preceding line   _c_ Or _My
prayer turned back_   _d_ Cn Compare Gk: Heb _like
the profanest of mockers of a cake_

35:10 _You deliver the weak from those too
strong for them._ A key point of trust and praise
in this song detailing the scheming and gleeful
attacks by the psalmist's enemies. Perhaps the
weak know better than others that trusting God
is the _only_ plan, not the backup plan.

Responding
35:13 FASTING. Obviously in this
instance the psalmist refers to fasting
from food. What is interesting is that he does so
in response to the sickness of his enemies. How
difficult would it be to deny ourselves one of
life's pleasures so that we could spend extra time
praying for the health of someone we don't like
and may even consider an enemy? As time
permits, examine your life and identify those
people you genuinely dislike. Then deny yourself
something you thoroughly enjoy—reading the
paper, watching a movie, attending an athletic
event—and use the time to pray for your
"enemies." _See also_ Spiritual Disciplines Index.

22 You have seen, O LORD; do not be silent!
   O Lord, do not be far from me!
23 Wake up! Bestir yourself for my defense,
   for my cause, my God and my Lord!
24 Vindicate me, O LORD, my God,
   according to your righteousness,
   and do not let them rejoice over me.
25 Do not let them say to themselves,
   "Aha, we have our heart's desire."
   Do not let them say, "We have
   swallowed you*a* up."

26 Let all those who rejoice at my calamity
   be put to shame and confusion;
   let those who exalt themselves against
   me
   be clothed with shame and dishonor.

27 Let those who desire my vindication
   shout for joy and be glad,
   and say evermore,
   "Great is the LORD,
   who delights in the welfare of his
   servant."
28 Then my tongue shall tell of your
   righteousness
   and of your praise all day long.

Psalm 36

Human Wickedness and Divine Goodness

To the leader. Of David, the servant of
the LORD.

1 Transgression speaks to the wicked
   deep in their hearts;
   there is no fear of God
   before their eyes.
2 For they flatter themselves in their own
   eyes
   that their iniquity cannot be found
   out and hated.

3 The words of their mouths are mischief
   and deceit;
   they have ceased to act wisely and do
   good.
4 They plot mischief while on their beds;
   they are set on a way that is not good;
   they do not reject evil.

5 Your steadfast love, O LORD, extends to
   the heavens,
   your faithfulness to the clouds.
6 Your righteousness is like the mighty
   mountains,
   your judgments are like the great
   deep;
   you save humans and animals alike,
   O LORD.

7 How precious is your steadfast love,
   O God!
   All people may take refuge in the
   shadow of your wings.
8 They feast on the abundance of your
   house,
   and you give them drink from the
   river of your delights.
9 For with you is the fountain of life;
   in your light we see light.

10 O continue your steadfast love to those
   who know you,
   and your salvation to the upright of
   heart!
11 Do not let the foot of the arrogant tread
   on me,
   or the hand of the wicked drive me
   away.
12 There the evildoers lie prostrate;
   they are thrust down, unable to rise.

a Heb *him*

35:27 SERVICE—*See* Spiritual Disciplines
Index.
36:1–12 *Transgression speaks to the wicked.*
The sharp contrast between the arrogance of
the wicked and the generous love of God sets
up the closing appeal for God's deliverance
(v 11).
36:1–4 *they do not reject evil.* How ironic that
those who even on their beds are plotting
mischief and who constantly deceive are also
flattering and fooling themselves, thinking
they're clever enough to get away with it.
36:5–9 *with you is the fountain of life.* The
blind arrogance of the wicked pales next to the
steadfast love and righteousness of God, which
govern the whole world.

Psalm 37

Exhortation to Patience and Trust

Of David.

1 Do not fret because of the wicked;
  do not be envious of wrongdoers,
2 for they will soon fade like the grass,
  and wither like the green herb.

3 Trust in the LORD, and do good;
  so you will live in the land, and enjoy
    security.
4 Take delight in the LORD,
  and he will give you the desires of
    your heart.

5 Commit your way to the LORD;
  trust in him, and he will act.
6 He will make your vindication shine
    like the light,
  and the justice of your cause like the
    noonday.

7 Be still before the LORD, and wait
    patiently for him;
  do not fret over those who prosper in
    their way,
  over those who carry out evil devices.

8 Refrain from anger, and forsake wrath.
  Do not fret—it leads only to evil.
9 For the wicked shall be cut off,
  but those who wait for the LORD shall
    inherit the land.

10 Yet a little while, and the wicked will be
    no more;
  though you look diligently for their
    place, they will not be there.
11 But the meek shall inherit the land,
  and delight themselves in abundant
    prosperity.

12 The wicked plot against the righteous,
  and gnash their teeth at them;
13 but the LORD laughs at the wicked,
  for he sees that their day is coming.

14 The wicked draw the sword and bend
    their bows
  to bring down the poor and needy,
  to kill those who walk uprightly;
15 their sword shall enter their own heart,
  and their bows shall be broken.

16 Better is a little that the righteous
    person has
  than the abundance of many wicked.
17 For the arms of the wicked shall be
    broken,
  but the LORD upholds the righteous.

18 The LORD knows the days of the
    blameless,
  and their heritage will abide forever;
19 they are not put to shame in evil times,
  in the days of famine they have
    abundance.

20 But the wicked perish,
  and the enemies of the LORD are like
    the glory of the pastures;
  they vanish—like smoke they vanish
    away.

21 The wicked borrow, and do not pay
    back,
  but the righteous are generous and
    keep giving;
22 for those blessed by the LORD shall
    inherit the land,
  but those cursed by him shall be cut
    off.

23 Our steps *a* are made firm by the LORD,
  when he delights in our *b* way;

a Heb *A man's steps*   *b* Heb *his*

37:1–2 *Do not fret because of the wicked.* The simple formula "Do good and prosper, ignore God and fail" often doesn't work, and we wonder why good things happen to bad people. The psalmist says not to worry about it. God will take care of them soon enough (e.g., vv 2, 9, 13).

37:3–6 *trust in him, and he will act.* Instead of fretting, we should trust, even "delight" in, God, who will protect and provide generously for those who do (cf. vv 23–26).

24 though we stumble,[a] we[b] shall not fall
        headlong,
    for the LORD holds us[c] by the hand.

25 I have been young, and now am old,
    yet I have not seen the righteous
        forsaken
    or their children begging bread.
26 They are ever giving liberally and
        lending,
    and their children become a blessing.

27 Depart from evil, and do good;
    so you shall abide forever.
28 For the LORD loves justice;
    he will not forsake his faithful ones.

    The righteous shall be kept safe forever,
        but the children of the wicked shall
            be cut off.

29 The righteous shall inherit the land,
    and live in it forever.

30 The mouths of the righteous utter
        wisdom,
    and their tongues speak justice.
31 The law of their God is in their hearts;
    their steps do not slip.

32 The wicked watch for the righteous,
    and seek to kill them.
33 The LORD will not abandon them to
        their power,
    or let them be condemned when they
        are brought to trial.

34 Wait for the LORD, and keep to his way,
    and he will exalt you to inherit the
        land;
    you will look on the destruction of
        the wicked.

35 I have seen the wicked oppressing,
    and towering like a cedar of
        Lebanon.[d]

36 Again I[e] passed by, and they were no
        more;
    though I sought them, they could not
        be found.
37 Mark the blameless, and behold the
        upright,
    for there is posterity for the
        peaceable.
38 But transgressors shall be altogether
        destroyed;
    the posterity of the wicked shall be
        cut off.

39 The salvation of the righteous is from
        the LORD;
    he is their refuge in the time of
        trouble.
40 The LORD helps them and rescues them;
    he rescues them from the wicked, and
        saves them,
    because they take refuge in him.

Psalm 38

A Penitent Sufferer's Plea for Healing

A Psalm of David, for the memorial offering.

1 O LORD, do not rebuke me in your anger,
    or discipline me in your wrath.
2 For your arrows have sunk into me,
    and your hand has come down on
        me.

3 There is no soundness in my flesh
        because of your indignation;
    there is no health in my bones
        because of my sin.
4 For my iniquities have gone over my
        head;
    they weigh like a burden too heavy
        for me.

a Heb he stumbles   b Heb he   c Heb him
d Gk: Meaning of Heb uncertain   e Gk Syr
Jerome: Heb he

37:27–28 *For the LORD loves justice.* Here are
the basics in a nutshell. Live and love justice too.
    38:1–22 *O LORD, do not rebuke me in your
anger.* This song of repentance sets up the
singer's confession with a long, detailed list of
aches and pains. Unlike Job, who in his distress
rightly defended his integrity, this psalmist takes
his illness as a sign of God's judgment.

5 My wounds grow foul and fester
   because of my foolishness;
6 I am utterly bowed down and prostrate;
   all day long I go around mourning.
7 For my loins are filled with burning,
   and there is no soundness in my flesh.
8 I am utterly spent and crushed;
   I groan because of the tumult of my
   heart.

9 O Lord, all my longing is known to you;
   my sighing is not hidden from you.
10 My heart throbs, my strength fails me;
   as for the light of my eyes—it also has
   gone from me.
11 My friends and companions stand aloof
   from my affliction,
   and my neighbors stand far off.

12 Those who seek my life lay their snares;
   those who seek to hurt me speak of
   ruin,
   and meditate treachery all day long.

13 But I am like the deaf, I do not hear;
   like the mute, who cannot speak.
14 Truly, I am like one who does not hear,
   and in whose mouth is no retort.

15 But it is for you, O LORD, that I wait;
   it is you, O Lord my God, who will
   answer.
16 For I pray, "Only do not let them rejoice
   over me,
   those who boast against me when my
   foot slips."

17 For I am ready to fall,
   and my pain is ever with me.
18 I confess my iniquity;
   I am sorry for my sin.

19 Those who are my foes without cause[a]
   are mighty,
   and many are those who hate me
   wrongfully.
20 Those who render me evil for good
   are my adversaries because I follow
   after good.

21 Do not forsake me, O LORD;
   O my God, do not be far from me;
22 make haste to help me,
   O Lord, my salvation.

Psalm 39

Prayer for Wisdom and Forgiveness

To the leader: to Jeduthun. A Psalm of David.

1 I said, "I will guard my ways
   that I may not sin with my
   tongue;
   I will keep a muzzle on my mouth
   as long as the wicked are in my
   presence."
2 I was silent and still;
   I held my peace to no avail;
   my distress grew worse,
3   my heart became hot within me.
   While I mused, the fire burned;
   then I spoke with my tongue:

4 "LORD, let me know my end,
   and what is the measure of my days;
   let me know how fleeting my life is.
5 You have made my days a few
   handbreadths,
   and my lifetime is as nothing in your
   sight.

a Q Ms: MT *my living foes*

38:18 *I am sorry for my sin.* This simple, unqualified confession models what it means to accept full responsibility without excuses or blaming. "I did it. I'm sorry" is all we need.

38:18 CONFESSION—*See* Spiritual Disciplines Index.

39:1–3 *I will keep a muzzle on my mouth.* The Psalms and the rest of the Bible warn us that our mouths can get us in a lot of trouble. The singer here has worked hard to avoid that, even shutting down whatever damning words he would like to say about the wicked.

39:4–13 *LORD, let me know my end.* But then anguished questions spill out, some echoing the language of Ecclesiastes. Life is so fragile, so short, like a puff of air, a passing shadow. How long do I have? What does it mean anyway? (v 6). Can't you back off a bit, God? (vv 10, 13).

Surely everyone stands as a mere breath.
                                    Selah

6   Surely everyone goes about like a
        shadow.
    Surely for nothing they are in
        turmoil;
        they heap up, and do not know who
            will gather.

7   "And now, O Lord, what do I wait for?
        My hope is in you.
8   Deliver me from all my
        transgressions.
    Do not make me the scorn of the
        fool.
9   I am silent; I do not open my mouth,
        for it is you who have done it.
10 Remove your stroke from me;
        I am worn down by the blows*a* of
            your hand.

11 "You chastise mortals
        in punishment for sin,
    consuming like a moth what is dear to
        them;
        surely everyone is a mere breath.
                                    Selah

12 "Hear my prayer, O LORD,
        and give ear to my cry;
    do not hold your peace at my tears.
    For I am your passing guest,
        an alien, like all my forebears.
13 Turn your gaze away from me, that I
        may smile again,
        before I depart and am no more."

Psalm 40

Thanksgiving for Deliverance and Prayer for Help

To the leader. Of David. A Psalm.

1   I waited patiently for the LORD;
        he inclined to me and heard my cry.
2   He drew me up from the desolate pit,*b*
        out of the miry bog,
    and set my feet upon a rock,
        making my steps secure.
3   He put a new song in my mouth,
        a song of praise to our God.
    Many will see and fear,
        and put their trust in the LORD.

4   Happy are those who make
        the LORD their trust,
    who do not turn to the proud,
        to those who go astray after false
            gods.
5   You have multiplied, O LORD my God,
        your wondrous deeds and your
            thoughts toward us;
        none can compare with you.
    Were I to proclaim and tell of them,
        they would be more than can be
            counted.

6   Sacrifice and offering you do not
        desire,
        but you have given me an open ear.*c*
    Burnt offering and sin offering
        you have not required.

a Heb *hostility*   *b* Cn: Heb *pit of tumult*
c Heb *ears you have dug for me*

39:7–8 *My hope is in you.* But the singer also hopes in God (v 7) and seeks deliverance from sin (v 8). Loose-end questions and hope in God often exist together in the one who seeks a life with God.

39:9 SILENCE—*See* Spiritual Disciplines Index.

39:12 PRAYER—*See* Spiritual Disciplines Index.

40:6–8 *Burnt offering and sin offering you have not required.* Religious ritual isn't the point. God wants people who "delight" to do God's will and have it operate at their very core where transformation has taken root.

Responding
40:6–8 SACRIFICE. For those of us raised with the idea that our great sacrifices and big offerings make us more acceptable to God, this verse seems almost heretical. According to verse 8, what does God require? How can we get to the point where God's law is in our heart and we delight to do his will? *See also* Spiritual Disciplines Index.

7 Then I said, "Here I am;
    in the scroll of the book it is written
        of me. *a*
8 I delight to do your will, O my God;
    your law is within my heart."

9 I have told the glad news of deliverance
    in the great congregation;
see, I have not restrained my lips,
    as you know, O Lord.
10 I have not hidden your saving help
        within my heart,
    I have spoken of your faithfulness and
        your salvation;
    I have not concealed your steadfast love
        and your faithfulness
    from the great congregation.

11 Do not, O Lord, withhold
        your mercy from me;
    let your steadfast love and your
        faithfulness
    keep me safe forever.
12 For evils have encompassed me
        without number;
my iniquities have overtaken me,
    until I cannot see;
they are more than the hairs of my
        head,
    and my heart fails me.

13 Be pleased, O Lord, to deliver me;
    O Lord, make haste to help me.
14 Let all those be put to shame and
        confusion
    who seek to snatch away my life;
let those be turned back and brought to
        dishonor
    who desire my hurt.
15 Let those be appalled because of their
        shame
    who say to me, "Aha, Aha!"

16 But may all who seek you
    rejoice and be glad in you;
may those who love your salvation
    say continually, "Great is the Lord!"
17 As for me, I am poor and needy,
    but the Lord takes thought for me.
You are my help and my deliverer;
    do not delay, O my God.

Psalm 41

Assurance of God's Help and a Plea for Healing

To the leader. A Psalm of David.

1 Happy are those who consider the
        poor; *b*
    the Lord delivers them in the day of
        trouble.
2 The Lord protects them and keeps them
        alive;
    they are called happy in the land.
    You do not give them up to the will of
        their enemies.
3 The Lord sustains them on their
        sickbed;
    in their illness you heal all their
        infirmities. *c*

4 As for me, I said, "O Lord, be gracious to
        me;
    heal me, for I have sinned against you."
5 My enemies wonder in malice
    when I will die, and my name perish.
6 And when they come to see me, they
        utter empty words,
    while their hearts gather mischief;
    when they go out, they tell it abroad.
7 All who hate me whisper together about
        me;
    they imagine the worst for me.

a Meaning of Heb uncertain   *b* Or *weak*
c Heb *you change all his bed*

40:11–12 *my heart fails me.* In saying that
his iniquities "are more than the hairs of [his]
head," the singer conveys his sense of the power and depth of sin. In confessing he rightly
appeals to God's steadfast love.

41:1–3 *Happy are those who consider the
poor.* Those who care for the weak will be cared

for in their own weakness.

41:4–12 *O Lord, be gracious to me.* The
singer confesses his sin and pleads for God's
help in his own illness. God heals and delivers.
Everyone else, including close friends, have
abandoned him and wished him the worst. God
doesn't give up on us.

8 They think that a deadly thing has
    fastened on me,
  that I will not rise again from where I
    lie.
9 Even my bosom friend in whom I
    trusted,
  who ate of my bread, has lifted the
    heel against me.
10 But you, O LORD, be gracious to me,
  and raise me up, that I may repay
    them.

11 By this I know that you are pleased with
    me;
  because my enemy has not
    triumphed over me.
12 But you have upheld me because of my
    integrity,
  and set me in your presence forever.

13 Blessed be the LORD, the God of Israel,
  from everlasting to everlasting.
      Amen and Amen.

BOOK II

(Psalms 42–72)

Psalm 42

Longing for God and His Help in Distress

To the leader. A Maskil of the Korahites.

1 As a deer longs for flowing streams,
    so my soul longs for you, O God.
2 My soul thirsts for God,
    for the living God.
  When shall I come and behold
    the face of God?
3 My tears have been my food

  day and night,
  while people say to me continually,
    "Where is your God?"

4 These things I remember,
    as I pour out my soul:
  how I went with the throng,[a]
    and led them in procession to the
      house of God,
  with glad shouts and songs of
    thanksgiving,
  a multitude keeping festival.
5 Why are you cast down, O my soul,
    and why are you disquieted within
      me?
  Hope in God; for I shall again praise him,
    my help 6and my God.

  My soul is cast down within me;
    therefore I remember you
  from the land of Jordan and of Hermon,
    from Mount Mizar.
7 Deep calls to deep
    at the thunder of your cataracts;
  all your waves and your billows
    have gone over me.
8 By day the LORD commands his
      steadfast love,
    and at night his song is with me,
    a prayer to the God of my life.

9 I say to God, my rock,
    "Why have you forgotten me?
  Why must I walk about mournfully
    because the enemy oppresses me?"
10 As with a deadly wound in my body,
    my adversaries taunt me,

a Meaning of Heb uncertain

41:13 *Blessed be the LORD.* This little doxology ends the first of the five books of the Psalms.

42:1–43:5 *As a deer longs for flowing streams.* Psalms 42 and 43 are often read together as a single psalm. They share common themes and even common refrains (42:3, 11; with 43:5; 42:9; with 43:2). They may have emerged from the anguish and separation of the Babylonian exile.

42:1–3 *My soul thirsts for God.* The powerful images of thirst and eagerness to be in God's

presence ("behold the face of God") point to the very core of our life with God.

42:5, 11–12 *Why are you cast down, O my soul? . . . Hope in God.* Choosing to hope is difficult in hard times, but it's the heart's way to say God will prevail, we will praise.

42:6–8 *all your waves and your billows have gone over me.* In the midst of discouragement, the rivers of God's life wash over the singer, soaking him in love and quenching his thirst.

42:8 PRAYER—See Spiritual Disciplines Index.

while they say to me continually,
"Where is your God?"

11 Why are you cast down, O my soul,
and why are you disquieted within
me?
Hope in God; for I shall again praise
him,
my help and my God.

Psalm 43

Prayer to God in Time of Trouble

1 Vindicate me, O God, and defend my
cause
against an ungodly people;
from those who are deceitful and unjust
deliver me!
2 For you are the God in whom I take
refuge;
why have you cast me off?
Why must I walk about mournfully
because of the oppression of the
enemy?

3 O send out your light and your truth;
let them lead me;
let them bring me to your holy hill
and to your dwelling.
4 Then I will go to the altar of God,
to God my exceeding joy;
and I will praise you with the harp,
O God, my God.

5 Why are you cast down, O my soul,
and why are you disquieted within
me?
Hope in God; for I shall again praise
him,
my help and my God.

Psalm 44

National Lament and Prayer for Help

To the leader. Of the Korahites. A Maskil.

1 We have heard with our ears, O God,
our ancestors have told us,
what deeds you performed in their days,
in the days of old:
2 you with your own hand drove out the
nations,
but them you planted;
you afflicted the peoples,
but them you set free;
3 for not by their own sword did they win
the land,
nor did their own arm give them
victory;
but your right hand, and your arm,
and the light of your countenance,
for you delighted in them.

4 You are my King and my God;
you command[a] victories for Jacob.
5 Through you we push down our foes;
through your name we tread down
our assailants.
6 For not in my bow do I trust,
nor can my sword save me.
7 But you have saved us from our foes,
and have put to confusion those who
hate us.
8 In God we have boasted continually,
and we will give thanks to your name
forever.   *Selah*

9 Yet you have rejected us and abased us,
and have not gone out with our armies.

a Gk Syr: Heb *You are my King, O God; command*

43:1–5 *Vindicate me, O God.* See note on
42:1–43:5. Psalm 43 is an appeal for God to
exercise justice and deliverance from enemies.

44:1–26 *We have heard with our ears, O God.*
Psalm 44 is a community song seeking God's
help in a time of confusion and desperation. A
key turning point is: "In God we have boasted
continually. . . . Yet you have rejected us" (vv
8–9). The people's trust and God's habit of
deliverance are recalled (vv 1–8). Terrible

defeats are described, times when Israel became
a laughingstock among the nations (vv 9–16).

44:17–22 *yet we have not forgotten you.* The
painfully puzzling question is why defeat has
come about. The community insists that it has
been faithful and that it may even be their
faithfulness ("Because of you") that has brought
disaster (v 22).

44:23–26 *Why do you sleep, O Lord?* A strong
appeal for God's attention and rescue.

10 You made us turn back from the foe,
    and our enemies have gotten spoil.
11 You have made us like sheep for
        slaughter,
    and have scattered us among the
        nations.
12 You have sold your people for a trifle,
    demanding no high price for them.

13 You have made us the taunt of our
        neighbors,
    the derision and scorn of those
        around us.
14 You have made us a byword among the
        nations,
    a laughingstock[a] among the peoples.
15 All day long my disgrace is before me,
    and shame has covered my face
16 at the words of the taunters and revilers,
    at the sight of the enemy and the
        avenger.

17 All this has come upon us,
    yet we have not forgotten you,
    or been false to your covenant.
18 Our heart has not turned back,
    nor have our steps departed from
        your way,
19 yet you have broken us in the haunt of
        jackals,
    and covered us with deep darkness.

20 If we had forgotten the name of our God,
    or spread out our hands to a strange
        god,

21 would not God discover this?
    For he knows the secrets of the heart.
22 Because of you we are being killed all
        day long,
    and accounted as sheep for the
        slaughter.

23 Rouse yourself! Why do you sleep,
        O Lord?
    Awake, do not cast us off forever!
24 Why do you hide your face?
    Why do you forget our affliction and
        oppression?
25 For we sink down to the dust;
    our bodies cling to the ground.
26 Rise up, come to our help.
    Redeem us for the sake of your
        steadfast love.

Psalm 45

Ode for a Royal Wedding

To the leader: according to Lilies. Of the
    Korahites. A Maskil. A love song.

1 My heart overflows with a goodly
        theme;
    I address my verses to the king;
    my tongue is like the pen of a ready
        scribe.

2 You are the most handsome of men;
    grace is poured upon your lips;
    therefore God has blessed you forever.

a Heb a shaking of the head

45:1–17 *My heart overflows with a goodly theme.* Taken literally, this song celebrates a king's wedding. Any ruler would love the singer's description of him (whether fawning or sincere). The king is handsome, strong, righteous, rich, and even fragrant (vv 2–9). The bride should and will yield to him gladly, much to her own good (vv 10–15). As with the Song of Solomon, this psalm has often come to be interpreted allegorically: Christ as King receives the Church as his bride.

Responding
45:1–17 CELEBRATION. If you are a fan of period movies, you can readily imagine the pomp and circumstance surrounding this royal wedding—the groom decked out in his best clothes with a sword on his thigh, the bride wearing a gold gown and accompanied by her attendants—as they process to the palace. All the while joy and gladness permeate the air. In *Celebration of Discipline* Richard Foster writes: "God's normal means of bringing his joy is by redeeming and sanctifying the ordinary junctures of life." As you go about your normal routine today, be especially aware of God's redeeming presence in the most menial job. Then at the end of the day, reflect on how that brought joy into your life. *See also* Spiritual Disciplines Index.

3 Gird your sword on your thigh,
  O mighty one,
  in your glory and majesty.

4 In your majesty ride on victoriously
  for the cause of truth and to defend[a]
  the right;
  let your right hand teach you dread
  deeds.
5 Your arrows are sharp
  in the heart of the king's enemies;
  the peoples fall under you.

6 Your throne, O God,[b] endures forever
  and ever.
  Your royal scepter is a scepter of
  equity;
7 you love righteousness and hate
  wickedness.
Therefore God, your God, has anointed
  you
  with the oil of gladness beyond your
  companions;
8 your robes are all fragrant with myrrh
  and aloes and cassia.
From ivory palaces stringed
  instruments make you glad;
9 daughters of kings are among your
  ladies of honor;
  at your right hand stands the queen
  in gold of Ophir.

10 Hear, O daughter, consider and incline
  your ear;
  forget your people and your father's
  house,
11 and the king will desire your beauty.
  Since he is your lord, bow to him;
12 the people[c] of Tyre will seek your
  favor with gifts,
  the richest of the people 13with all
  kinds of wealth.

The princess is decked in her chamber
  with gold-woven robes;[d]
14 in many-colored robes she is led to
  the king;
  behind her the virgins, her
  companions, follow.
15 With joy and gladness they are led
  along
  as they enter the palace of the king.

16 In the place of ancestors you, O king,[e]
  shall have sons;
  you will make them princes in all the
  earth.
17 I will cause your name to be celebrated
  in all generations;
  therefore the peoples will praise you
  forever and ever.

Psalm 46

God's Defense of His City and People

To the leader. Of the Korahites. According to
  Alamoth. A Song.

1 God is our refuge and strength,
  a very present[f] help in trouble.
2 Therefore we will not fear, though the
  earth should change,
  though the mountains shake in the
  heart of the sea;
3 though its waters roar and foam,
  though the mountains tremble with
  its tumult.   Selah

4 There is a river whose streams make
  glad the city of God,
  the holy habitation of the Most High.

a Cn: Heb *and the meekness of*   b Or *Your throne
is a throne of God, it*   c Heb *daughter*
d Or *people.* 13*All glorious is the princess within, gold
embroidery is her clothing*   e Heb lacks *O king*
f Or *well proved*

45:6 *Your throne, O God.* Addressing the king as God puzzles interpreters, for Israel did not regard the king as divine (as some of its neighbors did). Perhaps NRSV's alternate reading, "Your throne is a throne of God," helps. Or we may see the king as part of God's court, just as 2:7 sees him in some way as God's "son."

46:1–3 *God is our refuge and strength.* Martin Luther's hymn "A Mighty Fortress Is Our God," based on this psalm, captures its boldness. What boldness it takes to declare "we will not fear" when, according to these verses, the whole world was falling apart!

5 God is in the midst of the city;[a] it shall
    not be moved;
  God will help it when the morning
    dawns.
6 The nations are in an uproar, the
    kingdoms totter;
  he utters his voice, the earth melts.
7 The LORD of hosts is with us;
  the God of Jacob is our refuge.[b]   *Selah*

8 Come, behold the works of the LORD;
  see what desolations he has brought
    on the earth.
9 He makes wars cease to the end of the
    earth;
  he breaks the bow, and shatters the
    spear;
  he burns the shields with fire.
10 "Be still, and know that I am God!
  I am exalted among the nations,
  I am exalted in the earth."
11 The LORD of hosts is with us;
  the God of Jacob is our refuge.[b]   *Selah*

Psalm 47

God's Rule over the Nations

To the leader. Of the Korahites. A Psalm.

1 Clap your hands, all you peoples;
  shout to God with loud songs of joy.
2 For the LORD, the Most High, is awesome,
  a great king over all the earth.
3 He subdued peoples under us,

and nations under our feet.
4 He chose our heritage for us,
  the pride of Jacob whom he loves.
                                            Selah

5 God has gone up with a shout,
  the LORD with the sound of a trumpet.
6 Sing praises to God, sing praises;
  sing praises to our King, sing praises.
7 For God is the king of all the earth;
  sing praises with a psalm.[c]

8 God is king over the nations;
  God sits on his holy throne.
9 The princes of the peoples gather
  as the people of the God of Abraham.
For the shields of the earth belong to
    God;
  he is highly exalted.

Psalm 48

The Glory and Strength of Zion

A Song. A Psalm of the Korahites.

1 Great is the LORD and greatly to be praised
  in the city of our God.
His holy mountain, 2beautiful in
    elevation,
  is the joy of all the earth,
Mount Zion, in the far north,
  the city of the great King.

a Heb *of it*   b Or *fortress*   c Heb *Maskil*

46:4–9 *God is in the midst of the city.* The reason for confidence is that no catastrophe threatens God's rule at the heart of the world itself.

46:10 *Be still, and know that I am God!* More than silence, this is pausing, stepping back, and letting go of panic attacks by recognizing God's presence and power. Breathe.

47:1–9 *Clap your hands.* This is one of the "enthronement psalms," songs that celebrate God's rule as "king of all the earth" (v 7). Just as Israel rejoices that Yahweh rules over all, so it calls all peoples to join in "loud songs of joy" (v 1). To gladly acknowledge this unrivaled King puts us in a place where we can feel secure, learn, and hope.

48:1–14 *Great is the LORD.* This song praises

Zion as the seat of God's power and, because of that, as a fortress that makes kings who come to assault it tremble and flee (vv 4–7). The lavish praise of Zion points toward the sure, just rule of God.

48:2 *Mount Zion, in the far north.* In the word "north" the Hebrew poets echo the name of the mountain their Canaanite neighbors saw as the home of their gods (Mt. Zaphon, which means "north" in Hebrew). This points to Zion as symbolically central (though not geographically in the north), just as Isa 2:2 calls Zion the highest of the mountains, though even its near neighbor the Mount of Olives is taller. Zion is at the center of the world as the seat of the world's great King (cf. 46:4–7). We still sing songs of Zion as we participate in hope in God's rule.

3 Within its citadels God
   has shown himself a sure defense.

4 Then the kings assembled,
   they came on together.
5 As soon as they saw it, they were
      astounded;
   they were in panic, they took to
      flight;
6 trembling took hold of them there,
   pains as of a woman in labor,
7 as when an east wind shatters
   the ships of Tarshish.
8 As we have heard, so have we seen
   in the city of the LORD of hosts,
in the city of our God,
   which God establishes forever.   *Selah*

9 We ponder your steadfast love, O God,
   in the midst of your temple.
10 Your name, O God, like your praise,
   reaches to the ends of the earth.
Your right hand is filled with victory.
11   Let Mount Zion be glad,
let the towns *a* of Judah rejoice
   because of your judgments.

12 Walk about Zion, go all around it,
   count its towers,
13 consider well its ramparts;
   go through its citadels,
that you may tell the next generation
14   that this is God,
our God forever and ever.
   He will be our guide forever.

Psalm 49

The Folly of Trust in Riches

To the leader. Of the Korahites. A Psalm.

1 Hear this, all you peoples;
   give ear, all inhabitants of the world,
2 both low and high,
   rich and poor together.

3 My mouth shall speak wisdom;
   the meditation of my heart shall be
      understanding.
4 I will incline my ear to a proverb;
   I will solve my riddle to the music of
      the harp.

5 Why should I fear in times of trouble,
   when the iniquity of my persecutors
      surrounds me,
6 those who trust in their wealth
   and boast of the abundance of their
      riches?
7 Truly, no ransom avails for one's life, *b*
   there is no price one can give to God
      for it.
8 For the ransom of life is costly,
   and can never suffice,
9 that one should live on forever
   and never see the grave. *c*

10 When we look at the wise, they die;
   fool and dolt perish together
   and leave their wealth to others.
11 Their graves *d* are their homes forever,
   their dwelling places to all
      generations,
   though they named lands their own.
12 Mortals cannot abide in their pomp;
   they are like the animals that perish.

13 Such is the fate of the foolhardy,
   the end of those *e* who are pleased
      with their lot.   *Selah*
14 Like sheep they are appointed for Sheol;
   Death shall be their shepherd;
   straight to the grave they descend, *f*
   and their form shall waste away;
   Sheol shall be their home. *g*

a Heb *daughters*   *b* Another reading is *no one can ransom a brother*   *c* Heb *the pit*   *d* Gk Syr Compare Tg: Heb *their inward* (thought)   *e* Tg: Heb *after them*   *f* Cn: Heb *the upright shall have dominion over them in the morning*   *g* Meaning of Heb uncertain

---

49:1–20 *Hear this, all you peoples.* This song reflects wisdom themes. To some it may seem a bit morbid, but it shows refreshing realism in recognizing the fragility of life.

49:10–11 *leave their wealth.* The reality is we can't take it with us. Even when we do name lands and estates after ourselves, no money can buy immortality.

15 But God will ransom my soul from the
      power of Sheol,
    for he will receive me.   *Selah*

16 Do not be afraid when some become
      rich,
    when the wealth of their houses
      increases.
17 For when they die they will carry
      nothing away;
    their wealth will not go down after
      them.
18 Though in their lifetime they count
      themselves happy
    —for you are praised when you do
      well for yourself—
19 they*a* will go to the company of their
      ancestors,
    who will never again see the light.
20 Mortals cannot abide in their pomp;
    they are like the animals that perish.

Psalm 50

The Acceptable Sacrifice

A Psalm of Asaph.

1 The mighty one, God the LORD,
    speaks and summons the earth
    from the rising of the sun to its
      setting.
2 Out of Zion, the perfection of beauty,
    God shines forth.

3 Our God comes and does not keep
      silence,
    before him is a devouring fire,
    and a mighty tempest all around him.
4 He calls to the heavens above

and to the earth, that he may judge
      his people:
5 "Gather to me my faithful ones,
    who made a covenant with me by
      sacrifice!"
6 The heavens declare his righteousness,
    for God himself is judge.   *Selah*

7 "Hear, O my people, and I will speak,
    O Israel, I will testify against you.
    I am God, your God.
8 Not for your sacrifices do I rebuke you;
    your burnt offerings are continually
      before me.
9 I will not accept a bull from your house,
    or goats from your folds.
10 For every wild animal of the forest is
      mine,
    the cattle on a thousand hills.
11 I know all the birds of the air,*b*
    and all that moves in the field is
      mine.

12 "If I were hungry, I would not tell
      you,
    for the world and all that is in it is
      mine.
13 Do I eat the flesh of bulls,
    or drink the blood of goats?
14 Offer to God a sacrifice of
      thanksgiving,*c*
    and pay your vows to the Most
      High.
15 Call on me in the day of trouble;
    I will deliver you, and you shall
      glorify me."

---

a Cn: Heb *you*   *b* Gk Syr Tg: Heb *mountains*
c Or *make thanksgiving your sacrifice to God*

50:1–23 *The mighty one, God the LORD.* How interesting to see that the Israelites regularly sang a song in worship reminding them that going through the motions of worship isn't enough, even if they are very fine motions. This "prophetic" psalm echoes great passages from the prophets such as Isa 1:10–17; Amos 5:21–24; Mic 6:8. We would do well to take to heart its warnings against hollow worship.

50:4, 7–8, 14, 16–21 *he may judge his people.*

God calls heaven and earth as witnesses in a court where he brings charges against the Israelites. This is a common speech form in the prophets.

50:9–13 *all that moves in the field is mine.* Israel's Mesopotamian neighbors offer sacrifices to their gods to feed them. In dismissing that view and rebuking the Israelites, Yahweh reminds the Israelites that he won't go hungry without their offerings.

16 But to the wicked God says:
"What right have you to recite my
statutes,
or take my covenant on your lips?
17 For you hate discipline,
and you cast my words behind you.
18 You make friends with a thief when you
see one,
and you keep company with adulterers.

19 "You give your mouth free rein for evil,
and your tongue frames deceit.
20 You sit and speak against your kin;
you slander your own mother's child.
21 These things you have done and I have
been silent;
you thought that I was one just like
yourself.
But now I rebuke you, and lay the
charge before you.

22 "Mark this, then, you who forget God,
or I will tear you apart, and there will
be no one to deliver.
23 Those who bring thanksgiving as their
sacrifice honor me;
to those who go the right way *a*
I will show the salvation of God."

Psalm 51

Prayer for Cleansing and Pardon

To the leader. A Psalm of David, when the
prophet Nathan came to him, after he had
gone in to Bathsheba.

1 Have mercy on me, O God,

according to your steadfast love;
according to your abundant mercy
blot out my transgressions.
2 Wash me thoroughly from my
iniquity,
and cleanse me from my sin.

3 For I know my transgressions,
and my sin is ever before me.
4 Against you, you alone, have I
sinned,
and done what is evil in your sight,
so that you are justified in your
sentence
and blameless when you pass
judgment.
5 Indeed, I was born guilty,
a sinner when my mother conceived
me.

6 You desire truth in the inward
being; *b*
therefore teach me wisdom in my
secret heart.
7 Purge me with hyssop, and I shall be
clean;
wash me, and I shall be whiter than
snow.
8 Let me hear joy and gladness;
let the bones that you have crushed
rejoice.
9 Hide your face from my sins,
and blot out all my iniquities.

a Heb *who set a way*   *b* Meaning of Heb
uncertain

50:16–22 *What right have you?* A sharp
rebuke to those who pay lip service, but don't
live faithfully (cf. Jer 7:1–15).

50:23 SACRIFICE—*See* Spiritual Disciplines
Index.

51:1–19 *Have mercy on me, O God.* Psalm 51
is a song of repentance with a moving appeal to
God's steadfast love and mercy.

51:3–5 *I was born guilty.* The singer offers a
radical sense of how sinful he is, admitting full
blameworthiness. Surely to be understood as
hyperbole, his claim is that he was even a
wicked zygote. How deeply do we feel the
power of sin?

Responding
51:6 SECRECY. We normally think of
secrecy as being able to keep a secret,
but Dallas Willard in *The Spirit of the Disciplines*
writes: "In the discipline of secrecy . . . we
abstain from causing our good deeds and
qualities to be known." What connection does
this have to the psalmist's request that God
teach him wisdom in his "secret" heart? Might it
be that if we have wisdom in the depths of our
being, we will be able to easily practice the
Spiritual Discipline of secrecy? *See also* Spiritual
Disciplines Index.

[handwritten: REDEEM RESTORE BY TRIAL]

10 Create in me a clean heart, O God,
   and put a new and right[a] spirit within
      me.
11 Do not cast me away from your
      presence,
   and do not take your holy spirit from
      me.
12 Restore to me the joy of your
      salvation,
   and sustain in me a willing[b] spirit.

13 Then I will teach transgressors your
      ways,
   and sinners will return to you.
14 Deliver me from bloodshed, O God,
   O God of my salvation,
   and my tongue will sing aloud of your
      deliverance.

15 O Lord, open my lips,
   and my mouth will declare your
      praise.
16 For you have no delight in sacrifice;
   if I were to give a burnt offering, you
      would not be pleased.
17 The sacrifice acceptable to God[c] is a
      broken spirit;
   a broken and contrite heart, O God,
   you will not despise.

18 Do good to Zion in your good
      pleasure;
   rebuild the walls of Jerusalem,
19 then you will delight in right
      sacrifices,
   in burnt offerings and whole burnt
      offerings;
   then bulls will be offered on your
      altar.

Psalm 52

Judgment on the Deceitful

*To the leader. A Maskil of David, when Doeg
the Edomite came to Saul and said to him,
"David has come to the house of
Ahimelech."*

1 Why do you boast, O mighty one,
   of mischief done against the godly?[d]
   All day long 2you are plotting
      destruction.
   Your tongue is like a sharp razor,
   you worker of treachery.
3 You love evil more than good,
   and lying more than speaking the
      truth.   *Selah*
4 You love all words that devour,
   O deceitful tongue.

5 But God will break you down forever;
   he will snatch and tear you from your
      tent;
   he will uproot you from the land of
      the living.   *Selah*
6 The righteous will see, and fear,
   and will laugh at the evildoer,[e]
      saying,
7 "See the one who would not take
      refuge in God,
   but trusted in abundant riches,
   and sought refuge in wealth!"[f]

8 But I am like a green olive tree
   in the house of God.
   I trust in the steadfast love of God
   forever and ever.

a Or *steadfast*   *b* Or *generous*   *c* Or *My
sacrifice, O God,*   *d* Cn Compare Syr: Heb *the
kindness of God*   *e* Heb *him*   *f* Syr Tg: Heb *in his
destruction*

51:6–12 *Purge me . . . wash me.* Using heavy-
duty laundry words, the singer asks God to scrub
him up, to "create" (yes, the same word as in
Gen 1) in him a clean heart.

51:13–17 *my tongue will sing aloud of your
deliverance.* The singer is eager to share God's
goodness with others. Note how similar verses
16–17 are to the prophetic tone of Psalm 50.

51:16–19 SACRIFICE—*See* Spiritual
Disciplines Index.

52:1–9 *Why do you boast?* Psalm 52 is a sharp
word against the wicked. The boastful and
apparently successful one who "love[s] evil more
than good" (vv 1–4) will be broken down, uprooted, and made an object of ridicule (vv 5–7).
His arrogant self-sufficiency is set over against
the singer's simple rootedness in God (vv 8–9).

⁹ I will thank you forever,
    because of what you have done.
In the presence of the faithful
    I will proclaim *a* your name, for it is
        good.

Psalm 53

Denunciation of Godlessness

To the leader: according to Mahalath.
A Maskil of David.

¹ Fools say in their hearts, "There is no
    God."
They are corrupt, they commit
    abominable acts;
there is no one who does good.

² God looks down from heaven on
    humankind
to see if there are any who are wise,
who seek after God.

³ They have all fallen away, they are all
    alike perverse;
there is no one who does good,
    no, not one.

⁴ Have they no knowledge, those
    evildoers,
who eat up my people as they eat
    bread,
and do not call upon God?

⁵ There they shall be in great terror,
    in terror such as has not been.
For God will scatter the bones of the
    ungodly;*b*
they will be put to shame,*c* for God
    has rejected them.

⁶ O that deliverance for Israel would
    come from Zion!

When God restores the fortunes of his
    people,
Jacob will rejoice; Israel will be
    glad.

Psalm 54

Prayer for Vindication

To the leader: with stringed instruments.
A Maskil of David, when the Ziphites went
and told Saul, "David is in hiding among us."

¹ Save me, O God, by your name,
    and vindicate me by your might.
² Hear my prayer, O God;
    give ear to the words of my mouth.

³ For the insolent have risen against me,
    the ruthless seek my life;
    they do not set God before them.
                                      Selah

⁴ But surely, God is my helper;
    the Lord is the upholder of*d* my life.
⁵ He will repay my enemies for their
        evil.
    In your faithfulness, put an end to
        them.

⁶ With a freewill offering I will sacrifice to
        you;
    I will give thanks to your name,
        O Lord, for it is good.
⁷ For he has delivered me from every
        trouble,
    and my eye has looked in triumph on
        my enemies.

a Cn: Heb *wait for*   *b* Cn Compare Gk Syr: Heb
him who encamps against you   *c* Gk: Heb *you have
put (them) to shame*   *d* Gk Syr Jerome: Heb *is of
those who uphold* or *is with those who uphold*

53:1–6 *Fools say in their hearts.* God looks for
wise folk, but finds only fools. The fools' self-
assurance that "there is no God" is less atheism
and more a denial that God has any effective
power and presence. Though they have no
"knowledge of God," they will be shamed when
they discover how wrong they are. The psalm is

a forceful reminder that the "wise" are those
"who seek after God."

55:3–11 *My heart is in anguish within me.*
This is high-pitched complaint—noise and
clamor, trembling and horror, violence and
strife, oppression and fraud. No wonder the
singer wants to run away. Wouldn't we?

Psalm 55

Complaint about a Friend's Treachery

To the leader: with stringed instruments.
A Maskil of David.

1 Give ear to my prayer, O God;
   do not hide yourself from my
      supplication.
2 Attend to me, and answer me;
   I am troubled in my complaint.
I am distraught 3by the noise of the
      enemy,
   because of the clamor of the wicked.
For they bring*ᵃ* trouble upon me,
   and in anger they cherish enmity
      against me.

4 My heart is in anguish within me,
   the terrors of death have fallen upon
      me.
5 Fear and trembling come upon me,
   and horror overwhelms me.
6 And I say, "O that I had wings like a
      dove!
   I would fly away and be at rest;
7 truly, I would flee far away;
   I would lodge in the wilderness; *Selah*
8 I would hurry to find a shelter for
      myself
   from the raging wind and tempest."

9 Confuse, O Lord, confound their
      speech;
   for I see violence and strife in the city.
10 Day and night they go around it
   on its walls,
and iniquity and trouble are within it;
11   ruin is in its midst;
oppression and fraud
   do not depart from its marketplace.

12 It is not enemies who taunt me—
   I could bear that;
it is not adversaries who deal insolently
      with me—

I could hide from them.
13 But it is you, my equal,
   my companion, my familiar friend,
14 with whom I kept pleasant company;
   we walked in the house of God with
      the throng.
15 Let death come upon them;
   let them go down alive to Sheol;
   for evil is in their homes and in their
      hearts.

16 But I call upon God,
   and the LORD will save me.
17 Evening and morning and at noon
   I utter my complaint and moan,
   and he will hear my voice.
18 He will redeem me unharmed
   from the battle that I wage,
   for many are arrayed against me.
19 God, who is enthroned from of old,
                    Selah

   will hear, and will humble them—
because they do not change,
   and do not fear God.

20 My companion laid hands on a friend
   and violated a covenant with me*ᵇ*
21 with speech smoother than butter,
   but with a heart set on war;
with words that were softer than oil,
   but in fact were drawn swords.

22 Cast your burden*ᶜ* on the LORD,
   and he will sustain you;
he will never permit
   the righteous to be moved.

23 But you, O God, will cast them down
   into the lowest pit;
   the bloodthirsty and treacherous
      shall not live out half their days.
But I will trust in you.

a Cn Compare Gk: Heb *they cause to totter*
b Heb lacks *with me*   *c* Or *Cast what he has given you*

55:22 *Cast your burden . . . and he will sustain you.* Here we have a key word of assurance even when chaos reigns and friends betray. Instead of "What can I do now?" it is simply "Cast your burden on the LORD." Shrill anxiety can turn into deep rest for the psalmist—and for us (cf. Matt 11:28–30).

Psalm 56

Trust in God under Persecution

To the leader: according to The Dove on Far-
off Terebinths. Of David. A Miktam, when
the Philistines seized him in Gath.

1 Be gracious to me, O God, for people
        trample on me;
    all day long foes oppress me;
2 my enemies trample on me all day long,
        for many fight against me.
    O Most High, ³when I am afraid,
    I put my trust in you.
4 In God, whose word I praise,
        in God I trust; I am not afraid;
    what can flesh do to me?

5 All day long they seek to injure my
        cause;
    all their thoughts are against me for
        evil.
6 They stir up strife, they lurk,
        they watch my steps.
    As they hoped to have my life,
7   so repay *a* them for their crime;
    in wrath cast down the peoples,
        O God!

8 You have kept count of my tossings;
        put my tears in your bottle.
    Are they not in your record?
9 Then my enemies will retreat
        in the day when I call.
    This I know, that *b* God is for me.
10 In God, whose word I praise,
        in the LORD, whose word I praise,

11 in God I trust; I am not afraid.
        What can a mere mortal do to me?

12 My vows to you I must perform, O God;
        I will render thank offerings to you.
13 For you have delivered my soul from
        death,
    and my feet from falling,
    so that I may walk before God
        in the light of life.

Psalm 57

Praise and Assurance under Persecution

To the leader: Do Not Destroy. Of David. A
Miktam, when he fled from Saul, in the cave.

1 Be merciful to me, O God, be merciful
        to me,
    for in you my soul takes refuge;
    in the shadow of your wings I will take
        refuge,
    until the destroying storms pass by.
2 I cry to God Most High,
        to God who fulfills his purpose for me.
3 He will send from heaven and save me,
        he will put to shame those who
            trample on me.   *Selah*
    God will send forth his steadfast love
        and his faithfulness.

4 I lie down among lions
        that greedily devour *c* human prey;
    their teeth are spears and arrows,
        their tongues sharp swords.

a Cn: Heb *rescue*   *b* Or *because*   *c* Cn: Heb *are
aflame for*

56:1–13 *Be gracious to me, O God.* A prayer
for deliverance from persistent, troublemaking
enemies, though it contains more confidence
than desperation.

56:4, 10–11 *In God, whose word I praise.*
When the singer praises God's "word" here we
should not think of it as letters on a book page,
but as words and actions, as how God has
spoken and acted. The Psalms are full of such
praise. The heart of confidence is this: "Fearless
now, I trust in God. What can mere mortals
do?" (*The Message*). Praise strengthens our
trust, again by recalling God's faithful action

on behalf of the faithful.

56:8 *count . . . tossings; put my tears in your
bottle.* What striking images. How can we not
trust in the God who keeps such careful and
tender watch over his people?

57:1–11 *Be exalted, O God, above the
heavens.* Though there are clear appeals for
deliverance from dangerous enemies, the
striking feature of this psalm is a high sense of
praise; God's love is most expansive (vv 5,
10–11) and the psalmist is eager to sing it out—
"I will awake the dawn" (v 8). Such enthusiasm
challenges prim and proper boundaries.

5 Be exalted, O God, above the
      heavens.
   Let your glory be over all the earth.

6 They set a net for my steps;
      my soul was bowed down.
   They dug a pit in my path,
      but they have fallen into it
         themselves.   *Selah*
7 My heart is steadfast, O God,
      my heart is steadfast.
   I will sing and make melody.
8   Awake, my soul!
   Awake, O harp and lyre!
      I will awake the dawn.
9 I will give thanks to you, O Lord, among
      the peoples;
   I will sing praises to you among the
      nations.
10 For your steadfast love is as high as the
      heavens;
   your faithfulness extends to the
      clouds.

11 Be exalted, O God, above the
      heavens.
   Let your glory be over all the earth.

Psalm 58

Prayer for Vengeance

To the leader: Do Not Destroy. Of David.
A Miktam.

1 Do you indeed decree what is right, you
      gods? *a*
   Do you judge people fairly?
2 No, in your hearts you devise wrongs;
      your hands deal out violence on
         earth.

3 The wicked go astray from the womb;
      they err from their birth, speaking
         lies.
4 They have venom like the venom of a
      serpent,
   like the deaf adder that stops its
      ear,
5 so that it does not hear the voice of
      charmers
   or of the cunning enchanter.

6 O God, break the teeth in their
      mouths;
   tear out the fangs of the young lions,
      O LORD!
7 Let them vanish like water that runs
      away;
   like grass let them be trodden down *b*
      and wither.
8 Let them be like the snail that dissolves
      into slime;
   like the untimely birth that never sees
      the sun.
9 Sooner than your pots can feel the heat
      of thorns,
   whether green or ablaze, may he
      sweep them away!

10 The righteous will rejoice when they see
      vengeance done;
   they will bathe their feet in the blood
      of the wicked.
11 People will say, "Surely there is a reward
      for the righteous;
   surely there is a God who judges on
      earth."

a Or *mighty lords*   *b* Cn: Meaning of Heb
uncertain

58:1–11 *Do you indeed decree what is right,*
you gods? This song rises out of the dismay at
how badly people are being governed on earth.
There is no real justice; leaders "devise wrongs"
and "deal out violence" (v 2). In light of the
concluding verse (v 11) in praise of a God who
judges on earth, some may favor the NRSV
alternate translation "mighty lords" in verse 1.

58:6–11 *O God, break the teeth in their*
mouths. Those who live under corrupt rule
appeal to God to set things right again, which is
the general sense of the word we translate a bit
misleadingly as "vengeance" (see "The 'Cursing'
Psalms" in the Introduction). The psalmist
wishes not for revenge, but for justice. The
righteous will rejoice to see justice prevail. Does
that include you and me?

Psalm 59

Prayer for Deliverance from Enemies

To the leader: Do Not Destroy. Of David. A Miktam, when Saul ordered his house to be watched in order to kill him.

1   Deliver me from my enemies, O my
       God;
    protect me from those who rise up
       against me.
2   Deliver me from those who work evil;
       from the bloodthirsty save me.

3   Even now they lie in wait for my life;
       the mighty stir up strife against me.
    For no transgression or sin of mine,
       O LORD,
4   for no fault of mine, they run and
       make ready.

    Rouse yourself, come to my help and
       see!
5   You, LORD God of hosts, are God of
       Israel.
    Awake to punish all the nations;
       spare none of those who
       treacherously plot evil.   *Selah*

6   Each evening they come back,
       howling like dogs
       and prowling about the city.
7   There they are, bellowing with their
       mouths,
    with sharp words*a* on their lips—
       for "Who," they think,*b* "will hear
       us?"

8   But you laugh at them, O LORD;
       you hold all the nations in derision.
9   O my strength, I will watch for you;
       for you, O God, are my fortress.
10 My God in his steadfast love will meet
       me;
    my God will let me look in triumph
       on my enemies.

11 Do not kill them, or my people may
       forget;
    make them totter by your power, and
       bring them down,
    O Lord, our shield.
12 For the sin of their mouths, the words
       of their lips,
    let them be trapped in their pride.
    For the cursing and lies that they utter,
13   consume them in wrath;
    consume them until they are no more.
    Then it will be known to the ends of the
       earth
       that God rules over Jacob.   *Selah*

14 Each evening they come back,
       howling like dogs
       and prowling about the city.
15 They roam about for food,
       and growl if they do not get their fill.

16 But I will sing of your might;
       I will sing aloud of your steadfast love
       in the morning.
    For you have been a fortress for me
       and a refuge in the day of my distress.
17 O my strength, I will sing praises to you,
       for you, O God, are my fortress,
       the God who shows me steadfast love.

Psalm 60

Prayer for National Victory after Defeat

To the leader: according to the Lily of the Covenant. A Miktam of David; for instruction; when he struggled with Aram-naharaim and with Aram-zobah, and when Joab on his return killed twelve thousand Edomites in the Valley of Salt.

1   O God, you have rejected us, broken our
       defenses;
    you have been angry; now restore us!

a Heb *with swords*   *b* Heb lacks *they think*

59:8–13 *But you laugh at them, O LORD.* God laughs at the absurdity of the carefree oppressors. The psalmist wants God to let them get caught in this absurdity, to totter and fall rather than to get taken down too abruptly. There may be some delicious revenge in this, though the singer also promises to sing loudly of God's steadfast love (vv 15–17).

2 You have caused the land to quake; you
     have torn it open;
  repair the cracks in it, for it is
     tottering.
3 You have made your people suffer hard
     things;
  you have given us wine to drink that
     made us reel.

4 You have set up a banner for those who
     fear you,
  to rally to it out of bowshot.*a*   *Selah*
5 Give victory with your right hand, and
     answer us,*b*
  so that those whom you love may be
     rescued.

6 God has promised in his sanctuary:*c*
  "With exultation I will divide up
     Shechem,
  and portion out the Vale of
     Succoth.
7 Gilead is mine, and Manasseh is
     mine;
  Ephraim is my helmet;
  Judah is my scepter.
8 Moab is my washbasin;
  on Edom I hurl my shoe;
  over Philistia I shout in triumph."

9 Who will bring me to the fortified city?
  Who will lead me to Edom?
10 Have you not rejected us, O God?
  You do not go out, O God, with our
     armies.
11 O grant us help against the foe,
  for human help is worthless.
12 With God we shall do valiantly;
  it is he who will tread down our foes.

Psalm 61

Assurance of God's Protection

To the leader: with stringed instruments.
Of David.

1 Hear my cry, O God;
  listen to my prayer.
2 From the end of the earth I call to
     you,
  when my heart is faint.

Lead me to the rock
  that is higher than I;
3 for you are my refuge,
  a strong tower against the
     enemy.

4 Let me abide in your tent forever,
  find refuge under the shelter of your
     wings.   *Selah*
5 For you, O God, have heard my
     vows;
  you have given me the heritage of
     those who fear your name.

6 Prolong the life of the king;
  may his years endure to all
     generations!
7 May he be enthroned forever before
     God;
  appoint steadfast love and
     faithfulness to watch over him!

8 So I will always sing praises to your
     name,
  as I pay my vows day after day.

a Gk Syr Jerome: Heb *because of the truth*
b Another reading is *me*   *c* Or *by his holiness*

60:1–12 *O God, you have rejected us.* The song is full of ambiguity and longing. The claim that God has rejected them is followed by an appeal for rescue (vv 1–5). God assures that he controls the land they live in (vv 6–8). Then question and appeal appear together (vv 9–12). *The Message* translates verse 10, "You aren't giving up on us, are you, God?" That seems an apt expression of hopeful doubt, which leads to a confident appeal. It reflects well the ambivalence we sometimes feel in hard times.

61:1–8 *Hear my cry, O God.* As the singer appeals for God's help, he makes promises to keep the vows he is making (vv 5, 8). He has great confidence in God, "the rock that is higher than I" (v 2), and also looks to the security of God's blessing on the king (vv 6–7). Earthly rulers can be agents of God's good rule, and we can pray to that end.

Psalm 62

Song of Trust in God Alone

To the leader: according to Jeduthun.
A Psalm of David.

1 For God alone my soul waits in silence;
    from him comes my salvation.
2 He alone is my rock and my salvation,
    my fortress; I shall never be shaken.

3 How long will you assail a person,
    will you batter your victim, all of you,
    as you would a leaning wall, a
        tottering fence?
4 Their only plan is to bring down a
        person of prominence.
    They take pleasure in falsehood;
    they bless with their mouths,
    but inwardly they curse.   *Selah*

5 For God alone my soul waits in silence,
    for my hope is from him.
6 He alone is my rock and my salvation,
    my fortress; I shall not be shaken.
7 On God rests my deliverance and my
        honor;
    my mighty rock, my refuge is in God.

8 Trust in him at all times, O people;
    pour out your heart before him;
    God is a refuge for us.   *Selah*

9 Those of low estate are but a breath,
    those of high estate are a delusion;
    in the balances they go up;

they are together lighter than a
        breath.
10 Put no confidence in extortion,
    and set no vain hopes on robbery;
    if riches increase, do not set your
        heart on them.

11 Once God has spoken;
    twice have I heard this:
    that power belongs to God,
12 and steadfast love belongs to you,
        O Lord.
For you repay to all
    according to their work.

Psalm 63

Comfort and Assurance in God's Presence

A Psalm of David, when he was in the
        Wilderness of Judah.

1 O God, you are my God, I seek you,
    my soul thirsts for you;
my flesh faints for you,
    as in a dry and weary land where
        there is no water.
2 So I have looked upon you in the
        sanctuary,
    beholding your power and glory.
3 Because your steadfast love is better
        than life,
    my lips will praise you.
4 So I will bless you as long as I live;
    I will lift up my hands and call on
        your name.

62:1–12 *For God alone my soul waits in silence.* Psalm 62 is a strong call to trust in God alone. Note the repetition in verses 1 and 5. God the rock is far more trustworthy than people, rich or poor, who are "lighter than a breath" (v 9). It even warns those who may be tempted to be self-reliant as they grow prosperous. The Spiritual Discipline of simplicity helps focus attention and reliance on God.

Responding
62:1, 5 SILENCE. Too many times we take the attitude that it is a waste of time to "wait" on the Lord, much less quiet our soul while waiting. But the psalmist waits for

God and quiets his soul, because he recognizes that God fulfills all of his needs and hopes. Consider how waiting on God while quieting our soul changes our perception of God's provision; then set aside ten minutes to try it. What were the results? *See also* Spiritual Disciplines Index.

62:5 SOLITUDE—*See* Spiritual Disciplines Index.
63:1–11 *O God, you are my God.* Psalm 63 calls especially for focused attention on God. When the disciple looks upon God, thinks of him, and meditates on him, his "soul is satisfied as with a rich feast" (v 5).

5 My soul is satisfied as with a rich feast, *a*
  and my mouth praises you with
    joyful lips

6 when I think of you on my bed,
  and meditate on you in the watches
    of the night;

7 for you have been my help,
  and in the shadow of your wings I
    sing for joy.

8 My soul clings to you;
  your right hand upholds me.

9 But those who seek to destroy my life
  shall go down into the depths of the
    earth;

10 they shall be given over to the power of
  the sword,
  they shall be prey for jackals.

11 But the king shall rejoice in God;
  all who swear by him shall exult,
  for the mouths of liars will be
    stopped.

Psalm 64

Prayer for Protection from Enemies

To the leader. A Psalm of David.

1 Hear my voice, O God, in my
    complaint;
  preserve my life from the dread
    enemy.

2 Hide me from the secret plots of the
    wicked,
  from the scheming of evildoers,

3 who whet their tongues like swords,
  who aim bitter words like arrows,

4 shooting from ambush at the blameless;
  they shoot suddenly and without
    fear.

5 They hold fast to their evil purpose;
  they talk of laying snares secretly,
  thinking, "Who can see us? *b*

6   Who can search out our crimes? *c*

We have thought out a cunningly
    conceived plot."
For the human heart and mind are
    deep.

7 But God will shoot his arrow at them;
  they will be wounded suddenly.

8 Because of their tongue he will bring
    them to ruin; *d*
  all who see them will shake with
    horror.

9 Then everyone will fear;
  they will tell what God has brought
    about,
  and ponder what he has done.

10 Let the righteous rejoice in the LORD
  and take refuge in him.
Let all the upright in heart glory.

Psalm 65

Thanksgiving for Earth's Bounty

To the leader. A Psalm of David. A Song.

1 Praise is due to you,
  O God, in Zion;
and to you shall vows be performed,
2   O you who answer prayer!
To you all flesh shall come.
3 When deeds of iniquity overwhelm us,
  you forgive our transgressions.
4 Happy are those whom you choose and
    bring near
  to live in your courts.
We shall be satisfied with the goodness
    of your house,
  your holy temple.

a Heb *with fat and fatness*   *b* Syr: Heb *them*
c Cn: Heb *They search out crimes*   *d* Cn: Heb
*They will bring him to ruin, their tongue being against
them*

63:6 MEDITATION—*See* Spiritual Disciplines
Index.
64:7–10 *they will be wounded suddenly*. The
enemies' boast "Who can see us?" (v 5) makes
the suddenness of God's judgment even more
powerful. All of us should pay attention.

65:1–5 *Praise is due to you*. This hymn praises
God for answering prayer, for forgiveness, and
for deliverance. It is very expansive in noting "all
flesh" (v 2), "all the ends of the earth," and "the
farthest seas" (v 5).
65:2 PRAYER—*See* Spiritual Disciplines Index.

5 By awesome deeds you answer us with
      deliverance,
    O God of our salvation;
  you are the hope of all the ends of the
      earth
      and of the farthest seas.
6 By your*a* strength you established the
      mountains;
    you are girded with might.
7 You silence the roaring of the seas,
    the roaring of their waves,
    the tumult of the peoples.
8 Those who live at earth's farthest
      bounds are awed by your signs;
  you make the gateways of the morning
      and the evening shout for joy.

9 You visit the earth and water it,
    you greatly enrich it;
  the river of God is full of water;
    you provide the people with grain,
    for so you have prepared it.
10 You water its furrows abundantly,
      settling its ridges,
  softening it with showers,
    and blessing its growth.
11 You crown the year with your bounty;
    your wagon tracks overflow with
      richness.
12 The pastures of the wilderness
      overflow,
    the hills gird themselves with joy,
13 the meadows clothe themselves with
      flocks,
    the valleys deck themselves with
      grain,
  they shout and sing together for
      joy.

Psalm 66

Praise for God's Goodness to Israel

To the leader. A Song. A Psalm.

1 Make a joyful noise to God, all the
      earth;
2   sing the glory of his name;
    give to him glorious praise.
3 Say to God, "How awesome are your
      deeds!
  Because of your great power, your
      enemies cringe before you.
4 All the earth worships you;
    they sing praises to you,
    sing praises to your name."   *Selah*

5 Come and see what God has done:
    he is awesome in his deeds among
      mortals.
6 He turned the sea into dry land;
    they passed through the river on foot.
  There we rejoiced in him,
7   who rules by his might forever,
  whose eyes keep watch on the nations—
    let the rebellious not exalt
      themselves.   *Selah*

8 Bless our God, O peoples,
    let the sound of his praise be heard,
9 who has kept us among the living,
    and has not let our feet slip.
10 For you, O God, have tested us;
    you have tried us as silver is tried.
11 You brought us into the net;
    you laid burdens on our backs;
12 you let people ride over our heads;
    we went through fire and through
      water;

a Gk Jerome: Heb *his*

65:6–8 *you established the mountains.* The wide reach continues in recognizing God as Creator, who set up mountains and tamed watery chaos, a common creation theme.

65:9–13 *You visit the earth and water it.* The beautiful images of God's provision must have been even more powerful for Israelite farmers who knew their life itself depended on rain. Hills girded with joy, meadows clothed with flocks, and valleys decked with grain—the images are stunning. How good it is for us to enjoy God's fashion show!

66:1–12 *Make a joyful noise to God.* This thanksgiving song begins with a wide-reaching call to praise, including from "all the earth" and "O peoples." It notes God's action in bringing Israel to Canaan on dry land through the crossing of the sea in Exodus.

yet you have brought us out to a
     spacious place. *a*

13 I will come into your house with burnt
        offerings;
     I will pay you my vows,
14 those that my lips uttered
        and my mouth promised when I was
        in trouble.
15 I will offer to you burnt offerings of
        fatlings,
     with the smoke of the sacrifice of
        rams;
     I will make an offering of bulls and
        goats.   *Selah*

16 Come and hear, all you who fear God,
     and I will tell what he has done for
        me.
17 I cried aloud to him,
     and he was extolled with my tongue.
18 If I had cherished iniquity in my heart,
     the Lord would not have listened.
19 But truly God has listened;
     he has given heed to the words of my
        prayer.

20 Blessed be God,
     because he has not rejected my prayer
     or removed his steadfast love from
        me.

Psalm 67

The Nations Called to Praise God

To the leader: with stringed instruments.
     A Psalm. A Song.

1 May God be gracious to us and bless us

and make his face to shine upon us,
                                      Selah
2 that your way may be known upon
        earth,
     your saving power among all nations.
3 Let the peoples praise you, O God;
     let all the peoples praise you.

4 Let the nations be glad and sing for joy,
     for you judge the peoples with equity
     and guide the nations upon earth.
                                      Selah
5 Let the peoples praise you, O God;
     let all the peoples praise you.

6 The earth has yielded its increase;
     God, our God, has blessed us.
7 May God continue to bless us;
     let all the ends of the earth revere
        him.

Psalm 68

Praise and Thanksgiving

To the leader. Of David. A Psalm. A Song.

1 Let God rise up, let his enemies be
        scattered;
     let those who hate him flee before
        him.
2 As smoke is driven away, so drive them
        away;
     as wax melts before the fire,
     let the wicked perish before God.
3 But let the righteous be joyful;
     let them exult before God;
     let them be jubilant with joy.

a Cn Compare Gk Syr Jerome Tg: Heb *to a
saturation*

66:13–20 *I will tell you what he has done for
me.* In thanksgiving the singer here particularly
declares that God has listened, answered his
prayer, and continued to act in steadfast love.
Telling others of God's goodness toward us is
often part of what it means to thank God.

67:1–7 *May God be gracious to us.* Psalm 67
is a strong call to the nations and peoples to
praise God. Clearly God's particular blessing has
more than narrow effect. God's action includes
but reaches beyond a chosen people.

Responding
67:4 GUIDANCE. We are quick to
acknowledge that God can guide
individuals through things such as circumstances, signs, dreams, visions, and angels, but
we become uneasy when we consider that God
may be able to lead a whole people, and we
become even more uncomfortable when we talk
about the possibility of God's ability to "guide
the nations upon earth." Why do you think this
is so? *See also* Spiritual Disciplines Index.

4 Sing to God, sing praises to his name;
    lift up a song to him who rides upon
        the clouds [a]—
    his name is the Lord—
    be exultant before him.

5 Father of orphans and protector of
        widows
    is God in his holy habitation.
6 God gives the desolate a home to live
        in;
    he leads out the prisoners to
        prosperity,
    but the rebellious live in a parched
        land.

7 O God, when you went out before your
        people,
    when you marched through the
        wilderness,   Selah
8 the earth quaked, the heavens poured
        down rain
    at the presence of God, the God of
        Sinai,
    at the presence of God, the God of
        Israel.
9 Rain in abundance, O God, you
        showered abroad;
    you restored your heritage when it
        languished;
10 your flock found a dwelling in it;
    in your goodness, O God, you
        provided for the needy.

11 The Lord gives the command;
    great is the company of those [b] who
        bore the tidings:
12   "The kings of the armies, they flee,
        they flee!"
    The women at home divide the spoil,
13   though they stay among the
        sheepfolds—
    the wings of a dove covered with silver,
        its pinions with green gold.

14 When the Almighty [c] scattered kings
        there,
    snow fell on Zalmon.

15 O mighty mountain, mountain of
        Bashan;
    O many-peaked mountain, mountain
        of Bashan!
16 Why do you look with envy, O many-
        peaked mountain,
    at the mount that God desired for his
        abode,
    where the Lord will reside forever?
17 With mighty chariotry, twice ten
        thousand,
    thousands upon thousands,
    the Lord came from Sinai into the
        holy place. [d]
18 You ascended the high mount,
    leading captives in your train
    and receiving gifts from people,
    even from those who rebel against the
        Lord God's abiding there.
19 Blessed be the Lord,
    who daily bears us up;
    God is our salvation.   Selah
20 Our God is a God of salvation,
    and to God, the Lord, belongs escape
        from death.

21 But God will shatter the heads of his
        enemies,
    the hairy crown of those who walk in
        their guilty ways.
22 The Lord said,
    "I will bring them back from Bashan,
    I will bring them back from the depths
        of the sea,

a Or cast up a highway for him who rides through the
deserts   b Or company of the women
c Traditional rendering of Heb Shaddai
d Cn: Heb The Lord among them Sinai in the holy
(place)

68:7–20 *the earth quaked, the heavens poured
down rain.* This passage recalls how nature itself
blanched at God's marching in victory in the
exodus. It also questions Mt. Bashan (location
unknown) for envying God's choice of Zion as

the center of his rule.
68:24–27 *the singers in front.* The tribes of
Israel process with singers and musicians to
praise God, much like the liturgical processions
in churches today.

23 so that you may bathe[a] your feet in
      blood,
      so that the tongues of your dogs may
         have their share from the foe."

24 Your solemn processions are seen,[b]
      O God,
      the processions of my God, my King,
         into the sanctuary—
25 the singers in front, the musicians last,
      between them girls playing
         tambourines:
26 "Bless God in the great congregation,
      the LORD, O you who are of Israel's
         fountain!"
27 There is Benjamin, the least of them, in
      the lead,
      the princes of Judah in a body,
      the princes of Zebulun, the princes of
         Naphtali.

28 Summon your might, O God;
      show your strength, O God, as you
         have done for us before.
29 Because of your temple at Jerusalem
      kings bear gifts to you.
30 Rebuke the wild animals that live
      among the reeds,
      the herd of bulls with the calves of
         the peoples.
      Trample[c] under foot those who lust
         after tribute;
      scatter the peoples who delight in
         war.[d]
31 Let bronze be brought from Egypt;
      let Ethiopia[e] hasten to stretch out its
         hands to God.

32 Sing to God, O kingdoms of the earth;
      sing praises to the Lord,   Selah
33 O rider in the heavens, the ancient
         heavens;

listen, he sends out his voice, his
      mighty voice.
34 Ascribe power to God,
      whose majesty is over Israel;
      and whose power is in the skies.
35 Awesome is God in his[f] sanctuary,
      the God of Israel;
      he gives power and strength to his
         people.

Blessed be God!

Psalm 69

Prayer for Deliverance from Persecution

To the leader: according to Lilies. Of David.

1 Save me, O God,
      for the waters have come up to my
         neck.
2 I sink in deep mire,
      where there is no foothold;
   I have come into deep waters,
      and the flood sweeps over me.
3 I am weary with my crying;
      my throat is parched.
   My eyes grow dim
      with waiting for my God.

4 More in number than the hairs of my
         head
      are those who hate me without cause;
   many are those who would destroy me,
      my enemies who accuse me falsely.
   What I did not steal
      must I now restore?
5 O God, you know my folly;

a Gk Syr Tg: Heb *shatter*   b Or *have been seen*
c Cn: Heb *Trampling*   d Meaning of Heb of verse
30 is uncertain   e Or *Nubia*; Heb *Cush*
f Gk: Heb *from your*

68:33 *O rider in the heavens.* The application
of this phrase (echoing v 4) to God supersedes
any claim that Canaanite gods may lay to such
title and is one of several ways of pointing to
Yahweh unrivaled.

69:1–3, 13–15 *the waters have come up to my
neck.* In Hebrew thought, sinking into the mire
and coming into deep waters signal moving on

down toward Sheol, the Pit. The singer is in real
trouble.

69:6–12, 19–21 *do not let those who seek you
be dishonored because of me.* Here the psalmist's
faithfulness is misinterpreted and resisted. He
prays that this will not bring shame to others
who trust in God.

the wrongs I have done are not
   hidden from you.

6 Do not let those who hope in you be
      put to shame because of me,
   O Lord GOD of hosts;
do not let those who seek you be
      dishonored because of me,
   O God of Israel.
7 It is for your sake that I have borne
      reproach,
   that shame has covered my face.
8 I have become a stranger to my kindred,
   an alien to my mother's children.

9 It is zeal for your house that has
      consumed me;
   the insults of those who insult you
      have fallen on me.
10 When I humbled my soul with fasting,[a]
   they insulted me for doing so.
11 When I made sackcloth my clothing,
   I became a byword to them.
12 I am the subject of gossip for those who
      sit in the gate,
   and the drunkards make songs about
      me.

13 But as for me, my prayer is to you,
      O LORD.
   At an acceptable time, O God,
   in the abundance of your steadfast
      love, answer me.
With your faithful help 14rescue me
   from sinking in the mire;
   let me be delivered from my enemies
      and from the deep waters.
15 Do not let the flood sweep over me,
   or the deep swallow me up,
   or the Pit close its mouth over me.

16 Answer me, O LORD, for your steadfast
      love is good;
   according to your abundant mercy,
      turn to me.

17 Do not hide your face from your
      servant,
   for I am in distress—make haste to
      answer me.
18 Draw near to me, redeem me,
   set me free because of my enemies.

19 You know the insults I receive,
   and my shame and dishonor;
   my foes are all known to you.
20 Insults have broken my heart,
   so that I am in despair.
I looked for pity, but there was none;
   and for comforters, but I found none.
21 They gave me poison for food,
   and for my thirst they gave me
      vinegar to drink.

22 Let their table be a trap for them,
   a snare for their allies.
23 Let their eyes be darkened so that they
      cannot see,
   and make their loins tremble
      continually.
24 Pour out your indignation upon them,
   and let your burning anger overtake
      them.
25 May their camp be a desolation;
   let no one live in their tents.
26 For they persecute those whom you
      have struck down,
   and those whom you have wounded,
      they attack still more.[b]
27 Add guilt to their guilt;
   may they have no acquittal from you.
28 Let them be blotted out of the book of
      the living;
   let them not be enrolled among the
      righteous.
29 But I am lowly and in pain;
   let your salvation, O God, protect me.

a Gk Syr: Heb I wept, with fasting my soul, or I made
my soul mourn with fasting   b Gk Syr: Heb recount
the pain of

69:10 FASTING—*See* Spiritual Disciplines
Index.
   69:13 PRAYER—*See* Spiritual Disciplines
Index.
   69:30–36 *This will please the LORD more.* The

singer's glad praise and thanksgiving are even
more pleasing to God than sacrifices of oxen or
bulls (v 31). Praising God may give courage to
the needy who are also troubled by doubt (vv
32–33).

30 I will praise the name of God with a
        song;
    I will magnify him with
        thanksgiving.
31 This will please the LORD more than an
        ox
    or a bull with horns and hoofs.
32 Let the oppressed see it and be glad;
    you who seek God, let your hearts
        revive.
33 For the LORD hears the needy,
    and does not despise his own that are
        in bonds.

34 Let heaven and earth praise him,
    the seas and everything that moves in
        them.
35 For God will save Zion
    and rebuild the cities of Judah;
and his servants shall live*a* there and
        possess it;
36   the children of his servants shall
        inherit it,
    and those who love his name shall
        live in it.

Psalm 70

Prayer for Deliverance from Enemies

To the leader. Of David, for the memorial
offering.

1 Be pleased, O God, to deliver me.
    O LORD, make haste to help me!
2 Let those be put to shame and
        confusion
    who seek my life.
Let those be turned back and brought to
        dishonor
    who desire to hurt me.
3 Let those who say, "Aha, Aha!"
    turn back because of their shame.

4 Let all who seek you

rejoice and be glad in you.
Let those who love your salvation
    say evermore, "God is great!"
5 But I am poor and needy;
    hasten to me, O God!
You are my help and my deliverer;
    O LORD, do not delay!

Psalm 71

Prayer for Lifelong Protection and Help

1 In you, O LORD, I take refuge;
    let me never be put to shame.
2 In your righteousness deliver me and
        rescue me;
    incline your ear to me and save me.
3 Be to me a rock of refuge,
    a strong fortress,*b* to save me,
    for you are my rock and my fortress.

4 Rescue me, O my God, from the hand of
        the wicked,
    from the grasp of the unjust and cruel.
5 For you, O Lord, are my hope,
    my trust, O LORD, from my youth.
6 Upon you I have leaned from my birth;
    it was you who took me from my
        mother's womb.
My praise is continually of you.

7 I have been like a portent to many,
    but you are my strong refuge.
8 My mouth is filled with your praise,
    and with your glory all day long.
9 Do not cast me off in the time of old
        age;
    do not forsake me when my strength
        is spent.
10 For my enemies speak concerning me,
    and those who watch for my life
        consult together.

a Syr: Heb *and they shall live*   b Gk Compare
31.3: Heb *to come continually you have commanded*

71:1–24 *In you, O LORD, I take refuge.* The
context suggests that an aging person brings
this call for God's help. He has a history of
relying on God, from birth (v 6) to now in old
age (v 9). "So even to old age and gray hairs,
O God, do not forsake me" (v 18). A lifelong
memory of God's faithfulness helps the singer
rely on God in today's distress (vv 19–20). This
is a fitting prayer for folks who know that "old
age is not for sissies." The song is also filled
with promises to praise God for continued
faithfulness.

11 They say, "Pursue and seize that person
    whom God has forsaken,
    for there is no one to deliver."

12 O God, do not be far from me;
    O my God, make haste to help me!
13 Let my accusers be put to shame and
        consumed;
    let those who seek to hurt me
    be covered with scorn and disgrace.
14 But I will hope continually,
    and will praise you yet more and
        more.
15 My mouth will tell of your righteous
        acts,
    of your deeds of salvation all day
        long,
    though their number is past my
        knowledge.
16 I will come praising the mighty deeds of
        the Lord GOD,
    I will praise your righteousness, yours
        alone.

17 O God, from my youth you have taught
        me,
    and I still proclaim your wondrous
        deeds.
18 So even to old age and gray hairs,
    O God, do not forsake me,
    until I proclaim your might
    to all the generations to come.ᵃ
    Your power ¹⁹and your righteousness,
        O God,
    reach the high heavens.

    You who have done great things,
    O God, who is like you?
20 You who have made me see many
        troubles and calamities
    will revive me again;
    from the depths of the earth
        you will bring me up again.
21 You will increase my honor,
    and comfort me once again.

22 I will also praise you with the harp
    for your faithfulness, O my God;
    I will sing praises to you with the lyre,
    O Holy One of Israel.
23 My lips will shout for joy
    when I sing praises to you;
    my soul also, which you have rescued.
24 All day long my tongue will talk of your
        righteous help,
    for those who tried to do me harm
    have been put to shame, and disgraced.

Psalm 72

Prayer for Guidance and Support for the King

Of Solomon.

1 Give the king your justice, O God,
    and your righteousness to a king's son.
2 May he judge your people with
        righteousness,
    and your poor with justice.
3 May the mountains yield prosperity for
        the people,
    and the hills, in righteousness.
4 May he defend the cause of the poor of
        the people,
    give deliverance to the needy,
    and crush the oppressor.

5 May he live ᵇ while the sun endures,
    and as long as the moon, throughout
        all generations.
6 May he be like rain that falls on the
        mown grass,
    like showers that water the earth.
7 In his days may righteousness flourish
    and peace abound, until the moon is
        no more.

8 May he have dominion from sea to sea,
    and from the River to the ends of the
        earth.

a Gk Compare Syr: Heb *to a generation, to all that
come*   b Gk: Heb *may they fear you*

72:1–17 *Give the king your justice.* This royal
psalm asks for God's blessing on the king and
empowerment to bring genuinely just rule, the
nature of which is particularly noted in verses
5–7 and 12–14.

9 May his foes[a] bow down before him,
    and his enemies lick the dust.
10 May the kings of Tarshish and of the
    isles
    render him tribute,
    may the kings of Sheba and Seba
    bring gifts.
11 May all kings fall down before him,
    all nations give him service.

12 For he delivers the needy when they
    call,
    the poor and those who have no
    helper.
13 He has pity on the weak and the needy,
    and saves the lives of the needy.
14 From oppression and violence he
    redeems their life;
    and precious is their blood in his
    sight.

15 Long may he live!
    May gold of Sheba be given to him.
    May prayer be made for him
    continually,
    and blessings invoked for him all day
    long.
16 May there be abundance of grain in the
    land;
    may it wave on the tops of the
    mountains;
    may its fruit be like Lebanon;
    and may people blossom in the cities
    like the grass of the field.
17 May his name endure forever,
    his fame continue as long as the sun.
    May all nations be blessed in him;[b]
    may they pronounce him happy.

18 Blessed be the LORD, the God of Israel,
    who alone does wondrous things.

19 Blessed be his glorious name forever;
    may his glory fill the whole earth.
    Amen and Amen.

20 The prayers of David son of Jesse are
    ended.

BOOK III

(Psalms 73–89)

Psalm 73

Plea for Relief from Oppressors

A Psalm of Asaph.

1 Truly God is good to the upright,[c]
    to those who are pure in heart.
2 But as for me, my feet had almost
    stumbled;
    my steps had nearly slipped.
3 For I was envious of the arrogant;
    I saw the prosperity of the wicked.

4 For they have no pain;
    their bodies are sound and sleek.
5 They are not in trouble as others are;
    they are not plagued like other
    people.
6 Therefore pride is their necklace;
    violence covers them like a garment.
7 Their eyes swell out with fatness;
    their hearts overflow with follies.
8 They scoff and speak with malice;
    loftily they threaten oppression.
9 They set their mouths against heaven,
    and their tongues range over the
    earth.

a Cn: Heb *those who live in the wilderness*
b Or *bless themselves by him*   c Or *good to Israel*

72:15 PRAYER—*See* Spiritual Disciplines Index.

72:8–11, 15–17 *May he have dominion from sea to sea.* Here the song includes a grand, wide view of how the king's power and blessing will extend to the nations. This is an extension of the blessings God intends for the peoples of the world (going back to Abraham) through the people of Israel.

72:18–20 *Blessed be the LORD.* A doxology and notes mark the end of the second book in the Psalms.

73:1–14 *All in vain I have kept my heart clean.* Here the singer explores the question of why good things happen to bad people. After all, he's been good, but struggles, while the bad guys prosper.

10 Therefore the people turn and praise
    them, *a*
    and find no fault in them. *b*
11 And they say, "How can God know?
    Is there knowledge in the Most High?"
12 Such are the wicked;
    always at ease, they increase in riches.
13 All in vain I have kept my heart clean
    and washed my hands in innocence.
14 For all day long I have been plagued,
    and am punished every morning.

15 If I had said, "I will talk on in this way,"
    I would have been untrue to the circle
    of your children.
16 But when I thought how to understand
    this,
    it seemed to me a wearisome task,
17 until I went into the sanctuary of God;
    then I perceived their end.
18 Truly you set them in slippery places;
    you make them fall to ruin.
19 How they are destroyed in a moment,
    swept away utterly by terrors!
20 They are *c* like a dream when one awakes;
    on awaking you despise their
    phantoms.

21 When my soul was embittered,
    when I was pricked in heart,
22 I was stupid and ignorant;
    I was like a brute beast toward you.
23 Nevertheless I am continually with you;
    you hold my right hand.
24 You guide me with your counsel,
    and afterward you will receive me
    with honor. *d*
25 Whom have I in heaven but you?
    And there is nothing on earth that I
    desire other than you.
26 My flesh and my heart may fail,
    but God is the strength *e* of my heart
    and my portion forever.

27 Indeed, those who are far from you will
    perish;
    you put an end to those who are false
    to you.
28 But for me it is good to be near God;
    I have made the Lord GOD my refuge,
    to tell of all your works.

Psalm 74

Plea for Help in Time of National Humiliation

A Maskil of Asaph.

1 O God, why do you cast us off forever?
    Why does your anger smoke against
    the sheep of your pasture?
2 Remember your congregation, which
    you acquired long ago,
    which you redeemed to be the tribe of
    your heritage.
    Remember Mount Zion, where you
    came to dwell.
3 Direct your steps to the perpetual ruins;
    the enemy has destroyed everything
    in the sanctuary.

4 Your foes have roared within your holy
    place;
    they set up their emblems there.
5 At the upper entrance they hacked
    the wooden trellis with axes. *f*
6 And then, with hatchets and hammers,
    they smashed all its carved work.
7 They set your sanctuary on fire;
    they desecrated the dwelling place of
    your name,
    bringing it to the ground.

a Cn: Heb *his people return here*   *b* Cn: Heb
abundant waters are drained by them   *c* Cn: Heb
Lord   *d* Or *to glory*   *e* Heb *rock*
f Cn Compare Gk Syr: Meaning of Heb uncertain

73:15–28 *my soul was embittered.* The singer
catches himself in this bitter attitude and sees it
as dangerous. The evil will be treated justly. As
for himself, he comes to declare loyalty in
stirring affirmations (vv 25–26).

73:24 GUIDANCE—*See* Spiritual Disciplines
Index.

74:1–23 *O God, why do you cast us off
forever?* The community cries out for God's
help, apparently with Jerusalem sitting in ruins.
Mt. Zion, God's "dwelling place," now lies
devastated. The concluding verses appeal to
God to act against the "uproar of [his]
adversaries" (vv 20–23).

8 They said to themselves, "We will
        utterly subdue them";
    they burned all the meeting places of
        God in the land.

9 We do not see our emblems;
    there is no longer any prophet,
    and there is no one among us who
        knows how long.

10 How long, O God, is the foe to scoff?
    Is the enemy to revile your name
        forever?

11 Why do you hold back your hand;
    why do you keep your hand in[a] your
        bosom?

12 Yet God my King is from of old,
    working salvation in the earth.

13 You divided the sea by your might;
    you broke the heads of the dragons in
        the waters.

14 You crushed the heads of Leviathan;
    you gave him as food[b] for the
        creatures of the wilderness.

15 You cut openings for springs and
        torrents;
    you dried up ever-flowing streams.

16 Yours is the day, yours also the night;
    you established the luminaries[c] and
        the sun.

17 You have fixed all the bounds of the
        earth;
    you made summer and winter.

18 Remember this, O LORD, how the enemy
        scoffs,
    and an impious people reviles your
        name.

19 Do not deliver the soul of your dove to
        the wild animals;
    do not forget the life of your poor
        forever.

20 Have regard for your[d] covenant,
    for the dark places of the land are full
        of the haunts of violence.

21 Do not let the downtrodden be put to
        shame;
    let the poor and needy praise your
        name.

22 Rise up, O God, plead your cause;
    remember how the impious scoff at
        you all day long.

23 Do not forget the clamor of your foes,
    the uproar of your adversaries that
        goes up continually.

Psalm 75

Thanksgiving for God's Wondrous Deeds

To the leader: Do Not Destroy. A Psalm of
Asaph. A Song.

1 We give thanks to you, O God;
    we give thanks; your name is near.
    People tell of your wondrous deeds.

2 At the set time that I appoint
    I will judge with equity.

3 When the earth totters, with all its
        inhabitants,
    it is I who keep its pillars steady. *Selah*

4 I say to the boastful, "Do not boast,"
    and to the wicked, "Do not lift up
        your horn;

5 do not lift up your horn on high,
    or speak with insolent neck."

6 For not from the east or from the west
    and not from the wilderness comes
        lifting up;

7 but it is God who executes judgment,

a Cn: Heb *do you consume your right hand from*
b Heb *food for the people*   c Or *moon*; Heb *light*
d Gk Syr: Heb *the*

74:9–11 *there is no longer any prophet.* The
hiddenness of God's presence and purpose adds
to the pain and confusion.

74:12–17 *Yet God my King is from of old,
working salvation in the earth.* These verses
recall the power of God as Creator and as
fully capable of salvation. The reference to
"Leviathan" (v 14) is a poetic reference to God's
overcoming in creation the powers of chaos
represented allegorically by sea monsters, here
Leviathan. Note also 104:26, where Leviathan is
not a threat, but a pet.

75:2–5, 10 *I will judge with equity.* The
promise of judgment comes in the voice of God,
probably through a prophet or priest leading in
worship.

putting down one and lifting up
another.

8 For in the hand of the LORD there is a
cup
with foaming wine, well mixed;
he will pour a draught from it,
and all the wicked of the earth
shall drain it down to the dregs.

9 But I will rejoice[a] forever;
I will sing praises to the God of Jacob.

10 All the horns of the wicked I will cut off,
but the horns of the righteous shall
be exalted.

Psalm 76

Israel's God—Judge of All the Earth

*To the leader: with stringed instruments.
A Psalm of Asaph. A Song.*

1 In Judah God is known,
his name is great in Israel.
2 His abode has been established in
Salem,
his dwelling place in Zion.
3 There he broke the flashing arrows,
the shield, the sword, and the
weapons of war.   *Selah*

4 Glorious are you, more majestic
than the everlasting mountains.[b]
5 The stouthearted were stripped of their
spoil;
they sank into sleep;
none of the troops
was able to lift a hand.
6 At your rebuke, O God of Jacob,
both rider and horse lay stunned.

7 But you indeed are awesome!
Who can stand before you
when once your anger is roused?
8 From the heavens you uttered
judgment;
the earth feared and was still
9 when God rose up to establish judgment,
to save all the oppressed of the earth.
Selah

10 Human wrath serves only to praise you,
when you bind the last bit of your[c]
wrath around you.
11 Make vows to the LORD your God, and
perform them;
let all who are around him bring gifts
to the one who is awesome,
12 who cuts off the spirit of princes,
who inspires fear in the kings of the
earth.

Psalm 77

God's Mighty Deeds Recalled

*To the leader: according to Jeduthun.
Of Asaph. A Psalm.*

1 I cry aloud to God,
aloud to God, that he may hear me.
2 In the day of my trouble I seek the Lord;
in the night my hand is stretched out
without wearying;
my soul refuses to be comforted.
3 I think of God, and I moan;
I meditate, and my spirit faints.   *Selah*

4 You keep my eyelids from closing;
I am so troubled that I cannot speak.

a Gk: Heb *declare*   *b* Gk: Heb *the mountains of
prey*   *c* Heb lacks *your*

75:6–9 *For in the hand of the LORD there is a
cup.* God forces the wicked to drink to the dregs
a frothy draught that brings about the sure
justice of God (cf. Isa 51:17; Jer 25:15–16; Hab
2:16).

76:1–12 *In Judah, God is known.* This song of
Zion accords even greater attention to its most
glorious Inhabitant. Dwelling in Zion (or Salem,
an even older name for Jerusalem), God makes it
secure. God breaks the weapons of those who

attack it, puts them into a deep sleep, and even
stuns horse and rider. Again, this is a universal
reign, intending in part to "save all the oppressed
of the earth" (v 9). The song reminds us forcefully
of the power and good purposes of God's rule.

77:1–10 *I think of God, and I moan.* The stark
words here portray the deep anguish of the
singer. Moaning at the thought of God (v 3) and
wondering if God's steadfast love has ceased
forever (v 8) are apt examples of this darkness.

5 I consider the days of old,
    and remember the years of long ago.
6 I commune*a* with my heart in the
    night;
    I meditate and search my spirit:*b*
7 "Will the Lord spurn forever,
    and never again be favorable?
8 Has his steadfast love ceased forever?
    Are his promises at an end for all
    time?
9 Has God forgotten to be gracious?
    Has he in anger shut up his
    compassion?"   *Selah*
10 And I say, "It is my grief
    that the right hand of the Most High
    has changed."

11 I will call to mind the deeds of the LORD;
    I will remember your wonders of old.
12 I will meditate on all your work,
    and muse on your mighty deeds.
13 Your way, O God, is holy.
    What god is so great as our God?
14 You are the God who works wonders;
    you have displayed your might
    among the peoples.
15 With your strong arm you redeemed
    your people,
    the descendants of Jacob and Joseph.
                                        Selah

16 When the waters saw you, O God,

when the waters saw you, they were
    afraid;
    the very deep trembled.
17 The clouds poured out water;
    the skies thundered;
    your arrows flashed on every side.
18 The crash of your thunder was in the
    whirlwind;
    your lightnings lit up the world;
    the earth trembled and shook.
19 Your way was through the sea,
    your path, through the mighty
    waters;
    yet your footprints were unseen.
20 You led your people like a flock
    by the hand of Moses and Aaron.

Psalm 78

God's Goodness and Israel's Ingratitude

A Maskil of Asaph.

1 Give ear, O my people, to my teaching;
    incline your ears to the words of my
    mouth.
2 I will open my mouth in a parable;
    I will utter dark sayings from of old,
3 things that we have heard and known,
    that our ancestors have told us.
4 We will not hide them from their
    children;

a Gk Syr: Heb *My music*   *b* Syr Jerome: Heb *my spirit searches*

77:6 MEDITATION—*See* Spiritual Disciplines Index.

77:11–20 *I will call to mind the deeds of the LORD.* This hymn follows directly after the anguished words. The singer proposes to remember God's acts of deliverance and, in particular, to "meditate" and "muse" on them (v 12). The dramatic report of God's victory that follows would be stirring for us to ponder as we seek to recover hope in our dangerous world.

Responding
77:12 MEDITATION. In verse 6 the singer is meditating and searching his spirit in an effort to find the reasons for his misfortune. Now in this verse he is meditating on all of God's work and musing on his mighty

deeds. It seems the singer was suffering from grief about his situation and the recitation of God's deeds was a way to overcome it. Try to describe a time when your soul was bowed down from grief. If you tried meditating on God and his deeds during that time, what effect did it have on your soul? If you didn't meditate on them then, try to remember to do so the next time your soul is weary. *See also* Spiritual Disciplines Index.

78:1–8 *I will utter dark sayings from of old.* The opening verses of this historical psalm (cf. Pss 105; 106; 136) tell why God's action and the people's response should be retold—the next generation should know of them so that they will know how to respond wisely.

we will tell to the coming generation
    the glorious deeds of the LORD, and his
        might,
    and the wonders that he has done.

5 He established a decree in Jacob,
    and appointed a law in Israel,
which he commanded our ancestors
    to teach to their children;
6 that the next generation might know
        them,
    the children yet unborn,
and rise up and tell them to their
        children,
7   so that they should set their hope in
        God,
    and not forget the works of God,
        but keep his commandments;
8 and that they should not be like their
        ancestors,
    a stubborn and rebellious generation,
a generation whose heart was not
        steadfast,
    whose spirit was not faithful to God.

9 The Ephraimites, armed with *a* the bow,
    turned back on the day of battle.
10 They did not keep God's covenant,
    but refused to walk according to his
        law.
11 They forgot what he had done,
    and the miracles that he had shown
        them.
12 In the sight of their ancestors he worked
        marvels
    in the land of Egypt, in the fields of
        Zoan.
13 He divided the sea and let them pass
        through it,
    and made the waters stand like a
        heap.

14 In the daytime he led them with a
        cloud,
    and all night long with a fiery light.
15 He split rocks open in the wilderness,
    and gave them drink abundantly as
        from the deep.
16 He made streams come out of the rock,
    and caused waters to flow down like
        rivers.

17 Yet they sinned still more against him,
    rebelling against the Most High in the
        desert.
18 They tested God in their heart
    by demanding the food they craved.
19 They spoke against God, saying,
    "Can God spread a table in the
        wilderness?
20 Even though he struck the rock so that
        water gushed out
    and torrents overflowed,
can he also give bread,
    or provide meat for his people?"

21 Therefore, when the LORD heard, he was
        full of rage;
    a fire was kindled against Jacob,
    his anger mounted against Israel,
22 because they had no faith in God,
    and did not trust his saving power.
23 Yet he commanded the skies above,
    and opened the doors of heaven;
24 he rained down on them manna to eat,
    and gave them the grain of heaven.
25 Mortals ate of the bread of angels;
    he sent them food in abundance.
26 He caused the east wind to blow in the
        heavens,

---

a Heb *armed with shooting*

78:9-66 *They did not keep God's covenant.*
The stories are told for a variety of purposes—
here as a cautionary tale against rebelling
against God's goodness. God acted in wondrous
power, but the people "forgot what God had
done" (v 11), they spoke against God (v 19),
they did not trust God (v 22), they were dishonest with God (v 36), and they were not
true to the covenant of God (v 37). The story

becomes a history of rebellion and should
remind us not to scoff at or presume grace.
    78:9-10, 67-72 *he rejected the tent of Joseph.*
The psalm also moves to the rejection of the
leadership of the Northern tribes (the tribes of
Joseph, made up of those named after his sons,
Ephraim and Manasseh, anticipated in v 9, "the
Ephraimites"), in favor of the Southern tribe of
Judah and God's "servant David."

and by his power he led out the south
wind;

27 he rained flesh upon them like dust,
winged birds like the sand of the seas;

28 he let them fall within their camp,
all around their dwellings.

29 And they ate and were well filled,
for he gave them what they craved.

30 But before they had satisfied their
craving,
while the food was still in their
mouths,

31 the anger of God rose against them
and he killed the strongest of them,
and laid low the flower of Israel.

32 In spite of all this they still sinned;
they did not believe in his wonders.

33 So he made their days vanish like a
breath,
and their years in terror.

34 When he killed them, they sought for
him;
they repented and sought God
earnestly.

35 They remembered that God was their
rock,
the Most High God their redeemer.

36 But they flattered him with their
mouths;
they lied to him with their tongues.

37 Their heart was not steadfast toward
him;
they were not true to his covenant.

38 Yet he, being compassionate,
forgave their iniquity,
and did not destroy them;
often he restrained his anger,
and did not stir up all his wrath.

39 He remembered that they were but
flesh,
a wind that passes and does not come
again.

40 How often they rebelled against him in
the wilderness
and grieved him in the desert!

41 They tested God again and again,
and provoked the Holy One of Israel.

42 They did not keep in mind his power,
or the day when he redeemed them
from the foe;

43 when he displayed his signs in Egypt,
and his miracles in the fields of Zoan.

44 He turned their rivers to blood,
so that they could not drink of their
streams.

45 He sent among them swarms of flies,
which devoured them,
and frogs, which destroyed them.

46 He gave their crops to the caterpillar,
and the fruit of their labor to the
locust.

47 He destroyed their vines with hail,
and their sycamores with frost.

48 He gave over their cattle to the hail,
and their flocks to thunderbolts.

49 He let loose on them his fierce anger,
wrath, indignation, and distress,
a company of destroying angels.

50 He made a path for his anger;
he did not spare them from death,
but gave their lives over to the plague.

51 He struck all the firstborn in Egypt,
the first issue of their strength in the
tents of Ham.

52 Then he led out his people like sheep,
and guided them in the wilderness
like a flock.

53 He led them in safety, so that they were
not afraid;
but the sea overwhelmed their
enemies.

54 And he brought them to his holy hill,
to the mountain that his right hand
had won.

55 He drove out nations before them;
he apportioned them for a possession
and settled the tribes of Israel in their
tents.

56 Yet they tested the Most High God,
and rebelled against him.
They did not observe his decrees,

57 but turned away and were faithless like
their ancestors;
they twisted like a treacherous bow.

58 For they provoked him to anger with
their high places;
they moved him to jealousy with
their idols.

59 When God heard, he was full of wrath,
and he utterly rejected Israel.

60 He abandoned his dwelling at Shiloh,
　　the tent where he dwelt among
　　　mortals,
61 and delivered his power to captivity,
　　his glory to the hand of the foe.
62 He gave his people to the sword,
　　and vented his wrath on his
　　　heritage.
63 Fire devoured their young men,
　　and their girls had no marriage
　　　song.
64 Their priests fell by the sword,
　　and their widows made no
　　　lamentation.
65 Then the Lord awoke as from sleep,
　　like a warrior shouting because of
　　　wine.
66 He put his adversaries to rout;
　　he put them to everlasting
　　　disgrace.

67 He rejected the tent of Joseph,
　　he did not choose the tribe of
　　　Ephraim;
68 but he chose the tribe of Judah,
　　Mount Zion, which he loves.
69 He built his sanctuary like the high
　　　heavens,
　　like the earth, which he has founded
　　　forever.
70 He chose his servant David,
　　and took him from the sheepfolds;
71 from tending the nursing ewes he
　　　brought him
　　to be the shepherd of his people
　　　Jacob,
　　of Israel, his inheritance.
72 With upright heart he tended them,
　　and guided them with skillful hand.

Psalm 79

Plea for Mercy for Jerusalem

A Psalm of Asaph.

1 O God, the nations have come into
　　your inheritance;
　　they have defiled your holy temple;
　　they have laid Jerusalem in ruins.
2 They have given the bodies of your
　　　servants
　　to the birds of the air for food,
　　the flesh of your faithful to the wild
　　　animals of the earth.
3 They have poured out their blood like
　　　water
　　all around Jerusalem,
　　and there was no one to bury them.
4 We have become a taunt to our
　　　neighbors,
　　mocked and derided by those around
　　　us.

5 How long, O Lord? Will you be angry
　　forever?
　　Will your jealous wrath burn like fire?
6 Pour out your anger on the nations
　　that do not know you,
　　and on the kingdoms
　　that do not call on your name.
7 For they have devoured Jacob
　　and laid waste his habitation.

8 Do not remember against us the
　　　iniquities of our ancestors;
　　let your compassion come speedily to
　　　meet us,
　　for we are brought very low.
9 Help us, O God of our salvation,
　　for the glory of your name;
　　deliver us, and forgive our sins,
　　for your name's sake.

79:1–13 *O God, the nations have come into your inheritance.* The community prays for God's help, apparently in the aftermath of the terrible destruction of Jerusalem and its people in 587/586 BC. The loss was so overwhelming that no one was left to bury the dead (vv 2–3), a proverbial tragedy, but also quite literal. The people had lost everything—their nation, their Davidic king, their Temple, their glorious capital city, maybe even their covenant with God (see Lam 5:19–22). On top of these losses, their neighbors pillaged and taunted them.

79:5–13 *deliver us . . . for your name's sake.* The people's appeals for God's help may not be entirely out of self-interest. God's action to deliver, to show compassion, to act against the

10 Why should the nations say,
    "Where is their God?"
  Let the avenging of the outpoured
    blood of your servants
    be known among the nations before
    our eyes.

11 Let the groans of the prisoners come
    before you;
    according to your great power
    preserve those doomed to die.

12 Return sevenfold into the bosom of our
    neighbors
    the taunts with which they taunted
    you, O Lord!

13 Then we your people, the flock of your
    pasture,
    will give thanks to you forever;
    from generation to generation we will
    recount your praise.

Psalm 80

Prayer for Israel's Restoration

To the leader: on Lilies, a Covenant.
Of Asaph. A Psalm.

1 Give ear, O Shepherd of Israel,
    you who lead Joseph like a flock!
  You who are enthroned upon the
    cherubim, shine forth
2   before Ephraim and Benjamin and
    Manasseh.
  Stir up your might,
    and come to save us!

3 Restore us, O God;
    let your face shine, that we may be
    saved.

4 O Lord God of hosts,
    how long will you be angry with your
    people's prayers?

5 You have fed them with the bread of
    tears,
    and given them tears to drink in full
    measure.

6 You make us the scorn[a] of our
    neighbors;
    our enemies laugh among themselves.

7 Restore us, O God of hosts;
    let your face shine, that we may be
    saved.

8 You brought a vine out of Egypt;
    you drove out the nations and
    planted it.

9 You cleared the ground for it;
    it took deep root and filled the land.

10 The mountains were covered with its
    shade,
    the mighty cedars with its branches;

11 it sent out its branches to the sea,
    and its shoots to the River.

12 Why then have you broken down its
    walls,
    so that all who pass along the way
    pluck its fruit?

13 The boar from the forest ravages it,
    and all that move in the field feed on it.

14 Turn again, O God of hosts;
    look down from heaven, and see;
    have regard for this vine,

15   the stock that your right hand
    planted.[b]

a Syr: Heb strife   b Heb adds from verse 17 and
upon the one whom you made strong for yourself

---

oppressors will be "for the glory of [God's]
name." The nations have also taunted God
(vv 10, 12). In this devastating situation, it is
instructive for us to consider both their anguish
("How long, O Lord?") and their anticipation of
again praising God (v 13).

80:3, 7, 19 *Restore us, . . . let your face shine,
that we may be saved.* The psalm repeats this
powerful refrain. Often God's shining "glory"
shows in God's deliverance and presence among

his people. It also recalls the blessing of Num
6:25: "The Lord make his face to shine upon
you, and be gracious to you."

80:8–18 *You brought a vine out of Egypt.* The
psalm uses the powerful metaphor of a well-
tended vineyard that prospers (noting the
extent of the borders of Solomon's kingdom, the
Mediterranean to the Euphrates, v 11), but then
fails (cf. "The Song of the Vineyard" in Isa
5:1–10).

16 They have burned it with fire, they have
   cut it down; [a]
      may they perish at the rebuke of your
      countenance.
17 But let your hand be upon the one at
   your right hand,
      the one whom you made strong for
      yourself.
18 Then we will never turn back from
   you;
      give us life, and we will call on your
      name.

19 Restore us, O LORD God of hosts;
      let your face shine, that we may be
      saved.

Psalm 81

God's Appeal to Stubborn Israel

To the leader: according to The Gittith.
Of Asaph.

1 Sing aloud to God our strength;
      shout for joy to the God of Jacob.
2 Raise a song, sound the tambourine,
      the sweet lyre with the harp.
3 Blow the trumpet at the new moon,
      at the full moon, on our festal day.
4 For it is a statute for Israel,
      an ordinance of the God of Jacob.
5 He made it a decree in Joseph,
      when he went out over [b] the land of
      Egypt.

   I hear a voice I had not known:
6 "I relieved your [c] shoulder of the
      burden;
      your [c] hands were freed from the
      basket.

7 In distress you called, and I rescued
      you;
      I answered you in the secret place of
      thunder;
      I tested you at the waters of Meribah.
                                    Selah
8 Hear, O my people, while I admonish
      you;
      O Israel, if you would but listen to me!
9 There shall be no strange god among
      you;
      you shall not bow down to a foreign
      god.
10 I am the LORD your God,
      who brought you up out of the land
      of Egypt.
      Open your mouth wide and I will
      fill it.

11 "But my people did not listen to my
      voice;
      Israel would not submit to me.
12 So I gave them over to their stubborn
      hearts,
      to follow their own counsels.
13 O that my people would listen to me,
      that Israel would walk in my ways!
14 Then I would quickly subdue their
      enemies,
      and turn my hand against their foes.
15 Those who hate the LORD would cringe
      before him,
      and their doom would last forever.
16 I would feed you [d] with the finest of the
      wheat,
      and with honey from the rock I
      would satisfy you."

a Cn: Heb *it is cut down*   b Or *against*
c Heb *his*   d Cn Compare verse 16b: Heb *he
would feed him*

81:1–5 *Raise a song.* The context signals a song used for a feast day, perhaps the fall Feast of Tabernacles. This is scheduled praise to celebrate God's saving power, particularly noting God's deliverance of Israel from Egypt.
   81:8–10, 16 *Open your mouth wide and I will fill it.* God invites the people to reap the benefits of his adequacy and generosity. Trust wholeheartedly, open wide, and you'll get all you

need. Even more, you'll get the best there is.

Responding

81:11 SUBMISSION. How was Israel defiant and unsubmissive to God? What lessons can we learn from its example for our own nation? For our church? For our family? For ourselves? How do we apply what we learn? *See also* Spiritual Disciplines Index.

Psalm 82

A Plea for Justice

A Psalm of Asaph.

1 God has taken his place in the divine
    council;
  in the midst of the gods he holds
    judgment:
2 "How long will you judge unjustly
  and show partiality to the wicked?
                    Selah
3 Give justice to the weak and the
    orphan;
  maintain the right of the lowly and
    the destitute.
4 Rescue the weak and the needy;
  deliver them from the hand of the
    wicked."

5 They have neither knowledge nor
    understanding,
  they walk around in darkness;
  all the foundations of the earth are
    shaken.

6 I say, "You are gods,
  children of the Most High, all of
    you;
7 nevertheless, you shall die like
    mortals,
  and fall like any prince."[a]

8 Rise up, O God, judge the earth;
  for all the nations belong to
    you!

Psalm 83

Prayer for Judgment on Israel's Foes

A Song. A Psalm of Asaph.

1 O God, do not keep silence;
  do not hold your peace or be still,
    O God!
2 Even now your enemies are in tumult;
  those who hate you have raised their
    heads.
3 They lay crafty plans against your people;
  they consult together against those
    you protect.
4 They say, "Come, let us wipe them out
    as a nation;
  let the name of Israel be remembered
    no more."
5 They conspire with one accord;
  against you they make a covenant—
6 the tents of Edom and the Ishmaelites,
  Moab and the Hagrites,
7 Gebal and Ammon and Amalek,
  Philistia with the inhabitants of Tyre;
8 Assyria also has joined them;
  they are the strong arm of the
    children of Lot.   *Selah*

9 Do to them as you did to Midian,
  as to Sisera and Jabin at the Wadi
    Kishon,
10 who were destroyed at En-dor,
  who became dung for the ground.
11 Make their nobles like Oreb and Zeeb,
  all their princes like Zebah and
    Zalmunna,

a Or *fall as one man, O princes*

82:1, 6–7 *his place in the divine council.* Israel knew God to be the supreme judge. The song shows God holding court (for the "divine council," cf. Job 1:6; 1 Kings 22:19–23; see note on Ps 89:5). The gods of the nations are in attendance, but Israel's God clearly holds authority over all others gathered there. They have failed to do what God requires and so are condemned to "die like mortals."

82:3–5 *Give justice to the weak.* The gods' failure to act rightly—without knowledge or understanding—has shaken the foundations of the earth! Question: What shakes the earth so?

Answer: Failing to act justly on behalf of the weak, the orphaned, the destitute, the vulnerable. Part of true worship is to appeal to God to bring about this compassionate justice.

83:1–8 *those who hate you have raised their heads.* Appeals to God to act against his enemies, apparently here a coalition from Syria-Palestine that includes Assyria from Mesopotamia.

83:9–12 *Do to them as you did to Midian.* God's victories over Israel's enemies during the period of the judges are recalled.

12 who said, "Let us take the pastures of
        God
    for our own possession."

13 O my God, make them like whirling
        dust,*a*
    like chaff before the wind.
14 As fire consumes the forest,
        as the flame sets the mountains
            ablaze,
15 so pursue them with your tempest
        and terrify them with your hurricane.
16 Fill their faces with shame,
        so that they may seek your name,
            O Lord.
17 Let them be put to shame and dismayed
        forever;
    let them perish in disgrace.
18 Let them know that you alone,
        whose name is the Lord,
    are the Most High over all the earth.

Psalm 84

The Joy of Worship in the Temple

To the leader: according to The Gittith.
    Of the Korahites. A Psalm.

1 How lovely is your dwelling place,
        O Lord of hosts!
2 My soul longs, indeed it faints
        for the courts of the Lord;
    my heart and my flesh sing for joy
        to the living God.

3 Even the sparrow finds a home,
        and the swallow a nest for herself,
    where she may lay her young,
    at your altars, O Lord of hosts,
        my King and my God.
4 Happy are those who live in your house,
        ever singing your praise.   *Selah*

5 Happy are those whose strength is in
        you;
    in whose heart are the highways to
        Zion.*b*
6 As they go through the valley of Baca
        they make it a place of springs;
    the early rain also covers it with
        pools.
7 They go from strength to strength;
    the God of gods will be seen in Zion.

8 O Lord God of hosts, hear my prayer;
        give ear, O God of Jacob!   *Selah*
9 Behold our shield, O God;
        look on the face of your anointed.

10 For a day in your courts is better
        than a thousand elsewhere.
    I would rather be a doorkeeper in the
        house of my God
    than live in the tents of wickedness.
11 For the Lord God is a sun and shield;
        he bestows favor and honor.
    No good thing does the Lord withhold
        from those who walk uprightly.
12 O Lord of hosts,
        happy is everyone who trusts in you.

Psalm 85

Prayer for the Restoration of God's Favor

To the leader. Of the Korahites. A Psalm.

1 Lord, you were favorable to your land;
        you restored the fortunes of Jacob.
2 You forgave the iniquity of your people;
        you pardoned all their sin.   *Selah*
3 You withdrew all your wrath;
        you turned from your hot anger.

a Or *a tumbleweed*   *b* Heb lacks *to Zion*

84:1–12 *How lovely is your dwelling place,
O Lord of hosts!* This song reflects the sheer
delight at being in the Temple in Jerusalem, a
joy that extends in pilgrimage even to the
prospect of arriving there (vv 5–7).
    84:10 *For a day in your courts is better.* The
psalmist is glad to be just a doorkeeper at the

Temple. Perhaps we hear a note of envy of the
sparrow (v 3), who gets to build a nest and raise
her young in God's house.
    84:11–12 *happy is everyone who trusts in you.*
Enjoying God's presence and goodness extends
well beyond Temple courts, of course. Relaxing
in God and dwelling there brings joy as well.

4 Restore us again, O God of our
        salvation,
    and put away your indignation
        toward us.
5 Will you be angry with us forever?
    Will you prolong your anger to all
        generations?
6 Will you not revive us again,
    so that your people may rejoice in
        you?
7 Show us your steadfast love, O LORD,
    and grant us your salvation.

8 Let me hear what God the LORD will
        speak,
    for he will speak peace to his people,
    to his faithful, to those who turn to
        him in their hearts. a
9 Surely his salvation is at hand for those
        who fear him,
    that his glory may dwell in our land.

10 Steadfast love and faithfulness will
        meet;
    righteousness and peace will kiss each
        other.
11 Faithfulness will spring up from the
        ground,
    and righteousness will look down
        from the sky.
12 The LORD will give what is good,
    and our land will yield its increase.
13 Righteousness will go before him,
    and will make a path for his steps.

Psalm 86

Supplication for Help against Enemies

A Prayer of David.

1 Incline your ear, O LORD, and answer me,
    for I am poor and needy.
2 Preserve my life, for I am devoted to
        you;
    save your servant who trusts in you.
    You are my God; 3 be gracious to me,
        O Lord,
    for to you do I cry all day long.
4 Gladden the soul of your servant,
    for to you, O Lord, I lift up my soul.
5 For you, O Lord, are good and forgiving,
    abounding in steadfast love to all who
        call on you.
6 Give ear, O LORD, to my prayer;
    listen to my cry of supplication.
7 In the day of my trouble I call on you,
    for you will answer me.

8 There is none like you among the gods,
        O Lord,
    nor are there any works like yours.
9 All the nations you have made shall
        come
    and bow down before you, O Lord,
    and shall glorify your name.
10 For you are great and do wondrous
        things;
    you alone are God.
11 Teach me your way, O LORD,
    that I may walk in your truth;

a Gk: Heb but let them not turn back to folly

85:6 *Will you not revive us again?*
Remembering God's power and propensity to
forgive, the singers ask again for God's
restoration.

85:9–13 *Steadfast love and faithfulness . . .
righteousness and peace.* With the promise of
renewal comes a stirring vision of what happens
when God's "glory" dwells in the land. It is the
realm of the "peaceable kingdom" governed by
steadfast love, faithfulness, righteousness, and
peace. These characterize God, certainly, but
are also what God requires of all of us who
would live faithfully. God delights in these
virtues (see Jer 9:23–24).

86:2 *Preserve my life, for I am devoted to you.*
The psalmist calls out for deliverance, confident
both in his own goodness and in God's steady
love.

86:8–11 *There is none like you among the
gods.* With the surrounding nations worshiping
many gods, the psalmist declares the God of
Israel unrivaled, God alone. Even the polytheistic nations will eventually come to bow
down and glorify God. The singer asks help to
remain single-minded and wholehearted in this
pluralistic environment, not hedging or waffling
as he (and we) might be tempted to do.

give me an undivided heart to revere
　　your name.
12 I give thanks to you, O Lord my God,
　　with my whole heart,
　and I will glorify your name forever.
13 For great is your steadfast love toward
　　me;
　you have delivered my soul from the
　　depths of Sheol.

14 O God, the insolent rise up against me;
　a band of ruffians seeks my life,
　and they do not set you before them.
15 But you, O Lord, are a God merciful and
　　gracious,
　　slow to anger and abounding in
　　steadfast love and faithfulness.
16 Turn to me and be gracious to me;
　　give your strength to your servant;
　　save the child of your serving girl.
17 Show me a sign of your favor,
　　so that those who hate me may see it
　　and be put to shame,
　because you, LORD, have helped me
　　and comforted me.

Psalm 87

The Joy of Living in Zion

Of the Korahites. A Psalm. A Song.

1　On the holy mount stands the city he
　　founded;

2　the LORD loves the gates of Zion
　　more than all the dwellings of Jacob.
3　Glorious things are spoken of you,
　　O city of God.　　　　　　　　　Selah

4　Among those who know me I mention
　　　Rahab and Babylon;
　　Philistia too, and Tyre, with
　　　Ethiopia [a]—
　"This one was born there," they say.

5　And of Zion it shall be said,
　"This one and that one were born in
　　it";
　for the Most High himself will
　　establish it.
6　The LORD records, as he registers the
　　peoples,
　"This one was born there."　　　Selah

7　Singers and dancers alike say,
　"All my springs are in you."

Psalm 88

Prayer for Help in Despondency

A Song. A Psalm of the Korahites. To the
leader: according to Mahalath Leannoth.
A Maskil of Heman the Ezrahite.

1　O LORD, God of my salvation,

a Or Nubia; Heb Cush

86:15 *But you, O LORD, are a God merciful and gracious.* This is one of the dearest confessions of the Old Testament people, going back to when God gave his name to Moses in Exod 34:6 and often echoed in the biblical texts. Relying on such a God of love gives us great hope.

87:1–7 *Glorious things are spoken of you [Zion], O city of God.* This song celebrates Zion (Jerusalem) not only as the place God specially chose, but also as the center and emblem of God's power and purpose. Ultimately, the birth certificates of all the nations show Zion as their birthplace, signifying that they are all subject to the Most High, who creates and sustains all people and nations. God's loving purposes are wide enough to encompass all nations.

87:7 *Singers and dancers alike say.* In difficult times as well as good, we can join singers and dancers who celebrate and rely on God's nurturing and sovereign presence.

88:1–18 *O LORD, God of my salvation.* This lament song is unusually desperate and gloomy, even to the point of leaving out any words of praise. The singer is nearly among the dead in Sheol or the Pit. God has acted against him and turned friends against him. Yet despite asking why God has hidden his face from him (v 14), the psalmist prays all the time—at night (v 1), in the morning (v 13), every day (v 9). Even in the darkest time, he acts in hope that the Lord is still the "God of my salvation" (v 1) and that there is still reason to declare God's "steadfast love" (v 11). Lament songs, even the darkest of them, don't give up—a vital lesson for our formation education.

when, at night, I cry out in your
    presence,
2 let my prayer come before you;
    incline your ear to my cry.

3 For my soul is full of troubles,
    and my life draws near to Sheol.
4 I am counted among those who go
    down to the Pit;
  I am like those who have no help,
5 like those forsaken among the dead,
  like the slain that lie in the grave,
  like those whom you remember no more,
  for they are cut off from your hand.
6 You have put me in the depths of the Pit,
  in the regions dark and deep.
7 Your wrath lies heavy upon me,
  and you overwhelm me with all your
    waves.   *Selah*

8 You have caused my companions to
    shun me;
  you have made me a thing of horror
    to them.
  I am shut in so that I cannot escape;
9   my eye grows dim through sorrow.
  Every day I call on you, O LORD;
  I spread out my hands to you.
10 Do you work wonders for the dead?
  Do the shades rise up to praise you?
               Selah
11 Is your steadfast love declared in the
    grave,
  or your faithfulness in Abaddon?
12 Are your wonders known in the darkness,
  or your saving help in the land of
    forgetfulness?

13 But I, O LORD, cry out to you;
  in the morning my prayer comes
    before you.

14 O LORD, why do you cast me off?
  Why do you hide your face from me?
15 Wretched and close to death from my
    youth up,
  I suffer your terrors; I am desperate. *a*
16 Your wrath has swept over me;
  your dread assaults destroy me.
17 They surround me like a flood all day
    long;
  from all sides they close in on me.
18 You have caused friend and neighbor to
    shun me;
  my companions are in darkness.

Psalm 89

God's Covenant with David

A Maskil of Ethan the Ezrahite.

1 I will sing of your steadfast love,
  O LORD, *b* forever;
  with my mouth I will proclaim your
    faithfulness to all generations.
2 I declare that your steadfast love is
    established forever;
  your faithfulness is as firm as the
    heavens.

3 You said, "I have made a covenant with
    my chosen one,
  I have sworn to my servant David:
4 'I will establish your descendants forever,
  and build your throne for all
    generations.' "   *Selah*

5 Let the heavens praise your wonders,
  O LORD,
  your faithfulness in the assembly of
    the holy ones.

a Meaning of Heb uncertain   *b* Gk: Heb *the
steadfast love of the* LORD

89:1–52 *I will sing of your steadfast love.*
God's "steadfast love" and "faithfulness" anchor
this psalm, even when it concludes with bitter
lament. This is God's love that "endures forever,"
that "never quits," that pursues us all the days
of our lives (23:6).
  89:5 *in the assembly of the holy ones.* Living
among polytheistic neighbors, Israel often
speaks of a realm of divine beings, but Yahweh,

"the LORD," stands above them and leaves them
awestruck. One reason is the Lord's mastery of
creation, even crushing Rahab, the mythical
monster of chaotic waters who most threatens
creation (vv 9–10). Another reason is that, unlike
other heavenly beings, God's rule is established
in righteousness, justice, faithfulness, and
steadfast love (v 14). This one alone is the God
to rely on and rejoice in (vv 15–16).

6 For who in the skies can be compared to
the LORD?
Who among the heavenly beings is
like the LORD,
7 a God feared in the council of the holy
ones,
great and awesome[a] above all that are
around him?
8 O LORD God of hosts,
who is as mighty as you, O LORD?
Your faithfulness surrounds you.
9 You rule the raging of the sea;
when its waves rise, you still them.
10 You crushed Rahab like a carcass;
you scattered your enemies with your
mighty arm.
11 The heavens are yours, the earth also is
yours;
the world and all that is in it—you
have founded them.
12 The north and the south[b]—you created
them;
Tabor and Hermon joyously praise
your name.
13 You have a mighty arm;
strong is your hand, high your right
hand.
14 Righteousness and justice are the
foundation of your throne;
steadfast love and faithfulness go
before you.
15 Happy are the people who know the
festal shout,
who walk, O LORD, in the light of your
countenance;
16 they exult in your name all day long,
and extol[c] your righteousness.
17 For you are the glory of their strength;
by your favor our horn is exalted.
18 For our shield belongs to the LORD,
our king to the Holy One of Israel.

19 Then you spoke in a vision to your
faithful one, and said:
"I have set the crown[d] on one who is
mighty,
I have exalted one chosen from the
people.
20 I have found my servant David;
with my holy oil I have anointed him;
21 my hand shall always remain with him;

my arm also shall strengthen him.
22 The enemy shall not outwit him,
the wicked shall not humble him.
23 I will crush his foes before him
and strike down those who hate him.
24 My faithfulness and steadfast love shall
be with him;
and in my name his horn shall be
exalted.
25 I will set his hand on the sea
and his right hand on the rivers.
26 He shall cry to me, 'You are my Father,
my God, and the Rock of my
salvation!'
27 I will make him the firstborn,
the highest of the kings of the earth.
28 Forever I will keep my steadfast love for
him,
and my covenant with him will stand
firm.
29 I will establish his line forever,
and his throne as long as the heavens
endure.
30 If his children forsake my law
and do not walk according to my
ordinances,
31 if they violate my statutes
and do not keep my commandments,
32 then I will punish their transgression
with the rod
and their iniquity with scourges;
33 but I will not remove from him my
steadfast love,
or be false to my faithfulness.
34 I will not violate my covenant,
or alter the word that went forth from
my lips.
35 Once and for all I have sworn by my
holiness;
I will not lie to David.
36 His line shall continue forever,
and his throne endure before me like
the sun.
37 It shall be established forever like the
moon,
an enduring witness in the skies."
                                        Selah

a Gk Syr: Heb *greatly awesome*   b Or *Zaphon and
Yamin*   c Cn: Heb *are exalted in*   d Cn: Heb
help

38 But now you have spurned and rejected
     him;
   you are full of wrath against your
     anointed.
39 You have renounced the covenant with
     your servant;
   you have defiled his crown in the
     dust.
40 You have broken through all his walls;
   you have laid his strongholds in
     ruins.
41 All who pass by plunder him;
   he has become the scorn of his
     neighbors.
42 You have exalted the right hand of his
     foes;
   you have made all his enemies rejoice.
43 Moreover, you have turned back the
     edge of his sword,
   and you have not supported him in
     battle.
44 You have removed the scepter from his
     hand,*a*
   and hurled his throne to the ground.
45 You have cut short the days of his
     youth;
   you have covered him with shame.
                                        Selah

46 How long, O LORD? Will you hide
     yourself forever?
   How long will your wrath burn like
     fire?
47 Remember how short my time is—*b*
   for what vanity you have created all
     mortals!
48 Who can live and never see death?
   Who can escape the power of Sheol?
                                        Selah

49 Lord, where is your steadfast love of
     old,
   which by your faithfulness you swore
     to David?
50 Remember, O Lord, how your servant is
     taunted;
   how I bear in my bosom the insults of
     the peoples,*c*
51 with which your enemies taunt, O LORD,
   with which they taunted the
     footsteps of your anointed.

52 Blessed be the LORD forever.
     Amen and Amen.

BOOK IV

(Psalms 90–106)

Psalm 90

God's Eternity and Human Frailty

A Prayer of Moses, the man of God.

1 Lord, you have been our dwelling place*d*
   in all generations.
2 Before the mountains were brought
     forth,
   or ever you had formed the earth and
     the world,
   from everlasting to everlasting you are
     God.

3 You turn us*e* back to dust,
   and say, "Turn back, you mortals."
4 For a thousand years in your sight

a Cn: Heb *removed his cleanness*   *b* Meaning of
Heb uncertain   *c* Cn: Heb *bosom all of many
peoples*   *d* Another reading is *our refuge*
e Heb *humankind*

89:49–51 LORD, *where is your steadfast love of
old?* God had chosen David and his descendants
to rule over Israel, to be "the highest of the
kings of the earth" (v 27), supporting this with a
promise of steadfast love. The crushing defeat
of the monarchy troubles the psalmist deeply.
Yet even the cry "How long, O LORD?" (v 46)
reveals the deep conviction that God's steadfast
love never ends. Though we should not presume
on it, it will never fail.

89:52 *Blessed be the* LORD *forever.* This
doxology ends Book III.

90:1–17 *Lord, you have been our dwelling
place.* We may often sense the sharp tension
this psalm presents between God's overwhelming power and our fragility. God endures
from everlasting to everlasting, long before
creation, completely confounding any sense
of time (vv 2, 4). Humans easily return to dust,
sprout and wither in a day like grass, pass like
a sigh (vv 3, 5–6, 9).

are like yesterday when it is past,
or like a watch in the night.

5 You sweep them away; they are like a
dream,
like grass that is renewed in the
morning;
6 in the morning it flourishes and is
renewed;
in the evening it fades and withers.

7 For we are consumed by your anger;
by your wrath we are overwhelmed.
8 You have set our iniquities before you,
our secret sins in the light of your
countenance.

9 For all our days pass away under your
wrath;
our years come to an end *a* like a sigh.
10 The days of our life are seventy years,
or perhaps eighty, if we are strong;
even then their span *b* is only toil and
trouble;
they are soon gone, and we fly away.

11 Who considers the power of your anger?
Your wrath is as great as the fear that
is due you.
12 So teach us to count our days
that we may gain a wise heart.

13 Turn, O Lord! How long?
Have compassion on your servants!

14 Satisfy us in the morning with your
steadfast love,
so that we may rejoice and be glad all
our days.
15 Make us glad as many days as you have
afflicted us,
and as many years as we have seen
evil.
16 Let your work be manifest to your
servants,
and your glorious power to their
children.
17 Let the favor of the Lord our God be
upon us,
and prosper for us the work of our
hands—
O prosper the work of our hands!

Psalm 91

Assurance of God's Protection

1 You who live in the shelter of the Most
High,
who abide in the shadow of the
Almighty, *c*
2 will say to the Lord, "My refuge and my
fortress;
my God, in whom I trust."
3 For he will deliver you from the snare of
the fowler
and from the deadly pestilence;

a Syr: Heb *we bring our years to an end*
b Cn Compare Gk Syr Jerome Tg: Heb *pride*
c Traditional rendering of Heb *Shaddai*

90:12 *teach us to count our days.*
Acknowledging our weakness and frailty is a
step toward wisdom.

90:13 *Have compassion!* Rather than
suffering due penalty, the singer asks for
compassion, for the steadfast love that brings
gladness. Ps 103:13–14 supports this hope,
reminding us that the Lord "remembers that we
are dust" and shows compassion.

91:1 *You who live in the shelter of the Most
High.* Living in God, making the Most High our
"dwelling place" (v 9), shows a deep trust, a
stability that inspires the confidence of this
psalm. For us to dwell in God as a refuge differs
sharply from merely scampering into shelter
when trouble strikes.

Responding
91:1 SECRECY. Living "in the shadow
of the Almighty" reminds us of a child
walking with a parent and making every effort
to stay in the parent's shadow. It also hints of a
condition where the child is so uninhibited and
in love with the parent that he or she has no
desire for public recognition. How difficult has it
been for you to place your "public relations
department entirely in the hands of God," as
Dallas Willard puts it in *The Spirit of the Disciplines*? If you are having trouble abstaining
from the compulsion to make your good deeds
and qualities known, take it before your heavenly Father and ask for healing in this area of
your life. *See also* Spiritual Disciplines Index.

4 he will cover you with his pinions,
    and under his wings you will find
        refuge;
    his faithfulness is a shield and buckler.
5 You will not fear the terror of the night,
    or the arrow that flies by day,
6 or the pestilence that stalks in darkness,
    or the destruction that wastes at
        noonday.

7 A thousand may fall at your side,
    ten thousand at your right hand,
    but it will not come near you.
8 You will only look with your eyes
    and see the punishment of the
        wicked.

9 Because you have made the LORD your
        refuge,[a]
    the Most High your dwelling place,
10 no evil shall befall you,
    no scourge come near your tent.

11 For he will command his angels
        concerning you
    to guard you in all your ways.
12 On their hands they will bear you up,
    so that you will not dash your foot
        against a stone.
13 You will tread on the lion and the
        adder,
    the young lion and the serpent you
        will trample under foot.

14 Those who love me, I will deliver;
    I will protect those who know my
        name.
15 When they call to me, I will answer
        them;
    I will be with them in trouble,
    I will rescue them and honor them.
16 With long life I will satisfy them,
    and show them my salvation.

Psalm 92

Thanksgiving for Vindication

A Psalm. A Song for the Sabbath Day.

1 It is good to give thanks to the LORD,
    to sing praises to your name, O Most
        High;
2 to declare your steadfast love in the
        morning,
    and your faithfulness by night,
3 to the music of the lute and the harp,
    to the melody of the lyre.
4 For you, O LORD, have made me glad by
        your work;
    at the works of your hands I sing for
        joy.

5 How great are your works, O LORD!
    Your thoughts are very deep!
6 The dullard cannot know,
    the stupid cannot understand this:
7 though the wicked sprout like grass
    and all evildoers flourish,
    they are doomed to destruction
        forever,
8 but you, O LORD, are on high
        forever.
9 For your enemies, O LORD,
    for your enemies shall perish;
    all evildoers shall be scattered.

10 But you have exalted my horn like that
        of the wild ox;
    you have poured over me[b] fresh oil.
11 My eyes have seen the downfall of my
        enemies;
    my ears have heard the doom of my
        evil assailants.

a Cn: Heb *Because you, LORD, are my refuge; you have made*   *b* Syr: Meaning of Heb uncertain

---

91:11–12 *he will command his angels concerning you.* Jesus rebuked the devil for tempting him to use these promises of God's care presumptuously (Luke 4:9–12).

91:14 *Those who love me, I will deliver.* Note the change of voice to God's direct assurances of presence and care.

91:16 THE WITH-GOD LIFE—*See* Spiritual Disciplines Index.

92:1 *It is good to give thanks, . . . to sing praises.* Singing day and night of God's steady love and faithfulness is the right response to reality, but also reminds us of the truth of God's goodness. Making a habit of praise keeps our eyes open.

12 The righteous flourish like the palm
    tree,
    and grow like a cedar in Lebanon.
13 They are planted in the house of the
    LORD;
    they flourish in the courts of our
    God.
14 In old age they still produce fruit;
    they are always green and full of sap,
15 showing that the LORD is upright;
    he is my rock, and there is no
    unrighteousness in him.

Psalm 93

The Majesty of God's Rule

1 The LORD is king, he is robed in
    majesty;
    the LORD is robed, he is girded with
    strength.
He has established the world; it shall
    never be moved;
2   your throne is established from of
    old;
    you are from everlasting.

3 The floods have lifted up, O LORD,
    the floods have lifted up their voice;
    the floods lift up their roaring.
4 More majestic than the thunders of
    mighty waters,
    more majestic than the waves*a* of the
    sea,
    majestic on high is the LORD!

5 Your decrees are very sure;

holiness befits your house,
O LORD, forevermore.

Psalm 94

God the Avenger of the Righteous

1 O LORD, you God of vengeance,
    you God of vengeance, shine forth!
2 Rise up, O judge of the earth;
    give to the proud what they deserve!
3 O LORD, how long shall the wicked,
    how long shall the wicked exult?

4 They pour out their arrogant words;
    all the evildoers boast.
5 They crush your people, O LORD,
    and afflict your heritage.
6 They kill the widow and the stranger,
    they murder the orphan,
7 and they say, "The LORD does not see;
    the God of Jacob does not perceive."

8 Understand, O dullest of the people;
    fools, when will you be wise?
9 He who planted the ear, does he not
    hear?
    He who formed the eye, does he not see?
10 He who disciplines the nations,
    he who teaches knowledge to
    humankind,
    does he not chastise?
11   The LORD knows our thoughts,*b*
    that they are but an empty breath.

a Cn: Heb *majestic are the waves*   *b* Heb *the thoughts of humankind*

92:12–15 *The righteous flourish like the palm tree.* Being planted to flourish in the royal arboretum is God's choice, not ours. It's another reason to sing for joy.

93:1–5 *The LORD is king.* This, along with Pss 29; 47; 95–99, is one of the enthronement psalms, which celebrate God as King.

93:1–2 *He has established the world; it shall never be moved.* The Lord's kingship is established here through the creative power that makes the world unshakable.

93:3–4 *the floods have lifted up their voice.* "The floods," still roaring yet overcome by God's majesty, may well be the primordial waters God

brought to order in creation. When chaos rattles our foundations, admiring God's power in creation can strengthen our stability and hope.

94:1 *God of vengeance, shine forth!* In the Old Testament, the idea of "vengeance" does not point to revenge, getting even, but to justice, acting to set things right to overcome the distortion of reality that oppression brings. Ultimately this is God's job.

94:3–11 *The LORD knows.* The arrogant wicked crush and kill the vulnerable people, believing themselves unseen by God, but the One who created the eye does see and will discipline.

12 Happy are those whom you discipline,
      O LORD,
    and whom you teach out of your law,
13 giving them respite from days of
      trouble,
    until a pit is dug for the wicked.
14 For the LORD will not forsake his people;
    he will not abandon his heritage;
15 for justice will return to the righteous,
    and all the upright in heart will
      follow it.

16 Who rises up for me against the wicked?
    Who stands up for me against
      evildoers?
17 If the LORD had not been my help,
    my soul would soon have lived in the
      land of silence.
18 When I thought, "My foot is slipping,"
    your steadfast love, O LORD, held me
      up.
19 When the cares of my heart are many,
    your consolations cheer my soul.
20 Can wicked rulers be allied with you,
    those who contrive mischief by
      statute?
21 They band together against the life of
      the righteous,
    and condemn the innocent to death.
22 But the LORD has become my
      stronghold,
    and my God the rock of my refuge.
23 He will repay them for their iniquity
    and wipe them out for their
      wickedness;
    the LORD our God will wipe them out.

Psalm 95

A Call to Worship and Obedience

1 O come, let us sing to the LORD;
    let us make a joyful noise to the rock
      of our salvation!
2 Let us come into his presence with
      thanksgiving;
    let us make a joyful noise to him with
      songs of praise!
3 For the LORD is a great God,
    and a great King above all gods.
4 In his hand are the depths of the earth;
    the heights of the mountains are his
      also.
5 The sea is his, for he made it,
    and the dry land, which his hands
      have formed.

6 O come, let us worship and bow down,
    let us kneel before the LORD, our
      Maker!
7 For he is our God,
    and we are the people of his pasture,
    and the sheep of his hand.

  O that today you would listen to his
      voice!
8   Do not harden your hearts, as at
      Meribah,
    as on the day at Massah in the
      wilderness,
9 when your ancestors tested me,
    and put me to the proof, though they
      had seen my work.
10 For forty years I loathed that generation

94:18–23 *your steadfast love, O LORD, held me up.* When evil threatens and seems to prevail, God is still a sure refuge. Often rulers act corruptly, even making evil, oppressive practices law (v 20). In many places the victims of legal thugs have only God to rely on. Faith says God will set things right. We can sing with victims in their plight in order to identify with them and overcome our own numbness to evil.

95:1–5 *let us make a joyful noise!* The call to energy and enthusiasm in worship, to extravagant celebration, is only fitting for the Lord who is Creator and "a great King above all gods."

95:6–7 *let us worship and bow down.* Submission joins celebration when we recognize that the Creator is also the Shepherd. Here the sheep—the People of God—are called to be ready to be fed and to be led.

95:9 *your ancestors tested me . . . though they had seen my work.* Israel was often warned to remember, not to forget God's power and faithfulness. Yet it's easy to trust our own plans and resources, to stray from relying on God. Joyful praise and active memory help us follow the Shepherd.

and said, "They are a people whose
    hearts go astray,
and they do not regard my ways."
11 Therefore in my anger I swore,
    "They shall not enter my rest."

Psalm 96

Praise to God Who Comes in Judgment

1 O sing to the LORD a new song;
    sing to the LORD, all the earth.
2 Sing to the LORD, bless his name;
    tell of his salvation from day to day.
3 Declare his glory among the nations,
    his marvelous works among all the
    peoples.
4 For great is the LORD, and greatly to be
    praised;
    he is to be revered above all gods.
5 For all the gods of the peoples are idols,
    but the LORD made the heavens.
6 Honor and majesty are before him;
    strength and beauty are in his
    sanctuary.

7 Ascribe to the LORD, O families of the
    peoples,
    ascribe to the LORD glory and
    strength.

8 Ascribe to the LORD the glory due his
    name;
    bring an offering, and come into his
    courts.
9 Worship the LORD in holy splendor;
    tremble before him, all the earth.

10 Say among the nations, "The LORD is
    king!
    The world is firmly established; it
    shall never be moved.
    He will judge the peoples with equity."
11 Let the heavens be glad, and let the
    earth rejoice;
    let the sea roar, and all that fills it;
12   let the field exult, and everything in
    it.
    Then shall all the trees of the forest sing
    for joy
13   before the LORD; for he is coming,
    for he is coming to judge the earth.
    He will judge the world with
    righteousness,
    and the peoples with his truth.

Psalm 97

The Glory of God's Reign

1 The LORD is king! Let the earth rejoice;
    let the many coastlands be glad!

96:9 *tremble before him, all the earth.* This phrase captures the sense of the very expansive call to praise in this psalm, calling nations, all the peoples, all the earth to praise. Psalm 98 shares this broad call, including the call to nature itself to offer exuberant praise.

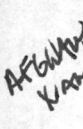
Responding
96:9 WORSHIP. People who followed the teaching and preaching of George Fox in the seventeenth century were called Quakers, an invective at that time, because they "quaked" while they worshiped the Lord. Why do you think Quakers were viewed with such derision? Can you name any groups today that face the same negative attitudes because they worship in ways outside the mainstream? If your attitude toward them is negative, take a moment now to confess that to God and ask for forgiveness. *See also* Spiritual Disciplines Index.

96:10 *The LORD is king!* Yahweh's kingship is based on his unrivaled power in creation, making the heavens (v 5) and establishing the world (v 10), and on the upright character of his rule (vv 10, 13).

96:11–13 *Then shall all the trees of the forest sing.* Creation itself, which often groans under arrogant, evil rulers (see, e.g., Isa 14:5–8), rejoices at God's just rule. The word "judge" here does not refer narrowly to one who determines judicial matters, but to a king who governs rightly.

97:1–12 *The LORD is king!* The Lord, who reigns, comes with such piercing brilliance ("glory"), such displays of power, and such a wondrous entourage (righteousness and justice) that everyone sees it and even the mountains melt like wax. Such shimmering glory exposes all that is false, dark, and distorted.

2 Clouds and thick darkness are all
        around him;
    righteousness and justice are the
        foundation of his throne.
3 Fire goes before him,
    and consumes his adversaries on
        every side.
4 His lightnings light up the world;
    the earth sees and trembles.
5 The mountains melt like wax before the
        LORD,
    before the Lord of all the earth.

6 The heavens proclaim his
        righteousness;
    and all the peoples behold his
        glory.
7 All worshipers of images are put to
        shame,
    those who make their boast in
        worthless idols;
    all gods bow down before him.
8 Zion hears and is glad,
    and the towns*a* of Judah rejoice,
    because of your judgments,
        O God.
9 For you, O LORD, are most high over all
        the earth;
    you are exalted far above all gods.

10 The LORD loves those who hate*b* evil;
    he guards the lives of his faithful;
    he rescues them from the hand of the
        wicked.
11 Light dawns*c* for the righteous,
    and joy for the upright in heart.
12 Rejoice in the LORD, O you
        righteous,
    and give thanks to his holy
        name!

Psalm 98

Praise the Judge of the World

A Psalm.

1 O sing to the LORD a new song,
    for he has done marvelous things.
His right hand and his holy arm
    have gotten him victory.
2 The LORD has made known his victory;
    he has revealed his vindication in the
        sight of the nations.
3 He has remembered his steadfast love
        and faithfulness
    to the house of Israel.
All the ends of the earth have seen
    the victory of our God.

4 Make a joyful noise to the LORD, all the
        earth;
    break forth into joyous song and sing
        praises.
5 Sing praises to the LORD with the lyre,
    with the lyre and the sound of melody.
6 With trumpets and the sound of the
        horn
    make a joyful noise before the King,
        the LORD.

7 Let the sea roar, and all that fills it;
    the world and those who live in it.
8 Let the floods clap their hands;
    let the hills sing together for joy
9 at the presence of the LORD, for he is
        coming
    to judge the earth.
He will judge the world with
        righteousness,
    and the peoples with equity.

a Heb *daughters*   *b* Cn: Heb *You who love the
LORD hate*   *c* Gk Syr Jerome: Heb *is sown*

97:8–12 *the towns of Judah rejoice, because
of your judgments.* The righteous don't shrink
back, but welcome and join in God's just rule.

98:1–9 *O sing to the LORD.* Compare Psalm
96, which has very similar themes. Rather than
creation (as in Ps 96), the main reason for a
victory song here is the "marvelous things"
God has done to deliver Israel. As in Psalm 96,
though, the whole creation rejoices because

of God's just rule.

98:4–9 *Make a joyful noise to the LORD, all the
earth.* The glad music of trumpet, horns, and a
big string band join the seas roaring, wild waters
clapping their hands, and hills singing for joy!
These images form the background of Isaac
Watts's great hymn "Joy to the World," in which
"fields and floods, rocks, hills and plains repeat
the sounding joy."

Psalm 99

Praise to God for His Holiness

1 The LORD is king; let the peoples tremble!
  He sits enthroned upon the
      cherubim; let the earth quake!
2 The LORD is great in Zion;
  he is exalted over all the peoples.
3 Let them praise your great and awesome
      name.
  Holy is he!
4 Mighty King, *a* lover of justice,
  you have established equity;
  you have executed justice
  and righteousness in Jacob.
5 Extol the LORD our God;
  worship at his footstool.
  Holy is he!

6 Moses and Aaron were among his priests,
  Samuel also was among those who
      called on his name.
  They cried to the LORD, and he
      answered them.
7 He spoke to them in the pillar of cloud;
  they kept his decrees,
  and the statutes that he gave them.

8 O LORD our God, you answered them;
  you were a forgiving God to them,
  but an avenger of their wrongdoings.
9 Extol the LORD our God,
  and worship at his holy mountain;
  for the LORD our God is holy.

Psalm 100

All Lands Summoned to Praise God

A Psalm of thanksgiving.

1 Make a joyful noise to the LORD, all the
      earth.
2   Worship the LORD with gladness;
  come into his presence with
      singing.

3 Know that the LORD is God.
  It is he that made us, and we are his; *b*
  we are his people, and the sheep of
      his pasture.

4 Enter his gates with thanksgiving,
  and his courts with praise.
  Give thanks to him, bless his name.

5 For the LORD is good;
  his steadfast love endures forever,
  and his faithfulness to all
      generations.

Psalm 101

A Sovereign's Pledge of Integrity and Justice

Of David. A Psalm.

1 I will sing of loyalty and of justice;
  to you, O LORD, I will sing.

a Cn: Heb *And a king's strength*   *b* Another
reading is *and not we ourselves*

99:1–9 *Holy is he!* The last in this series of
enthronement psalms, this song repeatedly calls
the People of God to worship, to tremble, to be
overwhelmed by the God who is with us but is
set apart from us (vv 3, 5, 9).

99:4–5 *Mighty King, lover of justice.* Other
songs celebrating God as King point to acts of
creation and deliverance. This one focuses more
on God's character as one who is just, who
answers those who call for help, who forgives
and establishes justice all at once, who is holy.
One way to "worship at his footstool" is to
admire who God is.

99:5 WORSHIP—*See* Spiritual Disciplines
Index.

100:1–2 *Worship the LORD with gladness.*
This is a joyous, universal call to praise and
thanksgiving. Its old hymn setting captures its
gladness: "Him serve with mirth, his praise
forthtell."

100:3 *Know that the LORD is God. . . . and we
are his.* The call to joyful noise (v 1) includes
relaxing and being creatures who are well
tended by the Creator-Shepherd. When we
accept our place and trust God's goodness, we
take a giant step toward wholeness.

100:5 *his steadfast love endures forever.*
Entering into worship with deep gladness
and living with liberating trust take root here.
Confessing that God's steadfast love and faithfulness will never fail opens the way to joy.

2 I will study the way that is blameless.
   When shall I attain it?

I will walk with integrity of heart
   within my house;
3 I will not set before my eyes
   anything that is base.

I hate the work of those who fall away;
   it shall not cling to me.
4 Perverseness of heart shall be far from
    me;
   I will know nothing of evil.

5 One who secretly slanders a neighbor
   I will destroy.
A haughty look and an arrogant heart
   I will not tolerate.

6 I will look with favor on the faithful in
    the land,
   so that they may live with me;
whoever walks in the way that is
    blameless
   shall minister to me.

7 No one who practices deceit
   shall remain in my house;
no one who utters lies
   shall continue in my presence.

8 Morning by morning I will destroy
   all the wicked in the land,
cutting off all evildoers
   from the city of the LORD.

Psalm 102

Prayer to the Eternal King for Help

*A prayer of one afflicted, when faint and
pleading before the LORD.*

1 Hear my prayer, O LORD;
   let my cry come to you.
2 Do not hide your face from me
   in the day of my distress.
Incline your ear to me;
   answer me speedily in the day when I
    call.

3 For my days pass away like smoke,
   and my bones burn like a furnace.
4 My heart is stricken and withered like
    grass;
   I am too wasted to eat my bread.
5 Because of my loud groaning
   my bones cling to my skin.
6 I am like an owl of the wilderness,
   like a little owl of the waste places.
7 I lie awake;
   I am like a lonely bird on the
    housetop.
8 All day long my enemies taunt me;
   those who deride me use my name for
    a curse.
9 For I eat ashes like bread,
   and mingle tears with my drink,
10 because of your indignation and anger;
   for you have lifted me up and thrown
    me aside.
11 My days are like an evening shadow;
   I wither away like grass.

101:1–2 *I will sing of loyalty and of justice.*
Kings and presidents routinely promise their
people that they will be compassionate and just.
This song makes that promise to God. The king
wants to be a godly leader, shaped steadily
toward what God delights in—loyal love, justice,
righteousness (see Jer 9:23–24). For God's rule
to prevail, all leaders should thrill to actively
love what God loves.

   Responding
101:2 STUDY. How do we "study the
way that is blameless"? What do we
study? Why should we study it? *See also*
Spiritual Disciplines Index.

101:5–8 *No one who practices deceit shall
remain in my house.* The godly leader steadily
roots out slander, twisted behavior, and
arrogance.
   102:1–11, 23–28 *My heart is stricken and
withered like grass.* Theses passages form a
prayer for help by an individual who describes
deep affliction. The other part of the poem
portrays Jerusalem in ruins, waiting to be
restored. Perhaps the individual's affliction is
connected with the people's loss.

12 But you, O Lord, are enthroned forever;
    your name endures to all generations.
13 You will rise up and have compassion
    on Zion,
    for it is time to favor it;
    the appointed time has come.
14 For your servants hold its stones dear,
    and have pity on its dust.
15 The nations will fear the name of the
    Lord,
    and all the kings of the earth your
    glory.
16 For the Lord will build up Zion;
    he will appear in his glory.
17 He will regard the prayer of the
    destitute,
    and will not despise their prayer.

18 Let this be recorded for a generation to
    come,
    so that a people yet unborn may
    praise the Lord:
19 that he looked down from his holy
    height,
    from heaven the Lord looked at the
    earth,
20 to hear the groans of the prisoners,
    to set free those who were doomed to
    die;
21 so that the name of the Lord may be
    declared in Zion,
    and his praise in Jerusalem,
22 when peoples gather together,
    and kingdoms, to worship the Lord.

23 He has broken my strength in midcourse;
    he has shortened my days.
24 "O my God," I say, "do not take me away
    at the midpoint of my life,
    you whose years endure
    throughout all generations."

25 Long ago you laid the foundation of the
    earth,
    and the heavens are the work of your
    hands.
26 They will perish, but you endure;
    they will all wear out like a garment.
    You change them like clothing, and
    they pass away;
27 but you are the same, and your years
    have no end.
28 The children of your servants shall live
    secure;
    their offspring shall be established in
    your presence.

Psalm 103

Thanksgiving for God's Goodness

Of David.

1 Bless the Lord, O my soul,
    and all that is within me,
    bless his holy name.
2 Bless the Lord, O my soul,
    and do not forget all his benefits—
3 who forgives all your iniquity,
    who heals all your diseases,
4 who redeems your life from the Pit,
    who crowns you with steadfast love
    and mercy,
5 who satisfies you with good as long as
    you live [a]
    so that your youth is renewed like the
    eagle's.

6 The Lord works vindication
    and justice for all who are oppressed.
7 He made known his ways to Moses,
    his acts to the people of Israel.

a Meaning of Heb uncertain

102:12–22 *You will rise up and have compassion on Zion.* These verses express confidence that God will rebuild Zion even in the midst of tragedy. Israel will see the fulfillment of its dearest hopes, that even the nations will gather in Zion to worship and obey God (v 22; cf. Isa 2:1–4; Mic 4:1–4). The God who is "enthroned forever" (v 12) and outlasts heaven and earth (vv 25–27) will see to it. Such

faith builds hope when disaster would tear us down.

102:17 PRAYER—*See* Spiritual Disciplines Index.

103:1–22 *Bless the Lord, O my soul.* This expansive recounting of God's goodness makes this hymn an "Amazing Grace" of the Old Testament, focusing intensely here on what the Israelites frequently witnessed.

8 The LORD is merciful and gracious,
   slow to anger and abounding in
      steadfast love.
9 He will not always accuse,
   nor will he keep his anger forever.
10 He does not deal with us according to
      our sins,
   nor repay us according to our
      iniquities.
11 For as the heavens are high above the
      earth,
   so great is his steadfast love toward
      those who fear him;
12 as far as the east is from the west,
   so far he removes our transgressions
      from us.
13 As a father has compassion for his
      children,
   so the LORD has compassion for those
      who fear him.
14 For he knows how we were made;
   he remembers that we are dust.

15 As for mortals, their days are like grass;
   they flourish like a flower of the field;
16 for the wind passes over it, and it is
      gone,
   and its place knows it no more.
17 But the steadfast love of the LORD is
      from everlasting to everlasting
   on those who fear him,
      and his righteousness to children's
         children,
18 to those who keep his covenant

and remember to do his
   commandments.

19 The LORD has established his throne in
      the heavens,
   and his kingdom rules over all.
20 Bless the LORD, O you his angels,
   you mighty ones who do his bidding,
      obedient to his spoken word.
21 Bless the LORD, all his hosts,
   his ministers that do his will.
22 Bless the LORD, all his works,
   in all places of his dominion.
   Bless the LORD, O my soul.

Psalm 104

God the Creator and Provider

1 Bless the LORD, O my soul.
   O LORD my God, you are very great.
   You are clothed with honor and majesty,
2   wrapped in light as with a garment.
   You stretch out the heavens like a tent,
3   you set the beams of your[a] chambers
         on the waters,
   you make the clouds your[a] chariot,
      you ride on the wings of the wind,
4   you make the winds your[a] messengers,
      fire and flame your[a] ministers.

5 You set the earth on its foundations,
   so that it shall never be shaken.

a Heb his

103:8 *The LORD is merciful and gracious, slow to anger and abounding in steadfast love.* This verse echoes the occasion when at Sinai God proclaimed the divine name, Yahweh ("the LORD"), to Moses (Exod 34:6). It is central to Israel's confession (see Num 14:8; Neh 9:17; Pss 86:15; 145:8; Jon 4:2).

103:10 *does not deal with us according to our sins.* Reflecting the themes of God as deliverer of Israel (v 7) and as Creator (v 14), the psalmist shows how God's love never quits. Though God is just (v 6), we don't suffer what we deserve (v 10). Though human life is fragile, God's love is rock solid (vv 15–18). To "bless the LORD" (vv 20–22) for this deepens our trust in God and produces a relaxed confidence at the heart of faith.

104:1–9 *You stretch out the heavens like a tent.* The first part of this stirring hymn praising God as Creator takes up many of the bold word pictures of the creation texts: stretching out the heavens like a tent (v 2; cf. Isa 40:22); setting the earth on firm foundations (v 5; cf. Job 38:4–6); proclaiming boundaries to threatening seas (v 9; cf. Job 38:8–11). Verse 7 echoes Genesis 1, but with more pizzazz, as at God's command the deeps that cover the earth scurry to their appointed places. A playful footnote to this witness to God's unrivaled power is in verse 26, where "Leviathan," sometimes portrayed as a chaotic monster threatening creation, is pictured as merely a playful creature, perhaps even God's pet.

6 You cover it with the deep as with a
    garment;
  the waters stood above the
    mountains.
7 At your rebuke they flee;
  at the sound of your thunder they
    take to flight.
8 They rose up to the mountains, ran
    down to the valleys
  to the place that you appointed for
    them.
9 You set a boundary that they may not
    pass,
  so that they might not again cover
    the earth.

10 You make springs gush forth in the
    valleys;
  they flow between the hills,
11 giving drink to every wild animal;
  the wild asses quench their thirst.
12 By the streams *a* the birds of the air have
    their habitation;
  they sing among the branches.
13 From your lofty abode you water the
    mountains;
  the earth is satisfied with the fruit of
    your work.

14 You cause the grass to grow for the
    cattle,
  and plants for people to use, *b*
  to bring forth food from the earth,
15   and wine to gladden the human
    heart,
  oil to make the face shine,
    and bread to strengthen the human
    heart.
16 The trees of the LORD are watered
    abundantly,
  the cedars of Lebanon that he
    planted.
17 In them the birds build their nests;
  the stork has its home in the fir trees.

18 The high mountains are for the wild
    goats;
  the rocks are a refuge for the coneys.
19 You have made the moon to mark the
    seasons;
  the sun knows its time for setting.
20 You make darkness, and it is night,
  when all the animals of the forest
    come creeping out.
21 The young lions roar for their prey,
  seeking their food from God.
22 When the sun rises, they withdraw
  and lie down in their dens.
23 People go out to their work
  and to their labor until the evening.

24 O LORD, how manifold are your works!
  In wisdom you have made them all;
  the earth is full of your creatures.
25 Yonder is the sea, great and wide,
  creeping things innumerable are
    there,
  living things both small and great.
26 There go the ships,
  and Leviathan that you formed to
    sport in it.

27 These all look to you
  to give them their food in due season;
28 when you give to them, they gather it
    up;
  when you open your hand, they are
    filled with good things.
29 When you hide your face, they are
    dismayed;
  when you take away their breath,
    they die
  and return to their dust.
30 When you send forth your spirit, *c* they
    are created;
  and you renew the face of the ground.

a Heb *By them*   *b* Or *to cultivate*   *c* Or *your breath*

104:10–30 *You make springs gush. . . . You cause the grass to grow.* God's lavish and orderly care for all the creatures brings them joy, and they rely on this steady care day-to-day (vv 27–30). We do well to marvel at the creation and bless God for the power, wisdom, and generosity we see in it. It can help ward off complacency, self-sufficiency, and even a false sense of entitlement. We do well to remember that each moment, each breath, is a gift.

31 May the glory of the LORD endure
        forever;
    may the LORD rejoice in his works—
32 who looks on the earth and it trembles,
    who touches the mountains and they
        smoke.
33 I will sing to the LORD as long as I live;
    I will sing praise to my God while I
        have being.
34 May my meditation be pleasing to him,
    for I rejoice in the LORD.
35 Let sinners be consumed from the
        earth,
    and let the wicked be no more.
    Bless the LORD, O my soul.
    Praise the LORD!

Psalm 105

God's Faithfulness to Israel

1 O give thanks to the LORD, call on his
        name,
    make known his deeds among the
        peoples.
2 Sing to him, sing praises to him;
    tell of all his wonderful works.
3 Glory in his holy name;
    let the hearts of those who seek the
        LORD rejoice.
4 Seek the LORD and his strength;
    seek his presence continually.
5 Remember the wonderful works he has
        done,
    his miracles, and the judgments he
        has uttered,
6 O offspring of his servant Abraham,[a]
    children of Jacob, his chosen ones.

7 He is the LORD our God;
    his judgments are in all the earth.

8 He is mindful of his covenant forever,
    of the word that he commanded, for a
        thousand generations,
9 the covenant that he made with
        Abraham,
    his sworn promise to Isaac,
10 which he confirmed to Jacob as a
        statute,
    to Israel as an everlasting covenant,
11 saying, "To you I will give the land of
        Canaan
    as your portion for an inheritance."

12 When they were few in number,
    of little account, and strangers in it,
13 wandering from nation to nation,
    from one kingdom to another people,
14 he allowed no one to oppress them;
    he rebuked kings on their account,
15 saying, "Do not touch my anointed ones;
    do my prophets no harm."

16 When he summoned famine against
        the land,
    and broke every staff of bread,
17 he had sent a man ahead of them,
    Joseph, who was sold as a slave.
18 His feet were hurt with fetters,
    his neck was put in a collar of iron;
19 until what he had said came to pass,
    the word of the LORD kept testing him.
20 The king sent and released him;
    the ruler of the peoples set him free.
21 He made him lord of his house,
    and ruler of all his possessions,
22 to instruct[b] his officials at his pleasure,
    and to teach his elders wisdom.

a Another reading is *Israel* (compare 1 Chr 16.13)
b Gk Syr Jerome: Heb *to bind*

105:1–45 *O give thanks to the LORD.* Historical psalms focus our attention on how God is at work in our ordinary experience. The placement of Psalm 105 joins it with seeing God as the Creator who steadily sustains life (Ps 104) and God who steadily acts in our "real world" (Ps 106). This psalm emphasizes God's faithfulness in keeping promises to Abraham and his descendants.
105:7–15 *the covenant that he made with Abraham, his sworn promise to Isaac.* God was at work even while Israel's first families lived as marginalized people in the land promised to them. The fulfillment of big promises sometimes has small beginnings.
105:16–25 *Joseph, who was sold as a slave.* God provides in desperate times and through unlikely means. In faithfulness behind the scenes God still acts, even when we struggle and doubt.

23 Then Israel came to Egypt;
    Jacob lived as an alien in the land of
        Ham.
24 And the LORD made his people very
        fruitful,
    and made them stronger than their
        foes,
25 whose hearts he then turned to hate his
        people,
    to deal craftily with his servants.

26 He sent his servant Moses,
    and Aaron whom he had chosen.
27 They performed his signs among them,
    and miracles in the land of Ham.
28 He sent darkness, and made the land
        dark;
    they rebelled *a* against his words.
29 He turned their waters into blood,
    and caused their fish to die.
30 Their land swarmed with frogs,
    even in the chambers of their kings.
31 He spoke, and there came swarms of
        flies,
    and gnats throughout their country.
32 He gave them hail for rain,
    and lightning that flashed through
        their land.
33 He struck their vines and fig trees,
    and shattered the trees of their
        country.
34 He spoke, and the locusts came,
    and young locusts without number;
35 they devoured all the vegetation in
        their land,
    and ate up the fruit of their ground.
36 He struck down all the firstborn in their
        land,
    the first issue of all their strength.

37 Then he brought Israel *b* out with silver
        and gold,

and there was no one among their
        tribes who stumbled.
38 Egypt was glad when they departed,
    for dread of them had fallen upon it.
39 He spread a cloud for a covering,
    and fire to give light by night.
40 They asked, and he brought quails,
    and gave them food from heaven in
        abundance.
41 He opened the rock, and water gushed
        out;
    it flowed through the desert like a
        river.
42 For he remembered his holy promise,
    and Abraham, his servant.

43 So he brought his people out with joy,
    his chosen ones with singing.
44 He gave them the lands of the nations,
    and they took possession of the
        wealth of the peoples,
45 that they might keep his statutes
    and observe his laws.
Praise the LORD!

Psalm 106

A Confession of Israel's Sins

1 Praise the LORD!
    O give thanks to the LORD, for he is
        good;
    for his steadfast love endures forever.
2 Who can utter the mighty doings of the
        LORD,
    or declare all his praise?
3 Happy are those who observe justice,
    who do righteousness at all times.

a Cn Compare Gk Syr: Heb *they did not rebel*
b Heb *them*

105:26–42 *He spoke, and there came swarms of flies.* No subtle presence here. God acts with "signs and wonders" in the plagues on Egypt (see 78:12–13, 42–53; Exod 7:8–12:32) and with generous provision in the wilderness.

105:43–45 *that they might keep his statutes.* In rejoicing over God's faithfulness that finally gave them the land promised to Abraham, the people are reminded that the right response is obedience and praise.

106:1–48 *Praise the LORD!* This historical psalm both confesses Israel's blatant failure to trust God and proclaims God's compassion. Given this history of rebellion and mercy, the singer asks again for rescue (vv 4–5, 47).

4 Remember me, O Lord, when you show
      favor to your people;
   help me when you deliver them;
5 that I may see the prosperity of your
      chosen ones,
   that I may rejoice in the gladness of
      your nation,
   that I may glory in your heritage.

6 Both we and our ancestors have sinned;
   we have committed iniquity, have
      done wickedly.
7 Our ancestors, when they were in
      Egypt,
   did not consider your wonderful
      works;
   they did not remember the abundance
      of your steadfast love,
   but rebelled against the Most High *a* at
      the Red Sea. *b*
8 Yet he saved them for his name's sake,
   so that he might make known his
      mighty power.
9 He rebuked the Red Sea, *b* and it became
      dry;
   he led them through the deep as
      through a desert.
10 So he saved them from the hand of the
      foe,
   and delivered them from the hand of
      the enemy.
11 The waters covered their adversaries;
   not one of them was left.
12 Then they believed his words;
   they sang his praise.

13 But they soon forgot his works;
   they did not wait for his counsel.
14 But they had a wanton craving in the
      wilderness,
   and put God to the test in the desert;

15 he gave them what they asked,
   but sent a wasting disease among
      them.

16 They were jealous of Moses in the camp,
   and of Aaron, the holy one of the
      Lord.
17 The earth opened and swallowed up
      Dathan,
   and covered the faction of Abiram.
18 Fire also broke out in their company;
   the flame burned up the wicked.

19 They made a calf at Horeb
   and worshiped a cast image.
20 They exchanged the glory of God *c*
   for the image of an ox that eats grass.
21 They forgot God, their Savior,
   who had done great things in Egypt,
22 wondrous works in the land of Ham,
   and awesome deeds by the Red Sea. *b*
23 Therefore he said he would destroy
      them—
   had not Moses, his chosen one,
   stood in the breach before him,
   to turn away his wrath from
      destroying them.

24 Then they despised the pleasant land,
   having no faith in his promise.
25 They grumbled in their tents,
   and did not obey the voice of the
      Lord.
26 Therefore he raised his hand and swore
      to them
   that he would make them fall in the
      wilderness,

---

a Cn Compare 78.17, 56: Heb *rebelled at the sea*
b Or *Sea of Reeds*   *c* Compare Gk Mss: Heb
exchanged their glory

106:6 *Both we and our ancestors have sinned.*
Though the story tells the history of rebellion, it
is not merely a blame game. The psalmist owns
and confesses failures both past and present.

106:7–12 *Our ancestors . . . did not consider
your wonderful works.* Even in the midst of the
full display of God's delivering power, the
people feared, doubted, grumbled, rebelled
(see Exod 14:10–12). The risks of freedom and

change can too easily make familiar bondage
seem comfortable.

106:13 *they soon forgot his works.* In
uncertain times especially it is important to
"remember" God's abundant love (v 7), not to
"forget" God's "awesome deeds" (vv 21–22).
Deliberate remembering gives a context for
confidence.

27 and would disperse[a] their descendants
     among the nations,
       scattering them over the lands.

28 Then they attached themselves to the
     Baal of Peor,
       and ate sacrifices offered to the dead;
29 they provoked the LORD to anger with
     their deeds,
       and a plague broke out among them.
30 Then Phinehas stood up and
     interceded,
       and the plague was stopped.
31 And that has been reckoned to him as
     righteousness
       from generation to generation
         forever.

32 They angered the LORD[b] at the waters of
     Meribah,
       and it went ill with Moses on their
         account;
33 for they made his spirit bitter,
       and he spoke words that were rash.

34 They did not destroy the peoples,
       as the LORD commanded them,
35 but they mingled with the nations
       and learned to do as they did.
36 They served their idols,
       which became a snare to them.
37 They sacrificed their sons
       and their daughters to the demons;
38 they poured out innocent blood,
       the blood of their sons and daughters,
         whom they sacrificed to the idols of
           Canaan;
       and the land was polluted with blood.
39 Thus they became unclean by their acts,
       and prostituted themselves in their
         doings.

40 Then the anger of the LORD was kindled
     against his people,
       and he abhorred his heritage;

41 he gave them into the hand of the
     nations,
       so that those who hated them ruled
         over them.
42 Their enemies oppressed them,
       and they were brought into
         subjection under their power.
43 Many times he delivered them,
       but they were rebellious in their
         purposes,
       and were brought low through their
         iniquity.
44 Nevertheless he regarded their distress
       when he heard their cry.
45 For their sake he remembered his
     covenant,
       and showed compassion according to
         the abundance of his steadfast
           love.
46 He caused them to be pitied
       by all who held them captive.

47 Save us, O LORD our God,
       and gather us from among the nations,
     that we may give thanks to your holy
       name
       and glory in your praise.

48 Blessed be the LORD, the God of Israel,
       from everlasting to everlasting.
     And let all the people say, "Amen."
       Praise the LORD!

BOOK V

(Psalms 107–150)

Psalm 107

Thanksgiving for Deliverance from Many Troubles

1 O give thanks to the LORD, for he is good;
       for his steadfast love endures forever.

a Syr Compare Ezek 20.23: Heb cause to fall
b Heb him

106:34–46 *They served their idols.* Unlike the previous stanzas, which point to rebellion in the wilderness, these refer to Israel's settlement and disloyalty in Canaan during the period of the judges. God's compassion in this repeated cycle of disobedience and deliverance (vv 43–45) gives reason for hope.

106:48 *let all the people say, "Amen."* Doxology and praise close this, the fourth book of the Psalter.

² Let the redeemed of the LORD say so,
    those he redeemed from trouble
³ and gathered in from the lands,
    from the east and from the west,
    from the north and from the south. *a*

⁴ Some wandered in desert wastes,
    finding no way to an inhabited town;
⁵ hungry and thirsty,
    their soul fainted within them.
⁶ Then they cried to the LORD in their
        trouble,
    and he delivered them from their
        distress;
⁷ he led them by a straight way,
    until they reached an inhabited
        town.
⁸ Let them thank the LORD for his
        steadfast love,
    for his wonderful works to
        humankind.
⁹ For he satisfies the thirsty,
    and the hungry he fills with good
        things.

¹⁰ Some sat in darkness and in gloom,
    prisoners in misery and in irons,
¹¹ for they had rebelled against the words
        of God,
    and spurned the counsel of the Most
        High.
¹² Their hearts were bowed down with
        hard labor;
    they fell down, with no one to help.
¹³ Then they cried to the LORD in their
        trouble,
    and he saved them from their distress;
¹⁴ he brought them out of darkness and
        gloom,
    and broke their bonds asunder.
¹⁵ Let them thank the LORD for his
        steadfast love,
    for his wonderful works to
        humankind.

¹⁶ For he shatters the doors of bronze,
    and cuts in two the bars of iron.

¹⁷ Some were sick *b* through their sinful
        ways,
    and because of their iniquities
        endured affliction;
¹⁸ they loathed any kind of food,
    and they drew near to the gates of
        death.
¹⁹ Then they cried to the LORD in their
        trouble,
    and he saved them from their distress;
²⁰ he sent out his word and healed them,
    and delivered them from destruction.
²¹ Let them thank the LORD for his
        steadfast love,
    for his wonderful works to
        humankind.
²² And let them offer thanksgiving
        sacrifices,
    and tell of his deeds with songs of joy.

²³ Some went down to the sea in ships,
    doing business on the mighty
        waters;
²⁴ they saw the deeds of the LORD,
    his wondrous works in the deep.
²⁵ For he commanded and raised the
        stormy wind,
    which lifted up the waves of the sea.
²⁶ They mounted up to heaven, they went
        down to the depths;
    their courage melted away in their
        calamity;
²⁷ they reeled and staggered like
        drunkards,
    and were at their wits' end.
²⁸ Then they cried to the LORD in their
        trouble,
    and he brought them out from their
        distress;

a Cn: Heb *sea*   *b* Cn: Heb *fools*

107:1–43 *O give thanks to the LORD.* This thanksgiving song celebrates rescue from four specific dangers: the desert, prison, sickness, and the stormy sea. In each case two verses are repeated as a refrain. In distress "they cried to the LORD in their trouble, and he delivered them" (vv 6, 13, 19, 28). In response to rescue, "Let them thank the LORD for his steadfast love . . ." (vv 8, 15, 21, 31). Thanksgiving remembers God's action, but even more gives witness to God's character.

29 he made the storm be still,
  and the waves of the sea were hushed.
30 Then they were glad because they had
    quiet,
  and he brought them to their desired
    haven.
31 Let them thank the LORD for his
    steadfast love,
  for his wonderful works to
    humankind.
32 Let them extol him in the congregation
    of the people,
  and praise him in the assembly of the
    elders.

33 He turns rivers into a desert,
  springs of water into thirsty ground,
34 a fruitful land into a salty waste,
  because of the wickedness of its
    inhabitants.
35 He turns a desert into pools of water,
  a parched land into springs of water.
36 And there he lets the hungry live,
  and they establish a town to live in;
37 they sow fields, and plant vineyards,
  and get a fruitful yield.
38 By his blessing they multiply greatly,
  and he does not let their cattle
    decrease.

39 When they are diminished and brought
    low
  through oppression, trouble, and
    sorrow,
40 he pours contempt on princes
  and makes them wander in trackless
    wastes;
41 but he raises up the needy out of
    distress,
  and makes their families like flocks.
42 The upright see it and are glad;
  and all wickedness stops its mouth.
43 Let those who are wise give heed to
    these things,

and consider the steadfast love of the
  LORD.

Psalm 108

Praise and Prayer for Victory

A Song. A Psalm of David.

1 My heart is steadfast, O God, my heart
    is steadfast;[a]
  I will sing and make melody.
  Awake, my soul![b]
2 Awake, O harp and lyre!
  I will awake the dawn.
3 I will give thanks to you, O LORD,
    among the peoples,
  and I will sing praises to you among
    the nations.
4 For your steadfast love is higher than
    the heavens,
  and your faithfulness reaches to the
    clouds.

5 Be exalted, O God, above the heavens,
  and let your glory be over all the
    earth.
6 Give victory with your right hand, and
    answer me,
  so that those whom you love may be
    rescued.

7 God has promised in his sanctuary:[c]
  "With exultation I will divide up
    Shechem,
  and portion out the Vale of Succoth.
8 Gilead is mine; Manasseh is mine;
  Ephraim is my helmet;
  Judah is my scepter.
9 Moab is my washbasin;
  on Edom I hurl my shoe;
  over Philistia I shout in triumph."

a Heb Mss Gk Syr: MT lacks *my heart is steadfast*
b Compare 57.8: Heb *also my soul*　　c Or *by his holiness*

107:33–43 *he lets the hungry live.* These stanzas praise God, especially for caring for the needy and oppressed. God loves and watches out for people at risk.
　107:43 *consider the steadfast love of the LORD.* Mull it over. Let it capture your attention. Learn

to know the love that is beyond knowing (see Eph 3:18–19).
　108:1–5 *My heart is steadfast.* These verses repeat 57:7–11. See note on 57:1–11.
　108:6–13 *Give the victory.* These verses repeat 60:5–12. See note on 60:1–12.

10 Who will bring me to the fortified city?
　　Who will lead me to Edom?
11 Have you not rejected us, O God?
　　You do not go out, O God, with our
　　　armies.
12 O grant us help against the foe,
　　for human help is worthless.
13 With God we shall do valiantly;
　　it is he who will tread down our foes.

Psalm 109

Prayer for Vindication and Vengeance

To the leader. Of David. A Psalm.

1 Do not be silent, O God of my praise.
2 For wicked and deceitful mouths are
　　opened against me,
　　speaking against me with lying
　　tongues.
3 They beset me with words of hate,
　　and attack me without cause.
4 In return for my love they accuse me,
　　even while I make prayer for them. a
5 So they reward me evil for good,
　　and hatred for my love.

6 They say, b "Appoint a wicked man
　　against him;
　　let an accuser stand on his right.
7 When he is tried, let him be found guilty;
　　let his prayer be counted as sin.
8 May his days be few;
　　may another seize his position.
9 May his children be orphans,
　　and his wife a widow.
10 May his children wander about and
　　beg;
　　may they be driven out of c the ruins
　　they inhabit.
11 May the creditor seize all that he has;
　　may strangers plunder the fruits of his
　　toil.

12 May there be no one to do him a
　　kindness,
　　nor anyone to pity his orphaned
　　children.
13 May his posterity be cut off;
　　may his name be blotted out in the
　　second generation.
14 May the iniquity of his father d be
　　remembered before the LORD,
　　and do not let the sin of his mother
　　be blotted out.
15 Let them be before the LORD
　　continually,
　　and may his e memory be cut off from
　　the earth.
16 For he did not remember to show
　　kindness,
　　but pursued the poor and needy
　　and the brokenhearted to their death.
17 He loved to curse; let curses come on
　　him.
　　He did not like blessing; may it be far
　　from him.
18 He clothed himself with cursing as his
　　coat,
　　may it soak into his body like water,
　　like oil into his bones.
19 May it be like a garment that he wraps
　　around himself,
　　like a belt that he wears every day."

20 May that be the reward of my accusers
　　from the LORD,
　　of those who speak evil against my
　　life.
21 But you, O LORD my Lord,
　　act on my behalf for your name's sake;
　　because your steadfast love is good,
　　deliver me.

a Syr: Heb I prayer　　b Heb lacks They say
c Gk: Heb and seek　　d Cn: Heb fathers
e Gk: Heb their

109:1–19 *They beset me with words of hate.*
Puzzled and distraught, the psalmist catalogs the
crimes of those who want to kill him. They return
attack for kindness, try to corrupt the court, wish
for the ruin of his family, and lie constantly.
109:4 PRAYER—*See* Spiritual Disciplines
Index.

109:20 *May that be the reward of my accusers
from the LORD.* Appealing to God's steadfast love
and care for the needy, the singer wants God to
turn the evil back toward his oppressors. As is
typical of the lament, the singer leaves justice in
God's hands rather than acting vengefully on his
own—a valuable word for us today.

22 For I am poor and needy,
  and my heart is pierced within me.
23 I am gone like a shadow at evening;
  I am shaken off like a locust.
24 My knees are weak through fasting;
  my body has become gaunt.
25 I am an object of scorn to my accusers;
  when they see me, they shake their
    heads.

26 Help me, O LORD my God!
  Save me according to your steadfast
    love.
27 Let them know that this is your hand;
  you, O LORD, have done it.
28 Let them curse, but you will bless.
  Let my assailants be put to shame;ᵃ
    may your servant be glad.
29 May my accusers be clothed with
    dishonor;
  may they be wrapped in their own
    shame as in a mantle.
30 With my mouth I will give great thanks
    to the LORD;
  I will praise him in the midst of the
    throng.
31 For he stands at the right hand of the
    needy,
  to save them from those who would
    condemn them to death.

Psalm 110

Assurance of Victory for God's Priest-King

Of David. A Psalm.

1 The LORD says to my lord,
  "Sit at my right hand

until I make your enemies your
    footstool."
2 The LORD sends out from Zion
  your mighty scepter.
  Rule in the midst of your foes.
3 Your people will offer themselves
    willingly
  on the day you lead your forces
  on the holy mountains.ᵇ
From the womb of the morning,
  like dew, your youthᶜ will come to you.
4 The LORD has sworn and will not
    change his mind,
  "You are a priest forever according to
    the order of Melchizedek."ᵈ

5 The Lord is at your right hand;
  he will shatter kings on the day of his
    wrath.
6 He will execute judgment among the
    nations,
  filling them with corpses;
he will shatter heads
  over the wide earth.
7 He will drink from the stream by the
    path;
  therefore he will lift up his head.

Psalm 111

Praise for God's Wonderful Works

1 Praise the LORD!

a Gk: Heb *They have risen up and have been put to
shame*   b Another reading is *in holy splendor*
c Cn: Heb *the dew of your youth*   d Or *forever, a
rightful king by my edict*

Responding
109:24 FASTING. The contrast
between fasting from food for spiritual
reasons and fasting from food for political
reasons is huge. The first fast focuses on God;
the second is about manipulation. The goal of
the first is intense spiritual activity; the purpose
of the second is to force other people to do
what the person fasting desires. To learn more
about spiritual fasting, read *God's Chosen
Fast* by Arthur Wallis. *See also* Spiritual
Disciplines Index.

110:1–7 *The LORD says to my lord.* This royal
psalm recognizes the Davidic monarch's
authority as both king and priest, roles not
ultimately separated in ancient Israel. The New
Testament often uses this psalm to refer to
Jesus as the Anointed One (Messiah) in the
continuing dynasty of David. It refers both to
the kingly role (v 1; see, e.g., Acts 2:34–35) and
the priestly role (v 4; see, e.g., Heb 5:6). This
new Messiah defeated and disarmed the powers
("rulers and authorities") and paraded them as
conquered enemies (Col 2:15; cf. Ps 110:5–6).

I will give thanks to the LORD with my
   whole heart,
   in the company of the upright, in the
     congregation.
2 Great are the works of the LORD,
   studied by all who delight in
     them.
3 Full of honor and majesty is his
   work,
   and his righteousness endures
     forever.
4 He has gained renown by his wonderful
   deeds;
   the LORD is gracious and merciful.
5 He provides food for those who fear
   him;
   he is ever mindful of his covenant.
6 He has shown his people the power of
   his works,
   in giving them the heritage of the
     nations.
7 The works of his hands are faithful and
   just;
   all his precepts are trustworthy.
8 They are established forever and ever,
   to be performed with faithfulness and
     uprightness.
9 He sent redemption to his people;
   he has commanded his covenant
     forever.
   Holy and awesome is his name.
10 The fear of the LORD is the beginning of
   wisdom;
   all those who practice it*a* have a good
     understanding.
   His praise endures forever.

Psalm 112

Blessings of the Righteous

1 Praise the LORD!
   Happy are those who fear the LORD,
   who greatly delight in his
     commandments.
2 Their descendants will be mighty in the
     land;
   the generation of the upright will be
     blessed.
3 Wealth and riches are in their houses,
   and their righteousness endures
     forever.
4 They rise in the darkness as a light for
     the upright;
   they are gracious, merciful, and
     righteous.
5 It is well with those who deal
     generously and lend,
   who conduct their affairs with justice.
6 For the righteous will never be
     moved;
   they will be remembered forever.
7 They are not afraid of evil tidings;
   their hearts are firm, secure in the
     LORD.
8 Their hearts are steady, they will not be
     afraid;
   in the end they will look in triumph
     on their foes.
9 They have distributed freely, they have
     given to the poor;
   their righteousness endures forever;
   their horn is exalted in honor.

a Gk Syr: Heb *them*

111:1–10 *Praise the LORD!* This hymn of thanksgiving and praise seems particularly suited to teaching. In Hebrew it is an alphabetic acrostic poem, in which the first line begins with the first letter of the alphabet, the second line with the second letter, and so on. This helps with memorization. The word "wisdom" (v 10) also suggests the song is especially intended to teach. So also the content reminds hearers of many of the main reasons to praise God. The song will reward patient, attentive reading.
111:2 STUDY—*See* Spiritual Disciplines Index.

112:1–10 *Praise the LORD!* This psalm, also an alphabetic acrostic, may well partner with Psalm 111 for teaching purposes. The songs are bridged by the use of "fear of the LORD" in 111:10 and 112:1. This psalm shifts from God's character to the traits of those who fear the Lord and "greatly delight in his commandments" (v 1). Compare Psalms 1; 19; 119, but also compare summaries of right, wisdom-guided behavior in Job 29–31; Prov 31:10–31. People who learn from this song to do the right thing (practice righteousness) will last and be honored, much to the annoyance of the wicked.

10 The wicked see it and are angry;
     they gnash their teeth and melt away;
     the desire of the wicked comes to
          nothing.

Psalm 113

God the Helper of the Needy

1 Praise the LORD!
  Praise, O servants of the LORD;
     praise the name of the LORD.

2 Blessed be the name of the LORD
     from this time on and forevermore.
3 From the rising of the sun to its
          setting
     the name of the LORD is to be praised.
4 The LORD is high above all nations,
     and his glory above the heavens.

5 Who is like the LORD our God,
     who is seated on high,
6 who looks far down
     on the heavens and the earth?
7 He raises the poor from the dust,
     and lifts the needy from the ash
          heap,
8 to make them sit with princes,
     with the princes of his people.
9 He gives the barren woman a home,
     making her the joyous mother of
          children.
  Praise the LORD!

Psalm 114

God's Wonders at the Exodus

1 When Israel went out from Egypt,
     the house of Jacob from a people of
          strange language,
2 Judah became God's*a* sanctuary,
     Israel his dominion.

3 The sea looked and fled;
     Jordan turned back.
4 The mountains skipped like rams,
     the hills like lambs.

5 Why is it, O sea, that you flee?
     O Jordan, that you turn back?
6 O mountains, that you skip like rams?
     O hills, like lambs?

7 Tremble, O earth, at the presence of the
          LORD,
     at the presence of the God of Jacob,
8 who turns the rock into a pool of water,
     the flint into a spring of water.

Psalm 115

The Impotence of Idols and the Greatness of God

1 Not to us, O LORD, not to us, but to your
          name give glory,

a Heb *his*

Responding
113:1 SERVICE. Contrary to this
psalm, which says God raises the poor
and lifts the needy, Jesus taught that we are to
bring his love and healing to the hungry, thirsty,
strangers, needy, ill, and imprisoned (see Matt
25). Are the teachings in these two passages at
odds with each other? Can they be reconciled
or are they just indicative of the struggle all
of us experience in serving those we find
"unlovable"? Try this week to become more
sensitive to the needs of people you find un-
deserving by giving food to a local food bank
or making a special effort to be friendly to
someone you don't know. *See also* Spiritual
Disciplines Index.

113:1–9 *Praise the LORD!* The Lord who is
high above the heavens looks far down to see
and care for the folk most people don't notice at
all—the poor and the needy in ash heaps and
garbage dumps. It should open the eyes of
"servants of the LORD."

114:1–8 *When Israel went out from Egypt.*
This playful hymn recounts God's wonders in
bringing Israel from Egypt to Canaan—splitting
the sea, providing water in the wilderness,
backing up the Jordan River. Rejoicing in God's
overwhelming power, the song teases elements
of nature for their quick compliance with God
on the march. "Why, O mountains, did you skip
like rams?" (cf. 29:6; 77:16). We can admire and
delight in God's wonders.

for the sake of your steadfast love and
  your faithfulness.
2 Why should the nations say,
  "Where is their God?"

3 Our God is in the heavens;
  he does whatever he pleases.
4 Their idols are silver and gold,
  the work of human hands.
5 They have mouths, but do not speak;
  eyes, but do not see.
6 They have ears, but do not hear;
  noses, but do not smell.
7 They have hands, but do not feel;
  feet, but do not walk;
  they make no sound in their throats.
8 Those who make them are like them;
  so are all who trust in them.

9 O Israel, trust in the LORD!
  He is their help and their shield.
10 O house of Aaron, trust in the LORD!
  He is their help and their shield.
11 You who fear the LORD, trust in the
  LORD!
  He is their help and their shield.

12 The LORD has been mindful of us; he
  will bless us;
  he will bless the house of Israel;
  he will bless the house of Aaron;
13 he will bless those who fear the LORD,
  both small and great.

14 May the LORD give you increase,
  both you and your children.
15 May you be blessed by the LORD,
  who made heaven and earth.

16 The heavens are the LORD's heavens,

but the earth he has given to human
  beings.
17 The dead do not praise the LORD,
  nor do any that go down into
  silence.
18 But we will bless the LORD
  from this time on and forevermore.
Praise the LORD!

Psalm 116

Thanksgiving for Recovery from Illness

1 I love the LORD, because he has heard
  my voice and my supplications.
2 Because he inclined his ear to me,
  therefore I will call on him as long as I
  live.
3 The snares of death encompassed me;
  the pangs of Sheol laid hold on me;
  I suffered distress and anguish.
4 Then I called on the name of the LORD:
  "O LORD, I pray, save my life!"

5 Gracious is the LORD, and righteous;
  our God is merciful.
6 The LORD protects the simple;
  when I was brought low, he saved me.
7 Return, O my soul, to your rest,
  for the LORD has dealt bountifully
  with you.

8 For you have delivered my soul from
  death,
  my eyes from tears,
  my feet from stumbling.
9 I walk before the LORD
  in the land of the living.
10 I kept my faith, even when I said,
  "I am greatly afflicted";
11 I said in my consternation,
  "Everyone is a liar."

115:1–18 *Not to us, O LORD.* This prayer of
the people declares that Yahweh, the God of
Israel, is the only one to trust. The structure of
the song suggests choruses singing and speakers
answering antiphonally.

115:2–8 *Their idols are silver and gold, the
work of human hands.* Though the nations
challenge Yahweh, their gods are sad specimens,

handmade and powerless. We today still vainly
trust in security schemes of our own making.

116:1–11 *I love the LORD, because he has
heard my voice.* The first part of this fine
example of the thanksgiving song shows the
singer's desperate situation, his anguished cry
for help, and God's gracious rescue. It describes
God's particular action and, even more, God's
character.

12 What shall I return to the LORD
    for all his bounty to me?
13 I will lift up the cup of salvation
    and call on the name of the LORD,
14 I will pay my vows to the LORD
    in the presence of all his people.
15 Precious in the sight of the LORD
    is the death of his faithful ones.
16 O LORD, I am your servant;
    I am your servant, the child of your
        serving girl.
    You have loosed my bonds.
17 I will offer to you a thanksgiving
        sacrifice
    and call on the name of the LORD.
18 I will pay my vows to the LORD
    in the presence of all his people,
19 in the courts of the house of the LORD,
    in your midst, O Jerusalem.
    Praise the LORD!

Psalm 117

Universal Call to Worship

1 Praise the LORD, all you nations!
    Extol him, all you peoples!
2 For great is his steadfast love toward us,
    and the faithfulness of the LORD
        endures forever.
    Praise the LORD!

Psalm 118

A Song of Victory

1 O give thanks to the LORD, for he is
        good;
    his steadfast love endures forever!

2 Let Israel say,
    "His steadfast love endures forever."
3 Let the house of Aaron say,
    "His steadfast love endures forever."
4 Let those who fear the LORD say,
    "His steadfast love endures forever."

5 Out of my distress I called on the LORD;
    the LORD answered me and set me in a
        broad place.
6 With the LORD on my side I do not fear.
    What can mortals do to me?
7 The LORD is on my side to help me;
    I shall look in triumph on those who
        hate me.
8 It is better to take refuge in the LORD
    than to put confidence in mortals.
9 It is better to take refuge in the LORD
    than to put confidence in princes.

10 All nations surrounded me;
    in the name of the LORD I cut them
        off!
11 They surrounded me, surrounded me
        on every side;
    in the name of the LORD I cut them
        off!
12 They surrounded me like bees;
    they blazed[a] like a fire of thorns;
    in the name of the LORD I cut them
        off!
13 I was pushed hard,[b] so that I was falling,
    but the LORD helped me.
14 The LORD is my strength and my might;
    he has become my salvation.

a Gk: Heb *were extinguished*   b Gk Syr Jerome:
Heb *You pushed me hard*

116:12–19 *What shall I return to the LORD for all his bounty?* Often in the cries for help in lament songs, the singer promises praise or sacrifices when God delivers him. The singer's gladness in paying his vows also reminds us of the importance of taking our promises to God seriously and of giving glad thanks.

117:1–2 *Praise the LORD, all you nations!* This, the shortest psalm of all, is compact, but packed. It has the complete form of the hymn of praise: call to praise, reason for praise, renewed call. It also has the magnificent bare-bones message: everybody, praise God for matchless love, praise the Lord!

118:1–29 *O give thanks to the LORD!* This individual song of thanksgiving is set in the context of community worship, complete with antiphonal singing (vv 2–4) and evidence of procession (vv 19–20, 27). It opens and closes with a familiar and central witness to God's steadfast love (vv 1, 29).

118:5–9 *The LORD is on my side.* Bold reminders for us about who to trust.

15 There are glad songs of victory in the
      tents of the righteous:
   "The right hand of the LORD does
      valiantly;
16   the right hand of the LORD is exalted;
      the right hand of the LORD does
      valiantly."
17 I shall not die, but I shall live,
      and recount the deeds of the LORD.
18 The LORD has punished me severely,
      but he did not give me over to death.

19 Open to me the gates of righteousness,
      that I may enter through them
      and give thanks to the LORD.

20 This is the gate of the LORD;
      the righteous shall enter through it.

21 I thank you that you have answered me
      and have become my salvation.
22 The stone that the builders rejected
      has become the chief cornerstone.
23 This is the LORD's doing;
      it is marvelous in our eyes.
24 This is the day that the LORD has made;
      let us rejoice and be glad in it. *a*
25 Save us, we beseech you, O LORD!

   O LORD, we beseech you, give us
      success!

26 Blessed is the one who comes in the
      name of the LORD. *b*
   We bless you from the house of the
      LORD.
27 The LORD is God,
      and he has given us light.
   Bind the festal procession with
      branches,
   up to the horns of the altar. *c*

28 You are my God, and I will give thanks
      to you;
   you are my God, I will extol you.

29 O give thanks to the LORD, for he is good,
      for his steadfast love endures forever.

Psalm 119

The Glories of God's Law

1 Happy are those whose way is
      blameless,
   who walk in the law of the LORD.

a Or *in him*   *b* Or *Blessed in the name of the LORD
is the one who comes*   *c* Meaning of Heb uncertain

118:22–24 *This is the LORD's doing.* God's
deliverance beat the odds, rescued and honored
the unlikely. It's only right to rejoice and
celebrate such remarkable acts.

119:1–176 *Happy are those whose way is
blameless.* This psalm explores the wonders of
God's provision through the law (Torah; see Ps
19) and the delight of living under its guidance.
It's easy to neglect this psalm. It's long. The
acrostic poetic device, in which the eight lines
of each stanza begin with the same letter,
sometimes hinders the flow. It frequently
repeats themes and especially eight words that
serve as poetic variants in referring to the law
(commandments, statutes, ordinances, decrees,
words, precepts, promise, law). But the psalm
deserves rumination, thoughtful brooding.
Psalm 119 is a wide-ranging A–Z reflection on
living gladly under God's rule. It includes praise
and thanksgiving, frequent admiration of God's
wisdom and generosity in giving the Torah,
pleas for deliverance and renewal, and much

more. People who have been taught that the
Israelites suffered under or were burdened
by Torah may be surprised at the psalm's
joyfulness. It brims over with how precious
Torah is and with eagerness to be shaped
toward the life it portrays.

Responding
119:1–176 STUDY and MEDITATION.
Written to instruct readers, this psalm
emphasizes that we should meditate on God's
precepts (v 15), statutes (v 23), works (v 27),
law (v 97), decrees (v 99), and promise (v 148).
In five out of the six references, the psalmist has
studied extensively, so that God's words come
readily to mind. Try this week to set aside time
first to meditate on the psalm, then to study it
in depth, and then to meditate on it again.
Which was easier, meditating on the psalm
before or after the study? *See also* Spiritual
Disciplines Index.

2 Happy are those who keep his decrees,
  who seek him with their whole heart,
3 who also do no wrong,
  but walk in his ways.
4 You have commanded your precepts
  to be kept diligently.
5 O that my ways may be steadfast
  in keeping your statutes!
6 Then I shall not be put to shame,
  having my eyes fixed on all your
    commandments.
7 I will praise you with an upright heart,
  when I learn your righteous
    ordinances.
8 I will observe your statutes;
  do not utterly forsake me.

9 How can young people keep their way
    pure?
  By guarding it according to your
    word.
10 With my whole heart I seek you;
  do not let me stray from your
    commandments.
11 I treasure your word in my heart,
  so that I may not sin against you.
12 Blessed are you, O LORD;
  teach me your statutes.
13 With my lips I declare
  all the ordinances of your mouth.
14 I delight in the way of your decrees
  as much as in all riches.
15 I will meditate on your precepts,
  and fix my eyes on your ways.
16 I will delight in your statutes;
  I will not forget your word.

17 Deal bountifully with your servant,
  so that I may live and observe your
    word.
18 Open my eyes, so that I may behold
  wondrous things out of your law.
19 I live as an alien in the land;
  do not hide your commandments
    from me.
20 My soul is consumed with longing
  for your ordinances at all times.
21 You rebuke the insolent, accursed ones,
  who wander from your
    commandments;
22 take away from me their scorn and
    contempt,
  for I have kept your decrees.
23 Even though princes sit plotting against
    me,
  your servant will meditate on your
    statutes.
24 Your decrees are my delight,
  they are my counselors.

25 My soul clings to the dust;
  revive me according to your word.
26 When I told of my ways, you answered
    me;
  teach me your statutes.
27 Make me understand the way of your
    precepts,
  and I will meditate on your wondrous
    works.
28 My soul melts away for sorrow;
  strengthen me according to your
    word.
29 Put false ways far from me;
  and graciously teach me your law.
30 I have chosen the way of faithfulness;
  I set your ordinances before me.
31 I cling to your decrees, O LORD;
  let me not be put to shame.
32 I run the way of your commandments,
  for you enlarge my understanding.

33 Teach me, O LORD, the way of your
    statutes,
  and I will observe it to the end.
34 Give me understanding, that I may keep
    your law
  and observe it with my whole heart.
35 Lead me in the path of your
    commandments,
  for I delight in it.
36 Turn my heart to your decrees,
  and not to selfish gain.

119:26–27 *teach me . . . Make me understand.*
In these ways and others throughout this song
("Open my eyes," v 18; "Turn my heart," v 36),
the psalmist asks God to teach him. This points
to a dynamic, continuing relationship between
God and the singer, not to a bookishness that
serves erudition and keeping rules. It appeals to
practical, ongoing guidance and transformation.

37 Turn my eyes from looking at vanities;
    give me life in your ways.
38 Confirm to your servant your promise,
    which is for those who fear you.
39 Turn away the disgrace that I dread,
    for your ordinances are good.
40 See, I have longed for your precepts;
    in your righteousness give me life.

41 Let your steadfast love come to me,
    O Lord,
    your salvation according to your
    promise.
42 Then I shall have an answer for those
    who taunt me,
    for I trust in your word.
43 Do not take the word of truth utterly
    out of my mouth,
    for my hope is in your ordinances.
44 I will keep your law continually,
    forever and ever.
45 I shall walk at liberty,
    for I have sought your precepts.
46 I will also speak of your decrees before
    kings,
    and shall not be put to shame;
47 I find my delight in your
    commandments,
    because I love them.
48 I revere your commandments, which I
    love,
    and I will meditate on your statutes.

49 Remember your word to your servant,
    in which you have made me hope.
50 This is my comfort in my distress,
    that your promise gives me life.
51 The arrogant utterly deride me,
    but I do not turn away from your law.
52 When I think of your ordinances from
    of old,
    I take comfort, O Lord.
53 Hot indignation seizes me because of
    the wicked,

    those who forsake your law.
54 Your statutes have been my songs
    wherever I make my home.
55 I remember your name in the night,
    O Lord,
    and keep your law.
56 This blessing has fallen to me,
    for I have kept your precepts.

57 The Lord is my portion;
    I promise to keep your words.
58 I implore your favor with all my heart;
    be gracious to me according to your
    promise.
59 When I think of your ways,
    I turn my feet to your decrees;
60 I hurry and do not delay
    to keep your commandments.
61 Though the cords of the wicked ensnare
    me,
    I do not forget your law.
62 At midnight I rise to praise you,
    because of your righteous
    ordinances.
63 I am a companion of all who fear you,
    of those who keep your precepts.
64 The earth, O Lord, is full of your
    steadfast love;
    teach me your statutes.

65 You have dealt well with your servant,
    O Lord, according to your word.
66 Teach me good judgment and
    knowledge,
    for I believe in your commandments.
67 Before I was humbled I went astray,
    but now I keep your word.
68 You are good and do good;
    teach me your statutes.
69 The arrogant smear me with lies,
    but with my whole heart I keep your
    precepts.
70 Their hearts are fat and gross,
    but I delight in your law.

119:59 *When I think of your ways.* Much of the singer's delight and devotion come from reflecting on God's own character and action— among others, God's faithfulness, steadfast love, creative power, and deliverance.

119:70 *I delight in your law.* Note throughout the psalm the language of delight, desire, longing, panting, joy, pleasure (sweeter than honey, better than money). The range and intensity of these images offer an inviting challenge for us to be as eager.

71 It is good for me that I was humbled,
    so that I might learn your statutes.
72 The law of your mouth is better to me
    than thousands of gold and silver
    pieces.

73 Your hands have made and fashioned
    me;
    give me understanding that I may
    learn your commandments.
74 Those who fear you shall see me and
    rejoice,
    because I have hoped in your word.
75 I know, O LORD, that your judgments
    are right,
    and that in faithfulness you have
    humbled me.
76 Let your steadfast love become my
    comfort
    according to your promise to your
    servant.
77 Let your mercy come to me, that I may
    live;
    for your law is my delight.
78 Let the arrogant be put to shame,
    because they have subverted me with
    guile;
    as for me, I will meditate on your
    precepts.
79 Let those who fear you turn to me,
    so that they may know your decrees.
80 May my heart be blameless in your
    statutes,
    so that I may not be put to shame.

81 My soul languishes for your salvation;
    I hope in your word.
82 My eyes fail with watching for your
    promise;
    I ask, "When will you comfort me?"
83 For I have become like a wineskin in the
    smoke,
    yet I have not forgotten your statutes.
84 How long must your servant endure?
    When will you judge those who
    persecute me?
85 The arrogant have dug pitfalls for me;
    they flout your law.
86 All your commandments are enduring;
    I am persecuted without cause; help
    me!

87 They have almost made an end of me
    on earth;
    but I have not forsaken your precepts.
88 In your steadfast love spare my life,
    so that I may keep the decrees of your
    mouth.

89 The LORD exists forever;
    your word is firmly fixed in heaven.
90 Your faithfulness endures to all
    generations;
    you have established the earth, and it
    stands fast.
91 By your appointment they stand today,
    for all things are your servants.
92 If your law had not been my delight,
    I would have perished in my misery.
93 I will never forget your precepts,
    for by them you have given me life.
94 I am yours; save me,
    for I have sought your precepts.
95 The wicked lie in wait to destroy me,
    but I consider your decrees.
96 I have seen a limit to all perfection,
    but your commandment is
    exceedingly broad.

97 Oh, how I love your law!
    It is my meditation all day long.
98 Your commandment makes me wiser
    than my enemies,
    for it is always with me.
99 I have more understanding than all my
    teachers,
    for your decrees are my meditation.
100 I understand more than the aged,
    for I keep your precepts.
101 I hold back my feet from every evil way,
    in order to keep your word.
102 I do not turn away from your ordinances,
    for you have taught me.
103 How sweet are your words to my taste,
    sweeter than honey to my mouth!
104 Through your precepts I get
    understanding;
    therefore I hate every false way.

105 Your word is a lamp to my feet
    and a light to my path.
106 I have sworn an oath and confirmed it,
    to observe your righteous ordinances.

107 I am severely afflicted;
  give me life, O LORD, according to
    your word.
108 Accept my offerings of praise, O LORD,
  and teach me your ordinances.
109 I hold my life in my hand continually,
  but I do not forget your law.
110 The wicked have laid a snare for me,
  but I do not stray from your precepts.
111 Your decrees are my heritage forever;
  they are the joy of my heart.
112 I incline my heart to perform your
    statutes
  forever, to the end.

113 I hate the double-minded,
  but I love your law.
114 You are my hiding place and my shield;
  I hope in your word.
115 Go away from me, you evildoers,
  that I may keep the commandments
    of my God.
116 Uphold me according to your promise,
    that I may live,
  and let me not be put to shame in my
    hope.
117 Hold me up, that I may be safe
  and have regard for your statutes
    continually.
118 You spurn all who go astray from your
    statutes;
  for their cunning is in vain.
119 All the wicked of the earth you count as
    dross;
  therefore I love your decrees.
120 My flesh trembles for fear of you,
  and I am afraid of your judgments.

121 I have done what is just and right;
  do not leave me to my oppressors.
122 Guarantee your servant's well-being;
  do not let the godless oppress me.
123 My eyes fail from watching for your
    salvation,
  and for the fulfillment of your
    righteous promise.
124 Deal with your servant according to
    your steadfast love,
  and teach me your statutes.
125 I am your servant; give me
    understanding,

so that I may know your decrees.
126 It is time for the LORD to act,
  for your law has been broken.
127 Truly I love your commandments
  more than gold, more than fine gold.
128 Truly I direct my steps by all your
    precepts;[a]
  I hate every false way.

129 Your decrees are wonderful;
  therefore my soul keeps them.
130 The unfolding of your words gives light;
  it imparts understanding to the
    simple.
131 With open mouth I pant,
  because I long for your
    commandments.
132 Turn to me and be gracious to me,
  as is your custom toward those who
    love your name.
133 Keep my steps steady according to your
    promise,
  and never let iniquity have dominion
    over me.
134 Redeem me from human oppression,
  that I may keep your precepts.
135 Make your face shine upon your
    servant,
  and teach me your statutes.
136 My eyes shed streams of tears
  because your law is not kept.

137 You are righteous, O LORD,
  and your judgments are right.
138 You have appointed your decrees in
    righteousness
  and in all faithfulness.
139 My zeal consumes me
  because my foes forget your words.
140 Your promise is well tried,
  and your servant loves it.
141 I am small and despised,
  yet I do not forget your precepts.
142 Your righteousness is an everlasting
    righteousness,
  and your law is the truth.
143 Trouble and anguish have come upon
    me,

a Gk Jerome: Meaning of Heb uncertain

but your commandments are my
    delight.
144 Your decrees are righteous forever;
    give me understanding that I may
    live.

145 With my whole heart I cry; answer me,
    O Lord.
    I will keep your statutes.
146 I cry to you; save me,
    that I may observe your decrees.
147 I rise before dawn and cry for help;
    I put my hope in your words.
148 My eyes are awake before each watch of
    the night,
    that I may meditate on your promise.
149 In your steadfast love hear my voice;
    O Lord, in your justice preserve my
    life.
150 Those who persecute me with evil
    purpose draw near;
    they are far from your law.
151 Yet you are near, O Lord,
    and all your commandments are
    true.
152 Long ago I learned from your decrees
    that you have established them
    forever.

153 Look on my misery and rescue me,
    for I do not forget your law.
154 Plead my cause and redeem me;
    give me life according to your
    promise.
155 Salvation is far from the wicked,
    for they do not seek your statutes.
156 Great is your mercy, O Lord;
    give me life according to your justice.
157 Many are my persecutors and my
    adversaries,
    yet I do not swerve from your decrees.
158 I look at the faithless with disgust,
    because they do not keep your
    commands.
159 Consider how I love your precepts;
    preserve my life according to your
    steadfast love.
160 The sum of your word is truth;
    and every one of your righteous
    ordinances endures forever.

161 Princes persecute me without cause,
    but my heart stands in awe of your
    words.
162 I rejoice at your word
    like one who finds great spoil.
163 I hate and abhor falsehood,
    but I love your law.
164 Seven times a day I praise you
    for your righteous ordinances.
165 Great peace have those who love your
    law;
    nothing can make them stumble.
166 I hope for your salvation, O Lord,
    and I fulfill your commandments.
167 My soul keeps your decrees;
    I love them exceedingly.
168 I keep your precepts and decrees,
    for all my ways are before you.

169 Let my cry come before you, O Lord;
    give me understanding according to
    your word.
170 Let my supplication come before you;
    deliver me according to your promise.
171 My lips will pour forth praise,
    because you teach me your statutes.
172 My tongue will sing of your promise,
    for all your commandments are right.
173 Let your hand be ready to help me,
    for I have chosen your precepts.
174 I long for your salvation, O Lord,
    and your law is my delight.
175 Let me live that I may praise you,
    and let your ordinances help me.
176 I have gone astray like a lost sheep; seek
    out your servant,
    for I do not forget your
    commandments.

Psalm 120

Prayer for Deliverance from Slanderers

A Song of Ascents.

1 In my distress I cry to the Lord,
    that he may answer me:
2 "Deliver me, O Lord,
    from lying lips,
    from a deceitful tongue."

3 What shall be given to you?
    And what more shall be done to you,

you deceitful tongue?
4 A warrior's sharp arrows,
    with glowing coals of the broom
        tree!

5 Woe is me, that I am an alien in
        Meshech,
    that I must live among the tents of
        Kedar.
6 Too long have I had my dwelling
    among those who hate peace.
7 I am for peace;
    but when I speak,
    they are for war.

Psalm 121

Assurance of God's Protection

A Song of Ascents.

1 I lift up my eyes to the hills—
    from where will my help come?
2 My help comes from the LORD,
    who made heaven and earth.

3 He will not let your foot be moved;
    he who keeps you will not slumber.
4 He who keeps Israel
    will neither slumber nor sleep.

5 The LORD is your keeper;
    the LORD is your shade at your right
        hand.
6 The sun shall not strike you by day,
    nor the moon by night.

7 The LORD will keep you from all evil;
    he will keep your life.

8 The LORD will keep
    your going out and your coming in
    from this time on and forevermore.

Psalm 122

Song of Praise and Prayer for Jerusalem

A Song of Ascents. Of David.

1 I was glad when they said to me,
    "Let us go to the house of the LORD!"
2 Our feet are standing
    within your gates, O Jerusalem.

3 Jerusalem—built as a city
    that is bound firmly together.
4 To it the tribes go up,
    the tribes of the LORD,
as was decreed for Israel,
    to give thanks to the name of the
        LORD.
5 For there the thrones for judgment were
        set up,
    the thrones of the house of David.

6 Pray for the peace of Jerusalem:
    "May they prosper who love you.
7 Peace be within your walls,
    and security within your towers."
8 For the sake of my relatives and
        friends
    I will say, "Peace be within you."
9 For the sake of the house of the LORD
        our God,
    I will seek your good.

120:1–7 *I cry to the LORD.* This is the first of fourteen "Songs of Ascent," likely pilgrimage songs for traveling to Jerusalem. Here the singer appeals to God to rescue him from those who hate peace. Today, beyond remote Meshech and Kedar, many seem to serve deceit and violence rather than peace. Only God can help us do otherwise.

121:1–3 *My help comes from the LORD.* The singer recognizes the true source of help, the Creator, who is alert to our need.

121:5–8 *The LORD is your keeper.* Psalm 121 repeatedly uses a Hebrew word meaning "to keep," "to guard," or "to watch over," like those who keep watch from city walls. It invites trust in God's steady attention to our need and condition.

122:1–5 *Our feet are standing within your gates, O Jerusalem.* To be in Jerusalem (often "Zion") is to be in God's presence and at the heart of God's just rule.

122:6–9 *Peace be within your walls.* We can gladly pray for the peace of Jerusalem, so troubled today. But metaphorically we can pray for and enter into God's rule and its blessings on all it reaches.

Psalm 123

Supplication for Mercy

A Song of Ascents.

1 To you I lift up my eyes,
  O you who are enthroned in the
    heavens!
2 As the eyes of servants
    look to the hand of their master,
  as the eyes of a maid
    to the hand of her mistress,
  so our eyes look to the LORD our God,
    until he has mercy upon us.

3 Have mercy upon us, O LORD, have
    mercy upon us,
  for we have had more than enough of
    contempt.
4 Our soul has had more than its fill
    of the scorn of those who are at ease,
    of the contempt of the proud.

Psalm 124

Thanksgiving for Israel's Deliverance

A Song of Ascents. Of David.

1 If it had not been the LORD who was on
    our side
  —let Israel now say—

2 if it had not been the LORD who was on
    our side,
  when our enemies attacked us,
3 then they would have swallowed us up
    alive,
  when their anger was kindled against
    us;
4 then the flood would have swept us
    away,
  the torrent would have gone over us;
5 then over us would have gone
    the raging waters.

6 Blessed be the LORD,
  who has not given us
    as prey to their teeth.
7 We have escaped like a bird
    from the snare of the fowlers;
  the snare is broken,
    and we have escaped.

8 Our help is in the name of the LORD,
  who made heaven and earth.

Psalm 125

The Security of God's People

A Song of Ascents.

1 Those who trust in the LORD are like
    Mount Zion,

123:1–4 *To you I lift up my eyes.* A prayer for God's mercy on the community that suffers scorn from the proud who have their ease at the community's expense. People of faith who are at ease today may well enter into such prayers on behalf of the faithful around the world who still suffer oppression and contempt.

Responding
123:3 PRAYER. This verse is similar to the Jesus Prayer—"Lord Jesus Christ, Son of God, have mercy on me, a sinner"— prayed by members of Orthodox churches. There is one difference: this is the prayer of a community asking for God's mercy. Try silently praying the Jesus Prayer throughout worship this Sunday except change it to reflect the prayer of a community—"Lord Jesus Christ, Son of God, have mercy on us, a gathering of

sinners." What changes did this exercise bring in your perception of the community you worship with? *See also* Spiritual Disciplines Index.

124:1–8 *If it had not been the LORD.* This thanksgiving song gives credit where credit is due—to the Lord. Once we've been delivered from trouble, it's easy to forget how it happened. Steadily practicing thanksgiving and praise helps our memory and focus. "Our help is in the name of the LORD" (v 8).

125:1–5 *Those who trust in the LORD are like Mount Zion.* The simile "like Mount Zion" offers a powerful image. Those who trust God enter into a towering security where evil neither has sway nor corrupts, where God's goodness and peace prevail. Our vision of what's possible in life with God should include such Zionlike stability.

which cannot be moved, but abides
  forever.
2 As the mountains surround Jerusalem,
  so the LORD surrounds his people,
  from this time on and forevermore.
3 For the scepter of wickedness shall not
  rest
    on the land allotted to the righteous,
  so that the righteous might not stretch
  out
    their hands to do wrong.
4 Do good, O LORD, to those who are
  good,
  and to those who are upright in their
  hearts.
5 But those who turn aside to their own
  crooked ways
  the LORD will lead away with
  evildoers.
  Peace be upon Israel!

Psalm 126

A Harvest of Joy

A Song of Ascents.

1 When the LORD restored the fortunes of
  Zion, [a]
  we were like those who dream.
2 Then our mouth was filled with
  laughter,
  and our tongue with shouts of joy;
  then it was said among the nations,

"The LORD has done great things for
  them."
3 The LORD has done great things for us,
  and we rejoiced.
4 Restore our fortunes, O LORD,
  like the watercourses in the Negeb.
5 May those who sow in tears
  reap with shouts of joy.
6 Those who go out weeping,
  bearing the seed for sowing,
  shall come home with shouts of joy,
  carrying their sheaves.

Psalm 127

God's Blessings in the Home

A Song of Ascents. Of Solomon.

1 Unless the LORD builds the house,
  those who build it labor in vain.
  Unless the LORD guards the city,
  the guard keeps watch in vain.
2 It is in vain that you rise up early
  and go late to rest,
  eating the bread of anxious toil;
  for he gives sleep to his beloved. [b]

3 Sons are indeed a heritage from the
  LORD,
  the fruit of the womb a reward.

a Or *brought back those who returned to Zion*
b Or *for he provides for his beloved during sleep*

126:1–3 *When the LORD restored . . . we were like those who dream.* This reflects, perhaps, the return of exiles from Babylon. In any event, it bursts with joy when the too-good-to-be-true actually comes true. Laughter, full of surprise and wonder, brims over and spills out over lips filled with song. God's marvels on our behalf deserve extravagant celebration.

Responding
126:2 CELEBRATION. "What soap is to the body, so laughter is to the soul," according to a Yiddish proverb. How does laughter cleanse our soul? Make a special effort this week to gather together a group of people you know who can have a hilarious time telling stories and laughing at themselves. Afterward,

reflect on how your soul was affected by the joy and laughter. *See also* Spiritual Disciplines Index.

126:4–6 *Restore our fortunes.* These verses appeal for yet another deliverance that will turn weeping into shouts of joy.

127:1–2 *Unless the LORD. . . . It is in vain.* Without dismissing hard work, this song puts it in perspective. We can't be self-sufficient. We can't make ourselves safe. Worry and workaholic lifestyles don't help a bit. God alone provides, guards, gives peace.

127:3–5 *the fruit of the womb a reward.* In Old Testament times, as in many cultures today, having many children was a sign of God's blessing and security.

4 Like arrows in the hand of a
    warrior
    are the sons of one's youth.
5 Happy is the man who has
    his quiver full of them.
  He shall not be put to shame
    when he speaks with his enemies in
    the gate.

Psalm 128

The Happy Home of the Faithful

A Song of Ascents.

1 Happy is everyone who fears the
    LORD,
    who walks in his ways.
2 You shall eat the fruit of the labor of
    your hands;
    you shall be happy, and it shall go
    well with you.

3 Your wife will be like a fruitful
    vine
    within your house;
  your children will be like olive
    shoots
    around your table.
4 Thus shall the man be blessed
    who fears the LORD.

5 The LORD bless you from Zion.
    May you see the prosperity of
    Jerusalem
    all the days of your life.
6 May you see your children's
    children.
    Peace be upon Israel!

Psalm 129

Prayer for the Downfall of Israel's Enemies

A Song of Ascents.

1 "Often have they attacked me from my
    youth"
    —let Israel now say—
2 "often have they attacked me from my
    youth,
    yet they have not prevailed against
    me.
3 The plowers plowed on my back;
    they made their furrows long."
4 The LORD is righteous;
    he has cut the cords of the wicked.
5 May all who hate Zion
    be put to shame and turned backward.
6 Let them be like the grass on the
    housetops
    that withers before it grows up,
7 with which reapers do not fill their
    hands
    or binders of sheaves their arms,
8 while those who pass by do not say,
    "The blessing of the LORD be upon
    you!
    We bless you in the name of the
    LORD!"

Psalm 130

Waiting for Divine Redemption

A Song of Ascents.

1 Out of the depths I cry to you, O LORD.
2 Lord, hear my voice!
  Let your ears be attentive
    to the voice of my supplications!

128:1–6 *Happy is everyone who fears the
LORD.* This song of blessing is especially related
to home and family. It shares the language from
wisdom literature of "fearing the LORD" and
"walking in his ways" (cf. Pss 1; 34; 37 for similar
themes). These are steady, practical choices we
can make.

129:1–4 *he has cut the cords of the wicked.*
The people proclaim that in righteousness God
has delivered them from repeated attacks.

129:5–8 *May all who hate Zion be put to
shame.* This passage shows confidence that
these wicked oppressors, the "haters of Zion,"
will never succeed. They failed in plowing
Israel's back and will fail to harvest their own
crops. To hate Zion may well mean to resist
God's good purposes for all, since this is the seat
of God's rule. God will prevail.

130:1–8 *Out of the depths I cry to you.* This
song of repentance appeals to God's "steadfast
love" (v 7).

3 If you, O LORD, should mark iniquities,
   Lord, who could stand?
4 But there is forgiveness with you,
   so that you may be revered.

5 I wait for the LORD, my soul waits,
   and in his word I hope;
6 my soul waits for the Lord
   more than those who watch for the
      morning,
   more than those who watch for the
      morning.

7 O Israel, hope in the LORD!
   For with the LORD there is steadfast
      love,
   and with him is great power to
      redeem.
8 It is he who will redeem Israel
   from all its iniquities.

Psalm 131

Song of Quiet Trust

A Song of Ascents. Of David.

1 O LORD, my heart is not lifted up,
   my eyes are not raised too high;
   I do not occupy myself with things
   too great and too marvelous for me.
2 But I have calmed and quieted my soul,
   like a weaned child with its mother;
   my soul is like the weaned child that
      is with me. [a]

3 O Israel, hope in the LORD
   from this time on and forevermore.

Psalm 132

The Eternal Dwelling of God in Zion

A Song of Ascents.

1 O LORD, remember in David's favor
   all the hardships he endured;
2 how he swore to the LORD
   and vowed to the Mighty One of
      Jacob,
3 "I will not enter my house
   or get into my bed;
4 I will not give sleep to my eyes
   or slumber to my eyelids,
5 until I find a place for the LORD,
   a dwelling place for the Mighty One
      of Jacob."

6 We heard of it in Ephrathah;
   we found it in the fields of Jaar.
7 "Let us go to his dwelling place;
   let us worship at his footstool."

8 Rise up, O LORD, and go to your resting
      place,
   you and the ark of your might.
9 Let your priests be clothed with
      righteousness,
   and let your faithful shout for joy.

a Or *my soul within me is like a weaned child*

130:3–4 *who could stand?* These verses note clearly an understanding of the enormity of sin—if God were an accountant, we would all be doomed. The wonder of God's grace was just as vivid then as now.

130:5–8 *my soul waits for the Lord.* The interplay between waiting and hoping comes through here in eagerness to receive the generosity of God's grace. The psalm reminds us neither to trivialize sin nor to underestimate God's love.

131:1–3 *my eyes are not raised too high.* An ode to humility. One of the core obstacles to spiritual maturity and life at its best is over-reaching ambition. The need to run the world, to control what happens, saps our energy and sabotages our ability to trust.

Responding
131:2 SILENCE. What surroundings are necessary to achieve a calm and quiet soul? How can these be cultivated? *See also* Spiritual Disciplines Index.

132:1–18 *O LORD, remember in David's favor.* This royal psalm celebrates God's selection of both David and his descendants as king and Zion (Jerusalem) as God's "habitation" on earth.

132:1–10 *remember in David's favor.* David not only conquered Jerusalem, but also brought the ark of the covenant there to renew its importance in Israel's worship. Of course this also enhanced the importance of David's new capital.

10 For your servant David's sake
    do not turn away the face of your
        anointed one.

11 The LORD swore to David a sure oath
    from which he will not turn back:
    "One of the sons of your body
    I will set on your throne.
12 If your sons keep my covenant
    and my decrees that I shall teach
        them,
    their sons also, forevermore,
    shall sit on your throne."

13 For the LORD has chosen Zion;
    he has desired it for his habitation:
14 "This is my resting place forever;
    here I will reside, for I have
        desired it.
15 I will abundantly bless its provisions;
    I will satisfy its poor with bread.
16 Its priests I will clothe with
        salvation,
    and its faithful will shout for joy.
17 There I will cause a horn to sprout up
        for David;
    I have prepared a lamp for my
        anointed one.
18 His enemies I will clothe with
        disgrace,
    but on him, his crown will gleam."

Psalm 133

The Blessedness of Unity

A Song of Ascents.

1 How very good and pleasant it is
    when kindred live together in unity!
2 It is like the precious oil on the head,
    running down upon the beard,
on the beard of Aaron,
    running down over the collar of his
        robes.
3 It is like the dew of Hermon,
    which falls on the mountains of Zion.
For there the LORD ordained his blessing,
    life forevermore.

Psalm 134

Praise in the Night

A Song of Ascents.

1 Come, bless the LORD, all you servants
    of the LORD,
who stand by night in the house of
    the LORD!
2 Lift up your hands to the holy place,
    and bless the LORD.

3 May the LORD, maker of heaven and
        earth,
    bless you from Zion.

132:11–12 *If your sons keep my covenant.* A restatement of God's covenant with David, here clearly noting that its future depends on obedience (cf. 2 Sam 7:14–15; Pss 89:34–37; 110).

132:13–18 *here I will reside.* God's presence in Zion assures the blessings of his rule. The New Testament's renewed use of the themes of the "anointed one" as David's descendant and of God in Zion bring us heightened forms of blessing and joy.

133:1–3 *How very good and pleasant it is!* Perhaps sung by pilgrims gathered from across Israel in festivals of worship, this psalm celebrates the unity of God's people. It's better than the generous anointing of a guest's head with oil (cf. 23:5), better than the abundant dews of beautiful Mt. Hermon, the highest mountain in the whole region. It reminds us to celebrate and work for such refreshing unity.

Responding
133:1–3 FELLOWSHIP. "Kindred" (v 1) means those people who could trace their ancestry to Abraham, Isaac, and Jacob, but in our day it can refer to our "kindred" in Christ. Dallas Willard writes in *The Spirit of the Disciplines:* "Personalities united can contain more of God and sustain the force of his greater presence much better than scattered individuals." How essential is fellowship in promoting unity? *See also* Spiritual Disciplines Index.

134:1–3 *Come, bless the LORD.* Perhaps used at the beginning of a festival, this psalm is a call to bless and receive blessing! "Bless the Lord" is another way to say "Praise the Lord."

134:1 SERVICE—*See* Spiritual Disciplines Index.

Psalm 135

Praise for God's Goodness and Might

1 Praise the LORD!
   Praise the name of the LORD;
   give praise, O servants of the LORD,
2 you that stand in the house of the LORD,
   in the courts of the house of our God.
3 Praise the LORD, for the LORD is good;
   sing to his name, for he is gracious.
4 For the LORD has chosen Jacob for
         himself,
   Israel as his own possession.

5 For I know that the LORD is great;
   our Lord is above all gods.
6 Whatever the LORD pleases he does,
   in heaven and on earth,
   in the seas and all deeps.
7 He it is who makes the clouds rise at the
         end of the earth;
   he makes lightnings for the rain
   and brings out the wind from his
         storehouses.

8 He it was who struck down the firstborn
         of Egypt,
   both human beings and animals;
9 he sent signs and wonders
   into your midst, O Egypt,
   against Pharaoh and all his servants.
10 He struck down many nations
   and killed mighty kings—

11 Sihon, king of the Amorites,
   and Og, king of Bashan,
   and all the kingdoms of Canaan—
12 and gave their land as a heritage,
   a heritage to his people Israel.

13 Your name, O LORD, endures forever,
   your renown, O LORD, throughout all
         ages.
14 For the LORD will vindicate his people,
   and have compassion on his servants.

15 The idols of the nations are silver and
         gold,
   the work of human hands.
16 They have mouths, but they do not
         speak;
   they have eyes, but they do not see;
17 they have ears, but they do not hear,
   and there is no breath in their
         mouths.
18 Those who make them
   and all who trust them
   shall become like them.

19 O house of Israel, bless the LORD!
   O house of Aaron, bless the LORD!
20 O house of Levi, bless the LORD!
   You that fear the LORD, bless the LORD!
21 Blessed be the LORD from Zion,
   he who resides in Jerusalem.
   Praise the LORD!

134:3 *May the LORD . . . bless you.* God's blessing on us brings life, wholeness, and joy. Gathered as God's people, we can join in praying such blessing for one another.

135:1–3, 19–21 *Praise the LORD! . . . Blessed be the LORD.* Hymns of praise such as this open and conclude with a call to praise. All kinds of people are called—worshipers, Israelites, priestly families, and people who "fear the LORD" (perhaps non-Israelites who have become servants of Yahweh).

135:4–18 *our LORD is above all gods.* The reasons for praise are many. God is Creator (vv 5–7). God acted in Israel's history (vv 8–11; cf. 136:10–22). God is compassionate (v 14). God is unrivaled (vv 15–18, cf. 115:4–8). Declaring the many reasons to praise God reminds us of how grandly God embraces our lives with love.

136:1–26 *O give thanks to the LORD.* The Old Testament frequently repeats the phrase "[God's] steadfast love endures forever." Here it appears to be an affirming antiphonal response in a song of worship. After a rousing call to praise (vv 1–4), the psalm recalls the "wonders" of God's work in creation (vv 4–9) and God's action in Israel's history (vv 10–22), ending with a summary call to praise (vv 23–25). Naming God's specific acts of faithfulness in our own lives and responding with "God's love [or, Your love] never quits" offers a powerful pattern for personal reflection and prayer, especially when we're spiritually out of sorts and things seem to be going badly. It reframes our distress in the context of God's love.

Psalm 136

God's Work in Creation and in History

1 O give thanks to the LORD, for he is
      good,
   for his steadfast love endures forever.
2 O give thanks to the God of gods,
   for his steadfast love endures forever.
3 O give thanks to the Lord of lords,
   for his steadfast love endures forever;

4 who alone does great wonders,
   for his steadfast love endures forever;
5 who by understanding made the
      heavens,
   for his steadfast love endures forever;
6 who spread out the earth on the waters,
   for his steadfast love endures forever;
7 who made the great lights,
   for his steadfast love endures forever;
8 the sun to rule over the day,
   for his steadfast love endures forever;
9 the moon and stars to rule over the
      night,
   for his steadfast love endures forever;

10 who struck Egypt through their
      firstborn,
   for his steadfast love endures forever;
11 and brought Israel out from among
      them,
   for his steadfast love endures forever;
12 with a strong hand and an outstretched
      arm,
   for his steadfast love endures forever;
13 who divided the Red Sea[a] in two,
   for his steadfast love endures forever;
14 and made Israel pass through the midst
      of it,
   for his steadfast love endures forever;
15 but overthrew Pharaoh and his army in
      the Red Sea,[a]
   for his steadfast love endures forever;
16 who led his people through the
      wilderness,

   for his steadfast love endures forever;
17 who struck down great kings,
   for his steadfast love endures forever;
18 and killed famous kings,
   for his steadfast love endures forever;
19 Sihon, king of the Amorites,
   for his steadfast love endures forever;
20 and Og, king of Bashan,
   for his steadfast love endures forever;
21 and gave their land as a heritage,
   for his steadfast love endures forever;
22 a heritage to his servant Israel,
   for his steadfast love endures forever.

23 It is he who remembered us in our low
      estate,
   for his steadfast love endures forever;
24 and rescued us from our foes,
   for his steadfast love endures forever;
25 who gives food to all flesh,
   for his steadfast love endures forever.

26 O give thanks to the God of heaven,
   for his steadfast love endures forever.

Psalm 137

Lament over the Destruction of Jerusalem

1 By the rivers of Babylon—
      there we sat down and there we wept
      when we remembered Zion.
2 On the willows[b] there
      we hung up our harps.
3 For there our captors
      asked us for songs,
   and our tormentors asked for mirth,
      saying,
      "Sing us one of the songs of Zion!"

4 How could we sing the LORD's song
      in a foreign land?
5 If I forget you, O Jerusalem,
      let my right hand wither!

a Or *Sea of Reeds*   b Or *poplars*

137:1–9 *By the rivers of Babylon.* This song of
great sadness recalls Babylon's destruction of
Jerusalem and the years of exile after this
devastating loss.

137:2–4 *we hung up our harps.* Apparently
renowned for music, the captive Israelites could
hardly sing glad "songs of Zion" in the wake of
losing their Temple, their capital, their nation,
perhaps even their covenant with God.

6 Let my tongue cling to the roof of my
       mouth,
   if I do not remember you,
   if I do not set Jerusalem
   above my highest joy.

7 Remember, O LORD, against the
       Edomites
   the day of Jerusalem's fall,
   how they said, "Tear it down! Tear it
       down!
   Down to its foundations!"
8 O daughter Babylon, you devastator![a]
   Happy shall they be who pay you
       back
   what you have done to us!
9 Happy shall they be who take your little
       ones
   and dash them against the rock!

Psalm 138

Thanksgiving and Praise

Of David.

1 I give you thanks, O LORD, with my
       whole heart;
   before the gods I sing your praise;
2 I bow down toward your holy temple
   and give thanks to your name for
       your steadfast love and your
       faithfulness;
   for you have exalted your name and
       your word
   above everything.[b]
3 On the day I called, you answered me,

you increased my strength of soul.[c]

4 All the kings of the earth shall praise
       you, O LORD,
   for they have heard the words of your
       mouth.
5 They shall sing of the ways of the LORD,
   for great is the glory of the LORD.
6 For though the LORD is high, he regards
       the lowly;
   but the haughty he perceives from far
       away.

7 Though I walk in the midst of trouble,
   you preserve me against the wrath of
       my enemies;
   you stretch out your hand,
   and your right hand delivers me.
8 The LORD will fulfill his purpose for me;
   your steadfast love, O LORD, endures
       forever.
   Do not forsake the work of your
       hands.

Psalm 139

The Inescapable God

To the leader. Of David. A Psalm.

1 O LORD, you have searched me and
       known me.

a Or you who are devastated   b Cn: Heb you have
exalted your word above all your name   c Syr
Compare Gk Tg: Heb you made me arrogant in my
soul with strength

137:7–9 *Happy shall they be who take your
little ones and dash them against the rock!* Bitter
words ask God to repay in kind the cruelty of
the Babylonians and the Edomites (Judah's
neighbors who joined in this disaster). Though
they are hard to read and all but impossible to
pray (especially in light of the revelation we
have in Christ), listening to such words may
reveal our own brokenness, vulnerability, and
even anger. God meets and transforms us in
these places too.

138:1–8 *with my whole heart.* This exuberant
song of thanksgiving and praise has a wide
reach. The speaker will sing God's praise
"before the gods." This may refer to the beings

in God's heavenly court or it might be the gods
of the nations, which Israel clearly subordinates
to Yahweh (see Ps 82). Even more, "All the kings
of the earth" sing in praise of God's ways.

138:6 *though the LORD is high, he regards the
lowly.* God attends to the needs of the humble
and, repeatedly in the biblical tradition, pulls
down the proud, whom he has figured out from
miles away.

138:7–8 *you preserve me.* Such lavish praise
provides the context for utter confidence that
God's purposes for even individual lives cannot
be thwarted. Neither heavenly nor earthly
powers stand in the way of God's loving purpose
(cf. Rom 8:37–39).

2 You know when I sit down and when I
      rise up;
   you discern my thoughts from far
      away.
3 You search out my path and my lying
      down,
   and are acquainted with all my ways.
4 Even before a word is on my tongue,
   O LORD, you know it completely.
5 You hem me in, behind and before,
   and lay your hand upon me.
6 Such knowledge is too wonderful for
      me;
   it is so high that I cannot attain it.

7 Where can I go from your spirit?
   Or where can I flee from your
      presence?
8 If I ascend to heaven, you are there;
   if I make my bed in Sheol, you are
      there.
9 If I take the wings of the morning
   and settle at the farthest limits of the
      sea,
10 even there your hand shall lead me,
   and your right hand shall hold me
      fast.
11 If I say, "Surely the darkness shall cover
      me,
   and the light around me become
      night,"
12 even the darkness is not dark to you;
   the night is as bright as the day,
   for darkness is as light to you.

13 For it was you who formed my inward
      parts;
   you knit me together in my mother's
      womb.

14 I praise you, for I am fearfully and
      wonderfully made.
   Wonderful are your works;
   that I know very well.
15   My frame was not hidden from you,
   when I was being made in secret,
      intricately woven in the depths of the
      earth.
16 Your eyes beheld my unformed
      substance.
   In your book were written
      all the days that were formed for me,
      when none of them as yet existed.
17 How weighty to me are your thoughts,
      O God!
   How vast is the sum of them!
18 I try to count them—they are more
      than the sand;
   I come to the end *a*—I am still with you.

19 O that you would kill the wicked, O God,
   and that the bloodthirsty would
      depart from me—
20 those who speak of you maliciously,
   and lift themselves up against you for
      evil! *b*
21 Do I not hate those who hate you,
      O LORD?
   And do I not loathe those who rise up
      against you?
22 I hate them with perfect hatred;
   I count them my enemies.
23 Search me, O God, and know my heart;
   test me and know my thoughts.
24 See if there is any wicked *c* way in me,
   and lead me in the way everlasting. *d*

a Or *I awake*   b Cn: Meaning of Heb uncertain
c Heb *hurtful*   d Or *the ancient way.* Compare Jer
6.16

139:1–6 *O LORD, you have searched me
and known me.* This phrase might be better
understood in a more ongoing way: "You
continue to search me and know me." At the
outset the singer observes that God does this
and even knows us better than we know
ourselves (cf. vv 13–18). But the idea of God's
knowing all the dark secrets of our hearts may
not be comforting. We may fear and even want
to avoid being known that well. We may want
some respite from the searching.

139:7–12 *where can I flee?* Even if we try to
avoid God's gaze, there is no place to hide. In
the Israelite understanding of the world, God
has every corner covered, side to side and top
to bottom. The futility of hiding can pull us
toward honest vulnerability.

139:23–24 *Search me.* Reticence turns to
invitation. The language is now an imperative
form. The wholeheartedness here suggests
being willing to listen, to be malleable, to be
changed.

Psalm 140

Prayer for Deliverance from Enemies

To the leader. A Psalm of David.

1 Deliver me, O Lord, from evildoers;
    protect me from those who are
        violent,
2 who plan evil things in their minds
    and stir up wars continually.
3 They make their tongue sharp as a
        snake's,
    and under their lips is the venom of
        vipers.   *Selah*

4 Guard me, O Lord, from the hands of
        the wicked;
    protect me from the violent
    who have planned my downfall.
5 The arrogant have hidden a trap for me,
    and with cords they have spread a
        net,*a*
    along the road they have set snares
        for me.   *Selah*

6 I say to the Lord, "You are my God;
    give ear, O Lord, to the voice of my
        supplications."
7 O Lord, my Lord, my strong deliverer,
    you have covered my head in the day
        of battle.
8 Do not grant, O Lord, the desires of the
        wicked;
    do not further their evil plot.*b*   *Selah*

9 Those who surround me lift up their
        heads;*c*
    let the mischief of their lips
        overwhelm them!

10 Let burning coals fall on them!
    Let them be flung into pits, no more
        to rise!
11 Do not let the slanderer be established
        in the land;
    let evil speedily hunt down the
        violent!

12 I know that the Lord maintains the
        cause of the needy,
    and executes justice for the poor.
13 Surely the righteous shall give thanks to
        your name;
    the upright shall live in your
        presence.

Psalm 141

Prayer for Preservation from Evil

A Psalm of David.

1 I call upon you, O Lord; come quickly
        to me;
    give ear to my voice when I call to
        you.
2 Let my prayer be counted as incense
        before you,
    and the lifting up of my hands as an
        evening sacrifice.

3 Set a guard over my mouth, O Lord;
    keep watch over the door of my lips.
4 Do not turn my heart to any evil,
    to busy myself with wicked deeds

a Or *they have spread cords as a net*   *b* Heb adds
they are exalted   *c* Cn Compare Gk: Heb *those
who surround me are uplifted in head*; Heb divides
verses 8 and 9 differently

140:1–8 *those who . . . stir up wars continually.*
Sometimes the psalmists' descriptions of enemies
exaggerate dramatically, but here the singer tells
of people constantly planning evil, stirring up
war, setting traps, and devising clever lies about
it. We know these people, up close and at a
distance. How could one not pray for protection
(vv 1, 6–8)?

140:9–13 *Let burning coals fall on them!*
Though the psalmist would eagerly like to see
this happen, it is God who confounds evil, who

protects the vulnerable.

141:1–10 *I call upon you, O Lord.* In contrast
to praying that God will bring swift judgment
on the wicked, here we have a prayer for God
to prevent us from joining them. This psalm
powerfully reminds us that evil is seductive and
that we're all vulnerable. The traps and snares
(v 9) and the "delicacies" (v 4) of the wicked
might well draw us in. Inviting God to guard
mouth and heart, such crucial gateways, is wise
(vv 3–4; cf. 19:14).

in company with those who work
　　iniquity;
　　do not let me eat of their delicacies.

5 Let the righteous strike me;
　　let the faithful correct me.
　Never let the oil of the wicked anoint
　　my head, *a*
　　for my prayer is continually *b* against
　　their wicked deeds.
6 When they are given over to those who
　　shall condemn them,
　　then they shall learn that my words
　　were pleasant.
7 Like a rock that one breaks apart and
　　shatters on the land,
　　so shall their bones be strewn at the
　　mouth of Sheol. *c*

8 But my eyes are turned toward you,
　　O GOD, my Lord;
　　in you I seek refuge; do not leave me
　　defenseless.
9 Keep me from the trap that they have
　　laid for me,
　　and from the snares of evildoers.
10 Let the wicked fall into their own nets,
　　while I alone escape.

Psalm 142

Prayer for Deliverance from Persecutors

A Maskil of David. When he was in the cave.
A Prayer.

1 With my voice I cry to the LORD;
　　with my voice I make supplication to
　　the LORD.

2 I pour out my complaint before him;
　　I tell my trouble before him.
3 When my spirit is faint,
　　you know my way.

In the path where I walk
　　they have hidden a trap for me.
4 Look on my right hand and see—
　　there is no one who takes notice of me;
　no refuge remains to me;
　　no one cares for me.

5 I cry to you, O LORD;
　　I say, "You are my refuge,
　　my portion in the land of the living."
6 Give heed to my cry,
　　for I am brought very low.

Save me from my persecutors,
　　for they are too strong for me.
7 Bring me out of prison,
　　so that I may give thanks to your
　　　　name.
The righteous will surround me,
　　for you will deal bountifully with me.

Psalm 143

Prayer for Deliverance from Enemies

A Psalm of David.

1 Hear my prayer, O LORD;
　　give ear to my supplications in your
　　faithfulness;
　　answer me in your righteousness.

a Gk: Meaning of Heb uncertain   *b* Cn: Heb *for
continually and my prayer*   *c* Meaning of Heb of
verses 5-7 is uncertain

Responding

141:2 PRAYER. As a reminder that
your prayers are visible to God, burn
incense during your times of prayer this week.
Also try lifting your hands as you pray. If this is
not possible, sit in a chair that will allow you to
hold your hands with palms up on your lap.
What effect did these two actions have on your
times alone with God? *See also* Spiritual
Disciplines Index.

142:1–7 *With my voice I cry to the LORD.* This

short song illustrates the flow of the lament
song. Address to God and a plea for help
intermingle (vv 1–3a). The description of
trouble (vv 3b–4) is followed by a confession
of trust (v 5). Then comes the petition for
help (vv 6–7a), followed by a vow of praise for
deliverance (v 7b). Confessing trust gives hope
and strength to the appeal, all the more sharply
here because this singer sees God as his only
resource (v 4). Remembering God's power and
love can help us make an honest appeal when
we're scared to death.

² Do not enter into judgment with your
      servant,
   for no one living is righteous before
      you.

³ For the enemy has pursued me,
   crushing my life to the ground,
   making me sit in darkness like those
      long dead.
⁴ Therefore my spirit faints within me;
   my heart within me is appalled.

⁵ I remember the days of old,
   I think about all your deeds,
   I meditate on the works of your
      hands.
⁶ I stretch out my hands to you;
   my soul thirsts for you like a parched
      land.   *Selah*

⁷ Answer me quickly, O LORD;
   my spirit fails.
   Do not hide your face from me,
      or I shall be like those who go down
         to the Pit.
⁸ Let me hear of your steadfast love in the
      morning,
   for in you I put my trust.
   Teach me the way I should go,
      for to you I lift up my soul.

⁹ Save me, O LORD, from my enemies;
   I have fled to you for refuge. *^a*
¹⁰ Teach me to do your will,
   for you are my God.

   Let your good spirit lead me
      on a level path.

¹¹ For your name's sake, O LORD, preserve
      my life.
   In your righteousness bring me out of
      trouble.
¹² In your steadfast love cut off my enemies,
   and destroy all my adversaries,
   for I am your servant.

Psalm 144

Prayer for National Deliverance and Security

Of David.

¹ Blessed be the LORD, my rock,
   who trains my hands for war, and my
      fingers for battle;
² my rock *^b* and my fortress,
   my stronghold and my deliverer,
   my shield, in whom I take refuge,
   who subdues the peoples *^c* under me.

³ O LORD, what are human beings that
      you regard them,
   or mortals that you think of them?
⁴ They are like a breath;
   their days are like a passing shadow.

⁵ Bow your heavens, O LORD, and come
      down;

^a One Heb Ms Gk: MT *to you I have hidden*
^b With 18.2 and 2 Sam 22.2: Heb *my steadfast love*
^c Heb Mss Syr Aquila Jerome: MT *my people*

143:1–12 *Hear my prayer, O LORD.* The phrase
"no one living is righteous before you" (v 2)
brings this psalm into the group of penitential
psalms, although most of the psalm pleads for
God to deliver the singer from enemies. The
Psalms show paradox. In a variety of ways they
recognize people as truly righteous, but here
such righteousness is overwhelmed by the sense
of God's holiness, much as in Isaiah's call (see Isa
6:1–7). Spiritual maturity holds the two at once—
genuine faithfulness, on the one hand, and a
vision of God's unmatched holiness, on the other.
   143:1 PRAYER—*See* Spiritual Disciplines
Index.

   143:5 MEDITATION—*See* Spiritual
Disciplines Index.
   144:1–11 *Rescue.* This prayer for national
deliverance is often associated with David (v 10).
The psalm reflects Israel's understanding that it
is God who empowers, protects, and rescues.
Human device and activity in themselves are
weak (see 118:5–9; 146:3; Isa 31:1–3).
   144:3–4 *what are human beings that you
regard them?* Echoing 8:4, these verses
acknowledge human frailty and set up God's
dramatic action in verses 5–8.
   144:5–8 *Bow your heavens, O LORD.* On this
powerful language, see note on 18:7–19.

touch the mountains so that they
    smoke.
6 Make the lightning flash and scatter
    them;
    send out your arrows and rout
    them.
7 Stretch out your hand from on high;
    set me free and rescue me from the
    mighty waters,
    from the hand of aliens,
8 whose mouths speak lies,
    and whose right hands are false.

9 I will sing a new song to you, O God;
    upon a ten-stringed harp I will play to
    you,
10 the one who gives victory to kings,
    who rescues his servant David.
11 Rescue me from the cruel sword,
    and deliver me from the hand of
    aliens,
    whose mouths speak lies,
    and whose right hands are false.

12 May our sons in their youth
    be like plants full grown,
    our daughters like corner pillars,
    cut for the building of a palace.
13 May our barns be filled,
    with produce of every kind;
    may our sheep increase by thousands,
    by tens of thousands in our fields,
14   and may our cattle be heavy with
    young.

May there be no breach in the walls, *a*
    no exile,
    and no cry of distress in our streets.

15 Happy are the people to whom such
    blessings fall;
    happy are the people whose God is
    the LORD.

Psalm 145

The Greatness and the Goodness of God

Praise. Of David.

1 I will extol you, my God and King,
    and bless your name forever and ever.
2 Every day I will bless you,
    and praise your name forever and ever.
3 Great is the LORD, and greatly to be
    praised;
    his greatness is unsearchable.

4 One generation shall laud your works to
    another,
    and shall declare your mighty acts.
5 On the glorious splendor of your majesty,
    and on your wondrous works, I will
    meditate.
6 The might of your awesome deeds shall
    be proclaimed,
    and I will declare your greatness.
7 They shall celebrate the fame of your
    abundant goodness,

a Heb lacks *in the walls*

144:12–15 *May our sons . . . be like plants full grown.* An appeal for the blessings of abundance and security for the people whose God is Yahweh.

145:1–21 *I will extol you, my God and King.* This is the first of the six hymns of praise that conclude the Psalter. Though it keeps the first person "I," the singer points to great choruses of praise from "one generation . . . to another" (v 4), "all your works" (v 10), and "all flesh" (v 21).

145:5 *I will meditate.* The singer not only declares, but "meditates" on the many reasons for praise offered in this psalm—God's splendor, compassion, generous provision, just rule, protection. Pausing to ponder and give steady

attention to these realities keeps us from trivializing God in thought and speech.

145:5 MEDITATION—*See* Spiritual Disciplines Index.

Responding
145:7 CELEBRATION. Many of us tend to limit our celebration of God's goodness to us to the holidays of Christmas and Easter. Make a list this week of the ways God has blessed and been good to you. Then try to think of some way you can pass your memories on to the next generation in your family or to people in your community of faith. This could take the form of a letter or a discussion that you initiate. *See also* Spiritual Disciplines Index.

and shall sing aloud of your
  righteousness.

8 The LORD is gracious and merciful,
  slow to anger and abounding in
    steadfast love.
9 The LORD is good to all,
  and his compassion is over all that he
    has made.

10 All your works shall give thanks to you,
  O LORD,
  and all your faithful shall bless you.
11 They shall speak of the glory of your
    kingdom,
  and tell of your power,
12 to make known to all people your[a]
    mighty deeds,
  and the glorious splendor of your[b]
    kingdom.
13 Your kingdom is an everlasting
    kingdom,
  and your dominion endures
    throughout all generations.

  The LORD is faithful in all his words,
  and gracious in all his deeds.[c]
14 The LORD upholds all who are
    falling,
  and raises up all who are bowed
    down.
15 The eyes of all look to you,
  and you give them their food in due
    season.
16 You open your hand,
  satisfying the desire of every living
    thing.
17 The LORD is just in all his ways,
  and kind in all his doings.
18 The LORD is near to all who call on him,
  to all who call on him in truth.
19 He fulfills the desire of all who fear him;

he also hears their cry, and saves
  them.
20 The LORD watches over all who love him,
  but all the wicked he will destroy.

21 My mouth will speak the praise of the
    LORD,
  and all flesh will bless his holy name
    forever and ever.

Psalm 146

Praise for God's Help

1 Praise the LORD!
  Praise the LORD, O my soul!
2 I will praise the LORD as long as I live;
  I will sing praises to my God all my
    life long.

3 Do not put your trust in princes,
  in mortals, in whom there is no help.
4 When their breath departs, they return
    to the earth;
  on that very day their plans perish.

5 Happy are those whose help is the God
    of Jacob,
  whose hope is in the LORD their God,
6 who made heaven and earth,
  the sea, and all that is in them;
  who keeps faith forever;
7 who executes justice for the oppressed;
  who gives food to the hungry.

  The LORD sets the prisoners free;
8   the LORD opens the eyes of the blind.
  The LORD lifts up those who are bowed
    down;
  the LORD loves the righteous.

a Gk Jerome Syr: Heb *his*   b Heb *his*   c These
two lines supplied by Q Ms Gk Syr

145:12 *the glorious splendor of your kingdom.*
This phrase reminds us that God's rule is and
always has been ultimate.

146:3–6a *Do not put your trust in.* A sharp
reminder to us about who to rely on. The
"happy" or "blessed" folk are those who rely on
the Creator rather than on frail mortals, who
return to dust.

146:6b–9 *who executes justice . . . gives food
. . . lifts up.* People mature in faith come to
understand how devoted God is to bringing
justice, to restoring the weak, to protecting
the vulnerable, who are so easily overrun by
the wicked. God's love draws us to share in
this, knowing that these matters cannot be
peripheral or optional for true disciples.

9 The LORD watches over the strangers;
  he upholds the orphan and the
    widow,
  but the way of the wicked he brings to
    ruin.

10 The LORD will reign forever,
  your God, O Zion, for all generations.
  Praise the LORD!

Psalm 147

Praise for God's Care for Jerusalem

1 Praise the LORD!
  How good it is to sing praises to our
    God;
    for he is gracious, and a song of praise
      is fitting.
2 The LORD builds up Jerusalem;
  he gathers the outcasts of Israel.
3 He heals the brokenhearted,
  and binds up their wounds.
4 He determines the number of the stars;
  he gives to all of them their names.
5 Great is our Lord, and abundant in
    power;
  his understanding is beyond measure.
6 The LORD lifts up the downtrodden;
  he casts the wicked to the ground.

7 Sing to the LORD with thanksgiving;
  make melody to our God on the lyre.
8 He covers the heavens with clouds,
  prepares rain for the earth,
  makes grass grow on the hills.
9 He gives to the animals their food,
  and to the young ravens when they
    cry.
10 His delight is not in the strength of the
    horse,

nor his pleasure in the speed of a
    runner; *a*
11 but the LORD takes pleasure in those
  who fear him,
  in those who hope in his steadfast
    love.

12 Praise the LORD, O Jerusalem!
  Praise your God, O Zion!
13 For he strengthens the bars of your
    gates;
  he blesses your children within you.
14 He grants peace *b* within your borders;
  he fills you with the finest of wheat.
15 He sends out his command to the earth;
  his word runs swiftly.
16 He gives snow like wool;
  he scatters frost like ashes.
17 He hurls down hail like crumbs—
  who can stand before his cold?
18 He sends out his word, and melts them;
  he makes his wind blow, and the
    waters flow.
19 He declares his word to Jacob,
  his statutes and ordinances to Israel.
20 He has not dealt thus with any other
    nation;
  they do not know his ordinances.
  Praise the LORD!

Psalm 148

Praise for God's Universal Glory

1 Praise the LORD!
  Praise the LORD from the heavens;
  praise him in the heights!
2 Praise him, all his angels;
  praise him, all his host!

a Heb *legs of a person*   *b* Or *prosperity*

147:1–20 *Praise the LORD!* This psalm calls for songs of praise to honor God for compassion, provision, creative power, and other themes widely shared. It notes particularly the building up, no doubt restoration, of Jerusalem. Some Christian interpreters have also seen in it the glories of the new Jerusalem under God's rule.

148:1–14 *Praise the LORD!* The call to praise section in hymns usually answers the question "Who?" or "How?" This psalm calls virtually all of creation to praise God—the cosmos, sea monsters and all creatures, weather, all kinds of people. It is exhilarating to join all of creation in praise to God. Read it out gladly and join in. For even more fun, use the similar but much longer song of the three young Hebrews in Nebuchadnezzar's furnace in Pr of Azar 28–68.

3 Praise him, sun and moon;
    praise him, all you shining stars!
4 Praise him, you highest heavens,
    and you waters above the heavens!

5 Let them praise the name of the LORD,
    for he commanded and they were
        created.
6 He established them forever and ever;
    he fixed their bounds, which cannot
        be passed. *a*

7 Praise the LORD from the earth,
    you sea monsters and all deeps,
8 fire and hail, snow and frost,
    stormy wind fulfilling his
        command!

9 Mountains and all hills,
    fruit trees and all cedars!
10 Wild animals and all cattle,
    creeping things and flying birds!

11 Kings of the earth and all peoples,
    princes and all rulers of the earth!
12 Young men and women alike,
    old and young together!

13 Let them praise the name of the LORD,
    for his name alone is exalted;
    his glory is above earth and heaven.
14 He has raised up a horn for his
        people,
    praise for all his faithful,
    for the people of Israel who are close
        to him.
    Praise the LORD!

Psalm 149

Praise for God's Goodness to Israel

1 Praise the LORD!
Sing to the LORD a new song,
    his praise in the assembly of the
        faithful.
2 Let Israel be glad in its Maker;
    let the children of Zion rejoice in
        their King.
3 Let them praise his name with dancing,
    making melody to him with
        tambourine and lyre.
4 For the LORD takes pleasure in his people;
    he adorns the humble with victory.
5 Let the faithful exult in glory;
    let them sing for joy on their couches.
6 Let the high praises of God be in their
        throats
    and two-edged swords in their hands,
7 to execute vengeance on the nations
    and punishment on the peoples,
8 to bind their kings with fetters
    and their nobles with chains of iron,
9 to execute on them the judgment
        decreed.
    This is glory for all his faithful ones.
    Praise the LORD!

Psalm 150

Praise for God's Surpassing Greatness

1 Praise the LORD!
Praise God in his sanctuary;
    praise him in his mighty firmament! *b*

a Or *he set a law that cannot pass away*
b Or *dome*

149:1–4 *with dancing . . . tambourine and lyre.* The call to singing, dancing, and using instruments may suggest forms of worship for a particular occasion, here maybe celebration in anticipation of God's ultimate victory.

149:5–9 *Let the faithful exult in glory.* The worshipers are eager to see and share in God's victory, when his kingdom comes in its fullness and wicked nations are overcome. Two-edged swords in our hands or not, we can joyfully share the hope of God's just rule fully come.

150:1–6 *Praise the LORD!* In concluding the Psalter, this call to praise describes how praise is to be offered. It basically says, "Be unrestrained and rambunctious. Let it all out!" "Praise him according to his surpassing greatness" (v 2) suggests that big bands, drums, and dancing may not even be exuberant enough. When our own worship traditions aren't quite cut-loose enough, we can still enter such praise with bursting hearts, full voices, clapping hands, and joyful feet as we listen and join musical settings of the psalm from great chorales to Duke Ellington's "Praise God and Dance." "Let everything that breathes praise the LORD!" (v 6). Oh, yes!

2 Praise him for his mighty deeds;
   praise him according to his
      surpassing greatness!

3 Praise him with trumpet sound;
   praise him with lute and harp!
4 Praise him with tambourine and dance;

   praise him with strings and pipe!
5 Praise him with clanging cymbals;
   praise him with loud clashing
      cymbals!
6 Let everything that breathes praise the
   LORD!
   Praise the LORD!

VIII. The People of God in Daily Life

Scriptures: *Proverbs, Ecclesiastes, Song of Solomon*

Deuterocanonical Books: *Wisdom of Solomon, Wisdom of Jesus Son of Sirach (Ecclesiasticus)*

> *The aim of God in history is the creation of an all-inclusive community of loving persons with God himself at the very center of this community as its prime Sustainer and most glorious Inhabitant (Eph 2:19–22; 3:10). The Bible traces the formation of this community from the creation in the Garden of Eden all the way to the new heaven and the new earth. Come, join us as we explore the many dimensions of this with-God history—from individual to family to tribe to people to nation to all humanity—and apply what we learn to our own spiritual formation.*

Previously, we saw the ways God used prayer and worship to advance the formation of an all-inclusive community of loving persons. In these Scriptures, we discover how the People of God are able to move forward in this process of formation through the wisdom gleaned from reflection on daily life.

God's Action

In the biblical wisdom literature we find principles governing daily living that, when rightly understood, can lead us to God. These principles, given by a loving God through the means of natural human wisdom, reveal God's will for our lives and how we can live harmoniously in the world. The book of Proverbs begins, "The proverbs of Solomon . . . for learning about wisdom and instruction" and for finding "the knowledge of God" (1:1–2; 2:5).

Through these passages God, much like a parent advising a child, reveals the patterns that help us gain an understanding of our own personal life (Prov 4:11–12), work with one another (15:1), and ultimately discover God himself (2:5–11; 24:21–22). They emphasize normative patterns of living (chap 14). They teach us that joy and happiness, sorrow and despair are a direct result of the life we lead and the choices we make (7:21–27). "Whoever loves discipline loves knowledge, but those who hate to be rebuked are stupid" (12:1). They represent a stored treasure of human experiences that reveal the wisdom and grace of God (3:5–8).

These wisdom sayings ultimately lay the responsibility for the "good life" at our own feet as we exercise the freedom God gave us to know and to serve him. "Happy are those who find wisdom, and those who get understanding. . . . The Lord by wisdom founded the earth; by understanding he established the heavens. . . . My child, do not let these escape from your sight" (Prov 3:13, 19–21).

These Scriptures focus on the practical choices we make in life and the consequences that flow from these choices. In contrast to other parts of Scripture, they do not focus on the more dominant biblical theme of salvation history—how we overcome our alienation from God. As a result of this shift of emphasis, some overlook the importance of these teachings. But in neglecting this wisdom literature we miss an important God-given resource for practical instruction on how to live a better life in the everyday world.

In clever, poetic, pithy or "catchy" sayings, these books emphasize a basic moral orientation that guides us in all aspects of daily living (Prov 2:1–5). They teach us the "things that are true on the whole and for the most part." The writers' confidence in life's moral order gives rise to the cause-and-effect reasoning that dominates these Scriptures. If we are good, then good will befall us: "A generous person will be enriched, and one who gives water will get water" (Prov 11:25). If we are evil, then evil will befall us: "Wisdom will not enter a deceitful soul, or dwell in a body enslaved to sin" (Wisd of Sol 1:4). The wisdom tradition of the Bible focuses on building character, promoting virtue, condemning vice, and teaching us ways in which we can do the right thing, for the right reason, at the right time, and in the right way.

Human Reaction

In wisdom literature we find three basic attitudes: a drive to develop moral values, a confidence in human moral development, and a commitment to participate and persevere in the moral order of this world. In ancient Israel, we see some, like Samuel, who internalized these teachings in such a way that they governed their actions. Others, like Samson, did not. King Solomon is an interesting example of a person who started out following the precepts of the wisdom teaching and then later lost his moral footing—with disastrous results.

To the ancient Hebrews, life was a seamless garment, and the wisdom tradition emphasizes this interconnectedness of all aspects of life. There was no separation of sacred and secular or of public and private. Those who memorized and followed the precepts of Proverbs did not retreat from life, for they adhered to a natural moral framework that guided them in their daily living.

Biblical wisdom literature completes the revelation we receive from the Scriptures illuminating salvation history; the former should not take a backseat to the latter, as so often occurs today. Does this explain why there are so many foolish Christians today? The wisdom tradition, while emphasizing the practical concerns of everyday life, also recognizes the supernatural moral order we find in God, who teaches us how to live rightly under divine authority. "O God, . . . who . . . by your wisdom have formed humankind to have dominion over the creatures you have made, and rule the world in holiness and righteousness, and pronounce judgment in uprightness of soul, give me the wisdom that sits by your throne, and do not reject me from among your servants" (Wisd of Sol 9:1–4). This moral order in both its natural and its supernatural aspects sustained the nation of Israel even as it encountered adversity and setbacks, and it continues to sustain the People of God to this day.

Blessings and Benefits for Our Formation

Often we begin seeking wisdom as a counterbalance to the tremendous power of the emotions and feelings that overtake our attitudes and actions, ruling our lives. What are our emotional needs? How do we channel such powerful random feelings? How can we genuinely attend to the needs of others? These questions, and others like them, can evoke profound responses that lead us to seek the clarity and goodness that come from counsel that produces wise conduct. "The fear of the LORD is the beginning of knowledge" (Prov 1:7), and the fear of the Lord leads us to the moral life.

The moral life, moreover, helps us understand the way in which the choices we make really do shape our destiny. It applies timeless principles to our time-bound situations. It demonstrates the way in which the eternal principles of God connect with our everyday living.

Ultimately, the wisdom tradition provides us the great benefit of being able to learn from the mistakes of others without having to repeat those same mistakes. We can take to heart such practical advice as: "To guarantee loans for a stranger brings trouble, but there is safety in refusing to do so" (Prov 11:15). Or the easily remembered call to service: "Those who oppress the poor insult their Maker, but those who are kind to the needy honor him" (14:31). Or we can save ourselves enormous heartache by heeding the cryptic warning, "One who hates a rebuke will die" (15:10).

In biblical times the Israelites memorized the wisdom sayings, as have Christians over the centuries even to our day. Being short and pithy, they are easy to learn. Hence, the proverbs have become timeless, portable teachers that have provided guidance in the wise way to live for many generations.

Limits and Liabilities for Our Formation

Although the wisdom writings are meant to lead us to God, they can become a substitute for the grace and forgiveness we seek. Rather than using them as a means to help us live in grace, we can turn them into an end in themselves. But they should never become a substitute for our personal relationship with God. They are designed to awaken us to our need for God and illustrate, in very specific terms, the gaps that exist between our need for God and our personal experience of him.

Alongside this first limitation is a second problem: the wisdom tradition's deemphasis of history. There is no reference in these writings to the exodus, the conquest of Canaan, the reign of David, or the exile. The wisdom tradition's exclusive focus on how to find the good and fulfilling life can, when divorced from an historical and social context, tempt us to treat them as rigid, universal laws. In ordinary circumstances this problem would not arise, but in extraordinary times of personal and social upheaval, the wisdom sayings can be misapplied. For example, parents who are having difficulty with a rebellious child could interpret Prov 13:24, from which we get the modern paraphrase "Spare the rod and spoil the child," as license for serious abuse.

Finally, throughout the history of the Church these passages have often been

The With-God Life

devalued because of their close parallel with the works of ancient pagan writers and their lack of a clear emphasis upon our need for God. Because of their strong tendency to emphasize that virtue has its own reward, bringing blessing to the righteous and condemnation to the wicked, many people think that wisdom literature communicates a sense of self-sufficiency that sets us apart from any need for or reliance upon God. But this is simply not the case. What many fail to recognize is the role human wisdom plays in our life with God. Unlike Aristotle, who elevates natural reason as the primary source of wisdom, Scripture teaches that the wisdom that guides our day-to-day life originates in God. The wisdom that is from God provides practical guidance in life while also connecting us to the broader landscape of the full intent of Scripture.

Insights and Instructions for Our Formation

Today, we face a crisis of confidence in moral living. We do not often see and even less often believe that adhering to a moral order will make any difference in our life. Does virtue have its own reward, as the ancient Greeks believed and the Scriptures teach? We often fail to act as if it does. Because there has been a wholesale loss of commitment to basic morality, individuals now focus on how they can promote their own welfare while satisfying their desires apart from God. The wisdom tradition can help us overcome the moral morass of contemporary society and give feet to our faith, providing specific insights for our own formation.

First of all, the wisdom writings teach us the enormous value of ordinary life. They underscore for us that our with-God life develops first and foremost in the middle of everyday tasks and everyday relationships. This is where we will find God and develop a life with God and nowhere else. We learn from the wisdom tradition to discover a life "with God" in our children, our work, and our play.

Second, the wisdom tradition makes the necessary link between the ethical teachings of the Torah and daily living. We can so easily force a wedge between our religious duties and the tasks of ordinary living. But the wisdom tradition will have none of it. Always it forces us to connect our religious rituals to the common ventures of life: the children we nurture, the friendships we cherish, the neighbors we meet, and the dead we bury.

Third, reading and meditating on specific counsels and warnings can have a guiding, instructing effect upon us as we seek to integrate this wisdom into our life. "A tranquil mind gives life to the flesh, but passion makes the bones rot" can remind us of David's ill health after his adulterous tryst with Bathsheba and can help us seek to do everything possible to avoid a similar fate (Prov 14:30; Ps 38).

Finally, the wisdom of the Old Testament always points us beyond ourselves to others and ultimately to God. To be sure, certain proverbs focus on individual foibles and failures—"If one gives answer before hearing, it is folly and shame" (Prov 18:13). But true wisdom expands our vision to account for the relationships we have with each other and ultimately to the relationship we have with God himself: "For the LORD will be your confidence and will keep your foot from being caught" (3:26). May we catch this vision as we study the wisdom writings and apply their insights to our everyday life.

PROVERBS

The book of Proverbs is a book of encouragement, offering us steadiness, stability, and comfort. Although Proverbs warns against the snares of wickedness, it also assures us that wisdom guides us in right paths. For this reason, Proverbs is considered more cheerful than other wisdom books such as Job and Ecclesiastes. The strong motif throughout Proverbs is that God's ways are superior to ours. Therefore, we must be in close relationship to God in order to live the virtuous life. Moreover, Proverbs insists the virtuous life is practical and will make us more contented and better off in every way.

Wisdom Literature and Spiritual Formation

Proverbs is a prime example of the wisdom literature of both the Old Testament and the Deuterocanonicals. Traditionally attributed to Solomon, more than likely in an honorary sense, its collections of sayings are now thought to have originated with the sages, a social class that served as teachers during the Divided Kingdom. The sayings were edited well after Solomon's time, in the postexilic period of the sixth century BC and later.

As a group, these writings serve as effective catalysts for our life with God. First, wisdom teaches that the most important foundation we build in life is a moral character that honors God. Wisdom reminds and teaches us that there is a right way and a wrong way to conduct life. And we are blessed if we find and follow the right way. "So that your trust may be in the LORD. . . . have I not written for you thirty sayings . . . to show you what is right and true" (Prov 22:19–21).

Second, wisdom shows the necessity for cause-and-effect reasoning. Such reasoning requires us to confront the consequences of our moral choices. It reminds us that if we are good, then good must follow; but if we are evil, then our whole life will fall apart. In Proverbs alone 117 verses contrast the righteous with the wicked.

See also *"The With-God Life" essay for this section of the Bible, "The People of God in Daily Life," pp. 901–4.*

Wisdom also demonstrates the overall providence of God. Even when God's influence is not obvious, God is always present through the ethical decisions we make.

Third, wisdom teaches us how to succeed in our human relationships. It shows that life begins and ends in community. From the wisdom books we learn what it means to live life fully aware of God. It also helps us grasp that our degree of success in close relationships will influence our chances of finding success in life. (The biblical writers are speaking of authentic, not worldly, success.) Wisdom gives us the self-awareness we need to find the love and happiness we long for.

Fourth, wisdom teaches us that human experience should not be the only source of our moral perspective. Even our experience of God, in and of itself, can confuse us. But Scripture interprets our experience of God with clarity and insight. The wisdom of God shows us how to lead a meaningful life.

Finally, wisdom provides a clear assessment of how things are, how they should be, and how we can live up to our God-given responsibilities. Taking note of the toughest aspects of life, wisdom invites us to turn what is into what should be. Wisdom does not sidestep difficult issues; it doesn't shrink from strong rebuke. The success of human life is at stake. Courageous right teaching must lead us to right conduct. Only then can we have a happy and exemplary life.

In each of these ways, wisdom plays a vital role in anchoring our life to God. It helps us to define the patterns in life that bring about success. Ultimately, it empowers us to find the greatest possible meaning in life by discovering and deepening our life with God.

How Should We Use Proverbs?

No doubt in past times the wisdom sayings of Proverbs were committed to memory, to be summoned up in times of need. Elders might use these sayings to instruct or reprove. Younger people might soak up these counsels as a way of growing in spiritual strength.

How can contemporary people follow suit? As Christians we understand that virtue is undergirded by grace. But we also know we must intend to do good and to be good, with God's support. If we read the book of Proverbs often, and devotionally, certain texts will speak to us. Sometimes they hit so hard they even make us laugh. With open, well-formed hearts, we will hear God's voice. Such attentive study is rather like the ancient practice of *lectio divina,* "holy reading." We read slowly and prayerfully, letting the Lord speak to us through the text. Intentional reading will help us to grow stronger in the virtuous life.

What Are These Sayings Driving At?

Proverbs offers a fine collection (in fact, several collections) of short, witty epigrams and sayings. These pointed, quotable quotes are something like the "sound bites" of our own time. What are they driving at? These sayings mean to strip away the false glamour of evil. They seek to entice us to good behavior with sharp insight.

The sayings of Proverbs hold up some virtues one by one. Let us consider a few of them.

Trust in God. "Trust in the LORD with all your heart, and do not rely on your own insight. In all your ways acknowledge him, and he will make straight your paths" (3:5–6). Over and over the sovereignty of God is mentioned. God's power is the most important factor in cultivating the virtuous life.

Attention to Parental Wisdom. The view that young people should learn from both mothers and fathers is pervasive throughout Proverbs. Family solidarity is often praised: "A wise child makes a glad father, but a foolish child is a mother's grief" (10:1).

Fidelity. Many wise sayings of Proverbs warn against the snares of sexual temptation, emphasizing the rewards of remaining faithful in marriage. "He who commits adultery has no sense; he who does it destroys himself" (6:32).

Straightforwardness. "Whoever winks the eye causes trouble, but the one who rebukes boldly makes peace" (10:10). The direct path of correction or settling a quarrel will work much better than a devious or sarcastic approach.

Discipline. "Whoever loves discipline loves knowledge, but those who hate to be rebuked are stupid" (12:1). Proverbs emphasizes discipline and open-minded learning. Growth in virtue begins with a willing heart and a mind eager to learn.

Friendship. Friendship is extolled throughout Proverbs. True and false friends are contrasted: "Some friends play at friendship but a true friend sticks closer than one's nearest kin" (18:24).

Temperance. Proverbs condemns drunkenness in no uncertain terms. "Wine is a mocker, strong drink a brawler, and whoever is led astray by it is not wise" (20:1). Words like these are good antidotes to an "everybody does it" mentality. Another sort of temperance, forbearance, is praised in the saying, "A soft answer turns away wrath, but a harsh word stirs up anger" (15:1).

Diligence. One oft-quoted passage in Proverbs praises hard work: "Go to the ant, you lazybones; consider its ways, and be wise" (6:6). This counsel about the diligence of the ants is intended to hit us where we live. How long will we laze around? Don't we have any self-respect? Where are our priorities?

Simplicity. Some texts in Proverbs make prosperity seem to be virtue's reward. But the wisdom writer reminds us that we do not earn God's favor by our deeds. "Better to be poor and walk in integrity than to be crooked in one's ways even though rich" (28:6).

These may be obvious truths to some, but the virtuous life does not just happen. It has to be cultivated, with God's grace and generous helpings of common sense.

An Instruction Book on Virtue

Taken as a whole, Proverbs is an instruction book on virtue, much of it addressed to men with the intention of keeping them out of trouble. Trouble, in Proverbs, usually takes the form of an attractive, licentious woman. In the many passages cautioning against adultery, provocative women go to great lengths to tempt sexually charged men. "I have perfumed my bed with myrrh, aloes, and cinnamon," says one (7:17). These women make extravagant promises about nights of sexual excess. "Come, let us take our fill of love until morning; let us delight ourselves with love" (7:18). Writing with an audience of young men in mind, the biblical writers focus on scolding not the intemperate women, but the intemperate men. They express little concern for these wicked women, but simply warn young men to stay away from them. "For many are those she [the wanton woman] has laid low, and numerous are her victims" (7:26). Although women don't come off very well in passages like these, virtue is also characterized in feminine form, namely, in the two heroines of Proverbs, Lady Wisdom and the ideal woman, the virtuous wife.

These two women personify the strong teaching motifs at work in Proverbs. The first is Wisdom (Sophia) embodied as a divinely inspired woman, our teacher and guide in the virtuous life. Lady Wisdom appears first in 1:20, crying aloud in the street and raising her voice in the market squares. Throughout much of the early part of Proverbs she speaks with divine authority, lecturing, reproving, and encouraging the wayward and uncertain, reminding them of their proper course of action.

Beginning in Proverbs 8 we begin to see a portrait of Lady Wisdom as God's agent on our behalf. She takes her stand at the crossroads, near the city gates, crying out (8:1-3). The point is that wisdom is widely available knowledge. God cares for us and wants to keep us out of trouble. So virtue is not a matter of arcane knowledge or obscure teaching. It is accessible to everyone.

A deeper meaning is also present here. God's spirit of Wisdom is a life-giving spirit (8:34-35) who has existed from the beginning. "The LORD created me at the beginning of his work," she says, "I was set up . . . before the beginning of the earth" (8:22-23). Wisdom is speaking directly to anyone who will listen. And she has godly authority. The connection between the creator God and Wisdom is elaborated in 8:22-31.

This long passage (8:22-31) is considered a key text in Christology. Some interpreters see the figure of Wisdom (Sophia) as connected to or even synonymous with the Logos or Word, which (as we read in John 1) was from the beginning. Prov 8:29-31 tells us God the creator has one who is "beside him, like a master worker." As God marks out the foundations of the earth this figure of Wisdom is "daily his delight" and rejoices in God's inhabited world. Taken together with John 1, this text becomes a rich resource for Christian reflection. God's interaction with Wisdom provides a joyful sense of the life-giving creative spirit of God, who delights in the human race.

Ideal Wife, Ideal Marriage

The second strong figure is that of the ideal wife, often referred to as "the woman of Proverbs," who provides us with a fine role model for the virtuous life (31:10-31). Here the virtue of wife and husband are intertwined. This teaching concerns a harmonious marriage and a strong family. As Christians we need to understand that this virtuous wife is a woman who lives in response to the grace of God, but who has her own struggles and challenges. She is not a plaster saint. First of all, she is in a trusting relationship with her husband and family. Her husband has faith in her, and his confidence is justified. This woman has personal gifts and skills, expressed in terms of spinning, sewing, and handicrafts.

Notice that this faithful woman is running a rather large household. She is a good manager. She gets up early and uses her time well. She also delegates; she plans things for others in the household to do. Her fields are planted and well supervised. She makes a profit from her property.

The wife of Proverbs is also socially concerned. She "opens her hand to the poor" (v 20). She is in a good position to be generous, because her house is in good order. Her husband is a prominent citizen, and she supports his activities. Yet she is also a full contributor to community life.

This famous passage describes the ordinary happiness to be gained through virtuous living. The woman's children call her "happy." Her husband thinks she is outstanding. But "charm" and "beauty" are not her watchwords. The virtuous person has an inner beauty that comes from serving God and others.

Although most of us cannot exemplify all these qualities, the point of the woman in Proverbs 31 is to identify an ideal—specifically, what qualities should be lifted up and praised. And it is clear that God is pleased with powerful, accomplished, compassionate, caring, and active women!

Humor and a Common Touch

Virtues and joys are promised to us in Proverbs as we pursue the life of spiritual formation and transformation. This wise book speaks in vigorous language, with humor and a common touch that still hits us right where we live. Proverbs can profitably be studied verse by verse, with pauses for reflection. There is much insight here about what God has in mind for us and the practical human circumstances in which God's plan of righteous living can be daily carried out.

—Emilie Griffin

1

The proverbs of Solomon son of David, king of Israel:

Prologue

2 For learning about wisdom and instruction,
for understanding words of insight,
3 for gaining instruction in wise dealing,
righteousness, justice, and equity;
4 to teach shrewdness to the simple,
knowledge and prudence to the young—
5 let the wise also hear and gain in learning,
and the discerning acquire skill,
6 to understand a proverb and a figure,
the words of the wise and their riddles.

7 The fear of the LORD is the beginning of knowledge;
fools despise wisdom and instruction.

Warnings against Evil Companions

8 Hear, my child, your father's instruction,
and do not reject your mother's teaching;
9 for they are a fair garland for your head,
and pendants for your neck.

10 My child, if sinners entice you,
do not consent.
11 If they say, "Come with us, let us lie in wait for blood;
let us wantonly ambush the innocent;
12 like Sheol let us swallow them alive
and whole, like those who go down to the Pit.
13 We shall find all kinds of costly things;
we shall fill our houses with booty.
14 Throw in your lot among us;
we will all have one purse"—
15 my child, do not walk in their way,
keep your foot from their paths;
16 for their feet run to evil,
and they hurry to shed blood.
17 For in vain is the net baited
while the bird is looking on;
18 yet they lie in wait—to kill themselves!
and set an ambush—for their own lives!
19 Such is the end[a] of all who are greedy for gain;
it takes away the life of its possessors.

The Call of Wisdom

20 Wisdom cries out in the street;
in the squares she raises her voice.

a Gk: Heb are the ways

1:1–6 *The proverbs of Solomon son of David.* The prologue explains what the book is for: it is not just a collection of clever sayings. No, these sayings—proverbs, parables, and riddles—are to educate the young and inexperienced and to shape them in right conduct. Proverbs, in short, is a book of spiritual and moral formation.

1:2 *For learning about wisdom.* The NIV translates this "for attaining wisdom and discipline." Discipline in this case means, not punishment, but training or formation in good living.

1:4 *to teach shrewdness to the simple.* In other contexts simplicity might be seen as desirable modesty and meekness, but not so here. In this context simplicity is a negative trait. The simple, naïve person can easily be led astray.

1:7 *The fear of the LORD.* In biblical usage, the "fear of the LORD" does not convey fright, being afraid of God. Instead, it means living in reverential awe of God's sovereignty, goodness, and mercy and in obedience to and relationship with him.

1:8–19 *Hear, my child, your father's instruction.* Bad companions will expose a person to various temptations, but the scriptural writer also notes (v 19) that those who lead others astray will be harshly judged by God in the end.

Responding
1:8–9; 6:20–21 SUBMISSION. Our parents are often the first persons with whom we practice submission. Reflect on your relationship with your mother and father. In what ways did you submit to their authority and in what ways did you reject it? What did they teach you about submission? *See also* Spiritual Disciplines Index.

21 At the busiest corner she cries out;
  at the entrance of the city gates she
    speaks:
22 "How long, O simple ones, will you love
    being simple?
  How long will scoffers delight in their
    scoffing
  and fools hate knowledge?
23 Give heed to my reproof;
  I will pour out my thoughts to you;
  I will make my words known to you.
24 Because I have called and you refused,
    have stretched out my hand and no
    one heeded,
25 and because you have ignored all my
    counsel
  and would have none of my reproof,
26 I also will laugh at your calamity;
  I will mock when panic strikes you,
27 when panic strikes you like a storm,
    and your calamity comes like a
    whirlwind,
  when distress and anguish come
    upon you.
28 Then they will call upon me, but I will
    not answer;
  they will seek me diligently, but will
    not find me.
29 Because they hated knowledge
  and did not choose the fear of the
    LORD,
30 would have none of my counsel,
  and despised all my reproof,
31 therefore they shall eat the fruit of their
    way
  and be sated with their own devices.
32 For waywardness kills the simple,
  and the complacency of fools
    destroys them;
33 but those who listen to me will be secure
  and will live at ease, without dread of
    disaster."

The Value of Wisdom

2 My child, if you accept my words
    and treasure up my commandments
      within you,
2 making your ear attentive to wisdom
    and inclining your heart to
      understanding;
3 if you indeed cry out for insight,
    and raise your voice for
      understanding;
4 if you seek it like silver,
    and search for it as for hidden
      treasures—
5 then you will understand the fear of the
    LORD
  and find the knowledge of God.
6 For the LORD gives wisdom;
    from his mouth come knowledge and
      understanding;
7 he stores up sound wisdom for the
    upright;
  he is a shield to those who walk
    blamelessly,
8 guarding the paths of justice
    and preserving the way of his faithful
      ones.
9 Then you will understand
    righteousness and justice
  and equity, every good path;
10 for wisdom will come into your heart,
    and knowledge will be pleasant to
      your soul;
11 prudence will watch over you;
    and understanding will guard you.
12 It will save you from the way of evil,
    from those who speak perversely,
13 who forsake the paths of uprightness
    to walk in the ways of darkness,
14 who rejoice in doing evil
    and delight in the perverseness of evil;
15 those whose paths are crooked,
    and who are devious in their ways.

1:20–33 *Wisdom cries out in the street.* Wisdom is personified as a woman with divine authority who roams the town, proclaiming the righteous ways of God wherever people gather.

2:1–7:27 *My child, if you accept my words.* Chapters 2–7 offer a well-planned discussion on virtue and good conduct. Chapter 2 lays out the four major themes for the sage's instruction to his student: (1) service to God; (2) the search for wisdom; (3) avoiding bad companions among men; and (4) avoiding bad companions among women. The fourth section is longer than the rest because these instructions, meant principally for young men, are more detailed and forceful.

2:2–3 *wisdom . . . understanding . . . insight.* These are all names for the same divine gift.

16 You will be saved from the loose[a]
    woman,
    from the adulteress with her smooth
        words,
17 who forsakes the partner of her youth
    and forgets her sacred covenant;
18 for her way[b] leads down to death,
    and her paths to the shades;
19 those who go to her never come back,
    nor do they regain the paths of life.

20 Therefore walk in the way of the good,
    and keep to the paths of the just.
21 For the upright will abide in the land,
    and the innocent will remain in it;
22 but the wicked will be cut off from the
    land,
    and the treacherous will be rooted out
        of it.

Admonition to Trust and Honor God

3 My child, do not forget my teaching,
    but let your heart keep my
        commandments;
2 for length of days and years of life
    and abundant welfare they will give
        you.

3 Do not let loyalty and faithfulness
        forsake you;
    bind them around your neck,
    write them on the tablet of your
        heart.
4 So you will find favor and good repute
    in the sight of God and of people.

5 Trust in the LORD with all your heart,
    and do not rely on your own insight.
6 In all your ways acknowledge him,
    and he will make straight your paths.
7 Do not be wise in your own eyes;
    fear the LORD, and turn away from
        evil.
8 It will be a healing for your flesh

and a refreshment for your body.
9 Honor the LORD with your substance
    and with the first fruits of all your
        produce;
10 then your barns will be filled with
        plenty,
    and your vats will be bursting with
        wine.

11 My child, do not despise the LORD's
        discipline
    or be weary of his reproof,
12 for the LORD reproves the one he loves,
    as a father the son in whom he
        delights.

The True Wealth

13 Happy are those who find wisdom,
    and those who get understanding,
14 for her income is better than silver,
    and her revenue better than gold.
15 She is more precious than jewels,
    and nothing you desire can compare
        with her.
16 Long life is in her right hand;
    in her left hand are riches and honor.
17 Her ways are ways of pleasantness,
    and all her paths are peace.
18 She is a tree of life to those who lay hold
        of her;
    those who hold her fast are called
        happy.

God's Wisdom in Creation

19 The LORD by wisdom founded the earth;
    by understanding he established the
        heavens;
20 by his knowledge the deeps broke open,
    and the clouds drop down the dew.

a Heb strange   b Cn: Heb house

3:1–12 *My child, do not forget.* There are
many rewards for trust in God and faithfulness
to him. Since Proverbs is largely a cheerful book,
we find the statement that the Lord's reproof is
a sign of his love (vv 11–12).
3:25–35 *Do not be afraid of sudden panic.*

Confidently serving God requires serving one's
neighbor (vv 27–28), being at peace with those
who are good (v 29), and not being envious of
the wicked (v 31), because the Lord's friendship
is entirely on the side of the just and against
evildoers.

The True Security

21 My child, do not let these escape from
  your sight:
  keep sound wisdom and prudence,
22 and they will be life for your soul
  and adornment for your neck.
23 Then you will walk on your way
  securely
  and your foot will not stumble.
24 If you sit down,*a* you will not be afraid;
  when you lie down, your sleep will be
  sweet.
25 Do not be afraid of sudden panic,
  or of the storm that strikes the
  wicked;
26 for the LORD will be your confidence
  and will keep your foot from being
  caught.

27 Do not withhold good from those to
  whom it is due,*b*
  when it is in your power to do it.
28 Do not say to your neighbor, "Go, and
  come again,
  tomorrow I will give it"—when you
  have it with you.
29 Do not plan harm against your
  neighbor
  who lives trustingly beside you.
30 Do not quarrel with anyone without
  cause,
  when no harm has been done to you.
31 Do not envy the violent
  and do not choose any of their ways;
32 for the perverse are an abomination to
  the LORD,
  but the upright are in his confidence.
33 The LORD's curse is on the house of the
  wicked,

but he blesses the abode of the
  righteous.
34 Toward the scorners he is scornful,
  but to the humble he shows favor.
35 The wise will inherit honor,
  but stubborn fools, disgrace.

Parental Advice

4 Listen, children, to a father's
  instruction,
  and be attentive, that you may gain*c*
  insight;
2 for I give you good precepts:
  do not forsake my teaching.
3 When I was a son with my father,
  tender, and my mother's favorite,
4 he taught me, and said to me,
  "Let your heart hold fast my words;
  keep my commandments, and live.
5 Get wisdom; get insight: do not forget,
  nor turn away
  from the words of my mouth.
6 Do not forsake her, and she will keep you;
  love her, and she will guard you.
7 The beginning of wisdom is this: Get
  wisdom,
  and whatever else you get, get insight.
8 Prize her highly, and she will exalt you;
  she will honor you if you embrace her.
9 She will place on your head a fair garland;
  she will bestow on you a beautiful
  crown."

Admonition to Keep to the Right Path

10 Hear, my child, and accept my words,
  that the years of your life may be
  many.

a Gk: Heb *lie down*   *b* Heb *from its owners*
c Heb *know*

Responding

3:27–28 SERVICE. We have all hurried
by a friend or a stranger in need, telling
ourselves that we would help if only we had
more time, more money, more courage. "Next
time," we say to ourselves, knowing full well
that there may not be an opportunity tomorrow.
Ask forgiveness for any sins of omission that you
have committed, and ask God for the will to put

your own desires aside in order to serve in the
present. *See also* Spiritual Disciplines Index.

4:1–9 *Listen, children, to a father's instruction.*
The sage's tone is very earnest. This is a life-or-
death matter requiring full attention.

4:10–27 *Hear, my child, and accept my words.*
The way of wisdom leads to life; the path of
goodness is a brilliant, shining path. Singleness
of heart is essential to right living.

11 I have taught you the way of wisdom;
    I have led you in the paths of
        uprightness.
12 When you walk, your step will not be
        hampered;
    and if you run, you will not stumble.
13 Keep hold of instruction; do not let go;
    guard her, for she is your life.
14 Do not enter the path of the wicked,
    and do not walk in the way of
        evildoers.
15 Avoid it; do not go on it;
    turn away from it and pass on.
16 For they cannot sleep unless they have
        done wrong;
    they are robbed of sleep unless they
        have made someone stumble.
17 For they eat the bread of wickedness
    and drink the wine of violence.
18 But the path of the righteous is like the
        light of dawn,
    which shines brighter and brighter
        until full day.
19 The way of the wicked is like deep
        darkness;
    they do not know what they stumble
        over.
20 My child, be attentive to my words;
    incline your ear to my sayings.
21 Do not let them escape from your sight;
    keep them within your heart.
22 For they are life to those who find
        them,
    and healing to all their flesh.
23 Keep your heart with all vigilance,
    for from it flow the springs of life.
24 Put away from you crooked speech,
    and put devious talk far from you.
25 Let your eyes look directly forward,
    and your gaze be straight before you.
26 Keep straight the path of your feet,
    and all your ways will be sure.
27 Do not swerve to the right or to the
        left;
    turn your foot away from evil.

Warning against Impurity and Infidelity

5 My child, be attentive to my wisdom;
    incline your ear to my understanding,
2 so that you may hold on to prudence,
    and your lips may guard knowledge.
3 For the lips of a loose *a* woman drip
        honey,
    and her speech is smoother than oil;
4 but in the end she is bitter as
        wormwood,
    sharp as a two-edged sword.
5 Her feet go down to death;
    her steps follow the path to Sheol.
6 She does not keep straight to the path of
        life;
    her ways wander, and she does not
        know it.

7 And now, my child, *b* listen to me,
    and do not depart from the words of
        my mouth.
8 Keep your way far from her,
    and do not go near the door of her
        house;
9 or you will give your honor to others,
    and your years to the merciless,
10 and strangers will take their fill of your
        wealth,
    and your labors will go to the house
        of an alien;
11 and at the end of your life you will
        groan,
    when your flesh and body are
        consumed,
12 and you say, "Oh, how I hated
        discipline,
    and my heart despised reproof!
13 I did not listen to the voice of my
        teachers
    or incline my ear to my instructors.
14 Now I am at the point of utter ruin
    in the public assembly."

15 Drink water from your own cistern,
    flowing water from your own well.

a Heb *strange*   *b* Gk Vg: Heb *children*

5:1–23 *My child, be attentive.* A strong
warning against the dangers of adultery. The
stratagems of the "loose woman" lead to bitter

conflict, bloodshed, and death. Married love
and fidelity will, on the other hand, bring secure
happiness (vv 15–20).

16 Should your springs be scattered abroad,
   streams of water in the streets?
17 Let them be for yourself alone,
   and not for sharing with strangers.
18 Let your fountain be blessed,
   and rejoice in the wife of your youth,
19   a lovely deer, a graceful doe.
   May her breasts satisfy you at all times;
   may you be intoxicated always by her
      love.
20 Why should you be intoxicated, my
      son, by another woman
   and embrace the bosom of an
      adulteress?
21 For human ways are under the eyes of
      the LORD,
   and he examines all their paths.
22 The iniquities of the wicked ensnare
      them,
   and they are caught in the toils of
      their sin.
23 They die for lack of discipline,
   and because of their great folly they
      are lost.

Practical Admonitions

6 My child, if you have given your
      pledge to your neighbor,
   if you have bound yourself to another, *a*
2 you are snared by the utterance of your
      lips, *b*
   caught by the words of your mouth.
3 So do this, my child, and save yourself,
   for you have come into your
      neighbor's power:
   go, hurry, *c* and plead with your
      neighbor.
4 Give your eyes no sleep
   and your eyelids no slumber;
5 save yourself like a gazelle from the
      hunter, *d*
   like a bird from the hand of the
      fowler.

6 Go to the ant, you lazybones;
   consider its ways, and be wise.
7 Without having any chief
   or officer or ruler,
8 it prepares its food in summer,
   and gathers its sustenance in harvest.
9 How long will you lie there,
      O lazybones?
   When will you rise from your sleep?
10 A little sleep, a little slumber,
   a little folding of the hands to rest,
11 and poverty will come upon you like a
      robber,
   and want, like an armed warrior.

12 A scoundrel and a villain
   goes around with crooked speech,
13 winking the eyes, shuffling the feet,
   pointing the fingers,
14 with perverted mind devising evil,
   continually sowing discord;
15 on such a one calamity will descend
      suddenly;
   in a moment, damage beyond repair.

16 There are six things that the LORD hates,
   seven that are an abomination to
      him:

a Or *a stranger*   *b* Cn Compare Gk Syr: Heb *the words of your mouth*   *c* Or *humble yourself*   *d* Cn: Heb *from the hand*

Responding

5:15–22 CHASTITY. Even those of us who are married are meant to remain chaste, in the sense of remaining faithful to one's husband or wife—in thought, word, *and* deed. With the advent of the Internet, sexual temptation is sometimes literally at our fingertips. Is there a sexual temptation in your life? How can you focus on rejoicing in your spouse? *See also* Spiritual Disciplines Index.

6:6 *Go to the ant, you lazybones.* The ant is held up as an example of the virtuous and industrious life. The idler is being admonished here.

6:16–19 *six things that the LORD hates, seven that are an abomination.* Seven evil tendencies are enumerated, mostly in terms of bodily organs: the eyes embody pride, the tongue tells lies, hands do murder, hearts concoct evil plans, feet carry out these wicked plans. False witnessing, that is, lying in a court of law, is worse perhaps than ordinary lying; and the seventh vice is stirring up hatred within families.

17 haughty eyes, a lying tongue,
   and hands that shed innocent blood,
18 a heart that devises wicked plans,
   feet that hurry to run to evil,
19 a lying witness who testifies falsely,
   and one who sows discord in a family.

20 My child, keep your father's
      commandment,
   and do not forsake your mother's
      teaching.
21 Bind them upon your heart always;
   tie them around your neck.
22 When you walk, they*a* will lead you;
   when you lie down, they*a* will watch
      over you;
   and when you awake, they*a* will talk
      with you.
23 For the commandment is a lamp and
      the teaching a light,
   and the reproofs of discipline are the
      way of life,
24 to preserve you from the wife of
      another,*b*
   from the smooth tongue of the
      adulteress.
25 Do not desire her beauty in your heart,
   and do not let her capture you with
      her eyelashes;
26 for a prostitute's fee is only a loaf of
      bread,*c*
   but the wife of another stalks a man's
      very life.
27 Can fire be carried in the bosom
   without burning one's clothes?
28 Or can one walk on hot coals
   without scorching the feet?
29 So is he who sleeps with his neighbor's
      wife;
   no one who touches her will go
      unpunished.
30 Thieves are not despised who steal only
   to satisfy their appetite when they are
      hungry.

31 Yet if they are caught, they will pay
      sevenfold;
   they will forfeit all the goods of their
      house.
32 But he who commits adultery has no
      sense;
   he who does it destroys himself.
33 He will get wounds and dishonor,
   and his disgrace will not be wiped
      away.
34 For jealousy arouses a husband's fury,
   and he shows no restraint when he
      takes revenge.
35 He will accept no compensation,
   and refuses a bribe no matter how
      great.

The False Attractions of Adultery

7 My child, keep my words
   and store up my commandments
      with you;
2 keep my commandments and live,
   keep my teachings as the apple of
      your eye;
3 bind them on your fingers,
   write them on the tablet of your heart.
4 Say to wisdom, "You are my sister,"
   and call insight your intimate friend,
5 that they may keep you from the loose*d*
      woman,
   from the adulteress with her smooth
      words.

6 For at the window of my house
   I looked out through my lattice,
7 and I saw among the simple ones,
   I observed among the youths,
   a young man without sense,
8 passing along the street near her corner,
   taking the road to her house

a Heb *it*   *b* Gk: MT *the evil woman*
c Cn Compare Gk Syr Vg Tg: Heb *for because of a
harlot to a piece of bread*   *d* Heb *strange*

6:20–7:27 *My child, keep your father's
commandment.* This is a second stern warning
against adultery that begins by pointing out
the importance of a mother's and a father's
teaching. This long and vividly worded caution
dramatizes the evil consequences of breaking

the marriage code, especially the effects of the
husband's rage.

7:7 *a young man without sense.* The sage
ridicules the young man who is preyed upon by
the harlot.

9 in the twilight, in the evening,
   at the time of night and darkness.

10 Then a woman comes toward him,
   decked out like a prostitute, wily of
   heart. *a*
11 She is loud and wayward;
   her feet do not stay at home;
12 now in the street, now in the squares,
   and at every corner she lies in wait.
13 She seizes him and kisses him,
   and with impudent face she says to
   him:
14 "I had to offer sacrifices,
   and today I have paid my vows;
15 so now I have come out to meet you,
   to seek you eagerly, and I have found
   you!
16 I have decked my couch with coverings,
   colored spreads of Egyptian linen;
17 I have perfumed my bed with myrrh,
   aloes, and cinnamon.
18 Come, let us take our fill of love until
   morning;
   let us delight ourselves with love.
19 For my husband is not at home;
   he has gone on a long journey.
20 He took a bag of money with him;
   he will not come home until full
   moon."

21 With much seductive speech she
   persuades him;
   with her smooth talk she compels him.
22 Right away he follows her,
   and goes like an ox to the slaughter,
   or bounds like a stag toward the trap *b*
23   until an arrow pierces its entrails.
   He is like a bird rushing into a snare,
   not knowing that it will cost him his
   life.

24 And now, my children, listen to me,
   and be attentive to the words of my
   mouth.

25 Do not let your hearts turn aside to her
   ways;
   do not stray into her paths.
26 For many are those she has laid low,
   and numerous are her victims.
27 Her house is the way to Sheol,
   going down to the chambers of
   death.

The Gifts of Wisdom

8 Does not wisdom call,
   and does not understanding raise her
   voice?
2 On the heights, beside the way,
   at the crossroads she takes her stand;
3 beside the gates in front of the town,
   at the entrance of the portals she cries
   out:
4 "To you, O people, I call,
   and my cry is to all that live.
5 O simple ones, learn prudence;
   acquire intelligence, you who lack it.
6 Hear, for I will speak noble things,
   and from my lips will come what is
   right;
7 for my mouth will utter truth;
   wickedness is an abomination to my
   lips.
8 All the words of my mouth are
   righteous;
   there is nothing twisted or crooked in
   them.
9 They are all straight to one who
   understands
   and right to those who find
   knowledge.
10 Take my instruction instead of silver,
   and knowledge rather than choice
   gold;
11 for wisdom is better than jewels,
   and all that you may desire cannot
   compare with her.

a Meaning of Heb uncertain   *b* Cn Compare
Gk: Meaning of Heb uncertain

8:1–36 *Does not wisdom call?* This entire chapter depicts wisdom as a woman with godly authority. She speaks in a challenging and inspiring way, assuring all who listen of God's blessings and rewards for following the right path. But the personification of wisdom is not meant to suggest that a second deity, even a lesser deity, is on hand. Rather, wisdom is an aspect of God.

12 I, wisdom, live with prudence,*a*
    and I attain knowledge and
        discretion.
13 The fear of the LORD is hatred of evil.
    Pride and arrogance and the way of evil
        and perverted speech I hate.
14 I have good advice and sound wisdom;
    I have insight, I have strength.
15 By me kings reign,
    and rulers decree what is just;
16 by me rulers rule,
    and nobles, all who govern rightly.
17 I love those who love me,
    and those who seek me diligently find
        me.
18 Riches and honor are with me,
    enduring wealth and prosperity.
19 My fruit is better than gold, even fine
        gold,
    and my yield than choice silver.
20 I walk in the way of righteousness,
    along the paths of justice,
21 endowing with wealth those who love
        me,
    and filling their treasuries.

Wisdom's Part in Creation

22 The LORD created me at the beginning*b*
    of his work,*c*
        the first of his acts of long ago.
23 Ages ago I was set up,
    at the first, before the beginning of
        the earth.
24 When there were no depths I was
        brought forth,
    when there were no springs
        abounding with water.
25 Before the mountains had been shaped,
    before the hills I was brought forth—
26 when he had not yet made earth and
        fields,*a*

27 When he established the heavens, I was
        there,
    when he drew a circle on the face of
        the deep,
28 when he made firm the skies above,
    when he established the fountains of
        the deep,
29 when he assigned to the sea its limit,
    so that the waters might not
        transgress his command,
    when he marked out the foundations of
        the earth,
30 then I was beside him, like a master
        worker;*d*
    and I was daily his*e* delight,
        rejoicing before him always,
31 rejoicing in his inhabited world
    and delighting in the human race.

32 "And now, my children, listen to me:
    happy are those who keep my ways.
33 Hear instruction and be wise,
    and do not neglect it.
34 Happy is the one who listens to me,
    watching daily at my gates,
    waiting beside my doors.
35 For whoever finds me finds life
    and obtains favor from the LORD;
36 but those who miss me injure
        themselves;
    all who hate me love death."

Wisdom's Feast

9 Wisdom has built her house,
    she has hewn her seven pillars.

a Meaning of Heb uncertain   *b* Or *me as the beginning*   *c* Heb *way*   *d* Another reading is *little child*   *e* Gk: Heb lacks *his*

8:22–31 *The LORD created me.* This text, which connects God as creator with the creativity of wisdom, is considered an important text in Christology. Some interpreters see Wisdom (Sophia) as connected to or synonymous with the Logos, or Word, which John 1 describes as with God in the beginning. God here is portrayed as life-giving, and Wisdom, "daily his delight," joins with him in rejoicing in the creation.

8:32–36 *Happy is the one who listens to me.* Here we learn that to find wisdom is to gain divine favor. "Wisdom" and "divine favor" are nearly synonyms.
9:1–12 *Wisdom has built her house.* The biblical writer continues to develop the figure of personified Wisdom. Wisdom's house of seven pillars consists of her teachings. It is possible that chapters 2–7 correspond to different rooms

2 She has slaughtered her animals, she
   has mixed her wine,
   she has also set her table.
3 She has sent out her servant-girls, she
   calls
   from the highest places in the town,
4 "You that are simple, turn in here!"
   To those without sense she says,
5 "Come, eat of my bread
   and drink of the wine I have mixed.
6 Lay aside immaturity,[a] and live,
   and walk in the way of insight."

General Maxims

7 Whoever corrects a scoffer wins abuse;
   whoever rebukes the wicked gets hurt.
8 A scoffer who is rebuked will only hate
   you;
   the wise, when rebuked, will love
   you.
9 Give instruction[b] to the wise, and they
   will become wiser still;
   teach the righteous and they will gain
   in learning.
10 The fear of the LORD is the beginning of
   wisdom,

and the knowledge of the Holy One is
   insight.
11 For by me your days will be multiplied,
   and years will be added to your life.
12 If you are wise, you are wise for yourself;
   if you scoff, you alone will bear it.

Folly's Invitation and Promise

13 The foolish woman is loud;
   she is ignorant and knows nothing.
14 She sits at the door of her house,
   on a seat at the high places of the
   town,
15 calling to those who pass by,
   who are going straight on their way,
16 "You who are simple, turn in here!"
   And to those without sense she says,
17 "Stolen water is sweet,
   and bread eaten in secret is
   pleasant."
18 But they do not know that the dead[c] are
   there,
   that her guests are in the depths of
   Sheol.

a Or *simpleness*   b Heb lacks *instruction*
c Heb *shades*

---

in Wisdom's house or temple. (A parallel may
be seen in the seven mansions or dwelling
places of Teresa of Avila's *Interior Castle*.) However, the biblical writer may also be writing a
coded "description" of the Temple at Jerusalem. Chapter 1 would thus correspond to the
vestibule of the Temple, and chapter 8 would
be the Holy of Holies. Wisdom literature sometimes works on this symbolic level, so it is not
out of the question for a symbolic "ground
plan" of Solomon's Temple to be represented
in chapters 1–9. These nine chapters combine
and interweave priestly material, prophetic
material, and Wisdom's counsel. Doubtless
there are several levels of meaning here.

9:13–18 *The foolish woman is loud*. Wisdom's
opposite appears, an inane and strident woman.
Like Wisdom, she is trying to win converts from
among the passers-by. The foolish woman is
also inviting guests to a banquet, a lesser one
with only bread and water compared to the
meat and wine at Wisdom's feast. The water is
stolen, sweet because it is forbidden, and the

bread is to be eaten in secret, in contrast to the
bread openly set out by Wisdom. But even sins
done in secret are seen by God. The foolish
woman is inviting her guests under false pre-
tenses; she is drawing them into the world of
death.

9:14. *She sits at the door of her house.*
Wisdom's house in verse 1 is described as
having seven pillars, while the foolish woman's
house is where she sits "at the high places
of the town." Two ways of life are being contrasted. The Jerusalem Temple with its worship
of Yahweh stresses the blessing of life. The
foolish woman's house is the temple of cult
prostitutes, where sexual rites confer only
spiritual death upon those who take part.

9:18 *But they do not know that the dead are
there.* The foolish woman is inviting her guests
into "the depths of Sheol." Sheol is not exactly
a hell of torment; it is the netherworld of the
departed, something like the underworld of
Greek and Roman myth. However, it is not a
pleasant place.

Wise Sayings of Solomon

375 prov of Solomon

10 The proverbs of Solomon.

A wise child makes a glad father,
  but a foolish child is a mother's grief.
2 Treasures gained by wickedness do not
    profit,
  but righteousness delivers from death.
3 The LORD does not let the righteous go
    hungry,
  but he thwarts the craving of the
    wicked.
4 A slack hand causes poverty,
  but the hand of the diligent makes
    rich.
5 A child who gathers in summer is
    prudent,
  but a child who sleeps in harvest
    brings shame.
6 Blessings are on the head of the
    righteous,
  but the mouth of the wicked conceals
    violence.
7 The memory of the righteous is a
    blessing,
  but the name of the wicked will rot.
8 The wise of heart will heed
    commandments,
  but a babbling fool will come to ruin.
9 Whoever walks in integrity walks
    securely,
  but whoever follows perverse ways
    will be found out.
10 Whoever winks the eye causes trouble,
  but the one who rebukes boldly
    makes peace. *a*

11 The mouth of the righteous is a
    fountain of life,
  but the mouth of the wicked conceals
    violence.
12 Hatred stirs up strife,
  but love covers all offenses.
13 On the lips of one who has
    understanding wisdom is
    found,
  but a rod is for the back of one who
    lacks sense.
14 The wise lay up knowledge,
  but the babbling of a fool brings ruin
    near.
15 The wealth of the rich is their fortress;
  the poverty of the poor is their ruin.
16 The wage of the righteous leads to
    life,
  the gain of the wicked to sin.
17 Whoever heeds instruction is on the
    path to life,
  but one who rejects a rebuke goes
    astray.
18 Lying lips conceal hatred,
  and whoever utters slander is a fool.
19 When words are many, transgression is
    not lacking,
  but the prudent are restrained in
    speech.
20 The tongue of the righteous is choice
    silver;
  the mind of the wicked is of little
    worth.
21 The lips of the righteous feed many,
  but fools die for lack of sense.

a Gk: Heb *but a babbling fool will come to ruin*

10:1–22:16 *A wise child makes a glad father.* The first collection of Solomon's proverbs contains 375 proverbs, mostly directed toward matters affecting the lives of individuals. These proverbs make use of parallelism, a poetic and rhetorical device in which a precept is stated positively in the first line and repeated in the reverse or negative mode in the next: "A scoffer who is rebuked will only hate you; the wise, when rebuked, will love you" (9:8); "A slack hand causes poverty, but the hand of the diligent makes rich" (10:4). Each one of these proverbs is meant to stand on its own, distinct from the rest; yet they have a cumulative effect when read one after another, because similar content links them all. These chapters build upon one another toward a climactic sense of the consequence of ignoring God's plan for virtuous living: "A good name is to be chosen rather than great riches, and favor is better than silver or gold" (22:1).

10:12 *Hatred stirs up strife, but love covers all offenses.* This sentiment is echoed in 17:9. Also, this observation is a favorite in the New Testament (cf. 1 Cor 13:7; James 5:20; 1 Pet 4:8).

22 The blessing of the LORD makes rich,
   and he adds no sorrow with it. *a*
23 Doing wrong is like sport to a fool,
   but wise conduct is pleasure to a
     person of understanding.
24 What the wicked dread will come upon
   them,
   but the desire of the righteous will be
     granted.
25 When the tempest passes, the wicked
   are no more,
   but the righteous are established
     forever.
26 Like vinegar to the teeth, and smoke to
   the eyes,
   so are the lazy to their employers.
27 The fear of the LORD prolongs life,
   but the years of the wicked will be
     short.
28 The hope of the righteous ends in
   gladness,
   but the expectation of the wicked
     comes to nothing.
29 The way of the LORD is a stronghold for
   the upright,
   but destruction for evildoers.
30 The righteous will never be removed,
   but the wicked will not remain in the
     land.
31 The mouth of the righteous brings
   forth wisdom,
   but the perverse tongue will be cut
     off.
32 The lips of the righteous know what is
   acceptable,
   but the mouth of the wicked what is
     perverse.

11 A false balance is an abomination to
   the LORD,
   but an accurate weight is his delight.

2 When pride comes, then comes
   disgrace;
   but wisdom is with the humble.
3 The integrity of the upright guides
   them,
   but the crookedness of the
     treacherous destroys them.
4 Riches do not profit in the day of
   wrath,
   but righteousness delivers from
     death.
5 The righteousness of the blameless
   keeps their ways straight,
   but the wicked fall by their own
     wickedness.
6 The righteousness of the upright saves
   them,
   but the treacherous are taken captive
     by their schemes.
7 When the wicked die, their hope
   perishes,
   and the expectation of the godless
     comes to nothing.
8 The righteous are delivered from
   trouble,
   and the wicked get into it
     instead.
9 With their mouths the godless would
   destroy their neighbors,
   but by knowledge the righteous are
     delivered.
10 When it goes well with the righteous,
   the city rejoices;
   and when the wicked perish, there is
     jubilation.
11 By the blessing of the upright a city is
   exalted,
   but it is overthrown by the mouth of
     the wicked.

a Or *and toil adds nothing to it*

10:22 *The blessing of the LORD makes rich.* It is striking that, although many proverbs exhort others to be hardworking and industrious, this proverb says that God's blessing is the real reason behind a person's prosperity.

11:1–31 *A false balance is an abomination.* This chapter continues the theme of right behavior. The just and the unjust are contrasted with regard to personal attitudes (vv 2–8) and the social implications of behavior (vv 9–15).

11:4 *Riches do not profit in the day of wrath.* What counts with God is a devoted heart. This sentiment has something in common with Ps 40:6: "Sacrifice and offering you do not desire, but you have given me an open ear." The Lord's blessing is not to be earned. God showers his blessing on the just, but not because they have earned his approval.

12 Whoever belittles another lacks sense,
   but an intelligent person remains
      silent.
13 A gossip goes about telling secrets,
   but one who is trustworthy in spirit
      keeps a confidence.
14 Where there is no guidance, a nation[a]
      falls,
   but in an abundance of counselors
      there is safety.
15 To guarantee loans for a stranger brings
      trouble,
   but there is safety in refusing to do so.
16 A gracious woman gets honor,
   but she who hates virtue is covered
      with shame.[b]
   The timid become destitute,[c]
   but the aggressive gain riches.
17 Those who are kind reward themselves,
   but the cruel do themselves harm.
18 The wicked earn no real gain,
   but those who sow righteousness get
      a true reward.
19 Whoever is steadfast in righteousness
      will live,
   but whoever pursues evil will die.
20 Crooked minds are an abomination to
      the Lord,
   but those of blameless ways are his
      delight.
21 Be assured, the wicked will not go
      unpunished,
   but those who are righteous will
      escape.
22 Like a gold ring in a pig's snout
   is a beautiful woman without good
      sense.
23 The desire of the righteous ends only in
      good;
   the expectation of the wicked in
      wrath.
24 Some give freely, yet grow all the richer;

others withhold what is due, and
   only suffer want.
25 A generous person will be enriched,
   and one who gives water will get water.
26 The people curse those who hold back
      grain,
   but a blessing is on the head of those
      who sell it.
27 Whoever diligently seeks good seeks
      favor,
   but evil comes to the one who
      searches for it.
28 Those who trust in their riches will
      wither,[d]
   but the righteous will flourish like
      green leaves.
29 Those who trouble their households
      will inherit wind,
   and the fool will be servant to the wise.
30 The fruit of the righteous is a tree of life,
   but violence[e] takes lives away.
31 If the righteous are repaid on earth,
   how much more the wicked and the
      sinner!

12 Whoever loves discipline loves
      knowledge,
   but those who hate to be rebuked are
      stupid.
2 The good obtain favor from the Lord,
   but those who devise evil he
      condemns.
3 No one finds security by wickedness,
   but the root of the righteous will
      never be moved.
4 A good wife is the crown of her husband,
   but she who brings shame is like
      rottenness in his bones.

a Or an army   b Compare Gk Syr: Heb lacks but
she . . . shame   c Gk: Heb lacks The timid . . .
destitute   d Cn: Heb fall   e Cn Compare Gk
Syr: Heb a wise man

Responding

11:12 SILENCE. Silence is a Spiritual
Discipline to be practiced not just in
meditation when we are alone and listening for
God's guiding voice, but also when we are with
others and need to hold back words that are
harsh, hurtful, or boastful. This week, try to be
aware of ways in which you might need to

practice silence in your relationships. *See also*
Spiritual Disciplines Index.

12:1–28 *Whoever loves discipline.* Here, as
elsewhere in Proverbs, knowledge and virtue
are equated. The beginner is encouraged to
grow in virtue through a number of contrasting
examples of good and bad behavior.

5 The thoughts of the righteous are just;
   the advice of the wicked is
      treacherous.
6 The words of the wicked are a deadly
      ambush,
   but the speech of the upright delivers
      them.
7 The wicked are overthrown and are no
      more,
   but the house of the righteous will
      stand.
8 One is commended for good sense,
   but a perverse mind is despised.
9 Better to be despised and have a servant,
   than to be self-important and lack
      food.
10 The righteous know the needs of their
      animals,
   but the mercy of the wicked is cruel.
11 Those who till their land will have
      plenty of food,
   but those who follow worthless
      pursuits have no sense.
12 The wicked covet the proceeds of
      wickedness, *a*
   but the root of the righteous bears
      fruit.
13 The evil are ensnared by the
      transgression of their lips,
   but the righteous escape from
      trouble.
14 From the fruit of the mouth one is filled
      with good things,
   and manual labor has its reward.
15 Fools think their own way is right,
   but the wise listen to advice.
16 Fools show their anger at once,
   but the prudent ignore an insult.
17 Whoever speaks the truth gives honest
      evidence,
   but a false witness speaks deceitfully.
18 Rash words are like sword thrusts,
   but the tongue of the wise brings
      healing.
19 Truthful lips endure forever,

   but a lying tongue lasts only a
      moment.
20 Deceit is in the mind of those who plan
      evil,
   but those who counsel peace have joy.
21 No harm happens to the righteous,
   but the wicked are filled with trouble.
22 Lying lips are an abomination to the
      LORD,
   but those who act faithfully are his
      delight.
23 One who is clever conceals knowledge,
   but the mind of a fool *b* broadcasts
      folly.
24 The hand of the diligent will rule,
   while the lazy will be put to forced
      labor.
25 Anxiety weighs down the human heart,
   but a good word cheers it up.
26 The righteous gives good advice to
      friends, *c*
   but the way of the wicked leads astray.
27 The lazy do not roast *d* their game,
   but the diligent obtain precious
      wealth. *d*
28 In the path of righteousness there is
      life,
   in walking its path there is no death.

13 A wise child loves discipline, *e*
   but a scoffer does not listen to
      rebuke.
2 From the fruit of their words good
      persons eat good things,
   but the desire of the treacherous is for
      wrongdoing.
3 Those who guard their mouths preserve
      their lives;
   those who open wide their lips come
      to ruin.
4 The appetite of the lazy craves, and gets
      nothing,

a Or *covet the catch of the wicked*   *b* Heb *the heart
of fools*   *c* Syr: Meaning of Heb uncertain
d Meaning of Heb uncertain   *e* Cn: Heb *A wise
child the discipline of his father*

12:5 *The thoughts of the righteous are just.*
This verse insists upon the importance of the
intentional life and significance of the desires of
the heart.

13:2–12 *From the fruit of their words good
persons eat good things.* These verses develop
the first major theme of this chapter, namely, the
dangers of uncontrolled desires and appetites.

while the appetite of the diligent is
  richly supplied.
5 The righteous hate falsehood,
  but the wicked act shamefully and
    disgracefully.
6 Righteousness guards one whose way is
    upright,
  but sin overthrows the wicked.
7 Some pretend to be rich, yet have
    nothing;
  others pretend to be poor, yet have
    great wealth.
8 Wealth is a ransom for a person's life,
  but the poor get no threats.
9 The light of the righteous rejoices,
  but the lamp of the wicked goes out.
10 By insolence the heedless make strife,
  but wisdom is with those who take
    advice.
11 Wealth hastily gotten *a* will dwindle,
  but those who gather little by little
    will increase it.
12 Hope deferred makes the heart sick,
  but a desire fulfilled is a tree of life.
13 Those who despise the word bring
    destruction on themselves,
  but those who respect the
    commandment will be rewarded.
14 The teaching of the wise is a fountain of
    life,
  so that one may avoid the snares of
    death.
15 Good sense wins favor,
  but the way of the faithless is their
    ruin. *b*
16 The clever do all things intelligently,
  but the fool displays folly.
17 A bad messenger brings trouble,
  but a faithful envoy, healing.
18 Poverty and disgrace are for the one
    who ignores instruction,
  but one who heeds reproof is
    honored.

19 A desire realized is sweet to the soul,
  but to turn away from evil is an
    abomination to fools.
20 Whoever walks with the wise becomes
    wise,
  but the companion of fools suffers
    harm.
21 Misfortune pursues sinners,
  but prosperity rewards the righteous.
22 The good leave an inheritance to their
    children's children,
  but the sinner's wealth is laid up for
    the righteous.
23 The field of the poor may yield much
    food,
  but it is swept away through injustice.
24 Those who spare the rod hate their
    children,
  but those who love them are diligent
    to discipline them.
25 The righteous have enough to satisfy
    their appetite,
  but the belly of the wicked is empty.

14 The wise woman *c* builds her house,
  but the foolish tears it down with
    her own hands.
2 Those who walk uprightly fear the LORD,
  but one who is devious in conduct
    despises him.
3 The talk of fools is a rod for their backs, *d*
  but the lips of the wise preserve them.
4 Where there are no oxen, there is no
    grain;
  but abundant crops come by the strength
    of the ox.
5 A faithful witness does not lie,
  but a false witness breathes out lies.
6 A scoffer seeks wisdom in vain,
  but knowledge is easy for one who
    understands.

a Gk Vg: Heb *from vanity*   *b* Cn Compare Gk Syr
Vg Tg: Heb *is enduring*   *c* Heb *Wisdom of women*
d Cn: Heb *a rod of pride*

13:13–25 *Those who despise the word bring
destruction on themselves.* The second theme of
the chapter unfolds in these verses: the choices
each person makes will determine his or her
quality of life.

14:2 *Those who walk uprightly fear the LORD.*
"Fear of the LORD" is mentioned again in verses

26–27. This fear is not a matter of being
frightened, but rather of awe, being moved by
God's transcendent power and majesty. Trust in
and love for the divine power and the resulting
obedience and relationship are implied by this
"fear of the LORD."

7 Leave the presence of a fool,
   for there you do not find words of
      knowledge.
8 It is the wisdom of the clever to
      understand where they go,
   but the folly of fools misleads.
9 Fools mock at the guilt offering, *a*
   but the upright enjoy God's favor.
10 The heart knows its own bitterness,
   and no stranger shares its joy.
11 The house of the wicked is destroyed,
   but the tent of the upright flourishes.
12 There is a way that seems right to a
      person,
   but its end is the way to death. *b*
13 Even in laughter the heart is sad,
   and the end of joy is grief.
14 The perverse get what their ways
      deserve,
   and the good, what their deeds
      deserve. *c*
15 The simple believe everything,
   but the clever consider their steps.
16 The wise are cautious and turn away
      from evil,
   but the fool throws off restraint and is
      careless.
17 One who is quick-tempered acts
      foolishly,
   and the schemer is hated.
18 The simple are adorned with *d* folly,
   but the clever are crowned with
      knowledge.
19 The evil bow down before the good,
   the wicked at the gates of the
      righteous.
20 The poor are disliked even by their
      neighbors,
   but the rich have many friends.
21 Those who despise their neighbors are
      sinners,
   but happy are those who are kind to
      the poor.
22 Do they not err that plan evil?
   Those who plan good find loyalty and
      faithfulness.
23 In all toil there is profit,
   but mere talk leads only to poverty.

24 The crown of the wise is their wisdom, *e*
   but folly is the garland *f* of fools.
25 A truthful witness saves lives,
   but one who utters lies is a betrayer.
26 In the fear of the LORD one has strong
      confidence,
   and one's children will have a refuge.
27 The fear of the LORD is a fountain of life,
   so that one may avoid the snares of
      death.
28 The glory of a king is a multitude of
      people;
   without people a prince is ruined.
29 Whoever is slow to anger has great
      understanding,
   but one who has a hasty temper exalts
      folly.
30 A tranquil mind gives life to the flesh,
   but passion makes the bones rot.
31 Those who oppress the poor insult their
      Maker,
   but those who are kind to the needy
      honor him.
32 The wicked are overthrown by their
      evildoing,
   but the righteous find a refuge in
      their integrity. *g*
33 Wisdom is at home in the mind of one
      who has understanding,
   but it is not *h* known in the heart of
      fools.
34 Righteousness exalts a nation,
   but sin is a reproach to any people.
35 A servant who deals wisely has the
      king's favor,
   but his wrath falls on one who acts
      shamefully.

15 A soft answer turns away wrath,
   but a harsh word stirs up anger.
2 The tongue of the wise dispenses
      knowledge, *i*
   but the mouths of fools pour out
      folly.

a Meaning of Heb uncertain   *b* Heb *ways of
death*   *c* Cn: Heb *from upon him*   *d* Or *inherit*
e Cn Compare Gk: Heb *riches*   *f* Cn: Heb *is the
folly*   *g* Gk Syr: Heb *in their death*   *h* Gk Syr:
Heb lacks *not*   *i* Cn: Heb *makes knowledge good*

14:17 *One who is quick-tempered acts foolishly.*
Rash, hot-tempered behavior is never praised in

Proverbs. This is one of the most common
themes in Middle Eastern wisdom.

3 The eyes of the LORD are in every place,
    keeping watch on the evil and the
        good.
4 A gentle tongue is a tree of life,
    but perverseness in it breaks the
        spirit.
5 A fool despises a parent's instruction,
    but the one who heeds admonition is
        prudent.
6 In the house of the righteous there is
        much treasure,
    but trouble befalls the income of the
        wicked.
7 The lips of the wise spread knowledge;
    not so the minds of fools.
8 The sacrifice of the wicked is an
        abomination to the LORD,
    but the prayer of the upright is his
        delight.
9 The way of the wicked is an
        abomination to the LORD,
    but he loves the one who pursues
        righteousness.
10 There is severe discipline for one who
        forsakes the way,
    but one who hates a rebuke will die.
11 Sheol and Abaddon lie open before the
        LORD,
    how much more human hearts!
12 Scoffers do not like to be rebuked;
    they will not go to the wise.
13 A glad heart makes a cheerful
        countenance,
    but by sorrow of heart the spirit is
        broken.
14 The mind of one who has
        understanding seeks knowledge,
    but the mouths of fools feed on folly.
15 All the days of the poor are hard,
    but a cheerful heart has a continual
        feast.
16 Better is a little with the fear of the LORD
    than great treasure and trouble with it.
17 Better is a dinner of vegetables where
        love is

than a fatted ox and hatred with it.
18 Those who are hot-tempered stir up
        strife,
    but those who are slow to anger calm
        contention.
19 The way of the lazy is overgrown with
        thorns,
    but the path of the upright is a level
        highway.
20 A wise child makes a glad father,
    but the foolish despise their mothers.
21 Folly is a joy to one who has no sense,
    but a person of understanding walks
        straight ahead.
22 Without counsel, plans go wrong,
    but with many advisers they succeed.
23 To make an apt answer is a joy to
        anyone,
    and a word in season, how good it is!
24 For the wise the path of life leads
        upward,
    in order to avoid Sheol below.
25 The LORD tears down the house of the
        proud,
    but maintains the widow's
        boundaries.
26 Evil plans are an abomination to the
        LORD,
    but gracious words are pure.
27 Those who are greedy for unjust gain
        make trouble for their
        households,
    but those who hate bribes will live.
28 The mind of the righteous ponders how
        to answer,
    but the mouth of the wicked pours
        out evil.
29 The LORD is far from the wicked,
    but he hears the prayer of the
        righteous.
30 The light of the eyes rejoices the heart,
    and good news refreshes the body.
31 The ear that heeds wholesome
        admonition
    will lodge among the wise.

15:11 *Sheol and Abaddon lie open before the
LORD.* This unusually positive reference to the
world of departed spirits suggests that the Lord
cares for even the dead.

15:15–17 *All the days of the poor are hard.* By

and large, wisdom teachers do not praise
poverty, but these consoling words comfort
those who know God in the midst of poverty.

15:29 PRAYER—*See* Spiritual Disciplines
Index.

32 Those who ignore instruction despise
    themselves,
    but those who heed admonition gain
    understanding.
33 The fear of the LORD is instruction in
    wisdom,
    and humility goes before honor.

16 The plans of the mind belong to
    mortals,
    but the answer of the tongue is from
    the LORD.
2 All one's ways may be pure in one's own
    eyes,
    but the LORD weighs the spirit.
3 Commit your work to the LORD,
    and your plans will be established.
4 The LORD has made everything for its
    purpose,
    even the wicked for the day of
    trouble.
5 All those who are arrogant are an
    abomination to the LORD;
    be assured, they will not go
    unpunished.
6 By loyalty and faithfulness iniquity is
    atoned for,
    and by the fear of the LORD one avoids
    evil.
7 When the ways of people please the
    LORD,
    he causes even their enemies to be at
    peace with them.
8 Better is a little with righteousness
    than large income with injustice.
9 The human mind plans the way,
    but the LORD directs the steps.
10 Inspired decisions are on the lips of a
    king;
    his mouth does not sin in judgment.
11 Honest balances and scales are the
    LORD's;
    all the weights in the bag are his
    work.
12 It is an abomination to kings to do evil,
    for the throne is established by
    righteousness.

13 Righteous lips are the delight of a king,
    and he loves those who speak what is
    right.
14 A king's wrath is a messenger of death,
    and whoever is wise will appease it.
15 In the light of a king's face there is life,
    and his favor is like the clouds that
    bring the spring rain.
16 How much better to get wisdom than
    gold!
    To get understanding is to be chosen
    rather than silver.
17 The highway of the upright avoids evil;
    those who guard their way preserve
    their lives.
18 Pride goes before destruction,
    and a haughty spirit before a fall.
19 It is better to be of a lowly spirit among
    the poor
    than to divide the spoil with the
    proud.
20 Those who are attentive to a matter will
    prosper,
    and happy are those who trust in the
    LORD.
21 The wise of heart is called perceptive,
    and pleasant speech increases
    persuasiveness.
22 Wisdom is a fountain of life to one who
    has it,
    but folly is the punishment of fools.
23 The mind of the wise makes their
    speech judicious,
    and adds persuasiveness to their lips.
24 Pleasant words are like a honeycomb,
    sweetness to the soul and health to
    the body.
25 Sometimes there is a way that seems to
    be right,
    but in the end it is the way to death.
26 The appetite of workers works for them;
    their hunger urges them on.
27 Scoundrels concoct evil,
    and their speech is like a scorching fire.
28 A perverse person spreads strife,
    and a whisperer separates close
    friends.

16:10–15 *Inspired decisions are on the lips of
a king.* These five verses focus on the proper
behavior of rulers. Rulers were thought to have
a special intimacy with God and were obliged to
share God's concern for justice.

29 The violent entice their neighbors,
    and lead them in a way that is not
        good.
30 One who winks the eyes plans *a* perverse
        things;
    one who compresses the lips brings
        evil to pass.
31 Gray hair is a crown of glory;
    it is gained in a righteous life.
32 One who is slow to anger is better than
        the mighty,
    and one whose temper is controlled
        than one who captures a city.
33 The lot is cast into the lap,
    but the decision is the LORD's alone.

17 Better is a dry morsel with quiet
    than a house full of feasting with
        strife.
2 A slave who deals wisely will rule over a
        child who acts shamefully,
    and will share the inheritance as one
        of the family.
3 The crucible is for silver, and the
        furnace is for gold,
    but the LORD tests the heart.
4 An evildoer listens to wicked lips;
    and a liar gives heed to a mischievous
        tongue.
5 Those who mock the poor insult their
        Maker;
    those who are glad at calamity will
        not go unpunished.
6 Grandchildren are the crown of the
        aged,
    and the glory of children is their
        parents.
7 Fine speech is not becoming to a fool;
    still less is false speech to a ruler. *b*
8 A bribe is like a magic stone in the eyes
        of those who give it;
    wherever they turn they prosper.
9 One who forgives an affront fosters
        friendship,
    but one who dwells on disputes will
        alienate a friend.

10 A rebuke strikes deeper into a discerning
        person
    than a hundred blows into a fool.
11 Evil people seek only rebellion,
    but a cruel messenger will be sent
        against them.
12 Better to meet a she-bear robbed of its
        cubs
    than to confront a fool immersed in
        folly.
13 Evil will not depart from the house
    of one who returns evil for good.
14 The beginning of strife is like letting out
        water;
    so stop before the quarrel breaks out.
15 One who justifies the wicked and one
        who condemns the righteous
    are both alike an abomination to the
        LORD.
16 Why should fools have a price in hand
    to buy wisdom, when they have no
        mind to learn?
17 A friend loves at all times,
    and kinsfolk are born to share
        adversity.
18 It is senseless to give a pledge,
    to become surety for a neighbor.
19 One who loves transgression loves strife;
    one who builds a high threshold
        invites broken bones.
20 The crooked of mind do not prosper,
    and the perverse of tongue fall into
        calamity.
21 The one who begets a fool gets trouble;
    the parent of a fool has no joy.
22 A cheerful heart is a good medicine,
    but a downcast spirit dries up the
        bones.
23 The wicked accept a concealed bribe
    to pervert the ways of justice.
24 The discerning person looks to wisdom,
    but the eyes of a fool to the ends of
        the earth.

a Gk Syr Vg Tg: Heb *to plan*   *b* Or *a noble person*

17:8 *A bribe is like a magic stone.* Though the biblical writer understands that a bribe may at first seem to get results, Scripture is clear that bribery undermines the social order (see also v 23).

17:16 *Why should fools have a price in hand to buy wisdom?* Here (as in vv 10, 12, 21, 24, 25) the fool is depicted not as a simple-minded fellow, but as one who gets in the way of a just and harmonious social order.

25 Foolish children are a grief to their
father
and bitterness to her who bore them.
26 To impose a fine on the innocent is not
right,
or to flog the noble for their integrity.
27 One who spares words is
knowledgeable;
one who is cool in spirit has
understanding.
28 Even fools who keep silent are
considered wise;
when they close their lips, they are
deemed intelligent.

18 The one who lives alone is
self-indulgent,
showing contempt for all who have
sound judgment. *a*
2 A fool takes no pleasure in
understanding,
but only in expressing personal
opinion.
3 When wickedness comes, contempt
comes also;
and with dishonor comes disgrace.
4 The words of the mouth are deep
waters;
the fountain of wisdom is a gushing
stream.
5 It is not right to be partial to the guilty,
or to subvert the innocent in
judgment.
6 A fool's lips bring strife,
and a fool's mouth invites a flogging.
7 The mouths of fools are their ruin,
and their lips a snare to themselves.
8 The words of a whisperer are like
delicious morsels;
they go down into the inner parts of
the body.
9 One who is slack in work
is close kin to a vandal.
10 The name of the LORD is a strong tower;
the righteous run into it and are safe.
11 The wealth of the rich is their strong
city;

in their imagination it is like a high
wall.
12 Before destruction one's heart is
haughty,
but humility goes before honor.
13 If one gives answer before hearing,
it is folly and shame.
14 The human spirit will endure sickness;
but a broken spirit—who can bear?
15 An intelligent mind acquires
knowledge,
and the ear of the wise seeks
knowledge.
16 A gift opens doors;
it gives access to the great.
17 The one who first states a case seems
right,
until the other comes and cross-
examines.
18 Casting the lot puts an end to disputes
and decides between powerful
contenders.
19 An ally offended is stronger than a
city; *b*
such quarreling is like the bars of a
castle.
20 From the fruit of the mouth one's
stomach is satisfied;
the yield of the lips brings
satisfaction.
21 Death and life are in the power of the
tongue,
and those who love it will eat its
fruits.
22 He who finds a wife finds a good thing,
and obtains favor from the LORD.
23 The poor use entreaties,
but the rich answer roughly.
24 Some *c* friends play at friendship *d*
but a true friend sticks closer than
one's nearest kin.

a Meaning of Heb uncertain   *b* Gk Syr Vg Tg:
Meaning of Heb uncertain   *c* Syr Tg: Heb *A man
of*   *d* Cn Compare Syr Vg Tg: Meaning of Heb
uncertain

18:1–24 *The one who lives alone.* A number
of sayings in chapter 18 emphasize the dangers
of the unguarded tongue, for example, insensitivity to others (v 1) and foolishly expressing

an opinion without listening (v 2).
18:21 *Death and life are in the power of the
tongue.* Some have likened these admonitions
to those in James 3:1–12.

19

Better the poor walking in integrity
than one perverse of speech who is
a fool.

2 Desire without knowledge is not good,
and one who moves too hurriedly
misses the way.

3 One's own folly leads to ruin,
yet the heart rages against the LORD.

4 Wealth brings many friends,
but the poor are left friendless.

5 A false witness will not go unpunished,
and a liar will not escape.

6 Many seek the favor of the generous,
and everyone is a friend to a giver of
gifts.

7 If the poor are hated even by their kin,
how much more are they shunned by
their friends!
When they call after them, they are not
there. [a]

8 To get wisdom is to love oneself;
to keep understanding is to prosper.

9 A false witness will not go unpunished,
and the liar will perish.

10 It is not fitting for a fool to live in
luxury,
much less for a slave to rule over
princes.

11 Those with good sense are slow to
anger,
and it is their glory to overlook an
offense.

12 A king's anger is like the growling of a
lion,
but his favor is like dew on the grass.

13 A stupid child is ruin to a father,
and a wife's quarreling is a continual
dripping of rain.

14 House and wealth are inherited from
parents,
but a prudent wife is from the LORD.

15 Laziness brings on deep sleep;
an idle person will suffer hunger.

16 Those who keep the commandment
will live;

those who are heedless of their ways
will die.

17 Whoever is kind to the poor lends to
the LORD,
and will be repaid in full.

18 Discipline your children while there is
hope;
do not set your heart on their
destruction.

19 A violent tempered person will pay the
penalty;
if you effect a rescue, you will only
have to do it again. [a]

20 Listen to advice and accept instruction,
that you may gain wisdom for the
future.

21 The human mind may devise many
plans,
but it is the purpose of the LORD that
will be established.

22 What is desirable in a person is loyalty,
and it is better to be poor than a liar.

23 The fear of the LORD is life indeed;
filled with it one rests secure
and suffers no harm.

24 The lazy person buries a hand in the
dish,
and will not even bring it back to the
mouth.

25 Strike a scoffer, and the simple will learn
prudence;
reprove the intelligent, and they will
gain knowledge.

26 Those who do violence to their father
and chase away their mother
are children who cause shame and
bring reproach.

27 Cease straying, my child, from the
words of knowledge,
in order that you may hear
instruction.

28 A worthless witness mocks at justice,
and the mouth of the wicked devours
iniquity.

a Meaning of Heb uncertain

19:1–29 *Better the poor walking in integrity.*
Although no particular subject dominates this
chapter, advice about the danger of wealth is
prominent.

19:20 *Listen to advice and accept instruction.*
Sometimes these words are connected with the
virtue of "counsel," which includes good political advice.

²⁹ Condemnation is ready for scoffers,
    and flogging for the backs of fools.

20 Wine is a mocker, strong drink a
    brawler,
    and whoever is led astray by it is not
      wise.
² The dread anger of a king is like the
    growling of a lion;
    anyone who provokes him to anger
      forfeits life itself.
³ It is honorable to refrain from strife,
    but every fool is quick to quarrel.
⁴ The lazy person does not plow in
    season;
    harvest comes, and there is nothing
      to be found.
⁵ The purposes in the human mind are
    like deep water,
    but the intelligent will draw them
      out.
⁶ Many proclaim themselves loyal,
    but who can find one worthy of trust?
⁷ The righteous walk in integrity—
    happy are the children who follow
      them!
⁸ A king who sits on the throne of
    judgment
    winnows all evil with his eyes.
⁹ Who can say, "I have made my heart
    clean;
    I am pure from my sin"?
¹⁰ Diverse weights and diverse measures
    are both alike an abomination to the
      LORD.
¹¹ Even children make themselves known
    by their acts,
    by whether what they do is pure and
      right.
¹² The hearing ear and the seeing eye—
    the LORD has made them both.
¹³ Do not love sleep, or else you will come
    to poverty;
    open your eyes, and you will have
      plenty of bread.
¹⁴ "Bad, bad," says the buyer,

    then goes away and boasts.
¹⁵ There is gold, and abundance of costly
    stones;
    but the lips informed by knowledge
      are a precious jewel.
¹⁶ Take the garment of one who has given
    surety for a stranger;
    seize the pledge given as surety for
      foreigners.
¹⁷ Bread gained by deceit is sweet,
    but afterward the mouth will be full
      of gravel.
¹⁸ Plans are established by taking advice;
    wage war by following wise guidance.
¹⁹ A gossip reveals secrets;
    therefore do not associate with a
      babbler.
²⁰ If you curse father or mother,
    your lamp will go out in utter darkness.
²¹ An estate quickly acquired in the
    beginning
    will not be blessed in the end.
²² Do not say, "I will repay evil";
    wait for the LORD, and he will help you.
²³ Differing weights are an abomination to
    the LORD,
    and false scales are not good.
²⁴ All our steps are ordered by the LORD;
    how then can we understand our own
      ways?
²⁵ It is a snare for one to say rashly, "It is
    holy,"
    and begin to reflect only after making
      a vow.
²⁶ A wise king winnows the wicked,
    and drives the wheel over them.
²⁷ The human spirit is the lamp of the
    LORD,
    searching every inmost part.
²⁸ Loyalty and faithfulness preserve the
    king,
    and his throne is upheld by
      righteousness. ͣ

a Gk: Heb *loyalty*

20:12 *The hearing ear and the seeing eye—the LORD has made them both.* Some commentators interpret this verse as relating to God's good intentions and the need for human beings to shape their intentions accordingly.

20:22 *Do not say, "I will repay evil."* Another good instance of the way God's power and insight are constantly interwoven with human wisdom.

29 The glory of youths is their strength,
  but the beauty of the aged is their
    gray hair.
30 Blows that wound cleanse away evil;
  beatings make clean the innermost
    parts.

21 The king's heart is a stream of water
  in the hand of the LORD;
  he turns it wherever he will.
2 All deeds are right in the sight of the
    doer,
  but the LORD weighs the heart.
3 To do righteousness and justice
  is more acceptable to the LORD than
    sacrifice.
4 Haughty eyes and a proud heart—
  the lamp of the wicked—are sin.
5 The plans of the diligent lead surely to
    abundance,
  but everyone who is hasty comes only
    to want.
6 The getting of treasures by a lying
    tongue
  is a fleeting vapor and a snare *a* of
    death.
7 The violence of the wicked will sweep
    them away,
  because they refuse to do what is just.
8 The way of the guilty is crooked,
  but the conduct of the pure is right.
9 It is better to live in a corner of the
    housetop
  than in a house shared with a
    contentious wife.
10 The souls of the wicked desire evil;
  their neighbors find no mercy in their
    eyes.
11 When a scoffer is punished, the simple
    become wiser;
  when the wise are instructed, they
    increase in knowledge.
12 The Righteous One observes the house
    of the wicked;
  he casts the wicked down to ruin.
13 If you close your ear to the cry of the
    poor,

  you will cry out and not be heard.
14 A gift in secret averts anger;
  and a concealed bribe in the bosom,
    strong wrath.
15 When justice is done, it is a joy to the
    righteous,
  but dismay to evildoers.
16 Whoever wanders from the way of
    understanding
  will rest in the assembly of the dead.
17 Whoever loves pleasure will suffer want;
  whoever loves wine and oil will not be
    rich.
18 The wicked is a ransom for the
    righteous,
  and the faithless for the upright.
19 It is better to live in a desert land
  than with a contentious and fretful
    wife.
20 Precious treasure remains *b* in the house
    of the wise,
  but the fool devours it.
21 Whoever pursues righteousness and
    kindness
  will find life *c* and honor.
22 One wise person went up against a city
    of warriors
  and brought down the stronghold in
    which they trusted.
23 To watch over mouth and tongue
  is to keep out of trouble.
24 The proud, haughty person, named
    "Scoffer,"
  acts with arrogant pride.
25 The craving of the lazy person is fatal,
  for lazy hands refuse to labor.
26 All day long the wicked covet, *d*
  but the righteous give and do not
    hold back.
27 The sacrifice of the wicked is an
    abomination;

a Gk: Heb *seekers*   *b* Gk: Heb *and oil*
c Gk: Heb *life and righteousness*   *d* Gk: Heb *all
day long one covets covetously*

21:3 SACRIFICE—*See* Spiritual Disciplines
Index.
  21:9 *It is better to live in a corner of the housetop.* The contentious and fretful wife comes in

for her share of criticism (see also v 19).
  21:13 *If you close your ear to the cry of the
poor.* Once again, God's concern for the poor
requires that we learn charity.

how much more when brought with
    evil intent.
28 A false witness will perish,
    but a good listener will testify
      successfully.
29 The wicked put on a bold face,
    but the upright give thought to[a] their
      ways.
30 No wisdom, no understanding, no
    counsel,
    can avail against the LORD.
31 The horse is made ready for the day of
    battle,
    but the victory belongs to the LORD.

22 A good name is to be chosen rather
    than great riches,
    and favor is better than silver or gold.
2 The rich and the poor have this in
    common:
    the LORD is the maker of them all.
3 The clever see danger and hide;
    but the simple go on, and suffer for it.
4 The reward for humility and fear of the
    LORD
    is riches and honor and life.
5 Thorns and snares are in the way of the
    perverse;
    the cautious will keep far from them.
6 Train children in the right way,
    and when old, they will not stray.
7 The rich rule over the poor,
    and the borrower is the slave of the
      lender.
8 Whoever sows injustice will reap
    calamity,
    and the rod of anger will fail.
9 Those who are generous are blessed,
    for they share their bread with the
      poor.
10 Drive out a scoffer, and strife goes out;
    quarreling and abuse will cease.
11 Those who love a pure heart and are
    gracious in speech
    will have the king as a friend.

12 The eyes of the LORD keep watch over
    knowledge,
    but he overthrows the words of the
      faithless.
13 The lazy person says, "There is a lion
    outside!
    I shall be killed in the streets!"
14 The mouth of a loose[b] woman is a deep
    pit;
    he with whom the LORD is angry falls
      into it.
15 Folly is bound up in the heart of a boy,
    but the rod of discipline drives it far
      away.
16 Oppressing the poor in order to enrich
    oneself,
    and giving to the rich, will lead only
      to loss.

Sayings of the Wise

17   The words of the wise:

Incline your ear and hear my words,[c]
    and apply your mind to my teaching;
18 for it will be pleasant if you keep them
    within you,
    if all of them are ready on your lips.
19 So that your trust may be in the LORD,
    I have made them known to you
      today—yes, to you.
20 Have I not written for you thirty
    sayings
    of admonition and knowledge,
21 to show you what is right and true,
    so that you may give a true answer to
      those who sent you?

22 Do not rob the poor because they are
    poor,
    or crush the afflicted at the gate;

a Another reading is *establish*   b Heb *strange*
c Cn Compare Gk: Heb *Incline your ear, and hear the
words of the wise*

22:14 *The mouth of a loose woman.* (See NRSV
translation note.) Some commentators think
that "loose" is better translated "strange" or
"foreign." Israel must shun the customs of less
holy and honorable nations.

22:17–29 *The words of the wise: Incline your
ear.* These verses are an extended message
about the stored-up treasury of wisdom available
in Israel's tradition. People of faith need not
invent their own rules of conduct. They can
access the wisdom already laid up for them.

23 for the LORD pleads their cause
  and despoils of life those who despoil
    them.
24 Make no friends with those given to
    anger,
  and do not associate with hotheads,
25 or you may learn their ways
  and entangle yourself in a snare.
26 Do not be one of those who give
    pledges,
  who become surety for debts.
27 If you have nothing with which to pay,
  why should your bed be taken from
    under you?
28 Do not remove the ancient landmark
  that your ancestors set up.
29 Do you see those who are skillful in
    their work?
  They will serve kings;
  they will not serve common people.

23 When you sit down to eat with a
    ruler,
  observe carefully what *a* is before you,
2 and put a knife to your throat
  if you have a big appetite.
3 Do not desire the ruler's *b* delicacies,
  for they are deceptive food.
4 Do not wear yourself out to get rich;
  be wise enough to desist.
5 When your eyes light upon it, it is
    gone;
  for suddenly it takes wings to itself,
  flying like an eagle toward heaven.
6 Do not eat the bread of the stingy;
  do not desire their delicacies;
7 for like a hair in the throat, so are they. *c*
  "Eat and drink!" they say to you;
  but they do not mean it.
8 You will vomit up the little you have
    eaten,
  and you will waste your pleasant
    words.
9 Do not speak in the hearing of a fool,
  who will only despise the wisdom of
    your words.
10 Do not remove an ancient landmark
  or encroach on the fields of orphans,

11 for their redeemer is strong;
  he will plead their cause against you.
12 Apply your mind to instruction
  and your ear to words of knowledge.
13 Do not withhold discipline from your
    children;
  if you beat them with a rod, they will
    not die.
14 If you beat them with the rod,
  you will save their lives from Sheol.
15 My child, if your heart is wise,
  my heart too will be glad.
16 My soul will rejoice
  when your lips speak what is right.
17 Do not let your heart envy sinners,
  but always continue in the fear of the
    LORD.
18 Surely there is a future,
  and your hope will not be cut off.

19 Hear, my child, and be wise,
  and direct your mind in the way.
20 Do not be among winebibbers,
  or among gluttonous eaters of meat;
21 for the drunkard and the glutton will
    come to poverty,
  and drowsiness will clothe them with
    rags.

22 Listen to your father who begot you,
  and do not despise your mother when
    she is old.
23 Buy truth, and do not sell it;
  buy wisdom, instruction, and
    understanding.
24 The father of the righteous will greatly
    rejoice;
  he who begets a wise son will be glad
    in him.
25 Let your father and mother be glad;
  let her who bore you rejoice.

26 My child, give me your heart,
  and let your eyes observe *d* my ways.
27 For a prostitute is a deep pit;

a Or *who*   *b* Heb *his*   *c* Meaning of Heb
uncertain   *d* Another reading is *delight in*

23:1–35 *When you sit down to eat.* These
rules of decorum and propriety are more than

common sense. They represent humility and
other desirable virtues.

an adulteress^a is a narrow well.
28 She lies in wait like a robber
and increases the number of the
faithless.

29 Who has woe? Who has sorrow?
Who has strife? Who has
complaining?
Who has wounds without cause?
Who has redness of eyes?
30 Those who linger late over wine,
those who keep trying mixed wines.
31 Do not look at wine when it is red,
when it sparkles in the cup
and goes down smoothly.
32 At the last it bites like a serpent,
and stings like an adder.
33 Your eyes will see strange things,
and your mind utter perverse things.
34 You will be like one who lies down in
the midst of the sea,
like one who lies on the top of a
mast.^b
35 "They struck me," you will say,^c "but I
was not hurt;
they beat me, but I did not feel it.
When shall I awake?
I will seek another drink."

24 Do not envy the wicked,
nor desire to be with them;
2 for their minds devise violence,
and their lips talk of mischief.

3 By wisdom a house is built,
and by understanding it is
established;
4 by knowledge the rooms are filled
with all precious and pleasant riches.
5 Wise warriors are mightier than strong
ones,^d
and those who have knowledge than
those who have strength;
6 for by wise guidance you can wage your
war,
and in abundance of counselors there
is victory.
7 Wisdom is too high for fools;

in the gate they do not open their
mouths.

8 Whoever plans to do evil
will be called a mischief-maker.
9 The devising of folly is sin,
and the scoffer is an abomination to
all.

10 If you faint in the day of adversity,
your strength being small;
11 if you hold back from rescuing those
taken away to death,
those who go staggering to the
slaughter;
12 if you say, "Look, we did not know
this"—
does not he who weighs the heart
perceive it?
Does not he who keeps watch over your
soul know it?
And will he not repay all according to
their deeds?

13 My child, eat honey, for it is good,
and the drippings of the honeycomb
are sweet to your taste.
14 Know that wisdom is such to your soul;
if you find it, you will find a future,
and your hope will not be cut off.

15 Do not lie in wait like an outlaw against
the home of the righteous;
do no violence to the place where the
righteous live;
16 for though they fall seven times, they
will rise again;
but the wicked are overthrown by
calamity.

17 Do not rejoice when your enemies fall,
and do not let your heart be glad
when they stumble,

a Heb *an alien woman*   b Meaning of Heb
uncertain   c Gk Syr Vg Tg: Heb lacks *you will say*
d Gk Compare Syr Tg: Heb *A wise man is strength*

23:27 *For a prostitute is a deep pit.* Another allusion to the alien or foreign woman may be found here; see note on 22:14.

24:5–6 *Wise warriors are mightier.* Israel's ideal is wisdom and strength combined. David and Solomon, in combination, represent this ideal.

18 or else the LORD will see it and be
displeased,
and turn away his anger from them.

19 Do not fret because of evildoers.
Do not envy the wicked;
20 for the evil have no future;
the lamp of the wicked will go out.

21 My child, fear the LORD and the king,
and do not disobey either of them;[a]
22 for disaster comes from them suddenly,
and who knows the ruin that both
can bring?

Further Sayings of the Wise

23 These also are sayings of the wise:

Partiality in judging is not good.
24 Whoever says to the wicked, "You are
innocent,"
will be cursed by peoples, abhorred by
nations;
25 but those who rebuke the wicked will
have delight,
and a good blessing will come upon
them.
26 One who gives an honest answer
gives a kiss on the lips.

27 Prepare your work outside,
get everything ready for you in the
field;
and after that build your house.

28 Do not be a witness against your
neighbor without cause,
and do not deceive with your lips.
29 Do not say, "I will do to others as they
have done to me;
I will pay them back for what they
have done."

30 I passed by the field of one who was
lazy,

by the vineyard of a stupid person;
31 and see, it was all overgrown with
thorns;
the ground was covered with nettles,
and its stone wall was broken down.
32 Then I saw and considered it;
I looked and received instruction.
33 A little sleep, a little slumber,
a little folding of the hands to rest,
34 and poverty will come upon you like a
robber,
and want, like an armed warrior.

Further Wise Sayings of Solomon

25 These are other proverbs of Solomon
that the officials of King Hezekiah of
Judah copied.

2 It is the glory of God to conceal things,
but the glory of kings is to search
things out.
3 Like the heavens for height, like the
earth for depth,
so the mind of kings is unsearchable.
4 Take away the dross from the silver,
and the smith has material for a
vessel;
5 take away the wicked from the presence
of the king,
and his throne will be established in
righteousness.
6 Do not put yourself forward in the
king's presence
or stand in the place of the great;
7 for it is better to be told, "Come up
here,"
than to be put lower in the presence
of a noble.

What your eyes have seen
8 do not hastily bring into court;
for[b] what will you do in the end,

a Gk: Heb do not associate with those who change
b Cn: Heb or else

24:30–32 *I passed by the field of one who was lazy.* This is one of the most creatively expressed cautions against laziness in Proverbs.
25:1–28 *These are other proverbs.* This chapter contains a highly structured group

of admonitions and sayings for kings and leaders.
25:2 *the glory of kings is to search things out.* Note how the idea is developed that kings have greater wisdom and greater responsibility.

when your neighbor puts you to
    shame?
9 Argue your case with your neighbor
    directly,
  and do not disclose another's secret;
10 or else someone who hears you will
    bring shame upon you,
  and your ill repute will have no end.

11 A word fitly spoken
  is like apples of gold in a setting of
    silver.
12 Like a gold ring or an ornament of gold
  is a wise rebuke to a listening ear.
13 Like the cold of snow in the time of
    harvest
  are faithful messengers to those who
    send them;
  they refresh the spirit of their
    masters.
14 Like clouds and wind without rain
  is one who boasts of a gift never
    given.
15 With patience a ruler may be
    persuaded,
  and a soft tongue can break bones.
16 If you have found honey, eat only
    enough for you,
  or else, having too much, you will
    vomit it.
17 Let your foot be seldom in your
    neighbor's house,
  otherwise the neighbor will become
    weary of you and hate you.
18 Like a war club, a sword, or a sharp
    arrow
  is one who bears false witness against
    a neighbor.
19 Like a bad tooth or a lame foot
  is trust in a faithless person in time of
    trouble.
20 Like vinegar on a wound [a]
  is one who sings songs to a heavy
    heart.
  Like a moth in clothing or a worm in
    wood,
  sorrow gnaws at the human heart. [b]

21 If your enemies are hungry, give them
    bread to eat;
  and if they are thirsty, give them
    water to drink;
22 for you will heap coals of fire on their
    heads,
  and the LORD will reward you.
23 The north wind produces rain,
  and a backbiting tongue, angry
    looks.
24 It is better to live in a corner of the
    housetop
  than in a house shared with a
    contentious wife.
25 Like cold water to a thirsty soul,
  so is good news from a far country.
26 Like a muddied spring or a polluted
    fountain
  are the righteous who give way before
    the wicked.
27 It is not good to eat much honey,
  or to seek honor on top of honor.
28 Like a city breached, without walls,
  is one who lacks self-control.

26 Like snow in summer or rain in
    harvest,
  so honor is not fitting for a fool.
2 Like a sparrow in its flitting, like a
    swallow in its flying,
  an undeserved curse goes nowhere.
3 A whip for the horse, a bridle for the
    donkey,
  and a rod for the back of fools.
4 Do not answer fools according to their
    folly,
  or you will be a fool yourself.
5 Answer fools according to their folly,
  or they will be wise in their own eyes.
6 It is like cutting off one's foot and
    drinking down violence,
  to send a message by a fool.
7 The legs of a disabled person hang limp;
  so does a proverb in the mouth of a
    fool.

a Gk: Heb *Like one who takes off a garment on a cold
day, like vinegar on lye*   b Gk Syr Tg: Heb lacks *Like
a moth . . . human heart*

26:1–28 *Like snow in summer.* This chapter
is low on religious content, but covers three
popular subjects of wisdom literature: the fool,
the lazy person, and the evil-talking person.

8 It is like binding a stone in a sling
   to give honor to a fool.
9 Like a thornbush brandished by the
   hand of a drunkard
   is a proverb in the mouth of a fool.
10 Like an archer who wounds everybody
   is one who hires a passing fool or
   drunkard. [a]
11 Like a dog that returns to its vomit
   is a fool who reverts to his folly.
12 Do you see persons wise in their own
   eyes?
   There is more hope for fools than for
   them.
13 The lazy person says, "There is a lion in
   the road!
   There is a lion in the streets!"
14 As a door turns on its hinges,
   so does a lazy person in bed.
15 The lazy person buries a hand in the
   dish,
   and is too tired to bring it back to the
   mouth.
16 The lazy person is wiser in self-esteem
   than seven who can answer discreetly.
17 Like somebody who takes a passing dog
   by the ears
   is one who meddles in the quarrel of
   another.
18 Like a maniac who shoots deadly
   firebrands and arrows,
19 so is one who deceives a neighbor
   and says, "I am only joking!"
20 For lack of wood the fire goes out,
   and where there is no whisperer,
   quarreling ceases.
21 As charcoal is to hot embers and wood
   to fire,
   so is a quarrelsome person for
   kindling strife.
22 The words of a whisperer are like
   delicious morsels;
   they go down into the inner parts of
   the body.
23 Like the glaze [b] covering an earthen
   vessel
   are smooth [c] lips with an evil heart.

24 An enemy dissembles in speaking
   while harboring deceit within;
25 when an enemy speaks graciously, do
   not believe it,
   for there are seven abominations
   concealed within;
26 though hatred is covered with guile,
   the enemy's wickedness will be
   exposed in the assembly.
27 Whoever digs a pit will fall into it,
   and a stone will come back on the
   one who starts it rolling.
28 A lying tongue hates its victims,
   and a flattering mouth works ruin.

27 Do not boast about tomorrow,
   for you do not know what a day
   may bring.
2 Let another praise you, and not your
   own mouth—
   a stranger, and not your own lips.
3 A stone is heavy, and sand is weighty,
   but a fool's provocation is heavier
   than both.
4 Wrath is cruel, anger is overwhelming,
   but who is able to stand before
   jealousy?
5 Better is open rebuke
   than hidden love.
6 Well meant are the wounds a friend
   inflicts,
   but profuse are the kisses of an
   enemy.
7 The sated appetite spurns honey,
   but to a ravenous appetite even the
   bitter is sweet.
8 Like a bird that strays from its nest
   is one who strays from home.
9 Perfume and incense make the heart
   glad,
   but the soul is torn by trouble. [d]
10 Do not forsake your friend or the friend
   of your parent;

a Meaning of Heb uncertain   b Cn: Heb *silver of
dross*   c Gk: Heb *burning*   d Gk: Heb *the
sweetness of a friend is better than one's own counsel*

26:27 *Whoever digs a pit will fall into it.* Another example of rough humor in Proverbs. It is easy to imagine these sayings being spoken aloud, to the laughter of the crowd.

do not go to the house of your
kindred in the day of your
calamity.
Better is a neighbor who is nearby
than kindred who are far away.

11 Be wise, my child, and make my heart
glad,
so that I may answer whoever
reproaches me.
12 The clever see danger and hide;
but the simple go on, and suffer for it.
13 Take the garment of one who has given
surety for a stranger;
seize the pledge given as surety for
foreigners. *a*
14 Whoever blesses a neighbor with a loud
voice,
rising early in the morning,
will be counted as cursing.
15 A continual dripping on a rainy day
and a contentious wife are alike;
16 to restrain her is to restrain the wind
or to grasp oil in the right hand. *b*
17 Iron sharpens iron,
and one person sharpens the wits *c* of
another.
18 Anyone who tends a fig tree will eat its
fruit,
and anyone who takes care of a
master will be honored.
19 Just as water reflects the face,
so one human heart reflects another.
20 Sheol and Abaddon are never satisfied,
and human eyes are never satisfied.
21 The crucible is for silver, and the
furnace is for gold,
so a person is tested *d* by being
praised.
22 Crush a fool in a mortar with a pestle
along with crushed grain,
but the folly will not be driven out.

23 Know well the condition of your flocks,
and give attention to your herds;
24 for riches do not last forever,
nor a crown for all generations.
25 When the grass is gone, and new
growth appears,

and the herbage of the mountains is
gathered,
26 the lambs will provide your clothing,
and the goats the price of a field;
27 there will be enough goats' milk for
your food,
for the food of your household
and nourishment for your servant-
girls.

28 The wicked flee when no one
pursues,
but the righteous are as bold as a lion.
2 When a land rebels
it has many rulers;
but with an intelligent ruler
there is lasting order. *b*
3 A ruler *e* who oppresses the poor
is a beating rain that leaves no food.
4 Those who forsake the law praise the
wicked,
but those who keep the law struggle
against them.
5 The evil do not understand justice,
but those who seek the LORD
understand it completely.
6 Better to be poor and walk in integrity
than to be crooked in one's ways even
though rich.
7 Those who keep the law are wise
children,
but companions of gluttons shame
their parents.
8 One who augments wealth by
exorbitant interest
gathers it for another who is kind to
the poor.
9 When one will not listen to the law,
even one's prayers are an
abomination.
10 Those who mislead the upright into evil
ways
will fall into pits of their own making,
but the blameless will have a goodly
inheritance.

a Vg and 20.16: Heb *for a foreign woman*
b Meaning of Heb uncertain   *c* Heb *face*
d Heb lacks *is tested*   *e* Cn: Heb *A poor person*

28:1 *the righteous are as bold as a lion.* Since
much wisdom writing seems to focus on wrong-

doing, it is good to find the righteous person
celebrated as bold and strong.

11 The rich is wise in self-esteem,
   but an intelligent poor person sees
     through the pose.
12 When the righteous triumph, there is
     great glory,
   but when the wicked prevail, people
     go into hiding.
13 No one who conceals transgressions
     will prosper,
   but one who confesses and forsakes
     them will obtain mercy.
14 Happy is the one who is never without
     fear,
   but one who is hard-hearted will fall
     into calamity.
15 Like a roaring lion or a charging bear
   is a wicked ruler over a poor people.
16 A ruler who lacks understanding is a
     cruel oppressor;
   but one who hates unjust gain will
     enjoy a long life.
17 If someone is burdened with the blood
     of another,
   let that killer be a fugitive until death;
   let no one offer assistance.
18 One who walks in integrity will be safe,
   but whoever follows crooked ways
     will fall into the Pit. *a*
19 Anyone who tills the land will have
     plenty of bread,
   but one who follows worthless
     pursuits will have plenty of
     poverty.
20 The faithful will abound with blessings,
   but one who is in a hurry to be rich
     will not go unpunished.
21 To show partiality is not good—
   yet for a piece of bread a person may
     do wrong.

22 The miser is in a hurry to get rich
   and does not know that loss is sure to
     come.
23 Whoever rebukes a person will
   afterward find more favor
   than one who flatters with the
     tongue.
24 Anyone who robs father or mother
   and says, "That is no crime,"
   is partner to a thug.
25 The greedy person stirs up strife,
   but whoever trusts in the LORD will be
     enriched.
26 Those who trust in their own wits are
     fools;
   but those who walk in wisdom come
     through safely.
27 Whoever gives to the poor will lack
     nothing,
   but one who turns a blind eye will get
     many a curse.
28 When the wicked prevail, people go
     into hiding;
   but when they perish, the righteous
     increase.

29 One who is often reproved, yet
     remains stubborn,
   will suddenly be broken beyond
     healing.
2 When the righteous are in authority,
     the people rejoice;
   but when the wicked rule, the people
     groan.
3 A child who loves wisdom makes a
     parent glad,
   but to keep company with prostitutes
     is to squander one's substance.

a Syr: Heb *fall all at once*

Responding
28:9, 13 CONFESSION and PRAYER.
Have you ever had a prayer block? A
reluctance to pray stemming from a deep-down
fear that something you're doing is wrong and
that God will tell you so? Attempting to conceal
a sin from God is the worst kind of folly, yet we
sometimes fear confession because, once we
admit to a sin, the next step is to forsake it.
Prayerfully consider a chronic sin, one that
you have confessed before but have trouble
forsaking. Write the sin or draw a symbol of it
on a piece of paper. In a fireplace or wherever
you can do so safely, light the paper on fire.
Confess the sin as you watch the paper darken,
shrink, and fade into ash. Ask God to bring his
refining fire into your life. *See also* Spiritual
Disciplines Index.

28:28 *When the wicked prevail, people go into
hiding.* Notice the social dimension in this advice.
It pertains to public as well as private life.

4 By justice a king gives stability to the
   land,
   but one who makes heavy exactions
      ruins it.
5 Whoever flatters a neighbor
   is spreading a net for the neighbor's
      feet.
6 In the transgression of the evil there is a
      snare,
   but the righteous sing and rejoice.
7 The righteous know the rights of the
      poor;
   the wicked have no such
      understanding.
8 Scoffers set a city aflame,
   but the wise turn away wrath.
9 If the wise go to law with fools,
   there is ranting and ridicule without
      relief.
10 The bloodthirsty hate the blameless,
   and they seek the life of the upright.
11 A fool gives full vent to anger,
   but the wise quietly holds it back.
12 If a ruler listens to falsehood,
   all his officials will be wicked.
13 The poor and the oppressor have this in
      common:
   the LORD gives light to the eyes of
      both.
14 If a king judges the poor with equity,
   his throne will be established forever.
15 The rod and reproof give wisdom,
   but a mother is disgraced by a
      neglected child.
16 When the wicked are in authority,
      transgression increases,
   but the righteous will look upon their
      downfall.
17 Discipline your children, and they will
      give you rest;
   they will give delight to your heart.
18 Where there is no prophecy, the people
      cast off restraint,

but happy are those who keep the
   law.
19 By mere words servants are not
      disciplined,
   for though they understand, they will
      not give heed.
20 Do you see someone who is hasty in
      speech?
   There is more hope for a fool than for
      anyone like that.
21 A slave pampered from childhood
   will come to a bad end. *a*
22 One given to anger stirs up strife,
   and the hothead causes much
      transgression.
23 A person's pride will bring humiliation,
   but one who is lowly in spirit will
      obtain honor.
24 To be a partner of a thief is to hate one's
      own life;
   one hears the victim's curse, but
      discloses nothing. *b*
25 The fear of others *c* lays a snare,
   but one who trusts in the LORD is
      secure.
26 Many seek the favor of a ruler,
   but it is from the LORD that one gets
      justice.
27 The unjust are an abomination to the
      righteous,
   but the upright are an abomination
      to the wicked.

Sayings of Agur

30 The words of Agur son of Jakeh. An
      oracle.

Thus says the man: I am weary, O God,
   I am weary, O God. How can I
      prevail? *d*

a Vg: Meaning of Heb uncertain   *b* Meaning of
Heb uncertain   *c* Or *human fear*   *d* Or *I am
spent.* Meaning of Heb uncertain

29:14 *If a king judges the poor with equity.*
Again, the good ruler is held up for admiration,
and God's love for the poor is manifested.

   29:26 *Many seek the favor of a ruler.* The proverb reminds us that the ultimate power of a
ruler is the power of God.

30:1–33 *The words of Agur.* A different tone
is struck in this discourse, written in the first
person. There is a sense of weariness and
discouragement, but the writer is clearly in
search of the consolation of divine wisdom.

2 Surely I am too stupid to be human;
    I do not have human understanding.
3 I have not learned wisdom,
    nor have I knowledge of the holy
      ones. *a*

4 Who has ascended to heaven and come
      down?
    Who has gathered the wind in the
      hollow of the hand?
    Who has wrapped up the waters in a
      garment?
    Who has established all the ends of
      the earth?
    What is the person's name?
    And what is the name of the person's
      child?
    Surely you know!

5 Every word of God proves true;
    he is a shield to those who take refuge
      in him.
6 Do not add to his words,
    or else he will rebuke you, and you
      will be found a liar.

7 Two things I ask of you;
    do not deny them to me before I die:
8 Remove far from me falsehood and
      lying;
    give me neither poverty nor riches;
    feed me with the food that I need,
9 or I shall be full, and deny you,
    and say, "Who is the LORD?"
    or I shall be poor, and steal,
    and profane the name of my God.

10 Do not slander a servant to a master,
    or the servant will curse you, and you
      will be held guilty.

11 There are those who curse their fathers
    and do not bless their mothers.
12 There are those who are pure in their
      own eyes
    yet are not cleansed of their filthiness.
13 There are those—how lofty are their eyes,
    how high their eyelids lift!—

14 there are those whose teeth are swords,
      whose teeth are knives,
    to devour the poor from off the earth,
      the needy from among mortals.

15 The leech *b* has two daughters;
    "Give, give," they cry.
  Three things are never satisfied;
    four never say, "Enough":
16 Sheol, the barren womb,
    the earth ever thirsty for water,
    and the fire that never says,
      "Enough." *b*

17 The eye that mocks a father
    and scorns to obey a mother
  will be pecked out by the ravens of the
      valley
    and eaten by the vultures.

18 Three things are too wonderful for me;
    four I do not understand:
19 the way of an eagle in the sky,
    the way of a snake on a rock,
    the way of a ship on the high seas,
    and the way of a man with a girl.

20 This is the way of an adulteress:
    she eats, and wipes her mouth,
    and says, "I have done no wrong."

21 Under three things the earth trembles;
    under four it cannot bear up:
22 a slave when he becomes king,
    and a fool when glutted with food;
23 an unloved woman when she gets a
      husband,
    and a maid when she succeeds her
      mistress.

24 Four things on earth are small,
    yet they are exceedingly wise:
25 the ants are a people without strength,
    yet they provide their food in the
      summer;

a Or *Holy One*   *b* Meaning of Heb uncertain

30:21–23 *Under three things . . . under four.*
Numerical sayings are used several times in
chapter 30. Here four kinds of undesirable
behavior are reproved. In later numerical sayings
(vv 24–28, 29–31) various creatures are held up
as examples of wisdom.

26 the badgers are a people without power,
   yet they make their homes in the
      rocks;
27 the locusts have no king,
   yet all of them march in rank;
28 the lizard*a* can be grasped in the hand,
   yet it is found in kings' palaces.

29 Three things are stately in their stride;
   four are stately in their gait:
30 the lion, which is mightiest among wild
      animals
   and does not turn back before any;
31 the strutting rooster,*b* the he-goat,
   and a king striding before*c* his people.

32 If you have been foolish, exalting
      yourself,
   or if you have been devising evil,
      put your hand on your mouth.
33 For as pressing milk produces curds,
   and pressing the nose produces
      blood,
   so pressing anger produces strife.

The Teaching of King Lemuel's Mother

31 The words of King Lemuel. An oracle
   that his mother taught him:

2 No, my son! No, son of my womb!
   No, son of my vows!
3 Do not give your strength to women,
   your ways to those who destroy kings.
4 It is not for kings, O Lemuel,
   it is not for kings to drink wine,
   or for rulers to desire*d* strong drink;
5 or else they will drink and forget what
      has been decreed,

and will pervert the rights of all the
      afflicted.
6 Give strong drink to one who is
      perishing,
   and wine to those in bitter distress;
7 let them drink and forget their poverty,
   and remember their misery no more.
8 Speak out for those who cannot speak,
   for the rights of all the destitute.*e*
9 Speak out, judge righteously,
   defend the rights of the poor and
      needy.

Ode to a Capable Wife

10 A capable wife who can find?
   She is far more precious than jewels.
11 The heart of her husband trusts in her,
   and he will have no lack of gain.
12 She does him good, and not harm,
   all the days of her life.
13 She seeks wool and flax,
   and works with willing hands.
14 She is like the ships of the merchant,
   she brings her food from far away.
15 She rises while it is still night
   and provides food for her household
   and tasks for her servant-girls.
16 She considers a field and buys it;
   with the fruit of her hands she plants
      a vineyard.
17 She girds herself with strength,
   and makes her arms strong.
18 She perceives that her merchandise is
      profitable.
   Her lamp does not go out at night.

a Or *spider*   *b* Gk Syr Tg Compare Vg: Meaning
of Heb uncertain   *c* Meaning of Heb uncertain
d Cn: Heb *where*   *e* Heb *all children of passing
away*

31:10–31 *A capable wife who can find?* This
fine passage is an acrostic poem in praise of the
virtuous wife. The acrostic is one of the stylized
poems (in which the initial or final letters of
each line spell a word or phrase) found in
wisdom literature.

31:13 *She seeks wool and flax.* Wool and flax
were the common textile fibers of Palestine,
Mesopotamia, and Greece.

R e s p o n d i n g
31:15 SERVICE. So often we view
service as something we perform for
strangers, something that occurs outside the
home, but some of our best opportunities to
serve come every day among those we love.
Today take an opportunity to serve someone
with whom you live or help out at a friend's
home. Wash the dishes out of turn, or do
another chore normally done by someone else.
See also Spiritual Disciplines Index.

19 She puts her hands to the distaff,
  and her hands hold the spindle.
20 She opens her hand to the poor,
  and reaches out her hands to the
    needy.
21 She is not afraid for her household
    when it snows,
  for all her household are clothed in
    crimson.
22 She makes herself coverings;
  her clothing is fine linen and purple.
23 Her husband is known in the city gates,
  taking his seat among the elders of
    the land.
24 She makes linen garments and sells
    them;
  she supplies the merchant with
    sashes.
25 Strength and dignity are her clothing,

  and she laughs at the time to come.
26 She opens her mouth with wisdom,
  and the teaching of kindness is on her
    tongue.
27 She looks well to the ways of her
    household,
  and does not eat the bread of idleness.
28 Her children rise up and call her happy;
  her husband too, and he praises her:
29 "Many women have done excellently,
  but you surpass them all."
30 Charm is deceitful, and beauty is vain,
  but a woman who fears the LORD is to
    be praised.
31 Give her a share in the fruit of her
    hands,
  and let her works praise her in the city
    gates.

31:19 *She puts her hand to the distaff.* The distaff represents the female realm. Ancient portraits of noblewomen show that women of all classes were proficient in spinning and weaving.

31:24 *She makes linen garments.* The wife also produces cloth for the market as well as

outfitting her own family handsomely. Textile production was an important industry in biblical times.

31:30 *a woman who fears the LORD is to be praised.* The last verses of the book of Proverbs remind us that God is sovereign over our daily lives.

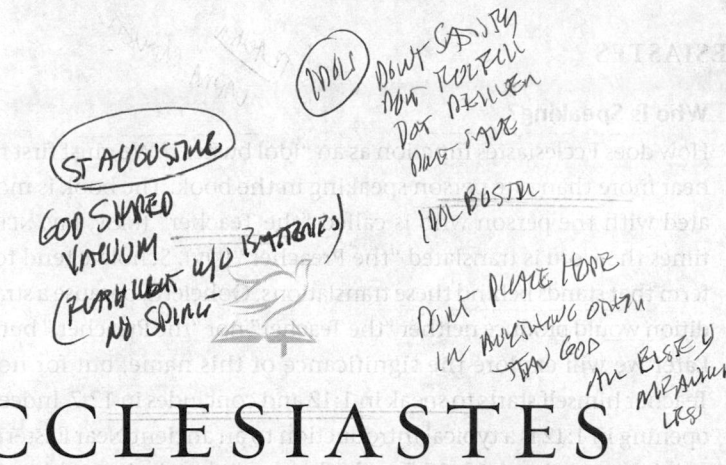

ECCLESIASTES

Ecclesiastes was written to warn us against placing our hope in anyone or anything other than God. It does so by pointing out the meaninglessness of life lived "under the sun," a phrase that could be replaced by "apart from God." At its conclusion, the book directs readers to "fear God," "keep his commandments," and expect his judgment (Eccl 12:13–14). Ecclesiastes may be regarded as an "idol buster," because it surveys the uselessness of many of the things in which we place our confidence, only to be let down by them.

Breaking the Idols

John Calvin rightly described the human mind as a "factory of idols"—it is constantly elevating created things or persons to places of utmost importance in our lives (Rom 1:21–25). These are things we plan our life around, devote our energy to, and sacrifice other things to achieve. Typically the Old Testament describes idols as the gods of the nations, deities with names such as Baal, Marduk, and Istar. However, Ecclesiastes, without once using the word "idol," clearly understands that more abstract concepts and impersonal objects such as wealth, status, power, relationships, pleasure, wisdom, and even religion itself can achieve idolatrous status in a person's life.

It is right here that Ecclesiastes has enormous value for our thinking about spiritual formation. The "Teacher," to whom the book is credited (1:1), becomes for us the ultimate iconoclast, smashing into pieces every object of ultimate trust. Money, sex, power, position, human wisdom, even our attempts to become righteous (see 7:15)—all are "vanity of vanities" (1:2). Nothing satisfies. Nothing delivers the goods. Nothing fulfills. Nothing. It is only when we have genuinely given up on everything, absolutely everything, that we can become candidates for growth in grace. Then, and only then, are we prepared to truly hear the "end of the matter," which is, "Fear God, and keep his commandments; for that is the whole duty of everyone" (12:13).

See also *"The With-God Life"* essays for this section of the Bible, *"The People of God in Travail,"* pp. 717–20, and *"The People of God in Daily Life,"* pp. 901–4.

Who Is Speaking?

How does Ecclesiastes function as an "idol buster"? We must first recognize that we hear more than one person speaking in the book. The book is most closely associated with the person who is called "the Teacher" (NRSV, NIV, NLT), though sometimes the word is translated "the Preacher" (KJV). Scholars tend to use the Hebrew term that stands behind these translations, Qoheleth, because a straightforward rendition would produce neither "the Teacher" nor "the Preacher," but "the Assembler." Later we will explore the significance of this name, but for now note that the Teacher himself starts to speak in 1:12 and concludes in 12:7. Indeed, the distinctive opening in 1:12 is a typical introduction to an ancient Near Eastern autobiography, so it is best to view 1:12–12:7 as the Teacher's description of his spiritual journey to find meaning in life.

The Teacher's words are framed by those of a second wisdom teacher who talks about the Teacher in the third person (1:1–11; 12:8–14). In 12:12, we observe that he is addressing his comments to his son, in traditional wisdom style. In essence, the book of Ecclesiastes is a lengthy quotation of the words of the Teacher to the second wise person's son along with evaluation and an ultimate conclusion.

Thinking "Under the Sun"

Who is the Teacher and what is he saying? The superscription of the book identifies the Teacher as the "son of David." This and a number of other hints in the book have contributed to the traditional view that the Teacher is Solomon. Even the name Qoheleth, which we have already seen literally means "the Assembler," may provide a link back to the story of Solomon where, during the dedication of the Temple (1 Kings 8), the verb "to assemble" is used repeatedly. In the final analysis it appears that this figure's story is constructed loosely on the life of Solomon rather than being the actual story of Solomon. By using the nickname Qoheleth, the writer is telling readers to think of Solomon as they hear of the Teacher, who can find no meaning in wealth, power, or even wisdom itself. After all, if Solomon couldn't have done so, then how can anyone else who has these things in far less quantity (2:12)?

The Teacher's message boiled down to a single phrase is "Life is difficult, and then you die." Or equally true, stated from the opposite perspective, "Because you die, there is no meaning in life, so nothing really matters."

The Teacher's thinking may be illustrated by looking at 2:12–17. Here he brings up wisdom as something that may provide meaning in life. He was, after all, a wisdom teacher, so one would expect that this area might prove fruitful to him. Indeed, as the passage opens, he affirms the value of wisdom over folly. Wisdom allows us to live life with eyes open as opposed to stumbling around blind like fools do. However, in verse 14 he remembers death. Death comes to both the wise and the foolish, so the Teacher sees that wisdom has no advantage over folly in the long run. Thus, "All is meaningless."

The Teacher's failure to find meaning under the sun leads him from time to time to advocate enjoying what measure of pleasure one can find in the world. In reading these passages, sometimes called *carpe diem* ("seize the day") texts since they encourage grabbing whatever gusto one can out of life (2:24–26; 3:12–14; 3:22; 5:18–20; 8:15; 9:7–10), one should, however, hear a tone of resignation. Even when a person is able to find such enjoyment in life (and this is rare), the benefit of the joy is to temporarily blot out the pain of the harshness of life as it truly is (5:20). In other words, it is a Novocain shot to the soul.

Finally, the Teacher's honest look at life leads to troubling comments concerning God's justice in the world. As a wisdom teacher, he expected that the godly would be rewarded and the wicked would be punished, but as a text such as 7:15–18 indicates, that is not what the Teacher saw in the world. The lack of proper retribution instilled in him a dark attitude toward life and skepticism toward the benefit of righteous behavior ("Do not be too righteous," 7:16).

Moving "Above the Sun"

This viewpoint is unexpected in the Bible and has led many to question the book's inclusion in the canon. However, the unnamed second wisdom teacher has rightly recognized its importance for his son's spiritual education. After all, the Teacher is only too right. "Under the sun" life is hard, then you die, end of the story. With its many allusions to Genesis 3, we rightly read the Teacher's speech as reflecting the truth of a fallen world.

Even so, the conclusion to the book does not just affirm the Teacher's analysis; it points beyond it to what is truly important. In spite of or even because of the darkness of the fallen world, the final words of the father call his son beyond "under the sun" to fear and obey God in the light of the expected judgment (12:13–14).

Reading Ecclesiastes from a New Testament Perspective

The New Testament never explicitly quotes or comments on Ecclesiastes. However, it is interesting to read Ecclesiastes in the light of Paul's comments in Rom 8:18–25. Paul here talks about how God has subjected the creation to "futility," using the same Greek word (*mataiotes*) that the Greek translation of the Old Testament uses to render the Hebrew word "meaningless" (*hebel*) in Ecclesiastes. It appears that Paul is reflecting on the effects of the fall (Gen 3) when he describes the "sufferings of the present time," and we have already noted that the Teacher's view of life "under the sun" may be understood as life affected by the curse. The recognition that life is "futile" deeply discouraged the Teacher, but it provides for Paul the foundation for hope, because he recognizes that God subjected the world to futility "in hope that the creation itself will be set free from its bondage to decay" and that it "will obtain the freedom of the glory of the children of God."

Paul's comments invite us to read Jesus' story in the light of Ecclesiastes. When we do so, we see that Jesus subjected himself to a meaningless world in order to free us from it. The famous hymn in Phil 2:6–11 describes how Jesus "emptied himself" and subjected himself to the life of a "slave," even dying on the cross.

As we meditate on the life of Christ, we see that he experienced the "meaninglessness" of life "under the sun." He was the very Word of God, but the world did not honor him as such (John 1:10). The synoptic Gospels tell us that he was born in a manger, not a palace. Toward the end of his life, not only the crowds but also those to whom he was closest abandoned him. Judas betrayed him, and Peter denied him. However, it was when he was on the cross that he experienced the "meaninglessness" of the fallen world in a way that the Teacher could only have imagined as he cried out, "My God, my God, why have you forsaken me?" (Matt 27:46).

In sum, using the language of Gal 3:13, Jesus became a curse to redeem us from the curse of the law. Jesus defeated death by dying on the cross and being resurrected (1 Cor 15). Jesus, in other words, defeated death, the very thing that most disturbed the Teacher's confidence in the meaning of life.

Reading Ecclesiastes in the light of the New Testament realities suggests that ultimate meaning is found in God through Christ, who defeats death and thus brings meaning to life. When Christ is preeminent, the One in whom we find our meaning, then other aspects of our life, including our work, pleasure, and wealth, can occupy appropriate places of significance.

—*Tremper Longman III*

Reflections of a Royal Philosopher

1 The words of the Teacher,[a] the son of David, king in Jerusalem.

2 Vanity of vanities, says the Teacher,[a]
   vanity of vanities! All is vanity.

3 What do people gain from all the toil
   at which they toil under the sun?

4 A generation goes, and a generation
   comes,
   but the earth remains forever.

5 The sun rises and the sun goes down,
   and hurries to the place where it rises.

6 The wind blows to the south,

a Heb *Qoheleth*, traditionally rendered *Preacher*

1:1 *The words of the Teacher.* The superscription announces that the words to follow (in 1:12–12:7) are from the Teacher, who is identified as a son of David. As explained in the Introduction, this title initiates a strategy of association (not identification) between this figure and King Solomon. Later, as the Teacher explores pleasure, wisdom, power, wealth, and status as potential avenues to ultimate meaning in life, we are reminded of the story of Solomon in 1 Kings and the fact that, though he had these things in abundance, he ended his life a failure. Readers should understand that if someone like Solomon could not find significance in these areas, neither will they.

1:2 *Vanity of vanities.* The word translated "vanity" (*hebel*) is repeated more than forty times throughout the book and represents the

Teacher's final conclusion about life. The word literally means "bubble, vapor" and signifies emptiness. In the context of Ecclesiastes it always means "devoid of meaning." The Teacher's search for meaning in life "under the sun" ends up empty. As we will see, the conclusion to the book moves us beyond the Teacher's "under the sun" thinking and points us to God (12:13–14). **1:3** *under the sun.* This phrase occurs twenty-nine times in the book and shows that the Teacher is conducting his search for meaning in the realm of earthly activity rather than appealing to heaven or to divine revelation. Why he so restricts himself is a matter of speculation, but the fact that he does so and comes up empty informs us that ultimate meaning in life is not to be found on earth.

and goes around to the north;
  round and round goes the wind,
    and on its circuits the wind
      returns.
7 All streams run to the sea,
    but the sea is not full;
  to the place where the streams flow,
    there they continue to flow.
8 All things*a* are wearisome;
    more than one can express;
  the eye is not satisfied with seeing,
    or the ear filled with hearing.
9 What has been is what will be,
    and what has been done is what will
      be done;
  there is nothing new under the sun.
10 Is there a thing of which it is said,
    "See, this is new"?
  It has already been,
    in the ages before us.
11 The people of long ago are not
      remembered,
    nor will there be any remembrance
  of people yet to come
    by those who come after them.

The Futility of Seeking Wisdom

12 I, the Teacher,*b* when king over Israel in Jerusalem, 13 applied my mind to seek and to search out by wisdom all that is done under heaven; it is an unhappy business that God has given to human beings to be busy with. 14 I saw all the deeds that are done under the sun; and see, all is vanity and a chasing after wind.*c*

15 What is crooked cannot be made
      straight,
    and what is lacking cannot be
      counted.

16 I said to myself, "I have acquired great wisdom, surpassing all who were over Jerusalem before me; and my mind has had great experience of wisdom and knowledge." 17 And I applied my mind to know wisdom and to know madness and folly. I perceived that this also is but a chasing after wind.*c*

18 For in much wisdom is much vexation,

a Or *words*   *b* Heb *Qoheleth*, traditionally rendered *Preacher*   *c* Or *a feeding on wind*. See Hos 12.1

1:4–10 *All things are wearisome*. Examples are given of much activity, but no real progress. The sun comes up and goes down, the wind goes round and round. The streams run to the sea, but the sea is never full. Such profitless activity illustrates the meaninglessness of life in spite of appearances, including human activity (v 10). We might think that something is new, but further thought or research will show that it is just a rehash of something from the past. Human experience is dull and unsatisfying.

1:11 *people of long ago are not remembered*. The Teacher struggled with the significance of life. We are born, labor hard, perhaps even rise in significance during our lifetime. However, once we die, we are soon forgotten. It is as if we never existed. Such reflections lead thoughtful people to question the meaning of life.

1:12 *I, the Teacher*. The form of this verse is typical of the opening of an autobiography in the ancient Near East. The previous verses have set the stage and the mood for the Teacher's ruminations, but now for the first time he himself speaks. His comments continue until 12:7.

1:13 *applied my mind*. The Teacher here sets his agenda, which is to examine his life to find

meaning. Even as he informs us about his intentions, he indicates his negative conclusions as he speaks of the "unhappy business" with which God occupies his human creatures.

1:14 *chasing after wind*. This phrase is another frequent refrain found in the Teacher's speech. "Chasing after wind" is a metaphor for vanity. Trying to catch the wind is a fruitless task, because one can never catch it. It's there, we can feel it, but it is just beyond our grasp. The Teacher says the search to find meaning is just as fruitless.

1:15 *What is crooked*. With this proverb, the Teacher acknowledges that there is something fundamentally wrong with the world "under the sun" and whatever it is cannot be fixed. Reading in the light of the rest of the canon, we can affirm that the Teacher's assessment is appropriate to a world experiencing the curses of the fall (Gen 3).

1:16 *surpassing all who were over Jerusalem*. The Teacher's wisdom is great. We again note the association with Solomon, whose wisdom was legendary (1 Kings 4:20–34). Thus, if the Teacher (and Solomon) cannot discover meaning and satisfaction in life under the sun, the rest of us will certainly fail.

and those who increase knowledge
increase sorrow.

The Futility of Self-Indulgence

2 I said to myself, "Come now, I will make a test of pleasure; enjoy yourself." But again, this also was vanity. 2I said of laughter, "It is mad," and of pleasure, "What use is it?" 3I searched with my mind how to cheer my body with wine—my mind still guiding me with wisdom—and how to lay hold on folly, until I might see what was good for mortals to do under heaven during the few days of their life. 4I made great works; I built houses and planted vineyards for myself; 5I made myself gardens and parks, and planted in them all kinds of fruit trees. 6I made myself pools from which to water the forest of growing trees. 7I bought male and female slaves, and had slaves who were born in my house; I also had great possessions of herds and flocks, more than any who had been before me in Jerusalem. 8I also gathered for myself silver and gold and the treasure of kings and of the provinces; I got singers, both men and women, and delights of the flesh, and many concubines.a

9 So I became great and surpassed all who were before me in Jerusalem; also my wisdom remained with me. 10Whatever my eyes desired I did not keep from them; I kept my heart from no pleasure, for my heart found pleasure in all my toil, and this was my reward for all my toil. 11Then I considered all that my hands had done and the toil I had spent in

doing it, and again, all was vanity and a chasing after wind,b and there was nothing to be gained under the sun.

Wisdom and Joy Given to One Who Pleases God

12 So I turned to consider wisdom and madness and folly; for what can the one do who comes after the king? Only what has already been done. 13Then I saw that wisdom excels folly as light excels darkness.

14 The wise have eyes in their head,
    but fools walk in darkness.

Yet I perceived that the same fate befalls all of them. 15Then I said to myself, "What happens to the fool will happen to me also; why then have I been so very wise?" And I said to myself that this also is vanity. 16For there is no enduring remembrance of the wise or of fools, seeing that in the days to come all will have been long forgotten. How can the wise die just like fools? 17So I hated life, because what is done under the sun was grievous to me; for all is vanity and a chasing after wind.b

18 I hated all my toil in which I had toiled under the sun, seeing that I must leave it to those who come after me 19—and who knows whether they will be wise or foolish? Yet they will be master of all for which I toiled and used my wisdom under the sun. This also is vanity. 20So I turned and gave my heart up to despair concerning all the toil of my labors under the sun, 21because sometimes one who

a Meaning of Heb uncertain   b Or a feeding on wind. See Hos 12.1

2:1–11 *I will make a test of pleasure.* The Teacher tries to find ultimate meaning and satisfaction in the pursuit of pleasure. He explores different forms of pleasure, some of it sensual (alcohol and women) and some of it from achievements and possessions (building great houses, acquiring slaves and livestock). His final conclusion, though, is that pleasure does not satisfy. It does not provide meaning in life.

2:12–17 *no enduring remembrance of the wise or of fools.* These verses explore the possibility of finding meaning in wisdom. The Teacher was a wise man and a book such as Proverbs places a high premium on the acquisition of wisdom. However, the Teacher ultimately must conclude

that even wisdom cannot provide meaning in the light of death. Wise people die as well as foolish people. In the long run what good is wisdom? Again, the Teacher's reasoning will require that we look beyond his "under the sun" reasoning if we are to find true meaning.

2:18–19 *I hated all my toil.* The Teacher for the first, but not the last, time raises the possibility that toil will provide meaning in life. Certainly today many people work hard with the idea that their efforts will justify their existence. However, here too the Teacher notices that you can't take it with you. Once you are dead, the fruits of your labors will go to someone who may be a fool.

has toiled with wisdom and knowledge and skill must leave all to be enjoyed by another who did not toil for it. This also is vanity and a great evil. 22What do mortals get from all the toil and strain with which they toil under the sun? 23For all their days are full of pain, and their work is a vexation; even at night their minds do not rest. This also is vanity.

24 There is nothing better for mortals than to eat and drink, and find enjoyment in their toil. This also, I saw, is from the hand of God; 25for apart from him *a* who can eat or who can have enjoyment? 26For to the one who pleases him God gives wisdom and knowledge and joy; but to the sinner he gives the work of gathering and heaping, only to give to one who pleases God. This also is vanity and a chasing after wind. *b*

Everything Has Its Time

3 For everything there is a season, and a time for every matter under heaven:
2 a time to be born, and a time to die;
a time to plant, and a time to pluck up what is planted;
3 a time to kill, and a time to heal;
a time to break down, and a time to build up;

4 a time to weep, and a time to laugh;
a time to mourn, and a time to dance;
5 a time to throw away stones, and a time to gather stones together;
a time to embrace, and a time to refrain from embracing;
6 a time to seek, and a time to lose;
a time to keep, and a time to throw away;
7 a time to tear, and a time to sew;
a time to keep silence, and a time to speak;
8 a time to love, and a time to hate;
a time for war, and a time for peace.

The God-Given Task

9 What gain have the workers from their toil? 10I have seen the business that God has given to everyone to be busy with. 11He has made everything suitable for its time; moreover he has put a sense of past and future into their minds, yet they cannot find out what God has done from the beginning to the end. 12I know that there is nothing better for them than to be happy and enjoy themselves as long as they live; 13moreover, it is

a Gk Syr: Heb *apart from me*   *b* Or *a feeding on wind.* See Hos 12.1

2:23 *even at night their minds do not rest.* Days full of pain, frustrating work, anxious nights. This description is an accurate portrayal of the life of many modern readers. The Teacher reports what he experiences and observes and what he says conforms with the description of the effects of the curse in Genesis 3. Ecclesiastes is realistic and accurate about life experience, but ultimately it will point us beyond the difficulties of life under the sun to a relationship with God (12:13–14).

2:24–26 *There is nothing better.* After exploring pleasure, wisdom, and toil for meaning and coming up empty, the Teacher now commends what might be called the simple pleasures of life: eating, drinking, and toil. Here we are not speaking of ultimate meaning and significance, but rather of diversions from the harsh realities of life. This passage and related ones (3:12–14; 3:22; 5:18–20; 8:15; 9:7–10) are often called *carpe diem* ("seize the day") passages, because the Teacher encourages his hearers to grab

whatever enjoyment they can in the midst of a painful "under the sun" existence.

3:1–8 *a time for every matter.* The Teacher acknowledges that God made an orderly world. Everything has its proper place, and life has a number of rhythms. Later he affirms that God "made everything suitable for its time" (v 11). On the surface, this thought is comforting and indeed is at the heart of the wisdom enterprise. The wise person must know the proper time for the right action or the right statement. However, what appears comforting turns dark in the Teacher's response to this truth (see note on 3:11).

3:11 *yet they cannot find out.* God has made everything suitable for its time; everything has its place. However, God does not let his human creatures in on the secret. One cannot be wise, since no one can read the circumstances in order to know the right way to act or to speak. The Teacher thus again vents his frustration with the way the world works.

God's gift that all should eat and drink and take pleasure in all their toil. [14]I know that whatever God does endures forever; nothing can be added to it, nor anything taken from it; God has done this, so that all should stand in awe before him. [15]That which is, already has been; that which is to be, already is; and God seeks out what has gone by. [a]

Judgment and the Future Belong to God

16 Moreover I saw under the sun that in the place of justice, wickedness was there, and in the place of righteousness, wickedness was there as well. [17]I said in my heart, God will judge the righteous and the wicked, for he has appointed a time for every matter, and for every work. [18]I said in my heart with regard to human beings that God is testing them to show that they are but animals. [19]For the fate of humans and the fate of animals is the same; as one dies, so dies the other. They all have the same breath, and humans have no advantage over the animals; for all is vanity. [20]All go to one place; all are from the dust, and all turn to dust again. [21]Who knows whether the human spirit goes upward and the spirit of animals goes downward to the earth? [22]So I saw that there is nothing better than that all should enjoy their work, for that is their lot; who can bring them to see what will be after them?

4 Again I saw all the oppressions that are practiced under the sun. Look, the tears of the oppressed—with no one to comfort them! On the side of their oppressors there was power—with no one to comfort them.

[2]And I thought the dead, who have already died, more fortunate than the living, who are still alive; [3]but better than both is the one who has not yet been, and has not seen the evil deeds that are done under the sun.

4 Then I saw that all toil and all skill in work come from one person's envy of another. This also is vanity and a chasing after wind. [b]

5 Fools fold their hands
   and consume their own flesh.

6 Better is a handful with quiet
   than two handfuls with toil,
   and a chasing after wind. [b]

7 Again, I saw vanity under the sun: [8]the case of solitary individuals, without sons or brothers; yet there is no end to all their toil, and their eyes are never satisfied with riches. "For whom am I toiling," they ask, "and depriving myself of pleasure?" This also is vanity and an unhappy business.

The Value of a Friend

9 Two are better than one, because they have a good reward for their toil. [10]For if they fall, one will lift up the other; but woe to one who is alone and falls and does not have another to help. [11]Again, if two lie together, they keep warm; but how can one keep warm alone? [12]And though one might prevail against another, two will withstand one. A threefold cord is not quickly broken.

13 Better is a poor but wise youth than

a Heb what is pursued   b Or a feeding on wind. See Hos 12.1

3:16 *in the place of justice, wickedness was there.* The Teacher's experience ("I saw") of the world raises fundamental questions about justice. Even though in 2:17 he asserts a traditional belief in God's ultimate reward for the righteous and punishment for the wicked, his later comments (see especially 7:15–18; 8:9–14) show just how difficult it was for him to affirm God's just rule in the world in the light of his experience.

3:19–20 *All go to one place.* The Teacher raises the universality of death, a reality that throughout the book makes him question the possibility of finding lasting meaning in life. Here he asserts his doubt that human beings

are any different from animals in this regard.

4:1–2 *all the oppressions.* The Teacher's experience of the world has taught him that life is fundamentally unfair; the powerful take advantage of the powerless. Such inequity leads him to prefer death over life.

4:9–12 *a threefold cord.* Life is hard and to face its difficulties alone is enough to break the spirit of any man or woman. Companionship provides solace in a tough world that has no ultimate meaning. Two are better than one, and even better is a group of three. Ultimate meaning is not found in relationship, only some comfort in the midst of a fallen world.

an old but foolish king, who will no longer take advice. [14]One can indeed come out of prison to reign, even though born poor in the kingdom. [15]I saw all the living who, moving about under the sun, follow that[a] youth who replaced the king;[b] [16]there was no end to all those people whom he led. Yet those who come later will not rejoice in him. Surely this also is vanity and a chasing after wind.[c]

Reverence, Humility, and Contentment

5 [d] Guard your steps when you go to the house of God; to draw near to listen is better than the sacrifice offered by fools; for they do not know how to keep from doing evil. [e] [2f] Never be rash with your mouth, nor let your heart be quick to utter a word before God, for God is in heaven, and you upon earth; therefore let your words be few.

3 For dreams come with many cares, and a fool's voice with many words.

4 When you make a vow to God, do not delay fulfilling it; for he has no pleasure in fools. Fulfill what you vow. [5]It is better that you should not vow than that you should vow and not fulfill it. [6]Do not let your mouth lead you into sin, and do not say before the messenger that it was a mistake; why should God be angry at your words, and destroy the work of your hands?

7 With many dreams come vanities and a multitude of words;[g] but fear God.

8 If you see in a province the oppression of the poor and the violation of justice and right, do not be amazed at the matter; for the high official is watched by a higher, and there are yet higher ones over them. [9]But all things considered, this is an advantage for a land: a king for a plowed field.[g]

10 The lover of money will not be satisfied with money; nor the lover of wealth, with gain. This also is vanity.

11 When goods increase, those who eat them increase; and what gain has their owner but to see them with his eyes?

a Heb *the second*   b Heb *him*   c Or *a feeding on wind.* See Hos 12.1   d Ch 4.17 in Heb   e Cn: Heb *they do not know how to do evil*   f Ch 5.1 in Heb   g Meaning of Heb uncertain

---

4:13–16 *Better is a poor but wise youth.* Through this imaginative story the relative value of wisdom over age, wealth, and status is affirmed. However, in the long run even wisdom loses its value.

5:1–2 *Guard your steps when you go to the house of God.* Throughout his spiritual autobiography (1:12–12:7) the Teacher displays a rather distant relationship with God. We need to remember that he restricts his observations to what he sees "under the sun," so that his comments about God reflect his deductions based on what he sees out there rather than on divine revelation. From what he sees elsewhere (see 7:15–18) he concludes that an intimate relationship with God doesn't get one too far. The wicked prosper and the godly perish. Thus, he advises great care if one approaches God at all. After all, not even the righteous and wise know "whether it is love or hate" that awaits them (9:1). Though the final speaker of the book will urge his son to move beyond this attitude to proper reverence of God (12:13–14), the Teacher's words are an important warning that we should not presume or even expect that our best spiritual efforts will result in some kind of immediate prosperity. They may even plunge us into more difficulty. God is not a quick-fix artist.

5:10 *The lover of money will not be satisfied.* Many people today try to find their satisfaction in life by making a lot of money. The Teacher has gone before us and tells us that wealth in itself does not bring contentment. Money is not the source of ultimate meaning. Those who love money will never have enough, and they will wear themselves out before they ever come close to being satisfied.

Responding
5:10 SIMPLICITY. The Teacher wrote that we will not be satisfied if we love money, and Paul advised Timothy that "the love of money is a root of all kinds of evil" (1 Tim 6:10). Yet the American tycoon John D. Rockefeller reportedly was asked once how much money was enough. His answer? "Just a little more." Why is money so seductive? How can its allure be broken, so that we can live in simplicity of heart and spirit? *See also* Spiritual Disciplines Index.

12 Sweet is the sleep of laborers, whether they eat little or much; but the surfeit of the rich will not let them sleep.

13 There is a grievous ill that I have seen under the sun: riches were kept by their owners to their hurt, [14]and those riches were lost in a bad venture; though they are parents of children, they have nothing in their hands. [15]As they came from their mother's womb, so they shall go again, naked as they came; they shall take nothing for their toil, which they may carry away with their hands. [16]This also is a grievous ill: just as they came, so shall they go; and what gain do they have from toiling for the wind? [17]Besides, all their days they eat in darkness, in much vexation and sickness and resentment.

18 This is what I have seen to be good: it is fitting to eat and drink and find enjoyment in all the toil with which one toils under the sun the few days of the life God gives us; for this is our lot. [19]Likewise all to whom God gives wealth and possessions and whom he enables to enjoy them, and to accept their lot and find enjoyment in their toil—this is the gift of God. [20]For they will scarcely brood over the days of their lives, because God keeps them occupied with the joy of their hearts.

The Frustration of Desires

6 There is an evil that I have seen under the sun, and it lies heavy upon humankind: [2]those to whom God gives wealth, possessions, and honor, so that they lack nothing of all that they desire, yet God does not enable them to enjoy these things, but a stranger enjoys them. This is vanity; it is a grievous ill. [3]A man may beget a hundred children, and live many years; but however many are the days of his years, if he does not enjoy life's good things, or has no burial, I say that a stillborn child is better off than he. [4]For it comes into vanity and goes into darkness, and in darkness its name is covered; [5]moreover it has not seen the sun or known anything; yet it finds rest rather than he. [6]Even though he should live a thousand years twice over, yet enjoy no good—do not all go to one place?

7 All human toil is for the mouth, yet the appetite is not satisfied. [8]For what advantage

---

5:12 *Sweet is the sleep of laborers.* Though the Teacher has concluded that work is not the source of ultimate meaning in life, it is relatively better than riches. Those who are wealthy and don't have to work often have trouble sleeping, but not laborers who work hard.

5:13–17 *just as they came, so shall they go.* The Teacher tells us why wealth doesn't bring lasting satisfaction and ultimate meaning. It is easily lost. In this case, he cites a "bad venture." So the person who works hard to amass a fortune can easily and quickly lose it. Jesus reminds his followers that they have "an unfailing treasure in heaven" (Luke 12:33).

5:20 *they will scarcely brood over the days of their lives.* In another *carpe diem* passage (see note on 2:24–26), the Teacher tells us the "advantage" that comes to those who are able to enjoy the simple pleasures in life. Enjoying one's food and drink distracts people from the harsh realities of life "under the sun."

6:2 *God does not enable them to enjoy these things.* Though some people can at least momentarily be distracted from the harsh realities of life by simple pleasures, the Teacher is well aware that many people simply don't have the constitution to be lulled into a state that forgets what awaits them: death. Indeed, it appears that the Teacher himself is such a person. His own struggles teach us that the simple pleasures can provide no more than a superficial distraction from the real problems of life.

6:3 *may beget a hundred children.* Numerous children and a long life were taken as great blessings during the Old Testament period. Today, we might feel the same if we have a good family life, some measure of prosperity, and our health. However, the Teacher points out that even people who experience such a "blessed life" are ultimately going to have their bubble burst by death. "All go to one place" (v 6), namely, the tomb. Our ultimate happiness is not to be found in family, prosperity, and health.

6:7 *All human toil is for the mouth.* Why do people work so hard, or even work at all? The Teacher suggests it is because of our own appetite. However, we work for more than survival or even to be comfortable. The urge for more never stops, and that means the work never stops either. Accordingly, work never brings us the ultimate fulfillment for which we yearn.

have the wise over fools? And what do the poor have who know how to conduct themselves before the living? 9Better is the sight of the eyes than the wandering of desire; this also is vanity and a chasing after wind. *a*

10 Whatever has come to be has already been named, and it is known what human beings are, and that they are not able to dispute with those who are stronger. 11The more words, the more vanity, so how is one the better? 12For who knows what is good for mortals while they live the few days of their vain life, which they pass like a shadow? For who can tell them what will be after them under the sun?

A Disillusioned View of Life

7 A good name is better than precious
    ointment,
        and the day of death, than the day of
        birth.
2 It is better to go to the house of
        mourning
    than to go to the house of feasting;
        for this is the end of everyone,
        and the living will lay it to heart.
3 Sorrow is better than laughter,
        for by sadness of countenance the
        heart is made glad.
4 The heart of the wise is in the house of
        mourning;
    but the heart of fools is in the house
        of mirth.
5 It is better to hear the rebuke of the wise
    than to hear the song of fools.

6 For like the crackling of thorns under a
        pot,
    so is the laughter of fools;
        this also is vanity.
7 Surely oppression makes the wise
        foolish,
    and a bribe corrupts the heart.
8 Better is the end of a thing than its
        beginning;
    the patient in spirit are better than
        the proud in spirit.
9 Do not be quick to anger,
    for anger lodges in the bosom of fools.
10 Do not say, "Why were the former days
        better than these?"
    For it is not from wisdom that you ask
        this.
11 Wisdom is as good as an inheritance,
    an advantage to those who see the
        sun.
12 For the protection of wisdom is like the
        protection of money,
    and the advantage of knowledge is
        that wisdom gives life to the one
        who possesses it.
13 Consider the work of God;
    who can make straight what he has
        made crooked?

14 In the day of prosperity be joyful, and in the day of adversity consider; God has made the one as well as the other, so that mortals may not find out anything that will come after them.

a Or *a feeding on wind.* See Hos 12.1

7:1 *the day of death.* To the Teacher the day of death is better than the day of birth, because death ends a meaningless and oppressive life under the sun. Birth is often surrounded by hope, but it is, in his opinion, a false hope that life itself will dampen.

7:5 *the rebuke of the wise.* The rebuke of the wise is better than the song of fools, because the former gets at the truth, while the latter is simply pretense. The Teacher prefers the truth, though painful, over false but happy illusions. "Under the sun," life is hard and death is inevitable, but most of us would like to repress those thoughts.

7:10 *Why were the former days better than*

these? Even today, we hear this. Although the present day has deep and unsettling problems, it is wrong to think of previous times as more moral or less dangerous. No, according to the Teacher, the past is as bad as the present ("there is nothing new under the sun," 1:9), and the future will be no better.

7:14 *mortals may not find out anything that will come after them.* We would like to think that God has established a strict moral order in which good people are rewarded and evil people are punished, but good or bad, in this life we have no guarantees. So the Teacher's advice is to enjoy the good days and roll with the punches of hard days.

The Riddles of Life

15 In my vain life I have seen everything; there are righteous people who perish in their righteousness, and there are wicked people who prolong their life in their evildoing. 16Do not be too righteous, and do not act too wise; why should you destroy yourself? 17Do not be too wicked, and do not be a fool; why should you die before your time? 18It is good that you should take hold of the one, without letting go of the other; for the one who fears God shall succeed with both.

19 Wisdom gives strength to the wise more than ten rulers that are in a city.

20 Surely there is no one on earth so righteous as to do good without ever sinning.

21 Do not give heed to everything that people say, or you may hear your servant cursing you; 22your heart knows that many times you have yourself cursed others.

23 All this I have tested by wisdom; I said, "I will be wise," but it was far from me. 24That which is, is far off, and deep, very deep; who can find it out? 25I turned my mind to know and to search out and to seek wisdom and the sum of things, and to know that wickedness is folly and that foolishness is madness. 26I found more bitter than death the woman who is a trap, whose heart is snares and nets, whose hands are fetters; one who pleases God escapes her, but the sinner is taken by her. 27See, this is what I found, says the Teacher,*a* adding one thing to another to find the sum, 28which my mind has sought repeatedly, but I have not found. One man among a thousand I found, but a woman among all these I have not found. 29See, this alone I found, that God made human beings straightforward, but they have devised many schemes.

Obey the King and Enjoy Yourself

8 Who is like the wise man?
    And who knows the interpretation of a
        thing?
    Wisdom makes one's face shine,
        and the hardness of one's
            countenance is changed.

2 Keep*a* the king's command because of your sacred oath. 3Do not be terrified; go from his presence, do not delay when the matter is unpleasant, for he does whatever he pleases. 4For the word of the king is powerful, and who can say to him, "What are you doing?" 5Whoever obeys a command will meet no harm, and the wise mind will know the time and way. 6For every matter has its time and way, although the troubles of mortals lie heavy upon them. 7Indeed, they do not know what is to be, for who can tell them how it will be? 8No one has power over the wind*b* to restrain the wind,*c* or power over the day of death; there is no discharge from the battle, nor does wickedness deliver

---

a Qoheleth, traditionally rendered *Preacher*
a Heb *I keep*   *c* Or *breath*

7:16 *Do not be too righteous.* The Teacher's advice is rather shocking. We wouldn't find it in the book of Proverbs. But, like him, we too have seen good people suffer and bad people prosper (v 15), which makes us question whether obeying God is worth it. In the short run, it may not be. However, in the final verses (12:13–14), we will hear the second wise teacher encouraging his son to obey God in the light of the future judgment.

7:28–29 *One man among a thousand.* The point of this passage is that it is hard to find anyone who is "straightforward." We are put off by the fact that the Teacher admits it as a possibility, though small, among males, while denying it altogether to females. At this point, we need to remember that the Teacher does not represent the final position of the book or normative biblical teaching, but speaks of his own life as he experienced it "under the sun."

8:6 *the troubles of mortals lie heavy upon them.* The Teacher affirms again (see 3:1–8) that there is a proper time for everything. God has created an orderly world. However, the Teacher expresses his frustration in spite of this insight. Elsewhere he expresses his sadness over the fact that God has not allowed people to know the right time for an action (3:11b). This likely is what is on his mind when he talks about the "troubles of mortals." Indeed, it is true to experience that we are often paralyzed from taking action because we don't know the proper course to take from our limited human perspective.

those who practice it. 9All this I observed, applying my mind to all that is done under the sun, while one person exercises authority over another to the other's hurt.

God's Ways Are Inscrutable

10 Then I saw the wicked buried; they used to go in and out of the holy place, and were praised in the city where they had done such things. *a* This also is vanity. 11Because sentence against an evil deed is not executed speedily, the human heart is fully set to do evil. 12Though sinners do evil a hundred times and prolong their lives, yet I know that it will be well with those who fear God, because they stand in fear before him, 13but it will not be well with the wicked, neither will they prolong their days like a shadow, because they do not stand in fear before God.

14 There is a vanity that takes place on earth, that there are righteous people who are treated according to the conduct of the wicked, and there are wicked people who are treated according to the conduct of the righteous. I said that this also is vanity. 15So I commend enjoyment, for there is nothing better for people under the sun than to eat, and drink, and enjoy themselves, for this will go with them in their toil through the days of life that God gives them under the sun.

16 When I applied my mind to know wisdom, and to see the business that is done on earth, how one's eyes see sleep neither day nor night, 17then I saw all the work of God, that no one can find out what is happening under the sun. However much they may toil in seeking, they will not find it out; even though those who are wise claim to know, they cannot find it out.

Take Life as It Comes

9 All this I laid to heart, examining it all, how the righteous and the wise and their deeds are in the hand of God; whether it is love or hate one does not know. Everything that confronts them 2is vanity, *b* since the same fate comes to all, to the righteous and the wicked, to the good and the evil, *c* to the clean and the unclean, to those who sacrifice and those who do not sacrifice. As are the good, so are the sinners; those who swear are like those who shun an oath. 3This is an evil in all that happens under the sun, that the same fate comes to everyone. Moreover, the hearts of all are full of evil; madness is in their hearts while they live, and after that they go to the dead. 4But whoever is joined with all the living has hope, for a living dog

a Meaning of Heb uncertain   *b* Syr Compare Gk: Heb *Everything that confronts them 2is everything*
c Gk Syr Vg: Heb lacks *and the evil*

8:8 *No one has power over the wind.* We all feel the frustration of trying to keep control of life in a fallen world. But trying to control life is like trying to master the wind—impossible. Just take death—no one can delay it forever no matter how hard they try.

Responding
8:8 SUBMISSION. Many people are very nervous during airplane flights. For some, the nervousness is caused by having absolutely no control over what happens. Those who recognize this have two choices: either they can continue to be miserable, or they can release everything to God and submit to the expertise of the company that made the airplane, the abilities of the controller monitoring its flight path, and the experience of the flight crew to get them safely to their destination. Can you

name some other problems we experience when we will not submit to those things that are unavoidable and inevitable? What can we do to lessen their effect on our lives? *See also* Spiritual Disciplines Index.

9:2 *since the same fate comes to all.* The Teacher feels no comfort in the fact that we are in the "hand of God" (v 1), because that does not assure anyone, whether godly or evil, of a pain-free life and certainly does not allow one to escape the "fate" that comes to everyone—death.

9:3 *madness is in their hearts while they live.* This verse clearly states the Teacher's fundamental complaint: life is difficult, and then comes death. Such a view of life under the sun leads him to conclude it is "vain" or "meaningless."

is better than a dead lion. 5The living know that they will die, but the dead know nothing; they have no more reward, and even the memory of them is lost. 6Their love and their hate and their envy have already perished; never again will they have any share in all that happens under the sun.

7 Go, eat your bread with enjoyment, and drink your wine with a merry heart; for God has long ago approved what you do. 8Let your garments always be white; do not let oil be lacking on your head. 9Enjoy life with the wife whom you love, all the days of your vain life that are given you under the sun, because that is your portion in life and in your toil at which you toil under the sun. 10Whatever your hand finds to do, do with your might; for there is no work or thought or knowledge or wisdom in Sheol, to which you are going.

11 Again I saw that under the sun the race is not to the swift, nor the battle to the strong, nor bread to the wise, nor riches to the intelligent, nor favor to the skillful; but time and chance happen to them all. 12For no one can anticipate the time of disaster. Like fish taken in a cruel net, and like birds caught in a snare, so mortals are snared at a time of calamity, when it suddenly falls upon them.

Wisdom Superior to Folly

13 I have also seen this example of wisdom under the sun, and it seemed great to me. 14There was a little city with few people in it. A great king came against it and besieged it, building great siegeworks against it. 15Now there was found in it a poor wise man, and he by his wisdom delivered the city. Yet no one remembered that poor man. 16So I said, "Wisdom is better than might; yet the poor man's wisdom is despised, and his words are not heeded."

17 The quiet words of the wise are more to
  be heeded
    than the shouting of a ruler among
      fools.
18 Wisdom is better than weapons of war,
    but one bungler destroys much good.

Miscellaneous Observations

10 Dead flies make the perfumer's
      ointment give off a foul odor;
    so a little folly outweighs wisdom and
      honor.
2 The heart of the wise inclines to the
      right,
    but the heart of a fool to the left.
3 Even when fools walk on the road, they
      lack sense,
    and show to everyone that they are
      fools.
4 If the anger of the ruler rises against
      you, do not leave your post,
    for calmness will undo great offenses.

5 There is an evil that I have seen under the sun, as great an error as if it proceeded from the ruler: 6folly is set in many high places, and the rich sit in a low place. 7I have seen slaves on horseback, and princes walking on foot like slaves.

8 Whoever digs a pit will fall into it;
    and whoever breaks through a wall
      will be bitten by a snake.

9:11 *the race is not to the swift.* Many people live with the illusion that the more skill we have, the harder we work, or the smarter we are, the better off life will be for us. From his observation and experience the Teacher knows better. Life comes with no guarantees.

9:12 *Like fish taken in a cruel net.* We can't predict when we will die. Often we live with the fiction that death is restricted to old age and before that we don't have to think about it. We can live our lives with abandon, and then when we grow older we can think about the serious questions. The Teacher doesn't allow this luxury, but constantly reminds us that we

could die at any moment.

10:1 *Dead flies.* The sad truth is that it takes just a pinch of folly to ruin a basically honorable life. One crucial mistake and a person's reputation can be ruined. It hardly seems fair, but then the Teacher hardly feels that life is fair.

10:8–9 *Whoever digs a pit.* Four normal activities prone to accidents are listed. They are not punishments for bad behavior, and they are not mentioned so that the wise can avoid them. They are unavoidable accidents. No matter how careful people are, they may be surprised by a snake on the other side of the wall. Life cannot be controlled.

9 Whoever quarries stones will be hurt by
   them;
   and whoever splits logs will be
   endangered by them.
10 If the iron is blunt, and one does not
   whet the edge,
   then more strength must be exerted;
   but wisdom helps one to succeed.
11 If the snake bites before it is charmed,
   there is no advantage in a charmer.

12 Words spoken by the wise bring them
   favor,
   but the lips of fools consume them.
13 The words of their mouths begin in
   foolishness,
   and their talk ends in wicked
   madness;
14 yet fools talk on and on.
   No one knows what is to happen,
   and who can tell anyone what the
   future holds?
15 The toil of fools wears them out,
   for they do not even know the way to
   town.

16 Alas for you, O land, when your king is a
   servant, *a*
   and your princes feast in the
   morning!
17 Happy are you, O land, when your king
   is a nobleman,
   and your princes feast at the proper
   time—
   for strength, and not for
   drunkenness!
18 Through sloth the roof sinks in,
   and through indolence the house
   leaks.
19 Feasts are made for laughter;

   wine gladdens life,
   and money meets every need.
20 Do not curse the king, even in your
   thoughts,
   or curse the rich, even in your
   bedroom;
   for a bird of the air may carry your
   voice,
   or some winged creature tell the
   matter.

The Value of Diligence

11 Send out your bread upon the
   waters,
   for after many days you will get it
   back.
2 Divide your means seven ways, or even
   eight,
   for you do not know what disaster
   may happen on earth.
3 When clouds are full,
   they empty rain on the earth;
   whether a tree falls to the south or to
   the north,
   in the place where the tree falls, there
   it will lie.
4 Whoever observes the wind will not
   sow;
   and whoever regards the clouds will
   not reap.
5 Just as you do not know how the breath
comes to the bones in the mother's womb, so
you do not know the work of God, who
makes everything.
6 In the morning sow your seed, and at
evening do not let your hands be idle; for
you do not know which will prosper, this or
that, or whether both alike will be good.

a Or a child

10:11 *no advantage in a charmer.* All the skill
in the world won't protect people from harm. To
be able to charm a snake is great, but when a
charmer is bitten by a snake, skill is to no avail.
Wisdom and skill have their limits.

11:2 *Divide your means seven ways, or even
eight.* The advice to "send out your bread upon
the waters" (v 1) is properly understood as an
encouragement to get involved in trade with the
hope of a material return. However, verse 2

urges people to diversify their investments as a
way of protecting against failure. If one or two
investments fold, then one won't be left high
and dry. The point the Teacher is trying to make
is that life in general is not predictable and is
subject to chance (9:11).

11:6 *do not let your hands be idle.* Again, the
Teacher shows his keen awareness that success
and failure are the result of chance. We are not
capable of controlling life. This viewpoint could

Youth and Old Age

7 Light is sweet, and it is pleasant for the eyes to see the sun.

8 Even those who live many years should rejoice in them all; yet let them remember that the days of darkness will be many. All that comes is vanity.

9 Rejoice, young man, while you are young, and let your heart cheer you in the days of your youth. Follow the inclination of your heart and the desire of your eyes, but know that for all these things God will bring you into judgment.

10 Banish anxiety from your mind, and put away pain from your body; for youth and the dawn of life are vanity.

12 Remember your creator in the days of your youth, before the days of trouble come, and the years draw near when you will say, "I have no pleasure in them"; 2before the sun and the light and the moon and the stars are darkened and the clouds return with *a* the rain; 3in the day when the guards of the house tremble, and the strong men are bent, and the women who grind cease working because they are few, and those who look through the windows see dimly; 4when the doors on the street are shut, and the sound of the grinding is low, and one rises up at the sound of a bird, and all the daughters of song are brought low; 5when one is afraid of heights, and terrors are in the road; the almond tree blossoms, the grasshopper drags itself along *b* and desire fails; because all must go to their eternal home, and the mourners will go about the streets; 6before the silver cord is snapped, *c* and the golden bowl is broken, and the pitcher is broken at the fountain, and the wheel broken at the cistern, 7and the dust returns to the earth as it was, and the breath *d* returns to God who gave it. 8Vanity of vanities, says the Teacher; *e* all is vanity.

Epilogue

9 Besides being wise, the Teacher *e* also taught the people knowledge, weighing and

a Or *after*; Heb *'ahar*   *b* Or *is a burden*   *c* Syr Vg Compare Gk: Heb *is removed*   *d* Or *the spirit*   *e* *Qoheleth*, traditionally rendered *Preacher*

---

lead to complete paralysis or else to increased labor, so that the balance of success might improve.

11:8 *the days of darkness will be many.* People should live life in the knowledge that our few days here on earth will be vastly outweighed by the time spent in the grave.

11:9 *Follow the inclination of your heart.* The Teacher gives with one hand and takes away with the other. At first he says, essentially, "Do whatever you desire, young man." Assuming young men were the same during the Old Testament period as today, at least in their basic impulses, that would lead to obvious, and not necessarily godly, results. But then the Teacher continues, "Just remember you will be judged for what you do." Some rabbis noted the contradiction between this verse and Num 15:39, and this led a minority of them to question the authoritative status of Ecclesiastes.

12:1–7 *the women who grind cease working because they are few.* The Teacher offers a final, somber meditation on death. He specifically uses a metaphor that compares the languishing of a house and its inhabitants to the gradual weakening of the body as it grows older and approaches death (v 3). It is even possible, though not universally accepted, that each of the four types of inhabitants of the house represent a part of the body that becomes increasingly ineffective with age. The women who grind grain would seem to represent the loss of teeth, while those who look through the window might signify the loss of eyesight. In any case, for the Teacher, whose perspective is "under the sun," death is the ultimate and sad end of human existence. It is with this depressing thought that his speech comes to a close, and the narrative gives way to the voice of a second wise man.

12:8 *all is vanity.* At this point we have the transition from the Teacher's speech to that of a second, unnamed wise man who is using the words of the Teacher to instruct his son (12:12) concerning life "under the sun." And his first words summarize the message of the Teacher—all is vanity.

Responding

12:9 ~~STUDY.~~ Besides carefully studying, the Teacher weighed (which implies careful evaluation) and arranged (which

studying and arranging many proverbs. [10]The Teacher[a] sought to find pleasing words, and he wrote words of truth plainly.

11 The sayings of the wise are like goads, and like nails firmly fixed are the collected sayings that are given by one shepherd.[b] [12]Of anything beyond these, my child, beware. Of making many books there is no end, and much study is a weariness of the flesh.

13 The end of the matter; all has been heard. Fear God, and keep his commandments; for that is the whole duty of everyone. [14]For God will bring every deed into judgment, including[c] every secret thing, whether good or evil.

a Qoheleth, traditionally rendered Preacher
b Meaning of Heb uncertain   c Or into the judgment on

---

implies systematic categories) many proverbs. Even though you may not have intensely studied anything for a long time, this week try to set aside a half hour each day and systematically study Proverbs 13. First take a couple of days to read it several times, taking time to evaluate it. Then write all of the self-contained sayings on separate slips of paper. Next, arrange the slips of paper into categories that are similar, for example, those that concentrate on relationships in one category, and those that focus on personal behavior in another. Last, read the proverb in its rearranged form. How did this exercise help you learn the proverb? *See also* Spiritual Disciplines Index.

12:10 *he wrote words of truth plainly.* The second wise man commends the Teacher to his son for the quality of his insight. It might be asked how the Teacher's words could be seen as true. The answer is to be found in his restricted perspective. Time and time again the Teacher

stated that he was observing things "under the sun." As he looked at the fallen world and how it worked, he rightly concluded that life is hard and then comes death. As we will see, though, the second wise man uses this conclusion to push his son beyond an "under the sun" perspective.

12:13 *The end of the matter; all has been heard.* The abruptness of these words gives the impression that the second wisdom teacher now moves on to what is really important. Over against the under-the-sun perspective of the Teacher, he encourages his son to have a proper relationship with God ("fear God"), maintain that relationship through obeying his will ("keep his commandments"), and live in the expectation of a future judgment. In a word, the second wisdom teacher affirms the Teacher's conclusion that ultimate meaning cannot be found "under the sun." He uses that insight to steer his son toward a proper relationship with God.

SONG OF SOLOMON

"Let him kiss me with the kisses of his mouth!" Thus begins the deeply sensual book known as the Song of Solomon, or the Song of Songs. The former title comes from the song's honorary attribution to Solomon (the actual author is unknown), but the latter title is perhaps the most apt, making the bold claim that this is no ordinary song, but a particularly sublime one. It may also hint at the fact that the book is a song that is composed of a multiplicity of songs. It is indeed a song, explaining the impression of unity created by the consistency of speakers (a man, a woman, and a group of women) and occasional repeated refrains. But it is also a collection of many songs, an insight that helps us see why attempts to provide an overarching plot structure to the book have proved such a failure.

A Full-Bodied Spirituality

The presence of such a passionate and intimate book in the canon of sacred Scripture has troubled Jewish and Christian interpreters for as long as we have records of interpretation. Most, however, did not attempt to eject the book from the canon; they rather questioned whether the book actually concerned what the language on the surface suggests—human love and intimacy. Thus, from the earliest known interpretations, around AD 100, until the mid-nineteenth century, a strategy of allegorical interpretation was utilized to "desexualize" the book. Indeed, more than one type of allegorical interpretation developed in the early centuries of known interpretation, but the main framework of such a view identifies God (or Jesus) as the man and Israel (or the Church or the individual Christian) as the woman. In such an interpretive approach, the book has nothing to do with intimate relationship between a man and a woman, but with one's relationship with God. Although few

See also "The With-God Life" essay for this section of the Bible,
"The People of God in Daily Life," pp. 901–4.

professional interpreters continue in this line of thinking, it is still often found in contemporary pulpits.

In the past century and a half readers of the Song have come to terms with the lack of any evidence within the book itself that it is an allegory. Allegories are not subtle, after all (consider the popular book *Pilgrim's Progress* by John Bunyan), and nowhere, as an example, does the book prod its readers to consider the kiss of Song of Sol 1:2 as anything other than a kiss.

From a historical distance, it appears that the allegorical approach to the Song was the result of the influence of contemporary culture and philosophy on the early Church and synagogue. In particular, Neoplatonic philosophy insisted that body and soul were separate entities. Some New Testament passages read in the light of this philosophy might seem to affirm its teaching (Matt 10:28). Consequently, the Church came to believe that the soul could thrive only if the body were ignored, or worse. After these ideas gained acceptance, it is not surprising that the early and medieval Church promoted the idea of a celibate priesthood, established monasteries, and allowed for the punishment of the body as a remedy for sexual arousal.

Though our own age surely has its blind spots in interpreting the Bible, the modern era is better suited to recover the sexual frankness of the Song. For the most part, theology better appreciates the fundamental unity of the human person. The language of "body," "soul," and "spirit" is used today to discuss different aspects of a whole person rather than separate parts. Taking the Song at face value is part of the remedy against treating body, emotions, and sex as somehow distinct from spirituality. The Song is an incarnational celebration of our spirituality.

After all, the intimate relationship between a man and a woman is not the result of the fall, but rather a gift of the creation. As a matter of fact, the Song, with all of its garden imagery and country settings, intends to remind us of the days in Eden when Adam and Eve were naked in the garden and feeling no shame. Adam proclaimed that Eve was flesh of his flesh. "Therefore a man leaves his father and his mother and clings to his wife, and they become one flesh" (Gen 2:24). The presence of the Song in the canon reminds us that God is interested in us as whole people. To read the Song as spiritual devotion is not at all at odds with reading it as pertaining to sensual pleasure.

The Redemption of Intimacy

However, remembering the harmony between Adam and Eve in the garden also reminds us of the fall. The sin was not specifically sexual; it was an assertion of moral autonomy, an act through which Adam and Eve demonstrated their belief that they could define what was wrong and right over against God's declaration. This act not only broke fellowship with God, but had ramifications for the easy intimacy of the man and the woman. They could no longer stand naked before each other without shame. Rather, they covered themselves with clothing.

Read in the light of Genesis 2–3, the Song of Solomon may be seen as a poem celebrating the redemption of sexuality. The man and the woman are once again naked in the garden and enjoying each other's presence. As with all aspects of our redemption before the final day, however, our sexual harmony enjoys an already/not-yet redemption. Although most of the book contains poems that rejoice in the union between the man and the woman, a few songs recognize continuing difficulties (5:2–6:3).

Illuminating the Divine-Human Relationship

The allegorical interpretation completely bypassed the idea that the Song is a collection of poems that celebrate and caution concerning human love. However, it would be wrong to swing the pendulum too far the other way. When read in the context of the canon, the Song has a clear and obvious relevance to the divine-human relationship. Throughout the Bible, our relationship to God is likened to a marriage.

Malachi speaks of marriage as a covenant (2:14), a legal form that is also used as perhaps the most pervasive metaphor of our relationship with God throughout the Bible. The prophets Jeremiah, Ezekiel, and Hosea all assume that Israel's relationship with God has the intimacy of a marriage, and all three of them also recognize that Israel has betrayed that relationship, so that its idolatry is likened to adultery (Jer 2:1–3; 3:1–5; Ezek 16; 23; Hos 1–3). The New Testament uses this imagery of intimacy to describe the Church's relationship to Christ (Eph 5:21–33) and the glory of the final consummation (Rev 19:6–8).

Read in the light of the rest of the canon, the Song then becomes a resource not only for our understanding of male-female relationships, but also for a more profound understanding of the intimacy and exclusivity of our relationship with God.

—*Tremper Longman III*

1

The Song of Songs, which is Solomon's.

Colloquy of Bride and Friends

2 Let him kiss me with the kisses of his
       mouth!
For your love is better than wine,
3   your anointing oils are fragrant,
your name is perfume poured out;
    therefore the maidens love you.

4 Draw me after you, let us make haste.
    The king has brought me into his
        chambers.
We will exult and rejoice in you;
    we will extol your love more than
        wine;
    rightly do they love you.

5 I am black and beautiful,
    O daughters of Jerusalem,

1:2 *your love is better than wine.* The Song is a sensuous book, reveling in God's good gifts of both spiritual and physical intimacy. All the senses participate in the description of the pleasures of love. Wine is a sensuous liquid, leaving a long aftertaste on the tongue, like the kisses of one's beloved. More than that, wine and love both leave one lightheaded.

Responding
1:4 CELEBRATION. What a wonderful way of celebrating God has given us with his good gift of sexuality! The entire book of Song of Solomon is a beautiful description of young lovers taking great joy in one another. Consider writing down or telling your spouse just how you delight in and appreciate him or her. *See also* Spiritual Disciplines Index.

like the tents of Kedar,
  like the curtains of Solomon.
6 Do not gaze at me because I am dark,
  because the sun has gazed on me.
My mother's sons were angry with me;
  they made me keeper of the
    vineyards,
  but my own vineyard I have not kept!
7 Tell me, you whom my soul loves,
  where you pasture your flock,
  where you make it lie down at noon;
for why should I be like one who is
    veiled
  beside the flocks of your
    companions?

8 If you do not know,
  O fairest among women,
follow the tracks of the flock,
  and pasture your kids
  beside the shepherds' tents.

Colloquy of Bridegroom, Friends, and Bride

9 I compare you, my love,
  to a mare among Pharaoh's chariots.
10 Your cheeks are comely with
    ornaments,
  your neck with strings of jewels.
11 We will make you ornaments of gold,
  studded with silver.

12 While the king was on his couch,
  my nard gave forth its fragrance.
13 My beloved is to me a bag of myrrh
  that lies between my breasts.
14 My beloved is to me a cluster of henna
    blossoms
  in the vineyards of En-gedi.

15 Ah, you are beautiful, my love;
  ah, you are beautiful;
  your eyes are doves.

16 Ah, you are beautiful, my beloved,
  truly lovely.
Our couch is green;
17   the beams of our house are cedar,
  our rafters[a] are pine.

2 I am a rose[b] of Sharon,
  a lily of the valleys.

2 As a lily among brambles,
  so is my love among maidens.

3 As an apple tree among the trees of the
    wood,
  so is my beloved among young men.
With great delight I sat in his shadow,
  and his fruit was sweet to my taste.

a Meaning of Heb uncertain   b Heb crocus

1:6 *My mother's sons were angry with me.* In ancient Israelite culture, a woman's brothers were charged with the protection of her sexuality (Gen 34). However, here and in 8:8–9, they are described as being overprotective. The woman's passion makes her feisty with her brothers, and in spite of their attempts to reign her in, she pursues her man, arranging a private tryst as he shepherds his flock outside the city (v 7).

1:10 *Your cheeks are comely with ornaments.* Compared to the virtue of "fear of the LORD," a woman's beauty is "vain" (see Prov 31:30). However, the Song extols the physical beauty of not only the woman, but also the man (see 5:10–16). The man's compliment to the woman here also suggests that there is nothing wrong and everything right with enhancing that beauty with jewelry.

1:13 *a bag of myrrh that lies between my breasts.* Early interpreters (Cyril of Alexandria)

understood the bag of myrrh as Jesus Christ who spans the Old and New Testaments (the breasts), a type of interpretation that demonstrates the desperation of the allegorical method. The image the woman conjures of the man as a fragrant object in such a personal and pleasurable place on her body highlights her desire for intimate physical union with the man.

1:16–17 *Our couch is green.* The couch is the soft grass of the countryside. The man and the woman lie on the grass, shaded by cedar and pine trees, which provide privacy. Throughout the Song, the countryside is the place of intimacy and the city hostile to their love. These are not descriptions of actual events, but poetic descriptions that encourage love in couples who read them. In reality, intimacy may be found in the city as well as the country. The important point is that intimacy requires privacy.

⁴ He brought me to the banqueting
　　house,
　　and his intention toward me was love.
⁵ Sustain me with raisins,
　　refresh me with apples;
　　for I am faint with love.
⁶ O that his left hand were under my
　　head,
　　and that his right hand embraced me!
⁷ I adjure you, O daughters of Jerusalem,
　　by the gazelles or the wild does:
　do not stir up or awaken love
　　until it is ready!

Springtime Rhapsody

⁸ The voice of my beloved!
　　Look, he comes,
　leaping upon the mountains,
　　bounding over the hills.
⁹ My beloved is like a gazelle
　　or a young stag.
Look, there he stands
　　behind our wall,
　gazing in at the windows,
　　looking through the lattice.
¹⁰ My beloved speaks and says to me:

"Arise, my love, my fair one,
　　and come away;
¹¹ for now the winter is past,
　　the rain is over and gone.
¹² The flowers appear on the earth;
　　the time of singing has come,
　and the voice of the turtledove
　　is heard in our land.
¹³ The fig tree puts forth its figs,
　　and the vines are in blossom;
　　they give forth fragrance.
Arise, my love, my fair one,
　　and come away.
¹⁴ O my dove, in the clefts of the rock,
　　in the covert of the cliff,
　let me see your face,
　　let me hear your voice;
　for your voice is sweet,
　　and your face is lovely.
¹⁵ Catch us the foxes,
　　the little foxes,
　that ruin the vineyards—
　　for our vineyards are in blossom."

¹⁶ My beloved is mine and I am his;
　　he pastures his flock among the lilies.

2:6 *O that his left hand were under my head.* The woman describes her desire to be in the man's embrace (see also 8:3). Throughout the Song, the woman does not hesitate to express her hope for physical intimacy with the man and vice versa. The best understanding of the verse is that they are lying down and the man has slipped his left arm under her head, and, as he cradles her head on his arm, he reaches over and pulls her toward him. According to Genesis 2, God created Eve to dispel Adam's loneliness. The Song thus acknowledges human yearning for intimacy with others. It is an incarnational witness to community at its deepest and most intimate level.

2:7 *do not stir up or awaken love until it is ready!* The description of the woman's intimacy with the man in the previous verses is so enticing that she feels that she must charge the daughters of Jerusalem not to jump into a passionate relationship prematurely. The daughters of Jerusalem play multiple roles in the Song; one dominant one is as the woman's disciples in love. This refrain occurs here as well

as in 3:5 and 8:4, all passages that conclude particularly passionate encounters between the man and the woman.

2:10–13 *the time of singing has come.* Springtime is the time for love. It is a time to be outdoors in a private garden setting. It is a time to remove clothes, not put them on. It is a time of new growth and fertility, as well as fragrant smells. In this delightful poem the woman quotes the man, who expresses his desire to be with the object of his desire.

2:15 *Catch us the foxes.* This verse comes at the end of a poem in which the man expresses his desire to be in the garden of love with the woman. Out of nowhere comes the warning about foxes that destroy the vineyard. The significance of the foxes is left intentionally ambiguous, but surely stands for those people and things that might disturb the tranquillity of the love between the man and the woman. The Song of Solomon is a realistic book. Although it celebrates love and sensual pleasure, it poetically recognizes the threats and obstacles to them that people encounter in life (see also 5:2–6:3).

¹⁷ Until the day breathes
    and the shadows flee,
turn, my beloved, be like a gazelle
    or a young stag on the cleft
       mountains. ^a

Love's Dream

3 Upon my bed at night
    I sought him whom my soul loves;
I sought him, but found him not;
    I called him, but he gave no answer. ^b
² "I will rise now and go about the city,
    in the streets and in the squares;
I will seek him whom my soul loves."
    I sought him, but found him not.
³ The sentinels found me,
    as they went about in the city.
"Have you seen him whom my soul
       loves?"
⁴ Scarcely had I passed them,
    when I found him whom my soul
       loves.
I held him, and would not let him go
    until I brought him into my mother's
       house,
    and into the chamber of her that
       conceived me.
⁵ I adjure you, O daughters of Jerusalem,
    by the gazelles or the wild does:
do not stir up or awaken love
    until it is ready!

The Groom and His Party Approach

⁶ What is that coming up from the
    wilderness,

like a column of smoke,
perfumed with myrrh and
    frankincense,
    with all the fragrant powders of the
       merchant?
⁷ Look, it is the litter of Solomon!
    Around it are sixty mighty men
       of the mighty men of Israel,
⁸ all equipped with swords
    and expert in war,
each with his sword at his thigh
    because of alarms by night.
⁹ King Solomon made himself a
       palanquin
    from the wood of Lebanon.
¹⁰ He made its posts of silver,
    its back of gold, its seat of purple;
its interior was inlaid with love. ^c
    Daughters of Jerusalem,
¹¹   come out.
Look, O daughters of Zion,
    at King Solomon,
at the crown with which his mother
       crowned him
    on the day of his wedding,
    on the day of the gladness of his heart.

The Bride's Beauty Extolled

4 How beautiful you are, my love,
    how very beautiful!
Your eyes are doves
    behind your veil.

^a Or *on the mountains of Bether*; meaning of Heb
uncertain   ^b Gk: Heb lacks this line
^c Meaning of Heb uncertain

3:1–5 *I sought him, but found him not.* In this
poem, the woman experiences the loneliness
that God's institution of marriage is intended
to dispel. However, after the fall and before
heaven, nothing completely transcends the
alienation introduced into relationship by our
sin. This poem describes how the woman moves
from her sense of loneliness to union with the
man she loves (v 4), though she has to move
through the dangerous city in order to be
with him.
3:6–11 *the crown with which his mother
crowned him.* This poem describes the opulence
that surrounds the wedding of Solomon. The
purpose is not to tell the story of Solomon, but

rather to express poetically the dignity and
honor that surround the intimate union of a
man and a woman.
4:1–16 *How beautiful you are, my love.* In this
lengthy descriptive poem the man describes the
physical beauty of the woman (see 5:10–16 for
a comparable description of the man by the
woman). He compliments her beauty starting
with her head and moving down to the ultimate
object of his attention, the garden that represents the most private part of her body. These
types of descriptive songs are known also from
ancient Egyptian love poetry and even modern
Arabic wedding songs. They are highly sensual
preludes to lovemaking.

Your hair is like a flock of goats,
 moving down the slopes of Gilead.
2 Your teeth are like a flock of shorn ewes
 that have come up from the washing,
all of which bear twins,
 and not one among them is bereaved.
3 Your lips are like a crimson thread,
 and your mouth is lovely.
Your cheeks are like halves of a
  pomegranate
behind your veil.
4 Your neck is like the tower of David,
 built in courses;
on it hang a thousand bucklers,
 all of them shields of warriors.
5 Your two breasts are like two fawns,
 twins of a gazelle,
 that feed among the lilies.
6 Until the day breathes
 and the shadows flee,
I will hasten to the mountain of myrrh
 and the hill of frankincense.
7 You are altogether beautiful, my love;
 there is no flaw in you.
8 Come with me from Lebanon, my
  bride;
 come with me from Lebanon.
Depart*a* from the peak of Amana,
 from the peak of Senir and Hermon,
from the dens of lions,
 from the mountains of leopards.

9 You have ravished my heart, my sister,
 my bride,
 you have ravished my heart with a
  glance of your eyes,
 with one jewel of your necklace.
10 How sweet is your love, my sister, my
 bride!

how much better is your love than
 wine,
 and the fragrance of your oils than
  any spice!
11 Your lips distill nectar, my bride;
 honey and milk are under your
  tongue;
 the scent of your garments is like the
  scent of Lebanon.
12 A garden locked is my sister, my bride,
 a garden locked, a fountain sealed.
13 Your channel*b* is an orchard of
  pomegranates
 with all choicest fruits,
 henna with nard,
14 nard and saffron, calamus and
  cinnamon,
 with all trees of frankincense,
myrrh and aloes,
 with all chief spices—
15 a garden fountain, a well of living water,
 and flowing streams from Lebanon.

16 Awake, O north wind,
 and come, O south wind!
Blow upon my garden
 that its fragrance may be wafted
  abroad.
Let my beloved come to his garden,
 and eat its choicest fruits.

5 I come to my garden, my sister, my
  bride;
 I gather my myrrh with my spice,
 I eat my honeycomb with my honey,
 I drink my wine with my milk.

a Or *Look*   *b* Meaning of Heb uncertain

4:8 *from the mountains of leopards*. The man encourages the woman to come to him from a variety of places that are rugged and dangerous (Lebanon, Amana, Hermon, Senir, the dens of lions, and the mountains of leopards). We are not to imagine a real woman tucked away in a lion's den. The poet uses these locations to suggest that the woman apart from the man is in a lonely and threatening place. For shelter, she should come into his protecting arms.

4:12–15 *A garden locked*. The man's descrip-

tive poem began by lovingly praising the woman's eyes, hair, teeth, lips, and cheeks. He then moved down her body to her neck and breasts. Now he describes the fragrant wonders of her garden with its fountain. This tastefully described watery garden represents the most private and sensuous part of her body. The garden is "locked"; the fountain "sealed." However, this wonderful place will soon be opened, so that the man may come in and enjoy "its choicest fruits" (v 16).

Eat, friends, drink,
and be drunk with love.

Another Dream

2 I slept, but my heart was awake.
Listen! my beloved is knocking.
"Open to me, my sister, my love,
my dove, my perfect one;
for my head is wet with dew,
my locks with the drops of the
night."
3 I had put off my garment;
how could I put it on again?
I had bathed my feet;
how could I soil them?
4 My beloved thrust his hand into the
opening,
and my inmost being yearned for
him.
5 I arose to open to my beloved,
and my hands dripped with myrrh,
my fingers with liquid myrrh,
upon the handles of the bolt.
6 I opened to my beloved,
but my beloved had turned and was
gone.
My soul failed me when he spoke.
I sought him, but did not find him;
I called him, but he gave no answer.
7 Making their rounds in the city
the sentinels found me;
they beat me, they wounded me,
they took away my mantle,
those sentinels of the walls.
8 I adjure you, O daughters of Jerusalem,
if you find my beloved,
tell him this:
I am faint with love.

Colloquy of Friends and Bride

9 What is your beloved more than
another beloved,
O fairest among women?
What is your beloved more than
another beloved,
that you thus adjure us?

10 My beloved is all radiant and ruddy,
distinguished among ten thousand.
11 His head is the finest gold;
his locks are wavy,
black as a raven.
12 His eyes are like doves
beside springs of water,
bathed in milk,
fitly set. *a*
13 His cheeks are like beds of spices,
yielding fragrance.
His lips are lilies,
distilling liquid myrrh.
14 His arms are rounded gold,
set with jewels.
His body is ivory work, *a*
encrusted with sapphires. *b*
15 His legs are alabaster columns,
set upon bases of gold.
His appearance is like Lebanon,
choice as the cedars.
16 His speech is most sweet,
and he is altogether desirable.
This is my beloved and this is my friend,
O daughters of Jerusalem.

6 Where has your beloved gone,
O fairest among women?
Which way has your beloved turned,
that we may seek him with you?

a Meaning of Heb uncertain   *b* Heb *lapis lazuli*

5:2–6:3 *my beloved had turned and was gone.* This poem imaginatively expresses the difficulty that a man and a woman have in moving intimately toward one another. He appears at her door and knocks (5:2), but she at first repels his advances. By the time she is ready to receive him ("my inmost being yearned for him," 5:4), he has left. The rest of the poem narrates her passionate and successful pursuit of the man.

5:14 *His body is ivory work.* This tasteful English translation may obscure the sensuous object under description. The word translated "body" suggests a more sexual part of the male body, while the "ivory work" could just as easily be understood to be an "ivory tusk." The Song, while discreet in its use of metaphor, nonetheless is not prudish in its approach to sexuality. The man and the woman are in the garden and, like Adam and Eve before the fall, do not feel shame as they stand naked before each other.

2 My beloved has gone down to his
    garden,
  to the beds of spices,
  to pasture his flock in the gardens,
    and to gather lilies.
3 I am my beloved's and my beloved is
    mine;
  he pastures his flock among the lilies.

The Bride's Matchless Beauty

4 You are beautiful as Tirzah, my love,
    comely as Jerusalem,
    terrible as an army with banners.
5 Turn away your eyes from me,
    for they overwhelm me!
  Your hair is like a flock of goats,
    moving down the slopes of Gilead.
6 Your teeth are like a flock of ewes,
    that have come up from the washing;
  all of them bear twins,
    and not one among them is bereaved.
7 Your cheeks are like halves of a
      pomegranate
    behind your veil.
8 There are sixty queens and eighty
      concubines,
    and maidens without number.
9 My dove, my perfect one, is the only one,
    the darling of her mother,
    flawless to her that bore her.
  The maidens saw her and called her
      happy;
    the queens and concubines also, and
      they praised her.
10 "Who is this that looks forth like the
      dawn,
    fair as the moon, bright as the sun,
    terrible as an army with banners?"

11 I went down to the nut orchard,
    to look at the blossoms of the valley,
  to see whether the vines had budded,

whether the pomegranates were in
    bloom.
12 Before I was aware, my fancy set me
  in a chariot beside my prince. *a*

13 *b* Return, return, O Shulammite!
  Return, return, that we may look
    upon you.

Why should you look upon the
    Shulammite,
  as upon a dance before two armies? *c*

Expressions of Praise

7 How graceful are your feet in sandals,
    O queenly maiden!
  Your rounded thighs are like jewels,
    the work of a master hand.
2 Your navel is a rounded bowl
    that never lacks mixed wine.
  Your belly is a heap of wheat,
    encircled with lilies.
3 Your two breasts are like two fawns,
    twins of a gazelle.
4 Your neck is like an ivory tower.
  Your eyes are pools in Heshbon,
    by the gate of Bath-rabbim.
  Your nose is like a tower of Lebanon,
    overlooking Damascus.
5 Your head crowns you like Carmel,
    and your flowing locks are like purple;
    a king is held captive in the tresses. *d*

6 How fair and pleasant you are,
    O loved one, delectable maiden! *e*
7 You are stately *f* as a palm tree,
    and your breasts are like its clusters.
8 I say I will climb the palm tree

---

a Cn: Meaning of Heb uncertain   b Ch 7.1 in
Heb   c Or *dance of Mahanaim*   d Meaning of
Heb uncertain   e Syr: Heb *in delights*
f Heb *This your stature is*

6:4 *terrible as an army with banners.* That the
effect of the woman's beauty on the man is compared to the fear instilled by an army (see also
6:10) seems odd at first. Upon reflection we understand that the beauty of the woman is so overpowering that it arouses fear as well as joy. One
cannot take one's eyes off an army on the march,
and the same is true for the object of one's love.

7:7–8 *I will climb the palm tree.* The man
likens the woman to a palm tree, slender but
bulging with fruit representing her breasts. The
man proclaims his desire for intimate touch by
expressing his intention to climb this palm tree
and grasp its fruit. He longs for physical intimacy with the woman he loves.

and lay hold of its branches.
O may your breasts be like clusters of
  the vine,
  and the scent of your breath like
  apples,
9 and your kisses *a* like the best wine
  that goes down *b* smoothly,
  gliding over lips and teeth. *c*

10 I am my beloved's,
  and his desire is for me.
11 Come, my beloved,
  let us go forth into the fields,
  and lodge in the villages;
12 let us go out early to the vineyards,
  and see whether the vines have
  budded,
  whether the grape blossoms have
  opened
  and the pomegranates are in
  bloom.
  There I will give you my love.
13 The mandrakes give forth fragrance,
  and over our doors are all choice
  fruits,
  new as well as old,
  which I have laid up for you, O my
  beloved.

8 O that you were like a brother to me,
  who nursed at my mother's breast!

If I met you outside, I would kiss you,
  and no one would despise me.
2 I would lead you and bring you
  into the house of my mother,
  and into the chamber of the one who
  bore me. *d*
  I would give you spiced wine to drink,
  the juice of my pomegranates.
3 O that his left hand were under my
  head,
  and that his right hand embraced me!
4 I adjure you, O daughters of Jerusalem,
  do not stir up or awaken love
  until it is ready!

Homecoming

5 Who is that coming up from the
  wilderness,
  leaning upon her beloved?

Under the apple tree I awakened you.
There your mother was in labor with
  you;
  there she who bore you was in labor.

6 Set me as a seal upon your heart,
  as a seal upon your arm;

a Heb *palate*   *b* Heb *down for my lover*
c Gk Syr Vg: Heb *lips of sleepers*   *d* Gk Syr: Heb
my mother; she (or *you*) *will teach me*

7:10 *I am my beloved's.* This phrase is repeated with some variation in 2:16 and 7:10. It is a statement of the mutual affection shared by the man and the woman. She gives herself wholly to him in this exclusive relationship.

Responding
7:10 CHASTITY. Married love is exclusive. Spouses belong to one another in a way they do not belong to any other person on earth. The exclusive fidelity of a marriage is a form of chastity, a sacred commitment that can sometimes be eroded as time passes. To give your commitment the attention it deserves, consider copying out your marriage vows or this line of Scripture on an index card or piece of paper. Place it somewhere where you will see it often—in your Bible as a bookmark, in your wallet, in your medicine cabinet. Each time you see it, as you are able,

reflect on how well you are honoring your vows. *See also* Spiritual Disciplines Index.

8:6 *Set me as a seal upon your heart.* The woman desires that the man take full possession of her. She surrenders herself to him, yearning for "one flesh" union. The seal in ancient Israelite society was typically a stamp that was pressed on soft clay to leave an impression that served as a person's identification. She wants to be marked as belonging to her beloved, with all her inward ("your heart") and outward ("your arm") being. Our own sense of individuality often rebels against this idea, and the danger is great in a fallen world, but the woman expresses a desire that we all have to be intimate and safe in the presence of another. Such an intense feeling explains why the ideal relationship between a man and a woman serves so well as a metaphor for our relationship with God.

for love is strong as death,
    passion fierce as the grave.
Its flashes are flashes of fire,
    a raging flame.
7 Many waters cannot quench love,
    neither can floods drown it.
If one offered for love
    all the wealth of one's house,
    it would be utterly scorned.

8 We have a little sister,
    and she has no breasts.
What shall we do for our sister,
    on the day when she is spoken for?
9 If she is a wall,
    we will build upon her a battlement
      of silver;
but if she is a door,
    we will enclose her with boards of
      cedar.
10 I was a wall,
    and my breasts were like towers;
then I was in his eyes

as one who brings*a* peace.
11 Solomon had a vineyard at Baal-
      hamon;
he entrusted the vineyard to keepers;
each one was to bring for its fruit a
      thousand pieces of silver.
12 My vineyard, my very own, is for
      myself;
you, O Solomon, may have the
      thousand,
and the keepers of the fruit two
      hundred!

13 O you who dwell in the gardens,
    my companions are listening for your
      voice;
    let me hear it.

14 Make haste, my beloved,
    and be like a gazelle
or a young stag
    upon the mountains of spices!

a Or *finds*

8:14 *Make haste, my beloved.* It is of great significance that the Song ends with an expression of yearning desire and not satisfaction. The abrupt end of the Song mirrors love itself, which is never satisfied with enough, but longs for more.

IX. The People of God in Rebellion

Scriptures: *1 Kings 12 to 2 Kings 25:10, 2 Chronicles 10–36:19, Isaiah, Jeremiah 1–36, Hosea, Joel, Amos, Jonah, Micah, Nahum, Habakkuk, Zephaniah*

Deuterocanonical Books: *Judith, Prayer of Manasseh*

> *The aim of God in history is the creation of an all-inclusive community of loving persons with God himself at the very center of this community as its prime Sustainer and most glorious Inhabitant (Eph 2:19–22; 3:10). The Bible traces the formation of this community from the creation in the Garden of Eden all the way to the new heaven and the new earth. Come, join us as we explore the many dimensions of this with-God history—from individual to family to tribe to people to nation to all humanity—and apply what we learn to our own spiritual formation.*

In the Scriptures listed above we will see the ways God continues to form an all-inclusive community through a nation under siege and a divided kingdom that faces imminent dispersion and captivity.

God's Action

When God gave the Mosaic law to Israel at Sinai, it was supposed to be a lasting record of his action in history that would mediate his presence and guide the people's moral and religious lives. Initially Moses, a prophet and judge, lived in their midst as a clear example of God's grace and a conduit of that grace to the People of God. Aaron, Moses' brother, presided over the tent of meeting as God's visible presence hovers over the Holy of Holies.

Once the Israelites entered and scattered throughout the Promised Land, God established judges as the primary means of mediating his presence. They settled disputes between individuals and the twelve tribes, led armies to secure their borders, and took action against centers of pagan worship. With the people's rejection of God as their king, God allowed a monarchy to be established and it, along with the priesthood, became the primary means through which God revealed his presence. The nation reached its apex during the reign of Solomon, when the Temple, with its worship liturgies, sacrificial rituals, and seasonal celebrations, became the center of religious life and the symbol of God's visible presence.

But after Solomon's death, the once-unified nation divided into two rival kingdoms—Israel to the north and Judah to the south. During the period of a broken and divided kingdom, God calls forth an old group—the prophets—in a new capacity to mediate God's presence to the people and their leaders. Since the time of Moses prophets had proclaimed God's word to the Israelites, but often they had fulfilled dual roles—prophet and priest, or prophet and judge—and never in a strained relationship with political power. But now the days were long gone in which Samuel held prophetic claim over the actions and office of King Saul. During this new era, the prophetic role becomes separated from and opposed to a rebellious political structure. The prophets become an "outsider" force in order to declare God's judgment on individuals and the state, calling them to radical repentance. The prophets interpret for the Israelites how God is acting through historical events and relay God's warning of the nation's imminent collapse and their bondage if they do not repent of their sins against God and each other.

These warnings fall on deaf ears, as the two political kingdoms, Israel and Judah, find themselves under siege and threatened with dispersion as captives by the expansionist nations. In the beginning, God banished humanity from its primitive garden, Eden. This time he draws upon Israel's rival kingdoms to deport the people of Israel from their new Garden of Eden, the Promised Land. This will mark the end of God's direct use of theocratic political structures.

Human Reaction

The breakup of the nation is a time of profound moral testing. The prophets react by declaring the word of the Lord in the midst of the people's great suffering, division, and national alienation brought on by their own idolatry and national disobedience. The prophets' chastisement of the people when they go astray is always moderated by the hope of the eventual return of the faithful to their land and the larger expectation of God's active presence in the future in the person of a redeemer, the Messiah.

Set apart to become a blessing to all humanity, the People of God are now coming to the point of inevitable judgment. They are now on the verge of being dispersed into exile in order to emerge, through suffering, capable of deeper forms of learning inaccessible by any other means. In this dire setting, the prophets faithfully explain all of the coming events despite being the targets of intense persecution and suffering themselves. Through their faithful proclamation of God's message and their clear apprehension of God's nature, they bring human moral consciousness to its highest point in history, a peak that stands yet today.

How do the people respond to these warnings? By turning a deaf ear. The glory of the Solomonic kingdom lingered over the landscape, but also contributed to the corruption of the ruling kings. When the people of Israel asked Solomon's son and successor to lighten "the hard service of your father and his heavy yoke that he placed on us," Rehoboam refused and instead added to their burdens (1 Kings 12:1–15). This prompted ten tribes to rebel and set up their own government in the north, headed by Jeroboam. Even though Israel was divided into the Northern and Southern Kingdoms, the memory and promise of relatively good times was strong

and still seductive. As we have seen from the beginnings of the nation, prosperity quickly exposes corruption and the limits of unformed character.

The Israelites also continue to fall away from God and his commandments and worship other gods. Idol worship reaches an all-time high during the Divided Kingdom. Not only do the people worship idols (1 Kings 18:21–24; 19:18; 2 Kings 10:21–24), but so do their kings (1 Kings 16:31; 22:53; 2 Kings 21:3). Not even the glorious Temple in Jerusalem, the stunning worship, the redemptive sacrifices, or the promise of God to remain faithful to the Israelites could soften the people to be faithful. And so the warnings of the prophets do not deter the Israelites from "whoring" after other gods. The prophetess Huldah "declared to them, 'Thus says the Lord, . . . Because they have abandoned me and have made offerings to other gods . . . therefore my wrath will be kindled against this place, and it will not be quenched'" (2 Kings 22:16–17).

Blessings and Benefits for Our Formation

In the challenge of foreign powers to Israel's national continuity and identity, we come to see that God works in history above and beyond the individual, the family, the tribe, and even the nation. Now we witness God working even through the unbelieving peoples, the nations, the Gentiles. God uses the nations to judge and chastise his own people. His hammer of judgment comes down upon the Israelites, wielded by the very nations harassing Israel and Judah. God's presence is being reconceived and redefined beyond the national framework of the Israelites to include all nations. He is at work everywhere. God is the God of heaven and earth.

One of the emerging blessings in this period for the formation of our character as a People of God is the understanding that we must reject any religion or morality too closely tied to a particular cultural and national identity. In this part of the biblical narrative, it becomes increasingly clear that non-Jews can also be good people, often showing greater spiritual sensitivity. "When the news reached the king of Nineveh, he rose from his throne, removed his robe, covered himself with sackcloth, and sat in ashes. . . . 'All shall turn from their evil ways and from the violence that is in their hands'" (Jon 3:6–8). But many of the Israelites were slow to learn this lesson, as demonstrated by Jonah, who pouts because the Ninevites repent and are spared from being overthrown.

In a similar vein, these Scriptures teach us that the kingdom of God has a separate identity from earthly kingdoms, even David's divinely ordained kingdom and lineage. This is a huge benefit to all people who are outside the Jewish faith and heritage and yet are faithful to God and his kingdom. Later it becomes clear through the ministry of Jesus that God's kingdom transcends all limitations imposed by human political and religious institutions. As Jesus pointed out to Pilate, "My kingdom is not from this world. If my kingdom were from this world, my followers would be fighting to keep me from being handed over to the Jews. But as it is, my kingdom is not from here" (John 18:36). However, during the time of rebellion, this was an entirely new concept.

The ordination of lone prophets to warn the Israelites to "turn away from the wickedness they have committed and do what is lawful and right" (Ezek 18:27) reveals, even in this stage of with-God life, that God's presence continues to be mediated through individuals. The Temple and its resident priesthood and supporting monarchy are certainly essential structures in the development of an all-inclusive community. Yet from the beginning of time the individual person responding to divine purpose still occupies a central place in God's plan to bring all humanity into a loving relationship with himself.

Another blessing of this waning period of the security of the monarchy is that the people have had the opportunity to become formed through generations of study of and submission to the law, enabling many individuals to develop the kind of character that could receive the divine call reserved only for the truly faithful and the remnant. This created a kind of democratization of well-ordered spiritual practice, which meant God was not confined to calling people who were affiliated with a certain tribe, a particular order in the Temple, or even a specific social class. For example, God called a lowly shepherd and "dresser of sycamore trees," Amos of Tekoa, to pronounce coming judgment upon the nations and upon Israel and its priesthood (Amos 1:1; 7:14). God was also free to call a member of the priestly class, Jeremiah, to deliver oracles of judgment against Judah and the gentile nations in addition to prophecies of restoration and comfort: "But as for you, have no fear, my servant Jacob, and do not be dismayed, O Israel; for I am going to save you from far away, and your offspring from the land of their captivity" (Jer 46:27). One person with God can still be a majority.

Limits and Liabilities for Our Formation

In the growing conflict between temporal power and divine purpose we see better than before how true prophets of God come to be despised, rejected, ignored, killed, or silenced. The messengers whom God sends to speak his word under deteriorating historical, political, and social conditions are considered pariahs, traitors, and even enemies. Contrary to the false prophets whom people adore, God's prophets are loners without institutional backing or approval. The people and their leaders love to hear false consolations, but prophets like Hosea and Amos speak the truth, God's truth, about the real condition of the Israelites' nation and religion. "You have plowed wickedness, you have reaped injustice, you have eaten the fruit of lies" (Hos 10:13). "I hate, I despise your festivals, and I take no delight in your solemn assemblies. Even though you offer me your burnt offerings and grain offerings, I will not accept them" (Amos 5:21–22). The people prefer to take solace in the false prophets' pleasant words rather than face the harsh words of the prophets of God. The errant people are in need of the discipline of guidance, something missing at this stage of their with-God life, but instead of listening they try to tame the correcting will of God by silencing the prophets. Meanwhile, the establishment tries to tame authentic prophecy by supporting false prophets.

In such a situation, these lone prophets of God proclaim a message that can be easily ignored and co-opted. Numerous times a prophet delivers God's word only to be demeaned. When Micaiah predicted Ahab's death at Ramoth-gilead, Ahab had him imprisoned: "Put this fellow in prison, and feed him on reduced rations of bread and water until I come in peace." Micaiah responded: "If you return in peace, the LORD has not spoken by me" (1 Kings 22:27–28). At other times prophets deliver God's word only to be contradicted by false prophets. Prophets now become the continuity in the with-God life clear up to the coming of the Messiah. Isaiah and Jeremiah, Joel and Amos, Micah and Nahum, Zechariah and Malachi, and all those in between show the way forward with God, forming a kind of "paradigm of faithfulness" for the long years of exile and beyond. And they peer into God's great future, pointing to the "stone cut without hands" that becomes "a great mountain filling the whole earth" (Dan 2:31–35).

Insights and Instructions for Our Formation

The prophets provide profound models for our formation because they worked in a context so similar to our own. They followed God's voice and provided guidance to God's people at a time when the culture at large did not want to hear their message.

First, through the prophets we learn that righteousness comes from the heart renewed in faith, not from outward ritual or legal obedience. We are called to a renewal of the covenant from the heart, not merely from the perspective of the formal observance of the law. God requires justice, mercy, and love, not merely outward sacrifice or formal obedience.

Second, in listening to the experience of the prophets and the people of Israel in this difficult period, we learn that even though we may resist God actively, he does not abandon us. Like the Israelites, we may choose to dismiss God's word to us. Yet out of their dismissal and ensuing suffering the vision of the messianic suffering servant came to the People of God. God now will choose to come to Israel not in the form of one who is powerful and popular, but instead through the lowly, enslaved, rejected, and despised. So God comes to us still.

Third, we learn that God is present with us during all of life's stages. God was with the Israelites as he disciplined them and allowed them to be conquered and deported from their homeland. God was also with the Israelites in the prophets' announcements of judgment and redemption, condemnation of external worship and lawlessness, denunciations of wickedness and faithlessness, and pronouncements of God's love for the poor and God's hatred for bloodshed.

Finally, we see that genuine goodness comes from a well-ordered inner life. In such a life, the growth of character is expressed in the effortless expression of good works and compassion, despite the prevailing circumstances. Reading about the Israelites' faithlessness and wickedness during their rebellion should not depress us, but instead should remind us of how quickly and easily all of us can forget the grace and love of God and the need for the continuous transformation of our character.

The With-God Life

ISAIAH

The book of Isaiah is an extended, complex prophetic meditation upon the city of Jerusalem and its meaning for the faith of ancient Israel and, by extension, for our faith as well. Thus when we read Isaiah, we need to think deeply about the significance of the city of Jerusalem for biblical faith. We find that Jerusalem is at the same time the location of the Temple, where the God of Israel has promised to be present, and the seat of the royal dynasty of David, to whom God has made profound promises and commitments. The city of Jerusalem, in the imagination of Israel and in our faith, is invested with profound theological depth and importance.

At the same time, however, we realize that Jerusalem is also a real urban center with political practices, international entanglements, and temptations to military adventurism. As a result the city—and all that it represents—was endlessly placed in jeopardy and kept under threat by the larger states surrounding it. Over the span of the book of Isaiah, the city is in turn affected by the ominous Assyrian Empire (745–712 BC), the Babylonian Empire (615–540 BC), and eventually the Persian Empire (540–333 BC).

Our reading of Isaiah focuses upon the relationship between the theological reality of Jerusalem and the political reality of Jerusalem, a relationship that is not always clear-cut. That is to say, the prophetic tradition works to interpret in imaginative, poetic ways the reality of urban life with reference to the God of Israel, who is known in the memory of Israel long before Isaiah. Isaiah invites us to study the interrelation of life and faith, a relationship that is for us never as easy or obvious as we may imagine.

Promise and Judgment

The poetic, imaginative tradition of Isaiah shows us how to reconstrue the destiny of Jerusalem in relationship to the God of Israel. In Isaiah we hear two theological accents that are in deep tension with each other. On the one hand, we know that

*See also "The With-God Life" essay for this section of the Bible,
"The People of God in Rebellion," pp. 975–79.*

981

Yahweh, the God of Israel, has made deep and abiding promises to protect and sustain Jerusalem for the sake of the Temple and the Davidic dynasty. The theme of promise is pervasive in the tradition of Isaiah and is understood to be deep and unconditional (see 2:2–4). The promises are particularly carried by the Davidic dynasty (as in 9:2–7; 11:1–9). But later on, after the dynasty of David has been terminated, Yahweh makes promises that are to be kept either directly by divine intervention (as in 65:17–25) or through the agency of Cyrus the Persian, a non-Jew (45:1). Isaiah presses constantly toward the fulfillment of God's promises and is very sure that no historical vagary can disrupt or nullify the ultimate fruition of divine promises. In 701 BC, the city was indeed "miraculously" delivered from the Assyrian military threat, so that the promises of God seemed vindicated (37:33–38). We are invited to stand in awe and wonder at the way in which God keeps promises.

The other theme we find in the book of Isaiah is an awareness that Jerusalem was endlessly a city short of fulfilled promises and constantly in jeopardy as a result of Yahweh's judgment. A century after the wondrous deliverance of 701 BC, the city was sacked by the Babylonians and the leading inhabitants of the city deported into exile (39:6–8). After that traumatic Babylonian incursion in 598 BC and after another in 587 BC, the city remained at best a shabby, destabilized community that evidenced none of the splendor of God's promises. In that season of shabbiness and failure, Isaiah invites us to ponder Jerusalem, to grieve its loss, but more important, to anticipate a restored, renovated, revivified Jerusalem. We are drawn into the reality of grief and hope. The buoyant expectation of the Isaiah tradition is grounded, not in perceived reality, but in the promises of God, which can be trusted and which continue to prevail in every circumstance.

Thus the themes of divine judgment and divine promise dominate Isaiah, themes that provide a way for us to think about the world differently. In this way, our deepest faith convictions are continually connected to lived reality. In large sweep, the book of Isaiah is divided into two parts:

- Chapters 1–39 (and especially chaps 1–12, 28–31, 36–39) are about loss and are closely linked to the eighth-century BC prophet Isaiah. In these chapters we are made aware that God will judge the city and its wayward economic and military policies, which are rooted in unfaith. In thinking on this theme, we come to realize that all our favorite arrangements of the world stand under divine judgment.

- Chapters 40–66 articulate hope, the conviction that the deportation of the sixth century BC will end soon and the speedy recovery of the city of Jerusalem will be glorious. Thus chapters 40–55, formed well after the time of Isaiah the prophet, anticipate the glorious return of the exiles on a new superhighway. Chapters 56–66, still about hope, reflect the struggle after the return of the exiles to order the restored city in ways that are faithful. Specifically, the inclusiveness urged in chapter 56 and the neighborliness advocated in chapter 58 constitute an important vision of the demands and permits of faith. Studying this material provides us with a basis for hope. As readers of Isaiah we are focused on the good future God will yet give us.

In the Gap

This ordering of the book of Isaiah into two parts means that as readers of Isaiah we may imagine ourselves precisely in the gap between 39:8 and 40:1. It is a historical gap of two hundred years during which Jerusalem was devastated. It is a literary gap that moves prophetic utterance into new modes of discourse. Finally, it is a theological gap that moves us from divine judgment to divine promise.

Judgment and hope, which are writ large in chapters 1–39 and 40–66, respectively, are also given repeated expression in lesser patterns throughout Isaiah. Judgment and hope become for us the great pivot points as we read our common life through the text of Isaiah. Thus in chapters 1–12 we can see that a persistent message of divine judgment over the city is punctuated in 2:2–4; 4:2–6; 9:2–7; and 11:1–9 by divine promises. We can trust that God's last word to us is always promise; it is, however, characteristically a promise that comes after judgment and not in place of judgment.

It is of great importance that the early Church—in its effort to bear witness to Jesus Christ—found the book of Isaiah especially important and useful. As Christians who read Isaiah, we can see how our faith makes connections to these texts. It is right to say that the tradition of Isaiah does not "predict" Jesus. Nonetheless, the early Church, in its interpretive imagination under the inspiration of God the Spirit, found the utterances of this tradition especially important for its testimony to Jesus. We may notice two points in particular. First, the "royal oracle" of Isa 9:2–6 was readily transposed in Christian reading, so that "the son who is given" according to the poem is Jesus as "Son of God," the real King who is to come (see Matt 4:15–16). Second, the Song of the Servant in 52:13–53:12 was taken in the early Church to be testimony to the suffering of Jesus that answered for the transgressions of the world (see Acts 8:32–33).

Beyond such particular texts, moreover, the twofold message of judgment and hope, of exile and homecoming—reflected in the twofold structure of the book in chapters 1–39 and chapters 40–66—is readily transposed for us in Christian reading into the crucifixion of Jesus and the resurrection of Jesus. Thus the narrative of Jesus reiterates and replicates the narrative of Jerusalem. In our own Christian faith and worship, we focus in turn on loss (of a Friday kind) and the capacity of God to work a newness (of an Easter kind). We ourselves can move from the book of Isaiah to the main claims of our faith.

It is relatively easy in Christian imagination to transpose the concrete reality of Jerusalem in Isaiah into a claim for Jesus of Nazareth. In this reading, the city of Jerusalem comes to function in metaphorical ways, though care must be taken never to forfeit the concrete historical reality of the city of Jerusalem. Once we make a shift from merely a literal interpretation to a metaphorical one, then it is possible for faithful people like us to carry the image of Jerusalem farther, to see that the cipher "Jerusalem" pertains not only to the ancient city and not only derivatively to the person of Jesus; in further extrapolation, the cipher "Jerusalem" functions for us as a metaphor for any centered symbol system—political, economic, psychological, or ecclesiastical. Seen in this interpretive extrapolation, the focus of Isaiah upon Jerusalem takes on immense pastoral power in our own contemporary faith. We come to realize that our best historical treasures stand under God's judgment and must be appropriately relinquished in order to be received back from God, having been transformed by the power of the faithful God.

Thus Isaiah shows us that God is powerfully and decisively—though hiddenly— engaged everywhere in the reality of the world. Once we acknowledge this claim, then the work of our faith is to relinquish in life, personal and public, all that contradicts the reality and purpose of God and to receive from God what we cannot generate for ourselves.

In interpreting Isaiah we must pay particular attention to the four poems that speak of Yahweh's "servant" (42:1–9; 49:1–7; 50:4–11; 52:13–53:12). The Church has taken these poems to refer to Jesus, even though it seems unmistakably clear that the primary reference in these poems is to Israel as God's servant. Nonetheless, it is possible for us as contemporary readers to imagine ourselves, in the middle of these poems of loss and hope, to be the carriers of God's transformative will in the world. Isaiah focuses upon the sovereign capacity of God to make all things new. That future, however, is not simply a divine gift. It is at the same time a human task given to people like us. The Isaiah tradition variously reflects on the human work of the Davidic king, on the work of the Persian king, and then on the human responsibility to practice a community life characterized by inclusiveness and neighborliness. Our reading causes us to ponder what tasks we are given in faith. Isaiah provides us with an opportunity to reflect on our mission and mandate as a "light to the nations" and "covenant to the people" (see 42:6; 49:6), as the one "anointed" to transform social relationships (61:1–4) and so to be a redemptive force in the newness that God is about to give. The book of Isaiah invites us to accept this calling to obedience in the world.

Isaiah calls upon us to attest to both the grandeur of God in compassionate sovereignty and the pastoral reality of being God's people who are mandated to be unafraid in the world (as in 43:1), because the world belongs to the God who is doing a new thing (43:18–19). May the book of Isaiah empower us to be unafraid of our calling.

—*Walter Brueggemann*

1

The vision of Isaiah son of Amoz, which he saw concerning Judah and Jerusalem in the days of Uzziah, Jotham, Ahaz, and Hezekiah, kings of Judah.

The Wickedness of Judah

2 Hear, O heavens, and listen, O earth;
  for the LORD has spoken:
I reared children and brought them up,
  but they have rebelled against me.
3 The ox knows its owner,
  and the donkey its master's crib;
but Israel does not know,
  my people do not understand.

4 Ah, sinful nation,
  people laden with iniquity,
offspring who do evil,
  children who deal corruptly,
who have forsaken the LORD,
  who have despised the Holy One of
    Israel,
  who are utterly estranged!

5 Why do you seek further beatings?
  Why do you continue to rebel?
The whole head is sick,
  and the whole heart faint.
6 From the sole of the foot even to the
    head,
  there is no soundness in it,

but bruises and sores
  and bleeding wounds;
they have not been drained, or bound
    up,
  or softened with oil.

7 Your country lies desolate,
  your cities are burned with fire;
in your very presence
  aliens devour your land;
it is desolate, as overthrown by
  foreigners.
8 And daughter Zion is left
  like a booth in a vineyard,
like a shelter in a cucumber field,
  like a besieged city.
9 If the LORD of hosts
  had not left us a few survivors,
we would have been like Sodom,
  and become like Gomorrah.

10 Hear the word of the LORD,
  you rulers of Sodom!
Listen to the teaching of our God,
  you people of Gomorrah!
11 What to me is the multitude of your
    sacrifices?
  says the LORD;
I have had enough of burnt offerings of
  rams
  and the fat of fed beasts;

1:1–12:6 *The vision of Isaiah.* The series of texts included in this first section of First Isaiah (chaps 1–39) contains terrible judgments that are to come upon Judah and Jerusalem; in each case, however, the oracle of judgment is followed by a positive oracle about a future after the judgment. These promises are placed in 2:2–4; 4:2–6; 9:2–7; and 11:1–9. This pattern of judgment followed by hope is characteristic of the structure of the book of Isaiah and forms a theological principle that says that God's people may expect a future congruent with God's own will for justice and well-being in the world.

1:1 *in the days of Uzziah, Jotham, Ahaz, and Hezekiah.* The listing of the four kings of Judah reminds us that biblical faith never occurs in a vacuum; faith occurs in a context, including the real and contested world of politics and economics. It is the vocation of prophetic faith

to interact with the socioeconomic and political realities of the day.

1:3 *The ox knows its owner.* The book of Isaiah opens with a powerful metaphor comparing Israel's relationship to God to the relationship of an ox or a donkey to its owner. But although the ox and donkey naturally know their owner, Israel unnaturally turns away from God. The first section of the book of Isaiah (chaps 1–12) is a meditation upon the costs and risks of turning away from God.

1:9 *we would have been like Sodom.* The poet imagines Jerusalem to be not unlike Sodom and Gomorrah, those most wicked of all cities (Gen 19). The metaphor causes us to look again at the religious practices and certitudes on which we count uncritically. Even Jerusalem, even our best faith, may be seen differently in prophetic perspective.

I do not delight in the blood of bulls,
   or of lambs, or of goats.

12 When you come to appear before me, [a]
   who asked this from your hand?
   Trample my courts no more;
13 bringing offerings is futile;
   incense is an abomination to me.
   New moon and sabbath and calling of
      convocation—
   I cannot endure solemn assemblies
      with iniquity.
14 Your new moons and your appointed
      festivals
   my soul hates;
   they have become a burden to me,
   I am weary of bearing them.
15 When you stretch out your hands,
   I will hide my eyes from you;
   even though you make many prayers,
   I will not listen;
   your hands are full of blood.
16 Wash yourselves; make yourselves
      clean;
   remove the evil of your doings
   from before my eyes;
   cease to do evil,
17   learn to do good;
   seek justice,
      rescue the oppressed,
   defend the orphan,
      plead for the widow.

18 Come now, let us argue it out,
   says the LORD:
   though your sins are like scarlet,

they shall be like snow;
   though they are red like crimson,
   they shall become like wool.
19 If you are willing and obedient,
   you shall eat the good of the land;
20 but if you refuse and rebel,
   you shall be devoured by the sword;
   for the mouth of the LORD has
      spoken.

The Degenerate City

21 How the faithful city
   has become a whore!
   She that was full of justice,
   righteousness lodged in her—
   but now murderers!
22 Your silver has become dross,
   your wine is mixed with water.
23 Your princes are rebels
   and companions of thieves.
   Everyone loves a bribe
   and runs after gifts.
   They do not defend the orphan,
   and the widow's cause does not come
      before them.

24 Therefore says the Sovereign, the LORD
      of hosts, the Mighty One of Israel:
   Ah, I will pour out my wrath on my
      enemies,
   and avenge myself on my foes!
25 I will turn my hand against you;
   I will smelt away your dross as with
      lye
   and remove all your alloy.

a Or see my face

1:12–17 *seek justice, rescue the oppressed, defend the orphan, plead for the widow.* The prophet contrasts two kinds of religion. In verses 12–15, a religion that is essentially manipulative (in its belief that following rituals guarantees God's blessing) is rejected. In verses 16–17, commended is a religion that focuses on a series of imperatives summoning God's people to obedience, focusing particularly on justice toward the oppressed, widows, and orphans, all categories of people who are exceedingly vulnerable and without ordinary social protection. This is a call to make sure our "traditions" are still vitally connected to the kingdom work to which God calls us.

1:21–26 *Afterward you shall be called the city of righteousness.* The poet describes the history of the city of Jerusalem, which begins as a faithful city but becomes disobedient and will be destroyed. Most remarkably, the strong word "afterward" (v 26) indicates the prophetic expectation that after its destruction there will be a new future for the city. This simple "afterward" bespeaks profound prophetic faith and invites us to ponder the ways in which God may cause an end to things we cherish or newness when we thought no newness was possible.

26 And I will restore your judges as at the
    first,
      and your counselors as at the
        beginning.
    Afterward you shall be called the city of
      righteousness,
      the faithful city.

27 Zion shall be redeemed by justice,
    and those in her who repent, by
      righteousness.
28 But rebels and sinners shall be
      destroyed together,
    and those who forsake the LORD shall
      be consumed.
29 For you shall be ashamed of the oaks
      in which you delighted;
    and you shall blush for the gardens
      that you have chosen.
30 For you shall be like an oak
      whose leaf withers,
    and like a garden without water.
31 The strong shall become like tinder,
      and their work[a] like a spark;
    they and their work shall burn together,
      with no one to quench them.

The Future House of God

2 The word that Isaiah son of Amoz saw
   concerning Judah and Jerusalem.

2 In days to come
    the mountain of the LORD's house
  shall be established as the highest of the
    mountains,
    and shall be raised above the hills;

all the nations shall stream to it.
3   Many peoples shall come and say,
    "Come, let us go up to the mountain of
      the LORD,
      to the house of the God of Jacob;
    that he may teach us his ways
      and that we may walk in his paths."
  For out of Zion shall go forth
    instruction,
    and the word of the LORD from
      Jerusalem.
4 He shall judge between the nations,
    and shall arbitrate for many peoples;
  they shall beat their swords into
      plowshares,
    and their spears into pruning hooks;
  nation shall not lift up sword against
    nation,
    neither shall they learn war any
    more.

Judgment Pronounced on Arrogance

5   O house of Jacob,
      come, let us walk
      in the light of the LORD!
6 For you have forsaken the ways of[b] your
        people,
      O house of Jacob.
  Indeed they are full of diviners[c] from
      the east
    and of soothsayers like the Philistines,
    and they clasp hands with foreigners.
7 Their land is filled with silver and gold,
    and there is no end to their treasures;

a Or *its makers*   b Heb lacks *the ways of*
c Cn: Heb lacks *of diviners*

Responding

1:26 MEDITATION. Consider what
your life would be like if there were no
market for your job skills. What effect would
that have on your personal history? What kinds
of things would come to an end? How would
you feel? *See also* Spiritual Disciplines Index.

2:6–4:1 *For you have forsaken the ways of
your people.* This extended unit is a prophetic
poem that anticipates the destruction and
demise of the city of Jerusalem and the collapse
of the political and economic system that was
seated in Jerusalem. It begins with an indictment

of Jerusalem's disobedience in the form of its
preoccupation with silver and gold, horses and
chariots, and idols (2:6–8). The poem then
moves to the powerful intervention by Yahweh
to cause the destruction of all things that were
treasured. The irony is that Jerusalem, which
thought itself to be the beloved city of God, now
becomes the disobedient city that receives God's
judgment. The ferociousness of "the day" ("a
day" in prophetic faith refers to the time when
God will fully assert God's rule in judgment and
in salvation) that is anticipated is reinforced by
the phrase "the LORD of hosts," which refers to
God as a leader of military troops (2:12).

their land is filled with horses,
 and there is no end to their chariots.
8 Their land is filled with idols;
 they bow down to the work of their
  hands,
 to what their own fingers have made.
9 And so people are humbled,
 and everyone is brought low—
 do not forgive them!
10 Enter into the rock,
 and hide in the dust
from the terror of the LORD,
 and from the glory of his majesty.
11 The haughty eyes of people shall be
  brought low,
 and the pride of everyone shall be
  humbled;
and the LORD alone will be exalted on
 that day.
12 For the LORD of hosts has a day
 against all that is proud and lofty,
 against all that is lifted up and high;*a*
13 against all the cedars of Lebanon,
 lofty and lifted up;
 and against all the oaks of Bashan;
14 against all the high mountains,
 and against all the lofty hills;
15 against every high tower,
 and against every fortified wall;
16 against all the ships of Tarshish,
 and against all the beautiful craft.*b*
17 The haughtiness of people shall be
  humbled,
 and the pride of everyone shall be
  brought low;
 and the LORD alone will be exalted on
  that day.
18 The idols shall utterly pass away.
19 Enter the caves of the rocks
 and the holes of the ground,
from the terror of the LORD,
 and from the glory of his majesty,
 when he rises to terrify the earth.
20 On that day people will throw away

to the moles and to the bats
 their idols of silver and their idols of
  gold,
 which they made for themselves to
  worship,
21 to enter the caverns of the rocks
 and the clefts in the crags,
from the terror of the LORD,
 and from the glory of his majesty,
 when he rises to terrify the earth.
22 Turn away from mortals,
 who have only breath in their
  nostrils,
 for of what account are they?

3 For now the Sovereign, the LORD of
  hosts,
 is taking away from Jerusalem and
  from Judah
support and staff—
 all support of bread,
 and all support of water—
2 warrior and soldier,
 judge and prophet,
 diviner and elder,
3 captain of fifty
 and dignitary,
counselor and skillful magician
 and expert enchanter.
4 And I will make boys their princes,
 and babes shall rule over them.
5 The people will be oppressed,
 everyone by another
 and everyone by a neighbor;
the youth will be insolent to the elder,
 and the base to the honorable.

6 Someone will even seize a relative,
 a member of the clan, saying,
"You have a cloak;
 you shall be our leader,
and this heap of ruins

---

a Cn Compare Gk: Heb *low* *b* Compare Gk:
Meaning of Heb uncertain

3:1, 18 *the Sovereign . . . is taking away . . .
the Lord will take away.* The prophet twice uses
the words "take away" to talk about loss in Jerusalem as divine judgment. The verb in verse 1
refers to the loss of the whole social fabric of
the city. The same verb in verse 18 refers to the
loss of all of the finery, which symbolizes the
urban elite's immense self-indulgence. All of
chapter 3 invites us to meditate on the dismay
and demise that come when life is out of sync
with the will of the sovereign God.

shall be under your rule."

7 But the other will cry out on that day,
    saying,
  "I will not be a healer;
    in my house there is neither bread
      nor cloak;
  you shall not make me
    leader of the people."

8 For Jerusalem has stumbled
    and Judah has fallen,
  because their speech and their deeds are
    against the LORD,
    defying his glorious presence.

9 The look on their faces bears witness
    against them;
  they proclaim their sin like Sodom,
    they do not hide it.
  Woe to them!
    For they have brought evil on
      themselves.

10 Tell the innocent how fortunate they
     are,
   for they shall eat the fruit of their
     labors.

11 Woe to the guilty! How unfortunate
     they are,
   for what their hands have done shall
     be done to them.

12 My people—children are their
     oppressors,
   and women rule over them.
   O my people, your leaders mislead you,
     and confuse the course of your paths.

13 The LORD rises to argue his case;
     he stands to judge the peoples.

14 The LORD enters into judgment
     with the elders and princes of his
       people:
   It is you who have devoured the
     vineyard;
     the spoil of the poor is in your houses.

15 What do you mean by crushing my
     people,
   by grinding the face of the poor? says
     the Lord GOD of hosts.

16 The LORD said:
   Because the daughters of Zion are
     haughty

and walk with outstretched necks,
  glancing wantonly with their eyes,
  mincing along as they go,
    tinkling with their feet;
17 the Lord will afflict with scabs
    the heads of the daughters of Zion,
    and the LORD will lay bare their secret
      parts.

18 In that day the Lord will take away the
finery of the anklets, the headbands, and the
crescents; 19the pendants, the bracelets, and
the scarfs; 20the headdresses, the armlets, the
sashes, the perfume boxes, and the amulets;
21the signet rings and nose rings; 22the festal
robes, the mantles, the cloaks, and the hand-
bags; 23the garments of gauze, the linen garments, the turbans, and the veils.

24 Instead of perfume there will be a
      stench;
   and instead of a sash, a rope;
   and instead of well-set hair, baldness;
   and instead of a rich robe, a binding
     of sackcloth;
   instead of beauty, shame. *a*

25 Your men shall fall by the sword
     and your warriors in battle.

26 And her gates shall lament and mourn;
     ravaged, she shall sit upon the
       ground.

4 Seven women shall take hold of one man
   in that day, saying,
 "We will eat our own bread and wear
     our own clothes;
   just let us be called by your name;
     take away our disgrace."

The Future Glory of the Survivors in Zion

2 On that day the branch of the LORD shall
be beautiful and glorious, and the fruit of
the land shall be the pride and glory of the
survivors of Israel. 3Whoever is left in Zion
and remains in Jerusalem will be called holy,
everyone who has been recorded for life in Jerusalem, 4once the Lord has washed away
the filth of the daughters of Zion and
cleansed the bloodstains of Jerusalem from its
midst by a spirit of judgment and by a spirit
of burning. 5Then the LORD will create over
the whole site of Mount Zion and over its

a Q Ms: MT lacks *shame*

places of assembly a cloud by day and smoke and the shining of a flaming fire by night. Indeed over all the glory there will be a canopy. 6It will serve as a pavilion, a shade by day from the heat, and a refuge and a shelter from the storm and rain.

The Song of the Unfruitful Vineyard

5 Let me sing for my beloved
  my love-song concerning his vineyard:
My beloved had a vineyard
  on a very fertile hill.
2 He dug it and cleared it of stones,
  and planted it with choice vines;
he built a watchtower in the midst of it,
  and hewed out a wine vat in it;
he expected it to yield grapes,
  but it yielded wild grapes.

3 And now, inhabitants of Jerusalem
  and people of Judah,
judge between me
  and my vineyard.
4 What more was there to do for my
  vineyard
  that I have not done in it?
When I expected it to yield grapes,
  why did it yield wild grapes?

5 And now I will tell you
  what I will do to my vineyard.
I will remove its hedge,
  and it shall be devoured;
I will break down its wall,

and it shall be trampled down.
6 I will make it a waste;
  it shall not be pruned or hoed,
  and it shall be overgrown with briers
    and thorns;
I will also command the clouds
  that they rain no rain upon it.

7 For the vineyard of the LORD of hosts
  is the house of Israel,
and the people of Judah
  are his pleasant planting;
he expected justice,
  but saw bloodshed;
righteousness,
  but heard a cry!

Social Injustice Denounced

8 Ah, you who join house to house,
  who add field to field,
until there is room for no one but you,
  and you are left to live alone
  in the midst of the land!
9 The LORD of hosts has sworn in my
    hearing:
Surely many houses shall be desolate,
  large and beautiful houses, without
    inhabitant.
10 For ten acres of vineyard shall yield but
    one bath,
  and a homer of seed shall yield a mere
    ephah. a

a The Heb bath, homer, and ephah are measures of quantity

5:1–7 *why did it yield wild grapes?* This poem is a parable that features God as the vineyard keeper and Israel as the vineyard. Through the course of the parable the vineyard keeper goes to great pains to take good care of the vineyard; when the vineyard produces "wild grapes," the keeper abandons the vineyard. This abandonment refers to the exile and the complete abandonment of the city of Jerusalem by God. This imagery of vine keeper and vineyard is picked up and reused in the New Testament in John 15 to describe the relationship between God and the community gathered around Jesus. In both places, the same two points are accented: that the vine is completely dependent upon the vine tree, and that the vine must bear fruit.

5:8–23 *Ah, you who.* The six "woes" in this poem are supplemented by an additional woe in 10:1–7. It is widely thought that the seven together constitute a series. The word "woe" is variously translated "ah" or "alas." It asserts that there is trouble or death to come. In this series of woes, the distorted forms of behavior range from economic exploitation (vv 8–10) to excessive self-indulgence (vv 11–12) to distortion of truth (v 18) and distorted descriptions of reality (vv 20–21). All are acts of disobedience that will evoke God's harsh judgment against the city. The theological point is that the sovereignty of God is strong and clear and cannot be evaded.

ISAIAH

The Charismatic Visionary

Selected Scriptures: *Isaiah 1; 6; 9; 13; 32; 40; 42–44; 53; 57; 65–66*

The holiness of God, judgment, hope, a people transformed by the Spirit of God: these are not only the core of Isaiah's message to Israel; they are the truths God first impressed on Isaiah himself. In his grand vision of God, Isaiah saw God filling the Temple and heard seraphs speaking of God's great holiness. Filled with unworthiness, Isaiah cried out, "Woe is me!" (Isa 6:5), only to find a seraph touching his lips with a live coal from the altar of God, purifying him from his sin.

"Whom shall I send, and who will go for us?" God asked. "Here am I; send me!" Isaiah replied (6:8). He went on to proclaim God's judgment on Israel for its continued unfaithfulness, and then to promise hope for release from the coming captivity and for the future of God's people. Through his vision of God's holiness, his confession of his own sin, and his acceptance of God's cleansing and call, Isaiah received the Spirit to guide him in offering many of the most moving and hope-filled words of the Bible. The Church sees many of Isaiah's prophecies ultimately fulfilled in the person and ministry of Jesus Christ, through whom God did "new things" (42:9) and who came "to bring good news to the oppressed, to bind up the brokenhearted, to proclaim liberty to the captives, and release to the prisoners" (61:1).

Today we might call Isaiah a mystic or a charismatic, or even a Pentecostal. His early vision of God served as vital preparation for his later work. And although he lived many centuries before Pentecost, Isaiah clearly was directed by God's Spirit to carry out his work. Through Isaiah God finally introduced an answer to his people's inability to serve him well. A Savior would come and forever change their relationship to God. Isaiah had a pivotal assignment, and he allowed God to prepare and equip him in powerful ways.

God still uses similar means to guide his people. He may call us to a ministry that is beyond our reach and then, through visions and radical movements of his Spirit, guide us in carrying out that work. Such was the way for William Seymour. Born in the South just after the Civil War, Seymour educated himself and later felt a call to begin a preaching ministry in the North within a denomination committed to holiness and racial inclusiveness. Later he accepted a call to pastor a church in California, and it was here that he experienced a spiritual breakthrough that would help usher in the Azusa Street Revival, the foundational event for the Pentecostal movement.

At a prayer meeting that lasted three days, people were filled with the Holy Spirit and overwhelmed with joy. Many began speaking in tongues, and some were healed. On the third night, Seymour himself had a vision of God's "white-hot brilliance" and divine love. God spoke healing and encouragement to him.

PROFILE

PROFILE

Soon this small group of common working people was joined by crowds of both black and white Christians from every social class, and then nearly every nationality, meeting three times a day. It became a "revolutionary new type of Christian community," born through the power of the Holy Spirit. People began leaving as missionaries to all parts of the world, and a newspaper Seymour started grew to worldwide distribution.

Born to slaves, Seymour "understood Pentecost as a new Jubilee requiring the release of the broken and the bruised from their oppression." He saw the tongues of fire on that occasion to be a sign of an Isaiah-like reconciliation among races and nations and cultures. He also believed all should be free to participate in leadership in response to God's call, irrespective of education, color, or gender. Women were among the most powerful leaders in the Azusa Mission.

Most important, Seymour stressed divine love as the "standard" for all that God was doing. Love was more important than glossolalia (speaking in tongues), for it was the source of all the Spirit's work. Without love anything that might be attributed to the Spirit became meaningless.

Isaiah prophesied in his time, but it would be many years before God's people would take hold of all God intended through his words. Even today Christians lose sight of their call to loose the bonds of injustice, let the oppressed go free, share bread with the hungry, and care for the homeless (58:6–7)—in essence, to live in love. The Azusa movement as well began to find it difficult to live up to the ideal of a revolutionary Christian community. Even before Seymour died, his mission encountered dissension due to the return of racial disunity, and today Seymour's vision for a Body of Christ with no divisions often remains more a dream than a reality.

In light of the work still to be done, may we follow the leading of Isaiah and commit ourselves to being changed by the holiness of God. May we be moved by God's judgment and encouraged by his promises of hope. And may we open ourselves to the Spirit's ministry of love and power in our lives. God has called each of us to a specific work of love in the world, and he awaits our reply. Then, surely, as God promised through Isaiah, God's "light shall break forth like the dawn, and [his] healing shall spring up quickly" (58:8).

Personal Reflection

- Have you experienced anything like Isaiah's vision of God (Isa 6)? How would you compare Isaiah's encounters with God (and his response) to your own experiences of God?
- What has been your understanding of the Holy Spirit's work in the lives of believers? How open are you to letting the Spirit move in powerful and new ways in your life?
- As you consider God's work for you in the world, how you can keep love central in all you do?

11 Ah, you who rise early in the morning
  in pursuit of strong drink,
who linger in the evening
  to be inflamed by wine,
12 whose feasts consist of lyre and harp,
  tambourine and flute and wine,
but who do not regard the deeds of the
  LORD,
  or see the work of his hands!
13 Therefore my people go into exile
  without knowledge;
their nobles are dying of hunger,
  and their multitude is parched with
  thirst.

14 Therefore Sheol has enlarged its
  appetite
and opened its mouth beyond
  measure;
the nobility of Jerusalem*a* and her
  multitude go down,
  her throng and all who exult in her.
15 People are bowed down, everyone is
  brought low,
and the eyes of the haughty are
  humbled.
16 But the LORD of hosts is exalted by
  justice,
  and the Holy God shows himself holy
  by righteousness.
17 Then the lambs shall graze as in their
  pasture,
  fatlings and kids*b* shall feed among
  the ruins.

18 Ah, you who drag iniquity along with
  cords of falsehood,
  who drag sin along as with cart ropes,
19 who say, "Let him make haste,
  let him speed his work
  that we may see it;
let the plan of the Holy One of Israel
  hasten to fulfillment,
  that we may know it!"
20 Ah, you who call evil good
  and good evil,
who put darkness for light
  and light for darkness,
who put bitter for sweet
  and sweet for bitter!
21 Ah, you who are wise in your own eyes,

and shrewd in your own sight!
22 Ah, you who are heroes in drinking
  wine
  and valiant at mixing drink,
23 who acquit the guilty for a bribe,
  and deprive the innocent of their
  rights!

Foreign Invasion Predicted

24 Therefore, as the tongue of fire devours
  the stubble,
  and as dry grass sinks down in the
  flame,
so their root will become rotten,
  and their blossom go up like dust;
for they have rejected the instruction of
  the LORD of hosts,
and have despised the word of the
  Holy One of Israel.

25 Therefore the anger of the LORD was
  kindled against his people,
  and he stretched out his hand against
  them and struck them;
the mountains quaked,
  and their corpses were like refuse
  in the streets.
For all this his anger has not turned
  away,
  and his hand is stretched out still.

26 He will raise a signal for a nation far
  away,
  and whistle for a people at the ends of
  the earth;
Here they come, swiftly, speedily!
27 None of them is weary, none stumbles,
  none slumbers or sleeps,
not a loincloth is loose,
  not a sandal-thong broken;
28 their arrows are sharp,
  all their bows bent,
their horses' hoofs seem like flint,
  and their wheels like the whirlwind.
29 Their roaring is like a lion,
  like young lions they roar;
they growl and seize their prey,
  they carry it off, and no one can
  rescue.

a Heb *her nobility*   *b* Cn Compare Gk: Heb *aliens*

30 They will roar over it on that day,
  like the roaring of the sea.
And if one look to the land—
  only darkness and distress;
and the light grows dark with clouds.

A Vision of God in the Temple

6 In the year that King Uzziah died, I saw
  the Lord sitting on a throne, high and
lofty; and the hem of his robe filled the temple. 2Seraphs were in attendance above him;
each had six wings: with two they covered
their faces, and with two they covered their
feet, and with two they flew. 3And one called
to another and said:

  "Holy, holy, holy is the LORD of hosts;
    the whole earth is full of his glory."

4The pivots a on the thresholds shook at the
voices of those who called, and the house
filled with smoke. 5And I said: "Woe is me! I
am lost, for I am a man of unclean lips, and I
live among a people of unclean lips; yet my
eyes have seen the King, the LORD of hosts!"

6 Then one of the seraphs flew to me,
holding a live coal that had been taken from
the altar with a pair of tongs. 7The seraph b
touched my mouth with it and said: "Now
that this has touched your lips, your guilt
has departed and your sin is blotted out."
8Then I heard the voice of the Lord saying,
"Whom shall I send, and who will go for us?"
And I said, "Here am I; send me!" 9And he
said, "Go and say to this people:

  'Keep listening, but do not
      comprehend;
  keep looking, but do not understand.'
10 Make the mind of this people dull,
    and stop their ears,
    and shut their eyes,
  so that they may not look with their
      eyes,

and listen with their ears,
  and comprehend with their minds,
  and turn and be healed.'"
11 Then I said, "How long, O Lord?" And
  he said:
"Until cities lie waste
    without inhabitant,
  and houses without people,
    and the land is utterly desolate;
12 until the LORD sends everyone far away,
    and vast is the emptiness in the midst
      of the land.
13 Even if a tenth part remain in it,
    it will be burned again,
  like a terebinth or an oak
    whose stump remains standing
    when it is felled." a
The holy seed is its stump.

Isaiah Reassures King Ahaz

7 In the days of Ahaz son of Jotham son
  of Uzziah, king of Judah, King Rezin of
Aram and King Pekah son of Remaliah of
Israel went up to attack Jerusalem, but could
not mount an attack against it. 2When the
house of David heard that Aram had allied
itself with Ephraim, the heart of Ahaz c and
the heart of his people shook as the trees of
the forest shake before the wind.

3 Then the LORD said to Isaiah, Go out to
meet Ahaz, you and your son Shear-jashub, d
at the end of the conduit of the upper pool on
the highway to the Fuller's Field, 4and say to
him, Take heed, be quiet, do not fear, and do
not let your heart be faint because of these
two smoldering stumps of firebrands, because
of the fierce anger of Rezin and Aram and
the son of Remaliah. 5Because Aram—with

a Meaning of Heb uncertain   b Heb He
c Heb his heart   d That is A remnant shall return

6:1–13 *I saw the Lord sitting on a throne.* This
chapter offers a report of Isaiah's "call" describing how he was commissioned into prophetic
ministry. Isaiah's vision of God, articulated in a
great panorama of the heavenly court where
God is ministered to by angels, is summed up in
"Holy, holy, holy," the song sung by the angels
(v 3). Isaiah's response to that vision of God's
holiness is his awareness of his uncleanness, lack
of qualification, and inadequacy. Before the awesome holiness of God, we all stand incompetent
and unqualified to serve. In Isaiah's vision, the
Lord asks the assembly of the heavenly court
whom to send; the prophet answers immediately, "Here am I; send me!" (v 8). God is Isaiah's
competence. And here he models how men and
women of faith are called into ministry. This is
spiritual formation in action.

Ephraim and the son of Remaliah—has plotted evil against you, saying, 6Let us go up against Judah and cut off Jerusalem*a* and conquer it for ourselves and make the son of Tabeel king in it; 7therefore thus says the Lord GOD:

It shall not stand,
    and it shall not come to pass.
8 For the head of Aram is Damascus,
    and the head of Damascus is Rezin.
(Within sixty-five years Ephraim will be shattered, no longer a people.)
9 The head of Ephraim is Samaria,
    and the head of Samaria is the son of Remaliah.
If you do not stand firm in faith,
    you shall not stand at all.

Isaiah Gives Ahaz the Sign of Immanuel

10 Again the LORD spoke to Ahaz, saying, 11Ask a sign of the LORD your God; let it be deep as Sheol or high as heaven. 12But Ahaz said, I will not ask, and I will not put the LORD to the test. 13Then Isaiah*b* said: "Hear then, O house of David! Is it too little for you to weary mortals, that you weary my God also? 14Therefore the Lord himself will give you a sign. Look, the young woman*c* is with child and shall bear a son, and shall name him Immanuel.*d* 15He shall eat curds and honey by the time he knows how to refuse the evil and choose the good. 16For before the child knows

how to refuse the evil and choose the good, the land before whose two kings you are in dread will be deserted. 17The LORD will bring on you and on your people and on your ancestral house such days as have not come since the day that Ephraim departed from Judah—the king of Assyria."

18 On that day the LORD will whistle for the fly that is at the sources of the streams of Egypt, and for the bee that is in the land of Assyria. 19And they will all come and settle in the steep ravines, and in the clefts of the rocks, and on all the thornbushes, and on all the pastures.

20 On that day the Lord will shave with a razor hired beyond the River—with the king of Assyria—the head and the hair of the feet, and it will take off the beard as well.

21 On that day one will keep alive a young cow and two sheep, 22and will eat curds because of the abundance of milk that they give; for everyone that is left in the land shall eat curds and honey.

23 On that day every place where there used to be a thousand vines, worth a thousand shekels of silver, will become briers and thorns. 24With bow and arrows one will go there, for all the land will be briers and thorns; 25and as for all the hills that used to

a Heb *cut it off*   *b* Heb *he*   *c* Gk *the virgin*
d That is *God is with us*

7:1–9 *If you do not stand firm in faith, you shall not stand at all.* The encounter between Isaiah and King Ahaz takes place while Jerusalem is surrounded by hostile armies and, consequently, faces an acute water shortage. The king is consumed with anxiety and fear. The oracle in verses 7–9 is intended to reassure the king that he and Jerusalem will be safe. Particular attention should be paid to the last two lines of verse 9, because they are commonly taken to be among the most characteristic, almost signature verses, of the prophet Isaiah. They tell us that faithful trust in Yahweh is required in order to be safe at all in the world. Faith here is not simply an emotional or psychological assurance; rather, it pertains directly to the public policy questions at hand.

7:14 *the young woman is with child and shall*

bear a son, and shall name him Immanuel. This verse is among the most famous and curious verses in all of the book of Isaiah. Note that the name shall be Immanuel. It means "God with us." The prophet Isaiah, more than any other, wants to affirm that God is indeed present with and for Jerusalem.

Responding
7:14 THE WITH-GOD LIFE. As the prophet affirmed that God was present with and for Jerusalem, Christians affirm that Jesus Christ is Immanuel, "God with us." At the next meeting of your small group or with a special friend describe a time when God made a difference in the life of your church or community with his presence. *See also* Spiritual Disciplines Index.

be hoed with a hoe, you will not go there for fear of briers and thorns; but they will become a place where cattle are let loose and where sheep tread.

Isaiah's Son a Sign of the Assyrian Invasion

8 Then the LORD said to me, Take a large tablet and write on it in common characters, "Belonging to Maher-shalal-hash-baz," [a] 2and have it attested [b] for me by reliable witnesses, the priest Uriah and Zechariah son of Jeberechiah. 3And I went to the prophetess, and she conceived and bore a son. Then the LORD said to me, Name him Maher-shal-al-hash-baz; 4for before the child knows how to call "My father" or "My mother," the wealth of Damascus and the spoil of Samaria will be carried away by the king of Assyria.

5 The LORD spoke to me again: 6Because this people has refused the waters of Shiloah that flow gently, and melt in fear before [c] Rezin and the son of Remaliah; 7therefore, the Lord is bringing up against it the mighty flood waters of the River, the king of Assyria and all his glory; it will rise above all its channels and overflow all its banks; 8it will sweep on into Judah as a flood, and, pouring over, it will reach up to the neck; and its outspread wings will fill the breadth of your land, O Immanuel.

9 Band together, you peoples, and be dismayed;
　　listen, all you far countries;
　　gird yourselves and be dismayed;
　　gird yourselves and be dismayed!
10 Take counsel together, but it shall be brought to naught;
　　speak a word, but it will not stand,
　　for God is with us. [d]

11 For the LORD spoke thus to me while his hand was strong upon me, and warned me not to walk in the way of this people, saying: 12Do not call conspiracy all that this people calls conspiracy, and do not fear what it fears, or be in dread. 13But the LORD of hosts, him you shall regard as holy; let him be your fear, and let him be your dread. 14He will become a sanctuary, a stone one strikes against; for both houses of Israel he will become a rock one stumbles over—a trap and a snare for the inhabitants of Jerusalem. 15And many among them shall stumble; they shall fall and be broken; they shall be snared and taken.

Disciples of Isaiah

16 Bind up the testimony, seal the teaching among my disciples. 17I will wait for the LORD, who is hiding his face from the house of Jacob, and I will hope in him. 18See, I and the children whom the LORD has given me are signs and portents in Israel from the LORD of hosts, who dwells on Mount Zion. 19Now if people say to you, "Consult the ghosts and

a That is *The spoil speeds, the prey hastens*
b Q Ms Gk Syr: MT *and I caused to be attested*
c Cn: Meaning of Heb uncertain
d Heb *immanu el*

8:1–4 *Maher-shalal-hash-baz.* In this passage, the prophet is preoccupied with communicating to the Jerusalem leadership that Assyria is being dispatched by God to judge and destroy the city. One rhetorical strategy for announcing that coming threat is to name the prophet's own children with slogans that allude to the military trouble to come. Thus the name "Maher-shalal-hash-baz" is in fact four Hebrew words strung together, meaning "spoil speeds, prey hastens" (v 1). With great speed the plunderers from Assyria are coming. They will plunder the city of Jerusalem and take away the valuable spoils they seek. This name, then, is quite ominous and is to be seen alongside the name Immanuel in 7:14, where

the same rhetorical strategy of naming is employed.

8:5–10 *this people has refused the waters of Shiloah.* This prophetic oracle nicely contrasts the "waters of Shiloah that flow gently" and "the mighty flood waters of the River [Euphrates], the king of Assyria and all his glory." Had Jerusalem chosen to be obedient to Yahweh, it would have in fact chosen a gentle stream of *shalom* ("peace"); since it did not, Jerusalem will, instead, receive the torrential, raging waters of the Euphrates, a metaphor for the king of Assyria, who is coming soon to threaten the city of Jerusalem. Jerusalem, charged with choosing life or death in terms of Yahweh's will, has now forfeited its chance to choose life.

the familiar spirits that chirp and mutter; should not a people consult their gods, the dead on behalf of the living, [20]for teaching and for instruction?" surely, those who speak like this will have no dawn! [21]They will pass through the land,[a] greatly distressed and hungry; when they are hungry, they will be enraged and will curse[b] their king and their gods. They will turn their faces upward, [22]or they will look to the earth, but will see only distress and darkness, the gloom of anguish; and they will be thrust into thick darkness.[c]

The Righteous Reign of the Coming King

9[d] But there will be no gloom for those who were in anguish. In the former time he brought into contempt the land of Zebulun and the land of Naphtali, but in the latter time he will make glorious the way of the sea, the land beyond the Jordan, Galilee of the nations.

[2][e] The people who walked in darkness
       have seen a great light;
    those who lived in a land of deep
       darkness—
       on them light has shined.
[3] You have multiplied the nation,

you have increased its joy;
they rejoice before you
    as with joy at the harvest,
    as people exult when dividing
       plunder.
[4] For the yoke of their burden,
    and the bar across their shoulders,
    the rod of their oppressor,
    you have broken as on the day of
       Midian.
[5] For all the boots of the tramping
       warriors
    and all the garments rolled in blood
    shall be burned as fuel for the fire.
[6] For a child has been born for us,
    a son given to us;
    authority rests upon his shoulders;
    and he is named
    Wonderful Counselor, Mighty God,
       Everlasting Father, Prince of Peace.
[7] His authority shall grow continually,
    and there shall be endless peace
    for the throne of David and his
       kingdom.
    He will establish and uphold it

a Heb *it*   b Or *curse by*   c Meaning of Heb uncertain   d Ch 8.23 in Heb   e Ch 9.1 in Heb

---

9:2–7 *Wonderful Counselor.* This well-known oracle of promise stands in sharp contrast to the ominous threats delivered in chapter 8. This divine oracle announces that there will be a new king in Jerusalem who will have the authority and the muscle to fend off the "rod of their oppressor," which in context is probably Assyria. A radical transformation is about to happen— from darkness to light, from sadness to joy, from oppression to freedom, from war to peace (vv 2–5). The reason for this newness is the birth of a child (v 6). In its original context this probably refers to the birth or the coronation of a new king, most likely Hezekiah, who succeeded his father, Ahab, who was not a very effective king. The four titles at the end of verse 6, made familiar to us through Handel's *Messiah*, are characteristic royal titles that would have been used in a coronation ceremony. They are not unlike the elaborate titles of imperial majesty assigned to Queen Victoria in the high days of the British Empire. The final verse, then, anticipates the expansion of the new king's kingdom, which will be marked by justice and righteousness, a governance accomplished by God's own will. In Christian reading this promise of a king in Jerusalem from the Davidic dynasty has been reread with reference to Jesus, as though the prophet were anticipating the coming of Jesus. Although a reference to Jesus is clearly a secondary interpretive maneuver that does not pertain to the historical intention of the prophet himself, it is a long-established and useful reading in church practice. Often referred to in interpretive theory as the "prophetic perspective," this approach sees a double fulfillment in the prophet's words— the primary and immediate historical context and also a more distant messianic reference. We may see in this passage (with reference both to Hezekiah and then to Jesus the Messiah) that God designates human agents whom he empowers and authorizes in the public process of history. Such human agents designated by Yahweh turn the public reality of politics and economics toward the will of Yahweh.

praise god

with justice and with righteousness
  from this time onward and
    forevermore.
The zeal of the LORD of hosts will do
  this.

Judgment on Arrogance and Oppression

8 The Lord sent a word against Jacob,
    and it fell on Israel;
9 and all the people knew it—
    Ephraim and the inhabitants of
      Samaria—
    but in pride and arrogance of heart
      they said:
10 "The bricks have fallen,
    but we will build with dressed
      stones;
    the sycamores have been cut down,
    but we will put cedars in their
      place."
11 So the LORD raised adversaries*a* against
      them,
    and stirred up their enemies,
12 the Arameans on the east and the
      Philistines on the west,
    and they devoured Israel with open
      mouth.
For all this his anger has not turned
      away;
    his hand is stretched out still.

13 The people did not turn to him who
      struck them,
    or seek the LORD of hosts.
14 So the LORD cut off from Israel head and
      tail,
    palm branch and reed in one day—
15 elders and dignitaries are the head,
    and prophets who teach lies are the
      tail;
16 for those who led this people led them
      astray,
    and those who were led by them were
      left in confusion.
17 That is why the Lord did not have pity
    on*b* their young people,
    or compassion on their orphans and
      widows;
for everyone was godless and an
      evildoer,
    and every mouth spoke folly.

For all this his anger has not turned
      away;
    his hand is stretched out still.

18 For wickedness burned like a fire,
    consuming briers and thorns;
    it kindled the thickets of the forest,
    and they swirled upward in a column
      of smoke.
19 Through the wrath of the LORD of hosts
    the land was burned,
    and the people became like fuel for the
      fire;
    no one spared another.
20 They gorged on the right, but still were
      hungry,
    and they devoured on the left, but
      were not satisfied;
    they devoured the flesh of their own
      kindred;*c*
21 Manasseh devoured Ephraim, and
      Ephraim Manasseh,
    and together they were against
      Judah.
For all this his anger has not turned
      away;
    his hand is stretched out still.

10 Ah, you who make iniquitous
      decrees,
    who write oppressive statutes,
2 to turn aside the needy from justice
    and to rob the poor of my people of
      their right,
    that widows may be your spoil,
    and that you may make the orphans
      your prey!
3 What will you do on the day of
      punishment,
    in the calamity that will come from
      far away?
To whom will you flee for help,
    and where will you leave your wealth,
4 so as not to crouch among the prisoners
    or fall among the slain?
For all this his anger has not turned
      away;
    his hand is stretched out still.

a Cn: Heb *the adversaries of Rezin*   *b* Q Ms: MT
rejoice over   *c* Or *arm*

Arrogant Assyria Also Judged

5 Ah, Assyria, the rod of my anger—
        the club in their hands is my fury!
6 Against a godless nation I send him,
        and against the people of my wrath I
            command him,
    to take spoil and seize plunder,
        and to tread them down like the mire
            of the streets.
7 But this is not what he intends,
        nor does he have this in mind;
    but it is in his heart to destroy,
        and to cut off nations not a few.
8 For he says:
    "Are not my commanders all kings?
9 Is not Calno like Carchemish?
        Is not Hamath like Arpad?
        Is not Samaria like Damascus?
10 As my hand has reached to the
            kingdoms of the idols
        whose images were greater than those
            of Jerusalem and Samaria,
11 shall I not do to Jerusalem and her idols
        what I have done to Samaria and her
            images?"

12 When the Lord has finished all his work
on Mount Zion and on Jerusalem, he*a* will
punish the arrogant boasting of the king of
Assyria and his haughty pride. 13For he says:
    "By the strength of my hand I have
            done it,
        and by my wisdom, for I have
            understanding;
    I have removed the boundaries of
            peoples,
        and have plundered their treasures;
        like a bull I have brought down those
            who sat on thrones.
14 My hand has found, like a nest,
        the wealth of the peoples;

and as one gathers eggs that have been
        forsaken,
    so I have gathered all the earth;
    and there was none that moved a wing,
        or opened its mouth, or chirped."

15 Shall the ax vaunt itself over the one
        who wields it,
        or the saw magnify itself against the
            one who handles it?
    As if a rod should raise the one who lifts
        it up,
        or as if a staff should lift the one who
            is not wood!
16 Therefore the Sovereign, the LORD of
            hosts,
        will send wasting sickness among his
            stout warriors,
    and under his glory a burning will be
            kindled,
        like the burning of fire.
17 The light of Israel will become a fire,
        and his Holy One a flame;
    and it will burn and devour
        his thorns and briers in one day.
18 The glory of his forest and his fruitful
            land
        the LORD will destroy, both soul and
            body,
    and it will be as when an invalid
            wastes away.
19 The remnant of the trees of his forest
        will be so few
        that a child can write them down.

The Repentant Remnant of Israel

20 On that day the remnant of Israel and
the survivors of the house of Jacob will no
more lean on the one who struck them, but

a Heb *I*

10:5–19 *Ah, Assyria, the rod of my anger.* This
oracle is a critical prophetic reflection upon
God's relationship to foreign powers. This
particular oracle reveals that God has recruited
Assyria, the great superpower of the eighth
century BC in the Fertile Crescent, to punish
God's people Israel. The accusation against
Assyria, however, is that Assyria did not respect
the limits or the intention of Yahweh and acted
in arrogance, so that the superpower in turn
stands under the judgment of God. The
extended oracle suggests that God's sovereignty
keeps the political and military ambitions of all
states penultimate. The relationship of such a
state to God is like the ax and the one who
wields the ax (v 15). This is a harsh and
concrete reflection on the sovereignty of God
over the public process.

will lean on the LORD, the Holy One of Israel, in truth. ²¹A remnant will return, the remnant of Jacob, to the mighty God. ²²For though your people Israel were like the sand of the sea, only a remnant of them will return. Destruction is decreed, overflowing with righteousness. ²³For the Lord GOD of hosts will make a full end, as decreed, in all the earth. ᵃ

24 Therefore thus says the Lord GOD of hosts: O my people, who live in Zion, do not be afraid of the Assyrians when they beat you with a rod and lift up their staff against you as the Egyptians did. ²⁵For in a very little while my indignation will come to an end, and my anger will be directed to their destruction. ²⁶The LORD of hosts will wield a whip against them, as when he struck Midian at the rock of Oreb; his staff will be over the sea, and he will lift it as he did in Egypt. ²⁷On that day his burden will be removed from your shoulder, and his yoke will be destroyed from your neck.

He has gone up from Rimmon, ᵇ
28   he has come to Aiath;
   he has passed through Migron,
      at Michmash he stores his baggage;
²⁹ they have crossed over the pass,
      at Geba they lodge for the night;
   Ramah trembles,
      Gibeah of Saul has fled.
³⁰ Cry aloud, O daughter Gallim!
   Listen, O Laishah!
   Answer her, O Anathoth!
³¹ Madmenah is in flight,
      the inhabitants of Gebim flee for
      safety.
³² This very day he will halt at Nob,

he will shake his fist
   at the mount of daughter Zion,
   the hill of Jerusalem.

³³ Look, the Sovereign, the LORD of hosts,
   will lop the boughs with terrifying
      power;
   the tallest trees will be cut down,
      and the lofty will be brought low.
³⁴ He will hack down the thickets of the
      forest with an ax,
   and Lebanon with its majestic trees ᶜ
      will fall.

The Peaceful Kingdom

11 A shoot shall come out from the
   stump of Jesse,
and a branch shall grow out of his
   roots.
² The spirit of the LORD shall rest on him,
   the spirit of wisdom and
      understanding,
   the spirit of counsel and might,
   the spirit of knowledge and the fear of
      the LORD.
³ His delight shall be in the fear of the
   LORD.

He shall not judge by what his eyes see,
   or decide by what his ears hear;
⁴ but with righteousness he shall judge
      the poor,
   and decide with equity for the meek
      of the earth;
he shall strike the earth with the rod of
   his mouth,

a Or *land*   b Cn: Heb *and his yoke from your neck, and a yoke will be destroyed because of fatness*
c Cn Compare Gk Vg: Heb *with a majestic one*

10:20–23 *survivors.* This reflection on the remnant of Israel indicates that after the terrible calamity of the exile there will continue to be a faithful community of Israel. Although the oracle is an assurance to Israel, the main claim is that God is trustworthy even amid the deepest calamity of God's people.
11:1–9 *The spirit of the LORD shall rest on him.* This oracle anticipates a new king coming out of the line of Jesse, who was the father of David. It seems to reflect a time when the monarchy had

failed; still, it promises that the dynasty of David will continue. The early Church reinterpreted this promise as a promise of the coming Messiah (see Rom 15:12). The oracle describes the expected and long-awaited king as one who will be infused with God's Spirit and who will practice justice and righteousness toward the needy of the earth. A special dimension of this promise is that the coming expected king will not only rejuvenate the social process but also heal creation and cause all of creation to be reconciled (vv 6–9).

and with the breath of his lips he
    shall kill the wicked.
5 Righteousness shall be the belt around
    his waist,
    and faithfulness the belt around his
        loins.

6 The wolf shall live with the lamb,
    the leopard shall lie down with the
        kid,
    the calf and the lion and the fatling
        together,
    and a little child shall lead them.
7 The cow and the bear shall graze,
    their young shall lie down together;
    and the lion shall eat straw like the
        ox.
8 The nursing child shall play over the
        hole of the asp,
    and the weaned child shall put its
        hand on the adder's den.
9 They will not hurt or destroy
    on all my holy mountain;
    for the earth will be full of the
        knowledge of the LORD
    as the waters cover the sea.

Return of the Remnant of Israel and Judah

10 On that day the root of Jesse shall stand
as a signal to the peoples; the nations shall
inquire of him, and his dwelling shall be glorious.

11 On that day the Lord will extend his
hand yet a second time to recover the remnant that is left of his people, from Assyria,
from Egypt, from Pathros, from Ethiopia,[a]
from Elam, from Shinar, from Hamath, and
from the coastlands of the sea.
12 He will raise a signal for the nations,
    and will assemble the outcasts of
        Israel,
    and gather the dispersed of Judah
        from the four corners of the earth.
13 The jealousy of Ephraim shall depart,
    the hostility of Judah shall be cut off;
    Ephraim shall not be jealous of Judah,

and Judah shall not be hostile towards
        Ephraim.
14 But they shall swoop down on the backs
        of the Philistines in the west,
    together they shall plunder the
        people of the east.
    They shall put forth their hand against
        Edom and Moab,
    and the Ammonites shall obey them.
15 And the LORD will utterly destroy
    the tongue of the sea of Egypt;
    and will wave his hand over the River
        with his scorching wind;
    and will split it into seven channels,
    and make a way to cross on foot;
16 so there shall be a highway from Assyria
    for the remnant that is left of his
        people,
    as there was for Israel
    when they came up from the land of
        Egypt.

Thanksgiving and Praise

12 You will say in that day:
    I will give thanks to you, O LORD,
    for though you were angry with me,
    your anger turned away,
    and you comforted me.

2 Surely God is my salvation;
    I will trust, and will not be afraid,
    for the LORD GOD[b] is my strength and
        my might;
    he has become my salvation.

3 With joy you will draw water from the
wells of salvation. 4And you will say in that
day:
    Give thanks to the LORD,
        call on his name;
    make known his deeds among the
        nations;
    proclaim that his name is exalted.

a Or *Nubia*; Heb *Cush*   b Heb *for Yah, the* LORD

12:1–6 *I will give thanks.* This brief hymnic
poem concludes the first section of the book of
Isaiah. This particular oracle celebrates the

coming goodness by the phrase "in that day"
(vv 1, 4). The God of the Bible is indeed the God
of the good future.

5 Sing praises to the LORD, for he has done
  gloriously;
    let this be known[a] in all the earth.
6 Shout aloud and sing for joy, O royal[b]
  Zion,
    for great in your midst is the Holy
      One of Israel.

Proclamation against Babylon

13 The oracle concerning Babylon that
     Isaiah son of Amoz saw.

2 On a bare hill raise a signal,
    cry aloud to them;
  wave the hand for them to enter
    the gates of the nobles.
3 I myself have commanded my
    consecrated ones,
  have summoned my warriors, my
    proudly exulting ones,
  to execute my anger.

4 Listen, a tumult on the mountains
    as of a great multitude!
  Listen, an uproar of kingdoms,
    of nations gathering together!
  The LORD of hosts is mustering
    an army for battle.
5 They come from a distant land,
    from the end of the heavens,
  the LORD and the weapons of his
    indignation,
  to destroy the whole earth.

6 Wail, for the day of the LORD is near;
    it will come like destruction from the
      Almighty![c]
7 Therefore all hands will be feeble,

and every human heart will melt,
8   and they will be dismayed.
  Pangs and agony will seize them;
    they will be in anguish like a woman
      in labor.
  They will look aghast at one another;
    their faces will be aflame.
9 See, the day of the LORD comes,
    cruel, with wrath and fierce anger,
  to make the earth a desolation,
    and to destroy its sinners from it.
10 For the stars of the heavens and their
      constellations
    will not give their light;
  the sun will be dark at its rising,
    and the moon will not shed its light.
11 I will punish the world for its evil,
    and the wicked for their iniquity;
  I will put an end to the pride of the
      arrogant,
    and lay low the insolence of tyrants.
12 I will make mortals more rare than fine
      gold,
    and humans than the gold of Ophir.
13 Therefore I will make the heavens
      tremble,
  and the earth will be shaken out of its
      place,
  at the wrath of the LORD of hosts
    in the day of his fierce anger.
14 Like a hunted gazelle,
    or like sheep with no one to gather
      them,
  all will turn to their own people,
    and all will flee to their own lands.

a Or this is made known   b Or O inhabitant of
c Traditional rendering of Heb Shaddai

13:1–23:18 *The oracle concerning.* The
oracles in this second section of the book are a
part of the recurring genre "oracles against the
nations" (see also Jer 46–51; Ezek 25–32; Amos
1–2). By enumerating many of the nation-states
around Judah, each of which stands under
judgment from God, the oracles make the
theological point that all nations are subject to
the sovereign will of God and look to a time
when the whole world will be brought under
God's good rule. Therefore, all nations are
candidates for the judgment of God, because

they have not been responsive to God's will,
have been arrogant in their power, and have
operated with a false sense of autonomy. The
importance of these texts for theological
reflection is that readers rethink the public
dimension of biblical faith in which God is
indeed a key player in the affairs of the nations.

13:1–22 *to execute my anger.* It is of course
not unimportant or accidental that the first of
the oracles against the nations is against Babylon,
the imperial state that most preoccupied the
tradition of Isaiah.

¹⁵ Whoever is found will be thrust
        through,
    and whoever is caught will fall by the
        sword.
¹⁶ Their infants will be dashed to pieces
        before their eyes;
    their houses will be plundered,
        and their wives ravished.
¹⁷ See, I am stirring up the Medes against
        them,
    who have no regard for silver
        and do not delight in gold.
¹⁸ Their bows will slaughter the young
        men;
    they will have no mercy on the fruit
        of the womb;
    their eyes will not pity children.
¹⁹ And Babylon, the glory of kingdoms,
        the splendor and pride of the
        Chaldeans,
    will be like Sodom and Gomorrah
        when God overthrew them.
²⁰ It will never be inhabited
        or lived in for all generations;
    Arabs will not pitch their tents there,
        shepherds will not make their flocks
        lie down there.
²¹ But wild animals will lie down there,
        and its houses will be full of howling
        creatures;
    there ostriches will live,
        and there goat-demons will dance.
²² Hyenas will cry in its towers,
        and jackals in the pleasant palaces;
    its time is close at hand,
        and its days will not be prolonged.

Restoration of Judah

14 But the LORD will have compassion on
        Jacob and will again choose Israel, and
will set them in their own land; and aliens
will join them and attach themselves to the
house of Jacob. ²And the nations will take
them and bring them to their place, and the
house of Israel will possess the nations[a] as
male and female slaves in the LORD's land; they

will take captive those who were their captors,
and rule over those who oppressed them.

Downfall of the King of Babylon

3 When the LORD has given you rest from
your pain and turmoil and the hard service
with which you were made to serve, ⁴you
will take up this taunt against the king of
Babylon:

    How the oppressor has ceased!
        How his insolence[b] has ceased!
⁵ The LORD has broken the staff of the
        wicked,
    the scepter of rulers,
⁶ that struck down the peoples in wrath
        with unceasing blows,
    that ruled the nations in anger
        with unrelenting persecution.
⁷ The whole earth is at rest and quiet;
        they break forth into singing.
⁸ The cypresses exult over you,
        the cedars of Lebanon, saying,
    "Since you were laid low,
        no one comes to cut us down."
⁹ Sheol beneath is stirred up
        to meet you when you come;
    it rouses the shades to greet you,
        all who were leaders of the earth;
    it raises from their thrones
        all who were kings of the nations.
¹⁰ All of them will speak
        and say to you:
    "You too have become as weak as we!
        You have become like us!"
¹¹ Your pomp is brought down to Sheol,
        and the sound of your harps;
    maggots are the bed beneath you,
        and worms are your covering.

¹² How you are fallen from heaven,
        O Day Star, son of Dawn!
    How you are cut down to the ground,
        you who laid the nations low!

a Heb *them*   b Q Ms Compare Gk Syr Vg:
Meaning of MT uncertain

13:19 *Babylon . . . will be like Sodom and
Gomorrah.* It is shocking that the oracle would
liken the capital city of Babylon to Sodom and
Gomorrah. We have already seen in 1:10 that

Jerusalem is also reckoned to be like Sodom and
Gomorrah. In both cases the usage of "Sodom
and Gomorrah" signifies the practice of extreme
evil and the fate of extreme judgment.

13 You said in your heart,
  "I will ascend to heaven;
 I will raise my throne
   above the stars of God;
 I will sit on the mount of assembly
   on the heights of Zaphon; *a*
14 I will ascend to the tops of the clouds,
   I will make myself like the Most
     High."
15 But you are brought down to Sheol,
   to the depths of the Pit.
16 Those who see you will stare at you,
   and ponder over you:
 "Is this the man who made the earth
     tremble,
   who shook kingdoms,
17 who made the world like a desert
   and overthrew its cities,
   who would not let his prisoners go
     home?"
18 All the kings of the nations lie in glory,
   each in his own tomb;
19 but you are cast out, away from your
     grave,
   like loathsome carrion, *b*
 clothed with the dead, those pierced by
     the sword,
   who go down to the stones of the Pit,
   like a corpse trampled underfoot.
20 You will not be joined with them in
     burial,
   because you have destroyed your
     land,
   you have killed your people.

 May the descendants of evildoers
   nevermore be named!
21 Prepare slaughter for his sons
   because of the guilt of their father. *c*
 Let them never rise to possess the earth
   or cover the face of the world with
     cities.

22 I will rise up against them, says the
LORD of hosts, and will cut off from Babylon
name and remnant, offspring and posterity,
says the LORD. 23And I will make it a possession of the hedgehog, and pools of water,
and I will sweep it with the broom of destruction, says the LORD of hosts.

An Oracle concerning Assyria

24 The LORD of hosts has sworn:
 As I have designed,
   so shall it be;
 and as I have planned,
   so shall it come to pass:
25 I will break the Assyrian in my land,
   and on my mountains trample him
     under foot;
 his yoke shall be removed from them,
   and his burden from their shoulders.
26 This is the plan that is planned
   concerning the whole earth;
 and this is the hand that is stretched
     out
   over all the nations.
27 For the LORD of hosts has planned,
   and who will annul it?
 His hand is stretched out,
   and who will turn it back?

An Oracle concerning Philistia

28In the year that King Ahaz died this oracle
came:

29 Do not rejoice, all you Philistines,
   that the rod that struck you is broken,
 for from the root of the snake will come
     forth an adder,
   and its fruit will be a flying fiery
     serpent.
30 The firstborn of the poor will graze,
   and the needy lie down in safety;
 but I will make your root die of famine,
   and your remnant I *d* will kill.
31 Wail, O gate; cry, O city;
   melt in fear, O Philistia, all of you!
 For smoke comes out of the north,
   and there is no straggler in its ranks.

a Or *assembly in the far north*   *b* Cn Compare
Gk: Heb *like a loathed branch*   *c* Syr Compare Gk:
Heb *fathers*   *d* Q Ms Vg: MT *he*

14:26–27. *This is the plan.* The use of the word
"plan" does not indicate a predetermined scheme
of things. Rather, it points to the intentionality
of God for the well-being of the earth, an
intentionality that cannot be resisted by any
rebellious nation-state.

32 What will one answer the messengers of
      the nation?
   "The LORD has founded Zion,
      and the needy among his people
      will find refuge in her."

An Oracle concerning Moab ③

15
   An oracle concerning Moab.

   Because Ar is laid waste in a night,
      Moab is undone;
   because Kir is laid waste in a night,
      Moab is undone.
2 Dibon*a* has gone up to the temple,
      to the high places to weep;
   over Nebo and over Medeba
      Moab wails.
   On every head is baldness,
      every beard is shorn;
3 in the streets they bind on sackcloth;
      on the housetops and in the squares
      everyone wails and melts in tears.
4 Heshbon and Elealeh cry out,
      their voices are heard as far as Jahaz;
   therefore the loins of Moab quiver;*b*
      his soul trembles.
5 My heart cries out for Moab;
      his fugitives flee to Zoar,
      to Eglath-shelishiyah.
   For at the ascent of Luhith
      they go up weeping;
   on the road to Horonaim
      they raise a cry of destruction;
6 the waters of Nimrim
      are a desolation;
   the grass is withered, the new growth
         fails,
      the verdure is no more.
7 Therefore the abundance they have
         gained
      and what they have laid up
   they carry away
      over the Wadi of the Willows.
8 For a cry has gone
      around the land of Moab;
   the wailing reaches to Eglaim,
      the wailing reaches to Beer-elim.
9 For the waters of Dibon*c* are full of
         blood;
      yet I will bring upon Dibon*c* even
         more—

a lion for those of Moab who escape,
   for the remnant of the land.

16
   Send lambs
   to the ruler of the land,
   from Sela, by way of the desert,
      to the mount of daughter Zion.
2 Like fluttering birds,
      like scattered nestlings,
   so are the daughters of Moab
      at the fords of the Arnon.
3 "Give counsel,
      grant justice;
   make your shade like night
      at the height of noon;
   hide the outcasts,
      do not betray the fugitive;
4 let the outcasts of Moab
      settle among you;
   be a refuge to them
      from the destroyer."

   When the oppressor is no more,
      and destruction has ceased,
   and marauders have vanished from the
         land,
5 then a throne shall be established in
         steadfast love
      in the tent of David,
   and on it shall sit in faithfulness
   a ruler who seeks justice
      and is swift to do what is right.

6 We have heard of the pride of Moab
      —how proud he is!—
   of his arrogance, his pride, and his
         insolence;
      his boasts are false.
7 Therefore let Moab wail,
      let everyone wail for Moab.
   Mourn, utterly stricken,
      for the raisin cakes of Kir-hareseth.

8 For the fields of Heshbon languish,
      and the vines of Sibmah,
   whose clusters once made drunk
      the lords of the nations,
   reached to Jazer
      and strayed to the desert;

a Cn: Heb *the house and Dibon*   b Cn Compare
Gk Syr: Heb *the armed men of Moab cry aloud*
c Q Ms Vg Compare Syr: MT *Dimon*

their shoots once spread abroad
    and crossed over the sea.
9 Therefore I weep with the weeping of
    Jazer
  for the vines of Sibmah;
I drench you with my tears,
  O Heshbon and Elealeh;
for the shout over your fruit harvest
  and your grain harvest has ceased.
10 Joy and gladness are taken away
    from the fruitful field;
and in the vineyards no songs are sung,
  no shouts are raised;
no treader treads out wine in the
    presses;
  the vintage-shout is hushed. *a*
11 Therefore my heart throbs like a harp
    for Moab,
  and my very soul for Kir-heres.

12 When Moab presents himself, when
he wearies himself upon the high place, when
he comes to his sanctuary to pray, he will not
prevail.

13 This was the word that the LORD spoke
concerning Moab in the past. 14 But now the
LORD says, In three years, like the years of a
hired worker, the glory of Moab will be
brought into contempt, in spite of all its great
multitude; and those who survive will be
very few and feeble.

An Oracle concerning Damascus

17 An oracle concerning Damascus.

See, Damascus will cease to be a city,
  and will become a heap of ruins.
2 Her towns will be deserted forever; *b*
  they will be places for flocks,
which will lie down, and no one will
    make them afraid.
3 The fortress will disappear from
    Ephraim,
  and the kingdom from Damascus;
and the remnant of Aram will be
  like the glory of the children of Israel,
    says the LORD of hosts.

4 On that day
  the glory of Jacob will be brought low,
  and the fat of his flesh will grow lean.
5 And it shall be as when reapers gather
    standing grain
  and their arms harvest the ears,
and as when one gleans the ears of
    grain
  in the Valley of Rephaim.
6 Gleanings will be left in it,
  as when an olive tree is beaten—
two or three berries
  in the top of the highest bough,
four or five
  on the branches of a fruit tree,
    says the LORD God of Israel.

7 On that day people will regard their
Maker, and their eyes will look to the Holy
One of Israel; 8 they will not have regard for
the altars, the work of their hands, and they
will not look to what their own fingers have
made, either the sacred poles *c* or the altars of
incense.

9 On that day their strong cities will be
like the deserted places of the Hivites and
the Amorites, *d* which they deserted because
of the children of Israel, and there will be
desolation.

10 For you have forgotten the God of your
    salvation,
  and have not remembered the Rock of
    your refuge;
therefore, though you plant pleasant
    plants
  and set out slips of an alien god,
11 though you make them grow on the
    day that you plant them,
  and make them blossom in the
    morning that you sow;

a Gk: Heb *I have hushed*   *b* Cn Compare Gk: Heb
the cities of Aroer are deserted   *c* Heb *Asherim*
d Cn Compare Gk: Heb *places of the wood and the
highest bough*

17:4 *the glory of Jacob.* While the surrounding
verses offer a theological critique of the several
nations around Jerusalem, this verse indicates
the "glory of Jacob" is also under threat. This
phrase surely refers to God's people either in the
Northern Kingdom or eventually in the environs
of Jerusalem.

yet the harvest will flee away
  in a day of grief and incurable pain.

12 Ah, the thunder of many peoples,
  they thunder like the thundering of
    the sea!
Ah, the roar of nations,
  they roar like the roaring of mighty
    waters!
13 The nations roar like the roaring of
    many waters,
  but he will rebuke them, and they will
    flee far away,
chased like chaff on the mountains
    before the wind
  and whirling dust before the storm.
14 At evening time, lo, terror!
  Before morning, they are no more.
This is the fate of those who despoil us,
  and the lot of those who plunder us.

An Oracle concerning Ethiopia

18 Ah, land of whirring wings
    beyond the rivers of Ethiopia,[a]
2 sending ambassadors by the Nile
  in vessels of papyrus on the waters!
Go, you swift messengers,
  to a nation tall and smooth,
to a people feared near and far,
  a nation mighty and conquering,
  whose land the rivers divide.

3 All you inhabitants of the world,
  you who live on the earth,
when a signal is raised on the
    mountains, look!
When a trumpet is blown, listen!
4 For thus the LORD said to me:
I will quietly look from my dwelling
  like clear heat in sunshine,
  like a cloud of dew in the heat of
    harvest.
5 For before the harvest, when the
    blossom is over
  and the flower becomes a ripening
    grape,
he will cut off the shoots with pruning
    hooks,
  and the spreading branches he will
    hew away.
6 They shall all be left

to the birds of prey of the mountains
  and to the animals of the earth.
And the birds of prey will summer on
    them,
  and all the animals of the earth will
    winter on them.

7 At that time gifts will be brought to the
LORD of hosts from[b] a people tall and smooth,
from a people feared near and far, a nation
mighty and conquering, whose land the
rivers divide, to Mount Zion, the place of the
name of the LORD of hosts.

An Oracle concerning Egypt

19 An oracle concerning Egypt.

See, the LORD is riding on a swift cloud
  and comes to Egypt;
the idols of Egypt will tremble at his
    presence,
  and the heart of the Egyptians will
    melt within them.
2 I will stir up Egyptians against Egyptians,
  and they will fight, one against the
    other,
  neighbor against neighbor,
  city against city, kingdom against
    kingdom;
3 the spirit of the Egyptians within them
    will be emptied out,
  and I will confound their plans;
they will consult the idols and the
    spirits of the dead
  and the ghosts and the familiar
    spirits;
4 I will deliver the Egyptians
  into the hand of a hard master;
a fierce king will rule over them,
  says the Sovereign, the LORD of hosts.

5 The waters of the Nile will be dried up,
  and the river will be parched and dry;
6 its canals will become foul,
  and the branches of Egypt's Nile will
    diminish and dry up,
  reeds and rushes will rot away.
7 There will be bare places by the Nile,
  on the brink of the Nile;

a Or *Nubia*; Heb *Cush* b Q Ms Gk Vg: MT *of*

and all that is sown by the Nile will dry
        up,
    be driven away, and be no more.
8 Those who fish will mourn;
    all who cast hooks in the Nile will
        lament,
    and those who spread nets on the
        water will languish.
9 The workers in flax will be in despair,
    and the carders and those at the loom
        will grow pale.
10 Its weavers will be dismayed,
    and all who work for wages will be
        grieved.

11 The princes of Zoan are utterly foolish;
    the wise counselors of Pharaoh give
        stupid counsel.
    How can you say to Pharaoh,
    "I am one of the sages,
        a descendant of ancient kings"?
12 Where now are your sages?
    Let them tell you and make known
    what the LORD of hosts has planned
        against Egypt.
13 The princes of Zoan have become fools,
    and the princes of Memphis are
        deluded;
    those who are the cornerstones of its
        tribes
    have led Egypt astray.
14 The LORD has poured into them[a]
    a spirit of confusion;
    and they have made Egypt stagger in all
        its doings
    as a drunkard staggers around in
        vomit.
15 Neither head nor tail, palm branch or
        reed,
    will be able to do anything for Egypt.

16 On that day the Egyptians will be like
women, and tremble with fear before the
hand that the LORD of hosts raises against
them. 17 And the land of Judah will become a
terror to the Egyptians; everyone to whom it
is mentioned will fear because of the plan
that the LORD of hosts is planning against
them.

Egypt, Assyria, and Israel Blessed

18 On that day there will be five cities in
the land of Egypt that speak the language of
Canaan and swear allegiance to the LORD of
hosts. One of these will be called the City of
the Sun.

19 On that day there will be an altar to
the LORD in the center of the land of Egypt,
and a pillar to the LORD at its border. 20 It will
be a sign and a witness to the LORD of hosts in
the land of Egypt; when they cry to the LORD
because of oppressors, he will send them a
savior, and will defend and deliver them.
21 The LORD will make himself known to the
Egyptians; and the Egyptians will know the
LORD on that day, and will worship with sacrifice and burnt offering, and they will make
vows to the LORD and perform them. 22 The
LORD will strike Egypt, striking and healing;
they will return to the LORD, and he will listen to their supplications and heal them.

23 On that day there will be a highway
from Egypt to Assyria, and the Assyrian will
come into Egypt, and the Egyptian into Assyria, and the Egyptians will worship with
the Assyrians.

24 On that day Israel will be the third with
Egypt and Assyria, a blessing in the midst of
the earth, 25 whom the LORD of hosts has

a Gk Compare Tg: Heb it

19:18–25 *the Egyptians will know the LORD.*
Although all of the nations are condemned
for their arrogance and refusal to submit to
Yahweh, it is remarkable that in the oracle on
Egypt judgment is not the last word. To be sure,
verses 1–17 pronounce harsh judgment, but the
verses that follow include promises that God
will heal Israel and Egypt. Thus the oracle on
Egypt holds out a positive hope that is without
parallel in the oracles on the other nations.

Responding
19:23 WORSHIP. This oracle includes
the remarkable image of the Egyptians
and Assyrians, bitter enemies, worshiping
together. It's difficult to hate someone with
whom you pray. Consider attending a worship
service of another denomination or faith, one
that seems very foreign to you. See what you
learn about what you share and where you
differ. *See also* Spiritual Disciplines Index.

blessed, saying, "Blessed be Egypt my people, and Assyria the work of my hands, and Israel my heritage."

Isaiah Dramatizes the Conquest of Egypt and Ethiopia

20 In the year that the commander-in-chief, who was sent by King Sargon of Assyria, came to Ashdod and fought against it and took it—²at that time the LORD had spoken to Isaiah son of Amoz, saying, "Go, and loose the sackcloth from your loins and take your sandals off your feet," and he had done so, walking naked and barefoot. ³Then the LORD said, "Just as my servant Isaiah has walked naked and barefoot for three years as a sign and a portent against Egypt and Ethiopia, *a* ⁴so shall the king of Assyria lead away the Egyptians as captives and the Ethiopians *b* as exiles, both the young and the old, naked and barefoot, with buttocks uncovered, to the shame of Egypt. ⁵And they shall be dismayed and confounded because of Ethiopia *a* their hope and of Egypt their boast. ⁶In that day the inhabitants of this coastland will say, 'See, this is what has happened to those in whom we hoped and to whom we fled for help and deliverance from the king of Assyria! And we, how shall we escape?' "

Oracles concerning Babylon, Edom, and Arabia

21 The oracle concerning the wilderness of the sea.

As whirlwinds in the Negeb sweep on,
 it comes from the desert,
 from a terrible land.
² A stern vision is told to me;
 the betrayer betrays,
 and the destroyer destroys.
Go up, O Elam,

lay siege, O Media;
all the sighing she has caused
 I bring to an end.
³ Therefore my loins are filled with
 anguish;
 pangs have seized me,
 like the pangs of a woman in labor;
I am bowed down so that I cannot hear,
 I am dismayed so that I cannot see.
⁴ My mind reels, horror has appalled me;
 the twilight I longed for
 has been turned for me into trembling.
⁵ They prepare the table,
 they spread the rugs,
 they eat, they drink.
Rise up, commanders,
 oil the shield!
⁶ For thus the Lord said to me:
"Go, post a lookout,
 let him announce what he sees.
⁷ When he sees riders, horsemen in pairs,
 riders on donkeys, riders on camels,
let him listen diligently,
 very diligently."
⁸ Then the watcher *c* called out:
"Upon a watchtower I stand, O Lord,
 continually by day,
and at my post I am stationed
 throughout the night.
⁹ Look, there they come, riders,
 horsemen in pairs!"
Then he responded,
 "Fallen, fallen is Babylon;
and all the images of her gods
 lie shattered on the ground."
¹⁰ O my threshed and winnowed one,
 what I have heard from the LORD of
 hosts,
 the God of Israel, I announce to you.

a Or *Nubia*; Heb *Cush*   *b* Or *Nubians*; Heb *Cushites*   *c* Q Ms: MT *a lion*

19:24–25 *Israel will be the third with Egypt and Assyria.* This oracle is among the most remarkable in all of Scripture, because it anticipates a time in the future when Egypt and Assyria, the two great imperial powers of the eighth century BC, will be treated along with Israel as God's chosen peoples. "My people," "the work of my hands," and "my heritage"—all phrases that characteristically refer to Israel as God's beloved people—are redistributed so that Egypt and Assyria are also God's favored peoples. These lines are of immense importance, because they show the vision of the Old Testament reaching well beyond ethnic parochialism to the world of the Gentiles, who are also cared for by God.

11   The oracle concerning Dumah.

One is calling to me from Seir,
  "Sentinel, what of the night?
  Sentinel, what of the night?"
12 The sentinel says:
  "Morning comes, and also the night.
    If you will inquire, inquire;
    come back again."

13   The oracle concerning the desert plain.

In the scrub of the desert plain you will
    lodge,
    O caravans of Dedanites.
14 Bring water to the thirsty,
    meet the fugitive with bread,
    O inhabitants of the land of
      Tema.
15 For they have fled from the swords,
    from the drawn sword,
  from the bent bow,
    and from the stress of battle.

16   For thus the Lord said to me: Within a
year, according to the years of a hired worker, all the glory of Kedar will come to an end;
17and the remaining bows of Kedar's warriors
will be few; for the Lord, the God of Israel, has
spoken.

A Warning of Destruction of Jerusalem

22 The oracle concerning the valley of
      vision.

What do you mean that you have gone
      up,
    all of you, to the housetops,
2   you that are full of shoutings,
    tumultuous city, exultant town?
Your slain are not slain by the
      sword,
    nor are they dead in battle.
3   Your rulers have all fled together;
    they were captured without the use of
      a bow.a
All of you who were found were
    captured,
    though they had fled far away.b
4   Therefore I said:
Look away from me,
    let me weep bitter tears;

do not try to comfort me
  for the destruction of my beloved
    people.

5   For the Lord God of hosts has a day
    of tumult and trampling and
      confusion
  in the valley of vision,
a battering down of walls
  and a cry for help to the mountains.
6   Elam bore the quiver
    with chariots and cavalry,c
    and Kir uncovered the shield.
7   Your choicest valleys were full of
      chariots,
    and the cavalry took their stand at
      the gates.
8   He has taken away the covering of
      Judah.

On that day you looked to the weapons of
the House of the Forest, 9and you saw that
there were many breaches in the city of David, and you collected the waters of the lower pool. 10You counted the houses of Jerusalem, and you broke down the houses to
fortify the wall. 11You made a reservoir between the two walls for the water of the old
pool. But you did not look to him who did it,
or have regard for him who planned it long
ago.

12 In that day the Lord God of hosts
    called to weeping and mourning,
    to baldness and putting on
      sackcloth;
13 but instead there was joy and
      festivity,
    killing oxen and slaughtering sheep,
    eating meat and drinking wine.
"Let us eat and drink,
    for tomorrow we die."
14 The Lord of hosts has revealed himself
      in my ears:
Surely this iniquity will not be forgiven
    you until you die,
  says the Lord God of hosts.

a Or *without their bows*   b Gk Syr Vg: Heb *fled
from far away*   c Meaning of Heb uncertain

Denunciation of Self-Seeking Officials

15 Thus says the Lord GOD of hosts: Come, go to this steward, to Shebna, who is master of the household, and say to him: 16 What right do you have here? Who are your relatives here, that you have cut out a tomb here for yourself, cutting a tomb on the height, and carving a habitation for yourself in the rock? 17 The LORD is about to hurl you away violently, my fellow. He will seize firm hold on you, 18 whirl you round and round, and throw you like a ball into a wide land; there you shall die, and there your splendid chariots shall lie, O you disgrace to your master's house! 19 I will thrust you from your office, and you will be pulled down from your post.

20 On that day I will call my servant Eliakim son of Hilkiah, 21 and will clothe him with your robe and bind your sash on him. I will commit your authority to his hand, and he shall be a father to the inhabitants of Jerusalem and to the house of Judah. 22 I will place on his shoulder the key of the house of David; he shall open, and no one shall shut; he shall shut, and no one shall open. 23 I will fasten him like a peg in a secure place, and he will become a throne of honor to his ancestral house. 24 And they will hang on him the whole weight of his ancestral house, the offspring and issue, every small vessel, from the cups to all the flagons. 25 On that day, says the LORD of hosts, the peg that was fastened in a secure place will give way; it will be cut down and fall, and the load that was on it will perish, for the LORD has spoken.

An Oracle concerning Tyre

23 The oracle concerning Tyre.

Wail, O ships of Tarshish,
    for your fortress is destroyed.[a]
When they came in from Cyprus
    they learned of it.
2 Be still, O inhabitants of the coast,
    O merchants of Sidon,
    your messengers crossed over the sea[b]

3 and were on the mighty waters;
your revenue was the grain of Shihor,
    the harvest of the Nile;
    you were the merchant of the
        nations.
4 Be ashamed, O Sidon, for the sea has
        spoken,
    the fortress of the sea, saying:
"I have neither labored nor given birth,
    I have neither reared young men
    nor brought up young women."
5 When the report comes to Egypt,
    they will be in anguish over the
        report about Tyre.
6 Cross over to Tarshish—
    wail, O inhabitants of the coast!
7 Is this your exultant city
    whose origin is from days of old,
whose feet carried her
    to settle far away?
8 Who has planned this
    against Tyre, the bestower of crowns,
whose merchants were princes,
    whose traders were the honored of
        the earth?
9 The LORD of hosts has planned it—
    to defile the pride of all glory,
    to shame all the honored of the earth.
10 Cross over to your own land,
    O ships of[c] Tarshish;
    this is a harbor[d] no more.
11 He has stretched out his hand over the
        sea,
    he has shaken the kingdoms;
the LORD has given command
        concerning Canaan
    to destroy its fortresses.
12 He said:
You will exult no longer,
    O oppressed virgin daughter Sidon;
rise, cross over to Cyprus—
    even there you will have no rest.

a Cn Compare verse 14: Heb *for it is destroyed, without houses*   b Q Ms: MT *crossing over the sea, they replenished you*   c Cn Compare Gk: Heb *like the Nile, daughter*   d Cn: Heb *restraint*

22:15 *steward . . . master of the household.* This verse suggests a way to think about stewardship; that is, that the steward is one who is responsible for the proper functioning of the whole household.

13 Look at the land of the Chaldeans! This is the people; it was not Assyria. They destined Tyre for wild animals. They erected their siege towers, they tore down her palaces, they made her a ruin. *a*

14 Wail, O ships of Tarshish,
for your fortress is destroyed.

15 From that day Tyre will be forgotten for seventy years, the lifetime of one king. At the end of seventy years, it will happen to Tyre as in the song about the prostitute:

16 Take a harp,
go about the city,
you forgotten prostitute!
Make sweet melody,
sing many songs,
that you may be remembered.

17 At the end of seventy years, the LORD will visit Tyre, and she will return to her trade, and will prostitute herself with all the kingdoms of the world on the face of the earth. 18 Her merchandise and her wages will be dedicated to the LORD; her profits *b* will not be stored or hoarded, but her merchandise will supply abundant food and fine clothing for those who live in the presence of the LORD.

Impending Judgment on the Earth

24 Now the LORD is about to lay waste the earth and make it desolate, and he will twist its surface and scatter its inhabitants.
2 And it shall be, as with the people, so with the priest;
as with the slave, so with his master;
as with the maid, so with her mistress;
as with the buyer, so with the seller;

as with the lender, so with the
borrower;
as with the creditor, so with the debtor.
3 The earth shall be utterly laid waste and
utterly despoiled;
for the LORD has spoken this word.

4 The earth dries up and withers,
the world languishes and withers;
the heavens languish together with
the earth.
5 The earth lies polluted
under its inhabitants;
for they have transgressed laws,
violated the statutes,
broken the everlasting covenant.
6 Therefore a curse devours the earth,
and its inhabitants suffer for their
guilt;
therefore the inhabitants of the earth
dwindled,
and few people are left.
7 The wine dries up,
the vine languishes,
all the merry-hearted sigh.
8 The mirth of the timbrels is stilled,
the noise of the jubilant has ceased,
the mirth of the lyre is stilled.
9 No longer do they drink wine with
singing;
strong drink is bitter to those who
drink it.
10 The city of chaos is broken down,
every house is shut up so that no one
can enter.

a Meaning of Heb uncertain   *b* Heb *it*

23:18 *dedicated to the LORD.* It is curious that at the end of this typical judgment speech the oracle looks beyond the destruction of the Mediterranean coastal city of Tyre to anticipate that its great commercial wealth will be "dedicated to the LORD." Thus this oracle by its end imagines that Tyre will act responsibly toward Yahweh. By implication the oracle anticipates the goods of Tyre being given for the benefit of Israel.

24:1–27:13 *Now the LORD is about to lay waste.* It is worth noting that in this third section of the book there is a complete lack of historical

specificity. This suggests that this is a very late part of the text in which the vision of biblical faith grows very large and concentrates on the immense sovereignty of Yahweh over the entire world. It is Yahweh, the God of Israel, who comes in judgment and in rescue.

24:5 *broken the everlasting covenant.* This phrase most likely refers to the covenant God made with all of creation after the flood (Gen 9) to sustain its well-being. Here, however, it is asserted that the earth has become so polluted that even that most elemental sustenance of the earth promised by God is placed in jeopardy.

11 There is an outcry in the streets for lack
    of wine;
      all joy has reached its eventide;
      the gladness of the earth is banished.
12 Desolation is left in the city,
      the gates are battered into ruins.
13 For thus it shall be on the earth
      and among the nations,
    as when an olive tree is beaten,
      as at the gleaning when the grape
        harvest is ended.

14 They lift up their voices, they sing for joy;
      they shout from the west over the
        majesty of the LORD.
15 Therefore in the east give glory to the
      LORD;
      in the coastlands of the sea glorify the
        name of the LORD, the God of
        Israel.
16 From the ends of the earth we hear
      songs of praise,
      of glory to the Righteous One.
    But I say, I pine away,
      I pine away. Woe is me!
    For the treacherous deal treacherously,
      the treacherous deal very
        treacherously.

17 Terror, and the pit, and the snare
      are upon you, O inhabitant of the
        earth!
18 Whoever flees at the sound of the terror
      shall fall into the pit;
    and whoever climbs out of the pit
      shall be caught in the snare.
    For the windows of heaven are opened,
      and the foundations of the earth
        tremble.
19 The earth is utterly broken,
      the earth is torn asunder,
      the earth is violently shaken.
20 The earth staggers like a drunkard,
      it sways like a hut;
    its transgression lies heavy upon it,
      and it falls, and will not rise again.

21 On that day the LORD will punish
      the host of heaven in heaven,
      and on earth the kings of the earth.
22 They will be gathered together
      like prisoners in a pit;
    they will be shut up in a prison,
      and after many days they will be
        punished.
23 Then the moon will be abashed,
      and the sun ashamed;
    for the LORD of hosts will reign
      on Mount Zion and in Jerusalem,
    and before his elders he will manifest
      his glory.

Praise for Deliverance from Oppression

25 O LORD, you are my God;
      I will exalt you, I will praise your
        name;
    for you have done wonderful things,
      plans formed of old, faithful and
        sure.
2 For you have made the city a heap,
      the fortified city a ruin;
    the palace of aliens is a city no more,
      it will never be rebuilt.
3 Therefore strong peoples will glorify
        you;
      cities of ruthless nations will fear you.
4 For you have been a refuge to the poor,
      a refuge to the needy in their distress,
      a shelter from the rainstorm and a
        shade from the heat.
    When the blast of the ruthless was like a
        winter rainstorm,
5   the noise of aliens like heat in a dry
        place,
    you subdued the heat with the shade of
        clouds;
      the song of the ruthless was stilled.

6 On this mountain the LORD of hosts will
      make for all peoples
    a feast of rich food, a feast of well-
        aged wines,

25:6–10a *a feast of rich food.* This poetic unit
is a spectacular promise of God's ultimate
defeat of death. The text is much used in the
Church to celebrate God's victory over death
that has been accomplished in the Easter
resurrection of Jesus. The prophet here
imagines a great festival of well-being in which
all of God's faithful people get to "wine and
dine" with the Lord of hosts, who is the giver of
the great banquet in the perfect age to come.

of rich food filled with marrow, of
  well-aged wines strained clear.
7 And he will destroy on this mountain
  the shroud that is cast over all
    peoples,
  the sheet that is spread over all
    nations;
8   he will swallow up death forever.
Then the Lord GOD will wipe away the
    tears from all faces,
  and the disgrace of his people he will
    take away from all the earth,
  for the LORD has spoken.
9 It will be said on that day,
  Lo, this is our God; we have waited for
    him, so that he might save us.
  This is the LORD for whom we have
    waited;
  let us be glad and rejoice in his
    salvation.
10 For the hand of the LORD will rest on
    this mountain.

The Moabites shall be trodden down in
    their place
  as straw is trodden down in a dung-
    pit.
11 Though they spread out their hands in
    the midst of it,
  as swimmers spread out their hands
    to swim,
  their pride will be laid low despite the
    struggle*a* of their hands.
12 The high fortifications of his walls will
    be brought down,
  laid low, cast to the ground, even to
    the dust.

Judah's Song of Victory

26 On that day this song will be sung
  in the land of Judah:
We have a strong city;
  he sets up victory
  like walls and bulwarks.
2 Open the gates,

so that the righteous nation that
  keeps faith
  may enter in.
3 Those of steadfast mind you keep in
    peace—
  in peace because they trust in you.
4 Trust in the LORD forever,
  for in the LORD GOD*b*
  you have an everlasting rock.
5 For he has brought low
  the inhabitants of the height;
  the lofty city he lays low.
He lays it low to the ground,
  casts it to the dust.
6 The foot tramples it,
  the feet of the poor,
  the steps of the needy.

7 The way of the righteous is level;
  O Just One, you make smooth the
    path of the righteous.
8 In the path of your judgments,
  O LORD, we wait for you;
your name and your renown
  are the soul's desire.
9 My soul yearns for you in the night,
  my spirit within me earnestly seeks
    you.
For when your judgments are in the
    earth,
  the inhabitants of the world learn
    righteousness.
10 If favor is shown to the wicked,
  they do not learn righteousness;
in the land of uprightness they deal
    perversely
  and do not see the majesty of the
    LORD.
11 O LORD, your hand is lifted up,
  but they do not see it.
Let them see your zeal for your people,
  and be ashamed.

a Meaning of Heb uncertain   *b* Heb *in Yah, the
LORD*

25:8 *swallow up death forever.* The imagery
here of death is not simply the fact of mortality.
Rather, "death" is understood as a great
devastating monster who stalks the earth and
seeks to undo all of the structures of life. In the
imagery of this verse, it is argued that God is an
even stronger power who, with great force and
brutality, will simply swallow death, chew it up,
and spit it out in complete nullification.

Let the fire for your adversaries
consume them.
12 O LORD, you will ordain peace for us,
for indeed, all that we have done, you
have done for us.
13 O LORD our God,
other lords besides you have ruled
over us,
but we acknowledge your name
alone.
14 The dead do not live;
shades do not rise—
because you have punished and
destroyed them,
and wiped out all memory of them.
15 But you have increased the nation,
O LORD,
you have increased the nation; you
are glorified;
you have enlarged all the borders of
the land.

16 O LORD, in distress they sought you,
they poured out a prayer[a]
when your chastening was on them.
17 Like a woman with child,
who writhes and cries out in her
pangs
when she is near her time,
so were we because of you, O LORD;
18 we were with child, we writhed,
but we gave birth only to wind.
We have won no victories on earth,

and no one is born to inhabit the
world.
19 Your dead shall live, their corpses[b] shall
rise.
O dwellers in the dust, awake and sing
for joy!
For your dew is a radiant dew,
and the earth will give birth to those
long dead.[c]

20 Come, my people, enter your
chambers,
and shut your doors behind you;
hide yourselves for a little while
until the wrath is past.
21 For the LORD comes out from his place
to punish the inhabitants of the earth
for their iniquity;
the earth will disclose the blood shed
on it,
and will no longer cover its slain.

Israel's Redemption

27 On that day the LORD with his cruel
and great and strong sword will punish Leviathan the fleeing serpent, Leviathan
the twisting serpent, and he will kill the dragon that is in the sea.

2 On that day:
A pleasant vineyard, sing about it!

a Meaning of Heb uncertain   b Cn Compare Syr
Tg: Heb *my corpse*   c Heb *to the shades*

Responding

26:16 PRAYER. The prayer described
here is one of pain, the desperate
prayer of last resort offered when things have
gotten so bad God is the only one left to turn to.
Were there times in your life when you found
yourself offering this prayer? Reflect on the role
of God in life's sufferings. *See also* Spiritual
Disciplines Index.

26:19 *Your dead shall live.* For the most part,
the Old Testament does not have on its horizon
the resurrection of the dead or life beyond
death. But two texts, both late, clearly attest
to Israel's emerging conviction about the
resurrection of the dead: this one and Dan 12:2.
In this text, it is anticipated that God's ultimate

triumph will rescue and revivify even those who
are long since dead. It is clearly this strain of Old
Testament faith that is the background for the
New Testament affirmation of the resurrection
of Jesus. Resurrection clearly does not mean
simply the resuscitation of corpses; it means,
rather, the renewal and revivification of well-
being under the rule of God.

26:20 *hide yourselves for a little while.* "A
little while" is a characteristic phrase for Israel
when it is waiting for God's action. It is not a
statement about length of time; it means that
the triumph of God is guaranteed and, therefore,
the faithful can wait with eager longing. No
matter how long the wait, it is only "a little
while" because it is very sure (see John 16:19).

3   I, the LORD, am its keeper;
       every moment I water it.
    I guard it night and day
       so that no one can harm it;
4   I have no wrath.
    If it gives me thorns and briers,
       I will march to battle against it.
       I will burn it up.
5   Or else let it cling to me for protection,
       let it make peace with me,
       let it make peace with me.

6   In days to come^a Jacob shall take root,
       Israel shall blossom and put forth
          shoots,
       and fill the whole world with fruit.

7   Has he struck them down as he struck
          down those who struck them?
    Or have they been killed as their
          killers were killed?
8   By expulsion,^b by exile you struggled
          against them;
       with his fierce blast he removed them
          in the day of the east wind.
9   Therefore by this the guilt of Jacob will
          be expiated,
       and this will be the full fruit of the
          removal of his sin:
    when he makes all the stones of the
          altars
       like chalkstones crushed to pieces,
       no sacred poles^c or incense altars will
          remain standing.
10 For the fortified city is solitary,
       a habitation deserted and forsaken,
          like the wilderness;
       the calves graze there,

there they lie down, and strip its
          branches.
11 When its boughs are dry, they are
          broken;
       women come and make a fire of
          them.
    For this is a people without
          understanding;
       therefore he that made them will not
          have compassion on them,
       he that formed them will show them
          no favor.

12 On that day the LORD will thresh from the channel of the Euphrates to the Wadi of Egypt, and you will be gathered one by one, O people of Israel. 13And on that day a great trumpet will be blown, and those who were lost in the land of Assyria and those who were driven out to the land of Egypt will come and worship the LORD on the holy mountain at Jerusalem.

Judgment on Corrupt Rulers, Priests, and Prophets

28 Ah, the proud garland of the
       drunkards of Ephraim,
    and the fading flower of its glorious
          beauty,
       which is on the head of those bloated
          with rich food, of those overcome
          with wine!
2   See, the Lord has one who is mighty
          and strong;

a Heb *Those to come*   b Meaning of Heb uncertain   c Heb *Asherim*

27:2–5 *I have no wrath.* In these verses the Isaiah tradition returns to the imagery of God as the vine keeper and Israel as the vineyard. Here it is announced that the vine keeper (Yahweh) will have great patience and attentiveness toward the vineyard (Israel), so it will eventually prosper. Thus the Isaiah tradition in this unit circles back upon the harsh judgment of 5:1–7 and indicates that harsh judgment is not the last word; the last word is God's desire for the well-being of God's beloved people and God's beloved city.

27:12 *On that day . . . you will be gathered.*

"On that day" signals future restoration and well-being that are unspecified, but quite certain and guaranteed by God's own promise. That rhetorical sign of the future is here combined with the word "gathered," which signifies the termination of exile and the bringing home of all of the Israelites who had been scattered far from the Land of Promise. Thus the great anticipation of the Isaiah tradition and of the Old Testament generally is one of a homecoming that will be buoyant, triumphant, and joyous.

like a storm of hail, a destroying
    tempest,
like a storm of mighty, overflowing
    waters;
with his hand he will hurl them down
    to the earth.
3 Trampled under foot will be
    the proud garland of the drunkards of
        Ephraim.
4 And the fading flower of its glorious
        beauty,
    which is on the head of those bloated
        with rich food,
    will be like a first-ripe fig before the
        summer;
    whoever sees it, eats it up
    as soon as it comes to hand.

5 In that day the LORD of hosts will be a
        garland of glory,
    and a diadem of beauty, to the
        remnant of his people;
6 and a spirit of justice to the one who sits
        in judgment,
    and strength to those who turn back
        the battle at the gate.

7 These also reel with wine
    and stagger with strong drink;
    the priest and the prophet reel with
        strong drink,
    they are confused with wine,
    they stagger with strong drink;
    they err in vision,
    they stumble in giving judgment.

8 All tables are covered with filthy
        vomit;
    no place is clean.

9 "Whom will he teach knowledge,
    and to whom will he explain the
        message?
    Those who are weaned from milk,
        those taken from the breast?
10 For it is precept upon precept, precept
        upon precept,
    line upon line, line upon line,
    here a little, there a little." *a*

11 Truly, with stammering lip
    and with alien tongue
    he will speak to this people,
12   to whom he has said,
    "This is rest;
        give rest to the weary;
    and this is repose";
        yet they would not hear.
13 Therefore the word of the LORD will be
        to them,
    "Precept upon precept, precept upon
        precept,
    line upon line, line upon line,
    here a little, there a little;" *a*
    in order that they may go, and fall
        backward,
    and be broken, and snared, and taken.

a Meaning of Heb of this verse uncertain

28:1–31:9 *Ah, the proud.* Chapters 28–31
form a new section of First Isaiah. Although
Isaiah will move later (chronologically and
theologically) into hope, these chapters likely
come earlier in the tradition, probably from the
prophet during the reign of Hezekiah at the end
of the eighth century BC. For the most part,
these chapters announce harsh judgment upon
the city of Jerusalem. The harsh judgment is
God's response to the Jerusalem government's
policy of making alliances with other people
rather than trusting in Yahweh. The sign of the
harsh judgment is the fact that in 28:1; 29:1;
29:15; 30:1; and 31:1 the oracles are all
introduced by a particular rhetorical marker

that used to be translated "woe," though it is
now translated in other ways ("ah," "ha," "oh,"
"alas"). This particular Hebrew particle puts
listeners on alert that big trouble is about to be
announced. These oracles uniformly announce
that big trouble is to come upon disobedient
Jerusalem.

28:5–6 *In that day.* The writer is looking to a
sure future in God's hands; that future, moreover, concerns the remnant of God's people,
that is, the faithful who will survive exile and
be restored. These verses are a clear example
of the way in which the Isaiah proclamation is
twofold: first judgment, then promises of
restoration.

14 Therefore hear the word of the LORD,
        you scoffers
    who rule this people in Jerusalem.
15 Because you have said, "We have made
        a covenant with death,
    and with Sheol we have an
        agreement;
    when the overwhelming scourge passes
        through
    it will not come to us;
    for we have made lies our refuge,
        and in falsehood we have taken
        shelter";
16 therefore thus says the Lord GOD,
    See, I am laying in Zion a foundation
        stone,
    a tested stone,
    a precious cornerstone, a sure
        foundation.
    "One who trusts will not panic."
17 And I will make justice the line,
        and righteousness the plummet;
    hail will sweep away the refuge of lies,
        and waters will overwhelm the
        shelter.

18 Then your covenant with death will be
        annulled,
    and your agreement with Sheol will
        not stand;
    when the overwhelming scourge passes
        through
    you will be beaten down by it.
19 As often as it passes through, it will take
        you;
    for morning by morning it will pass
        through,
        by day and by night;
    and it will be sheer terror to understand
        the message.
20 For the bed is too short to stretch
        oneself on it,
    and the covering too narrow to wrap
        oneself in it.
21 For the LORD will rise up as on Mount
        Perazim,
    he will rage as in the valley of Gibeon
    to do his deed—strange is his deed!—
        and to work his work—alien is his
        work!
22 Now therefore do not scoff,

28:15, 18 *covenant with death.* This phrase likely refers to the fact that the Jerusalem government has made covenants in the form of political and military alliances instead of trusting its covenant with Yahweh. The Isaiah tradition views all such political alliances as foolhardy attempts on Israel's part to secure its own existence, when in fact its real security can come only from submission to and trust in Yahweh. It is clear in covenantal theology that the king in Jerusalem is to be son and servant only of Yahweh and of no other power. It is no wonder, then, that the prophetic tradition maintains that the king's choosing other alliances will only lead to death and destruction.

Responding

28:15–18 SUBMISSION. This week when reading the newspaper or listening to the news, note how many times nations depend on alliances and the reasons behind them. Consider the ways the world would be different if every nation submitted to and trusted in God alone for the security and safety of its citizens. *See also* Spiritual Disciplines Index.

28:16 *precious cornerstone.* The prophetic oracle turns from harsh indictment to a promise that God will lay a "precious cornerstone" that will be the pivot point for the rebuilding and restoration of Jerusalem and God's people. The phrase is itself enigmatic and clearly appeals to architectural imagery. It is plausible that the precious cornerstone here anticipated is rock-bottom faith out of which newness is possible. The early Church, in pondering this text, took over the phrase and understood Jesus of Nazareth to be the cornerstone for God's newness in the world (see 1 Pet 2:4–8).

28:21 *alien is his work!* This refers to God's action in harsh judgment and punishment. Martin Luther understood well that judgment and punishment are alien to God's own propensity. God's preference is always forgiveness, compassion, mercy, and reconciliation; the circumstances of a recalcitrant people and a recalcitrant earth, however, require God to commit acts of judgment that are inimical to God's own character and inclination. Thus, the "alien work" of God points to realism about coming judgment from God, but also awareness that this is not the true or preferred work of God.

or your bonds will be made stronger;
for I have heard a decree of destruction
    from the Lord GOD of hosts upon the
    whole land.

23 Listen, and hear my voice;
    Pay attention, and hear my speech.
24 Do those who plow for sowing plow
    continually?
    Do they continually open and harrow
    their ground?
25 When they have leveled its surface,
    do they not scatter dill, sow cummin,
and plant wheat in rows
    and barley in its proper place,
    and spelt as the border?
26 For they are well instructed;
    their God teaches them.

27 Dill is not threshed with a threshing
    sledge,
    nor is a cart wheel rolled over
    cummin;
but dill is beaten out with a stick,
    and cummin with a rod.
28 Grain is crushed for bread,
    but one does not thresh it forever;
one drives the cart wheel and horses
    over it,
    but does not pulverize it.
29 This also comes from the LORD of hosts;
    he is wonderful in counsel,
    and excellent in wisdom.

The Siege of Jerusalem

29 Ah, Ariel, Ariel,
the city where David encamped!
    Add year to year;
    let the festivals run their round.
2 Yet I will distress Ariel,
    and there shall be moaning and
    lamentation,
    and Jerusalem *a* shall be to me like an
    Ariel. *b*
3 And like David *c* I will encamp against
    you;
    I will besiege you with towers
    and raise siegeworks against you.
4 Then deep from the earth you shall
    speak,

from low in the dust your words shall
    come;
    your voice shall come from the ground
    like the voice of a ghost,
    and your speech shall whisper out of
    the dust.

5 But the multitude of your foes *d* shall be
    like small dust,
    and the multitude of tyrants like
    flying chaff.
And in an instant, suddenly,
6   you will be visited by the LORD of
    hosts
with thunder and earthquake and great
    noise,
    with whirlwind and tempest, and the
    flame of a devouring fire.
7 And the multitude of all the nations
    that fight against Ariel,
    all that fight against her and her
    stronghold, and who distress her,
    shall be like a dream, a vision of the
    night.
8 Just as when a hungry person dreams of
    eating
    and wakes up still hungry,
or a thirsty person dreams of drinking
    and wakes up faint, still thirsty,
so shall the multitude of all the nations
    be
    that fight against Mount Zion.

9 Stupefy yourselves and be in a stupor,
    blind yourselves and be blind!
Be drunk, but not from wine;
    stagger, but not from strong drink!
10 For the LORD has poured out upon you
    a spirit of deep sleep;
    he has closed your eyes, you prophets,
    and covered your heads, you seers.

11 The vision of all this has become for you like the words of a sealed document. If it is given to those who can read, with the command, "Read this," they say, "We cannot, for it is sealed." 12 And if it is given to those who cannot read, saying, "Read this," they say, "We cannot read."

---

a Heb *she*   *b* Probable meaning, *altar hearth*;
compare Ezek 43.15   *c* Gk: Meaning of Heb
uncertain   *d* Cn: Heb *strangers*

13 The Lord said:
　Because these people draw near with
　　their mouths
　and honor me with their lips,
　　while their hearts are far from me,
　and their worship of me is a human
　　commandment learned by rote;
14 so I will again do
　　amazing things with this people,
　　shocking and amazing.
　The wisdom of their wise shall perish,
　and the discernment of the
　　discerning shall be hidden.

15 Ha! You who hide a plan too deep for
　　the LORD,
　whose deeds are in the dark,
　and who say, "Who sees us? Who
　　knows us?"
16 You turn things upside down!
　Shall the potter be regarded as the
　　clay?
　Shall the thing made say of its maker,
　　"He did not make me";
　or the thing formed say of the one who
　　formed it,
　　"He has no understanding"?

Hope for the Future

17 Shall not Lebanon in a very little while
　　become a fruitful field,
　and the fruitful field be regarded as a
　　forest?
18 On that day the deaf shall hear
　　the words of a scroll,
　and out of their gloom and darkness
　　the eyes of the blind shall see.

19 The meek shall obtain fresh joy in the
　　LORD,
　and the neediest people shall exult in
　　the Holy One of Israel.
20 For the tyrant shall be no more,
　and the scoffer shall cease to be;
　all those alert to do evil shall be cut
　　off—
21 those who cause a person to lose a
　　lawsuit,
　who set a trap for the arbiter in the
　　gate,
　and without grounds deny justice to
　　the one in the right.

22 Therefore thus says the LORD, who redeemed Abraham, concerning the house of
Jacob:
　No longer shall Jacob be ashamed,
　　no longer shall his face grow pale.
23 For when he sees his children,
　　the work of my hands, in his midst,
　　they will sanctify my name;
　they will sanctify the Holy One of Jacob,
　　and will stand in awe of the God of
　　Israel.
24 And those who err in spirit will come to
　　understanding,
　and those who grumble will accept
　　instruction.

The Futility of Reliance on Egypt

30 Oh, rebellious children, says the
　　LORD,
　who carry out a plan, but not mine;
　who make an alliance, but against my
　　will,

Responding

29:13 WORSHIP. The words of this
verse hit home. Each of us has sat in
church with our mind far from God or prayed a
familiar prayer with our lips and not our heart.
There is a beauty in familiarity, but it can also
lead to boredom or, worse, contempt. If your
worship routine has grown stagnant, consider
refreshing it with a new worship ritual, prayer
posture, or different type of prayer. *See also*
Spiritual Disciplines Index.

30:1–2 *rebellious children.* Israel, at the end

of the eighth century BC, obviously does not
believe that reliance upon Yahweh is adequate
and seeks to carry out its own "plan" for
security that is rooted in a military alliance with
Egypt and with Pharaoh. Such political alliances
are held in the Isaiah tradition to be foolishness,
because they are the antithesis of trust in
Yahweh. In this particular way, the Isaiah
tradition mounts a massive and sustained
critique against all attempts to secure our own
existence through political posturing and
military expansionism. In the long run, such
ventures are destructive and will not work.

adding sin to sin;

2 who set out to go dow[n]
without asking for my [...]
to take refuge in the protectio[n ...]
Pharaoh,
and to seek shelter in the shadow of
Egypt;

3 Therefore the protection of Pharaoh
shall become your shame,
and the shelter in the shadow of
Egypt your humiliation.

4 For though his officials are at Zoan
and his envoys reach Hanes,

5 everyone comes to shame
through a people that cannot profit
them,
that brings neither help nor profit,
but shame and disgrace.

6 An oracle concerning the animals of the
Negeb.
Through a land of trouble and distress,
of lioness and roaring*a* lion,
of viper and flying serpent,
they carry their riches on the backs of
donkeys,
and their treasures on the humps of
camels,
to a people that cannot profit them.

7 For Egypt's help is worthless and empty,
therefore I have called her,
"Rahab who sits still."*b*

A Rebellious People

8 Go now, write it before them on a
tablet,
and inscribe it in a book,
so that it may be for the time to come
as a witness forever.

they are a rebellious people,
[fai]thless children,
who will not hear
[the instr]uction of the LORD;

[10 who say to the] seers, "Do not see";
to the pro[p]hets, "Do not
11 leave the [...]
[tell] us what is right;
let us hear [pleas]ings,
[...] One of Israel [...] from the path,

12 Therefore thus says the [...] the Holy
[One of] Israel:
Because you reject this word,
and put your trust in oppression and
deceit,
and rely on them;

13 therefore this iniquity shall become for
you
like a break in a high wall, bulging
out, and about to collapse,
whose crash comes suddenly, in an
instant;

14 its breaking is like that of a potter's
vessel
that is smashed so ruthlessly
that among its fragments not a sherd is
found
for taking fire from the hearth,
or dipping water out of the cistern.

15 For thus said the Lord GOD, the Holy
One of Israel:
In returning and rest you shall be saved;
in quietness and in trust shall be your
strength.

a Cn: Heb *from them*   *b* Meaning of Heb
uncertain

[handwritten annotations: TRUE, SECURITY, circled; "7:9 IF YOU DON'T STAND IN FAITH YOU WILL NOT STAND AT ALL."]

30:15 *in quietness and in trust shall be your strength.* The lines of this verse, along with 7:9, constitute what is probably the most significant affirmation of the prophet Isaiah in the eighth century BC. Both 7:9 and this text urge complete reliance upon Yahweh as the alternative to frantic, anxious military and political posturing. Isaiah is not a pacifist; rather, he believes that trust in Yahweh is the taproot of security. All trust in armaments and alliances, he reasons, is an act of mistrust and idolatry that will only lead to destruction. The assurance of faith is the conviction that anxious self-securing does not work in the real world. The phrase "returning and rest" is an affirmation that faith is quiet confidence, which is decisive for being safe and well in the world. The oracle goes on to say that those who rely on armaments will finally be routed by armaments (vv 16–17). An arms race ultimately cannot be won!

30:15 SILENCE—*See* Spiritual Disciplines Index.

ISAIAH 30:16–33

But you refused ¹⁶and _ swift!
"No! We will flee up_reat of
therefore you sh_
and, "We will rid_
therefore you shall flee,
¹⁷ A thousand s_
one_ on the top of a
at the t_
until you_in,
like_al on a hill.

_romise to Zion

¹⁸ Therefore the LORD waits to be gracious
   to you;
   therefore he will rise up to show
      mercy to you.
For the LORD is a God of justice;
   blessed are all those who wait for him.
19 Truly, O people in Zion, inhabitants of Jerusalem, you shall weep no more. He will surely be gracious to you at the sound of your cry; when he hears it, he will answer you. ²⁰Though the Lord may give you the bread of adversity and the water of affliction, yet your Teacher will not hide himself any more, but your eyes shall see your Teacher. ²¹And when you turn to the right or when you turn to the left, your ears shall hear a word behind you, saying, "This is the way; walk in it." ²²Then you will defile your silver-covered idols and your gold-plated images. You will scatter them like filthy rags; you will say to them, "Away with you!"

23 He will give rain for the seed with which you sow the ground, and grain, the produce of the ground, which will be rich and plenteous. On that day your cattle will graze in broad pastures; ²⁴and the oxen and donkeys that till the ground will eat silage, which has been winnowed with shovel and fork. ²⁵On every lofty mountain and every high hill there will be brooks running with

_—on a day of the great slaughter, when the towers fall. ²⁶Moreover the light of the moon will be like the light of the sun, and the light of the sun will be sevenfold, like the light of seven days, on the day when the LORD binds up the injuries of his people, and heals the wounds inflicted by his blow.

Judgment on Assyria

27 See, the name of the LORD comes from
      far away,
   burning with his anger, and in thick
      rising smoke; ᵃ
his lips are full of indignation,
   and his tongue is like a devouring
      fire;
²⁸ his breath is like an overflowing stream
      that reaches up to the neck—
to sift the nations with the sieve of
      destruction,
   and to place on the jaws of the
      peoples a bridle that leads them
      astray.

29 You shall have a song as in the night when a holy festival is kept; and gladness of heart, as when one sets out to the sound of the flute to go to the mountain of the LORD, to the Rock of Israel. ³⁰And the LORD will cause his majestic voice to be heard and the descending blow of his arm to be seen, in furious anger and a flame of devouring fire, with a cloudburst and tempest and hailstones. ³¹The Assyrian will be terror-stricken at the voice of the LORD, when he strikes with his rod. ³²And every stroke of the staff of punishment that the LORD lays upon him will be to the sound of timbrels and lyres; battling with brandished arm he will fight with him. ³³For his burning place ᵇ has long been prepared; truly it is made ready for the king, ᶜ its

a Meaning of Heb uncertain   b Or Topheth
c Or Molech

Responding

30:20–21 GUIDANCE. It is often difficult to hear that voice guiding us to the right path. In his _Rules for the Discernment of Spirits_, Ignatius of Loyola states that good influences provide courage and strength and

produce peace and a greater feeling of love, while choices influenced by evil can be counted on to cause regret, sadness, and disquiet. Reflect on his words. Are there any paths in your life that don't stand up to this test of discernment? _See also_ Spiritual Disciplines Index.

pyre made deep and wide, with fire and wood in abundance; the breath of the LORD, like a stream of sulfur, kindles it.

Alliance with Egypt Is Futile

31 Alas for those who go down to
  Egypt for help
 and who rely on horses,
who trust in chariots because they are
  many
 and in horsemen because they are
  very strong,
but do not look to the Holy One of
  Israel
 or consult the LORD!
2 Yet he too is wise and brings disaster;
 he does not call back his words,
but will rise against the house of the
  evildoers,
 and against the helpers of those who
  work iniquity.
3 The Egyptians are human, and not God;
 their horses are flesh, and not spirit.
When the LORD stretches out his hand,
 the helper will stumble, and the one
  helped will fall,
 and they will all perish together.

4 For thus the LORD said to me,
As a lion or a young lion growls over its
  prey,
 and—when a band of shepherds is
  called out against it—
is not terrified by their shouting
 or daunted at their noise,
so the LORD of hosts will come down

to fight upon Mount Zion and upon
  its hill.
5 Like birds hovering overhead, so the
  LORD of hosts
 will protect Jerusalem;
he will protect and deliver it,
 he will spare and rescue it.

6 Turn back to him whom you[a] have deeply betrayed, O people of Israel. 7For on that day all of you shall throw away your idols of silver and idols of gold, which your hands have sinfully made for you.
8 "Then the Assyrian shall fall by a sword,
  not of mortals;
 and a sword, not of humans, shall
  devour him;
he shall flee from the sword,
 and his young men shall be put to
  forced labor.
9 His rock shall pass away in terror,
 and his officers desert the standard in
  panic,"
says the LORD, whose fire is in Zion,
 and whose furnace is in Jerusalem.

Government with Justice Predicted

32 See, a king will reign in
  righteousness,
 and princes will rule with justice.
2 Each will be like a hiding place from the
  wind,
 a covert from the tempest,
 like streams of water in a dry place,

a Heb *they*

31:1–4 *Alas for those who go down to Egypt for help.* The prophet urges a radical either/or choice upon the Jerusalem government. "Egypt" is here a metaphor for all reliance upon political, military posturing. The reason that the Egyptians are no adequate source of reliance in the real world is that they are human and not God; they are flesh and not spirit. Yahweh, the God of Israel, however, is spirit—that is, he has the capacity to make all things new.

32:1–35:10 *See, a king will reign.* In this next section, the tradition of Isaiah moves forward in time and theologically toward hope.

32:1 *a king will reign in righteousness.* The Isaiah tradition keeps one eye on the Davidic dynasty and believes that, in contrast to the failed kings of the eighth century BC, there will come a king who will rule in righteousness and justice. This is consistent with the oracular anticipations of chapters 9 and 11. It is believed, in the Isaiah tradition, that such a king will make possible in the world new life in which there will be safety and well-being and joy. Such promises became the root of messianic hope in the New Testament, which easily identified Jesus as the coming king who would make all things new.

like the shade of a great rock in a
 weary land.
3 Then the eyes of those who have sight
 will not be closed,
 and the ears of those who have
 hearing will listen.
4 The minds of the rash will have good
 judgment,
 and the tongues of stammerers will
 speak readily and distinctly.
5 A fool will no longer be called noble,
 nor a villain said to be honorable.
6 For fools speak folly,
 and their minds plot iniquity:
to practice ungodliness,
 to utter error concerning the LORD,
to leave the craving of the hungry
 unsatisfied,
 and to deprive the thirsty of drink.
7 The villainies of villains are evil;
 they devise wicked devices
to ruin the poor with lying words,
 even when the plea of the needy is
 right.
8 But those who are noble plan noble
 things,
 and by noble things they stand.

Complacent Women Warned of Disaster

9 Rise up, you women who are at ease,
 hear my voice;
 you complacent daughters, listen to
 my speech.
10 In little more than a year
 you will shudder, you complacent
 ones;
for the vintage will fail,
 the fruit harvest will not come.
11 Tremble, you women who are at ease,

shudder, you complacent ones;
 strip, and make yourselves bare,
 and put sackcloth on your loins.
12 Beat your breasts for the pleasant fields,
 for the fruitful vine,
13 for the soil of my people
 growing up in thorns and briers;
yes, for all the joyous houses
 in the jubilant city.
14 For the palace will be forsaken,
 the populous city deserted;
the hill and the watchtower
 will become dens forever,
the joy of wild asses,
 a pasture for flocks;
15 until a spirit from on high is poured out
 on us,
 and the wilderness becomes a fruitful
 field,
 and the fruitful field is deemed a
 forest.

The Peace of God's Reign

16 Then justice will dwell in the
 wilderness,
 and righteousness abide in the
 fruitful field.
17 The effect of righteousness will be
 peace,
 and the result of righteousness,
 quietness and trust forever.
18 My people will abide in a peaceful
 habitation,
 in secure dwellings, and in quiet
 resting places.
19 The forest will disappear completely,[a]
 and the city will be utterly laid low.

a Cn: Heb And it will hail when the forest comes down

32:15–20 *peaceful habitation.* Again it
is promised, after so much judgment and
punishment, that the ultimate outcome for
God's people will be justice and righteousness,
and peace. The earlier part of this chapter
had imagined that this would come through
the Davidic dynasty. In these verses, however,
there is no mention of such a king. It is simply
the case that God will work such a newness
and such a goodness; the People of God
are urged to have confidence to wait for

the good gifts that God will yet give in the
future.

Responding
32:17 SILENCE. What does it mean for
righteousness to result in quietness?
Close your eyes. Picture the complete quietness
of your soul. Feel the peace settling over you, a
glimpse of the kingdom to come. How can you
better cultivate quietness? *See also* Spiritual
Disciplines Index.

20 Happy will you be who sow beside every
    stream,
  who let the ox and the donkey range
    freely.

A Prophecy of Deliverance from Foes

33 Ah, you destroyer,
    who yourself have not been
    destroyed;
  you treacherous one,
    with whom no one has dealt
      treacherously!
  When you have ceased to destroy,
    you will be destroyed;
  and when you have stopped dealing
      treacherously,
    you will be dealt with treacherously.

2 O Lord, be gracious to us; we wait for
    you.
  Be our arm every morning,
    our salvation in the time of trouble.
3 At the sound of tumult, peoples fled;
    before your majesty, nations
      scattered.
4 Spoil was gathered as the caterpillar
    gathers;
    as locusts leap, they leaped*a* upon it.
5 The Lord is exalted, he dwells on high;
    he filled Zion with justice and
      righteousness;
6 he will be the stability of your times,
    abundance of salvation, wisdom, and
      knowledge;
    the fear of the Lord is Zion's
      treasure.*b*

7 Listen! the valiant*a* cry in the streets;
    the envoys of peace weep bitterly.
8 The highways are deserted,
    travelers have quit the road.

  The treaty is broken,
    its oaths*c* are despised,
    its obligation*d* is disregarded.
9 The land mourns and languishes;
    Lebanon is confounded and withers
      away;
  Sharon is like a desert;
    and Bashan and Carmel shake off
      their leaves.

10 "Now I will arise," says the Lord,
    "now I will lift myself up;
    now I will be exalted.
11 You conceive chaff, you bring forth
      stubble;
    your breath is a fire that will consume
      you.
12 And the peoples will be as if burned to
      lime,
    like thorns cut down, that are burned
      in the fire."

13 Hear, you who are far away, what I have
      done;
    and you who are near, acknowledge
      my might.
14 The sinners in Zion are afraid;
    trembling has seized the godless:
  "Who among us can live with the
      devouring fire?
  Who among us can live with
      everlasting flames?"
15 Those who walk righteously and speak
      uprightly,
    who despise the gain of oppression,
  who wave away a bribe instead of
      accepting it,

a Meaning of Heb uncertain   *b* Heb *his treasure*;
meaning of Heb uncertain   *c* Q Ms: MT *cities*
d Or *everyone*

33:5–6 *he will be the stability of your times.*
Here hope rests on God's direct capacity to give
justice and righteousness, which will issue in
security, stability, and salvation. There is no
mention here of the Davidic king, for now there
is anticipation of God's direct rule and
intervention.
  33:15–16 *Those who walk righteously . . . will
live on the heights.* These verses articulate in

succinct fashion one of the primary ethical
traditions of the Old Testament, a tradition that
is also sounded in Pss 15; 24; Job 31. It is clear
that an ethic of responsibility focuses particularly
on fair and generous economic transactions with
one's neighbors. It is characteristically promised
in the Old Testament that those who practice
such an ethic will live a life of abundance, well-
being, and security.

who stop their ears from hearing of
    bloodshed
and shut their eyes from looking on
    evil,
16 they will live on the heights;
    their refuge will be the fortresses of
        rocks;
    their food will be supplied, their
        water assured.

The Land of the Majestic King

17 Your eyes will see the king in his beauty;
    they will behold a land that stretches
        far away.
18 Your mind will muse on the terror:
    "Where is the one who counted?
    Where is the one who weighed the
        tribute?
    Where is the one who counted the
        towers?"
19 No longer will you see the insolent
        people,
    the people of an obscure speech that
        you cannot comprehend,
    stammering in a language that you
        cannot understand.
20 Look on Zion, the city of our appointed
        festivals!
    Your eyes will see Jerusalem,
    a quiet habitation, an immovable
        tent,
    whose stakes will never be pulled up,
    and none of whose ropes will be
        broken.
21 But there the LORD in majesty will be for
        us
    a place of broad rivers and streams,
    where no galley with oars can go,
    nor stately ship can pass.
22 For the LORD is our judge, the LORD is
        our ruler,
    the LORD is our king; he will save us.

23 Your rigging hangs loose;
    it cannot hold the mast firm in its
        place,
    or keep the sail spread out.

Then prey and spoil in abundance will
    be divided;
    even the lame will fall to plundering.
24 And no inhabitant will say, "I am sick";
    the people who live there will be
        forgiven their iniquity.

Judgment on the Nations

34 Draw near, O nations, to hear;
    O peoples, give heed!
Let the earth hear, and all that fills it;
    the world, and all that comes from it.
2 For the LORD is enraged against all the
        nations,
    and furious against all their hordes;
    he has doomed them, has given them
        over for slaughter.
3 Their slain shall be cast out,
    and the stench of their corpses shall
        rise;
    the mountains shall flow with their
        blood.
4 All the host of heaven shall rot away,
    and the skies roll up like a scroll.
All their host shall wither
    like a leaf withering on a vine,
    or fruit withering on a fig tree.

5 When my sword has drunk its fill in the
        heavens,
    lo, it will descend upon Edom,
    upon the people I have doomed to
        judgment.
6 The LORD has a sword; it is sated with
        blood,
    it is gorged with fat,
    with the blood of lambs and goats,

34:1–17, *the* LORD *is enraged.* Chapters 34–35
form a sharp and complete contrast. Chapter 34
is unmitigated vengeance on the part of God,
who will work complete annihilation on the
unspecified nations who have been recalcitrant
and rebellious (see particularly vv 2, 5, 8). The
poetry imagines devastation so complete that
these once proud and buoyant nations are

reduced to nesting places for owls and buzzards.
The imagery thus alludes to places of filth and
defilement where none can live adequately (see
v 15). This poetry, almost too tough to hear, is
extreme rhetoric describing God's undoing of
those parts of creation that refuse to accept the
sovereignty of God.

with the fat of the kidneys of rams.
For the LORD has a sacrifice in Bozrah,
    a great slaughter in the land of Edom.
7 Wild oxen shall fall with them,
    and young steers with the mighty
        bulls.
Their land shall be soaked with blood,
    and their soil made rich with fat.

8 For the LORD has a day of vengeance,
    a year of vindication by Zion's cause. *a*
9 And the streams of Edom *b* shall be
        turned into pitch,
    and her soil into sulfur;
    her land shall become burning pitch.
10 Night and day it shall not be quenched;
    its smoke shall go up forever.
From generation to generation it shall
        lie waste;
    no one shall pass through it forever
        and ever.
11 But the hawk *c* and the hedgehog *c* shall
        possess it;
    the owl *c* and the raven shall live in it.
He shall stretch the line of confusion
        over it,
    and the plummet of chaos over *d* its
        nobles.
12 They shall name it No Kingdom There,
    and all its princes shall be nothing.
13 Thorns shall grow over its strongholds,
    nettles and thistles in its fortresses.
It shall be the haunt of jackals,
    an abode for ostriches.
14 Wildcats shall meet with hyenas,
    goat-demons shall call to each other;
there too Lilith shall repose,
    and find a place to rest.
15 There shall the owl nest

and lay and hatch and brood in its
        shadow;
there too the buzzards shall gather,
    each one with its mate.
16 Seek and read from the book of the
        LORD:
    Not one of these shall be missing;
    none shall be without its mate.
For the mouth of the LORD has
        commanded,
    and his spirit has gathered them.
17 He has cast the lot for them,
    his hand has portioned it out to them
        with the line;
they shall possess it forever,
    from generation to generation they
        shall live in it.

The Return of the Redeemed to Zion

35 The wilderness and the dry land
        shall be glad,
    the desert shall rejoice and blossom;
like the crocus 2 it shall blossom
        abundantly,
    and rejoice with joy and singing.
The glory of Lebanon shall be given to
        it,
    the majesty of Carmel and Sharon.
They shall see the glory of the LORD,
    the majesty of our God.

3 Strengthen the weak hands,
    and make firm the feeble knees.
4 Say to those who are of a fearful heart,
    "Be strong, do not fear!
Here is your God.
    He will come with vengeance,

a Or *of recompense by Zion's defender*   *b* Heb *her
streams*   *c* Identification uncertain
d Heb lacks *over*

Responding
35:1 SOLITUDE. The wilderness and
the desert are classic symbols of
solitude. For modern Christians, retreating to
such locales for meditation and prayer may not
be a possibility. Choose a place where you know
you can experience solitude and treat it as your
own personal wilderness. Set aside several times
this week to visit it. *See also* Spiritual Disciplines
Index.

35:1–10 *the desert shall rejoice and blossom*.
Chapter 35 is a lyrical, visionary expectation
that God's people, as a result of the devastation
of the enemy in chapter 34, will be permitted to
come home to Jerusalem in well-being and joy.
It is likely that the poetry wants to relate the
historical revivification of Jerusalem to the
revivification of all of the earth, the latter
probably to be given by the promise of great
rain.

with terrible recompense.
  He will come and save you."

5 Then the eyes of the blind shall be
    opened,
  and the ears of the deaf unstopped;
6 then the lame shall leap like a deer,
  and the tongue of the speechless sing
    for joy.
  For waters shall break forth in the
    wilderness,
  and streams in the desert;
7 the burning sand shall become a pool,
  and the thirsty ground springs of
    water;
  the haunt of jackals shall become a
    swamp,[a]
  the grass shall become reeds and
    rushes.

8 A highway shall be there,
  and it shall be called the Holy Way;
  the unclean shall not travel on it,[b]
  but it shall be for God's people;[c]
  no traveler, not even fools, shall go
    astray.
9 No lion shall be there,
  nor shall any ravenous beast come up
    on it;
  they shall not be found there,
  but the redeemed shall walk there.

10 And the ransomed of the LORD shall
    return,
  and come to Zion with singing;
  everlasting joy shall be upon their
    heads;
  they shall obtain joy and gladness,
  and sorrow and sighing shall flee
    away.

Sennacherib Threatens Jerusalem

36 In the fourteenth year of King Hezekiah, King Sennacherib of Assyria
came up against all the fortified cities of Judah and captured them. 2The king of Assyria sent the Rabshakeh from Lachish to King
Hezekiah at Jerusalem, with a great army. He
stood by the conduit of the upper pool on the
highway to the Fuller's Field. 3And there
came out to him Eliakim son of Hilkiah, who
was in charge of the palace, and Shebna the
secretary, and Joah son of Asaph, the
recorder.

4 The Rabshakeh said to them, "Say to
Hezekiah: Thus says the great king, the king
of Assyria: On what do you base this confidence of yours? 5Do you think that mere
words are strategy and power for war? On
whom do you now rely, that you have rebelled against me? 6See, you are relying on

a Cn: Heb *in the haunt of jackals is her resting place*
b Or *pass it by*   c Cn: Heb *for them*

35:5–7 *the lame shall leap like a deer.* The
return trip to Jerusalem will be so buoyant that
even the disabled will be able to come home
and be restored to full function; the blind, the
deaf, the lame, and the mute are all given back
their lives. Reference should be made to Luke
7:22, in which Jesus is identified as the one who
enacts all of these anticipated transformations.
The transformation of the disabled among
God's people is matched by the transformation
of the thirsty ground through rain. It is to be
remembered that the events of the Bible take
place in an arid climate, and therefore the gift of
rain is exactly the gift of God that revivifies the
whole earth.
  35:8–10 *the Holy Way.* The poet imagines
a new superhighway, from exile in Babylon to
Jerusalem, that will be so broad, wide, and clear
that not even foolish, careless travelers can get

lost. All will travel home without threat or
anxiety. Those who come home are marked as
the "redeemed" and the "ransomed," the ones
to whom God has been particularly attentive.
  36:1–39:8 *Sennacherib . . . captured.* This
section, chapters 36–39, consists of a kind of
material very different both from what precedes
and from the great visions of restoration that
follow. This material probably looks back to the
experiences and utterances of Isaiah, near the
end of his prophetic career, during a crisis in
Jerusalem in 701 BC under King Hezekiah. In
that year, the aggressive armies of the empire
of Assyria, led by Sennacherib, laid siege to
the city of Jerusalem and placed it in acute
jeopardy. The ultimate threat, of course,
is Yahweh himself, who has moved decisively
against God's people.

adding sin to sin;

2 who set out to go down to Egypt
    without asking for my counsel,
  to take refuge in the protection of
      Pharaoh,
  and to seek shelter in the shadow of
      Egypt;
3 Therefore the protection of Pharaoh
      shall become your shame,
  and the shelter in the shadow of
      Egypt your humiliation.
4 For though his officials are at Zoan
    and his envoys reach Hanes,
5 everyone comes to shame
    through a people that cannot profit
      them,
  that brings neither help nor profit,
    but shame and disgrace.

6 An oracle concerning the animals of the
Negeb.
  Through a land of trouble and distress,
    of lioness and roaring*a* lion,
    of viper and flying serpent,
  they carry their riches on the backs of
      donkeys,
    and their treasures on the humps of
      camels,
    to a people that cannot profit them.
7 For Egypt's help is worthless and empty,
    therefore I have called her,
    "Rahab who sits still."*b*

A Rebellious People

8 Go now, write it before them on a
      tablet,
  and inscribe it in a book,
    so that it may be for the time to come
      as a witness forever.

9 For they are a rebellious people,
    faithless children,
  children who will not hear
    the instruction of the LORD;
10 who say to the seers, "Do not see";
    and to the prophets, "Do not
      prophesy to us what is right;
  speak to us smooth things,
    prophesy illusions,
11 leave the way, turn aside from the path,
    let us hear no more about the Holy
      One of Israel."
12 Therefore thus says the Holy One of
      Israel:
  Because you reject this word,
    and put your trust in oppression and
      deceit,
    and rely on them;
13 therefore this iniquity shall become for
      you
  like a break in a high wall, bulging
    out, and about to collapse,
  whose crash comes suddenly, in an
      instant;
14 its breaking is like that of a potter's
      vessel
  that is smashed so ruthlessly
  that among its fragments not a sherd is
      found
  for taking fire from the hearth,
    or dipping water out of the cistern.

15 For thus said the Lord GOD, the Holy
      One of Israel:
  In returning and rest you shall be saved;
    in quietness and in trust shall be your
      strength.

a Cn: Heb *from them* *b* Meaning of Heb
uncertain

30:15 *in quietness and in trust shall be your
strength.* The lines of this verse, along with 7:9,
constitute what is probably the most significant
affirmation of the prophet Isaiah in the eighth
century BC. Both 7:9 and this text urge complete
reliance upon Yahweh as the alternative to
frantic, anxious military and political posturing.
Isaiah is not a pacifist; rather, he believes that
trust in Yahweh is the taproot of security. All
trust in armaments and alliances, he reasons, is
an act of mistrust and idolatry that will only lead
to destruction. The assurance of faith is the
conviction that anxious self-securing does not
work in the real world. The phrase "returning
and rest" is an affirmation that faith is quiet
confidence, which is decisive for being safe and
well in the world. The oracle goes on to say that
those who rely on armaments will finally be
routed by armaments (vv 16–17). An arms race
ultimately cannot be won!
30:15 SILENCE—*See* Spiritual Disciplines
Index.

But you refused [16]and said,
"No! We will flee upon horses"—
    therefore you shall flee!
and, "We will ride upon swift steeds"—
    therefore your pursuers shall be swift!
[17] A thousand shall flee at the threat of
        one,
    at the threat of five you shall flee,
until you are left
    like a flagstaff on the top of a
        mountain,
    like a signal on a hill.

God's Promise to Zion

[18] Therefore the LORD waits to be gracious
        to you;
    therefore he will rise up to show
        mercy to you.
    For the LORD is a God of justice;
        blessed are all those who wait for him.

[19] Truly, O people in Zion, inhabitants of
Jerusalem, you shall weep no more. He will
surely be gracious to you at the sound of your
cry; when he hears it, he will answer you.
[20]Though the Lord may give you the bread of
adversity and the water of affliction, yet your
Teacher will not hide himself any more, but
your eyes shall see your Teacher. [21]And when
you turn to the right or when you turn to
the left, your ears shall hear a word behind
you, saying, "This is the way; walk in it."
[22]Then you will defile your silver-covered
idols and your gold-plated images. You will
scatter them like filthy rags; you will say to
them, "Away with you!"

[23] He will give rain for the seed with
which you sow the ground, and grain, the
produce of the ground, which will be rich
and plenteous. On that day your cattle will
graze in broad pastures; [24]and the oxen and
donkeys that till the ground will eat silage,
which has been winnowed with shovel and
fork. [25]On every lofty mountain and every
high hill there will be brooks running with
water—on a day of the great slaughter, when
the towers fall. [26]Moreover the light of the
moon will be like the light of the sun, and the
light of the sun will be sevenfold, like the
light of seven days, on the day when the LORD
binds up the injuries of his people, and heals
the wounds inflicted by his blow.

Judgment on Assyria

[27] See, the name of the LORD comes from
        far away,
    burning with his anger, and in thick
        rising smoke;[a]
his lips are full of indignation,
    and his tongue is like a devouring
        fire;
[28] his breath is like an overflowing stream
    that reaches up to the neck—
to sift the nations with the sieve of
        destruction,
    and to place on the jaws of the
        peoples a bridle that leads them
        astray.

[29] You shall have a song as in the night
when a holy festival is kept; and gladness of
heart, as when one sets out to the sound of
the flute to go to the mountain of the LORD,
to the Rock of Israel. [30]And the LORD will
cause his majestic voice to be heard and the
descending blow of his arm to be seen, in furious anger and a flame of devouring fire,
with a cloudburst and tempest and hailstones. [31]The Assyrian will be terror-stricken
at the voice of the LORD, when he strikes with
his rod. [32]And every stroke of the staff of punishment that the LORD lays upon him will be
to the sound of timbrels and lyres; battling
with brandished arm he will fight with him.
[33]For his burning place[b] has long been prepared; truly it is made ready for the king,[c] its

a Meaning of Heb uncertain   b Or Topheth
c Or Molech

Responding

30:20–21 GUIDANCE. It is often
difficult to hear that voice guiding us to
the right path. In his *Rules for the Discernment
of Spirits*, Ignatius of Loyola states that good
influences provide courage and strength and
produce peace and a greater feeling of love,
while choices influenced by evil can be counted
on to cause regret, sadness, and disquiet. Reflect
on his words. Are there any paths in your life
that don't stand up to this test of discernment?
See also Spiritual Disciplines Index.

pyre made deep and wide, with fire and wood in abundance; the breath of the LORD, like a stream of sulfur, kindles it.

Alliance with Egypt Is Futile

31 Alas for those who go down to Egypt for help
and who rely on horses,
who trust in chariots because they are many
and in horsemen because they are very strong,
but do not look to the Holy One of Israel
or consult the LORD!
2 Yet he too is wise and brings disaster;
he does not call back his words,
but will rise against the house of the evildoers,
and against the helpers of those who work iniquity.
3 The Egyptians are human, and not God;
their horses are flesh, and not spirit.
When the LORD stretches out his hand,
the helper will stumble, and the one helped will fall,
and they will all perish together.

4 For thus the LORD said to me,
As a lion or a young lion growls over its prey,
and—when a band of shepherds is called out against it—
is not terrified by their shouting
or daunted at their noise,
so the LORD of hosts will come down
to fight upon Mount Zion and upon its hill.
5 Like birds hovering overhead, so the
LORD of hosts
will protect Jerusalem;
he will protect and deliver it,
he will spare and rescue it.

6 Turn back to him whom you[a] have deeply betrayed, O people of Israel. 7For on that day all of you shall throw away your idols of silver and idols of gold, which your hands have sinfully made for you.
8 "Then the Assyrian shall fall by a sword, not of mortals;
and a sword, not of humans, shall devour him;
he shall flee from the sword,
and his young men shall be put to forced labor.
9 His rock shall pass away in terror,
and his officers desert the standard in panic,"
says the LORD, whose fire is in Zion,
and whose furnace is in Jerusalem.

Government with Justice Predicted

32 See, a king will reign in righteousness,
and princes will rule with justice.
2 Each will be like a hiding place from the wind,
a covert from the tempest,
like streams of water in a dry place,

a Heb *they*

31:1–4 *Alas for those who go down to Egypt for help.* The prophet urges a radical either/or choice upon the Jerusalem government. "Egypt" is here a metaphor for all reliance upon political, military posturing. The reason that the Egyptians are no adequate source of reliance in the real world is that they are human and not God; they are flesh and not spirit. Yahweh, the God of Israel, however, is spirit—that is, he has the capacity to make all things new.

32:1–35:10 *See, a king will reign.* In this next section, the tradition of Isaiah moves forward in time and theologically toward hope.

32:1 *a king will reign in righteousness.* The Isaiah tradition keeps one eye on the Davidic dynasty and believes that, in contrast to the failed kings of the eighth century BC, there will come a king who will rule in righteousness and justice. This is consistent with the oracular anticipations of chapters 9 and 11. It is believed, in the Isaiah tradition, that such a king will make possible in the world new life in which there will be safety and well-being and joy. Such promises became the root of messianic hope in the New Testament, which easily identified Jesus as the coming king who would make all things new.

like the shade of a great rock in a
        weary land.
3 Then the eyes of those who have sight
        will not be closed,
    and the ears of those who have
        hearing will listen.
4 The minds of the rash will have good
        judgment,
    and the tongues of stammerers will
        speak readily and distinctly.
5 A fool will no longer be called noble,
    nor a villain said to be honorable.
6 For fools speak folly,
    and their minds plot iniquity:
to practice ungodliness,
    to utter error concerning the LORD,
to leave the craving of the hungry
        unsatisfied,
    and to deprive the thirsty of drink.
7 The villainies of villains are evil;
    they devise wicked devices
to ruin the poor with lying words,
    even when the plea of the needy is
        right.
8 But those who are noble plan noble
        things,
    and by noble things they stand.

Complacent Women Warned of Disaster

9 Rise up, you women who are at ease,
        hear my voice;
    you complacent daughters, listen to
        my speech.
10 In little more than a year
    you will shudder, you complacent
        ones;
for the vintage will fail,
    the fruit harvest will not come.
11 Tremble, you women who are at ease,

shudder, you complacent ones;
strip, and make yourselves bare,
    and put sackcloth on your loins.
12 Beat your breasts for the pleasant fields,
    for the fruitful vine,
13 for the soil of my people
    growing up in thorns and briers;
yes, for all the joyous houses
    in the jubilant city.
14 For the palace will be forsaken,
    the populous city deserted;
the hill and the watchtower
    will become dens forever,
the joy of wild asses,
    a pasture for flocks;
15 until a spirit from on high is poured out
        on us,
    and the wilderness becomes a fruitful
        field,
    and the fruitful field is deemed a
        forest.

The Peace of God's Reign

16 Then justice will dwell in the
        wilderness,
    and righteousness abide in the
        fruitful field.
17 The effect of righteousness will be
        peace,
    and the result of righteousness,
        quietness and trust forever.
18 My people will abide in a peaceful
        habitation,
    in secure dwellings, and in quiet
        resting places.
19 The forest will disappear completely, *a*
    and the city will be utterly laid low.

a Cn: Heb *And it will hail when the forest comes down*

32:15–20 *peaceful habitation.* Again it
is promised, after so much judgment and
punishment, that the ultimate outcome for
God's people will be justice and righteousness,
and peace. The earlier part of this chapter
had imagined that this would come through
the Davidic dynasty. In these verses, however,
there is no mention of such a king. It is simply
the case that God will work such a newness
and such a goodness; the People of God
are urged to have confidence to wait for

the good gifts that God will yet give in the
future.

Responding
32:17 **SILENCE.** What does it mean for
righteousness to result in quietness?
Close your eyes. Picture the complete quietness
of your soul. Feel the peace settling over you, a
glimpse of the kingdom to come. How can you
better cultivate quietness? *See also* Spiritual
Disciplines Index.

20 Happy will you be who sow beside every
  stream,
  who let the ox and the donkey range
   freely.

A Prophecy of Deliverance from Foes

33 Ah, you destroyer,
  who yourself have not been
   destroyed;
 you treacherous one,
  with whom no one has dealt
   treacherously!
 When you have ceased to destroy,
  you will be destroyed;
 and when you have stopped dealing
   treacherously,
  you will be dealt with treacherously.

2 O Lord, be gracious to us; we wait for
   you.
  Be our arm every morning,
  our salvation in the time of trouble.
3 At the sound of tumult, peoples fled;
  before your majesty, nations
   scattered.
4 Spoil was gathered as the caterpillar
   gathers;
  as locusts leap, they leaped*a* upon it.
5 The Lord is exalted, he dwells on high;
  he filled Zion with justice and
   righteousness;
6 he will be the stability of your times,
  abundance of salvation, wisdom, and
   knowledge;
  the fear of the Lord is Zion's
   treasure.*b*

7 Listen! the valiant*a* cry in the streets;
  the envoys of peace weep bitterly.
8 The highways are deserted,
  travelers have quit the road.

 The treaty is broken,
  its oaths*c* are despised,
  its obligation*d* is disregarded.
9 The land mourns and languishes;
  Lebanon is confounded and withers
   away;
 Sharon is like a desert;
  and Bashan and Carmel shake off
   their leaves.

10 "Now I will arise," says the Lord,
  "now I will lift myself up;
  now I will be exalted.
11 You conceive chaff, you bring forth
   stubble;
  your breath is a fire that will consume
   you.
12 And the peoples will be as if burned to
   lime,
  like thorns cut down, that are burned
   in the fire."

13 Hear, you who are far away, what I have
   done;
  and you who are near, acknowledge
   my might.
14 The sinners in Zion are afraid;
  trembling has seized the godless:
 "Who among us can live with the
   devouring fire?
 Who among us can live with
   everlasting flames?"
15 Those who walk righteously and speak
   uprightly,
  who despise the gain of oppression,
 who wave away a bribe instead of
   accepting it,

a Meaning of Heb uncertain   *b* Heb *his treasure*;
meaning of Heb uncertain   *c* Q Ms: MT *cities*
d Or *everyone*

33:5–6 *he will be the stability of your times.*
Here hope rests on God's direct capacity to give
justice and righteousness, which will issue in
security, stability, and salvation. There is no
mention here of the Davidic king, for now there
is anticipation of God's direct rule and
intervention.
 33:15–16 *Those who walk righteously . . . will
live on the heights.* These verses articulate in

succinct fashion one of the primary ethical
traditions of the Old Testament, a tradition that
is also sounded in Pss 15; 24; Job 31. It is clear
that an ethic of responsibility focuses particularly
on fair and generous economic transactions with
one's neighbors. It is characteristically promised
in the Old Testament that those who practice
such an ethic will live a life of abundance, well-
being, and security.

who stop their ears from hearing of
     bloodshed
and shut their eyes from looking on
     evil,
16 they will live on the heights;
     their refuge will be the fortresses of
          rocks;
     their food will be supplied, their
          water assured.

The Land of the Majestic King

17 Your eyes will see the king in his beauty;
     they will behold a land that stretches
          far away.
18 Your mind will muse on the terror:
     "Where is the one who counted?
     Where is the one who weighed the
          tribute?
     Where is the one who counted the
          towers?"
19 No longer will you see the insolent
          people,
     the people of an obscure speech that
          you cannot comprehend,
     stammering in a language that you
          cannot understand.
20 Look on Zion, the city of our appointed
          festivals!
     Your eyes will see Jerusalem,
     a quiet habitation, an immovable
          tent,
     whose stakes will never be pulled up,
     and none of whose ropes will be
          broken.
21 But there the LORD in majesty will be for
          us
     a place of broad rivers and streams,
     where no galley with oars can go,
     nor stately ship can pass.
22 For the LORD is our judge, the LORD is
          our ruler,
     the LORD is our king; he will save us.

23 Your rigging hangs loose;
     it cannot hold the mast firm in its
          place,
     or keep the sail spread out.

Then prey and spoil in abundance will
          be divided;
     even the lame will fall to plundering.
24 And no inhabitant will say, "I am sick";
     the people who live there will be
          forgiven their iniquity.

Judgment on the Nations

34 Draw near, O nations, to hear;
     O peoples, give heed!
Let the earth hear, and all that fills it;
     the world, and all that comes from it.
2 For the LORD is enraged against all the
          nations,
     and furious against all their hordes;
     he has doomed them, has given them
          over for slaughter.
3 Their slain shall be cast out,
     and the stench of their corpses shall
          rise;
     the mountains shall flow with their
          blood.
4 All the host of heaven shall rot away,
     and the skies roll up like a scroll.
All their host shall wither
     like a leaf withering on a vine,
     or fruit withering on a fig tree.

5 When my sword has drunk its fill in the
          heavens,
     lo, it will descend upon Edom,
     upon the people I have doomed to
          judgment.
6 The LORD has a sword; it is sated with
          blood,
     it is gorged with fat,
     with the blood of lambs and goats,

34:1–17 *the LORD is enraged.* Chapters 34–35 form a sharp and complete contrast. Chapter 34 is unmitigated vengeance on the part of God, who will work complete annihilation on the unspecified nations who have been recalcitrant and rebellious (see particularly vv 2, 5, 8). The poetry imagines devastation so complete that these once proud and buoyant nations are reduced to nesting places for owls and buzzards. The imagery thus alludes to places of filth and defilement where none can live adequately (see v 15). This poetry, almost too tough to hear, is extreme rhetoric describing God's undoing of those parts of creation that refuse to accept the sovereignty of God.

with the fat of the kidneys of rams.
For the LORD has a sacrifice in Bozrah,
   a great slaughter in the land of Edom.
7 Wild oxen shall fall with them,
   and young steers with the mighty
      bulls.
Their land shall be soaked with blood,
   and their soil made rich with fat.

8 For the LORD has a day of vengeance,
   a year of vindication by Zion's cause. *a*
9 And the streams of Edom *b* shall be
      turned into pitch,
   and her soil into sulfur;
   her land shall become burning pitch.
10 Night and day it shall not be quenched;
   its smoke shall go up forever.
From generation to generation it shall
      lie waste;
   no one shall pass through it forever
      and ever.
11 But the hawk *c* and the hedgehog *c* shall
      possess it;
   the owl *c* and the raven shall live in it.
He shall stretch the line of confusion
      over it,
   and the plummet of chaos over *d* its
      nobles.
12 They shall name it No Kingdom There,
   and all its princes shall be nothing.
13 Thorns shall grow over its strongholds,
   nettles and thistles in its fortresses.
It shall be the haunt of jackals,
   an abode for ostriches.
14 Wildcats shall meet with hyenas,
   goat-demons shall call to each other;
there too Lilith shall repose,
   and find a place to rest.
15 There shall the owl nest

and lay and hatch and brood in its
      shadow;
there too the buzzards shall gather,
   each one with its mate.
16 Seek and read from the book of the
      LORD:
   Not one of these shall be missing;
   none shall be without its mate.
For the mouth of the LORD has
      commanded,
   and his spirit has gathered them.
17 He has cast the lot for them,
   his hand has portioned it out to them
      with the line;
they shall possess it forever,
   from generation to generation they
      shall live in it.

The Return of the Redeemed to Zion

35 The wilderness and the dry land
      shall be glad,
   the desert shall rejoice and blossom;
like the crocus *2* it shall blossom
      abundantly,
   and rejoice with joy and singing.
The glory of Lebanon shall be given to
      it,
   the majesty of Carmel and Sharon.
They shall see the glory of the LORD,
   the majesty of our God.

3 Strengthen the weak hands,
   and make firm the feeble knees.
4 Say to those who are of a fearful heart,
   "Be strong, do not fear!
Here is your God.
   He will come with vengeance,

a Or *of recompense by Zion's defender*   b Heb *her
streams*   c Identification uncertain
d Heb lacks *over*

Responding

35:1 SOLITUDE. The wilderness and
the desert are classic symbols of
solitude. For modern Christians, retreating to
such locales for meditation and prayer may not
be a possibility. Choose a place where you know
you can experience solitude and treat it as your
own personal wilderness. Set aside several times
this week to visit it. *See also* Spiritual Disciplines
Index.

35:1–10 *the desert shall rejoice and blossom.*
Chapter 35 is a lyrical, visionary expectation
that God's people, as a result of the devastation
of the enemy in chapter 34, will be permitted to
come home to Jerusalem in well-being and joy.
It is likely that the poetry wants to relate the
historical revivification of Jerusalem to the
revivification of all of the earth, the latter
probably to be given by the promise of great
rain.

with terrible recompense.
  He will come and save you."

⁵ Then the eyes of the blind shall be
    opened,
  and the ears of the deaf unstopped;
⁶ then the lame shall leap like a deer,
  and the tongue of the speechless sing
    for joy.
  For waters shall break forth in the
    wilderness,
  and streams in the desert;
⁷ the burning sand shall become a pool,
  and the thirsty ground springs of
    water;
  the haunt of jackals shall become a
    swamp, ᵃ
  the grass shall become reeds and
    rushes.

⁸ A highway shall be there,
  and it shall be called the Holy Way;
  the unclean shall not travel on it, ᵇ
  but it shall be for God's people; ᶜ
  no traveler, not even fools, shall go
    astray.
⁹ No lion shall be there,
  nor shall any ravenous beast come up
    on it;
  they shall not be found there,
  but the redeemed shall walk there.

¹⁰ And the ransomed of the LORD shall
    return,
  and come to Zion with singing;
  everlasting joy shall be upon their
    heads;
  they shall obtain joy and gladness,
  and sorrow and sighing shall flee
    away.

Sennacherib Threatens Jerusalem

36 In the fourteenth year of King Hezekiah, King Sennacherib of Assyria came up against all the fortified cities of Judah and captured them. ²The king of Assyria sent the Rabshakeh from Lachish to King Hezekiah at Jerusalem, with a great army. He stood by the conduit of the upper pool on the highway to the Fuller's Field. ³And there came out to him Eliakim son of Hilkiah, who was in charge of the palace, and Shebna the secretary, and Joah son of Asaph, the recorder.

4 The Rabshakeh said to them, "Say to Hezekiah: Thus says the great king, the king of Assyria: On what do you base this confidence of yours? ⁵Do you think that mere words are strategy and power for war? On whom do you now rely, that you have rebelled against me? ⁶See, you are relying on

a Cn: Heb *in the haunt of jackals is her resting place*
b Or *pass it by*   c Cn: Heb *for them*

35:5–7 *the lame shall leap like a deer.* The return trip to Jerusalem will be so buoyant that even the disabled will be able to come home and be restored to full function; the blind, the deaf, the lame, and the mute are all given back their lives. Reference should be made to Luke 7:22, in which Jesus is identified as the one who enacts all of these anticipated transformations. The transformation of the disabled among God's people is matched by the transformation of the thirsty ground through rain. It is to be remembered that the events of the Bible take place in an arid climate, and therefore the gift of rain is exactly the gift of God that revivifies the whole earth.

35:8–10 *the Holy Way.* The poet imagines a new superhighway, from exile in Babylon to Jerusalem, that will be so broad, wide, and clear that not even foolish, careless travelers can get

lost. All will travel home without threat or anxiety. Those who come home are marked as the "redeemed" and the "ransomed," the ones to whom God has been particularly attentive.

36:1–39:8 *Sennacherib . . . captured.* This section, chapters 36–39, consists of a kind of material very different both from what precedes and from the great visions of restoration that follow. This material probably looks back to the experiences and utterances of Isaiah, near the end of his prophetic career, during a crisis in Jerusalem in 701 BC under King Hezekiah. In that year, the aggressive armies of the empire of Assyria, led by Sennacherib, laid siege to the city of Jerusalem and placed it in acute jeopardy. The ultimate threat, of course, is Yahweh himself, who has moved decisively against God's people.

Egypt, that broken reed of a staff, which will pierce the hand of anyone who leans on it. Such is Pharaoh king of Egypt to all who rely on him. 7But if you say to me, 'We rely on the LORD our God,' is it not he whose high places and altars Hezekiah has removed, saying to Judah and to Jerusalem, 'You shall worship before this altar'? 8Come now, make a wager with my master the king of Assyria: I will give you two thousand horses, if you are able on your part to set riders on them. 9How then can you repulse a single captain among the least of my master's servants, when you rely on Egypt for chariots and for horsemen? 10Moreover, is it without the LORD that I have come up against this land to destroy it? The LORD said to me, Go up against this land, and destroy it."

11 Then Eliakim, Shebna, and Joah said to the Rabshakeh, "Please speak to your servants in Aramaic, for we understand it; do not speak to us in the language of Judah within in the hearing of the people who are on the wall." 12But the Rabshakeh said, "Has my master sent me to speak these words to your master and to you, and not to the people sitting on the wall, who are doomed with you to eat their own dung and drink their own urine?"

13 Then the Rabshakeh stood and called out in a loud voice in the language of Judah,

"Hear the words of the great king, the king of Assyria! 14Thus says the king: 'Do not let Hezekiah deceive you, for he will not be able to deliver you. 15Do not let Hezekiah make you rely on the LORD by saying, The LORD will surely deliver us; this city will not be given into the hand of the king of Assyria.' 16Do not listen to Hezekiah; for thus says the king of Assyria: 'Make your peace with me and come out to me; then every one of you will eat from your own vine and your own fig tree and drink water from your own cistern, 17until I come and take you away to a land like your own land, a land of grain and wine, a land of bread and vineyards. 18Do not let Hezekiah mislead you by saying, The LORD will save us. Has any of the gods of the nations saved their land out of the hand of the king of Assyria? 19Where are the gods of Hamath and Arpad? Where are the gods of Sepharvaim? Have they delivered Samaria out of my hand? 20Who among all the gods of these countries have saved their countries out of my hand, that the LORD should save Jerusalem out of my hand?' "

21 But they were silent and answered him not a word, for the king's command was, "Do not answer him." 22Then Eliakim son of Hilkiah, who was in charge of the palace, and Shebna the secretary, and Joah son of Asaph, the recorder, came to Hezekiah with their

---

36:4–10 *On whom do you now rely?* This passage constitutes the first of three speeches that the prophetic tradition has placed on the lips of the Assyrian king or his official (see also 36:13–20; 37:10–13). These three taunting speeches seek to talk Jerusalem and Hezekiah out of faith in Yahweh. The Rabshakeh's speech revolves around the use of the word "rely" and asks Hezekiah and the Jerusalem leaders whether they can really rely on Yahweh or whether they must finally rely on the immense military power of Assyria.

36:13–20 *he will not be able to deliver you.* The Rabshakeh's second speech again urges the city of Jerusalem to surrender to Assyria rather than be destroyed, since no god has been able to withstand the military aggressiveness of Assyria. The implicit claim of Isaiah, of course, is that Yahweh, unlike the other gods, is able to

save. The whole of the rhetorical exchange functions as a meditation upon faith and whether the People of God are able to trust God in real circumstances of threat and anxiety.

Responding
36:15 PRAYER. Try an experiment in which you pray for the safety of a person you know who comes in harm's way—police officer, firefighter, soldier, missionary—while keeping in mind the following example. During World War II the village church of Poughill, England, scheduled a member to pray each hour of the day, seven days a week for the safety of those serving in the military from their community. Because none were killed, to this day the villagers believe God heard and answered their prayers. *See also* Spiritual Disciplines Index.

clothes torn, and told him the words of the Rabshakeh.

Hezekiah Consults Isaiah

37 When King Hezekiah heard it, he tore his clothes, covered himself with sackcloth, and went into the house of the LORD. 2And he sent Eliakim, who was in charge of the palace, and Shebna the secretary, and the senior priests, covered with sackcloth, to the prophet Isaiah son of Amoz. 3They said to him, "Thus says Hezekiah, This day is a day of distress, of rebuke, and of disgrace; children have come to the birth, and there is no strength to bring them forth. 4It may be that the LORD your God heard the words of the Rabshakeh, whom his master the king of Assyria has sent to mock the living God, and will rebuke the words that the LORD your God has heard; therefore lift up your prayer for the remnant that is left."

5 When the servants of King Hezekiah came to Isaiah, 6Isaiah said to them, "Say to your master, 'Thus says the LORD: Do not be afraid because of the words that you have heard, with which the servants of the king of Assyria have reviled me. 7I myself will put a spirit in him, so that he shall hear a rumor, and return to his own land; I will cause him to fall by the sword in his own land.' "

8 The Rabshakeh returned, and found the king of Assyria fighting against Libnah; for he had heard that the king had left Lachish. 9Now the king[a] heard concerning King Tirhakah of Ethiopia,[b] "He has set out to fight against you." When he heard it, he sent messengers to Hezekiah, saying, 10"Thus shall you speak to King Hezekiah of Judah: Do not let your God on whom you rely deceive you by promising that Jerusalem will not be given into the hand of the king of Assyria. 11See, you have heard what the kings of Assyria have done to all lands, destroying them utterly. Shall you be delivered? 12Have the gods of the nations delivered them, the nations that my predecessors destroyed, Gozan, Haran, Rezeph, and the people of Eden who were in Telassar? 13Where is the king of Hamath, the king of Arpad, the king of the city of Sepharvaim, the king of Hena, or the king of Ivvah?"

Hezekiah's Prayer

14 Hezekiah received the letter from the hand of the messengers and read it; then Hezekiah went up to the house of the LORD and spread it before the LORD. 15And Hezekiah prayed to the LORD, saying: 16"O LORD of hosts, God of Israel, who are enthroned above the cherubim, you are God, you alone, of all the kingdoms of the earth; you have made heaven and earth. 17Incline your ear, O LORD, and hear; open your eyes, O LORD, and see; hear all the words of Sennacherib, which he has sent to mock the living God. 18Truly, O LORD, the kings of Assyria have laid waste all the nations and their lands, 19and have hurled their gods into the fire, though they were no gods, but the work of human hands—wood and stone—and so they were destroyed. 20So now, O LORD our God, save us from his hand, so that all the kingdoms of the earth may know that you alone are the LORD."

21 Then Isaiah son of Amoz sent to Heze-

a Heb he   b Or Nubia; Heb Cush

37:6-7 *Do not be afraid.* King Hezekiah is appropriately anxious and fearful in the face of the imperial threat. He has no adequate response to the Assyrian taunt. However, what the king cannot do, the prophet Isaiah is able to do. The prophet offers an immense assurance to King Hezekiah: the Assyrian armies will be taken away and the holy city will be made safe. The prophet invites the king to have trust and confidence even in the face of immense threat.

37:15 *Hezekiah prayed to the LORD.* In the midst of his anxiety and fear, Hezekiah is here shown to be a man of prayer and represented as one of the model kings in the Old Testament. The response he makes to the threefold taunting by the Assyrians is to pray to God that God now save him and the city—finally coming to the insight that Isaiah has been urging, namely, that the only source of comfort and strength is indeed the rule of Yahweh, upon whom the king must risk everything.

37:21-22 PRAYER—*See* Spiritual Disciplines Index.

kiah, saying: "Thus says the LORD, the God of
Israel: Because you have prayed to me concerning King Sennacherib of Assyria, 22this is
the word that the LORD has spoken concerning him:

She despises you, she scorns you—
virgin daughter Zion;
she tosses her head—behind your back,
daughter Jerusalem.

23 "Whom have you mocked and reviled?
Against whom have you raised your
voice
and haughtily lifted your eyes?
Against the Holy One of Israel!
24 By your servants you have mocked the
Lord,
and you have said, 'With my many
chariots
I have gone up the heights of the
mountains,
to the far recesses of Lebanon;
I felled its tallest cedars,
its choicest cypresses;
I came to its remotest height,
its densest forest.
25 I dug wells
and drank waters,
I dried up with the sole of my foot
all the streams of Egypt.'

26 "Have you not heard
that I determined it long ago?
I planned from days of old
what now I bring to pass,
that you should make fortified cities

crash into heaps of ruins,
27 while their inhabitants, shorn of
strength,
are dismayed and confounded;
they have become like plants of the field
and like tender grass,
like grass on the housetops,
blighted a before it is grown.

28 "I know your rising up b and your sitting
down,
your going out and coming in,
and your raging against me.
29 Because you have raged against me
and your arrogance has come to my
ears,
I will put my hook in your nose
and my bit in your mouth;
I will turn you back on the way
by which you came.

30 "And this shall be the sign for you: This
year eat what grows of itself, and in the second year what springs from that; then in the
third year sow, reap, plant vineyards, and eat
their fruit. 31The surviving remnant of the
house of Judah shall again take root downward, and bear fruit upward; 32for from Jerusalem a remnant shall go out, and from
Mount Zion a band of survivors. The zeal of
the LORD of hosts will do this.

33 "Therefore thus says the LORD concerning the king of Assyria: He shall not come into
this city, shoot an arrow there, come before it

a With 2 Kings 19.26: Heb field   b Q Ms Gk: MT
lacks your rising up

37:21–35 *I bring to pass.* The interface
between political taunts by the empire and
prophetic responses on behalf of Yahweh
constitutes a great dramatic interface that
articulates a primary claim of the Isaiah tradition. It is affirmed over and over again that the
real governor of the public process of history is
Yahweh; any power in Jerusalem or among the
nations that thinks and acts otherwise is
destined for trouble.

37:33–35 *He shall not come into this city.* This
prose oracle by the prophet Isaiah represents the
high point in the Isaiah tradition's affirmation of
God's commitment to the city of Jerusalem. That

God's commitment will keep the city safe is
promised in the most exacting terms. This high
Jerusalem theology growing out of the Isaiah
tradition constituted an immense theological
problem a century later in the time of Jeremiah.
That later prophet had to announce that God
was about to destroy the city and therefore had
to contradict the theological claim of the Isaiah
tradition (see Jer 7:1–15). The different messages that had to be delivered by the Isaiah
tradition and the Jeremiah tradition indicate
how biblical faith is always geared to the
discernment of the new truth of God in particular historical circumstances.

with a shield, or cast up a siege ramp against it. ³⁴By the way that he came, by the same he shall return; he shall not come into this city, says the LORD. ³⁵For I will defend this city to save it, for my own sake and for the sake of my servant David."

Sennacherib's Defeat and Death

36 Then the angel of the LORD set out and struck down one hundred eighty-five thousand in the camp of the Assyrians; when morning dawned, they were all dead bodies. ³⁷Then King Sennacherib of Assyria left, went home, and lived at Nineveh. ³⁸As he was worshiping in the house of his god Nisroch, his sons Adrammelech and Sharezer killed him with the sword, and they escaped into the land of Ararat. His son Esar-haddon succeeded him.

Hezekiah's Illness

38 In those days Hezekiah became sick and was at the point of death. The prophet Isaiah son of Amoz came to him, and said to him, "Thus says the LORD: Set your house in order, for you shall die; you shall not recover." ²Then Hezekiah turned his face to the wall, and prayed to the LORD: ³"Remember now, O LORD, I implore you, how I have walked before you in faithfulness with a whole heart, and have done what is good in your sight." And Hezekiah wept bitterly.

4 Then the word of the LORD came to Isaiah: ⁵"Go and say to Hezekiah, Thus says the LORD, the God of your ancestor David: I have heard your prayer, I have seen your tears; I will add fifteen years to your life. ⁶I will deliver you and this city out of the hand of the king of Assyria, and defend this city.

7 "This is the sign to you from the LORD, that the LORD will do this thing that he has promised: ⁸See, I will make the shadow cast by the declining sun on the dial of Ahaz turn back

---

37:36–38 *the angel of the LORD . . . struck down . . . the Assyrians.* The prophet Isaiah has now delivered four oracles, a prose oracle in verses 6–7, a poetic oracle in verses 26–29, and two prose oracles in verses 33–35. Now the narrator here reports that the prophetic assurances given to Hezekiah all came true. Scholars speculate that the withdrawal of the Assyrian armies from the siege of Jerusalem happened because either a plague struck and decimated the armies or Sennacherib had to hurry home to save his throne from his rebellious sons. Either way, the Isaiah tradition insists that these historical events were indeed connected to the rule of Yahweh. The rhetorical "connector" between the rule of Yahweh and actual historical happenings is the phrase "the angel of the LORD," which is one way in which the Bible talks about the linkage between the rule of heaven and the circumstances on earth. In any case, in 701 BC Isaiah's promises concerning the deliverance of Jerusalem by Yahweh were completely vindicated. Jerusalem turned out to be safe from the imperial threat of Assyria, even though it had no resources of its own to secure its future.

38:1–21 *Remember now, O LORD.* King Hezekiah, a man of great faith, is smitten with an illness that places his life in jeopardy. Note the pastoral tone in which the sick king of honest faith prays passionately to God. He appeals to God on the basis of his faithfulness and obedience (v 3). Then the poetic utterance is a celebration of healing that comes to him (vv 10–20). This affirmation culminates in thanksgiving and testimony to the children that God is the one who saves (v 19). Thus we are able to watch a man of faith struggle through the fear and anxiety of terminal illness and the surprise and gratitude of healing. On a theological level, the text confirms that God is the Lord of all healing in personal matters, even as Isaiah has attested that God is the Lord of the future in public political matters. The public and the personal are always kept together in Isaiah, as indeed they are in the person of Hezekiah, who is both a powerful king and a man of faith. The prayer of Hezekiah attests that candid petition and buoyant gratitude are appropriate appeals to the God of all healings.

Responding

38:3–7 PRAYER. From a cursory reading, Hezekiah's prayer seems very self-serving, but God still spared his life. Why do you think God let Hezekiah live an additional fifteen years? How should this example affect the way we pray? *See also* Spiritual Disciplines Index.

ten steps." So the sun turned back on the dial the ten steps by which it had declined. *a*

9 A writing of King Hezekiah of Judah, after he had been sick and had recovered from his sickness:

10 I said: In the noontide of my days
    I must depart;
I am consigned to the gates of Sheol
    for the rest of my years.
11 I said, I shall not see the LORD
    in the land of the living;
I shall look upon mortals no more
    among the inhabitants of the world.
12 My dwelling is plucked up and removed
    from me
    like a shepherd's tent;
like a weaver I have rolled up my life;
    he cuts me off from the loom;
from day to night you bring me to an
    end; *a*
13   I cry for help *b* until morning;
like a lion he breaks all my bones;
    from day to night you bring me to an
    end. *a*

14 Like a swallow or a crane *a* I clamor,
    I moan like a dove.
My eyes are weary with looking upward.
    O Lord, I am oppressed; be my security!
15 But what can I say? For he has spoken to
    me,
    and he himself has done it.
All my sleep has fled *c*
    because of the bitterness of my soul.

16 O Lord, by these things people live,
    and in all these is the life of my spirit. *a*
Oh, restore me to health and make
    me live!
17 Surely it was for my welfare
    that I had great bitterness;
but you have held back *d* my life
    from the pit of destruction,
for you have cast all my sins
    behind your back.
18 For Sheol cannot thank you,

    death cannot praise you;
those who go down to the Pit cannot
    hope
    for your faithfulness.
19 The living, the living, they thank you,
    as I do this day;
fathers make known to children
    your faithfulness.

20 The LORD will save me,
    and we will sing to stringed
      instruments *e*
all the days of our lives,
    at the house of the LORD.

21 Now Isaiah had said, "Let them take a lump of figs, and apply it to the boil, so that he may recover." 22 Hezekiah also had said, "What is the sign that I shall go up to the house of the LORD?"

Envoys from Babylon Welcomed

39 At that time King Merodach-baladan son of Baladan of Babylon sent envoys with letters and a present to Hezekiah, for he heard that he had been sick and had recovered. 2 Hezekiah welcomed them; he showed them his treasure house, the silver, the gold, the spices, the precious oil, his whole armory, all that was found in his storehouses. There was nothing in his house or in all his realm that Hezekiah did not show them. 3 Then the prophet Isaiah came to King Hezekiah and said to him, "What did these men say? From where did they come to you?" Hezekiah answered, "They have come to me from a far country, from Babylon." 4 He said, "What have they seen in your house?" Hezekiah answered, "They have seen all that is in my house; there is nothing in my storehouses that I did not show them."

5 Then Isaiah said to Hezekiah, "Hear the word of the LORD of hosts: 6 Days are coming

a Meaning of Heb uncertain   *b* Cn: Meaning of Heb uncertain   *c* Cn Compare Syr: Heb *I will walk slowly all my years*   *d* Cn Compare Gk Vg: Heb *loved*   *e* Heb *my stringed instruments*

39:1–8 *Days are coming.* This chapter concludes the first half of the book of Isaiah.

Although Babylon has been mentioned in the oracles of chapters 13, 14, and 21, for the most

*160 YEARS
WAS BABYLON*

when all that is in your house, and that which your ancestors have stored up until this day, shall be carried to Babylon; nothing shall be left, says the LORD. ⁷Some of your own sons who are born to you shall be taken away; they shall be eunuchs in the palace of the king of Babylon." ⁸Then Hezekiah said to Isaiah, "The word of the LORD that you have spoken is good." For he thought, "There will be peace and security in my days."

God's People Are Comforted

40 Comfort, O comfort my people,
says your God.
² Speak tenderly to Jerusalem,
and cry to her
that she has served her term,
that her penalty is paid,
that she has received from the LORD's
hand
double for all her sins.

---

part the first half of Isaiah takes place during the time of Assyrian dominance. By the end of the eighth century BC, however, the Assyrian Empire was growing weak, and one of its colonies, Babylon, was beginning to assert itself. In this chapter, we may imagine that Babylon was beginning to mobilize allies against the old power Assyria. Clearly our text reports a diplomatic mission in which King Hezekiah hosted the visiting dignitaries in pursuit of a new alliance. Hezekiah is apparently a ready ally for any who would oppose Assyria. The key substance of the chapter, for which verses 1–4 provide context, however, is the prophetic oracle of verses 6–7. In those verses the prophet Isaiah announces to Hezekiah that the Jerusalem establishment and the Davidic dynasty will be deported to Babylon; the sons of the royal house will be humiliated and will be made subservient eunuchs in the royal palaces of Babylon. This oracle is a stunning announcement of the failure of the entire Jerusalem establishment. God has now finally decided to give over to Jerusalem's enemies the whole city to which Yahweh had been committed.

39:8 *There will be peace and security in my days.* Hezekiah's response may be read a cynical reaction, as though he concluded that the judgment would happen after his lifetime and he wouldn't have to worry about it. There is, however, an alternative reading that suggests that Hezekiah is such a man of faith that his response is an acceptance of and a submission to God's will for the future. In either case, the book of Isaiah reaches a moment of complete shutdown at 39:8. It is likely that this oracle was given about 700 BC, at the end of the reign of Hezekiah. When we take up chapter 40, 160 years have elapsed, during which time the city of Jerusalem has been destroyed and the leading citizens of the city have been exiled to

Babylon. Thus, at 39:8, we must wait in silence for a long time until there is a new utterance of the gospel of God. This structuring of Isaiah is an affirmation that in moments of loss and silence there can only be faithful waiting and confidence in God.

40:1–55:13 *she has served her term.* Many scholars label these chapters "Second Isaiah," because this material is an extension of the tradition that obviously runs beyond the prophet and events of the eighth century BC. Chapters 40–55 are thought to be the poetic utterance of a prophetic figure situated in Babylon in 540 BC, just at the moment when the Persians, led by their king, Cyrus, are about to overturn what is left of Babylonian rule. The coming of the Persians against Babylon means that the Jews will be free to go home, because Babylon no longer has the power to restrain them. In the theological interpretation of this poetic tradition, the rise of Cyrus the Persian is understood to be an act of Yahweh, who sends Cyrus to be a deliverer of the Jews. Thus the decisive theme of this poetry is homecoming, which is a counterpoint to the judgment of deportation, which was the dominant emphasis of chapters 1–39.

40:1–2 *O comfort my people.* The verb here is a plural imperative, "Comfort Ye," whereby God appears to address the angels and messengers who are gathered around the heavenly throne. The decisive announcement is that it is now time for all of the Jews to be able to go home, because the punishment has been completed. Thus the news is that God's anger that provoked deportation has now been satisfied; the Jews in Babylon who remain get a new lease on life. They return home, and in the decades that follow new forms of the Jewish faith emerge.

HOME COMING REVERSALS

3 A voice cries out:
   "In the wilderness prepare the way of
        the LORD,
      make straight in the desert a highway
        for our God.
4 Every valley shall be lifted up,
      and every mountain and hill be made
        low;
   the uneven ground shall become level,
      and the rough places a plain.
5 Then the glory of the LORD shall be
        revealed,
      and all people shall see it together,
   for the mouth of the LORD has
        spoken."

6 A voice says, "Cry out!"
   And I said, "What shall I cry?"
   All people are grass,
      their constancy is like the flower of
        the field.
7 The grass withers, the flower fades,
      when the breath of the LORD blows
        upon it;
      surely the people are grass.
8 The grass withers, the flower fades;
      but the word of our God will stand
        forever.
9 Get you up to a high mountain,
      O Zion, herald of good tidings; *a*

   lift up your voice with strength,
      O Jerusalem, herald of good
        tidings, *b*
   lift it up, do not fear;
   say to the cities of Judah,
      "Here is your God!"
10 See, the Lord GOD comes with might,
      and his arm rules for him;
   his reward is with him,
      and his recompense before him.
11 He will feed his flock like a shepherd;
      he will gather the lambs in his arms,
   and carry them in his bosom,
      and gently lead the mother sheep.

12 Who has measured the waters in the
        hollow of his hand
   and marked off the heavens with a
        span,
   enclosed the dust of the earth in a
        measure,
      and weighed the mountains in scales
      and the hills in a balance?
13 Who has directed the spirit of the
        LORD,
      or as his counselor has instructed
        him?

a Or *O herald of good tidings to Zion*
b Or *O herald of good tidings to Jerusalem*

40:3–4 *prepare the way of the LORD.* The intention of the divine plan for homecoming is to construct a great highway on which there can be a triumphal entry. The theme of the highway home is picked up from 35:8–10. What is envisioned is a great procession of Jews coming home in exuberance, led by the glory of God. These verses are used in the New Testament in all four of the Gospel narratives about the coming of Jesus (Matt 3:3; Mark 1:3; Luke 3:4–6; John 1:23). The text is used in each case with the initiative of John the Baptist. In that context, the "great highway" has to do with the coming of King Jesus, who now is the sovereign Lord who will institute a great homecoming. It can be argued that the Gospel traditions that narrate the teachings and miracles of Jesus are in fact acts of homecoming whereby Jesus restores people to full functioning in life.

40:9 *lift up your voice.* The writer reports the

commissioning of a messenger, presumably Second Isaiah. The double use of the phrase "herald of good tidings" is of particular interest, because it contains the first use in the Bible of a term that has the meaning of "gospel"—good news. The substance of the gospel in terse form is "Here is your God." The messenger announces that the God of Israel is back in play after having been sidelined by Babylonian hegemony. It is the reassertion of Yahweh—as we shall see—through Cyrus the Persian that makes possible a new lease on life for the displaced inhabitants of Jerusalem.

40:10–11 *his arm rules for him . . . he will gather the lambs in his arms.* The combination of the image of a mighty ruler and that of a gentle nursemaid is of importance for understanding the rich complexity of the character of Yahweh in this poetry (see Deut 1:30–31).

14 Whom did he consult for his
    enlightenment,
  and who taught him the path of
    justice?
Who taught him knowledge,
  and showed him the way of
    understanding?
15 Even the nations are like a drop from a
    bucket,
  and are accounted as dust on the
    scales;
  see, he takes up the isles like fine dust.
16 Lebanon would not provide fuel
    enough,
  nor are its animals enough for a burnt
    offering.
17 All the nations are as nothing before
    him;
  they are accounted by him as less
    than nothing and emptiness.

18 To whom then will you liken God,
  or what likeness compare with him?
19 An idol?—A workman casts it,
  and a goldsmith overlays it with
    gold,
  and casts for it silver chains.
20 As a gift one chooses mulberry wood *a*
  —wood that will not rot—
then seeks out a skilled artisan
  to set up an image that will not
    topple.

21 Have you not known? Have you not
    heard?
  Has it not been told you from the
    beginning?
  Have you not understood from the
    foundations of the earth?
22 It is he who sits above the circle of the
    earth,
  and its inhabitants are like
    grasshoppers;
who stretches out the heavens like a
    curtain,

and spreads them like a tent to
    live in;
23 who brings princes to naught,
  and makes the rulers of the earth as
    nothing.

24 Scarcely are they planted, scarcely
    sown,
  scarcely has their stem taken root in
    the earth,
when he blows upon them, and they
    wither,
  and the tempest carries them off like
    stubble.

25 To whom then will you compare me,
  or who is my equal? says the Holy
    One.
26 Lift up your eyes on high and see:
  Who created these?
He who brings out their host and
    numbers them,
  calling them all by name;
because he is great in strength,
  mighty in power,
  not one is missing.

27 Why do you say, O Jacob,
  and speak, O Israel,
"My way is hidden from the LORD,
  and my right is disregarded by my
    God"?
28 Have you not known? Have you not
    heard?
The LORD is the everlasting God,
  the Creator of the ends of the earth.
He does not faint or grow weary;
  his understanding is unsearchable.
29 He gives power to the faint,
  and strengthens the powerless.
30 Even youths will faint and be weary,
  and the young will fall exhausted;

a Meaning of Heb uncertain

40:18 *To whom then will you liken God?*
Although there are other gods who claim to
have divine power, they are all impotent, weak,
and powerless in the face of Yahweh. Israel's
future depends on recognizing the incomparable

power coupled with the incomparable fidelity
of Yahweh. All hope for the future in the Isaiah
tradition is rooted in the character of God, who
has the capacity to do something utterly new.

31 but those who wait for the LORD shall
    renew their strength,
  they shall mount up with wings like
    eagles,
  they shall run and not be weary,
  they shall walk and not faint.

Israel Assured of God's Help

41 Listen to me in silence,
    O coastlands;
let the peoples renew their strength;
let them approach, then let them speak;
let us together draw near for
  judgment.

2 Who has roused a victor from the east,
  summoned him to his service?
He delivers up nations to him,
  and tramples kings under foot;
he makes them like dust with his sword,
  like driven stubble with his bow.
3 He pursues them and passes on safely,
  scarcely touching the path with his
  feet.
4 Who has performed and done this,
  calling the generations from the
  beginning?
I, the LORD, am first,
  and will be with the last.
5 The coastlands have seen and are afraid,

the ends of the earth tremble;
  they have drawn near and come.
6 Each one helps the other,
  saying to one another, "Take
  courage!"
7 The artisan encourages the goldsmith,
  and the one who smooths with the
  hammer encourages the one who
  strikes the anvil,
saying of the soldering, "It is good";
  and they fasten it with nails so that it
  cannot be moved.
8 But you, Israel, my servant,
  Jacob, whom I have chosen,
  the offspring of Abraham, my friend;
9 you whom I took from the ends of the
  earth,
  and called from its farthest corners,
saying to you, "You are my servant,
  I have chosen you and not cast you
  off";
10 do not fear, for I am with you,
  do not be afraid, for I am your God;
I will strengthen you, I will help you,
  I will uphold you with my victorious
  right hand.

11 Yes, all who are incensed against you
  shall be ashamed and disgraced;
  those who strive against you

40:29–31 *those who wait for the LORD shall renew their strength.* The newness that Yahweh is able to enact is outlined here: Yahweh causes a complete reversal of fortune for those who trust in Yahweh. Thus homecoming is a complete reversal of the circumstance of exile, a reversal that is accomplished by Yahweh's incomparable, inestimable power. In addition to the historical theme of homecoming, this famous passage is pregnant with the spiritual formation themes of waiting, renewing, running, and walking.

41:2–4 *He delivers up nations.* "A victor from the east" is a reference to the Persian king Cyrus, who will be named later (see 44:28; 45:1). The self-announcement of God (v 4) is a boast that it is Yahweh and none other who has caused the upheaval in world history through the rise of Persia. Typical of Second Isaiah, these verses show the way in which prophetic poetry links the rule of God to the concrete realities of

political life. Although Cyrus the Persian is the key political player in the regional economy, he serves as such at the behest of the God of Israel, who is the real ruler of the historical process.

41:10 *do not fear . . . do not be afraid.* These phrases are characteristic announcements of divine presence. The recurring promise of God's presence is the most fundamental assurance given in gospel faith. God *is* with us: ours is a with-God life. The announcement itself radically transforms situations by inspiring an awareness of God's presence. In the Gospel presentation of Jesus' life, the same "Do not be afraid" is used at key points. The birth and the resurrection of Jesus are decisive events in the history of the world that evoke from God this transformative announcement of his presence (Luke 2:10; Matt 28:5).

41:10 THE WITH-GOD LIFE—*See* Spiritual Disciplines Index.

shall be as nothing and shall perish.
12 You shall seek those who contend with
you,
but you shall not find them;
those who war against you
shall be as nothing at all.
13 For I, the LORD your God,
hold your right hand;
it is I who say to you, "Do not fear,
I will help you."

14 Do not fear, you worm Jacob,
you insect[a] Israel!
I will help you, says the LORD;
your Redeemer is the Holy One of
Israel.
15 Now, I will make of you a threshing
sledge,
sharp, new, and having teeth;
you shall thresh the mountains and
crush them,
and you shall make the hills like
chaff.
16 You shall winnow them and the wind
shall carry them away,
and the tempest shall scatter them.
Then you shall rejoice in the LORD;
in the Holy One of Israel you shall
glory.

17 When the poor and needy seek water,
and there is none,
and their tongue is parched with thirst,
I the LORD will answer them,
I the God of Israel will not forsake
them.
18 I will open rivers on the bare heights,[b]
and fountains in the midst of the
valleys;
I will make the wilderness a pool of
water,
and the dry land springs of water.

19 I will put in the wilderness the cedar,
the acacia, the myrtle, and the olive;
I will set in the desert the cypress,
the plane and the pine together,
20 so that all may see and know,
all may consider and understand,
that the hand of the LORD has done this,
the Holy One of Israel has created it.

The Futility of Idols

21 Set forth your case, says the LORD;
bring your proofs, says the King of
Jacob.
22 Let them bring them, and tell us
what is to happen.
Tell us the former things, what they are,
so that we may consider them,
and that we may know their outcome;
or declare to us the things to come.
23 Tell us what is to come hereafter,
that we may know that you are gods;
do good, or do harm,
that we may be afraid and terrified.
24 You, indeed, are nothing
and your work is nothing at all;
whoever chooses you is an
abomination.

25 I stirred up one from the north, and he
has come,
from the rising of the sun he was
summoned by name.[c]
He shall trample[d] on rulers as on
mortar,
as the potter treads clay.
26 Who declared it from the beginning, so
that we might know,

a Syr: Heb *men of*   b Or *trails*   c Cn Compare
Q Ms Gk: MT *and he shall call on my name*
d Cn: Heb *come*

41:17–20 *I the LORD will answer them.* Here
the writer is announcing the homecoming of
exiled Jews to Jerusalem due to the miraculous
emancipation caused by Yahweh, who also
transforms the dry and unproductive environment into a fruitful and luxurious one. The
savior of Israel is also the creator of the world
and can bring the whole world to newness.

Thus, not only does Israel rejoice and sing praise
to God, but all creatures join in that praise to
the creator.

41:25 *I stirred up one from the north.* The
claim here is that God is an active subject who
can initiate new realities in the public world, in
contrast to the Babylonian gods, which are
mute, passive, and impotent.

My servant sur not well
Israel servant people

and beforehand, so that we might say,
        "He is right"?
There was no one who declared it, none
        who proclaimed,
    none who heard your words.
27 I first have declared it to Zion,[a]
        and I give to Jerusalem a herald of
        good tidings.
28 But when I look there is no one;
        among these there is no
        counselor
    who, when I ask, gives an answer.
29 No, they are all a delusion;
        their works are nothing;
    their images are empty wind.

The Servant, a Light to the Nations

42 Here is my servant, whom I uphold,
        my chosen, in whom my soul
        delights;
    I have put my spirit upon him;
        he will bring forth justice to the
        nations.
2 He will not cry or lift up his voice,
        or make it heard in the street;
3 a bruised reed he will not break,
        and a dimly burning wick he will not
        quench;
    he will faithfully bring forth
        justice.
4 He will not grow faint or be crushed
        until he has established justice in the
        earth;
    and the coastlands wait for his
        teaching.

5 Thus says God, the LORD,
        who created the heavens and
        stretched them out,
    who spread out the earth and what
        comes from it,
    who gives breath to the people upon it
        and spirit to those who walk in it:
6 I am the LORD, I have called you in
        righteousness,
    I have taken you by the hand and kept
        you;
    I have given you as a covenant to the
        people,[b]
        a light to the nations,
7   to open the eyes that are blind,
    to bring out the prisoners from the
        dungeon,
        from the prison those who sit in
        darkness.
8 I am the LORD, that is my name;
        my glory I give to no other,
        nor my praise to idols.
9 See, the former things have come to pass,
        and new things I now declare;
    before they spring forth,
        I tell you of them.

A Hymn of Praise

10 Sing to the LORD a new song,
        his praise from the end of the earth!
    Let the sea roar[c] and all that fills it,
        the coastlands and their inhabitants.

a Cn: Heb *First to Zion—Behold, behold them*
b Meaning of Heb uncertain   *c* Cn Compare Ps
96.11; 98.7: Heb *Those who go down to the sea*

41:27 *good tidings.* See note on 40:9. The
good news that this portion of Isaiah announces
is that the God of creation and salvation is
engaged on behalf of God's people in a massive,
transformative act.

42:1–9 *Here is my servant.* Israel, as Yahweh's
servant, is mandated to enact God's transformative healing and mending of the whole world.
In such rhetoric Israel, as the People of God,
exists for the well-being of the world. In verses
6–7 the vocation of Israel as Yahweh's servant
becomes even more specific. Israel is to be "a
covenant to the people, a light to the nations."
This magisterial phrasing suggests that Israel has

a particular vocation to enhance the life of the
whole world. This kind of language perhaps
reaches all the way back to the promise to
Abraham in Gen 12:3 that the existence of
Israel should be "a blessing" to the rest of
the nations of the world.

42:1–4 *my chosen . . . will bring forth justice
to the nations.* The term "justice" is used three
times in this passage. The poet imagines that
all over the world people live in circumstances
of exploitation and oppression. In all such
circumstances there is an eager waiting for the
restoration of equitable living that can come
only through the intervention of God.

11 Let the desert and its towns lift up their
        voice,
    the villages that Kedar inhabits;
let the inhabitants of Sela sing for joy,
    let them shout from the tops of the
        mountains.
12 Let them give glory to the LORD,
    and declare his praise in the
        coastlands.
13 The LORD goes forth like a soldier,
    like a warrior he stirs up his fury;
he cries out, he shouts aloud,
    he shows himself mighty against his
        foes.

14 For a long time I have held my peace,
    I have kept still and restrained myself;
now I will cry out like a woman in labor,
    I will gasp and pant.
15 I will lay waste mountains and hills,
    and dry up all their herbage;
I will turn the rivers into islands,
    and dry up the pools.
16 I will lead the blind
    by a road they do not know,
by paths they have not known
        I will guide them.
I will turn the darkness before them
        into light,
    the rough places into level ground.
These are the things I will do,
    and I will not forsake them.
17 They shall be turned back and utterly
        put to shame—
those who trust in carved images,
who say to cast images,
    "You are our gods."

18 Listen, you that are deaf;
    and you that are blind, look up and
        see!
19 Who is blind but my servant,
    or deaf like my messenger whom I
        send?

Who is blind like my dedicated one,
    or blind like the servant of the LORD?
20 He sees many things, but does[a] not
        observe them;
    his ears are open, but he does not
        hear.

Israel's Disobedience

21 The LORD was pleased, for the sake of his
        righteousness,
    to magnify his teaching and make it
        glorious.
22 But this is a people robbed and
        plundered,
    all of them are trapped in holes
    and hidden in prisons;
they have become a prey with no one to
        rescue,
    a spoil with no one to say, "Restore!"
23 Who among you will give heed to this,
    who will attend and listen for the
        time to come?
24 Who gave up Jacob to the spoiler,
    and Israel to the robbers?
Was it not the LORD, against whom we
        have sinned,
    in whose ways they would not walk,
    and whose law they would not obey?
25 So he poured upon him the heat of his
        anger
    and the fury of war;
it set him on fire all around, but he did
        not understand;
    it burned him, but he did not take it
        to heart.

Restoration and Protection Promised

43 But now thus says the LORD,
    he who created you, O Jacob,
    he who formed you, O Israel:
Do not fear, for I have redeemed you;

a Heb *You see many things but do*

42:16 GUIDANCE—*See* Spiritual Disciplines
Index.

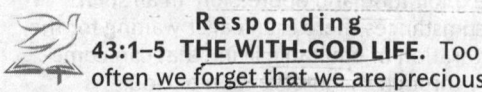

**Responding
43:1–5 THE WITH-GOD LIFE.** Too
often we forget that we are precious

in the Lord's sight, honored, and loved. Read
these reminding words every day for a week.
See what they do for your sense of security
in God's love. *See also* Spiritual Disciplines
Index.

I have called you by name, you are
    mine.
2 When you pass through the waters, I
    will be with you;
  and through the rivers, they shall not
    overwhelm you;
  when you walk through fire you shall
    not be burned,
  and the flame shall not consume you.
3 For I am the LORD your God,
  the Holy One of Israel, your Savior.
I give Egypt as your ransom,
  Ethiopia a and Seba in exchange for
    you.
4 Because you are precious in my sight,
  and honored, and I love you,
I give people in return for you,
  nations in exchange for your life.
5 Do not fear, for I am with you;
  I will bring your offspring from the
    east,
  and from the west I will gather you;
6 I will say to the north, "Give them up,"
  and to the south, "Do not withhold;
bring my sons from far away
  and my daughters from the end of the
    earth—
7 everyone who is called by my name,
  whom I created for my glory,
  whom I formed and made."

8 Bring forth the people who are blind,
    yet have eyes,
  who are deaf, yet have ears!
9 Let all the nations gather together,
  and let the peoples assemble.
Who among them declared this,
  and foretold to us the former things?
Let them bring their witnesses to justify
    them,
  and let them hear and say, "It is true."
10 You are my witnesses, says the LORD,
  and my servant whom I have chosen,
so that you may know and believe me
  and understand that I am he.
Before me no god was formed,
  nor shall there be any after me.
11 I, I am the LORD,
  and besides me there is no savior.
12 I declared and saved and proclaimed,
  when there was no strange god
    among you;
  and you are my witnesses, says the
    LORD.
13 I am God, and also henceforth I am He;
  there is no one who can deliver from
    my hand;
  I work and who can hinder it?

a Or *Nubia*; Heb *Cush*

43:3 *I give Egypt as your ransom.* This
remarkable use of the word "ransom" suggests
that God is willing to give the population of
Egypt and Ethiopia to "buy" the precious
Israelites, who are held in hock by the empire. It
is likely that this use of the word "ransom" is
taken up in Mark 10:45, where Jesus announces
that his own life is to be a "ransom" for many
who are powerless to change themselves.

43:9–13 *bring their witnesses to justify them.*
The middle portion of the book of Isaiah (chaps
40–55) imagines a contested claim between the
power of Babylon and the weakness of Israel or,
conversely, the power of the Babylonian gods
and the power of Yahweh, the God of Israel. In
this passage the matter is presented as a
courtroom scene, where evidence is provided
and a decision is to be made about the true
God. Thus, in poetic imagination, witnesses
are invited to give an account of the gods of

Babylon (v 9). The Israelite exiles are summoned to court to be witnesses on behalf of
Yahweh. The witnesses are told exactly what
they are to say, namely, that this God is the only
God and all other gods are fakes who have no
power (vv 10–13). This concept of witness in the
poetic imagery of a trial scene is what has
produced the whole notion of "martyrs" in the
New Testament. The Greek term from which we
get "martyr" simply means "witness"; witnesses
are those who are willing to die for their version
of the truth. In extrapolation from that notion
of witness comes the whole notion of an evangelist, that is, a witness to the good news of
God's victory over the power of evil. Thus the
notion of witnesses in this poetic unit has
immense significance for identifying the
vocation of Israel to tell the truth about God
and, derivatively, the vocation of the Church to
tell the truth about Jesus Christ.

14 Thus says the LORD,
    your Redeemer, the Holy One of
        Israel:
    For your sake I will send to Babylon
        and break down all the bars,
        and the shouting of the Chaldeans
            will be turned to lamentation. *a*
15 I am the LORD, your Holy One,
    the Creator of Israel, your King.
16 Thus says the LORD,
    who makes a way in the sea,
    a path in the mighty waters,
17 who brings out chariot and horse,
    army and warrior;
    they lie down, they cannot rise,
        they are extinguished, quenched like
            a wick:
18 Do not remember the former things,
    or consider the things of old.
19 I am about to do a new thing;
    now it springs forth, do you not
        perceive it?
    I will make a way in the wilderness
        and rivers in the desert.
20 The wild animals will honor me,
    the jackals and the ostriches;
    for I give water in the wilderness,
        rivers in the desert,
    to give drink to my chosen people,
21   the people whom I formed for myself
    so that they might declare my praise.

22 Yet you did not call upon me, O Jacob;

but you have been weary of me,
    O Israel!
23 You have not brought me your sheep for
        burnt offerings,
    or honored me with your sacrifices.
    I have not burdened you with offerings,
        or wearied you with frankincense.
24 You have not bought me sweet cane
        with money,
    or satisfied me with the fat of your
        sacrifices.
    But you have burdened me with your
        sins;
    you have wearied me with your
        iniquities.

25 I, I am He
    who blots out your transgressions for
        my own sake,
    and I will not remember your sins.
26 Accuse me, let us go to trial;
    set forth your case, so that you may be
        proved right.
27 Your first ancestor sinned,
    and your interpreters transgressed
        against me.
28 Therefore I profaned the princes of the
        sanctuary,
    I delivered Jacob to utter destruction,
    and Israel to reviling.

a Meaning of Heb uncertain

43:18–19 *I am about to do a new thing.* These verses are a spectacular point of accent in the center of the book of Isaiah. It is the burden of this poet in exile to announce that the new thing is God's intervention on behalf of exiles to bring them home. Although this miraculous deliverance is understood as a replication of the old exodus narrative, remarkably Israel is directed to forget the old exodus narrative in order to notice the new narrative of departure from Babylonian exile. The "new thing" is not only more contemporary, but also more spectacular, and exhibits the power of God in more effective ways. These verses demonstrate the theological continuity and discontinuity between Israel's earlier memory and its present experience. In these verses all the accent is upon the new experience, which pushes the old memory aside. It may be worth noting that in the relationship between the Old Testament and the New Testament, insofar as Christians are concerned, the same accent is upon the new at the expense of the old. Our God is doing a new thing.

43:25 *I will not remember your sins.* Here is yet another dramatic statement of God's forgiveness of the people's sin that resulted in the exile. This statement is congruent with the initial exilic announcement of 40:1–2. The new beginning for Israel is based on God's readiness to forgive and, therefore, to break the old cycle of alienation and judgment.

God's Blessing on Israel

44 But now hear, O Jacob my servant,
Israel whom I have chosen!
2 Thus says the LORD who made you,
who formed you in the womb and
will help you:
Do not fear, O Jacob my servant,
Jeshurun whom I have chosen.
3 For I will pour water on the thirsty land,
and streams on the dry ground;
I will pour my spirit upon your
descendants,
and my blessing on your offspring.
4 They shall spring up like a green
tamarisk,
like willows by flowing streams.
5 This one will say, "I am the LORD's,"
another will be called by the name of
Jacob,
yet another will write on the hand,
"The LORD's,"
and adopt the name of Israel.

6 Thus says the LORD, the King of Israel,
and his Redeemer, the LORD of hosts:
I am the first and I am the last;
besides me there is no god.
7 Who is like me? Let them proclaim it,
let them declare and set it forth before
me.
Who has announced from of old the
things to come?*a*
Let them tell us*b* what is yet to be.
8 Do not fear, or be afraid;
have I not told you from of old and
declared it?
You are my witnesses!
Is there any god besides me?

There is no other rock; I know not
one.

The Absurdity of Idol Worship

9 All who make idols are nothing, and the
things they delight in do not profit; their
witnesses neither see nor know. And so they
will be put to shame. 10Who would fashion a
god or cast an image that can do no good?
11Look, all its devotees shall be put to shame;
the artisans too are merely human. Let them
all assemble, let them stand up; they shall
be terrified, they shall all be put to shame.

12 The ironsmith fashions it*c* and works it
over the coals, shaping it with hammers, and
forging it with his strong arm; he becomes
hungry and his strength fails, he drinks no
water and is faint. 13The carpenter stretches
a line, marks it out with a stylus, fashions it
with planes, and marks it with a compass;
he makes it in human form, with human
beauty, to be set up in a shrine. 14He cuts
down cedars or chooses a holm tree or an
oak and lets it grow strong among the trees of
the forest. He plants a cedar and the rain
nourishes it. 15Then it can be used as fuel.
Part of it he takes and warms himself; he kindles a fire and bakes bread. Then he makes a
god and worships it, makes it a carved image and bows down before it. 16Half of it he
burns in the fire; over this half he roasts meat,
eats it and is satisfied. He also warms himself
and says, "Ah, I am warm, I can feel the fire!"
17The rest of it he makes into a god, his idol,

a Cn: Heb *from my placing an eternal people and
things to come*   *b* Tg: Heb *them*   *c* Cn: Heb *an ax*

44:8 *Do not fear. . . . You are my witnesses!*
This verse combines two remarkable phrases
that we have already seen (see notes on 41:10;
43:9–13). It is yet another "salvation oracle" with
the familiar formula "Do not fear," as well as
another affirmation that Israel is to be Yahweh's
witness and to tell the truth about Yahweh. It is
important that the salvation oracle is used to
undergird the vocation of witnesses. This leads
us to imagine that the witnesses might indeed
be fearful and anxious, for telling the truth about
Yahweh in the Babylonian environment could be

dangerous. Indeed, when the truth is being told
about the biblical God, it is always in a context
of anxiety and fear, because the gods of the
empire all around are resistant to such truth.

44:9–20 *their witnesses neither see nor know.*
It is acknowledged that the other gods have
witnesses as well, but those witnesses are
completely dysfunctional. The reason they are
dysfunctional, as the passage goes on to say, is
that they have nothing about which to bear
witness, because the gods whose claims they
defend are nothing more than empty ciphers.

bows down to it and worships it; he prays to it and says, "Save me, for you are my god!"

18 They do not know, nor do they comprehend; for their eyes are shut, so that they cannot see, and their minds as well, so that they cannot understand. ¹⁹No one considers, nor is there knowledge or discernment to say, "Half of it I burned in the fire; I also baked bread on its coals, I roasted meat and have eaten. Now shall I make the rest of it an abomination? Shall I fall down before a block of wood?" ²⁰He feeds on ashes; a deluded mind has led him astray, and he cannot save himself or say, "Is not this thing in my right hand a fraud?"

Israel Is Not Forgotten

²¹ Remember these things, O Jacob,
    and Israel, for you are my servant;
I formed you, you are my servant;
    O Israel, you will not be forgotten by
        me.
²² I have swept away your transgressions
        like a cloud,
    and your sins like mist;
    return to me, for I have redeemed you.

²³ Sing, O heavens, for the LORD has done
        it;
    shout, O depths of the earth;
break forth into singing, O mountains,
    O forest, and every tree in it!
For the LORD has redeemed Jacob,
    and will be glorified in Israel.

²⁴ Thus says the LORD, your Redeemer,
    who formed you in the womb:
I am the LORD, who made all things,
    who alone stretched out the heavens,
    who by myself spread out the earth;
²⁵ who frustrates the omens of liars,
    and makes fools of diviners;
who turns back the wise,
    and makes their knowledge foolish;
²⁶ who confirms the word of his servant,
    and fulfills the prediction of his
        messengers;
who says of Jerusalem, "It shall be
        inhabited,"
    and of the cities of Judah, "They shall
        be rebuilt,
    and I will raise up their ruins";
²⁷ who says to the deep, "Be dry—
    I will dry up your rivers";
²⁸ who says of Cyrus, "He is my shepherd,
    and he shall carry out all my purpose";
and who says of Jerusalem, "It shall be
        rebuilt,"
    and of the temple, "Your foundation
        shall be laid."

Cyrus, God's Instrument

45 Thus says the LORD to his anointed,
        to Cyrus,
    whose right hand I have grasped
to subdue nations before him
    and strip kings of their robes,
to open doors before him—
    and the gates shall not be closed:

44:28 *Cyrus . . . shall carry out all my purpose.* This verse is the first explicit reference to the Persian king Cyrus, alluded to in 41:2 and 41:25 and here identified as the one who will carry the mandates of Yahweh for the overthrow of Babylon and the emancipation of Israel. The designation of Cyrus as "my shepherd" refers to his royal office, as is customary in the Old Testament (e.g., Ezek 34). Here it is anticipated that Cyrus will be the one who will rebuild Jerusalem. And indeed, in the text of Ezra and Nehemiah, it is clear that the Jewish rebuilders of Jerusalem are mandated by Persia and financed out of the Persian royal treasury.

45:1 *Thus says the LORD to his anointed, to Cyrus.* Although Cyrus is named in 44:28 as the

one designated to carry Yahweh's mandate in the world, this verse is even more spectacular because it refers to Cyrus as "his anointed." This statement means that Yahweh has designated a Gentile to do the work of emancipation. In Hebrew the word "anointed" is the one from which we get "messiah," so Cyrus the Gentile is the Jewish messiah. The matter is even more spectacular if we remember that in Greek this same word is translated as "Christ," so that Cyrus is a "Christ" who will do God's work in the world and emancipate God's people. This exceedingly daring theological affirmation was required by the demanding circumstances in which the poet lived and worked.

CYRUS AND DARIUS

God's Unwitting Instruments

Selected Scriptures: *Isaiah 44:28–45:8; Ezra 1; 3:7; 4:3–5; 5:6–6:15*

Although God loves to use his people to do his work, God also uses some unlikely figures. Two pagan rulers of Persia took active roles in furthering the national life of Israel and preparing it for the coming Messiah. Their actions brought an end to the prophesied seventy years of captivity for Israel's Southern Kingdom, Judah.

Captivity had come as divine judgment for Israel's unfaithfulness and idolatry, yet, as God promised through the prophet Jeremiah, the captivity would last only seventy years and then God would regather his people to their land. He promised to make a new covenant with Israel unlike the Mosaic covenant engraved in stone: he would engrave his law on the hearts of his people (Jer 31:33–34). All this would come to fulfillment in part through the leadership of two kings, Cyrus and Darius, who would never share in the promise.

Cyrus, as king of Persia, decreed that all people who had been deported from other lands were free to return to their homelands; he even encouraged them to rebuild their houses of worship. Therefore Jews living in Babylon began to return to Jerusalem, and under Darius they rebuilt the Temple. Yet neither king sincerely worshiped Israel's God. Although Cyrus spoke of the "God of heaven," declaring that God had "given [him] all the kingdoms of the earth" (Ezra 1:2), he spoke similarly to other nations about their gods. A wise and diplomatic ruler, he seemed to know how best to gain the allegiance of his subject nations.

God not only used these rulers; he said of Cyrus, "He is my shepherd, and he shall carry out all my purpose" (Isa 44:28). He went on to call Cyrus his "anointed, . . . whose right hand I have grasped to subdue nations before him" (45:1).

As we see time and time again throughout the Old Testament, God went to great lengths to express his love for his people and to show them his faithfulness. But often he worked his will through surprising and mysterious means. He chose people whose lives were not committed to him to display his power and the breadth of his dominion. "I arm you, though you do not know me, so that they may know, from the rising of the sun and from the west, that there is no one besides me; I am the LORD, and there is no other" (45:5–6).

Personal Reflection

- When has God used someone in a significant way in your life who was not committed to God? Did you credit God at the time? How is it clear now that God was behind it?
- How aware are you usually of God's sovereign movement among both those who follow him and those who don't?

PROFILE

2 I will go before you
  and level the mountains, *a*
I will break in pieces the doors of
    bronze
  and cut through the bars of iron,
3 I will give you the treasures of
    darkness
  and riches hidden in secret places,
so that you may know that it is I, the
    LORD,
  the God of Israel, who call you by
    your name.
4 For the sake of my servant Jacob,
  and Israel my chosen,
I call you by your name,
  I surname you, though you do not
    know me.
5 I am the LORD, and there is no other;
  besides me there is no god.
I arm you, though you do not know
    me,
6 so that they may know, from the rising
    of the sun
  and from the west, that there is no
    one besides me;
I am the LORD, and there is no other.
7 I form light and create darkness,
  I make weal and create woe;
I the LORD do all these things.

8 Shower, O heavens, from above,
  and let the skies rain down
    righteousness;
let the earth open, that salvation may
    spring up, *b*
  and let it cause righteousness to
    sprout up also;
  I the LORD have created it.

9 Woe to you who strive with your Maker,
  earthen vessels with the potter! *c*
Does the clay say to the one who fashions
    it, "What are you making"?
  or "Your work has no handles"?
10 Woe to anyone who says to a father,
  "What are you begetting?"
  or to a woman, "With what are you in
    labor?"
11 Thus says the LORD,
  the Holy One of Israel, and its Maker:
Will you question me *d* about my
    children,
  or command me concerning the work
    of my hands?
12 I made the earth,
  and created humankind upon it;
it was my hands that stretched out the
    heavens,
  and I commanded all their host.
13 I have aroused Cyrus *e* in righteousness,
  and I will make all his paths straight;
he shall build my city
  and set my exiles free,
not for price or reward,
  says the LORD of hosts.
14 Thus says the LORD:
The wealth of Egypt and the
    merchandise of Ethiopia, *f*
  and the Sabeans, tall of stature,
shall come over to you and be yours,
  they shall follow you;

a Q Ms Gk: MT *the swellings*   *b* Q Ms: MT *that
they may bring forth salvation*   *c* Cn: Heb *with
the potsherds,* or *with the potters*   *d* Cn: Heb
Ask me of things to come*   *e* Heb *him*
f Or *Nubia*; Heb *Cush*

45:3 SECRECY—*See* Spiritual Disciplines
Index.
45:9–10 *Woe to you who strive with your
Maker.* It may be that some in the Jewish exilic
community resisted the notion that they should
be saved by a gentile messiah and that verse 9 is
a chiding of such resistance to God's purpose.
First, God is portrayed as the potter and Israel
as the clay, which is expected to be responsive
to the demands and intentions of the potter.
However, the clay defies the potter, as Israel
may be defying Yahweh. This same imagery of

clay and potter turns up in Jeremiah 18–19
and famously in 2 Cor 4:7. The second image
of recalcitrance is even more earthy, for it
imagines a father in sexual intercourse or a
mother in labor and the recalcitrant semen or
fetus resisting what the father or mother is
about to do. Such an image is, of course,
ludicrous; the poet means to say that in the
same way it is ludicrous for Israel to resist the
purposes of Yahweh.
45:14–15 THE WITH-GOD LIFE—*See*
Spiritual Disciplines Index.

they shall come over in chains and
    bow down to you.
They will make supplication to you,
    saying,
"God is with you alone, and there is
    no other;
there is no god besides him."
15 Truly, you are a God who hides himself,
    O God of Israel, the Savior.
16 All of them are put to shame and
    confounded,
    the makers of idols go in confusion
    together.
17 But Israel is saved by the Lord
    with everlasting salvation;
you shall not be put to shame or
    confounded
    to all eternity.

18 For thus says the Lord,
who created the heavens
    (he is God!),
who formed the earth and made it
    (he established it;
he did not create it a chaos,
    he formed it to be inhabited!):
I am the Lord, and there is no other.
19 I did not speak in secret,
    in a land of darkness;
I did not say to the offspring of Jacob,
    "Seek me in chaos."
I the Lord speak the truth,
    I declare what is right.

Idols Cannot Save Babylon

20 Assemble yourselves and come
    together,
    draw near, you survivors of the
    nations!
They have no knowledge—
    those who carry about their wooden
    idols,
and keep on praying to a god
    that cannot save.
21 Declare and present your case;
    let them take counsel together!
Who told this long ago?
    Who declared it of old?
Was it not I, the Lord?
    There is no other god besides me,
a righteous God and a Savior;
    there is no one besides me.

22 Turn to me and be saved,
    all the ends of the earth!
For I am God, and there is no other.
23 By myself I have sworn,
    from my mouth has gone forth in
    righteousness
    a word that shall not return:
"To me every knee shall bow,
    every tongue shall swear."

24 Only in the Lord, it shall be said of me,
    are righteousness and strength;
all who were incensed against him
    shall come to him and be ashamed.
25 In the Lord all the offspring of Israel
    shall triumph and glory.

45:15 *a God who hides himself.* The poet accepts that the God of Israel as the true God is one who remains hidden and is not readily available and transparent in the workings of creation. This statement is the foundation of an important theological trajectory that became crucial for the theological revolution of Martin Luther. The notion of *Deus absconditus*, the God who is hidden, was a correction to easier notions of God in which, when God revealed himself, everything was inexhaustibly known and available about God. Against that, the theology that grew out of the work of Martin Luther insists that apart from God's self-revelation in Jesus

Christ, God retains unto his own self the ultimate mystery of his life and character. The hiddenness of God is a way of speaking about the theological awareness that God is not at the beck and call of human beings.

45:23 *every knee shall bow.* In this verse God issues a summons to all of the nations and expects them to bow down. The last two lines are famously reiterated in the great hymn to Christ in Phil 2:10–11. In the lyrical doxology of the early Church, the summons to praise Yahweh is transposed into a summons to praise Jesus Christ.

46 Bel bows down, Nebo stoops,
their idols are on beasts and cattle;
these things you carry are loaded
as burdens on weary animals.
2 They stoop, they bow down together;
they cannot save the burden,
but themselves go into captivity.

3 Listen to me, O house of Jacob,
all the remnant of the house of
Israel,
who have been borne by me from your
birth,
carried from the womb;
4 even to your old age I am he,
even when you turn gray I will carry
you.
I have made, and I will bear;
I will carry and will save.

5 To whom will you liken me and make
me equal,
and compare me, as though we were
alike?
6 Those who lavish gold from the purse,
and weigh out silver in the scales—
they hire a goldsmith, who makes it
into a god;
then they fall down and worship!
7 They lift it to their shoulders, they
carry it,
they set it in its place, and it stands
there;
it cannot move from its place.

If one cries out to it, it does not answer
or save anyone from trouble.

8 Remember this and consider, *a*
recall it to mind, you transgressors,
9 remember the former things of old;
for I am God, and there is no other;
I am God, and there is no one like me,
10 declaring the end from the beginning
and from ancient times things not yet
done,
saying, "My purpose shall stand,
and I will fulfill my intention,"
11 calling a bird of prey from the east,
the man for my purpose from a far
country.
I have spoken, and I will bring it to pass;
I have planned, and I will do it.

12 Listen to me, you stubborn of heart,
you who are far from deliverance:
13 I bring near my deliverance, it is not far
off,
and my salvation will not tarry;
I will put salvation in Zion,
for Israel my glory.

The Humiliation of Babylon

47 Come down and sit in the dust,
virgin daughter Babylon!
Sit on the ground without a throne,
daughter Chaldea!

a Meaning of Heb uncertain

46:1–13 *they cannot save . . . I will carry you.* In this chapter the poet contrasts Yahweh, the God of Israel, with Bel and Nebo, the gods of Babylon. The point is that Yahweh is incomparable. Israel in exile, even in Babylon, can well trust Yahweh and should not use any of its energy on the weak and untrustworthy Babylonian gods. The images of Bel and Nebo are on the backs of donkeys in something like a Rose Bowl parade; every time the donkey in the parade takes a step, the idol on the back of the donkey sways, and this is understood to be a sign of weakness and dependence (vv 1–2). In contrast, Yahweh does not need to be carried (vv 3–4). Notice the verbs of which Yahweh is the subject: "made," "bear," "carry," "save" (v 4). All of that leads to the

conclusion that Yahweh is incomparable (v 5); consequently, Israel in exile is right to "repent" of its loyalty to the Babylonian gods in order to recommit to its loyalty to Yahweh.

47:1–15 *Sit on the ground without a throne!* After chapter 46 exposes the fraudulent character of the Babylonian gods, chapter 47, in turn, exposes the fraudulent character of Babylonian politics. Thus the two chapters together exhibit the inescapable interface of politics and religion in biblical faith. In this chapter it is anticipated—and accomplished in poetic imagination—that the great superpower Babylon will soon be leveled. This conviction is at the center of the poetry of Second Isaiah with the expectation that the Persian king Cyrus will

For you shall no more be called
    tender and delicate.
2 Take the millstones and grind meal,
    remove your veil,
strip off your robe, uncover your legs,
    pass through the rivers.
3 Your nakedness shall be uncovered,
    and your shame shall be seen.
I will take vengeance,
    and I will spare no one.
4 Our Redeemer—the LORD of hosts is his
        name—
    is the Holy One of Israel.

5 Sit in silence, and go into darkness,
    daughter Chaldea!
For you shall no more be called
    the mistress of kingdoms.
6 I was angry with my people,
    I profaned my heritage;
I gave them into your hand,
    you showed them no mercy;
on the aged you made your yoke
    exceedingly heavy.
7 You said, "I shall be mistress forever,"
    so that you did not lay these things to
        heart
    or remember their end.

8 Now therefore hear this, you lover of
        pleasures,
    who sit securely,
who say in your heart,
    "I am, and there is no one besides me;
I shall not sit as a widow
    or know the loss of children"—
9 both these things shall come upon you
    in a moment, in one day:
the loss of children and widowhood
    shall come upon you in full measure,
in spite of your many sorceries
    and the great power of your
        enchantments.

10 You felt secure in your wickedness;
    you said, "No one sees me."

Your wisdom and your knowledge
    led you astray,
and you said in your heart,
    "I am, and there is no one besides
        me."
11 But evil shall come upon you,
    which you cannot charm away;
disaster shall fall upon you,
    which you will not be able to ward
        off;
and ruin shall come on you suddenly,
    of which you know nothing.

12 Stand fast in your enchantments
    and your many sorceries,
    with which you have labored from
        your youth;
perhaps you may be able to succeed,
    perhaps you may inspire terror.
13 You are wearied with your many
        consultations;
    let those who study *a* the heavens
stand up and save you,
    those who gaze at the stars,
and at each new moon predict
    what *b* shall befall you.

14 See, they are like stubble,
    the fire consumes them;
they cannot deliver themselves
    from the power of the flame.
No coal for warming oneself is this,
    no fire to sit before!
15 Such to you are those with whom you
        have labored,
    who have trafficked with you from
        your youth;
they all wander about in their own
        paths;
    there is no one to save you.

a Meaning of Heb uncertain   *b* Gk Syr Compare
Vg: Heb *from what*

---

move soon against Babylon. The reason that
Babylon will soon be toppled is that the empire
showed "no mercy" to Jerusalem and the
community of Yahweh's faithful (see v 6).

Although Babylon brags about its autonomy, the
reality is that Babylon, like every superpower, is
eventually accountable to Yahweh, who is the
Lord of history.

God the Creator and Redeemer

48 Hear this, O house of Jacob,
who are called by the name of
Israel,
and who came forth from the loins[a]
of Judah;
who swear by the name of the LORD,
and invoke the God of Israel,
but not in truth or right.
2 For they call themselves after the holy
city,
and lean on the God of Israel;
the LORD of hosts is his name.

3 The former things I declared long
ago,
they went out from my mouth and I
made them known;
then suddenly I did them and they
came to pass.
4 Because I know that you are
obstinate,
and your neck is an iron sinew
and your forehead brass,
5 I declared them to you from long ago,
before they came to pass I announced
them to you,
so that you would not say, "My idol did
them,
my carved image and my cast image
commanded them."

6 You have heard; now see all this;
and will you not declare it?
From this time forward I make you hear
new things,
hidden things that you have not
known.
7 They are created now, not long ago;
before today you have never heard of
them,
so that you could not say, "I already
knew them."
8 You have never heard, you have never
known,
from of old your ear has not been
opened.
For I knew that you would deal very
treacherously,
and that from birth you were called a
rebel.

9 For my name's sake I defer my anger,
for the sake of my praise I restrain it
for you,
so that I may not cut you off.
10 See, I have refined you, but not like[b]
silver;
I have tested you in the furnace of
adversity.
11 For my own sake, for my own sake, I do
it,
for why should my name[c] be
profaned?
My glory I will not give to another.

12 Listen to me, O Jacob,
and Israel, whom I called:
I am He; I am the first,
and I am the last.
13 My hand laid the foundation of the
earth,
and my right hand spread out the
heavens;
when I summon them,
they stand at attention.

14 Assemble, all of you, and hear!
Who among them has declared these
things?
The LORD loves him;
he shall perform his purpose on
Babylon,
and his arm shall be against the
Chaldeans.
15 I, even I, have spoken and called him,
I have brought him, and he will
prosper in his way.
16 Draw near to me, hear this!
From the beginning I have not spoken
in secret,
from the time it came to be I have
been there.
And now the Lord GOD has sent me and
his spirit.

17 Thus says the LORD,
your Redeemer, the Holy One of
Israel:
I am the LORD your God,

a Cn: Heb *waters*   b Cn: Heb *with*   c Gk Old
Latin: Heb *for why should it*

who teaches you for your own good,
who leads you in the way you should
    go.
18 O that you had paid attention to my
    commandments!
Then your prosperity would have
    been like a river,
and your success like the waves of the
    sea;
19 your offspring would have been like the
    sand,
and your descendants like its grains;
their name would never be cut off
    or destroyed from before me.

20 Go out from Babylon, flee from Chaldea,
    declare this with a shout of joy,
        proclaim it,
send it forth to the end of the earth;
    say, "The LORD has redeemed his
        servant Jacob!"
21 They did not thirst when he led them
        through the deserts;
he made water flow for them from the
        rock;
he split open the rock and the water
        gushed out.

22 "There is no peace," says the LORD, "for
        the wicked."

The Servant's Mission

49 Listen to me, O coastlands,
    pay attention, you peoples from far
        away!

The LORD called me before I was born,
    while I was in my mother's womb he
        named me.
2 He made my mouth like a sharp sword,
    in the shadow of his hand he
        hid me;
he made me a polished arrow,
    in his quiver he hid me away.
3 And he said to me, "You are my
        servant,
    Israel, in whom I will be glorified."
4 But I said, "I have labored in vain,
    I have spent my strength for nothing
        and vanity;
yet surely my cause is with the LORD,
    and my reward with my God."

5 And now the LORD says,
    who formed me in the womb to be his
        servant,
to bring Jacob back to him,
    and that Israel might be gathered to
        him,
for I am honored in the sight of the
        LORD,
    and my God has become my
        strength—
6 he says,
"It is too light a thing that you should
        be my servant
    to raise up the tribes of Jacob
    and to restore the survivors of Israel;
I will give you as a light to the nations,
    that my salvation may reach to the
        end of the earth."

49:1–7 *I will give you as a light to the nations.* The poet again speaks of Yahweh's "servant." As indicated in the note on 42:1–9, it is almost certain that the servant refers to Israel. In verse 6 here there is the curious sense that servant Israel has a ministry and mission to Israel. Thus it must be the case that the poet anticipates a faithful subcommunity of Israel with a mission to the larger community of Israel. Be that as it may, this poetic articulation looks beyond the rescue of Israel and indicates that Israel has a much larger service to perform: to be "a light to the nations." This phrasing is already familiar to us from 42:6 and indicates the large theological horizon of Isaiah. The God of Israel is indeed the God of all the nations. Again, it is worth noticing that the mandate given to Israel here is already included in the initial mandate given to Abraham in Gen 12:3. Israel does not exist for its own sake. Israel exists as an instrument whereby God's governance of all of the nations of the world will produce the happy outcome of rescue, salvation, and well-being. The missionary impetus of this vision is immensely important for the self-understanding of Israel. It is, moreover, astonishing that this missionary mandate is given precisely in the dark days of exile. Of course, this claim is transposed in the Christian reading of the text to the missionary impetus of the Church.

7 Thus says the LORD,
    the Redeemer of Israel and his Holy
        One,
to one deeply despised, abhorred by the
        nations,
    the slave of rulers,
"Kings shall see and stand up,
    princes, and they shall prostrate
        themselves,
because of the LORD, who is faithful,
    the Holy One of Israel, who has
        chosen you."

Zion's Children to Be Brought Home

8 Thus says the LORD:
    In a time of favor I have answered you,
        on a day of salvation I have helped you;
    I have kept you and given you
        as a covenant to the people,*a*
    to establish the land,
        to apportion the desolate heritages;
9 saying to the prisoners, "Come out,"
    to those who are in darkness, "Show
        yourselves."
    They shall feed along the ways,
        on all the bare heights*b* shall be their
            pasture;
10 they shall not hunger or thirst,
    neither scorching wind nor sun shall
        strike them down,

for he who has pity on them will lead
        them,
    and by springs of water will guide
        them.
11 And I will turn all my mountains into a
        road,
    and my highways shall be raised up.
12 Lo, these shall come from far away,
    and lo, these from the north and
        from the west,
    and these from the land of Syene.*c*

13 Sing for joy, O heavens, and exult,
        O earth;
    break forth, O mountains, into
        singing!
For the LORD has comforted his people,
    and will have compassion on his
        suffering ones.

14 But Zion said, "The LORD has forsaken
        me,
    my Lord has forgotten me."
15 Can a woman forget her nursing child,
    or show no compassion for the child
        of her womb?
Even these may forget,
    yet I will not forget you.

a Meaning of Heb uncertain   *b* Or *the trails*
c Q Ms: MT *Sinim*

Responding

49:6 SERVICE. The note on 49:1–7 says that being a light to the nations means that "Israel does not exist for its own sake." What does this mean for us as Christians? For whose sake do we exist and how can we better fulfill our mandate? *See also* Spiritual Disciplines Index.

49:8–9 *prisoners.* The large responsibility of Israel is reiterated. The phrase "as a covenant to the people" is repeated from 42:6. The rest of verses 8–9, then, explains what this momentous phrase might mean in terms of reestablishing the exiles and emancipating prisoners. Since in the ancient world prisoners tended to be the poor and the marginalized, we see that Israel's mandate is particularly against every culture's practice of dismissing the marginalized, who are incapable of emancipating themselves.

49:14–15 *I will not forget you.* The poet quotes Zion, who apparently has issued a complaint against God, perhaps in a regular liturgical service, that God has forsaken and forgotten it. This language may be borrowed from Lam 5:20. Lamentations 5 is a long poem of grief over the loss of Jerusalem. In the poetry of Lamentations Israel is convinced that the reason for being in exile is Yahweh's forgetting and forsaking. The same sentiment is expressed here in verse 14. What is most remarkable is that in verse 15 God directly answers and refutes the charge made in verse 14. God answers the word "forget" and makes a particular play on the words "compassion" and "womb," which are the same word in Hebrew but with different vowels. Thus it is asserted that a mother nursing a child cannot and will not forget the child—not simply because of love, but because a nursing mother will have very sore breasts if she does not let the

16 See, I have inscribed you on the palms
    of my hands;
  your walls are continually before me.
17 Your builders outdo your destroyers, *a*
    and those who laid you waste go away
    from you.
18 Lift up your eyes all around and see;
    they all gather, they come to you.
  As I live, says the LORD,
    you shall put all of them on like an
    ornament,
  and like a bride you shall bind them
    on.

19 Surely your waste and your desolate
    places
  and your devastated land—
surely now you will be too crowded for
    your inhabitants,
  and those who swallowed you up will
    be far away.
20 The children born in the time of your
    bereavement
  will yet say in your hearing:
  "The place is too crowded for me;
  make room for me to settle."
21 Then you will say in your heart,
  "Who has borne me these?
  I was bereaved and barren,
    exiled and put away—
    so who has reared these?
  I was left all alone—
  where then have these come from?"

22 Thus says the Lord GOD:
  I will soon lift up my hand to the
    nations,
    and raise my signal to the peoples;
  and they shall bring your sons in their
    bosom,
  and your daughters shall be carried
    on their shoulders.
23 Kings shall be your foster fathers,
    and their queens your nursing
    mothers.

With their faces to the ground they
    shall bow down to you,
  and lick the dust of your feet.
Then you will know that I am the LORD;
  those who wait for me shall not be
    put to shame.

24 Can the prey be taken from the mighty,
    or the captives of a tyrant *b* be
    rescued?
25 But thus says the LORD:
Even the captives of the mighty shall be
    taken,
  and the prey of the tyrant be rescued;
for I will contend with those who
    contend with you,
  and I will save your children.
26 I will make your oppressors eat their
    own flesh,
  and they shall be drunk with their
    own blood as with wine.
Then all flesh shall know
  that I am the LORD your Savior,
  and your Redeemer, the Mighty One
    of Jacob.

50 Thus says the LORD:
  Where is your mother's bill of
    divorce
  with which I put her away?
Or which of my creditors is it
  to whom I have sold you?
No, because of your sins you were sold,
  and for your transgressions your
    mother was put away.
2 Why was no one there when I came?
  Why did no one answer when I
    called?
Is my hand shortened, that it cannot
    redeem?
Or have I no power to deliver?
By my rebuke I dry up the sea,

a Or *Your children come swiftly; your destroyers*
b Q Ms Syr Vg: MT *of a righteous person*

---

child suckle. The poet then ups the ante in the
last part of verse 15 to allow for the extreme
case in which a mother may forget such a child
and counters that, even were that to happen,
Yahweh will not forget Israel. Thus God's answer

exploits the imagery of mother and child, but
then moves beyond it to make a more radical
claim for God's abiding fidelity toward Israel.
  50:2 *Is my hand shortened? . . . . Or have I no
power to deliver?* These last two of the four

I make the rivers a desert;
   their fish stink for lack of water,
   and die of thirst. *a*
3 I clothe the heavens with blackness,
   and make sackcloth their covering.

The Servant's Humiliation and Vindication

4 The Lord GOD has given me
   the tongue of a teacher, *b*
that I may know how to sustain
   the weary with a word.
Morning by morning he wakens—
   wakens my ear
to listen as those who are taught.
5 The Lord GOD has opened my ear,
   and I was not rebellious,
   I did not turn backward.
6 I gave my back to those who struck me,
   and my cheeks to those who pulled
     out the beard;
I did not hide my face
   from insult and spitting.

7 The Lord GOD helps me;
   therefore I have not been disgraced;
therefore I have set my face like flint,
   and I know that I shall not be put to
     shame;
8   he who vindicates me is near.
Who will contend with me?
   Let us stand up together.
Who are my adversaries?
   Let them confront me.

9 It is the Lord GOD who helps me;
   who will declare me guilty?
All of them will wear out like a garment;
   the moth will eat them up.

10 Who among you fears the LORD
   and obeys the voice of his servant,
who walks in darkness
   and has no light,
yet trusts in the name of the LORD
   and relies upon his God?
11 But all of you are kindlers of fire,
   lighters of firebrands. *c*
Walk in the flame of your fire,
   and among the brands that you have
     kindled!
This is what you shall have from my
   hand:
   you shall lie down in torment.

Blessings in Store for God's People

51 Listen to me, you that pursue
     righteousness,
  you that seek the LORD.
Look to the rock from which you were
   hewn,
  and to the quarry from which you
    were dug.
2 Look to Abraham your father
  and to Sarah who bore you;

a Or *die on the thirsty ground*   *b* Cn: Heb *of those who are taught*   *c* Syr: Heb *you gird yourselves with firebrands*

---

rhetorical questions seem to be a defiant self-assertion by God in answer to accusations and complaints that must have been issued by people in the exile. Thus the defiant question "Is my hand shortened?" is in response to a complaint by Israel that "Yahweh's hand is shortened." In the exodus tradition it is said doxologically that God has rescued Israel "with a mighty hand and an outstretched arm" (e.g., Deut 5:15). Thus, in exile, Israel had imagined Yahweh to be weak, and that is why Israel was left in exile. The Isaiah tradition wants to reassert the power of Yahweh and, therefore, has Yahweh defiantly refute the accusation that he is weak. The implication is that Yahweh has immense power and that power is about to move toward liberating Israel for its homecoming, reminiscent of the exodus tradition.

50:4–9 *he who vindicates me is near.* Another poem concerning the servant who is summoned, empowered, and helped by God to do his work in the world. The judicial language in verses 8–9 is important. It is asserted that God "vindicates," which means in legal terms "acquits," and that if God vindicates, then no one else can bring a charge of guilt. This rhetoric recurs in Rom 8:33–34, where it is asserted in parallel language that God "justifies" and, therefore, no one can "condemn." In both cases it is asserted that the power of God to make his beloved free and innocent cannot be overturned by any hostile force.

51:2 *Look to Abraham.* In 43:18–19 the poet admonishes Israel in exile to forget the old tradition of the exodus. In this verse, conversely,

for he was but one when I called him,
    but I blessed him and made him many.
3 For the Lord will comfort Zion;
    he will comfort all her waste places,
and will make her wilderness like Eden,
    her desert like the garden of the Lord;
joy and gladness will be found in her,
    thanksgiving and the voice of song.

4 Listen to me, my people,
    and give heed to me, my nation;
for a teaching will go out from me,
    and my justice for a light to the
      peoples.
5 I will bring near my deliverance swiftly,
    my salvation has gone out
    and my arms will rule the peoples;
the coastlands wait for me,
    and for my arm they hope.
6 Lift up your eyes to the heavens,
    and look at the earth beneath;
for the heavens will vanish like smoke,
    the earth will wear out like a garment,
    and those who live on it will die like
      gnats;ᵃ
but my salvation will be forever,
    and my deliverance will never be
      ended.

7 Listen to me, you who know
    righteousness,
you people who have my teaching in
    your hearts;
do not fear the reproach of others,
    and do not be dismayed when they
      revile you.
8 For the moth will eat them up like a
    garment,
    and the worm will eat them like
      wool;
but my deliverance will be forever,
    and my salvation to all generations.

9 Awake, awake, put on strength,
    O arm of the Lord!
Awake, as in days of old,
    the generations of long ago!
Was it not you who cut Rahab in
      pieces,
    who pierced the dragon?
10 Was it not you who dried up the sea,
    the waters of the great deep;
who made the depths of the sea a way
    for the redeemed to cross over?
11 So the ransomed of the Lord shall
      return,

a Or in like manner

---

the poet summons Israel in exile to remember the Genesis traditions of promise and the figures of Abraham and Sarah, who were carriers of that promise. If we consider 43:18–19 and this verse together, we can see that there is a tricky mandate both to remember and to forget. In this verse, the point is that Israel is not rootless and abandoned, but must stay rooted in God's promise. The most important reality for Israel in exile is that God's promises are at work even in exile.

51:7–8 *you people who have my teaching in your hearts.* Here again is a salvation oracle: "Do not fear." In this particular case the reason for being fearless is that the teaching of Yahweh is in one's "heart." Being rooted in Torah teachings of the God of Israel makes one fearless in a world of jeopardy and threat.

51:11 *the ransomed of the Lord shall return.* Again, the word "ransom" is used (see note on 43:3). The usage here is not yet explicitly theological; it is simply a metaphor for the purchase of captives' freedom. It becomes

theological later on, but continues the intent of the image of emancipation of captives.

Responding
51:11 CELEBRATION. Celebration may well be the most overlooked of the Spiritual Disciplines, but it is indeed a discipline meant to be practiced. Reaching for everlasting joy through singing, dancing, and praising is essential even and perhaps especially in times of sadness, because it returns our focus to God. As Dallas Willard writes in *The Spirit of the Disciplines:* "Celebration heartily done makes our deprivation and sorrows seem small, and we find in it great strength to do the will of our God, because his goodness becomes so real to us." The next time you find yourself dwelling in sorrow, do your best to remember the myriad goodnesses of God, to shift your focus from yourself and your pain to the Author of all of your blessings. *See also* Spiritual Disciplines Index.

and come to Zion with singing;
  everlasting joy shall be upon their
    heads;
  they shall obtain joy and gladness,
  and sorrow and sighing shall flee
    away.

12 I, I am he who comforts you;
  why then are you afraid of a mere
    mortal who must die,
  a human being who fades like grass?
13 You have forgotten the LORD, your
    Maker,
  who stretched out the heavens
  and laid the foundations of the earth.
You fear continually all day long
  because of the fury of the oppressor,
  who is bent on destruction.
  But where is the fury of the
    oppressor?
14 The oppressed shall speedily be
    released;
  they shall not die and go down to the
    Pit,
  nor shall they lack bread.
15 For I am the LORD your God,
  who stirs up the sea so that its waves
    roar—
  the LORD of hosts is his name.
16 I have put my words in your mouth,
  and hidden you in the shadow of my
    hand,
  stretching out*a* the heavens
  and laying the foundations of the
    earth,
  and saying to Zion, "You are my
    people."

17 Rouse yourself, rouse yourself!
  Stand up, O Jerusalem,
you who have drunk at the hand of the
    LORD
  the cup of his wrath,
who have drunk to the dregs
  the bowl of staggering.
18 There is no one to guide her
  among all the children she has borne;
there is no one to take her by the hand
  among all the children she has
    brought up.
19 These two things have befallen you

—who will grieve with you?—
devastation and destruction, famine
    and sword—
  who will comfort you?*b*
20 Your children have fainted,
  they lie at the head of every street
  like an antelope in a net;
they are full of the wrath of the LORD,
  the rebuke of your God.

21 Therefore hear this, you who are
    wounded, *c*
  who are drunk, but not with wine:
22 Thus says your Sovereign, the LORD,
  your God who pleads the cause of his
    people:
See, I have taken from your hand the
    cup of staggering;
  you shall drink no more
    from the bowl of my wrath.
23 And I will put it into the hand of your
    tormentors,
  who have said to you,
  "Bow down, that we may walk on
    you";
and you have made your back like the
    ground
  and like the street for them to walk
    on.

Let Zion Rejoice

52 Awake, awake,
  put on your strength, O Zion!
Put on your beautiful garments,
  O Jerusalem, the holy city;
for the uncircumcised and the unclean
  shall enter you no more.
2 Shake yourself from the dust, rise up,
  O captive*d* Jerusalem;
loose the bonds from your neck,
  O captive daughter Zion!

3 For thus says the LORD: You were sold
for nothing, and you shall be redeemed without money. 4For thus says the Lord GOD: Long
ago, my people went down into Egypt to reside there as aliens; the Assyrian, too, has oppressed them without cause. 5Now therefore

a Syr: Heb *planting*   *b* Q Ms Gk Syr Vg: MT *how
may I comfort you?*   *c* Or *humbled*   *d* Cn: Heb
rise up, sit

what am I doing here, says the LORD, seeing that my people are taken away without cause? Their rulers howl, says the LORD, and continually, all day long, my name is despised. 6Therefore my people shall know my name; therefore in that day they shall know that it is I who speak; here am I.

7 How beautiful upon the mountains
   are the feet of the messenger who
      announces peace,
   who brings good news,
   who announces salvation,
   who says to Zion, "Your God reigns."
8 Listen! Your sentinels lift up their voices,
   together they sing for joy;
   for in plain sight they see
   the return of the LORD to Zion.
9 Break forth together into singing,
   you ruins of Jerusalem;
   for the LORD has comforted his people,
   he has redeemed Jerusalem.
10 The LORD has bared his holy arm

before the eyes of all the nations;
and all the ends of the earth shall see
   the salvation of our God.

11 Depart, depart, go out from there!
   Touch no unclean thing;
   go out from the midst of it, purify
      yourselves,
   you who carry the vessels of the LORD.
12 For you shall not go out in haste,
   and you shall not go in flight;
   for the LORD will go before you,
   and the God of Israel will be your rear
      guard.

The Suffering Servant

13 See, my servant shall prosper;
   he shall be exalted and lifted up,
   and shall be very high.
14 Just as there were many who were
      astonished at him a

a Syr Tg Heb you

52:7 *How beautiful . . . are the feet of the messenger who announces peace.* This familiar text uses the imagery of a messenger running from Babylon to Jerusalem to announce the victory of Yahweh over the Babylonian gods that will permit the return of Israel to Jerusalem. It is clear that such a messenger running six hundred miles over the sand would not have "beautiful feet"; the phrasing probably means that the feet are welcome, because one can tell by the way the messenger runs that the news is good. This text is the third usage, along with 40:9 and 41:27, of the word "good news," or "gospel," in a more or less technical sense. The substance of the good news is that "your God reigns," or "your God has just become king," by defeating the other powers. This announcement of the new rule of God is taken up in parallel fashion in the initial announcement of Jesus in Mark that "the kingdom of God has come near" (1:14–15), which means that the rule of God has displaced all other rules through Jesus, who embodies and enacts the new rule of God.

52:13–53:12 *See, my servant shall prosper.* The most extensive and best known of the Servant Songs. We have already seen that in 42:1 and 49:6 the servant is probably Israel (see notes on 42:1–9; 49:1–7). It is certainly the case,

nonetheless, that in the early Church this poem was taken up and understood as an anticipatory reference to Jesus Christ, who would suffer in saving and redemptive ways. That particular connection of this imagery to Jesus is explicit in Acts 8. There Isa 53:7–8 is quoted (8:32–33) and Philip the evangelist offers an interpretation that specifically connects the Isaiah text to Jesus (8:34–35). This "second reading" moves past the initial reading of Judaism, in which the servant clearly refers to Israel. Two things may be particularly noticed about this poem. First, it is declared that the servant, by his suffering, will be "wounded for our transgressions" (53:4–5). This remarkable statement that the servant may take on himself the suffering of others has been important in some interpretations of Jesus. Second, at the end of the poem (53:10–12), there seems to be a notion of the recovery and well-being of the servant, who has died, so there may also be an inchoate notion of resurrection here. If that is the case, then the dramatic movement of the entire poem is to move into the abyss and then out of it into well-being and triumph. Such a twofold movement, of course, squares easily with the Christian narrative of Jesus' crucifixion and resurrection.

—so marred was his appearance,
  beyond human semblance,
  and his form beyond that of mortals—
15 so he shall startle [a] many nations;
  kings shall shut their mouths because
    of him;
  for that which had not been told them
    they shall see,
  and that which they had not heard
    they shall contemplate.

53 Who has believed what we have
    heard?
  And to whom has the arm of the LORD
    been revealed?
2 For he grew up before him like a young
    plant,
  and like a root out of dry ground;
  he had no form or majesty that we
    should look at him,
  nothing in his appearance that we
    should desire him.
3 He was despised and rejected by others;
  a man of suffering [b] and acquainted
    with infirmity;
  and as one from whom others hide
    their faces [c]
  he was despised, and we held him of
    no account.

4 Surely he has borne our infirmities
  and carried our diseases;
  yet we accounted him stricken,
    struck down by God, and afflicted.
5 But he was wounded for our
    transgressions,
  crushed for our iniquities;
  upon him was the punishment that
    made us whole,
  and by his bruises we are healed.
6 All we like sheep have gone astray;
  we have all turned to our own way,
  and the LORD has laid on him
    the iniquity of us all.

7 He was oppressed, and he was afflicted,
  yet he did not open his mouth;

like a lamb that is led to the slaughter,
  and like a sheep that before its
    shearers is silent,
  so he did not open his mouth.
8 By a perversion of justice he was taken
    away.
  Who could have imagined his future?
  For he was cut off from the land of the
    living,
  stricken for the transgression of my
    people.
9 They made his grave with the wicked
  and his tomb [d] with the rich, [e]
  although he had done no violence,
  and there was no deceit in his mouth.

10 Yet it was the will of the LORD to crush
    him with pain. [f]
  When you make his life an offering for
    sin, [a]
  he shall see his offspring, and shall
    prolong his days;
  through him the will of the LORD shall
    prosper.
11 Out of his anguish he shall see light; [g]
  he shall find satisfaction through his
    knowledge.
  The righteous one, [h] my servant, shall
    make many righteous,
  and he shall bear their iniquities.
12 Therefore I will allot him a portion with
    the great,
  and he shall divide the spoil with the
    strong;
  because he poured out himself to death,
  and was numbered with the
    transgressors;
  yet he bore the sin of many,

a Meaning of Heb uncertain   b Or a man of
sorrows   c Or as one who hides his face from us
d Q Ms: MT and in his death   e Cn: Heb with a
rich person   f Or by disease; meaning of Heb
uncertain   g Q Mss: MT lacks light   h Or and
he shall find satisfaction. Through his knowledge, the
righteous one

Responding
53:7 SILENCE. Reflect on the silence
of the lamb led to slaughter and the
sheep before the shearers. What light do these
images shed on Jesus' sacrifice? What is the
significance of suffering in silence? *See also*
Spiritual Disciplines Index.

and made intercession for the
transgressors.

The Eternal Covenant of Peace

54 Sing, O barren one who did not
bear;
burst into song and shout,
you who have not been in labor!
For the children of the desolate woman
will be more
than the children of her that is
married, says the LORD.
2 Enlarge the site of your tent,
and let the curtains of your
habitations be stretched out;
do not hold back; lengthen your cords
and strengthen your stakes.
3 For you will spread out to the right and
to the left,
and your descendants will possess the
nations
and will settle the desolate towns.

4 Do not fear, for you will not be
ashamed;
do not be discouraged, for you will
not suffer disgrace;
for you will forget the shame of your
youth,
and the disgrace of your widowhood
you will remember no more.
5 For your Maker is your husband,
the LORD of hosts is his name;
the Holy One of Israel is your Redeemer,
the God of the whole earth he is
called.
6 For the LORD has called you
like a wife forsaken and grieved in
spirit,
like the wife of a man's youth when she
is cast off,
says your God.
7 For a brief moment I abandoned you,
but with great compassion I will
gather you.

54:1–3 *Sing, O barren one!* In the ancient world the lyrical imagery of the barren woman having many children signifies a coming blessing of prosperity and well-being. Thus the poet imagines, through the figure of the woman, the complete reversal of the fortunes of Israel, from exile to homecoming. The imagery of the barren woman is no doubt rooted in the Genesis references, particularly to Sarah, but then also to Rebekah and Rachel, for in every generation of Genesis the mother of Israel is barren until the eleventh hour, when an heir is miraculously given (Gen 11:30; 25:21; 29:31). As we read back to Genesis in this text, so we also read forward in Christian tradition to where the text is taken up and quoted in Gal 4:27. In the allegory of Hagar and Sarah in the Letter to the Galatians, Paul transposes the imagery into gospel and law, so that the fruitful woman with a future is the gospel and the woman without a future is the law. Thus this Isaiah text stands at the center of a very long and complex theological tradition.

54:4–6 *you will not be ashamed.* Again, there is a salvation oracle in the parallel "Do not fear" and "Do not be discouraged." The salvation oracle here, however, makes use of the image of marriage. In a patriarchal society it was particularly scandalous for a woman to be abandoned by a husband. In this text the

scandal of rejection and reembrace is used in parallel to verses 1–3 to talk about the abandonment of Israel by God in exile and then the immediate prospect that Yahweh, the husband, will again restore the wife, Israel. Israel in exile is shamed as an abandoned woman in a patriarchal society. Now Israel, as the recovered and reloved woman, is celebrated and enhanced by Yahweh, who again loves Israel and restores her to dignity, honor, and well-being. In both verses 1–3 and verses 4–6 the agile poetic capacity of the poet is evident in the use of these images of intimate family relationships to announce the good news of God's gift of a future to exilic Israel.

54:7–8 *I abandoned you.* These verses are spectacular because they are the direct, explicit, unambiguous announcement by God that he has indeed abandoned Israel in exile. The notion of abandonment (v 7) is paralleled by the hiding of God's face (v 8), for the hiding of God's face means that Israel cannot live. Of course in many Psalms, notably in Ps 22:1, Israel had complained that God had abandoned Israel. Here, however, the acknowledgment of abandonment is on God's own lips. In the full expression of the two verses, the acknowledgment of abandonment and the hiding of the face in exile are mentioned in order that the second half of each verse can

8 In overflowing wrath for a moment
    I hid my face from you,
  but with everlasting love I will have
      compassion on you,
    says the LORD, your Redeemer.

9 This is like the days of Noah to me:
    Just as I swore that the waters of Noah
      would never again go over the earth,
  so I have sworn that I will not be angry
      with you
    and will not rebuke you.
10 For the mountains may depart
    and the hills be removed,
  but my steadfast love shall not depart
      from you,
  and my covenant of peace shall not
      be removed,
    says the LORD, who has compassion
      on you.

11 O afflicted one, storm-tossed, and not
      comforted,
  I am about to set your stones in
      antimony,
  and lay your foundations with
      sapphires. a
12 I will make your pinnacles of rubies,
    your gates of jewels,
  and all your wall of precious stones.
13 All your children shall be taught by the
      LORD,
  and great shall be the prosperity of
      your children.

14 In righteousness you shall be
      established;
  you shall be far from oppression, for
      you shall not fear;
  and from terror, for it shall not come
      near you.
15 If anyone stirs up strife,
    it is not from me;
  whoever stirs up strife with you
    shall fall because of you.
16 See it is I who have created the smith
    who blows the fire of coals,
    and produces a weapon fit for its
      purpose;
  I have also created the ravager to
      destroy.
17 No weapon that is fashioned against
    you shall prosper,
  and you shall confute every tongue
      that rises against you in
      judgment.
This is the heritage of the servants of
    the LORD
  and their vindication from me, says
      the LORD.

An Invitation to Abundant Life

55 Ho, everyone who thirsts,
    come to the waters;
  and you that have no money,
    come, buy and eat!
Come, buy wine and milk
    without money and without price.

a Or lapis lazuli

announce the good news that the abandonment
is over. Thus the poet characteristically looks to a
future that will be filled with God's love for Israel.
Note that in both verses the term "compassion"
is the key word (see 49:14–15). Israel has a future
after abandonment precisely because Yahweh
loves Israel like a mother loves a vulnerable
baby.

54:9–10 *like the days of Noah.* In a daring
poetic connection the poet suggests that the
experience of the exile is parallel to the
experience of Noah in the flood, for both flood
and exile are experiences of chaos. What counts
in these verses, however, is not the experience
of the flood but the fact that God has sworn

that such an abandonment of Israel would
happen "never again," the same "never again"
used in the flood narrative (Gen 9:11). Thus, in
both cases, Israel may be confident that it is, by
God's own promise, immune from any such
threat in the future.

55:1–13 *everyone who thirsts, come to the
waters.* The middle portion of Isaiah (chaps
40–55) culminates here in a great summons to
Israel in exile to give up all of its fascinations
with Babylonian power and Babylonian gods
and to return to the free, gracious, and
compassionate gift of Yahweh, who will bring
the exiles home. This chapter begins with a
summons that sounds much like one that might

2 Why do you spend your money for that
        which is not bread,
    and your labor for that which does
        not satisfy?
    Listen carefully to me, and eat what is
        good,
    and delight yourselves in rich food.
3 Incline your ear, and come to me;
        listen, so that you may live.
    I will make with you an everlasting
        covenant,
    my steadfast, sure love for David.
4 See, I made him a witness to the
        peoples,
    a leader and commander for the
        peoples.
5 See, you shall call nations that you do
        not know,
    and nations that do not know you
        shall run to you,
    because of the LORD your God, the Holy
        One of Israel,
    for he has glorified you.

6 Seek the LORD while he may be found,
    call upon him while he is near;
7 let the wicked forsake their way,
    and the unrighteous their thoughts;

let them return to the LORD, that he
        may have mercy on them,
    and to our God, for he will
        abundantly pardon.
8 For my thoughts are not your
        thoughts,
    nor are your ways my ways, says the
        LORD.
9 For as the heavens are higher than the
        earth,
    so are my ways higher than your ways
    and my thoughts than your thoughts.

10 For as the rain and the snow come
        down from heaven,
    and do not return there until they
        have watered the earth,
    making it bring forth and sprout,
        giving seed to the sower and bread to
        the eater,
11 so shall my word be that goes out from
        my mouth;
    it shall not return to me empty,
    but it shall accomplish that which I
        purpose,
    and succeed in the thing for which I
        sent it.

---

come from a street vendor in Damascus or
Jerusalem who is selling water and inviting
people to come and buy. The cry of the street
vendor is in the mouth of Yahweh, however,
who invites the listeners to have free wine and
milk and bread. Such free bread, wine, and milk
bespeak God's incredible generosity and for
Christians may form an imaginative background
for an understanding of the Eucharist. In
contrast, in the Babylonian economy, where
Jews tried to make their way, bread, wine, and
milk were very expensive. With such demanding
prices, people labor mightily for economic
success and then discover that they are not
satisfied with what they finally get. Although the
text is obviously addressed to the sixth-century
BC exiles, it takes no imagination to see that the
same issue is at stake for many employees in the
capitalist system who work and work to earn
what is promised and then discover that the
consumer goods of the system are not at all
satisfying. The good news is that there is an

alternative offered in the gospel (see Matt
11:28–30).

55:8–11 *my thoughts are not your thoughts*. A
contrast is made between the "thoughts" of
Israel in exile and the "thoughts" of Yahweh (vv
8–9). The word translated "thought" can also be
translated "plan" or "intention." The thoughts or
intentions of the Israelites in exile were that they
were in exile in perpetuity, without hope. The
good news (gospel) announced by the poet is
that there is another "plan"; the plan of Yahweh
is that there will be immediate homecoming.
This massive statement of faith articulates the
conviction of faithful people that there is a divine
intention for the future that transcends our plans,
which are often conceived in fear or in anxiety.
God's good intention for the exiles overrides
their own sense of despair. Additionally, the
images of rain and snow for the life-giving gentleness and unobtrusiveness of God's ways (v 10)
are a dramatic contrast to the thoughts and ways
of human ingenuity and manipulation.

12 For you shall go out in joy,
    and be led back in peace;
the mountains and the hills before you
    shall burst into song,
    and all the trees of the field shall clap
        their hands.
13 Instead of the thorn shall come up the
        cypress;
    instead of the brier shall come up the
        myrtle;
    and it shall be to the LORD for a
        memorial,
        for an everlasting sign that shall not
            be cut off.

The Covenant Extended to All Who Obey

56 Thus says the LORD:
    Maintain justice, and do what is
        right,
    for soon my salvation will come,
        and my deliverance be revealed.

2 Happy is the mortal who does this,
    the one who holds it fast,
who keeps the sabbath, not profaning it,
    and refrains from doing any evil.

3 Do not let the foreigner joined to the
        LORD say,
    "The LORD will surely separate me
        from his people";
and do not let the eunuch say,
    "I am just a dry tree."
4 For thus says the LORD:
To the eunuchs who keep my sabbaths,
    who choose the things that please me
    and hold fast my covenant,
5 I will give, in my house and within my
        walls,
    a monument and a name
        better than sons and daughters;
I will give them an everlasting name
    that shall not be cut off.

55:12–13 *go out in joy.* The culmination of Second Isaiah (chaps 40–55) in these two verses envisions a mighty procession coming back to Jerusalem in joy and *shalom* ("peace") and triumph. Thus these verses are a match to 40:3–5 at the beginning of Second Isaiah; both texts imagine a great triumphal return home to Jerusalem. The reference to the cypress and myrtle in place of thorns and briars is perhaps an allusion to the curse of Gen 3:18. If that connection is a valid one, then it means that God not only restores Israel to a new kind of *shalom;* God also restores creation to its proper productive, fruitful functioning.

56:1–66:24 *Maintain justice.* The material in chapters 56–66, termed "Third Isaiah," is probably dated somewhere between 520 and 480 BC and reflects the status of the Jerusalem community after the Jews had returned home from exile at the behest of the Persians. The city of Jerusalem and its infrastructure of faith had to be reconstructed, and there was predictably great dispute about how to do that. It is clear that Third Isaiah represents one voice and one party to that dispute. The beginning point for Third Isaiah is to announce that the maintenance of justice is the condition of well-being for the community that is to be reconstructed. Justice here undoubtedly

means a concern for the economic welfare of the disadvantaged and the disinherited. This advocacy is probably in tension with an alternative one, voiced by Ezekiel, that champions holiness as the primary way to identify God's people. The vision of Third Isaiah is not confined to the proper ordering of cultic matters, but concerns public welfare in the reorganization of the economy.

56:3–6 *shall not be cut off.* One of the disputes in the reconstruction period after the exile was the matter of who was eligible to be a member of the community. Although some wanted to be exclusivist and keep out disqualified people, these verses make clear that Third Isaiah advocates an inclusive policy that is extended to eunuchs and foreigners. It is thought by some scholars that these verses intend precisely to contradict the exclusionary Torah regulation of Deut 23:1–7. Reference to "eunuchs" is of particular interest, because the term probably refers to Jews who had violated their own person in order to advance themselves in the power structure of the Persian environment. Particular reference might be made to Isa 39:7, the next-to-last verse of First Isaiah, which anticipates that royal princes from Jerusalem will be carried away and made eunuchs who will be subservient in Babylon.

6 And the foreigners who join themselves
        to the LORD,
    to minister to him, to love the name
        of the LORD,
    and to be his servants,
all who keep the sabbath, and do not
        profane it,
    and hold fast my covenant—
7 these I will bring to my holy mountain,
    and make them joyful in my house of
        prayer;
their burnt offerings and their sacrifices
    will be accepted on my altar;
for my house shall be called a house of
        prayer
    for all peoples.
8 Thus says the Lord GOD,
    who gathers the outcasts of Israel,
I will gather others to them
    besides those already gathered. *a*

The Corruption of Israel's Rulers

9 All you wild animals,
    all you wild animals in the forest,
        come to devour!
10 Israel's *b* sentinels are blind,
    they are all without knowledge;
they are all silent dogs
    that cannot bark;
dreaming, lying down,
    loving to slumber.
11 The dogs have a mighty appetite;
    they never have enough.

The shepherds also have no
        understanding;
    they have all turned to their own way,
        to their own gain, one and all.
12 "Come," they say, "let us *c* get wine;
    let us fill ourselves with strong drink.
And tomorrow will be like today,
    great beyond measure."

Israel's Futile Idolatry

57 The righteous perish,
        and no one takes it to heart;
the devout are taken away,
    while no one understands.
For the righteous are taken away from
        calamity,
2   and they enter into peace;
    those who walk uprightly
        will rest on their couches.
3 But as for you, come here,
    you children of a sorceress,
    you offspring of an adulterer and a
        whore. *d*
4 Whom are you mocking?
    Against whom do you open your
        mouth wide
    and stick out your tongue?
Are you not children of transgression,
    the offspring of deceit—

a Heb *besides his gathered ones*   *b* Heb *His*
c Q Ms Syr Vg Tg: MT *me*   *d* Heb *an adulterer and
she plays the whore*

Thus it is not impossible that this first text in
Third Isaiah, which concerns the inclusion of
Jewish eunuchs, looks back to the last section of
First Isaiah and that they are to be understood
together. The inclusion of eunuchs, which Torah
regulation (Deut 23) would exclude, is paralleled
to the inclusion of foreigners. The only requirement for both eunuchs and foreigners is that
they must keep Sabbath and keep covenant.
This inclusion is in contrast to the tradition that
is represented, for example, in Ezekiel and Ezra.
    56:7 *my house shall be called a house of
prayer for all peoples.* This inclusive advocacy
urges that all people be welcomed to the
Temple, which was reconstructed in 520–516 BC.
It is worth noting that this phrase is taken up by
Jesus in Matt 21:13, where the statement from

Isaiah is combined with another prophetic
statement from Jer 7:11 about the Temple
becoming "a den for robbers." Jesus' use of
texts from Isaiah and Jeremiah shows the way
in which he was schooled in the prophetic
tradition, which continues the critical practice
of the prophetic tradition.

Responding
56:7 PRAYER. Meditation, confession,
and repentance are proper attitudes for
prayer, but so is joy, as this verse reminds us. Joy
is also one of the fruits of the spirit (Gal 5:22). If
you have trouble bringing joy to your time of
prayer, consider beginning or ending your
prayer time with a favorite celebratory hymn or
praise song. *See also* Spiritual Disciplines Index.

5 you that burn with lust among the
        oaks,
    under every green tree;
    you that slaughter your children in the
        valleys,
    under the clefts of the rocks?
6 Among the smooth stones of the valley
        is your portion;
    they, they, are your lot;
    to them you have poured out a drink
        offering,
    you have brought a grain offering.
    Shall I be appeased for these things?
7 Upon a high and lofty mountain
    you have set your bed,
    and there you went up to offer
        sacrifice.
8 Behind the door and the doorpost
    you have set up your symbol;
    for, in deserting me,[a] you have
        uncovered your bed,
    you have gone up to it,
    you have made it wide;
    and you have made a bargain for
        yourself with them,
    you have loved their bed,
    you have gazed on their nakedness.[b]
9 You journeyed to Molech[c] with oil,
    and multiplied your perfumes;
    you sent your envoys far away,
    and sent down even to Sheol.
10 You grew weary from your many
        wanderings,
    but you did not say, "It is useless."
    You found your desire rekindled,
    and so you did not weaken.

11 Whom did you dread and fear
    so that you lied,

and did not remember me
    or give me a thought?
Have I not kept silent and closed my
    eyes,[d]
and so you do not fear me?
12 I will concede your righteousness and
        your works,
    but they will not help you.
13 When you cry out, let your collection of
        idols deliver you!
    The wind will carry them off,
    a breath will take them away.
    But whoever takes refuge in me shall
        possess the land
    and inherit my holy mountain.

A Promise of Help and Healing

14 It shall be said,
    "Build up, build up, prepare the way,
        remove every obstruction from my
        people's way."
15 For thus says the high and lofty one
    who inhabits eternity, whose name is
        Holy:
    I dwell in the high and holy place,
    and also with those who are contrite
        and humble in spirit,
    to revive the spirit of the humble,
    and to revive the heart of the
        contrite.
16 For I will not continually accuse,
    nor will I always be angry;
    for then the spirits would grow faint
        before me,
    even the souls that I have made.

a Meaning of Heb uncertain   b Or their phallus;
Heb the hand   c Or the king   d Gk Vg: Heb
silent even for a long time

57:15 *high and lofty one.* This particular poetic formulation sees God as holy, high, and lofty, one who dwells remote from the earth. What is staggering about this theological characterization of God is that this same God who is remote and who dwells on high keeps company with the humble, the contrite, and the poor in spirit. This statement reflects a primal conviction of the Old Testament about a God who is both far off and near (see Jer 23:23). It is clear that in Christian tradition the same

dialectic is at work in the person of Jesus, who is the very Word of God and yet has special friends among the socially unacceptable (Mark 2:16). Holding these two aspects together is of immense importance; biblical faith is put at risk anytime there is a god solely transcendent and unconnected to the world or anytime there is a god who dwells solely in the world without transcendence. The latter temptation is particularly apparent in many "New Age" religious articulations.

17 Because of their wicked covetousness I
     was angry;
  I struck them, I hid and was angry;
  but they kept turning back to their
     own ways.
18 I have seen their ways, but I will heal
     them;
  I will lead them and repay them with
     comfort,
  creating for their mourners the fruit
     of the lips. *a*
19 Peace, peace, to the far and the near,
     says the LORD;
  and I will heal them.
20 But the wicked are like the tossing sea
     that cannot keep still;
  its waters toss up mire and mud.
21 There is no peace, says my God, for the
     wicked.

False and True Worship

58 Shout out, do not hold back!
     Lift up your voice like a trumpet!
  Announce to my people their rebellion,
     to the house of Jacob their sins.

2 Yet day after day they seek me
  and delight to know my ways,
as if they were a nation that practiced
     righteousness
  and did not forsake the ordinance of
     their God;
they ask of me righteous judgments,
  they delight to draw near to God.
3 "Why do we fast, but you do not see?
  Why humble ourselves, but you do
     not notice?"
Look, you serve your own interest on
     your fast day,
  and oppress all your workers.
4 Look, you fast only to quarrel and to
     fight
  and to strike with a wicked fist.
Such fasting as you do today
  will not make your voice heard on
     high.
5 Is such the fast that I choose,
  a day to humble oneself?

a Meaning of Heb uncertain

57:18 *I will.* This verse, dominated by first-person verbs with God as the subject, indicates an immense divine resolve. The angry, punishing God of verse 17 reverses course and resolves to heal, comfort, and forgive. God's capacity to articulate and enact a newness is the good news that breaks the vicious cycle of sin and suffering.

58:3 SERVICE—*See* Spiritual Disciplines Index.

Responding
58:3–6 **FASTING.** Fasting—indeed, any one of the Spiritual Disciplines—does us no good when we engage in it for the wrong reasons and with the wrong attitude. The next time you choose to fast, dedicate and prepare yourself with a period of prayer. Pray for right intentions, for right reverence. *See also* Spiritual Disciplines Index.

58:5–7 *the fast that I choose.* Here the prophetic tradition advocates an understanding of religion that is focused primarily on neighbor love. A fast is a religious discipline, but the kind of "fast"—religious discipline—God would like to see has to do with the breaking of oppression and with concern for the suffering of those who lack food, clothing, and shelter. Indeed, the last phrase of verse 7, in Hebrew, goes beyond calling the poor and the homeless "your own kin," as in English, to calling them "your own flesh." That is, the ones addressed by the poetry must stand in profound solidarity with the needy. This imagined scenario of true religion (echoed in James 1:27) is contrasted by the preceding verses (vv 1–4), in which a phony kind of religion is punctilious about liturgical and pious practices, but at the same time is economically exploitative of workers who work for low pay and are gouged by high interest charges. Thus the negative critique of verses 1–4 and the positive alternative of verses 5–7 articulate a profound either/or that is at the heart of prophetic understandings of covenantal faith. It is clear that this either/or is still on the table for men and women of faith in the Christian tradition, for there is a great temptation to make religion a nice, sweet thing that is detached from economic reality. The sentiment of this poem would find that scandalous and unacceptable.

Is it to bow down the head like a
  bulrush,
    and to lie in sackcloth and ashes?
Will you call this a fast,
  a day acceptable to the Lord?

6 Is not this the fast that I choose:
    to loose the bonds of injustice,
    to undo the thongs of the yoke,
  to let the oppressed go free,
    and to break every yoke?
7 Is it not to share your bread with the
    hungry,
    and bring the homeless poor into
      your house;
  when you see the naked, to cover them,
    and not to hide yourself from your
      own kin?
8 Then your light shall break forth like
    the dawn,
    and your healing shall spring up
      quickly;
  your vindicator[a] shall go before you,
    the glory of the Lord shall be your
      rear guard.
9 Then you shall call, and the Lord will
    answer;
  you shall cry for help, and he will say,
    Here I am.

If you remove the yoke from among
  you,
  the pointing of the finger, the
    speaking of evil,
10 if you offer your food to the hungry
  and satisfy the needs of the afflicted,
  then your light shall rise in the darkness
  and your gloom be like the noonday.

11 The Lord will guide you continually,
  and satisfy your needs in parched
    places,
  and make your bones strong;
and you shall be like a watered garden,
  like a spring of water,
  whose waters never fail.
12 Your ancient ruins shall be rebuilt;
  you shall raise up the foundations of
    many generations;
you shall be called the repairer of the
    breach,
  the restorer of streets to live in.

13 If you refrain from trampling the
    sabbath,
  from pursuing your own interests on
    my holy day;
if you call the sabbath a delight
  and the holy day of the Lord
    honorable;
if you honor it, not going your own
    ways,
  serving your own interests, or
    pursuing your own affairs;[b]
14 then you shall take delight in the Lord,
  and I will make you ride upon the
    heights of the earth;
I will feed you with the heritage of your
    ancestor Jacob,
  for the mouth of the Lord has spoken.

Injustice and Oppression to Be Punished

59 See, the Lord's hand is not too
    short to save,
    nor his ear too dull to hear.

a Or vindication   b Heb or speaking words

58:9 *the Lord will answer.* The consequence
of true religion as it is detailed in verses 5–7 is
the immediate attentiveness and presence of
God. The implication of verses 5–9, taken all
together, is that neighbor love is a precondition
of the attentiveness of God, who will hear
prayers and intervene according to the practice
of the faithful.
58:11 GUIDANCE—*See* Spiritual Disciplines
Index.
58:13–14 *refrain from trampling the sabbath.*
These verses, not unlike verses 5–9a and verses

9b–12, are organized in an "if-then" format.
The primary condition articulated is that the
Sabbath must be honored. When the Sabbath is
properly honored, then there will be prosperity
and security. It is likely that this insistence on
the Sabbath is connected to verses 3–4, which
have to do with exploitation of workers who are
not given good pay or adequate time for rest
and enjoyment of life. Thus the entire chapter is
a powerful statement of the interface between
economic responsibility and effective religious
practice.

2 Rather, your iniquities have been
    barriers
    between you and your God,
and your sins have hidden his face from
    you
    so that he does not hear.
3 For your hands are defiled with blood,
    and your fingers with iniquity;
your lips have spoken lies,
    your tongue mutters wickedness.
4 No one brings suit justly,
    no one goes to law honestly;
they rely on empty pleas, they speak lies,
    conceiving mischief and begetting
    iniquity.
5 They hatch adders' eggs,
    and weave the spider's web;
whoever eats their eggs dies,
    and the crushed egg hatches out a
    viper.
6 Their webs cannot serve as clothing;
    they cannot cover themselves with
    what they make.
Their works are works of iniquity,
    and deeds of violence are in their
    hands.
7 Their feet run to evil,
    and they rush to shed innocent
    blood;
their thoughts are thoughts of iniquity,
    desolation and destruction are in
    their highways.
8 The way of peace they do not know,
    and there is no justice in their paths.
Their roads they have made crooked;
    no one who walks in them knows
    peace.

9 Therefore justice is far from us,
    and righteousness does not reach us;

we wait for light, and lo! there is
    darkness;
    and for brightness, but we walk in
    gloom.
10 We grope like the blind along a wall,
    groping like those who have no eyes;
we stumble at noon as in the twilight,
    among the vigorous[a] as though we
    were dead.
11 We all growl like bears;
    like doves we moan mournfully.
We wait for justice, but there is none;
    for salvation, but it is far from us.
12 For our transgressions before you are
    many,
    and our sins testify against us.
Our transgressions indeed are with us,
    and we know our iniquities:
13 transgressing, and denying the LORD,
    and turning away from following our
    God,
talking oppression and revolt,
    conceiving lying words and uttering
    them from the heart.
14 Justice is turned back,
    and righteousness stands at a
    distance;
for truth stumbles in the public square,
    and uprightness cannot enter.
15 Truth is lacking,
    and whoever turns from evil is
    despoiled.

The LORD saw it, and it displeased him
    that there was no justice.
16 He saw that there was no one,
    and was appalled that there was no
    one to intervene;

a Meaning of Heb uncertain

59:1–8 *no justice in their paths.* After the harsh indictment of verses 1–7, verse 8 draws the conclusion that the community here indicted for distortion and disobedience will never find the way to *shalom* ("peace") and well-being. The term *shalom* is used at the beginning and end of the verse. Notice that between them stands the word "justice"; the real indictment is that the community's political and economic practices are not ordered to guarantee the equity and harmony of its members. The argument is that the community will have no well-being if it tries to organize power and wealth in unjust ways. The "deeds of violence" (v 6) are perhaps not muggings on the street, but tax laws and other systems that gouge the powerless. The theme of justice continues in verses 9, 11, and 14. This prophetic polemic concerns a disordered society that cannot, through religious disciplines, find well-being.

HOPE!

so his own arm brought him victory,
and his righteousness upheld him.
17 He put on righteousness like a
breastplate,
and a helmet of salvation on his head;
he put on garments of vengeance for
clothing,
and wrapped himself in fury as in a
mantle.
18 According to their deeds, so will he
repay;
wrath to his adversaries, requital to
his enemies;
to the coastlands he will render
requital.
19 So those in the west shall fear the name
of the Lord,
and those in the east, his glory;
for he will come like a pent-up stream
that the wind of the Lord drives on.

20 And he will come to Zion as Redeemer,
to those in Jacob who turn from
transgression, says the Lord.
21 And as for me, this is my covenant with
them, says the Lord: my spirit that is upon
you, and my words that I have put in your
mouth, shall not depart out of your mouth,
or out of the mouths of your children, or out
of the mouths of your children's children,
says the Lord, from now on and forever.

The Ingathering of the Dispersed

60 Arise, shine; for your light has
come,
and the glory of the Lord has risen
upon you.
2 For darkness shall cover the earth,
and thick darkness the peoples;
but the Lord will arise upon you,
and his glory will appear over you.
3 Nations shall come to your light,
and kings to the brightness of your
dawn.

4 Lift up your eyes and look around;
they all gather together, they come to
you;
your sons shall come from far away,
and your daughters shall be carried
on their nurses' arms.
5 Then you shall see and be radiant;
your heart shall thrill and rejoice, *a*
because the abundance of the sea shall
be brought to you,
the wealth of the nations shall come
to you.
6 A multitude of camels shall cover you,
the young camels of Midian and
Ephah;
all those from Sheba shall come.

a Heb *be enlarged*

59:20 *he will come to Zion as Redeemer.*
Chapter 59, for the most part, is quite harsh in
its judgment and promises justice from God
for those who have been disobedient. It is
remarkable, given that tone, that the last word
of the chapter is an offer of well-being. It is an
announcement that even Israel's distorted
society, in the purview of the poet, is still an
arena in which the saving God may come. The
condition of the redeemer's entry into the city of
Jerusalem, however, is that there must be a
"turn." The purpose of the address is to summon
Israel to get its "neighbor practices" in order,
because such practices become the matrix in
which the presence of God is possible. Thus
verse 20, which promises the redeemer on the
basis of "turning," is, in its argument, very much
like the "if-then" articulations of chapter 58.
60:1–62:12 *Arise, shine.* Chapters 60–62 are
among the most lyrical and eloquent of all of
the poetry of Third Isaiah. They are the most
forceful articulation of hope and, in terms of
their lyrical power, have most in common with
Second Isaiah. Chapter 60 is a great summons to
hope; parallel to 9:2, it announces that the light
of God's goodness and blessing in the form of an
amazing economic revival will soon displace the
darkness of misery, despondency, and malaise
in the community. In what follows the poet
envisions a scenario in which the great wealth
of the nations shall flow to Israel, so that
Jerusalem will again be the economic center of
the Near East, as it was for a brief moment in
the time of Solomon in the tenth century BC.
The recovery of commerce is a concrete form
of God's blessing; the creator gives gifts in the
economic mode as well as in the other modes
of creation.

They shall bring gold and frankincense,
   and shall proclaim the praise of the
   LORD.
7 All the flocks of Kedar shall be gathered
     to you,
   the rams of Nebaioth shall minister to
     you;
they shall be acceptable on my altar,
   and I will glorify my glorious house.

8 Who are these that fly like a cloud,
   and like doves to their windows?
9 For the coastlands shall wait for me,
   the ships of Tarshish first,
to bring your children from far away,
   their silver and gold with them,
for the name of the LORD your God,
   and for the Holy One of Israel,
   because he has glorified you.
10 Foreigners shall build up your walls,
   and their kings shall minister to you;
for in my wrath I struck you down,
   but in my favor I have had mercy on
     you.
11 Your gates shall always be open;
   day and night they shall not be shut,
so that nations shall bring you their
     wealth,
   with their kings led in procession.
12 For the nation and kingdom
   that will not serve you shall perish;
   those nations shall be utterly laid
     waste.
13 The glory of Lebanon shall come to
     you,
   the cypress, the plane, and the pine,
to beautify the place of my sanctuary;

and I will glorify where my feet rest.
14 The descendants of those who
     oppressed you
   shall come bending low to you,
and all who despised you
   shall bow down at your feet;
they shall call you the City of the LORD,
   the Zion of the Holy One of Israel.
15 Whereas you have been forsaken and
     hated,
   with no one passing through,
I will make you majestic forever,
   a joy from age to age.
16 You shall suck the milk of nations,
   you shall suck the breasts of kings;
and you shall know that I, the LORD, am
     your Savior
   and your Redeemer, the Mighty One
     of Jacob.

17 Instead of bronze I will bring gold,
   instead of iron I will bring silver;
instead of wood, bronze,
   instead of stones, iron.
I will appoint Peace as your overseer
   and Righteousness as your
     taskmaster.
18 Violence shall no more be heard in your
     land,
   devastation or destruction within
     your borders;
you shall call your walls Salvation,
   and your gates Praise.

God the Glory of Zion
19 The sun shall no longer be
   your light by day,

60:6–11 *A multitude of camels.* Verse 6
envisions great caravans of camels loaded with
goods that will enhance the economy of
Jerusalem. The reference to Sheba is a nice
connection to the prosperity of Solomon
(1 Kings 10:1–13). More interesting, however, is
the reference to gold and frankincense as
particularly precious commodities that will
come to the revivified city. The imagery of these
precious commodities is taken up again in
Matthew's narrative of the visit to the Christ
child by the wise men, who bring gifts of "gold,
frankincense and myrrh" (2:11). Notice, more-

over, that in Matthew, as here, these goods are
brought by "Gentiles" to enhance the "Jewish"
center of reality. The lavish recovery of the
economy of Jerusalem that is anticipated also
includes the "ships of Tarshish" (v 9), indicating
great sea commerce. Moreover, it is anticipated
that the commercial enterprise of Jerusalem
will stay open day and night because there will
be so much traffic (v 11). The exuberance of
this economic recovery is astonishing, and it is
closely tied to the transformative intrusion of
God into what is presently a dismal situation for
Judaism.

nor for brightness shall the moon
   give light to you by night; [a]
but the LORD will be your everlasting
   light,
   and your God will be your glory.
20 Your sun shall no more go down,
   or your moon withdraw itself;
for the LORD will be your everlasting
   light,
   and your days of mourning shall be
     ended.
21 Your people shall all be righteous;
   they shall possess the land forever.
They are the shoot that I planted, the
     work of my hands,
   so that I might be glorified.
22 The least of them shall become a clan,
   and the smallest one a mighty nation;
I am the LORD;
   in its time I will accomplish it quickly.

The Good News of Deliverance

61 The spirit of the Lord GOD is upon
   me,
   because the LORD has anointed me;
he has sent me to bring good news to
     the oppressed,
   to bind up the brokenhearted,
   to proclaim liberty to the captives,
   and release to the prisoners;
2 to proclaim the year of the LORD's favor,

and the day of vengeance of our God;
   to comfort all who mourn;
3 to provide for those who mourn in
     Zion—
   to give them a garland instead of
     ashes,
the oil of gladness instead of mourning,
   the mantle of praise instead of a faint
     spirit.
They will be called oaks of
     righteousness,
   the planting of the LORD, to display
     his glory.
4 They shall build up the ancient ruins,
   they shall raise up the former
     devastations;
they shall repair the ruined cities,
   the devastations of many
     generations.

5 Strangers shall stand and feed your
     flocks,
   foreigners shall till your land and
     dress your vines;
6 but you shall be called priests of the
     LORD,
   you shall be named ministers of our
     God;

a Q Ms Gk Old Latin Tg: MT lacks *by night*

60:21 *they shall possess the land forever.* At the end of this lyrical prospect for the future, the old promises of land from Genesis are reiterated. This promise of land is of immense importance to this generation of Jews who have known landlessness and deportation. Thus homecoming, according to God's promise, is a precondition of all of the extravagant economic expectation of the chapter.

61:1–11 *The spirit of the Lord GOD is upon me.* The lyrical possibility of the future voiced in chapter 60 is continued in chapter 61. This time, however, it is not the direct intervention of God that will produce well-being but, rather, the intervention of a human agent who is anointed and authorized by God. The identification of the one who is so anointed is not given, but it is clear that this is someone who will make a massive difference in the life of recovering Jerusalem. The

anointing anticipated here is reminiscent of royal anointings of the past, indicating that this un-named figure is someone who is entrusted with great and legitimate power. The coming of that anointed one, moreover, is "good news"—a fourth use of the technical term for "gospel" (see 40:9; 41:27; 52:7). The first verses of this poem then go on to specify the good work of social transformation to be done by this anointed one in language not unlike that of 42:6 and 49:6. The particular phrasing of verse 2 concerning "the year of the LORD's favor" is commonly taken to be a reference to the old Torah provision of Jubilee in Leviticus 25. Thus a radical restitution of the economy is here anticipated. Verses 1–2a are the ones Jesus selects and reads aloud in the synagogue in Luke 4:18–19. It is clear that Jesus is understood as the fulfillment and actualization of the promise of this text.

you shall enjoy the wealth of the
    nations,
and in their riches you shall glory.
7 Because their[a] shame was double,
    and dishonor was proclaimed as their
        lot,
therefore they shall possess a double
        portion;
    everlasting joy shall be theirs.

8 For I the LORD love justice,
    I hate robbery and wrongdoing;[b]
I will faithfully give them their
        recompense,
    and I will make an everlasting
        covenant with them.
9 Their descendants shall be known
        among the nations,
    and their offspring among the
        peoples;
all who see them shall acknowledge
    that they are a people whom the LORD
        has blessed.
10 I will greatly rejoice in the LORD,
    my whole being shall exult in my
        God;
for he has clothed me with the
    garments of salvation,
he has covered me with the robe of
        righteousness,
as a bridegroom decks himself with a
        garland,
    and as a bride adorns herself with her
        jewels.
11 For as the earth brings forth its shoots,
    and as a garden causes what is sown
        in it to spring up,
so the Lord GOD will cause
    righteousness and praise
to spring up before all the nations.

The Vindication and Salvation of Zion

62 For Zion's sake I will not keep silent,
    and for Jerusalem's sake I will not rest,

until her vindication shines out like the
        dawn,
    and her salvation like a burning
        torch.
2 The nations shall see your vindication,
    and all the kings your glory;
and you shall be called by a new name
    that the mouth of the LORD will give.
3 You shall be a crown of beauty in the
        hand of the LORD,
    and a royal diadem in the hand of
        your God.
4 You shall no more be termed Forsaken,[c]
    and your land shall no more be
        termed Desolate;[d]
but you shall be called My Delight Is in
        Her,[e]
    and your land Married;[f]
for the LORD delights in you,
    and your land shall be married.
5 For as a young man marries a young
        woman,
    so shall your builder[g] marry you,
and as the bridegroom rejoices over the
        bride,
    so shall your God rejoice over you.
6 Upon your walls, O Jerusalem,
    I have posted sentinels;
all day and all night
    they shall never be silent.
You who remind the LORD,
    take no rest,
7 and give him no rest
    until he establishes Jerusalem
and makes it renowned throughout
        the earth.
8 The LORD has sworn by his right hand
    and by his mighty arm:
I will not again give your grain
    to be food for your enemies,

a Heb your   b Or robbery with a burnt offering
c Heb Azubah   d Heb Shemamah
e Heb Hephzibah   f Heb Beulah   g Cn: Heb
your sons

62:1–4 *I will not keep silent.* After the exile
and the long dormancy of Yahweh, the prospect
of hope for the community of faith is possible
because Yahweh breaks the silence. As in 42:14,
God breaks the silence by speaking in a sovereign way that completely transforms the social
prospects of the community. In particular, it is
anticipated that the unproductive land will now
be made fruitful in a revivification of the processes of creation (v 4).

and foreigners shall not drink the wine
    for which you have labored;
9 but those who garner it shall eat it
    and praise the LORD,
and those who gather it shall drink it
    in my holy courts.

10 Go through, go through the gates,
    prepare the way for the people;
build up, build up the highway,
    clear it of stones,
    lift up an ensign over the peoples.
11 The LORD has proclaimed
    to the end of the earth:
Say to daughter Zion,
    "See, your salvation comes;
his reward is with him,
    and his recompense before him."
12 They shall be called, "The Holy People,
    The Redeemed of the LORD";
and you shall be called, "Sought Out,
    A City Not Forsaken."

Vengeance on Edom

63 "Who is this that comes from
    Edom,
    from Bozrah in garments stained
      crimson?
Who is this so splendidly robed,
    marching in his great might?"

"It is I, announcing vindication,
    mighty to save."

2 "Why are your robes red,
    and your garments like theirs who
      tread the wine press?"

3 "I have trodden the wine press alone,
    and from the peoples no one was
      with me;
I trod them in my anger
    and trampled them in my wrath;
their juice spattered on my garments,
    and stained all my robes.
4 For the day of vengeance was in my
    heart,

and the year for my redeeming work
    had come.
5 I looked, but there was no helper;
    I stared, but there was no one to
      sustain me;
so my own arm brought me victory,
    and my wrath sustained me.
6 I trampled down peoples in my anger,
    I crushed them in my wrath,
    and I poured out their lifeblood on
      the earth."

God's Mercy Remembered

7 I will recount the gracious deeds of the
    LORD,
    the praiseworthy acts of the LORD,
because of all that the LORD has done for
    us,
    and the great favor to the house of
      Israel
that he has shown them according to
      his mercy,
    according to the abundance of his
      steadfast love.
8 For he said, "Surely they are my people,
    children who will not deal falsely";
and he became their savior
9   in all their distress.
It was no messenger[a] or angel
    but his presence that saved them;[b]
in his love and in his pity he redeemed
      them;
he lifted them up and carried them
    all the days of old.

10 But they rebelled
    and grieved his holy spirit;
therefore he became their enemy;
    he himself fought against them.
11 Then they[c] remembered the days of
    old,
    of Moses his servant.[d]
Where is the one who brought them up
    out of the sea
    with the shepherds of his flock?

a Gk: Heb *anguish*   b Or *savior.* *9In all their*
distress he was distressed; the angel of his presence
saved them;   c Heb *he*   d Cn: Heb *his people*

63:11–13 THE WITH-GOD LIFE—*See* Spiritual Disciplines Index.

Where is the one who put within them
   his holy spirit,
12 who caused his glorious arm
   to march at the right hand of Moses,
who divided the waters before them
   to make for himself an everlasting
      name,
13 who led them through the depths?
Like a horse in the desert,
   they did not stumble.
14 Like cattle that go down into the valley,
   the spirit of the LORD gave them rest.
Thus you led your people,
   to make for yourself a glorious name.

A Prayer of Penitence

15 Look down from heaven and see,
   from your holy and glorious
      habitation.
Where are your zeal and your might?
   The yearning of your heart and your
      compassion?
   They are withheld from me.
16 For you are our father,
   though Abraham does not know us
   and Israel does not acknowledge us;
you, O LORD, are our father;
   our Redeemer from of old is your
      name.
17 Why, O LORD, do you make us stray
   from your ways
   and harden our heart, so that we do
      not fear you?
Turn back for the sake of your servants,
   for the sake of the tribes that are your
      heritage.
18 Your holy people took possession for a
      little while;
   but now our adversaries have
      trampled down your sanctuary.
19 We have long been like those whom
      you do not rule,
   like those not called by your name.

64 O that you would tear open the
      heavens and come down,
so that the mountains would quake at
   your presence—
2a as when fire kindles brushwood
   and the fire causes water to boil—
to make your name known to your
      adversaries,
   so that the nations might tremble at
      your presence!
3 When you did awesome deeds that we
      did not expect,
   you came down, the mountains
      quaked at your presence.
4 From ages past no one has heard,
   no ear has perceived,
no eye has seen any God besides you,
   who works for those who wait for
      him.
5 You meet those who gladly do right,
   those who remember you in your
      ways.
But you were angry, and we sinned;
   because you hid yourself we
      transgressed.b
6 We have all become like one who is
      unclean,
   and all our righteous deeds are like a
      filthy cloth.
We all fade like a leaf,
   and our iniquities, like the wind, take
      us away.
7 There is no one who calls on your
      name,
   or attempts to take hold of you;
for you have hidden your face from us,
   and have deliveredc us into the hand
      of our iniquity.
8 Yet, O LORD, you are our Father;

a Ch 64.1 in Heb   b Meaning of Heb uncertain
c Gk Syr Old Latin Tg: Heb *melted*

63:15–16 *you are our father.* This is a prayer
of some segment of the Jewish community
that is being oppressed by other segments of
the community. Since this segment of the
community cannot find solace in the power
structure of the community, it looks beyond
the community in a direct appeal to God. The
reference to God as "our father" suggests
both an intimate connection and probably an
obligation on the part of God the father to look
after these needy children. In Christian context,
this petitionary address to "our father" will be
understood as an anticipation of Jesus' model
prayer (Matt 6:9–13).

we are the clay, and you are our
potter;
we are all the work of your hand.
9 Do not be exceedingly angry, O Lord,
and do not remember iniquity
forever.
Now consider, we are all your people.
10 Your holy cities have become a
wilderness,
Zion has become a wilderness,
Jerusalem a desolation.
11 Our holy and beautiful house,
where our ancestors praised you,
has been burned by fire,
and all our pleasant places have
become ruins.
12 After all this, will you restrain yourself,
O Lord?
Will you keep silent, and punish us so
severely?

The Righteousness of God's Judgment

65 I was ready to be sought out by
those who did not ask,
to be found by those who did not
seek me.
I said, "Here I am, here I am,"
to a nation that did not call on my
name.
2 I held out my hands all day long
to a rebellious people,
who walk in a way that is not good,
following their own devices;
3 a people who provoke me
to my face continually,
sacrificing in gardens
and offering incense on bricks;
4 who sit inside tombs,
and spend the night in secret places;
who eat swine's flesh,
with broth of abominable things in
their vessels;
5 who say, "Keep to yourself,

do not come near me, for I am too
holy for you."
These are a smoke in my nostrils,
a fire that burns all day long.
6 See, it is written before me:
I will not keep silent, but I will
repay;
I will indeed repay into their laps
7   their *a* iniquities and their *a* ancestors'
iniquities together,
says the Lord;
because they offered incense on the
mountains
and reviled me on the hills,
I will measure into their laps
full payment for their actions.
8 Thus says the Lord:
As the wine is found in the cluster,
and they say, "Do not destroy it,
for there is a blessing in it,"
so I will do for my servants' sake,
and not destroy them all.
9 I will bring forth descendants *b* from
Jacob,
and from Judah inheritors *c* of my
mountains;
my chosen shall inherit it,
and my servants shall settle there.
10 Sharon shall become a pasture for
flocks,
and the Valley of Achor a place for
herds to lie down,
for my people who have sought me.
11 But you who forsake the Lord,
who forget my holy mountain,
who set a table for Fortune
and fill cups of mixed wine for Destiny;
12 I will destine you to the sword,
and all of you shall bow down to the
slaughter;

a Gk Syr: Heb *your*   *b* Or *a descendant*
c Or *an inheritor*

64:8 *we are all the work of your hand.* Again,
as in 63:16, God is addressed as "our Father."
The reference is reinforced by a second image,
of Israel as clay that is amenable to God as
potter. In the image in 45:9 the clay was resistant to the potter. In contrast, here Israel as
clay is now completely dependent upon and
readily responsive to God as potter. Israel is fully
prepared to trust in the good gifts of the father
God. This text demonstrates the imaginative
way in which Israel can mobilize fresh imagery
to probe nuances of its rich relationship with
Yahweh.

because, when I called, you did not
answer,
when I spoke, you did not listen,
but you did what was evil in my sight,
and chose what I did not delight in.
13 Therefore thus says the Lord GOD:
My servants shall eat,
but you shall be hungry;
my servants shall drink,
but you shall be thirsty;
my servants shall rejoice,
but you shall be put to shame;
14 my servants shall sing for gladness of
heart,
but you shall cry out for pain of heart,
and shall wail for anguish of spirit.
15 You shall leave your name to my chosen
to use as a curse,
and the Lord GOD will put you to
death;
but to his servants he will give a
different name.
16 Then whoever invokes a blessing in the
land

shall bless by the God of faithfulness,
and whoever takes an oath in the land
shall swear by the God of faithfulness;
because the former troubles are forgotten
and are hidden from my sight.

The Glorious New Creation

17 For I am about to create new heavens
and a new earth;
the former things shall not be
remembered
or come to mind.
18 But be glad and rejoice forever
in what I am creating;
for I am about to create Jerusalem as a joy,
and its people as a delight.
19 I will rejoice in Jerusalem,
and delight in my people;
no more shall the sound of weeping be
heard in it,
or the cry of distress.
20 No more shall there be in it
an infant that lives but a few days,

65:17–25 *create new heavens and a new earth.* This promissory oracle is one of the most sweeping, eloquent, and profound in all of the Old Testament. This lyrical articulation asserts that God does not simply extrapolate newness from what is given in the world. Yahweh as creator has the capacity to work completely *ex nihilo* ("from nothing") in order to do something quite new that is not derived from what was before. The poem begins with the sweeping "new heaven and a new earth," so that Israel is invited in its poetic imagination to move out from all that is broken and dysfunctional in the old world. This promissory phrase is picked up and reiterated in Rev 21:1 as the ultimate, most sweeping promise of the entire New Testament. In Isaiah the prospect of "new heavens and a new earth" is seconded by adding to it a new Jerusalem (v 18), a point reiterated in Rev 21:2. Thus Jerusalem is reckoned in prophetic imagination to be the epicenter of God's future in the world. Jerusalem is recognized as the place of the presence of the holy God; it is also the reference point to which all nations come for instruction. This oracle near the end of the book of Isaiah is undoubtedly placed as a counterpoint to the beginning oracle of 2:2–4,

which envisions all nations coming to Jerusalem. Thus Jerusalem is understood here, not simply as a place of Jewish power, but as a place where all the nations can have access to the goodness and guidance of God. The remainder of this oracle then details what the new heavens, the new earth, and the new city will look like, each point of which is in contrast to the failed former Jerusalem: no more infant mortality (v 20); no more economic usurpation (vv 21–22); no more pain in childbirth, perhaps a text that is counterpoint to the curse of Gen 3:16 (v 23). There will be a kind of immediate communication between God and Israel in its petition (v 24). Indeed, in 58:9 we have seen that God will answer the call of Israel; in this text, however, God not only will answer the call but will hear the call before it is even uttered. This way of putting the matter suggests the intense immediacy of the relationship and the intensity of Yahweh's affinity for the city and its inhabitants. In sum, this poem lays out a future in which God's governance is fully and completely established, a governance that is characteristically named in the Bible the kingdom of God.

or an old person who does not live
    out a lifetime;
for one who dies at a hundred years will
    be considered a youth,
and one who falls short of a hundred
    will be considered accursed.
21 They shall build houses and inhabit
    them;
    they shall plant vineyards and eat
        their fruit.
22 They shall not build and another
    inhabit;
    they shall not plant and another eat;
for like the days of a tree shall the days
    of my people be,
and my chosen shall long enjoy the
    work of their hands.
23 They shall not labor in vain,
    or bear children for calamity; *a*
for they shall be offspring blessed by
    the LORD—
and their descendants as well.
24 Before they call I will answer,
    while they are yet speaking I will
        hear.
25 The wolf and the lamb shall feed
    together,
    the lion shall eat straw like the ox;
but the serpent—its food shall be
    dust!
They shall not hurt or destroy
    on all my holy mountain,
                says the LORD.

The Worship-God Demands

66 Thus says the LORD:
Heaven is my throne
   and the earth is my footstool;
what is the house that you would build
    for me,
   and what is my resting place?
2 All these things my hand has made,
   and so all these things are mine, *b*
                says the LORD.
But this is the one to whom I will look,
   to the humble and contrite in spirit,
   who trembles at my word.

3 Whoever slaughters an ox is like one
    who kills a human being;

whoever sacrifices a lamb, like one
   who breaks a dog's neck;
whoever presents a grain offering, like
   one who offers swine's blood; *c*
whoever makes a memorial offering
   of frankincense, like one who
   blesses an idol.
These have chosen their own ways,
   and in their abominations they take
   delight;
4 I also will choose to mock *d* them,
   and bring upon them what they
   fear;
because, when I called, no one
   answered,
   when I spoke, they did not listen;
but they did what was evil in my
   sight,
   and chose what did not please me.

The LORD Vindicates Zion

5 Hear the word of the LORD,
   you who tremble at his word:
Your own people who hate you
   and reject you for my name's sake
have said, "Let the LORD be
   glorified,
   so that we may see your joy";
but it is they who shall be put to
   shame.

6 Listen, an uproar from the city!
   A voice from the temple!
The voice of the LORD,
   dealing retribution to his
   enemies!

7 Before she was in labor
   she gave birth;
before her pain came upon her
   she delivered a son.
8 Who has heard of such a thing?
   Who has seen such things?
Shall a land be born in one day?
   Shall a nation be delivered in one
   moment?
Yet as soon as Zion was in labor

---

a Or *sudden terror*   *b* Gk Syr: Heb *these things
came to be*   *c* Meaning of Heb uncertain
d Or *to punish*

she delivered her children.

9 Shall I open the womb and not
      deliver?
    says the LORD;
    shall I, the one who delivers, shut the
      womb?
    says your God.

10 Rejoice with Jerusalem, and be glad for
      her,
    all you who love her;
    rejoice with her in joy,
    all you who mourn over her—
11 that you may nurse and be satisfied
      from her consoling breast;
    that you may drink deeply with
      delight
    from her glorious bosom.

12 For thus says the LORD:
    I will extend prosperity to her like a
      river,
    and the wealth of the nations like an
      overflowing stream;
    and you shall nurse and be carried on
      her arm,
    and dandled on her knees.
13 As a mother comforts her child,
    so I will comfort you;
    you shall be comforted in
      Jerusalem.

The Reign and Indignation of God

14 You shall see, and your heart shall
      rejoice;
    your bodies*a* shall flourish like the
      grass;
    and it shall be known that the hand of
      the LORD is with his servants,
    and his indignation is against his
      enemies.
15 For the LORD will come in fire,
    and his chariots like the whirlwind,

to pay back his anger in fury,
    and his rebuke in flames of fire.
16 For by fire will the LORD execute
      judgment,
    and by his sword, on all flesh;
    and those slain by the LORD shall be
      many.

17 Those who sanctify and purify themselves to go into the gardens, following the
one in the center, eating the flesh of pigs,
vermin, and rodents, shall come to an end together, says the LORD.

18 For I know*b* their works and their
thoughts, and I am*c* coming to gather all nations and tongues; and they shall come and
shall see my glory, 19and I will set a sign
among them. From them I will send survivors
to the nations, to Tarshish, Put,*d* and Lud—
which draw the bow—to Tubal and Javan, to
the coastlands far away that have not heard
of my fame or seen my glory; and they shall
declare my glory among the nations. 20They
shall bring all your kindred from all the nations as an offering to the LORD, on horses,
and in chariots, and in litters, and on mules,
and on dromedaries, to my holy mountain Jerusalem, says the LORD, just as the Israelites
bring a grain offering in a clean vessel to the
house of the LORD. 21And I will also take some
of them as priests and as Levites, says the
LORD.

22 For as the new heavens and the new
      earth,
    which I will make,
    shall remain before me, says the LORD;
    so shall your descendants and your
      name remain.

---

a Heb *bones*   b Gk Syr: Heb lacks *know*
c Gk Syr Vg Tg: Heb *it is*   d Gk: Heb *Pul*

66:7–13 *she delivered her children.* The
book of Isaiah moves toward its culmination
by portraying God in poignant and powerful
maternal images. Thus God is the mother God,
an image we have already seen in 49:15. It is this
mother God who will nurse and comfort (v 13;
see 40:1–2). The book of Isaiah began in chapters

1–3 with a harsh condemnation of old, failed
Jerusalem. As the tradition comes to its fruition
and completion in these latter chapters, now
a new Jerusalem is envisioned, a city greatly
beloved and cared for by a tender, gentle,
attentive mother God.

23 From new moon to new moon,
    and from sabbath to sabbath,
  all flesh shall come to worship
        before me,
  says the LORD.

24 And they shall go out and look at the
dead bodies of the people who have rebelled
against me; for their worm shall not die, their
fire shall not be quenched, and they shall be
an abhorrence to all flesh.

Responding

66:23 WORSHIP. We often think of
worship as occurring in our spirits, in
our hearts. Yet this reference is very deliberately
to "flesh," which in biblical terminology signifies
weakness, corruption, and need. What does it
mean for all flesh to come to worship God? *See
also* Spiritual Disciplines Index.

66:23–24 *all flesh shall come to worship.* The
penultimate verse of Isaiah imagines that
Jerusalem is an inclusive place of worship that is
open and available for "all flesh." It is noted by
many commentators that the final verse, 24, is
in contrast to verse 23. The last verse is filled
with anger and hostility. As a consequence, the
practice in regular synagogue reading of this
text is to read straight through verse 24, then
circle back and read verse 23 again. This way
the hearing of the tradition of Isaiah, unlike the
written form of the book, finishes with a great
affirmation that "all flesh shall come to worship
before" the Lord. Such a reading practice is an
indication of the way in which the community of
faith must practice interpretive imagination in
handling the written text. The book of Isaiah
ends with a vision of Jerusalem as the center of
well-being that God gives to the earth. It is no
wonder that the faithful can regularly hope
"next year in Jerusalem."

JEREMIAH

Tough times demand tough words. Whenever the community suffers a difficult blow, we quite naturally ask, "Why?" or, more to the point of the faith community, "What is God doing in our pain?" These are the basic pastoral questions that concern any community of faith when it is about its most serious business. And these are the questions that concern many in our culture today. The Church after September 11, 2001, after the falling towers and a changed world, or the Church that lives in circumstances of marginalization and disenfranchisement is a Church that will find, in the words of Jeremiah, honest words that we need to hear—even if they can sometimes be words we do not want to hear.

As the initial verse of the book of Jeremiah states, here are the "words of Jeremiah," some of the most eloquent, anguished words in all of the Bible. (There is of course a certain irony in this designation since, throughout, it is the "word of the LORD" that prompts Jeremiah to speak.) Jeremiah's words tend to be symbolic, metaphorical, and prophetic—highly charged and emotional words. The prophets of Israel, like Jeremiah, are not to be thought of primarily as social reformers, predictors of the future, or leftist social critics. They were poets. Through words, through vivid metaphor and poetic simile, they make our deepest hopes, our worst fears, our yearning faith heard.

The first verses of the book of Jeremiah also tell us that all this took place during the reigns of the last four kings of Judah (1:1–3). That means that this is a book about endings, a book that deals with what the faith community thinks about when an old world is passing and a new world is not yet seen. There is therefore much mourning and grief in Jeremiah, for that is the way people respond to endings and to death and relinquishment. There is also much anger and hurt, for that is the way people often feel when a once-predictable, known world is being wrenched from their hands. Because we live in a time when many have given up hope for the promises of the old, conventional, expected world, the book of Jeremiah has a message for us

See also *"The With-God Life" essays for this section of the Bible, "The People of God in Rebellion,"*
pp. 975–79, and "The People of God in Exile," pp. 1171–74.

in their grief and loss. For many, our age is an age of relinquishment and dislocation. The false gods are losing their grip over our imagination. Our misplaced hopes are being exposed for their lies. Now, where do we turn?

The Literature of Exiles

We do not know a great deal about the faith community of Jeremiah's time, but we do know that it was going through a tough, painful time. Judah had been overrun by some "enemy from the north," possibly the Babylonian Empire. Jerusalem fell in 597 BC, and by 587 the whole nation was in ruin. Cities were laid waste, national hopes were dashed, and the faith of the people was in crisis as they were carted off into Babylonian captivity. What was the ultimate meaning of all this tragedy?

The book of Jeremiah is the literature of exiles, people who had lost their home and their future and who tried to make sense of the present age. The faith community used Jeremiah's interpretation of the present situation as well as his laying of blame to make sense of a great tragedy. Sections like 4:13–18 and 26:1–6 are keys to understanding Jeremiah's theological reading of the community's sad circumstances. The Church at its best is a community that attempts to read the world through the lens of theology, constantly raising the God question. Therefore we must ask not simply, "Why did this happen?" but, "What is God up to in all this?"

Jeremiah is stunningly relevant to our present time. Homelessness has become a metaphor for our age. People feel uprooted, uncertain about the future, fearful in the present, ridden with guilt about the past. The Church, having once been culturally significant in North America, now feels pushed to the margins. In listening to Jeremiah attempt to make sense of the events of his day, today's faith community can find interpretive resources for thinking about the faith challenges of our age.

Poetry, Prose, and Prophecy

Though Jeremiah contains some of the most eloquent literature of the Old Testament, reading Jeremiah can be difficult. The book sometimes seems disorganized, switching back and forth from poetry to biography, from history to strange visions. There is no discernible plot or story line. Instead we find a mix of oracles, laments, sermons, biography, and even a letter. The intended audience for the book likewise seems mixed. Sometimes the prophet talks to kings, sometimes to other nations, sometimes to God, and sometimes to the people as a whole. We are able to listen in on all these speeches and to become, in our own place and time, part of the conversation.

Jeremiah begins (1:1–3) in straightforward prose. We appear to be reading history, a sort of biography with names and dates. But then, with "the word of the LORD came to me" (1:4), the language breaks open into poetry, the pace quickens, and we enter a dramatic, conflicted world where God continually assaults and assails the community in a flood of vivid words. Most of the poetry in Jeremiah is grouped in chapters 1–25 and 46–51. And most of that poetry is in the form of prophetic oracle, poetry in which God directly addresses the faith community by saying, "I . . ." Most of these oracles sound like accusations delivered in a law court. The Lord has a complaint against Israel, and through the prophet Jeremiah that complaint is made manifest.

Most of the speech in Jeremiah is harsh, honest, and judgmental (to this day we call a fierce, critical speech a "jeremiad"). In today's Church, we don't hear much talk like Jeremiah's—most of our religious communicators tend toward more soothing, reassuring, and placid speech.

But there are also some breathtakingly beautiful moments in which God's love for Israel and God's grace become manifest. The popular conception that Jeremiah contains unrelenting judgment and condemnation of Israel is not true. The same God who judges Israel is also the God who has done great things for the covenant community in the past and longs to do great things even now. Jeremiah speaks those good words too. God only rebukes Israel in order to win back and to bless Israel.

Many have noted that the book of Jeremiah sounds discordant and disjointed. There are different voices. Poetry clashes with prose. Parts of Jeremiah appear to have been composed by different people and at different times. We ought to remember that this is literature from a dark and difficult time in Israel's history. As Jeremiah shuttles back and forth between hopefulness and despair, perhaps we ought to admit that this is exactly the way we sometimes react to national trauma. The sometimes jagged quality of the narrative is an honest depiction of how badly shaken people sometimes feel. Here are words from God and words spoken to God that have not been cleaned and prettied up for church. In the book of Jeremiah, greater stress has been put on honest, heartfelt expression than on noble religious sentiment.

We witness Jeremiah moving back and forth between complete despair and sweeping hope, between strong commitment to God and anger against God's demands. One moment he gives up hope, calls it quits, and attempts to end the conversation. Then, in the very next verse, the conversation resumes, and Jeremiah returns to the fray and speaks again. Even for those as close to the heart of God as Jeremiah, we see that it is possible one day to feel firm hope and confidence in the goodness of God and the next day to feel complete forsakenness and despair. Here is a very honest, very revealing book of the Bible. Rather than polite, superficial speech, everyone smiling, everyone positive, upbeat, happy, and content, Jeremiah provides us with a wonderful invitation to passionate, honest relationship with the God who has called our faith community to be a community not only of love and hope but also of truth and realism. This is at the heart of any true spiritual formation work.

Suffering and Spiritual Formation

When you think about it, the theology of suffering and tragedy represented in Jeremiah is rather startling, particularly in our present theological context. The question on many of our modern minds when we encounter communal tragedy is, "Why do bad things happen to good people (like us!)?" We tend to see ourselves as innocent victims of undeserved suffering, often in the form of bodily pain, health crises, and personal problems. "Why me, God?"

Jeremiah addresses suffering, hurting, exiled Israel with a repeated refrain: "Your present troubles are the direct result of your past infidelities. God has called you for a great mission to all the nations. With that calling comes a great responsibility. Because you have failed in your vocation, because you have cheapened your vocation by hankering after false gods, you have brought your ruin upon yourselves. Your pain is punishment from a hurt and offended God. There will be no restoration and recovery until you honestly take responsibility for your situation, repent—that is, *change*—and return to the love and service of the God who loved and created you."

That message is a long way from the "prosperity gospel" that infects many churches today. Jeremiah's proclamation reminds us that our God is alive, demanding, and sovereign and that our community stands in the succession of Israel, a great people who dared to be in conversation with and in service to so great a God.

Exchanges between Jeremiah and God are heated, passionate, and sometimes adversarial, accusatory, and touchingly beautiful. Here is a God who has been passionately committed to the faith community and who feels deeply offended by the community's apostasy. The God of Israel is not some dispassionate, detached heavenly bureaucrat just following the rules, treating all nations just the same. This God has staked a great deal upon the covenant community, freeing it from Egyptian slavery, giving it a good Land of Promise, commissioning it to be a light to all the nations.

And here is a prophet, a spokesperson for God, who has been enlisted when still a mere youth to say difficult words of judgment to the community. Jeremiah speaks because he has been summoned, commissioned, called to speak. He speaks not necessarily what he wants to speak, but what God wants the community to hear. And what is the response of the faith community to this faithful divine speaking? Mostly rejection. Jeremiah is a person caught in the middle between a demanding God and an evasive, unfaithful community. Jeremiah is in service to the faith community, listening and telling them what he hears, but as a result he suffers fierce resentment and rejection from the community. Faithful servants of God in today's faith community who find themselves caught in similar circumstances will find a truthful naming of their situation in the life of Jeremiah and great encouragement in their present struggles to speak the truth in love.

Here are some questions. Do you think the contemporary faith community can withstand such truthful testimony? Are we still able to hear such honesty from God's messengers? Is it possible for us to move from our self-pitying sense of victimization and innocent, undeserved suffering to an acceptance of our moral responsibility for much of the mess in which we find ourselves?

—*William H. Willimon*

TOUGH WORDS FOR TOUGH TIMES

1 The words of Jeremiah son of Hilkiah, of the priests who were in Anathoth in the land of Benjamin, 2to whom the word of the LORD came in the days of King Josiah son of Amon of Judah, in the thirteenth year of his reign. 3It came also in the days of King Jehoiakim son of Josiah of Judah, and until the end of the eleventh year of King Zedekiah son of Josiah of Judah, until the captivity of Jerusalem in the fifth month.

Jeremiah's Call and Commission

4 Now the word of the LORD came to me saying,
5 "Before I formed you in the womb I knew you,
and before you were born I consecrated you;
I appointed you a prophet to the nations."
6Then I said, "Ah, Lord GOD! Truly I do not know how to speak, for I am only a boy." 7But the LORD said to me,
"Do not say, 'I am only a boy';
for you shall go to all to whom I send you,
and you shall speak whatever I command you.
8 Do not be afraid of them,
for I am with you to deliver you,
says the LORD."
9Then the LORD put out his hand and touched my mouth; and the LORD said to me,
"Now I have put my words in your mouth.
10 See, today I appoint you over nations and over kingdoms,

1:4 *the word of the LORD came to me.* In this book noted for its prophetic words—fierce, fiery, and wonderful—the first word is God's. The prophet's words begin, not with the prophet having something inside him that needs to be expressed, but rather with God's word coming to him. This is what Martin Luther referred to as the "external word," a word that is not self-derived, a word that comes as an intrusion, a gift from the outside, from a God who will not leave us in silence. It is therefore somewhat of a misnomer to speak of this book as the "book of Jeremiah," as if this book mostly contained the words of a man. It is perhaps better entitled the "book of God," because it is God who begins this conversation and God's words that are Jeremiah's main concern.

1:5 *Before I formed you in the womb I knew you.* The word of the Lord that comes to Jeremiah is not only a gift but also a vocation. Even before he was born Jeremiah had been set aside, commandeered, consecrated for service to the Lord. In a sense, every word from the Lord is also a call from the Lord. We read every verse of Scripture lovingly and attentively, because every verse is a potential summons from God. Perhaps when we read, we ought not to ask ourselves, "What do these words mean?" but "What is God summoning me to do through these words?" God speaks a word because God has an assignment for us.

1:6 *I do not know how to speak, for I am only a boy.* When the prophet speaks, in response to the call of God, his first word is a word of resistance. The one called for divine work immediately senses his limitations for that work. He tries to beg off, listing his inadequacies. Jeremiah was not being modest in saying "I am only a boy"; he was simply being truthful. This is quite typical of the call for divine service, and quite beside the point. God tends, it would appear from stories of vocation in Scripture, almost always to call people who are too young, too timid, too old, or too immoral. The story is not about the singular virtues of the one being called. The story is about a risk-taking, bold sort of God who reaches in and calls people for divine service, giving them what they need for that service (vv 7–8). Jeremiah need not work alone. God equips and stands beside those whom God calls. This is the sort of God who says, in effect, "I'm getting ready to change, revolutionize, renovate, and reorient the whole world—and guess who's going to help me?"

Responding
1:6–8 GUIDANCE. Too often we also think we are too young or too old, too busy or too underqualified to do God's work— or simply that someone else will. What limitations are you nursing as excuses for ignoring your divine vocation? *See also* Spiritual Disciplines Index.

to pluck up and to pull down,
to destroy and to overthrow,
to build and to plant."

11 The word of the LORD came to me, saying, "Jeremiah, what do you see?" And I said, "I see a branch of an almond tree." [a] 12 Then the LORD said to me, "You have seen well, for I am watching [b] over my word to perform it." 13 The word of the LORD came to me a second time, saying, "What do you see?" And I said, "I see a boiling pot, tilted away from the north."

14 Then the LORD said to me: Out of the north disaster shall break out on all the inhabitants of the land. 15 For now I am calling all the tribes of the kingdoms of the north, says the LORD; and they shall come and all of them shall set their thrones at the entrance of the gates of Jerusalem, against all its surrounding walls and against all the cities of Judah. 16 And I will utter my judgments against them, for all their wickedness in forsaking me; they have made offerings to other gods, and worshiped the works of their own hands. 17 But you, gird up your loins; stand up and tell them everything that I command you. Do not break down before them, or I will break you before them. 18 And I for my part have made you today a fortified city, an iron pillar, and a bronze wall, against the whole land—against the kings of Judah, its princes, its priests, and the people of the land. 19 They will fight against you; but they shall not prevail against you, for I am with you, says the LORD, to deliver you.

God Pleads with Israel to Repent

2 The word of the LORD came to me, saying: 2 Go and proclaim in the hearing of Jerusalem, Thus says the LORD:

I remember the devotion of your youth,
  your love as a bride,
how you followed me in the wilderness,
  in a land not sown.
3 Israel was holy to the LORD,
  the first fruits of his harvest.
All who ate of it were held guilty;
  disaster came upon them,
                            says the LORD.

4 Hear the word of the LORD, O house of Jacob, and all the families of the house of Israel. 5 Thus says the LORD:

What wrong did your ancestors find
  in me
that they went far from me,

a Heb shaqed   b Heb shoqed

1:10 *today I appoint you over nations and over kingdoms.* Though "only a boy," Jeremiah is put in charge of the downfall and rise of kingdoms, the task of destroying and creating cultures. That's some power to place in the hands of a young preacher! What God wants Jeremiah to do is not small. Furthermore, the renovation of the community is not a painless affair. Something must be plucked up in order for something to be planted. The word that brings new life is also the word that destroys and overthrows. The intrusion of the word of God is not a placid or pleasant affair. Time and again, the community must relearn the potentially disruptive, disconcerting, and even destructive power of the word of the living God. Jesus began his ministry in Luke 4 with a confrontational sermon and an angry congregational response. The beginning of the book of Jeremiah implies that God acts and moves in to make a new future, a new world, by speaking,

by giving a word to the world through the prophet. God's standard way of making a new world is through speech (see Gen 1).

1:19 *They will fight against you.* No false advertising here. The task that God has called young Jeremiah to perform will not be easy. Nothing less than the tearing down of the old order and the building of a new world is involved in the prophet's speaking the word of God. There will be resistance, for the world does not eagerly, receptively hear God's truth. The word of God comes into the world, and the world receives it not (John 1:10). Yet along with the fair warning comes a strong promise of divine presence and support. Success, popularity, and visible results are not promised. What is promised is sustaining presence. God is with those whom God commissions. Though the task ahead is full of peril, it is also a task that is sustained by a promise: God says, "I am with you."

and went after worthless things, and
   became worthless themselves?
6 They did not say, "Where is the LORD
   who brought us up from the land of
      Egypt,
   who led us in the wilderness,
      in a land of deserts and pits,
   in a land of drought and deep darkness,
      in a land that no one passes through,
         where no one lives?"
7 I brought you into a plentiful land
      to eat its fruits and its good things.
   But when you entered you defiled my
      land,
      and made my heritage an
         abomination.
8 The priests did not say, "Where is the
   LORD?"
   Those who handle the law did not
      know me;
   the rulers[a] transgressed against me;
      the prophets prophesied by Baal,
      and went after things that do not
         profit.

9 Therefore once more I accuse you,
                              says the LORD,
   and I accuse your children's children.
10 Cross to the coasts of Cyprus and look,

send to Kedar and examine with care;
   see if there has ever been such a
      thing.
11 Has a nation changed its gods,
      even though they are no gods?
   But my people have changed their glory
      for something that does not profit.
12 Be appalled, O heavens, at this,
   be shocked, be utterly desolate,
                              says the LORD,
13 for my people have committed two evils:
   they have forsaken me,
   the fountain of living water,
      and dug out cisterns for themselves,
   cracked cisterns
      that can hold no water.

14 Is Israel a slave? Is he a homeborn
      servant?
   Why then has he become plunder?
15 The lions have roared against him,
      they have roared loudly.
   They have made his land a waste;
      his cities are in ruins, without
         inhabitant.
16 Moreover, the people of Memphis and
      Tahpanhes
   have broken the crown of your head.

a Heb shepherds

2:5 *What wrong did your ancestors find in me?* God reminds the community that they are not just any people; they are a people owned, consecrated, and accountable to God. They are the People of God as a result of God's amazing act of liberation and deliverance in the exodus. God is passionately partisan when it comes to dealings with Israel. Yet despite that gracious, divinely initiated origin, Israel "went after worthless things." (Whenever we read "Israel" in the testimony of Jeremiah, it is a fair analogy to also read "Church.") How sad when a people, once called to divine purpose, forsake that purpose and put themselves in service to false gods. The picture of our own culture grows more clear. We pray, "God bless America." God has already blessed America with so many good gifts. Yet millions hanker after "worthless things." Jeremiah says that those who frantically seek rubbish become refuse themselves.

2:13 *my people have committed two evils.*

Jeremiah, like most of Israel's prophets, tends to speak in highly charged metaphor. When someone has something important, difficult, sweeping, or tough to say, prose tends to give way to poetry. The modern atheistic question ("Is there a God?") is hardly ever asked in the Bible. The Bible's issue is invariably idolatry ("Who is the god who is there?"). Here God accuses Israel of idolatry, of forsaking the Creator, who has steadfastly loved Israel. Forsaking that love, that "fountain of living water," people instead dig their own wells, seeking water that is self-derived. Does this not remind us of our current situation, in which many, in what some have called an "Age of the Spirit," subjectively, individually seek all sorts of spiritual consolation, spiritual fads, and spiritual benefits by forsaking the historic, corporate faith of the saints? What we might charitably call "spiritual seeking" Jeremiah might name idolatry.

¹⁷ Have you not brought this upon
          yourself
     by forsaking the LORD your God,
        while he led you in the way?
¹⁸ What then do you gain by going to
          Egypt,
     to drink the waters of the Nile?
     Or what do you gain by going to
          Assyria,
        to drink the waters of the Euphrates?
¹⁹ Your wickedness will punish you,
     and your apostasies will convict you.
     Know and see that it is evil and bitter
        for you to forsake the LORD your God;
     the fear of me is not in you,
                    says the Lord GOD of hosts.

²⁰ For long ago you broke your yoke
     and burst your bonds,
        and you said, "I will not serve!"
     On every high hill
        and under every green tree
     you sprawled and played the whore.
²¹ Yet I planted you as a choice vine,
     from the purest stock.
     How then did you turn degenerate
        and become a wild vine?
²² Though you wash yourself with lye
        and use much soap,
     the stain of your guilt is still before
          me,
                    says the Lord GOD.
²³ How can you say, "I am not defiled,
     I have not gone after the Baals"?
     Look at your way in the valley;
        know what you have done—
     a restive young camel interlacing her
          tracks,
²⁴   a wild ass at home in the wilderness,
     in her heat sniffing the wind!
        Who can restrain her lust?

None who seek her need weary
          themselves;
     in her month they will find her.
²⁵ Keep your feet from going unshod
     and your throat from thirst.
     But you said, "It is hopeless,
        for I have loved strangers,
     and after them I will go."

²⁶ As a thief is shamed when caught,
     so the house of Israel shall be
          shamed—
     they, their kings, their officials,
        their priests, and their prophets,
²⁷ who say to a tree, "You are my father,"
     and to a stone, "You gave me birth."
     For they have turned their backs to me,
        and not their faces.
     But in the time of their trouble they say,
        "Come and save us!"
²⁸ But where are your gods
        that you made for yourself?
     Let them come, if they can save you,
        in your time of trouble;
     for you have as many gods
        as you have towns, O Judah.

²⁹ Why do you complain against me?
     You have all rebelled against me,
                    says the LORD.
³⁰ In vain I have struck down your
          children;
     they accepted no correction.
     Your own sword devoured your
          prophets
        like a ravening lion.
³¹ And you, O generation, behold the
          word of the LORD!^a
     Have I been a wilderness to Israel,
        or a land of thick darkness?

_____
^a Meaning of Heb uncertain

_____
2:28 *But where are your gods that you made
for yourself?* The Lord mocks the false faith of
Judah. The people are derided and scorned by
the God who loved and cherished them. Who
are our "gods"? Where do we turn in our "time
of trouble"? High-tech medicine, money, sex,
the nation, the military, the corporation. We
have "as many gods" as there are towns in our
nation. As Martin Luther once said, "Whatever
you fix your heart upon and rely upon, that is
your God." Today, many resources and much
energy are going into a quest for "national
security." But this verse points out that there is
no security in time of trouble except in the arms
of the true and living God.

Why then do my people say, "We are
      free,
   we will come to you no more"?
32 Can a girl forget her ornaments,
      or a bride her attire?
   Yet my people have forgotten me,
      days without number.

33 How well you direct your course
      to seek lovers!
   So that even to wicked women
      you have taught your ways.
34 Also on your skirts is found
      the lifeblood of the innocent poor,
   though you did not catch them
            breaking in.
      Yet in spite of all these things[a]
35 you say, "I am innocent;
      surely his anger has turned from me."
   Now I am bringing you to judgment
      for saying, "I have not sinned."
36 How lightly you gad about,
      changing your ways!
   You shall be put to shame by Egypt
      as you were put to shame by Assyria.
37 From there also you will come away
      with your hands on your head;
   for the LORD has rejected those in whom
         you trust,
      and you will not prosper through
         them.

Unfaithful Israel

3 If[b] a man divorces his wife
      and she goes from him
   and becomes another man's wife,
      will he return to her?
   Would not such a land be greatly
         polluted?

You have played the whore with many
      lovers;
   and would you return to me?
                        says the LORD.
2 Look up to the bare heights,[c] and see!
      Where have you not been lain with?
   By the waysides you have sat waiting for
         lovers,
      like a nomad in the wilderness.
   You have polluted the land
      with your whoring and wickedness.
3 Therefore the showers have been
         withheld,
      and the spring rain has not come;
   yet you have the forehead of a whore,
      you refuse to be ashamed.
4 Have you not just now called to me,
      "My Father, you are the friend of my
         youth—
5 will he be angry forever,
      will he be indignant to the end?"
   This is how you have spoken,
      but you have done all the evil that
         you could.

A Call to Repentance

6 The LORD said to me in the days of King
Josiah: Have you seen what she did, that
faithless one, Israel, how she went up on
every high hill and under every green tree,
and played the whore there? 7 And I thought,
"After she has done all this she will return to
me"; but she did not return, and her false sister Judah saw it. 8 She[d] saw that for all the
adulteries of that faithless one, Israel, I had
sent her away with a decree of divorce; yet her
false sister Judah did not fear, but she too

a Meaning of Heb uncertain   b Q Ms Gk Syr:
MT *Saying, If*   c Or *the trails*   d Q Ms Gk Mss
Syr: MT *I*

3:1 *You have played the whore with many
lovers.* Admittedly, this is not the most genteel
language in the Bible. Judah is compared to a
"whore with many lovers." Conversations
between the covenant community and God
become quickly overheated. The Lord is
passionately connected to the community and
has placed a great deal of faith and trust in it.
Therefore, when the community breaks that
relationship, betrays that trust, the language

becomes heated and fierce. So many times we
construe our relationship with God as a matter
of belief, a matter of affirming certain biblical
truths. Jeremiah depicts that relationship as
analogous to the relationship of husband and
wife in marriage. More than mere intellectual
assent is involved here. Nothing less than
marital love, with its accompanying fidelity or
infidelity, is similar to the love between God and
the community of faith.

went and played the whore. 9Because she took her whoredom so lightly, she polluted the land, committing adultery with stone and tree. 10Yet for all this her false sister Judah did not return to me with her whole heart, but only in pretense, says the LORD.

11 Then the LORD said to me: Faithless Israel has shown herself less guilty than false Judah. 12Go, and proclaim these words toward the north, and say:
Return, faithless Israel,
says the LORD.
I will not look on you in anger,
for I am merciful,
says the LORD;
I will not be angry forever.
13 Only acknowledge your guilt,
that you have rebelled against the
LORD your God,
and scattered your favors among
strangers under every green tree,
and have not obeyed my voice,
says the LORD.
14 Return, O faithless children,
says the LORD,
for I am your master;
I will take you, one from a city and two
from a family,
and I will bring you to Zion.

15 I will give you shepherds after my own heart, who will feed you with knowledge and understanding. 16And when you have multi-

plied and increased in the land, in those days, says the LORD, they shall no longer say, "The ark of the covenant of the LORD." It shall not come to mind, or be remembered, or missed; nor shall another one be made. 17At that time Jerusalem shall be called the throne of the LORD, and all nations shall gather to it, to the presence of the LORD in Jerusalem, and they shall no longer stubbornly follow their own evil will. 18In those days the house of Judah shall join the house of Israel, and together they shall come from the land of the north to the land that I gave your ancestors for a heritage.

19 I thought
how I would set you among my
children,
and give you a pleasant land,
the most beautiful heritage of all the
nations.
And I thought you would call me, My
Father,
and would not turn from following me.
20 Instead, as a faithless wife leaves her
husband,
so you have been faithless to me,
O house of Israel,
says the LORD.

21 A voice on the bare heights a is heard,
the plaintive weeping of Israel's
children,

a Or the trails

3:12–13 *Return, faithless Israel.* Some think of Jeremiah as constantly condemnatory and judgmental, but that is unfair to the prophet's total testimony. In these verses we hear the point of the prophet's fierce divine judgment and rebuke—the restoration of relationship. God keeps wavering between separation and reunion, divorce and renewal of wedding vows. Behind Jeremiah's words is the assumption that there can be no reunion, no renovation without first being honest. God tells the Israelites the truth so that, in facing the truth of their waywardness, they might "return," might again embrace the God who has in the past so graciously embraced them. If the prophet's words sound harsh and hard, let us be reminded that there is no sustained, truly loving relation-

ship that is not based on honesty. In our own permissive, anything-goes age, honesty often sounds harsh and hard to our compromised ears. Truth often feels cruel to the deceitful.

3:15 *I will give you shepherds after my own heart.* Throughout the prophecy of Jeremiah is the recurring theme of contrast between false and true religious leaders. There is criticism of lying, false "shepherds" who will tickle the ears of the people and tell their congregations anything they want to hear. In this verse God promises to give the community true leaders who will speak the truth, even when the truth hurts. Truthful leaders, honest preachers, and bold prophets are gifts of God to the faith community.

because they have perverted their way,
  they have forgotten the LORD their
    God:
22 Return, O faithless children,
  I will heal your faithlessness.

"Here we come to you;
  for you are the LORD our God.
23 Truly the hills are[a] a delusion,
  the orgies on the mountains.
Truly in the LORD our God
  is the salvation of Israel.
24 "But from our youth the shameful
thing has devoured all for which our ancestors had labored, their flocks and their herds,
their sons and their daughters. 25Let us lie
down in our shame, and let our dishonor
cover us; for we have sinned against the LORD
our God, we and our ancestors, from our
youth even to this day; and we have not
obeyed the voice of the LORD our God."

4 If you return, O Israel,
                              says the LORD,
  if you return to me,
  if you remove your abominations from
      my presence,
    and do not waver,
2 and if you swear, "As the LORD lives!"
    in truth, in justice, and in
      uprightness,
  then nations shall be blessed[b] by him,
    and by him they shall boast.
3 For thus says the LORD to the people of
Judah and to the inhabitants of Jerusalem:
  Break up your fallow ground,
    and do not sow among thorns.
4 Circumcise yourselves to the LORD,
  remove the foreskin of your hearts,
  O people of Judah and inhabitants of
      Jerusalem,
  or else my wrath will go forth like fire,

and burn with no one to quench it,
  because of the evil of your doings.

Invasion and Desolation of Judah Threatened

5 Declare in Judah, and proclaim in Jerusalem, and say:
  Blow the trumpet through the land;
    shout aloud[c] and say,
  "Gather together, and let us go
    into the fortified cities!"
6 Raise a standard toward Zion,
    flee for safety, do not delay,
  for I am bringing evil from the north,
    and a great destruction.
7 A lion has gone up from its thicket,
    a destroyer of nations has set out;
    he has gone out from his place
  to make your land a waste;
    your cities will be ruins
    without inhabitant.
8 Because of this put on sackcloth,
    lament and wail:
  "The fierce anger of the LORD
    has not turned away from us."

9On that day, says the LORD, courage shall
fail the king and the officials; the priests shall
be appalled and the prophets astounded.
10Then I said, "Ah, Lord GOD, how utterly
you have deceived this people and Jerusalem, saying, 'It shall be well with you,' even
while the sword is at the throat!"

11 At that time it will be said to this people and to Jerusalem: A hot wind comes from
me out of the bare heights[d] in the desert toward my poor people, not to winnow or

a Gk Syr Vg: Heb *Truly from the hills is*
b Or *shall bless themselves*   c Or *shout, take your
weapons*: Heb *shout, fill* (your hand)   d Or *the
trails*

4:1 *If you return, O Israel.* Although the Lord
expresses strong anger against Israel and even
threatens to break off the relationship with it,
here we gaze into the heart of God on this
matter of Israel's sin and infidelity. All of the
judgment, condemnation, and rebuke is in the
hope of return, renovation, and renewal. Though
the situation is tragic, sad, and serious, all is not

lost. Something can be done. Israel is invited to
return, to restore its original covenant with God,
with the one true God who encourages new
beginning, conversion, transformation, and
rebirth. A favorite prophetic word is "return."
God grants the people a second chance. And if
spiritual formation means anything, it means
returning, conversion, transformation.

cleanse— ¹²a wind too strong for that. Now it is I who speak in judgment against them.

¹³ Look! He comes up like clouds,
  his chariots like the whirlwind;
his horses are swifter than eagles—
  woe to us, for we are ruined!
¹⁴ O Jerusalem, wash your heart clean of
    wickedness
  so that you may be saved.
How long shall your evil schemes
  lodge within you?
¹⁵ For a voice declares from Dan
  and proclaims disaster from Mount
    Ephraim.
¹⁶ Tell the nations, "Here they are!"
  Proclaim against Jerusalem,
"Besiegers come from a distant land;
  they shout against the cities of Judah.
¹⁷ They have closed in around her like
    watchers of a field,
  because she has rebelled against me,
              says the LORD.
¹⁸ Your ways and your doings
  have brought this upon you.
This is your doom; how bitter it is!
  It has reached your very heart."

Sorrow for a Doomed Nation

¹⁹ My anguish, my anguish! I writhe in
    pain!
  Oh, the walls of my heart!
My heart is beating wildly;
  I cannot keep silent;
for I ᵃ hear the sound of the trumpet,
  the alarm of war.
²⁰ Disaster overtakes disaster,
  the whole land is laid waste.
Suddenly my tents are destroyed,
  my curtains in a moment.
²¹ How long must I see the standard,
  and hear the sound of the trumpet?
²² "For my people are foolish,
    they do not know me;
  they are stupid children,
    they have no understanding.
They are skilled in doing evil,
  but do not know how to do good."

²³ I looked on the earth, and lo, it was
    waste and void;

and to the heavens, and they had no
    light.
²⁴ I looked on the mountains, and lo, they
    were quaking,
  and all the hills moved to and fro.
²⁵ I looked, and lo, there was no one at all,
  and all the birds of the air had fled.
²⁶ I looked, and lo, the fruitful land was a
    desert,
  and all its cities were laid in ruins
  before the LORD, before his fierce
    anger.

27 For thus says the LORD: The whole land shall be a desolation; yet I will not make a full end.
²⁸ Because of this the earth shall mourn,
  and the heavens above grow black;
for I have spoken, I have purposed;
  I have not relented nor will I turn
    back.

²⁹ At the noise of horseman and archer
  every town takes to flight;
they enter thickets; they climb among
    rocks;
  all the towns are forsaken,
  and no one lives in them.
³⁰ And you, O desolate one,
  what do you mean that you dress in
    crimson,
    that you deck yourself with
      ornaments of gold,
    that you enlarge your eyes with
      paint?
In vain you beautify yourself.
  Your lovers despise you;
  they seek your life.
³¹ For I heard a cry as of a woman in labor,
  anguish as of one bringing forth her
    first child,
the cry of daughter Zion gasping for
    breath,
  stretching out her hands,
"Woe is me! I am fainting before
    killers!"

The Utter Corruption of God's People

5 Run to and fro through the streets of
  Jerusalem,

a Another reading is *for you, O my soul,*

JEREMIAH

The Weeping Prophet

Selected Scriptures: *Jeremiah 1–3; 10–11; 15; 17–18; 20; 23; 31; 35; 37–44*

In the darkest biblical period of Israel's life, God gave Jeremiah the unpleasant job of conveying God's white-hot anger and announcing the nation's destruction.

The Israelites rejected both Jeremiah and his message. They viewed Jeremiah as a traitor; they beat him, put him in stocks, imprisoned him, and once even threw him into a muddy cistern (Jer 37:15–16). Yet he probably suffered more intensely in his spirit. "Why is my pain unceasing, my wound incurable, refusing to be healed?" he cried to God (15:18). Jeremiah poured out his anguish at what his own people had committed against God and at what he too was suffering at their hands.

Yet he could no more stop his prophesying than he could stop his tears. Jeremiah felt the urgency of his call: "There is something like a burning fire shut up in my bones; I am weary with holding it in, and I cannot" (20:9). Still he grieved as he saw his words and warnings ignored by his very own people.

Jeremiah carried out God's call for his life without ever seeing outward success. Judah had lived long practicing idolatry and injustice—Manasseh's fifty-five-year reign had helped instill roving and self-centered hearts that even godly King Josiah couldn't change for long. God knew that only their own destruction would bring his people back to him, and he asked Jeremiah to deliver this message.

In *Subversive Spirituality*, Eugene Peterson describes Jeremiah as a good "ascetical theologian" who illustrated the difference between those who will find life in God and those who won't. "The kind of lives we lead, who we *are*, not just what we *do*, are huge factors influencing our access to truth, any truth but especially the Truth that is God. . . . Ascetical theology gives its attention to conditions, conditions which are congenial to developing God-awareness as over against growing God-calluses, looking out for rivers and steering away from deserts [as illustrated in Jer 17:5–10]. The way we are—the way we spend our money, eat our meals, read a book, treat a stranger—affects our capacity to see the beauty of holiness, hear the word of absolution, feel the touch of love, enter into a life of prayer."

Jeremiah lived "God-aware" and grieved for those who did not. Surely he anticipated with nearly as much joy as God the time of the new covenant he prophesied: "I will put my law within them, and I will write it on their hearts; and I will be their God, and they shall be my people" (31:33). Not yet has that covenant come in all its fullness. Like Jeremiah, we too may live as weeping prophets, grieving ministers.

Personal Reflection

- When have you sensed, as Jeremiah did, a call in your life as a "fire shut up in [your] bones" that you could not hold in?
- When have you experienced grief over the apparent failure of your ministry or calling? What might be God's perspective on this failure?

PROFILE

look around and take note!
Search its squares and see
    if you can find one person
who acts justly
    and seeks truth—
so that I may pardon Jerusalem. *a*

2 Although they say, "As the LORD lives,"
    yet they swear falsely.
3 O LORD, do your eyes not look for truth?
You have struck them,
    but they felt no anguish;
you have consumed them,
    but they refused to take correction.
They have made their faces harder than
        rock;
    they have refused to turn back.

4 Then I said, "These are only the poor,
    they have no sense;
for they do not know the way of the
        LORD,
    the law of their God.
5 Let me go to the rich *b*
    and speak to them;
surely they know the way of the LORD,
    the law of their God."
But they all alike had broken the yoke,
    they had burst the bonds.

6 Therefore a lion from the forest shall kill
        them,
    a wolf from the desert shall destroy
        them.
A leopard is watching against their
        cities;
    everyone who goes out of them shall
        be torn in pieces—
because their transgressions are many,
    their apostasies are great.

7 How can I pardon you?
    Your children have forsaken me,

and have sworn by those who are no
        gods.
When I fed them to the full,
    they committed adultery
    and trooped to the houses of
        prostitutes.
8 They were well-fed lusty stallions,
    each neighing for his neighbor's wife.
9 Shall I not punish them for these things?
                            says the LORD;
    and shall I not bring retribution
    on a nation such as this?

10 Go up through her vine-rows and
        destroy,
    but do not make a full end;
strip away her branches,
    for they are not the LORD's.
11 For the house of Israel and the house of
        Judah
    have been utterly faithless to me,
                            says the LORD.
12 They have spoken falsely of the LORD,
    and have said, "He will do nothing.
No evil will come upon us,
    and we shall not see sword or
        famine."
13 The prophets are nothing but wind,
    for the word is not in them.
Thus shall it be done to them!

14 Therefore thus says the LORD, the God
        of hosts:
Because they *c* have spoken this word,
I am now making my words in your
        mouth a fire,
    and this people wood, and the fire
        shall devour them.
15 I am going to bring upon you

a Heb *it*   *b* Or *the great*   *c* Heb *you*

5:12 *No evil will come upon us.* False prophets are repeatedly criticized in Jeremiah. Not every religious spokesperson speaks for God. In Jeremiah, false prophets tend to specialize in sweet-sounding, easily comforting words that are "deceptive" (7:8). A true spokesperson for God speaks God's truth, even when it hurts. Alas, too many contemporary religious leaders seem to specialize in soothing, rather than honest, speech. Or, as Jeremiah puts it, they are "nothing but wind" (v 13). The true prophet is more concerned to make God's word heard than to evoke popular acclaim. Would your church want a preacher like Jeremiah? Would any church?

a nation from far away, O house of
 Israel,
                                    says the LORD.
It is an enduring nation,
 it is an ancient nation,
a nation whose language you do not
 know,
 nor can you understand what they say.
16 Their quiver is like an open tomb;
 all of them are mighty warriors.
17 They shall eat up your harvest and your
 food;
 they shall eat up your sons and your
 daughters;
 they shall eat up your flocks and your
 herds;
 they shall eat up your vines and your
 fig trees;
 they shall destroy with the sword
 your fortified cities in which you
 trust.

18 But even in those days, says the LORD,
I will not make a full end of you. 19And when
your people say, "Why has the LORD our God
done all these things to us?" you shall say to
them, "As you have forsaken me and served
foreign gods in your land, so you shall serve
strangers in a land that is not yours."

20 Declare this in the house of Jacob,
 proclaim it in Judah:
21 Hear this, O foolish and senseless
 people,
 who have eyes, but do not see,
 who have ears, but do not hear.
22 Do you not fear me? says the LORD;
 Do you not tremble before me?
I placed the sand as a boundary for the
 sea,
 a perpetual barrier that it cannot pass;
though the waves toss, they cannot
 prevail,
 though they roar, they cannot pass
 over it.
23 But this people has a stubborn and
 rebellious heart;

they have turned aside and gone
 away.
24 They do not say in their hearts,
 "Let us fear the LORD our God,
who gives the rain in its season,
 the autumn rain and the spring rain,
and keeps for us
 the weeks appointed for the harvest."
25 Your iniquities have turned these away,
 and your sins have deprived you of
 good.
26 For scoundrels are found among my
 people;
 they take over the goods of others.
Like fowlers they set a trap; a
 they catch human beings.
27 Like a cage full of birds,
 their houses are full of treachery;
therefore they have become great and
 rich,
28   they have grown fat and sleek.
They know no limits in deeds of
 wickedness;
 they do not judge with justice
the cause of the orphan, to make it
 prosper,
 and they do not defend the rights of
 the needy.
29 Shall I not punish them for these things?
                                    says the LORD,
 and shall I not bring retribution
 on a nation such as this?

30 An appalling and horrible thing
 has happened in the land:
31 the prophets prophesy falsely,
 and the priests rule as the prophets
 direct; b
my people love to have it so,
 but what will you do when the end
 comes?

The Imminence and Horror of the Invasion

6 Flee for safety, O children of Benjamin,
 from the midst of Jerusalem!

a Meaning of Heb uncertain   b Or rule by their
own authority

6:1 *Flee for safety!* Jeremiah speaks of the
coming of the great adversary from the north.

This is a somber warning of impending doom.
The situation is desperate. The prophet has

Blow the trumpet in Tekoa,
   and raise a signal on Beth-haccherem;
for evil looms out of the north,
   and great destruction.
2 I have likened daughter Zion
   to the loveliest pasture. *a*
3 Shepherds with their flocks shall come
     against her.
   They shall pitch their tents around
     her;
   they shall pasture, all in their places.
4 "Prepare war against her;
   up, and let us attack at noon!"
"Woe to us, for the day declines,
   the shadows of evening lengthen!"
5 "Up, and let us attack by night,
   and destroy her palaces!"
6 For thus says the LORD of hosts:
Cut down her trees;
   cast up a siege ramp against
     Jerusalem.
This is the city that must be punished; *b*
   there is nothing but oppression
     within her.
7 As a well keeps its water fresh,
   so she keeps fresh her wickedness;
violence and destruction are heard
     within her;
   sickness and wounds are ever before
     me.
8 Take warning, O Jerusalem,
   or I shall turn from you in disgust,
and make you a desolation,
   an uninhabited land.

9 Thus says the LORD of hosts:
Glean *c* thoroughly as a vine
   the remnant of Israel;
like a grape-gatherer, pass your hand
     again
   over its branches.

10 To whom shall I speak and give warning,
   that they may hear?
See, their ears are closed, *d*
   they cannot listen.
The word of the LORD is to them an
     object of scorn;
   they take no pleasure in it.
11 But I am full of the wrath of the LORD;
   I am weary of holding it in.

Pour it out on the children in the street,
   and on the gatherings of young men
     as well;
both husband and wife shall be taken,
   the old folk and the very aged.
12 Their houses shall be turned over to
     others,
   their fields and wives together;
for I will stretch out my hand
   against the inhabitants of the land,
          says the LORD.

13 For from the least to the greatest of
     them,
   everyone is greedy for unjust gain;
and from prophet to priest,
   everyone deals falsely.
14 They have treated the wound of my
     people carelessly,
   saying, "Peace, peace,"
   when there is no peace.
15 They acted shamefully, they committed
     abomination;
   yet they were not ashamed,
   they did not know how to blush.
Therefore they shall fall among those
     who fall;

a Or *I will destroy daughter Zion, the loveliest pasture*
b Or *the city of license*   *c* Cn: Heb *They shall glean*
d Heb *are uncircumcised*

---

gone looking for a few virtuous people who might turn the situation around, but has found none. It is fitting that we in the contemporary faith community, which rests content in a situation of uneasy peace and prosperity, should hear this word of alarm, should be reminded that many of our sisters and brothers in the faith face horrible situations. In our present circumstances, we may be at ease. But Scripture unites us with those who suffer and particularly those who suffer because of their faith. Some have noted that in the last century more Christians may have been martyred than in all the previous centuries combined. It is a sober thought, but the Bible does not avoid such sober thoughts. Scripture places the contemporary faith community in solidarity with sisters and brothers who suffer evil.

at the time that I punish them, they
    shall be overthrown,
                says the LORD.
16 Thus says the LORD:
Stand at the crossroads, and look,
    and ask for the ancient paths,
where the good way lies; and walk in it,
    and find rest for your souls.
But they said, "We will not walk in it."
17 Also I raised up sentinels for you:
    "Give heed to the sound of the
        trumpet!"
But they said, "We will not give heed."
18 Therefore hear, O nations,
    and know, O congregation, what will
        happen to them.
19 Hear, O earth; I am going to bring
      disaster on this people,
    the fruit of their schemes,
because they have not given heed to my
      words;
    and as for my teaching, they have
      rejected it.
20 Of what use to me is frankincense that
      comes from Sheba,
    or sweet cane from a distant land?
Your burnt offerings are not acceptable,
    nor are your sacrifices pleasing to me.
21 Therefore thus says the LORD:
See, I am laying before this people
    stumbling blocks against which they
      shall stumble;
parents and children together,
    neighbor and friend shall perish.

22 Thus says the LORD:
See, a people is coming from the land of
      the north,
    a great nation is stirring from the
      farthest parts of the earth.
23 They grasp the bow and the javelin,
    they are cruel and have no mercy,
    their sound is like the roaring sea;
they ride on horses,

equipped like a warrior for battle,
    against you, O daughter Zion!

24 "We have heard news of them,
    our hands fall helpless;
anguish has taken hold of us,
    pain as of a woman in labor.
25 Do not go out into the field,
    or walk on the road;
for the enemy has a sword,
    terror is on every side."

26 O my poor people, put on sackcloth,
    and roll in ashes;
make mourning as for an only child,
    most bitter lamentation:
for suddenly the destroyer
    will come upon us.

27 I have made you a tester and a refiner[a]
      among my people
    so that you may know and test their
      ways.
28 They are all stubbornly rebellious,
    going about with slanders;
they are bronze and iron,
    all of them act corruptly.
29 The bellows blow fiercely,
    the lead is consumed by the fire;
in vain the refining goes on,
    for the wicked are not removed.
30 They are called "rejected silver,"
    for the LORD has rejected them.

Jeremiah Proclaims God's Judgment on the Nation

7 The word that came to Jeremiah from
the LORD: 2Stand in the gate of the LORD's
house, and proclaim there this word, and
say, Hear the word of the LORD, all you people
of Judah, you that enter these gates to worship the LORD. 3Thus says the LORD of hosts,

a Or a fortress

7:1–15 *Stand in the gate of the LORD's house,
and proclaim there this word.* Jeremiah moves to
the Temple, where he stands at the front door
and preaches a sermon. He would have had
difficulty getting all the way into the pulpit for a
sermon like this! The situation is ironic. Here is

the Temple, that holy place where God's word
ought to be found, but Jeremiah gets just as far
as the front door with the word from God that
he has to speak. The Temple, so large, so sound
and secure, was surely seen by the populace as
a place of divine strength, as solid proof that

the God of Israel: Amend your ways and your doings, and let me dwell with you*a* in this place. 4Do not trust in these deceptive words: "This is*b* the temple of the LORD, the temple of the LORD, the temple of the LORD."

5 For if you truly amend your ways and your doings, if you truly act justly one with another, 6if you do not oppress the alien, the orphan, and the widow, or shed innocent blood in this place, and if you do not go after other gods to your own hurt, 7then I will dwell with you in this place, in the land that I gave of old to your ancestors forever and ever.

8 Here you are, trusting in deceptive words to no avail. 9Will you steal, murder, commit adultery, swear falsely, make offerings to Baal, and go after other gods that you have not known, 10and then come and stand before me in this house, which is called by my name, and say, "We are safe!"—only to go on doing all these abominations? 11Has this house, which is called by my name, become a den of robbers in your sight? You know, I too am watching, says the LORD. 12Go now to my place that was in Shiloh, where I made my name dwell at first, and see what I did to it for the wickedness of my people Israel. 13And now, because you have done all these things, says the LORD, and when I spoke to you persistently, you did not listen, and when I called you, you did not answer, 14therefore I will do to the house that is called by my name, in which you trust, and to the place that I gave to you and to your ancestors, just what I did to Shiloh. 15And I will cast you out of my sight, just as I cast out all your kinsfolk, all the offspring of Ephraim.

The People's Disobedience

16 As for you, do not pray for this people, do not raise a cry or prayer on their behalf, and do not intercede with me, for I will not hear you. 17Do you not see what they are doing in the towns of Judah and in the streets of Jerusalem? 18The children gather wood, the fathers kindle fire, and the women knead dough, to make cakes for the queen of heaven; and they pour out drink offerings to other gods, to provoke me to anger. 19Is it I whom they provoke? says the LORD. Is it not themselves, to their own hurt? 20Therefore thus says the Lord GOD: My anger and my wrath shall be poured out on this place, on human beings and animals, on the trees of the field and the fruit of the ground; it will burn and not be quenched.

21 Thus says the LORD of hosts, the God of Israel: Add your burnt offerings to your sacrifices, and eat the flesh. 22For in the day that I brought your ancestors out of the land of Egypt, I did not speak to them or command them concerning burnt offerings and sacrifices. 23But this command I gave them, "Obey my voice, and I will be your God, and you shall be my people; and walk only in the way that I command you, so that it may be well with you." 24Yet they did not obey or incline their ear, but, in the stubbornness of their evil will, they walked in their own counsels, and looked backward rather than forward. 25From the day that your ancestors came out of the land of Egypt until this day, I have persistently sent all my servants the prophets to them, day after day; 26yet they did not listen to me, or pay attention, but they stiffened their necks. They did worse than their ancestors did.

27 So you shall speak all these words to them, but they will not listen to you. You shall call to them, but they will not answer

a Or *and I will let you dwell*   *b* Heb *They are*

Israel possessed a strong God who would protect the nation. The Temple was a great architectural reassurance that "we are safe" (v 10). And yet it is there that Jeremiah predicts the unthinkable: the Temple shall be destroyed (v 14). This is the same passage that Jesus quoted when he cleansed the Temple (v 11; see Matt 21:13). If we are capable of perverting even the house of God for our own idolatrous purposes, what other good thing do we pervert? This passage surely causes us to ask ourselves: In what ways have we used our houses of God, our beloved temples, as a defense against God, as a false assurance that, because we have this place—solid, eternal, secure—we do not have to worry too much about serving God? The great theologian Karl Barth said, "Christians go to church to make their last stand against God."

you. 28You shall say to them: This is the nation that did not obey the voice of the LORD their God, and did not accept discipline; truth has perished; it is cut off from their lips.

29 Cut off your hair and throw it away;
    raise a lamentation on the bare
        heights,ᵃ
  for the LORD has rejected and forsaken
    the generation that provoked his
        wrath.

30 For the people of Judah have done evil in my sight, says the LORD; they have set their abominations in the house that is called by my name, defiling it. 31And they go on building the high placeᵇ of Topheth, which is in the valley of the son of Hinnom, to burn their sons and their daughters in the fire—which I did not command, nor did it come into my mind. 32Therefore, the days are surely coming, says the LORD, when it will no more be called Topheth, or the valley of the son of Hinnom, but the valley of Slaughter: for they will bury in Topheth until there is no more room. 33The corpses of this people will be food for the birds of the air, and for the animals of the earth; and no one will frighten them away. 34And I will bring to an end the sound of mirth and gladness, the voice of the bride and bridegroom in the cities of Judah and in the streets of Jerusalem; for the land shall become a waste.

8 At that time, says the LORD, the bones of the kings of Judah, the bones of its officials, the bones of the priests, the bones of the prophets, and the bones of the inhabitants of Jerusalem shall be brought out of their tombs; 2and they shall be spread before the sun and the moon and all the host of heaven, which they have loved and served, which they have followed, and which they have inquired of and worshiped; and they shall not be gathered or buried; they shall be like dung on the surface of the ground. 3Death shall be preferred to life by all the remnant that remains of this evil family in all the places where I have driven them, says the LORD of hosts.

The Blind Perversity of the Whole Nation

4 You shall say to them, Thus says the
    LORD:
  When people fall, do they not get up
    again?
    If they go astray, do they not turn
      back?
5 Why then has this peopleᶜ turned away
    in perpetual backsliding?
  They have held fast to deceit,
    they have refused to return.
6 I have given heed and listened,
    but they do not speak honestly;
  no one repents of wickedness,
    saying, "What have I done!"
  All of them turn to their own course,
    like a horse plunging headlong into
      battle.
7 Even the stork in the heavens
    knows its times;
  and the turtledove, swallow, and craneᵈ
    observe the time of their coming;
  but my people do not know
    the ordinance of the LORD.

8 How can you say, "We are wise,
    and the law of the LORD is with us,"
  when, in fact, the false pen of the
      scribes
    has made it into a lie?
9 The wise shall be put to shame,
    they shall be dismayed and taken;
  since they have rejected the word of the
    LORD,
    what wisdom is in them?
10 Therefore I will give their wives to
    others
    and their fields to conquerors,
  because from the least to the greatest
    everyone is greedy for unjust gain;
  from prophet to priest
    everyone deals falsely.
11 They have treated the wound of my
      people carelessly,
  saying, "Peace, peace,"
    when there is no peace.
12 They acted shamefully, they committed
    abomination;

a Or the trails   b Gk Tg: Heb high places
c One Ms Gk: MT this people, Jerusalem,
d Meaning of Heb uncertain

yet they were not at all ashamed,
    they did not know how to blush.
Therefore they shall fall among those
    who fall;
    at the time when I punish them, they
        shall be overthrown,
                says the LORD.
13 When I wanted to gather them, says the
    LORD,
there are *a* no grapes on the vine,
    nor figs on the fig tree;
even the leaves are withered,
    and what I gave them has passed away
        from them. *b*

14 Why do we sit still?
    Gather together, let us go into the
        fortified cities
    and perish there;
for the LORD our God has doomed us to
    perish,
    and has given us poisoned water to
        drink,
    because we have sinned against the
        LORD.
15 We look for peace, but find no good,
    for a time of healing, but there is
        terror instead.

16 The snorting of their horses is heard
        from Dan;
    at the sound of the neighing of their
        stallions
    the whole land quakes.
They come and devour the land and all
        that fills it,
    the city and those who live in it.
17 See, I am letting snakes loose among
        you,
    adders that cannot be charmed,
    and they shall bite you,
                says the LORD.

The Prophet Mourns for the People

18 My joy is gone, grief is upon me,
    my heart is sick.
19 Hark, the cry of my poor people
    from far and wide in the land:
    "Is the LORD not in Zion?
    Is her King not in her?"
("Why have they provoked me to anger
    with their images,
    with their foreign idols?")
20 "The harvest is past, the summer is
    ended,
    and we are not saved."
21 For the hurt of my poor people I am
    hurt,
    I mourn, and dismay has taken hold
        of me.

22 Is there no balm in Gilead?
    Is there no physician there?
Why then has the health of my poor
        people
    not been restored?

9 *c* O that my head were a spring of water,
    and my eyes a fountain of tears,
so that I might weep day and night
    for the slain of my poor people!
2 *d* O that I had in the desert
    a traveler's lodging place,
that I might leave my people
    and go away from them!
For they are all adulterers,
    a band of traitors.
3 They bend their tongues like bows;
    they have grown strong in the land
        for falsehood, and not for truth;
    for they proceed from evil to evil,

a Or *I will make an end of them, says the* LORD. *There are*   *b* Meaning of Heb uncertain   *c* Ch 8.23 in Heb   *d* Ch 9.1 in Heb

---

9:1 *O that my head were a spring of water.* Grief is a prophetic activity. Kings put a happy face on everything, tell the people this is the best of all possible worlds and they never had it so good. It takes a truthful prophet to have the guts to grieve societal disaster. Tears are a sign of relinquishment, a letting go of false hopes and false gods, an admission that we are in sad shape and in need of deliverance. The community that is faithful to the truth is always the place where we go to grieve, where we are given the space and the permission to weep. Grief is not the final prophetic act, but it may be the first—an honest admission that we are a people who need a God who loves and saves. Tears are thus a prelude to openness to the possibility of divine deliverance.

and they do not know me, says the
LORD.

4 Beware of your neighbors,
    and put no trust in any of your kin;*a*
for all your kin*b* are supplanters,
    and every neighbor goes around like a
        slanderer.
5 They all deceive their neighbors,
    and no one speaks the truth;
they have taught their tongues to speak
        lies;
    they commit iniquity and are too
        weary to repent.*c*
6 Oppression upon oppression, deceit*d*
    upon deceit!
They refuse to know me, says the LORD.

7 Therefore thus says the LORD of hosts:
I will now refine and test them,
    for what else can I do with my sinful
        people?*e*
8 Their tongue is a deadly arrow;
    it speaks deceit through the mouth.
They all speak friendly words to their
        neighbors,
    but inwardly are planning to lay an
        ambush.
9 Shall I not punish them for these
        things? says the LORD;
    and shall I not bring retribution
on a nation such as this?

10 Take up*f* weeping and wailing for the
        mountains,
    and a lamentation for the pastures of
        the wilderness,
because they are laid waste so that no
        one passes through,
    and the lowing of cattle is not heard;
both the birds of the air and the
        animals
    have fled and are gone.
11 I will make Jerusalem a heap of ruins,
    a lair of jackals;
and I will make the towns of Judah a
        desolation,
    without inhabitant.

12 Who is wise enough to understand
this? To whom has the mouth of the LORD

spoken, so that they may declare it? Why is
the land ruined and laid waste like a wilderness, so that no one passes through? 13And
the LORD says: Because they have forsaken
my law that I set before them, and have not
obeyed my voice, or walked in accordance
with it, 14but have stubbornly followed their
own hearts and have gone after the Baals, as
their ancestors taught them. 15Therefore thus
says the LORD of hosts, the God of Israel: I
am feeding this people with wormwood, and
giving them poisonous water to drink. 16I
will scatter them among nations that neither they nor their ancestors have known;
and I will send the sword after them, until I
have consumed them.

The People Mourn in Judgment

17 Thus says the LORD of hosts:
    Consider, and call for the mourning
        women to come;
    send for the skilled women to come;
18 let them quickly raise a dirge over us,
    so that our eyes may run down with
        tears,
    and our eyelids flow with water.
19 For a sound of wailing is heard from
        Zion:
    "How we are ruined!
    We are utterly shamed,
because we have left the land,
    because they have cast down our
        dwellings."

20 Hear, O women, the word of the LORD,
    and let your ears receive the word of
        his mouth;
teach to your daughters a dirge,
    and each to her neighbor a lament.
21 "Death has come up into our windows,
    it has entered our palaces,
to cut off the children from the streets
    and the young men from the
        squares."
22 Speak! Thus says the LORD:
    "Human corpses shall fall

a Heb *in a brother*   *b* Heb *for every brother*
c Cn Compare Gk: Heb *they weary themselves with
iniquity.* 6*Your dwelling*   *d* Cn: Heb *Your dwelling
in the midst of deceit*   *e* Or *my poor people*
f Gk Syr: Heb *I will take up*

like dung upon the open field,
like sheaves behind the reaper,
and no one shall gather them."

23 Thus says the LORD: Do not let the wise boast in their wisdom, do not let the mighty boast in their might, do not let the wealthy boast in their wealth; 24but let those who boast boast in this, that they understand and know me, that I am the LORD; I act with steadfast love, justice, and righteousness in the earth, for in these things I delight, says the LORD.

25 The days are surely coming, says the LORD, when I will attend to all those who are circumcised only in the foreskin: 26Egypt, Judah, Edom, the Ammonites, Moab, and all those with shaven temples who live in the desert. For all these nations are uncircumcised, and all the house of Israel is uncircumcised in heart.

Idolatry Has Brought Ruin on Israel

10 Hear the word that the LORD speaks to you, O house of Israel. 2Thus says the LORD:

Do not learn the way of the nations,
or be dismayed at the signs of the
heavens;
for the nations are dismayed at them.
3 For the customs of the peoples are false:
a tree from the forest is cut down,
and worked with an ax by the hands
of an artisan;
4 people deck it with silver and gold;
they fasten it with hammer and nails
so that it cannot move.
5 Their idols*a* are like scarecrows in a
cucumber field,
and they cannot speak;
they have to be carried,
for they cannot walk.
Do not be afraid of them,
for they cannot do evil,
nor is it in them to do good.

6 There is none like you, O LORD;
you are great, and your name is great
in might.
7 Who would not fear you, O King of the
nations?

For that is your due;
among all the wise ones of the nations
and in all their kingdoms
there is no one like you.
8 They are both stupid and foolish;
the instruction given by idols
is no better than wood!*b*
9 Beaten silver is brought from Tarshish,
and gold from Uphaz.
They are the work of the artisan and of
the hands of the goldsmith;
their clothing is blue and purple;
they are all the product of skilled
workers.
10 But the LORD is the true God;
he is the living God and the
everlasting King.
At his wrath the earth quakes,
and the nations cannot endure his
indignation.

11 Thus shall you say to them: The gods who did not make the heavens and the earth shall perish from the earth and from under the heavens.*c*

12 It is he who made the earth by his
power,
who established the world by his
wisdom,
and by his understanding stretched
out the heavens.
13 When he utters his voice, there is a
tumult of waters in the heavens,
and he makes the mist rise from the
ends of the earth.
He makes lightnings for the rain,
and he brings out the wind from his
storehouses.
14 Everyone is stupid and without
knowledge;
goldsmiths are all put to shame by
their idols;
for their images are false,
and there is no breath in them.
15 They are worthless, a work of delusion;
at the time of their punishment they
shall perish.

a Heb *They*   *b* Meaning of Heb uncertain
c This verse is in Aramaic

16 Not like these is the LORD, *a* the portion
      of Jacob,
   for he is the one who formed all things,
   and Israel is the tribe of his inheritance;
   the LORD of hosts is his name.

The Coming Exile

17 Gather up your bundle from the ground,
      O you who live under siege!
18 For thus says the LORD:
   I am going to sling out the inhabitants
      of the land
      at this time,
   and I will bring distress on them,
      so that they shall feel it.

19 Woe is me because of my hurt!
      My wound is severe.
   But I said, "Truly this is my punishment,
      and I must bear it."
20 My tent is destroyed,
      and all my cords are broken;
   my children have gone from me,
      and they are no more;
   there is no one to spread my tent again,
      and to set up my curtains.
21 For the shepherds are stupid,
      and do not inquire of the LORD;
   therefore they have not prospered,
      and all their flock is scattered.

22 Hear, a noise! Listen, it is coming—
      a great commotion from the land of
         the north
   to make the cities of Judah a desolation,
      a lair of jackals.

23 I know, O LORD, that the way of human
      beings is not in their control,

that mortals as they walk cannot
      direct their steps.
24 Correct me, O LORD, but in just measure;
      not in your anger, or you will bring
      me to nothing.

25 Pour out your wrath on the nations that
      do not know you,
   and on the peoples that do not call on
      your name;
   for they have devoured Jacob;
      they have devoured him and
         consumed him,
   and have laid waste his habitation.

Israel and Judah Have Broken the Covenant

11 The word that came to Jeremiah from the LORD: 2 Hear the words of this covenant, and speak to the people of Judah and the inhabitants of Jerusalem. 3 You shall say to them, Thus says the LORD, the God of Israel: Cursed be anyone who does not heed the words of this covenant, 4 which I commanded your ancestors when I brought them out of the land of Egypt, from the iron-smelter, saying, Listen to my voice, and do all that I command you. So shall you be my people, and I will be your God, 5 that I may perform the oath that I swore to your ancestors, to give them a land flowing with milk and honey, as at this day. Then I answered, "So be it, LORD."

6 And the LORD said to me: Proclaim all these words in the cities of Judah, and in the streets of Jerusalem: Hear the words of this covenant and do them. 7 For I solemnly warned your ancestors when I brought them

a Heb lacks *the* LORD

11:1–17 *So shall you be my people, and I will be your God.* The prophets of Israel were rarely radical innovators; more typically they were great traditionalists. A favorite prophetic word is "remember," followed by "return." In this passage, Jeremiah speaks for God, specifically asking the people to remember the covenant that God made with Israel many years ago. That covenant was exclusively at God's initiative. It can be summed up in the majestic pronouncement, "So shall you shall be my people, and I will be your God." That covenant is the basis for all that Jeremiah has said. It is because God owns Israel, loves Israel, and calls Israel that God is so demanding of Israel. The people of faith stand in a unique relationship with God, a relationship of call and response. God has faithfully promised; we are to respond in faith. Some of the community's best work of renovation and renewal is covenant remembrance. Some of the best sermons for a community to hear can be summed up as, "Remember who you are."

up out of the land of Egypt, warning them persistently, even to this day, saying, Obey my voice. [8]Yet they did not obey or incline their ear, but everyone walked in the stubbornness of an evil will. So I brought upon them all the words of this covenant, which I commanded them to do, but they did not.

9 And the LORD said to me: Conspiracy exists among the people of Judah and the inhabitants of Jerusalem. [10]They have turned back to the iniquities of their ancestors of old, who refused to heed my words; they have gone after other gods to serve them; the house of Israel and the house of Judah have broken the covenant that I made with their ancestors. [11]Therefore, thus says the LORD, assuredly I am going to bring disaster upon them that they cannot escape; though they cry out to me, I will not listen to them. [12]Then the cities of Judah and the inhabitants of Jerusalem will go and cry out to the gods to whom they make offerings, but they will never save them in the time of their trouble. [13]For your gods have become as many as your towns, O Judah; and as many as the streets of Jerusalem are the altars to shame you have set up, altars to make offerings to Baal.

14 As for you, do not pray for this people, or lift up a cry or prayer on their behalf, for I will not listen when they call to me in the time of their trouble. [15]What right has my beloved in my house, when she has done vile deeds? Can vows[a] and sacrificial flesh avert your doom? Can you then exult? [16]The LORD once called you, "A green olive tree, fair with goodly fruit"; but with the roar of a great tempest he will set fire to it, and its branches will be consumed. [17]The LORD of hosts, who planted you, has pronounced evil against you, because of the evil that the house of Israel and the house of Judah have done, provoking me to anger by making offerings to Baal.

Jeremiah's Life Threatened

[18] It was the LORD who made it known to
        me, and I knew;
    then you showed me their evil deeds.
[19] But I was like a gentle lamb
        led to the slaughter.
    And I did not know it was against me
        that they devised schemes, saying,
    "Let us destroy the tree with its fruit,
        let us cut him off from the land of the
            living,
        so that his name will no longer be
            remembered!"
[20] But you, O LORD of hosts, who judge
        righteously,
    who try the heart and the mind,
    let me see your retribution upon them,
        for to you I have committed my cause.

21 Therefore thus says the LORD concerning the people of Anathoth, who seek your life, and say, "You shall not prophesy in the name of the LORD, or you will die by our hand"—[22]therefore thus says the LORD of hosts: I am going to punish them; the young men shall die by the sword; their sons and their daughters shall die by famine; [23]and not even a remnant shall be left of them. For I will bring disaster upon the people of Anathoth, the year of their punishment.

Jeremiah Complains to God

12 You will be in the right, O LORD,
        when I lay charges against you;
    but let me put my case to you.

---

a Gk: Heb *Can many*

12:1–4 *let me put my case to you.* Here we are given an extraordinary glimpse into the soul of the prophet. This passage is one of Jeremiah's personal laments, in which the prophet complains about the ill treatment that he has received because he dared to speak for God. A plot has been hatched against his life. Jeremiah preached to the people the word that he had been given, "yet they did not obey or incline their ear" (11:8). The prophet is depressed. So Jeremiah becomes a prosecuting attorney putting the case against God. The prophet is so intimately connected with God that he can actually criticize and accuse God. It is important for contemporary servants of God to hear Jeremiah complain to God. God does not punish Jeremiah for his accusations. Rather, God receives the complaint, and the prophet and his God go on together. Anger, even anger directed against God, is not unthinkable in a prophet.

Why does the way of the guilty prosper?
Why do all who are treacherous
thrive?

2 You plant them, and they take root;
they grow and bring forth fruit;
you are near in their mouths
yet far from their hearts.

3 But you, O LORD, know me;
You see me and test me—my heart is
with you.
Pull them out like sheep for the
slaughter,
and set them apart for the day of
slaughter.

4 How long will the land mourn,
and the grass of every field wither?
For the wickedness of those who live in
it
the animals and the birds are swept
away,
and because people said, "He is blind
to our ways." a

God Replies to Jeremiah

5 If you have raced with foot-runners and
they have wearied you,
how will you compete with horses?
And if in a safe land you fall down,
how will you fare in the thickets of
the Jordan?

6 For even your kinsfolk and your own
family,
even they have dealt treacherously
with you;
they are in full cry after you;
do not believe them,

though they speak friendly words to
you.

7 I have forsaken my house,
I have abandoned my heritage;
I have given the beloved of my heart
into the hands of her enemies.

8 My heritage has become to me
like a lion in the forest;
she has lifted up her voice against me—
therefore I hate her.

9 Is the hyena greedy b for my heritage at
my command?
Are the birds of prey all around her?
Go, assemble all the wild animals;
bring them to devour her.

10 Many shepherds have destroyed my
vineyard,
they have trampled down my
portion,
they have made my pleasant portion
a desolate wilderness.

11 They have made it a desolation;
desolate, it mourns to me.
The whole land is made desolate,
but no one lays it to heart.

12 Upon all the bare heights c in the desert
spoilers have come;
for the sword of the LORD devours
from one end of the land to the other;
no one shall be safe.

13 They have sown wheat and have reaped
thorns,

a Gk: Heb to our future   b Cn: Heb Is the hyena,
the bird of prey   c Or the trails

12:1 Why does the way of the guilty prosper? The persistently repeated biblical question is rarely, "Why do bad things happen to good people?" but rather, "Why do good things keep happening to bad people?" At the beginning of chapter 12 Jeremiah does much complaining to God about the abuse that he has suffered, but first he complains about all the good things that have happened to his enemies and foes. God has some explaining to do! Note that God's response does not address Jeremiah's question. We hope therefore that Jeremiah at least feels somewhat better about the situation after his ranting and venting, because he has gotten no satisfactory response to his accusations and complaints. Sometimes, it's therapeutic just to be able to complain, though it does little for one's spiritual formation.

Responding
12:1 PRAYER. Jeremiah's question for God was why good things happen to bad people. Take time today to make a list of your most central God questions, your most troublesome gaps in understanding. Pray with your most pressing question at the forefront of your mind. Did you learn from the asking? See also Spiritual Disciplines Index.

they have tired themselves out but
   profit nothing.
They shall be ashamed of their[a]
   harvests
because of the fierce anger of the
   LORD.

14 Thus says the LORD concerning all my evil neighbors who touch the heritage that I have given my people Israel to inherit: I am about to pluck them up from their land, and I will pluck up the house of Judah from among them. 15And after I have plucked them up, I will again have compassion on them, and I will bring them again to their heritage and to their land, every one of them. 16And then, if they will diligently learn the ways of my people, to swear by my name, "As the LORD lives," as they taught my people to swear by Baal, then they shall be built up in the midst of my people. 17But if any nation will not listen, then I will completely uproot it and destroy it, says the LORD.

The Linen Loincloth

13 Thus said the LORD to me, "Go and buy yourself a linen loincloth, and put it on your loins, but do not dip it in water." 2So I bought a loincloth according to the word of the LORD, and put it on my loins. 3And the word of the LORD came to me a second time, saying, 4"Take the loincloth that you bought and are wearing, and go now to the Euphrates,[b] and hide it there in a cleft of the rock." 5So I went, and hid it by the Euphrates,[c] as the LORD commanded me. 6And after many days the LORD said to me, "Go now to the Euphrates,[b] and take from there the loincloth that I commanded you to hide

there." 7Then I went to the Euphrates,[b] and dug, and I took the loincloth from the place where I had hidden it. But now the loincloth was ruined; it was good for nothing.

8 Then the word of the LORD came to me: 9Thus says the LORD: Just so I will ruin the pride of Judah and the great pride of Jerusalem. 10This evil people, who refuse to hear my words, who stubbornly follow their own will and have gone after other gods to serve them and worship them, shall be like this loincloth, which is good for nothing. 11For as the loincloth clings to one's loins, so I made the whole house of Israel and the whole house of Judah cling to me, says the LORD, in order that they might be for me a people, a name, a praise, and a glory. But they would not listen.

Symbol of the Wine-Jars

12 You shall speak to them this word: Thus says the LORD, the God of Israel: Every wine-jar should be filled with wine. And they will say to you, "Do you think we do not know that every wine-jar should be filled with wine?" 13Then you shall say to them: Thus says the LORD: I am about to fill all the inhabitants of this land—the kings who sit on David's throne, the priests, the prophets, and all the inhabitants of Jerusalem—with drunkenness. 14And I will dash them one against another, parents and children together, says the LORD. I will not pity or spare or have compassion when I destroy them.

a Heb your   b Or to Parah; Heb perath   c Or by Parah; Heb perath

---

13:1–14 *a linen loincloth . . . every wine-jar.* These obscure parables seem to be somehow speaking to the issue of Babylonian supremacy over Judah, but it is difficult to say for sure just what they mean. Why would God speak to us with such obscure stories? Why did Jesus love to tell obscure parables that few people seemed able to understand? Perhaps such strange, enigmatic stories are reminders that God is God and we are not. Hard-to-understand Scripture reminds us of the gap between God and us.

Perhaps what God is trying to say to us is so high, so deep, and so grand that small minds like ours just can't get it. How do you like working with a God who refuses to put everything on the bottom shelf, who sometimes talks to us in ways that are far beyond our powers of comprehension? Is an enigmatic, difficult-to-interpret passage of Scripture a threat to us? Or is it an opportunity to savor the mystery, the gap between us and God?

Exile Threatened

15 Hear and give ear; do not be haughty,
   for the LORD has spoken.
16 Give glory to the LORD your God
      before he brings darkness,
   and before your feet stumble
      on the mountains at twilight;
   while you look for light,
      he turns it into gloom
      and makes it deep darkness.
17 But if you will not listen,
      my soul will weep in secret for your
         pride;
   my eyes will weep bitterly and run
         down with tears,
      because the LORD's flock has been
         taken captive.

18 Say to the king and the queen mother:
      "Take a lowly seat,
   for your beautiful crown
      has come down from your head."a
19 The towns of the Negeb are shut up
      with no one to open them;
   all Judah is taken into exile,
      wholly taken into exile.

20 Lift up your eyes and see
      those who come from the north.
   Where is the flock that was given you,
      your beautiful flock?
21 What will you say when they set as
         head over you
      those whom you have trained
      to be your allies?
   Will not pangs take hold of you,
      like those of a woman in labor?
22 And if you say in your heart,
      "Why have these things come upon
         me?"
   it is for the greatness of your iniquity
      that your skirts are lifted up,
      and you are violated.
23 Can Ethiopiansb change their skin
      or leopards their spots?
   Then also you can do good
      who are accustomed to do evil.
24 I will scatter youc like chaff
      driven by the wind from the desert.
25 This is your lot,

the portion I have measured out to
      you, says the LORD,
   because you have forgotten me
      and trusted in lies.
26 I myself will lift up your skirts over your
         face,
      and your shame will be seen.
27 I have seen your abominations,
      your adulteries and neighings, your
         shameless prostitutions
      on the hills of the countryside.
   Woe to you, O Jerusalem!
      How long will it be
   before you are made clean?

The Great Drought

14 The word of the LORD that came to
   Jeremiah concerning the drought:
2 Judah mourns
      and her gates languish;
   they lie in gloom on the ground,
      and the cry of Jerusalem goes up.
3 Her nobles send their servants for
         water;
      they come to the cisterns,
   they find no water,
      they return with their vessels empty.
   They are ashamed and dismayed
      and cover their heads,
4 because the ground is cracked.
   Because there has been no rain on the
         land
   the farmers are dismayed;
      they cover their heads.
5 Even the doe in the field forsakes her
         newborn fawn
      because there is no grass.
6 The wild asses stand on the bare
         heights,d
      they pant for air like jackals;
   their eyes fail
      because there is no herbage.

7 Although our iniquities testify against
         us,
      act, O LORD, for your name's sake;
   our apostasies indeed are many,
      and we have sinned against you.

---

a Gk Syr Vg: Meaning of Heb uncertain
b Or *Nubians*; Heb *Cushites*   c Heb *them*
d Or *the trails*

8 O hope of Israel,
      its savior in time of trouble,
   why should you be like a stranger in the
         land,
      like a traveler turning aside for the
         night?
9 Why should you be like someone
         confused,
      like a mighty warrior who cannot give
         help?
   Yet you, O LORD, are in the midst of us,
      and we are called by your name;
      do not forsake us!

10 Thus says the LORD concerning this
         people:
   Truly they have loved to wander,
      they have not restrained their feet;
   therefore the LORD does not accept
         them,
      now he will remember their iniquity
   and punish their sins.

11 The LORD said to me: Do not pray for the
welfare of this people. 12Although they fast,
I do not hear their cry, and although they
offer burnt offering and grain offering, I do
not accept them; but by the sword, by famine,
and by pestilence I consume them.

Denunciation of Lying Prophets

13 Then I said: "Ah, Lord GOD! Here are the
prophets saying to them, 'You shall not see
the sword, nor shall you have famine, but I
will give you true peace in this place.'" 14And
the LORD said to me: The prophets are prophesying lies in my name; I did not send them,
nor did I command them or speak to them.
They are prophesying to you a lying vision,
worthless divination, and the deceit of their
own minds. 15Therefore thus says the LORD
concerning the prophets who prophesy in
my name though I did not send them, and
who say, "Sword and famine shall not come
on this land": By sword and famine those
prophets shall be consumed. 16And the people to whom they prophesy shall be thrown
out into the streets of Jerusalem, victims of
famine and sword. There shall be no one to
bury them—themselves, their wives, their
sons, and their daughters. For I will pour out
their wickedness upon them.

17 You shall say to them this word:
   Let my eyes run down with tears night
         and day,
      and let them not cease,
   for the virgin daughter—my people—is
         struck down with a crushing
         blow,
      with a very grievous wound.
18 If I go out into the field,
      look—those killed by the sword!
   And if I enter the city,
      look—those sick with a famine!
   For both prophet and priest ply their
         trade throughout the land,
      and have no knowledge.

The People Plead for Mercy

19 Have you completely rejected Judah?
      Does your heart loathe Zion?
   Why have you struck us down
      so that there is no healing for us?
   We look for peace, but find no good;
      for a time of healing, but there is
         terror instead.
20 We acknowledge our wickedness,
         O LORD,
      the iniquity of our ancestors,
      for we have sinned against you.
21 Do not spurn us, for your name's sake;
      do not dishonor your glorious throne;
      remember and do not break your
         covenant with us.
22 Can any idols of the nations bring rain?
      Or can the heavens give showers?
   Is it not you, O LORD our God?
      We set our hope on you,
      for it is you who do all this.

Punishment Is Inevitable

15 Then the LORD said to me: Though
      Moses and Samuel stood before me,
yet my heart would not turn toward this peo-

a Heb look—the sicknesses of

14:12 FASTING—See Spiritual Disciplines Index.

ple. Send them out of my sight, and let them go! [2]And when they say to you, "Where shall we go?" you shall say to them: Thus says the LORD:

> Those destined for pestilence, to
> pestilence,
> and those destined for the sword, to
> the sword;
> those destined for famine, to famine,
> and those destined for captivity, to
> captivity.

[3]And I will appoint over them four kinds of destroyers, says the LORD: the sword to kill, the dogs to drag away, and the birds of the air and the wild animals of the earth to devour and destroy. [4]I will make them a horror to all the kingdoms of the earth because of what King Manasseh son of Hezekiah of Judah did in Jerusalem.

> [5] Who will have pity on you,
>   O Jerusalem,
>   or who will bemoan you?
> Who will turn aside
>   to ask about your welfare?
> [6] You have rejected me, says the LORD,
>   you are going backward;
> so I have stretched out my hand against
>   you and destroyed you—
>   I am weary of relenting.
> [7] I have winnowed them with a
>   winnowing fork
>   in the gates of the land;
> I have bereaved them, I have destroyed
>   my people;
>   they did not turn from their ways.
> [8] Their widows became more numerous
>   than the sand of the seas;
> I have brought against the mothers of
>   youths

> a destroyer at noonday;
> I have made anguish and terror
>   fall upon her suddenly.
> [9] She who bore seven has languished;
>   she has swooned away;
> her sun went down while it was yet day;
>   she has been shamed and disgraced.
> And the rest of them I will give to the
>   sword
>   before their enemies,
>   says the LORD.

Jeremiah Complains Again and Is Reassured

[10] Woe is me, my mother, that you ever bore me, a man of strife and contention to the whole land! I have not lent, nor have I borrowed, yet all of them curse me. [11]The LORD said: Surely I have intervened in your life[a] for good, surely I have imposed enemies on you in a time of trouble and in a time of distress.[b] [12]Can iron and bronze break iron from the north?

[13] Your wealth and your treasures I will give as plunder, without price, for all your sins, throughout all your territory. [14]I will make you serve your enemies in a land that you do not know, for in my anger a fire is kindled that shall burn forever.

> [15] O LORD, you know;
>   remember me and visit me,
>   and bring down retribution for me on
>   my persecutors.
>   In your forbearance do not take me away;
>   know that on your account I suffer
>   insult.
> [16] Your words were found, and I ate them,

a Heb intervened with you   b Meaning of Heb uncertain

15:16–18 *Your words were found, and I ate them.* Jeremiah has been made a prophet, a spokesperson for the truth, because God's word came to him. At first that word was sweet delight. He devoured those good words. Yet because the prophet has dared to utter those words—all of them, including the ones not so sweet—he bears a heavy burden; he is alone. He has had to deliver the hard news that Israel is about to go into exile (chaps 13–14). Here we hear about the cost of fidelity to the truth of God. The blessing of divine vocation can also be a great burden. Those who work for God, who dare to say yes to the divine summons, who dare to speak up for God, are often persecuted, victimized, and made lonely. It is good for us to be reminded, by Jeremiah's lament, of the cost of faithful discipleship and good to ask ourselves: Are we prepared to bear such a burden?

and your words became to me a joy
and the delight of my heart;
for I am called by your name,
O Lord, God of hosts.
17 I did not sit in the company of
merrymakers,
nor did I rejoice;
under the weight of your hand I sat
alone,
for you had filled me with
indignation.
18 Why is my pain unceasing,
my wound incurable,
refusing to be healed?
Truly, you are to me like a deceitful
brook,
like waters that fail.

19 Therefore thus says the Lord:
If you turn back, I will take you back,
and you shall stand before me.
If you utter what is precious, and not
what is worthless,
you shall serve as my mouth.
It is they who will turn to you,
not you who will turn to them.
20 And I will make you to this people
a fortified wall of bronze;
they will fight against you,
but they shall not prevail over you,
for I am with you
to save you and deliver you,
says the Lord.
21 I will deliver you out of the hand of the
wicked,
and redeem you from the grasp of the
ruthless.

Jeremiah's Celibacy and Message

16 The word of the Lord came to me: 2You shall not take a wife, nor shall you have sons or daughters in this place. 3For thus says the Lord concerning the sons and daughters who are born in this place, and concerning the mothers who bear them and the fathers who beget them in this land: 4They shall die of deadly diseases. They shall not be lamented, nor shall they be buried; they shall become like dung on the surface of the ground. They shall perish by the sword and by famine, and their dead bodies shall become food for the birds of the air and for the wild animals of the earth.

5 For thus says the Lord: Do not enter the house of mourning, or go to lament, or bemoan them; for I have taken away my peace from this people, says the Lord, my steadfast love and mercy. 6Both great and small shall die in this land; they shall not be buried, and no one shall lament for them; there shall be no gashing, no shaving of the head for them. 7No one shall break bread*a* for the mourner, to offer comfort for the dead; nor shall anyone give them the cup of consolation to drink for their fathers or their mothers. 8You shall not go into the house of feasting to sit with them, to eat and drink. 9For thus says the Lord of hosts, the God of Israel: I am going to banish from this place, in your days and before your eyes, the voice of mirth and the voice of gladness, the voice of the bridegroom and the voice of the bride.

10 And when you tell this people all these words, and they say to you, "Why has the Lord pronounced all this great evil against us? What is our iniquity? What is the sin that

a Two Mss Gk: MT *break for them*

Responding

15:16–18 SOLITUDE. As the lives of the prophets so richly illustrate, divine vocation does not always lead to earthly happiness, but it does often lead to solitude. Why are those so close to God so intimate with solitude? What is the difference between loneliness and solitude as experienced by the prophets? *See also* Spiritual Disciplines Index.

15:19–21 *If you utter what is precious.* God follows up on Jeremiah's eloquent lament with reiterated demands. Though the going is hard for the prophet, God continues to demand great things from his servant of the word. Discipleship is not easy, not filled with rewards. People will fight against the truth. Yet the promise is also reiterated: God shall not desert those who are faithful and love God's truth more than public praise.

we have committed against the LORD our God?" 11then you shall say to them: It is because your ancestors have forsaken me, says the LORD, and have gone after other gods and have served and worshiped them, and have forsaken me and have not kept my law; 12and because you have behaved worse than your ancestors, for here you are, every one of you, following your stubborn evil will, refusing to listen to me. 13Therefore I will hurl you out of this land into a land that neither you nor your ancestors have known, and there you shall serve other gods day and night, for I will show you no favor.

God Will Restore Israel

14 Therefore, the days are surely coming, says the LORD, when it shall no longer be said, "As the LORD lives who brought the people of Israel up out of the land of Egypt," 15but "As the LORD lives who brought the people of Israel up out of the land of the north and out of all the lands where he had driven them." For I will bring them back to their own land that I gave to their ancestors.

16 I am now sending for many fishermen, says the LORD, and they shall catch them; and afterward I will send for many hunters, and they shall hunt them from every mountain and every hill, and out of the clefts of the rocks. 17For my eyes are on all their ways; they are not hidden from my presence, nor is their iniquity concealed from my sight. 18And a I will doubly repay their iniquity and their sin, because they have polluted my land with the carcasses of their detestable idols, and have filled my inheritance with their abominations.

19 O LORD, my strength and my
      stronghold,
   my refuge in the day of trouble,
to you shall the nations come
      from the ends of the earth and say:
Our ancestors have inherited nothing
      but lies,
   worthless things in which there is no
      profit.
20 Can mortals make for themselves gods?
   Such are no gods!

21 "Therefore I am surely going to teach them, this time I am going to teach them my power and my might, and they shall know that my name is the LORD."

Judah's Sin and Punishment

17 The sin of Judah is written with an iron pen; with a diamond point it is engraved on the tablet of their hearts, and on the horns of their altars, 2while their children remember their altars and their sacred poles, b beside every green tree, and on the high hills, 3on the mountains in the open country. Your wealth and all your treasures I will give for spoil as the price of your sin c throughout all your territory. 4By your own act you shall lose the heritage that I gave you, and I will make you serve your enemies in a land that you do not know, for in my anger a fire is kindled d that shall burn forever.

5 Thus says the LORD:
   Cursed are those who trust in mere
      mortals
      and make mere flesh their strength,
      whose hearts turn away from the
         LORD.
6 They shall be like a shrub in the desert,
      and shall not see when relief comes.
   They shall live in the parched places of
         the wilderness,
      in an uninhabited salt land.

7 Blessed are those who trust in the LORD,
      whose trust is the LORD.
8 They shall be like a tree planted by
         water,
      sending out its roots by the stream.
   It shall not fear when heat comes,
      and its leaves shall stay green;
   in the year of drought it is not anxious,
      and it does not cease to bear fruit.

9 The heart is devious above all else;
      it is perverse—
      who can understand it?
10 I the LORD test the mind
      and search the heart,

a Gk: Heb *And first*   b Heb *Asherim*
c Cn: Heb *spoil your high places for sin*   d Two
Mss Theodotion: *you kindled*

to give to all according to their ways,
  according to the fruit of their doings.

11 Like the partridge hatching what it did
    not lay,
  so are all who amass wealth unjustly;
in mid-life it will leave them,
  and at their end they will prove to be
    fools.

12 O glorious throne, exalted from the
    beginning,
  shrine of our sanctuary!
13 O hope of Israel! O LORD!
  All who forsake you shall be put to
    shame;
  those who turn away from you[a] shall be
    recorded in the underworld,[b]
  for they have forsaken the fountain of
    living water, the LORD.

Jeremiah Prays for Vindication

14 Heal me, O LORD, and I shall be healed;
  save me, and I shall be saved;
  for you are my praise.
15 See how they say to me,
  "Where is the word of the LORD?
  Let it come!"
16 But I have not run away from being a
    shepherd[c] in your service,
  nor have I desired the fatal day.
  You know what came from my lips;
  it was before your face.
17 Do not become a terror to me;
  you are my refuge in the day of
    disaster;
18 Let my persecutors be shamed,
  but do not let me be shamed;
let them be dismayed,
  but do not let me be dismayed;
bring on them the day of disaster;
  destroy them with double
    destruction!

Hallow the Sabbath Day

19 Thus said the LORD to me: Go and stand
in the People's Gate, by which the kings of Ju-

dah enter and by which they go out, and in
all the gates of Jerusalem, 20and say to them:
Hear the word of the LORD, you kings of Judah, and all Judah, and all the inhabitants of
Jerusalem, who enter by these gates. 21Thus
says the LORD: For the sake of your lives, take
care that you do not bear a burden on the
sabbath day or bring it in by the gates of Jerusalem. 22And do not carry a burden out of
your houses on the sabbath or do any work,
but keep the sabbath day holy, as I commanded your ancestors. 23Yet they did not listen or incline their ear; they stiffened their
necks and would not hear or receive instruction.

24 But if you listen to me, says the LORD,
and bring in no burden by the gates of this
city on the sabbath day, but keep the sabbath day holy and do no work on it, 25then
there shall enter by the gates of this city
kings[d] who sit on the throne of David, riding
in chariots and on horses, they and their officials, the people of Judah and the inhabitants of Jerusalem; and this city shall be inhabited forever. 26And people shall come
from the towns of Judah and the places
around Jerusalem, from the land of Benjamin, from the Shephelah, from the hill country, and from the Negeb, bringing burnt offerings and sacrifices, grain offerings and
frankincense, and bringing thank offerings to
the house of the LORD. 27But if you do not
listen to me, to keep the sabbath day holy,
and to carry in no burden through the gates
of Jerusalem on the sabbath day, then I will
kindle a fire in its gates; it shall devour the palaces of Jerusalem and shall not be quenched.

The Potter and the Clay

18 The word that came to Jeremiah from
the LORD: 2"Come, go down to the
potter's house, and there I will let you hear
my words." 3So I went down to the potter's
house, and there he was working at his wheel.

a Heb *me*   b Or *in the earth*   c Meaning of
Heb uncertain   d Cn: Heb *kings and officials*

18:1–6 *Come, go down to the potter's house.*
The prophets specialize in not only vivid speech
but also vivid actions. Jeremiah is told to observe

a potter at work and to take this as a symbol
for God's work with the covenant community.
Paul will use the same image, relating it to the

⁴The vessel he was making of clay was spoiled in the potter's hand, and he reworked it into another vessel, as seemed good to him.

5 Then the word of the LORD came to me: ⁶Can I not do with you, O house of Israel, just as this potter has done? says the LORD. Just like the clay in the potter's hand, so are you in my hand, O house of Israel. ⁷At one moment I may declare concerning a nation or a kingdom, that I will pluck up and break down and destroy it, ⁸but if that nation, concerning which I have spoken, turns from its evil, I will change my mind about the disaster that I intended to bring on it. ⁹And at another moment I may declare concerning a nation or a kingdom that I will build and plant it, ¹⁰but if it does evil in my sight, not listening to my voice, then I will change my mind about the good that I had intended to do to it. ¹¹Now, therefore, say to the people of Judah and the inhabitants of Jerusalem: Thus says the LORD: Look, I am a potter shaping evil against you and devising a plan against you. Turn now, all of you from your evil way, and amend your ways and your doings.

Israel's Stubborn Idolatry

12 But they say, "It is no use! We will follow our own plans, and each of us will act according to the stubbornness of our evil will."

¹³ Therefore thus says the LORD:
  Ask among the nations:
    Who has heard the like of this?
  The virgin Israel has done
    a most horrible thing.
¹⁴ Does the snow of Lebanon leave
    the crags of Sirion?ᵃ
  Do the mountainᵇ waters run dry,ᶜ
    the cold flowing streams?
¹⁵ But my people have forgotten me,

they burn offerings to a delusion;
  theyᵈ have stumbledᵈ in their ways,
    in the ancient roads,
  and have gone into bypaths,
    not the highway,
¹⁶ making their land a horror,
    a thing to be hissed at forever.
  All who pass by it are horrified
    and shake their heads.
¹⁷ Like the wind from the east,
    I will scatter them before the enemy.
  I will show them my back, not my face,
    in the day of their calamity.

A Plot against Jeremiah

18 Then they said, "Come, let us make plots against Jeremiah—for instruction shall not perish from the priest, nor counsel from the wise, nor the word from the prophet. Come, let us bring charges against him,ᵉ and let us not heed any of his words."

¹⁹ Give heed to me, O LORD,
    and listen to what my adversaries say!
²⁰ Is evil a recompense for good?
    Yet they have dug a pit for my life.
  Remember how I stood before you
    to speak good for them,
    to turn away your wrath from them.
²¹ Therefore give their children over to
        famine;
  hurl them out to the power of the
        sword,
  let their wives become childless and
        widowed.
  May their men meet death by
        pestilence,

ᵃ Cn: Heb *of the field*   ᵇ Cn: Heb *foreign*
ᶜ Cn: Heb *Are . . . plucked up?*   ᵈ Gk Syr Vg: Heb
they made them stumble   ᵉ Heb *strike him with the
tongue*

Church, in Rom 9:20–24. God is busy molding, forming, pushing, and pulling Israel into shape, just as a potter shapes clay. God is not passive, but actively forming the community in unseen and unacknowledged but powerful ways. Jeremiah's words to the faithless but potentially faithful community are themselves an example of a creative, resourceful God at work. In the next chapter (19:1–2, 10) Jeremiah will be told to

buy a pot, stand in a public place in Jerusalem, and throw the pot to the ground, smashing it into pieces—this is what God is going to do to a faithless nation. But for now, he is to watch a potter at work. See the potter knead, pound, pull, then lovingly and delicately shape the clay into a beautiful, useful, durable vessel? That's what God is doing with us! That's the work of spiritual formation!

their youths be slain by the sword in
    battle.
22 May a cry be heard from their houses,
    when you bring the marauder
      suddenly upon them!
For they have dug a pit to catch me,
    and laid snares for my feet.
23 Yet you, O LORD, know
    all their plotting to kill me.
Do not forgive their iniquity,
    do not blot out their sin from your
      sight.
Let them be tripped up before you;
    deal with them while you are angry.

The Broken Earthenware Jug

19 Thus said the LORD: Go and buy a potter's earthenware jug. Take with you*a*
some of the elders of the people and some of
the senior priests, 2and go out to the valley of
the son of Hinnom at the entry of the Potsherd Gate, and proclaim there the words
that I tell you. 3You shall say: Hear the word
of the LORD, O kings of Judah and inhabitants of Jerusalem. Thus says the LORD of
hosts, the God of Israel: I am going to bring
such disaster upon this place that the ears of
everyone who hears of it will tingle. 4Because
the people have forsaken me, and have profaned this place by making offerings in it to
other gods whom neither they nor their ancestors nor the kings of Judah have known,
and because they have filled this place with
the blood of the innocent, 5and gone on
building the high places of Baal to burn their
children in the fire as burnt offerings to Baal,
which I did not command or decree, nor did
it enter my mind; 6therefore the days are surely coming, says the LORD, when this place
shall no more be called Topheth, or the valley of the son of Hinnom, but the valley of
Slaughter. 7And in this place I will make void
the plans of Judah and Jerusalem, and will
make them fall by the sword before their enemies, and by the hand of those who seek
their life. I will give their dead bodies for food
to the birds of the air and to the wild animals of the earth. 8And I will make this city
a horror, a thing to be hissed at; everyone
who passes by it will be horrified and will
hiss because of all its disasters. 9And I will

make them eat the flesh of their sons and
the flesh of their daughters, and all shall eat
the flesh of their neighbors in the siege, and
in the distress with which their enemies and
those who seek their life afflict them.

10 Then you shall break the jug in the
sight of those who go with you, 11and shall
say to them: Thus says the LORD of hosts: So
will I break this people and this city, as one
breaks a potter's vessel, so that it can never be
mended. In Topheth they shall bury until
there is no more room to bury. 12Thus will I
do to this place, says the LORD, and to its inhabitants, making this city like Topheth.
13And the houses of Jerusalem and the houses
of the kings of Judah shall be defiled like the
place of Topheth—all the houses upon whose
roofs offerings have been made to the whole
host of heaven, and libations have been
poured out to other gods.

14 When Jeremiah came from Topheth,
where the LORD had sent him to prophesy, he
stood in the court of the LORD's house and
said to all the people: 15Thus says the LORD of
hosts, the God of Israel: I am now bringing
upon this city and upon all its towns all the
disaster that I have pronounced against it,
because they have stiffened their necks, refusing to hear my words.

Jeremiah Persecuted by Pashhur

20 Now the priest Pashhur son of Immer, who was chief officer in the
house of the LORD, heard Jeremiah prophesying these things. 2Then Pashhur struck the
prophet Jeremiah, and put him in the stocks
that were in the upper Benjamin Gate of the
house of the LORD. 3The next morning when
Pashhur released Jeremiah from the stocks,
Jeremiah said to him, The LORD has named
you not Pashhur but "Terror-all-around." 4For
thus says the LORD: I am making you a terror
to yourself and to all your friends; and they
shall fall by the sword of their enemies while
you look on. And I will give all Judah into
the hand of the king of Babylon; he shall carry them captive to Babylon, and shall kill
them with the sword. 5I will give all the
wealth of this city, all its gains, all its prized

a Syr Tg Compare Gk: Heb lacks *take with you*

belongings, and all the treasures of the kings of Judah into the hand of their enemies, who shall plunder them, and seize them, and carry them to Babylon. 6And you, Pashhur, and all who live in your house, shall go into captivity, and to Babylon you shall go; there you shall die, and there you shall be buried, you and all your friends, to whom you have prophesied falsely.

Jeremiah Denounces His Persecutors

7 O Lord, you have enticed me,
    and I was enticed;
  you have overpowered me,
    and you have prevailed.
  I have become a laughingstock all day
      long;
    everyone mocks me.
8 For whenever I speak, I must cry out,
    I must shout, "Violence and
        destruction!"
  For the word of the Lord has become for
      me
    a reproach and derision all day long.
9 If I say, "I will not mention him,
    or speak any more in his name,"
  then within me there is something like
      a burning fire

shut up in my bones;
  I am weary with holding it in,
    and I cannot.
10 For I hear many whispering:
    "Terror is all around!
  Denounce him! Let us denounce him!"
    All my close friends
    are watching for me to stumble.
  "Perhaps he can be enticed,
    and we can prevail against him,
    and take our revenge on him."
11 But the Lord is with me like a dread
      warrior;
  therefore my persecutors will
      stumble,
    and they will not prevail.
  They will be greatly shamed,
    for they will not succeed.
  Their eternal dishonor
    will never be forgotten.
12 O Lord of hosts, you test the righteous,
    you see the heart and the mind;
  let me see your retribution upon them,
    for to you I have committed my cause.

13 Sing to the Lord;
    praise the Lord!

20:7–9 *I have become a laughingstock all day long.* This is an eloquent depiction of the prophet's plight. He accuses God of seducing him, of wrestling him into submission (exchanges between God and his servants can be passionate and honest). As a result of God's enticement, the prophet is mocked by the world. His pain is more than private. Just as God has staked much on Israel, so God stakes much on the words and deeds of the prophet. The world looks on and mocks. Most of the news that Jeremiah has to deliver is bad news and the world, in its ways, does not gladly receive bad news. Yet despite the public abuse, the prophet can't keep silent. God's word is like "a burning fire" within him, and he must speak. The People of God tell the truth about the world not because they like to, but because they must.

20:12–14 *you test the righteous . . . praise the Lord! . . . Cursed be the day.* Consistency and constancy are not the highest virtues, particularly for people like Jeremiah who are

under terrible threat and in much distress. In the short space of three verses Jeremiah shuttles from accusation against God for putting his servants to the test, to singing praise to the Lord, then to cursing the very day on which he was born. This movement forms the transition between two of Jeremiah's laments. His faith is anything but "firm," "solid," and "unwavering," those virtues that we often ascribe to folk of faith. Jeremiah's faith is best called honest. When assailed by foes without and fears within, this is how faithful people often feel. They are able to move from accusation to praise to depression—all in the space of a day! Is this a sign of uncertain, unsteady faith or a sign of deep, truthful, honest relationship with God? Let us claim the latter. Let us be formed by the candor of Jeremiah in his conversations with God. Let us pray for an equally honest relationship with our Creator, Redeemer, and Sustainer, even when God's creativity, redemption, and sustenance hurt.

For he has delivered the life of the
 needy
   from the hands of evildoers.

14 Cursed be the day
   on which I was born!
The day when my mother bore me,
   let it not be blessed!
15 Cursed be the man
   who brought the news to my father,
      saying,
"A child is born to you, a son,"
   making him very glad.
16 Let that man be like the cities
   that the LORD overthrew without pity;
let him hear a cry in the morning
   and an alarm at noon,
17 because he did not kill me in the womb;
   so my mother would have been my
      grave,
   and her womb forever great.
18 Why did I come forth from the womb
   to see toil and sorrow,
      and spend my days in shame?

Jerusalem Will Fall to Nebuchadrezzar

21 This is the word that came to Jeremiah
   from the LORD, when King Zedekiah
sent to him Pashhur son of Malchiah and the
priest Zephaniah son of Maaseiah, saying,
2 "Please inquire of the LORD on our behalf, for
King Nebuchadrezzar of Babylon is making
war against us; perhaps the LORD will perform
a wonderful deed for us, as he has often done,
and will make him withdraw from us."

3 Then Jeremiah said to them: 4 Thus you
shall say to Zedekiah: Thus says the LORD,
the God of Israel: I am going to turn back the
weapons of war that are in your hands and
with which you are fighting against the king
of Babylon and against the Chaldeans who
are besieging you outside the walls; and I will
bring them together into the center of this
city. 5 I myself will fight against you with outstretched hand and mighty arm, in anger, in
fury, and in great wrath. 6 And I will strike
down the inhabitants of this city, both human beings and animals; they shall die of a
great pestilence. 7 Afterward, says the LORD, I
will give King Zedekiah of Judah, and his servants, and the people in this city—those who
survive the pestilence, sword, and famine—
into the hands of King Nebuchadrezzar of
Babylon, into the hands of their enemies,
into the hands of those who seek their lives.
He shall strike them down with the edge of
the sword; he shall not pity them, or spare
them, or have compassion.

8 And to this people you shall say: Thus
says the LORD: See, I am setting before you
the way of life and the way of death. 9 Those
who stay in this city shall die by the sword, by

21:1–10 *King Nebuchadrezzar of Babylon is
making war against us.* The prophets of Israel
do not speak words just about religion. They
talk about everything. Nothing in the life of this
world is excluded from the prophetic purview,
even politics. Suddenly Jeremiah shifts from
high-flown poetry about his relationship with
God (chap 20) to the grubby realities of political
maneuvering. King Zedekiah is desperate. He
has his back against the wall. So now he turns
to God, sending Jeremiah to inquire of Pashhur
and a priest named Zephaniah. But what
Jeremiah has to say to the scheming king is not
what the king wants to hear. (Those were the
days when preachers did not mind confronting
politicians and telling them off, no matter what.)
Jeremiah tells the king it is too late for such
calculated use of religion for political ends—
God is sovereign and will not be enlisted in

national projects. God even says that he will
take up arms against the covenant people and
fight on the side of the Babylonians (vv 5–6)! In
a day in which our own nation seeks "national
security" in our weapons, arms, and armies, let
us heed the politics of Jeremiah. The God
proclaimed here is not a national patron, a pet
for our national aspirations, or a guard against
our national fears. This God is free, sovereign,
and true. In times of national difficulty, the
rulers turn to God, invoking his name and
praying for his blessings. But this God will not
be so used and abused. The rulers go to God
asking for more blessings and benefits only to
hear God say, through the prophet, "I will punish
you according to the fruit of your doings" (v 14).
It's then that the politicians often tell the
preacher to "stick to religion and stay out of
politics."

famine, and by pestilence; but those who go out and surrender to the Chaldeans who are besieging you shall live and shall have their lives as a prize of war. [10]For I have set my face against this city for evil and not for good, says the LORD: it shall be given into the hands of the king of Babylon, and he shall burn it with fire.

Message to the House of David

[11] To the house of the king of Judah say: Hear the word of the LORD, [12]O house of David! Thus says the LORD:

Execute justice in the morning,
    and deliver from the hand of the
        oppressor
anyone who has been robbed,
    or else my wrath will go forth like fire,
    and burn, with no one to quench it,
    because of your evil doings.

[13] See, I am against you, O inhabitant of
        the valley,
    O rock of the plain,
                    says the LORD;
you who say, "Who can come down
        against us,
    or who can enter our places of refuge?"
[14] I will punish you according to the fruit
        of your doings,
                    says the LORD;
I will kindle a fire in its forest,
    and it shall devour all that is around it.

Exhortation to Repent

22 Thus says the LORD: Go down to the house of the king of Judah, and speak there this word, [2]and say: Hear the word of the LORD, O King of Judah sitting on the throne of David—you, and your servants, and your people who enter these gates. [3]Thus says the LORD: Act with justice and righteousness, and deliver from the hand of the oppressor anyone who has been robbed. And do no wrong or violence to the alien, the orphan, and the widow, or shed innocent blood

in this place. [4]For if you will indeed obey this word, then through the gates of this house shall enter kings who sit on the throne of David, riding in chariots and on horses, they, and their servants, and their people. [5]But if you will not heed these words, I swear by myself, says the LORD, that this house shall become a desolation. [6]For thus says the LORD concerning the house of the king of Judah:

You are like Gilead to me,
    like the summit of Lebanon;
but I swear that I will make you a desert,
    an uninhabited city. [a]
[7] I will prepare destroyers against you,
    all with their weapons;
they shall cut down your choicest cedars
    and cast them into the fire.

[8] And many nations will pass by this city, and all of them will say one to another, "Why has the LORD dealt in this way with that great city?" [9]And they will answer, "Because they abandoned the covenant of the LORD their God, and worshiped other gods and served them."

[10] Do not weep for him who is dead,
    nor bemoan him;
weep rather for him who goes away,
    for he shall return no more
    to see his native land.

Message to the Sons of Josiah

[11] For thus says the LORD concerning Shallum son of King Josiah of Judah, who succeeded his father Josiah, and who went away from this place: He shall return here no more, [12]but in the place where they have carried him captive he shall die, and he shall never see this land again.

[13] Woe to him who builds his house by
        unrighteousness,
    and his upper rooms by injustice;
who makes his neighbors work for
        nothing,

a Cn: Heb *uninhabited cities*

22:13–17 *Woe to him who builds his house by unrighteousness.* Once again, the prophets of Israel do not confine themselves to matters of

religion. Having wandered into the cesspool that is politics, now the prophet attacks economics. What the covenant community is apt to interpret

and does not give them their wages;
14 who says, "I will build myself a spacious
      house
    with large upper rooms,"
  and who cuts out windows for it,
    paneling it with cedar,
    and painting it with vermilion.
15 Are you a king
    because you compete in cedar?
  Did not your father eat and drink
    and do justice and righteousness?
  Then it was well with him.
16 He judged the cause of the poor and
      needy;
    then it was well.
  Is not this to know me?
    says the LORD.
17 But your eyes and heart
    are only on your dishonest gain,
  for shedding innocent blood,
    and for practicing oppression and·
      violence.
18 Therefore thus says the LORD concerning King Jehoiakim son of Josiah of Judah:
  They shall not lament for him, saying,
    "Alas, my brother!" or "Alas, sister!"
  They shall not lament for him, saying,
    "Alas, lord!" or "Alas, his majesty!"
19 With the burial of a donkey he shall be
      buried—
    dragged off and thrown out beyond
      the gates of Jerusalem.

20 Go up to Lebanon, and cry out,
    and lift up your voice in Bashan;
  cry out from Abarim,
    for all your lovers are crushed.

21 I spoke to you in your prosperity,
    but you said, "I will not listen."
  This has been your way from your youth,
    for you have not obeyed my voice.
22 The wind shall shepherd all your
      shepherds,
    and your lovers shall go into captivity;
  then you will be ashamed and dismayed
    because of all your wickedness.
23 O inhabitant of Lebanon,
    nested among the cedars,
  how you will groan *a* when pangs come
      upon you,
    pain as of a woman in labor!

Judgment on Coniah (Jehoiachin)

24 As I live, says the LORD, even if King
Coniah son of Jehoiakim of Judah were the
signet ring on my right hand, even from there
I would tear you off 25and give you into the
hands of those who seek your life, into the
hands of those of whom you are afraid, even
into the hands of King Nebuchadrezzar of
Babylon and into the hands of the Chaldeans. 26I will hurl you and the mother who
bore you into another country, where you
were not born, and there you shall die. 27But
they shall not return to the land to which
they long to return.
28 Is this man Coniah a despised broken
      pot,
    a vessel no one wants?
  Why are he and his offspring hurled out
    and cast away in a land that they do
      not know?

a Gk Vg Syr: Heb *will be pitied*

---

as a temporary national setback, a crisis in
homeland security, a time of governmental
instability, the prophet calls a failure to worship
the true and living God. We say, "Business is
business." The prophet says, "All our business is
God's business." The prophet will not allow
matters of economics to be kept sealed off and
safe from the judging, searing gaze of God. The
faith community that allows its religious
imagination to become mired in things
exclusively "spiritual," that confines issues of
"spirit" to those relatively insignificant personal,
private, and subjective concerns, is not being

faithful to the God who speaks through
Jeremiah. For Jesus, bread is a spiritual issue.
Where our money is, our hearts are. Jesus was,
in this, a true prophet in the lineage of
Jeremiah. Imagine a preacher asking, in a
sermon, "Do you want to know why our nation
suffered the terrorist attack of 9/11? I'll tell you.
Because of our treatment of the poor, because
of the inequities in our economic life, the
disparities between executive salaries and those
of the workers—that is why we are in the fix we
are in." Imagine that sort of sermon and you will
realize why Jeremiah's life is in danger.

²⁹ O land, land, land,
     hear the word of the LORD!
³⁰ Thus says the LORD:
   Record this man as childless,
      a man who shall not succeed in his
         days;
   for none of his offspring shall succeed
      in sitting on the throne of David,
      and ruling again in Judah.

Restoration after Exile

23 Woe to the shepherds who destroy
and scatter the sheep of my pasture!
says the LORD. ²Therefore thus says the LORD,
the God of Israel, concerning the shepherds
who shepherd my people: It is you who have
scattered my flock, and have driven them
away, and you have not attended to them.
So I will attend to you for your evil doings,
says the LORD. ³Then I myself will gather the
remnant of my flock out of all the lands
where I have driven them, and I will bring
them back to their fold, and they shall be
fruitful and multiply. ⁴I will raise up shepherds over them who will shepherd them,
and they shall not fear any longer, or be dismayed, nor shall any be missing, says the
LORD.

The Righteous Branch of David

5 The days are surely coming, says the
LORD, when I will raise up for David a righteous Branch, and he shall reign as king and
deal wisely, and shall execute justice and righteousness in the land. ⁶In his days Judah will
be saved and Israel will live in safety. And
this is the name by which he will be called:
"The LORD is our righteousness."

7 Therefore, the days are surely coming,
says the LORD, when it shall no longer be said,
"As the LORD lives who brought the people of
Israel up out of the land of Egypt," ⁸but "As
the LORD lives who brought out and led the
offspring of the house of Israel out of the
land of the north and out of all the lands
where he ^a had driven them." Then they shall
live in their own land.

False Prophets of Hope Denounced

9 Concerning the prophets:
   My heart is crushed within me,
      all my bones shake;
   I have become like a drunkard,
      like one overcome by wine,
   because of the LORD
      and because of his holy words.
¹⁰ For the land is full of adulterers;
      because of the curse the land mourns,
      and the pastures of the wilderness are
         dried up.
   Their course has been evil,
      and their might is not right.
¹¹ Both prophet and priest are ungodly;
      even in my house I have found their
         wickedness,
                              says the LORD.
¹² Therefore their way shall be to them
      like slippery paths in the darkness,

a Gk: Heb *I*

23:1, 9, 11 *Woe to the shepherds . . . the
prophets . . . prophet and priest.* From economics
to politics to matters of professional ethics the
prophet moves. Leadership—civic and religious—
is a moral issue, according to Jeremiah. The
people have been betrayed by their leaders and
now they shall suffer for it. But, even more sadly,
God has been betrayed by the leaders. Leadership, whether in the government or in the faith
community, is a divine vocation, a spiritual responsibility. The sins of the general populace
receive attention from the prophet, but the sins
of the rulers, the dignitaries, and those in power
receive special attention and particular condemnation. The false prophet is known from the true,

at least in the book of Jeremiah, because of the
false prophet's propensity to tell the world what
it wants to hear. "Do not listen to the words of
the prophets . . . ; they are deluding you" (v 16).
Leaders, both civic and religious, are held to a
high standard of accountability because leadership is a high vocation. Jeremiah obviously would
not understand our contemporary distinction
between "private" and "public" morality,
between "personal" moral matters and "public"
matters. For the prophet, it is all of one piece—
behavior in a bedroom or a boardroom, ethics
in the House of Representatives or at our
house—it is all a matter of fidelity or infidelity
to God.

into which they shall be driven and
    fall;
for I will bring disaster upon them
    in the year of their punishment,
                  says the LORD.
13 In the prophets of Samaria
    I saw a disgusting thing:
they prophesied by Baal
    and led my people Israel astray.
14 But in the prophets of Jerusalem
    I have seen a more shocking thing:
they commit adultery and walk in lies;
    they strengthen the hands of
        evildoers,
so that no one turns from wickedness;
all of them have become like Sodom to
    me,
    and its inhabitants like Gomorrah.
15 Therefore thus says the LORD of hosts
    concerning the prophets:
"I am going to make them eat
    wormwood,
    and give them poisoned water to drink;
for from the prophets of Jerusalem
    ungodliness has spread throughout
        the land."

16 Thus says the LORD of hosts: Do not listen to the words of the prophets who prophesy to you; they are deluding you. They speak visions of their own minds, not from the mouth of the LORD. 17They keep saying to those who despise the word of the LORD, "It shall be well with you"; and to all who stubbornly follow their own stubborn hearts, they say, "No calamity shall come upon you."

18 For who has stood in the council of the
    LORD
    so as to see and to hear his word?
    Who has given heed to his word so as
        to proclaim it?
19 Look, the storm of the LORD!
    Wrath has gone forth,
a whirling tempest;
    it will burst upon the head of the
        wicked.
20 The anger of the LORD will not turn back
    until he has executed and
        accomplished
    the intents of his mind.

In the latter days you will understand it
    clearly.

21 I did not send the prophets,
    yet they ran;
I did not speak to them,
    yet they prophesied.
22 But if they had stood in my council,
    then they would have proclaimed my
        words to my people,
and they would have turned them from
    their evil way,
    and from the evil of their doings.

23 Am I a God near by, says the LORD, and not a God far off? 24Who can hide in secret places so that I cannot see them? says the LORD. Do I not fill heaven and earth? says the LORD. 25I have heard what the prophets have said who prophesy lies in my name, saying, "I have dreamed, I have dreamed!" 26How long? Will the hearts of the prophets ever turn back—those who prophesy lies, and who prophesy the deceit of their own heart? 27They plan to make my people forget my name by their dreams that they tell one another, just as their ancestors forgot my name for Baal. 28Let the prophet who has a dream tell the dream, but let the one who has my word speak my word faithfully. What has straw in common with wheat? says the LORD. 29Is not my word like fire, says the LORD, and like a hammer that breaks a rock in pieces? 30See, therefore, I am against the prophets, says the LORD, who steal my words from one another. 31See, I am against the prophets, says the LORD, who use their own tongues and say, "Says the LORD." 32See, I am against those who prophesy lying dreams, says the LORD, and who tell them, and who lead my people astray by their lies and their recklessness, when I did not send them or appoint them; so they do not profit this people at all, says the LORD.

33 When this people, or a prophet, or a priest asks you, "What is the burden of the LORD?" you shall say to them, "You are the burden,a and I will cast you off, says the LORD." 34And as for the prophet, priest, or

a Gk Vg: Heb What burden

the people who say, "The burden of the LORD," I will punish them and their households. 35Thus shall you say to one another, among yourselves, "What has the LORD answered?" or "What has the LORD spoken?" 36But "the burden of the LORD" you shall mention no more, for the burden is everyone's own word, and so you pervert the words of the living God, the LORD of hosts, our God. 37Thus you shall ask the prophet, "What has the LORD answered you?" or "What has the LORD spoken?" 38But if you say, "the burden of the LORD," thus says the LORD: Because you have said these words, "the burden of the LORD," when I sent to you, saying, You shall not say, "the burden of the LORD," 39therefore, I will surely lift you up*a* and cast you away from my presence, you and the city that I gave to you and your ancestors. 40And I will bring upon you everlasting disgrace and perpetual shame, which shall not be forgotten.

The Good and the Bad Figs

24 The LORD showed me two baskets of figs placed before the temple of the LORD. This was after King Nebuchadrezzar of Babylon had taken into exile from Jerusalem King Jeconiah son of Jehoiakim of Judah, together with the officials of Judah, the artisans, and the smiths, and had brought them to Babylon. 2One basket had very good figs, like first-ripe figs, but the other basket had very bad figs, so bad that they could not be eaten. 3And the LORD said to me, "What do you see, Jeremiah?" I said, "Figs, the good figs very good, and the bad figs very bad, so bad that they cannot be eaten."

4 Then the word of the LORD came to me: 5Thus says the LORD, the God of Israel: Like these good figs, so I will regard as good the exiles from Judah, whom I have sent away from this place to the land of the Chaldeans. 6I will set my eyes upon them for good, and I will bring them back to this land. I will build them up, and not tear them down; I will plant them, and not pluck them up. 7I will give them a heart to know that I am the LORD; and they

shall be my people and I will be their God, for they shall return to me with their whole heart.

8 But thus says the LORD: Like the bad figs that are so bad they cannot be eaten, so will I treat King Zedekiah of Judah, his officials, the remnant of Jerusalem who remain in this land, and those who live in the land of Egypt. 9I will make them a horror, an evil thing, to all the kingdoms of the earth—a disgrace, a byword, a taunt, and a curse in all the places where I shall drive them. 10And I will send sword, famine, and pestilence upon them, until they are utterly destroyed from the land that I gave to them and their ancestors.

The Babylonian Captivity Foretold

25 The word that came to Jeremiah concerning all the people of Judah, in the fourth year of King Jehoiakim son of Josiah of Judah (that was the first year of King Nebuchadrezzar of Babylon), 2which the prophet Jeremiah spoke to all the people of Judah and all the inhabitants of Jerusalem: 3For twenty-three years, from the thirteenth year of King Josiah son of Amon of Judah, to this day, the word of the LORD has come to me, and I have spoken persistently to you, but you have not listened. 4And though the LORD persistently sent you all his servants the prophets, you have neither listened nor inclined your ears to hear 5when they said, "Turn now, every one of you, from your evil way and wicked doings, and you will remain upon the land that the LORD has given to you and your ancestors from of old and forever; 6do not go after other gods to serve and worship them, and do not provoke me to anger with the work of your hands. Then I will do you no harm." 7Yet you did not listen to me, says the LORD, and so you have provoked me to anger with the work of your hands to your own harm.

8 Therefore thus says the LORD of hosts: Because you have not obeyed my words, 9I am going to send for all the tribes of the north, says the LORD, even for King Nebuchadrezzar of Babylon, my servant, and I will bring them

a Heb Mss Gk Vg: MT *forget you*

25:9 *I am going to send for all the tribes of the north.* Here is an astounding, curious claim. God

says that he will send the armies of Babylon against his own covenant people, armies led by

against this land and its inhabitants, and against all these nations around; I will utterly destroy them, and make them an object of horror and of hissing, and an everlasting disgrace. *a* 10And I will banish from them the sound of mirth and the sound of gladness, the voice of the bridegroom and the voice of the bride, the sound of the millstones and the light of the lamp. 11This whole land shall become a ruin and a waste, and these nations shall serve the king of Babylon seventy years. 12Then after seventy years are completed, I will punish the king of Babylon and that nation, the land of the Chaldeans, for their iniquity, says the LORD, making the land an everlasting waste. 13I will bring upon that land all the words that I have uttered against it, everything written in this book, which Jeremiah prophesied against all the nations. 14For many nations and great kings shall make slaves of them also; and I will repay them according to their deeds and the work of their hands.

The Cup of God's Wrath

15 For thus the LORD, the God of Israel, said to me: Take from my hand this cup of the wine of wrath, and make all the nations to whom I send you drink it. 16They shall drink and stagger and go out of their minds because of the sword that I am sending among them.

17 So I took the cup from the LORD's hand, and made all the nations to whom the LORD sent me drink it: 18Jerusalem and the towns of Judah, its kings and officials, to make them a desolation and a waste, an object of hissing

and of cursing, as they are today; 19Pharaoh king of Egypt, his servants, his officials, and all his people; 20all the mixed people; *b* all the kings of the land of Uz; all the kings of the land of the Philistines—Ashkelon, Gaza, Ekron, and the remnant of Ashdod; 21Edom, Moab, and the Ammonites; 22all the kings of Tyre, all the kings of Sidon, and the kings of the coastland across the sea; 23Dedan, Tema, Buz, and all who have shaven temples; 24all the kings of Arabia and all the kings of the mixed peoples *b* that live in the desert; 25all the kings of Zimri, all the kings of Elam, and all the kings of Media; 26all the kings of the north, far and near, one after another, and all the kingdoms of the world that are on the face of the earth. And after them the king of Sheshach *c* shall drink.

27 Then you shall say to them, Thus says the LORD of hosts, the God of Israel: Drink, get drunk and vomit, fall and rise no more, because of the sword that I am sending among you.

28 And if they refuse to accept the cup from your hand to drink, then you shall say to them: Thus says the LORD of hosts: You must drink! 29See, I am beginning to bring disaster on the city that is called by my name, and how can you possibly avoid punishment? You shall not go unpunished, for I am summoning a sword against all the inhabitants of the earth, says the LORD of hosts.

a Gk Compare Syr: Heb *and everlasting desolations*
b Meaning of Heb uncertain   *c* *Sheshach* is a cryptogram for *Babel*, Babylon

---

"King Nebuchadrezzar of Babylon, my servant." How could this be? Nebuchadrezzar is a pagan king who presumes to be a god. And yet the Lord says that he has enlisted the help of this king to send a message to his own people. Israel has brought just destruction upon itself. And the agent of that destruction will be the Babylonian king. This is an astounding claim, but it is a claim derived from the faith of Israel. Each day when Jews pray, "Hear, O Israel: The LORD our God, the LORD is one" (Deut 6:4, NIV), they assert that the truth is not that the Babylonians have their gods and Israel has its God; rather, there is only one God, whether the Babylonians know it or not. And this God is over all. This

God works both sides of the street. This God has plans for not just the covenant people but all peoples. This God is sovereign, even over the Babylonians. So the claim is an assertion not so much of the power of the Babylonians, but rather of the sovereign power of the Lord. Can we today believe that God can work even through our enemies? Must we keep relearning the truth of the sweeping claim, "Hear, O Israel: The LORD our God, the LORD is one"? We are bound with the Babylonians, even with our enemies, not in some common humanity, but rather in a common sovereign God. Here is a God great enough even to address a hostile pagan ruler by the designation "my servant."

30 You, therefore, shall prophesy against them all these words, and say to them:
The LORD will roar from on high,
and from his holy habitation utter his voice;
he will roar mightily against his fold,
and shout, like those who tread grapes,
against all the inhabitants of the earth.
31 The clamor will resound to the ends of the earth,
for the LORD has an indictment against the nations;
he is entering into judgment with all flesh,
and the guilty he will put to the sword,
says the LORD.

32 Thus says the LORD of hosts:
See, disaster is spreading from nation to nation,
and a great tempest is stirring from the farthest parts of the earth!
33 Those slain by the LORD on that day shall extend from one end of the earth to the other. They shall not be lamented, or gathered, or buried; they shall become dung on the surface of the ground.
34 Wail, you shepherds, and cry out;
roll in ashes, you lords of the flock,
for the days of your slaughter have come—and your dispersions, *a*
and you shall fall like a choice vessel.
35 Flight shall fail the shepherds,
and there shall be no escape for the lords of the flock.
36 Hark! the cry of the shepherds,
and the wail of the lords of the flock!
For the LORD is despoiling their pasture,
37 and the peaceful folds are devastated,
because of the fierce anger of the LORD.
38 Like a lion he has left his covert;
for their land has become a waste
because of the cruel sword,
and because of his fierce anger.

Jeremiah's Prophecies in the Temple

26 At the beginning of the reign of King Jehoiakim son of Josiah of Judah, this word came from the LORD: 2Thus says the LORD: Stand in the court of the LORD's house, and speak to all the cities of Judah that come to worship in the house of the LORD; speak to them all the words that I command you; do not hold back a word. 3It may be that they will listen, all of them, and will turn from their evil way, that I may change my mind about the disaster that I intend to bring on

a Meaning of Heb uncertain

26:1–9 *speak to all the cities of Judah.* In the very middle of the book of Jeremiah, we have a sermon. Much of Jeremiah's prophecy appears to be delivered out in the streets and up at the Temple. Now we go into the house of God. God strictly charges the spokesperson, Jeremiah, to not "hold back a word." We are not given a detailed report on the sermon, only a description of the response. When Jeremiah finished preaching his great sermon in the Temple, the priests, the religious functionaries, and all the people joined together in unison, "You shall die!" Surely this is the story that Luke had in mind when he reported on Jesus' inaugural sermon at his hometown synagogue in Nazareth (4:14–30). We have already noted that, although we call this the book of Jeremiah, the most interesting character in it may be, not the prophet Jeremiah, but the Lord. But here, in

this passage, we are right to notice the crowd—the priests and the people—the ones who have our faces. Isn't it ironic that we come to church asking, "Is there any word from the Lord?" and yet when God sends his word through a fierce teller of the truth like Jeremiah, we wish he were dead? Take this episode as a parable of Sunday morning in almost any church. Let us measure ourselves against this passage and see how our faith community shapes up. In reading these Bible texts, it makes all the difference where we sit. Surely we are not meant to be up in the pulpit, with Jeremiah, haranguing the people. Rather, we are to find our place among the hearers at the Temple that day, with a people who were spoken to by a loquacious, loving God, but who refused to hear. And the congregation rose and with one voice repeated the persistent congregational response, "Kill him!"

them because of their evil doings. ⁴You shall say to them: Thus says the LORD: If you will not listen to me, to walk in my law that I have set before you, ⁵and to heed the words of my servants the prophets whom I send to you urgently—though you have not heeded—⁶then I will make this house like Shiloh, and I will make this city a curse for all the nations of the earth.

7 The priests and the prophets and all the people heard Jeremiah speaking these words in the house of the LORD. ⁸And when Jeremiah had finished speaking all that the LORD had commanded him to speak to all the people, then the priests and the prophets and all the people laid hold of him, saying, "You shall die! ⁹Why have you prophesied in the name of the LORD, saying, 'This house shall be like Shiloh, and this city shall be desolate, without inhabitant'?" And all the people gathered around Jeremiah in the house of the LORD.

10 When the officials of Judah heard these things, they came up from the king's house to the house of the LORD and took their seat in the entry of the New Gate of the house of the LORD. ¹¹Then the priests and the prophets said to the officials and to all the people, "This man deserves the sentence of death, because he has prophesied against this city, as you have heard with your own ears."

12 Then Jeremiah spoke to all the officials and all the people, saying, "It is the LORD who sent me to prophesy against this house and this city all the words you have heard. ¹³Now therefore amend your ways and your doings, and obey the voice of the LORD your God, and the LORD will change his mind about the disaster that he has pronounced against you. ¹⁴But as for me, here I am in your hands. Do with me as seems good and right to you. ¹⁵Only know for certain that if you put me to death, you will be bringing innocent blood upon yourselves and upon this city and its inhabitants, for in truth the LORD sent me to you to speak all these words in your ears."

16 Then the officials and all the people said to the priests and the prophets, "This man does not deserve the sentence of death, for he has spoken to us in the name of the LORD our God." ¹⁷And some of the elders of the land arose and said to all the assembled people, ¹⁸"Micah of Moresheth, who prophesied during the days of King Hezekiah of Judah, said to all the people of Judah: 'Thus says the LORD of hosts,

Zion shall be plowed as a field;
   Jerusalem shall become a heap of
      ruins,
   and the mountain of the house a
      wooded height.'

¹⁹Did King Hezekiah of Judah and all Judah actually put him to death? Did he not fear the LORD and entreat the favor of the LORD, and did not the LORD change his mind about the disaster that he had pronounced against them? But we are about to bring great disaster on ourselves!"

20 There was another man prophesying in the name of the LORD, Uriah son of Shemaiah from Kiriath-jearim. He prophesied against this city and against this land in words exactly like those of Jeremiah. ²¹And when King Jehoiakim, with all his warriors and all the officials, heard his words, the king sought to put him to death; but when Uriah heard of it, he was afraid and fled and escaped to Egypt. ²²Then King Jehoiakim sent ᵃ Elnathan son of Achbor and men with him to Egypt, ²³and they took Uriah from Egypt and brought him to King Jehoiakim, who struck him down with the sword and threw his dead body into the burial place of the common people.

24 But the hand of Ahikam son of Shaphan was with Jeremiah so that he was not given over into the hands of the people to be put to death.

The Sign of the Yoke

27 In the beginning of the reign of King Zedekiah ᵇ son of Josiah of Judah, this word came to Jeremiah from the LORD. ²Thus the LORD said to me: Make yourself a yoke of straps and bars, and put them on your neck. ³Send word ᶜ to the king of Edom, the king of Moab, the king of the Ammonites, the king of Tyre, and the king of Sidon by the hand of the envoys who have come to Jerusalem to King Zedekiah of Judah. ⁴Give them this charge for their masters: Thus says the LORD

a Heb adds *men to Egypt*   b Another reading is *Jehoiakim*   c Cn: Heb *send them*

of hosts, the God of Israel: This is what you shall say to your masters: [5]It is I who by my great power and my outstretched arm have made the earth, with the people and animals that are on the earth, and I give it to whomever I please. [6]Now I have given all these lands into the hand of King Nebuchadnezzar of Babylon, my servant, and I have given him even the wild animals of the field to serve him. [7]All the nations shall serve him and his son and his grandson, until the time of his own land comes; then many nations and great kings shall make him their slave.

8 But if any nation or kingdom will not serve this king, Nebuchadnezzar of Babylon, and put its neck under the yoke of the king of Babylon, then I will punish that nation with the sword, with famine, and with pestilence, says the LORD, until I have completed its[a] destruction by his hand. [9]You, therefore, must not listen to your prophets, your diviners, your dreamers,[b] your soothsayers, or your sorcerers, who are saying to you, "You shall not serve the king of Babylon." [10]For they are prophesying a lie to you, with the result that you will be removed far from your land; I will drive you out, and you will perish. [11]But any nation that will bring its neck under the yoke of the king of Babylon and serve him, I will leave on its own land, says the LORD, to till it and live there.

12 I spoke to King Zedekiah of Judah in the same way: Bring your necks under the yoke of the king of Babylon, and serve him and his people, and live. [13]Why should you and your people die by the sword, by famine, and by pestilence, as the LORD has spoken concerning any nation that will not serve the king of Babylon? [14]Do not listen to the words of the prophets who are telling you not to serve the king of Babylon, for they are prophesying a lie to you. [15]I have not sent them, says the LORD, but they are prophesying falsely in my name, with the result that I will drive you out and you will perish, you and the prophets who are prophesying to you.

16 Then I spoke to the priests and to all this people, saying, Thus says the LORD: Do not listen to the words of your prophets who are prophesying to you, saying, "The vessels of the LORD's house will soon be brought back from Babylon," for they are prophesying a lie to you. [17]Do not listen to them; serve the king of Babylon and live. Why should this city become a desolation? [18]If indeed they are prophets, and if the word of the LORD is with them, then let them intercede with the LORD of hosts, that the vessels left in the house of the LORD, in the house of the king of Judah, and in Jerusalem may not go to Babylon. [19]For thus says the LORD of hosts concerning the pillars, the sea, the stands, and the rest of the vessels that are left in this city, [20]which King Nebuchadnezzar of Babylon did not take away when he took into exile from Jerusalem to Babylon King Jeconiah son of Jehoiakim of Judah, and all the nobles of Judah and Jerusalem— [21]thus says the LORD of hosts, the God of Israel, concerning the vessels left in the house of the LORD, in the house of the king of Judah, and in Jerusalem: [22]They shall be carried to Babylon, and there they shall stay, until the day when I give attention to them, says the LORD. Then I will bring them up and restore them to this place.

a Heb their　　b Gk Syr Vg: Heb dreams

27:1 *this word came to Jeremiah from the LORD.* You have to hand it to the Lord; God is persistent. With rhythmic repetition, this phrase appears again and again throughout the book of Jeremiah. And you also have to hand it the Lord. When it comes to criticizing politicians, the Lord does not play favorites. The Lord manages to lambaste all the kings—Josiah, Jehoiakim, Coniah, and Zedekiah. The community of faith needs to be even-handed in its political criticism. It is not that there are some "good" kings and some "bad" kings. The situation seems to be that kings, by their very nature, on either side of the aisle, seem to get confused. They forget that they are servants of God and start taking on airs, acting like God. And then, in the unkindest cut of all, Jeremiah tells these kings that the king of Babylon, Nebuchadrezzar, will be their master, will impose a "yoke" (v 8) around their necks. It is sad that the nation that was blessed with so much, chosen by God for particular witness and service, now becomes the servant of the pagans. Now the judgment.

Hananiah Opposes Jeremiah and Dies

28 In that same year, at the beginning of the reign of King Zedekiah of Judah, in the fifth month of the fourth year, the prophet Hananiah son of Azzur, from Gibeon, spoke to me in the house of the LORD, in the presence of the priests and all the people, saying, 2"Thus says the LORD of hosts, the God of Israel: I have broken the yoke of the king of Babylon. 3Within two years I will bring back to this place all the vessels of the LORD's house, which King Nebuchadnezzar of Babylon took away from this place and carried to Babylon. 4I will also bring back to this place King Jeconiah son of Jehoiakim of Judah, and all the exiles from Judah who went to Babylon, says the LORD, for I will break the yoke of the king of Babylon."

5 Then the prophet Jeremiah spoke to the prophet Hananiah in the presence of the priests and all the people who were standing in the house of the LORD; 6and the prophet Jeremiah said, "Amen! May the LORD do so; may the LORD fulfill the words that you have prophesied, and bring back to this place from Babylon the vessels of the house of the LORD, and all the exiles. 7But listen now to this word that I speak in your hearing and in the hearing of all the people. 8The prophets who preceded you and me from ancient times prophesied war, famine, and pestilence against many countries and great kingdoms. 9As for the prophet who prophesies peace, when the word of that prophet comes true, then it will be known that the LORD has truly sent the prophet."

10 Then the prophet Hananiah took the yoke from the neck of the prophet Jeremiah, and broke it. 11And Hananiah spoke in the presence of all the people, saying, "Thus says the LORD: This is how I will break the yoke of King Nebuchadnezzar of Babylon from the neck of all the nations within two years." At this, the prophet Jeremiah went his way.

12 Sometime after the prophet Hananiah had broken the yoke from the neck of the prophet Jeremiah, the word of the LORD came to Jeremiah: 13Go, tell Hananiah, Thus says the LORD: You have broken wooden bars only to forge iron bars in place of them! 14For thus says the LORD of hosts, the God of Israel: I have put an iron yoke on the neck of all these nations so that they may serve King Nebuchadnezzar of Babylon, and they shall indeed serve him; I have even given him the wild animals. 15And the prophet Jeremiah said to the prophet Hananiah, "Listen, Hananiah, the LORD has not sent you, and you made this people trust in a lie. 16Therefore thus says the LORD: I am going to send you off the face of the earth. Within this year you will be dead, because you have spoken rebellion against the LORD."

17 In that same year, in the seventh month, the prophet Hananiah died.

Jeremiah's Letter to the Exiles in Babylon

29 These are the words of the letter that the prophet Jeremiah sent from Jerusalem to the remaining elders among the exiles, and to the priests, the prophets, and all

---

29:1–23 *the letter that the prophet Jeremiah sent from Jerusalem.* Jeremiah has used many linguistic devices to get the word of the Lord across—invective, oracles, sermons, parables, and symbolic actions. Here is a letter sent to those in exile. And to these forlorn people, languishing in Babylon, homes destroyed, families uprooted and lost, Jeremiah says that the exile will be long. He tells them not to listen to the false prophets who tell them that this is only a temporary setback. Rather, they need to adapt and adjust to the exilic situation. Although they are to remain God's chosen, covenant people, they are to pray for the welfare of Babylon; they are to take up life there, build houses and plant gardens, and do the best they can. Jeremiah does not stop being the truthful prophet, even during the exile. Even though disaster has befallen the people, Jeremiah still dares to speak the truth to them. It takes courage to speak to prosperous, powerful people, but it takes even more courage to speak truth to victimized, hurting, suffering people. Jeremiah tells them that they are to faithfully make the best of a bad situation. They are not merely to whine and protest their condition; rather, they are to make life and a home where they are. Mobile, uprooted, dislocated people need to hear this word. They

the people, whom Nebuchadnezzar had taken into exile from Jerusalem to Babylon. ²This was after King Jeconiah, and the queen mother, the court officials, the leaders of Judah and Jerusalem, the artisans, and the smiths had departed from Jerusalem. ³The letter was sent by the hand of Elasah son of Shaphan and Gemariah son of Hilkiah, whom King Zedekiah of Judah sent to Babylon to King Nebuchadnezzar of Babylon. It said: ⁴Thus says the LORD of hosts, the God of Israel, to all the exiles whom I have sent into exile from Jerusalem to Babylon: ⁵Build houses and live in them; plant gardens and eat what they produce. ⁶Take wives and have sons and daughters; take wives for your sons, and give your daughters in marriage, that they may bear sons and daughters; multiply there, and do not decrease. ⁷But seek the welfare of the city where I have sent you into exile, and pray to the LORD on its behalf, for in its welfare you will find your welfare. ⁸For thus says the LORD of hosts, the God of Israel: Do not let the prophets and the diviners who are among you deceive you, and do not listen to the dreams that they dream,ᵃ ⁹for it is a lie that they are prophesying to you in my name; I did not send them, says the LORD.

10 For thus says the LORD: Only when Babylon's seventy years are completed will I visit you, and I will fulfill to you my promise and bring you back to this place. ¹¹For surely I know the plans I have for you, says the

LORD, plans for your welfare and not for harm, to give you a future with hope. ¹²Then when you call upon me and come and pray to me, I will hear you. ¹³When you search for me, you will find me; if you seek me with all your heart, ¹⁴I will let you find me, says the LORD, and I will restore your fortunes and gather you from all the nations and all the places where I have driven you, says the LORD, and I will bring you back to the place from which I sent you into exile.

15 Because you have said, "The LORD has raised up prophets for us in Babylon,"— ¹⁶Thus says the LORD concerning the king who sits on the throne of David, and concerning all the people who live in this city, your kinsfolk who did not go out with you into exile: ¹⁷Thus says the LORD of hosts, I am going to let loose on them sword, famine, and pestilence, and I will make them like rotten figs that are so bad they cannot be eaten. ¹⁸I will pursue them with the sword, with famine, and with pestilence, and will make them a horror to all the kingdoms of the earth, to be an object of cursing, and horror, and hissing, and a derision among all the nations where I have driven them, ¹⁹because they did not heed my words, says the LORD, when I persistently sent to you my servants the prophets, but theyᵇ would not listen, says the LORD. ²⁰But now, all you exiles whom I

a Cn: Heb *your dreams that you cause to dream*
b Syr: Heb *you*

do not have to be at home, back in Israel, to be with God. God promises, "When you call upon me and come and pray to me, I will hear you" (v 12). Some of Jeremiah's words prepare people to go into exile. Other words of Jeremiah speak to those who are already in exile. Where does the contemporary faith community find itself today, and what word do we most need to hear?

Responding
29:7 **PRAYER and SERVICE.** This verse beautifully illustrates the interconnectedness of the Spiritual Disciplines. Prayer and service are mutually strengthening, and both enhance our own well-being. Take an inventory of the Spiritual Disciplines in your life. Which are you practicing well? Which could you

practice more or in a different manner? *See also* Spiritual Disciplines Index.

Responding
29:11–13 PRAYER. The images of searching and seeking are powerful metaphors for prayer. Since the twelfth century Christians have used prayer labyrinths to seek God. The physical action of walking through a maze and stopping at various prayer stations symbolizes a contemplative journey. This ancient meditation has experienced a recent renaissance. Visit a labyrinth walk, or if you can't find one nearby, try an online labyrinth or create your own version of a walking meditation. *See also* Spiritual Disciplines Index.

sent away from Jerusalem to Babylon, hear the word of the LORD: 21 Thus says the LORD of hosts, the God of Israel, concerning Ahab son of Kolaiah and Zedekiah son of Maaseiah, who are prophesying a lie to you in my name: I am going to deliver them into the hand of King Nebuchadrezzar of Babylon, and he shall kill them before your eyes. 22 And on account of them this curse shall be used by all the exiles from Judah in Babylon: "The LORD make you like Zedekiah and Ahab, whom the king of Babylon roasted in the fire," 23 because they have perpetrated outrage in Israel and have committed adultery with their neighbors' wives, and have spoken in my name lying words that I did not command them; I am the one who knows and bears witness, says the LORD.

The Letter of Shemaiah

24 To Shemaiah of Nehelam you shall say: 25 Thus says the LORD of hosts, the God of Israel: In your own name you sent a letter to all the people who are in Jerusalem, and to the priest Zephaniah son of Maaseiah, and to all the priests, saying, 26 The LORD himself has made you priest instead of the priest Jehoiada, so that there may be officers in the house of the LORD to control any madman who plays the prophet, to put him in the stocks and the collar. 27 So now why have you not rebuked Jeremiah of Anathoth who plays the prophet for you? 28 For he has actually sent to us in Babylon, saying, "It will be a long time;

build houses and live in them, and plant gardens and eat what they produce."

29 The priest Zephaniah read this letter in the hearing of the prophet Jeremiah. 30 Then the word of the LORD came to Jeremiah: 31 Send to all the exiles, saying, Thus says the LORD concerning Shemaiah of Nehelam: Because Shemaiah has prophesied to you, though I did not send him, and has led you to trust in a lie, 32 therefore thus says the LORD: I am going to punish Shemaiah of Nehelam and his descendants; he shall not have anyone living among this people to see[a] the good that I am going to do to my people, says the LORD, for he has spoken rebellion against the LORD.

Restoration Promised for Israel and Judah

30 The word that came to Jeremiah from the LORD: 2 Thus says the LORD, the God of Israel: Write in a book all the words that I have spoken to you. 3 For the days are surely coming, says the LORD, when I will restore the fortunes of my people, Israel and Judah, says the LORD, and I will bring them back to the land that I gave to their ancestors and they shall take possession of it.

4 These are the words that the LORD spoke concerning Israel and Judah:

5 Thus says the LORD:
   We have heard a cry of panic,
      of terror, and no peace.

a Gk: Heb and he shall not see

30:1–31:40 *I will restore the fortunes of my people.* After so much judgment and condemnation, at last we receive consolation from Jeremiah. Jeremiah has a reputation for being one of the most condemnatory of all the prophets, but his reputation is not fully deserved. These words are some of the most comforting, reassuring promises in all of Scripture. God will not, cannot desert his covenant community. The exile may be long and it may be bitter, but the day will come when Israel will be over. During some of Israel's darkest days, Israel voiced some of its most sweeping, extravagant claims for the ultimate goodness of God. These words were probably written in exile. They are not a statement of present reality, but rather a future hope.

What a testament of faith! When the community lifts itself up from the ashes and the rubble and dares to sing a doxology, this is faith. It takes courage to speak words of judgment to people, and Jeremiah has done that. But it also takes great courage to speak of the goodness of God to people who have been battered about by life and suffered tragedy. Sometimes those who have given up hope don't appreciate talk of hope. It can be offensive to those who are in the grip of sadness to hear talk of joy. And yet the faith community is renewed by daring to speak hopeful truth, even amid the rubble. To be honest and hopeful at the same time is a great challenge of faith.

6 Ask now, and see,
    can a man bear a child?
Why then do I see every man
    with his hands on his loins like a
        woman in labor?
Why has every face turned pale?
7 Alas! that day is so great
    there is none like it;
it is a time of distress for Jacob;
    yet he shall be rescued from it.
8 On that day, says the LORD of hosts, I
will break the yoke from off his*a* neck, and I
will burst his*a* bonds, and strangers shall no
more make a servant of him. 9But they shall
serve the LORD their God and David their
king, whom I will raise up for them.

10 But as for you, have no fear, my servant
        Jacob, says the LORD,
    and do not be dismayed, O Israel;
for I am going to save you from far away,
    and your offspring from the land of
        their captivity.
Jacob shall return and have quiet and
        ease,
    and no one shall make him afraid.
11 For I am with you, says the LORD, to save
        you;
I will make an end of all the nations
        among which I scattered you,
    but of you I will not make an end.
I will chastise you in just measure,
    and I will by no means leave you
        unpunished.

12 For thus says the LORD:
Your hurt is incurable,
    your wound is grievous.
13 There is no one to uphold your cause,
    no medicine for your wound,
    no healing for you.
14 All your lovers have forgotten you;
    they care nothing for you;
for I have dealt you the blow of an
        enemy,
    the punishment of a merciless foe,
because your guilt is great,
    because your sins are so numerous.
15 Why do you cry out over your hurt?
    Your pain is incurable.
Because your guilt is great,

because your sins are so numerous,
    I have done these things to you.
16 Therefore all who devour you shall be
        devoured,
    and all your foes, every one of them,
        shall go into captivity;
those who plunder you shall be
        plundered,
    and all who prey on you I will make a
        prey.
17 For I will restore health to you,
    and your wounds I will heal,
                            says the LORD,
because they have called you an outcast:
    "It is Zion; no one cares for her!"

18 Thus says the LORD:
I am going to restore the fortunes of the
        tents of Jacob,
    and have compassion on his
        dwellings;
the city shall be rebuilt upon its mound,
    and the citadel set on its rightful site.
19 Out of them shall come thanksgiving,
    and the sound of merrymakers.
I will make them many, and they shall
        not be few;
    I will make them honored, and they
        shall not be disdained.
20 Their children shall be as of old,
    their congregation shall be
        established before me;
    and I will punish all who oppress them.
21 Their prince shall be one of their own,
    their ruler shall come from their
        midst;
I will bring him near, and he shall
        approach me,
    for who would otherwise dare to
        approach me?
                            says the LORD.
22 And you shall be my people,
    and I will be your God.

23 Look, the storm of the LORD!
    Wrath has gone forth,
a whirling*b* tempest;
    it will burst upon the head of the
        wicked.

a Cn: Heb *your*   *b* One Ms: Meaning of MT
uncertain

24 The fierce anger of the LORD will not
     turn back
  until he has executed and
     accomplished
  the intents of his mind.
In the latter days you will understand
     this.

The Joyful Return of the Exiles

31 At that time, says the LORD, I will be
the God of all the families of Israel,
and they shall be my people.
2 Thus says the LORD:
The people who survived the sword
     found grace in the wilderness;
  when Israel sought for rest,
3   the LORD appeared to him *a* from far
        away. *b*
  I have loved you with an everlasting
     love;
     therefore I have continued my
        faithfulness to you.
4 Again I will build you, and you shall be
     built,
  O virgin Israel!
Again you shall take *c* your tambourines,

and go forth in the dance of the
     merrymakers.
5 Again you shall plant vineyards
  on the mountains of Samaria;
  the planters shall plant,
     and shall enjoy the fruit.
6 For there shall be a day when sentinels
        will call
  in the hill country of Ephraim:
  "Come, let us go up to Zion,
     to the LORD our God."

7 For thus says the LORD:
Sing aloud with gladness for Jacob,
  and raise shouts for the chief of the
        nations;
  proclaim, give praise, and say,
  "Save, O LORD, your people,
     the remnant of Israel."
8 See, I am going to bring them from the
        land of the north,
  and gather them from the farthest
        parts of the earth,

a Gk: Heb *me*   *b* Or *to him long ago*
c Or *adorn yourself with*

31:2 *The people . . . found grace in the
wilderness.* Grace! Even in the wilderness.
The wilderness for Israel is a place of sin and
desolation, that forty-year wandering that came
after the exodus. The wilderness is a place of
hunger and depravation, a place where hope is
in short supply along with everything else
needed for life. And yet Jeremiah claims that it
was in the wilderness that Israel found the
depths of the love of God. In the wilderness,
God remained steadfast to his promises to the
covenant people. Though the faith community
failed to keep its promises to God in the
wilderness, there God demonstrated the
persistence and resilience of his gracious care.
The prophets of Israel often use the wilderness
as a metaphor, comparing that time to Israel's
time of exile. The wilderness is a place no
one wants to go to, but eventually in this life
everyone must. Wilderness is that shadowy
place where we are apt to lose our way, where
there is that day-to-day struggle just to survive.
And yet the prophet makes the exuberant claim
that, even in the wilderness, especially in the
wilderness, the grace of God is experienced.

The implication is that anytime the community
of faith finds itself in some "wilderness," we are
to look up, to be attentive and expectant. Even
there, especially there, there can be grace.

31:8 *I am going to bring them from the land
of the north.* For the people who have lost their
home, the people who live nowhere, there shall
be homecoming. For all the people, the weakest
and the most vulnerable, there shall be home.
Homelessness has become a predominant
metaphor for our age. People seem to lack
anywhere to be at home, at rest, and at peace.
All of the suffering and trouble that people
endure has as its end result, not permanent
uprootedness and despair, but home. Sometimes the faith community speaks of this homecoming as "salvation," being "born again," being
"saved." Whenever this homecoming happens,
it is seen as a great gift of God, perhaps God's
greatest gift. The proclamation is twofold here:
there is a home for you, and you can, by the
grace of God, come home. This is at least part, a
very big part, of what Jesus called "good news."
For people in our age, it may be the very best
good news.

among them the blind and the lame,
    those with child and those in labor,
      together;
    a great company, they shall return
      here.
9 With weeping they shall come,
    and with consolations*a* I will lead
      them back,
I will let them walk by brooks of water,
    in a straight path in which they shall
      not stumble;
for I have become a father to Israel,
    and Ephraim is my firstborn.

10 Hear the word of the LORD, O nations,
    and declare it in the coastlands far
      away;
    say, "He who scattered Israel will gather
      him,
    and will keep him as a shepherd a
      flock."
11 For the LORD has ransomed Jacob,
    and has redeemed him from hands
      too strong for him.
12 They shall come and sing aloud on the
      height of Zion,
    and they shall be radiant over the
      goodness of the LORD,
over the grain, the wine, and the oil,
    and over the young of the flock and
      the herd;
their life shall become like a watered
      garden,
    and they shall never languish again.

13 Then shall the young women rejoice in
      the dance,
    and the young men and the old shall
      be merry.
I will turn their mourning into joy,
    I will comfort them, and give them
      gladness for sorrow.
14 I will give the priests their fill of fatness,
    and my people shall be satisfied with
      my bounty,

                  says the LORD.

15 Thus says the LORD:
A voice is heard in Ramah,
    lamentation and bitter weeping.
Rachel is weeping for her children;
    she refuses to be comforted for her
      children,
    because they are no more.
16 Thus says the LORD:
Keep your voice from weeping,
    and your eyes from tears;
for there is a reward for your work,
                says the LORD:
    they shall come back from the land of
      the enemy;
17 there is hope for your future,
                says the LORD:
    your children shall come back to their
      own country.

18 Indeed I heard Ephraim pleading:

a Gk Compare Vg Tg: Heb *supplications*

31:16 *there is a reward for your work.* This verse follows the great expression of desolation (v 15) that Matthew cites in his Gospel when the boy babies are massacred at Jesus' birth (2:18). Rivers of tears have been cried, and now the Lord promises joy. Specifically, the Lord promises "reward for your work." We may have some misgivings about a religion that is based on threat of punishment or promise of reward, but the Bible does not have these misgivings. Although there may be no one-to-one correlation between the good that we do for God and the good that we get from God, there is a repeated promise here, and in many places of Scripture, that there shall be reward. Faithfulness shall be noted by God and blessed.

Jeremiah has spoken the truth, and many have rejected that truth. But to those who receive the truth and embody it in their lives, Jeremiah hears God promise sure reward. God rewards those whose lives demonstrate their love for God. Sometimes those rewards do not come as quickly as we would like; sometimes they are not in the form that we would wish, but nevertheless there is the promise that they will come. Of course, not enough is said about reward here to make it the main reason for obedience to God. We serve God for many different reasons, primarily love for God. Expectation of reward may not be the main motivation for our fidelity to God; however, it is promised, and it is a motivation.

"You disciplined me, and I took the
    discipline;
    I was like a calf untrained.
Bring me back, let me come back,
    for you are the LORD my God.
19 For after I had turned away I repented;
    and after I was discovered, I struck my
      thigh;
    I was ashamed, and I was dismayed
    because I bore the disgrace of my
      youth."
20 Is Ephraim my dear son?
    Is he the child I delight in?
As often as I speak against him,
    I still remember him.
Therefore I am deeply moved for him;
    I will surely have mercy on him,
            says the LORD.

21 Set up road markers for yourself,
    make yourself signposts;
consider well the highway,
    the road by which you went.
Return, O virgin Israel,
    return to these your cities.
22 How long will you waver,
    O faithless daughter?
For the LORD has created a new thing on
    the earth:
    a woman encompasses*a* a man.

23 Thus says the LORD of hosts, the God of
Israel: Once more they shall use these words
in the land of Judah and in its towns when I
restore their fortunes:
    "The LORD bless you, O abode of
      righteousness,
    O holy hill!"
24 And Judah and all its towns shall live there
together, and the farmers and those who
wander*b* with their flocks.
25 I will satisfy the weary,
    and all who are faint I will replenish.
26 Thereupon I awoke and looked, and
my sleep was pleasant to me.

Individual Retribution

27 The days are surely coming, says the
LORD, when I will sow the house of Israel and
the house of Judah with the seed of humans
and the seed of animals. 28 And just as I have
watched over them to pluck up and break
down, to overthrow, destroy, and bring evil,
so I will watch over them to build and to
plant, says the LORD. 29 In those days they
shall no longer say:
    "The parents have eaten sour grapes,
    and the children's teeth are set on
      edge."
30 But all shall die for their own sins; the teeth
of everyone who eats sour grapes shall be set
on edge.

A New Covenant

31 The days are surely coming, says the
LORD, when I will make a new covenant with
the house of Israel and the house of Judah.
32 It will not be like the covenant that I made
with their ancestors when I took them by
the hand to bring them out of the land of
Egypt—a covenant that they broke, though
I was their husband,*c* says the LORD. 33 But
this is the covenant that I will make with the
house of Israel after those days, says the LORD:
I will put my law within them, and I will
write it on their hearts; and I will be their
God, and they shall be my people. 34 No
longer shall they teach one another, or say to
each other, "Know the LORD," for they shall
all know me, from the least of them to the
greatest, says the LORD; for I will forgive their
iniquity, and remember their sin no more.

35 Thus says the LORD,
    who gives the sun for light by day
      and the fixed order of the moon and
        the stars for light by night,
    who stirs up the sea so that its waves
      roar—
    the LORD of hosts is his name:
36 If this fixed order were ever to cease
    from my presence, says the LORD,
then also the offspring of Israel would
    cease
    to be a nation before me forever.

37 Thus says the LORD:
    If the heavens above can be measured,
      and the foundations of the earth
        below can be explored,

a Meaning of Heb uncertain   *b* Cn Compare Syr
Vg Tg: Heb *and they shall wander*   *c* Or *master*

then I will reject all the offspring of
   Israel
   because of all they have done,
               says the LORD.

Jerusalem to Be Enlarged

38 The days are surely coming, says the
LORD, when the city shall be rebuilt for the
LORD from the tower of Hananel to the Corner Gate. 39 And the measuring line shall go
out farther, straight to the hill Gareb, and
shall then turn to Goah. 40 The whole valley
of the dead bodies and the ashes, and all the
fields as far as the Wadi Kidron, to the corner
of the Horse Gate toward the east, shall be sacred to the LORD. It shall never again be uprooted or overthrown.

Jeremiah Buys a Field During the Siege

32 The word that came to Jeremiah from
the LORD in the tenth year of King
Zedekiah of Judah, which was the eighteenth
year of Nebuchadrezzar. 2 At that time the
army of the king of Babylon was besieging Jerusalem, and the prophet Jeremiah was confined in the court of the guard that was in the
palace of the king of Judah, 3 where King Zedekiah of Judah had confined him. Zedekiah
had said, "Why do you prophesy and say:
Thus says the LORD: I am going to give this
city into the hand of the king of Babylon,
and he shall take it; 4 King Zedekiah of Judah
shall not escape out of the hands of the
Chaldeans, but shall surely be given into the
hands of the king of Babylon, and shall speak
with him face to face and see him eye to eye;
5 and he shall take Zedekiah to Babylon, and
there he shall remain until I attend to him,
says the LORD; though you fight against the
Chaldeans, you shall not succeed?"

6 Jeremiah said, The word of the LORD
came to me. 7 Hanamel son of your uncle
Shallum is going to come to you and say,
"Buy my field that is at Anathoth, for the
right of redemption by purchase is yours."
8 Then my cousin Hanamel came to me in
the court of the guard, in accordance with the
word of the LORD, and said to me, "Buy my
field that is at Anathoth in the land of Benjamin, for the right of possession and redemption is yours; buy it for yourself." Then
I knew that this was the word of the LORD.

9 And I bought the field at Anathoth from
my cousin Hanamel, and weighed out the
money to him, seventeen shekels of silver.
10 I signed the deed, sealed it, got witnesses,
and weighed the money on scales. 11 Then I
took the sealed deed of purchase, containing the terms and conditions, and the open
copy; 12 and I gave the deed of purchase to
Baruch son of Neriah son of Mahseiah, in
the presence of my cousin Hanamel, in the
presence of the witnesses who signed the
deed of purchase, and in the presence of all
the Judeans who were sitting in the court of
the guard. 13 In their presence I charged Baruch, saying, 14 Thus says the LORD of hosts,
the God of Israel: Take these deeds, both this
sealed deed of purchase and this open deed,
and put them in an earthenware jar, in order
that they may last for a long time. 15 For thus
says the LORD of hosts, the God of Israel:
Houses and fields and vineyards shall again
be bought in this land.

Jeremiah Prays for Understanding

16 After I had given the deed of purchase
to Baruch son of Neriah, I prayed to the LORD,
saying: 17 Ah Lord GOD! It is you who made
the heavens and the earth by your great

32:6–15 *I bought the field.* In the midst of so
much destruction, desecration, and uncertainty,
Jeremiah does something very bold. He buys a
piece of land and makes sure that his purchase
is public. Buying a piece of land in such an
uncertain time is a visible, concrete sign of faith
in the future. God's faithful are so sure of the
promises of God that they can do things like
plant gardens, build houses, have children, and
perform all the other acts that are dependent

upon faith in the future. A beautiful new church
built in the heart of a decaying inner-city landscape, a mission begun in a country torn apart
by civil war, attention given to a troubled soul
who is still in the grip of addiction: through such
concrete, public gestures, the faith community
shows its conviction that the promises of God
are trustworthy and, although we do not always
know what the future holds, we know who
holds the future.

power and by your outstretched arm. Nothing is too hard for you. 18You show steadfast love to the thousandth generation,*a* but repay the guilt of parents into the laps of their children after them, O great and mighty God whose name is the LORD of hosts, 19great in counsel and mighty in deed; whose eyes are open to all the ways of mortals, rewarding all according to their ways and according to the fruit of their doings. 20You showed signs and wonders in the land of Egypt, and to this day in Israel and among all humankind, and have made yourself a name that continues to this very day. 21You brought your people Israel out of the land of Egypt with signs and wonders, with a strong hand and outstretched arm, and with great terror; 22and you gave them this land, which you swore to their ancestors to give them, a land flowing with milk and honey; 23and they entered and took possession of it. But they did not obey your voice or follow your law; of all you commanded them to do, they did nothing. Therefore you have made all these disasters come upon them. 24See, the siege ramps have been cast up against the city to take it, and the city, faced with sword, famine, and pestilence, has been given into the hands of the Chaldeans who are fighting against it. What you spoke has happened, as you yourself can see. 25Yet you, O Lord GOD, have said to me, "Buy the field for money and get witnesses"— though the city has been given into the hands of the Chaldeans.

God's Assurance of the People's Return

26 The word of the LORD came to Jeremiah: 27See, I am the LORD, the God of all flesh; is anything too hard for me? 28Therefore, thus says the LORD: I am going to give this city into the hands of the Chaldeans and into the hand of King Nebuchadrezzar of Babylon, and he shall take it. 29The Chaldeans who are fighting against this city shall come, set it on fire, and burn it, with the houses on whose roofs offerings have been made to Baal and libations have been poured out to other gods, to provoke me to anger. 30For the people of Israel and the people of Judah have done nothing but evil in my sight from their youth; the people of Israel have done noth-

ing but provoke me to anger by the work of their hands, says the LORD. 31This city has aroused my anger and wrath, from the day it was built until this day, so that I will remove it from my sight 32because of all the evil of the people of Israel and the people of Judah that they did to provoke me to anger—they, their kings and their officials, their priests and their prophets, the citizens of Judah and the inhabitants of Jerusalem. 33They have turned their backs to me, not their faces; though I have taught them persistently, they would not listen and accept correction. 34They set up their abominations in the house that bears my name, and defiled it. 35They built the high places of Baal in the valley of the son of Hinnom, to offer up their sons and daughters to Molech, though I did not command them, nor did it enter my mind that they should do this abomination, causing Judah to sin.

36 Now therefore thus says the LORD, the God of Israel, concerning this city of which you say, "It is being given into the hand of the king of Babylon by the sword, by famine, and by pestilence": 37See, I am going to gather them from all the lands to which I drove them in my anger and my wrath and in great indignation; I will bring them back to this place, and I will settle them in safety. 38They shall be my people, and I will be their God. 39I will give them one heart and one way, that they may fear me for all time, for their own good and the good of their children after them. 40I will make an everlasting covenant with them, never to draw back from doing good to them; and I will put the fear of me in their hearts, so that they may not turn from me. 41I will rejoice in doing good to them, and I will plant them in this land in faithfulness, with all my heart and all my soul.

42 For thus says the LORD: Just as I have brought all this great disaster upon this people, so I will bring upon them all the good fortune that I now promise them. 43Fields shall be bought in this land of which you are saying, It is a desolation, without human beings or animals; it has been given into the hands of the Chaldeans. 44Fields shall be bought for money, and deeds shall be signed and sealed and witnessed, in the land of Ben-

a Or *to thousands*

jamin, in the places around Jerusalem, and in the cities of Judah, of the hill country, of the Shephelah, and of the Negeb; for I will restore their fortunes, says the LORD.

Healing after Punishment

33 The word of the LORD came to Jeremiah a second time, while he was still confined in the court of the guard: ²Thus says the LORD who made the earth,ᵃ the LORD who formed it to establish it—the LORD is his name: ³Call to me and I will answer you, and will tell you great and hidden things that you have not known. ⁴For thus says the LORD, the God of Israel, concerning the houses of this city and the houses of the kings of Judah that were torn down to make a defense against the siege ramps and before the sword:ᵇ ⁵The Chaldeans are coming in to fightᶜ and to fill them with the dead bodies of those whom I shall strike down in my anger and my wrath, for I have hidden my face from this city because of all their wickedness. ⁶I am going to bring it recovery and healing; I will heal them and reveal to them abundanceᵇ of prosperity and security. ⁷I will restore the fortunes of Judah and the fortunes of Israel, and rebuild them as they were at first. ⁸I will cleanse them from all the guilt of their sin against me, and I will forgive all the guilt of their sin and rebellion against me. ⁹And this cityᵈ shall be to me a name of joy, a praise and a glory before all the nations of the earth who shall hear of all the good that I do for them; they shall fear and tremble because of all the good and all the prosperity I provide for it.

10 Thus says the LORD: In this place of which you say, "It is a waste without human beings or animals," in the towns of Judah and the streets of Jerusalem that are desolate, without inhabitants, human or animal, there shall once more be heard ¹¹the voice of mirth and the voice of gladness, the voice of the bridegroom and the voice of the bride, the voices of those who sing, as they bring thank offerings to the house of the LORD:

"Give thanks to the LORD of hosts,
  for the LORD is good,
  for his steadfast love endures forever!"

For I will restore the fortunes of the land as at first, says the LORD.

12 Thus says the LORD of hosts: In this place that is waste, without human beings or animals, and in all its towns there shall again be pasture for shepherds resting their flocks. ¹³In the towns of the hill country, of the Shephelah, and of the Negeb, in the land of Benjamin, the places around Jerusalem, and in the towns of Judah, flocks shall again pass under the hands of the one who counts them, says the LORD.

The Righteous Branch and the Covenant with David

14 The days are surely coming, says the LORD, when I will fulfill the promise I made to the house of Israel and the house of Judah. ¹⁵In those days and at that time I will cause a righteous Branch to spring up for David; and he shall execute justice and righteousness in the land. ¹⁶In those days Judah will be saved and Jerusalem will live in safety. And this is the name by which it will be called: "The LORD is our righteousness."

17 For thus says the LORD: David shall never lack a man to sit on the throne of the house of Israel, ¹⁸and the levitical priests shall never lack a man in my presence to offer burnt offerings, to make grain offerings, and to make sacrifices for all time.

19 The word of the LORD came to Jeremiah: ²⁰Thus says the LORD: If any of you could break my covenant with the day and my covenant with the night, so that day and night would not come at their appointed time, ²¹only then could my covenant with my servant David be broken, so that he would not have a son to reign on his throne, and my covenant with my ministers the Levites. ²²Just as the host of heaven cannot be numbered and the sands of the sea cannot be measured, so I will increase the offspring of my servant David, and the Levites who minister to me.

23 The word of the LORD came to Jeremiah: ²⁴Have you not observed how these people say, "The two families that the LORD chose

---

a Gk: Heb *it*   b Meaning of Heb uncertain
c Cn: Heb *They are coming in to fight against the*
Chaldeans   d Heb *And it*

have been rejected by him," and how they hold my people in such contempt that they no longer regard them as a nation? 25Thus says the LORD: Only if I had not established my covenant with day and night and the ordinances of heaven and earth, 26would I reject the offspring of Jacob and of my servant David and not choose any of his descendants as rulers over the offspring of Abraham, Isaac, and Jacob. For I will restore their fortunes, and will have mercy upon them.

Death in Captivity Predicted for Zedekiah

34 The word that came to Jeremiah from the LORD, when King Nebuchadrezzar of Babylon and all his army and all the kingdoms of the earth and all the peoples under his dominion were fighting against Jerusalem and all its cities: 2Thus says the LORD, the God of Israel: Go and speak to King Zedekiah of Judah and say to him: Thus says the LORD: I am going to give this city into the hand of the king of Babylon, and he shall burn it with fire. 3And you yourself shall not escape from his hand, but shall surely be captured and handed over to him; you shall see the king of Babylon eye to eye and speak with him face to face; and you shall go to Babylon. 4Yet hear the word of the LORD, O King Zedekiah of Judah! Thus says the LORD concerning you: You shall not die by the sword; 5you shall die in peace. And as spices were burned*a* for your ancestors, the earlier kings who preceded you, so they shall burn spices*b* for you and lament for you, saying, "Alas, lord!" For I have spoken the word, says the LORD.

6 Then the prophet Jeremiah spoke all these words to Zedekiah king of Judah, in Jerusalem, 7when the army of the king of Babylon was fighting against Jerusalem and against all the cities of Judah that were left, Lachish and Azekah; for these were the only fortified cities of Judah that remained.

Treacherous Treatment of Slaves

8 The word that came to Jeremiah from the LORD, after King Zedekiah had made a covenant with all the people in Jerusalem to make a proclamation of liberty to them— 9that all should set free their Hebrew slaves, male and female, so that no one should hold another Judean in slavery. 10And they obeyed, all the officials and all the people who had entered into the covenant that all would set free their slaves, male or female, so that they would not be enslaved again; they obeyed and set them free. 11But afterward they turned around and took back the male and female slaves they had set free, and brought them again into subjection as slaves. 12The word of the LORD came to Jeremiah from the LORD: 13Thus says the LORD, the God of Israel: I myself made a covenant with your ancestors when I brought them out of the land of Egypt, out of the house of slavery, saying, 14"Every seventh year each of you must set free any Hebrews who have been sold to you and have served you six years; you must set them free from your service." But your ancestors did not listen to me or incline their ears to me. 15You yourselves recently repented and did what was right in my sight by proclaiming liberty to one another, and you made a covenant before me in the house that is called by my name; 16but then you turned around and profaned my name when each of you took back your male and female slaves, whom you had set free according to their desire, and you brought them again into subjection to be your slaves. 17Therefore, thus says the LORD: You have not obeyed me by granting a release to your neighbors and friends; I am going to grant a release to you, says the LORD—a release to the sword, to pestilence, and to famine. I will make you a horror to all the kingdoms of the earth. 18And those who transgressed my covenant and did not keep the terms of the covenant that they made before me, I will make like*c* the calf when they cut it in two and passed between its parts: 19the officials of Judah, the officials of Jerusalem, the eunuchs, the priests, and all the people of the land who passed between the parts of the calf 20shall be handed over to their enemies and to those who seek their lives. Their corpses shall become food for the birds of the air and the wild animals of the earth. 21And as for King Zedekiah of Judah and his officials, I will hand them over to their enemies and to those who seek their

a Heb *as there was burning*   b Heb *shall burn*
c Cn: Heb lacks *like*

lives, to the army of the king of Babylon, which has withdrawn from you. 22I am going to command, says the LORD, and will bring them back to this city; and they will fight against it, and take it, and burn it with fire. The towns of Judah I will make a desolation without inhabitant.

The Rechabites Commended

35 The word that came to Jeremiah from the LORD in the days of King Jehoiakim son of Josiah of Judah: 2Go to the house of the Rechabites, and speak with them, and bring them to the house of the LORD, into one of the chambers; then offer them wine to drink. 3So I took Jaazaniah son of Jeremiah son of Habazziniah, and his brothers, and all his sons, and the whole house of the Rechabites. 4I brought them to the house of the LORD into the chamber of the sons of Hanan son of Igdaliah, the man of God, which was near the chamber of the officials, above the chamber of Maaseiah son of Shallum, keeper of the threshold. 5Then I set before the Rechabites pitchers full of wine, and cups; and I said to them, "Have some wine." 6But they answered, "We will drink no wine, for our ancestor Jonadab son of Rechab commanded us, 'You shall never drink wine, neither you nor your children; 7nor shall you ever build a house, or sow seed; nor shall you plant a vineyard, or even own one; but you shall live in tents all your days, that you may live many days in the land where you reside.' 8We have obeyed the charge of our ancestor Jonadab son of Rechab in all that he commanded us, to drink no wine all our days, ourselves, our wives, our sons, or our daughters, 9and not to build houses to live in. We have no vineyard or field or seed; 10but we have lived in tents, and have obeyed and done all that our ancestor Jonadab commanded us. 11But when King Nebuchadrezzar of Babylon came up against the land, we said, 'Come, and let us go to Jerusalem for fear of the army of the Chaldeans and the army of the Arameans.' That is why we are living in Jerusalem."

12 Then the word of the LORD came to Jeremiah: 13Thus says the LORD of hosts, the God of Israel: Go and say to the people of Ju-

dah and the inhabitants of Jerusalem, Can you not learn a lesson and obey my words? says the LORD. 14The command has been carried out that Jonadab son of Rechab gave to his descendants to drink no wine; and they drink none to this day, for they have obeyed their ancestor's command. But I myself have spoken to you persistently, and you have not obeyed me. 15I have sent to you all my servants the prophets, sending them persistently, saying, "Turn now every one of you from your evil way, and amend your doings, and do not go after other gods to serve them, and then you shall live in the land that I gave to you and your ancestors." But you did not incline your ear or obey me. 16The descendants of Jonadab son of Rechab have carried out the command that their ancestor gave them, but this people has not obeyed me. 17Therefore, thus says the LORD, the God of hosts, the God of Israel: I am going to bring on Judah and on all the inhabitants of Jerusalem every disaster that I have pronounced against them; because I have spoken to them and they have not listened, I have called to them and they have not answered.

18 But to the house of the Rechabites Jeremiah said: Thus says the LORD of hosts, the God of Israel: Because you have obeyed the command of your ancestor Jonadab, and kept all his precepts, and done all that he commanded you, 19therefore thus says the LORD of hosts, the God of Israel: Jonadab son of Rechab shall not lack a descendant to stand before me for all time.

The Scroll Read in the Temple

36 In the fourth year of King Jehoiakim son of Josiah of Judah, this word came to Jeremiah from the LORD: 2Take a scroll and write on it all the words that I have spoken to you against Israel and Judah and all the nations, from the day I spoke to you, from the days of Josiah until today. 3It may be that when the house of Judah hears of all the disasters that I intend to do to them, all of them may turn from their evil ways, so that I may forgive their iniquity and their sin.

4 Then Jeremiah called Baruch son of Neriah, and Baruch wrote on a scroll at Jeremiah's dictation all the words of the LORD that

he had spoken to him. ⁵And Jeremiah ordered Baruch, saying, "I am prevented from entering the house of the Lord; ⁶so you go yourself, and on a fast day in the hearing of the people in the Lord's house you shall read the words of the Lord from the scroll that you have written at my dictation. You shall read them also in the hearing of all the people of Judah who come up from their towns. ⁷It may be that their plea will come before the Lord, and that all of them will turn from their evil ways, for great is the anger and wrath that the Lord has pronounced against this people." ⁸And Baruch son of Neriah did all that the prophet Jeremiah ordered him about reading from the scroll the words of the Lord in the Lord's house.

9 In the fifth year of King Jehoiakim son of Josiah of Judah, in the ninth month, all the people in Jerusalem and all the people who came from the towns of Judah to Jerusalem proclaimed a fast before the Lord. ¹⁰Then, in the hearing of all the people, Baruch read the words of Jeremiah from the scroll, in the house of the Lord, in the chamber of Gemariah son of Shaphan the secretary, which was in the upper court, at the entry of the New Gate of the Lord's house.

The Scroll Read in the Palace

11 When Micaiah son of Gemariah son of Shaphan heard all the words of the Lord from the scroll, ¹²he went down to the king's house, into the secretary's chamber; and all the officials were sitting there: Elishama the secretary, Delaiah son of Shemaiah, Elnathan son of Achbor, Gemariah son of Shaphan, Zedekiah son of Hananiah, and all the officials. ¹³And Micaiah told them all the words that he had heard, when Baruch read the scroll in the hearing of the people. ¹⁴Then all the officials sent Jehudi son of Nethaniah son of Shelemiah son of Cushi to say to Baruch, "Bring the scroll that you read in the hearing of the people, and come." So Baruch son of Neriah took the scroll in his hand and came to them. ¹⁵And they said to him, "Sit down and read it to us." So Baruch read it to them. ¹⁶When they heard all the words, they turned to one another in alarm, and said to Baruch, "We certainly must report all these words to the king." ¹⁷Then they questioned Baruch, "Tell us now, how did you write all these words? Was it at his dictation?" ¹⁸Baruch answered them, "He dictated all these words to me, and I wrote them with ink on the scroll." ¹⁹Then the officials said to Baruch, "Go and hide, you and Jeremiah, and let no one know where you are."

Jehoiakim Burns the Scroll

20 Leaving the scroll in the chamber of Elishama the secretary, they went to the court of the king; and they reported all the words to the king. ²¹Then the king sent Jehudi to get the scroll, and he took it from the chamber of Elishama the secretary; and Jehudi read it to the king and all the officials who stood beside the king. ²²Now the king was sitting in his winter apartment (it was the ninth month), and there was a fire burning in the brazier before him. ²³As Jehudi read three or four columns, the king[a] would cut them off with a penknife and throw them into the fire in the brazier, until the entire scroll was consumed in the fire that was in the brazier. ²⁴Yet neither the king, nor any of his servants who heard all these words, was alarmed, nor did they tear their garments. ²⁵Even when Elnathan and Delaiah and Gemariah urged the king not to burn the scroll, he would not listen to them. ²⁶And the king commanded Jerahmeel the king's son and Seraiah son of Azriel and Shelemiah son of Abdeel to arrest the secretary Baruch and the prophet Jeremiah. But the Lord hid them.

Jeremiah Dictates Another

27 Now, after the king had burned the scroll with the words that Baruch wrote at Jeremiah's dictation, the word of the Lord came to Jeremiah: ²⁸Take another scroll and write on it all the former words that were in the first scroll, which King Jehoiakim of Judah has burned. ²⁹And concerning King Jehoiakim of Judah you shall say: Thus says the Lord, You have dared to burn this scroll, saying, Why have you written in it that the king of Babylon will certainly come and destroy this land, and will cut off from it human beings and animals? ³⁰Therefore thus says

a Heb *he*

the LORD concerning King Jehoiakim of Judah: He shall have no one to sit upon the throne of David, and his dead body shall be cast out to the heat by day and the frost by night. 31And I will punish him and his offspring and his servants for their iniquity; I will bring on them, and on the inhabitants of Jerusalem, and on the people of Judah, all the disasters with which I have threatened them—but they would not listen.

32 Then Jeremiah took another scroll and gave it to the secretary Baruch son of Neriah, who wrote on it at Jeremiah's dictation all the words of the scroll that King Jehoiakim of Judah had burned in the fire; and many similar words were added to them.

Zedekiah's Vain Hope

37 Zedekiah son of Josiah, whom King Nebuchadrezzar of Babylon made king in the land of Judah, succeeded Coniah son of Jehoiakim. 2But neither he nor his servants nor the people of the land listened to the words of the LORD that he spoke through the prophet Jeremiah.

3 King Zedekiah sent Jehucal son of Shelemiah and the priest Zephaniah son of Maaseiah to the prophet Jeremiah saying, "Please pray for us to the LORD our God." 4Now Jeremiah was still going in and out among the people, for he had not yet been put in prison. 5Meanwhile, the army of Pharaoh had come out of Egypt; and when the Chaldeans who were besieging Jerusalem heard news of them, they withdrew from Jerusalem.

6 Then the word of the LORD came to the prophet Jeremiah: 7Thus says the LORD, God of Israel: This is what the two of you shall say to the king of Judah, who sent you to me to inquire of me: Pharaoh's army, which set out to help you, is going to return to its own land, to Egypt. 8And the Chaldeans shall return and fight against this city; they shall take it and burn it with fire. 9Thus says the LORD: Do not deceive yourselves, saying, "The Chaldeans will surely go away from us," for they will not go away. 10Even if you defeated the whole army of Chaldeans who are fighting against you, and there remained of them only wounded men in their tents, they would rise up and burn this city with fire.

Jeremiah Is Imprisoned

11 Now when the Chaldean army had withdrawn from Jerusalem at the approach of Pharaoh's army, 12Jeremiah set out from Jerusalem to go to the land of Benjamin to receive his share of property *a* among the people there. 13When he reached the Benjamin Gate, a sentinel there named Irijah son of Shelemiah son of Hananiah arrested the prophet Jeremiah saying, "You are deserting to the Chaldeans." 14And Jeremiah said, "That is a lie; I am not deserting to the Chaldeans." But Irijah would not listen to him, and arrested Jeremiah and brought him to the officials. 15The officials were enraged at Jeremiah, and they beat him and imprisoned him in the house of the secretary Jonathan, for it had been made a prison. 16Thus Jeremiah was put in the cistern house, in the cells, and remained there many days.

17 Then King Zedekiah sent for him, and received him. The king questioned him secretly in his house, and said, "Is there any word from the LORD?" Jeremiah said, "There is!" Then he said, "You shall be handed over to the king of Babylon." 18Jeremiah also said to King Zedekiah, "What wrong have I done

---

a Meaning of Heb uncertain

37:1–38:28 *King Zedekiah sent . . . to the prophet Jeremiah.* Chapters 37–38 report the prophet's interactions with the vacillating and weak King Zedekiah. The Babylonians are at the gates. Three times Zedekiah sends for Jeremiah, but each time Jeremiah foresees defeat and advises capitulation, something Zedekiah doesn't want to hear. Let's face it. The Bible does not deal too generously with powerful, political people. Behind this story is not simply the affirmation that politics can often be a dirty business, but rather the repeated, politically significant, biblical insistence that it is God, not kings, who rules the world. Powerful political leaders, even in their power, are accountable to a higher power, namely, the Lord of heaven and earth. This is a hard lesson for kings to learn, a lesson that King Zedekiah avoids to the very end.

to you or your servants or this people, that you have put me in prison? 19Where are your prophets who prophesied to you, saying, 'The king of Babylon will not come against you and against this land'? 20Now please hear me, my lord king: be good enough to listen to my plea, and do not send me back to the house of the secretary Jonathan to die there." 21So King Zedekiah gave orders, and they committed Jeremiah to the court of the guard; and a loaf of bread was given him daily from the bakers' street, until all the bread of the city was gone. So Jeremiah remained in the court of the guard.

Jeremiah in the Cistern

38 Now Shephatiah son of Mattan, Gedaliah son of Pashhur, Jucal son of Shelemiah, and Pashhur son of Malchiah heard the words that Jeremiah was saying to all the people, 2Thus says the LORD, Those who stay in this city shall die by the sword, by famine, and by pestilence; but those who go out to the Chaldeans shall live; they shall have their lives as a prize of war, and live. 3Thus says the LORD, This city shall surely be handed over to the army of the king of Babylon and be taken. 4Then the officials said to the king, "This man ought to be put to death, because he is discouraging the soldiers who are left in this city, and all the people, by speaking such words to them. For this man is not seeking the welfare of this people, but their harm." 5King Zedekiah said, "Here he is; he is in your hands; for the king is powerless against you." 6So they took Jeremiah and threw him into the cistern of Malchiah, the king's son, which was in the court of the guard, letting Jeremiah down by ropes. Now there was no water in the cistern, but only mud, and Jeremiah sank in the mud.

Jeremiah Is Rescued by Ebed-melech

7 Ebed-melech the Ethiopian, *a* a eunuch in the king's house, heard that they had put Jeremiah into the cistern. The king happened to be sitting at the Benjamin Gate, 8So Ebed-melech left the king's house and spoke to the king, 9"My lord king, these men have acted wickedly in all they did to the prophet Jeremiah by throwing him into the cistern to

die there of hunger, for there is no bread left in the city." 10Then the king commanded Ebed-melech the Ethiopian, *a* "Take three men with you from here, and pull the prophet Jeremiah up from the cistern before he dies." 11So Ebed-melech took the men with him and went to the house of the king, to a wardrobe of *b* the storehouse, and took from there old rags and worn-out clothes, which he let down to Jeremiah in the cistern by ropes. 12Then Ebed-melech the Ethiopian *a* said to Jeremiah, "Just put the rags and clothes between your armpits and the ropes." Jeremiah did so. 13Then they drew Jeremiah up by the ropes and pulled him out of the cistern. And Jeremiah remained in the court of the guard.

Zedekiah Consults Jeremiah Again

14 King Zedekiah sent for the prophet Jeremiah and received him at the third entrance of the temple of the LORD. The king said to Jeremiah, "I have something to ask you; do not hide anything from me." 15Jeremiah said to Zedekiah, "If I tell you, you will put me to death, will you not? And if I give you advice, you will not listen to me." 16So King Zedekiah swore an oath in secret to Jeremiah, "As the LORD lives, who gave us our lives, I will not put you to death or hand you over to these men who seek your life."

17 Then Jeremiah said to Zedekiah, "Thus says the LORD, the God of hosts, the God of Israel, If you will only surrender to the officials of the king of Babylon, then your life shall be spared, and this city shall not be burned with fire, and you and your house shall live. 18But if you do not surrender to the officials of the king of Babylon, then this city shall be handed over to the Chaldeans, and they shall burn it with fire, and you yourself shall not escape from their hand." 19King Zedekiah said to Jeremiah, "I am afraid of the Judeans who have deserted to the Chaldeans, for I might be handed over to them and they would abuse me." 20Jeremiah said, "That will not happen. Just obey the voice of the LORD in what I say to you, and it shall go well with you, and your life shall be

a Or *Nubian*; Heb *Cushite*   *b* Cn: Heb *to under*

spared. 21But if you are determined not to surrender, this is what the LORD has shown me— 22a vision of all the women remaining in the house of the king of Judah being led out to the officials of the king of Babylon and saying,

'Your trusted friends have seduced you
　　and have overcome you;
Now that your feet are stuck in the
　　mud,
　　they desert you.'

23All your wives and your children shall be led out to the Chaldeans, and you yourself shall not escape from their hand, but shall be seized by the king of Babylon; and this city shall be burned with fire."

24 Then Zedekiah said to Jeremiah, "Do not let anyone else know of this conversation, or you will die. 25If the officials should hear that I have spoken with you, and they should come and say to you, 'Just tell us what you said to the king; do not conceal it from us, or we will put you to death. What did the king say to you?' 26then you shall say to them, 'I was presenting my plea to the king not to send me back to the house of Jonathan to die there.' " 27All the officials did come to Jeremiah and questioned him; and he answered them in the very words the king had commanded. So they stopped questioning him, for the conversation had not been overheard. 28And Jeremiah remained in the court of the guard until the day that Jerusalem was taken.

The Fall of Jerusalem

39 In the ninth year of King Zedekiah of Judah, in the tenth month, King Nebuchadrezzar of Babylon and all his army came against Jerusalem and besieged it; 2in the eleventh year of Zedekiah, in the fourth month, on the ninth day of the month, a breach was made in the city. 3When Jerusalem was taken, a all the officials of the king of Babylon came and sat in the middle gate: Nergal-sharezer, Samgar-nebo, Sarsechim the Rabsaris, Nergal-sharezer the Rabmag, with all the rest of the officials of the king of Babylon. 4When King Zedekiah of Judah and all the soldiers saw them, they fled, going out of the city at night by way of the king's garden through the gate between the two walls; and they went toward the Arabah. 5But the army of the Chaldeans pursued them, and overtook Zedekiah in the plains of Jericho; and when they had taken him, they brought him up to King Nebuchadrezzar of Babylon, at Riblah, in the land of Hamath; and he passed sentence on him. 6The king of Babylon slaughtered the sons of Zedekiah at Riblah before his eyes; also the king of Babylon slaughtered all the nobles of Judah. 7He put out the eyes of Zedekiah, and bound him in fetters to take him to Babylon. 8The Chaldeans burned the king's house and the houses of the people, and broke down the walls of Jerusalem. 9Then Nebuzaradan the captain of the guard exiled to Babylon the rest of the people who were left in the city, those who had deserted to him, and the people who remained. 10Nebuzaradan the captain of the guard left in the land of Judah some of the poor people who owned nothing, and gave them vineyards and fields at the same time.

Jeremiah, Set Free, Remembers Ebed-melech

11 King Nebuchadrezzar of Babylon gave command concerning Jeremiah through Nebuzaradan, the captain of the guard, saying, 12"Take him, look after him well and do him no harm, but deal with him as he may ask you." 13So Nebuzaradan the captain of the guard, Nebushazban the Rabsaris, Nergal-sharezer the Rabmag, and all the chief officers of the king of Babylon sent 14and took Jeremiah from the court of the guard. They entrusted him to Gedaliah son of Ahikam son of Shaphan to be brought home. So he stayed with his own people.

15 The word of the LORD came to Jeremiah while he was confined in the court of the guard: 16Go and say to Ebed-melech the Ethiopian: b Thus says the LORD of hosts, the God of Israel: I am going to fulfill my words against this city for evil and not for good, and they shall be accomplished in your presence on that day. 17But I will save you on that day, says the LORD, and you shall not be handed over to those whom you dread. 18For I will

a This clause has been transposed from 38.28
b Or *Nubian*; Heb *Cushite*

surely save you, and you shall not fall by the sword; but you shall have your life as a prize of war, because you have trusted in me, says the Lord.

Jeremiah with Gedaliah the Governor

40 The word that came to Jeremiah from the Lord after Nebuzaradan the captain of the guard had let him go from Ramah, when he took him bound in fetters along with all the captives of Jerusalem and Judah who were being exiled to Babylon. ²The captain of the guard took Jeremiah and said to him, "The Lord your God threatened this place with this disaster; ³and now the Lord has brought it about, and has done as he said, because all of you sinned against the Lord and did not obey his voice. Therefore this thing has come upon you. ⁴Now look, I have just released you today from the fetters on your hands. If you wish to come with me to Babylon, come, and I will take good care of you; but if you do not wish to come with me to Babylon, you need not come. See, the whole land is before you; go wherever you think it good and right to go. ⁵If you remain,ᵃ then return to Gedaliah son of Ahikam son of Shaphan, whom the king of Babylon appointed governor of the towns of Judah, and stay with him among the people; or go wherever you think it right to go." So the captain of the guard gave him an allowance of food and a present, and let him go. ⁶Then Jeremiah went to Gedaliah son of Ahikam at Mizpah, and stayed with him among the people who were left in the land.

7 When all the leaders of the forces in the open country and their troops heard that the king of Babylon had appointed Gedaliah son of Ahikam governor in the land, and had committed to him men, women, and children, those of the poorest of the land who had not been taken into exile to Babylon, ⁸they went to Gedaliah at Mizpah—Ishmael son of Nethaniah, Johanan son of Kareah, Seraiah son of Tanhumeth, the sons of Ephai the Netophathite, Jezaniah son of the Maacathite, they and their troops. ⁹Gedaliah son of Ahikam son of Shaphan swore to them and their troops, saying, "Do not be afraid to serve the Chaldeans. Stay in the land and

serve the king of Babylon, and it shall go well with you. ¹⁰As for me, I am staying at Mizpah to represent you before the Chaldeans who come to us; but as for you, gather wine and summer fruits and oil, and store them in your vessels, and live in the towns that you have taken over." ¹¹Likewise, when all the Judeans who were in Moab and among the Ammonites and in Edom and in other lands heard that the king of Babylon had left a remnant in Judah and had appointed Gedaliah son of Ahikam son of Shaphan as governor over them, ¹²then all the Judeans returned from all the places to which they had been scattered and came to the land of Judah, to Gedaliah at Mizpah; and they gathered wine and summer fruits in great abundance.

13 Now Johanan son of Kareah and all the leaders of the forces in the open country came to Gedaliah at Mizpah ¹⁴and said to him, "Are you at all aware that Baalis king of the Ammonites has sent Ishmael son of Nethaniah to take your life?" But Gedaliah son of Ahikam would not believe them. ¹⁵Then Johanan son of Kareah spoke secretly to Gedaliah at Mizpah, "Please let me go and kill Ishmael son of Nethaniah, and no one else will know. Why should he take your life, so that all the Judeans who are gathered around you would be scattered, and the remnant of Judah would perish?" ¹⁶But Gedaliah son of Ahikam said to Johanan son of Kareah, "Do not do such a thing, for you are telling a lie about Ishmael."

Insurrection against Gedaliah

41 In the seventh month, Ishmael son of Nethaniah son of Elishama, of the royal family, one of the chief officers of the king, came with ten men to Gedaliah son of Ahikam, at Mizpah. As they ate bread together there at Mizpah, ²Ishmael son of Nethaniah and the ten men with him got up and struck down Gedaliah son of Ahikam son of Shaphan with the sword and killed him, because the king of Babylon had appointed him governor in the land. ³Ishmael also killed all the Judeans who were with Gedaliah at Mizpah, and the Chaldean soldiers who happened to be there.

ᵃ Syr: Meaning of Heb uncertain

4 On the day after the murder of Gedaliah, before anyone knew of it, [5]eighty men arrived from Shechem and Shiloh and Samaria, with their beards shaved and their clothes torn, and their bodies gashed, bringing grain offerings and incense to present at the temple of the Lord. [6]And Ishmael son of Nethaniah came out from Mizpah to meet them, weeping as he came. As he met them, he said to them, "Come to Gedaliah son of Ahikam." [7]When they reached the middle of the city, Ishmael son of Nethaniah and the men with him slaughtered them, and threw them[a] into a cistern. [8]But there were ten men among them who said to Ishmael, "Do not kill us, for we have stores of wheat, barley, oil, and honey hidden in the fields." So he refrained, and did not kill them along with their companions.

9 Now the cistern into which Ishmael had thrown all the bodies of the men whom he had struck down was the large cistern[b] that King Asa had made for defense against King Baasha of Israel; Ishmael son of Nethaniah filled that cistern with those whom he had killed. [10]Then Ishmael took captive all the rest of the people who were in Mizpah, the king's daughters and all the people who were left at Mizpah, whom Nebuzaradan, the captain of the guard, had committed to Gedaliah son of Ahikam. Ishmael son of Nethaniah took them captive and set out to cross over to the Ammonites.

11 But when Johanan son of Kareah and all the leaders of the forces with him heard of all the crimes that Ishmael son of Nethaniah had done, [12]they took all their men and went to fight against Ishmael son of Nethaniah. They came upon him at the great pool that is in Gibeon. [13]And when all the people who were with Ishmael saw Johanan son of Kareah and all the leaders of the forces with him, they were glad. [14]So all the people whom Ishmael had carried away captive from Mizpah turned around and came back, and went to Johanan son of Kareah. [15]But Ishmael son of Nethaniah escaped from Johanan with eight men, and went to the Ammonites. [16]Then Johanan son of Kareah and all the leaders of the forces with him took all the rest of the people whom Ishmael son of Nethaniah had

carried away captive[c] from Mizpah after he had slain Gedaliah son of Ahikam—soldiers, women, children, and eunuchs, whom Johanan brought back from Gibeon. [d] [17]And they set out, and stopped at Geruth Chimham near Bethlehem, intending to go to Egypt [18]because of the Chaldeans; for they were afraid of them, because Ishmael son of Nethaniah had killed Gedaliah son of Ahikam, whom the king of Babylon had made governor over the land.

Jeremiah Advises Survivors Not to Migrate

42 Then all the commanders of the forces, and Johanan son of Kareah and Azariah[e] son of Hoshaiah, and all the people from the least to the greatest, approached [2]the prophet Jeremiah and said, "Be good enough to listen to our plea, and pray to the Lord your God for us—for all this remnant. For there are only a few of us left out of many, as your eyes can see. [3]Let the Lord your God show us where we should go and what we should do." [4]The prophet Jeremiah said to them, "Very well: I am going to pray to the Lord your God as you request, and whatever the Lord answers you I will tell you; I will keep nothing back from you." [5]They in their turn said to Jeremiah, "May the Lord be a true and faithful witness against us if we do not act according to everything that the Lord your God sends us through you. [6]Whether it is good or bad, we will obey the voice of the Lord our God to whom we are sending you, in order that it may go well with us when we obey the voice of the Lord our God."

7 At the end of ten days the word of the Lord came to Jeremiah. [8]Then he summoned Johanan son of Kareah and all the commanders of the forces who were with him, and all the people from the least to the greatest, [9]and said to them, "Thus says the Lord, the God of Israel, to whom you sent me to present your plea before him: [10]If you will

a Syr: Heb lacks *and threw them*; compare verse 9
b Gk: Heb *whom he had killed by the hand of Gedaliah*   c Cn: Heb *whom he recovered from Ishmael son of Nethaniah*   d Meaning of Heb uncertain   e Gk: Heb *Jezaniah*

only remain in this land, then I will build you up and not pull you down; I will plant you, and not pluck you up; for I am sorry for the disaster that I have brought upon you. [11]Do not be afraid of the king of Babylon, as you have been; do not be afraid of him, says the LORD, for I am with you, to save you and to rescue you from his hand. [12]I will grant you mercy, and he will have mercy on you and restore you to your native soil. [13]But if you continue to say, 'We will not stay in this land,' thus disobeying the voice of the LORD your God [14]and saying, 'No, we will go to the land of Egypt, where we shall not see war, or hear the sound of the trumpet, or be hungry for bread, and there we will stay,' [15]then hear the word of the LORD, O remnant of Judah. Thus says the LORD of hosts, the God of Israel: If you are determined to enter Egypt and go to settle there, [16]then the sword that you fear shall overtake you there, in the land of Egypt; and the famine that you dread shall follow close after you into Egypt; and there you shall die. [17]All the people who have determined to go to Egypt to settle there shall die by the sword, by famine, and by pestilence; they shall have no remnant or survivor from the disaster that I am bringing upon them.

18 "For thus says the LORD of hosts, the God of Israel: Just as my anger and my wrath were poured out on the inhabitants of Jerusalem, so my wrath will be poured out on you when you go to Egypt. You shall become an object of execration and horror, of cursing and ridicule. You shall see this place no more. [19]The LORD has said to you, O remnant of Judah, Do not go to Egypt. Be well aware that I have warned you today [20]that you have made a fatal mistake. For you yourselves sent me to the LORD your God, saying, 'Pray for us to the LORD our God, and whatever the LORD our God says, tell us and we will do it.' [21]So I have told you today, but you have not obeyed the voice of the LORD your God in anything that he sent me to tell you. [22]Be well aware, then, that you shall die by the sword, by famine, and by pestilence in the place where you desire to go and settle."

Taken to Egypt, Jeremiah Warns of Judgment

43 When Jeremiah finished speaking to all the people all these words of the LORD their God, with which the LORD their God had sent him to them, [2]Azariah son of Hoshaiah and Johanan son of Kareah and all the other insolent men said to Jeremiah, "You are telling a lie. The LORD our God did not send you to say, 'Do not go to Egypt to settle there'; [3]but Baruch son of Neriah is inciting you against us, to hand us over to the Chaldeans, in order that they may kill us or take us into exile in Babylon." [4]So Johanan son of Kareah and all the commanders of the forces and all the people did not obey the voice of the LORD, to stay in the land of Judah. [5]But Johanan son of Kareah and all the commanders of the forces took all the remnant of Judah who had returned to settle in the land of Judah from all the nations to which they had been driven— [6]the men, the women, the children, the princesses, and everyone whom Nebuzaradan the captain of the guard had left with Gedaliah son of Ahikam son of Shaphan; also the prophet Jeremiah and Baruch son of Neriah. [7]And they came into the land of Egypt, for they did not obey the voice of the LORD. And they arrived at Tahpanhes.

8 Then the word of the LORD came to Jeremiah in Tahpanhes: [9]Take some large stones in your hands, and bury them in the clay pavement[a] that is at the entrance to Pharaoh's palace in Tahpanhes. Let the Judeans see you do it, [10]and say to them, Thus says the LORD of hosts, the God of Israel: I am going to send and take my servant King Nebuchadrezzar of Babylon, and he[b] will set his throne above these stones that I have buried, and he will spread his royal canopy over them. [11]He shall come and ravage the land of Egypt, giving

> those who are destined for pestilence, to pestilence,
> and those who are destined for captivity, to captivity,
> and those who are destined for the sword, to the sword.

[12]He[c] shall kindle a fire in the temples of the

---

a Meaning of Heb uncertain   b Gk Syr: Heb I
c Gk Syr Vg: Heb I

gods of Egypt; and he shall burn them and carry them away captive; and he shall pick clean the land of Egypt, as a shepherd picks his cloak clean of vermin; and he shall depart from there safely. [13]He shall break the obelisks of Heliopolis, which is in the land of Egypt; and the temples of the gods of Egypt he shall burn with fire.

Denunciation of Persistent Idolatry

44 The word that came to Jeremiah for all the Judeans living in the land of Egypt, at Migdol, at Tahpanhes, at Memphis, and in the land of Pathros, [2]Thus says the LORD of hosts, the God of Israel: You yourselves have seen all the disaster that I have brought on Jerusalem and on all the towns of Judah. Look at them; today they are a desolation, without an inhabitant in them, [3]because of the wickedness that they committed, provoking me to anger, in that they went to make offerings and serve other gods that they had not known, neither they, nor you, nor your ancestors. [4]Yet I persistently sent to you all my servants the prophets, saying, "I beg you not to do this abominable thing that I hate!" [5]But they did not listen or incline their ear, to turn from their wickedness and make no offerings to other gods. [6]So my wrath and my anger were poured out and kindled in the towns of Judah and in the streets of Jerusalem; and they became a waste and a desolation, as they still are today. [7]And now thus says the LORD God of hosts, the God of Israel: Why are you doing such great harm to yourselves, to cut off man and woman, child and infant, from the midst of Judah, leaving yourselves without a remnant? [8]Why do you provoke me to anger with the works of your hands, making offerings to other gods in the land of Egypt where you have come to settle? Will you be cut off and become an object of cursing and ridicule among all the nations of the earth? [9]Have you forgotten the crimes of your ancestors, of the kings of Judah, of their[a] wives, your own crimes and those of your wives, which they committed in the land of Judah and in the streets of Jerusalem? [10]They have shown no contrition or fear to this day, nor have they walked in my law and my statutes that I set before you and before your ancestors.

11   Therefore thus says the LORD of hosts, the God of Israel: I am determined to bring disaster on you, to bring all Judah to an end. [12]I will take the remnant of Judah who are determined to come to the land of Egypt to settle, and they shall perish, everyone; in the land of Egypt they shall fall; by the sword and by famine they shall perish; from the least to the greatest, they shall die by the sword and by famine; and they shall become an object of execration and horror, of cursing and ridicule. [13]I will punish those who live in the land of Egypt, as I have punished Jerusalem, with the sword, with famine, and with pestilence, [14]so that none of the remnant of Judah who have come to settle in the land of Egypt shall escape or survive or return to the land of Judah. Although they long to go back to live there, they shall not go back, except some fugitives.

15   Then all the men who were aware that their wives had been making offerings to other gods, and all the women who stood by, a great assembly, all the people who lived in Pathros in the land of Egypt, answered Jeremiah: [16]"As for the word that you have spo-

a Heb his

44:4–5 *I persistently sent to you . . . the prophets.* For forty chapters, ruin has been predicted by the prophet. The sad truth has been told. And now that great, long-anticipated wrath has come. The results of the infidelity of the covenant people are everywhere to be seen. And yet it did not have to be so. Servants were sent to proclaim the truth, but the people did not listen. This is an old story, a story that the community of faith reenacts in our own time. So in the writings of the prophets, it is not simply the ancient exiles, hiding out in Egypt, who are meant to learn from Jeremiah's words, but we modern-day readers as well. There is punishment, not simply sent by the hand of God, but punishment that we bring on ourselves, consequences of our behavior. It may not be a story that we want to hear. It may be a story that we have spent great resources in avoiding. Nevertheless, this sad story of "truth and consequences" is true.

ken to us in the name of the LORD, we are not going to listen to you. [17]Instead, we will do everything that we have vowed, make offerings to the queen of heaven and pour out libations to her, just as we and our ancestors, our kings and our officials, used to do in the towns of Judah and in the streets of Jerusalem. We used to have plenty of food, and prospered, and saw no misfortune. [18]But from the time we stopped making offerings to the queen of heaven and pouring out libations to her, we have lacked everything and have perished by the sword and by famine." [19]And the women said,[a] "Indeed we will go on making offerings to the queen of heaven and pouring out libations to her; do you think that we made cakes for her, marked with her image, and poured out libations to her without our husbands' being involved?"

20 Then Jeremiah said to all the people, men and women, all the people who were giving him this answer: [21]"As for the offerings that you made in the towns of Judah and in the streets of Jerusalem, you and your ancestors, your kings and your officials, and the people of the land, did not the LORD remember them? Did it not come into his mind? [22]The LORD could no longer bear the sight of your evil doings, the abominations that you committed; therefore your land became a desolation and a waste and a curse, without inhabitant, as it is to this day. [23]It is because you burned offerings, and because you sinned against the LORD and did not obey the voice of the LORD or walk in his law and in his statutes and in his decrees, that this disaster has befallen you, as is still evident today."

24 Jeremiah said to all the people and all the women, "Hear the word of the LORD, all you Judeans who are in the land of Egypt, [25]Thus says the LORD of hosts, the God of Israel: You and your wives have accomplished in deeds what you declared in words, saying, 'We are determined to perform the vows that we have made, to make offerings to the queen of heaven and to pour out libations to her.' By

all means, keep your vows and make your libations! [26]Therefore hear the word of the LORD, all you Judeans who live in the land of Egypt: Lo, I swear by my great name, says the LORD, that my name shall no longer be pronounced on the lips of any of the people of Judah in all the land of Egypt, saying, 'As the Lord GOD lives.' [27]I am going to watch over them for harm and not for good; all the people of Judah who are in the land of Egypt shall perish by the sword and by famine, until not one is left. [28]And those who escape the sword shall return from the land of Egypt to the land of Judah, few in number; and all the remnant of Judah, who have come to the land of Egypt to settle, shall know whose words will stand, mine or theirs! [29]This shall be the sign to you, says the LORD, that I am going to punish you in this place, in order that you may know that my words against you will surely be carried out: [30]Thus says the LORD, I am going to give Pharaoh Hophra, king of Egypt, into the hands of his enemies, those who seek his life, just as I gave King Zedekiah of Judah into the hand of King Nebuchadrezzar of Babylon, his enemy who sought his life."

A Word of Comfort to Baruch

45 The word that the prophet Jeremiah spoke to Baruch son of Neriah, when he wrote these words in a scroll at the dictation of Jeremiah, in the fourth year of King Jehoiakim son of Josiah of Judah: [2]Thus says the LORD, the God of Israel, to you, O Baruch: [3]You said, "Woe is me! The LORD has added sorrow to my pain; I am weary with my groaning, and I find no rest." [4]Thus you shall say to him, "Thus says the LORD: I am going to break down what I have built, and pluck up what I have planted—that is, the whole land. [5]And you, do you seek great things for yourself? Do not seek them; for I am going to bring disaster upon all flesh, says the LORD; but I will give you your life as a prize of war in every place to which you may go."

a Compare Syr: Heb lacks *And the women said*

45:5 SERVICE—*See* Spiritual Disciplines Index.

Judgment on Egypt

46 The word of the LORD that came to the prophet Jeremiah concerning the nations.

2 Concerning Egypt, about the army of Pharaoh Neco, king of Egypt, which was by the river Euphrates at Carchemish and which King Nebuchadrezzar of Babylon defeated in the fourth year of King Jehoiakim son of Josiah of Judah:

3 Prepare buckler and shield,
    and advance for battle!
4 Harness the horses;
    mount the steeds!
Take your stations with your helmets,
    whet your lances,
    put on your coats of mail!
5 Why do I see them terrified?
    They have fallen back;
their warriors are beaten down,
    and have fled in haste.
They do not look back—
    terror is all around!
                                    says the LORD.
6 The swift cannot flee away,
    nor can the warrior escape;
in the north by the river Euphrates
    they have stumbled and fallen.

7 Who is this, rising like the Nile,
    like rivers whose waters surge?
8 Egypt rises like the Nile,
    like rivers whose waters surge.
It said, Let me rise, let me cover the
        earth,
    let me destroy cities and their
        inhabitants.
9 Advance, O horses,
    and dash madly, O chariots!
Let the warriors go forth:
    Ethiopia*a* and Put who carry the
        shield,
    the Ludim, who draw*b* the bow.
10 That day is the day of the Lord GOD of
        hosts,
    a day of retribution,
    to gain vindication from his foes.
The sword shall devour and be sated,
    and drink its fill of their blood.
For the Lord GOD of hosts holds a
        sacrifice

in the land of the north by the river
        Euphrates.
11 Go up to Gilead, and take balm,
    O virgin daughter Egypt!
In vain you have used many medicines;
    there is no healing for you.
12 The nations have heard of your shame,
    and the earth is full of your cry;
for warrior has stumbled against warrior;
    both have fallen together.

Babylonia Will Strike Egypt

13 The word that the LORD spoke to the prophet Jeremiah about the coming of King Nebuchadrezzar of Babylon to attack the land of Egypt:

14 Declare in Egypt, and proclaim in
        Migdol;
    proclaim in Memphis and Tahpanhes;
Say, "Take your stations and be ready,
    for the sword shall devour those
        around you."
15 Why has Apis fled?*c*
    Why did your bull not stand?
    —because the LORD thrust him down.
16 Your multitude stumbled*d* and fell,
    and one said to another,*e*
"Come, let us go back to our own
        people
    and to the land of our birth,
    because of the destroying sword."
17 Give Pharaoh, king of Egypt, the name
    "Braggart who missed his chance."

18 As I live, says the King,
    whose name is the LORD of hosts,
one is coming
    like Tabor among the mountains,
    and like Carmel by the sea.
19 Pack your bags for exile,
    sheltered daughter Egypt!
For Memphis shall become a waste,
    a ruin, without inhabitant.

20 A beautiful heifer is Egypt—
    a gadfly from the north lights upon
        her.

a Or *Nubia*; Heb *Cush*   *b* Cn: Heb *who grasp, who draw*   *c* Gk: Heb *Why was it swept away*
d Gk: Meaning of Heb uncertain   *e* Gk: Heb *and fell one to another and they said*

21 Even her mercenaries in her midst
     are like fatted calves;
they too have turned and fled
     together,
     they did not stand;
for the day of their calamity has come
     upon them,
     the time of their punishment.

22 She makes a sound like a snake gliding
     away;
     for her enemies march in force,
and come against her with axes,
     like those who fell trees.
23 They shall cut down her forest,
                    says the LORD,
     though it is impenetrable,
because they are more numerous
     than locusts;
     they are without number.
24 Daughter Egypt shall be put to shame;
     she shall be handed over to a people
          from the north.

25 The LORD of hosts, the God of Israel,
said: See, I am bringing punishment upon
Amon of Thebes, and Pharaoh, and Egypt
and her gods and her kings, upon Pharaoh
and those who trust in him. 26 I will hand
them over to those who seek their life, to
King Nebuchadrezzar of Babylon and his officers. Afterward Egypt shall be inhabited as
in the days of old, says the LORD.

God Will Save Israel

27 But as for you, have no fear, my servant
     Jacob,
and do not be dismayed, O Israel;

for I am going to save you from far
     away,
and your offspring from the land of
     their captivity.
Jacob shall return and have quiet and
     ease,
and no one shall make him afraid.
28 As for you, have no fear, my servant
     Jacob,
                    says the LORD,
     for I am with you.
I will make an end of all the nations
     among which I have banished you,
     but I will not make an end of you!
I will chastise you in just measure,
     and I will by no means leave you
          unpunished.

Judgment on the Philistines

47 The word of the LORD that came to
the prophet Jeremiah concerning the
Philistines, before Pharaoh attacked Gaza:
2 Thus says the LORD:
See, waters are rising out of the north
     and shall become an overflowing
          torrent;
they shall overflow the land and all that
     fills it,
     the city and those who live in it.
People shall cry out,
     and all the inhabitants of the land
          shall wail.
3 At the noise of the stamping of the
          hoofs of his stallions,
     at the clatter of his chariots, at the
          rumbling of their wheels,
parents do not turn back for children,
     so feeble are their hands,

46:28 *I will make an end of all the nations . . .
but I will not make an end of you!* Though God
has used even the pagan nations to teach his
covenant people a bitter lesson, God makes
clear that the covenant continues. All of the
pagan nations that so raged against and so
terribly devastated the faith community shall
have their day. One by one, the nations are
named in a great roll call of all of Israel's pagan
enemies—Egypt, Philistia, Moab, Ammon,
Edom, and so on (chaps 46–51). In their own
ways, they were all great nations, but no more.

They may have had great armies and great
economies, but they lacked what the faith
community has—the steadfast love of God,
the promise of God never to desert it. God can
use even pagan Babylon for his purposes, but
God can also punish Babylon, and will. Yet
the promise, and the people the promise has
engendered, continues. Even in the darkest and
most difficult times, even when all hope seems
lost, the little community of faith clings to the
great promise, "I will not make an end of you."

4 because of the day that is coming
   to destroy all the Philistines,
to cut off from Tyre and Sidon
   every helper that remains.
For the LORD is destroying the
      Philistines,
   the remnant of the coastland of
      Caphtor.
5 Baldness has come upon Gaza,
   Ashkelon is silenced.
O remnant of their power!*a*
   How long will you gash yourselves?
6 Ah, sword of the LORD!
   How long until you are quiet?
Put yourself into your scabbard,
   rest and be still!
7 How can it*b* be quiet,
   when the LORD has given it an order?
Against Ashkelon and against the
      seashore—
   there he has appointed it.

Judgment on Moab

48 Concerning Moab.

Thus says the LORD of hosts, the God of Israel:
   Alas for Nebo, it is laid waste!
      Kiriathaim is put to shame, it is taken;
   the fortress is put to shame and broken
      down;
2   the renown of Moab is no more.
   In Heshbon they planned evil against
      her:
   "Come, let us cut her off from being a
      nation!"
   You also, O Madmen, shall be brought
      to silence;*c*
   the sword shall pursue you.

3 Hark! a cry from Horonaim,
   "Desolation and great destruction!"
4 "Moab is destroyed!"
   her little ones cry out.
5 For at the ascent of Luhith
   they go*d* up weeping bitterly;
for at the descent of Horonaim
   they have heard the distressing cry of
      anguish.
6 Flee! Save yourselves!
   Be like a wild ass*e* in the desert!

7 Surely, because you trusted in your
      strongholds*f* and your treasures,
   you also shall be taken;
Chemosh shall go out into exile,
   with his priests and his attendants.
8 The destroyer shall come upon every
      town,
   and no town shall escape;
the valley shall perish,
   and the plain shall be destroyed,
   as the LORD has spoken.

9 Set aside salt for Moab,
   for she will surely fall;
her towns shall become a desolation,
   with no inhabitant in them.

10 Accursed is the one who is slack in doing
the work of the LORD; and accursed is the one
who keeps back the sword from bloodshed.

11 Moab has been at ease from his youth,
   settled like wine*g* on its dregs;
he has not been emptied from vessel to
      vessel,
   nor has he gone into exile;
therefore his flavor has remained
   and his aroma is unspoiled.

12 Therefore, the time is surely coming,
says the LORD, when I shall send to him de-
canters to decant him, and empty his vessels, and break his*h* jars in pieces. 13Then
Moab shall be ashamed of Chemosh, as the
house of Israel was ashamed of Bethel, their
confidence.

14 How can you say, "We are heroes
   and mighty warriors"?
15 The destroyer of Moab and his towns
      has come up,
   and the choicest of his young men
      have gone down to slaughter,
   says the King, whose name is the
      LORD of hosts.
16 The calamity of Moab is near at hand
   and his doom approaches swiftly.

---

a Gk: Heb *their valley*   *b* Gk Vg: Heb *you*
c The place-name *Madmen* sounds like the Hebrew
verb *to be silent*   *d* Cn: Heb *he goes*
e Gk Aquila: Heb *like Aroer*   *f* Gk: Heb *works*
g Heb lacks *like wine*   *h* Gk Aquila: Heb *their*

17 Mourn over him, all you his neighbors,
and all who know his name;
say, "How the mighty scepter is broken,
the glorious staff!"

18 Come down from glory,
and sit on the parched ground,
enthroned daughter Dibon!
For the destroyer of Moab has come up
against you;
he has destroyed your strongholds.
19 Stand by the road and watch,
you inhabitant of Aroer!
Ask the man fleeing and the woman
escaping;
say, "What has happened?"
20 Moab is put to shame, for it is broken
down;
wail and cry!
Tell it by the Arnon,
that Moab is laid waste.

21 Judgment has come upon the tableland, upon Holon, and Jahzah, and Mephaath, 22and Dibon, and Nebo, and Beth-diblathaim, 23and Kiriathaim, and Beth-gamul, and Beth-meon, 24and Kerioth, and Bozrah, and all the towns of the land of Moab, far and near. 25The horn of Moab is cut off, and his arm is broken, says the LORD.

26 Make him drunk, because he magnified himself against the LORD; let Moab wallow in his vomit; he too shall become a laughingstock. 27Israel was a laughingstock for you, though he was not caught among thieves; but whenever you spoke of him you shook your head!

28 Leave the towns, and live on the rock,
O inhabitants of Moab!
Be like the dove that nests
on the sides of the mouth of a gorge.
29 We have heard of the pride of Moab—
he is very proud—
of his loftiness, his pride, and his
arrogance,
and the haughtiness of his heart.
30 I myself know his insolence, says the
LORD;
his boasts are false,
his deeds are false.

31 Therefore I wail for Moab;
I cry out for all Moab;
for the people of Kir-heres I mourn.
32 More than for Jazer I weep for you,
O vine of Sibmah!
Your branches crossed over the sea,
reached as far as Jazer; a
upon your summer fruits and your
vintage
the destroyer has fallen.
33 Gladness and joy have been taken away
from the fruitful land of Moab;
I have stopped the wine from the wine
presses;
no one treads them with shouts of
joy;
the shouting is not the shout of joy.

34 Heshbon and Elealeh cry out; b as far as Jahaz they utter their voice, from Zoar to Horonaim and Eglath-shelishiyah. For even the waters of Nimrim have become desolate. 35And I will bring to an end in Moab, says the LORD, those who offer sacrifice at a high place and make offerings to their gods. 36Therefore my heart moans for Moab like a flute, and my heart moans like a flute for the people of Kir-heres; for the riches they gained have perished.

37 For every head is shaved and every beard cut off; on all the hands there are gashes, and on the loins sackcloth. 38On all the housetops of Moab and in the squares there is nothing but lamentation; for I have broken Moab like a vessel that no one wants, says the LORD. 39How it is broken! How they wail! How Moab has turned his back in shame! So Moab has become a derision and a horror to all his neighbors.

40 For thus says the LORD:
Look, he shall swoop down like an
eagle,
and spread his wings against Moab;
41 the towns c shall be taken
and the strongholds seized.
The hearts of the warriors of Moab, on
that day,

a Two Mss and Isa 16.8: MT *the sea of Jazer*
b Cn: Heb *From the cry of Heshbon to Elealeh*
c Or *Kerioth*

shall be like the heart of a woman in
  labor.
42 Moab shall be destroyed as a people,
  because he magnified himself against
    the LORD.
43 Terror, pit, and trap
  are before you, O inhabitants of Moab!
              says the LORD.
44 Everyone who flees from the terror
  shall fall into the pit,
and everyone who climbs out of the pit
  shall be caught in the trap.
For I will bring these things*a* upon
  Moab
  in the year of their punishment,
             says the LORD.

45 In the shadow of Heshbon
  fugitives stop exhausted;
for a fire has gone out from Heshbon,
  a flame from the house of Sihon;
it has destroyed the forehead of Moab,
  the scalp of the people of tumult. *b*
46 Woe to you, O Moab!
  The people of Chemosh have
    perished,
for your sons have been taken captive,
  and your daughters into captivity.
47 Yet I will restore the fortunes of Moab
  in the latter days, says the LORD.
Thus far is the judgment on Moab.

Judgment on the Ammonites

49
Concerning the Ammonites.

Thus says the LORD:
  Has Israel no sons?
  Has he no heir?
Why then has Milcom dispossessed
  Gad,
  and his people settled in its towns?
2 Therefore, the time is surely coming,
  says the LORD,
when I will sound the battle alarm
  against Rabbah of the Ammonites;
it shall become a desolate mound,
  and its villages shall be burned with
    fire;
then Israel shall dispossess those who
  dispossessed him,
  says the LORD.

3 Wail, O Heshbon, for Ai is laid waste!
  Cry out, O daughters*c* of Rabbah!
Put on sackcloth,
  lament, and slash yourselves with
    whips! *d*
For Milcom shall go into exile,
  with his priests and his attendants.
4 Why do you boast in your strength?
  Your strength is ebbing,
O faithless daughter.
  You trusted in your treasures, saying,
    "Who will attack me?"
5 I am going to bring terror upon you,
  says the Lord GOD of hosts,
  from all your neighbors,
and you will be scattered, each
    headlong,
  with no one to gather the fugitives.
6 But afterward I will restore the fortunes
of the Ammonites, says the LORD.

Judgment on Edom

7 Concerning Edom.

Thus says the LORD of hosts:
  Is there no longer wisdom in Teman?
  Has counsel perished from the
    prudent?
  Has their wisdom vanished?
8 Flee, turn back, get down low,
  inhabitants of Dedan!
For I will bring the calamity of Esau
    upon him,
  the time when I punish him.
9 If grape-gatherers came to you,
  would they not leave gleanings?
If thieves came by night,
  even they would pillage only what
    they wanted.
10 But as for me, I have stripped Esau
    bare,
  I have uncovered his hiding places,
  and he is not able to conceal himself.
His offspring are destroyed, his kinsfolk
  and his neighbors; and he is no
    more.
11 Leave your orphans, I will keep them
    alive;
  and let your widows trust in me.

---

a Gk Syr: Heb *bring upon it*   *b* Or *of Shaon*
c Or *villages*   *d* Cn: Meaning of Heb uncertain

12 For thus says the LORD: If those who do not deserve to drink the cup still have to drink it, shall you be the one to go unpunished? You shall not go unpunished; you must drink it. 13For by myself I have sworn, says the LORD, that Bozrah shall become an object of horror and ridicule, a waste, and an object of cursing; and all her towns shall be perpetual wastes.

14 I have heard tidings from the LORD,
and a messenger has been sent among
the nations:
"Gather yourselves together and come
against her,
and rise up for battle!"
15 For I will make you least among the
nations,
despised by humankind.
16 The terror you inspire
and the pride of your heart have
deceived you,
you who live in the clefts of the rock, a
who hold the height of the hill.
Although you make your nest as high as
the eagle's,
from there I will bring you down,
says the LORD.

17 Edom shall become an object of horror; everyone who passes by it will be horrified and will hiss because of all its disasters. 18As when Sodom and Gomorrah and their neighbors were overthrown, says the LORD, no one shall live there, nor shall anyone settle in it. 19Like a lion coming up from the thickets of the Jordan against a perennial pasture, I will suddenly chase Edom b away from it; and I will appoint over it whomever I choose. c For who is like me? Who can summon me? Who is the shepherd who can stand before me? 20Therefore hear the plan that the LORD has made against Edom and the purposes that he has formed against the inhabitants of Teman: Surely the little ones of the flock shall be dragged away; surely their fold shall be appalled at their fate. 21At the sound of their fall the earth shall tremble; the sound of their cry shall be heard at the Red Sea. d 22Look, he shall mount up and swoop down like an eagle, and spread his wings against Bozrah, and the heart of the warriors of Edom in that day shall be like the heart of a woman in labor.

Judgment on Damascus

23 Concerning Damascus.

Hamath and Arpad are confounded,
for they have heard bad news;
they melt in fear, they are troubled like
the sea e
that cannot be quiet.
24 Damascus has become feeble, she
turned to flee,
and panic seized her;
anguish and sorrows have taken hold of
her,
as of a woman in labor.
25 How the famous city is forsaken, f
the joyful town! g
26 Therefore her young men shall fall in
her squares,
and all her soldiers shall be destroyed
in that day,
says the LORD of hosts.
27 And I will kindle a fire at the wall of
Damascus,
and it shall devour the strongholds of
Ben-hadad.

Judgment on Kedar and Hazor

28 Concerning Kedar and the kingdoms of Hazor that King Nebuchadrezzar of Babylon defeated.

Thus says the LORD:
Rise up, advance against Kedar!
Destroy the people of the east!
29 Take their tents and their flocks,
their curtains and all their goods;
carry off their camels for yourselves,
and a cry shall go up: "Terror is all
around!"
30 Flee, wander far away, hide in deep
places,
O inhabitants of Hazor!
says the LORD.
For King Nebuchadrezzar of Babylon
has made a plan against you
and formed a purpose against you.

a Or of Sela   b Heb him   c Or and I will single
out the choicest of his rams: Meaning of Heb
uncertain   d Or Sea of Reeds   e Cn: Heb there
is trouble in the sea   f Vg: Heb is not forsaken
g Syr Vg Tg: Heb the town of my joy

31 Rise up, advance against a nation at
    ease,
  that lives secure,
                   says the LORD,
  that has no gates or bars,
    that lives alone.
32 Their camels shall become booty,
    their herds of cattle a spoil.
  I will scatter to every wind
    those who have shaven temples,
  and I will bring calamity
    against them from every side,
                  says the LORD.
33 Hazor shall become a lair of jackals,
    an everlasting waste;
  no one shall live there,
    nor shall anyone settle in it.

Judgment on Elam

34 The word of the LORD that came to the prophet Jeremiah concerning Elam, at the beginning of the reign of King Zedekiah of Judah.

35 Thus says the LORD of hosts: I am going to break the bow of Elam, the mainstay of their might; 36and I will bring upon Elam the four winds from the four quarters of heaven; and I will scatter them to all these winds, and there shall be no nation to which the exiles from Elam shall not come. 37I will terrify Elam before their enemies, and before those who seek their life; I will bring disaster upon them, my fierce anger, says the LORD. I will send the sword after them, until I have consumed them; 38and I will set my throne in Elam, and destroy their king and officials, says the LORD.

39 But in the latter days I will restore the fortunes of Elam, says the LORD.

Judgment on Babylon

50 The word that the LORD spoke concerning Babylon, concerning the land of the Chaldeans, by the prophet Jeremiah:

2 Declare among the nations and
    proclaim,
  set up a banner and proclaim,
  do not conceal it, say:
  Babylon is taken,
    Bel is put to shame,

    Merodach is dismayed.
  Her images are put to shame,
    her idols are dismayed.

3 For out of the north a nation has come up against her; it shall make her land a desolation, and no one shall live in it; both human beings and animals shall flee away.

4 In those days and in that time, says the LORD, the people of Israel shall come, they and the people of Judah together; they shall come weeping as they seek the LORD their God. 5They shall ask the way to Zion, with faces turned toward it, and they shall come and join[a] themselves to the LORD by an everlasting covenant that will never be forgotten.

6 My people have been lost sheep; their shepherds have led them astray, turning them away on the mountains; from mountain to hill they have gone, they have forgotten their fold. 7All who found them have devoured them, and their enemies have said, "We are not guilty, because they have sinned against the LORD, the true pasture, the LORD, the hope of their ancestors."

8 Flee from Babylon, and go out of the land of the Chaldeans, and be like male goats leading the flock. 9For I am going to stir up and bring against Babylon a company of great nations from the land of the north; and they shall array themselves against her; from there she shall be taken. Their arrows are like the arrows of a skilled warrior who does not return empty-handed. 10Chaldea shall be plundered; all who plunder her shall be sated, says the LORD.

11 Though you rejoice, though you exult,
    O plunderers of my heritage,
  though you frisk about like a heifer on
      the grass,
    and neigh like stallions,
12 your mother shall be utterly shamed,
    and she who bore you shall be
      disgraced.
  Lo, she shall be the last of the nations,
    a wilderness, dry land, and a desert.

a Gk: Heb toward it. Come! They shall join

13 Because of the wrath of the LORD she
    shall not be inhabited,
  but shall be an utter desolation;
  everyone who passes by Babylon shall
    be appalled
  and hiss because of all her wounds.
14 Take up your positions around Babylon,
    all you that bend the bow;
  shoot at her, spare no arrows,
    for she has sinned against the LORD.
15 Raise a shout against her from all sides,
    "She has surrendered;
  her bulwarks have fallen,
    her walls are thrown down."
  For this is the vengeance of the LORD:
    take vengeance on her,
    do to her as she has done.
16 Cut off from Babylon the sower,
    and the wielder of the sickle in time
      of harvest;
  because of the destroying sword
    all of them shall return to their own
      people,
    and all of them shall flee to their own
      land.

17 Israel is a hunted sheep driven away by
lions. First the king of Assyria devoured it,
and now at the end King Nebuchadrezzar of
Babylon has gnawed its bones. 18Therefore,
thus says the LORD of hosts, the God of Israel: I am going to punish the king of Babylon
and his land, as I punished the king of Assyria. 19I will restore Israel to its pasture, and
it shall feed on Carmel and in Bashan, and on
the hills of Ephraim and in Gilead its hunger
shall be satisfied. 20In those days and at that
time, says the LORD, the iniquity of Israel shall
be sought, and there shall be none; and the
sins of Judah, and none shall be found; for I
will pardon the remnant that I have spared.

21 Go up to the land of Merathaim;a
    go up against her,
  and attack the inhabitants of Pekodb
    and utterly destroy the last of them,c
                        says the LORD;
    do all that I have commanded you.
22 The noise of battle is in the land,
    and great destruction!
23 How the hammer of the whole earth

  is cut down and broken!
  How Babylon has become
    a horror among the nations!
24 You set a snare for yourself and you were
    caught, O Babylon,
    but you did not know it;
  you were discovered and seized,
    because you challenged the LORD.
25 The LORD has opened his armory,
    and brought out the weapons of his
      wrath,
  for the Lord GOD of hosts has a task to do
    in the land of the Chaldeans.
26 Come against her from every quarter;
    open her granaries;
  pile her up like heaps of grain, and
      destroy her utterly;
    let nothing be left of her.
27 Kill all her bulls,
    let them go down to the slaughter.
  Alas for them, their day has come,
    the time of their punishment!

28 Listen! Fugitives and refugees from the
land of Babylon are coming to declare in Zion
the vengeance of the LORD our God,
vengeance for his temple.

29 Summon archers against Babylon, all
who bend the bow. Encamp all around her;
let no one escape. Repay her according to her
deeds; just as she has done, do to her—for
she has arrogantly defied the LORD, the Holy
One of Israel. 30Therefore her young men
shall fall in her squares, and all her soldiers
shall be destroyed on that day, says the LORD.

31 I am against you, O arrogant one,
    says the Lord GOD of hosts;
  for your day has come,
    the time when I will punish you.
32 The arrogant one shall stumble and fall,
    with no one to raise him up,
  and I will kindle a fire in his cities,
    and it will devour everything around
      him.

33 Thus says the LORD of hosts: The people
of Israel are oppressed, and so too are the

a Or of Double Rebellion   b Or of Punishment
c Tg: Heb destroy after them

people of Judah; all their captors have held them fast and refuse to let them go. 34Their Redeemer is strong; the LORD of hosts is his name. He will surely plead their cause, that he may give rest to the earth, but unrest to the inhabitants of Babylon.

35 A sword against the Chaldeans, says the
LORD,
and against the inhabitants of
Babylon,
and against her officials and her
sages!
36 A sword against the diviners,
so that they may become fools!
A sword against her warriors,
so that they may be destroyed!
37 A sword against her*a* horses and against
her*a* chariots,
and against all the foreign troops in
her midst,
so that they may become women!
A sword against all her treasures,
that they may be plundered!
38 A drought*b* against her waters,
that they may be dried up!
For it is a land of images,
and they go mad over idols.

39 Therefore wild animals shall live with hyenas in Babylon,*c* and ostriches shall inhabit her; she shall never again be peopled, or inhabited for all generations. 40As when God overthrew Sodom and Gomorrah and their neighbors, says the LORD, so no one shall live there, nor shall anyone settle in her.

41 Look, a people is coming from the
north;
a mighty nation and many kings
are stirring from the farthest parts of
the earth.
42 They wield bow and spear,
they are cruel and have no mercy.
The sound of them is like the roaring
sea;
they ride upon horses,
set in array as a warrior for battle,
against you, O daughter Babylon!

43 The king of Babylon heard news of
them,
and his hands fell helpless;
anguish seized him,
pain like that of a woman in labor.

44 Like a lion coming up from the thickets of the Jordan against a perennial pasture, I will suddenly chase them away from her; and I will appoint over her whomever I choose.*d* For who is like me? Who can summon me? Who is the shepherd who can stand before me? 45Therefore hear the plan that the LORD has made against Babylon, and the purposes that he has formed against the land of the Chaldeans: Surely the little ones of the flock shall be dragged away; surely their*e* fold shall be appalled at their fate. 46At the sound of the capture of Babylon the earth shall tremble, and her cry shall be heard among the nations.

51 Thus says the LORD:
I am going to stir up a destructive
wind*f*
against Babylon
and against the inhabitants of Leb-
qamai;*g*
2 and I will send winnowers to Babylon,
and they shall winnow her.
They shall empty her land
when they come against her from
every side
on the day of trouble.
3 Let not the archer bend his bow,
and let him not array himself in his
coat of mail.
Do not spare her young men;
utterly destroy her entire army.
4 They shall fall down slain in the land of
the Chaldeans,
and wounded in her streets.
5 Israel and Judah have not been forsaken
by their God, the LORD of hosts,
though their land is full of guilt
before the Holy One of Israel.

a Cn: Heb *his*   b Another reading is *A sword*
c Heb lacks *in Babylon*   d Or *and I will single out the choicest of her rams*: Meaning of Heb uncertain
e Syr Gk Tg Compare 49.20: Heb lacks *their*
f Or *stir up the spirit of a destroyer*   g Leb-qamai is a cryptogram for *Kasdim*, Chaldea

6 Flee from the midst of Babylon,
　　save your lives, each of you!
Do not perish because of her guilt,
　　for this is the time of the LORD's
　　　vengeance;
　　he is repaying her what is due.
7 Babylon was a golden cup in the LORD's
　　hand,
　　making all the earth drunken;
the nations drank of her wine,
　　and so the nations went mad.
8 Suddenly Babylon has fallen and is
　　　shattered;
　　wail for her!
Bring balm for her wound;
　　perhaps she may be healed.
9 We tried to heal Babylon,
　　but she could not be healed.
Forsake her, and let each of us go
　　to our own country;
for her judgment has reached up to
　　heaven
　　and has been lifted up even to the
　　　skies.
10 The LORD has brought forth our
　　　vindication;
　　come, let us declare in Zion
　　the work of the LORD our God.

11 Sharpen the arrows!
　　Fill the quivers!
The LORD has stirred up the spirit of the kings
of the Medes, because his purpose concerning Babylon is to destroy it, for that is the
vengeance of the LORD, vengeance for his
temple.
12 Raise a standard against the walls of
　　　Babylon;
　　make the watch strong;
　　post sentinels;
　　prepare the ambushes;
　　for the LORD has both planned and done
　　what he spoke concerning the
　　　inhabitants of Babylon.
13 You who live by mighty waters,
　　rich in treasures,
　　your end has come,
　　the thread of your life is cut.
14 The LORD of hosts has sworn by himself:
　　Surely I will fill you with troops like a
　　　swarm of locusts,

and they shall raise a shout of victory
　　over you.

15 It is he who made the earth by his
　　　power,
　　who established the world by his
　　　wisdom,
　　and by his understanding stretched out
　　　the heavens.
16 When he utters his voice there is a
　　　tumult of waters in the heavens,
　　and he makes the mist rise from the
　　　ends of the earth.
He makes lightnings for the rain,
　　and he brings out the wind from his
　　　storehouses.
17 Everyone is stupid and without
　　　knowledge;
　　goldsmiths are all put to shame by
　　　their idols;
　　for their images are false,
　　and there is no breath in them.
18 They are worthless, a work of delusion;
　　at the time of their punishment they
　　　shall perish.
19 Not like these is the LORD,ª the portion
　　of Jacob,
　　for he is the one who formed all
　　　things,
and Israel is the tribe of his inheritance;
　　the LORD of hosts is his name.

Israel the Creator's Instrument

20 You are my war club, my weapon of
　　　battle:
　　with you I smash nations;
　　with you I destroy kingdoms;
21 with you I smash the horse and its rider;
　　with you I smash the chariot and the
　　　charioteer;
22 with you I smash man and woman;
　　with you I smash the old man and the
　　　boy;
　　with you I smash the young man and
　　　the girl;
23 　　with you I smash shepherds and their
　　　flocks;
　　with you I smash farmers and their
　　　teams;

a Heb lacks the LORD

with you I smash governors and
     deputies.

The Doom of Babylon

24 I will repay Babylon and all the inhabitants of Chaldea before your very eyes for
all the wrong that they have done in Zion,
says the LORD.

25 I am against you, O destroying mountain,
                              says the LORD,
     that destroys the whole earth;
     I will stretch out my hand against you,
        and roll you down from the crags,
        and make you a burned-out
           mountain.
26 No stone shall be taken from you for a
        corner
     and no stone for a foundation,
     but you shall be a perpetual waste,
        says the LORD.

27 Raise a standard in the land,
     blow the trumpet among the nations;
     prepare the nations for war against her,
        summon against her the kingdoms,
        Ararat, Minni, and Ashkenaz;
     appoint a marshal against her,
        bring up horses like bristling locusts.
28 Prepare the nations for war against her,
     the kings of the Medes, with their
        governors and deputies,
     and every land under their dominion.
29 The land trembles and writhes,
     for the LORD's purposes against
        Babylon stand,
     to make the land of Babylon a
        desolation,
     without inhabitant.
30 The warriors of Babylon have given up
        fighting,
     they remain in their strongholds;
     their strength has failed,
        they have become women;
     her buildings are set on fire,
        her bars are broken.
31 One runner runs to meet another,
     and one messenger to meet another,
     to tell the king of Babylon
     that his city is taken from end to end:
32 the fords have been seized,

the marshes have been burned with
     fire,
     and the soldiers are in panic.
33 For thus says the LORD of hosts, the God
        of Israel:
     Daughter Babylon is like a threshing
        floor
     at the time when it is trodden;
     yet a little while
     and the time of her harvest will come.

34 "King Nebuchadrezzar of Babylon has
        devoured me,
        he has crushed me;
     he has made me an empty vessel,
        he has swallowed me like a monster;
     he has filled his belly with my
        delicacies,
        he has spewed me out.
35 May my torn flesh be avenged on
        Babylon,"
        the inhabitants of Zion shall say.
     "May my blood be avenged on the
           inhabitants of Chaldea,"
     Jerusalem shall say.
36 Therefore thus says the LORD:
     I am going to defend your cause
        and take vengeance for you.
     I will dry up her sea
        and make her fountain dry;
37 and Babylon shall become a heap of
        ruins,
     a den of jackals,
     an object of horror and of hissing,
        without inhabitant.

38 Like lions they shall roar together;
     they shall growl like lions' whelps.
39 When they are inflamed, I will set out
        their drink
     and make them drunk, until they
           become merry
     and then sleep a perpetual sleep
        and never wake, says the LORD.
40 I will bring them down like lambs to the
        slaughter,
     like rams and goats.

41 How Sheshach[a] is taken,
     the pride of the whole earth seized!

a *Sheshach* is a cryptogram for *Babel*, Babylon

How Babylon has become
  an object of horror among the
    nations!
42 The sea has risen over Babylon;
  she has been covered by its
    tumultuous waves.
43 Her cities have become an object of
    horror,
  a land of drought and a desert,
a land in which no one lives,
  and through which no mortal passes.
44 I will punish Bel in Babylon,
  and make him disgorge what he has
    swallowed.
The nations shall no longer stream to
    him;
  the wall of Babylon has fallen.

45 Come out of her, my people!
  Save your lives, each of you,
    from the fierce anger of the LORD!
46 Do not be fainthearted or fearful
    at the rumors heard in the land—
one year one rumor comes,
  the next year another,
rumors of violence in the land
  and of ruler against ruler.

47 Assuredly, the days are coming
    when I will punish the images of
      Babylon;
  her whole land shall be put to shame,
    and all her slain shall fall in her
      midst.
48 Then the heavens and the earth,
  and all that is in them,
    shall shout for joy over Babylon;
  for the destroyers shall come against
    them out of the north,
      says the LORD.
49 Babylon must fall for the slain of
    Israel,
  as the slain of all the earth have fallen
    because of Babylon.

50 You survivors of the sword,
  go, do not linger!
Remember the LORD in a distant land,
  and let Jerusalem come into your
    mind:
51 We are put to shame, for we have heard
    insults;
  dishonor has covered our face,
for aliens have come
  into the holy places of the LORD's
    house.

52 Therefore the time is surely coming,
    says the LORD,
  when I will punish her idols,
and through all her land
  the wounded shall groan.
53 Though Babylon should mount up to
    heaven,
  and though she should fortify her
    strong height,
from me destroyers would come upon
    her,
  says the LORD.

51:50 *Remember the LORD in a distant land.*
What do you do when you are far from home, exiled, strangers in a strange land, having lost so much? You remember. You bring to mind your true home. You nurture those practices of remembrance that sustain you in a difficult time. Much of the faith community's best work is remembrance, the loving nurture of the memory of our true origin, our true identity, and our true vocation. The community of faith is sometimes accused of being anachronistic, old-fashioned, and out of touch. But the faith community has learned, down through the ages, that without remembrance, it perishes. Remembrance of our true home gives us

courage in the present exile. Having remembered whose we are and whence we have come, we are given courage and confidence in the present. Think of this reading of Scripture, this study of the book of Jeremiah, as a courageous, life-giving act of remembrance.

Responding
51:50 STUDY. Some of the faith community's essential work is remembrance, which we can do through study of the Scriptures. How might it change your Bible study to view it as your duty to remember the history of the People of God? *See also* Spiritual Disciplines Index.

54 Listen!—a cry from Babylon!
    A great crashing from the land of the
        Chaldeans!
55 For the LORD is laying Babylon waste,
    and stilling her loud clamor.
Their waves roar like mighty waters,
    the sound of their clamor resounds;
56 for a destroyer has come against her,
    against Babylon;
her warriors are taken,
    their bows are broken;
for the LORD is a God of recompense,
    he will repay in full.
57 I will make her officials and her sages
        drunk,
    also her governors, her deputies, and
        her warriors;
they shall sleep a perpetual sleep and
        never wake,
    says the King, whose name is the
        LORD of hosts.

58 Thus says the LORD of hosts:
The broad wall of Babylon
    shall be leveled to the ground,
and her high gates
    shall be burned with fire.
The peoples exhaust themselves for
        nothing,
    and the nations weary themselves
        only for fire. a

Jeremiah's Command to Seraiah

59 The word that the prophet Jeremiah
commanded Seraiah son of Neriah son of
Mahseiah, when he went with King Zedekiah of Judah to Babylon, in the fourth year of
his reign. Seraiah was the quartermaster.
60 Jeremiah wrote in a b scroll all the disasters that would come on Babylon, all these
words that are written concerning Babylon.
61 And Jeremiah said to Seraiah: "When you
come to Babylon, see that you read all these
words, 62 and say, 'O LORD, you yourself
threatened to destroy this place so that neither human beings nor animals shall live in
it, and it shall be desolate forever.' 63 When
you finish reading this scroll, tie a stone to it,
and throw it into the middle of the Euphrates, 64 and say, 'Thus shall Babylon sink, to

rise no more, because of the disasters that I
am bringing on her.' " c
Thus far are the words of Jeremiah.

The Destruction of Jerusalem Reviewed

52 Zedekiah was twenty-one years old
when he began to reign; he reigned
eleven years in Jerusalem. His mother's name
was Hamutal daughter of Jeremiah of Libnah.
2 He did what was evil in the sight of the LORD,
just as Jehoiakim had done. 3 Indeed, Jerusalem and Judah so angered the LORD that he
expelled them from his presence.
Zedekiah rebelled against the king of Babylon. 4 And in the ninth year of his reign, in
the tenth month, on the tenth day of the
month, King Nebuchadrezzar of Babylon
came with all his army against Jerusalem, and
they laid siege to it; they built siegeworks
against it all around. 5 So the city was besieged
until the eleventh year of King Zedekiah. 6 On
the ninth day of the fourth month the famine
became so severe in the city that there was no
food for the people of the land. 7 Then a
breach was made in the city wall; d and all the
soldiers fled and went out from the city by
night by the way of the gate between the two
walls, by the king's garden, though the
Chaldeans were all around the city. They went
in the direction of the Arabah. 8 But the army
of the Chaldeans pursued the king, and overtook Zedekiah in the plains of Jericho; and all
his army was scattered, deserting him. 9 Then
they captured the king, and brought him up
to the king of Babylon at Riblah in the land of
Hamath, and he passed sentence on him.
10 The king of Babylon killed the sons of Zedekiah before his eyes, and also killed all the officers of Judah at Riblah. 11 He put out the eyes
of Zedekiah, and bound him in fetters, and
the king of Babylon took him to Babylon, and
put him in prison until the day of his death.
12 In the fifth month, on the tenth day of
the month—which was the nineteenth year
of King Nebuchadrezzar, king of Babylon—
Nebuzaradan the captain of the bodyguard
who served the king of Babylon, entered Jeru-

a Gk Syr Compare Hab 2.13: Heb and the nations for
fire, and they are weary   b Or one   c Gk: Heb on
her. And they shall weary themselves   d Heb lacks
wall

salem. [13]He burned the house of the LORD, the king's house, and all the houses of Jerusalem; every great house he burned down. [14]All the army of the Chaldeans, who were with the captain of the guard, broke down all the walls around Jerusalem. [15]Nebuzaradan the captain of the guard carried into exile some of the poorest of the people and the rest of the people who were left in the city and the deserters who had defected to the king of Babylon, together with the rest of the artisans. [16]But Nebuzaradan the captain of the guard left some of the poorest people of the land to be vinedressers and tillers of the soil.

17 The pillars of bronze that were in the house of the LORD, and the stands and the bronze sea that were in the house of the LORD, the Chaldeans broke in pieces, and carried all the bronze to Babylon. [18]They took away the pots, the shovels, the snuffers, the basins, the ladles, and all the vessels of bronze used in the temple service. [19]The captain of the guard took away the small bowls also, the firepans, the basins, the pots, the lampstands, the ladles, and the bowls for libation, both those of gold and those of silver. [20]As for the two pillars, the one sea, the twelve bronze bulls that were under the sea, and the stands,[a] which King Solomon had made for the house of the LORD, the bronze of all these vessels was beyond weighing. [21]As for the pillars, the height of the one pillar was eighteen cubits, its circumference was twelve cubits; it was hollow and its thickness was four fingers. [22]Upon it was a capital of bronze; the height of the capital was five cubits; latticework and pomegranates, all of bronze, encircled the top of the capital. And the second pillar had the same, with pomegranates. [23]There were ninety-six pomegranates on the sides; all the pomegranates encircling the latticework numbered one hundred.

24 The captain of the guard took the chief priest Seraiah, the second priest Zephaniah, and the three guardians of the threshold; [25]and from the city he took an officer who had been in command of the soldiers, and seven men of the king's council who were found in the city; the secretary of the commander of the army who mustered the people of the land; and sixty men of the people of the land who were found inside the city. [26]Then Nebuzaradan the captain of the guard took them, and brought them to the king of Babylon at Riblah. [27]And the king of Babylon struck them down, and put them to death at Riblah in the land of Hamath. So Judah went into exile out of its land.

28 This is the number of the people whom Nebuchadrezzar took into exile: in the seventh year, three thousand twenty-three Judeans; [29]in the eighteenth year of Nebuchadrezzar he took into exile from Jerusalem eight hundred thirty-two persons; [30]in the twenty-third year of Nebuchadrezzar, Nebuzaradan the captain of the guard took into exile of the Judeans seven hundred forty-five persons; all the persons were four thousand six hundred.

Jehoiachin Favored in Captivity

31 In the thirty-seventh year of the exile of King Jehoiachin of Judah, in the twelfth month, on the twenty-fifth day of the month, King Evil-merodach of Babylon, in the year he began to reign, showed favor to King Jehoiachin of Judah and brought him out of prison; [32]he spoke kindly to him, and gave him a seat above the seats of the other kings who were with him in Babylon. [33]So Jehoiachin put aside his prison clothes, and every day of his life he dined regularly at the king's table. [34]For his allowance, a regular daily allowance was given him by the king of Babylon, as long as he lived, up to the day of his death.

a Cn: Heb *that were under the stands*

52:34 *a regular daily allowance was given him . . . up to the day of his death.* The book of Jeremiah is known for its rather ragged, unsatisfactory ending. After so many marvelous, dramatic events, the book seems to just dribble off with a rather anticlimactic conclusion. After so much poetry and so many stirring, dramatic events, this is the end? Perhaps the book is not meant to "end." Perhaps the story continues in your faith community and mine. Even as you read these words, the story does not end, but lives and breathes in the present age. The word of the Lord is forever a living word.

LAMENTATIONS

After our great national trauma on September 11, 2001, when the towers fell, so many died, and the goodness of the future was called into question, many Christian communities, in their hurt, horror, and despair, turned for solace and guidance to an ancient and rather obscure book of the Bible—Lamentations. In this book we journey into the dark, dusty, despairing corners of human hearts, into those times in our collective experience that we would rather forget or avoid. Yet as people of faith we believe that our God gives us the resources to help us refrain from avoiding or denying the pain and tragedy. We can grieve, cry out, clench our fists, and ask God why under the conviction that our God cares for us and loves us enough to speak to us, even in tragedy. How is it possible for people like us—so skilled in putting a happy face on even the worst of circumstances, so desirous of cheap consolation—to stare tragedy in the face and to tell the truth about it? It is because Christians believe that, on the cross, Jesus gave a powerful answer to the questions raised by this book of the Bible. In the midst of the most desperate lamentation, mourning the worst tragedies, our God is there, with us.

Psalms of Lament

Israel was known for its psalms of lament—those poetic complaints that are honestly laid before God. Israel loved God enough, felt close enough to God, to be able, in times of tragedy, to clench its fists and cry out to God, to complain, to accuse, and to weep. Some may believe that, as Christians, we must always feel joy, must always have smiles on our faces. Lamentations, however, is the literature of those who have a much deeper, more honest experience of our relationship with God. Its laments know that there is no way always to be happy and joyful. To say to contemporary believers, "If you have faith, you will always be filled with joy and delight," is to place an intolerable burden on them. This life is too full of heartache for us to expect to somehow bypass genuine grief. Either we are in grief over our own losses or, loving our neighbor

---

See also "The With-God Life" essays for this section of the Bible, "The People of God in Travail,"
pp. 717–20, and "The People of God in Exile," pp. 1171–74.

as ourselves, we feel grief at our neighbor's loss. Perpetually joyful believers who never need Lamentations are self-centered, self-consumed believers who feel none of the pain of the rest of the world. The psalms of lament provide good Jewish ballast to our sometimes superficial and just a bit too cheerful Christian piety.

In Lamentations we have a poetic collection that consists entirely of the community's dirges and psalms of lament. Tradition has sometimes ascribed these psalms to the prophet Jeremiah, and sometimes passages of Lamentations do sound like some of Jeremiah's laments. But few today believe that Jeremiah wrote or edited these psalms. The specific cause of grief is the horribly cataclysmic destruction of Jerusalem in 587 BC. Jerusalem was the center of the nation's faith, the great gift that God had given Israel. Jerusalem's ruin presents not only a national, economic, and political disaster, but also a huge crisis in faith. If God has allowed Jerusalem to be destroyed, how is it possible to speak of the fidelity of God to the covenant community? If God did not step in and prevent this disaster, what on earth might God be expected to do in other calamities?

The stanzas of the poetry in Lamentations are arranged according to the twenty-two letters of the Hebrew alphabet, thus indicating that this poetry was meant for public recitation, probably in worship assemblies on days of national fasting and mourning. Lamentations is thus a hymn book for Israel. The arrangement of Lamentations indicates that here we have the bold public processing of pain, "grief work." Lamentations consists of mostly unrelieved cries of grief. The closest the book comes to hope is the expression of trust that ultimately, in the end, the Lord shall redeem the Lord's people (chap 3). Lamentations is our deepest grief, our greatest despair brought out of the closet, pulled out in the open, made audible. Today, when the contemporary Church reads Lamentations, the disciplines of mourning are being taught by a people who have experienced the worst of disaster to a people who tend to avoid grief at all possible cost.

The Art of Eloquent Grief

People often say, "What are funerals for? They can't much help the person who has died." Funerals are for everyone since, at any given moment within the community, everyone there is either grieving or preparing to grieve. The deceased's family and friends are experiencing the immediate crisis of acute grief. But almost everyone is dealing with some past grief, and everyone is preparing for future grief. Life is full of necessary losses, closed doors, dashed hopes, and collapsed towers. Lamentations is the saints from the past teaching us how to grieve in the present. It is training in the art of eloquent grieving.

When it comes time to be in grief, people who have never before attended a funeral are at a real disadvantage. They don't know what to expect, and they don't feel permission to be angry, hurt, empty, hopeless, or experience any and all of the other emotions that accompany any realistic, truthful grieving.

Having lived through what many have called the bloodiest century in all of human history, the twentieth century, with its wars, massacres, genocides, and inhumanity (and the present century does not seem to be off to a promising start), today's faith community needs Lamentations more than ever. There will be no recovery, no renovation, and no rebirth until there is first the legitimate expression of grief, the public processing of pain, and honest admission of our true situation. Lamentations is the part of the Bible that teaches us how to grieve, how to be angry with God when we need to be, how to weep when tears are necessary.

In reading Lamentations we would do well to consider certain questions of examination. How is it that grief forms us spiritually? What is it about genuine, gut-wrenching grief that drives us deeper into the heart of God? Why does the dark journey into grief often cause such radical character transformation? Are there disciplines of mourning that we need to experience, personally and corporately?

—*William H. Willimon*

The Deserted City

1 How lonely sits the city
   that once was full of people!
How like a widow she has become,
   she that was great among the
      nations!
She that was a princess among the
      provinces
   has become a vassal.

2 She weeps bitterly in the night,
   with tears on her cheeks;
among all her lovers
   she has no one to comfort her;
all her friends have dealt treacherously
      with her,
   they have become her enemies.

3 Judah has gone into exile with
      suffering
   and hard servitude;
she lives now among the nations,
   and finds no resting place;
her pursuers have all overtaken her
   in the midst of her distress.

4 The roads to Zion mourn,
   for no one comes to the festivals;
all her gates are desolate,
   her priests groan;
her young girls grieve, *a*
   and her lot is bitter.

5 Her foes have become the masters,
   her enemies prosper,

a Meaning of Heb uncertain

1:1 *How lonely sits the city that once was full of people!* Lamentations begins in deserted streets, ashes, and ruin. The city that once was a gathering place for people, a safe and vibrant place, has become a desolate wasteland. Many people in our day live in a culture of forlorn, deserted cities and a time of dashed dreams. The honest words of Lamentations tell these people to bring their despair to church, lay it on the altar, place it before the faith community, and thus have their pain redeemed.

1:5 *her enemies prosper.* Tragedy causes a crisis of faith. If God is good and has created a good world, then why do the wicked prosper?

Furthermore, Lamentations raises the frightening question of the responsibility of God for our pain. Does our God really make us suffer because of our transgressions? This is an ancient, difficult question for people of faith. Lamentations dares to assert an unpopular conviction—very unpopular in our day—that, yes, God is involved even in the sorrow and pain of the world and, yes, our wrong actions do have bad consequences. Israel demonstrates, in Lamentations, that it is a great enough people even to take responsibility for its failures, even to see in its worst national events the wise workings of God.

because the LORD has made her suffer
  for the multitude of her
    transgressions;
her children have gone away,
  captives before the foe.

6 From daughter Zion has departed
  all her majesty.
Her princes have become like stags
  that find no pasture;
they fled without strength
  before the pursuer.

7 Jerusalem remembers,
  in the days of her affliction and
    wandering,
all the precious things
  that were hers in days of old.
When her people fell into the hand of
    the foe,
  and there was no one to help her,
the foe looked on mocking
  over her downfall.

8 Jerusalem sinned grievously,
  so she has become a mockery;
all who honored her despise her,
  for they have seen her nakedness;
she herself groans,
  and turns her face away.

9 Her uncleanness was in her skirts;
  she took no thought of her future;
her downfall was appalling,
  with none to comfort her.
"O LORD, look at my affliction,
  for the enemy has triumphed!"

10 Enemies have stretched out their hands
  over all her precious things;
she has even seen the nations
  invade her sanctuary,

those whom you forbade
  to enter your congregation.

11 All her people groan
  as they search for bread;
they trade their treasures for food
  to revive their strength.
Look, O LORD, and see
  how worthless I have become.

12 Is it nothing to you,[a] all you who pass
    by?
Look and see
if there is any sorrow like my sorrow,
  which was brought upon me,
which the LORD inflicted
  on the day of his fierce anger.

13 From on high he sent fire;
  it went deep into my bones;
he spread a net for my feet;
  he turned me back;
he has left me stunned,
  faint all day long.

14 My transgressions were bound[a] into a
    yoke;
  by his hand they were fastened
    together;
they weigh on my neck,
  sapping my strength;
the Lord handed me over
  to those whom I cannot withstand.

15 The LORD has rejected
  all my warriors in the midst of me;
he proclaimed a time against me
  to crush my young men;
the Lord has trodden as in a wine press
  the virgin daughter Judah.

a Meaning of Heb uncertain

1:12 *Look and see if there is any sorrow like my sorrow.* This passage is read in some churches on Good Friday. It evokes the image of the beaten Christ, carrying his cross through the crowds on the way to Calvary. Anyone in deep grief tends to feel like a spectacle to the world. When we experience some terrible trauma, for us time comes to a halt. But the world keeps passing by, oblivious to our pain. Is there any sorrow like my sorrow? Probably not. Grief tends to be very personal, private, and individual. Yet Lamentations urges grief to "go public," to be articulated and shared with the community and thus to be spread around with others. Even the worst of sorrows can be borne if they are shared.

16 For these things I weep;
      my eyes flow with tears;
   for a comforter is far from me,
      one to revive my courage;
   my children are desolate,
      for the enemy has prevailed.

17 Zion stretches out her hands,
      but there is no one to comfort her;
   the LORD has commanded against Jacob
      that his neighbors should become his
         foes;
   Jerusalem has become
      a filthy thing among them.

18 The LORD is in the right,
      for I have rebelled against his word;
   but hear, all you peoples,
      and behold my suffering;
   my young women and young men
      have gone into captivity.

19 I called to my lovers
      but they deceived me;
   my priests and elders
      perished in the city
   while seeking food
      to revive their strength.

20 See, O LORD, how distressed I am;
      my stomach churns,
   my heart is wrung within me,
      because I have been very rebellious.
   In the street the sword bereaves;
      in the house it is like death.

21 They heard how I was groaning,
      with no one to comfort me.
   All my enemies heard of my trouble;
      they are glad that you have done it.
   Bring on the day you have announced,
      and let them be as I am.

22 Let all their evil doing come before you;
      and deal with them
   as you have dealt with me
      because of all my transgressions;
   for my groans are many
      and my heart is faint.

God's Warnings Fulfilled

2 How the Lord in his anger
      has humiliated[a] daughter Zion!
   He has thrown down from heaven to
         earth
      the splendor of Israel;
   he has not remembered his footstool
      in the day of his anger.

2 The Lord has destroyed without mercy
      all the dwellings of Jacob;
   in his wrath he has broken down
      the strongholds of daughter Judah;
   he has brought down to the ground in
         dishonor
      the kingdom and its rulers.

3 He has cut down in fierce anger
      all the might of Israel;
   he has withdrawn his right hand from
         them
      in the face of the enemy;
   he has burned like a flaming fire in Jacob,
      consuming all around.

4 He has bent his bow like an enemy,
      with his right hand set like a foe;
   he has killed all in whom we took pride
      in the tent of daughter Zion;
   he has poured out his fury like fire.

5 The Lord has become like an enemy;
      he has destroyed Israel.
   He has destroyed all its palaces,
      laid in ruins its strongholds,
   and multiplied in daughter Judah
      mourning and lamentation.

6 He has broken down his booth like a
         garden,
      he has destroyed his tabernacle;
   the LORD has abolished in Zion
      festival and sabbath,
   and in his fierce indignation has
         spurned
      king and priest.

7 The Lord has scorned his altar,
      disowned his sanctuary;

a Meaning of Heb uncertain

he has delivered into the hand of the
enemy
the walls of her palaces;
a clamor was raised in the house of the
LORD
as on a day of festival.

8 The LORD determined to lay in ruins
the wall of daughter Zion;
he stretched the line;
he did not withhold his hand from
destroying;
he caused rampart and wall to
lament;
they languish together.

9 Her gates have sunk into the ground;
he has ruined and broken her bars;
her king and princes are among the
nations;
guidance is no more,
and her prophets obtain
no vision from the LORD.

10 The elders of daughter Zion
sit on the ground in silence;
they have thrown dust on their heads
and put on sackcloth;
the young girls of Jerusalem
have bowed their heads to the
ground.

11 My eyes are spent with weeping;
my stomach churns;
my bile is poured out on the ground
because of the destruction of my
people,
because infants and babes faint
in the streets of the city.

12 They cry to their mothers,
"Where is bread and wine?"
as they faint like the wounded
in the streets of the city,
as their life is poured out
on their mothers' bosom.

13 What can I say for you, to what
compare you,
O daughter Jerusalem?
To what can I liken you, that I may
comfort you,
O virgin daughter Zion?
For vast as the sea is your ruin;
who can heal you?

14 Your prophets have seen for you
false and deceptive visions;
they have not exposed your iniquity
to restore your fortunes,
but have seen oracles for you
that are false and misleading.

15 All who pass along the way
clap their hands at you;
they hiss and wag their heads
at daughter Jerusalem;
"Is this the city that was called
the perfection of beauty,
the joy of all the earth?"

16 All your enemies
open their mouths against you;
they hiss, they gnash their teeth,
they cry: "We have devoured her!
Ah, this is the day we longed for;
at last we have seen it!"

17 The LORD has done what he purposed,
he has carried out his threat;
as he ordained long ago,
he has demolished without pity;
he has made the enemy rejoice over
you,
and exalted the might of your foes.

2:14 *Your prophets have seen for you false and underlined deceptive visions.* Jeremiah complained of false prophets who healed the wounds of people lightly. False prophets do not tell the truth. They always see positive, warm, fuzzy visions; people love such lies. The community of faith is frighteningly in need of truthful prophets who will honestly expose wrongs and tell the truth about the situation. Even in times of grief, the community of faith is distinguished as one of the few places where the truth can be told. Take that as a test for a true church; it is the place where true and exposing visions can be seen.

18 Cry aloud[a] to the Lord!
  O wall of daughter Zion!
Let tears stream down like a torrent
  day and night!
Give yourself no rest,
  your eyes no respite!

19 Arise, cry out in the night,
  at the beginning of the watches!
Pour out your heart like water
  before the presence of the Lord!
Lift your hands to him
  for the lives of your children,
who faint for hunger
  at the head of every street.

20 Look, O LORD, and consider!
  To whom have you done this?
Should women eat their offspring,
  the children they have borne?
Should priest and prophet be killed
  in the sanctuary of the Lord?

21 The young and the old are lying
  on the ground in the streets;
my young women and my young men
  have fallen by the sword;
in the day of your anger you have killed
    them,
  slaughtering without mercy.

22 You invited my enemies from all
    around
  as if for a day of festival;
and on the day of the anger of the LORD
  no one escaped or survived;
those whom I bore and reared
  my enemy has destroyed.

God's Steadfast Love Endures

3 I am one who has seen affliction
  under the rod of God's[b] wrath;
2 he has driven and brought me
  into darkness without any light;
3 against me alone he turns his hand,
  again and again, all day long.

4 He has made my flesh and my skin
    waste away,
  and broken my bones;
5 he has besieged and enveloped me

with bitterness and tribulation;
6 he has made me sit in darkness
  like the dead of long ago.

7 He has walled me about so that I cannot
    escape;
  he has put heavy chains on me;
8 though I call and cry for help,
  he shuts out my prayer;
9 he has blocked my ways with hewn
    stones,
  he has made my paths crooked.

10 He is a bear lying in wait for me,
  a lion in hiding;
11 he led me off my way and tore me to
    pieces;
  he has made me desolate;
12 he bent his bow and set me
  as a mark for his arrow.

13 He shot into my vitals
  the arrows of his quiver;
14 I have become the laughingstock of all
    my people,
  the object of their taunt-songs all day
    long.
15 He has filled me with bitterness,
  he has sated me with wormwood.

16 He has made my teeth grind on gravel,
  and made me cower in ashes;
17 my soul is bereft of peace;
  I have forgotten what happiness is;
18 so I say, "Gone is my glory,
  and all that I had hoped for from the
    LORD."

19 The thought of my affliction and my
    homelessness
  is wormwood and gall!
20 My soul continually thinks of it
  and is bowed down within me.
21 But this I call to mind,
  and therefore I have hope:

22 The steadfast love of the LORD never
    ceases,[c]
  his mercies never come to an end;

a Cn: Heb *Their heart cried*   b Heb *his*   c Syr
Tg: Heb LORD, *we are not cut off*

23 they are new every morning;
    great is your faithfulness.
24 "The LORD is my portion," says my soul,
    "therefore I will hope in him."

25 The LORD is good to those who wait for
    him,
    to the soul that seeks him.
26 It is good that one should wait quietly
    for the salvation of the LORD.
27 It is good for one to bear
    the yoke in youth,
28 to sit alone in silence
    when the Lord has imposed it,
29 to put one's mouth to the dust
    (there may yet be hope),
30 to give one's cheek to the smiter,
    and be filled with insults.

AMEN! HE IS THERE IN OUR SUFFERING

31 For the Lord will not
    reject forever.
32 Although he causes grief, he will have
    compassion
    according to the abundance of his
    steadfast love;
33 for he does not willingly afflict
    or grieve anyone.

34 When all the prisoners of the land
    are crushed under foot,
35 when human rights are perverted
    in the presence of the Most High,
36 when one's case is subverted
    —does the Lord not see it?

37 Who can command and have it done,
    if the Lord has not ordained it?
38 Is it not from the mouth of the Most
    High

that good and bad come?
39 Why should any who draw breath
    complain
    about the punishment of their sins?

40 Let us test and examine our ways,
    and return to the LORD.
41 Let us lift up our hearts as well as our
    hands
    to God in heaven.
42 We have transgressed and rebelled,
    and you have not forgiven.

43 You have wrapped yourself with anger
    and pursued us,
    killing without pity;
44 you have wrapped yourself with a cloud
    so that no prayer can pass through.
45 You have made us filth and rubbish
    among the peoples.

46 All our enemies
    have opened their mouths against us;
47 panic and pitfall have come upon us,
    devastation and destruction.
48 My eyes flow with rivers of tears
    because of the destruction of my
    people.

49 My eyes will flow without ceasing,
    without respite,
50 until the LORD from heaven
    looks down and sees.
51 My eyes cause me grief
    at the fate of all the young women in
    my city.

52 Those who were my enemies without
    cause

3:22–23 *The steadfast love of the LORD never ceases.* Even in the middle of soul-searing lament, there is doxology, praise. Is this statement of God's love only a pious fraud? Does this grieving community really feel that God is loving, merciful, and faithful? Perhaps it is only after honest, heartfelt grief that we are able to sing doxology. Here, in the middle of Lamentations, is an extraordinary statement of faith, faith that is born of doubt, despair, and tears. Perhaps that is the best sort of faith.

3:26 SILENCE—*See* Spiritual Disciplines index.

Responding
3:44 PRAYER. In his despair, the writer of Lamentations accuses God of deliberately erecting a barrier that no prayer of the Israelites could pass through. Is this a valid complaint? Why or why not? *See also* Spiritual Disciplines Index.

have hunted me like a bird;
53 they flung me alive into a pit
and hurled stones on me;
54 water closed over my head;
I said, "I am lost."

55 I called on your name, O LORD,
from the depths of the pit;
56 you heard my plea, "Do not close your
ear
to my cry for help, but give me
relief!"
57 You came near when I called on you;
you said, "Do not fear!"

58 You have taken up my cause, O Lord,
you have redeemed my life.
59 You have seen the wrong done to me,
O LORD;
judge my cause.
60 You have seen all their malice,
all their plots against me.

61 You have heard their taunts, O LORD,
all their plots against me.
62 The whispers and murmurs of my
assailants
are against me all day long.
63 Whether they sit or rise—see,
I am the object of their taunt-songs.

64 Pay them back for their deeds, O LORD,
according to the work of their hands!
65 Give them anguish of heart;
your curse be on them!
66 Pursue them in anger and destroy them
from under the LORD's heavens.

The Punishment of Zion

4 How the gold has grown dim,
how the pure gold is changed!
The sacred stones lie scattered
at the head of every street.

2 The precious children of Zion,
worth their weight in fine gold—
how they are reckoned as earthen pots,
the work of a potter's hands!

3 Even the jackals offer the breast
and nurse their young,

but my people has become cruel,
like the ostriches in the wilderness.

4 The tongue of the infant sticks
to the roof of its mouth for thirst;
the children beg for food,
but no one gives them anything.

5 Those who feasted on delicacies
perish in the streets;
those who were brought up in purple
cling to ash heaps.

6 For the chastisement a of my people has
been greater
than the punishment b of Sodom,
which was overthrown in a moment,
though no hand was laid on it. c

7 Her princes were purer than snow,
whiter than milk;
their bodies were more ruddy than coral,
their hair c like sapphire. d

8 Now their visage is blacker than soot;
they are not recognized in the streets.
Their skin has shriveled on their bones;
it has become as dry as wood.

9 Happier were those pierced by the sword
than those pierced by hunger,
whose life drains away, deprived
of the produce of the field.

10 The hands of compassionate women
have boiled their own children;
they became their food
in the destruction of my people.

11 The LORD gave full vent to his wrath;
he poured out his hot anger,
and kindled a fire in Zion
that consumed its foundations.

12 The kings of the earth did not believe,
nor did any of the inhabitants of the
world,
that foe or enemy could enter
the gates of Jerusalem.

a Or *iniquity*   b Or *sin*   c Meaning of Heb
uncertain   d Or *lapis lazuli*

13 It was for the sins of her prophets
   and the iniquities of her priests,
  who shed the blood of the righteous
   in the midst of her.

14 Blindly they wandered through the
    streets,
  so defiled with blood
  that no one was able
   to touch their garments.

15 "Away! Unclean!" people shouted at
    them;
  "Away! Away! Do not touch!"
  So they became fugitives and
    wanderers;
  it was said among the nations,
  "They shall stay here no longer."

16 The LORD himself has scattered them,
  he will regard them no more;
  no honor was shown to the priests,
  no favor to the elders.

17 Our eyes failed, ever watching
   vainly for help;
  we were watching eagerly
   for a nation that could not save.

18 They dogged our steps
   so that we could not walk in our
    streets;
  our end drew near; our days were
    numbered;
   for our end had come.

19 Our pursuers were swifter
   than the eagles in the heavens;
  they chased us on the mountains,
   they lay in wait for us in the
    wilderness.

20 The LORD's anointed, the breath of our
    life,
  was taken in their pits—

the one of whom we said, "Under his
    shadow
  we shall live among the nations."

21 Rejoice and be glad, O daughter Edom,
  you that live in the land of Uz;
  but to you also the cup shall pass;
  you shall become drunk and strip
   yourself bare.

22 The punishment of your iniquity,
  O daughter Zion, is
    accomplished,
  he will keep you in exile no longer;
  but your iniquity, O daughter Edom, he
    will punish,
  he will uncover your sins.

A Plea for Mercy

5 Remember, O LORD, what has befallen
   us;
  look, and see our disgrace!
2 Our inheritance has been turned over to
    strangers,
  our homes to aliens.
3 We have become orphans, fatherless;
  our mothers are like widows.
4 We must pay for the water we drink;
  the wood we get must be bought.
5 With a yoke *a* on our necks we are hard
    driven;
  we are weary, we are given no rest.
6 We have made a pact with *b* Egypt and
    Assyria,
  to get enough bread.
7 Our ancestors sinned; they are no more,
  and we bear their iniquities.
8 Slaves rule over us;
  there is no one to deliver us from
   their hand.
9 We get our bread at the peril of our
    lives,

a Symmachus: Heb lacks *With a yoke*
b Heb *have given the hand to*

5:7 *Our ancestors sinned; . . . and we bear
their iniquities.* Is it fair for us to "bear the
iniquities" of our ancestors? Perhaps not fair,
but certainly it is true. We really do, in a deep
sense, pay for the sins of our forebears. The past
has a way of making us pay, even if it was not
our responsibility. Some of our pain is not self-
induced. This is a difficult insight, but true.
Lamentations specializes in the practice of
telling the truth.

because of the sword in the
   wilderness.

10 Our skin is black as an oven
   from the scorching heat of famine.

11 Women are raped in Zion,
   virgins in the towns of Judah.

12 Princes are hung up by their hands;
   no respect is shown to the elders.

13 Young men are compelled to grind,
   and boys stagger under loads of wood.

14 The old men have left the city gate,
   the young men their music.

15 The joy of our hearts has ceased;
   our dancing has been turned to
   mourning.

16 The crown has fallen from our head;
   woe to us, for we have sinned!

17 Because of this our hearts are sick,

because of these things our eyes have
   grown dim:

18 because of Mount Zion, which lies
   desolate;
   jackals prowl over it.

19 But you, O LORD, reign forever;
   your throne endures to all
   generations.

20 Why have you forgotten us completely?
   Why have you forsaken us these
   many days?

21 Restore us to yourself, O LORD, that we
   may be restored;
   renew our days as of old—

22 unless you have utterly rejected us,
   and are angry with us beyond
   measure.

5:19 *But you, O LORD, reign forever.* People in grief report that they have "good days and bad days"; they oscillate between firm, faithful confidence and tearful despair. So does Lamentations. This Scripture is so helpful to the community in the time of grief in that it honestly mirrors what it really feels like to be in grief. Lamentations thereby gives us permission to express our sorrow as we do, not as we ought to do. It is permitted to have sure faith in God one moment and to be cast down in doubt the next. It takes strong faith in the secure love of God to be able honestly to admit our anger and disappointment with God.

X. The People of God in Exile

Scriptures: *2 Kings 25:11–30, 2 Chronicles 36:20–23, Jeremiah 37–52, Lamentations, Ezekiel, Daniel, Obadiah*

Deuterocanonical Books: *Baruch, Letter of Jeremiah, Additions to Daniel (Prayer of Azariah and the Song of the Three Jews, Susanna, Bel and the Dragon)*

> *The aim of God in history is the creation of an all-inclusive community of loving persons with God himself at the very center of this community as its prime Sustainer and most glorious Inhabitant (Eph 2:19–22; 3:10). The Bible traces the formation of this community from the creation in the Garden of Eden all the way to the new heaven and the new earth. Come, join us as we explore the many dimensions of this with-God history—from individual to family to tribe to people to nation to all humanity—and apply what we learn to our own spiritual formation.*

Previously we saw the nation of Israel rebel against God. In the Scriptures listed above we will see the ways God continues the process of forming an all-inclusive community as God sends his people from the Promised Land into exile.

God's Action

In the exile we see God's faithfulness to his people in judgment upon them. Judgment, however, does not mean that they are forsaken: "The Lord disciplines those whom he loves" (Heb 12:6). Through the tragic but necessary means of judgment the law is upheld and the supremacy of Yahweh as the only God is driven home. The Jewish people are stripped of all the externals they had come to believe were the substance of their lives: their king, their Temple, their city, and their land.

The people, unable to look to these externals, are left with what they can carry on their backs and hold within their hearts: mainly their sacred writings and their memories and customs. Retaining and refining these, they learn—much against their will—of the greatness and goodness of God far beyond anything they had known before. They learn what they had long been told: that God is available to, and totally sufficient for, the individual heart devoted to him, no matter what the circumstances. Further, they learn that God is acting and working far beyond their own Jewish culture, that "The eyes of the Lord range throughout the entire earth, to strengthen those whose heart is true to him" (2 Chron 16:9). And they learn in deeper ways than ever before that experiencing "The Lord is my shepherd, I shall not want" is not limited by circumstances (Ps 23:1).

Thus, in judgment there is blessing. So the way forward is to accept the judgment, side with God, and "kiss the rod" of affliction. As a result, during the exile when Jews are dispersed "from India to Ethiopia" (Esther 8:9), the Jewish religion and culture survives in its essential features through God alone and without any political or geographical base.

God blesses the exiled people in their personal walk with him. The immediacy of the divine-human relationship reemerges, but now it is all the more stable on the human side, incorporating within it a holy history extending all the way back to creation. Esther and Daniel know who they are in relation to God in a way that Adam or Moses never could. The riches of the previous "with-God" life now come to rest in the individual, and this human finitude is supplemented by the continuing influences of the law, the family, the developing synagogue system, and numerous communal customs.

The individual prophet is now an established central fixture in how God is "with" his people. "Believe in the LORD your God and you will be established; believe his prophets" (2 Chron 20:20). The radical independence of the prophet from any "establishment"—even from a Jewish establishment—is more strongly imprinted upon the People of God than ever during this period, even though the prophet as "outsider" had always been a major thread woven into the fabric of Israel. From Jeremiah and Ezekiel to John the Baptist, the right of the prophet to "come out of nowhere" and speak for God is confirmed. The people welcome the prophets and expect them to fulfill their role. But the leaders, whose own authority and right to lead is constantly challenged by the prophets, withhold their support.

Finally, Yahweh is identified as "the God of heaven" which, like the air surrounding us—the "first heaven" in biblical terms—is over all and directly and sufficiently available to all (2 Chron 36:23; Ezra 1:2; Neh 1:4; Dan 2:17–19, 28).

Hammered out in the cauldron of exile, this new understanding of where God is in relation to us develops into the language of "the kingdom of the heavens." Later, Jesus uses and expands this new understanding of "the kingdom of the heavens" to proclaim salvation to all, beyond any "official" religious or political arrangement. The experience of the exile and of how God was with his people in judgment proves essential to the new and more adequate understanding of how "[our] God reigns" (Isa 52:7).

Human Reaction

God's people first respond to exile with denial, anguish, lamentation, confusion, bitterness, and the rejection of exile and judgment as God's will. This negative reaction feeds the problem of false prophets, which begins late in the period of the Divided Kingdom. Of them Jeremiah famously says, "They have treated the wound of my people carelessly, saying 'Peace, peace,' when there is no peace" (6:14). The true prophets perceive and accept God's hand in judgment, seeing through and beyond it to God's ultimate blessing. The false prophets deny the reality of God's judgment and insist that Israel's blessing comes from its continuation as a separate nation.

A major part of the true blessing in and beyond judgment is the emergence of "the law and the prophets" as the heart of the covenant relationship with God. This makes possible the development of institutions and rituals of family and community that can stand free of all human arrangements and ultimately survive the collapse and destruction of those human arrangements. These developments are central to the spiritual formation of the People of God during the exile. They will also prove essential to later Jewish dispersions, as well as to how Christian fellowships would think of themselves as nonethnic, spiritual bodies, independent of human arrangements.

In the exile and afterward the Jewish people finally get monotheism and the keeping of the law down pat as an absolute demand. They firmly accept this demand, though misinterpretation of its exact meaning clouds reception of the later moves of God upon his people, up to today.

Blessings and Benefits for Our Formation

The great advantage of this form of mediation is the emphasis it places on individual responsibility—on personal holiness and faithfulness to the law and to God. This stands out in stark relief with figures like Daniel and Esther and appears in similar stories such as Bel and the Dragon, Susanna, and Judith. Here the primary emphasis is on the faithfulness of the individual to God and God's faithfulness to the individual.

Also, the Israelites are now forced to become citizens of the world, not a people hidden in an ethnic enclave. God, who transcends national identity, appoints his people to be a blessing to all peoples among whom they dwell. They seek the welfare of "Babylon" under God, and do this without themselves losing contact with God—indeed, they are able to do this precisely because of God's presence with them (Jer 29:4–7). All the peoples of the earth must come to know that Yahweh is God, and Israel has the role of bringing this to pass. The Israelites were from the outset assigned to be witnesses to all the nations; and in the exile and dispersion this significantly does come to pass even though, as the story of Jonah clearly reveals, the nation as a whole fails in this task. Now, in ways unexpected and unanticipated, the Abrahamic covenant moves forward: "In you all the families of the earth shall be blessed" (Gen 12:3).

Limits and Liabilities for Our Formation

However, in themselves exile and dispersion are not enough to open up the People of God to the world and to free its individuals from cultural self-righteousness. Much good is accomplished, but the overall outcome of the exile and subsequent return to the land is an increasingly repressive system of external rules that dictate personal behavior and public ritual. It is this stifling externalization that Jesus so thoroughly exposes and condemns.

Also, such brutal events as befell the Jewish people in the years of exile are surely not the best way to learn the ways of God, nor something he would have

The With-God Life

chosen unless it was absolutely necessary. "Why will you die, O house of Israel? For I have no pleasure in the death of anyone, says the Lord GOD. Turn, then, and live" (Ezek 18:31–32). The Israelites as a whole could not be a light to the Gentiles when crushed and oppressed, though occasionally individuals succeeded in burning brightly on the world stage. Suffering can be redemptive when received in faith, but it is not intrinsically good. There is a better way to get to where it brings us, if only we will take it, so that we can avoid the pain and tears of Lamentations. This is important for us to remember when we are in the rigorous process of being spiritually formed. There is a better way than "no pain, no gain": "God's kindness is meant to lead you to repentance" (Rom 2:4).

Insights and Instructions for Our Formation

What can we learn from this dimension of God-with-us? Well, first, we learn we *can* sing the Lord's song in a foreign land (Ps 137:4). And we must, for God is the God of all peoples, not just of one nation or one culture. Indeed, God is most likely in places and events and people that we have already written off. And we should look for and expect to find God there.

Second, if we are to succeed in fulfilling the law, we must not aim just to refine our external actions, but to become the kind of person inwardly from whom the deeds of the law flow naturally. We cannot keep the law by trying to keep the law. Here again indirection is the key. What things can we do so that keeping the law will be a grace-filled side effect of who we have become? Appropriate disciplines of the spiritual life show us the way. By living in such Spiritual Disciplines as part of an overall plan for our life "in Christ," we can prevent the keeping of the law from becoming a senseless, grinding fetish that brings death, as it did in postexilic Israel.

Finally, we learn that God is with us in our failures and beyond our failures. Indeed, he uses even our failures for our good. "Weeping may linger for the night, but joy comes with the morning" (Ps 30:5). There is always a morning with God . . . a morning different and far better than we can ever imagine. Even the darkness and death endured by the Israelites throughout the centuries will one day be broken and dispersed. "The dawn from on high will break upon us, to give light to those who sit in darkness and in the shadow of death" (Luke 1:78–79).

The With-God Life

EZEKIEL

E zekiel's life bridged the great cataclysm of 586 BC, when Jerusalem—God's own city—was completely destroyed by the Babylonians and its population exiled. Ezekiel, a priest, had been taken to Babylon after the initial capture of the city in the first deportation of exiles in 598 BC. There, on the banks of the river Chebar, Ezekiel the priest from Jerusalem became Ezekiel the prophet of the exiles. The people Ezekiel addressed were traumatized. They had witnessed the brutality of war and had lost loved ones to massacre. They exhibited the symptoms of war-torn refugees and were dazed and stupefied by the terror that had overcome their everyday lives. Ezekiel's graphic depictions of violence rightly trouble contemporary readers who live in relative ease. But set in the midst of a community that could not erase living memories of terror, these terrible portrayals are closer to everyday reality than we realize.

In the exile the people wrestled with the theological problem of how to live after "the city has fallen" (33:21; lit., "the city was struck down" or "smashed"). The end of Jerusalem resulted in the destruction of the Temple, home of the presence of God among the People of God. The disciplines of the spiritual life had required the Temple. Without it, living with God seemed no longer possible. In the face of such a calamity the exilic community was tempted to give up on life with God and adopt the ways of life of its Babylonian captors. Ezekiel was convinced that was not the answer. He saw a way forward with God. In receiving Ezekiel's message we discover that there can be a future life with God after the world crashes in calamity and nothing familiar remains.

Eating the Word of God

Confronted with such an inexplicable event, Ezekiel began with what he had inherited—the long story of God's presence with the people. Faced with evidence that the story had come to an end, Ezekiel revisited the familiar tale of God with Israel.

See also *"The With-God Life" essay for this section of the Bible,*
"The People of God in Exile," pp. 1171–74.

But when Ezekiel retold the old story, he set it in a different key. In his retelling the story was not marked by a litany of God's mighty deeds but by a long record of Israel's rebellious acts (chaps 16, 20, 23). Faced with a radically new situation, Ezekiel reread the script of the People of God and found a word from God that had not been heard before. Here lie the origins of the practice of the synagogue (lit., "the gathering" or "the congregation"). The exiles discovered that the presence of God was as close as a gathering that reads the Scripture closely. Arriving at the dead end of a way of life we, like the exiles, congregate to practice the Spiritual Disciplines and to discover a life with God that has gone long unnoticed.

Ezekiel ate Scripture (3:1–3). His close reading of God's word was both physical and spiritual. The Scripture became a part of him, body and soul. In digesting God's word Ezekiel was transformed. He was nourished in ways that gave him new eyes to see and ears to hear what life with God would mean in his time and place. In swallowing "words of lamentation and mourning and woe" (2:10), Ezekiel discovered that the collapse of the way of life of the people with God was no surprise. It had been a long time in coming. He saw that the true story of the People of God was a tale of ignoring, betraying, and mocking God that brought a crashing end to the relationship with God as it had been. Life could not go on like this. God's destruction of the nation, the city, and the Temple was inevitable.

Discerning True Prophecy

Ezekiel's blunt words shocked his compatriots, who could not imagine that he was speaking the truth (3:7–11). The people were accustomed to the benign words of those who delivered comforting sermons. Ezekiel called these crowd-pleasers false prophets who only pretended that they heard the word of God (13:1–16). They whitewashed the real trouble that confronted the people in their relationship with God, "saying 'Peace,' when there is no peace" (13:10–12). The exiles were in widespread denial and could not face the painful truth that Ezekiel voiced. To break through this thick shell of denial Ezekiel used dramatic signs (4:1–17; 5:1–4; 12:1–16; 21:1–7; 24:15–24) and outrageous metaphors (chap 23).

The exilic community was challenged by one of the most difficult dilemmas that can face the People of God—discerning true from false prophecy. Ezekiel's prophetic voice did not sound sensible. In fact, it was rude and horrifying, and initially Ezekiel's preaching was rejected as foolishness. But the exile lasted a long time. The prophet stayed in the midst of the people and staked his life on the claim that, on the other side of terrible judgment, God had not given up on the people. Over time the exiles changed their verdict and judged Ezekiel's testimony to be the truth. The communal practice of discernment—rooted in the Spiritual Disciplines—demands long-term patience and daring openness to an unexpected, even unwanted, word.

The Hinge of Renewal

Denial was the spiritual blindness confronting Ezekiel (chaps 1–24). The exilic community could not see the truth about God's righteous anger. But once the people opened their eyes to the roots of their trouble, Ezekiel was faced with a community whose despair made it deaf to hope (chaps 33–48). The disciplines of the spiritual life seek to overcome the blindness of denial and the deafness of despair. The People of God in exile began to see again when they said: "Our transgressions and our sins weigh upon us, and we waste away because of them; how then can we live?" (33:10). Telling the truth was the first step in the healing journey of repentance. The people saw the terrible damage they had caused in their relationship with God and could not imagine that it could be repaired in their lifetime. Ezekiel saw something else. He saw that new life with God was as close as a turn to the way of the Lord. In the absence of the Temple and the system of repairing the relationship with God through sacrifice, what was required was a personal and communal decision to live rightly with God and neighbor. God's desire was for a people who returned to obedience: "For I have no pleasure in the death of anyone, says the Lord GOD. Turn, then, and live" (18:32).

At the lowest ebb of the spiritual journey of the exiled People of God they emerged from deep denial only to be confronted with suffocating despair. This bleak moment is the surprising hinge of renewal that lies at the heart of the book of Ezekiel and of the Spiritual Disciplines. This movement is a cruciform pattern rooted deeply in the liturgical life of the Church. Worship begins with a truthful confession that reveals the people's deep denial. In the singing of "*Kyrie eleison*" ("Lord, have mercy") the personal and communal cry of exilic despair is given voice. Then a surprising and unexpected word is delivered: "A new heart I will give you, and a new spirit I will put within you; . . . and you shall be my people, and I will be your God" (36:26, 28). This impossible word of hope was as unbelievable to the exilic community as was the word of judgment that broke through their determined denial. The people were spiritually dead. They had no source of life or vitality. No strategies for renewal, no techniques for improvement could revive the remnant of Israel. They spoke the truth when they said: "Our bones are dried up, and our hope is lost; we are cut off completely" (37:11). A new future was only possible through an inexplicable gift of God: "Thus says the Lord GOD to these bones: I will cause breath to enter you, and you shall live" (37:5). In a mysterious way, the prophetic vision of revival was itself the first breath of newness in the dry bones of the exiled People of God. The new future began with one who dared to utter an alternative to the triumph of death.

The Danger and Wonder of God's Holiness

It is impossible to read Ezekiel without noticing his priestly vision. For Ezekiel the presence of God was an almost material reality. He spoke of the glory of God (Hebrew *kavod*) as a deafening, blinding force that resided in the Temple (1:4–28). When he portrayed the horror of Jerusalem's fall, he described the exit of God's glory from the Temple as God abandoning the holy place of the People of God (8:6; 10:18–19; 11:22–25). When Ezekiel saw the future he glimpsed a day when the glory of God returns to the Temple (43:1–5) and waters the land (47:1–12) so that the city can be named: "The LORD is There" (48:35). Being with God was, for Ezekiel, an awesome and overwhelming experience (1:28; 43:3). Priests were accustomed to living in the neighborhood of the glory of God and of dealing with the dangerous reality of God's holiness. The Temple was carefully organized to be a place where the people could safely meet the holiness of God. God's holiness is the manifestation of God's presence and character. It is something like high-voltage electricity or nuclear radiation. Those who get close to God's holiness must be careful, lest there be circuit overloads or deadly contamination.

Ezekiel saw that the judgment of Jerusalem and the destruction of the Temple were the result of the ways in which the people had ignored the risk of mishandling God's holiness. They had taken God for granted. They had imagined that God existed for their benefit. They had reduced God to slogans like "God loves you" and "In God we trust." They were not in awe of God's freedom to speak independently of their opinions, biases, or certainties. They were no longer prepared for God to be holy, free, or other than what they had already decided God was allowed to be. In other words, they had grown accustomed to living as if God was theirs to control and manipulate in order to satisfy their version of events and their needs and wants. Ezekiel called this for what it was—idolatry and an abomination.

The People of God in our day are tempted to imagine that Ezekiel's priestly language is antiquated, superseded by later theological discoveries. But the disciplines of the spiritual life—prayer, Scripture, worship, fasting, hospitality—intend to remind a people tempted by idolatrous technology that God is beyond control, that God is holy. Ezekiel boldly declares that God gives people new life beyond death, because God is God and needs to preserve his good name and holy reputation (36:22–32). In the end, the renewal of the People of God is a result of the holiness of God.

This is the testimony of African American spirituals that find in Ezekiel a contemporary exile. They sing that the glory of God—the "wheel within a wheel a-rolling way in the middle of the sky"—is the source of faith ("the big wheel rolled by the faith") and of grace ("the little wheel rolled by the grace of God") for a people enslaved far from home. They live in the incredible conviction that "dem bones are gonna rise again." Here we glimpse the ways in which the spiritual identity of both Jews and Christians is profoundly shaped by Ezekiel's prophecy among the exiles. Whenever the Church finds itself living between the terror of Good Friday's horrible ending and the wonder of Easter Sunday's impossible homecoming, it recognizes what it is to be a people exiled on a long Holy Saturday between denial and the truth, between despair and hope. In a season of absence when the glory of God is far, far away the People of God are called to "eat the scroll" of Ezekiel, to digest its hard truth and to be sustained by its nourishing hope.

—*Edwin Searcy*

The Vision of the Chariot

1 In the thirtieth year, in the fourth month, on the fifth day of the month, as I was among the exiles by the river Chebar, the heavens were opened, and I saw visions of God. 2On the fifth day of the month (it was the fifth year of the exile of King Jehoiachin), 3the word of the LORD came to the priest Ezekiel son of Buzi, in the land of the Chaldeans by the river Chebar; and the hand of the LORD was on him there.

4 As I looked, a stormy wind came out of the north: a great cloud with brightness around it and fire flashing forth continually, and in the middle of the fire, something like gleaming amber. 5In the middle of it was something like four living creatures. This was their appearance: they were of human form. 6Each had four faces, and each of them had four wings. 7Their legs were straight, and the soles of their feet were like the sole of a calf's foot; and they sparkled like burnished bronze. 8Under their wings on their four sides they had human hands. And the four had their faces and their wings thus: 9their wings touched one another; each of them moved straight ahead, without turning as they moved. 10As for the appearance of their faces: the four had the face of a human being, the face of a lion on the right side, the face of an ox on the left side, and the face of an eagle; 11such were their faces. Their wings were spread out above; each creature had two wings, each of which touched the wing of another, while two covered their bodies. 12Each moved straight ahead; wherever the spirit would go, they went, without turning as they went. 13In the middle of*a* the living creatures there was something that looked like burning coals of fire, like torches moving to and fro among the living creatures; the fire was bright, and lightning issued from the fire. 14The living creatures darted to and fro, like a flash of lightning.

15 As I looked at the living creatures, I saw a wheel on the earth beside the living creatures, one for each of the four of them. *b* 16As for the appearance of the wheels and their construction: their appearance was like the gleaming of beryl; and the four had the same form, their construction being something like a wheel within a wheel. 17When they moved, they moved in any of the four directions without veering as they moved. 18Their rims were tall and awesome, for the rims of all four were full of eyes all around. 19When the living creatures moved, the wheels moved beside them; and when the living creatures rose from the earth, the wheels rose. 20Wherever the spirit would go, they went, and the wheels rose along with them; for the spirit of the living creatures was in the wheels. 21When they

a Gk OL: Heb *And the appearance of*   *b* Heb *of their faces*

1:1 *and I saw visions of God.* Ezekiel is witness to an extraordinary sight. Exiled from Jerusalem, living in a detention center for deportees, he sees the heavens opened and God revealed. As a priest, Ezekiel is practiced at a ritual life with God. Now Ezekiel discovers life with God far removed from the safety and familiarity of the Temple. Contrary to the available evidence, God has not abandoned Israel. Ezekiel is to speak for God in the midst of unimaginable trauma and desperate circumstances.

1:4 *in the middle of the fire, something like.* This God is too expansive for words. Ezekiel must find pictures that are "something like" the overwhelming vision he has seen and heard. He portrays another dimension of existence in which strange living creatures and wheels within wheels and wings that sound like thunder surround the throne of God, who is "something that looked like fire" (v 27). Ezekiel is describing the holiness of God. To say that God is holy is to be reminded that God is, by definition, beyond all of our categories and beyond our control.

1:10 *the face of a human being . . . lion . . . ox . . . eagle.* The "four living creatures" (v 5) that Ezekiel sees surrounding the throne of God (cf. 10:14) are glimpsed in John's vision (Rev 4:7). Early Christian writers connected the four Evangelists (Matthew, Mark, Luke, and John) with the four living creatures (human being, lion, ox, and eagle) in various combinations. In this way the early Church testified that the God who had spoken through Ezekiel was revealed in Jesus Christ.

No must be afraid

moved, the others moved; when they stopped, the others stopped; and when they rose from the earth, the wheels rose along with them; for the spirit of the living creatures was in the wheels.

22 Over the heads of the living creatures there was something like a dome, shining like crystal,*a* spread out above their heads. 23Under the dome their wings were stretched out straight, one toward another; and each of the creatures had two wings covering its body. 24When they moved, I heard the sound of their wings like the sound of mighty waters, like the thunder of the Almighty,*b* a sound of tumult like the sound of an army; when they stopped, they let down their wings. 25And there came a voice from above the dome over their heads; when they stopped, they let down their wings.

26 And above the dome over their heads there was something like a throne, in appearance like sapphire;*c* and seated above the likeness of a throne was something that seemed like a human form. 27Upward from what appeared like the loins I saw something like gleaming amber, something that looked like fire enclosed all around; and downward from what looked like the loins I saw something that looked like fire, and there was a splendor all around. 28Like the bow in a cloud on a rainy day, such was the appearance of the splendor all around. This was the appearance of the likeness of the glory of the LORD.

When I saw it, I fell on my face, and I heard the voice of someone speaking.

The Vision of the Scroll

2 He said to me: O mortal,*d* stand up on your feet, and I will speak with you. 2And when he spoke to me, a spirit entered into me and set me on my feet; and I heard him speaking to me. 3He said to me, Mortal, I am sending you to the people of Israel, to a nation*e* of rebels who have rebelled against me; they and their ancestors have transgressed against me to this very day. 4The descendants are impudent and stubborn. I am sending you to them, and you shall say to them, "Thus says the Lord GOD." 5Whether they hear or refuse to hear (for they are a rebellious house), they shall know that there has been a prophet among them. 6And you, O mortal, do not be afraid of them, and do not be afraid of their words, though briers and thorns surround you and you live among scorpions; do not be afraid of their words, and do not be dismayed at their looks, for they are a rebellious house. 7You shall speak my words to them, whether they hear or refuse to hear; for they are a rebellious house.

8 But you, mortal, hear what I say to you; do not be rebellious like that rebellious house; open your mouth and eat what I give you.

a Gk: Heb *like the awesome crystal* *b* Traditional rendering of Heb *Shaddai* *c* Or *lapis lazuli* *d* Or *son of man*; Heb *ben adam* (and so throughout the book when Ezekiel is addressed) *e* Syr: Heb *to nations*

1:28 *the glory of the LORD.* The glory of the Lord is the shining, potent, almost material presence of God. Coming close to the glory of God causes Ezekiel to fall on his face before such high-voltage energy. Being with God in such intensity overpowers the prophet in awe and fear.

Responding
1:28 WORSHIP. Like Ezekiel, minister and theologian A. W. Tozer felt the only response to God was simply to fall on one's face. Tozer would spend four to five hours at a time lying face down on the floor, saying nothing. As you are able, try worshiping God in this

position. Bask in God's glory; meditate on your relationship to him. Listen. *See also* Spiritual Disciplines Index.

2:1 *O mortal.* God addresses Ezekiel as "mortal" (lit., "son of man"; see NRSV note). He is not God. He is a finite and insignificant creature. Only God is holy. The relationship with God is always marked by this massive inequity in power, though we are tempted to imagine otherwise.

2:2 *and set me on my feet.* Ezekiel's response to God is inspired, from the start, by God's own speech. When God speaks, the Spirit enters the prophet and stands him up. God's call energizes and encourages risky prophetic speech and life.

EZEKIEL

A Dramatic Submission

Selected Scriptures: *Ezekiel 1–3; 37; 47*

Early on, God asked Ezekiel to take extreme measures to warn Israel of disaster due to their unfaithfulness. As if psychotic, Ezekiel shaved his head and burned his hair (Ezek 5:1). He lay on his side for a year, eating food cooked on cow dung (4:15). He clapped his hands and stomped his feet. He crawled through a hole in his house, carrying his belongings, and then, when his wife died, appeared apathetic, forbidden to mourn (24:16). Despite his urgent warning, the people persisted in their idolatry.

Then Jerusalem fell under siege and was destroyed, and Ezekiel became silent. After thirteen years, God moved him again to prophesy (33:22). This time his message spoke hope. Israel would finally give up its fascination with other gods. It would "know that I am the LORD." These words ring out more than fifty times in Ezekiel's recorded message. Israel's future was, indeed, hopeful, for the Lord, Yahweh— "the One Who Is Always Present"—would finally draw his people to himself through their suffering in exile. God's presence with them would not wane, despite their displacement. And the message Ezekiel lived out, "God with us," would finally sink in.

Ezekiel declared, "The hand of the LORD was upon me" (e.g., 1:3; 3:14; 3:22). He sensed God's intent to use him and, in disciplined submission, he cooperated. Ezekiel became a theatrical expression of God's message to his people, exhibiting the Immanuel presence of God. Late in his prophecy, Ezekiel described a restored Temple and renewed worship of God. In his vision, a river flows from underneath the Temple toward the Dead Sea, and "when it enters the sea, the sea of stagnant waters, the water will become fresh; . . . and everything will live where the river goes" (47:8–9).

Like Ezekiel, we also can submit ourselves to God's hand upon us. God may not call us to theatrics, but we will move with Life from outside ourselves, for we will find ourselves swept into the River of God. Richard Foster celebrates this marvelous vision in a letter he once wrote: "The River of God is flowing today. No one can stop it, and no one can contain it. It is a deep River of divine intimacy, a powerful River of holy living, a dancing River of jubilation in the Spirit, and a wide River of unconditional love for all peoples. And the promise is that everything the River touches will live! Oh, my friend, may I urge you . . . to step into the flow of this mighty River of God. . . . and then determine never to step out. This is a consciously chosen course of action that involves both group and individual life. Let it be for us, as Jesus says, that streams of living water will ever flow out of our innermost being."

Personal Reflection
- Looking back, when could you say, "the hand of the Lord was upon me"? What kind of message or work did God offer through you?
- How regularly do you practice submission to God's movement in and through you? How willing are you to be used by God as he wills?

9I looked, and a hand was stretched out to me, and a written scroll was in it. 10He spread it before me; it had writing on the front and on the back, and written on it were words of lamentation and mourning and woe.

3 He said to me, O mortal, eat what is offered to you; eat this scroll, and go, speak to the house of Israel. 2So I opened my mouth, and he gave me the scroll to eat. 3He said to me, Mortal, eat this scroll that I give you and fill your stomach with it. Then I ate it; and in my mouth it was as sweet as honey.

4 He said to me: Mortal, go to the house of Israel and speak my very words to them. 5For you are not sent to a people of obscure speech and difficult language, but to the house of Israel— 6not to many peoples of obscure speech and difficult language, whose words you cannot understand. Surely, if I sent you to them, they would listen to you. 7But the house of Israel will not listen to you, for they are not willing to listen to me; because all the house of Israel have a hard forehead and a stubborn heart. 8See, I have made your face hard against their faces, and your forehead hard against their foreheads. 9Like the hardest stone, harder than flint, I have made your forehead; do not fear them or be dismayed at their looks, for they are a rebellious house. 10He said to me: Mortal, all my words that I shall speak to you receive in your heart and hear with your ears; 11then go to the exiles, to your people, and speak to them. Say to them, "Thus says the Lord GOD"; whether they hear or refuse to hear.

Ezekiel at the River Chebar

12 Then the spirit lifted me up, and as the glory of the LORD rose *a* from its place, I heard behind me the sound of loud rumbling; 13it was the sound of the wings of the living creatures brushing against one another, and the sound of the wheels beside them, that sounded like a loud rumbling. 14The spirit lifted me up and bore me away; I went in bitterness in the heat of my spirit, the hand of the LORD being strong upon me. 15I came to the exiles at Tel-abib, who lived by the river Chebar.*b* And I sat there among them, stunned, for seven days.

16 At the end of seven days, the word of the LORD came to me: 17Mortal, I have made you a sentinel for the house of Israel; when-

a Cn: Heb *and blessed be the glory of the LORD*
b Two Mss Syr: Heb *Chebar, and to where they lived.* Another reading is *Chebar, and I sat where they sat*

3:1 *eat this scroll.* The prophet eats—literally and figuratively—a message of "lamentation and mourning and woe" (2:10). Ezekiel internalizes the word of God until it becomes a part of his being. This word of ache and loss nourishes Ezekiel's body and soul. The bitter news tastes surprisingly sweet, a reminder of the sweetness of the law (Ps 19:10) and of another scroll that is eaten by John (Rev 10:10). As Ezekiel eats the word, we glimpse the purpose of the disciplines of the spiritual life. Through prayer and study, worship and service, we regularly digest God's word into the core of our being, where it feeds and transforms us.

Responding
3:1–3 STUDY. Despite its content, God's word tasted sweet in Ezekiel's mouth. Jeremiah also ate God's word, which became to him "the delight of [his] heart" (15:16). Copy one or both of these passages onto a bookmark to read each time you open your Bible, as a dedication for your study. *See also* Spiritual Disciplines Index.

3:7 *a hard forehead and a stubborn heart.* The conversation between God and the people has broken down. The problem is not language (v 5). The problem is the refusal of the people to listen. They are in denial. They would rather ignore God than face the truth about the trouble that is real and imminent. Ezekiel can have no illusions about the lack of desire of God's own people to be with God now.

3:16–21 *have made you a sentinel.* Ezekiel is commissioned as a sentinel over Israel to alert the people to approaching danger. Yet Israel cannot comprehend that this danger comes from God, who will not be mocked. The prophet is not responsible for the response of the people, but only for the call to turn toward righteous living. With Israel, we today must regularly choose whether to trust or ignore the sentry's warning. Do we want a life with God?

O mortal you are a SENTINEL to warn

ever you hear a word from my mouth, you shall give them warning from me. 18If I say to the wicked, "You shall surely die," and you give them no warning, or speak to warn the wicked from their wicked way, in order to save their life, those wicked persons shall die for their iniquity; but their blood I will require at your hand. 19But if you warn the wicked, and they do not turn from their wickedness, or from their wicked way, they shall die for their iniquity; but you will have saved your life. 20Again, if the righteous turn from their righteousness and commit iniquity, and I lay a stumbling block before them, they shall die; because you have not warned them, they shall die for their sin, and their righteous deeds that they have done shall not be remembered; but their blood I will require at your hand. 21If, however, you warn the righteous not to sin, and they do not sin, they shall surely live, because they took warning; and you will have saved your life.

Ezekiel Isolated and Silenced

22 Then the hand of the LORD was upon me there; and he said to me, Rise up, go out into the valley, and there I will speak with you. 23So I rose up and went out into the valley; and the glory of the LORD stood there, like the glory that I had seen by the river Chebar; and I fell on my face. 24The spirit entered into me, and set me on my feet; and he spoke with me and said to me: Go, shut yourself inside your house. 25As for you, mortal, cords shall be placed on you, and you shall be bound with them, so that you cannot go out among the people; 26and I will make your tongue cling to the roof of your mouth, so that you shall be speechless and unable to

reprove them; for they are a rebellious house. 27But when I speak with you, I will open your mouth, and you shall say to them, "Thus says the Lord GOD"; let those who will hear, hear; and let those who refuse to hear, refuse; for they are a rebellious house.

The Siege of Jerusalem Portrayed

4 And you, O mortal, take a brick and set it before you. On it portray a city, Jerusalem; 2and put siegeworks against it, and build a siege wall against it, and cast up a ramp against it; set camps also against it, and plant battering rams against it all around. 3Then take an iron plate and place it as an iron wall between you and the city; set your face toward it, and let it be in a state of siege, and press the siege against it. This is a sign for the house of Israel.

4 Then lie on your left side, and place the punishment of the house of Israel upon it; you shall bear their punishment for the number of the days that you lie there. 5For I assign to you a number of days, three hundred ninety days, equal to the number of the years of their punishment; and so you shall bear the punishment of the house of Israel. 6When you have completed these, you shall lie down a second time, but on your right side, and bear the punishment of the house of Judah; forty days I assign you, one day for each year. 7You shall set your face toward the siege of Jerusalem, and with your arm bared you shall prophesy against it. 8See, I am putting cords on you so that you cannot turn from one side to the other until you have completed the days of your siege.

9 And you, take wheat and barley, beans and lentils, millet and spelt; put them into

---

3:25–27 *you shall be bound.* God shuts the sentinel up. Called to warn the people, Ezekiel finds his voice muted. He will not ramble on or speak without cause. In due time God will use his voice, but not now. The prophet's voice is not his own.

4:1–3 *take a brick and set it before you.* God instructs Ezekiel to use symbolic acts as signs that portray the truth about Jerusalem's future. This "sign language" offers stark, compelling images that function as embodied prophetic

speech. Ezekiel enacts the message in bold street theater.

4:4–11 *Then lie on your left side.* The prophet participates in the suffering that is coming upon the people. He lies down, symbolically bearing the weight of Israel's punishment while eating the skimpy rations of besieged Jerusalem. As God's sentinel the prophet is both with God and with the people. He knows the burden of judgment and the hunger of his compatriots in his body.

one vessel, and make bread for yourself. During the number of days that you lie on your side, three hundred ninety days, you shall eat it. ¹⁰The food that you eat shall be twenty shekels a day by weight; at fixed times you shall eat it. ¹¹And you shall drink water by measure, one-sixth of a hin; at fixed times you shall drink. ¹²You shall eat it as a barley-cake, baking it in their sight on human dung. ¹³The LORD said, "Thus shall the people of Israel eat their bread, unclean, among the nations to which I will drive them." ¹⁴Then I said, "Ah Lord GOD! I have never defiled myself; from my youth up until now I have never eaten what died of itself or was torn by animals, nor has carrion flesh come into my mouth." ¹⁵Then he said to me, "See, I will let you have cow's dung instead of human dung, on which you may prepare your bread."

16 Then he said to me, Mortal, I am going to break the staff of bread in Jerusalem; they shall eat bread by weight and with fearfulness; and they shall drink water by measure and in dismay. ¹⁷Lacking bread and water, they will look at one another in dismay, and waste away under their punishment.

A Sword against Jerusalem

5 And you, O mortal, take a sharp sword; use it as a barber's razor and run it over your head and your beard; then take balances for weighing, and divide the hair. ²One third of the hair you shall burn in the fire inside the city, when the days of the siege are completed; one third you shall take and strike with the sword all around the city;ᵃ and one third you shall scatter to the wind, and I will un-

sheathe the sword after them. ³Then you shall take from these a small number, and bind them in the skirts of your robe. ⁴From these, again, you shall take some, throw them into the fire and burn them up; from there a fire will come out against all the house of Israel.

5 Thus says the Lord GOD: This is Jerusalem; I have set her in the center of the nations, with countries all around her. ⁶But she has rebelled against my ordinances and my statutes, becoming more wicked than the nations and the countries all around her, rejecting my ordinances and not following my statutes. ⁷Therefore thus says the Lord GOD: Because you are more turbulent than the nations that are all around you, and have not followed my statutes or kept my ordinances, but have acted according to the ordinances of the nations that are all around you; ⁸therefore thus says the Lord GOD: I, I myself, am coming against you; I will execute judgments among you in the sight of the nations. ⁹And because of all your abominations, I will do to you what I have never yet done, and the like of which I will never do again. ¹⁰Surely, parents shall eat their children in your midst, and children shall eat their parents; I will execute judgments on you, and any of you who survive I will scatter to every wind. ¹¹Therefore, as I live, says the Lord GOD, surely, because you have defiled my sanctuary with all your detestable things and with all your abominations—therefore I will cut you down;ᵇ my eye will not spare, and I will have

---

a Heb *it*   *b* Another reading is *I will withdraw*

5:5–9 *I will do to you what I have never yet done.* The horror of what is to take place is now in plain view. Jerusalem—footstool of God—has broken covenant with God. Zion has abandoned God's ordinances and statutes in favor of the ways of the world that surrounds it. This is not a simple misdemeanor. Jerusalem has committed such abominations that God is enraged and determined to leave the city of David in desolate ruins. This is nearly unimaginable for God, who has never done this before and who expects never to do it again. Here we confront the holy otherness of God, which is not tamed by slogans

that insist "God loves you." God's fury has broken the leash of all attempts at domesticating his holy freedom. Sensing the impending disaster, the people imagine that God is not strong enough to deter the armies and gods of Babylon. Jerusalem suspects that God is weaker than it had realized. Ezekiel has a different story to tell. He sees that God is the perpetrator of the terror that now befalls his homeland. The terrible events that are bringing the nation and the city to an end are the inevitable result of broken covenant promises. The awful truth is that God is wreaking havoc on his own people and city.

no pity. ¹²One third of you shall die of pestilence or be consumed by famine among you; one third shall fall by the sword around you; and one third I will scatter to every wind and will unsheathe the sword after them.

13 My anger shall spend itself, and I will vent my fury on them and satisfy myself; and they shall know that I, the LORD, have spoken in my jealousy, when I spend my fury on them. ¹⁴Moreover I will make you a desolation and an object of mocking among the nations around you, in the sight of all that pass by. ¹⁵You shall be[a] a mockery and a taunt, a warning and a horror, to the nations around you, when I execute judgments on you in anger and fury, and with furious punishments—I, the LORD, have spoken— ¹⁶when I loose against you[b] my deadly arrows of famine, arrows for destruction, which I will let loose to destroy you, and when I bring more and more famine upon you, and break your staff of bread. ¹⁷I will send famine and wild animals against you, and they will rob you of your children; pestilence and bloodshed shall pass through you; and I will bring the sword upon you. I, the LORD, have spoken.

Judgment on Idolatrous Israel

6 The word of the LORD came to me: ²O mortal, set your face toward the mountains of Israel, and prophesy against them, ³and say, You mountains of Israel, hear the word of the Lord GOD! Thus says the Lord GOD to the mountains and the hills, to the ravines and the valleys: I, I myself will bring a sword upon you, and I will destroy your high places. ⁴Your altars shall become desolate, and your incense stands shall be broken; and I will throw down your slain in front of your idols. ⁵I will lay the corpses of the people of Israel in front of their idols; and I will scatter your bones around your altars. ⁶Wherever you live, your towns shall be waste and your high places ruined, so that your altars will be waste and ruined,[c] your idols broken and destroyed, your incense stands cut down, and your works wiped out. ⁷The slain shall fall in your midst; then you shall know that I am the LORD.

8 But I will spare some. Some of you shall escape the sword among the nations and be scattered through the countries. ⁹Those of you who escape shall remember me among the nations where they are carried captive, how I was crushed by their wanton heart that turned away from me, and their wanton eyes that turned after their idols. Then they will be loathsome in their own sight for the evils that they have committed, for all their abominations. ¹⁰And they shall know that I am the LORD; I did not threaten in vain to bring this disaster upon them.

a Gk Syr Vg Tg: Heb *It shall be*   b Heb *them*
c Syr Vg Tg: Heb *and be made guilty*

6:2–6 *prophesy against them.* God's sentinel turns his attention to the centers of worship that dot the hilltops of Israel beyond Jerusalem. The problem in the land is not atheism, but idolatry. The people place their trust and their lives in gods that have no glory. Ezekiel is to set his face toward this deep communal delusion. He is to confront the fraudulent idols head on. And what about us? Are we prepared to confront the fraudulent idols of postmodern culture: racism, sexism, militarism, consumerism, relativism, and a hundred other isms that call for our allegiance today?

6:7 *then you shall know that I am the LORD.* The people have amnesia. In spite of their claims to worship God, they are no longer living in relationship with "the LORD" (in Hebrew, YHWH), whose name was first revealed to Moses (Exod 3:14). The phrase "then you shall know that I am LORD" appears eighty-six times in the book of Ezekiel. At the core of the awful judgment is God's deep desire to be known for who God is. The people have become accustomed to using God to justify all manner of their favorite policies, projects, and positions. They dare not allow God the freedom to be God. Ezekiel understands that the heart of renewal for the People of God is coming to know the Lord in their bones.

6:8–10 *But I will spare some.* Looking back to Israel from exile in Babylon, Ezekiel sees that some residents of the land will survive to tell the story of destruction. The survivors are key witnesses whose truth telling among the nations will shape the reformation of the People of God in exile. A remnant will tell the next generation the causes of the catastrophe.

Day of the Lord Anger Nsa

11 Thus says the Lord GOD: Clap your hands and stamp your foot, and say, Alas for all the vile abominations of the house of Israel! For they shall fall by the sword, by famine, and by pestilence. 12 Those far off shall die of pestilence; those nearby shall fall by the sword; and any who are left and are spared shall die of famine. Thus I will spend my fury upon them. 13 And you shall know that I am the LORD, when their slain lie among their idols around their altars, on every high hill, on all the mountain tops, under every green tree, and under every leafy oak, wherever they offered pleasing odor to all their idols. 14 I will stretch out my hand against them, and make the land desolate and waste, throughout all their settlements, from the wilderness to Riblah.*a* Then they shall know that I am the LORD.

Impending Disaster

7 The word of the LORD came to me: 2 You, O mortal, thus says the Lord GOD to the land of Israel:

An end! The end has come
  upon the four corners of the land.
3 Now the end is upon you,
  I will let loose my anger upon you;
  I will judge you according to your ways,
  I will punish you for all your
    abominations.
4 My eye will not spare you, I will have no
    pity.
  I will punish you for your ways,
  while your abominations are among
    you.
Then you shall know that I am the LORD.
5 Thus says the Lord GOD:

Disaster after disaster! See, it comes.
6 An end has come, the end has come.
It has awakened against you; see, it
    comes!
7 Your doom *b* has come to you,
  O inhabitant of the land.
The time has come, the day is near—
  of tumult, not of reveling on the
    mountains.
8 Soon now I will pour out my wrath
    upon you;
  I will spend my anger against you.
I will judge you according to your ways,
  and punish you for all your
    abominations.
9 My eye will not spare; I will have no
    pity.
  I will punish you according to your
    ways,
  while your abominations are among
    you.
Then you shall know that it is I the LORD who
strike.
10 See, the day! See, it comes!
  Your doom *b* has gone out.
The rod has blossomed, pride has
    budded.
11 Violence has grown into a rod of
    wickedness.
None of them shall remain,
  not their abundance, not their
    wealth;
  no pre-eminence among them. *b*
12 The time has come, the day draws near;

a Another reading is Diblah   *b Meaning of Heb uncertain*

7:2–4 *upon the four corners of the land.* Ezekiel's warning moves beyond Jerusalem and the idolatrous shrines on the mountaintops of Israel. Everything is now at "an end." Life in the Promised Land is now over for the People of God. They have been rooted in this soil, but their organic connection with the earth has now been broken. Naming this ending as the handiwork of God is crucial. Like an addict in denial whose life finally crumbles into disaster and bankruptcy, the people cannot be restored to life until confronted with the dead end of their reliance on false gods and empty hopes.

7:7–12 *not of reveling on the mountains.* With Amos (5:18–20), Ezekiel turns Israel's longing for the "day of the LORD" on its head. The people have been praying to be with God. They have longed for Immanuel. Now their prayer is answered, but it is not what they had expected. The day of God's coming is tumultuous. There is no dancing. God's day is a disaster for the People of God. This is a sobering reminder. We too pray for renewal. We too want to be with God. We too long for "the day of the LORD." And so we too must ask: Are we prepared for God's answer to come in God's way?

let not the buyer rejoice, nor the seller
mourn,
for wrath is upon all their multitude.
13 For the sellers shall not return to what has
been sold as long as they remain alive. For the
vision concerns all their multitude; it shall
not be revoked. Because of their iniquity, they
cannot maintain their lives. *a*
14 They have blown the horn and made
everything ready;
but no one goes to battle,
for my wrath is upon all their
multitude.
15 The sword is outside, pestilence and
famine are inside;
those in the field die by the sword;
those in the city—famine and
pestilence devour them.
16 If any survivors escape,
they shall be found on the mountains
like doves of the valleys,
all of them moaning over their iniquity.
17 All hands shall grow feeble,
all knees turn to water.
18 They shall put on sackcloth,
horror shall cover them.
Shame shall be on all faces,
baldness on all their heads.
19 They shall fling their silver into the
streets,
their gold shall be treated as unclean.
Their silver and gold cannot save them on
the day of the wrath of the LORD. They shall
not satisfy their hunger or fill their stomachs
with it. For it was the stumbling block of their
iniquity. 20 From their *b* beautiful ornament,
in which they took pride, they made their
abominable images, their detestable things;
therefore I will make of it an unclean thing to
them.
21 I will hand it over to strangers as booty,
to the wicked of the earth as plunder;
they shall profane it.
22 I will avert my face from them,

so that they may profane my
treasured *c* place;
the violent shall enter it,
they shall profane it.
23 Make a chain! *a*
For the land is full of bloody crimes;
the city is full of violence.
24 I will bring the worst of the nations
to take possession of their houses.
I will put an end to the arrogance of the
strong,
and their holy places shall be
profaned.
25 When anguish comes, they will seek
peace,
but there shall be none.
26 Disaster comes upon disaster,
rumor follows rumor;
they shall keep seeking a vision from
the prophet;
instruction shall perish from the
priest,
and counsel from the elders.
27 The king shall mourn,
the prince shall be wrapped in
despair,
and the hands of the people of the
land shall tremble.
According to their way I will deal with
them;
according to their own judgments I
will judge them.
And they shall know that I am the LORD.

Abominations in the Temple

8 In the sixth year, in the sixth month,
on the fifth day of the month, as I sat in
my house, with the elders of Judah sitting
before me, the hand of the Lord GOD fell
upon me there. 2 I looked, and there was a
figure that looked like a human being; *d* below

a Meaning of Heb uncertain   b Syr Symmachus:
Heb *its*   c Or *secret*   d Gk: Heb *like fire*

7:26 *seeking a vision from the prophet . . .
priest . . . elders.* In the midst of the disasters
and the rumors the people turn to prophet,
priest, and elder seeking vision, instruction, and
counsel. They turn, in a panic, hoping for an
answer. But these wise visionaries do not have

anything to say. This calamity is beyond their
capacity to explain. Finally, even the politicians—the king and the prince (v 27)—can
only grieve. Even the spin doctors throw up
their hands in despair. There are no answers.
This problem cannot be solved. It is the end.

what appeared to be its loins it was fire, and above the loins it was like the appearance of brightness, like gleaming amber. ³It stretched out the form of a hand, and took me by a lock of my head; and the spirit lifted me up between earth and heaven, and brought me in visions of God to Jerusalem, to the entrance of the gateway of the inner court that faces north, to the seat of the image of jealousy, which provokes to jealousy. ⁴And the glory of the God of Israel was there, like the vision that I had seen in the valley.

5 Then God*ᵃ* said to me, "O mortal, lift up your eyes now in the direction of the north." So I lifted up my eyes toward the north, and there, north of the altar gate, in the entrance, was this image of jealousy. ⁶He said to me, "Mortal, do you see what they are doing, the great abominations that the house of Israel are committing here, to drive me far from my sanctuary? Yet you will see still greater abominations."

7 And he brought me to the entrance of the court; I looked, and there was a hole in the wall. ⁸Then he said to me, "Mortal, dig through the wall"; and when I dug through the wall, there was an entrance. ⁹He said to me, "Go in, and see the vile abominations that they are committing here." ¹⁰So I went in and looked; there, portrayed on the wall all around, were all kinds of creeping things, and loathsome animals, and all the idols of the house of Israel. ¹¹Before them stood seventy of the elders of the house of Israel, with Jaazaniah son of Shaphan standing among

them. Each had his censer in his hand, and the fragrant cloud of incense was ascending. ¹²Then he said to me, "Mortal, have you seen what the elders of the house of Israel are doing in the dark, each in his room of images? For they say, 'The LORD does not see us, the LORD has forsaken the land.' " ¹³He said also to me, "You will see still greater abominations that they are committing."

14 Then he brought me to the entrance of the north gate of the house of the LORD; women were sitting there weeping for Tammuz. ¹⁵Then he said to me, "Have you seen this, O mortal? You will see still greater abominations than these."

16 And he brought me into the inner court of the house of the LORD; there, at the entrance of the temple of the LORD, between the porch and the altar, were about twenty-five men, with their backs to the temple of the LORD, and their faces toward the east, prostrating themselves to the sun toward the east. ¹⁷Then he said to me, "Have you seen this, O mortal? Is it not bad enough that the house of Judah commits the abominations done here? Must they fill the land with violence, and provoke my anger still further? See, they are putting the branch to their nose! ¹⁸Therefore I will act in wrath; my eye will not spare, nor will I have pity; and though they cry in my hearing with a loud voice, I will not listen to them."

a Heb *he*

8:2–18 *drive me far from my sanctuary.* Ezekiel has a stunning vision of the Temple and of Jerusalem, his home. He sees "the glory of the God of Israel" there (v 4), but then learns that God is about to be driven out of his own sanctuary. Even the Temple is no longer a safe preserve for the holy. In Jerusalem's final days the elders take it for granted that God has left them to their own devices (v 12). They assume that God is long gone from the Temple precincts. Idolatry has now made its way from the hilltop shrines into the sanctuary of the Lord. At the Temple's north gate the god Tammuz is being worshiped (v 14); at the Temple's entrance sun worship is practiced (vv 16–18). And all of this

is taking place in the full presence of the glory of the Lord. Yet no one notices the mismatch between the ritual practices of the people and the holy presence of Yahweh. The sacred place has become profane. Charged with maintaining the ritual cleanness of the Temple, the priests are complicit in its contamination. In spite of all the hymns and prayers and offerings, God is being driven away by the stench of idolatry. Here Ezekiel glimpses something new. He sees that God may now be available beyond the sacred Holy of Holies. Like the exiles, God is also on the move. Unlike the exiles, God is free to come and go.

The Slaughter of the Idolaters

9 Then he cried in my hearing with a loud voice, saying, "Draw near, you executioners of the city, each with his destroying weapon in his hand." ²And six men came from the direction of the upper gate, which faces north, each with his weapon for slaughter in his hand; among them was a man clothed in linen, with a writing case at his side. They went in and stood beside the bronze altar.

3 Now the glory of the God of Israel had gone up from the cherub on which it rested to the threshold of the house. The LORD called to the man clothed in linen, who had the writing case at his side; ⁴and said to him, "Go through the city, through Jerusalem, and put a mark on the foreheads of those who sigh and groan over all the abominations that are committed in it." ⁵To the others he said in my hearing, "Pass through the city after him, and kill; your eye shall not spare, and you shall show no pity. ⁶Cut down old men, young men and young women, little children and women, but touch no one who has the mark. And begin at my sanctuary." So they began with the elders who were in front of the house. ⁷Then he said to them, "Defile the house, and fill the courts with the slain. Go!" So they went out and killed in the city. ⁸While they were killing, and I was left alone, I fell prostrate on my face and cried out, "Ah Lord GOD! will you destroy all who remain of Israel as you pour out your wrath upon Jerusalem?" ⁹He said to me, "The guilt of the house of Israel and Judah is exceedingly great; the land is full of bloodshed and the city full of perversity; for they say, 'The LORD has forsaken the land, and the LORD does not see.' ¹⁰As for me, my eye will not spare, nor will I have pity, but I will bring down their deeds upon their heads."

11 Then the man clothed in linen, with the writing case at his side, brought back word, saying, "I have done as you commanded me."

God's Glory Leaves Jerusalem

10 Then I looked, and above the dome that was over the heads of the cherubim there appeared above them something like a sapphire, *a* in form resembling a throne. ²He said to the man clothed in linen, "Go within the wheelwork underneath the cherubim; fill your hands with burning coals from among the cherubim, and scatter them over the city." He went in as I looked on. ³Now the cherubim were standing on the south side of the house when the man went in; and a cloud filled the inner court. ⁴Then the glory of the LORD rose up from the cherub to the threshold of the house; the house was filled with the cloud, and the court was full of the brightness of the glory of the LORD. ⁵The sound of the wings of the cherubim was heard as far as the outer court, like the voice of God Almighty *b* when he speaks.

6 When he commanded the man clothed in linen, "Take fire from within the wheelwork, from among the cherubim," he went in and stood beside a wheel. ⁷And a cherub stretched out his hand from among the cher-

a Or *lapis lazuli*   *b* Traditional rendering of Heb *El Shaddai*

9:4 *those who sigh and groan over all the abominations.* In the midst of the devastation there is protection for those who are against the abominations. Telling the truth about the trouble is safe. Lying about the trouble is deadly.

9:8–10 *will you destroy all?* To this point Ezekiel has been speaking for God. Here he speaks to God on behalf of the people. The prophet desires an end to the awful judgment. He is not eager for Jerusalem's demise. But God will not be dissuaded. The nation imagines that God "does not see" the bloodshed and perversity that abounds (v 9). It is about to learn otherwise. Ezekiel cannot prevent the inevitable calamity that now befalls a people who have easily presumed to be with God.

10:2 *burning coals . . . scatter them over the city.* Now the man clothed in linen who marked some for survival (9:4) is sent to set the city ablaze. The inhabitants of Jerusalem assume that the fire is started by the Babylonians. Ezekiel dares another explanation. He announces that God is setting fire to Jerusalem with coals from the altar. God will cleanse the city at all costs. The people cannot delay the end intended by God any longer.

ubim to the fire that was among the cherubim, took some of it and put it into the hands
of the man clothed in linen, who took it and
went out. 8The cherubim appeared to have
the form of a human hand under their wings.

9 I looked, and there were four wheels beside the cherubim, one beside each cherub;
and the appearance of the wheels was like
gleaming beryl. 10And as for their appearance,
the four looked alike, something like a wheel
within a wheel. 11When they moved, they
moved in any of the four directions without
veering as they moved; but in whatever direction the front wheel faced, the others followed
without veering as they moved. 12Their entire body, their rims, their spokes, their wings,
and the wheels—the wheels of the four of
them—were full of eyes all around. 13As for
the wheels, they were called in my hearing
"the wheelwork." 14Each one had four faces:
the first face was that of the cherub, the second
face was that of a human being, the third that
of a lion, and the fourth that of an eagle.

15 The cherubim rose up. These were the
living creatures that I saw by the river Chebar.
16When the cherubim moved, the wheels
moved beside them; and when the cherubim
lifted up their wings to rise up from the earth,
the wheels at their side did not veer. 17When
they stopped, the others stopped, and when
they rose up, the others rose up with them; for
the spirit of the living creatures was in them.

18 Then the glory of the LORD went out
from the threshold of the house and stopped
above the cherubim. 19The cherubim lifted
up their wings and rose up from the earth in
my sight as they went out with the wheels beside them. They stopped at the entrance of
the east gate of the house of the LORD; and the
glory of the God of Israel was above them.

20 These were the living creatures that
I saw underneath the God of Israel by the
river Chebar; and I knew that they were cherubim. 21Each had four faces, each four wings,
and underneath their wings something like
human hands. 22As for what their faces were
like, they were the same faces whose appearance I had seen by the river Chebar. Each
one moved straight ahead.

Judgment on Wicked Counselors

11 The spirit lifted me up and brought
me to the east gate of the house of the
LORD, which faces east. There, at the entrance
of the gateway, were twenty-five men; among
them I saw Jaazaniah son of Azzur, and Pelatiah son of Benaiah, officials of the people.
2He said to me, "Mortal, these are the men
who devise iniquity and who give wicked
counsel in this city; 3they say, 'The time is not
near to build houses; this city is the pot, and
we are the meat.' 4Therefore prophesy against
them; prophesy, O mortal."

5 Then the spirit of the LORD fell upon me,
and he said to me, "Say, Thus says the LORD:
This is what you think, O house of Israel; I
know the things that come into your mind.
6You have killed many in this city, and have
filled its streets with the slain. 7Therefore
thus says the Lord GOD: The slain whom you
have placed within it are the meat, and this
city is the pot; but you shall be taken out of

10:9–19 *four wheels beside the cherubim.*
Ezekiel again sees a vision of four wheels within
wheels (1:15–21)—"the wheelwork" (10:13).
But now the wheelwork is on the move. God's
glory is departing and will not be easily available. God is not trapped in the ritual confines
of worship. The congregation cannot presume
that God is always present in the sanctuary.
Ezekiel sees that God is free to walk away. In
this dramatic evacuation God terminates commitment to the way things have been, because
the people have abandoned God. They are
interested only in God's usefulness, in the ways
they can use God to meet their needs. But God

does not exist to be useful, to meet needs, or
to serve causes. God exists for his own sake. So
God departs, leaving the Temple an empty shell
(v 18). There is no glory in the sanctuary any
longer. The Spirit has fled. All that is left are the
trappings of religion. There is no energy to heal
and no power to transform. Now Ezekiel sees
the awesome glory of God as he had seen by
the river Chebar in polluted Babylon (vv 20, 22).
God has fled Jerusalem, but has not abandoned
Israel. And what about us? Dare we ask the
unasked question of our day: Are our elaborate
sanctuaries empty shells, devoid of the *shekinah*
glory of God?

it. 8 You have feared the sword; and I will bring the sword upon you, says the Lord GOD. 9 I will take you out of it and give you over to the hands of foreigners, and execute judgments upon you. 10 You shall fall by the sword; I will judge you at the border of Israel. And you shall know that I am the LORD. 11 This city shall not be your pot, and you shall not be the meat inside it; I will judge you at the border of Israel. 12 Then you shall know that I am the LORD, whose statutes you have not followed, and whose ordinances you have not kept, but you have acted according to the ordinances of the nations that are around you."

13 Now, while I was prophesying, Pelatiah son of Benaiah died. Then I fell down on my face, cried with a loud voice, and said, "Ah Lord GOD! will you make a full end of the remnant of Israel?"

God Will Restore Israel

14 Then the word of the LORD came to me: 15 Mortal, your kinsfolk, your own kin, your fellow exiles, *a* the whole house of Israel, all of them, are those of whom the inhabitants of Jerusalem have said, "They have gone far from the LORD; to us this land is given for a possession." 16 Therefore say: Thus says the Lord GOD: Though I removed them far away among the nations, and though I scattered them among the countries, yet I have been a sanctuary to them for a little while *b* in the countries where they have gone. 17 Therefore say: Thus says the Lord GOD: I will gather you from the peoples, and assemble you out of the countries where you have been scattered, and I will give you the land of Israel. 18 When they come there, they will remove from it all its detestable things and all its abominations. 19 I will give them one *c* heart, and put a new spirit within them; I will remove the heart of stone from their flesh and give them a heart of flesh, 20 so that they may follow my statutes

a Gk Syr: Heb *people of your kindred*   *b* Or *to some extent*   *c* Another reading is *a new*

11:13 *Pelatiah . . . died.* At the conclusion of his second vision (8:1–11:25) Ezekiel is overcome by the news of a death in the exiled community. His vision has revealed the terrible ending that will soon befall Jerusalem. Now the death of Pelatiah (lit., "refugee of God") leaves him doubtful of the future of the exilic remnant in Babylon. Perhaps it too is soon at an end. And with the remnant's ending there will be no hope for any future for Israel. To this point Ezekiel has glimpsed no sign of a future after the exile for the People of God. The fall of Jerusalem is, it seems, the end of Israel's story with God. Now Ezekiel asks if the remnant too will come to a "full end."

11:14–20 *I will gather you.* In these verses Ezekiel sees something other than a final ending. Here is his first glimpse of an unexpected future. This is an extraordinary vision. For all of the harshness of his visions of judgment, Ezekiel's description of the collapse of Jerusalem and of Israel sounds all too commonplace. The world knows more than its share of ruthless catastrophes and brutal captivities. But the emergence of a deep hope for homecoming and renewal comes as if out of nowhere. The exilic community has no evidence on which to base any hope. The relatives back home in Jerusalem say

that their cousins in exile "have gone far from the LORD" (v 15). But Ezekiel hears God say that this is not true. The exiles are actually close to God because they are being given divine sanctuary in their dispersion among foreign nations (v 16). In this terribly discouraging place Ezekiel announces God's astounding and far-reaching promises. This tiny and marginalized community will yet form a renewed People of God to whom God will give "one heart" and a "new spirit" (v 19; cf. Ps 51:10). This radical reorientation of life is to be the free and unmerited gift of God. The exiles do not deserve a future any more than do the inhabitants of Jerusalem. This makes God's promise to be present in relationship even more striking: "Then they shall be my people, and I will be their God" (v 20; 14:11; 36:28; 37:23, 27). God intends to live intimately with, and to be known by, Israel. There is a future beyond the terrible ending of Jerusalem's destruction. That future is located among the scattered exiles, who imagine that they are the last of a dying breed. Instead, they are amazed to discover that God is in exile with them and is already fashioning a future beyond all expectation. Can we hope for such a future for ourselves as well?

and keep my ordinances and obey them. Then they shall be my people, and I will be their God. [21]But as for those whose heart goes after their detestable things and their abominations, *a* I will bring their deeds upon their own heads, says the Lord GOD.

22 Then the cherubim lifted up their wings, with the wheels beside them; and the glory of the God of Israel was above them. [23]And the glory of the LORD ascended from the middle of the city, and stopped on the mountain east of the city. [24]The spirit lifted me up and brought me in a vision by the spirit of God into Chaldea, to the exiles. Then the vision that I had seen left me. [25]And I told the exiles all the things that the LORD had shown me.

Judah's Captivity Portrayed

12 The word of the LORD came to me: [2]Mortal, you are living in the midst of a rebellious house, who have eyes to see but do not see, who have ears to hear but do not hear; [3]for they are a rebellious house. Therefore, mortal, prepare for yourself an exile's baggage, and go into exile by day in their sight; you shall go like an exile from your place to another place in their sight. Perhaps they will understand, though they are a rebellious house. [4]You shall bring out your baggage by day in their sight, as baggage for exile; and you shall go out yourself at evening in their sight, as those do who go into exile. [5]Dig through the wall in their sight, and car-

ry the baggage through it. [6]In their sight you shall lift the baggage on your shoulder, and carry it out in the dark; you shall cover your face, so that you may not see the land; for I have made you a sign for the house of Israel.

7 I did just as I was commanded. I brought out my baggage by day, as baggage for exile, and in the evening I dug through the wall with my own hands; I brought it out in the dark, carrying it on my shoulder in their sight.

8 In the morning the word of the LORD came to me: [9]Mortal, has not the house of Israel, the rebellious house, said to you, "What are you doing?" [10]Say to them, "Thus says the Lord GOD: This oracle concerns the prince in Jerusalem and all the house of Israel in it." [11]Say, "I am a sign for you: as I have done, so shall it be done to them; they shall go into exile, into captivity." [12]And the prince who is among them shall lift his baggage on his shoulder in the dark, and shall go out; he *b* shall dig through the wall and carry it through; he shall cover his face, so that he may not see the land with his eyes. [13]I will spread my net over him, and he shall be caught in my snare; and I will bring him to Babylon, the land of the Chaldeans, yet he shall not see it; and he shall die there. [14]I will scatter to every wind all who are around him, his helpers and all his troops; and I will unsheathe the sword behind them.

a Cn: Heb *And to the heart of their detestable things and their abominations their heart goes*   *b* Gk Syr: Heb *they*

11:23–25 *I told the exiles all the things.* God's glory rises above Jerusalem and hovers east of the city. In his vision Ezekiel is brought back to the deportees in Chaldea. Here he tells the exiles what he has seen. We are reminded that Ezekiel's visions are for an exiled people who have seen the old order crumble and who cannot fathom what it means. They are tempted to believe the surrounding culture when it points to the ending of their glory days and when it mocks their God. Ezekiel's visions offer the exiled community an alternative truth. He testifies that it is God who has ended the old glory days and that God is already shaping a new future. The exiled community is left to decide who, and what, to believe.

12:3–11 *a sign for the house of Israel.* Ezekiel performs a symbolic act of street theater. The exiles are "a rebellious house" (v 3). They cannot see Jerusalem's certain doom and do not hear that it is God's intention (v 2). Ezekiel is instructed to reenact his flight into exile. He does so without saying a word. In the morning he answers his neighbors' question: "What are you doing?" They may hope that it is a sign of their impending return home. But Ezekiel says it is a sign of the end for Israel's prince, who will die in exile. There will be no quick and easy homecoming. Mercy waits on the far side of a judgment that will leave the land "a desolation" (v 20).

15And they shall know that I am the LORD, when I disperse them among the nations and scatter them through the countries. 16But I will let a few of them escape from the sword, from famine and pestilence, so that they may tell of all their abominations among the nations where they go; then they shall know that I am the LORD.

Judgment Not Postponed

17 The word of the LORD came to me: 18Mortal, eat your bread with quaking, and drink your water with trembling and with fearfulness; 19and say to the people of the land, Thus says the Lord GOD concerning the inhabitants of Jerusalem in the land of Israel: They shall eat their bread with fearfulness, and drink their water in dismay, because their land shall be stripped of all it contains, on account of the violence of all those who live in it. 20The inhabited cities shall be laid waste, and the land shall become a desolation; and you shall know that I am the LORD.

21 The word of the LORD came to me: 22Mortal, what is this proverb of yours about the land of Israel, which says, "The days are prolonged, and every vision comes to nothing"? 23Tell them therefore, "Thus says the Lord GOD: I will put an end to this proverb, and they shall use it no more as a proverb in Israel." But say to them, The days are near, and the fulfillment of every vision. 24For there shall no longer be any false vision or flattering divination within the house of Israel. 25But I the LORD will speak the word that I speak, and it will be fulfilled. It will no longer be delayed; but in your days, O rebellious house, I will speak the word and fulfill it, says the Lord GOD.

26 The word of the LORD came to me: 27Mortal, the house of Israel is saying, "The vi-sion that he sees is for many years ahead; he prophesies for distant times." 28Therefore say to them, Thus says the Lord GOD: None of my words will be delayed any longer, but the word that I speak will be fulfilled, says the Lord GOD.

False Prophets Condemned

13 The word of the LORD came to me: 2Mortal, prophesy against the prophets of Israel who are prophesying; say to those who prophesy out of their own imagination: "Hear the word of the LORD!" 3Thus says the Lord GOD, Alas for the senseless prophets who follow their own spirit, and have seen nothing! 4Your prophets have been like jackals among ruins, O Israel. 5You have not gone up into the breaches, or repaired a wall for the house of Israel, so that it might stand in battle on the day of the LORD. 6They have envisioned falsehood and lying divination; they say, "Says the LORD," when the LORD has not sent them, and yet they wait for the fulfillment of their word! 7Have you not seen a false vision or uttered a lying divination, when you have said, "Says the LORD," even though I did not speak?

8 Therefore thus says the Lord GOD: Because you have uttered falsehood and envisioned lies, I am against you, says the Lord GOD. 9My hand will be against the prophets who see false visions and utter lying divinations; they shall not be in the council of my people, nor be enrolled in the register of the house of Israel, nor shall they enter the land of Israel; and you shall know that I am the Lord GOD. 10Because, in truth, because they have misled my people, saying, "Peace," when there is no peace; and because, when the people build a wall, these prophets*a* smear whitewash on it. 11Say to those who

a Heb *they*

13:1–23 *those who prophesy out of their own imagination*. In these verses the prophet confronts false prophets. The exiles hear conflicting testimony from those who claim to speak for God. They do not know what to believe. A similar conflict is played out between Jeremiah and Hananiah (Jer 27–28). The dilemma created by false prophecy persists in every generation and is never easily resolved.

13:10 *these prophets smear whitewash on it*. Ezekiel names the nature of false prophecy. He identifies the prophets who prop up the status quo as liars. They are eager to mollify the people by preaching "peace when there is no peace." Instead of telling the truth these so-called prophets fabricate falsehoods. They "whitewash" over the cracks and cover up the flaws in the walls of Israelite society. These self-

smear whitewash on it that it shall fall. There will be a deluge of rain, *a* great hailstones will fall, and a stormy wind will break out. 12When the wall falls, will it not be said to you, "Where is the whitewash you smeared on it?" 13Therefore thus says the Lord GOD: In my wrath I will make a stormy wind break out, and in my anger there shall be a deluge of rain, and hailstones in wrath to destroy it. 14I will break down the wall that you have smeared with whitewash, and bring it to the ground, so that its foundation will be laid bare; when it falls, you shall perish within it; and you shall know that I am the LORD. 15Thus I will spend my wrath upon the wall, and upon those who have smeared it with whitewash; and I will say to you, The wall is no more, nor those who smeared it— 16the prophets of Israel who prophesied concerning Jerusalem and saw visions of peace for it, when there was no peace, says the Lord GOD.

17 As for you, mortal, set your face against the daughters of your people, who prophesy out of their own imagination; prophesy against them 18and say, Thus says the Lord GOD: Woe to the women who sew bands on all wrists, and make veils for the heads of persons of every height, in the hunt for human lives! Will you hunt down lives among my people, and maintain your own lives? 19You have profaned me among my people for handfuls of barley and for pieces of bread, putting to death persons who should not die and keeping alive persons who should not live, by your lies to my people, who listen to lies.

20 Therefore thus says the Lord GOD: I am against your bands with which you hunt lives;*b* I will tear them from your arms, and let the lives go free, the lives that you hunt down like birds. 21I will tear off your veils, and save my people from your hands; they shall no longer be prey in your hands; and you shall know that I am the LORD. 22Because you have disheartened the righteous falsely, although I have not disheartened them, and you have encouraged the wicked not to turn from their wicked way and save their lives; 23therefore you shall no longer see false visions or practice divination; I will save my people from your hand. Then you will know that I am the LORD.

God's Judgments Justified

14 Certain elders of Israel came to me and sat down before me. 2And the word of the LORD came to me: 3Mortal, these men have taken their idols into their hearts, and placed their iniquity as a stumbling block before them; shall I let myself be consulted by them? 4Therefore speak to them, and say to them, Thus says the Lord GOD: Any of those of the house of Israel who take their idols into their hearts and place their iniquity as a stumbling block before them, and yet come to the prophet—I the LORD will answer those who come with the multitude of their idols, 5in order that I may take hold of the hearts of the house of Israel, all of whom are estranged from me through their idols.

6 Therefore say to the house of Israel, Thus says the Lord GOD: Repent and turn away from your idols; and turn away your faces from all your abominations. 7For any of those of the house of Israel, or of the aliens who reside in Israel, who separate themselves from me, taking their idols into their hearts and placing their iniquity as a stumbling block before them, and yet come to a prophet to inquire of me by him, I the LORD will answer

---

a Heb *rain and you*   *b* Gk Syr: Heb *lives for birds*

---

made prophets delude the people with phony promises that ignore the blunt realities of the requirements of God. Preachers who speak for God are called to risk the truth, not to whitewash over trouble. Without the truth, the people will not know they are living a lie. Without a prophet who dares to speak the truth, there will be no chance to turn back to God's ways.

14:1–5 *Certain elders of Israel came.* Elders come for a consultation with the prophet, but they have taken "their idols into their hearts." They are under the sway of other gods, trusting not in God, but in various techniques and methods for crafting prosperity and security. To have interiorized idolatry is to be estranged from God (v 5) and so to be cut off from the people. Being with God requires being with no other gods.

them myself. [8]I will set my face against them; I will make them a sign and a byword and cut them off from the midst of my people; and you shall know that I am the LORD.

9 If a prophet is deceived and speaks a word, I, the LORD, have deceived that prophet, and I will stretch out my hand against him, and will destroy him from the midst of my people Israel. [10]And they shall bear their punishment—the punishment of the inquirer and the punishment of the prophet shall be the same— [11]so that the house of Israel may no longer go astray from me, nor defile themselves any more with all their transgressions. Then they shall be my people, and I will be their God, says the Lord GOD.

12 The word of the LORD came to me: [13]Mortal, when a land sins against me by acting faithlessly, and I stretch out my hand against it, and break its staff of bread and send famine upon it, and cut off from it human beings and animals, [14]even if Noah, Daniel,[a] and Job, these three, were in it, they would save only their own lives by their righteousness, says the Lord GOD. [15]If I send wild animals through the land to ravage it, so that it is made desolate, and no one may pass through because of the animals; [16]even if these three men were in it, as I live, says the Lord GOD, they would save neither sons nor daughters; they alone would be saved, but the land would be desolate. [17]Or if I bring a sword upon that land and say, "Let a sword pass through the land," and I cut off human beings and animals from it; [18]though these three men were in it, as I live, says the Lord GOD, they would save neither sons nor daughters, but they alone would be saved. [19]Or if I send a pestilence into that land, and pour out my wrath upon it with blood, to cut off humans and animals from it; [20]even if Noah, Daniel,[a] and Job were in it, as I live, says the Lord GOD, they would save neither son nor daughter; they would save only their own lives by their righteousness.

21 For thus says the Lord GOD: How much more when I send upon Jerusalem my four deadly acts of judgment, sword, famine, wild animals, and pestilence, to cut off humans and animals from it! [22]Yet, survivors shall be left in it, sons and daughters who will be brought out; they will come out to you. When you see their ways and their deeds, you will be consoled for the evil that I have brought upon Jerusalem, for all that I have brought upon it. [23]They shall console you, when you see their ways and their deeds; and you shall know that it was not without cause that I did all that I have done in it, says the Lord GOD.

The Useless Vine

15 The word of the LORD came to me:
2 O mortal, how does the wood of
    the vine surpass all other wood—
the vine branch that is among the
    trees of the forest?
3 Is wood taken from it to make anything?
    Does one take a peg from it on which
      to hang any object?
4 It is put in the fire for fuel;
    when the fire has consumed both
      ends of it
    and the middle of it is charred,
    is it useful for anything?
5 When it was whole it was used for
      nothing;
    how much less—when the fire has
      consumed it,

a Or, as otherwise read, Danel

14:13–20 *Noah, Daniel, and Job.* The sin of the land is so dire that even heroic and righteous characters like these three would be able to save only their own skins in such a time. (The Daniel mentioned here and in 28:3 is apparently a different character from Ezekiel's exilic contemporary depicted in the book of Daniel.) The three are heroic models known throughout the ancient Near East. Surely their very presence would have an effect on the land in which they lived, providing some protection from judgment. Not a chance, says Ezekiel. Not even the children of such heroic figures would be spared. As it is, the survivors who will arrive in exile will not be models of righteous living. Instead, "their ways and their deeds" (v 22) will give the exiles all the evidence they need to understand the calamity that is befalling Jerusalem. The judgment of the land and its people is relentless and all-encompassing. There is no way out.

and it is charred—
can it ever be used for anything!

6 Therefore thus says the Lord GOD: Like the wood of the vine among the trees of the forest, which I have given to the fire for fuel, so I will give up the inhabitants of Jerusalem. [7]I will set my face against them; although they escape from the fire, the fire shall still consume them; and you shall know that I am the LORD, when I set my face against them. [8]And I will make the land desolate, because they have acted faithlessly, says the Lord GOD.

God's Faithless Bride

16 The word of the LORD came to me: [2]Mortal, make known to Jerusalem her abominations, [3]and say, Thus says the Lord GOD to Jerusalem: Your origin and your birth were in the land of the Canaanites; your father was an Amorite, and your mother a Hittite. [4]As for your birth, on the day you were born your navel cord was not cut, nor were you washed with water to cleanse you, nor rubbed with salt, nor wrapped in cloths. [5]No eye pitied you, to do any of these things for you out of compassion for you; but you were thrown out in the open field, for you were abhorred on the day you were born.

6 I passed by you, and saw you flailing about in your blood. As you lay in your blood, I said to you, "Live! [7]and grow up[a] like a plant of the field." You grew up and became tall and arrived at full womanhood;[b] your breasts were formed, and your hair had grown; yet you were naked and bare.

8 I passed by you again and looked on you; you were at the age for love. I spread the edge of my cloak over you, and covered your nakedness: I pledged myself to you and entered into a covenant with you, says the Lord GOD, and you became mine. [9]Then I bathed you with water and washed off the blood from you, and anointed you with oil. [10]I clothed you with embroidered cloth and with sandals of fine leather; I bound you in fine linen and covered you with rich fabric.[c] [11]I adorned you with ornaments: I put bracelets on your arms, a chain on your neck, [12]a ring on your nose, earrings in your ears, and a beautiful crown upon your head. [13]You were adorned with gold and silver, while your clothing was of fine linen, rich fabric,[c] and embroidered cloth. You had choice flour and honey and oil for food. You grew exceedingly beautiful, fit to be a queen. [14]Your fame spread among the nations on account of your beauty, for it was perfect because of my splendor that I had bestowed on you, says the Lord GOD.

15 But you trusted in your beauty, and played the whore because of your fame, and lavished your whorings on any passer-by.[d]

a Gk Syr: Heb Live! I made you a myriad
b Cn: Heb ornament of ornaments   c Meaning of Heb uncertain   d Heb adds let it be his

---

16:3–14 *your origin and your birth . . . Amorite . . . Hittite.* The beginning of this lengthy allegory retells the history of Jerusalem as an orphan foundling, abandoned by her parents and left to die. God found Jerusalem, cared for her, and adopted her into the covenant by marriage. The pattern of adoption is a common description of the life of the people with God. Israel was adopted as God's firstborn child (Exod 4:22; Jer 31:9; Rom 9:4). Paul speaks of the inclusion of the Gentiles in the same terms (Rom 8:15, 23; Gal 4:5; Eph 1:5). To be in covenant with God is to have received the great gift of birthright through adoption.

16:15–34 *But you . . . played the whore.* Now the history of Jerusalem takes a shocking turn. The city, like every city, has an official, sanitized version of its past. Jerusalem has convinced itself that it has long been God's faithful covenant partner. Ezekiel begs to differ. The prophet offers a radical new telling of Jerusalem's relationship with God. He offends his audience, calling the royal city a "whore." Jerusalem has been unfaithful with other gods and other nations. The children of the city have been sacrificed to other gods (v 20). In other words, they have been raised to place their trust and their future in the hands of gods that are frauds. At the same time the leaders of Jerusalem have been secretly having liaisons with the Egyptians (v 26), the Assyrians (v 28), and the Chaldeans (v 29). Jerusalem has been unfaithful to God in its worship and in its politics. The threat to Jerusalem's covenant with God is both a spiritual and a political crisis.

16 You took some of your garments, and made for yourself colorful shrines, and on them played the whore; nothing like this has ever been or ever shall be. *a* 17 You also took your beautiful jewels of my gold and my silver that I had given you, and made for yourself male images, and with them played the whore; 18 and you took your embroidered garments to cover them, and set my oil and my incense before them. 19 Also my bread that I gave you—I fed you with choice flour and oil and honey—you set it before them as a pleasing odor; and so it was, says the Lord GOD. 20 You took your sons and your daughters, whom you had borne to me, and these you sacrificed to them to be devoured. As if your whorings were not enough! 21 You slaughtered my children and delivered them up as an offering to them. 22 And in all your abominations and your whorings you did not remember the days of your youth, when you were naked and bare, flailing about in your blood.

23 After all your wickedness (woe, woe to you! says the Lord GOD), 24 you built yourself a platform and made yourself a lofty place in every square; 25 at the head of every street you built your lofty place and prostituted your beauty, offering yourself to every passer-by, and multiplying your whoring. 26 You played the whore with the Egyptians, your lustful neighbors, multiplying your whoring, to provoke me to anger. 27 Therefore I stretched out my hand against you, reduced your rations, and gave you up to the will of your enemies, the daughters of the Philistines, who were ashamed of your lewd behavior. 28 You played the whore with the Assyrians, because you were insatiable; you played the whore with them, and still you were not satisfied. 29 You multiplied your whoring with Chaldea, the land of merchants; and even with this you were not satisfied.

30 How sick is your heart, says the Lord GOD, that you did all these things, the deeds of a brazen whore; 31 building your platform at the head of every street, and making your lofty place in every square! Yet you were not like a whore, because you scorned payment. 32 Adulterous wife, who receives strangers instead of her husband! 33 Gifts are given to all whores; but you gave your gifts to all your lovers, bribing them to come to you from all around for your whorings. 34 So you were different from other women in your whorings: no one solicited you to play the whore; and you gave payment, while no payment was given to you; you were different.

35 Therefore, O whore, hear the word of the LORD: 36 Thus says the Lord GOD, Because your lust was poured out and your nakedness uncovered in your whoring with your lovers, and because of all your abominable idols, and because of the blood of your children that you gave to them, 37 therefore, I will gather all your lovers, with whom you took pleasure, all those you loved and all those you hated; I will gather them against you from all around, and will uncover your nakedness to them, so that they may see all your nakedness. 38 I will judge you as women who commit adultery and shed blood are judged, and bring blood upon you in wrath and jealousy. 39 I will deliver you into their hands, and they shall throw down your platform and break down your lofty places; they shall strip you of your clothes and take your beautiful objects and leave you naked and bare. 40 They shall bring up a mob against you, and they shall stone you and cut you to

a Meaning of Heb uncertain

Responding

16:15 SECRECY. In our day and age we can so easily find ourselves "lavishing [our] whorings on any passer-by" with our unguarded speech. We live in a world that clings to values that, frankly, are not God's values, and so we can quickly get sucked into bragging about those things we unconsciously treat as idols—our possessions, money, influence, accomplishments. And what we say about these things often reveals unhealthy attachments. Do we, for example, talk about our position, our home, or our "important connections" with an unbecoming pride? In the next few weeks watch your own words about these matters. When you find excessive pride, swallow the words and examine them carefully. See what you learn about yourself and your idols. *See also* Spiritual Disciplines Index.

pieces with their swords. ⁴¹They shall burn your houses and execute judgments on you in the sight of many women; I will stop you from playing the whore, and you shall also make no more payments. ⁴²So I will satisfy my fury on you, and my jealousy shall turn away from you; I will be calm, and will be angry no longer. ⁴³Because you have not remembered the days of your youth, but have enraged me with all these things; therefore, I have returned your deeds upon your head, says the Lord GOD.

Have you not committed lewdness beyond all your abominations? ⁴⁴See, everyone who uses proverbs will use this proverb about you, "Like mother, like daughter." ⁴⁵You are the daughter of your mother, who loathed her husband and her children; and you are the sister of your sisters, who loathed their husbands and their children. Your mother was a Hittite and your father an Amorite. ⁴⁶Your elder sister is Samaria, who lived with her daughters to the north of you; and your younger sister, who lived to the south of you, is Sodom with her daughters. ⁴⁷You not only followed their ways, and acted according to their abominations; within a very little time you were more corrupt than they in all your ways. ⁴⁸As I live, says the Lord GOD, your sister Sodom and her daughters have not done as you and your daughters have done. ⁴⁹This was the guilt of your sister Sodom: she and her daughters had pride, excess of food, and prosperous ease, but did not aid the poor and needy. ⁵⁰They were haughty, and did abominable things before me; therefore I removed them when I saw it. ⁵¹Samaria has not committed half your sins; you have committed more abominations than they, and have made your sisters appear righteous by all the abominations that you have committed. ⁵²Bear your disgrace, you also, for you have brought about for your sisters a more favorable judgment; because of your sins in which you acted more abominably than they, they are more in the right than you. So be ashamed, you also, and bear your disgrace, for you have made your sisters appear righteous.

53 I will restore their fortunes, the fortunes of Sodom and her daughters and the fortunes of Samaria and her daughters, and I will restore your own fortunes along with theirs, ⁵⁴in order that you may bear your disgrace and be ashamed of all that you have done, becoming a consolation to them. ⁵⁵As for your sisters, Sodom and her daughters shall return to their former state, Samaria and her daughters shall return to their former state, and you and your daughters shall return to your former state. ⁵⁶Was not your sister Sodom a byword in your mouth in the day of your pride, ⁵⁷before your wickedness was uncovered? Now you are a mockery to the daughters of Aram ᵃ and all her neighbors, and to the daughters of the Philistines, those all around who despise you. ⁵⁸You must bear the penalty of your lewdness and your abominations, says the LORD.

An Everlasting Covenant

59 Yes, thus says the Lord GOD: I will deal with you as you have done, you who have despised the oath, breaking the covenant; ⁶⁰yet I will remember my covenant with you

a Another reading is *Edom*

16:35–43 *I will satisfy my fury on you.* Ezekiel confronts a God enraged in jealousy and mad passion. Jerusalem's existence with God is now awful and terrifying. God is the gravest threat to Jerusalem's life. The love of God cannot easily be managed. Being with God in covenant is a dangerous proposition.

16:44–58 *Your elder sister is Samaria.* Here Ezekiel humbles Jerusalem, naming it as more corrupt than its two siblings—Samaria in the north and Sodom in the south. Both cities were long regarded by Jerusalem as poor cousins who deserved the harsh judgment that had come upon them in the past. Jerusalem had long remained proud of its purity and faithfulness to God. But now "they are more in the right" than Jerusalem is (v 52). Jerusalem's history has been completely rewritten; its name no longer suggests virtue and clean living but, instead, connotes disgust. Humility begins with humiliation, with a deep recognition that the city and its people have no special claim on life with God.

in the days of your youth, and I will establish with you an everlasting covenant. 61 Then you will remember your ways, and be ashamed when I *a* take your sisters, both your elder and your younger, and give them to you as daughters, but not on account of my *b* covenant with you. 62 I will establish my covenant with you, and you shall know that I am the LORD, 63 in order that you may remember and be confounded, and never open your mouth again because of your shame, when I forgive you all that you have done, says the Lord GOD.

The Two Eagles and the Vine

17 The word of the LORD came to me: 2 O mortal, propound a riddle, and speak an allegory to the house of Israel. 3 Say: Thus says the Lord GOD:

A great eagle, with great wings and long pinions,
  rich in plumage of many colors,
  came to the Lebanon.
He took the top of the cedar,
4   broke off its topmost shoot;
  he carried it to a land of trade,
  set it in a city of merchants.
5 Then he took a seed from the land,
  placed it in fertile soil;
a plant *c* by abundant waters,
  he set it like a willow twig.
6 It sprouted and became a vine
  spreading out, but low;
its branches turned toward him,
  its roots remained where it stood.
So it became a vine;
  it brought forth branches,
  put forth foliage.

7 There was another great eagle,
  with great wings and much plumage.
And see! This vine stretched out
  its roots toward him;

it shot out its branches toward him,
  so that he might water it.
From the bed where it was planted
8   it was transplanted
to good soil by abundant waters,
  so that it might produce branches
  and bear fruit
  and become a noble vine.
9 Say: Thus says the Lord GOD:
  Will it prosper?
Will he not pull up its roots,
  cause its fruit to rot *c* and wither,
  its fresh sprouting leaves to fade?
No strong arm or mighty army will be needed
  to pull it from its roots.
10 When it is transplanted, will it thrive?
When the east wind strikes it,
  will it not utterly wither,
  wither on the bed where it grew?

11 Then the word of the LORD came to me: 12 Say now to the rebellious house: Do you not know what these things mean? Tell them: The king of Babylon came to Jerusalem, took its king and its officials, and brought them back with him to Babylon. 13 He took one of the royal offspring and made a covenant with him, putting him under oath (he had taken away the chief men of the land), 14 so that the kingdom might be humble and not lift itself up, and that by keeping his covenant it might stand. 15 But he rebelled against him by sending ambassadors to Egypt, in order that they might give him horses and a large army. Will he succeed? Can one escape who does such things? Can he break the covenant and yet escape? 16 As I live, says the Lord GOD, surely in the place where the king resides who made him king, whose oath he despised, and whose covenant with him he broke—in

a Syr: Heb *you*   *b* Heb lacks *my*   *c* Meaning of Heb uncertain

---

16:59–63 *an everlasting covenant.* The "yet" that begins verse 60 catches us by complete surprise. There is no obvious explanation for God's about-face from judgment to promise, from a final ending to a new beginning. Nonetheless, it is clear that Jerusalem's future rests utterly in God's change of heart. Israel knows

this about God's sudden turning (cf. Isa 54:7–8; Jer 30:12–13, 16–17). Such unexpected amazing grace confounds (v 63) the people even as it makes life with God a possibility beyond the closure of judgment. Dare we today hope for God's sudden turning, for God's amazing grace?

Babylon he shall die. [17]Pharaoh with his mighty army and great company will not help him in war, when ramps are cast up and siege walls built to cut off many lives. [18]Because he despised the oath and broke the covenant, because he gave his hand and yet did all these things, he shall not escape. [19]Therefore thus says the Lord GOD: As I live, I will surely return upon his head my oath that he despised, and my covenant that he broke. [20]I will spread my net over him, and he shall be caught in my snare; I will bring him to Babylon and enter into judgment with him there for the treason he has committed against me. [21]All the pick[a] of his troops shall fall by the sword, and the survivors shall be scattered to every wind; and you shall know that I, the LORD, have spoken.

Israel Exalted at Last

22 Thus says the Lord GOD:
   I myself will take a sprig
      from the lofty top of a cedar;
   I will set it out.
   I will break off a tender one
      from the topmost of its young twigs;
   I myself will plant it
      on a high and lofty mountain.
23 On the mountain height of Israel
   I will plant it,

in order that it may produce boughs
      and bear fruit,
   and become a noble cedar.
Under it every kind of bird will live;
   in the shade of its branches will nest
      winged creatures of every kind.
24 All the trees of the field shall know
      that I am the LORD.
I bring low the high tree,
   I make high the low tree;
I dry up the green tree
   and make the dry tree flourish.
I the LORD have spoken;
   I will accomplish it.

Individual Retribution

18 The word of the LORD came to me: [2]What do you mean by repeating this proverb concerning the land of Israel, "The parents have eaten sour grapes, and the children's teeth are set on edge"? [3]As I live, says the Lord GOD, this proverb shall no more be used by you in Israel. [4]Know that all lives are mine; the life of the parent as well as the life of the child is mine: it is only the person who sins that shall die.

5 If a man is righteous and does what is lawful and right— [6]if he does not eat upon the mountains or lift up his eyes to the idols

---

a Another reading is *fugitives*

17:22 *I . . will take a sprig from the lofty top of a cedar.* The kings of Egypt and Babylon have been taking Israel's king like an eagle takes the top shoot of a cedar tree (vv 3, 7). This political intrigue has led Israel into deep trouble. Now Ezekiel breaks into the messages of doom with news that God will step into the political fray. There will yet be a new messiah, a branch from the Davidic line. The text jumps over the bleak horizon of history and glimpses a distant promise.

18:2–9 *sour grapes . . . teeth are set on edge.* The exilic community is quoting an old proverb that links the actions of one generation with the lives of the generation that follows (cf. Jer 31:29–30). In this new setting the proverb has the effect of shutting down new possibility for the People of God. Left unchallenged, it leads to paralysis, the belief that there is no way out of the situation that has been handed down by the previous generation. Ezekiel announces that this

generation is not paralyzed by the past. He warns about idolatry (v 6a), about sexual and marital faithfulness (v 6b), and about economic faithfulness (vv 7–8a). This catalog of righteousness provides the shape of life with God after the cataclysm of Israel's destruction. The exiles are not doomed to live in the shadow of judgment. It is within their capacity to enter into relationship with God after the Temple is gone. The shape of that relationship is grounded in the covenantal obligation to love God and neighbor—hence no idolatry (no loving other gods), no infidelity (no breaking of the marital covenant), and no economic oppression (no taking what rightfully belongs to the neighbor). This is what is needed in order to lose the taste of the "sour grapes" eaten by the previous generation. The children of the exile are free to taste new life by living rightly with God and with one another.

of the house of Israel, does not defile his neighbor's wife or approach a woman during her menstrual period, [7]does not oppress anyone, but restores to the debtor his pledge, commits no robbery, gives his bread to the hungry and covers the naked with a garment, [8]does not take advance or accrued interest, withholds his hand from iniquity, executes true justice between contending parties, [9]follows my statutes, and is careful to observe my ordinances, acting faithfully—such a one is righteous; he shall surely live, says the Lord GOD.

10 If he has a son who is violent, a shedder of blood, [11]who does any of these things (though his father[a] does none of them), who eats upon the mountains, defiles his neighbor's wife, [12]oppresses the poor and needy, commits robbery, does not restore the pledge, lifts up his eyes to the idols, commits abomination, [13]takes advance or accrued interest; shall he then live? He shall not. He has done all these abominable things; he shall surely die; his blood shall be upon himself.

14 But if this man has a son who sees all the sins that his father has done, considers, and does not do likewise, [15]who does not eat upon the mountains or lift up his eyes to the idols of the house of Israel, does not defile his neighbor's wife, [16]does not wrong anyone, exacts no pledge, commits no robbery, but gives his bread to the hungry and covers the naked with a garment, [17]withholds his hand from iniquity,[b] takes no advance or accrued interest, observes my ordinances, and follows my statutes; he shall not die for his father's iniquity; he shall surely live. [18]As for his father, because he practiced extortion, robbed his brother, and did what is not good among his people, he dies for his iniquity.

19 Yet you say, "Why should not the son suffer for the iniquity of the father?" When the son has done what is lawful and right, and has been careful to observe all my statutes, he shall surely live. [20]The person who sins shall die. A child shall not suffer for the iniquity of a parent, nor a parent suffer for the iniquity of a child; the righteousness of the righteous shall be his own, and the wickedness of the wicked shall be his own.

21 But if the wicked turn away from all their sins that they have committed and keep all my statutes and do what is lawful and right, they shall surely live; they shall not die. [22]None of the transgressions that they have committed shall be remembered against them; for the righteousness that they have done they shall live. [23]Have I any pleasure in the death of the wicked, says the Lord GOD, and not rather that they should turn from their ways and live? [24]But when the righteous turn away from their righteousness and commit iniquity and do the same abominable things that the wicked do, shall they live? None of the righteous deeds that they have done shall be remembered; for the treachery of which they are guilty and the sin they have committed, they shall die.

25 Yet you say, "The way of the Lord is unfair." Hear now, O house of Israel: Is my way unfair? Is it not your ways that are unfair? [26]When the righteous turn away from their righteousness and commit iniquity, they shall die for it; for the iniquity that they have committed they shall die. [27]Again, when the wicked turn away from the wickedness they have committed and do what is lawful and right, they shall save their life. [28]Because they

---

a Heb *he*   *b* Gk: Heb *the poor*

18:21–32 *they shall not die.* Just as the past history of the community does not trap the coming generation in judgment, so the past history of the wicked does not condemn them to death. The future does not depend on the past, but on the choices to be made in the present. Life can continue in the same habitual ruts, ignoring the alternate path cut by the way (the Torah) of the Lord, or life can take a sharp turn and follow the way of the Lord, the ordi-

nances and statues of God. This repentant turn to the Lord's way of life is God's intense desire: "Turn, then, and live" (v 32). No amount of transgression in the past will make it impossible to get a "new heart and a new spirit" (v 31). John's baptism of repentance (Mark 1:4) and Jesus' call to repent and live under God's reign (Mark 1:15) echo Ezekiel's urging to respond to the holiness of God with lives turned around to the ways of God.

considered and turned away from all the transgressions that they had committed, they shall surely live; they shall not die. 29Yet the house of Israel says, "The way of the Lord is unfair." O house of Israel, are my ways unfair? Is it not your ways that are unfair?

30 Therefore I will judge you, O house of Israel, all of you according to your ways, says the Lord GOD. Repent and turn from all your transgressions; otherwise iniquity will be your ruin. a 31Cast away from you all the transgressions that you have committed against me, and get yourselves a new heart and a new spirit! Why will you die, O house of Israel? 32For I have no pleasure in the death of anyone, says the Lord GOD. Turn, then, and live.

Israel Degraded

19 As for you, raise up a lamentation for the princes of Israel, 2and say:
What a lioness was your mother
    among lions!
She lay down among young lions,
    rearing her cubs.
3 She raised up one of her cubs;
    he became a young lion,
and he learned to catch prey;
    he devoured humans.
4 The nations sounded an alarm against
        him;
    he was caught in their pit;
and they brought him with hooks
    to the land of Egypt.
5 When she saw that she was thwarted,
    that her hope was lost,
she took another of her cubs
    and made him a young lion.
6 He prowled among the lions;
    he became a young lion,
and he learned to catch prey;
    he devoured people.
7 And he ravaged their strongholds, b
    and laid waste their towns;
the land was appalled, and all in it,
    at the sound of his roaring.
8 The nations set upon him
    from the provinces all around;
they spread their net over him;
    he was caught in their pit.
9 With hooks they put him in a cage,

and brought him to the king of
        Babylon;
they brought him into custody,
so that his voice should be heard no
        more
    on the mountains of Israel.
10 Your mother was like a vine in a
        vineyard c
    transplanted by the water,
fruitful and full of branches
    from abundant water.
11 Its strongest stem became
    a ruler's scepter; d
it towered aloft
    among the thick boughs;
it stood out in its height
    with its mass of branches.
12 But it was plucked up in fury,
    cast down to the ground;
the east wind dried it up;
    its fruit was stripped off,
its strong stem was withered;
    the fire consumed it.
13 Now it is transplanted into the
        wilderness,
    into a dry and thirsty land.
14 And fire has gone out from its stem,
    has consumed its branches and fruit,
so that there remains in it no strong
        stem,
    no scepter for ruling.

This is a lamentation, and it is used as a lamentation.

Israel's Continuing Rebellion

20 In the seventh year, in the fifth month, on the tenth day of the month, certain elders of Israel came to consult the LORD, and sat down before me. 2And the word of the LORD came to me: 3Mortal, speak to the elders of Israel, and say to them: Thus says the Lord GOD: Why are you coming? To consult me? As I live, says the Lord GOD, I will not be consulted by you. 4Will you judge them, mortal, will you judge them? Then let them know the abominations of

a Or so that they shall not be a stumbling block of iniquity to you   b Heb his widows   c Cn: Heb in your blood   d Heb Its strongest stems became rulers' scepters

their ancestors, 5and say to them: Thus says the Lord GOD: On the day when I chose Israel, I swore to the offspring of the house of Jacob—making myself known to them in the land of Egypt—I swore to them, saying, I am the LORD your God. 6On that day I swore to them that I would bring them out of the land of Egypt into a land that I had searched out for them, a land flowing with milk and honey, the most glorious of all lands. 7And I said to them, Cast away the detestable things your eyes feast on, every one of you, and do not defile yourselves with the idols of Egypt; I am the LORD your God. 8But they rebelled against me and would not listen to me; not one of them cast away the detestable things their eyes feasted on, nor did they forsake the idols of Egypt.

Then I thought I would pour out my wrath upon them and spend my anger against them in the midst of the land of Egypt. 9But I acted for the sake of my name, that it should not be profaned in the sight of the nations among whom they lived, in whose sight I made myself known to them in bringing them out of the land of Egypt. 10So I led them out of the land of Egypt and brought them into the wilderness. 11I gave them my statutes and showed them my ordinances, by whose observance everyone shall live. 12Moreover I gave them my sabbaths, as a sign between me and them, so that they might know that I the LORD sanctify them. 13But the house of Israel rebelled against me in the wilderness; they did not observe my statutes but rejected my ordinances, by whose observance everyone shall live; and my sabbaths they greatly profaned.

Then I thought I would pour out my wrath upon them in the wilderness, to make an end of them. 14But I acted for the sake of my name, so that it should not be profaned in the sight of the nations, in whose sight I had brought them out. 15Moreover I swore to them in the wilderness that I would not bring them into the land that I had given them, a land flowing with milk and honey, the most glorious of all lands, 16because they rejected my ordinances and did not observe my statutes, and profaned my sabbaths; for their heart went after their idols. 17Nevertheless my eye spared them, and I did not destroy them or make an end of them in the wilderness.

18 I said to their children in the wilderness, Do not follow the statutes of your parents, nor observe their ordinances, nor defile yourselves with their idols. 19I the LORD am your God; follow my statutes, and be careful to observe my ordinances, 20and hallow my sabbaths that they may be a sign between me and you, so that you may know that I the LORD am your God. 21But the children rebelled against me; they did not follow my statutes, and were not careful to observe my ordinances, by whose observance everyone shall live; they profaned my sabbaths.

Then I thought I would pour out my wrath upon them and spend my anger against them in the wilderness. 22But I withheld my hand, and acted for the sake of my name, so that it should not be profaned in the sight of the nations, in whose sight I had brought them out. 23Moreover I swore to them in the wilderness that I would scatter them among the nations and disperse them through the countries, 24because they had not executed my ordinances, but had rejected my statutes and profaned my sabbaths, and their eyes were set on their ancestors' idols. 25Moreover I gave them statutes

---

20:5–29 *On the day when I chose Israel.* Having rewritten the history of Jerusalem in chapter 16, Ezekiel now rewrites the national history of Israel. The prophet rereads the beloved tradition in light of the strange new world of life in exile. The traditional memory had been a recital of God's mighty acts (Deut 26:5–9). In Ezekiel's hands the story is inverted into a litany of the ways in which the people have abused the covenant life with God. Ezekiel notices that the

terrible ending that now faces Israel is the result of long-term unfaithfulness. The exiles cannot comprehend how God could allow this cataclysm to occur. But when the prophet traces Israel's history of rebellion, he seems almost surprised that God has not acted in judgment sooner.

20:9 *for the sake of my name.* God remains in covenant for the sake of his reputation. Israel has been saved because of God's self-concern, not because of its faithfulness (see 36:22–32).

that were not good and ordinances by which they could not live. [26]I defiled them through their very gifts, in their offering up all their firstborn, in order that I might horrify them, so that they might know that I am the LORD.

27 Therefore, mortal, speak to the house of Israel and say to them, Thus says the Lord GOD: In this again your ancestors blasphemed me, by dealing treacherously with me. [28]For when I had brought them into the land that I swore to give them, then wherever they saw any high hill or any leafy tree, there they offered their sacrifices and presented the provocation of their offering; there they sent up their pleasing odors, and there they poured out their drink offerings. [29](I said to them, What is the high place to which you go? So it is called Bamah[a] to this day.) [30]Therefore say to the house of Israel, Thus says the Lord GOD: Will you defile yourselves after the manner of your ancestors and go astray after their detestable things? [31]When you offer your gifts and make your children pass through the fire, you defile yourselves with all your idols to this day. And shall I be consulted by you, O house of Israel? As I live, says the Lord GOD, I will not be consulted by you.

32 What is in your mind shall never happen—the thought, "Let us be like the nations, like the tribes of the countries, and worship wood and stone."

God Will Restore Israel

33 As I live, says the Lord GOD, surely with a mighty hand and an outstretched arm, and with wrath poured out, I will be king over you. [34]I will bring you out from the peoples and gather you out of the countries where you are scattered, with a mighty hand and an outstretched arm, and with wrath poured out; [35]and I will bring you into the wilderness of the peoples, and there I will enter into judgment with you face to face. [36]As I entered into judgment with your ancestors in the wilderness of the land of Egypt, so I will enter into judgment with you, says the Lord GOD. [37]I will make you pass under the staff, and will bring you within the bond of the covenant. [38]I will purge out the rebels among you, and those who transgress against me; I will bring them out of the land where they reside as aliens, but they shall not enter the land of Israel. Then you shall know that I am the LORD.

39 As for you, O house of Israel, thus says the Lord GOD: Go serve your idols, every one of you now and hereafter, if you will not listen to me; but my holy name you shall no more profane with your gifts and your idols.

40 For on my holy mountain, the mountain height of Israel, says the Lord GOD, there all the house of Israel, all of them, shall serve me in the land; there I will accept them, and there I will require your contributions and the choicest of your gifts, with all your sacred things. [41]As a pleasing odor I will accept you, when I bring you out from the peoples, and gather you out of the countries where you have been scattered; and I will manifest my holiness among you in the sight of the nations. [42]You shall know that I am the LORD, when I bring you into the land of Israel, the country that I swore to give to your ancestors. [43]There you shall remember your ways and all the deeds by which you have polluted yourselves; and you shall loathe yourselves for all the evils that you have committed. [44]And you shall know that I am the LORD, when I deal with you for my name's sake, not according to your evil ways, or corrupt deeds, O house of Israel, says the Lord GOD.

A Prophecy against the Negeb

45[b] The word of the LORD came to me: [46]Mortal, set your face toward the south,

a That is *High Place*   b Ch 21.1 in Heb

20:32 *worship wood and stone.* The people's ongoing temptation and the root of their idolatry is the longing to "be like the nations." The nations worship other gods, have other sources of security, and rely on other means of prosperity. The nations believe, "The gods help those who help themselves" (*Aesop's Fables*).

But the People of God are to be a peculiar people. They worship the God who helps those who cannot help themselves. God will yet act to gather the scattered remnants of the people (v 34), to judge and make covenant with them (vv 36–37), and to shape a holy people, set apart from the nations, once more (v 41).

preach against the south, and prophesy against the forest land in the Negeb; [47]say to the forest of the Negeb, Hear the word of the LORD: Thus says the Lord GOD, I will kindle a fire in you, and it shall devour every green tree in you and every dry tree; the blazing flame shall not be quenched, and all faces from south to north shall be scorched by it. [48]All flesh shall see that I the LORD have kindled it; it shall not be quenched. [49]Then I said, "Ah Lord GOD! they are saying of me, 'Is he not a maker of allegories?' "

The Drawn Sword of God

21 [a] The word of the LORD came to me: [2]Mortal, set your face toward Jerusalem and preach against the sanctuaries; prophesy against the land of Israel [3]and say to the land of Israel, Thus says the LORD: I am coming against you, and will draw my sword out of its sheath, and will cut off from you both righteous and wicked. [4]Because I will cut off from you both righteous and wicked, therefore my sword shall go out of its sheath against all flesh from south to north; [5]and all flesh shall know that I the LORD have drawn my sword out of its sheath; it shall not be sheathed again. [6]Moan therefore, mortal; moan with breaking heart and bitter grief before their eyes. [7]And when they say to you, "Why do you moan?" you shall say, "Because of the news that has come. Every heart will melt and all hands will be feeble, every spirit will faint and all knees will turn to water. See, it comes and it will be fulfilled," says the Lord GOD.

[8] And the word of the LORD came to me: [9]Mortal, prophesy and say: Thus says the Lord; Say:

A sword, a sword is sharpened,
　　it is also polished;
[10] it is sharpened for slaughter,
　　honed to flash like lightning!
How can we make merry?

You have despised the rod,
　　and all discipline. [b]
[11] The sword [c] is given to be polished,
　　to be grasped in the hand;
it is sharpened, the sword is polished,
　　to be placed in the slayer's hand.
[12] Cry and wail, O mortal,
　　for it is against my people;
it is against all Israel's princes;
　　they are thrown to the sword,
　　together with my people.
Ah! Strike the thigh!
[13]For consider: What! If you despise the rod, will it not happen? [b] says the Lord GOD.
[14] And you, mortal, prophesy;
　　strike hand to hand.
Let the sword fall twice, thrice;
　　it is a sword for killing.
A sword for great slaughter—
　　it surrounds them;
[15] therefore hearts melt
　　and many stumble.
At all their gates I have set
　　the point [b] of the sword.
Ah! It is made for flashing,
　　it is polished [d] for slaughter.
[16] Attack to the right!
　　Engage to the left!
　　—wherever your edge is directed.
[17] I too will strike hand to hand,
　　I will satisfy my fury;
　　I the LORD have spoken.

[18] The word of the LORD came to me: [19]Mortal, mark out two roads for the sword of the king of Babylon to come; both of them shall issue from the same land. And make a signpost, make it for a fork in the road leading to a city; [20]mark out the road for the sword to come to Rabbah of the Ammonites or to Judah and to [e] Jerusalem the fortified.

a Ch 21.6 in Heb　　*b* Meaning of Heb uncertain
c Heb *It*　　*d* Tg: Heb *wrapped up*　　*e* Gk Syr: Heb *Judah in*

21:6–7 *moan with breaking heart and bitter grief.* The prophet enacts a sign of the terrible end that now befalls Jerusalem and Israel. Brokenhearted, Ezekiel moans and grieves in front of the exiles. His public display of lamentation invites questions from the crowd.

Moaning is all that can be uttered in the face of God's assault on the People of God (vv 3–5). The violence that befalls the land and the city is not God's undoing, but God's doing. The prophet of God is reduced to bitter grief, a broken heart, and deep moans.

21For the king of Babylon stands at the parting of the way, at the fork in the two roads, to use divination; he shakes the arrows, he consults the teraphim, *a* he inspects the liver. 22Into his right hand comes the lot for Jerusalem, to set battering rams, to call out for slaughter, for raising the battle cry, to set battering rams against the gates, to cast up ramps, to build siege towers. 23But to them it will seem like a false divination; they have sworn solemn oaths; but he brings their guilt to remembrance, bringing about their capture.

24   Therefore thus says the Lord GOD: Because you have brought your guilt to remembrance, in that your transgressions are uncovered, so that in all your deeds your sins appear—because you have come to remembrance, you shall be taken in hand. *b*

25 As for you, vile, wicked prince of Israel,
     you whose day has come,
       the time of final punishment,
26 thus says the Lord GOD:
     Remove the turban, take off the crown;
       things shall not remain as they are.
     Exalt that which is low,
       abase that which is high.
27 A ruin, a ruin, a ruin—
     I will make it!
     (Such has never occurred.)
     Until he comes whose right it is;
       to him I will give it.

28   As for you, mortal, prophesy, and say, Thus says the Lord GOD concerning the Ammonites, and concerning their reproach; say:
     A sword, a sword! Drawn for slaughter,
       polished to consume, *c* to flash like
         lightning.
29 Offering false visions for you,
     divining lies for you,
       they place you over the necks

of the vile, wicked ones—
     those whose day has come,
       the time of final punishment.
30 Return it to its sheath!
     In the place where you were created,
       in the land of your origin,
         I will judge you.
31 I will pour out my indignation upon
       you,
     with the fire of my wrath
     I will blow upon you.
   I will deliver you into brutish hands,
     those skillful to destroy.
32 You shall be fuel for the fire,
     your blood shall enter the earth;
   you shall be remembered no more,
     for I the LORD have spoken.

The Bloody City

22   The word of the LORD came to me: 2You, mortal, will you judge, will you judge the bloody city? Then declare to it all its abominable deeds. 3You shall say, Thus says the Lord GOD: A city! Shedding blood within itself; its time has come; making its idols, defiling itself. 4You have become guilty by the blood that you have shed, and defiled by the idols that you have made; you have brought your day near, the appointed time of your years has come. Therefore I have made you a disgrace before the nations, and a mockery to all the countries. 5Those who are near and those who are far from you will mock you, you infamous one, full of tumult.

6   The princes of Israel in you, everyone according to his power, have been bent on shedding blood. 7Father and mother are treated with contempt in you; the alien residing

a Or *the household gods*   *b* Or *be taken captive*
c Cn: Heb *to contain*

22:2–12 *judge the bloody city.* Here God takes legal action against Jerusalem. The city is arraigned in God's courtroom (v 2) and the evidence of its guilt is presented. The list of offenses is read (vv 6–12). It details crimes of violence that break the ethical injunctions of Deuteronomy as well as ritual violations that break the codes of Leviticus. The offenses include social, liturgical, sexual, and economic misconduct. Taken together the evidence leads to the damning conclusion of the prosecutor's case: Jerusalem is guilty of forgetting God (v 12). Its bloody life (v 2) reveals that it does not remember the covenant it has made with God. That covenant of life with God requires a people who do not forget their obligation to live in God's way (according to God's Torah).

within you suffers extortion; the orphan and the widow are wronged in you. 8You have despised my holy things, and profaned my sabbaths. 9In you are those who slander to shed blood, those in you who eat upon the mountains, who commit lewdness in your midst. 10In you they uncover their fathers' nakedness; in you they violate women in their menstrual periods. 11One commits abomination with his neighbor's wife; another lewdly defiles his daughter-in-law; another in you defiles his sister, his father's daughter. 12In you, they take bribes to shed blood; you take both advance interest and accrued interest, and make gain of your neighbors by extortion; and you have forgotten me, says the Lord GOD.

13 See, I strike my hands together at the dishonest gain you have made, and at the blood that has been shed within you. 14Can your courage endure, or can your hands remain strong in the days when I shall deal with you? I the LORD have spoken, and I will do it. 15I will scatter you among the nations and disperse you through the countries, and I will purge your filthiness out of you. 16And I*a* shall be profaned through you in the sight of the nations; and you shall know that I am the LORD.

17 The word of the LORD came to me: 18Mortal, the house of Israel has become dross to me; all of them, silver,*b* bronze, tin, iron, and lead. In the smelter they have become dross. 19Therefore thus says the Lord GOD: Because you have all become dross, I will gather you into the midst of Jerusalem. 20As one gathers silver, bronze, iron, lead, and tin into a smelter, to blow the fire upon them in order to melt them; so I will gather you in my anger and in my wrath, and I will put

you in and melt you. 21I will gather you and blow upon you with the fire of my wrath, and you shall be melted within it. 22As silver is melted in a smelter, so you shall be melted in it; and you shall know that I the LORD have poured out my wrath upon you.

23 The word of the LORD came to me: 24Mortal, say to it: You are a land that is not cleansed, not rained upon in the day of indignation. 25Its princes*c* within it are like a roaring lion tearing the prey; they have devoured human lives; they have taken treasure and precious things; they have made many widows within it. 26Its priests have done violence to my teaching and have profaned my holy things; they have made no distinction between the holy and the common, neither have they taught the difference between the unclean and the clean, and they have disregarded my sabbaths, so that I am profaned among them. 27Its officials within it are like wolves tearing the prey, shedding blood, destroying lives to get dishonest gain. 28Its prophets have smeared whitewash on their behalf, seeing false visions and divining lies for them, saying, "Thus says the Lord GOD," when the LORD has not spoken. 29The people of the land have practiced extortion and committed robbery; they have oppressed the poor and needy, and have extorted from the alien without redress. 30And I sought for anyone among them who would repair the wall and stand in the breach before me on behalf of the land, so that I would not destroy it; but I found no one. 31Therefore I have poured out my indignation upon them; I

a Gk Syr Vg: Heb *you*   *b* Transposed from the end of the verse; compare verse 20   *c* Gk: Heb *indignation.* 25*A conspiracy of its prophets*

22:23–30 *You are a land that is not cleansed.* God can find no civil or religious leaders who have "[stood] in the breach" (v 30) to prevent God's judgment on the land (cf. 13:5). The list of leaders includes princes (v 25), priests (v 26), officials (v 27), prophets (v 28), and landowners (v 29). In every case those in positions of authority have abused their power—the princes have stolen, the priests have profaned the holy, the officials have made dishonest gain, the prophets

have lied, and the landowners have practiced extortion. Contrary to the prophet's earlier testimony (14:12–20), there were some whose righteousness could have prevented the calamity that is now befalling Israel. The leaders of the People of God have particular responsibility to keep the covenant and to remember the ways of life with God. May such leaders arise in our day!

have consumed them with the fire of my wrath; I have returned their conduct upon their heads, says the Lord GOD.

Oholah and Oholibah

23 The word of the LORD came to me: ²Mortal, there were two women, the daughters of one mother; ³they played the whore in Egypt; they played the whore in their youth; their breasts were caressed there, and their virgin bosoms were fondled. ⁴Oholah was the name of the elder and Oholibah the name of her sister. They became mine, and they bore sons and daughters. As for their names, Oholah is Samaria, and Oholibah is Jerusalem.

5 Oholah played the whore while she was mine; she lusted after her lovers the Assyrians, warriors *a* ⁶clothed in blue, governors and commanders, all of them handsome young men, mounted horsemen. ⁷She bestowed her favors upon them, the choicest men of Assyria all of them; and she defiled herself with all the idols of everyone for whom she lusted. ⁸She did not give up her whorings that she had practiced since Egypt; for in her youth men had lain with her and fondled her virgin bosom and poured out their lust upon her. ⁹Therefore I delivered her into the hands of her lovers, into the hands of the Assyrians, for whom she lusted. ¹⁰These uncovered her nakedness; they seized her sons and her daughters; and they killed her with the

sword. Judgment was executed upon her, and she became a byword among women.

11 Her sister Oholibah saw this, yet she was more corrupt than she in her lusting and in her whorings, which were worse than those of her sister. ¹²She lusted after the Assyrians, governors and commanders, warriors *a* clothed in full armor, mounted horsemen, all of them handsome young men. ¹³And I saw that she was defiled; they both took the same way. ¹⁴But she carried her whorings further; she saw male figures carved on the wall, images of the Chaldeans portrayed in vermilion, ¹⁵with belts around their waists, with flowing turbans on their heads, all of them looking like officers—a picture of Babylonians whose native land was Chaldea. ¹⁶When she saw them she lusted after them, and sent messengers to them in Chaldea. ¹⁷And the Babylonians came to her into the bed of love, and they defiled her with their lust; and after she defiled herself with them, she turned from them in disgust. ¹⁸When she carried on her whorings so openly and flaunted her nakedness, I turned in disgust from her, as I had turned from her sister. ¹⁹Yet she increased her whorings, remembering the days of her youth, when she played the whore in the land of Egypt ²⁰and lusted after her paramours there, whose members were like those of donkeys, and whose emission was like that of stallions. ²¹Thus you longed for the lewdness of your

a Meaning of Heb uncertain

23:2–49 *there were two women.* Again Ezekiel rewrites the familiar history of Israel in order to rewrite the exiles' reading of the catastrophe that is befalling them. As in chapters 16 and 20 he undertakes to recast the conventional story of the People of God in a radically unconventional way. Now that the destruction of Jerusalem draws near, Ezekiel's portrayals of that event become even more shocking. In this chapter he describes the failed political alliances of Israel's two great capitals—Samaria and Jerusalem—through the allegory of two sisters—Oholah and Oholibah (lit., "my tent" and "my tent is in it"). The narrative turns the cherished stories of Israel's faithfulness upside down once more. These two sacred sites are described in the most

offensive language possible. The destruction of both cities is portrayed as the stoning of two women caught in adultery. Contemporary readers are rightly shocked at the level of domestic violence that this reveals in God's own household. Ezekiel intends the people to find the text abhorrent. They dare not believe that God's mad passion could spill out in such cataclysmic violence. The prophet, however, has digested (3:1–13) the terrible truth that God is attacking the people. Ezekiel will use every rhetorical device possible to tell this truth to the community in exile. He will not whitewash the trouble—the trouble with the people and the trouble with God.

youth, when the Egyptians*a* fondled your bosom and caressed*b* your young breasts.

22 Therefore, O Oholibah, thus says the Lord God: I will rouse against you your lovers from whom you turned in disgust, and I will bring them against you from every side: 23the Babylonians and all the Chaldeans, Pekod and Shoa and Koa, and all the Assyrians with them, handsome young men, governors and commanders all of them, officers and warriors,*c* all of them riding on horses. 24They shall come against you from the north*d* with chariots and wagons and a host of peoples; they shall set themselves against you on every side with buckler, shield, and helmet, and I will commit the judgment to them, and they shall judge you according to their ordinances. 25I will direct my indignation against you, in order that they may deal with you in fury. They shall cut off your nose and your ears, and your survivors shall fall by the sword. They shall seize your sons and your daughters, and your survivors shall be devoured by fire. 26They shall also strip you of your clothes and take away your fine jewels. 27So I will put an end to your lewdness and your whoring brought from the land of Egypt; you shall not long for them, or remember Egypt any more. 28For thus says the Lord God: I will deliver you into the hands of those whom you hate, into the hands of those from whom you turned in disgust; 29and they shall deal with you in hatred, and take away all the fruit of your labor, and leave you naked and bare, and the nakedness of your whorings shall be exposed. Your lewdness and your whorings 30have brought this upon you, because you played the whore with the nations, and polluted yourself with their idols. 31You have gone the way of your sister; therefore I will give her cup into your hand. 32Thus says the Lord God:

You shall drink your sister's cup,
    deep and wide;
you shall be scorned and derided,
    it holds so much.
33 You shall be filled with drunkenness
    and sorrow.
A cup of horror and desolation
    is the cup of your sister Samaria;
34 you shall drink it and drain it out,

and gnaw its sherds,
    and tear out your breasts;

for I have spoken, says the Lord God. 35Therefore thus says the Lord God: Because you have forgotten me and cast me behind your back, therefore bear the consequences of your lewdness and whorings.

36 The Lord said to me: Mortal, will you judge Oholah and Oholibah? Then declare to them their abominable deeds. 37For they have committed adultery, and blood is on their hands; with their idols they have committed adultery; and they have even offered up to them for food the children whom they had borne to me. 38Moreover this they have done to me: they have defiled my sanctuary on the same day and profaned my sabbaths. 39For when they had slaughtered their children for their idols, on the same day they came into my sanctuary to profane it. This is what they did in my house.

40 They even sent for men to come from far away, to whom a messenger was sent, and they came. For them you bathed yourself, painted your eyes, and decked yourself with ornaments; 41you sat on a stately couch, with a table spread before it on which you had placed my incense and my oil. 42The sound of a raucous multitude was around her, with many of the rabble brought in drunken from the wilderness; and they put bracelets on the arms*e* of the women, and beautiful crowns upon their heads.

43 Then I said, Ah, she is worn out with adulteries, but they carry on their sexual acts with her. 44For they have gone in to her, as one goes in to a whore. Thus they went in to Oholah and to Oholibah, wanton women. 45But righteous judges shall declare them guilty of adultery and of bloodshed; because they are adulteresses and blood is on their hands.

46 For thus says the Lord God: Bring up an assembly against them, and make them an object of terror and of plunder. 47The assembly shall stone them and with their swords they shall cut them down; they shall kill their

a Two Mss: MT *from Egypt*   *b* Cn: Heb *for the sake of*   *c* Compare verses 6 and 12: Heb *officers and called ones*   *d* Gk: Meaning of Heb uncertain   *e* Heb *hands*

sons and their daughters, and burn up their houses. 48Thus will I put an end to lewdness in the land, so that all women may take warning and not commit lewdness as you have done. 49They shall repay you for your lewdness, and you shall bear the penalty for your sinful idolatry; and you shall know that I am the Lord GOD.

The Boiling Pot

24 In the ninth year, in the tenth month, on the tenth day of the month, the word of the LORD came to me: 2Mortal, write down the name of this day, this very day. The king of Babylon has laid siege to Jerusalem this very day. 3And utter an allegory to the rebellious house and say to them, Thus says the Lord GOD:

Set on the pot, set it on,
    pour in water also;
4 put in it the pieces,
    all the good pieces, the thigh and the
        shoulder;
    fill it with choice bones.
5 Take the choicest one of the flock,
    pile the logs*g* under it;
    boil its pieces,*b*
    seethe*c* also its bones in it.

6 Therefore thus says the Lord GOD:
Woe to the bloody city,
    the pot whose rust is in it,
    whose rust has not gone out of it!
Empty it piece by piece,
    making no choice at all.*d*
7 For the blood she shed is inside it;
    she placed it on a bare rock;
    she did not pour it out on the ground,

to cover it with earth.
8 To rouse my wrath, to take vengeance,
    I have placed the blood she shed
    on a bare rock,
    so that it may not be covered.
9Therefore thus says the Lord GOD:
    Woe to the bloody city!
    I will even make the pile great.
10 Heap up the logs, kindle the fire;
    boil the meat well, mix in the spices,
    let the bones be burned.
11 Stand it empty upon the coals,
    so that it may become hot, its copper
        glow,
    its filth melt in it, its rust be
        consumed.
12 In vain I have wearied myself;*e*
    its thick rust does not depart.
    To the fire with its rust!*f*
13 Yet, when I cleansed you in your filthy
        lewdness,
    you did not become clean from your
        filth;
    you shall not again be cleansed
        until I have satisfied my fury upon
            you.
14I the LORD have spoken; the time is coming,
I will act. I will not refrain, I will not spare, I will
not relent. According to your ways and your
doings I will judge you, says the Lord GOD.

Ezekiel's Bereavement

15 The word of the LORD came to me:
16Mortal, with one blow I am about to take

a Compare verse 10: Heb *the bones*   *b* Two Mss:
Heb *its boilings*   *c* Cn: Heb *its bones seethe*
d Heb *piece, no lot has fallen on it*   *e* Cn: Meaning
of Heb uncertain   *f* Meaning of Heb uncertain

24:2 *this very day.* Three times in one verse the prophet notes that "this day" is the day that Jerusalem is besieged. The text has been preparing the exiles for this day, though they have been in disbelief that their world could ever come to this. On this day it comes to pass.

24:15–24 *you shall not mourn.* Ezekiel enacts a final sign before the destruction of Jerusalem. His beloved wife dies and he does not mourn in public. She is the delight of his eyes (v 16) and her death brings a great, aching sigh, but there is to be no public display of grief. When asked

why he acts this way, the prophet says that Jerusalem—"the delight of [their] eyes" (v 21)—is also about to die. That death will elicit deep groaning and guilt, but there is to be no public mourning among the exiles for their beloved city. The city's devastation is God's doing. It is God who "will profane [the] sanctuary" (v 21), not the Babylonians. The prohibition of public grief at the fall of Jerusalem is meant as a sign of faith in the power of God's purposes and promises in history.

away from you the delight of your eyes; yet you shall not mourn or weep, nor shall your tears run down. 17Sigh, but not aloud; make no mourning for the dead. Bind on your turban, and put your sandals on your feet; do not cover your upper lip or eat the bread of mourners.a 18So I spoke to the people in the morning, and at evening my wife died. And on the next morning I did as I was commanded.

19 Then the people said to me, "Will you not tell us what these things mean for us, that you are acting this way?" 20Then I said to them: The word of the LORD came to me: 21Say to the house of Israel, Thus says the Lord GOD: I will profane my sanctuary, the pride of your power, the delight of your eyes, and your heart's desire; and your sons and your daughters whom you left behind shall fall by the sword. 22And you shall do as I have done; you shall not cover your upper lip or eat the bread of mourners.a 23Your turbans shall be on your heads and your sandals on your feet; you shall not mourn or weep, but you shall pine away in your iniquities and groan to one another. 24Thus Ezekiel shall be a sign to you; you shall do just as he has done. When this comes, then you shall know that I am the Lord GOD.

25 And you, mortal, on the day when I take from them their stronghold, their joy and glory, the delight of their eyes and their heart's affection, and alsob their sons and their daughters, 26on that day, one who has escaped will come to you to report to you the news. 27On that day your mouth shall be opened to the one who has escaped, and you shall speak and no longer be silent. So you shall be a sign to them; and they shall know that I am the LORD.

Proclamation against Ammon

25 The word of the LORD came to me: 2Mortal, set your face toward the Ammonites and prophesy against them. 3Say to the Ammonites, Hear the word of the Lord GOD: Thus says the Lord GOD, Because you said, "Aha!" over my sanctuary when it was profaned, and over the land of Israel when it was made desolate, and over the house of Judah when it went into exile; 4therefore I am handing you over to the people of the east for a possession. They shall set their encampments among you and pitch their tents in your midst; they shall eat your fruit, and they shall drink your milk. 5I will make Rabbah a pasture for camels and Ammon a fold for flocks. Then you shall know that I am the LORD. 6For thus says the Lord GOD: Because

a Vg Tg: Heb of men   b Heb lacks and also

24:27 *On that day your mouth shall be opened.* Ezekiel has nothing else to say to Israel until news arrives of Jerusalem's destruction (v 26). On that day the prophet will again have a voice. But until that day (33:21–22) he will remain mute among the exiles. There is nothing that can be said. No words can express the great ache in awaiting the dreaded news. This is the turning point in the book of Ezekiel. The covenanted right living expected of the people has not been forthcoming. The glory of God has departed because God has been mocked. The holy city is soon to be a desolate ruin. Now even the prophetic voice is mute. Grieving silence is the only sound that tells the truth on such a day.

25:1–32:32 *and prophesy against them.* Chapters 25–32 form an interlude in Ezekiel's prophetic speech to the exiles. With Ezekiel the people wait in silence for the fall of Jerusalem. In the meantime, in these chapters the prophet pronounces oracles against other nations (cf. Isa 13–23; Jer 46–51; Amos 1–2; Zeph 2). He announces that the God of Israel is also the God of international relations (Ps 86:9)—from Israel's local neighbors (chap 25), to the wealthy city-states Tyre and Sidon (chaps 26–28), to the huge superpowers Egypt and Assyria (chaps 29–32). The absence of Babylon from this list may be an act of prudence in light of the Babylonian captivity of the exilic community. Ezekiel's claim that tiny Israel's God is the God of every nation is a bold one. Yet these oracles assert that there is more at work in international politics and economics than simply brute force. The just and righteous ways of the God of Israel are God's intention for the People of God and for the world of nations. The prophet testifies that God brings down even the greatest powers when they imagine that their security can be self-assured and their ways can be made self-righteous.

you have clapped your hands and stamped your feet and rejoiced with all the malice within you against the land of Israel, 7therefore I have stretched out my hand against you, and will hand you over as plunder to the nations. I will cut you off from the peoples and will make you perish out of the countries; I will destroy you. Then you shall know that I am the LORD.

Proclamation against Moab

8 Thus says the Lord GOD: Because Moab*a* said, The house of Judah is like all the other nations, 9therefore I will lay open the flank of Moab from the towns*b* on its frontier, the glory of the country, Beth-jeshimoth, Baal-meon, and Kiriathaim. 10I will give it along with Ammon to the people of the east as a possession. Thus Ammon shall be remembered no more among the nations, 11and I will execute judgments upon Moab. Then they shall know that I am the LORD.

Proclamation against Edom

12 Thus says the Lord GOD: Because Edom acted revengefully against the house of Judah and has grievously offended in taking vengeance upon them, 13therefore thus says the Lord GOD, I will stretch out my hand against Edom, and cut off from it humans and animals, and I will make it desolate; from Teman even to Dedan they shall fall by the sword. 14I will lay my vengeance upon Edom by the hand of my people Israel; and they shall act in Edom according to my anger and according to my wrath; and they shall know my vengeance, says the Lord GOD.

Proclamation against Philistia

15 Thus says the Lord GOD: Because with unending hostilities the Philistines acted in vengeance, and with malice of heart took re-

venge in destruction; 16therefore thus says the Lord GOD, I will stretch out my hand against the Philistines, cut off the Cherethites, and destroy the rest of the seacoast. 17I will execute great vengeance on them with wrathful punishments. Then they shall know that I am the LORD, when I lay my vengeance on them.

Proclamation against Tyre

26 In the eleventh year, on the first day of the month, the word of the LORD came to me: 2Mortal, because Tyre said concerning Jerusalem,

"Aha, broken is the gateway of the
    peoples;
  it has swung open to me;
I shall be replenished,
  now that it is wasted,"

3therefore, thus says the Lord GOD:
  See, I am against you, O Tyre!
  I will hurl many nations against you,
  as the sea hurls its waves.
4 They shall destroy the walls of Tyre
  and break down its towers.
  I will scrape its soil from it
  and make it a bare rock.
5 It shall become, in the midst of the sea,
  a place for spreading nets.
I have spoken, says the Lord GOD.
  It shall become plunder for the nations,
6   and its daughter-towns in the country
  shall be killed by the sword.
Then they shall know that I am the LORD.

7 For thus says the Lord GOD: I will bring against Tyre from the north King Nebuchadrezzar of Babylon, king of kings, together with horses, chariots, cavalry, and a great and powerful army.

a Gk Old Latin: Heb *Moab and Seir*   *b* Heb *towns from its towns*

25:5 *Then you shall know that I am* the LORD. The judgments against the nations, like the judgment against Israel (see 6:1–7), are not intended to result in their extinction, but so that they will come to know that Yahweh is God. The final intentions of God for the nations lie beyond judgment when they know, and are known, by Yahweh.

26:2 *the gateway . . . has swung open to me.* Tyre is home to a thriving economy based on global trade. It is alert to every opportunity for gain and spies in Jerusalem's loss a chance for quick profit. Such a blatant attempt at illicit gain is cause for this lengthy oracle of judgment and lament (chaps 26–28).

8 Your daughter-towns in the country
 he shall put to the sword.
He shall set up a siege wall against you,
 cast up a ramp against you,
 and raise a roof of shields against you.
9 He shall direct the shock of his
  battering rams against your walls
 and break down your towers with his
  axes.
10 His horses shall be so many
 that their dust shall cover you.
At the noise of cavalry, wheels, and
 chariots
your very walls shall shake,
when he enters your gates
 like those entering a breached city.
11 With the hoofs of his horses
 he shall trample all your streets.
He shall put your people to the sword,
 and your strong pillars shall fall to the
  ground.
12 They will plunder your riches
 and loot your merchandise;
they shall break down your walls
 and destroy your fine houses.
Your stones and timber and soil
 they shall cast into the water.
13 I will silence the music of your songs;
 the sound of your lyres shall be heard
  no more.
14 I will make you a bare rock;
 you shall be a place for spreading
  nets.
You shall never again be rebuilt,
 for I the LORD have spoken,
 says the Lord GOD.

15 Thus says the Lord GOD to Tyre: Shall not the coastlands shake at the sound of your fall, when the wounded groan, when slaughter goes on within you? 16 Then all the princes of the sea shall step down from their thrones; they shall remove their robes and strip off their embroidered garments. They shall clothe themselves with trembling, and shall sit on the ground; they shall tremble every moment, and be appalled at you. 17 And they shall raise a lamentation over you, and say to you:

How you have vanished[a] from the seas,
 O city renowned,
once mighty on the sea,
 you and your inhabitants,[b]
who imposed your[c] terror
 on all the mainland![d]
18 Now the coastlands tremble
 on the day of your fall;
the coastlands by the sea
 are dismayed at your passing.

Earthquake!

19 For thus says the Lord GOD: When I make you a city laid waste, like cities that are not inhabited, when I bring up the deep over you, and the great waters cover you, 20 then I will thrust you down with those who descend into the Pit, to the people of long ago, and I will make you live in the world below, among primeval ruins, with those who go down to the Pit, so that you will not be inhabited or have a place[e] in the land of the living. 21 I will bring you to a dreadful end, and you shall be no more; though sought for, you will never be found again, says the Lord GOD.

Lamentation over Tyre

27 The word of the LORD came to me: 2 Now you, mortal, raise a lamentation over Tyre, 3 and say to Tyre, which sits at the entrance to the sea, merchant of the peoples on many coastlands, Thus says the Lord GOD:

 O Tyre, you have said,
  "I am perfect in beauty."

a Gk OL Aquila: Heb *have vanished, O inhabited one,*
b Heb *it and its inhabitants* c Heb *their*
d Cn: Heb *its inhabitants* e Gk: Heb *I will give beauty*

26:16 *They shall clothe themselves with trembling.* Faced with the impossible and unprecedented collapse of Tyre's economic juggernaut, the bosses of an international economy based on shipping ("princes of the sea") tremble, tremble, tremble (vv 16, 18). If Tyre is not safe from Yahweh, then there is no economy that can escape the judgment of the God of Israel.

27:3 *I am perfect in beauty.* Tyre is awed at its productive capacity. Its skilled workers are unsurpassed (v 4). Its trading partners are part of a vast global network (vv 12–25). Yet the entire elaborate system will "sink into the heart of the seas" (v 27) when God brings it to an end.

4 Your borders are in the heart of the seas;
      your builders made perfect your
         beauty.
5 They made all your planks
      of fir trees from Senir;
   they took a cedar from Lebanon
      to make a mast for you.
6 From oaks of Bashan
      they made your oars;
   they made your deck of pines*a*
      from the coasts of Cyprus,
      inlaid with ivory.
7 Of fine embroidered linen from Egypt
      was your sail,
      serving as your ensign;
   blue and purple from the coasts of
         Elishah
      was your awning.
8 The inhabitants of Sidon and Arvad
      were your rowers;
   skilled men of Zemer*b* were within you,
      they were your pilots.
9 The elders of Gebal and its artisans were
         within you,
      caulking your seams;
   all the ships of the sea with their
         mariners were within you,
      to barter for your wares.
10 Paras*c* and Lud and Put
      were in your army,
      your mighty warriors;
   they hung shield and helmet in you;
      they gave you splendor.
11 Men of Arvad and Helech*d*
      were on your walls all around;
      men of Gamad were at your towers.
   They hung their quivers all around your
         walls;
      they made perfect your beauty.
12 Tarshish did business with you out of
the abundance of your great wealth; silver,
iron, tin, and lead they exchanged for your
wares. 13Javan, Tubal, and Meshech traded
with you; they exchanged human beings and
vessels of bronze for your merchandise.
14Beth-togarmah exchanged for your wares
horses, war horses, and mules. 15The Rhodi-
ans*e* traded with you; many coastlands were
your own special markets; they brought you
in payment ivory tusks and ebony. 16Edom*f*
did business with you because of your abun-

dant goods; they exchanged for your wares
turquoise, purple, embroidered work, fine
linen, coral, and rubies. 17Judah and the land
of Israel traded with you; they exchanged
for your merchandise wheat from Minnith,
millet,*g* honey, oil, and balm. 18Damascus
traded with you for your abundant goods—
because of your great wealth of every kind—
wine of Helbon, and white wool. 19Vedan
and Javan from Uzal*g* entered into trade for
your wares; wrought iron, cassia, and sweet
cane were bartered for your merchandise.
20Dedan traded with you in saddlecloths for
riding. 21Arabia and all the princes of Kedar
were your favored dealers in lambs, rams, and
goats; in these they did business with you.
22The merchants of Sheba and Raamah traded with you; they exchanged for your wares
the best of all kinds of spices, and all precious stones, and gold. 23Haran, Canneh,
Eden, the merchants of Sheba, Asshur, and
Chilmad traded with you. 24These traded
with you in choice garments, in clothes of
blue and embroidered work, and in carpets of
colored material, bound with cords and made
secure; in these they traded with you.*h* 25The
ships of Tarshish traveled for you in your
trade.

   So you were filled and heavily laden
      in the heart of the seas.
26 Your rowers have brought you
      into the high seas.
   The east wind has wrecked you
      in the heart of the seas.
27 Your riches, your wares, your
         merchandise,
      your mariners and your pilots,
      your caulkers, your dealers in
         merchandise,
      and all your warriors within you,
      with all the company
         that is with you,
      sink into the heart of the seas
      on the day of your ruin.
28 At the sound of the cry of your pilots
      the countryside shakes,

a Or *boxwood*   *b* Cn Compare Gen 10.18: Heb
your skilled men, O Tyre   *c* Or *Persia*   *d* Or *and
your army*   *e* Gk: Heb *The Dedanites*
f Another reading is *Aram*   *g* Meaning of Heb
uncertain   *h* Cn: Heb *in your market*

29 and down from their ships
          come all that handle the oar.
     The mariners and all the pilots of the
          sea
     stand on the shore
30 and wail aloud over you,
          and cry bitterly.
     They throw dust on their heads
          and wallow in ashes;
31 they make themselves bald for you,
          and put on sackcloth,
     and they weep over you in bitterness of
          soul,
          with bitter mourning.
32 In their wailing they raise a
          lamentation for you,
          and lament over you:
     "Who was ever destroyed*a* like Tyre
          in the midst of the sea?
33 When your wares came from the seas,
          you satisfied many peoples;
     with your abundant wealth and
          merchandise
     you enriched the kings of the earth.
34 Now you are wrecked by the seas,
          in the depths of the waters;
     your merchandise and all your crew
          have sunk with you.
35 All the inhabitants of the coastlands
          are appalled at you;
     and their kings are horribly afraid,
          their faces are convulsed.
36 The merchants among the peoples hiss
          at you;
     you have come to a dreadful end
          and shall be no more forever."

Proclamation against the King of Tyre

28 The word of the LORD came to me:
     2Mortal, say to the prince of Tyre,
Thus says the Lord GOD:
     Because your heart is proud
          and you have said, "I am a god;
     I sit in the seat of the gods,
          in the heart of the seas,"

yet you are but a mortal, and no god,
          though you compare your mind
          with the mind of a god.
3 You are indeed wiser than Daniel;*b*
          no secret is hidden from you;
4 by your wisdom and your
          understanding
     you have amassed wealth for yourself,
     and have gathered gold and silver
          into your treasuries.
5 By your great wisdom in trade
          you have increased your wealth,
     and your heart has become proud in
          your wealth.
6 Therefore thus says the Lord GOD:
     Because you compare your mind
          with the mind of a god,
7 therefore, I will bring strangers against
          you,
          the most terrible of the nations;
     they shall draw their swords against the
          beauty of your wisdom
          and defile your splendor.
8 They shall thrust you down to the Pit,
          and you shall die a violent death
          in the heart of the seas.
9 Will you still say, "I am a god,"
          in the presence of those who kill you,
     though you are but a mortal, and no
          god,
          in the hands of those who wound
          you?
10 You shall die the death of the
          uncircumcised
          by the hand of foreigners;
     for I have spoken, says the Lord GOD.

Lamentation over the King of Tyre

11 Moreover the word of the LORD came to
me: 12Mortal, raise a lamentation over the
king of Tyre, and say to him, Thus says the
Lord GOD:

a Tg Vg: Heb *like silence*   *b* Or, as otherwise read,
Danel

28:2 *you are but a mortal, and no god.* The
root cause of Tyre's inevitable fall is its self-
deification. It has grown accustomed to being in
control. It bows to no one and to nothing. Tyre
idolizes itself, saying in its heart, "I am a god." It

has mistaken great wisdom (vv 3–5) for
the power to create and to shape life. Tyre is
arrogant. Its necessary humbling can only occur
through the humiliation of losing control to "the
most terrible of the nations" (v 7).

You were the signet of perfection, *a*
   full of wisdom and perfect in beauty.
13 You were in Eden, the garden of God;
   every precious stone was your
      covering,
   carnelian, chrysolite, and moonstone,
   beryl, onyx, and jasper,
   sapphire, *b* turquoise, and emerald;
   and worked in gold were your settings
   and your engravings. *a*
   On the day that you were created
   they were prepared.
14 With an anointed cherub as guardian I
     placed you; *a*
   you were on the holy mountain of
     God;
   you walked among the stones of fire.
15 You were blameless in your ways
   from the day that you were created,
   until iniquity was found in you.
16 In the abundance of your trade
   you were filled with violence, and you
     sinned;
   so I cast you as a profane thing from the
     mountain of God,
   and the guardian cherub drove you out
   from among the stones of fire.
17 Your heart was proud because of your
     beauty;
   you corrupted your wisdom for the
     sake of your splendor.
   I cast you to the ground;
   I exposed you before kings,
   to feast their eyes on you.
18 By the multitude of your iniquities,
   in the unrighteousness of your trade,
   you profaned your sanctuaries.
   So I brought out fire from within you;
   it consumed you,
   and I turned you to ashes on the earth
   in the sight of all who saw you.

19 All who know you among the peoples
   are appalled at you;
   you have come to a dreadful end
   and shall be no more forever.

Proclamation against Sidon

20 The word of the LORD came to me: 21 Mortal, set your face toward Sidon, and prophesy against it, 22 and say, Thus says the Lord GOD:
   I am against you, O Sidon,
   and I will gain glory in your midst.
   They shall know that I am the LORD
   when I execute judgments in it,
   and manifest my holiness in it;
23 for I will send pestilence into it,
   and bloodshed into its streets;
   and the dead shall fall in its midst,
   by the sword that is against it on
     every side.
   And they shall know that I am the LORD.

24 The house of Israel shall no longer find a pricking brier or a piercing thorn among all their neighbors who have treated them with contempt. And they shall know that I am the Lord GOD.

Future Blessing for Israel

25 Thus says the Lord GOD: When I gather the house of Israel from the peoples among whom they are scattered, and manifest my holiness in them in the sight of the nations, then they shall settle on their own soil that I gave to my servant Jacob. 26 They shall live in safety in it, and shall build houses and plant vineyards. They shall live in safety, when I execute judgments upon all their neighbors who have treated them with contempt. And they shall know that I am the LORD their God.

a Meaning of Heb uncertain   *b* Or *lapis lazuli*

28:12–19 *raise a lamentation over the king of Tyre.* This song of woe casts Tyre's ruler in the role of Adam, God's beloved earthling in Eden. In this version of the ancient story, God's primal human—Tyre's king—is expelled from the garden for disobedience to God that is revealed in abusive trade practices (vv 16, 18).

28:25–26 *When I gather the house of Israel.* Here is a glimmer of hope for an exiled, de-feated remnant. The judgments on Israel's neighbors will result in Israel's restoration and the exiles' homecoming. But this is not the reason God intends the defeat of the nations. Ezekiel announces that Israel's salvation is a secondary by-product of Yahweh's desire to be known among the nations as incomparably glorious and holy beyond measure.

Proclamation against Egypt

29 In the tenth year, in the tenth month, on the twelfth day of the month, the word of the LORD came to me: [2]Mortal, set your face against Pharaoh king of Egypt, and prophesy against him and against all Egypt; [3]speak, and say, Thus says the Lord GOD:

I am against you,
    Pharaoh king of Egypt,
the great dragon sprawling
    in the midst of its channels,
saying, "My Nile is my own;
    I made it for myself."
[4] I will put hooks in your jaws,
    and make the fish of your channels
        stick to your scales.
I will draw you up from your channels,
    with all the fish of your channels
        sticking to your scales.
[5] I will fling you into the wilderness,
    you and all the fish of your channels;
you shall fall in the open field,
    and not be gathered and buried.
To the animals of the earth and to the
        birds of the air
I have given you as food.
[6] Then all the inhabitants of Egypt shall
        know
    that I am the LORD
because you[a] were a staff of reed
    to the house of Israel;
[7] when they grasped you with the hand,
        you broke,
    and tore all their shoulders;
and when they leaned on you, you
        broke,

and made all their legs unsteady.[b]

[8] Therefore, thus says the Lord GOD: I will bring a sword upon you, and will cut off from you human being and animal; [9]and the land of Egypt shall be a desolation and a waste. Then they shall know that I am the LORD.

Because you[c] said, "The Nile is mine, and I made it," [10]therefore, I am against you, and against your channels, and I will make the land of Egypt an utter waste and desolation, from Migdol to Syene, as far as the border of Ethiopia.[d] [11]No human foot shall pass through it, and no animal foot shall pass through it; it shall be uninhabited forty years. [12]I will make the land of Egypt a desolation among desolated countries; and her cities shall be a desolation forty years among cities that are laid waste. I will scatter the Egyptians among the nations, and disperse them among the countries.

[13] Further, thus says the Lord GOD: At the end of forty years I will gather the Egyptians from the peoples among whom they were scattered; [14]and I will restore the fortunes of Egypt, and bring them back to the land of Pathros, the land of their origin; and there they shall be a lowly kingdom. [15]It shall be the most lowly of the kingdoms, and never again exalt itself above the nations; and I will make them so small that they will never again rule over the nations. [16]The Egyptians[e] shall never again be the reliance of the house of Israel; they will recall their iniquity, when they

---

a Gk Syr Vg: Heb *they*   b Syr: Heb *stand*
c Gk Syr Vg: Heb *he*   d Or *Nubia*; Heb *Cush*
e Heb *It*

29:2–12 *My Nile is my own; I made it for myself.* Ezekiel now addresses mighty Pharaoh, ruler of superpower Egypt. The king of Egypt is a "great dragon sprawling" in the Nile, claiming ownership and autonomy as a self-made power (vv 3, 9). But Pharaoh is to become food for wild animals (v 5) because, when impoverished Israel reached out for aid and assistance, Egypt responded by tearing the shoulders and breaking the legs of the People of God (v 7). The text argues that there is no autonomy from the purposes of God in the world.

29:13–16 *At the end of forty years.* Egypt's diaspora will not last forever. Its people will live for forty years scattered as foreigners and resident aliens among the wilderness of the nations (as Israel wandered for forty years after the exodus before arriving home in the Promised Land). God will "restore the fortunes of Egypt" (v 14) after its wilderness wanderings. But there will be one difference. Pharaoh's superpower is destined to exist among the nations as a "lowly kingdom" (v 14) and so to finally know that Yahweh is God (v 16) and that self-sufficiency is not possible.

turned to them for aid. Then they shall know that I am the Lord GOD.

Babylonia Will Plunder Egypt

17 In the twenty-seventh year, in the first month, on the first day of the month, the word of the LORD came to me: 18Mortal, King Nebuchadrezzar of Babylon made his army labor hard against Tyre; every head was made bald and every shoulder was rubbed bare; yet neither he nor his army got anything from Tyre to pay for the labor that he had expended against it. 19Therefore thus says the Lord GOD: I will give the land of Egypt to King Nebuchadrezzar of Babylon; and he shall carry off its wealth and despoil it and plunder it; and it shall be the wages for his army. 20I have given him the land of Egypt as his payment for which he labored, because they worked for me, says the Lord GOD.

21 On that day I will cause a horn to sprout up for the house of Israel, and I will open your lips among them. Then they shall know that I am the LORD.

Lamentation for Egypt

30 The word of the LORD came to me: 2Mortal, prophesy, and say, Thus says the Lord GOD:
Wail, "Alas for the day!"
3   For a day is near,
      the day of the LORD is near;
    it will be a day of clouds,
      a time of doom a for the nations.
4   A sword shall come upon Egypt,
      and anguish shall be in Ethiopia, b
    when the slain fall in Egypt,
      and its wealth is carried away,
      and its foundations are torn down.
5Ethiopia, b and Put, and Lud, and all Arabia, and Libya, c and the people of the allied land d shall fall with them by the sword.

6   Thus says the LORD:
    Those who support Egypt shall fall,
      and its proud might shall come down;
    from Migdol to Syene
      they shall fall within it by the sword,
    says the Lord GOD.
7   They shall be desolated among other
        desolated countries,

and their cities shall lie among cities
        laid waste.
8   Then they shall know that I am the
        LORD,
    when I have set fire to Egypt,
      and all who help it are broken.
9 On that day, messengers shall go out from me in ships to terrify the unsuspecting Ethiopians; e and anguish shall come upon them on the day of Egypt's doom; f for it is coming!

10   Thus says the Lord GOD:
    I will put an end to the hordes of Egypt,
      by the hand of King Nebuchadrezzar
        of Babylon.
11   He and his people with him, the most
        terrible of the nations,
      shall be brought in to destroy the
        land;
    and they shall draw their swords against
        Egypt,
      and fill the land with the slain.
12   I will dry up the channels,
      and will sell the land into the hand of
        evildoers;
    I will bring desolation upon the land
        and everything in it
      by the hand of foreigners;
    I the LORD have spoken.

13   Thus says the Lord GOD:
    I will destroy the idols
      and put an end to the images in
        Memphis;
    there shall no longer be a prince in the
        land of Egypt;
      so I will put fear in the land of Egypt.
14   I will make Pathros a desolation,
      and will set fire to Zoan,
      and will execute acts of judgment on
        Thebes.
15   I will pour my wrath upon Pelusium,
      the stronghold of Egypt,
      and cut off the hordes of Thebes.
16   I will set fire to Egypt;
      Pelusium shall be in great agony;

a Heb lacks *of doom*   b Or *Nubia*; Heb *Cush*
c Compare Gk Syr Vg: Heb *Cub*   d Meaning of Heb uncertain   e Or *Nubians*; Heb *Cush*
f Heb *the day of Egypt*

Thebes shall be breached,
 and Memphis face adversaries by day.
17 The young men of On and of Pi-beseth
 shall fall by the sword;
 and the cities themselves*a* shall go
  into captivity.
18 At Tehaphnehes the day shall be dark,
 when I break there the dominion of
  Egypt,
 and its proud might shall come to an
  end;
 the city*b* shall be covered by a cloud,
 and its daughter-towns shall go into
  captivity.
19 Thus I will execute acts of judgment on
 Egypt.
 Then they shall know that I am the
  LORD.

Proclamation against Pharaoh

20 In the eleventh year, in the first month, on the seventh day of the month, the word of the LORD came to me: 21Mortal, I have broken the arm of Pharaoh king of Egypt; it has not been bound up for healing or wrapped with a bandage, so that it may become strong to wield the sword. 22Therefore thus says the Lord GOD: I am against Pharaoh king of Egypt, and will break his arms, both the strong arm and the one that was broken; and I will make the sword fall from his hand. 23I will scatter the Egyptians among the nations, and disperse them throughout the lands. 24I will strengthen the arms of the king of Babylon, and put my sword in his hand; but I will break the arms of Pharaoh, and he will groan before him with the groans of one mortally wounded. 25I will strengthen the arms of the king of Babylon, but the arms of Pharaoh

shall fall. And they shall know that I am the LORD, when I put my sword into the hand of the king of Babylon. He shall stretch it out against the land of Egypt, 26and I will scatter the Egyptians among the nations and disperse them throughout the countries. Then they shall know that I am the LORD.

The Lofty Cedar

31 In the eleventh year, in the third month, on the first day of the month, the word of the LORD came to me: 2Mortal, say to Pharaoh king of Egypt and to his hordes:
 Whom are you like in your greatness?
3 Consider Assyria, a cedar of Lebanon,
 with fair branches and forest shade,
  and of great height,
  its top among the clouds.*c*
4 The waters nourished it,
 the deep made it grow tall,
 making its rivers flow*d*
 around the place it was planted,
 sending forth its streams
 to all the trees of the field.
5 So it towered high
 above all the trees of the field;
 its boughs grew large
 and its branches long,
 from abundant water in its shoots.
6 All the birds of the air
 made their nests in its boughs;
 under its branches all the animals of the
  field
 gave birth to their young;
 and in its shade
 all great nations lived.

a Heb *and they* *b* Heb *she* *c* Gk: Heb *thick boughs* *d* Gk: Heb *rivers going*

30:24 *I will strengthen the arms of the king of Babylon.* The purposes of God among the nations will be advanced by Israel's captor— the king of Babylon. Here Ezekiel continues the stunning claim that the archenemy of the People of God is, in fact, empowered by God to carry out the judgments of God.

31:3–17 *Assyria, a cedar of Lebanon.* Ezekiel portrays toppled Assyria as a glorious cedar of Lebanon, "the envy of all the trees of Eden" (v 9). It is felled because it "towered high," a

skyscraper whose "heart was proud of its height" (v 10). This is a warning to Egypt and to all nations. No people is intended to tower over others (v 14). No nation—no tree (even the wondrous trees in Eden, the garden of God, Gen 2:9)—is greater than God. Every attempt to replace God's glory with human accomplishment will result in being brought down "to the world below" (v 18). But people who live in close relationship with God will be like trees that bear fruit beyond all expectation (Ps 1; Jer 17:5–10).

[handwritten: Morals on Lebanon!]

7 It was beautiful in its greatness,
  in the length of its branches;
for its roots went down
  to abundant water.
8 The cedars in the garden of God could
    not rival it,
  nor the fir trees equal its boughs;
the plane trees were as nothing
  compared with its branches;
no tree in the garden of God
  was like it in beauty.
9 I made it beautiful
  with its mass of branches,
the envy of all the trees of Eden
  that were in the garden of God.

10 Therefore thus says the Lord GOD: Because it[a] towered high and set its top among the clouds,[b] and its heart was proud of its height, 11I gave it into the hand of the prince of the nations; he has dealt with it as its wickedness deserves. I have cast it out. 12Foreigners from the most terrible of the nations have cut it down and left it. On the mountains and in all the valleys its branches have fallen, and its boughs lie broken in all the watercourses of the land; and all the peoples of the earth went away from its shade and left it.
13 On its fallen trunk settle
  all the birds of the air,
and among its boughs lodge
  all the wild animals.
14All this is in order that no trees by the waters may grow to lofty height or set their tops among the clouds,[b] and that no trees that drink water may reach up to them in height.
  For all of them are handed over to
    death,
  to the world below;
along with all mortals,
  with those who go down to the Pit.

15 Thus says the Lord GOD: On the day it went down to Sheol I closed the deep over it and covered it; I restrained its rivers, and its mighty waters were checked. I clothed Lebanon in gloom for it, and all the trees of the field fainted because of it. 16I made the nations quake at the sound of its fall, when I cast it down to Sheol with those who go down to the Pit; and all the trees of Eden, the choice and best of Lebanon, all that were well watered, were consoled in the world below.

17They also went down to Sheol with it, to those killed by the sword, along with its allies,[c] those who lived in its shade among the nations.

18 Which among the trees of Eden was like you in glory and in greatness? Now you shall be brought down with the trees of Eden to the world below; you shall lie among the uncircumcised, with those who are killed by the sword. This is Pharaoh and all his horde, says the Lord GOD.

Lamentation over Pharaoh and Egypt

32 In the twelfth year, in the twelfth month, on the first day of the month, the word of the LORD came to me: 2Mortal, raise a lamentation over Pharaoh king of Egypt, and say to him:
  You consider yourself a lion among the
    nations,
  but you are like a dragon in the seas;
you thrash about in your streams,
  trouble the water with your feet,
  and foul your[d] streams.
3 Thus says the Lord GOD:
  In an assembly of many peoples
  I will throw my net over you;
  and I[e] will haul you up in my dragnet.
4 I will throw you on the ground,
  on the open field I will fling you,
and will cause all the birds of the air to
    settle on you,
  and I will let the wild animals of the
    whole earth gorge themselves
    with you.
5 I will strew your flesh on the
    mountains,
  and fill the valleys with your carcass.[f]
6 I will drench the land with your flowing
    blood
  up to the mountains,
  and the watercourses will be filled
    with you.
7 When I blot you out, I will cover the
    heavens,
  and make their stars dark;
I will cover the sun with a cloud,
  and the moon shall not give its light.

a Syr Vg: Heb *you*   b Gk: Heb *thick boughs*
c Heb *its arms*   d Heb *their*   e Gk Vg: Heb *they*
f Symmachus Syr Vg: Heb *your height*

8 All the shining lights of the heavens
    I will darken above you,
  and put darkness on your land,
                          says the Lord GOD.
9 I will trouble the hearts of many
        peoples,
    as I carry you captive*a* among the
        nations,
    into countries you have not known.
10 I will make many peoples appalled at
        you;
    their kings shall shudder because of
        you.
  When I brandish my sword before
        them,
    they shall tremble every moment
  for their lives, each one of them,
    on the day of your downfall.
11 For thus says the Lord GOD:
  The sword of the king of Babylon shall
        come against you.
12 I will cause your hordes to fall
    by the swords of mighty ones,
    all of them most terrible among the
        nations.
  They shall bring to ruin the pride of
        Egypt,
    and all its hordes shall perish.
13 I will destroy all its livestock
    from beside abundant waters;
  and no human foot shall trouble them
        any more,
    nor shall the hoofs of cattle trouble
        them.
14 Then I will make their waters clear,
    and cause their streams to run like oil,
        says the Lord GOD.
15 When I make the land of Egypt desolate
  and when the land is stripped of all
        that fills it,
  when I strike down all who live in it,
    then they shall know that I am the
        LORD.
16 This is a lamentation; it shall be
        chanted.

  The women of the nations shall chant
        it.
  Over Egypt and all its hordes they shall
        chant it,
    says the Lord GOD.

Dirge over Egypt

17 In the twelfth year, in the first month,*b*
on the fifteenth day of the month, the word
of the LORD came to me:
18 Mortal, wail over the hordes of Egypt,
    and send them down,
  with Egypt*c* and the daughters of
        majestic nations,
  to the world below,
    with those who go down to the Pit.
19 "Whom do you surpass in beauty?
    Go down! Be laid to rest with the
        uncircumcised!"
20 They shall fall among those who are killed
by the sword. Egypt*c* has been handed over to
the sword; carry away both it and its hordes.
21 The mighty chiefs shall speak of them, with
their helpers, out of the midst of Sheol: "They
have come down, they lie still, the uncircumcised, killed by the sword."

22 Assyria is there, and all its company,
their graves all around it, all of them killed,
fallen by the sword. 23 Their graves are set in
the uttermost parts of the Pit. Its company is
all around its grave, all of them killed, fallen
by the sword, who spread terror in the land
of the living.

24 Elam is there, and all its hordes around
its grave; all of them killed, fallen by the
sword, who went down uncircumcised into
the world below, who spread terror in the
land of the living. They bear their shame
with those who go down to the Pit. 25 They
have made Elam*c* a bed among the slain with
all its hordes, their graves all around it, all of
them uncircumcised, killed by the sword; for
terror of them was spread in the land of the

---

a Gk: Heb *bring your destruction*   *b* Gk: Heb lacks
in the first month   *c* Heb *it*

32:22–32 *Their graves are set in . . . the Pit.*
The conclusion of the oracles against the
nations portrays the death of global terrorism.
The litany of nations who have "spread terror in

the land of the living" (v 32) is read aloud at
their resting place in the massive graveyard in
the Pit. It is worth considering what a contemporary litany of nations would look like.

living, and they bear their shame with those who go down to the Pit; they are placed among the slain.

26 Meshech and Tubal are there, and all their multitude, their graves all around them, all of them uncircumcised, killed by the sword; for they spread terror in the land of the living. [27] And they do not lie with the fallen warriors of long ago[a] who went down to Sheol with their weapons of war, whose swords were laid under their heads, and whose shields[b] are upon their bones; for the terror of the warriors was in the land of the living. [28] So you shall be broken and lie among the uncircumcised, with those who are killed by the sword.

29 Edom is there, its kings and all its princes, who for all their might are laid with those who are killed by the sword; they lie with the uncircumcised, with those who go down to the Pit.

30 The princes of the north are there, all of them, and all the Sidonians, who have gone down in shame with the slain, for all the terror that they caused by their might; they lie uncircumcised with those who are killed by the sword, and bear their shame with those who go down to the Pit.

31 When Pharaoh sees them, he will be consoled for all his hordes—Pharaoh and all his army, killed by the sword, says the Lord GOD. [32] For he[c] spread terror in the land of the living; therefore he shall be laid to rest among the uncircumcised, with those who are slain by the sword—Pharaoh and all his multitude, says the Lord GOD.

Ezekiel Israel's Sentry

33 The word of the LORD came to me: [2] O Mortal, speak to your people and say to them, If I bring the sword upon a land, and the people of the land take one of their number as their sentinel; [3] and if the sentinel sees the sword coming upon the land and blows the trumpet and warns the people; [4] then if any who hear the sound of the trumpet do not take warning, and the sword comes and takes them away, their blood shall be upon their own heads. [5] They heard the sound of the trumpet and did not take warning; their blood shall be upon themselves. But if they had taken warning, they would have saved their lives. [6] But if the sentinel sees the sword coming and does not blow the trumpet, so that the people are not warned, and the sword comes and takes any of them, they are taken away in their iniquity, but their blood I will require at the sentinel's hand.

7 So you, mortal, I have made a sentinel for the house of Israel; whenever you hear a word from my mouth, you shall give them warning from me. [8] If I say to the wicked, "O wicked ones, you shall surely die," and you do not speak to warn the wicked to turn from their ways, the wicked shall die in their iniquity, but their blood I will require at your hand. [9] But if you warn the wicked to turn from their ways, and they do not turn from their ways, the wicked shall die in their iniquity, but you will have saved your life.

God's Justice and Mercy

10 Now you, mortal, say to the house of Israel, Thus you have said: "Our transgressions and our sins weigh upon us, and we waste

a Gk Old Latin: Heb of the uncircumcised
b Cn: Heb iniquities   c Cn: Heb I

33:10 *our sins weigh upon us.* For the first time the exilic community tells the truth about its situation. Its prayer of confession is a longing acknowledgment that the weight of past sin is so great that the community is dying. Denial now turns to despair. Ezekiel preaches a recurrent sermon (chap 18) that offers a way into the future through a sharp turn to the ways and doings of God (v 11). The People of God are at their lowest ebb and, yet, on the verge of renewal.

Responding
33:10 CONFESSION. The People of God are burdened by their sin. Many of us are similarly burdened by sins we need to confess. Sometimes confessing privately to God can leave us still aching with pain and shame, not sure we have confessed properly or that we deserve forgiveness. Consider asking a trusted friend or pastor, one who is wise and compassionate, to hear your specific confession. *See also* Spiritual Disciplines Index.

away because of them; how then can we live?" 11Say to them, As I live, says the Lord God, I have no pleasure in the death of the wicked, but that the wicked turn from their ways and live; turn back, turn back from your evil ways; for why will you die, O house of Israel? 12And you, mortal, say to your people, The righteousness of the righteous shall not save them when they transgress; and as for the wickedness of the wicked, it shall not make them stumble when they turn from their wickedness; and the righteous shall not be able to live by their righteousness *a* when they sin. 13Though I say to the righteous that they shall surely live, yet if they trust in their righteousness and commit iniquity, none of their righteous deeds shall be remembered; but in the iniquity that they have committed they shall die. 14Again, though I say to the wicked, "You shall surely die," yet if they turn from their sin and do what is lawful and right— 15if the wicked restore the pledge, give back what they have taken by robbery, and walk in the statutes of life, committing no iniquity—they shall surely live, they shall not die. 16None of the sins that they have committed shall be remembered against them; they have done what is lawful and right, they shall surely live.

17 Yet your people say, "The way of the Lord is not just," when it is their own way that is not just. 18When the righteous turn from their righteousness, and commit iniquity, they shall die for it. *b* 19And when the wicked turn from their wickedness, and do what is lawful and right, they shall live by it. *b* 20Yet you say, "The way of the Lord is not just." O house of Israel, I will judge all of you according to your ways!

The Fall of Jerusalem

21 In the twelfth year of our exile, in the tenth month, on the fifth day of the month,

someone who had escaped from Jerusalem came to me and said, "The city has fallen." 22Now the hand of the Lord had been upon me the evening before the fugitive came; but he had opened my mouth by the time the fugitive came to me in the morning; so my mouth was opened, and I was no longer unable to speak.

The Survivors in Judah

23 The word of the Lord came to me: 24Mortal, the inhabitants of these waste places in the land of Israel keep saying, "Abraham was only one man, yet he got possession of the land; but we are many; the land is surely given us to possess." 25Therefore say to them, Thus says the Lord God: You eat flesh with the blood, and lift up your eyes to your idols, and shed blood; shall you then possess the land? 26You depend on your swords, you commit abominations, and each of you defiles his neighbor's wife; shall you then possess the land? 27Say this to them, Thus says the Lord God: As I live, surely those who are in the waste places shall fall by the sword; and those who are in the open field I will give to the wild animals to be devoured; and those who are in strongholds and in caves shall die by pestilence. 28I will make the land a desolation and a waste, and its proud might shall come to an end; and the mountains of Israel shall be so desolate that no one will pass through. 29Then they shall know that I am the Lord, when I have made the land a desolation and a waste because of all their abominations that they have committed.

30 As for you, mortal, your people who talk together about you by the walls, and at the doors of the houses, say to one another, each to a neighbor, "Come and hear what the word is that comes from the Lord."

a Heb *by it*   *b* Heb *them*

33:22 *my mouth was opened.* Here, at 586 BC, we are at the hinge of the book of Ezekiel. News arrives in the exilic community that "the city has fallen" (v 21). With this news the prophet regains his ability to speak. The death of Jerusalem has been acknowledged. There is no more denial. The end has come. Now, out of the loss

and the silence and the numbness, Ezekiel speaks startling hope amid widespread despair. The tradition of holy city and Promised Land has been broken. Out of this broken tradition Ezekiel speaks of the possibility of new life with God.

31They come to you as people come, and they sit before you as my people, and they hear your words, but they will not obey them. For flattery is on their lips, but their heart is set on their gain. 32To them you are like a singer of love songs, *a* one who has a beautiful voice and plays well on an instrument; they hear what you say, but they will not do it. 33When this comes—and come it will!—then they shall know that a prophet has been among them.

Israel's False Shepherds

34 The word of the LORD came to me: 2Mortal, prophesy against the shepherds of Israel: prophesy, and say to them— to the shepherds: Thus says the Lord GOD: Ah, you shepherds of Israel who have been feeding yourselves! Should not shepherds feed the sheep? 3You eat the fat, you clothe yourselves with the wool, you slaughter the fatlings; but you do not feed the sheep. 4You have not strengthened the weak, you have not healed the sick, you have not bound up the injured, you have not brought back the strayed, you have not sought the lost, but with force and harshness you have ruled them. 5So they were scattered, because there was no shepherd; and scattered, they became food for all the wild animals. 6My sheep were scattered, they wandered over all the mountains and on every high hill; my sheep were scattered over all the face of the earth, with no one to search or seek for them.

7 Therefore, you shepherds, hear the word of the LORD: 8As I live, says the Lord GOD, because my sheep have become a prey, and my sheep have become food for all the wild animals, since there was no shepherd; and because my shepherds have not searched for my sheep, but the shepherds have fed themselves, and have not fed my sheep; 9therefore, you shepherds, hear the word of the LORD: 10Thus says the Lord GOD, I am against the shepherds; and I will demand my sheep at their hand, and put a stop to their feeding the sheep; no longer shall the shepherds feed themselves. I will rescue my sheep from their mouths, so that they may not be food for them.

God, the True Shepherd

11 For thus says the Lord GOD: I myself will search for my sheep, and will seek them out. 12As shepherds seek out their flocks when they are among their scattered sheep, so I will seek out my sheep. I will rescue them from all the places to which they have been scattered on a day of clouds and thick darkness. 13I will bring them out from the peoples and gather them from the countries, and will bring them into their own land; and I will feed them on the mountains of Israel, by the watercourses, and in all the inhabited parts of the land. 14I will feed them with good pasture, and the mountain heights of Israel shall be their pasture; there they shall lie down in good grazing land, and they shall feed on

a Cn: Heb *like a love song*

34:2–10 *prophesy against the shepherds of Israel.* The future of the People of God after the end of everything that they have ever known begins with prophetic critique of its leaders. The ancient world called its leadership elite the "shepherds" of the people. Ezekiel speaks against the leaders' irresponsibility. The flock of Israel has been scattered and left unprotected because of a massive failure in leadership. Disgraced kings Jehoiachin and Zedekiah have fleeced the flock of Israel. They have enjoyed the perks of power, but abandoned their obligations. They have not cared for the weak, the sick, the injured, the strayed, and the lost (v 4). So God now turns against the

leadership of the People of God (v 10).
34:11–22 *I myself will search for my sheep.* With the leadership of the People of God in disarray, God steps forward to take the lead (cf. Isa 40:11; Jer 31:10). God's response to the crisis of leadership takes two forms. God will find the lost sheep (cf. Luke 15:3–7) and will care for them faithfully (vv 12–16), bringing the flock to green pastures (cf. Ps 23). But God will also attend to injustices within the flock, protecting the vulnerable while disciplining the abusive (vv 17–22). This good shepherd is the pastor (lit., "shepherd") of the People of God, who provides and models pastoral care within the congregation of Israel.

rich pasture on the mountains of Israel. 15I myself will be the shepherd of my sheep, and I will make them lie down, says the Lord GOD. 16I will seek the lost, and I will bring back the strayed, and I will bind up the injured, and I will strengthen the weak, but the fat and the strong I will destroy. I will feed them with justice.

17 As for you, my flock, thus says the Lord GOD: I shall judge between sheep and sheep, between rams and goats: 18Is it not enough for you to feed on the good pasture, but you must tread down with your feet the rest of your pasture? When you drink of clear water, must you foul the rest with your feet? 19And must my sheep eat what you have trodden with your feet, and drink what you have fouled with your feet?

20 Therefore, thus says the Lord GOD to them: I myself will judge between the fat sheep and the lean sheep. 21Because you pushed with flank and shoulder, and butted at all the weak animals with your horns until you scattered them far and wide, 22I will save my flock, and they shall no longer be ravaged; and I will judge between sheep and sheep.

23 I will set up over them one shepherd, my servant David, and he shall feed them: he shall feed them and be their shepherd. 24And I, the LORD, will be their God, and my servant David shall be prince among them; I, the LORD, have spoken.

25 I will make with them a covenant of peace and banish wild animals from the land, so that they may live in the wild and sleep in the woods securely. 26I will make them and the region around my hill a blessing; and I will send down the showers in their season; they shall be showers of blessing. 27The trees of the field shall yield their fruit, and the earth shall yield its increase. They shall be secure on their soil; and they shall know that I am the LORD, when I break the bars of their yoke, and save them from the hands of those who enslaved them. 28They shall no more be plunder for the nations, nor shall the animals of the land devour them; they shall live in safety, and no one shall make them afraid. 29I will provide for them a splendid vegetation so that they shall no more be consumed with hunger in the land, and no longer suffer the insults of the nations. 30They shall know that I, the LORD their God, am with them, and that they, the house of Israel, are my people, says the Lord GOD. 31You are my sheep, the sheep of my pasture a and I am your God, says the Lord GOD.

Judgment on Mount Seir

35 The word of the LORD came to me: 2Mortal, set your face against Mount Seir, and prophesy against it, 3and say to it, Thus says the Lord GOD:

I am against you, Mount Seir;
I stretch out my hand against you
to make you a desolation and a waste.

a Gk OL: Heb *pasture, you are people*

34:18 *is it not enough for you?* Within the flock of God there is constant jockeying for position. The strongest take the best pasture and, in the process, do not care for the land or its water. Even within the People of God there is injustice that must be stopped and relationships that must be set right. Pastoral care includes seeing that justice is done.

34:23 *I will set up over them one shepherd.* The People of God will no longer have divided loyalties between the two kingdoms, Ephraim in the north and Judah in the south. There will be one ruler, another David, who will feed a united flock. The Church glimpses here a sign of the promised good shepherd that it meets in Jesus, offspring of the line of David (John 10:11–18).

34:25–31 *a covenant of peace.* The exilic community has been showered with trouble, making it vulnerable and afraid. Now it hears an extraordinary promise of security (vv 25, 27), showers of blessing (v 26), and safe sanctuary (v 28). The text moves from a description ("They shall know that I, the LORD their God, am with them," v 30) to a direct promise ("You are my sheep, the sheep of my pasture and I am your God," v 31). The scattered people now hear the voice of God as a flock hears its shepherd. Turning in response, they are called back into life with God in obedience and gratitude.

4 I lay your towns in ruins;
    you shall become a desolation,
    and you shall know that I am the
    LORD.

5Because you cherished an ancient enmity, and gave over the people of Israel to the power of the sword at the time of their calamity, at the time of their final punishment; 6therefore, as I live, says the Lord GOD, I will prepare you for blood, and blood shall pursue you; since you did not hate bloodshed, bloodshed shall pursue you. 7I will make Mount Seir a waste and a desolation; and I will cut off from it all who come and go. 8I will fill its mountains with the slain; on your hills and in your valleys and in all your watercourses those killed with the sword shall fall. 9I will make you a perpetual desolation, and your cities shall never be inhabited. Then you shall know that I am the LORD.

10 Because you said, "These two nations and these two countries shall be mine, and we will take possession of them,"—although the LORD was there— 11therefore, as I live, says the Lord GOD, I will deal with you according to the anger and envy that you showed because of your hatred against them; and I will make myself known among you,*a* when I judge you. 12You shall know that I, the LORD, have heard all the abusive speech that you uttered against the mountains of Israel, saying, "They are laid desolate, they are given us to devour." 13And you magnified yourselves against me with your mouth, and multiplied your words against me; I heard it. 14Thus says the Lord GOD: As the whole earth rejoices, I will make you desolate. 15As you rejoiced over the inheritance of the house of Israel, because it was desolate, so I will deal with you; you shall be desolate, Mount Seir, and all Edom, all of it. Then they shall know that I am the LORD.

Blessing on Israel

36 And you, mortal, prophesy to the mountains of Israel, and say: O mountains of Israel, hear the word of the LORD. 2Thus says the Lord GOD: Because the enemy said of you, "Aha!" and, "The ancient heights have become our possession," 3therefore prophesy, and say: Thus says the Lord GOD: Because they made you desolate indeed, and crushed you from all sides, so that you became the possession of the rest of the nations, and you became an object of gossip and slander among the people; 4therefore, O mountains of Israel, hear the word of the Lord GOD: Thus says the Lord GOD to the mountains and the hills, the watercourses and the valleys, the desolate wastes and the deserted towns, which have become a source of plunder and an object of derision to the rest of the nations all around; 5therefore thus says the Lord GOD: I am speaking in my hot jealousy against the rest of the nations, and against all Edom, who, with wholehearted joy and utter contempt, took my land as their possession, because of its pasture, to plunder it. 6Therefore prophesy concerning the land of Israel, and say to the mountains and hills, to the watercourses and valleys, Thus says the Lord GOD: I am speaking in my jealous wrath, because you have suffered the insults of the nations; 7therefore thus says the Lord GOD: I swear that the nations that are all around you shall themselves suffer insults.

8 But you, O mountains of Israel, shall shoot out your branches, and yield your fruit to my people Israel; for they shall soon come home. 9See now, I am for you; I will turn to you, and you shall be tilled and sown; 10and I will multiply your population, the whole house of Israel, all of it; the towns shall be inhabited and the waste places rebuilt; 11and I will multiply human beings and animals upon you. They shall increase and be fruitful; and I will cause you to be inhabited as in your former times, and will do more good to you than ever before. Then you shall know that I

a Gk: Heb *them*

36:1–15 *prophesy to the mountains of Israel.* Ezekiel is commanded to prophesy to the mountains of Israel, because the surrounding nations have made the land into occupied territory. God's reputation among the nations is at stake. So the soil is promised fertility, habitation, and safety (vv 8–12). The land will no longer be subject to insults and disgrace, nor will it cause the people to suffer awful grief (vv 14–15).

am the LORD. 12I will lead people upon you—
my people Israel—and they shall possess you,
and you shall be their inheritance. No longer
shall you bereave them of children.

13 Thus says the Lord GOD: Because they
say to you, "You devour people, and you bereave your nation of children," 14therefore
you shall no longer devour people and no
longer bereave your nation of children, says
the Lord GOD; 15and no longer will I let you
hear the insults of the nations, no longer
shall you bear the disgrace of the peoples;
and no longer shall you cause your nation
to stumble, says the Lord GOD.

The Renewal of Israel

16 The word of the LORD came to me:
17Mortal, when the house of Israel lived on
their own soil, they defiled it with their ways
and their deeds; their conduct in my sight
was like the uncleanness of a woman in her
menstrual period. 18So I poured out my wrath
upon them for the blood that they had shed
upon the land, and for the idols with which
they had defiled it. 19I scattered them among
the nations, and they were dispersed through
the countries; in accordance with their conduct and their deeds I judged them. 20But
when they came to the nations, wherever
they came, they profaned my holy name, in
that it was said of them, "These are the peo-

ple of the LORD, and yet they had to go out of
his land." 21But I had concern for my holy
name, which the house of Israel had profaned among the nations to which they
came.

22 Therefore say to the house of Israel,
Thus says the Lord GOD: It is not for your
sake, O house of Israel, that I am about to
act, but for the sake of my holy name, which
you have profaned among the nations to
which you came. 23I will sanctify my great
name, which has been profaned among the
nations, and which you have profaned
among them; and the nations shall know
that I am the LORD, says the Lord GOD, when
through you I display my holiness before
their eyes. 24I will take you from the nations,
and gather you from all the countries, and
bring you into your own land. 25I will sprinkle clean water upon you, and you shall be
clean from all your uncleannesses, and from
all your idols I will cleanse you. 26A new
heart I will give you, and a new spirit I will
put within you; and I will remove from your
body the heart of stone and give you a heart
of flesh. 27I will put my spirit within you,
and make you follow my statutes and be
careful to observe my ordinances. 28Then
you shall live in the land that I gave to your
ancestors; and you shall be my people, and
I will be your God. 29I will save you from all

36:22–32 *for the sake of my holy name.*
Ezekiel outlines the surprising ground of Israel's
hope. This hope centers on the promises of
what God is about to do (vv 24–30). God will
take the people home and will give them a new
heart and a new spirit for obedience (v 26). The
intimate relation of life with God will be restored (v 28). Creation itself will be renewed
(vv 29–30). But this promise is not the result of
any substantive change or massive change in
the people. They have "profaned" God's name
in the world (vv 20–23). They have cheapened
and trivialized God by the way they have lived,
by their "evil ways" and "abominable deeds,"
their bloodshed and idolatry (vv 17–18, 31). God
intends new life, but the people have played no
part in making this possible. God's capacity to
love this rebellious people is exhausted. Israel's
long history of bad behavior has pushed God

beyond all limits of compassion. What now?
Now God acts not for their sake, but for the
sake of his "holy name" (v 22; see also 20:9).
God will bring the people home for the sake
of maintaining God's good name among the
nations. The ground of Israel's hope is the by-
product of God's desire to be holy, of God's
need to be God. God saves the people not out
of deep affection or devotion, but out of concern for his own reputation. It was tempting for
the exiles to believe that they would return
home because they were the righteous remnant
of an otherwise unrighteous people. They might
have assumed that God was obligated to restore
the Temple and the royal dynasty because of
their righteousness. But Ezekiel announces that
God is under no obligation to bring the people
home. Their homecoming is to be an inexplicable gift, the result of God's holiness.

your uncleannesses, and I will summon the grain and make it abundant and lay no famine upon you. 30I will make the fruit of the tree and the produce of the field abundant, so that you may never again suffer the disgrace of famine among the nations. 31Then you shall remember your evil ways, and your dealings that were not good; and you shall loathe yourselves for your iniquities and your abominable deeds. 32It is not for your sake that I will act, says the Lord GOD; let that be known to you. Be ashamed and dismayed for your ways, O house of Israel.

33 Thus says the Lord GOD: On the day that I cleanse you from all your iniquities, I will cause the towns to be inhabited, and the waste places shall be rebuilt. 34The land that was desolate shall be tilled, instead of being the desolation that it was in the sight of all who passed by. 35And they will say, "This land that was desolate has become like the garden of Eden; and the waste and desolate and ruined towns are now inhabited and fortified." 36Then the nations that are left all around you shall know that I, the LORD, have rebuilt the ruined places, and replanted that which was desolate; I, the LORD, have spoken, and I will do it.

37 Thus says the Lord GOD: I will also let the house of Israel ask me to do this for them: to increase their population like a flock. 38Like the flock for sacrifices,*a* like the flock at Jerusalem during her appointed festivals, so shall the ruined towns be filled with flocks of people. Then they shall know that I am the LORD.

The Valley of Dry Bones

37 The hand of the LORD came upon me, and he brought me out by the spirit of the LORD and set me down in the middle of a valley; it was full of bones. 2He led me all around them; there were very many lying in the valley, and they were very dry. 3He said to me, "Mortal, can these bones live?" I answered, "O Lord GOD, you know." 4Then he said to me, "Prophesy to these bones, and say to them: O dry bones, hear the word of the LORD. 5Thus says the Lord GOD to these bones: I will cause breath*b* to enter you, and you shall live. 6I will lay sinews on you, and will cause flesh to come upon you, and cover you with skin, and put breath*b* in you, and you shall live; and you shall know that I am the LORD."

7 So I prophesied as I had been commanded; and as I prophesied, suddenly there was a noise, a rattling, and the bones came together, bone to its bone. 8I looked, and there were sinews on them, and flesh had come upon them, and skin had covered them; but there was no breath in them. 9Then he said to me, "Prophesy to the breath, prophesy, mortal, and say to the breath:*c* Thus says the Lord GOD: Come from the four winds, O breath,*c* and breathe upon these slain, that they may live." 10I prophesied as he commanded me, and the breath came into them, and they lived, and stood on their feet, a vast multitude.

11 Then he said to me, "Mortal, these bones are the whole house of Israel. They say,

a Heb *flock of holy things*   *b* Or *spirit*
c Or *wind* or *spirit*

37:1–10 *it was full of bones.* Ezekiel is set down in a valley of skeletal remains, a cruel reminder of the horrific scenes of corpses that the exiles witnessed before their departure from Israel. He is told to speak a daring new word of God to the bones. The speech of the prophet is unexpected, a sign of the freedom of God to act in unpredictable ways. The bones come to life in two stages. First they are fleshed out and only then are they given *ruah* (Hebrew meaning "breath," "wind," or "spirit"). Initially Ezekiel prophesies to the bones, telling them of God's

intention to restore them to life. Upon hearing the sounds and seeing the signs of God's promised revival (vv 7–8), Ezekiel preaches to the Spirit/breath/wind, calling it to enter the waiting lifeless bodies (v 10). The bones do nothing to restore themselves to life. They are the recipients of a future they cannot possibly produce. To share this spiritual journey with God is to discover that life on the other side of death and despair is inevitably a response of abiding gratitude to the One who makes life with God possible again.

'Our bones are dried up, and our hope is lost; we are cut off completely.' [12]Therefore prophesy, and say to them, Thus says the Lord GOD: I am going to open your graves, and bring you up from your graves, O my people; and I will bring you back to the land of Israel. [13]And you shall know that I am the LORD, when I open your graves, and bring you up from your graves, O my people. [14]I will put my spirit within you, and you shall live, and I will place you on your own soil; then you shall know that I, the LORD, have spoken and will act, says the LORD."

The Two Sticks

15 The word of the LORD came to me: [16]Mortal, take a stick and write on it, "For Judah, and the Israelites associated with it"; then take another stick and write on it, "For Joseph (the stick of Ephraim) and all the house of Israel associated with it"; [17]and join them together into one stick, so that they may become one in your hand. [18]And when your people say to you, "Will you not show us what you mean by these?" [19]say to them, Thus says the Lord GOD: I am about to take the stick of Joseph (which is in the hand of Ephraim) and the tribes of Israel associated with it; and I will put the stick of Judah upon it,[a] and make them one stick, in order that they may be one in my hand. [20]When the sticks on which you write are in your hand before their eyes, [21]then say to them, Thus says the Lord GOD: I will take the people of Israel from the nations among which they have gone, and will gather them from every quarter, and bring them to their own land. [22]I will make them one nation in the land, on the mountains of Israel; and one king shall be king over them all. Never again shall they be two nations, and never again shall they be divided into two kingdoms. [23]They shall never again defile themselves with their idols and their detestable things, or with any of their transgressions. I will save them from all the apostasies into which they have fallen,[b] and will cleanse them. Then they shall be my people, and I will be their God.

24 My servant David shall be king over them; and they shall all have one shepherd. They shall follow my ordinances and be careful to observe my statutes. [25]They shall live in the land that I gave to my servant Jacob, in which your ancestors lived; they and their children and their children's children shall live there forever; and my servant David shall be their prince forever. [26]I will make a covenant of peace with them; it shall be an ever-

a Heb *I will put them upon it*   *b* Another reading is *from all the settlements in which they have sinned*

37:11–14 *we are cut off completely.* Now Ezekiel is given an interpretation of the vision. The exiles are in despair (lit., "without spirit"). They can see no future. Ezekiel is instructed to preach to a dead community. There is no life in it. Note that the prophet's sermon is not filled with techniques for improvement or strategies for growth. He announces that God is going to revive the people by putting flesh back on the dry bones of their life together and by inspiring them with the Spirit (cf. Gen 2:7). They will emerge from the grave of their captivity and live again in freedom. This revival of the people will be God's doing alone; it will not be fashioned by Ezekiel's powerful preaching or by any other human endeavor. Then the people will know that it is the Lord who speaks and acts (v 14). This is a spiritual transformation of the People of God. It is divinely inspired personal rebirth and social renewal of life with God. Christian readers of this text notice here the fingerprints of the God whose Spirit breathes amazing vitality into the People of God at the birth of the Church on Pentecost (Acts 2:1–21). This vision of the valley of dry bones and their return to life by the power of God has resonated repeatedly throughout the history of the People of God. How often have we felt the desolation and are thrown upon the resources of God for life to come?

37:16–23 *become one in your hand.* The Southern Kingdom, Judah, has a Northern sibling—Ephraim—sent into exile a century and a half before Jerusalem's devastation. The two have been perennial rivals, unable to live in harmony. Now Ezekiel enacts a sign of their impending reunion, never again to be divided. The People of God habitually split into rival camps, unwilling and unable to live as one. But Ezekiel points ahead to the promise of a reconciled life with God.

lasting covenant with them; and I will bless[a] them and multiply them, and will set my sanctuary among them forevermore. 27My dwelling place shall be with them; and I will be their God, and they shall be my people. 28Then the nations shall know that I the LORD sanctify Israel, when my sanctuary is among them forevermore.

Invasion by Gog

38 The word of the LORD came to me: 2Mortal, set your face toward Gog, of the land of Magog, the chief prince of Meshech and Tubal. Prophesy against him 3and say: Thus says the Lord GOD: I am against you, O Gog, chief prince of Meshech and Tubal; 4I will turn you around and put hooks into your jaws, and I will lead you out with all your army, horses and horsemen, all of them clothed in full armor, a great company, all of them with shield and buckler, wielding swords. 5Persia, Ethiopia,[b] and Put are with them, all of them with buckler and helmet; 6Gomer and all its troops; Beth-togarmah from the remotest parts of the north with all its troops—many peoples are with you.

7 Be ready and keep ready, you and all the companies that are assembled around you, and hold yourselves in reserve for them. 8After many days you shall be mustered; in the latter years you shall go against a land restored from war, a land where people were gathered

from many nations on the mountains of Israel, which had long lain waste; its people were brought out from the nations and now are living in safety, all of them. 9You shall advance, coming on like a storm; you shall be like a cloud covering the land, you and all your troops, and many peoples with you.

10 Thus says the Lord GOD: On that day thoughts will come into your mind, and you will devise an evil scheme. 11You will say, "I will go up against the land of unwalled villages; I will fall upon the quiet people who live in safety, all of them living without walls, and having no bars or gates"; 12to seize spoil and carry off plunder; to assail the waste places that are now inhabited, and the people who were gathered from the nations, who are acquiring cattle and goods, who live at the center[c] of the earth. 13Sheba and Dedan and the merchants of Tarshish and all its young warriors[d] will say to you, "Have you come to seize spoil? Have you assembled your horde to carry off plunder, to carry away silver and gold, to take away cattle and goods, to seize a great amount of booty?"

14 Therefore, mortal, prophesy, and say to Gog: Thus says the Lord GOD: On that day when my people Israel are living securely, you will rouse yourself[e] 15and come from your

---

a Tg: Heb give   b Or Nubia; Heb Cush
c Heb navel   d Heb young lions   e Gk: Heb will you not know?

37:24–28 *a covenant of peace.* God will sign a peace treaty with Israel. The people will live rightly. The king will be a faithful shepherd. God will once again dwell in the sanctuary. Ezekiel envisions God's will done, God's kingdom come. He glimpses a future transformation that is rooted in the purposes of God, not in the available evidence. The people are free to choose where to place their trust—in the despair of the available evidence or in the daring intentions of God.

Responding
37:27–28 THE WITH-GOD LIFE. The dwelling place of God, the Temple, was understandably a central preoccupation of the exiled people of Israel. How is God with us today? Are our church buildings his sanctuary? *See also* Spiritual Disciplines Index.

38:1–39:29 *Gog, of the land of Magog.* In chapters 38–39 Ezekiel is given a vision of a cataclysmic battle in the distant future between God and dark, powerful forces from the north led by a monstrous creature named Gog. God's triumph in the apocalyptic confrontation (38:19–23) will reveal once and for all God's holiness and covenant loyalty to Israel. The exiles live under the thumb of a great empire. They are traumatized by the horror that they have been through. Dark forces out of the north have ravaged their country and their homes. They are living a nightmare. Ezekiel's prophecy of God's eventual triumph over Gog, so that the people can live safely and securely, is a poem of faith. It roots the People of God in expectancy, not fear, as the way forward into life with God.

MY HOLY NAME
KNOWN +
No DEFILE

place out of the remotest parts of the north, you and many peoples with you, all of them riding on horses, a great horde, a mighty army; [16]you will come up against my people Israel, like a cloud covering the earth. In the latter days I will bring you against my land, so that the nations may know me, when through you, O Gog, I display my holiness before their eyes.

Judgment on Gog

17 Thus says the Lord GOD: Are you he of whom I spoke in former days by my servants the prophets of Israel, who in those days prophesied for years that I would bring you against them? [18]On that day, when Gog comes against the land of Israel, says the Lord GOD, my wrath shall be aroused. [19]For in my jealousy and in my blazing wrath I declare: On that day there shall be a great shaking in the land of Israel; [20]the fish of the sea, and the birds of the air, and the animals of the field, and all creeping things that creep on the ground, and all human beings that are on the face of the earth, shall quake at my presence, and the mountains shall be thrown down, and the cliffs shall fall, and every wall shall tumble to the ground. [21]I will summon the sword against Gog[a] in[b] all my mountains, says the Lord GOD; the swords of all will be against their comrades. [22]With pestilence and bloodshed I will enter into judgment with him; and I will pour down torrential rains and hailstones, fire and sulfur, upon him and his troops and the many peoples that are with him. [23]So I will display my greatness and my holiness and make myself known in the eyes of many nations. Then they shall know that I am the LORD.

Gog's Armies Destroyed

39 And you, mortal, prophesy against Gog, and say: Thus says the Lord GOD: I am against you, O Gog, chief prince of Meshech and Tubal! [2]I will turn you around and drive you forward, and bring you up from the remotest parts of the north, and lead you against the mountains of Israel. [3]I will strike your bow from your left hand, and will make your arrows drop out of your right hand. [4]You shall fall on the mountains of Israel, you and all your troops and the peoples that are with

you; I will give you to birds of prey of every kind and to the wild animals to be devoured. [5]You shall fall in the open field; for I have spoken, says the Lord GOD. [6]I will send fire on Magog and on those who live securely in the coastlands; and they shall know that I am the LORD.

7 My holy name I will make known among my people Israel; and I will not let my holy name be profaned any more; and the nations shall know that I am the LORD, the Holy One in Israel. [8]It has come! It has happened, says the Lord GOD. This is the day of which I have spoken.

9 Then those who live in the towns of Israel will go out and make fires of the weapons and burn them—bucklers and shields, bows and arrows, handpikes and spears—and they will make fires of them for seven years. [10]They will not need to take wood out of the field or cut down any trees in the forests, for they will make their fires of the weapons; they will despoil those who despoiled them, and plunder those who plundered them, says the Lord GOD.

The Burial of Gog

11 On that day I will give to Gog a place for burial in Israel, the Valley of the Travelers[c] east of the sea; it shall block the path of the travelers, for there Gog and all his horde will be buried; it shall be called the Valley of Hamon-gog. [d] [12]Seven months the house of Israel shall spend burying them, in order to cleanse the land. [13]All the people of the land shall bury them; and it will bring them honor on the day that I show my glory, says the Lord GOD. [14]They will set apart men to pass through the land regularly and bury any invaders[e] who remain on the face of the land, so as to cleanse it; for seven months they shall make their search. [15]As the searchers[e] pass through the land, anyone who sees a human bone shall set up a sign by it, until the buriers have buried it in the Valley of Hamon-gog. [d] [16](A city Hamonah[f] is there also.) Thus they shall cleanse the land.

17 As for you, mortal, thus says the Lord

a Heb him   b Heb to or for   c Or of the Abarim
d That is, the Horde of Gog   e Heb travelers
f That is The Horde

GOD: Speak to the birds of every kind and to all the wild animals: Assemble and come, gather from all around to the sacrificial feast that I am preparing for you, a great sacrificial feast on the mountains of Israel, and you shall eat flesh and drink blood. 18 You shall eat the flesh of the mighty, and drink the blood of the princes of the earth—of rams, of lambs, and of goats, of bulls, all of them fatlings of Bashan. 19 You shall eat fat until you are filled, and drink blood until you are drunk, at the sacrificial feast that I am preparing for you. 20 And you shall be filled at my table with horses and charioteers, a with warriors and all kinds of soldiers, says the Lord GOD.

Israel Restored to the Land

21 I will display my glory among the nations; and all the nations shall see my judgment that I have executed, and my hand that I have laid on them. 22 The house of Israel shall know that I am the LORD their God, from that day forward. 23 And the nations shall know that the house of Israel went into captivity for their iniquity, because they dealt treacherously with me. So I hid my face from them and gave them into the hand of their adversaries, and they all fell by the sword. 24 I dealt with them according to their uncleanness and their transgressions, and hid my face from them.

25 Therefore thus says the Lord GOD: Now I will restore the fortunes of Jacob, and have mercy on the whole house of Israel; and I will be jealous for my holy name. 26 They shall forget b their shame, and all the treachery they have practiced against me, when they live securely in their land with no one to make them afraid, 27 when I have brought

them back from the peoples and gathered them from their enemies' lands, and through them have displayed my holiness in the sight of many nations. 28 Then they shall know that I am the LORD their God because I sent them into exile among the nations, and then gathered them into their own land. I will leave none of them behind; 29 and I will never again hide my face from them, when I pour out my spirit upon the house of Israel, says the Lord GOD.

The Vision of the New Temple

40 In the twenty-fifth year of our exile, at the beginning of the year, on the tenth day of the month, in the fourteenth year after the city was struck down, on that very day, the hand of the LORD was upon me, and he brought me there. 2 He brought me, in visions of God, to the land of Israel, and set me down upon a very high mountain, on which was a structure like a city to the south. 3 When he brought me there, a man was there, whose appearance shone like bronze, with a linen cord and a measuring reed in his hand; and he was standing in the gateway. 4 The man said to me, "Mortal, look closely and listen attentively, and set your mind upon all that I shall show you, for you were brought here in order that I might show it to you; declare all that you see to the house of Israel."

5 Now there was a wall all around the outside of the temple area. The length of the measuring reed in the man's hand was six long cubits, each being a cubit and a handbreadth in length; so he measured the thick-

---

a Heb chariots   b Another reading is They shall bear

40:1–42:20 *he brought me there.* Twenty-five years into the long exile, Ezekiel has a vision that takes him to a renewed holy city in which everything is perfectly ordered. The society, the priesthood, and the Temple are no longer marked by rebellion and abomination. The lengthy and careful description of the Temple provided here reflects Ezekiel's vision of a people who take great care with the holy in their midst. The Temple is the location where the common and holy meet. This meeting must be managed with

great care. Worship that encounters the holy is full of risk. Yet God's holiness is also the source of Israel's past, present, and future. Everything relies upon God and upon sustaining the elemental encounter between God and the people. The sanctuary must be a safe space for God to be with the people. Ezekiel sees that if the Temple is made a sanctuary for a living relationship between God and the people, then worship as a communal Spiritual Discipline will be rekindled with vitality in the days to come.

ness of the wall, one reed; and the height, one reed. 6Then he went into the gateway facing east, going up its steps, and measured the threshold of the gate, one reed deep. *a* There were 7recesses, and each recess was one reed wide and one reed deep; and the space between the recesses, five cubits; and the threshold of the gate by the vestibule of the gate at the inner end was one reed deep. 8Then he measured the inner vestibule of the gateway, one cubit. 9Then he measured the vestibule of the gateway, eight cubits; and its pilasters, two cubits; and the vestibule of the gate was at the inner end. 10There were three recesses on either side of the east gate; the three were of the same size; and the pilasters on either side were of the same size. 11Then he measured the width of the opening of the gateway, ten cubits; and the width of the gateway, thirteen cubits. 12There was a barrier before the recesses, one cubit on either side; and the recesses were six cubits on either side. 13Then he measured the gate from the back*b* of the one recess to the back*b* of the other, a width of twenty-five cubits, from wall to wall. *c* 14He measured*d* also the vestibule, twenty cubits; and the gate next to the pilaster on every side of the court. *e* 15From the front of the gate at the entrance to the end of the inner vestibule of the gate was fifty cubits. 16The recesses and their pilasters had windows, with shutters*e* on the inside of the gateway all around, and the vestibules also had windows on the inside all around; and on the pilasters were palm trees.

17 Then he brought me into the outer court; there were chambers there, and a pavement, all around the court; thirty chambers fronted on the pavement. 18The pavement ran along the side of the gates, corresponding to the length of the gates; this was the lower pavement. 19Then he measured the distance from the inner front of*f* the lower gate to the outer front of the inner court, one hundred cubits.*g*

20 Then he measured the gate of the outer court that faced north—its depth and width. 21Its recesses, three on either side, and its pilasters and its vestibule were of the same size as those of the first gate; its depth was fifty cubits, and its width twenty-five cubits. 22Its windows, its vestibule, and its palm trees were of the same size as those of the gate that faced toward the east. Seven steps led up to it; and its vestibule was on the inside. *h* 23Opposite the gate on the north, as on the east, was a gate to the inner court; he measured from gate to gate, one hundred cubits.

24 Then he led me toward the south, and there was a gate on the south; and he measured its pilasters and its vestibule; they had the same dimensions as the others. 25There were windows all around in it and in its vestibule, like the windows of the others; its depth was fifty cubits, and its width twenty-five cubits. 26There were seven steps leading up to it; its vestibule was on the inside. *h* It had palm trees on its pilasters, one on either side. 27There was a gate on the south of the inner court; and he measured from gate to gate toward the south, one hundred cubits.

28 Then he brought me to the inner court by the south gate, and he measured the south gate; it was of the same dimensions as the others. 29Its recesses, its pilasters, and its vestibule were of the same size as the others; and there were windows all around in it and in its vestibule; its depth was fifty cubits, and its width twenty-five cubits. 30There were vestibules all around, twenty-five cubits deep and five cubits wide. 31Its vestibule faced the outer court, and palm trees were on its pilasters, and its stairway had eight steps.

32 Then he brought me to the inner court on the east side, and he measured the gate; it was of the same size as the others. 33Its recesses, its pilasters, and its vestibule were of the same dimensions as the others; and there were windows all around in it and in its vestibule; its depth was fifty cubits, and its width twenty-five cubits. 34Its vestibule faced the outer court, and it had palm trees on its pilasters, on either side; and its stairway had eight steps.

35 Then he brought me to the north gate, and he measured it; it had the same dimen-

a Heb *deep, and one threshold, one reed deep*
b Gk: Heb *roof*   c Heb *opening facing opening*
d Heb *made*   e Meaning of Heb uncertain
f Compare Gk: Heb *from before*   g Heb adds *the east and the north*   h Gk: Heb *before them*

sions as the others. [36]Its recesses, its pilasters, and its vestibule were of the same size as the others;[a] and it had windows all around. Its depth was fifty cubits, and its width twenty-five cubits. [37]Its vestibule[b] faced the outer court, and it had palm trees on its pilasters, on either side; and its stairway had eight steps.

38 There was a chamber with its door in the vestibule of the gate,[c] where the burnt offering was to be washed. [39]And in the vestibule of the gate were two tables on either side, on which the burnt offering and the sin offering and the guilt offering were to be slaughtered. [40]On the outside of the vestibule[d] at the entrance of the north gate were two tables; and on the other side of the vestibule of the gate were two tables. [41]Four tables were on the inside, and four tables on the outside of the side of the gate, eight tables, on which the sacrifices were to be slaughtered. [42]There were also four tables of hewn stone for the burnt offering, a cubit and a half long, and one cubit and a half wide, and one cubit high, on which the instruments were to be laid with which the burnt offerings and the sacrifices were slaughtered. [43]There were pegs, one handbreadth long, fastened all around the inside. And on the tables the flesh of the offering was to be laid.

44 On the outside of the inner gateway there were chambers for the singers in the inner court, one[e] at the side of the north gate facing south, the other at the side of the east gate facing north. [45]He said to me, "This chamber that faces south is for the priests who have charge of the temple, [46]and the chamber that faces north is for the priests who have charge of the altar; these are the descendants of Zadok, who alone among the descendants of Levi may come near to the LORD to minister to him." [47]He measured the court, one hundred cubits deep, and one hundred cubits wide, a square; and the altar was in front of the temple.

The Temple

48 Then he brought me to the vestibule of the temple and measured the pilasters of the vestibule, five cubits on either side; and the width of the gate was fourteen cubits; and

the sidewalls of the gate were three cubits[f] on either side. [49]The depth of the vestibule was twenty cubits, and the width twelve[g] cubits; ten steps led up[h] to it; and there were pillars beside the pilasters on either side.

41 Then he brought me to the nave, and measured the pilasters; on each side six cubits was the width of the pilasters.[i] [2]The width of the entrance was ten cubits; and the sidewalls of the entrance were five cubits on either side. He measured the length of the nave, forty cubits, and its width, twenty cubits. [3]Then he went into the inner room and measured the pilasters of the entrance, two cubits; and the width of the entrance, six cubits; and the sidewalls[j] of the entrance, seven cubits. [4]He measured the depth of the room, twenty cubits, and its width, twenty cubits, beyond the nave. And he said to me, This is the most holy place.

5 Then he measured the wall of the temple, six cubits thick; and the width of the side chambers, four cubits, all around the temple. [6]The side chambers were in three stories, one over another, thirty in each story. There were offsets[k] all around the wall of the temple to serve as supports for the side chambers, so that they should not be supported by the wall of the temple. [7]The passageway[l] of the side chambers widened from story to story; for the structure was supplied with a stairway all around the temple. For this reason the structure became wider from story to story. One ascended from the bottom story to the uppermost story by way of the middle one. [8]I saw also that the temple had a raised platform all around; the foundations of the side chambers measured a full reed of six long cubits. [9]The thickness of the outer wall of the side chambers was five cubits; and the free space between the side chambers of the temple [10]and the chambers of the court

a One Ms: Compare verses 29 and 33: MT lacks *were of the same size as the others*   b Gk Vg Compare verses 26, 31, 34: Heb *pilasters*
c Cn: Heb *at the pilasters of the gates*   d Cn: Heb *to him who goes up*   e Heb lacks *one*   f Gk: Heb *and the width of the gate was three cubits*
g Gk: Heb *eleven*   h Gk: Heb *and by steps that went up*   i Compare Gk: Heb *tent*   j Gk: Heb *width*   k Gk Compare 1 Kings 6.6: Heb *they entered*   l Cn: Heb *it was surrounded*

was a width of twenty cubits all around the temple on every side. [11]The side chambers opened onto the area left free, one door toward the north, and another door toward the south; and the width of the part that was left free was five cubits all around.

12 The building that was facing the temple yard on the west side was seventy cubits wide; and the wall of the building was five cubits thick all around, and its depth ninety cubits.

13 Then he measured the temple, one hundred cubits deep; and the yard and the building with its walls, one hundred cubits deep; [14]also the width of the east front of the temple and the yard, one hundred cubits.

15 Then he measured the depth of the building facing the yard at the west, together with its galleries[a] on either side, one hundred cubits.

The nave of the temple and the inner room and the outer[b] vestibule [16]were paneled,[c] and, all around, all three had windows with recessed[d] frames. Facing the threshold the temple was paneled with wood all around, from the floor up to the windows (now the windows were covered), [17]to the space above the door, even to the inner room, and on the outside. And on all the walls all around in the inner room and the nave there was a pattern.[e] [18]It was formed of cherubim and palm trees, a palm tree between cherub and cherub. Each cherub had two faces: [19]a human face turned toward the palm tree on the one side, and the face of a young lion turned toward the palm tree on the other side. They were carved on the whole temple all around; [20]from the floor to the area above the door, cherubim and palm trees were carved on the wall.[f]

21 The doorposts of the nave were square. In front of the holy place was something resembling [22]an altar of wood, three cubits high, two cubits long, and two cubits wide;[g] its corners, its base,[h] and its walls were of wood. He said to me, "This is the table that stands before the LORD." [23]The nave and the holy place had each a double door. [24]The doors had two leaves apiece, two swinging leaves for each door. [25]On the doors of the nave were carved cherubim and palm trees,

such as were carved on the walls; and there was a canopy of wood in front of the vestibule outside. [26]And there were recessed windows and palm trees on either side, on the sidewalls of the vestibule.[i]

The Holy Chambers and the Outer Wall

42 Then he led me out into the outer court, toward the north, and he brought me to the chambers that were opposite the temple yard and opposite the building on the north. [2]The length of the building that was on the north side[j] was[k] one hundred cubits, and the width fifty cubits. [3]Across the twenty cubits that belonged to the inner court, and facing the pavement that belonged to the outer court, the chambers rose[l] gallery[m] by gallery[m] in three stories. [4]In front of the chambers was a passage on the inner side, ten cubits wide and one hundred cubits deep,[n] and its[o] entrances were on the north. [5]Now the upper chambers were narrower, for the galleries[m] took more away from them than from the lower and middle chambers in the building. [6]For they were in three stories, and they had no pillars like the pillars of the outer[p] court; for this reason the upper chambers were set back from the ground more than the lower and the middle ones. [7]There was a wall outside parallel to the chambers, toward the outer court, opposite the chambers, fifty cubits long. [8]For the chambers on the outer court were fifty cubits long, while those opposite the temple were one hundred cubits long. [9]At the foot of these chambers ran a passage that one entered from the east in order to enter them from the outer court. [10]The width of the passage[q] was fixed by the wall of the court.

On the south[r] also, opposite the vacant area and opposite the building, there were

a Cn: Meaning of Heb uncertain   b Gk: Heb of the court   c Gk: Heb the thresholds
d Cn Compare Gk 1 Kings 6.4: Meaning of Heb uncertain   e Heb measures   f Cn Compare verse 25: Heb and the wall   g Gk: Heb lacks two cubits wide   h Gk: Heb length   i Cn: Heb vestibule. And the side chambers of the temple and the canopies   j Gk: Heb door   k Gk: Heb before the length   l Heb lacks the chambers rose
m Meaning of Heb uncertain   n Gk Syr: Heb a way of one cubit   o Heb their   p Gk: Heb lacks outer   q Heb lacks of the passage   r Gk: Heb east

chambers [11] with a passage in front of them; they were similar to the chambers on the north, of the same length and width, with the same exits [a] and arrangements and doors. [12] So the entrances of the chambers to the south were entered through the entrance at the head of the corresponding passage, from the east, along the matching wall. [b]

13 Then he said to me, "The north chambers and the south chambers opposite the vacant area are the holy chambers, where the priests who approach the LORD shall eat the most holy offerings; there they shall deposit the most holy offerings—the grain offering, the sin offering, and the guilt offering—for the place is holy. [14] When the priests enter the holy place, they shall not go out of it into the outer court without laying there the vestments in which they minister, for these are holy; they shall put on other garments before they go near to the area open to the people."

15 When he had finished measuring the interior of the temple area, he led me out by the gate that faces east, and measured the temple area all around. [16] He measured the east side with the measuring reed, five hundred cubits by the measuring reed. [17] Then he turned and measured [c] the north side, five hundred cubits by the measuring reed. [18] Then he turned and measured [c] the south side, five hundred cubits by the measuring reed. [19] Then he turned to the west side and measured, five hundred cubits by the measuring reed. [20] He measured it on the four sides. It had a wall around it, five hundred cubits long and five hundred cubits wide, to make a separation between the holy and the common.

The Divine Glory Returns to the Temple

43 Then he brought me to the gate, the gate facing east. [2] And there, the glory of the God of Israel was coming from the east; the sound was like the sound of mighty waters; and the earth shone with his glory. [3] The [d] vision I saw was like the vision that I had seen when he came to destroy the city, and [e] like the vision that I had seen by the river Chebar; and I fell upon my face. [4] As the glory of the LORD entered the temple by the gate facing east, [5] the spirit lifted me up, and brought me into the inner court; and the glory of the LORD filled the temple.

6 While the man was standing beside me, I heard someone speaking to me out of the temple. [7] He said to me: Mortal, this is the place of my throne and the place for the soles of my feet, where I will reside among the people of Israel forever. The house of Israel shall no more defile my holy name, neither they nor their kings, by their whoring, and by the corpses of their kings at their death. [f][8] When they placed their threshold by my threshold and their doorposts beside my doorposts, with only a wall between me and them, they were defiling my holy name by their abominations that they committed; therefore I have consumed them in my anger. [9] Now let them put away their idolatry and the corpses of their kings far from me, and I will reside among them forever.

10 As for you, mortal, describe the temple to the house of Israel, and let them measure the pattern; and let them be ashamed of their iniquities. [11] When they are ashamed of all that they have done, make known to them the plan of the temple, its arrangement, its exits and its entrances, and its whole form—all its ordinances and its entire plan and all its

a Heb *and all their exits*   b Meaning of Heb uncertain   c Gk: Heb *measuring reed all around. He measured*   d Gk: Heb *Like the vision* e Syr: Heb *and the visions*   f Or *on their high places*

43:2–5 *the earth shone with his glory.* After careful preparation the Temple is perfectly ordered and ready for the return of God's glory (chap. 10). After a history of so much disorder and dislocation, this is a sight for sore eyes—human and divine. Ezekiel sees a blaze of glory and hears the thundering presence of the holy. As he did when he first saw the vision of the fire and of the wheels within wheels, he falls on his face (1:28). This is the long-awaited day of the Lord. It is the return of the presence of God among the People of God. This is Ezekiel's priestly version of the messianic hope. With Ezekiel, the inheritors of the New Testament share a deep longing for the return of the holy one (cf. Rev 22:20).

laws; and write it down in their sight, so that they may observe and follow the entire plan and all its ordinances. 12 This is the law of the temple: the whole territory on the top of the mountain all around shall be most holy. This is the law of the temple.

The Altar

13 These are the dimensions of the altar by cubits (the cubit being one cubit and a handbreadth): its base shall be one cubit high,[a] and one cubit wide, with a rim of one span around its edge. This shall be the height of the altar: 14 From the base on the ground to the lower ledge, two cubits, with a width of one cubit; and from the smaller ledge to the larger ledge, four cubits, with a width of one cubit; 15 and the altar hearth, four cubits; and from the altar hearth projecting upward, four horns. 16 The altar hearth shall be square, twelve cubits long by twelve wide. 17 The ledge also shall be square, fourteen cubits long by fourteen wide, with a rim around it half a cubit wide, and its surrounding base, one cubit. Its steps shall face east.

18 Then he said to me: Mortal, thus says the Lord GOD: These are the ordinances for the altar: On the day when it is erected for offering burnt offerings upon it and for dashing blood against it, 19 you shall give to the levitical priests of the family of Zadok, who draw near to me to minister to me, says the Lord GOD, a bull for a sin offering. 20 And you shall take some of its blood, and put it on the four horns of the altar, and on the four corners of the ledge, and upon the rim all around; thus you shall purify it and make atonement for it. 21 You shall also take the bull of the sin offering, and it shall be burnt in the appointed place belonging to the temple, outside the sacred area.

22 On the second day you shall offer a male goat without blemish for a sin offering; and the altar shall be purified, as it was purified with the bull. 23 When you have finished purifying it, you shall offer a bull without blemish and a ram from the flock without blemish. 24 You shall present them before the LORD, and the priests shall throw salt on them and offer them up as a burnt offering to the LORD. 25 For seven days you shall provide daily a goat for a sin offering; also a bull and a ram from the flock, without blemish, shall be provided. 26 Seven days shall they make atonement for the altar and cleanse it, and so consecrate it. 27 When these days are over, then from the eighth day onward the priests shall offer upon the altar your burnt offerings and your offerings of well-being; and I will accept you, says the Lord GOD.

The Closed Gate

44 Then he brought me back to the outer gate of the sanctuary, which faces east; and it was shut. 2 The LORD said to me: This gate shall remain shut; it shall not be opened, and no one shall enter by it; for the LORD, the God of Israel, has entered by it; therefore it shall remain shut. 3 Only the prince, because he is a prince, may sit in it to eat food before the LORD; he shall enter by way of the vestibule of the gate, and shall go out by the same way.

Admission to the Temple

4 Then he brought me by way of the north gate to the front of the temple; and I looked, and lo! the glory of the LORD filled the temple of the LORD; and I fell upon my face. 5 The LORD said to me: Mortal, mark well, look closely, and listen attentively to all that I shall tell you concerning all the ordinances of the temple of the LORD and all its laws; and mark well those who may be admitted to[b] the temple and all those who are to be excluded from the sanctuary. 6 Say to the rebellious house,[c]

a Gk: Heb lacks *high*   b Cn: Heb *the entrance of*
c Gk: Heb lacks *house*

44:4 *fell upon my face.* Ezekiel is overcome once more by the glory of the Lord. God's presence is now at home in the Temple, filling its sacred space. God's own entrance to the Temple has been sealed (v 2). It is reserved for God's use and is shut in expectation that there will never again be an exit of the glory of God from the Temple.

44:5—46:24 *the ordinances of the temple . . . and all its laws.* The vision now moves from the architecture of the Temple to the organization of the Temple and of the society—its ordinances

to the house of Israel, Thus says the Lord GOD: O house of Israel, let there be an end to all your abominations 7in admitting foreigners, uncircumcised in heart and flesh, to be in my sanctuary, profaning my temple when you offer to me my food, the fat and the blood. You*a* have broken my covenant with all your abominations. 8And you have not kept charge of my sacred offerings; but you have appointed foreigners*b* to act for you in keeping my charge in my sanctuary.

9 Thus says the Lord GOD: No foreigner, uncircumcised in heart and flesh, of all the foreigners who are among the people of Israel, shall enter my sanctuary. 10But the Levites who went far from me, going astray from me after their idols when Israel went astray, shall bear their punishment. 11They shall be ministers in my sanctuary, having oversight at the gates of the temple, and serving in the temple; they shall slaughter the burnt offering and the sacrifice for the people, and they shall attend on them and serve them. 12Because they ministered to them before their idols and made the house of Israel stumble into iniquity, therefore I have sworn concerning them, says the Lord GOD, that they shall bear their punishment. 13They shall not come near to me, to serve me as priest, nor come near any of my sacred offerings, the things that are most sacred; but they shall bear their shame, and the consequences of the abominations that they have committed. 14Yet I will appoint them to keep charge of the temple, to do all its chores, all that is to be done in it.

The Levitical Priests

15 But the levitical priests, the descendants of Zadok, who kept the charge of my sanctuary when the people of Israel went astray from me, shall come near to me to minister to me; and they shall attend me to offer me the fat and the blood, says the Lord GOD. 16It is they who shall enter my sanctuary, it is they who shall approach my table,

to minister to me, and they shall keep my charge. 17When they enter the gates of the inner court, they shall wear linen vestments; they shall have nothing of wool on them, while they minister at the gates of the inner court, and within. 18They shall have linen turbans on their heads, and linen undergarments on their loins; they shall not bind themselves with anything that causes sweat. 19When they go out into the outer court to the people, they shall remove the vestments in which they have been ministering, and lay them in the holy chambers; and they shall put on other garments, so that they may not communicate holiness to the people with their vestments. 20They shall not shave their heads or let their locks grow long; they shall only trim the hair of their heads. 21No priest shall drink wine when he enters the inner court. 22They shall not marry a widow, or a divorced woman, but only a virgin of the stock of the house of Israel, or a widow who is the widow of a priest. 23They shall teach my people the difference between the holy and the common, and show them how to distinguish between the unclean and the clean. 24In a controversy they shall act as judges, and they shall decide it according to my judgments. They shall keep my laws and my statutes regarding all my appointed festivals, and they shall keep my sabbaths holy. 25They shall not defile themselves by going near to a dead person; for father or mother, however, and for son or daughter, and for brother or unmarried sister they may defile themselves. 26After he has become clean, they shall count seven days for him. 27On the day that he goes into the holy place, into the inner court, to minister in the holy place, he shall offer his sin offering, says the Lord GOD.

28 This shall be their inheritance: I am their inheritance; and you shall give them no holding in Israel; I am their holding.

a Gk Syr Vg: Heb *They*   *b* Heb lacks *foreigners*

---

and laws that are intended to keep the holy free from contamination. The presence of the glory of God is nothing to trifle with. Ezekiel envisions the day when the People of God take great care to organize their life in order to host the awesome presence of the holy in their midst. This is a priestly vision of the kingdom of God.

29They shall eat the grain offering, the sin offering, and the guilt offering; and every devoted thing in Israel shall be theirs. 30The first of all the first fruits of all kinds, and every offering of all kinds from all your offerings, shall belong to the priests; you shall also give to the priests the first of your dough, in order that a blessing may rest on your house. 31The priests shall not eat of anything, whether bird or animal, that died of itself or was torn by animals.

The Holy District

45 When you allot the land as an inheritance, you shall set aside for the LORD a portion of the land as a holy district, twenty-five thousand cubits long and twenty*a* thousand cubits wide; it shall be holy throughout its entire extent. 2Of this, a square plot of five hundred by five hundred cubits shall be for the sanctuary, with fifty cubits for an open space around it. 3In the holy district you shall measure off a section twenty-five thousand cubits long and ten thousand wide, in which shall be the sanctuary, the most holy place. 4It shall be a holy portion of the land; it shall be for the priests, who minister in the sanctuary and approach the LORD to minister to him; and it shall be both a place for their houses and a holy place for the sanctuary. 5Another section, twenty-five thousand cubits long and ten thousand cubits wide, shall be for the Levites who minister at the temple, as their holding for cities to live in.*b*

6 Alongside the portion set apart as the holy district you shall assign as a holding for the city an area five thousand cubits wide, and twenty-five thousand cubits long; it shall belong to the whole house of Israel.

7 And to the prince shall belong the land on both sides of the holy district and the holding of the city, alongside the holy district and the holding of the city, on the west and on the east, corresponding in length to one of the tribal portions, and extending from the western to the eastern boundary 8of the land. It is to be his property in Israel. And my princes shall no longer oppress my people; but they shall let the house of Israel have the land according to their tribes.

9 Thus says the Lord GOD: Enough, O princes of Israel! Put away violence and oppression, and do what is just and right. Cease your evictions of my people, says the Lord GOD.

Weights and Measures

10 You shall have honest balances, an honest ephah, and an honest bath.*c* 11The ephah and the bath shall be of the same measure, the bath containing one-tenth of a homer, and the ephah one-tenth of a homer; the homer shall be the standard measure. 12The shekel shall be twenty gerahs. Twenty shekels, twenty-five shekels, and fifteen shekels shall make a mina for you.

Offerings

13 This is the offering that you shall make: one-sixth of an ephah from each homer of wheat, and one-sixth of an ephah from each homer of barley, 14and as the fixed portion of oil,*d* one-tenth of a bath from each cor (the cor,*e* like the homer, contains ten baths); 15and one sheep from every flock of two hundred, from the pastures of Israel. This is the offering for grain offerings, burnt offerings, and offerings of well-being, to make atonement for them, says the Lord GOD. 16All the people of the land shall join with the prince in Israel in making this offering. 17But this shall be the obligation of the prince regarding the burnt offerings, grain offerings, and drink offerings, at the festivals, the new moons, and the sabbaths, all the appointed

a Gk: Heb *ten*   *b* Gk: Heb *as their holding, twenty chambers*   *c* A Heb measure of volume   *d* Cn: Heb *oil, the bath the oil*   *e* Vg: Heb *homer*

45:13–17 *All the people . . . shall join . . . in making this offering.* The prophet sees a time when the People of God have recovered the Spiritual Discipline of offering precious gifts of food and sustenance to God, who sustains all of life. The carefully organized system of sacrifice envisioned here embeds this Spiritual Discipline deep within the mind and heart of the People of God, lest they forget who, and whose, they are.

festivals of the house of Israel: he shall provide the sin offerings, grain offerings, the burnt offerings, and the offerings of well-being, to make atonement for the house of Israel.

Festivals

18 Thus says the Lord GOD: In the first month, on the first day of the month, you shall take a young bull without blemish, and purify the sanctuary. 19The priest shall take some of the blood of the sin offering and put it on the doorposts of the temple, the four corners of the ledge of the altar, and the posts of the gate of the inner court. 20You shall do the same on the seventh day of the month for anyone who has sinned through error or ignorance; so you shall make atonement for the temple.

21 In the first month, on the fourteenth day of the month, you shall celebrate the festival of the passover, and for seven days unleavened bread shall be eaten. 22On that day the prince shall provide for himself and all the people of the land a young bull for a sin offering. 23And during the seven days of the festival he shall provide as a burnt offering to the LORD seven young bulls and seven rams without blemish, on each of the seven days; and a male goat daily for a sin offering. 24He shall provide as a grain offering an ephah for each bull, an ephah for each ram, and a hin of oil to each ephah. 25In the seventh month, on the fifteenth day of the month and for the seven days of the festival, he shall make the same provision for sin offerings, burnt offerings, and grain offerings, and for the oil.

Miscellaneous Regulations

46 Thus says the Lord GOD: The gate of the inner court that faces east shall remain closed on the six working days; but on the sabbath day it shall be opened and on the day of the new moon it shall be opened. 2The prince shall enter by the vestibule of the gate from outside, and shall take his stand by the post of the gate. The priests shall offer his burnt offering and his offerings of well-being, and he shall bow down at the threshold of the gate. Then he shall go out, but the gate shall not be closed until evening. 3The peo-

ple of the land shall bow down at the entrance of that gate before the LORD on the sabbaths and on the new moons. 4The burnt offering that the prince offers to the LORD on the sabbath day shall be six lambs without blemish and a ram without blemish; 5and the grain offering with the ram shall be an ephah, and the grain offering with the lambs shall be as much as he wishes to give, together with a hin of oil to each ephah. 6On the day of the new moon he shall offer a young bull without blemish, and six lambs and a ram, which shall be without blemish; 7as a grain offering he shall provide an ephah with the bull and an ephah with the ram, and with the lambs as much as he wishes, together with a hin of oil to each ephah. 8When the prince enters, he shall come in by the vestibule of the gate, and he shall go out by the same way.

9 When the people of the land come before the LORD at the appointed festivals, whoever enters by the north gate to worship shall go out by the south gate; and whoever enters by the south gate shall go out by the north gate: they shall not return by way of the gate by which they entered, but shall go out straight ahead. 10When they come in, the prince shall come in with them; and when they go out, he shall go out.

11 At the festivals and the appointed seasons the grain offering with a young bull shall be an ephah, and with a ram an ephah, and with the lambs as much as one wishes to give, together with a hin of oil to an ephah. 12When the prince provides a freewill offering, either a burnt offering or offerings of well-being as a freewill offering to the LORD, the gate facing east shall be opened for him; and he shall offer his burnt offering or his offerings of well-being as he does on the sabbath day. Then he shall go out, and after he has gone out the gate shall be closed.

13 He shall provide a lamb, a yearling, without blemish, for a burnt offering to the LORD daily; morning by morning he shall provide it. 14And he shall provide a grain offering with it morning by morning regularly, one-sixth of an ephah, and one-third of a hin of oil to moisten the choice flour, as a grain offering to the LORD; this is the ordi-

nance for all time. [15]Thus the lamb and the grain offering and the oil shall be provided, morning by morning, as a regular burnt offering.

16 Thus says the Lord GOD: If the prince makes a gift to any of his sons out of his inheritance,[a] it shall belong to his sons, it is their holding by inheritance. [17]But if he makes a gift out of his inheritance to one of his servants, it shall be his to the year of liberty; then it shall revert to the prince; only his sons may keep a gift from his inheritance. [18]The prince shall not take any of the inheritance of the people, thrusting them out of their holding; he shall give his sons their inheritance out of his own holding, so that none of my people shall be dispossessed of their holding.

19 Then he brought me through the entrance, which was at the side of the gate, to the north row of the holy chambers for the priests; and there I saw a place at the extreme western end of them. [20]He said to me, "This is the place where the priests shall boil the guilt offering and the sin offering, and where they shall bake the grain offering, in order not to bring them out into the outer court and so communicate holiness to the people."

21 Then he brought me out to the outer court, and led me past the four corners of the court; and in each corner of the court there was a court— [22]in the four corners of the court were small[b] courts, forty cubits long and thirty wide; the four were of the same size. [23]On the inside, around each of the four courts[c] was a row of masonry, with hearths made at the bottom of the rows all around.

[24]Then he said to me, "These are the kitchens where those who serve at the temple shall boil the sacrifices of the people."

Water Flowing from the Temple

47 Then he brought me back to the entrance of the temple; there, water was flowing from below the threshold of the temple toward the east (for the temple faced east); and the water was flowing down from below the south end of the threshold of the temple, south of the altar. [2]Then he brought me out by way of the north gate, and led me around on the outside to the outer gate that faces toward the east;[d] and the water was coming out on the south side.

3 Going on eastward with a cord in his hand, the man measured one thousand cubits, and then led me through the water; and it was ankle-deep. [4]Again he measured one thousand, and led me through the water; and it was knee-deep. Again he measured one thousand, and led me through the water; and it was up to the waist. [5]Again he measured one thousand, and it was a river that I could not cross, for the water had risen; it was deep enough to swim in, a river that could not be crossed. [6]He said to me, "Mortal, have you seen this?"

Then he led me back along the bank of the river. [7]As I came back, I saw on the bank of the river a great many trees on the one side and on the other. [8]He said to me, "This water flows toward the eastern region and goes

a Gk: Heb *it is his inheritance*   b Gk Syr Vg: Meaning of Heb uncertain   c Heb *the four of them*   d Meaning of Heb uncertain

---

47:1–12 *water was flowing from below . . . the temple.* The book of Ezekiel draws to a close with an extraordinary sight. In his vision the prophet sees water flowing from the Temple. The glory of God has returned to the Temple, but it is no longer restricted to the Temple precincts. It pours out in a great river of life that grows from a trickle into a stream and then into a river that cannot be crossed (v 5). The river swarms with fish and wildlife (v 9) and is surrounded by trees with fruit that is always ripe for the picking (v 12). Finally, the river flows into the Dead Sea and makes even that stagnant salted sea into a great freshwater lake (v 8). Because the Temple and the society are carefully constructed to host the glory of God, the People of God now see the effects of the presence of God's glory upon every living thing (cf. Rev 22:1–2). Ezekiel's priestly vision is a vision of ecological renewal. He sees that Israel's house of worship is to overflow with life and healing for all living things. Worship is for the adoration of God's holiness, not for the betterment of humankind. Yet the holiness of God pours out of worship, spreading life in the kingdom of God for the sake of God's name (see 36:22–32).

down into the Arabah; and when it enters the sea, the sea of stagnant waters, the water will become fresh. 9 Wherever the river goes, [a] every living creature that swarms will live, and there will be very many fish, once these waters reach there. It will become fresh; and everything will live where the river goes. 10 People will stand fishing beside the sea [b] from En-gedi to En-eglaim; it will be a place for the spreading of nets; its fish will be of a great many kinds, like the fish of the Great Sea. 11 But its swamps and marshes will not become fresh; they are to be left for salt. 12 On the banks, on both sides of the river, there will grow all kinds of trees for food. Their leaves will not wither nor their fruit fail, but they will bear fresh fruit every month, because the water for them flows from the sanctuary. Their fruit will be for food, and their leaves for healing."

The New Boundaries of the Land

13 Thus says the Lord GOD: These are the boundaries by which you shall divide the land for inheritance among the twelve tribes of Israel. Joseph shall have two portions. 14 You shall divide it equally; I swore to give it to your ancestors, and this land shall fall to you as your inheritance.

15 This shall be the boundary of the land: On the north side, from the Great Sea by way of Hethlon to Lebo-hamath, and on to Zedad, [c] 16 Berothah, Sibraim (which lies between the border of Damascus and the border of Hamath), as far as Hazer-hatticon, which is on the border of Hauran. 17 So the boundary shall run from the sea to Hazar-enon, which is north of the border of Damascus, with the border of Hamath to the north. [d] This shall be the north side.

18 On the east side, between Hauran and Damascus; along the Jordan between Gilead and the land of Israel; to the eastern sea and as far as Tamar. [e] This shall be the east side.

19 On the south side, it shall run from Tamar as far as the waters of Meribath-kadesh, from there along the Wadi of Egypt [f] to the Great Sea. This shall be the south side.

20 On the west side, the Great Sea shall be the boundary to a point opposite Lebo-hamath. This shall be the west side.

21 So you shall divide this land among you according to the tribes of Israel. 22 You shall allot it as an inheritance for yourselves and for the aliens who reside among you and have begotten children among you. They shall be to you as citizens of Israel; with you they shall be allotted an inheritance among the tribes of Israel. 23 In whatever tribe aliens reside, there you shall assign them their inheritance, says the Lord GOD.

The Tribal Portions

48 These are the names of the tribes: Beginning at the northern border, on the Hethlon road, [g] from Lebo-hamath, as far as Hazar-enon (which is on the border of Damascus, with Hamath to the north), and [h] extending from the east side to the west, [i] Dan, one portion. 2 Adjoining the territory of Dan, from the east side to the west, Asher, one portion. 3 Adjoining the territory of Asher, from the east side to the west, Naphtali, one portion. 4 Adjoining the territory of Naphtali, from the east side to the west, Manasseh, one portion. 5 Adjoining the territory of Manasseh, from the east side to the west, Ephraim, one portion. 6 Adjoining the territory of Ephraim, from the east side to the west, Reuben, one portion. 7 Adjoining the territory of Reuben, from the east side to the west, Judah, one portion.

8 Adjoining the territory of Judah, from

---

a Gk Syr Vg Tg: Heb *the two rivers go*   b Heb *it*
c Gk: Heb *Lebo-zedad,* 16 *Hamath*   d Meaning of
Heb uncertain   e Compare Syr: Heb *you shall
measure*   f Heb lacks *of Egypt*   g Compare
47.15: Heb *by the side of the way*   h Cn: Heb *and
they shall be his*   i Gk Compare verses 2-8: Heb
the east side the west

47:22–23 *the aliens . . . shall be to you as citizens.* Here the prophet notes that a restored People of God will offer radical hospitality to resident aliens. Not only are resident aliens to be protected (Lev 19:33–34) and given access to food (Deut 24:17–22), now they are accorded full legal citizenship in the tribes of Israel. To be with God in holiness is to be bound to neighbor and stranger in community. It is a word of reconciliation and unity. It is a word for us today.

the east side to the west, shall be the portion that you shall set apart, twenty-five thousand cubits in width, and in length equal to one of the tribal portions, from the east side to the west, with the sanctuary in the middle of it. 9The portion that you shall set apart for the LORD shall be twenty-five thousand cubits in length, and twenty[a] thousand in width. 10These shall be the allotments of the holy portion: the priests shall have an allotment measuring twenty-five thousand cubits on the northern side, ten thousand cubits in width on the western side, ten thousand in width on the eastern side, and twenty-five thousand in length on the southern side, with the sanctuary of the LORD in the middle of it. 11This shall be for the consecrated priests, the descendants[b] of Zadok, who kept my charge, who did not go astray when the people of Israel went astray, as the Levites did. 12It shall belong to them as a special portion from the holy portion of the land, a most holy place, adjoining the territory of the Levites. 13Alongside the territory of the priests, the Levites shall have an allotment twenty-five thousand cubits in length and ten thousand in width. The whole length shall be twenty-five thousand cubits and the width twenty[c] thousand. 14They shall not sell or exchange any of it; they shall not transfer this choice portion of the land, for it is holy to the LORD.

15 The remainder, five thousand cubits in width and twenty-five thousand in length, shall be for ordinary use for the city, for dwellings and for open country. In the middle of it shall be the city; 16and these shall be its dimensions: the north side four thousand five hundred cubits, the south side four thousand five hundred, the east side four thousand five hundred, and the west side four thousand five hundred. 17The city shall have open land: on the north two hundred fifty cubits, on the south two hundred fifty, on the east two hundred fifty, on the west two hundred fifty. 18The remainder of the length alongside the holy portion shall be ten thousand cubits to the east, and ten thousand to the west, and it shall be alongside the holy portion. Its produce shall be food for the workers of the city. 19The workers of the city, from all the tribes of Israel, shall cultivate it. 20The whole portion that you shall set apart shall be twenty-five thousand cubits square, that is, the holy portion together with the property of the city.

21 What remains on both sides of the holy portion and of the property of the city shall belong to the prince. Extending from the twenty-five thousand cubits of the holy portion to the east border, and westward from the twenty-five thousand cubits to the west border, parallel to the tribal portions, it shall belong to the prince. The holy portion with the sanctuary of the temple in the middle of it, 22and the property of the Levites and of the city, shall be in the middle of that which belongs to the prince. The portion of the prince shall lie between the territory of Judah and the territory of Benjamin.

23 As for the rest of the tribes: from the east side to the west, Benjamin, one portion. 24Adjoining the territory of Benjamin, from the east side to the west, Simeon, one portion. 25Adjoining the territory of Simeon, from the east side to the west, Issachar, one portion. 26Adjoining the territory of Issachar,

---

a Compare 45.1: Heb *ten*   b One Ms Gk: Heb *of the descendants*   c Gk: Heb *ten*

48:15–35 *In the middle of it shall be the city.* Nowhere in this final vision has Ezekiel named the city that he is describing. It is not Jerusalem reconstructed. It is a new sacred city, one with twelve gates, within a new and harmonious creation. The seer John will glimpse this city "coming down out of heaven from God" in a revelation of the end of time (Rev 21:2). The conclusion of the book of Ezekiel reveals the name of this holy city. It is to be called "The LORD is There" (v 35). Jerusalem was once such a city, but it has become a desolation best called "God is Gone" (see 10:18–19; 11:22–25). Now the exiles long for home. That home will be the city that is home to the God of Abraham and Sarah. Ezekiel's dream of the coming city of God, home to the People of God, is a compelling vision of hope for wandering pilgrims who live in dispersion and exile to this day (cf. Heb 11:13–16).

from the east side to the west, Zebulun, one portion. [27] Adjoining the territory of Zebulun, from the east side to the west, Gad, one portion. [28] And adjoining the territory of Gad to the south, the boundary shall run from Tamar to the waters of Meribath-kadesh, from there along the Wadi of Egypt[a] to the Great Sea. [29] This is the land that you shall allot as an inheritance among the tribes of Israel, and these are their portions, says the Lord God.

30   These shall be the exits of the city: On the north side, which is to be four thousand five hundred cubits by measure, [31] three gates, the gate of Reuben, the gate of Judah, and the gate of Levi, the gates of the city being named after the tribes of Israel. [32] On the east side, which is to be four thousand five hundred cubits, three gates, the gate of Joseph, the gate of Benjamin, and the gate of Dan. [33] On the south side, which is to be four thousand five hundred cubits by measure, three gates, the gate of Simeon, the gate of Issachar, and the gate of Zebulun. [34] On the west side, which is to be four thousand five hundred cubits, three gates,[b] the gate of Gad, the gate of Asher, and the gate of Naphtali. [35] The circumference of the city shall be eighteen thousand cubits. And the name of the city from that time on shall be, The Lord is There.

a Heb lacks of Egypt   b One Ms Gk Syr: MT their gates three

DANIEL *MYSTERIOUS*

Hungry lions, fiery furnaces, kings with unpronounceable names. Dreams and visions, apocalyptic battles between nations, death and salvation in unlikely places—the stories in Daniel are familiar, but odd. Like King Belshazzar (chap 5), we have seen "the writing on the wall" (this is where the phrase comes from) or at least the writing on the pages of our Bibles. But do we know what to make of it all?

Indeed, mystery surrounds the book of Daniel. We do not know who wrote it or exactly when it was written, although its portrayal of Daniel and his friends as Jewish exiles in Babylon indicates that it was most likely partially written during Antiochus IV Epiphanes' persecution of the Jews in Babylon, which began with the desecration of the Temple in 167 BC. Daniel is also unusual for being written partly in Hebrew (1:1–2:4a; 8:1–12:13) and partly in Aramaic (2:4b–7:28). Even its genre—half stories, half visions—is mysterious. Unfortunately, the book of Daniel rarely appears in Christian worship, so little guidance for understanding it is likely to be found there. The common lectionary followed by many congregations turns to Daniel only once every three years (All Saints' Day, year C).

So how might we take a meaningful look at this Scripture? For the purpose of this volume, we will treat Daniel as a book of case studies in which people practice their faith while living in a culture that ignores or opposes their beliefs. Each chapter, roughly, poses a new crisis. Exile is at the root of these crises and holds the stories together. Babylon, we discover, makes it hard to remain true to God and offers enticements to serve other gods. Yet in every crisis and temptation, Daniel and friends hold fast to God. More important, God stands with them not only in extreme settings, like lions' dens and fiery furnaces, but in familiar activities, for example, in eating food, telling the truth, and showing mercy. God rewards their faith and allows it to spread, sometimes even to the kings who keep them in exile.

The repeating gospel, or "good news," of Daniel is that God is sovereign, governing all the world. Thus, even in exile, personal practices of spiritual formation

---

See also *"The With-God Life"* essays for this section of the Bible, *"The People of God in Exile,"* pp. 1171–74, and *"The People of God in Restoration,"* pp. 1355–59.

CRISES THAT
LEAD TO SPIRITUAL DISCIPLINE

result in public and political re-formation. Through these practices, Daniel's character is formed, so that he can be trusted to respond to all the challenges set before him. As we shall see, Spiritual Disciplines not only enrich one's inner life, they humanize and transform life for others.

Holy Simplicity

The crisis in the first chapter arises from Daniel's refusal to eat the king's rations. This refusal puts Daniel's life at risk, yet affirms that life depends on more than what any human (or king) can provide. In biblical times, to accept food from another's table was to place oneself under the protection of the host. By eating simple vegetables from God's earth instead of rich food from the king's table, Daniel indicates which "host" he trusts for salvation, protection, and life's daily necessities.

Food-based Spiritual Disciplines have existed at least since the Israelites left the bread they ate by Pharaoh's fleshpots in favor of manna in the desert. The Jewish practice of keeping kosher, Muslim fasting during Ramadan, and the Christian Eucharist are parallel disciplines that affirm humanity's reliance on God for the essential gifts of life.

Related practices need not pertain to food, however. Refusing to define ourselves as "consumers" may help orient our attention toward God and away from material goods. The Amish rejection of modern conveniences and Roman Catholic vows of "chastity, poverty, and obedience" focus attention on God's providence. Tithing is comparable as a Spiritual Discipline too, insofar as it decreases self-indulgence and raises our awareness that everything we have is God's gift.

Telling the Truth

On the surface, the second chapter concerns the interpretation of a dream. Of course, in the Bible, dreams are never just dreams. They are avenues for revealing truth (Gen 28:10–22; Matt 2:19–22). Thus, the crisis in this chapter has to do with the king who *won't* tell the truth (about the dream) and his advisers who *can't* tell the truth (without knowing the dream). This suppression of truth in government circles leads to threats of brutality (in the text and always). The king vows to kill all the learned people of his realm (2:5, 12). Violence is averted only when Daniel tells the truth by revealing the dream.

What makes telling the truth a Spiritual Discipline? First, the truth is not blurted out immediately. Like any discipline, it requires patience and time (2:16). Second, telling the truth involves a time of "small-group sharing" by Daniel with his friends and their subsequent prayers (2:17–18). Third, Daniel's truth asserts the sovereignty of God over all other rulers (2:44). Throughout, Daniel's grounding in the spiritual life is evidenced in his ability to sleep peacefully during the ordeal (2:19) while the king loses sleep (2:1)!

No Other Gods

In the third chapter, Daniel is no longer at the center of the crisis. Fellow exiles Shadrach, Meshach, and Abednego are coerced by law to worship a giant statue of the king. Their refusal to do so means almost certain death in the king's furnace. Yet this trio does not practice Spiritual Disciplines for personal gain. If protection is all they want from a god, bowing to Nebuchadnezzar's statue will save them from the flames as surely as God will—and sooner! What matters more than life to them, however, is keeping the first commandment: "You shall have no other gods before me" (Exod 20:3; Deut 5:7).

Keeping this commandment as a Spiritual Discipline means more than trusting God to answer prayer. They trust God, whether or not prayers are answered and whether or not their lives are spared. "If our God . . . is able to deliver us," they say, "let him. . . . But if not . . . we will not serve your gods" (3:17–18). Theirs is a God for the long run—for life and death. In effect, theirs is a resurrection faith, for it does not end at the grave. As the apostle Paul will later say: "If we live, we live to the Lord, and if we die, we die to the Lord; so then, whether we live or whether we die, we are the Lord's" (Rom 14:8).

The faith of Shadrach, Meshach, and Abednego does not depend on their rescue from the furnace; however, their escape does produce a miraculous transformation in Nebuchadnezzar. The same king who warned them to worship his god or die ends up praising their God—and commanding others to do likewise!

Righteousness and Mercy

Crisis strikes again in chapter 4. This time it affects not the exiles, but Babylon's king, the epitome of power and prestige. Nebuchadnezzar considers himself a self-made man, the proud possessor of everything he sees from his rooftop (4:29–30). Yet after imagining that the whole world exists to provide for him, he winds up unable even to provide for himself (4:32–33).

Daniel tells the king how to put his life back in order. "O king," he says, "atone for your sins with righteousness, and your iniquities with mercy to the oppressed, so that your prosperity may be prolonged" (4:27). Daniel knows that the "prosperity" of one person depends on others prospering too. No one "makes it alone."

"Righteousness" here has nothing to do with abstract piety; it parallels "mercy to the oppressed." Both righteousness and mercy call for concrete acts of justice and generosity toward persons in need. In effect, Daniel is telling the king (and readers) to get down off the rooftop and into the street, where human needs can be met. Taking part in mission and ministry to others is the Spiritual Discipline espoused in this chapter.

We don't know if Nebuchadnezzar practiced what Daniel preached. But we know he got the message well enough to repeat it. At the end of the chapter, he praises God, whose "ways are justice; and [who] is able to bring low those who walk in pride" (4:37).

Reading the Writing on the Wall

Any Spiritual Disciplines in the fifth chapter are visible only in contrast to the utter lack of discipline (spiritual or otherwise) at Belshazzar's table. This so-called son of Nebuchadnezzar (history books disagree) hosts a raucous feast for a thousand lords. In a drunken state, he uses holy vessels looted from Jerusalem's Temple (1:2) to praise the gods of gold, silver, bronze, iron, wood, and stone. A strange (disembodied?) hand writes on the palace wall for all to see. When the king offers a reward to anyone who can interpret it, Daniel reads "the writing on the wall" as a death sentence against the foolish monarch.

Daniel's condemnation has three parts. First, as he rejected Nebuchadnezzar's rich food in chapter 1, he rebuffs Belshazzar's offer of extravagant rewards here (5:17). He refuses to be beholden to his captors or any earthly power. The ability to say no to coercive economic interests is a Spiritual Discipline of the first order and permits openness to God.

Second, Daniel reprimands Belshazzar (5:18–22) for not learning from his father, Nebuchadnezzar, who had come to know and worship God (chap 4). In effect, Belshazzar has violated the commandment to honor father and mother (Exod 20:12; Deut 5:16). This commandment requires more than devotion to one's immediate family. It calls for reverence for the wisdom, traditions, values, and experiences of prior generations—a reverence Belshazzar ignored.

Third, Daniel indicts Belshazzar most severely for using sacred vessels from one religion to worship the gods of another (5:23). The king's misuse of the Temple treasures causes his downfall. Daniel declares that the king's reign is ended and his kingdom forfeited to others (5:24–28). Implicitly condemned are all practices that defile the beliefs, principles, and holy objects of faiths that worship the one true God.

Blameless Among the Lyin'

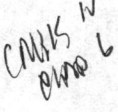

The final story, in chapter 6, puts the book's namesake at the center again. Regardless of what we learned as children, Daniel's crisis here is not with lions per se, but with lying. The wild beasts pose little threat and do him no harm (6:23). Jealous and deceitful co-workers, however, nearly cause his destruction.

These "presidents and satraps" trick the king into signing a law Daniel will break, then they testify against him in the king's court. In so doing, they break the law against bearing "false witness" (Exod 20:16; Deut 5:20). Daniel is sent to the lions' den but survives, because he is blameless before God and the king (6:22). His integrity—public (6:3–4) and private (6:10)—saves him from lions and liars alike. Daniel's enemies don't fare as well. They are fed to the lions (6:24), while God is exalted (6:26–27) and Daniel is honored (6:28).

Is Daniel's blamelessness an unrealistic ideal? Perhaps. But seeking to live blamelessly in response to God's love—not as a precondition—is good spiritual practice.

Concrete Hope

The latter half of the book of Daniel takes the form of apocalyptic visions. Daniel, the man, remains present as the seer and interpreter of these visions, yet the personalized stories of faith in prior chapters give way to sweeping vistas of political upheaval—nations in conflict and powers waging war. Still, the message of these chapters is like that of the earlier accounts: God governs the world as surely as God governs our personal lives. The same God who accompanied certain people into exile governs all people for justice and peace, even at great sacrifice.

Hope, in these chapters, is not abstract or "sweet by-and-by," but concrete. Hope is political, global, and substantial in what it says and those it addresses. Hope speaks specifically to people in exile, especially to those who do not have access to the royal courts and power as Daniel did; and it assures them that their spiritual practices are not in vain. Though the Spiritual Disciplines themselves do not bring salvation, the God they meet through them does. This God is trustworthy to make all things right. Kings come and go, kingdoms fall and rise, yet God remains— as do those who follow God's ways.

—*James M. Rand*

Four Young Israelites at the Babylonian Court

1 In the third year of the reign of King Jehoiakim of Judah, King Nebuchadnezzar of Babylon came to Jerusalem and besieged it. ²The Lord let King Jehoiakim of Judah fall into his power, as well as some of the vessels of the house of God. These he brought to the land of Shinar,ᵃ and placed the vessels in the treasury of his gods.

3 Then the king commanded his palace master Ashpenaz to bring some of the Israelites of the royal family and of the nobility, ⁴young men without physical defect and handsome, versed in every branch of wisdom, endowed with knowledge and insight, and competent to serve in the king's palace; they were to be taught the literature and language of the Chaldeans. ⁵The king assigned them a daily portion of the royal rations of food and wine. They were to be educated for three years, so that at the end of that time they could be stationed in the king's court. ⁶Among them were Daniel, Hananiah, Mishael, and Azariah, from the tribe of Judah. ⁷The palace master gave them other names: Daniel he called Belteshazzar, Hananiah he

a Gk Theodotion: Heb adds *to the house of his own gods*

1:1–2 *The Lord let King Jehoiakim of Judah fall.* The book of Daniel opens on the "eve of destruction"—the eve of the exile. The end of Judah is in sight; Jehoiakim's short reign is nearly over. The impending defeat of God's people seems to signal God's defeat. Can God be trusted when everything falls apart? Who practices faith when God is absent? But wait! God is not absent or defeated! Visible only to the eyes of faith, "The Lord let[s] King Jehoiakim . . . fall" (see also v 9). Nebuchadnezzar does not act under his own power. God determines the destiny of nations and kings (as we shall see again and again in chaps 7–12). The conviction that God is sovereign over Israel *and* other nations compels us to turn our lives toward God. Despite setbacks and defeat, God's redemptive purpose lives on. There *is* reason to practice faith! God is still with his people.

1:2 *some of the vessels of the house of God.* These vessels will play a key role in chapter 5.

1:4 *young men without physical defect and handsome. Who decides what is beautiful?* If Babylon does, Nebuchadnezzar and his cohorts may exploit young and intelligent Israelites however they please. If modern advertising and entertainment choose, we are bound to fall short. Yet when God judges beauty, even exiles and others "rejected by mortals" become "precious in God's sight" (1 Pet 2:4). Thankfully, "the LORD does not see as mortals see; they look on the outward appearance, but the LORD looks on the heart" (1 Sam 16:7). God, give us eyes to see!

1:5 *a daily portion of the royal rations.* The king intends to strip the Jewish people of their identity by supplying them with everything else: food, education, names, and career advancement. Lacking an identity, these persons will be docile, compliant servants of the king— exactly what he wants. The king understands how material goods can block one's relationship with God.

called Shadrach, Mishael he called Meshach, and Azariah he called Abednego.

8 But Daniel resolved that he would not defile himself with the royal rations of food and wine; so he asked the palace master to allow him not to defile himself. 9Now God allowed Daniel to receive favor and compassion from the palace master. 10The palace master said to Daniel, "I am afraid of my lord the king; he has appointed your food and your drink. If he should see you in poorer condition than the other young men of your own age, you would endanger my head with the king." 11Then Daniel asked the guard whom the palace master had appointed over Daniel, Hananiah, Mishael, and Azariah: 12"Please test your servants for ten days. Let us be given vegetables to eat and water to drink. 13You can then compare our appearance with the appearance of the young men who eat the royal rations, and deal with your servants according to what you observe." 14So he agreed to this proposal and tested them for ten days. 15At the end of ten days it was observed that they appeared better and fatter than all the young men who had been eating the royal rations. 16So the guard continued to withdraw their royal rations and the wine they were to drink, and gave them vegetables. 17To these four young men God gave knowledge and skill in every aspect of literature and wisdom; Daniel also had insight into all visions and dreams.

18 At the end of the time that the king had set for them to be brought in, the palace master brought them into the presence of Nebuchadnezzar, 19and the king spoke with them. And among them all, no one was found to compare with Daniel, Hananiah, Mishael, and Azariah; therefore they were stationed in the king's court. 20In every matter of wisdom and understanding concerning which the king inquired of them, he found them ten times better than all the magicians and enchanters in his whole kingdom. 21And Daniel continued there until the first year of King Cyrus.

Nebuchadnezzar's Dream

2 In the second year of Nebuchadnezzar's reign, Nebuchadnezzar dreamed such dreams that his spirit was troubled and his sleep left him. 2So the king commanded that the magicians, the enchanters, the sorcerers, and the Chaldeans be summoned to tell the king his dreams. When they came in and stood before the king, 3he said to them, "I have had such a dream that my spirit is troubled by the desire to understand it." 4The Chaldeans said to the king (in Aramaic),a "O king, live forever! Tell your servants the dream, and we will reveal the interpretation." 5The king answered the Chaldeans, "This is a public decree: if you do not tell me both the dream and its inter-

a The text from this point to the end of chapter 7 is in Aramaic

---

1:8 *Daniel . . . would not defile himself with the royal rations.* Daniel rejects the king's offer of a "Eucharist" that would bind him to Babylon and distance him from God. He knows that faithfulness is accompanied by a constant craving that the world cannot meet. As Jesus said, "Blessed are those who hunger and thirst for righteousness" (Matt 5:6).

1:9 *God allowed.* The one who shapes global politics (v 2) directs individual lives too.

1:10 *I am afraid of my lord the king.* Fear blocks the spiritual life and limits choices. Daniel must find a way around fear and around those who are fearful.

1:12 *Let us be given vegetables . . . and water.* Daniel's choice to receive food from God's earth instead of the king's table shows who he trusts

to provide for his needs.

1:19 *no one was found to compare with Daniel, Hananiah, Mishael, and Azariah.* Though Babylonian names were imposed (v 7), their Jewish names remain. Spiritual practices help to maintain one's true, God-given identity.

2:1 *his sleep left him.* Nebuchadnezzar's anxious spirit robs him of sleep. Daniel's nurtured spirit allows him to sleep (v 19) and receive a needed vision.

2:2 *the magicians, the enchanters, the sorcerers, and the Chaldeans.* Magic, enchantment, and sorcery are often mocked in this book. The king calls such practices "lying and misleading" (v 9), though he seeks them out. The Chaldeans too confess the shortcomings of efforts at divination (v 10).

pretation, you shall be torn limb from limb, and your houses shall be laid in ruins. 6But if you do tell me the dream and its interpretation, you shall receive from me gifts and rewards and great honor. Therefore tell me the dream and its interpretation." 7They answered a second time, "Let the king first tell his servants the dream, then we can give its interpretation." 8The king answered, "I know with certainty that you are trying to gain time, because you see I have firmly decreed: 9if you do not tell me the dream, there is but one verdict for you. You have agreed to speak lying and misleading words to me until things take a turn. Therefore, tell me the dream, and I shall know that you can give me its interpretation." 10The Chaldeans answered the king, "There is no one on earth who can reveal what the king demands! In fact no king, however great and powerful, has ever asked such a thing of any magician or enchanter or Chaldean. 11The thing that the king is asking is too difficult, and no one can reveal it to the king except the gods, whose dwelling is not with mortals."

12 Because of this the king flew into a violent rage and commanded that all the wise men of Babylon be destroyed. 13The decree was issued, and the wise men were about to be executed; and they looked for Daniel and his companions, to execute them. 14Then Daniel responded with prudence and discretion to Arioch, the king's chief executioner, who had gone out to execute the wise men of Babylon; 15he asked Arioch, the royal official, "Why is the decree of the king so urgent?" Arioch then explained the matter to Daniel. 16So Daniel went in and requested that the king give him time and he would tell the king the interpretation.

God Reveals Nebuchadnezzar's Dream

17 Then Daniel went to his home and informed his companions, Hananiah, Mishael, and Azariah, 18and told them to seek mercy from the God of heaven concerning this mystery, so that Daniel and his companions with the rest of the wise men of Babylon might not perish. 19Then the mystery was revealed to Daniel in a vision of the night, and Daniel blessed the God of heaven.

20 Daniel said:

"Blessed be the name of God from age
   to age,
  for wisdom and power are his.
21 He changes times and seasons,
   deposes kings and sets up kings;
he gives wisdom to the wise
  and knowledge to those who have
   understanding.
22 He reveals deep and hidden things;
  he knows what is in the darkness,
  and light dwells with him.
23 To you, O God of my ancestors,
  I give thanks and praise,
for you have given me wisdom and
   power,
  and have now revealed to me what we
   asked of you,
for you have revealed to us what the
   king ordered."

Daniel Interprets the Dream

24 Therefore Daniel went to Arioch, whom the king had appointed to destroy the

---

2:5 *you shall be torn limb from limb.* The king governs with threats and rewards. Daniel's spirituality, however, utilizes prudence and discretion (v 14), cooperation (v 17), prayer, and a desire to save rather than harm (v 18).

2:11 *too difficult.* Unlike these spiritual impostors, Abraham and Sarah (Gen 18:12–14) and Mary (Luke 1:34–37) know that "nothing [is] impossible with God." *whose dwelling is not with mortals.* Jewish and Christian spirituality finds God among mortals: Immanuel, God-with-us (Isa 7:14, Matt 1:23). The magicians' and enchanters' gods are remote; yet Jewish and

Christian faith invites believers to "call upon [the LORD] while he is near" (Isa 55:6).

2:14 *Daniel responded . . . to the king's chief executioner.* Daniel speaks face-to-face with his foe (2:24 also). Jesus (Matt 5:44–45) and Paul (Rom 12:20) urge similar disciplines for living faithfully with enemies.

2:18–19 *the rest of the wise men.* Daniel cares about others' safety as well as his own. After Daniel spoke out for the larger community, "the mystery was revealed." Is there a connection between concern for others and the ability to hear what God wants to say?

wise men of Babylon, and said to him, "Do not destroy the wise men of Babylon; bring me in before the king, and I will give the king the interpretation."

25 Then Arioch quickly brought Daniel before the king and said to him: "I have found among the exiles from Judah a man who can tell the king the interpretation." 26The king said to Daniel, whose name was Belteshazzar, "Are you able to tell me the dream that I have seen and its interpretation?" 27Daniel answered the king, "No wise men, enchanters, magicians, or diviners can show to the king the mystery that the king is asking, 28but there is a God in heaven who reveals mysteries, and he has disclosed to King Nebuchadnezzar what will happen at the end of days. Your dream and the visions of your head as you lay in bed were these: 29To you, O king, as you lay in bed, came thoughts of what would be hereafter, and the revealer of mysteries disclosed to you what is to be. 30But as for me, this mystery has not been revealed to me because of any wisdom that I have more than any other living being, but in order that the interpretation may be known to the king and that you may understand the thoughts of your mind.

31 "You were looking, O king, and lo! there was a great statue. This statue was huge, its brilliance extraordinary; it was standing before you, and its appearance was frightening. 32The head of that statue was of fine gold, its chest and arms of silver, its middle and thighs of bronze, 33its legs of iron, its feet partly of iron and partly of clay. 34As you looked on, a stone was cut out, not by human hands, and it struck the statue on its feet of iron and clay and broke them in pieces. 35Then the iron, the clay, the bronze, the silver, and the gold, were all broken in pieces and became like the chaff of the summer threshing floors; and the wind carried them away, so that not a trace of them could be found. But the stone that struck the statue became a great mountain and filled the whole earth.

36 "This was the dream; now we will tell the king its interpretation. 37You, O king, the king of kings—to whom the God of heaven has given the kingdom, the power, the might, and the glory, 38into whose hand he has given human beings, wherever they live, the wild animals of the field, and the birds of the air, and whom he has established as ruler over them all—you are the head of gold. 39After you shall arise another kingdom inferior to yours, and yet a third kingdom of bronze, which shall rule over the whole earth. 40And there shall be a fourth kingdom, strong as iron; just as iron crushes and smashes everything,[a] it shall crush and shatter all these. 41As you saw the feet and toes partly of potter's clay and partly of iron, it shall be a divided kingdom; but some of the strength of iron shall be in it, as you saw the iron mixed with the clay. 42As the toes of the feet were part iron and part clay, so the kingdom shall be partly strong and partly brittle. 43As you saw the iron mixed with clay, so will they mix with one another in marriage,[b] but they will not hold together, just as iron does not mix with clay. 44And in the days of those kings the God of heaven will set up a kingdom that shall never be destroyed, nor shall this kingdom be left to another people. It shall crush all these kingdoms and bring them to an end, and it shall stand forever; 45just as you saw that a stone was cut from the mountain not by hands, and that it crushed the iron, the bronze, the clay, the silver, and the gold. The great God has informed the king what shall be hereafter. The dream is certain, and its interpretation trustworthy."

Daniel and His Friends Promoted

46 Then King Nebuchadnezzar fell on his face, worshiped Daniel, and commanded that

---

a Gk Theodotion Syr Vg: Aram adds *and like iron that crushes*   b Aram *by human seed*

2:32–33 *gold . . . silver . . . bronze . . . iron . . . clay.* The elements that make up the statue in the king's dream are almost the same as the elements Belshazzar will toast as "gods" (5:4).

2:44 *a kingdom that shall never be destroyed.* Kings rise and fall. The truth Daniel reveals to Nebuchadnezzar is that only God is forever. This conviction enables persistent Spiritual Disciplines in trying times.

DANIEL

Freed by Discipline

Selected Scripture: *Daniel 1–6*

Exiled from his homeland at a young age and placed in political service to the empires of Babylon and Persia, Daniel served in humility and strength, never seeking honor or personal gain. He didn't waver in his trust in God or in fulfilling the unusual types of service to which God called him.

He landed in a life situation he would not have chosen, and yet Daniel remained committed to worshiping God where he was without succumbing to the pursuits of the world around him. Daniel served kings, interpreted their dreams, deciphered mysterious God-etched writing on a wall, ate and drank according to God's command, and accepted his fate in a lions' den rather than give up praying daily. Daniel grew in the knowledge of his day while at the same time gaining supernatural knowledge as God had occasion to give it.

Perhaps better than any other Old Testament character, Daniel modeled a person committed to a life of unceasing discipline, and he experienced great freedoms as a result. His disciplined, God-directed eating and drinking habits produced the freedom of a healthy, robust body and his appointment to rule over others. His discipline of study achieved respect within the king's inner circle and the freedom to influence the ruler. His discipline of service kept him in a position to assist future kings and fulfill the first clearly eschatological role in the Old Testament, prophesying the course of events for future world empires, the coming of the Messiah, and Christ's second coming. As Daniel portrays, discipline need not be burdensome. Rather, when performed as a route to a deeper relationship with God, it can prove life-giving.

Dietrich Bonhoeffer knew this as well. Imprisoned under Hitler, this German pastor and teacher became an exile in his own country. Bonhoeffer experienced circumstances more extreme even than Daniel. His prior commitment to a disciplined life likely enabled him to keep faith in God throughout an ordeal that ended in execution. "If there is no element of asceticism in our lives, if we give free rein to the desires of the flesh, . . . we shall find it hard to train for the service of Christ. When the flesh is satisfied it is hard to pray with cheerfulness or to devote oneself to a life of service which calls for much self-renunciation," Bonhoeffer explains in his classic work *The Cost of Discipleship*.

And yet we resist a disciplined life. Bonhoeffer continues: "We claim liberty from all legal compulsion, from self-martyrdom and mortification, and play this off against the proper evangelical use of discipline and asceticism; we thus excuse our self-indulgence and irregularity in prayer, in meditation, and in our bodily life. But the contrast between our behavior and the word of Jesus is all too painfully evident."

PROFILE: DANIEL

We forget that discipleship means estrangement from the world, and *we forget the real joy and freedom which are the outcome of a devout rule of life*" (italics added).

Daniel left the lions' den unharmed. Dietrich Bonhoeffer was executed in a prison just days before Germany was liberated. Though one man lived and one died, their spirits shared an undying commitment to God, built and strengthened by a life of discipline, or discipleship. Daniel set a course for responsible spiritual freedom. May we follow, as Bonhoeffer and others have done, finding freedom and depth in God through a life of discipline.

Personal Reflection

- When have you landed in a life situation you would not have chosen? In what way did you sense God's call to faithful and holy living despite the circumstances?

- Although Daniel served kings, he refused to conform to their worldly lifestyles. What influences make it difficult for you to live "in the world and not of it"? (John 17:16; Rom 12:2) Your job? Friendships? Family? Volunteer work? Your neighborhood? The pull of the media? What worldly ways are most tempting to you?

- How much is discipline a committed part of your life? Consider an area of your life in which God might be asking you to practice greater discipline. How could this discipline influence your relationship with God?

a grain offering and incense be offered to him. 47The king said to Daniel, "Truly, your God is God of gods and Lord of kings and a revealer of mysteries, for you have been able to reveal this mystery!" 48Then the king promoted Daniel, gave him many great gifts, and made him ruler over the whole province of Babylon and chief prefect over all the wise men of Babylon. 49Daniel made a request of the king, and he appointed Shadrach, Meshach, and Abednego over the affairs of the province of Babylon. But Daniel remained at the king's court.

The Golden Image

3 King Nebuchadnezzar made a golden statue whose height was sixty cubits and whose width was six cubits; he set it up on the plain of Dura in the province of Babylon. 2Then King Nebuchadnezzar sent for the satraps, the prefects, and the governors, the counselors, the treasurers, the justices, the magistrates, and all the officials of the provinces, to assemble and come to the dedication of the statue that King Nebuchadnezzar had set up. 3So the satraps, the prefects, and the governors, the counselors, the treasurers, the justices, the magistrates, and all the officials of the provinces, assembled for the dedication of the statue that King Nebuchadnezzar had set up. When they were standing before the statue that Nebuchadnezzar had set up, 4the herald proclaimed aloud, "You are commanded, O peoples, nations, and languages, 5that when you hear the sound of the horn, pipe, lyre, trigon, harp, drum, and entire musical ensemble, you are to fall down and worship the golden statue that King Nebuchadnezzar has set up. 6Whoever does not fall down and worship

3:2–7 *the statue that King Nebuchadnezzar had set up.* Five times in these six verses, Daniel reminds us who made the idol. This repetition becomes sarcastic and taunting, providing a singsong refrain to the verses (see also vv 14, 15, 18). Also repeated are the lists of instruments and government officials. The text laughs at these things, playfully reminding us that our ultimate obedience and loyalty are not with any of them.

shall immediately be thrown into a furnace of blazing fire." [7]Therefore, as soon as all the peoples heard the sound of the horn, pipe, lyre, trigon, harp, drum, and entire musical ensemble, all the peoples, nations, and languages fell down and worshiped the golden statue that King Nebuchadnezzar had set up.

[8] Accordingly, at this time certain Chaldeans came forward and denounced the Jews. [9]They said to King Nebuchadnezzar, "O king, live forever! [10]You, O king, have made a decree, that everyone who hears the sound of the horn, pipe, lyre, trigon, harp, drum, and entire musical ensemble, shall fall down and worship the golden statue, [11]and whoever does not fall down and worship shall be thrown into a furnace of blazing fire. [12]There are certain Jews whom you have appointed over the affairs of the province of Babylon: Shadrach, Meshach, and Abednego. These pay no heed to you, O king. They do not serve your gods and they do not worship the golden statue that you have set up."

[13] Then Nebuchadnezzar in furious rage commanded that Shadrach, Meshach, and Abednego be brought in; so they brought those men before the king. [14]Nebuchadnezzar said to them, "Is it true, O Shadrach, Meshach, and Abednego, that you do not serve my gods and you do not worship the golden statue that I have set up? [15]Now if you are ready when you hear the sound of the horn, pipe, lyre, trigon, harp, drum, and entire musical en-

semble to fall down and worship the statue that I have made, well and good. [a] But if you do not worship, you shall immediately be thrown into a furnace of blazing fire, and who is the god that will deliver you out of my hands?"

[16] Shadrach, Meshach, and Abednego answered the king, "O Nebuchadnezzar, we have no need to present a defense to you in this matter. [17]If our God whom we serve is able to deliver us from the furnace of blazing fire and out of your hand, O king, let him deliver us. [b] [18]But if not, be it known to you, O king, that we will not serve your gods and we will not worship the golden statue that you have set up."

The Fiery Furnace

[19] Then Nebuchadnezzar was so filled with rage against Shadrach, Meshach, and Abednego that his face was distorted. He ordered the furnace heated up seven times more than was customary, [20]and ordered some of the strongest guards in his army to bind Shadrach, Meshach, and Abednego and to throw them into the furnace of blazing fire. [21]So the men were bound, still wearing their tunics, [c] their trousers, [c] their hats, and their other garments, and they were thrown into the furnace of blazing fire. [22]Because the

a Aram lacks *well and good*   b Or *If our God whom we serve is able to deliver us, he will deliver us from the furnace of blazing fire and out of your hand, O king.*
c Meaning of Aram word uncertain

Responding
3:12 WORSHIP. Golden statues aside, minister and theologian A. W. Tozer says, "The essence of idolatry is the entertainment of thoughts about God that are unworthy of him." Consider this statement. If worship is at its essence appreciation of God, are any unworthy thoughts hindering your worship? Spend some of your prayer time meditating on who God is; ask him to illuminate for you those misunderstandings you hold about his character. *See also* Spiritual Disciplines Index.

3:17–18 *If our God . . . is able to deliver us.* This is a towering statement of monotheistic faith. The exiles refuse to put their lives ahead of God. They would rather yield up their own

bodies than worship an idol (v 28). Again, their declaration is playfully tongue-in-cheek: if God does not save them, they sure won't worship a statue when they are dead! This is not unlike Ps 30:9, which inquires, "What profit is there in my death? . . . Will the dust praise you?" In life and in death, Shadrach, Meshach, and Abednego will bless God (see Ps 63:4).

Responding
3:17–18 SERVICE. Shadrach, Meshach, and Abednego understood that true service is giving without expecting in return. Do you serve those around you with no expectation of reciprocity? Today seek to serve someone anonymously, so that credit cannot be given. *See also* Spiritual Disciplines Index.

king's command was urgent and the furnace was so overheated, the raging flames killed the men who lifted Shadrach, Meshach, and Abednego. 23But the three men, Shadrach, Meshach, and Abednego, fell down, bound, into the furnace of blazing fire.

24 Then King Nebuchadnezzar was astonished and rose up quickly. He said to his counselors, "Was it not three men that we threw bound into the fire?" They answered the king, "True, O king." 25He replied, "But I see four men unbound, walking in the middle of the fire, and they are not hurt; and the fourth has the appearance of a god." a 26Nebuchadnezzar then approached the door of the furnace of blazing fire and said, "Shadrach, Meshach, and Abednego, servants of the Most High God, come out! Come here!" So Shadrach, Meshach, and Abednego came out from the fire. 27And the satraps, the prefects, the governors, and the king's counselors gathered together and saw that the fire had not had any power over the bodies of those men; the hair of their heads was not singed, their tunics b were not harmed, and not even the smell of fire came from them. 28Nebuchadnezzar said, "Blessed be the God of Shadrach, Meshach, and Abednego, who has sent his angel and delivered his servants who trusted in him. They disobeyed the king's command and yielded up their bodies rather than serve and worship any god except their own God. 29Therefore I make a decree: Any people, nation, or language that utters blasphemy against the God of Shadrach, Meshach, and Abednego shall be torn limb from limb, and their houses laid in ruins; for there is no other god who is able to deliver in this way." 30Then the king promoted Shadrach, Meshach, and Abednego in the province of Babylon.

Nebuchadnezzar's Second Dream

4 c King Nebuchadnezzar to all peoples, nations, and languages that live throughout the earth: May you have abundant prosperity! 2The signs and wonders that the Most High God has worked for me I am pleased to recount.

3 How great are his signs,
    how mighty his wonders!
  His kingdom is an everlasting kingdom,
    and his sovereignty is from
      generation to generation.

4 d I, Nebuchadnezzar, was living at ease in my home and prospering in my palace. 5I saw a dream that frightened me; my fantasies in bed and the visions of my head terrified me. 6So I made a decree that all the wise men of Babylon should be brought before me, in order that they might tell me the interpretation of the dream. 7Then the magicians, the enchanters, the Chaldeans, and the diviners came in, and I told them the dream, but they could not tell me its interpretation. 8At last Daniel came in before me—he who was named Belteshazzar after the name of my god, and who is endowed with a spirit of the holy gods e—and I told him the dream: 9"O Belteshazzar, chief of the magicians, I know that you are endowed with a spirit of the holy gods e and that no mystery is too difficult for you. Hear f the dream that I saw; tell me its interpretation.

10 g Upon my bed this is what I saw;
    there was a tree at the center of the
      earth,

a Aram *a son of the gods*   b Meaning of Aram word uncertain   c Ch 3.31 in Aram   d Ch 4.1 in Aram   e Or *a holy, divine spirit*   f Theodotion: Aram *The visions of*   g Theodotion Syr Compare Gk: Aram adds *The visions of my head*

3:25 THE WITH-GOD LIFE—*See* Spiritual Disciplines Index.
  3:28–29 *Blessed be the God of Shadrach, Meshach, and Abednego.* Nebuchadnezzar decides to no longer worship his own statue (image), but to praise the God of the Israelites. He is a changed man—but not completely. In his next breath he threatens to "tear limb from limb" anyone who fails to worship this God. Once a king always a king, perhaps.

  4:3 *How great are his signs!* The doxology continues the king's adoration of God from chapter 3.
  4:5 *visions of my head.* While "prospering in [his] palace" (v 4), Nebuchadnezzar has "visions" in his head. Which state is true and which is an illusion? In the Bible, dreams always reveal truth. The king's waking life (of luxury) is what is unreal.

and its height was great.

11 The tree grew great and strong,
   its top reached to heaven,
   and it was visible to the ends of the
      whole earth.
12 Its foliage was beautiful,
   its fruit abundant,
   and it provided food for all.
   The animals of the field found shade
      under it,
   the birds of the air nested in its
      branches,
   and from it all living beings were fed.

13 "I continued looking, in the visions of my head as I lay in bed, and there was a holy watcher, coming down from heaven. 14 He cried aloud and said:

'Cut down the tree and chop off its
      branches,
   strip off its foliage and scatter its fruit.
   Let the animals flee from beneath it
   and the birds from its branches.
15 But leave its stump and roots in the
      ground,
   with a band of iron and bronze,
   in the tender grass of the field.
   Let him be bathed with the dew of
      heaven,
   and let his lot be with the animals of
      the field
   in the grass of the earth.
16 Let his mind be changed from that of a
      human,
   and let the mind of an animal be
      given to him.
   And let seven times pass over him.
17 The sentence is rendered by decree of
      the watchers,
   the decision is given by order of the
      holy ones,
   in order that all who live may know
   that the Most High is sovereign over
      the kingdom of mortals;
   he gives it to whom he will

and sets over it the lowliest of human
      beings.'

18 "This is the dream that I, King Nebuchadnezzar, saw. Now you, Belteshazzar, declare the interpretation, since all the wise men of my kingdom are unable to tell me the interpretation. You are able, however, for you are endowed with a spirit of the holy gods." a

Daniel Interprets the Second Dream

19 Then Daniel, who was called Belteshazzar, was severely distressed for a while. His thoughts terrified him. The king said, "Belteshazzar, do not let the dream or the interpretation terrify you." Belteshazzar answered, "My lord, may the dream be for those who hate you, and its interpretation for your enemies! 20 The tree that you saw, which grew great and strong, so that its top reached to heaven and was visible to the end of the whole earth, 21 whose foliage was beautiful and its fruit abundant, and which provided food for all, under which animals of the field lived, and in whose branches the birds of the air had nests— 22 it is you, O king! You have grown great and strong. Your greatness has increased and reaches to heaven, and your sovereignty to the ends of the earth. 23 And whereas the king saw a holy watcher coming down from heaven and saying, 'Cut down the tree and destroy it, but leave its stump and roots in the ground, with a band of iron and bronze, in the grass of the field; and let him be bathed with the dew of heaven, and let his lot be with the animals of the field, until seven times pass over him'— 24 this is the interpretation, O king, and it is a decree of the Most High that has come upon my lord the king: 25 You shall be driven away from human society, and your dwelling shall be with the wild animals. You shall be made to eat grass like oxen, you shall be bathed with the dew of heaven, and seven times shall pass

a Or a holy, divine spirit

4:17 that the Most High is sovereign. Nebuchadnezzar is stripped of his sovereignty in order to learn that God is sovereign. His sovereignty (v 22) is subordinate to "the Most High," who "gives it to whom he will" (v 25). The power of humans is always limited by what God permits.

over you, until you have learned that the Most High has sovereignty over the kingdom of mortals, and gives it to whom he will. 26As it was commanded to leave the stump and roots of the tree, your kingdom shall be re-established for you from the time that you learn that Heaven is sovereign. 27Therefore, O king, may my counsel be acceptable to you: atone for[a] your sins with righteousness, and your iniquities with mercy to the oppressed, so that your prosperity may be prolonged."

Nebuchadnezzar's Humiliation

28 All this came upon King Nebuchadnezzar. 29At the end of twelve months he was walking on the roof of the royal palace of Babylon, 30and the king said, "Is this not magnificent Babylon, which I have built as a royal capital by my mighty power and for my glorious majesty?" 31While the words were still in the king's mouth, a voice came from heaven: "O King Nebuchadnezzar, to you it is declared: The kingdom has departed from you! 32You shall be driven away from human society, and your dwelling shall be with the animals of the field. You shall be made to eat grass like oxen, and seven times shall pass over you, until you have learned that the Most High has sovereignty over the kingdom of mortals and gives it to whom he will." 33Immediately the sentence was fulfilled against Nebuchadnezzar. He was driven away from human society, ate grass like oxen, and his body was bathed with the dew of heaven, until his hair grew as long as eagles' feathers and his nails became like birds' claws.

Nebuchadnezzar Praises God

34 When that period was over, I, Nebuchadnezzar, lifted my eyes to heaven, and my reason returned to me.
    I blessed the Most High,

and praised and honored the one
    who lives forever.
For his sovereignty is an everlasting sovereignty,
and his kingdom endures from
    generation to generation.
35 All the inhabitants of the earth are
    accounted as nothing,
    and he does what he wills with the
        host of heaven
    and the inhabitants of the earth.
There is no one who can stay his hand
    or say to him, "What are you doing?"
36At that time my reason returned to me; and my majesty and splendor were restored to me for the glory of my kingdom. My counselors and my lords sought me out, I was re-established over my kingdom, and still more greatness was added to me. 37Now I, Nebuchadnezzar, praise and extol and honor the King of heaven,
    for all his works are truth,
        and his ways are justice;
    and he is able to bring low
        those who walk in pride.

Belshazzar's Feast

5 King Belshazzar made a great festival for a thousand of his lords, and he was drinking wine in the presence of the thousand.
2 Under the influence of the wine, Belshazzar commanded that they bring in the vessels of gold and silver that his father Nebuchadnezzar had taken out of the temple in Jerusalem, so that the king and his lords, his wives and his concubines might drink from them. 3So they brought in the vessels of gold and silver[b] that had been taken out of the temple, the house of God in Jerusalem, and

a Aram break off   b Theodotion Vg: Aram lacks and silver

4:27 *righteousness and . . . mercy.* The king's hubris allows him to imagine he is independent, owning everything he sees (v 30). Daniel reminds him that an established life is not isolated from others, but requires righteousness and mercy—concrete acts that address one's neighbors. A lifetime of Spiritual Disciplines has enabled Daniel to live an established life.

4:34 *his sovereignty is an everlasting sovereignty.* Nebuchadnezzar also discovers that an established life must acknowledge the one whose sovereignty is over all. Thus, he blesses, praises, and honors the Most High.
    5:2 *vessels . . . taken out of the temple.* See note on 1:2.

the king and his lords, his wives, and his concubines drank from them. 4They drank the wine and praised the gods of gold and silver, bronze, iron, wood, and stone.

The Writing on the Wall

5 Immediately the fingers of a human hand appeared and began writing on the plaster of the wall of the royal palace, next to the lampstand. The king was watching the hand as it wrote. 6Then the king's face turned pale, and his thoughts terrified him. His limbs gave way, and his knees knocked together. 7The king cried aloud to bring in the enchanters, the Chaldeans, and the diviners; and the king said to the wise men of Babylon, "Whoever can read this writing and tell me its interpretation shall be clothed in purple, have a chain of gold around his neck, and rank third in the kingdom." 8Then all the king's wise men came in, but they could not read the writing or tell the king the interpretation. 9Then King Belshazzar became greatly terrified and his face turned pale, and his lords were perplexed.

10 The queen, when she heard the discussion of the king and his lords, came into the banqueting hall. The queen said, "O king, live forever! Do not let your thoughts terrify you or your face grow pale. 11There is a man in your kingdom who is endowed with a spirit of the holy gods.a In the days of your father he was found to have enlightenment, understanding, and wisdom like the wisdom of

the gods. Your father, King Nebuchadnezzar, made him chief of the magicians, enchanters, Chaldeans, and diviners,b 12because an excellent spirit, knowledge, and understanding to interpret dreams, explain riddles, and solve problems were found in this Daniel, whom the king named Belteshazzar. Now let Daniel be called, and he will give the interpretation."

The Writing on the Wall Interpreted

13 Then Daniel was brought in before the king. The king said to Daniel, "So you are Daniel, one of the exiles of Judah, whom my father the king brought from Judah? 14I have heard of you that a spirit of the godsc is in you, and that enlightenment, understanding, and excellent wisdom are found in you. 15Now the wise men, the enchanters, have been brought in before me to read this writing and tell me its interpretation, but they were not able to give the interpretation of the matter. 16But I have heard that you can give interpretations and solve problems. Now if you are able to read the writing and tell me its interpretation, you shall be clothed in purple, have a chain of gold around your neck, and rank third in the kingdom."

17 Then Daniel answered in the presence of the king, "Let your gifts be for yourself, or give your rewards to someone else! Nevertheless I will read the writing to the king and

a Or *a holy, divine spirit*   b Aram adds *the king your father*   c Or *a divine spirit*

5:4 *gods of gold and silver, bronze, iron, wood, and stone.* See note on 2:32.

5:6 *his knees knocked together.* More comic relief (see note on 3:2–7). Laughing at earthly authorities reminds us where true power resides and liberates us to speak truth to power as Daniel does in verse 17.

5:10–12 *The queen said.* This is the only woman to act or speak in Daniel. In a culture dominated by men, she demonstrates more wisdom than the men around her. She knows where to turn for spiritual direction—not to mortals, but to one "who is endowed with a spirit of the holy gods" (v 11).

5:17 *give your rewards to someone else!* What Belshazzar can give is nothing compared to

what God has given (recounted in v 18). Daniel remembers who is the source of all blessings.

Responding
5:17 SIMPLICITY. Daniel rejects the king's offers of costly clothing, jewelry, and influence in his community. He must have been tempted by some or all of the offers, but Daniel understood that material possessions (and certainly professional success) can get in the way of our relationship with God. Challenge yourself to identify some possessions to which you are a little too attached and take the step of giving some away, to a friend or to a charitable organization. *See also* Spiritual Disciplines Index.

let him know the interpretation. 18O king, the Most High God gave your father Nebuchadnezzar kingship, greatness, glory, and majesty. 19And because of the greatness that he gave him, all peoples, nations, and languages trembled and feared before him. He killed those he wanted to kill, kept alive those he wanted to keep alive, honored those he wanted to honor, and degraded those he wanted to degrade. 20But when his heart was lifted up and his spirit was hardened so that he acted proudly, he was deposed from his kingly throne, and his glory was stripped from him. 21He was driven from human society, and his mind was made like that of an animal. His dwelling was with the wild asses, he was fed grass like oxen, and his body was bathed with the dew of heaven, until he learned that the Most High God has sovereignty over the kingdom of mortals, and sets over it whomever he will. 22And you, Belshazzar his son, have not humbled your heart, even though you knew all this! 23You have exalted yourself against the Lord of heaven! The vessels of his temple have been brought in before you, and you and your lords, your wives and your concubines have been drinking wine from them. You have praised the gods of silver and gold, of bronze, iron, wood, and stone, which do not see or hear or know; but the God in whose power is your very breath, and to whom belong all your ways, you have not honored.

24 "So from his presence the hand was sent and this writing was inscribed. 25And this is the writing that was inscribed: MENE, MENE, TEKEL, and PARSIN. 26This is the interpretation of the matter: MENE, God has numbered the days of*a* your kingdom and brought it to an end; 27TEKEL, you have been weighed on the scales and found wanting; 28PERES,*b* your kingdom is divided and given to the Medes and Persians."

29 Then Belshazzar gave the command, and Daniel was clothed in purple, a chain of gold was put around his neck, and a proclamation was made concerning him that he should rank third in the kingdom.

30 That very night Belshazzar, the Chaldean king, was killed. 31*c* And Darius the Mede received the kingdom, being about sixty-two years old.

The Plot against Daniel

6 It pleased Darius to set over the kingdom one hundred twenty satraps, stationed throughout the whole kingdom, 2and over them three presidents, including Daniel; to these the satraps gave account, so that the king might suffer no loss. 3Soon Daniel distinguished himself above all the other presidents and satraps because an excellent spirit was in him, and the king planned to appoint him over the whole kingdom. 4So the presidents and the satraps tried to find grounds for complaint against Daniel in connection with the kingdom. But they could find no grounds for complaint or any corruption, because he was faithful, and no negligence or corruption could be found in him. 5The men said, "We shall not find any ground for complaint against this Daniel unless we find it in connection with the law of his God."

a Aram lacks *the days of*   *b* The singular of *Parsin*
c Ch 6.1 in Aram

5:23 *the God in whose power is your very breath.* Again, Daniel distinguishes between the gods that can do nothing and the one who gives the power of breath and life.

5:26 *has numbered the days.* Even though God's work against Belshazzar is not finished, Daniel reports it as a done deal. Daniel's trust in God's future transforms the present for him.

5:29–30 *Belshazzar, the Chaldean king, was killed.* Both Daniel and Belshazzar get their just reward! The prophecy Daniel announced is accomplished. Daniel, who knows the source

and limits of power, succeeds in government and endures. Belshazzar, unable to say no to himself, is destroyed.

6:4 *no negligence or corruption could be found in him.* Daniel's blamelessness is established in these verses. But being blameless is no guarantee of safety. Anyone who was picked on in school knows that upright behavior invites trouble. Right attitudes and actions are properly motivated not by the desire for personal benefit, but right relations with God.

6 So the presidents and satraps conspired and came to the king and said to him, "O King Darius, live forever! [7]All the presidents of the kingdom, the prefects and the satraps, the counselors and the governors are agreed that the king should establish an ordinance and enforce an interdict, that whoever prays to anyone, divine or human, for thirty days, except to you, O king, shall be thrown into a den of lions. [8]Now, O king, establish the interdict and sign the document, so that it cannot be changed, according to the law of the Medes and the Persians, which cannot be revoked." [9]Therefore King Darius signed the document and interdict.

Daniel in the Lions' Den

10 Although Daniel knew that the document had been signed, he continued to go to his house, which had windows in its upper room open toward Jerusalem, and to get down on his knees three times a day to pray to his God and praise him, just as he had done previously. [11]The conspirators came and found Daniel praying and seeking mercy before his God. [12]Then they approached the king and said concerning the interdict, "O king! Did you not sign an interdict, that

anyone who prays to anyone, divine or human, within thirty days except to you, O king, shall be thrown into a den of lions?" The king answered, "The thing stands fast, according to the law of the Medes and Persians, which cannot be revoked." [13]Then they responded to the king, "Daniel, one of the exiles from Judah, pays no attention to you, O king, or to the interdict you have signed, but he is saying his prayers three times a day."

14 When the king heard the charge, he was very much distressed. He was determined to save Daniel, and until the sun went down he made every effort to rescue him. [15]Then the conspirators came to the king and said to him, "Know, O king, that it is a law of the Medes and Persians that no interdict or ordinance that the king establishes can be changed."

16 Then the king gave the command, and Daniel was brought and thrown into the den of lions. The king said to Daniel, "May your God, whom you faithfully serve, deliver you!" [17]A stone was brought and laid on the mouth of the den, and the king sealed it with his own signet and with the signet of his lords, so that nothing might be changed concerning Daniel. [18]Then the king went to his palace

---

6:10 *just as he had done previously.* Daniel's enemies attack him precisely at the point of his reliability—his prayer practice. Daniel's prayer life is exemplified in a few brief phrases. It is private (in his house), yet public (with windows open). He prays in a room facing "toward Jerusalem" as Muslims today pray toward Mecca; and he does so several times a day. Though in exile and under watch, he includes "praise." Most important, Daniel is steadfast in prayer, doing "as he had done previously." Kneeling is also mentioned, yet is only one of many positions for prayer in the Bible. Other postures include spreading or raising one's arms, bowing down, lying prostrate, standing, and sitting.

Responding
6:10 PRAYER. Consider making a commitment this week to pray on your knees three times each day at predetermined times. What do you learn from planning your

prayer times in this way? How does it differ from more spontaneous prayer? *See also* Spiritual Disciplines Index.

6:13 *he is saying his prayers three times a day.* The ninth commandment (Exod 20:16; Deut 5:20) prohibits bearing "false witness." The law is concerned with more than just telling a lie; it is intended to protect the innocent from destructive testimony in courts of law. Daniel's conspirators, however, shade the truth in order to ruin one who is blameless. Perhaps Jesus was thinking of Daniel when he said, "Blessed are you when people . . . utter all kinds of evil against you falsely on my account, . . . for in the same way they persecuted the prophets" (Matt 5:11–12).

6:17 *sealed it with his own signet.* This is reminiscent of the sealing of Jesus' tomb by the guards (Matt 27:66). The lions' den is as much a grave for Daniel as the tomb is for Jesus, and his emergence from it prefigures Christ's resurrection.

and spent the night fasting; no food was brought to him, and sleep fled from him.

Daniel Saved from the Lions

19 Then, at break of day, the king got up and hurried to the den of lions. 20When he came near the den where Daniel was, he cried out anxiously to Daniel, "O Daniel, servant of the living God, has your God whom you faithfully serve been able to deliver you from the lions?" 21Daniel then said to the king, "O king, live forever! 22My God sent his angel and shut the lions' mouths so that they would not hurt me, because I was found blameless before him; and also before you, O king, I have done no wrong." 23Then the king was exceedingly glad and commanded that Daniel be taken up out of the den. So Daniel was taken up out of the den, and no kind of harm was found on him, because he had trusted in his God. 24The king gave a command, and those who had accused Daniel were brought and thrown into the den of lions—they, their children, and their wives. Before they reached the bottom of the den the lions overpowered them and broke all their bones in pieces.

25 Then King Darius wrote to all peoples and nations of every language throughout the whole world: "May you have abundant prosperity! 26I make a decree, that in all my royal dominion people should tremble and fear before the God of Daniel:

For he is the living God,
    enduring forever.
His kingdom shall never be destroyed,
    and his dominion has no end.
27 He delivers and rescues,

he works signs and wonders in
    heaven and on earth;
for he has saved Daniel
    from the power of the lions."
28So this Daniel prospered during the reign of Darius and the reign of Cyrus the Persian.

Visions of the Four Beasts

7 In the first year of King Belshazzar of Babylon, Daniel had a dream and visions of his head as he lay in bed. Then he wrote down the dream:*a* 2I,*b* Daniel, saw in my vision by night the four winds of heaven stirring up the great sea, 3and four great beasts came up out of the sea, different from one another. 4The first was like a lion and had eagles' wings. Then, as I watched, its wings were plucked off, and it was lifted up from the ground and made to stand on two feet like a human being; and a human mind was given to it. 5Another beast appeared, a second one, that looked like a bear. It was raised up on one side, had three tusks*c* in its mouth among its teeth and was told, "Arise, devour many bodies!" 6After this, as I watched, another appeared, like a leopard. The beast had four wings of a bird on its back and four heads; and dominion was given to it. 7After this I saw in the visions by night a fourth beast, terrifying and dreadful and exceedingly strong. It had great iron teeth and was devouring, breaking in pieces, and stamping what was left with its feet. It was different from all the beasts that preceded it, and it had ten horns. 8I was considering the horns, when another horn appeared, a little one coming up among

a Q Ms Theodotion: MT adds *the beginning of the words; he said*   *b* Theodotion: Aram *Daniel answered and said, I*   *c* Or *ribs*

6:18 **FASTING**—*See* Spiritual Disciplines Index.

6:20 **SERVICE**—*See* Spiritual Disciplines Index.

6:22–23 **THE WITH-GOD LIFE**—*See* Spiritual Disciplines Index.

6:23 *because he had trusted in his God.* Daniel is unscathed, ostensibly due to his trust in God. Jesus trusted God equally, but was bloodied and killed. Again we note that blamelessness alone does not save.

6:26–27 *he has saved Daniel from the power of the lions.* As if to correct any perception that Daniel saved himself, this doxology rejoices over the One who "delivers and rescues."

7:2 *the four winds of heaven stirring up the great sea.* Though still in exile in Babylon, Daniel begins to have visions that extend beyond national borders. If the first six chapters showed that God is able to save Israel, the question from here forward is whether God can save an entire world beset by "beasts" and dangers.

them; to make room for it, three of the earlier horns were plucked up by the roots. There were eyes like human eyes in this horn, and a mouth speaking arrogantly.

Judgment before the Ancient One

9 As I watched,
> thrones were set in place,
>> and an Ancient One[a] took his throne,
> his clothing was white as snow,
>> and the hair of his head like pure wool;
> his throne was fiery flames,
>> and its wheels were burning fire.
10 A stream of fire issued
> and flowed out from his presence.
A thousand thousands served him,
> and ten thousand times ten thousand
>> stood attending him.
The court sat in judgment,
> and the books were opened.

11 I watched then because of the noise of the arrogant words that the horn was speaking. And as I watched, the beast was put to death, and its body destroyed and given over to be burned with fire. 12 As for the rest of the beasts, their dominion was taken away, but their lives were prolonged for a season and a time. 13 As I watched in the night visions,

> I saw one like a human being[b]
>> coming with the clouds of heaven.
> And he came to the Ancient One[a]
>> and was presented before him.
14 To him was given dominion
> and glory and kingship,
that all peoples, nations, and languages
> should serve him.
His dominion is an everlasting dominion

that shall not pass away,
> and his kingship is one
>> that shall never be destroyed.

Daniel's Visions Interpreted

15 As for me, Daniel, my spirit was troubled within me,[c] and the visions of my head terrified me. 16 I approached one of the attendants to ask him the truth concerning all this. So he said that he would disclose to me the interpretation of the matter: 17 "As for these four great beasts, four kings shall arise out of the earth. 18 But the holy ones of the Most High shall receive the kingdom and possess the kingdom forever—forever and ever."

19 Then I desired to know the truth concerning the fourth beast, which was different from all the rest, exceedingly terrifying, with its teeth of iron and claws of bronze, and which devoured and broke in pieces, and stamped what was left with its feet; 20 and concerning the ten horns that were on its head, and concerning the other horn, which came up and to make room for which three of them fell out—the horn that had eyes and a mouth that spoke arrogantly, and that seemed greater than the others. 21 As I looked, this horn made war with the holy ones and was prevailing over them, 22 until the Ancient One[a] came; then judgment was given for the holy ones of the Most High, and the time arrived when the holy ones gained possession of the kingdom.

23 This is what he said: "As for the fourth beast,

a Aram *an Ancient of Days* | b Aram *one like a son of man* | c Aram *troubled in its sheath*

7:13 *like a human being.* As the great arrogant, devouring beasts are destroyed, a new, saving figure who is "like a son of man" (Aramaic *bar* enash) appears. The use of a poetic simile ("like") has led to many different interpretations of this person, yet some conclusions can be made. First, he is allied with, not opposed to, the "Ancient One" (God). Second, his arrival inaugurates an era of justice and peace for the world and a new eschatological age for humankind. In the New Testament Gospels, Jesus calls himself "the Son of Man" eighty-one times, indicating that he and the early Church

saw him as the fulfillment of Daniel's vision.

7:14 *that shall never be destroyed.* Destruction comes to those who are bent on destroying others. Those who "serve" fare far better than those who seek dominion and power for themselves.

7:15 *the visions of my head terrified me.* Daniel makes a refreshing admission of his emotional state. His ability to confess his "troubled" spirit and "terrified" head reflects spiritual strength. Unlike the beasts (vv 8, 11), Daniel lacks arrogance. His hope rests in "the Most High," not in himself.

there shall be a fourth kingdom on earth
    that shall be different from all the
        other kingdoms;
it shall devour the whole earth,
    and trample it down, and break it to
        pieces.
24 As for the ten horns,
    out of this kingdom ten kings shall arise,
    and another shall arise after them.
This one shall be different from the
        former ones,
    and shall put down three kings.
25 He shall speak words against the Most
        High,
    shall wear out the holy ones of the
        Most High,
    and shall attempt to change the
        sacred seasons and the law;
and they shall be given into his power
    for a time, two times,*a* and half a time.
26 Then the court shall sit in judgment,
    and his dominion shall be taken away,
    to be consumed and totally destroyed.
27 The kingship and dominion
    and the greatness of the kingdoms
        under the whole heaven
shall be given to the people of the
        holy ones of the Most High;
    their kingdom shall be an everlasting
        kingdom,
    and all dominions shall serve and
        obey them."

28 Here the account ends. As for me, Daniel, my thoughts greatly terrified me, and my face turned pale; but I kept the matter in my mind.

Vision of a Ram and a Goat

8 In the third year of the reign of King Belshazzar a vision appeared to me, Daniel, after the one that had appeared to me at first. 2In the vision I was looking and saw myself in Susa the capital, in the province of Elam,*b* and I was by the river Ulai.*c* 3I looked up and saw a ram standing beside the river.*d* It had two horns. Both horns were long, but one was longer than the other, and the longer one came up second. 4I saw the ram charging westward and northward and southward. All beasts were powerless to withstand it, and no one could rescue from its power; it did as it pleased and became strong.

5 As I was watching, a male goat appeared from the west, coming across the face of the whole earth without touching the ground. The goat had a horn*e* between its eyes. 6It came toward the ram with the two horns that I had seen standing beside the river,*d* and it ran at it with savage force. 7I saw it approaching the ram. It was enraged against it and struck the ram, breaking its two horns. The ram did not have power to withstand it; it threw the ram down to the ground and trampled upon it, and there was no one who could rescue the ram from its power. 8Then the male goat grew exceedingly great; but at the height of its power, the great horn was broken, and in its place there came up four prominent horns toward the four winds of heaven.

9 Out of one of them came another*f* horn, a little one, which grew exceedingly great toward the south, toward the east, and toward the beautiful land. 10It grew as high as the host of heaven. It threw down to the earth some of the host and some of the stars, and trampled on them. 11Even against the prince of the host it acted arrogantly; it took the regular burnt of-

a Aram *a time, times*   *b* Gk Theodotion: MT
Q Ms repeat *in the vision I was looking*   *c* Or *the
Ulai Gate*   *d* Or *gate*   *e* Theodotion: Gk *one
horn*; Heb *a horn of vision*   *f* Cn Compare 7.8:
Heb *one*

7:26–27 *his dominion shall be taken away.*
The vision of this chapter looks past the apparent realities of the world. It believes that the "beasts" of the present will not rule forever, that the ways of destruction are ending. A new dominion "shall be given to the . . . holy ones of the Most High." Daniel's view of the future is not unlike that of Jesus, who foresaw that "the meek . . . will inherit the earth" (Matt 5:5).

8:5 *across the face of the whole earth.* If today's world seems to be in a precarious state, Daniel reminds us that it always has been. Yet, from our perspective, there is cause for hope. If marauding "rams" and "goats" did not destroy the earth two and a half millennia ago, perhaps our warring world will be stopped short of total annihilation too.

fering away from him and overthrew the place of his sanctuary. [12]Because of wickedness, the host was given over to it together with the regular burnt offering;[a] it cast truth to the ground, and kept prospering in what it did. [13]Then I heard a holy one speaking, and another holy one said to the one that spoke, "For how long is this vision concerning the regular burnt offering, the transgression that makes desolate, and the giving over of the sanctuary and host to be trampled?"[a] [14]And he answered him,[b] "For two thousand three hundred evenings and mornings; then the sanctuary shall be restored to its rightful state."

Gabriel Interprets the Vision

15 When I, Daniel, had seen the vision, I tried to understand it. Then someone appeared standing before me, having the appearance of a man, [16]and I heard a human voice by the Ulai, calling, "Gabriel, help this man understand the vision." [17]So he came near where I stood; and when he came, I became frightened and fell prostrate. But he said to me, "Understand, O mortal,[c] that the vision is for the time of the end."

18 As he was speaking to me, I fell into a trance, face to the ground; then he touched me and set me on my feet. [19]He said, "Listen, and I will tell you what will take place later in the period of wrath; for it refers to the appointed time of the end. [20]As for the ram that you saw with the two horns, these are the kings of Media and Persia. [21]The male goat[d] is the king of Greece, and the great horn between its eyes is the first king. [22]As for the horn that was broken, in place of which four others arose, four kingdoms shall arise from his[e] nation, but not with his power.

23 At the end of their rule,
  when the transgressions have reached
    their full measure,
  a king of bold countenance shall arise,
    skilled in intrigue.
24 He shall grow strong in power,[f]
  shall cause fearful destruction,
  and shall succeed in what he does.
He shall destroy the powerful
  and the people of the holy ones.
25 By his cunning
  he shall make deceit prosper under
    his hand,
  and in his own mind he shall be great.
Without warning he shall destroy many
  and shall even rise up against the
    Prince of princes.
But he shall be broken, and not by
    human hands.
[26]The vision of the evenings and the mornings that has been told is true. As for you, seal up the vision, for it refers to many days from now."

27 So I, Daniel, was overcome and lay sick for some days; then I arose and went about the king's business. But I was dismayed by the vision and did not understand it.

[a] Meaning of Heb uncertain   [b] Gk Theodotion Syr Vg: Heb *me*   [c] Heb *son of man*   [d] Or *shaggy male goat*   [e] Gk Theodotion Vg: Heb *the*   [f] Theodotion and one Gk Ms: Heb repeats (from 8.22) *but not with his power*

8:16 *Gabriel.* This archangel, second only to Michael in Christian lore, is frequently the herald of new beginnings. He visits Mary to announce the birth of her child (Luke 1:26) and is traditionally identified as the one who will sound the trumpet at Christ's return (1 Thess 4:16). Here too he proclaims a new era and new dynasty to redress evil.

8:18 *set me on my feet.* Daniel's falling to the ground and being "set on [his] feet" has overtones of dying and rising. Not only does this have New Testament implications; it also mirrors the suffering and salvation of the nations in this chapter.

8:19 *time of the end.* What seems like the end may not be, despite Gabriel's prediction. As Jesus tells his disciples, no one knows about that day or hour, not even the angels (Mark 13:32). Looking too closely for signs of the end may keep us from seeing God's saving work.

8:25 *and not by human hands.* A single sentence in this chapter asserts God's role in history, ensuring that evil shall not prevail.

8:27 *I arose and went about the king's business.* Though dismayed, confused, and "sick" over the world's condition, Daniel does not surrender or retreat. He goes about his business diligently. Faith is the call to keep going despite adversity.

Daniel's Prayer for the People

9 In the first year of Darius son of Ahasuerus, by birth a Mede, who became king over the realm of the Chaldeans— 2in the first year of his reign, I, Daniel, perceived in the books the number of years that, according to the word of the LORD to the prophet Jeremiah, must be fulfilled for the devastation of Jerusalem, namely, seventy years.

3 Then I turned to the Lord God, to seek an answer by prayer and supplication with fasting and sackcloth and ashes. 4I prayed to the LORD my God and made confession, saying,

"Ah, Lord, great and awesome God, keeping covenant and steadfast love with those who love you and keep your commandments, 5we have sinned and done wrong, acted wickedly and rebelled, turning aside from your commandments and ordinances. 6We have not listened to your servants the prophets, who spoke in your name to our kings, our princes, and our ancestors, and to all the people of the land.

7 "Righteousness is on your side, O Lord, but open shame, as at this day, falls on us, the people of Judah, the inhabitants of Jerusalem, and all Israel, those who are near and those who are far away, in all the lands to which you have driven them, because of the treachery that they have committed against you. 8Open shame, O LORD, falls on us, our kings, our officials, and our ancestors, because we have sinned against you. 9To the Lord our God belong mercy and forgiveness, for we have rebelled against him, 10and have not obeyed the voice of the LORD our God by following his laws, which he set before us by his servants the prophets.

11 "All Israel has transgressed your law and turned aside, refusing to obey your voice. So the curse and the oath written in the law of Moses, the servant of God, have been poured out upon us, because we have sinned against you. 12He has confirmed his words, which he spoke against us and against our rulers, by bringing upon us a calamity so great that what has been done against Jerusalem has never before been done under the whole heaven. 13Just as it is written in the law of Moses, all this calamity has come upon us. We did not entreat the favor of the LORD our God, turning from our iniquities and reflecting on his[a] fidelity. 14So the LORD kept watch over this calamity until he brought it upon us. Indeed, the LORD our God is right in all that he has done; for we have disobeyed his voice.

15 "And now, O Lord our God, who brought your people out of the land of Egypt with a mighty hand and made your name renowned even to this day—we have sinned, we have done wickedly. 16O Lord, in view of all your righteous acts, let your anger and wrath, we pray, turn away from your city

a Heb your

9:1–27 seventy years. The two previous chapters dealt with crises involving politics and powers. This chapter concerns a crisis of timing and delayed expectations. Around 587 BC Jeremiah announced that Israel's exile would last seventy years. But, at the time of this writing, nearly five hundred years have passed! Is Jeremiah's prophecy not trustworthy? Daniel seeks an answer through prayer (v 3) based not in human righteousness, but God's "great mercies" (v 18). Like the father of the prodigal son (Luke 15:20–24), God hastens to reply (v 23). Through Gabriel, God announces not seventy years of exile, but "seventy weeks of years" (v 24, RSV), or 490 years in all. In other words, the time of exile is almost over. The time of God's coming is near, says the prophet.

9:3 FASTING—See Spiritual Disciplines Index.

Responding
9:3–21 PRAYER and CONFESSION. In this prayer Daniel confesses his own sin and also the sin of the People of God, one of many biblical examples of confession by proxy. Although it can never take the place of confession of our individual and specific sins, we should not overlook corporate confession in our own practice. During your next prayer time, contemplate the sin of your family, your church, your nation; confess these too and ask God's forgiveness even for those sins in which you have been unwittingly complicit. See also Spiritual Disciplines Index.

Jerusalem, your holy mountain; because of our sins and the iniquities of our ancestors, Jerusalem and your people have become a disgrace among all our neighbors. 17Now therefore, O our God, listen to the prayer of your servant and to his supplication, and for your own sake, Lord,*a* let your face shine upon your desolated sanctuary. 18Incline your ear, O my God, and hear. Open your eyes and look at our desolation and the city that bears your name. We do not present our supplication before you on the ground of our righteousness, but on the ground of your great mercies. 19O Lord, hear; O Lord, forgive; O Lord, listen and act and do not delay! For your own sake, O my God, because your city and your people bear your name!"

The Seventy Weeks

20 While I was speaking, and was praying and confessing my sin and the sin of my people Israel, and presenting my supplication before the Lord my God on behalf of the holy mountain of my God— 21while I was speaking in prayer, the man Gabriel, whom I had seen before in a vision, came to me in swift flight at the time of the evening sacrifice. 22He came*b* and said to me, "Daniel, I have now come out to give you wisdom and understanding. 23At the beginning of your supplications a word went out, and I have come to declare it, for you are greatly beloved. So consider the word and understand the vision:

24 "Seventy weeks are decreed for your people and your holy city: to finish the transgression, to put an end to sin, and to atone for iniquity, to bring in everlasting righteousness, to seal both vision and prophet, and to anoint a most holy place.*c* 25Know therefore and understand: from the time that the word went out to restore and rebuild Jerusalem until the time of an anointed prince, there shall

be seven weeks; and for sixty-two weeks it shall be built again with streets and moat, but in a troubled time. 26After the sixty-two weeks, an anointed one shall be cut off and shall have nothing, and the troops of the prince who is to come shall destroy the city and the sanctuary. Its*d* end shall come with a flood, and to the end there shall be war. Desolations are decreed. 27He shall make a strong covenant with many for one week, and for half of the week he shall make sacrifice and offering cease; and in their place*e* shall be an abomination that desolates, until the decreed end is poured out upon the desolator."

Conflict of Nations and Heavenly Powers

10 In the third year of King Cyrus of Persia a word was revealed to Daniel, who was named Belteshazzar. The word was true, and it concerned a great conflict. He understood the word, having received understanding in the vision.

2 At that time I, Daniel, had been mourning for three weeks. 3I had eaten no rich food, no meat or wine had entered my mouth, and I had not anointed myself at all, for the full three weeks. 4On the twenty-fourth day of the first month, as I was standing on the bank of the great river (that is, the Tigris), 5I looked up and saw a man clothed in linen, with a belt of gold from Uphaz around his waist. 6His body was like beryl, his face like lightning, his eyes like flaming torches, his arms and legs like the gleam of burnished bronze, and the sound of his words like the roar of a multitude. 7I, Daniel, alone saw the vision; the people who were with me did not see the vision, though a great trembling fell

a Theodotion Vg Compare Syr: Heb *for the Lord's sake*   *b* Gk Syr: Heb *He made to understand*   *c* Or *thing* or *one*   *d* Or *His*   *e* Cn: Meaning of Heb uncertain

---

10:1–21 He *understood the word*. This chapter, part of a unit with chapters 11–12, contains many marks common to a prophet's call: divine confrontation (v 7), introductory word (v 11), commission (v 14), the prophet's objection (v 17), divine reassurance (vv 18–19), and the prophet's acceptance (v 19b). Several features, however,

make this call unique. Physical touch is prominent (vv 10, 16, 18). The one called is twice identified as "greatly beloved" (vv 11, 19). And, most notably, Daniel is called less to speak God's word than to "understand what is to happen" (v 14). This understanding is the basis for the final two chapters.

upon them, and they fled and hid themselves. [8]So I was left alone to see this great vision. My strength left me, and my complexion grew deathly pale, and I retained no strength. [9]Then I heard the sound of his words; and when I heard the sound of his words, I fell into a trance, face to the ground.

10 But then a hand touched me and roused me to my hands and knees. [11]He said to me, "Daniel, greatly beloved, pay attention to the words that I am going to speak to you. Stand on your feet, for I have now been sent to you." So while he was speaking this word to me, I stood up trembling. [12]He said to me, "Do not fear, Daniel, for from the first day that you set your mind to gain understanding and to humble yourself before your God, your words have been heard, and I have come because of your words. [13]But the prince of the kingdom of Persia opposed me twenty-one days. So Michael, one of the chief princes, came to help me, and I left him there with the prince of the kingdom of Persia,[a] [14]and have come to help you understand what is to happen to your people at the end of days. For there is a further vision for those days."

15 While he was speaking these words to me, I turned my face toward the ground and was speechless. [16]Then one in human form touched my lips, and I opened my mouth to speak, and said to the one who stood before me, "My lord, because of the vision such pains have come upon me that I retain no strength. [17]How can my lord's servant talk with my lord? For I am shaking,[b] no strength remains in me, and no breath is left in me."

18 Again one in human form touched me and strengthened me. [19]He said, "Do not fear, greatly beloved, you are safe. Be strong and courageous!" When he spoke to me, I was strengthened and said, "Let my lord speak, for

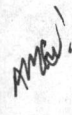

you have strengthened me." [20]Then he said, "Do you know why I have come to you? Now I must return to fight against the prince of Persia, and when I am through with him, the prince of Greece will come. [21]But I am to tell you what is inscribed in the book of truth. There is no one with me who contends against these princes except Michael, your prince.

11 [1]As for me, in the first year of Darius the Mede, I stood up to support and strengthen him.

2 "Now I will announce the truth to you. Three more kings shall arise in Persia. The fourth shall be far richer than all of them, and when he has become strong through his riches, he shall stir up all against the kingdom of Greece. [3]Then a warrior king shall arise, who shall rule with great dominion and take action as he pleases. [4]And while still rising in power, his kingdom shall be broken and divided toward the four winds of heaven, but not to his posterity, nor according to the dominion with which he ruled; for his kingdom shall be uprooted and go to others besides these.

5 "Then the king of the south shall grow strong, but one of his officers shall grow stronger than he and shall rule a realm greater than his own realm. [6]After some years they shall make an alliance, and the daughter of the king of the south shall come to the king of the north to ratify the agreement. But she shall not retain her power, and his offspring shall not endure. She shall be given up, she and her attendants and her child and the one who supported her.

"In those times [7]a branch from her roots shall rise up in his place. He shall come against the army and enter the fortress of the

---

a Gk Theodotion: Heb *I was left there with the kings of Persia*   *b* Gk: Heb *from now*

11:1–45 *Three more kings shall arise in Persia.* In contrast to the allegorical beasts of chapters 7–8, the material here is plainly reported. The nations of Persia, Greece, Egypt, Libya, and Ethiopia are named. The exploits, intrigues, and alliances of kings are detailed and are generally verifiable by historians. The chaos and suffering evident in prior chapters is unabated, however,

and abominations and idolatry remain. Yet "the people who are loyal to their God shall stand firm and take action" (v 32). Faith in the sovereign God translates into concrete action by believers. Not so for the wicked and power-hungry rulers. They shall come to their end with no one to help them (v 45b).

king of the north, and he shall take action against them and prevail. 8Even their gods, with their idols and with their precious vessels of silver and gold, he shall carry off to Egypt as spoils of war. For some years he shall refrain from attacking the king of the north; 9then the latter shall invade the realm of the king of the south, but will return to his own land.

10 "His sons shall wage war and assemble a multitude of great forces, which shall advance like a flood and pass through, and again shall carry the war as far as his fortress. 11Moved with rage, the king of the south shall go out and do battle against the king of the north, who shall muster a great multitude, which shall, however, be defeated by his enemy. 12When the multitude has been carried off, his heart shall be exalted, and he shall overthrow tens of thousands, but he shall not prevail. 13For the king of the north shall again raise a multitude, larger than the former, and after some years*a* he shall advance with a great army and abundant supplies.

14 "In those times many shall rise against the king of the south. The lawless among your own people shall lift themselves up in order to fulfill the vision, but they shall fail. 15Then the king of the north shall come and throw up siegeworks, and take a well-fortified city. And the forces of the south shall not stand, not even his picked troops, for there shall be no strength to resist. 16But he who comes against him shall take the actions he pleases, and no one shall withstand him. He shall take a position in the beautiful land, and all of it shall be in his power. 17He shall set his mind to come with the strength of his whole kingdom, and he shall bring terms of peace*b* and perform them. In order to destroy the kingdom,*c* he shall give him a woman in marriage; but it shall not succeed or be to his advantage. 18Afterward he shall turn to the coastlands, and shall capture many. But a commander shall put an end to his insolence; indeed,*d* he shall turn his insolence back upon him. 19Then he shall turn back toward the fortresses of his own land, but he shall stumble and fall, and shall not be found.

20 "Then shall arise in his place one who

shall send an official for the glory of the kingdom; but within a few days he shall be broken, though not in anger or in battle. 21In his place shall arise a contemptible person on whom royal majesty had not been conferred; he shall come in without warning and obtain the kingdom through intrigue. 22Armies shall be utterly swept away and broken before him, and the prince of the covenant as well. 23And after an alliance is made with him, he shall act deceitfully and become strong with a small party. 24Without warning he shall come into the richest parts*e* of the province and do what none of his predecessors had ever done, lavishing plunder, spoil, and wealth on them. He shall devise plans against strongholds, but only for a time. 25He shall stir up his power and determination against the king of the south with a great army, and the king of the south shall wage war with a much greater and stronger army. But he shall not succeed, for plots shall be devised against him 26by those who eat of the royal rations. They shall break him, his army shall be swept away, and many shall fall slain. 27The two kings, their minds bent on evil, shall sit at one table and exchange lies. But it shall not succeed, for there remains an end at the time appointed. 28He shall return to his land with great wealth, but his heart shall be set against the holy covenant. He shall work his will, and return to his own land.

29 "At the time appointed he shall return and come into the south, but this time it shall not be as it was before. 30For ships of Kittim shall come against him, and he shall lose heart and withdraw. He shall be enraged and take action against the holy covenant. He shall turn back and pay heed to those who forsake the holy covenant. 31Forces sent by him shall occupy and profane the temple and fortress. They shall abolish the regular burnt offering and set up the abomination that makes desolate. 32He shall seduce with intrigue those who violate the covenant; but the people who are loyal to their God shall

---

a Heb *and at the end of the times years*   *b* Gk: Heb *kingdom, and upright ones with him*   *c* Heb *it*
d Meaning of Heb uncertain   *e* Or *among the richest men*

stand firm and take action. ³³The wise among the people shall give understanding to many; for some days, however, they shall fall by sword and flame, and suffer captivity and plunder. ³⁴When they fall victim, they shall receive a little help, and many shall join them insincerely. ³⁵Some of the wise shall fall, so that they may be refined, purified, and cleansed, *a* until the time of the end, for there is still an interval until the time appointed.

36 "The king shall act as he pleases. He shall exalt himself and consider himself greater than any god, and shall speak horrendous things against the God of gods. He shall prosper until the period of wrath is completed, for what is determined shall be done. ³⁷He shall pay no respect to the gods of his ancestors, or to the one beloved by women; he shall pay no respect to any other god, for he shall consider himself greater than all. ³⁸He shall honor the god of fortresses instead of these; a god whom his ancestors did not know he shall honor with gold and silver, with precious stones and costly gifts. ³⁹He shall deal with the strongest fortresses by the help of a foreign god. Those who acknowledge him he shall make more wealthy, and shall appoint them as rulers over many, and shall distribute the land for a price.

The Time of the End

40 "At the time of the end the king of the south shall attack him. But the king of the north shall rush upon him like a whirlwind, with chariots and horsemen, and with many ships. He shall advance against countries and pass through like a flood. ⁴¹He shall come into the beautiful land, and tens of thousands shall fall victim, but Edom and Moab and the main part of the Ammonites shall escape from his power. ⁴²He shall stretch out his hand against the countries, and the land of Egypt shall not escape. ⁴³He shall become

ruler of the treasures of gold and of silver, and all the riches of Egypt; and the Libyans and the Ethiopians *b* shall follow in his train. ⁴⁴But reports from the east and the north shall alarm him, and he shall go out with great fury to bring ruin and complete destruction to many. ⁴⁵He shall pitch his palatial tents between the sea and the beautiful holy mountain. Yet he shall come to his end, with no one to help him.

The Resurrection of the Dead

12 "At that time Michael, the great prince, the protector of your people, shall arise. There shall be a time of anguish, such as has never occurred since nations first came into existence. But at that time your people shall be delivered, everyone who is found written in the book. ²Many of those who sleep in the dust of the earth *c* shall awake, some to everlasting life, and some to shame and everlasting contempt. ³Those who are wise shall shine like the brightness of the sky, *d* and those who lead many to righteousness, like the stars forever and ever. ⁴But you, Daniel, keep the words secret and the book sealed until the time of the end. Many shall be running back and forth, and evil *e* shall increase."

5 Then I, Daniel, looked, and two others appeared, one standing on this bank of the stream and one on the other. ⁶One of them said to the man clothed in linen, who was upstream, "How long shall it be until the end of these wonders?" ⁷The man clothed in linen, who was upstream, raised his right hand and his left hand toward heaven. And I heard him swear by the one who lives forever that it would be for a time, two times, and half a

a Heb *made them white*   *b* Or *Nubians;* Heb *Cushites*   *c* Or *the land of dust*   *d* Or *dome*   *e* Cn Compare Gk: Heb *knowledge*

12:1 *protector of your people.* Michael, like Gabriel, is a guardian angel not only for individuals, but for the whole nation.

12:2 *those who sleep in the dust of the earth shall awake.* This is one of very few explicit references to resurrection in the Hebrew Bible and is perhaps the most clear. It attests to God's

ultimate victory not only over despotic kings, but over the last enemy, death (1 Cor 15:26). Though rare in this literature, resurrection attests to Daniel's understanding of God's dominion over *all* of creation and is a suitable "reward" for God's people as they "persevere," "rest," and "rise" each day in a hostile world (vv 12–13).

time,[a] and that when the shattering of the power of the holy people comes to an end, all these things would be accomplished. 8I heard but could not understand; so I said, "My lord, what shall be the outcome of these things?" 9He said, "Go your way, Daniel, for the words are to remain secret and sealed until the time of the end. 10Many shall be purified, cleansed, and refined, but the wicked shall continue to act wickedly. None of the wicked shall understand, but those who are wise shall understand. 11From the time that the regular burnt offering is taken away and the abomination that desolates is set up, there shall be one thousand two hundred ninety days. 12Happy are those who persevere and attain the thousand three hundred thirty-five days. 13But you, go your way,[b] and rest; you shall rise for your reward at the end of the days."

a Heb *a time, times, and a half*
b Gk Theodotion: Heb adds *to the end*

HOSEA

H osea is historically placed "in the days" of the Divided Kingdom during the eighth century BC (1:1)—a significant placement because Hosea's message represents a last call from God to the Northern Kingdom, Israel, before its destruction and exile at the hands of the Assyrian Empire in 722/721 BC. The book of Hosea is canonically placed first in the Hebrew Bible's Book of the Twelve (or the Minor Prophets, as named in Christian Scripture)—a strategic position insofar as the sweep of its message, as laid out in its first three chapters, introduces a dramatic preview of the implicit story line of the People of God throughout the rest of the Book of the Twelve. It is a line that moves from covenant betrayal to punishment to restoration.

Adulterous Israel

This drama unfolds in a painful, real-life marital experience that Hosea undergoes at God's command: he marries a "wife of whoredom," names and accommodates the "children of whoredom" she bears, and finally takes back the unfaithful wife. God directs these extreme acts in order to bring forth through this prophet a message concerning the parallel experiences that God sees in his own "marital" relationship with Israel. The book's second verse captures this two-step movement, which corresponds with the book's two-part literary structure: "When the LORD first spoke through Hosea, the LORD said to Hosea . . ." (1:2). Chapters 1–3 focus on God's words to Hosea (see 1:1, 4, 6, 9; 3:1); then 4:1 introduces the remaining chapters of the book (4–14) as a word that comes through the prophet to address God's people: "Hear the word of the LORD, O people of Israel; for the LORD has an indictment against the inhabitants of the land. There is no faithfulness or loyalty, and no knowledge of God in the land."

Here the primary form of the remaining chapters is identified as legal indictment or covenant lawsuit and the primary theme as the charge of unfaithfulness and absence of the knowledge of God. This theme is sounded repeatedly (4:6; 5:4; 6:6; 11:3),

See also *"The With-God Life" essay for this section of the Bible,*
"The People of God in Rebellion," pp. 975–79.

and takes on special conjugal associations within the marital context that Hosea has taken up. Thus Hosea, in divorce-court fashion, moves to the summarizing verdict: "My people are destroyed for lack of knowledge" (4:6). This is not about intellectual knowledge, but rather the intimacy and intercourse with God that constitute faithful covenantal relations (cf. Gen 4:1)—those relations capable of producing children who, unlike Hosea's own representative children (1:4–9), bear the names and reflect the character of covenant identity. Poetically expressed, the ensuing case lays out how loss of intimacy with God has produced illicit, illegitimate, and unjust relations with others.

A Call to Know God

Yet, incredibly, just as Hosea is directed beyond his broken home toward a restored family (3:1–5), God in the end appeals his own final verdict and points beyond Israel's exile to reclamation of his beloved (14:4–7; cf. 2:14–20) and offspring (11:7–9; cf. 1:10–11; 2:21–23), but not without the wrenching internal struggle that Hosea himself undergoes firsthand (see note to 11:8).

Thus in Hosea we encounter one of Scripture's most poignant calls to "know God." In this prophet we find a model instance of radical spiritual formation and also a message that probes the dynamics and depths of spiritual transformation as it moves dramatically and poetically from the passions, pains, and promises of Hosea's family affairs to the covenant relations exposed in the very heart of God and his people.

This call to "know God" echoes down through the centuries and into our churches and families and lives. We today stand under judgment, for we too have gone "whoring" after other gods, gods of wealth and prestige and power. And Yahweh's call to repentance comes to us. Not a superficial, ritual repentance, mind you; "I desire steadfast love and not sacrifice, the knowledge of God rather than burnt offerings" (6:6). No, God has been leading us "with cords of human kindness, with bands of love" (11:4), and our response needs to be one of utter, compassionate surrender, a response of heart and soul and mind and strength.

—*Rickie D. Moore*

---

1 The word of the LORD that came to Hosea son of Beeri, in the days of Kings Uzziah, Jotham, Ahaz, and Hezekiah of Judah, and in the days of King Jeroboam son of Joash of Israel.

The Family of Hosea

2 When the LORD first spoke through Hosea, the LORD said to Hosea, "Go, take for yourself a wife of whoredom and have children of whoredom, for the land commits

---

1:1 *The word . . . came . . . in the days . . . of Judah and . . . of Israel.* The divine word cuts into our history and across our political divisions. By referring to the national dating systems of both Israel and Judah, the prophetic word here, as elsewhere (e.g., Ezek 37:15–28), refuses to

concede the divorce between the North and South as final, as will become explicit in v 11. We are put on notice right away, even before we get to Hosea's divorce, that God's word can challenge the finality of our most settled divisions.

great whoredom by forsaking the LORD." [3]So he went and took Gomer daughter of Diblaim, and she conceived and bore him a son.

4 And the LORD said to him, "Name him Jezreel;[a] for in a little while I will punish the house of Jehu for the blood of Jezreel, and I will put an end to the kingdom of the house of Israel. [5]On that day I will break the bow of Israel in the valley of Jezreel."

6 She conceived again and bore a daughter. Then the LORD said to him, "Name her Lo-ruhamah,[b] for I will no longer have pity on the house of Israel or forgive them. [7]But I will have pity on the house of Judah, and I will save them by the LORD their God; I will not save them by bow, or by sword, or by war, or by horses, or by horsemen."

8 When she had weaned Lo-ruhamah, she conceived and bore a son. [9]Then the LORD said, "Name him Lo-ammi,[c] for you are not my people and I am not your God."[d]

The Restoration of Israel

10[e] Yet the number of the people of Israel shall be like the sand of the sea, which can be neither measured nor numbered; and in the place where it was said to them, "You are not my people," it shall be said to them, "Children of the living God." [11]The people of Judah and the people of Israel shall be gathered together, and they shall appoint for themselves one head; and they shall take possession of[f] the land, for great shall be the day of Jezreel.

2[g] Say to your brother,[h] Ammi,[i] and to your sister,[j] Ruhamah.[k]

Israel's Infidelity, Punishment, and Redemption

2 Plead with your mother, plead—
　for she is not my wife,
　　and I am not her husband—
　　　that she put away her whoring from her
　　　　face,

a That is *God sows*　　b That is *Not pitied*　　c That is *Not my people*　　d Heb *I am not yours*　　e Ch 2.1 in Heb　　f Heb *rise up from*　　g Ch 2.3 in Heb　　h Gk: Heb *brothers*　　i That is *My people*　　j Gk Vg: Heb *sisters*　　k That is *Pitied*

1:2 *the LORD said to Hosea.* The word *to* the prophet is preparatory to the word that will be spoken *through* the prophet. The messenger's life must bear the message before his lips are ready to speak it. Thus, God's word is about more than simply conveying information; it is about effecting formation and evoking transformation. *take for yourself a wife of whoredom and have children of whoredom.* God resorts here to drastic, even scandalous measures to reach a covenant people who have themselves scandalized the sacred covenant. God's word, God's prophet, even God's own reputation are all put at risk in God's desperate desire for relationship with his people.

Responding

1:2 CHASTITY. The scandal of Hosea, with its shocking directive from God to marry a "wife of whoredom," illustrates just how important it is to govern our sexual impulses. According to Dallas Willard, chastity is not necessarily complete abstinence, but rather the state that results when we turn away from dwelling on the sexual dimensions of our relationships and focus instead on the other positive aspects of our interactions with those around us. "To practice chastity, then, we must first practice love, practice seeking the good of those of the opposite sex we come in contact with," he writes in *The Spirit of the Disciplines*. Contemplate the role of chastity in your own life. *See also* Spiritual Disciplines Index.

1:9 *Name him Lo-ammi, for you are not my people.* The covenant unfaithfulness of the People of God will inevitably come to mark their children's identity, or rather the loss of their identity, in what amounts to an "x-ing" out of chosenness that leaves only a vacuous stigma, not unlike the name "Generation X" in our own culture.

2:2 *she is not my wife, and I am not her husband.* God here parallels his own "marital" (covenant) status with Israel to Hosea's in what is virtually an announcement of divorce. The bad news must be named, uncovered (see 1:3, 10), and elaborated (even to the children; see 2:1–13) against all inclinations to cover up, whitewash, and deny. Such prophetic oracles witness against our "cheap grace" spiritualities that presume to lay claim to the "good news" without ever having faced the bad.

and her adultery from between her
        breasts,
3 or I will strip her naked
        and expose her as in the day she was
            born,
        and make her like a wilderness,
        and turn her into a parched land,
        and kill her with thirst.
4 Upon her children also I will have no
        pity,
        because they are children of
            whoredom.
5 For their mother has played the whore;
        she who conceived them has acted
            shamefully.
        For she said, "I will go after my lovers;
        they give me my bread and my water,
        my wool and my flax, my oil and my
            drink."
6 Therefore I will hedge up her*a* way with
        thorns;
        and I will build a wall against her,
        so that she cannot find her paths.
7 She shall pursue her lovers,
        but not overtake them;
        and she shall seek them,
        but shall not find them.
        Then she shall say, "I will go
        and return to my first husband,
        for it was better with me then than
            now."
8 She did not know
        that it was I who gave her
        the grain, the wine, and the oil,
        and who lavished upon her silver
        and gold that they used for Baal.
9 Therefore I will take back
        my grain in its time,
        and my wine in its season,
        and I will take away my wool and my
            flax,
        which were to cover her nakedness.
10 Now I will uncover her shame
        in the sight of her lovers,

and no one shall rescue her out of my
        hand.
11 I will put an end to all her mirth,
        her festivals, her new moons, her
            sabbaths,
        and all her appointed festivals.
12 I will lay waste her vines and her fig
        trees,
        of which she said,
    "These are my pay,
        which my lovers have given me."
    I will make them a forest,
        and the wild animals shall devour
            them.
13 I will punish her for the festival days of
        the Baals,
        when she offered incense to them
    and decked herself with her ring and
            jewelry,
        and went after her lovers,
        and forgot me, says the LORD.

14 Therefore, I will now allure her,
        and bring her into the wilderness,
        and speak tenderly to her.
15 From there I will give her her vineyards,
        and make the Valley of Achor a door
            of hope.
    There she shall respond as in the days of
        her youth,
        as at the time when she came out of
            the land of Egypt.
16 On that day, says the LORD, you will call
me, "My husband," and no longer will you
call me, "My Baal."*b* 17 For I will remove the
names of the Baals from her mouth, and they
shall be mentioned by name no more. 18 I will
make for you*c* a covenant on that day with
the wild animals, the birds of the air, and the
creeping things of the ground; and I will abolish*d* the bow, the sword, and war from the
land; and I will make you lie down in safety.

a Gk Syr: Heb *your*   *b* That is, *"My master"*
c Heb *them*   *d* Heb *break*

2:14 *Therefore, I will now allure her.* This
startling turn in God's intention from condemnation to mercy is made all the more surprising by
its being introduced with the word "therefore."
Far from following as a logical consequence, this
move of divine grace is diametrically opposed to
what has preceded it. Yet does not God's grace
do just that, coming to us in ways that fly in the
face of all rhyme and reason? No wonder we
call it amazing!

HOSEA

A Faithful Lover

Selected Scriptures: *Hosea 1–6; 11–14*

Containing some of the most emotion-filled language of the Bible, Hosea's words to Israel pulse with God's passion and his raging, intense, unfailing love for the people he made. Hosea also reveals God's jealousy, his disgust at Israel's whoredom, and his anger at its outright spurning of his pure love. As a visible, earthy demonstration, God asked Hosea to live out on a human scale what God was experiencing on a divine scale. "Go, take for yourself a wife of whoredom, . . . for the land commits great whoredom by forsaking the LORD" (Hos 1:2). Hosea agreed to marry and love a prostitute, Gomer, to bring her into his home, and to care for her despite her unfaithfulness.

Through Hosea's experiences with Gomer, we see the reaches of God's anguished, heartrending commitment to his people. As both thwarted lover and deserted parent, God pours out his heart's emotion toward Israel, reminiscing, chastising, lamenting, warning of Israel's grim future, and, finally, promising to take her back, heal her, and cause her to flourish. "I will now allure her, and bring her into the wilderness, and speak tenderly to her" (2:14).

Hosea modeled God's commitment to his people and his unfailing love despite their waywardness. God holds the same love for each one of us. Just as the Israelites turned their back on God, enticed by the gods around them or prompted by fear to seek other promises of security, we too step away from our lives with God, turning to other relationships, money, or status to meet our soul's needs.

God experiences the same anguish today as he did in Hosea's day: "A wind has wrapped them in its wings, and they shall be ashamed because of their altars" (4:19). "Their deeds do not permit them to return to their God. For the spirit of whoredom is within them, and they do not know the LORD" (5:4). We, like Israel, are "silly and without sense" (7:11). Yet God, the most faithful lover, cannot let us go: "How can I give you up . . . ? How can I hand you over . . . ?" (11:8).

In the end, it was a prayer of repentance and a living prayer of love God asked of his people. "Take words with you and return to the LORD . . . [offering] the fruit of [your] lips" (14:2), Hosea directed them.

Hosea awaited Gomer's plea for forgiveness and her spoken love. He then yearned to see her words lived out in their life together. God too waits to hear us voice our love, ask for forgiveness, and express a loyal commitment to live with him and only him. Then he waits to see our very lives become a prayer to him.

Personal Reflection

- Reflect quietly, prayerfully, upon the story of Hosea and Gomer, God and you. What do you learn?
- Has God ever asked you to love someone sacrificially in any way similar to what he asked of Hosea? How did you respond?

PROFILE

[19]And I will take you for my wife forever; I will take you for my wife in righteousness and in justice, in steadfast love, and in mercy. [20]I will take you for my wife in faithfulness; and you shall know the LORD.

[21] On that day I will answer, says the LORD,
  I will answer the heavens
  and they shall answer the earth;
[22] and the earth shall answer the grain,
    the wine, and the oil,
  and they shall answer Jezreel;[a]
[23] and I will sow him[b] for myself in the
    land.
  And I will have pity on Lo-ruhamah,[c]
  and I will say to Lo-ammi,[d] "You are
    my people";
  and he shall say, "You are my God."

Further Assurances of God's Redeeming Love

3 The LORD said to me again, "Go, love a woman who has a lover and is an adulteress, just as the LORD loves the people of Israel, though they turn to other gods and love raisin cakes." [2]So I bought her for fifteen shekels of silver and a homer of barley and a measure of wine.[e] [3]And I said to her, "You must remain as mine for many days; you shall not play the whore, you shall not have intercourse with a man, nor I with you." [4]For the Israelites shall remain many days without king or prince, without sacrifice or pillar, without ephod or teraphim. [5]Afterward the Israelites shall return and seek the LORD their God, and David their king; they shall come in awe to the LORD and to his goodness in the latter days.

God Accuses Israel

4 Hear the word of the LORD, O people of
    Israel;
  for the LORD has an indictment against
    the inhabitants of the land.
There is no faithfulness or loyalty,
  and no knowledge of God in the land.
[2] Swearing, lying, and murder,
  and stealing and adultery break out;
  bloodshed follows bloodshed.
[3] Therefore the land mourns,
  and all who live in it languish;
together with the wild animals
  and the birds of the air,
  even the fish of the sea are perishing.

[4] Yet let no one contend,
  and let none accuse,
  for with you is my contention,
    O priest.[f]

---

a That is God sows   b Cn: Heb her   c That is Not pitied   d That is Not my people   e Gk: Heb a homer of barley and a lethech of barley   f Cn: Meaning of Heb uncertain

---

2:23 *I will say to Lo-ammi, "You are my people."* This is the final step in a stunning promise that depicts God's extravagant restoration of his broken marriage and home. A tender courtship (vv 14–15) followed by a glorious wedding day (vv 16–20) that will include a housewarming shower (vv 21–22) especially devoted to the children. All of this will then be crowned by an adoption of the children, every one of them (v 23), by this husband who intends to remove the stigma of their illegitimacy by renaming them after himself. To forgive adultery is one thing; to embrace the children that issued from it is another. There is no greater depiction of God's amazing grace in all of Scripture, as Paul seems to agree in his appropriation of this text (Rom 9:25–26).

3:1 *The LORD said to me again, "Go, love a woman who has a lover."* Could a more demanding call to forgive be imagined?! Hosea's account of his compliance does not romanticize his full accomplishment of this demand. He reports only that "I bought her" (v 2) and "I said to her, 'You must remain as mine for many days'" (v 3)—actions that do not yet claim the achievement of love. However, taking concrete steps that are at least in line with such a tall order may represent the true extent of the work that we are able do, even as we look to the power of God's example ("just as the LORD loves," v 1) that is at work in us "both to will and to work for his good pleasure" (Phil 2:12–13).

4:3 *Therefore the land mourns.* The prophets understood that betraying the covenant with God (v 1) would inevitably bring violations of social relationships (v 2) and even, as here, the breaching of the ecological order.

5 You shall stumble by day;
    the prophet also shall stumble with
        you by night,
    and I will destroy your mother.
6 My people are destroyed for lack of
        knowledge;
    because you have rejected knowledge,
    I reject you from being a priest to me.
    And since you have forgotten the law of
        your God,
    I also will forget your children.

7 The more they increased,
    the more they sinned against me;
    they changed *a* their glory into
        shame.
8 They feed on the sin of my people;
    they are greedy for their iniquity.
9 And it shall be like people, like priest;
    I will punish them for their ways,
    and repay them for their deeds.
10 They shall eat, but not be satisfied;
    they shall play the whore, but not
        multiply;
    because they have forsaken the LORD
    to devote themselves to 11whoredom.

The Idolatry of Israel

    Wine and new wine
    take away the understanding.
12 My people consult a piece of wood,
    and their divining rod gives them
        oracles.
For a spirit of whoredom has led them
    astray,
    and they have played the whore,
    forsaking their God.
13 They sacrifice on the tops of the
    mountains,
    and make offerings upon the hills,
under oak, poplar, and terebinth,
    because their shade is good.

Therefore your daughters play the
    whore,

and your daughters-in-law commit
    adultery.
14 I will not punish your daughters when
    they play the whore,
    nor your daughters-in-law when they
    commit adultery;
for the men themselves go aside with
    whores,
    and sacrifice with temple prostitutes;
thus a people without understanding
    comes to ruin.

15 Though you play the whore, O Israel,
    do not let Judah become guilty.
Do not enter into Gilgal,
    or go up to Beth-aven,
    and do not swear, "As the LORD lives."
16 Like a stubborn heifer,
    Israel is stubborn;
can the LORD now feed them
    like a lamb in a broad pasture?

17 Ephraim is joined to idols—
    let him alone.
18 When their drinking is ended, they
        indulge in sexual orgies;
    they love lewdness more than their
        glory. *b*
19 A wind has wrapped them *c* in its wings,
    and they shall be ashamed because of
        their altars. *d*

Impending Judgment on Israel and Judah

5   Hear this, O priests!
    Give heed, O house of Israel!
Listen, O house of the king!
    For the judgment pertains to you;
for you have been a snare at Mizpah,
    and a net spread upon Tabor,
2 and a pit dug deep in Shittim; *e*
    but I will punish all of them.

a Ancient Heb tradition: MT *I will change*
b Cn Compare Gk: Meaning of Heb uncertain
c Heb *her*   *d* Gk Syr: Heb *sacrifices*
e Cn: Meaning of Heb uncertain

4:6 *My people are destroyed for lack of knowledge.* This is the knowledge of marital intimacy (see Gen 4:1) with God that is rejected and replaced by carnal knowledge with other gods (vv 10–19; cf. 5:4). Knowledge that would have produced legitimate children, indeed children marked with the identity of the knowledge of God, is traded for the kind that yields orphaned children (v 6b) and even sterility (v 10; cf. 9:11–16).

3 I know Ephraim,
 and Israel is not hidden from me;
for now, O Ephraim, you have played
  the whore;
 Israel is defiled.
4 Their deeds do not permit them
 to return to their God.
For the spirit of whoredom is within
  them,
 and they do not know the LORD.

5 Israel's pride testifies against him;
 Ephraim[a] stumbles in his guilt;
 Judah also stumbles with them.
6 With their flocks and herds they shall
  go
 to seek the LORD,
but they will not find him;
 he has withdrawn from them.
7 They have dealt faithlessly with the
  LORD;
 for they have borne illegitimate
  children.
 Now the new moon shall devour
  them along with their fields.

8 Blow the horn in Gibeah,
 the trumpet in Ramah.
Sound the alarm at Beth-aven;
 look behind you, Benjamin!
9 Ephraim shall become a desolation
 in the day of punishment;
among the tribes of Israel
 I declare what is sure.
10 The princes of Judah have become
 like those who remove the landmark;
on them I will pour out
 my wrath like water.

11 Ephraim is oppressed, crushed in
  judgment,
 because he was determined to go after
  vanity.[b]
12 Therefore I am like maggots to Ephraim,
 and like rottenness to the house of
  Judah.
13 When Ephraim saw his sickness,
 and Judah his wound,
then Ephraim went to Assyria,
 and sent to the great king.[c]
But he is not able to cure you
 or heal your wound.
14 For I will be like a lion to Ephraim,
 and like a young lion to the house of
  Judah.
I myself will tear and go away;
 I will carry off, and no one shall
  rescue.
15 I will return again to my place
 until they acknowledge their guilt
  and seek my face.
In their distress they will beg my
  favor:

A Call to Repentance

6 "Come, let us return to the LORD;
 for it is he who has torn, and he will
  heal us;
 he has struck down, and he will bind
  us up.
2 After two days he will revive us;
 on the third day he will raise us up,
 that we may live before him.
3 Let us know, let us press on to know the
  LORD;

a Heb *Israel and Ephraim*   b Gk: Meaning of Heb
uncertain   c Cn: Heb *to a king who will contend*

5:13 *When Ephraim saw his sickness, . . . then Ephraim went to Assyria.* In addition to illicit religious relations (e.g., 4:17), Israel seeks to find remedy in illicit political liaisons (cf. 7:11; 8:9–10)—certainly not the last time that a people would be found pursuing the idols of personal indulgence in tandem with the idols of public power. Just read the headlines of any newspaper on any day of the year.

6:2 *on the third day he will raise us up.* Is this confession part of a sincere act of repentance, initiated by the words, "Come, let us return to the LORD" (v 1)? Despite its orthodox line, it appears that this confident expectation of revival ("as sure as the dawn," v 3) is only the empty wish of a shallow repentance that God dismisses in v 4 with the words, "Your love is like a morning cloud, like the dew that goes away early." Hosea, like many revivalists, was alert to the problem of superficial, quick-fix repentance (see also 5:6; 6:6; 7:14; 8:2). False worship of God, however rightly scripted, is no better than worship of false gods.

his appearing is as sure as the dawn;
   he will come to us like the showers,
      like the spring rains that water the
         earth.”

Impenitence of Israel and Judah

4 What shall I do with you, O Ephraim?
   What shall I do with you, O Judah?
   Your love is like a morning cloud,
      like the dew that goes away early.
5 Therefore I have hewn them by the
      prophets,
   I have killed them by the words of my
      mouth,
   and my*a* judgment goes forth as the
      light.
6 For I desire steadfast love and not
      sacrifice,
   the knowledge of God rather than
      burnt offerings.

7 But at*b* Adam they transgressed the
      covenant;
   there they dealt faithlessly with me.
8 Gilead is a city of evildoers,
   tracked with blood.
9 As robbers lie in wait*c* for someone,
   so the priests are banded together;*d*
   they murder on the road to Shechem,
      they commit a monstrous crime.
10 In the house of Israel I have seen a
      horrible thing;
   Ephraim's whoredom is there, Israel is
      defiled.

11 For you also, O Judah, a harvest is
      appointed.

When I would restore the fortunes of
      my people,
7 ¹when I would heal Israel,
   the corruption of Ephraim is revealed,
   and the wicked deeds of Samaria;
for they deal falsely,
   the thief breaks in,
   and the bandits raid outside.
2 But they do not consider
   that I remember all their wickedness.

Now their deeds surround them,
   they are before my face.
3 By their wickedness they make the king
      glad,
   and the officials by their treachery.
4 They are all adulterers;
   they are like a heated oven,
whose baker does not need to stir the
      fire,
   from the kneading of the dough until
      it is leavened.
5 On the day of our king the officials
   became sick with the heat of wine;
   he stretched out his hand with
      mockers.
6 For they are kindled*e* like an oven, their
      heart burns within them;
   all night their anger smolders;
   in the morning it blazes like a flaming
      fire.
7 All of them are hot as an oven,
   and they devour their rulers.
All their kings have fallen;
   none of them calls upon me.

8 Ephraim mixes himself with the peoples;
   Ephraim is a cake not turned.
9 Foreigners devour his strength,
   but he does not know it;
gray hairs are sprinkled upon him,
   but he does not know it.
10 Israel's pride testifies against*f* him;
   yet they do not return to the LORD
      their God,
   or seek him, for all this.

Futile Reliance on the Nations

11 Ephraim has become like a dove,
   silly and without sense;
   they call upon Egypt, they go to
      Assyria.
12 As they go, I will cast my net over them;
   I will bring them down like birds of
      the air;

a Gk Syr: Heb *your*   *b* Cn: Heb *like*
c Cn: Meaning of Heb uncertain   *d* Syr: Heb *are*
a company   *e* Gk Syr: Heb *brought near*
f Or *humbles*

6:6 SACRIFICE—*See* Spiritual Disciplines Index.

I will discipline them according to the
report made to their assembly. *a*

13 Woe to them, for they have strayed
from me!
Destruction to them, for they have
rebelled against me!
I would redeem them,
but they speak lies against me.

14 They do not cry to me from the heart,
but they wail upon their beds;
they gash themselves for grain and
wine;
they rebel against me.

15 It was I who trained and strengthened
their arms,
yet they plot evil against me.

16 They turn to that which does not
profit;*b*
they have become like a defective
bow;
their officials shall fall by the sword
because of the rage of their tongue.
So much for their babbling in the land
of Egypt.

Israel's Apostasy

8 Set the trumpet to your lips!
One like a vulture *a* is over the house
of the LORD,
because they have broken my covenant,
and transgressed my law.

2 Israel cries to me,
"My God, we—Israel—know you!"

3 Israel has spurned the good;
the enemy shall pursue him.

4 They made kings, but not through me;
they set up princes, but without my
knowledge.
With their silver and gold they made
idols
for their own destruction.

5 Your calf is rejected, O Samaria.
My anger burns against them.

How long will they be incapable of
innocence?

6 For it is from Israel,
an artisan made it;
it is not God.
The calf of Samaria
shall be broken to pieces. *c*

7 For they sow the wind,
and they shall reap the whirlwind.
The standing grain has no heads,
it shall yield no meal;
if it were to yield,
foreigners would devour it.

8 Israel is swallowed up;
now they are among the nations
as a useless vessel.

9 For they have gone up to Assyria,
a wild ass wandering alone;
Ephraim has bargained for lovers.

10 Though they bargain with the nations,
I will now gather them up.
They shall soon writhe
under the burden of kings and
princes.

11 When Ephraim multiplied altars to
expiate sin,
they became to him altars for sinning.

12 Though I write for him the multitude of
my instructions,
they are regarded as a strange thing.

13 Though they offer choice sacrifices, *b*
though they eat flesh,
the LORD does not accept them.
Now he will remember their iniquity,
and punish their sins;
they shall return to Egypt.

14 Israel has forgotten his Maker,
and built palaces;
and Judah has multiplied fortified
cities;

a Meaning of Heb uncertain   *b* Cn: Meaning of
Heb uncertain   *c* Or *shall go up in flames*

7:13 *Destruction to them, for they have
rebelled against me!* Having enumerated God's
indictments against his people, Hosea will now
increasingly present God's sentence (cf. 8:1,
8,14; 9:17). The reality of divine judgment
registers prominently in the prophets of Israel,
as it will among any generation of God's people
who have not lost their sense of ethical and
moral seriousness.

but I will send a fire upon his cities,
and it shall devour his strongholds.

Punishment for Israel's Sin

9 Do not rejoice, O Israel!
  Do not exult[a] as other nations do;
for you have played the whore,
    departing from your God.
You have loved a prostitute's pay
  on all threshing floors.
2 Threshing floor and wine vat shall not
    feed them,
  and the new wine shall fail them.
3 They shall not remain in the land of the
    LORD;
  but Ephraim shall return to Egypt,
  and in Assyria they shall eat unclean
    food.

4 They shall not pour drink offerings of
    wine to the LORD,
  and their sacrifices shall not please
    him.
Such sacrifices shall be like mourners'
    bread;
  all who eat of it shall be defiled;
for their bread shall be for their hunger
    only;
  it shall not come to the house of the
    LORD.

5 What will you do on the day of
    appointed festival,
  and on the day of the festival of the
    LORD?
6 For even if they escape destruction,
  Egypt shall gather them,
  Memphis shall bury them.
Nettles shall possess their precious
    things of silver;[b]
  thorns shall be in their tents.

7 The days of punishment have come,
  the days of recompense have come;
  Israel cries,[c]

"The prophet is a fool,
  the man of the spirit is mad!"
Because of your great iniquity,
  your hostility is great.
8 The prophet is a sentinel for my God
    over Ephraim,
yet a fowler's snare is on all his ways,
  and hostility in the house of his God.
9 They have deeply corrupted themselves
  as in the days of Gibeah;
he will remember their iniquity,
  he will punish their sins.

10 Like grapes in the wilderness,
  I found Israel.
Like the first fruit on the fig tree,
  in its first season,
  I saw your ancestors.
But they came to Baal-peor,
  and consecrated themselves to a
    thing of shame,
  and became detestable like the thing
    they loved.
11 Ephraim's glory shall fly away like a
    bird—
  no birth, no pregnancy, no
    conception!
12 Even if they bring up children,
  I will bereave them until no one is left.
Woe to them indeed
  when I depart from them!
13 Once I saw Ephraim as a young palm
    planted in a lovely meadow,[b]
  but now Ephraim must lead out his
    children for slaughter.
14 Give them, O LORD—
  what will you give?
Give them a miscarrying womb
  and dry breasts.

15 Every evil of theirs began at Gilgal;
  there I came to hate them.

a Gk: Heb *To exultation*   b Meaning of Heb
uncertain   c Cn Compare Gk: Heb *shall know*

9:1 *Do not rejoice, O Israel!* It may be harvest time in Israel (see 9:2, 4–5, 10, 16), but Hosea knows that all the festivity, even though it is on the religious calendar, will only serve to keep Israel from knowing what time it is. The prophets were keen on the fact that there is a time to laugh as well as to weep (cf. Eccl 3:4), but upbeat religious observance all too often serves as a hedge against the expression of lament, until any place for it is denied in our spiritual life.

Because of the wickedness of their deeds
  I will drive them out of my house.
I will love them no more;
  all their officials are rebels.

16 Ephraim is stricken,
  their root is dried up,
  they shall bear no fruit.
Even though they give birth,
  I will kill the cherished offspring of
    their womb.
17 Because they have not listened to him,
  my God will reject them;
  they shall become wanderers among
    the nations.

Israel's Sin and Captivity

10 Israel is a luxuriant vine
  that yields its fruit.
The more his fruit increased
  the more altars he built;
as his country improved,
  he improved his pillars.
2 Their heart is false;
  now they must bear their guilt.
The LORD^a will break down their altars,
  and destroy their pillars.

3 For now they will say:
  "We have no king,
for we do not fear the LORD,
  and a king—what could he do for us?"
4 They utter mere words;
  with empty oaths they make
    covenants;
so litigation springs up like poisonous
    weeds
  in the furrows of the field.
5 The inhabitants of Samaria tremble
  for the calf^b of Beth-aven.
Its people shall mourn for it,
  and its idolatrous priests shall wail^c
    over it,
  over its glory that has departed from it.

6 The thing itself shall be carried to
    Assyria
  as tribute to the great king.^d
Ephraim shall be put to shame,
  and Israel shall be ashamed of his
    idol.^e

7 Samaria's king shall perish
  like a chip on the face of the waters.
8 The high places of Aven, the sin of
    Israel,
  shall be destroyed.
Thorn and thistle shall grow up
  on their altars.
They shall say to the mountains, Cover
    us,
  and to the hills, Fall on us.

9 Since the days of Gibeah you have
    sinned, O Israel;
  there they have continued.
  Shall not war overtake them in
    Gibeah?
10 I will come^f against the wayward people
    to punish them;
  and nations shall be gathered against
    them
  when they are punished^g for their
    double iniquity.

11 Ephraim was a trained heifer
  that loved to thresh,
  and I spared her fair neck;
but I will make Ephraim break the
    ground;
  Judah must plow;
  Jacob must harrow for himself.
12 Sow for yourselves righteousness;
  reap steadfast love;
  break up your fallow ground;

a Heb he   b Gk Syr: Heb *calves*   c Cn: Heb
exult   d Cn: Heb *to a king who will contend*
e Cn: Heb *counsel*   f Cn Compare Gk: Heb *In my
desire*   g Gk: Heb *bound*

10:12 *break up your fallow ground.* In this
chapter the harvest of divine judgment is announced (vv 1, 4, 13–15), but even in this late
hour a call is given to start over with the chance
for a new planting of righteousness (v 12a). Yet

such reformation must start with hard plowing
(cf. v 11) that goes deep and breaks up the
hardened crusts of habit and heart. This late
offer of divine grace will entail a breaking, not
an escape from it.

for it is time to seek the LORD,
    that he may come and rain
        righteousness upon you.

13 You have plowed wickedness,
    you have reaped injustice,
    you have eaten the fruit of lies.
Because you have trusted in your power
    and in the multitude of your warriors,
14 therefore the tumult of war shall rise
        against your people,
    and all your fortresses shall be
        destroyed,
    as Shalman destroyed Beth-arbel on the
        day of battle
    when mothers were dashed in pieces
        with their children.
15 Thus it shall be done to you, O Bethel,
    because of your great wickedness.
    At dawn the king of Israel
        shall be utterly cut off.

God's Compassion Despite Israel's Ingratitude

11 When Israel was a child, I loved him,
        and out of Egypt I called my son.
2 The more I [a] called them,
    the more they went from me; [b]
    they kept sacrificing to the Baals,
        and offering incense to idols.

3 Yet it was I who taught Ephraim to
        walk,
    I took them up in my [c] arms;
    but they did not know that I healed
        them.
4 I led them with cords of human
        kindness,
    with bands of love.
I was to them like those
    who lift infants to their cheeks. [d]

I bent down to them and fed them.

5 They shall return to the land of Egypt,
    and Assyria shall be their king,
    because they have refused to return to
        me.
6 The sword rages in their cities,
    it consumes their oracle-priests,
    and devours because of their schemes.
7 My people are bent on turning away
        from me.
    To the Most High they call,
    but he does not raise them up at all. [e]

8 How can I give you up, Ephraim?
    How can I hand you over, O Israel?
    How can I make you like Admah?
    How can I treat you like Zeboiim?
My heart recoils within me;
    my compassion grows warm and
        tender.
9 I will not execute my fierce anger;
    I will not again destroy Ephraim;
for I am God and no mortal,
    the Holy One in your midst,
    and I will not come in wrath. [e]

10 They shall go after the LORD,
    who roars like a lion;
when he roars,
    his children shall come trembling
        from the west.
11 They shall come trembling like birds
        from Egypt,
    and like doves from the land of
        Assyria;
    and I will return them to their homes,
        says the LORD.

a Gk: Heb they   b Gk: Heb them   c Gk Syr Vg:
Heb his   d Or who ease the yoke on their jaws
e Meaning of Heb uncertain

11:8 *How can I give you up, Ephraim?* In the amazing confession in this verse we see God describing the wrenching passions of his own inner life. These words stand between the execution of his sentence of judgment (vv 5–7) and his own appeal and commutation of this sentence, "I will not execute my fierce anger; I will not again destroy Ephraim" (v 9). This depiction of the depths of divine mercy here— a heart attack ("My heart recoils within me") and the womb stirrings of a mother's love (associated with the Hebrew term for "compassion")—link with the surging familial passions evoked in the family affairs of Hosea in chapters 1–3. Such revelations of God's heart are undoubtedly decisive in making possible the transformation of our own.

12 *a* Ephraim has surrounded me with lies,
  and the house of Israel with deceit;
but Judah still walks *b* with God,
  and is faithful to the Holy One.

12 Ephraim herds the wind,
  and pursues the east wind all day
    long;
they multiply falsehood and violence;
  they make a treaty with Assyria,
  and oil is carried to Egypt.

The Long History of Rebellion

2 The LORD has an indictment against
    Judah,
  and will punish Jacob according to
    his ways,
  and repay him according to his deeds.
3 In the womb he tried to supplant his
    brother,
  and in his manhood he strove with
    God.
4 He strove with the angel and prevailed,
  he wept and sought his favor;
he met him at Bethel,
  and there he spoke with him. *c*
5 The LORD the God of hosts,
  the LORD is his name!
6 But as for you, return to your God,
  hold fast to love and justice,
  and wait continually for your God.

7 A trader, in whose hands are false
    balances,
  he loves to oppress.
8 Ephraim has said, "Ah, I am rich,
  I have gained wealth for myself;
in all of my gain
  no offense has been found in me
  that would be sin." *d*
9 I am the LORD your God
  from the land of Egypt;
I will make you live in tents again,
  as in the days of the appointed
    festival.

10 I spoke to the prophets;
  it was I who multiplied visions,
  and through the prophets I will bring
    destruction.
11 In Gilead *e* there is iniquity,
  they shall surely come to nothing.
In Gilgal they sacrifice bulls,
  so their altars shall be like stone heaps
  on the furrows of the field.
12 Jacob fled to the land of Aram,
  there Israel served for a wife,
  and for a wife he guarded sheep. *f*
13 By a prophet the LORD brought Israel up
    from Egypt,
  and by a prophet he was guarded.
14 Ephraim has given bitter offense,
  so his Lord will bring his crimes down
    on him
  and pay him back for his insults.

Relentless Judgment on Israel

13 When Ephraim spoke, there was
    trembling;
he was exalted in Israel;
  but he incurred guilt through Baal
    and died.
2 And now they keep on sinning
  and make a cast image for themselves,
idols of silver made according to their
    understanding,
  all of them the work of artisans.
"Sacrifice to these," they say. *g*
  People are kissing calves!
3 Therefore they shall be like the
    morning mist
  or like the dew that goes away early,
like chaff that swirls from the threshing
    floor
  or like smoke from a window.

a Ch 12.1 in Heb   *b* Heb *roams* or *rules*
c Gk Syr: Heb *us*   *d* Meaning of Heb uncertain
e Compare Syr: Heb *Gilead*   *f* Heb lacks *sheep*
g Cn Compare Gk: Heb *To these they say sacrifices of*
people

12:2 *The LORD . . . will punish Jacob according to his ways.* This verse affirms the principle of divine retribution (the punishment fits the crime) and also introduces a section that is dominated by a series of historical retrospectives on Israel's sinful life course (indeed "his ways"; see vv 3–4, 12–14; 13:1, 4–6). There are times when persons and peoples must come to terms with their own sin histories as well as God's salvation history if there is to be any hope for restoration.

4 Yet I have been the LORD your God
    ever since the land of Egypt;
you know no God but me,
    and besides me there is no savior.
5 It was I who fed[a] you in the wilderness,
    in the land of drought.
6 When I fed[b] them, they were satisfied;
    they were satisfied, and their heart
        was proud;
    therefore they forgot me.
7 So I will become like a lion to them,
    like a leopard I will lurk beside the
        way.
8 I will fall upon them like a bear robbed
        of her cubs,
    and will tear open the covering of
        their heart;
    there I will devour them like a lion,
        as a wild animal would mangle them.

9 I will destroy you, O Israel;
    who can help you?[c]
10 Where now is[d] your king, that he may
        save you?
    Where in all your cities are your
        rulers,
of whom you said,
    "Give me a king and rulers"?
11 I gave you a king in my anger,
    and I took him away in my wrath.

12 Ephraim's iniquity is bound up;
    his sin is kept in store.
13 The pangs of childbirth come for him,
    but he is an unwise son;
for at the proper time he does not
        present himself
    at the mouth of the womb.

14 Shall I ransom them from the power of
        Sheol?
    Shall I redeem them from Death?
O Death, where are[e] your plagues?
    O Sheol, where is[e] your destruction?
    Compassion is hidden from my eyes.

15 Although he may flourish among
        rushes,[f]
    the east wind shall come, a blast from
        the LORD,
    rising from the wilderness;
and his fountain shall dry up,
    his spring shall be parched.
It shall strip his treasury
    of every precious thing.
16[g] Samaria shall bear her guilt,
    because she has rebelled against her
        God;
they shall fall by the sword,
    their little ones shall be dashed in
        pieces,
    and their pregnant women ripped
        open.

A Plea for Repentance

14 Return, O Israel, to the LORD your
    God,
    for you have stumbled because of
        your iniquity.
2 Take words with you
    and return to the LORD;
say to him,
    "Take away all guilt;

a Gk Syr: Heb knew   b Cn: Heb according to their
pasture   c Gk Syr: Heb for in me is your help
d Gk Syr Vg: Heb I will be   e Gk Syr: Heb I will be
f Or among brothers   g Ch 14.1 in Heb

14:2 *Take words with you and return to the*
LORD. Although repentance is about doing
something (the Hebrew verb is "to turn/return")
rather than just saying something, it often begins
with the speaking of words. Yet the very wrongs
for which repentance is needed can keep us
from seeing the right words. The grace of this
passage, however, is that the divine command to
"take words" is immediately followed by the
divine provision of the very words that are to be
taken. The divine grace that responds to our
confession of sin is already at work in eliciting it.

Responding
14:2 CONFESSION. Our words, the
"fruit of our lips," are all we need to
confess and receive forgiveness. Where once
animal sacrifice was required, now we can
confess personally to God with nothing more to
offer than our repentance. What a blessing!
Take time today to respond to God's grace with
a sincere confession of your heart. *See also*
Spiritual Disciplines Index.

accept that which is good,
and we will offer
the fruit^a of our lips.
3 Assyria shall not save us;
we will not ride upon horses;
we will say no more, 'Our God,'
to the work of our hands.
In you the orphan finds mercy."

Assurance of Forgiveness

4 I will heal their disloyalty;
I will love them freely,
for my anger has turned from them.
5 I will be like the dew to Israel;
he shall blossom like the lily,
he shall strike root like the forests of
Lebanon.^b
6 His shoots shall spread out;
his beauty shall be like the olive tree,
and his fragrance like that of
Lebanon.

7 They shall again live beneath my^c
shadow,
they shall flourish as a garden;^d
they shall blossom like the vine,
their fragrance shall be like the wine
of Lebanon.
8 O Ephraim, what have I^e to do with
idols?
It is I who answer and look after you.^f
I am like an evergreen cypress;
your faithfulness^g comes from me.
9 Those who are wise understand these
things;
those who are discerning know them.
For the ways of the LORD are right,
and the upright walk in them,
but transgressors stumble in them.

a Gk Syr: Heb *bulls*   b Cn: Heb *like Lebanon*
c Heb *his*   d Cn: Heb *they shall grow grain*
e Or *What more has Ephraim*   f Heb *him*
g Heb *your fruit*

14:8 *your faithfulness comes from me.* Either this phrase or its alternative Hebrew rendering, "your fruit comes from me" (see NRSV note), expresses a fitting conclusion to Hosea's final presentation of God's promise to restore his people (vv 3–8), for we have both a picture of restored covenant (marital) faithfulness (vv 3–4) and the fruit that (super)naturally springs from it (vv 5–8). Striking here is the realization that God not only rewards our faithfulness, but also engenders it in the first place (cf. v 4, "I will heal their disloyalty"). Thus our life from God is known to be, even long before the New Testament, a work of divine grace from start to finish (see Eph 2:8).

JOEL

Whether national, local, or individual, a disaster dismantles life. The agony of living through each day rips through our souls. How shall we endure? By stoic denial? Emotional withdrawal? Or is there a life-giving way through the pain of life-devouring events?

The prophet Joel conveys understanding and hope to the desolated People of God during a national cataclysm. Unlike most prophets, Joel does not warn of impending doom; he interprets a doom that is already present. Joel discloses the power, holiness, and mercy of God in a manner that restores intimacy between God and his people.

Joel says very little about himself, and the date of his prophecy is difficult to fix. Writing between the eighth and second centuries before Christ, Joel experienced one of the worst natural disasters in Judah's history. Joel's references to the Temple and its practices, coupled with his lack of reference to a king, indicate that Joel may have lived in or near Jerusalem after the Babylonian exile, about 500 BC. Joel's words echo other, and presumably earlier, prophetic speeches, lending further credence to a postexilic date.

A Forewarning of the Day of the Lord

In the pre-pesticide environment of the ancient Near East, devouring locusts have ravaged the land. Drought intensifies the trouble. Fires burn out of control across the dry and denuded landscape. Wild animals and domesticated herds begin to thirst and starve. Famine threatens God's people. The nation of Judah looks and feels like a war zone.

There is no prospect of human help, no simple path to recovery, little vision of hope. In addition to physical and emotional suffering, the people suffer spiritually. Worship services are suspended because there is not enough grain or wine to make

---

See also *"The With-God Life" essay for this section of the Bible,*
"The People of God in Rebellion," pp. 975–79.

the daily offerings. There are only bugs, dust, terror, and destruction. God's people wonder if God has forsaken them.

Joel perceives the disaster as a forewarning of the day of the Lord. He anticipates that God will someday intervene in human affairs with a cataclysm so decisive that God's salvation and judgment will end the present age. Similarly, the current crisis expresses God's judgment and triggers repentance. Through disaster, God reforms and reinvigorates the attachment of God's people to him. With nothing but God to rely upon, God's people begin to experience him more intensely. Faith, which had deteriorated into mere external conformity, is revived. Covenant loyalty is strengthened, wandering hearts are reoriented to God, and people actively experience God's deliverance.

A foretaste of God's final judgment accomplishes its purpose of bringing people to repentance. The shared participation in God's deliverance forms the People of God into a community that delights in his presence. The pledged outpouring of the Holy Spirit will launch supernatural fullness of life for all who call on the Lord.

Holiness through Judgment

In contrast, those who have mistreated God's people will endure the impending day of the Lord as a terrible day of final retribution for sin. Through acts of judgment, God's holiness will shine upon all nations. On that day, the Lord will be a refuge for his people. By judgment, God will set everything right, ushering in a new and wonderful era when God is overwhelmingly present among his people.

When life is hard, God pleads with us to unveil to him our sadness, our sin, and our innermost selves in holy mourning. He invites us to reorient ourselves toward him and his deliverance, toward his mercy and willingness to bless his people. God asks us to stake our helpless and hopeless souls on his capacity to enrich and fulfill our ravaged lives.

—Barbara M. Musselman

---

1 The word of the Lord that came to Joel son of Pethuel:

Lament over the Ruin of the Country

2 Hear this, O elders,
　give ear, all inhabitants of the land!
Has such a thing happened in your days,
　or in the days of your ancestors?
3 Tell your children of it,
　and let your children tell their children,
　and their children another generation.

4 What the cutting locust left,
　the swarming locust has eaten.
What the swarming locust left,
　the hopping locust has eaten,
and what the hopping locust left,
　the destroying locust has eaten.

5 Wake up, you drunkards, and weep;
　and wail, all you wine-drinkers,
over the sweet wine,
　for it is cut off from your mouth.

1:2–3 *Hear this, O elders.* A command to hear, and to tell, how the country is ruined by the worst locust plague in history.

1:5 *Wake up, you drunkards.* Wine is a symbol of joy and God's blessing, but disaster has severed the people from both.

6 For a nation has invaded my land,
    powerful and innumerable;
its teeth are lions' teeth,
    and it has the fangs of a lioness.
7 It has laid waste my vines,
    and splintered my fig trees;
it has stripped off their bark and thrown
        it down;
    their branches have turned white.

8 Lament like a virgin dressed in sackcloth
    for the husband of her youth.
9 The grain offering and the drink
        offering are cut off
    from the house of the LORD.
The priests mourn,
    the ministers of the LORD.
10 The fields are devastated,
    the ground mourns;
for the grain is destroyed,
    the wine dries up,
    the oil fails.

11 Be dismayed, you farmers,
    wail, you vinedressers,
over the wheat and the barley;
    for the crops of the field are ruined.
12 The vine withers,

the fig tree droops.
Pomegranate, palm, and apple—
    all the trees of the field are dried up;
surely, joy withers away
    among the people.

A Call to Repentance and Prayer

13 Put on sackcloth and lament, you
        priests;
    wail, you ministers of the altar.
Come, pass the night in sackcloth,
    you ministers of my God!
Grain offering and drink offering
    are withheld from the house of your
        God.

14 Sanctify a fast,
    call a solemn assembly.
Gather the elders
    and all the inhabitants of the land
to the house of the LORD your God,
    and cry out to the LORD.

15 Alas for the day!
For the day of the LORD is near,
    and as destruction from the
        Almighty [a] it comes.

a Traditional rendering of Heb *Shaddai*

1:6–7 *For a nation has invaded my land.* Joel compares the insects to a powerful invading army. Successive swarms of hopping, walking, and flying insects leave no surviving vegetation (v 4).

1:8 *Lament like a virgin.* Judah mourns for a pleasant future now lost, like a betrothed woman mourning her beloved. Hope is dead.

1:9 *The grain . . . and the drink offering.* Due to the failed harvest, there is no grain or wine to use for the daily offerings expressing devotion to God. The disaster means God's people cannot even worship appropriately.

1:10 *The fields are devastated.* Fertile ground, grain, wine, and oil are signs of covenant blessing (Deut 11:13–17) and their scarcity is a sign of the covenant curses (Deut 28:51). How do the people understand God's presence when every outward sign of covenant blessing is stripped from them? How do we? And how do the devastating experiences of life grow the soul?

1:13 *Put on sackcloth and lament.* God requires holiness, and Judah's sin is serious. Not only do the people need to repent, but so do the priests.

1:14 *Sanctify a fast.* Joel summons the people to make their mourning and desperation holy by turning to God for help. The discipline of fasting, entered into with a whole heart, imparts a spiritual vulnerability to God. God transforms the hearts of those willing to take this radical step toward him. Joel instructs the people to gather in God's house and purposefully devote their laments to God. Those who suffer have no difficulty immersing themselves in agony, but the People of God are to carry their pain into God's presence. Authentic turning to God is the only fruitful activity in times of horrible calamity.

1:15–16 *Alas for the day!* Moses had warned that God would answer covenant breaking with locusts and loss (Deut 28:38–45). The manifestation of these covenant curses is evidence that the day of the Lord is coming.

16 Is not the food cut off
        before our eyes,
    joy and gladness
        from the house of our God?

17 The seed shrivels under the clods, *a*
        the storehouses are desolate;
    the granaries are ruined
        because the grain has failed.
18 How the animals groan!
        The herds of cattle wander about
    because there is no pasture for them;
        even the flocks of sheep are dazed. *b*

19 To you, O Lord, I cry.
    For fire has devoured
        the pastures of the wilderness,
    and flames have burned
        all the trees of the field.
20 Even the wild animals cry to you
        because the watercourses are
            dried up,
    and fire has devoured
        the pastures of the wilderness.

2 Blow the trumpet in Zion;
        sound the alarm on my holy
            mountain!
    Let all the inhabitants of the land
            tremble,
        for the day of the Lord is coming, it is
            near—
2 a day of darkness and gloom,
        a day of clouds and thick darkness!
    Like blackness spread upon the
            mountains
        a great and powerful army comes;
    their like has never been from of old,
        nor will be again after them
    in ages to come.

3 Fire devours in front of them,
        and behind them a flame burns.
    Before them the land is like the garden
            of Eden,
        but after them a desolate wilderness,
        and nothing escapes them.

4 They have the appearance of horses,
        and like war-horses they charge.
5 As with the rumbling of chariots,
        they leap on the tops of the
            mountains,
    like the crackling of a flame of fire
        devouring the stubble,
    like a powerful army
        drawn up for battle.

6 Before them peoples are in anguish,
        all faces grow pale. *a*
7 Like warriors they charge,
        like soldiers they scale the wall.
    Each keeps to its own course,
        they do not swerve from *c* their paths.
8 They do not jostle one another,
        each keeps to its own track;
    they burst through the weapons
        and are not halted.
9 They leap upon the city,
        they run upon the walls;
    they climb up into the houses,
        they enter through the windows like
            a thief.

10 The earth quakes before them,
        the heavens tremble.
    The sun and the moon are darkened,
        and the stars withdraw their shining.
11 The Lord utters his voice

a Meaning of Heb uncertain   *b* Compare Gk Syr
Vg: Meaning of Heb uncertain   *c* Gk Syr Vg: Heb
they do not take a pledge along

Contrary to conventional wisdom, it will be a terrible day of destruction, not only for Judah's enemies, but also for Judah itself.

1:17–20 *the storehouses are desolate.* Joel does not deny any facet of reality. The people have no stored resources on which to depend. They are utterly destitute. Their only hope is God.

2:1 *Blow the trumpet!* Sentinels sounded the alarm to warn of enemy invasions. God is the sentinel sounding this alarm, alerting the people to see his hand at work in this crisis.

2:2–11 *a day of darkness.* The locusts foreshadow the day of the Lord, which will be even more destructive. People will be appropriately terrified. God's judgment will be as powerful and devastating as an invading army or fire.

at the head of his army;
how vast is his host!
    Numberless are those who obey his
        command.
Truly the day of the LORD is great;
    terrible indeed—who can endure it?

12 Yet even now, says the LORD,
    return to me with all your heart,
with fasting, with weeping, and with
        mourning;
13   rend your hearts and not your
        clothing.
Return to the LORD, your God,
    for he is gracious and merciful,
slow to anger, and abounding in
        steadfast love,
    and relents from punishing.
14 Who knows whether he will not turn
        and relent,
    and leave a blessing behind him,
a grain offering and a drink offering
    for the LORD, your God?

15 Blow the trumpet in Zion;
    sanctify a fast;
call a solemn assembly;
16   gather the people.
Sanctify the congregation;
    assemble the aged;
gather the children,
    even infants at the breast.

Let the bridegroom leave his room,
    and the bride her canopy.
17 Between the vestibule and the altar
    let the priests, the ministers of the
        LORD, weep.
Let them say, "Spare your people,
        O LORD,
    and do not make your heritage a
        mockery,
    a byword among the nations.
Why should it be said among the
        peoples,
    'Where is their God?' "

God's Response and Promise

18 Then the LORD became jealous for his
        land,
    and had pity on his people.
19 In response to his people the LORD said:
I am sending you
    grain, wine, and oil,
    and you will be satisfied;
and I will no more make you
    a mockery among the nations.

20 I will remove the northern army far
        from you,
    and drive it into a parched and
        desolate land,
its front into the eastern sea,
    and its rear into the western sea;

2:12–13 *Yet even now.* Even though judgment is at hand, there is hope. It is not too late to change God's mind. Ancient Near Eastern people expressed mourning by tearing their clothing and putting on sackcloth. God exhorts the people to convert external actions into a radical reorientation of the heart and mind and will. The antidote for spiritual destitution is still the same. God invites his people into passionate communion with him through fasting, weeping, mourning, and the rending of our hearts.

Responding
2:12–13 FASTING. God calls his people to return to him through the external discipline of fasting. Why is fasting such a powerful means of reconciliation? *See also* Spiritual Disciplines Index.

2:13 *Return to the LORD.* God's steadfast love motivates him to impart blessing and mercy rather than punishment. God is emotionally attached to his people and hopes that they will cry out to him for help and mercy and turn from their indifference and sin.

2:15 FASTING—*See* Spiritual Disciplines Index.

2:16 *gather the people.* The people are to attend to God, interrupting even the most life-giving human events to seek God's mercy.

2:18–24 *Then the LORD became jealous.* God seeks his people's exclusive love. The people amend their hearts, and God responds with a series of promises for safety, abundant life, and intimacy with him.

its stench and foul smell will rise up.
  Surely he has done great things!

21 Do not fear, O soil;
    be glad and rejoice,
  for the LORD has done great things!
22 Do not fear, you animals of the field,
    for the pastures of the wilderness are
      green;
  the tree bears its fruit,
    the fig tree and vine give their full
      yield.

23 O children of Zion, be glad
    and rejoice in the LORD your God;
  for he has given the early rain*a* for your
      vindication,
  he has poured down for you
    abundant rain,
  the early and the later rain, as before.
24 The threshing floors shall be full of
      grain,
  the vats shall overflow with wine and
    oil.

25 I will repay you for the years
    that the swarming locust has eaten,
  the hopper, the destroyer, and the
    cutter,
  my great army, which I sent against
      you.

26 You shall eat in plenty and be satisfied,
    and praise the name of the LORD your
      God,
  who has dealt wondrously with you.

And my people shall never again be put
  to shame.
27 You shall know that I am in the midst of
    Israel,
  and that I, the LORD, am your God
    and there is no other.
And my people shall never again be put
  to shame.

God's Spirit Poured Out

28 *b* Then afterward
  I will pour out my spirit on all flesh;
  your sons and your daughters shall
    prophesy,
  your old men shall dream dreams,
  and your young men shall see visions.
29 Even on the male and female slaves,
    in those days, I will pour out my
      spirit.

30 I will show portents in the heavens and
on the earth, blood and fire and columns of
smoke. 31 The sun shall be turned to darkness,
and the moon to blood, before the great and
terrible day of the LORD comes. 32 Then everyone who calls on the name of the LORD shall
be saved; for in Mount Zion and in Jerusalem
there shall be those who escape, as the LORD
has said, and among the survivors shall be
those whom the LORD calls.

3 *c* For then, in those days and at that time,
  when I restore the fortunes of Judah and
Jerusalem, 2 I will gather all the nations and
bring them down to the valley of Jehosha-

a Meaning of Heb uncertain   *b* Ch 3.1 in Heb
c Ch 4.1 in Heb

2:25–27 *I will repay you.* God foretells the
restoration of all that has been lost in a healed
future full of covenant blessings. Throughout
history people of faith who literally have lost
everything have clung to this passage as a
promise of God's healing, restoring purposes.

2:26–27 *You shall eat in plenty.* Experiencing
God's presence follows receiving God's deliverance from judgment. God's positive intervention
will silence the unbelieving who accuse God of
abandoning his people.

2:28–32 *I will pour out my spirit on all flesh.*
This is the glorious eschatological passage
quoted by the apostle Peter in his sermon at

Pentecost (Acts 2:14–21). Peter applies it to the
outpouring of the Holy Spirit upon all kinds of
people irrespective of gender or age or social
class. Note that only half of Joel's prophecy
comes to pass in Peter's day: the cataclysmic
blood and fire and smoke await future fulfillment to usher in "the great and terrible day
of the LORD."

2:32 *Then everyone who calls on the . . . LORD
shall be saved.* God calls out to people through
disaster and delivers from judgment those who
respond to him in repentance and belief. The
day of the Lord will be a day of salvation for
those who call on the Lord.

phat, and I will enter into judgment with them there, on account of my people and my heritage Israel, because they have scattered them among the nations. They have divided my land, ³and cast lots for my people, and traded boys for prostitutes, and sold girls for wine, and drunk it down.

4 What are you to me, O Tyre and Sidon, and all the regions of Philistia? Are you paying me back for something? If you are paying me back, I will turn your deeds back upon your own heads swiftly and speedily. ⁵For you have taken my silver and my gold, and have carried my rich treasures into your temples.ᵃ ⁶You have sold the people of Judah and Jerusalem to the Greeks, removing them far from their own border. ⁷But now I will rouse them to leave the places to which you have sold them, and I will turn your deeds back upon your own heads. ⁸I will sell your sons and your daughters into the hand of the people of Judah, and they will sell them to the Sabeans, to a nation far away; for the LORD has spoken.

Judgment in the Valley of Jehoshaphat

⁹ Proclaim this among the nations:
    Prepare war,ᵇ
    stir up the warriors.
Let all the soldiers draw near,
    let them come up.
¹⁰ Beat your plowshares into swords,
    and your pruning hooks into spears;
    let the weakling say, "I am a warrior."

¹¹ Come quickly,ᶜ
    all you nations all around,
    gather yourselves there.
Bring down your warriors, O LORD.
¹² Let the nations rouse themselves,
    and come up to the valley of
        Jehoshaphat;
for there I will sit to judge
    all the neighboring nations.

¹³ Put in the sickle,
    for the harvest is ripe.
Go in, tread,
    for the wine press is full.
The vats overflow,
    for their wickedness is great.

¹⁴ Multitudes, multitudes,
    in the valley of decision!
For the day of the LORD is near
    in the valley of decision.
¹⁵ The sun and the moon are darkened,
    and the stars withdraw their shining.

¹⁶ The LORD roars from Zion,
    and utters his voice from Jerusalem,
    and the heavens and the earth shake.
But the LORD is a refuge for his people,
    a stronghold for the people of Israel.

The Glorious Future of Judah

¹⁷ So you shall know that I, the LORD your
        God,
    dwell in Zion, my holy mountain.
And Jerusalem shall be holy,
    and strangers shall never again pass
        through it.

ᵃ Or *palaces*   ᵇ Heb *sanctify war*   ᶜ Meaning of Heb uncertain

---

3:4–8 *What are you to me?* The day of the Lord will not be redemptive for those who reject God, and justice will certainly triumph over evil. God will chastise the nations who have abused Judah. God's judgment will be in proportion to the crimes committed. Those who sold God's people into slavery will themselves be enslaved.
3:9–10 *Prepare war.* Judgment is a life-or-death struggle.
3:13 *Put in the sickle.* The harvest and wine press are classic images of God's final judgment against evil. The wine vat is a picture of over-flowing wickedness. The harvest of the day of the Lord separates God's people from God's enemies.
3:14 *Multitudes . . . in the valley of decision!* It is not human decision that so many await. It is the Lord's judgment.
3:16 *The LORD roars.* Though God is powerful and frightens the arrogant, God is a safe haven for those with penitent hearts.
3:17 *So you shall know.* God's people will enjoy his life-giving and holy presence, living in harmony with God in a glorious Edenic paradise.

18 In that day
  the mountains shall drip sweet wine,
    the hills shall flow with milk,
  and all the stream beds of Judah
    shall flow with water;
  a fountain shall come forth from the
    house of the LORD
  and water the Wadi Shittim.

19 Egypt shall become a desolation
  and Edom a desolate wilderness,

because of the violence done to the
    people of Judah,
  in whose land they have shed
    innocent blood.
20 But Judah shall be inhabited forever,
  and Jerusalem to all generations.
21 I will avenge their blood, and I will not
    clear the guilty, *a*
  for the LORD dwells in Zion.

a Gk Syr: Heb *I will hold innocent their blood that I
have not held innocent*

3:18 *In that day.* Joel reassures the suffering
that a coming age of the Spirit follows God's
judgment. The house of the Lord will be a
refreshing source of life and blessing.

Handwritten annotations:
(1) ANGER OVER SOCIAL INJUSTICE
(2) COMPASSION FOR OPPRESSED HUMANS

AMOS

When Amos the Judahite was sent by God to Samaria, then the capital city of Israel, the Northern Kingdom, around the year 755 BC, Israel had politically dominated Judah, the Southern Kingdom, for more than a hundred years. Amos arrived as an outsider, but he came to a people who had witnessed prophets at work before. Yet perhaps not since Moses had there been a less likely candidate for this historical fork in the road or one more filled with Spirit and divine speech than this tough keeper of sheep and sycamore trees from Tekoa. Moses' most daunting charge was to wield the power of God's word against Pharaoh, but Amos's charge was to wield the word against his own kin.

The stunning nature of Amos's calling and the explosive force of God's message through him—like the reverberating roar of a lion (1:2)—must have compelled faithful scribes to collect his words into the Bible's first book of prophecies. Amos's activity slightly precedes that of the great eighth-century prophets Hosea, Isaiah, and Micah. He is the spiritual progenitor of this type of lyric prophet, who is vigilantly allegiant to God and most passionate to express God's anger over social injustice and compassion for oppressed humans. Such passion is certainly the fruit of an intimate, spiritual walk with God.

Faithful Listening and Realpolitik

That Amos apparently first criticized Israel's neighboring nations (1:1–2:3) and then followed with judgments against Judah and Israel (2:4–9:10) is a bit striking when compared to the pattern in other prophetic books, which usually reverse this order. We may suppose that this order suggests the prophet's dutiful listening to God's guidance and the courage to convey a very unwelcome message, for a certain political savvy guided the message to the ears of shrewd politicians. The enduring king of Israel was Jeroboam II, a pro-Assyrian who had over the course of nearly forty years

See also *"The With-God Life"* essay for this section of the Bible,
"The People of God in Rebellion," pp. 975–79.

wrestled back territory from neighboring nations, expanded Israelite borders, and brought peace and prosperity to both the kingdom and its wealthy class.

However, by 755 his major ally, Assyria, had declined considerably (if temporarily), and his opportunistic neighbors mustered themselves to retake border territory. Meanwhile, rival politicians in Samaria and a disgruntled elite accustomed to privilege began murmuring and pushing for change, namely, a fortuitous alliance with neighbors other than Assyria. This internal faction was led by Pekah, an Israelite rival chomping at the bit to take over Jeroboam's throne. Not coincidentally, Pekah was backed by political leaders in Damascus, Syria, who wanted to put him in power and exploit his reign.

For Transgressions Foreign and at Home

Perhaps when Amos fired off his first speeches in the royal city, criticizing injustices of the foreign coalition leaders one by one (Damascus, Gaza, Tyre), it was a psychological ploy to gain the beleaguered King Jeroboam's sympathetic ear (1:3–10). "Ah!" thought the king. "He is telling me what I want to hear!" After all, these threatening nations were guilty of excesses of injustice and arrogance in their ruthless grasping after Jeroboam's territory and after the futile security of believing they could take on a declining Assyria. And Jeroboam's kingdom had God on its side, who would not stand for the barbaric, foreign travesties Amos described.

The Israelite king's sense of righteous indignation may have soared even higher when Amos moved next to critique the king's vassal, Judah, and that tiresome Jerusalem: "For three transgressions of Judah, and for four," Amos railed, "I will not revoke the punishment; because they have rejected the law of the LORD. . . . I will send a fire on Judah, and it shall devour the strongholds of Jerusalem" (2:4–5). Yet the divine message Amos was duty-bound to convey next would not allow the Israelite head of state to rest content with the idea that his national interests and party politics were necessarily equal to the will of God.

Not hesitancy, but charged readiness marked Amos's last and lengthiest judgment speech—indeed, against Israel! Perhaps the king and his men turned pale. With anger fueled by compassion, Amos announced for God: "For three transgressions of Israel, and for four, I will not revoke the punishment; because they sell the righteous for silver, and the needy for a pair of sandals—they who trample the head of the poor into the dust of the earth" (2:6–7). In hurting the poor by the excesses of its privileged class, said Amos soberly, Israel is no better morally and will not be favored politically. This is what God cares about most—the suffering, oppressed poor—not power, not politics, not who is king. Therefore, if God judges the other nations for humanitarian wrongs, how much more will God bring the Israelites to justice when they run roughshod over their own people!

Spiritual Strength of Character

No doubt also within hearing range of Amos were Israel's shrewd and powerful politicians who had internally pressed for their new national leader, Pekah, and who had long courted coalition partners in order to protect the nation. That their ill-conceived and shortsighted plan of aggression could actually jeopardize the nation's very existence, bring about its invasion and collapse, was nothing less than a grandiose miscalculation. Yet this was indeed the outcome in the coming years, when the coalition, led by Pekah of Israel and Rezin of Damascus, finally provoked a force greater than it could handle. The sleeping giant, Assyria, under Tiglath-pileser III, arose and wiped Israel as a nation off the map forty years after Amos made his prophecy. Only human hindsight, or God's prophetic foresight in 755, could have told the Israelite leaders and people of the dangers waiting to be unleashed just down the road. Amos, in the face of ridicule and persecution, was given the spiritual strength to raise his voice with God's message for "such a time as this."

—*Nancy C. Lee*

---

1 The words of Amos, who was among the shepherds of Tekoa, which he saw concerning Israel in the days of King Uzziah of Judah and in the days of King Jeroboam son of Joash of Israel, two years*a* before the earthquake.

Judgment on Israel's Neighbors

2And he said:

The LORD roars from Zion,
  and utters his voice from Jerusalem;
the pastures of the shepherds wither,
  and the top of Carmel dries up.

3 Thus says the LORD:
For three transgressions of Damascus,
  and for four, I will not revoke the
    punishment;*b*
because they have threshed Gilead
  with threshing sledges of iron.
4 So I will send a fire on the house of
    Hazael,
  and it shall devour the strongholds of
    Ben-hadad.
5 I will break the gate bars of Damascus,

a Or during two years   b Heb cause it to return

1:1 *the earthquake.* In a time when devastating natural phenomena were understood as caused by divine anger, it is not surprising that an earthquake was associated with God's prophetic word of judgment reverberating through the powerful capital city of Samaria. Archaeologists have found evidence of damage from a major earthquake around 753 BC in Samaria and Hazor, and Zechariah also refers to it (14:5).

1:2 *The LORD roars from Zion.* Amos utters what he "saw": like a lion's sudden roar, the hot blast of God's speech dries up the natural landscape, which now bears witness to God's threatening and tangible presence. Our sophisticated theologies should not abandon the idea or distance us from the feeling that God can indeed be angry over injustice and consequent human suffering.

1:3–5 *For three transgressions of Damascus, and for four.* God pays close attention to the actions of nations. Wrongs are noted, and there will be consequences. This formula, repeated in the following speeches, suggests that it is not for a single transgression, but for numerous ones, that God will judge each nation. Amos utters a type of rhetoric regarded as the standard prophetic judgment speech in the Old Testament. He specifies why God is critical of Israel's most powerful neighbor (because Damascus "threshed," pulverized, or brutally "took apart" Gilead in defeat). The second part of the prophet's judgment speech then gives God's specific punishment (he will destroy the royal house of Damascus and its people will go into exile). The power a nation holds is a privilege; if it is abused, God will take it away. Here God has Amos shake the confidence of any Israelite counting on an alliance with Damascus, including Pekah, who is backed by Syrian insurgents who want to exploit his future reign.

and cut off the inhabitants from the
    Valley of Aven,
and the one who holds the scepter from
    Beth-eden;
and the people of Aram shall go into
    exile to Kir,   says the LORD.

6 Thus says the LORD:
For three transgressions of Gaza,
    and for four, I will not revoke the
        punishment; *a*
because they carried into exile entire
    communities,
to hand them over to Edom.
7 So I will send a fire on the wall of Gaza,
    fire that shall devour its strongholds.
8 I will cut off the inhabitants from
    Ashdod,
and the one who holds the scepter
    from Ashkelon;
I will turn my hand against Ekron,
and the remnant of the Philistines
    shall perish,   says the Lord GOD.

9 Thus says the LORD:
For three transgressions of Tyre,
    and for four, I will not revoke the
        punishment; *a*
because they delivered entire
    communities over to Edom,
and did not remember the covenant
    of kinship.
10 So I will send a fire on the wall of Tyre,
    fire that shall devour its strongholds.

11 Thus says the LORD:
For three transgressions of Edom,
    and for four, I will not revoke the
        punishment; *a*
because he pursued his brother with the
    sword
and cast off all pity;
he maintained his anger perpetually, *b*
and kept his wrath *c* forever.
12 So I will send a fire on Teman,
and it shall devour the strongholds of
    Bozrah.

13 Thus says the LORD:
For three transgressions of the
    Ammonites,
and for four, I will not revoke the
    punishment; *a*
because they have ripped open
    pregnant women in Gilead
in order to enlarge their territory.
14 So I will kindle a fire against the wall of
    Rabbah,
fire that shall devour its strongholds,
with shouting on the day of battle,
with a storm on the day of the
    whirlwind;
15 then their king shall go into exile,
he and his officials together,
                says the LORD.

---

a Heb *cause it to return*   *b* Syr Vg: Heb *and his anger tore perpetually*   *c* Gk Syr Vg: Heb *and his wrath kept*

1:6–10 *For three transgressions of Gaza, . . . of Tyre, and for four.* God's judgment against Gaza, key city of the Philistines, and against Tyre, key city of the Phoenicians, occurred because they captured entire communities and handed them over to the Edomites in a kind of slave trade. Such blatant injustice against another people in international dealings will not stand; God promises to cut down these powerful nations for their actions. In light of later historical events such as the Holocaust, we might well ask: Where is God's intervention when the inhumane violations are most egregious? It turns out that this is not only a modern question. God's intervention and justice are sometimes agonizingly delayed,

arriving in their own time, or in eternity. Damascus did not fall to the Assyrians for another twenty-five years.

1:11 *he pursued his brother.* This phrase suggests Edom attacked Israel in some way in Amos's time, forsook brotherly compassion, and allowed anger to simmer. The ancestry of these peoples is traced back to the troubled relationship between Jacob (Israel) and Esau (Edom; Gen 25; 27).

1:13–15 *For three transgressions of the Ammonites, and for four.* Like a laser beam, God's vision sees each major wrong; here it illumines the Ammonites' inhumane attack on pregnant women while engaging in an offensive war.

2 Thus says the LORD:
  For three transgressions of Moab,
    and for four, I will not revoke the
      punishment;*a*
  because he burned to lime
    the bones of the king of Edom.
2 So I will send a fire on Moab,
    and it shall devour the strongholds of
      Kerioth,
  and Moab shall die amid uproar,
    amid shouting and the sound of the
      trumpet;
3 I will cut off the ruler from its midst,
    and will kill all its officials with him,
                                says the LORD.

Judgment on Judah

4 Thus says the LORD:
  For three transgressions of Judah,
    and for four, I will not revoke the
      punishment;*a*
  because they have rejected the law of
    the LORD,
    and have not kept his statutes,

but they have been led astray by the
    same lies
  after which their ancestors walked.
5 So I will send a fire on Judah,
    and it shall devour the strongholds of
      Jerusalem.

Judgment on Israel

6 Thus says the LORD:
  For three transgressions of Israel,
    and for four, I will not revoke the
      punishment;*a*
  because they sell the righteous for
    silver,
    and the needy for a pair of sandals—
7 they who trample the head of the poor
    into the dust of the earth,
    and push the afflicted out of the way;
  father and son go in to the same girl,
    so that my holy name is profaned;
8 they lay themselves down beside every
    altar
    on garments taken in pledge;

a Heb *cause it to return*

2:1–3 *For three transgressions of Moab, and for four.* The ruler of Moab is judged for burning to dust the bones of the king of Edom. In each case thus far, God unveils and judges the neighboring nations for war atrocities. An implicit critique throughout for Amos's hearers must have been that Israel surely did not want to align itself within a coalition of nations that violated the most basic ethics of how nations should treat each other. Today's international war ethics found in "just war" theories would disapprove of the nations' abuses cited by Amos here, for "just war" is limited to proportionate acts of self-defense, among other things. Burning the enemy king's bones to dust is not a "just measure" in responding to his attack.

2:4–5 *For three transgressions of Judah, and for four.* Here Amos, using the same formulaic speech, now judges Judah. As with the six previous nations, God judges Judah in just one verse, but it is a devastating critique: it has rejected the law (Torah) of Yahweh (though how is not precisely defined).

2:6–8 *For three transgressions of Israel, and for four.* Now Amos's circling verbal attack finally zeros in on Israel, on Jeroboam's kingdom

and the privileged wealthy class that abuses the poor. *because they sell the righteous for silver.* "Righteous" (those in the right morally or legally) may also be translated as "innocent." The line may be interpreted in different ways: the innocent are sold as slaves to a debtor when they cannot pay, or the wealthy who own slaves sell them simply to get money. *sell . . . the needy for a pair of sandals.* This line may mean the poor are so desperate for sandals (or any necessary commodity) that they sell themselves into slavery to an overlord unethical enough to make such an exchange; or it may mean a slave is such a cheap commodity that the price the owner gets for the slave will bring only enough for a needed pair of sandals. Either way, the slave is regarded not as a human being but as a cheap commodity.

Responding
2:6–8 SERVICE Israel's overwhelming sin is taking advantage of the poor— quite the opposite of what God charges us to do. Is our society's treatment of the poor cause for similar outrage? Explain. *See also* Spiritual Disciplines Index.

and in the house of their God they
> drink
wine bought with fines they imposed.

9 Yet I destroyed the Amorite before
> them,
whose height was like the height of
> cedars,
and who was as strong as oaks;
I destroyed his fruit above,
and his roots beneath.
10 Also I brought you up out of the land of
> Egypt,
and led you forty years in the
> wilderness,
to possess the land of the Amorite.
11 And I raised up some of your children to
> be prophets
and some of your youths to be
> nazirites. *a*
Is it not indeed so, O people of Israel?
> says the LORD.

12 But you made the nazirites *a* drink wine,
and commanded the prophets,
saying, "You shall not prophesy."

13 So, I will press you down in your place,
just as a cart presses down
when it is full of sheaves. *b*
14 Flight shall perish from the swift,
and the strong shall not retain their
> strength,
nor shall the mighty save their lives;

15 those who handle the bow shall not
> stand,
and those who are swift of foot shall
> not save themselves,
nor shall those who ride horses save
> their lives;
16 and those who are stout of heart among
> the mighty
shall flee away naked in that day,
> says the LORD.

Israel's Guilt and Punishment

3 Hear this word that the LORD has spoken against you, O people of Israel,
against the whole family that I brought up
out of the land of Egypt:
2 You only have I known
of all the families of the earth;
therefore I will punish you
for all your iniquities.

3 Do two walk together
unless they have made an
> appointment?
4 Does a lion roar in the forest,
when it has no prey?
Does a young lion cry out from its den,
if it has caught nothing?
5 Does a bird fall into a snare on the
> earth,
when there is no trap for it?
Does a snare spring up from the
> ground,

a That is, *those separated* or *those consecrated*
b Meaning of Heb uncertain

2:8 *garments taken in pledge*. This line also refers to a practice that exploits the poor. Those who cannot pay their debt must relinquish their garments in the sanctuary, where the wealthy lounge about with little regard for them, for their owners, or apparently for the Israelite law that forbade keeping a person's pledged garment overnight (Exod 22:26–27). This is Amos's first suggestion to beware of the Temple, a locale for neglect of justice and exploiting the poor, a kind of pawnshop where magistrates and creditors also pushed for "collections" of debts and taxes.

2:9–16 *Yet I destroyed the Amorite*. God reminds the Israelites that when they were weak and helpless, it was God's divine power

that brought them (note the shift in pronoun from "they" in vv 6–9 to "you" in vv 10–13 for emphasis) safely out of Egypt and into the land, thus also implying that God will be on the side of the downtrodden faithful. Now, however, God will disempower a haughty people who want to silence the prophets (see also 3:7–8).

3:2 *You only have I known of all the families of the earth*. Later, in 9:7, Amos will say, "Are you not like the Ethiopians to me, O people of Israel?" There Israel is paralleled with the Philistines and Arameans, whom God also brought into their land. From those to whom much is given, much is expected, but Israel is not the only nation that has received from God.

AMOS

A Cry for Justice

Selected Scriptures: *Amos 2:4–8; 5; 8; 9:8–15*

Amos spent most of his life overseeing herds of animals and caring for fig trees in the hill country of Tekoa in Judah. Yet during one particular year of his life, God took Amos out of the hills and gave him a weighty message to carry to the Northern Kingdom, Israel. Both Judah and Israel were comfortable: material wealth abounded and the two kingdoms were stable, even expanding their borders. However, this prosperity led them to forget their God and his laws.

Amid their prosperity, the Israelites were selling the poor into slavery because of debts owed, and they denied the powerless justice in the courts. "They sell the righteous for silver, . . . they . . . trample the head of the poor into the dust of the earth" (Amos 2:6–7). They were openly promiscuous, with father and son even sharing a prostitute or concubine (2:7). They defiled their worship by drinking wine acquired with money from their unjust fines against the poor in God's own house (2:8).

God grew enraged and spoke his judgments through Amos. He would no longer tolerate the people's masquerade of devotion to him. Although the Israelites performed their rituals of worship, their lack of love for those in need around them revealed the superficiality of their worship. Amos pronounced God's response: "I hate, I despise your festivals, and I take no delight in your solemn assemblies. . . . I will not listen to the melody of your harps" (5:21, 23).

The call for justice rings louder in Amos than in any other book. "Let justice roll down like waters, and righteousness like an ever-flowing stream," cried Amos on God's behalf (5:24). This is God's vision for his people. While the Israelites were concerning themselves with expansion of territory and wealth, God wanted his people to live a simple life, looking out for each other as well as for the poor and oppressed. Amos's prophetic message resounded with God's demand not only for honorable, generous treatment of the poor and needy but also for holy relationships and true worship of the One God. "Prepare to meet your God, O Israel!" (4:12): God would bring judgment on his people if they did not return to his simple, just, and holy ways.

John Woolman, a Quaker businessman and preacher, held Amos's words up to the eighteenth-century society in which he lived and, consequently, took up the cause for the abolition of slavery. His passionate writing and speaking became the impetus causing the Society of Friends not only to end slavery in their midst but also to reimburse their slaves for their time in bondage. So convinced was Woolman of the demands of justice outlined in the Bible that he moved many Southern Friends to accept financial bankruptcy and migrate to the North in order to emancipate their slaves.

PROFILE: AMOS

Woolman wrote: "I was renewedly confirmed in my mind that the Lord (whose tender mercies are over all his works, and whose ear is open to the cries and groans of the oppressed) is graciously moving in the hearts of people to draw them off from the desire of wealth and to bring them into such an humble, lowly way of living that they may see their way clearly to repair to the standard of true righteousness, and may not only break the yoke of oppression, but may know him to be their strength and support in times of outward affliction" (*The Journal of John Woolman*).

God cares about how we live our lives. The reminders that Amos provided for Israel prove no less essential today. By protecting justice, by generosity, simple living, and holy relationships, we will find ourselves living with God and extending his kingdom.

Personal Reflection

- The discipline of simplicity underlies Amos's call for justice and righteousness. In what way can simple living help you act generously toward the poor? Justly toward the oppressed? With holiness in your relationships?
- As the story of the Quakers illustrates, a commitment to justice may mean increased difficulty in daily living. How might this be true for you?

when it has taken nothing?
6 Is a trumpet blown in a city,
   and the people are not afraid?
Does disaster befall a city,
   unless the LORD has done it?
7 Surely the Lord GOD does nothing,
   without revealing his secret
   to his servants the prophets.
8 The lion has roared;
   who will not fear?
The Lord GOD has spoken;
   who can but prophesy?

9 Proclaim to the strongholds in
      Ashdod,
   and to the strongholds in the land of
      Egypt,
and say, "Assemble yourselves on
      Mount *a* Samaria,
   and see what great tumults are within
      it,
   and what oppressions are in its
      midst."
10 They do not know how to do right, says
      the LORD,
   those who store up violence and
      robbery in their strongholds.
11 Therefore thus says the Lord GOD:
An adversary shall surround the
      land,
   and strip you of your defense;
   and your strongholds shall be
      plundered.

12 Thus says the LORD: As the shepherd rescues from the mouth of the lion two legs, or a piece of an ear, so shall the people of Israel who live in Samaria be rescued, with the corner of a couch and part *b* of a bed.

a Gk Syr: Heb *the mountains of*   *b* Meaning of Heb uncertain

---

3:11–15 *An adversary shall surround the land.* Beyond disempowering Israel's warriors and leaders, God now announces total destruction by an adversarial nation as Israel's punishment. God will tear down the religious sanctuary at Bethel, along with the luxurious royal palaces, ending the Israelites' immoral complicities.

13 Hear, and testify against the house of
Jacob,
   says the Lord God, the God of hosts:
14 On the day I punish Israel for its
transgressions,
   I will punish the altars of Bethel,
and the horns of the altar shall be cut
off
   and fall to the ground.
15 I will tear down the winter house as well
as the summer house;
   and the houses of ivory shall perish,
and the great houses*a* shall come to an
end,
                        says the Lord.

4 Hear this word, you cows of Bashan
   who are on Mount Samaria,
who oppress the poor, who crush the
needy,
   who say to their husbands, "Bring
something to drink!"
2 The Lord God has sworn by his
holiness:
   The time is surely coming upon you,
when they shall take you away with
hooks,
   even the last of you with fishhooks.
3 Through breaches in the wall you shall
leave,
   each one straight ahead;
and you shall be flung out into
Harmon,*b*   says the Lord.
4 Come to Bethel—and transgress;
   to Gilgal—and multiply transgression;
bring your sacrifices every morning,
   your tithes every three days;
5 bring a thank offering of leavened
bread,
   and proclaim freewill offerings,
publish them;
   for so you love to do, O people of
Israel!
                        says the Lord God.

Israel Rejects Correction

6 I gave you cleanness of teeth in all your
cities,
   and lack of bread in all your places,
yet you did not return to me,
                        says the Lord.

7 And I also withheld the rain from you
   when there were still three months to
the harvest;
I would send rain on one city,
   and send no rain on another city;
one field would be rained upon,
   and the field on which it did not rain
withered;
8 so two or three towns wandered to one
town
   to drink water, and were not
satisfied;
yet you did not return to me,
                        says the Lord.

9 I struck you with blight and mildew;
   I laid waste*c* your gardens and your
vineyards;
   the locust devoured your fig trees and
your olive trees;
yet you did not return to me,
                        says the Lord.

10 I sent among you a pestilence after the
manner of Egypt;
   I killed your young men with the
sword;
I carried away your horses;*d*
   and I made the stench of your camp
go up into your nostrils;
yet you did not return to me,
                        says the Lord.

a Or *many houses*   b Meaning of Heb uncertain
c Cn: Heb *the multitude of*   d Heb *with the
captivity of your horses*

4:1–11 *Hear this word, you cows of Bashan . . .
who oppress the poor.* Amos further denounces
the wealthy lifestyle that thrives on the backs of
the poor. He sarcastically calls upon the wealthy
to keep bringing their sacrifices and tithes to
Bethel—not in exchange for forgiveness or to
please God, but in order to transgress! God had
tried in vain to get the Israelites' attention, but
their self-absorbed ways have dulled them to
God's voice, to compassion for the poor, and to
a coming justice to be exacted by the Creator of
all the earth.

11 I overthrew some of you,
    as when God overthrew Sodom and
        Gomorrah,
    and you were like a brand snatched
        from the fire;
    yet you did not return to me,
                  says the LORD.

12 Therefore thus I will do to you, O Israel;
    because I will do this to you,
    prepare to meet your God, O Israel!

13 For lo, the one who forms the
        mountains, creates the wind,
    reveals his thoughts to mortals,
  makes the morning darkness,
    and treads on the heights of the
        earth—
    the LORD, the God of hosts, is his
    name!

A Lament for Israel's Sin

5 Hear this word that I take up over you in
  lamentation, O house of Israel:
2 Fallen, no more to rise,
    is maiden Israel;
forsaken on her land,
    with no one to raise her up.

3 For thus says the Lord GOD:
The city that marched out a thousand
    shall have a hundred left,
and that which marched out a hundred
    shall have ten left. *a*

4 For thus says the LORD to the house of
    Israel:
Seek me and live;
5   but do not seek Bethel,
  and do not enter into Gilgal
  or cross over to Beer-sheba;
for Gilgal shall surely go into exile,
  and Bethel shall come to nothing.

6 Seek the LORD and live,
  or he will break out against the house
    of Joseph like fire,
  and it will devour Bethel, with no one
    to quench it.
7 Ah, you that turn justice to wormwood,
  and bring righteousness to the ground!

8 The one who made the Pleiades and
    Orion,
  and turns deep darkness into the
    morning,
  and darkens the day into night,
who calls for the waters of the sea,
  and pours them out on the surface of
    the earth,
  the LORD is his name,
9 who makes destruction flash out
    against the strong,
  so that destruction comes upon the
    fortress.

10 They hate the one who reproves in the
    gate,
  and they abhor the one who speaks
    the truth.
11 Therefore because you trample on the
    poor
  and take from them levies of grain,
you have built houses of hewn stone,
  but you shall not live in them;
you have planted pleasant vineyards,
  but you shall not drink their wine.
12 For I know how many are your
    transgressions,
  and how great are your sins—
you who afflict the righteous, who take
    a bribe,
  and push aside the needy in the gate.
13 Therefore the prudent will keep silent
    in such a time;
  for it is an evil time.

a Heb adds *to the house of Israel*

5:1–14 *Hear this word that I take up over you in lamentation.* Here Amos utters a national dirge, a stunning technique used by the prophets to announce the death of the personified nation ahead of time as a warning of impending doom if the people do not straighten up (see also 5:16–17). He follows with intensifying imperatives by God: "Seek me and live!" (v 4). Amos says, practice justice and *live,* so that "the LORD, the God of hosts, will be with you" (v 14). Here the with-God life requires justice as a matter of life and death.

14 Seek good and not evil,
   that you may live;
and so the LORD, the God of hosts, will
      be with you,
   just as you have said.
15 Hate evil and love good,
   and establish justice in the gate;
it may be that the LORD, the God of hosts,
   will be gracious to the remnant of
      Joseph.

16 Therefore thus says the LORD, the God
      of hosts, the Lord:
In all the squares there shall be wailing;
   and in all the streets they shall say,
      "Alas! alas!"
They shall call the farmers to
      mourning,
   and those skilled in lamentation, to
      wailing;
17 in all the vineyards there shall be
      wailing,
   for I will pass through the midst of
      you,
                              says the LORD.

The Day of the LORD a Dark Day

18 Alas for you who desire the day of the
      LORD!
   Why do you want the day of the LORD?
It is darkness, not light;
19   as if someone fled from a lion,
      and was met by a bear;
   or went into the house and rested a
         hand against the wall,
      and was bitten by a snake.
20 Is not the day of the LORD darkness, not
      light,
   and gloom with no brightness in it?

21 I hate, I despise your festivals,
   and I take no delight in your solemn
      assemblies.

22 Even though you offer me your burnt
         offerings and grain offerings,
   I will not accept them;
and the offerings of well-being of your
      fatted animals
   I will not look upon.
23 Take away from me the noise of your
      songs;
   I will not listen to the melody of your
      harps.
24 But let justice roll down like waters,
   and righteousness like an ever-
      flowing stream.

25 Did you bring to me sacrifices and offerings the forty years in the wilderness,
O house of Israel? 26 You shall take up Sakkuth
your king, and Kaiwan your star-god, your
images, *a* which you made for yourselves;
27 therefore I will take you into exile beyond
Damascus, says the LORD, whose name is the
God of hosts.

Complacent Self-Indulgence Will Be Punished

6 Alas for those who are at ease in Zion,
   and for those who feel secure on
      Mount Samaria,
   the notables of the first of the nations,
      to whom the house of Israel resorts!
2 Cross over to Calneh, and see;
   from there go to Hamath the great;
      then go down to Gath of the
         Philistines.
Are you better *b* than these kingdoms?
   Or is your *c* territory greater than
      their *d* territory,
3 O you that put far away the evil day,
   and bring near a reign of violence?

a Heb *your images, your star-god*   *b* Or *Are they better*   *c* Heb *their*   *d* Heb *your*

5:21–23 *I hate, I despise your festivals. . . . Take away from me the noise of your songs. . . . But let justice roll down like waters, and righteousness like an ever-flowing stream.* Famous lines by Amos, made yet more famous by Martin Luther King, Jr. In this dramatic critique, God despises the pretense of hypocritical worship lacking justice.

6:1–8 *Alas for those who are at ease.* Prophets usually use the word "Alas" (see also v 4) when uttering a dirge for the coming destruction of a people. Those who have long lived in oblivious comfort (graphically described in vv 4–6) do not see their way of life coming to an end.

4 Alas for those who lie on beds of ivory,
    and lounge on their couches,
and eat lambs from the flock,
    and calves from the stall;
5 who sing idle songs to the sound of the
        harp,
    and like David improvise on
        instruments of music;
6 who drink wine from bowls,
    and anoint themselves with the finest
        oils,
    but are not grieved over the ruin of
        Joseph!
7 Therefore they shall now be the first to
        go into exile,
    and the revelry of the loungers shall
        pass away.

8 The Lord God has sworn by himself
    (says the Lord, the God of hosts):
I abhor the pride of Jacob
    and hate his strongholds;
    and I will deliver up the city and all
        that is in it.

9 If ten people remain in one house, they
shall die. 10 And if a relative, one who burns
the dead, [a] shall take up the body to bring it
out of the house, and shall say to someone in
the innermost parts of the house, "Is anyone else with you?" the answer will come,
"No." Then the relative[b] shall say, "Hush!
We must not mention the name of the Lord."

11 See, the Lord commands,
    and the great house shall be shattered
        to bits,
    and the little house to pieces.
12 Do horses run on rocks?
    Does one plow the sea with oxen?[c]
But you have turned justice into poison
    and the fruit of righteousness into
        wormwood—
13 you who rejoice in Lo-debar,[d]
    who say, "Have we not by our own
        strength
    taken Karnaim[e] for ourselves?"

14 Indeed, I am raising up against you a
        nation,
    O house of Israel, says the Lord, the
        God of hosts,
    and they shall oppress you from Lebo-
        hamath
    to the Wadi Arabah.

Locusts, Fire, and a Plumb Line

7 This is what the Lord God showed me: he
was forming locusts at the time the lat-
ter-growth began to sprout (it was the latter
growth after the king's mowings). 2 When
they had finished eating the grass of the land,
I said,
    "O Lord God, forgive, I beg you!
        How can Jacob stand?
        He is so small!"
3 The Lord relented concerning this;
    "It shall not be," said the Lord.

4 This is what the Lord God showed me:
the Lord God was calling for a shower of fire,[f]
and it devoured the great deep and was eating up the land. 5 Then I said,
    "O Lord God, cease, I beg you!
        How can Jacob stand?
        He is so small!"
6 The Lord relented concerning this;
    "This also shall not be," said the Lord
        God.

7 This is what he showed me: the Lord
was standing beside a wall built with a plumb
line, with a plumb line in his hand. 8 And the
Lord said to me, "Amos, what do you see?"
And I said, "A plumb line." Then the Lord
said,
    "See, I am setting a plumb line
        in the midst of my people Israel;
    I will never again pass them by;
9 the high places of Isaac shall be made
        desolate,

a Or who makes a burning for him   b Heb he
c Or Does one plow them with oxen   d Or in
a thing of nothingness   e Or horns
f Or for a judgment by fire

7:2–9 *O Lord God, forgive, I beg you!* Twice
(vv 2, 5) Amos offers intercessory lament
prayers to God on behalf of "Jacob" (Israel), as

the three visions alarm him about the
diminishing size of the kingdom.

and the sanctuaries of Israel shall be
  laid waste,
and I will rise against the house of
  Jeroboam with the sword."

Amaziah Complains to the King

10 Then Amaziah, the priest of Bethel,
sent to King Jeroboam of Israel, saying,
"Amos has conspired against you in the very
center of the house of Israel; the land is not
able to bear all his words. 11For thus Amos
has said,

'Jeroboam shall die by the sword,
  and Israel must go into exile
  away from his land.' "

12And Amaziah said to Amos, "O seer, go,
flee away to the land of Judah, earn your
bread there, and prophesy there; 13but never
again prophesy at Bethel, for it is the king's
sanctuary, and it is a temple of the kingdom."

14 Then Amos answered Amaziah, "I am*a*
no prophet, nor a prophet's son; but I am*a* a
herdsman, and a dresser of sycamore trees,
15and the LORD took me from following the
flock, and the LORD said to me, 'Go, prophesy to my people Israel.'

16 "Now therefore hear the word of the
  LORD.
You say, 'Do not prophesy against Israel,
  and do not preach against the house
    of Isaac.'
17 Therefore thus says the LORD:
'Your wife shall become a prostitute in
  the city,
and your sons and your daughters
  shall fall by the sword,
and your land shall be parceled out by
  line;
you yourself shall die in an unclean
  land,

and Israel shall surely go into exile
  away from its land.' "

The Basket of Fruit

8 This is what the Lord GOD showed me—
  a basket of summer fruit.*b* 2He said,
"Amos, what do you see?" And I said, "A basket of summer fruit."*b* Then the LORD said to
me,

"The end*c* has come upon my people
  Israel;
I will never again pass them by.
3 The songs of the temple*d* shall become
  wailings in that day,"
                              says the Lord GOD;
"the dead bodies shall be many,
  cast out in every place. Be silent!"

4 Hear this, you that trample on the
  needy,
  and bring to ruin the poor of the
    land,
5 saying, "When will the new moon be
    over
  so that we may sell grain;
and the sabbath,
  so that we may offer wheat for sale?
We will make the ephah small and the
    shekel great,
  and practice deceit with false
    balances,
6 buying the poor for silver
  and the needy for a pair of sandals,
  and selling the sweepings of the
    wheat."

7 The LORD has sworn by the pride of
    Jacob:

a Or *was*   *b* Heb *qayits*   *c* Heb *qets*
d Or *palace*

7:9–17 *I will rise against the house of Jero-*
boam. Amos predicts the end of Jeroboam's
reign; this seems to prompt paranoia in the king
and his priest in Bethel that the prophet may be
conspiring with the pro-Damascus coalition to
remove him in favor of Pekah. Thus the priest,
sent by the king, says to Amos, "O seer, go, flee
away to the land of Judah; . . . but never again
prophesy at Bethel." Amos replies with his
famous biographical statement, "I am no

prophet," but in the face of this royal directive
from a priest who has sold his holy office for
political power Amos proceeds to prophesy!

8:1–3 *The end has come.* The fourth vision
God gives Amos, a basket of summer fruit,
serves simply as a wordplay to suggest the word
"end." As the nation expires, with mourning and
wailing, those who "trample on the needy" (v 4)
still continue going about that business, blind to
the whole society collapsing around them.

Surely I will never forget any of their
    deeds.
8 Shall not the land tremble on this
        account,
    and everyone mourn who lives in it,
    and all of it rise like the Nile,
        and be tossed about and sink again,
            like the Nile of Egypt?

9 On that day, says the Lord GOD,
    I will make the sun go down at noon,
        and darken the earth in broad
            daylight.
10 I will turn your feasts into mourning,
        and all your songs into lamentation;
    I will bring sackcloth on all loins,
        and baldness on every head;
    I will make it like the mourning for an
            only son,
        and the end of it like a bitter day.

11 The time is surely coming, says the Lord
        GOD,
    when I will send a famine on the
            land;
    not a famine of bread, or a thirst for
            water,
    but of hearing the words of the LORD
12 They shall wander from sea to sea,
        and from north to east;
    they shall run to and fro, seeking the
            word of the LORD,
        but they shall not find it.

13 In that day the beautiful young women
            and the young men
        shall faint for thirst.
14 Those who swear by Ashimah of
            Samaria,
        and say, "As your god lives, O Dan,"
    and, "As the way of Beer-sheba lives"—
        they shall fall, and never rise again.

The Destruction of Israel

9 I saw the LORD standing beside[a] the
        altar, and he said:
    Strike the capitals until the thresholds
            shake,
        and shatter them on the heads of all
            the people;[b]
    and those who are left I will kill with
            the sword;
        not one of them shall flee away,
        not one of them shall escape.

2 Though they dig into Sheol,
        from there shall my hand take them;
    though they climb up to heaven,
        from there I will bring them down.
3 Though they hide themselves on the
            top of Carmel,
        from there I will search out and take
            them;
    and though they hide from my sight at
            the bottom of the sea,
        there I will command the sea-serpent,
            and it shall bite them.
4 And though they go into captivity in
            front of their enemies,
        there I will command the sword, and
            it shall kill them;
    and I will fix my eyes on them
        for harm and not for good.

5 The Lord, GOD of hosts,
    he who touches the earth and it melts,
        and all who live in it mourn,
    and all of it rises like the Nile,
        and sinks again, like the Nile of Egypt;
6 who builds his upper chambers in the
            heavens,
        and founds his vault upon the earth;
    who calls for the waters of the sea,
        and pours them out upon the surface
            of the earth—
    the LORD is his name.

a Or on   b Heb all of them

9:1–10 *I saw the LORD standing beside the altar.* In a final vision, Amos sees God standing by the altar calling for its destruction and the destruction of the people. Such direct violence upon the people by God is unsettling to say the least, but this kind of graphic imagery of destruction is typical of the prophets in their zeal to describe God's punishment of recalcitrant injustice.

7 Are you not like the Ethiopians[a] to me,
    O people of Israel? says the LORD.
  Did I not bring Israel up from the land
      of Egypt,
    and the Philistines from Caphtor and
      the Arameans from Kir?
8 The eyes of the Lord GOD are upon the
      sinful kingdom,
    and I will destroy it from the face of
      the earth
  —except that I will not utterly destroy
    the house of Jacob,

                                says the LORD.

9 For lo, I will command,
    and shake the house of Israel among
      all the nations
  as one shakes with a sieve,
    but no pebble shall fall to the ground.
10 All the sinners of my people shall die by
      the sword,
    who say, "Evil shall not overtake or
      meet us."

The Restoration of David's Kingdom

11 On that day I will raise up
    the booth of David that is fallen,
  and repair its[b] breaches,
    and raise up its[c] ruins,
    and rebuild it as in the days of old;

12 in order that they may possess the
      remnant of Edom
    and all the nations who are called by
      my name,
  says the LORD who does this.

13 The time is surely coming, says the
      LORD,
    when the one who plows shall
      overtake the one who reaps,
    and the treader of grapes the one who
      sows the seed;
  the mountains shall drip sweet wine,
    and all the hills shall flow with it.
14 I will restore the fortunes of my people
      Israel,
    and they shall rebuild the ruined
      cities and inhabit them;
  they shall plant vineyards and drink
      their wine,
    and they shall make gardens and eat
      their fruit.
15 I will plant them upon their land,
    and they shall never again be plucked
      up
  out of the land that I have given
      them,

                    says the LORD your God.

a Or Nubians; Heb Cushites   b Gk: Heb their
c Gk: Heb his

9:11–15 *On that day I will raise up the booth of David that is fallen.* This promise of God's restoration of the Davidic kingdom might possibly come from a later time period than Amos's (perhaps from the Babylonian exile); nevertheless, exiled Israel's hope will reside in the root of Jesse (Isa 11:1, 10).

OBADIAH

Afll Scripture is inspired by God and profitable for spiritual formation, even the shortest, most obscure book in the Old Testament—Obadiah. We know nothing about Obadiah, a common name that means "servant of the Lord," except that he must have lived in Judah since he prophesies in relation to Jerusalem. The vision of Obadiah is most likely set in the early exilic period, shortly after the destruction of Jerusalem around 587 BC. The wider context is the long-standing history of antagonism between Israel and Edom, which serves as the prophecy's framework. The Edomites (who lived to the southeast of the Dead Sea) were the descendants of Esau, the older twin of Jacob, who was cheated out of his birthright by his younger brother, also called Israel (Gen 25:21–34; 27:41). The prolonged conflict between these two nations resulted in the Edomites' refusal to allow the Israelites passage through their land en route to the Promised Land (Num 20:14–21). Saul (1 Sam 14:47), David (2 Sam 8:13–14), and Solomon (1 Kings 11:14–22) all had problems with the Edomites, and now, Obadiah tells us, these people actively rejoiced over the capture of Jerusalem (Ps 137:7) and gloated over the misfortune of Judah.

The prophecy of Obadiah divides into two parts. In verses 1–15 we read the oracle against Edom for its pride, self-assurance, and shameful indifference toward Israel and the announcement of coming judgment upon it as a consequence. Then in verses 16–21 a message of hope speaks of a retribution that is justified, when Edom will be humiliated and utterly despised. The promises made long ago to Abraham, Isaac, and Jacob that they and their descendants would possess the land will not be frustrated, as Israel is gloriously restored with expanded territory.

Trusting in God

Obadiah serves as a warning to God's people. The message against Edom was in part condemnation against its perceived wisdom and sense of pride. The prophetic message is always a judgment on purely human wisdom. Scripture reminds us that the

See also *"The With-God Life" essay for this section of the Bible,*
"The People of God in Exile," pp. 1171–74.

foolishness of God is wiser than human wisdom. We do well to examine whose wisdom we are trusting. Obadiah also offers hope and encouragement to God's people in all periods of history. When unbelievers mock us in our weakness, when they take advantage of us, God's anger rises against them. After they have had opportunities to turn back to him, perhaps through the witness of the people they ridicule or persecute, God will ensure that they are justly dealt with for their sin. So there's no need for us to seek vengeance; we can get on with more positive and fruitful activities and leave God's enemies to God himself (see Ps 22:27–28).

Through New Testament eyes we can see a much larger fulfillment than Obadiah was able to see. With the coming of the Messiah, the People of God are not limited to the Jewish remnant. "There is no longer Jew or Greek, there is no longer slave or free, there is no longer male and female; for all of you are one in Christ Jesus. And if you belong to Christ, then you are Abraham's offspring, heirs according to the promise" (Gal 3:28–29). Rom 4:13 reminds us that the descendants of Abraham will inherit the whole world, not just a part of the Holy Land. And Jesus said, "Blessed are the meek, for they will inherit the earth" (Matt 5:5). This is the same promise clearly stated in God's last word through Obadiah, that "the kingdom shall be the Lord's" (Obad 21).

—*Trevor Miller*

Proud Edom Will Be Brought Low

1 The vision of Obadiah.

Thus says the Lord God concerning
   Edom:
We have heard a report from the Lord,
   and a messenger has been sent among
      the nations:

"Rise up! Let us rise against it for battle!"
2 I will surely make you least among the
      nations;
   you shall be utterly despised.
3 Your proud heart has deceived you,
   you that live in the clefts of the rock,[a]
   whose dwelling is in the heights.

a Or *clefts of Sela*

---

1 *a messenger has been sent.* We know nothing of the man, only his message, but the fact that he was a messenger from God is all-important. In order to pass on the report we must first listen to God's voice.

about sins we see in their lives. Similarly, we also must listen to the counsel of those we trust. Is there a situation in your life about which you need to take action? *See also* Spiritual Disciplines Index.

Responding
1 GUIDANCE. Being a messenger of God can be a lonely job, for God's messages are often hard for humans to hear. No one wants to be the one telling others that their behavior is wrong, much less that there will be consequences. We are decidedly not meant to go around smugly pointing out others' foibles, but there are times when, after much praying and searching for discernment, we are called to take the serious step of confronting friends

2 *I will surely make you least.* As the Judge of all the earth, God will always do right, and as with the Edomites, our pride, self-assurance, and shameful indifference will all succumb to God's righteous judgment. Choice brings consequence, and all who listen to God and who speak for God (like Obadiah) will encounter times when doing the right thing and saying the right thing are hard. God cannot act against his own just nature, and those who speak for him must speak for him.

You say in your heart,
   "Who will bring me down to the
        ground?"
4 Though you soar aloft like the eagle,
   though your nest is set among the
        stars,
   from there I will bring you down, says
        the LORD.

Pillage and Slaughter Will Repay Edom's Cruelty

5 If thieves came to you,
   if plunderers by night
   —how you have been destroyed!—
   would they not steal only what they
        wanted?
   If grape-gatherers came to you,
   would they not leave gleanings?
6 How Esau has been pillaged,
   his treasures searched out!
7 All your allies have deceived you,
   they have driven you to the border;
   your confederates have prevailed
        against you;
   those who ate a your bread have set a
        trap for you—
   there is no understanding of it.
8 On that day, says the LORD,
   I will destroy the wise out of Edom,
   and understanding out of Mount
        Esau.

9 Your warriors shall be shattered,
        O Teman,
   so that everyone from Mount Esau
        will be cut off.

Edom Mistreated His Brother

10 For the slaughter and violence done to
        your brother Jacob,
   shame shall cover you,
   and you shall be cut off forever.
11 On the day that you stood aside,
   on the day that strangers carried off
        his wealth,
   and foreigners entered his gates
   and cast lots for Jerusalem,
   you too were like one of them.
12 But you should not have gloated b over c
        your brother
   on the day of his misfortune;
   you should not have rejoiced over the
        people of Judah
   on the day of their ruin;
   you should not have boasted
   on the day of distress.
13 You should not have entered the gate of
        my people
   on the day of their calamity;
   you should not have joined in the
        gloating over Judah's d disaster

a Cn: Heb lacks those who ate   b Heb But do not
gloat (and similarly through verse 14)   c Heb on
the day of   d Heb his

---

3 *Your proud heart has deceived you.* Pride is the most deadly of all sins because it affects who one is, the whole person. It colors everything and makes discernment impossible, destroying other virtues along the way. Pride turns the self away from God and results in an "I know best, no one can tell me anything" attitude. The consequences are defiance, disloyalty, unbelief, and a false sense of self-sufficiency. Humility destroys pride, and humility is fed by Spiritual Disciplines and daily living that cultivates awareness of God and watchfulness over self.

3–4 *you that live in the clefts of the rock.* The Edomites boasted about being in an impregnable place, hence their pride and insolence. Their self-sufficiency made them say, "Who will bring [us] down to the ground?"

and God answered, "I will" (v 8). Their sense of security was deceptive—although impregnable to human forces, they were still vulnerable to the power of God. No one is safe from the ultimate justice of God.

12–14 *you should not have gloated.* God cannot act against his own nature; he cannot fail to be just. As if showing a series of newsreel pictures flashing scene after scene before the Edomites' eyes, Obadiah lists examples of their vindictive, unforgiving, gloating response to their brother's misfortune. "You should not have" occurs eight times in these verses and proceeds from the general to the particular. You knew the right thing, but you chose the wrong thing. Choice always brings consequence; hence a foundational Spiritual Discipline is to continually choose life.

on the day of his calamity;
you should not have looted his goods
on the day of his calamity.
14 You should not have stood at the
crossings
to cut off his fugitives;
you should not have handed over his
survivors
on the day of distress.

15 For the day of the LORD is near against
all the nations.
As you have done, it shall be done to
you;
your deeds shall return on your own
head.
16 For as you have drunk on my holy
mountain,
all the nations around you shall
drink;
they shall drink and gulp down,[a]
and shall be as though they had never
been.

Israel's Final Triumph

17 But on Mount Zion there shall be those
that escape,
and it shall be holy;
and the house of Jacob shall take
possession of those who
dispossessed them.

18 The house of Jacob shall be a fire,
the house of Joseph a flame,
and the house of Esau stubble;
they shall burn them and consume
them,
and there shall be no survivor of the
house of Esau;
for the LORD has spoken.
19 Those of the Negeb shall possess Mount
Esau,
and those of the Shephelah the land
of the Philistines;
they shall possess the land of Ephraim
and the land of Samaria,
and Benjamin shall possess Gilead.
20 The exiles of the Israelites who are in
Halah[b]
shall possess[c] Phoenicia as far as
Zarephath;
and the exiles of Jerusalem who are in
Sepharad
shall possess the towns of the Negeb.
21 Those who have been saved[d] shall go up
to Mount Zion
to rule Mount Esau;
and the kingdom shall be the LORD's.

a Meaning of Heb uncertain   b Cn: Heb in this
army   c Cn: Meaning of Heb uncertain
d Or Saviors

---

15 *As you have done, it shall be done to you.*
The punishment will always fit the crime—
"your deeds shall return" (see Matt 7:1–2; Gal
6:7–8; Ps 7:14–16).

JONAH

[handwritten note: GOD SHOWS MERCY ON WHOM HE PLEASE]

G od is on a quest to forgive people and reconcile them to himself. In the biographical narrative of Jonah, God stretches toward those who are far from him and toward those who are nearby. He takes a chance on brutal and spiritually ignorant Nineveh and, even more intriguing, on spiritually arrogant and malicious Jonah. God insists on showing mercy to whomever he pleases. This message has unfortunately sometimes been lost in debates over the improbability of a person surviving ingestion by a sea creature and the unanimous repentance of the Ninevites. Regardless of the historicity of the book of Jonah, the import remains the same.

The book of Jonah gives no internal evidence for its authorship or date. A prophet named Jonah son of Amittai is mentioned in 2 Kings 14:25. If this person is the prophet of Jonah, the book is set in the eighth century BC, before Nineveh directly threatened Israel. Unique among prophetic books, Jonah is a narrative containing no prophetic pronouncements for Israel.

God's Method of Formation

God employs ministry as the pathway of growth for Jonah. He directs Jonah to proclaim his message of judgment in Nineveh, the capital city of militaristic Assyria. Jonah refuses to go. Unlike with other reluctant prophets, Jonah's unwillingness to obey God's command does not stem from his personal insecurities. Jonah rebuffs God because he is outraged at the possibility that the Ninevites will repent and God will forswear punishing them.

God's call to Jonah challenges Jonah's self-sufficiency, arrogance, and indifference. God gives Jonah a ministry to the sailors who unwittingly help him flee from God and a ministry to violent Nineveh. Each of Jonah's ministries introduces him to people with hearts softer toward the Lord than his own. In spite of Jonah's insubordination, God impressively uses Jonah to bring both the sailors and the Ninevites to a yielding humility before the Lord.

See also *"The With-God Life" essay for this section of the Bible,*
"The People of God in Rebellion," pp. 975–79.

Still Jonah relentlessly continues to relate to God only on his own terms. He is convinced that his way is better than God's way. Although Jonah's doctrine is impeccable, nothing inside Jonah intends to submit to the Lord. Jonah recognizes God as the Creator of the world. He understands that God is merciful. He hears God and speaks with God. Yet Jonah is much more difficult for God to touch than any of the Gentiles described in the narrative. Jonah is not seeking a fuller experience of God, and he does not want to grow. Nevertheless, God persistently presses Jonah to mature. Each ministry experience leads to an intense personal encounter between Jonah and God.

A Theology of Mercy

The narrative illuminates the relationship between judgment and mercy. Signs of God's judgment turn out to be expressions of God's grace. Through the life-threatening storm instigated by God, the frightened sailors come to personally experience and worship the Lord, who created and rules the sea. The gigantic sea creature sent by God to swallow Jonah delivers him from death and begets in him a temporary humility. A message of impending doom kindles genuine and complete repentance in Nineveh. In none of these instances does the mercy of God "feel" good. Yet each time the threat of judgment results in a reorientation toward God. Furthermore, God's dealings with Jonah, Nineveh, and the sailors dispel the notion that anyone ever merits God's mercy. Mercy is an utter gift from God. Nevertheless, those who humbly submit to God's authority and seek his mercy are not disappointed.

Jesus referred to Jonah's ministry, stating that only "the sign of the prophet Jonah" was to be given Israel (Matt 12:38–41). The positive response of the Gentiles to Jesus' message and the tragic disobedience of many who first received his message parallel events in the story of Jonah.

Ultimately, Jonah's unenthusiastic ministry among the Gentiles transforms many lives. Tragically, the formation of Jonah himself remains a question to the very end. But that is not the point of the book; rather, in this narrative we witness the depth and breadth of God's forgiving heart as he works in and through even a reluctant prophet, offering mercy and grace both to one nearby and to those far off.

—Barbara M. Musselman

Jonah Tries to Run Away from God

1 Now the word of the LORD came to Jonah son of Amittai, saying, 2"Go at once to Nineveh, that great city, and cry out against it; for their wickedness has come up before me." 3But Jonah set out to flee to Tarshish from the presence of the LORD. He went down to Joppa and found a ship going to Tarshish;

1:1 *Jonah son of Amittai.* The prophet is aptly named. In Hebrew, Jonah means "dove," and Amittai means "truth," "truth telling," or "truth of God."

1:2 *Go at once to Nineveh.* From Jonah's perspective, the Ninevites are not God's people; they do not have the law, and they are ruthless killers. God's assessment of their wickedness would seem an understatement to Jonah, who despises the Ninevites.

so he paid his fare and went on board, to go with them to Tarshish, away from the presence of the LORD.

4 But the LORD hurled a great wind upon the sea, and such a mighty storm came upon the sea that the ship threatened to break up. 5Then the mariners were afraid, and each cried to his god. They threw the cargo that was in the ship into the sea, to lighten it for them. Jonah, meanwhile, had gone down into the hold of the ship and had lain down, and was fast asleep. 6The captain came and said to him, "What are you doing sound asleep? Get up, call on your god! Perhaps the god will spare us a thought so that we do not perish."

7 The sailors*a* said to one another, "Come, let us cast lots, so that we may know on whose account this calamity has come upon us." So they cast lots, and the lot fell on Jonah. 8Then they said to him, "Tell us why this calamity has come upon us. What is your occupation? Where do you come from? What is your country? And of what people are you?" 9"I am a Hebrew," he replied. "I worship the LORD, the God of heaven, who made the sea and the dry land." 10Then the men were even more afraid, and said to him, "What is this that you have done!" For the men knew that he was fleeing from the presence of the LORD, because he had told them so.

11 Then they said to him, "What shall we do to you, that the sea may quiet down for us?" For the sea was growing more and more tempestuous. 12He said to them, "Pick me up and throw me into the sea; then the sea will quiet down for you; for I know it is because of me that this great storm has come upon you." 13Nevertheless the men rowed hard to bring the ship back to land, but they could not, for the sea grew more and more stormy against them. 14Then they cried out to the LORD, "Please, O LORD, we pray, do not let us perish on account of this man's life. Do not make us guilty of innocent blood; for you, O LORD, have done as it pleased you." 15So they picked Jonah up and threw him into the sea; and the sea ceased from its raging. 16Then the men feared the LORD even more, and they offered a sacrifice to the LORD and made vows.

17*b* But the LORD provided a large fish to swallow up Jonah; and Jonah was in the belly of the fish three days and three nights.

a Heb *They*   *b* Ch 2.1 in Heb

1:3 *But Jonah set out to flee.* Jonah is appalled that God intends to give the Ninevites a chance to reform. He wants them to suffer. Instead of traveling east toward landlocked Nineveh, Jonah books passage on a gentile trading vessel heading west. Hebrew people understood the sea as a place of chaos, danger, and evil. Jonah expects to find a locale completely hostile to God.

1:6 *Get up, call on your god!* The gentile sailors have a deeper sensitivity to their need for mercy than Jonah does. Though deeply uncertain about the character of God, the sailors are willing to risk more on less.

1:7 *let us cast lots.* Discerning unseen truth by casting lots was conventional behavior for ancient Near Eastern peoples.

1:8 *Tell us why.* Rather than kill him first and ask questions later, the sailors charitably seek to confirm their discernment by questioning Jonah about his circumstances.

1:9 *I worship the LORD.* Jonah's doctrine is flawless. He states that he worships (lit., "fears") God, who made the whole earth and rules the heavens. In reality, Jonah fears very little, least of all God.

1:11–12 *What shall we do?* The sailors defer to Jonah's knowledge of God and ask him how to appease God. Jonah understands God too well to believe any ritual act could compensate for his disobedience.

1:14 *Then they cried out to the LORD.* The sailors do not want to die, nor do they want to do wrong. Finally, they ask God not to hold them responsible for Jonah's death, and they throw Jonah into the sea. Jonah's assessment of what God required was correct, and the sea stops raging.

1:16 *Then the men feared the LORD.* Whatever doubts the pagan sailors may have harbored about God dissolve. With their new understanding, they wholeheartedly worship God. By way of the storm and Jonah's testimony, the sailors have come to know God, who created and rules the sea.

A Psalm of Thanksgiving

2 Then Jonah prayed to the LORD his God from the belly of the fish, ²saying,
"I called to the LORD out of my distress,
  and he answered me;
out of the belly of Sheol I cried,
  and you heard my voice.
³ You cast me into the deep,
  into the heart of the seas,
  and the flood surrounded me;
all your waves and your billows
  passed over me.
⁴ Then I said, 'I am driven away
  from your sight;
how *a* shall I look again
  upon your holy temple?'
⁵ The waters closed in over me;
  the deep surrounded me;
weeds were wrapped around my head
⁶   at the roots of the mountains.
I went down to the land
  whose bars closed upon me forever;
yet you brought up my life from the Pit,
  O LORD my God.
⁷ As my life was ebbing away,
  I remembered the LORD;
and my prayer came to you,
  into your holy temple.
⁸ Those who worship vain idols
  forsake their true loyalty,
⁹ But I with the voice of thanksgiving
  will sacrifice to you;
what I have vowed I will pay.
  Deliverance belongs to the LORD!"
¹⁰Then the LORD spoke to the fish, and it spewed Jonah out upon the dry land.

Conversion of Nineveh

3 The word of the LORD came to Jonah a second time, saying, ²"Get up, go to Nineveh, that great city, and proclaim to it the message that I tell you." ³So Jonah set out and went to Nineveh, according to the word of the LORD. Now Nineveh was an exceedingly large city, a three days' walk across. ⁴Jonah began to go into the city, going a day's walk. And he cried out, "Forty days more, and Nineveh shall be overthrown!" ⁵And the people of Nineveh believed God; they proclaimed a fast, and everyone, great and small, put on sackcloth.

6 When the news reached the king of Nineveh, he rose from his throne, removed his

a Theodotion: Heb *surely*

2:1–9 *Then Jonah prayed.* Once Jonah is captive inside the fish, his distress awakens him to God as nothing else has been able to do. For the first time, he recognizes that the God of Israel is a God of rescue and deliverance.

Responding
2:1–9 PRAYER. Jonah resists God for a long time, but once he is in the belly of the fish, he can do nothing else but pray. And once he starts to turn to God, he begins, albeit slowly, to change. As Richard Foster writes, "Our prayer muscles need to be limbered up a bit, and once the blood-flow of intercession begins, we will find that we feel like praying." Challenge yourself to commit to daily prayer, even when you don't feel like it. See if you can limber up your prayer muscles. *See also* Spiritual Disciplines Index.

2:9 *But I with the voice of thanksgiving.* Jonah comes to the spiritually vital place the gentile sailors had reached earlier. This is apparently the first time heartfelt worship infuses Jonah's theological understanding. He yields to God, and God delivers him out of the fish. Jonah recognizes that God's mercy has saved him. Jonah has the opportunity to make this the defining moment of his life.

3:1 *The word of the LORD came to Jonah a second time.* God gives Jonah a second chance to obey. This time Jonah goes to Nineveh as God commands.

Responding
3:5 FASTING. Even the notoriously sinful Ninevites hear God and know how to respond—with fasting. Consider undertaking a fast this week in the name of those people in your life who don't know God. *See also* Spiritual Disciplines Index.

3:6 *When the news reached the king.* Jonah does not prophesy directly to the king, though kings are typical recipients of such prophetic oracles. Nevertheless, the king becomes a

PROFILE

Jonah: Displeased with God's Mercy

Selected Scriptures: *Jonah 1–4*

God chose for Jonah a difficult task: prophesying not to his own people, Israel, but to the enemy. The Ninevites, residents of the capital of the Assyrian empire, were idolatrous and known for heinous acts of violence and cruelty. They were also the ones God had said would later overtake Israel. Considering Nineveh's reputation and its relationship to Israel, it's no wonder Jonah struggled with God's command to go and preach judgment.

Although another prophet may have been more than willing to pronounce Nineveh's sure destruction, Jonah felt reluctant to follow God's command. It was not that Jonah was afraid to enter Nineveh (although that would have been reasonable)—it was because he knew God too well. He knew God to be "a gracious God and merciful, slow to anger, and abounding in steadfast love, and ready to relent from punishing" (Jon 4:2). If the Ninevites should repent, Jonah reasoned, God would forgive. This was not acceptable to Jonah and made him angry (4:1).

Jonah may have possessed a keen understanding of God's mercy on one level, but at a deeper level he didn't understand holy mercy at all. Indeed, Jonah himself experienced this same mercy after running from God and his implausible task and being thrown into the sea. "As my life was ebbing away," he prayed inside the fish, "I remembered the LORD; and my prayer came to you. . . . Deliverance belongs to the LORD!" (2:7, 9). Jonah could thank God for the mercy he received. He could expect mercy toward Israel, which also had proven idolatrous and periodically cruel. Yet he could not tolerate God's mercy offered to the other side, the enemy. Had he really understood the stunning depth of God's mercy, Jonah would have shared God's love even for the vile Ninevites.

A man who lived long after Jonah received a call from God to go to a people similarly idolatrous and cruel. His story resembles Jonah's in many ways, but unlike Jonah, he came to understand God's mercy and to share God's love for the enemy. Patrick was captured at age sixteen by a band of Celtic pirates and taken from his home in England to Ireland, where he was sold into slavery. A nominal Christian, Patrick experienced a great deepening in his with-God life during six years of captivity. In living with his captors he came to understand the Celtic people, learning their language and experiencing their culture. He grew to love them.

One night, in a dream, Patrick heard a voice telling him a ship was ready to take him home. The next day he escaped to the coast, boarded a ship, and made it back to England. Patrick served the Church until the age of forty-eight, when he had another dream that changed the course of his life. In it, an angel read a letter from his

PROFILE: JONAH

former Irish captors, who cried, "We appeal to you, holy servant boy, to come and walk among us." Interpreting the dream as God's call for him to return voluntarily to the Celtic peoples of Ireland, Patrick launched an Irish Christian movement, likely baptizing tens of thousands of people and planting hundreds of churches. His evangelistic approach grew even more successful in the generations following his death.

Unlike with Jonah, captivity fostered in Patrick a God-shaped mercy for all people, even his enemies. We can choose to be like Jonah, stingy with our grace and generous with our judgment, or we can recall God's lavish forgiveness and love, keeping his mercy ever before us as our guide.

Personal Reflection

- Jonah insisted on focusing not on his own sin but on the Ninevites'. Why are we so often blind to the depths of our own sin?

- Is there a person or group you are prone to criticize or someone who has hurt or threatened you? Would your reaction be more like Jonah's or Patrick's if God asked you to minister to that person or group in some way?

robe, covered himself with sackcloth, and sat in ashes. 7Then he had a proclamation made in Nineveh: "By the decree of the king and his nobles: No human being or animal, no herd or flock, shall taste anything. They shall not feed, nor shall they drink water. 8Human beings and animals shall be covered with sackcloth, and they shall cry mightily to God. All shall turn from their evil ways and from the violence that is in their hands. 9Who knows? God may relent and change his mind; he may turn from his fierce anger, so that we do not perish."

10 When God saw what they did, how they turned from their evil ways, God changed his mind about the calamity that he had said he would bring upon them; and he did not do it.

Jonah's Anger

4 But this was very displeasing to Jonah, and he became angry. 2He prayed to the

model of faithful leadership in the Hebrew pattern (Deut 17:19–20). He models spiritual responsiveness to God for his people, humbly clothing himself in sackcloth, sitting in ashes, and proclaiming an absolute fast throughout the land.

3:7–8 *No human being or animal . . . shall taste anything. . . . nor shall they drink water.* In sharp contrast to Jonah, the Ninevites respond immediately to God's message with a penitence that is extreme. Even the animals are clad in sackcloth, and everyone abstains from water as well as food. Fasting expresses devotion and repentance, but also sharpens it. Israel in its best moments never responded with such zealous devotion.

3:8 *All shall turn . . . from the violence.* Incredibly, the brutal Assyrians are convinced to forsake their customary violence. They willingly risk a complete redirection of life even though their knowledge of God is minimal.

3:10 *When God saw what they did.* God is sensitive to the evil in the world and promises to mete out justice. At the same time, God forgives even the notoriously wicked, like the Ninevites, when they repent and renounce evil. God offers his mercy across all human and national barriers, altering his plans in response to prayers and repentant hearts.

LORD and said, "O LORD! Is not this what I said while I was still in my own country? That is why I fled to Tarshish at the beginning; for I knew that you are a gracious God and merciful, slow to anger, and abounding in steadfast love, and ready to relent from punishing. ³And now, O LORD, please take my life from me, for it is better for me to die than to live." ⁴And the LORD said, "Is it right for you to be angry?" ⁵Then Jonah went out of the city and sat down east of the city, and made a booth for himself there. He sat under it in the shade, waiting to see what would become of the city.

6 The LORD God appointed a bush,ᵃ and made it come up over Jonah, to give shade over his head, to save him from his discomfort; so Jonah was very happy about the bush. ⁷But when dawn came up the next day, God appointed a worm that attacked the bush, so that it withered. ⁸When the sun rose, God prepared a sultry east wind, and the sun beat down on the head of Jonah so that he was faint and asked that he might die. He said, "It is better for me to die than to live."

Jonah Is Reproved

9 But God said to Jonah, "Is it right for you to be angry about the bush?" And he said, "Yes, angry enough to die." ¹⁰Then the LORD said, "You are concerned about the bush, for which you did not labor and which you did not grow; it came into being in a night and perished in a night. ¹¹And should I not be concerned about Nineveh, that great city, in which there are more than a hundred and twenty thousand persons who do not know their right hand from their left, and also many animals?"

a Heb *qiqayon*, possibly *the castor bean plant*

4:1 *But this was very displeasing to Jonah.* Jonah completes his mission to the Ninevites, but the sight of God sparing them causes his gnawing bitterness to resurface. Though Jonah has been obedient to God, his attitude toward the Ninevites remains unchanged. An unrepentant nationalism prevents Jonah from seeing the Ninevites as candidates for God's mercy.

4:2–3 *He prayed to the LORD.* Jonah complains directly to God, and God listens. God willingly engages Jonah's thoughts and feelings, although Jonah does not appear to appreciate the massive generosity of this gift. Jonah has a personal relationship with God and knows many truths about God, but in spite of these privileges he does not yield to God. *for I knew that you are a gracious God and merciful.* Jonah has a flawless understanding of God's character (see Exod 34:6) and a recent experience of God's mercy. Nevertheless, he condemns God based upon his own estimation of what is just and consistent. He does not want God to be who God is. He does not approve of a God who is just *and* merciful, sovereign *and yet* responsive to human supplication. Hate and bitterness consume Jonah, and he wishes he were dead.

Responding
4:2–3 PRAYER. Like Jonah, we are displeased when God's grace does not match our own sense of justice, which is aimed most often at those we do not know or do not like. Today pray for God to replace your thirst for "justice" with his steadfast love. *See also* Spiritual Disciplines Index.

4:5 *Then Jonah . . . sat down east of the city.* Jonah withdraws from the city, stubbornly hopeful that God will eventually see things his way. He looks down on Nineveh to view the destruction from a front-row seat. God uses the material at hand to shape Jonah's spiritual understanding, in this instance a plant (vv 6–8).

4:9 *But God said to Jonah.* God continues his conversation with Jonah. Jonah believes God has been unfair. Jonah believes he deserves God's favor in ways that Nineveh does not merit. If God will not change to suit Jonah, Jonah would rather die.

4:10 *Then the LORD said.* God makes it clear that Jonah is full of self-interest rather than the devotion to justice he claims. Unlike Jonah, God cares for all peoples. God's love and mercy extend beyond the borders of Israel, a reality Jonah never grasps. Jonah represents all of us who, in spite of having a direct relationship with God, fail to grasp and submit to God's true character.

MICAH

Micah (whose name means "Who is like Yahweh?") was a native of More-sheth, a village some twenty miles from Jerusalem. A contemporary of Isaiah and Hosea, he prophesied to both the Northern Kingdom (Israel) and the Southern Kingdom (Judah) during the latter half of the eighth century BC, a period of self-serving rulers, corrupt judges, false prophets, and idolatrous people. Israel failed to heed Micah's message and so was conquered by the Assyrians in 722/721 BC. In contrast, Judah under King Hezekiah experienced a revival and was spared judgment for another hundred years. Micah's prophecy exemplifies four leading themes for the spiritual formation of the erring People of God.

① Four leading themes of Micah prophecy

The Wages of Sin

The culture Micah addressed was riddled with false worship (1:7; 5:13–14), fraud (2:2), cultic prostitution (1:7), bribery (3:11; 7:3), occult practices (5:12), and other evils. "The faithful have disappeared from the land, and there is no one left who is upright" (7:2). Consequently, God's face was hidden from the people (3:4), their souls were barren (6:13–15), their prayers went unanswered (3:4, 7), and judgment lay at the door (e.g., 1:6–7; 2:3; 3:12). From this we learn that communion with God is clouded and social *shalom,* or well-being, forfeited by the sins we are so prone to commit.

The Compassionate Shepherd ②

Sheep are among the least intelligent of animals. They readily stray from the fold, injure themselves, or fall prey to wild beasts. We humans are like lost sheep, prone to wander and exposed to manifold perils (Isa 53:6). But God is the faithful shepherd (Mic 2:12; 5:4; 7:14) who gathers up his people, guides their steps, protects them from harm, and nurtures new life. Micah points to the coming Messiah, the compassionate shepherd who "shall stand and feed his flock in the strength of the LORD" (5:4). The apostle John describes this "good shepherd" (John 10:11, 14) as the one who will lay

---

See also *"The With-God Life" essay for this section of the Bible,*
"The People of God in Rebellion," pp. 975–79.

---

down his life for the sheep and, after taking it up again, will live among and care for his flock through the Comforter, whom he will send (John 14:16, KJV). Micah offers us a vision of the compassionate Shepherd, who shelters us from danger, directs our paths, and nurtures our souls.

Fundamentals of a Redeemed Life ③

Against the backdrop of endemic evil, Micah outlines the essentials of a righteous life. The Lord is a God of mercy (Mic 7:18), compassion (7:19), and faithfulness (7:20). On his side, God forgives sins (7:18–19); redeems from spiritual bondage (4:10; 6:4); bestows righteousness, or right standing with himself (7:9); and blesses with peace (5:5). On the human side, one must exercise continual faith (7:7–9), remember God's mighty deeds (6:5), devote oneself to prayer (7:7), and bless others as dew graces the grass (5:7). Perfecting holiness and godliness is the stuff of spiritual formation.

Compassionate Social Engagement ④

Micah 6:8

The best-known words of Micah's prophecy occur in 6:8: "He has told you, O mortal, what is good; and what does the LORD require of you but to do justice, and to love kindness, and to walk humbly with your God?" The Lord despises empty religious rituals. For their part, God's people must uphold the rights of the poor and downtrodden in society, embody good-heartedness and mercy in relation to others, and live in close communion with God. Christian spiritual formation ought not and, indeed, cannot be divorced from compassionate social engagement.

—*Bruce Demarest*

---

1 The word of the LORD that came to Micah of Moresheth in the days of Kings Jotham, Ahaz, and Hezekiah of Judah, which he saw concerning Samaria and Jerusalem.

Judgment Pronounced against Samaria

2 Hear, you peoples, all of you;
    listen, O earth, and all that is in it;
and let the Lord GOD be a witness
        against you,
    the Lord from his holy temple.
3 For lo, the LORD is coming out of his
        place,
    and will come down and tread upon
        the high places of the earth.
4 Then the mountains will melt under
        him
    and the valleys will burst open,
like wax near the fire,
    like waters poured down a steep place.
5 All this is for the transgression of Jacob

and for the sins of the house of Israel.
    What is the transgression of Jacob?
        Is it not Samaria?
    And what is the high place*a* of Judah?
        Is it not Jerusalem?
6 Therefore I will make Samaria a heap in
        the open country,
    a place for planting vineyards.
I will pour down her stones into the
        valley,
    and uncover her foundations.
7 All her images shall be beaten to pieces,
    all her wages shall be burned with
        fire,
    and all her idols I will lay waste;
for as the wages of a prostitute she
        gathered them,
    and as the wages of a prostitute they
        shall again be used.

a Heb *what are the high places*

The Doom of the Cities of Judah

8 For this I will lament and wail;
    I will go barefoot and naked;
    I will make lamentation like the jackals,
    and mourning like the ostriches.
9 For her wound[a] is incurable.
    It has come to Judah;
    it has reached to the gate of my people,
    to Jerusalem.

10 Tell it not in Gath,
    weep not at all;
    in Beth-leaphrah
    roll yourselves in the dust.
11 Pass on your way,
    inhabitants of Shaphir,
    in nakedness and shame;
    the inhabitants of Zaanan
    do not come forth;
    Beth-ezel is wailing
    and shall remove its support from
    you.
12 For the inhabitants of Maroth
    wait anxiously for good,
    yet disaster has come down from the
    LORD
    to the gate of Jerusalem.
13 Harness the steeds to the chariots,
    inhabitants of Lachish;
    it was the beginning of sin
    to daughter Zion,
    for in you were found
    the transgressions of Israel.
14 Therefore you shall give parting gifts
    to Moresheth-gath;
    the houses of Achzib shall be a
    deception
    to the kings of Israel.
15 I will again bring a conqueror upon
    you,
    inhabitants of Mareshah;
    the glory of Israel
    shall come to Adullam.

16 Make yourselves bald and cut off your
    hair
    for your pampered children;
    make yourselves as bald as the eagle,
    for they have gone from you into
    exile.

Social Evils Denounced

2 Alas for those who devise wickedness
    and evil deeds[b] on their beds!
  When the morning dawns, they
    perform it,
    because it is in their power.
2 They covet fields, and seize them;
    houses, and take them away;
    they oppress householder and house,
    people and their inheritance.
3 Therefore thus says the LORD:
  Now, I am devising against this family
    an evil
    from which you cannot remove your
    necks;
  and you shall not walk haughtily,
    for it will be an evil time.
4 On that day they shall take up a taunt
    song against you,
    and wail with bitter lamentation,
  and say, "We are utterly ruined;
    the LORD[c] alters the inheritance of my
    people;
  how he removes it from me!
    Among our captors[d] he parcels out
    our fields."
5 Therefore you will have no one to cast
    the line by lot
    in the assembly of the LORD.

6 "Do not preach"—thus they preach—
    "one should not preach of such
    things;

a Gk Syr Vg: Heb *wounds*   b Cn: Heb *work evil*
c Heb *he*   d Cn: Heb *the rebellious*

2:1, 3 *Alas for those who devise wickedness
. . . I am devising against this family an evil.* The
parallelism in these verses, which uphold God's
righteousness, is striking. Whereas evildoers
plot wicked schemes, God plots (the same
verb) judgment upon their heads—but not of
the metaphysical sort; instead, it is a very real

material-economic judgment. The land that is
unfairly seized (v 2) will be redistributed by God
(vv 4–5). This announcement of just retribution
reinforces the prophecy of chapter 1. God's
people must be alert and sensitive to the enticements of sin, which distances the soul from
God and incurs his holy discipline.

disgrace will not overtake us."
7 Should this be said, O house of Jacob?
  Is the LORD's patience exhausted?
  Are these his doings?
Do not my words do good
  to one who walks uprightly?
8 But you rise up against my people[a] as an
      enemy;
  you strip the robe from the peaceful,[b]
from those who pass by trustingly
  with no thought of war.
9 The women of my people you drive out
  from their pleasant houses;
from their young children you take away
  my glory forever.
10 Arise and go;
  for this is no place to rest,
because of uncleanness that destroys
  with a grievous destruction.[c]
11 If someone were to go about uttering
      empty falsehoods,
  saying, "I will preach to you of wine
      and strong drink,"
  such a one would be the preacher for
      this people!

A Promise for the Remnant of Israel

12 I will surely gather all of you, O Jacob,
  I will gather the survivors of Israel;
I will set them together
  like sheep in a fold,
like a flock in its pasture;
  it will resound with people.
13 The one who breaks out will go up
      before them;
  they will break through and pass the
      gate,
going out by it.
Their king will pass on before them,
  the LORD at their head.

Wicked Rulers and Prophets

3 And I said:
  Listen, you heads of Jacob
  and rulers of the house of Israel!

Should you not know justice?—
2   you who hate the good and love the
      evil,
  who tear the skin off my people,[d]
      and the flesh off their bones;
3 who eat the flesh of my people,
  flay their skin off them,
break their bones in pieces,
  and chop them up like meat[e] in a
      kettle,
  like flesh in a caldron.

4 Then they will cry to the LORD,
  but he will not answer them;
he will hide his face from them at that
      time,
  because they have acted wickedly.

5 Thus says the LORD concerning the
      prophets
  who lead my people astray,
who cry "Peace"
  when they have something to eat,
but declare war against those
  who put nothing into their mouths.
6 Therefore it shall be night to you,
      without vision,
  and darkness to you, without
      revelation.
The sun shall go down upon the
      prophets,
  and the day shall be black over them;
7 the seers shall be disgraced,
  and the diviners put to shame;
they shall all cover their lips,
  for there is no answer from God.
8 But as for me, I am filled with power,
  with the spirit of the LORD,
  and with justice and might,
to declare to Jacob his transgression
  and to Israel his sin.

a Cn: Heb *But yesterday my people rose*   b Cn: Heb
from before a garment   c Meaning of Heb
uncertain   d Heb *from them*   e Gk: Heb *as*

2:12–13 *I will surely gather all of you.* A
common pattern in Micah and in other biblical
prophets is the announcement of judgment
followed by blessing. The godly in the fallen
world often suffer innocently along with the
ungodly. Nevertheless, God is acutely aware of
their anguished cries. The coming Shepherd-
King assuredly will gather up, protect, and
comfort his people.

3:8 *But as for me, I am filled with power.* In

9 Hear this, you rulers of the house of
        Jacob
    and chiefs of the house of Israel,
    who abhor justice
    and pervert all equity,
10 who build Zion with blood
    and Jerusalem with wrong!
11 Its rulers give judgment for a bribe,
    its priests teach for a price,
    its prophets give oracles for money;
    yet they lean upon the LORD and say,
    "Surely the LORD is with us!
    No harm shall come upon us."
12 Therefore because of you
    Zion shall be plowed as a field;
Jerusalem shall become a heap of ruins,
    and the mountain of the house a
        wooded height.

Peace and Security through Obedience

4 In days to come
    the mountain of the LORD's house
shall be established as the highest of the
        mountains,
    and shall be raised up above the hills.
Peoples shall stream to it,
2   and many nations shall come and say:
"Come, let us go up to the mountain of
        the LORD,
    to the house of the God of Jacob;
that he may teach us his ways
    and that we may walk in his paths."
For out of Zion shall go forth instruction,

and the word of the LORD from
        Jerusalem.
3 He shall judge between many peoples,
    and shall arbitrate between strong
        nations far away;
they shall beat their swords into
        plowshares,
    and their spears into pruning hooks;
nation shall not lift up sword against
        nation,
    neither shall they learn war any more;
4 but they shall all sit under their own
        vines and under their own fig trees,
    and no one shall make them afraid;
for the mouth of the LORD of hosts
        has spoken.

5 For all the peoples walk,
    each in the name of its god,
but we will walk in the name of the
        LORD our God
forever and ever.

Restoration Promised after Exile

6 In that day, says the LORD,
    I will assemble the lame
and gather those who have been driven
        away,
    and those whom I have afflicted.
7 The lame I will make the remnant,
    and those who were cast off, a strong
        nation;

---

contrast to the spineless and people-pleasing
false prophets, Micah is an effective spokesman
for God because he is filled with the life-giving
Spirit. God's people will grow spiritually and
minister fruitfully when they walk humbly in
dependence upon him. A lifestyle of faith and
prayer releases a power from above that far
transcends our human resources.

4:1–5 *In days to come the mountain of the
LORD's house shall be established.* The dark
night of judgment announced in chapter 3 will
be followed by the bright morning of worldwide
regathering under the Messiah. The coming
kingdom of God will be characterized by freedom from ignorance (v 2), war (v 3), and fear
(v 4). In the future new order, "the freedom of
the glory of the children of God" (Rom 8:21)

will be fully manifested. The New Testament
enjoins those who possess this hope to pursue
holiness of life (2 Pet 3:11; 1 John 3:3), that is,
to work intentionally on their spiritual formation, both personally and in community.

4:7 *The lame I will make the remnant, and
those who were cast off, a strong nation.* The
"remnant" is an important theme in Micah's
prophecy (see also 2:12; 5:7–8; 7:18). The
covenant-keeping King will gather out of the
world a remnant of believing people for his
praise. The truth is that individuals within this
redeemed solidarity need each other in order to
grow spiritually and minister effectively. We are
born anew as individuals, but we grow together.
The royal road to knowing God runs through
human community.

and the LORD will reign over them in
Mount Zion
now and forevermore.

8 And you, O tower of the flock,
hill of daughter Zion,
to you it shall come,
the former dominion shall come,
the sovereignty of daughter
Jerusalem.

9 Now why do you cry aloud?
Is there no king in you?
Has your counselor perished,
that pangs have seized you like a
woman in labor?
10 Writhe and groan, *a* O daughter Zion,
like a woman in labor;
for now you shall go forth from the city
and camp in the open country;
you shall go to Babylon.
There you shall be rescued,
there the LORD will redeem you
from the hands of your enemies.

11 Now many nations
are assembled against you,
saying, "Let her be profaned,
and let our eyes gaze upon Zion."
12 But they do not know
the thoughts of the LORD;
they do not understand his plan,
that he has gathered them as sheaves
to the threshing floor.
13 Arise and thresh,
O daughter Zion,
for I will make your horn iron
and your hoofs bronze;
you shall beat in pieces many peoples,
and shall *b* devote their gain to the
LORD,
their wealth to the Lord of the whole
earth.

5 *c* Now you are walled around with a wall; *d*
siege is laid against us;
with a rod they strike the ruler of Israel
upon the cheek.

The Ruler from Bethlehem

2 *e* But you, O Bethlehem of Ephrathah,
who are one of the little clans of
Judah,
from you shall come forth for me
one who is to rule in Israel,
whose origin is from of old,
from ancient days.
3 Therefore he shall give them up until
the time
when she who is in labor has brought
forth;
then the rest of his kindred shall return
to the people of Israel.
4 And he shall stand and feed his flock in
the strength of the LORD,
in the majesty of the name of the
LORD his God.
And they shall live secure, for now he
shall be great
to the ends of the earth;
5 and he shall be the one of peace.

If the Assyrians come into our land
and tread upon our soil, *f*
we will raise against them seven
shepherds
and eight installed as rulers.
6 They shall rule the land of Assyria with
the sword,
and the land of Nimrod with the
drawn sword; *g*
they *h* shall rescue us from the Assyrians

a Meaning of Heb uncertain   *b* Gk Syr Tg:
Heb *and I will*   *c* Ch 4.14 in Heb
d Cn Compare Gk: Meaning of Heb uncertain
e Ch 5.1 in Heb   *f* Gk: Heb *in our palaces*
g Cn: Heb *in its entrances*   *h* Heb *he*

Responding
4:7 FELLOWSHIP. "Without community our hearts close up and die,"
says Jean Vanier, founder of the worldwide
L'Arche ministry. Today, prayerfully explore how
you can exchange the Western world's rugged

individualism and self-reliance for the powerful
sense of community that existed in the early
Church (Acts 2:42–47; 4:32–35). Remember
that Scripture describes the People of God as
a family, a household, a body, a flock, a holy
nation. *See also* Spiritual Disciplines Index.

if they come into our land
  or tread within our border.

The Future Role of the Remnant

7 Then the remnant of Jacob,
  surrounded by many peoples,
shall be like dew from the LORD,
  like showers on the grass,
which do not depend upon people
  or wait for any mortal.
8 And among the nations the remnant of
    Jacob,
  surrounded by many peoples,
shall be like a lion among the animals
    of the forest,
  like a young lion among the flocks of
    sheep,
which, when it goes through, treads
    down
  and tears in pieces, with no one to
    deliver.
9 Your hand shall be lifted up over your
    adversaries,
  and all your enemies shall be cut off.

10 In that day, says the LORD,
  I will cut off your horses from among
    you
  and will destroy your chariots;
11 and I will cut off the cities of your land
  and throw down all your strongholds;
12 and I will cut off sorceries from your
    hand,
  and you shall have no more
    soothsayers;
13 and I will cut off your images
  and your pillars from among you,
and you shall bow down no more
  to the work of your hands;
14 and I will uproot your sacred poles*a*
    from among you
  and destroy your towns.

15 And in anger and wrath I will execute
    vengeance
  on the nations that did not obey.

God Challenges Israel

6 Hear what the LORD says:
  Rise, plead your case before the
    mountains,
  and let the hills hear your voice.
2 Hear, you mountains, the controversy
    of the LORD,
  and you enduring foundations of the
    earth;
for the LORD has a controversy with his
    people,
  and he will contend with Israel.

3 "O my people, what have I done to you?
  In what have I wearied you? Answer
    me!
4 For I brought you up from the land of
    Egypt,
  and redeemed you from the house of
    slavery;
and I sent before you Moses,
  Aaron, and Miriam.
5 O my people, remember now what King
    Balak of Moab devised,
  what Balaam son of Beor answered
    him,
and what happened from Shittim to
    Gilgal,
  that you may know the saving acts of
    the LORD."

What God Requires

6 "With what shall I come before the
    LORD,
  and bow myself before God on high?

a Heb *Asherim*

5:2–5 *O Bethlehem . . . from you shall come forth for me one who is to rule in Israel.* Against the backdrop of faithless and corrupt rulers, Micah peers seven hundred years into the future to contemplate the Bethlehem birth of Jesus, the perfect ruler. The strong messianic King will gently shepherd, or nurture, his beleaguered people now and forever. In a fractured and anxiety-ridden world, the Shepherd-King will be his people's peace (*shalom*). As Paul unequivocally states, "He [Christ Jesus] is our peace" (Eph 2:14). Peace with God and experiential peace of heart represent, respectively, the foundational datum and comforting reality of the spiritual life.

Shall I come before him with burnt
  offerings,
  with calves a year old?
7 Will the LORD be pleased with
    thousands of rams,
  with ten thousands of rivers of oil?
Shall I give my firstborn for my
    transgression,
  the fruit of my body for the sin of my
    soul?"
8 He has told you, O mortal, what is good;
  and what does the LORD require of
    you
but to do justice, and to love kindness,
  and to walk humbly with your God?

Cheating and Violence to Be Punished

9 The voice of the LORD cries to the city
    (it is sound wisdom to fear your name):
  Hear, O tribe and assembly of the city! *a*
10   Can I forget *b* the treasures of
        wickedness in the house of the
        wicked,
    and the scant measure that is
        accursed?
11 Can I tolerate wicked scales
    and a bag of dishonest weights?
12 Your *c* wealthy are full of violence;
    your *d* inhabitants speak lies,
    with tongues of deceit in their
        mouths.
13 Therefore I have begun *e* to strike you
        down,
    making you desolate because of your
        sins.
14 You shall eat, but not be satisfied,
    and there shall be a gnawing hunger
        within you;
  you shall put away, but not save,
    and what you save, I will hand over to
        the sword.
15 You shall sow, but not reap;
    you shall tread olives, but not anoint
        yourselves with oil;
    you shall tread grapes, but not drink
        wine.

16 For you have kept the statutes of Omri *f*
    and all the works of the house of
        Ahab,
    and you have followed their counsels.
Therefore I will make you a desolation,
    and your *g* inhabitants an object
        of hissing;
  so you shall bear the scorn of my
    people.

The Total Corruption of the People

7 Woe is me! For I have become like one
    who,
    after the summer fruit has been
        gathered,
    after the vintage has been gleaned,
  finds no cluster to eat;
    there is no first-ripe fig for which I
        hunger.
2 The faithful have disappeared from the
        land,
    and there is no one left who is
        upright;
  they all lie in wait for blood,
    and they hunt each other with nets.
3 Their hands are skilled to do evil;
    the official and the judge ask for a
        bribe,
    and the powerful dictate what they
        desire;
    thus they pervert justice. *h*
4 The best of them is like a brier,
    the most upright of them a thorn
        hedge.
  The day of their *i* sentinels, of their *i*
        punishment, has come;
    now their confusion is at hand.
5 Put no trust in a friend,
    have no confidence in a loved one;
  guard the doors of your mouth
    from her who lies in your embrace;

a Cn Compare Gk: Heb *tribe, and who has appointed
it yet?*   *b* Cn: Meaning of Heb uncertain
c Heb *Whose*   *d* Heb *whose*   *e* Gk Syr Vg: Heb
have made sick   *f* Gk Syr Vg Tg: Heb *the statutes of
Omri are kept*   *g* Heb *its*   *h* Cn: Heb *they weave
it*   *i* Heb *your*

Responding
6:6–8 SACRIFICE. It sounds so simple,
and so lovely, to do these things God
asks of us. How well are you fulfilling God's
requirements? *See also* Spiritual Disciplines
Index.

6 for the son treats the father with
        contempt,
    the daughter rises up against her
        mother,
    the daughter-in-law against her mother-
        in-law;
    your enemies are members of your
        own household.
7 But as for me, I will look to the Lord,
    I will wait for the God of my
        salvation;
    my God will hear me.

Penitence and Trust in God
8 Do not rejoice over me, O my enemy;
    when I fall, I shall rise;
    when I sit in darkness,
        the Lord will be a light to me.
9 I must bear the indignation of the Lord,
        because I have sinned against him,
    until he takes my side
        and executes judgment for me.
    He will bring me out to the light;
        I shall see his vindication.
10 Then my enemy will see,
        and shame will cover her who said to
            me,
    "Where is the Lord your God?"
    My eyes will see her downfall;a
        now she will be trodden down
            like the mire of the streets.

A Prophecy of Restoration
11 A day for the building of your walls!
        In that day the boundary shall be far
            extended.
12 In that day they will come to you
        from Assyria tob Egypt,

    and from Egypt to the River,
        from sea to sea and from mountain to
            mountain.
13 But the earth will be desolate
        because of its inhabitants,
    for the fruit of their doings.

14 Shepherd your people with your staff,
        the flock that belongs to you,
    which lives alone in a forest
        in the midst of a garden land;
    let them feed in Bashan and Gilead
        as in the days of old.
15 As in the days when you came out of
        the land of Egypt,
    show usc marvelous things.
16 The nations shall see and be ashamed
        of all their might;
    they shall lay their hands on their
            mouths;
        their ears shall be deaf;
17 they shall lick dust like a snake,
        like the crawling things of the earth;
    they shall come trembling out of their
            fortresses;
    they shall turn in dread to the Lord
            our God,
        and they shall stand in fear of you.

God's Compassion and Steadfast Love
18 Who is a God like you, pardoning
            iniquity
    and passing over the transgression
        of the remnant of yourd possession?
    He does not retain his anger forever,

a Heb lacks downfall   b One Ms: MT Assyria and
cities of   c Cn: Heb I will show him   d Heb his

7:7–9 *I will look to the Lord.* In a culture of gloom, Micah and the remnant wait expectantly upon their God, confident that he will answer their prayers and revive their souls. As we deepen our relationship with Christ, we become assured of his ability to sustain and succor our soul when the going gets tough. When groping about in personal or communal darkness, we look trustingly to the One who can bring us into the brightness of a glorious spiritual illumination (cf. Ps 27:1).

7:18–20 *Who is a God like you, . . . passing*

over the transgression? Micah closes his prophecy with an impassioned doxology of praise to the God of mercy, forgiving grace, and covenantal faithfulness. For the People of God, the story always ends with blessing. When we meditate on the mysterious ways in which the Father is conforming us to the image of his beloved Son, we too will raise our voices in heartfelt gratitude and praise. "For his anger is but for a moment; his favor is for a lifetime. Weeping may linger for the night, but joy comes with the morning" (Ps 30:5).

because he delights in showing
    clemency.
19 He will again have compassion upon us;
    he will tread our iniquities under foot.
You will cast all our *a* sins
    into the depths of the sea.

20 You will show faithfulness to Jacob
    and unswerving loyalty to Abraham,
as you have sworn to our ancestors
    from the days of old.

a Gk Syr Vg Tg: Heb *their*

NAHUM

The book of Nahum contains a stern and somber prophecy foretelling the fall of Nineveh, the great and seemingly indestructible capital of Assyria.

Judah had lived through more than a century of terror, torture, and oppression at the hands of the dominating Assyrians, who were renowned for their evil and oppressive ways. Assyria represented everything that Judah dreaded: paganism, oppression, violence, injustice, wealth, and brutality. Winds of hatred and cruelty blow through the pages of this book.

Nahum, whose name means "comfort" or "consolation," foretells that Nineveh's end will come. God has heard the cry of his people, he has witnessed the evil Assyrian regime, and he is going to act powerfully in judging and obliterating Nineveh and all it stands for.

The prophecy was written sometime after the destruction of the Egyptian city of Thebes (3:8–10), which occurred around the year 663 BC, and before the fall of Nineveh in 612 BC. Nahum was prophesying at the same time as Jeremiah, Habakkuk, and Zephaniah.

Religious Reform in Judah

Under the reign of the young king Josiah, who followed God's ways, Judah had begun to reform and free itself from Assyrian religious practices. In 621 the "book of the law" was found while the Temple in Jerusalem was being repaired (see 2 Chron 34:8–21). Its discovery accelerated the religious and cultural reforms, and Josiah was able to oversee the abolition of pagan worship, the removal of false priests, and the purging of the pagan altar at Bethel. He reinstituted the Passover and spurred a return to the true worship of God.

Despite these reforms and accompanying renewal of faith, an additional period of waiting required the people of Judah to hold on to faith in the midst of suffering and injustice. This is the context in which Nahum prophesied. The prophecy is full

See also *"The With-God Life" essay for this section of the Bible,*
"The People of God in Rebellion," pp. 975–79.

of vivid, dramatic poetry, possibly the finest in the Old Testament. The prologue in chapter 1 begins with a recalling of the nature and character of God before revealing his anger against Nineveh. Chapters 2 and 3 relate the main prophecy, describing the downfall coming to Nineveh together with its causes and consequences.

One Universal God

Nahum's message declares that the God of Israel is not merely a national deity but the true sovereign God, whose power extends over all the nations. We know from Nah 1:12 and from the prophecies of Isaiah and Micah that God had used the experience of domination by Assyria to judge his people for their sins, because they had been unfaithful to the covenant. But now Assyria would be judged, as all nations who pursue evil and cruelty will be judged, eventually reaping what was sown and harvesting the seeds of their own destruction.

The book of Nahum is not an easy or comfortable book, for it addresses a world gripped by evil and suffering oppression at the hands of a wicked and ungodly nation. It does, however, reveal the triumph of faith in a time of faltering devotion.

—Roy Searle

---

1 An oracle concerning Nineveh. The book of the vision of Nahum of Elkosh.

The Consuming Wrath of God

2 A jealous and avenging God is the LORD,
   the LORD is avenging and wrathful;
the LORD takes vengeance on his
      adversaries
   and rages against his enemies.
3 The LORD is slow to anger but great in
      power,
   and the LORD will by no means clear
   the guilty.

His way is in whirlwind and storm,
   and the clouds are the dust of his feet.
4 He rebukes the sea and makes it dry,
   and he dries up all the rivers;
Bashan and Carmel wither,
   and the bloom of Lebanon fades.
5 The mountains quake before him,
   and the hills melt;
the earth heaves before him,
   the world and all who live in it.

6 Who can stand before his indignation?
   Who can endure the heat of his anger?
His wrath is poured out like fire,

1:2–8 *God is the LORD.* In Nahum, we have to reckon with a God who is both loving and compassionate yet also, in the light of evil in the world, a God of justice, judgment, and righteous anger. Nahum portrays God as one who hates human violence, abuse, oppression, and exploitation. Reflecting on this aspect of God's nature, believers are compelled to reflect on those attributes and actions in the human heart that need to be renounced and dealt with. A genuine commitment to right beliefs will, by its very nature, lead to righteous behavior.

1:2 *A jealous and avenging God.* God is a jealous God who tolerates no rivals. Idolatry is disobedience to God and invokes his anger. He punishes those who contravene, disobey, and proliferate evil. His goodness (v 7) demands a just response, to right what is wrong.

1:3 *The LORD is slow to anger but great in power.* God is not quick-tempered, but patient and slow to anger. Anger is not the first or most important attribute of God. In fact, God's anger is far down the list and comes out only slowly and reluctantly. God's heart is filled with compassion (much higher on the list), which is the grounds upon which sinners can appeal to his mercy.

and by him the rocks are broken in
    pieces.
7 The LORD is good,
    a stronghold in a day of trouble;
he protects those who take refuge in him,
8   even in a rushing flood.
He will make a full end of his
    adversaries, [a]
and will pursue his enemies into
    darkness.
9 Why do you plot against the LORD?
He will make an end;
    no adversary will rise up twice.
10 Like thorns they are entangled,
    like drunkards they are drunk;
they are consumed like dry straw.
11 From you one has gone out
    who plots evil against the LORD,
    one who counsels wickedness.

Good News for Judah

12 Thus says the LORD,
    "Though they are at full strength and
        many, [b]

they will be cut off and pass away.
    Though I have afflicted you,
    I will afflict you no more.
13 And now I will break off his yoke from
        you
    and snap the bonds that bind you."

14 The LORD has commanded concerning
        you:
    "Your name shall be perpetuated no
        longer;
from the house of your gods I will cut off
    the carved image and the cast image.
I will make your grave, for you are
    worthless."

15 [c] Look! On the mountains the feet of one
    who brings good tidings,
    who proclaims peace!
Celebrate your festivals, O Judah,
    fulfill your vows,

a Gk: Heb *of her place*   b Meaning of Heb
uncertain   c Ch 2.1 in Heb

1:7 *a stronghold in a day of trouble.* God is
with his people in the hard times. Often it is
on the anvil of the hard places that we learn
more about God and ourselves. Automatic,
unguarded reactions under pressure often
reveal what is in the heart. It is in such moments
and through such seasons of pressure and trial
that we need to throw ourselves on God's mercy
and realize his compassion and goodness in
seeking to liberate us from those things that
taint our hearts and destroy us. His desire to
liberate us brings hope to the human soul and
explains why he serves as our "stronghold."

1:12-13 *I will break off his yoke from you.* God
is a liberator of his people. His nature leads him
to save and redeem. A message that should
have been indelibly written in the hearts of his
people from the time of the exodus is that the
Lord will set his people free. To everyone who
knows oppression, bondage, cruelty, and
slavery, the message of God's power to liberate
is good news.

1:14 *The LORD has commanded concerning
you.* What is good news for the righteous is
terrible news for those who are under God's
judgment. The righteous anger of God is
revealed against the evil of those who falsely

believe that they can act with impunity and
treat other people so cruelly. Any nation that
dares to do what Assyria did will eventually
write its own obituary. In the divine purposes
evil will be punished.

1:15 *Celebrate your festivals, O Judah.* Feasts
and festivals of faith are important components
in the life of believers. God's people gather
together to hear stories of faith, remember the
acts of God, offer thanksgiving, and renew vows
(Isa 40:9). Observing the Christian calendar,
with its various feasts and saints' days, festivals
and seasons, is a building block of faith.

Responding
1:15 CELEBRATION. One of the most
important festivals of the Jewish calendar year is Passover, the celebration of the
deliverance of the People of God from slavery
in ancient Egypt. At the seder, or special meal,
celebrants eat particular kinds of food, each
with its own significance, and read aloud passages from Exodus. Consider researching and
preparing a Passover seder this April for your
family and friends to commemorate God's
deliverance of his people. *See also* Spiritual
Disciplines Index.

for never again shall the wicked invade
  you;
  they are utterly cut off.

The Destruction of the Wicked City

2 A shatterer[a] has come up against you.
    Guard the ramparts;
    watch the road;
  gird your loins;
    collect all your strength.

2 (For the LORD is restoring the majesty of
      Jacob,
    as well as the majesty of Israel,
  though ravagers have ravaged them
    and ruined their branches.)

3 The shields of his warriors are red;
    his soldiers are clothed in crimson.
  The metal on the chariots flashes
    on the day when he musters them;
    the chargers[b] prance.
4 The chariots race madly through the
      streets,
    they rush to and fro through the
      squares;
  their appearance is like torches,
    they dart like lightning.
5 He calls his officers;
    they stumble as they come forward;
  they hasten to the wall,
    and the mantelet[c] is set up.
6 The river gates are opened,
    the palace trembles.
7 It is decreed[c] that the city[d] be exiled,
    its slave women led away,
  moaning like doves
    and beating their breasts.

8 Nineveh is like a pool
    whose waters[e] run away.
  "Halt! Halt!"—
    but no one turns back.
9 "Plunder the silver,
    plunder the gold!
  There is no end of treasure!
    An abundance of every precious
      thing!"

10 Devastation, desolation, and
      destruction!
  Hearts faint and knees tremble,
    all loins quake,
    all faces grow pale!
11 What became of the lions' den,
    the cave[f] of the young lions,
  where the lion goes,
    and the lion's cubs, with no one to
      disturb them?
12 The lion has torn enough for his whelps
    and strangled prey for his lionesses;
  he has filled his caves with prey
    and his dens with torn flesh.

13 See, I am against you, says the LORD of
hosts, and I will burn your[g] chariots in smoke,
and the sword shall devour your young lions; I will cut off your prey from the earth,
and the voice of your messengers shall be
heard no more.

a Cn: Heb scatterer   b Cn Compare Gk Syr: Heb
cypresses   c Meaning of Heb uncertain
d Heb it   e Cn Compare Gk: Heb a pool, from the
days that she has become, and they   f Cn: Heb
pasture   g Heb her

2:1–13 *A shatterer has come up against you.*
The destruction of Nineveh represents the
conquering of evil. Sin and evil manifested in
countless different ways will inevitably evoke
God's opposition. The frailty of human pride and
arrogance is seen in the folly of the Assyrians. To
deepen our faith and grow spiritually, we must
seek after the "city of God," not the "Ninevehs"
of this world. In the Western world, influenced by
modernity's scientific rationalism, it is relatively
easy to be beguiled by the false notion that we
are masters of our own destiny. The idea that we
have the power to determine life and outcomes
is rife, despite the threats posed to such a belief
by recent historical events, for example, September 11, 2001. What is regarded as impregnable is
as nothing to God. Human pride allied to a belief
in one's self-sufficiency is arrogant and an affront
to God, since it presupposes there is no need of
God. It leads to ruin in both individual lives and
the life of the nation. Great cultures have come
and gone, many dashed on the rocks of self-
belief—the city of God, in contrast, remains,
founded on righteousness.

Ruin Imminent and Inevitable

3 Ah! City of bloodshed,
  utterly deceitful, full of booty—
  no end to the plunder!
2 The crack of whip and rumble of wheel,
  galloping horse and bounding chariot!
3 Horsemen charging,
  flashing sword and glittering spear,
  piles of dead,
  heaps of corpses,
  dead bodies without end—
  they stumble over the bodies!
4 Because of the countless debaucheries
      of the prostitute,
  gracefully alluring, mistress of sorcery,
  who enslaves*a* nations through her
      debaucheries,
  and peoples through her sorcery,
5 I am against you,
  says the LORD of hosts,
  and will lift up your skirts over your
      face;
  and I will let nations look on your
      nakedness
  and kingdoms on your shame.
6 I will throw filth at you
  and treat you with contempt,
  and make you a spectacle.
7 Then all who see you will shrink from
      you and say,

"Nineveh is devastated; who will
      bemoan her?"
  Where shall I seek comforters for you?

8 Are you better than Thebes*b*
  that sat by the Nile,
  with water around her,
  her rampart a sea,
  water her wall?
9 Ethiopia*c* was her strength,
  Egypt too, and that without limit;
  Put and the Libyans were her*d*
      helpers.

10 Yet she became an exile,
  she went into captivity;
  even her infants were dashed in pieces
      at the head of every street;
  lots were cast for her nobles,
  all her dignitaries were bound in
      fetters.
11 You also will be drunken,
  you will go into hiding;*e*
  you will seek
  a refuge from the enemy.
12 All your fortresses are like fig trees
  with first-ripe figs—

a Heb *sells*   b Heb *No-amon*   c Or *Nubia*; Heb
Cush   d Gk: Heb *your*   e Meaning of Heb
uncertain

3:1–7 *Ah! City of bloodshed!* Many people have been enticed by the false promises and temptations of a rich, powerful culture that promises much but delivers little. The Scriptures frequently describe cities such as Rome, Babylon, and Nineveh as "harlots," because they draw people away from the simplicity of life and faith through the alluring attraction of money, sex, power, influence, and success. Such allurements will be exposed by God (v 5). The problem of the human heart remains a key issue in spiritual formation (see Prov 4:23). The heart, with its capacity to both give and receive, is assailed constantly by the attractions and trappings associated with money, sex, and power. These elements, made stronger today by a "consumer rights" society, tempt and ruin the lives of many. We are called to both guard our hearts and give our hearts—to guard them from the constant temptations of money, sex, and power and to give them completely to God and his purposes. Such giving affords true meaning, perspective, beauty, and order to life. Embracing the simplicity of faith frees us from the slavery of temptation and allows us to keep our hearts focused on God amid the pressures, pains, and pleasures of the world.

3:11–19 *All your fortresses are like fig trees.* When our enemies are defeated and our redemption is realized, there is cause for much rejoicing. Spiritual formation calls for an appreciation and celebration of the goodness and grace of God. The power of praise works wonders in the development of believers' faith—not the pie-in-the-sky, empty triumphalism that denies reality, but the sure conviction that sees the goodness of God in the midst of adversity. Life is often wounding, hurts are carried, and memories are inevitably both good and bad, but God remains good and he will conquer our enemies. Remember to celebrate such good news.

if shaken they fall
    into the mouth of the eater.
13 Look at your troops:
    they are women in your midst.
The gates of your land
    are wide open to your foes;
    fire has devoured the bars of your
        gates.

14 Draw water for the siege,
    strengthen your forts;
trample the clay,
    tread the mortar,
    take hold of the brick mold!
15 There the fire will devour you,
    the sword will cut you off.
    It will devour you like the locust.

Multiply yourselves like the locust,
    multiply like the grasshopper!
16 You increased your merchants
    more than the stars of the heavens.

The locust sheds its skin and flies
    away.
17 Your guards are like grasshoppers,
    your scribes like swarms *a* of locusts
settling on the fences
    on a cold day—
when the sun rises, they fly away;
    no one knows where they have gone.

18 Your shepherds are asleep,
    O king of Assyria;
    your nobles slumber.
Your people are scattered on the
        mountains
    with no one to gather them.
19 There is no assuaging your hurt,
    your wound is mortal.
All who hear the news about you
    clap their hands over you.
For who has ever escaped
    your endless cruelty?

a Meaning of Heb uncertain

HABAKKUK

"**I**t just isn't right!" We find ourselves exclaiming these words repeatedly over the course of our lives. The observation is especially poignant when family, friends, or leaders whom we expect to act honorably and for our welfare betray our trust. Our sense of betrayal deepens when we witness transgressors enjoying the fruits of their wrongdoing. We struggle to understand why God does not hold them accountable sooner.

The prophet Habakkuk brings such observations and complaints to God. Habakkuk identifies himself as a prophet, but no further information is known about him. Central to his prophecy is the developing power of the Chaldeans, founders of the Neo-Babylonian Empire. Utterly defeating the Egyptian army in 605 BC, the Chaldeans eventually drove the Egyptians out of Asia. Habakkuk was probably a contemporary of Jeremiah, Zephaniah, and Nahum, prophesying to Judah in the decades prior to the destruction of Jerusalem and the exile of its citizens in 587 BC. A puppet of the Egyptian pharaohs, King Jehoiakim of Judah reigned until the Chaldean army occupied Jerusalem in 597 BC. Through vice and repressive policies, he deepened the spiritual crisis in Judah (Jer 22:13-19). Habakkuk observes that the leaders of God's people are corrupt. They are indifferent to the laws of God, justice, and the well-being of the people; their sins materially and spiritually harm those they are charged with helping. Idolatry and immorality have become agreeable in Judah. Evil is rampant among God's people. Habakkuk questions why God appears to be idle in the face of this iniquity and unmoved by the sufferings of the righteous.

Trusting God When He Doesn't Seem to Make Sense

God assures Habakkuk that he fervently opposes evil and intends to chastise the guilty. He is preparing the Chaldeans to execute justice in Judah on his behalf. Habakkuk observes that this plan will reinforce control by the wicked and increase the

---

See also *"The With-God Life" essay for this section of the Bible,*
"The People of God in Rebellion," pp. 975–79.

---

anguish of the blameless. The knowledge deepens Habakkuk's confusion and theological dilemma.

Deeply committed to comprehending God, Habakkuk actively waits for God. God responds to Habakkuk, but does not fully engage all his questions. Instead, God affirms that when circumstances are bleak and God's ways seem bewildering, the righteous live by faith. God's faithful people learn to frame events in terms of the redeeming character and power of God. They understand that God is always working toward the right and good, even in and through devastating events. In spite of what they may see and experience in the time prior to God's appearing, the upright choose to be oriented toward God in faithfulness, especially when God does not appear to make sense.

The authenticity and promises of God ultimately satisfy Habakkuk. He responds with praise and trust in God.

Spiritual Formation through Bewilderment and Affliction

Habakkuk's experience demonstrates that bewilderment and affliction are not signs of spiritual immaturity or unfortunate distractions from faith. Instead, these episodes contribute to the development of strong faith and are the raw materials of prayer and worship. With God's people, the prophet suffers in the period before the end and through the coming judgment. How the faithful shall live in such an "in-between" time is Habakkuk's concern. Troubled by the possibility that God assents to oppression, Habakkuk wrestles with God in the face of overwhelming disaster. By challenging and questioning God, Habakkuk learns submission to the intentions and purposes of God, becoming a joyful example of one who lives by faith alone.

Many of us assume that doubts about God's fairness or sovereignty mean that we have left, at least momentarily, the life of faith, that we are questioning our belief system. But Habakkuk demonstrates that asking probing questions that challenge God is very much a part of the life of faith. Habakkuk is a model for boldly going to God with our questions and confusion about what does not make sense to us. God wants to be in conversation with us, as he is with Habakkuk.

Also, Habakkuk's faithfulness is not law keeping, but trust in God's word in the face of overwhelming disaster. Habakkuk is an example of the kind of faith that justifies, a faith that the apostle Paul advances several hundred years later (Rom 1:17; Gal 3:11).

—*Barbara M. Musselman*

1

The oracle that the prophet Habakkuk saw.

The Prophet's Complaint

2 O LORD, how long shall I cry for help,
  and you will not listen?
  Or cry to you "Violence!"
  and you will not save?
3 Why do you make me see wrongdoing
  and look at trouble?
  Destruction and violence are before me;
  strife and contention arise.
4 So the law becomes slack
  and justice never prevails.
  The wicked surround the righteous—
  therefore judgment comes forth
  perverted.

5 Look at the nations, and see!
  Be astonished! Be astounded!
  For a work is being done in your days
  that you would not believe if you were
  told.
6 For I am rousing the Chaldeans,
  that fierce and impetuous nation,
  who march through the breadth of the
  earth
  to seize dwellings not their own.
7 Dread and fearsome are they;
  their justice and dignity proceed from
  themselves.
8 Their horses are swifter than leopards,
  more menacing than wolves at dusk;
  their horses charge.
  Their horsemen come from far away;
  they fly like an eagle swift to devour.
9 They all come for violence,
  with faces pressing*a* forward;
  they gather captives like sand.
10 At kings they scoff,
  and of rulers they make sport.
  They laugh at every fortress,
  and heap up earth to take it.
11 Then they sweep by like the wind;
  they transgress and become guilty;
  their own might is their god!

12 Are you not from of old,
  O LORD my God, my Holy One?
  You*b* shall not die.
  O LORD, you have marked them for
  judgment;
  and you, O Rock, have established
  them for punishment.
13 Your eyes are too pure to behold evil,
  and you cannot look on wrongdoing;
  why do you look on the treacherous,
  and are silent when the wicked
  swallow
  those more righteous than they?
14 You have made people like the fish of
  the sea,
  like crawling things that have no
  ruler.

15 The enemy*c* brings all of them up with
  a hook;
  he drags them out with his net,
  he gathers them in his seine;
  so he rejoices and exults.
16 Therefore he sacrifices to his net
  and makes offerings to his seine;

a Meaning of Heb uncertain   *b* Ancient Heb tradition: MT *We*   *c* Heb *He*

1:2–4 *O LORD, how long?* In dialogue with God, Habakkuk wonders why God does not promptly intervene to terminate injustice and oppression. God does not seem interested in helping his people, upholding the law, or even defending his own good name. Instead, God allows destruction, violence, and injustice to flourish among his people. Even though God's people have disciplined themselves to offer intercessory prayer, God does not appear to hear. Habakkuk is disappointed by the Lord's seeming indifference and by the dearth of expected rewards for the faithful. Clearly, God refuses to be manipulated or controlled.

1:5–11 *Look at the nations!* God answers Habakkuk's complaint with astonishing news. He has been hard at work behind the scenes preparing the Chaldeans to chastise Judah. Violence, captives, and rubble will be the outcome.

1:12–17 *Are you not from of old?* Habakkuk is baffled. How can a holy God award victory to a ruthless people even less righteous than Judah? How can God's solution allow the suffering of the righteous to increase? Habakkuk is not shy in sharing his pointed questions with God.

for by them his portion is lavish,
 and his food is rich.
17 Is he then to keep on emptying his net,
 and destroying nations without
  mercy?

God's Reply to the Prophet's Complaint

2 I will stand at my watchpost,
 and station myself on the rampart;
I will keep watch to see what he will say
 to me,
 and what he *a* will answer concerning
  my complaint.
2 Then the LORD answered me and said:
Write the vision;
 make it plain on tablets,
 so that a runner may read it.
3 For there is still a vision for the
  appointed time;
 it speaks of the end, and does not lie.
If it seems to tarry, wait for it;
 it will surely come, it will not delay.
4 Look at the proud!
 Their spirit is not right in them,
 but the righteous live by their faith. *b*
5 Moreover, wealth *c* is treacherous;
 the arrogant do not endure.
They open their throats wide as Sheol;
 like Death they never have enough.
They gather all nations for themselves,
 and collect all peoples as their own.

The Woes of the Wicked

6 Shall not everyone taunt such people
and, with mocking riddles, say about them,

"Alas for you who heap up what is not
 your own!"
How long will you load yourselves
 with goods taken in pledge?
7 Will not your own creditors suddenly
 rise,
 and those who make you tremble
  wake up?
Then you will be booty for them.
8 Because you have plundered many
 nations,
 all that survive of the peoples shall
  plunder you—
because of human bloodshed, and
  violence to the earth,
 to cities and all who live in them.

9 "Alas for you who get evil gain for your
 house,
 setting your nest on high
 to be safe from the reach of harm!"
10 You have devised shame for your house
 by cutting off many peoples;
 you have forfeited your life.
11 The very stones will cry out from the
 wall,
 and the plaster *d* will respond from
  the woodwork.

12 "Alas for you who build a town by
 bloodshed,
 and found a city on iniquity!"
13 Is it not from the LORD of hosts

a Syr: Heb *I* *b* Or *faithfulness* *c* Other Heb
Mss read *wine* *d* Or *beam*

2:1 *I will stand at my watchpost.* Habakkuk longs to come to terms with God's ways. He understands that the reply will not come instantly. He is prepared to actively watch and wait for God to respond to his troubled misgivings. He waits in a place and posture that position him to receive God's answer.

2:2–3 *Then the LORD answered.* God's message is true and permanent. He instructs Habakkuk to write down the message so others who wish to understand can read it.

2:3 *If it seems to tarry.* Confidence that God's plans are right, beneficial, and reliable, even when they seem not to make sense, is more sustaining than a detailed knowledge of God's plans. Waiting for God is never futile. The vision will not fail to arrive in its due time.

2:4 *Look at the proud!* The arrogant are internally frail and cannot last, but God fulfills and strengthens those who belong to him with life-giving faith.

2:6–13 *Alas for you who heap up what is not your own!* God holds Judah's conquerors accountable. He is firmly opposed to evil and conveys consequences for their wickedness in five visions of woe ("Alas," vv 6, 9, 12, 15, 19). Though the times are violent and evil seems to triumph, eventually the wicked will be judged and brought to an end.

that peoples labor only to feed the
　　flames,
and nations weary themselves for
　　nothing?
14 But the earth will be filled
　　with the knowledge of the glory of
　　　the LORD,
　　as the waters cover the sea.

15 "Alas for you who make your neighbors
　　drink,
　　pouring out your wrath[a] until they
　　　are drunk,
　　in order to gaze on their nakedness!"
16 You will be sated with contempt instead
　　of glory.
　　Drink, you yourself, and stagger![b]
The cup in the LORD's right hand
　　will come around to you,
　　and shame will come upon your glory!
17 For the violence done to Lebanon will
　　overwhelm you;
　　the destruction of the animals will
　　　terrify you—[c]
because of human bloodshed and
　　violence to the earth,
　　to cities and all who live in them.

18 What use is an idol
　　once its maker has shaped it—
　　a cast image, a teacher of lies?
For its maker trusts in what has been
　　made,
　　though the product is only an idol
　　　that cannot speak!
19 Alas for you who say to the wood,
　　"Wake up!"

to silent stone, "Rouse yourself!"
　　Can it teach?
See, it is gold and silver plated,
　　and there is no breath in it at all.

20 But the LORD is in his holy temple;
　　let all the earth keep silence before
　　　him!

3 A prayer of the prophet Habakkuk ac-
　　cording to Shigionoth.

The Prophet's Prayer

2 O LORD, I have heard of your renown,
　　and I stand in awe, O LORD, of your
　　　work.
In our own time revive it;
　　in our own time make it known;
　　in wrath may you remember mercy.
3 God came from Teman,
　　the Holy One from Mount Paran.

　　　　　　　　　　　　　　　　　Selah

His glory covered the heavens,
　　and the earth was full of his praise.
4 The brightness was like the sun;
　　rays came forth from his hand,
　　where his power lay hidden.
5 Before him went pestilence,
　　and plague followed close behind.
6 He stopped and shook the earth;
　　he looked and made the nations
　　　tremble.
The eternal mountains were shattered;
　　along his ancient pathways
　　the everlasting hills sank low.

a Or poison　　b Q Ms Gk: MT be uncircumcised
c Gk Syr: Meaning of Heb uncertain

2:14 *the earth will be filled with the knowledge
. . . of the LORD.* This describes the great eschatological vision of the entire earth filled with the
knowledge of God. With the coming of Jesus,
the Word of God incarnate, we see the beginnings of this prophecy coming to pass. The full
consummation, however, awaits Christ's return
and millennial reign.

2:20 *let all the earth keep silence.* Silence
before God is the appropriate response to God's
holiness. It is a Spiritual Discipline of the first
order.

Responding
2:20 SILENCE. Challenge yourself to
spend two to four hours in silence with
God. Take a journal and write down the insights
that come to you. *See also* Spiritual Disciplines
Index.

3:2–19 *O LORD, I have heard.* A liturgical psalm
in which Habakkuk prays with praise and trust
in God.

3:3–15 *God came from Teman.* God aids his
people, routing their adversaries like a battling
warrior.

7 I saw the tents of Cushan under
       affliction;
    the tent-curtains of the land of
       Midian trembled.
8 Was your wrath against the rivers,*a*
       O LORD?
    Or your anger against the rivers,*a*
    or your rage against the sea,*b*
    when you drove your horses,
    your chariots to victory?
9 You brandished your naked bow,
    sated*c* were the arrows at your
       command.*d*   Selah
    You split the earth with rivers.
10 The mountains saw you, and writhed;
    a torrent of water swept by;
    the deep gave forth its voice.
    The sun*e* raised high its hands;
11 the moon*f* stood still in its exalted
       place,
    at the light of your arrows speeding
       by,
    at the gleam of your flashing spear.
12 In fury you trod the earth,
    in anger you trampled nations.
13 You came forth to save your people,
    to save your anointed.
    You crushed the head of the wicked
       house,
    laying it bare from foundation to
       roof.*d*   Selah
14 You pierced with their*g* own arrows the
       head*h* of his warriors,*i*
    who came like a whirlwind to scatter
       us,*j*
    gloating as if ready to devour the poor
    who were in hiding.

15 You trampled the sea with your horses,
    churning the mighty waters.

16 I hear, and I tremble within;
    my lips quiver at the sound.
    Rottenness enters into my bones,
    and my steps tremble*k* beneath me.
    I wait quietly for the day of calamity
    to come upon the people who attack
       us.

Trust and Joy in the Midst of Trouble

17 Though the fig tree does not blossom,
    and no fruit is on the vines;
    though the produce of the olive fails,
    and the fields yield no food;
    though the flock is cut off from the
       fold,
    and there is no herd in the stalls,
18 yet I will rejoice in the LORD;
    I will exult in the God of my
       salvation.
19 GOD, the Lord, is my strength;
    he makes my feet like the feet of a
       deer,
    and makes me tread upon the
       heights.*l*

    To the leader: with stringed*m*
       instruments.

a Or *against River*   *b* Or *against Sea*
c Cn: Heb *oaths*   *d* Meaning of Heb uncertain
e Heb *It*   *f* Heb *sun, moon*   *g* Heb *his*
h Or *leader*   *i* Vg Compare Gk Syr: Meaning of
Heb uncertain   *j* Heb *me*   *k* Cn Compare Gk:
Meaning of Heb uncertain   *l* Heb *my heights*
m Heb *my stringed*

3:16 *I hear, and I tremble.* Habakkuk yields to God's rigorous, yet merciful, method of revival with gratitude. Habakkuk is convinced that God is at work even in events that do not seem desirable when isolated from the larger stream of God's purpose in history.

3:17–19 *yet I will rejoice in the LORD.* Habakkuk's devotion to honest engagement with God has ripened into a trusting intimacy with God. Although Habakkuk comprehends the coming calamity, his joy and peace in God overflow. Habakkuk's newfound thanksgiving and praise are motivated solely by the character and faithfulness of God. Devastating circumstances cannot inhibit Habakkuk's faith. God has enabled Habakkuk to wholeheartedly rejoice in God.

WAKE UP CALL

ZEPHANIAH

To an old, sick, and suffering nation a young Zephaniah came bearing a prophecy of judgment and hope. Under the long and violent reign of Manasseh (696–642 BC), who had defied God in his ambition to become rich and powerful, Judah had fallen away from God. The nation's spiritual life was corrupt and characterized by a commingling of beliefs and practices that included sexual immorality, fertility rites, astrology, superstition, and pagan nature worship.

The picture painted by the book of Zephaniah is one of a people indifferent toward God, living as though he didn't really exist and looking after themselves independent from him—a form of practical atheism. Neglect of the law led to all kinds of spiritual and social ills, such as idolatry, pride, covetousness, theft, violence, and various forms of abuse.

Social life was characterized by self-sufficiency and the pursuit of riches. In its wake lay many evidences of fraud, deception, apathy, government failures, immoral leadership, indifference, social injustice, and unrighteousness.

A Prophetic Wake-Up Call

Zephaniah's prophecy, which followed a period of almost fifty years when no voice was heard from the Lord, was a wake-up call to a nation that had assumed that God wouldn't intervene or do anything. Addressing the popular notion that "The LORD will not do good, nor will he do harm" (1:12), the prophet declares God's intention emphatically seven times in the opening verses, "I will" (1:2–4). Those who think and act as though God won't touch them will be forced to rethink.

The main part of the prophecy deals with God's plans to bring judgment upon the nation (1:2–3:8). The focal point throughout is Zephaniah's proclamation of the "day of the LORD" (1:14). Gripped by the awesome nature of this terrible day of reckoning, Zephaniah speaks of the causes and conditions that have led to God's judgment (1:15–17).

See also *"The With-God Life"* essay for this section of the Bible,
"The People of God in Rebellion," pp. 975–79.

1347

What Zephaniah perceived was God's holiness. Humanity's rejection of God and its embracing of idolatry and independence, which led to all kinds of evil, inevitably called forth God's judgment. Such evil could not go unchecked forever; it was bound to invoke the wrath and anger of a holy and righteous God, and the impact of that would be known throughout the earth (1:18). On that day God's abhorrence of evil and passion for justice will be at long last realized.

God's Restoration of His People

The final section of the book (3:9–20) speaks of hope, as Zephaniah sees the world that God will usher in after judgment. Having proclaimed God's judgment, he now speaks of God's mercy and portrays a time when the Lord will restore his people. They will offer true worship to God, experience a new unity, and be freed from fear, oppression, and the pursuit of those things that corrupt and spoil. Believers will know that they are loved and secure in God.

The book of Zephaniah reminds us that we should never take God's holiness for granted. Our gracious acceptance by God is premised on his going to extraordinary lengths to save us from a fearful judgment. It also reveals that having a right relationship with God requires a commitment to living a righteous life.

—*Roy Searle*

---

1 The word of the LORD that came to Zephaniah son of Cushi son of Gedaliah son of Amariah son of Hezekiah, in the days of King Josiah son of Amon of Judah.

The Coming Judgment on Judah

2 I will utterly sweep away everything from the face of the earth, says the LORD.

3 I will sweep away humans and animals;

I will sweep away the birds of the air
    and the fish of the sea.
I will make the wicked stumble.*
I will cut off humanity
    from the face of the earth, says the LORD.

4 I will stretch out my hand against Judah,

a Cn: Heb *sea, and those who cause the wicked to stumble*

1:1 *Zephaniah son of Cushi.* When the nation was young, old men led it. Now that the nation is old, God uses young men like Zephaniah, Jeremiah, and King Josiah to lead his people in the ways of righteousness. Growing in grace requires humility and an openness to God's use of those younger than ourselves. Through a new, younger generation, God brought a sick, older, complacent generation back to himself. Are we listening to the heart of God and his call as it comes through the lives of others, many of whom may speak to us from beyond our tradition and experience? By tracing his lineage back to King Hezekiah (see 2 Kings 18:5–7), Zephaniah is able to look back to a time, in contrast to his complacent contemporary culture, when his ancestors lived among a People of God who were renewed and vibrant in their faith. We should be thankful and appreciative when our family history has included a godly inheritance and seek to build new and renewed faith on the foundations that come to us from our forefathers and foremothers in the faith.

1:2–3 *I will utterly sweep away everything.* (See also v 18; 2:13.) God speaks through life's storms, devastating happenings, and terrors. It is important to keep our eyes of faith open to the signs of God's presence and the activity of his kingdom in the happenings of life and world events.

and against all the inhabitants of
    Jerusalem;
and I will cut off from this place every
    remnant of Baal
and the name of the idolatrous
    priests; *a*

5 those who bow down on the roofs
    to the host of the heavens;
those who bow down and swear to the
    LORD,
but also swear by Milcom; *b*
6 those who have turned back from
    following the LORD,
who have not sought the LORD or
    inquired of him.

7 Be silent before the Lord GOD!
    For the day of the LORD is at hand;
the LORD has prepared a sacrifice,
    he has consecrated his guests.
8 And on the day of the LORD's sacrifice
    I will punish the officials and the king's
    sons

and all who dress themselves in
    foreign attire.
9 On that day I will punish
    all who leap over the threshold,
who fill their master's house
    with violence and fraud.

10 On that day, says the LORD,
    a cry will be heard from the Fish Gate,
a wail from the Second Quarter,
    a loud crash from the hills.
11 The inhabitants of the Mortar wail,
    for all the traders have perished;
all who weigh out silver are cut off.
12 At that time I will search Jerusalem with
    lamps,
and I will punish the people
    who rest complacently *c* on their dregs,
those who say in their hearts,

a Compare Gk: Heb *the idolatrous priests with the
priests*   *b* Gk Mss Syr Vg: Heb *Malcam* (or, *their
king*)   *c* Heb *who thicken*

1:4–6 *those who have turned back from following the LORD.* Failing to live as though God mattered, the nation neglected his law and consequently fell into disobedience. Neglect of God's word leads people away from his will and purposes. The practice of *lectio divina,* the daily reading of Scripture, is a neglected yet vital discipline for believers. The Scriptures are our "memory book"; they are God's covenantal text. Reading, meditating, and saturating ourselves with the Bible both aids faith development and deepens our understanding of God and his ways and will for our lives. Picking and mixing religious beliefs and practices lead to idolatry and the judgment of God, a consequence of neglect of God's word.

1:7 *Be silent before the Lord GOD!* The summons to be silent is a call to listen and acknowledge the Lord. Activity can preclude hearing what God is saying and doing. Busyness and being driven by a culture that overvalues what can be achieved, where worth is associated by what is done, can hinder believers' "being" with God. The call to silence is the contemplative call to pay attention to God, to be still in the midst of life's activities, and to draw near to the One in whom we "live and move and have our being" (Acts 17:28).

Responding
1:7 SILENCE. Try the experiment of living an entire day in silence. As you find new ways to express yourself to those around you, think about the role of words in your life. Where are words strengthening your relationship with God and others? Where are words obscuring and hindering? *See also* Spiritual Disciplines Index.

1:11 *all the traders have perished.* (See also vv 13, 18.) The lure and hold that the pursuit of money has upon people are powerful enemies of spiritual formation. It is impossible to love both God and money (see Matt 6:24; 1 Tim 6:10). Belief in our self-sufficiency keeps us from recognizing our dependency upon God. Money will be of no use on the day of judgment.

1:12 *the people who rest complacently on their dregs.* Complacency and apathy lead to judgment. Complacency—self-satisfaction—is a very dangerous issue for Christians. Nothing can weaken or destroy spiritual life more. Complacency prevents us from becoming all that God longs to see us be; it tires our soul and fatigues our spirit. God's warning against complacency must be heeded (Prov 1:32; Rev 3:15–19).

"The LORD will not do good,
    nor will he do harm."
13 Their wealth shall be plundered,
    and their houses laid waste.
Though they build houses,
    they shall not inhabit them;
though they plant vineyards,
    they shall not drink wine from
        them.

The Great Day of the LORD

14 The great day of the LORD is near,
    near and hastening fast;
the sound of the day of the LORD is
        bitter,
    the warrior cries aloud there.
15 That day will be a day of wrath,
    a day of distress and anguish,
a day of ruin and devastation,
    a day of darkness and gloom,
a day of clouds and thick darkness,
16   a day of trumpet blast and battle cry
against the fortified cities
    and against the lofty battlements.

17 I will bring such distress upon people
    that they shall walk like the blind;
    because they have sinned against the
        LORD,
their blood shall be poured out like
        dust,
    and their flesh like dung.
18 Neither their silver nor their gold
    will be able to save them
    on the day of the LORD's wrath;
in the fire of his passion
    the whole earth shall be consumed;
for a full, a terrible end
    he will make of all the inhabitants of
        the earth.

Judgment on Israel's Enemies

2 Gather together, gather,
    O shameless nation,
2 before you are driven away
    like the drifting chaff,[a]
before there comes upon you

the fierce anger of the LORD,
before there comes upon you
    the day of the LORD's wrath.
3 Seek the LORD, all you humble of the
        land,
    who do his commands;
seek righteousness, seek humility;
    perhaps you may be hidden
    on the day of the LORD's wrath.
4 For Gaza shall be deserted,
    and Ashkelon shall become a
        desolation;
Ashdod's people shall be driven out at
        noon,
    and Ekron shall be uprooted.

5 Ah, inhabitants of the seacoast,
    you nation of the Cherethites!
The word of the LORD is against you,
    O Canaan, land of the Philistines;
    and I will destroy you until no
        inhabitant is left.
6 And you, O seacoast, shall be
        pastures,
    meadows for shepherds
    and folds for flocks.
7 The seacoast shall become the
        possession
    of the remnant of the house of Judah,
    on which they shall pasture,
and in the houses of Ashkelon
    they shall lie down at evening.
For the LORD their God will be mindful
        of them
    and restore their fortunes.

8 I have heard the taunts of Moab
    and the revilings of the Ammonites,
how they have taunted my people
    and made boasts against their
        territory.
9 Therefore, as I live, says the LORD of
        hosts,
    the God of Israel,

a Cn Compare Gk Syr: Heb *before a decree is born;*
like chaff a day has passed away

2:3 *Seek the LORD.* The first mandate is that
the people humbly seek the Lord and in so doing
obey his commands and live righteously. Only
such actions are able to avert the righteous wrath
and judgments of God and to make possible the
receipt of a future hope (Matt 5:5–8).

Moab shall become like Sodom
  and the Ammonites like Gomorrah,
a land possessed by nettles and salt pits,
  and a waste forever.
The remnant of my people shall
    plunder them,
  and the survivors of my nation shall
    possess them.
10 This shall be their lot in return for their
    pride,
  because they scoffed and boasted
  against the people of the LORD of
    hosts.
11 The LORD will be terrible against them;
  he will shrivel all the gods of the
    earth,
and to him shall bow down,
  each in its place,
  all the coasts and islands of the
    nations.

12 You also, O Ethiopians, *a*
  shall be killed by my sword.

13 And he will stretch out his hand against
    the north,
  and destroy Assyria;
and he will make Nineveh a desolation,
  a dry waste like the desert.
14 Herds shall lie down in it,
  every wild animal; *b*
the desert owl *c* and the screech owl *c*
  shall lodge on its capitals;
the owl *d* shall hoot at the window,
  the raven *e* croak on the threshold;
  for its cedar work will be laid bare.
15 Is this the exultant city
  that lived secure,

that said to itself,
  "I am, and there is no one else"?
What a desolation it has become,
  a lair for wild animals!
Everyone who passes by it
  hisses and shakes the fist.

The Wickedness of Jerusalem

3 Ah, soiled, defiled,
    oppressing city!
2 It has listened to no voice;
  it has accepted no correction.
It has not trusted in the LORD;
  it has not drawn near to its God.

3 The officials within it
  are roaring lions;
its judges are evening wolves
  that leave nothing until the
    morning.
4 Its prophets are reckless,
  faithless persons;
its priests have profaned what is sacred,
  they have done violence to the law.
5 The LORD within it is righteous;
  he does no wrong.
Every morning he renders his
    judgment,
  each dawn without fail;
  but the unjust knows no shame.

6 I have cut off nations;
  their battlements are in ruins;
I have laid waste their streets
  so that no one walks in them;

a Or *Nubians*; Heb *Cushites*   *b* Tg Compare Gk:
Heb *nation*   *c* Meaning of Heb uncertain
d Cn: Heb *a voice*   *e* Gk Vg: Heb *desolation*

2:9–15 *Moab shall become like Sodom.* What
God decrees he does! Nations and cities,
thinking themselves invincible, are literally
brought to ground by the power of God. Moab,
Ammon, Sodom, Gomorrah, and Nineveh are
reduced to nothing.

3:2 *It has listened to no voice.* Jerusalem was
failing to listen, being closed to any correction,
showing disregard for God, and having no desire
to seek him that caused the demise and desecration of the city (see Eph 5:15).

3:4 *its priests have profaned what is sacred.*
Profaning what is sacred and violating the law
lead to ruin. The purpose of the law of the Lord
is not to act as a killjoy, but to help us live the
life that God intends and that is best for us.

3:5 *The LORD within it is righteous.* The nature
of God is goodness and righteousness, which
stand in contrast to the qualities of those whose
rebellion and disregard for him lead to shameless actions. Seeking God and honoring him lead
to life; disobedience and indifference lead to
ruin, spiritually and socially.

their cities have been made desolate,
  without people, without inhabitants.
7 I said, "Surely the city[a] will fear me,
    it will accept correction;
  it will not lose sight[b]
    of all that I have brought upon it."
But they were the more eager
    to make all their deeds corrupt.

Punishment and Conversion of the Nations

8 Therefore wait for me, says the LORD,
    for the day when I arise as a witness.
For my decision is to gather nations,
    to assemble kingdoms,
  to pour out upon them my indignation,
    all the heat of my anger;
  for in the fire of my passion
    all the earth shall be consumed.

9 At that time I will change the speech of
      the peoples
    to a pure speech,
  that all of them may call on the name
      of the LORD
    and serve him with one accord.
10 From beyond the rivers of Ethiopia[c]
    my suppliants, my scattered ones,
    shall bring my offering.

11 On that day you shall not be put to
      shame
    because of all the deeds by which you
      have rebelled against me;
  for then I will remove from your midst
    your proudly exultant ones,
  and you shall no longer be haughty
    in my holy mountain.

12 For I will leave in the midst of you
    a people humble and lowly.
  They shall seek refuge in the name of
      the LORD—
13   the remnant of Israel;
    they shall do no wrong
    and utter no lies,
  nor shall a deceitful tongue
    be found in their mouths.
  Then they will pasture and lie down,
    and no one shall make them afraid.

A Song of Joy

14 Sing aloud, O daughter Zion;
    shout, O Israel!
  Rejoice and exult with all your heart,
    O daughter Jerusalem!
15 The LORD has taken away the judgments
      against you,
    he has turned away your enemies.
  The king of Israel, the LORD, is in your
      midst;
    you shall fear disaster no more.
16 On that day it shall be said to
      Jerusalem:
  Do not fear, O Zion;
    do not let your hands grow weak.
17 The LORD, your God, is in your midst,
    a warrior who gives victory;
  he will rejoice over you with gladness,
    he will renew you[d] in his love;
  he will exult over you with loud
      singing
18   as on a day of festival.[e]

a Heb it   b Gk Syr: Heb its dwelling will not be cut
off   c Or Nubia; Heb Cush   d Gk Syr: Heb he
will be silent   e Gk Syr: Meaning of Heb uncertain

3:8–9 *Therefore wait for me.* Two sides of God's nature are revealed in these verses—his righteous judgment and his eternal mercy. Beyond judgment lay a day of restoration and new life for the people. Thus Zephaniah paints images of both the horrific and the hopeful; the source of the prophet's despair comes from his understanding of sinful human nature and his hope arises from his appreciation of God's infinite mercy.

3:13 *the remnant of Israel; they shall do no wrong.* (See also vv 15–16.) Trust in God renders believers free from fear and secure and safe in the knowledge of his love and protection. The people of Judah lived their lives independently of God and built on the false securities of wealth, position, status, and power.

3:17 *he will rejoice over you with gladness.* On the day of new beginnings God rejoices over his people, renewing us by his love. A remarkable concept to meditate on is that believers, children of God, can bring delight to the heart of God; that our lives can bring pleasure (as well as pain) to the God who created us, who loves us, and who in his mercy and commitment to us brings us back into right relationship with himself.

I will remove disaster from you, ^{a}
    so that you will not bear reproach for
      it.
19 I will deal with all your oppressors
    at that time.
And I will save the lame
    and gather the outcast,
and I will change their shame into praise
    and renown in all the earth.

20 At that time I will bring you home,
    at the time when I gather you;
for I will make you renowned and
    praised
    among all the peoples of the earth,
when I restore your fortunes
    before your eyes, says the LORD.

a Cn: Heb *I will remove from you; they were*

3:20 *I will bring you home.* To a wayward, rebellious, and negligent people—a prodigal people—God issues the compassionate invitation to come "home." There is a welcome in the heart of God to those who return "home." Such a homecoming results in a restoration of unity and purity of heart (v 9), humility (vv 11–12), integrity and honesty (v 13), and security (vv 13, 17a). In essence the heart of faith, relationship with God, is restored. Life is found in knowing God.

I will remove disaster from you,
so that you will not bear reproach for

I will deal with all your oppressors
at that time.
And I will save the lame
and gather the outcast,
and I will change their shame into praise,
and renown in all the earth.

¹⁸ And that day I will bring you home,
at the time
for I will make you renowned and
praised
among all the peoples of the earth,
when I restore your fortunes
before your eyes, says the LORD.

3:20 ... bring you home ... to every land,
rebellious, and ... trouble ... prophet ...
people. God sends the compassionate invitation
... to come home. "These is a welcome in the heart
of God, to those who room "home." Such a

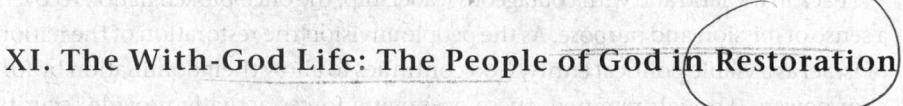

XI. The With-God Life: The People of God in Restoration

Scriptures: *Ezra, Nehemiah, Esther, Daniel, Haggai, Zechariah, Malachi*

Deuterocanonical Books: *Additions to Esther, 1 Esdras 2–9 & 2 Esdras, 1, 2, 3, & 4 Maccabees, Tobit, Additions to Daniel (Prayer of Azariah and the Song of the Three Jews, Susanna, Bel and the Dragon)*

The aim of God in history is the creation of an all-inclusive community of loving persons with God himself at the very center of this community as its prime Sustainer and most glorious Inhabitant (Eph 2:19–22; 3:10). The Bible traces the formation of this community from the creation in the Garden of Eden all the way to the new heaven and the new earth. Come, join us as we explore the many dimensions of this with-God history—from individual to family to tribe to people to nation to all humanity—and apply what we learn to our own spiritual formation.

In the previous section, we discovered the way in which God used the exile to bring his people closer to the nonethnic, all-inclusive community he is creating in history. In these Scriptures we will see how God continues this formation by returning the people to the land and restoring the liturgical life of Israel.

God's Action

After the fall of Jerusalem and the demise of Judah, we find the people of Israel scattered across the vast expanse of the Babylonian Empire. There they have been left to ponder their fate and find God. Out of the dark abyss of the loss of their nation, land, Temple, and community life, they begin to consider God's original promise to Abraham. Are they not the chosen people? Why is God punishing them in this way? Why this long? What does God want?

The answers come in surprising and ironic ways. During the exile, in the midst of utter despair, the Israelites receive assurance from God that they *will* return to their desolate land, rebuild their ruined cities, and restore their cherished Temple. Unexpectedly, God uses this despair and a foreign power to achieve his divine purposes.

Following the exile God continues to influence pagan rulers so that the survival of Abraham's descendants, the lineage from which the promised one, the Messiah, will spring, can be realized. Gentile rulers give Ezra and Nehemiah permission to return to Israel and rebuild the Temple and the walls of Jerusalem (Ezra 1:1–4; Neh 2:1–9). Esther successfully pleads with the king of Persia to protect the Israelites: "Let my life be given me . . . and the lives of my people" (7:3). Through the generosity and kindness of foreign rulers, the Israelites survive and return to their land to rebuild their crumbled Temple and restore their religious practices.

Back in the land and with courageous leadership, the once-broken nation recovers a sense of mission and purpose. As the people envision the restoration of the nation of Israel as a viable political entity, God continues to allow their domination by foreign powers. Though resented, these occupying forces actually provide security and stability in a time of political upheaval in the Mediterranean world, giving the Israelites freedom to recover their religious heritage. At God's initiation, the law is restored, the Temple is rebuilt, and the people rediscover the security they so desperately seek—not now in an army or a nation, but in faith in the Lord God, the Almighty. God, in calling Israel to return in faithfulness, offers it the renewing power of his forgiveness, the free gift of his grace, and the blessed opportunity of a new beginning.

After the people are home, but still under the domination of foreign powers, God ordains two institutions to stand at the heart of Jewish religious life: the synagogue, where devout God-followers can cultivate and express sincere and sustaining faith in him, and the restored Temple, where the daily rituals required by the law are the guiding force. In the villages the synagogues become the focus of regular local worship. From them arise the rabbis, teachers who interpret the Scriptures and become the caretakers of a Jewish culture centered in Torah, and the Pharisees, who represent the more flexible tradition of the synagogue.

Through the institution of the Temple the people of Israel discover the security of continuity with the past and stability in the present. Here the pilgrimage holidays are celebrated, the priestly class is reestablished, and liturgy flourishes. And a new group, the Sadducees, become indicative of those who believe that God can be worshiped only in Jerusalem. They seek to preserve the Temple worship that generations of devout Jews had worked so hard to recover.

Human Reaction

The idea of God's restoration of the people of Israel is one of the most striking themes in all of Scripture. Equally striking is the response of the Israelites, driven by prophetic promise and messianic hope, as they return to rebuild the walls of Jerusalem and the Temple and to establish a faithful community based on obedience to the law. "O Lord God of heaven, the great and awesome God," Nehemiah begins, "We have offended you deeply, failing to keep the commandments. . . . Remember the word that you commanded your servant Moses, 'If you are unfaithful, I will scatter you among the peoples; but if you return to me and keep my commandments and do them, though your outcasts are under the farthest skies, I will gather them from there and bring them to the place at which I have chosen to establish my name'" (1:5–9). From their exile experience, the Israelites learn to trust in the God who fulfills covenant promises, restores his people, and resolves the paradoxes of history. They come to see that, although the promise of God does not evaporate, it can go dormant. Another striking response is the Israelites' fidelity to the word of the prophets.

During the exile, the prophet Ezekiel had called for a new order, a holy community, in which an ordered priesthood and a regulated liturgy would recover God's favor for the fallen nation. During the restoration the prophets look back on a once-proud history and conclude that the people had gone astray by rejecting God and pursuing the pagan idols of their neighbors. With Ezekiel's call to make God the sole center of Israel's allegiance and the later prophets' insights into the reasons for Israel's fall, radical monotheism captures the imagination of the people of Israel. Thus, monotheism becomes the acid test of devotion and calls forth the total loyalty of all God's people.

The exile had not only caused a rupture in Israel's continued presence in the land; it had caused a break in the continuity of Israelite culture as well. Upon the return, a new culture has to be established. The Israelites develop this new way of life centered on the family, the synagogue, and the community—a way of life that survives the numerous foreign occupations, political intrigues, religious wars, and insurrections that envelop the land for centuries. When the city of Jerusalem falls to the Romans in AD 70 and the Jews disperse all over the Mediterranean basin, their culture continues to survive and even flourish. Today we see it in every corner of the earth.

Also, out of the dark abyss of national calamity and foreign exile, Israel comes to anticipate the dawning of a "day of the LORD," a day when God's apocalyptic judgment will come and Israel will be restored to its original stature and greatness. Ultimately, the people of Israel embrace God's redemptive purposes for all history.

A spiritual downside to the exile is the hardening of the Israelites' hearts. They had rejected God before the exile by worshiping other gods and oppressing the poor. This rejection continues after the exile, but in a different way. By concentrating so intently on the law and its interpretation, they lose that aspect of God that is always reaching out, always inclusive, always loving, always redeeming. This overreaction becomes a rigid system of laws and regulations focused on its own survival rather than a way for people to enter into a with-God life.

Blessings and Benefits for Our Formation

Through the process of exile and restoration, the Israelites discover that God is not limited to a particular time or a specific place. God can be worshiped at any time and in any place. Daniel "continued to go to his house . . . and to get down on his knees three times a day to pray to his God and praise him" (6:10). God, they learn, is not far off or removed from interaction with the finite world. Yahweh is the God of this world, even though existing distinct from it.

Although the Israelites are forced to live under the domination of foreign nations, the fact that they are able to reestablish their religious faith makes it unmistakably clear that a life with God is not dependent upon human governments. The Israelites had to learn this all-important lesson through the tragedy of exile. We can only hope that our learning will be less destructive.

The With-God Life

The period of restoration is also a harbinger of the later message of Jesus of "the kingdom of the heavens," a nonmaterial kingdom without borders. Daniel speaks prophetically of a stone cut "not by human hands," a stone that overcomes all human governments, a stone that "became a great mountain and filled the whole earth" (2:34–35). This Living Stone, says Peter, is "a cornerstone chosen and precious; and whoever believes in him will not be put to shame" (1 Pet 2:6). Jesus Christ, the Living Stone, has brought his invisible kingdom to earth in the form of love and power, truth and righteousness, a spiritual kingdom that is here now but is not yet fully realized.

Limits and Liabilities for Our Formation

But limitations abound. The preoccupation with ritual purity during this period creates a violent backlash as insidious as anything experienced during the exile. The divorce and abandonment of non-Jewish wives, for example, not only create a violation of God's law, but also precipitate a national crisis. Nehemiah exclaims, "When the people heard the law, they separated from Israel all those of foreign descent. . . . Shall we . . . act treacherously against our God by marrying foreign women?" (13:3, 27). This attitude provides the context for some of Jesus' most profound teaching: "It was also said, 'Whoever divorces his wife, let him give her a certificate of divorce.' But I say to you that anyone who divorces his wife, except on the ground of unchastity, causes her to commit adultery; and whoever marries a divorced woman commits adultery" (Matt 5:31–32).

Further, the Israelites discover that dealing with informal entities is often harder than dealing with a formal government. Although the Persians occupied the land and gave Nehemiah official permission to return and rebuild the walls of Jerusalem, local residents and "rulers" resist the Israelites' efforts. The situation grows so grave that half "worked on construction, and half held the spears, shields, bows, and body-armor; and the leaders posted themselves behind the whole house of Judah, who were building the wall" (Neh 4:16–17). Their experience should motivate us to pray for the stability of nations and for those who are in positions of authority in government (1 Tim 2:2).

Another liability occurs when the Israelites lose control of their destiny and become pawns in the hands of occupying nations and a religious establishment on which there is no check. Losing control over one's destiny sounds strange to our ears, because the freedom to do what we want or worship wherever we wish is so ingrained in our psyches. However, in Israel's village-based agrarian culture dominated by foreign powers, the lack of control is a critical factor in the development of numerous nationalistic movements and breakaway sects in the two centuries immediately preceding the birth of Jesus.

Insights and Instructions for Our Formation

The insights for our own formation are many and varied. First of all, we learn to look to God and God's future for our care and security instead of to any earthly kingdom.

Human governments are to fulfill their God-ordained task of maintaining order and ensuring justice, but they can never compare to the assurance of a present lived under and in the power of God or of an eternity with God.

Second, we need to affirm the vital importance of homes, faith gatherings, and local communities in providing social cohesion. The exiled Israelites kept their faith and culture alive by reciting their communal history in their homes and religious gatherings. In the restoration children received informal religious instruction on the laps of their parents, and the people received formal religious instruction at the feet of the rabbis. The entire community of faith affirmed and lived out its common faith. Can we do any less?

Third, we should encourage those who have the gift of leadership, a gift necessary for our growth and edification. When their neighbors threatened the Israelites, Nehemiah found a practical and effective solution: half of the people worked on the wall while the other half provided protection from enemies. In our day, practical wisdom—what is often called "common sense"—is in short supply. We would be wise to listen to those who have the gift of wisdom and express it through responsible leadership.

Fourth, we relearn that worship needs to stand at the very center of our life together. The restoration of Israel began when King Cyrus of Persia charged the first group of exiles to rebuild the Temple, the focal point of Jewish ritual and belief. After the people returned to Jerusalem, they gathered at the site of the preexilic Temple and "set up the altar on its foundation, . . . From the first day of the seventh month they began to offer burnt offerings to the LORD. But the foundation of the temple of the LORD was not yet laid" (Ezra 3:3, 6). The people worshiped under adverse circumstances in the extreme. So can we.

Finally, we ought to lift high the messianic themes we find in the literature of the restoration. They are too numerous and too specific to ignore. "And he will come to Zion as Redeemer, to those in Jacob who turn from transgression, says the LORD" (Isa 59:20). "The spirit of the Lord GOD is upon me, because the LORD has anointed me" (Isa 61:1). "Lo, your king comes to you; triumphant and victorious is he, humble and riding on a donkey, on a colt, the foal of a donkey" (Zech 9:9). "The messenger of the covenant in whom you delight—indeed, he is coming" (Mal 3:1). These, and other passages like them, cultivate a deep and abiding hope in the dawning "day of the LORD." It is this very hope, a hope in a coming Messiah, that generates the tremendous passion and belief in God's ultimate promise of restoration.

It is within the framework of this hope for restoration that Jesus challenges Judaism's legalism; unleashes the love, truth, and power of God into the world; and becomes the light of the nations and the redemption of the world. From this witness, God's purposes in history are ultimately fulfilled.

The With-God Life

HAGGAI

The book of Haggai is a series of prophetic messages to the People of God after their return from exile. Like us, they are seeking comfortable lives under economic hardship, and their time is consumed with meeting their physical needs. However, while the people have been concerned with their own households, they have ignored the time for reconstructing the "house of the LORD" (1:14). Thus, much like other prophets, Haggai brings a message of both reprimand and promise, giving the people concrete instruction to rebuild and consecrate the Temple so that the spiritual community might be reformed. Despite their return to Jerusalem, God's people cannot be fully restored from exile until they have reestablished the Lord's house as their center.

Rebuke and Assurance

The text refers to the second year of King Darius I (520 BC), acknowledging the reality that the people live under a foreign (Persian) government. However, addressing the governor Zerubbabel and the high priest Joshua, Haggai indicates that this should not have kept the children of Israel from rebuilding the Temple. The people have apparently had opportunity and resources, as they have acquired paneled houses, food, drink, clothing, and wages for themselves. But because they left the Lord's house "in ruins" (1:9), the people have not found contentment and their labors have not been fruitful; Yahweh has punished them with a drought (1:11).

Haggai's rebuke is effective: the governor, high priest, and people begin construction (1:14). At this point, the text turns from reproach to reassurance, as the Lord reminds the people that he delivered their ancestors from Egypt, is still their God, and will continue to be with them (2:4–5). Yahweh promises to "shake the heavens and the earth and the sea and the dry land" to make the Temple glorious (2:6), and when the foundation stone is laid (2:18), the Lord promises to reverse the people's agricultural misfortune and to bless them with prosperity. Finally, speaking through

See also *"The With-God Life"* essay for this section of the Bible,
"The People of God in Restoration," pp. 1355–59.

Haggai to Zerubbabel, a descendant of David, the Lord promises a coming day—at the shaking of the heavens and the earth—when the political order will be overthrown and the Lord's chosen will reign as king (2:23).

Haggai's message of admonishment and hope holds meaning for our lives and faith as well. The prophet communicates the need for a space dedicated to God and his worship. And in contrast to their "own houses" that the people hurry to (1:9), that space—the Lord's house—should be central to the community. Rebuilding and dedicating the Temple are necessary for the Israelites' spiritual reformation, as the people are connected in their worship of God. Along with the returned exiles, we hear the prophet's charge to reorder our lives and are reminded that priority belongs to God and blessing is God's to give. But we may also "take courage" (2:4) for the "work" we are called to, for we are the People of God and God's promises endure throughout history.

—*Rebekah Close LeMon*

The Command to Rebuild the Temple

1 In the second year of King Darius, in the sixth month, on the first day of the month, the word of the LORD came by the prophet Haggai to Zerubbabel son of Shealtiel, governor of Judah, and to Joshua son of Jehozadak, the high priest. ²Thus says the LORD of hosts: These people say the time has not yet come to rebuild the LORD's house. ³Then the word of the LORD came by the prophet Haggai, saying: ⁴Is it a time for you yourselves to live in your paneled houses, while this house lies in ruins? ⁵Now therefore thus says the LORD of hosts: Consider how you have fared. ⁶You have sown much, and harvested little; you eat, but you never have

---

1:1 *In the second year of King Darius*. This unusually specific time reference places Haggai's first address in August or September of 520 BC and reminds us of the real context of Jerusalem under Persian rule. Haggai's first prophetic message is spoken to the governor Zerubbabel and the high priest Joshua. Their fathers are also named, connecting this book to the people's long history of faith that preceded the return of the exiles. Zerubbabel is descended from David, though he was appointed to a civic post by a Persian king. These are Haggai's only messages, though he is twice named as a prophet in Ezra (5:1; 6:14). Haggai's name, derived from a root word meaning "to journey, to make a pilgrimage," alludes to a theme of this book—the faith journey of the People of God, return from exile, and restoration of the Temple and worship.

1:2 *Thus says the LORD of hosts*. This phrase portrays God as the powerful Commander of heaven. "The LORD of hosts" appears fourteen times in Haggai, reminding us that God is more powerful than human circumstances.

1:2–11 *the time has not yet come to rebuild the LORD's house.* The people have put off building the Temple, but have built houses for themselves (paneled ones, suggesting wealth). The metaphor of earning wages but putting them into "a bag with holes" (v 6) suggests that the people's efforts will be wasted until they construct the Temple, since they have apparently worked, but still have not fared well. This message calls us to replace our self-concern with right worship.

Responding
1:2–11 SIMPLICITY/FRUGALITY. The Lord here reprimands the People of God for putting their money and resources in their own homes, their own interests. Where in your life have you invested for yourself what belongs to God? Are you giving enough of what you have to the community and to the work of the Lord? *See also* Spiritual Disciplines Index.

enough; you drink, but you never have your fill; you clothe yourselves, but no one is warm; and you that earn wages earn wages to put them into a bag with holes.

7 Thus says the LORD of hosts: Consider how you have fared. 8Go up to the hills and bring wood and build the house, so that I may take pleasure in it and be honored, says the LORD. 9You have looked for much, and, lo, it came to little; and when you brought it home, I blew it away. Why? says the LORD of hosts. Because my house lies in ruins, while all of you hurry off to your own houses. 10Therefore the heavens above you have withheld the dew, and the earth has withheld its produce. 11And I have called for a drought on the land and the hills, on the grain, the new wine, the oil, on what the soil produces, on human beings and animals, and on all their labors.

12 Then Zerubbabel son of Shealtiel, and Joshua son of Jehozadak, the high priest, with all the remnant of the people, obeyed the voice of the LORD their God, and the words of the prophet Haggai, as the LORD their God had sent him; and the people feared the LORD. 13Then Haggai, the messenger of the LORD, spoke to the people with the LORD's message, saying, I am with you, says the LORD. 14And the LORD stirred up the spirit of Zerubbabel son of Shealtiel, governor of Judah, and the spirit of Joshua son of Jehozadak, the high priest, and the spirit of all the remnant of the people; and they came and worked on the house of the LORD of hosts, their God, 15on the twenty-fourth day of the month, in the sixth month.

The Future Glory of the Temple

2 In the second year of King Darius, 1in the seventh month, on the twenty-first day of the month, the word of the LORD came by the prophet Haggai, saying: 2Speak now to Zerubbabel son of Shealtiel, governor of Judah, and to Joshua son of Jehozadak, the high priest, and to the remnant of the people, and say, 3Who is left among you that saw this house in its former glory? How does it look to you now? Is it not in your sight as nothing? 4Yet now take courage, O Zerubbabel, says the LORD; take courage, O Joshua, son of Jehozadak, the high priest; take courage, all you people of the land, says the LORD; work, for I am with you, says the LORD of hosts, 5according to the promise that I made you when you came out of Egypt. My spirit abides among you; do not fear. 6For thus says the LORD of hosts: Once again, in a little while, I will shake the heavens and the earth and the sea and the dry land; 7and I will shake all the nations, so that the treasure of all nations shall come, and I will fill this house with splendor, says the LORD of hosts. 8The silver is mine, and the gold is mine, says the LORD of hosts. 9The latter splendor of this house shall be greater than the former, says the LORD of hosts; and in this place I will give prosperity, says the LORD of hosts.

A Rebuke and a Promise

10 On the twenty-fourth day of the ninth month, in the second year of Darius, the word of the LORD came by the prophet Haggai, saying: 11Thus says the LORD of hosts: Ask the priests for a ruling: 12If one carries consecrated meat in the fold of one's garment,

---

2:3 *Who is left among you that saw this house?* This Temple's future glory is contrasted with that of the First Temple (Solomon's Temple), before its destruction in 587 BC. God promises action in order to realize the Second Temple's glory, and the Lord's active presence encourages the people.

2:5 *according to the promise that I made you.* Recalling the exodus from Egypt, God reminds the people that he has always been and will always be with them.

2:6–9 *Once again, in a little while, I will shake.*

The phrase "in a little while" appears in several Old Testament texts (see Ps 37:10; Isa 10:25; 29:17; Hos 1:4). It is not a vague time reference, but an indicator of the apocalyptic promise that God will set the world right; here it assures the returned exiles that God will bring a new era. God's pledge to shake the earth and all the nations, like the repeated epithet "LORD of hosts," depicts God's ultimate power. With the cosmic reordering to come, all the nations' wealth will be given in offering to God, and the Temple will be made glorious.

and with the fold touches bread, or stew, or wine, or oil, or any kind of food, does it become holy? The priests answered, "No." ¹³Then Haggai said, "If one who is unclean by contact with a dead body touches any of these, does it become unclean?" The priests answered, "Yes, it becomes unclean." ¹⁴Haggai then said, So is it with this people, and with this nation before me, says the LORD; and so with every work of their hands; and what they offer there is unclean. ¹⁵But now, consider what will come to pass from this day on. Before a stone was placed upon a stone in the LORD's temple, ¹⁶how did you fare?*ᵃ* When one came to a heap of twenty measures, there were but ten; when one came to the wine vat to draw fifty measures, there were but twenty. ¹⁷I struck you and all the products of your toil with blight and mildew and hail; yet you did not return to me, says the LORD. ¹⁸Consider from this day on, from the twenty-fourth day of the ninth month. Since the day that the foundation of the LORD's temple was laid, consider: ¹⁹Is there

any seed left in the barn? Do the vine, the fig tree, the pomegranate, and the olive tree still yield nothing? From this day on I will bless you.

God's Promise to Zerubbabel

20 The word of the LORD came a second time to Haggai on the twenty-fourth day of the month: ²¹Speak to Zerubbabel, governor of Judah, saying, I am about to shake the heavens and the earth, ²²and to overthrow the throne of kingdoms; I am about to destroy the strength of the kingdoms of the nations, and overthrow the chariots and their riders; and the horses and their riders shall fall, every one by the sword of a comrade. ²³On that day, says the LORD of hosts, I will take you, O Zerubbabel my servant, son of Shealtiel, says the LORD, and make you like a signet ring; for I have chosen you, says the LORD of hosts.

ᵃ Gk: Heb *since they were*

2:11–14 *Ask the priests for a ruling.* The prophet communicates a message by posing questions to the community priests. The priests answer that even if meat has been consecrated, it cannot make other food holy, while uncleanness can be communicated by contact. Verse 14 clarifies the meaning of these questions: the people may build the Temple, but what is offered to God there will not be clean until the Temple is consecrated. Again, the people must not only construct the Temple building, but rededicate it, their community, and themselves to God. Likewise, our work is not acceptable to God if it is motion without dedication.

2:15–19 *from this day on.* The prophet contrasts the want in the land before work on the Temple began with the economic prosperity the Lord promises upon the laying of the Temple's

foundation. By beginning construction, the people have turned to God, and God responds with blessing.

2:21–23 *Speak to Zerubbabel.* Haggai's final address envisions a restored monarchy and affirms God's promise to David's ancestors (2 Sam 7:16); verse 23 indicates that Zerubbabel will be given the authority, symbolized by a signet ring, of one chosen by the king. Yet monarchy was a disputed institution, and other prophecies envision alternate political futures; Ezekiel depicts a Temple-centered life without a king (Ezek 40–48), and Zechariah presents the possibility of a religious and a political figure sharing leadership (Zech 4). Thus, even with its tone of promise, Haggai's address is embedded in the often-contentious reality of political life.

ZECHARIAH

The prophet Zechariah is closely associated with Haggai, as they are mentioned together in Ezra (Ezra 5:1; 6:14). The two books also share a political and historical context—Judah under Persian rule—though their forms are quite different; unlike Haggai's, Zechariah's prophecy includes dramatic visions. Also, the much longer book, Zechariah, presents at least two voices; chapters 1–8 and 9–14, often called First and Second Zechariah, are distinguishable by differences in tone, style, and time reference.

Content and Message

Like Haggai, the book of Zechariah calls the people of Israel (back) to God-centered community, even under Persian government, and is characterized by both judgment for past failures and the promise of restoration. Concerned with the daily lives of God's people after the exile, Zechariah calls for the reconstruction of the Temple: "Thus says the Lord of hosts: Let your hands be strong" (8:9). But this prophet's words also look beyond the community's immediate context, alluding to the people's history while projecting hope for the fulfillment of God's promises for their future. The diverse text of Zechariah includes visions tracing the changes to come in the world (1:1–6:15), instructions for true faithfulness (7:8–10; 8:16–17), descriptions of the good life in store for the chosen Jerusalem (8:1–8, 14–15; 12:8–9), celebration of God's lordship (8:20–23; 9:9–17), depictions of God humbling cities and nations to gather his scattered people (9:1–8; 11:1–3), the coming punishment of bad leaders (10:1–12; 11:4–17), the purging of false prophets and purification of the people (10:2; 13:1–6), the approach of the "day of the Lord" (12:1–9; 13:1–4; 14:1–21), and allusions to the coming Messiah and the peace he will bring (9:9–10; 12:10–12; 13:7–9).

God is active in this book, participating in the community's history as it moves from exile toward restoration and a time of peace, when "old men and old women shall again sit in the streets of Jerusalem. . . . And the streets of the city shall be full

See also *"The With-God Life"* essay for this section of the Bible,
"The People of God in Restoration," pp. 1355–59.

of boys and girls playing" (8:4–5). In fact, the name Zechariah means "Yahweh has remembered," and a central message in this book is Yahweh's desire for his children's *return*—to worship of their God, to a rebuilt city and Temple, and ultimately to the wonderful realization of God's promises for them.

Through the vivid language and imagery of this book, we may also be spiritually formed. We receive a call we constantly and profoundly need—God's call desiring relationship with us, calling us to return to him. We are reminded of the ultimate hope of our faith, in the Messiah who commands "peace to the nations" (9:10). We are promised newness, enduring community, and God's movement in the world on our behalf, even as we are reminded of the necessity of our action as well. May we participate in the community God is building of people "from nations of every language" (8:23), seeking in our lives and faith to "render . . . judgments that are true and make for peace" and to "show kindness and mercy to one another" (8:16; 7:9).

—*Rebekah Close LeMon*

Israel Urged to Repent

1 In the eighth month, in the second year of Darius, the word of the LORD came to the prophet Zechariah son of Berechiah son of Iddo, saying: ²The LORD was very angry with your ancestors. ³Therefore say to them, Thus says the LORD of hosts: Return to me, says the LORD of hosts, and I will return to you, says the LORD of hosts. ⁴Do not be like your ancestors, to whom the former prophets proclaimed, "Thus says the LORD of hosts, Return from your evil ways and from your evil deeds." But they did not hear or heed me, says the LORD. ⁵Your ancestors, where are they? And the prophets, do they live forever? ⁶But my words and my statutes, which I commanded my servants the prophets, did

they not overtake your ancestors? So they repented and said, "The LORD of hosts has dealt with us according to our ways and deeds, just as he planned to do."

First Vision: The Horsemen

7 On the twenty-fourth day of the eleventh month, the month of Shebat, in the second year of Darius, the word of the LORD came to the prophet Zechariah son of Berechiah son of Iddo; and Zechariah*ᵃ* said, ⁸In the night I saw a man riding on a red horse! He was standing among the myrtle trees in the glen; and behind him were red, sorrel, and white horses. ⁹Then I said, "What are these, my lord?" The

a Heb *and he*

1:2–6 *The LORD was very angry with your ancestors.* With the mention of the people's ancestors, we are reminded of the long history of the faith. We are also reminded that despite past failures, God seeks us and initiates relationship with us. Though their ancestors chose evil, God calls the people of Israel to return.

1:7–6:8 *In the night I saw.* Zechariah's eight visions, contained in these chapters, include vivid and varied imagery and symbolism. As a whole, the visions depict a progression in the history of Israel from foreshadowed restoration of Jerusalem to particular roles for the high

priest Joshua and governor Zerubbabel, to purification of the people and their worship, to a world set right by God. God is at work in history and among us, actively restoring his people.

1:7–17 *I saw a man riding on a red horse!* Zechariah's first vision includes a heavenly patrol, which finds the earth at peace. Yet the angel alludes to what is to come, asking "how long" mercy will be withheld from Jerusalem and the cities of Judah (v 12). The Lord responds with "gracious and comforting words" indicating that the Jerusalem Temple will be rebuilt and prosperity restored (vv 13–17).

angel who talked with me said to me, "I will show you what they are." [10]So the man who was standing among the myrtle trees answered, "They are those whom the LORD has sent to patrol the earth." [11]Then they spoke to the angel of the LORD who was standing among the myrtle trees, "We have patrolled the earth, and lo, the whole earth remains at peace." [12]Then the angel of the LORD said, "O LORD of hosts, how long will you withhold mercy from Jerusalem and the cities of Judah, with which you have been angry these seventy years?" [13]Then the LORD replied with gracious and comforting words to the angel who talked with me. [14]So the angel who talked with me said to me, Proclaim this message: Thus says the LORD of hosts; I am very jealous for Jerusalem and for Zion. [15]And I am extremely angry with the nations that are at ease; for while I was only a little angry, they made the disaster worse. [16]Therefore, thus says the LORD, I have returned to Jerusalem with compassion; my house shall be built in it, says the LORD of hosts, and the measuring line shall be stretched out over Jerusalem. [17]Proclaim further: Thus says the LORD of hosts: My cities shall again overflow with prosperity; the LORD will again comfort Zion and again choose Jerusalem.

Second Vision: The Horns and the Smiths

[18][a] And I looked up and saw four horns. [19]I asked the angel who talked with me, "What are these?" And he answered me, "These are the horns that have scattered Judah, Israel, and Jerusalem." [20]Then the LORD showed me four blacksmiths. [21]And I asked, "What are they coming to do?" He answered, "These are the horns that scattered Judah, so that no head could be raised; but these have come to terrify them, to strike down the horns of the nations that lifted up their horns against the land of Judah to scatter its people." [b]

Third Vision: The Man with a Measuring Line

2 [c] I looked up and saw a man with a measuring line in his hand. [2]Then I asked, "Where are you going?" He answered me, "To measure Jerusalem, to see what is its width and what is its length." [3]Then the angel who talked with me came forward, and another angel came forward to meet him, [4]and said to him, "Run, say to that young man: Jerusalem shall be inhabited like villages without walls, because of the multitude of people and animals in it. [5]For I will be a wall of fire all around it, says the LORD, and I will be the glory within it."

Interlude: An Appeal to the Exiles

6 Up, up! Flee from the land of the north, says the LORD; for I have spread you abroad like the four winds of heaven, says the LORD. [7]Up! Escape to Zion, you that live with daughter Babylon. [8]For thus said the LORD of hosts (after his glory [d] sent me) regarding the nations that plundered you: Truly, one who touches you touches the apple of my eye. [e] [9]See now, I am going to raise [f] my hand against them,

a Ch 2.1 in Heb   b Heb it   c Ch 2.5 in Heb
d Cn: Heb after glory he   e Heb his eye
f Or wave

1:18–21 *I . . . saw four horns.* Building toward the restoration promised in the first vision, Zechariah's second vision depicts four horns, representing the nations that scattered the Israelites, along with four blacksmiths (which are stronger than horns) who have come to strike those nations down. God is going to demonstrate his might over those who oppress his people.

2:1–5 *I . . . saw a man with a measuring line.* Zechariah's third vision. A man measuring Jerusalem, presumably so that its walls can be rebuilt, is stopped by the instruction of an angel.

2:4–5 *Jerusalem shall be inhabited.* The third vision indicates that greatness will come to

Jerusalem. It will be well inhabited and will not need conventional walls because God will protect it as a "wall of fire." God also pledges to dwell in Jerusalem, to be the "glory within it," an image that refers to the rebuilt Temple and God's promise of presence with his people.

2:8–9 *Truly, one who touches you.* The imagery here is intimate, reminding us that God holds us close. *the apple of my eye.* This phrase portrays the personal, cherished nature of our relationship with God, including the protective care God shows for his people. The Lord pledges to raise a hand against those who bring them harm.

and they shall become plunder for their own slaves. Then you will know that the LORD of hosts has sent me. [10]Sing and rejoice, O daughter Zion! For lo, I will come and dwell in your midst, says the LORD. [11]Many nations shall join themselves to the LORD on that day, and shall be my people; and I will dwell in your midst. And you shall know that the LORD of hosts has sent me to you. [12]The LORD will inherit Judah as his portion in the holy land, and will again choose Jerusalem.

13 Be silent, all people, before the LORD; for he has roused himself from his holy dwelling.

Fourth Vision: Joshua and Satan

3 Then he showed me the high priest Joshua standing before the angel of the LORD, and Satan[a] standing at his right hand to accuse him. [2]And the LORD said to Satan,[a] "The LORD rebuke you, O Satan![a] The LORD who has chosen Jerusalem rebuke you! Is not this man a brand plucked from the fire?" [3]Now Joshua was dressed with filthy clothes as he stood before the angel. [4]The angel said to those who were standing before him, "Take off his filthy clothes." And to him he said, "See, I have taken your guilt away from you,

and I will clothe you with festal apparel." [5]And I said, "Let them put a clean turban on his head." So they put a clean turban on his head and clothed him with the apparel; and the angel of the LORD was standing by.

6 Then the angel of the LORD assured Joshua, saying [7]"Thus says the LORD of hosts: If you will walk in my ways and keep my requirements, then you shall rule my house and have charge of my courts, and I will give you the right of access among those who are standing here. [8]Now listen, Joshua, high priest, you and your colleagues who sit before you! For they are an omen of things to come: I am going to bring my servant the Branch. [9]For on the stone that I have set before Joshua, on a single stone with seven facets, I will engrave its inscription, says the LORD of hosts, and I will remove the guilt of this land in a single day. [10]On that day, says the LORD of hosts, you shall invite each other to come under your vine and fig tree."

Fifth Vision: The Lampstand and Olive Trees

4 The angel who talked with me came again, and wakened me, as one is wak-

a Or the Accuser; Heb the Adversary

2:11–12 *Many nations shall join.* Zechariah alludes not only to the restoration of Jerusalem but also to God's sovereignty in all the world. The community of God will not be limited to Judah, but "many nations shall join themselves to the LORD" and will be claimed as God's people.

3:1–10 *Then he showed me the high priest.* Zechariah's fourth vision focuses on Joshua, the high priest, and, by extension, the Temple in Jerusalem. Joshua also received Haggai's prophecy (Hag 1:1, 12; 2:2, 4).

3:4–5 *I have taken your guilt away from you.* The removal of the high priest's "filthy clothes" symbolizes purification and the preparation of the people for their restored city. Removing dirty garments and replacing them with "festal apparel" and "a clean turban" might also represent the end of the Israelites' ordeal. In this way, the exile and their time away from right relationship with God are being removed from them and replaced with newness and cleanness.

3:7 *then you shall rule my house.* God here indicates that the priest Joshua will "rule [his]

house." Yet this, like our callings to God's service, requires right living. We, like Joshua, must walk in God's ways and keep his requirements.

3:8 *my servant the Branch.* Isa 11:1 refers to "a shoot . . . from the stump of Jesse, and a branch [that] shall grow out of his roots." The "branch" referred to in Zechariah (see also 6:12) alludes to God's promise that a descendant of David would rule as king. Zechariah, like Haggai, speaks to Zerubbabel, the Persian-appointed governor of Judah, who is of the Davidic line. Zerubbabel may be the "branch" here, though this language has significance beyond the postexilic Judean community. The "branch from the house of David" was interpreted by the early Church as a promise of the coming Messiah, consistent with the Lord's promise to "remove the guilt of this land in a single day" (v 9).

3:8 SERVICE—*See* Spiritual Disciplines Index.

4:1–10 *The angel who talked with me.* After the fourth vision's depiction of Joshua, the fifth speaks of the governor, Zerubbabel, who also received Haggai's prophecy (Hag 1:1; 2:2, 21).

PROFILE

Zechariah: The Prophet of Small Things

Selected Scriptures: *Zechariah 1–14*

A remnant of the Jewish people had just returned to Jerusalem from captivity in Babylon. They were eager to rebuild the Temple. Yet after they built an altar and laid the foundation for the new Temple, outside oppression quickly dampened their spirits and the work of rebuilding lost all momentum. The Temple foundation lay untouched for almost twenty years.

Zechariah, born in Babylon, had traveled back with the governor, Zerubbabel. As both prophet and priest, the young Zechariah became God's voice of encouragement to rebuild. The people would soon learn what God had taught their ancestors many times before. Young Zechariah reminded them that God would accomplish all he had promised, "not by might, nor by power, but by my spirit, says the LORD" (Zech 4:6).

Indeed, "whoever has despised the day of small things shall rejoice," God declared to the people through Zechariah (4:10). Zerubbabel had laid the foundation of the Temple and, though not a leader of stature like David or Solomon, he would see the building to completion as just the beginning of all God would carry out according to his word. God had even more in mind than restoring his Temple; he wanted to restore his people as well. The Israelites needed to join God in celebrating their future rather than grieving their past. Rather than focusing on the rituals of fasting in remembrance of Jerusalem's fall, the people needed to focus on living for God every day and celebrating his goodness.

"I have purposed in these days to do good to Jerusalem," God said. "Do not be afraid. These are the things that you shall do: Speak the truth to one another, render in your gates judgments that are true and make for peace, do not devise evil in your hearts against one another, and love no false oath; for all these are things that I hate" (8:15–17). God's examples were the common stuff of everyday life, the "small" areas of daily conversation and business, the attitudes of the mind, and promises made.

The early-nineteenth-century author Hannah More wrote passionately on the topic of small things: "It is important to practice the smaller virtues, to avoid scrupulously the lesser sins, and to bear patiently with minor trials. The acquisition of even the smallest virtue is actually a conquest over the opposite vice and doubles our moral strength. The spiritual enemy has one subject less, and the conqueror one virtue more. By being negligent in small things, we are not aware how much we injure Christianity in the eyes of the world. How can we expect people to believe that we are in earnest in great points when they see that we cannot withstand a trivial temptation?

"But there is a still more serious point of view to consider. Do small faults, continually repeated, always retain their original weakness? Is a bad temper which is never repressed not worse after years of indulgence than when we first gave the reins to it? . . . Before we positively determine that small faults are innocent, we must try to prove that they shall never outgrow their primitive dimensions. We must make certain that the infant shall never become a giant."

Richard Foster comments on the themes of Zechariah and More, urging Christians to consider them with "utmost seriousness": "Frankly the battle is won or lost precisely in the trifling areas of life. . . . It is the small fidelities that are most helpful in training the heart toward God. These thousands upon thousands of little actions of righteousness and peace and joy in the Holy Spirit slowly but surely change our heart. More than any other thing the small corners of life reveal who we truly are. The large virtues most often occur in a public forum and usually we are able to put on a good front when we know others are watching. It is in the unguarded moment, however, when no one is watching that what is really in our heart comes to the surface. And may the revelation of our heart be a cause for rejoicing in the goodness of God" (*Spiritual Classics*).

Surely, Zechariah faithfully proclaimed, if the people would come back to God and love him in even the small areas of their lives, they would find cause for rejoicing.

Personal Reflection

- How attentive are you to the "small" areas of your life, such as your thought life, your conversation, your truthfulness, your business life? How much do your daily habits affect your overall character and spiritual life, habits such as eating, smoking, watching television? Consider now whether God is asking you to let him rebuild you in any of these areas.

- Early on, Zechariah reminds the people of three characteristics of their ancestors: disobedience, delay in repenting, and doubt that God would follow through with what he said (1:4–6). Hannah More warns Christians against the "small" fault of "trifling," devoting our time to activities of little importance: "A life devoted to trifles not only takes away the inclination, but the capacity for higher pursuits." How might a life devoted to activities of little importance lead to disobedience, delay, or doubt? Is there an area of your life where you may need to guard against trifling?

ened from sleep. ²He said to me, "What do you see?" And I said, "I see a lampstand all of gold, with a bowl on the top of it; there are seven lamps on it, with seven lips on each of the lamps that are on the top of it. ³And by it there are two olive trees, one on the right of the bowl and the other on its left." ⁴I said to the angel who talked with me, "What are these, my lord?" ⁵Then the angel who talked with me answered me, "Do you not know what these are?" I said, "No, my lord." ⁶He said to me, "This is the word of the LORD to Zerubbabel: Not by might, nor by power, but by my spirit, says the LORD of hosts. ⁷What are you, O great mountain? Before Zerubbabel you shall become a plain; and he shall bring out the top stone amid shouts of 'Grace, grace to it!'"

8 Moreover the word of the LORD came to me, saying, ⁹"The hands of Zerubbabel have laid the foundation of this house; his hands shall also complete it. Then you will know that the LORD of hosts has sent me to you. ¹⁰For whoever has despised the day of small things shall rejoice, and shall see the plummet in the hand of Zerubbabel.

"These seven are the eyes of the LORD, which range through the whole earth." ¹¹Then I said to him, "What are these two olive trees on the right and the left of the lampstand?" ¹²And a second time I said to him,

"What are these two branches of the olive trees, which pour out the oil^a through the two golden pipes?" ¹³He said to me, "Do you not know what these are?" I said, "No, my lord." ¹⁴Then he said, "These are the two anointed ones who stand by the Lord of the whole earth."

Sixth Vision: The Flying Scroll

5 Again I looked up and saw a flying scroll. ²And he said to me, "What do you see?" I answered, "I see a flying scroll; its length is twenty cubits, and its width ten cubits." ³Then he said to me, "This is the curse that goes out over the face of the whole land; for everyone who steals shall be cut off according to the writing on one side, and everyone who swears falsely^b shall be cut off according to the writing on the other side. ⁴I have sent it out, says the LORD of hosts, and it shall enter the house of the thief, and the house of anyone who swears falsely by my name; and it shall abide in that house and consume it, both timber and stones."

Seventh Vision: The Woman in a Basket

5 Then the angel who talked with me came forward and said to me, "Look up and see what this is that is coming out." ⁶I said, "What is it?"

a Cn: Heb *gold* b The word *falsely* added from verse 4

4:6–9 *Not by might.* The foundation of the new Temple has been laid under the leadership of Zerubbabel (v 9; cf. Hag 2:18). Yet we are reminded that human strength or authority (even ingenuity) cannot make the Temple glorious or defend the people (vv 6–7). This is utterly a work of the Spirit of Yahweh, which accounts for the ritual shouts of, "Grace, grace to it" (e.g., gift). The "great mountain," perhaps a proud nation or personal foe of Zerubbabel, will indeed be humbled (made "a plain"), but by the Lord's Spirit, not by human effort. The "top stone" may be a part of the Temple (see Hag 2:15–19). Even as this vision renews God's promises to the people, it also reminds us that it is not human might that fulfills those promises, but the Lord.

4:14 *These are the two anointed ones.* In the explanation of the fifth vision, the symbolism of

the two olive trees is explained. The "two anointed ones" probably refers to Zerubbabel and Joshua, who received and obeyed God's command to rebuild the Temple and were therefore instrumental in the restoration of Jerusalem.

5:1–4 *I . . . saw a flying scroll.* The sixth vision depicts a scroll with writing on both sides. Those who steal and swear falsely will be "cut off," or punished, according to its writing. We may infer that God's commandments are written on the scroll and are thus reminded of the centrality of God's law in the life of faith.

5:5–11 *see what this is that is coming out.* In the seventh vision, the "iniquity" and "wickedness" of Israel are symbolized by a woman in a basket with a weighted cover, which is carried away by two winged women. This is perhaps a symbolic purification: sin is contained, even

He said, "This is a basket*a* coming out." And he said, "This is their iniquity*b* in all the land." [7]Then a leaden cover was lifted, and there was a woman sitting in the basket! *a* [8]And he said, "This is Wickedness." So he thrust her back into the basket,*a* and pressed the leaden weight down on its mouth. [9]Then I looked up and saw two women coming forward. The wind was in their wings; they had wings like the wings of a stork, and they lifted up the basket*a* between earth and sky. [10]Then I said to the angel who talked with me, "Where are they taking the basket?" *a* [11]He said to me, "To the land of Shinar, to build a house for it; and when this is prepared, they will set the basket*a* down there on its base."

Eighth Vision: Four Chariots

6 And again I looked up and saw four chariots coming out from between two mountains—mountains of bronze. [2]The first chariot had red horses, the second chariot black horses, [3]the third chariot white horses, and the fourth chariot dappled gray*c* horses. [4]Then I said to the angel who talked with me, "What are these, my lord?" [5]The angel answered me, "These are the four winds*d* of heaven going out, after presenting themselves before the Lord of all the earth. [6]The chariot with the black horses goes toward the north country, the white ones go toward the west country,*e* and the dappled ones go toward the south country." [7]When the steeds came out, they were impatient to get off and patrol the earth. And he said, "Go, patrol the earth." So they patrolled the earth. [8]Then he cried out to me, "Lo, those who go toward the north country have set my spirit at rest in the north country."

The Coronation of the Branch

[9]The word of the Lord came to me: [10]Collect silver and gold*f* from the exiles—from Heldai, Tobijah, and Jedaiah—who have arrived from Babylon; and go the same day to the house of Josiah son of Zephaniah. [11]Take the silver and gold and make a crown,*g* and set it on the head of the high priest Joshua son of Jehozadak; [12]say to him: Thus says the Lord of hosts: Here is a man whose name is Branch: for he shall branch out in his place, and he shall build the temple of the Lord. [13]It is he that shall build the temple of the Lord; he shall bear royal honor, and shall sit upon his throne and rule. There shall be a priest by his throne, with peaceful understanding between the two of them. [14]And the crown*h* shall be in the care of Heldai,*i* Tobijah, Jedaiah, and Josiah*j* son of Zephaniah, as a memorial in the temple of the Lord.

[15]Those who are far off shall come and help to build the temple of the Lord; and you shall know that the Lord of hosts has sent me to you. This will happen if you diligently obey the voice of the Lord your God.

Hypocritical Fasting Condemned

7 In the fourth year of King Darius, the word of the Lord came to Zechariah on the fourth day of the ninth month, which is Chislev. [2]Now the people of Bethel had sent

---

a Heb *ephah*   *b* Gk Compare Syr: Heb *their eye*
c Compare Gk: Meaning of Heb uncertain
d Or *spirits*   *e* Cn: Heb *go after them*
f Cn Compare verse 11: Heb lacks *silver and gold*
g Gk Mss Syr Tg: Heb *crowns*   *h* Gk Syr: Heb *crowns*   *i* Syr Compare verse 10: Heb *Helem*
j Syr Compare verse 10: Heb *Hen*

---

captured, and then removed altogether. The winged women take the basket to the land of Shinar (mentioned in Gen 11:2 as the location of the Tower of Babel and in Isa 11:11 as one of the places to which Israel was scattered), where a house will apparently be built for it. This symbolic vision thus alludes to the division in the people's history, intimating that it has been contained and that God's community is soon to be reconsolidated.

6:1–8 *I . . . saw four chariots.* Zechariah's eighth and final vision is reminiscent of his first;

it includes horses, now with chariots, that patrol the earth. Yet, in contrast to the foreshadowed restoration in the first vision, God has now established harmony in all the land.

6:12–15 *he shall branch out in his place.* See the note on 3:8. This oracle depicts the rebuilding of the Temple as a task not limited to the Judean community. Demonstrating the progression in this text toward God's all-inclusive community, even people "far off" will come to help with the construction, confirming the truth of Zechariah's prophecy.

Sharezer and Regem-melech and their men, to entreat the favor of the LORD, ³and to ask the priests of the house of the LORD of hosts and the prophets, "Should I mourn and practice abstinence in the fifth month, as I have done for so many years?" ⁴Then the word of the LORD of hosts came to me: ⁵Say to all the people of the land and the priests: When you fasted and lamented in the fifth month and in the seventh, for these seventy years, was it for me that you fasted? ⁶And when you eat and when you drink, do you not eat and drink only for yourselves? ⁷Were not these the words that the LORD proclaimed by the former prophets, when Jerusalem was inhabited and in prosperity, along with the towns around it, and when the Negeb and the Shephelah were inhabited?

Punishment for Rejecting God's Demands

8 The word of the LORD came to Zechariah, saying: ⁹Thus says the LORD of hosts: Render true judgments, show kindness and mercy to one another; ¹⁰do not oppress the widow, the orphan, the alien, or the poor; and do not devise evil in your hearts against one another. ¹¹But they refused to listen, and turned a stubborn shoulder, and stopped their ears in order not to hear. ¹²They made their hearts adamant in order not to hear the law and the words that the LORD of hosts had sent by his spirit through the former prophets. Therefore great wrath came from the LORD of hosts. ¹³Just as, when I ᵃ called, they would not hear, so, when they called, I would not hear, says the LORD of hosts, ¹⁴and I scattered them with a whirlwind among all the nations that they had not known. Thus the land they left was desolate, so that no one went to and fro, and a pleasant land was made desolate.

God's Promises to Zion

8 The word of the LORD of hosts came to me, saying: ²Thus says the LORD of hosts: I am jealous for Zion with great jealousy, and I am jealous for her with great wrath. ³Thus says the LORD: I will return to Zion, and will dwell in the midst of Jerusalem; Jerusalem shall be called the faithful city, and the mountain of the LORD of hosts shall be called the holy mountain. ⁴Thus says the LORD of hosts: Old men and old women shall again sit in the streets of Jerusalem, each with staff in hand because of their great age. ⁵And the streets of the city shall be full of boys and girls playing in its streets. ⁶Thus says the LORD of hosts: Even though it seems impossible to the remnant of this people in these days, should it also seem impossible to me, says the LORD of hosts? ⁷Thus says the LORD of hosts: I will save my people from the east country and from the west country; ⁸and I will bring them to live in Jerusalem. They shall be my people and I will be their God, in faithfulness and in righteousness.

a Heb *he*

7:3–10 *was it for me that you fasted?* This oracle describes the community's religious practices—mourning, fasting, and lament. Yet these have apparently become empty, performed not for the Lord, but for the people themselves. We are reminded of the hollowness of piety if it is not for the Lord's worship. Along with the people, we are told that devout faith is demonstrated, not in rote ritual, but in rendering "true judgments, . . . kindness and mercy" (v 9). We are to act on behalf of the powerless in our world, taking particular care not to do harm to widows, orphans, aliens, and the poor.

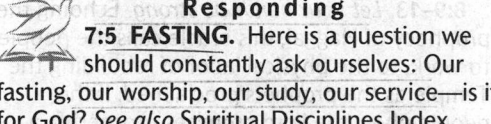

Responding
7:5 FASTING. Here is a question we should constantly ask ourselves: Our fasting, our worship, our study, our service—is it for God? *See also* Spiritual Disciplines Index.

8:1–5 *I will return to Zion.* Description of the Lord as "jealous" and full of "wrath" indicates that God will take action on behalf of Zion. This will bring the new Jerusalem, in which life will be good. The old and young alike will have prosperity and joy.
8:6–8 *Even though it seems impossible.* A reminder that even what seems impossible (according to human capability) is utterly possible with God.

9 Thus says the LORD of hosts: Let your hands be strong—you that have recently been hearing these words from the mouths of the prophets who were present when the foundation was laid for the rebuilding of the temple, the house of the LORD of hosts. 10For before those days there were no wages for people or for animals, nor was there any safety from the foe for those who went out or came in, and I set them all against one another. 11But now I will not deal with the remnant of this people as in the former days, says the LORD of hosts. 12For there shall be a sowing of peace; the vine shall yield its fruit, the ground shall give its produce, and the skies shall give their dew; and I will cause the remnant of this people to possess all these things. 13Just as you have been a cursing among the nations, O house of Judah and house of Israel, so I will save you and you shall be a blessing. Do not be afraid, but let your hands be strong.

14 For thus says the LORD of hosts: Just as I purposed to bring disaster upon you, when your ancestors provoked me to wrath, and I did not relent, says the LORD of hosts, 15so again I have purposed in these days to do good to Jerusalem and to the house of Judah; do not be afraid. 16These are the things that you shall do: Speak the truth to one another, render in your gates judgments that are true and make for peace, 17do not devise evil in your hearts against one another, and love

no false oath; for all these are things that I hate, says the LORD.

Joyful Fasting

18 The word of the LORD of hosts came to me, saying: 19Thus says the LORD of hosts: The fast of the fourth month, and the fast of the fifth, and the fast of the seventh, and the fast of the tenth, shall be seasons of joy and gladness, and cheerful festivals for the house of Judah: therefore love truth and peace.

Many Peoples Drawn to Jerusalem

20 Thus says the LORD of hosts: Peoples shall yet come, the inhabitants of many cities; 21the inhabitants of one city shall go to another, saying, "Come, let us go to entreat the favor of the LORD, and to seek the LORD of hosts; I myself am going." 22Many peoples and strong nations shall come to seek the LORD of hosts in Jerusalem, and to entreat the favor of the LORD. 23Thus says the LORD of hosts: In those days ten men from nations of every language shall take hold of a Jew, grasping his garment and saying, "Let us go with you, for we have heard that God is with you."

Judgment on Israel's Enemies

9   An Oracle.

The word of the LORD is against the land of Hadrach
and will rest upon Damascus.

8:9–13 *Let your hands be strong.* Echoing the prophecy of Haggai, this oracle calls the people to work, to the physical labor of rebuilding the Temple as the prophets proclaimed. If the people obey, the Lord promises prosperity, a reversal of their former misfortune. Faithfulness brings favor. The Lord intends to save the people so that they will "be a blessing" (v 13).

8:16–17 *These are the things.* As in 7:9–10, the Lord calls the people to speak truth, make peace, and avoid evil and false oaths. These instructions tell us how we are to be "a blessing" (v 13) as well.

8:18–19 *The fast . . . shall be seasons of joy and gladness.* Here we find an interesting conjoining of two Spiritual Disciplines not

usually thought of as going together: fasting and celebration.

Responding

8:19 FASTING. Dallas Willard writes, "In fasting, we learn how to suffer happily as we feast on God." Consider undertaking a fast as a thank-you to God for a blessing in your life. Think of it as a way to concentrate your joy. *See also* Spiritual Disciplines Index.

8:20–23 *Peoples shall yet come.* God's community grows through the addition of peoples from all nations to form a truly all-inclusive community, reminding us that God's lordship and blessing are universal.

For to the LORD belongs the capital[a] of
　　Aram,[b]
　　as do all the tribes of Israel;
2 Hamath also, which borders on it,
　　Tyre and Sidon, though they are very
　　　wise.
3 Tyre has built itself a rampart,
　　and heaped up silver like dust,
　　and gold like the dirt of the streets.
4 But now, the Lord will strip it of its
　　possessions
　　and hurl its wealth into the sea,
　　and it shall be devoured by fire.

5 Ashkelon shall see it and be afraid;
　　Gaza too, and shall writhe in anguish;
　　Ekron also, because its hopes are
　　　withered.
　The king shall perish from Gaza;
　　Ashkelon shall be uninhabited;
6 a mongrel people shall settle in Ashdod,
　　and I will make an end of the pride of
　　　Philistia.
7 I will take away its blood from its mouth,
　　and its abominations from between
　　　its teeth;
　it too shall be a remnant for our God;
　　it shall be like a clan in Judah,
　　and Ekron shall be like the Jebusites.
8 Then I will encamp at my house as a
　　guard,
　　so that no one shall march to and fro;
　no oppressor shall again overrun them,
　　for now I have seen with my own
　　　eyes.

The Coming Ruler of God's People

9 Rejoice greatly, O daughter Zion!
　　Shout aloud, O daughter Jerusalem!

Lo, your king comes to you;
　　triumphant and victorious is he,
　humble and riding on a donkey,
　　on a colt, the foal of a donkey.
10 He[c] will cut off the chariot from Ephraim
　　and the war-horse from Jerusalem;
　and the battle bow shall be cut off,
　　and he shall command peace to the
　　　nations;
　his dominion shall be from sea to sea,
　　and from the River to the ends of the
　　　earth.

11 As for you also, because of the blood of
　　my covenant with you,
　　I will set your prisoners free from the
　　　waterless pit.
12 Return to your stronghold, O prisoners
　　of hope;
　　today I declare that I will restore to
　　　you double.
13 For I have bent Judah as my bow;
　　I have made Ephraim its arrow.
　I will arouse your sons, O Zion,
　　against your sons, O Greece,
　　and wield you like a warrior's sword.

14 Then the LORD will appear over them,
　　and his arrow go forth like lightning;
　the Lord GOD will sound the trumpet
　　and march forth in the whirlwinds of
　　　the south.
15 The LORD of hosts will protect them,
　　and they shall devour and tread down
　　　the slingers;[d]
　they shall drink their blood[e] like wine,

a Heb eye   b Cn: Heb of Adam (or of humankind)
c Gk: Heb I   d Cn: Heb the slingstones
e Gk: Heb shall drink

9:1–8 *The word of the LORD is against the land
of Hadrach.* The beginning of the chapters
referred to as Second Zechariah (9–14) portrays
God's strength. God is a warrior, fighting to
reassemble the scattered Israelites, stripping the
cities' wealth, humbling them (as with the
"pride of Philistia," v 6), and correcting their
"abominations" (as with the Philistines' consuming blood, v 7). The oracle promises that
no foe will overtake Judah again.

9:9–11 *Lo, your king comes.* After the battles

promised in verses 1–8, the assurance of these
verses is peace. A humble king comes not with
fanfare, but on a colt (v 9). With universal
authority ("dominion . . . from sea to sea"), he
will end warfare and instead "command peace to
the nations" (v 10). The Gospels of Matthew and
John use the same description of a king riding a
donkey in presenting Jesus entering the city on
Palm Sunday. The overthrow of nations and
sowing of peace occur because of the covenant
between the Lord and the people (v 11).

and be full like a bowl,
    drenched like the corners of the altar.

16 On that day the LORD their God will
    save them
    for they are the flock of his people;
for like the jewels of a crown
    they shall shine on his land.
17 For what goodness and beauty are his!
    Grain shall make the young men
      flourish,
    and new wine the young women.

Restoration of Judah and Israel

10 Ask rain from the LORD
    in the season of the spring rain,
from the LORD who makes the storm
      clouds,
who gives showers of rain to you, *a*
    the vegetation in the field to everyone.
2 For the teraphim *b* utter nonsense,
    and the diviners see lies;
the dreamers tell false dreams,
    and give empty consolation.
Therefore the people wander like sheep;
    they suffer for lack of a shepherd.

3 My anger is hot against the shepherds,
    and I will punish the leaders; *c*
for the LORD of hosts cares for his flock,
      the house of Judah,
and will make them like his proud
      war-horse.
4 Out of them shall come the
      cornerstone,
    out of them the tent peg,
out of them the battle bow,
    out of them every commander.
5 Together they shall be like warriors in
      battle,

trampling the foe in the mud of the
      streets;
they shall fight, for the LORD is with
      them,
    and they shall put to shame the riders
      on horses.

6 I will strengthen the house of Judah,
    and I will save the house of Joseph.
I will bring them back because I have
      compassion on them,
    and they shall be as though I had not
      rejected them;
for I am the LORD their God and I will
      answer them.
7 Then the people of Ephraim shall
      become like warriors,
    and their hearts shall be glad as with
      wine.
Their children shall see it and rejoice,
    their hearts shall exult in the LORD.

8 I will signal for them and gather them
      in,
    for I have redeemed them,
    and they shall be as numerous as they
      were before.
9 Though I scattered them among the
      nations,
    yet in far countries they shall
      remember me,
    and they shall rear their children and
      return.
10 I will bring them home from the land of
      Egypt,
    and gather them from Assyria;
I will bring them to the land of Gilead
      and to Lebanon,

a Heb *them*   *b* Or *household gods*   *c* Or *male goats*

10:2–5 *For the teraphim utter nonsense.* After a description of God's wonderful provision for the earth (v 1), accusation is made against those who offer the people false prophecy, misleading them, confusing them, and leaving them like sheep without a shepherd (v 2). But the false prophets are not the only ones to anger God. The Lord is furious with the shepherds as well; Israel's leaders have failed to care for the people, so God will punish them (vv 3–5).

10:6–12 *I will strengthen.* In contrast to human leaders, the Lord will take action in caring for his flock. These verses use the pronoun "I" thirteen times, emphasizing God's active involvement with his people, strengthening, having compassion, answering, signaling, gathering, and bringing them home. The message of Yahweh's remembering is visible here, as is the call for us to respond to our God; the people will remember their God and will therefore return (v 9).

until there is no room for them.
¹¹ They*a* shall pass through the sea of
distress,
and the waves of the sea shall be
struck down,
and all the depths of the Nile dried up.
The pride of Assyria shall be laid low,
and the scepter of Egypt shall depart.
¹² I will make them strong in the LORD,
and they shall walk in his name,
says the LORD.

11

Open your doors, O Lebanon,
so that fire may devour your cedars!
² Wail, O cypress, for the cedar has fallen,
for the glorious trees are ruined!
Wail, oaks of Bashan,
for the thick forest has been felled!
³ Listen, the wail of the shepherds,
for their glory is despoiled!
Listen, the roar of the lions,
for the thickets of the Jordan are
destroyed!

Two Kinds of Shepherds

4 Thus said the LORD my God: Be a shepherd of the flock doomed to slaughter. ⁵ Those who buy them kill them and go unpunished; and those who sell them say, "Blessed be the LORD, for I have become rich"; and their own shepherds have no pity on them. ⁶ For I will no longer have pity on the inhabitants of the earth, says the LORD. I will cause them, every one, to fall each into the hand of a neighbor, and each into the hand of the king; and they shall devastate the earth, and I will deliver no one from their hand.

7 So, on behalf of the sheep merchants, I became the shepherd of the flock doomed to slaughter. I took two staffs; one I named Favor, the other I named Unity, and I tended the sheep. ⁸ In one month I disposed of the three shepherds, for I had become impatient with them, and they also detested me. ⁹ So I said, "I will not be your shepherd. What is to die, let it die; what is to be destroyed, let it be destroyed; and let those that are left devour the flesh of one another!" ¹⁰ I took my staff Favor and broke it, annulling the covenant that I had made with all the peoples. ¹¹ So it was annulled on that day, and the sheep merchants, who were watching me, knew that it was the word of the LORD. ¹² I then said to them, "If it seems right to you, give me my wages; but if not, keep them." So they weighed out as my wages thirty shekels of silver. ¹³ Then the LORD said to me, "Throw it into the treasury"*b*—this lordly price at which I was valued by them. So I took the thirty shekels of silver and threw them into the treasury*b* in the house of the LORD. ¹⁴ Then I broke my second staff Unity, annulling the family ties between Judah and Israel.

15 Then the LORD said to me: Take once more the implements of a worthless shepherd. ¹⁶ For I am now raising up in the land a shepherd who does not care for the perishing, or seek the wandering,*c* or heal the maimed, or nourish the healthy,*d* but devours the flesh of the fat ones, tearing off even their hoofs.
¹⁷ Oh, my worthless shepherd,
who deserts the flock!
May the sword strike his arm
and his right eye!
Let his arm be completely withered,
his right eye utterly blinded!

Jerusalem's Victory

12

An Oracle.

The word of the LORD concerning Israel:
Thus says the LORD, who stretched out the

a Gk: Heb *He*   *b* Syr: Heb *it to the potter*   *c* Syr Compare Gk Vg: Heb *the youth*   *d* Meaning of Heb uncertain

---

11:1–3 *Open your doors.* A message of humbling the proud, symbolized by the trees of Lebanon—cedars and oaks that stand strong and tall. Lebanon is invited to open its doors, but the Lord intends to devour and fell its proud trees.

11:7–14 *I became the shepherd.* A lengthy meditation on the "shepherds" of Judah. Breaking the staffs of "Favor" and "Unity"

repeats the message that the Lord will be their shepherd, breaking trust with failed leaders.

12:1–14:21 *The word of the LORD.* The tone of chapters 12–14 is one of building, impending action. The repeated references to "that day" and the "day of the LORD" refer to a coming day when God will act in judgment as well as salvation, reigning sovereign.

heavens and founded the earth and formed the human spirit within: 2See, I am about to make Jerusalem a cup of reeling for all the surrounding peoples; it will be against Judah also in the siege against Jerusalem. 3On that day I will make Jerusalem a heavy stone for all the peoples; all who lift it shall grievously hurt themselves. And all the nations of the earth shall come together against it. 4On that day, says the LORD, I will strike every horse with panic, and its rider with madness. But on the house of Judah I will keep a watchful eye, when I strike every horse of the peoples with blindness. 5Then the clans of Judah shall say to themselves, "The inhabitants of Jerusalem have strength through the LORD of hosts, their God."

6 On that day I will make the clans of Judah like a blazing pot on a pile of wood, like a flaming torch among sheaves; and they shall devour to the right and to the left all the surrounding peoples, while Jerusalem shall again be inhabited in its place, in Jerusalem. 7 And the LORD will give victory to the tents of Judah first, that the glory of the house of David and the glory of the inhabitants of Jerusalem may not be exalted over that of Judah. 8On that day the LORD will shield the inhabitants of Jerusalem so that the feeblest among them on that day shall be like David, and the house of David shall be like God, like the angel of the LORD, at their head. 9And on that day I will seek to destroy all the nations that come against Jerusalem.

Mourning for the Pierced One

10 And I will pour out a spirit of compassion and supplication on the house of David and the inhabitants of Jerusalem, so that, when they look on the one*a* whom they have pierced, they shall mourn for him, as one mourns for an only child, and weep bitterly over him, as one weeps over a firstborn. 11On that day the mourning in Jerusalem will be as great as the mourning for Hadad-rimmon in the plain of Megiddo. 12The land shall mourn, each family by itself; the family of the house of David by itself, and their wives by themselves; the family of the house of Nathan by itself, and their wives by themselves; 13the family of the house of Levi by itself, and their wives by themselves; the family of the Shimeites by itself, and their wives by themselves; 14and all the families that are left, each by itself, and their wives by themselves.

13 On that day a fountain shall be opened for the house of David and the inhabitants of Jerusalem, to cleanse them from sin and impurity.

Idolatry Cut Off

2 On that day, says the LORD of hosts, I will cut off the names of the idols from the land, so that they shall be remembered no more; and also I will remove from the land the prophets and the unclean spirit. 3And if

a Heb *on me*

12:2–5 *I am about to make Jerusalem.* In these verses, Jerusalem will be purged (and refined) in a battle, fortified by the "LORD of hosts," an image of God as warrior. The city will then be like a "heavy stone" (v 3), strong enough to withstand any opposition.

12:8–9 *On that day.* Another reference to the coming "day of the LORD"—God will protect the inhabitants of Jerusalem and defeat its enemies. These verses also indicate a partiality for the weakest among the people; God intends to make the "feeblest . . . like David." God's care is particular and individual as well as concerned with the whole of the community.

12:10 *the one whom they have pierced, they shall mourn.* God's protection of Jerusalem is

here an expression of compassion. Although it is not explicit who the pierced one is, some consider this an allusion to the "suffering servant" often depicted in Scripture (see Isa 52:13–53:12). If the pierced one is the Lord himself, this verse is unmistakably messianic.

13:1–3 *On that day a fountain shall be opened.* The need for the purification of Jerusalem is repeated. The cleansing will come by the water of a fountain as well as the Lord's action. The theme of memory is significant here, as Yahweh will erase the names of idols, so that the people cannot remember (and therefore cannot worship) them. The purification will include the false prophets who have been condemned in this book as well.

any prophets appear again, their fathers and mothers who bore them will say to them, "You shall not live, for you speak lies in the name of the LORD"; and their fathers and their mothers who bore them shall pierce them through when they prophesy. 4On that day the prophets will be ashamed, every one, of their visions when they prophesy; they will not put on a hairy mantle in order to deceive, 5but each of them will say, "I am no prophet, I am a tiller of the soil; for the land has been my possession*a* since my youth." 6And if anyone asks them, "What are these wounds on your chest?"*b* the answer will be "The wounds I received in the house of my friends."

The Shepherd Struck, the Flock Scattered

7   "Awake, O sword, against my shepherd,
      against the man who is my associate,"
            says the LORD of hosts.
  Strike the shepherd, that the sheep may
      be scattered;
  I will turn my hand against the little
      ones.
8 In the whole land, says the LORD,
      two-thirds shall be cut off and perish,
      and one-third shall be left alive.
9 And I will put this third into the fire,
      refine them as one refines silver,
      and test them as gold is tested.
  They will call on my name,
      and I will answer them.
  I will say, "They are my people";
      and they will say, "The LORD is our
      God."

Future Warfare and Final Victory

14 See, a day is coming for the LORD, when the plunder taken from you will be divided in your midst. 2For I will gather all the nations against Jerusalem to battle, and the city shall be taken and the houses looted and the women raped; half the city shall go into exile, but the rest of the people shall not be cut off from the city. 3Then the LORD will go forth and fight against those nations as when he fights on a day of battle. 4On that day his feet shall stand on the Mount of Olives, which lies before Jerusalem on the east; and the Mount of Olives shall be split in two from east to west by a very wide valley; so that one half of the Mount shall withdraw northward, and the other half southward. 5And you shall flee by the valley of the LORD's mountain,*c* for the valley between the mountains shall reach to Azal;*d* and you shall flee as you fled from the earthquake in the days of King Uzziah of Judah. Then the LORD my God will come, and all the holy ones with him.

6 On that day there shall not be*e* either cold or frost.*f* 7And there shall be continuous day (it is known to the LORD), not day and not night, for at evening time there shall be light.

8 On that day living waters shall flow out from Jerusalem, half of them to the eastern

a Cn: Heb *for humankind has caused me to possess*
b Heb *wounds between your hands*   *c* Heb *my mountains*   *d* Meaning of Heb uncertain
e Cn: Heb *there shall not be light*   *f* Compare Gk Syr Vg Tg: Meaning of Heb uncertain

---

13:5 *I am no prophet.* After the indictment of verses 3–4, prophets will disavow their profession and instead call themselves "tiller[s] of the soil." Amos also spoke these words (Amos 7:14). They could indicate humility, fear, or a changing social order that rejected prophecy because it had been falsely used.

13:7–9 *Awake, O sword.* A final message spoken against the Lord's shepherd, though the identity of the "associate" (v 7) is unclear. The land will be purged and those remaining will be "refined," or purified. The Lord will be with them, promising to answer if they call on his name. Repeating an important message in

this book, God again claims the people as his own (v 9).

14:1 *a day is coming.* The coming "day of the LORD" continues to be depicted The day will be ominous for those who bear it, bringing radical changes in the world. Though the description includes fearful images, it also demonstrates God's might and ultimate sovereignty in the cosmos.

14:8–10 *living waters shall flow.* A second water image (see 13:1), these waters are "living," doing God's cleansing, renewing work over all the earth, from the "eastern sea . . . to the western sea," and ushering in God's universal reign.

On that day!!!

sea and half of them to the western sea; it shall continue in summer as in winter.

9 And the LORD will become king over all the earth; on that day the LORD will be one and his name one.

10 The whole land shall be turned into a plain from Geba to Rimmon south of Jerusalem. But Jerusalem shall remain aloft on its site from the Gate of Benjamin to the place of the former gate, to the Corner Gate, and from the Tower of Hananel to the king's wine presses. [11]And it shall be inhabited, for never again shall it be doomed to destruction; Jerusalem shall abide in security.

12 This shall be the plague with which the LORD will strike all the peoples that wage war against Jerusalem: their flesh shall rot while they are still on their feet; their eyes shall rot in their sockets, and their tongues shall rot in their mouths. [13]On that day a great panic from the LORD shall fall on them, so that each will seize the hand of a neighbor, and the hand of the one will be raised against the hand of the other; [14]even Judah will fight at Jerusalem. And the wealth of all the surrounding nations shall be collected—gold, silver, and garments in great abundance. [15]And a plague like this plague shall fall on the horses, the mules, the camels, the donkeys, and whatever animals may be in those camps.

16 Then all who survive of the nations that have come against Jerusalem shall go up year after year to worship the King, the LORD of hosts, and to keep the festival of booths.*a* [17]If any of the families of the earth do not go up to Jerusalem to worship the King, the LORD of hosts, there will be no rain upon them. [18]And if the family of Egypt do not go up and present themselves, then on them shall*b* come the plague that the LORD inflicts on the nations that do not go up to keep the festival of booths.*a* [19]Such shall be the punishment of Egypt and the punishment of all the nations that do not go up to keep the festival of booths.*a*

20 On that day there shall be inscribed on the bells of the horses, "Holy to the LORD." And the cooking pots in the house of the LORD shall be as holy as*c* the bowls in front of the altar; [21]and every cooking pot in Jerusalem and Judah shall be sacred to the LORD of hosts, so that all who sacrifice may come and use them to boil the flesh of the sacrifice. And there shall no longer be traders*d* in the house of the LORD of hosts on that day.

a Or *tabernacles*; Heb *succoth*　　*b* Gk Syr: Heb *shall not*　　*c* Heb *shall be like*　　*d* Or *Canaanites*

14:17 *If any . . . do not go up . . . to worship.* After the promise of Jerusalem's eternal security in verse 11, this verse reminds Judah and us today that God's activity demands human response. As in Haggai, this verse indicates that those who do not turn to God in worship will not receive blessing. We may be comforted by this book's often-repeated assurance that God is acting for us, but we must not lose sight of our responsibility as participants in covenant with God. We are called to worship. It is among the most central of the Spiritual Disciplines.

MALACHI

First-generation believers are often passionate for God, whereas subsequent generations may grow cold and indifferent. This was so with the Jews returning from Babylonian captivity. Zerubbabel led the first group of exiles to the homeland in 537 BC, followed by a second under Ezra in 458, and a third under Nehemiah in 445. When Malachi (whose name means "my messenger") wrote, about 430 BC, the Temple had been rebuilt, the sacrifices reinstituted, and Jerusalem's walls restored. But after a generation or two the Jews had forgotten the painful lessons of their captivity. Priests became corrupt, and the people became hard-hearted and cynical. Men divorced their wives, withheld tithes, and insulted God with false accusations. God raised up Malachi to call priests and people back into relationship with himself. This prophecy contains four themes of spiritual formation for the wayward community.

God's Unconditional Love

God's first word to his erring people was a tender declaration of love (1:2a): God unconditionally gives himself and gifts for sinners' blessing. Divine love is not kindled by any worth or quenched by any unworthiness in us. We languish spiritually without experiential awareness of God's unconditional love for us just as we are. "The LORD, your God . . . will renew you in his love" (Zeph 3:17). Our consciousness of God's love motivates us to love him and others in return (cf. Deut 6:5; 1 John 4:19).

Responsibilities of Leadership

God was forming the returning exiles spiritually through godly leaders such as Ezra, Haggai, and Nehemiah. But the hearts of the priests drifted from vital relationship with Yahweh. Consequently, they offered unacceptable sacrifices, and their faithless teaching caused many to stumble (Mal 2:8). God looks for leaders who will walk with him, provide edifying instruction, and direct people closer to, not away from, his heart.

See also *"The With-God Life" essay for this section of the Bible,*
"The People of God in Restoration," pp. 1355–59.

Practice of Spiritual Disciplines

Malachi summoned the backslidden people to renew spiritual practices, beginning with repentance: "Return to me, and I will return to you, says the LORD of hosts" (3:7). Repentance is foreign to postmodern culture, where "What is right for me is right." But God blesses those who confess and forsake sin and return to him (3:16b–17). Another renewing discipline is meditation; the faithful in Malachi's day "thought on [God's] name" (3:16c). Pondering God's words, character, and works refreshes the heart with spiritual manna. Malachi also commended the discipline of encouragement, for "those who revered the LORD spoke with one another" (3:16a). Growing saints bless one another with words of exhortation and spiritual guidance. The prophet also emphasized the centrality of worship, in which we acknowledge God's worth and respond obediently to his leading.

Kindling of Hope

In response to the question, "Where is the God of justice?" (2:17), God promises to send one who will prepare the way for "the Lord," "the messenger of the covenant" (3:1). The Church has traditionally seen these expectations met in the coming of Jesus as God's Messiah. The Messiah's coming gives us firm hope and encourages us to persevere in the challenging pursuit of spiritual maturity and godliness.

—*Bruce Demarest*

---

1 An oracle. The word of the LORD to Israel by Malachi. *a*

Israel Preferred to Edom

2 I have loved you, says the LORD. But you say, "How have you loved us?" Is not Esau Jacob's brother? says the LORD. Yet I have loved Jacob 3but I have hated Esau; I have made his hill country a desolation and his heritage a desert for jackals. 4If Edom says, "We are shattered but we will rebuild the ruins," the LORD of hosts says: They may build, but I will tear down, until they are called the wicked country, the people with whom the LORD is angry forever. 5Your own eyes shall see this, and you shall say, "Great is the LORD beyond the borders of Israel!"

Corruption of the Priesthood

6 A son honors his father, and servants their master. If then I am a father, where is the honor due me? And if I am a master, where is the respect due me? says the LORD of hosts to you, O priests, who despise my name. You say, "How have we despised your name?" 7By offering polluted food on my altar. And you say, "How have we polluted it?" *b* By thinking that the LORD's table may be despised. 8When you offer blind animals in sacrifice, is that

a Or *by my messenger*   *b* Gk: Heb *you*

1:2–3 *I have hated Esau.* As Jacob's elder brother, Esau should have received preferential treatment. But as this reference to Genesis recalls, God sovereignly chose Jacob over Esau as a demonstration of his ravishing love for Israel. Here the mention of Jacob and Esau is meant to point us to the larger issue of ethnicity—to God's preference for Israel and his condemnation of the Edomites, the descendants of Esau. The Hebrew word translated "hate" means to love less highly or bestow fewer favors on (Gen 29:30–31; cf. Luke 14:26).

not wrong? And when you offer those that are lame or sick, is that not wrong? Try presenting that to your governor; will he be pleased with you or show you favor? says the LORD of hosts. ⁹And now implore the favor of God, that he may be gracious to us. The fault is yours. Will he show favor to any of you? says the LORD of hosts. ¹⁰Oh, that someone among you would shut the temple*a* doors, so that you would not kindle fire on my altar in vain! I have no pleasure in you, says the LORD of hosts, and I will not accept an offering from your hands. ¹¹For from the rising of the sun to its setting my name is great among the nations, and in every place incense is offered to my name, and a pure offering; for my name is great among the nations, says the LORD of hosts. ¹²But you profane it when you say that the Lord's table is polluted, and the food for it*b* may be despised. ¹³"What a weariness this is," you say, and you sniff at me,*c* says the LORD of hosts. You bring what has been taken by violence or is lame or sick, and this you bring as your offering! Shall I accept that from your hand? says the LORD. ¹⁴Cursed be the cheat who has a male in the flock and vows to give it, and yet sacrifices to the Lord what is blemished; for I am a great King, says the LORD of hosts, and my name is reverenced among the nations.

2 And now, O priests, this command is for you. ²If you will not listen, if you will not lay it to heart to give glory to my name,

says the LORD of hosts, then I will send the curse on you and I will curse your blessings; indeed I have already cursed them,*d* because you do not lay it to heart. ³I will rebuke your offspring, and spread dung on your faces, the dung of your offerings, and I will put you out of my presence.*e*

4 Know, then, that I have sent this command to you, that my covenant with Levi may hold, says the LORD of hosts. ⁵My covenant with him was a covenant of life and well-being, which I gave him; this called for reverence, and he revered me and stood in awe of my name. ⁶True instruction was in his mouth, and no wrong was found on his lips. He walked with me in integrity and uprightness, and he turned many from iniquity. ⁷For the lips of a priest should guard knowledge, and people should seek instruction from his mouth, for he is the messenger of the LORD of hosts. ⁸But you have turned aside from the way; you have caused many to stumble by your instruction; you have corrupted the covenant of Levi, says the LORD of hosts, ⁹and so I make you despised and abased before all the people, inasmuch as you have not kept my ways but have shown partiality in your instruction.

---

a Heb lacks *temple*   *b* Compare Syr Tg: Heb *its fruit, its food*   *c* Another reading is *at it*   *d* Heb *it*   *e* Cn Compare Gk Syr: Heb *and he shall bear you to it*

1:8 *will he be pleased with you or show you favor?* God challenges the spiritually indifferent priests to present their second-rate sacrifices to the Persian governor. If the civil ruler will not accept these, how much less will the jealous God? To offer the Almighty less than our costly and wholehearted devotion is to insult his majesty.

Responding
1:8, 14 SACRIFICE. God asks us for the first fruits, the best and most perfect we have, yet too often what we give to God is lame, blemished, or second-rate. This distinction applies to our prayer and worship, our tithes and service. Consider your prayer time, for example. Do you pray when you are at

your most refreshed and awake, when you can focus and concentrate? How can you give God the best you have to offer? *See also* Spiritual Disciplines Index.

1:10 *shut the temple doors.* God will be no partner to a cheap religion that seeks his favor with the least expenditure of diligence. In order to deepen relationship with God, we must invest time and treasure worthy of the awesome God of creation and redemption.

2:2 *If you will not listen.* Relationship develops as we silence distractions and devote focused attention to the other person and his or her words. We must listen attentively, for God customarily speaks, not with a loud shout, but by "a sound of sheer silence" (1 Kings 19:12).

The Covenant Profaned by Judah

10 Have we not all one father? Has not one God created us? Why then are we faithless to one another, profaning the covenant of our ancestors? [11] Judah has been faithless, and abomination has been committed in Israel and in Jerusalem; for Judah has profaned the sanctuary of the LORD, which he loves, and has married the daughter of a foreign god. [12] May the LORD cut off from the tents of Jacob anyone who does this—any to witness[a] or answer, or to bring an offering to the LORD of hosts.

13 And this you do as well: You cover the LORD's altar with tears, with weeping and groaning because he no longer regards the offering or accepts it with favor at your hand. [14] You ask, "Why does he not?" Because the LORD was a witness between you and the wife of your youth, to whom you have been faithless, though she is your companion and your wife by covenant. [15] Did not one God make her?[b] Both flesh and spirit are his.[c] And what does the one God[d] desire? Godly offspring. So look to yourselves, and do not let anyone be faithless to the wife of his youth. [16] For I hate[e] divorce, says the LORD, the God of Israel, and covering one's garment with violence, says the LORD of hosts. So take heed to yourselves and do not be faithless.

17 You have wearied the LORD with your words. Yet you say, "How have we wearied him?" By saying, "All who do evil are good in the sight of the LORD, and he delights in them." Or by asking, "Where is the God of justice?"

The Coming Messenger

3 See, I am sending my messenger to prepare the way before me, and the Lord whom you seek will suddenly come to his temple. The messenger of the covenant in whom you delight—indeed, he is coming, says the LORD of hosts. [2] But who can endure the day of his coming, and who can stand when he appears?

For he is like a refiner's fire and like fullers' soap; [3] he will sit as a refiner and purifier of silver, and he will purify the descendants of Levi and refine them like gold and silver, until they present offerings to the LORD in righteousness.[f] [4] Then the offering of Judah and Jerusalem will be pleasing to the LORD as in the days of old and as in former years.

5 Then I will draw near to you for judgment; I will be swift to bear witness against the sorcerers, against the adulterers, against those who swear falsely, against those who oppress the hired workers in their wages, the widow and the orphan, against those who thrust aside the alien, and do not fear me, says the LORD of hosts.

6 For I the LORD do not change; therefore you, O children of Jacob, have not perished. [7] Ever since the days of your ancestors you have turned aside from my statutes and have not kept them. Return to me, and I will return to you, says the LORD of hosts. But you say, "How shall we return?"

Do Not Rob God

8 Will anyone rob God? Yet you are robbing me! But you say, "How are we robbing you?" In your tithes and offerings! [9] You are cursed with a curse, for you are robbing me—the whole nation of you! [10] Bring the full tithe

---

a Cn Compare Gk: Heb *arouse*   b Or *Has he not made one?*   c Cn: Heb *and a remnant of spirit was his*   d Heb *he*   e Cn: Heb *he hates*   f Or *right offerings to the LORD*

2:14–15 *do not let anyone be faithless to the wife of his youth.* Many backslidden men of Jerusalem broke faith with their wives. The quality of our relationship with God will be no better than the quality of our relationships with others.

3:2 *who can stand when he appears?* For God's people, the appearance of the Messiah is not punitive, but purifying. God cleanses the souls of his people that they may worship him acceptably. We must welcome and cooperate with the Lord's sanctifying work in our lives.

3:5 *against those who . . . do not fear me, says the LORD of hosts.* The sins Christ will judge at his coming are social crimes—oppressing wage earners, mistreating widows and orphans, and casting aside immigrants. The taproot of these social evils, however, is a deficiency of soul—absence of fear of the Lord.

into the storehouse, so that there may be food in my house, and thus put me to the test, says the LORD of hosts; see if I will not open the windows of heaven for you and pour down for you an overflowing blessing. [11]I will rebuke the locust[a] for you, so that it will not destroy the produce of your soil; and your vine in the field shall not be barren, says the LORD of hosts. [12]Then all nations will count you happy, for you will be a land of delight, says the LORD of hosts.

13 You have spoken harsh words against me, says the LORD. Yet you say, "How have we spoken against you?" [14]You have said, "It is vain to serve God. What do we profit by keeping his command or by going about as mourners before the LORD of hosts? [15]Now we count the arrogant happy; evildoers not only prosper, but when they put God to the test they escape."

The Reward of the Faithful

16 Then those who revered the LORD spoke with one another. The LORD took note and listened, and a book of remembrance was written before him of those who revered the LORD and thought on his name. [17]They shall be mine, says the LORD of hosts, my special possession on the day when I act, and I will spare them as parents spare their children who

serve them. [18]Then once more you shall see the difference between the righteous and the wicked, between one who serves God and one who does not serve him.

The Great Day of the LORD

4[b] See, the day is coming, burning like an oven, when all the arrogant and all evildoers will be stubble; the day that comes shall burn them up, says the LORD of hosts, so that it will leave them neither root nor branch. [2]But for you who revere my name the sun of righteousness shall rise, with healing in its wings. You shall go out leaping like calves from the stall. [3]And you shall tread down the wicked, for they will be ashes under the soles of your feet, on the day when I act, says the LORD of hosts.

4 Remember the teaching of my servant Moses, the statutes and ordinances that I commanded him at Horeb for all Israel.

5 Lo, I will send you the prophet Elijah before the great and terrible day of the LORD comes. [6]He will turn the hearts of parents to their children and the hearts of children to their parents, so that I will not come and strike the land with a curse.[c]

a Heb devourer   b Ch 4.1-6 are Ch 3.19-24 in Heb
c Or a ban of utter destruction

3:12 *you will be a land of delight, says the LORD of hosts.* Material prosperity in itself does not produce soul satisfaction. Many with abundant possessions are spiritually desolate. We must labor for what nourishes our hearts—disciplined pursuit of the divine Lover and fulfilling our covenant obligations.

Responding
3:17–18 SERVICE. What sets you apart as one who serves God? *See also* Spiritual Disciplines Index.

4:2 *healing in its wings.* God promises that "the sun of righteousness" will bring healing to

his people. During his earthly ministry Jesus bound up physical wounds and healed sin-scarred souls. When he appears a second time, the healing we long for will be completed. All that has been darkened by sin will become light in the Lord.

4:5–6 *strike the land with a curse.* The Old Testament closes with God's promise to send one like the great prophet Elijah. More than four hundred years later the rugged desert preacher John the Baptist would proclaim the familiar alternatives of a blessing or a curse (cf. Deut 11:26–29)—but in the form of new life in Jesus or of fearful judgment.

THE
DEUTEROCANONICAL

BOOKS

The books and parts of books from Tobit through 2 Maccabees are recognized as Deuterocanonical Scripture by the Roman Catholic, Greek, and Russian Orthodox Churches.

Additions to Esther
Judith
1 Maccabees
2 Maccabees
Wisdom of Solomon
Wisdom of Jesus Son of Sirach (Ecclesiasticus)
Baruch
Letter of Jeremiah
Tobit
Additions to Daniel
  Prayer of Azariah and the Song of the Three Jews
  Susanna
  Bel and the Dragon

The books from 1 Esdras through 3 Maccabees are recognized as Deuterocanonical Scripture by the Greek and the Russian Orthodox Churches. They are not so recognized by the Roman Catholic Church, but 1 Esdras and the Prayer of Manasseh (together with 2 Esdras) are placed in an appendix to the Latin Vulgate Bible.

1 Esdras
3 Maccabees
Psalm 151
Prayer of Manasseh

The following book is included in the Slavonic Bible as 3 Esdras, but is not found in the Greek. It is included in the Appendix to the Latin Vulgate Bible as 4 Esdras.

2 Esdras
(Note: In the Latin Vulgate, Ezra-Nehemiah = 1 and 2 Esdras)

The following book appears in an appendix to the Greek Bible.

4 Maccabees

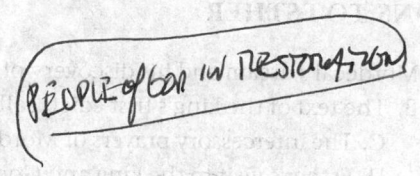

ESTHER

(THE GREEK VERSION CONTAINING
THE ADDITIONAL CHAPTERS)

There are actually two different biblical versions of the book of Esther. The Hebrew version, which forms the basis of most English translations, is the canonical book of Esther for the Jewish and Protestant traditions. The Greek version, which is the basis of St. Jerome's Latin Vulgate translation, is the canonical book of Esther for the Roman Catholic and Orthodox Christian traditions. The Greek version is basically a translation (with some alterations) of the Hebrew version to which six major additions (labeled A through F), comprising a total of 107 verses, have been made.

Although the Greek and Hebrew versions of the Esther narrative are closely related, in their final forms they are very different stories. In the Hebrew book of Esther, there is no mention whatsoever of God or any specifically Jewish religious practice (e.g., prayer, observance of the law). The Greek version, by contrast, is a deeply religious narrative. The six additions include more than fifty references to God and present Mordecai and Esther as models of faith, devotion, and adherence to the laws of Torah. Its main text also contains added religious references, such as Mordecai's advice to Esther to "fear God and keep his laws" (2:20) and to "call upon the Lord" (4:8) and the proclamation by Haman's companions that "the living God" is with Mordecai (6:13).

Overall, the Greek version of Esther places a strong emphasis on God's providential control over the events taking place in the story. The narrative moves from a crisis of the Jewish people to intercessory prayers on their behalf, to divine deliverance as an answer to those prayers. This movement is particularly clear in the layout of the six additions:

See also *"The With-God Life" essay for this section of the Bible, "The People of God in Restoration," pp. 1355–59.*

A. Mordecai's dream and his discovery of the assassination plot against the king

  B. The text of the king's first edict, calling for Jewish genocide

    C. The intercessory prayers of Mordecai and Esther

    D. Esther's visit to the king and God's conversion of the king's spirit

  E. The text of the king's second edict, undoing the earlier edict against the Jews

F. Mordecai's interpretation of his dream (Addition A) in light of the events of this story

Notice that the six additions are organized into three pairs that together create a symmetrical structure within the narrative: A and F concern the dream, with F providing the interpretation of A; B and E present the two royal edicts, with E working to counteract B; and at the center, constituting the turning point in the narrative, C and D present the prayers of Mordecai and Esther and God's answer to those prayers, with D responding to C.

We may read the Greek version of Esther as a response to the Hebrew version or even as an attempt to complete what was felt to be theologically incomplete. Indeed, for many readers, the lack of any reference to God in the Hebrew version seems to cry out for some kind of assurance of divine providence.

No doubt some readers will prefer this explicitly theological retelling of the tale, finding in it a strong affirmation of God's guidance even in the most grim of circumstances. Others will prefer the Hebrew version, finding its insistence on leaving the question of divine presence unresolved to be truer to the ambiguities of life in this world. But we need not choose one version over the other. Instead, we might reflect on the two together as different interpretations of the same story. One affirms God's presence, and one leaves it an open question. One answers the other's questions, and one questions the other's answers. Is this not an ongoing conversation within each of us as we struggle to live by faith in what is believed but not seen?

—*Timothy K. Beal*

Note: *The Deuterocanonical portions of the Book of Esther are translated from the Greek version (Septuagint) and comprise one hundred and seven additional verses that have been inserted at the appropriate places in the translation of the Hebrew form of the book. The disordered chapter numbers come from the displacement of the additions to the end of the Hebrew form of the Book of Esther by St. Jerome in his Latin Vulgate translation and from the subsequent division of the Bible into chapters by Stephen Langton, who numbered the additions consecutively as though they formed a direct continuation of the Hebrew text. The Deuterocanonical portions are given in the order found in the Greek text so that they may be read in their proper context, but the chapter and verse numbers conform to those of the King James or Authorized Version. Proper names are given according to their Hebrew rather than their Greek form; for example, Ahasuerus and Mordecai instead of Artaxerxes and Mardocheus. The additions, conveniently indicated by the letters A–F, are located as follows: A, before 1.1; B, after 3.13; C and D, after 4.17; E, after 8.12; F after 10.3.*

Mordecai's Dream

11 *a* 2In the second year of the reign of Artaxerxes the Great, on the first day of Nisan, Mordecai son of Jair son of Shimei *b* son of Kish, of the tribe of Benjamin, had a dream. 3He was a Jew living in the city of Susa, a great man, serving in the court of the king. 4He was one of the captives whom King Nebuchadnezzar of Babylon had brought from Jerusalem with King Jeconiah of Judea. And this was his dream: 5Noises *c* and confusion, thunders and earthquake, tumult on the earth! 6Then two great dragons came forward, both ready to fight, and they roared terribly. 7At their roaring every nation prepared for war, to fight against the righteous nation. 8It was a day of darkness and gloom, of tribulation and distress, affliction and great tumult on the earth! 9And the whole righteous nation was troubled; they feared the evils that threatened them, *d* and were ready to perish. 10Then they cried out to God; and at their outcry, as though from a tiny spring, there came a great river, with abundant water; 11light came, and the sun rose, and the lowly were exalted and devoured those held in honor.

12 Mordecai saw in this dream what God had determined to do, and after he awoke he had it on his mind, seeking all day to understand it in every detail.

A Plot against the King

12 Now Mordecai took his rest in the courtyard with Gabatha and Tharra, the two eunuchs of the king who kept watch in the courtyard. 2He overheard their conversation and inquired into their purposes, and learned that they were preparing to lay hands on King Artaxerxes; and he informed the king concerning them. 3Then the king examined the two eunuchs, and after they had confessed it, they were led away to execution. 4The king made a permanent record of these things, and Mordecai wrote an account of them. 5And the king ordered Mordecai to serve in the court, and rewarded him for these things. 6But Haman son of Hammedatha, a Bougean, who was in great honor with the king, determined to injure Mordecai and his people because of the two eunuchs of the king.

END OF ADDITION A

Arataxerxes' Banquet

1 It was after this that the following things happened in the days of Artaxerxes, the same Artaxerxes who ruled over one hundred twenty-seven provinces from India to Ethiopia. *e* 2In those days, when King Artaxerxes was enthroned in the city of Susa, 3in the third year of his reign, he gave a banquet for his Friends and other persons of various nations, the Persians and Median nobles, and the governors of the provinces. 4After this, when he had displayed to them the riches of his kingdom and the splendor of his bountiful celebration during the course of one hundred eighty days, 5at the end of the festivity *f* the king gave a drinking party for the people of various nations who lived in the city. This was held for six days in the courtyard of the royal palace, 6which was adorned with curtains of fine linen and cotton, held

a Chapters 11.2—12.6 correspond to chapter A 1-17 in some translations.   *b* Gk *Semeios*
c Or *Voices*   *d* Gk *their own evils*   *e* Other ancient authorities lack *to Ethiopia*
f Gk *marriage feast*

11:5–11 *Two great dragons came forward.* In Addition A, Mordecai's dream of dragons and a world war of apocalyptic proportions is presented as a divine revelation of what is to come. In the final addition (F), Mordecai will interpret his dream in light of the events of the story: he and Haman are the dragons; Esther is the tiny spring that becomes a river; and the Jews are the lowly nation that overcomes its oppressors. Thus Additions A and F place the entire story of Esther within a framework of divine revelation. Everything is anticipated ahead of time. Everything will make sense in retrospect. Nothing is left to chance. Nothing is left ambiguous.

by cords of purple linen attached to gold and silver blocks on pillars of marble and other stones. Gold and silver couches were placed on a mosaic floor of emerald, mother-of-pearl, and marble. There were coverings of gauze, embroidered in various colors, with roses arranged around them. 7 The cups were of gold and silver, and a miniature cup was displayed, made of ruby, worth thirty thousand talents. There was abundant sweet wine, such as the king himself drank. 8 The drinking was not according to a fixed rule; but the king wished to have it so, and he commanded his stewards to comply with his pleasure and with that of the guests.

9 Meanwhile, Queen Vashti *a* gave a drinking party for the women in the palace where King Artaxerxes was.

Dismissal of Queen Vashti

10 On the seventh day, when the king was in good humor, he told Haman, Bazan, Tharra, Boraze, Zatholtha, Abataza, and Tharaba, the seven eunuchs who served King Artaxerxes, 11 to escort the queen to him in order to proclaim her as queen and to place the diadem on her head, and to have her display her beauty to all the governors and the people of various nations, for she was indeed a beautiful woman. 12 But Queen Vashti *a* refused to obey him and would not come with the eunuchs. This offended the king and he became furious. 13 He said to his Friends, "This is how Vashti *a* has answered me. *b* Give therefore your ruling and judgment on this matter." 14 Arkesaeus, Sarsathaeus, and Malesear, then the governors of the Persians and Medes who were closest to the king—Arkesaeus, Sarsathaeus, and Malesear, who sat beside him in the chief seats—came to him 15 and told him what must be done to Queen Vashti *a* for not obeying the order that the king had sent her by the eunuchs. 16 Then Muchaeus said to the king and the governors, "Queen Vashti *a* has insulted not only the king but also all the king's governors and officials" 17 (for he had reported to them what the queen had said and how she had defied the king). "And just as she defied King Artaxerxes, 18 so now the other ladies who are wives of the Persian and Median governors,

on hearing what she has said to the king, will likewise dare to insult their husbands. 19 If therefore it pleases the king, let him issue a royal decree, inscribed in accordance with the laws of the Medes and Persians so that it may not be altered, that the queen may no longer come into his presence; but let the king give her royal rank to a woman better than she. 20 Let whatever law the king enacts be proclaimed in his kingdom, and thus all women will give honor to their husbands, rich and poor alike." 21 This speech pleased the king and the governors, and the king did as Muchaeus had recommended. 22 The king sent the decree into all his kingdom, to every province in its own language, so that in every house respect would be shown to every husband.

Esther Becomes Queen

2 After these things, the king's anger abated, and he no longer was concerned about Vashti *a* or remembered what he had said and how he had condemned her. 2 Then the king's servants said, "Let beautiful and virtuous girls be sought out for the king. 3 The king shall appoint officers in all the provinces of his kingdom, and they shall select beautiful young virgins to be brought to the harem in Susa, the capital. Let them be entrusted to the king's eunuch who is in charge of the women, and let ointments and whatever else they need be given them. 4 And the woman who pleases the king shall be queen instead of Vashti." *a* This pleased the king, and he did so.

5 Now there was a Jew in Susa the capital whose name was Mordecai son of Jair son of Shimei *c* son of Kish, of the tribe of Benjamin; 6 he had been taken captive from Jerusalem among those whom King Nebuchadnezzar of Babylon had captured. 7 And he had a foster child, the daughter of his father's brother, Aminadab, and her name was Esther. When her parents died, he brought her up to womanhood as his own. The girl was beautiful in appearance. 8 So, when the decree of the king was proclaimed, and many girls were gathered in Susa the capital in custody

a Gk *Astin*   *b* Gk *Astin has said thus and so*
c Gk *Semeios*

of Gai, Esther also was brought to Gai, who had custody of the women. [9]The girl pleased him and won his favor, and he quickly provided her with ointments and her portion of food,[a] as well as seven maids chosen from the palace; he treated her and her maids with special favor in the harem. [10]Now Esther had not disclosed her people or country, for Mordecai had commanded her not to make it known. [11]And every day Mordecai walked in the courtyard of the harem, to see what would happen to Esther.

12 Now the period after which a girl was to go to the king was twelve months. During this time the days of beautification are completed—six months while they are anointing themselves with oil of myrrh, and six months with spices and ointments for women. [13]Then she goes in to the king; she is handed to the person appointed, and goes with him from the harem to the king's palace. [14]In the evening she enters and in the morning she departs to the second harem, where Gai the king's eunuch is in charge of the women; and she does not go in to the king again unless she is summoned by name.

15 When the time was fulfilled for Esther daughter of Aminadab, the brother of Mordecai's father, to go in to the king, she neglected none of the things that Gai, the eunuch in charge of the women, had commanded. Now Esther found favor in the eyes of all who saw her. [16]So Esther went in to King Artaxerxes in the twelfth month, which is Adar, in the seventh year of his reign. [17]And the king loved Esther and she found favor beyond all the other virgins, so he put on her the queen's diadem. [18]Then the king gave a banquet lasting seven days for all his Friends and the officers to celebrate his marriage to Esther; and he granted a remission of taxes to those who were under his rule.

The Plot Discovered

19 Meanwhile Mordecai was serving in the courtyard. [20]Esther had not disclosed her country—such were the instructions of Mordecai; but she was to fear God and keep his laws, just as she had done when she was with him. So Esther did not change her mode of life.

21 Now the king's eunuchs, who were chief bodyguards, were angry because of Mordecai's advancement, and they plotted to kill King Artaxerxes. [22]The matter became known to Mordecai, and he warned Esther, who in turn revealed the plot to the king. [23]He investigated the two eunuchs and hanged them. Then the king ordered a memorandum to be deposited in the royal library in praise of the goodwill shown by Mordecai.

Mordecai Refuses to Do Obeisance

3 After these events King Artaxerxes promoted Haman son of Hammedatha, a Bougean, advancing him and granting him precedence over all the king's[b] Friends. [2]So all who were at court used to do obeisance to Haman,[c] for so the king had commanded to be done. Mordecai, however, did not do obeisance. [3]Then the king's courtiers said to Mordecai, "Mordecai, why do you disobey the king's command?" [4]Day after day they spoke to him, but he would not listen to them. Then they informed Haman that Mordecai was resisting the king's command. Mordecai had told them that he was a Jew. [5]So when Haman learned that Mordecai was not doing obeisance to him, he became furiously angry, [6]and plotted to destroy all the Jews under Artaxerxes' rule.

7 In the twelfth year of King Artaxerxes Haman[d] came to a decision by casting lots, taking the days and the months one by one, to fix on one day to destroy the whole race of Mordecai. The lot fell on the fourteenth[e] day of the month of Adar.

Decree against the Jews

8 Then Haman[d] said to King Artaxerxes, "There is a certain nation scattered among the other nations in all your kingdom; their laws are different from those of every other nation, and they do not keep the laws of the king. It is not expedient for the king to tolerate them. [9]If it pleases the king, let it be decreed that they are to be destroyed, and I will pay ten thousand talents of silver into the king's treasury." [10]So the king took off his

a Gk lacks *of food*   b Gk *all his*   c Gk *him*
d Gk *he*   e Other ancient witnesses read
thirteenth; see 8.12

signet ring and gave it to Haman to seal the decree[a] that was to be written against the Jews. [11]The king told Haman, "Keep the money, and do whatever you want with that nation."

12 So on the thirteenth day of the first month the king's secretaries were summoned, and in accordance with Haman's instructions they wrote in the name of King Artaxerxes to the magistrates and the governors in every province from India to Ethiopia. There were one hundred twenty-seven provinces in all, and the governors were addressed each in his own language. [13]Instructions were sent by couriers throughout all the empire of Artaxerxes to destroy the Jewish people on a given day of the twelfth month, which is Adar, and to plunder their goods.

Addition B

The King's Letter

13 [b] This is a copy of the letter: "The Great King, Artaxerxes, writes the following to the governors of the hundred twenty-seven provinces from India to Ethiopia and to the officials under them:

2 "Having become ruler of many nations and master of the whole world (not elated with presumption of authority but always acting reasonably and with kindness), I have determined to settle the lives of my subjects in lasting tranquility and, in order to make my kingdom peaceable and open to travel throughout all its extent, to restore the peace desired by all people.

3 "When I asked my counselors how this might be accomplished, Haman—who excels among us in sound judgment, and is distinguished for his unchanging goodwill and steadfast fidelity, and has attained the second place in the kingdom— [4]pointed out to us that among all the nations in the world there is scattered a certain hostile people, who have laws contrary to those of every nation and continually disregard the ordinances of kings, so that the unifying of the kingdom that we honorably intend cannot be brought about. [5]We understand that this people, and it alone, stands constantly in opposition to every nation, perversely following a strange manner of life and laws, and is ill-disposed to our government, doing all the harm they can so that our kingdom may not attain stability.

6 "Therefore we have decreed that those indicated to you in the letters written by Haman, who is in charge of affairs and is our second father, shall all—wives and children included—be utterly destroyed by the swords of their enemies, without pity or restraint, on the fourteenth day of the twelfth month, Adar, of this present year, [7]so that those who have long been hostile and remain so may in a single day go down in violence to Hades, and leave our government completely secure and untroubled hereafter."

End of Addition B

3 [14]Copies of the document were posted in every province, and all the nations were ordered to be prepared for that day. [15]The matter was expedited also in Susa. And while the king and Haman caroused together, the city of Susa[c] was thrown into confusion.

Mordecai Seeks Esther's Aid

4 When Mordecai learned of all that had been done, he tore his clothes, put on sackcloth, and sprinkled himself with ashes; then he rushed through the street of the city, shouting loudly: "An innocent nation is being destroyed!" [2]He got as far as the king's gate, and there he stopped, because no one was allowed to enter the courtyard clothed in sackcloth and ashes. [3]And in every province where the king's proclamation had been posted there was a loud cry of mourning and lamentation among the Jews, and they put on sackcloth and ashes. [4]When the queen's[d] maids and eunuchs came and told her, she was deeply troubled by what she heard had happened, and sent some clothes to Mordecai to put on instead of sackcloth; but he would not consent. [5]Then Esther summoned

a Gk lacks *the decree*   b Chapter 13.1-7 corresponds to chapter B 1-7 in some translations. c Gk *the city*   d Gk *When her*

Hachratheus, the eunuch who attended her, and ordered him to get accurate information for her from Mordecai. [a]

7 So Mordecai told him what had happened and how Haman had promised to pay ten thousand talents into the royal treasury to bring about the destruction of the Jews. [8]He also gave him a copy of what had been posted in Susa for their destruction, to show to Esther; and he told him to charge her to go in to the king and plead for his favor in behalf of the people. "Remember," he said, "the days when you were an ordinary person, being brought up under my care—for Haman, who stands next to the king, has spoken against us and demands our death. Call upon the Lord; then speak to the king in our behalf, and save us from death."

9 Hachratheus went in and told Esther all these things. [10]And she said to him, "Go to Mordecai and say, [11]'All nations of the empire know that if any man or woman goes to the king inside the inner court without being called, there is no escape for that person. Only the one to whom the king stretches out the golden scepter is safe—and it is now thirty days since I was called to go to the king.' "

12 When Hachratheus delivered her entire message to Mordecai, [13]Mordecai told him to go back and say to her, "Esther, do not say to yourself that you alone among all the Jews will escape alive. [14]For if you keep quiet at such a time as this, help and protection will come to the Jews from another quarter, but you and your father's family will perish. Yet, who knows whether it was not for such a time as this that you were made queen?" [15]Then Esther gave the messenger this answer to take back to Mordecai: [16]"Go and gather all the Jews who are in Susa and fast on my behalf; for three days and nights do not eat or drink, and my maids and I will also go without food. After that I will go to the king, contrary to the law, even if I must die." [17]So Mordecai went away and did what Esther had told him to do.

ADDITION C

Mordecai's Prayer

13 [8 b]Then Mordecai[c] prayed to the Lord, calling to remembrance all the works of the Lord.

9 He said, "O Lord, Lord, you rule as King over all things, for the universe is in your power and there is no one who can oppose you when it is your will to save Israel, [10]for you have made heaven and earth and every wonderful thing under heaven. [11]You are Lord of all, and there is no one who can resist you, the Lord. [12]You know all things; you know, O Lord, that it was not in insolence or pride or for any love of glory that I did this, and refused to bow down to this proud Haman; [13]for I would have been willing to kiss the soles of his feet to save Israel! [14]But I did this so that I might not set human glory above the glory of God, and I will not bow down to anyone but you, who are my Lord; and I will not do these things in pride. [15]And now, O Lord God and King, God of Abraham, spare your people; for the eyes of our foes are upon us[d] to annihilate us, and they desire to

a Other ancient witnesses add [6]*So Hachratheus went out to Mordecai in the street of the city opposite the city gate.   b* Chapters 13.8—15.16 correspond to chapters C 1-30 and D 1-16 in some translations. *c* Gk *he   d* Gk *for they are eying us*

13:8–14:19 *O Lord, Lord.* In Addition C, Mordecai's (13:8–18) and Esther's (14:1–19) prayers of intercession to God on behalf of the Jews are written in a style typical of other biblical prayers of intercession. Both emphasize God's providential control over all creation and all human powers, and both recall God's deliverance of the Israelites from slavery in Egypt in order to move God to a similar act of deliverance now. Mordecai's closing line, "O Lord; do not destroy the lips of those who praise you" (13:17), is a particularly poignant plea for divine compassion and mindfulness. Esther's request that God "put eloquent speech in my mouth before the lion" (14:13), her insistence that she abhors being married to a Gentile, and her refusal to eat from Haman's table identify her with Daniel, another exiled Jew who struggled to maintain the law while living in exile among ungodly enemies.

destroy the inheritance that has been yours from the beginning. 16Do not neglect your portion, which you redeemed for yourself out of the land of Egypt. 17Hear my prayer, and have mercy upon your inheritance; turn our mourning into feasting that we may live and sing praise to your name, O Lord; do not destroy the lips*a* of those who praise you."

18 And all Israel cried out mightily, for their death was before their eyes.

Esther's Prayer

14 Then Queen Esther, seized with deadly anxiety, fled to the Lord. 2She took off her splendid apparel and put on the garments of distress and mourning, and instead of costly perfumes she covered her head with ashes and dung, and she utterly humbled her body; every part that she loved to adorn she covered with her tangled hair. 3She prayed to the Lord God of Israel, and said: "O my Lord, you only are our king; help me, who am alone and have no helper but you, 4for my danger is in my hand. 5Ever since I was born I have heard in the tribe of my family that you, O Lord, took Israel out of all the nations, and our ancestors from among all their forebears, for an everlasting inheritance, and that you did for them all that you promised. 6And now we have sinned before you, and you have handed us over to our enemies 7because we glorified their gods. You are righteous, O Lord! 8And now they are not satisfied that we are in bitter slavery, but they have covenanted with their idols 9to abolish what your mouth has ordained, and to destroy your inheritance, to stop the mouths of those who praise you and to quench your altar and the glory of your house, 10to open the mouths of the nations for the praise of vain idols, and to magnify forever a mortal king.

11 "O Lord, do not surrender your scepter to what has no being; and do not let them laugh at our downfall; but turn their plan against them, and make an example of him who began this against us. 12Remember, O Lord; make yourself known in this time of our affliction, and give me courage, O King of the gods and Master of all dominion! 13Put eloquent speech in my mouth before the lion, and turn his heart to hate the man who is fighting against us, so that there may be an end of him and those who agree with him. 14But save us by your hand, and help me, who am alone and have no helper but you, O Lord. 15You have knowledge of all things, and you know that I hate the splendor of the wicked and abhor the bed of the uncircumcised and of any alien. 16You know my necessity—that I abhor the sign of my proud position, which is upon my head on days when I appear in public. I abhor it like a filthy rag, and I do not wear it on the days when I am at leisure. 17And your servant has not eaten at Haman's table, and I have not honored the king's feast or drunk the wine of libations. 18Your servant has had no joy since the day that I was brought here until now, except in you, O Lord God of Abraham. 19O God, whose might is over all, hear the voice of the despairing, and save us from the hands of evildoers. And save me from my fear!"

END OF ADDITION C

ADDITION D

Esther Is Received by the King

15 On the third day, when she ended her prayer, she took off the garments in which she had worshiped, and arrayed herself in splendid attire. 2Then, majestically adorned, after invoking the aid of the all-seeing God and Savior, she took two maids with

a Gk *mouth*

Responding

14:1–3 PRAYER. This description of Esther's ritual preparation for prayer is extraordinary. She covers her head with ashes and dung and covers the rest of her body with her tangled hair. Considered in the context of the larger story, it may be seen as an explicit denunciation of all the careful grooming that has brought her to her position. Consider this attitude of Esther's. What do you hold dear for the sake of the world? What must you cast aside to grow closer to God in prayer? *See also* Spiritual Disciplines Index.

her; [3]on one she leaned gently for support, [4]while the other followed, carrying her train. [5]She was radiant with perfect beauty, and she looked happy, as if beloved, but her heart was frozen with fear. [6]When she had gone through all the doors, she stood before the king. He was seated on his royal throne, clothed in the full array of his majesty, all covered with gold and precious stones. He was most terrifying.

[7] Lifting his face, flushed with splendor, he looked at her in fierce anger. The queen faltered, and turned pale and faint, and collapsed on the head of the maid who went in front of her. [8]Then God changed the spirit of the king to gentleness, and in alarm he sprang from his throne and took her in his arms until she came to herself. He comforted her with soothing words, and said to her, [9]"What is it, Esther? I am your husband. [a] Take courage; [10]You shall not die, for our law applies only to our subjects. [b] Come near."

[11] Then he raised the golden scepter and touched her neck with it; [12]he embraced her, and said, "Speak to me." [13]She said to him, "I saw you, my lord, like an angel of God, and my heart was shaken with fear at your glory. [14]For you are wonderful, my lord, and your countenance is full of grace." [15]And while she was speaking, she fainted and fell. [16]Then the king was agitated, and all his servants tried to comfort her.

END OF ADDITION D

5 [c] [3]The king said to her, "What do you wish, Esther? What is your request? It shall be given you, even to half of my kingdom." [4]And Esther said, "Today is a special day for me. If it pleases the king, let him and Haman come to the dinner that I shall prepare today." [5]Then the king said, "Bring Ha-

man quickly, so that we may do as Esther desires." So they both came to the dinner that Esther had spoken about. [6]While they were drinking wine, the king said to Esther, "What is it, Queen Esther? It shall be granted you." [7]She said, "My petition and request is: [8]if I have found favor in the sight of the king, let the king and Haman come to the dinner that I shall prepare them, and tomorrow I will do as I have done today."

Haman's Plot against Mordecai

[9] So Haman went out from the king joyful and glad of heart. But when he saw Mordecai the Jew in the courtyard, he was filled with anger. [10]Nevertheless, he went home and summoned his friends and his wife Zosara. [11]And he told them about his riches and the honor that the king had bestowed on him, and how he had advanced him to be the first in the kingdom. [12]And Haman said, "The queen did not invite anyone to the dinner with the king except me; and I am invited again tomorrow. [13]But these things give me no pleasure as long as I see Mordecai the Jew in the courtyard." [14]His wife Zosara and his friends said to him, "Let a gallows be made, fifty cubits high, and in the morning tell the king to have Mordecai hanged on it. Then, go merrily with the king to the dinner." This advice pleased Haman, and so the gallows was prepared.

Mordecai's Reward from the King

6 That night the Lord took sleep from the king, so he gave orders to his secretary to bring the book of daily records, and to read to him. [2]He found the words written about Mordecai, how he had told the king about the two royal eunuchs who were on guard and

---

a Gk *brother*   *b* Meaning of Gk uncertain
c In Greek, Chapter D replaces verses 1 and 2 in Hebrew.

15:8 *Then God changed the spirit of the king to gentleness.* Here in Addition D an answer to the intercessory prayers of Mordecai and Esther (Addition C) is given when God converts the spirit of the king from rage to gentleness in relation to Esther. What results is his offer to grant her wish (5:3). In this way, the king's

answer to Esther's request follows God's answer to her and Mordecai's prayers. Unlike in the Hebrew version of the story, the turning point in this narrative is not the king's favorable response to Esther, but God's favorable response to Esther and Mordecai.

sought to lay hands on King Artaxerxes. [3]The king said, "What honor or dignity did we bestow on Mordecai?" The king's servants said, "You have not done anything for him." [4]While the king was inquiring about the goodwill shown by Mordecai, Haman was in the courtyard. The king asked, "Who is in the courtyard?" Now Haman had come to speak to the king about hanging Mordecai on the gallows that he had prepared. [5]The servants of the king answered, "Haman is standing in the courtyard." And the king said, "Summon him." [6]Then the king said to Haman, "What shall I do for the person whom I wish to honor?" And Haman said to himself, "Whom would the king wish to honor more than me?" [7]So he said to the king, "For a person whom the king wishes to honor, [8]let the king's servants bring out the fine linen robe that the king has worn, and the horse on which the king rides, [9]and let both be given to one of the king's honored Friends, and let him robe the person whom the king loves and mount him on the horse, and let it be proclaimed through the open square of the city, saying, 'Thus shall it be done to everyone whom the king honors.' " [10]Then the king said to Haman, "You have made an excellent suggestion! Do just as you have said for Mordecai the Jew, who is on duty in the courtyard. And let nothing be omitted from what you have proposed." [11]So Haman got the robe and the horse; he put the robe on Mordecai and made him ride through the open square of the city, proclaiming, "Thus shall it be done to everyone whom the king wishes to honor." [12]Then Mordecai returned to the courtyard, and Haman hurried back to his house, mourning and with his head covered. [13]Haman told his wife Zosara and his friends what had befallen him. His friends and his wife said to him, "If Mordecai is of the Jewish people, and you have begun to be humiliated before him, you will surely fall. You will not be able to defend yourself, because the living God is with him."

Haman at Esther's Banquet

14 While they were still talking, the eunuchs arrived and hurriedly brought Haman to the banquet that Esther had prepared.

7 [1]So the king and Haman went in to drink with the queen. [2]And the second day, as they were drinking wine, the king said, "What is it, Queen Esther? What is your petition and what is your request? It shall be granted to you, even to half of my kingdom." [3]She answered and said, "If I have found favor with the king, let my life be granted me at my petition, and my people at my request. [4]For we have been sold, I and my people, to be destroyed, plundered, and made slaves—we and our children—male and female slaves. This has come to my knowledge. Our antagonist brings shame on[a] the king's court." [5]Then the king said, "Who is the person that would dare to do this thing?" [6]Esther said, "Our enemy is this evil man Haman!" At this, Haman was terrified in the presence of the king and queen.

Punishment of Haman

7 The king rose from the banquet and went into the garden, and Haman began to beg for his life from the queen, for he saw that he was in serious trouble. [8]When the king returned from the garden, Haman had thrown himself on the couch, pleading with the queen. The king said, "Will he dare even assault my wife in my own house?" Haman, when he heard, turned away his face. [9]Then Bugathan, one of the eunuchs, said to the king, "Look, Haman has even prepared a gallows for Mordecai, who gave information of concern to the king; it is standing at Haman's house, a gallows fifty cubits high." So the king said, "Let Haman be hanged on that." [10]So Haman was hanged on the gallows he had prepared for Mordecai. With that the anger of the king abated.

Royal Favor Shown the Jews

8 On that very day King Artaxerxes granted to Esther all the property of the persecutor[b] Haman. Mordecai was summoned by the king, for Esther had told the king[c] that he was related to her. [2]The king took the ring that had been taken from Haman, and gave it to Mordecai; and Esther set Mordecai over everything that had been Haman's.

a Gk *is not worthy of*   b Gk *slanderer*
c Gk *him*

3 Then she spoke once again to the king and, falling at his feet, she asked him to avert all the evil that Haman had planned against the Jews. 4The king extended his golden scepter to Esther, and she rose and stood before the king. 5Esther said, "If it pleases you, and if I have found favor, let an order be sent rescinding the letters that Haman wrote and sent to destroy the Jews in your kingdom. 6How can I look on the ruin of my people? How can I be safe if my ancestral nation*a* is destroyed?" 7The king said to Esther, "Now that I*b* have granted all of Haman's property to you and have hanged him on a tree because he acted against the Jews, what else do you request? 8Write in my name what you think best and seal it with my ring; for whatever is written at the king's command and sealed with my ring cannot be contravened."

9 The secretaries were summoned on the twenty-third day of the first month, that is, Nisan, in the same year; and all that he commanded with respect to the Jews was given in writing to the administrators and governors of the provinces from India to Ethiopia, one hundred twenty-seven provinces, to each province in its own language. 10The edict was written*c* with the king's authority and sealed with his ring, and sent out by couriers. 11He ordered the Jews in every city to observe their own laws, to defend themselves, and to act as they wished against their opponents and enemies 12on a certain day, the thirteenth of the twelfth month, which is Adar, throughout all the kingdom of Artaxerxes.

ADDITION E

The Decree of Artaxerxes

16 *d* The following is a copy of this letter: "The Great King, Artaxerxes, to the governors of the provinces from India to Ethiopia, one hundred twenty-seven provinces, and to those who are loyal to our government, greetings.

2 "Many people, the more they are honored with the most generous kindness of their benefactors, the more proud do they become, 3and not only seek to injure our subjects, but in their inability to stand prosperity, they even undertake to scheme against their own benefactors. 4They not only take away thankfulness from others, but, carried away by the boasts of those who know nothing of goodness, they even assume that they will escape the evil-hating justice of God, who always sees everything. 5And often many of those who are set in places of authority have been made in part responsible for the shedding of innocent blood, and have been involved in irremediable calamities, by the persuasion of friends who have been entrusted with the administration of public affairs, 6when these persons by the false trickery of their evil natures beguile the sincere goodwill of their sovereigns.

7 "What has been wickedly accomplished through the pestilent behavior of those who exercise authority unworthily can be seen, not so much from the more ancient records that we hand on, as from investigation of matters close at hand.*e* 8In the future we will take care to render our kingdom quiet and peaceable for all, 9by changing our methods and always judging what comes before our eyes with more equitable consideration. 10For Haman son of Hammedatha, a Macedonian (really an alien to the Persian blood, and quite devoid of our kindliness), having become our guest, 11enjoyed so fully the goodwill that we have for every nation that he was called our father and was continually bowed down to by all as the person second to the royal throne. 12But, unable to restrain his arrogance, he undertook to deprive us of our kingdom and our life,*f* 13and with intricate craft and deceit asked for the destruction of Mordecai, our savior and perpetual benefactor, and of Esther, the blameless partner of our kingdom, together with their whole nation. 14He thought that by these methods he would catch us undefended and would transfer the kingdom of the Persians to the Macedonians.

15 "But we find that the Jews, who were consigned to annihilation by this thrice-accursed man, are not evildoers, but are

---

a Gk *country*   *b* Gk *If I*   *c* Gk *It was written*
d Chapter 16.1-24 corresponds to chapter E 1-24 in some translations.   *e* Gk *matters beside* (your) *feet*
f Gk *our spirit*

governed by most righteous laws [16]and are children of the living God, most high, most mighty,[a] who has directed the kingdom both for us and for our ancestors in the most excellent order.

17 "You will therefore do well not to put in execution the letters sent by Haman son of Hammedatha, [18]since he, the one who did these things, has been hanged at the gate of Susa with all his household—for God, who rules over all things, has speedily inflicted on him the punishment that he deserved.

19 "Therefore post a copy of this letter publicly in every place, and permit the Jews to live under their own laws. [20]And give them reinforcements, so that on the thirteenth day of the twelfth month, Adar, on that very day, they may defend themselves against those who attack them at the time of oppression. [21]For God, who rules over all things, has made this day to be a joy for his chosen people instead of a day of destruction for them.

22 "Therefore you shall observe this with all good cheer as a notable day among your commemorative festivals, [23]so that both now and hereafter it may represent deliverance for you[b] and the loyal Persians, but that it may be a reminder of destruction for those who plot against us.

24 "Every city and country, without exception, that does not act accordingly shall be destroyed in wrath with spear and fire. It shall be made not only impassable for human beings, but also most hateful to wild animals and birds for all time.

END OF ADDITION E

8 [13]"Let copies of the decree be posted conspicuously in all the kingdom, and let all the Jews be ready on that day to fight against their enemies."

14 So the messengers on horseback set out with all speed to perform what the king had commanded; and the decree was published also in Susa. [15]Mordecai went out dressed in the royal robe and wearing a gold crown and a turban of purple linen. The people in Susa rejoiced on seeing him. [16]And the Jews had

light and gladness [17]in every city and province wherever the decree was published; wherever the proclamation was made, the Jews had joy and gladness, a banquet and a holiday. And many of the Gentiles were circumcised and became Jews out of fear of the Jews.

Victory of the Jews

9 Now on the thirteenth day of the twelfth month, which is Adar, the decree written by the king arrived. [2]On that same day the enemies of the Jews perished; no one resisted, because they feared them. [3]The chief provincial governors, the princes, and the royal secretaries were paying honor to the Jews, because fear of Mordecai weighed upon them. [4]The king's decree required that Mordecai's name be held in honor throughout the kingdom.[c] [6]Now in the city of Susa the Jews killed five hundred people, [7]including Pharsannestain, Delphon, Phasga, [8]Pharadatha, Barea, Sarbacha, [9]Marmasima, Aruphaeus, Arsaeus, Zabutheus, [10]the ten sons of Haman son of Hammedatha, the Bougean, the enemy of the Jews—and they indulged[d] themselves in plunder.

11 That very day the number of those killed in Susa was reported to the king. [12]The king said to Esther, "In Susa, the capital, the Jews have destroyed five hundred people. What do you suppose they have done in the surrounding countryside? Whatever more you ask will be done for you." [13]And Esther said to the king, "Let the Jews be allowed to do the same tomorrow. Also, hang up the bodies of Haman's ten sons." [14]So he permitted this to be done, and handed over to the Jews of the city the bodies of Haman's sons to hang up. [15]The Jews who were in Susa gathered on the fourteenth and killed three hundred people, but took no plunder.

16 Now the other Jews in the kingdom gathered to defend themselves, and got relief from their enemies. They destroyed fifteen

a Gk *greatest*   *b* Other ancient authorities read *for us*   *c* Meaning of Gk uncertain. Some ancient authorities add verse 5, *So the Jews struck down all their enemies with the sword, killing and destroying them, and they did as they pleased to those who hated them.*   *d* Other ancient authorities read *did not indulge*

thousand of them, but did not engage in plunder. [17] On the fourteenth day they rested and made that same day a day of rest, celebrating it with joy and gladness. [18] The Jews who were in Susa, the capital, came together also on the fourteenth, but did not rest. They celebrated the fifteenth with joy and gladness. [19] On this account then the Jews who are scattered around the country outside Susa keep the fourteenth of Adar as a joyful holiday, and send presents of food to one another, while those who live in the large cities keep the fifteenth day of Adar as their joyful holiday, also sending presents to one another.

The Festival of Purim

20 Mordecai recorded these things in a book, and sent it to the Jews in the kingdom of Artaxerxes both near and far, [21] telling them that they should keep the fourteenth and fifteenth days of Adar, [22] for on these days the Jews got relief from their enemies. The whole month (namely, Adar), in which their condition had been changed from sorrow into gladness and from a time of distress to a holiday, was to be celebrated as a time for feasting[a] and gladness and for sending presents of food to their friends and to the poor. 23 So the Jews accepted what Mordecai had written to them [24]—how Haman son of Hammedatha, the Macedonian,[b] fought against them, how he made a decree and cast lots[c] to destroy them, [25] and how he went in to the king, telling him to hang Mordecai; but the wicked plot he had devised against the Jews came back upon himself, and he and his sons were hanged. [26] Therefore these days were called "Purim," because of the lots (for in their language this is the word that means "lots"). And so, because of what was written in this letter, and because of what they had experienced in this affair and what had befallen them, Mordecai established this festi-

val,[d] [27] and the Jews took upon themselves, upon their descendants, and upon all who would join them, to observe it without fail.[e] These days of Purim should be a memorial and kept from generation to generation, in every city, family, and country. [28] These days of Purim were to be observed for all time, and the commemoration of them was never to cease among their descendants.

29 Then Queen Esther daughter of Aminadab along with Mordecai the Jew wrote down what they had done, and gave full authority to the letter about Purim.[f] [31] And Mordecai and Queen Esther established this decision on their own responsibility, pledging their own well-being to the plan.[e] [32] Esther established it by a decree forever, and it was written for a memorial.

10 The king levied a tax upon his kingdom both by land and sea. [2] And as for his power and bravery, and the wealth and glory of his kingdom, they were recorded in the annals of the kings of the Persians and the Medes. [3] Mordecai acted with authority on behalf of King Artaxerxes and was great in the kingdom, as well as honored by the Jews. His way of life was such as to make him beloved to his whole nation.

ADDITION F

Mordecai's Dream Fulfilled

4[g] And Mordecai said, "These things have come from God; [5] for I remember the dream that I had concerning these matters, and

a Gk of weddings   b Other ancient witnesses read the Bougean   c Gk a lot   d Gk he established (it)   e Meaning of Gk uncertain   f Verse 30 in Heb is lacking in Gk: Letters were sent to all the Jews, to the one hundred twenty-seven provinces of the kingdom of Ahasuerus, in words of peace and truth.   g Chapter 10.4-13 and 11.1 correspond to chapter F 1-11 in some translations.

10:4–13 *These things have come from God.* Here in Addition F Mordecai now explains the riddle of his dream (11:5–11 in Addition A). Thus the entire narrative is framed by the divine revelation of the dream and its interpretation. Throughout his interpretation, moreover, Mordecai emphasizes that it was God, not himself or Esther, who delivered the people. Indeed, the fact that all the events of the story had been predicted in Mordecai's dream is given as further proof that nothing was an accident or left to chance. All was part of God's providential plan.

none of them has failed to be fulfilled. [6]There was the little spring that became a river, and there was light and sun and abundant water—the river is Esther, whom the king married and made queen. [7]The two dragons are Haman and myself. [8]The nations are those that gathered to destroy the name of the Jews. [9]And my nation, this is Israel, who cried out to God and was saved. The Lord has saved his people; the Lord has rescued us from all these evils; God has done great signs and wonders, wonders that have never happened among the nations. [10]For this purpose he made two lots, one for the people of God and one for all the nations, [11]and these two lots came to the hour and moment and day of decision before God and among all the nations. [12]And God remembered his people and vindicated his inheritance. [13]So they will observe these days in the month of Adar, on the fourteenth and fifteenth[a] of that month, with an assembly and joy and gladness before God, from generation to generation forever among his people Israel."

Postscript

11 [1]In the fourth year of the reign of Ptolemy and Cleopatra, Dositheus, who said that he was a priest and a Levite,[b] and his son Ptolemy brought to Egypt[c] the preceding Letter about Purim, which they said was authentic and had been translated by Lysimachus son of Ptolemy, one of the residents of Jerusalem.

END OF ADDITION F

a Other ancient authorities lack *and fifteenth*
b Or *priest, and Levitas*   c Cn: Gk *brought in*

1 ESDRAS

The book of 1 Esdras retells the story of 2 Chronicles 35–36, Ezra, and Nehemiah 8. The opening six chapters contain many chronological contradictions, the result of the author's clumsy attempt to bring the figure of Zerubbabel, a descendant of David, to greater prominence. The author rearranges the events found in the book of Ezra (Esdras is the Greek form of this Hebrew name) to introduce a court tale, the tale of the three bodyguards, from which Zerubbabel will emerge as the hero. His intervention in the court of King Darius reinitiates the reconstruction of the Temple. Moreover, the work of Nehemiah is overlooked entirely, so as to make the restoration of Jerusalem Zerubbabel's achievement. Making a descendant of David a key player in the restoration after the exile is the author's way of showing how God has indeed been faithful to his promises to David's dynasty, restoring the "booth of David that is fallen" (Amos 9:11). This would have appealed to early Christians, moreover, since it glorified one of Jesus' ancestors (see Matt 1:12–13; Luke 3:27)

A Priesthood of Pedigree

This book underscores the importance of genealogical pedigree, of lineage, for belonging to the People of God and for one's role in the People of God. Only those who can demonstrate their connection with a family known from preexilic Israel are included in the People of God, and priesthood is strictly a matter of family pedigree. Moreover, the bloodlines of Israel cannot be mixed with those of the "peoples of the land" (8:92) through intermarriage (a group that included not only Gentiles, but also many Jews left behind during the exile, who were now cut off from the "congregation of the exile," which returned and took power during the reforms). 1 Esdras thus represents the stream against which early Christians would swim as they proclaimed that trusting in Jesus could make Gentiles part of Israel and descendants of Abraham (see Gal 3:26–29; Matt 3:7–10; John 8:33–41). The idea that "fleshly qualifications" were essential for priesthood would also be swept aside by the author of Hebrews in

See also *"The With-God Life" essays for this section of the Bible, "The People of God as a Nation,"*
pp. 391–96, and "The People of God in Restoration," pp. 1355–59.

favor of the high-priesthood of Jesus, qualified not by bloodline but by virtue of an indestructible life (Heb 7:5, 13–16).

Renewal Through Festivals

The book of 1 Esdras is structured around the observance of two key religious festivals, Passover and Booths (Succoth). The book begins with Josiah's observance of the Passover in Jerusalem; the Festival of Booths punctuates the return of the exiles and the beginning of work on the Temple (5:47–73); and the observance of Passover marks the completion of the Temple after significant obstacles have been overcome (7:1–15). The ending of the book has almost certainly been lost, as it breaks off in midsentence. In the original form, the book would have told at least of the observance of the Festival of Booths, the episode begun in 1 Esd 9:55 ("they came together") and narrated in full in Neh 8:13–18.

The rhythms of 1 Esdras show a people connecting their experience of God's working in their midst with the story of God's past acts of salvation celebrated in the liturgical year. The structure of the book invites us to consider how the rhythms of our liturgical year (Advent, Christmas, Lent, Holy Week, Pentecost) structure and lend meaning to our own lives, and how they provide opportunities for our own spiritual renewal as we intentionally invite God's mighty acts of deliverance anew into our lives each year.

—David A. deSilva

Josiah Celebrates the Passover

1 Josiah kept the passover to his Lord in Jerusalem; he killed the passover lamb on the fourteenth day of the first month, 2having placed the priests according to their divisions, arrayed in their vestments, in the temple of the Lord. 3He told the Levites, the temple servants of Israel, that they should sanctify themselves to the Lord and put the holy ark of the Lord in the house that King Solomon, son of David, had built; 4and he said, "You need no longer carry it on your shoulders. Now worship the Lord your God and serve his people Israel; prepare yourselves by your families and kindred, 5in accordance with the directions of King David of Israel and the magnificence of his son Solomon. Stand in order in the temple according to the groupings of the ancestral houses of you Levites, who minister before your kindred the people of Israel, 6and kill the passover lamb and prepare the sacrifices for your kindred, and keep the passover according to

---

1:1 *Josiah kept the passover to his Lord.* (See also vv 20–22.) The story of Josiah's Passover appears here without a context; in 2 Chronicles it is the climax of a reign that has been marked by the rediscovery of the law and wholehearted commitment to bringing the people back in line with God's vision for them and their relationship with their covenant God. Passover is ideally suited for a time of recommitment to God, as the people remember how God liberated them from Egypt and redeemed them to be God's special possession. The Christian liturgical year offers many such opportunities to reflect on God's acts on our behalf in Jesus (Christmas, Holy Week, Easter) and in the giving of the Spirit (Pentecost) and also offers us seasons of renewal and rededication (Advent, Lent) during which to heighten our attention to the spiritual life. Keeping these festivals "to our Lord," making the most of these opportunities to take Jesus' life into our lives, is a Spiritual Discipline not to be neglected.

the commandment of the Lord that was given to Moses."

7 To the people who were present Josiah gave thirty thousand lambs and kids, and three thousand calves; these were given from the king's possessions, as he promised, to the people and the priests and Levites. 8Hilkiah, Zechariah, and Jehiel,*a* the chief officers of the temple, gave to the priests for the passover two thousand six hundred sheep and three hundred calves. 9And Jeconiah and Shemaiah and his brother Nethanel, and Hashabiah and Ochiel and Joram, captains over thousands, gave the Levites for the passover five thousand sheep and seven hundred calves.

10 This is what took place. The priests and the Levites, having the unleavened bread, stood in proper order according to kindred 11and the grouping of the ancestral houses, before the people, to make the offering to the Lord as it is written in the book of Moses; this they did in the morning. 12They roasted the passover lamb with fire, as required; and they boiled the sacrifices in bronze pots and caldrons, with a pleasing odor, 13and carried them to all the people. Afterward they prepared the passover for themselves and for their kindred the priests, the sons of Aaron, 14because the priests were offering the fat until nightfall; so the Levites prepared it for themselves and for their kindred the priests, the sons of Aaron. 15The temple singers, the sons of Asaph, were in their place according to the arrangement made by David, and also Asaph, Zechariah, and Eddinus, who represented the king. 16The gatekeepers were at each gate; no one needed to interrupt his daily duties, for their kindred the Levites prepared the passover for them.

17 So the things that had to do with the sacrifices to the Lord were accomplished that day: the passover was kept 18and the sacri-

fices were offered on the altar of the Lord, according to the command of King Josiah. 19And the people of Israel who were present at that time kept the passover and the festival of unleavened bread seven days. 20No passover like it had been kept in Israel since the times of the prophet Samuel; 21none of the kings of Israel had kept such a passover as was kept by Josiah and the priests and Levites and the people of Judah and all of Israel who were living in Jerusalem. 22In the eighteenth year of the reign of Josiah this passover was kept.

The End of Josiah's Reign

23 And the deeds of Josiah were upright in the sight of the Lord, for his heart was full of godliness. 24In ancient times the events of his reign have been recorded—concerning those who sinned and acted wickedly toward the Lord beyond any other people or kingdom, and how they grieved the Lord*b* deeply, so that the words of the Lord fell upon Israel.

25 After all these acts of Josiah, it happened that Pharaoh, king of Egypt, went to make war at Carchemish on the Euphrates, and Josiah went out against him. 26And the king of Egypt sent word to him saying, "What have we to do with each other, O king of Judea? 27I was not sent against you by the Lord God, for my war is at the Euphrates. And now the Lord is with me! The Lord is with me, urging me on! Stand aside, and do not oppose the Lord."

28 Josiah, however, did not turn back to his chariot, but tried to fight with him, and did not heed the words of the prophet Jeremiah from the mouth of the Lord. 29He joined battle with him in the plain of Megiddo, and the commanders came down

a Gk *Esyelus*   *b* Gk *him*

1:28 *the words of the prophet Jeremiah from the mouth of the Lord.* (See also vv 47, 50–52.) God is present for his people through the words of the prophets who speak in God's name. Through these words, God will shepherd his people to safety. The second half of chapter 1, however, is dominated by a series of tragedies that result when the People of God do not submit

their own desires and agendas to the word they receive from God. The fact that this fatal mistake could claim the life of the righteous and God-loving king Josiah as well as the self-promoting and godless opportunist Zedekiah warns us that it is all too easy even for God-seekers to become more closely attached to their plans and dreams than to the path God calls them to follow.

against King Josiah. [30]The king said to his servants, "Take me away from the battle, for I am very weak." And immediately his servants took him out of the line of battle. [31]He got into his second chariot; and after he was brought back to Jerusalem he died, and was buried in the tomb of his ancestors.

[32] In all Judea they mourned for Josiah. The prophet Jeremiah lamented for Josiah, and the principal men, with the women,[a] have made lamentation for him to this day; it was ordained that this should always be done throughout the whole nation of Israel. [33]These things are written in the book of the histories of the kings of Judea; and every one of the acts of Josiah, and his splendor, and his understanding of the law of the Lord, and the things that he had done before, and these that are now told, are recorded in the book of the kings of Israel and Judah.

The Last Kings of Judah

[34] The men of the nation took Jeconiah[b] son of Josiah, who was twenty-three years old, and made him king in succession to his father Josiah. [35]He reigned three months in Judah and Jerusalem. Then the king of Egypt deposed him from reigning in Jerusalem, [36]and fined the nation one hundred talents of silver and one talent of gold. [37]The king of Egypt made his brother Jehoiakim king of Judea and Jerusalem. [38]Jehoiakim put the nobles in prison, and seized his brother Zarius and brought him back from Egypt.

[39] Jehoiakim was twenty-five years old when he began to reign in Judea and Jerusalem; he did what was evil in the sight of the Lord. [40]King Nebuchadnezzar of Babylon came up against him; he bound him with a chain of bronze and took him away to Babylon. [41]Nebuchadnezzar also took some holy vessels of the Lord, and carried them away, and stored them in his temple in Babylon. [42]But the things that are reported about Jehoiakim,[c] and his uncleanness and impiety, are written in the annals of the kings.

[43] His son Jehoiachin[d] became king in his place; when he was made king he was eighteen years old, [44]and he reigned three months and ten days in Jerusalem. He did what was evil in the sight of the Lord. [45]A year later Nebuchadnezzar sent and removed him to Babylon, with the holy vessels of the Lord, [46]and made Zedekiah king of Judea and Jerusalem.

The Fall of Jerusalem

Zedekiah was twenty-one years old, and he reigned eleven years. [47]He also did what was evil in the sight of the Lord, and did not heed the words that were spoken by the prophet Jeremiah from the mouth of the Lord. [48]Although King Nebuchadnezzar had made him swear by the name of the Lord, he broke his oath and rebelled; he stiffened his neck and hardened his heart and transgressed the laws of the Lord, the God of Israel. [49]Even the leaders of the people and of the priests committed many acts of sacrilege and lawlessness beyond all the unclean deeds of all the nations, and polluted the temple of the Lord in Jerusalem—the temple that God had made holy. [50]The God of their ancestors sent his messenger to call them back, because he would have spared them and his dwelling place. [51]But they mocked his messengers, and whenever the Lord spoke, they scoffed at his prophets, [52]until in his anger against his people because of their ungodly acts he gave command to bring against them the kings of the Chaldeans. [53]These killed their young men with the sword around their holy temple, and did not spare young man or young woman,[e] old man or child, for he gave them all into their hands. [54]They took all the holy vessels of the Lord, great and small, the treasure chests of the Lord, and the royal stores, and carried them away to Babylon. [55]They burned the house of the Lord, broke down the walls of Jerusalem, burned their towers with fire, [56]and utterly destroyed all its glorious things. The survivors he led away to Babylon with the sword, [57]and they were servants to him and to his sons until the Persians began to reign, in fulfillment of the word of the Lord by the mouth of Jeremiah, [58]saying, "Until the land has enjoyed its sabbaths, it shall keep sabbath all the time of its desolation until the completion of seventy years."

a Or their wives   b 2 Kings 23.30; 2 Chr 36.1 Jehoahaz   c Gk him   d Gk Jehoiakim
e Gk virgin

Cyrus Permits the Exiles to Return

2 In the first year of Cyrus as king of the Persians, so that the word of the Lord by the mouth of Jeremiah might be accomplished— 2the Lord stirred up the spirit of King Cyrus of the Persians, and he made a proclamation throughout all his kingdom and also put it in writing:

3 "Thus says Cyrus king of the Persians: The Lord of Israel, the Lord Most High, has made me king of the world, 4and he has commanded me to build him a house at Jerusalem, which is in Judea. 5If any of you, therefore, are of his people, may your Lord be with you; go up to Jerusalem, which is in Judea, and build the house of the Lord of Israel—he is the Lord who dwells in Jerusalem— 6and let each of you, wherever you may live, be helped by the people of your place with gold and silver, 7with gifts and with horses and cattle, besides the other things added as votive offerings for the temple of the Lord that is in Jerusalem."

8 Then arose the heads of families of the tribes of Judah and Benjamin, and the priests and the Levites, and all whose spirit the Lord had stirred to go up to build the house in Jerusalem for the Lord; 9their neighbors helped them with everything, with silver and gold, with horses and cattle, and with a very great number of votive offerings from many whose hearts were stirred.

10 King Cyrus also brought out the holy vessels of the Lord that Nebuchadnezzar had carried away from Jerusalem and stored in his temple of idols. 11When King Cyrus of the Persians brought these out, he gave them to Mithridates, his treasurer, 12and by him they were given to Sheshbazzar,a the governor of Judea. 13The number of these was: one thousand gold cups, one thousand silver cups, twenty-nine silver censers, thirty gold bowls, two thousand four hundred ten silver bowls, and one thousand other vessels. 14All the vessels were handed over, gold and silver, five thousand four hundred sixty-nine, 15and they were carried back by Sheshbazzar

with the returning exiles from Babylon to Jerusalem.

Opposition to Rebuilding Jerusalem

16 In the time of King Artaxerxes of the Persians, Bishlam, Mithridates, Tabeel, Rehum, Beltethmus, the scribe Shimshai, and the rest of their associates, living in Samaria and other places, wrote him the following letter, against those who were living in Judea and Jerusalem:

17 "To King Artaxerxes our lord, your servants the recorder Rehum and the scribe Shimshai and the other members of their council, and the judges in Coelesyria and Phoenicia: 18Let it now be known to our lord the king that the Jews who came up from you to us have gone to Jerusalem and are building that rebellious and wicked city, repairing its market places and walls and laying the foundations for a temple. 19Now if this city is built and the walls finished, they will not only refuse to pay tribute but will even resist kings. 20Since the building of the temple is now going on, we think it best not to neglect such a matter, 21but to speak to our lord the king, in order that, if it seems good to you, search may be made in the records of your ancestors. 22You will find in the annals what has been written about them, and will learn that this city was rebellious, troubling both kings and other cities, 23and that the Jews were rebels and kept setting up blockades in it from of old. That is why this city was laid waste. 24Therefore we now make known to you, O lord and king, that if this city is built and its walls finished, you will no longer have access to Coelesyria and Phoenicia."

25 Then the king, in reply to the recorder Rehum, Beltethmus, the scribe Shimshai, and the others associated with them and living in Samaria and Syria and Phoenicia, wrote as follows:

26 "I have read the letter that you sent me. So I ordered search to be made, and it has been found that this city from of old has

a Gk Sanabassaros

2:2 the Lord stirred up the spirit of King Cyrus. God is present for his people in rulers who do

what is just, who release people from conditions of oppression, exile, and alienation.

fought against kings, 27that the people in it were given to rebellion and war, and that mighty and cruel kings ruled in Jerusalem and exacted tribute from Coelesyria and Phoenicia. 28Therefore I have now issued orders to prevent these people from building the city and to take care that nothing more be done 29and that such wicked proceedings go no further to the annoyance of kings."

30 Then, when the letter from King Artaxerxes was read, Rehum and the scribe Shimshai and their associates went quickly to Jerusalem, with cavalry and a large number of armed troops, and began to hinder the builders. And the building of the temple in Jerusalem stopped until the second year of the reign of King Darius of the Persians.

The Debate of the Three Bodyguards

3 Now King Darius gave a great banquet for all that were under him, all that were born in his house, and all the nobles of Media and Persia, 2and all the satraps and generals and governors that were under him in the hundred twenty-seven satrapies from India to Ethiopia. 3They ate and drank, and when they were satisfied they went away, and King Darius went to his bedroom; he went to sleep, but woke up again.

4 Then the three young men of the bodyguard, who kept guard over the person of the king, said to one another, 5"Let each of us state what one thing is strongest; and to the one whose statement seems wisest, King Darius will give rich gifts and great honors of victory. 6He shall be clothed in purple, and drink from gold cups, and sleep on a gold bed, a and have a chariot with gold bridles, and a turban of fine linen, and a necklace around his neck; 7and because of his wisdom he shall sit next to Darius and shall be called Kinsman of Darius."

8 Then each wrote his own statement, and they sealed them and put them under the pillow of King Darius, 9and said, "When the king wakes, they will give him the writing; and to the one whose statement the king and the three nobles of Persia judge to be wisest the victory shall be given according to what is written." 10The first wrote, "Wine is strongest." 11The second wrote, "The king is strongest." 12The third wrote, "Women are strongest, but above all things truth is victor." b

13 When the king awoke, they took the writing and gave it to him, and he read it. 14Then he sent and summoned all the nobles of Persia and Media and the satraps and generals and governors and prefects, 15and he took his seat in the council chamber, and the writing was read in their presence. 16He said, "Call the young men, and they shall explain their statements." So they were summoned, and came in. 17They said to them, "Explain to us what you have written."

The Speech about Wine

Then the first, who had spoken of the strength of wine, began and said: 18"Gentlemen, how is wine the strongest? It leads astray the minds of all who drink it. 19It makes equal the mind of the king and the orphan, of the slave and the free, of the poor and the rich. 20It turns every thought to feasting and mirth, and forgets all sorrow and debt. 21It makes all hearts feel rich, forgets kings and satraps, and makes everyone talk in millions. c 22When people drink they forget to be friendly with friends and kindred, and before long they draw their swords. 23And when they recover from the wine, they do not remember what they have done. 24Gentlemen, is not wine the strongest, since it forces people to do these things?" When he had said this, he stopped speaking.

a Gk on gold   b Or but truth is victor over all things
c Gk talents

3:18–24 *how is wine the strongest?* People in sorrow, anxiety, or pain can turn to healthful and healing resources, like God and the community of faith, or to resources that mask the pain. Wine (and alcohol and other substances more broadly) is such a painkiller. But like all painkillers, it neither makes the realities of life any better nor equips users to deal with those realities, and even tacks on its own surcharge (here through subverting the mind's grasp on reality and injuring relationships).

The Speech about the King

4 Then the second, who had spoken of the strength of the king, began to speak: ²"Gentlemen, are not men strongest, who rule over land and sea and all that is in them? ³But the king is stronger; he is their lord and master, and whatever he says to them they obey. ⁴If he tells them to make war on one another, they do it; and if he sends them out against the enemy, they go, and conquer mountains, walls, and towers. ⁵They kill and are killed, and do not disobey the king's command; if they win the victory, they bring everything to the king—whatever spoil they take and everything else. ⁶Likewise those who do not serve in the army or make war but till the soil; whenever they sow and reap, they bring some to the king; and they compel one another to pay taxes to the king. ⁷And yet he is only one man! If he tells them to kill, they kill; if he tells them to release, they release; ⁸if he tells them to attack, they attack; if he tells them to lay waste, they lay waste; if he tells them to build, they build; ⁹if he tells them to cut down, they cut down; if he tells them to plant, they plant. ¹⁰All his people and his armies obey him. Furthermore, he reclines, he eats and drinks and sleeps, ¹¹but they keep watch around him, and no one may go away to attend to his own affairs, nor do they disobey him. ¹²Gentlemen, why is not the king the strongest, since he is to be obeyed in this fashion?" And he stopped speaking.

The Speech about Women

13 Then the third, who had spoken of women and truth (and this was Zerubbabel), began to speak: ¹⁴"Gentlemen, is not the king great, and are not men many, and is not wine strong? Who is it, then, that rules them, or has the mastery over them? Is it not women? ¹⁵Women gave birth to the king and to every people that rules over sea and land. ¹⁶From women they came; and women brought up the very men who plant the vineyards from which comes wine. ¹⁷Women make men's clothes; they bring men glory; men cannot ex-ist without women. ¹⁸If men gather gold and silver or any other beautiful thing, and then see a woman lovely in appearance and beauty, ¹⁹they let all those things go, and gape at her, and with open mouths stare at her, and all prefer her to gold or silver or any other beautiful thing. ²⁰A man leaves his own father, who brought him up, and his own country, and clings to his wife. ²¹With his wife he ends his days, with no thought of his father or his mother or his country. ²²Therefore you must realize that women rule over you!

"Do you not labor and toil, and bring everything and give it to women? ²³A man takes his sword, and goes out to travel and rob and steal and to sail the sea and rivers; ²⁴he faces lions, and he walks in darkness, and when he steals and robs and plunders, he brings it back to the woman he loves. ²⁵A man loves his wife more than his father or his mother. ²⁶Many men have lost their minds because of women, and have become slaves because of them. ²⁷Many have perished, or stumbled, or sinned because of women. ²⁸And now do you not believe me?

"Is not the king great in his power? Do not all lands fear to touch him? ²⁹Yet I have seen him with Apame, the king's concubine, the daughter of the illustrious Bartacus; she would sit at the king's right hand ³⁰and take the crown from the king's head and put it on her own, and slap the king with her left hand. ³¹At this the king would gaze at her with mouth agape. If she smiles at him, he laughs; if she loses her temper with him, he flatters her, so that she may be reconciled to him. ³²Gentlemen, why are not women strong, since they do such things?"

The Speech about Truth

33 Then the king and the nobles looked at one another; and he began to speak about truth: ³⁴"Gentlemen, are not women strong? The earth is vast, and heaven is high, and the sun is swift in its course, for it makes the circuit of the heavens and returns to its place in one day. ³⁵Is not the one who does these things great? But truth is great, and stronger than all things. ³⁶The whole earth calls upon

---

4:36–41 *The whole earth calls upon truth.* The concept of "truth" in this court tale is closely related to the concept of "cosmic order," that which lies behind and provides the foundation for the world of sense experience, which is, by contrast, "ephemeral" or "fleeting"

truth, and heaven blesses it. All God's works[a] quake and tremble, and with him there is nothing unrighteous. 37 Wine is unrighteous, the king is unrighteous, women are unrighteous, all human beings are unrighteous, all their works are unrighteous, and all such things. There is no truth in them and in their unrighteousness they will perish. 38 But truth endures and is strong forever, and lives and prevails forever and ever. 39 With it there is no partiality or preference, but it does what is righteous instead of anything that is unrighteous or wicked. Everyone approves its deeds, 40 and there is nothing unrighteous in its judgment. To it belongs the strength and the kingship and the power and the majesty of all the ages. Blessed be the God of truth!" 41 When he stopped speaking, all the people shouted and said, "Great is truth, and strongest of all!"

Zerubbabel's Reward

42 Then the king said to him, "Ask what you wish, even beyond what is written, and we will give it to you, for you have been found to be the wisest. You shall sit next to me, and be called my Kinsman." 43 Then he said to the king, "Remember the vow that you made on the day when you became king, to build Jerusalem, 44 and to send back all the vessels that were taken from Jerusalem, which Cyrus set apart when he began[b] to destroy Babylon, and vowed to send them back there. 45 You also vowed to build the temple, which the Edomites burned when Judea was laid waste by the Chaldeans. 46 And now, O lord the king, this is what I ask and request of you, and this befits your greatness. I pray therefore that you fulfill the vow whose fulfillment you vowed to the King of heaven with your own lips."

47 Then King Darius got up and kissed him, and wrote letters for him to all the treasurers and governors and generals and satraps, that they should give safe conduct to him and to all who were going up with him to build Jerusalem. 48 And he wrote letters to all the governors in Coelesyria and Phoenicia and to those in Lebanon, to bring cedar timber from Lebanon to Jerusalem, and to help him build the city. 49 He wrote in behalf of all the Jews who were going up from his kingdom to Judea, in the interest of their freedom, that no officer or satrap or governor or treasurer should forcibly enter their doors; 50 that all the country that they would occupy should be theirs without tribute; that the Idumeans should give up the villages of the Jews that they held; 51 that twenty talents a year should be given for the building of the temple until it was completed, 52 and an additional ten talents a year for burnt offerings to be offered on the altar every day, in accordance with the commandment to make seventeen offerings; 53 and that all who came from Babylonia to build the city should have their freedom, they and their children and all the priests who came. 54 He wrote also concerning their support and the priests' vestments in which[c] they were to minister. 55 He wrote that the support for the Levites should be provided until the day when the temple would be finished and Jerusalem built. 56 He wrote that land and wages should be provided for all who guarded the city. 57 And he sent back from Babylon all the vessels that Cyrus had set apart; everything that Cyrus had ordered to be done, he also commanded to be done and to be sent to Jerusalem.

a Gk *All the works*   b Cn: Gk *vowed*   c Gk *in what priestly vestments*

(the real sense of "unrighteous," as established by the contrast in v 36). Those things that give us escape or pleasure are fleeting; those human beings who seem to have the most power are fleeting. It is only God's ordering and just rule, God's enduring providence, that truly endure and bring stability. Staying connected with God and rooting our lives in God's unshakable ordering of the world emerges thus as the path to stability and security in the midst of unstable, ephemeral, unreliable realities.

4:43–46 *Then he said to the king.* How Zerubbabel uses the privilege, position, and favor that come to him is instructive. Having risen to prominence in Darius's court and been presented with the possibility of gaining anything he asks from Darius, Zerubbabel seeks out what will most honor God and benefit all of God's people, making sure all his sisters and brothers share in his favor and fortune.

Zerubbabel's Prayer

58 When the young man went out, he lifted up his face to heaven toward Jerusalem, and praised the King of heaven, saying, [59]"From you comes the victory; from you comes wisdom, and yours is the glory. I am your servant. [60]Blessed are you, who have given me wisdom; I give you thanks, O Lord of our ancestors."

61 So he took the letters, and went to Babylon and told this to all his kindred. [62]And they praised the God of their ancestors, because he had given them release and permission [63]to go up and build Jerusalem and the temple that is called by his name; and they feasted, with music and rejoicing, for seven days.

List of the Returning Exiles

5 After this the heads of ancestral houses were chosen to go up, according to their tribes, with their wives and sons and daughters, and their male and female servants, and their livestock. [2]And Darius sent with them a thousand cavalry to take them back to Jerusalem in safety, with the music of drums and flutes; [3]all their kindred were making merry. And he made them go up with them.

4 These are the names of the men who went up, according to their ancestral houses in the tribes, over their groups: [5]the priests, the descendants of Phinehas son of Aaron; Jeshua son of Jozadak son of Seraiah and Joakim son of Zerubbabel son of Shealtiel, of the house of David, of the lineage of Phares, of the tribe of Judah, [6]who spoke wise words before King Darius of the Persians, in the second year of his reign, in the month of Nisan, the first month.

7 These are the Judeans who came up out of their sojourn in exile, whom King Nebuchadnezzar of Babylon had carried away to Babylon [8]and who returned to Jerusalem and the rest of Judea, each to his own town. They came with Zerubbabel and Jeshua, Nehemiah, Seraiah, Resaiah, Eneneus, Mordecai, Beelsarus, Aspharasus, Reeliah, Rehum, and Baanah, their leaders.

9 The number of those of the nation and their leaders: the descendants of Parosh, two thousand one hundred seventy-two. The descendants of Shephatiah, four hundred seventy-two. [10]The descendants of Arah, seven hundred fifty-six. [11]The descendants of Pahath-moab, of the descendants of Jeshua and Joab, two thousand eight hundred twelve. [12]The descendants of Elam, one thousand two hundred fifty-four. The descendants of Zattu, nine hundred forty-five. The descendants of Chorbe, seven hundred five. The descendants of Bani, six hundred forty-eight. [13]The descendants of Bebai, six hundred twenty-three. The descendants of Azgad, one thousand three hundred twenty-two. [14]The descendants of Adonikam, six hundred sixty-seven. The descendants of Bigvai, two thousand sixty-six. The descendants of Adin, four hundred fifty-four. [15]The descendants of Ater, namely of Hezekiah, ninety-two. The descendants of Kilan and Azetas, sixty-seven.

4:58–63 *From you comes the victory.* Zerubbabel's request (vv 43–46) exhibited a God-centeredness that sanctifies his position and his fortunes, seen here in his expression of awareness of God's presence with him and God's power working through him in the contest of the three bodyguards for the purpose of advancing God's will. He has also transformed an occasion in which he might have sought a way to bless himself into an opportunity to give his people occasion to bless the God who was at work in Zerubbabel and for their deliverance. The joy that is shared by the People of God at the close of the chapter is far greater than the satisfaction Zerubbabel could ever have had from seeking his own advancement from King Darius; we should be inspired to discover ways to bring our sisters and brothers in Christ into the blessing and favor that come our way as well.

5:1 *the heads of ancestral houses were chosen to go up.* God is present in faithfulness to his promises to restore the exiled Judeans to their homeland, making the hope nurtured by Isa 35:1–10 and 40:1–5 real in the life circumstances of the returnees. Knowing God's promises, a knowledge acquired through meditation upon Scripture, helps us direct our hopes and yearnings as well as recognize when God is breaking into our lives to act on our behalf.

The descendants of Azaru, four hundred thirty-two. [16]The descendants of Annias, one hundred one. The descendants of Arom. The descendants of Bezai, three hundred twenty-three. The descendants of Arsiphurith, one hundred twelve. [17]The descendants of Baiterus, three thousand five. The descendants of Bethlomon, one hundred twenty-three. [18]Those from Netophah, fifty-five. Those from Anathoth, one hundred fifty-eight. Those from Bethasmoth, forty-two. [19]Those from Kriatharim, twenty-five. Those from Chephirah and Beeroth, seven hundred forty-three. [20]The Chadiasans and Ammidians, four hundred twenty-two. Those from Kirama and Geba, six hundred twenty-one. [21]Those from Macalon, one hundred twenty-two. Those from Betolio, fifty-two. The descendants of Niphish, one hundred fifty-six. [22]The descendants of the other Calamolalus and Ono, seven hundred twenty-five. The descendants of Jerechus, three hundred forty-five. [23]The descendants of Senaah, three thousand three hundred thirty.

24 The priests: the descendants of Jedaiah son of Jeshua, of the descendants of Anasib, nine hundred seventy-two. The descendants of Immer, one thousand and fifty-two. [25]The descendants of Pashhur, one thousand two hundred forty-seven. The descendants of Charme, one thousand seventeen.

26 The Levites: the descendants of Jeshua and Kadmiel and Bannas and Sudias, seventy-four. [27]The temple singers: the descendants of Asaph, one hundred twenty-eight. [28]The gatekeepers: the descendants of Shallum, the descendants of Ater, the descendants of Talmon, the descendants of Akkub, the descendants of Hatita, the descendants of Shobai, in all one hundred thirty-nine.

29 The temple servants: the descendants of Esau, the descendants of Hasupha, the descendants of Tabbaoth, the descendants of Keros, the descendants of Sua, the descendants of Padon, the descendants of Lebanah,

the descendants of Hagabah, [30]the descendants of Akkub, the descendants of Uthai, the descendants of Ketab, the descendants of Hagab, the descendants of Subai, the descendants of Hana, the descendants of Cathua, the descendants of Geddur, [31]the descendants of Jairus, the descendants of Daisan, the descendants of Noeba, the descendants of Chezib, the descendants of Gazera, the descendants of Uzza, the descendants of Phinoe, the descendants of Hasrah, the descendants of Basthai, the descendants of Asnah, the descendants of Maani, the descendants of Nephisim, the descendants of Acuph,[a] the descendants of Hakupha, the descendants of Asur, the descendants of Pharakim, the descendants of Bazluth, [32]the descendants of Mehida, the descendants of Cutha, the descendants of Charea, the descendants of Barkos, the descendants of Serar, the descendants of Temah, the descendants of Neziah, the descendants of Hatipha.

33 The descendants of Solomon's servants: the descendants of Assaphioth, the descendants of Peruda, the descendants of Jaalah, the descendants of Lozon, the descendants of Isdael, the descendants of Shephatiah, [34]the descendants of Agia, the descendants of Pochereth-hazzebaim, the descendants of Sarothie, the descendants of Masiah, the descendants of Gas, the descendants of Addus, the descendants of Subas, the descendants of Apherra, the descendants of Barodis, the descendants of Shaphat, the descendants of Allon.

35 All the temple servants and the descendants of Solomon's servants were three hundred seventy-two.

36 The following are those who came up from Tel-melah and Tel-harsha, under the leadership of Cherub, Addan, and Immer, [37]though they could not prove by their ancestral houses or lineage that they belonged

a Other ancient authorities read *Acub* or *Acum*

5:37 *prove by their ancestral houses . . . that they belonged to Israel.* One of the more radical facets of the gospel was the conviction that the fundamental criterion defining the People of God had shifted from an ethnic and genealogical

one (being born Jewish) to a universal one (being born of God by receiving the Holy Spirit as a result of trusting in Jesus; see John 1:11–13; 3:3–8; Gal 3:26–29; 4:6–7). The Jewish Christians, especially, had to accept that the price

to Israel: the descendants of Delaiah son of Tobiah, and the descendants of Nekoda, six hundred fifty-two.

38 Of the priests the following had assumed the priesthood but were not found registered: the descendants of Habaiah, the descendants of Hakkoz, and the descendants of Jaddus who had married Agia, one of the daughters of Barzillai, and was called by his name. 39When a search was made in the register and the genealogy of these men was not found, they were excluded from serving as priests. 40And Nehemiah and Attharias*a* told them not to share in the holy things until a high priest should appear wearing Urim and Thummim.*b*

41 All those of Israel, twelve or more years of age, besides male and female servants, were forty-two thousand three hundred sixty; 42their male and female servants were seven thousand three hundred thirty-seven; there were two hundred forty-five musicians and singers. 43There were four hundred thirty-five camels, and seven thousand thirty-six horses, two hundred forty-five mules, and five thousand five hundred twenty-five donkeys.

44 Some of the heads of families, when they came to the temple of God that is in Jerusalem, vowed that, to the best of their ability, they would erect the house on its site, 45and that they would give to the sacred treasury for the work a thousand minas of gold, five thousand minas of silver, and one hundred priests' vestments.

46 The priests, the Levites, and some of the people*c* settled in Jerusalem and its vicinity; and the temple singers, the gatekeepers, and all Israel in their towns.

Worship Begins Again

47 When the seventh month came, and the Israelites were all in their own homes, they gathered with a single purpose in the square before the first gate toward the east. 48Then Jeshua son of Jozadak, with his fellow priests, and Zerubbabel son of Shealtiel, with his kinsmen, took their places and prepared the altar of the God of Israel, 49to offer burnt offerings upon it, in accordance with the directions in the book of Moses the man of God. 50And some joined them from the other peoples of the land. And they erected the altar in its place, for all the peoples of the land were hostile to them and were stronger than they; and they offered sacrifices at the proper times and burnt offerings to the Lord morning and evening. 51They kept the festival of booths, as it is commanded in the law, and offered the proper sacrifices every day, 52and thereafter the regular offerings and sacrifices on sabbaths and at new moons and at all the consecrated feasts. 53And all who had made any vow to God began to offer sacrifices to God, from the new moon of the seventh month, though the temple of God was not yet built. 54They gave money to the masons and the carpenters, and food and drink 55and carts*d* to the Sidonians and the Tyrians, to bring cedar logs from Lebanon and convey them in rafts to the harbor of Joppa, according to the decree that they had in writing from King Cyrus of the Persians.

The Foundations of the Temple Laid

56 In the second year after their coming to the temple of God in Jerusalem, in the second

a Or *the governor*   *b* Gk *Manifestation and Truth*
c Or *those who were of the people*   *d* Meaning of Gk uncertain

---

of becoming a blessing to all nations would be giving up a sense of ethnic privilege—in a sense, a kind of dying to self so that others might experience new life. The pattern of the Messiah was thus replicated in their experience and continues to challenge us today; in our spiritual growth we need to discover ways in which we are being called to die to self for the sake of extending God's promise to others.

5:47–53 *When the seventh month came.* We come to the second festival that punctuates this

narrative. The Festival of Booths is an especially appropriate one to be highlighted at this point, before the Temple has been rebuilt, for it takes the worshipers back to the years spent in the wilderness after the exodus. During that time, Israel lived in tents, but knew the provision of God and his shepherding of the people to their destiny. Just so, the returnees are reminded that God's presence and leading are real and vibrant even without the Temple structure.

month, Zerubbabel son of Shealtiel and Jeshua son of Jozadak made a beginning, together with their kindred and the levitical priests and all who had come back to Jerusalem from exile; [57]and they laid the foundation of the temple of God on the new moon of the second month in the second year after they came to Judea and Jerusalem. [58]They appointed the Levites who were twenty or more years of age to have charge of the work of the Lord. And Jeshua arose, and his sons and kindred and his brother Kadmiel and the sons of Jeshua Emadabun and the sons of Joda son of Iliadun, with their sons and kindred, all the Levites, pressing forward the work on the house of God with a single purpose.

So the builders built the temple of the Lord. [59]And the priests stood arrayed in their vestments, with musical instruments and trumpets, and the Levites, the sons of Asaph, with cymbals, [60]praising the Lord and blessing him, according to the directions of King David of Israel; [61]they sang hymns, giving thanks to the Lord, "For his goodness and his glory are forever upon all Israel." [62]And all the people sounded trumpets and shouted with a great shout, praising the Lord for the erection of the house of the Lord. [63]Some of the levitical priests and heads of ancestral houses, old men who had seen the former house, came to the building of this one with outcries and loud weeping, [64]while many came with trumpets and a joyful noise, [65]so that the people could not hear the trumpets because of the weeping of the people.

For the multitude sounded the trumpets loudly, so that the sound was heard far away; [66]and when the enemies of the tribe of Judah and Benjamin heard it, they came to find out what the sound of the trumpets meant. [67]They learned that those who had returned from exile were building the temple for the Lord God of Israel. [68]So they approached Zerubbabel and Jeshua and the heads of the ancestral houses and said to them, "We will build with you. [69]For we obey your Lord just as you do and we have been sacrificing to him ever since the days of King Esar-haddon[a] of the Assyrians, who brought us here." [70]But Zerubbabel and Jeshua and the heads of the ancestral houses in Israel said to them, "You have nothing to do with us in building the house for the Lord our God, [71]for we alone will build it for the Lord of Israel, as Cyrus, the king of the Persians, has commanded us." [72]But the peoples of the land pressed hard[b] upon those in Judea, cut off their supplies, and hindered their building; [73]and by plots and demagoguery and uprisings they prevented the completion of the building as long as King Cyrus lived. They were kept from building for two years, until the reign of Darius.

Work on the Temple Begins Again

6 Now in the second year of the reign of Darius, the prophets Haggai and Zechariah son of Iddo prophesied to the Jews who

a Gk Asbasareth   b Meaning of Gk uncertain

5:58–62 *work on the house of God with a single purpose.* The image of people working together with one spirit to build God's house, surrounded and spurred on by psalms and hymns of praise to God, presents us with an ideal well pursued now as we press forward to build up God's new Temple. As a community of faith, we are challenged to discern God's vision with such clarity that all can embrace it and invest in it with one mind and heart. Our work as the community of God is all too often accompanied by criticism, murmuring, or lack of enthusiasm. When we take care to create an atmosphere of praise and celebration of what God accomplishes as we invest in his vision,

however, the spirits of all concerned are uplifted, and each becomes aware of how God is present in and through the work of his people.

5:70–72 *You have nothing to do with us.* One cannot help but wonder if there was a missed opportunity here, one that might have resulted in unifying the people of the land with the congregation of the exile, bringing the former into a closer conformity with the way of life laid down in Torah. The ethnic tensions exhibited here are transcended in the early Church, in which the holiness of the People of God is preserved as outsiders are transformed and included. Here outsiders are systematically excluded and denied the possibility of redemption or transformation.

were in Judea and Jerusalem; they prophesied to them in the name of the Lord God of Israel. [2]Then Zerubbabel son of Shealtiel and Jeshua son of Jozadak began to build the house of the Lord that is in Jerusalem, with the help of the prophets of the Lord who were with them.

3 At the same time Sisinnes the governor of Syria and Phoenicia and Sathrabuzanes and their associates came to them and said, [4]"By whose order are you building this house and this roof and finishing all the other things? And who are the builders that are finishing these things?" [5]Yet the elders of the Jews were dealt with kindly, for the providence of the Lord was over the captives; [6]they were not prevented from building until word could be sent to Darius concerning them and a report made.

7 A copy of the letter that Sisinnes the governor of Syria and Phoenicia, and Sathrabuzanes, and their associates the local rulers in Syria and Phoenicia, wrote and sent to Darius:

8 "To King Darius, greetings. Let it be fully known to our lord the king that, when we went to the country of Judea and entered the city of Jerusalem, we found the elders of the Jews, who had been in exile, [9]building in the city of Jerusalem a great new house for the Lord, of hewn stone, with costly timber laid in the walls. [10]These operations are going on rapidly, and the work is prospering in their hands and being completed with all splendor and care. [11]Then we asked these elders, 'At whose command are you building this house and laying the foundations of this structure?' [12]In order that we might inform you in writing who the leaders are, we questioned them and asked them for a list of the names of those who are at their head. [13]They answered us, 'We are the servants of the Lord who created the heaven and the earth. [14]The house was built many years ago by a king of Israel

who was great and strong, and it was finished. [15]But when our ancestors sinned against the Lord of Israel who is in heaven, and provoked him, he gave them over into the hands of King Nebuchadnezzar of Babylon, king of the Chaldeans; [16]and they pulled down the house, and burned it, and carried the people away captive to Babylon. [17]But in the first year that Cyrus reigned over the country of Babylonia, King Cyrus wrote that this house should be rebuilt. [18]And the holy vessels of gold and of silver, which Nebuchadnezzar had taken out of the house in Jerusalem and stored in his own temple, these King Cyrus took out again from the temple in Babylon, and they were delivered to Zerubbabel and Sheshbazzar[a] the governor [19]with the command that he should take all these vessels back and put them in the temple at Jerusalem, and that this temple of the Lord should be rebuilt on its site. [20]Then this Sheshbazzar, after coming here, laid the foundations of the house of the Lord that is in Jerusalem. Although it has been in process of construction from that time until now, it has not yet reached completion.' [21]Now therefore, O king, if it seems wise to do so, let search be made in the royal archives of our lord[b] the king that are in Babylon; [22]if it is found that the building of the house of the Lord in Jerusalem was done with the consent of King Cyrus, and if it is approved by our lord the king, let him send us directions concerning these things."

Official Permission Granted

23 Then Darius commanded that search be made in the royal archives that were deposited in Babylon. And in Ecbatana, the fortress that is in the country of Media, a scroll[c] was found in which this was recorded:

a Gk Sanabassarus   b Other ancient authorities read of Cyrus   c Other authorities read passage

---

6:1–2 the help of the prophets . . . who were with them. God supports the doing of his work through the ministry of people who listen for and speak God's word to the people. Haggai and Zechariah make God present to the people as they reveal his will within the situation and

declare how God is moving in their midst.
6:5 the elders of the Jews were dealt with kindly. Again, God's presence is signaled when his people are dealt with kindly by those in authority. Peace for the People of God is a favor from the Lord.

24 "In the first year of the reign of King Cyrus, he ordered the building of the house of the Lord in Jerusalem, where they sacrifice with perpetual fire; 25 its height to be sixty cubits and its width sixty cubits, with three courses of hewn stone and one course of new native timber; the cost to be paid from the treasury of King Cyrus; 26 and that the holy vessels of the house of the Lord, both of gold and of silver, which Nebuchadnezzar took out of the house in Jerusalem and carried away to Babylon, should be restored to the house in Jerusalem, to be placed where they had been."

27 So Darius[a] commanded Sisinnes the governor of Syria and Phoenicia, and Sathrabuzanes, and their associates, and those who were appointed as local rulers in Syria and Phoenicia, to keep away from the place, and to permit Zerubbabel, the servant of the Lord and governor of Judea, and the elders of the Jews to build this house of the Lord on its site. 28 "And I command that it be built completely, and that full effort be made to help those who have returned from the exile of Judea, until the house of the Lord is finished; 29 and that out of the tribute of Coelesyria and Phoenicia a portion be scrupulously given to these men, that is, to Zerubbabel the governor, for sacrifices to the Lord, for bulls and rams and lambs, 30 and likewise wheat and salt and wine and oil, regularly every year, without quibbling, for daily use as the priests in Jerusalem may indicate, 31 in order that libations may be made to the Most High God for the king and his children, and prayers be offered for their lives."

32 He commanded that if anyone should transgress or nullify any of the things herein written,[b] a beam should be taken out of the house of the perpetrator, who then should be impaled upon it, and all property forfeited to the king. 33 "Therefore may the Lord, whose name is there called upon, destroy every king and nation that shall stretch out their hands to

hinder or damage that house of the Lord in Jerusalem.

34 "I, King Darius, have decreed that it be done with all diligence as here prescribed."

The Temple Is Dedicated

7 Then Sisinnes the governor of Coelesyria and Phoenicia, and Sathrabuzanes, and their associates, following the orders of King Darius, 2 supervised the holy work with very great care, assisting the elders of the Jews and the chief officers of the temple. 3 The holy work prospered, while the prophets Haggai and Zechariah prophesied; 4 and they completed it by the command of the Lord God of Israel. So with the consent of Cyrus and Darius and Artaxerxes, kings of the Persians, 5 the holy house was finished by the twenty-third day of the month of Adar, in the sixth year of King Darius. 6 And the people of Israel, the priests, the Levites, and the rest of those who returned from exile who joined them, did according to what was written in the book of Moses. 7 They offered at the dedication of the temple of the Lord one hundred bulls, two hundred rams, four hundred lambs, 8 and twelve male goats for the sin of all Israel, according to the number of the twelve leaders of the tribes of Israel; 9 and the priests and the Levites stood arrayed in their vestments, according to kindred, for the services of the Lord God of Israel in accordance with the book of Moses; and the gatekeepers were at each gate.

The Passover

10 The people of Israel who came from exile kept the passover on the fourteenth day of the first month, after the priests and the Levites were purified together. 11 Not all of the returned captives were purified, but the Levites were all purified together,[c] 12 and they

a Gk he   b Other authorities read stated above or added in writing   c Meaning of Gk uncertain

---

6:28 I command . . . that full effort be made to help. See notes on 2:2; 6:5.

6:31 libations may be made to the Most High God for the king and his children. When rulers are indeed enforcing policies that allow the

People of God to flourish and to pursue God's vision for human community, it is certainly appropriate to remember them before God and acknowledge his provision of peace through them (see also 8:21; 1 Tim 2:1–4).

sacrificed the passover lamb for all the returned captives and for their kindred the priests and for themselves. 13 The people of Israel who had returned from exile ate it, all those who had separated themselves from the abominations of the peoples of the land and sought the Lord. 14 They also kept the festival of unleavened bread seven days, rejoicing before the Lord, 15 because he had changed the will of the king of the Assyrians concerning them, to strengthen their hands for the service of the Lord God of Israel.

Ezra Arrives in Jerusalem

8 After these things, when Artaxerxes, the king of the Persians, was reigning, Ezra came, the son of Seraiah, son of Azariah, son of Hilkiah, son of Shallum, 2 son of Zadok, son of Ahitub, son of Amariah, son of Uzzi, son of Bukki, son of Abishua, son of Phineas, son of Eleazar, son of Aaron the high *a* priest. 3 This Ezra came up from Babylon as a scribe skilled in the law of Moses, which was given by the God of Israel; 4 and the king showed him honor, for he found favor before the king *b* in all his requests. 5 There came up with him to Jerusalem some of the people of Israel and some of the priests and Levites and temple singers and gatekeepers and temple servants, 6 in the seventh year of the reign of Artaxerxes, in the fifth month (this was the king's seventh year); for they left Babylon on the new moon of the first month and arrived in Jerusalem on the new moon of the fifth month, by the prosperous journey that the Lord gave them. *c* 7 For Ezra possessed great knowledge, so that he omitted nothing from the law of the Lord or the commandments, but taught all Israel all the ordinances and judgments.

The King's Mandate

8 The following is a copy of the written commission from King Artaxerxes that was delivered to Ezra the priest and reader of the law of the Lord:

9 "King Artaxerxes to Ezra the priest and reader of the law of the Lord, greeting. 10 In accordance with my gracious decision, I have given orders that those of the Jewish nation and of the priests and Levites and others in our realm, those who freely choose to do so, may go with you to Jerusalem. 11 Let as many as are so disposed, therefore, leave with you, just as I and the seven Friends who are my counselors have decided, 12 in order to look into matters in Judea and Jerusalem, in accordance with what is in the law of the Lord, 13 and to carry to Jerusalem the gifts for the Lord of Israel that I and my Friends have vowed, and to collect for the Lord in Jerusalem all the gold and silver that may be found in the country of Babylonia, 14 together with what is given by the nation for the temple of their Lord that is in Jerusalem, both gold and silver for bulls and rams and lambs and what goes with them, 15 so as to offer sacrifices on the altar of their Lord that is in Jerusalem. 16 Whatever you and your kindred are minded to do with the gold and silver, perform it in accordance with the will of your God; 17 deliver the holy vessels of the Lord that are given you for the use of the temple of your God that is in Jerusalem. 18 And whatever else occurs to you as necessary for the temple of your God, you may provide out of the royal treasury.

19 "I, King Artaxerxes, have commanded the treasurers of Syria and Phoenicia that whatever Ezra the priest and reader of the law of the Most High God sends for, they shall take care to give him, 20 up to a hundred talents of silver, and likewise up to a hundred cors of wheat, a hundred baths of wine, and salt in abundance. 21 Let all things prescribed in the law of God be scrupulous-

a Gk *the first*   *b* Gk *him*   *c* Other authorities add *for him* or *upon him*

8:3,7 *This Ezra came up from Babylon.* Ezra emerges near the end of the story, bringing the fruits of the detailed study of the law to the restored people and Temple. Ezra's ministry assures that, just as the people's former disobe- dience to the law resulted in destruction and exile, the people's renewed obedience to the law would result in ongoing security in the land of Israel.

ly fulfilled for the Most High God, so that wrath may not come upon the kingdom of the king and his sons. 22You are also informed that no tribute or any other tax is to be laid on any of the priests or Levites or temple singers or gatekeepers or temple servants or persons employed in this temple, and that no one has authority to impose any tax on them.

23 "And you, Ezra, according to the wisdom of God, appoint judges and justices to judge all those who know the law of your God, throughout all Syria and Phoenicia; and you shall teach it to those who do not know it. 24All who transgress the law of your God or the law of the kingdom shall be strictly punished, whether by death or some other punishment, either fine or imprisonment."

Ezra Praises God

25 Then Ezra the scribe said,[a] "Blessed be the Lord alone, who put this into the heart of the king, to glorify his house that is in Jerusalem, 26and who honored me in the sight of the king and his counselors and all his Friends and nobles. 27I was encouraged by the help of the Lord my God, and I gathered men from Israel to go up with me."

The Leaders Who Returned

28 These are the leaders, according to their ancestral houses and their groups, who went up with me from Babylon, in the reign of King Artaxerxes: 29Of the descendants of Phineas, Gershom. Of the descendants of Ithamar, Gamael. Of the descendants of David, Hattush son of Shecaniah. 30Of the descendants of Parosh, Zechariah, and with him a hundred fifty men enrolled. 31Of the descendants of Pahath-moab, Eliehoenai son of Zerahiah, and with him two hundred men. 32Of the descendants of Zattu, Shecaniah son of Jahaziel, and with him three hundred men. Of the descendants of Adin, Obed son of Jonathan, and with him two hundred fifty men. 33Of the descendants of Elam, Jeshaiah son of Gotholiah, and with him seventy men. 34Of the descendants of Shephatiah, Zeraiah son of Michael, and with him seventy men. 35Of the descendants of Joab, Obadiah son of Jehiel, and with him two hundred twelve men. 36Of the descendants of Bani, Shelomith son of Josiphiah, and with him a hundred sixty men. 37Of the descendants of Bebai, Zechariah son of Bebai, and with him twenty-eight men. 38Of the descendants of Azgad, Johanan son of Hakkatan, and with him a hundred ten men. 39Of the descendants of Adonikam, the last ones, their names being Eliphelet, Jeuel, and Shemaiah, and with them seventy men. 40Of the descendants of Bigvai, Uthai son of Istalcurus, and with him seventy men.

41 I assembled them at the river called Theras, and we encamped there three days, and I inspected them. 42When I found there none of the descendants of the priests or of the Levites, 43I sent word to Eliezar, Iduel, Maasmas, 44Elnathan, Shemaiah, Jarib, Nathan, Elnathan, Zechariah, and Meshullam, who were leaders and men of understanding; 45I told them to go to Iddo, who was the leading man at the place of the treasury, 46and ordered them to tell Iddo and his kindred and the treasurers at that place to send us men to serve as priests in the house of our Lord. 47And by the mighty hand of our Lord they brought us competent men of the descendants of Mahli son of Levi, son of Israel, namely Sherebiah[b] with his descendants and kinsmen, eighteen; 48also Hashabiah and Annunus and his brother Jeshaiah, of the descendants of Hananiah, and their descendants, twenty men; 49and of the temple servants, whom David and the leaders had given for the service of the Levites, two hundred twenty temple servants; the list of all their names was reported.

---

a Other ancient authorities lack *Then Ezra the scribe said*   b Gk *Asbebias*

8:25–27 *Blessed be the Lord alone.* The favors granted to the congregation of the returnees by Artaxerxes (vv 9–22) are understood yet again as a sign of God's presence with and actions on behalf of his people: the help from Artaxerxes is nothing less than the "help of the Lord."

Ezra Proclaims a Fast

50 There I proclaimed a fast for the young men before our Lord, to seek from him a prosperous journey for ourselves and for our children and the livestock that were with us. [51]For I was ashamed to ask the king for foot soldiers and cavalry and an escort to keep us safe from our adversaries; [52]for we had said to the king, "The power of our Lord will be with those who seek him, and will support them in every way." [53]And again we prayed to our Lord about these things, and we found him very merciful.

The Gifts for the Temple

54 Then I set apart twelve of the leaders of the priests, Sherebiah and Hashabiah, and ten of their kinsmen with them; [55]and I weighed out to them the silver and the gold and the holy vessels of the house of our Lord, which the king himself and his counselors and the nobles and all Israel had given. [56]I weighed and gave to them six hundred fifty talents of silver, and silver vessels worth a hundred talents, and a hundred talents of gold, [57]and twenty golden bowls, and twelve bronze vessels of fine bronze that glittered like gold. [58]And I said to them, 'You are holy to the Lord, and the vessels are holy, and the silver and the gold are vowed to the Lord, the Lord of our ancestors. [59]Be watchful and on guard until you deliver them to the leaders of the priests and the Levites, and to the heads of the ancestral houses of Israel, in Jerusalem, in the chambers of the house of our Lord." [60]So the priests and the Levites who took the silver and the gold and the vessels that had been in Jerusalem carried them to the temple of the Lord.

The Return to Jerusalem

61 We left the river Theras on the twelfth day of the first month; and we arrived in Jerusalem by the mighty hand of our Lord, which was upon us; he delivered us from every enemy on the way, and so we came to Jerusalem. [62]When we had been there three days, the silver and the gold were weighed and delivered in the house of our Lord to the priest Meremoth son of Uriah; [63]with him was Eleazar son of Phinehas, and with them were Jozabad son of Jeshua and Moeth son of Binnui,[a] the Levites. [64]The whole was counted and weighed, and the weight of everything was recorded at that very time. [65]And those who had returned from exile offered sacrifices to the Lord, the God of Israel, twelve bulls for all Israel, ninety-six rams, [66]seventy-two lambs, and as a thank offering twelve male goats—all as a sacrifice to the Lord. [67]They delivered the king's orders to the royal stewards and to the governors of Coelesyria and Phoenicia; and these officials[b] honored the people and the temple of the Lord.

Ezra's Prayer

68 After these things had been done, the leaders came to me and said, [69]"The people of

a Gk *Sabannus*   b Gk *they*

Responding
8:50 FASTING. Consider engaging in a short fast to prepare for your next business trip or family vacation. Pray for a safe and prosperous journey. *See also* Spiritual Disciplines Index.

8:50–53 *There I proclaimed a fast.* Ezra refuses to mouth platitudes about God's presence and guidance in one moment and then turn to human resources for protection and security in the next. Rather, he and his company seek to walk in congruity with their convictions about God's love and favor toward them. The Spiritual Disciplines of prayer and fasting as means of seeking God's face again emerge as fundamental practices for life with God. Ezra's clarity on this point (vv 51–52) is a challenge to us to examine where we are in fact building our security or seeking our firm foundation—in the wealth and power of this world or in God's face and favor.

8:58–59 *You are holy to the Lord.* The image of a consecrated people entrusted with holy things and a task to perform for God resonates strongly with our task as disciples. What has God entrusted to us, who have ourselves been consecrated to God, to guard and deliver for his purposes? How do we discharge our trust from God in our use of our spiritual gifts and natural resources, exercising watchful stewardship?

Israel and the rulers and the priests and the Levites have not put away from themselves the alien peoples of the land and their pollutions, the Canaanites, the Hittites, the Perizzites, the Jebusites, the Moabites, the Egyptians, and the Edomites. [70]For they and their descendants have married the daughters of these people, [a] and the holy race has been mixed with the alien peoples of the land; and from the beginning of this matter the leaders and the nobles have been sharing in this iniquity."

[71] As soon as I heard these things I tore my garments and my holy mantle, and pulled out hair from my head and beard, and sat down in anxiety and grief. [72]And all who were ever moved at [b] the word of the Lord of Israel gathered around me, as I mourned over this iniquity, and I sat grief-stricken until the evening sacrifice. [73]Then I rose from my fast, with my garments and my holy mantle torn, and kneeling down and stretching out my hands to the Lord [74]I said,

"O Lord, I am ashamed and confused before your face. [75]For our sins have risen higher than our heads, and our mistakes have mounted up to heaven [76]from the times of our ancestors, and we are in great sin to this day. [77]Because of our sins and the sins of our ancestors, we with our kindred and our kings and our priests were given over to the kings of the earth, to the sword and exile and plundering, in shame until this day. [78]And now in some measure mercy has come to us from you, O Lord, to leave to us a root and a name in your holy place, [79]and to uncover a light for us in the house of the Lord our God, and to give us food in the time of our servitude. [80]Even in our bondage we were not forsaken by our Lord, but he brought us into favor with the kings of the Persians, so that they have given us food [81]and glorified the temple of our Lord, and raised Zion from desolation, to give us a stronghold in Judea and Jerusalem.

[82] "And now, O Lord, what shall we say, when we have these things? For we have transgressed your commandments, which you gave by your servants the prophets, saying, [83]'The land that you are entering to take possession of is a land polluted with the pollution of the aliens of the land; and they have filled it with their uncleanness. [84]Therefore do not give your daughters in marriage to their descendants, and do not take their daughters for your descendants; [85]do not seek ever to have peace with them, so that you may be strong and eat the good things of the land and leave it for an inheritance to your children forever.' [86]And all that has happened to us has come about because of our evil deeds and our great sins. For you, O Lord, lifted the burden of our sins [87]and gave us such a root as this; but we turned back again to transgress your law by mixing with the uncleanness of the peoples of the land. [88]Were you not angry enough with us to destroy us without leaving a root or seed or name? [89]O Lord of Israel, you are faithful; for we are left as a root to this day. [90]See, we are now before you in our iniquities; for we can no longer stand in your presence because of these things."

a Gk *their daughters*   *b* Or *zealous for*

8:71–73 *I tore my garments and my holy mantle.* Ezra models for us the level of openness and honesty before God in prayer that allows our spirit to connect with God's Spirit at our point of deepest need. Again he models the use of Spiritual Disciplines (fasting, prayer vigils) as part of his relationship with God (see also 9:2).

8:83–85 *a land polluted with the pollution of the aliens of the land.* Ezra appears to have Lev 18:19–30 in mind in this inexact quotation. Applied to the conquest of Canaan, this command did help ensure that the Hebrews would not lose their identity or their fidelity to God; as Ezra reapplies it in 515 BC, this command appears to have led the "congregation of the exile" to cut themselves off from fellow Israelites who had simply been separated from them during the time of the exile. This conveys a double-edged message to disciples of Jesus. On the one hand, we are reminded that we too are called to remain faithful to God by not participating in the sins of the non-Christians around us. On the other hand, we are cautioned not to draw our boundaries so tightly that we cut ourselves off from other Christians with whom the Spirit of God would join us.

The Plan for Ending Mixed Marriages

91 While Ezra was praying and making his confession, weeping and lying on the ground before the temple, there gathered around him a very great crowd of men and women and youths from Jerusalem; for there was great weeping among the multitude. 92Then Shecaniah son of Jehiel, one of the men of Israel, called out, and said to Ezra, "We have sinned against the Lord, and have married foreign women from the peoples of the land; but even now there is hope for Israel. 93Let us take an oath to the Lord about this, that we will put away all our foreign wives, with their children, 94as seems good to you and to all who obey the law of the Lord. 95Rise up*a* and take action, for it is your task, and we are with you to take strong measures." 96Then Ezra rose up and made the leaders of the priests and Levites of all Israel swear that they would do this. And they swore to it.

The Expulsion of Foreign Wives

9 Then Ezra set out and went from the court of the temple to the chamber of Jehohanan son of Eliashib, 2and spent the night there; and he did not eat bread or drink water, for he was mourning over the great iniquities of the multitude. 3And a proclamation was made throughout Judea and Jerusalem to all who had returned from exile that they should assemble at Jerusalem, 4and that if any did not meet there within two or three days, in accordance with the decision of the ruling elders, their livestock would be seized for sacrifice and the men themselves*b* expelled from the multitude of those who had returned from the captivity.

5 Then the men of the tribe of Judah and Benjamin assembled at Jerusalem within three days; this was the ninth month, on the twentieth day of the month. 6All the multitude sat in the open square before the temple, shivering because of the bad weather that prevailed. 7Then Ezra stood up and said to them, "You have broken the law and married foreign women, and so have increased the sin of Israel. 8Now then make confession and give glory to the Lord the God of our ancestors, 9and do his will; separate yourselves from the peoples of the land and from your foreign wives."

10 Then all the multitude shouted and said with a loud voice, "We will do as you have said. 11But the multitude is great and it is winter, and we are not able to stand in the open air. This is not a work we can do in one day or two, for we have sinned too much in these things. 12So let the leaders of the multitude stay, and let all those in our settlements who have foreign wives come at the

a Other ancient authorities read *as seems good to you." And all who obeyed the law of the Lord rose and said to Ezra, 95"Rise up*   *b* Gk *he himself*

8:91 **PRAYER**—*See* Spiritual Disciplines Index.

Responding
8:91 **CONFESSION.** The scene described here is a very public one. Confession is often appropriately relegated to private quarters, but some confessions are necessarily public. If you have done something wrong that affects your entire family, church, or office, consider whether God is calling you to publicly admit your sin. *See also* Spiritual Disciplines Index.

9:3 *all who had returned from exile.* Just as "Israel" is being redefined throughout this book as "all who had returned from exile" (though many descendants of Jacob had remained in the land), so the early Church would come to redefine Israel as those who heed the One whom God raised up, Jesus Christ. Paul, indeed, would marvel at the way spiritual Israel had always been selected out from among the natural descendants of Abraham (see Rom 9).

9:7–10, 36 *You have broken the law.* When confronted with sinning against God's law, the returnees are willing to admit their guilt and take the steps to move back into obedience to God—even though it involved what must have been a tremendously painful sacrifice. Our own spiritual growth will also depend on our willingness to be confronted by God's call to holiness by the Word, by fellow Christians, and by the Spirit and to sacrifice those parts of our lives that do not reflect Christlikeness, however painful and difficult that may be.

time appointed, 13with the elders and judges of each place, until we are freed from the wrath of the Lord over this matter."

14 Jonathan son of Asahel and Jahzeiah son of Tikvah*a* undertook the matter on these terms, and Meshullam and Levi and Shabbethai served with them as judges. 15And those who had returned from exile acted in accordance with all this.

16 Ezra the priest chose for himself the leading men of their ancestral houses, all of them by name; and on the new moon of the tenth month they began their sessions to investigate the matter. 17And the cases of the men who had foreign wives were brought to an end by the new moon of the first month.

18 Of the priests, those who were brought in and found to have foreign wives were: 19of the descendants of Jeshua son of Jozadak and his kindred, Maaseiah, Eliezar, Jarib, and Jodan. 20They pledged themselves to put away their wives, and to offer rams in expiation of their error. 21Of the descendants of Immer: Hanani and Zebadiah and Maaseiah and Shemaiah and Jehiel and Azariah. 22Of the descendants of Pashhur: Elioenai, Maaseiah, Ishmael, and Nathanael, and Gedaliah, and Salthas.

23 And of the Levites: Jozabad and Shimei and Kelaiah, who was Kelita, and Pethahiah and Judah and Jonah. 24Of the temple singers: Eliashib and Zaccur.*b* 25Of the gatekeepers: Shallum and Telem.*c*

26 Of Israel: of the descendants of Parosh: Ramiah, Izziah, Malchijah, Mijamin, and Eleazar, and Asibias, and Benaiah. 27Of the descendants of Elam: Mattaniah and Zechariah, Jezrielus and Abdi, and Jeremoth and Elijah. 28Of the descendants of Zamoth: Eliadas, Eliashib, Othoniah, Jeremoth, and Zabad and Zerdaiah. 29Of the descendants of Bebai: Jehohanan and Hananiah and Zabbai and

Emathis. 30Of the descendants of Mani: Olamus, Mamuchus, Adaiah, Jashub, and Sheal and Jeremoth. 31Of the descendants of Addi: Naathus and Moossias, Laccunus and Naidus, and Bescaspasmys and Sesthel, and Belnuus and Manasseas. 32Of the descendants of Annan, Elionas and Asaias and Melchias and Sabbaias and Simon Chosamaeus. 33Of the descendants of Hashum: Mattenai and Mattattah and Zabad and Eliphelet and Manasseh and Shimei. 34Of the descendants of Bani: Jeremai, Momdius, Maerus, Joel, Mamdai and Bedeiah and Vaniah, Carabasion and Eliashib and Mamitanemus, Eliasis, Binnui, Elialis, Shimei, Shelemiah, Nethaniah. Of the descendants of Ezora: Shashai, Azarel, Azael, Samatus, Zambris, Joseph. 35Of the descendants of Nooma: Mazitias, Zabad, Iddo, Joel, Benaiah. 36All these had married foreign women, and they put them away together with their children.

Ezra Reads the Law to the People

37 The priests and the Levites and the Israelites settled in Jerusalem and in the country. On the new moon of the seventh month, when the people of Israel were in their settlements, 38the whole multitude gathered with one accord in the open square before the east gate of the temple; 39they told Ezra the chief priest and reader to bring the law of Moses that had been given by the Lord God of Israel. 40So Ezra the chief priest brought the law, for all the multitude, men and women, and all the priests to hear the law, on the new moon of the seventh month. 41He read aloud in the open square before the gate of the temple from early morning until midday, in the presence of both men and women; and all the

a Gk *Thocanos*   b Gk *Bacchurus*
c Gk *Tolbanes*

9:40–41, 48 *for all . . . to hear the law.* The heart of spiritual renewal is the reading and study of God's Word, attending to it in private and in community, devoting to it the time that it merits. Committing to not only grow in the Word ourselves, but also to help our sisters and brothers— and our children in the Lord—hear and understand the Word is an essential investment of

ourselves for the life of the community of faith.

Responding
9:40–41, 48 **STUDY.** Is God calling you to share your knowledge about Scripture? Consider asking an acquaintance to join in a Bible study with you. *See also* Spiritual Disciplines Index.

multitude gave attention to the law. [42]Ezra the priest and reader of the law stood on the wooden platform that had been prepared; [43]and beside him stood Mattathiah, Shema, Ananias, Azariah, Uriah, Hezekiah, and Baalsamus on his right, [44]and on his left Pedaiah, Mishael, Malchijah, Lothasubus, Nabariah, and Zechariah. [45]Then Ezra took up the book of the law in the sight of the multitude, for he had the place of honor in the presence of all. [46]When he opened the law, they all stood erect. And Ezra blessed the Lord God Most High, the God of hosts, the Almighty, [47]and the multitude answered, "Amen." They lifted up their hands, and fell to the ground and worshiped the Lord. [48]Jeshua and Anniuth and Sherebiah, Jadinus, Akkub, Shabbethai, Hodiah, Maiannas and Kelita, Azariah and Jozabad, Hanan, Pelaiah, the Levites, taught the law of the Lord,[a] at the same time explaining what was read.

49 Then Attharates[b] said to Ezra the chief priest and reader, and to the Levites who were teaching the multitude, and to all, [50]"This day is holy to the Lord"—now they were all weeping as they heard the law— [51]"so go your way, eat the fat and drink the sweet, and send portions to those who have none; [52]for the day is holy to the Lord; and do not be sorrowful, for the Lord will exalt you." [53]The Levites commanded all the people, saying, "This day is holy; do not be sorrowful." [54]Then they all went their way, to eat and drink and enjoy themselves, and to give portions to those who had none, and to make great rejoicing; [55]because they were inspired by the words which they had been taught. And they came together.[c]

a Other ancient authorities add *and read the law of the Lord to the multitude*   b Or *the governor*
c The Greek text ends abruptly: compare Neh 8.13

9:50–53 *This day is holy to the Lord.* It is appropriate for a book that has focused on the rhythms of the liturgical year to offer advice on how to keep the liturgical festivals. Even though the people were right to be sorrowful for their own failure to keep the law, it was a time to set personal sorrows aside and to honor God by giving God their full attention. The festivals of our liturgical year are times to focus on what God has done and continues to do on behalf of his people and to rejoice in God together. The Christian calendar offers us many opportunities to reflect together as families and congregations on the ways in which God has been, continues to be, and will yet be present and active in our lives and to find joy in these times of reflection on our life with God.

2 ESDRAS

COMPRISING WHAT IS SOMETIMES CALLED
5 EZRA (CHAPTERS 1-2), 4 EZRA (CHAPTERS 3-14), AND
6 EZRA (CHAPTERS 15-16)

The book of 2 Esdras grew to its present form in stages. The heart of the book (2 Esdras 3–14, often called 4 Ezra—a difference in Hebrew and Greek nomenclature) is a Jewish apocalypse from the end of the first century AD. The author writes in the wake of seeing Jerusalem destroyed (probably personally, as the work gives evidence of being written in Hebrew and within the land of Israel) and seeing Rome continue to grow and prosper for decades after the fact without any sign of God's intervention to judge and punish. Writing in the name of Ezra, who lived and worked in the period after the destruction of the First Temple, a Jewish author wrestles with the "big questions" he must face if the core of his theology—the belief that God chose Israel, that Torah is God's provision of the way to life, that God judges the earth with justice, that being careful to do God's law actually makes a positive difference—is to have any meaning in the decades after the disasters of AD 70.

What is the meaning of "election" when Israel is again under the boot of a godless nation? Why does God allow Rome to prosper after destroying Jerusalem, when Rome's neglect of God is so much more egregious than Israel's ever was? What meaning is there in trying to keep the covenant, when Israel has never been able to keep the covenant successfully? The book is broadly reminiscent of Job in its persistent questioning of God's justice, emphasis on the limits of human comprehension, and conviction that the answer must involve God's self-revelation.

Seeking God

The everyday world of sense experience fails to provide meaningful answers for the author, so he reaches beyond to the bigger picture, that invisible sacred canopy of

See also *"The With-God Life" essay for this section of the Bible, "The People of God in Restoration," pp. 1355–59.*

God's realm and activity, for a perspective that might make the with-God life in this world viable once more. This is precisely the power of an apocalypse, whether it is Daniel, Revelation, 4 Ezra, or any of several dozen other specimens from the turn of the era that attempt to give readers a glimpse of the "really real." By opening our eyes to the world beyond our experience (in terms of the activities in the spaces of God and his angels and the larger struggles against the forces of darkness) and the time beyond our time (in terms of primordial and future history), apocalypses set our experiences, challenges, and temptations within a broader context that interprets and sheds new light on them. So often, this is precisely what we need most and what we would profitably seek from God by whatever venue he chooses to communicate with us about our experiences. One of the first contributions 2 Esdras can make to our spiritual formation, then, is to urge us to keep seeking "apocalyptic adjustments" to our perception of our world, to keep seeking God's mind and perspective on the situations around us and how we can respond faithfully within them.

When "Ezra" pours out his heart before God and asks the big questions, it is important for us to observe the nature of the "therapy" he receives. He does not always get answers to his questions. Rather, he receives an experience of God, an opportunity to pour out all his questions and frustrations before God, hear the word from God that he needs (even if it does not match all his questions), and receive assurances of God's justice and goodness until he rediscovers his center in God. Again, this speaks directly to our spiritual formation as we wrestle with the big questions of "why" with God and receive in the end, as our answer, "Peace; persist."

It was the early Church, rather than the synagogue, that maintained an interest in apocalypses. 4 Ezra continued to fuel Christian faith and hope long after the last of the eagle's wings (the emperors Nerva and Trajan) disappeared and continued to be replaced by more of the same rather than the kingdom of God. The same can be seen from the ongoing power of Revelation today, long after its Babylon (i.e., Rome) passed from the earth. Apocalypses retain their power because they remain windows into a larger vista than we enjoy in our daily lives, through which we need to keep looking to remember that God and the world that God will re-create are the ultimate realities that undergird our lives.

A Christian author appended a two-chapter introduction (2 Esdras 1–2, often called 5 Ezra) in the mid-second century. In it, he affirms that the Church is the successor to a disobedient Israel in the plan of God, but also affirms that those who have come to God in Christ must embody the grateful response to God that Israel did not. 5 Ezra concludes with a vision of God's redeemed from every nation making up the full number of Israel and gathered around the Son of God. Another Christian writer added a conclusion (2 Esdras 15–16, called 6 Ezra) in the mid to late third century, in the wake of the Decian persecution. In it, he prepares Christians to remain faithful in spite of ongoing persecution, denouncing the repressive systems that suppress God's truth and oppose his justice with promises of God's coming judgment upon them.

Experiencing God

The book of 2 Esdras raises an important question about how God communicates with human beings and about alternative ways in which we might experience God. This is a book about visions, dreams, and conversations with angels and other supernatural beings. Although apocalypses are not *merely* reports about ecstatic experiences (they are also the fruit of deep reflection on Scripture and how it can be brought to bear on new situations), it is difficult to deny that some genuine ecstatic experiences stand behind their composition in some way. As such, they stand in continuity with God's use of dreams, visions, and other ecstatic experiences to communicate with his people both in Israel and in the early Church. 2 Esdras challenges us to invite God to enter our lives and impact our consciousness in both rational and nonrational ways and to watch for God's presence and word coming in a grander variety of ways than our world teaches us to expect.

—David A. deSilva

The Genealogy of Ezra

1 The book*a* of the prophet Ezra son of Seraiah, son of Azariah, son of Hilkiah, son of Shallum, son of Zadok, son of Ahitub, 2son of Ahijah, son of Phinehas, son of Eli, son of Amariah, son of Azariah, son of Meraimoth, son of Arna, son of Uzzi, son of Borith, son of Abishua, son of Phinehas, son of Eleazar, 3son of Aaron, of the tribe of Levi, who was a captive in the country of the Medes in the reign of Artaxerxes, king of the Persians. *b*

Ezra's Prophetic Call

4 The word of the Lord came to me, saying, 5"Go, declare to my people their evil deeds, and to their children the iniquities that they have committed against me, so that they may tell*c* their children's children 6that the sins of their parents have increased in them, for they have forgotten me and have offered sacrifices to strange gods. 7Was it not I who brought them out of the land of Egypt, out of the house of bondage? But they have angered me and despised my counsels. 8Now you, pull out the hair of your head and hurl*d* all evils upon them, for they have not obeyed my

law—they are a rebellious people. 9How long shall I endure them, on whom I have bestowed such great benefits? 10For their sake I have overthrown many kings; I struck down Pharaoh with his servants and all his army. 11I destroyed all nations before them, and scattered in the east the peoples of two provinces, *e* Tyre and Sidon; I killed all their enemies.

God's Mercies to Israel

12 "But speak to them and say, Thus says the Lord: 13Surely it was I who brought you through the sea, and made safe highways for you where there was no road; I gave you Moses as leader and Aaron as priest; 14I provided light for you from a pillar of fire, and did great wonders among you. Yet you have forgotten me, says the Lord.

a Other ancient authorities read *The second book*
b Other ancient authorities, which place chapters 1 and 2 after 16.78, lack verses 1-3 and begin the chapter: *The word of the Lord that came to Ezra son of Chusi in the days of King Nebuchadnezzar, saying, "Go,*
c Other ancient authorities read *nourish*
d Other ancient authorities read *and shake out*
e Other ancient authorities read *Did I not destroy the city of Bethsaida because of you, and to the south burn two cities . . . ?*

1:4–37 *Go, declare to my people their evil deeds.* This indictment of Israel provides the negative image of how the author would encourage us to relate to God. Put positively,

we should always keep God's gifts, help, and commitment to us in mind and embody a grateful response to God in all aspects of the life he has given us.

15 "Thus says the Lord Almighty:[a] The quails were a sign to you; I gave you camps for your protection, and in them you complained. [16]You have not exulted in my name at the destruction of your enemies, but to this day you still complain.[b] [17]Where are the benefits that I bestowed on you? When you were hungry and thirsty in the wilderness, did you not cry out to me, [18]saying, 'Why have you led us into this wilderness to kill us? It would have been better for us to serve the Egyptians than to die in this wilderness.' [19]I pitied your groanings and gave you manna for food; you ate the bread of angels. [20]When you were thirsty, did I not split the rock so that waters flowed in abundance? Because of the heat I clothed you with the leaves of trees.[c] [21]I divided fertile lands among you; I drove out the Canaanites, the Perizzites, and the Philistines[d] before you. What more can I do for you? says the Lord. [22]Thus says the Lord Almighty:[a] When you were in the wilderness, at the bitter stream, thirsty and blaspheming my name, [23]I did not send fire on you for your blasphemies, but threw a tree into the water and made the stream sweet.

Israel's Disobedience and Rejection

24 "What shall I do to you, O Jacob? You, Judah, would not obey me. I will turn to other nations and will give them my name, so that they may keep my statutes. [25]Because you have forsaken me, I also will forsake you. When you beg mercy of me, I will show you no mercy. [26]When you call to me, I will not listen to you; for you have defiled your hands with blood, and your feet are swift to commit murder. [27]It is not as though you had forsaken me; you have forsaken yourselves, says the Lord.

28 "Thus says the Lord Almighty: Have I not entreated you as a father entreats his sons

a Other ancient authorities lack *Almighty*
b Other ancient authorities read verse 16, *Your pursuer with his army I sank in the sea, but still the people complain also concerning their own destruction.*
c Other ancient authorities read *I made for you trees with leaves*   d Other ancient authorities read *Perizzites and their children*

1:17 *Where are the benefits that I bestowed on you?* Having received God's favors during the period of the exodus, the wilderness wandering, the conquest of Canaan, and the sending of the prophets to call Israel to repent and return (vv 4–32), the people of Israel ought to have responded by honoring God and living the law. Their failure to do so opens up the way for a newly formed people, having received God's favor in Jesus, now to do what the first people did not (v 37). God's question about the benefits bestowed invites us to consider how we can keep God's gifts to us present in our lives and in our relationship with God. We are invited to remain mindful of them, to meditate upon the kindnesses and help of God in the past, in the present, and yet to come until our hearts radiate with gratitude toward God. We are invited to set that gratitude in the center of our hearts, so that it will shape our lives for obedience, service, and witness. In this way, God's gifts take root and bear fruit, remaining present for us and returning to God in a beautiful and God-honoring way.

1:24 *I will turn to other nations.* The author announces here the theme of transfer, especially in light of the first nation's unwillingness to

bear the appropriate fruits and the assurance that the new nation will. In this he agrees with Matt 21:33–43 (esp. 21:40, 43), by whom he appears to have been informed. 5 Ezra, in fact, is a study in how Matthew and Revelation nurtured the thought and hopes of a particular second-century Christian (cf., e.g., how vv 30, 33 reflect Matt 23:37–38 and how v 32 recalls Matt 23:34–35). As in Matthew, however, the indictment of Israel and the Church's succession to a place in God's favor challenge us with a picture of our responsibility to God to bear the fruits of righteousness and covenant loyalty for which God looks (notably in acts of love and service; see 2:20–24).

1:27 *you have forsaken yourselves.* When we are most busy with the daily concerns of our lives, we think we are indeed doing what is necessary to look after ourselves. But if we are so busy that we neglect God, we are in turn neglecting ourselves in all that busyness. To the extent that we neglect our relationship with God and fail to put our response to God's grace in the forefront of our lives, we lose ourselves and leave ourselves at the mercy of spiritual and earthly enemies.

or a mother her daughters or a nurse her children, [29]so that you should be my people and I should be your God, and that you should be my children and I should be your father? [30]I gathered you as a hen gathers her chicks under her wings. But now, what shall I do to you? I will cast you out from my presence. [31]When you offer oblations to me, I will turn my face from you; for I have rejected your[a] festal days, and new moons, and circumcisions of the flesh.[b] [32]I sent you my servants the prophets, but you have taken and killed them and torn their bodies[c] in pieces; I will require their blood of you, says the Lord.[d]

33 "Thus says the Lord Almighty: Your house is desolate; I will drive you out as the wind drives straw; [34]and your sons will have no children, because with you[e] they have neglected my commandment and have done what is evil in my sight. [35]I will give your houses to a people that will come, who without having heard me will believe. Those to whom I have shown no signs will do what I have commanded. [36]They have seen no prophets, yet will recall their former state.[f] [37]I call to witness the gratitude of the people that is to come, whose children rejoice with gladness;[g] though they do not see me with bodily eyes, yet with the spirit they will believe the things I have said.

38 "And now, father,[h] look with pride and see the people coming from the east; [39]to them I will give as leaders Abraham, Isaac, and Jacob, and Hosea and Amos and Micah and Joel and Obadiah and Jonah [40]and Nahum and Habakkuk, Zephaniah, Haggai, Zechariah and Malachi, who is also called the messenger of the Lord.[i]

God's Judgment on Israel

2 "Thus says the Lord: I brought this people out of bondage, and I gave them commandments through my servants the prophets; but they would not listen to them, and made my counsels void. [2]The mother who bore them[j] says to them, 'Go, my children, because I am a widow and forsaken. [3]I brought you up with gladness; but with mourning and sorrow I have lost you, because you have sinned before the Lord God and have done what is evil in my sight.[k] [4]But now what can I do for you? For I am a widow and forsaken. Go, my children, and ask for mercy from the Lord.' [5]Now I call upon you, father, as a witness in addition to

a Other ancient authorities read *I have not commanded for you*   b Other ancient authorities lack *of the flesh*   c Other ancient authorities read *the bodies of the apostles*   d Other ancient authorities add *Thus says the Lord Almighty: Recently you also laid hands on me, crying out before the judge's seat for him to deliver me to you. You took me as a sinner, not as a father who freed you from slavery, and you delivered me to death by hanging me on the tree; these are the things you have done. Therefore, says the Lord, let my Father and his angels return and judge between you and me; if I have not kept the commandment of the Father, if I have not nourished you, if I have not done the things my Father commanded, I will contend in judgment with you, says the Lord.*   e Other ancient authorities lack *with you*   f Other ancient authorities read *their iniquities*   g Other ancient authorities read *The apostles bear witness to the coming people with joy*   h Other ancient authorities read *brother*   i Other ancient authorities read *and Jacob, Elijah and Enoch, Zechariah and Hosea, Amos, Joel, Micah, Obadiah, Zephaniah,* [40]*Nahum, Jonah, Mattia (or Mattathias), Habakkuk, and twelve angels with flowers*   j Other ancient authorities read *They begat for themselves a mother who*   k Other ancient authorities read *in his sight*

1:37 *the gratitude of the people that is to come.* Gratitude, as was well known at the turn of the era, meant honoring the giver through public testimony to one's experience of favor, showing loyalty to the giver, and offering some kind of response to the giver (usually acts of service). Applied to our relationship with God, the concept of gratitude removes all tension between "grace" and "works": the latter are always a response to the former, but they remain a necessary response as well.

Responding
1:37 **WORSHIP.** As part of the "people that is to come," what kind of witness does our gratitude bear? How does our response to God justify, in a sense, God's confidence in us as recipients of God's mercy and kindness? *See also* Spiritual Disciplines Index.

1:39–40 *to them I will give as leaders.* We are given Abraham, Isaac, and Jacob as "leaders" as we are rooted in the promises given to them by

the mother of the children, because they would not keep my covenant, 6so that you may bring confusion on them and bring their mother to ruin, so that they may have no offspring. 7Let them be scattered among the nations; let their names be blotted out from the earth, because they have despised my covenant.

8 "Woe to you, Assyria, who conceal the unrighteous within you! O wicked nation, remember what I did to Sodom and Gomorrah, 9whose land lies in lumps of pitch and heaps of ashes.ª That is what I will do to those who have not listened to me, says the Lord Almighty."

10 Thus says the Lord to Ezra: "Tell my people that I will give them the kingdom of Jerusalem, which I was going to give to Israel. 11Moreover, I will take back to myself their glory, and will give to these others the everlasting habitations, which I had prepared for Israel.ᵇ 12The tree of life shall give them fragrant perfume, and they shall neither toil nor become weary. 13Goᶜ and you will receive; pray that your days may be few, that they may be shortened. The kingdom is already prepared for you; be on the watch! 14Call, O call heaven and earth to witness: I set aside evil and created good; for I am the Living One, says the Lord.

Exhortation to Good Works

15 "Mother, embrace your children; bring them up with gladness, as does a dove; strengthen their feet, because I have chosen you, says the Lord. 16And I will raise up the dead from their places, and bring them out from their tombs, because I recognize my name in them. 17Do not fear, mother of children, for I have chosen you, says the Lord. 18I will send you help, my servants Isaiah and Jeremiah. According to their counsel I have consecrated and prepared for you twelve trees loaded with various fruits, 19and the same number of springs flowing with milk and honey, and seven mighty mountains on which roses and lilies grow; by these I will fill your children with joy.

20 "Guard the rights of the widow, secure justice for the ward, give to the needy, defend the orphan, clothe the naked, 21care for the injured and the weak, do not ridicule the lame, protect the maimed, and let the blind have a vision of my splendor. 22Protect the old and the young within your walls. 23When you find any who are dead, commit them to the grave and mark it,ᵈ and I will

a Other ancient authorities read Gomorrah, whose land descends to hell   b Lat for those   c Other ancient authorities read Seek   d Or seal it; or mark them and commit them to the grave

---

our trust in Jesus (cf. Gal 3:6–29); we receive the twelve prophets as leaders as we are rooted in the Scriptures, in which we continue to hear the living word of God in the prophets.

2:15 Mother, embrace your children. (See also vv 30–32.) Addressing the Church as a whole as a "mother" speaks to the character that the Church is to embody for individual believers. We are invited to be a nurturing community, one in which each disciple finds the embrace of something greater and through which we are assured of God's merciful character and unfailing favor. Creating a community that is able to "embrace" each member, we make God's presence, promises, and character real for one another.

2:18–19 I will send you help, my servants Isaiah and Jeremiah. Isaiah and Jeremiah, like the twelve minor prophets (see 1:39–40), are sent as help by keeping our hope fixed on the

good things God has prepared and by teaching us rather directly about the kind of response God expects from the people he has formed for himself. When we dedicate ourselves to the study of Scripture, the text comes to life and God is able to bring us vision and to lead us anew through the Word of God.

2:20–24 Guard the rights of the widow. Deuteronomy, the prophets, Jesus, and the apostles (notably James; see James 1:27) all bear witness to the fact that genuine knowledge of God transforms human relationships and breaks forth into works of love and mercy. The poetic injunction to "let the blind have a vision of my splendor" is a poignant way of expressing the fact that God's goodness and love can be made visible and palpable to people in distress as God's love takes on flesh in our bodies and impacts the lives of those to whom we reach out in love and restorative care.

give you the first place in my resurrection. [ESCHATOLOGY] [24]Pause and be quiet, my people, because your rest will come.

25 "Good nurse, nourish your children; strengthen their feet. [26]Not one of the servants[a] whom I have given you will perish, for I will require them from among your number. [27]Do not be anxious, for when the day of tribulation and anguish comes, others shall weep and be sorrowful, but you shall rejoice and have abundance. [28]The nations shall envy you, but they shall not be able to do anything against you, says the Lord. [29]My power will protect[b] you, so that your children may not see hell.[c]

30 "Rejoice, O mother, with your children, because I will deliver you, says the Lord. [31]Remember your children that sleep, because I will bring them out of the hiding places of the earth, and will show mercy to them; for I am merciful, says the Lord Almighty. [32]Embrace your children until I come, and proclaim mercy to them; because my springs run over, and my grace will not fail."

[ESCHATOLOGY]

Ezra on Mount Horeb

33 I, Ezra, received a command from the Lord on Mount Horeb to go to Israel. When I came to them they rejected me and refused the Lord's commandment. [34]Therefore I say to you, O nations that hear and understand,

"Wait for your shepherd; he will give you everlasting rest, because he who will come at the end of the age is close at hand. [35]Be ready for the rewards of the kingdom, because perpetual light will shine on you forevermore. [36]Flee from the shadow of this age, receive the joy of your glory; I publicly call on my savior to witness.[d] [37]Receive what the Lord has entrusted to you and be joyful, giving thanks to him who has called you to the celestial kingdoms. [38]Rise, stand erect and see the number of those who have been sealed at the feast of the Lord. [39]Those who have departed from the shadow of this age have received glorious garments from the Lord. [40]Take again your full number, O Zion, and close the list of your people who are clothed in white, who have fulfilled the law of the Lord. [41]The number of your children, whom you desired, is now complete; implore the Lord's authority that your people, who have been called from the beginning, may be made holy."

Ezra Sees the Son of God

42 I, Ezra, saw on Mount Zion a great multitude that I could not number, and they all were praising the Lord with songs. [43]In their

a Or slaves   b Lat hands will cover   c Lat Gehenna   d Other ancient authorities read I testify that my savior has been commissioned by the Lord

---

2:33–48 *Wait for your shepherd.* This passage, bearing the imprint of Rev 7:4–17, calls us to look ahead to the way in which we will be fully and finally "with God." It orients us toward this present life as to a fleeting shadow and teaches us to yearn for the embrace and the glory that God will give us in the age to come. What is "real" and what is "shadow" is quite the opposite here from what we are taught (e.g., about "the real world").

2:39–40 *glorious garments from the Lord.* (See also v 45.) The Scriptures' use of the imagery of "garments" is quite rich. Here we think first of the gift of immortality, which we will put on like a garment at the last day (vv 39, 45), when we will be "fully clothed," after we have shed the body of mortality like a worn-out garment (see 1 Cor 15:53–54; 2 Cor 5:2–5). But we also think

of the cleansing we have received from our sins by Christ, by whose blood we have washed our garments and made them white (Rev 7:14); we think of the righteous deeds God has allowed us to do, which become our clothing and the bridal gown of the whole Church (Rev 19:7–8); we think of the summons to keep our lives undefiled by compromise with the powers of this world and the cravings of our own flesh, so that we may walk in white (Rev 3:4–5). Finally, we cannot help but think about the invitation to put on Christ and to clothe ourselves with love and kindness (Gal 3:27; Col 3:12–17). These images lend themselves well to meditation, even to symbolic action as a means of apprehending the spiritual gift offered to us by the new life in Christ.

midst was a young man of great stature, taller than any of the others, and on the head of each of them he placed a crown, but he was more exalted than they. And I was held spellbound. 44Then I asked an angel, "Who are these, my lord?" 45He answered and said to me, "These are they who have put off mortal clothing and have put on the immortal, and have confessed the name of God. Now they are being crowned, and receive palms." 46Then I said to the angel, "Who is that young man who is placing crowns on them and putting palms in their hands?" 47He answered and said to me, "He is the Son of God, whom they confessed in the world." So I began to praise those who had stood valiantly for the name of the Lord. a 48Then the angel said to me, "Go, tell my people how great and how many are the wonders of the Lord God that you have seen."

Ezra's Prayer of Complaint

3 In the thirtieth year after the destruction of the city, I was in Babylon—I, Salathiel, who am also called Ezra. I was troubled as I lay on my bed, and my thoughts welled up in my heart, 2because I saw the desolation of Zion and the wealth of those who lived in Babylon. 3My spirit was greatly agitated, and I began to speak anxious words to the Most High, and said, 4"O sovereign Lord, did you not speak at the beginning when you planted b the earth—and that without help—and commanded the dust c 5and it gave you Adam, a lifeless body? Yet he was the

creation of your hands, and you breathed into him the breath of life, and he was made alive in your presence. 6And you led him into the garden that your right hand had planted before the earth appeared. 7And you laid upon him one commandment of yours; but he transgressed it, and immediately you appointed death for him and for his descendants. From him there sprang nations and tribes, peoples and clans without number. 8And every nation walked after its own will; they did ungodly things in your sight and rejected your commands, and you did not hinder them. 9But again, in its time you brought the flood upon the inhabitants of the world and destroyed them. 10And the same fate befell all of them: just as death came upon Adam, so the flood upon them. 11But you left one of them, Noah with his household, and all the righteous who have descended from him.

12 "When those who lived on earth began to multiply, they produced children and peoples and many nations, and again they began to be more ungodly than were their ancestors. 13And when they were committing iniquity in your sight, you chose for yourself one of them, whose name was Abraham; 14you loved him, and to him alone you revealed the end of the times, secretly by night. 15You made an everlasting covenant with him, and promised him that you would never forsake his descendants; and you gave him Isaac, and to Isaac you gave Jacob and Esau. 16You set apart

a Other ancient authorities read to praise and glorify the Lord   b Other ancient authorities read formed   c Syr Ethiop: Lat people or world

---

3:1–14:48 *In the thirtieth year after the destruction of the city.* In these chapters, the older Jewish apocalypse called 4 Ezra, the model of "Ezra," through whose persona the real author writes, teaches us that the difficult questions we would ask of God will only be answered when we are willing to give significant time and energy to seeking God's face. A quick prayer of "Why, God, why?!" and then a return to business as usual will not suffice. Instead, God invites us to come into his presence for extended conversations, during which God imparts himself and his perspective to us. As we read through this book,

we will be struck by Ezra's honesty and openness in prayer. He holds back no question, no emotion. This is essential to experiencing God's healing in times of distress and grief. Ezra also does not leave the place of prayer until he has heard from God and experienced God's presence, which is even more essential. We short-circuit our own engagement with prayer when we neglect either part of this equation. We have probably all been where Ezra is at the start of this book, tossing in bed with troubled thoughts. But have we perceived this experience as God's invitation to conversation in prayer?

Jacob for yourself, but Esau you rejected; and Jacob became a great multitude. [17]And when you led his descendants out of Egypt, you brought them to Mount Sinai. [18]You bent down the heavens and shook[a] the earth, and moved the world, and caused the depths to tremble, and troubled the times. [19]Your glory passed through the four gates of fire and earthquake and wind and ice, to give the law to the descendants of Jacob, and your commandment to the posterity of Israel.

20 "Yet you did not take away their evil heart from them, so that your law might produce fruit in them. [21]For the first Adam, burdened with an evil heart, transgressed and was overcome, as were also all who were descended from him. [22]Thus the disease became permanent; the law was in the hearts of the people along with the evil root; but what was good departed, and the evil remained. [23]So the times passed and the years were completed, and you raised up for yourself a servant, named David. [24]You commanded him to build a city for your name, and there to offer you oblations from what is yours. [25]This was done for many years; but the inhabitants of the city transgressed, [26]in everything doing just as Adam and all his descendants had done, for they also had the evil heart. [27]So you handed over your city to your enemies.

Babylon Compared with Zion

28 "Then I said in my heart, Are the deeds of those who inhabit Babylon any better? Is that why it has gained dominion over Zion? [29]For when I came here I saw ungodly deeds without number, and my soul has seen many sinners during these thirty years.[b] And my heart failed me, [30]because I have seen how you endure those who sin, and have spared those who act wickedly, and have destroyed your people, and protected your enemies, [31]and have not shown to anyone how your way may be comprehended.[c] Are the deeds of Babylon better than those of Zion? [32]Or has another nation known you besides Israel? Or what tribes have so believed the covenants as these tribes of Jacob? [33]Yet their reward has not appeared and their labor has borne no fruit. For I have traveled widely among the nations and have seen that they abound in wealth, though they are unmindful of your commandments. [34]Now therefore weigh in a balance our iniquities and those of the inhabitants of the world; and it will be found which way the turn of the scale will incline. [35]When have the inhabitants of the earth not sinned in your sight? Or what nation has kept your commandments so well? [36]You may indeed find individuals who have kept your commandments, but nations you will not find."

a Syr Ethiop Arab 1 Georg: Lat *set fast*   b Ethiop Arab 1 Arm: Lat Syr *in this thirtieth year*   c Syr; compare Ethiop: Lat *how this way should be forsaken*

3:20–22 *Yet you did not take away their evil heart from them.* The author's reading of Genesis 3 is consonant with Paul's in Rom 5:12–21. The basic human problem is that our hearts are divided between following self and sin and following God. The author faults God for not removing the evil inclination from the human heart; Paul would praise God for planting his Holy Spirit within our hearts, to guide us into and empower us for an undivided pursuit of life with God. Ezekiel's promise of a new heart and a new spirit (Ezek 36:25–27) comes to fulfillment here in our reception of and life with the Holy Spirit.

3:28–36 *Are the deeds of those who inhabit Babylon any better?* The author wrestles here with the basic question, "Why do good things happen to bad people?" asked also in Psalm 73. If God has chastened Israel for its sins, why does God not punish Rome for its far worse sins? The author of Psalm 73 had to look to the end of life for an answer; the author here looks to the horizon of God's forthcoming apocalyptic interventions. At the root of each answer is the conviction that God will always prove, in the end, to be just. As we watch Ezra throughout these opening conversations, we see the cathartic effect of raising in prayer the hard questions that trouble us upon our beds and the importance of taking this first step if God is to be allowed to deal with our deep needs. No question is too hard for God, no feeling hidden from him—but God can only deal with those things we openly bring before him for his healing and help.

Limitations of the Human Mind

4 Then the angel that had been sent to me, whose name was Uriel, answered [2]and said to me, "Your understanding has utterly failed regarding this world, and do you think you can comprehend the way of the Most High?" [3]Then I said, "Yes, my lord." And he replied to me, "I have been sent to show you three ways, and to put before you three problems. [4]If you can solve one of them for me, then I will show you the way you desire to see, and will teach you why the heart is evil."

5 I said, "Speak, my lord."

And he said to me, "Go, weigh for me the weight of fire, or measure for me a blast[a] of wind, or call back for me the day that is past."

6 I answered and said, "Who of those that have been born can do that, that you should ask me about such things?"

7 And he said to me, "If I had asked you, 'How many dwellings are in the heart of the sea, or how many streams are at the source of the deep, or how many streams are above the firmament, or which are the exits of Hades, or which are the entrances[b] of paradise?' [8]perhaps you would have said to me, 'I never went down into the deep, nor as yet into Hades, neither did I ever ascend into heaven.' [9]But now I have asked you only about fire and wind and the day—things that you have experienced and from which you cannot be separated, and you have given me no answer about them." [10]He said to me, "You cannot understand the things with which you have grown up; [11]how then can your mind comprehend the way of the Most High? And how can one who is already worn out[c] by the corrupt world understand incorruption?"[d] When I heard this, I fell on my face[e] [12]and said to him, "It would have been better for us not to be here than to come here and live in ungodliness, and to suffer and not understand why."

Parable of the Forest and the Sea

13 He answered me and said, "I went into a forest of trees of the plain, and they made a plan [14]and said, 'Come, let us go and make war against the sea, so that it may recede before us and so that we may make for ourselves more forests.' [15]In like manner the waves of the sea also made a plan and said, 'Come, let us go up and subdue the forest of the plain so that there also we may gain more territory for ourselves.' [16]But the plan of the forest was in vain, for the fire came and consumed it;

a Syr Ethiop Arab 1 Arab 2 Georg *a measure*
b Syr Compare Ethiop Arab 2 Arm: Lat lacks *of Hades, or which are the entrances*   c Meaning of Lat uncertain   d Syr Ethiop *the way of the incorruptible?*   e Syr Ethiop Arab 1: Meaning of Lat uncertain

---

4:1 *the angel that had been sent to me, whose name was Uriel.* The angel Uriel's answers in the upcoming chapters often do not directly answer Ezra's questions, and they are often redundant—but this is part of the therapy Ezra needs. God knows that what we often really need is not the answer to the question we are posing; God also knows that we need to be reaffirmed and taken repeatedly back to the information we need to hear and internalize. The repetition of basic truths we may hear from God is not God's avoidance of our questions, but his calming reassurance of what we need most to hear. Perhaps the most important ingredient in Ezra's journey through difficulty to a new integrated wholeness is not merely the content, but the experience of God that dominates this book.

4:9–11 *You cannot understand the things with which you have grown up.* The responses Ezra receives often recall God's response to Job. Humility with regard to the limitations of human understanding where God is concerned is necessary, given the fact that we cannot even claim to have mastered knowledge of and power over all the phenomena even of this world. More to the point, it is ultimately not understanding, but presence—the companionship and love of God—that we need most in our deep questioning.

4:12 *to suffer and not understand why.* Victor Frankl, the author of *Man's Search for Meaning,* well understood that suffering was not the human problem, but suffering without meaning. We can tolerate much hardship and anguish if we can find meaning in the midst of it. Ezra models the way to lay hold of this meaning—his restless search drives him closer and closer to the heart of God.

17likewise also the plan of the waves of the sea was in vain,[a] for the sand stood firm and blocked it. 18If now you were a judge between them, which would you undertake to justify, and which to condemn?"

19 I answered and said, "Each made a foolish plan, for the land has been assigned to the forest, and the locale of the sea a place to carry its waves."

20 He answered me and said, "You have judged rightly, but why have you not judged so in your own case? 21For as the land has been assigned to the forest and the sea to its waves, so also those who inhabit the earth can understand only what is on the earth, and he who is[b] above the heavens can understand what is above the height of the heavens."

The New Age Will Make All Things Clear

22 Then I answered and said, "I implore you, my lord, why[c] have I been endowed with the power of understanding? 23For I did not wish to inquire about the ways above, but about those things that we daily experience: why Israel has been given over to the Gentiles in disgrace; why the people whom you loved has been given over to godless tribes, and the law of our ancestors has been brought to destruction and the written covenants no longer exist. 24We pass from the world like locusts, and our life is like a mist,[d] and we are not worthy to obtain mercy. 25But what will he do for his[e] name that is invoked over us? It is about these things that I have asked."

26 He answered me and said, "If you are alive, you will see, and if you live long,[f] you will often marvel, because the age is hurrying swiftly to its end. 27It will not be able to bring the things that have been promised to the righteous in their appointed times, because this age is full of sadness and infirmities. 28For the evil about which[g] you ask me has been sown, but the harvest of it has not yet come. 29If therefore that which has been sown is not reaped, and if the place where the evil has been sown does not pass away, the field where the good has been sown will not come. 30For a grain of evil seed was sown in Adam's heart from the beginning, and how much ungodliness it has produced until now—and will produce until the time of threshing comes! 31Consider now for yourself how much fruit of ungodliness a grain of evil seed has produced. 32When heads of grain without number are sown, how great a threshing floor they will fill!"

When Will the New Age Come?

33 Then I answered and said, "How long?[g] When will these things be? Why are our years few and evil?" 34He answered me and said, "Do not be in a greater hurry than the Most High. You, indeed, are in a hurry for yourself,[h] but the Highest is in a hurry on behalf of many. 35Did not the souls of the righteous in their chambers ask about these matters, saying, 'How long are we to remain here?[i] And when will the harvest of our reward

a Lat lacks *was in vain*   b Or *those who are*
c Syr Ethiop Arm: Meaning of Lat uncertain
d Syr Ethiop Arab Georg: Lat *a trembling*
e Ethiop adds *holy*   f Syr: Lat *live*   g Syr
Ethiop: Meaning of Lat uncertain   h Syr Ethiop
Arab Arm: Meaning of Lat uncertain   i Syr
Ethiop Arab 2 Georg: Lat *How long do I hope thus?*

4:28–31 *the evil about which you ask me has been sown.* Uriel imparts an important insight about the ways in which evil multiplies like a harvest from a seed. For this reason, it is so imperative not to sow the seeds of malice, discontent, slander, lust, greed, and the like in our lives and communities, for the evil takes on a life of its own and becomes fruitful beyond our imagination. Although the author looks ahead only to the age to come for a world in which the harvest of the good seeds that are sown can spring up, those seeds of life, love, and healing are sown now in the midst of our broken world. Out of these will be born the life of the world to come.

4:35–37 *How long are we to remain here?* This text is highly reminiscent of Rev 6:9–11, a near contemporary vision. The message of both is clear: God's vision and plan for this world are larger than our personal fates, and we will only find peace as we entrust ourselves to God's goodness and allow our frustration and impatience to dissolve in the sea of his good timing.

come?' [36]And the archangel Jeremiel answered and said, 'When the number of those like yourselves is completed;[a] for he has weighed the age in the balance, [37]and measured the times by measure, and numbered the times by number; and he will not move or arouse them until that measure is fulfilled.' "

38 Then I answered and said, "But, O sovereign Lord, all of us also are full of ungodliness. [39]It is perhaps on account of us that the time of threshing is delayed for the righteous—on account of the sins of those who inhabit the earth."

40 He answered me and said, "Go and ask a pregnant woman whether, when her nine months have been completed, her womb can keep the fetus within her any longer."

41 And I said, "No, lord, it cannot."

He said to me, "In Hades the chambers of the souls are like the womb. [42]For just as a woman who is in labor makes haste to escape the pangs of birth, so also do these places hasten to give back those things that were committed to them from the beginning. [43]Then the things that you desire to see will be disclosed to you."

How Much Time Remains?

44 I answered and said, "If I have found favor in your sight, and if it is possible, and if I am worthy, [45]show me this also: whether more time is to come than has passed, or whether for us the greater part has gone by. [46]For I know what has gone by, but I do not know what is to come."

47 And he said to me, "Stand at my right side, and I will show you the interpretation of a parable."

48 So I stood and looked, and lo, a flaming furnace passed by before me, and when the flame had gone by I looked, and lo, the smoke remained. [49]And after this a cloud full of water passed before me and poured down a heavy and violent rain, and when the violent rainstorm had passed, drops still remained in the cloud.[b]

50 He said to me, "Consider it for yourself; for just as the rain is more than the drops, and the fire is greater than the smoke, so the quantity that passed was far greater; but drops and smoke remained."

51 Then I prayed and said, "Do you think that I shall live until those days? Or who will be alive in those days?"

52 He answered me and said, "Concerning the signs about which you ask me, I can tell you in part; but I was not sent to tell you concerning your life, for I do not know.

Signs of the End

5 "Now concerning the signs: lo, the days are coming when those who inhabit the earth shall be seized with great terror,[c] and the way of truth shall be hidden, and the land shall be barren of faith. [2]Unrighteousness shall be increased beyond what you yourself see, and beyond what you heard of formerly. [3]And the land that you now see ruling shall be a trackless waste, and people shall see it desolate. [4]But if the Most High grants that you live, you shall see it thrown into confusion after the third period;[d]

and the sun shall suddenly begin to
    shine at night,
    and the moon during the day.
[5] Blood shall drip from wood,
    and the stone shall utter its voice;
    the peoples shall be troubled,
    and the stars shall fall.[e]

[6]And one shall reign whom those who inhabit the earth do not expect, and the birds shall fly away together; [7]and the Dead Sea[f] shall cast up fish; and one whom the many do not know shall make his voice heard by night, and all shall hear his voice.[g] [8]There shall be chaos also in many places, fire shall often break out, the wild animals shall roam beyond their haunts, and menstruous women shall bring forth monsters. [9]Salt waters shall be found in the sweet, and all friends shall conquer one another; then shall reason hide itself, and wisdom shall withdraw into its

a Syr Ethiop Arab 2: Lat *number of seeds is completed for you*   *b* Lat *in it*   *c* Syr Ethiop: Meaning of Lat uncertain   *d* Literally *after the third*; Ethiop *after three months*; Arm *after the third vision*; Georg *after the third day*   *e* Ethiop Compare Syr and Arab: Meaning of Lat uncertain   *f* Lat *Sea of Sodom*   *g* Cn: Lat *fish; and it shall make its voice heard by night, which the many have not known, but all shall hear its voice.*

chamber, [10]and it shall be sought by many but shall not be found, and unrighteousness and unrestraint shall increase on earth. [11]One country shall ask its neighbor, 'Has righteousness, or anyone who does right, passed through you?' And it will answer, 'No.' [12]At that time people shall hope but not obtain; they shall labor, but their ways shall not prosper. [13]These are the signs that I am permitted to tell you, and if you pray again, and weep as you do now, and fast for seven days, you shall hear yet greater things than these."

Conclusion of the Vision

14 Then I woke up, and my body shuddered violently, and my soul was so troubled that it fainted. [15]But the angel who had come and talked with me held me and strengthened me and set me on my feet.

16 Now on the second night Phaltiel, a chief of the people, came to me and said, "Where have you been? And why is your face sad? [17]Or do you not know that Israel has been entrusted to you in the land of their exile? [18]Rise therefore and eat some bread, and do not forsake us, like a shepherd who leaves the flock in the power of savage wolves."

19 Then I said to him, "Go away from me and do not come near me for seven days; then you may come to me."

He heard what I said and left me. [20]So I fasted seven days, mourning and weeping, as the angel Uriel had commanded me.

Ezra's Second Prayer of Complaint

21 After seven days the thoughts of my heart were very grievous to me again. [22]Then my soul recovered the spirit of understanding, and I began once more to speak words in the presence of the Most High. [23]I said, "O sovereign Lord, from every forest of the earth and from all its trees you have chosen one vine, [24]and from all the lands of the world you have chosen for yourself one region, [a] and from all the flowers of the world you have chosen for yourself one lily, [25]and from all the depths of the sea you have filled for yourself one river, and from all the cities that have been built you have consecrated Zion for yourself, [26]and from all the birds that have been created you have named for yourself one dove, and from all the flocks that have been made you have provided for yourself one sheep, [27]and from all the multitude of peoples you have gotten for yourself one people; and to this people, whom you have loved, you have given the law that is approved by all. [28]And now, O Lord, why have you handed the one over to the many, and dishonored [b] the one root beyond the others, and scattered your only one among the many? [29]And those who opposed your promises have trampled on those who believed your covenants. [30]If you really hate your people, they should be punished at your own hands."

Response to Ezra's Complaints

31 When I had spoken these words, the angel who had come to me on a previous night was sent to me. [32]He said to me, "Listen

a Ethiop: Lat pit   b Syr Ethiop Arab: Lat prepared

5:13, 20 *if you pray again . . . and fast for seven days.* This book underscores the intentionality and investment required of those who would encounter God at their points of deepest struggle. Ezra commits entire weeks in succession to fasting, heartfelt prayer, and solitude in order to meet God and be met by God. Do we make enough room in our lives for these disciplines, given the burdens we carry in our own hearts?

Responding
5:13, 20 FASTING. If you feel called to fast from food for seven days, as Ezra does here, start slowly, with several twenty-four-hour periods of fasting from lunch to lunch, and work your way up to a full day (thirty-six hours) and then three days. When you are ready for the seven days, prepare your body by eating lighter meals for the day or two before you begin. Then write in your journal about your experience. Don't worry too much about the results one way or the other. When you have completed the seven days, break your fast with fruit juice, then fruits and vegetables, and work your way up to heavier foods. *See also* Spiritual Disciplines Index.

to me, and I will instruct you; pay attention to me, and I will tell you more."

33 Then I said, "Speak, my lord." And he said to me, "Are you greatly disturbed in mind over Israel? Or do you love him more than his Maker does?"

34 I said, "No, my lord, but because of my grief I have spoken; for every hour I suffer agonies of heart, while I strive to understand the way of the Most High and to search out some part of his judgment."

35 He said to me, "You cannot." And I said, "Why not, my lord? Why then was I born? Or why did not my mother's womb become my grave, so that I would not see the travail of Jacob and the exhaustion of the people of Israel?"

36 He said to me, "Count up for me those who have not yet come, and gather for me the scattered raindrops, and make the withered flowers bloom again for me; 37 open for me the closed chambers, and bring out for me the winds shut up in them, or show me the picture of a voice; and then I will explain to you the travail that you ask to understand." [a]

38 I said, "O sovereign Lord, who is able to know these things except him whose dwelling is not with mortals? 39 As for me, I am without wisdom, and how can I speak concerning the things that you have asked me?"

40 He said to me, "Just as you cannot do one of the things that were mentioned, so you cannot discover my judgment, or the goal of the love that I have promised to my people."

Why Successive Generations Have Been Created

41 I said, "Yet, O Lord, you have charge of those who are alive at the end, but what will those do who lived before me, or we, ourselves, or those who come after us?"

42 He said to me, "I shall liken my judgment to a circle; [b] just as for those who are last there is no slowness, so for those who are first there is no haste."

43 Then I answered and said, "Could you not have created at one time those who have been and those who are and those who will be, so that you might show your judgment the sooner?"

44 He replied to me and said, "The creation cannot move faster than the Creator, nor can the world hold at one time those who have been created in it."

45 I said, "How have you said to your servant that you [c] will certainly give life at one time to your creation? If therefore all creatures will live at one time [d] and the creation will sustain them, it might even now be able to support all of them present at one time."

46 He said to me, "Ask a woman's womb, and say to it, 'If you bear ten [e] children, why one after another?' Request it therefore to produce ten at one time."

47 I said, "Of course it cannot, but only each in its own time."

48 He said to me, "Even so I have given the womb of the earth to those who from time to time are sown in it. 49 For as an infant does not bring forth, and a woman who has become old does not bring forth any longer, so I have made the same rule for the world that I created."

When and How Will the End Come?

50 Then I inquired and said, "Since you have now given me the opportunity, let me speak before you. Is our mother, of whom you have told me, still young? Or is she now approaching old age?"

51 He replied to me, "Ask a woman who bears children, and she will tell you. 52 Say to her, 'Why are those whom you have borne recently not like those whom you bore before, but smaller in stature?' 53 And she herself will answer you, 'Those born in the strength of youth are different from those born during the time of old age, when the womb is failing.' 54 Therefore you also should consider that you and your contemporaries are small-

a Lat *see*   b Or *crown*   c Syr Ethiop Arab 1:
Meaning of Lat uncertain   d Lat lacks *If . . . one
time*   e Syr Ethiop Arab 2 Arm: Meaning of Lat
uncertain

5:33-35, 40 *I strive to understand the way of the Most High.* See note on 4:9-11.

5:44 *the creation cannot move faster than the Creator.* See note on 4:35-37.

er in stature than those who were before you, [55]and those who come after you will be smaller than you, as born of a creation that already is aging and passing the strength of youth."

56 I said, "I implore you, O Lord, if I have found favor in your sight, show your servant through whom you will visit your creation."

6 He said to me, "At the beginning of the circle of the earth, before[a] the portals of the world were in place, and before the assembled winds blew, [2]and before the rumblings of thunder sounded, and before the flashes of lightning shone, and before the foundations of paradise were laid, [3]and before the beautiful flowers were seen, and before the powers of movements[b] were established, and before the innumerable hosts of angels were gathered together, [4]and before the heights of the air were lifted up, and before the measures of the firmaments were named, and before the footstool of Zion was established, [5]and before the present years were reckoned and before the imaginations of those who now sin were estranged, and before those who stored up treasures of faith were sealed— [6]then I planned these things, and they were made through me alone and not through another; just as the end shall come through me alone and not through another."

The Dividing of the Times

7 I answered and said, "What will be the dividing of the times? Or when will be the end of the first age and the beginning of the age that follows?"

8 He said to me, "From Abraham to Isaac,[c] because from him were born Jacob and Esau, for Jacob's hand held Esau's heel from the beginning. [9]Now Esau is the end of this age, and Jacob is the beginning of the age that follows. [10]The beginning of a person is the hand, and the end of a person is the heel;[d] seek for nothing else, Ezra, between the heel and the hand, Ezra!"

More Signs of the End

11 I answered and said, "O sovereign Lord, if I have found favor in your sight, [12]show

your servant the last of your signs of which you showed me a part on a previous night."

13 He answered and said to me, "Rise to your feet and you will hear a full, resounding voice. [14]And if the place where you are standing is greatly shaken [15]while the voice is speaking, do not be terrified; because the word concerns the end, and the foundations of the earth will understand [16]that the speech concerns them. They will tremble and be shaken, for they know that their end must be changed."

17 When I heard this, I got to my feet and listened; a voice was speaking, and its sound was like the sound of mighty[e] waters. [18]It said, "The days are coming when I draw near to visit the inhabitants of the earth, [19]and when I require from the doers of iniquity the penalty of their iniquity, and when the humiliation of Zion is complete. [20]When the seal is placed upon the age that is about to pass away, then I will show these signs: the books shall be opened before the face of the firmament, and all shall see my judgment[f] together. [21]Children a year old shall speak with their voices, and pregnant women shall give birth to premature children at three and four months, and these shall live and leap about. [22]Sown places shall suddenly appear unsown, and full storehouses shall suddenly be found to be empty; [23]the trumpet shall sound aloud, and when all hear it, they shall suddenly be terrified. [24]At that time friends shall make war on friends like enemies, the earth and those who inhabit it shall be terrified, and the springs of the fountains shall stand still, so that for three hours they shall not flow.

25 "It shall be that whoever remains after all that I have foretold to you shall be saved and shall see my salvation and the end of my world. [26]And they shall see those who were taken up, who from their birth have not tast-

a Meaning of Lat uncertain: Compare Syr *The beginning by the hand of humankind, but the end by my own hands. For as before the land of the world existed there, and before*; Ethiop: *At first by the Son of Man, and afterwards I myself. For before the earth and the lands were created, and before*   b Or *earthquakes*
c Other ancient authorities read *to Abraham*
d Syr: Meaning of Lat uncertain   e Lat *many*
f Syr: Lat lacks *my judgment*

ed death; and the heart of the earth's[a] inhabitants shall be changed and converted to a different spirit. 27For evil shall be blotted out, and deceit shall be quenched; 28faithfulness shall flourish, and corruption shall be overcome, and the truth, which has been so long without fruit, shall be revealed."

Conclusion of the Second Vision

29 While he spoke to me, little by little the place where I was standing began to rock to and fro.[b] 30And he said to me, "I have come to show you these things this night.[c] 31If therefore you will pray again and fast again for seven days, I will again declare to you greater things than these,[d] 32because your voice has surely been heard by the Most High; for the Mighty One has seen your uprightness and has also observed the purity that you have maintained from your youth. 33Therefore he sent me to show you all these things, and to say to you: 'Believe and do not be afraid! 34Do not be quick to think vain thoughts concerning the former times; then you will not act hastily in the last times.' "

The Third Vision

35 Now after this I wept again and fasted seven days in the same way as before, in order to complete the three weeks that had been prescribed for me. 36Then on the eighth night my heart was troubled within me again, and I began to speak in the presence of the Most High. 37My spirit was greatly aroused, and my soul was in distress.

God's Work in Creation

38 I said, "O Lord, you spoke at the beginning of creation, and said on the first day, 'Let heaven and earth be made,' and your word accomplished the work. 39Then the spirit was blowing, and darkness and silence embraced everything; the sound of human voices was not yet there.[e] 40Then you commanded a ray of light to be brought out from your store-chambers, so that your works could be seen.

41 "Again, on the second day, you created the spirit of the firmament, and commanded it to divide and separate the waters, so that one part might move upward and the other part remain beneath.

42 "On the third day you commanded the waters to be gathered together in a seventh part of the earth; six parts you dried up and kept so that some of them might be planted and cultivated and be of service before you. 43For your word went forth, and at once the work was done. 44Immediately fruit came forth in endless abundance and of varied appeal to the taste, and flowers of inim-

a Syr Compare Ethiop Arab 1 Arm: Lat lacks *earth's*
b Syr Ethiop Compare Arab Arm: Meaning of Lat uncertain   c Syr Compare Ethiop: Meaning of Lat uncertain   d Syr Ethiop Arab 1 Arm: Lat adds *by day*   e Syr Ethiop: Lat *was not yet from you*

6:26–28 *And they shall see those who were taken up.* The People of God are consistently called to live in the light of that future day when God will manifest himself to all and when God's values will prevail (see, e.g., Rom 13:11–14; 1 Thess 5:1–9). Here, once again, we are called to godly nonconformity, keeping ourselves from allowing the corruption, hard-heartedness, and self-centeredness of this world to shape our own hearts and lives, living instead as witnesses to the "different spirit" that God imparts and nurtures.

6:31–32, 35 *If therefore you will pray again and fast for seven days.* See note on 5:13, 20. There is an intimate connection between conversation with God and holiness of life. If we are committed to seeking God's answers and healing for our deepest needs, we must also be committed to walking in the ways that lead to God and are consonant with "life with God."

6:31–35 FASTING—*See* Spiritual Disciplines Index.

6:34 *Do not . . . think vain thoughts concerning the former times.* A sound understanding and confident perception of how God has been at work in history and in our own lives provide us with wisdom that will keep us steady in the midst of present and future turbulence. Meditating regularly on the former, then, prepares us for a spiritually mature approach to the latter.

6:36 *my heart was troubled . . . and I began to speak.* See note on 3:1–14:48.

itable color, and odors of inexpressible fragrance. These were made on the third day.

45 "On the fourth day you commanded the brightness of the sun, the light of the moon, and the arrangement of the stars to come into being; 46and you commanded them to serve humankind, about to be formed.

47 "On the fifth day you commanded the seventh part, where the water had been gathered together, to bring forth living creatures, birds, and fishes; and so it was done. 48The dumb and lifeless water produced living creatures, as it was commanded, so that therefore the nations might declare your wondrous works.

49 "Then you kept in existence two living creatures;a the one you called Behemothb and the name of the other Leviathan. 50And you separated one from the other, for the seventh part where the water had been gathered together could not hold them both. 51And you gave Behemothb one of the parts that had been dried up on the third day, to live in it, where there are a thousand mountains; 52but to Leviathan you gave the seventh part, the watery part; and you have kept them to be eaten by whom you wish, and when you wish.

53 "On the sixth day you commanded the earth to bring forth before you cattle, wild animals, and creeping things; 54and over these you placed Adam, as ruler over all the works that you had made; and from him we have all come, the people whom you have chosen.

Why Do God's People Suffer?

55 "All this I have spoken before you, O Lord, because you have said that it was for

us that you created this world.c 56As for the other nations that have descended from Adam, you have said that they are nothing, and that they are like spittle, and you have compared their abundance to a drop from a bucket. 57And now, O Lord, these nations, which are reputed to be as nothing, domineer over us and devour us. 58But we your people, whom you have called your firstborn, only begotten, zealous for you,d and most dear, have been given into their hands. 59If the world has indeed been created for us, why do we not possess our world as an inheritance? How long will this be so?"

Response to Ezra's Questions

7 When I had finished speaking these words, the angel who had been sent to me on the former nights was sent to me again. 2He said to me, "Rise, Ezra, and listen to the words that I have come to speak to you."

3 I said, "Speak, my lord." And he said to me, "There is a sea set in a wide expanse so that it is deep and vast, 4but it has an entrance set in a narrow place, so that it is like a river. 5If there are those who wish to reach the sea, to look at it or to navigate it, how can they come to the broad part unless they pass through the narrow part? 6Another example: There is a city built and set on a plain, and it is full of all good things; 7but the entrance to it is narrow and set in a precipitous place, so that there is fire on the right hand and deep water on the left. 8There is only

a Syr Ethiop: Lat two souls   b Other Lat authorities read Enoch   c Syr Ethiop Arab 2: Lat the firstborn world Compare Arab 1 first world
d Meaning of Lat uncertain

6:55–59 it was for us that you created this world. The author's reading of Genesis 1 (vv 38–54) is joined to his conviction that God created the world to benefit ethnic Israel, that part of creation specially chosen by God to be his own possession. This collides, of course, with his experience of Rome's destruction of Jerusalem and the turmoil that had once again engulfed Israel. Of course, Paul would not affirm the author's position. God is not only the God of the Jews, but also the God of the Gentiles (Rom 3:29–30). The latter are not "like spittle" to God, but are equally the object of God's redeeming love. However, the apostolic witnesses would agree with the angel's answer (in chaps 7–8) that our inheritance is not this world and its treasures, but God and the riches of his kindness and companionship forever in the age to come (see Heb 11:13–16; 13:13–14). This hope sustains disciples as they endure the difficulties of the present age, the path they must traverse to their inheritance with God (7:6–14).

one path lying between them, that is, between the fire and the water, so that only one person can walk on the path. 9If now the city is given to someone as an inheritance, how will the heir receive the inheritance unless by passing through the appointed danger?"

10 I said, "That is right, lord." He said to me, "So also is Israel's portion. 11For I made the world for their sake, and when Adam transgressed my statutes, what had been made was judged. 12And so the entrances of this world were made narrow and sorrowful and toilsome; they are few and evil, full of dangers and involved in great hardships. 13But the entrances of the greater world are broad and safe, and yield the fruit of immortality. 14Therefore unless the living pass through the difficult and futile experiences, they can never receive those things that have been reserved for them. 15Now therefore why are you disturbed, seeing that you are to perish? Why are you moved, seeing that you are mortal? 16Why have you not considered in your mind what is to come, rather than what is now present?"

The Fate of the Ungodly

17 Then I answered and said, "O sovereign Lord, you have ordained in your law that the righteous shall inherit these things, but that the ungodly shall perish. 18The righteous, therefore, can endure difficult circumstances while hoping for easier ones; but those who have done wickedly have suffered the difficult circumstances and will never see the easier ones."

19 He said to me, "You are not a better judge than the Lord, a or wiser than the Most High! 20Let many perish who are now living, rather than that the law of God that is set before them be disregarded! 21For the Lord b strictly commanded those who came into the world, when they came, what they should do to live, and what they should observe to avoid punishment. 22Nevertheless they were not obedient, and spoke against him;

> they devised for themselves vain
>   thoughts,
> 23   and proposed to themselves wicked
>   frauds;
> they even declared that the Most High
>   does not exist,
>   and they ignored his ways.
> 24 They scorned his law,
>   and denied his covenants;
> they have been unfaithful to his
>   statutes,
>   and have not performed his works.

25That is the reason, Ezra, that empty things are for the empty, and full things are for the full.

The Temporary Messianic Kingdom

26 "For indeed the time will come, when the signs that I have foretold to you will come to pass, that the city that now is not seen shall appear, c and the land that now is hidden shall be disclosed. 27Everyone who has been delivered from the evils that I have foretold shall see my wonders. 28For my son the Messiah d shall be revealed with those who are with him, and those who remain shall rejoice four hundred years. 29After those years my son the Messiah shall die, and all who draw human breath. e 30Then the world shall be turned back to primeval silence for seven days, as it was at the first beginnings, so that no one shall be left. 31After seven days the world that is not yet awake shall be roused,

a Other ancient authorities read God; Ethiop Georg *the only One*   b Other ancient authorities read *God*   c Arm: Lat Syr *that the bride shall appear, even the city appearing*   d Syr Arab 1: Ethiop *my Messiah*; Arab 2 *the Messiah*; Arm *the Messiah of God*; Lat *my son Jesus*   e Arm *all who have continued in faith and in patience*

7:20–25 *the Lord strictly commanded those who came into the world.* Respecting God's honor and obeying God's law are inextricably linked. How we walk from day to day will reflect either our dedication to please and honor God with our lives or our neglect of the honor due our Creator and Redeemer. Convictions about divine judgment and punishment are related not merely to the magnitude of the evils that people might do, but to the contempt for God that such actions and lifestyles display.

and that which is corruptible shall perish. 32The earth shall give up those who are asleep in it, and the dust those who rest there in silence; and the chambers shall give up the souls that have been committed to them. 33The Most High shall be revealed on the seat of judgment, and compassion shall pass away, and patience shall be withdrawn.*a* 34Only judgment shall remain, truth shall stand, and faithfulness shall grow strong. 35Recompense shall follow, and the reward shall be manifested; righteous deeds shall awake, and unrighteous deeds shall not sleep.*b* 36The pit*c* of torment shall appear, and opposite it shall be the place of rest; and the furnace of hell*d* shall be disclosed, and opposite it the paradise of delight. 37Then the Most High will say to the nations that have been raised from the dead, 'Look now, and understand whom you have denied, whom you have not served, whose commandments you have despised. 38Look on this side and on that; here are delight and rest, and there are fire and torments.' Thus he will*e* speak to them on the day of judgment— 39a day that has no sun or moon or stars, 40or cloud or thunder or lightning, or wind or water or air, or darkness or evening or morning, 41or summer or spring or heat or winter*f* or frost or cold, or hail or rain or dew, 42or noon or night, or dawn or shining or brightness or light, but only the splendor of the glory of the Most High, by which all shall see what has been destined. 43It will last as though for a week of years. 44This is my judgment and its prescribed order; and to you alone I have shown these things."

Only a Few Will Be Saved

45I answered and said, "O sovereign Lord, I said then and*g* I say now: Blessed are those who are alive and keep your commandments! 46But what of those for whom I prayed? For who among the living is there that has not sinned, or who is there among mortals that has not transgressed your covenant? 47And now I see that the world to come will bring delight to few, but torments to many. 48For an evil heart has grown up in us, which has alienated us from God,*h* and has brought us into corruption and the ways of death, and has shown us the paths of perdition and removed us far from life—and that not merely for a few but for almost all who have been created."

49He answered me and said, "Listen to me, Ezra,*i* and I will instruct you, and will admonish you once more. 50For this reason the Most High has made not one world but two. 51Inasmuch as you have said that the righteous are not many but few, while the ungodly abound, hear the explanation for this.

a Lat *shall gather together*   *b* The passage from verse 36 to verse 105, formerly missing, has been restored to the text   *c* Syr Ethiop: Lat *place*
d Lat Syr Ethiop *Gehenna*   *e* Syr Ethiop Arab 1: Lat *you shall*   *f* Or *storm*   *g* Syr: Lat *And I answered, "I said then, O Lord, and*   *h* Cn: Lat Syr Ethiop *from these*   *i* Syr Arab 1 Georg: Lat Ethiop lack *Ezra*

7:33–34 *compassion shall pass away, and patience shall be withdrawn.* God deals with the world—and with us—now with patience, and it is incumbent upon us to make a good and salvific use of God's patience. The testimony of Rom 2:4 and 2 Pet 3:9 is that God's present mercy in delaying judgment is meant to make space for repentance and amendment of life. To regard God's delay as an invitation to sin would be a perverse misuse of the gift that is "today," a day given by God for reconciliation and reform.
7:37–38 *Look now, and understand whom you have denied.* The author invites us to look ahead to the day of God's self-manifestation to *all,* so that we will be empowered to keep living in line with God's self-manifestation to *us,* looking ahead to the day when our experience of God shall be vindicated in a universal experience of God.
7:47–48 *the world to come will bring delight to few.* The cry of this author reminds us of the immensity of Christ's gift to us. By his death on our behalf, he overcame the alienation from God that this author laments, cleansing our conscience and washing away the memory of our sins from God's presence as well (Heb 9:11–14; 10:11–18), restoring our life with God.

52 "If you have just a few precious stones, will you add to them lead and clay?"[a] 53 I said, "Lord, how could that be?" 54 And he said to me, "Not only that, but ask the earth and she will tell you; defer to her, and she will declare it to you. 55 Say to her, 'You produce gold and silver and bronze, and also iron and lead and clay; 56 but silver is more abundant than gold, and bronze than silver, and iron than bronze, and lead than iron, and clay than lead.' 57 Judge therefore which things are precious and desirable, those that are abundant or those that are rare?"

58 I said, "O sovereign Lord, what is plentiful is of less worth, for what is more rare is more precious."

59 He answered me and said, "Consider within yourself[b] what you have thought, for the person who has what is hard to get rejoices more than the person who has what is plentiful. 60 So also will be the judgment[c] that I have promised; for I will rejoice over the few who shall be saved, because it is they who have made my glory to prevail now, and through them my name has now been honored. 61 I will not grieve over the great number of those who perish; for it is they who are now like a mist, and are similar to a flame and smoke—they are set on fire and burn hotly, and are extinguished."

Lamentation of Ezra, with Response

62 I replied and said, "O earth, what have you brought forth, if the mind is made out of the dust like the other created things? 63 For it would have been better if the dust itself had not been born, so that the mind might not have been made from it. 64 But now the mind grows with us, and therefore we are tormented, because we perish and we know it. 65 Let the human race lament, but let the wild animals of the field be glad; let all who have been born lament, but let the cattle and the flocks rejoice. 66 It is much better with them than with us; for they do not look for a judgment, and they do not know of any torment or salvation promised to them after death. 67 What does it profit us that we shall be preserved alive but cruelly tormented? 68 For all who have been born are entangled in[d] iniquities, and are full of sins and burdened with transgressions. 69 And if after death we were not to come into judgment, perhaps it would have been better for us."

70 He answered me and said, "When the Most High made the world and Adam and all who have come from him, he first prepared the judgment and the things that pertain to the judgment. 71 But now, understand from your own words—for you have said that the mind grows with us. 72 For this reason, therefore, those who live on earth shall be tormented, because though they had understanding, they committed iniquity; and though they received the commandments, they did not keep them; and though they obtained the law, they dealt unfaithfully with what they received. 73 What, then, will they have to say in the judgment, or how will they answer in the last times? 74 How

a Arab 1: Meaning of Lat Syr Ethiop uncertain
b Syr Ethiop Arab 1: Meaning of Lat uncertain
c Syr Arab 1: Lat *creation*   d Syr *defiled with*

7:52–61 *If you have just a few precious stones.* (See also 8:1–3.) What gives a person value or makes for a worthwhile life? How do we measure it? Here, it is measured in terms of fulfilling the purpose for which we were made, namely, living in line with God's character and purpose. Making God's honor prevail in the world establishes our own honor and worth (see also Sir 10:19–24). This passage encourages us to continue to distinguish ourselves in discipleship, affirming that our godly nonconformity makes us shine out like gold against clay, delighting the God who made us. However, the author once seems to fall short of reflecting God's heart at verse 61. This is not the attitude of the God who desires that none be lost and who sent his Son to offer to everyone the hope of life with God (1 Tim 2:4). Nor is this the attitude of Jesus, who compared himself to a shepherd who would leave the many who were righteous to seek out the one who was lost and in danger of perishing (Matt 18:10–14).

7:74 *How long the Most High has been patient!* Again the author's words are at odds with those of other witnesses of God, who speak of God's delays of punishment as the result of God's commitment to people, not to an inflexible timetable (see Rom 2:4; 2 Pet 3:9).

long the Most High has been patient with those who inhabit the world!—and not for their sake, but because of the times that he has foreordained."

State of the Dead before Judgment

75 I answered and said, "If I have found favor in your sight, O Lord, show this also to your servant: whether after death, as soon as everyone of us yields up the soul, we shall be kept in rest until those times come when you will renew the creation, or whether we shall be tormented at once?"

76 He answered me and said, "I will show you that also, but do not include yourself with those who have shown scorn, or number yourself among those who are tormented. 77 For you have a treasure of works stored up with the Most High, but it will not be shown to you until the last times. 78 Now concerning death, the teaching is: When the decisive decree has gone out from the Most High that a person shall die, as the spirit leaves the body to return again to him who gave it, first of all it adores the glory of the Most High. 79 If it is one of those who have shown scorn and have not kept the way of the Most High, who have despised his law and hated those who fear God— 80 such spirits shall not enter into habitations, but shall immediately wander about in torments, always grieving and sad, in seven ways. 81 The first way, because they have scorned the law of the Most High. 82 The second way, because they cannot now make a good repentance so that they may live. 83 The third way, they shall see the reward laid up for those who have trusted the covenants of the Most High. 84 The fourth way, they shall consider the torment laid up for themselves in the last days. 85 The fifth way, they shall see how the habitations of the others are guarded by angels in profound quiet. 86 The sixth way, they shall see how some of them will cross over[a] into torments. 87 The seventh way, which is worse[b] than all the ways that have been mentioned, because they shall utterly waste away in confusion and be consumed with shame,[c] and shall wither with fear at seeing the glory of the Most High in whose presence they sinned while they were alive, and in whose presence they are to be judged in the last times.

88 "Now this is the order of those who have kept the ways of the Most High, when they shall be separated from their mortal body.[d] 89 During the time that they lived in it,[c] they laboriously served the Most High, and withstood danger every hour so that they might keep the law of the Lawgiver perfectly. 90 Therefore this is the teaching concerning them: 91 First of all, they shall see with great joy the glory of him who receives them, for they shall have rest in seven orders. 92 The first order, because they have striven with great effort to overcome the evil thought that was formed with them, so that it might not lead them astray from life into death. 93 The second order, because they see the perplexity in which the souls of the ungodly wander and the punishment that awaits them. 94 The third order, they see the witness that he who formed them bears concerning them, that throughout their life they kept the law with

a Cn: Meaning of Lat uncertain   b Lat Syr Ethiop greater   c Syr Ethiop: Meaning of Lat uncertain   d Lat the corruptible vessel

---

7:77 For you have a treasure of works stored up with the Most High. Jesus would also direct our ambitions toward laying up treasure for ourselves in heaven, gained by investing ourselves in acts of love and kindness toward our fellow humans in need (see Luke 12:33–34; see also Shepherd of Hermas, Similitude 1). The hidden quality of this treasure may present a stumbling block for people who like to watch their investments grow or see the tangible fruits of their labors. The life of faith, of course, invites us to walk in trust rather than sight on these points, so that we will find our treasure to be rich and full for eternity.

7:78–80 first of all it adores the glory of the Most High. All must worship God and acknowledge his claim on our whole being after death; it is therefore essential to do this throughout life as well, so that our encounter with God beyond death will be the continuation of a long friendship with God begun in our life and not confrontation with a long neglected and dishonored Judge.

7:91–92 to overcome the evil thought that was formed with them. See note on 7:127–29.

which they were entrusted. *95* The fourth order, they understand the rest that they now enjoy, being gathered into their chambers and guarded by angels in profound quiet, and the glory waiting for them in the last days. *96* The fifth order, they rejoice that they have now escaped what is corruptible and shall inherit what is to come; and besides they see the straits and toil *a* from which they have been delivered, and the spacious liberty that they are to receive and enjoy in immortality. *97* The sixth order, when it is shown them how their face is to shine like the sun, and how they are to be made like the light of the stars, being incorruptible from then on. *98* The seventh order, which is greater than all that have been mentioned, because they shall rejoice with boldness, and shall be confident without confusion, and shall be glad without fear, for they press forward to see the face of him whom they served in life and from whom they are to receive their reward when glorified. *99* This is the order of the souls of the righteous, as henceforth is announced; *b* and the previously mentioned are the ways of torment that those who would not give heed shall suffer hereafter."

100 Then I answered and said, "Will time therefore be given to the souls, after they have been separated from the bodies, to see what you have described to me?"

101 He said to me, "They shall have freedom for seven days, so that during these seven days they may see the things of which you have been told, and afterwards they shall be gathered in their habitations."

No Intercession for the Ungodly

102 I answered and said, "If I have found favor in your sight, show further to me, your servant, whether on the day of judgment the righteous will be able to intercede for the ungodly or to entreat the Most High for them— *103* fathers for sons or sons for parents, brothers for brothers, relatives for their kindred, or friends for those who are most dear."

104 He answered me and said, "Since you have found favor in my sight, I will show you this also. The day of judgment is decisive *c* and displays to all the seal of truth. Just as now a father does not send his son, or a son his father, or a master his servant, or a friend his dearest friend, to be ill *d* or sleep or eat or be healed in his place, *105* so no one shall ever pray for another on that day, neither shall anyone lay a burden on another; *e* for then all shall bear their own righteousness and unrighteousness."

36 *106* I answered and said, "How then do we find that first Abraham prayed for the people of Sodom, and Moses for our ancestors who sinned in the desert, 37 *107* and Joshua after him for Israel in the days of Achan, 38 *108* and Samuel in the days of Saul, *f* and David for the plague, and Solomon for those at the dedication, 39 *109* and Elijah for those who received the rain, and for the one who was dead, that he might live, 40 *110* and Hezekiah for the people in the days of Sennacherib, and many others prayed for many? 41 *111* So if now, when corruption has increased and unrighteousness has multiplied, the righteous have prayed for the ungodly, why will it not be so then as well?"

42 *112* He answered me and said, "This present world is not the end; the full glory does not *g* remain in it; *h* therefore those who were strong prayed for the weak. 43 *113* But

a Syr Ethiop: Lat *fullness*   *b* Syr: Meaning of Lat uncertain   *c* Lat *bold*   *d* Syr Ethiop Arm: Lat *to understand*   *e* Syr Ethiop: Lat lacks *on that . . . another*   *f* Syr Ethiop Arab 1: Lat Arab 2 Arm lack *in the days of Saul*   *g* Lat lacks *not*   *h* Or *the glory does not continuously abide in it*

7:98 *they press forward to see the face of him whom they served in life.* The eagerness with which the souls of the righteous strain forward to meet God face-to-face contrasts powerfully with the desire of the souls of the ungodly to avoid God's face and the shame and fear his gaze brings (v 87). Cultivation of the life with God now plants anticipation of joy and fulfillment then when we fly to God's full presence; pressing forward to seek God's face through prayer and the other Spiritual Disciplines initiates a movement that is joyfully consummated across the threshold of death.

7:110–12 PRAYER—*See* Spiritual Disciplines Index.

the day of judgment will be the end of this age and the beginning*a* of the immortal age to come, in which corruption has passed away, 44 *114* sinful indulgence has come to an end, unbelief has been cut off, and righteousness has increased and truth has appeared. 45 *115* Therefore no one will then be able to have mercy on someone who has been condemned in the judgment, or to harm*b* someone who is victorious."

Lamentation over the Fate of Most People

46 *116* I answered and said, "This is my first and last comment: it would have been better if the earth had not produced Adam, or else, when it had produced him, had restrained him from sinning. 47 *117* For what good is it to all that they live in sorrow now and expect punishment after death? 48 *118* O Adam, what have you done? For though it was you who sinned, the fall was not yours alone, but ours also who are your descendants. 49 *119* For what good is it to us, if an immortal time has been promised to us, but we have done deeds that bring death? 50 *120* And what good is it that an everlasting hope has been promised to us, but we have miserably failed? 51 *121* Or that safe and healthful habitations have been reserved for us, but we have lived wickedly? 52 *122* Or that the glory of the Most High will defend those who have led a pure life, but we have walked in the most wicked ways? 53 *123* Or that a paradise shall be revealed, whose fruit remains unspoiled and in which are abundance and healing, but we shall not enter it 54 *124* because we have lived in perverse ways?*c* 55 *125* Or that the faces of those who practiced

self-control shall shine more than the stars, but our faces shall be blacker than darkness? 56 *126* For while we lived and committed iniquity we did not consider what we should suffer after death."

57 *127* He answered and said, "This is the significance of the contest that all who are born on earth shall wage: 58 *128* if they are defeated they shall suffer what you have said, but if they are victorious they shall receive what I have said.*d* 59 *129* For this is the way of which Moses, while he was alive, spoke to the people, saying, 'Choose life for yourself, so that you may live!' 60 *130* But they did not believe him or the prophets after him, or even myself who have spoken to them. 61 *131* Therefore there shall not be*e* grief at their destruction, so much as joy over those to whom salvation is assured."

Ezra Appeals to God's Mercy

62 *132* I answered and said, "I know, O Lord, that the Most High is now called merciful, because he has mercy on those who have not yet come into the world; 63 *133* and gracious, because he is gracious to those who turn in repentance to his law; 64 *134* and patient, because he shows patience toward those who have sinned, since they are his own creatures; 65 *135* and bountiful, because he would rather give than take away;*f* 66 *136* and abundant in compassion, because he makes his compassions abound more and

a Syr Ethiop: Lat lacks *the beginning*   *b* Syr Ethiop: Lat *overwhelm*   *c* Cn: Lat Syr *places*
d Syr Ethiop Arab 1: Lat *what I say*   *e* Syr: Lat *there was not*   *f* Or *he is ready to give according to requests*

7:127–29 *This is the significance of the contest.* This author finds the "meaning of life" in our struggle against the evil inclination within us and our efforts to decide for obedience to God against the yearnings of our flesh, the world, and the devil. The apocalyptic visions of God's judgment and the rewards and punishments laid up for humanity serve to prioritize this "contest" above every temporal contest (e.g., the "rat race") in which we find ourselves competing. In verse 129, the angel quotes Deut 30:19 to affirm that victory is indeed possible. Doing

what pleases God is difficult and requires discipline and hard work; hence it is a contest that engages our best efforts. Victory is all the more accessible, however, insofar as God has equipped us with the Holy Spirit to guide, empower, and work Christlikeness within us (see Rom 8:2–4; Gal 5:16–25).

7:132–40 *the Most High is now called merciful.* See note on 7:47–48. God indeed set forward Jesus as the one in whom pardon of sins could be offered and God's compassion and mercy (see Exod 34:6–7) made effective.

more to those now living and to those who are gone and to those yet to come— 67 137 for if he did not make them abound, the world with those who inhabit it would not have life— 68 138 and he is called the giver, because if he did not give out of his goodness so that those who have committed iniquities might be relieved of them, not one ten-thousandth of humankind could have life; 69 139 and the judge, because if he did not pardon those who were created by his word and blot out the multitude of their sins, *a* 70 140 there would probably be left only very few of the innumerable multitude."

8 He answered me and said, "The Most High made this world for the sake of many, but the world to come for the sake of only a few. 2 But I tell you a parable, Ezra. Just as, when you ask the earth, it will tell you that it provides a large amount of clay from which earthenware is made, but only a little dust from which gold comes, so is the course of the present world. 3 Many have been created, but only a few shall be saved."

Ezra Again Appeals to God's Mercy

4 I answered and said, "Then drink your fill of understanding, *b* O my soul, and drink wisdom, O my heart. 5 For not of your own will did you come into the world, *c* and against your will you depart, for you have been given only a short time to live. 6 O Lord above us, grant to your servant that we may pray before you, and give us a seed for our heart and cultivation of our understanding so that fruit may be produced, by which every mortal who bears the likeness *d* of a human being may be able to live. 7 For you alone exist, and we are a work of your hands, as you have declared. 8 And because you give life to the body that is now fashioned in the womb, and furnish it with members, what you have created is preserved amid fire and water, and for nine months the womb *e* endures your creature that has been created in it. 9 But that which keeps and that which is kept shall both be kept by your keeping. *c* And when the

womb gives up again what has been created in it, 10 you have commanded that from the members themselves (that is, from the breasts) milk, the fruit of the breasts, should be supplied, 11 so that what has been fashioned may be nourished for a time; and afterwards you will still guide it in your mercy. 12 You have nurtured it in your righteousness, and instructed it in your law, and reproved it in your wisdom. 13 You put it to death as your creation, and make it live as your work. 14 If then you will suddenly and quickly *f* destroy what with so great labor was fashioned by your command, to what purpose was it made? 15 And now I will speak out: About all humankind you know best; but I will speak about your people, for whom I am grieved, 16 and about your inheritance, for whom I lament, and about Israel, for whom I am sad, and about the seed of Jacob, for whom I am troubled. 17 Therefore I will pray before you for myself and for them, for I see the failings of us who inhabit the earth; 18 and now also *g* I have heard of the swiftness of the judgment that is to come. 19 Therefore hear my voice and understand my words, and I will speak before you."

Ezra's Prayer

The beginning of the words of Ezra's prayer, *h* before he was taken up. He said: 20 "O Lord, you who inhabit eternity, *i* whose eyes are exalted *j* and whose upper chambers are in the air, 21 whose throne is beyond measure and whose glory is beyond comprehension, before whom the hosts of angels stand trembling 22 and at whose command they are changed to wind and fire, *k* whose word is sure and whose utterances are certain, whose

a Lat *contempts*   *b* Syr: Lat *Then release understanding*   *c* Syr: Meaning of Lat uncertain
d Syr: Lat *place*   *e* Lat *what you have formed*
f Syr: Lat *will with a light command*   *g* Lat *but*
h Syr Ethiop; Lat *beginning of Ezra's words*
i Or *you who abide forever*   *j* Another Lat text reads *whose are the highest heavens*   *k* Syr: Lat *they whose service takes the form of wind and fire*

8:6 *give us a seed for our heart.* The author's plea for "a seed for our heart" that will produce understanding and righteous fruit is answered in

the gift of the Holy Spirit of God (Rom 8:2–4; Gal 5:16–25).

command is strong and whose ordinance is terrible, 23whose look dries up the depths and whose indignation makes the mountains melt away, and whose truth is established*a* forever— 24hear, O Lord, the prayer of your servant, and give ear to the petition of your creature; attend to my words. 25For as long as I live I will speak, and as long as I have understanding I will answer. 26O do not look on the sins of your people, but on those who serve you in truth. 27Do not take note of the endeavors of those who act wickedly, but of the endeavors of those who have kept your covenants amid afflictions. 28Do not think of those who have lived wickedly in your sight, but remember those who have willingly acknowledged that you are to be feared. 29Do not will the destruction of those who have the ways of cattle, but regard those who have gloriously taught your law.*b* 30Do not be angry with those who are deemed worse than wild animals, but love those who have always put their trust in your glory. 31For we and our ancestors have passed our lives in ways that bring death;*c* but it is because of us sinners that you are called merciful. 32For if you have desired to have pity on us, who have no works of righteousness, then you will be called merciful. 33For the righteous, who have many works laid up with you, shall receive their reward in consequence of their own deeds. 34But what are mortals, that you are angry with them; or what is a corruptible race, that you are so bitter against it? 35For in truth there is no one among those who have been born who has not acted wickedly; among those who have existed*d* there is no one who has not done wrong. 36For in this, O Lord, your righteousness and goodness will be declared, when you are merciful to those who have no store of good works."

Response to Ezra's Prayer

37 He answered me and said, "Some things you have spoken rightly, and it will turn out according to your words. 38For indeed I will not concern myself about the fashioning of those who have sinned, or about their death, their judgment, or their destruction; 39but I will rejoice over the creation of the righteous, over their pilgrimage also, and their salvation, and their receiving their reward. 40As I have spoken, therefore, so it shall be.

41 "For just as the farmer sows many seeds in the ground and plants a multitude of seedlings, and yet not all that have been sown will come up*e* in due season, and not all that were planted will take root; so also those who have been sown in the world will not all be saved."

42 I answered and said, "If I have found favor in your sight, let me speak. 43If the farmer's seed does not come up, because it has not received your rain in due season, or if it has been ruined by too much rain, it perishes.*f* 44But people, who have been formed by your hands and are called your own image because they are made like you, and for whose sake you have formed all things—have you also made them like the farmer's seed? 45Surely not, O Lord*g* above! But spare your people and have mercy on your inheritance, for you have mercy on your own creation."

Ezra's Final Appeal for Mercy

46 He answered me and said, "Things that are present are for those who live now, and

a Arab 2: Other authorities read *truth bears witness*
b Syr *have received the brightness of your law*
c Syr Ethiop: Meaning of Lat uncertain   *d* Syr: Meaning of Lat uncertain   *e* Syr Ethiop *will live*; Lat *will be saved*   *f* Cn: Compare Syr Arab 1 Arm Georg 2: Meaning of Lat uncertain   *g* Ethiop Arab Compare Syr: Lat lacks *O Lord*

8:26–36 *O do not look on the sins of your people.* Ezra has been invoking God's justice; now that he finds out how just God is, he cries for God's mercy. But God cannot choose between love and righteousness as Ezra would have him. He loves his creation more than his human interrogators ever could (5:33; 8:47), yet God's love cannot express itself unjustly. Paul would argue that the author's plea that God regard not the sins of the people but the obedience of the righteous had already been answered in Jesus, whose perfect offering of righteousness won forgiveness and the hope of righteousness for all who would be joined to him (Rom 5:16–19).

things that are future are for those who will live hereafter. [47]For you come far short of being able to love my creation more than I love it. But you have often compared yourself[a] to the unrighteous. Never do so! [48]But even in this respect you will be praiseworthy before the Most High, [49]because you have humbled yourself, as is becoming for you, and have not considered yourself to be among the righteous. You will receive the greatest glory, [50]for many miseries will affect those who inhabit the world in the last times, because they have walked in great pride. [51]But think of your own case, and inquire concerning the glory of those who are like yourself, [52]because it is for you that paradise is opened, the tree of life is planted, the age to come is prepared, plenty is provided, a city is built, rest is appointed,[b] goodness is established and wisdom perfected beforehand. [53]The root of evil[c] is sealed up from you, illness is banished from you, and death[d] is hidden; Hades has fled and corruption has been forgotten;[e] [54]sorrows have passed away, and in the end the treasure of immortality is made manifest. [55]Therefore do not ask any more questions about the great number of those who perish. [56]For when they had opportunity to choose, they despised the Most High, and were contemptuous of his law, and abandoned his ways. [57]Moreover, they have even trampled on his righteous ones, [58]and said in their hearts that there is no God—though they knew well that they must die. [59]For just as the things that I have predicted await[f] you, so the thirst and torment that are prepared await them. For the Most High did not intend that anyone should be destroyed; [60]but those who were

created have themselves defiled the name of him who made them, and have been ungrateful to him who prepared life for them now. [61]Therefore my judgment is now drawing near; [62]I have not shown this to all people, but only to you and a few like you."

Then I answered and said, [63]"O Lord, you have already shown me a great number of the signs that you will do in the last times, but you have not shown me when you will do them."

More about the Signs of the End

9 He answered me and said, "Measure carefully in your mind, and when you see that some of the predicted signs have occurred, [2]then you will know that it is the very time when the Most High is about to visit the world that he has made. [3]So when there shall appear in the world earthquakes, tumult of peoples, intrigues of nations, wavering of leaders, confusion of princes, [4]then you will know that it was of these that the Most High spoke from the days that were of old, from the beginning. [5]For just as with everything that has occurred in the world, the beginning is evident,[g] and the end manifest; [6]so also are the times of the Most High: the beginnings are manifest in wonders and mighty works, and the end in penalties[h] and in signs.

a Syr Ethiop: Lat *brought yourself near*   b Syr Ethiop: Lat *allowed*   c Lat lacks *of evil*   d Syr Ethiop Arm: Lat lacks *death*   e Syr: Lat *Hades and corruption have fled into oblivion*; or *corruption has fled into Hades to be forgotten*   f Syr: Lat *will receive*   g Syr: Ethiop *is in the word*; Meaning of Lat uncertain   h Syr: Lat Ethiop *in effects*

8:56 *For when they had opportunity to choose.* Freedom of choice heightens the significance of our choices. The disciplined life is one in which we consistently exercise freedom of choice to pursue the path that honors God and falls in line with God's values.

8:60–61 *those who were created . . . have been ungrateful to him who prepared life for them.* The ingratitude of the creature is what makes sin and disobedience so odious. God's presence and kindness are evident in the gift of life and the nurturing and sustaining of life (see vv 4–14).

Given the gift of life, how should we live, if not to honor and please and serve the Giver? Scripture consistently connects our behavior with the honor or dishonor that falls upon God's name. Paul, following Isaiah, understands Israel's disobedience to have brought reproach upon the name of Israel's God (Rom 2:24; Isa 52:5). When God's people live in obedience to his character and righteousness, God's name is honored (Matt 5:16; 1 Pet 2:12). In gratitude for God's gift of life and redemption, it is only appropriate for us to live in a way that graces God's name in return.

7 "It shall be that all who will be saved and will be able to escape on account of their works, or on account of the faith by which they have believed, [8]will survive the dangers that have been predicted, and will see my salvation in my land and within my borders, which I have sanctified for myself from the beginning. [9]Then those who have now abused my ways shall be amazed, and those who have rejected them with contempt shall live in torments. [10]For as many as did not acknowledge me in their lifetime, though they received my benefits, [11]and as many as scorned my law while they still had freedom, and did not understand but despised it[a] while an opportunity of repentance was still open to them, [12]these must in torment acknowledge it[a] after death. [13]Therefore, do not continue to be curious about how the ungodly will be punished; but inquire how the righteous will be saved, those to whom the age belongs and for whose sake the age was made."[b]

The Argument Recapitulated

14 I answered and said, [15]"I said before, and I say now, and will say it again: there are more who perish than those who will be saved, [16]as a wave is greater than a drop of water."

17 He answered me and said, "As is the field, so is the seed; and as are the flowers, so are the colors; and as is the work, so is the product; and as is the farmer, so is the threshing floor. [18]For there was a time in this age when I was preparing for those who now exist, before the world was made for them to live in, and no one opposed me then, for no one

existed; [19]but now those who have been created in this world, which is supplied both with an unfailing table and an inexhaustible pasture,[c] have become corrupt in their ways. [20]So I considered my world, and saw that it was lost. I saw that my earth was in peril because of the devices of those who[d] had come into it. [21]And I saw and spared some[e] with great difficulty, and saved for myself one grape out of a cluster, and one plant out of a great forest.[f] [22]So let the multitude perish that has been born in vain, but let my grape and my plant be saved, because with much labor I have perfected them.

23 "Now, if you will let seven days more pass—do not, however, fast during them, [24]but go into a field of flowers where no house has been built, and eat only of the flowers of the field, and taste no meat and drink no wine, but eat only flowers— [25]and pray to the Most High continually, then I will come and talk with you."

The Abiding Glory of the Mosaic Law

26 So I went, as he directed me, into the field that is called Ardat;[g] there I sat among the flowers and ate of the plants of the field, and the nourishment they afforded satisfied me. [27]After seven days, while I lay on the grass, my heart was troubled again as it was before. [28]Then my mouth was opened, and I began to speak before the Most High, and said,

---

a Or me   b Syr: Lat *saved, and whose is the age and for whose sake the age was made and when* c Cn: Lat *law*   d Cn: Lat *devices that*   e Lat *them*   f Syr Ethiop Arab 1: Lat *tribe*   g Syr Ethiop *Arpad*; Arm *Ardab*

9:10 *For as many as did not acknowledge me in their lifetime.* Throughout life, we experience God's generosity and benefits; the responsibility is now ours to respond as grateful and appreciative recipients of God's bounty by honoring his just claim on our lives and conduct. By responding well to God's gifts now and meeting grace with a grace-full response, we will continue to enjoy God's favor into the future age (7:60).
9:22 *with much labor I have perfected them.* Ezra began by complaining, in effect, about where God was to be found in the midst of a world racked with injustice. Here God is found

laboring alongside righteous disciples, perfecting them in God's ways in the midst of a world that cannot hold all the good things God has prepared for those who love him. This verse also introduces an important counterbalance to the book's emphasis on human effort and to Ezra's complaint about the presence of the "evil inclination" within us. God may not remove the latter and may demand righteousness from his people, but God partners with disciples against the evil inclination and works within us to bring about the righteousness he seeks.

29"O Lord, you showed yourself among us, to our ancestors in the wilderness when they came out from Egypt and when they came into the untrodden and unfruitful wilderness; 30and you said, 'Hear me, O Israel, and give heed to my words, O descendants of Jacob. 31For I sow my law in you, and it shall bring forth fruit in you, and you shall be glorified through it forever.' 32But though our ancestors received the law, they did not keep it and did not observe the*a* statutes; yet the fruit of the law did not perish—for it could not, because it was yours. 33Yet those who received it perished, because they did not keep what had been sown in them. 34Now this is the general rule that, when the ground has received seed, or the sea a ship, or any dish food or drink, and when it comes about that what was sown or what was launched or what was put in is destroyed, 35they are destroyed, but the things that held them remain; yet with us it has not been so. 36For we who have received the law and sinned will perish, as well as our hearts that received it; 37the law, however, does not perish but survives in its glory."

The Vision of a Weeping Woman

38 When I said these things in my heart, I looked around,*b* and on my right I saw a woman; she was mourning and weeping with a loud voice, and was deeply grieved at heart; her clothes were torn, and there were ashes on her head. 39Then I dismissed the thoughts with which I had been engaged, and turned to her 40and said to her, "Why are you weeping, and why are you grieved at heart?"

41 She said to me, "Let me alone, my lord, so that I may weep for myself and continue to mourn, for I am greatly embittered in spirit and deeply distressed."

42 I said to her, "What has happened to you? Tell me."

43 And she said to me, "Your servant was barren and had no child, though I lived with my husband for thirty years. 44Every hour and every day during those thirty years I prayed to the Most High, night and day. 45And after thirty years God heard your servant, and looked upon my low estate, and considered my distress, and gave me a son. I rejoiced greatly over him, I and my husband and all my neighbors;*c* and we gave great glory to the Mighty One. 46And I brought him up with much care. 47So when he grew up and I came to take a wife for him, I set a day for the marriage feast.

10 "But it happened that when my son entered his wedding chamber, he fell down and died. 2So all of us put out our lamps, and all my neighbors*c* attempted to console me; I remained quiet until the evening of the second day. 3But when all of them had stopped consoling me, encouraging me to be quiet, I got up in the night and fled, and I came to this field, as you see. 4And now I intend not to return to the town, but to stay here; I will neither eat nor drink, but will mourn and fast continually until I die."

5 Then I broke off the reflections with which I was still engaged, and answered her in anger and said, 6"You most foolish of women, do you not see our mourning, and what has happened to us? 7For Zion, the mother of us all, is in deep grief and great distress. 8It is most appropriate to mourn

---

a Lat *my*   *b* Syr Arab Arm: Lat *I looked about me with my eyes*   *c* Literally *all my citizens*

Responding
9:43–45 PRAYER. Do you have a prayer request that has so far gone unanswered? Meditate on this story from Ezra's vision to help you wait for God's time. *See also* Spiritual Disciplines Index.

10:8–20 *It is most appropriate to mourn now.* As Ezra begins to console the grieving "woman," who will turn out to be Jerusalem, he shows that he has moved to a place where he grieves for all humanity in its alienation from God as

well as for Israel's particular loss and pain. The consolation he offers is that each of us can find strength to bear private pain when we feel it in solidarity with the pain and grief of humanity and creation itself. The experience of private grief, indeed, can drive us deeper into solidarity with those who grieve; the experience of injustice can drive us toward solidarity with those who suffer injustice. Discovering our solidarity in pain, we discover our solidarity in the universal longing for God's intervention and help.

now, because we are all mourning, and to be sorrowful, because we are all sorrowing; you are sorrowing for one son, but we, the whole world, for our mother. *a* 9Now ask the earth, and she will tell you that it is she who ought to mourn over so many who have come into being upon her. 10From the beginning all have been born of her, and others will come; and, lo, almost all go *b* to perdition, and a multitude of them will come to doom. 11Who then ought to mourn the more, she who lost so great a multitude, or you who are grieving for one alone? 12But if you say to me, 'My lamentation is not like the earth's, for I have lost the fruit of my womb, which I brought forth in pain and bore in sorrow; 13but it is with the earth according to the way of the earth—the multitude that is now in it goes as it came'; 14then I say to you, 'Just as you brought forth in sorrow, so the earth also has from the beginning given her fruit, that is, humankind, to him who made her.' 15Now, therefore, keep your sorrow to yourself, and bear bravely the troubles that have come upon you. 16For if you acknowledge the decree of God to be just, you will receive your son back in due time, and will be praised among women. 17Therefore go into the town to your husband."

18 She said to me, "I will not do so; I will not go into the city, but I will die here."

19 So I spoke again to her, and said, 20"Do not do that, but let yourself be persuaded—for how many are the adversities of Zion?—and be consoled because of the sorrow of Jerusalem. 21For you see how our sanctuary has been laid waste, our altar thrown down, our temple destroyed; 22our harp has been laid low, our song has been silenced, and our rejoicing has been ended; the light of our lampstand has been put out, the ark of our covenant has been plundered, our holy things have been polluted, and the name by which we are called has been almost profaned; our children *c* have suffered abuse, our priests have been burned to death, our Levites have gone into exile, our virgins have been defiled, and our wives have been ravished; our righteous men *d* have been carried off, our little ones have been cast out, our young men have been enslaved and our strong men made powerless. 23And, worst of all, the seal of Zion has been deprived of its glory, and given over into the hands of those that hate us. 24Therefore shake off your great sadness and lay aside your many sorrows, so that the Mighty One may be merciful to you again, and the Most High may give you rest, a respite from your troubles."

25 While I was talking to her, her face suddenly began to shine exceedingly; her countenance flashed like lightning, so that I was too frightened to approach her, and my heart was terrified. While *e* I was wondering what this meant, 26she suddenly uttered a loud and fearful cry, so that the earth shook at the sound. 27When I looked up, the woman was no longer visible to me, but a city was being

a Compare Syr: Meaning of Lat uncertain
b Literally *walk*   *c* Ethiop *free men*   *d* Syr *our seers*   *e* Syr Ethiop Arab 1: Lat lacks *I was too . . . terrified. While*

10:16 *For if you acknowledge the decree of God to be just.* The advice Ezra gives the "woman" reflects the position Ezra himself has been internalizing only with difficulty (namely, affirming God's goodness and justice in the midst of his questions and trusting in God's ultimate provisions for good). Ezra must finally yield to "the way things are" if he is to move forward. In our remonstrations with God, it must be our goal to discover God's mind, not change it and insist that things be other than they are. At some point, we must submit our limited understanding to the limitless goodness and wisdom of God, acknowledging "the decree of God to be just."

Far from being intellectually dishonest, this position recognizes that our intellects are limited and that the peace of resignation is what our spirits need. This is but one aspect of the "resignation to divine providence" held up by many spiritual directors through the centuries as a component of mature discipleship.

10:27 *a city was being built.* Zion still has a glorious future in God's plan, and this is the assurance Ezra needed. The vision does not answer the author's difficult questions about "why," but it assures him of a much needed "that" in God's forthcoming interventions in the life of his people.

built,[a] and a place of huge foundations showed itself. I was afraid, and cried with a loud voice and said, 28"Where is the angel Uriel, who came to me at first? For it was he who brought me into this overpowering bewilderment; my end has become corruption, and my prayer a reproach."

Uriel's Interpretation of the Vision

29 While I was speaking these words, the angel who had come to me at first came to me, and when he saw me 30lying there like a corpse, deprived of my understanding, he grasped my right hand and strengthened me and set me on my feet, and said to me, 31"What is the matter with you? And why are you troubled? And why are your understanding and the thoughts of your mind troubled?"

32 I said, "It was because you abandoned me. I did as you directed, and went out into the field, and lo, what I have seen and can still see, I am unable to explain."

33 He said to me, "Stand up like a man, and I will instruct you."

34 I said, "Speak, my lord; only do not forsake me, so that I may not die before my time.[b] 35For I have seen what I did not know, and I hear[c] what I do not understand 36—or is my mind deceived, and my soul dreaming? 37Now therefore I beg you to give your servant an explanation of this bewildering vision."

38 He answered me and said, "Listen to me, and I will teach you, and tell you about the things that you fear; for the Most High has revealed many secrets to you. 39He has seen your righteous conduct, and that you have sorrowed continually for your people and mourned greatly over Zion. 40This therefore is the meaning of the vision. 41The woman who appeared to you a little while ago, whom you saw mourning and whom you began to console 42(you do not now see the form of a woman, but there appeared to you a city being built)[d] 43and who told you about the misfortune of her son—this is the interpretation: 44The woman whom you saw is Zion, which you now behold as a city being built.[e] 45And as for her telling you that she was barren for thirty years, the reason is that there were three thousand[f] years in the world before any offering was offered in it.[g] 46And after three thousand[h] years Solomon built the city, and offered offerings; then it was that the barren woman bore a son. 47And as for her telling you that she brought him up with much care, that was the period of residence in Jerusalem. 48And as for her saying to you, 'My son died as he entered his wedding chamber,' and that misfortune had overtaken her,[i] this was the destruction that befell Jerusalem. 49So you saw her likeness, how she mourned for her son, and you began to console her for what had happened.[j] 50For now the Most High, seeing that you are sincerely grieved and profoundly distressed for her, has shown you the brilliance of her glory, and the loveliness of her beauty. 51Therefore I told you to remain in the field where no house had been built, 52for I knew that the Most High would reveal these things to you. 53Therefore I told you to go into the field where there was no foundation of any building, 54because no work of human construc-

a Lat: Syr Ethiop Arab 1 Arab 2 Arm *but there was an established city*　　b Syr Ethiop Arab: Lat *die to no purpose*　　c Other ancient authorities read *have heard*　　d Lat: Syr Ethiop Arab 1 Arab 2 Arm *an established city*　　e Cn: Lat *an established city*　　f Most Lat Mss read *three*　　g Cn: Lat Syr Arab Arm *her*　　h Syr Ethiop Arab Arm: Lat *three*　　i Or *him*　　j Most Lat Mss and Arab 1 add *These were the things to be opened to you*

10:39, 50 *you have sorrowed continually for your people.* Acknowledging and feeling our pain in the presence of God opens us up to receive his profound comfort, as is the case for Ezra in this episode.

10:54 *no work of human construction.* The angel reminds us that our so seemingly solid world with its grand edifices and projection of being "absolute" is ultimately shakable and destined for shaking (see Heb 12:26–29). Only what is built and founded by God is permanent, and it is therefore always advantageous to invest our energies, resources, and selves in this life in what will bear fruit "where the city of the Most High" will be revealed (cf. Heb 13:13–14).

tion could endure in a place where the city of the Most High was to be revealed.

55 "Therefore do not be afraid, and do not let your heart be terrified; but go in and see the splendor or[a] the vastness of the building, as far as it is possible for your eyes to see it, [56]and afterward you will hear as much as your ears can hear. [57]For you are more blessed than many, and you have been called to be with[b] the Most High as few have been. [58]But tomorrow night you shall remain here, [59]and the Most High will show you in those dream visions what the Most High will do to those who inhabit the earth in the last days."

So I slept that night and the following one, as he had told me.

The Vision of the Eagle

11 On the second night I had a dream: I saw rising from the sea an eagle that had twelve feathered wings and three heads. [2]I saw it spread its wings over[c] the whole earth, and all the winds of heaven blew upon it, and the clouds were gathered around it. [d] [3]I saw that out of its wings there grew opposing wings; but they became little, puny wings. [4]But its heads were at rest; the middle head was larger than the other heads, but it too was at rest with them. [5]Then I saw that the eagle flew with its wings, and it reigned over the earth and over those who inhabit it. [6]And I saw how all things under heaven were subjected to it, and no one spoke against it— not a single creature that was on the earth. [7]Then I saw the eagle rise upon its talons, and it uttered a cry to its wings, saying, [8]"Do not all watch at the same time; let each sleep in its own place, and watch in its turn; [9]but let the heads be reserved for the last."

10 I looked again and saw that the voice did not come from its heads, but from the middle of its body. [11]I counted its rival wings, and there were eight of them. [12]As I watched, one wing on the right side rose up, and it reigned over all the earth. [13]And after a time its reign came to an end, and it disappeared, so that even its place was no longer visible. Then the next wing rose up and reigned, and it continued to reign a long time. [14]While it was reigning its end came also, so that it disappeared like the first. [15]And a voice sounded, saying to it, [16]"Listen to me, you who have ruled the earth all this time; I announce this to you before you disappear. [17]After you no one shall rule as long as you have ruled, not even half as long."

18 Then the third wing raised itself up, and held the rule as the earlier ones had done, and it also disappeared. [19]And so it went with all the wings; they wielded power one after another and then were never seen again. [20]I kept looking, and in due time the wings that followed[e] also rose up on the right[f] side, in order to rule. There were some of them that ruled, yet disappeared suddenly; [21]and others of them rose up, but did not hold the rule.

22 And after this I looked and saw that the twelve wings and the two little wings had disappeared, [23]and nothing remained on the eagle's body except the three heads that were at rest and six little wings.

24 As I kept looking I saw that two little wings separated from the six and remained under the head that was on the right side; but four remained in their place. [25]Then I saw that these little wings[g] planned to set themselves up and hold the rule. [26]As I kept looking, one was set up, but suddenly disappeared; [27]a second also, and this disappeared more quickly than the first. [28]While I continued to look the two that remained were planning between themselves to reign together; [29]and while they were planning, one of the heads that were at rest (the one that

---

a Other ancient authorities read *and* 　 b Or *been named by* 　 c Arab 2 Arm: Lat Syr Ethiop *in* 　 d Syr: Compare Ethiop Arab: Lat lacks *the clouds and around it* 　 e Syr Arab 2 *the little wings* 　 f Some Ethiop Mss read *left* 　 g Syr: Lat *underwings*

10:58–59 *tomorrow night you shall remain here.* Again we see the connection between Ezra's experience of divine revelation and his willingness to spend time in God's presence, to devote days and nights to waiting for God and following the promptings of God and his agents. The visions of what God will yet do allow Ezra to interpret his present situation in light of God's future interventions, which will resolve the tensions he feels so deeply.

was in the middle) suddenly awoke; it was greater than the other two heads. 30And I saw how it allied the two heads with itself, 31and how the head turned with those that were with it and devoured the two little wings*a* that were planning to reign. 32Moreover this head gained control of the whole earth, and with much oppression dominated its inhabitants; it had greater power over the world than all the wings that had gone before.

33 After this I looked again and saw the head in the middle suddenly disappear, just as the wings had done. 34But the two heads remained, which also in like manner ruled over the earth and its inhabitants. 35And while I looked, I saw the head on the right side devour the one on the left.

A Lion Roused from the Forest

36 Then I heard a voice saying to me, "Look in front of you and consider what you see." 37When I looked, I saw what seemed to be a lion roused from the forest, roaring; and I heard how it uttered a human voice to the eagle, and spoke, saying, 38"Listen and I will speak to you. The Most High says to you, 39'Are you not the one that remains of the four beasts that I had made to reign in my world, so that the end of my times might come through them? 40You, the fourth that has come, have conquered all the beasts that have gone before; and you have held sway over the world with great terror, and over all the earth with grievous oppression; and for so long you have lived on the earth with deceit.*b* 41You have judged the earth, but not with truth, 42for you have oppressed the meek and injured the peaceable; you have hated those who tell the truth, and have loved liars; you have destroyed the homes of those who brought forth fruit, and have laid low the walls of those who did you no harm. 43Your insolence has come up before the Most High, and your pride to the Mighty One. 44The Most High has looked at his times; now they have ended, and his ages have reached completion. 45Therefore you, eagle, will surely disappear, you and your terrifying wings, your most evil little wings, your malicious heads, your most evil talons, and your whole worthless body, 46so that the whole earth, freed from your violence, may be refreshed and relieved, and may hope for the judgment and mercy of him who made it.' "

12 While the lion was saying these words to the eagle, I looked 2and saw that the remaining head had disappeared. The two wings that had gone over to it rose up and*c* set themselves up to reign, and their reign was brief and full of tumult. 3When I looked again, they were already vanishing.

a Syr: Lat *underwings*   *b* Syr Arab Arm: Lat Ethiop *The fourth came, however, and conquered . . . and held sway . . . and for so long lived*   *c* Ethiop: Lat lacks *rose up and*

11:36–46 *you have held sway over the world.* Rome was lauded by its own poets and prophets as the bringer of law, order, peace, and prosperity, the vehicle chosen by the gods for the stable rule of humankind. The author calls attention to the underside of empire, the violence, the economic and ecological burden, the silencing of dissenting voices. The Messiah's main task is to indict Rome for its injustice and to execute God's judgment upon it. The faith nurtured here, as in Daniel and Revelation, is no opiate for people living under an oppressive or unjust regime. Its visions of a world beyond our present experience do not distract its readers from their situation in this world or defuse the energy of critique and reform. Rather, these visions provide the perspective and empower-ment for prophetic critique and resistance. Our faith has not been fully formed by Scripture until we are brought to the place where we too refuse to whitewash a government's oppressive methods of ensuring security and prosperity, even if we benefit from them.

12:3–6 *you search out the ways of the Most High.* At any step of our spiritual journey, we can meet with perplexity; especially in the process of seeing God deal with our deepest wounds and needs, our strength can fail. Ezra models for us the importance—and the resource—of being able to take all of these things back to God for his sustaining grace and his help, so that we can press through to the good end that God has for us.

The whole body of the eagle was burned, and the earth was exceedingly terrified.

Then I woke up in great perplexity of mind and great fear, and I said to my spirit, [4]"You have brought this upon me, because you search out the ways of the Most High. [5]I am still weary in mind and very weak in my spirit, and not even a little strength is left in me, because of the great fear with which I have been terrified tonight. [6]Therefore I will now entreat the Most High that he may strengthen me to the end."

The Interpretation of the Vision

7 Then I said, "O sovereign Lord, if I have found favor in your sight, and if I have been accounted righteous before you beyond many others, and if my prayer has indeed come up before your face, [8]strengthen me and show me, your servant, the interpretation and meaning of this terrifying vision so that you may fully comfort my soul. [9]For you have judged me worthy to be shown the end of the times and the last events of the times."

10 He said to me, "This is the interpretation of this vision that you have seen: [11]The eagle that you saw coming up from the sea is the fourth kingdom that appeared in a vision to your brother Daniel. [12]But it was not explained to him as I now explain to you or have explained it. [13]The days are coming when a kingdom shall rise on earth, and it shall be more terrifying than all the kingdoms that have been before it. [14]And twelve kings shall reign in it, one after another. [15]But the second that is to reign shall hold sway for a longer time than any other one of the twelve. [16]This is the interpretation of the twelve wings that you saw.

17 "As for your hearing a voice that spoke, coming not from the eagle's[a] heads but from the midst of its body, this is the interpretation: [18]In the midst of[b] the time of that kingdom great struggles shall arise, and it shall be in danger of falling; nevertheless it shall not fall then, but shall regain its former power.[c] [19]As for your seeing eight little wings[d] clinging to its wings, this is the interpretation: [20]Eight kings shall arise in it, whose times shall be short and their years swift; [21]two of them shall perish when the middle of its time draws near; and four shall be kept for the time when its end approaches, but two shall be kept until the end.

22 "As for your seeing three heads at rest, this is the interpretation: [23]In its last days the Most High will raise up three kings,[e] and they[f] shall renew many things in it, and shall rule the earth [24]and its inhabitants more oppressively than all who were before them. Therefore they are called the heads of the eagle, [25]because it is they who shall sum up his wickedness and perform his last actions. [26]As for your seeing that the large head disappeared, one of the kings[g] shall die in his bed, but in agonies. [27]But as for the two who remained, the sword shall devour them. [28]For the sword of one shall devour him who was with him; but he also shall fall by the sword in the last days.

29 "As for your seeing two little wings[h]

a Lat *his*   b Syr Arm: Lat *After*   c Ethiop Arab 1 Arm: Lat Syr *its beginning*   d Syr: Lat *underwings*   e Syr Ethiop Arab Arm: Lat *kingdoms*   f Syr Ethiop Arm: Lat *he*   g Lat *them*   h Arab 1: Lat *underwings*

12:11–12 *The eagle that you saw.* The eagle vision has been presented as a reformulation of the vision of Daniel 7, which led up to Antiochus IV as the great enemy of the People of God (see 1 & 2 Maccabees). The author seeks to understand his present situation in light of God's earlier revelations, which continue to shed light on our existence in the world long after the first meaning for the first audience has been exhausted. That the author has Rome in mind is clear from the choice of symbol (the eagle was Rome's symbol for itself), the fact that the second ruler (Augustus) reigned twice as long as any of his successors, the correlation of the murmuring in the eagle's body with a civil war in the midst of Rome's rule in the first century (AD 68–69), and the story of the three heads (which match the emperors Vespasian, Titus, and Domitian very well). The fact that the eagle's rule does not end as predicted is no obstacle: this text joins the many biblical voices in calling world empires to account before God and in assuring the People of God that the domination systems of the world will never have the last word.

passing over to[a] the head which was on the right side, [30]this is the interpretation: It is these whom the Most High has kept for the eagle's[b] end; this was the reign which was brief and full of tumult, as you have seen.

31 "And as for the lion whom you saw rousing up out of the forest and roaring and speaking to the eagle and reproving him for his unrighteousness, and as for all his words that you have heard, [32]this is the Messiah[c] whom the Most High has kept until the end of days, who will arise from the offspring of David, and will come and speak[d] with them. He will denounce them for their ungodliness and for their wickedness, and will display before them their contemptuous dealings. [33]For first he will bring them alive before his judgment seat, and when he has reproved them, then he will destroy them. [34]But in mercy he will set free the remnant of my people, those who have been saved throughout my borders, and he will make them joyful until the end comes, the day of judgment, of which I spoke to you at the beginning. [35]This is the dream that you saw, and this is its interpretation. [36]And you alone were worthy to learn this secret of the Most High. [37]Therefore write all these things that you have seen in a book, put it[e] in a hidden place; [38]and you shall teach them to the wise among your people, whose hearts you know are able to comprehend and keep these secrets. [39]But as for you, wait here seven days more, so that you may be shown whatever it pleases the Most High to show you." Then he left me.

The People Come to Ezra

40 When all the people heard that the seven days were past and I had not returned to the city, they all gathered together, from the least to the greatest, and came to me and

spoke to me, saying, [41]"How have we offended you, and what harm have we done you, that you have forsaken us and sit in this place? [42]For of all the prophets you alone are left to us, like a cluster of grapes from the vintage, and like a lamp in a dark place, and like a haven for a ship saved from a storm. [43]Are not the disasters that have befallen us enough? [44]Therefore if you forsake us, how much better it would have been for us if we also had been consumed in the burning of Zion. [45]For we are no better than those who died there." And they wept with a loud voice.

Then I answered them and said, [46]"Take courage, O Israel; and do not be sorrowful, O house of Jacob; [47]for the Most High has you in remembrance, and the Mighty One has not forgotten you in your struggle. [48]As for me, I have neither forsaken you nor withdrawn from you; but I have come to this place to pray on account of the desolation of Zion, and to seek mercy on account of the humiliation of our[f] sanctuary. [49]Now go to your homes, every one of you, and after these days I will come to you." [50]So the people went into the city, as I told them to do. [51]But I sat in the field seven days, as the angel[g] had commanded me; and I ate only of the flowers of the field, and my food was of plants during those days.

The Man from the Sea

13 After seven days I dreamed a dream in the night. [2]And lo, a wind arose from the sea and stirred up[h] all its waves. [3]As I kept looking the wind made something like the

a Syr Ethiop: Lat lacks to   b Lat his
c Literally anointed one   d Syr: Lat lacks of
days . . . and speak   e Ethiop Arab 1 Arab 2 Arm:
Lat Syr them   f Syr Ethiop: Lat your   g Literally
he   h Other ancient authorities read I saw a wind
arise from the sea and stir up

12:31–32 *this is the Messiah.* See note on 11:36–46.

12:39, 51 *wait here seven days more.* Ezra's commitment to solitude, waiting for God, and prayer (now with a partial rather than total fast) continues.

12:42–44 *of all the prophets you alone are left to us.* The reactions of the people to Ezra's

departure to seek a word from God remind us that the people around us also desperately need a word from the Lord. When we wait for God and seek his face, we do so not only for ourselves, but also to share the light and peace we receive with those around us, drawing them closer to God and involving them more deeply in their own discipleship.

figure of a man come up out of the heart of the sea. And I saw[a] that this man flew[b] with the clouds of heaven; and wherever he turned his face to look, everything under his gaze trembled, [4]and whenever his voice issued from his mouth, all who heard his voice melted as wax melts[c] when it feels the fire.

[5] After this I looked and saw that an innumerable multitude of people were gathered together from the four winds of heaven to make war against the man who came up out of the sea. [6]And I looked and saw that he carved out for himself a great mountain, and flew up on to it. [7]And I tried to see the region or place from which the mountain was carved, but I could not.

[8] After this I looked and saw that all who had gathered together against him, to wage war with him, were filled with fear, and yet they dared to fight. [9]When he saw the onrush of the approaching multitude, he neither lifted his hand nor held a spear or any weapon of war; [10]but I saw only how he sent forth from his mouth something like a stream of fire, and from his lips a flaming breath, and from his tongue he shot forth a storm of sparks.[d] [11]All these were mingled together, the stream of fire and the flaming breath and the great storm, and fell on the onrushing multitude that was prepared to fight, and burned up all of them, so that suddenly nothing was seen of the innumerable multitude but only the dust of ashes and the smell of smoke. When I saw it, I was amazed.

[12] After this I saw the same man come down from the mountain and call to himself another multitude that was peaceable. [13]Then many people[e] came to him, some of whom were joyful and some sorrowful; some of them were bound, and some were bringing others as offerings.

The Interpretation of the Vision

Then I woke up in great terror, and prayed to the Most High, and said, [14]"From the beginning you have shown your servant these wonders, and have deemed me worthy to have my prayer heard by you; [15]now show me the interpretation of this dream also. [16]For as I consider it in my mind, alas for those who will be left in those days! And still more, alas for those who are not left! [17]For those who are not left will be sad [18]because they understand the things that are reserved for the last days, but cannot attain them. [19]But alas for those also who are left, and for that very reason! For they shall see great dangers and much distress, as these dreams show. [20]Yet it is better[f] to come into these things,[g] though incurring peril, than to pass from the world like a cloud, and not to see what will happen in the last days."

He answered me and said, [21]"I will tell you the interpretation of the vision, and I will also explain to you the things that you have mentioned. [22]As for what you said about those who survive, and concerning those who do not survive,[h] this is the interpretation: [23]The one who brings the peril at that time will protect those who fall into peril, who have works and faith toward the Almighty. [24]Understand therefore that those

a Syr: Lat lacks *the wind . . . I saw*   b Syr Ethiop Arab Arm: Lat *grew strong*   c Syr: Lat *burned as the earth rests*   d Meaning of Lat uncertain   e Lat Syr Arab 2 literally *the faces of many people*   f Ethiop Compare Arab 2: Lat *easier*   g Syr: Lat *this*   h Syr Arab 1: Lat lacks *and . . . not survive*

13:3–4, 10–11 *the figure of a man.* The author attributes characteristics of God (whose gaze makes the earth tremble in Ps 104:32, whose voice makes creation melt like wax in Ps 97:5, whose fiery breath makes his enemies die in Pss 18:8; 97:3) to the Messiah figure, who is invested with the power and authority of God. Even though he himself does not identify Jesus as the Messiah, he indirectly feeds the Christian understanding of God revealing himself in Jesus and of the Son sharing in the essential nature of the Father.

13:23 The one who brings the peril . . . will protect those who fall into peril. As in the exodus, where the People of God did not experience the plagues poured out on Egypt, and in Revelation 7, where the People of God are sealed to be protected from the wrath God will yet pour out, this author affirms the conviction that those who have walked in the fear of the Lord have nothing to fear from God when he comes to judge the world.

who are left are more blessed than those who have died.

25 "This is the interpretation of the vision: As for your seeing a man come up from the heart of the sea, [26]this is he whom the Most High has been keeping for many ages, who will himself deliver his creation; and he will direct those who are left. [27]And as for your seeing wind and fire and a storm coming out of his mouth, [28]and as for his not holding a spear or weapon of war, yet destroying the onrushing multitude that came to conquer him, this is the interpretation: [29]The days are coming when the Most High will deliver those who are on the earth. [30]And bewilderment of mind shall come over those who inhabit the earth. [31]They shall plan to make war against one another, city against city, place against place, people against people, and kingdom against kingdom. [32]When these things take place and the signs occur that I showed you before, then my Son will be revealed, whom you saw as a man coming up from the sea. [a]

33 "Then, when all the nations hear his voice, all the nations shall leave their own lands and the warfare that they have against one another; [34]and an innumerable multitude shall be gathered together, as you saw, wishing to come and conquer him. [35]But he shall stand on the top of Mount Zion. [36]And Zion shall come and be made manifest to all people, prepared and built, as you saw the mountain carved out without hands. [37]Then he, my Son, will reprove the assembled nations for their ungodliness (this was symbolized by the storm), [38]and will reproach them to their face with their evil thoughts and the torments with which they are to be tortured (which were symbolized by the

flames), and will destroy them without effort by means of the law [b] (which was symbolized by the fire).

39 "And as for your seeing him gather to himself another multitude that was peaceable, [40]these are the nine [c] tribes that were taken away from their own land into exile in the days of King Hoshea, whom Shalmaneser, king of the Assyrians, made captives; he took them across the river, and they were taken into another land. [41]But they formed this plan for themselves, that they would leave the multitude of the nations and go to a more distant region, where no human beings had ever lived, [42]so that there at least they might keep their statutes that they had not kept in their own land. [43]And they went in by the narrow passages of the Euphrates river. [44]For at that time the Most High performed signs for them, and stopped the channels of the river until they had crossed over. [45]Through that region there was a long way to go, a journey of a year and a half; and that country is called Arzareth. [d]

46 "Then they lived there until the last times; and now, when they are about to come again, [47]the Most High will stop [e] the channels of the river again, so that they may be able to cross over. Therefore you saw the multitude gathered together in peace. [48]But those who are left of your people, who are found within my holy borders, shall be saved. [f] [49]Therefore when he destroys the multitude of the nations that are gathered together, he

a Syr and most Lat Mss lack *from the sea*
b Syr: Lat *effort and the law*   c Other Lat Mss *ten*; Syr Ethiop Arab 1 Arm *nine and a half*   d That is *Another Land*   e Syr: Lat *stops*   f Syr: Lat lacks *shall be saved*

13:39–42 *they would leave the multitude of the nations and go to a more distant region.* The myth of the exiled nine tribes of the Northern Kingdom provides a praiseworthy model for the author's audience. They may not be able to physically remove themselves from their current context, but they can recommit themselves to keep their ways separate from those of the Gentiles around them and to perform God's law now in the diaspora more zealously than their

ancestors had done in Israel. In a similar vein, the disciples of Jesus in the "new Israel" are continually called to live as strangers in the world, to preserve clear boundaries between themselves and the "nations" around them (e.g., through the avoidance of all idolatry and a commitment to sexual purity), and to commit themselves to following Jesus' ways (see 1 Pet 1:13–19; 2:11–12; 4:1–4).

will defend the people who remain. ⁵⁰And then he will show them very many wonders."

51 I said, "O sovereign Lord, explain this to me: Why did I see the man coming up from the heart of the sea?"

52 He said to me, "Just as no one can explore or know what is in the depths of the sea, so no one on earth can see my Son or those who are with him, except in the time of his day.ᵃ ⁵³This is the interpretation of the dream that you saw. And you alone have been enlightened about this, ⁵⁴because you have forsaken your own ways and have applied yourself to mine, and have searched out my law; ⁵⁵for you have devoted your life to wisdom, and called understanding your mother. ⁵⁶Therefore I have shown you these things; for there is a reward laid up with the Most High. For it will be that after three more days I will tell you other things, and explain weighty and wondrous matters to you."

57 Then I got up and walked in the field, giving great glory and praise to the Most High for the wonders that he doesᵇ from time to time, ⁵⁸and because he governs the times and whatever things come to pass in their seasons. And I stayed there three days.

The Lord Commissions Ezra

14 On the third day, while I was sitting under an oak, suddenly a voice came out of a bush opposite me and said, "Ezra, Ezra!" ²And I answered, "Here I am, Lord," and I rose to my feet. ³Then he said to me, "I revealed myself in a bush and spoke to Moses when my people were in bondage in Egypt; ⁴and I sent him and ledᶜ my people out of Egypt; and I led him up on Mount Sinai, where I kept him with me many days. ⁵I told him many wondrous things, and showed him

the secrets of the times and declared to himᵈ the end of the times. Then I commanded him, saying, ⁶'These words you shall publish openly, and these you shall keep secret.' ⁷And now I say to you: ⁸Lay up in your heart the signs that I have shown you, the dreams that you have seen, and the interpretations that you have heard; ⁹for you shall be taken up from among humankind, and henceforth you shall live with my Son and with those who are like you, until the times are ended. ¹⁰The age has lost its youth, and the times begin to grow old. ¹¹For the age is divided into twelve parts, and nineᵉ of its parts have already passed, ¹²as well as half of the tenth part; so two of its parts remain, besides half of the tenth part.ᶠ ¹³Now therefore, set your house in order, and reprove your people; comfort the lowly among them, and instruct those that are wise.ᵍ And now renounce the life that is corruptible, ¹⁴and put away from you mortal thoughts; cast away from you the burdens of humankind, and divest yourself now of your weak nature; ¹⁵lay to one side the thoughts that are most grievous to you, and hurry to escape from these times. ¹⁶For evils worse than those that you have now seen happen shall take place hereafter. ¹⁷For the weaker the world becomes through old age, the more shall evils be increased upon its inhabitants. ¹⁸Truth shall go farther away, and falsehood shall come near. For the eagleʰ that you saw in the vision is already hurrying to come."

---

a Syr: Ethiop *except when his time and his day have come.* Lat lacks *his*   *b* Lat *did*   *c* Syr Arab 1 Arab 2 *he led*   *d* Syr Ethiop Arab Arm: Lat lacks *declared to him*   *e* Cn: Lat Ethiop *ten*   *f* Syr lacks verses 11, 12: Ethiop *For the world is divided into ten parts, and has come to the tenth, and half of the tenth remains. Now . . .*   *g* Lat lacks *and . . . wise*   *h* Syr Ethiop Arab Arm: Meaning of Lat uncertain

---

13:57–58 *giving great glory and praise to the Most High.* Ezra arrives at the place where he can glorify God and affirm his justice, but it has been a long process. First he had to move through blaming God and questioning his justice. In a second phase, he still experienced grief, but also began to rediscover trust. Only as he persisted in seeking God, devoting large amounts of time and of himself to the process, did he arrive at the place where God's goodness

and trustworthiness emerged again as the center of his life.

14:1–2 *suddenly a voice came out of a bush opposite me.* God appears to Ezra as he had appeared to Moses, suggesting a continuity to God's self-revelation. As we meditate on the many ways in which God revealed himself, his heart, and his movement toward the People of God in the past, we are alerted to ways in which to look for his self-revelations in the present.

Ezra's Concern to Restore the Scriptures

19 Then I answered and said, "Let me speak[a] in your presence, Lord. 20For I will go, as you have commanded me, and I will reprove the people who are now living; but who will warn those who will be born hereafter? For the world lies in darkness, and its inhabitants are without light. 21For your law has been burned, and so no one knows the things which have been done or will be done by you. 22If then I have found favor with you, send the holy spirit into me, and I will write everything that has happened in the world from the beginning, the things that were written in your law, so that people may be able to find the path, and that those who want to live in the last days may do so."

23 He answered me and said, "Go and gather the people, and tell them not to seek you for forty days. 24But prepare for yourself many writing tablets, and take with you Sarea, Dabria, Selemia, Ethanus, and Asiel— these five, who are trained to write rapidly; 25and you shall come here, and I will light in your heart the lamp of understanding, which shall not be put out until what you are about to write is finished. 26And when you have finished, some things you shall make public, and some you shall deliver in secret to the wise; tomorrow at this hour you shall begin to write."

Ezra's Last Words to the People

27 Then I went as he commanded me, and I gathered all the people together, and said, 28"Hear these words, O Israel. 29At first our ancestors lived as aliens in Egypt, and they were liberated from there 30and received the law of life, which they did not keep, which you also have transgressed after them. 31Then land was given to you for a possession in the land of Zion; but you and your ancestors committed iniquity and did not keep the ways that the Most High commanded you. 32And since he is a righteous judge, in due time he took from you what he had given. 33And now you are here, and your people[b] are farther in the interior.[c] 34If you, then, will rule over your minds and discipline your hearts, you shall be kept alive, and after death you shall obtain mercy. 35For after death the judgment will come, when we shall live again; and then the names of the righteous shall become manifest, and the deeds of the ungodly shall be disclosed. 36But let no one come to me now, and let no one seek me for forty days."

The Restoration of the Scriptures

37 So I took the five men, as he commanded me, and we proceeded to the field, and remained there. 38And on the next day a voice called me, saying, "Ezra, open your mouth and drink what I give you to drink." 39So I opened my mouth, and a full cup was offered to me; it was full of something like water, but its color was like fire. 40I took it and drank; and when I had drunk it, my heart poured forth understanding, and wisdom increased in my breast, for my spirit retained its memory, 41and my mouth was opened and was no longer closed. 42Moreover, the Most High gave understanding to the five men, and by turns they wrote what was dictated, using characters that they did not know.[d] They sat forty days; they wrote during the daytime, and ate their bread at night. 43But as

a Most Lat Mss lack *Let me speak*　　b Lat *brothers* c Syr Ethiop Arm: Lat *are among you*　　d Syr Compare Ethiop Arab 2 Arm: Meaning of Lat uncertain

---

14:22 *send the holy spirit into me.* The climax of 4 Ezra is the restoration of the Scriptures after the exile. The image of Ezra's drinking a fiery bowl handed to him by God (vv 38–40) speaks of the purity and the power lying behind and flowing through the Word. It has proven throughout the millennia to be the surest guide to the path that leads to God and to life (see Ps 119:105, 130, 144).

14:34 *If you, then, will rule over your minds and discipline your hearts.* The path to life involves "ruling" our thoughts and "disciplining" our hearts (our desires, drives, etc.). This is, of course, a recurrent theme in the spiritual formation of the People of God (see 4 Maccabees; Gal 5:16–25; Rom 6:1–14). The Spiritual Disciplines are all meant to help us heighten our responsiveness to God's Spirit and decrease our captivity to our undisciplined nature.

for me, I spoke in the daytime and was not silent at night. [44]So during the forty days, ninety-four[a] books were written. [45]And when the forty days were ended, the Most High spoke to me, saying, "Make public the twenty-four[b] books that you wrote first, and let the worthy and the unworthy read them; [46]but keep the seventy that were written last, in order to give them to the wise among your people. [47]For in them is the spring of understanding, the fountain of wisdom, and the river of knowledge." [48]And I did so.[c]

Vengeance on the Wicked

15[d] Speak in the ears of my people the words of the prophecy that I will put in your mouth, says the Lord, [2]and cause them to be written on paper; for they are trustworthy and true. [3]Do not fear the plots against you, and do not be troubled by the unbelief of those who oppose you. [4]For all unbelievers shall die in their unbelief.[e]

[5] Beware, says the Lord, I am bringing evils upon the world, the sword and famine, death and destruction, [6]because iniquity has spread throughout every land, and their harmful doings have reached their limit. [7]Therefore, says the Lord, [8]I will be silent no longer concerning their ungodly acts that they impiously commit, neither will I tolerate their wicked practices. Innocent and righteous blood cries out to me, and the souls of the righteous cry out continually. [9]I will surely avenge them, says the Lord, and will receive to myself all the innocent blood from among them. [10]See, my people are being led like a flock to the slaughter; I will not allow them to live any longer in the land of Egypt, [11]but I will bring them out with a mighty hand and with an uplifted arm, and will strike Egypt with plagues, as before, and will destroy all its land.

[12] Let Egypt mourn, and its foundations, because of the plague of chastisement and castigation that the Lord will bring upon it. [13]Let the farmers that till the ground mourn, because their seed shall fail to grow[f] and their trees shall be ruined by blight and hail and by a terrible tempest. [14]Alas for the world and for

a Syr Ethiop Arab 1 Arm: Meaning of Lat uncertain   b Syr Arab 1: Lat lacks *twenty-four*   c Syr adds *in the seventh year of the sixth week, five thousand years and three months and twelve days after creation. At that time Ezra was caught up, and taken to the place of those who are like him, after he had written all these things. And he was called the scribe of the knowledge of the Most High for ever and ever.* Ethiop Arab 1 Arm have a similar ending   d Chapters 15 and 16 (except 15.57-59, which has been found in Greek) are extant only in Lat   e Other ancient authorities add *and all who believe shall be saved by their faith*   f Lat lacks *to grow*

14:45–47 *Make public the twenty-four books that you wrote first.* Scripture, of course, remains foundational for our spiritual nurture, a source of understanding and wisdom for all who study and meditate prayerfully on it. The author also commends, however, extrabiblical texts (no doubt including the one he has written) as secondary sources of guidance and inspiration for those who are sufficiently grounded in the primary canon. We continue today to derive much help from works that profess to impart spiritual wisdom and direction; it is all too often the case, however, that the extrabiblical texts are consumed by people who have not acquired a foundation for discernment by prayerful study of God's word to them in Scripture. The angel's warning about caution in distributing the "esoteric" wisdom of the seventy books suggests we should also be cautious about building our faith on anything but the foundation of the Scriptures and give those primary place in our spiritual formation.

15:3, 8–11 *Do not fear the plots against you.* The Christian author of 2 Esdras 15–16 encourages Christians facing the harsh persecutions of the third century to persevere in faith in God, here by assuring Christians that God will keep faith with them. God's past acts on behalf of his people (seen, e.g., in the plagues sent upon Egypt and the deliverance of the Hebrews in the exodus) reveal God's unchanging character and show how he can be counted upon to act in the future. He will judge their cause and intervene on their behalf.

15:14–19 *Alas for the world.* God can be present in the turmoil that comes upon repressive regimes and countries, providing for a changed situation for the oppressed and those who live in it! 15For the sword and misery draw near them, and nation shall rise up to fight against nation, with swords in their hands. 16For there shall be unrest among people; growing strong against one another, they shall in their might have no respect for their king or the chief of their leaders. 17For a person will desire to go into a city, and shall not be able to do so. 18Because of their pride the cities shall be in confusion, the houses shall be destroyed, and people shall be afraid. 19People shall have no pity for their neighbors, but shall make an assault upon*a* their houses with the sword, and plunder their goods, because of hunger for bread and because of great tribulation.

20 See how I am calling together all the kings of the earth to turn to me, says God, from the rising sun and from the south, from the east and from Lebanon; to turn and repay what they have given them. 21Just as they have done to my elect until this day, so I will do, and will repay into their bosom. Thus says the Lord God: 22My right hand will not spare the sinners, and my sword will not cease from those who shed innocent blood on earth. 23And a fire went forth from his wrath, and consumed the foundations of the earth and the sinners, like burnt straw. 24Alas for those who sin and do not observe my commandments, says the Lord;*b* 25I will not spare them. Depart, you faithless children! Do not pollute my sanctuary. 26For God*c* knows all who sin against him; therefore he will hand them over to death and slaughter. 27Already calamities have come upon the whole earth, and you shall remain in them; God*c* will not deliver you, because you have sinned against him.

A Terrifying Vision of Warfare

28 What a terrifying sight, appearing from the east! 29The nations of the dragons of Arabia shall come out with many chariots, and from the day that they set out, their hissing shall spread over the earth, so that all who hear them will fear and tremble. 30Also the Carmonians, raging in wrath, shall go forth like wild boars*d* from the forest, and with great power they shall come and engage them in battle, and with their tusks they shall devastate a portion of the land of the Assyrians with their teeth. 31And then the dragons,*e* remembering their origin, shall become still stronger; and if they combine in great power and turn to pursue them, 32then these shall be disorganized and silenced by their power, and shall turn and flee.*f* 33And from the land of the Assyrians an enemy in ambush shall attack them and destroy one of them, and fear and trembling shall come upon their army, and indecision upon their kings.

Judgment on Babylon

34 See the clouds from the east, and from the north to the south! Their appearance is exceedingly threatening, full of wrath and storm. 35They shall clash against one another and shall pour out a heavy tempest on the earth, and their own tempest;*g* and there shall be blood from the sword as high as a horse's belly 36and a man's thigh and a camel's hock. 37And there shall be fear and great trembling on the earth; those who see that wrath shall be horror-stricken, and they shall be seized with trembling. 38After that, heavy storm clouds shall be stirred up from the south, and from the north, and another part from the west. 39But the winds from the east shall prevail over the cloud that was*h* raised in wrath, and shall dispel it; and the tempest*g* that was to cause destruction by the east wind shall be driven violently to-

---

a Cn: Lat *shall empty*   *b* Other ancient authorities read *God*   *c* Other ancient authorities read *the Lord*   *d* Other ancient authorities lack *like wild boars*   *e* Cn: Lat *dragon*   *f* Other ancient authorities read *turn their face to the north*   *g* Meaning of Lat uncertain   *h* Literally *that he*

---

harassed People of God. The author paints a picture here of the anticommunity: when pressure and hardship come upon a domination system, that system and its relationships deteriorate into chaos. The Christian community, on the other hand, is consistently called to model unity and solidarity in the face of calamity, its members remaining committed to each other rather than self.

ward the south and west. 40Great and mighty clouds, full of wrath and tempest, shall rise and destroy all the earth and its inhabitants, and shall pour out upon every high and lofty place*a* a terrible tempest, 41fire and hail and flying swords and floods of water, so that all the fields and all the streams shall be filled with the abundance of those waters. 42They shall destroy cities and walls, mountains and hills, trees of the forests, and grass of the meadows, and their grain. 43They shall go on steadily to Babylon and blot it out. 44They shall come to it and surround it; they shall pour out on it the tempest*b* and all its fury;*c* then the dust and smoke shall reach the sky, and all who are around it shall mourn for it. 45And those who survive shall serve those who have destroyed it.

Judgment on Asia

46 And you, Asia, who share in the splendor of Babylon and the glory of her person— 47woe to you, miserable wretch! For you have made yourself like her; you have decked out your daughters for prostitution to please and glory in your lovers, who have always lusted after you. 48You have imitated that hateful one in all her deeds and devices.*d* Therefore God*e* says, 49I will send evils upon you: widowhood, poverty, famine, sword, and pestilence, bringing ruin to your houses, bringing destruction and death. 50And the glory of your strength shall wither like a flower when the heat shall rise that is sent upon you. 51You shall be weakened like a wretched woman who is beaten and wounded, so that you cannot receive your mighty lovers. 52Would I have dealt with you so violently, says the Lord, 53if you had not killed my chosen people continually, exulting and clapping your hands and talking about their death when you were drunk?

54 Beautify your face! 55The reward of a prostitute is in your lap; therefore you shall receive your recompense. 56As you will do to my chosen people, says the Lord, so God will do to you, and will hand you over to adversities. 57Your children shall die of hunger, and you shall fall by the sword; your cities shall be wiped out, and all your people who are in the open country shall fall by the sword. 58Those who are in the mountains and highlands*f* shall perish of hunger, and they shall eat their own flesh in hunger for bread and drink their own blood in thirst for water. 59Unhappy above all others, you shall come and suffer fresh miseries. 60As they pass by they shall crush the hateful*g* city, and shall destroy a part of your land and abolish a portion of your glory, when they return from devastated Babylon. 61You shall be broken down by them like stubble,*h* and they shall be like fire to you. 62They shall devour you and your cities, your land and your mountains; they shall burn with fire all your forests and your fruitful trees. 63They shall carry your children away captive, plunder your wealth, and mar the glory of your countenance.

Further Denunciations

16 Woe to you, Babylon and Asia! Woe to you, Egypt and Syria! 2Bind on sackcloth and cloth of goats' hair,*i* and wail for your children, and lament for them; for your

a Or *eminent person*   *b* Meaning of Lat uncertain   *c* Other ancient authorities add *until they destroy it to its foundations*   *d* Other ancient authorities read *devices, and you have followed after that one about to gratify her magnates and leaders so that you may be made proud and be pleased by her fornications*   *e* Other ancient authorities read *the Lord*   *f* Gk: Lat omits *and highlands*   *g* Another reading is *idle* or *unprofitable*   *h* Other ancient authorities read *like dry straw*   *i* Other ancient authorities lack *cloth of goats' hair*

15:46–48 *And you, Asia, who share in the splendor of Babylon.* The author indicts the province of Asia Minor for allowing the prospect of prosperity to seduce it into adopting Rome's ideology and policies. The language of harlotry as an image for imperialism is well known from Revelation 17–18. The text points out the dangers of "getting in bed" with a "Babylonian" domination system and allowing the comforts and benefits it offers to lead us to approve and support its exploitative economy. We find ourselves sleeping with God's enemy, rather than keeping ourselves pure for our marriage to the Lamb.

16:1–16 *Woe to you.* See note on 15:14–19.

destruction is at hand. ³The sword has been sent upon you, and who is there to turn it back? ⁴A fire has been sent upon you, and who is there to quench it? ⁵Calamities have been sent upon you, and who is there to drive them away? ⁶Can one drive off a hungry lion in the forest, or quench a fire in the stubble once it has started to burn?ᵃ ⁷Can one turn back an arrow shot by a strong archer? ⁸The Lord God sends calamities, and who will drive them away? ⁹Fire will go forth from his wrath, and who is there to quench it? ¹⁰He will flash lightning, and who will not be afraid? He will thunder, and who will not be terrified? ¹¹The Lord will threaten, and who will not be utterly shattered at his presence? ¹²The earth and its foundations quake, the sea is churned up from the depths, and its waves and the fish with them shall be troubled at the presence of the Lord and the glory of his power. ¹³For his right hand that bends the bow is strong, and his arrows that he shoots are sharp and when they are shot to the ends of the world will not miss once. ¹⁴Calamities are sent forth and shall not return until they come over the earth. ¹⁵The fire is kindled, and shall not be put out until it consumes the foundations of the earth. ¹⁶Just as an arrow shot by a mighty archer does not return, so the calamities that are sent upon the earth shall not return. ¹⁷Alas for me! Alas for me! Who will deliver me in those days?

The Horror of the Last Days

18 The beginning of sorrows, when there shall be much lamentation; the beginning of famine, when many shall perish; the beginning of wars, when the powers shall be terrified; the beginning of calamities, when all shall tremble. What shall they do, when the calamities come? ¹⁹Famine and plague, tribulation and anguish are sent as scourges for the correction of humankind. ²⁰Yet for all this they will not turn from their iniquities, or ever be mindful of the scourges. ²¹Indeed, provisions will be so cheap upon earth that people will imagine that peace is assured for them, and then calamities shall spring up on the earth—the sword, famine, and great confusion. ²²For many of those who live on the earth shall perish by famine; and those who

survive the famine shall die by the sword. ²³And the dead shall be thrown out like dung, and there shall be no one to console them; for the earth shall be left desolate, and its cities shall be demolished. ²⁴No one shall be left to cultivate the earth or to sow it. ²⁵The trees shall bear fruit, but who will gather it? ²⁶The grapes shall ripen, but who will tread them? For in all places there shall be great solitude; ²⁷a person will long to see another human being, or even to hear a human voice. ²⁸For ten shall be left out of a city; and two, out of the field, those who have hidden themselves in thick groves and clefts in the rocks. ²⁹Just as in an olive orchard three or four olives may be left on every tree, ³⁰or just as, when a vineyard is gathered, some clusters may be leftᵇ by those who search carefully through the vineyard, ³¹so in those days three or four shall be left by those who search their houses with the sword. ³²The earth shall be left desolate, and its fields shall be plowed up,ᶜ and its roads and all its paths shall bring forth thorns, because no sheep will go along them. ³³Virgins shall mourn because they have no bridegrooms; women shall mourn because they have no husbands; their daughters shall mourn, because they have no help. ³⁴Their bridegrooms shall be killed in war, and their husbands shall perish of famine.

God's People Must Prepare for the End

35 Listen now to these things, and understand them, you who are servants of the Lord. ³⁶This is the word of the Lord; receive it and do not disbelieve what the Lord says.ᵈ ³⁷The calamities draw near, and are not delayed. ³⁸Just as a pregnant woman, in the ninth month when the time of her delivery draws near, has great pains around her womb for two or three hours beforehand, but when the child comes forth from the womb, there will not be a moment's delay, ³⁹so the calamities will not delay in coming upon the earth, and the world will groan, and pains will seize it on every side.

ᵃ Other ancient authorities read *fire when dry straw has been set on fire*   ᵇ Other ancient authorities read *a cluster may remain exposed*   ᶜ Other ancient authorities read *be for briers*   ᵈ Cn: Lat *do not believe the gods of whom the Lord speaks*

40 Hear <u>my words</u>, O my people; prepare for battle, an<u>d in the midst of the calamities</u> be like str<u>angers on the earth. </u>41<u>Let the one</u> who sells be <u>like one who will flee; let the</u> one who buys <u>be like one who will lose; </u>42let the one who does business be like one who will not make a profit; and let the one who builds a house be like one who will not live in it; 43let the one who sows be like one who will not reap; so also the one who prunes the vines, like one who will not gather the grapes; 44those who marry, like those who will have no children; and those who do not marry, like those who are widowed. 45Because of this, those who labor, labor in vain; 46for strangers shall gather their fruits, and plunder their goods, overthrow their houses, and take their children captive; for in captivity and famine they will produce their children.*a* 47Those who conduct business, do so only to have it plundered; the more they adorn their cities, their houses and possessions, and their persons, 48the more angry I will be with them for their sins, says the Lord. 49Just as a respectable and virtuous woman abhors a prostitute, 50so righteousness shall abhor iniquity, when she decks herself out, and shall accuse her to her face when he comes who will defend the one who searches out every sin on earth.

The Power and Wisdom of God

51 Therefore do not be like her or her works. 52For in a very short time iniquity will be removed from the earth, and righteousness will reign over us. 53Sinners must not say that they have not sinned;*b* for God*c* will burn coals of fire on the head of everyone who says, "I have <u>not sinned before God</u> and his glory." 54<u>The Lord</u>*d* <u>certainly knows</u> every<u>thing that people do; he knows their imagi</u>nat<u>ions and their thoughts and their hearts.</u> 55<u>He said, "Let the earth be made," and</u> it was <u>made, and "Let the heaven be made</u>," and <u>it was made. </u>56<u>At his word the stars w</u>ere fixed <u>in their places, and he knows the num</u>ber o<u>f the stars. </u>57<u>He searches the abyss </u>and its tre<u>asures; he has measured the sea and its</u> contents<u>; </u>58<u>he has confined the sea </u>in the midst of the waters;*e* and by his word he has suspended the <u>earth over the water. </u>59He has spread out the heaven like a dome and made it secure upon the waters; 60he has put springs of water in the desert, and pools on the tops of the mountains, so as to send rivers from

a Other ancient authorities read *therefore those who are married may know that they will produce children for captivity and famine*   *b* Other ancient authorities add *or the unjust done injustice*   *c* Lat *for he*   *d* Other ancient authorities read *Lord God*   *e* Other ancient authorities read *confined the world between the waters and the waters*

16:40–42 <u>be *like strangers on the earth*.</u> This passage, modeled on 1 Cor 7:29–31, teaches disciples to remain detached in their inner person in their involvements with the economies and systems of the world. Here, specifically, the fact that the latter stand under God's judgment tells us that the world's economy is not permanent or ultimate. It provides a shaky foundation and a poor anchorage for our lives. Our hearts are to be set on our life with God, the pillars of our soul and self sunk deep into that bedrock that will not be shaken by the calamities that must befall all secular systems.

16:51 *Therefore do not be like her or her works*. Like the voice from heaven in Rev 18:4–8, this author summons us not to conform our lives to the roles and values imposed upon us by the domination systems in which we live (see note on 15:46–48). The judgments that God will pour out upon all injustice drive us to conform our

lives to God's vision for a just and whole community.

16:54–63 *The Lord . . . knows everything that people do*. God's presence with us extends into the deepest, most private areas of our being. How we respond to this fact makes the difference between wholeness and life, and denial and death. We invite God to examine us now (see Ps 139:23–24), to lay bare our areas of sin and dysfunction, and we seek God's forgiveness and restoration, so that he will not need to examine us then as Judge. Our openness to God's examination of our consciences and lives now will lead to healing, growth, and freedom. There is no shame in this process now, no need to hide our deepest selves from God. But if we neglect God's healing here and try to hide our inner selves from God, we will be exposed to shame on the last day (vv 65–66), when the hidden and unhealed is brought to light.

the heights to water the earth. 61He formed human beings and put a heart in the midst of each body, and gave each person breath and life and understanding 62and the spirit*a* of Almighty God,*b* who surely made all things and searches out hidden things in hidden places. 63He knows your imaginations and what you think in your hearts! Woe to those who sin and want to hide their sins! 64The Lord will strictly examine all their works, and will make a public spectacle of all of you. 65You shall be put to shame when your sins come out before others, and your own iniquities shall stand as your accusers on that day. 66What will you do? Or how will you hide your sins before the Lord and his glory? 67Indeed, God*c* is the judge; fear him! Cease from your sins, and forget your iniquities, never to commit them again; so God*c* will lead you forth and deliver you from all tribulation.

Impending Persecution of God's People

68 The burning wrath of a great multitude is kindled over you; they shall drag some of you away and force you to eat what was sacrificed to idols. 69And those who consent to eat shall be held in derision and contempt, and shall be trampled under foot. 70For in many places*d* and in neighboring cities there shall be a great uprising against those who fear the Lord. 71They shall*e* be like maniacs, sparing no one, but plundering and destroying those who continue to fear the Lord.*f* 72For they shall destroy and plunder their goods, and drive them out of house and home. 73Then the tested quality of my elect shall be manifest, like gold that is tested by fire.

Promise of Divine Deliverance

74 Listen, my elect ones, says the Lord; the days of tribulation are at hand, but I will deliver you from them. 75Do not fear or doubt, for God*c* is your guide. 76You who keep my commandments and precepts, says the Lord God, must not let your sins weigh you down, or your iniquities prevail over you. 77Woe to those who are choked by their sins and overwhelmed by their iniquities! They are like a field choked with underbrush and its path*g* overwhelmed with thorns, so that no one can pass through. 78It is shut off and given up to be consumed by fire.

a Or *breath*   *b* Other ancient authorities read *of the Lord Almighty*   *c* Other ancient authorities read *the Lord*   *d* Meaning of Lat uncertain   *e* Other ancient authorities read *For people, because of their misfortunes, shall*   *f* Other ancient authorities read *fear God*   *g* Other ancient authorities read *seed*

16:73–75 *Then the tested quality of my elect shall be manifest.* Encountering hardship for the sake of God and our obedience to God are understood not as an experience of victimization, but as a trial or test, an opportunity to be proven and found genuine (see 1 Pet 1:6–7). God is present as a guide in the midst of hardships suffered for his sake, empowering us to engage them as a trial, assured of his companionship and his promise of deliverance throughout the ordeal.

JUDITH

The book of Judith is a tightly constructed, edifying, and entertaining Jewish novella describing Israel's deliverance from the fury of a foreign power through the hand of a woman, Judith. Of uncertain date, but probably written between 150 and 50 BC, the book teaches not so much by doctrinal exposition or sage advice as by the story of the people's distress, their cry to God, and the bold and wily ways of their deliverer.

Distress and Deliverance

The narrative begins with an apparently unrelated battle between King Nebuchadnezzar and the Medes hundreds of miles east of Israel (chap 1). However, the ambition of the pagan king, whose will is carried out by his general, Holofernes, knows no bounds, and soon Israel is implicated in his strategies for conquest (2–4). The noose tightens around the people as they are unwilling to yield to his threats (5–6). The first part of the book closes with the people immured in a mountain village with the water supply cut off, facing certain death and in "great misery" (7:32).

Like a biblical judge, Judith arises from mourning for her deceased husband, exchanges the garments of sorrow for the accoutrements of war, beautifies herself so that she might use all her feminine charm to insinuate herself into the good graces of the enemy, and earnestly implores the help of the God of Israel (chaps 8–9). Her beauty and deceptive words to the enemy will be the two weapons that gain her access to Holofernes' tent (10–11).

While there, she seemingly acquiesces in all of his suggestions, but does so only to further enflame Holofernes' heart for her. His lust is fueled by a great quantity of wine, "much more than he had ever drunk in any one day since he was born" (12:20). The servants leave his presence, and Judith uses his sword to slice off his head (chap 13). Upon arriving back among her people, Judith displays the head, causing great celebration among her people and resultant panic among the enemy (14).

See also *"The With-God Life"* essay for this section of the Bible, *"The People of God in Rebellion,"* pp. 975–79.

Deliverance is assured as the enemy flees in confusion. Her story is then sung by the people, much like Deborah's was sung a thousand years earlier (16; Judg 5).

The book of Judith is a joyous and triumphant book. It revels in the unexpected way the People of God are delivered. Crucial to the deliverance is both the religious devotion and the crafty manner of Judith. This basic ambiguity in her character, from the perspective of the twenty-first century, contributes to the allure of Judith today. She draws us to her by her uncompromising fidelity and devotion to God; she arrests us by her unabashed use of physical charms and deceptive words to disarm an enemy. Once again God is blessing those with faithful and shrewd hearts.

—*William R. Long*

Arphaxad Fortifies Ecbatana

1 It was the twelfth year of the reign of Nebuchadnezzar, who ruled over the Assyrians in the great city of Nineveh. In those days Arphaxad ruled over the Medes in Ecbatana. [2]He built walls around Ecbatana with hewn stones three cubits thick and six cubits long; he made the walls seventy cubits high and fifty cubits wide. [3]At its gates he raised towers one hundred cubits high and sixty cubits wide at the foundations. [4]He made its gates seventy cubits high and forty cubits wide to allow his armies to march out in force and his infantry to form their ranks. [5]Then King Nebuchadnezzar made war against King Arphaxad in the great plain that is on the borders of Ragau. [6]There rallied to him all the people of the hill country and all those who lived along the Euphrates, the Tigris, and the Hydaspes, and, on the plain, Arioch, king of the Elymeans. Thus, many nations joined the forces of the Chaldeans.[a]

Nebuchadnezzar Issues Ultimatum

[7] Then Nebuchadnezzar, king of the Assyrians, sent messengers to all who lived in Persia and to all who lived in the west, those who lived in Cilicia and Damascus, Lebanon and Antilebanon, and all who lived along the seacoast, [8]and those among the nations of Carmel and Gilead, and Upper Galilee and the great plain of Esdraelon, [9]and all who were in Samaria and its towns, and beyond the Jordan as far as Jerusalem and Bethany and Chelous and Kadesh and the river of Egypt, and Tahpanhes and Raamses and the whole land of Goshen, [10]even beyond Tanis and Memphis, and all who lived in Egypt as far as the borders of Ethiopia. [11]But all who lived in the whole region disregarded the summons of Nebuchadnezzar, king of the Assyrians, and refused to join him in the war; for they were not afraid of him, but regarded him as only one man.[b] So they sent back his messengers empty-handed and in disgrace.

[12] Then Nebuchadnezzar became very angry with this whole region, and swore by his throne and kingdom that he would take revenge on the whole territory of Cilicia and Damascus and Syria, that he would kill with his sword also all the inhabitants of the land

a Syr: Gk *Cheleoudites*   *b* Or *a man*

1:1 *the reign of Nebuchadnezzar, who ruled over the Assyrians in . . . Nineveh.* The novella opens with references to Nebuchadnezzar the Assyrian, even though history says he was a Babylonian; he ruled in Nineveh, though history says he ruled in Babylonia; he set out against Arphaxad, whom history does not know. The effect is to put readers in the remote past, sealing them off from history and preparing them to listen to the flow of the narrative.

1:11 *all . . . in the whole region disregarded the summons.* Disregarding a royal summons is an act of disrespect, a slight that almost invites retaliation. It is akin to a taunt, a sneering refusal to play the game of power politics.

of Moab, and the people of Ammon, and all Judea, and every one in Egypt, as far as the coasts of the two seas.

Arphaxad Is Defeated

13 In the seventeenth year he led his forces against King Arphaxad and defeated him in battle, overthrowing the whole army of Arphaxad and all his cavalry and all his chariots. 14Thus he took possession of his towns and came to Ecbatana, captured its towers, plundered its markets, and turned its glory into disgrace. 15He captured Arphaxad in the mountains of Ragau and struck him down with his spears, thus destroying him once and for all. 16Then he returned to Nineveh, he and all his combined forces, a vast body of troops; and there he and his forces rested and feasted for one hundred twenty days.

The Expedition against the West

2 In the eighteenth year, on the twenty-second day of the first month, there was talk in the palace of Nebuchadnezzar, king of the Assyrians, about carrying out his revenge on the whole region, just as he had said. 2He summoned all his ministers and all his nobles and set before them his secret plan and recounted fully, with his own lips, all the wickedness of the region. *a* 3They decided that every one who had not obeyed his command should be destroyed.

4 When he had completed his plan, Nebuchadnezzar, king of the Assyrians, called Holofernes, the chief general of his army,

second only to himself, and said to him, 5"Thus says the Great King, the lord of the whole earth: Leave my presence and take with you men confident in their strength, one hundred twenty thousand foot soldiers and twelve thousand cavalry. 6March out against all the land to the west, because they disobeyed my orders. 7Tell them to prepare earth and water, for I am coming against them in my anger, and will cover the whole face of the earth with the feet of my troops, to whom I will hand them over to be plundered. 8Their wounded shall fill their ravines and gullies, and the swelling river shall be filled with their dead. 9I will lead them away captive to the ends of the whole earth. 10You shall go and seize all their territory for me in advance. They must yield themselves to you, and you shall hold them for me until the day of their punishment. 11But to those who resist show no mercy, but hand them over to slaughter and plunder throughout your whole region. 12For as I live, and by the power of my kingdom, what I have spoken I will accomplish by my own hand. 13And you— take care not to transgress any of your lord's commands, but carry them out exactly as I have ordered you; do it without delay."

Campaign of Holofernes

14 So Holofernes left the presence of his lord, and summoned all the commanders, generals, and officers of the Assyrian army.

a Meaning of Gk uncertain

1:12 *Nebuchadnezzar became very angry.* Like the stereotypical Eastern tyrant in ancient literature, Nebuchadnezzar flies into a rage at the slight. His anger knows no bounds. The whole western region, as far as Egypt, must be put to the sword.

1:16 *he and his forces rested and feasted.* The first foray against Arphaxad has ended in victory. Engaged readers know, however, that Nebuchadnezzar is like a crouching lion, ready to spring against its prey at its pleasure.

2:3 *every one who had not obeyed his command should be destroyed.* Six years later Nebuchadnezzar springs. No mercy is offered

the inhabitants of the west. Those who didn't obey him would be destroyed.

2:4 *Holofernes, the chief general of his army.* This is our first meeting with the ill-starred general of Nebuchadnezzar's troops. He will represent the interests of Nebuchadnezzar and direct the huge army (120,000 troops).

2:7 *I am coming against them.* A seeming development in Nebuchadnezzar's policy toward those who rebuffed him earlier. If the people submit to Holofernes, they are to be held for Nebuchadnezzar until the day of punishment (v 10). If, however, they continue to resist, Holofernes is to slaughter and plunder them, showing no mercy (v 11).

15He mustered the picked troops by divisions as his lord had ordered him to do, one hundred twenty thousand of them, together with twelve thousand archers on horseback, 16and he organized them as a great army is marshaled for a campaign. 17He took along a vast number of camels and donkeys and mules for transport, and innumerable sheep and oxen and goats for food; 18also ample rations for everyone, and a huge amount of gold and silver from the royal palace.

19 Then he set out with his whole army, to go ahead of King Nebuchadnezzar and to cover the whole face of the earth to the west with their chariots and cavalry and picked foot soldiers. 20Along with them went a mixed crowd like a swarm of locusts, like the dust*a* of the earth—a multitude that could not be counted.

21 They marched for three days from Nineveh to the plain of Bectileth, and camped opposite Bectileth near the mountain that is to the north of Upper Cilicia. 22From there Holofernes*b* took his whole army, the infantry, cavalry, and chariots, and went up into the hill country. 23He ravaged Put and Lud, and plundered all the Rassisites and the Ishmaelites on the border of the desert, south of the country of the Chelleans. 24Then he followed*c* the Euphrates and passed through Mesopotamia and destroyed all the fortified towns along the brook Abron, as far as the sea. 25He also seized the territory of Cilicia, and killed everyone who resisted him. Then he came to the southern borders of Japheth, facing Arabia. 26He surrounded all the Midianites, and burned their tents and plundered their sheepfolds.

27Then he went down into the plain of Damascus during the wheat harvest, and burned all their fields and destroyed their flocks and herds and sacked their towns and ravaged their lands and put all their young men to the sword.

28 So fear and dread of him fell upon all the people who lived along the seacoast, at Sidon and Tyre, and those who lived in Sur and Ocina and all who lived in Jamnia. Those who lived in Azotus and Ascalon feared him greatly.

Entreaties for Peace

3 They therefore sent messengers to him to sue for peace in these words: 2"We, the servants of Nebuchadnezzar, the Great King, lie prostrate before you. Do with us whatever you will. 3See, our buildings and all our land and all our wheat fields and our flocks and herds and all our encampments*d* lie before you; do with them as you please. 4Our towns and their inhabitants are also your slaves; come and deal with them as you see fit."

5 The men came to Holofernes and told him all this. 6Then he went down to the seacoast with his army and stationed garrisons in the fortified towns and took picked men from them as auxiliaries. 7These people and all in the countryside welcomed him with garlands and dances and tambourines. 8Yet he demolished all their shrines*e* and cut down their sacred groves; for he had been commissioned to destroy all the gods of the land, so that all nations should worship Nebuchadnezzar alone,

a Gk *sand*   *b* Gk *he*   *c* Or *crossed*   *d* Gk *all the sheepfolds of our tents*   *e* Syr: Gk *borders*

2:15–18 *one hundred twenty thousand of them.* The huge number of troops is given again. Camels, donkeys, mules, and innumerable sheep and oxen also are prepared. A full-scale attack of monumental proportions on the western region impends. Familiar biblical phrases for the great number of troops follow: "like a swarm of locusts, like the dust of the earth—a multitude that could not be counted" (v 20).

2:28 *fear and dread of him fell upon all the people.* As Holofernes gets closer to Israel, the tension mounts. Names that only a few verses earlier would have been unfamiliar to readers now ring loud in their ears. Sidon and Tyre were just north of Israel, along the Mediterranean. Azotus and Ascalon were in the land of Israel itself. The vise is tightening.

3:8 *worship Nebuchadnezzar.* Nebuchadnezzar's making the nations submit to him is another way of saying that they should worship him, which is the ultimate goal of his foreign policy. Just below the surface of the text rages the battle not between the troops of Holofernes and other armies, but between the idolatry of Nebuchadnezzar and the true worship of the God of Israel.

and that all their dialects and tribes should call upon him as a god.

9 Then he came toward Esdraelon, near Dothan, facing the great ridge of Judea; [10]he camped between Geba and Scythopolis, and remained for a whole month in order to collect all the supplies for his army.

Judea on the Alert

4 When the Israelites living in Judea heard of everything that Holofernes, the general of Nebuchadnezzar, the king of the Assyrians, had done to the nations, and how he had plundered and destroyed all their temples, [2]they were therefore greatly terrified at his approach; they were alarmed both for Jerusalem and for the temple of the Lord their God. [3]For they had only recently returned from exile, and all the people of Judea had just now gathered together, and the sacred vessels and the altar and the temple had been consecrated after their profanation. [4]So they sent word to every district of Samaria, and to Kona, Beth-horon, Belmain, and Jericho, and to Choba and Aesora, and the valley of Salem. [5]They immediately seized all the high hilltops and fortified the villages on them and stored up food in preparation for war—since their fields had recently been harvested.

6 The high priest, Joakim, who was in Jerusalem at the time, wrote to the people of Bethulia and Betomesthaim, which faces Esdraelon opposite the plain near Dothan, [7]ordering them to seize the mountain passes, since by them Judea could be invaded; and it would be easy to stop any who tried to enter, for the approach was narrow, wide enough for only two at a time to pass.

Prayer and Penance

8 So the Israelites did as they had been ordered by the high priest Joakim and the senate of the whole people of Israel, in session at Jerusalem. [9]And every man of Israel cried out to God with great fervor, and they humbled themselves with much fasting. [10]They and their wives and their children and their cattle and every resident alien and hired laborer and purchased slave—they all put sackcloth around their waists. [11]And all the Israelite men, women, and children living at Jerusalem prostrated themselves before the temple and put ashes on their heads and spread out their sackcloth before the Lord. [12]They even draped the altar with sackcloth and cried out in unison, praying fervently to the God of Israel not to allow their infants to be carried off and their wives to be taken as booty, and the towns

---

3:9 *facing the great ridge of Judea.* The danger arrives at Israel's gates. A one-month pause in the action strengthens Holofernes and tests the mettle of the People of God. It took only three chapters to get from Nineveh to Judea. Now the action will slow to a crawl as internal, rather than external, movements are emphasized. The war within the heart and the war within the community are now the focus.

4:3 *they had only recently returned from exile.* The author sets his work at a time when the memory of exile and return was still fresh. It was an experience no one wanted to repeat. It would have been akin to facing a second holocaust when the embers were still warm from the first. Israel's every sinew will be stretched to meet the foe.

4:7 *seize the mountain passes.* The people of Israel, through the high priest Joakim, would do all in their power to prepare militarily and spiritually for the battle. The classic battle maneuver

is to seize high places and the adjoining mountain passes, thereby reducing to almost nil the effectiveness of even a huge army.

4:9 *every man of Israel cried out to God, . . . with much fasting.* The Spiritual Disciplines were also essential for a full defense. Repentance, mourning, fasting, and calling on God were the Israelites' spiritual preparations. We err if we think that spiritual preparation is one whit less important than professional competence, experience, or skill for the battles we face.

Responding
4:9–13 FASTING. The Israelites react to the news about Holofernes without hesitation. Immediately they turn to fasting. And God responds. The next time you receive bad news or hear of something terrible happening in the world, consider responding with a fast. *See also* Spiritual Disciplines Index.

they had inherited to be destroyed, and the sanctuary to be profaned and desecrated to the malicious joy of the Gentiles.

13 The Lord heard their prayers and had regard for their distress; for the people fasted many days throughout Judea and in Jerusalem before the sanctuary of the Lord Almighty. 14The high priest Joakim and all the priests who stood before the Lord and ministered to the Lord, with sackcloth around their loins, offered the daily burnt offerings, the votive offerings, and freewill offerings of the people. 15With ashes on their turbans, they cried out to the Lord with all their might to look with favor on the whole house of Israel.

Council against the Israelites

5 It was reported to Holofernes, the general of the Assyrian army, that the people of Israel had prepared for war and had closed the mountain passes and fortified all the high hilltops and set up barricades in the plains. 2In great anger he called together all the princes of Moab and the commanders of Ammon and all the governors of the coastland, 3and said to them, "Tell me, you Canaanites, what people is this that lives in the hill country? What towns do they inhabit? How large is their army, and in what does their power and strength consist? Who rules over them as king and leads their army? 4And why have they alone, of all who live in the west, refused to come out and meet me?"

Achior's Report

5 Then Achior, the leader of all the Ammonites, said to him, "May my lord please listen to a report from the mouth of your servant, and I will tell you the truth about this people that lives in the mountain district near you. No falsehood shall come from your servant's mouth. 6These people are descended from the Chaldeans. 7At one time they lived in Mesopotamia, because they did not wish to follow the gods of their ancestors who were in Chaldea. 8Since they had abandoned the ways of their ancestors, and worshiped the God of heaven, the God they had come to know, their ancestors*a* drove them out from the presence of their gods. So they fled to Mesopotamia, and lived there for a long time. 9Then their God commanded them to leave the place where they were living and go to the land of Canaan. There they settled, and grew very prosperous in gold and silver and very much livestock. 10When a famine spread over the land of Canaan they went down to Egypt and lived there as long as they had food. There they became so great a multitude that their race could not be counted. 11So the king of Egypt became hostile to them; he exploited them and forced them to make bricks. 12They cried out to their God, and he afflicted the whole land of Egypt with incurable plagues. So the Egyptians drove them out of their sight. 13Then God dried up the Red Sea before them, 14and he led them by the way of Sinai and Kadesh-barnea. They drove out all the people of the desert, 15and took up residence in the land of the Amorites, and by their might destroyed all the inhabitants of Heshbon; and crossing over the Jordan they took possession of all the

a Gk *they*

4:13 *The Lord heard their prayers and had regard for their distress.* Like the prayer of Tobit and Sarah in their need (Tob 3:16), so the prayer of the People of God was heard. However, unlike in Tobit, an angel isn't sent to deliver, nor is assurance of deliverance given immediately. That God "had regard for their distress" is reminiscent of the language of Exodus, where God saw the suffering of the people and "took notice of them" (2:25).

5:2 *In great anger.* Like commander, like general. Nebuchadnezzar's rage is mirrored in Holofernes' anger. Yet here the anger is a controlled boil. Holofernes gathers intelligence about Israel in order to exploit its weaknesses.

5:5–21 *I will tell you.* A "foreigner," an Ammonite (the Israelites had had chilly relations with the Ammonites for centuries), testifies to the greatness of the God of Israel. How intimately aware of the details of Israel's sacred history is this foreigner! Would our friends, much less our traditional enemies, be able to tell *our* spiritual story, God's dealing with us, in such a sympathetic spirit?

hill country. ¹⁶They drove out before them the Canaanites, the Perizzites, the Jebusites, the Shechemites, and all the Gergesites, and lived there a long time.

17 "As long as they did not sin against their God they prospered, for the God who hates iniquity is with them. ¹⁸But when they departed from the way he had prescribed for them, they were utterly defeated in many battles and were led away captive to a foreign land. The temple of their God was razed to the ground, and their towns were occupied by their enemies. ¹⁹But now they have returned to their God, and have come back from the places where they were scattered, and have occupied Jerusalem, where their sanctuary is, and have settled in the hill country, because it was uninhabited.

20 "So now, my master and lord, if there is any oversight in this people and they sin against their God and we find out their offense, then we can go up and defeat them. ²¹But if they are not a guilty nation, then let my lord pass them by; for their Lord and God will defend them, and we shall become the laughingstock of the whole world."

22 When Achior had finished saying these things, all the people standing around the tent began to complain; Holofernes' officers and all the inhabitants of the seacoast and Moab insisted that he should be cut to pieces. ²³They said, "We are not afraid of the Israelites; they are a people with no strength or power for making war. ²⁴Therefore let us go ahead, Lord Holofernes, and your vast army will swallow them up."

Achior Handed over to the Israelites

6 When the disturbance made by the people outside the council had died down, Holofernes, the commander of the Assyrian army, said to Achior*ᵃ* in the presence of all the foreign contingents:

2 "Who are you, Achior and you mercenaries of Ephraim, to prophesy among us as you have done today and tell us not to make war against the people of Israel because their God will defend them? What god is there except Nebuchadnezzar? He will send his forces and destroy them from the face of the earth. Their God will not save them; ³we the king's*ᵇ* servants will destroy them as one man. They cannot resist the might of our cavalry. ⁴We will overwhelm them;*ᶜ* their mountains will be drunk with their blood, and their fields will be full of their dead. Not even their footprints will survive our attack; they will utterly perish. So says King Nebuchadnezzar, lord of the whole earth. For he has spoken; none of his words shall be in vain.

5 "As for you, Achior, you Ammonite mercenary, you have said these words in a moment of perversity; you shall not see my face again from this day until I take revenge on this race that came out of Egypt. ⁶Then at my return the sword of my army and the spear*ᵈ* of my servants shall pierce your sides, and you shall fall among their wounded. ⁷Now my slaves are going to take you back into the hill country and put you in one of

ᵃ Other ancient authorities add *and to all the Moabites*   *ᵇ* Gk *his*   *ᶜ* Other ancient authorities add *with it*   *ᵈ* Lat Syr: Gk *people*

5:17 *As long as they did not sin.* This is the key to the entire history of Israel. God's blessing and the people's fidelity are inextricably linked. This theology, taught so brilliantly in Deuteronomy, gave explanations for disasters, fueled hope in distress, and encouraged fidelity when trouble threatened. The scriptural authors consistently reject a secular, power-politics view of world history.

6:2 *What god is there except Nebuchadnezzar? . . . Their God will not save them.* Achior's story is a stinging rebuke to Nebuchadnezzar, for Achior contended that Holofernes' victory would depend on the people's loyalty to God; if the people did

not sin, God would protect them (5:20–21). Holofernes responds to this stinging rebuke to Nebuchadnezzar by angrily dismissing the God of Israel. The battle is now starkly defined as a struggle between two divinities.

6:5 *you shall not see my face again . . . until I take revenge.* Achior's testimony, though true, exposes him to personal danger. He will be put in one of the targeted Israelite towns. "See if Israel's God defends you there!" is Holofernes' approach. Would we stand up for a person outside of the covenant community when to do so might court danger for us? Achior is a permanent witness to the courage of the outsider.

the towns beside the passes. 8You will not die until you perish along with them. 9If you really hope in your heart that they will not be taken, then do not look downcast! I have spoken, and none of my words shall fail to come true."

10 Then Holofernes ordered his slaves, who waited on him in his tent, to seize Achior and take him away to Bethulia and hand him over to the Israelites. 11So the slaves took him and led him out of the camp into the plain, and from the plain they went up into the hill country and came to the springs below Bethulia. 12When the men of the town saw them,a they seized their weapons and ran out of the town to the top of the hill, and all the slingers kept them from coming up by throwing stones at them. 13So having taken shelter below the hill, they bound Achior and left him lying at the foot of the hill, and returned to their master.

14 Then the Israelites came down from their town and found him; they untied him and brought him into Bethulia and placed him before the magistrates of their town, 15who in those days were Uzziah son of Micah, of the tribe of Simeon, and Chabris son of Gothoniel, and Charmis son of Melchiel. 16They called together all the elders of the town, and all their young men and women ran to the assembly. They set Achior in the midst of all their people, and Uzziah questioned him about what had happened. 17He answered and told them what had taken place at the council of Holofernes, and all that he had said in the presence of the Assyrian leaders, and all that Holofernes had boasted he would do against the house of Israel. 18Then the people fell down and worshiped God, and cried out:

19 "O Lord God of heaven, see their arrogance, and have pity on our people in their

humiliation, and look kindly today on the faces of those who are consecrated to you."

20 Then they reassured Achior, and praised him highly. 21Uzziah took him from the assembly to his own house and gave a banquet for the elders; and all that night they called on the God of Israel for help.

The Campaign against Bethulia

7 The next day Holofernes ordered his whole army, and all the allies who had joined him, to break camp and move against Bethulia, and to seize the passes up into the hill country and make war on the Israelites. 2So all their warriors marched off that day; their fighting forces numbered one hundred seventy thousand infantry and twelve thousand cavalry, not counting the baggage and the foot soldiers handling it, a very great multitude. 3They encamped in the valley near Bethulia, beside the spring, and they spread out in breadth over Dothan as far as Balbaim and in length from Bethulia to Cyamon, which faces Esdraelon.

4 When the Israelites saw their vast numbers, they were greatly terrified and said to one another, "They will now strip clean the whole land; neither the high mountains nor the valleys nor the hills will bear their weight." 5Yet they all seized their weapons, and when they had kindled fires on their towers, they remained on guard all that night.

6 On the second day Holofernes led out all his cavalry in full view of the Israelites in Bethulia. 7He reconnoitered the approaches to their town, and visited the springs that supplied their water; he seized them and set guards of soldiers over them, and then returned to his army.

8 Then all the chieftains of the Edomites

a Other ancient authorities add *on the top of the hill*

6:18–19 *see their arrogance and have pity on our people in their humiliation.* Israel's fidelity in worshiping and crying out to God constrasts starkly with the pride of the opposing forces.

7:1 *The next day.* Instead of years passing as in 2:1, we have a day. The action, which has been slowing, now grinds to a standstill. The battle between Yahweh and Nebuchadnezzar, to be

fought through subordinates, is about to begin.

7:8–15 *all the chieftains . . . and all the leaders . . . came to him.* Other traditional foes of Israel report to Holofernes. Having seen what happened to Achior, they are much more upbeat in their assessment of Holofernes' chances. "Cut off the water supply," they say, "and capitulation will soon follow."

and all the leaders of the Moabites and the commanders of the coastland came to him and said, 9"Listen to what we have to say, my lord, and your army will suffer no losses. 10This people, the Israelites, do not rely on their spears but on the height of the mountains where they live, for it is not easy to reach the tops of their mountains. 11Therefore, my lord, do not fight against them in regular formation, and not a man of your army will fall. 12Remain in your camp, and keep all the men in your forces with you; let your servants take possession of the spring of water that flows from the foot of the mountain, 13for this is where all the people of Bethulia get their water. So thirst will destroy them, and they will surrender their town. Meanwhile, we and our people will go up to the tops of the nearby mountains and camp there to keep watch to see that no one gets out of the town. 14They and their wives and children will waste away with famine, and before the sword reaches them they will be strewn about in the streets where they live. 15Thus you will pay them back with evil, because they rebelled and did not receive you peaceably."

16 These words pleased Holofernes and all his attendants, and he gave orders to do as they had said. 17So the army of the Ammonites moved forward, together with five thousand Assyrians, and they encamped in the valley and seized the water supply and the springs of the Israelites. 18And the Edomites and Ammonites went up and encamped in the hill country opposite Dothan; and they sent some of their men toward the south and the east, toward Egrebeh, which is near Chusi beside the Wadi Mochmur. The rest of the Assyrian army encamped in the plain, and covered the whole face of the land. Their tents and supply trains spread out in great number, and they formed a vast multitude.

The Distress of the Israelites

19 The Israelites then cried out to the Lord their God, for their courage failed, because all their enemies had surrounded them, and there was no way of escape from them. 20The whole Assyrian army, their infantry, chariots, and cavalry, surrounded them for thirty-four days, until all the water containers of every inhabitant of Bethulia were empty; 21their cisterns were going dry, and on no day did they have enough water to drink, for their drinking water was rationed. 22Their children were listless, and the women and young men fainted from thirst and were collapsing in the streets of the town and in the gateways; they no longer had any strength.

23 Then all the people, the young men, the women, and the children, gathered around Uzziah and the rulers of the town and cried out with a loud voice, and said before all the elders, 24"Let God judge between you and us! You have done us a great injury in not making peace with the Assyrians. 25For now we have no one to help us; God has sold us into their hands, to be strewn before them in thirst and exhaustion. 26Now summon them and surrender the whole town as booty to the army of Holofernes and to all his forces. 27For it would be better for us to be captured by them.*a We shall indeed become slaves, but our lives will be spared, and we shall not witness our little ones dying before our eyes, and our wives and children drawing their last breath. 28We call to witness against you heaven and earth and our God, the Lord of our ancestors, who punishes us for our sins and the sins of our ancestors; do today the things that we have described!"

29 Then great and general lamentation arose throughout the assembly, and they cried out to the Lord God with a loud voice.

a Other ancient authorities add *than to die of thirst*

7:19 *there was no way of escape.* The noose is tightening around Israel. No way of escape presents itself. Water containers were going empty (v 20); children were weak and strength melted away (v 22). This is the dramatic center of the novella.

7:24 *You have done us a great injury.* In their distress the people attack their town leader, Uzziah, for not striking a deal with Holofernes. Uzziah tried to buy time by requesting five more days before surrendering (v 30). Extremity drives us to compromise, to desperation, to hasty accusation.

30But Uzziah said to them, "Courage, my brothers and sisters!a Let us hold out for five days more; by that time the Lord our God will turn his mercy to us again, for he will not forsake us utterly. 31But if these days pass by, and no help comes for us, I will do as you say."

32 Then he dismissed the people to their various posts, and they went up on the walls and towers of their town. The women and children he sent home. In the town they were in great misery.

The Character of Judith

8 Now in those days Judith heard about these things: she was the daughter of Merari son of Ox son of Joseph son of Oziel son of Elkiah son of Ananias son of Gideon son of Raphain son of Ahitub son of Elijah son of Hilkiah son of Eliab son of Nathanael son of Salamiel son of Sarasadai son of Israel. 2Her husband Manasseh, who belonged to her tribe and family, had died during the barley harvest. 3For as he stood overseeing those who were binding sheaves in the field, he was overcome by the burning heat, and took to his bed and died in his town Bethulia. So they buried him with his ancestors in the field between Dothan and Balamon. 4Judith remained as a widow for three years and four months 5at home where she set up a tent for herself on the roof of her house. She put sackcloth around her waist and dressed in widow's clothing. 6She fasted all the days of her widowhood, except the day before the sabbath and the sabbath itself, the day before the new moon and the day of the new moon, and the festivals and days of rejoicing of the house of Israel. 7She was beautiful in appearance, and was very lovely to behold. Her husband Manasseh had left her gold and silver, men and women slaves, livestock, and fields; and she maintained this estate. 8No one spoke ill of her, for she feared God with great devotion.

Judith and the Elders

9 When Judith heard the harsh words spoken by the people against the ruler, because they were faint for lack of water, and when she heard all that Uzziah said to them, and how he promised them under oath to surrender the town to the Assyrians after five days, 10she sent her maid, who was in charge of all she possessed, to summon Uzziah andb Chabris and Charmis, the elders of her town. 11They came to her, and she said to them:

"Listen to me, rulers of the people of Bethulia! What you have said to the people today is not right; you have even sworn and pro-

a Gk Courage, brothers   b Other ancient authorities lack Uzziah and (see verses 28 and 35)

7:32 *they were in great misery.* "Misery" is the last word of the first part of the book. Fidelity appears to be fruitless. It yields only misery. The fortunes of the people are at their nadir.

8:1 *she was the daughter of.* Judith is introduced with the fanfare of a genealogy, the only woman with an extended genealogical listing in the Scriptures. Genealogy ties people together; it is the invisible cord linking Judith with the people's common destiny and hope. It gives her a place in the world, a location from which to deliver the people.

8:4–8 *Judith remained as a widow.* Several aspects of Judith's life are stressed. She is a widow (vv 4–6), beautiful and wealthy (v 7), and well regarded among the people (v 8). Her piety is noteworthy (v 8). It is exemplified through her extended time of mourning for her dead husband (v 4). She combines beauty, piety, wealth, devotion to the people, and maturity.

Responding
8:6 FASTING. Judith's exemplary fasting practice prepared her well for the task before her. Take some time to reflect on what kind of experiences God is preparing you for. What Spiritual Disciplines do you need to work at more? *See also* Spiritual Disciplines Index.

8:9–13 *When Judith heard the harsh words.* Judith sends her maid to the rulers to report her dissatisfaction with their plan to surrender the town unless deliverance appears within five days. This action is reminiscent of the tests to which the people of Israel put God in the wilderness. Such tests might buy time from human pressure, but they attempt to limit God.

nounced this oath between God and you, promising to surrender the town to our enemies unless the Lord turns and helps us within so many days. 12Who are you to put God to the test today, and to set yourselves up in the place of*a* God in human affairs? 13You are putting the Lord Almighty to the test, but you will never learn anything! 14You cannot plumb the depths of the human heart or understand the workings of the human mind; how do you expect to search out God, who made all these things, and find out his mind or comprehend his thought? No, my brothers, do not anger the Lord our God. 15For if he does not choose to help us within these five days, he has power to protect us within any time he pleases, or even to destroy us in the presence of our enemies. 16Do not try to bind the purposes of the Lord our God; for God is not like a human being, to be threatened, or like a mere mortal, to be won over by pleading. 17Therefore, while we wait for his deliverance, let us call upon him to help us, and he will hear our voice, if it pleases him.

18 "For never in our generation, nor in these present days, has there been any tribe or family or people or town of ours that worships gods made with hands, as was done in days gone by. 19That was why our ancestors were handed over to the sword and to pillage, and so they suffered a great catastrophe before our enemies. 20But we know no other god but him, and so we hope that he will not disdain us or any of our nation. 21For if we are captured, all Judea will be captured and our sanctuary will be plundered; and he will make us pay for its desecration with our blood. 22The slaughter of our kindred and the captivity of the land and the desolation of our inheritance—all this he will bring on our heads among the Gentiles, wherever we serve as slaves; and we shall be an offense and a disgrace in the eyes of those who acquire us. 23For our slavery will not bring us into favor, but the Lord our God will turn it to dishonor.

24 "Therefore, my brothers, let us set an example for our kindred, for their lives depend upon us, and the sanctuary—both the temple and the altar—rests upon us. 25In spite of everything let us give thanks to the Lord our God, who is putting us to the test as he did our ancestors. 26Remember what he did with Abraham, and how he tested Isaac, and what happened to Jacob in Syrian Mesopotamia, while he was tending the sheep of Laban, his mother's brother. 27For he has not tried us with fire, as he did them, to search their hearts, nor has he taken vengeance on us; but the Lord scourges those who are close to him in order to admonish them."

28 Then Uzziah said to her, "All that you have said was spoken out of a true heart, and there is no one who can deny your words. 29Today is not the first time your wisdom has been shown, but from the beginning of your life all the people have recognized your understanding, for your heart's disposition is right. 30But the people were so thirsty that they compelled us to do for them what we have promised, and made us take an oath that we cannot break. 31Now since you are a God-fearing woman, pray for us, so that the Lord may send us rain to fill our cisterns. Then we will no longer feel faint from thirst."

32 Then Judith said to them, "Listen to me.

a Or *above*

8:14 *You cannot plumb the depths of the human heart.* Our constant desire to plan our lives, avoid distress, eliminate the problems that beset us, and give God an "easy" way to show the divine glory all reflect the shallowness of our thinking, the limitations of our minds, and the pride of our hearts.

8:25 *In spite of everything let us give thanks.* Instead of giving in to the forces of defeat and negativism, Judith thanks God for the test the people face. God tests people and has done so since time immemorial; he admonishes "those who are close to him" (v 27). What prevents us from recognizing the difficulties we face as divine chastenings?

8:29 *all the people have recognized your understanding.* Judith's capacities grow before our eyes. She not only is beautiful, religious, and wealthy, but her wisdom shows that her heart's "disposition is right." Wisdom comes from the faithful attempt to honor God in the midst of trying circumstances.

I am about to do something that will go down through all generations of our descendants. [33]Stand at the town gate tonight so that I may go out with my maid; and within the days after which you have promised to surrender the town to our enemies, the Lord will deliver Israel by my hand. [34]Only, do not try to find out what I am doing; for I will not tell you until I have finished what I am about to do."

35 Uzziah and the rulers said to her, "Go in peace, and may the Lord God go before you, to take vengeance on our enemies." [36]So they returned from the tent and went to their posts.

The Prayer of Judith

9 Then Judith prostrated herself, put ashes on her head, and uncovered the sackcloth she was wearing. At the very time when the evening incense was being offered in the house of God in Jerusalem, Judith cried out to the Lord with a loud voice, and said,

2 "O Lord God of my ancestor Simeon, to whom you gave a sword to take revenge on those strangers who had torn off a virgin's clothing[a] to defile her, and exposed her thighs to put her to shame, and polluted her womb to disgrace her; for you said, 'It shall not be done'—yet they did it; [3]so you gave up their rulers to be killed, and their bed, which was ashamed of the deceit they had practiced, was stained with blood, and you struck down slaves along with princes, and princes on their thrones. [4]You gave up their wives for booty and their daughters to captivity, and all their booty to be divided among your beloved children who burned with zeal for you and abhorred the pollution of their blood and called on you for help. O God, my God, hear me also, a widow.

5 "For you have done these things and those that went before and those that followed. You have designed the things that are now, and those that are to come. What you had in mind has happened; [6]the things you decided on presented themselves and said, 'Here we are!' For all your ways are prepared in advance, and your judgment is with foreknowledge.

7 "Here now are the Assyrians, a greatly increased force, priding themselves in their horses and riders, boasting in the strength of their foot soldiers, and trusting in shield and spear, in bow and sling. They do not know that you are the Lord who crushes wars; the Lord is your name. [8]Break their strength by your might, and bring down their power in your anger; for they intend to defile your sanctuary, and to pollute the tabernacle where your glorious name resides, and to break off the horns[b] of your altar with the sword. [9]Look at their pride, and send your wrath upon their heads. Give to me, a widow, the strong hand to do what I plan. [10]By the deceit of my lips strike down the slave with the prince and the prince with his servant; crush their arrogance by the hand of a woman.

a Cn: Gk *loosed her womb*   b Syr: Gk *horn*

8:33 *the Lord will deliver.* Note the contrast between Judith's and Uzziah's words. Here Judith says that God will deliver the people by her hand within five days. Earlier Uzziah said that God will be merciful within the five days, *but* if no help comes, the people ought to be ready to surrender (7:30–31). Judith's wisdom rests in not having a backup plan where God's glory is concerned.

9:1 *Judith prostrated herself, put ashes on her head.* Before embarking on the perilous journey that leads to deliverance, Judith worships and prays. While the community is offering incense, she is offering herself to God. Effective service begins with consecration to God and to the task.

9:2–4 *my ancestor Simeon, to whom you gave a sword to take revenge on those strangers.*

Judith's unusual prayer begins with a reference to a violent act from her tribal history. Jacob's daughter, Dinah, was raped by Shechemites (Gen 34). Her brothers lured the Shechemite males into circumcision. While they were healing from the operation, the brothers massacred them. This story energizes Judith as she prays. She will assume the role of avenger, as her forefathers did generations ago.

9:10 *By the deceit of my lips strike down.* Deceit will be the means by which Judith is enabled to exact the vengeance inspired by her ancestors (v 13). This strong woman smashes almost all of our preconceived categories of deliverance: deliverance by a woman, deliverance through deceit, deliverance through calculated violence, and deliverance through seduction (11:16).

11 "For your strength does not depend on numbers, nor your might on the powerful. But you are the God of the lowly, helper of the oppressed, upholder of the weak, protector of the forsaken, savior of those without hope. 12Please, please, God of my father, God of the heritage of Israel, Lord of heaven and earth, Creator of the waters, King of all your creation, hear my prayer! 13Make my deceitful words bring wound and bruise on those who have planned cruel things against your covenant, and against your sacred house, and against Mount Zion, and against the house your children possess. 14Let your whole nation and every tribe know and understand that you are God, the God of all power and might, and that there is no other who protects the people of Israel but you alone!"

Judith Prepares to Go to Holofernes

10 When Judith*a* had stopped crying out to the God of Israel, and had ended all these words, 2she rose from where she lay prostrate. She called her maid and went down into the house where she lived on sabbaths and on her festal days. 3She removed the sackcloth she had been wearing, took off her widow's garments, bathed her body with water, and anointed herself with precious ointment. She combed her hair, put on a tiara, and dressed herself in the festive attire that she used to wear while her husband Manasseh was living. 4She put sandals on her feet, and put on her anklets, bracelets, rings, earrings, and all her other jewelry. Thus she made herself very beautiful, to entice the eyes of all

the men who might see her. 5She gave her maid a skin of wine and a flask of oil, and filled a bag with roasted grain, dried fig cakes, and fine bread;*b* then she wrapped up all her dishes and gave them to her to carry.

6 Then they went out to the town gate of Bethulia and found Uzziah standing there with the elders of the town, Chabris and Charmis. 7When they saw her transformed in appearance and dressed differently, they were very greatly astounded at her beauty and said to her, 8"May the God of our ancestors grant you favor and fulfill your plans, so that the people of Israel may glory and Jerusalem may be exalted." She bowed down to God.

9 Then she said to them, "Order the gate of the town to be opened for me so that I may go out and accomplish the things you have just said to me." So they ordered the young men to open the gate for her, as she requested. 10When they had done this, Judith went out, accompanied by her maid. The men of the town watched her until she had gone down the mountain and passed through the valley, where they lost sight of her.

Judith Is Captured

11 As the women*c* were going straight on through the valley, an Assyrian patrol met her 12and took her into custody. They asked her, "To what people do you belong, and where are you coming from, and where are you going?" She replied, "I am a daughter of the Hebrews, but I am fleeing from them, for

a Gk *she*   *b* Other ancient authorities add *and cheese*   *c* Gk *they*

9:11 *you are the God of the lowly.* Judith justifies her brazen plan because of the nature of the God she serves: God of the lowly, oppressed, and weak. Here are strong echoes of Hannah's song (1 Sam 2:1–10), which we also hear later in Mary's Magnificat (Luke 1:46–55).

10:4 *she made herself very beautiful, to entice the eyes of all the men.* New garments are required for the new task, and the author many times emphasizes Judith's beauty (vv 7, 14, 19, 23). She will have no compunctions against using every measure of feminine charm to wriggle her way into the good graces of Holofernes.

10:9 *the gate of the town to be opened for me.* As Judith heads from one world to the other, from the covenant community to the enemy, she passes through the gate of the town. The gate represents the great transitions of life, dangerous barriers through which one must go in order to fulfill one's calling.

10:12 *I am a daughter of the Hebrews, but I am fleeing from them.* The first of Judith's ambiguous words. She gains access to Holofernes' tent by virtue of her claim to special knowledge and the impression she gives that she defected from Israel. Her beauty will help her make her case to Holofernes.

they are about to be handed over to you to be devoured. [13]I am on my way to see Holofernes the commander of your army, to give him a true report; I will show him a way by which he can go and capture all the hill country without losing one of his men, captured or slain."

14 When the men heard her words, and observed her face—she was in their eyes marvelously beautiful—they said to her, [15]"You have saved your life by hurrying down to see our lord. Go at once to his tent; some of us will escort you and hand you over to him. [16]When you stand before him, have no fear in your heart, but tell him what you have just said, and he will treat you well."

17 They chose from their number a hundred men to accompany her and her maid, and they brought them to the tent of Holofernes. [18]There was great excitement in the whole camp, for her arrival was reported from tent to tent. They came and gathered around her as she stood outside the tent of Holofernes, waiting until they told him about her. [19]They marveled at her beauty and admired the Israelites, judging them by her. They said to one another, "Who can despise these people, who have women like this among them? It is not wise to leave one of their men alive, for if we let them go they will be able to beguile the whole world!"

Judith Is Brought before Holofernes

20 Then the guards of Holofernes and all his servants came out and led her into the tent. [21]Holofernes was resting on his bed under a canopy that was woven with purple and gold, emeralds and other precious stones. [22]When they told him of her, he came to the front of the tent, with silver lamps carried before him. [23]When Judith came into the presence of Holofernes[a] and his servants, they all marveled at the beauty of her face. She prostrated herself and did obeisance to him, but his slaves raised her up.

11 Then Holofernes said to her, "Take courage, woman, and do not be afraid in your heart, for I have never hurt anyone who chose to serve Nebuchadnezzar, king of all the earth. [2]Even now, if your people who live in the hill country had not slighted me, I would never have lifted my spear against them. They have brought this on themselves. [3]But now tell me why you have fled from them and have come over to us. In any event, you have come to safety. Take courage! You will live tonight and ever after. [4]No one will hurt you. Rather, all will treat you well, as they do the servants of my lord King Nebuchadnezzar."

Judith Explains Her Presence

5 Judith answered him, "Accept the words of your slave, and let your servant speak in your presence. I will say nothing false to my lord this night. [6]If you follow out the words of your servant, God will accomplish something through you, and my lord will not fail to achieve his purposes. [7]By the life of Nebuchadnezzar, king of the whole earth, and by the power of him who has sent you to direct every living being! Not only do human beings

a Gk him

10:17–20 *they brought them to the tent of Holofernes.* Within a scant seven verses from her departure, Judith is at another gate: the entrance of Holofernes' tent. So ravishingly beautiful is she that the enemy soldiers recognize her capacity for deception and beguilement (v 19). This is the first of many ironies in the next several chapters. It is almost as if the adversaries are willing dupes, easily charmed by the seductive powers of Judith.

10:22 *he came to the front of the tent, with silver lamps carried before him.* The silver lamps are a nice touch. Holofernes lives with a constant awareness of his proximity to the throne. The bright colors and wealth attending him are perfect foils for the bloody plot hatched by Judith.

11:5 *I will say nothing false to my lord this night.* Probably the most fatefully ambiguous of Judith's messages. By listening to Judith, Holofernes will not fail to accomplish the purpose of "my lord." Of course, Holofernes hears "my lord" as referring to himself; Judith means it to refer to the God of Israel. Readers are delighted, knowing that the God of Israel will have the last word over human tyrants.

serve him because of you, but also the animals of the field and the cattle and the birds of the air will live, because of your power, under Nebuchadnezzar and all his house. 8For we have heard of your wisdom and skill, and it is reported throughout the whole world that you alone are the best in the whole kingdom, the most informed and the most astounding in military strategy.

9 "Now as for Achior's speech in your council, we have heard his words, for the people of Bethulia spared him and he told them all he had said to you. 10Therefore, lord and master, do not disregard what he said, but keep it in your mind, for it is true. Indeed our nation cannot be punished, nor can the sword prevail against them, unless they sin against their God.

11 "But now, in order that my lord may not be defeated and his purpose frustrated, death will fall upon them, for a sin has overtaken them by which they are about to provoke their God to anger when they do what is wrong. 12Since their food supply is exhausted and their water has almost given out, they have planned to kill their livestock and have determined to use all that God by his laws has forbidden them to eat. 13They have decided to consume the first fruits of the grain and the tithes of the wine and oil, which they had consecrated and set aside for the priests who minister in the presence of our God in Jerusalem—things it is not lawful for any of the people even to touch with their hands. 14Since even the people in Jerusalem have been doing this, they have sent messengers there in order to bring back permis-

sion from the council of the elders. 15When the response reaches them and they act upon it, on that very day they will be handed over to you to be destroyed.

16 "So when I, your slave, learned all this, I fled from them. God has sent me to accomplish with you things that will astonish the whole world wherever people shall hear about them. 17Your servant is indeed God-fearing and serves the God of heaven night and day. So, my lord, I will remain with you; but every night your servant will go out into the valley and pray to God. He will tell me when they have committed their sins. 18Then I will come and tell you, so that you may go out with your whole army, and not one of them will be able to withstand you. 19Then I will lead you through Judea, until you come to Jerusalem; there I will set your throne.a You will drive them like sheep that have no shepherd, and no dog will so much as growl at you. For this was told me to give me foreknowledge; it was announced to me, and I was sent to tell you."

20 Her words pleased Holofernes and all his servants. They marveled at her wisdom and said, 21"No other woman from one end of the earth to the other looks so beautiful or speaks so wisely!" 22Then Holofernes said to her, "God has done well to send you ahead of the people, to strengthen our hands and bring destruction on those who have despised my lord. 23You are not only beautiful in appearance, but wise in speech. If you do as you have said, your God shall be my God,

a Or chariot

11:9–11 *do not disregard what he said, but keep it in your mind, for it is true.* Judith cleverly uses Achior's speech to undermine Holofernes' hope. Achior was correct about Israel being unconquerable if loyal to God. Yet she claims she knows of Israel's disloyalty in this circumstance (v 11). Thus, she lulls Holofernes into a false sense of security. His later drunkenness will mirror the mental seduction of this chapter.

11:16 *God has sent me to accomplish with you things that will astonish the whole world.* The beguilement continues. The results of what will take place will astonish the world.

Holofernes so arrogantly assumes he knows what Judith means that he asks for no clarification.

11:17 *every night your servant will go out into the valley and pray to God.* Judith is making her escape plans. She has to establish a pattern of unhindered access to and departure from Holofernes' tent. Her prayer outside the enemy camp is the means to do this.

11:19 *your throne.* Judith creates mental pictures for Holofernes of his throne in Jerusalem. No wonder her words "pleased Holofernes" (v 20).

and you shall live in the palace of King Nebuchadnezzar and be renowned throughout the whole world."

Judith as a Guest of Holofernes

12 Then he commanded them to bring her in where his silver dinnerware was kept, and ordered them to set a table for her with some of his own delicacies, and with some of his own wine to drink. 2But Judith said, "I cannot partake of them, or it will be an offense; but I will have enough with the things I brought with me." 3Holofernes said to her, "If your supply runs out, where can we get you more of the same? For none of your people are here with us." 4Judith replied, "As surely as you live, my lord, your servant will not use up the supplies I have with me before the Lord carries out by my hand what he has determined."

5 Then the servants of Holofernes brought her into the tent, and she slept until midnight. Toward the morning watch she got up 6and sent this message to Holofernes: "Let my lord now give orders to allow your servant to go out and pray." 7So Holofernes commanded his guards not to hinder her. She remained in the camp three days. She went out each night to the valley of Bethulia, and bathed at the spring in the camp.*a* 8After bathing, she prayed the Lord God of Israel to direct her way for the triumph of his*b* people. 9Then she returned purified and stayed in the tent until she ate her food toward evening.

Judith Attends Holofernes' Banquet

10 On the fourth day Holofernes held a banquet for his personal attendants only, and did not invite any of his officers. 11He said to Bagoas, the eunuch who had charge of his personal affairs, "Go and persuade the Hebrew woman who is in your care to join us and to eat and drink with us. 12For it would be a disgrace if we let such a woman go without having intercourse with her. If we do not seduce her, she will laugh at us."

13 So Bagoas left the presence of Holofernes, and approached her and said, "Let this pretty girl not hesitate to come to my lord to be honored in his presence, and to enjoy drinking wine with us, and to become today like one of the Assyrian women who serve in the palace of Nebuchadnezzar." 14Judith replied, "Who am I to refuse my lord? Whatever pleases him I will do at once, and it will be a joy to me until the day of my death." 15So she proceeded to dress herself in all her woman's finery. Her maid went ahead and spread for her on the ground before Holofernes the lambskins she had received from Bagoas for her daily use in reclining.

16 Then Judith came in and lay down. Holofernes' heart was ravished with her and his passion was aroused, for he had been wait-

a Other ancient authorities lack *in the camp*
b Other ancient authorities read *her*

12:6 *allow your servant to go out and pray.* Judith establishes a pattern that will hold her in good stead after her daring plan to kill the enemy general. Threefold repetition established a pattern of daily prayer (v 7). Prayer, purification (vv 8–9), and kosher diet (v 2) are the triad of Judith's practices preparing her for her great deed of deliverance.

Responding
12:6–9 SOLITUDE. Judith goes into the valley alone and purifies herself with a bath followed by a period of prayer. In biblical times and among Orthodox Jews today immersion in a *mikvah*, ritual bath, filled with *mayim chayim*, living water, is an important rite of

purification (Lev 11:36). The *mikvah* represents a time of change—impure to pure, non-Jew to Jew, single to married. As you shower or bathe today, think about the role of water in Christian thought. What does water represent to you? Does it make you think of purification, of baptism? *See also* Spiritual Disciplines Index.

12:14 *Whatever pleases him I will do at once.* Judith's titillating response to Holofernes' invitation raises the intensity of her encounter with him in his tent. She drinks with him, lies down on the lambskins, and gets Holofernes to drink "much more than he had ever drunk in any one day since he was born" (v 20). The stage is set for the main event.

ing for an opportunity to seduce her from the day he first saw her. ¹⁷So Holofernes said to her, "Have a drink and be merry with us!" ¹⁸Judith said, "I will gladly drink, my lord, because today is the greatest day in my whole life." ¹⁹Then she took what her maid had prepared and ate and drank before him. ²⁰Holofernes was greatly pleased with her, and drank a great quantity of wine, much more than he had ever drunk in any one day since he was born.

Judith Beheads Holofernes

13 When evening came, his slaves quickly withdrew. Bagoas closed the tent from outside and shut out the attendants from his master's presence. They went to bed, for they all were weary because the banquet had lasted so long. ²But Judith was left alone in the tent, with Holofernes stretched out on his bed, for he was dead drunk.

3 Now Judith had told her maid to stand outside the bedchamber and to wait for her to come out, as she did on the other days; for she said she would be going out for her prayers. She had said the same thing to Bagoas. ⁴So everyone went out, and no one, either small or great, was left in the bedchamber. Then Judith, standing beside his bed, said in her heart, "O Lord God of all might, look in this hour on the work of my hands for the exaltation of Jerusalem. ⁵Now indeed is the time to help your heritage and to carry out my design to destroy the enemies who have risen up against us."

6 She went up to the bedpost near Holofernes' head, and took down his sword

that hung there. ⁷She came close to his bed, took hold of the hair of his head, and said, "Give me strength today, O Lord God of Israel!" ⁸Then she struck his neck twice with all her might, and cut off his head. ⁹Next she rolled his body off the bed and pulled down the canopy from the posts. Soon afterward she went out and gave Holofernes' head to her maid, ¹⁰who placed it in her food bag.

Judith Returns to Bethulia

Then the two of them went out together, as they were accustomed to do for prayer. They passed through the camp, circled around the valley, and went up the mountain to Bethulia, and came to its gates. ¹¹From a distance Judith called out to the sentries at the gates, "Open, open the gate! God, our God, is with us, still showing his power in Israel and his strength against our enemies, as he has done today!"

12 When the people of her town heard her voice, they hurried down to the town gate and summoned the elders of the town. ¹³They all ran together, both small and great, for it seemed unbelievable that she had returned. They opened the gate and welcomed them. Then they lit a fire to give light, and gathered around them. ¹⁴Then she said to them with a loud voice, "Praise God, O praise him! Praise God, who has not withdrawn his mercy from the house of Israel, but has destroyed our enemies by my hand this very night!"

15 Then she pulled the head out of the bag and showed it to them, and said, "See here, the head of Holofernes, the commander

---

13:4–5 *Judith, standing beside his bed, said in her heart, "O Lord God."* When she needs her greatest strength and determination she calls upon God. As a latter-day example of a biblical judge who will deliver the people through skillful warfare, Judith will strike a strategic blow against the foe.

13:8 *cut off his head.* This is the decisive event, depicted in art and music for the last several centuries. The scene has elements of the grotesque and erotic. Judith cuts off Holofernes' head with the sword hanging by his bedpost; she carries his head in a food bag through the

lines of the unsuspecting enemy; when the body is discovered, it is twice mentioned that Holofernes' body has no head (14:15, 18). The imagery is unmistakable: Holofernes' "sword" was the cause of his losing his "head."

13:11 *Open, open the gate!* The gate represents the boundary between the sacred community and the world. Judith's reentry reintegrates her into her people, whom she had left on her daring adventure. An echo of Ps 24:7 may be intended. Her return symbolizes God's powerful return to the People of God.

of the Assyrian army, and here is the canopy beneath which he lay in his drunken stupor. The Lord has struck him down by the hand of a woman. 16 As the Lord lives, who has protected me in the way I went, I swear that it was my face that seduced him to his destruction, and that he committed no sin with me, to defile and shame me."

17 All the people were greatly astonished. They bowed down and worshiped God, and said with one accord, "Blessed are you our God, who have this day humiliated the enemies of your people."

18 Then Uzziah said to her, "O daughter, you are blessed by the Most High God above all other women on earth; and blessed be the Lord God, who created the heavens and the earth, who has guided you to cut off the head of the leader of our enemies. 19 Your praise*a* will never depart from the hearts of those who remember the power of God. 20 May God grant this to be a perpetual honor to you, and may he reward you with blessings, because you risked your own life when our nation was brought low, and you averted our ruin, walking in the straight path before our God." And all the people said, "Amen. Amen."

Judith's Counsel

14 Then Judith said to them, "Listen to me, my friends. Take this head and hang it upon the parapet of your wall. 2 As soon as day breaks and the sun rises on the earth, each of you take up your weapons, and let every able-bodied man go out of the town; set a captain over them, as if you were going down to the plain against the Assyrian outpost; only do not go down. 3 Then they will seize their arms and go into the camp and rouse the officers of the Assyrian army. They will rush into the tent of Holofernes and will

not find him. Then panic will come over them, and they will flee before you. 4 Then you and all who live within the borders of Israel will pursue them and cut them down in their tracks. 5 But before you do all this, bring Achior the Ammonite to me so that he may see and recognize the man who despised the house of Israel and sent him to us as if to his death."

6 So they summoned Achior from the house of Uzziah. When he came and saw the head of Holofernes in the hand of one of the men in the assembly of the people, he fell down on his face in a faint. 7 When they raised him up he threw himself at Judith's feet, and did obeisance to her, and said, "Blessed are you in every tent of Judah! In every nation those who hear your name will be alarmed. 8 Now tell me what you have done during these days."

So Judith told him in the presence of the people all that she had done, from the day she left until the moment she began speaking to them. 9 When she had finished, the people raised a great shout and made a joyful noise in their town. 10 When Achior saw all that the God of Israel had done, he believed firmly in God. So he was circumcised, and joined the house of Israel, remaining so to this day.

Holofernes' Death Is Discovered

11 As soon as it was dawn they hung the head of Holofernes on the wall. Then they all took their weapons, and they went out in companies to the mountain passes. 12 When the Assyrians saw them they sent word to their commanders, who then went to the generals and the captains and to all their other officers. 13 They came to Holofernes' tent and said to the steward in charge of all

a Other ancient authorities read *hope*

13:15–16 *The Lord has struck him down by the hand of a woman.* It is Judith's face that seduced Holofernes, her hand that slew him, his head that was in her bag. She joins the ranks of other famous biblical women of power: Deborah, who delivered the people (Judg 4); Jael, who slew Sisera (Judg 4, 5); and the woman whose wisdom averted destruction of her city (2 Sam 20:14–22).

14:10 *When Achior saw . . . he believed.* When Achior the Ammonite saw the great things God had done, he converted to Judaism. The harsh words prohibiting Ammonite membership in the People of God (Deut 23:3) are seemingly ignored, perhaps because of the way that Achior's words provided fuel for Judith's mission to Holofernes.

his personal affairs, "Wake up our lord, for the slaves have been so bold as to come down against us to give battle, to their utter destruction."

14 So Bagoas went in and knocked at the entry of the tent, for he supposed that he was sleeping with Judith. 15But when no one answered, he opened it and went into the bedchamber and found him sprawled on the floor dead, with his head missing. 16He cried out with a loud voice and wept and groaned and shouted, and tore his clothes. 17Then he went to the tent where Judith had stayed, and when he did not find her, he rushed out to the people and shouted, 18"The slaves have tricked us! One Hebrew woman has brought disgrace on the house of King Nebuchadnezzar. Look, Holofernes is lying on the ground, and his head is missing!"

19 When the leaders of the Assyrian army heard this, they tore their tunics and were greatly dismayed, and their loud cries and shouts rose up throughout the camp.

The Assyrians Flee in Panic

15 When the men in the tents heard it, they were amazed at what had happened. 2Overcome with fear and trembling, they did not wait for one another, but with one impulse all rushed out and fled by every path across the plain and through the hill country. 3Those who had camped in the hills around Bethulia also took to flight. Then the Israelites, everyone that was a soldier, rushed out upon them. 4Uzziah sent men to Beto-masthaim[a] and Choba and Kola, and to all the frontiers of Israel, to tell what had taken place and to urge all to rush out upon the enemy to destroy them. 5When the Israelites heard it, with one accord they fell upon the enemy,[b] and cut them down as far as Choba. Those in Jerusalem and all the hill country also came, for they were told what had happened in the camp of the enemy. The men in Gilead and in Galilee outflanked them with great slaughter, even beyond Damascus and its borders. 6The rest of the people of Bethulia fell upon the Assyrian camp and plundered it, acquiring great riches. 7And the Israelites, when they returned from the slaughter, took possession of what remained. Even the villages and towns in the hill country and in the plain got a great amount of booty, since there was a vast quantity of it.

The Israelites Celebrate Their Victory

8 Then the high priest Joakim and the elders of the Israelites who lived in Jerusalem came to witness the good things that the Lord had done for Israel, and to see Judith and to wish her well. 9When they met her, they all blessed her with one accord and said to her, "You are the glory of Jerusalem, you are the great boast of Israel, you are the great pride of our nation! 10You have done all this with your own hand; you have done great good to Israel, and God is well pleased with it. May the Almighty Lord bless you forever!" And all the people said, "Amen."

11 All the people plundered the camp for thirty days. They gave Judith the tent of Holofernes and all his silver dinnerware, his beds, his bowls, and all his furniture. She took them and loaded her mules and hitched up her carts and piled the things on them.

12 All the women of Israel gathered to see her, and blessed her, and some of them performed a dance in her honor. She took ivy-wreathed wands in her hands and distributed them to the women who were with her; 13and she and those who were with her crowned themselves with olive wreaths. She went before all the people in the dance, lead-

a Other ancient authorities add *and Bebai*
b Gk *them*

15:2 *all rushed out and fled.* As Judith had surmised, when Holofernes' men realized that their leader was slain, they fell into a panic. It is reminiscent of the panic induced by Gideon's troops smashing their jars and blowing their trumpets (Judg 7:19–23). As here, a much larger army is scattered through this stratagem.

15:11 *All the people plundered the camp.* The thirty-day plundering party in the camp is reminiscent of Holofernes' thirty days of collecting supplies in camp before his assault against the people (3:10). Celebration should continue for as many days as the buildup of fear.

ing all the women, while all the men of Israel followed, bearing their arms and wearing garlands and singing hymns.

Judith Offers Her Hymn of Praise

14 Judith began this thanksgiving before all Israel, and all the people loudly sang this

16 song of praise. ¹And Judith said,
Begin a song to my God with tambourines,
> sing to my Lord with cymbals.
> Raise to him a new psalm;*a*
> exalt him, and call upon his name.

2 For the Lord is a God who crushes wars;
> he sets up his camp among his people;
> he delivered me from the hands of my pursuers.

3 The Assyrian came down from the mountains of the north;
> he came with myriads of his warriors;
> their numbers blocked up the wadis, and their cavalry covered the hills.

4 He boasted that he would burn up my territory,
> and kill my young men with the sword,
> and dash my infants to the ground, and seize my children as booty, and take my virgins as spoil.

5 But the Lord Almighty has foiled them by the hand of a woman.*b*

6 For their mighty one did not fall by the hands of the young men,
> nor did the sons of the Titans strike him down,
> nor did tall giants set upon him;
> but Judith daughter of Merari with the beauty of her countenance undid him.

7 For she put away her widow's clothing to exalt the oppressed in Israel.
> She anointed her face with perfume;

8 she fastened her hair with a tiara
> and put on a linen gown to beguile him.

9 Her sandal ravished his eyes,
> her beauty captivated his mind,
> and the sword severed his neck!

10 The Persians trembled at her boldness,
> the Medes were daunted at her daring.

11 Then my oppressed people shouted;
> my weak people cried out,*c* and the enemy*d* trembled;
> they lifted up their voices, and the enemy*d* were turned back.

12 Sons of slave-girls pierced them through and wounded them like the children of fugitives;
> they perished before the army of my Lord.

13 I will sing to my God a new song:
O Lord, you are great and glorious, wonderful in strength, invincible.

14 Let all your creatures serve you,
for you spoke, and they were made.
You sent forth your spirit,*e* and it formed them;*f*
> there is none that can resist your voice.

15 For the mountains shall be shaken to their foundations with the waters;

a Other ancient authorities read *a psalm and praise*
b Other ancient authorities add *he has confounded them*   *c* Other ancient authorities read *feared*
d Gk *they*   *e* Or *breath*   *f* Other ancient authorities read *they were created*

16:1–17 *Begin a song to my God.* Like the song of celebration in Judges 5 or the Song at the Sea in Exodus 15, a song of praise follows deliverance here as well. Three themes emerge in the song: praise to God for deliverance (vv 1–4), narration of the story of deliverance (vv 5–12), singing a new song to God and woe to the nations (vv 13–17). Every great act of victory requires a song to complete it.

Responding
16:1–17 CELEBRATION. Consider writing your own song of praise to God. Choose favorite portions from the Psalms or other biblical songs of praise and add praises from your own life experience. *See also* Spiritual Disciplines Index.

before your glance the rocks shall
    melt like wax.
But to those who fear you
    you show mercy.
16 For every sacrifice as a fragrant offering
        is a small thing,
    and the fat of all whole burnt
        offerings to you is a very little
        thing;
    but whoever fears the Lord is great
        forever.

17 Woe to the nations that rise up against
        my people!
    The Lord Almighty will take
        vengeance on them in the day of
        judgment;
    he will send fire and worms into their
        flesh;
    they shall weep in pain forever.

18 When they arrived at Jerusalem, they
worshiped God. As soon as the people were
purified, they offered their burnt offerings,
their freewill offerings, and their gifts. 19Ju-
dith also dedicated to God all the possessions
of Holofernes, which the people had given
her; and the canopy that she had taken for
herself from his bedchamber she gave as a
votive offering. 20For three months the people continued feasting in Jerusalem before
the sanctuary, and Judith remained with
them.

The Renown and Death of Judith

21 After this they all returned home to
their own inheritances. Judith went to Bethulia, and remained on her estate. For the rest
of her life she was honored throughout the
whole country. 22Many desired to marry her,
but she gave herself to no man all the days of
her life after her husband Manasseh died and
was gathered to his people. 23She became
more and more famous, and grew old in her
husband's house, reaching the age of one
hundred five. She set her maid free. She died
in Bethulia, and they buried her in the cave
of her husband Manasseh; 24and the house of
Israel mourned her for seven days. Before she
died she distributed her property to all those
who were next of kin to her husband Manasseh, and to her own nearest kindred. 25No
one ever again spread terror among the Israelites during the lifetime of Judith, or for a
long time after her death.

16:6 *the beauty of her countenance undid
him.* Not from the hands of the young men or
the warriors did deliverance come, but through
the hands of Judith, who used her beauty to
defeat the enemy. Does our faith have room for
unexpected means of triumph?

16:17 *Woe to the nations that rise up against
my people!* Those who know that they battle not
against flesh and blood know that even dramatic
victories are only signposts along the greater
road of struggle, setback, and victory. The last
word is not unhindered praise, but a warning to
the nations. Like the beautiful Psalms 137 and
110, which end with images of violence, so the
hymn of Judith ends with a judgment scene.

16:25 *No one ever again spread terror among
the Israelites during the lifetime of Judith.* Israel
is safe for Judith's lifetime and a good long time
afterwards. Readers close the book with gratitude to God for the present peace and hope
that God will raise up deliverers if other dangers
arise.

1 MACCABEES

The book of 1 Maccabees tells the story of the greatest threat to the identity of the People of God since the Babylonian exile and how God preserved his people. Jewish elites, in collusion with the Hellenistic king Antiochus IV Epiphanes (r. 175–164 BC), planned to transform Jerusalem into a Greek city with a Greek constitution, a cosmopolitan atmosphere, and a pluralistic worldview in which Gentiles would feel equally at home. Introducing gentile rituals into the Temple itself—the "desolating sacrilege" (1:54; "abomination that desolates," Dan 9:27; 12:11)—came to be remembered as the climax of these "reforms." This plan promised to put Jerusalem on the political and economic map in an exciting, new way, but at the cost of Israel's distinctive identity, found in its commitment to living according to the Torah in obedience to the One God.

Revolution from Below

Massive popular resistance led Antiochus IV to "pacify" the city with brutal force and barbaric cruelty. A priest named Mattathias and his five sons, the most celebrated of which is Judas "Maccabeus," the "Hammer," led a successful revolt against the armies of Antiochus IV and his successors. They eventually restored political independence to Israel, gaining for themselves and their descendants the titles of high priest and king. Their dynasty, known as the Hasmoneans, ruled Israel until 63 BC, when Pompey led the Roman legions into Judea. These events are directly reflected in Daniel, *1 Enoch,* several of the Dead Sea Scrolls, and 1, 2, & 4 Maccabees. They continued to exert a powerful influence on Jewish and Christian literature written in the first centuries after Christ and shaped Jewish nationalism and messianic expectations through the second century AD.

First Maccabees was written by a loyal supporter of the Hasmonean dynasty in an atmosphere of mixed sentiments about a dynasty that did not have hereditary claims to the title of either high priest or king. A history glorifying the courageous

See also *"The With-God Life"* essay for this section of the Bible,
"The People of God in Restoration," pp. 1355–59.

and self-sacrificial deeds undertaken by this family for the benefit of the nation would serve to legitimate their continuing authority over a new generation. He wrote originally in Hebrew within a few decades, or perhaps merely years, after the death of John Hyrcanus I (104 BC), the last hero to be celebrated in this history. He writes in the language and idiom of the historical books of the Old Testament, expressing the conviction that God continues to work in similar ways in new generations of his people. The "classic" interventions of God we read about in Scripture continue to surface in the ongoing story of his people, particularly through the exploits of Judas and his brothers, who come collectively to be known as the "Maccabees" in the early Church.

Spiritual Formation in 1 Maccabees

Reading 1 Maccabees, a story about an insurgent movement that achieves its ends by violence, as a resource for spiritual formation presents several challenges. On its own or in light of the Old Testament conquest narratives, it could support wars of liberation and the use of violent force as a means of achieving God's purposes or, worse, provide a charter for co-opting the name of God for a violent coup. Reading the book in a canonical context, one that includes the New Testament, however, gives us important guidance about appropriating its message in light of the revelation of God in Jesus Christ.

Judas Maccabeus is lauded as the "savior of Israel" (9:21) and represents a major way in which God was understood to be present with God's people: through military power bringing political independence. "Savior" often served as a title for military deliverers. The term was used to acclaim the Greek general Demetrius, who liberated Athens from a siege, and Augustus, whose rise to power brought an end to Roman civil war. The paradigm of a "savior of Israel" who would be a political and military leader dominated messianic hopes at the turn of the era (see *Psalms of Solomon* 17–18 for some striking testimonies). In the fifty years before and after Christ, revolutionary movements gathered around self-proclaimed "messiahs" of this military kind, who promised political independence for Israel and revenge against the Gentiles. Jesus' own disciples kept trying to understand him and his mission in these terms. James and John thought they could enjoy positions of power in the new political order that Jesus would usher in (Mark 10:35–45). Even after the resurrection, the disciples were looking for Jesus to bring political independence to Israel (Acts 1:6). This ideology led ultimately to the first and second Jewish revolts against Rome (AD 66–70, 132–35) and spelled utter desolation for Jerusalem.

Jesus defied this set of expectations. He came indeed as a conqueror, but not with a view toward exterminating individual human beings. Jesus engaged Satan, who kept human beings in slavery through the fear of death (Heb 2:14–15), in mortal combat. Jesus took on the domination systems of imperialism and economic injustice, which undermine human community and deprive many of dignity and the necessities of life. As "Savior of the world," and not merely "of Israel," Jesus challenged the ethnocentrism of the People of God. But human opponents were still to be loved and redeemed. People were to be challenged to think about how to secure the well-being of all people, rather than allow political and economic ideologies to cut them off from concern for everyone. Only then would they experience wholeness themselves. His strategy of conquest involved prophetic announcement of God's vision for how we are to live together in human community, indictment of all that stood in the way of that vision, and the selfless giving of himself for others in love and service.

Just as the model of the "savior" was transformed by Jesus, so the model of the warrior in the cause of God must be transformed by Jesus' mode of conquest and his command to love one's enemies. Once we do this, 1 Maccabees can offer us great insight into, and help embolden us for, the campaigns to which we as Christians are called. The fire of the Maccabees focused through the lens of Jesus can illumine important dimensions of our own formation as warriors in the cause of God, as we offer ourselves to God as agents for the wholeness and peace of the People of God in every place.

—*David A. deSilva*

Alexander the Great

1 After Alexander son of Philip, the Macedonian, who came from the land of Kittim, had defeated*a* King Darius of the Persians and the Medes, he succeeded him as king. (He had previously become king of Greece.) ²He fought many battles, conquered strongholds, and put to death the kings of the earth. ³He advanced to the ends of the earth, and plundered many nations. When the earth became quiet before him, he was exalted, and his heart was lifted up. ⁴He gathered a very strong army and ruled over countries, nations, and princes, and they became tributary to him.

5 After this he fell sick and perceived that he was dying. ⁶So he summoned his most honored officers, who had been brought up with him from youth, and divided his king-dom among them while he was still alive. ⁷And after Alexander had reigned twelve years, he died.

8 Then his officers began to rule, each in his own place. ⁹They all put on crowns after his death, and so did their descendants after them for many years; and they caused many evils on the earth.

Antiochus Epiphanes and Renegade Jews

10 From them came forth a sinful root, Antiochus Epiphanes, son of King Antiochus; he had been a hostage in Rome. He began to reign in the one hundred thirty-seventh year of the kingdom of the Greeks. *b*

11 In those days certain renegades came out from Israel and misled many, saying, "Let us go and make a covenant with the Gen-

a Gk adds *and he defeated* b 175 B.C.

1:8–9 *they caused many evils.* The feuding Hellenistic kings who divided Alexander's empire represent the worst evils of domination systems. Their military expeditions against one another in vain attempts to annex each other's territories display the wastefulness and systemic evils of imperialism, of national war machines, and of the ecological and economic ravages that accompany them. Such systems have continu-ally opposed God's vision for human community and wholeness, promoting brokenness instead.

1:11–15 *certain renegades came out . . . and misled many.* The "renegades" from Israel pursue a mistaken strategy for attaining security and prosperity. They believe that becoming more like the dominant Hellenistic culture, and thus making it easier for that culture's representa-tives to understand Judeans and treat them as

tiles around us, for since we separated from them many disasters have come upon us." [12]This proposal pleased them, [13]and some of the people eagerly went to the king, who authorized them to observe the ordinances of the Gentiles. [14]So they built a gymnasium in Jerusalem, according to Gentile custom, [15]and removed the marks of circumcision, and abandoned the holy covenant. They joined with the Gentiles and sold themselves to do evil.

Antiochus in Egypt

16 When Antiochus saw that his kingdom was established, he determined to become king of the land of Egypt, in order that he might reign over both kingdoms. [17]So he invaded Egypt with a strong force, with chariots and elephants and cavalry and with a large fleet. [18]He engaged King Ptolemy of Egypt in battle, and Ptolemy turned and fled before him, and many were wounded and fell. [19]They captured the fortified cities in the land of Egypt, and he plundered the land of Egypt.

Persecution of the Jews

20 After subduing Egypt, Antiochus returned in the one hundred forty-third year.[a] He went up against Israel and came to Jerusa-

lem with a strong force. [21]He arrogantly entered the sanctuary and took the golden altar, the lampstand for the light, and all its utensils. [22]He took also the table for the bread of the Presence, the cups for drink offerings, the bowls, the golden censers, the curtain, the crowns, and the gold decoration on the front of the temple; he stripped it all off. [23]He took the silver and the gold, and the costly vessels; he took also the hidden treasures that he found. [24]Taking them all, he went into his own land.

> He shed much blood,
>   and spoke with great arrogance.
> [25] Israel mourned deeply in every
>   community,
> [26]   rulers and elders groaned,
>   young women and young men became
>   faint,
>   the beauty of the women faded.
> [27] Every bridegroom took up the lament;
>   she who sat in the bridal chamber was
>   mourning.
> [28] Even the land trembled for its
>   inhabitants,
>   and all the house of Jacob was clothed
>   with shame.

a 169 B.C.

---

allies in the empire, was worth leaving behind the distinctive way of life (the life of "holiness") into which God had called them. But abundance and peace come not from joining in with gentile imperialism, but from moving toward a more just peace, where domination and power yield to cooperation and protection of mutual interests, and from living out the covenant with God more broadly and deeply. Examining ourselves to discern to what extent we try to become "like the nations," conforming our lives and practices to what the world values, is vital to our spiritual health. When we retreat from these things and order our lives more fully around what honors God and what God values, we discover a form of liberation greater than that provided by Judas and his brothers.

1:16 *he determined to become king of the land of Egypt.* The doctrine of perpetual expansion is built into the ideology of all domination

systems, but this "more" mentality represents a tremendous threat to spiritual growth. How different it would have been for Antiochus if he sought to rule not "more," but "better," to expand his ability to rule justly, to deepen the experience of peace and social holiness throughout his kingdom.

1:20–23 *He arrogantly entered the sanctuary.* Coming to the Temple in Jerusalem, Antiochus fails to see a holy place in which to encounter the living God and to be invited into a quality of life beyond his deepest hopes. Instead, in line with his own imperialistic ideology, he sees the Temple merely as a repository of material resources to be exploited. His failure challenges us to work at remaining open to ways of encountering God, rather than having our vision limited to what is materially at hand and temporally at stake in any given circumstance.

The Occupation of Jerusalem

29 Two years later the king sent to the cities of Judah a chief collector of tribute, and he came to Jerusalem with a large force. 30Deceitfully he spoke peaceable words to them, and they believed him; but he suddenly fell upon the city, dealt it a severe blow, and destroyed many people of Israel. 31He plundered the city, burned it with fire, and tore down its houses and its surrounding walls. 32They took captive the women and children, and seized the livestock. 33Then they fortified the city of David with a great strong wall and strong towers, and it became their citadel. 34They stationed there a sinful people, men who were renegades. These strengthened their position; 35they stored up arms and food, and collecting the spoils of Jerusalem they stored them there, and became a great menace,

36 for the citadel*a* became an ambush
        against the sanctuary,
    an evil adversary of Israel at all times.
37 On every side of the sanctuary they
        shed innocent blood;
    they even defiled the sanctuary.
38 Because of them the residents of
        Jerusalem fled;
    she became a dwelling of strangers;
    she became strange to her offspring,
    and her children forsook her.
39 Her sanctuary became desolate like a
        desert;

her feasts were turned into mourning,
    her sabbaths into a reproach,
    her honor into contempt.
40 Her dishonor now grew as great as her
        glory;
    her exaltation was turned into
        mourning.

Installation of Gentile Cults

41 Then the king wrote to his whole kingdom that all should be one people, 42and that all should give up their particular customs. 43All the Gentiles accepted the command of the king. Many even from Israel gladly adopted his religion; they sacrificed to idols and profaned the sabbath. 44And the king sent letters by messengers to Jerusalem and the towns of Judah; he directed them to follow customs strange to the land, 45to forbid burnt offerings and sacrifices and drink offerings in the sanctuary, to profane sabbaths and festivals, 46to defile the sanctuary and the priests, 47to build altars and sacred precincts and shrines for idols, to sacrifice swine and other unclean animals, 48and to leave their sons uncircumcised. They were to make themselves abominable by everything unclean and profane, 49so that they would forget the law and change all the ordinances. 50He added,*b* "And whoever does not obey the command of the king shall die."

51 In such words he wrote to his whole

a Gk it   *b* Gk lacks *He added*

1:28, 39–40 *the house of Jacob was clothed with shame.* The attempt to improve Jerusalem's political prestige does not have the results for which the "renegades" hoped. Instead, Jerusalem is "clothed with shame" and desolation. The story is putting forward an argument in narrative form: honor can never be gained by breaking faith with God. Any attempt to gain prestige in the eyes of the world at the cost of honoring God will ultimately result in shame.

1:41–50 *all should be one people.* Even though it is historically unlikely that Antiochus IV tried to impose cultural and religious uniformity upon all peoples in his kingdom, it is likely that he understood the Judeans' dedication to the law and the One God to be problematic for the unity of his kingdom. In a similar way, many regimes

continue to regard Christians within their borders as subversive elements and seek to enforce apostasy and force conformity. Whence the threat to the powers that be? The witness of the People of God to an authority beyond any earthly power and to a vision for human community that often stands opposed to the practices by which domination systems perpetuate themselves makes their "differences" especially threatening. Their distinctive way of life (in Judaism, reflected in circumcision, the avoidance of certain foods, and observing the Sabbath—all prominent in 1 Macc 1–2) is a perpetual reminder of their distinctive convictions. Thus the spiritual battle takes on the form of pushing or resisting conformity.

kingdom. He appointed inspectors over all the people and commanded the towns of Judah to offer sacrifice, town by town. ⁵²Many of the people, everyone who forsook the law, joined them, and they did evil in the land; ⁵³they drove Israel into hiding in every place of refuge they had.

54 Now on the fifteenth day of Chislev, in the one hundred forty-fifth year,ᵃ they erected a desolating sacrilege on the altar of burnt offering. They also built altars in the surrounding towns of Judah, ⁵⁵and offered incense at the doors of the houses and in the streets. ⁵⁶The books of the law that they found they tore to pieces and burned with fire. ⁵⁷Anyone found possessing the book of the covenant, or anyone who adhered to the law, was condemned to death by decree of the king. ⁵⁸They kept using violence against Israel, against those who were found month after month in the towns. ⁵⁹On the twenty-fifth day of the month they offered sacrifice on the altar that was on top of the altar of burnt offering. ⁶⁰According to the decree, they put to death the women who had their children circumcised, ⁶¹and their families and those who circumcised them; and they hung the infants from their mothers' necks.

62 But many in Israel stood firm and were resolved in their hearts not to eat unclean food. ⁶³They chose to die rather than to be defiled by food or to profane the holy covenant;

and they did die. ⁶⁴Very great wrath came upon Israel.

Mattathias and His Sons

2 In those days Mattathias son of John son of Simeon, a priest of the family of Joarib, moved from Jerusalem and settled in Modein. ²He had five sons, John surnamed Gaddi, ³Simon called Thassi, ⁴Judas called Maccabeus, ⁵Eleazar called Avaran, and Jonathan called Apphus. ⁶He saw the blasphemies being committed in Judah and Jerusalem, ⁷and said,

"Alas! Why was I born to see this,
    the ruin of my people, the ruin of the
        holy city,
    and to live there when it was given over
        to the enemy,
    the sanctuary given over to aliens?
8 Her temple has become like a person
        without honor;ᵇ
9   her glorious vessels have been carried
        into exile.
    Her infants have been killed in her
        streets,
    her youths by the sword of the foe.
10 What nation has not inherited her
        palacesᶜ
    and has not seized her spoils?
11 All her adornment has been taken away;

a 167 B.C.   b Meaning of Gk uncertain
c Other ancient authorities read has not had a part
in her kingdom

1:53 *they drove Israel into hiding.* The People of God retain their identity as "Israel" by walking with integrity in relation to God. Even though they are marginalized in dramatic ways, they remain "Israel": they remain themselves. Although the "renegades" may be spared these trials and come and go in Jerusalem, they become a dramatic embodiment of what it means to gain the world but lose their own souls.

1:56–63 *They kept using violence against Israel.* The martyrs, though executed as insubordinate subjects defying the king, stand as monuments to what is truly valuable and most to be prized. Keeping faith with God, standing in integrity, remaining true to who we are as members of God's people—these give value and beauty to life. To sacrifice them even for

length of life would be to lose all that gives that life value and all that gives us self-respect. The martyrs teach the surpassing value of remaining in fellowship with God, and soberly admonish us not to compromise this for any of the rewards with which the world often tempts disciples.

2:7–14 *Alas! Why was I born to see this?* Mattathias's lament exhibits a deep passion for the honor of Jerusalem, a deep connectedness with the suffering of the People of God and the city. Part of our spiritual formation consists in allowing ourselves truly to "see" (rather than avoid) the suffering and pain of others, so that we feel a spiritual connection with them and are filled with a deep passion for their plight and vindication. Such holy passions, in turn, guide us to meaningful interventions for God's cause.

no longer free, she has become a slave.
12 And see, our holy place, our beauty,
    and our glory have been laid waste;
  the Gentiles have profaned them.
13   Why should we live any longer?"

14 Then Mattathias and his sons tore their clothes, put on sackcloth, and mourned greatly.

Pagan Worship Refused

15 The king's officers who were enforcing the apostasy came to the town of Modein to make them offer sacrifice. 16Many from Israel came to them; and Mattathias and his sons were assembled. 17Then the king's officers spoke to Mattathias as follows: "You are a leader, honored and great in this town, and supported by sons and brothers. 18Now be the first to come and do what the king commands, as all the Gentiles and the people of Judah and those that are left in Jerusalem have done. Then you and your sons will be numbered among the Friends of the king, and you and your sons will be honored with silver and gold and many gifts."

19 But Mattathias answered and said in a loud voice: "Even if all the nations that live under the rule of the king obey him, and have chosen to obey his commandments, every one of them abandoning the religion of their ancestors, 20I and my sons and my brothers will continue to live by the covenant of our ancestors. 21Far be it from us to desert the law and the ordinances. 22We will not obey the king's words by turning aside from our religion to the right hand or to the left."

23 When he had finished speaking these words, a Jew came forward in the sight of all to offer sacrifice on the altar in Modein, according to the king's command. 24When Mattathias saw it, he burned with zeal and his heart was stirred. He gave vent to righteous anger; he ran and killed him on the altar. 25At the same time he killed the king's officer who was forcing them to sacrifice, and he tore down the altar. 26Thus he burned with zeal for the law, just as Phinehas did against Zimri son of Salu.

27 Then Mattathias cried out in the town with a loud voice, saying: "Let every one who is zealous for the law and supports the covenant come out with me!" 28Then he and his sons fled to the hills and left all that they had in the town.

29 At that time many who were seeking righteousness and justice went down to the wilderness to live there, 30they, their sons,

---

2:17–18 *do what the king commands.* Mattathias is offered personal security, even prosperity, for supporting an arrogant regime. Domination systems stay in place because individuals are willing to place a higher value on their own security than the *shalom,* or peace, wholeness-in-community, of the larger human community. This is an area for constant vigilance and self-examination as well as careful consideration of how we will use whatever respect and public regard we have—to promote adherence to the status quo or to the cause of God.

2:19–20 *I . . will continue to live by the covenant.* Mattathias further models the independence from the court of popular opinion that is necessary for consistently faithful action. We must honor and obey God and preserve the health of our soul, even if no other human being affirms us in this commitment.

2:24–26 *He gave vent to righteous anger.* Mattathias's "zeal for the law" manifests itself in the execution of an apostate and the gentile tempter, connecting him with Phinehas (Num 25:6–15), who also won the priesthood for his family by such action. In Christ, "righteous anger" can no longer be manifested as violence against another human being, for the enemy is to be loved; it can and should, however, continue to drive us to purify the People of God of injustice and unholiness.

2:27–30 *went down to the wilderness.* Maintaining faithfulness to God and avoidance of entanglement in compromise may sometimes require withdrawal. The discipline of retreat, whether alone or in community with those who are also seeking God and discerning God's call, is a helpful means of determining how our life has become entangled and what changes in attitudes or behaviors God is calling for. Discerning how we are called to distance ourselves from the culture around us in order to remain faithful is a task that perpetually engages the People of God (see, e.g., Rev 18:4–5).

their wives, and their livestock, because troubles pressed heavily upon them. [31]And it was reported to the king's officers, and to the troops in Jerusalem the city of David, that those who had rejected the king's command had gone down to the hiding places in the wilderness. [32]Many pursued them, and overtook them; they encamped opposite them and prepared for battle against them on the sabbath day. [33]They said to them, "Enough of this! Come out and do what the king commands, and you will live." [34]But they said, "We will not come out, nor will we do what the king commands and so profane the sabbath day." [35]Then the enemy[a] quickly attacked them. [36]But they did not answer them or hurl a stone at them or block up their hiding places, [37]for they said, "Let us all die in our innocence; heaven and earth testify for us that you are killing us unjustly." [38]So they attacked them on the sabbath, and they died, with their wives and children and livestock, to the number of a thousand persons.

[39] When Mattathias and his friends learned of it, they mourned for them deeply. [40]And all said to their neighbors: "If we all do as our kindred have done and refuse to fight with the Gentiles for our lives and for our ordinances, they will quickly destroy us from the earth." [41]So they made this decision that day: "Let us fight against anyone who comes to attack us on the sabbath day; let us not all die as our kindred died in their hiding places."

Counter-Attack

[42] Then there united with them a company of Hasideans, mighty warriors of Israel, all who offered themselves willingly for the law. [43]And all who became fugitives to escape their troubles joined them and reinforced them. [44]They organized an army, and struck down sinners in their anger and renegades in their wrath; the survivors fled to the Gentiles for safety. [45]And Mattathias and his friends went around and tore down the altars; [46]they forcibly circumcised all the uncircumcised boys that they found within the borders of Israel. [47]They hunted down the arrogant, and the work prospered in their hands. [48]They rescued the law out of the hands of the Gentiles and kings, and they never let the sinner gain the upper hand.

The Last Words of Mattathias

[49] Now the days drew near for Mattathias to die, and he said to his sons: "Arrogance and scorn have now become strong; it is a time of ruin and furious anger. [50]Now, my children, show zeal for the law, and give your lives for the covenant of our ancestors.

[51] "Remember the deeds of the ancestors, which they did in their generations; and you will receive great honor and an everlasting name. [52]Was not Abraham found faithful when tested, and it was reckoned to him as righteousness? [53]Joseph in the time of his distress kept the commandment, and became lord of Egypt. [54]Phinehas our ancestor, be-

a Gk *they*

2:34–41 *Let us not all die.* Though he reveres the martyrs for their witness to the ultimate value of following God's commands, Mattathias and his party must look to what will best secure the integrity of the whole People of God. Decisions either to keep God's commands rigidly or to relax them for the sake of God's larger purposes may reflect equal fidelity and call for discernment.

2:51–60 *Remember the deeds of the ancestors.* An important spiritual resource is the memory of those who have lived and died in the faith, when remembering leads to following their example and allowing our story to be shaped by

sacred history. Abraham kept faith with God even when the stakes were critically high (he did not just "believe God," but acted faithfully in his relationship with God), and in each of the examples that follow "keeping faith" with God and remaining obedient to the commandments is central to the characters' success. This is even the case with David (the Greek word behind "mercy" is often used to translate the Hebrew word for "covenant faithfulness," no doubt the original meaning here). These witnesses help us to reflect on the path we should follow and to trust that the path toward God is always better than the path away from God.

cause he was deeply zealous, received the covenant of everlasting priesthood. [55]Joshua, because he fulfilled the command, became a judge in Israel. [56]Caleb, because he testified in the assembly, received an inheritance in the land. [57]David, because he was merciful, inherited the throne of the kingdom forever. [58]Elijah, because of great zeal for the law, was taken up into heaven. [59]Hananiah, Azariah, and Mishael believed and were saved from the flame. [60]Daniel, because of his innocence, was delivered from the mouth of the lions.

[61] "And so observe, from generation to generation, that none of those who put their trust in him will lack strength. [62]Do not fear the words of sinners, for their splendor will turn into dung and worms. [63]Today they will be exalted, but tomorrow they will not be found, because they will have returned to the dust, and their plans will have perished. [64]My children, be courageous and grow strong in the law, for by it you will gain honor.

[65] "Here is your brother Simeon who, I know, is wise in counsel; always listen to him; he shall be your father. [66]Judas Maccabeus has been a mighty warrior from his youth; he shall command the army for you and fight the battle against the peoples.[a] [67]You shall rally around you all who observe the law, and avenge the wrong done to your people. [68]Pay back the Gentiles in full, and obey the commands of the law."

[69] Then he blessed them, and was gathered to his ancestors. [70]He died in the one hundred forty-sixth year[b] and was buried in the tomb of his ancestors at Modein. And all Israel mourned for him with great lamentation.

The Early Victories of Judas

3 Then his son Judas, who was called Maccabeus, took command in his place. [2]All his brothers and all who had joined his father helped him; they gladly fought for Israel.

[3] He extended the glory of his people.
  Like a giant he put on his breastplate;
he bound on his armor of war and
    waged battles,
  protecting the camp by his sword.
[4] He was like a lion in his deeds,
  like a lion's cub roaring for prey.
[5] He searched out and pursued those who
    broke the law;
  he burned those who troubled his
    people.
[6] Lawbreakers shrank back for fear of him;
  all the evildoers were confounded;
  and deliverance prospered by his
    hand.
[7] He embittered many kings,
  but he made Jacob glad by his deeds,
  and his memory is blessed forever.
[8] He went through the cities of Judah;
  he destroyed the ungodly out of the
    land;[c]
  thus he turned away wrath from
    Israel.
[9] He was renowned to the ends of the
    earth;
  he gathered in those who were
    perishing.

a Or of the people   b 166 B.C.   c Gk it

2:61–64 *you will gain honor.* This chapter has powerfully raised the issue of what kind of honor and name we might seek and from whom (see also 2:17–18, 51). If we are sensitive to how worldly-minded people evaluate us, our commitment to walk in God's ways will be compromised. But if we seek to be approved and valued by God above all, single-hearted commitment to grow in discipleship and to be available for God's work will be enhanced.

3:3–9 *Like a giant he put on his breastplate.* One of the goals of spiritual formation is to equip us to be warriors for the cause of God. God calls us collectively to identify sources of ungodliness within the community of faith and to move toward greater holiness, toward more complete commitment to walk in God's ways, thus always turning away wrath and moving more fully into the shadow of God's favor. He raises us up, like Judas, to work toward advancing the honor of God's people in every place where they are treated with less respect than is due. Our weapons are not instruments of violence, but God's provisions for discernment and healing; our opponents are not objects for violence, but people like ourselves to be redeemed.

10 Apollonius now gathered together Gentiles and a large force from Samaria to fight against Israel. [11]When Judas learned of it, he went out to meet him, and he defeated and killed him. Many were wounded and fell, and the rest fled. [12]Then they seized their spoils; and Judas took the sword of Apollonius, and used it in battle the rest of his life.

13 When Seron, the commander of the Syrian army, heard that Judas had gathered a large company, including a body of faithful soldiers who stayed with him and went out to battle, [14]he said, "I will make a name for myself and win honor in the kingdom. I will make war on Judas and his companions, who scorn the king's command." [15]Once again a strong army of godless men went up with him to help him, to take vengeance on the Israelites.

16 When he approached the ascent of Beth-horon, Judas went out to meet him with a small company. [17]But when they saw the army coming to meet them, they said to Judas, "How can we, few as we are, fight against so great and so strong a multitude? And we are faint, for we have eaten nothing today." [18]Judas replied, "It is easy for many to be hemmed in by few, for in the sight of Heaven there is no difference between saving by many or by few. [19]It is not on the size of the army that victory in battle depends, but strength comes from Heaven. [20]They come against us in great insolence and lawlessness to destroy us and our wives and our children, and to despoil us; [21]but we fight for our lives and our laws. [22]He himself will crush them before us; as for you, do not be afraid of them."

23 When he finished speaking, he rushed suddenly against Seron and his army, and they were crushed before him. [24]They pursued them[a] down the descent of Beth-horon to the plain; eight hundred of them fell, and the rest fled into the land of the Philistines. [25]Then Judas and his brothers began to be feared, and terror fell on the Gentiles all around them. [26]His fame reached the king, and the Gentiles talked of the battles of Judas.

The Policy of Antiochus

27 When King Antiochus heard these reports, he was greatly angered; and he sent and gathered all the forces of his kingdom, a very strong army. [28]He opened his coffers and gave a year's pay to his forces, and ordered them to be ready for any need. [29]Then he saw that the money in the treasury was exhausted, and that the revenues from the country were small because of the dissension and disaster that he had caused in the land by abolishing the laws that had existed from the earliest days. [30]He feared that he might not have such funds as he had before for his expenses and for the gifts that he used to give more lavishly than preceding kings. [31]He was greatly perplexed in mind; then he determined to go to Persia and collect the revenues from those regions and raise a large fund.

32 He left Lysias, a distinguished man of royal lineage, in charge of the king's affairs

a Other ancient authorities read him

3:12 *seized their spoils.* God's people are equipped for further battles against injustice and the domination systems of the world by what they take from each previous struggle.

3:18–22 *strength comes from Heaven.* Judas reminds his armies, and us, of a principle first learned in 1 Sam 14:6. How many battles do God's people fail to engage by overestimating the strength and resources of the oppressive system and underestimating the strength and resources of God? Faith takes its stand, however, based on what is right in God's sight, rather than assurance of success calculated in terms of human strength

and resources, and leaves the results to God.

3:27–31 *the money in the treasury was exhausted.* Here we see the sheer waste caused by domination systems and their war machines and the incredible resources that must be appropriated from more constructive enterprises to sustain them. Rather than reflecting and seeking wisdom, perhaps even repenting of his policies in Judea, Antiochus IV blindly throws more and more resources behind his anger. The logic of the domination system means deprivation not only for its enemies, but also for the mass of its supporters.

from the river Euphrates to the borders of Egypt. ³³Lysias was also to take care of his son Antiochus until he returned. ³⁴And he turned over to Lysias*a* half of his forces and the elephants, and gave him orders about all that he wanted done. As for the residents of Judea and Jerusalem, ³⁵Lysias was to send a force against them to wipe out and destroy the strength of Israel and the remnant of Jerusalem; he was to banish the memory of them from the place, ³⁶settle aliens in all their territory, and distribute their land by lot. ³⁷Then the king took the remaining half of his forces and left Antioch his capital in the one hundred and forty-seventh year.*b* He crossed the Euphrates river and went through the upper provinces.

Preparations for Battle

38 Lysias chose Ptolemy son of Dorymenes, and Nicanor and Gorgias, able men among the Friends of the king, ³⁹and sent with them forty thousand infantry and seven thousand cavalry to go into the land of Judah and destroy it, as the king had commanded. ⁴⁰So they set out with their entire force, and when they arrived they encamped near Emmaus in the plain. ⁴¹When the traders of the region heard what was said to them, they took silver and gold in immense amounts, and fetters,*c* and went to the camp to get the Israelites for slaves. And forces from Syria and the land of the Philistines joined with them.

42 Now Judas and his brothers saw that misfortunes had increased and that the forces were encamped in their territory. They also learned what the king had commanded to do to the people to cause their final destruction. ⁴³But they said to one another, "Let us restore the ruins of our people, and fight for our people and the sanctuary." ⁴⁴So the congregation assembled to be ready for battle, and to pray and ask for mercy and compassion.

⁴⁵ Jerusalem was uninhabited like a
    wilderness;
  not one of her children went in or
    out.
  The sanctuary was trampled down,
    and aliens held the citadel;
  it was a lodging place for the Gentiles.
  Joy was taken from Jacob;
    the flute and the harp ceased to play.

46 Then they gathered together and went to Mizpah, opposite Jerusalem, because Israel formerly had a place of prayer in Mizpah. ⁴⁷They fasted that day, put on sackcloth and sprinkled ashes on their heads, and tore their clothes. ⁴⁸And they opened the book of the law to inquire into those matters about which

a Gk *him*   *b* 165 B.C.   *c* Syr: Gk Mss, Vg *slaves*

3:41 *went to the camp to get the Israelites for slaves.* People who regard those in misery and on the verge of greater misfortune merely as spoils to be gobbled up and transformed into profit are opportunists of the worst sort. Setting material gain above the human connection with those who stand to be injured by our gain is a persistent obstacle to realizing God's vision for human community.

3:46–53 *They fasted that day.* Judas and his armies engage in an array of Spiritual Disciplines in preparation for their engagement with the enemies of the People of God. They fast, an act of spiritual dedication. They mourn, allowing themselves to touch their own pain and the pain of their people. They search the Scriptures and examine themselves, their commitments, and their motives in light of what they read, in an attempt to discern if their hearts are truly in line with God. They gather around themselves signs of the people's faithfulness to God (the tithes and offerings yet to be delivered to the Temple and the Nazirites who have completed their vows to God) and signs of God's commitment to be available to this people (the priestly vestments). Thus prepared, they arrive at the discernment of God's cause in the midst of their present circumstances (the need to make provision for the people's covenant loyalty by regaining the Temple, and the need to vindicate the honor of God's house). First Maccabees consistently challenges us to align ourselves with God's vision for his people, to lay ourselves on the line as God leads us for the sake of that vision, and to have the courage in faith to bring what we learn from the Spiritual Disciplines of prayer, fasting, meditation upon Scripture, and holy conversation into the forefront of our lives.

the Gentiles consulted the likenesses of their gods. ⁴⁹They also brought the vestments of the priesthood and the first fruits and the tithes, and they stirred up the nazirites*a* who had completed their days; ⁵⁰and they cried aloud to Heaven, saying,

"What shall we do with these?
    Where shall we take them?
⁵¹ Your sanctuary is trampled down and
        profaned,
    and your priests mourn in
        humiliation.
⁵² Here the Gentiles are assembled against
        us to destroy us;
    you know what they plot against us.
⁵³ How will we be able to withstand them,
        if you do not help us?"

⁵⁴ Then they sounded the trumpets and gave a loud shout. ⁵⁵After this Judas appointed leaders of the people, in charge of thousands and hundreds and fifties and tens. ⁵⁶Those who were building houses, or were about to be married, or were planting a vineyard, or were fainthearted, he told to go home again, according to the law. ⁵⁷Then the army marched out and encamped to the south of Emmaus.

⁵⁸ And Judas said, "Arm yourselves and be courageous. Be ready early in the morning to fight with these Gentiles who have assembled against us to destroy us and our sanctu-ary. ⁵⁹It is better for us to die in battle than to see the misfortunes of our nation and of the sanctuary. ⁶⁰But as his will in heaven may be, so shall he do."

The Battle at Emmaus

4 Now Gorgias took five thousand infantry and one thousand picked cavalry, and this division moved out by night ²to fall upon the camp of the Jews and attack them suddenly. Men from the citadel were his guides. ³But Judas heard of it, and he and his warriors moved out to attack the king's force in Emmaus ⁴while the division was still absent from the camp. ⁵When Gorgias entered the camp of Judas by night, he found no one there, so he looked for them in the hills, because he said, "These men are running away from us."

⁶ At daybreak Judas appeared in the plain with three thousand men, but they did not have armor and swords such as they desired. ⁷And they saw the camp of the Gentiles, strong and fortified, with cavalry all around it; and these men were trained in war. ⁸But Judas said to those who were with him, "Do not fear their numbers or be afraid when they charge. ⁹Remember how our ancestors were saved at the Red Sea, when Pharaoh with his forces pursued them. ¹⁰And now, let us cry to Heaven, to see whether he will favor us and

a That is *those separated* or *those consecrated*

Responding

3:47, 48 FASTING and STUDY. What counterintuitive ways to prepare for battle! Instead of practicing maneuvers and resting, instead of eating to strengthen their bodies for battle, Judas and his armies pray, fast, and study God's word. Reflect on how you prepare for important events in your life. The next time you are in preparations, consider fasting and studying the Bible as part of your training. *See also* Spiritual Disciplines Index.

3:53, 59–60 *It is better for us to die in battle.* Only God's help will bring about victory for those who fight in God's cause, but faithful warriors must be willing to stand by the right, whatever God may dispose. Our responsibility is always faithfulness, not victory.

4:6 *they did not have armor and swords.* God equips his people with what they need to bring God's will to pass on earth. Indeed, as we are equipped by God—gaining competencies, receiving spiritual gifts, being strategically placed by God for enacting his will—we become more certain of God's commitment to claim victory over all the spiritual forces of wickedness.

4:8–11 *Remember how our ancestors were saved.* Once again Judas models how reflection on God's character and our hope for God's interventions in the present (how God will be "with us" now) can be informed by reflection on his actions on behalf of his people in the past, here particularly the deliverance at the Red Sea. Verse 11 puts the primary focus on witness rather than on outcome. In the Maccabean literature, both the martyr and the military hero win the victory of bringing honor to God and advancing his cause through their witness.

remember his covenant with our ancestors and crush this army before us today. [11]Then all the Gentiles will know that there is one who redeems and saves Israel."

12 When the foreigners looked up and saw them coming against them, [13]they went out from their camp to battle. Then the men with Judas blew their trumpets [14]and engaged in battle. The Gentiles were crushed, and fled into the plain, [15]and all those in the rear fell by the sword. They pursued them to Gazara, and to the plains of Idumea, and to Azotus and Jamnia; and three thousand of them fell. [16]Then Judas and his force turned back from pursuing them, [17]and he said to the people, "Do not be greedy for plunder, for there is a battle before us; [18]Gorgias and his force are near us in the hills. But stand now against our enemies and fight them, and afterward seize the plunder boldly."

19 Just as Judas was finishing this speech, a detachment appeared, coming out of the hills. [20]They saw that their army[a] had been put to flight, and that the Jews[a] were burning the camp, for the smoke that was seen showed what had happened. [21]When they perceived this, they were greatly frightened, and when they also saw the army of Judas drawn up in the plain for battle, [22]they all fled into the land of the Philistines. [23]Then Judas returned to plunder the camp, and they seized a great amount of gold and silver, and cloth dyed blue and sea purple, and great riches. [24]On their return they sang hymns and praises to Heaven—"For he is good, for his mercy endures forever." [25]Thus Israel had a great deliverance that day.

First Campaign of Lysias

26 Those of the foreigners who escaped went and reported to Lysias all that had happened. [27]When he heard it, he was perplexed and discouraged, for things had not happened to Israel as he had intended, nor had they turned out as the king had ordered. [28]But the next year he mustered sixty thousand picked infantry and five thousand cavalry to subdue them. [29]They came into Idumea and encamped at Beth-zur, and Judas met them with ten thousand men.

30 When he saw that their army was strong, he prayed, saying, "Blessed are you, O Savior of Israel, who crushed the attack of the mighty warrior by the hand of your servant David, and gave the camp of the Philistines into the hands of Jonathan son of Saul, and of the man who carried his armor. [31]Hem in this army by the hand of your people Israel, and let them be ashamed of their troops and their cavalry. [32]Fill them with cowardice; melt the boldness of their strength; let them tremble in their destruction. [33]Strike them down with the sword of those who love you, and let all who know your name praise you with hymns."

34 Then both sides attacked, and there fell of the army of Lysias five thousand men; they fell in action.[b] [35]When Lysias saw the rout of his troops and observed the boldness that inspired those of Judas, and how ready they were either to live or to die nobly, he withdrew to Antioch and enlisted merce-

---

a Gk *they*   *b* Or *and some fell on the opposite side*

4:17–18 *Do not be greedy for plunder.* In many causes, we may be distracted from pursuing God's course to the end by the unexpected opportunities for temporal gain along the way. How many warriors in the cause for a just peace lose the vision and stop when they begin to obtain posts, authority, and a share in the wealth of the domination system they previously opposed!

4:24–25 *they sang hymns.* In every victory over sin or the forces of wickedness, in every deliverance, it is essential to discern and acknowledge how God's hand has been at work

and to offer the sacrifice of praise. This keeps us mindful of God's presence with us and for us, as well as reminding us of our utter dependence upon him for every advance we make.

4:30–33 *he prayed.* Judas's prayer recalls David's defeat of Goliath (1 Sam 17) and Jonathan's routing of the Philistine camp (1 Sam 14:6–15). This again models how we are to allow the memory of who God is and how God has acted before to guide and shape our present responses and to embolden courageous action in the cause of God's kingdom.

naries in order to invade Judea again with an even larger army.

Cleansing and Dedication of the Temple

36 Then Judas and his brothers said, "See, our enemies are crushed; let us go up to cleanse the sanctuary and dedicate it." [37]So all the army assembled and went up to Mount Zion. [38]There they saw the sanctuary desolate, the altar profaned, and the gates burned. In the courts they saw bushes sprung up as in a thicket, or as on one of the mountains. They saw also the chambers of the priests in ruins. [39]Then they tore their clothes and mourned with great lamentation; they sprinkled themselves with ashes [40]and fell face down on the ground. And when the signal was given with the trumpets, they cried out to Heaven.

41 Then Judas detailed men to fight against those in the citadel until he had cleansed the sanctuary. [42]He chose blameless priests devoted to the law, [43]and they cleansed the sanctuary and removed the defiled stones to an unclean place. [44]They deliberated what to do about the altar of burnt offering, which had been profaned. [45]And they thought it best to tear it down, so that it would not be a lasting shame to them that the Gentiles had defiled it. So they tore down the altar, [46]and stored the stones in a convenient place on the temple hill until a prophet should come to tell what to do with them. [47]Then they took unhewn[a] stones, as the law directs, and built a new altar like the former one. [48]They also rebuilt the sanctuary and the interior of the temple, and consecrated the courts. [49]They made new holy vessels, and brought the lampstand, the altar of incense, and the table into the temple. [50]Then they offered incense on the altar and lit the lamps on the lampstand, and these gave light in the temple. [51]They placed the bread on the table and hung up the curtains. Thus they finished all the work they had undertaken.

52 Early in the morning on the twenty-fifth day of the ninth month, which is the month of Chislev, in the one hundred forty-eighth year,[b] [53]they rose and offered sacrifice, as the law directs, on the new altar of burnt offering that they had built. [54]At the very season and on the very day that the Gentiles had profaned it, it was dedicated with songs and harps and lutes and cymbals.

a Gk whole   b 164 B.C.

4:36–58 *cleanse the sanctuary and dedicate it.* The dramatic episode of the rededication of the Temple, the renewal of the sacred space, signals the removal of the "disgrace" inflicted by the domination systems of Antiochus IV upon the People of God. Clearing out the signs of defilement and thus purging the memory of disgrace, renewing the accoutrements of Temple worship, selecting the anniversary of the tragedy as the occasion for a new beginning—all of these have paradigmatic value for the renewal of the worshiping community at any level (individual, congregational, denominational, global). In the transformation of God's sacred space, we ourselves become God's temple, individually (as in 1 Cor 3:16–17; 6:19) or collectively (as in 1 Pet 2:4–5). As such, we are called regularly to search out, acknowledge, and lament how ungodly influences, practices, values, and ambitions have defiled the new temple of God. We are called regularly to remove the defilements and renew ourselves and our communities of faith in such a way that we are free from the shame of the past and liberated for a new, holy, God-centered future.

4:52–54 *the twenty-fifth day.* Judas's choice of a date for the rededication ceremony invites us to think carefully about ways to "redeem" significant dates, places, or other points at which ungodliness and shame have entered our individual or collective lives and to transform these points into occasions for celebrating the renewing and healing power of God.

Responding
4:54–58 **CELEBRATION.** In *The Spirit of the Disciplines* Dallas Willard describes celebration as "the completion of worship, for it dwells on the greatness of God as shown in his goodness *to us.*" List all the ways God has been good to his people and to you personally. Add to your list and turn to it often, whenever you need to dwell on how good God is to us. *See also* Spiritual Disciplines Index.

55All the people fell on their faces and worshiped and blessed Heaven, who had prospered them. 56So they celebrated the dedication of the altar for eight days, and joyfully offered burnt offerings; they offered a sacrifice of well-being and a thanksgiving offering. 57They decorated the front of the temple with golden crowns and small shields; they restored the gates and the chambers for the priests, and fitted them with doors. 58There was very great joy among the people, and the disgrace brought by the Gentiles was removed.

59 Then Judas and his brothers and all the assembly of Israel determined that every year at that season the days of dedication of the altar should be observed with joy and gladness for eight days, beginning with the twenty-fifth day of the month of Chislev.

60 At that time they fortified Mount Zion with high walls and strong towers all around, to keep the Gentiles from coming and trampling them down as they had done before. 61Judasa stationed a garrison there to guard it; he also fortified Beth-zur to guard it, so that the people might have a stronghold that faced Idumea.

Wars with Neighboring Peoples

5 When the Gentiles all around heard that the altar had been rebuilt and the sanctuary dedicated as it was before, they became very angry, 2and they determined to destroy the descendants of Jacob who lived among them. So they began to kill and destroy among the people. 3But Judas made war on the descendants of Esau in Idumea, at Akrabattene, because they kept lying in wait for Israel. He dealt them a heavy blow and humbled them and despoiled them. 4He also remembered the wickedness of the sons of Baean, who were a trap and a snare to the people and ambushed them on the highways. 5They were shut up by him in theirb towers; and he encamped against them, vowed their complete destruction, and burned with fire their towers and all who were in them. 6Then he crossed over to attack the Ammonites, where he found a strong band and many people, with Timothy as their leader. 7He engaged in many battles with them, and they were crushed before him; he struck them down. 8He also took Jazer and its villages; then he returned to Judea.

Liberation of Galilean Jews

9 Now the Gentiles in Gilead gathered together against the Israelites who lived in their territory, and planned to destroy them. But they fled to the stronghold of Dathema, 10and sent to Judas and his brothers a letter that said, "The Gentiles around us have gathered together to destroy us. 11They are preparing to come and capture the stronghold to which we have fled, and Timothy is leading their forces. 12Now then, come and rescue us from their hands, for many of us have fallen, 13and all our kindred who were in the

a Gk He   b Gk her

4:59 every year at that season the . . . dedication . . . should be observed. The institution of Hanukkah as an annual festival is significant as a means of keeping the people's hearts committed to remaining on their renewed path and not slipping back into the errors of 1:11–15. This suggests that we reflect on the meaning of the Christian liturgical calendar, supplemented with significant anniversaries commemorating key markers in our own spiritual pilgrimage. Such reminders of where we have been with God help keep our feet on the path forward with God.

5:1 they became very angry. The restoration of holiness, difference, "otherness" to the temple of God signals a threat to the worldly powers around it. The Temple and its people are no longer "tamed" or "domesticated" for life in the Gentile-dominated world, and those domination systems respond in their customary way.

5:2 they determined to destroy the descendants of Jacob. What happens to God's people in one place (here, the successes of Judas) affects the experience of God's people in other places (here, a heightened threat of destruction for other Jews). This calls for solidarity and the responsibility on the part of those who have enjoyed liberation and renewal to stand beside and aid those whose situation has become more precarious.

land of Tob have been killed; the enemy[a] have captured their wives and children and goods, and have destroyed about a thousand persons there."

14 While the letter was still being read, other messengers, with their garments torn, came from Galilee and made a similar report; [15]they said that the people of Ptolemais and Tyre and Sidon, and all Galilee of the Gentiles,[b] had gathered together against them "to annihilate us." [16]When Judas and the people heard these messages, a great assembly was called to determine what they should do for their kindred who were in distress and were being attacked by enemies.[c] [17]Then Judas said to his brother Simon, "Choose your men and go and rescue your kindred in Galilee; Jonathan my brother and I will go to Gilead." [18]But he left Joseph, son of Zechariah, and Azariah, a leader of the people, with the rest of the forces, in Judea to guard it; [19]and he gave them this command, "Take charge of this people, but do not engage in battle with the Gentiles until we return." [20]Then three thousand men were assigned to Simon to go to Galilee, and eight thousand to Judas for Gilead.

21 So Simon went to Galilee and fought many battles against the Gentiles, and the Gentiles were crushed before him. [22]He pursued them to the gate of Ptolemais; as many as three thousand of the Gentiles fell, and he despoiled them. [23]Then he took the Jews[d] of Galilee and Arbatta, with their wives and children, and all they possessed, and led them to Judea with great rejoicing.

Judas and Jonathan in Gilead

24 Judas Maccabeus and his brother Jonathan crossed the Jordan and made three days' journey into the wilderness. [25]They encountered the Nabateans, who met them peaceably and told them all that had happened to their kindred in Gilead: [26]"Many of them have been shut up in Bozrah and Bosor, in Alema and Chaspho, Maked and Carnaim"—all these towns were strong and large— [27]"and some have been shut up in the other towns of Gilead; the enemy[a] are getting ready to attack the strongholds tomorrow and capture and destroy all these people in a single day."

28 Then Judas and his army quickly turned back by the wilderness road to Bozrah; and he took the town, and killed every male by the edge of the sword; then he seized all its spoils and burned it with fire. [29]He left the place at night, and they went all the way to the stronghold of Dathema.[e] [30]At dawn they looked out and saw a large company, which could not be counted, carrying ladders and engines of war to capture the stronghold, and attacking the Jews within.[f] [31]So Judas saw that the battle had begun and that the cry of the town went up to Heaven, with trumpets and loud shouts, [32]and he said to the men of his forces, "Fight today for your kindred!" [33]Then he came up behind them in three companies, who sounded their trumpets and cried aloud in prayer. [34]And when the army of Timothy realized that it was Maccabeus, they fled before him, and he dealt them a heavy blow. As many as eight thousand of them fell that day.

35 Next he turned aside to Maapha,[g] and fought against it and took it; and he killed every male in it, plundered it, and burned it with fire. [36]From there he marched on and took Chaspho, Maked, and Bosor, and the other towns of Gilead.

37 After these things Timothy gathered another army and encamped opposite Raphon, on the other side of the stream. [38]Judas sent men to spy out the camp, and they reported to him, "All the Gentiles around us have gathered to him; it is a very large force. [39]They also have hired Arabs to help them, and they are encamped across the stream,

a Gk they   b Gk aliens   c Gk them
d Gk those   e Gk lacks of Dathema. See verse 9
f Gk and they were attacking them   g Other
ancient authorities read Alema

5:16–17, 21–23, 45 *what they should do for their kindred.* Judas and his forces are not content with having attained security in their own land; they continue to labor for the security and wholeness of the People of God abroad. None have rest until all have rest and enjoy *shalom* (peace, wholeness-in-community).

ready to come and fight against you." And Judas went to meet them.

40 Now as Judas and his army drew near to the stream of water, Timothy said to the officers of his forces, "If he crosses over to us first, we will not be able to resist him, for he will surely defeat us. 41 But if he shows fear and camps on the other side of the river, we will cross over to him and defeat him." 42 When Judas approached the stream of water, he stationed the officers*a* of the army at the stream and gave them this command, "Permit no one to encamp, but make them all enter the battle." 43 Then he crossed over against them first, and the whole army followed him. All the Gentiles were defeated before him, and they threw away their arms and fled into the sacred precincts at Carnaim. 44 But he took the town and burned the sacred precincts with fire, together with all who were in them. Thus Carnaim was conquered; they could stand before Judas no longer.

The Return to Jerusalem

45 Then Judas gathered together all the Israelites in Gilead, the small and the great, with their wives and children and goods, a very large company, to go to the land of Judah. 46 So they came to Ephron. This was a large and very strong town on the road, and they could not go around it to the right or to the left; they had to go through it. 47 But the people of the town shut them out and blocked up the gates with stones.

48 Judas sent them this friendly message, "Let us pass through your land to get to our land. No one will do you harm; we will simply pass by on foot." But they refused to open to him. 49 Then Judas ordered proclamation to be made to the army that all should encamp where they were. 50 So the men of the forces encamped, and he fought against the town all that day and all the night, and the town was delivered into his hands. 51 He destroyed every male by the edge of the sword, and razed and plundered the town. Then he passed through the town over the bodies of the dead.

52 Then they crossed the Jordan into the large plain before Beth-shan. 53 Judas kept rallying the laggards and encouraging the people all the way until he came to the land of Judah. 54 So they went up to Mount Zion with joy and gladness, and offered burnt offerings, because they had returned in safety; not one of them had fallen.

Joseph and Azariah Defeated

55 Now while Judas and Jonathan were in Gilead and their*b* brother Simon was in Galilee before Ptolemais, 56 Joseph son of Zechariah, and Azariah, the commanders of the forces, heard of their brave deeds and of the heroic war they had fought. 57 So they said, "Let us also make a name for ourselves; let us go and make war on the Gentiles around us." 58 So they issued orders to the men of the forces that were with them and marched against Jamnia. 59 Gorgias and his men came out of the town to meet them in battle. 60 Then Joseph and Azariah were routed, and were pursued to the borders of Judea; as many as two thousand of the people of Israel fell that day. 61 Thus the people suffered a great rout because, thinking to do a brave deed, they did not listen to Judas and

a Or *scribes*   *b* Gk *his*

5:40–41 *if he shows fear.* Boldness in the cause of God (see 1 Sam 14:8–10; Phil 1:27–28) is a witness to the power and victory of the One whom we serve.

5:48–51 *they refused to open to him.* Opposition to the new "exodus" from places of oppression is familiar from the first exodus (see Num 20:17–21; 21:21–24). But God once again opens the way forward and removes the obstacle.

5:55–62, 67 *Let us also make a name for ourselves.* Although these passages clearly serve to legitimate the Hasmonean dynasty as God's chosen family, they also teach an essential lesson. The battles we engage can never be driven by the desire to make a name for ourselves. Spiritual engagements are not the arena for self-serving ambitions. We must be sure that we are called by God to take some action and undertake it out of obedience to God and a desire to see God's purposes for his people advanced. God, not our ambitions, must always lead.

his brothers. 62But they did not belong to the family of those men through whom deliverance was given to Israel.

63 The man Judas and his brothers were greatly honored in all Israel and among all the Gentiles, wherever their name was heard. 64People gathered to them and praised them.

Success at Hebron and Philistia

65 Then Judas and his brothers went out and fought the descendants of Esau in the land to the south. He struck Hebron and its villages and tore down its strongholds and burned its towers on all sides. 66Then he marched off to go into the land of the Philistines, and passed through Marisa.*a* 67On that day some priests, who wished to do a brave deed, fell in battle, for they went out to battle unwisely. 68But Judas turned aside to Azotus in the land of the Philistines; he tore down their altars, and the carved images of their gods he burned with fire; he plundered the towns and returned to the land of Judah.

The Last Days of Antiochus Epiphanes

6 King Antiochus was going through the upper provinces when he heard that Elymais in Persia was a city famed for its wealth in silver and gold. 2Its temple was very rich, containing golden shields, breastplates, and weapons left there by Alexander son of Philip, the Macedonian king who first reigned over the Greeks. 3So he came and tried to take the city and plunder it, but he could not because his plan had become known to the citizens 4and they withstood him in battle. So he fled and in great disappointment left there to return to Babylon.

5 Then someone came to him in Persia and reported that the armies that had gone into the land of Judah had been routed; 6that Lysias had gone first with a strong force, but had turned and fled before the Jews;*b* that the Jews*c* had grown strong from the arms,

supplies, and abundant spoils that they had taken from the armies they had cut down; 7that they had torn down the abomination that he had erected on the altar in Jerusalem; and that they had surrounded the sanctuary with high walls as before, and also Beth-zur, his town.

8 When the king heard this news, he was astounded and badly shaken. He took to his bed and became sick from disappointment, because things had not turned out for him as he had planned. 9He lay there for many days, because deep disappointment continually gripped him, and he realized that he was dying. 10So he called all his Friends and said to them, "Sleep has departed from my eyes and I am downhearted with worry. 11I said to myself, 'To what distress I have come! And into what a great flood I now am plunged! For I was kind and beloved in my power.' 12But now I remember the wrong I did in Jerusalem. I seized all its vessels of silver and gold, and I sent to destroy the inhabitants of Judah without good reason. 13I know that it is because of this that these misfortunes have come upon me; here I am, perishing of bitter disappointment in a strange land."

14 Then he called for Philip, one of his Friends, and made him ruler over all his kingdom. 15He gave him the crown and his robe and the signet, so that he might guide his son Antiochus and bring him up to be king. 16Thus King Antiochus died there in the one hundred forty-ninth year.*d* 17When Lysias learned that the king was dead, he set up Antiochus the king's*e* son to reign. Lysias*f* had brought him up from boyhood; he named him Eupator.

a Other ancient authorities read *Samaria*
b Gk *them*   *c* Gk *they*   *d* 163 B.C.   *e* Gk *his*
f Gk *He*

6:8–11 *became sick from disappointment.* Antiochus's death is not a picture of repentance (godly sorrow), but of that regret, that "sorrow unto death," that consumes a person near the end of a life that has not been lived with attention to God and matters of ultimate value.

Antiochus's despair over failed and impermanent ventures (Persia and Judea) impress upon him the waste he has made of his life. This is the final reward for those who have played by the rules of the game of domination systems, even if one has been at the top of such a system.

Renewed Attacks from Syria

18 Meanwhile the garrison in the citadel kept hemming Israel in around the sanctuary. They were trying in every way to harm them and strengthen the Gentiles. 19Judas therefore resolved to destroy them, and assembled all the people to besiege them. 20They gathered together and besieged the citadel*a* in the one hundred fiftieth year;*b* and he built siege towers and other engines of war. 21But some of the garrison escaped from the siege and some of the ungodly Israelites joined them. 22They went to the king and said, "How long will you fail to do justice and to avenge our kindred? 23We were happy to serve your father, to live by what he said, and to follow his commands. 24For this reason the sons of our people besieged the citadel*c* and became hostile to us; moreover, they have put to death as many of us as they have caught, and they have seized our inheritances. 25It is not against us alone that they have stretched out their hands; they have also attacked all the lands on their borders. 26And see, today they have encamped against the citadel in Jerusalem to take it; they have fortified both the sanctuary and Beth-zur; 27unless you quickly prevent them, they will do still greater things, and you will not be able to stop them."

28 The king was enraged when he heard this. He assembled all his Friends, the commanders of his forces and those in authority.*d* 29Mercenary forces also came to him from other kingdoms and from islands of the seas. 30The number of his forces was one hundred thousand foot soldiers, twenty thousand horsemen, and thirty-two elephants accustomed to war. 31They came through Idumea and encamped against Beth-zur, and for many days they fought and built engines of war; but the Jews*e* sallied out and burned these with fire, and fought courageously.

The Battle at Beth-zechariah

32 Then Judas marched away from the citadel and encamped at Beth-zechariah, opposite the camp of the king. 33Early in the morning the king set out and took his army by a forced march along the road to Beth-zechariah, and his troops made ready for bat-

tle and sounded their trumpets. 34They offered the elephants the juice of grapes and mulberries, to arouse them for battle. 35They distributed the animals among the phalanxes; with each elephant they stationed a thousand men armed with coats of mail, and with brass helmets on their heads; and five hundred picked horsemen were assigned to each beast. 36These took their position beforehand wherever the animal was; wherever it went, they went with it, and they never left it. 37On the elephants*f* were wooden towers, strong and covered; they were fastened on each animal by special harness, and on each were four*d* armed men who fought from there, and also its Indian driver. 38The rest of the cavalry were stationed on either side, on the two flanks of the army, to harass the enemy while being themselves protected by the phalanxes. 39When the sun shone on the shields of gold and brass, the hills were ablaze with them and gleamed like flaming torches.

40 Now a part of the king's army was spread out on the high hills, and some troops were on the plain, and they advanced steadily and in good order. 41All who heard the noise made by their multitude, by the marching of the multitude and the clanking of their arms, trembled, for the army was very large and strong. 42But Judas and his army advanced to the battle, and six hundred of the king's army fell. 43Now Eleazar, called Avaran, saw that one of the animals was equipped with royal armor. It was taller than all the others, and he supposed that the king was on it. 44So he gave his life to save his people and to win for himself an everlasting name. 45He courageously ran into the midst of the phalanx to reach it; he killed men right and left, and they parted before him on both sides. 46He got under the elephant, stabbed it from beneath, and killed it; but it fell to the ground upon him and he died. 47When the Jews*e* saw the royal might and the fierce attack of the forces, they turned away in flight.

a Gk *it*   *b* 162 B.C.   *c* Meaning of Gk uncertain   *d* Gk *those over the reins*   *e* Gk *they* *f* Gk *them*   *g* Cn: Some authorities read *thirty*; others *thirty-two*

The Siege of the Temple

48 The soldiers of the king's army went up to Jerusalem against them, and the king encamped in Judea and at Mount Zion. 49He made peace with the people of Beth-zur, and they evacuated the town because they had no provisions there to withstand a siege, since it was a sabbatical year for the land. 50So the king took Beth-zur and stationed a guard there to hold it. 51Then he encamped before the sanctuary for many days. He set up siege towers, engines of war to throw fire and stones, machines to shoot arrows, and catapults. 52The Jews*a* also made engines of war to match theirs, and fought for many days. 53But they had no food in storage,*b* because it was the seventh year; those who had found safety in Judea from the Gentiles had consumed the last of the stores. 54Only a few men were left in the sanctuary; the rest scattered to their own homes, for the famine proved too much for them.

Syria Offers Terms

55 Then Lysias heard that Philip, whom King Antiochus while still living had appointed to bring up his son Antiochus to be king, 56had returned from Persia and Media with the forces that had gone with the king, and that he was trying to seize control of the government. 57So he quickly gave orders to withdraw, and said to the king, to the commanders of the forces, and to the troops, "Daily we grow weaker, our food supply is scant, the place against which we are fighting is strong, and the affairs of the kingdom press urgently on us. 58Now then let us come to terms with these people, and make peace with them and with all their nation. 59Let

us agree to let them live by their laws as they did before; for it was on account of their laws that we abolished that they became angry and did all these things."

60 The speech pleased the king and the commanders, and he sent to the Jews*c* an offer of peace, and they accepted it. 61So the king and the commanders gave them their oath. On these conditions the Jews*a* evacuated the stronghold. 62But when the king entered Mount Zion and saw what a strong fortress the place was, he broke the oath he had sworn and gave orders to tear down the wall all around. 63Then he set off in haste and returned to Antioch. He found Philip in control of the city, but he fought against him, and took the city by force.

Expedition of Bacchides and Alcimus

7 In the one hundred fifty-first year*d* Demetrius son of Seleucus set out from Rome, sailed with a few men to a town by the sea, and there began to reign. 2As he was entering the royal palace of his ancestors, the army seized Antiochus and Lysias to bring them to him. 3But when this act became known to him, he said, "Do not let me see their faces!" 4So the army killed them, and Demetrius took his seat on the throne of his kingdom.

5 Then there came to him all the renegade and godless men of Israel; they were led by Alcimus, who wanted to be high priest. 6They brought to the king this accusation against the people: "Judas and his brothers have destroyed all your Friends, and have driven us out of our land. 7Now then send a

---

a Gk *they*   *b* Other ancient authorities read *in the sanctuary*   *c* Gk *them*   *d* 161 B.C.

6:51–59 *Daily we grow weaker.* The competitive, self-seeking, and factious spirit nurtured by domination systems introduces serious weaknesses into these systems. They become "houses divided" and must make unnecessary compromises with the enemy (here, Judas), so as to fight internal battles. This is precisely why factiousness, rivalry, and self-seeking must be excluded from the People of God (Phil 1:27–2:4). Otherwise, we will likewise continue to make compromises with, and

accommodations to, our spiritual enemies, placing an unhealthy and destructive priority on winning our battles within the Church rather than on winning God's cause in the world.

7:5–7 *Then there came to him all the renegade and godless men.* A continuing threat to the *shalom,* or peace, wholeness-in-community, of God's people are those who are committed to their own internal agendas (here, promoting Alcimus) and use unholy resources and strategies to eliminate the opposition.

man whom you trust; let him go and see all the ruin that Judas[a] has brought on us and on the land of the king, and let him punish them and all who help them."

8 So the king chose Bacchides, one of the king's Friends, governor of the province Beyond the River; he was a great man in the kingdom and was faithful to the king. [9]He sent him, and with him he sent the ungodly Alcimus, whom he made high priest; and he commanded him to take vengeance on the Israelites. [10]So they marched away and came with a large force into the land of Judah; and he sent messengers to Judas and his brothers with peaceable but treacherous words. [11]But they paid no attention to their words, for they saw that they had come with a large force.

12 Then a group of scribes appeared in a body before Alcimus and Bacchides to ask for just terms. [13]The Hasideans were first among the Israelites to seek peace from them, [14]for they said, "A priest of the line of Aaron has come with the army, and he will not harm us." [15]Alcimus[b] spoke peaceable words to them and swore this oath to them, "We will not seek to injure you or your friends." [16]So they trusted him; but he seized sixty of them and killed them in one day, in accordance with the word that was written,

[17]   "The flesh of your faithful ones and
            their blood
        they poured out all around Jerusalem,
            and there was no one to bury them."

[18]Then the fear and dread of them fell on all the people, for they said, "There is no truth or justice in them, for they have violated the agreement and the oath that they swore."

19 Then Bacchides withdrew from Jerusalem and encamped in Beth-zaith. And he sent and seized many of the men who had deserted to him,[c] and some of the people, and killed them and threw them into a great pit. [20]He placed Alcimus in charge of the country and left with him a force to help him; then Bacchides went back to the king.

21 Alcimus struggled to maintain his high priesthood, [22]and all who were troubling their people joined him. They gained control of the land of Judah and did great damage in Israel. [23]And Judas saw all the wrongs that Alcimus and those with him had done among the Israelites; it was more than the Gentiles had done. [24]So Judas[a] went out into all the surrounding parts of Judea, taking vengeance on those who had deserted and preventing those in the city[d] from going out into the country. [25]When Alcimus saw that Judas and those with him had grown strong, and realized that he could not withstand them, he returned to the king and brought malicious charges against them.

Nicanor in Judea

26 Then the king sent Nicanor, one of his honored princes, who hated and detested Israel, and he commanded him to destroy the people. [27]So Nicanor came to Jerusalem with a large force, and treacherously sent to Judas and his brothers this peaceable message, [28]"Let there be no fighting between you and me; I shall come with a few men to see you face to face in peace."

29 So he came to Judas, and they greeted one another peaceably; but the enemy were preparing to kidnap Judas. [30]It became known to Judas that Nicanor[a] had come to him with treacherous intent, and he was afraid of him and would not meet him again.

---

a Gk he   b Gk He   c Or many of his men who had deserted   d Gk and they were prevented

---

7:12–18 *So they trusted him; but he seized sixty of them and killed them.* Those who have been in the forefront of advancing God's kingdom agenda may not find it easy or safe to return to a peaceable coexistence with the powers that be. The tragedies and suffering that befell God's people in their sacred history, and not merely their victories, continue to be reenacted in their ongoing story. Here, the Hasideans' fate is connected with the sorrows of the first siege of Jerusalem in Ps 79:2–3. We can keep returning to these stories, lament psalms, and woe oracles as a means of finding meaning in the adverse circumstances that fall upon us now as the People of God. The Scriptures remain a primary resource as we experience new pains and call out for God's presence and restoration.

31When Nicanor learned that his plan had been disclosed, he went out to meet Judas in battle near Caphar-salama. 32About five hundred of the army of Nicanor fell, and the rest[a] fled into the city of David.

Nicanor Threatens the Temple

33 After these events Nicanor went up to Mount Zion. Some of the priests from the sanctuary and some of the elders of the people came out to greet him peaceably and to show him the burnt offering that was being offered for the king. 34But he mocked them and derided them and defiled them and spoke arrogantly, 35and in anger he swore this oath, "Unless Judas and his army are delivered into my hands this time, then if I return safely I will burn up this house." And he went out in great anger. 36At this the priests went in and stood before the altar and the temple; they wept and said,

37 "You chose this house to be called by
     your name,
   and to be for your people a house of
        prayer and supplication.
38 Take vengeance on this man and on his
        army,
   and let them fall by the sword;
  remember their blasphemies,
     and let them live no longer."

The Death of Nicanor

39 Now Nicanor went out from Jerusalem and encamped in Beth-horon, and the Syrian army joined him. 40Judas encamped in Adasa with three thousand men. Then Judas prayed and said, 41"When the messengers from the king spoke blasphemy, your angel went out and struck down one hundred eighty-five thousand of the Assyrians.[b] 42So also crush this army before us today; let the rest learn that Nicanor[c] has spoken wickedly against the sanctuary, and judge him according to this wickedness."

43 So the armies met in battle on the thirteenth day of the month of Adar. The army of Nicanor was crushed, and he himself was the first to fall in the battle. 44When his army saw that Nicanor had fallen, they threw down their arms and fled. 45The Jews[a] pursued them a day's journey, from Adasa as far as Gazara, and as they followed they kept sounding the battle call on the trumpets. 46People came out of all the surrounding villages of Judea, and they outflanked the enemy[d] and drove them back to their pursuers,[e] so that they all fell by the sword; not even one of them was left. 47Then the Jews[a] seized the spoils and the plunder; they cut off Nicanor's head and the right hand that he had so arrogantly stretched out, and brought them and displayed them just outside Jerusalem. 48The people rejoiced greatly and celebrated that day as a day of great gladness. 49They decreed that this day should be celebrated each year on the thirteenth day of Adar. 50So the land of Judah had rest for a few days.

A Eulogy of the Romans

8 Now Judas heard of the fame of the Romans, that they were very strong and were well-disposed toward all who made an alliance with them, that they pledged friendship to those who came to them, 2and that they were very strong. He had been told of their wars and of the brave deeds that they were doing among the Gauls, how they had defeated them and forced them to pay tribute, 3and what they had done in the land of Spain to get control of the silver and gold mines there, 4and how they had gained con-

a Gk they   b Gk of them   c Gk he
d Gk them   e Gk these

7:35–42 *in anger he swore this oath.* Nicanor's arrogance is typical of the representatives of the successive domination systems that impact God's people in Judea, from Assyria (see 2 Kings 19:8–37) to Babylon (see Jer 50–51) to Rome (see Rev 18). Where people act arrogantly (that is, without the fear of God) with regard to God's people, whether exploiting them, marginalizing them, or mistreating them, the temple of God is being profaned. We are challenged to take up the posture of the priests, who see and name the arrogance in prayer before God, learning to burn in holy indignation, and the posture of Judas and his forces, who zealously put themselves in harm's way for the sake of God's holy people in every place.

trol of the whole region by their planning and patience, even though the place was far distant from them. They also subdued the kings who came against them from the ends of the earth, until they crushed them and inflicted great disaster on them; the rest paid them tribute every year. 5They had crushed in battle and conquered Philip, and King Perseus of the Macedonians, *a* and the others who rose up against them. 6They also had defeated Antiochus the Great, king of Asia, who went to fight against them with one hundred twenty elephants and with cavalry and chariots and a very large army. He was crushed by them; 7they took him alive and decreed that he and those who would reign after him should pay a heavy tribute and give hostages and surrender some of their best provinces, 8the countries of India, Media, and Lydia. These they took from him and gave to King Eumenes. 9The Greeks planned to come and destroy them, 10but this became known to them, and they sent a general against the Greeks *b* and attacked them. Many of them were wounded and fell, and the Romans *c* took captive their wives and children; they plundered them, conquered the land, tore down their strongholds, and enslaved them to this day. 11The remaining kingdoms and islands, as many as ever opposed them, they destroyed and enslaved; 12but with their friends and those who rely on them they have kept friendship. They have subdued kings far and near, and as many as have heard of their fame have feared them. 13Those whom they wish to help and to make kings, they make kings, and those whom they wish to depose; and they have been greatly ex-

alted. 14Yet for all this not one of them has put on a crown or worn purple as a mark of pride, 15but they have built for themselves a senate chamber, and every day three hundred twenty senators constantly deliberate concerning the people, to govern them well. 16They trust one man each year to rule over them and to control all their land; they all heed the one man, and there is no envy or jealousy among them.

An Alliance with Rome

17 So Judas chose Eupolemus son of John son of Accos, and Jason son of Eleazar, and sent them to Rome to establish friendship and alliance, 18and to free themselves from the yoke; for they saw that the kingdom of the Greeks was enslaving Israel completely. 19They went to Rome, a very long journey; and they entered the senate chamber and spoke as follows: 20"Judas, who is also called Maccabeus, and his brothers and the people of the Jews have sent us to you to establish alliance and peace with you, so that we may be enrolled as your allies and friends." 21The proposal pleased them, 22and this is a copy of the letter that they wrote in reply, on bronze tablets, and sent to Jerusalem to remain with them there as a memorial of peace and alliance:

23 "May all go well with the Romans and with the nation of the Jews at sea and on land forever, and may sword and enemy be far from them. 24If war comes first to Rome or to any of their allies in all their dominion, 25the nation of the Jews shall act as their allies

---

a Or *Kittim*   *b* Gk *them*   *c* Gk *they*

8:1–16 *the fame of the Romans.* Despite the rosy picture of Rome painted here, it is the domination system par excellence. It intrudes in the governance of other nations to suit its own interests (v 13). It "crushes" and "conquers" other kingdoms. Even when it seeks alliances, those alliances are simply a peaceful and relatively inexpensive means of extending its influence. Knowing that we see in this chapter a picture of the "beast rising out of the sea" that will be denounced in Revelation 13 and 18 calls for circumspection on the part of the People of

God in regard to their endorsement of imperialism in any form.

8:17–32 *to establish friendship and alliance.* Judas uses Rome's power as leverage against the more immediate threat from the Greco-Syrian king, and perhaps shows a certain savvy in so doing. But it is an alliance that is fraught with danger, as it entangles Judea further in existing domination systems (e.g., the pledge to help the Romans in any way, vv 24–26) and eventually leads to Roman domination of Judea.

wholeheartedly, as the occasion may indicate to them. 26To the enemy that makes war they shall not give or supply grain, arms, money, or ships, just as Rome has decided; and they shall keep their obligations without receiving any return. 27In the same way, if war comes first to the nation of the Jews, the Romans shall willingly act as their allies, as the occasion may indicate to them. 28And to their enemies there shall not be given grain, arms, money, or ships, just as Rome has decided; and they shall keep these obligations and do so without deceit. 29Thus on these terms the Romans make a treaty with the Jewish people. 30If after these terms are in effect both parties shall determine to add or delete anything, they shall do so at their discretion, and any addition or deletion that they may make shall be valid.

31 "Concerning the wrongs that King Demetrius is doing to them, we have written to him as follows, 'Why have you made your yoke heavy on our friends and allies the Jews? 32If now they appeal again for help against you, we will defend their rights and fight you on sea and on land.' "

Bacchides Returns to Judea

9 When Demetrius heard that Nicanor and his army had fallen in battle, he sent Bacchides and Alcimus into the land of Judah a second time, and with them the right wing of the army. 2They went by the road that leads to Gilgal and encamped against Mesaloth in Arbela, and they took it and killed many people. 3In the first month of the one hundred fifty-second year[a] they encamped against Jerusalem; 4then they marched off and went to Berea with twenty thousand foot soldiers and two thousand cavalry.

5 Now Judas was encamped in Elasa, and with him were three thousand picked men. 6When they saw the huge number of the enemy forces, they were greatly frightened, and many slipped away from the camp, until no more than eight hundred of them were left.

7 When Judas saw that his army had slipped away and the battle was imminent, he was crushed in spirit, for he had no time to assemble them. 8He became faint, but he said to those who were left, "Let us get up and go against our enemies. We may have the strength to fight them." 9But they tried to dissuade him, saying, "We do not have the strength. Let us rather save our own lives now, and let us come back with our kindred and fight them; we are too few." 10But Judas said, "Far be it from us to do such a thing as to flee from them. If our time has come, let us die bravely for our kindred, and leave no cause to question our honor."

The Last Battle of Judas

11 Then the army of Bacchides[b] marched out from the camp and took its stand for the encounter. The cavalry was divided into two companies, and the slingers and the archers went ahead of the army, as did all the chief warriors. 12Bacchides was on the right wing. Flanked by the two companies, the phalanx advanced to the sound of the trumpets; and the men with Judas also blew their trumpets. 13The earth was shaken by the noise of the armies, and the battle raged from morning until evening.

14 Judas saw that Bacchides and the strength of his army were on the right; then all the stouthearted men went with him, 15and they crushed the right wing, and he pursued them as far as Mount Azotus. 16When those on the left wing saw that the right wing was crushed, they turned and followed close behind Judas and his men. 17The battle became desperate, and many on both sides were wounded and fell. 18Judas also fell, and the rest fled.

19 Then Jonathan and Simon took their brother Judas and buried him in the tomb of their ancestors at Modein, 20and wept for

a 160 B.C.   b Gk lacks of Bacchides

9:9–10: *If our time has come, let us die bravely.* Having said many times before that victory depends on God rather than on numbers, Judas has to live by that maxim when the situation seems hopeless even to him. His courage in the face of battle for God's people never depends on assurances of victory: he is as willing to die for God's cause as to enjoy victory in it (see 3:59–60).

him. All Israel made great lamentation for him; they mourned many days and said,

21 "How is the mighty fallen,
     the savior of Israel!"

22Now the rest of the acts of Judas, and his wars and the brave deeds that he did, and his greatness, have not been recorded, but they were very many.

Jonathan Succeeds Judas

23 After the death of Judas, the renegades emerged in all parts of Israel; all the wrongdoers reappeared. 24In those days a very great famine occurred, and the country went over to their side. 25Bacchides chose the godless and put them in charge of the country. 26They made inquiry and searched for the friends of Judas, and brought them to Bacchides, who took vengeance on them and made sport of them. 27So there was great distress in Israel, such as had not been since the time that prophets ceased to appear among them.

28 Then all the friends of Judas assembled and said to Jonathan, 29"Since the death of your brother Judas there has been no one like him to go against our enemies and Bacchides, and to deal with those of our nation who hate us. 30Now therefore we have chosen you today to take his place as our ruler and leader, to fight our battle." 31So Jonathan accepted the leadership at that time in place of his brother Judas.

The Campaigns of Jonathan

32 When Bacchides learned of this, he tried to kill him. 33But Jonathan and his brother Simon and all who were with him heard of it, and they fled into the wilderness of Tekoa and camped by the water of the pool of Asphar. 34Bacchides found this out on the

sabbath day, and he with all his army crossed the Jordan.

35 So Jonathan *a* sent his brother as leader of the multitude and begged the Nabateans, who were his friends, for permission to store with them the great amount of baggage that they had. 36But the family of Jambri from Medeba came out and seized John and all that he had, and left with it.

37 After these things it was reported to Jonathan and his brother Simon, "The family of Jambri are celebrating a great wedding, and are conducting the bride, a daughter of one of the great nobles of Canaan, from Nadabath with a large escort." 38Remembering how their brother John had been killed, they went up and hid under cover of the mountain. 39They looked out and saw a tumultuous procession with a great amount of baggage; and the bridegroom came out with his friends and his brothers to meet them with tambourines and musicians and many weapons. 40Then they rushed on them from the ambush and began killing them. Many were wounded and fell, and the rest fled to the mountain; and the Jews *b* took all their goods. 41So the wedding was turned into mourning and the voice of their musicians into a funeral dirge. 42After they had fully avenged the blood of their brother, they returned to the marshes of the Jordan.

43 When Bacchides heard of this, he came with a large force on the sabbath day to the banks of the Jordan. 44And Jonathan said to those with him, "Let us get up now and fight for our lives, for today things are not as they were before. 45For look! the battle is in front of us and behind us; the water of the Jordan is on this side and on that, with marsh and

a Gk *he*   *b* Gk *they*

9:23–27 *the renegades emerged.* The rededication of the Temple was far from the end of the campaign. The People of God need to be prepared for the ebb and flow of setbacks and victories. Ultimate victory in the cause of God depends on the community's and its leaders' determination to keep pressing forward (9:28–31) rather than allow the most serious of setbacks to erode their commitment.

9:24 *a very great famine occurred.* Famine and want often drive people to cower before the domination system that controls supply (v 52) even against their moral judgment. This should lead us to consider how we can mobilize our resources to bring relief to God's people in their desperation, so that they are not pressed to betray their consciences or God's cause for bread.

thicket; there is no place to turn. [46]Cry out now to Heaven that you may be delivered from the hands of our enemies." [47]So the battle began, and Jonathan stretched out his hand to strike Bacchides, but he eluded him and went to the rear. [48]Then Jonathan and the men with him leaped into the Jordan and swam across to the other side, and the enemy[a] did not cross the Jordan to attack them. [49]And about one thousand of Bacchides' men fell that day.

Bacchides Builds Fortifications

50 Then Bacchides[b] returned to Jerusalem and built strong cities in Judea: the fortress in Jericho, and Emmaus, and Bethhoron, and Bethel, and Timnath, and[c] Pharathon, and Tephon, with high walls and gates and bars. [51]And he placed garrisons in them to harass Israel. [52]He also fortified the town of Beth-zur, and Gazara, and the citadel, and in them he put troops and stores of food. [53]And he took the sons of the leading men of the land as hostages and put them under guard in the citadel at Jerusalem.

54 In the one hundred and fifty-third year,[d] in the second month, Alcimus gave orders to tear down the wall of the inner court of the sanctuary. He tore down the work of the prophets! [55]But he only began to tear it down, for at that time Alcimus was stricken and his work was hindered; his mouth was stopped and he was paralyzed, so that he could no longer say a word or give commands concerning his house. [56]And Alcimus died at that time in great agony. [57]When Bacchides saw that Alcimus was dead, he returned to the king, and the land of Judah had rest for two years.

The End of the War

58 Then all the lawless plotted and said, "See! Jonathan and his men are living in quiet and confidence. So now let us bring Bac-

chides back, and he will capture them all in one night." [59]And they went and consulted with him. [60]He started to come with a large force, and secretly sent letters to all his allies in Judea, telling them to seize Jonathan and his men; but they were unable to do it, because their plan became known. [61]And Jonathan's men[a] seized about fifty of the men of the country who were leaders in this treachery, and killed them.

62 Then Jonathan with his men, and Simon, withdrew to Bethbasi in the wilderness; he rebuilt the parts of it that had been demolished, and they fortified it. [63]When Bacchides learned of this, he assembled all his forces, and sent orders to the men of Judea. [64]Then he came and encamped against Bethbasi; he fought against it for many days and made machines of war.

65 But Jonathan left his brother Simon in the town, while he went out into the country; and he went with only a few men. [66]He struck down Odomera and his kindred and the people of Phasiron in their tents. [67]Then he[e] began to attack and went into battle with his forces; and Simon and his men sallied out from the town and set fire to the machines of war. [68]They fought with Bacchides, and he was crushed by them. They pressed him very hard, for his plan and his expedition had been in vain. [69]So he was very angry at the renegades who had counseled him to come into the country, and he killed many of them. Then he decided to go back to his own land.

70 When Jonathan learned of this, he sent ambassadors to him to make peace with him and obtain release of the captives. [71]He agreed, and did as he said; and he swore to Jonathan[f] that he would not try to harm him as long as he lived. [72]He restored to him the

a Gk *they*   b Gk *he*   c Some authorities omit *and*   d 159 B.C.   e Other ancient authorities read *they*   f Gk *him*

9:54–56 *Alcimus was stricken.* Alcimus's fate illustrates the spiritual dangers of tearing down the temple of God (1 Cor 3:17) and not taking heed how one builds upon the foundation (1 Cor 3:10). His ill-advised renovations call us to discern "the work of the prophets" in ourselves, our families, and the broader community of faith (the Temple) and to treat one another as holy places, guarding against sacrilege and safeguarding the good work God has done in each person and congregation.

captives whom he had taken previously from the land of Judah; then he turned and went back to his own land, and did not come again into their territory. [73]Thus the sword ceased from Israel. Jonathan settled in Michmash and began to judge the people; and he destroyed the godless out of Israel.

Revolt of Alexander Epiphanes

10 In the one hundred sixtieth year[a] Alexander Epiphanes, son of Antiochus, landed and occupied Ptolemais. They welcomed him, and there he began to reign. [2]When King Demetrius heard of it, he assembled a very large army and marched out to meet him in battle. [3]Demetrius sent Jonathan a letter in peaceable words to honor him; [4]for he said to himself, "Let us act first to make peace with him[b] before he makes peace with Alexander against us, [5]for he will remember all the wrongs that we did to him and to his brothers and his nation." [6]So Demetrius[c] gave him authority to recruit troops, to equip them with arms, and to become his ally; and he commanded that the hostages in the citadel should be released to him.

7 Then Jonathan came to Jerusalem and read the letter in the hearing of all the people and of those in the citadel. [8]They were greatly alarmed when they heard that the king had given him authority to recruit troops. [9]But those in the citadel released the hostages to Jonathan, and he returned them to their parents.

10 And Jonathan took up residence in Jerusalem and began to rebuild and restore the city. [11]He directed those who were doing the work to build the walls and encircle Mount Zion with squared stones, for better fortification; and they did so.

12 Then the foreigners who were in the strongholds that Bacchides had built fled; [13]all of them left their places and went back to their own lands. [14]Only in Beth-zur did some remain who had forsaken the law and the commandments, for it served as a place of refuge.

15 Now King Alexander heard of all the promises that Demetrius had sent to Jonathan, and he heard of the battles that Jona-

than[c] and his brothers had fought, of the brave deeds that they had done, and of the troubles that they had endured. [16]So he said, "Shall we find another such man? Come now, we will make him our friend and ally." [17]And he wrote a letter and sent it to him, in the following words:

Jonathan Becomes High Priest

18 "King Alexander to his brother Jonathan, greetings. [19]We have heard about you, that you are a mighty warrior and worthy to be our friend. [20]And so we have appointed you today to be the high priest of your nation; you are to be called the king's Friend and you are to take our side and keep friendship with us." He also sent him a purple robe and a golden crown.

21 So Jonathan put on the sacred vestments in the seventh month of the one hundred sixtieth year,[d] at the festival of booths,[e] and he recruited troops and equipped them with arms in abundance. [22]When Demetrius heard of these things he was distressed and said, [23]"What is this that we have done? Alexander has gotten ahead of us in forming a friendship with the Jews to strengthen himself. [24]I also will write them words of encouragement and promise them honor and gifts, so that I may have their help." [25]So he sent a message to them in the following words:

A Letter from Demetrius to Jonathan

"King Demetrius to the nation of the Jews, greetings. [26]Since you have kept your agreement with us and have continued your friendship with us, and have not sided with our enemies, we have heard of it and rejoiced. [27]Now continue still to keep faith with us, and we will repay you with good for what you do for us. [28]We will grant you many immunities and give you gifts.

29 "I now free you and exempt all the Jews from payment of tribute and salt tax and crown levies, [30]and instead of collecting the third of the grain and the half of the fruit of the trees that I should receive, I release them from this day and henceforth. I will not col-

a 152 B.C.   *b* Gk *them*   *c* Gk *he*   *d* 152 B.C.
e Or *tabernacles*

lect them from the land of Judah or from the three districts added to it from Samaria and Galilee, from this day and for all time. 31Jerusalem and its environs, its tithes and its revenues, shall be holy and free from tax. 32I release also my control of the citadel in Jerusalem and give it to the high priest, so that he may station in it men of his own choice to guard it. 33And everyone of the Jews taken as a captive from the land of Judah into any part of my kingdom, I set free without payment; and let all officials cancel also the taxes on their livestock.

34 "All the festivals and sabbaths and new moons and appointed days, and the three days before a festival and the three after a festival—let them all be days of immunity and release for all the Jews who are in my kingdom. 35No one shall have authority to exact anything from them or annoy any of them about any matter.

36 "Let Jews be enrolled in the king's forces to the number of thirty thousand men, and let the maintenance be given them that is due to all the forces of the king. 37Let some of them be stationed in the great strongholds of the king, and let some of them be put in positions of trust in the kingdom. Let their officers and leaders be of their own number, and let them live by their own laws, just as the king has commanded in the land of Judah.

38 "As for the three districts that have been added to Judea from the country of Samaria, let them be annexed to Judea so that they may be considered to be under one ruler and obey no other authority than the high priest. 39Ptolemais and the land adjoining it I have given as a gift to the sanctuary in Jerusalem, to meet the necessary expenses of the sanctuary. 40I also grant fifteen thousand shekels of silver yearly out of the king's revenues from appropriate places. 41And all the additional funds that the government officials have not paid as they did in the first years,*a* they shall give from now on for the service of the temple.*b* 42Moreover, the five thousand shekels of silver that my officials*c* have received every year from the income of the services of the temple, this too is canceled, because it belongs to the priests who minister there. 43And all who take refuge at

the temple in Jerusalem, or in any of its precincts, because they owe money to the king or are in debt, let them be released and receive back all their property in my kingdom.

44 "Let the cost of rebuilding and restoring the structures of the sanctuary be paid from the revenues of the king. 45And let the cost of rebuilding the walls of Jerusalem and fortifying it all around, and the cost of rebuilding the walls in Judea, also be paid from the revenues of the king."

Death of Demetrius

46 When Jonathan and the people heard these words, they did not believe or accept them, because they remembered the great wrongs that Demetrius*d* had done in Israel and how much he had oppressed them. 47They favored Alexander, because he had been the first to speak peaceable words to them, and they remained his allies all his days.

48 Now King Alexander assembled large forces and encamped opposite Demetrius. 49The two kings met in battle, and the army of Demetrius fled, and Alexander*e* pursued him and defeated them. 50He pressed the battle strongly until the sun set, and on that day Demetrius fell.

Treaty of Ptolemy and Alexander

51 Then Alexander sent ambassadors to Ptolemy king of Egypt with the following message: 52"Since I have returned to my kingdom and have taken my seat on the throne of my ancestors, and established my rule—for I crushed Demetrius and gained control of our country; 53I met him in battle, and he and his army were crushed by us, and we have taken our seat on the throne of his kingdom— 54now therefore let us establish friendship with one another; give me now your daughter as my wife, and I will become your son-in-law, and will make gifts to you and to her in keeping with your position."

55 Ptolemy the king replied and said, "Happy was the day on which you returned

a Meaning of Gk uncertain   *b* Gk *house*
c Gk *they*   *d* Gk *he*   *e* Other ancient authorities read *Alexander fled, and Demetrius*

to the land of your ancestors and took your seat on the throne of their kingdom. ⁵⁶And now I will do for you as you wrote, but meet me at Ptolemais, so that we may see one another, and I will become your father-in-law, as you have said."

57 So Ptolemy set out from Egypt, he and his daughter Cleopatra, and came to Ptolemais in the one hundred sixty-second year.ᵃ ⁵⁸King Alexander met him, and Ptolemyᵇ gave him his daughter Cleopatra in marriage, and celebrated her wedding at Ptolemais with great pomp, as kings do.

59 Then King Alexander wrote to Jonathan to come and meet him. ⁶⁰So he went with pomp to Ptolemais and met the two kings; he gave them and their Friends silver and gold and many gifts, and found favor with them. ⁶¹A group of malcontents from Israel, renegades, gathered together against him to accuse him; but the king paid no attention to them. ⁶²The king gave orders to take off Jonathan's garments and to clothe him in purple, and they did so. ⁶³The king also seated him at his side; and he said to his officers, "Go out with him into the middle of the city and proclaim that no one is to bring charges against him about any matter, and let no one annoy him for any reason." ⁶⁴When his accusers saw the honor that was paid him, in accord with the proclamation, and saw him clothed in purple, they all fled. ⁶⁵Thus the king honored him and enrolled him among his chiefᶜ Friends, and made him general and governor of the province. ⁶⁶And Jonathan returned to Jerusalem in peace and gladness.

Apollonius Is Defeated by Jonathan

67 In the one hundred sixty-fifth yearᵈ Demetrius son of Demetrius came from Crete to the land of his ancestors. ⁶⁸When King Alexander heard of it, he was greatly distressed and returned to Antioch. ⁶⁹And Demetrius appointed Apollonius the governor of Coelesyria, and he assembled a large force and encamped against Jamnia. Then he sent the following message to the high priest Jonathan:

70 "You are the only one to rise up against us, and I have fallen into ridicule and disgrace because of you. Why do you assume authority against us in the hill country? ⁷¹If you now have confidence in your forces, come down to the plain to meet us, and let us match strength with each other there, for I have with me the power of the cities. ⁷²Ask and learn who I am and who the others are that are helping us. People will tell you that you cannot stand before us, for your ancestors were twice put to flight in their own land. ⁷³And now you will not be able to withstand my cavalry and such an army in the plain, where there is no stone or pebble, or place to flee."

74 When Jonathan heard the words of Apollonius, his spirit was aroused. He chose ten thousand men and set out from Jerusalem, and his brother Simon met him to help him. ⁷⁵He encamped before Joppa, but the people of the city closed its gates, for Apollonius had a garrison in Joppa. ⁷⁶So they fought against it, and the people of the city became afraid and opened the gates, and Jonathan gained possession of Joppa.

77 When Apollonius heard of it, he mustered three thousand cavalry and a large army, and went to Azotus as though he were going farther. At the same time he advanced into the plain, for he had a large troop of cav-

ᵃ 150 B.C.   ᵇ Gk *he*   ᶜ Gk *first*   ᵈ 147 B.C.

10:59–66 *Then King Alexander wrote to Jonathan.* Without sacrificing the covenant between Israel and God, Jonathan enjoyed more than the "renegades" of 1:11–15 ever hoped to gain by forsaking the covenant. The path of faithfulness may not always preclude enjoyment of gain—but we are called always to make the path of faithfulness, and not the enjoyment of gain, the object of our intentions and ambitions.

10:70 *You are the only one.* God frequently asks his representatives to take a bold, uncomfortable, exposed, and often lonely stand against the powers that be. Standing as God directs makes us an affront to those powers and their self-assurance; our continued existence becomes a mark of shame against them. Thus the conflict begins anew, as it did for Jonathan.

alry and put confidence in it. [78]Jonathan[a] pursued him to Azotus, and the armies engaged in battle. [79]Now Apollonius had secretly left a thousand cavalry behind them. [80]Jonathan learned that there was an ambush behind him, for they surrounded his army and shot arrows at his men from early morning until late afternoon. [81]But his men stood fast, as Jonathan had commanded, and the enemy's[b] horses grew tired.

82 Then Simon brought forward his force and engaged the phalanx in battle (for the cavalry was exhausted); they were overwhelmed by him and fled, [83]and the cavalry was dispersed in the plain. They fled to Azotus and entered Beth-dagon, the temple of their idol, for safety. [84]But Jonathan burned Azotus and the surrounding towns and plundered them; and the temple of Dagon, and those who had taken refuge in it, he burned with fire. [85]The number of those who fell by the sword, with those burned alive, came to eight thousand.

86 Then Jonathan left there and encamped against Askalon, and the people of the city came out to meet him with great pomp.

87 He and those with him then returned to Jerusalem with a large amount of booty. [88]When King Alexander heard of these things, he honored Jonathan still more; [89]and he sent to him a golden buckle, such as it is the custom to give to the King's Kinsmen. He also gave him Ekron and all its environs as his possession.

Ptolemy Invades Syria

11 Then the king of Egypt gathered great forces, like the sand by the seashore, and many ships; and he tried to get possession of Alexander's kingdom by trickery and add it to his own kingdom. [2]He set out for Syria with peaceable words, and the people of the towns opened their gates to him and went to meet him, for King Alexander had commanded them to meet him, since he was Alexander's[c] father-in-law. [3]But when Ptolemy entered the towns he stationed forces as a garrison in each town.

4 When he[d] approached Azotus, they showed him the burnt-out temple of Dagon, and Azotus and its suburbs destroyed, and the corpses lying about, and the charred bodies of those whom Jonathan[a] had burned in the war, for they had piled them in heaps along his route. [5]They also told the king what Jonathan had done, to throw blame on him; but the king kept silent. [6]Jonathan met the king at Joppa with pomp, and they greeted one another and spent the night there. [7]And Jonathan went with the king as far as the river called Eleutherus; then he returned to Jerusalem.

8 So King Ptolemy gained control of the coastal cities as far as Seleucia by the sea, and he kept devising wicked designs against Alexander. [9]He sent envoys to King Demetrius, saying, "Come, let us make a covenant with each other, and I will give you in marriage my daughter who was Alexander's wife, and you shall reign over your father's kingdom. [10]I now regret that I gave him my daughter, for he has tried to kill me." [11]He threw blame on Alexander[e] because he coveted his kingdom. [12]So he took his daughter away from him and gave her to Demetrius. He was estranged from Alexander, and their enmity became manifest.

13 Then Ptolemy entered Antioch and put on the crown of Asia. Thus he put two crowns on his head, the crown of Egypt and that of Asia. [14]Now King Alexander was in Cilicia at that time, because the people of that region were in revolt. [15]When Alexander heard of it, he came against him in battle. Ptolemy

a Gk he   b Gk their   c Gk his   d Other ancient authorities read they   e Gk him

---

11:8–12 *he kept devising wicked designs against Alexander.* At many points, the gentile players model the values of the "anticommunity," the strategies that erode and betray community, and thus can help us see more clearly the brokenness in human community that God wants to overcome and heal. Demetrius put a higher value on securing the throne than the lives of kin (7:1–4). Here, Ptolemy uses marriage to his daughter as a political tool. Ambition and desire for power are valued more highly than family ties, with the result that these families deprive themselves of the constant love and support available in the family.

marched out and met him with a strong force, and put him to flight. ¹⁶So Alexander fled into Arabia to find protection there, and King Ptolemy was triumphant. ¹⁷Zabdiel the Arab cut off the head of Alexander and sent it to Ptolemy. ¹⁸But King Ptolemy died three days later, and his troops in the strongholds were killed by the inhabitants of the strongholds. ¹⁹So Demetrius became king in the one hundred sixty-seventh year. *a*

Jonathan's Diplomacy

20 In those days Jonathan assembled the Judeans to attack the citadel in Jerusalem, and he built many engines of war to use against it. ²¹But certain renegades who hated their nation went to the king and reported to him that Jonathan was besieging the citadel. ²²When he heard this he was angry, and as soon as he heard it he set out and came to Ptolemais; and he wrote Jonathan not to continue the siege, but to meet him for a conference at Ptolemais as quickly as possible.

23 When Jonathan heard this, he gave orders to continue the siege. He chose some of the elders of Israel and some of the priests, and put himself in danger, ²⁴for he went to the king at Ptolemais, taking silver and gold and clothing and numerous other gifts. And he won his favor. ²⁵Although certain renegades of his nation kept making complaints against him, ²⁶the king treated him as his predecessors had treated him; he exalted him in the presence of all his Friends. ²⁷He confirmed him in the high priesthood and in as many other honors as he had formerly had, and caused him to be reckoned among his chief *b* Friends. ²⁸Then Jonathan asked the king to free Judea and the three districts of Samaria *c* from tribute, and promised him three hundred talents. ²⁹The king consented, and wrote a letter to Jonathan about all these things; its contents were as follows:

30 "King Demetrius to his brother Jonathan and to the nation of the Jews, greetings. ³¹This copy of the letter that we wrote concerning you to our kinsman Lasthenes we have written to you also, so that you may know what it says. ³²'King Demetrius to his father Lasthenes, greetings. ³³We have determined to do good to the nation of the Jews, who are our friends and fulfill their obligations to us, because of the goodwill they show toward us. ³⁴We have confirmed as their possession both the territory of Judea and the three districts of Aphairema and Lydda and Rathamin; the latter, with all the region bordering them, were added to Judea from Samaria. To all those who offer sacrifice in Jerusalem we have granted release from *d* the royal taxes that the king formerly received from them each year, from the crops of the land and the fruit of the trees. ³⁵And the other payments henceforth due to us of the tithes, and the taxes due to us, and the salt pits and the crown taxes due to us—from all these we shall grant them release. ³⁶And not one of these grants shall be canceled from this time on forever. ³⁷Now therefore take care to make a copy of this, and let it be given to Jonathan and put up in a conspicuous place on the holy mountain.' "

The Intrigue of Trypho

38 When King Demetrius saw that the land was quiet before him and that there was no opposition to him, he dismissed all his troops, all of them to their own homes, except the foreign troops that he had recruited from the islands of the nations. So all the troops who had served under his predecessors hated him. ³⁹A certain Trypho had formerly been one of Alexander's supporters; he saw

a 145 B.C.   *b* Gk *first*   *c* Cn: Gk *the three districts and Samaria*   *d* Or *Samaria, for all those who offer sacrifice in Jerusalem, in place of*

11:38–40 *A certain Trypho had formerly been one of Alexander's supporters.* When one finally secures one's place in a competitive system, someone else emerges, watching for a sign of weakness and an opportunity to deprive one of his or her position and prosperity. There can be no peace as long as people act as rivals and enemies rather than as kin who cooperate reliably for one another's good. Corporations are beginning to learn what God has been trying to teach for millennia: the doctrine of the survival of the fittest individual is not the best policy for a collective group, since it is extremely stressful, alienating, and ultimately wasteful.

that all the troops were grumbling against Demetrius. So he went to Imalkue the Arab, who was bringing up Antiochus, the young son of Alexander, [40]and insistently urged him to hand Antiochus[a] over to him, to become king in place of his father. He also reported to Imalkue[a] what Demetrius had done and told of the hatred that the troops of Demetrius[b] had for him; and he stayed there many days.

41 Now Jonathan sent to King Demetrius the request that he remove the troops of the citadel from Jerusalem, and the troops in the strongholds; for they kept fighting against Israel. [42]And Demetrius sent this message back to Jonathan: "Not only will I do these things for you and your nation, but I will confer great honor on you and your nation, if I find an opportunity. [43]Now then you will do well to send me men who will help me, for all my troops have revolted." [44]So Jonathan sent three thousand stalwart men to him at Antioch, and when they came to the king, the king rejoiced at their arrival.

45 Then the people of the city assembled within the city, to the number of a hundred and twenty thousand, and they wanted to kill the king. [46]But the king fled into the palace. Then the people of the city seized the main streets of the city and began to fight. [47]So the king called the Jews to his aid, and they all rallied around him and then spread out through the city; and they killed on that day about one hundred thousand. [48]They set fire to the city and seized a large amount of spoil on that day, and saved the king. [49]When the people of the city saw that the Jews had gained control of the city as they pleased, their courage failed and they cried out to the king with this entreaty: [50]"Grant us peace, and make the Jews stop fighting against us and our city." [51]And they threw down their arms and made peace. So the Jews gained glory in the sight of the king and of all the people in his kingdom, and they returned to Jerusalem with a large amount of spoil.

52 So King Demetrius sat on the throne of his kingdom, and the land was quiet before him. [53]But he broke his word about all that he had promised; he became estranged from Jonathan and did not repay the favors that

Jonathan[c] had done him, but treated him very harshly.

Trypho Seizes Power

54 After this Trypho returned, and with him the young boy Antiochus who began to reign and put on the crown. [55]All the troops that Demetrius had discharged gathered around him; they fought against Demetrius,[a] and he fled and was routed. [56]Trypho captured the elephants[d] and gained control of Antioch. [57]Then the young Antiochus wrote to Jonathan, saying, "I confirm you in the high priesthood and set you over the four districts and make you one of the king's Friends." [58]He also sent him gold plates and a table service, and granted him the right to drink from gold cups and dress in purple and wear a gold buckle. [59]He appointed Jonathan's[e] brother Simon governor from the Ladder of Tyre to the borders of Egypt.

Campaigns of Jonathan and Simon

60 Then Jonathan set out and traveled beyond the river and among the towns, and all the army of Syria gathered to him as allies. When he came to Askalon, the people of the city met him and paid him honor. [61]From there he went to Gaza, but the people of Gaza shut him out. So he besieged it and burned its suburbs with fire and plundered them. [62]Then the people of Gaza pleaded with Jonathan, and he made peace with them, and took the sons of their rulers as hostages and sent them to Jerusalem. And he passed through the country as far as Damascus.

63 Then Jonathan heard that the officers of Demetrius had come to Kadesh in Galilee with a large army, intending to remove him from office. [64]He went to meet them, but left his brother Simon in the country. [65]Simon encamped before Beth-zur and fought against it for many days and hemmed it in. [66]Then they asked him to grant them terms of peace, and he did so. He removed them from there, took possession of the town, and set a garrison over it.

67 Jonathan and his army encamped by the waters of Gennesaret. Early in the morn-

a Gk him   b Gk his troops   c Gk he
d Gk animals   e Gk his

ing they marched to the plain of Hazor, 68and there in the plain the army of the foreigners met him; they had set an ambush against him in the mountains, but they themselves met him face to face. 69Then the men in ambush emerged from their places and joined battle. 70All the men with Jonathan fled; not one of them was left except Mattathias son of Absalom and Judas son of Chalphi, commanders of the forces of the army. 71Jonathan tore his clothes, put dust on his head, and prayed. 72Then he turned back to the battle against the enemy*a* and routed them, and they fled. 73When his men who were fleeing saw this, they returned to him and joined him in the pursuit as far as Kadesh, to their camp, and there they encamped. 74As many as three thousand of the foreigners fell that day. And Jonathan returned to Jerusalem.

Alliances with Rome and Sparta

12 Now when Jonathan saw that the time was favorable for him, he chose men and sent them to Rome to confirm and renew the friendship with them. 2He also sent letters to the same effect to the Spartans and to other places. 3So they went to Rome and entered the senate chamber and said, "The high priest Jonathan and the Jewish nation have sent us to renew the former friendship and alliance with them." 4And the Romans*b* gave them letters to the people in every place, asking them to provide for the envoys*a* safe conduct to the land of Judah.

5 This is a copy of the letter that Jonathan wrote to the Spartans: 6"The high priest Jonathan, the senate of the nation, the priests, and the rest of the Jewish people to their brothers the Spartans, greetings. 7Already in time past a letter was sent to the high priest Onias from Arius,*c* who was king among you, stating that you are our brothers, as the appended copy shows. 8Onias welcomed the envoy with honor, and received the letter, which contained a clear declaration of alliance and friendship. 9Therefore, though we have no need of these things, since we have as encouragement the holy books that

a Gk *them*　　*b* Gk *they*　　*c* Vg Compare verse 20: Gk *Darius*

11:71 *Jonathan tore his clothes.* Like Judas in 9:10, Jonathan is brought back to the place where he cannot put his trust in his army, his former victories, or his titles, but must rediscover the ground of all his confidence in God alone. Part of the rhythm of spiritual formation involves returning to this point again and again in prayer and humility before God, so that we never lose sight of our Rock and only Redeemer. It is significant that Jonathan is flanked by a Mattathias and a Judas—loyal friends on whom he can rely in a time of spiritual stress, and also reminders of Jonathan's father and brother, who provide examples of the way forward.

12:1–23 *he chose men and sent them to Rome.* The treaties and letters in this passage are laced with two important themes. First, Jonathan looks to God for help and encouragement, not to political alliances. Scripture provides encouragement in the midst of "many trials and many wars" (v 13), for in these texts we read of the Ally whose purposes are never ultimately thwarted, whose reliability is beyond question. We discern that Ally's purposes in the

present and, in fact, make ourselves allies with God in his cause rather than the reverse. Jonathan reminds us that God is active and real, as much as any human ally (vv 14–15). Second, these letters display a willingness to redefine "kinship" beyond the ethnic lines defining Israel by looking back to Abraham, the father of many nations (v 21). Paul will also look to Abraham as the one in whom Gentiles and Jews have equal place in the family of God (Gal 3:6–29), as many as join themselves to the "offspring," Christ, who is heir to Abraham's promise. God is the one to determine the boundaries of God's family, not human beings. Within those boundaries, we are being shaped by God to act as family to one another by acts of love and service, by constant vigilance in prayer (v 11), and through the sharing of possessions (the import of v 23). As surprising as it is to see Jews and Spartans discussing their kinship, so surprising will it continue to be for us to discover the breadth of God's family in Christ and our mutual obligations toward one another.

are in our hands, 10we have undertaken to send to renew our family ties and friendship with you, so that we may not become estranged from you, for considerable time has passed since you sent your letter to us. 11We therefore remember you constantly on every occasion, both at our festivals and on other appropriate days, at the sacrifices that we offer and in our prayers, as it is right and proper to remember brothers. 12And we rejoice in your glory. 13But as for ourselves, many trials and many wars have encircled us; the kings around us have waged war against us. 14We were unwilling to annoy you and our other allies and friends with these wars, 15for we have the help that comes from Heaven for our aid, and so we were delivered from our enemies, and our enemies were humbled. 16We therefore have chosen Numenius son of Antiochus and Antipater son of Jason, and have sent them to Rome to renew our former friendship and alliance with them. 17We have commanded them to go also to you and greet you and deliver to you this letter from us concerning the renewal of our family ties. 18And now please send us a reply to this."

19 This is a copy of the letter that they sent to Onias: 20"King Arius of the Spartans, to the high priest Onias, greetings. 21It has been found in writing concerning the Spartans and the Jews that they are brothers and are of the family of Abraham. 22And now that we have learned this, please write us concerning your welfare; 23we on our part write to you that your livestock and your property belong to us, and ours belong to you. We therefore command that our envoys*a* report to you accordingly."

Further Campaigns of Jonathan and Simon

24 Now Jonathan heard that the commanders of Demetrius had returned, with a larger force than before, to wage war against

him. 25So he marched away from Jerusalem and met them in the region of Hamath, for he gave them no opportunity to invade his own country. 26He sent spies to their camp, and they returned and reported to him that the enemy*a* were being drawn up in formation to attack the Jews*b* by night. 27So when the sun had set, Jonathan commanded his troops to be alert and to keep their arms at hand so as to be ready all night for battle, and he stationed outposts around the camp. 28When the enemy heard that Jonathan and his troops were prepared for battle, they were afraid and were terrified at heart; so they kindled fires in their camp and withdrew. *c* 29But Jonathan and his troops did not know it until morning, for they saw the fires burning. 30Then Jonathan pursued them, but he did not overtake them, for they had crossed the Eleutherus river. 31So Jonathan turned aside against the Arabs who are called Zabadeans, and he crushed them and plundered them. 32Then he broke camp and went to Damascus, and marched through all that region.

33 Simon also went out and marched through the country as far as Askalon and the neighboring strongholds. He turned aside to Joppa and took it by surprise, 34for he had heard that they were ready to hand over the stronghold to those whom Demetrius had sent. And he stationed a garrison there to guard it.

35 When Jonathan returned he convened the elders of the people and planned with them to build strongholds in Judea, 36to build the walls of Jerusalem still higher, and to erect a high barrier between the citadel and the city to separate it from the city, in order to isolate it so that its garrison*d* could neither buy nor sell. 37So they gathered together

a Gk *they*   *b* Gk *them*   *c* Other ancient authorities omit *and withdrew*   *d* Gk *they*

12:35–38 *build the walls of Jerusalem still higher.* The repeated attention given to the fortifications of Jerusalem (see 4:60; 10:11; 13:10, 52) teaches two things. First, in any campaign, we must give constant attention to our fortifications for defense. Second, temporal fortifications are never completely secure, or

to rebuild the city; part of the wall on the valley to the east had fallen, and he repaired the section called Chaphenatha. 38Simon also built Adida in the Shephelah; he fortified it and installed gates with bolts.

Trypho Captures Jonathan

39 Then Trypho attempted to become king in Asia and put on the crown, and to raise his hand against King Antiochus. 40He feared that Jonathan might not permit him to do so, but might make war on him, so he kept seeking to seize and kill him, and he marched out and came to Beth-shan. 41Jonathan went out to meet him with forty thousand picked warriors, and he came to Beth-shan. 42When Trypho saw that he had come with a large army, he was afraid to raise his hand against him. 43So he received him with honor and commended him to all his Friends, and he gave him gifts and commanded his Friends and his troops to obey him as they would himself. 44Then he said to Jonathan, "Why have you put all these people to so much trouble when we are not at war? 45Dismiss them now to their homes and choose for yourself a few men to stay with you, and come with me to Ptolemais. I will hand it over to you as well as the other strongholds and the remaining troops and all the officials, and will turn around and go home. For that is why I am here."

46 Jonathan*a* trusted him and did as he said; he sent away the troops, and they returned to the land of Judah. 47He kept with himself three thousand men, two thousand of whom he left in Galilee, while one thou-

sand accompanied him. 48But when Jonathan entered Ptolemais, the people of Ptolemais closed the gates and seized him, and they killed with the sword all who had entered with him.

49 Then Trypho sent troops and cavalry into Galilee and the Great Plain to destroy all Jonathan's soldiers. 50But they realized that Jonathan had been seized and had perished along with his men, and they encouraged one another and kept marching in close formation, ready for battle. 51When their pursuers saw that they would fight for their lives, they turned back. 52So they all reached the land of Judah safely, and they mourned for Jonathan and his companions and were in great fear; and all Israel mourned deeply. 53All the nations around them tried to destroy them, for they said, "They have no leader or helper. Now therefore let us make war on them and blot out the memory of them from humankind."

Simon Takes Command

13 Simon heard that Trypho had assembled a large army to invade the land of Judah and destroy it, 2and he saw that the people were trembling with fear. So he went up to Jerusalem, and gathering the people together 3he encouraged them, saying to them, "You yourselves know what great things my brothers and I and the house of my father have done for the laws and the sanctuary; you know also the wars and the difficulties that my brothers and I have seen. 4By

a Gk *he*

---

else there would not be that constant nagging sense that we ought always to be shoring them up somehow (more resources, more energy, more insulation). For this reason, the People of God began seriously to look at God as their fortress (e.g., Pss 18:2; 31:2–3; 59:9, 16–17; 61:3; 71:3; 91:2). God is a far more adequate tower of defense than the imaginary fortifications the rich think they have in their wealth, for example (Prov 18:10–11). Through prayer, attention to the Scriptures, hearing God's promises, and leaning on God's presence, we find the only

adequate fortifications against the assaults of the world, the flesh, and the devil.

12:53 *They have no leader.* "Interregnum" periods, times without a "leader" (*archegos*), are especially dangerous times (see also 9:21–27), since the people are easily thrown into confusion. God has provided for his people in Christ, however, a leader (*archegos,* Acts 3:15; 5:31) who will never leave his people without guidance, empowerment, and vision. We are challenged thus to keep gathering around our leader in prayer and collective worship, so as to remain clear about our "marching orders."

reason of this all my brothers have perished for the sake of Israel, and I alone am left. [5]And now, far be it from me to spare my life in any time of distress, for I am not better than my brothers. [6]But I will avenge my nation and the sanctuary and your wives and children, for all the nations have gathered together out of hatred to destroy us."

7 The spirit of the people was rekindled when they heard these words, [8]and they answered in a loud voice, "You are our leader in place of Judas and your brother Jonathan. [9]Fight our battles, and all that you say to us we will do." [10]So he assembled all the warriors and hurried to complete the walls of Jerusalem, and he fortified it on every side. [11]He sent Jonathan son of Absalom to Joppa, and with him a considerable army; he drove out its occupants and remained there.

Deceit and Treachery of Trypho

12 Then Trypho left Ptolemais with a large army to invade the land of Judah, and Jonathan was with him under guard. [13]Simon encamped in Adida, facing the plain. [14]Trypho learned that Simon had risen up in place of his brother Jonathan, and that he was about to join battle with him, so he sent envoys to him and said, [15]"It is for the money that your brother Jonathan owed the royal treasury, in connection with the offices he held, that we are detaining him. [16]Send now one hundred talents of silver and two of his sons as hostages, so that when released he will not revolt against us, and we will release him."

17 Simon knew that they were speaking deceitfully to him, but he sent to get the money and the sons, so that he would not arouse great hostility among the people, who might say, [18]"It was because Simon[a] did not send him the money and the sons, that Jonathan[b] perished." [19]So he sent the sons and the hundred talents, but Trypho[b] broke his word and did not release Jonathan.

20 After this Trypho came to invade the country and destroy it, and he circled around by the way to Adora. But Simon and his army kept marching along opposite him to every place he went. [21]Now the men in the citadel kept sending envoys to Trypho urging him to come to them by way of the wilderness and to send them food. [22]So Trypho got all his cavalry ready to go, but that night a very heavy snow fell, and he did not go because of the snow. He marched off and went into the land of Gilead. [23]When he approached Baskama, he killed Jonathan, and he was buried there. [24]Then Trypho turned and went back to his own land.

Jonathan's Tomb

25 Simon sent and took the bones of his brother Jonathan, and buried him in Modein, the city of his ancestors. [26]All Israel bewailed him with great lamentation, and mourned

a Gk I   b Gk he

13:3–5 *far be it from me to spare my life in any time of distress.* Simon remains committed to labor on in the campaign fought by his father and brothers in the pursuit of the wholeness and peace of the People of God. His noble stance challenges us to consider ways in which God is inviting us to participate more fully and faithfully in the campaigns waged by our sisters and brothers and mothers and fathers in the faith, and to find our strength and vision in solidarity with them. We need to study closely the lives of men and women of faith who have laid down their lives for the sake of God's people, serving the cause of justice and peace, witnessing prophetically to ungodliness and injustice, and servicing the needs of the weak, in order that we may remain alert to ways in which God will call us to do likewise.

13:17–19 *Simon knew that they were speaking deceitfully to him.* How important it is not to give the people whom we would reach for God occasion to doubt our sincerity or our motives! How often the enemy uses suspicions of impropriety to undermine great works of God in the community of faith! Simon was willing to pay a ransom he knew would never be honored just to keep his own integrity above question and thus to preserve the unity and strength of God's people. Integrity is the only "credit rating" we have when it comes to witnessing, to nurturing the People of God, to being able and authorized to stand up for God in the community of faith.

for him many days. ²⁷And Simon built a monument over the tomb of his father and his brothers; he made it high so that it might be seen, with polished stone at the front and back. ²⁸He also erected seven pyramids, opposite one another, for his father and mother and four brothers. ²⁹For the pyramids ᵃ he devised an elaborate setting, erecting about them great columns, and on the columns he put suits of armor for a permanent memorial, and beside the suits of armor he carved ships, so that they could be seen by all who sail the sea. ³⁰This is the tomb that he built in Modein; it remains to this day.

Judea Gains Independence

31 Trypho dealt treacherously with the young King Antiochus; he killed him ³²and became king in his place, putting on the crown of Asia; and he brought great calamity on the land. ³³But Simon built up the strongholds of Judea and walled them all around, with high towers and great walls and gates and bolts, and he stored food in the strongholds. ³⁴Simon also chose emissaries and sent them to King Demetrius with a request to grant relief to the country, for all that Trypho did was to plunder. ³⁵King Demetrius sent him a favorable reply to this request, and wrote him a letter as follows, ³⁶"King Demetrius to Simon, the high priest and friend of kings, and to the elders and nation of the Jews, greetings. ³⁷We have received the gold crown and the palm branch that you ᵇ sent, and we are ready to make a general peace with you and to write to our officials to grant you release from tribute. ³⁸All the grants that we have made to you remain valid, and let the strongholds that you have built be your possession. ³⁹We pardon any errors and offenses committed to this day, and cancel the crown tax that you owe; and whatever other tax has been collected in Jerusalem shall be collected no longer. ⁴⁰And if any of you are qualified to be enrolled in our bodyguard, ᶜ let them be enrolled, and let there be peace between us."

41 In the one hundred seventieth year ᵈ the yoke of the Gentiles was removed from Israel, ⁴²and the people began to write in their documents and contracts, "In the first year of Simon the great high priest and commander and leader of the Jews."

The Capture of Gazara by Simon

43 In those days Simon ᵉ encamped against Gazara ᶠ and surrounded it with troops. He made a siege engine, brought it up to the city, and battered and captured one tower. ⁴⁴The men in the siege engine leaped out into the city, and a great tumult arose in the city. ⁴⁵The men in the city, with their wives and children, went up on the wall with their clothes torn, and they cried out with a loud voice, asking Simon to make peace with them; ⁴⁶they said, "Do not treat us according to our wicked acts but according to your mercy." ⁴⁷So Simon reached an agreement with them and stopped fighting against them. But

---

a Gk For these   b The word you in verses 37-40 is plural   c Or court   d 142 B.C.   e Gk he   f Cn: Gk Gaza

---

13:25–30 Simon built a monument. People might criticize Simon's erection of the monuments as a wasteful employment of a war-torn country's resources and as part of a self-serving political agenda. But the text suggests that God's people need to remain mindful of those who have embodied God's values, whose memory provides guideposts pointing us to holiness, righteousness, and the nobility of walking with God no matter where that leads. Our forward-looking culture jeopardizes our own connectedness with the vision, the example, and the resources of our forerunners in this race of faith, but Scripture calls us to linger over their headstones, remember their example, and walk in their paths (see Heb 11:1–12:3; 13:7).

13:41–42 the people began to write in their documents. The Judeans marked their discovery of a new freedom with a new system of dating. This kept them in touch with the power of that turning point and kept them mindful of the new trajectory on which God had set them, so that they might not wander back into captivity. Many evangelical Christians talk about the date on which they were "born again" or "met Jesus" to the same effect, wanting to remember and remain steady in a new trajectory.

he expelled them from the city and cleansed the houses in which the idols were located, and then entered it with hymns and praise. [48]He removed all uncleanness from it, and settled in it those who observed the law. He also strengthened its fortifications and built in it a house for himself.

Simon Regains the Citadel at Jerusalem

49 Those who were in the citadel at Jerusalem were prevented from going in and out to buy and sell in the country. So they were very hungry, and many of them perished from famine. [50]Then they cried to Simon to make peace with them, and he did so. But he expelled them from there and cleansed the citadel from its pollutions. [51]On the twenty-third day of the second month, in the one hundred seventy-first year,[a] the Jews[b] entered it with praise and palm branches, and with harps and cymbals and stringed instruments, and with hymns and songs, because a great enemy had been crushed and removed from Israel. [52]Simon[c] decreed that every year they should celebrate this day with rejoicing. He strengthened the fortifications of the temple hill alongside the citadel, and he and his men lived there. [53]Simon saw that his son John had reached manhood, and so he made him commander of all the forces; and he lived at Gazara.

Capture of Demetrius

14 In the one hundred seventy-second year[d] King Demetrius assembled his forces and marched into Media to obtain help, so that he could make war against Trypho. [2]When King Arsaces of Persia and Media heard that Demetrius had invaded his territory, he sent one of his generals to take him alive. [3]The general[c] went and defeated the army of Demetrius, and seized him and took him to Arsaces, who put him under guard.

Eulogy of Simon

4 The land[e] had rest all the days of Simon.
  He sought the good of his nation;
 his rule was pleasing to them,
    as was the honor shown him, all his days.
5 To crown all his honors he took Joppa for a harbor,
    and opened a way to the isles of the sea.
6 He extended the borders of his nation,
    and gained full control of the country.
7 He gathered a host of captives;
  he ruled over Gazara and Beth-zur and the citadel,
    and he removed its uncleanness from it;
    and there was none to oppose him.

a 141 B.C.   b Gk they   c Gk He   d 140 B.C.
e Other ancient authorities add of Judah

13:49–51 *Those who were in the citadel.* The "citadel" was the garrison of gentile and heterodox Jewish soldiers initially planted under Antiochus IV (1:33–34), the last stronghold of domination by the ungodly that plagued Jerusalem long past Judas's rededication of the Temple (see 6:18–21; 11:20, 41; 13:21). Identifying, besieging, taking, and cleansing strongholds continues to be part of the calling of Christian disciples (see 2 Cor 10:3–5), wherever the worldly mind-set still dominates aspects of Christian community and mission, constraining our freedom in Christ and sapping our collective strength at critical moments.
  14:4–15 *The land had rest all the days of Simon.* This poetic celebration of Simon's reign combines many images of the quality of life God

wants for his people. It is painted with Old Testament phrases that make this poem wax messianic. "Rest" from violence (see 1 Kings 5:4), the safe pursuit of agriculture and the provision of food for all (see Ezek 34:27; Zech 8:12), the peaceful enjoyment of community (see Zech 8:4–5), and the connection of every family with the means of production necessary to sustain life (Mic 4:4) are persistent snapshots of God's vision for the whole human community. The vision calls us to seek out and support the ways in which the vision is being realized, but also to inquire into the places where this vision is being resisted or betrayed. This would help us discover where God would move us to bear witness and to take up his cause on behalf of his people in every place.

8 They tilled their land in peace;
   the ground gave its increase,
   and the trees of the plains their fruit.
9 Old men sat in the streets;
   they all talked together of good
      things,
   and the youths put on splendid
      military attire.
10 He supplied the towns with food,
   and furnished them with the means
      of defense,
   until his renown spread to the ends of
      the earth.
11 He established peace in the land,
   and Israel rejoiced with great joy.
12 All the people sat under their own vines
      and fig trees,
   and there was none to make them
      afraid.
13 No one was left in the land to fight
      them,
   and the kings were crushed in those
      days.
14 He gave help to all the humble among
      his people;
   he sought out the law,
   and did away with all the renegades
      and outlaws.
15 He made the sanctuary glorious,
   and added to the vessels of the
      sanctuary.

Diplomacy with Rome and Sparta

16 It was heard in Rome, and as far away as
Sparta, that Jonathan had died, and they
were deeply grieved. 17 When they heard that
his brother Simon had become high priest
in his stead, and that he was ruling over the
country and the towns in it, 18 they wrote to
him on bronze tablets to renew with him the
friendship and alliance that they had established with his brothers Judas and Jonathan.
19 And these were read before the assembly
in Jerusalem.

20 This is a copy of the letter that the Spartans sent:

"The rulers and the city of the Spartans to
the high priest Simon and to the elders and
the priests and the rest of the Jewish people,
our brothers, greetings. 21 The envoys who
were sent to our people have told us about
your glory and honor, and we rejoiced at
their coming. 22 We have recorded what they
said in our public decrees, as follows, 'Numenius son of Antiochus and Antipater son
of Jason, envoys of the Jews, have come to us
to renew their friendship with us. 23 It has
pleased our people to receive these men with
honor and to put a copy of their words in
the public archives, so that the people of the
Spartans may have a record of them. And
they have sent a copy of this to the high priest
Simon.' "

24 After this Simon sent Numenius to
Rome with a large gold shield weighing one
thousand minas, to confirm the alliance with
the Romans. *a*

Official Honors for Simon

25 When the people heard these things
they said, "How shall we thank Simon and his
sons? 26 For he and his brothers and the house
of his father have stood firm; they have
fought and repulsed Israel's enemies and established its freedom." 27 So they made a
record on bronze tablets and put it on pillars
on Mount Zion.

This is a copy of what they wrote: "On the
eighteenth day of Elul, in the one hundred
seventy-second year, *b* which is the third

a Gk *them*   *b* 140 B.C.

14:25–49 *How shall we thank Simon and his
sons?* The public decrees of honors and powers
for Simon reflect a proper response to the benefactions of Simon and his family on behalf of the
whole people. This is a familiar dynamic in the
ancient world, where those who bring great
benefits are met with great gratitude in the form
of honor, loyalty, and service. Similar questions
are asked, and "decrees" made, in regard to
God's benefactions, as in Ps 116:12–19. The
response to Simon models for us, as from a
lesser case to a greater one, what kind of honors
we should confer upon Christ for all his benefits,
and how we should enact that response of
gratitude by giving up ourselves to his service,
thus acknowledging the claim over our whole
lives that is his by right (see 2 Cor 5:15).

year of the great high priest Simon, [28]in Asaramel,[a] in the great assembly of the priests and the people and the rulers of the nation and the elders of the country, the following was proclaimed to us:

29 "Since wars often occurred in the country, Simon son of Mattathias, a priest of the sons[b] of Joarib, and his brothers, exposed themselves to danger and resisted the enemies of their nation, in order that their sanctuary and the law might be preserved; and they brought great glory to their nation. [30]Jonathan rallied the[c] nation, became their high priest, and was gathered to his people. [31]When their enemies decided to invade their country and lay hands on their sanctuary, [32]then Simon rose up and fought for his nation. He spent great sums of his own money; he armed the soldiers of his nation and paid them wages. [33]He fortified the towns of Judea, and Beth-zur on the borders of Judea, where formerly the arms of the enemy had been stored, and he placed there a garrison of Jews. [34]He also fortified Joppa, which is by the sea, and Gazara, which is on the borders of Azotus, where the enemy formerly lived. He settled Jews there, and provided in those towns[d] whatever was necessary for their restoration.

35 "The people saw Simon's faithfulness[e] and the glory that he had resolved to win for his nation, and they made him their leader and high priest, because he had done all these things and because of the justice and loyalty that he had maintained toward his nation. He sought in every way to exalt his people. [36]In his days things prospered in his hands, so that the Gentiles were put out of the[c] country, as were also those in the city of David in Jerusalem, who had built themselves a citadel from which they used to sally forth and defile the environs of the sanctuary, doing great damage to its purity. [37]He settled Jews in it and fortified it for the safety of the country and of the city, and built the walls of Jerusalem higher.

38 "In view of these things King Demetrius confirmed him in the high priesthood, [39]made him one of his Friends, and paid him high honors. [40]For he had heard that the Jews were addressed by the Romans as friends and allies and brothers, and that the Romans[f] had received the envoys of Simon with honor.

41 "The Jews and their priests have resolved that Simon should be their leader and high priest forever, until a trustworthy prophet should arise, [42]and that he should be governor over them and that he should take charge of the sanctuary and appoint officials over its tasks and over the country and the weapons and the strongholds, and that he should take charge of the sanctuary, [43]and that he should be obeyed by all, and that all contracts in the country should be written in his name, and that he should be clothed in purple and wear gold.

44 "None of the people or priests shall be permitted to nullify any of these decisions or to oppose what he says, or to convene an assembly in the country without his permission, or to be clothed in purple or put on a gold buckle. [45]Whoever acts contrary to these decisions or rejects any of them shall be liable to punishment."

46 All the people agreed to grant Simon the right to act in accordance with these decisions. [47]So Simon accepted and agreed to be high priest, to be commander and ethnarch of the Jews and priests, and to be protector of them all.[g] [48]And they gave orders to inscribe this decree on bronze tablets, to put them up in a conspicuous place in the precincts of the sanctuary, [49]and to deposit copies of them in the treasury, so that Simon and his sons might have them.

Letter of Antiochus VII

15 Antiochus, son of King Demetrius, sent a letter from the islands of the sea to Simon, the priest and ethnarch of the Jews, and to all the nation; [2]its contents were as follows: "King Antiochus to Simon the high priest and ethnarch and to the nation of the Jews, greetings. [3]Whereas certain scoundrels have gained control of the kingdom of our ancestors, and I intend to lay claim to the

---

a This word resembles the Hebrew words for *the court of the people of God* or *the prince of the people of God*   *b* Meaning of Gk uncertain   *c* Gk *their*   *d* Gk *them*   *e* Other ancient authorities read *conduct*   *f* Gk *they*   *g* Or *to preside over them all*

kingdom so that I may restore it as it formerly was, and have recruited a host of mercenary troops and have equipped warships, [4]and intend to make a landing in the country so that I may proceed against those who have destroyed our country and those who have devastated many cities in my kingdom, [5]now therefore I confirm to you all the tax remissions that the kings before me have granted you, and a release from all the other payments from which they have released you. [6]I permit you to mint your own coinage as money for your country, [7]and I grant freedom to Jerusalem and the sanctuary. All the weapons that you have prepared and the strongholds that you have built and now hold shall remain yours. [8]Every debt you owe to the royal treasury and any such future debts shall be canceled for you from henceforth and for all time. [9]When we gain control of our kingdom, we will bestow great honor on you and your nation and the temple, so that your glory will become manifest in all the earth."

10 In the one hundred seventy-fourth year[a] Antiochus set out and invaded the land of his ancestors. All the troops rallied to him, so that there were only a few with Trypho. [11]Antiochus pursued him, and Trypho[b] came in his flight to Dor, which is by the sea; [12]for he knew that troubles had converged on him, and his troops had deserted him. [13]So Antiochus encamped against Dor, and with him were one hundred twenty thousand warriors and eight thousand cavalry. [14]He surrounded the town, and the ships joined battle from the sea; he pressed the town hard from land and sea, and permitted no one to leave or enter it.

Rome Supports the Jews

15 Then Numenius and his companions arrived from Rome, with letters to the kings and countries, in which the following was written: [16]"Lucius, consul of the Romans, to King Ptolemy, greetings. [17]The envoys of the Jews have come to us as our friends and allies to renew our ancient friendship and alliance. They had been sent by the high priest Simon and by the Jewish people [18]and have brought a gold shield weighing one thousand minas.

[19]We therefore have decided to write to the kings and countries that they should not seek their harm or make war against them and their cities and their country, or make alliance with those who war against them. [20]And it has seemed good to us to accept the shield from them. [21]Therefore if any scoundrels have fled to you from their country, hand them over to the high priest Simon, so that he may punish them according to their law."

22 The consul[c] wrote the same thing to King Demetrius and to Attalus and Ariarathes and Arsaces, [23]and to all the countries, and to Sampsames,[d] and to the Spartans, and to Delos, and to Myndos, and to Sicyon, and to Caria, and to Samos, and to Pamphylia, and to Lycia, and to Halicarnassus, and to Rhodes, and to Phaselis, and to Cos, and to Side, and to Aradus and Gortyna and Cnidus and Cyprus and Cyrene. [24]They also sent a copy of these things to the high priest Simon.

Antiochus VII Threatens Simon

25 King Antiochus besieged Dor for the second time, continually throwing his forces against it and making engines of war; and he shut Trypho up and kept him from going out or in. [26]And Simon sent to Antiochus[e] two thousand picked troops, to fight for him, and silver and gold and a large amount of military equipment. [27]But he refused to receive them, and broke all the agreements he formerly had made with Simon, and became estranged from him. [28]He sent to him Athenobius, one of his Friends, to confer with him, saying, "You hold control of Joppa and Gazara and the citadel in Jerusalem; they are cities of my kingdom. [29]You have devastated their territory, you have done great damage in the land, and you have taken possession of many places in my kingdom. [30]Now then, hand over the cities that you have seized and the tribute money of the places that you have conquered outside the borders of Judea; [31]or else pay me five hundred talents of silver for the destruction that you have caused and five hundred talents more for the tribute

a 138 B.C.   *b* Gk *he*   *c* Gk *He*   *d* The name is uncertain   *e* Gk *him* money of the cities. Otherwise we will come and make war on you."

32 So Athenobius, the king's Friend, came to Jerusalem, and when he saw the splendor of Simon, and the sideboard with its gold and silver plate, and his great magnificence, he was amazed. When he reported to him the king's message, 33Simon said to him in reply: "We have neither taken foreign land nor seized foreign property, but only the inheritance of our ancestors, which at one time had been unjustly taken by our enemies. 34Now that we have the opportunity, we are firmly holding the inheritance of our ancestors. 35As for Joppa and Gazara, which you demand, they were causing great damage among the people and to our land; for them we will give you one hundred talents."

Athenobius*a* did not answer him a word, 36but returned in wrath to the king and reported to him these words, and also the splendor of Simon and all that he had seen. And the king was very angry.

Victory over Cendebeus

37 Meanwhile Trypho embarked on a ship and escaped to Orthosia. 38Then the king made Cendebeus commander-in-chief of the coastal country, and gave him troops of infantry and cavalry. 39He commanded him to encamp against Judea, to build up Kedron and fortify its gates, and to make war on the people; but the king pursued Trypho. 40So Cendebeus came to Jamnia and began to provoke the people and invade Judea and take the people captive and kill them. 41He built up Kedron and stationed horsemen and troops there, so that they might go out and make raids along the highways of Judea, as the king had ordered him.

16 John went up from Gazara and reported to his father Simon what Cendebeus had done. 2And Simon called in his two eldest sons Judas and John, and said to them: "My brothers and I and my father's house have fought the wars of Israel from our youth until this day, and things have prospered in our hands so that we have delivered Israel many times. 3But now I have grown old, and you by Heaven's*b* mercy are mature in years. Take my place and my brother's, and go out and fight for our nation, and may the help that comes from Heaven be with you."

4 So John*c* chose out of the country twenty thousand warriors and cavalry, and they marched against Cendebeus and camped for the night in Modein. 5Early in the morning they started out and marched into the plain, where a large force of infantry and cavalry

a Gk *He*   b Gk *his*   c Other ancient authorities read *he*

15:33 *the inheritance of our ancestors.* Simon defends his conquest of neighboring lands as an attempt to regain Israel's ancestral inheritance, the boundaries of the Davidic kingdom at its zenith. In Christ, the "booth of David that is fallen" (Amos 9:11) is restored in a way unexpected by Simon and the Maccabees. Jesus and his disciples first reached out to the Jewish people (Acts 9:31; 15:16–18), which opened up the way for the inclusion of all nations among God's people. We must look to God for how he is reclaiming his inheritance among all peoples, guiding us as we reach out to bring people from every place into communion with God and with one another.

16:2–3 *Simon called in his two eldest sons.* Simon invites his sons to consider the witness of their father and his brothers and to take their place in the line of warriors who pursue the peace and security of the People of God. The passing along of the vision for God's people and the calling to labor for the realization and preservation of that vision are part of the task of every generation and, in many ways, the most important inheritance one generation bequeaths to the next. In mentoring and equipping younger disciples to stand up and give courageous leadership to the People of God, we embody God's provision for the future of his people. In this process, it is important to teach them how to derive strength and guidance from the examples of their teachers and of the larger cloud of witnesses who have led God's people throughout the millennia and especially to know how to seek and find "the help that comes from Heaven" in the midst of their new campaigns for justice and wholeness.

was coming to meet them; and a stream lay between them. 6Then he and his army lined up against them. He saw that the soldiers were afraid to cross the stream, so he crossed over first; and when his troops saw him, they crossed over after him. 7Then he divided the army and placed the cavalry in the center of the infantry, for the cavalry of the enemy were very numerous. 8They sounded the trumpets, and Cendebeus and his army were put to flight; many of them fell wounded and the rest fled into the stronghold. 9At that time Judas the brother of John was wounded, but John pursued them until Cendebeus[a] reached Kedron, which he had built. 10They also fled into the towers that were in the fields of Azotus, and John[a] burned it with fire, and about two thousand of them fell. He then returned to Judea safely.

Murder of Simon and His Sons

11 Now Ptolemy son of Abubus had been appointed governor over the plain of Jericho; he had a large store of silver and gold, 12for he was son-in-law of the high priest. 13His heart was lifted up; he determined to get control of the country, and made treacherous plans against Simon and his sons, to do away with them. 14Now Simon was visiting the towns of the country and attending to their needs, and he went down to Jericho with his sons Mattathias and Judas, in the one hundred seventy-seventh year,[b] in the eleventh month, which is the month of Shebat. 15The son of Abubus received them treacherously in the little stronghold called Dok, which he

had built; he gave them a great banquet, and hid men there. 16When Simon and his sons were drunk, Ptolemy and his men rose up, took their weapons, rushed in against Simon in the banquet hall and killed him and his two sons, as well as some of his servants. 17So he committed an act of great treachery and returned evil for good.

John Succeeds Simon

18 Then Ptolemy wrote a report about these things and sent it to the king, asking him to send troops to aid him and to turn over to him the towns and the country. 19He sent other troops to Gazara to do away with John; he sent letters to the captains asking them to come to him so that he might give them silver and gold and gifts; 20and he sent other troops to take possession of Jerusalem and the temple hill. 21But someone ran ahead and reported to John at Gazara that his father and brothers had perished, and that "he has sent men to kill you also." 22When he heard this, he was greatly shocked; he seized the men who came to destroy him and killed them, for he had found out that they were seeking to destroy him.

23 The rest of the acts of John and his wars and the brave deeds that he did, and the building of the walls that he completed, and his achievements, 24are written in the annals of his high priesthood, from the time that he became high priest after his father.

a Gk he   b 134 B.C.

16:6 *he crossed over first.* John Hyrcanus I models that tenet that we can only lead others as far as we are willing to go ourselves. If we desire to motivate commitment to spiritual growth in the lives of others and to see what God can do in a community of people committed to deeper discipleship, we need to go first and model what such a life looks like. Particularly if we are faced with engaging the powers in some way (whether seeking to live a lifestyle that witnesses to Jesus' values for human community, rather than the self-centered, consumption-oriented values of society, or campaigning for justice for those who suffer abuse,

deprivation, or marginalization at the hands of others), God looks for those who are willing to cross the stream first, who will thus embolden others by example.

Responding
16:6 GUIDANCE. Think about who in your life might be watching and waiting for your example. Is God calling you to guide someone? Consider joining a local program such as Big Brothers/Big Sisters of America or engaging in a less formal mentorship with someone you know from church or from work. *See also* Spiritual Disciplines Index.

2 MACCABEES

Second Maccabees tells essentially the same story as 1 Maccabees 1–7, but from a very different perspective. This author is much more interested in the involvement of the Jewish high priests Jason and Menelaus and the Jewish aristocracy in the transformation of Jerusalem from a city governed by the Torah into a Greek city. He wants to provide a "before" and "after" perspective on this radical hellenization, contrasting how God protects the Temple and people under Onias III, who championed devout adherence to the Torah, with how God allows the Temple and people to be afflicted under Jason and Menelaus, who repressed observance of the Torah. He moves the martyrs, those who were faithful to God unto death, to center stage as the heroes of the story; without their sacrifice Judas and his brothers would never have enjoyed success.

Commitment to the Covenant

These changes serve what appears to be the author's main purpose, namely, to demonstrate that the philosophy of history taught by Deuteronomy continues to be true in the recent past and, by implication, the author's and his readers' present. This theme pervades the Deuterocanonical books (see especially Tobit, Judith, Prayer of Azariah, and Baruch). The message of Deuteronomy was simple. Faithful observance of the covenant with God will lead to the enjoyment of collective *shalom,* well-being and security. Violation, neglect, and abandonment of the covenant (sin) signify an intent to break the covenant relationship with God. God will respond by punishing those whom God has blessed with the experience of the curses of Deuteronomy 28–29 if they show themselves to be ungrateful and disloyal. Repentance and renewed obedience, however, can bring an end to God's wrath and stem the tide of national misfortune.

The attractions of an "alien way of life" continued to lure Jews away from commitment to their distinctive lifestyle shaped by the commandments of God.

See also "The With-God Life" essay for this section of the Bible,
"The People of God in Restoration," pp. 1355–59.

As he looks back and interprets the hellenization crisis in light of Deuteronomy's theology of the covenant (with its blessings and curses), the author of 2 Maccabees promotes continued commitment to walking in the way of God's covenant as the only secure path to prosperity and security for the people of Israel. Of first importance was the people's relationship with the God who protects his Temple and people.

Another major theological contribution of 2 Maccabees is the well-developed doctrine of the resurrection of the body (7:9, 11, 14, 23, 29; 12:43–45; 14:46). By giving life beyond death to God's faithful ones, God can be faithful both to the nation (e.g., punishing them collectively for their disobedience) and to the individual (e.g., rewarding with life those who die for the sake of God in the midst of a disobedient nation). This hope for life beyond death helped the People of God to invest themselves fully in their life with God and the actions to which God called them, even when this would have been disadvantageous from a temporal, worldly perspective. It continues to help us prioritize faithful response to God's call above every other consideration.

God's Continued Deliverance of His People

Two letters have been added at the beginning of 2 Maccabees, which originally started at 2:19. An earlier letter, which may represent the only surviving piece of correspondence bearing the name of Judas Maccabeus, is found in 1:10–2:18. A later letter (1:1–9), written in 124/123 BC, serves as a cover letter for the whole work as it now stands. In both of these letters, Judean Jews are seen trying to get their sisters and brothers in Egypt to acknowledge and celebrate God's deliverance of the Temple from the desecration under Antiochus IV. They are promoting, in effect, the observance of Hanukkah. In connection with these letters, the story told in 2 Maccabees becomes the record of how God was reconciled to and delivered his people—a continuation of God's saving acts on behalf of his people contained in the Old Testament and worthy of similar commemoration.

—*David A. deSilva*

A Letter to the Jews in Egypt

1 The Jews in Jerusalem and those in the land of Judea,

To their Jewish kindred in Egypt,

Greetings and true peace.

2 May God do good to you, and may he remember his covenant with Abraham and Isaac and Jacob, his faithful servants. 3May he give you all a heart to worship him and to do his will with a strong heart and a willing spirit. 4May he open your heart to his law and his commandments, and may he bring peace. 5May he hear your prayers and be reconciled to you, and may he not forsake you in time of evil. 6We are now praying for you here.

7 In the reign of Demetrius, in the one hundred sixty-ninth year, *a* we Jews wrote to you, in the critical distress that came upon us in those years after Jason and his company revolted from the holy land and the kingdom 8and burned the gate and shed innocent blood. We prayed to the Lord and were heard, and we offered sacrifice and grain offering, and we lit the lamps and set out the loaves. 9And now see that you keep the festival of booths in the month of Chislev, in the one hundred eighty-eighth year. *b*

A Letter to Aristobulus

10 The people of Jerusalem and of Judea and the senate and Judas,

To Aristobulus, who is of the family of the

a 143 B.C.   *b* 124 B.C.

1:2–6 *May God do good to you.* An important dimension of the discipline of prayer is the development of spiritual connection among the People of God over great distances by praying for one another. This prayer, offered by Judean Jews for their sisters and brothers in Egypt, suggests several focal points for our own prayers: the spiritual renewal and sustenance of God's people here and beyond our national borders; the well-being of God's people in every place; the deliverance of God's people in the midst of the trials that confront them (which can often be severe and oppressive indeed, especially in restricted nations). Like the authors of this letter, however, we also need to communicate to our sisters and brothers abroad our mindfulness of them in prayer (which will be a source of great encouragement) and seek out ways to be used by God to meet their needs (see 2 Cor 8:13–14).

Responding

1:2–6 PRAYER. Copy out these verses and keep them at hand the next time you read the newspaper or watch the television news. When a story about people in other parts of the country or the world speaks to your heart, pray these words aloud for them. *See also* Spiritual Disciplines Index.

1:5 *May he hear your prayers and be reconciled to you.* The diaspora—the scattering of Jews beyond the boundaries of Israel and their ongoing residence in gentile lands—was a result of exile and hence regarded as an experience of punishment. The authors of this first letter (1:1–9) consider their fellow Jews in Egypt to be in need of being reconciled to God, while they themselves are confident of their own relationship with God ("we prayed . . . and were heard," v 8). 3 Maccabees will counter this ideology, affirming instead that God hears his people in every land and is distant from none of them—an important development toward liberating the concept of God's saving purposes from being bound to a particular patch of territory.

1:9 *see that you keep the festival of booths.* The two letters that preface 2 Maccabees (1:1–9; 1:10–2:18) have as their primary goal getting the Egyptian Jews to put Hanukkah on their liturgical calendar (see also 2:16–18). These letters admittedly promote political agendas (asserting the authority of Jerusalem over Jews living abroad in religious matters; winning acknowledgment for the Hasmonean dynasty that God was indeed at work through them on behalf of God's people), but they also present a spiritual challenge. What God does for his people in one place has import for God's people in every place. Celebrating what God has done for our sisters and brothers in another place affirms our connectedness with them, as we share in their joys, and affirms God's care for them to be as great and important to us as God's care for us. These letters challenge us to be alert to God's purposes at work for his people across the globe and to let God broaden the horizons of our interest and concern accordingly.

anointed priests, teacher of King Ptolemy, and to the Jews in Egypt,

Greetings and good health.

11 Having been saved by God out of grave dangers we thank him greatly for taking our side against the king,[a] 12for he drove out those who fought against the holy city. 13When the leader reached Persia with a force that seemed irresistible, they were cut to pieces in the temple of Nanea by a deception employed by the priests of the goddess[b] Nanea. 14On the pretext of intending to marry her, Antiochus came to the place together with his Friends, to secure most of its treasures as a dowry. 15When the priests of the temple of Nanea had set out the treasures and Antiochus had come with a few men inside the wall of the sacred precinct, they closed the temple as soon as he entered it. 16Opening a secret door in the ceiling, they threw stones and struck down the leader and his men; they dismembered them and cut off their heads and threw them to the people outside. 17Blessed in every way be our God, who has brought judgment on those who have behaved impiously.

Fire Consumes Nehemiah's Sacrifice

18 Since on the twenty-fifth day of Chislev we shall celebrate the purification of the temple, we thought it necessary to notify you, in order that you also may celebrate the festival of booths and the festival of the fire given when Nehemiah, who built the temple and the altar, offered sacrifices.

19 For when our ancestors were being led captive to Persia, the pious priests of that time took some of the fire of the altar and secretly hid it in the hollow of a dry cistern, where they took such precautions that the place was unknown to anyone. 20But after many years had passed, when it pleased God, Nehemiah, having been commissioned by the king of Persia, sent the descendants of the priests who had hidden the fire to get it. And when they reported to us that they had not found fire but only a thick liquid, he ordered them to dip it out and bring it. 21When the materials for the sacrifices were presented, Nehemiah ordered the priests to sprinkle the liquid on the wood and on the things laid upon it. 22When this had been done and some time had passed, and when the sun, which had been clouded over, shone out, a great fire blazed up, so that all marveled. 23And while the sacrifice was being consumed, the priests offered prayer—the priests and everyone. Jonathan led, and the rest responded, as did Nehemiah. 24The prayer was to this effect:

"O Lord, Lord God, Creator of all things, you are awe-inspiring and strong and just and merciful, you alone are king and are kind, 25you alone are bountiful, you alone are just and almighty and eternal. You rescue Israel from every evil; you chose the ancestors and consecrated them. 26Accept this sacrifice on behalf of all your people Israel and preserve your portion and make it holy. 27Gather together our scattered people, set free those who are slaves among the Gentiles, look on those who are rejected and despised, and let

a Cn: Gk *as those who array themselves against a king*
b Gk lacks *the goddess*

1:19–22 *when our ancestors were being led captive to Persia.* The second letter seems preoccupied with looking for signs of continuity between the First Temple, built by Solomon, and the Second Temple, rebuilt after the exile. Although some of what was lost (e.g., the ark of the covenant) has not been restored, the second altar was connected with the first by the holy fire (see Lev 10:1–3 and the prohibition against using "unholy fire"), the authentic fire preserved miraculously from Solomon's Temple. This story speaks of the importance of spiritual continuity, of connection with our heritage in the faith. This is something all too easily overlooked in a climate that emphasizes "contemporary" worship experiences to the exclusion of mining the deep and rich veins of spiritual and theological insight running down to the core of Christian experience. New forms must still burn with the authentic, ancient fire, which we continue to find as we connect with God in Scripture, read the spiritual guidance offered by saints touched by God's fire through the centuries, and encounter the Holy Spirit, who kindles within us that same fire.

the Gentiles know that you are our God. [28]Punish those who oppress and are insolent with pride. [29]Plant your people in your holy place, as Moses promised."

30 Then the priests sang the hymns. [31]After the materials of the sacrifice had been consumed, Nehemiah ordered that the liquid that was left should be poured on large stones. [32]When this was done, a flame blazed up; but when the light from the altar shone back, it went out. [33]When this matter became known, and it was reported to the king of the Persians that, in the place where the exiled priests had hidden the fire, the liquid had appeared with which Nehemiah and his associates had burned the materials of the sacrifice, [34]the king investigated the matter, and enclosed the place and made it sacred. [35]And with those persons whom the king favored he exchanged many excellent gifts. [36]Nehemiah and his associates called this "nephthar," which means purification, but by most people it is called naphtha.[a]

Jeremiah Hides the Tent, Ark, and Altar

2 One finds in the records that the prophet Jeremiah ordered those who were being deported to take some of the fire, as has been mentioned, [2]and that the prophet, after giving them the law, instructed those who were being deported not to forget the commandments of the Lord, or to be led astray in their thoughts on seeing the gold and silver statues and their adornment. [3]And with other similar words he exhorted them that the law should not depart from their hearts.

4 It was also in the same document that the prophet, having received an oracle, ordered that the tent and the ark should follow with him, and that he went out to the mountain where Moses had gone up and had seen the inheritance of God. [5]Jeremiah came and found a cave-dwelling, and he brought there the tent and the ark and the altar of incense; then he sealed up the entrance. [6]Some of those who followed him came up intending to mark the way, but could not find it. [7]When Jeremiah learned of it, he rebuked them and declared: "The place shall remain unknown until God gathers his people together again and shows his mercy. [8]Then the Lord will disclose these things, and the glory of the Lord and the cloud will appear, as they were shown in the case of Moses, and as Solomon asked that the place should be specially consecrated."

9 It was also made clear that being possessed of wisdom Solomon[b] offered sacrifice for the dedication and completion of the temple. [10]Just as Moses prayed to the Lord, and fire came down from heaven and consumed the sacrifices, so also Solomon prayed, and the fire came down and consumed the whole burnt offerings. [11]And Moses said, "They were consumed because the sin offering had not been eaten." [12]Likewise Solomon also kept the eight days.

13 The same things are reported in the records and in the memoirs of Nehemiah, and also that he founded a library and collected the books about the kings and prophets, and the writings of David, and letters of kings about votive offerings. [14]In the same way Judas also collected all the books that had been lost on account of the war that had

a Gk nephthai   b Gk he

2:14–15 *Judas also collected all the books that had been lost.* Depriving the people of their sacred books and the connection with God and the guidance they offered was central to the attack on the People of God in 167 BC. It remains an ongoing strategy of the political and spiritual enemies of God's people. The letter memorializes an overlooked aspect of Judas's campaign of restoration, as he gathered and reconstituted the Scriptures and took steps to make sure other communities (e.g., in Egypt) had access to them as well. This offer could be seen as another

attempt by Jerusalem Jews to centralize their religious authority (i.e., by claiming to have *the* authoritative version of the Scriptures over against the texts in use by Alexandrian Jews). Nevertheless, it reminds us of our obligation to do all we can to help keep the Scriptures available to all our sisters and brothers worldwide, especially those suffering the same repressive measures that Antiochus brought to bear on the Jews. It is a precious spiritual formation resource that none can afford to be without.

come upon us, and they are in our possession. [15]So if you have need of them, send people to get them for you.

16 Since, therefore, we are about to celebrate the purification, we write to you. Will you therefore please keep the days? [17]It is God who has saved all his people, and has returned the inheritance to all, and the kingship and the priesthood and the consecration, [18]as he promised through the law. We have hope in God that he will soon have mercy on us and will gather us from everywhere under heaven into his holy place, for he has rescued us from great evils and has purified the place.

The Compiler's Preface

19 The story of Judas Maccabeus and his brothers, and the purification of the great temple, and the dedication of the altar, [20]and further the wars against Antiochus Epiphanes and his son Eupator, [21]and the appearances that came from heaven to those who fought bravely for Judaism, so that though few in number they seized the whole land and pursued the barbarian hordes, [22]and regained possession of the temple famous throughout the world, and liberated the city, and reestablished the laws that were about to be abolished, while the Lord with great kindness became gracious to them— [23]all this, which has been set forth by Jason of Cyrene in five volumes, we shall attempt to condense into a single book. [24]For considering the flood of statistics involved and the difficulty there is for those who wish to enter upon the narratives of history because of the mass of material, [25]we have aimed to please those who wish to read, to make it easy for those who are inclined to memorize, and to profit all readers. [26]For us who have undertaken the toil of abbreviating, it is no light matter but calls for sweat and loss of sleep, [27]just as it is not easy for one who prepares a banquet and seeks the benefit of others. Nevertheless, to secure the gratitude of many we will gladly endure the uncomfortable toil, [28]leaving the responsibility for exact details to the compiler, while devoting our effort to arriving at the outlines of the condensation. [29]For as the master builder of a new house must be concerned with the whole construction, while the one who undertakes its painting and decoration has to consider only what is suitable for its adornment, such in my judgment is the case with us. [30]It is the duty of the original historian to occupy the ground, to discuss matters from every side, and to take trouble with details, [31]but the one who recasts the narrative should be allowed to strive for brevity of expression and to forego exhaustive treatment. [32]At this point therefore let us begin our narrative, without adding any more to what has already been said; for it would be foolish to lengthen the preface while cutting short the history itself.

Arrival of Heliodorus in Jerusalem

3 While the holy city was inhabited in unbroken peace and the laws were strictly observed because of the piety of the high priest Onias and his hatred of wickedness,

---

2:20–21 *wars against Antiochus Epiphanes . . . the appearances that came from heaven.* There is a meaningful pun between "Epiphanes," the divine title Antiochus IV claimed for himself, and the Greek word from which we get "epiphanies," here translated "appearances." The first represents the godless arrogance of human domination systems; the second, the help that God gives to his people, empowering them to take their stand against those self-glorifying powers.

2:21 *pursued the barbarian hordes.* Greek cultural imperialism is clearly expressed by the term "barbarian," the word used by Greeks to denote all who lived by non-Greek, and hence inferior, customs. The author turns this word back against the representatives of Greek culture, accusing Antiochus and his forces of being the real enemies of virtue and civilized society (see also 10:4; 13:9) and affirming the Jewish way of life as the way honorable and civilized people live. In so doing, he provides a fine example of how to let God's leading, and not the dominant culture's labels, set the agenda for how we are to live and behave.

3:1 *the laws were strictly observed.* Walking in God's ways as a community leads to "unbroken peace," *shalom.* Attempts to "get ahead" outside God's ways and purposes, even in violation of

²it came about that the kings themselves honored the place and glorified the temple with the finest presents, ³even to the extent that King Seleucus of Asia defrayed from his own revenues all the expenses connected with the service of the sacrifices.

4 But a man named Simon, of the tribe of Benjamin, who had been made captain of the temple, had a disagreement with the high priest about the administration of the city market. ⁵Since he could not prevail over Onias, he went to Apollonius of Tarsus,ᵃ who at that time was governor of Coelesyria and Phoenicia, ⁶and reported to him that the treasury in Jerusalem was full of untold sums of money, so that the amount of the funds could not be reckoned, and that they did not belong to the account of the sacrifices, but that it was possible for them to fall under the control of the king. ⁷When Apollonius met the king, he told him of the money about which he had been informed. The kingᵇ chose Heliodorus, who was in charge of his affairs, and sent him with commands to effect the removal of the reported wealth. ⁸Heliodorus at once set out on his journey, ostensibly to make a tour of inspection of the cities of Coelesyria and Phoenicia, but in fact to carry out the king's purpose.

9 When he had arrived at Jerusalem and had been kindly welcomed by the high priest ofᶜ the city, he told about the disclosure that had been made and stated why he had come, and he inquired whether this really was the situation. ¹⁰The high priest explained that there were some deposits belonging to widows and orphans, ¹¹and also some money of Hyrcanus son of Tobias, a man of very prominent position, and that it totaled in all four hundred talents of silver and two hundred of gold. To such an extent the impious Simon had misrepresented the facts. ¹²And he said that it was utterly impossible that wrong should be done to those people who had trusted in the holiness of the place and in the sanctity and inviolability of the temple that is honored throughout the whole world.

Heliodorus Plans to Rob the Temple

13 But Heliodorus, because of the orders he had from the king, said that this money must in any case be confiscated for the king's treasury. ¹⁴So he set a day and went in to direct the inspection of these funds.

There was no little distress throughout the whole city. ¹⁵The priests prostrated themselves before the altar in their priestly vestments and called toward heaven upon him who had given the law about deposits, that he should keep them safe for those who had deposited them. ¹⁶To see the appearance of the high priest was to be wounded at heart, for his face and the change in his color disclosed the anguish of his soul. ¹⁷For terror and bodily trembling had come over the man, which plainly showed to those who looked at him the pain lodged in his heart. ¹⁸People also hurried out of their houses in crowds to make

ᵃ Gk *Apollonius son of Tharseas*   ᵇ Gk *He*
ᶜ Other ancient authorities read *and*

God's ways, lead to regret and disgrace. This announces the author's principal point: as God's people we can only ultimately enjoy security and wholeness by living in line with God's leading, making the virtues of the new covenant real in our interactions with one another and with the world around us.

3:12 *the sanctity and inviolability of the temple.* Money deposited in the Temple treasury was held to be sacred and inviolable on account of the holiness of the place and the honor of the God who dwelt in it. Forces from within (Simon) and without (Heliodorus) now threaten the honor of God and the Temple by betraying the trust of those who deposited those sums of money there. What of the temple of God formed by the Spirit? Like Timothy, we too are admonished to "guard the good treasure . . . with the help of the Holy Spirit living in us" (2 Tim 1:14; cf. 1 Tim 6:20), to contend for the faith God entrusted to the saints (Jude 3-4). The life-giving message of Jesus, the gifts of the Spirit, the gift of one another in community, the hope and means of transformation into the image of Christ—such "deposits," and many others besides, entrusted to us by God must be cherished and kept inviolable with the same zeal as the residents of Jerusalem show in the verses that follow.

a general supplication because the holy place was about to be brought into dishonor. [19]Women, girded with sackcloth under their breasts, thronged the streets. Some of the young women who were kept indoors ran together to the gates, and some to the walls, while others peered out of the windows. [20]And holding up their hands to heaven, they all made supplication. [21]There was something pitiable in the prostration of the whole populace and the anxiety of the high priest in his great anguish.

The Lord Protects His Temple

[22] While they were calling upon the Almighty Lord that he would keep what had been entrusted safe and secure for those who had entrusted it, [23]Heliodorus went on with what had been decided. [24]But when he arrived at the treasury with his bodyguard, then and there the Sovereign of spirits and of all authority caused so great a manifestation that all who had been so bold as to accompany him were astounded by the power of God, and became faint with terror. [25]For there appeared to them a magnificently caparisoned horse, with a rider of frightening mien; it rushed furiously at Heliodorus and struck at him with its front hoofs. Its rider was seen to have armor and weapons of gold. [26]Two young men also appeared to him, remarkably strong, gloriously beautiful and splendidly dressed, who stood on either side of him and flogged him continuously, inflicting many blows on him. [27]When he suddenly fell to the ground and deep darkness came over him, his men took him up, put him on a stretcher, [28]and carried him away—this man who had just entered the aforesaid

treasury with a great retinue and all his bodyguard but was now unable to help himself. They recognized clearly the sovereign power of God.

Onias Prays for Heliodorus

[29] While he lay prostrate, speechless because of the divine intervention and deprived of any hope of recovery, [30]they praised the Lord who had acted marvelously for his own place. And the temple, which a little while before was full of fear and disturbance, was filled with joy and gladness, now that the Almighty Lord had appeared.

[31] Some of Heliodorus's friends quickly begged Onias to call upon the Most High to grant life to one who was lying quite at his last breath. [32]So the high priest, fearing that the king might get the notion that some foul play had been perpetrated by the Jews with regard to Heliodorus, offered sacrifice for the man's recovery. [33]While the high priest was making an atonement, the same young men appeared again to Heliodorus dressed in the same clothing, and they stood and said, "Be very grateful to the high priest Onias, since for his sake the Lord has granted you your life. [34]And see that you, who have been flogged by heaven, report to all people the majestic power of God." Having said this they vanished.

The Conversion of Heliodorus

[35] Then Heliodorus offered sacrifice to the Lord and made very great vows to the Savior of his life, and having bidden Onias farewell, he marched off with his forces to the king. [36]He bore testimony to all concerning the deeds of the supreme God, which

---

3:16–21 *they all made supplication.* We are reminded here of the power of corporate prayer, as we seek God's interventions on behalf of the community in solidarity with one another before God. Whether God manifests himself for deliverance from trial, for sustaining his people in the midst of challenges, or for empowering them to go forward and act on his behalf (as in Acts 4:29–31), God does seem to delight in manifesting himself where his people gather together in unity and fervency.

3:34,36 *report to all people the majestic power of God.* In the ancient world, it was expected that recipients of favors would express their gratitude by telling others about it, thus extending the fame and enhancing the prestige of the giver. The testimony we can give to our own experiences of God's power to correct and reform, to heal and deliver, is the essence of witness and evangelism. When we speak of what God has done for us in particular, our witness is most authentic and effective.

he had seen with his own eyes. [37]When the king asked Heliodorus what sort of person would be suitable to send on another mission to Jerusalem, he replied, [38]"If you have any enemy or plotter against your government, send him there, for you will get him back thoroughly flogged, if he survives at all; for there is certainly some power of God about the place. [39]For he who has his dwelling in heaven watches over that place himself and brings it aid, and he strikes and destroys those who come to do it injury." [40]This was the outcome of the episode of Heliodorus and the protection of the treasury.

Simon Accuses Onias

4 The previously mentioned Simon, who had informed about the money against[a] his own country, slandered Onias, saying that it was he who had incited Heliodorus and had been the real cause of the misfortune. [2]He dared to designate as a plotter against the government the man who was the benefactor of the city, the protector of his compatriots, and a zealot for the laws. [3]When his hatred progressed to such a degree that even murders were committed by one of Simon's approved agents, [4]Onias recognized that the rivalry was serious and that Apollonius son of Menestheus,[b] and governor of Coelesyria and Phoenicia, was intensifying the malice of Simon. [5]So he appealed to the king, not accusing his compatriots but having in view the welfare, both public and private, of all the people. [6]For he saw that without the king's attention public affairs could not again reach a peaceful settlement, and that Simon would not stop his folly.

Jason's Reforms

[7] When Seleucus died and Antiochus, who was called Epiphanes, succeeded to the kingdom, Jason the brother of Onias obtained the high priesthood by corruption, [8]promising the king at an interview[c] three hundred sixty talents of silver, and from another source of revenue eighty talents. [9]In addition to this he promised to pay one hundred fifty more if permission were given to establish by his authority a gymnasium and a body of youth for it, and to enroll the people of Jerusalem as citizens of Antioch. [10]When the king assented and Jason[d] came to office, he at once shifted his compatriots over to the Greek way of life.

[11] He set aside the existing royal concessions to the Jews, secured through John the father of Eupolemus, who went on the mission to establish friendship and alliance with the Romans; and he destroyed the lawful ways of living and introduced new customs contrary to the law. [12]He took delight in establishing a gymnasium right under the citadel, and he induced the noblest of the young men to wear the Greek hat. [13]There was such an extreme of Hellenization and increase in the adoption of foreign ways because of the surpassing wickedness of Jason, who was ungodly and no true[e] high priest, [14]that the priests were no longer intent upon their service at the altar. Despising the sanctuary and neglecting the sacrifices, they hurried to take part in the unlawful proceedings in the wrestling arena after the signal for the

a Gk and   b Vg Compare verse 21: Meaning of Gk uncertain   c Or by a petition   d Gk he
e Gk lacks true

4:5–6 *having in view the welfare . . . of all the people.* Onias acts consistently with a view to securing the welfare of the People of God, not advancing his personal cause against his rivals. The spiritually well-formed keep their eyes on the health of the community and direct their attention there rather than allowing themselves to be caught in personal rivalries and jealousies (cf. Phil 1:15–18).
4:13–17 *the surpassing wickedness of Jason.* Jason and the priestly aristocracy model for us

the dangers of valuing the world's forms of prestige more than what has value in God's sight. In their situation, pursuing the former meant not only neglecting to do what brought eternal honor in God's sight, but failing to honor God with the loyal obedience that God merited. This is a persistent threat to spiritual growth. How often have we neglected our relationship with God and the service God seeks from us, because we have chosen to invest our time and energies in attaining worldly forms of prestige?

discus-throwing, 15disdaining the honors prized by their ancestors and putting the highest value upon Greek forms of prestige. 16For this reason heavy disaster overtook them, and those whose ways of living they admired and wished to imitate completely became their enemies and punished them. 17It is no light thing to show irreverence to the divine laws—a fact that later events will make clear.

Jason Introduces Greek Customs

18 When the quadrennial games were being held at Tyre and the king was present, 19the vile Jason sent envoys, chosen as being Antiochian citizens from Jerusalem, to carry three hundred silver drachmas for the sacrifice to Hercules. Those who carried the money, however, thought best not to use it for sacrifice, because that was inappropriate, but to expend it for another purpose. 20So this money was intended by the sender for the sacrifice to Hercules, but by the decision of its carriers it was applied to the construction of triremes.

21 When Apollonius son of Menestheus was sent to Egypt for the coronation*a* of Philometor as king, Antiochus learned that Philometor*b* had become hostile to his government, and he took measures for his own security. Therefore upon arriving at Joppa he proceeded to Jerusalem. 22He was welcomed magnificently by Jason and the city, and ushered in with a blaze of torches and with shouts. Then he marched his army into Phoenicia.

Menelaus Becomes High Priest

23 After a period of three years Jason sent Menelaus, the brother of the previously mentioned Simon, to carry the money to the king and to complete the records of essential business. 24But he, when presented to the king, extolled him with an air of authority, and secured the high priesthood for himself, outbidding Jason by three hundred talents of silver. 25After receiving the king's orders he returned, possessing no qualification for the high priesthood, but having the hot temper of a cruel tyrant and the rage of a savage wild beast. 26So Jason, who after supplanting his own brother was supplanted by another man, was driven as a fugitive into the land of Ammon. 27Although Menelaus continued to hold the office, he did not pay regularly any of the money promised to the king. 28When Sostratus the captain of the citadel kept requesting payment—for the collection of the revenue was his responsibility—the two of them were summoned by the king on account of this issue. 29Menelaus left his own brother Lysimachus as deputy in the high priesthood, while Sostratus left Crates, the commander of the Cyprian troops.

The Murder of Onias

30 While such was the state of affairs, it happened that the people of Tarsus and of Mallus revolted because their cities had been given as a present to Antiochis, the king's concubine. 31So the king went hurriedly to settle the trouble, leaving Andronicus, a man of high rank, to act as his deputy. 32But Menelaus, thinking he had obtained a suitable opportunity, stole some of the gold vessels of the temple and gave them to Andronicus; other vessels, as it happened, he had sold to Tyre and the neighboring cities. 33When Onias became fully aware of these acts, he publicly exposed them, having first

---

a Meaning of Gk uncertain   *b* Gk *he*

4:33 *he publicly exposed them.* Onias remains involved in looking after the peace and sanctity of the Temple. Even though he has been forced from power and twice supplanted, he does not withdraw his concern for the Temple out of bitterness. His focus and commitment again model how the spiritually mature continue to work for the health of the community of faith, even after being wronged.

Responding
4:33 SERVICE. Service to the community can take many forms, including exposing and speaking out against evil. Is there a wrong in your community or church that needs to be brought to light or protested publicly? *See also* Spiritual Disciplines Index.

withdrawn to a place of sanctuary at Daphne near Antioch. [34]Therefore Menelaus, taking Andronicus aside, urged him to kill Onias. Andronicus[a] came to Onias, and resorting to treachery, offered him sworn pledges and gave him his right hand; he persuaded him, though still suspicious, to come out from the place of sanctuary; then, with no regard for justice, he immediately put him out of the way.

Andronicus Is Punished

35 For this reason not only Jews, but many also of other nations, were grieved and displeased at the unjust murder of the man. [36]When the king returned from the region of Cilicia, the Jews in the city[b] appealed to him with regard to the unreasonable murder of Onias, and the Greeks shared their hatred of the crime. [37]Therefore Antiochus was grieved at heart and filled with pity, and wept because of the moderation and good conduct of the deceased. [38]Inflamed with anger, he immediately stripped off the purple robe from Andronicus, tore off his clothes, and led him around the whole city to that very place where he had committed the outrage against Onias, and there he dispatched the bloodthirsty fellow. The Lord thus repaid him with the punishment he deserved.

Unpopularity of Lysimachus and Menelaus

39 When many acts of sacrilege had been committed in the city by Lysimachus with the connivance of Menelaus, and when report of them had spread abroad, the populace gathered against Lysimachus, because many of the gold vessels had already been stolen. [40]Since the crowds were becoming aroused and filled with anger, Lysimachus armed about three thousand men and launched an unjust attack, under the leadership of a cer-

tain Auranus, a man advanced in years and no less advanced in folly. [41]But when the Jews[c] became aware that Lysimachus was attacking them, some picked up stones, some blocks of wood, and others took handfuls of the ashes that were lying around, and threw them in wild confusion at Lysimachus and his men. [42]As a result, they wounded many of them, and killed some, and put all the rest to flight; the temple robber himself they killed close by the treasury.

43 Charges were brought against Menelaus about this incident. [44]When the king came to Tyre, three men sent by the senate presented the case before him. [45]But Menelaus, already as good as beaten, promised a substantial bribe to Ptolemy son of Dorymenes to win over the king. [46]Therefore Ptolemy, taking the king aside into a colonnade as if for refreshment, induced the king to change his mind. [47]Menelaus, the cause of all the trouble, he acquitted of the charges against him, while he sentenced to death those unfortunate men, who would have been freed uncondemned if they had pleaded even before Scythians. [48]And so those who had spoken for the city and the villages[d] and the holy vessels quickly suffered the unjust penalty. [49]Therefore even the Tyrians, showing their hatred of the crime, provided magnificently for their funeral. [50]But Menelaus, because of the greed of those in power, remained in office, growing in wickedness, having become the chief plotter against his compatriots.

Jason Tries to Regain Control

5 About this time Antiochus made his second invasion of Egypt. [2]And it happened that, for almost forty days, there appeared

a Gk He   b Or in each city   c Gk they
d Other ancient authorities read the people

4:49 even the Tyrians . . . provided magnificently for their funeral. God calls us to stand for and witness to what is just—and to denounce what is unjust. Spiritual formation leads to prophetic witness. The Tyrians' witness invites us to ask ourselves: Whom can we honor in death as a witness to the nobility of their lives,

the justice of their cause, and (as in the case of many sisters and brothers in restricted nations) the injustice of their demise? If our efforts to keep them in life fail, we can still prevent the purveyors of injustice from pronouncing the last word.

over all the city golden-clad cavalry charging through the air, in companies fully armed with lances and drawn swords— [3] troops of cavalry drawn up, attacks and counterattacks made on this side and on that, brandishing of shields, massing of spears, hurling of missiles, the flash of golden trappings, and armor of all kinds. [4] Therefore everyone prayed that the apparition might prove to have been a good omen.

5 When a false rumor arose that Antiochus was dead, Jason took no fewer than a thousand men and suddenly made an assault on the city. When the troops on the wall had been forced back and at last the city was being taken, Menelaus took refuge in the citadel. [6] But Jason kept relentlessly slaughtering his compatriots, not realizing that success at the cost of one's kindred is the greatest misfortune, but imagining that he was setting up trophies of victory over enemies and not over compatriots. [7] He did not, however, gain control of the government; in the end he got only disgrace from his conspiracy, and fled again into the country of the Ammonites. [8] Finally he met a miserable end. Accused[a] before Aretas the ruler of the Arabs, fleeing from city to city, pursued by everyone, hated as a rebel against the laws, and abhorred as the executioner of his country and his compatriots, he was cast ashore in Egypt. [9] There he who had driven many from their own country into exile died in exile, having embarked to go to the Lacedaemonians in hope

of finding protection because of their kinship. [10] He who had cast out many to lie unburied had no one to mourn for him; he had no funeral of any sort and no place in the tomb of his ancestors.

11 When news of what had happened reached the king, he took it to mean that Judea was in revolt. So, raging inwardly, he left Egypt and took the city by storm. [12] He commanded his soldiers to cut down relentlessly everyone they met and to kill those who went into their houses. [13] Then there was massacre of young and old, destruction of boys, women, and children, and slaughter of young girls and infants. [14] Within the total of three days eighty thousand were destroyed, forty thousand in hand-to-hand fighting, and as many were sold into slavery as were killed.

Pillage of the Temple

15 Not content with this, Antiochus[b] dared to enter the most holy temple in all the world, guided by Menelaus, who had become a traitor both to the laws and to his country. [16] He took the holy vessels with his polluted hands, and swept away with profane hands the votive offerings that other kings had made to enhance the glory and honor of the place. [17] Antiochus was elated in spirit, and did not perceive that the Lord was angered for a little while because of the sins of those who lived in the city, and that this

a Cn: Gk Imprisoned   b Gk he

5:2–4 *there appeared over all the city golden-clad cavalry.* Manifestations of the supernatural, from private dream visions (15:12–16) to public apparitions (see 10:29, 11:6–10; 12:22), distinguish 2 Maccabees from 1 Maccabees. Unlike the latter, the former challenges us to be open to "intrusions" of the divine in nonrational, yet nevertheless authentic and spiritually empowering ways.

5:6 *Jason kept relentlessly slaughtering his compatriots.* Jason embodies the antithesis of Onias, who refused to put his own personal success and cause above those of the community. Too often, however, we fall into Jason's pattern, losing sight of the fact that our fellow Christians are our family and any hostility

against them, any action that beats one of them down, injures our own kin.

5:17 *did not perceive that the Lord was angered.* The arrogance and godlessness of the gentile nations God uses to chasten his own people is commonplace in Scripture (see, e.g., Isa 10:5–19; 47:6–15) and intertestamental literature (2 Esd 3:28–36). The instruments of God's punishment of his own people appear as senseless "tools" in his hands, lacking any understanding of God's purposes. The example of Antiochus serves as a warning to us to be aware of God's hand at work and look for ways in which to serve God's purposes, lest we too become so "elated in heart" that we think our own agenda, and not God's, is driving our history.

was the reason he was disregarding the holy place. [18]But if it had not happened that they were involved in many sins, this man would have been flogged and turned back from his rash act as soon as he came forward, just as Heliodorus had been, whom King Seleucus sent to inspect the treasury. [19]But the Lord did not choose the nation for the sake of the holy place, but the place for the sake of the nation. [20]Therefore the place itself shared in the misfortunes that befell the nation and afterward participated in its benefits; and what was forsaken in the wrath of the Almighty was restored again in all its glory when the great Lord became reconciled.

21 So Antiochus carried off eighteen hundred talents from the temple, and hurried away to Antioch, thinking in his arrogance that he could sail on the land and walk on the sea, because his mind was elated. [22]He left governors to oppress the people: at Jerusalem, Philip, by birth a Phrygian and in character more barbarous than the man who appointed him; [23]and at Gerizim, Andronicus; and besides these Menelaus, who lorded it over his compatriots worse than the others did. In his malice toward the Jewish citizens,[a] [24]Antiochus[b] sent Apollonius, the captain of the Mysians, with an army of twenty-two thousand, and commanded him to kill all the grown men and to sell the women and boys

as slaves. [25]When this man arrived in Jerusalem, he pretended to be peaceably disposed and waited until the holy sabbath day; then, finding the Jews not at work, he ordered his troops to parade under arms. [26]He put to the sword all those who came out to see them, then rushed into the city with his armed warriors and killed great numbers of people.

27 But Judas Maccabeus, with about nine others, got away to the wilderness, and kept himself and his companions alive in the mountains as wild animals do; they continued to live on what grew wild, so that they might not share in the defilement.

The Suppression of Judaism

6 Not long after this, the king sent an Athenian[c] senator[d] to compel the Jews to forsake the laws of their ancestors and no longer to live by the laws of God; [2]also to pollute the temple in Jerusalem and to call it the temple of Olympian Zeus, and to call the one in Gerizim the temple of Zeus-the-Friend-of-Strangers, as did the people who lived in that place.

3 Harsh and utterly grievous was the onslaught of evil. [4]For the temple was filled

---

a Or worse than the others did in his malice toward the Jewish citizens   b Gk he   c Other ancient authorities read Antiochian   d Or Geron an Athenian

---

5:18 But if it had not happened that they were involved in many sins. This verse points out the danger of permitting apostates or renegades to enter into the midst of the covenant community. The Temple was profaned not because of Antiochus's power or God's powerlessness, but because of the disobedience of some portion of the people. 1 Maccabees regards Judas's actions against apostate Jews as the means by which God's wrath was turned away from the nation (3:5–8). 2 Maccabees, however, regards the faithfulness of the covenant people, especially those who are faithful unto death, as the means by which God's wrath is averted (7:38; 8:5). Paul followed Judas's example prior to his conversion; Jesus followed the example of the martyrs in being "obedient to the point of death" (Phil 2:8), making his death "a ransom for many" (Mark 10:45). Jesus' example has rendered all "witch

hunts" inappropriate. Our task now is not to purge the renegades in our midst, but to nurture communities of faith in which God is so fully and powerfully present that any "renegades" are convicted and turned by God's own Spirit (1 Cor 14:24–25).

5:19–20 the Lord did not choose the nation for the sake of the holy place. The author recognizes that the holiness and faithfulness of the People of God is of primary importance. The requirements of holiness cannot be localized or externalized to sacred places, but must be lived out in the spaces of our own lives. God has chosen us to be his holy place, above any geographic locale.

5:27 got away to the wilderness. See note on 1 Macc 2:27–30.

6:1–2, 7–9 to compel the Jews to forsake the laws. See note on 1 Macc 1:41–50.

with debauchery and reveling by the Gentiles, who dallied with prostitutes and had intercourse with women within the sacred precincts, and besides brought in things for sacrifice that were unfit. 5 The altar was covered with abominable offerings that were forbidden by the laws. 6 People could neither keep the sabbath, nor observe the festivals of their ancestors, nor so much as confess themselves to be Jews.

7 On the monthly celebration of the king's birthday, the Jews[a] were taken, under bitter constraint, to partake of the sacrifices; and when a festival of Dionysus was celebrated, they were compelled to wear wreaths of ivy and to walk in the procession in honor of Dionysus. 8 At the suggestion of the people of Ptolemais[b] a decree was issued to the neighboring Greek cities that they should adopt the same policy toward the Jews and make them partake of the sacrifices, 9 and should kill those who did not choose to change over to Greek customs. One could see, therefore, the misery that had come upon them. 10 For example, two women were brought in for having circumcised their children. They publicly paraded them around the city, with their babies hanging at their breasts, and then hurled them down headlong from the wall. 11 Others who had assembled in the caves nearby, in order to observe the seventh day secretly, were betrayed to Philip and were all burned together, because their piety kept them from defending

themselves, in view of their regard for that most holy day.

Providential Significance of the Persecution

12 Now I urge those who read this book not to be depressed by such calamities, but to recognize that these punishments were designed not to destroy but to discipline our people. 13 In fact, it is a sign of great kindness not to let the impious alone for long, but to punish them immediately. 14 For in the case of the other nations the Lord waits patiently to punish them until they have reached the full measure of their sins; but he does not deal in this way with us, 15 in order that he may not take vengeance on us afterward when our sins have reached their height. 16 Therefore he never withdraws his mercy from us. Although he disciplines us with calamities, he does not forsake his own people. 17 Let what we have said serve as a reminder; we must go on briefly with the story.

The Martyrdom of Eleazar

18 Eleazar, one of the scribes in high position, a man now advanced in age and of noble presence, was being forced to open his mouth to eat swine's flesh. 19 But he, welcoming death with honor rather than life with pollution, went up to the rack of his own accord, spitting out the flesh, 20 as all ought to go who have the courage to refuse

a Gk they   b Cn: Gk suggestion of the Ptolemies (or of Ptolemy)

6:10–11 hurled them down . . . from the wall. See note on 1 Macc 1:56–63.

6:12–17 these punishments were designed . . . to discipline our people. Following Deuteronomy, the author interprets national misfortune as God's hand disciplining his people, driving them to repentance so that their sins will not reach the point of no return. Unlike the author of the Wisdom of Solomon, this author does not believe that God shows such care to the gentile nations, whom he simply leaves alone until he wipes them out (cf. Wisd of Sol 11:24; 12:2, 8–10, 20). The Wisdom of Solomon, like the early Church, which revered that book, reflects a God who is God of both Jew and Gentile (Rom 3:29). In light of that revelation, we can no longer

pretend that God shows favoritism, but rather must recognize that he includes all people in his outreaching care.

6:18–20 death with honor rather than life with pollution. Lev 20:22–26 reveals the significance of Israel's concern to distinguish between clean and unclean foods, eating only the former: by this practice they mirrored God's actions, who had made a distinction between Israel and the other nations, separating the former out as "clean" and "holy" to himself. Eating pork, then, becomes a potent symbol for the renunciation of ethnic distinctiveness and privilege, a rejection of the lines of clean and unclean that had kept the Jews distinct and separate from the nations.

things that it is not right to taste, even for the natural love of life.

21 Those who were in charge of that unlawful sacrifice took the man aside because of their long acquaintance with him, and privately urged him to bring meat of his own providing, proper for him to use, and to pretend that he was eating the flesh of the sacrificial meal that had been commanded by the king, 22so that by doing this he might be saved from death, and be treated kindly on account of his old friendship with them. 23But making a high resolve, worthy of his years and the dignity of his old age and the gray hairs that he had reached with distinction and his excellent life even from childhood, and moreover according to the holy God-given law, he declared himself quickly, telling them to send him to Hades.

24 "Such pretense is not worthy of our time of life," he said, "for many of the young might suppose that Eleazar in his ninetieth year had gone over to an alien religion, 25and through my pretense, for the sake of living a brief moment longer, they would be led astray because of me, while I defile and disgrace my old age. 26Even if for the present I would avoid the punishment of mortals, yet whether I live or die I will not escape the hands of the Almighty. 27Therefore, by bravely giving up my life now, I will show myself worthy of my old age 28and leave to the young a noble example of how to die a good death willingly and nobly for the revered and holy laws."

When he had said this, he went[a] at once to the rack. 29Those who a little before had acted toward him with goodwill now changed to ill will, because the words he had uttered were in their opinion sheer madness.[b] 30When he was about to die under the blows, he groaned aloud and said: "It is clear to the Lord in his holy knowledge that, though I might have been saved from death, I am enduring terrible sufferings in my body under this beating, but in my soul I am glad to suffer these things because I fear him."

31 So in this way he died, leaving in his death an example of nobility and a memorial of courage, not only to the young but to the great body of his nation.

The Martyrdom of Seven Brothers

7 It happened also that seven brothers and their mother were arrested and were being compelled by the king, under torture with whips and thongs, to partake of unlawful

a Other ancient authorities read *was dragged*
b Meaning of Gk uncertain

6:24–28 *Such pretense is not worthy of our time of life.* There can be no saving of our private conscience if our public witness is compromised. When we "pretend" to go along with something that is against our conscience, either by our actions or our politic silences, we defile ourselves—no matter how we might privately try to distance ourselves and reason how we remain "pure in God's sight." Eleazar challenges us to keep our focus on God, the ultimate judge, and not be cowed into unholy accommodations or compromises.

6:29–31 *leaving in his death an example of nobility.* The tortures are inflicted by Antiochus as a measure of his contempt for the Jewish way of life and for those who cling to it. From his perspective, an "honorable" person would embrace his values and his way of life instead. From the author's perspective, the truly noble person is the one who puts his or her obligation to honor and obey God first, whatever external circumstances press on such a person. Making progress in discipleship will often depend on our ability not to accept society's evaluation of our choices and our lives when these do not make sense to the worldly mind, but to make God's positive evaluation of our lives the first priority and order our lives accordingly. The examples of contemporary martyrs for Christ continue to offer encouragement to those of us facing our own trials, whether equal or considerably less grievous, if we pay attention to their stories.

7:1–42 *seven brothers and their mother were arrested.* This chapter is very difficult for the sensitive to read. At first, the experiences described here may seem remote, belonging to a distant and barbarous time. Yet many Christians in restricted nations continue to be tortured and killed, because they have broken with the majority and allowed God to make of them a distinct people. If this story moves us, how should it mobilize us to support our sisters

swine's flesh. 2One of them, acting as their spokesman, said, "What do you intend to ask and learn from us? For we are ready to die rather than transgress the laws of our ancestors."

3 The king fell into a rage, and gave orders to have pans and caldrons heated. 4These were heated immediately, and he commanded that the tongue of their spokesman be cut out and that they scalp him and cut off his hands and feet, while the rest of the brothers and the mother looked on. 5When he was utterly helpless, the king*a* ordered them to take him to the fire, still breathing, and to fry him in a pan. The smoke from the pan spread widely, but the brothers*b* and their mother encouraged one another to die nobly, saying, 6"The Lord God is watching over us and in truth has compassion on us, as Moses declared in his song that bore witness against the people to their faces, when he said, 'And he will have compassion on his servants.' "*c*

7 After the first brother had died in this way, they brought forward the second for their sport. They tore off the skin of his head with the hair, and asked him, "Will you eat rather than have your body punished limb by limb?" 8He replied in the language of his ancestors and said to them, "No." Therefore he in turn underwent tortures as the first brother had done. 9And when he was at his last breath, he said, "You accursed wretch, you dismiss us from this present life, but the King of the universe will raise us up to an everlasting renewal of life, because we have died for his laws."

10 After him, the third was the victim of their sport. When it was demanded, he quickly put out his tongue and courageously stretched forth his hands, 11and said nobly, "I got these from Heaven, and because of his laws I disdain them, and from him I hope to get them back again." 12As a result the king himself and those with him were astonished at the young man's spirit, for he regarded his sufferings as nothing.

a Gk *he*   *b* Gk *they*   *c* Gk *slaves*

---

and brothers? We enter here again into the global dimension of spiritual formation, which cannot remain just about "my walk with God," but must grow to include "my solidarity with, and care for, all the People of God" (see Matt 25:31–46; 1 John 3:16–18).

7:2 *we are ready to die rather than transgress.* The first brother refuses to be "schooled" by Antiochus and his strategies of coercion. He is fully settled in his mind concerning the ultimate value of walking in God's ways and will "teach" Antiochus about this value. He comes to the scene as a witness, not a victim.

7:6 *The Lord God is watching over us.* When they might have felt most forsaken by God in the time of trial, the mother and her sons see how, despite all appearances, God is in fact present and moving and thus how their trials have meaning in light of this. Scripture, here specifically Deut 32:36–43, proves again an essential resource.

7:7, 10 *they brought forward the second for their sport.* Treating torture as a "sport" displays the degree of inhumanity possessing Antiochus and his enforcers. This signifies not strength, as worldly minds might suppose, but an extreme lack of connectedness with their fellow human beings whom they were abusing and, therefore, their alienation from their own humanity. God leads us, rather, toward connection with both ourselves and others as a vehicle for growth and a measure of spiritual maturity.

7:9 *an everlasting renewal of life.* The author of Hebrews would hold up these martyrs as praiseworthy examples for Christians to follow, specifically in their choice of enduring difficulties now rather than relinquishing their hold on God's promise of everlasting life in God's presence (Heb 11:35b). The hope for immortality, seen here as the gift of the mighty God who creates worlds out of nothing (vv 28–29), can be a powerful focal point for setting priorities and decision making in this life. Here, in the Deuterocanonicals, the idea of eternal life, which takes on full expression in the New Testament, is introduced.

7:11, 23 *I got these from Heaven.* The martyrs exhibit firm convictions regarding reciprocity in their relationship with God. Life in these bodies is a gift from God; life in the body is to be used to honor and serve God; God will perpetually renew his gift of life to those who thus use their lives. Paul will also place reciprocity—our obligation to honor our Redeemer, who gave his life for ours, by living our lives for him—at the heart of discipleship (2 Cor 5:15).

13 After he too had died, they maltreated and tortured the fourth in the same way. [14]When he was near death, he said, "One cannot but choose to die at the hands of mortals and to cherish the hope God gives of being raised again by him. But for you there will be no resurrection to life!"

15 Next they brought forward the fifth and maltreated him. [16]But he looked at the king,[a] and said, "Because you have authority among mortals, though you also are mortal, you do what you please. But do not think that God has forsaken our people. [17]Keep on, and see how his mighty power will torture you and your descendants!"

18 After him they brought forward the sixth. And when he was about to die, he said, "Do not deceive yourself in vain. For we are suffering these things on our own account, because of our sins against our own God. Therefore[b] astounding things have happened. [19]But do not think that you will go unpunished for having tried to fight against God!"

20 The mother was especially admirable and worthy of honorable memory. Although she saw her seven sons perish within a single day, she bore it with good courage because of her hope in the Lord. [21]She encouraged each of them in the language of their ancestors. Filled with a noble spirit, she reinforced her woman's reasoning with a man's courage, and said to them, [22]"I do not know how you came into being in my womb. It was not I who gave you life and breath, nor I who set in order the elements within each of you. [23]Therefore the Creator of the world, who shaped the beginning of humankind and devised the origin of all things, will in his mercy give life and breath back to you again, since you now forget yourselves for the sake of his laws."

24 Antiochus felt that he was being treated with contempt, and he was suspicious of her reproachful tone. The youngest brother being still alive, Antiochus[c] not only appealed to him in words, but promised with oaths that he would make him rich and enviable if he would turn from the ways of his ancestors, and that he would take him for his Friend and entrust him with public affairs. [25]Since the young man would not listen to him at all, the king called the mother to him and urged her to advise the youth to save himself. [26]After much urging on his part, she undertook to persuade her son. [27]But, leaning close to him, she spoke in their native language as follows, deriding the cruel tyrant: "My son, have pity on me. I carried you nine months in my womb, and nursed you for three years, and have reared you and brought you up to this point in your life, and have taken care of you.[d] [28]I beg you, my child, to look at the heaven and the earth and see everything that is in them, and recognize that God did not make them out of things that existed.[e] And in the same way the hu-

a Gk at him   b Lat: Other ancient authorities lack Therefore   c Gk he   d Or have borne the burden of your education   e Or God made them out of things that did not exist

---

7:18–19, 33–35 *do not think that you will go unpunished.* (See also 9:5–12.) Human oppressors commonly carry on as if they will never be held accountable to God's standards of justice, imposing their own will by whatever means they deem expedient. The belief that all are accountable to God enables both endurance in discipleship and prophetic witness against oppressors.

7:22–23 *It was not I who gave you life.* The mother regards her own family, even her own children, not as her own, but as God's. As she displays, our first duty as family is to help one another find and pursue the path of faithfulness to God. Attachment and possession reflect a faulty understanding of relationships and distort them. We are more healthfully bound together by ties of common discipleship than by ownership.

7:24 *promised with oaths that he would make him rich.* The enemies of our soul can weaken our spirit and undermine discipleship as effectively with promises of prosperity as with threats of adversity. This has been especially the case in the Western world.

7:28 *God did not make them out of things that existed.* This is perhaps the earliest text giving clear expression to the conviction that God created the heavens and the earth *ex nihilo*, "out of nothing" (thus creating both

man race came into being. ²⁹Do not fear this butcher, but prove worthy of your brothers. Accept death, so that in God's mercy I may get you back again along with your brothers."

30 While she was still speaking, the young man said, "What are you*a* waiting for? I will not obey the king's command, but I obey the command of the law that was given to our ancestors through Moses. ³¹But you,*b* who have contrived all sorts of evil against the Hebrews, will certainly not escape the hands of God. ³²For we are suffering because of our own sins. ³³And if our living Lord is angry for a little while, to rebuke and discipline us, he will again be reconciled with his own servants.*c* ³⁴But you, unholy wretch, you most defiled of all mortals, do not be elated in vain and puffed up by uncertain hopes, when you raise your hand against the children of heaven. ³⁵You have not yet escaped the judgment of the almighty, all-seeing God. ³⁶For our brothers after enduring a brief suffering have drunk*d* of ever-flowing life, under God's covenant; but you, by the judgment of God, will receive just punishment for your arrogance.

³⁷I, like my brothers, give up body and life for the laws of our ancestors, appealing to God to show mercy soon to our nation and by trials and plagues to make you confess that he alone is God, ³⁸and through me and my brothers to bring to an end the wrath of the Almighty that has justly fallen on our whole nation."

39 The king fell into a rage, and handled him worse than the others, being exasperated at his scorn. ⁴⁰So he died in his integrity, putting his whole trust in the Lord.

41 Last of all, the mother died, after her sons.

42 Let this be enough, then, about the eating of sacrifices and the extreme tortures.

The Revolt of Judas Maccabeus

8 Meanwhile Judas, who was also called Maccabeus, and his companions secretly entered the villages and summoned their kindred and enlisted those who had continued in the Jewish faith, and so they gathered about six thousand. ²They implored the Lord

---

a The Gk here for *you* is plural   *b* The Gk here for *you* is singular   *c* Gk *slaves*   *d* Cn: Gk *fallen*

---

substance and form), rather than from preexisting material (thus giving form, but not substance). At first sight this belief might seem to be disconnected from the life-threatening situation in which the mother and her youngest son find themselves. On the contrary, however, the mother uses this conviction to encourage her young son to die for the sake of God, knowing that the God who made the universe out of nothing can and will re-create the young boy's life in the age to come, no matter what happens to the substance of his body in the tyrant's arena. As real to our senses as this world is, which we confess to exist only by God's word, so real is also the promise of the life beyond death, which shall also be granted by the power of his word to God's faithful servants. This conviction continues to embolden radical commitment to walk in obedience and faithfulness to God in the face of harsh opposition and temporal loss.

7:37–38 *I . . . give up body and life.* The martyrs' obedience to the point of death is a means by which God can be reconciled to his

formerly disobedient people. It is the token of obedience and commitment that aligns with Deut 30:2–3; it is the example by which zeal for the covenant spreads again throughout the people and holiness is restored. Such an understanding of the voluntary self-sacrifice of a righteous person clearly informed early Christian reflection on the death of Jesus, whose death also averted God's wrath, allowed the disobedient to be reconciled to God, and enabled obedience to the covenant from the heart.

8:2–4 *They implored the Lord.* A recurring theme throughout Scripture is that prayer is most powerfully engaged when we discern God's character (here, God's "hatred of evil" and commitment to help those unjustly oppressed) and God's interests (the preservation of the honor of God's name, embodied in the Temple and his people), and when we pray in line with who God is and what God does. This is the reverse of the misplaced attempt to get God "on board" with our character and interests in prayer.

to look upon the people who were oppressed by all; and to have pity on the temple that had been profaned by the godless; ³to have mercy on the city that was being destroyed and about to be leveled to the ground; to hearken to the blood that cried out to him; ⁴to remember also the lawless destruction of the innocent babies and the blasphemies committed against his name; and to show his hatred of evil.

5 As soon as Maccabeus got his army organized, the Gentiles could not withstand him, for the wrath of the Lord had turned to mercy. ⁶Coming without warning, he would set fire to towns and villages. He captured strategic positions and put to flight not a few of the enemy. ⁷He found the nights most advantageous for such attacks. And talk of his valor spread everywhere.

8 When Philip saw that the man was gaining ground little by little, and that he was pushing ahead with more frequent successes, he wrote to Ptolemy, the governor of Coelesyria and Phoenicia, to come to the aid of the king's government. ⁹Then Ptolemy*a* promptly appointed Nicanor son of Patroclus, one of the king's chief*b* Friends, and sent him, in command of no fewer than twenty thousand Gentiles of all nations, to wipe out the whole race of Judea. He associated with him Gorgias, a general and a man of experience in military service. ¹⁰Nicanor determined to make up for the king the tribute due to the Romans, two thousand talents, by selling the captured Jews into slavery. ¹¹So he immediately sent to the towns on the seacoast, inviting them to buy Jewish slaves and promising to hand over ninety slaves for a talent, not expecting the judgment from the Almighty that was about to overtake him.

Preparation for Battle

12 Word came to Judas concerning Nicanor's invasion; and when he told his companions of the arrival of the army, ¹³those who were cowardly and distrustful of God's justice ran off and got away. ¹⁴Others sold all their remaining property, and at the same time implored the Lord to rescue those who had been sold by the ungodly Nicanor before he ever met them, ¹⁵if not for their own sake, then for the sake of the covenants made with their ancestors, and because he had called them by his holy and glorious name. ¹⁶But Maccabeus gathered his forces together, to the number six thousand, and exhorted them not to be frightened by the enemy and not to fear the great multitude of Gentiles who were wickedly coming against them, but to fight nobly, ¹⁷keeping before their eyes the lawless outrage that the Gentiles*c* had committed against the holy place, and the torture of the derided city, and besides, the overthrow of their ancestral way of life. ¹⁸"For they trust to arms and acts of daring," he said, "but we trust in the Almighty God, who is able with a single nod to strike down those who are coming against us, and even, if necessary, the whole world."

19 Moreover, he told them of the occasions when help came to their ancestors; how, in the time of Sennacherib, when one hundred eighty-five thousand perished, ²⁰and the time of the battle against the

a Gk *he*   *b* Gk *one of the first*   *c* Gk *they*

8:5 *the Gentiles could not withstand him.* Judas and his armies can only succeed because of the martyrs' loyalty to God. Their display of fidelity satisfied God's wrath and aroused his compassion for his people, whose devotion to God has become evident.

8:14–15 *for the sake of the covenants made with their ancestors.* The connection between God's honor and the fate of his people is a common one in the intertestamental period (see also Jth 9:8; 3 Macc 2:9; Bar 2:15, 26; Pr of Azar 20). Knowing that we are the bearers of God's honor in this world spurs us on to safeguard that honor by our own commitment to loyalty and holiness (see Rom 2:23–24), but it also assures us that God safeguards our honor and dignity whenever it is assaulted on account of our faithful walk with God.

8:18 *we trust in the Almighty God.* This author shares with the author of 1 Maccabees the conviction, deeply rooted in Scripture, that deliverance comes from God's help rather than human force of arms (see Ps 20:7). See also note on 1 Macc 3:18–22.

Galatians that took place in Babylonia, when eight thousand Jews[a] fought along with four thousand Macedonians; yet when the Macedonians were hard pressed, the eight thousand, by the help that came to them from heaven, destroyed one hundred twenty thousand Galatians[b] and took a great amount of booty.

Judas Defeats Nicanor

21 With these words he filled them with courage and made them ready to die for their laws and their country; then he divided his army into four parts. 22He appointed his brothers also, Simon and Joseph and Jonathan, each to command a division, putting fifteen hundred men under each. 23Besides, he appointed Eleazar to read aloud[c] from the holy book, and gave the watchword, "The help of God"; then, leading the first division himself, he joined battle with Nicanor.

24 With the Almighty as their ally, they killed more than nine thousand of the enemy, and wounded and disabled most of Nicanor's army, and forced them all to flee. 25They captured the money of those who had come to buy them as slaves. After pursuing them for some distance, they were obliged to return because the hour was late. 26It was the day before the sabbath, and for that reason they did not continue their pursuit. 27When they had collected the arms of the enemy and stripped them of their spoils, they kept the sabbath, giving great praise

and thanks to the Lord, who had preserved them for that day and allotted it to them as the beginning of mercy. 28After the sabbath they gave some of the spoils to those who had been tortured and to the widows and orphans, and distributed the rest among themselves and their children. 29When they had done this, they made common supplication and implored the merciful Lord to be wholly reconciled with his servants.[d]

Judas Defeats Timothy and Bacchides

30 In encounters with the forces of Timothy and Bacchides they killed more than twenty thousand of them and got possession of some exceedingly high strongholds, and they divided a very large amount of plunder, giving to those who had been tortured and to the orphans and widows, and also to the aged, shares equal to their own. 31They collected the arms of the enemy,[e] and carefully stored all of them in strategic places; the rest of the spoils they carried to Jerusalem. 32They killed the commander of Timothy's forces, a most wicked man, and one who had greatly troubled the Jews. 33While they were celebrating the victory in the city of their ancestors, they burned those who had set fire to the sacred gates, Callisthenes and some others, who had fled into one little house; so these received the proper reward for their impiety.[c]

a Gk lacks *Jews* b Gk lacks *Galatians*
c Meaning of Gk uncertain d Gk *slaves*
e Gk *their arms*

8:23 *the watchword, "The help of God."* A "watchword" is a kind of password given in military camps. In the dark of night, this would be the only way to know if a friend or enemy was approaching. Judas chooses watchwords that remind the soldiers of their dependence upon and hope in God (see also 13:15); they would repeat these to one another throughout the night as a reminder of their great Ally and source of confidence. A well-chosen "watchword," sometimes in the form of a two- or three-word maxim or prayer that we can use throughout the day as a reminder to ourselves and perhaps others, can provide spiritual focus and direction for our thoughts and energies, keeping us on track toward growth or renewal. Replacing

casual greetings with seasonal watchwords (e.g., "Christ is coming" during Advent or "Christ is risen" during Easter, following our Greek Orthodox sisters and brothers) can also provide occasions for redirecting our thoughts and hearts to the great mysteries of faith throughout the day and night.

8:28, 30 *gave some of the spoils to those who had been tortured.* Judas and his armies provide consistently for the needs of the victims of the dominant culture's repressive measures. Disciples of God will be more emboldened to offer costly witness and remain faithful to God when they know that the larger family of God will continue to supply their families' needs in their absence or inability to provide.

34 The thrice-accursed Nicanor, who had brought the thousand merchants to buy the Jews, 35having been humbled with the help of the Lord by opponents whom he regarded as of the least account, took off his splendid uniform and made his way alone like a runaway slave across the country until he reached Antioch, having succeeded chiefly in the destruction of his own army! 36So he who had undertaken to secure tribute for the Romans by the capture of the people of Jerusalem proclaimed that the Jews had a Defender, and that therefore the Jews were invulnerable, because they followed the laws ordained by him.

The Last Campaign of Antiochus Epiphanes

9 About that time, as it happened, Antiochus had retreated in disorder from the region of Persia. 2He had entered the city called Persepolis and attempted to rob the temples and control the city. Therefore the people rushed to the rescue with arms, and Antiochus and his army were defeated,*a* with the result that Antiochus was put to flight by the inhabitants and beat a shameful retreat. 3While he was in Ecbatana, news came to him of what had happened to Nicanor and the forces of Timothy. 4Transported with rage, he conceived the idea of turning upon the Jews the injury done by those who had put him to flight; so he ordered his charioteer to drive without stopping until he completed the journey. But the judgment of heaven rode with him! For in his arrogance he said, "When I get there I will make Jerusalem a cemetery of Jews."

5 But the all-seeing Lord, the God of Israel, struck him with an incurable and invisible blow. As soon as he stopped speaking he was seized with a pain in his bowels, for which there was no relief, and with sharp internal tortures— 6and that very justly, for he had tortured the bowels of others with many and strange inflictions. 7Yet he did not in any way stop his insolence, but was even more filled with arrogance, breathing fire in his rage against the Jews, and giving orders to drive even faster. And so it came about that he fell out of his chariot as it was rushing along, and the fall was so hard as to torture every limb of his body. 8Thus he who only a little while before had thought in his superhuman arrogance that he could command the waves of the sea, and had imagined that he could weigh the high mountains in a balance, was brought down to earth and carried in a litter, making the power of God manifest to all. 9And so the ungodly man's body swarmed with worms, and while he was still living in anguish and pain, his flesh rotted away, and because of the stench the whole army felt revulsion at his decay. 10Because of his intolerable stench no one was able to carry the man who a little while before had thought that he could touch the stars of heaven. 11Then it was that, broken in spirit, he began to lose much of his arrogance and to come to his senses under the scourge of God, for he was tortured with pain every moment. 12And when he could not endure his own stench, he uttered these words, "It is right to be subject to God; mortals should not think that they are equal to God."*b*

Antiochus Makes a Promise to God

13 Then the abominable fellow made a vow to the Lord, who would no longer have mercy on him, stating 14that the holy city,

a Gk they were defeated   b Or not think thoughts proper only to God

---

8:36 *the Jews had a Defender.* Jerusalem is shown once again to be invulnerable in the Nicanor episode, after commitment to live by God's covenant is restored in the land (3:39; 5:17–20).

9:11–12 *come to his senses under the scourge of God.* The more rebellious we are against God's just demands on our lives, the more strict the discipline required to bring us around to understanding who we are before God. Such life lessons are painful, but, if they lead us to a spiritual conversion such as Antiochus is depicted as having, then they are shown to have come from the hand of a loving God who draws us to himself by all means necessary.

9:13–18 *made a vow to the Lord.* Even though we may truly wonder if Antiochus himself made these vows, we do see a reflection of how God

which he was hurrying to level to the ground and to make a cemetery, he was now declaring to be free; [15]and the Jews, whom he had not considered worth burying but had planned to throw out with their children for the wild animals and for the birds to eat, he would make, all of them, equal to citizens of Athens; [16]and the holy sanctuary, which he had formerly plundered, he would adorn with the finest offerings; and all the holy vessels he would give back, many times over; and the expenses incurred for the sacrifices he would provide from his own revenues; [17]and in addition to all this he also would become a Jew and would visit every inhabited place to proclaim the power of God. [18]But when his sufferings did not in any way abate, for the judgment of God had justly come upon him, he gave up all hope for himself and wrote to the Jews the following letter, in the form of a supplication. This was its content:

Antiochus's Letter and Death

19 "To his worthy Jewish citizens, Antiochus their king and general sends hearty greetings and good wishes for their health and prosperity. [20]If you and your children are well and your affairs are as you wish, I am glad. As my hope is in heaven, [21]I remember with affection your esteem and goodwill. On my way back from the region of Persia I suffered an annoying illness, and I have deemed it necessary to take thought for the general security of all. [22]I do not despair of my condition, for I have good hope of recovering from my illness, [23]but I observed that my father, on the occasions when he made expeditions into the upper country, appointed his successor, [24]so that, if anything unexpected happened or any unwelcome news came, the people throughout the realm would not be troubled, for they would know to whom the government was left. [25]Moreover, I understand how the princes along the borders and the neighbors of my kingdom keep watching for opportunities and waiting to see what will happen. So I have appointed my son Antiochus to be king, whom I have often entrusted and commended to most of you when I hurried off to the upper provinces; and I have written to him what is written here. [26]I therefore urge and beg you to remember the public and private services rendered to you and to maintain your present goodwill, each of you, toward me and my son. [27]For I am sure that he will follow my policy and will treat you with moderation and kindness."

28 So the murderer and blasphemer, having endured the more intense suffering, such as he had inflicted on others, came to the end of his life by a most pitiable fate, among the mountains in a strange land. [29]And Philip, one of his courtiers, took his body home; then, fearing the son of Antiochus, he withdrew to Ptolemy Philometor in Egypt.

Purification of the Temple

10 Now Maccabeus and his followers, the Lord leading them on, recovered the temple and the city; [2]they tore down the altars that had been built in the public square by the foreigners, and also destroyed the sacred precincts. [3]They purified the sanctuary, and made another altar of sacrifice; then, striking fire out of flint, they offered sacrifices, after a lapse of two years, and they offered incense and lighted lamps and set out the bread of the Presence. [4]When they had done this, they fell prostrate and implored the Lord that they might never again fall into such misfortunes, but that, if they should ever sin, they might be disciplined by him with forbearance and not be handed over to blasphemous and barbarous nations. [5]It happened that on the same day on which the sanctuary had been profaned by the foreigners,

---

works with us in this passage. We too may have found ourselves at some point bargaining with God, promising a completely reformed life and many specific acts of service, if God would but spare us some trouble. God knows, however, that our spiritual health and growth may require passing through these troubles rather than escaping them. Thus God allows Antiochus to continue to suffer in humility, to face the pain of what his life has become rather than to escape it, and to meet God there in that pain.

10:1–4 *purified the sanctuary.* See note on 1 Macc 4:36–58.

the purification of the sanctuary took place, that is, on the twenty-fifth day of the same month, which was Chislev. [6]They celebrated it for eight days with rejoicing, in the manner of the festival of booths, remembering how not long before, during the festival of booths, they had been wandering in the mountains and caves like wild animals. [7]Therefore, carrying ivy-wreathed wands and beautiful branches and also fronds of palm, they offered hymns of thanksgiving to him who had given success to the purifying of his own holy place. [8]They decreed by public edict, ratified by vote, that the whole nation of the Jews should observe these days every year.

9 Such then was the end of Antiochus, who was called Epiphanes.

Accession of Antiochus Eupator

10 Now we will tell what took place under Antiochus Eupator, who was the son of that ungodly man, and will give a brief summary of the principal calamities of the wars. [11]This man, when he succeeded to the kingdom, appointed one Lysias to have charge of the government and to be chief governor of Coelesyria and Phoenicia. [12]Ptolemy, who was called Macron, took the lead in showing justice to the Jews because of the wrong that had been done to them, and attempted to maintain peaceful relations with them. [13]As a result he was accused before Eupator by the king's Friends. He heard himself called a traitor at every turn, because he had abandoned Cyprus, which Philometor had entrusted to him, and had gone over to Antiochus Epiphanes. Unable to command the respect due his office,[a] he took poison and ended his life.

Campaign in Idumea

14 When Gorgias became governor of the region, he maintained a force of mercenaries, and at every turn kept attacking the Jews.

[15]Besides this, the Idumeans, who had control of important strongholds, were harassing the Jews; they received those who were banished from Jerusalem, and endeavored to keep up the war. [16]But Maccabeus and his forces, after making solemn supplication and imploring God to fight on their side, rushed to the strongholds of the Idumeans. [17]Attacking them vigorously, they gained possession of the places, and beat off all who fought upon the wall, and slaughtered those whom they encountered, killing no fewer than twenty thousand.

18 When at least nine thousand took refuge in two very strong towers well equipped to withstand a siege, [19]Maccabeus left Simon and Joseph, and also Zacchaeus and his troops, a force sufficient to besiege them; and he himself set off for places where he was more urgently needed. [20]But those with Simon, who were money-hungry, were bribed by some of those who were in the towers, and on receiving seventy thousand drachmas let some of them slip away. [21]When word of what had happened came to Maccabeus, he gathered the leaders of the people, and accused these men of having sold their kindred for money by setting their enemies free to fight against them. [22]Then he killed these men who had turned traitor, and immediately captured the two towers. [23]Having success at arms in everything he undertook, he destroyed more than twenty thousand in the two strongholds.

Judas Defeats Timothy

24 Now Timothy, who had been defeated by the Jews before, gathered a tremendous force of mercenaries and collected the cavalry from Asia in no small number. He came on, intending to take Judea by storm. [25]As he drew near, Maccabeus and his men sprinkled

_a_ Cn: Meaning of Gk uncertain

10:5 _the twenty-fifth day._ See note on 1 Macc 4:52–54.
10:8 _observe these days every year._ See note on 1 Macc 4:59.
10:25–28 _sprinkled dust on their heads._ On the eve of battle, Judas and his forces do not

"pump one another up" with vain boasts about their strength as warriors, but rather humble themselves before God with acts of repentance and seek God's face. Their confidence proceeds always from the renewal of their relationship with God.

dust on their heads and girded their loins with sackcloth, in supplication to God. 26Falling upon the steps before the altar, they implored him to be gracious to them and to be an enemy to their enemies and an adversary to their adversaries, as the law declares. 27And rising from their prayer they took up their arms and advanced a considerable distance from the city; and when they came near the enemy they halted. 28Just as dawn was breaking, the two armies joined battle, the one having as pledge of success and victory not only their valor but also their reliance on the Lord, while the other made rage their leader in the fight.

29 When the battle became fierce, there appeared to the enemy from heaven five resplendent men on horses with golden bridles, and they were leading the Jews. 30Two of them took Maccabeus between them, and shielding him with their own armor and weapons, they kept him from being wounded. They showered arrows and thunderbolts on the enemy, so that, confused and blinded, they were thrown into disorder and cut to pieces. 31Twenty thousand five hundred were slaughtered, besides six hundred cavalry.

32 Timothy himself fled to a stronghold called Gazara, especially well garrisoned, where Chaereas was commander. 33Then Maccabeus and his men were glad, and they besieged the fort for four days. 34The men within, relying on the strength of the place, kept blaspheming terribly and uttering wicked words. 35But at dawn of the fifth day, twenty young men in the army of Maccabeus, fired with anger because of the blasphemies, bravely stormed the wall and with savage fury cut down everyone they met. 36Others who came up in the same way wheeled around against the defenders and set fire to the towers; they kindled fires and burned the blasphemers alive. Others broke open the gates and let in the rest of the force, and they occupied the city. 37They killed Timothy, who was hiding in a cistern, and his brother Chaereas, and Apollophanes. 38When they had accomplished these things, with hymns and thanksgivings they blessed the Lord who shows great kindness to Israel and gives them the victory.

Lysias Besieges Beth-zur

11 Very soon after this, Lysias, the king's guardian and kinsman, who was in charge of the government, being vexed at what had happened, 2gathered about eighty thousand infantry and all his cavalry and came against the Jews. He intended to make the city a home for Greeks, 3and to levy tribute on the temple as he did on the sacred places of the other nations, and to put up the high priesthood for sale every year. 4He took no account whatever of the power of God, but was elated with his ten thousands of infantry, and his thousands of cavalry, and his eighty elephants. 5Invading Judea, he approached Beth-zur, which was a fortified place about five stadia a from Jerusalem, and pressed it hard.

6 When Maccabeus and his men got word that Lysias b was besieging the strongholds, they and all the people, with lamentations and tears, prayed the Lord to send a good angel to save Israel. 7Maccabeus himself was the first to take up arms, and he urged the others to risk their lives with him to aid their kindred. Then they eagerly rushed off together. 8And there, while they were still near Jerusalem, a horseman appeared at their

a Meaning of Gk uncertain   b Gk he

10:29 *there appeared to the enemy from heaven.* Visions of the activities of heavenly armies are prominent in 2 Maccabees (see also 11:8–10; 12:22), frequent reminders that victory comes from God and that his help is no less real than help from temporal quarters. Inferior numbers and resources do not deter Judas and his armies when they realize that God is on their side—not that God endorses a human cause; rather, the people have discerned God's cause

and made it their own.

10:38 *with hymns and thanksgivings they blessed the Lord.* The expression of gratitude to God is not only just and proper, but it is also an effective reminder to all concerned that God has indeed acted on behalf of his people, that God is in their midst and working out his good purposes among them (see also 8:27).

11:8–10 *a horseman appeared.* See note on 10:29.

head, clothed in white and brandishing weapons of gold. [9]And together they all praised the merciful God, and were strengthened in heart, ready to assail not only humans but the wildest animals or walls of iron. [10]They advanced in battle order, having their heavenly ally, for the Lord had mercy on them. [11]They hurled themselves like lions against the enemy, and laid low eleven thousand of them and sixteen hundred cavalry, and forced all the rest to flee. [12]Most of them got away stripped and wounded, and Lysias himself escaped by disgraceful flight.

Lysias Makes Peace with the Jews

[13] As he was not without intelligence, he pondered over the defeat that had befallen him, and realized that the Hebrews were invincible because the mighty God fought on their side. So he sent to them [14]and persuaded them to settle everything on just terms, promising that he would persuade the king, constraining him to be their friend. [a] [15]Maccabeus, having regard for the common good, agreed to all that Lysias urged. For the king granted every request in behalf of the Jews which Maccabeus delivered to Lysias in writing.

[16] The letter written to the Jews by Lysias was to this effect:

"Lysias to the people of the Jews, greetings. [17]John and Absalom, who were sent by you, have delivered your signed communication and have asked about the matters indicated in it. [18]I have informed the king of everything that needed to be brought before him, and he has agreed to what was possible. [19]If you will maintain your goodwill toward the government, I will endeavor in the future to help promote your welfare. [20]And concerning such matters and their details, I have ordered these men and my representatives to confer with you. [21]Farewell. The one hundred forty-eighth year, [b] Dioscorinthius twenty-fourth."

[22] The king's letter ran thus:

"King Antiochus to his brother Lysias, greetings. [23]Now that our father has gone on to the gods, we desire that the subjects of the kingdom be undisturbed in caring for their own affairs. [24]We have heard that the Jews do not consent to our father's change to Greek customs, but prefer their own way of living and ask that their own customs be allowed them. [25]Accordingly, since we choose that this nation also should be free from disturbance, our decision is that their temple be restored to them and that they shall live according to the customs of their ancestors. [26]You will do well, therefore, to send word to them and give them pledges of friendship, so that they may know our policy and be of good cheer and go on happily in the conduct of their own affairs."

[27] To the nation the king's letter was as follows:

"King Antiochus to the senate of the Jews and to the other Jews, greetings. [28]If you are well, it is as we desire. We also are in good health. [29]Menelaus has informed us that you wish to return home and look after your own affairs. [30]Therefore those who go home by the thirtieth of Xanthicus will have our pledge of friendship and full permission [31]for the Jews to enjoy their own food and laws, just as formerly, and none of them shall be molested in any way for what may have been done in ignorance. [32]And I have also sent Menelaus to encourage you. [33]Farewell. The one hundred forty-eighth year, [b] Xanthicus fifteenth."

[34] The Romans also sent them a letter, which read thus:

"Quintus Memmius and Titus Manius, envoys of the Romans, to the people of the Jews, greetings. [35]With regard to what Lysias the kinsman of the king has granted you, we also give consent. [36]But as to the matters that he decided are to be referred to the king, as soon as you have considered them, send some one promptly so that we may make proposals appropriate for you. For we are on our way to Antioch. [37]Therefore make haste and send messengers so that we may have your judgment. [38]Farewell. The one hundred forty-eighth year, [b] Xanthicus fifteenth."

Incidents at Joppa and Jamnia

12 When this agreement had been reached, Lysias returned to the king, and the Jews went about their farming.

a Meaning of Gk uncertain   b 164 B.C.

2 But some of the governors in various places, Timothy and Apollonius son of Gennaeus, as well as Hieronymus and Demophon, and in addition to these Nicanor the governor of Cyprus, would not let them live quietly and in peace. 3And the people of Joppa did so ungodly a deed as this: they invited the Jews who lived among them to embark, with their wives and children, on boats that they had provided, as though there were no ill will to the Jews;*a* 4and this was done by public vote of the city. When they accepted, because they wished to live peaceably and suspected nothing, the people of Joppa*b* took them out to sea and drowned them, at least two hundred. 5When Judas heard of the cruelty visited on his compatriots, he gave orders to his men 6and, calling upon God, the righteous judge, attacked the murderers of his kindred. He set fire to the harbor by night, burned the boats, and massacred those who had taken refuge there. 7Then, because the city's gates were closed, he withdrew, intending to come again and root out the whole community of Joppa. 8But learning that the people in Jamnia meant in the same way to wipe out the Jews who were living among them, 9he attacked the Jamnites by night and set fire to the harbor and the fleet, so that the glow of the light was seen in Jerusalem, thirty miles*c* distant.

The Campaign in Gilead

10 When they had gone more than a mile*d* from there, on their march against Timothy, at least five thousand Arabs with five hundred cavalry attacked them. 11After a hard fight, Judas and his companions, with God's help, were victorious. The defeated nomads begged Judas to grant them pledges of friendship, promising to give him livestock and to help his people*e* in all other ways. 12Judas, realizing that they might indeed be useful in many ways, agreed to make peace with them; and after receiving his pledges they went back to their tents.

13 He also attacked a certain town that was strongly fortified with earthworks*f* and walls, and inhabited by all sorts of Gentiles. Its name was Caspin. 14Those who were within, relying on the strength of the walls and on their supply of provisions, behaved most insolently toward Judas and his men, railing at them and even blaspheming and saying unholy things. 15But Judas and his men, calling upon the great Sovereign of the world, who without battering rams or engines of war overthrew Jericho in the days of Joshua, rushed furiously upon the walls. 16They took the town by the will of God, and slaughtered untold numbers, so that the adjoining lake, a quarter of a mile*g* wide, appeared to be running over with blood.

Judas Defeats Timothy's Army

17 When they had gone ninety-five miles*h* from there, they came to Charax, to the Jews who are called Toubiani. 18They did not find Timothy in that region, for he had by then left there without accomplishing anything, though in one place he had left a very strong garrison. 19Dositheus and Sosipater, who were captains under Maccabeus, marched out and destroyed those whom Timothy had left in the stronghold, more than ten thousand men. 20But Maccabeus arranged his army in divisions, set men*e* in command of the divisions, and hurried after Timothy, who had with him one hundred twenty thousand infantry and two thousand five hundred cavalry. 21When Timothy learned of the approach of Judas, he sent off the women and the children and also the baggage to a place called Carnaim; for that place was hard to besiege and difficult of access because of the narrowness of all the approaches. 22But when Judas's first division appeared, terror and fear came over the enemy at the manifestation to them of him who

a Gk *to them*   *b* Gk *they*   *c* Gk *two hundred forty stadia*   *d* Gk *nine stadia*   *e* Gk *them*
f Meaning of Gk uncertain   *g* Gk *two stadia*
h Gk *seven hundred fifty stadia*

12:8-9 *the Jews who were living among them.* See note on 1 Macc 5:16–17, 21–23, 45.

12:15 *who . . . overthrew Jericho in the days of Joshua.* An important recurring motif throughout the Maccabean literature is that the God who

revealed his power and character in past acts of deliverance on behalf of his people or judgment against the insolent remains the same God who continues to act in this world.

sees all things. In their flight they rushed headlong in every direction, so that often they were injured by their own men and pierced by the points of their own swords. ²³Judas pressed the pursuit with the utmost vigor, putting the sinners to the sword, and destroyed as many as thirty thousand.

24 Timothy himself fell into the hands of Dositheus and Sosipater and their men. With great guile he begged them to let him go in safety, because he held the parents of most of them, and the brothers of some, to whom no consideration would be shown. ²⁵And when with many words he had confirmed his solemn promise to restore them unharmed, they let him go, for the sake of saving their kindred.

Judas Wins Other Victories

26 Then Judas*a* marched against Carnaim and the temple of Atargatis, and slaughtered twenty-five thousand people. ²⁷After the rout and destruction of these, he marched also against Ephron, a fortified town where Lysias lived with multitudes of people of all nationalities. *b* Stalwart young men took their stand before the walls and made a vigorous defense; and great stores of war engines and missiles were there. ²⁸But the Jews*c* called upon the Sovereign who with power shatters the might of his enemies, and they got the town into their hands, and killed as many as twenty-five thousand of those who were in it.

29 Setting out from there, they hastened to Scythopolis, which is seventy-five miles*d* from Jerusalem. ³⁰But when the Jews who lived there bore witness to the goodwill that the people of Scythopolis had shown them and their kind treatment of them in times of misfortune, ³¹they thanked them and exhorted them to be well disposed to their race in the future also. Then they went up to Jerusalem, as the festival of weeks was close at hand.

Judas Defeats Gorgias

32 After the festival called Pentecost, they hurried against Gorgias, the governor of Idumea, ³³who came out with three thousand infantry and four hundred cavalry. ³⁴When they joined battle, it happened that a few of the Jews fell. ³⁵But a certain Dositheus, one of Bacenor's men, who was on horseback and was a strong man, caught hold of Gorgias, and grasping his cloak was dragging him off by main strength, wishing to take the accursed man alive, when one of the Thracian cavalry bore down on him and cut off his arm; so Gorgias escaped and reached Marisa.

36 As Esdris and his men had been fighting for a long time and were weary, Judas called upon the Lord to show himself their ally and leader in the battle. ³⁷In the language of their ancestors he raised the battle cry, with hymns; then he charged against Gorgias's troops when they were not expecting it, and put them to flight.

Prayers for Those Killed in Battle

38 Then Judas assembled his army and went to the city of Adullam. As the seventh day was coming on, they purified themselves according to the custom, and kept the sabbath there.

39 On the next day, as had now become necessary, Judas and his men went to take up the bodies of the fallen and to bring them back to lie with their kindred in the sepulchres of their ancestors. ⁴⁰Then under the tunic of each one of the dead they found sacred tokens of the idols of Jamnia, which the

a Gk he   *b* Meaning of Gk uncertain
c Gk they   *d* Gk six hundred stadia

12:29–31 *they hastened to Scythopolis.* Judas uses his power to liberate the People of God in non-Judean territories from oppression by Gentiles (see note on 1 Macc 5:16–17, 21–23, 45), while making friends with gentile cities showing themselves well disposed to the People of God in their midst. How well do we use what power we have (e.g., coordinating economic embargoes) to work toward bringing relief and toleration for persecuted disciples living under repressive regimes?

12:39–40 *sacred tokens of the idols of Jamnia.* Looking for help both from God and from idols amounts to "limping with two different opinions" (1 Kings 18:21)—with disastrous results. Those who try to build their security in both God and some other source are really trusting in neither.

law forbids the Jews to wear. And it became clear to all that this was the reason these men had fallen. [41]So they all blessed the ways of the Lord, the righteous judge, who reveals the things that are hidden; [42]and they turned to supplication, praying that the sin that had been committed might be wholly blotted out. The noble Judas exhorted the people to keep themselves free from sin, for they had seen with their own eyes what had happened as the result of the sin of those who had fallen. [43]He also took up a collection, man by man, to the amount of two thousand drachmas of silver, and sent it to Jerusalem to provide for a sin offering. In doing this he acted very well and honorably, taking account of the resurrection. [44]For if he were not expecting that those who had fallen would rise again, it would have been superfluous and foolish to pray for the dead. [45]But if he was looking to the splendid reward that is laid up for those who fall asleep in godliness, it was a holy and pious thought. Therefore he made atonement for the dead, so that they might be delivered from their sin.

Menelaus Is Put to Death

13 In the one hundred forty-ninth year[a] word came to Judas and his men that Antiochus Eupator was coming with a great army against Judea, [2]and with him Lysias, his guardian, who had charge of the government. Each of them had a Greek force of one hundred ten thousand infantry, five thousand three hundred cavalry, twenty-two elephants, and three hundred chariots armed with scythes.

3 Menelaus also joined them and with utter hypocrisy urged Antiochus on, not for the sake of his country's welfare, but because he thought that he would be established in office. [4]But the King of kings aroused the anger of Antiochus against the scoundrel; and when Lysias informed him that this man was to blame for all the trouble, he ordered them to take him to Beroea and to put him to death by the method that is customary in that place. [5]For there is a tower there, fifty cubits high, full of ashes, and it has a rim running around it that on all sides inclines precipitously into the ashes. [6]There they all push to destruction anyone guilty of sacrilege or notorious for other crimes. [7]By such a fate it came about that Menelaus the lawbreaker died, without even burial in the earth. [8]And this was eminently just; because he had committed many sins against the altar whose fire and ashes were holy, he met his death in ashes.

A Battle Near the City of Modein

9 The king with barbarous arrogance was coming to show the Jews things far worse than those that had been done[b] in his father's time. [10]But when Judas heard of this, he ordered the people to call upon the Lord day and night, now if ever to help those who were on the point of being deprived of the law and their country and the holy temple, [11]and not to let the people who had just begun to revive fall into the hands of the blasphemous Gentiles. [12]When they had all joined in the same petition and had implored the merciful Lord with weeping and fasting and lying

a 163 B.C.   b Or the worst of the things that had been done

12:42–45 *He also took up a collection . . . for a sin offering.* The author may have misunderstood Judas's actions here. Rather than trying to make atonement for the dead so that they would have a place in the resurrection, Judas was more probably seeking to preserve the surviving soldiers from being punished by God on account of the idolatry that had been committed in their midst. Nevertheless, the author commends the practice of offering prayers and other acts of atonement on behalf of the dead, confident of God's mercy beyond the grave. Remembering the dead in prayer before God remains a mainstay of many Christian denominations and serves as a reminder that the communion of saints transcends death.

13:3 *with utter hypocrisy urged Antiochus on.* Menelaus puts his own interests ahead of those of the community of faith, making him the anti-model of nobility and a threat to the welfare of the People of God (cf. Onias's spiritually mature example in 4:4–6).

13:10–12 *call upon the Lord day and night.* The importance of the discipline of corporate prayer is again underscored (see 3:16–21). God's people find God's power and direction and learn

prostrate for three days without ceasing, Judas exhorted them and ordered them to stand ready.

13 After consulting privately with the elders, he determined to march out and decide the matter by the help of God before the king's army could enter Judea and get possession of the city. ¹⁴So, committing the decision to the Creator of the world and exhorting his troops to fight bravely to the death for the laws, temple, city, country, and commonwealth, he pitched his camp near Modein. ¹⁵He gave his troops the watchword, "God's victory," and with a picked force of the bravest young men, he attacked the king's pavilion at night and killed as many as two thousand men in the camp. He stabbed*ᵃ* the leading elephant and its rider. ¹⁶In the end they filled the camp with terror and confusion and withdrew in triumph. ¹⁷This happened, just as day was dawning, because the Lord's help protected him.

Antiochus Makes a Treaty with the Jews

18 The king, having had a taste of the daring of the Jews, tried strategy in attacking their positions. ¹⁹He advanced against Bethzur, a strong fortress of the Jews, was turned back, attacked again,*ᵇ* and was defeated. ²⁰Judas sent in to the garrison whatever was necessary. ²¹But Rhodocus, a man from the ranks of the Jews, gave secret information to the enemy; he was sought for, caught, and put in prison. ²²The king negotiated a second time with the people in Beth-zur, gave pledges, received theirs, withdrew, attacked Judas and his men, was defeated; ²³he got word that Philip, who had been left in charge of the government, had revolted in Antioch; he was dismayed, called in the Jews, yielded and swore to observe all their rights, settled with

them and offered sacrifice, honored the sanctuary and showed generosity to the holy place. ²⁴He received Maccabeus, left Hegemonides as governor from Ptolemais to Gerar, ²⁵and went to Ptolemais. The people of Ptolemais were indignant over the treaty; in fact they were so angry that they wanted to annul its terms.*ᵃ* ²⁶Lysias took the public platform, made the best possible defense, convinced them, appeased them, gained their goodwill, and set out for Antioch. This is how the king's attack and withdrawal turned out.

Alcimus Speaks against Judas

14 Three years later, word came to Judas and his men that Demetrius son of Seleucus had sailed into the harbor of Tripolis with a strong army and a fleet, ²and had taken possession of the country, having made away with Antiochus and his guardian Lysias.

3 Now a certain Alcimus, who had formerly been high priest but had willfully defiled himself in the times of separation,*ᶜ* realized that there was no way for him to be safe or to have access again to the holy altar, ⁴and went to King Demetrius in about the one hundred fifty-first year,*ᵈ* presenting to him a crown of gold and a palm, and besides these some of the customary olive branches from the temple. During that day he kept quiet. ⁵But he found an opportunity that furthered his mad purpose when he was invited by Demetrius to a meeting of the council and was asked about the attitude and intentions of the Jews. He answered:

6 "Those of the Jews who are called

---

a Meaning of Gk uncertain   *b* Or *faltered*
c Other ancient authorities read *of mixing*
d 161 B.C.

---

how to move in step with God through dedication to prayer individually and as a body. It is noteworthy that this prayer vigil lasted for several days. Those whose times of prayer never exceed an hour have not plumbed the depths of intimacy with God and the People of God that comes from more extended times of devotion together.

Responding

13:10–12 PRAYER. Challenge yourself by continually lengthening your prayer time by several minutes each time. Does this change your attitude toward prayer? *See also* Spiritual Disciplines Index.

13:12 FASTING—*See* Spiritual Disciplines Index.

Hasideans, whose leader is Judas Maccabeus, are keeping up war and stirring up sedition, and will not let the kingdom attain tranquility. [7]Therefore I have laid aside my ancestral glory—I mean the high priesthood—and have now come here, [8]first because I am genuinely concerned for the interests of the king, and second because I have regard also for my compatriots. For through the folly of those whom I have mentioned our whole nation is now in no small misfortune. [9]Since you are acquainted, O king, with the details of this matter, may it please you to take thought for our country and our hard-pressed nation with the gracious kindness that you show to all. [10]For as long as Judas lives, it is impossible for the government to find peace." [11]When he had said this, the rest of the king's Friends,[a] who were hostile to Judas, quickly inflamed Demetrius still more. [12]He immediately chose Nicanor, who had been in command of the elephants, appointed him governor of Judea, and sent him off [13]with orders to kill Judas and scatter his troops, and to install Alcimus as high priest of the great[b] temple. [14]And the Gentiles throughout Judea, who had fled before[c] Judas, flocked to join Nicanor, thinking that the misfortunes and calamities of the Jews would mean prosperity for themselves.

Nicanor Makes Friends with Judas

[15] When the Jews[d] heard of Nicanor's coming and the gathering of the Gentiles, they sprinkled dust on their heads and prayed to him who established his own people forever and always upholds his own heritage by manifesting himself. [16]At the command of the leader, they[e] set out from there immediately and engaged them in battle at a village called Dessau.[c] [17]Simon, the brother of Judas, had encountered Nicanor, but had been temporarily[f] checked because of the sudden consternation created by the enemy.

[18] Nevertheless Nicanor, hearing of the valor of Judas and his troops and their courage in battle for their country, shrank from deciding the issue by bloodshed. [19]Therefore he sent Posidonius, Theodotus, and Mattathias to give and receive pledges of friendship. [20]When the terms had been fully considered, and the leader had informed the people, and it had appeared that they were of one mind, they agreed to the covenant. [21]The leaders[g] set a day on which to meet by themselves. A chariot came forward from each army; seats of honor were set in place; [22]Judas posted armed men in readiness at key places to prevent sudden treachery on the part of the enemy; so they duly held the consultation.

[23] Nicanor stayed on in Jerusalem and did nothing out of the way, but dismissed the flocks of people that had gathered. [24]And he kept Judas always in his presence; he was warmly attached to the man. [25]He urged him to marry and have children; so Judas[e] married, settled down, and shared the common life.

Nicanor Turns against Judas

[26] But when Alcimus noticed their goodwill for one another, he took the covenant that had been made and went to Demetrius. He told him that Nicanor was disloyal to the government, since he had appointed that conspirator against the kingdom, Judas, to be his successor. [27]The king became excited and, provoked by the false accusations of that

a Gk of the Friends   b Gk greatest   c Meaning of Gk uncertain   d Gk they   e Gk he
f Other ancient authorities read slowly
g Gk They

14:15 *prayed to him who established his own people forever.* The Anglican collect is a form of prayer that begins with a declaration of some attribute of God and follows it with a petition that grows out of that attribute. The prayers in the Maccabean literature are the distant forebears of this powerful kind of prayer, in which God's character, as revealed in Scripture or previous acts of deliverance, informs how we hope and trust God will manifest himself anew in our lives. See also note on 8:2–4.

14:18–20 *hearing of the valor of Judas and his troops.* When we can look upon our "enemies," perceive their humanity, and even find respect and appreciation for their qualities, God is at work leading us away from conflict toward a less wasteful and destructive way forward.

depraved man, wrote to Nicanor, stating that he was displeased with the covenant and commanding him to send Maccabeus to Antioch as a prisoner without delay.

28 When this message came to Nicanor, he was troubled and grieved that he had to annul their agreement when the man had done no wrong. [29]Since it was not possible to oppose the king, he watched for an opportunity to accomplish this by a stratagem. [30]But Maccabeus, noticing that Nicanor was more austere in his dealings with him and was meeting him more rudely than had been his custom, concluded that this austerity did not spring from the best motives. So he gathered not a few of his men, and went into hiding from Nicanor. [31]When the latter became aware that he had been cleverly outwitted by the man, he went to the great[a] and holy temple while the priests were offering the customary sacrifices, and commanded them to hand the man over. [32]When they declared on oath that they did not know where the man was whom he wanted, [33]he stretched out his right hand toward the sanctuary, and swore this oath: "If you do not hand Judas over to me as a prisoner, I will level this shrine of God to the ground and tear down the altar, and build here a splendid temple to Dionysus."

34 Having said this, he went away. Then the priests stretched out their hands toward heaven and called upon the constant Defender of our nation, in these words: [35]"O Lord of all, though you have need of nothing, you were pleased that there should be a temple for your habitation among us; [36]so now, O holy One, Lord of all holiness, keep undefiled forever this house that has been so recently purified."

Razis Dies for His Country

37 A certain Razis, one of the elders of Jerusalem, was denounced to Nicanor as a man who loved his compatriots and was very well thought of and for his goodwill was called father of the Jews. [38]In former times, when there was no mingling with the Gentiles, he had been accused of Judaism, and he had most zealously risked body and life for Judaism. [39]Nicanor, wishing to exhibit the enmity that he had for the Jews, sent more than five hundred soldiers to arrest him; [40]for he thought that by arresting[b] him he would do them an injury. [41]When the troops were about to capture the tower and were forcing the door of the courtyard, they ordered that fire be brought and the doors burned. Being surrounded, Razis[c] fell upon his own sword, [42]preferring to die nobly rather than to fall into the hands of sinners and suffer outrages unworthy of his noble birth. [43]But in the heat of the struggle he did not hit exactly, and the crowd was now rushing in through the doors. He courageously ran up on the wall, and bravely threw himself down into the crowd. [44]But as they quickly drew back, a space opened and he fell in the middle of the empty space. [45]Still alive and aflame with anger, he rose, and though his blood gushed forth and his wounds were severe he ran through the crowd; and standing upon a steep rock, [46]with his blood now completely drained from him, he tore out his entrails, took them in both hands and hurled them at the crowd, calling upon the Lord of life and spirit to give them back to him again. This was the manner of his death.

Nicanor's Arrogance

15 When Nicanor heard that Judas and his troops were in the region of Samaria, he made plans to attack them with complete safety on the day of rest. [2]When the Jews who were compelled to follow him said, "Do not destroy so savagely and barbarously, but show respect for the day that he who sees all things has honored and hallowed above other days," [3]the thrice-accursed wretch asked if there were a sovereign in heaven who had commanded the keeping of the sabbath day. [4]When they declared, "It is the living Lord himself, the Sovereign in heaven,

a Gk greatest   b Meaning of Gk uncertain
c Gk he

14:32–36 swore this oath. See note on 1 Macc 7:35–42.

15:3–5 the Sovereign in heaven. Obedience to the heavenly sovereign has often brought the

who ordered us to observe the seventh day," [5]he replied, "But I am a sovereign also, on earth, and I command you to take up arms and finish the king's business." Nevertheless, he did not succeed in carrying out his abominable design.

Judas Prepares the Jews for Battle

6 This Nicanor in his utter boastfulness and arrogance had determined to erect a public monument of victory over Judas and his forces. [7]But Maccabeus did not cease to trust with all confidence that he would get help from the Lord. [8]He exhorted his troops not to fear the attack of the Gentiles, but to keep in mind the former times when help had come to them from heaven, and so to look for the victory that the Almighty would give them. [9]Encouraging them from the law and the prophets, and reminding them also of the struggles they had won, he made them the more eager. [10]When he had aroused their courage, he issued his orders, at the same time pointing out the perfidy of the Gentiles and their violation of oaths. [11]He armed each of them not so much with confidence in shields and spears as with the inspiration of brave words, and he cheered them all by re-

lating a dream, a sort of vision,[a] which was worthy of belief.

12 What he saw was this: Onias, who had been high priest, a noble and good man, of modest bearing and gentle manner, one who spoke fittingly and had been trained from childhood in all that belongs to excellence, was praying with outstretched hands for the whole body of the Jews. [13]Then in the same fashion another appeared, distinguished by his gray hair and dignity, and of marvelous majesty and authority. [14]And Onias spoke, saying, "This is a man who loves the family of Israel and prays much for the people and the holy city—Jeremiah, the prophet of God." [15]Jeremiah stretched out his right hand and gave to Judas a golden sword, and as he gave it he addressed him thus: [16]"Take this holy sword, a gift from God, with which you will strike down your adversaries."

17 Encouraged by the words of Judas, so noble and so effective in arousing valor and awaking courage in the souls of the young, they determined not to carry on a campaign[b] but to attack bravely, and to decide the matter by fighting hand to hand with all courage,

a Meaning of Gk uncertain   b Or to remain in camp

People of God into conflict with the demands of temporal authorities. Regular communion with God and stepping out in obedience to God in small ways in times of tranquillity are the best preparation for standing boldly for God and his commandments when the temporal authorities try to impose their will by violent force.

15:7–9 *times when help had come to them from heaven . . . the law and the prophets.* Judas indicates two perpetually helpful resources for spiritual encouragement in the face of new trials: remembrance of the People of God's individual or collective experience of God's help and guidance in the past and recollection of Scripture.

Responding
15:9 STUDY. Judas's command of Scripture was so strong that he could draw upon it to encourage those around him. Knowledge like this comes from a great deal of study. If regular Bible study is a challenge for

you, consider asking a friend or your spouse to study the Bible with you and hold you accountable for your study time. *See also* Spiritual Disciplines Index.

15:12–16 *What he saw was this.* This passage becomes a warrant for the belief that the saints now in God's presence intercede on behalf of their sisters and brothers still facing the trials of this life. It also encourages us to be receptive to nonrational ways in which God might choose to communicate timely and helpful messages to us, dreams and visions being frequent means for divine revelation throughout the witness of Scripture.

Responding
15:12–16 GUIDANCE. Consider keeping a journal by your bed in which to record your dreams. As you write each dream down, ask God to reveal its significance. *See also* Spiritual Disciplines Index.

because the city and the sanctuary and the temple were in danger. [18]Their concern for wives and children, and also for brothers and sisters[a] and relatives, lay upon them less heavily; their greatest and first fear was for the consecrated sanctuary. [19]And those who had to remain in the city were in no little distress, being anxious over the encounter in the open country.

The Defeat and Death of Nicanor

20 When all were now looking forward to the coming issue, and the enemy was already close at hand with their army drawn up for battle, the elephants[b] strategically stationed and the cavalry deployed on the flanks, [21]Maccabeus, observing the masses that were in front of him and the varied supply of arms and the savagery of the elephants, stretched out his hands toward heaven and called upon the Lord who works wonders; for he knew that it is not by arms, but as the Lord[c] decides, that he gains the victory for those who deserve it. [22]He called upon him in these words: "O Lord, you sent your angel in the time of King Hezekiah of Judea, and he killed fully one hundred eighty-five thousand in the camp of Sennacherib. [23]So now, O Sovereign of the heavens, send a good angel to spread terror and trembling before us. [24]By the might of your arm may these blasphemers who come against your holy people be struck down." With these words he ended his prayer.

25 Nicanor and his troops advanced with trumpets and battle songs, [26]but Judas and his troops met the enemy in battle with invocations to God and prayers. [27]So, fighting with their hands and praying to God in their hearts, they laid low at least thirty-five thousand, and were greatly gladdened by God's manifestation.

28 When the action was over and they were returning with joy, they recognized Nicanor, lying dead, in full armor. [29]Then there was shouting and tumult, and they blessed the Sovereign Lord in the language of their ancestors. [30]Then the man who was ever in body and soul the defender of his people, the man who maintained his youthful goodwill toward his compatriots, ordered them to cut off Nicanor's head and arm and carry them to Jerusalem. [31]When he arrived there and had called his compatriots together and stationed the priests before the altar, he sent for those who were in the citadel. [32]He showed them the vile Nicanor's head and that profane man's arm, which had been boastfully stretched out against the holy house of the Almighty. [33]He cut out the tongue of the ungodly Nicanor and said that he would feed it piecemeal to the birds and would hang up these rewards of his folly opposite the sanctuary. [34]And they all, looking to heaven, blessed the Lord who had manifested himself, saying, "Blessed is he who has kept his own place undefiled!" [35]Judas[d] hung Nicanor's head from the citadel, a clear and conspicuous sign to everyone of the help of the Lord. [36]And they all decreed by public vote never to let this day go unobserved, but to celebrate the thirteenth day of the twelfth month—which is called Adar in the Aramaic language—the day before Mordecai's day.

37 This, then, is how matters turned out with Nicanor, and from that time the city has been in the possession of the Hebrews. So I will here end my story.

a Gk *for brothers*   b Gk *animals*   c Gk *he*
d Gk *He*

15:27 *fighting with their hands and praying to God in their hearts.* As disciples of Jesus, who taught us to love, pray for, and show kindness to our enemies (Matt 5:43–48; Luke 6:35–36), the shape of our "fighting" changes dramatically. Nevertheless, this portion of the verse provides an apt motto for those seeking spiritual maturity; we keep ourselves in constant conversation with God and set ourselves ever at his disposal, even as we fully engage the tasks God has placed before us in our vocation and mission.

15:36 *never to let this day go unobserved.* New deliverances by God's hand call for new festivals for collective expressions of gratitude to God for his mighty acts, by which they can become part of the memory of the People of God and continue to fuel faith for the future. See also note on 1 Macc 4:59.

The Compiler's Epilogue

38 If it is well told and to the point, that is what I myself desired; if it is poorly done and mediocre, that was the best I could do. 39For just as it is harmful to drink wine alone, or, again, to drink water alone, while wine mixed with water is sweet and delicious and enhances one's enjoyment, so also the style of the story delights the ears of those who read the work. And here will be the end.

3 MACCABEES

The book of 3 Maccabees is best described as a work of historical fiction. Characters, locations, and situations from real history appear in its pages, but not to recount a true history. The author appears to have combined the true story of the defeat of Antiochus III at the Battle of Raphia, the Heliodorus episode from 2 Maccabees 3 (without the motives of plundering the Temple), reminiscences of Pompey's unauthorized tour of the holy places, an actual (but more local) persecution of Jews under a later Ptolemy, and purely fictional elements (like forced apostasy from Judaism to the cult of Dionysus) into a dramatic and stirring tale of deliverance. This book was probably written in Egypt, perhaps even Alexandria, during the early Roman period (between 30 BC and AD 50). The tensions between Jews and the indigenous population reflected in the story accord well with what we know of the friction between Jews and Gentiles in that area (including the issue of whether Jews are to be considered "citizens" of Alexandria).

Third Maccabees very closely parallels the story of 2 Maccabees. A gentile leader intends to profane the Temple, setting the Jews in an uproar (2 Macc 3:1–21; 3 Macc 1:1–29); a high priest offers an effective prayer (2 Macc 3:31–34; 3 Macc 2:1–20); God stops the arrogant Gentile in his tracks (2 Macc 3:22–30; 3 Macc 2:21–24). Thereafter, a gentile king tries to force apostasy upon a Jewish population (2 Macc 4:7–17; 6:1–11; 3 Macc 2:25–33); persecution of the faithful ensues (2 Macc 6:12–7:42; 3 Macc 3:1–5:51); an elderly, steadfast priest named Eleazar and other faithful Jews pray for God's help (2 Macc 6:26–30; 7:37–38; 8:2–4; 3 Macc 6:1–17); God and his angels rescue God's people (2 Macc 8:5–9:29; 11:6–12; 15:22–24; 3 Macc 6:18–21); and the Jews establish an annual festival commemorating their deliverance (2 Macc 10:1–8; 3 Macc 6:30–40). The author of 3 Maccabees provides Egyptian Jews with a saga similar to the one in 2 Maccabees to assure them that they share in the fortunes of the Temple just as much as Jews in Israel and that God cares for his people "in the land of their enemies" (Lev 26:44, quoted in 3 Macc 6:15) just as carefully and

See also *"The With-God Life"* essay for this section of the Bible, *"The People of God in Restoration,"* pp. 1355–59.

decisively as God does for his people in the land of Israel. Exile from the land in no way implies exile from God's presence or help—or a spiritually inferior position in any regard.

Knowledge of God

This book underscores the importance of knowing who God is and how God acts, knowledge that comes through the study of the sacred story recorded in the Scriptures. This knowledge, a foundation that needs to be laid while life is on an even keel, becomes the basis for hope and the direction for prayer and action amid the crises of life. The book also highlights the importance of recognizing how God is presently at work in our lives and communities, discerning God's hand "behind the scenes," as it were, so that we are more aware of and assured by God's presence and care. The ethnocentrism of the book is unmistakable, a legacy the early Christians would overcome as they proclaimed that the One God of the Jews was also the God of the Gentiles.

—*David A. deSilva*

The Battle of Raphia

1 When Philopator learned from those who returned that the regions that he had controlled had been seized by Antiochus, he gave orders to all his forces, both infantry and cavalry, took with him his sister Arsinoë, and marched out to the region near Raphia, where the army of Antiochus was encamped. 2But a certain Theodotus, determined to carry out the plot he had devised, took with him the best of the Ptolemaic arms that had been previously issued to him,*a* and crossed over by night to the tent of Ptolemy, intending single-handed to kill him and thereby end the war. 3But Dositheus, known as the son of Drimylus, a Jew by birth who later changed his religion and apostatized from the ancestral traditions, had led the king away and arranged that a certain insignificant man should sleep in the tent; and so it turned out that this man incurred the vengeance meant for the king.*b* 4When a bitter fight resulted, and matters were turning out rather in favor of Antiochus, Arsinoë went to the troops with wailing and tears, her locks all disheveled, and exhorted them to defend themselves and their children and wives bravely, promising to give them each two minas of gold if they won the battle. 5And so it came about that the enemy was routed in

the action, and many captives also were taken. 6Now that he had foiled the plot, Ptolemy*c* decided to visit the neighboring cities and encourage them. 7By doing this, and by endowing their sacred enclosures with gifts, he strengthened the morale of his subjects.

Philopator Attempts to Enter the Temple

8 Since the Jews had sent some of their council and elders to greet him, to bring him gifts of welcome, and to congratulate him on what had happened, he was all the more eager to visit them as soon as possible. 9After he had arrived in Jerusalem, he offered sacrifice to the supreme God*d* and made thank offerings and did what was fitting for the holy place.*e* Then, upon entering the place and being impressed by its excellence and its beauty, 10he marveled at the good order of the temple, and conceived a desire to enter the sanctuary. 11When they said that this was not permitted, because not even members of their own nation were allowed to enter, not even all of the priests, but only the high priest who was pre-eminent over all—and he only once a year—the king was by no means per-

a Or *the best of the Ptolemaic soldiers previously put under his command*   *b* Gk *that one*   *c* Gk *he*   *d* Gk *the greatest God*   *e* Gk *the place*

suaded. [12]Even after the law had been read to him, he did not cease to maintain that he ought to enter, saying, "Even if those men are deprived of this honor, I ought not to be." [13]And he inquired why, when he entered every other temple,[a] no one there had stopped him. [14]And someone answered thoughtlessly that it was wrong to take that as a portent.[b] [15]"But since this has happened," the king[c] said, "why should not I at least enter, whether they wish it or not?"

Jewish Resistance to Ptolemy

16 Then the priests in all their vestments prostrated themselves and entreated the supreme God[d] to aid in the present situation and to avert the violence of this evil design, and they filled the temple with cries and tears; [17]those who remained behind in the city were agitated and hurried out, supposing that something mysterious was occurring. [18]Young women who had been secluded in their chambers rushed out with their mothers, sprinkled their hair with dust,[e] and filled the streets with groans and lamentations. [19]Those women who had recently been arrayed for marriage abandoned the bridal chambers[f] prepared for wedded union, and, neglecting proper modesty, in a disorderly rush flocked together in the city. [20]Mothers and nurses abandoned even newborn children here and there, some in houses and some in the streets, and without a backward look they crowded together at the most high temple. [21]Various were the supplications of those gathered there because of what the king was profanely plotting. [22]In addition, the bolder of the citizens would not tolerate the completion of his plans or the fulfillment of his intended purpose. [23]They shouted to their compatriots to take arms and die courageously for the ancestral law, and created a considerable disturbance in the holy place;[g] and being barely restrained by the old men and the elders,[h] they resorted to the same posture of supplication as the others. [24]Meanwhile the crowd, as before, was engaged in prayer, [25]while the elders near the king tried in various ways to change his arrogant mind from the plan that he had conceived. [26]But

a Or *entered the temple precincts*   b Or *to boast of this*   c Gk *he*   d Gk *the greatest God*   e Other ancient authorities add *and ashes*   f Or *the canopies*   g Gk *the place*   h Other ancient authorities read *priests*

1:11–12 *not even members of their own nation were allowed to enter.* The strict limitations on access to the Holy of Holies—being permitted only to one man and that only once each year—does not mean that Jews regarded God as distant and inaccessible. Indeed, one of the principal themes of 3 Maccabees is that, even in the land of Egypt, far away from the Temple, God is near to his people and readily accessible through fervent prayer. We are reminded, however, that Jesus ushered in a decisively new stage in human-divine relationships when he opened up God's heavenly Holy of Holies to the many sons and daughters who follow Christ (Heb 9:6–14; 10:19–25). Our times of prayer (Heb 4:14–16), corporate worship (Heb 10:19–25; 13:15), and Christian service (Heb 13:16) all anticipate and culminate in our welcome into the full and unveiled presence of God.

1:18–21 *filled the streets with groans and lamentations.* Observing the frenzied response of the citizens of Jerusalem to the threat to the Temple may remind us of the benefits we have received: we no longer depend on a vulnerable sacred space for our connection with God, since Christ entered heaven itself and purified us to be a living, global temple. Their passionate response, however, also raises the question: What should command our attention, our concern, our immediate investment of ourselves, to the point where we too would cast considerations even of propriety aside? Where is God's temple—the Body of Christ—in danger of profanation now on account of human arrogance and ignorance of God's justice, and how are we called to seek God's intervention?

1:23 *to take arms and die courageously.* Violent action requires a measure of courage; submitting a situation to God in fervent prayer and seeking how God would intervene can require both greater courage and faith. In the world of the story, of course, the results of the latter course of action are far better, preserving life and establishing a more secure peace in the end.

he, in his arrogance, took heed of nothing, and began now to approach, determined to bring the aforesaid plan to a conclusion. 27When those who were around him observed this, they turned, together with our people, to call upon him who has all power to defend them in the present trouble and not to overlook this unlawful and haughty deed. 28The continuous, vehement, and concerted cry of the crowds[a] resulted in an immense uproar; 29for it seemed that not only the people but also the walls and the whole earth around echoed, because indeed all at that time[b] preferred death to the profanation of the place.

The Prayer of the High Priest Simon

2 Then the high priest Simon, facing the sanctuary, bending his knees and extending his hands with calm dignity, prayed as follows:[c] 2"Lord, Lord, king of the heavens, and sovereign of all creation, holy among the holy ones, the only ruler, almighty, give attention to us who are suffering grievously from an impious and profane man, puffed up in his audacity and power. 3For you, the creator of all things and the governor of all, are a just Ruler, and you judge those who

have done anything in insolence and arrogance. 4You destroyed those who in the past committed injustice, among whom were even giants who trusted in their strength and boldness, whom you destroyed by bringing on them a boundless flood. 5You consumed with fire and sulfur the people of Sodom who acted arrogantly, who were notorious for their vices;[d] and you made them an example to those who should come afterward. 6You made known your mighty power by inflicting many and varied punishments on the audacious Pharaoh who had enslaved your holy people Israel. 7And when he pursued them with chariots and a mass of troops, you overwhelmed him in the depths of the sea, but carried through safely those who had put their confidence in you, the Ruler over the whole creation. 8And when they had seen works of your hands, they praised you, the Almighty. 9You, O King, when you had created the boundless and immeasurable earth, chose this city and sanctified this place for

a Other ancient authorities read *vehement cry of the assembled crowds*   b Other ancient authorities lack *at that time*   c Other ancient authorities lack verse 1   d Other ancient authorities read *secret in their vices*

2:2–20 *Lord, Lord, king of the heavens.* The prayer of Simon the high priest (2:2–20), like the prayer of the priestly Eleazar (6:2–15), looks to the story of God's past acts of deliverance as the basis for expecting God's deliverance in the present. These prayers (like many of the psalms that follow the same pattern) teach us that God's past acts express something about his unchanging character and that this in turn provides the basis for understanding what God will do in the present situation. Reading and reflecting on Scripture is such an important Spiritual Discipline, in part, because it shapes our expectations and prepares us for encounters with God in the present and future. Reading and reflecting on the traces of God's hand in our own lives and in the story of our faith community provide another vital and empowering resource for the same.

Responding
2:2–20 STUDY. What does this prayer teach us about the purpose of study?

Reflect on your favorite Bible story. Why is it your favorite? What does it teach you about the nature of God? *See also* Spiritual Disciplines Index.

2:3–8 *you judge those who have done anything in insolence and arrogance.* Simon focuses his prayer on the perception that God judges those who act insolently or arrogantly, something he has learned from God's punishment of the giants by the flood (v 4; see Gen 6:1–4 and its extensive development in *1 Enoch* 6–36, which are presupposed here), the destruction of Sodom (v 5; see Gen 19:16–28), and the punishment of Pharaoh (vv 6–8; see Exod 1–14). It is by means of crushing the arrogant that God makes his honor known and recognized in the world, another principle that fuels prayer for God's ongoing interventions on behalf of his oppressed people.

2:9–10 *You . . . chose this city.* The Temple is understood as a gift from God to Israel, a means by which God has made himself accessible to

your name, though you have no need of anything; and when you had glorified it by your magnificent manifestation,[a] you made it a firm foundation for the glory of your great and honored name. 10And because you love the house of Israel, you promised that if we should have reverses and tribulation should overtake us, you would listen to our petition when we come to this place and pray. 11And indeed you are faithful and true. 12And because oftentimes when our fathers were oppressed you helped them in their humiliation, and rescued them from great evils, 13see now, O holy King, that because of our many and great sins we are crushed with suffering, subjected to our enemies, and overtaken by helplessness. 14In our downfall this audacious and profane man undertakes to violate the holy place on earth dedicated to your glorious name. 15For your dwelling is the heaven of heavens, unapproachable by human beings. 16But because you graciously bestowed your glory on your people Israel, you sanctified this place. 17Do not punish us for the defilement committed by these men, or call us to account for this profanation, otherwise the transgressors will boast in their wrath and exult in the arrogance of their tongue, saying, 18'We have trampled down the house of the sanctuary as the houses of the abominations are trampled down.' 19Wipe away our sins and disperse our errors, and reveal your mercy at this hour. 20Speedily let your mercies overtake us, and put praises in the mouth of those who are downcast and broken in spirit, and give us peace."

God's Punishment of Ptolemy

21 Thereupon God, who oversees all things, the first Father of all, holy among the holy ones, having heard the lawful supplication, scourged him who had exalted himself in insolence and audacity. 22He shook him on this side and that as a reed is shaken by the wind, so that he lay helpless on the ground and, besides being paralyzed in his limbs, was unable even to speak, since he was smitten[b] by a righteous judgment. 23Then both friends and bodyguards, seeing the severe punishment that had overtaken him, and fearing that he would lose his life, quickly dragged him out, panic-stricken in their exceedingly great fear. 24After a while he recovered, and though he had been punished, he by no means repented, but went away uttering bitter threats.

Hostile Measures against the Jews

25 When he arrived in Egypt, he increased in his deeds of malice, abetted by the previously mentioned drinking companions and comrades, who were strangers to everything just. 26He was not content with his uncounted licentious deeds, but even continued with such audacity that he framed evil reports in the various localities; and many of his friends, intently observing the king's purpose, themselves also followed his will. 27He proposed to inflict public disgrace on the Jewish community,[c] and he set up a stone[d] on the tower in the courtyard with this inscrip-

a Or *epiphany*   b Other ancient authorities read *pierced*   c Gk *the nation*   d Gk *stele*

---

his people. It is not based on a false view that God is only present in the Temple or that God has need of a human-made dwelling. Sacred space is a gift to human beings, to facilitate our approach to the divine. Far from limiting God, sacred space helps us overcome our own limitations. Identifying sacred spaces can be an aid to us. Moving toward and entering them with our bodies can serve as an aid to moving toward God in our intentions and preparing to encounter God.

2:25 *abetted by . . . drinking companions.* The author provides a brief reminder that we can be spurred on in our baser or nobler designs by the

company with which we surround ourselves. A cadre of friends committed to growing in discipleship is a means of grace by which our own spiritual formation is promoted and empowered.

**Responding
2:25–26 FELLOWSHIP.** Is someone in your life causing you to stumble? What is it about the relationship that makes it a negative influence? Can your relationship be made healthy or is it better severed? *See also* Spiritual Disciplines Index.

tion: [28]"None of those who do not sacrifice shall enter their sanctuaries, and all Jews shall be subjected to a registration involving poll tax and to the status of slaves. Those who object to this are to be taken by force and put to death; [29]those who are registered are also to be branded on their bodies by fire with the ivy-leaf symbol of Dionysus, and they shall also be reduced to their former limited status." [30]In order that he might not appear to be an enemy of all, he inscribed below: "But if any of them prefer to join those who have been initiated into the mysteries, they shall have equal citizenship with the Alexandrians."

[31] Now some, however, with an obvious abhorrence of the price to be exacted for maintaining the religion of their city,[a] readily gave themselves up, since they expected to enhance their reputation by their future association with the king. [32]But the majority acted firmly with a courageous spirit and did not abandon their religion; and by paying money in exchange for life they confidently attempted to save themselves from the registration. [33]They remained resolutely hopeful of obtaining help, and they abhorred those who separated themselves from them, considering them to be enemies of the Jewish nation,[b] and depriving them of companionship and mutual help.

The Jews and Their Neighbors

3 When the impious king comprehended this situation, he became so infuriated that not only was he enraged against those Jews who lived in Alexandria, but was still more bitterly hostile toward those in the countryside; and he ordered that all should promptly be gathered into one place, and put to death by the most cruel means. [2]While these matters were being arranged, a hostile rumor was circulated against the Jewish nation by some who conspired to do them ill, a pretext being given by a report that they hindered others[c] from the observance of their customs. [3]The Jews, however, continued to maintain goodwill and unswerving loyalty toward the dynasty; [4]but because they worshiped God and conducted themselves by his law, they kept their separateness with respect to foods. For this reason they appeared hateful to some; [5]but since they adorned their style of life with the good deeds of upright people, they were established in good repute with everyone. [6]Nevertheless those of other races paid no heed to their good service

a Meaning of Gk uncertain   b Gk the nation
c Gk them

2:33 *depriving them of companionship and mutual help.* The response of the faithful Jews toward the apostate Jews is important in this story. In this scene, we find a picture of the Jewish community exercising corporate discipline toward Jews who prefer to break faith with God and participate in idolatrous rites than bear the cost of fidelity (see vv 30–31). Several New Testament texts also raise the question of how the congregation of believers should serve as a resource for spiritual discipline, so as to facilitate the commitment of individual believers to persevere in faithful witness, holiness of life, and Christian service (see, e.g., Matt 18:10–20; 1 Cor 5:1–13; Gal 6:1; Col 3:16; Heb 3:12–14; 10:24–25). Our own spiritual formation is linked inextricably with our responsibility to, and responsibility for, one another in the family of faith.

3:3–7 *conducted themselves by his law.* The distinctive lifestyle of the Jews could inspire either admiration or disdain among non-Jews. Walking in line with Torah meant, practically, forming close-knit communities in which people produced their own food (necessary to be sure it was ritually clean and properly slaughtered), ate with one another, and avoided all settings where Gentiles would worship some idol (which would include most private parties, guild meetings, and civic festivals). The Jews came to be maligned as "atheists" (because they denied the many gods their due and because they refused any physical representation of Yahweh) and xenophobes (because they tended to mingle with their own). They sought, however, to counteract such perceptions with benevolent and honorable deeds, just as we Christians are advised to do (see 1 Pet 2:11–12, 15) when our way of life conforms so completely to God's values that we become an affront to the world around us.

to their nation, which was common talk among all; [7]instead they gossiped about the differences in worship and foods, alleging that these people were loyal neither to the king nor to his authorities, but were hostile and greatly opposed to his government. So they attached no ordinary reproach to them.

8 The Greeks in the city, though wronged in no way, when they saw an unexpected tumult around these people and the crowds that suddenly were forming, were not strong enough to help them, for they lived under tyranny. They did try to console them, being grieved at the situation, and expected that matters would change; [9]for such a great community ought not be left to its fate when it had committed no offense. [10]And already some of their neighbors and friends and business associates had taken some of them aside privately and were pledging to protect them and to exert more earnest efforts for their assistance.

Ptolemy's Decree That All Jews Be Arrested

11 Then the king, boastful of his present good fortune, and not considering the might of the supreme God,[a] but assuming that he would persevere constantly in his same purpose, wrote this letter against them:

12 "King Ptolemy Philopator to his generals and soldiers in Egypt and all its districts, greetings and good health:

13 "I myself and our government are faring well. [14]When our expedition took place in Asia, as you yourselves know, it was brought to conclusion, according to plan, by the gods' deliberate alliance with us in battle, [15]and we considered that we should not rule the nations inhabiting Coelesyria and Phoenicia by the power of the spear, but should

cherish them with clemency and great benevolence, gladly treating them well. [16]And when we had granted very great revenues to the temples in the cities, we came on to Jerusalem also, and went up to honor the temple of those wicked people, who never cease from their folly. [17]They accepted our presence by word, but insincerely by deed, because when we proposed to enter their inner temple and honor it with magnificent and most beautiful offerings, [18]they were carried away by their traditional arrogance, and excluded us from entering; but they were spared the exercise of our power because of the benevolence that we have toward all. [19]By maintaining their manifest ill-will toward us, they become the only people among all nations who hold their heads high in defiance of kings and their own benefactors, and are unwilling to regard any action as sincere.

20 "But we, when we arrived in Egypt victorious, accommodated ourselves to their folly and did as was proper, since we treat all nations with benevolence. [21]Among other things, we made known to all our amnesty toward their compatriots here, both because of their alliance with us and the myriad affairs liberally entrusted to them from the beginning; and we ventured to make a change, by deciding both to deem them worthy of Alexandrian citizenship and to make them participants in our regular religious rites.[b] [22]But in their innate malice they took this in a contrary spirit, and disdained what is good. Since they incline constantly to evil, [23]they not only spurn the priceless citizenship, but also both by speech and by silence they abom-

---

a Gk *the greatest God*　　　b Other ancient authorities read *partners of our regular priests*

3:18–19 *By maintaining their manifest ill-will toward us.* Ptolemy's interpretation of the Jews' pious and correct actions in regard to the Jerusalem Temple warn people of faith to prepare to be misunderstood. The strategy for correcting such misunderstanding prescribed by this text is to reach out in acts of kindness, act honorably in all things, and entrust all matters to God, who alone can change the mind of other human beings.

3:22–23 *disdained what is good.* As we seek to bring our lives into closer conformity with Christ's and as we follow God's call in our lives, we are going to be challenged to make a number of decisions showing that what the world holds most dear is not most dear to us. As we grow in discipleship, we need to be prepared to be accused of "disdaining what is good" in our neighbors' eyes for the sake of attaining what is best in God's sight.

inate those few among them who are sincerely disposed toward us; in every situation, in accordance with their infamous way of life, they secretly suspect that we may soon alter our policy. 24Therefore, fully convinced by these indications that they are ill-disposed toward us in every way, we have taken precautions so that, if a sudden disorder later arises against us, we shall not have these impious people behind our backs as traitors and barbarous enemies. 25Therefore we have given orders that, as soon as this letter arrives, you are to send to us those who live among you, together with their wives and children, with insulting and harsh treatment, and bound securely with iron fetters, to suffer the sure and shameful death that befits enemies. 26For when all of these have been punished, we are sure that for the remaining time the government will be established for ourselves in good order and in the best state. 27But those who shelter any of the Jews, whether old people or children or even infants, will be tortured to death with the most hateful torments, together with their families. 28Any who are willing to give information will receive the property of those who incur the punishment, and also two thousand drachmas from the royal treasury, and will be awarded their freedom. *a* 29Every place detected sheltering a Jew is to be made unapproachable and burned with fire, and shall become useless for all time to any mortal creature." 30The letter was written in the above form.

The Jews Deported to Alexandria

4 In every place, then, where this decree arrived, a feast at public expense was arranged for the Gentiles with shouts and gladness, for the inveterate enmity that had long ago been in their minds was now made evident and outspoken. 2But among the Jews there was incessant mourning, lamentation, and tearful cries; everywhere their hearts were burning, and they groaned because of the unexpected destruction that had suddenly been decreed for them. 3What district or city, or what habitable place at all, or what streets were not filled with mourning and wailing for them? 4For with such a harsh and ruthless spirit were they being sent off, all together, by the generals in the several cities, that at the sight of their unusual punishments, even some of their enemies, perceiving the common object of pity before their eyes, reflected on the uncertainty of life and shed tears at the most miserable expulsion of these people. 5For a multitude of gray-headed old men, sluggish and bent with age, was being led away, forced to march at a swift pace by the violence with which they were driven in such a shameful manner. 6And young women who had just entered the bridal chamber *b* to share married life exchanged joy for wailing, their myrrh-perfumed hair sprinkled with ashes, and were carried away unveiled, all together raising a lament instead of a wedding song, as they were torn by the harsh treatment of the heathen. *c* 7In bonds and in public view they were violently dragged along as far as the place of embarkation. 8Their husbands, in the prime of youth, their necks encircled

a Gk *crowned with freedom*   *b* Or *the canopy*
c Other ancient authorities read *as though torn by heathen whelps*

3:27, 29 *those who shelter any of the Jews.* Showing solidarity with and kindness toward the People of God can be very costly, especially under repressive regimes. These verses cannot help but recall the situation in Nazi Germany, and now the situation in many nations where Christianity is a prohibited religion. We who live in tolerant nations are challenged to pray that God would raise up people in every nation who will be willing to risk their lives to shelter victims of injustice, and seek out ways in which to create such shelter ourselves.

4:4 *even some of their enemies . . . reflected on the uncertainty of life.* The reversal of fortune experienced by the Jewish people becomes an object lesson in the "uncertainty of life," a common theme of Greek tragedy and a fact noted countless times in history. Given this fact, it is all the more essential to give adequate attention to building and maintaining an unshakable foundation for life that will sustain us through the chances and changes of life; hence the vital importance of the Spiritual Disciplines.

with ropes instead of garlands, spent the remaining days of their marriage festival in lamentations instead of good cheer and youthful revelry, seeing death immediately before them. [a] [9]They were brought on board like wild animals, driven under the constraint of iron bonds; some were fastened by the neck to the benches of the boats, others had their feet secured by unbreakable fetters, [10]and in addition they were confined under a solid deck, so that, with their eyes in total darkness, they would undergo treatment befitting traitors during the whole voyage.

The Jews Imprisoned at Schedia

11 When these people had been brought to the place called Schedia, and the voyage was concluded as the king had decreed, he commanded that they should be enclosed in the hippodrome that had been built with a monstrous perimeter wall in front of the city, and that was well suited to make them an obvious spectacle to all coming back into the city and to those from the city [b] going out into the country, so that they could neither communicate with the king's forces nor in any way claim to be inside the circuit of the city. [c] [12]And when this had happened, the king, hearing that the Jews' compatriots from the city frequently went out in secret to lament bitterly the ignoble misfortune of their kindred, [13]ordered in his rage that these people be dealt with in precisely the same fashion as the others, not omitting any detail of their punishment. [14]The entire race was to be registered individually, not for the hard labor that has been briefly mentioned before, but to be tortured with the outrages that he had ordered, and at the end to be destroyed in the space of a single day. [15]The registration of these people was therefore conducted with bitter haste and zealous intensity from the rising of the sun until its setting, coming to an end after forty days but still uncompleted.

16 The king was greatly and continually filled with joy, organizing feasts in honor of all his idols, with a mind alienated from truth and with a profane mouth, praising speechless things that are not able even to communicate or to come to one's help, and uttering improper words against the supreme God. [d] [17]But after the previously mentioned interval of time the scribes declared to the king that they were no longer able to take the census of the Jews because of their immense number, [18]though most of them were still in the country, some still residing in their homes, and some at the place; [e] the task was impossible for all the generals in Egypt. [19]After he had threatened them severely, charging that they had been bribed to contrive a means of escape, he was clearly convinced about the matter [20]when they said and proved that both the paper [f] and the pens they used for writing had already given out. [21]But this was an act of the invincible providence of him who was aiding the Jews from heaven.

Execution of the Jews Is Twice Thwarted

5 Then the king, completely inflexible, was filled with overpowering anger and wrath; so he summoned Hermon, keeper of the elephants, [2]and ordered him on the following day to drug all the elephants—five hundred in number—with large handfuls of

a Gk *seeing Hades already lying at their feet*
b Gk *those of them*   c Or *claim protection of the walls*; meaning of Gk uncertain   d Gk *the greatest God*   e Other ancient authorities read *on the way*
f Or *paper factory*

4:9–10 *They were brought on board like wild animals.* Such suffering as the Jews endured in the story (the literary details of which cannot help but recall the sufferings of African people in the "Middle Passage," the slave trade) is calculated to break the spirit of human beings, but it can also become the crucible in which deep and invincible spirituality is refined. What human beings intend for evil, God can transform for good.

4:21 *an act of the invincible providence.* (See also 5:11–13; 5:28–30; 6:18–21.) God's providential care for the Jews in Egypt is manifested in each of the three times the execution attempt is thwarted. What might seem like tedious ebb and flow in the plot actually underscores the main theological point of the story.

frankincense and plenty of unmixed wine, and to drive them in, maddened by the lavish abundance of drink, so that the Jews might meet their doom. ³When he had given these orders he returned to his feasting, together with those of his Friends and of the army who were especially hostile toward the Jews. ⁴And Hermon, keeper of the elephants, proceeded faithfully to carry out the orders. ⁵The servants in charge of the Jews *a* went out in the evening and bound the hands of the wretched people and arranged for their continued custody through the night, convinced that the whole nation would experience its final destruction. ⁶For to the Gentiles it appeared that the Jews were left without any aid, ⁷because in their bonds they were forcibly confined on every side. But with tears and a voice hard to silence they all called upon the Almighty Lord and Ruler of all power, their merciful God and Father, praying ⁸that he avert with vengeance the evil plot against them and in a glorious manifestation rescue them from the fate now prepared for them. ⁹So their entreaty ascended fervently to heaven.

10 Hermon, however, when he had drugged the pitiless elephants until they had been filled with a great abundance of wine and satiated with frankincense, presented himself at the courtyard early in the morning to report to the king about these preparations. ¹¹But the Lord *b* sent upon the king a portion of sleep, that beneficence that from the beginning, night and day, is bestowed by him who grants it to whomever he wishes. ¹²And

by the action of the Lord he was overcome by so pleasant and deep a sleep *c* that he quite failed in his lawless purpose and was completely frustrated in his inflexible plan. ¹³Then the Jews, since they had escaped the appointed hour, praised their holy God and again implored him who is easily reconciled to show the might of his all-powerful hand to the arrogant Gentiles.

14 But now, since it was nearly the middle of the tenth hour, the person who was in charge of the invitations, seeing that the guests were assembled, approached the king and nudged him. ¹⁵And when he had with difficulty roused him, he pointed out that the hour of the banquet was already slipping by, and he gave him an account of the situation. ¹⁶The king, after considering this, returned to his drinking, and ordered those present for the banquet to recline opposite him. ¹⁷When this was done he urged them to give themselves over to revelry and to make the present *d* portion of the banquet joyful by celebrating all the more. ¹⁸After the party had been going on for some time, the king summoned Hermon and with sharp threats demanded to know why the Jews had been allowed to remain alive through the present day. ¹⁹But when he, with the corroboration of the king's *e* Friends, pointed out that while it was still night he had carried out completely the order given him, ²⁰the king, *b* possessed by

a Gk *them*   *b* Gk *he*   *c* Other ancient authorities add *from evening until the ninth hour*   *d* Other ancient authorities read *delayed* (Gk *untimely*)   *e* Gk *his*

5:7–8, 11 *in a glorious manifestation rescue them.* The people pray for deliverance by means of a "glorious manifestation," but God's first act in response to their prayer is simply to have King Ptolemy sleep a few extra hours past the appointed time—not a very impressive display, but still very effective. The author would train us not to miss the "miraculous" in the mundane or ordinary, wherever God is at work.

Responding
5:7–9 PRAYER. The People of God prayed with the full expectation that God would answer their prayer if they pre-

sented it with the right action and right attitude. As Richard Foster writes in *Celebration of Discipline:* "We can determine if we are praying correctly if the requests come to pass. If not, we look for the 'block'; perhaps we are praying wrongly, perhaps something within us needs changing, perhaps there are new principles of prayer to be learned, perhaps patience and persistence are needed. We listen, make the necessary adjustments, and try again." Reflect on these words. Are your prayers being answered? If not, what is your block? *See also* Spiritual Disciplines Index.

a savagery worse than that of Phalaris, said that the Jews[a] were benefited by today's sleep, "but," he added, "tomorrow without delay prepare the elephants in the same way for the destruction of the lawless Jews!" 21When the king had spoken, all those present readily and joyfully with one accord gave their approval, and all went to their own homes. 22But they did not so much employ the duration of the night in sleep as in devising all sorts of insults for those they thought to be doomed.

23 Then, as soon as the cock had crowed in the early morning, Hermon, having equipped[b] the animals, began to move them along in the great colonnade. 24The crowds of the city had been assembled for this most pitiful spectacle and they were eagerly waiting for daybreak. 25But the Jews, at their last gasp—since the time had run out—stretched their hands toward heaven and with most tearful supplication and mournful dirges implored the supreme God[c] to help them again at once. 26The rays of the sun were not yet shed abroad, and while the king was receiving his Friends, Hermon arrived and invited him to come out, indicating that what the king desired was ready for action. 27But he, on receiving the report and being struck by the unusual invitation to come out—since he had been completely overcome by incomprehension—inquired what the matter was for which this had been so zealously completed for him. 28This was the act of God who rules over all things, for he had implanted in the king's mind a forgetfulness of the things he had previously devised. 29Then Hermon and all the king's Friends[d] pointed out that the animals and the armed forces were ready, "O king, according to your eager purpose."[e] 30But at these words he was filled with an overpowering wrath, because by the providence of God his whole mind had been deranged concerning these matters; and with a threatening look he said, 31"If your parents or children were present, I would have prepared them to be a rich feast for the savage animals instead of the Jews, who give me no ground for complaint and have exhibited to an extraordinary degree a full and firm loyalty to my ancestors. 32In fact you would have been deprived of life instead of these, if it were not for an affection arising from our nurture in common and your usefulness." 33So Hermon suffered an unexpected and dangerous threat, and his eyes wavered and his face fell. 34The king's Friends one by one sullenly slipped away and dismissed[f] the assembled people to their own occupations. 35Then the Jews, on hearing what the king had said, praised the manifest Lord God, King of kings, since this also was his aid that they had received.

36 The king, however, reconvened the party in the same manner and urged the guests to return to their celebrating. 37After summoning Hermon he said in a threatening tone, "How many times, you poor wretch, must I give you orders about these things? 38Equip[g] the elephants now once more for the destruction of the Jews tomorrow!" 39But the officials who were at table with him, wondering at his instability of mind, remonstrated as follows: 40"O king, how long will you put us to the test, as though we are idiots, ordering now for a third time that they be destroyed, and again revoking your decree in the matter?[h] 41As a result the city is in a tumult because of its expectation; it is crowded with masses of people, and also in constant danger of being plundered."

42 At this the king, a Phalaris in everything and filled with madness, took no account of the changes of mind that had come about within him for the protection of the Jews, and he firmly swore an irrevocable oath that he would send them to death[i] without

a Gk they   b Or armed   c Gk the greatest God
d Gk all the Friends   e Other ancient authorities read pointed to the beasts and the armed forces, saying, "They are ready, O king, according to your eager purpose."   f Other ancient authorities read he dismissed   g Or Arm   h Other ancient authorities read when the matter is in hand   i Gk Hades

---

5:28, 30 *This was the act of God.* The second act of deliverance involves a temporary derangement of the king's mind. The author again underscores how God can be seen at work "behind the scenes" to protect his people.

delay, mangled by the knees and feet of the animals, [43]and would also march against Judea and rapidly level it to the ground with fire and spear, and by burning to the ground the temple inaccessible to him[a] would quickly render it forever empty of those who offered sacrifices there. [44]Then the Friends and officers departed with great joy, and they confidently posted the armed forces at the places in the city most favorable for keeping guard.

45 Now when the animals had been brought virtually to a state of madness, so to speak, by the very fragrant draughts of wine mixed with frankincense and had been equipped with frightful devices, the elephant keeper [46]entered at about dawn into the courtyard—the city now being filled with countless masses of people crowding their way into the hippodrome—and urged the king on to the matter at hand. [47]So he, when he had filled his impious mind with a deep rage, rushed out in full force along with the animals, wishing to witness, with invulnerable heart and with his own eyes, the grievous and pitiful destruction of the aforementioned people.

48 When the Jews saw the dust raised by the elephants going out at the gate and by the following armed forces, as well as by the trampling of the crowd, and heard the loud and tumultuous noise, [49]they thought that this was their last moment of life, the end of their most miserable suspense, and giving way to lamentation and groans they kissed each other, embracing relatives and falling into one another's arms[b]—parents and children, mothers and daughters, and others with babies at their breasts who were drawing their last milk. [50]Not only this, but when they considered the help that they had received before

from heaven, they prostrated themselves with one accord on the ground, removing the babies from their breasts, [51]and cried out in a very loud voice, imploring the Ruler over every power to manifest himself and be merciful to them, as they stood now at the gates of death.[c]

The Prayer of Eleazar

6 Then a certain Eleazar, famous among the priests of the country, who had attained a ripe old age and throughout his life had been adorned with every virtue, directed the elders around him to stop calling upon the holy God, and he prayed as follows: [2]"King of great power, Almighty God Most High, governing all creation with mercy, [3]look upon the descendants of Abraham, O Father, upon the children of the sainted Jacob, a people of your consecrated portion who are perishing as foreigners in a foreign land. [4]Pharaoh with his abundance of chariots, the former ruler of this Egypt, exalted with lawless insolence and boastful tongue, you destroyed together with his arrogant army by drowning them in the sea, manifesting the light of your mercy on the nation of Israel. [5]Sennacherib exulting in his countless forces, oppressive king of the Assyrians, who had already gained control of the whole world by the spear and was lifted up against your holy city, speaking grievous words with boasting and insolence, you, O Lord, broke in pieces, showing your power to many nations. [6]The three companions in Babylon who had voluntarily surrendered their lives to the flames so as not to serve vain things, you res-

a Gk *us*   *b* Gk *falling upon their necks*
c Gk *Hades*

5:50 *when they considered the help that they had received.* The faithful Jews are emboldened to pray by their recollection of God's recent acts on their behalf (vv 13, 35), again highlighting for us the importance of our remaining mindful of the traces of God's hand in our lives, whether that hand has painted in bold, dramatic strokes or brushed lightly. As such, it commends to us the disciplines of daily reflection and journal writing, returning frequently to review how God

has been at work in our lives.

6:4–5 *Pharaoh with his abundance of chariots.* The stories of Pharaoh and Sennacherib (Exod 14–15; 2 Kings 18–19) teach that those who come against God's people with "boasting and insolence" also give God an opportunity to manifest his power, justice, and deliverance. Scripture teaches that our hope in every such situation is that God's salvation, and not human arrogance, will have the last word.

cued unharmed, even to a hair, moistening the fiery furnace with dew and turning the flame against all their enemies. [7]Daniel, who through envious slanders was thrown down into the ground to lions as food for wild animals, you brought up to the light unharmed. [8]And Jonah, wasting away in the belly of a huge, sea-born monster, you, Father, watched over and restored[a] unharmed to all his family. [9]And now, you who hate insolence, all-merciful and protector of all, reveal yourself quickly to those of the nation of Israel[b]— who are being outrageously treated by the abominable and lawless Gentiles.

10 "Even if our lives have become entangled in impieties in our exile, rescue us from the hand of the enemy, and destroy us, Lord, by whatever fate you choose. [11]Let not the vain-minded praise their vanities[c] at the destruction of your beloved people, saying, 'Not even their god has rescued them.' [12]But you, O Eternal One, who have all might and all power, watch over us now and have mercy on us who by the senseless insolence of the lawless are being deprived of life in the manner of traitors. [13]And let the Gentiles cower today in fear of your invincible might, O honored One, who have power to save the nation of Jacob. [14]The whole throng of infants and their parents entreat you with tears. [15]Let it be shown to all the Gentiles that you are with us,

O Lord, and have not turned your face from us; but just as you have said, 'Not even when they were in the land of their enemies did I neglect them,' so accomplish it, O Lord."

Two Angels Rescue the Jews

16 Just as Eleazar was ending his prayer, the king arrived at the hippodrome with the animals and all the arrogance of his forces. [17]And when the Jews observed this they raised great cries to heaven so that even the nearby valleys resounded with them and brought an uncontrollable terror upon the army. [18]Then the most glorious, almighty, and true God revealed his holy face and opened the heavenly gates, from which two glorious angels of fearful aspect descended, visible to all but the Jews. [19]They opposed the forces of the enemy and filled them with confusion and terror, binding them with immovable shackles. [20]Even the king began to shudder bodily, and he forgot his sullen insolence. [21]The animals turned back upon the armed forces following them and began trampling and destroying them.

22 Then the king's anger was turned to pity and tears because of the things that he

a Other ancient authorities read *rescued and restored*; others, *mercifully restored*   b Other ancient authorities read *to the saints of Israel*   c Or *bless their vain gods*

6:6–7 *The three companions in Babylon.* The stories of the three young men, who refused idolatrous worship like the majority of Jews in 3 Maccabees (Dan 3, see 3 Macc 2:30–32; 3:21), and Daniel, who also came to trial on account of slander (Dan 6, see 3 Macc 3:2–7), are especially suited to the situation of the Jews in this story. They model how to remain faithful to God and to entrust one's cause to a just Judge (cf. 1 Pet 2:23; 4:19).

6:10–11 *rescue us from the hand of the enemy.* God's honor and presence in the world are bound up inseparably with the fate of the People of God, those few in the world who call upon the name of the One God (see Dan 9:15–19 for another example of this argument emerging in a Jewish prayer). Being bearers of God's honor both challenges us to live accordingly (cf. 1 Pet 2:12; Rom 2:23–24) and gives us

assurance of vindication when that honor is threatened by human evil.

6:15 *you are with us . . . just as you have said.* Eleazar discovers a timely and appropriate word for his people's situation in Lev 26:44. The study of Scripture and the discipline of prayer come together in powerful ways as we search out and cling to God's promises in Scripture and wrestle with God in prayer concerning their applicability to current life situations.

6:18 *visible to all but the Jews.* The people of faith do not need to see marvelous sights as evidence of God's miraculous interventions; it is enough to experience God's deliverance. See the downplaying of the "marvelous" in 5:8, 11 as well.

6:20, 22 *the king's anger was turned to pity and tears.* Ptolemy evidences the change of heart—the *metanoia*—that only God can work,

had devised beforehand. 23For when he heard the shouting and saw them all fallen headlong to destruction, he wept and angrily threatened his Friends, saying, 24"You are committing treason and surpassing tyrants in cruelty; and even me, your benefactor, you are now attempting to deprive of dominion and life by secretly devising acts of no advantage to the kingdom. 25Who has driven from their homes those who faithfully kept our country's fortresses, and foolishly gathered every one of them here? 26Who is it that has so lawlessly encompassed with outrageous treatment those who from the beginning differed from*a* all nations in their goodwill toward us and often have accepted willingly the worst of human dangers? 27Loose and untie their unjust bonds! Send them back to their homes in peace, begging pardon for your former actions!*b* 28Release the children of the almighty and living God of heaven, who from the time of our ancestors until now has granted an unimpeded and notable stability to our government." 29These then were the things he said; and the Jews, immediately released, praised their holy God and Savior, since they now had escaped death.

The Jews Celebrate Their Deliverance

30 Then the king, when he had returned to the city, summoned the official in charge of the revenues and ordered him to provide to the Jews both wines and everything else needed for a festival of seven days, deciding that they should celebrate their rescue with all joyfulness in that same place in which they had expected to meet their destruction. 31Accordingly those disgracefully treated and near to death,*c* or rather, who stood at its gates, arranged for a banquet of deliverance instead of a bitter and lamentable death, and full of joy they apportioned to celebrants the place that had been prepared for their destruction and burial. 32They stopped their chanting of dirges and took up the song of their ancestors, praising God, their Savior and worker of wonders. *d* Putting an end to all mourning and wailing, they formed choruses*e* as a sign of peaceful joy. 33Likewise also the king, after convening a great banquet to celebrate these events, gave thanks to heaven unceasingly and lavishly for the unexpected rescue that he*f* had experienced. 34Those who had previously believed that the Jews would be destroyed and become food for birds, and had joyfully registered them, groaned as they themselves were overcome by disgrace, and their fire-breathing boldness was ignominiously*g* quenched.

35 The Jews, as we have said before, arranged the aforementioned choral group*h* and passed the time in feasting to the accompaniment of joyous thanksgiving and psalms. 36And when they had ordained a public rite for these things in their whole community and for their descendants, they

a Or *excelled above*   *b* Other ancient authorities read *revoking your former commands*   *c* Gk *Hades* *d* Other ancient authorities read *praising Israel and the wonder-working God*; or *praising Israel's Savior, the wonder-working God*   *e* Or *dances*   *f* Other ancient authorities read *they*   *g* Other ancient authorities read *completely*   *h* Or *dance*

---

a complete change of mind and renewal of a true perspective on one's situation in life. As the starting place for spiritual wisdom and maturity, we are encouraged to seek in prayer and meditation the renewal of this gift from God in ourselves and in others.

6:30 *a festival of seven days.* See note on 1 Macc 4:52-54.

6:32 *took up the song of their ancestors.* The traditional hymns of our spiritual forebears find new life and new meaning in the light of new experiences of God's power; and in turn they breathe significance into those new experiences by connecting them with the acts God has consistently performed to benefit his people.

6:36 *a festival, not for drinking and gluttony, but because of the deliverance.* The social and temporal aspects of holidays, however enjoyable, can threaten to rob us of their deeper contributions to our spiritual growth as individuals, families, and communities. Holidays—holy days—are a means of grace when we use them foremost as occasions to joyfully and prayerfully celebrate God's acts of deliverance.

instituted the observance of the aforesaid days as a festival, not for drinking and gluttony, but because of the deliverance that had come to them through God. 37Then they petitioned the king, asking for dismissal to their homes. 38So their registration was carried out from the twenty-fifth of Pachon to the fourth of Epeiph,*a* for forty days; and their destruction was set for the fifth to the seventh of Epeiph,*b* the three days 39on which the Lord of all most gloriously revealed his mercy and rescued them all together and unharmed. 40Then they feasted, being provided with everything by the king, until the fourteenth day,*c* on which also they made the petition for their dismissal. 41The king granted their request at once and wrote the following letter for them to the generals in the cities, magnanimously expressing his concern:

Ptolemy's Letter on Behalf of the Jews

7 "King Ptolemy Philopator to the generals in Egypt and all in authority in his government, greetings and good health:

2 "We ourselves and our children are faring well, the great God guiding our affairs according to our desire. 3Certain of our friends, frequently urging us with malicious intent, persuaded us to gather together the Jews of the kingdom in a body and to punish them with barbarous penalties as traitors; 4for they declared that our government would never be firmly established until this was accomplished, because of the ill-will that these people had toward all nations. 5They also led them out with harsh treatment as slaves, or rather as traitors, and, girding themselves with a cruelty more savage than that of Scythian custom, they tried without any inquiry or examination to put them to death.

6But we very severely threatened them for these acts, and in accordance with the clemency that we have toward all people we barely spared their lives. Since we have come to realize that the God of heaven surely defends the Jews, always taking their part as a father does for his children, 7and since we have taken into account the friendly and firm goodwill that they had toward us and our ancestors, we justly have acquitted them of every charge of whatever kind. 8We also have ordered all people to return to their own homes, with no one in any place*d* doing them harm at all or reproaching them for the irrational things that have happened. 9For you should know that if we devise any evil against them or cause them any grief at all, we always shall have not a mortal but the Ruler over every power, the Most High God, in everything and inescapably as an antagonist to avenge such acts. Farewell."

The Jews Return Home with Joy

10 On receiving this letter the Jews*e* did not immediately hurry to make their departure, but they requested of the king that at their own hands those of the Jewish nation who had willfully transgressed against the holy God and the law of God should receive the punishment they deserved. 11They declared that those who for the belly's sake had transgressed the divine commandments would never be favorably disposed toward the king's government. 12The king*f* then, admitting and approving the truth of what they said, granted them a general license so that freely, and without royal authority or

a July 7—August 15   *b* August 16—18
c August 25   *d* Other ancient authorities read
way   *e* Gk *they*   *f* Gk *He*

---

supervision, they might destroy those everywhere in his kingdom who had transgressed the law of God. [13] When they had applauded him in fitting manner, their priests and the whole multitude shouted the Hallelujah and joyfully departed. [14] And so on their way they punished and put to a public and shameful death any whom they met of their compatriots who had become defiled. [15] In that day they put to death more than three hundred men; and they kept the day as a joyful festival, since they had destroyed the profaners. [16] But those who had held fast to God even to death and had received the full enjoyment of deliverance began their departure from the city, crowned with all sorts of very fragrant flowers, joyfully and loudly giving thanks to the one God of their ancestors, the eternal Savior[a] of Israel, in words of praise and all kinds of melodious songs.

17 When they had arrived at Ptolemais, called "rose-bearing" because of a characteristic of the place, the fleet waited for them, in accordance with the common desire, for seven days. [18] There they celebrated their deliverance,[b] for the king had generously provided all things to them for their journey until all of them arrived at their own houses. [19] And when they had all landed in peace with appropriate thanksgiving, there too in like manner they decided to observe these days as a joyous festival during the time of their stay. [20] Then, after inscribing them as holy on a pillar and dedicating a place of prayer at the site of the festival, they departed unharmed, free, and overjoyed, since at the king's command they had all of them been brought safely by land and sea and river to their own homes. [21] They also possessed greater prestige among their enemies, being held in honor and awe; and they were not subject at all to confiscation of their belongings by anyone. [22] Besides, they all recovered all of their property, in accordance with the registration, so that those who held any of it restored it to them with extreme fear.[c] So the supreme God perfectly performed great deeds for their deliverance. [23] Blessed be the Deliverer of Israel through all times! Amen.

a Other ancient authorities read the holy Savior; others, the holy one   b Gk they made a cup of deliverance   c Other ancient authorities read with a very large supplement

---

7:14–15 *they punished and put to a public and shameful death.* Although the people in the story are acting in line with the commands of the Torah to execute idolaters among the Jewish people, this course of action falls short of the ideals of the new covenant. God desires not the deaths of sinners, but their repentance, restoration, and transformation.

7:21 *possessed greater prestige among their enemies.* The conclusion of the story contrasts sharply with 3:2–7, teaching that the rewards of faithfulness include God's vindication of our allegiance to him. Our honor is most secure when it is established on the basis of faithfulness to God, avoiding opportunities for alleged "advancement" that lead us away from obedience to him.

4 MACCABEES

Fourth Maccabees was written in Greek probably during the first half of the first century AD. It is a product of the Jewish diaspora. Though the precise geographic location of its anonymous author remains uncertain (Syria and Cilicia remain the strongest candidates), his cultural location is quite clear. He is both thoroughly committed to the Jewish way of life and thoroughly adept in the Greek language, philosophical ethics, and rhetoric. His book, in fact, takes a very common Greek philosophical thesis—that reason can and should master the emotions—and gives it a distinctively Jewish spin. He writes to demonstrate that it is a mind and will trained by strict observance of Torah, the Jewish law, that alone fulfills this ethical ideal and empowers a person's perfect commitment to the ethical virtues praised in Greek culture. In an environment where Jews face significant prejudice because of their way of life and its peculiarities, the author writes to confirm Jews' commitment to following the Torah as the God-given tool for achieving the highest ideals even of their detractors.

Athletic Discipleship

This book contributes rather more directly to spiritual formation than 1, 2, & 3 Maccabees insofar as its author has a formational goal. He wants to encourage his audience to develop a will and rational faculty that can maintain the upper hand over feelings, impulses, desires, and physical sensations (all of these aspects of our experience are subsumed in the Greek word for "passions" or "emotions" in this book). The author of 4 Maccabees also promotes a clear strategy for attaining this goal, calling his audience to the rigorous training and exercise program known as the Mosaic law.

Thinking about growth in Christian discipleship in terms of "athletic training" goes all the way back to Paul (see 1 Cor 9:24–27; Phil 3:12–14) and other early Christian leaders (see Heb 12:1–4). These early Christian leaders shared the formational

See also *"The With-God Life" essay for this section of the Bible,*
"The People of God in Restoration," pp. 1355–59.

CHRISTIAN ASTHETICAL TRAINING VALUE TODAY

goal so deeply valued by this author (Rom 6:12–13; 7:5–6; Gal 5:16, 24; Titus 2:11–14; 3:3–7; 1 Pet 2:11). They understood that God had provided, however, a better trainer and "coach," as it were, in the Holy Spirit. Walking closely in line with the indwelling Spirit, believers are both led and empowered to attain mastery of the passions (Gal 5:16–25).

ATHLETIC IMAGE

Readers of 4 Maccabees will be struck by the author's penchant for using athletic imagery to describe the martyrs and their experiences at the hands of Antiochus's torturers. The martyrs are "noble athletes" or "contestants" (6:9–10; 17:13). Endurance of the torments becomes a "noble contest" or "competition" (11:20; 16:16; 17:11) played out in the "arena [lit., gymnasium] of sufferings" (11:20). The martyrs gain victory precisely by not succumbing to the torturers (their "antagonists," 17:14), thus not being defeated in their commitment to God (11:20). The prize awarded to those who have wrestled with their own weaknesses and overcome the pressures to break faith with God is nothing less than immortality (17:12). Athletic imagery also appears in 9:8, 23; 12:11, 14; 13:13, 15.

Athletic imagery well suits the author's view of a life lived with God, since, in his experience, God is at work training the People of God, so that they will be able to live out the values of covenant loyalty in every situation they encounter. In this respect, the author of 4 Maccabees would have found substantial agreement among Greek and Roman philosophers and ethicists. Most of these also used athletic imagery as a means of expressing the level of commitment required and the rigors involved if people truly wanted to become virtuous and live out their full potential as moral and noble beings. It was only through deliberate and consistent effort that people would be able to develop their moral faculty to the point that desires, impulses, emotions, and physical sensations no longer threatened their commitment to virtue. The result was a life of freedom—freedom from the tyranny of the passions of the flesh and from the tyranny of those who could use their power over their bodies to control their wills as well.

The Greek word for "athlete" is *askētēs* (12:11), and for "athletic training" *askēsis*, from which we derive the words "ascetic" and "asceticism." Ascetic practices have long held a place of honor in Christian spirituality as a means by which believers could discipline the flesh, assist the will to gain ascendancy over the flesh, and discover more and more of the spiritual resources that God puts at disciples' disposal.

MONASTIC ATHLETE

The early monastic movements and the desert fathers and mothers, for example, committed themselves to rigorous training in this regard, making frequent use of fasting, all-night prayer vigils, austere lifestyles, deprivation of "creature comforts," and even self-flagellation. Although some of these practices may be called into question (notably the last of these), many of them (and others besides) are still found to have value as we train ourselves for spiritual maturity and Christian service.

Training in the Life of the Spirit

If the martyrs' ability to withstand the most extreme pain seems unbelievable, this is because we have not made sufficient use of the Spiritual Disciplines at our disposal.

Spiritual Disciplines are actions that lie within our power to do regularly, but they become a means of grace by which God, through our regular attention to God and to training in the life of the Spirit, empowers us to do what lies far beyond our power. 4 Maccabees brings home the importance of practicing Spiritual Disciplines when life is calm and the sea untroubled. In the midst of the martyrs' trials, it would have been too late to begin to learn virtue or to expect to display the courage and integrity that preserve the soul. The crisis is the time in which to prove what years of rigorous spiritual and moral training have made possible. The martyrs are only "free" with regard to the tyrant and his instruments of compulsion and subjugation because they have lived with God closely before the trials, and so have been empowered by God through long acquaintance and work to face those trials. 4 Maccabees, then, invites us to seek out that regimen of Spiritual Disciplines that will facilitate our liberation from the debilitating power of the flesh, as well as to regard the uninvited challenges and temptations we face as opportunities to exercise our spirits and our wills now in preparation for greater victories later.

—*David A. deSilva*

The Author's Definition of His Task

1 The subject that I am about to discuss is most philosophical, that is, whether devout reason is sovereign over the emotions. So it is right for me to advise you to pay earnest attention to philosophy. 2For the subject is essential to everyone who is seeking knowledge, and in addition it includes the praise of the highest virtue—I mean, of course, rational judgment. 3If, then, it is evident that reason rules over those emotions that hinder self-control, namely, gluttony and lust, 4it is also clear that it masters the emotions that hinder one from justice, such as malice, and those that stand in the way of courage, namely, anger, fear, and pain. 5Some might perhaps ask, "If reason rules the emotions, why is it not sovereign over forgetfulness and ignorance?" Their attempt at argument is ridiculous![a] 6For reason does not rule its own emotions, but those that are opposed to justice, courage, and self-control;[b] and it is not for the purpose of destroying them, but so that one may not give way to them.

7 I could prove to you from many and various examples that reason[c] is dominant over the emotions, 8but I can demonstrate it best from the noble bravery of those who died for the sake of virtue, Eleazar and the seven

a Or *They are attempting to make my argument ridiculous!* b Other ancient authorities add *and rational judgment* c Other ancient authorities read *devout reason*

1:3–4, 6 *reason rules over those emotions that hinder self-control.* The author shares with Greco-Roman ethicists and with Paul an optimism about the human race, insofar as we can "will what is right" (see Rom 7:14–21). It is particularly the case that those who have studied God's word "know" in their minds what God requires (see vv 15–17). The pressing human predicament is that "knowledge" of the right is not enough, given the power of the inclinations of the flesh, here spoken of as the "emotions" (Greek *pathē*, a term that encompasses emotions, drives, inclinations, and sensations). The goal of "philosophy" was to empower the "reason" (our rational faculty and will) to persevere in virtue rather than allowing the "emotions" to lead us away from virtue. This is, again, in keeping with Paul (see Gal 5:16–25), though he discovered the ultimate solution to be not obedience to the Torah, but receiving and following the Holy Spirit.

1:7–9 *the noble bravery of those who died for . . . virtue.* The author uses the extreme case to prove the rule. If the martyrs who endured the

brothers and their mother. [9]All of these, by despising sufferings that bring death, demonstrated that reason controls the emotions. [10]On this anniversary[a] it is fitting for me to praise for their virtues those who, with their mother, died for the sake of nobility and goodness, but I would also call them blessed for the honor in which they are held. [11]All people, even their torturers, marveled at their courage and endurance, and they became the cause of the downfall of tyranny over their nation. By their endurance they conquered the tyrant, and thus their native land was purified through them. [12]I shall shortly have an opportunity to speak of this; but, as my custom is, I shall begin by stating my main principle, and then I shall turn to their story, giving glory to the all-wise God.

The Supremacy of Reason

[13]Our inquiry, accordingly, is whether reason is sovereign over the emotions. [14]We shall decide just what reason is and what emotion is, how many kinds of emotions there are, and whether reason rules over all these. [15]Now reason is the mind that with sound logic prefers the life of wisdom. [16]Wisdom, next, is the knowledge of divine and human matters and the causes of these. [17]This, in turn, is education in the law, by which we learn divine matters reverently and human affairs to our advantage. [18]Now the kinds of wisdom are rational judgment, justice, courage, and self-control. [19]Rational judgment is supreme over all of these, since by means of it reason rules over the emotions. [20]The two most comprehensive types[b] of the emotions are pleasure and pain; and each of these is by nature concerned with both body and soul. [21]The emotions of both pleasure and pain have many consequences. [22]Thus desire precedes pleasure and delight follows it. [23]Fear precedes pain and sorrow comes after. [24]Anger, as a person will see by reflecting on this experience, is an emotion embracing pleasure and pain. [25]In pleasure there exists even a malevolent tendency, which is the most complex of all the emotions. [26]In the soul it is boastfulness, covetousness, thirst for honor, rivalry, and malice; [27]in the body, indiscriminate eating, gluttony, and solitary gormandizing.

[28]Just as pleasure and pain are two plants growing from the body and the soul, so there are many offshoots of these plants,[c] [29]each of which the master cultivator, reason, weeds and

---

a Gk At this time   b Or sources   c Other ancient authorities read these emotions

---

most grievous emotions (fear for themselves, grief for one another) and sensations (intense physical sufferings) can achieve victory, then victory in the more ordinary contests against less powerful emotions and physical drives is more than possible and all excuses for weakness are eliminated.

1:10 *On this anniversary.* 4 Maccabees may well have been composed for an annual commemoration of the martyrs (see also 3:19), possibly linked to Hanukkah, possibly to the traditional date of the martyrdoms (August 1 in the Christian calendar). The commemoration of the "saints" has been a staple of Christian spirituality, providing opportunities throughout the year to remember the "witnesses" to faith in God who are also the "spectators" surrounding and watching us as we run our race (Heb 12:1–2). Remembering the way particular believers have lived throughout the centuries, reading selections from the devotional writings they have left to us, and reflecting on the dynamics of their life with God can enrich, empower, and renew our own.

Responding

1:10 STUDY. Turn to the Spiritual Formation Bibliography in the back of the book. Select one of the devotional books listed there, and plan some time to read and study it. What do the words of your brothers and sisters in Christ teach you about him? *See also* Spiritual Disciplines Index.

1:15–17 *reason is the mind that . . . prefers the life of wisdom.* At the heart of personal formation lies a choice: Do we commit to seeking a life of stability and integrity with "wisdom" as our guide, or do we yield to the direction of the passions and endure the unstable life that results? Wisdom is here construed as knowledge about what is the virtuous course of action in any situation—what is just and good in the sight of God and people of good conscience—gained specifically through studying God's Word.

prunes and ties up and waters and thoroughly irrigates, and so tames the jungle of habits and emotions. [30]For reason is the guide of the virtues, but over the emotions it is sovereign.

Observe now, first of all, that rational judgment is sovereign over the emotions by virtue of the restraining power of self-control. [31]Self-control, then, is dominance over the desires. [32]Some desires are mental, others are physical, and reason obviously rules over both. [33]Otherwise, how is it that when we are attracted to forbidden foods we abstain from the pleasure to be had from them? Is it not because reason is able to rule over appetites? I for one think so. [34]Therefore when we crave seafood and fowl and animals and all sorts of foods that are forbidden to us by the law, we abstain because of domination by reason. [35]For the emotions of the appetites are restrained, checked by the temperate mind, and all the impulses of the body are bridled by reason.

Compatibility of the Law with Reason

2 And why is it amazing that the desires of the mind for the enjoyment of beauty are rendered powerless? [2]It is for this reason, certainly, that the temperate Joseph is praised, because by mental effort[a] he overcame sexual desire. [3]For when he was young and in his prime for intercourse, by his reason he nullified the frenzy[b] of the passions. [4]Not only is reason proved to rule over the frenzied urge of sexual desire, but also over every desire.[c] [5]Thus the law says, "You shall not covet your neighbor's wife or anything that is your neighbor's." [6]In fact, since the law has told us not to covet, I could prove to you all the more that reason is able to control desires.

Just so it is with the emotions that hinder one from justice. [7]Otherwise how could it

a Other ancient authorities add *in reasoning*
b Or *gadfly*   c Or *all covetousness*

1:31–35 *we abstain because of domination by reason.* The dietary restrictions imposed by the Torah seemed especially baffling and backward to Gentiles (see 5:6–9) and invited their ridicule. This author tries to explain these food laws (see Lev 11:1–31) as an opportunity given to the Jews by God to learn and demonstrate "self-control," power over the natural appetites. Although the author here believes Jews are able to follow the Torah's restrictions on diet because their reason has mastered their inclinations, he recognizes more fundamentally that the day-by-day observance of God's law provides the training that makes it possible for reason to become more powerful than the drives of the flesh and of self (see 2:8–9; 5:22–24). The same benefits have long been held to come from certain Spiritual Disciplines. Fasting, by which we abstain from certain foods or from all food for a time, fixes in our minds, hearts, and bodies the priority of our life with God over our physical cravings and appetites. Prayer vigils through the night exercise the will to be with God over the natural inclination toward sleep. The discipline of simplicity trains us to resist all excessive desires and practice greater justice and love toward those in need. The discipline of almsgiving trains us against greed and cultivates generosity.

2:1–3 *by mental effort he overcame sexual desire.* Many people struggle with lust. The

author tells us that, though this "desire" is potently felt in both mind and body, it need not exercise power over our will. Rather, like Joseph, we can exercise our reason, calling to mind the goodness of the God for whose sake we abstain, the benefits of obedience, and the regret and shame of yielding to the moment.

Responding

2:1–3 CHASTITY. "Sex is like a river— it is a good and wonderful blessing when kept within its proper channel. A river that overflows its banks is a dangerous thing," writes Richard Foster in *Celebration of Discipline*. If you or someone you know is struggling with sexual temptation, pray for this person by visualizing a river that has overflowed its banks and asking God to bring it back to normal. *See also* Spiritual Disciplines Index.

2:5–6 *reason is able to control desires.* The author believes that God commands only what is possible, differing with Paul significantly (see Rom 7:7–8), who sees it less likely that we will use the law to overcome the passions and more likely that sin will use the law to overwhelm us with ungodly passions. Paul also knows that God has made the Spirit available and present within all who follow Christ. The Spirit is the first and best resource to turn to when beset by the passions.

be that someone who is habitually a solitary gormandizer, a glutton, or even a drunkard can learn a better way, unless reason is clearly lord of the emotions? [8]Thus, as soon as one adopts a way of life in accordance with the law, even though a lover of money, one is forced to act contrary to natural ways and to lend without interest to the needy and to cancel the debt when the seventh year arrives. [9]If one is greedy, one is ruled by the law through reason so that one neither gleans the harvest nor gathers the last grapes from the vineyard.

In all other matters we can recognize that reason rules the emotions. [10]For the law prevails even over affection for parents, so that virtue is not abandoned for their sakes. [11]It is superior to love for one's wife, so that one rebukes her when she breaks the law. [12]It takes precedence over love for children, so that one punishes them for misdeeds. [13]It is sovereign over the relationship of friends, so that one rebukes friends when they act wickedly. [14]Do not consider it paradoxical when reason, through the law, can prevail even over enmity. The fruit trees of the enemy are not cut down, but one preserves the property of enemies from marauders and helps raise up what has fallen. [a]

[15] It is evident that reason rules even [b] the more violent emotions: lust for power, vainglory, boasting, arrogance, and malice. [16]For the temperate mind repels all these malicious emotions, just as it repels anger—for it is sovereign over even this. [17]When Moses was angry with Dathan and Abiram, he did nothing against them in anger, but controlled his anger by reason. [18]For, as I have said, the temperate mind is able to get the better of the emotions, to correct some, and to render others powerless. [19]Why else did Jacob, our most wise father, censure the households of Simeon and Levi for their irrational slaughter of the entire tribe of the Shechemites, saying, "Cursed be their anger"? [20]For if reason could not control anger, he would not have spoken thus. [21]Now when God fashioned human beings, he planted in them emotions and inclinations, [22]but at the same time he enthroned the mind among the senses as a sacred governor over them all. [23]To the mind he gave the law; and one who lives subject to

a Or *the beasts that have fallen*   b Other ancient authorities read *through*

2:8–9 *a way of life in accordance with the law.* The nature of the Torah as "training" against our natural inclinations is evident here. Similarly, following the law of Christ and yielding to the new life the Spirit seeks to cultivate within us "forces us to act contrary to natural ways" while reshaping us into Christ's own image.

2:11–13 *one rebukes friends when they act wickedly.* Family and friends are called by the law to reinforce one another's commitment to virtue. Accountability to one another in Christian community (within the home or within other covenant relationships in the congregation) provides another essential Spiritual Discipline safeguarding our growth and progress in the Lord.

2:14 *reason, through the law, can prevail even over enmity.* The Torah sought to mitigate the passion of enmity both by restraining what one could inflict on an enemy's territory in war (Deut 20:19–20) and by commanding acts of neighborly kindness toward a personal enemy rather than standing by idly while he or she

suffers loss (Exod 23:4–5). Such pruning of the excess of enmity reaches its zenith in Jesus' command to "love" our enemies (Matt 5:44), an ideal achieved only through the work of the Spirit and the practice of acts of kindness toward our personal "enemies" whenever opportunity arises.

2:21–23 *he enthroned the mind among the senses as a sacred governor over them all.* These verses are key to understanding the author's conception of personal wholeness. Unlike some Stoic philosophers, he would never advocate the elimination of the emotions (see 3:2–5), since God planted emotions within the human person. In God's vision for humanity, however, the mind—trained by and subject to God's law—is to exercise governance over the emotions and inclinations. This vision, adapted in Christ to center on our submission to the Holy Spirit rather than the Torah, invites us to bring our lives in line with the order God intended for us in our creation. Rather than allowing the passions to continue to upset and revolt against

Reason is the master of emotions. No spirit is the master of emotions. Holy Spirit that uses God's word wise counsel mentor oxen.

this will rule a kingdom that is temperate, just, good, and courageous.

24 How is it then, one might say, that if reason is master of the emotions, it does not control forgetfulness and ignorance? **3** [1]But this argument is entirely ridiculous; for it is evident that reason rules not over its own emotions, but over those of the body. [2]No one of us[a] can eradicate that kind of desire, but reason can provide a way for us not to be enslaved by desire. [3]No one of us can eradicate anger from the mind, but reason can help to deal with anger. [4]No one of us can eradicate malice, but reason can fight at our side so that we are not overcome by malice. [5]For reason does not uproot the emotions but is their antagonist.

King David's Thirst

6 Now this can be explained more clearly by the story of King David's thirst. [7]David had been attacking the Philistines all day long, and together with the soldiers of his nation had killed many of them. [8]Then when evening fell, he[b] came, sweating and quite exhausted, to the royal tent, around which the whole army of our ancestors had encamped. [9]Now all the rest were at supper, [10]but the king was extremely thirsty, and though springs were plentiful there, he could not satisfy his thirst from them. [11]But a certain irrational desire for the water in the enemy's territory tormented and inflamed him, undid and consumed him. [12]When his guards complained bitterly because of the king's craving, two staunch young soldiers, respecting[c] the king's desire, armed themselves fully, and taking a pitcher climbed over the enemy's ramparts. [13]Eluding the sentinels at the gates, they went searching throughout the enemy camp [14]and found the spring, and from it boldly brought the king a drink. [15]But David,[d] though he was burning with thirst, considered it an altogether fearful danger to his soul to drink what was regarded as equivalent to blood. [16]Therefore, opposing reason to desire, he poured out the drink as an offering to God. [17]For the temperate mind can conquer the drives of the emotions and quench the flames of frenzied desires; [18]it can overthrow bodily agonies even when they are extreme, and by nobility of reason spurn all domination by the emotions.

target control

---

a Gk you b Other ancient authorities read *he hurried and*
c Or *embarrassed because of*
d Gk he

God's order, we are invited to keep yielding to the Spirit and the fruit it seeks to produce in our lives (see Gal 5:19–25).

3:2–5 *reason can provide a way for us not to be enslaved by desire.* The goal of the Spiritual Disciplines is not to eliminate the experience of anger or lust or other cravings; nor does the experience of these emotions cast a shadow over our discipleship. Rather, the author calls us to deal with these emotions and inclinations always in a way that honors God, namely, mastering them so that they do not lead us into sin.

3:15–16 *poured out the drink as an offering to God.* The strange story of David's thirst (modified somewhat from 2 Sam 23:13–17; 1 Chron 11:15–19) calls us to examine our desires and distinguish between what is natural and appropriate and what is excessive and inappropriate. It was appropriate for David to be thirsty; it was inappropriate for him to crave only the water that flowed from a particular spring in the enemy's camp and thus could only be acquired at great expense (in terms of the risk to life undertaken by the two brave soldiers). David knew that it would be an affront to God to spend something so costly and precious as the water they brought back on his excessive cravings, and so he offered it to God instead. The author invites us to consider what we spend on our desires, to search out and become sensitive to those excesses in which we indulge that could be the equivalent of life for somebody else. For example, many casual or extravagant purchases (representing needs that could be satisfied for much less, or representing no real need at all) could be forestalled and turned into aid to improve life or provide necessities for our brothers and sisters around us or abroad. Moving toward simplicity of life as a Spiritual Discipline again commends itself.

An Attempt on the Temple Treasury

19 The present occasion now invites us to a narrative demonstration of temperate reason.

20 At a time when our ancestors were enjoying profound peace because of their observance of the law and were prospering, so that even Seleucus Nicanor, king of Asia, had both appropriated money to them for the temple service and recognized their commonwealth— 21 just at that time certain persons attempted a revolution against the public harmony and caused many and various disasters.

4 Now there was a certain Simon, a political opponent of the noble and good man, Onias, who then held the high priesthood for life. When despite all manner of slander he was unable to injure Onias in the eyes of the nation, he fled the country with the purpose of betraying it. 2 So he came to Apollonius, governor of Syria, Phoenicia, and Cilicia, and said, 3 "I have come here because I am loyal to the king's government, to report that in the Jerusalem treasuries there are deposited tens of thousands in private funds, which are not the property of the temple but belong to King Seleucus." 4 When Apollonius learned the details of these things, he praised Simon for his service to the king and went up to Seleucus to inform him of the rich treasure. 5 On receiving authority to deal with this matter, he proceeded quickly to our country accompanied by the accursed Simon and a very strong military force. 6 He said that he had come with the king's authority to seize the private funds in the treasury. 7 The people indignantly protested his words, considering it outrageous that those who had committed deposits to the sacred treasury should be deprived of them, and did all that they could to prevent it. 8 But, uttering threats, Apollonius went on to the temple. 9 While the priests together with women and children were imploring God in the temple to shield the holy place that was being treated so contemptuously, 10 and while Apollonius was going up with his armed forces to seize the money, angels on horseback with lightning flashing from their weapons appeared from heaven, instilling in them great fear and trembling. 11 Then Apollonius fell down half dead in the temple area that was open to all, stretched out his hands toward heaven, and with tears begged the Hebrews to pray for him and propitiate the wrath of the heavenly army. 12 For he said that he had committed a sin deserving of death, and that if he were spared he would praise the blessedness of the holy place before all people. 13 Moved by these words, the high priest Onias, although otherwise he had scruples about doing so, prayed for him so that King Seleucus would not suppose that Apollonius had been overcome by human treachery and not by divine justice. 14 So Apollonius,[a] having been saved beyond all expectations, went away to report to the king what had happened to him.

Antiochus' Persecution of the Jews

15 When King Seleucus died, his son Antiochus Epiphanes succeeded to the throne, an arrogant and terrible man, 16 who removed Onias from the priesthood and appointed Onias's[b] brother Jason as high priest. 17 Jason[c] agreed that if the office were conferred on him he would pay the king three thousand six hundred sixty talents annually. 18 So the king appointed him high priest and ruler of the nation. 19 Jason[c] changed the nation's way of life and altered its form of government in complete violation of the law, 20 so that not only was a gymnasium constructed at the very citadel[d] of our native land, but also the temple service was abolished. 21 The divine justice was angered by these acts and caused Antiochus himself to make war on them. 22 For when he was warring against Ptolemy in Egypt, he heard that a rumor of his death had spread and that the people of Jerusalem had rejoiced greatly. He speedily

a Gk he   b Gk his   c Gk He   d Or high place

marched against them, 23and after he had plundered them he issued a decree that if any of them were found observing the ancestral law they should die. 24When, by means of his decrees, he had not been able in any way to put an end to the people's observance of the law, but saw that all his threats and punishments were being disregarded 25— even to the extent that women, because they had circumcised their sons, were thrown headlong from heights along with their infants, though they had known beforehand that they would suffer this— 26when, I say, his decrees were despised by the people, he himself tried through torture to compel everyone in the nation to eat defiling foods and to renounce Judaism.

Antiochus's Encounter with Eleazar

5 The tyrant Antiochus, sitting in state with his counselors on a certain high place, and with his armed soldiers standing around him, 2ordered the guards to seize each and every Hebrew and to compel them to eat pork and food sacrificed to idols. 3If any were not willing to eat defiling food, they were to be broken on the wheel and killed. 4When many persons had been rounded up, one man, Eleazar by name, leader of the flock, was brought *a* before the king. He was a man of priestly family, learned in the law, advanced in age, and known to many in the tyrant's court because of his philosophy. *b*

5 When Antiochus saw him he said, 6"Before I begin to torture you, old man, I would advise you to save yourself by eating pork, 7for I respect your age and your gray hairs. Although you have had them for so long a time, it does not seem to me that you are a philosopher when you observe the religion of the Jews. 8When nature has granted it to us, why should you abhor eating the very excellent meat of this animal? 9It is senseless not to enjoy delicious things that are not shameful, and wrong to spurn the gifts of nature. 10It seems to me that you will do something even more senseless if, by holding a vain opinion concerning the truth, you continue to despise me to your own hurt. 11Will you not awaken from your foolish philosophy, dispel your futile reasonings, adopt a mind appropriate to your years, philosophize according to the truth of what is beneficial, 12and have compassion on your old age by honoring my humane advice? 13For consider this: if there is some power watching over this religion of yours, it will excuse you from any transgression that arises out of compulsion."

14 When the tyrant urged him in this fashion to eat meat unlawfully, Eleazar asked to have a word. 15When he had received permission to speak, he began to address the people as follows: 16"We, O Antiochus, who have been persuaded to govern our lives by the divine law, think that there is no compulsion more powerful than our obedience to the law. 17Therefore we consider that we

---

a Or *was the first of the flock to be brought*
b Other ancient authorities read *his advanced age*

4:26 *tried through torture to compel everyone.* A recurring question that will dominate the narration of the martyrdoms that follow is whether any force would ever be sufficient to compel disobedience, or whether we can find sufficient strength from God's presence with us to stay the course of obedience and covenant loyalty with God. The presence of so many martyrs in the communion of saints strongly suggests that the latter is true (see 5:13,16).

5:9, 11 *It is senseless not to enjoy delicious things.* Disciples need to be prepared to be misunderstood by neighbors who do not live by the same values. If we follow Christ, we will naturally abstain from many pursuits and pleasures that the worldly-minded prize and give priority to. Our choices will appear senseless at many points, and we may be challenged to persevere in the face not only of ridicule, but of attempts to "help us come to our senses" and not miss out on life.

5:13, 16 *no compulsion more powerful than our obedience to the law.* See note on 4:26. Our deepest, most underlying drive or compulsion will ultimately determine our life choices, especially under pressure. One of the main goals of spiritual formation is to discover that drive as yearning for God and pleasing God, a drive that will yield the peaceful fruit of integrity in all aspects of life.

should not transgress it in any respect. [18]Even if, as you suppose, our law were not truly divine and we had wrongly held it to be divine, not even so would it be right for us to invalidate our reputation for piety. [19]Therefore do not suppose that it would be a petty sin if we were to eat defiling food; [20]to transgress the law in matters either small or great is of equal seriousness, [21]for in either case the law is equally despised. [22]You scoff at our philosophy as though living by it were irrational, [23]but it teaches us self-control, so that we master all pleasures and desires, and it also trains us in courage, so that we endure any suffering willingly; [24]it instructs us in justice, so that in all our dealings we act impartially,[a] and it teaches us piety, so that with proper reverence we worship the only living God.

25 "Therefore we do not eat defiling food; for since we believe that the law was established by God, we know that in the nature of things the Creator of the world in giving us the law has shown sympathy toward us. [26]He has permitted us to eat what will be most suitable for our lives,[b] but he has forbidden us to eat meats that would be contrary to this.

[27]It would be tyrannical for you to compel us not only to transgress the law, but also to eat in such a way that you may deride us for eating defiling foods, which are most hateful to us. [28]But you shall have no such occasion to laugh at me, [29]nor will I transgress the sacred oaths of my ancestors concerning the keeping of the law, [30]not even if you gouge out my eyes and burn my entrails. [31]I am not so old and cowardly as not to be young in reason on behalf of piety. [32]Therefore get your torture wheels ready and fan the fire more vehemently! [33]I do not so pity my old age as to break the ancestral law by my own act. [34]I will not play false to you, O law that trained me, nor will I renounce you, beloved self-control. [35]I will not put you to shame, philosophical reason, nor will I reject you, honored priesthood and knowledge of the law. [36]You, O king,[c] shall not defile the honorable mouth of my old age, nor my long life lived lawfully. [37]My ancestors will receive me as pure, as one who does not fear your violence even to death. [38]You may tyrannize the

a Or so that we hold in balance all our habitual inclinations   b Or souls   c Gk lacks O king

---

5:20–21 *to transgress the law in matters either small or great.* Stated positively, every temptation to sin or engage in self-serving behavior presents an opportunity to honor God and walk with him. Keeping the question, "How can I honor or show love for God in this moment?" ever before us will both make us more aware of God's presence with us and help us walk with God consistently.

5:22–24 *it teaches us self-control.* See note on 1:31–35. The Torah provided very practical ways in which to train in the virtues listed; the Spiritual Disciplines integrated into our day-to-day lives provide a similar and much needed regimen.

5:26 *He has permitted us to eat what would be most suitable.* If we are to submit fully to God and the life God seeks to nurture in us, we too must believe fundamentally that what God permits is in fact best suited to our wholeness and fulfillment, and that what God refuses or forbids is in fact contrary to the same. Any other posture results in the double-mindedness that hobbles all spiritual progress, as we "[limp] with two different opinions" (1 Kings 18:21) about

what will make for a satisfying and full life, first seeking it from God and then seeking it in the fulfillment of our carnal cravings.

Responding
5:26 SUBMISSION. Submitting to God's wishes is the only path to true happiness, yet we still often persist in trying to make ourselves happy. Today look for a way you can practice submission with another person. It may be as simple as taking on a task no one else wants to do or denying yourself in order to acquiesce to another's wishes. How does it feel to put your own desires aside? *See also* Spiritual Disciplines Index.

5:29, 34–37 *nor will I transgress the sacred oaths of my ancestors.* Remembering our heritage in the faith, our spiritual roots, and how God has been present with us in our pilgrimage thus far provides a constant resource for keeping our direction clear and our forward movement steady when temptations or trials upset our equanimity.

ungodly, but you shall not dominate my religious principles, either by words or through deeds."

Martyrdom of Eleazar

6 When Eleazar in this manner had made eloquent response to the exhortations of the tyrant, the guards who were standing by dragged him violently to the instruments of torture. [2]First they stripped the old man, though he remained adorned with the gracefulness of his piety. [3]After they had tied his arms on each side they flogged him, [4]while a herald who faced him cried out, "Obey the king's commands!" [5]But the courageous and noble man, like a true Eleazar, was unmoved, as though being tortured in a dream; [6]yet while the old man's eyes were raised to heaven, his flesh was being torn by scourges, his blood flowing, and his sides were being cut to pieces. [7]Although he fell to the ground because his body could not endure the agonies, he kept his reason upright and unswerving. [8]One of the cruel guards rushed at him and began to kick him in the side to make him get up again after he fell. [9]But he bore the pains and scorned the punishment and endured the tortures. [10]Like a noble athlete the old man, while being beaten, was victorious over his torturers; [11]in fact, with his face bathed in sweat, and gasping heavily for breath, he amazed even his torturers by his courageous spirit.

[12] At that point, partly out of pity for his old age, [13]partly out of sympathy from their acquaintance with him, partly out of admiration for his endurance, some of the king's retinue came to him and said, [14]"Eleazar, why are you so irrationally destroying yourself through these evil things? [15]We will set before you some cooked meat; save yourself by pretending to eat pork."

[16] But Eleazar, as though more bitterly tormented by this counsel, cried out: [17]"Never may we, the children of Abraham, [a] think so basely that out of cowardice we feign a role unbecoming to us! [18]For it would be irrational if having lived in accordance with truth up to old age and having maintained in accordance with law the reputation of such a life, we should now change our course [19]and ourselves become a pattern of impiety to the young by setting them an example in the eating of defiling food. [20]It would be shameful if we should survive for a little while and during that time be a laughingstock to all for our cowardice, [21]and be despised by the tyrant as unmanly by not contending even to death for our divine law. [22]Therefore, O children of Abraham, die nobly for your religion! [23]And you, guards of the tyrant, why do you delay?"

[24] When they saw that he was so courageous in the face of the afflictions, and that he had not been changed by their compassion, the guards brought him to the fire. [25]There they burned him with maliciously contrived instruments, threw him down, and poured stinking liquids into his nostrils. [26]When he was now burned to his very bones and about to expire, he lifted up his eyes to God and said, [27]"You know, O God, that though I might have saved myself, I am dying in burning torments for the sake of the law. [28]Be merciful to your people, and let our punishment suffice for them. [29]Make my blood their purification, and take my life in exchange for theirs." [30]After he said this, the

a Or *O children of Abraham*

5:38 *You may tyrannize the ungodly.* Identifying the forces that try to tyrannize and dominate us, jeopardizing our complete commitment to walk with God, is essential if we are to discern where the spiritual battle lies and how to resist and to seek help from God. In Eleazar's case, Antiochus presented the external force, but his own vulnerability to fear and pain could have been able internal accomplices.

6:2 *adorned with the gracefulness of his piety.*

Those who are stripped of their dignity because of their walk with God, as so many of our sisters and brothers are, need to be reminded constantly of the dignity and worth God has bestowed upon them. In a situation of reproach and abuse (see 1 Pet 2:12, 19–20; 4:4, 12–16), the first medicine is reassurance of one's value in God's sight (see 1 Pet 1:3–7; 2:9–10).

6:17–19 *feign a role.* See note on 2 Macc 6:24–28.

holy man died nobly in his tortures; even in the tortures of death he resisted, by virtue of reason, for the sake of the law.

31 Admittedly, then, devout reason is sovereign over the emotions. [32] For if the emotions had prevailed over reason, we would have testified to their domination. [33] But now that reason has conquered the emotions, we properly attribute to it the power to govern. [34] It is right for us to acknowledge the dominance of reason when it masters even external agonies. It would be ridiculous to deny it. [a] [35] I have proved not only that reason has mastered agonies, but also that it masters pleasures and in no respect yields to them.

An Encomium on Eleazar

7 For like a most skillful pilot, the reason of our father Eleazar steered the ship of religion over the sea of the emotions, [2] and though buffeted by the stormings of the tyrant and overwhelmed by the mighty waves of tortures, [3] in no way did he turn the rudder of religion until he sailed into the haven of immortal victory. [4] No city besieged with many ingenious war machines has ever held out as did that most holy man. Although his sacred life was consumed by tortures and racks, he conquered the besiegers with the shield of his devout reason. [5] For in setting his mind firm like a jutting cliff, our father Eleazar broke the maddening waves of the emotions. [6] O priest, worthy of the priesthood, you neither defiled your sacred teeth nor profaned your stomach, which had room only for reverence and purity, by eating defiling foods. [7] O man in harmony with the law and philosopher of divine life! [8] Such should be those who are administrators of the law, shielding it with their own blood and noble sweat in sufferings even to death. [9] You, father, strengthened our loyalty to the law through your glorious endurance, and you did not abandon the holiness that you praised, but by your deeds you made your words of divine [b] philosophy credible. [10] O aged man, more powerful than tortures; O elder, fiercer than fire; O supreme king over the passions, Eleazar! [11] For just as our father Aaron, armed with the censer, ran through the multitude of the people and conquered the fiery [c] angel, [12] so the descendant of Aaron, Eleazar, though being consumed by the fire, remained unmoved in his reason. [13] Most amazing, indeed, though he was an old man, his body no longer tense and firm, [d] his muscles flabby, his sinews feeble, he became young again [14] in spirit through reason; and by reason like that of Isaac he rendered the many-headed rack ineffective. [15] O man of blessed age and of venerable gray hair and

a Syr: Meaning of Gk uncertain   b Other ancient authorities lack *divine*   c Other ancient authorities lack *fiery*   d Gk *the tautness of the body already loosed*

6:28–29 *let our punishment suffice for them.* Self-sacrificial covenant faithfulness and obedience toward God effects atonement in 4 Maccabees, as God regards the fidelity of the few and, for their sake, has mercy on the many (see also 17:21–22). Such reflections help prepare for the early Christian interpretation of the death of Jesus, the obedient martyr who restored the possibility of the life of "God with us" for those who had been disobedient.

7:4 *he conquered the besiegers with the shield of his devout reason.* Conquering the enemies of our souls is a frequent topic in Scripture, but the shape of "conquering" is not always what we would recognize as such. Eleazar "conquers" because he holds on to faith in God, but from Antiochus's perspective he was merely a captive, a member of a conquered people, who was being tortured. Antiochus had won the battle that counted in the world's eyes when he conquered Jerusalem; Eleazar won the battle that counted for eternity when he kept faith with God in the face of every trial. We are thereby challenged to discern and invest ourselves in winning battles of the latter kind.

7:8–9 *those who are administrators of the law.* Leadership in the Christian community is always leadership by example. Leaders are especially charged with modeling choices that reinforce the belief that God's rewards are always better than the rewards of sin, and with making the call of Jesus "credible" and "real" in the midst of the challenges of life by their own integrity.

of law-abiding life, whom the faithful seal of death has perfected!

16 If, therefore, because of piety an aged man despised tortures even to death, most certainly devout reason is governor of the emotions. [17]Some perhaps might say, "Not all have full command of their emotions, because not all have prudent reason." [18]But as many as attend to religion with a whole heart, these alone are able to control the passions of the flesh, [19]since they believe that they, like our patriarchs Abraham and Isaac and Jacob, do not die to God, but live to God. [20]No contradiction therefore arises when some persons appear to be dominated by their emotions because of the weakness of their reason. [21]What person who lives as a philosopher by the whole rule of philosophy, and trusts in God, [22]and knows that it is blessed to endure any suffering for the sake of virtue, would not be able to overcome the emotions through godliness? [23]For only the wise and courageous are masters of their emotions.

Seven Brothers Defy the Tyrant

8 For this is why even the very young, by following a philosophy in accordance with devout reason, have prevailed over the most painful instruments of torture. [2]For when the tyrant was conspicuously defeated in his first attempt, being unable to compel an aged man to eat defiling foods, then in violent rage he commanded that others of

the Hebrew captives be brought, and that any who ate defiling food would be freed after eating, but if any were to refuse, they would be tortured even more cruelly.

3 When the tyrant had given these orders, seven brothers—handsome, modest, noble, and accomplished in every way—were brought before him along with their aged mother. [4]When the tyrant saw them, grouped about their mother as though a chorus, he was pleased with them. And struck by their appearance and nobility, he smiled at them, and summoned them nearer and said, [5]"Young men, with favorable feelings I admire each and every one of you, and greatly respect the beauty and the number of such brothers. Not only do I advise you not to display the same madness as that of the old man who has just been tortured, but I also exhort you to yield to me and enjoy my friendship. [6]Just as I am able to punish those who disobey my orders, so I can be a benefactor to those who obey me. [7]Trust me, then, and you will have positions of authority in my government if you will renounce the ancestral tradition of your national life. [8]Enjoy your youth by adopting the Greek way of life and by changing your manner of living. [9]But if by disobedience you rouse my anger, you will compel me to destroy each and every one of you with dreadful punishments through tortures. [10]Therefore take pity on yourselves. Even I, your enemy, have compassion for your youth and handsome

---

7:18–19 *as many as attend to religion with a whole heart.* A firm hope for the life of the world to come sustains commitment to keep up the hard work of restraining the passions, choosing the path that honors God, yielding to the Spirit rather than gratifying ourselves in ways that do not promote Christlikeness. Understanding that we were created for more than this life and that God has prepared eternal joys in his presence helps us refuse the temporal indulgences that trip us up in our discipleship.

8:8, 23 *Enjoy your youth.* A pressing distraction from spiritual growth is the ever present invitation to "enjoy ourselves" by indulging in the pleasures that cater to our senses and to our unregenerate mind. Acquiring luxury items,

seeking prestige, indulging in drink and food, satisfying the "desires of the mind for the enjoyment of beauty" (2:1) through sexual affairs, living for moments of indolence—our spiritual progress will be hindered if we think we are "missing out" on life by not making some room for these, especially if we are naturally suited to acquire them (vv 4–5). As Antiochus rightly perceives, such temptations are especially difficult for "youth," and we have almost come to expect that young people will have seasons of excess and indulgence before "settling down." This is again a place to seek the help of God and other disciples for the reinforcement of that single-mindedness that preserves integrity.

appearance. [11]Will you not consider this, that if you disobey, nothing remains for you but to die on the rack?"

12 When he had said these things, he ordered the instruments of torture to be brought forward so as to persuade them out of fear to eat the defiling food. [13]When the guards had placed before them wheels and joint-dislocators, rack and hooks[a] and catapults[b] and caldrons, braziers and thumbscrews and iron claws and wedges and bellows, the tyrant resumed speaking: [14]"Be afraid, young fellows; whatever justice you revere will be merciful to you when you transgress under compulsion."

15 But when they had heard the inducements and saw the dreadful devices, not only were they not afraid, but they also opposed the tyrant with their own philosophy, and by their right reasoning nullified his tyranny. [16]Let us consider, on the other hand, what arguments might have been used if some of them had been cowardly and unmanly. Would they not have been the following? [17]"O wretches that we are and so senseless! Since the king has summoned and exhorted us to accept kind treatment if we obey him, [18]why do we take pleasure in vain resolves and venture upon a disobedience that brings death? [19]O men and brothers, should we not fear the instruments of torture and consider the threats of torments, and give up this vain opinion and this arrogance that threatens to destroy us? [20]Let us take pity on our youth and have compassion on our mother's age; [21]and let us seriously consider that if we disobey we are dead! [22]Also, divine justice will excuse us for fearing the king when we are under compulsion. [23]Why do we banish ourselves from this most pleasant life and deprive ourselves of this delightful world? [24]Let us not struggle against compulsion[c] or take

hollow pride in being put to the rack. [25]Not even the law itself would arbitrarily put us to death for fearing the instruments of torture. [26]Why does such contentiousness excite us and such a fatal stubbornness please us, when we can live in peace if we obey the king?"

27 But the youths, though about to be tortured, neither said any of these things nor even seriously considered them. [28]For they were contemptuous of the emotions and sovereign over agonies, [29]so that as soon as the tyrant had ceased counseling them to eat defiling food, all with one voice together, as from one mind, said:

9 "Why do you delay, O tyrant? For we are ready to die rather than transgress our ancestral commandments; [2]we are obviously putting our forebears to shame unless we should practice ready obedience to the law and to Moses[d] our counselor. [3]Tyrant and counselor of lawlessness, in your hatred for us do not pity us more than we pity ourselves. [e] [4]For we consider this pity of yours, which insures our safety through transgression of the law, to be more grievous than death itself. [5]You are trying to terrify us by threatening us with death by torture, as though a short time ago you learned nothing from Eleazar. [6]And if the aged men of the Hebrews because of their religion lived piously[f] while enduring torture, it would be even more fitting that we young men should die despising your coercive tortures, which our aged instructor also overcame. [7]Therefore, tyrant, put us to the test; and if you take our lives because of our religion, do not suppose that you can in-

---

a Meaning of Gk uncertain   b Here and elsewhere in 4 Macc an instrument of torture
c Or *fate*   d Other ancient authorities read *knowledge*   e Meaning of Gk uncertain
f Other ancient authorities read *died*

8:14 *transgress under compulsion.* See notes on 4:26; 5:13, 16.

9:2, 6 *putting our forebears to shame.* Reflecting on the communion of saints throughout the millennia (see note on 1:10) has the further benefit of connecting us with their example and achievements in the faith, so that they become a source for spiritual fortitude as we face our

own trials and seek strength for a response of obedience.

9:7 *if you take our lives because of our religion.* In many circumstances, the disciple needs carefully to discern what would constitute true (or at least the greater) injury or loss. Gaining the whole world was not deemed by Jesus an acceptable compensation for losing one's own

jure us by torturing us. 8For we, through this severe suffering and endurance, shall have the prize of virtue and shall be with God, on whose account we suffer; 9but you, because of your bloodthirstiness toward us, will deservedly undergo from the divine justice eternal torment by fire."

The Torture of the First and Second Brothers

10 When they had said these things, the tyrant was not only indignant, as at those who are disobedient, but also infuriated, as at those who are ungrateful. 11Then at his command the guards brought forward the eldest, and having torn off his tunic, they bound his hands and arms with thongs on each side. 12When they had worn themselves out beating him with scourges, without accomplishing anything, they placed him upon the wheel. 13When the noble youth was stretched out around this, his limbs were dislocated, 14and with every member disjointed he denounced the tyrant, saying, 15"Most abominable tyrant, enemy of heavenly justice, savage of mind, you are mangling me in this manner, not because I am a murderer, or as one who acts impiously, but because I protect the divine law." 16And when the guards said, "Agree to eat so that you may be released from the tortures," 17he replied, "You abominable lackeys, your wheel is not so powerful as to strangle my reason. Cut my limbs, burn my flesh, and twist my joints; 18through all these tortures I will convince you that children of the Hebrews alone are invincible where virtue is concerned." 19While he was

saying these things, they spread fire under him, and while fanning the flames[a] they tightened the wheel further. 20The wheel was completely smeared with blood, and the heap of coals was being quenched by the drippings of gore, and pieces of flesh were falling off the axles of the machine. 21Although the ligaments joining his bones were already severed, the courageous youth, worthy of Abraham, did not groan, 22but as though transformed by fire into immortality, he nobly endured the rackings. 23"Imitate me, brothers," he said. "Do not leave your post in my struggle[b] or renounce our courageous family ties. 24Fight the sacred and noble battle for religion. Thereby the just Providence of our ancestors may become merciful to our nation and take vengeance on the accursed tyrant." 25When he had said this, the saintly youth broke the thread of life.

26 While all were marveling at his courageous spirit, the guards brought in the next eldest, and after fitting themselves with iron gauntlets having sharp hooks, they bound him to the torture machine and catapult. 27Before torturing him, they inquired if he were willing to eat, and they heard his noble decision.[c] 28These leopard-like beasts tore out his sinews with the iron hands, flayed all his flesh up to his chin, and tore away his scalp. But he steadfastly endured this agony and said, 29"How sweet is any kind of death for the religion of our ancestors!" 30To the

a Meaning of Gk uncertain   b Other ancient authorities read *post forever*   c Other ancient authorities read *having heard his noble decision, they tore him to shreds*

---

soul (Matt 16:26, KJV). We are thus invited to train ourselves to look first to the health of our souls and the integrity of our walk with God and to safeguard against injury there.

9:15 *because I protect the divine law.* These martyrs, like the Christians addressed by 1 Peter (see 4:13–16) and many other witnesses against injustice, know that they suffer because they are doing what is right in God's sight. Their walk with God and his inner assurance enable them to continue to use their bodies to protect God's honor and proclaim God's values in the world.

9:17–18 *through all these tortures I will*

convince you. Antiochus is trying to use the brothers' bodies (through fear and pain) as a means of gaining control over their wills. Even though steadfast faith in God does not deliver these young men from the oppressor's power over their bodies, it does prevent him from exercising power over their souls.

9:29–31 *How sweet is any kind of death.* Common to many martyrologies is some testimony to the way in which God enables his children to bear inhuman agonies and master their fear for his sake. Stephen was visited by a vision of the glorified Christ (Acts 7:55–56); the

tyrant he said, "Do you not think, you most savage tyrant, that you are being tortured more than I, as you see the arrogant design of your tyranny being defeated by our endurance for the sake of religion? [31]I lighten my pain by the joys that come from virtue, [32]but you suffer torture by the threats that come from impiety. You will not escape, you most abominable tyrant, the judgments of the divine wrath."

The Torture of the Third and Fourth Brothers

10 When he too had endured a glorious death, the third was led in, and many repeatedly urged him to save himself by tasting the meat. [2]But he shouted, "Do you not know that the same father begot me as well as those who died, and the same mother bore me, and that I was brought up on the same teachings? [3]I do not renounce the noble kinship that binds me to my brothers."[a] [5]Enraged by the man's boldness, they disjointed his hands and feet with their instruments, dismembering him by prying his limbs from their sockets, [6]and breaking his fingers and arms and legs and elbows. [7]Since they were not able in any way to break his spirit,[b] they abandoned the instruments[c] and scalped him with their fingernails in a Scythian fashion. [8]They immediately brought him to the wheel, and while his vertebrae were being dislocated by this, he saw his own flesh torn all around and drops of blood flowing from his entrails. [9]When he was about to die, he said, [10]"We, most abominable tyrant, are suffering because of our godly training and virtue, [11]but you, because of your impiety and bloodthirstiness, will undergo unceasing torments."

[12] When he too had died in a manner worthy of his brothers, they dragged in the fourth, saying, [13]"As for you, do not give way to the same insanity as your brothers, but obey the king and save yourself." [14]But he said to them, "You do not have a fire hot enough to make me play the coward. [15]No— by the blessed death of my brothers, by the eternal destruction of the tyrant, and by the everlasting life of the pious, I will not renounce our noble family ties. [16]Contrive tortures, tyrant, so that you may learn from them that I am a brother to those who have just now been tortured." [17]When he heard this, the bloodthirsty, murderous, and utterly abominable Antiochus gave orders to cut out his tongue. [18]But he said, "Even if you remove my organ of speech, God hears also those who are mute. [19]See, here is my tongue; cut it off, for in spite of this you will not make our reason speechless. [20]Gladly, for the sake of God, we let our bodily members be mutilated. [21]God will visit you swiftly, for you are cutting out a tongue that has been melodious with divine hymns."

The Torture of the Fifth and Sixth Brothers

11 When he too died, after being cruelly tortured, the fifth leaped up, saying, [2]"I will not refuse, tyrant, to be tortured for the sake of virtue. [3]I have come of my own accord, so that by murdering me you will incur punishment from the heavenly justice for even more crimes. [4]Hater of virtue, hater of humankind, for what act of ours are you de-

---

a Other ancient authorities add verse 4, *So if you have any instrument of torture, apply it to my body; for you cannot touch my soul, even if you wish."*
b Gk *to strangle him*   *c* Other ancient authorities read *they tore off his skin*

---

martyrs in this story arrive at what might almost be called an out-of-body experience as they fix their eyes on God (see 6:5–6). The God whose presence and strength sustains us in a thousand lesser trials throughout life can also be trusted to sustain us in the most difficult of trials, as martyrs around the world still discover.

10:21 *God will visit you swiftly.* God is present for the fourth brother in the assurance of vindication, since this brother is conscious of having

presented his bodily members as "instruments of righteousness" (Rom 6:13), especially of consecrating his organs of speech through employing them to worship God. As we consecrate our minds and bodies more fully to God's honor and service, consciously bringing more and more of our whole being into our walk with God, God's presence in our lives becomes proportionately more real and reaffirming.

stroying us in this way? [5]Is it because[a] we revere the Creator of all things and live according to his virtuous law? [6]But these deeds deserve honors, not tortures."[b] [9]While he was saying these things, the guards bound him and dragged him to the catapult; [10]they tied him to it on his knees, and fitting iron clamps on them, they twisted his back[c] around the wedge on the wheel,[d] so that he was completely curled back like a scorpion, and all his members were disjointed. [11]In this condition, gasping for breath and in anguish of body, [12]he said, "Tyrant, they are splendid favors that you grant us against your will, because through these noble sufferings you give us an opportunity to show our endurance for the law."

[13] When he too had died, the sixth, a mere boy, was led in. When the tyrant inquired whether he was willing to eat and be released, he said, [14]"I am younger in age than my brothers, but I am their equal in mind. [15]Since to this end we were born and bred, we ought likewise to die for the same principles. [16]So if you intend to torture me for not eating defiling foods, go on torturing!" [17]When he had said this, they led him to the wheel. [18]He was carefully stretched tight upon it, his back was broken, and he was roasted[e] from underneath. [19]To his back they applied sharp spits that had been heated in the fire, and pierced his ribs so that his entrails were burned through. [20]While being tortured he said, "O contest befitting holiness, in which so many of us brothers have been summoned to an arena of sufferings for religion, and in which we have not been defeated! [21]For religious knowledge, O tyrant, is invincible. [22]I also, equipped with nobility, will die with my brothers, [23]and I myself will bring a great avenger upon you, you inventor of tortures and enemy of those who are truly devout. [24]We six boys have paralyzed your tyranny. [25]Since you have not been able to persuade us to change our mind or to force us to eat defiling foods, is not this your downfall? [26]Your fire is cold to us, and the catapults painless, and your violence powerless. [27]For it is not the guards of the tyrant but those of the divine law that are set over us; therefore, unconquered, we hold fast to reason."

The Torture of the Seventh Brother

12 When he too, thrown into the caldron, had died a blessed death, the seventh and youngest of all came forward. [2]Even though the tyrant had been vehemently reproached by the brothers, he felt strong compassion for this child when he saw that he was already in fetters. He summoned him to come nearer and tried to persuade him, saying, [3]"You see the result of your brothers' stupidity, for they died in torments because of their

a Other ancient authorities read *Or does it seem evil to you that*   b Other authorities add verses 7 and 8, [7]*If you but understood human feelings and had hope of salvation from God*— [8]*but, as it is, you are a stranger to God and persecute those who serve him."*
c Gk *loins*   d Meaning of Gk uncertain
e Other ancient authorities add *by fire*

11:4–6 *live according to his virtuous law.* See note on 9:15.

11:12 *an opportunity to show our endurance for the law.* The author of 1 Peter will also encourage disciples to regard trials of their faith not as experiences of being victimized, but as opportunities to demonstrate the genuineness of their commitment to God, which carries great reward (see 1:6–7). Such an outlook can help empower us for a faithful outcome in any kind of temptation.

11:20 *O contest befitting holiness.* The imagery of the athletic competition or "contest" is frequently used to help oppressed groups see themselves as competitors rather than victims

(see, e.g., Heb 10:32; 12:1–4). Also see the Introduction to 4 Maccabees.

11:27 *not the guards of the tyrant but those of the divine law.* The author returns to the issue of 4:26 (see note). What force is acting more compellingly on the martyrs in their contest— the torturers or the martyrs' training in the law and their walk with God? Only insofar as they had invested throughout life in cultivating that walk with God and allowing the Spiritual Discipline of following Torah to shape their character and strengthen their will are they positioned to stand "unconquered" in the face of trials and maintain their integrity.

disobedience. [4]You too, if you do not obey, will be miserably tortured and die before your time, [5]but if you yield to persuasion you will be my friend and a leader in the government of the kingdom." [6]When he had thus appealed to him, he sent for the boy's mother to show compassion on her who had been bereaved of so many sons and to influence her to persuade the surviving son to obey and save himself. [7]But when his mother had exhorted him in the Hebrew language, as we shall tell a little later, [8]he said, "Let me loose, let me speak to the king and to all his friends that are with him." [9]Extremely pleased by the boy's declaration, they freed him at once. [10]Running to the nearest of the braziers, [11]he said, "You profane tyrant, most impious of all the wicked, since you have received good things and also your kingdom from God, were you not ashamed to murder his servants and torture on the wheel those who practice religion? [12]Because of this, justice has laid up for you intense and eternal fire and tortures, and these throughout all time[a] will never let you go. [13]As a man, were you not ashamed, you most savage beast, to cut out the tongues of men who have feelings like yours and are made of the same elements as you, and to maltreat and torture them in this way? [14]Surely they by dying nobly fulfilled their service to God, but you will wail bitterly for having killed without cause the contestants for virtue." [15]Then because he too was about to die, he said, [16]"I do not desert the excellent example[b] of my brothers, [17]and I call on the God of our ancestors to be merciful to our nation;[c] [18]but on you he will take vengeance both in this present life and when you are dead." [19]After he had uttered these imprecations, he flung himself into the braziers and so ended his life.[d]

Reason's Sovereignty in the Seven

13 Since, then, the seven brothers despised sufferings even unto death, everyone must concede that devout reason is sovereign over the emotions. [2]For if they had been slaves to their emotions and had eaten defiling food, we would say that they had been conquered by these emotions. [3]But in fact it was not so. Instead, by reason, which is praised before God, they prevailed over

a Gk throughout the whole age   b Other ancient authorities read the witness   c Other ancient authorities read my race   d Gk and so gave up; other ancient authorities read gave up his spirit or his soul

---

12:4–5 *if you yield . . . you will be my friend and a leader.* In addition to the threat of pain, the promise of favor is another favorite tool used by our spiritual and physical enemies to subvert our will (see also note on 2 Macc 7:24).

12:9 *they freed him at once.* The prospect of having won over at least the youngest of the seven brothers pleases Antiochus and the torturers, since it signals a victory for them at long last and, in large measure, eradicates the victories of the previous brothers over the tortures. The Roman general Agricola spurs his troops on to face yet another battle out of the fear of marring their past victories by a shameful defeat late in the campaign (Tacitus *Agricola* 33). So we need to remain mindful of the victories God has given us over our spiritual enemies of the flesh, the world, and the devil in the past, and to feel loath to give them the pleasure of a victory after so many failed attempts to subvert our commitment to honor God with our whole selves.

12:11–14 *were you not ashamed?* Oppressors of any kind are alienated from both piety and solidarity with other human beings, and thus indeed from God and their own humanity. If we allow ourselves to be alienated from either, our discipleship will be subverted little by little until the image of Christ is no longer recognizable in us or to us (in the face of another).

13:4 *The supremacy of the mind.* The author would have us give full attention to training and developing this inner faculty that God gave us to discipline ourselves and bring our whole selves in line with God's rule. Now in Christ, God provides the Holy Spirit as well to empower our "reason" and to guide us into Christlikeness. As we practice submitting to the Spirit's leading in prayer and in cultivating an awareness of the Spirit in our day-to-day interactions, we will find Paul's claims about the Spirit's ability to master the "passions and desires" of the flesh to be true as well (see Gal 5:16–25).

their emotions. [4]The supremacy of the mind over these cannot be overlooked, for the brothers[a] mastered both emotions and pains. [5]How then can one fail to confess the sovereignty of right reason over emotion in those who were not turned back by fiery agonies? [6]For just as towers jutting out over harbors hold back the threatening waves and make it calm for those who sail into the inner basin, [7]so the seven-towered right reason of the youths, by fortifying the harbor of religion, conquered the tempest of the emotions. [8]For they constituted a holy chorus of religion and encouraged one another, saying, [9]"Brothers, let us die like brothers for the sake of the law; let us imitate the three youths in Assyria who despised the same ordeal of the furnace. [10]Let us not be cowardly in the demonstration of our piety." [11]While one said, "Courage, brother," another said, "Bear up nobly," [12]and another reminded them, "Remember whence you came, and the father by whose hand Isaac would have submitted to being slain for the sake of religion." [13]Each of them and all of them together looking at one another, cheerful and undaunted, said, "Let us with all our hearts consecrate ourselves to God, who gave us our lives,[b] and let us use our bodies as a bulwark for the law. [14]Let us not fear him who thinks he is killing us, [15]for great is the struggle of the soul and the danger of eternal torment lying before those who transgress the commandment of God. [16]Therefore let us put on the full armor of self-control, which is divine reason. [17]For if we so die,[c] Abraham and Isaac and Jacob will welcome us, and all the fathers will praise us." [18]Those who were left behind said to each of the brothers who were being dragged away, "Do not put us to shame, brother, or betray the brothers who have died before us."

19 You are not ignorant of the affection of family ties, which the divine and all-wise Providence has bequeathed through the fathers to their descendants and which was implanted in the mother's womb. [20]There each of the brothers spent the same length of time and was shaped during the same period of time; and growing from the same blood

a Gk *they*   *b* Or *souls*   *c* Other ancient authorities read *suffer*

13:8–17 *a holy chorus of religion.* The image of the chorus, speaking in unison and reinforcing for one another the trustworthiness of God's promises and the value of obedience, reminds us of the importance of mutual encouragement among the People of God for the perseverance of any single member. We are time after time the means by which God becomes present to disciples facing temptation, flagging in their commitment, losing sight of the value of walking with God, relinquishing their hold on the prize of faithfulness. We too are called to help each other look into Scripture to recall timely words and examples, remind one another of the larger picture of this life and the next, in light of which our choices become clearer, and encourage one another to live with a view to the approval of God and the communion of saints. The life to come (viewed negatively as "eternal torment" and positively as a "welcome" by the "fathers"), the communion of saints, and the compelling logic of Scripture—these become real and present for each one of us when they are reflected and reinforced by fellow disciples who love us.

Responding
13:8–17 FELLOWSHIP. Today reach out to someone with an offer of fellowship. Offer a listening ear, a word of encouragement, or physical assistance to someone to whom you haven't reached out before. *See also* Spiritual Disciplines Index.

13:19–27 *the affection of family ties.* The author uses familiar topics about how love grows among siblings, heightening readers' appreciation of the emotions the brothers had to overcome in order to urge one another on to face pain and death. Following the emotion would have led the brothers to yield to the tyrant and spare each other the grief of loss. The early Church used the language of "sisters and brothers" to talk about relationships among Christians, now made kin by birth into God's family, new "blood relations" by the blood of Jesus. Such language was geared toward encouraging the growth of heartfelt love toward one another in the church, where we too are nurtured by the same Parent, educated in the same heritage, trained in the same way of life, directed toward shared goals, and through the same life, they were brought to the light of day. 21When they were born after an equal time of gestation, they drank milk from the same fountains. From such embraces brotherly-loving souls are nourished; 22and they grow stronger from this common nurture and daily companionship, and from both general education and our discipline in the law of God.

23 Therefore, when sympathy and brotherly affection had been so established, the brothers were the more sympathetic to one another. 24Since they had been educated by the same law and trained in the same virtues and brought up in right living, they loved one another all the more. 25A common zeal for nobility strengthened their goodwill toward one another, and their concord, 26because they could make their brotherly love more fervent with the aid of their religion. 27But although nature and companionship and virtuous habits had augmented the affection of family ties, those who were left endured for the sake of religion, while watching their brothers being maltreated and tortured to death.

14 Furthermore, they encouraged them to face the torture, so that they not only despised their agonies, but also mastered the emotions of brotherly love.

2 O reason,*a* more royal than kings and freer than the free! 3O sacred and harmonious concord of the seven brothers on behalf of religion! 4None of the seven youths proved coward or shrank from death, 5but all of them, as though running the course toward immortality, hastened to death by torture. 6Just as the hands and feet are moved in harmony with the guidance of the mind, so those holy youths, as though moved by an immortal spirit of devotion, agreed to go to death for its sake. 7O most holy seven, brothers in harmony! For just as the seven days of creation move in choral dance around religion, 8so these

youths, forming a chorus, encircled the sevenfold fear of tortures and dissolved it. 9Even now, we ourselves shudder as we hear of the suffering of these young men; they not only saw what was happening, not only heard the direct word of threat, but also bore the sufferings patiently, and in agonies of fire at that. 10What could be more excruciatingly painful than this? For the power of fire is intense and swift, and it consumed their bodies quickly.

An Encomium on the Mother of the Seven

11 Do not consider it amazing that reason had full command over these men in their tortures, since the mind of woman despised even more diverse agonies, 12for the mother of the seven young men bore up under the rackings of each one of her children.

13 Observe how complex is a mother's love for her children, which draws everything toward an emotion felt in her inmost parts. 14Even unreasoning animals, as well as human beings, have a sympathy and parental love for their offspring. 15For example, among birds, the ones that are tame protect their young by building on the housetops, 16and the others, by building at the tops of mountains and depths of chasms, in holes of trees, and on tree-tops, hatch the nestlings and ward off the intruder. 17If they are not able to keep the intruder*b* away, they do what they can to help their young by flying in circles around them in the anguish of love, warning them with their own calls. 18And why is it necessary to demonstrate sympathy for children by the example of unreasoning animals, 19since even bees at the time for making honeycombs defend themselves against intruders and, as though with an iron dart, sting those who approach their hive and defend it even to the death? 20But sympathy for her children

a Or *O minds*   *b* Gk *it*

---

and invited into a shared life and constant companionship. This kind of love, in turn, was expected to breed cooperation (rather than competition) in all ventures, sharing of resources, harmony, and forbearance. Allowing fellow Christians into our lives so closely, moreover, positions them well to encourage us in our own

discipleship in the face of any challenge, just as the seven brothers relied on one another for support in making a faithful response. Cultivating this level of Christian fellowship is an essential part of our collective spiritual formation as the Body of Christ.

14:8 *forming a chorus.* See note on 13:8–17.

did not sway the mother of the young men; she was of the same mind as Abraham.

15 O reason of the children, tyrant over the emotions! O religion, more desirable to the mother than her children! ²Two courses were open to this mother, that of religion, and that of preserving her seven sons for a time, as the tyrant had promised. ³She loved religion more, the religion that preserves them for eternal life according to God's promise.ᵃ ⁴In what manner might I express the emotions of parents who love their children? We impress upon the character of a small child a wondrous likeness both of mind and of form. Especially is this true of mothers, who because of their birth pangs have a deeper sympathy toward their offspring than do the fathers. ⁵Considering that mothers are the weaker sex and give birth to many, they are more devoted to their children.ᵇ ⁶The mother of the seven boys, more than any other mother, loved her children. In seven pregnancies she had implanted in herself tender love toward them, ⁷and because of the many pains she suffered with each of them she had sympathy for them; ⁸yet because of the fear of God she disdained the temporary safety of her children. ⁹Not only so, but also because of the nobility of her sons and their ready obedience to the law, she felt a greater tenderness toward them. ¹⁰For they were righteous and self-controlled and brave and mag-

nanimous, and loved their brothers and their mother, so that they obeyed her even to death in keeping the ordinances.

11 Nevertheless, though so many factors influenced the mother to suffer with them out of love for her children, in the case of none of them were the various tortures strong enough to pervert her reason. ¹²But each child separately and all of them together the mother urged on to death for religion's sake. ¹³O sacred nature and affection of parental love, yearning of parents toward offspring, nurture and indomitable suffering by mothers! ¹⁴This mother, who saw them tortured and burned one by one, because of religion did not change her attitude. ¹⁵She watched the flesh of her children being consumed by fire, their toes and fingers scatteredᶜ on the ground, and the flesh of the head to the chin exposed like masks.

16 O mother, tried now by more bitter pains than even the birth pangs you suffered for them! ¹⁷O woman, who alone gave birth to such complete devotion! ¹⁸When the firstborn breathed his last, it did not turn you aside, nor when the second in torments looked at you piteously nor when the third expired; ¹⁹nor did you weep when you looked at

ᵃ Gk *according to God*   ᵇ Or *For to the degree that mothers are weaker and the more children they bear, the more they are devoted to their children.*
ᶜ Or *quivering*

15:2–3, 8 *She loved religion more.* The mother models how the mind of faith evaluates advantage: nothing can be advantageous if it leads us away from God and from responding to God with loyal obedience. Conversely, whatever nurtures our connection with God has value for eternity. As we exercise ourselves in living out these priorities when the sea is calm, we train ourselves to remain true to them when the storms arise.

15:9, 17 *because of the nobility of her sons.* What are the values that shape our raising of the young (whether our children, our students, or others whom we mentor)? Do we train them for "success" or for "nobility"? The example of the mother commends the latter as the ultimate (and most fulfilling) goal, calling us to anchor the young in a relationship with God and to make

faithfulness to God, rather than "getting ahead" in any temporal sense, their first ambition.

15:18–22 *When the firstborn breathed his last.* The author invites us into the mother's pain and experience far more than we would no doubt wish, trying to make her experience as vivid as possible for readers. Just as we shy away from reading these verses, many Christians shy away from looking closely at the pains our sisters and brothers endure in nations where their confession of Jesus brings persecution. Many parents still must watch their children starve before their eyes, be taken from their custody to a government school, or be subjected to brutal torture and death. If we allow ourselves to enter into their pain, how would God move us to stand beside them, console them, and work fervently for the relief and

the eyes of each one in his tortures gazing boldly at the same agonies, and saw in their nostrils the signs of the approach of death. [20] When you saw the flesh of children burned upon the flesh of other children, severed hands upon hands, scalped heads upon heads, and corpses fallen on other corpses, and when you saw the place filled with many spectators of the torturings, you did not shed tears. [21] Neither the melodies of sirens nor the songs of swans attract the attention of their hearers as did the voices of the children in torture calling to their mother. [22] How great and how many torments the mother then suffered as her sons were tortured on the wheel and with the hot irons! [23] But devout reason, giving her heart a man's courage in the very midst of her emotions, strengthened her to disregard, for the time, her parental love.

24 Although she witnessed the destruction of seven children and the ingenious and various rackings, this noble mother disregarded all these[a] because of faith in God. [25] For as in the council chamber of her own soul she saw mighty advocates—nature, family, parental love, and the rackings of her children— [26] this mother held two ballots, one bearing death and the other deliverance for her children. [27] She did not approve the deliverance that would preserve the seven sons for a short time, [28] but as the daughter of God-fearing Abraham she remembered his fortitude.

29 O mother of the nation, vindicator of the law and champion of religion, who carried away the prize of the contest in your heart! [30] O more noble than males in steadfastness, and more courageous than men in endurance! [31] Just as Noah's ark, carrying the world in the universal flood, stoutly endured the waves, [32] so you, O guardian of the law, overwhelmed from every side by the flood of your emotions and the violent winds, the torture of your sons, endured nobly and withstood the wintry storms that assail religion.

16 If, then, a woman, advanced in years and mother of seven sons, endured seeing her children tortured to death, it must be admitted that devout reason is sovereign over the emotions. [2] Thus I have demonstrated not only that men have ruled over the emotions, but also that a woman has despised the fiercest tortures. [3] The lions surrounding Daniel were not so savage, nor was the raging fiery furnace of Mishael so intensely hot, as was her innate parental love, inflamed as she saw her seven sons tortured in such varied ways. [4] But the mother quenched so many and such great emotions by devout reason.

5 Consider this also: If this woman, though a mother, had been fainthearted, she would have mourned over them and perhaps spoken as follows: [6] "O how wretched am I and many times unhappy! After bearing seven children, I am now the mother of none! [7] O seven childbirths all in vain, seven profitless pregnancies, fruitless nurturings and wretched nursings! [8] In vain, my sons, I endured many birth pangs for you, and the more grievous anxieties of your upbringing. [9] Alas for my children, some unmarried, others married and without offspring.[b] I shall not see your children or have the happiness of being called grandmother. [10] Alas, I who had so many and beautiful children am a widow and alone, with many sorrows.[c] [11] And when I die, I shall have none of my sons to bury me."

12 Yet that holy and God-fearing mother did not wail with such a lament for any of them, nor did she dissuade any of them from dying, nor did she grieve as they were dying. [13] On the contrary, as though having a mind like adamant and giving rebirth for immortality to the whole number of her sons, she implored them and urged them on to death

a Other ancient authorities read *having bidden them farewell, surrendered them*   *b* Gk *without benefit*   *c* Or *much to be pitied*

---

deliverance of our sisters and brothers? This is an aspect of the formation of Christian community that this author would not have us neglect.

16:12–13 *nor did she grieve.* The mother knew in her heart what Jesus would teach as well: those who lose their lives for the sake of God are the ones who secure their lives forever

for the sake of religion. ¹⁴O mother, soldier of God in the cause of religion, elder and woman! By steadfastness you have conquered even a tyrant, and in word and deed you have proved more powerful than a man. ¹⁵For when you and your sons were arrested together, you stood and watched Eleazar being tortured, and said to your sons in the Hebrew language, ¹⁶"My sons, noble is the contest to which you are called to bear witness for the nation. Fight zealously for our ancestral law. ¹⁷For it would be shameful if, while an aged man endures such agonies for the sake of religion, you young men were to be terrified by tortures. ¹⁸Remember that it is through God that you have had a share in the world and have enjoyed life, ¹⁹and therefore you ought to endure any suffering for the sake of God. ²⁰For his sake also our father Abraham was zealous to sacrifice his son Isaac, the ancestor of our nation; and when Isaac saw his father's hand wielding a knife*a* and descending upon him, he did not cower. ²¹Daniel the righteous was thrown to the lions, and Hananiah, Azariah, and Mishael were hurled into the fiery furnace and endured it for the sake of God. ²²You too must have the same faith in God and not be grieved. ²³It is unreasonable for people who have religious knowledge not to withstand pain."

24 By these words the mother of the seven encouraged and persuaded each of her sons to die rather than violate God's commandment. ²⁵They knew also that those who die for the sake of God live to God, as do Abraham and Isaac and Jacob and all the patriarchs.

a Gk *sword*

(Matt 10:39). As we give ourselves over more and more to the leading of the Spirit and to the life that God nurtures within us, we do in fact give up much. We have to say no to many pleasurable things that others around us enjoy. We have to relinquish many of our "rights": to hold grudges, indulge anger, hoard resources. We may even be called to follow God to a place that will lead to an untimely death. But in all such "loss" there is no "grief," since God is present, lavishing the joys of his companionship and approval. As we spur one another on to endure losses of this kind, we participate in one another's "rebirth for immortality."

16:16 *noble is the contest to which you are called.* Martyrdom is not the only contest in which we are called to bear witness to the surpassing goodness of life with God. All of life is such an arena, and all our words, aspirations, and deeds bear witness to something. As Christ takes shape within us, he also takes shape for others through us. In this sense, we are called to be temples of God, bearing his Spirit within us and providing a constant testimony to God's presence, goodness, and vision for human community.

16:18–19 *through God . . . you have had a share in the world.* The logic here is the logic of patronage and reciprocity. If God gave us life, we must use life to honor God. Whatever good things we have enjoyed, we have enjoyed because of God's favor; therefore we owe God our complete loyalty and obedience. No temptation is too great to endure and overcome out of love for and loyalty to God; no loss is too awful to bear if loyalty to God requires it. Paul would continue this line of thinking in 2 Cor 5:15: since Christ died on our behalf to restore us to God, we owe it to him to live for him and not for ourselves. A focal question for our discipleship, then, can be: How can I show gratitude to God and to Christ in this circumstance?

16:21–22 *Daniel the righteous was thrown to the lions.* Daniel and the three young men were delivered from the lions and the furnace; the martyrs actually had to suffer the fires and the iron claws of their tormentors. As Augustine said, however, both those who escaped and those who suffered triumphed in the Eternal God. God was equally present for both in their trials, even though the outcomes were decidedly different; both are now present with God.

16:25 *those who die for the sake of God live to God.* A fundamental conviction about our life with God is that it is unending. Jesus would make a similar statement about Abraham, Isaac, and Jacob: those who identify themselves with God and with whom God identifies himself do not "die" in any ultimate sense (Matt 22:31–32). Because of this, connection with God becomes a more powerful force in life than fear of death (in any of its manifestations).

17 Some of the guards said that when she also was about to be seized and put to death she threw herself into the flames so that no one might touch her body.

2 O mother, who with your seven sons nullified the violence of the tyrant, frustrated his evil designs, and showed the courage of your faith! [3] Nobly set like a roof on the pillars of your sons, you held firm and unswerving against the earthquake of the tortures. [4] Take courage, therefore, O holy-minded mother, maintaining firm an enduring hope in God. [5] The moon in heaven, with the stars, does not stand so august as you, who, after lighting the way of your star-like seven sons to piety, stand in honor before God and are firmly set in heaven with them. [6] For your children were true descendants of father Abraham. [a]

The Effect of the Martyrdoms

7 If it were possible for us to paint the history of your religion as an artist might, would not those who first beheld it have shuddered as they saw the mother of the seven children enduring their varied tortures to death for the sake of religion? [8] Indeed it would be proper to inscribe on their tomb these words as a reminder to the people of our nation: [b]

9 "Here lie buried an aged priest and an aged woman and seven sons, because of the violence of the tyrant who wished to destroy the way of life of the Hebrews. [10] They vindicated their nation, looking to God and enduring torture even to death."

11 Truly the contest in which they were engaged was divine, [12] for on that day virtue gave the awards and tested them for their endurance. The prize was immortality in endless life. [13] Eleazar was the first contestant, the mother of the seven sons entered the competition, and the brothers contended. [14] The tyrant was the antagonist, and the world and the human race were the spectators. [15] Reverence for God was victor and gave the crown to its own athletes. [16] Who did not admire the athletes of the divine [c] legislation? Who were not amazed?

17 The tyrant himself and all his council marveled at their [d] endurance, [18] because of which they now stand before the divine throne and live the life of eternal blessedness. [19] For Moses says, "All who are consecrated are under your hands." [20] These, then, who have been consecrated for the sake of God, [e] are honored, not only with this honor, but also by the fact that because of them our enemies did not rule over our nation, [21] the tyrant was punished, and the homeland purified—they having become, as it were, a ransom for the sin of our nation. [22] And through the blood of those devout ones and their death as an atoning sacrifice, divine Providence preserved Israel that previously had been mistreated.

23 For the tyrant Antiochus, when he saw the courage of their virtue and their en-

a Gk For your childbearing was from Abraham the father; other ancient authorities read For . . . Abraham the servant   b Or as a memorial to the heroes of our people   c Other ancient authorities read true   d Other ancient authorities add virtue and   e Other ancient authorities lack for the sake of God

---

17:6 *true descendants of father Abraham.* There were significant debates over what made a person a "true descendant of father Abraham." Although this author and Paul would disagree about the role of Jesus in making as many Jews and Gentiles as believed in him heirs of the promise to Abraham (see Gal 3:14–18, 26–29), they would agree that Abraham's genuine descendants are those who exhibit the same faithfulness toward God and belief in God's promises that Abraham showed (Gal 3:6–9; Rom 4:11–12, 16, 20–25), especially in the face of death.

17:11–15 *Truly the contest . . . was divine.* Just as the martyrs, in the extreme case, discerned that God's honor was at stake and not merely their own temporal well-being, followers of Christ are similarly called to cultivate an awareness of the larger issues or battles that underlie our daily challenges and choices. If the choices are discovered to line up with a path that honors God |or one that does not (or even dishonors God), our desire to honor God with our whole person empowers us for those choices.

17:21–22 *an atoning sacrifice.* See note on 6:28–29.

durance under the tortures, proclaimed them to his soldiers as an example for their own endurance, 24and this made them brave and courageous for infantry battle and siege, and he ravaged and conquered all his enemies.

18 O Israelite children, offspring of the seed of Abraham, obey this law and exercise piety in every way, 2knowing that devout reason is master of all emotions, not only of sufferings from within, but also of those from without.

3 Therefore those who gave over their bodies in suffering for the sake of religion were not only admired by mortals, but also were deemed worthy to share in a divine inheritance. 4Because of them the nation gained peace, and by reviving observance of the law in the homeland they ravaged the enemy. 5The tyrant Antiochus was both punished on earth and is being chastised after his death. Since in no way whatever was he able to compel the Israelites to become pagans and to abandon their ancestral customs, he left Jerusalem and marched against the Persians.

The Mother's Address to Her Children

6 The mother of seven sons expressed also these principles to her children: 7"I was a pure virgin and did not go outside my father's house; but I guarded the rib from which woman was made. *a* 8No seducer corrupted me on a desert plain, nor did the destroyer, the deceitful serpent, defile the purity of my virginity. 9In the time of my maturity I remained with my husband, and when these sons had grown up their father died. A happy man was he, who lived out his life with good children, and did not have the grief of bereavement. 10While he was still with you, he taught you the law and the prophets. 11He read to you about Abel slain by Cain, and Isaac who was offered as a burnt offering, and about Joseph in prison. 12He told you of the zeal of Phinehas, and he taught you about Hananiah, Azariah, and Mishael in the fire. 13He praised Daniel in the den of the lions and blessed him. 14He reminded you of the scripture of Isaiah, which says, 'Even though you go through the fire, the flame shall not consume you.' 15He sang to you songs of the psalmist David, who said, 'Many are the afflictions of the righteous.' 16He recounted to you Solomon's proverb, 'There is a tree of life for those who do his will.' 17He confirmed the query of Ezekiel, 'Shall these dry bones live?' 18For he did not forget to teach you the song that Moses taught, which says, 19'I kill and I make alive: this is your life and the length of your days.' "

20 O bitter was that day—and yet not bitter—when that bitter tyrant of the Greeks quenched fire with fire in his cruel caldrons, and in his burning rage brought those seven sons of the daughter of Abraham to the catapult and back again to more *b* tortures, 21pierced the pupils of their eyes and cut out their tongues, and put them to death with various tortures. 22For these crimes divine justice pursued and will pursue the accursed tyrant. 23But the sons of Abraham with their victorious mother are gathered together into the chorus of the fathers, and have received pure and immortal *c* souls from God, 24to whom be glory forever and ever. Amen.

a Gk *the rib that was built*   *b* Other ancient authorities read *to all his*   *c* Other ancient authorities read *victorious*

18:10–19 *he taught you the law and the prophets*. The martyrs' training in their life with God began at an early age in their parents' home, which is also where we are to do our primary works of evangelism and making disciples (see Eph 6:4). If you are a parent, how do you use your time with your children? What foundation are you laying for their faithful response to God as you prepare them to face life's manifold contests? The father and mother of the martyrs challenge us to bring "life with God" intentionally into the home and the lives of our children (whether our own or others to whom we pledge our support by virtue of their baptism into Christ) through telling the stories about God and the people who walked with God, passing on our own experiences of God, and anchoring children in their spiritual heritage.

PSALM 151

P salm 151 is one of several psalms that we know from ancient texts but that are not part of Psalms in the Jewish and most Christian canons. However, Psalm 151 belongs to the Eastern Orthodox Christian canon and has long been known from ancient Greek, Latin, and Syriac texts of the Bible. In 1956 it was also found on a scroll of biblical psalms among the Dead Sea Scrolls, used by the pre-Christian Jewish community at Qumran. Found in Qumran Cave 11, the scroll (11QPsª) shows us that this community was using Psalm 151 in worship at least as early as the time of Jesus and suggests that it is older still, though scholars disagree widely over its date of origin.

Though there are variants in the ancient texts, the Greek version of the psalm is used in the Orthodox canon and here. The versions all put into song the themes about David from 1 Samuel 16–17. Their witness is consistent with common teaching in the Psalms and beyond about David's chosenness and God's calling out unlikely people and empowering them to do remarkable things.

—*Howard R. Macy*

See also *"The With-God Life" essay for this section of the Bible,*
"The People of God in Prayer and Worship," pp. 769–72.

This psalm is ascribed to David as his own composition (though it is outside the number[a]), after he had fought in single combat with Goliath.

1 I was small among my brothers,
    and the youngest in my father's house;
  I tended my father's sheep.

2 My hands made a harp;
    my fingers fashioned a lyre.

3 And who will tell my Lord?
    The Lord himself; it is he who hears.[b]

4 It was he who sent his messenger[c]
    and took me from my father's sheep,

and anointed me with his anointing oil.

5 My brothers were handsome and tall,
    but the Lord was not pleased with them.

6 I went out to meet the Philistine,[d]
    and he cursed me by his idols.

7 But I drew his own sword;
    I beheaded him, and took away
        disgrace from the people of Israel.

a Other ancient authorities add *of the one hundred fifty* (psalms)   b Other ancient authorities add *everything*; others add *me*; others read *who will hear me*   c Or *angel*   d Or *foreigner*

151:1–7 *I was small among my brothers.* Though the existing variant versions of this psalm differ in length and wording, the core content is the same. As a whole it affirms David's rightful role as God's chosen leader for Israel.

151:1–5 *I was small.* When Samuel ("[God's] messenger") was sent to Jesse's family, David wasn't even brought to the interview (see 1 Sam 16:1–13). He was the least likely to succeed—not tall and handsome like his brothers, but the youngest, left with the job reserved for the least important. Yet at God's initiative Samuel anointed (chose) him.

151:2–3 *My hands made a harp.* Perhaps in shepherd David's singing and praise God saw the "heart" that would make him a great leader (cf. 1 Sam 16:7). The textual variants of this section suggest that David used his voice and harp to glorify God.

151:6–7 *I went out to meet the Philistine.* The first demonstration that God had chosen and empowered David was the defeat of the giant Goliath (see 1 Sam 17). It witnesses not only to David as the next "anointed one," but also testifies to God's power to use unlikely people like us to do impossible things.

WISDOM OF SOLOMON

T he Wisdom of Solomon provides guidance for daily living. It moves wisdom beyond the worlds of rulers, philosophers, and holy men and women to the day-in, day-out lives of God's people. God wants the best life possible for us, which is why we pursue wisdom. "To fix one's thought on [wisdom] is perfect understanding, and one who is vigilant on her account will soon be free from care" (6:15).

Jesus drew heavily from the biblical wisdom tradition in his Sermon on the Mount. Beatitudes, loving enemies, instructions in piety, reminding us not to worry, identifying the kingdom-bound—all build up to the finale: "Everyone then who hears these words of mine and acts on them *will be like a wise man [or woman]* who built [a] house on rock" (Matt 7:24, italics added). Those who put Jesus' teaching into practice will become wise and live lives that rest on solid foundations. The sermon places wisdom at the center of Christian faith and practice. Growth in wisdom is a pillar of Christian discipleship.

The Wisdom of Solomon is not, however, a Christian document. It was likely written by a hellenized Jewish intellectual—a philosopher or teacher—in Alexandria, Egypt, around 30 BC. Although the motivations for writing cannot be fully known, the author likely required a text for interacting with Greek culture and contextualizing within it Yahweh's message. Despite the dispersion of the children of Abraham to every corner of the Mediterranean and beyond, the story of God's ongoing relationship with them was not finished. Yet it needed articulating anew for those more influenced by Hellenistic culture than by the story of the exodus. Over three hundred miles and nearly six hundred years removed from Jerusalem as the ongoing geographical center for Jewish formation, the Wisdom of Solomon provided guidance for growth in wisdom from the God of all gods.

See also *"The With-God Life" essay for this section of the Bible,*
"The People of God in Daily Life," pp. 901–4.

In turn, as heirs of the Jewish tradition, Christians are also heirs of the wisdom tradition. Although the New Testament contains the wisdom teaching of Jesus, the theological wisdom of Paul, and the practical wisdom of the Letters, for extended reflection on wisdom and its contribution to our formation we look to pre-Christian Scripture. (For more about wisdom literature, see "Wisdom Literature and Spiritual Formation" in the introduction to Proverbs.) In the Wisdom of Solomon we find themes helpful for Christian formation.

Wisdom Is a Presence

Although wisdom is often represented as an aspect of character or virtue, in the Wisdom of Solomon it is a proper noun: Wisdom is a presence with a life of her own. "Wisdom is radiant and unfading, and she is easily discerned by those who love her, and is found by those who seek her" (6:12). Wisdom delivers the Israelites from oppression (10:15), holds blasphemers accountable (1:6), was present in the beginning at the creation (9:9), and in the end is the carrier of salvation (9:18). Wisdom is everywhere and at all times, and, like Solomon, those who would be wise request an audience with her.

Wisdom Is Gained in Daily Living

"I loved her and sought her from my youth," writes the author, "I desired to take her for my bride" (8:2). The Wisdom of Solomon brings Wisdom into the first person of daily living. Always before us, she eventually moves from head to heart, from concept to comprehension. In so moving, every moment becomes pregnant with possibility for growth in godliness.

Wisdom Is Inclusive

Although Wisdom has no place for foolishness (something cannot include its opposite), she invites all of God's creation on her journey. "Although she is but one, she can do all things, and while remaining in herself, she renews all things" (7:27). As such, all that lives is prized (11:26), and God's "immortal spirit is in all things" (12:1). This includes even those who were foolish but could be wise, for example, Canaanites (12:3–11) and nature worshipers (13:1–9). Even though they are in error, Wisdom seeks them out. In every situation she steps back to assess how all creation can be included and responds accordingly. Wisdom errs in the direction of inclusion.

Wisdom Invites Us on a Journey

"She goes about seeking those worthy of her, and she graciously appears to them in their paths, and meets them in every thought" (6:16). As individuals, we are at a given place of maturity, but there is more maturing to be done. This is the case in all matters of living; we can grow relationally, spiritually, intellectually, and mentally. God calls us to become something we are not yet, a reflection of his heart and mind. Wisdom moves this process along by providing a vision for life and guiding our steps along the way. We are called to loving, caring, long suffering, and giving as modeled later in Jesus' life. Wisdom accompanies us on the journey.

Wisdom Takes a Long View

Often in our culture, temporal life is understood as the end of all life. Wisdom will have none of it. She knows there is a greater life, an eternal existence into which we are drawn. "In kinship with wisdom there is immortality" (8:17). This kinship is life with God, beginning each moment. The wise live as fully as possible in light of this reality. We become caught up in eternity, right now, moment by moment, setting the stage for wisdom's further nurturance.

Wisdom Is to Be Cultivated

Wisdom can come upon us by chance, but if we are to become full of God's wisdom we need to seek her out. First, as in the Wisdom of Solomon, we prize her. We ask for and befriend Wisdom in silence, in prayer, in thought, in reading. We make the search for Wisdom a priority. Second, we spend time with wise people. Wise ones are easy to find, but hard to notice. They ponder life's most important questions. They are eager to learn and slow to speak. They have depth of thought and heart. We would be wise to be in their presence. Finally, we develop a conscience and do our best to live by wisdom. We become more easily convicted of right and wrong, repenting when in error. A healthy skepticism oversees our actions, and we change course when needed.

Wisdom hopes to be part of our lives. The Wisdom of Solomon celebrates this and invites us to become a people at rest with God and one another, at home in the creation and living wisely in the midst of it.

—*Felicia and Lyle SmithGraybeal*

Exhortation to Uprightness

1 Love righteousness, you rulers of the
earth,
think of the Lord in goodness
and seek him with sincerity of heart;
² because he is found by those who do
not put him to the test,
and manifests himself to those who do
not distrust him.

³ For perverse thoughts separate people
from God,
and when his power is tested, it exposes
the foolish;
⁴ because wisdom will not enter a
deceitful soul,
or dwell in a body enslaved to sin.
⁵ For a holy and disciplined spirit will flee
from deceit,

1:1 *Love righteousness, you rulers of the earth.* Loving righteousness is the foundation for God's type of life and is especially vital for "rulers of the earth," but the actual audience is all of God's people.

1:2 *those who do not distrust him.* Those who assume God's care, who trust, find God. Distrusting God is living in isolation, either psychologically or physically, from God and others.

1:3-4 *perverse thoughts separate people from God.* The mind becomes what it dwells on. Wisdom cannot make a place in the mind and heart abiding in perversity. Try as it might to be outwardly proper, the foolish soul uses deceit for convincing others of its health.

1:5 *a holy and disciplined spirit.* Holiness comes through discipline. The holiness proceeding from discipline allows discernment between what is foolish and unrighteous and what is wise and righteous.

and will leave foolish thoughts behind,
and will be ashamed at the approach of
   unrighteousness.

6 For wisdom is a kindly spirit,
   but will not free blasphemers from the
      guilt of their words;
   because God is witness of their inmost
      feelings,
   and a true observer of their hearts, and
      a hearer of their tongues.
7 Because the spirit of the Lord has filled
      the world,
   and that which holds all things
      together knows what is said,
8 therefore those who utter unrighteous
      things will not escape notice,
   and justice, when it punishes, will not
      pass them by.
9 For inquiry will be made into the
      counsels of the ungodly,
   and a report of their words will come to
      the Lord,
   to convict them of their lawless deeds;
10 because a jealous ear hears all things,
   and the sound of grumbling does not
      go unheard.
11 Beware then of useless grumbling,
   and keep your tongue from slander;
   because no secret word is without
      result,a
   and a lying mouth destroys the soul.

12 Do not invite death by the error of your
      life,
   or bring on destruction by the works of
      your hands;
13 because God did not make death,
   and he does not delight in the death of
      the living.
14 For he created all things so that they
      might exist;
   the generative forcesb of the world are
      wholesome,
   and there is no destructive poison in
      them,
   and the dominionc of Hades is not on
      earth.
15 For righteousness is immortal.

Life as the Ungodly See It

16 But the ungodly by their words and
      deeds summoned death;d
   considering him a friend, they pined
      away
   and made a covenant with him,
   because they are fit to belong to his
      company.

2 For they reasoned unsoundly, saying
      to themselves,
   "Short and sorrowful is our life,
   and there is no remedy when a life
      comes to its end,

a Or will go unpunished   b Or the creatures
c Or palace   d Gk him

1:6 *a kindly spirit.* Wisdom is kind, but does
not save us from the results of our choices.

1:8 *those who utter unrighteous things.*
The words proceeding from a mouth—and the
thought in the mind connected to that mouth—
reflect the condition of the heart. A good heart
produces good, encouraging words. A bad heart
produces bad, hateful words.

1:9 *to convict them.* Judgment manifests itself
not from an outside entity—God or Church or
society—but from within, as actions bear their
inevitable fruit.

1:11 *keep your tongue from slander.* Again,
the emphasis is on the fact that our souls, our
words, and our actions are all of a piece. A lying
mouth is the result of a soul headed toward
destruction, and a habit of lying further ensures
this destruction. Sin or good actions reinforce

the current state of a soul; they also reveal the
soul's health.

1:13 *God did not make death.* We should be
on the side of life and all that lives in God's
creation. If something is celebrating the culture
of death, it cannot be from God.

1:16—2:24 *the ungodly.* This passage paints a
picture of unformed souls, "the ungodly" or
wicked, and their disposition and motivation.
The life of the ungodly contrasts with the life of
the "righteous" described in 3:1–9.

1:16 *summoned death.* Those not participating in the work of personal formation, whether
intentionally or by default, court death of spirit
and the loss of meaning for their lives. Whether
they realize it or not, they have made friends
with death itself.

and no one has been known to return
    from Hades.
2 For we were born by mere chance,
and hereafter we shall be as though we
    had never been,
for the breath in our nostrils is smoke,
and reason is a spark kindled by the
    beating of our hearts;
3 when it is extinguished, the body will
    turn to ashes,
and the spirit will dissolve like empty air.
4 Our name will be forgotten in time,
and no one will remember our works;
our life will pass away like the traces of a
    cloud,
and be scattered like mist
that is chased by the rays of the sun
and overcome by its heat.
5 For our allotted time is the passing of a
    shadow,
and there is no return from our death,
because it is sealed up and no one turns
    back.

6 "Come, therefore, let us enjoy the good
    things that exist,
and make use of the creation to the full
    as in youth.
7 Let us take our fill of costly wine and
    perfumes,

and let no flower of spring pass us by.
8 Let us crown ourselves with rosebuds
    before they wither.
9 Let none of us fail to share in our
    revelry;
everywhere let us leave signs of
    enjoyment,
because this is our portion, and this our
    lot.
10 Let us oppress the righteous poor man;
let us not spare the widow
or regard the gray hairs of the aged.
11 But let our might be our law of right,
for what is weak proves itself to be useless.

12 "Let us lie in wait for the righteous man,
because he is inconvenient to us and
    opposes our actions;
he reproaches us for sins against the
    law,
and accuses us of sins against our
    training.
13 He professes to have knowledge of God,
and calls himself a child*a* of the Lord.
14 He became to us a reproof of our
    thoughts;
15 the very sight of him is a burden to us,
because his manner of life is unlike that
    of others,

a Or *servant*

2:2–5 *and reason is a spark.* For the ungodly, wisdom and reason, even life itself, are accidental occurrences in a meaningless universe. These verses summarize a view of life that fits amazingly well with some angst-ridden, nihilistic subcultures we see today and reveal that this hip alternative crowd has not discovered anything new.

2:6 *let us enjoy the good things.* "Eat, drink, and be merry, for tomorrow we die"—this is the only option left if there is no future or motivation for maturing the soul. This philosophy makes a god of God's gift of pleasure.

2:9 *let us leave signs of enjoyment.* Without regard to the consequences they will meet in the future, the ungodly gain meaning as others see their "signs of enjoyment," the evidence of the carefree lifestyle they live and others cannot. They pursue lavish lives and think others are envious, making themselves the center of

attention. This is childish selfishness for adults, resulting in wasteful lifestyles and depriving the poor of the means for living.

2:10–11 *let our might be our law of right.* Oppression is achieved through force, violent or nonviolent, and is legitimized simply because it is possible. In "Might makes right" the thrill comes from seeing one's will imposed on others.

2:12–20 *the very sight of him is a burden to us.* Sometimes merely by being present in a situation, a righteous person can implicitly condemn the ways of the wicked, since their own hearts convict them. Even when not outwardly apparent, we still have an effect on the unrighteous when we pursue righteousness. They are insecure in the midst of their bluster and seek to test to make sure they are right. So they persecute the righteous to see if God "will help" them. The world is intensely curious about how God's people conduct themselves.

and his ways are strange.

16 We are considered by him as something
base,
and he avoids our ways as unclean;
he calls the last end of the righteous
happy,
and boasts that God is his father.

17 Let us see if his words are true,
and let us test what will happen at the
end of his life;

18 for if the righteous man is God's child,
he will help him,
and will deliver him from the hand of
his adversaries.

19 Let us test him with insult and torture,
so that we may find out how gentle he is,
and make trial of his forbearance.

20 Let us condemn him to a shameful
death,
for, according to what he says, he will
be protected."

Error of the Wicked

21 Thus they reasoned, but they were led
astray,
for their wickedness blinded them,

22 and they did not know the secret
purposes of God,
nor hoped for the wages of holiness,
nor discerned the prize for blameless
souls;

23 for God created us for incorruption,
and made us in the image of his own
eternity, [a]

24 but through the devil's envy death
entered the world,

and those who belong to his company
experience it.

The Destiny of the Righteous

3 But the souls of the righteous are in
the hand of God,
and no torment will ever touch them.

2 In the eyes of the foolish they seemed to
have died,
and their departure was thought to be a
disaster,

3 and their going from us to be their
destruction;
but they are at peace.

4 For though in the sight of others they
were punished,
their hope is full of immortality.

5 Having been disciplined a little, they
will receive great good,
because God tested them and found
them worthy of himself;

6 like gold in the furnace he tried them,
and like a sacrificial burnt offering he
accepted them.

7 In the time of their visitation they will
shine forth,
and will run like sparks through the
stubble.

8 They will govern nations and rule over
peoples,
and the Lord will reign over them
forever.

9 Those who trust in him will understand
truth,

[a] Other ancient authorities read nature

2:15 *his ways are strange.* For the outsider,
the life of the righteous is hard to fathom. We
should not expect applause for seeking to act
wisely.

2:20 *he will be protected.* The righteous are
safe with God. Conversely, the wicked are convinced there is no God when the righteous are
not saved by the only paradigm of salvation the
wicked know: the denial of death and pain-free
physical life. Yet again we see the sharp contrast
between the ways of God and earthly notions of
success.

3:1 *in the hand of God.* The righteous live

forever in God's care. This makes intentional
spiritual formation of vital importance, for "we
are now becoming what we will be forever."

3:2 *they seemed to have died.* We are all
destined for trials and hardships—even death.
This is the fate of all, but only the righteous are
aware of it.

3:5 *God tested them.* Although to the foolish
trials look like a curse, the wise understand
them as God "putting us through it" to discover
if we share a vision for a world reconciled to
God, an abiding hope in God's ultimate perseverance and triumph for good.

and the faithful will abide with him in
love,
because grace and mercy are upon his
holy ones,
and he watches over his elect. *a*

The Destiny of the Ungodly

10 But the ungodly will be punished as
their reasoning deserves,
those who disregarded the righteous *b*
and rebelled against the Lord;
11 for those who despise wisdom and
instruction are miserable.
Their hope is vain, their labors are
unprofitable,
and their works are useless.
12 Their wives are foolish, and their
children evil;
13 their offspring are accursed.

On Childlessness

For blessed is the barren woman who is
undefiled,
who has not entered into a sinful
union;
she will have fruit when God examines
souls.
14 Blessed also is the eunuch whose hands
have done no lawless deed,
and who has not devised wicked things
against the Lord;
for special favor will be shown him for
his faithfulness,
and a place of great delight in the
temple of the Lord.
15 For the fruit of good labors is renowned,

and the root of understanding does not
fail.
16 But children of adulterers will not come
to maturity,
and the offspring of an unlawful union
will perish.
17 Even if they live long they will be held
of no account,
and finally their old age will be without
honor.
18 If they die young, they will have no hope
and no consolation on the day of
judgment.
19 For the end of an unrighteous
generation is grievous.

4 Better than this is childlessness with
virtue,
for in the memory of virtue *c* is
immortality,
because it is known both by God and by
mortals.
2 When it is present, people imitate *d* it,
and they long for it when it has gone;
throughout all time it marches,
crowned in triumph,
victor in the contest for prizes that are
undefiled.
3 But the prolific brood of the ungodly
will be of no use,
and none of their illegitimate seedlings
will strike a deep root
or take a firm hold.

a Text of this line uncertain; omitted by some
ancient authorities. Compare 4.15   *b* Or *what is
right*   *c* Gk *it*   *d* Other ancient authorities
read *honor*

3:8 *They will govern nations.* The People of
God will persevere though the trials of this life,
be formed along the way, and live in community
with God, reigning over the universe forever
(see Rev 22:5).

3:11 *their works are useless.* Although the life
strategy of the wicked seemingly brings success,
ultimately their works are destined to burn as
"stubble" (v 7). This is the natural outcome of
events even if appearances show otherwise.

3:13–14 *blessed is the barren woman.* As
examples, the faithful barren woman and the
eunuch—"failures" in contemporary Jewish

society—enter God's rest in a way the wicked
can never imagine. This is a significant statement in a culture connecting the number of
offspring with God's favor.

4:1 *childlessness with virtue.* Better than the
temporal sign of many offspring is virtue, a
temporal and eternal reward. Virtue is recognized as an eternal good.

4:3 *the prolific brood of the ungodly.* The
children of the ungodly are a witness against
parents. Their lives are shallow and insecure, a
reflection of the shallowness and insecurity of
the parents' life.

4 For even if they put forth boughs for a
while,
standing insecurely they will be shaken
by the wind,
and by the violence of the winds they
will be uprooted.
5 The branches will be broken off before
they come to maturity,
and their fruit will be useless,
not ripe enough to eat, and good for
nothing.
6 For children born of unlawful unions
are witnesses of evil against their
parents when God examines
them. *a*
7 But the righteous, though they die
early, will be at rest.
8 For old age is not honored for length of
time,
or measured by number of years;
9 but understanding is gray hair for
anyone,
and a blameless life is ripe old age.

10 There were some who pleased God and
were loved by him,
and while living among sinners were
taken up.
11 They were caught up so that evil might
not change their understanding
or guile deceive their souls.
12 For the fascination of wickedness
obscures what is good,
and roving desire perverts the innocent
mind.
13 Being perfected in a short time, they
fulfilled long years;
14 for their souls were pleasing to the
Lord,
therefore he took them quickly from
the midst of wickedness.
15 Yet the peoples saw and did not
understand,
or take such a thing to heart,

that God's grace and mercy are with his
elect,
and that he watches over his holy ones.

The Triumph of the Righteous

16 The righteous who have died will
condemn the ungodly who are
living,
and youth that is quickly perfected *b*
will condemn the prolonged old
age of the unrighteous.
17 For they will see the end of the wise,
and will not understand what the Lord
purposed for them,
and for what he kept them safe.
18 The unrighteous *c* will see, and will have
contempt for them,
but the Lord will laugh them to scorn.
After this they will become dishonored
corpses,
and an outrage among the dead forever;
19 because he will dash them speechless to
the ground,
and shake them from the foundations;
they will be left utterly dry and barren,
and they will suffer anguish,
and the memory of them will perish.

The Final Judgment

20 They will come with dread when their
sins are reckoned up,
and their lawless deeds will convict
them to their face.

5 Then the righteous will stand with
great confidence
in the presence of those who have
oppressed them
and those who make light of their
labors.
2 When the unrighteous *d* see them, they
will be shaken with dreadful fear,

---

a Gk *at their examination*   *b* Or *ended*
c Gk *They*   *d* Gk *they*

4:7 *though they die early.* The righteous life is
not numbered in earth years. Eternal life has
already begun for those being formed in godliness, and so time is a meaningless measure.
Old age, even for the physically young, is

achieved through maturing in a life guided by
God's values.
4:15 *saw and did not understand.* The wicked
do not understand that life is for nurturing the
soul and being spiritually formed.

and they will be amazed at the
    unexpected salvation of the
    righteous.
3 They will speak to one another in
    repentance,
and in anguish of spirit they will groan,
    and say,
4 "These are persons whom we once held
    in derision
and made a byword of reproach—fools
    that we were!
We thought that their lives were
    madness
and that their end was without honor.
5 Why have they been numbered among
    the children of God?
And why is their lot among the saints?
6 So it was we who strayed from the way
    of truth,
and the light of righteousness did not
    shine on us,
and the sun did not rise upon us.
7 We took our fill of the paths of
    lawlessness and destruction,
and we journeyed through trackless
    deserts,
but the way of the Lord we have not
    known.
8 What has our arrogance profited us?
And what good has our boasted wealth
    brought us?

9 "All those things have vanished like a
    shadow,
and like a rumor that passes by;
10 like a ship that sails through the billowy
    water,
and when it has passed no trace can be
    found,
no track of its keel in the waves;
11 or as, when a bird flies through the air,
no evidence of its passage is found;

the light air, lashed by the beat of its
    pinions
and pierced by the force of its rushing
    flight,
is traversed by the movement of its
    wings,
and afterward no sign of its coming is
    found there;
12 or as, when an arrow is shot at a target,
the air, thus divided, comes together at
    once,
so that no one knows its pathway.
13 So we also, as soon as we were born,
    ceased to be,
and we had no sign of virtue to show,
but were consumed in our wickedness."
14 Because the hope of the ungodly is like
    thistledown *a* carried by the
    wind,
and like a light frost *b* driven away by a
    storm;
it is dispersed like smoke before the
    wind,
and it passes like the remembrance of a
    guest who stays but a day.

The Reward of the Righteous

15 But the righteous live forever,
and their reward is with the Lord;
the Most High takes care of them.
16 Therefore they will receive a glorious
    crown
and a beautiful diadem from the hand
    of the Lord,
because with his right hand he will
    cover them,
and with his arm he will shield them.
17 The Lord *c* will take his zeal as his whole
    armor,

a Other ancient authorities read *dust*   *b* Other
ancient authorities read *spider's web*   *c* Gk *He*

5:2 *they will be amazed.* At the judgment, the
unrighteous realize the righteous are living the
right kind of life and are surprised. For some
reason, they cannot fathom the logic of the
with-God life and will only see the light too late.

5:9–14 *like a shadow.* The efforts and lives of
the wicked go unremembered. All the metaphors

in this passage reinforce the idea that "the paths
of lawlessness and destruction" (v 7) make
no ultimate contribution to life, but are like a
shadow, a rumor, a wave from a boat, the path
of a bird in flight, smoke or thistledown dispersed in the wind—no evidence of their
passing is left.

and will arm all creation to repel[a] his
    enemies;
[18] he will put on righteousness as a
    breastplate,
and wear impartial justice as a helmet;
[19] he will take holiness as an invincible
    shield,
[20] and sharpen stern wrath for a sword,
and creation will join with him to fight
    against his frenzied foes.
[21] Shafts of lightning will fly with true
    aim,
and will leap from the clouds to the
    target, as from a well-drawn bow,
[22] and hailstones full of wrath will be
    hurled as from a catapult;
the water of the sea will rage against
    them,
and rivers will relentlessly overwhelm
    them;
[23] a mighty wind will rise against them,
and like a tempest it will winnow them
    away.
Lawlessness will lay waste the whole
    earth,
and evildoing will overturn the thrones
    of rulers.

Kings Should Seek Wisdom

6 Listen therefore, O kings, and
    understand;
learn, O judges of the ends of the earth.
[2] Give ear, you that rule over multitudes,
and boast of many nations.
[3] For your dominion was given you from
    the Lord,
and your sovereignty from the Most
    High;
he will search out your works and
    inquire into your plans.
[4] Because as servants of his kingdom you
    did not rule rightly,
or keep the law,

or walk according to the purpose of
    God,
[5] he will come upon you terribly and
    swiftly,
because severe judgment falls on those
    in high places.
[6] For the lowliest may be pardoned in
    mercy,
but the mighty will be mightily tested.
[7] For the Lord of all will not stand in awe
    of anyone,
or show deference to greatness;
because he himself made both small
    and great,
and he takes thought for all alike.
[8] But a strict inquiry is in store for the
    mighty.
[9] To you then, O monarchs, my words are
    directed,
so that you may learn wisdom and not
    transgress.
[10] For they will be made holy who observe
    holy things in holiness,
and those who have been taught them
    will find a defense.
[11] Therefore set your desire on my words;
long for them, and you will be
    instructed.

Description of Wisdom

[12] Wisdom is radiant and unfading,
and she is easily discerned by those who
    love her,
and is found by those who seek her.
[13] She hastens to make herself known to
    those who desire her.
[14] One who rises early to seek her will have
    no difficulty,
for she will be found sitting at the gate.
[15] To fix one's thought on her is perfect
    understanding,

a Or *punish*

5:17 *arm all creation.* Even the created order
works against the deeds of the unrighteous! It is
armed by God for battle (note similar language
in Eph 6:14–17).
    6:11 *set your desire on my words.* The words
of God—written, spoken, and lived; experienced

individually and in community—are our instructions for living. These words refer to both the
Bible and to Wisdom wherever we find her.
    6:12 *Wisdom . . . is easily discerned.* Wisdom—
a part of God's life—wants to be found. We will
find Wisdom if we seek her.

and one who is vigilant on her account
    will soon be free from care,
16 because she goes about seeking those
    worthy of her,
and she graciously appears to them in
    their paths,
and meets them in every thought.

17 The beginning of wisdom *a* is the most
    sincere desire for instruction,
and concern for instruction is love of
    her,
18 and love of her is the keeping of her
    laws,
and giving heed to her laws is assurance
    of immortality,
19 and immortality brings one near to
    God;
20 so the desire for wisdom leads to a
    kingdom.

21 Therefore if you delight in thrones and
    scepters, O monarchs over the
    peoples,
honor wisdom, so that you may reign
    forever.
22 I will tell you what wisdom is and how
    she came to be,
and I will hide no secrets from you,
but I will trace her course from the
    beginning of creation,
and make knowledge of her clear,
and I will not pass by the truth;
23 nor will I travel in the company of
    sickly envy,
for envy *b* does not associate with
    wisdom.
24 The multitude of the wise is the
    salvation of the world,

and a sensible king is the stability of any
    people.
25 Therefore be instructed by my words,
    and you will profit.

Solomon Like Other Mortals

7 I also am mortal, like everyone else,
    a descendant of the first-formed child
      of earth;
and in the womb of a mother I was
    molded into flesh,
2 within the period of ten months,
    compacted with blood,
from the seed of a man and the pleasure
    of marriage.
3 And when I was born, I began to
    breathe the common air,
and fell upon the kindred earth;
my first sound was a cry, as is true of all.
4 I was nursed with care in swaddling
    cloths.
5 For no king has had a different
    beginning of existence;
6 there is for all one entrance into life,
    and one way out.

Solomon's Respect for Wisdom

7 Therefore I prayed, and understanding
    was given me;
I called on God, and the spirit of
    wisdom came to me.
8 I preferred her to scepters and thrones,
and I accounted wealth as nothing in
    comparison with her.
9 Neither did I liken to her any priceless
    gem,
because all gold is but a little sand in her
    sight,

a Gk *Her beginning*   *b* Gk *this*

6:24 *the salvation of the world.* The wise have a vital role in the world; as "salt" (Matt 5:13), they preserve, or save, our life on earth.

7:5 *no king has had a different beginning.* Although Solomon had many advantages, he too began as a child who in time was faced with the choice of making wisdom or foolishness the foundation of his life. When it comes to wisdom, we all start at the same place and form our path by how well attuned to wisdom we become.

7:7 *I prayed, and understanding was given me.* Solomon asked God for wisdom, and this set the direction for his life. Wisdom is worth more than anything on earth.

Responding
7:7 PRAYER. Like Solomon's, is your prayer practice resulting in wisdom? Is wisdom always the purpose of prayer? *See also* Spiritual Disciplines Index.

and silver will be accounted as clay
    before her.
10 I loved her more than health and
    beauty,
and I chose to have her rather than
    light,
because her radiance never ceases.
11 All good things came to me along with
    her,
and in her hands uncounted wealth.
12 I rejoiced in them all, because wisdom
    leads them;
but I did not know that she was their
    mother.
13 I learned without guile and I impart
    without grudging;
I do not hide her wealth,
14 for it is an unfailing treasure for
    mortals;
those who get it obtain friendship with
    God,
commended for the gifts that come
    from instruction.

Solomon Prays for Wisdom

15 May God grant me to speak with
    judgment,
and to have thoughts worthy of what I
    have received;
for he is the guide even of wisdom
and the corrector of the wise.
16 For both we and our words are in his
    hand,
as are all understanding and skill in
    crafts.
17 For it is he who gave me unerring
    knowledge of what exists,
to know the structure of the world and
    the activity of the elements;
18 the beginning and end and middle of
    times,
the alternations of the solstices and the
    changes of the seasons,

19 the cycles of the year and the
    constellations of the stars,
20 the natures of animals and the tempers
    of wild animals,
the powers of spirits *a* and the thoughts
    of human beings,
the varieties of plants and the virtues of
    roots;
21 I learned both what is secret and what is
    manifest,
22 for wisdom, the fashioner of all things,
    taught me.

The Nature of Wisdom

There is in her a spirit that is intelligent,
    holy,
unique, manifold, subtle,
mobile, clear, unpolluted,
distinct, invulnerable, loving the good,
    keen,
irresistible, 23beneficent, humane,
steadfast, sure, free from anxiety,
all-powerful, overseeing all,
and penetrating through all spirits
that are intelligent, pure, and altogether
    subtle.
24 For wisdom is more mobile than any
    motion;
because of her pureness she pervades
    and penetrates all things.
25 For she is a breath of the power of God,
and a pure emanation of the glory of
    the Almighty;
therefore nothing defiled gains
    entrance into her.
26 For she is a reflection of eternal light,
a spotless mirror of the working of God,
and an image of his goodness.
27 Although she is but one, she can do all
    things,

a Or *winds*

7:15 GUIDANCE—*See* Spiritual Disciplines
Index.

7:15–22 *what I have received.* As part of his
encounter with wisdom, Solomon was taught
the way the world works in a host of disciplines:
ecology, botany, chemistry, metaphysics, psy-
chology, and so on. Many years of curiosity,

observation, study, and prayer created a wise
mind and heart.

7:22–23 *There is in her a spirit.* Listed are,
undoubtedly, many characteristics we want for
our own lives, which are the fruit of working
with God in our spiritual formation.

All the fountains of God's wisdom is in Christ

and while remaining in herself, she
    renews all things;
in every generation she passes into holy
    souls
and makes them friends of God, and
    prophets;
28 for God loves nothing so much as the
    person who lives with wisdom.
29 She is more beautiful than the sun,
and excels every constellation of the
    stars.
Compared with the light she is found to
    be superior,
30 for it is succeeded by the night,
but against wisdom evil does not
    prevail.

8 She reaches mightily from one end of
    the earth to the other,
and she orders all things well.

Solomon's Love for Wisdom

2 I loved her and sought her from my
    youth;
I desired to take her for my bride,
and became enamored of her beauty.
3 She glorifies her noble birth by living
    with God,
and the Lord of all loves her.
4 For she is an initiate in the knowledge
    of God,
and an associate in his works.
5 If riches are a desirable possession in life,
what is richer than wisdom, the active
    cause of all things?
6 And if understanding is effective,
who more than she is fashioner of what
    exists?
7 And if anyone loves righteousness,
her labors are virtues;
for she teaches self-control and
    prudence,
justice and courage;

nothing in life is more profitable for
    mortals than these.
8 And if anyone longs for wide
    experience,
she knows the things of old, and infers
    the things to come;
she understands turns of speech and
    the solutions of riddles;
she has foreknowledge of signs and
    wonders
and of the outcome of seasons and
    times.

Wisdom Indispensible to Rulers

9 Therefore I determined to take her to
    live with me,
knowing that she would give me good
    counsel
and encouragement in cares and grief.
10 Because of her I shall have glory among
    the multitudes
and honor in the presence of the elders,
    though I am young.
11 I shall be found keen in judgment,
and in the sight of rulers I shall be
    admired.
12 When I am silent they will wait for me,
and when I speak they will give heed;
if I speak at greater length,
they will put their hands on their
    mouths.
13 Because of her I shall have immortality,
and leave an everlasting remembrance
    to those who come after me.
14 I shall govern peoples,
and nations will be subject to me;
15 dread monarchs will be afraid of me
    when they hear of me;
among the people I shall show myself
    capable, and courageous in war.
16 When I enter my house, I shall find rest
    with her;

8:1 *she orders all things well.* Just as Wisdom coordinates, or "orders," her responsibilities well, we also should seek to order (or reorder) our world according to wisdom. Using wisdom, we should order our lives according to God's vision of what they should be.

8:7 *her labors are virtues.* Wisdom brings with her virtue: self-control, prudence, courage, and justice. Wisdom cannot be separated from righteousness. We can only be wise if our ends are good and worthwhile.

8:8 *she knows the things of old.* With wisdom comes the proper perspective on life situations— being aware of the relevant history, the dynamics, and the proper goals for each.

for companionship with her has no
    bitterness,
and life with her has no pain, but
    gladness and joy.
17 When I considered these things
    inwardly,
and pondered in my heart
that in kinship with wisdom there is
    immortality,
18 and in friendship with her, pure
    delight,
and in the labors of her hands,
    unfailing wealth,
and in the experience of her company,
    understanding,
and renown in sharing her words,
I went about seeking how to get her for
    myself.
19 As a child I was naturally gifted,
and a good soul fell to my lot;
20 or rather, being good, I entered an
    undefiled body.
21 But I perceived that I would not possess
    wisdom unless God gave her to
    me—
and it was a mark of insight to know
    whose gift she was—
so I appealed to the Lord and implored
    him,
and with my whole heart I said:

Solomon's Prayer for Wisdom

9 "O God of my ancestors and Lord of
    mercy,
who have made all things by your word,
2 and by your wisdom have formed
    humankind
to have dominion over the creatures
    you have made,
3 and rule the world in holiness and
    righteousness,
and pronounce judgment in
    uprightness of soul,

4 give me the wisdom that sits by your
    throne,
and do not reject me from among your
    servants.
5 For I am your servant[a] the son of your
    serving girl,
a man who is weak and short-lived,
with little understanding of judgment
    and laws;
6 for even one who is perfect among
    human beings
will be regarded as nothing without the
    wisdom that comes from you.
7 You have chosen me to be king of your
    people
and to be judge over your sons and
    daughters.
8 You have given command to build a
    temple on your holy mountain,
and an altar in the city of your
    habitation,
a copy of the holy tent that you
    prepared from the beginning.
9 With you is wisdom, she who knows
    your works
and was present when you made the
    world;
she understands what is pleasing in
    your sight
and what is right according to your
    commandments.
10 Send her forth from the holy heavens,
and from the throne of your glory send
    her,
that she may labor at my side,
and that I may learn what is pleasing to
    you.
11 For she knows and understands all
    things,
and she will guide me wisely in my
    actions

a Gk *slave*

8:21 *I appealed to the Lord.* We pray for wisdom and the spiritual formation it brings. Although some are naturally gifted, all of us need to be intentional in seeking Wisdom out, looking to God for her. Without God, there is no wisdom.

9:2 *dominion over the creatures you have made.* Once again, we are reminded God cre-

ated the earth and gave humans dominion. This makes the work of partnering with God for formation and transformation all the more vital.

9:10 *that I may learn.* God, through Wisdom, teaches just and right living. The path of wisdom requires that we are always learners.

and guard me with her glory.

¹² Then my works will be acceptable,
and I shall judge your people justly,
and shall be worthy of the throne ᵃ of
my father.

¹³ For who can learn the counsel of God?
Or who can discern what the Lord
wills?

¹⁴ For the reasoning of mortals is
worthless,
and our designs are likely to fail;

¹⁵ for a perishable body weighs down the
soul,
and this earthy tent burdens the
thoughtful ᵇ mind.

¹⁶ We can hardly guess at what is on
earth,
and what is at hand we find with
labor;
but who has traced out what is in the
heavens?

¹⁷ Who has learned your counsel,
unless you have given wisdom
and sent your holy spirit from on high?

¹⁸ And thus the paths of those on earth
were set right,
and people were taught what pleases
you,
and were saved by wisdom."

The Work of Wisdom from Adam to Moses

10 Wisdom ᶜ protected the first-formed
father of the world, when he
alone had been created;
she delivered him from his
transgression,

² and gave him strength to rule all things.

³ But when an unrighteous man departed
from her in his anger,
he perished because in rage he killed his
brother.

⁴ When the earth was flooded because of
him, wisdom again saved it,
steering the righteous man by a paltry
piece of wood.

⁵ Wisdom ᶜ also, when the nations in
wicked agreement had been put
to confusion,
recognized the righteous man and
preserved him blameless before
God,
and kept him strong in the face of his
compassion for his child.

⁶ Wisdom ᶜ rescued a righteous man when
the ungodly were perishing;
he escaped the fire that descended on
the Five Cities. ᵈ

⁷ Evidence of their wickedness still
remains:
a continually smoking wasteland,
plants bearing fruit that does not
ripen,
and a pillar of salt standing as a
monument to an unbelieving
soul.

⁸ For because they passed wisdom by,
they not only were hindered from
recognizing the good,
but also left for humankind a reminder
of their folly,
so that their failures could never go
unnoticed.

⁹ Wisdom rescued from troubles those
who served her.

¹⁰ When a righteous man fled from his
brother's wrath,

a Gk thrones   b Or anxious   c Gk She
d Or on Pentapolis

9:17 *sent your holy spirit.* The instilling of
wisdom is one of the essential works of the Holy
Spirit. As we open our minds to God through
prayer and reflection, in times of withdrawal
and times of engagement, the Holy Spirit becomes present and presents us with God's
perspective on our lives in community.

10:1 *first-formed father of the world.* Adam,
Noah, Abraham, Lot, Jacob, Joseph, Moses, the
nation of Israel—these are the archetypes of the
soul being formed in the ways of Wisdom. Cain,
Lot's wife, the nation of Egypt, Joseph's brothers,
Jacob's enemies—these are examples of living
without wisdom. We can gain much by reflecting on how they worked in partnership with,
or against, God.

10:9 SERVICE—*See* Spiritual Disciplines
Index.

she guided him on straight paths;
she showed him the kingdom of God,
and gave him knowledge of holy things;
she prospered him in his labors,
and increased the fruit of his toil.
11 When his oppressors were covetous,
she stood by him and made him rich.
12 She protected him from his enemies,
and kept him safe from those who lay in
wait for him;
in his arduous contest she gave him the
victory,
so that he might learn that godliness is
more powerful than anything else.

13 When a righteous man was sold,
wisdom[a] did not desert him,
but delivered him from sin.
She descended with him into the
dungeon,
14 and when he was in prison she did not
leave him,
until she brought him the scepter of a
kingdom
and authority over his masters.
Those who accused him she showed to
be false,
and she gave him everlasting honor.

Wisdom Led the Israelites out of Egypt

15 A holy people and blameless race
wisdom delivered from a nation of
oppressors.
16 She entered the soul of a servant of the
Lord,
and withstood dread kings with
wonders and signs.
17 She gave to holy people the reward of
their labors;
she guided them along a marvelous way,
and became a shelter to them by day,
and a starry flame through the night.
18 She brought them over the Red Sea,
and led them through deep waters;
19 but she drowned their enemies,

and cast them up from the depth of the
sea.
20 Therefore the righteous plundered the
ungodly;
they sang hymns, O Lord, to your holy
name,
and praised with one accord your
defending hand;
21 for wisdom opened the mouths of those
who were mute,
and made the tongues of infants speak
clearly.

Wisdom Led the Israelites through the Desert

11 Wisdom[b] prospered their works by
the hand of a holy prophet.
2 They journeyed through an
uninhabited wilderness,
and pitched their tents in untrodden
places.
3 They withstood their enemies and
fought off their foes.
4 When they were thirsty, they called
upon you,
and water was given them out of flinty
rock,
and from hard stone a remedy for their
thirst.
5 For through the very things by which
their enemies were punished,
they themselves received benefit in
their need.
6 Instead of the fountain of an ever-
flowing river,
stirred up and defiled with blood
7 in rebuke for the decree to kill the infants,
you gave them abundant water
unexpectedly,
8 showing by their thirst at that time
how you punished their enemies.
9 For when they were tried, though they
were being disciplined in mercy,

a Gk she   b Gk She

10:10 GUIDANCE—*See* Spiritual Disciplines
Index.
10:10–12 *a righteous man.* These verses
recount Jacob's protection and blessing by
Wisdom so that he could even wrestle a

powerful angel and live (Gen 32:22–30).
10:12 *godliness is more powerful.* Godliness
joined with wisdom creates an unmovable soul,
one lasting forever, and is more powerful than
we can imagine.

they learned how the ungodly were
    tormented when judged in
    wrath.

10 For you tested them as a parent[a] does in
    warning,
but you examined the ungodly[b] as a
    stern king does in condemnation.

11 Whether absent or present, they were
    equally distressed,

12 for a twofold grief possessed them,
and a groaning at the memory of what
    had occurred.

13 For when they heard that through their
    own punishments
the righteous[c] had received benefit,
    they perceived it was the Lord's
    doing.

14 For though they had mockingly
    rejected him who long before had
    been cast out and exposed,
at the end of the events they marveled
    at him,
when they felt thirst in a different way
    from the righteous.

Punishment of the Wicked

15 In return for their foolish and wicked
    thoughts,
which led them astray to worship
    irrational serpents and worthless
    animals,
you sent upon them a multitude of
    irrational creatures to punish
    them,

16 so that they might learn that one is
    punished by the very things by
    which one sins.

17 For your all-powerful hand,
which created the world out of formless
    matter,

did not lack the means to send upon
    them a multitude of bears, or
    bold lions,

18 or newly-created unknown beasts full of
    rage,
or such as breathe out fiery breath,
or belch forth a thick pall of smoke,
or flash terrible sparks from their eyes;

19 not only could the harm they did
    destroy people,[d]
but the mere sight of them could kill by
    fright.

20 Even apart from these, people[c] could
    fall at a single breath
when pursued by justice
and scattered by the breath of your
    power.
But you have arranged all things by
    measure and number and weight.

God Is Powerful and Merciful

21 For it is always in your power to show
    great strength,
and who can withstand the might of
    your arm?

22 Because the whole world before you is
    like a speck that tips the scales,
and like a drop of morning dew that
    falls on the ground.

23 But you are merciful to all, for you can
    do all things,
and you overlook people's sins, so that
    they may repent.

24 For you love all things that exist,
and detest none of the things that you
    have made,
for you would not have made anything
    if you had hated it.

a Gk a father   b Gk those   c Gk they
d Gk them

11:9 *disciplined in mercy.* If the trials of life do not kill us, they make us stronger. This is one of the many ways God uses life circumstances for the maturing of our hidden lives. This verse refers to the grumblings of the Israelites in the wilderness as God disciplined them and formed them as his people.

11:16 *one is punished.* Although Scripture shows there is judgment at the end of time, it is clear sin is its own punishment even in this life, as it creates dysfunction and heartache for the individual and the community.

11:24 *For you love all things.* God loves all of the creation. God would not create anything for hating. That is why God is slow to anger and act in judgment. He is patient because he loves his creation like a father loves his children.

25 How would anything have endured if
      you had not willed it?
   Or how would anything not called forth
      by you have been preserved?
26 You spare all things, for they are yours,
      O Lord, you who love the living.

12

For your immortal spirit is in all
      things.
2 Therefore you correct little by little
      those who trespass,
   and you remind and warn them of the
      things through which they sin,
   so that they may be freed from
      wickedness and put their trust in
      you, O Lord.

The Sins of the Canaanites

3 Those who lived long ago in your holy
      land
4 you hated for their detestable
      practices,
   their works of sorcery and unholy rites,
5 their merciless slaughter[a] of children,
   and their sacrificial feasting on human
      flesh and blood.
   These initiates from the midst of a
      heathen cult,[b]
6 these parents who murder helpless
      lives,
   you willed to destroy by the hands of
      our ancestors,
7 so that the land most precious of all to
      you
   might receive a worthy colony of the
      servants[c] of God.
8 But even these you spared, since they
      were but mortals,
   and sent wasps[d] as forerunners of your
      army

to destroy them little by little,
9 though you were not unable to give the
      ungodly into the hands of the
      righteous in battle,
   or to destroy them at one blow by dread
      wild animals or your stern word.
10 But judging them little by little you
      gave them an opportunity to
      repent,
   though you were not unaware that their
      origin[e] was evil
   and their wickedness inborn,
   and that their way of thinking would
      never change.
11 For they were an accursed race from the
      beginning,
   and it was not through fear of anyone
      that you left them unpunished
      for their sins.

God Is Sovereign

12 For who will say, "What have you
      done?"
   or will resist your judgment?
   Who will accuse you for the destruction
      of nations that you made?
   Or who will come before you to plead as
      an advocate for the unrighteous?
13 For neither is there any god besides you,
      whose care is for all people,[f]
   to whom you should prove that you
      have not judged unjustly;
14 nor can any king or monarch confront
      you about those whom you have
      punished.

a Gk slaughterers   b Meaning of Gk uncertain
c Or children   d Or hornets   e Or nature
f Or all things

12:2 *you correct little by little.* God is long-
suffering, encouraging our growth, always wanting freedom for us. What we experience as
punishment is often the fruit of our sin and an
opportunity to learn and grow in godliness. God
works with us even when we fail. He yearns for
us to grow.

Responding
12:2 GUIDANCE. What means is God
using in your life to correct you little by

little? How are you opening yourself to his
correction? *See also* Spiritual Disciplines
Index.

12:8–10 *even these you spared.* Even though
the practices of the Canaanites were an abomination to the Lord, God's punishment came
slowly, so they might have opportunity for
repentance. God's love is desperately hopeful
and merciful.

15 You are righteous and you rule all
     things righteously,
  deeming it alien to your power
     to condemn anyone who does not
        deserve to be punished.
16 For your strength is the source of
     righteousness,
  and your sovereignty over all causes you
     to spare all.
17 For you show your strength when
     people doubt the completeness of
     your power,
  and you rebuke any insolence among
     those who know it. *a*
18 Although you are sovereign in strength,
     you judge with mildness,
  and with great forbearance you govern
     us;
  for you have power to act whenever you
     choose.

God's Lessons for Israel

19 Through such works you have taught
     your people
  that the righteous must be kind,
  and you have filled your children with
     good hope,
  because you give repentance for sins.
20 For if you punished with such great care
     and indulgence *b*
  the enemies of your servants *c* and those
     deserving of death,
  granting them time and opportunity to
     give up their wickedness,
21 with what strictness you have judged
     your children,
  to whose ancestors you gave oaths and
     covenants full of good promises!

22 So while chastening us you scourge our
     enemies ten thousand times more,
  so that, when we judge, we may
     meditate upon your goodness,
  and when we are judged, we may expect
     mercy.

The Punishment of the Egyptians

23 Therefore those who lived
     unrighteously, in a life of folly,
  you tormented through their own
     abominations.
24 For they went far astray on the paths of
     error,
  accepting as gods those animals that
     even their enemies *d* despised;
  they were deceived like foolish infants.
25 Therefore, as though to children who
     cannot reason,
  you sent your judgment to mock them.
26 But those who have not heeded the
     warning of mild rebukes
  will experience the deserved judgment
     of God.
27 For when in their suffering they became
     incensed
  at those creatures that they had
     thought to be gods, being
     punished by means of them,
  they saw and recognized as the true
     God the one whom they had
     before refused to know.
  Therefore the utmost condemnation
     came upon them.

a Meaning of Gk uncertain   *b* Other ancient
authorities lack *and indulgence*; others read *and
entreaty*   *c* Or *children*   *d* Gk *they*

12:19 *the righteous must be kind.* Following
God's example of always showing mercy and
providing opportunities for second chances, we
too must be slow to judge and quick to discern
how to serve and to help. In so doing, we can
emulate God by showing kindness, being long-
suffering, and avoiding condemnation.

Responding
12:22 MEDITATION. Here we are
instructed to meditate upon God's
goodness when we judge. Good advice we can
follow at other times in our lives. Try meditating
on God's goodness when you are stuck in traffic
and late for an appointment, when your boss
asks you to stay late at work, when your spouse
or a friend does something unspeakably insen-
sitive. What do you learn? *See also* Spiritual
Disciplines Index.

The Foolishness of Nature Worship

13 For all people who were ignorant of
God were foolish by nature;
and they were unable from the good
things that are seen to know the
one who exists,
nor did they recognize the artisan while
paying heed to his works;
2 but they supposed that either fire or
wind or swift air,
or the circle of the stars, or turbulent
water,
or the luminaries of heaven were the
gods that rule the world.
3 If through delight in the beauty of these
things people assumed them to
be gods,
let them know how much better than
these is their Lord,
for the author of beauty created them.
4 And if people[a] were amazed at their
power and working,
let them perceive from them
how much more powerful is the one
who formed them.
5 For from the greatness and beauty of
created things
comes a corresponding perception of
their Creator.
6 Yet these people are little to be blamed,
for perhaps they go astray
while seeking God and desiring to find
him.
7 For while they live among his works,
they keep searching,

and they trust in what they see, because
the things that are seen are
beautiful.
8 Yet again, not even they are to be
excused;
9 for if they had the power to know so
much
that they could investigate the world,
how did they fail to find sooner the
Lord of these things?

The Foolishness of Idolatry

10 But miserable, with their hopes set on
dead things, are those
who give the name "gods" to the works
of human hands,
gold and silver fashioned with skill,
and likenesses of animals,
or a useless stone, the work of an
ancient hand.
11 A skilled woodcutter may saw down a
tree easy to handle
and skillfully strip off all its bark,
and then with pleasing workmanship
make a useful vessel that serves life's
needs,
12 and burn the cast-off pieces of his work
to prepare his food, and eat his fill.
13 But a cast-off piece from among them,
useful for nothing,
a stick crooked and full of knots,
he takes and carves with care in his
leisure,
and shapes it with skill gained in
idleness;[b]

a Gk they   b Other ancient authorities read with
intelligent skill

13:1 *were foolish by nature*. Certainly we
were not made "foolish." By "nature," the
author refers to those who are "ignorant of
God," and because of this foundation all their
actions become foolish as a result. Idolatry is
first of all foolish.

13:5 *a corresponding perception of their
Creator*. Wonder in creation is a primary resource for knowledge of God and thus for our
spiritual formation. To view the creation, to
study, to stand in awe, reflecting on the Creator
who made such marvels, lead to thanksgiving,
praise, and prayer. Although the creation is not

god, "The heavens are telling the glory of God"
(Ps 19:1).

13:7 *they keep searching*. Humanity in all
times and in all places has sought the presence
behind the objects stirring the senses.

13:10 *with their hopes set on dead things*.
Those who do not trust in God trust in the work
of human hands. Although we may no longer
worship idols fashioned from metal or rock or
wood, we are still tempted by idols. To trust
in the contemporary idols of money, sex, and
power is to put as ultimate "dead things" formed
by human hands.

he forms it in the likeness of a human
    being,
14 or makes it like some worthless animal,
    giving it a coat of red paint and coloring
        its surface red
    and covering every blemish in it with
        paint;
15 then he makes a suitable niche for it,
    and sets it in the wall, and fastens it
        there with iron.
16 He takes thought for it, so that it may
        not fall,
    because he knows that it cannot help
        itself,
    for it is only an image and has need of
        help.
17 When he prays about possessions and
        his marriage and children,
    he is not ashamed to address a lifeless
        thing.
18 For health he appeals to a thing that is
        weak;
    for life he prays to a thing that is dead;
    for aid he entreats a thing that is utterly
        inexperienced;
    for a prosperous journey, a thing that
        cannot take a step;
19 for money-making and work and
        success with his hands
    he asks strength of a thing whose hands
        have no strength.

Folly of a Navigator Praying to an Idol

14 Again, one preparing to sail and
        about to voyage over raging waves
    calls upon a piece of wood more fragile
        than the ship that carries him.
2 For it was desire for gain that planned
        that vessel,
    and wisdom was the artisan who built
        it;
3 but it is your providence, O Father, that
        steers its course,
    because you have given it a path in the
        sea,

and a safe way through the waves,
4 showing that you can save from every
        danger,
    so that even a person who lacks skill
        may put to sea.
5 It is your will that works of your wisdom
        should not be without effect;
    therefore people trust their lives even to
        the smallest piece of wood,
    and passing through the billows on a
        raft they come safely to land.
6 For even in the beginning, when
        arrogant giants were perishing,
    the hope of the world took refuge on a
        raft,
    and guided by your hand left to the
        world the seed of a new
        generation.
7 For blessed is the wood by which
        righteousness comes.

8 But the idol made with hands is
        accursed, and so is the one who
        made it—
    he for having made it, and the
        perishable thing because it was
        named a god.
9 For equally hateful to God are the
        ungodly and their ungodliness;
10 for what was done will be punished
        together with the one who did it.
11 Therefore there will be a visitation also
        upon the heathen idols,
    because, though part of what God
        created, they became an
        abomination,
    snares for human souls
    and a trap for the feet of the foolish.

The Origin and Evils of Idolatry

12 For the idea of making idols was the
        beginning of fornication,
    and the invention of them was the
        corruption of life;

14:3 *that steers its course.* Success in all
matters is dependent on God. No matter how
sure our plans, life can throw unanticipated
barriers and storms our way. At all times we
live under the grace and mercy of God. It is folly

to think otherwise.
14:12 *making idols.* Whatever our idols, they
serve as a filler for the human heart, a replace-
ment for God, who cannot be controlled or
manipulated.

13 for they did not exist from the
        beginning,
    nor will they last forever.
14 For through human vanity they entered
        the world,
    and therefore their speedy end has been
        planned.

15 For a father, consumed with grief at an
        untimely bereavement,
    made an image of his child, who had
        been suddenly taken from him;
    he now honored as a god what was once
        a dead human being,
    and handed on to his dependents secret
        rites and initiations.
16 Then the ungodly custom, grown
        strong with time, was kept as a
        law,
    and at the command of monarchs
        carved images were worshiped.
17 When people could not honor
        monarchs*a* in their presence,
        since they lived at a distance,
    they imagined their appearance far
        away,
    and made a visible image of the king
        whom they honored,
    so that by their zeal they might flatter
        the absent one as though present.

18 Then the ambition of the artisan
        impelled
    even those who did not know the king
        to intensify their worship.
19 For he, perhaps wishing to please his
        ruler,
    skillfully forced the likeness to take
        more beautiful form,
20 and the multitude, attracted by the
        charm of his work,
    now regarded as an object of worship
        the one whom shortly before
        they had honored as a human
        being.
21 And this became a hidden trap for
        humankind,

because people, in bondage to
        misfortune or to royal authority,
    bestowed on objects of stone or wood
        the name that ought not to be
        shared.

22 Then it was not enough for them to err
        about the knowledge of God,
    but though living in great strife due to
        ignorance,
    they call such great evils peace.
23 For whether they kill children in their
        initiations, or celebrate secret
        mysteries,
    or hold frenzied revels with strange
        customs,
24 they no longer keep either their lives or
        their marriages pure,
    but they either treacherously kill one
        another, or grieve one another by
        adultery,
25 and all is a raging riot of blood and
        murder, theft and deceit,
        corruption, faithlessness, tumult,
        perjury,
26 confusion over what is good,
        forgetfulness of favors,
    defiling of souls, sexual perversion,
    disorder in marriages, adultery, and
        debauchery.
27 For the worship of idols not to be
        named
    is the beginning and cause and end of
        every evil.
28 For their worshipers*b* either rave in
        exultation,
    or prophesy lies, or live unrighteously,
        or readily commit perjury;
29 for because they trust in lifeless idols
    they swear wicked oaths and expect to
        suffer no harm.
30 But just penalties will overtake them on
        two counts:
    because they thought wrongly about
        God in devoting themselves to
        idols,

a Gk *them*   *b* Gk *they*

14:22 *they call such great evils peace*. Even
goods like peace and security, if purchased

through aggression and blood, are idolatrous
and evil.

and because in deceit they swore
    unrighteously through contempt
    for holiness.
31 For it is not the power of the things by
    which people swear,[a]
but the just penalty for those who sin,
that always pursues the transgression of
    the unrighteous.

Benefits of Worshiping the True God

15 But you, our God, are kind and true,
    patient, and ruling all things[b] in
    mercy.
2 For even if we sin we are yours, knowing
    your power;
but we will not sin, because we know
    that you acknowledge us as yours.
3 For to know you is complete
    righteousness,
and to know your power is the root of
    immortality.
4 For neither has the evil intent of human
    art misled us,
nor the fruitless toil of painters,
a figure stained with varied colors,
5 whose appearance arouses yearning in
    fools,
so that they desire[c] the lifeless form of a
    dead image.
6 Lovers of evil things and fit for such
    objects of hope[d]
are those who either make or desire or
    worship them.

The Foolishness of Worshiping Clay Idols

7 A potter kneads the soft earth
and laboriously molds each vessel for
    our service,
fashioning out of the same clay
both the vessels that serve clean uses
and those for contrary uses, making all
    alike;
but which shall be the use of each of
    them
the worker in clay decides.
8 With misspent toil, these workers form
    a futile god from the same clay—

these mortals who were made of earth a
    short time before
and after a little while go to the earth
    from which all mortals are taken,
when the time comes to return the
    souls that were borrowed.
9 But the workers are not concerned that
    mortals are destined to die
or that their life is brief,
but they compete with workers in gold
    and silver,
and imitate workers in copper;
and they count it a glorious thing to
    mold counterfeit gods.
10 Their heart is ashes, their hope is
    cheaper than dirt,
and their lives are of less worth than
    clay,
11 because they failed to know the one
    who formed them
and inspired them with active souls
and breathed a living spirit into them.
12 But they considered our existence an
    idle game,
and life a festival held for profit,
for they say one must get money
    however one can, even by base
    means.
13 For these persons, more than all others,
    know that they sin
when they make from earthy matter
    fragile vessels and carved images.

14 But most foolish, and more miserable
    than an infant,
are all the enemies who oppressed your
    people.
15 For they thought that all their heathen
    idols were gods,
though these have neither the use of
    their eyes to see with,
nor nostrils with which to draw breath,
nor ears with which to hear,
nor fingers to feel with,

a Or of the oaths people swear   b Or ruling the
universe   c Gk and he desires   d Gk such hopes

15:2 *even if we sin.* Whether we sin or not,
we are God's. This assurance is a foundation for
Christian formation. He will not abandon us if

we fail. We remain his children, and he wants us
to grow and mature.

and their feet are of no use for walking.
16 For a human being made them,
and one whose spirit is borrowed
formed them;
for none can form gods that are like
themselves.
17 People are mortal, and what they make
with lawless hands is dead;
for they are better than the objects they
worship,
since[a] they have life, but the idols[b]
never had.

Serpents in the Desert

18 Moreover, they worship even the most
hateful animals,
which are worse than all others when
judged by their lack of
intelligence;
19 and even as animals they are not so
beautiful in appearance that one
would desire them,
but they have escaped both the praise of
God and his blessing.

16 Therefore those people[c] were
deservedly punished through
such creatures,
and were tormented by a multitude of
animals.
2 Instead of this punishment you showed
kindness to your people,
and you prepared quails to eat,
a delicacy to satisfy the desire of
appetite;
3 in order that those people, when they
desired food,
might lose the least remnant of
appetite[d]
because of the odious creatures sent to
them,
while your people,[c] after suffering want
a short time,
might partake of delicacies.

4 For it was necessary that upon those
oppressors inescapable want
should come,
while to these others it was merely
shown how their enemies were
being tormented.

5 For when the terrible rage of wild
animals came upon your people[e]
and they were being destroyed by the
bites of writhing serpents,
your wrath did not continue to the end;
6 they were troubled for a little while as a
warning,
and received a symbol of deliverance to
remind them of your law's
command.

7 For the one who turned toward it was
saved, not by the thing that was
beheld,
but by you, the Savior of all.
8 And by this also you convinced our
enemies
that it is you who deliver from every
evil.
9 For they were killed by the bites of
locusts and flies,
and no healing was found for them,
because they deserved to be punished
by such things.
10 But your children were not conquered
even by the fangs of venomous
serpents,
for your mercy came to their help and
healed them.
11 To remind them of your oracles they
were bitten,
and then were quickly delivered,

a Other ancient authorities read *of which*
b Gk *but they*   c Gk *they*   d Gk *loathed the necessary appetite*   e Gk *them*

16:6 *received a symbol*. Symbols, whether liturgical or everyday, are an important resource the Lord uses for our spiritual formation. Since God uses symbols to speak to his people, reflection and meditation are necessary disciplines for the with-God life.
16:7 *the one who turned toward it*. God

provides and protects us often without our knowledge or participation, but the with-God life requires that we turn away from what is destroying us (whether ideas, behaviors, or something else) and turn toward what gives us life. In so doing, we are God's partners in reconciliation (2 Cor 5:16–21).

so that they would not fall into deep
forgetfulness
and become unresponsive*a* to your
kindness.

12 For neither herb nor poultice cured
them,
but it was your word, O Lord, that heals
all people.

13 For you have power over life and death;
you lead mortals down to the gates of
Hades and back again.

14 A person in wickedness kills another,
but cannot bring back the departed
spirit,
or set free the imprisoned soul.

Disastrous Storms Strike Egypt

15 To escape from your hand is impossible;

16 for the ungodly, refusing to know you,
were flogged by the strength of your
arm,
pursued by unusual rains and hail and
relentless storms,
and utterly consumed by fire.

17 For—most incredible of all—in water,
which quenches all things,
the fire had still greater effect,
for the universe defends the righteous.

18 At one time the flame was restrained,
so that it might not consume the
creatures sent against the
ungodly,
but that seeing this they might know
that they were being pursued by the
judgment of God;

19 and at another time even in the midst
of water it burned more intensely
than fire,
to destroy the crops of the unrighteous
land.

The Israelites Receive Manna

20 Instead of these things you gave your
people food of angels,

and without their toil you supplied
them from heaven with bread
ready to eat,
providing every pleasure and suited to
every taste.

21 For your sustenance manifested your
sweetness toward your children;
and the bread, ministering*b* to the
desire of the one who took it,
was changed to suit everyone's liking.

22 Snow and ice withstood fire without
melting,
so that they might know that the crops
of their enemies
were being destroyed by the fire that
blazed in the hail
and flashed in the showers of rain;

23 whereas the fire,*c* in order that the
righteous might be fed,
even forgot its native power.

24 For creation, serving you who made it,
exerts itself to punish the
unrighteous,
and in kindness relaxes on behalf of
those who trust in you.

25 Therefore at that time also, changed
into all forms,
it served your all-nourishing bounty,
according to the desire of those who
had need,*d*

26 so that your children, whom you loved,
O Lord, might learn
that it is not the production of crops
that feeds humankind
but that your word sustains those who
trust in you.

27 For what was not destroyed by fire
was melted when simply warmed by a
fleeting ray of the sun,

---

a Meaning of Gk uncertain   *b* Gk *and it,
ministering*   *c* Gk *this*   *d* Or *who made
supplication*

16:26 *your word sustains.* It is easy to think
that the "production of crops"—our sophisticated business plan—is what meets our needs,
but the writer reminds us that this is not so. We
are dependent on God's word to sustain us. This
is so even for those who are ignorant of it. All of
life is dependent on God's deeper word, which
gives us direction, meaning, and hope and provides our motivation and power for living.

28 to make it known that one must rise
        before the sun to give you thanks,
    and must pray to you at the dawning of
        the light;
29 for the hope of an ungrateful person
        will melt like wintry frost,
    and flow away like waste water.

Terror Strikes the Egyptians at Night

17 Great are your judgments and hard
        to describe;
    therefore uninstructed souls have gone
        astray.
2 For when lawless people supposed that
        they held the holy nation in their
        power,
    they themselves lay as captives of
        darkness and prisoners of long
        night,
    shut in under their roofs, exiles from
        eternal providence.
3 For thinking that in their secret sins
        they were unobserved
    behind a dark curtain of forgetfulness,
    they were scattered, terribly*a* alarmed,
    and appalled by specters.
4 For not even the inner chamber that
        held them protected them from
        fear,
    but terrifying sounds rang out around
        them,
    and dismal phantoms with gloomy
        faces appeared.

5 And no power of fire was able to give
        light,
    nor did the brilliant flames of the stars
    avail to illumine that hateful night.
6 Nothing was shining through to them
        except a dreadful, self-kindled fire,
    and in terror they deemed the things
        that they saw
    to be worse than that unseen appearance.
7 The delusions of their magic art lay
        humbled,
    and their boasted wisdom was
        scornfully rebuked.
8 For those who promised to drive off the
        fears and disorders of a sick soul
    were sick themselves with ridiculous
        fear.
9 For even if nothing disturbing
        frightened them,
    yet, scared by the passing of wild
        animals and the hissing of snakes
10 they perished in trembling fear,
    refusing to look even at the air, though
        it nowhere could be avoided.
11 For wickedness is a cowardly thing,
        condemned by its own
        testimony;*b*
    distressed by conscience, it has always
        exaggerated*c* the difficulties.

a Other ancient authorities read *unobserved, they
were darkened behind a dark curtain of forgetfulness,
terribly*   *b* Meaning of Gk uncertain   *c* Other
ancient authorities read *anticipated*

16:28 *one must rise before the sun.* The
Spiritual Disciplines vary, but intention in our
life with God is essential. Whether we serve an
annoying neighbor, attend worship despite our
melancholy, or take time to engage in whatever
discipline we have chosen, the reality is that
God desires our fellowship, and in the Spiritual
Disciplines we create space for a growing friendship. A life with God requires our intentional,
conscious participation.

Responding
16:28 PRAYER. This verse recommends prayer before sunrise. Reflect
on your customary prayer time. Is it your best,
most alert time or a time when you are often
tired? Try praying at a different time of day than

usual. How does it affect your prayer? *See also*
Spiritual Disciplines Index.

17:3 *thinking that in their secret sins they
were unobserved.* There is no secret life; nothing
is hidden from God. It is an illusion to think we
can get away with our sins. We may fool those
closest to us, but in the end we are only fooling
ourselves.

17:4 *protected them from fear.* Although we
do our best to construct a life that isolates us
from want and concern, fear awaits the first
opening, reminding us there is no security apart
from life with God in community.

17:11 *condemned by its own testimony.* In the
end, wickedness turns on and condemns itself.
Sinfulness is often its own punishment.

¹² For fear is nothing but a giving up of the
     helps that come from reason;
¹³ and hope, defeated by this inward
     weakness,
   prefers ignorance of what causes the
     torment.
¹⁴ But throughout the night, which was
     really powerless
   and which came upon them from the
     recesses of powerless Hades,
   they all slept the same sleep,
¹⁵ and now were driven by monstrous
     specters,
   and now were paralyzed by their souls'
     surrender;
   for sudden and unexpected fear
     overwhelmed them.
¹⁶ And whoever was there fell down,
   and thus was kept shut up in a prison
     not made of iron;
¹⁷ for whether they were farmers or
     shepherds
   or workers who toiled in the wilderness,
   they were seized, and endured the
     inescapable fate;
   for with one chain of darkness they all
     were bound.
¹⁸ Whether there came a whistling wind,
   or a melodious sound of birds in wide-
     spreading branches,
   or the rhythm of violently rushing
     water,
¹⁹ or the harsh crash of rocks hurled
     down,
   or the unseen running of leaping
     animals,
   or the sound of the most savage roaring
     beasts,
   or an echo thrown back from a hollow
     of the mountains,

   it paralyzed them with terror.
²⁰ For the whole world was illumined with
     brilliant light,
   and went about its work unhindered,
²¹ while over those people alone heavy
     night was spread,
   an image of the darkness that was
     destined to receive them;
   but still heavier than darkness were
     they to themselves.

Light Shines on the Israelites

18 But for your holy ones there was
     very great light.
   Their enemies *a* heard their voices but
     did not see their forms,
   and counted them happy for not
     having suffered,
² and were thankful that your holy ones, *b*
     though previously wronged, were
     doing them no injury;
   and they begged their pardon for
     having been at variance with
     them. *b*
³ Therefore you provided a flaming pillar
     of fire
   as a guide for your people's *c* unknown
     journey,
   and a harmless sun for their glorious
     wandering.
⁴ For their enemies *d* deserved to be
     deprived of light and imprisoned
     in darkness,
   those who had kept your children
     imprisoned,

---

a Gk *They*   *b* Meaning of Gk uncertain
c Gk *their*   *d* Gk *those persons*

17:12 *fear is nothing.* Fear is foolish in a
universe created and sustained by a loving God
(1 John 4:18).

17:16 *a prison not made of iron.* Our fears
eventually place us in a prison of darkness. The
darkness is caused by our inability to see God
clearly.

17:21 *heavy night was spread.* Ultimately,
lives established in fear lead to individual and
social darkness, as our whole existence is lived

for "me" or "my family" or "my country," rather
than for God and neighbor. The Egyptians lived
for themselves only and were thus plagued by
darkness. The Israelites trusted God and so
could see. The Egyptians' hardship and Israel's
liberation were the results.

18:2 *were doing them no injury.* Wisdom led
the Israelites, though severely wronged, to forgo
revenge against Egypt.

through whom the imperishable light
of the law was to be given to the
world.

The Death of the Egyptian Firstborn

5 When they had resolved to kill the
    infants of your holy ones,
and one child had been abandoned and
    rescued,
you in punishment took away a
    multitude of their children;
and you destroyed them all together by
    a mighty flood.
6 That night was made known
    beforehand to our ancestors,
so that they might rejoice in sure
    knowledge of the oaths in which
    they trusted.
7 The deliverance of the righteous and
    the destruction of their enemies
were expected by your people.
8 For by the same means by which you
    punished our enemies
you called us to yourself and glorified
    us.
9 For in secret the holy children of good
    people offered sacrifices,
and with one accord agreed to the
    divine law,
so that the saints would share alike the
    same things,
both blessings and dangers;
and already they were singing the
    praises of the ancestors. a
10 But the discordant cry of their enemies
    echoed back,
and their piteous lament for their
    children was spread abroad.
11 The slave was punished with the same
    penalty as the master,
and the commoner suffered the same
    loss as the king;

12 and they all together, by the one form b
    of death,
had corpses too many to count.
For the living were not sufficient even
    to bury them,
since in one instant their most valued
    children had been destroyed.
13 For though they had disbelieved
    everything because of their magic
    arts,
yet, when their firstborn were
    destroyed, they acknowledged
    your people to be God's child.
14 For while gentle silence enveloped all
    things,
and night in its swift course was now
    half gone,
15 your all-powerful word leaped from
    heaven, from the royal throne,
into the midst of the land that was
    doomed,
a stern warrior
16 carrying the sharp sword of your
    authentic command,
and stood and filled all things with
    death,
and touched heaven while standing on
    the earth.
17 Then at once apparitions in dreadful
    dreams greatly troubled them,
and unexpected fears assailed them;
18 and one here and another there, hurled
    down half dead,
made known why they were dying;
19 for the dreams that disturbed them
    forewarned them of this,
so that they might not perish without
    knowing why they suffered.

a Other ancient authorities read *dangers, the*
ancestors already leading the songs of praise
b Gk *name*

18:4 *the imperishable light of the law*. With
their liberation from Egypt, the Israelites were
on a mission to bring the knowledge of God's
law, which brings peace and goodness, to all the
world—though this was not fulfilled until the
coming of Jesus Christ, who commissioned the
Church to bring his life and love to all humanity

(Matt 28:19–20; Rom 8:19–21).
    18:13 *acknowledged your people to be God's
child*. For the author the entire nation of Israel is
"God's child," a singular pronoun for a plural
people. What if the Church—encompassing
every tradition, every denomination—thought of
itself as God's singular child (see John 17:20–24)?

Threat of Annihilation in the Desert

20 The experience of death touched also
the righteous,
and a plague came upon the multitude
in the desert,
but the wrath did not long continue.
21 For a blameless man was quick to act as
their champion;
he brought forward the shield of his
ministry,
prayer and propitiation by incense;
he withstood the anger and put an end
to the disaster,
showing that he was your servant.
22 He conquered the wrath[a] not by
strength of body,
not by force of arms,
but by his word he subdued the
avenger,
appealing to the oaths and covenants
given to our ancestors.
23 For when the dead had already fallen on
one another in heaps,
he intervened and held back the wrath,
and cut off its way to the living.
24 For on his long robe the whole world
was depicted,
and the glories of the ancestors were
engraved on the four rows of
stones,
and your majesty was on the diadem
upon his head.
25 To these the destroyer yielded, these he[b]
feared;
for merely to test the wrath was
enough.

The Red Sea

19 But the ungodly were assailed to the
end by pitiless anger,
for God[c] knew in advance even their
future actions:

2 how, though they themselves had
permitted[d] your people to depart
and hastily sent them out,
they would change their minds and
pursue them.
3 For while they were still engaged in
mourning,
and were lamenting at the graves of
their dead,
they reached another foolish decision,
and pursued as fugitives those whom
they had begged and compelled
to leave.
4 For the fate they deserved drew them
on to this end,
and made them forget what had
happened,
in order that they might fill up the
punishment that their torments
still lacked,
5 and that your people might experience[e]
an incredible journey,
but they themselves might meet a
strange death.

God Guides and Protects His People

6 For the whole creation in its nature was
fashioned anew,
complying with your commands,
so that your children[f] might be kept
unharmed.
7 The cloud was seen overshadowing the
camp,
and dry land emerging where water had
stood before,
an unhindered way out of the Red Sea,
and a grassy plain out of the raging
waves,

a Cn: Gk *multitude*   *b* Other ancient authorities
read *they*   *c* Gk *he*   *d* Other ancient authorities
read *had changed their minds to permit*   *e* Other
ancient authorities read *accomplish*   *f* Or *servants*

18:19 *why they suffered.* The sin of the
Egyptians was the oppression of the Israelites.
Despite Moses' challenge and God's plagues,
this was not acknowledged until the death of
the firstborn males, an occurrence causing great
grief and much reflection. Often we do not
recognize our sin until revealed through times of
grief and reflection.

19:6 *the whole creation.* Release of the captive Israelites is facilitated by the release of the
creation working in their favor. It can be destructive, but ultimately nature is here for our good
and nurture.

8 where those protected by your hand
    passed through as one nation,
after gazing on marvelous wonders.
9 For they ranged like horses,
and leaped like lambs,
praising you, O Lord, who delivered
    them.
10 For they still recalled the events of their
    sojourn,
how instead of producing animals the
    earth brought forth gnats,
and instead of fish the river spewed out
    vast numbers of frogs.
11 Afterward they saw also a new kind*a* of
    birds,
when desire led them to ask for
    luxurious food;
12 for, to give them relief, quails came up
    from the sea.

The Punishment of the Egyptians

13 The punishments did not come upon
    the sinners
without prior signs in the violence of
    thunder,
for they justly suffered because of their
    wicked acts;
for they practiced a more bitter hatred
    of strangers.
14 Others had refused to receive strangers
    when they came to them,
but these made slaves of guests who
    were their benefactors.
15 And not only so—but, while
    punishment of some sort will
    come upon the former
for having received strangers with
    hostility,
16 the latter, having first received them
    with festal celebrations,
afterward afflicted with terrible
    sufferings

those who had already shared the same
    rights.
17 They were stricken also with loss of
    sight—
just as were those at the door of the
    righteous man—
when, surrounded by yawning
    darkness,
all of them tried to find the way
    through their own doors.

A New Harmony in Nature

18 For the elements changed*b* places with
    one another,
as on a harp the notes vary the nature
    of the rhythm,
while each note remains the same.*c*
This may be clearly inferred from the
    sight of what took place.
19 For land animals were transformed into
    water creatures,
and creatures that swim moved over to
    the land.
20 Fire even in water retained its normal
    power,
and water forgot its fire-quenching
    nature.
21 Flames, on the contrary, failed to
    consume
the flesh of perishable creatures that
    walked among them,
nor did they melt*d* the crystalline,
    quick-melting kind of heavenly
    food.

Conclusion

22 For in everything, O Lord, you have
    exalted and glorified your people,
and you have not neglected to help
    them at all times and in all places.

a Or *production*   *b* Gk *changing*   *c* Meaning of
Gk uncertain   *d* Cn: Gk *nor could be melted*

19:13 *hatred of strangers.* How we treat the stranger in our midst is a sign of the health of our personal and communal lives and a measure of our trust, or lack of trust, in God (Gen 19:1–11; Heb 13:2).

19:18 *the sight of what took place.* Freedom from oppression also brings about a new balance for nature, where depravation and destruction have ceased and God's goodness flows.

19:22 *help them at all times and in all places.* God wants nothing more than our good; he is available "at all times and in all places" for partnership in creating a world where the good of all is encouraged.

WISDOM OF JESUS SON OF

SIRACH

OR ECCLESIASTICUS

T he fragmentation of the Jewish people following the destruction of Jerusalem in 587 BC, anticipated by the fall of Samaria in 722/721 BC, resulted in three widely separated centers of Jewish life. A substantial number of those deported to Babylonia chose to remain there after their enforced diaspora became voluntary under the Persian ruler Cyrus. Some, however, found the appeal of the homeland irresistible and made the hazardous journey to Jerusalem and its immediate environs, only to face a hostile reception from other Jews who had occupied the land during the absence of the exiles. A third group migrated south to Egypt, perhaps as early as the sixth century BC, and eventually settled in Alexandria.

The author, Jesus ben Eleazar ben Sirach, was a teacher, probably in Jerusalem, during a crucial period of encounter with Hellenism that divided the priestly aristocracy into rival factions, the Tobiads and Oniads. In 198 BC a shift from Ptolemaic control of the region of Judea to Seleucid rule, based in Syria, soon generated anti-Jewish sentiment aimed at eradicating the religious practices peculiar to Judaism. Mattathias and his sons, defenders of ancestral tradition, eventually rebelled against Syrian hegemony. This resistance, the Maccabean revolt, began in 167 BC and culminated in the Hasmonean dynasty from 142 to 63 BC, when the Roman general Pompey marched into the region. Sirach was probably written shortly before the rebellion against Syria. The author, known as Ben Sira for convenience, lived under the high-priesthood of Simon "the Just" (219–196 BC).

Alexandrian Judaism played a dual role in the preservation of the book, first as the locale of its translation into Greek by Ben Sira's grandson, who arrived in the city in the thirty-eighth year of Ptolemy Euergetes (132 BC) and completed the translation soon

---

See also *"The With-God Life" essay for this section of the Bible,*
"The People of God in Daily Life," pp. 901–4.

after 117 BC, and later as the community that esteemed additional sacred writings in Greek, known as the Septuagint, along with the twenty-four books in the Hebrew Bible. Subsequent Jewish and Christian attitudes toward Sirach were ambivalent. Later reformers considered its teachings worthy of study, although the Catholic and Orthodox Churches gave it "Deuterocanonical" status. The book survived in its Greek form, which has been supplemented in the modern era by discoveries of about two-thirds of the Hebrew text, first in a synagogue storeroom for discarded holy books (a *genizah*) in Cairo and later at two sites near the Dead Sea, Masada and Qumran.

Alexandrian Judaism was highly Hellenized, judging from the writings of Philo, one of its most influential citizens. As a center of learning with an extraordinary library, Alexandria attracted leading philosophers, mathematicians, and rhetoricians. Affluent Jewish families sent their sons to study there. Jews who excelled in this curriculum ran the risk of exalting Greek learning over ancestral traditions. In Jerusalem, Ben Sira refused to abandon the old ways while openly embracing much that Hellenism offered. He serves as a prime example of a religious teacher who faces modernism without fear, welcoming its promise while adhering to the best, in his view, of traditional values. Examining the challenge of Hellenism and Ben Sira's response provides an entry into the book that offers insights into the modern confrontation between Christians and a secular society. Basically, Ben Sira grounds his teaching, sociologically and theologically, on the centrality of family and the truth of sacred narrative.

The Challenge and Promise of Hellenism

The diversity of the Hebrew Bible paved the way for embracing foreign insights. The primary inclination of the first two divisions, the Torah and the Prophets, was ethnocentric, even if ancient Near Eastern literary themes and forms were incorporated. The Mosaic teaching and subsequent prophetic revelation centered on a covenantal people. In the third division, the Writings, one section, wisdom literature (Proverbs, Job, and Ecclesiastes), goes in a different direction; it dwells on truths common to all peoples. These books are entirely silent about the traditions associated with the patriarchs Abraham, Isaac, and Jacob as well as Moses and David. Nothing in the story of the Lord's interaction with the kingdoms of Israel and Judah appears here. Ben Sira stands in this tradition, especially that represented by the book of Proverbs, whose style and content inform his teachings. In the end he breaks out of that tradition, melding the sacred narrative of Israel with general truths applicable to everyone.

Ben Sira's appreciation for Greek ways of life goes beyond assent to Stoic philosophical concepts pertaining to a rational principle governing the universe and undergirding virtue, even including that of opposing forces in nature to combat evil and reinforce the good. He unabashedly uses a Stoic formula describing God as "the all," and he freely takes up the struggle, not exclusively Greek, for prudent speech, athletic valor in the virtues, and the exercise of caution as an ethical stance. In matters of practice, Ben Sira advises his students to participate in banquets, occasions among the Greeks for intellectual display and sensual pleasure, and defends the medical profession.

Greek literature, especially the Homeric legends, the *Iliad* and the *Odyssey*, presented notable examples of courage and virtue. Nothing quite like them existed in

Jewish recorded history, and certainly no one like Plato and Aristotle. Compared to them, Moses and the ritual practices based on the revelation at Sinai seemed provincial. Ben Sira examined sacred narrative in an attempt to fill a national gallery with portraits of heroes to rival the Greeks', beginning with Enoch. A similar move occurs in the Letter to the Hebrews, which mentions many of the same people, now seen as heavenly witnesses summoning Christians to faithful living (Heb 11).

Remarkable features of this national gallery are the prominence of priestly figures and the significance of the Temple in determining those chosen for inclusion. Admiration for the priesthood culminates in an exuberant celebration of the final portrait, described in lavish detail, of Ben Sira's contemporary, the high priest Simon. Another striking feature is the absence of any women.

Ben Sira introduces readers to the problem facing all religious people: how to be in the world, but not of the world. As citizens of another realm, we Christians struggle to resist everything worldly that reduces our witness to the sublime. Not everything that falls under the heading "secular" need be avoided, for the human experiment over millennia has generated much truth. Other faiths too have garnered fresh insights into God's relationship with humankind, and honesty, coupled with modesty, compels us to listen to others. Ben Sira did just that, listening attentively to worthy Greek voices. In the modern world, dialogue across confessional lines in the everyday marketplace is perhaps the only hope left for bringing a modicum of harmony to a divided world. The key here is found in the word "listen." Others too have a story they treasure. Only by hearing their story and appreciating its power can we earn the right to transmit what we consider precious and transforming. In faithful witness to our story, we grow more like him whom it proclaims.

The Centrality of the Family

To fend off the seductive power of Hellenism, Ben Sira elevates the family and the values transmitted in the home. During the monarchy, the prominence of the extended family, central to rural life, dwindled as kings and administrators assumed greater control over the populace. The vacuum created by the collapse of the monarchy was partially filled by the priestly hierarchy, but the school also became a context for the formation of character, hence a powerful instrument of social control. Above all, the "house of instruction" (51:23), if the expression is not just a metaphor in the book of Sirach, was a center for training young men for the scribal profession.

As a teacher of young boys, Ben Sira sought to make them aware of social constraints on behavior. Possibly the most exacting demand involved honor and shame, for happiness depended in large part on one's reputation. Anything that brought shame to a family resulted in a corresponding decline in honor. Saving face meant a great deal in the ancient world, where adversity often implied disfavor before God. This concept partially explains Ben Sira's harsh remarks about daughters, for pregnancy outside marriage brought shame on the family that had failed to "control" the girl. The boys who disobeyed their fathers and behaved badly also contributed their share of disgrace to parents. Loss of honor was reflected in sociological status; falling into poverty that placed one at the mercy of others struck Ben

Sira as worse than death. Nevertheless, manual labor was not in itself dishonorable, for society depended on the fruit of such work.

Friendship too plays a significant role in Ben Sira's worldview, perhaps because of its place in Greek culture. He compares friends to wine, best when aged. The importance of loyal friends compensates somewhat for the diminishing bonds of the extended family. The New Testament advances this notion further, stressing the household of faith that unites in one family all those who confess discipleship to Jesus. Brothers and sisters have one Father, a conviction with universal implications that have the potential for uniting humankind. In both Christianity and Judaism the idea of a chosen people competes with a broader vision of equality under the Creator.

How does Ben Sira instill these values in his students, whom he calls sons according to the custom in the ancient Near East? He teaches a wide range of coping skills: etiquette, proper speech, sexual control, financial responsibility, moral values, humility, and charity, among others. At once both practical and existential, his instructions treat mundane situations and profound mysteries, including death. Drawing on precedent in Proverbs, Ben Sira stresses the erotic dimension of intellectual inquiry, identifying wisdom with a desirable woman whose love draws students to her. Indeed, she enjoys a special relationship with the Creator and is best portrayed in myth akin to the story of human beginnings in Genesis.

The importance of the family to Ben Sira, and to the Bible generally, is a strong link to the present. The intimacy within a household, the bond that helps families make it through all kinds of adversity and emerge stronger, has only one equal—the ardor arising from religious devotion. That is why the metaphor of marriage and the language of parenting best describe this relationship between believers and God. A moment's reflection on the larger family to which we belong, on the magnitude of obligation imposed on us to be worthy sons and daughters of a heavenly Parent, and on the providential implications of this lofty concept will surely inspire in us much gratitude and humility.

The Creator and Human Praise

The dominant theme in Sirach is the "fear of God," the ancient equivalent of the modern word "religion." Along with wisdom, which has its origin and goal in worship, the fear of the Lord defines the ideal relationship between humankind and God. Ben Sira frequently bursts into song, praising the Creator at times with cool mathematical detachment and at other times with emotional abandon. He even includes two prayers, rare within wisdom literature before his time, addressing God as father, shepherd, ruler, and judge. In the second of these prayers, he exposes a vindictive soul, asking for divine punishment to fall on specific enemies. The later stipulation that Christians desiring divine forgiveness must first pardon those who have wronged them points to an ideal not easily practiced. Perhaps that is why Sirach relies so heavily on God's mercy, as opposed to the book of Proverbs, where human merit suffices to bring well-being. Waning self-confidence, poignantly expressed in the books of Job and Ecclesiastes, may have prompted Ben Sira to place extraordinary emphasis on divine compassion.

Still, Ben Sira engages mightily in the defense of God's justice, appealing to the usual arguments, self-contradictory, that suffering results from sin, serves as discipline, and will be compensated in due time. To these, Ben Sira adds a philosophical argument that the universe consists of opposite forces and a psychological one that God uses emotional anxiety to punish the wicked. Nevertheless, Ben Sira refuses to endorse the newest argument, that of reward and punishment after death. Like the Sadducees in Jesus' day, Ben Sira considers death final. For Christians and Jews generally, belief in a blessed existence after death eases the double scandal of innocent suffering and the prosperity of the wicked.

Ben Sira opposes all speculation about divine mystery, whether astrological or apocalyptic. In his view, no one can ascertain the future by studying the stars, nor has anyone ever made a journey through the heavens to acquire secret knowledge. Wisdom is in the final analysis a gift of God, not the product of human inquiry. Even dreams, a medium of divine communication with humans in some circles, draw from Ben Sira a sharp response questioning their reliability. He believes that the Mosaic legislation and Scripture in particular sufficed, when combined with his own insights into reality. The Temple and its personnel are God's gift to a covenanted people, together with sacred Scripture. Their proper response is adoration of God and righteousness toward humans.

In short, Ben Sira resists Hellenism when it compromises ancestral tradition, but embraces its promise as well. He recognizes the sociological underpinnings of the family and reinforces concepts about honor and shame, moral values, and revered tradition. He also teaches the lasting worth of the spiritual legacy bequeathed through centuries of struggle to understand what is good and true. Like everyone, he has flaws, but even broken vessels can be used by God to inspire and instruct. From him we learn that wisdom's yoke is heavy. One greater than he uses similar imagery to invite followers to faithful discipleship (Matt 11:28–30).

Knowledge, for Ben Sira, has both an intellectual and a religious component. True wisdom is faith seeking understanding, to use a later formulation of the issue. Insight begins with worship, indeed finds its highest point there as well. For us too a worldview that allows room for creative intentionality in the universe guides all knowledge. The world did not originate as an accident, we believe, and from that premise we try to understand life's agony and ecstasy. Submitting to an external yoke both chastens and purifies us. In recognizing a will external to our own, we rise above selfish desire and aspire to nobler thoughts and deeds.

Moreover, genuine knowledge is not an end in itself for Ben Sira. His real goal is to offer praise to the Creator. For anyone who has eyes to see, the universe is alive with silent witness to divine generosity, which Ben Sira calls mercy. In this regard he offers a valid example to modern Christians. We are called to adore the One who crafted this wondrous universe and who lovingly sustains it despite our misguided efforts to achieve dominance. In the end, we may discover with Ben Sira that submissive praise best defines the with-God life.

—*James L. Crenshaw*

THE PROLOGUE

Many great teachings have been given to us through the Law and the Prophets and the others[a] that followed them, and for these we should praise Israel for instruction and wisdom. Now, those who read the scriptures must not only themselves understand them, but must also as lovers of learning be able through the spoken and written word to help the outsiders. So my grandfather Jesus, who had devoted himself especially to the reading of the Law and the Prophets and the other books of our ancestors, and had acquired considerable proficiency in them, was himself also led to write something pertaining to instruction and wisdom, so that by becoming familiar also with his book[b] those who love learning might make even greater progress in living according to the law.

You are invited therefore to read it with goodwill and attention, and to be indulgent in cases where, despite our diligent labor in translating, we may seem to have rendered some phrases imperfectly. For what was originally expressed in Hebrew does not have exactly the same sense when translated into another language. Not only this book, but even the Law itself, the Prophecies, and the rest of the books differ not a little when read in the original.

When I came to Egypt in the thirty-eighth year of the reign of Euergetes and stayed for some time, I found opportunity for no little instruction.[c] It seemed highly necessary that I should myself devote some diligence and labor to the translation of this book. During that time I have applied my skill day and night to complete and publish the book for those living abroad who wished to gain learning and are disposed to live according to the law.

In Praise of Wisdom

1 All wisdom is from the Lord,
    and with him it remains forever.
2 The sand of the sea, the drops of rain,
    and the days of eternity—who can
    count them?

---

a Or *other books*   b Gk *with these things*
c Other ancient authorities read *I found a copy affording no little instruction*

Prologue *You are invited.* Composed by Ben Sira's grandson, this elegant prologue explains why the original book was written and justifies its translation into Greek. The introduction praises the author for superior knowledge of the Jewish Scriptures in their threefold division of Law, Prophets, and an as yet undetermined third group called the "other books." Furthermore, it notes that translations are not exact replications, for every language is unique. It therefore urges patience. Finally, it locates the translation between 132 and 117 BC in Egypt. Contemporary readers of Scripture often take the Bible for granted, giving little or no thought to the long and costly process by which it has reached them. An original revelatory experience produced an oral and subsequently written testimony to God's presence and will. Later generations preserved that witness, updating it on the basis of their experiences before God. As a new language replaced the old, the Scriptures were translated into the new, often in competing renditions and against strong resistance. Some translators gave shape to new languages, for example the King James version to English,

Luther's translation to German, and Calvin's to French. Other translators were executed by ecclesial authorities because of their passion to render the Bible into the language of the masses. From the earliest Jewish scribes and later Masoretes to modern translators of the Bible into the languages and dialects spoken today, hosts of people have devoted their lives to rendering the Scriptures into all spoken languages. Like Ben Sira and his grandson, they believed that they were inspired to write so that others could know God's will for their lives.

1:1–10 *All wisdom is from the Lord.* The book opens with a brief hymn praising Wisdom reminiscent of Prov 1:20–33; 8:1–36. The source of Wisdom, and her Creator, is none other than the Lord. Ever generous, the enthroned Creator poured out Wisdom on all creation. Although given proportionately, she is not easily found, and only her Creator fully understands her. For others, she remains a mystery inviting them to engage in a lifelong search. Like other unknowns, she manifests herself only partially, even tantalizingly. She is not discovered through intellectual endeavor, but is granted by God to

3 The height of heaven, the breadth of
   the earth,
   the abyss, and wisdom *a*—who can
     search them out?
4 Wisdom was created before all other
   things,
   and prudent understanding from
     eternity. *b*
6 The root of wisdom—to whom has it
   been revealed?
   Her subtleties—who knows them? *c*
8 There is but one who is wise, greatly to
   be feared,
   seated upon his throne—the Lord.
9 It is he who created her;
   he saw her and took her measure;
   he poured her out upon all his works,
10 upon all the living according to his gift;
   he lavished her upon those who love
     him. *d*

Fear of the Lord Is True Wisdom

11 The fear of the Lord is glory and
   exultation,
   and gladness and a crown of
     rejoicing.
12 The fear of the Lord delights the heart,

and gives gladness and joy and long
   life. *e*
13 Those who fear the Lord will have a
   happy end;
   on the day of their death they will be
     blessed.

14 To fear the Lord is the beginning of
   wisdom;
   she is created with the faithful in the
     womb.
15 She made *f* among human beings an
   eternal foundation,
   and among their descendants she will
     abide faithfully.
16 To fear the Lord is fullness of wisdom;
   she inebriates mortals with her fruits;

a Other ancient authorities read *the depth of the
abyss*   *b* Other ancient authorities add as verse 5,
The source of wisdom is God's word in the highest
heaven, and her ways are the eternal commandments.
c Other ancient authorities add as verse 7, The
knowledge of wisdom—to whom was it manifested?
And her abundant experience—who has understood it?
d Other ancient authorities add Love of the Lord is
glorious wisdom; to those to whom he appears he
apportions her, that they may see him.*   e* Other
ancient authorities add The fear of the Lord is a gift
from the Lord; also for love he makes firm paths.
f Gk *made as a nest*

---

favored people, that is, Israel. The sense of awe
with which Ben Sira opens his book of instruction captures a sentiment often expressed in
Scripture. Divine mystery always remains, however much we think we have understood God's
nature. Human imagination succeeds only in
touching the hem of the divine garment, for God
is always far greater than we think. Like wisdom,
the depth of riches bestowed on humankind
cannot be measured (cf. Rom 11:33).

1:11–20 *To fear the Lord is the beginning of
wisdom.* What, then, is the root of wisdom,
that base from which it grows and flourishes
in people? That rare quality is worship, in contemporary jargon, piety. The "fear of the Lord"
functioned in the ancient world exactly like the
modern term "religion" does today. Ben Sira
thinks that religious devotion generates true
insight, for God has revealed truth to Israel
through Moses and the prophets. Religious
people acquire knowledge to the extent that
they devote their lives to the divine will made

known in the Bible. At the same time, they reap
additional benefits, specifically health, wealth,
and longevity. The simple belief that religion
brings rich reward in this life has reinforced
piety from time immemorial. In ancient Israel
the importance of the extended family enabled
people to overlook specific instances of injustice
against an individual since it was believed that
over time things would even out for the family.
But once individual rights came to the fore that
conviction became less and less persuasive. The
emphasis on individuality led to an insistence
on immediate justice. There is some truth in the
claim that religion pays, but the more one thinks
in terms of spiritual rewards rather than material
ones, the more convincing such claims become.
To think of riches and long life as indicators of
divine favor can lead to egregious error, as Job's
friends demonstrate so clearly by deducing that
he was wicked because of the grief that befell
him and his family.

17 she fills their^a whole house with
    desirable goods,
and their^a storehouses with her
    produce.
18 The fear of the Lord is the crown of
    wisdom,
making peace and perfect health to
    flourish.^b
19 She rained down knowledge and
    discerning comprehension,
and she heightened the glory of those
    who held her fast.
20 To fear the Lord is the root of wisdom,
    and her branches are long life.^c

22 Unjust anger cannot be justified,
    for anger tips the scale to one's ruin.
23 Those who are patient stay calm until
    the right moment,
and then cheerfulness comes back to
    them.
24 They hold back their words until the
    right moment;
then the lips of many tell of their
    good sense.

25 In the treasuries of wisdom are wise
    sayings,
but godliness is an abomination to a
    sinner.

26 If you desire wisdom, keep the
    commandments,
and the Lord will lavish her upon you.
27 For the fear of the Lord is wisdom and
    discipline,
fidelity and humility are his delight.

28 Do not disobey the fear of the Lord;
    do not approach him with a divided
    mind.
29 Do not be a hypocrite before others,
    and keep watch over your lips.
30 Do not exalt yourself, or you may fall
    and bring dishonor upon yourself.
The Lord will reveal your secrets
    and overthrow you before the whole
    congregation,
because you did not come in the fear of
    the Lord,
and your heart was full of deceit.

Duties toward God

2 My child, when you come to serve the
    Lord,
    prepare yourself for testing.^d

a Other ancient authorities read *her*   b Other
ancient authorities add *Both are gifts of God for
peace; glory opens out for those who love him. He saw
her and took her measure.*   c Other ancient
authorities add as verse 21, *The fear of the Lord drives
away sins; and where it abides, it will turn away all
anger.*   d Or *trials*

1:22–30 *If you desire wisdom, keep the commandments.* Wisdom makes a difference in how people behave; indeed, by keeping the commandments one has access to additional understanding. Certain character traits reveal a lack of knowledge, particularly uncontrolled anger, hypocrisy, pride, and deceit. Knowing when to speak will bring approval from other people and from the Lord. When society is well ordered, it can truly be said of others, as it was of Jesus, that they increase daily in favor with God and human beings (Luke 2:52). Ben Sira warns that the Lord will divulge one's secrets to the whole congregation, bringing humiliation. Christianity has turned that thought into a powerful nightmare about a final judgment when all human secrets will be made known. The motivational force of this idea, its capacity to encourage virtue, stems from the negative side of ethics.

It stresses the stick, or punishment, rather than the carrot, or reward. The cardinal virtues, according to the teachers of wisdom, consisted of timing, eloquence, restraint, and integrity. To know when to speak, and then being able to persuade others, while exercising control over one's passions and always speaking truthfully—this was virtue. Above all, however, virtue consisted of devotion to the law or, more correctly, to its source.

2:1 *My child.* This book has an audience, here indicated by direct address, as in the initial collection of Proverbs, chapters 1–9. Throughout the ancient Near East, sages addressed teachings to their sons. Originally, this designation indicated family lineage, but eventually it came to mean students in general. Only boys received education in the scribal arts, with the occasional exception of princesses in Egypt and Mesopotamia.

2 Set your heart right and be steadfast,
  and do not be impetuous in time of
    calamity.
3 Cling to him and do not depart,
  so that your last days may be
    prosperous.
4 Accept whatever befalls you,
  and in times of humiliation be
    patient.
5 For gold is tested in the fire,
  and those found acceptable, in the
    furnace of humiliation. *a*
6 Trust in him, and he will help you;
  make your ways straight, and hope in
    him.

7 You who fear the Lord, wait for his
    mercy;
  do not stray, or else you may fall.
8 You who fear the Lord, trust in him,
  and your reward will not be lost.
9 You who fear the Lord, hope for good
    things,

for lasting joy and mercy. *b*
10 Consider the generations of old and see:
  has anyone trusted in the Lord and
    been disappointed?
  Or has anyone persevered in the fear of
    the Lord*c* and been forsaken?
  Or has anyone called upon him and
    been neglected?
11 For the Lord is compassionate and
    merciful;
  he forgives sins and saves in time of
    distress.

12 Woe to timid hearts and to slack hands,
  and to the sinner who walks a double
    path!
13 Woe to the fainthearted who have no
    trust!
  Therefore they will have no shelter.

a Other ancient authorities add *in sickness and
poverty put your trust in him*   *b* Other ancient
authorities add *For his reward is an everlasting gift
with joy.*   *c* Gk *of him*

To some extent, this limitation of professional training to males explains the feminization of knowledge. Calling wisdom a bride or depicting her as the object of ardor invested the intellectual and moral quest with definite erotic fascination. Ben Sira warns his students of the difficulties associated with learning, comparing these tests with the process of refining gold. Scribal texts from Mesopotamia and Egypt frequently mention the rigorous requirements facing young students, along with the stiff punishment for slackers. In Egypt, the hieroglyph for a teacher is that of an arm holding a cane with which to punish lazy or incompetent boys. In Christian moral education, resisting temptation becomes a major emphasis, and temptation is considered the work of an energetic and ubiquitous rebel, Satan. In resisting him, Jesus resorts to Scripture and thus provides an example for Christians (Matt 4:1–11).

2:7–11 *You who fear the Lord, wait for his mercy.* Here for the first time Ben Sira refers to God's mercy, a theme that will become omnipresent until the end of the book. Earlier sages had not emphasized this quality, for they assumed that individuals earned the rewards or punishment they received. A new spirit seems to have dawned, with less optimism about human possibility and a keener sense of need for divine mercy. Here too Ben Sira introduces a stylistic feature for the first time, starting several verses with a common phrase. This type of instruction continues through verse 18, with four different introductory phrases being employed three times each ("You who fear the Lord," "Or has anyone," "Woe to," and "Those who fear the Lord"). Like teachers before him, Ben Sira appeals to ancient tradition, including Scripture. The compassionate nature of the Lord is proclaimed emphatically in Exod 34:6, but often elsewhere. For that reason, David chose to fall into the hands of the Lord rather than be subject to an impersonal force (2 Sam 24:14). His reason is clearly stated: "For his mercy is great." This concept of mercy is advanced all the more in the New Testament, where Jesus becomes the very incarnation of God's great mercy. Even more, he calls his disciples to exhibit this quality of life as well: "Blessed are the merciful, for they will receive mercy" (Matt 5:7). This is the basis for any genuine Christian spiritual transformation. It is all done within the accepting environment of God's overwhelming mercy toward us. We constantly cry out, as so many did during Jesus' earthly sojourn, "Jesus, Son of David, have mercy on me!" (Mark 10:47).

14 Woe to you who have lost your nerve!
  What will you do when the Lord's
    reckoning comes?

15 Those who fear the Lord do not disobey
    his words,
  and those who love him keep his
    ways.
16 Those who fear the Lord seek to please
    him,
  and those who love him are filled
    with his law.
17 Those who fear the Lord prepare their
    hearts,
  and humble themselves before him.
18 Let us fall into the hands of the Lord,
  but not into the hands of mortals;
  for equal to his majesty is his mercy,
  and equal to his name are his works. *a*

Duties toward Parents

3 Listen to me your father, O children;
    act accordingly, that you may be kept
      in safety.
2 For the Lord honors a father above his
    children,
  and he confirms a mother's right over
    her children.
3 Those who honor their father atone for
    sins,
4 and those who respect their mother
    are like those who lay up treasure.
5 Those who honor their father will have
    joy in their own children,
  and when they pray they will be
    heard.
6 Those who respect their father will have
    long life,

and those who honor *b* their mother
  obey the Lord;
7 they will serve their parents as their
    masters. *c*
8 Honor your father by word and deed,
  that his blessing may come upon you.
9 For a father's blessing strengthens the
    houses of the children,
  but a mother's curse uproots their
    foundations.
10 Do not glorify yourself by dishonoring
    your father,
  for your father's dishonor is no glory
    to you.
11 The glory of one's father is one's own
    glory,
  and it is a disgrace for children not to
    respect their mother.
12 My child, help your father in his old
    age,
  and do not grieve him as long as he
    lives;
13 even if his mind fails, be patient with
    him;
  because you have all your faculties do
    not despise him.
14 For kindness to a father will not be
    forgotten,
  and will be credited to you against
    your sins;
15 in the day of your distress it will be
    remembered in your favor;
  like frost in fair weather, your sins will
    melt away.

a Syr: Gk lacks this line   *b* Heb: Other ancient
authorities read *comfort*   *c* In other ancient
authorities this line is preceded by *Those who fear
the Lord honor their father,*

3:1–16 *Those who honor their father will have
joy.* Having reminded his students of the importance of religion, Ben Sira now turns to the
primary responsibility among humans, the
honoring of parents. Just as the Decalogue
moves from obligations toward God to those
toward parents, Ben Sira underscores the rewards for treating aged parents with respect,
even when their judgments have become impaired (v 13). He even thinks that successful
praying depends on just treatment of parents,

which has an atoning power. Here Ben Sira
becomes poetic: "Like frost in fair weather,
your sins will melt away" (v 15). Today's aging
population presents unprecedented problems
and increases the likelihood of having to deal
with parents who experience decreased mental
capacities along with the usual physical afflictions. Ben Sira's advice becomes therefore all
the more urgent. We cannot claim to honor the
heavenly Father unless we do the same for
earthly parents.

16 Whoever forsakes a father is like a
blasphemer,
and whoever angers a mother is
cursed by the Lord.

Humility

17 My child, perform your tasks with
humility;[a]
then you will be loved by those whom
God accepts.
18 The greater you are, the more you must
humble yourself;
so you will find favor in the sight of
the Lord.[b]
20 For great is the might of the Lord;
but by the humble he is glorified.
21 Neither seek what is too difficult for
you,
nor investigate what is beyond your
power.
22 Reflect upon what you have been
commanded,
for what is hidden is not your
concern.
23 Do not meddle in matters that are
beyond you,
for more than you can understand
has been shown you.
24 For their conceit has led many astray,
and wrong opinion has impaired
their judgment.

25 Without eyes there is no light;
without knowledge there is no
wisdom.[c]

26 A stubborn mind will fare badly at the
end,
and whoever loves danger will perish
in it.
27 A stubborn mind will be burdened by
troubles,
and the sinner adds sin to sins.
28 When calamity befalls the proud, there
is no healing,
for an evil plant has taken root in
him.
29 The mind of the intelligent appreciates
proverbs,
and an attentive ear is the desire of
the wise.

Alms for the Poor

30 As water extinguishes a blazing fire,
so almsgiving atones for sin.
31 Those who repay favors give thought to
the future;
when they fall they will find support.

Duties toward the Poor and the Oppressed

4 My child, do not cheat the poor of
their living,
and do not keep needy eyes waiting.
2 Do not grieve the hungry,
or anger one in need.
3 Do not add to the troubles of the
desperate,

a Heb: Gk *meekness*   b Other ancient authorities
add as verse 19, *Many are lofty and renowned, but to
the humble he reveals his secrets.*   c Heb: Other
ancient authorities lack verse 25

3:21–24 *Neither seek what is too difficult for
you.* Some puzzles cannot be solved, nor should
they be, according to Ben Sira. We should apply
that principle to intellectual tasks we commit
ourselves to, lest our studies bring unnecessary
perplexity. Ben Sira urges students to tackle
modest assignments, being content to remain in
the presence of mystery. Both in Jewish circles
and among the Greeks, the second century was
an age of increasing speculation about the secrets of the universe. Philosophical speculation
was matched by astrological and spiritual ruminations. Certain groups made strong claims to
have access to secret knowledge, and initiates
received exalted benefits, setting them apart

from the populace. Ben Sira discourages his
students from participating in such useless
speculations.
3:30 *so almsgiving atones for sin.* Just as
honoring one's parents atones for sin, almsgiving also brings forgiveness. Caring for the
poor was always central to biblical ethics, and
it lies at the heart of Ben Sira's teaching too.
The growing tendency to identify the powerless
with the righteous has taken root in Ben Sira's
advice, although he provides a negative justification for this conduct (a slighted needy person
could curse you and an attentive God bring it to
reality, 4:6).

or delay giving to the needy.
4 Do not reject a suppliant in distress,
   or turn your face away from the poor.
5 Do not avert your eye from the needy,
   and give no one reason to curse you;
6 for if in bitterness of soul some should
      curse you,
   their Creator will hear their prayer.

7 Endear yourself to the congregation;
   bow your head low to the great.
8 Give a hearing to the poor,
   and return their greeting politely.
9 Rescue the oppressed from the oppressor;
   and do not be hesitant in giving a
      verdict.
10 Be a father to orphans,
   and be like a husband to their
      mother;
   you will then be like a son of the Most
      High,
   and he will love you more than does
      your mother.

The Rewards of Wisdom

11 Wisdom teaches*a* her children
   and gives help to those who seek her.
12 Whoever loves her loves life,
   and those who seek her from early
      morning are filled with joy.
13 Whoever holds her fast inherits glory,
   and the Lord blesses the place she*b*
      enters.

14 Those who serve her minister to the
      Holy One;
   the Lord loves those who love her.
15 Those who obey her will judge the
      nations,
   and all who listen to her will live
      secure.
16 If they remain faithful, they will inherit
      her;
   their descendants will also obtain her.
17 For at first she will walk with them on
      tortuous paths;
   she will bring fear and dread upon
      them,
   and will torment them by her discipline
      until she trusts them, *c*
   and she will test them with her
      ordinances.
18 Then she will come straight back to
      them again and gladden them,
   and will reveal her secrets to them.
19 If they go astray she will forsake them,
   and hand them over to their ruin.

20 Watch for the opportune time, and
      beware of evil,
   and do not be ashamed to be yourself.
21 For there is a shame that leads to sin,
   and there is a shame that is glory and
      favor.

a Heb Syr: Gk *exalts*   *b* Or *he*   *c* Or *until they remain faithful in their heart*

4:10 *you will then be like a son of the Most High.* Several names for God occur in Sirach, but the "Most High" is a preferred title, recalling Elyon in earlier psalms and the narrative about the patriarchs, Abraham, Isaac, and Jacob. The Bible owns a rich array of epithets for God, among which are Yahweh, El, Eloah, Elohim, and El Shaddai. Metaphors for God are equally numerous, but Lord, shepherd, rock, refuge, redeemer, warrior, and healer appear often. Ben Sira uses the metaphor of father, rare in the Old Testament but customary in the New Testament.
4:11–19 *If they remain faithful, they will inherit her.* Returning to the feminine figure of Wisdom, Ben Sira also reverts to the idea of testing, this time inaugurated for the purpose of determining which students deserve her

approval. The rigors of learning are well documented, together with students' complaints about having to forego pleasures while busying themselves with practice exercises. The close association of knowledge and God reminds readers of the emphasis in Proverbs 8, where Wisdom is both the first creative act and the agent of all subsequent divine activity. In New Testament reflection on creation, Jesus as divine *logos* and *sophia,* Word and Wisdom, assists in the creative process and continues to sustain the universe.
4:21 *there is a shame that leads to sin, and there is a shame that is glory and favor.* This reference to shame anticipates what will be said later about things that should bring shame and other things that should not (41:17–42:8).

22 Do not show partiality, to your own
　　　harm,
　　or deference, to your downfall.
23 Do not refrain from speaking at the
　　　proper moment,[a]
　　and do not hide your wisdom.[b]
24 For wisdom becomes known through
　　　speech,
　　and education through the words of
　　　the tongue.
25 Never speak against the truth,
　　but be ashamed of your ignorance.
26 Do not be ashamed to confess your sins,
　　and do not try to stop the current of a
　　　river.
27 Do not subject yourself to a fool,
　　or show partiality to a ruler.
28 Fight to the death for truth,
　　and the Lord God will fight for you.

29 Do not be reckless in your speech,
　　or sluggish and remiss in your deeds.
30 Do not be like a lion in your home,
　　or suspicious of your servants.
31 Do not let your hand be stretched out to
　　　receive
　　and closed when it is time to give.

Precepts for Everyday Living

5 Do not rely on your wealth,
　　or say, "I have enough."
2 Do not follow your inclination and
　　　strength
　　in pursuing the desires of your heart.

3 Do not say, "Who can have power over
　　　me?"
　　for the Lord will surely punish you.

4 Do not say, "I sinned, yet what has
　　　happened to me?"
　　for the Lord is slow to anger.
5 Do not be so confident of forgiveness[c]
　　that you add sin to sin.
6 Do not say, "His mercy is great,
　　he will forgive[d] the multitude of my
　　　sins,"
　　for both mercy and wrath are with him,
　　and his anger will rest on sinners.
7 Do not delay to turn back to the Lord,
　　and do not postpone it from day to
　　　day;
　　for suddenly the wrath of the Lord will
　　　come upon you,
　　and at the time of punishment you
　　　will perish.
8 Do not depend on dishonest wealth,
　　for it will not benefit you on the day
　　　of calamity.

9 Do not winnow in every wind,
　　or follow every path.[e]
10 Stand firm for what you know,
　　and let your speech be consistent.

a Heb: Gk *at a time of salvation*　　b So some Gk
Mss and Heb Syr Lat: Other Gk Mss lack *and do not
hide your wisdom*　　c Heb: Gk *atonement*　　d Heb:
Gk *he* (or *it*) *will atone for*　　e Gk adds *so it is with
the double-tongued sinner* (see 6.1)

Responding

4:26 CONFESSION. Likened here to
the current of a river, confession is the
most natural of acts. Today honor this need of
your soul by taking a pen and paper and asking
God to reveal to you any sin that you have not
yet confessed. *See also* Spiritual Disciplines Index.

4:26–28 *Fight to the death for truth.* This
combination of proverbial saying and conventional wisdom comes to a climax in the service
of truth, which is celebrated beautifully in
another Deuterocanonical book, 1 Esdras (see
4:34–41). In both texts, the idea of truth is
closely associated with God, who is curiously
called by a combination of names in verse 28

(Yahweh, which is translated "Lord," and Elohim,
which is translated "God").

5:3–6 *Do not say . . . for.* This old formula of
debate appears here four times. Throughout the
ancient Near East, this formula seems to have
been used primarily in contexts dealing with
divine justice. Here Ben Sira argues against
excessive confidence in riches; we should not be
like the fool in the New Testament whose plans
for early retirement were cut short by death
(Luke 12:13–21). Even more serious, however, is
presumption about God's mercy, mistaking
divine patience for weakness or indulgence. Like
the apostle Paul, Ben Sira does not view God's
mercy as an invitation to sin more actively so
that grace might abound (Rom 6:1).

11 Be quick to hear,
 but deliberate in answering.
12 If you know what to say, answer your
  neighbor;
 but if not, put your hand over your
  mouth.

13 Honor and dishonor come from
  speaking,
 and the tongue of mortals may be
  their downfall.
14 Do not be called double-tongued[a]
 and do not lay traps with your
  tongue;
 for shame comes to the thief,
 and severe condemnation to the
  double-tongued.
15 In great and small matters cause no
  harm,[b]

6 ¹and do not become an enemy instead
 of a friend;
 for a bad name incurs shame and
  reproach;
 so it is with the double-tongued
  sinner.

2 Do not fall into the grip of passion,[c]
 or you may be torn apart as by a bull.[d]
3 Your leaves will be devoured and your
  fruit destroyed,
 and you will be left like a withered
  tree.
4 Evil passion destroys those who have it,
 and makes them the laughingstock of
  their enemies.

Friendship, False and True

5 Pleasant speech multiplies friends,
 and a gracious tongue multiplies
  courtesies.

6 Let those who are friendly with you be
  many,
 but let your advisers be one in a
  thousand.
7 When you gain friends, gain them
  through testing,
 and do not trust them hastily.
8 For there are friends who are such when
  it suits them,
 but they will not stand by you in time
  of trouble.
9 And there are friends who change into
  enemies,
 and tell of the quarrel to your
  disgrace.
10 And there are friends who sit at your
  table,
 but they will not stand by you in time
  of trouble.
11 When you are prosperous, they become
  your second self,
 and lord it over your servants;
12 but if you are brought low, they turn
  against you,
 and hide themselves from you.
13 Keep away from your enemies,
 and be on guard with your friends.

14 Faithful friends are a sturdy shelter:
 whoever finds one has found a
  treasure.
15 Faithful friends are beyond price;
 no amount can balance their worth.
16 Faithful friends are life-saving
  medicine;
 and those who fear the Lord will find
  them.

a Heb: Gk *a slanderer*   b Heb Syr: Gk *be ignorant*
c Heb: Meaning of Gk uncertain   d Meaning of
Gk uncertain

5:14 *Do not be called double-tongued.* Sages in various cultures railed against the abuse of speech, whether by duplicity or slander. The Letter of James joins this fight to control the organ of speech in a function that resembles a ship's rudder (1:26; 3:1–12). Ben Sira thinks of slander as lying in ambush.

6:6 *let your advisers be one in a thousand.* The expression "one in a thousand" occurs also in Job and Ecclesiastes as well as in Egyptian wisdom literature. Its precise sense beyond simple hyperbole, however, is unclear.

6:7–17 *When you gain friends.* One of several treatments of friendship in the book, this unit serves notice of its importance to Ben Sira. Greek writers also discuss this topic often. Friendship must be earned, and one must weed out false friends through testing. The true friend who comes through the period of testing with flying colors is priceless.

17 Those who fear the Lord direct their
    friendship aright,
  for as they are, so are their neighbors
    also.

Blessings of Wisdom

18 My child, from your youth choose
    discipline,
  and when you have gray hair you will
    still find wisdom.
19 Come to her like one who plows and
    sows,
  and wait for her good harvest.
  For when you cultivate her you will toil
    but little,
  and soon you will eat of her produce.
20 She seems very harsh to the
    undisciplined;
  fools cannot remain with her.
21 She will be like a heavy stone to test
    them,
  and they will not delay in casting her
    aside.
22 For wisdom is like her name;
  she is not readily perceived by many.

23 Listen, my child, and accept my
    judgment;
  do not reject my counsel.
24 Put your feet into her fetters,
  and your neck into her collar.
25 Bend your shoulders and carry her,
  and do not fret under her bonds.
26 Come to her with all your soul,

  and keep her ways with all your
    might.
27 Search out and seek, and she will
    become known to you;
  and when you get hold of her, do not
    let her go.
28 For at last you will find the rest she
    gives,
  and she will be changed into joy for
    you.
29 Then her fetters will become for you a
    strong defense,
  and her collar a glorious robe.
30 Her yoke*a* is a golden ornament,
  and her bonds a purple cord.
31 You will wear her like a glorious robe,
  and put her on like a splendid
    crown.*b*

32 If you are willing, my child, you can be
    disciplined,
  and if you apply yourself you will
    become clever.
33 If you love to listen you will gain
    knowledge,
  and if you pay attention you will
    become wise.
34 Stand in the company of the elders.
  Who is wise? Attach yourself to such
    a one.
35 Be ready to listen to every godly
    discourse,

a Heb: Gk *Upon her*   *b* Heb: Gk *crown of gladness*

6:22 *wisdom is like her name . . . not readily perceived.* This enigmatic statement about wisdom's intentional obscurity relies on a pun in Hebrew, one not easily rendered into English. Its larger context draws on imagery from agriculture (v 19) and perhaps footracing (v 21). One must put forth hard labor before enjoying a harvest, and a runner must practice with ankle weights to strengthen the feet. Once these weights are removed, the runner moves more rapidly than before using the weights.

6:23–31 *Bend your shoulders and carry her.* Continuing the idea of difficulty that becomes a blessing, Ben Sira compares education to oxen pulling a heavy yoke. Jesus uses the same image, inviting followers to put on his yoke,

which is surprisingly easy and affords rest (Matt 11:29–30). A certain irony clings to this comparison, for teachers also describe fools as brutish.

6:32–37 *If you love to listen you will gain knowledge.* Lacking reading materials, students were expected to learn by listening to intelligent conversation. Beyond that, eager learners are admonished to meditate on the commandments. According to Psalms, such reflection on the Torah brings endless joy (19:7–10; 119). That positive appreciation for divine instruction also permeated Jewish literature at Qumran, where additional psalms were discovered and where commentaries on Scripture were written around the time of Jesus.

and let no wise proverbs escape you.
36 If you see an intelligent person, rise
early to visit him;
let your foot wear out his doorstep.
37 Reflect on the statutes of the Lord,
and meditate at all times on his
commandments.
It is he who will give insight to[a] your
mind,
and your desire for wisdom will be
granted.

Miscellaneous Advice

7 Do no evil, and evil will never overtake
you.
2 Stay away from wrong, and it will
turn away from you.
3 Do[b] not sow in the furrows of injustice,
and you will not reap a sevenfold crop.

4 Do not seek from the Lord high office,
or the seat of honor from the king.
5 Do not assert your righteousness before
the Lord,
or display your wisdom before the king.
6 Do not seek to become a judge,
or you may be unable to root out
injustice;
you may be partial to the powerful,
and so mar your integrity.
7 Commit no offense against the public,

and do not disgrace yourself among
the people.
8 Do not commit a sin twice;
not even for one will you go
unpunished.
9 Do not say, "He will consider the great
number of my gifts,
and when I make an offering to the
Most High God, he will accept it."
10 Do not grow weary when you pray;
do not neglect to give alms.
11 Do not ridicule a person who is
embittered in spirit,
for there is One who humbles and
exalts.
12 Do not devise[c] a lie against your
brother,
or do the same to a friend.
13 Refuse to utter any lie,
for it is a habit that results in no good.
14 Do not babble in the assembly of the
elders,
and do not repeat yourself when you
pray.

15 Do not hate hard labor
or farm work, which was created by
the Most High.

a Heb: Gk *will confirm*   b Gk *My child, do*
c Heb: Gk *plow*

Responding
6:37 MEDITATION. Meditation is
described here as a discipline that
should be performed continually, not just done
for half an hour at a time. Pick a day this week
and seek to live it in constant meditation. Does
it change your outlook? *See also* Spiritual
Disciplines Index.

7:4 *Do not seek . . . the seat of honor from the
king.* This warning against a natural desire to be
perceived as important is also found in the New
Testament, where a mother asks that her sons
be honored and where followers are advised to
take a backseat (Matt 20:20–27).

Responding
7:10 PRAYER. If you fear growing
weary of your prayer practice, try

another form of prayer. Try praying while
walking, or try flash praying, in which you offer
a brief blessing for each person you drive by or
pass in the corridor. *See also* Spiritual Disciplines
Index.

7:14 *Do not babble in the assembly . . . and
do not repeat yourself when you pray.* Liturgical
prayers in postexilic literature tended to be
verbose (cf. Ezra 9; Neh 9; Dan 9). Ben Sira
advises against talking too much at any time,
knowing that the tongue can easily lead one
astray. Jesus also counseled his followers to
keep their prayers simple and sincere (Matt
6:5–8).

7:15–17 *Do not hate hard labor or farm
work, which was created by the Most High.*
Unlike some professionals who look down on
blue-collar workers, Ben Sira has a profound

16 Do not enroll in the ranks of sinners;
    remember that retribution does not
      delay.
17 Humble yourself to the utmost,
    for the punishment of the ungodly is
      fire and worms. *a*

Relations with Others

18 Do not exchange a friend for money,
    or a real brother for the gold of Ophir.
19 Do not dismiss *b* a wise and good wife,
    for her charm is worth more than
      gold.
20 Do not abuse slaves who work
      faithfully,
    or hired laborers who devote
      themselves to their task.
21 Let your soul love intelligent slaves; *c*
    do not withhold from them their
      freedom.

22 Do you have cattle? Look after them;
    if they are profitable to you, keep
      them.
23 Do you have children? Discipline them,
    and make them obedient *d* from their
      youth.
24 Do you have daughters? Be concerned
      for their chastity, *e*
    and do not show yourself too
      indulgent with them.
25 Give a daughter in marriage, and you
      complete a great task;
    but give her to a sensible man.
26 Do you have a wife who pleases you? *f*
      Do not divorce her;
    but do not trust yourself to one whom
      you detest.

27 With all your heart honor your father,
    and do not forget the birth pangs of
      your mother.
28 Remember that it was of your parents *g*
      you were born;
    how can you repay what they have
      given to you?

29 With all your soul fear the Lord,
    and revere his priests.
30 With all your might love your Maker,
    and do not neglect his ministers.
31 Fear the Lord and honor the priest,
    and give him his portion, as you have
      been commanded:
  the first fruits, the guilt offering, the
      gift of the shoulders,
  the sacrifice of sanctification, and the
      first fruits of the holy things.

32 Stretch out your hand to the poor,
    so that your blessing may be
      complete.
33 Give graciously to all the living;
    do not withhold kindness even from
      the dead.
34 Do not avoid those who weep,
    but mourn with those who mourn.
35 Do not hesitate to visit the sick,
    because for such deeds you will be
      loved.
36 In all you do, remember the end of your
      life,
    and then you will never sin.

a Heb *for the expectation of mortals is worms*
b Heb: Gk *deprive yourself of*   c Heb *Love a wise
slave as yourself*   d Gk *bend their necks*
e Gk *body*   f Heb Syr lack *who pleases you*
g Gk *them*

---

appreciation for those who work with their
hands, for that was God's assignment to the
|first couple in the garden. Ben Sira's additional
comment about the fate of the ungodly as fire
and worms marks a new departure, for in the
Old Testament only Isa 66:24 speculates about
eternal punishment (cf. Jth 16:17). By New
Testament times, this originally Persian concept
had become widely accepted within Jewish
circles.

7:24 CHASTITY—*See* Spiritual Disciplines
Index.

7:31 *the first fruits, the guilt offering, the gift
of the shoulders.* Seldom does Sirach mention
specific stipulations about the sacrificial system.
During the exilic period (587–539 BC) and until
the dedication of the restored Temple in 516,
sacrifice was replaced by prayer and the reading
of Scripture. Ben Sira's priestly interests were
contrary to this trend, which ultimately prevailed in synagogues.

Prudence and Common Sense

8 Do not contend with the powerful,
   or you may fall into their hands.
2 Do not quarrel with the rich,
   in case their resources outweigh
      yours;
   for gold has ruined many,
      and has perverted the minds of kings.
3 Do not argue with the loud of mouth,
   and do not heap wood on their fire.

4 Do not make fun of one who is ill-bred,
   or your ancestors may be insulted.
5 Do not reproach one who is turning
      away from sin;
   remember that we all deserve
      punishment.
6 Do not disdain one who is old,
   for some of us are also growing old.
7 Do not rejoice over anyone's death;
   remember that we must all die.

8 Do not slight the discourse of the sages,
   but busy yourself with their maxims;
   because from them you will learn
      discipline
   and how to serve princes.
9 Do not ignore the discourse of the aged,
   for they themselves learned from
      their parents; *a*
   from them you learn how to
      understand
   and to give an answer when the need
      arises.

10 Do not kindle the coals of sinners,
   or you may be burned in their
      flaming fire.
11 Do not let the insolent bring you to
      your feet,
   or they may lie in ambush against
      your words.

12 Do not lend to one who is stronger than
      you;
   but if you do lend anything, count it
      as a loss.
13 Do not give surety beyond your means;
   but if you give surety, be prepared to
      pay.

14 Do not go to law against a judge,
   for the decision will favor him
      because of his standing.
15 Do not go traveling with the reckless,
   or they will be burdensome to you;
   for they will act as they please,
   and through their folly you will
      perish with them.
16 Do not pick a fight with the quick-
      tempered,
   and do not journey with them
      through lonely country,
   because bloodshed means nothing to
      them,
   and where no help is at hand, they
      will strike you down.
17 Do not consult with fools,
   for they cannot keep a secret.
18 In the presence of strangers do nothing
      that is to be kept secret,
   for you do not know what they will
      divulge. *b*
19 Do not reveal your thoughts to anyone,
   or you may drive away your
      happiness. *c*

Advice concerning Women

9 Do not be jealous of the wife of your
      bosom,
   or you will teach her an evil lesson to
      your own hurt.
2 Do not give yourself to a woman

a Or *ancestors*   *b* Or *it will bring forth*   *c* Heb:
Gk *and let him not return a favor to you*

8:6–9 *Do not disdain one who is old.* Occasionally, Ben Sira exhibits a sense of humor; here he warns against looking down on an old person because "some of us" are growing old. He follows that bit of advice with a reminder of the human condition: everyone dies. Above all,

Ben Sira urges students to learn from the aged, people who have experienced life's many surprises. Such wisdom is to be viewed as supplementary, however, to the usual curriculum—the maxims of their teachers.

and let her trample down your
strength.

3 Do not go near a loose woman,
or you will fall into her snares.
4 Do not dally with a singing girl,
or you will be caught by her tricks.
5 Do not look intently at a virgin,
or you may stumble and incur
penalties for her.
6 Do not give yourself to prostitutes,
or you may lose your inheritance.
7 Do not look around in the streets of a
city,
or wander about in its deserted
sections.
8 Turn away your eyes from a shapely
woman,
and do not gaze at beauty belonging
to another;
many have been seduced by a woman's
beauty,
and by it passion is kindled like a fire.
9 Never dine with another man's wife,
or revel with her at wine;
or your heart may turn aside to her,
and in blood*a* you may be plunged
into destruction.

Choice of Friends

10 Do not abandon old friends,
for new ones cannot equal them.
A new friend is like new wine;
when it has aged, you can drink it
with pleasure.

11 Do not envy the success of sinners,
for you do not know what their end
will be like.
12 Do not delight in what pleases the
ungodly;
remember that they will not be held
guiltless all their lives.

13 Keep far from those who have power to
kill,
and you will not be haunted by the
fear of death.
But if you approach them, make no
misstep,
or they may rob you of your life.
Know that you are stepping among
snares,
and that you are walking on the city
battlements.

14 As much as you can, aim to know your
neighbors,
and consult with the wise.
15 Let your conversation be with
intelligent people,
and let all your discussion be about
the law of the Most High.
16 Let the righteous be your dinner
companions,
and let your glory be in the fear of the
Lord.

Concerning Rulers

17 A work is praised for the skill of the
artisan;
so a people's leader is proved wise by
his words.
18 The loud of mouth are feared in their
city,
and the one who is reckless in speech
is hated.

10 A wise magistrate educates his
people,
and the rule of an intelligent person
is well ordered.
2 As the people's judge is, so are his
officials;

a Heb: Gk by your spirit

9:1–9 *Do not be jealous of the wife.* How men
ought to relate to women is always a slippery
subject for moralists. Here Ben Sira offers some
advice about various types of women, mostly of
dubious virtue or belonging to a forbidden
category, such as virgins or other men's wives.
The fear of falling under a woman's power or
losing one's strength through sexual excess

already appears in Prov 31:3. The dangers posed
by prostitutes and the attraction of female figures
are standard teachings in the ancient world.

9:10 *when it has aged, you can drink it with
pleasure.* The comparison of an old friend to
wine that has aged well can hardly be matched.
Only those who have known such loyal friends
can fully appreciate it.

as the ruler of the city is, so are all its
  inhabitants.
3 An undisciplined king ruins his people,
  but a city becomes fit to live in
      through the understanding of its
      rulers.
4 The government of the earth is in the
      hand of the Lord,
  and over it he will raise up the right
      leader for the time.
5 Human success is in the hand of the
      Lord,
  and it is he who confers honor upon
      the lawgiver. *a*

The Sin of Pride

6 Do not get angry with your neighbor for
      every injury,
  and do not resort to acts of insolence.
7 Arrogance is hateful to the Lord and to
      mortals,
  and injustice is outrageous to both.
8 Sovereignty passes from nation to
      nation
      on account of injustice and insolence
      and wealth. *b*
9 How can dust and ashes be proud?
  Even in life the human body decays. *c*
10 A long illness baffles the physician; *d*
  the king of today will die tomorrow.
11 For when one is dead
  he inherits maggots and vermin *e* and
      worms.
12 The beginning of human pride is to
      forsake the Lord;
  the heart has withdrawn from its
      Maker.
13 For the beginning of pride is sin,

and the one who clings to it pours out
      abominations.
  Therefore the Lord brings upon them
      unheard-of calamities,
  and destroys them completely.
14 The Lord overthrows the thrones of
      rulers,
  and enthrones the lowly in their
      place.
15 The Lord plucks up the roots of the
      nations, *f*
  and plants the humble in their place.
16 The Lord lays waste the lands of the
      nations,
  and destroys them to the foundations
      of the earth.
17 He removes some of them and destroys
      them,
  and erases the memory of them from
      the earth.
18 Pride was not created for human beings,
  or violent anger for those born of
      women.

Persons Deserving Honor

19 Whose offspring are worthy of honor?
      Human offspring.
  Whose offspring are worthy of honor?
      Those who fear the Lord.
  Whose offspring are unworthy of
      honor?
      Human offspring.

a Heb: Gk *scribe*   *b* Other ancient authorities
add here or after verse 9a, *Nothing is more wicked
than one who loves money, for such a person puts his
own soul up for sale.*   *c* Heb: Meaning of Gk
uncertain   *d* Heb Lat: Meaning of Gk uncertain
e Heb: Gk *wild animals*   *f* Other ancient
authorities read *proud nations*

10:4 *The government of the earth is in the
hand of the Lord.* In a context about governing,
Ben Sira presents his political philosophy: God
rules the earth through human agents, choosing
the right person for the time. As a member of
the aristocracy, Ben Sira trusted those in authority; the New Testament also opts for submission
to rulers as administrators appointed by God
(Rom 13:1). The dangers of resisting ruthless
sovereigns are well documented, but submission
at any cost did not appeal to some segments of

Judean society, especially the Maccabeans, who
fought successfully against Syrian despotism.
Ambiguity toward kings has a long history in the
Bible, in both historical narrative and prophetic
texts.
    10:9–11 *How can dust and ashes be proud?*
"Dust and ashes" was the biblical way of acknowledging human littleness. Ben Sira pushes
the idea even farther. Kings of today die tomorrow; his majesty has merely become a feast for
creeping things, wild animals, and worms.

Whose offspring are unworthy of
    honor?
Those who break the
    commandments.
20 Among family members their leader is
    worthy of honor,
but those who fear the Lord are
    worthy of honor in his eyes. *a*
22 The rich, and the eminent, and the
    poor—
their glory is the fear of the Lord.
23 It is not right to despise one who is
    intelligent but poor,
and it is not proper to honor one who
    is sinful.
24 The prince and the judge and the ruler
    are honored,
but none of them is greater than the
    one who fears the Lord.
25 Free citizens will serve a wise servant,
    and an intelligent person will not
    complain.

Concerning Humility

26 Do not make a display of your wisdom
    when you do your work,
and do not boast when you are in need.
27 Better is the worker who has goods in
    plenty
than the boaster who lacks bread.

28 My child, honor yourself with humility,
    and give yourself the esteem you
    deserve.
29 Who will acquit those who condemn *b*
    themselves?
And who will honor those who
    dishonor themselves? *c*
30 The poor are honored for their
    knowledge,

while the rich are honored for their
    wealth.
31 One who is honored in poverty, how
    much more in wealth!
And one dishonored in wealth, how
    much more in poverty!

The Deceptiveness of Appearances

11 The wisdom of the humble lifts
    their heads high,
and seats them among the great.
2 Do not praise individuals for their good
    looks,
or loathe anyone because of
    appearance alone.
3 The bee is small among flying creatures,
    but what it produces is the best of
    sweet things.
4 Do not boast about wearing fine clothes,
    and do not exalt yourself when you
    are honored;
for the works of the Lord are wonderful,
    and his works are concealed from
    humankind.
5 Many kings have had to sit on the
    ground,
but one who was never thought of
    has worn a crown.
6 Many rulers have been utterly disgraced,
    and the honored have been handed
    over to others.

Deliberation and Caution

7 Do not find fault before you investigate;
    examine first, and then criticize.
8 Do not answer before you listen,

a Other ancient authorities add as verse 21, *The
fear of the Lord is the beginning of acceptance; obduracy
and pride are the beginning of rejection.*   *b* Heb: Gk
sin against   *c* Heb Lat: Gk *their own life*

10:19–24, 30 *those who fear the Lord are
worthy of honor.* True honor, Ben Sira insists,
comes only to God-fearers. Whether people are
rich or poor, eminent or lowly, the sole avenue
to honor is piety. Humans, therefore, face a
decision whether to be honorable or dishonorable. Honor may be achieved in more than one
way. The rich are esteemed because of their
wealth, but the knowledgeable poor receive
praise for intelligence.

11:3–6 *what it produces is the best of sweet
things.* The saying about a bee's tiny size and the
sweetness of the honey it produces is also found
in a Greek text, but the idea could readily occur
to anyone. Ancient Near Eastern sages warn
against ignoring small things, like a fire, given
their devastating consequences. The author of
Ecclesiastes also mentions a ruler who went from
rags to riches, a prison to a throne (Eccl 4:13–16),
vaguely reminiscent of the biblical Joseph.

and do not interrupt when another is
  speaking.
9 Do not argue about a matter that does
    not concern you,
  and do not sit with sinners when they
    judge a case.

10 My child, do not busy yourself with
    many matters;
  if you multiply activities, you will not
    be held blameless.
  If you pursue, you will not overtake,
  and by fleeing you will not escape.
11 There are those who work and struggle
    and hurry,
  but are so much the more in want.
12 There are others who are slow and need
    help,
  who lack strength and abound in
    poverty;
  but the eyes of the Lord look kindly
    upon them;
  he lifts them out of their lowly
    condition
13 and raises up their heads
  to the amazement of the many.

14 Good things and bad, life and death,
  poverty and wealth, come from the
    Lord.ᵃ
17 The Lord's gift remains with the devout,
  and his favor brings lasting success.
18 One becomes rich through diligence
    and self-denial,
  and the reward allotted to him is this:
19 when he says, "I have found rest,

and now I shall feast on my goods!"
  he does not know how long it will be
    until he leaves them to others and dies.

20 Stand by your agreement and attend to it,
  and grow old in your work.
21 Do not wonder at the works of a sinner,
  but trust in the Lord and keep at your
    job;
  for it is easy in the sight of the Lord
    to make the poor rich suddenly, in an
      instant.
22 The blessing of the Lord isᵇ the reward
    of the pious,
  and quickly God causes his blessing
    to flourish.
23 Do not say, "What do I need,
  and what further benefit can be
    mine?"
24 Do not say, "I have enough,
  and what harm can come to me now?"
25 In the day of prosperity, adversity is
    forgotten,
  and in the day of adversity, prosperity
    is not remembered.
26 For it is easy for the Lord on the day of
    death
  to reward individuals according to
    their conduct.

a Other ancient authorities add as verses 15 and 16,
¹⁵Wisdom, understanding, and knowledge of the law
come from the Lord; affection and the ways of good
works come from him. ¹⁶Error and darkness were created
with sinners; evil grows old with those who take pride in
malice.   b Heb: Gk is in

11:14 *Good things and bad . . . come from the
Lord.* In a monotheistic religion both good and
evil are attributed to the same God, as here (cf.
1 Sam 2:7; Job 1:21; Isa 45:7). The idea of an
adversary with extraordinary, although limited,
power arose as a means of softening the message
of a single deity doling out weal and woe. Christianity gives this figure a demonic zeal in pursuit
of its goals, comparing Satan to a lion stalking its
prey (1 Pet 5:8).
11:15–19 *One becomes rich through diligence
and self-denial.* This anecdote resembles Jesus'
story about the rich fool (Luke 12:16–21), which
encourages followers to lay up abiding treasures

in heaven rather than temporary rewards on
earth. (See NRSV note for vv 15–16.)
11:26–28 *by how he ends, a person becomes
known.* Ben Sira did not believe in life after
death; any delayed reward for good deeds had
to be made up before the moment of death.
Because riches did not necessarily imply virtue
on the part of this possessor, one had to reserve
judgment about a person until his or her departure from this life. The true indicator of
blessedness, in Ben Sira's view, was a long line
of descendants, provided that they feared God
(16:1–3; cf. Wisd of Sol 4:1).

BEN SIRA

Wisdom for a Virtuous Life

Selected Scriptures: *Sirach: Prologue; 1–5; 11–12; 14; 39; 51*

Ben Sira, or Jesus ben (son of) Sirach, became an important guide to the Jewish people during the four-hundred-year "silent" period between the death of the prophet Malachi and the coming of John the Baptist. At a time when the Jews were undergoing the transition from Egyptian to Seleucid rule, Ben Sira urged them to cling to their commitment to God and his law. Combining his love for wisdom and his conviction that the Jewish people must hold tightly to God's commands, Ben Sira wrote a collection of wisdom sayings and poetry to remind the Jews of their heritage as God's people and encourage them to live virtuous lives.

As one who loved learning, Ben Sira had studied the Hebrew Scriptures and had a good knowledge of Greek and Egyptian literature and thought. Having gained much wisdom himself through his disciplined study, he believed serious study to be the path to wisdom.

Ben Sira played the role of wise grandfather to a Jewish people with renewed commitment to God yet with no understanding of where God would take them in the future. Passionate about preserving purity as a people, Ben Sira shared his common-sense views on nearly every aspect of life, including instruction on reprimanding slaves, raising daughters, handling money, living in marriage, and associating with difficult people. He also provided deep spiritual principles: Remember God's faithfulness to past generations. Cling to God and expect suffering, knowing that God will bring help and joy. Live in humility. Don't take sin or forgiveness lightly. Learn from the aged and don't judge by appearances. Remember: "All the works of the Lord are good, and he will supply every need in its time" (Sir 39:33).

In following Ben Sira's example of serious, ongoing study of God's Word and a lifelong hunger for wisdom, we can be assured of making great strides in the life of discipleship. One who did so was Jan van Ruusbroec, a fifteenth-century Flemish contemplative who wrote about the life of devotion to God. Because he closely followed the path of contemplation, his teaching provides a valuable framework for living the life of virtue that Jesus ben Sirach encouraged. Ruusbroec calls Christians in one of his best-known works to "see" as Christ calls us to see, learning, in other words, Christ's wisdom. Ruusbroec names three things necessary for "seeing":

- the action of God's grace upon us as we seek him with an interior heart longing;
- a freeing of ourselves from outward attachments that would hinder an internal gaze of the soul upon God; and
- the turning of our will toward God.

PROFILE

PROFILE: BEN SIRA

Ruusbroec teaches the way to a virtuous and zealous interior life that is essential to living out the wisdom of God. And Ruusbroec assures us, as Ben Sira did, that our commitment to seeking God diligently and following in his ways will bring blessing. In *Spiritual Classics* Richard Foster writes about the fruit of contemplation: "As we continually and lovingly press our will toward God, the grace of God creates within us such an inward transformation of character that the moral virtues easily and naturally flow from us, in much the same way that beautiful music easily and naturally flows from an accomplished violinist. This is a goal worth our most earnest pursuit."

Personal Reflection

- Do you know anyone like Ben Sira who has actively pursued the seeking of wisdom and obedience to God's commands for a lifetime? Who like this speaks in your life and guides you in living wisely? Do you or will you fill this role for others who come after you?
- In reflecting on Ben Sira's life of committed study and Ruusbroec's life of committed contemplation, what link do you see between these two disciplines? Why is it unwise to practice one independent of the other?

---

27 An hour's misery makes one forget past delights,
  and at the close of one's life one's deeds are revealed.
28 Call no one happy before his death;
  by how he ends, a person becomes known. [a]

Care in Choosing Friends

29 Do not invite everyone into your home,
  for many are the tricks of the crafty.
30 Like a decoy partridge in a cage, so is the mind of the proud,
  and like spies they observe your weakness; [b]
31 for they lie in wait, turning good into evil,
  and to worthy actions they attach blame.
32 From a spark many coals are kindled,
  and a sinner lies in wait to shed blood.
33 Beware of scoundrels, for they devise evil,
  and they may ruin your reputation forever.
34 Receive strangers into your home and they will stir up trouble for you,
  and will make you a stranger to your own family.

12 If you do good, know to whom you do it,
  and you will be thanked for your good deeds.
2 Do good to the devout, and you will be repaid—
  if not by them, certainly by the Most High.

a Heb: Gk *and through his children a person becomes known*   b Heb: Gk *downfall*

12:1–7 *If you do good, know to whom you do it.* Giving assistance to sinners complicates reality; hence one should only bestow alms on worthy people. This criterion for charitable giving, when carried to an extreme, would grind benevolence to a halt. How can anyone really know the heart of a beggar? Ben Sira's stated reason for charitable acts comes close to sheer

3 No good comes to one who persists in
   evil
     or to one who does not give alms.
4 Give to the devout, but do not help the
   sinner.
5   Do good to the humble, but do not
       give to the ungodly;
   hold back their bread, and do not give it
     to them,
   for by means of it they might subdue
     you;
   then you will receive twice as much evil
     for all the good you have done to
     them.
6 For the Most High also hates sinners
     and will inflict punishment on the
     ungodly. *a*
7 Give to the one who is good, but do not
     help the sinner.
8 A friend is not known *b* in prosperity,
     nor is an enemy hidden in adversity.
9 One's enemies are friendly *c* when one
     prospers,
   but in adversity even one's friend
     disappears.
10 Never trust your enemy,
     for like corrosion in copper, so is his
     wickedness.
11 Even if he humbles himself and walks
     bowed down,
   take care to be on your guard against
     him.
   Be to him like one who polishes a
     mirror,
   to be sure it does not become
     completely tarnished.
12 Do not put him next to you,
     or he may overthrow you and take
     your place.
   Do not let him sit at your right hand,
     or else he may try to take your own
     seat,
   and at last you will realize the truth of
     my words,

and be stung by what I have said.

13 Who pities a snake charmer when he is
     bitten,
   or all those who go near wild
     animals?
14 So no one pities a person who associates
     with a sinner
   and becomes involved in the other's
     sins.
15 He stands by you for a while,
     but if you falter, he will not be there.
16 An enemy speaks sweetly with his lips,
     but in his heart he plans to throw you
     into a pit;
   an enemy may have tears in his eyes,
     but if he finds an opportunity he will
     never have enough of your blood.
17 If evil comes upon you, you will find
     him there ahead of you;
   pretending to help, he will trip you
     up.
18 Then he will shake his head, and clap
     his hands,
   and whisper much, and show his true
     face.

Caution Regarding Associates

13 Whoever touches pitch gets dirty,
     and whoever associates with a
     proud person becomes like him.
2 Do not lift a weight too heavy for you,
     or associate with one mightier and
     richer than you.
   How can the clay pot associate with the
     iron kettle?
   The pot will strike against it and be
     smashed.
3 A rich person does wrong, and even
     adds insults;

a Other ancient authorities add *and he is keeping
them for the day of their punishment*   *b* Other
ancient authorities read *punished*   *c* Heb: Gk
grieved

selfishness; one gives to be praised on earth and
to receive credit from God. Jesus advances the
discussion of almsgiving immeasurably by calling his disciples to give in secret from a heart
that has been transformed by the giving heart
of God (Matt 6:1–4).

13:3 *A rich person does wrong, and even adds
insults.* This sober observation about human
nature appears in a large section on the rich and
powerful (13:1–20). People of means can conduct themselves rudely and continue to receive
adulation, but persons lacking possessions suffer

a poor person suffers wrong, and
    must add apologies.
4 A rich person *a* will exploit you if you
    can be of use to him,
  but if you are in need he will abandon
    you.
5 If you own something, he will live with
    you;
  he will drain your resources without a
    qualm.
6 When he needs you he will deceive you,
    and will smile at you and encourage
    you;
  he will speak to you kindly and say,
    "What do you need?"
7 He will embarrass you with his
    delicacies,
  until he has drained you two or three
    times,
  and finally he will laugh at you.
  Should he see you afterwards, he will
    pass you by
  and shake his head at you.

8 Take care not to be led astray
  and humiliated when you are
    enjoying yourself. *b*
9 When an influential person invites you,
    be reserved,
  and he will invite you more
    insistently.
10 Do not be forward, or you may be
    rebuffed;
  do not stand aloof, or you will be
    forgotten.
11 Do not try to treat him as an equal,

or trust his lengthy conversations;
  for he will test you by prolonged talk,
    and while he smiles he will be
    examining you.
12 Cruel are those who do not keep your
    secrets;
  they will not spare you harm or
    imprisonment.
13 Be on your guard and very careful,
  for you are walking about with your
    own downfall. *c*

15 Every creature loves its like,
  and every person the neighbor.
16 All living beings associate with their
    own kind,
  and people stick close to those like
    themselves.
17 What does a wolf have in common with
    a lamb?
  No more has a sinner with the
    devout.
18 What peace is there between a hyena
    and a dog?
  And what peace between the rich and
    the poor?
19 Wild asses in the wilderness are the prey
    of lions;
  likewise the poor are feeding grounds
    for the rich.

a Gk *He*   *b* Other ancient authorities read *in your folly*   *c* Other ancient authorities add as verse 14, *When you hear these things in your sleep, wake up! During all your life love the Lord, and call on him for your salvation.*

---

one indignity after another. Choosing a powerful associate carries risk, like banging together clay pots and iron kettles. The Letter of James underscores this danger, noting that the rich pose a threat to the poor and thus should not be given special honor in the assembled congregation (2:1–7). We should recognize that using persons cuts both ways, for people with great wealth are often courted because of the favors they can bestow on others.

13:15–23 *Every creature loves its like.* The argument in this passage rests on a bad analogy, the distinction between species. Wolves do not associate with lambs; neither should the rich pal around with the poor. The problem is that rich and poor belong to the same species. Ben Sira wishes to say that the natural enmity between different kinds of animals is duplicated when opposite types of people, rich and poor, try to be intimate. The insights behind this description of people's reactions to comments made by the wealthy and by the poor show Ben Sira's keen observation of society. In short, the rich can do no wrong, and the poor deserve nothing but contempt. Having exposed such toadying to the movers and shakers of a community, Ben Sira hastens to concede that wealth as such is not a sin.

20 Humility is an abomination to the
     proud;
   likewise the poor are an abomination
     to the rich.

21 When the rich person totters, he is
     supported by friends,
   but when the humble a falls, he is
     pushed away even by friends.
22 If the rich person slips, many come to
     the rescue;
   he speaks unseemly words, but they
     justify him.
   If the humble person slips, they even
     criticize him;
   he talks sense, but is not given a
     hearing.
23 The rich person speaks and all are silent;
   they extol to the clouds what he says.
   The poor person speaks and they say,
     "Who is this fellow?"
   And should he stumble, they even
     push him down.
24 Riches are good if they are free from sin;
   poverty is evil only in the opinion of
     the ungodly.

25 The heart changes the countenance,
   either for good or for evil. b
26 The sign of a happy heart is a cheerful
     face,
   but to devise proverbs requires
     painful thinking.

14 Happy are those who do not
     blunder with their lips,
   and need not suffer remorse for sin.
2 Happy are those whose hearts do not
     condemn them,
   and who have not given up their
     hope.

Responsible Use of Wealth

3 Riches are inappropriate for a small-
     minded person;
   and of what use is wealth to a miser?
4 What he denies himself he collects for
     others;
   and others will live in luxury on his
     goods.
5 If one is mean to himself, to whom will
     he be generous?
   He will not enjoy his own riches.
6 No one is worse than one who is
     grudging to himself;
   this is the punishment for his
     meanness.
7 If ever he does good, it is by mistake;
   and in the end he reveals his
     meanness.
8 The miser is an evil person;
   he turns away and disregards people.
9 The eye of the greedy person is not
     satisfied with his share;
   greedy injustice withers the soul.
10 A miser begrudges bread,
   and it is lacking at his table.

11 My child, treat yourself well, according
     to your means,
   and present worthy offerings to the
     Lord.
12 Remember that death does not tarry,
   and the decree c of Hades has not been
     shown to you.
13 Do good to friends before you die,
   and reach out and give to them as
     much as you can.
14 Do not deprive yourself of a day's
     enjoyment;

a Other ancient authorities read *poor*   b Other
ancient authorities add *and a glad heart makes a
cheerful countenance*   c Heb Syr: Gk *covenant*

13:26 *to devise proverbs requires painful
thinking.* Ben Sira mentions the mental and
physical stress connected with scholarly activity
(cf. Eccl 12:12).
   14:14–19 *Do not deprive yourself of a day's
enjoyment.* Like the Teacher in Ecclesiastes
(2:24–26; 3:12–14), Ben Sira urges his students

to enjoy life to the fullest, knowing that a decree
stands over everyone: "You must die." A later
rabbinic saying captures this idea nicely: "Everyone will have to account for every good thing
left unenjoyed during life." In other words, we
insult the Creator when we refuse to take full
advantage of the many blessings that life offers.

do not let your share of desired good
     pass by you.
15 Will you not leave the fruit of your
     labors to another,
   and what you acquired by toil to be
     divided by lot?
16 Give, and take, and indulge yourself,
     because in Hades one cannot look for
     luxury.
17 All living beings become old like a
     garment,
   for the decree[a] from of old is, "You
     must die!"
18 Like abundant leaves on a spreading
     tree
   that sheds some and puts forth
     others,
   so are the generations of flesh and
     blood:
   one dies and another is born.
19 Every work decays and ceases to exist,
   and the one who made it will pass
     away with it.

The Happiness of Seeking Wisdom

20 Happy is the person who meditates on[b]
     wisdom
   and reasons intelligently,
21 who[c] reflects in his heart on her ways
   and ponders her secrets,
22 pursuing her like a hunter,
   and lying in wait on her paths;
23 who peers through her windows
   and listens at her doors;
24 who camps near her house
   and fastens his tent peg to her walls;

25 who pitches his tent near her,
   and so occupies an excellent lodging
     place;
26 who places his children under her
     shelter,
   and lodges under her boughs;
27 who is sheltered by her from the heat,
   and dwells in the midst of her glory.

15 Whoever fears the Lord will do this,
   and whoever holds to the law will
     obtain wisdom.[d]
2 She will come to meet him like a
     mother,
   and like a young bride she will
     welcome him.
3 She will feed him with the bread of
     learning,
   and give him the water of wisdom to
     drink.
4 He will lean on her and not fall,
   and he will rely on her and not be put
     to shame.
5 She will exalt him above his neighbors,
   and will open his mouth in the midst
     of the assembly.
6 He will find gladness and a crown of
     rejoicing,
   and will inherit an everlasting name.
7 The foolish will not obtain her,
   and sinners will not see her.
8 She is far from arrogance,
   and liars will never think of her.

a Heb: Gk covenant   b Other ancient authorities
read dies in   c The structure adopted in verses 21-
27 follows the Heb   d Gk her

The two illustrations of human mortality, leaves falling from a tree and the decaying of a garment, were also used in Greek literature with the same meaning. The author of Wisdom of Solomon encountered rogues who pressed the *carpe diem* ("seize the day") slogan too far, gathering rosebuds at the expense of others (Wisd of Sol 2:1–20). Similarities with the teachings in Ecclesiastes are obvious, but the differences are equally glaring. The fun lovers in the canonical book are not rogues like those in Wisdom of Solomon.

14:20 MEDITATION—*See* Spiritual Disciplines Index.

14:20–15:10 *Happy is the person who meditates on wisdom . . . pursuing her like a hunter.* This hymn in praise of Wisdom employs mixed images (a hunter and a lover). The latter image prevails, and the lover is advised to camp beside Wisdom's house, about which Prov 9:1–6 has more to say. Defying convention, he should peer into her windows and listen beside her doors. Willingly, she comes to the one who observes the law, like a mother and a wife, feeding him with the bread of understanding and the water of wisdom (cf. bread and wine in Prov 9:5; also Folly's offer of stolen water and bread eaten in secret in 9:17).

9 Praise is unseemly on the lips of a
      sinner,
   for it has not been sent from the Lord.
10 For in wisdom must praise be uttered,
   and the Lord will make it prosper.

Freedom of Choice

11 Do not say, "It was the Lord's doing that
      I fell away";
   for he does not do[a] what he hates.
12 Do not say, "It was he who led me
      astray";
   for he has no need of the sinful.
13 The Lord hates all abominations;
   such things are not loved by those
      who fear him.
14 It was he who created humankind in
      the beginning,
   and he left them in the power of their
      own free choice.
15 If you choose, you can keep the
      commandments,
   and to act faithfully is a matter of
      your own choice.
16 He has placed before you fire and water;
   stretch out your hand for whichever
      you choose.
17 Before each person are life and death,
   and whichever one chooses will be
      given.
18 For great is the wisdom of the Lord;
   he is mighty in power and sees
      everything;
19 his eyes are on those who fear him,
   and he knows every human action.
20 He has not commanded anyone to be
      wicked,
   and he has not given anyone
      permission to sin.

God's Punishment of Sinners

16 Do not desire a multitude of
      worthless[b] children,
   and do not rejoice in ungodly
      offspring.
2 If they multiply, do not rejoice in them,
   unless the fear of the Lord is in them.

3 Do not trust in their survival,
   or rely on their numbers;[c]
   for one can be better than a thousand,
   and to die childless is better than to
      have ungodly children.
4 For through one intelligent person a
      city can be filled with people,
   but through a clan of outlaws it
      becomes desolate.

5 Many such things my eye has seen,
   and my ear has heard things more
      striking than these.
6 In an assembly of sinners a fire is
      kindled,
   and in a disobedient nation wrath
      blazes up.
7 He did not forgive the ancient giants
   who revolted in their might.
8 He did not spare the neighbors of Lot,
   whom he loathed on account of their
      arrogance.
9 He showed no pity on the doomed
      nation,
   on those dispossessed because of their
      sins;[d]
10 or on the six hundred thousand foot
      soldiers
   who assembled in their
      stubbornness.[e]
11 Even if there were only one stiff-necked
      person,
   it would be a wonder if he remained
      unpunished.
   For mercy and wrath are with the Lord;[f]
   he is mighty to forgive—but he also
      pours out wrath.
12 Great as is his mercy, so also is his
      chastisement;

a Heb: Gk you ought not to do   b Heb: Gk
unprofitable   c Other ancient authorities add For
you will groan in untimely mourning, and will know of
their sudden end.   d Other ancient authorities
add All these things he did to the hard-hearted nations,
and by the multitude of his holy ones he was not
appeased.   e Other ancient authorities add
Chastising, showing mercy, striking, healing, the Lord
persisted in mercy and discipline.   f Gk him

15:15 *to act faithfully is a matter of your own choice.* Ben Sira affirms freedom of choice.
Everyone opts for life, or for death.

he judges a person according to his or
   her deeds.
13 The sinner will not escape with plunder,
   and the patience of the godly will not
      be frustrated.
14 He makes room for every act of mercy;
   everyone receives in accordance with
      his or her deeds. *a*

17 Do not say, "I am hidden from the Lord,
   and who from on high has me in
      mind?
   Among so many people I am unknown,
      for what am I in a boundless creation?
18 Lo, heaven and the highest heaven,
   the abyss and the earth, tremble at his
      visitation! *b*
19 The very mountains and the
      foundations of the earth
   quiver and quake when he looks
      upon them.
20 But no human mind can grasp this,
   and who can comprehend his ways?
21 Like a tempest that no one can see,
   so most of his works are concealed. *c*
22 Who is to announce his acts of justice?
   Or who can await them? For his
      decree *d* is far off." *e*
23 Such are the thoughts of one devoid of
      understanding;
   a senseless and misguided person
      thinks foolishly.

God's Wisdom Seen in Creation

24 Listen to me, my child, and acquire
      knowledge,
   and pay close attention to my words.
25 I will impart discipline precisely *f*
   and declare knowledge accurately.

26 When the Lord created *g* his works from
      the beginning,
   and, in making them, determined
      their boundaries,
27 he arranged his works in an eternal
      order,
   and their dominion *h* for all
      generations.
   They neither hunger nor grow weary,
      and they do not abandon their tasks.
28 They do not crowd one another,
   and they never disobey his word.
29 Then the Lord looked upon the earth,
   and filled it with his good things.
30 With all kinds of living beings he
      covered its surface,
   and into it they must return.

a Other ancient authorities add *15 The Lord hardened
Pharaoh so that he did not recognize him, in order that
his works might be known under heaven. 16 His mercy is
manifest to the whole of creation, and he divided his
light and darkness with a plumb line.*   *b* Other
ancient authorities add *The whole world past and
present is in his will.*   *c* Meaning of Gk uncertain:
Heb Syr *If I sin, no eye can see me, and if I am disloyal
all in secret, who is to know?*   *d* Heb *the decree*: Gk
the covenant   *e* Other ancient authorities add *and
a scrutiny for all comes at the end*   *f* Gk *by weight*
g Heb: Gk *judged*   *h* Or *elements*

16:21 *most of his works are concealed.* Observable reality is not all there is, for most of God's works remain hidden. Modern science has reinforced this observation, opening up vast regions of outer space and discovering wonders beneath the sea. The universe truly deserves the two-word description "surpassing wonder." Although Ben Sira places this sentiment about divine hiddenness in the mind of fools, who think they can get away with anything because of the distance between heaven and earth, it need not be limited to them. We can draw different conclusions from divine concealment, for example, that human eyes cannot gaze on holiness with impunity or that God is by necessity invisible to any but the spiritual eye.

16:24–17:14 *he arranged his works in an eternal order.* This hymn praises the Creator for the intricate design of the universe, its perfect order. The description of human origins mentions the image of God and concludes with reference to divine prohibitions placed within the backdrop of an eternal covenant. In this entire section Ben Sira merely alludes to the biblical narrative, assuming familiarity with it on the part of his readers. We do not know how this familiarity with the content of Scripture was acquired, whether through oral instruction at home and in synagogues or through personal study of written texts.

17 The Lord created human beings out
      of earth,
  and makes them return to it again.
2 He gave them a fixed number of days,
  but granted them authority over
    everything on the earth. *a*
3 He endowed them with strength like his
    own, *b*
  and made them in his own image.
4 He put the fear of them *c* in all living
    beings,
  and gave them dominion over beasts
    and birds. *d*
6 Discretion and tongue and eyes,
  ears and a mind for thinking he gave
    them.
7 He filled them with knowledge and
    understanding,
  and showed them good and evil.
8 He put the fear of him into *e* their hearts
  to show them the majesty of his
    works. *f*
10 And they will praise his holy name,
9   to proclaim the grandeur of his
    works.
11 He bestowed knowledge upon them,
  and allotted to them the law of life. *g*
12 He established with them an eternal
    covenant,
  and revealed to them his decrees.
13 Their eyes saw his glorious majesty,
  and their ears heard the glory of his
    voice.
14 He said to them, "Beware of all evil."
  And he gave commandment to each
    of them concerning the
    neighbor.
15 Their ways are always known to him;
  they will not be hid from his eyes. *h*
17 He appointed a ruler for every nation,
  but Israel is the Lord's own portion. *i*
19 All their works are as clear as the sun
    before him,
  and his eyes are ever upon their ways.
20 Their iniquities are not hidden from
    him,
  and all their sins are before the Lord. *j*
22 One's almsgiving is like a signet ring
    with the Lord, *k*
  and he will keep a person's kindness
    like the apple of his eye. *l*

23 Afterward he will rise up and repay
    them,
  and he will bring their recompense
    on their heads.
24 Yet to those who repent he grants a
    return,
  and he encourages those who are
    losing hope.

A Call to Repentance

25 Turn back to the Lord and forsake your
    sins;
  pray in his presence and lessen your
    offense.
26 Return to the Most High and turn away
    from iniquity, *m*
  and hate intensely what he abhors.
27 Who will sing praises to the Most High
    in Hades
  in place of the living who give
    thanks?
28 From the dead, as from one who does
    not exist, thanksgiving has
    ceased;
  those who are alive and well sing the
    Lord's praises.
29 How great is the mercy of the Lord,
  and his forgiveness for those who
    return to him!
30 For not everything is within human
    capability,

a Lat: Gk *it*   *b* Lat: Gk *proper to them*   *c* Syr: Gk
him   *d* Other ancient authorities add as verse 5,
They obtained the use of the five faculties of the Lord; as
sixth he distributed to them the gift of mind, and as
seventh, reason, the interpreter of one's faculties.
e Other ancient authorities read *He set his eye upon*
f Other ancient authorities add *and he gave them to*
boast of his marvels forever   *g* Other ancient
authorities add *so that they may know that they who*
are alive now are mortal   *h* Other ancient
authorities add *16Their ways from youth tend toward*
evil, and they are unable to make for themselves hearts
of flesh in place of their stony hearts. 17For in the
division of the nations of the whole earth, he appointed
i Other ancient authorities add as verse 18, *whom,*
being his firstborn, he brings up with discipline, and
allotting to him the light of his love, he does not neglect
him.   *j* Other ancient authorities add as verse 21,
But the Lord, who is gracious and knows how they are
formed, has neither left them nor abandoned them, but
has spared them.   *k* Gk *him*   *l* Other ancient
authorities add *apportioning repentance to his sons and*
daughters   *m* Other ancient authorities add *for he*
will lead you out of darkness to the light of health.

since human beings are not
immortal.
31 What is brighter than the sun? Yet it
can be eclipsed.
So flesh and blood devise evil.
32 He marshals the host of the height of
heaven;
but all human beings are dust and
ashes.

The Majesty of God

18 He who lives forever created the
whole universe;
2   the Lord alone is just. *a*
4 To none has he given power to proclaim
his works;
and who can search out his mighty
deeds?
5 Who can measure his majestic power?
And who can fully recount his
mercies?
6 It is not possible to diminish or increase
them,
nor is it possible to fathom the
wonders of the Lord.
7 When human beings have finished,
they are just beginning,
and when they stop, they are still
perplexed.
8 What are human beings, and of what
use are they?
What is good in them, and what is
evil?
9 The number of days in their life is great
if they reach one hundred years. *b*
10 Like a drop of water from the sea and a
grain of sand,
so are a few years among the days of
eternity.
11 That is why the Lord is patient with
them
and pours out his mercy upon them.
12 He sees and recognizes that their end is
miserable;

therefore he grants them forgiveness
all the more.
13 The compassion of human beings is for
their neighbors,
but the compassion of the Lord is for
every living thing.
He rebukes and trains and teaches
them,
and turns them back, as a shepherd
his flock.
14 He has compassion on those who
accept his discipline
and who are eager for his precepts.

The Right Spirit in Giving Alms

15 My child, do not mix reproach with
your good deeds,
or spoil your gift by harsh words.
16 Does not the dew give relief from the
scorching heat?
So a word is better than a gift.
17 Indeed, does not a word surpass a good
gift?
Both are to be found in a gracious
person.
18 A fool is ungracious and abusive,
and the gift of a grudging giver makes
the eyes dim.

The Need of Reflection and Self-control

19 Before you speak, learn;
and before you fall ill, take care of
your health.
20 Before judgment comes, examine
yourself;
and at the time of scrutiny you will
find forgiveness.
21 Before falling ill, humble yourself;

a Other ancient authorities add *and there is no other
beside him; 3he steers the world with the span of his
hand, and all things obey his will; for he is king of all
things by his power, separating among them the holy
things from the profane.*   *b* Other ancient
authorities add *but the death of each one is beyond the
calculation of all*

18:8–14 *What are human beings, and of what
use are they?* Like Psalm 8, this section reflects
on mortals. The picture of human grandeur is
missing, however, and the emphasis falls on
ephemerality and smallness. A drop of water, a
grain of sand—that is all we are. Because of the
end awaiting mortals, God has compassion,
shepherdlike, on the docile (note well, Ben Sira
does not say that such kindness extends to
sinners).

and when you have sinned, repent.

22 Let nothing hinder you from paying a
     vow promptly,
     and do not wait until death to be
        released from it.

23 Before making a vow, prepare yourself;
     do not be like one who puts the Lord
        to the test.

24 Think of his wrath on the day of death,
     and of the moment of vengeance
        when he turns away his face.

25 In the time of plenty think of the time
        of hunger;
     in days of wealth think of poverty and
        need.

26 From morning to evening conditions
        change;
     all things move swiftly before the
        Lord.

27 One who is wise is cautious in
        everything;
     when sin is all around, one guards
        against wrongdoing.

28 Every intelligent person knows wisdom,
     and praises the one who finds her.

29 Those who are skilled in words become
        wise themselves,
     and pour forth apt proverbs. *a*

SELF-CONTROL *b*

30 Do not follow your base desires,
     but restrain your appetites.

31 If you allow your soul to take pleasure in
        base desire,
     it will make you the laughingstock of
        your enemies.

32 Do not revel in great luxury,
     or you may become impoverished by
        its expense.

33 Do not become a beggar by feasting
        with borrowed money,
     when you have nothing in your
        purse. *c*

19 The one who does this *d* will not
        become rich;

one who despises small things will
     fail little by little.

2 Wine and women lead intelligent men
        astray,
     and the man who consorts with
        prostitutes is reckless.

3 Decay and worms will take possession
        of him,
     and the reckless person will be
        snatched away.

Against Loose Talk

4 One who trusts others too quickly has a
        shallow mind,
     and one who sins does wrong to
        himself.

5 One who rejoices in wickedness *e* will be
        condemned, *f*

6   but one who hates gossip has less evil.

7 Never repeat a conversation,
     and you will lose nothing at all.

8 With friend or foe do not report it,
     and unless it would be a sin for you,
        do not reveal it;

9 for someone may have heard you and
        watched you,
     and in time will hate you.

10 Have you heard something? Let it die
        with you.
     Be brave, it will not make you burst!

11 Having heard something, the fool
        suffers birth pangs
     like a woman in labor with a child.

12 Like an arrow stuck in a person's thigh,
     so is gossip inside a fool.

a Other ancient authorities add *Better is confidence
in the one Lord than clinging with a dead heart to a
dead one.*   *b* This heading is included in the Gk
text.   *c* Other ancient authorities add *for you will
be plotting against your own life*   *d* Heb: Gk A
worker who is a drunkard   *e* Other ancient
authorities read *heart*   *f* Other ancient
authorities add *but one who withstands pleasures
crowns his life.* 6*One who controls the tongue will live
without strife,*

19:2 *Wine and women lead intelligent men
astray.* This classic statement about wine and
women must be balanced by sayings elsewhere
in the book praising both.

19:10 *Be brave, it will not make you burst!*
This example of humor resembles the proverb
comparing gossip to delicious morsels (Prov
18:8).

13 Question a friend; perhaps he did not
       do it;
   or if he did, so that he may not do it
       again.
14 Question a neighbor; perhaps he did
       not say it;
   or if he said it, so that he may not
       repeat it.
15 Question a friend, for often it is slander;
   so do not believe everything you hear.
16 A person may make a slip without
       intending it.
   Who has not sinned with his tongue?
17 Question your neighbor before you
       threaten him;
   and let the law of the Most High take
       its course. *a*

True and False Wisdom

20 The whole of wisdom is fear of the Lord,
   and in all wisdom there is the
       fulfillment of the law. *b*
22 The knowledge of wickedness is not
       wisdom,
   nor is there prudence in the counsel
       of sinners.
23 There is a cleverness that is detestable,
   and there is a fool who merely lacks
       wisdom.
24 Better are the God-fearing who lack
       understanding
   than the highly intelligent who
       transgress the law.
25 There is a cleverness that is exact but
       unjust,
   and there are people who abuse favors
       to gain a verdict.
26 There is the villain bowed down in
       mourning,
   but inwardly he is full of deceit.
27 He hides his face and pretends not to
       hear,

but when no one notices, he will take
       advantage of you.
28 Even if lack of strength keeps him from
       sinning,
   he will nevertheless do evil when he
       finds the opportunity.
29 A person is known by his appearance,
   and a sensible person is known when
       first met, face to face.
30 A person's attire and hearty laughter,
   and the way he walks, show what he is.

Silence and Speech

20 There is a rebuke that is untimely,
     and there is the person who is wise
         enough to keep silent.
2 How much better it is to rebuke than to
       fume!
3 And the one who admits his fault will
       be kept from failure.
4 Like a eunuch lusting to violate a girl
   is the person who does right under
       compulsion.
5 Some people keep silent and are
       thought to be wise,
   while others are detested for being
       talkative.
6 Some people keep silent because they
       have nothing to say,
   while others keep silent because they
       know when to speak.
7 The wise remain silent until the right
       moment,

a Other ancient authorities add *and do not be angry.*
*18The fear of the Lord is the beginning of acceptance,
and wisdom obtains his love. 19The knowledge of the
Lord's commandments is life-giving discipline; and
those who do what is pleasing to him enjoy the fruit of
the tree of immortality.* *b* Other ancient
authorities add *and the knowledge of his omnipotence.*
*21When a slave says to his master, "I will not act as you
wish," even if later he does it, he angers the one who
supports him.*

19:24 *the highly intelligent who transgress the
law.* A rare acknowledgment that intelligent
scoundrels exist, this saying stresses the need
for distinguishing kinds of knowledge. The Bible
knows the shady side of wisdom, its use for
selfish and destructive ends.

Responding
20:1, 6 SILENCE. Deliberately holding
your tongue is a wonderful way to practice submission to those around you. The next
time you engage in a conversation with a friend,
make an effort to listen more than you speak.
See also Spiritual Disciplines Index.

but a boasting fool misses the right
   moment.
8 Whoever talks too much is detested,
   and whoever pretends to authority is
   hated. *a*

Paradoxes

9 There may be good fortune for a person
   in adversity,
   and a windfall may result in a loss.
10 There is the gift that profits you
   nothing,
   and the gift to be paid back double.
11 There are losses for the sake of glory,
   and there are some who have raised
   their heads from humble
   circumstances.
12 Some buy much for little,
   but pay for it seven times over.
13 The wise make themselves beloved by
   only few words, *b*
   but the courtesies of fools are wasted.
14 A fool's gift will profit you nothing, *c*
   for he looks for recompense
   sevenfold. *d*
15 He gives little and upbraids much;
   he opens his mouth like a town crier.
   Today he lends and tomorrow he asks it
   back;
   such a one is hateful to God and
   humans. *e*
16 The fool says, "I have no friends,
   and I get no thanks for my good
   deeds.
   Those who eat my bread are evil-
   tongued."
17 How many will ridicule him, and how
   often! *f*

Inappropriate Speech

18 A slip on the pavement is better than a
   slip of the tongue;
   the downfall of the wicked will occur
   just as speedily.
19 A coarse person is like an inappropriate
   story,

continually on the lips of the
   ignorant.
20 A proverb from a fool's lips will be
   rejected,
   for he does not tell it at the proper
   time.
21 One may be prevented from sinning by
   poverty;
   so when he rests he feels no remorse.
22 One may lose his life through shame,
   or lose it because of human respect. *g*
23 Another out of shame makes promises
   to a friend,
   and so makes an enemy for nothing.

Lying

24 A lie is an ugly blot on a person;
   it is continually on the lips of the
   ignorant.
25 A thief is preferable to a habitual liar,
   but the lot of both is ruin.
26 A liar's way leads to disgrace,
   and his shame is ever with him.

PROVERBIAL SAYINGS *h*
27 The wise person advances himself by
   his words,
   and one who is sensible pleases the
   great.
28 Those who cultivate the soil heap up
   their harvest,
   and those who please the great atone
   for injustice.
29 Favors and gifts blind the eyes of the
   wise;

a Other ancient authorities add *How good it is to
show repentance when you are reproved, for so you will
escape deliberate sin!* *b* Heb: Gk *by words*
c Other ancient authorities add *so it is with the
envious who give under compulsion* *d* Syr: Gk *he
has many eyes instead of one* *e* Other ancient
authorities lack *to God and humans* *f* Other
ancient authorities add *for he has not honestly
received what he has, and what he does not have is
unimportant to him* *g* Other ancient authorities
read *his foolish look* *h* This heading is included
in the Gk text.

20:21 *One may be prevented from sinning by poverty.* An Egyptian proverb points out that the
only thing keeping a fool from lying with a prostitute is his lack of money.

like a muzzle on the mouth they stop
reproofs.

30 Hidden wisdom and unseen treasure,
of what value is either?

31 Better are those who hide their folly
than those who hide their wisdom. *a*

Various Sins

21 Have you sinned, my child? Do so
no more,
but ask forgiveness for your past sins.

2 Flee from sin as from a snake;
for if you approach sin, it will bite
you.
Its teeth are lion's teeth,
and can destroy human lives.

3 All lawlessness is like a two-edged
sword;
there is no healing for the wound it
inflicts.

4 Panic and insolence will waste away
riches;
thus the house of the proud will be
laid waste. *b*

5 The prayer of the poor goes from their
lips to the ears of God, *c*
and his judgment comes speedily.

6 Those who hate reproof walk in the
sinner's steps,
but those who fear the Lord repent in
their heart.

7 The mighty in speech are widely
known;
when they slip, the sensible person
knows it.

8 Whoever builds his house with other
people's money
is like one who gathers stones for his
burial mound. *d*

9 An assembly of the wicked is like a
bundle of tow,
and their end is a blazing fire.

10 The way of sinners is paved with
smooth stones,
but at its end is the pit of Hades.

Wisdom and Foolishness

11 Whoever keeps the law controls his
thoughts,
and the fulfillment of the fear of the
Lord is wisdom.

12 The one who is not clever cannot be
taught,
but there is a cleverness that increases
bitterness.

13 The knowledge of the wise will increase
like a flood,
and their counsel like a life-giving
spring.

14 The mind *e* of a fool is like a broken jar;
it can hold no knowledge.

15 When an intelligent person hears a wise
saying,
he praises it and adds to it;
when a fool *f* hears it, he laughs at *g* it
and throws it behind his back.

16 A fool's chatter is like a burden on a
journey,
but delight is found in the speech of
the intelligent.

17 The utterance of a sensible person is
sought in the assembly,
and they ponder his words in their
minds.

18 Like a house in ruins is wisdom to a
fool,
and to the ignorant, knowledge is talk
that has no meaning.

19 To a senseless person education is fetters
on his feet,
and like manacles on his right hand.

20 A fool raises his voice when he laughs,
but the wise *h* smile quietly.

---

a Other ancient authorities add *32Unwearied
endurance in seeking the Lord is better than a masterless
charioteer of one's own life.* *b* Other ancient
authorities read *uprooted* *c* Gk *his ears*
d Other ancient authorities read *for the winter*
e Syr Lat: Gk *entrails* *f* Syr: Gk *reveler*
g Syr: Gk *dislikes* *h* Syr Lat: Gk *clever*

Responding
21:5 PRAYER. Why is the prayer of
poor people given special expedience?

What does this reveal about the nature of God?
What does it direct for our lives? *See also*
Spiritual Disciplines Index.

21 To the sensible person education is like
    a golden ornament,
  and like a bracelet on the right arm.

22 The foot of a fool rushes into a house,
  but an experienced person waits
    respectfully outside.
23 A boor peers into the house from the
    door,
  but a cultivated person remains
    outside.
24 It is ill-mannered for a person to listen
    at a door;
  the discreet would be grieved by the
    disgrace.

25 The lips of babblers speak of what is not
    their concern, *a*
  but the words of the prudent are
    weighed in the balance.
26 The mind of fools is in their mouth,
  but the mouth of the wise is in *b* their
    mind.
27 When an ungodly person curses an
    adversary, *c*
  he curses himself.
28 A whisperer degrades himself
  and is hated in his neighborhood.

The Idler

22 The idler is like a filthy stone,
    and every one hisses at his disgrace.
 2 The idler is like the filth of dunghills;
  anyone that picks it up will shake it
    off his hand.

Degenerate Children

 3 It is a disgrace to be the father of an
    undisciplined son,
  and the birth of a daughter is a loss.
 4 A sensible daughter obtains a husband
    of her own,
  but one who acts shamefully is a grief
    to her father.
 5 An impudent daughter disgraces father
    and husband,
  and is despised by both.
 6 Like music in time of mourning is ill-
    timed conversation,
  but a thrashing and discipline are at
    all times wisdom. *d*

Wisdom and Folly

 9 Whoever teaches a fool is like one who
    glues potsherds together,
  or who rouses a sleeper from deep
    slumber.
10 Whoever tells a story to a fool tells it to
    a drowsy man;
  and at the end he will say, "What is
    it?"
11 Weep for the dead, for he has left the
    light behind;
  and weep for the fool, for he has left
    intelligence behind.
  Weep less bitterly for the dead, for he is
    at rest;
  but the life of the fool is worse than
    death.
12 Mourning for the dead lasts seven days,
  but for the foolish or the ungodly it
    lasts all the days of their lives.

13 Do not talk much with a senseless
    person
  or visit an unintelligent person. *e*
  Stay clear of him, or you may have
    trouble,
  and be spattered when he shakes
    himself off.
  Avoid him and you will find rest,
  and you will never be wearied by his
    lack of sense.
14 What is heavier than lead?
  And what is its name except "Fool"?
15 Sand, salt, and a piece of iron
  are easier to bear than a stupid
    person.

16 A wooden beam firmly bonded into a
    building
  is not loosened by an earthquake;
  so the mind firmly resolved after due
    reflection
  will not be afraid in a crisis.

*a Other ancient authorities read of strangers speak
of these things   b Other ancient authorities omit
in   c Or curses Satan   d Other ancient
authorities add 7Children who are brought up in a
good life, conceal the lowly birth of their parents.
8Children who are disdainfully and boorishly haughty
stain the nobility of their kindred.   e Other ancient
authorities add For being without sense he will despise
everything about you*

17 A mind settled on an intelligent
        thought
    is like stucco decoration that makes a
        wall smooth.
18 Fences*a* set on a high place
    will not stand firm against the wind;
    so a timid mind with a fool's resolve
    will not stand firm against any fear.

The Preservation of Friendship

19 One who pricks the eye brings tears,
    and one who pricks the heart makes
        clear its feelings.
20 One who throws a stone at birds scares
        them away,
    and one who reviles a friend destroys
        a friendship.
21 Even if you draw your sword against a
        friend,
    do not despair, for there is a way back.
22 If you open your mouth against your
        friend,
    do not worry, for reconciliation is
        possible.
    But as for reviling, arrogance, disclosure
        of secrets, or a treacherous blow—
    in these cases any friend will take to
        flight.

23 Gain the trust of your neighbor in his
        poverty,
    so that you may rejoice with him in
        his prosperity.
    Stand by him in time of distress,
    so that you may share with him in his
        inheritance.*b*
24 The vapor and smoke of the furnace
        precede the fire;
    so insults precede bloodshed.
25 I am not ashamed to shelter a friend,
    and I will not hide from him.
26 But if harm should come to me because
    of him,

whoever hears of it will beware of
    him.

A Prayer for Help against Sinning

27 Who will set a guard over my mouth,
    and an effective seal upon my lips,
    so that I may not fall because of them,
    and my tongue may not destroy me?

23 O Lord, Father and Master of my
        life,
    do not abandon me to their designs,
    and do not let me fall because of
        them!
2 Who will set whips over my thoughts,
    and the discipline of wisdom over my
        mind,
    so as not to spare me in my errors,
    and not overlook my*c* sins?
3 Otherwise my mistakes may be
        multiplied,
    and my sins may abound,
    and I may fall before my adversaries,
    and my enemy may rejoice over me.*d*
4 O Lord, Father and God of my life,
    do not give me haughty eyes,
5   and remove evil desire from me.
6 Let neither gluttony nor lust overcome
        me,
    and do not give me over to shameless
        passion.

DISCIPLINE OF THE TONGUE*e*

7 Listen, my children, to instruction
        concerning the mouth;
    the one who observes it will never be
        caught.

---

a Other ancient authorities read *Pebbles*
b Other ancient authorities add *For one should not
always despise restricted circumstances, or admire a rich
person who is stupid.*   *c* Gk *their*   *d* Other
ancient authorities add *From them the hope of your
mercy is remote*   *e* This heading is included in the
Gk text.

22:27–23:6 *an effective seal upon my lips, so
that I may not fall because of them.* One of two
prayers in Sirach (the other is found in chap 36),
this petition begins with a request for a guard
to be placed over the mouth, assuring proper
speech, which prevents falling, a thematic word

in the prayer. The thought continues, this time
with a request for whips as discipline. God is
addressed as "Lord," "Father," and "Master of
my life" (or "God of my life"). Ben Sira seeks
deliverance from pride and lust, evil desire and
shamelessness.

8 Sinners are overtaken through their
      lips;
   by them the reviler and the arrogant
      are tripped up.
9 Do not accustom your mouth to oaths,
   nor habitually utter the name of the
      Holy One;
10 for as a servant who is constantly under
      scrutiny
   will not lack bruises,
   so also the person who always swears
      and utters the Name
   will never be cleansed *a* from sin.
11 The one who swears many oaths is full
      of iniquity,
   and the scourge will not leave his
      house.
   If he swears in error, his sin remains on
      him,
   and if he disregards it, he sins doubly;
   if he swears a false oath, he will not be
      justified,
   for his house will be filled with
      calamities.

Foul Language

12 There is a manner of speaking
      comparable to death; *b*
   may it never be found in the
      inheritance of Jacob!
   Such conduct will be far from the godly,
   and they will not wallow in sins.
13 Do not accustom your mouth to coarse,
      foul language,
   for it involves sinful speech.
14 Remember your father and mother
   when you sit among the great,
   or you may forget yourself in their
      presence,
   and behave like a fool through bad
      habit;
   then you will wish that you had never
      been born,

and you will curse the day of your
      birth.
15 Those who are accustomed to using
      abusive language
   will never become disciplined as long
      as they live.

Concerning Sexual Sins

16 Two kinds of individuals multiply sins,
   and a third incurs wrath.
   Hot passion that blazes like a fire
   will not be quenched until it burns
      itself out;
   one who commits fornication with his
      near of kin
   will never cease until the fire burns
      him up.
17 To a fornicator all bread is sweet;
   he will never weary until he dies.
18 The one who sins against his marriage
      bed
   says to himself, "Who can see me?
   Darkness surrounds me, the walls hide
      me,
   and no one sees me. Why should I
      worry?
   The Most High will not remember
      sins."
19 His fear is confined to human eyes
   and he does not realize that the eyes
      of the Lord
   are ten thousand times brighter than
      the sun;
   they look upon every aspect of human
      behavior
   and see into hidden corners.
20 Before the universe was created, it was
      known to him,
   and so it is since its completion.

a Syr *be free*   *b* Other ancient authorities read
clothed about with death

23:16–27 *the eyes of the Lord . . . look upon
every aspect of human behavior.* Fornicators
and adulterers count on darkness to hide their
lewdness, but they cannot hide from divine
scrutiny. Ben Sira reminds such practitioners
of evil that God's eyes are ten thousand times
brighter than the sun. Therefore, Ben Sira concludes, guilty men and women will be punished
for their adultery. The woman's offense is
deemed to have been a triple one: first, against
God; second, against her husband; and third,
against her progeny. In this instance, innocent
children also suffer.

21 This man will be punished in the streets
of the city,
   and where he least suspects it, he will
   be seized.

22 So it is with a woman who leaves her
husband
   and presents him with an heir by
   another man.
23 For first of all, she has disobeyed the law
of the Most High;
   second, she has committed an offense
   against her husband;
and third, through her fornication she
   has committed adultery
   and brought forth children by
   another man.
24 She herself will be brought before the
assembly,
   and her punishment will extend to
   her children.
25 Her children will not take root,
   and her branches will not bear fruit.
26 She will leave behind an accursed
memory
   and her disgrace will never be blotted
   out.
27 Those who survive her will recognize
   that nothing is better than the fear of
   the Lord,
   and nothing sweeter than to heed the
   commandments of the Lord. *a*

THE PRAISE OF WISDOM *b*

24 Wisdom praises herself,
   and tells of her glory in the midst of
   her people.
2 In the assembly of the Most High she
opens her mouth,
   and in the presence of his hosts she
   tells of her glory:

3 "I came forth from the mouth of the
Most High,
   and covered the earth like a mist.
4 I dwelt in the highest heavens,
   and my throne was in a pillar of cloud.
5 Alone I compassed the vault of heaven
   and traversed the depths of the abyss.
6 Over waves of the sea, over all the earth,
   and over every people and nation I
   have held sway. *c*
7 Among all these I sought a resting place;
   in whose territory should I abide?

8 "Then the Creator of all things gave me
a command,
   and my Creator chose the place for
   my tent.
He said, 'Make your dwelling in Jacob,
   and in Israel receive your
   inheritance.'
9 Before the ages, in the beginning, he
created me,
   and for all the ages I shall not cease to
   be.
10 In the holy tent I ministered before
him,
   and so I was established in Zion.
11 Thus in the beloved city he gave me a
resting place,
   and in Jerusalem was my domain.
12 I took root in an honored people,
   in the portion of the Lord, his
   heritage.

13 "I grew tall like a cedar in Lebanon,
   and like a cypress on the heights of
   Hermon.

a Other ancient authorities add as verse 28, *It is a
great honor to follow God, and to be received by him is
long life.   b* This heading is included in the Gk
text.   *c* Other ancient authorities read *I have
acquired a possession*

24:1–22 *my Creator chose the place for my
tent.* This hymn praising wisdom makes extensive use of the story about beginnings in Genesis
1–2, along with Prov 8:22–31. Issuing from the
divine mouth, Wisdom traveled everywhere in
search of a permanent dwelling place, at last
finding one in Jerusalem, where she ministers
in the Temple. There she took root like various
trees and vines, yielding abundant fruit. She
then invited people to taste her food and drink,
promising that they would want more. This
sumptuous repast is identified as the law
proclaimed to Israel by Moses (v 23). Ben Sira
does not deny that other nations possess some
wisdom, but for him wisdom resides primarily
in Jerusalem and more specifically in Torah.

14 I grew tall like a palm tree in En-gedi,ᵃ
   and like rosebushes in Jericho;
  like a fair olive tree in the field,
   and like a plane tree beside waterᵇ I
    grew tall.
15 Like cassia and camel's thorn I gave
   forth perfume,
  and like choice myrrh I spread my
   fragrance,
  like galbanum, onycha, and stacte,
   and like the odor of incense in the
    tent.
16 Like a terebinth I spread out my
   branches,
  and my branches are glorious and
   graceful.
17 Like the vine I bud forth delights,
  and my blossoms become glorious
   and abundant fruit.ᶜ

19 "Come to me, you who desire me,
   and eat your fill of my fruits.
20 For the memory of me is sweeter than
   honey,
  and the possession of me sweeter
   than the honeycomb.
21 Those who eat of me will hunger for
   more,
  and those who drink of me will thirst
   for more.
22 Whoever obeys me will not be put to
   shame,
  and those who work with me will not
   sin."

Wisdom and the Law

23 All this is the book of the covenant of
   the Most High God,
  the law that Moses commanded us
  as an inheritance for the
   congregations of Jacob.ᵈ
25 It overflows, like the Pishon, with
   wisdom,
  and like the Tigris at the time of the
   first fruits.

26 It runs over, like the Euphrates, with
   understanding,
  and like the Jordan at harvest time.
27 It pours forth instruction like the Nile,ᵉ
   like the Gihon at the time of vintage.
28 The first man did not know wisdomᶠ
   fully,
  nor will the last one fathom her.
29 For her thoughts are more abundant
   than the sea,
  and her counsel deeper than the great
   abyss.

30 As for me, I was like a canal from a river,
   like a water channel into a garden.
31 I said, "I will water my garden
   and drench my flower-beds."
  And lo, my canal became a river,
   and my river a sea.
32 I will again make instruction shine
   forth like the dawn,
  and I will make it clear from far away.
33 I will again pour out teaching like
   prophecy,
  and leave it to all future generations.
34 Observe that I have not labored for
   myself alone,
  but for all who seek wisdom.ᶠ

Those Who Are Worthy of Praise

25 I take pleasure in three things,
  and they are beautiful in the sight
  of God and of mortals:ᵍ

a Other ancient authorities read *on the beaches*
b Other ancient authorities omit *beside water*
c Other ancient authorities add as verse 18, *I am the mother of beautiful love, of fear, of knowledge, and of holy hope; being eternal, I am given to all my children, to those who are named by him.*   d Other ancient authorities add as verse 24, "Do not cease to be strong in the Lord, cling to him so that he may strengthen you; the Lord Almighty alone is God, and besides him there is no savior."*   e Syr: Gk It makes instruction shine forth like light*   f Gk her*   g Syr Lat: Gk In three things I was beautiful and I stood in beauty before the Lord and mortals.*

24:30–34 *my canal became a river, and my river a sea.* Having returned to the myth of origins and treated it creatively by naming various rivers flowing through the garden, Ben Sira appears to describe his own literary endeavor, likening it to a small brook that became increasingly larger. Inspired by its surprising success, he decided to expand the work for the benefit of those wishing to learn.

agreement among brothers and sisters,
   friendship among neighbors,
and a wife and a husband who live in
   harmony.
2 I hate three kinds of people,
   and I loathe their manner of life:
a pauper who boasts, a rich person who
   lies,
and an old fool who commits
   adultery.

3 If you gathered nothing in your youth,
   how can you find anything in your
   old age?
4 How attractive is sound judgment in
   the gray-haired,
and for the aged to possess good
   counsel!
5 How attractive is wisdom in the aged,
   and understanding and counsel in
   the venerable!
6 Rich experience is the crown of the
   aged,
and their boast is the fear of the Lord.

7 I can think of nine whom I would call
   blessed,
and a tenth my tongue proclaims:
a man who can rejoice in his children;
a man who lives to see the downfall of
   his foes.
8 Happy the man who lives with a
   sensible wife,
and the one who does not plow with
   ox and ass together. *a*
Happy is the one who does not sin with
   the tongue,
and the one who has not served an
   inferior.

9 Happy is the one who finds a friend, *b*
   and the one who speaks to attentive
   listeners.
10 How great is the one who finds wisdom!
   But none is superior to the one who
   fears the Lord.
11 Fear of the Lord surpasses everything;
   to whom can we compare the one
   who has it? *c*

Some Extreme Forms of Evil

13 Any wound, but not a wound of the
   heart!
Any wickedness, but not the
   wickedness of a woman!
14 Any suffering, but not suffering from
   those who hate!
And any vengeance, but not the
   vengeance of enemies!
15 There is no venom *d* worse than a
   snake's venom, *d*
and no anger worse than a woman's *e*
   wrath.

The Evil of a Wicked Woman

16 I would rather live with a lion and a
   dragon
than live with an evil woman.
17 A woman's wickedness changes her
   appearance,
and darkens her face like that of a
   bear.

a Heb Syr: Gk lacks *and the one who does not plow
with ox and ass together*   b Lat Syr: Gk *good sense*
c Other ancient authorities add as verse 12, *The fear
of the Lord is the beginning of love for him, and faith is
the beginning of clinging to him.*   d Syr: Gk *head*
e Other ancient authorities read *an enemy's*

25:3 *If you gathered nothing in your youth,
how can you find anything in your old age?* This
comment about an old man who thinks he is a
ladies' man reeks with sarcasm. If you could not
sway women in youth, how can you expect to
do so now? The futile effort to recapture one's
youth gives this observation special pathos. Ben
Sira therefore has genuine admiration for sensible
old people.
   25:7 *nine whom I would call blessed, and a
tenth.* This stylistic device, producing what are

called numerical proverbs, occurs in Canaanite
texts and occasionally elsewhere; in prophetic
and wisdom literature it often emphasizes the
final item, as here. Sometimes, however, the
numerical proverb lists only one item rather
than all of them (cf. Amos 1:3, 6, 9, 11, 13; 2:1).
   25:16 *I would rather live with a lion . . . than
live with an evil woman.* Similar sayings occur in
the book of Proverbs; obviously, the authors
were men. Women might have spoken about the
comparable difficulties that husbands present.

18 Her husband sits a among the
    neighbors,
    and he cannot help sighing b bitterly.
19 Any iniquity is small compared to a
    woman's iniquity;
    may a sinner's lot befall her!
20 A sandy ascent for the feet of the aged—
    such is a garrulous wife to a quiet
    husband.
21 Do not be ensnared by a woman's
    beauty,
    and do not desire a woman for her
    possessions. c
22 There is wrath and impudence and
    great disgrace
    when a wife supports her husband.
23 Dejected mind, gloomy face,
    and wounded heart come from an
    evil wife.
    Drooping hands and weak knees
    come from the wife who does not
    make her husband happy.
24 From a woman sin had its beginning,
    and because of her we all die.
25 Allow no outlet to water,
    and no boldness of speech to an evil
    wife.
26 If she does not go as you direct,
    separate her from yourself.

The Joy of a Good Wife

26 Happy is the husband of a good wife;
    the number of his days will be
    doubled.
2 A loyal wife brings joy to her husband,
    and he will complete his years in
    peace.
3 A good wife is a great blessing;

she will be granted among the
    blessings of the man who fears
    the Lord.
4 Whether rich or poor, his heart is
    content,
    and at all times his face is cheerful.

The Worst of Evils: A Wicked Wife

5 Of three things my heart is frightened,
    and of a fourth I am in great fear: d
    Slander in the city, the gathering of a
    mob,
    and false accusation—all these are
    worse than death.
6 But it is heartache and sorrow when a
    wife is jealous of a rival,
    and a tongue-lashing makes it known
    to all.
7 A bad wife is a chafing yoke;
    taking hold of her is like grasping a
    scorpion.
8 A drunken wife arouses great anger;
    she cannot hide her shame.
9 The haughty stare betrays an unchaste
    wife;
    her eyelids give her away.

10 Keep strict watch over a headstrong
    daughter,
    or else, when she finds liberty, she
    will make use of it.
11 Be on guard against her impudent eye,
    and do not be surprised if she sins
    against you.
12 As a thirsty traveler opens his mouth
    and drinks from any water near him,

a Heb Syr: Gk loses heart   b Other ancient
authorities read and listening he sighs   c Heb Syr:
Other Gk authorities read for her beauty
d Syr: Meaning of Gk uncertain

25:24 *because of her we all die.* Ben Sira
blames Eve for human mortality, forgetting that
in the story Adam joins her in transgressing the
divine prohibition. Male authors persisted in
foisting the blame on women, as in the Greek
tale of Pandora, whose curiosity led to the
opening of a box that released evils; its hasty
closing prevented hope from escaping to provide relief for those suddenly burdened with
nightmarish affliction.

26:10–12 *Be on guard.* Ben Sira's crude
description of a rebellious daughter explains
why he can consider the birth of a daughter a
loss (22:3). Greek antifeminism went farther, for
it grounded such nonsense in philosophy itself.
Since matter was evil, reproduction and everything connected with it was considered sinful.
This attitude permeated the early Church,
especially its Gnostic branch.

so she will sit in front of every tent peg
  and open her quiver to the arrow.

The Blessing of a Good Wife

13 A wife's charm delights her husband,
  and her skill puts flesh on his bones.
14 A silent wife is a gift from the Lord,
  and nothing is so precious as her self-
    discipline.
15 A modest wife adds charm to charm,
  and no scales can weigh the value of
    her chastity.
16 Like the sun rising in the heights of the
    Lord,
  so is the beauty of a good wife in her
    well-ordered home.
17 Like the shining lamp on the holy
    lampstand,
  so is a beautiful face on a stately figure.
18 Like golden pillars on silver bases,
  so are shapely legs and steadfast feet.

Other ancient authorities add verses 19-27:

19 *My child, keep sound the bloom of your
    youth,*
  and do not give your strength to strangers.
20 *Seek a fertile field within the whole plain,*
  and sow it with your own seed, trusting
    in your fine stock.
21 *So your offspring will prosper,*
  and, having confidence in their good
    descent, will grow great.
22 *A prostitute is regarded as spittle,*
  and a married woman as a tower of
    death to her lovers.
23 *A godless wife is given as a portion to a*
    lawless man,
  but a pious wife is given to the man who
    fears the Lord.

24 *A shameless woman constantly acts*
    disgracefully,
  but a modest daughter will even be
    embarrassed before her husband.
25 *A headstrong wife is regarded as a dog,*
  but one who has a sense of shame will
    fear the Lord.
26 *A wife honoring her husband will seem*
    wise to all,
  but if she dishonors him in her pride she
    will be known to all as ungodly.
  Happy is the husband of a good wife;
  for the number of his years will be
    doubled.
27 *A loud-voiced and garrulous wife is like a*
    trumpet sounding the charge,
  and every person like this lives in the
    anarchy of war.

Three Depressing Things

28 At two things my heart is grieved,
  and because of a third anger comes
    over me:
a warrior in want through poverty,
  intelligent men who are treated
    contemptuously,
and a man who turns back from
    righteousness to sin—
  the Lord will prepare him for the
    sword!

The Temptations of Commerce

29 A merchant can hardly keep from
    wrongdoing,
  nor is a tradesman innocent of sin.

27 Many have committed sin for gain,[a]
  and those who seek to get rich will
    avert their eyes.

---

a Other ancient authorities read *a trifle*

26:13–18 *A wife's charm . . . her skill . . . her
self-discipline.* Teachers described reality as they
saw it. Good wives also existed, and blessed
indeed was a man who had discovered one (cf.
36:26–30). Ben Sira's comparison of a beautiful
woman with a lamp on a sacred stand recalls
Prov 6:20–35, in which the Torah is likened to a
light. This idea became popular in Psalms and in
early Christology, where Jesus was identified as

the Word and Light of the World (Ps 119:105;
John 1:1–5).

Responding
26:15 CHASTITY. "Modesty" is a
term little discussed today. What is
the role of modesty in today's society? What is
the connection, if any, between chastity and
modesty? *See also* Spiritual Disciplines Index.

2 As a stake is driven firmly into a fissure
  between stones,
    so sin is wedged in between selling
    and buying.
3 If a person is not steadfast in the fear of
  the Lord,
    his house will be quickly overthrown.

Tests in Life

4 When a sieve is shaken, the refuse
  appears;
    so do a person's faults when he speaks.
5 The kiln tests the potter's vessels;
    so the test of a person is in his
    conversation.
6 Its fruit discloses the cultivation of a tree;
    so a person's speech discloses the
    cultivation of his mind.
7 Do not praise anyone before he speaks,
    for this is the way people are tested.

Reward and Retribution

8 If you pursue justice, you will attain it
    and wear it like a glorious robe.
9 Birds roost with their own kind,
    so honesty comes home to those who
    practice it.
10 A lion lies in wait for prey;
    so does sin for evildoers.

Varieties of Speech

11 The conversation of the godly is always
   wise,
     but the fool changes like the moon.
12 Among stupid people limit your time,
     but among thoughtful people linger
     on.
13 The talk of fools is offensive,
     and their laughter is wantonly sinful.
14 Their cursing and swearing make one's
   hair stand on end,
     and their quarrels make others stop
     their ears.

15 The strife of the proud leads to
   bloodshed,
     and their abuse is grievous to hear.

Betraying Secrets

16 Whoever betrays secrets destroys
   confidence,
     and will never find a congenial friend.
17 Love your friend and keep faith with
   him;
     but if you betray his secrets, do not
     follow after him.
18 For as a person destroys his enemy,
     so you have destroyed the friendship
     of your neighbor.
19 And as you allow a bird to escape from
   your hand,
     so you have let your neighbor go, and
     will not catch him again.
20 Do not go after him, for he is too far off,
     and has escaped like a gazelle from a
     snare.
21 For a wound may be bandaged,
     and there is reconciliation after abuse,
     but whoever has betrayed secrets is
     without hope.

Hypocrisy and Retribution

22 Whoever winks the eye plots mischief,
     and those who know him will keep
     their distance.
23 In your presence his mouth is all
   sweetness,
     and he admires your words;
   but later he will twist his speech
     and with your own words he will trip
     you up.
24 I have hated many things, but him
   above all;
     even the Lord hates him.
25 Whoever throws a stone straight up
     throws it on his own head,

26:29–27:2 *Many have committed sin for gain.* The ancient practice of barter opened the door for considerable profit, and Ben Sira believed that sellers were prone to excessive greed, like many CEOs today.

27:4–7 *the test of a person is in his conversation.* Intellectual criteria prevail in this section,

which values reason above everything.

27:25–29 *Whoever throws a stone straight up throws it on his own head.* The sages believed that actions had inevitable consequences. Once set in motion, a deed attained its natural goal, for good or ill, sometimes with no suggestion of divine implementation.

and a treacherous blow opens up
    many wounds.
26 Whoever digs a pit will fall into it,
    and whoever sets a snare will be
    caught in it.
27 If a person does evil, it will roll back
    upon him,
    and he will not know where it came
    from.
28 Mockery and abuse issue from the
    proud,
    but vengeance lies in wait for them
    like a lion.
29 Those who rejoice in the fall of the
    godly will be caught in a snare,
    and pain will consume them before
    their death.

Anger and Vengeance

30 Anger and wrath, these also are
    abominations,
    yet a sinner holds on to them.

28 The vengeful will face the Lord's
    vengeance,
    for he keeps a strict account of[a] their
    sins.
2 Forgive your neighbor the wrong he has
    done,
    and then your sins will be pardoned
    when you pray.
3 Does anyone harbor anger against
    another,
    and expect healing from the Lord?
4 If one has no mercy toward another like
    himself,
    can he then seek pardon for his own
    sins?
5 If a mere mortal harbors wrath,
    who will make an atoning sacrifice for
    his sins?
6 Remember the end of your life, and set
    enmity aside;
    remember corruption and death, and
    be true to the commandments.

7 Remember the commandments, and do
    not be angry with your neighbor;
    remember the covenant of the Most
    High, and overlook faults.
8 Refrain from strife, and your sins will be
    fewer;
    for the hot-tempered kindle strife,
9 and the sinner disrupts friendships
    and sows discord among those who
    are at peace.
10 In proportion to the fuel, so will the fire
    burn,
    and in proportion to the obstinacy, so
    will strife increase;[b]
in proportion to a person's strength will
    be his anger,
    and in proportion to his wealth he
    will increase his wrath.
11 A hasty quarrel kindles a fire,
    and a hasty dispute sheds blood.

The Evil Tongue

12 If you blow on a spark, it will glow;
    if you spit on it, it will be put out;
    yet both come out of your mouth.

13 Curse the gossips and the double-
    tongued,
    for they destroy the peace of many.
14 Slander[c] has shaken many,
    and scattered them from nation to
    nation;
    it has destroyed strong cities,
    and overturned the houses of the
    great.
15 Slander[d] has driven virtuous women
    from their homes,
    and deprived them of the fruit of
    their toil.

---

a Other ancient authorities read *for he firmly
establishes*   b Other ancient authorities read *burn*
c Gk *A third tongue*   d Gk *a third tongue*

28:2–5 *Forgive your neighbor . . . then your
sins will be pardoned.* Forgiveness is contingent
on one's readiness to pardon others. Jesus also
emphasized the necessity of forgiving offenders
before expecting God's gracious response (Matt
6:14).

28:13–26 *a blow of the tongue crushes the
bones.* The personification of the tongue ac-
centuates the debilitating effect of slander
within a community. Hyperbole underscores
the impact of hurtful words.

16 Those who pay heed to slander[a] will
          not find rest,
     nor will they settle down in peace.
17 The blow of a whip raises a welt,
     but a blow of the tongue crushes the
          bones.
18 Many have fallen by the edge of the
          sword,
     but not as many as have fallen
          because of the tongue.
19 Happy is the one who is protected from
          it,
     who has not been exposed to its anger,
who has not borne its yoke,
     and has not been bound with its
          fetters.
20 For its yoke is a yoke of iron,
     and its fetters are fetters of bronze;
21 its death is an evil death,
     and Hades is preferable to it.
22 It has no power over the godly;
     they will not be burned in its flame.
23 Those who forsake the Lord will fall
          into its power;
     it will burn among them and will not
          be put out.
It will be sent out against them like a
          lion;
     like a leopard it will mangle them.
24a   As you fence in your property
          with thorns,
25b so make a door and a bolt for your
          mouth.
24b   As you lock up your silver and
          gold,
25a so make balances and scales for your
          words.
26 Take care not to err with your tongue,[b]
     and fall victim to one lying in wait.

On Lending and Borrowing

29 The merciful lend to their neighbors;
          by holding out a helping hand they
          keep the commandments.

2 Lend to your neighbor in his time of
          need;
     repay your neighbor when a loan falls
          due.
3 Keep your promise and be honest with
          him,
     and on every occasion you will find
          what you need.
4 Many regard a loan as a windfall,
     and cause trouble to those who help
          them.
5 One kisses another's hands until he gets
          a loan,
     and is deferential in speaking of his
          neighbor's money;
but at the time for repayment he delays,
     and pays back with empty promises,
     and finds fault with the time.
6 If he can pay, his creditor[c] will hardly
          get back half,
     and will regard that as a windfall.
If he cannot pay, the borrower[c] has
          robbed the other of his money,
     and he has needlessly made him an
          enemy;
he will repay him with curses and
          reproaches,
     and instead of glory will repay him
          with dishonor.
7 Many refuse to lend, not because of
          meanness,
     but from fear[d] of being defrauded
          needlessly.

8 Nevertheless, be patient with someone
          in humble circumstances,
     and do not keep him waiting for your
          alms.
9 Help the poor for the commandment's
          sake,

a Gk *it*   *b* Gk *with it*   *c* Gk *he*   *d* Other
ancient authorities read *many refuse to lend,
therefore, because of such meanness; they are afraid*

29:1–7 *The merciful lend.* The astute depiction of posturing by a creditor reveals Ben Sira's keen powers of observation. Alert to the potential for making an enemy of the borrower, the considerate person lends to the needy anyway.

29:9 *Help the poor for the commandment's*

sake. The call to help the poor because it is commanded is advanced by Jesus to a call to help the poor because they need help. The move is from external obedience to the inner transformation of the heart (Mark 7:17–23; 10:21).

and in their need do not send them
away empty-handed.

10 Lose your silver for the sake of a brother
or a friend,
and do not let it rust under a stone
and be lost.

11 Lay up your treasure according to the
commandments of the Most
High,
and it will profit you more than gold.

12 Store up almsgiving in your treasury,
and it will rescue you from every
disaster;

13 better than a stout shield and a sturdy
spear,
it will fight for you against the enemy.

On Guaranteeing Debts

14 A good person will be surety for his
neighbor,
but the one who has lost all sense of
shame will fail him.

15 Do not forget the kindness of your
guarantor,
for he has given his life for you.

16 A sinner wastes the property of his
guarantor,

17   and the ungrateful person abandons
his rescuer.

18 Being surety has ruined many who were
prosperous,
and has tossed them about like waves
of the sea;
it has driven the influential into exile,
and they have wandered among
foreign nations.

19 The sinner comes to grief through
surety;
his pursuit of gain involves him in
lawsuits.

20 Assist your neighbor to the best of your
ability,
but be careful not to fall yourself.

Home and Hospitality

21 The necessities of life are water, bread,
and clothing,
and also a house to assure privacy.

22 Better is the life of the poor under their
own crude roof
than sumptuous food in the house of
others.

23 Be content with little or much,
and you will hear no reproach for
being a guest. *a*

24 It is a miserable life to go from house to
house;
as a guest you should not open your
mouth;

25 you will play the host and provide drink
without being thanked,
and besides this you will hear rude
words like these:

26 "Come here, stranger, prepare the
table;
let me eat what you have there."

27 "Be off, stranger, for an honored guest is
here;
my brother has come for a visit, and I
need the guest-room."

28 It is hard for a sensible person to bear
scolding about lodging *b* and the
insults of the moneylender.

Concerning Children *c*

30 He who loves his son will whip him
often,
so that he may rejoice at the way he
turns out.

2 He who disciplines his son will profit by
him,
and will boast of him among
acquaintances.

a Lat: Gk *reproach from your family*; other ancient
authorities lack this line   *b* Or *scolding from the
household*   *c* This heading is included in the Gk
text.

29:10 *Lose your silver for the sake of a brother.*
Hiding one's silver under a rock, the equivalent
today of hiding money in a mattress, does no
one any good. The proper use of wealth is to
help those in need.

29:21 *The necessities of life are.* What do
we really need? Ben Sira narrows down the
necessities of life to four things: water, bread,
clothing, and a house. In 39:26 he asks for a
little more comfort by adding fire, iron, salt,
milk, honey, wine, and oil.

3 He who teaches his son will make his
     enemies envious,
    and will glory in him among his
     friends.
4 When the father dies he will not seem
     to be dead,
    for he has left behind him one like
     himself,
5 whom in his life he looked upon with
     joy
    and at death, without grief.
6 He has left behind him an avenger
     against his enemies,
    and one to repay the kindness of his
     friends.

7 Whoever spoils his son will bind up his
     wounds,
    and will suffer heartache at every
     cry.
8 An unbroken horse turns out stubborn,
    and an unchecked son turns out
     headstrong.
9 Pamper a child, and he will terrorize
     you;
    play with him, and he will grieve you.
10 Do not laugh with him, or you will have
     sorrow with him,
    and in the end you will gnash your
     teeth.
11 Give him no freedom in his youth,
    and do not ignore his errors.
12 Bow down his neck in his youth, *a*
    and beat his sides while he is young,
   or else he will become stubborn and
     disobey you,
    and you will have sorrow of soul from
     him. *b*
13 Discipline your son and make his yoke
    heavy, *c*

so that you may not be offended by
    his shamelessness.

14 Better off poor, healthy, and fit
    than rich and afflicted in body.
15 Health and fitness are better than any
     gold,
    and a robust body than countless
     riches.
16 There is no wealth better than health of
     body,
    and no gladness above joy of heart.
17 Death is better than a life of misery,
    and eternal sleep *d* than chronic
     sickness.

Concerning Foods *e*

18 Good things poured out upon a mouth
     that is closed
    are like offerings of food placed upon
     a grave.
19 Of what use to an idol is a sacrifice?
    For it can neither eat nor smell.
  So is the one punished by the Lord;
20 he sees with his eyes and groans
    as a eunuch groans when embracing a
     girl. *f*

21 Do not give yourself over to sorrow,
    and do not distress yourself
     deliberately.
22 A joyful heart is life itself,
    and rejoicing lengthens one's life
     span.

a Other ancient authorities lack this line and the
preceding line   *b* Other ancient authorities lack
this line   *c* Heb: Gk *take pains with him*
d Other ancient authorities lack *eternal sleep*
e This heading is included in the Gk text; other
ancient authorities place the heading before verse
16   *f* Other ancient authorities add *So is the
person who does right under compulsion*

30:1–13 *He who loves his son will whip him
often.* Harsh discipline was practiced in the
ancient world, and Ben Sira subscribed to
corporal punishment as a way of building
character. He missed out on one of the real
joys of life, joining one's children in play. In this
matter, as in others, modern readers need to
consider cultural assumptions then and now,
which should prevent a literal application of

ancient practices in a thoroughly modern
situation.

30:19 *an idol . . . can neither eat nor smell.*
Idols have mouths, but cannot eat (cf. Ps
115:5–7); afflicted persons fare no better. Jewish authors mocked idols for their incapacity
to prevent theft, escape from fire, avoid being
touched by menstruating women, and keep
birds from defecating on them.

23 Indulge yourself[a] and take comfort,
   and remove sorrow far from you,
   for sorrow has destroyed many,
   and no advantage ever comes from it.
24 Jealousy and anger shorten life,
   and anxiety brings on premature old
      age.
25 Those who are cheerful and merry at
      table
   will benefit from their food.

Right Attitude toward Riches

31 Wakefulness over wealth wastes
   away one's flesh,
   and anxiety about it drives away
      sleep.
2 Wakeful anxiety prevents slumber,
   and a severe illness carries off sleep.[b]
3 The rich person toils to amass a fortune,
   and when he rests he fills himself
      with his dainties.
4 The poor person toils to make a meager
      living,
   and if ever he rests he becomes needy.

5 One who loves gold will not be justified;
   one who pursues money will be led
      astray[c] by it.
6 Many have come to ruin because of
      gold,
   and their destruction has met them
      face to face.
7 It is a stumbling block to those who are
      avid for it,
   and every fool will be taken captive by
      it.
8 Blessed is the rich person who is found
      blameless,
   and who does not go after gold.
9 Who is he, that we may praise him?
   For he has done wonders among his
      people.
10 Who has been tested by it and been
      found perfect?

Let it be for him a ground for
      boasting.
Who has had the power to transgress
      and did not transgress,
   and to do evil and did not do it?
11 His prosperity will be established,[d]
   and the assembly will proclaim his
      acts of charity.

Table Etiquette

12 Are you seated at the table of the great?[e]
   Do not be greedy at it,
   and do not say, "How much food
      there is here!"
13 Remember that a greedy eye is a bad
      thing.
   What has been created more greedy
      than the eye?
   Therefore it sheds tears for any reason.
14 Do not reach out your hand for
      everything you see,
   and do not crowd your neighbor[f] at
      the dish.
15 Judge your neighbor's feelings by your
      own,
   and in every matter be thoughtful.
16 Eat what is set before you like a well
      brought-up person,[g]
   and do not chew greedily, or you will
      give offense.
17 Be the first to stop, as befits good
      manners,
   and do not be insatiable, or you will
      give offense.
18 If you are seated among many persons,
   do not help yourself[h] before they do.

a Other ancient authorities read *Beguile yourself*
b Other ancient authorities read *sleep carries off a
severe illness*   c Heb Syr: Gk *pursues destruction
will be filled*   d Other ancient authorities add
because of this   e Heb Syr: Gk *at a great table*
f Gk *him*   g Heb: Gk *like a human being*
h Gk *reach out your hand*

31:12–18 *Eat what is set before you.* Wisdom literature frequently offers advice on table manners, indeed has often been compared to the work of columnists like Ann Landers and Dear Abby, to etiquette books like Emily Post's, and to books such as those by Dale Carnegie on winning friends. Like these modern authors, ancient sages hoped to help others cope in everyday circumstances.

19 How ample a little is for a
        well-disciplined person!
    He does not breathe heavily when in
        bed.
20 Healthy sleep depends on moderate
        eating;
    he rises early, and feels fit.
    The distress of sleeplessness and of
        nausea
    and colic are with the glutton.
21 If you are overstuffed with food,
        get up to vomit, and you will have
        relief.
22 Listen to me, my child, and do not
        disregard me,
    and in the end you will appreciate my
        words.
    In everything you do be moderate,ᵃ
    and no sickness will overtake
        you.
23 People bless the one who is liberal with
        food,
    and their testimony to his generosity
        is trustworthy.
24 The city complains of the one who is
        stingy with food,
    and their testimony to his stinginess
        is accurate.

Temperance in Drinking Wine

25 Do not try to prove your strength by
        wine-drinking,
    for wine has destroyed many.
26 As the furnace tests the work of the
        smith,ᵇ
    so wine tests hearts when the insolent
        quarrel.
27 Wine is very life to human beings
    if taken in moderation.
    What is life to one who is without
        wine?
    It has been created to make people
        happy.

28 Wine drunk at the proper time and in
        moderation
    is rejoicing of heart and gladness of
        soul.
29 Wine drunk to excess leads to bitterness
        of spirit,
    to quarrels and stumbling.
30 Drunkenness increases the anger of a
        fool to his own hurt,
    reducing his strength and adding
        wounds.
31 Do not reprove your neighbor at a
        banquet of wine,
    and do not despise him in his
        merrymaking;
    speak no word of reproach to him,
    and do not distress him by making
        demands of him.

Etiquette at a Banquet

32 If they make you master of the
        feast, do not exalt yourself;
    be among them as one of their
        number.
    Take care of them first and then sit
        down;
2   when you have fulfilled all your
        duties, take your place,
    so that you may be merry along with
        them
    and receive a wreath for your
        excellent leadership.

3   Speak, you who are older, for it is your
        right,
    but with accurate knowledge, and do
        not interrupt the music.
4   Where there is entertainment, do not
        pour out talk;
    do not display your cleverness at the
        wrong time.

ᵃ Heb Syr: Gk industrious   ᵇ Heb: Gk tests the
hardening of steel by dipping

31:25–32:13 *Do not try to prove your strength
by wine-drinking.* The first part of this section
deals with strong drink, both its pleasures and
its dangers. Then it offers advice about conduct
at a banquet. In Greco-Roman society, banquets
were occasions of intellectual stimulation and
were governed by strict rules of protocol. Chief
hosts were chosen, prayers were offered,
and music was provided. Above all, speeches
abounded. Seniority gave one distinct advantages at these banquets, as everywhere else in
the ancient world, unlike today in the West.

5 A ruby seal in a setting of gold
   is a concert of music at a banquet of
      wine.
6 A seal of emerald in a rich setting of
      gold
   is the melody of music with good
      wine.

7 Speak, you who are young, if you are
      obliged to,
   but no more than twice, and only if
      asked.
8 Be brief; say much in few words;
   be as one who knows and can still
      hold his tongue.
9 Among the great do not act as their
      equal;
   and when another is speaking, do not
      babble.

10 Lightning travels ahead of the
      thunder,
   and approval goes before one who is
      modest.
11 Leave in good time and do not be the
      last;
   go home quickly and do not linger.
12 Amuse yourself there to your heart's
      content,
   but do not sin through proud speech.
13 But above all bless your Maker,
   who fills you with his good gifts.

The Providence of God

14 The one who seeks God^a will accept his
      discipline,
   and those who rise early to seek him^b
      will find favor.
15 The one who seeks the law will be filled
      with it,
   but the hypocrite will stumble at it.
16 Those who fear the Lord will form true
      judgments,
   and they will kindle righteous deeds
      like a light.
17 The sinner will shun reproof,

and will find a decision according to
   his liking.

18 A sensible person will not overlook a
      thoughtful suggestion;
   an insolent^c and proud person will
      not be deterred by fear.^d
19 Do nothing without deliberation,
   but when you have acted, do not
      regret it.
20 Do not go on a path full of hazards,
   and do not stumble at an obstacle
      twice.^e
21 Do not be overconfident on a smooth^f
      road,
22   and give good heed to your paths.^g
23 Guard^h yourself in every act,
   for this is the keeping of the
      commandments.

24 The one who keeps the law preserves
      himself,ⁱ
   and the one who trusts the Lord will
      not suffer loss.

33 No evil will befall the one who fears
     the Lord,
   but in trials such a one will be rescued
      again and again.
2 The wise will not hate the law,
   but the one who is hypocritical about
      it is like a boat in a storm.
3 The sensible person will trust in the
      law;
   for such a one the law is as
      dependable as a divine oracle.

4 Prepare what to say, and then you will
      be listened to;

---

a Heb: Gk *who fears the Lord*   *b* Other ancient
authorities lack *to seek him*   *c* Heb: Gk *alien*
d Meaning of Gk uncertain. Other ancient
authorities add *and after acting, with him, without
deliberation*   *e* Heb: Gk *stumble on stony ground*
f Or *an unexplored*   *g* Heb Syr: Gk *and beware of
your children*   *h* Heb Syr: Gk *Trust*   *i* Heb: Gk
who believes the law heeds the commandments

33:3 *the law is as dependable as a divine oracle.*
Inquiry by casting sacred dice was thought to be
an exact science, reliable because it was over-

seen by the Lord. Ben Sira thinks of the law
as equally trustworthy, precisely because it
originated with God.

draw upon your training, and give
your answer.

5 The heart of a fool is like a cart wheel,
and his thoughts like a turning axle.

6 A mocking friend is like a stallion
that neighs no matter who the rider
is.

Differences in Nature and in Humankind

7 Why is one day more important than
another,
when all the daylight in the year is
from the sun?

8 By the Lord's wisdom they were
distinguished,
and he appointed the different
seasons and festivals.

9 Some days he exalted and hallowed,
and some he made ordinary days.

10 All human beings come from the
ground,
and humankind *a* was created out of
the dust.

11 In the fullness of his knowledge the
Lord distinguished them
and appointed their different ways.

12 Some he blessed and exalted,
and some he made holy and brought
near to himself;
but some he cursed and brought low,
and turned them out of their place.

13 Like clay in the hand of the potter,
to be molded as he pleases,
so all are in the hand of their Maker,
to be given whatever he decides.

14 Good is the opposite of evil,
and life the opposite of death;
so the sinner is the opposite of the
godly.

15 Look at all the works of the Most High;
they come in pairs, one the opposite
of the other.

16 Now I was the last to keep vigil;
I was like a gleaner following the
grape-pickers;

17 by the blessing of the Lord I arrived
first,
and like a grape-picker I filled my
wine press.

18 Consider that I have not labored for
myself alone,
but for all who seek instruction.

19 Hear me, you who are great among the
people,
and you leaders of the congregation,
pay heed!

The Advantage of Independence

20 To son or wife, to brother or friend,
do not give power over yourself, as
long as you live;
and do not give your property to
another,
in case you change your mind and
must ask for it.

21 While you are still alive and have breath
in you,
do not let anyone take your place.

22 For it is better that your children should
ask from you
than that you should look to the
hand of your children.

23 Excel in all that you do;
bring no stain upon your honor.

24 At the time when you end the days of
your life,
in the hour of death, distribute your
inheritance.

The Treatment of Slaves

25 Fodder and a stick and burdens for a
donkey;
bread and discipline and work for a
slave.

a Heb: Gk *Adam*

33:13 *Like clay in the hand of a potter.* The
Creator shapes vessels according to his wishes;
humans are like clay in God's hand. Earlier Ben
Sira emphasized free will. Jeremiah and Isaiah
also use the image of the divine potter who had
the power to shape human wills as desired (e.g.,
Isa 64:8; Jer 18:6), which stands in tension with
the equally widespread idea that humans are
responsible for their deeds.

33:16–18 *I was the last to keep vigil.* Once
again the author inserts a brief autobiographical
comment.

26 Set your slave to work, and you will find
      rest;
   leave his hands idle, and he will seek
      liberty.
27 Yoke and thong will bow the neck,
   and for a wicked slave there are racks
      and tortures.
28 Put him to work, in order that he may
      not be idle,
29   for idleness teaches much evil.
30 Set him to work, as is fitting for him,
   and if he does not obey, make his
      fetters heavy.
   Do not be overbearing toward anyone,
   and do nothing unjust.

31 If you have but one slave, treat him like
      yourself,
   because you have bought him with
      blood.
   If you have but one slave, treat him like
      a brother,
   for you will need him as you need
      your life.
32 If you ill-treat him, and he leaves you
      and runs away,
33   which way will you go to seek him?

Dreams Mean Nothing

34 The senseless have vain and false
      hopes,
   and dreams give wings to fools.
2 As one who catches at a shadow and
      pursues the wind,
   so is anyone who believes in*a* dreams.
3 What is seen in dreams is but a
      reflection,
   the likeness of a face looking at itself.

4 From an unclean thing what can be
      clean?
   And from something false what can
      be true?
5 Divinations and omens and dreams are
      unreal,
   and like a woman in labor, the mind
      has fantasies.
6 Unless they are sent by intervention
      from the Most High,
   pay no attention to them.
7 For dreams have deceived many,
   and those who put their hope in
      them have perished.
8 Without such deceptions the law will
      be fulfilled,
   and wisdom is complete in the mouth
      of the faithful.

Experience as a Teacher

9 An educated*b* person knows many
      things,
   and one with much experience
      knows what he is talking about.
10 An inexperienced person knows few
      things,
11   but he that has traveled acquires
      much cleverness.
12 I have seen many things in my travels,
   and I understand more than I can
      express.
13 I have often been in danger of death,
   but have escaped because of these
      experiences.

a Syr: Gk *pays heed to*   b Other ancient
authorities read *A traveled*

33:30–31 *If you have but one slave, treat
him like a brother.* Slavery was common in the
ancient world; here some of its horror is mitiga-
ted through compassion, even if guided by self-
interest. The viewpoint is that of the owner, not
the slave. Given the story of Egyptian bondage,
the very existence of slavery in Israel is an
anomaly.

34:1–8 *dreams give wings to fools.* Dreams
were an acceptable means of revelation in some
ancient texts, but a few prophets questioned their

veracity. Ben Sira follows them to some extent,
but he is not fully convinced that dreams are
useless. Like prophecy, a related phenomenon,
dreams had no means of validating their source.

34:9–12 *he that has traveled acquires much
cleverness.* Travel in Ben Sira's day was hazardous but instructive; some early Christians
seem to have moved about from city to city with
ease, despite the risks. Paul said he experienced
shipwreck several times on his frequent
journeys (2 Cor 11:25).

Fear the Lord

14 The spirit of those who fear the Lord
      will live,
15   for their hope is in him who saves
      them.
16 Those who fear the Lord will not be
      timid,
      or play the coward, for he is their hope.
17 Happy is the soul that fears the Lord!
18   To whom does he look? And who is
      his support?
19 The eyes of the Lord are on those who
      love him,
      a mighty shield and strong support,
      a shelter from scorching wind and a
      shade from noonday sun,
      a guard against stumbling and a help
      against falling.
20 He lifts up the soul and makes the eyes
      sparkle;
      he gives health and life and blessing.

Offering Sacrifices

21 If one sacrifices ill-gotten goods, the
      offering is blemished; *a*
22   the gifts *b* of the lawless are not
      acceptable.
23 The Most High is not pleased with the
      offerings of the ungodly,
      nor for a multitude of sacrifices does
      he forgive sins.
24 Like one who kills a son before his
      father's eyes
      is the person who offers a sacrifice
      from the property of the poor.
25 The bread of the needy is the life of the
      poor;
      whoever deprives them of it is a
      murderer.
26 To take away a neighbor's living is to
      commit murder;
27   to deprive an employee of wages is to
      shed blood.

28 When one builds and another tears
      down,
      what do they gain but hard work?
29 When one prays and another curses,
      to whose voice will the Lord listen?
30 If one washes after touching a corpse,
      and touches it again,
      what has been gained by washing?
31 So if one fasts for his sins,
      and goes again and does the same
      things,
      who will listen to his prayer?
      And what has he gained by humbling
      himself?

The Law and Sacrifices

35 The one who keeps the law makes
      many offerings;
2   one who heeds the commandments
      makes an offering of well-being.
3 The one who returns a kindness offers
      choice flour,
4   and one who gives alms sacrifices a
      thank offering.
5 To keep from wickedness is pleasing to
      the Lord,
      and to forsake unrighteousness is an
      atonement.
6 Do not appear before the Lord empty-
      handed,
7   for all that you offer is in fulfillment
      of the commandment.
8 The offering of the righteous enriches
      the altar,
      and its pleasing odor rises before the
      Most High.
9 The sacrifice of the righteous is
      acceptable,
      and it will never be forgotten.
10 Be generous when you worship the
      Lord,

a Other ancient authorities read *is made in mockery*
b Other ancient authorities read *mockeries*

34:21–24 SACRIFICE—*See* Spiritual Disciplines
Index.

34:21–27 *If one sacrifices ill-gotten goods.*
The source of earnings offered to God matters.
Utter obscenity adheres to an offering obtained
at the expense of the needy.

34:31 FASTING and PRAYER—*See* Spiritual
Disciplines Index.

35:4, 9 SACRIFICE—*See* Spiritual Disciplines
Index.

35:10 WORSHIP—*See* Spiritual Disciplines
Index.

and do not stint the first fruits of your
hands.

11 With every gift show a cheerful face,
and dedicate your tithe with gladness.

12 Give to the Most High as he has given to
you,
and as generously as you can afford.

13 For the Lord is the one who repays,
and he will repay you sevenfold.

Divine Justice

14 Do not offer him a bribe, for he will not
accept it;

15 and do not rely on a dishonest
sacrifice;
for the Lord is the judge,
and with him there is no partiality.

16 He will not show partiality to the poor;
but he will listen to the prayer of one
who is wronged.

17 He will not ignore the supplication of
the orphan,
or the widow when she pours out her
complaint.

18 Do not the tears of the widow run down
her cheek

19 as she cries out against the one who
causes them to fall?

20 The one whose service is pleasing to the
Lord will be accepted,
and his prayer will reach to the
clouds.

21 The prayer of the humble pierces the
clouds,
and it will not rest until it reaches its
goal;
it will not desist until the Most High
responds

22 and does justice for the righteous,
and executes judgment.

Indeed, the Lord will not delay,
and like a warrior*a* will not be patient
until he crushes the loins of the
unmerciful

23 and repays vengeance on the nations;
until he destroys the multitude of the
insolent,
and breaks the scepters of the
unrighteous;

24 until he repays mortals according to
their deeds,
and the works of all according to their
thoughts;

25 until he judges the case of his people
and makes them rejoice in his mercy.

26 His mercy is as welcome in time of
distress
as clouds of rain in time of drought.

A Prayer for God's People

36 Have mercy upon us, O God*b* of all,
2 and put all the nations in fear of
you.

3 Lift up your hand against foreign
nations
and let them see your might.

4 As you have used us to show your
holiness to them,
so use them to show your glory to us.

5 Then they will know,*c* as we have
known,
that there is no God but you, O Lord.

6 Give new signs, and work other
wonders;

7 make your hand and right arm
glorious.

a Heb: Gk *and with them*   *b* Heb: Gk *O Master,
the God*   *c* Heb: Gk *And let them know you*

35:17 *He will not ignore the supplication of
the orphan.* Nothing pierces the clouds like
the prayer of the humble (v 21), for God is the
champion of widows and orphans. Deuteronomy understands the Lord as supremely interested in the powerless members of society.
   35:20 SERVICE—*See* Spiritual Disciplines
Index.
   35:20–22 PRAYER—*See* Spiritual Disciplines
Index.

36:1–22 *Have mercy upon us, O God.* Like
many laments in Psalms, this prayer seeks
special exaltation of Israel before the nations.
A period in which God's hand appears to be
concealed is reflected in the perennial cry,
"Give new signs, and work other wonders" (v 6),
or "Hurry up and act to fulfill the prophetic
promises." Such is Ben Sira's fervent prayer on
behalf of Zion and its scattered people, who
await God's wondrous deliverance.

8 Rouse your anger and pour out your
    wrath;
9 destroy the adversary and wipe out
    the enemy.
10 Hasten the day, and remember the
    appointed time, *a*
    and let people recount your mighty
    deeds.
11 Let survivors be consumed in the fiery
    wrath,
    and may those who harm your people
    meet destruction.
12 Crush the heads of hostile rulers
    who say, "There is no one but
    ourselves."
13 Gather all the tribes of Jacob, *b*
16 and give them their inheritance, as at
    the beginning.
17 Have mercy, O Lord, on the people
    called by your name,
    on Israel, whom you have named *c*
    your firstborn,
18 Have pity on the city of your sanctuary, *d*
    Jerusalem, the place of your
    dwelling. *e*
19 Fill Zion with your majesty, *f*
    and your temple *g* with your glory.
20 Bear witness to those whom you created
    in the beginning,
    and fulfill the prophecies spoken in
    your name.
21 Reward those who wait for you
    and let your prophets be found
    trustworthy.
22 Hear, O Lord, the prayer of your
    servants, according to your
    goodwill toward *h* your people,
    and all who are on the earth will know
    that you are the Lord, the God of the
    ages.

Concerning Discrimination

23 The stomach will take any food,
    yet one food is better than another.
24 As the palate tastes the kinds of game,
    so an intelligent mind detects false
    words.
25 A perverse mind will cause grief,
    but a person with experience will pay
    him back.

26 A woman will accept any man as a
    husband,
    but one girl is preferable to another.
27 A woman's beauty lights up a man's
    face,
    and there is nothing he desires more.
28 If kindness and humility mark her
    speech,
    her husband is more fortunate than
    other men.
29 He who acquires a wife gets his best
    possession, *i*
    a helper fit for him and a pillar of
    support. *j*
30 Where there is no fence, the property
    will be plundered;
    and where there is no wife, a man will
    become a fugitive and a
    wanderer. *k*
31 For who will trust a nimble robber
    that skips from city to city?
    So who will trust a man that has no
    nest,
    but lodges wherever night overtakes
    him?

False Friends

37 Every friend says, "I too am a friend";
    but some friends are friends only in
    name.
2 Is it not a sorrow like that for death
    itself
    when a dear friend turns into an
    enemy?
3 O inclination to evil, why were you
    formed
    to cover the land with deceit?
4 Some companions rejoice in the
    happiness of a friend,

a Other ancient authorities read *remember your
oath*   *b* Owing to a dislocation in the Greek Mss
of Sirach, the verse numbers 14 and 15 are not used
in chapter 36, though no text is missing.
c Other ancient authorities read *you have likened to*
d Or *on your holy city*   *e* Heb: Gk *your rest*
f Heb Syr: Gk *the celebration of your wondrous deeds*
g Heb Syr: Gk Lat *people*   *h* Heb and two Gk
witnesses: Lat and most Gk witnesses read *according
to the blessing of Aaron for*   *i* Heb: Gk *enters upon a
possession*   *j* Heb: Gk *rest*   *k* Heb: Gk *wander
about and sigh*

but in time of trouble they are against
    him.

5 Some companions help a friend for
    their stomachs' sake,
    yet in battle they will carry his shield.

6 Do not forget a friend during the
    battle,[a]
and do not be unmindful of him
    when you distribute your spoils.[b]

Caution in Taking Advice

7 All counselors praise the counsel they
    give,
    but some give counsel in their own
    interest.

8 Be wary of a counselor,
    and learn first what is his interest,
    for he will take thought for himself.
He may cast the lot against you

9   and tell you, "Your way is good,"
    and then stand aside to see what
    happens to you.

10 Do not consult the one who regards you
    with suspicion;
    hide your intentions from those who
    are jealous of you.

11 Do not consult with a woman about her
    rival
    or with a coward about war,
with a merchant about business
    or with a buyer about selling,
with a miser about generosity[c]
    or with the merciless about
    kindness,
with an idler about any work
    or with a seasonal laborer about
    completing his work,
with a lazy servant about a big task—
    pay no attention to any advice they
    give.

12 But associate with a godly person
    whom you know to be a keeper of the
    commandments,
who is like-minded with yourself,
    and who will grieve with you if you
    fail.

13 And heed[d] the counsel of your own
    heart,
    for no one is more faithful to you
    than it is.

14 For our own mind sometimes keeps us
    better informed
    than seven sentinels sitting high on a
    watchtower.

15 But above all pray to the Most High
    that he may direct your way in truth.

True and False Wisdom

16 Discussion is the beginning of every
    work,
    and counsel precedes every
    undertaking.

17 The mind is the root of all conduct;

18   it sprouts four branches,[e]
good and evil, life and death;
    and it is the tongue that continually
    rules them.

19 Some people may be clever enough to
    teach many,
    and yet be useless to themselves.

20 A skillful speaker may be hated;
    he will be destitute of all food,

21 for the Lord has withheld the gift of
    charm,
    since he is lacking in all wisdom.

22 If a person is wise to his own advantage,
    the fruits of his good sense will be
    praiseworthy.[f]

23 A wise person instructs his own people,
    and the fruits of his good sense will
    endure.

24 A wise person will have praise heaped
    upon him,
    and all who see him will call him
    happy.

25 The days of a person's life are
    numbered,

a Heb: Gk *in your heart*   *b* Heb: Gk *him in your
wealth*   *c* Heb: Gk *gratitude*   *d* Heb: Gk
establish   *e* Heb: Gk *As a clue to changes of heart
four kinds of destiny appear*   *f* Other ancient
witnesses read *trustworthy*

37:7–15 *learn first what is his interest.* Choosing an adviser requires careful thinking to sort
out vested interests, but sometimes the choice
is obvious, like not asking a woman about her
rival or a coward about war. Better still, Ben Sira
says, is relying on one's own judgment.

but the days of Israel are without
     number.
26 One who is wise among his people will
     inherit honor,[a]
     and his name will live forever.

Concerning Moderation

27 My child, test yourself while you live;
     see what is bad for you and do not
       give in to it.
28 For not everything is good for everyone,
     and no one enjoys everything.
29 Do not be greedy for every delicacy,
     and do not eat without restraint;
30 for overeating brings sickness,
     and gluttony leads to nausea.
31 Many have died of gluttony,
     but the one who guards against it
       prolongs his life.

Concerning Physicians and Health

38 Honor physicians for their services,
     for the Lord created them;
 2 for their gift of healing comes from the
     Most High,
     and they are rewarded by the king.
 3 The skill of physicians makes them
     distinguished,
     and in the presence of the great they
       are admired.
 4 The Lord created medicines out of the
     earth,
     and the sensible will not despise
       them.
 5 Was not water made sweet with a tree
     in order that its[b] power might be
       known?
 6 And he gave skill to human beings
     that he[c] might be glorified in his
       marvelous works.

 7 By them the physician[d] heals and takes
     away pain;
 8   the pharmacist makes a mixture from
       them.
   God's[e] works will never be finished;
     and from him health[f] spreads over all
       the earth.

 9 My child, when you are ill, do not delay,
     but pray to the Lord, and he will heal
       you.
10 Give up your faults and direct your
     hands rightly,
     and cleanse your heart from all sin.
11 Offer a sweet-smelling sacrifice, and a
       memorial portion of choice flour,
     and pour oil on your offering, as
       much as you can afford.[g]
12 Then give the physician his place, for
       the Lord created him;
     do not let him leave you, for you need
       him.
13 There may come a time when recovery
       lies in the hands of physicians,[h]
14   for they too pray to the Lord
     that he grant them success in diagnosis[i]
       and in healing, for the sake of
         preserving life.
15 He who sins against his Maker,
     will be defiant toward the physician.[j]

On Mourning for the Dead

16 My child, let your tears fall for the dead,
     and as one in great pain begin the
       lament.

a Other ancient authorities read *confidence*
b Or *his*   c Or *they*   d Heb: Gk *he*   e Gk *His*
f Or *peace*   g Heb: Lat lacks *as much as you can
afford*; Meaning of Gk uncertain   h Gk *in their
hands*   i Heb: Gk *rest*   j Heb: Gk *may he fall
into the hands of the physician*

38:1–15 *their gift of healing comes from the
Most High.* Because sickness was thought to
be the result of sin, physicians appeared to
interfere with divine punishment. Ben Sira
defends the healing profession, arguing that
God made herbs and medicinal roots and that
doctors can pray for guidance in their work.
Medicine was in its infancy at the time of
Sirach.

Responding
38:9–14 PRAYER. Take time today to
pray for all those you know who are sick
in your family, church, and community. Then
pray for all those who are in the health-care
profession, that their hands may have the ability
to heal and their hearts the humility to recognize that their success comes from the Lord.
See also Spiritual Disciplines Index.

Lay out the body with due ceremony,
and do not neglect the burial.

17 Let your weeping be bitter and your
wailing fervent;
make your mourning worthy of the
departed,
for one day, or two, to avoid criticism;
then be comforted for your grief.

18 For grief may result in death,
and a sorrowful heart saps one's
strength.

19 When a person is taken away, sorrow is
over;
but the life of the poor weighs down
the heart.

20 Do not give your heart to grief;
drive it away, and remember your
own end.

21 Do not forget, there is no coming back;
you do the dead a no good, and you
injure yourself.

22 Remember his b fate, for yours is like it;
yesterday it was his, c and today it is
yours.

23 When the dead is at rest, let his
remembrance rest too,
and be comforted for him when his
spirit has departed.

Trades and Crafts

24 The wisdom of the scribe depends on
the opportunity of leisure;
only the one who has little business
can become wise.

25 How can one become wise who handles
the plow,
and who glories in the shaft of a
goad,
who drives oxen and is occupied with
their work,
and whose talk is about bulls?

26 He sets his heart on plowing furrows,
and he is careful about fodder for the
heifers.

27 So it is with every artisan and master
artisan
who labors by night as well as by day;
those who cut the signets of seals,
each is diligent in making a great
variety;
they set their heart on painting a lifelike
image,
and they are careful to finish their
work.

28 So it is with the smith, sitting by the
anvil,
intent on his iron-work;
the breath of the fire melts his flesh,
and he struggles with the heat of the
furnace;
the sound of the hammer deafens his
ears, d
and his eyes are on the pattern of the
object.
He sets his heart on finishing his
handiwork,
and he is careful to complete its
decoration.

29 So it is with the potter sitting at his
work
and turning the wheel with his feet;
he is always deeply concerned over his
products,
and he produces them in quantity.

30 He molds the clay with his arm
and makes it pliable with his feet;
he sets his heart to finish the glazing,
and he takes care in firing e the kiln.

31 All these rely on their hands,
and all are skillful in their own work.

a Gk *him* b Heb: Gk *my* c Heb: Gk *mine*
d Cn: Gk *renews his ear* e Cn: Gk *cleaning*

38:22–23 *When the dead is at rest, let his remembrance rest too.* This epitaph, like so many in ancient Egypt and Greece, has gallows humor. Grieve, Ben Sira suggests, but briefly and get on with life. This way one avoids falling into a state of depression after a serious loss, while nonetheless showing proper respect to the deceased.
38:24–39:11 *The wisdom of the scribe.* Like the Egyptian *Instructions of Duauf,* Sirach contrasts the scribes with other types of laborers—farmers, craftsmen, smiths, potters. Ben Sira does not disparage their contribution to society, but he thinks that scribes enjoy more prestige and power, even a lasting memorial. Some scribal texts lovingly refer to the implements of the trade, such as the reed pen, in erotic language.

32 Without them no city can be inhabited,
　　and wherever they live, they will not
　　　go hungry. *a*
　　Yet they are not sought out for the
　　　council of the people, *b*
33 　　nor do they attain eminence in the
　　　public assembly.
　　They do not sit in the judge's seat,
　　　nor do they understand the decisions
　　　　of the courts;
　　they cannot expound discipline or
　　　judgment,
　　and they are not found among the
　　　rulers. *c*
34 But they maintain the fabric of the
　　　world,
　　and their concern is for *d* the exercise
　　　of their trade.

The Activity of the Scribe

　　How different the one who devotes
　　　himself
　　　to the study of the law of the Most
　　　　High!

39 　He seeks out the wisdom of all the
　　　ancients,
　　and is concerned with prophecies;
2 　he preserves the sayings of the famous
　　and penetrates the subtleties of
　　　parables;
3 　he seeks out the hidden meanings of
　　　proverbs
　　and is at home with the obscurities of
　　　parables.
4 　He serves among the great
　　and appears before rulers;
　　he travels in foreign lands

and learns what is good and evil in
　　the human lot.
5 　He sets his heart to rise early
　　to seek the Lord who made him,
　　and to petition the Most High;
　　he opens his mouth in prayer
　　and asks pardon for his sins.

6 　If the great Lord is willing,
　　he will be filled with the spirit of
　　　understanding;
　　he will pour forth words of wisdom of
　　　his own
　　and give thanks to the Lord in prayer.
7 　The Lord *e* will direct his counsel and
　　　knowledge,
　　as he meditates on his mysteries.
8 　He will show the wisdom of what he
　　　has learned,
　　and will glory in the law of the Lord's
　　　covenant.
9 　Many will praise his understanding;
　　it will never be blotted out.
　　His memory will not disappear,
　　and his name will live through all
　　　generations.
10 Nations will speak of his wisdom,
　　and the congregation will proclaim
　　　his praise.
11 If he lives long, he will leave a name
　　　greater than a thousand,
　　and if he goes to rest, it is enough *f* for
　　　him.

a Syr: Gk *and people can neither live nor walk there*
b Most ancient authorities lack this line
c Cn: Gk *among parables*   *d* Syr: Gk *prayer is in*
e Gk *He himself*   *f* Cn: Meaning of Gk uncertain

38:34 STUDY—*See* Spiritual Disciplines Index.

Responding
39:5–6 PRAYER. Time and again early morning prayer is lauded in wisdom literature. If morning is not your normal prayer time, challenge yourself to rise a half hour earlier and spend the time in prayer. If you have trouble staying awake in early morning prayer, then try a walking meditation. *See also* Spiritual Disciplines Index.

Responding
39:7 MEDITATION. If you have not tried it before, give yourself the opportunity to experience God's direction through contemplative prayer. Sit in silence and try to empty your mind of all extraneous thoughts and fill it with the presence of God. If you find yourself losing your focus or being distracted by background noise, repeat a word or phrase, such as "Abba," "Jesus," or "Fill me," over and over. Start by praying for ten minutes and gradually increase your prayer time. *See also* Spiritual Disciplines Index.

A Hymn of Praise to God

12 I have more on my mind to express;
   I am full like the full moon.
13 Listen to me, my faithful children, and
      blossom
   like a rose growing by a stream of
      water.
14 Send out fragrance like incense,
   and put forth blossoms like a lily.
   Scatter the fragrance, and sing a hymn
      of praise;
   bless the Lord for all his works.
15 Ascribe majesty to his name
   and give thanks to him with praise,
   with songs on your lips, and with harps;
   this is what you shall say in
      thanksgiving:

16 "All the works of the Lord are very
      good,
   and whatever he commands will be
      done at the appointed time.
17 No one can say, 'What is this?' or 'Why
      is that?'—
   for at the appointed time all such
      questions will be answered.
   At his word the waters stood in a heap,
   and the reservoirs of water at the
      word of his mouth.
18 When he commands, his every purpose
      is fulfilled,
   and none can limit his saving power.
19 The works of all are before him,
   and nothing can be hidden from his
      eyes.
20 From the beginning to the end of time
      he can see everything,
   and nothing is too marvelous for
      him.
21 No one can say, 'What is this?' or 'Why
      is that?'—
   for everything has been created for its
      own purpose.

22 "His blessing covers the dry land like a
      river,
   and drenches it like a flood.
23 But his wrath drives out the nations,
   as when he turned a watered land
      into salt.
24 To the faithful his ways are straight,
   but full of pitfalls for the wicked.
25 From the beginning good things were
      created for the good,
   but for sinners good things and bad. a
26 The basic necessities of human life
   are water and fire and iron and salt
   and wheat flour and milk and honey,
   the blood of the grape and oil and
      clothing.
27 All these are good for the godly,
   but for sinners they turn into evils.

28 "There are winds created for vengeance,
   and in their anger they can dislodge
      mountains; b
   on the day of reckoning they will pour
      out their strength
   and calm the anger of their Maker.
29 Fire and hail and famine and pestilence,
   all these have been created for
      vengeance;
30 the fangs of wild animals and scorpions
      and vipers,
   and the sword that punishes the
      ungodly with destruction.
31 They take delight in doing his bidding,
   always ready for his service on earth;
   and when their time comes they
      never disobey his command."

32 So from the beginning I have been
      convinced of all this

a Heb Lat: Gk *sinners bad things*   b Heb Syr: Gk
can scourge mightily

39:12–35 *I have more on my mind to express.*
Another autobiographical intrusion paves the
way for hymnic praise, which follows. The concern here is to affirm the appropriateness of the
created order, which includes good things for
devout people and punishments for the wicked.
Ben Sira singles out some of these vengeful
agents: winds, fire, hail, famine, pestilence, wild
beasts, scorpions, vipers, and swords (vv 28–30).
Only the last of these is wielded by humans.
Divine and human punishment act in a syn-
ergistic relationship, he thinks. There is danger
here, especially when humans forget their minor
role in the scheme of things.

and have thought it out and left it in
   writing:

33 All the works of the Lord are good,
   and he will supply every need in its
      time.

34 No one can say, "This is not as good as
      that,"
   for everything proves good in its
      appointed time.

35 So now sing praise with all your heart
      and voice,
   and bless the name of the Lord.

Human Wretchedness

40 Hard work was created for everyone,
   and a heavy yoke is laid on the
      children of Adam,
from the day they come forth from
   their mother's womb
until the day they return to[a] the
   mother of all the living.[b]

2 Perplexities and fear of heart are theirs,
   and anxious thought of the day of
      their death.

3 From the one who sits on a splendid
      throne
   to the one who grovels in dust and
      ashes,

4 from the one who wears purple and a
      crown
   to the one who is clothed in burlap,

5 there is anger and envy and trouble and
      unrest,
   and fear of death, and fury and strife.
And when one rests upon his bed,
   his sleep at night confuses his mind.

6 He gets little or no rest;
   he struggles in his sleep as he did by
      day.[c]
He is troubled by the visions of his
      mind
   like one who has escaped from the
      battlefield.

7 At the moment he reaches safety he
      wakes up,
   astonished that his fears were
      groundless.

8 To all creatures, human and animal,
   but to sinners seven times more,

9 come death and bloodshed and strife
      and sword,
   calamities and famine and ruin and
      plague.

10 All these were created for the wicked,
   and on their account the flood came.

11 All that is of earth returns to earth,
   and what is from above returns
      above.[d]

Injustice Will Not Prosper

12 All bribery and injustice will be blotted
      out,
   but good faith will last forever.

13 The wealth of the unjust will dry up like
      a river,
   and crash like a loud clap of thunder
      in a storm.

14 As a generous person has cause to
      rejoice,
   so lawbreakers will utterly fail.

15 The children of the ungodly put out few
      branches;
   they are unhealthy roots on sheer
      rock.

16 The reeds by any water or river bank
   are plucked up before any grass;

17 but kindness is like a garden of
      blessings,
   and almsgiving endures forever.

The Joys of Life

18 Wealth and wages make life sweet,[e]
   but better than either is finding a
      treasure.

19 Children and the building of a city
      establish one's name,
   but better than either is the one who
      finds wisdom.

a Other Gk and Lat authorities read *are buried in*
b Heb: Gk *of all*   *c* Arm: Meaning of Gk
uncertain   *d* Heb Syr: Gk Lat *from the waters
returns to the sea*   *e* Heb: Gk *Life is sweet for the
self-reliant worker*

40:1–11 *Hard work was created for everyone.*
This section describes the oppressive nature of
human existence and concludes that psychic

distress afflicts sinners much more heavily than
decent people.

Cattle and orchards make one
   prosperous; *a*
but a blameless wife is accounted
   better than either.
20 Wine and music gladden the heart,
   but the love of friends *b* is better than
   either.
21 The flute and the harp make sweet
   melody,
but a pleasant voice is better than
   either.
22 The eye desires grace and beauty,
but the green shoots of grain more
   than either.
23 A friend or companion is always
   welcome,
but a sensible wife *c* is better than
   either.
24 Kindred and helpers are for a time of
   trouble,
but almsgiving rescues better than
   either.
25 Gold and silver make one stand firm,
but good counsel is esteemed more
   than either.
26 Riches and strength build up
   confidence,
but the fear of the Lord is better than
   either.
There is no want in the fear of the Lord,
and with it there is no need to seek for
   help.
27 The fear of the Lord is like a garden of
   blessing,
and covers a person better than any
   glory.

The Disgrace of Begging

28 My child, do not lead the life of a
   beggar;
it is better to die than to beg.
29 When one looks to the table of another,
one's way of life cannot be considered
   a life.
One loses self-respect with another
   person's food,

but one who is intelligent and well
   instructed guards against that.
30 In the mouth of the shameless begging
   is sweet,
but it kindles a fire inside him.

Concerning Death

41 O death, how bitter is the thought
   of you
to the one at peace among
   possessions,
who has nothing to worry about and is
   prosperous in everything,
and still is vigorous enough to enjoy
   food!
2 O death, how welcome is your sentence
to one who is needy and failing in
   strength,
worn down by age and anxious about
   everything;
to one who is contrary, and has lost
   all patience!
3 Do not fear death's decree for you;
remember those who went before you
   and those who will come after.
4 This is the Lord's decree for all flesh;
why then should you reject the will of
   the Most High?
Whether life lasts for ten years or a
   hundred or a thousand,
there are no questions asked in Hades.

The Fate of the Wicked

5 The children of sinners are abominable
   children,
and they frequent the haunts of the
   ungodly.
6 The inheritance of the children of
   sinners will perish,
and on their offspring will be a
   perpetual disgrace.
7 Children will blame an ungodly father,

a Heb Syr: Gk lacks *but better . . . prosperous*
b Heb: Gk *wisdom*   *c* Heb Compare Syr: Gk *wife
with her husband*

41:1–4 *O death, how bitter . . . how welcome!*
One's opinion of death varies depending on
circumstances. Death is welcome to people who
have lost the capacity to enjoy life, but odious to
those in full vigor.

for they suffer disgrace because of
   him.
8 Woe to you, the ungodly,
   who have forsaken the law of the
      Most High God!
9 If you have children, calamity will be
      theirs;
   you will beget them only for
      groaning.
When you stumble, there is lasting joy;*a*
   and when you die, a curse is your lot.
10 Whatever comes from earth returns to
      earth;
   so the ungodly go from curse to
      destruction.

11 The human body is a fleeting thing,
   but a virtuous name will never be
      blotted out.*b*
12 Have regard for your name, since it will
      outlive you
   longer than a thousand hoards of
      gold.
13 The days of a good life are numbered,
   but a good name lasts forever.

14 My children, be true to your training
      and be at peace;
   hidden wisdom and unseen treasure—
      of what value is either?

A Series of Contrasts

15 Better are those who hide their folly
      than those who hide their wisdom.
16 Therefore show respect for my words;
   for it is not good to feel shame in every
      circumstance,
   nor is every kind of abashment to be
      approved.*c*

17 Be ashamed of sexual immorality,
      before your father or mother;
   and of a lie, before a prince or a ruler;
18 of a crime, before a judge or magistrate;
   and of a breach of the law, before the
      congregation and the people;

of unjust dealing, before your partner or
      your friend;
19 and of theft, in the place where you
      live.
Be ashamed of breaking an oath or
      agreement,*d*
   and of leaning on your elbow at
      meals;
of surliness in receiving or giving,
20 and of silence, before those who greet
      you;
of looking at a prostitute,
21 and of rejecting the appeal of a
      relative;
of taking away someone's portion or
      gift,
   and of gazing at another man's wife;
22 of meddling with his servant-girl—
   and do not approach her bed;
of abusive words, before friends—
   and do not be insulting after making
      a gift.

42 Be ashamed of repeating what you
      hear,
   and of betraying secrets.
Then you will show proper shame,
   and will find favor with everyone.

Of the following things do not be
      ashamed,
   and do not sin to save face:
2 Do not be ashamed of the law of the
      Most High and his covenant,
   and of rendering judgment to acquit
      the ungodly;
3 of keeping accounts with a partner or
      with traveling companions,
   and of dividing the inheritance of
      friends;
4 of accuracy with scales and weights,
   and of acquiring much or little;
5 of profit from dealing with merchants,

a Heb: Meaning of Gk uncertain   *b* Heb: Gk
*People grieve over the death of the body, but the bad
name of sinners will be blotted out*   *c* Heb: Gk *and
not everything is confidently esteemed by everyone*
d Heb: Gk *before the truth of God and the covenant*

41:17—42:8 *Be ashamed of . . . Do not be
ashamed of.* Some acts bring disgrace, while
others bestow honor. Ben Sira names specific

occasions for proper shame and mentions actions
that one should avoid lest shame ensue.

and of frequent disciplining of
   children,
   and of drawing blood from the back
   of a wicked slave.
6 Where there is an untrustworthy wife, a
   seal is a good thing;
   and where there are many hands, lock
   things up.
7 When you make a deposit, be sure it is
   counted and weighed,
   and when you give or receive, put it
   all in writing.
8 Do not be ashamed to correct the stupid
   or foolish
   or the aged who are guilty of sexual
   immorality.
   Then you will show your sound
   training,
   and will be approved by all.

Daughters and Fathers
9 A daughter is a secret anxiety to her
   father,
   and worry over her robs him of sleep;
   when she is young, for fear she may not
   marry,
   or if married, for fear she may be
   disliked;
10 while a virgin, for fear she may be
   seduced
   and become pregnant in her father's
   house;
   or having a husband, for fear she may
   go astray,
   or, though married, for fear she may
   be barren.
11 Keep strict watch over a headstrong
   daughter,
   or she may make you a laughingstock
   to your enemies,

a byword in the city and the assembly
   of [a] the people,
   and put you to shame in public
   gatherings. [b]
See that there is no lattice in her room,
   no spot that overlooks the
   approaches to the house. [c]
12 Do not let her parade her beauty before
   any man,
   or spend her time among married
   women; [a]
13 for from garments comes the moth,
   and from a woman comes woman's
   wickedness.
14 Better is the wickedness of a man than a
   woman who does good;
   it is woman who brings shame and
   disgrace.

The Works of God in Nature
15 I will now call to mind the works of the
   Lord,
   and will declare what I have seen.
   By the word of the Lord his works are
   made;
   and all his creatures do his will. [d]
16 The sun looks down on everything with
   its light,
   and the work of the Lord is full of his
   glory.
17 The Lord has not empowered even his
   holy ones
   to recount all his marvelous works,
   which the Lord the Almighty has
   established
   so that the universe may stand firm in
   his glory.

a Heb: Meaning of Gk uncertain   b Heb: Gk to
shame before the great multitude   c Heb: Gk lacks
See . . . house   d Syr Compare Heb: most Gk
witnesses lack and all . . . will

42:9–14 *A daughter is a secret anxiety to her
father.* In Israelite society fathers were responsible for arranging a daughter's marriage, which
entailed considerable energy and expense. Because her virginity was deemed highly important, parents went to great lengths to protect it.
No reasonable person today subscribes to the
view expressed in verse 14.

42:15–43:33 *I will now call to mind the works
of the Lord.* Ben Sira sings the Creator's praises.
Everything is perfectly made, with opposites
balancing one another. Sun and moon, stars,
lightning, clouds, hail, rain, and snow—all these
and more manifest God's wisdom. Yet God is
greater than the sum of all his works, and no
account of his works can succeed in telling the
whole story.

18 He searches out the abyss and the
human heart;
he understands their innermost
secrets.
For the Most High knows all that may
be known;
he sees from of old the things that are
to come. *a*
19 He discloses what has been and what is
to be,
and he reveals the traces of hidden
things.
20 No thought escapes him,
and nothing is hidden from him.
21 He has set in order the splendors of his
wisdom;
he is from all eternity one and the
same.
Nothing can be added or taken away,
and he needs no one to be his
counselor.
22 How desirable are all his works,
and how sparkling they are to see! *b*
23 All these things live and remain forever;
each creature is preserved to meet a
particular need. *c*
24 All things come in pairs, one opposite
the other,
and he has made nothing
incomplete.
25 Each supplements the virtues of the
other.
Who could ever tire of seeing his
glory?

The Splendor of the Sun

43 The pride of the higher realms is
the clear vault of the sky,
as glorious to behold as the sight of
the heavens.
2 The sun, when it appears, proclaims as
it rises
what a marvelous instrument it is, the
work of the Most High.
3 At noon it parches the land,
and who can withstand its burning
heat?

4 A man tending *d* a furnace works in
burning heat,
but three times as hot is the sun
scorching the mountains;
it breathes out fiery vapors,
and its bright rays blind the eyes.
5 Great is the Lord who made it;
at his orders it hurries on its course.

The Splendor of the Moon

6 It is the moon that marks the changing
seasons, *e*
governing the times, their everlasting
sign.
7 From the moon comes the sign for
festal days,
a light that wanes when it completes
its course.
8 The new moon, as its name suggests,
renews itself; *f*
how marvelous it is in this change,
a beacon to the hosts on high,
shining in the vault of the heavens!

The Glory of the Stars and the Rainbow

9 The glory of the stars is the beauty of
heaven,
a glittering array in the heights of the
Lord.
10 On the orders of the Holy One they
stand in their appointed places;
they never relax in their watches.
11 Look at the rainbow, and praise him
who made it;
it is exceedingly beautiful in its
brightness.
12 It encircles the sky with its glorious arc;
the hands of the Most High have
stretched it out.

The Marvels of Nature

13 By his command he sends the driving
snow

a Heb: Gk *he sees the sign(s) of the age*   *b* Meaning
of Gk uncertain   *c* Heb: Gk *forever for every need,
and all are obedient*   *d* Other ancient authorities
read *blowing upon*   *e* Heb: Meaning of Gk
uncertain   *f* Heb: Gk *The month is named after the
moon*

42:18 SECRECY—*See* Spiritual Disciplines Index.

and speeds the lightnings of his
    judgment.
14 Therefore the storehouses are opened,
    and the clouds fly out like birds.
15 In his majesty he gives the clouds their
    strength,
    and the hailstones are broken in
    pieces.
17a   The voice of his thunder rebukes
    the earth;
16 when he appears, the mountains
    shake.
  At his will the south wind blows;
17b so do the storm from the north and
    the whirlwind.
  He scatters the snow like birds flying
    down,
    and its descent is like locusts alighting.
18 The eye is dazzled by the beauty of its
    whiteness,
    and the mind is amazed as it falls.
19 He pours frost over the earth like salt,
    and icicles form like pointed thorns.
20 The cold north wind blows,
    and ice freezes on the water;
  it settles on every pool of water,
    and the water puts it on like a
    breastplate.
21 He consumes the mountains and burns
    up the wilderness,
    and withers the tender grass like fire.
22 A mist quickly heals all things;
    the falling dew gives refreshment
    from the heat.

23 By his plan he stilled the deep
    and planted islands in it.
24 Those who sail the sea tell of its
    dangers,
    and we marvel at what we hear.
25 In it are strange and marvelous
    creatures,

all kinds of living things, and huge
    sea-monsters.
26 Because of him each of his messengers
    succeeds,
    and by his word all things hold
    together.

27 We could say more but could never say
    enough;
    let the final word be: "He is the all."
28 Where can we find the strength to
    praise him?
    For he is greater than all his works.
29 Awesome is the Lord and very great,
    and marvelous is his power.
30 Glorify the Lord and exalt him as much
    as you can,
    for he surpasses even that.
  When you exalt him, summon all your
    strength,
    and do not grow weary, for you
    cannot praise him enough.
31 Who has seen him and can describe him?
    Or who can extol him as he is?
32 Many things greater than these lie
    hidden,
    for I[a] have seen but few of his works.
33 For the Lord has made all things,
    and to the godly he has given
    wisdom.

HYMN IN HONOR OF OUR ANCESTORS[b]

44 Let us now sing the praises of
    famous men,
    our ancestors in their generations.
2 The Lord apportioned to them[c] great
    glory,
    his majesty from the beginning.

a Heb: Gk we   b This title is included in the Gk
text.   c Heb: Gk created

44:1–50:21 *Let us now sing the praises of famous men.* This section of the book integrates biblical tradition with wisdom literature, an innovation. The praise of ancient worthies begins with Enoch and concludes with the high priest Simon, a contemporary of Ben Sira. A glaring omission in this national portrait gallery, at least from modern perspectives, are feminine faces.

The heroes are not always the obvious choices, and pride of place goes to priestly representatives. Moreover, the things for which individuals are praised sometimes strike modern readers as strange. Prophets, for example, are not remembered for championing social justice or for specific oracles. The failure to mention the restoration figure Ezra has generated much

3 There were those who ruled in their
  kingdoms,
  and made a name for themselves by
    their valor;
  those who gave counsel because they
    were intelligent;
  those who spoke in prophetic oracles;
4 those who led the people by their
    counsels
  and by their knowledge of the
    people's lore;
  they were wise in their words of
    instruction;
5 those who composed musical tunes,
  or put verses in writing;
6 rich men endowed with resources,
  living peacefully in their homes—
7 all these were honored in their
    generations,
  and were the pride of their times.
8 Some of them have left behind a name,
  so that others declare their praise.
9 But of others there is no memory;
  they have perished as though they
    had never existed;
  they have become as though they had
    never been born,
  they and their children after them.
10 But these also were godly men,
  whose righteous deeds have not been
    forgotten;
11 their wealth will remain with their
    descendants,
  and their inheritance with their
    children's children. a
12 Their descendants stand by the
    covenants;
  their children also, for their sake.
13 Their offspring will continue forever,
  and their glory will never be blotted
    out.
14 Their bodies are buried in peace,
  but their name lives on generation
    after generation.

15 The assembly declares b their wisdom,
  and the congregation proclaims their
    praise.

Enoch

16 Enoch pleased the Lord and was taken
    up,
  an example of repentance to all
    generations.

Noah

17 Noah was found perfect and righteous;
  in the time of wrath he kept the race
    alive; c
  therefore a remnant was left on the
    earth
  when the flood came.
18 Everlasting covenants were made with
    him
  that all flesh should never again be
    blotted out by a flood.

Abraham

19 Abraham was the great father of a
    multitude of nations,
  and no one has been found like him
    in glory.
20 He kept the law of the Most High,
  and entered into a covenant with
    him;
  he certified the covenant in his flesh,
  and when he was tested he proved
    faithful.
21 Therefore the Lord d assured him with
    an oath
  that the nations would be blessed
    through his offspring;
  that he would make him as numerous
    as the dust of the earth,
  and exalt his offspring like the stars,

a Heb Compare Lat Syr: Meaning of Gk uncertain
b Heb: Gk *Peoples declare*   c Heb: Gk *was taken in
exchange*   d Gk *he*

---

speculation among scholars. Curiously, Abraham
is said to have kept the Mosaic law before it had
been proclaimed. A surprising entry is Phinehas,
a priest who showed exceptional zeal in the
cause of pure worship. Speculation about Elijah's
return (cf. Mal 4:5–6) is alive and well, as it was

in Jesus' day. The mention of Enoch in 49:14
introduces a possible gloss that pushes the list
all the way back to Adam. Clearly, Ben Sira was
profoundly impressed with the high priest in full
sartorial splendor.

and give them an inheritance from sea
   to sea
and from the Euphrates[a] to the ends
   of the earth.

Isaac and Jacob

22 To Isaac also he gave the same assurance
   for the sake of his father Abraham.
The blessing of all people and the
   covenant
23   he made to rest on the head of Jacob;
he acknowledged him with his
   blessings,
and gave him his inheritance;
he divided his portions,
   and distributed them among twelve
   tribes.

Moses

From his descendants the Lord[b]
   brought forth a godly man,
who found favor in the sight of all

45 1 and was beloved by God and people,
      Moses, whose memory is blessed.
2 He made him equal in glory to the holy
      ones,
   and made him great, to the terror of
      his enemies.
3 By his words he performed swift
      miracles;[c]
   the Lord[b] glorified him in the
      presence of kings.
He gave him commandments for his
   people,
   and revealed to him his glory.
4 For his faithfulness and meekness he
      consecrated him,
   choosing him out of all humankind.
5 He allowed him to hear his voice,
      and led him into the dark cloud,
and gave him the commandments face
      to face,
   the law of life and knowledge,
so that he might teach Jacob the
      covenant,
   and Israel his decrees.

Aaron

6 He exalted Aaron, a holy man like
      Moses[d]

who was his brother, of the tribe of
   Levi.
7 He made an everlasting covenant with
      him,
   and gave him the priesthood of the
      people.
He blessed him with stateliness,
   and put a glorious robe on him.
8 He clothed him in perfect splendor,
   and strengthened him with the
      symbols of authority,
   the linen undergarments, the long
      robe, and the ephod.
9 And he encircled him with
      pomegranates,
   with many golden bells all around,
to send forth a sound as he walked,
   to make their ringing heard in the
      temple
   as a reminder to his people;
10 with the sacred vestment, of gold and
      violet
   and purple, the work of an
      embroiderer;
with the oracle of judgment, Urim and
      Thummim;
11   with twisted crimson, the work of an
         artisan;
with precious stones engraved like seals,
   in a setting of gold, the work of a
      jeweler,
to commemorate in engraved letters
   each of the tribes of Israel;
12 with a gold crown upon his turban,
      inscribed like a seal with "Holiness,"
a distinction to be prized, the work of
      an expert,
   a delight to the eyes, richly adorned.
13 Before him such beautiful things did
      not exist.
   No outsider ever put them on,
but only his sons
   and his descendants in perpetuity.
14 His sacrifices shall be wholly burned
      twice every day continually.
15 Moses ordained him,
   and anointed him with holy oil;
it was an everlasting covenant for him

---

a Syr: Heb Gk *River*   *b* Gk *he*   *c* Heb: Gk
caused signs to cease   *d* Gk *him*

and for his descendants as long as the
    heavens endure,
to minister to the Lord[a] and serve as
    priest
and bless his people in his name.
16 He chose him out of all the living
    to offer sacrifice to the Lord,
incense and a pleasing odor as a
    memorial portion,
    to make atonement for the[b] people.
17 In his commandments he gave him
    authority and statutes and[c]
    judgments,
to teach Jacob the testimonies,
    and to enlighten Israel with his law.
18 Outsiders conspired against him,
    and envied him in the wilderness,
Dathan and Abiram and their followers
    and the company of Korah, in wrath
    and anger.
19 The Lord saw it and was not pleased,
    and in the heat of his anger they were
    destroyed;
he performed wonders against them
    to consume them in flaming fire.
20 He added glory to Aaron
    and gave him a heritage;
he allotted to him the best of the first
    fruits,
    and prepared bread of first fruits in
    abundance;
21 for they eat the sacrifices of the Lord,
    which he gave to him and his
    descendants.
22 But in the land of the people he has no
    inheritance,
    and he has no portion among the
    people;
for the Lord[d] himself is his[e] portion
    and inheritance.

Phinehas

23 Phinehas son of Eleazar ranks third in
    glory
    for being zealous in the fear of the
    Lord,
and standing firm, when the people
    turned away,
    in the noble courage of his soul;
    and he made atonement for Israel.

24 Therefore a covenant of friendship was
    established with him,
    that he should be leader of the
    sanctuary and of his people,
that he and his descendants should
    have
    the dignity of the priesthood forever.
25 Just as a covenant was established with
    David
    son of Jesse of the tribe of Judah,
that the king's heritage passes only
    from son to son,
    so the heritage of Aaron is for his
    descendants alone.

26 And now bless the Lord
    who has crowned you with glory.[f]
May the Lord[d] grant you wisdom of
    mind
    to judge his people with justice,
so that their prosperity may not vanish,
    and that their glory may endure
    through all their generations.

Joshua and Caleb

46 Joshua son of Nun was mighty in
    war,
    and was the successor of Moses in the
    prophetic office.
He became, as his name implies,
    a great savior of God's[g] elect,
to take vengeance on the enemies that
    rose against them,
    so that he might give Israel its
    inheritance.
2 How glorious he was when he lifted his
    hands
    and brandished his sword against the
    cities!
3 Who before him ever stood so firm?
    For he waged the wars of the Lord.
4 Was it not through him that the sun
    stood still
    and one day became as long as two?
5 He called upon the Most High, the
    Mighty One,

a Gk him   b Other ancient authorities read his
or your   c Heb: Gk authority in covenants of
d Gk he   e Other ancient authorities read your
f Heb: Gk lacks And . . . glory   g Gk his

when enemies pressed him on every side,
and the great Lord answered him
with hailstones of mighty power.
6 He overwhelmed that nation in battle,
and on the slope he destroyed his opponents,
so that the nations might know his armament,
that he was fighting in the sight of the Lord;
for he was a devoted follower of the Mighty One.
7 And in the days of Moses he proved his loyalty,
he and Caleb son of Jephunneh:
they opposed the congregation,*a*
restrained the people from sin,
and stilled their wicked grumbling.
8 And these two alone were spared
out of six hundred thousand infantry,
to lead the people*b* into their inheritance,
the land flowing with milk and honey.
9 The Lord gave Caleb strength,
which remained with him in his old age,
so that he went up to the hill country,
and his children obtained it for an inheritance,
10 so that all the Israelites might see
how good it is to follow the Lord.

The Judges

11 The judges also, with their respective names,
whose hearts did not fall into idolatry
and who did not turn away from the Lord—
may their memory be blessed!
12 May their bones send forth new life
from where they lie,
and may the names of those who have been honored
live again in their children!

13 Samuel was beloved by his Lord;
a prophet of the Lord, he established the kingdom
and anointed rulers over his people.
14 By the law of the Lord he judged the congregation,
and the Lord watched over Jacob.
15 By his faithfulness he was proved to be a prophet,
and by his words he became known as a trustworthy seer.
16 He called upon the Lord, the Mighty One,
when his enemies pressed him on every side,
and he offered in sacrifice a suckling lamb.
17 Then the Lord thundered from heaven,
and made his voice heard with a mighty sound;
18 he subdued the leaders of the enemy*c*
and all the rulers of the Philistines.
19 Before the time of his eternal sleep,
Samuel*d* bore witness before the Lord and his anointed:
"No property, not so much as a pair of shoes,
have I taken from anyone!"
And no one accused him.
20 Even after he had fallen asleep, he prophesied
and made known to the king his death,
and lifted up his voice from the ground
in prophecy, to blot out the wickedness of the people.

Nathan

47 After him Nathan rose up to prophesy in the days of David.

David

2 As the fat is set apart from the offering of well-being,
so David was set apart from the Israelites.
3 He played with lions as though they were young goats,
and with bears as though they were lambs of the flock.
4 In his youth did he not kill a giant,
and take away the people's disgrace,

---

a Other ancient authorities read *the enemy*
b Gk *them*   c Heb: Gk *leaders of the people of Tyre*
d Gk *he*

when he whirled the stone in the sling
and struck down the boasting
Goliath?
5 For he called on the Lord, the Most
High,
and he gave strength to his right arm
to strike down a mighty warrior,
and to exalt the power *a* of his people.
6 So they glorified him for the tens of
thousands he conquered,
and praised him for the blessings
bestowed by the Lord,
when the glorious diadem was given
to him.
7 For he wiped out his enemies on every
side,
and annihilated his adversaries the
Philistines;
he crushed their power *a* to our own
day.
8 In all that he did he gave thanks
to the Holy One, the Most High,
proclaiming his glory;
he sang praise with all his heart,
and he loved his Maker.
9 He placed singers before the altar,
to make sweet melody with their
voices. *b*
10 He gave beauty to the festivals,
and arranged their times throughout
the year, *c*
while they praised God's *d* holy name,
and the sanctuary resounded from
early morning.
11 The Lord took away his sins,
and exalted his power *a* forever;
he gave him a covenant of kingship
and a glorious throne in Israel.

Solomon

12 After him a wise son rose up
who because of him lived in security: *e*
13 Solomon reigned in an age of peace,
because God made all his borders
tranquil,
so that he might build a house in his
name
and provide a sanctuary to stand
forever.
14 How wise you were when you were
young!

You overflowed like the Nile *f* with
understanding.
15 Your influence spread throughout the
earth,
and you filled it with proverbs having
deep meaning.
16 Your fame reached to far-off islands,
and you were loved for your peaceful
reign.
17 Your songs, proverbs, and parables,
and the answers you gave astounded
the nations.
18 In the name of the Lord God,
who is called the God of Israel,
you gathered gold like tin
and amassed silver like lead.
19 But you brought in women to lie at your
side,
and through your body you were
brought into subjection.
20 You stained your honor,
and defiled your family line,
so that you brought wrath upon your
children,
and they were grieved *g* at your folly,
21 because the sovereignty was divided
and a rebel kingdom arose out of
Ephraim.
22 But the Lord will never give up his
mercy,
or cause any of his works to perish;
he will never blot out the descendants
of his chosen one,
or destroy the family line of him who
loved him.
So he gave a remnant to Jacob,
and to David a root from his own
family.

Rehoboam and Jeroboam

23 Solomon rested with his ancestors,
and left behind him one of his sons,
broad in *h* folly and lacking in sense,
Rehoboam, whose policy drove the
people to revolt.

a Gk *horn*   *b* Other ancient authorities add *and
daily they sing his praises*   *c* Gk *to completion*
d Gk *his*   *e* Heb: Gk *in a broad place*   *f* Heb:
Gk *a river*   *g* Other ancient authorities read *I was
grieved*   *h* Heb (with a play on the name
Rehoboam) Syr: Gk *the people's*

Then Jeroboam son of Nebat led Israel
 into sin
and started Ephraim on its sinful
 ways.
24 Their sins increased more and more,
 until they were exiled from their
 land.
25 For they sought out every kind of
 wickedness,
 until vengeance came upon them.

Elijah

48
Then Elijah arose, a prophet like
 fire,
and his word burned like a torch.
2 He brought a famine upon them,
 and by his zeal he made them few in
 number.
3 By the word of the Lord he shut up the
 heavens,
 and also three times brought down
 fire.
4 How glorious you were, Elijah, in your
 wondrous deeds!
 Whose glory is equal to yours?
5 You raised a corpse from death
 and from Hades, by the word of the
 Most High.
6 You sent kings down to destruction,
 and famous men, from their sickbeds.
7 You heard rebuke at Sinai
 and judgments of vengeance at
 Horeb.
8 You anointed kings to inflict
 retribution,
 and prophets to succeed you. *a*
9 You were taken up by a whirlwind of
 fire,
 in a chariot with horses of fire.
10 At the appointed time, it is written, you
 are destined *b*
 to calm the wrath of God before it
 breaks out in fury,
 to turn the hearts of parents to their
 children,
 and to restore the tribes of Jacob.
11 Happy are those who saw you
 and were adorned *c* with your love!
 For we also shall surely live. *d*

Elisha

12 When Elijah was enveloped in the
 whirlwind,
 Elisha was filled with his spirit.
He performed twice as many signs,
 and marvels with every utterance of
 his mouth. *e*
Never in his lifetime did he tremble
 before any ruler,
 nor could anyone intimidate him at
 all.
13 Nothing was too hard for him,
 and when he was dead, his body
 prophesied.
14 In his life he did wonders,
 and in death his deeds were
 marvelous.

15 Despite all this the people did not
 repent,
 nor did they forsake their sins,
until they were carried off as plunder
 from their land,
 and were scattered over all the earth.
The people were left very few in
 number,
 but with a ruler from the house of
 David.
16 Some of them did what was right,
 but others sinned more and more.

Hezekiah

17 Hezekiah fortified his city,
 and brought water into its midst;
he tunneled the rock with iron tools,
 and built cisterns for the water.
18 In his days Sennacherib invaded the
 country;
 he sent his commander *f* and
 departed;
he shook his fist against Zion,
 and made great boasts in his
 arrogance.
19 Then their hearts were shaken and their
 hands trembled,

---

a Heb: Gk *him*   *b* Heb: Gk *are for reproofs*
c Other ancient authorities read *and have died*
d Text and meaning of Gk uncertain   *e* Heb: Gk
lacks *He performed . . . mouth*   *f* Other ancient
authorities add *from Lachish*

and they were in anguish, like women
in labor.
20 But they called upon the Lord who is
merciful,
spreading out their hands toward
him.
The Holy One quickly heard them from
heaven,
and delivered them through Isaiah.
21 The Lord *a* struck down the camp of the
Assyrians,
and his angel wiped them out.
22 For Hezekiah did what was pleasing to
the Lord,
and he kept firmly to the ways of his
ancestor David,
as he was commanded by the prophet
Isaiah,
who was great and trustworthy in his
visions.

Isaiah

23 In Isaiah's *b* days the sun went
backward,
and he prolonged the life of the king.
24 By his dauntless spirit he saw the future,
and comforted the mourners in Zion.
25 He revealed what was to occur to the
end of time,
and the hidden things before they
happened.

Josiah and Other Worthies

49 The name *c* of Josiah is like blended
incense
prepared by the skill of the perfumer;
his memory *d* is as sweet as honey to
every mouth,
and like music at a banquet of wine.
2 He did what was right by reforming the
people,
and removing the wicked
abominations.
3 He kept his heart fixed on the Lord;
in lawless times he made godliness
prevail.

4 Except for David and Hezekiah and
Josiah,
all of them were great sinners,

for they abandoned the law of the Most
High;
the kings of Judah came to an end.
5 They *e* gave their power to others,
and their glory to a foreign nation,
6 who set fire to the chosen city of the
sanctuary,
and made its streets desolate,
as Jeremiah had foretold. *f*
7 For they had mistreated him,
who even in the womb had been
consecrated a prophet,
to pluck up and ruin and destroy,
and likewise to build and to plant.

8 It was Ezekiel who saw the vision of
glory,
which God *g* showed him above the
chariot of the cherubim.
9 For God *g* also mentioned Job
who held fast to all the ways of
justice. *h*
10 May the bones of the Twelve Prophets
send forth new life from where they
lie,
for they comforted the people of Jacob
and delivered them with confident
hope.

11 How shall we magnify Zerubbabel?
He was like a signet ring on the right
hand,
12 and so was Jeshua son of Jozadak;
in their days they built the house
and raised a temple *i* holy to the Lord,
destined for everlasting glory.
13 The memory of Nehemiah also is
lasting;
he raised our fallen walls,
and set up gates and bars,
and rebuilt our ruined houses.

Retrospect

14 Few have *j* ever been created on earth
like Enoch,
for he was taken up from the earth.

a Gk He   b Gk his   c Heb: Gk memory
d Heb: Gk it   e Heb He   f Gk by the hand of
Jeremiah   g Gk he   h Heb Compare Syr:
Meaning of Gk uncertain   i Other ancient
authorities read *people*   j Heb Syr: Gk *No one has*

15 Nor was anyone ever born like Joseph; *a*
    even his bones were cared for.
16 Shem and Seth and Enosh were
    honored, *b*
    but above every other created living
    being was Adam.

Simon Son of Onias

50 The leader of his brothers and the
    pride of his people *c*
    was the high priest, Simon son of
    Onias,
    who in his life repaired the house,
    and in his time fortified the temple.
2 He laid the foundations for the high
    double walls,
    the high retaining walls for the
    temple enclosure.
3 In his days a water cistern was dug, *d*
    a reservoir like the sea in
    circumference.
4 He considered how to save his people
    from ruin,
    and fortified the city against siege.
5 How glorious he was, surrounded by
    the people,
    as he came out of the house of the
    curtain.
6 Like the morning star among the
    clouds,
    like the full moon at the festal
    season; *d*
7 like the sun shining on the temple of
    the Most High,
    like the rainbow gleaming in splendid
    clouds;
8 like roses in the days of first fruits,
    like lilies by a spring of water,
    like a green shoot on Lebanon on a
    summer day;
9 like fire and incense in the censer,
    like a vessel of hammered gold
    studded with all kinds of precious
    stones;
10 like an olive tree laden with fruit,
    and like a cypress towering in the
    clouds.
11 When he put on his glorious robe

and clothed himself in perfect
    splendor,
    when he went up to the holy altar,
    he made the court of the sanctuary
    glorious.
12 When he received the portions from
    the hands of the priests,
    as he stood by the hearth of the altar
    with a garland of brothers around him,
    he was like a young cedar on Lebanon
    surrounded by the trunks of palm
    trees.
13 All the sons of Aaron in their splendor
    held the Lord's offering in their
    hands
    before the whole congregation of
    Israel.
14 Finishing the service at the altars, *e*
    and arranging the offering to the
    Most High, the Almighty,
15 he held out his hand for the cup
    and poured a drink offering of the
    blood of the grape;
    he poured it out at the foot of the altar,
    a pleasing odor to the Most High, the
    king of all.
16 Then the sons of Aaron shouted;
    they blew their trumpets of
    hammered metal;
    they sounded a mighty fanfare
    as a reminder before the Most High.
17 Then all the people together quickly
    fell to the ground on their faces
    to worship their Lord,
    the Almighty, God Most High.
18 Then the singers praised him with their
    voices
    in sweet and full-toned melody. *f*
19 And the people of the Lord Most High
    offered

a Heb Syr: Gk adds *the leader of his brothers, the
support of the people*   *b* Heb: Gk *Shem and Seth
were honored by people*   *c* Heb Syr: Gk lacks this
line. Compare 49.15   *d* Heb: Meaning of Gk
uncertain   *e* Other ancient authorities read *altar*
f Other ancient authorities read *in sweet melody
throughout the house*

50:17 WORSHIP—*See* Spiritual Disciplines Index.

their prayers before the Merciful One,
until the order of worship of the Lord
  was ended,
  and they completed his ritual.
20 Then Simon[a] came down and raised his
  hands
  over the whole congregation of
  Israelites,
  to pronounce the blessing of the Lord
  with his lips,
  and to glory in his name;
21 and they bowed down in worship a
  second time,
  to receive the blessing from the Most
  High.

A Benediction

22 And now bless the God of all,
  who everywhere works great wonders,
  who fosters our growth from birth,
  and deals with us according to his
  mercy.
23 May he give us[b] gladness of heart,
  and may there be peace in our[c] days
  in Israel, as in the days of old.
24 May he entrust to us his mercy,
  and may he deliver us in our[d] days!

Epilogue

25 Two nations my soul detests,
  and the third is not even a people:
26 Those who live in Seir,[e] and the
  Philistines,
  and the foolish people that live in
  Shechem.

27 Instruction in understanding and
  knowledge
  I have written in this book,

Jesus son of Eleazar son of Sirach[f] of
  Jerusalem,
  whose mind poured forth wisdom.
28 Happy are those who concern
  themselves with these things,
  and those who lay them to heart will
  become wise.
29 For if they put them into practice, they
  will be equal to anything,
  for the fear[g] of the Lord is their path.

PRAYER OF JESUS SON OF SIRACH[h]

51 I give you thanks, O Lord and King,
  and praise you, O God my Savior.
I give thanks to your name,
2   for you have been my protector and
    helper
  and have delivered me from destruction
  and from the trap laid by a slanderous
    tongue,
  from lips that fabricate lies.
In the face of my adversaries
  you have been my helper 3and
    delivered me,
  in the greatness of your mercy and of
    your name,
  from grinding teeth about to devour
    me,
  from the hand of those seeking my
    life,
  from the many troubles I endured,
4   from choking fire on every side,

a Gk *he*   b Other ancient authorities read *you*
c Other ancient authorities read *your*   d Other
ancient authorities read *his*   e Heb Compare Lat:
Gk *on the mountain of Samaria*   f Heb: Meaning
of Gk uncertain   g Heb: Other ancient
authorities read *light*   h This title is included in
the Gk text.

50:21 WORSHIP—*See* Spiritual Disciplines
Index.
50:25–26 *Two nations my soul detests.* Nationalism was not a feature of wisdom literature
until Ben Sira. Hatred toward Edomites and
Samaritans was current; hostility toward ancient
Philistines remained only in memory, for these
people had long since disappeared.
50:27–29 *I have written in this book, Jesus
son of Eleazar son of Sirach of Jerusalem.* Here

Ben Sira identifies himself in a rare act of autho-
rial pride. Until now, biblical authors were content to remain anonymous, although books
were attributed to various people like Solomon
and Daniel in the late postexilic period.
51:1–12 *you have been my protector and
helper.* This thanksgiving hymn, like many
psalms of that genre, expresses gratitude for
deliverance from distress.

and from the midst of fire that I had
    not kindled,
5 from the deep belly of Hades,
    from an unclean tongue and lying
        words—
6   the slander of an unrighteous tongue
        to the king.
My soul drew near to death,
    and my life was on the brink of Hades
        below.
7 They surrounded me on every side,
    and there was no one to help me;
I looked for human assistance,
    and there was none.
8 Then I remembered your mercy, O Lord,
    and your kindness[a] from of old,
for you rescue those who wait for you
    and save them from the hand of their
        enemies.
9 And I sent up my prayer from the earth,
    and begged for rescue from death.
10 I cried out, "Lord, you are my Father;[b]
    do not forsake me in the days of
        trouble,
    when there is no help against the
        proud.
11 I will praise your name continually,
    and will sing hymns of thanksgiving."
My prayer was heard,
12   for you saved me from destruction
    and rescued me in time of trouble.
For this reason I thank you and praise
        you,
    and I bless the name of the Lord.

Heb adds:
Give thanks to the LORD, for he is good,
    for his steadfast love endures forever;

Give thanks to the God of praises,
    for his steadfast love endures forever;

Give thanks to the guardian of Israel,
    for his steadfast love endures forever;

Give thanks to him who formed all things,
    for his steadfast love endures forever;

Give thanks to the redeemer of Israel,
    for his steadfast love endures forever;

Give thanks to him who gathers the
        dispersed of Israel,
    for his steadfast love endures forever;

Give thanks to him who rebuilt his city and
        his sanctuary,
    for his steadfast love endures forever;

Give thanks to him who makes a horn to
        sprout for the house of David,
    for his steadfast love endures forever;

Give thanks to him who has chosen the
        sons of Zadok to be priests,
    for his steadfast love endures forever;

Give thanks to the shield of Abraham,
    for his steadfast love endures forever;

Give thanks to the rock of Isaac,
    for his steadfast love endures forever;

Give thanks to the mighty one of Jacob,
    for his steadfast love endures forever;

Give thanks to him who has chosen Zion,
    for his steadfast love endures forever;

Give thanks to the King of the kings of
        kings,
    for his steadfast love endures forever;

He has raised up a horn for his people,
    praise for all his loyal ones.

For the children of Israel, the people close to
        him.
    Praise the LORD!

Autobiographical Poem on Wisdom

13 While I was still young, before I went on
    my travels,

a Other ancient authorities read *work*   b Heb:
Gk *the Father of my lord*

51:13 PRAYER—*See* Spiritual Disciplines Index.

I sought wisdom openly in my prayer.
14 Before the temple I asked for her,
　　and I will search for her until the end.

15 From the first blossom to the ripening
　　　　grape
　　my heart delighted in her;
　　my foot walked on the straight path;
　　from my youth I followed her steps.

16 I inclined my ear a little and received
　　　　her,
　　and I found for myself much
　　　　instruction.
17 I made progress in her;
　　to him who gives wisdom I will give
　　　　glory.

18 For I resolved to live according to
　　　　wisdom, *a*
　　and I was zealous for the good,
　　and I shall never be disappointed.
19 My soul grappled with wisdom, *a*
　　and in my conduct I was strict; *b*

I spread out my hands to the heavens,
　　and lamented my ignorance of her.
20 I directed my soul to her,
　　and in purity I found her.

With her I gained understanding from
　　　　the first;
　　therefore I will never be forsaken.
21 My heart was stirred to seek her;
　　therefore I have gained a prize
　　　　possession.

22 The Lord gave me my tongue as a
　　　　reward,
　　and I will praise him with it.

23 Draw near to me, you who are
　　　　uneducated,
　　and lodge in the house of instruction.
24 Why do you say you are lacking in these
　　　　things, *c*
　　and why do you endure such great
　　　　thirst?
25 I opened my mouth and said,
　　Acquire wisdom *d* for yourselves
　　　　without money.

26 Put your neck under her *e* yoke,
　　and let your souls receive instruction;
　　it is to be found close by.

27 See with your own eyes that I have
　　　　labored but little
　　and found for myself much serenity.
28 Hear but a little of my instruction,
　　and through me you will acquire
　　　　silver and gold. *f*

29 May your soul rejoice in God's *g* mercy,
　　and may you never be ashamed to
　　　　praise him.
30 Do your work in good time,
　　and in his own time God *h* will give
　　　　you your reward.

a Gk *her*　　*b* Meaning of Gk uncertain
c Cn Compare Heb Syr: Meaning of Gk uncertain
d Heb: Gk lacks *wisdom*　　*e* Heb: other ancient
authorities read *the*　　*f* Syr Compare Heb: Gk *Get
instruction with a large sum of silver, and you will gain
by it much gold.*　　*g* Gk *his*　　*h* Gk *he*

51:13–30 *Draw near to me, you who are
uneducated, and lodge in the house of instruction.* Ben Sira explains his interest in knowledge
and invites young students to lodge in his school
or, if the "house of instruction" is a metaphor
for the book of Sirach, to study it diligently. Like

modern colleges and universities, he argues that
an education at his school is cost-effective. His
final word rises above financial considerations,
coming to rest in the fullness of God's mercy
while anticipating future reward.

BARUCH

Although the book of Baruch was actually written much later, the setting is during the exile in the sixth century BC. Exile brings dislocation, disorientation, and questioning. Seemingly secure realities of life and faith are subject to special scrutiny. In this new reality, Baruch draws upon three streams of biblical tradition to challenge and exhort the People of God. The traditions most alive for the author are those of sin and repentance from Jeremiah and Deuteronomy, wisdom seeking from Job 28, and hopeful longing from Isaiah 40–66. Baruch teaches us that the biblical traditions are vital for us today, and that one of the goals of spiritual formation is to draw creatively upon these supple traditions to make us aware of our shortcomings, challenge our laziness, and inspire us in our longing.

Judgment, Exile, and Forgiveness

Each of these major themes or traditions provides the background for a distinct section of Baruch. After a brief introduction (1:1–14), the author of Baruch probes the deep dimensions of sin, exile, loss, and repentance (1:15–3:8). Echoes of Jeremiah 32 and Deuteronomy 28, especially, are behind the ideas of Israel's sinning against God (1:13), God's choice to judge Israel (1:15; 2:6), Israel's disobedience (1:21; 2:16), and the resultant calamity of exile. Finally, the exhortations to pray to God for forgiveness and the moving prayer presenting Israel's yearnings for forgiveness and wholeness (3:1–8) are drawn from the world of Jeremiah and Deuteronomy.

But the author does not leave readers, or the people in exile, in a state of confession. The second major section of the book (3:9–4:4) is largely drawn from ideas in Job 28 about the need for and value of seeking wisdom from God. Wisdom, as described in the Old Testament, is both a universal phenomenon as well as God's special gift to Israel. Baruch takes up the latter theme and uses it as a stimulus to exhort readers to learn where there is wisdom and understanding (3:14). Israel and others sought wisdom, but did not find it. No one really pays attention to the gift

See also *"The With-God Life" essay for this section of the Bible,*
"The People of God in Exile," pp. 1171–74.

of wisdom, but God knows the way to it and offers it to people (3:31–37). It is most clearly evident in the Scriptures (4:1). Wisdom will be the gift that beckons us from our cycle of sin and confession.

Hope Is the Last Word

But the author is not content to remain there. Baruch concludes with a clarion call to hope and the vivid expectation that restoration is imminent (4:5–5:9). There are no more powerful words in the Old Testament expressing hope than those found in Isaiah 40–66. Our author draws upon that language to urge courage on readers (4:21, 30), to tell them about the new name God will provide them (5:4), and to close the book with the stirring picture, derived from Isaiah 40, of the mountains being made low and the valleys filled up in aiding the quick return of the people to their Promised Land. Hope, therefore, is the last word.

—Glandion Carney and William R. Long

Baruch and the Jews in Babylon

1 These are the words of the book that Baruch son of Neriah son of Mahseiah son of Zedekiah son of Hasadiah son of Hilkiah wrote in Babylon, ²in the fifth year, on the seventh day of the month, at the time when the Chaldeans took Jerusalem and burned it with fire.

3 Baruch read the words of this book to Jeconiah son of Jehoiakim, king of Judah, and to all the people who came to hear the book, ⁴and to the nobles and the princes, and to the elders, and to all the people, small and great, all who lived in Babylon by the river Sud.

5 Then they wept, and fasted, and prayed before the Lord; ⁶they collected as much money as each could give, ⁷and sent it to Jerusalem to the high priest *a* Jehoiakim son of Hilkiah son of Shallum, and to the priests, and to all the people who were present with him in Jerusalem. ⁸At the same time, on the tenth day of Sivan, Baruch *b* took the vessels of the house of the Lord, which had been carried away from the temple, to return them to the land of Judah—the silver vessels that Zedekiah son of Josiah, king of Judah, had made, ⁹after King Nebuchadnezzar of Babylon had carried away from Jerusalem Jeconiah and the princes and the prisoners and the nobles and the people of the land, and brought them to Babylon.

A Letter to Jerusalem

10 They said: Here we send you money; so buy with the money burnt offerings and sin offerings and incense, and prepare a grain offering, and offer them on the altar of the Lord our God; ¹¹and pray for the life of King Nebuchadnezzar of Babylon, and for the life

a Gk *the priest* *b* Gk *he*

1:2 *fifth year.* The book of Baruch assumes a situation of exile. Jerusalem had been burned, and the Temple either destroyed or about to be destroyed. Great loss prevailed. Physical and political exile is mirrored in its spiritual counterpart. In spiritual exile our soul becomes famished, isolated, and distant from the sources of its familiar strength.

1:5 *Then they wept.* The ringing cadences of Baruch's book cut the people to their heart. Yet weeping was not their only reality. They responded with gifts of money for the Temple (v 6). The fourfold reality of a book read, a message heard, an emotion expressed, and a gift given characterizes the exiles' initial reaction.

1:5 FASTING—*See* Spiritual Disciplines Index.

1:11 *pray for the life of King Nebuchadnezzar.* The powerful Babylonian king who sacked Jerusalem and exiled its leading citizens was not a typical recipient of this kind of prayer, but exilic

of his son Belshazzar, so that their days on earth may be like the days of heaven. 12The Lord will give us strength, and light to our eyes; we shall live under the protection*a* of King Nebuchadnezzar of Babylon, and under the protection of his son Belshazzar, and we shall serve them many days and find favor in their sight. 13Pray also for us to the Lord our God, for we have sinned against the Lord our God, and to this day the anger of the Lord and his wrath have not turned away from us. 14And you shall read aloud this scroll that we are sending you, to make your confession in the house of the Lord on the days of the festivals and at appointed seasons.

Confession of Sins

15 And you shall say: The Lord our God is in the right, but there is open shame on us today, on the people of Judah, on the inhabitants of Jerusalem, 16and on our kings, our rulers, our priests, our prophets, and our ancestors, 17because we have sinned before the Lord. 18We have disobeyed him, and have not heeded the voice of the Lord our God, to walk in the statutes of the Lord that he set before us. 19From the time when the Lord brought our ancestors out of the land of Egypt until today, we have been disobedient to the Lord our God, and we have been negligent, in not heeding his voice. 20So to this day there have clung to us the calamities and the curse that the Lord declared through his servant Moses at the time when he brought our ancestors out of the land of Egypt to give to us a land flowing with milk and honey. 21We did not listen to the voice of the Lord our God in all the words of the prophets whom he sent to us, 22but all of us followed the intent of our own wicked hearts by serving other gods and doing what is evil in the sight of the Lord our God.

2 So the Lord carried out the threat he spoke against us: against our judges who ruled Israel, and against our kings and our rulers and the people of Israel and Judah. 2Under the whole heaven there has not been done the like of what he has done in Jerusalem, in accordance with the threats that were*b* written in the law of Moses. 3Some of us ate the flesh of their sons and others the flesh of their daughters. 4He made them subject to all the kingdoms around us, to be an object of scorn and a desolation among all the surrounding peoples, where the Lord has scattered them. 5They were brought down and not raised up, because our nation*c* sinned against the Lord our God, in not heeding his voice.

6 The Lord our God is in the right, but there is open shame on us and our ancestors this very day. 7All those calamities with which the Lord threatened us have come upon us. 8Yet we have not entreated the favor of the Lord by turning away, each of us, from the thoughts of our wicked hearts. 9And the Lord has kept the calamities ready, and the Lord has brought them upon us, for the Lord is just in all the works that he has commanded us to do. 10Yet we have not obeyed his voice, to walk in the statutes of the Lord that he set before us.

Prayer for Deliverance

11 And now, O Lord God of Israel, who brought your people out of the land of Egypt with a mighty hand and with signs and

---

a Gk *in the shadow*   *b* Gk *in accordance with what is*   *c* Gk *because we*

---

life brings a different prayer focus. The daunting realities of distance from the Promised Land lead not simply to longing for the land, but to a prayer that the secular ruler is preserved. People do seek the favor of the powers that be, even in exile.

1:21 *We did not listen.* Listening is not the same as hearing. In Hebrew, "listen" is a synonym for "obey." To listen is to obey, but our ears are full of the din of today; our mental inboxes are overflowing with information and competing demands. Have we heard all these messages, but neglected the most important one, the voice of God?

2:10 *we have not obeyed.* True spiritual formation begins with an honest assessment of our shortcomings. Painful as it is, our first step is a recognition that our lives have neither the discipline, the focus, nor the consistency that we would like. Confession chastens and opens the heart, however, to the secret work of the Spirit of God.

wonders and with great power and outstretched arm, and made yourself a name that continues to this day, [12]we have sinned, we have been ungodly, we have done wrong, O Lord our God, against all your ordinances. [13]Let your anger turn away from us, for we are left, few in number, among the nations where you have scattered us. [14]Hear, O Lord, our prayer and our supplication, and for your own sake deliver us, and grant us favor in the sight of those who have carried us into exile; [15]so that all the earth may know that you are the Lord our God, for Israel and his descendants are called by your name.

16 O Lord, look down from your holy dwelling, and consider us. Incline your ear, O Lord, and hear; [17]open your eyes, O Lord, and see, for the dead who are in Hades, whose spirit has been taken from their bodies, will not ascribe glory or justice to the Lord; [18]but the person who is deeply grieved, who walks bowed and feeble, with failing eyes and famished soul, will declare your glory and righteousness, O Lord.

19 For it is not because of any righteous deeds of our ancestors or our kings that we bring before you our prayer for mercy, O Lord our God. [20]For you have sent your anger and your wrath upon us, as you declared by your servants the prophets, saying: [21]Thus says the Lord: Bend your shoulders and serve the king of Babylon, and you will remain in the land that I gave to your ancestors. [22]But if you will not obey the voice of the Lord and will not serve the king of Babylon, [23]I will

make to cease from the towns of Judah and from the region around Jerusalem the voice of mirth and the voice of gladness, the voice of the bridegroom and the voice of the bride, and the whole land will be a desolation without inhabitants.

24 But we did not obey your voice, to serve the king of Babylon; and you have carried out your threats, which you spoke by your servants the prophets, that the bones of our kings and the bones of our ancestors would be brought out of their resting place; [25]and indeed they have been thrown out to the heat of day and the frost of night. They perished in great misery, by famine and sword and pestilence. [26]And the house that is called by your name you have made as it is today, because of the wickedness of the house of Israel and the house of Judah.

God's Promise Recalled

27 Yet you have dealt with us, O Lord our God, in all your kindness and in all your great compassion, [28]as you spoke by your servant Moses on the day when you commanded him to write your law in the presence of the people of Israel, saying, [29]"If you will not obey my voice, this very great multitude will surely turn into a small number among the nations, where I will scatter them. [30]For I know that they will not obey me, for they are a stiff-necked people. But in the land of their exile they will come to themselves [31]and know that I am the Lord their God. I will give them a heart that obeys and ears that hear;

Responding

2:10 CONFESSION. The next time you engage in confession, reflect on the causes of your disobedience. What external factors or triggers are leading to your mistakes? Ask God to show you which Spiritual Disciplines can help you to be more obedient. *See also* Spiritual Disciplines Index.

2:14 *Hear, O Lord.* Petition is the key hallmark of covenantal transaction, a practice old and defining in Israel. Sincere confession is only the first step. Then one must call on God. We ask God to hear not so much because we feel God may be deaf as to exhort ourselves to make

listening a more central part of our own formation. Even before a word is on our tongue, God knows it (Ps 139:4).

2:14 PRAYER—*See* Spiritual Disciplines Index.

2:31 *give them a heart.* In order to begin anew, to return from exile, one needs a new center, a new source of energy, a new orientation. Our hearts become tired, even damaged, as we experience our exile. Weariness, anger, grief, and bitterness overtake the heart. We cannot remake our own heart apart from the gracious gift of God. God's pulsating energy flow will pump fresh life to our damaged organ.

32they will praise me in the land of their exile, and will remember my name 33and turn from their stubbornness and their wicked deeds; for they will remember the ways of their ancestors, who sinned before the Lord. 34I will bring them again into the land that I swore to give to their ancestors, to Abraham, Isaac, and Jacob, and they will rule over it; and I will increase them, and they will not be diminished. 35I will make an everlasting covenant with them to be their God and they shall be my people; and I will never again remove my people Israel from the land that I have given them."

3 O Lord Almighty, God of Israel, the soul in anguish and the wearied spirit cry out to you. 2Hear, O Lord, and have mercy, for we have sinned before you. 3For you are enthroned forever, and we are perishing forever. 4O Lord Almighty, God of Israel, hear now the prayer of the people[a] of Israel, the children of those who sinned before you, who did not heed the voice of the Lord their God, so that calamities have clung to us. 5Do not remember the iniquities of our ancestors, but in this crisis remember your power and your name. 6For you are the Lord our God, and it is you, O Lord, whom we will praise. 7For you have put the fear of you in our hearts so that we would call upon your name; and we will praise you in our exile, for we have put away from our hearts all the iniquity of our ancestors who sinned against you. 8See, we are today in our exile where you have scattered us, to be reproached and cursed and punished for all the iniquities of our ancestors, who forsook the Lord our God.

In Praise of Wisdom

9   Hear the commandments of life,
      O Israel;
   give ear, and learn wisdom!

10 Why is it, O Israel, why is it that you are
      in the land of your enemies,
   that you are growing old in a foreign
      country,
   that you are defiled with the dead,
11   that you are counted among those in
      Hades?
12 You have forsaken the fountain of
      wisdom.
13 If you had walked in the way of God,
   you would be living in peace forever.
14 Learn where there is wisdom,
   where there is strength,
   where there is understanding,
   so that you may at the same time
      discern
   where there is length of days, and life,
   where there is light for the eyes, and
      peace.

15 Who has found her place?
   And who has entered her
      storehouses?
16 Where are the rulers of the nations,
   and those who lorded it over the
      animals on earth;
17 those who made sport of the birds of
      the air,
   and who hoarded up silver and gold
   in which people trust,
   and there is no end to their getting;
18 those who schemed to get silver, and
      were anxious,
   but there is no trace of their works?
19 They have vanished and gone down to
      Hades,
   and others have arisen in their place.

20 Later generations have seen the light of
      day,
   and have lived upon the earth;

a Gk dead

3:1–8 *we have sinned before you.* These verses give a short, direct, and earnest prayer. It is filled with confession (v 4), supplication (v 5), recognition (v 6), and longing (vv 7–8). The first great movement of this book closes with the anguished and weary soul still crying to God (v 1).

3:12 *fountain of wisdom.* The language now shifts from a confession or repentance cycle to reflections on wisdom. God is not only the judge of personal or communal shortcomings; he is also the giver of wisdom. Though we have forsaken wisdom, it is still there, beckoning to us, a gift from the God of Israel.

but they have not learned the way to
   knowledge,
      nor understood her paths,
      nor laid hold of her.
21 Their descendants have strayed far from
   her *a* way.
22 She has not been heard of in Canaan,
      or seen in Teman;
23 the descendants of Hagar, who seek for
   understanding on the earth,
      the merchants of Merran and Teman,
      the story-tellers and the seekers for
         understanding,
   have not learned the way to wisdom,
      or given thought to her paths.

24 O Israel, how great is the house of God,
      how vast the territory that he
         possesses!
25 It is great and has no bounds;
      it is high and immeasurable.
26 The giants were born there, who were
      famous of old,
      great in stature, expert in war.
27 God did not choose them,
      or give them the way to knowledge;
28 so they perished because they had no
      wisdom,
      they perished through their folly.

29 Who has gone up into heaven, and
      taken her,
   and brought her down from the
      clouds?
30 Who has gone over the sea, and found
      her,
   and will buy her for pure gold?

31 No one knows the way to her,
      or is concerned about the path to her.
32 But the one who knows all things
      knows her,
      he found her by his understanding.
   The one who prepared the earth for all
      time
      filled it with four-footed creatures;
33 the one who sends forth the light, and
      it goes;
      he called it, and it obeyed him,
         trembling;
34 the stars shone in their watches, and
      were glad;
      he called them, and they said, "Here
         we are!"
   They shone with gladness for him
      who made them.
35 This is our God;
      no other can be compared to him.
36 He found the whole way to knowledge,
      and gave her to his servant Jacob
      and to Israel, whom he loved.
37 Afterward she appeared on earth
      and lived with humankind.

4 She is the book of the commandments
   of God,
      the law that endures forever.
   All who hold her fast will live,
      and those who forsake her will die.
2 Turn, O Jacob, and take her;
      walk toward the shining of her light.
3 Do not give your glory to another,
      or your advantages to an alien people.

a Other ancient authorities read *their*

3:31–32 *no one knows the way to her.* Though
wisdom is available, no one finds it (v 15). Both
the international community and Israel are offered the gift, but no one accepts. No one really
searches it out (v 30). Why do we fly from the
divine gift? Perhaps because it is so rare. Information is everywhere, but wisdom is scarce. But
wisdom is what we need in our lives, and God
is the source of it.

4:1 *She is the book.* Wisdom is not some ethereal concept, inaccessible and removed from the
struggles of people. It is identified with the Book,
the Scriptures. What good news this is! Instead

of racking our brains for insight, guidance, and
comfort, we have it right before our eyes.

Responding

4:1 STUDY. Scheduling a large block
of time is the best way to foster the
concentration necessary to study Scripture.
Challenge yourself to set aside two or three
days for a private study retreat. Try to stay
where you will be undisturbed and create a
study plan in advance in order to be disciplined
with your time. *See also* Spiritual Disciplines
Index.

4 Happy are we, O Israel,
for we know what is pleasing to God.

Encouragement for Israel

5 Take courage, my people,
who perpetuate Israel's name!
6 It was not for destruction
that you were sold to the nations,
but you were handed over to your
enemies
because you angered God.
7 For you provoked the one who made
you
by sacrificing to demons and not to
God.
8 You forgot the everlasting God, who
brought you up,
and you grieved Jerusalem, who
reared you.
9 For she saw the wrath that came upon
you from God,
and she said:
Listen, you neighbors of Zion,
God has brought great sorrow upon
me;
10 for I have seen the exile of my sons and
daughters,
which the Everlasting brought upon
them.
11 With joy I nurtured them,
but I sent them away with weeping
and sorrow.
12 Let no one rejoice over me, a widow
and bereaved of many;
I was left desolate because of the sins of
my children,
because they turned away from the
law of God.
13 They had no regard for his statutes;
they did not walk in the ways of
God's commandments,
or tread the paths his righteousness
showed them.
14 Let the neighbors of Zion come;
remember the capture of my sons and
daughters,

which the Everlasting brought upon
them.
15 For he brought a distant nation against
them,
a nation ruthless and of a strange
language,
which had no respect for the aged
and no pity for a child.
16 They led away the widow's beloved
sons,
and bereaved the lonely woman of
her daughters.

17 But I, how can I help you?
18 For he who brought these calamities
upon you
will deliver you from the hand of your
enemies.
19 Go, my children, go;
for I have been left desolate.
20 I have taken off the robe of peace
and put on sackcloth for my
supplication;
I will cry to the Everlasting all my
days.

21 Take courage, my children, cry to God,
and he will deliver you from the
power and hand of the enemy.
22 For I have put my hope in the
Everlasting to save you,
and joy has come to me from the
Holy One,
because of the mercy that will soon
come to you
from your everlasting savior. *a*
23 For I sent you out with sorrow and
weeping,
but God will give you back to me with
joy and gladness forever.
24 For as the neighbors of Zion have now
seen your capture,
so they soon will see your salvation by
God,

a Or *from the Everlasting, your savior*

4:21 *Take courage.* A new theme is sounded in the third part of Baruch—deliverance is imminent. The last word is not sin and confession or even the gift of wisdom, but blessed return and deliverance from the hand of the enemy. The long night of political and spiritual exile can end. Dangers may accompany the return, and the journey of faith is not for the faint-hearted.

which will come to you with great glory
and with the splendor of the
Everlasting.
25 My children, endure with patience the
wrath that has come upon you
from God.
Your enemy has overtaken you,
but you will soon see their
destruction
and will tread upon their necks.
26 My pampered children have traveled
rough roads;
they were taken away like a flock
carried off by the enemy.

27 Take courage, my children, and cry to
God,
for you will be remembered by the
one who brought this upon you.
28 For just as you were disposed to go
astray from God,
return with tenfold zeal to seek him.
29 For the one who brought these
calamities upon you
will bring you everlasting joy with
your salvation.

Jerusalem Is Assured of Help

30 Take courage, O Jerusalem,
for the one who named you will
comfort you.
31 Wretched will be those who mistreated
you
and who rejoiced at your fall.
32 Wretched will be the cities that your
children served as slaves;
wretched will be the city that received
your offspring.
33 For just as she rejoiced at your fall
and was glad for your ruin,

so she will be grieved at her own
desolation.
34 I will take away her pride in her great
population,
and her insolence will be turned to
grief.
35 For fire will come upon her from the
Everlasting for many days,
and for a long time she will be
inhabited by demons.

36 Look toward the east, O Jerusalem,
and see the joy that is coming to you
from God.
37 Look, your children are coming, whom
you sent away;
they are coming, gathered from east
and west,
at the word of the Holy One,
rejoicing in the glory of God.

5 Take off the garment of your sorrow
and affliction, O Jerusalem,
and put on forever the beauty of the
glory from God.
2 Put on the robe of the righteousness
that comes from God;
put on your head the diadem of the
glory of the Everlasting;
3 for God will show your splendor
everywhere under heaven.
4 For God will give you evermore the
name,
"Righteous Peace, Godly Glory."

5 Arise, O Jerusalem, stand upon the
height;
look toward the east,
and see your children gathered from
west and east
at the word of the Holy One,

4:30 *Take courage.* Any good piece of advice is worth repeating. But here the author does not just promise deliverance. Comfort from the one who named us is assured. The daunting trip from exile to our proper land is now made less intimidating because of the intimate presence of our God.

5:1 *put on forever.* Deliverance is portrayed in terms of new clothing. Our clothes of distress, confession, and sin are no longer appropriate for the journey of hope and restoration. We clothe ourselves not simply with the armor of God (Eph 6:10–17), but with the robe of righteousness (v 2), the robe of beauty. Our new clothing is not simply functional, but beautiful. Beauty and freedom, intimacy with God and deliverance go hand in hand for the People of God.

rejoicing that God has remembered
them.

6 For they went out from you on foot,
led away by their enemies;
but God will bring them back to you,
carried in glory, as on a royal throne.

7 For God has ordered that every high
mountain and the everlasting
hills be made low
and the valleys filled up, to make level
ground,

so that Israel may walk safely in the
glory of God.

8 The woods and every fragrant tree
have shaded Israel at God's
command.

9 For God will lead Israel with joy,
in the light of his glory,
with the mercy and righteousness
that come from him.

5:7 *every high mountain.* The book closes in words derived from Isaiah 40 and celebrated in Handel's *Messiah.* Deliverance is nigh. Even the trip back to our Promised Land is now easy. Safety, fellowship, and restoration are hallmarks of our postexilic spiritual formation.

THE LETTER OF
JEREMIAH

There could be no more authoritative or comforting voice to the people of Israel in exile than that of Jeremiah. The brilliant and memorable teachings of the prophet from Anathoth were emblazoned on the hearts of the exilic community. His words of somber judgment, his anguished cries of personal dejection, and his unbridled hope in a vital future for the People of God provided an explanation for suffering as well as an expectation for a reversal of fortunes in the future.

The Futility of Idol Worship

One of the themes explored by the prophet Jeremiah was the futility and stupidity of the worship of idols—the gods of the nations (Jer 10:1–16). These idols are simply the work of artisans and goldsmiths. They have no life. To bow down and worship them is to partake of the foolishness of those who fashion the idols (10:1–9). The true God, the God of Israel, stands in stark contrast to these idols: "But the Lord is the true God; he is the living God and the everlasting King" (10:10).

The temptation to abandon one's own God in exile and to adopt the religion of the surrounding peoples was immense. Israel's Temple had been destroyed, sacrifice was no more, the regular priestly ritual was not celebrated, and the holidays could not properly be observed. All the external rhythms of religious life, Israel's Spiritual Disciplines, were curtailed by exile. There must have been many exiles who could echo the plaintive words of the psalmist, "How could we sing the Lord's song in a foreign land?" (Ps 137:4).

The Heart of the Letter of Jeremiah

The problem of idolatry lies at the heart of the Letter of Jeremiah. With seemingly

---

See also *"The With-God Life" essay for this section of the Bible,*
"The People of God in Exile," pp. 1171–74.

---

endless repetition, the exilic author, writing under the name of Jeremiah but composing his letter several centuries later during the Hellenistic period (fourth through second centuries BC), ridicules the idols and idol makers of the nations. The idols are "false and cannot speak" (v 8); their eyes are full of the dust stirred up by the feet of the priests (v 18); they are powerless to give wealth (v 35); "they cannot save" (v 49); and they "can neither curse nor bless" (v 66).

The enduring significance of the Letter of Jeremiah for today is as a warning against the debilitating force of activities or commitments that dilute our allegiance to the living God. There are the sudden or incremental allures of the bright lights of the culture in which we live. How easy it is to accommodate to the dominant cultural values, which invade our lives through the mass media. How tempting is the life of ease over a life of discipline. Even the "gods" of modern culture have power to form us spiritually. De-form may be more accurate. The stark and simple words of the Letter of Jeremiah exhort us to an uncompromising rejection of the lures of contemporary culture that would draw us away from the true God.

—*William R. Long*

6 *a* A copy of a letter that Jeremiah sent to those who were to be taken to Babylon as exiles by the king of the Babylonians, to give them the message that God had commanded him.

The People Face a Long Captivity

2 Because of the sins that you have committed before God, you will be taken to Babylon as exiles by Nebuchadnezzar, king of the Babylonians. ³Therefore when you have come to Babylon you will remain there for many years, for a long time, up to seven generations; after that I will bring you away from there in peace. ⁴Now in Babylon you will see gods made of silver and gold and wood, which people carry on their shoulders, and which cause the heathen to fear. ⁵So beware of becoming at all like the foreigners or of letting fear for these gods *b* possess you ⁶when you see the multitude before and behind them worshiping them. But say in your heart, "It is you, O Lord,

a The King James Version (like the Latin Vulgate) prints The Letter of Jeremiah as Chapter 6 of the Book of Baruch, and the chapter and verse numbers are here retained. In the Greek Septuagint, the Letter is separated from Baruch by the Book of Lamentations. *b* Gk *for them*

(In some traditions, the Letter of Jeremiah was added to Baruch as a sixth chapter.)

1 *A copy of a letter that Jeremiah sent.* The prophet Jeremiah sent a letter to exiles in Jeremiah 29, urging them to build homes, plant gardens, and adapt to exile. By appealing to the authority of Jeremiah in this letter, the author not only ties the people to their tradition, but gives encouragement to exiles. In our e-mail and cell-phone culture, a letter still carries immense weight.

3 *you will remain there for many years.* Exile often lasts longer than first anticipated. The challenges to exiles change after years become decades and decades turn into centuries. Is there such a thing as permanent exile? For what should one hope? Or is seven generations perhaps the "perfect number" of exilic generations, after which restoration will come?

6 *It is you, O Lord.* This letter probes competing allegiances. Our allegiance to the Lord God is shown in worship. We "must" worship our God; our life and health depend on it.

Responding
6 WORSHIP. What are the gods worshiped by the multitudes? Which of these gods are you most susceptible to? *See also* Spiritual Disciplines Index.

whom we must worship." ⁷For my angel is with you, and he is watching over your lives.

The Helplessness of Idols

8 Their tongues are smoothed by the carpenter, and they themselves are overlaid with gold and silver; but they are false and cannot speak. ⁹People*a* take gold and make crowns for the heads of their gods, as they might for a girl who loves ornaments. ¹⁰Sometimes the priests secretly take gold and silver from their gods and spend it on themselves, ¹¹or even give some of it to the prostitutes on the terrace. They deck their gods*b* out with garments like human beings—these gods of silver and gold and wood ¹²that cannot save themselves from rust and corrosion. When they have been dressed in purple robes, ¹³their faces are wiped because of the dust from the temple, which is thick upon them. ¹⁴One of them holds a scepter, like a district judge, but is unable to destroy anyone who offends it. ¹⁵Another has a dagger in its right hand, and an ax, but cannot defend itself from war and robbers. ¹⁶From this it is evident that they are not gods; so do not fear them.

17 For just as someone's dish is useless when it is broken, ¹⁸so are their gods when they have been set up in the temples. Their eyes are full of the dust raised by the feet of those who enter. And just as the gates are shut on every side against anyone who has offended a king, as though under sentence of death, so the priests make their temples secure with doors and locks and bars, in order that they may not be plundered by robbers.

¹⁹They light more lamps for them than they light for themselves, though their gods*c* can see none of them. ²⁰They are*d* just like a beam of the temple, but their hearts, it is said, are eaten away when crawling creatures from the earth devour them and their robes. They do not notice ²¹when their faces have been blackened by the smoke of the temple. ²²Bats, swallows, and birds alight on their bodies and heads; and so do cats. ²³From this you will know that they are not gods; so do not fear them.

24 As for the gold that they wear for beauty—it*e* will not shine unless someone wipes off the tarnish; for even when they were being cast, they did not feel it. ²⁵They are bought without regard to cost, but there is no breath in them. ²⁶Having no feet, they are carried on the shoulders of others, revealing to humankind their worthlessness. And those who serve them are put to shame ²⁷because, if any of these gods falls*f* to the ground, they themselves must pick it up. If anyone sets it upright, it cannot move itself; and if it is tipped over, it cannot straighten itself. Gifts are placed before them just as before the dead. ²⁸The priests sell the sacrifices that are offered to these gods*g* and use the money themselves. Likewise their wives preserve some of the meat*h* with salt, but give none to the poor or helpless. ²⁹Sacrifices to them may even be touched by women in their periods or at childbirth. Since you know by these

a Gk *They*　　*b* Gk *them*　　*c* Gk *they*　　*d* Gk *It is*　　*e* Lat Syr: Gk *they*　　*f* Gk *if they fall*　　*g* Gk *to them*　　*h* Gk *of them*

---

7 *my angel is with you.* God's presence through an angel is emphasized during the exodus (Exod 14:19; 23:20; 32:34). Now an angel is present during exile. For those in personal exile, far from the springs of life that water deeply buried roots, the angel of God's presence is the lifeline.

16 *it is evident that they are not gods.* A series of repeated verbal attacks on foreign gods culminates with the familiar refrain, "they are not gods." Even those who are not tempted to follow the allure of other masters like to hear the reassuring word that the promises of these masters are empty.

18 *in order that they may not be plundered.*

The author provides a humorous picture. The gods, who are supposed to protect the people, are themselves in need of protection, lest they get stolen. Either the dust gets in their eyes or they risk being carried off. What is the power of the so-called gods of our world?

28 *The priests sell . . . but give none to the poor.* The biblical measure of religion is how it cares for the poor and oppressed. The poor, crippled, blind, and lame receive invitations to the feast of the Son of God (Luke 14:21). Here the idols of the people are ridiculed because the food offered to them is sold for profit rather than distributed to the needy.

things that they are not gods, do not fear them.

30 For how can they be called gods? Women serve meals for gods of silver and gold and wood; [31] and in their temples the priests sit with their clothes torn, their heads and beards shaved, and their heads uncovered. [32] They howl and shout before their gods as some do at a funeral banquet. [33] The priests take some of the clothing of their gods[a] to clothe their wives and children. [34] Whether one does evil to them or good, they will not be able to repay it. They cannot set up a king or depose one. [35] Likewise they are not able to give either wealth or money; if one makes a vow to them and does not keep it, they will not require it. [36] They cannot save anyone from death or rescue the weak from the strong. [37] They cannot restore sight to the blind; they cannot rescue one who is in distress. [38] They cannot take pity on a widow or do good to an orphan. [39] These things that are made of wood and overlaid with gold and silver are like stones from the mountain, and those who serve them will be put to shame. [40] Why then must anyone think that they are gods, or call them gods?

The Foolishness of Worshiping Idols

Besides, even the Chaldeans themselves dishonor them; for when they see someone who cannot speak, they bring Bel and pray that the mute may speak, as though Bel[b] were able to understand! [41] Yet they themselves cannot perceive this and abandon them, for they have no sense. [42] And the women, with cords around them, sit along the passageways, burning bran for incense. [43] When one of them is led off by one of the passers-by and is taken to bed by him, she derides the woman next to her, because she was not as attractive as herself and her cord was not broken. [44] Whatever is done for these idols[c] is

false. Why then must anyone think that they are gods, or call them gods?

45 They are made by carpenters and goldsmiths; they can be nothing but what the artisans wish them to be. [46] Those who make them will certainly not live very long themselves; [47] how then can the things that are made by them be gods? They have left only lies and reproach for those who come after. [48] For when war or calamity comes upon them, the priests consult together as to where they can hide themselves and their gods. [c] [49] How then can one fail to see that these are not gods, for they cannot save themselves from war or calamity? [50] Since they are made of wood and overlaid with gold and silver, it will afterward be known that they are false. [51] It will be manifest to all the nations and kings that they are not gods but the work of human hands, and that there is no work of God in them. [52] Who then can fail to know that they are not gods? [d]

53 For they cannot set up a king over a country or give rain to people. [54] They cannot judge their own cause or deliver one who is wronged, for they have no power; [55] they are like crows between heaven and earth. When fire breaks out in a temple of wooden gods overlaid with gold or silver, their priests will flee and escape, but the gods[e] will be burned up like timbers. [56] Besides, they can offer no resistance to king or enemy. Why then must anyone admit or think that they are gods?

57 Gods made of wood and overlaid with silver and gold are unable to save themselves from thieves or robbers. [58] Anyone who can will strip them of their gold and silver and of the robes they wear, and go off with this booty, and they will not be able to help them-

a Gk some of their clothing   b Gk he
c Gk them   d Meaning of Gk uncertain
e Gk they

---

34 *They cannot set up a king or depose one.* Idols neither reward nor punish. The true God does both. God deposes and appoints kings. "The king's heart is a stream of water in the hand of the Lord; [God] turns it wherever he will" (Prov 21:1).

54 *they have no power.* There is no greater contrast between the power of the true God and an idol than in the contest between Elijah and the prophets of Baal (1 Kings 18:20–40). That passage also ridicules false gods, mocks them, and demonstrates the power of the true God, the God of Israel.

selves. 59So it is better to be a king who shows his courage, or a household utensil that serves its owner's need, than to be these false gods; better even the door of a house that protects its contents, than these false gods; better also a wooden pillar in a palace, than these false gods.

60 For sun and moon and stars are bright, and when sent to do a service, they are obedient. 61So also the lightning, when it flashes, is widely seen; and the wind likewise blows in every land. 62When God commands the clouds to go over the whole world, they carry out his command. 63And the fire sent from above to consume mountains and woods does what it is ordered. But these idols*a* are not to be compared with them in appearance or power. 64Therefore one must not think that they are gods, nor call them gods, for they are not able either to decide a case or to do good to anyone. 65Since you know then that they are not gods, do not fear them.

66 They can neither curse nor bless kings; 67they cannot show signs in the heavens for the nations, or shine like the sun or give light like the moon. 68The wild animals are better than they are, for they can flee to shelter and help themselves. 69So we have no evidence whatever that they are gods; therefore do not fear them.

70 Like a scarecrow in a cucumber bed, which guards nothing, so are their gods of wood, overlaid with gold and silver. 71In the same way, their gods of wood, overlaid with gold and silver, are like a thornbush in a garden on which every bird perches; or like a corpse thrown out in the darkness. 72From the purple and linen*b* that rot upon them you will know that they are not gods; and they will finally be consumed themselves, and be a reproach in the land. 73Better, therefore, is someone upright who has no idols; such a person will be far above reproach.

a Gk *these things*   *b* Cn: Gk *marble,* Syr *silk*

---

73 *Better, therefore, is someone upright who has no idols.* The final word is the value of right belief and conduct. God is praised in both.

PRAYER OF MANASSEH

The Prayer of Manasseh is included in Greek and Slavonic Bibles. This beautiful prayer, of uncertain date and authorship, draws on a rich array of biblical themes that have continuing value for the Spiritual Disciplines. Among these themes are the recognition of the creative power of God (v 2), God's splendor (v 5), God's judgment against sinners (v 5), God's measureless mercy (v 6), the need for repentance (v 8), the sense of human unworthiness before the divine grace (v 9), earnest supplication for God's kindness (v 11), and a vow to praise God all one's days (v 15).

Especially noteworthy are the repeated invocations of God's compassion. Although divine judgment is mentioned only once, God's mercy is stressed at least four times. God's mercy is "immeasurable and unsearchable" (v 6); God is a God "of great compassion" (v 7); God relents at human suffering (v 7); and God promises forgiveness to those who have sinned (v 7). It is on the basis of this appeal to God's mercy that the author confidently approaches God and confesses his sin.

The prayer is ascribed to Manasseh, the longest reigning monarch of Judah. His fifty-five-year reign is roundly condemned for its immorality and sin by the authors of 2 Kings 21 and 2 Chronicles 33. In the latter account, the author mentions that because Manasseh ignored the word of the Lord, the Lord brought Assyrian armies against Judah, and they took Manasseh captive in fetters (33:11). In this condition "he entreated the favor of the LORD his God and humbled himself greatly before the God of his ancestors" (33:12). God restored Manasseh to Jerusalem, and "then Manasseh knew that the LORD indeed was God" (33:13).

The reference to Manasseh's sudden and unexpected repentance no doubt stimulated the creative mind of an exilic author to pen this prayer. The prayer neatly falls

See also *"The With-God Life" essay for this section of the Bible, "The People of God in Rebellion," pp. 975–79.*

into three sections: an ascription of praise (1–7), a prayer of repentance (8–10), and a request for forgiveness (11–15). Its evident sincerity and deep longing for intimacy with God break through the familiar phrases like a jet breaking through the cloud layer and bursting into the brilliant sunlight. Stop and pray any verse. Each has the capacity to stimulate the heart. The prayer ends with a desire to praise God all the days of life (v 15). Our prayer mingles with the song of the heavenly host (v 15) to produce a beautiful symphony of praise to the God of Israel.

—*William R. Long*

Ascription of Praise

1 O Lord Almighty,
    God of our ancestors,
    of Abraham and Isaac and Jacob
    and of their righteous offspring;
2 you who made heaven and earth
    with all their order;
3 who shackled the sea by your word of
        command,
    who confined the deep
    and sealed it with your terrible and
        glorious name;
4 at whom all things shudder,
    and tremble before your power,
5 for your glorious splendor cannot be
        borne,
    and the wrath of your threat to sinners
        is unendurable;
6 yet immeasurable and unsearchable
    is your promised mercy,
7 for you are the Lord Most High,
    of great compassion, long-suffering,
        and very merciful,
    and you relent at human suffering.
    O Lord, according to your great
        goodness
    you have promised repentance and
        forgiveness

to those who have sinned against you,
    and in the multitude of your mercies
    you have appointed repentance for
        sinners,
    so that they may be saved. *a*
8 Therefore you, O Lord, God of the
        righteous,
    have not appointed repentance for the
        righteous,
    for Abraham and Isaac and Jacob, who
        did not sin against you,
    but you have appointed repentance for
        me, who am a sinner.

Confession of Sins

9 For the sins I have committed are more
        in number than the sand of the
        sea;
    my transgressions are multiplied,
        O Lord, they are multiplied!
    I am not worthy to look up and see the
        height of heaven
    because of the multitude of my
        iniquities.
10 I am weighted down with many an iron
        fetter,

a Other ancient authorities lack *O Lord, according . . . be saved*

---

3 *shackled the sea.* God's power is evident in the creation of the heavens above and the sea beneath. Once this vast theater is established, the focus is on God's splendor and actions in the human world. Nature and grace are two themes of a potent prayer.

8 *for me.* No practice of spiritual formation is real unless it relates the truths of the gospel to the heart of the individual. Illustrious figures from the past might inspire, but God's work

reaches those in every generation, including me.

Responding
8–15 CONFESSION. Confess your sins to God and petition him for forgiveness by copying out these verses and studying them. Then pray them aloud. Repeat the recitation as often as necessary. *See also* Spiritual Disciplines Index.

so that I am rejected *a* because of my
    sins,
and I have no relief;
for I have provoked your wrath
and have done what is evil in your
    sight,
setting up abominations and
    multiplying offenses.

Supplication for Pardon

11 And now I bend the knee of my heart,
    imploring you for your kindness.
12 I have sinned, O Lord, I have sinned,
    and I acknowledge my transgressions.
13 I earnestly implore you,
    forgive me, O Lord, forgive me!
Do not destroy me with my
    transgressions!

Do not be angry with me forever or
    store up evil for me;
do not condemn me to the depths of
    the earth.
For you, O Lord, are the God of those
    who repent,
14 and in me you will manifest your
    goodness;
for, unworthy as I am, you will save me
    according to your great mercy,
15 and I will praise you continually all the
    days of my life.
For all the host of heaven sings your
    praise,
and yours is the glory forever. Amen.

a Other ancient authorities read *so that I cannot lift up my head*

---

15 *I will praise you continually.* Praise is the fruit of forgiveness. The shackles on our heart fall away. The tongue is released to praise. The heavenly chorus joins in song. Praise becomes our way of life. Let nothing hinder your praise of God today. Glory to God!

TOBIT

The book of Tobit is a testament to the vitality and resilience of Israel's faith during the time of exile (sixth century BC). Written in the fourth or third century BC, Tobit teaches that fidelity to the living God even in the midst of exile will be rewarded. God so arranges events that independent actions of people geographically far removed from each other fit into God's larger plan of redemption for people. Though told in a sprightly narrative form with a few long prayers, Tobit is both an exhortation to the People of God to live faithfully and a yearning for a restored community in the future.

Faithful Life

Three movements in Tobit are replete with themes of spiritual formation. The first movement is the description of the faithful life of Tobit and his wife, Anna, in exile (chaps 1–3). They practice hospitality and give alms. They show their concern for their community by burying the dead of Israel that are cavalierly cast aside by the powers in control. They also suffer for their fidelity. Tobit is sought after for defying the ruler's decree. He goes blind while ministering to his community. He and Anna quarrel because of his suspicion that she has improperly obtained a young goat for food (2:11–14). In his distress, Tobit prays for his life to end (3:6). A mixed plaid of blessings attends the life of those who choose to live faithfully.

Journey

Second, the book describes the journey of Tobias, the son, to the east to redeem money held by Tobit's relative (chaps 4–10). Tobias is accompanied by an angel of God. What begins as a fairly straightforward journey turns into an occasion not only for getting the money, but also for Tobias to find both a wife and a remedy for Tobit's blindness. The lesson for spiritual formation is that in the journeys of our lives,

---

See also *"The With-God Life"* essays for this section of the Bible, *"The People of God in Travail,"* pp. 717–20, and *"The People of God in Restoration,"* pp. 1355–59.

when we think we are looking for one thing, God often brings many different things to minister to needs we did not think could ever be met.

Return

The final movement of Tobit is the return of Tobias and the angel to Tobit and Anna, the healing of Tobit, and the final blessing of God for his unexpected goodness (chaps 11–14). In a scene reminiscent of the parable of the prodigal son, Anna announces the return of Tobias and the angel (11:5–6). Excitement builds as Tobit's sight is restored, the family meets Tobias's new wife, Sarah, and the angel of God finally reveals his identity (chap 12). Prayers of gratitude and words of exhortation and satisfaction complete the book (chaps 13–14). Restoration, hopeful longing, and enjoyment are the results of faithful service.

In simple, straightforward, and powerful words, the book of Tobit teaches us that regular practice of the Spiritual Disciplines receives its reward, that suffering is not the last word in life, and that God's providential hand guides life even in the most unlikely of circumstances.

—William R. Long

1 This book tells the story of Tobit son of Tobiel son of Hananiel son of Aduel son of Gabael son of Raphael son of Raguel of the descendants[a] of Asiel, of the tribe of Naphtali, 2who in the days of King Shalmaneser[b] of the Assyrians was taken into captivity from Thisbe, which is to the south of Kedesh Naphtali in Upper Galilee, above Asher toward the west, and north of Phogor.

Tobit's Youth and Virtuous Life

3 I, Tobit, walked in the ways of truth and righteousness all the days of my life. I performed many acts of charity for my kindred and my people who had gone with me in exile to Nineveh in the land of the Assyrians. 4When I was in my own country, in the land of Israel, while I was still a young man, the whole tribe of my ancestor Naphtali deserted the house of David and Jerusalem. This city had been chosen from among all the tribes of Israel, where all the tribes of Israel should offer sacrifice and where the temple, the dwelling of God, had been consecrated and established for all generations forever.

5 All my kindred and our ancestral house of Naphtali sacrificed to the calf[c] that King Jeroboam of Israel had erected in Dan and on all the mountains of Galilee. 6But I alone went often to Jerusalem for the festivals, as it is prescribed for all Israel by an everlasting

a Other ancient authorities lack *of Raphael son of Raguel of the descendants*   b Gk *Enemessaros*   c Other ancient authorities read *heifer*

1:2 *who . . . was taken into captivity.* The challenge to all people of faith is to maintain faithfulness in exile. Spiritual exile can take place even without physical dislocation. It occurs when we have lost our moorings, when the predictable character of life and faith vanishes, when pain or confusion so fills our life that we feel adrift, passionless, angry, or oppressed. Exile measures us.

1:3–9 *I, Tobit, walked in the ways of truth and righteousness all the days of my life.* Tobit, however, exudes confidence in exile. He is described similarly to Job (Job 1:1), but here the language is in the first person. He describes his fidelity to God (v 6) in words reminiscent of Elijah (1 Kings 19:10). Thus, he combines in his intensity and faithfulness the diligence of the prophet and the sage. Regular, earnest piety is the order of the day.

decree. I would hurry off to Jerusalem with the first fruits of the crops and the firstlings of the flock, the tithes of the cattle, and the first shearings of the sheep. 7I would give these to the priests, the sons of Aaron, at the altar; likewise the tenth of the grain, wine, olive oil, pomegranates, figs, and the rest of the fruits to the sons of Levi who ministered at Jerusalem. Also for six years I would save up a second tenth in money and go and distribute it in Jerusalem. 8A third tenth a I would give to the orphans and widows and to the converts who had attached themselves to Israel. I would bring it and give it to them in the third year, and we would eat it according to the ordinance decreed concerning it in the law of Moses and according to the instructions of Deborah, the mother of my father Tobiel, b for my father had died and left me an orphan. 9When I became a man I married a woman, c a member of our own family, and by her I became the father of a son whom I named Tobias.

Taken Captive to Nineveh

10 After I was carried away captive to Assyria and came as a captive to Nineveh, everyone of my kindred and my people ate the food of the Gentiles, 11but I kept myself from eating the food of the Gentiles. 12Because I was mindful of God with all my heart, 13the Most High gave me favor and good standing with Shalmaneser, d and I used to buy everything he needed. 14Until his death I used to go into Media, and buy for him there. While in the country of Media I left bags of silver worth ten talents in trust with Gabael, the brother of Gabri. 15But when Shalmaneser d died, and his son Sennacherib reigned in his place, the highways into Media became unsafe and I could no longer go there.

Courage in Burying the Dead

16 In the days of Shalmaneser d I performed many acts of charity to my kindred, those of my tribe. 17I would give my food to the hungry and my clothing to the naked; and if I saw the dead body of any of my people thrown out behind the wall of Nineveh, I would bury it. 18I also buried any whom King Sennacherib put to death when he came fleeing from Judea in those days of judgment that the king of heaven executed upon him because of his blasphemies. For in his anger he put to death many Israelites; but I would secretly remove the bodies and bury them. So when Sennacherib looked for them he could not find them. 19Then one of the Ninevites went and informed the king about me, that I was burying them; so I hid myself. But when I realized that the king knew about me and that I was being searched for to be put to death, I was afraid and ran away. 20Then all my property was confiscated; nothing was left to me that was not taken into the royal treasury except my wife Anna and my son Tobias.

21 But not forty e days passed before two of Sennacherib's f sons killed him, and they fled to the mountains of Ararat, and his son Esar-haddon g reigned after him. He appointed Ahikar, the son of my brother Hanael h over all the accounts of his kingdom, and he had authority over the entire administration. 22Ahikar interceded for me, and I returned to Nineveh. Now Ahikar was chief cupbearer, keeper of the signet, and in charge of administration of the accounts under King Sennacherib of Assyria; so Esar-haddon g reappointed him. He was my nephew and so a close relative.

2 Then during the reign of Esar-haddon g I returned home, and my wife Anna and my son Tobias were restored to me. At our festival of Pentecost, which is the sacred festival of weeks, a good dinner was prepared for me

a A third tenth added from other ancient authorities   b Lat: Gk Hananiel   c Other ancient authorities add Anna   d Gk Enemessaros   e Other ancient authorities read either forty-five or fifty   f Gk his   g Gk Sacherdonos   h Other authorities read Hananael

---

1:19–20 I was being searched for to be put to death. Tobit's loyalty to God gets him into trouble with the authorities. He flees. His goods are confiscated. He must act secretly. Exile means that the rhythms of our life are determined by external forces, forces we cannot control, forces that expose and exploit our vulnerability.

and I reclined to eat. 2When the table was set for me and an abundance of food placed before me, I said to my son Tobias, "Go, my child, and bring whatever poor person you may find of our people among the exiles in Nineveh, who is wholeheartedly mindful of God,*a* and he shall eat together with me. I will wait for you, until you come back." 3So Tobias went to look for some poor person of our people. When he had returned he said, "Father!" And I replied, "Here I am, my child." Then he went on to say, "Look, father, one of our own people has been murdered and thrown into the market place, and now he lies there strangled." 4Then I sprang up, left the dinner before even tasting it, and removed the body*b* from the square*c* and laid it*b* in one of the rooms until sunset when I might bury it.*b* 5When I returned, I washed myself and ate my food in sorrow. 6Then I remembered the prophecy of Amos, how he said against Bethel,*d*

> "Your festivals shall be turned into mourning,
>   and all your songs into lamentation."

And I wept.

Tobit Becomes Blind

7 When the sun had set, I went and dug a grave and buried him. 8And my neighbors laughed and said, "Is he still not afraid? He has already been hunted down to be put to death for doing this, and he ran away; yet here he is again burying the dead!" 9That same night I washed myself and went into my courtyard and slept by the wall of the courtyard; and my face was uncovered because of the heat. 10I did not know that there were sparrows on the wall; their fresh droppings fell into my eyes and produced white films. I went to physicians to be healed, but the more they treated me with ointments the more my vision was obscured by the white films, until I became completely blind. For four years I remained unable to see. All my kindred were sorry for me, and Ahikar took care of me for two years before he went to Elymais.

Tobit's Wife Earns Their Livelihood

11 At that time, also, my wife Anna earned money at women's work. 12She used to send what she made to the owners and they would pay wages to her. One day, the seventh of Dystrus, when she cut off a piece she had woven and sent it to the owners, they paid her full wages and also gave her a young goat for a meal. 13When she returned to me, the goat began to bleat. So I called her and said, "Where did you get this goat? It is surely not stolen, is it? Return it to the owners; for we have no right to eat anything stolen." 14But she said to me, "It was given to me as a gift in addition to my wages." But I did not believe her, and told her to return it to the owners. I became flushed with anger against her over this. Then she replied to me, "Where are your acts of charity? Where are your righteous deeds? These things are known about you!"*e*

Tobit's Prayer

3 Then with much grief and anguish of heart I wept, and with groaning began to pray:
2 "You are righteous, O Lord,
    and all your deeds are just;
all your ways are mercy and truth;
    you judge the world.*f*

---

a Lat: Gk *wholeheartedly mindful*   *b* Gk *him*
c Other ancient authorities lack *from the square*
d Other ancient authorities read *against Bethlehem*
e Or *to you*; Gk *with you*   *f* Other ancient authorities read *you render true and righteous judgment forever*

2:10 *I became completely blind.* Once one trial is over, a new one arises. This one is seemingly more permanent and debilitating. In antiquity, blindness cut off one's ability to work and be productive. We often think that our biggest obstacles to faith come through the dislocation of exile, but Tobit teaches us that even in exile things can and often do get worse. Pains multiply.

2:11–14 *I did not believe her.* Tobit's fortunes reach their nadir when he accuses his wife of stealing a goat, since he thinks there was no way she could have legitimately earned enough to obtain one. Tobit's triple traumas in exile—loss of possessions, loss of physical health, conflict with wife—mirror the collapse of Job's world in Job 1–2.

3:1 **PRAYER**—*See* Spiritual Disciplines Index.

3 And now, O Lord, remember me
    and look favorably upon me.
Do not punish me for my sins
    and for my unwitting offenses
    and those that my ancestors
        committed before you.
They sinned against you,
4   and disobeyed your commandments.
So you gave us over to plunder, exile,
        and death,
    to become the talk, the byword, and
        an object of reproach
    among all the nations among whom
        you have dispersed us.
5 And now your many judgments are true
    in exacting penalty from me for my
        sins.
For we have not kept your
        commandments
    and have not walked in accordance
        with truth before you.
6 So now deal with me as you will;
    command my spirit to be taken from
        me,
    so that I may be released from the face
        of the earth and become dust.
For it is better for me to die than to live,
    because I have had to listen to
        undeserved insults,
    and great is the sorrow within me.
Command, O Lord, that I be released
        from this distress;
    release me to go to the eternal home,
    and do not, O Lord, turn your face
        away from me.
For it is better for me to die
    than to see so much distress in my life
    and to listen to insults."

Sarah Falsely Accused

7 On the same day, at Ecbatana in Media,
it also happened that Sarah, the daughter of
Raguel, was reproached by one of her father's
maids. 8For she had been married to seven
husbands, and the wicked demon Asmodeus
had killed each of them before they had been
with her as is customary for wives. So the
maid said to her, "You are the one who kills[a]
your husbands! See, you have already been
married to seven husbands and have not
borne the name of[b] a single one of them.
9Why do you beat us? Because your husbands
are dead? Go with them! May we never see a
son or daughter of yours!"

Sarah's Prayer for Death

10 On that day she was grieved in spirit
and wept. When she had gone up to her father's upper room, she intended to hang herself. But she thought it over and said, "Never shall they reproach my father, saying to
him, 'You had only one beloved daughter
but she hanged herself because of her distress.' And I shall bring my father in his old
age down in sorrow to Hades. It is better for
me not to hang myself, but to pray the Lord
that I may die and not listen to these reproaches anymore." 11At that same time,
with hands outstretched toward the window,
she prayed and said,
    "Blessed are you, merciful God!
        Blessed is your name forever;
        let all your works praise you forever.
12 And now, Lord, [c] I turn my face to you,
        and raise my eyes toward you.
13 Command that I be released from the
        earth
    and not listen to such reproaches any
        more.

a Other ancient authorities read strangles
b Other ancient authorities read have had no benefit
from   c Other ancient authorities lack Lord

3:6 *command my spirit to be taken from me.*
Tobit asks God to let him die. How often do
people, in the quiet of the night, racked with
bodily pain or internal anguish, tormented by
feelings of guilt, helplessness, worthlessness,
or aimlessness, feel that their life is over, that
any kind of purposive existence is no longer
possible? We enter the dark night of the soul.

3:7–9 *Sarah, the daughter of Raguel, was*
reproached. Seemingly unrelated events in far-
off places may be connected by the conduit
of the providence of God. Sarah lost several
husbands through the action of evil spiritual
forces. She, like Tobit, feels the sting of reproach
for her sorry condition.

3:11–15 *Command that I be released from the*
earth. Sarah prays a prayer similar to Tobit's.
Each person's anguish has its unique contours,

14 You know, O Master, that I am innocent
of any defilement with a man,
15 and that I have not disgraced my name
or the name of my father in the land
of my exile.
I am my father's only child;
he has no other child to be his heir;
and he has no close relative or other
kindred
for whom I should keep myself as
wife.
Already seven husbands of mine have
died.
Why should I still live?
But if it is not pleasing to you, O Lord,
to take my life,
hear me in my disgrace."

An Answer to Prayer

16 At that very moment, the prayers of
both of them were heard in the glorious presence of God. 17So Raphael was sent to heal
both of them: Tobit, by removing the white
films from his eyes, so that he might see God's
light with his eyes; and Sarah, daughter of
Raguel, by giving her in marriage to Tobias
son of Tobit, and by setting her free from the
wicked demon Asmodeus. For Tobias was entitled to have her before all others who had
desired to marry her. At the same time that
Tobit returned from the courtyard into his
house, Sarah daughter of Raguel came down
from her upper room.

Tobit Gives Instructions to His Son

4 That same day Tobit remembered the
money that he had left in trust with
Gabael at Rages in Media, 2and he said to
himself, "Now I have asked for death. Why do
I not call my son Tobias and explain to him
about the money before I die?" 3Then he
called his son Tobias, and when he came to
him he said, "My son, when I die, *a* give me a
proper burial. Honor your mother and do
not abandon her all the days of her life. Do
whatever pleases her, and do not grieve her in
anything. 4Remember her, my son, because
she faced many dangers for you while you
were in her womb. And when she dies, bury
her beside me in the same grave.

5 "Revere the Lord all your days, my son,
and refuse to sin or to transgress his commandments. Live uprightly all the days of

a Lat

---

though the common chord of the collective
chorus is often a request for death. Tobit's
debility is primarily physical; Sarah's pain is
psychological. They both ask for release from
this life. Can we calibrate the toll that physical
and psychic pain exacts on us?

Responding
3:11–16 PRAYER. Most of us are
taught that prayer should be confined
to asking God to intervene in situations to make
them better or to help people. But Tobit is so
grief-stricken and anguished over his losses that
he prays for his own death. What circumstances
in your life might lead you to pray to die? How
would you justify such a prayer? Consider Rom
8:18–25 as you ponder this question. *See also*
Spiritual Disciplines Index.

3:16 *the prayers of both of them were heard.*
Before they call on God, God is ready with
an answer. God will move heaven and earth,
through the ministry of the angel Raphael, to
alleviate the multiple torments of Tobit and
Sarah. It will take a while, and God will use
weak human instruments, but God's purpose
of healing will take place. Perhaps God's
restorative hand has already been raised on
your behalf.

4:2 *explain to him about the money.* Before
we get too carried away with the rich spiritual
principles illustrated in this story, we need to
recognize that money moves the story of Tobit
along. Tobit's deposit with a far-off kinsman will
be the means by which his son, Tobias, can live
after Tobit's death. God sends the most spiritual
of creatures—angels—on the most secular of
journeys—to get money—to attain the most
redemptive of purposes.

4:5 *Revere the Lord all your days.* Despite
Tobit's overwhelming grief and loss, he urges on
his son the same faithfulness that has characterized his own life. Is there an irony here? Maybe
the source of Tobit's strength is his realization
that fidelity to God even in distress is the only
basis for his hope.

your life, and do not walk in the ways of wrongdoing; 6for those who act in accordance with truth will prosper in all their activities. To all those who practice righteousness*a* 7give alms from your possessions, and do not let your eye begrudge the gift when you make it. Do not turn your face away from anyone who is poor, and the face of God will not be turned away from you. 8If you have many possessions, make your gift from them in proportion; if few, do not be afraid to give according to the little you have. 9So you will be laying up a good treasure for yourself against the day of necessity. 10For almsgiving delivers from death and keeps you from going into the Darkness. 11Indeed, almsgiving, for all who practice it, is an excellent offering in the presence of the Most High.

12 "Beware, my son, of every kind of fornication. First of all, marry a woman from among the descendants of your ancestors; do not marry a foreign woman, who is not of your father's tribe; for we are the descendants of the prophets. Remember, my son, that Noah, Abraham, Isaac, and Jacob, our ancestors of old, all took wives from among their kindred. They were blessed in their children, and their posterity will inherit the land. 13So now, my son, love your kindred, and in your heart do not disdain your kindred, the sons and daughters of your people, by refusing to take a wife for yourself from among them. For in pride there is ruin and great confusion. And in idleness there is loss and dire poverty, because idleness is the mother of famine.

14 "Do not keep over until the next day the wages of those who work for you, but pay them at once. If you serve God you will receive payment. Watch yourself, my son, in everything you do, and discipline yourself in all your conduct. 15And what you hate, do not do to anyone. Do not drink wine to excess

or let drunkenness go with you on your way. 16Give some of your food to the hungry, and some of your clothing to the naked. Give all your surplus as alms, and do not let your eye begrudge your giving of alms. 17Place your bread on the grave of the righteous, but give none to sinners. 18Seek advice from every wise person and do not despise any useful counsel. 19At all times bless the Lord God, and ask him that your ways may be made straight and that all your paths and plans may prosper. For none of the nations has understanding, but the Lord himself will give them good counsel; but if he chooses otherwise, he casts down to deepest Hades. So now, my child, remember these commandments, and do not let them be erased from your heart.

Money Left in Trust with Gabael

20 "And now, my son, let me explain to you that I left ten talents of silver in trust with Gabael son of Gabrias, at Rages in Media. 21Do not be afraid, my son, because we have become poor. You have great wealth if you fear God and flee from every sin and do what is good in the sight of the Lord your God."

The Angel Raphael

5 Then Tobias answered his father Tobit, "I will do everything that you have commanded me, father; 2but how can I obtain the money*b* from him, since he does not know me and I do not know him? What evidence*c* am I to give him so that he will recognize and trust me, and give me the money? Also,

---

a The text of codex Sinaiticus goes directly from verse 6 to verse 19, reading *To those who practice righteousness* 19*the Lord will give good counsel.* In order to fill the lacuna verses 7 to 18 are derived from other ancient authorities   b Gk *it*
c Gk *sign*

4:6 *those who act in accordance with truth.* "Truth" is a word that has suffered much in our day. Even before breaking news has a chance to settle, "spin doctors" enter in to massage the meaning of events in order to please their corporate or political sponsors. In addition, postmodernists blithely claim that truth is

merely a construction placed on wispy and evanescent perceptions. At times, however, truth clears its throat and will be heard. Recapture the language of truth. It is sturdy, positive, and rooted in God.

4:14 SERVICE—*See* Spiritual Disciplines Index.

I do not know the roads to Media, or how to get there." ³Then Tobit answered his son Tobias, "He gave me his bond and I gave him my bond. I*a* divided his in two; we each took one part, and I put one with the money. And now twenty years have passed since I left this money in trust. So now, my son, find yourself a trustworthy man to go with you, and we will pay him wages until you return. But get back the money from Gabael."*b*

4 So Tobias went out to look for a man to go with him to Media, someone who was acquainted with the way. He went out and found the angel Raphael standing in front of him; but he did not perceive that he was an angel of God. ⁵Tobias*c* said to him, "Where do you come from, young man?" "From your kindred, the Israelites," he replied, "and I have come here to work." Then Tobias*d* said to him, "Do you know the way to go to Media?" ⁶"Yes," he replied, "I have been there many times; I am acquainted with it and know all the roads. I have often traveled to Media, and would stay with our kinsman Gabael who lives in Rages of Media. It is a journey of two days from Ecbatana to Rages; for it lies in a mountainous area, while Ecbatana is in the middle of the plain." ⁷Then Tobias said to him, "Wait for me, young man, until I go in and tell my father; for I do need you to travel with me, and I will pay you your wages." ⁸He replied, "All right, I will wait; but do not take too long."

9 So Tobias*d* went in to tell his father Tobit and said to him, "I have just found a man who is one of our own Israelite kindred!" He replied, "Call the man in, my son, so that I may learn about his family and to what tribe he belongs, and whether he is trustworthy enough to go with you."

10 Then Tobias went out and called him, and said, "Young man, my father is calling for you." So he went in to him, and Tobit greeted him first. He replied, "Joyous greetings to you!" But Tobit retorted, "What joy is left for me any more? I am a man without eyesight; I cannot see the light of heaven, but I lie in darkness like the dead who no longer see the light. Although still alive, I am among the dead. I hear people but I cannot see them." But the young man*d* said, "Take courage; the time is near for God to heal you; take courage." Then Tobit said to him, "My son Tobias wishes to go to Media. Can you accompany him and guide him? I will pay your wages, brother." He answered, "I can go with him and I know all the roads, for I have often gone to Media and have crossed all its plains, and I am familiar with its mountains and all of its roads."

11 Then Tobit*d* said to him, "Brother, of what family are you and from what tribe? Tell me, brother." ¹²He replied, "Why do you need to know my tribe?" But Tobit*d* said, "I want to be sure, brother, whose son you are and what your name is." ¹³He replied, "I am Azariah, the son of the great Hananiah, one of your relatives." ¹⁴Then Tobit said to him, "Welcome! God save you, brother. Do not feel bitter toward me, brother, because I wanted to be sure about your ancestry. It turns out that you are a kinsman, and of good and noble lineage. For I knew Hananiah and Nathan,*e* the two sons of Shemeliah,*f* and they used to go with me to Jerusalem and worshiped with me there, and were not led astray. Your kindred are good people; you come of good stock. Hearty welcome!"

a Other authorities read *He*   *b* Gk *from him*
c Gk *He*   *d* Gk *he*   *e* Other ancient
authorities read *Jathan* or *Nathaniah*   *f* Other
ancient authorities read *Shemaiah*

5:4 *found the angel Raphael standing in front of him.* While looking for a human guide, Tobias meets an angelic messenger. The angel knows the way to the money. The angel will protect. The angel will orchestrate a visit along the route to Sarah and her family, which will lead to a marriage proposal by Tobias. When angels enter into our lives, things change. Look up. God's angel may be right in front of you.

5:9 *whether he is trustworthy enough to go with you.* The life of spiritual formation is confronted with innumerable opportunities for discernment. People stand before us. We must make judgments. We entrust valuable things into the hands of people we do not know well. Ask for the gift of discernment, to see if people are "trustworthy."

15 Then he added, "I will pay you a drachma a day as wages, as well as expenses for yourself and my son. So go with my son, [16]and[a] I will add something to your wages." Raphael[b] answered, "I will go with him; so do not fear. We shall leave in good health and return to you in good health, because the way is safe." [17]So Tobit[c] said to him, "Blessings be upon you, brother."

Then he called his son and said to him, "Son, prepare supplies for the journey and set out with your brother. May God in heaven bring you safely there and return you in good health to me; and may his angel, my son, accompany you both for your safety."

Before he went out to start his journey, he kissed his father and mother. Tobit then said to him, "Have a safe journey."

18 But his mother[d] began to weep, and said to Tobit, "Why is it that you have sent my child away? Is he not the staff of our hand as he goes in and out before us? [19]Do not heap money upon money, but let it be a ransom for our child. [20]For the life that is given to us by the Lord is enough for us." [21]Tobit[b] said to her, "Do not worry; our child will leave in good health and return to us in good health. Your eyes will see him on the day when he returns to you in good health. Say no more! Do not fear for them, my sister. [22]For a good angel will accompany him; his journey will be successful, and he will come back in good health." [1]So she stopped weeping.

Journey to Rages

The young man went out and the angel went with him; [2]and the dog came out with him and went along with them. So they both journeyed along, and when the first night overtook them they camped by the Tigris river. [3]Then the young man went down to wash his feet in the Tigris river. Suddenly a large fish leaped up from the water and tried to swallow the young man's foot, and he cried out. [4]But the angel said to the young man, "Catch hold of the fish and hang on to it!" So the young man grasped the fish and drew it up on the land. [5]Then the angel said to him, "Cut open the fish and take out its gall, heart, and liver. Keep them with you, but throw away the intestines. For its gall, heart, and liver are useful as medicine." [6]So after cutting open the fish the young man gathered together the gall, heart, and liver; then he roasted and ate some of the fish, and kept some to be salted.

The two continued on their way together until they were near Media.[e] [7]Then the young man questioned the angel and said to him, "Brother Azariah, what medicinal value is there in the fish's heart and liver, and in the gall?" [8]He replied, "As for the fish's heart and liver, you must burn them to make a smoke in the presence of a man or woman afflicted by a demon or evil spirit, and every affliction will flee away and never remain with that person any longer. [9]And as for the gall, anoint a person's eyes where white films have appeared on them; blow upon them, upon the white films, and the eyes[f] will be healed."

Raphael's Instructions

10 When he entered Media and already was approaching Ecbatana,[g] [11]Raphael said to the young man, "Brother Tobias." "Here I am," he answered. Then Raphael[c] said to him, "We must stay this night in the home of Raguel. He is your relative, and he has a daughter named Sarah. [12]He has no male heir and no daughter except Sarah only, and you, as next of kin to her, have before all other

---

a Other ancient authorities add *when you return safely*　　*b* Gk *He*　　*c* Gk *he*　　*d* Other ancient authorities add *Anna*　　*e* Other ancient authorities read *Ecbatana*　　*f* Gk *they*　　*g* Other ancient authorities read *Rages*

6:3–6 *a large fish leaped up from the water.* On the journey to the kinsman's house, Tobias learns that the fish that threatens will be the fish that heals. It will supply the ingredients to scare off demons and to heal blind eyes. And one can also eat the rest of the fish!

6:11–13 *Then Raphael said to him.* The secret plan of God's providence is at work when we are unaware of it. Sometimes, as here, it is explained to us. Other times we might remain oblivious to it. If we could only believe, in our distress and uncertainty, that God's forces are working for us in secret, then we would have peace like a river.

men a hereditary claim on her. Also it is right for you to inherit her father's possessions. Moreover, the girl is sensible, brave, and very beautiful, and her father is a good man." [13]He continued, "You have every right to take her in marriage. So listen to me, brother; tonight I will speak to her father about the girl, so that we may take her to be your bride. When we return from Rages we will celebrate her marriage. For I know that Raguel can by no means keep her from you or promise her to another man without incurring the penalty of death according to the decree of the book of Moses. Indeed he knows that you, rather than any other man, are entitled to marry his daughter. So now listen to me, brother, and tonight we shall speak concerning the girl and arrange her engagement to you. And when we return from Rages we will take her and bring her back with us to your house."

14 Then Tobias said in answer to Raphael, "Brother Azariah, I have heard that she already has been married to seven husbands and that they died in the bridal chamber. On the night when they went in to her, they would die. I have heard people saying that it was a demon that killed them. [15]It does not harm her, but it kills anyone who desires to approach her. So now, since I am the only son my father has, I am afraid that I may die and bring my father's and mother's life down to their grave, grieving for me—and they have no other son to bury them."

16 But Raphael[a] said to him, "Do you not remember your father's orders when he commanded you to take a wife from your father's house? Now listen to me, brother, and say no more about this demon. Take her. I know that this very night she will be given to you in marriage. [17]When you enter the bridal chamber, take some of the fish's liver and heart, and put them on the embers of the incense. An odor will be given off; [18]the demon will smell it and flee, and will never be seen near her any more. Now when you are about to go to bed with her, both of you must first stand up and pray, imploring the Lord of heaven that mercy and safety may be granted to you. Do not be afraid, for she was set apart for you before the world was made. You will save her, and she will go with you. I presume that you will have children by her, and they will be as brothers to you. Now say no more!" When Tobias heard the words of Raphael and learned that she was his kinswoman,[b] related through his father's lineage, he loved her very much, and his heart was drawn to her.

Arrival at Home of Raguel

7 Now when they[c] entered Ecbatana, Tobias[a] said to him, "Brother Azariah, take me straight to our brother Raguel." So he took him to Raguel's house, where they found him sitting beside the courtyard door. They greeted him first, and he replied, "Joyous greetings, brothers; welcome and good health!" Then he brought them into his house. [2]He said to his wife Edna, "How much the young man resembles my kinsman Tobit!" [3]Then Edna questioned them, saying, "Where are you from, brothers?" They answered, "We belong to the descendants of Naphtali who are exiles in Nineveh." [4]She said to them, "Do you know our kinsman Tobit?" And they replied, "Yes, we know him." Then she asked them, "Is he[d] in good health?" [5]They replied, "He is alive and in good health." And Tobias added, "He is my father!" [6]At that Raguel jumped up and kissed him and wept. [7]He also spoke to him as follows, "Blessings on you, my child, son of a good and noble father![e] O most miserable of

a Gk he   b Gk sister   c Other ancient authorities read he   d Other ancient authorities add alive and   e Other ancient authorities add When he heard that Tobit had lost his sight, he was stricken with grief and wept. Then he said,

---

6:14 *On the night when they went in to her, they would die.* The plan of God does not always seem to be a plan of grace. After all, Tobias might be Sarah's eighth victim if he marries her. Question the plan as it is presented to you. If it is from God, it can endure the questions.

6:18 *When Tobias heard the words of Raphael . . . he loved her very much.* God is the great interpreter, and God will make the situation plain. When Tobias understands and his fears are allayed, he embraces the plan with gratitude and joy. His heart soars.

calamities that such an upright and beneficent man has become blind!" He then embraced his kinsman Tobias and wept. ⁸His wife Edna also wept for him, and their daughter Sarah likewise wept. ⁹Then Raguel*ᵃ* slaughtered a ram from the flock and received them very warmly.

Marriage of Tobias and Sarah

When they had bathed and washed themselves and had reclined to dine, Tobias said to Raphael, "Brother Azariah, ask Raguel to give me my kinswoman*ᵇ* Sarah." ¹⁰But Raguel overheard it and said to the lad, "Eat and drink, and be merry tonight. For no one except you, brother, has the right to marry my daughter Sarah. Likewise I am not at liberty to give her to any other man than yourself, because you are my nearest relative. But let me explain to you the true situation more fully, my child. ¹¹I have given her to seven men of our kinsmen, and all died on the night when they went in to her. But now, my child, eat and drink, and the Lord will act on behalf of you both." But Tobias said, "I will neither eat nor drink anything until you settle the things that pertain to me." So Raguel said, "I will do so. She is given to you in accordance with the decree in the book of Moses, and it has been decreed from heaven that she be given to you. Take your kinswoman;*ᵇ* from now on you are her brother and she is your sister. She is given to you from today and forever. May the Lord of heaven, my child, guide and prosper you both this night and grant you mercy and

peace." ¹²Then Raguel summoned his daughter Sarah. When she came to him he took her by the hand and gave her to Tobias,*ᶜ* saying, "Take her to be your wife in accordance with the law and decree written in the book of Moses. Take her and bring her safely to your father. And may the God of heaven prosper your journey with his peace." ¹³Then he called her mother and told her to bring writing material; and he wrote out a copy of a marriage contract, to the effect that he gave her to him as wife according to the decree of the law of Moses. ¹⁴Then they began to eat and drink.

15 Raguel called his wife Edna and said to her, "Sister, get the other room ready, and take her there." ¹⁶So she went and made the bed in the room as he had told her, and brought Sarah*ᵈ* there. She wept for her daughter.*ᵈ* Then, wiping away the tears,*ᵉ* she said to her, "Take courage, my daughter; the Lord of heaven grant you joy*ᶠ* in place of your sorrow. Take courage, my daughter." Then she went out.

Tobias Routs the Demon

8 When they had finished eating and drinking they wanted to retire; so they took the young man and brought him into the bedroom. ²Then Tobias remembered the words of Raphael, and he took the fish's liver and heart out of the bag where he had them and put them on the embers of the

a Gk *he*   *b* Gk *sister*   *c* Gk *him*   *d* Gk *her*
e Other ancient authorities read *the tears of her*
daughter   *f* Other ancient authorities read *favor*

7:11 *until you settle the things that pertain to me.* The plan has its fulfillment in Tobias's marriage to Sarah. The plan is sealed by the sharing of common elements: food and drink. Readers have almost forgotten the money, which was the reason for embarking on the trip in the first place.

7:16 *Take courage, my daughter; the Lord of heaven grant you joy in place of your sorrow.* This is the prayer not simply for Tobias and Sarah, but for the world today. May there be joy in place of sorrow in our lives, in the tangled world of the Middle East, in the steppes of central Asia, in the hearts of all who genuinely call on God.

Responding
7:16 PRAYER. The conditions behind this marriage are far from normal; immediately prior to each of seven other weddings, the bride's future husband had died. At this wedding, we find the bride's mother praying that God would grant the bride "joy in place of [her] sorrow." Describe someone you know whose life has been steeped in sorrow. As the opportunity arises, gently ask the person if you could pray for him or her. *See also* Spiritual Disciplines Index.

incense. ³The odor of the fish so repelled the demon that he fled to the remotest parts *a* of Egypt. But Raphael followed him, and at once bound him there hand and foot.

4 When the parents *b* had gone out and shut the door of the room, Tobias got out of bed and said to Sarah, *c* "Sister, get up, and let us pray and implore our Lord that he grant us mercy and safety." ⁵So she got up, and they began to pray and implore that they might be kept safe. Tobias *d* began by saying,

"Blessed are you, O God of our
        ancestors,
    and blessed is your name in all
        generations forever.
Let the heavens and the whole creation
    bless you forever.
6 You made Adam, and for him you made
        his wife Eve
    as a helper and support.
From the two of them the human
    race has sprung.
You said, 'It is not good that the man
        should be alone;
    let us make a helper for him like
        himself.'
7 I now am taking this kinswoman of
        mine,
    not because of lust,
    but with sincerity.
Grant that she and I may find mercy
    and that we may grow old together."
⁸And they both said, "Amen, Amen." ⁹Then they went to sleep for the night.

But Raguel arose and called his servants to him, and they went and dug a grave, ¹⁰for he said, "It is possible that he will die and we will become an object of ridicule and derision." ¹¹When they had finished digging the grave, Raguel went into his house and called his wife, ¹²saying, "Send one of the maids and have her go in to see if he is alive. But if he is dead, let us bury him without anyone knowing it." ¹³So they sent the maid, lit a lamp, and opened the door; and she went in and found them sound asleep together. ¹⁴Then the maid came out and informed them that he was alive and that nothing was wrong. ¹⁵So they blessed the God of heaven, and Raguel *b* said,

"Blessed are you, O God, with every
        pure blessing;
    let all your chosen ones bless you. *e*
    Let them bless you forever.
16 Blessed are you because you have made
        me glad.
    It has not turned out as I expected,
    but you have dealt with us according
        to your great mercy.
17 Blessed are you because you had
        compassion
    on two only children.
Be merciful to them, O Master, and keep
        them safe;
    bring their lives to fulfillment
    in happiness and mercy."
¹⁸Then he ordered his servants to fill in the grave before daybreak.

Wedding Feast

19 After this he asked his wife to bake many loaves of bread; and he went out to the herd and brought two steers and four rams and ordered them to be slaughtered. So they began to make preparations. ²⁰Then he called for Tobias and swore on oath to him in these words: *f* "You shall not leave here for fourteen days, but shall stay here eating and drinking with me; and you shall cheer up my daughter, who has been depressed. ²¹Take at once half of what I own and return in safety to your father; the other half will be yours when my wife and I die. Take courage, my child. I am your father and Edna is your mother, and we belong to you as well as to your wife *g* now and forever. Take courage, my child."

a Or *fled through the air to the parts*   *b* Gk *they*
c Gk *her*   *d* Gk *He*   *e* Other ancient authorities lack this line   *f* Other ancient authorities read *Tobias and said to him*
g Gk *sister*

8:9 *dug a grave*. Touching dramatic irony. There is even an undercurrent of humor. When sorrow has laced our lives, we try to prepare for the next onset of anguish. We dig graves to hold the detritus of future tragedies, because we are so accustomed to loss that preparation for its next onslaught at least gives us something to do until it strikes.

The Money Recovered

9 Then Tobias called Raphael and said to him, [2]"Brother Azariah, take four servants and two camels with you and travel to Rages. Go to the home of Gabael, give him the bond, get the money, and then bring him with you to the wedding celebration. [4]For you know that my father must be counting the days, and if I delay even one day I will upset him very much. [3]You are witness to the oath Raguel has sworn, and I cannot violate his oath."[a] [5]So Raphael with the four servants and two camels went to Rages in Media and stayed with Gabael. Raphael[b] gave him the bond and informed him that Tobit's son Tobias had married and was inviting him to the wedding celebration. So Gabael[c] got up and counted out to him the money bags, with their seals intact; then they loaded them on the camels.[d] [6]In the morning they both got up early and went to the wedding celebration. When they came into Raguel's house they found Tobias reclining at table. He sprang up and greeted Gabael,[e] who wept and blessed him with the words, "Good and noble son of a father good and noble, upright and generous! May the Lord grant the blessing of heaven to you and your wife, and to your wife's father and mother. Blessed be God, for I see in Tobias the very image of my cousin Tobit."

Anxiety of the Parents

10 Now, day by day, Tobit kept counting how many days Tobias[c] would need for going and for returning. And when the days had passed and his son did not appear, [2]he said, "Is it possible that he has been detained? Or that Gabael has died, and there is no one to give him the money?" [3]And he began to worry. [4]His wife Anna said, "My child has perished and is no longer among the living." And she began to weep and mourn for her son, saying, [5]"Woe to me, my child, the light of my eyes, that I let you make

the journey." [6]But Tobit kept saying to her, "Be quiet and stop worrying, my dear;[f] he is all right. Probably something unexpected has happened there. The man who went with him is trustworthy and is one of our own kin. Do not grieve for him, my dear;[f] he will soon be here." [7]She answered him, "Be quiet yourself! Stop trying to deceive me! My child has perished." She would rush out every day and watch the road her son had taken, and would heed no one.[g] When the sun had set she would go in and mourn and weep all night long, getting no sleep at all.

Tobias and Sarah Start for Home

Now when the fourteen days of the wedding celebration had ended that Raguel had sworn to observe for his daughter, Tobias came to him and said, "Send me back, for I know that my father and mother do not believe that they will see me again. So I beg of you, father, to let me go so that I may return to my own father. I have already explained to you how I left him." [8]But Raguel said to Tobias, "Stay, my child, stay with me; I will send messengers to your father Tobit and they will inform him about you." [9]But he said, "No! I beg you to send me back to my father." [10]So Raguel promptly gave Tobias his wife Sarah, as well as half of all his property: male and female slaves, oxen and sheep, donkeys and camels, clothing, money, and household goods. [11]Then he saw them safely off; he embraced Tobias[e] and said, "Farewell, my child; have a safe journey. The Lord of heaven prosper you and your wife Sarah, and may I see children of yours before I die." [12]Then he kissed his daughter Sarah and said to her, "My daughter, honor your father-in-law and your mother-in-law,[h] since from now on they are as much your parents as

a In other ancient authorities verse 3 precedes verse 4   b Gk He   c Gk he   d Other ancient authorities lack on the camels   e Gk him f Gk sister   g Other ancient authorities read and she would eat nothing   h Other ancient authorities lack parts of Then . . . mother-in-law

---

10:1–3 *he began to worry.* Tobias did not return within the expected time. Hope deferred makes the heart sick. We have our timetables and woe to the world if it does not work accord-

ing to those timetables! Worry is the result. Worry eats at us, destroying our peace of mind, circumscribing our powers, telescoping our vision.

those who gave you birth. Go in peace, daughter, and may I hear a good report about you as long as I live." Then he bade them farewell and let them go. Then Edna said to Tobias, "My child and dear brother, the Lord of heaven bring you back safely, and may I live long enough to see children of you and of my daughter Sarah before I die. In the sight of the Lord I entrust my daughter to you; do nothing to grieve her all the days of your life. Go in peace, my child. From now on I am your mother and Sarah is your beloved wife.[a] May we all prosper together all the days of our lives." Then she kissed them both and saw them safely off. [13]Tobias parted from Raguel with happiness and joy, praising the Lord of heaven and earth, King over all, because he had made his journey a success. Finally, he blessed Raguel and his wife Edna, and said, "I have been commanded by the Lord to honor you all the days of my life."[b]

Homeward Journey

11 When they came near to Kaserin, which is opposite Nineveh, Raphael said, [2]"You are aware of how we left your father. [3]Let us run ahead of your wife and prepare the house while they are still on the way." [4]As they went on together Raphael[c] said to him, "Have the gall ready." And the dog[d] went along behind them.

[5] Meanwhile Anna sat looking intently down the road by which her son would come. [6]When she caught sight of him coming, she said to his father, "Look, your son is coming, and the man who went with him!"

Tobit's Sight Restored

[7] Raphael said to Tobias, before he had approached his father, "I know that his eyes will be opened. [8]Smear the gall of the fish on his eyes; the medicine will make the white films shrink and peel off from his eyes, and your father will regain his sight and see the light."

[9] Then Anna ran up to her son and threw her arms around him, saying, "Now that I have seen you, my child, I am ready to die." And she wept. [10]Then Tobit got up and came stumbling out through the courtyard door. Tobias went up to him, [11]with the gall of the fish in his hand, and holding him firmly, he blew into his eyes, saying, "Take courage, father." With this he applied the medicine on his eyes, [12]and it made them smart.[b] [13]Next, with both his hands he peeled off the white films from the corners of his eyes. Then Tobit[c] saw his son and[e] threw his arms around him, [14]and he wept and said to him, "I see you, my son, the light of my eyes!" Then he said,

"Blessed be God,
   and blessed be his great name,
   and blessed be all his holy angels.
May his holy name be blessed[f]
   throughout all the ages.
[15] Though he afflicted me,
   he has had mercy upon me.[g]
   Now I see my son Tobias!"

So Tobit went in rejoicing and praising God

a Gk *sister*   b Lat: Meaning of Gk uncertain
c Gk *he*   d Codex Sinaiticus reads *And the Lord*
e Other ancient authorities lack *saw his son and*
f Codex Sinaiticus reads *May his great name be upon us and blessed be all the angels*   g Lat: Gk lacks this line

---

11:6 *Look, your son is coming!* In language reminiscent of the parable of the prodigal son, Anna announces Tobias's arrival. All the waiting is suddenly forgotten. Time rushes together. The endless days and nights of prayer, hope, worry, frustration, and false hope have now ended. She thought that the biggest gift in store was the gift of Tobias's return. In fact, that was only a small portion of it.

11:8 *Smear the gall . . . and your father will regain his sight.* Tobias had already been told in 6:9 that the gall was to be applied to Tobit's eyes to restore his sight. The angel repeats the instructions here. There is often a considerable

gap in time between our knowledge of what needs to be done and the right time for its application. It is not enough to know the words or even the cure; we must have divine insight to use them on the right occasion. Words fitly spoken and acts fitly done are beams of the divine love.

11:13 *Then Tobit saw his son!* Not only has his son returned, but Tobit sees his son. Surely Tobit thought that his blindness was permanent. Do we truly believe that God is able to accomplish abundantly more than we even ask or imagine (Eph 3:20)?

at the top of his voice. Tobias reported to his father that his journey had been successful, that he had brought the money, that he had married Raguel's daughter Sarah, and that she was, indeed, on her way there, very near to the gate of Nineveh.

16 Then Tobit, rejoicing and praising God, went out to meet his daughter-in-law at the gate of Nineveh. When the people of Nineveh saw him coming, walking along in full vigor and with no one leading him, they were amazed. [17]Before them all, Tobit acknowledged that God had been merciful to him and had restored his sight. When Tobit met Sarah the wife of his son Tobias, he blessed her saying, "Come in, my daughter, and welcome. Blessed be your God who has brought you to us, my daughter. Blessed be your father and your mother, blessed be my son Tobias, and blessed be you, my daughter. Come in now to your home, and welcome, with blessing and joy. Come in, my daughter." So on that day there was rejoicing among all the Jews who were in Nineveh. [18]Ahikar and his nephew Nadab were also present to share Tobit's joy. With merriment they celebrated Tobias's wedding feast for seven days, and many gifts were given to him. [a]

Raphael's Wages

12 When the wedding celebration was ended, Tobit called his son Tobias and said to him, "My child, see to paying the wages of the man who went with you, and give him a bonus as well." [2]He replied, "Father, how much shall I pay him? It would do no harm to give him half of the possessions brought back with me. [3]For he has led me back to you safely, he cured my wife, he brought the money back with me, and he healed you. How much extra shall I give him as a bonus?" [4]Tobit said, "He deserves, my child, to receive half of all that he brought back." [5]So Tobias[b] called him

and said, "Take for your wages half of all that you brought back, and farewell."

Raphael's Exhortation

6 Then Raphael[b] called the two of them privately and said to them, "Bless God and acknowledge him in the presence of all the living for the good things he has done for you. Bless and sing praise to his name. With fitting honor declare to all people the deeds[c] of God. Do not be slow to acknowledge him. [7]It is good to conceal the secret of a king, but to acknowledge and reveal the works of God, and with fitting honor to acknowledge him. Do good and evil will not overtake you. [8]Prayer with fasting[d] is good, but better than both is almsgiving with righteousness. A little with righteousness is better than wealth with wrongdoing.[e] It is better to give alms than to lay up gold. [9]For almsgiving saves from death and purges away every sin. Those who give alms will enjoy a full life, [10]but those who commit sin and do wrong are their own worst enemies.

Raphael Discloses His Identity

11 "I will now declare the whole truth to you and will conceal nothing from you. Already I have declared it to you when I said, 'It is good to conceal the secret of a king, but to reveal with due honor the works of God.' [12]So now when you and Sarah prayed, it was I who brought and read[f] the record of your prayer before the glory of the Lord, and likewise whenever you would bury the dead. [13]And that time when you did not hesitate to get up and leave your dinner to go and bury the dead, [14]I was sent to you to test you. And at the same time God sent me to heal you and Sarah your daughter-in-law. [15]I am

a Other ancient authorities lack parts of this sentence   *b* Gk *he*   *c* Gk *words*; other ancient authorities read *words of the deeds*   *d* Codex Sinaiticus *with sincerity*   *e* Lat   *f* Lat: Gk lacks *and read*

Responding

12:8 FASTING. Similar to this verse is Matt 6:16–18, in which Jesus' teaching about fasting is given with the assumption that we will fast—"whenever you fast." He goes on to explain that we should go about our lives as we would on every other day and not call attention to the fact that we are fasting. Rather, we should do it in secret. What reason does Jesus give for keeping our fast a secret? Why is this important for the growth of our soul? *See also* Spiritual Disciplines Index.

Raphael, one of the seven angels who stand ready and enter before the glory of the Lord."

16 The two of them were shaken; they fell face down, for they were afraid. 17 But he said to them, "Do not be afraid; peace be with you. Bless God forevermore. 18 As for me, when I was with you, I was not acting on my own will, but by the will of God. Bless him each and every day; sing his praises. 19 Although you were watching me, I really did not eat or drink anything—but what you saw was a vision. 20 So now get up from the ground, *a* and acknowledge God. See, I am ascending to him who sent me. Write down all these things that have happened to you." And he ascended. 21 Then they stood up, and could see him no more. 22 They kept blessing God and singing his praises, and they acknowledged God for these marvelous deeds of his, when an angel of God had appeared to them.

Tobit's Thanksgiving to God

13 Then Tobit *b* said:
"Blessed be God who lives forever,
  because his kingdom *c* lasts
      throughout all ages.
2 For he afflicts, and he shows mercy;
  he leads down to Hades in the lowest
      regions of the earth,
  and he brings up from the great abyss, *d*
  and there is nothing that can escape
      his hand.
3 Acknowledge him before the nations,
      O children of Israel;
  for he has scattered you among them.
4 He has shown you his greatness even
      there.
Exalt him in the presence of every
      living being,
  because he is our Lord and he is our
      God;

he is our Father and he is God forever.
5 He will afflict *e* you for your iniquities,
  but he will again show mercy on all of
      you.
He will gather you from all the nations
  among whom you have been scattered.
6 If you turn to him with all your heart
      and with all your soul,
  to do what is true before him,
then he will turn to you
  and will no longer hide his face from
      you.
So now see what he has done for you;
  acknowledge him at the top of your
      voice.
Bless the Lord of righteousness,
  and exalt the King of the ages. *f*
In the land of my exile I acknowledge
      him,
  and show his power and majesty to a
      nation of sinners:
'Turn back, you sinners, and do what is
      right before him;
  perhaps he may look with favor upon
      you and show you mercy.'
7 As for me, I exalt my God,
  and my soul rejoices in the King of
      heaven.
8 Let all people speak of his majesty,
  and acknowledge him in Jerusalem.
9 O Jerusalem, the holy city,
  he afflicted *g* you for the deeds of your
      hands, *h*

a Other ancient authorities read *now bless the Lord on earth*   *b* Gk *he*   *c* Other ancient authorities read *forever, and his kingdom*   *d* Gk *from destruction*   *e* Other ancient authorities read *He afflicted*   *f* The lacuna in codex Sinaiticus, verses 6b to 10a, is filled in from other ancient authorities   *g* Other ancient authorities read *will afflict*   *h* Other ancient authorities read *your children*

12:15 *I am Raphael, one of the seven angels.* As the scales fall from Tobit's eyes, so the mystery of Raphael also falls away. Raphael's self-revelation neatly corresponds to Tobit's self-identification in 1:3. We often perceive God's presence in our life only after the events have occurred. Our long and dangerous journeys might stretch us to our limits, but occasionally we are given fresh draughts

of interpretive clarity. Praise God for those insights.

13:2 *For he afflicts, and he shows mercy.* We often feel most comfortable only with the second half of this sentence. But those who have been through the valleys of life are not afraid to say that God afflicts. God leads to Hades as well as brings up from the abyss. Why give God credit only for the easy times in life?

but will again have mercy on the
  children of the righteous.
10 Acknowledge the Lord, for he is good,ᵃ
  and bless the King of the ages,
  so that his tentᵇ may be rebuilt in you
    in joy.
May he cheer all those within you who
    are captives,
  and love all those within you who are
    distressed,
  to all generations forever.
11 A bright light will shine to all the ends
    of the earth;
  many nations will come to you from
    far away,
  the inhabitants of the remotest parts of
    the earth to your holy name,
  bearing gifts in their hands for the
    King of heaven.
Generation after generation will give
    joyful praise in you;
  the name of the chosen city will
    endure forever.
12 Cursed are all who speak a harsh word
    against you;
  cursed are all who conquer you
  and pull down your walls,
all who overthrow your towers
  and set your homes on fire.
But blessed forever will be all who
    revere you.ᶜ
13 Go, then, and rejoice over the children
    of the righteous,
  for they will be gathered together
  and will praise the Lord of the ages.
14 Happy are those who love you,
  and happy are those who rejoice in
    your prosperity.

Happy also are all people who grieve
    with you
  because of your afflictions;
for they will rejoice with you
  and witness all your glory forever.
15 My soul blessesᵈ the Lord, the great King!
16   For Jerusalem will be builtᵉ as his
      house for all ages.
How happy I will be if a remnant of my
      descendants should survive
  to see your glory and acknowledge
      the King of heaven.
The gates of Jerusalem will be built with
      sapphire and emerald,
  and all your walls with precious stones.
The towers of Jerusalem will be built
      with gold,
  and their battlements with pure gold.
The streets of Jerusalem will be paved
      with ruby and with stones of Ophir.
17 The gates of Jerusalem will sing hymns
      of joy,
  and all her houses will cry, 'Hallelujah!
Blessed be the God of Israel!'
  and the blessed will bless the holy
      name forever and ever."

Tobit's Final Counsel

14 So ended Tobit's words of praise.
2 Tobitᶠ died in peace when he was
one hundred twelve years old, and was buried
with great honor in Nineveh. He was sixty-
twoᵍ years old when he lost his eyesight, and
after regaining it he lived in prosperity, giv-

---

a Other ancient authorities read *Lord worthily*
b Or *tabernacle*   c Other ancient authorities read
who build you up   d Or *O my soul, bless*   e Other
ancient authorities add *for a city*   f Gk *He*
g Other ancient authorities read *fifty-eight*

13:5 *He will gather you.* Tobit no longer longs
for death. His experience of redemption makes
him yearn for the gathering of Israel, the return
to the land. Our small victories make us yearn
for the full satisfaction of the heart.

13:11 *A bright light will shine to all the ends
of the earth.* The biblical pattern of redemption
and restoration emphasizes the gathering of
Israel as the first step of the light of God going
out to the nations. That light then will attract
the nations to come to Israel. Our longings for

peace and harmony in our broken world are
encouraged in this passage. The quality of our
spiritual formation is related to the intensity and
quality of our longings.

14:2 *he lived in prosperity, giving alms and
continually blessing God.* Life goes on after the
maelstrom. Tobit's activity mirrors that of his
earlier life: faithful living and almsgiving. He
lives in hope (v 5) and dies in satisfaction. God
be praised!

ing alms and continually blessing God and acknowledging God's majesty.

3 When he was about to die, he called his son Tobias and the seven sons of Tobias[a] and gave this command: "My son, take your children [4]and hurry off to Media, for I believe the word of God that Nahum spoke about Nineveh, that all these things will take place and overtake Assyria and Nineveh. Indeed, everything that was spoken by the prophets of Israel, whom God sent, will occur. None of all their words will fail, but all will come true at their appointed times. So it will be safer in Media than in Assyria and Babylon. For I know and believe that whatever God has said will be fulfilled and will come true; not a single word of the prophecies will fail. All of our kindred, inhabitants of the land of Israel, will be scattered and taken as captives from the good land; and the whole land of Israel will be desolate, even Samaria and Jerusalem will be desolate. And the temple of God in it will be burned to the ground, and it will be desolate for a while.[b]

5 "But God will again have mercy on them, and God will bring them back into the land of Israel; and they will rebuild the temple of God, but not like the first one until the period when the times of fulfillment shall come. After this they all will return from their exile and will rebuild Jerusalem in splendor; and in it the temple of God will be rebuilt, just as the prophets of Israel have said concerning it. [6]Then the nations in the whole world will all be converted and worship God in truth. They will all abandon their idols, which deceitfully have led them into their error; [7]and in righteousness they will praise the eternal God. All the Israelites who are saved in those days and are truly mindful of God will be gathered together; they will go to Jerusalem and live in safety forever in the land of Abraham, and it will be given over to them. Those who sincerely love God will rejoice, but those who commit sin and injustice will vanish from all the earth. [8,9]So now, my children, I command you, serve God faithfully and do what is pleasing in his sight. Your children are also to be commanded to do what is right and to give alms, and to be mindful of God and to bless his name at all times with sin-

cerity and with all their strength. So now, my son, leave Nineveh; do not remain here. [10]On whatever day you bury your mother beside me, do not stay overnight within the confines of the city. For I see that there is much wickedness within it, and that much deceit is practiced within it, while the people are without shame. See, my son, what Nadab did to Ahikar who had reared him. Was he not, while still alive, brought down into the earth? For God repaid him to his face for this shameful treatment. Ahikar came out into the light, but Nadab went into the eternal darkness, because he tried to kill Ahikar. Because he gave alms, Ahikar[c] escaped the fatal trap that Nadab had set for him, but Nadab fell into it himself, and was destroyed. [11]So now, my children, see what almsgiving accomplishes, and what injustice does—it brings death! But now my breath fails me."

Death of Tobit and Anna

Then they laid him on his bed, and he died; and he received an honorable funeral. [12]When Tobias's mother died, he buried her beside his father. Then he and his wife and children[d] returned to Media and settled in Ecbatana with Raguel his father-in-law. [13]He treated his parents-in-law[e] with great respect in their old age, and buried them in Ecbatana of Media. He inherited both the property of Raguel and that of his father Tobit. [14]He died highly respected at the age of one hundred seventeen[f] years. [15]Before he died he heard[g] of the destruction of Nineveh, and he saw its prisoners being led into Media, those whom King Cyaxares[h] of Media had taken captive. Tobias[i] praised God for all he had done to the people of Nineveh and Assyria; before he died he rejoiced over Nineveh, and he blessed the Lord God forever and ever. Amen.[j]

a Lat: Gk lacks and the seven sons of Tobias   b Lat: Other ancient authorities read of God will be in distress and will be burned for a while   c Gk he; other ancient authorities read Manasses
d Codex Sinaiticus lacks and children   e Gk them
f Other authorities read other numbers
g Codex Sinaiticus reads saw and heard
h Cn: Codex Sinaiticus Ahikar; other ancient authorities read Nebuchadnezzar and Ahasuerus
i Gk He   j Other ancient authorities lack Amen

PRAYER OF AZARIAH AND THE SONG OF THE THREE JEWS

(Part of Chapter 3 of the Greek version of Daniel)

Sometime during the intertestamental period three additions to the book of Daniel were composed: the Prayer of Azariah and the Song of the Three Jews, Susanna, and Bel and the Dragon. Though written in the second or first century BC, all three stories are set in Babylon during the days of Daniel (sixth century BC). None of these stories are included in the Protestant Old Testament canon, but they have survived no doubt due to their powerful testimony to God's faithfulness to his people in exile.

Encouragement in Exile

Although they are situated in sixth-century BC Babylon, the overall purpose of these stories is to encourage Hellenistic Jews, who were likewise living in "exile." Many Jews were dispersed throughout the world, while those in ancient Palestine endured the humiliation and oppression of foreign rule in their homeland. The message that unites all three additions is the same: God has not forgotten his people. This message certainly has a dynamic personal dimension, but it also concerns Israel as a people, as a nation. What is of ultimate concern is not simply the survival of Jews

See also *"The With-God Life" essays for this section of the Bible, "The People of God in Exile,"* pp. 1171–74, *and "The People of God in Restoration,"* pp. 1355–59.

as individuals, but the continued survival and reinvigoration of the People of God, in their land, worshiping God in accordance with the law.

The setting for the Prayer of Azariah and the Song of the Three Jews is the opening chapters of the book of Daniel. There we read that Daniel's three companions, Hananiah, Mishael, and Azariah (given the Babylonian names Shadrach, Meshach, Abednego in Dan 1:7), refused to worship the gods and idols of Babylon. They were cast into a furnace (Dan 3:22–23), but delivered through the intervention of a fourth figure who had "the appearance of a god" (Dan 3:25). The Prayer of Azariah and the Song of the Three Jews recounts the prayer of Azariah (vv 3–22) and the song that he and his two companions sang in the fire (vv 29–68).

An Appeal for Deliverance

The contents of the prayer and song may be a bit surprising. One might expect Azariah to pray to God for their rescue from the fire. One might also expect the song to "bless the Lord" (virtually each line of the song begins this way) for their rescue. But one quickly recognizes that this is not their focus. The prayer is not for the deliverance of the three men from the fire, nor is the song simply praise for deliverance of the three individuals. Rather, the personal well-being of the three is the author's vehicle for addressing a larger issue.

Azariah's prayer is an appeal to God, for the sake of his name and his covenantal promise to Abraham (vv 11–12), to deliver Israel from Babylon. It is also an appeal to the Israelites to have a contrite heart and humble spirit (v 15), so that God will deliver them. So when the three men are delivered from the fire (vv 26–27), we should see not just the rescue of individuals, but a symbol of Israel's national deliverance from exile. By writing a story such as this, concerning Israel's faithfulness in Babylon, the author is appealing to the past to encourage the people and give them hope in their present state of exile. In other words, God delivered Israel once before from exile in Babylon, and he can do it again.

Blessing and Praise

The song of praise (vv 29–68) blesses God and calls upon all creation and all people to bless him as well. The song begins by blessing God for his exalted status (vv 29–34). It then calls upon all of creation to bless him, beginning with heavenly things (vv 35–41) and progressing to the elements and seasons (vv 42–51), the earth and its contents (vv 52–59), and all people (v 60). Finally it narrows its focus to Israel (vv 61–65) and then to the three Jews (v 66). It is only in verse 66 that we see any indication that the deliverance of the three is the cause for praise. The point is that our understanding of God as deliverer must be rooted in our understanding of God as creator. God is mighty to deliver because he is mighty to create. This linkage of God as redeemer and creator is a common theme of the Old Testament (e.g., see Isa 45:11–25, esp. vv 12, 18).

And although the song eventually narrows to the three men delivered from the fire, it would be a mistake to understand the song as speaking primarily to the question of the deliverance of individuals. To be sure, this story would encourage Hellenistic Jews to endure persecution and remain faithful to the God of Israel, but ancient Israelites did not think in individualistic terms, as modern Westerners often do. To be an Israelite, particularly in the "furnace" of foreign domination, meant to have a heightened sense of corporate identity. In other words, Israelites did not ask first and foremost, "When is God going to save me?" but, "When is God going to save us?" So when we read that the three were delivered "from Hades . . . the power of death" (v 66), we must keep the big picture in view. The story is meant to encourage Hellenistic Jews as they awaited national deliverance from the "fire" of foreign rule and oppression. This is not to say that individual suffering and "exile" were unimportant to this writer, only that individual exile must be understood in the context of corporate identity as the People of God.

                                                                —*Peter Enns*

(Additions to Daniel, inserted between 3.23 and 3.24)

The Prayer of Azariah in the Furnace

1 They[a] walked around in the midst of the flames, singing hymns to God and blessing the Lord. 2 Then Azariah stood still in the fire and prayed aloud:

3 "Blessed are you, O Lord, God of our
      ancestors, and worthy of praise;
   and glorious is your name forever!
4 For you are just in all you have done;
   all your works are true and your ways
      right,
   and all your judgments are true.

5 You have executed true judgments in all
      you have brought upon us
   and upon Jerusalem, the holy city of
      our ancestors;
   by a true judgment you have brought
      all this upon us because of our
      sins.
6 For we have sinned and broken your law
      in turning away from you;
   in all matters we have sinned
      grievously.
7 We have not obeyed your
      commandments,

a That is, Hananiah, Mishael, and Azariah (Dan 2.17), the original names of Shadrach, Meshach, and Abednego (Dan 1.6-7).

---

3 *God of our ancestors.* Azariah is "reminding" God of something he makes more explicit in verse 11, that God's faithfulness to his covenant with Abraham is the basis upon which God will act now. God's past actions are "proof" that he will deliver. He is faithful to his people through all time because he is a promise-keeping God.

4–10 *in all you have brought upon us and upon Jerusalem.* We clearly see (esp. in vv 5, 9) that the focus of Azariah's prayer is Israel's national state of exile. The Israelites are in Babylon because of their sin and disobedience (vv 6–7), and God was just to punish them (vv 8–10). Even though on one real level this is a story intended to encourage Jews individually, it should be read first against the backdrop of Israel's national predicament. Azariah and his two companions, living during the time of Daniel, are here symbolic of Israel's national struggle to come to grips with its meager status. Beginning with Abraham and extending throughout the Bible, God does not deliver individuals for their own sake. He means to deliver a people, recreated in his own image. For Christians, this national deliverance is realized in the Church, the new People of God, redeemed in Christ. So too our own individual struggles to live lives of faith must be seen within the context of the People of God as a whole, in its full depth and breadth, both historically and today.

we have not kept them or done what
you have commanded us for our
own good.
8 So all that you have brought upon us,
and all that you have done to us,
you have done by a true judgment.
9 You have handed us over to our
enemies, lawless and hateful
rebels,
and to an unjust king, the most
wicked in all the world.
10 And now we cannot open our mouths;
we, your servants who worship you,
have become a shame and a
reproach.
11 For your name's sake do not give us up
forever,
and do not annul your covenant.
12   Do not withdraw your mercy from us,
for the sake of Abraham your beloved
and for the sake of your servant Isaac
and Israel your holy one,
13 to whom you promised
to multiply their descendants like the
stars of heaven
and like the sand on the shore of the
sea.
14 For we, O Lord, have become fewer than
any other nation,

and are brought low this day in all the
world because of our sins.
15 In our day we have no ruler, or prophet,
or leader,
no burnt offering, or sacrifice, or
oblation, or incense,
no place to make an offering before
you and to find mercy.
16 Yet with a contrite heart and a humble
spirit may we be accepted,
17   as though it were with burnt offerings
of rams and bulls,
or with tens of thousands of fat
lambs;
such may our sacrifice be in your
sight today,
and may we unreservedly follow
you,[a]
for no shame will come to those who
trust in you.
18 And now with all our heart we follow
you;
we fear you and seek your presence.
19 Do not put us to shame,
but deal with us in your patience
and in your abundant mercy.
20 Deliver us in accordance with your
marvelous works,

a Meaning of Gk uncertain

11–14 *to whom you promised to multiply their descendants.* God is reminded that his covenant obligation to Abraham, Isaac, and Jacob requires him to be faithful to their descendants. After all, God promised to multiply their descendants. If he doesn't come to their aid now when their number has dwindled lower than that of any other nation (v 14), would that not render that promise null and void? Once again, the basis for God's present help is his character as a covenant-keeping God, one who is faithful to his promises. The security of God's people rests in the character of the God they worship.

15–17 *we have no ruler, or prophet, or leader, no burnt offering, or sacrifice.* The means by which the Israelites had formerly been able to reconcile with God, namely, mediation by proper spiritual leaders and Temple sacrifices, do not exist in exile. Now, in the absence of these things, they are called upon to be humble and contrite. Humility and contrition are then

accepted as if they were offerings (v 17). The realities of the exile dictate the means of reconciliation, and God is ready and willing to accept them. In fact, it may be that an attitude of humility is more important (see Hos 6:6).

Responding
16–17 SACRIFICE. Consider offering a sacrifice to God. It could be a sacrificial act of service, a financial donation, or an attitude of humility. *See also* Spiritual Disciplines Index.

18–27 *Deliver us.* Deliverance of the three men is a symbol of national deliverance, since such deliverance will make known the world over that Israel's God is glorious (v 22). This was an important concern in Hellenistic Judaism: the Jews' vindication to all that they were still the People of God, even though they were justly punished by God.

and bring glory to your name, O Lord.
21 Let all who do harm to your servants be
      put to shame;
   let them be disgraced and deprived of
      all power,
   and let their strength be broken.
22 Let them know that you alone are the
      Lord God,
   glorious over the whole world."

The Song of the Three Jews

23 Now the king's servants who threw
them in kept stoking the furnace with naphtha, pitch, tow, and brushwood. 24And the
flames poured out above the furnace forty-
nine cubits, 25and spread out and burned those
Chaldeans who were caught near the furnace.
26But the angel of the Lord came down into
the furnace to be with Azariah and his companions, and drove the fiery flame out of the
furnace, 27and made the inside of the furnace
as though a moist wind were whistling
through it. The fire did not touch them at all
and caused them no pain or distress.

28 Then the three with one voice praised
and glorified and blessed God in the furnace:
29 "Blessed are you, O Lord, God of our
      ancestors,
   and to be praised and highly exalted
      forever;
30 And blessed is your glorious, holy
      name,
   and to be highly praised and highly
      exalted forever.
31 Blessed are you in the temple of your
      holy glory,
   and to be extolled and highly
      glorified forever.

32 Blessed are you who look into the
      depths from your throne on the
      cherubim,
   and to be praised and highly exalted
      forever.
33 Blessed are you on the throne of your
      kingdom,
   and to be extolled and highly exalted
      forever.
34 Blessed are you in the firmament of
      heaven,
   and to be sung and glorified forever.

35 "Bless the Lord, all you works of the Lord;
   sing praise to him and highly exalt
      him forever.
36 Bless the Lord, you heavens;
   sing praise to him and highly exalt
      him forever.
37 Bless the Lord, you angels of the Lord;
   sing praise to him and highly exalt
      him forever.
38 Bless the Lord, all you waters above the
      heavens;
   sing praise to him and highly exalt
      him forever.
39 Bless the Lord, all you powers of the
      Lord;
   sing praise to him and highly exalt
      him forever.
40 Bless the Lord, sun and moon;
   sing praise to him and highly exalt
      him forever.
41 Bless the Lord, stars of heaven;
   sing praise to him and highly exalt
      him forever.
42 "Bless the Lord, all rain and dew;
   sing praise to him and highly exalt
      him forever.

28–34 *Blessed are you.* The song blesses the
Lord for a number of things. It begins by praising
the God who is enthroned in heaven (v 34).
Who God is is the primary basis for praise. And
it is because God is holy and exalted that he
hears the cries of his people. God's character
and actions are never divorced from each other.

35–41 *all you works of the Lord.* After praise
of God for his character, God is praised for his
works of creation. Those mentioned in this section are heavenly beings and bodies in language
derived from Genesis 1. The song has not yet
gotten to praising God for his act of deliverance.
First things first: God is to be praised because
he is holy (vv 28–34), then because he is the
Creator.

42–68 *sing praise to him.* There is a clear
progression from the heavenly realm of verses
35–41 to more "down to earth" elements: rain,
seasons, light (vv 42–51); mountains, vegetation,

43 Bless the Lord, all you winds;
  sing praise to him and highly exalt
    him forever.
44 Bless the Lord, fire and heat;
  sing praise to him and highly exalt
    him forever.
45 Bless the Lord, winter cold and summer
    heat;
  sing praise to him and highly exalt
    him forever.
46 Bless the Lord, dews and falling snow;
  sing praise to him and highly exalt
    him forever.
47 Bless the Lord, nights and days;
  sing praise to him and highly exalt
    him forever.
48 Bless the Lord, light and darkness;
  sing praise to him and highly exalt
    him forever.
49 Bless the Lord, ice and cold;
  sing praise to him and highly exalt
    him forever.
50 Bless the Lord, frosts and snows;
  sing praise to him and highly exalt
    him forever.
51 Bless the Lord, lightnings and clouds;
  sing praise to him and highly exalt
    him forever.

52 "Let the earth bless the Lord;
  let it sing praise to him and highly
    exalt him forever.
53 Bless the Lord, mountains and hills;
  sing praise to him and highly exalt
    him forever.
54 Bless the Lord, all that grows in the
    ground;
  sing praise to him and highly exalt
    him forever.
55 Bless the Lord, seas and rivers;

  sing praise to him and highly exalt
    him forever.
56 Bless the Lord, you springs;
  sing praise to him and highly exalt
    him forever.
57 Bless the Lord, you whales and all that
    swim in the waters;
  sing praise to him and highly exalt
    him forever.
58 Bless the Lord, all birds of the air;
  sing praise to him and highly exalt
    him forever.
59 Bless the Lord, all wild animals and
    cattle;
  sing praise to him and highly exalt
    him forever.

60 "Bless the Lord, all people on earth;
  sing praise to him and highly exalt
    him forever.
61 Bless the Lord, O Israel;
  sing praise to him and highly exalt
    him forever.
62 Bless the Lord, you priests of the Lord;
  sing praise to him and highly exalt
    him forever.
63 Bless the Lord, you servants of the Lord;
  sing praise to him and highly exalt
    him forever.
64 Bless the Lord, spirits and souls of the
    righteous;
  sing praise to him and highly exalt
    him forever.
65 Bless the Lord, you who are holy and
    humble in heart;
  sing praise to him and highly exalt
    him forever.

66 "Bless the Lord, Hananiah, Azariah, and
    Mishael;

---

animal life (vv 52–59); all people (v 60); Israel (vv 61–65); Hananiah, Azariah, and Mishael (vv 66–68). Reasons for praising God are all around us, and his people must be continually reminded—even amid the most trying of circumstances—that God is worthy of praise, regardless of their circumstances. That does not mean that suffering and oppression are irrelevant. Quite the opposite. Focusing first on God's character and creative power allows us to see

present struggles in proper perspective.

65 *holy and humble in heart.* Here we revisit the theme introduced in verse 16. Israel's deliverance from exile, as with the deliverance of the three from the fire, depends upon the recognition of one's status relative to the one who sits enthroned in heaven and created the world. To have a true understanding of such things is to be humble in heart.

sing praise to him and highly exalt
  him forever.
For he has rescued us from Hades and
  saved us from the power*a* of
  death,
and delivered us from the midst of
  the burning fiery furnace;
from the midst of the fire he has
  delivered us.

67 Give thanks to the Lord, for he is good,
  for his mercy endures forever.
68 All who worship the Lord, bless the God
  of gods,
  sing praise to him and give thanks to
  him,
  for his mercy endures forever."

a Gk *hand*

Responding
65 CELEBRATION. Try to find some
new ways of singing praise to God in
everyday life. You and your family or friends
could revive the tradition of gathering around
the piano and singing together. If you don't have
a piano, try an a cappella sing-along. *See also*
Spiritual Disciplines Index.

66–68 *he has rescued us from Hades.* The
deliverance of the three is likened to deliverance from death. Israel's national deliverance
from exile would likewise be a new lease on life
for God's people. It would be the great demonstration of the holy (vv 29–34), creator God
(vv 35–59), responding in his mercy (vv 67–68)
to his people who have humbled themselves.

SUSANNA

(CHAPTER 13 OF THE GREEK VERSION OF DANIEL)

Like the other two additions to Daniel, Susanna was written in the second or first century BC and is set in Babylon during the sixth-century BC exile of the Israelites. Unlike the other two stories, however, this one concerns the corruption of fellow Jews in power, rather than foreign oppression, and how the faithful are to respond. Susanna is a holy Jewish woman who maintains her trust in God's justice against the false accusations of two corrupt Israelite elders. These elders schemed to trap Susanna in an adulterous relationship. She could either consent and go free, but break God's law in doing so, or refuse the elders' advances, keep God's law, but be put to death by the elders, who would falsely charge her with adultery.

A God-Fearing Woman

The character of the elders is in stark contrast to that of Susanna. She fears God and follows the law. The elders are corrupt lawbreakers (they commit adultery and bear false witness). But because they are in power, the deck is stacked against Susanna having any chance at a fair hearing (see v 41). Still, Susanna's decision is straightforward. Rather than give in to their wishes, she would prefer to be unjustly put to death by the elders for being faithful to God's law. Even though she faced immediate death, "through her tears she looked up toward Heaven, for her heart trusted in the Lord" (v 35). Hers is a heart and life formed by the power of God in such a way that when on the spot she could respond appropriately.

Susanna is saved in the end through the wise and cunning intervention of Daniel. God stirs him to speak up in the assembly. He points out the simple fact that they are about to execute a respected member of their community, one with an impeccable reputation (see v 27), without bothering to investigate the charges. This is a rather obvious point, perhaps, but one that had been neglected, no doubt, because

See also "The With-God Life" essays for this section of the Bible, "The People of God In Exile," pp. 1171–74, and "The People of God in Restoration," pp. 1355–59.

of the elders' status in the community. The people recognize that God has given Daniel the "standing of an elder" (v 50). He proceeds to interrogate the elders separately. When their stories do not agree, their guilt is exposed, they are put to death, and Susanna is vindicated.

Nationalism and Identity

On one level this story certainly makes a point of accenting the strength of a woman of true, deep faith and God's deliverance of "those who hope in him" (v 60). But, as with the other additions to Daniel, there is an important nationalistic dimension to this story too. This story is a reminder to Hellenistic Jews to live on foreign soil as though they were in the land—that is, in accordance with God's law. The law of Moses is clearly an important element in this story, being either mentioned or clearly implied at several key points (vv 3, 9, 23, 43, 53, 61–62). The keeping of the Torah is what gives Jews their identity, especially in exile. They must remember that they are bound to it, not only in the face of foreign opposition (as we see in the other two additions to Daniel), but even in the face of the abuse of power by fellow Jews. Thus, the People of God in exile are reminded that, just like Susanna, God will deliver them if they keep their hope in him alone.

—*Peter Enns*

Susanna's Beauty Attracts Two Elders

1 There was a man living in Babylon whose name was Joakim. ²He married the daughter of Hilkiah, named Susanna, a very beautiful woman and one who feared the Lord. ³Her parents were righteous, and had trained their daughter according to the law of Moses. ⁴Joakim was very rich, and had a fine garden adjoining his house; the Jews used to come to him because he was the most honored of them all.

5 That year two elders from the people were appointed as judges. Concerning them the Lord had said: "Wickedness came forth from Babylon, from elders who were judges, who were supposed to govern the people." ⁶These men were frequently at Joakim's house, and all who had a case to be tried came to them there.

7 When the people left at noon, Susanna would go into her husband's garden to walk. ⁸Every day the two elders used to see her, going in and walking about, and they began to lust for her. ⁹They suppressed their consciences and turned away their eyes from looking to Heaven or remembering their duty to administer justice. ¹⁰Both were overwhelmed with passion for her, but they did

1–4 *a very beautiful woman and one who feared the Lord.* Susanna "feared the Lord," was trained "according to the law of Moses," and married a man, Joakim, who was honored more than his fellow Jews. The quality of Susanna's character will be quickly contrasted with those of the elders. She is living the exemplary life of an exilic Jew: she fears God, obeys the law, and has an impeccable reputation.

5 *Wickedness came forth from Babylon.* It is not clear precisely which biblical text is being cited here (although Jer 23:14–15 may provide some inspiration). The wickedness of those who are supposed to lead with honor and dignity is an ever present problem, then and now. If those who are expected to adjudicate cases among the people scheme against the weak, there is nowhere to turn. Power corrupts those who, unlike Susanna, do not fear God and do not walk according to his law. But God's people are to remain true, regardless.

7–14 *overwhelmed with passion for her.* The

not tell each other of their distress, [11]for they were ashamed to disclose their lustful desire to seduce her. [12]Day after day they watched eagerly to see her.

13 One day they said to each other, "Let us go home, for it is time for lunch." So they both left and parted from each other. [14]But turning back, they met again; and when each pressed the other for the reason, they confessed their lust. Then together they arranged for a time when they could find her alone.

The Elders Attempt to Seduce Susanna

15 Once, while they were watching for an opportune day, she went in as before with only two maids, and wished to bathe in the garden, for it was a hot day. [16]No one was there except the two elders, who had hidden themselves and were watching her. [17]She said to her maids, "Bring me olive oil and ointments, and shut the garden doors so that I can bathe." [18]They did as she told them: they shut the doors of the garden and went out by the side doors to bring what they had been commanded; they did not see the elders, because they were hiding.

19 When the maids had gone out, the two elders got up and ran to her. [20]They said, "Look, the garden doors are shut, and no one can see us. We are burning with desire for you; so give your consent, and lie with us. [21]If you refuse, we will testify against you that a young man was with you, and this was why you sent your maids away."

22 Susanna groaned and said, "I am completely trapped. For if I do this, it will mean death for me; if I do not, I cannot escape your hands. [23]I choose not to do it; I will fall into

---

two elders demonstrate a familiar pattern that leads to sinful actions. (1) They see Susanna every day. People are tempted by what they are familiar with, by what it is set before them every day. (2) Unchecked fixation leads to lust. Rather than fearing God and obeying the law of Moses by averting their eyes, they allow themselves to be led astray. (3) Their lust leads them to suppress their consciousness of God and their commitment to their godly duty. (4) Their guilty consciences still maintaining some grip on their behavior, they are ashamed to admit to each other what they are thinking. But rather than heed their consciences, they remain in the pattern of watching her day after day. (5) Deception is also part of the routine, but after they confess their lust to each other, finding confidence in partnership, rather than turning away from sin, they arrange for a time when they can find her alone.

Responding

14 CONFESSION. These men confessed their mutual sin not in order to repent, but to further suppress their consciences (v 9). Both were too mired in their own sin to acknowledge the sin of the other. Even without such personal bias, it's easy to dismiss or downplay a sin confessed to us. This kind of reaction is devastating to another person's spiritual health. If someone confesses a sin to you, honor that person's confession by treating the matter with the gravity it deserves. Fully hear the person out and pray together for forgiveness. Conversely, if you want to confess to another, choose that person carefully and let him or her know that you need your confession to be taken seriously. *See also* Spiritual Disciplines Index.

21 *we will testify against you.* The elders' plan apparently included not only hiding in the garden to catch Susanna alone, but "plan B" as well: what to do if she refuses. When those who rule—especially those who judge disputes—oppress those they are bound to protect, there is no place for the powerless to go. There is no one to hear their cause. But even there, God will show himself faithful to his people.

22–23 *I am completely trapped.* The elders' story, that Susanna was involved with another man, would be believed by the people (see v 41). Her choices are either disobey God and save her life or obey God and die, since the penalty for adultery is death. For Susanna, the options are simple. She can either sin and live or obey God and die. Note that she does not appeal to her innocence and call upon God to deliver her from the situation, at least not here. There is not a second of debate. Her obedience to God's law is immediate, even if it is costly. Obedience often carries with it a heavy cost. What is required, though, is to be faithful regardless of the cost.

your hands, rather than sin in the sight of the Lord."

24 Then Susanna cried out with a loud voice, and the two elders shouted against her. 25And one of them ran and opened the garden doors. 26When the people in the house heard the shouting in the garden, they rushed in at the side door to see what had happened to her. 27And when the elders told their story, the servants felt very much ashamed, for nothing like this had ever been said about Susanna.

The Elders Testify against Susanna

28 The next day, when the people gathered at the house of her husband Joakim, the two elders came, full of their wicked plot to have Susanna put to death. In the presence of the people they said, 29"Send for Susanna daughter of Hilkiah, the wife of Joakim." 30So they sent for her. And she came with her parents, her children, and all her relatives.

31 Now Susanna was a woman of great refinement and beautiful in appearance. 32As she was veiled, the scoundrels ordered her to be unveiled, so that they might feast their eyes on her beauty. 33Those who were with her and all who saw her were weeping.

34 Then the two elders stood up before the people and laid their hands on her head. 35Through her tears she looked up toward Heaven, for her heart trusted in the Lord. 36The elders said, "While we were walking in the garden alone, this woman came in with two maids, shut the garden doors, and dismissed the maids. 37Then a young man, who was hiding there, came to her and lay with her. 38We were in a corner of the garden, and when we saw this wickedness we ran to them. 39Although we saw them embracing, we could not hold the man, because he was stronger than we, and he opened the doors and got away. 40We did, however, seize this woman and asked who the young man was, 41but she would not tell us. These things we testify."

Because they were elders of the people and judges, the assembly believed them and condemned her to death.

42 Then Susanna cried out with a loud voice, and said, "O eternal God, you know what is secret and are aware of all things before they come to be; 43you know that these men have given false evidence against me. And now I am to die, though I have done none of the wicked things that they have charged against me!"

44 The Lord heard her cry. 45Just as she was being led off to execution, God stirred up the holy spirit of a young lad named Daniel, 46and he shouted with a loud voice, "I want no part in shedding this woman's blood!"

Daniel Rescues Susanna

47 All the people turned to him and asked, "What is this you are saying?" 48Taking his stand among them he said, "Are you such fools, O Israelites, as to condemn a daughter

---

27 *the servants felt very much ashamed.* This is the second time we see shame in this story: here and in verse 11. The only character who does not feel shame is Susanna. The elders were ashamed because of their sin. The servants are ashamed, perhaps because they believe the charges against Susanna, perhaps because they are so shocked at this turn of events. But we are not told what Susanna is feeling: her actions are the focus. As Susanna was introduced in verses 1–4, she is still a woman who fears God and obeys his law. The question the story asks is, "How will she fare as a result?"

32 *feast their eyes on her beauty.* Even as they knowingly condemn an innocent woman to death to save themselves, the elders lust after

Susanna. She is doubly persecuted, doubly oppressed.

35 *she looked up toward Heaven.* (Cf. v 9, where the elders "turned away their eyes from looking to Heaven.") Looking toward heaven was not a last-ditch effort on Susanna's part to extricate herself from the situation. It was her normal posture in life: "her heart trusted in the Lord."

42 *you know what is secret.* What sustains Susanna is the unflinching conviction that God is all-knowing. Even though we are caught by surprise, he is not. What is implied in her cry is that God is also all-compassionate toward his people.

of Israel without examination and without learning the facts? [49]Return to court, for these men have given false evidence against her."

50 So all the people hurried back. And the rest of the[a] elders said to him, "Come, sit among us and inform us, for God has given you the standing of an elder." [51]Daniel said to them, "Separate them far from each other, and I will examine them."

52 When they were separated from each other, he summoned one of them and said to him, "You old relic of wicked days, your sins have now come home, which you have committed in the past, [53]pronouncing unjust judgments, condemning the innocent and acquitting the guilty, though the Lord said, 'You shall not put an innocent and righteous person to death.' [54]Now then, if you really saw this woman, tell me this: Under what tree did you see them being intimate with each other?" He answered, "Under a mastic tree."[b] [55]And Daniel said, "Very well! This lie has cost you your head, for the angel of God has received the sentence from God and will immediately cut[c] you in two."

56 Then, putting him to one side, he ordered them to bring the other. And he said to him, "You offspring of Canaan and not of Judah, beauty has beguiled you and lust has perverted your heart. [57]This is how you have been treating the daughters of Israel, and they were intimate with you through fear;

but a daughter of Judah would not tolerate your wickedness. [58]Now then, tell me: Under what tree did you catch them being intimate with each other?" He answered, "Under an evergreen oak."[d] [59]Daniel said to him, "Very well! This lie has cost you also your head, for the angel of God is waiting with his sword to split[e] you in two, so as to destroy you both."

60 Then the whole assembly raised a great shout and blessed God, who saves those who hope in him. [61]And they took action against the two elders, because out of their own mouths Daniel had convicted them of bearing false witness; they did to them as they had wickedly planned to do to their neighbor. [62]Acting in accordance with the law of Moses, they put them to death. Thus innocent blood was spared that day.

63 Hilkiah and his wife praised God for their daughter Susanna, and so did her husband Joakim and all her relatives, because she was found innocent of a shameful deed. [64]And from that day onward Daniel had a great reputation among the people.

a Gk lacks *rest of the*   b The Greek words for *mastic tree* and *cut* are similar, thus forming an ironic wordplay   c The Greek words for *mastic tree* and *cut* are similar, thus forming an ironic wordplay   d The Greek words for *evergreen oak* and *split* are similar, thus forming an ironic wordplay   e The Greek words for *evergreen oak* and *split* are similar, thus forming an ironic wordplay

---

50 *God has given you the standing of an elder.* Daniel, who is wise and just, is given the status of elder by God. He is portrayed in stark contrast to the corrupt elders, who, although duly elected, have relinquished their divine right to hold such authority.

60 *God, who saves those who hope in him.* This is a summary of the message of the book. It is true on both a personal and a national level. It is not a vague "hope in hope." It is hope in a good, just, holy, creator God who is with his people.

62 *law of Moses.* The basis for the punishment of the elders is the law of Moses. The elders transgressed God's standard and so were punished by that same standard. The law was one of the marks of the Jewish people living on foreign soil, and acting according to it was both a reminder to themselves and a statement to non-Jews that they were a special people. Steadfastness to God's standards in a world that rejects these standards—either knowingly or unknowingly—is always a requirement of the People of God.

BEL AND THE DRAGON

(CHAPTER 14 OF THE GREEK VERSION OF DANIEL)

Written in the second or first century BC, Bel and the Dragon, the third addition to Daniel, is actually two stories in one. In the story of Bel (vv 1–22) Daniel exposes the religion of Babylonia as a sham during the Israelite exile there in the sixth century BC. The priests of Bel have been fooling the people into thinking that the idol of Bel located in the temple was real: the food the priests left for it every night was gone—presumably eaten—by morning. But Daniel outwits the Babylonians by proving that the food was eaten secretly by the priests and their families. He has his servants scatter ashes across the temple floor. The next morning, footprints of "men and women and children" (v 20) are seen: they had entered the temple through a secret entrance beneath the table (v 13). The king is enraged and orders the priests and their families put to death and the temple destroyed.

Daniel and the Dragon

In the second story (vv 23–42), Daniel proves that the "great dragon" (v 23)—a snake revered by the Babylonians—was not a god, but just an ordinary snake. He claims that he will be able to kill the snake "without sword or club" (v 26). He feeds it a strange concoction of "pitch, fat, and hair," after which it bursts open (v 27). Whereas exposing the schemes of some priests was rewarded by the king, killing one of their "live" gods was not looked upon as kindly. Daniel is thrown, once again (see Dan 6), into the lions' den.

See also *"The With-God Life"* essays for this section of the Bible, *"The People of God In Exile,"* pp. 1171–74, and *"The People of God in Restoration,"* pp. 1355–59.

After six days in the lions' den, and after they had stopped feeding the lions a ration of "two human bodies and two sheep" a day (v 32), Daniel's prospects look bleak. But God sends Daniel the prophet Habakkuk to provide food for him and—although this is not explicitly mentioned—to protect him from the now hungry lions. When Cyrus returns the next day, he finds Daniel safe, has him released immediately, and feeds his accusers to the lions.

One point of this story is a bit perplexing: Habakkuk lived in the late seventh century BC, while the story of Daniel takes place about a hundred years later. Why introduce such an element that is obviously out of chronological sequence? It is certainly not the case that the author did not know his biblical history. Rather, the presence of a biblical character from an earlier time helps express the lesson of this story: help in the present circumstances comes from appealing to the past; the same God active in the past is with the Israelites who are now living in exile. They too can say, with Daniel, "You have remembered me, O God, and have not forsaken those who love you" (v 38).

Bearing Witness in Exile

Like Susanna, this story also highlights Daniel's cunning and wisdom. But, as with the other additions to Daniel, there is a larger purpose for this story. Daniel's clear boldness and faith serve as examples for Israel's behavior in exile. The Israelites are to live in a way that bears witness to the true God; they, like Daniel, are not to "revere idols made with hands, but the living God, who created the heaven and earth and has dominion over all living creatures" (v 5). That dominion extends even over the foreign kings, who for the time being seem so strong in keeping Israel in exile. But while the Israelites are in exile, they are to live as God's people not only when the outcome is favorable (as in the story of Bel), but also when there is a price to pay (as in the story of the dragon).

—*Peter Enns*

Daniel and the Priests of Bel

1 When King Astyages was laid to rest with his ancestors, Cyrus the Persian succeeded to his kingdom. 2Daniel was a companion of the king, and was the most honored of all his Friends.

3 Now the Babylonians had an idol called Bel, and every day they provided for it twelve bushels of choice flour and forty sheep and six measures*a* of wine. 4The king revered it and went every day to worship it. But Daniel worshiped his own God.

So the king said to him, "Why do you not worship Bel?" 5He answered, "Because I do not revere idols made with hands, but the living God, who created heaven and earth and has dominion over all living creatures."

6 The king said to him, "Do you not think

a A little more than fifty gallons

---

4 *But Daniel worshiped his own God.* Even though Daniel was in a position of power in Babylon, he worshiped the true God rather than those of Babylon. In a society where religion and politics were linked closely, this was a risky—potentially life-threatening—position to take. But what is true must be held as true, regardless of personal cost.

that Bel is a living god? Do you not see how much he eats and drinks every day?" 7And Daniel laughed, and said, "Do not be deceived, O king, for this thing is only clay inside and bronze outside, and it never ate or drank anything."

8 Then the king was angry and called the priests of Bel[a] and said to them, "If you do not tell me who is eating these provisions, you shall die. 9But if you prove that Bel is eating them, Daniel shall die, because he has spoken blasphemy against Bel." Daniel said to the king, "Let it be done as you have said."

10 Now there were seventy priests of Bel, besides their wives and children. So the king went with Daniel into the temple of Bel. 11The priests of Bel said, "See, we are now going outside; you yourself, O king, set out the food and prepare the wine, and shut the door and seal it with your signet. 12When you return in the morning, if you do not find that Bel has eaten it all, we will die; otherwise Daniel will, who is telling lies about us." 13They were unconcerned, for beneath the table they had made a hidden entrance, through which they used to go in regularly and consume the provisions. 14After they had gone out, the king set out the food for Bel. Then Daniel ordered his servants to bring ashes, and they scattered them throughout the whole temple in the presence of the king alone. Then they went out, shut the door and sealed it with the king's signet, and departed. 15During the night the priests came as usual, with their wives and children, and they ate and drank everything.

16 Early in the morning the king rose and came, and Daniel with him. 17The king said, "Are the seals unbroken, Daniel?" He answered, "They are unbroken, O king." 18As soon as the doors were opened, the king looked at the table, and shouted in a loud voice, "You are great, O Bel, and in you there is no deceit at all!"

19 But Daniel laughed and restrained the king from going in. "Look at the floor," he said, "and notice whose footprints these are." 20The king said, "I see the footprints of men and women and children."

21 Then the king was enraged, and he arrested the priests and their wives and children.

a Gk *his priests*

Responding

4 WORSHIP. As Daniel shows, worship is central to Christian faith. Consider preparing yourself on Saturday night for your church worship service the next morning by studying the Bible verses that will be read, singing some of the songs that might be sung, examining your soul for sins that need to be confessed, and going to bed early. *See also* Spiritual Disciplines Index.

5 *has dominion over all living creatures.* As we see in the Prayer of Azariah and the Song of the Three Jews (see note on vv 28–34), the basis of Daniel's worship is who God is, namely, the Creator and Ruler of all that exists. In describing God this way, Daniel is not simply proclaiming his private belief in God. He is issuing a challenge to the king of Persia, who fancied himself as "ruler."

7 *it never ate or drank anything.* Daniel's challenge to the king goes so far as to laugh at the preposterous notion that an object of clay and iron can eat. As obvious as that might sound to us today, however, in the ancient world idols filled every house, town, and temple. Daniel's challenge went right to the heart of Babylonian religion. That is the function of true faith: to pierce and expose any cultural idolatry, and to do so with a boldness that comes from God. So it is today too.

9 *Let it be done as you have said.* Daniel's confidence in God is so strong he agrees with the king's counterchallenge: whoever is wrong will die. Faith in God, in a hostile culture, will often bring God's people into direct conflict with prevailing powers. But that is what it means to bear witness in the world that the true King reigns.

14 *Daniel ordered his servants to bring ashes.* Daniel is not fooled for a minute. It seems that Daniel, in his wisdom, already knew how the priests made it seem that the idol ate the food left for it. Daniel has set a trap for the king, and it is about to be sprung. The People of God are vigilant, observant. The eyes of the wise are wide open (or as Qoheleth puts it, "The wise have eyes in their head," Eccl 2:14).

They showed him the secret doors through which they used to enter to consume what was on the table. 22Therefore the king put them to death, and gave Bel over to Daniel, who destroyed it and its temple.

Daniel Kills the Dragon

23 Now in that place*a* there was a great dragon, which the Babylonians revered. 24The king said to Daniel, "You cannot deny that this is a living god; so worship him." 25Daniel said, "I worship the Lord my God, for he is the living God. 26But give me permission, O king, and I will kill the dragon without sword or club." The king said, "I give you permission."

27 Then Daniel took pitch, fat, and hair, and boiled them together and made cakes, which he fed to the dragon. The dragon ate them, and burst open. Then Daniel said, "See what you have been worshiping!"

28 When the Babylonians heard about it, they were very indignant and conspired against the king, saying, "The king has become a Jew; he has destroyed Bel, and killed the dragon, and slaughtered the priests." 29Going to the king, they said, "Hand Daniel over to us, or else we will kill you and your household." 30The king saw that they were pressing him hard, and under compulsion he handed Daniel over to them.

Daniel in the Lions' Den

31 They threw Daniel into the lions' den, and he was there for six days. 32There were seven lions in the den, and every day they had been given two human bodies and two sheep; but now they were given nothing, so that they would devour Daniel.

33 Now the prophet Habakkuk was in Judea; he had made a stew and had broken bread into a bowl, and was going into the field to take it to the reapers. 34But the angel of the Lord said to Habakkuk, "Take the food that you have to Babylon, to Daniel, in the lions' den." 35Habakkuk said, "Sir, I have never seen Babylon, and I know nothing about the den." 36Then the angel of the Lord took him by the crown of his head and carried him by his hair; with the speed of the wind*b* he set him down in Babylon, right over the den.

37 Then Habakkuk shouted, "Daniel, Daniel! Take the food that God has sent you." 38Daniel said, "You have remembered me, O God, and have not forsaken those who love you." 39So Daniel got up and ate. And the angel of God immediately returned Habakkuk to his own place.

40 On the seventh day the king came to mourn for Daniel. When he came to the den

a Other ancient authorities lack *in that place*
b Or *by the power of his spirit*

---

22 *gave Bel over to Daniel, who destroyed it and its temple.* What happened to the Israelites when they were taken into captivity is now happening to the Babylonians: their temple is destroyed. Here we see an additional indication that at least part of the purpose of this story goes beyond Daniel's vindication to speak to Israel's vindication among the nations. God's purpose is to maintain his people as a people, not just as individuals. For Hellenistic Jews living in exile, to read of the destruction of Babylon's temple would have reminded them that their God, the God of their ancestors, is on the move.

26 *I will kill the dragon without sword or club.* The dragon may be a "living" god and not an idol like Bel, but that is not the point. Daniel issues a second challenge: a true god cannot be killed.

28–30 *under compulsion he handed Daniel over.* The behavior of Babylon's king is in stark contrast to Daniel's. Daniel (just like Azariah and his companions, and Susanna) is prepared to die for his faith, but the king is looking out only for himself. True faith breeds true courage. But the king is intimidated by the people's threat to put him and his household to death. Perhaps there is no greater proof that the gods he worshiped are false and the God of Daniel is true: the king had no intention of losing his life over his "god." Dying for one's faith was an ever present threat for God's people in exile.

33–39 *Take the food that you have to Babylon, to Daniel, in the lions' den.* Habakkuk comes on the scene and provides Daniel with food. It is not clear how providing food for Daniel would have saved him from the lions' hunger, but the larger point should not be lost. It is God's intervention

he looked in, and there sat Daniel! [41] The king shouted with a loud voice, "You are great, O Lord, the God of Daniel, and there is no other besides you!" [42] Then he pulled Daniel[a] out, and threw into the den those who had attempted his destruction, and they were instantly eaten before his eyes.

a Gk *him*

---

that saved Daniel from his second stint in the lions' den. Why have the Lord send Habakkuk, who lived a hundred years before Daniel? Such a chronological "error" would have been plainly obvious to ancient readers. But it is no mistake. Instead, it provides a powerful lesson for the readers of this book. The God of the prophets, the God of the past, the God of Israel's glory days is still the God of Israel in exile. Our present circumstances do not determine who God is or what he does. Because he is the God of the past, he is the God of the present.

41 *The king shouted with a loud voice, "You are great, O Lord!"* The king's confession that the God of Daniel is the true God amounts to Israel's victory over its captors. God's glory will be known throughout the world, and all will confess his name. The Lord is the Creator of the universe, not the private god of an exiled people. It is through delivering his people from exile that God will be made known throughout the world. That is a pattern established at least as early as the exodus (Exod 9:15–16) and culminates in the final exodus, where Christ delivers his people from sin and death through his resurrection and redemption. And so all will confess "Jesus Christ is Lord, to the glory of God the Father" (Phil 2:11).

THE NEW
TESTAMENT

XII. The People of God with Immanuel

Scriptures: *Matthew, Mark, Luke, John*

> *The aim of God in history is the creation of an all-inclusive community of loving persons with God himself at the very center of this community as its prime Sustainer and most glorious Inhabitant (Eph 2:19–22; 3:10). The Bible traces the formation of this community from the creation in the Garden of Eden all the way to the new heaven and the new earth. Come, join us as we explore the many dimensions of this with-God history—from individual to family to tribe to people to nation to all humanity—and apply what we learn to our own spiritual formation.*

Previously we saw the people of Israel reoccupy the land while under the domination of foreign powers. In the Scriptures listed above we will see the ways God continues the process of forming an all-inclusive community through a dramatic new event in salvation history: the coming of Immanuel ("God with us").

God's Action

"And the Word became flesh and lived among us, and we have seen his glory, the glory as of a father's only son, full of grace and truth" (John 1:14). In the Gospels God is with us as a man among other human beings in ordinary human relationships. God is now acting in a uniquely direct and personal way through the incarnation—the life, ministry, death, and resurrection of Jesus. This pivotal chapter of history has all the directness and intimacy of God's presence in the Garden of Eden, but in a physical, human form. Jesus was a child, a teenager, and then a craftsman in his community; he was also a respected rabbi among the people. Although he was born an "outsider" (John 1:46) and ministered without any authority from recognized human institutions, it became obvious that there was more to Jesus than could be explained in merely human terms. The kingdom and power of God *in* him and *with* him began to draw others under the influence of the kingdom, which was directly and immediately available to them *through* him (Luke 16:16). God "anointed Jesus of Nazareth with the Holy Spirit and with power," and "he went about doing good and healing all who were oppressed by the devil, for God was with him" (Acts 10:38).

In the public square Jesus proclaims the good news of the kingdom of the heavens and teaches how to enter into its life and power. He ministers to all as well as trains selected individuals from among the huge number of people who respond to his person and work. These people, filled and empowered by the Holy Spirit, then become Jesus' continuing embodiment in the Church and go "to all the world"—again, fulfilling God's promise to Abraham.

The overall effect of Jesus' presence and teaching is the possibility, for humankind, of a personal knowledge of God and a fellowship of with him that had never been known before. As Jesus says in his great prayer to the Father, "I have made your name known to those whom you gave me from the world" (John 17:6). And people's union with one another through Jesus and the Father is of such a quality, Jesus continues, that "the world may know that you have sent me and have loved them even as you have loved me" (John 17:23).

We must never forget, however, that Jesus could only have come when he did and not before, because humankind had to be prepared for this greatest of all events in holy history. God accomplished this preparation by the ways he had been "with" his people through all the previous centuries and by all that they had lived through. But now "the time is fulfilled," it is the "fullness of time," and the One comes who can say, "Whoever has seen me has seen the Father" (Mark 1:15; Gal 4:4; John 14:9).

So Jesus deposits on public record, available to all, the most beautiful teachings about God and his world that have ever been given. At the same time he embodies and models this teaching in his own life. With his public death and resurrection, Jesus' name and face are inscribed on the drama of world history, and ever afterward he becomes the greatest historical figure in the whole of humanity. And by nurturing and cultivating a small group of carefully selected individuals, he initiates a society of God-inhabited people who carry God's salvation to the ends of the earth. Today, this task is still in progress and waits for each generation to take it up and carry it forward.

During the period covered by the Gospels, the primary mode of God-with-us is Jesus himself. He calls people to be his disciples. To be a disciple means to be a student or apprentice to someone, and Jesus calls his disciples to respond with a seamless faith in him for everything. In this context, discipleship to Jesus means learning to live life as Jesus would. Our need for transformation and character development has found its perfect answer.

We do not pick and choose what we will trust Jesus for. Through Jesus and his death and resurrection we receive life "from above" and the forgiveness of sins. But the very same confidence in Jesus that brings us forgiveness also leads us to receive him as Lord and, therefore, our constant Teacher. We become God-inhabited people who are students of Jesus—lovingly learning from him all that he teaches and forming countless societies of love, truth, and power that continuously spread the light of Christ into the darkness of the world.

So discipleship, or apprenticeship, to Jesus in kingdom living is the basic form of God's presence with his people in the Gospels. A distinctive historical entity, Christ's Church, emerges from this supernaturally sustained relationship. The business of Jesus' people is apprenticeship to him: we learn to live in the kingdom as if he were living our lives, and to bring others into apprenticeship to him.

The With-God Life

But this is not an easy and simple matter. Instead, it is constant warfare. The term "the Church Militant" (the union of believers on earth) is no joke. The presence and progress of the kingdom of God on earth is the most radical threat an arrogant, God-alienated humanity can face. So although apprenticeship to Jesus is the basic form of God's presence with us, its flip side is constant warfare with "the world, the flesh, and the devil" (see 1 John 2:16; Gal 5:16–17; 1 Pet 5:8). This is an essential part of spiritual formation, both in the Gospels and afterward (1 John 2:15). It goes hand in hand with discipleship. "Friendship with the world is enmity with God" (James 4:4).

The battle between what is of human origin and what is from heaven, which is fully engaged in the Gospels, was already an ancient conflict (Matt 21:25). Sadly, we find that religious institutions are often on the side of human rather than divine origin: "Jerusalem, Jerusalem, the city that kills the prophets and stones those who are sent to it!" (Luke 13:34; cf. Jer 35:14–15). And since Jesus spoke these words, religion regrettably has presided over the deaths of many who were sent from God. But this is not something we learn to do as apprentices of Jesus Christ.

Extending the People of God to include all of humanity was painful and profound, for it meant that no human cultural form was ultimate—not even a religious form. How shocking are the words, "Many will come from east and west and will eat with Abraham and Isaac and Jacob in the kingdom of heaven, while the heirs of the kingdom will be thrown into the outer darkness, where there will be weeping and gnashing of teeth" (Matt 8:11–12). Or "The Law and the Prophets *were* proclaimed until John; since then the gospel of the kingdom of God is preached, and every one is forcing [their] way into it" (Luke 16:16, NASB). Or "Therefore I tell you, the kingdom of God will be taken away from you and given to a people that produces the fruits of the kingdom" (Matt 21:43). These words are not spoken to the Jews alone, but to any cultural group that places itself above the active presence of the kingdom of God and the person of Jesus among human beings.

Human Reaction

Because of the prominence of the crucifixion in the Gospel story and the bitter battle leading up to it, the widespread acceptance of Jesus by the people of Israel is often overlooked. Indeed, from the human point of view it was precisely the overwhelming popularity of Jesus that led him into the conflict with the "authorities" that ended in his death. The time was indeed ripe for his coming, and there were many among the People of God who recognized him as the Messiah, the Savior of the world—though they did not yet fully understand what that meant.

Most important, Jesus' teaching was effectively put on public record for the entire world. He was "lifted up," and all kinds and classes of people were "drawn to him" (see John 12:32)—and still are. A suitable group of apprentices was formed, then transformed, and then molded (by the coming of the Spirit upon them soon after Jesus ascended into the heavens) into a self-replicating force for world revolution "to the end of the age" (Matt 28:20). These ordinary people—with no earthly kingdom,

The With-God Life

but with divine power—became his witnesses "unto the uttermost part of the earth" (Acts 1:8, KJV; cf. Acts 10:1—11:18).

Blessings and Benefits for Our Formation

At last it becomes absolutely clear what "spiritual formation" is all about: disciples are to teach "them to obey everything that I have commanded you" (Matt 28:20). Obedience means to bring our inner person into such a transformed condition that the deeds of Christ naturally arise out of it. It is not to focus on the actions themselves, for that way leads to deadly legalism, and surely we have had enough of that already. Instead, Christian spiritual formation focuses on becoming a "good tree" with the full assurance that "no good tree bears bad fruit" (Luke 6:43). The end result of such a process is a natural and "automatic" obedience to Christ and his way.

In a word, spiritual formation is "Christlikeness" from the inside out. It is this end to which God has been working since the beginning. Christlikeness does, in fact, create the all-inclusive community that genuinely unites and knits us together as one. It is the wholeness and holiness for which, by nature, the human heart hungers and which is displayed among the people of God through the fruit and the gifts of the Spirit. Qualified and powerful "ambassadors for Christ," we live here and now as "children of God without blemish in the midst of a crooked and perverse generation, in which [we] shine like stars in the world" (2 Cor 5:20; Phil 2:15).

Limits and Liabilities for Our Formation

The primary limitations of this form of God-with-us are twofold. First, social conditions shaped expectations in a manner that prevented many people from being able to receive Jesus as "Messiah." In the minds of nearly everyone the Messiah would bring a kind of radical political reform and restoration of national identity that was flatly incompatible with the realities of God's kingdom and the central teachings of Jesus. This prevented a correct understanding and reception of that kingdom and made the personal presence of Jesus, though extremely powerful and convincing, also confusing and enigmatic, even to his closest followers. Neither Jesus' behavior nor his teaching could be understood within the cultural assumptions at the time he lived; and to step outside those assumptions was almost impossible, even for the most well-intentioned hearers. Further mediation was needed.

Jesus, of course, understood all this, and provision was made for a correct understanding to develop, as the resurrection, Pentecost, and the story of the Church unfolds in the book of Acts and continues to unfold up to this very day.

The second limitation is the fact that "the Spirit was not yet *given*" (John 7:39, NASB). The death and departure of Jesus and the coming of the Spirit upon the disciples was, in point of fact, a liberation of Christ from the self-imposed limitations of the divine presence in the individual life of a Jewish teacher and healer (Phil 2:5–8). With this liberation the person of Christ became free to move with the word of the gospel of the kingdom throughout the inner life of the disciples and about the world at large (e.g., Acts 6:7; 19:20; 2 Tim 2:9; John 14:15–26; Col 3:16). But the

The With-God Life

Gospels do not provide the final and ultimately perfect way God will dwell in his people, as Acts, the Letters, and Revelation vividly reveal. History's work is not yet complete.

Insights and Instructions for Our Formation

What can we learn from this stage of God-with-us? First, the physical world, including the human body, is beautiful, powerful, and holy under God. The physical world is the dwelling place of spiritual life—and of God himself, when he became enfleshed in Jesus Christ. The physical world mediates the presence of God-with-us in many ways, but above all it is the place where we learn to live in union with the kingdom of God. We seek and find the kingdom of God, first, in Jesus himself, but then in every detail of ordinary life (Matt 6:33). The character of Jesus descends upon our body as we progress in spiritual formation, and it—that is, our body—becomes the bearer and showplace of the fruit of the Spirit.

Second, God's coming in the person of Jesus Christ, from the babe and the carpenter to the cross and the resurrection, was totally unexpected and incomprehensible to human ways of thinking. This reminds us that God can never be tamed or domesticated. In fact, we need to be immediately suspicious of proposals and arrangements that make perfect human sense. In human history and in individual lives, God is always entering at unexpected times and in unexpected ways: "My thoughts are not your thoughts, nor are your ways my ways, says the LORD" (Isa 55:8). God's revelation of his thoughts and ways in the person of the Nazarene carpenter-turned-rabbi sets for all time the boundaries of his thoughts and ways. But much still must be done before his people can fully enter into that revelation.

Finally, our discipleship is incarnational at all times, not just in religious moments. Inner Christlikeness does not just include our religious rituals and moral character. These are fundamental, to be sure, but real inner Christlikeness makes every act of family, business, and community a time of learning how to live our life as Jesus would live it. Remember, for all but the last few years Jesus' life was in domestic contexts much like our own. Under his tutelage we learn how to make heavenly friends by managing, under God, "mammon." Being faithful in the "very little" trains us for being faithful "in much," in "the true riches" that God possesses and will place in our charge when he knows we are ready (Luke 16:9–12). In the beginning, we were placed in a garden and were, under God's power, to take care of it. Our "garden" today may take many forms, but we are to be responsible where we are for what God has made. We are privileged to work under God's direction and power in everything we do (Col 3:17). Could this be our eternal destiny as well?

The With-God Life

THE GOSPEL ACCORDING TO

MATTHEW

The Gospel of Matthew was placed first in the New Testament canon for a reason. By the time the Church began to collect the books for the first official New Testament canon in the fourth century AD, it was the most popular and widely used Gospel. Although this book gives prominence and a special role to Peter (which appealed to the Western Church), it is also the most Jewish of the four canonical Gospels. The author not only deals with specifically Jewish issues, but he even seeks to conform his material to a reverential Jewish way of speaking. For example, unlike the authors of the other Gospels, who speak of the kingdom of God, he speaks of the kingdom of heaven. The Gospel of Matthew is a presentation of the story of Jesus and his followers viewed through the lens of a Jewish sapiential, or wisdom, approach to the believing and spiritual life. The Gospel seeks to give not merely information or inspiration, but wisdom for believing and living a godly life and, as such, it lends itself to being used in spiritually formative ways.

The Writing of a Gospel

The Gospel of Matthew was, in all likelihood, not the first Gospel to be written, even though canonically it is placed first. It is fairly certain that the Gospel of Matthew was composed using various written sources, including the Gospel of Mark, a now lost collection of Jesus' sayings known today as Q, and some special material uniquely its own (e.g., much of the birth-narrative material in Matthew 1–2). Its author is much like the scribe or wise teacher "who has been trained for the kingdom of heaven [and] is like the master of a household who brings out of his treasure what is new and what is old" (13:52). The Evangelist has skillfully woven together his source material to produce a compelling portrait of Jesus as both sage and Wisdom itself, as both the revealer of God and Immanuel ("God with us"). Though this Gospel is

---

See also *"The With-God Life" essay for this section of the Bible,*
"The People of God with Immanuel," pp. 1785–89.

formally anonymous, the superscript added later indicates it has some association with Matthew, presumably the disciple so named among the Twelve. It was likely composed in its final form in the 70s or 80s.

Matthew was written when there was still a living relationship between Jesus' followers and the Jewish community. There is considerable concern for the observance of the commandments and Mosaic law. Indeed, a famous, uniquely Matthean sentence even says that none of the law will pass away until all is accomplished (5:18). In short, this Gospel seems to be written by and for a community of Jesus' followers who were overwhelmingly Jewish, not only in ethnic extraction, but also in orientation and patterns of daily living.

It is plausible that the Gospel of Matthew arose out of a school setting and was used by Jewish Christian teachers as a teaching aid for their flock. It is no accident that Jesus is most clearly presented as a teacher with learners (the meaning of *mathetes,* which we translate "disciple") in this Gospel. For example, the term *mathetes,* which occurs only in the first five books of the New Testament, we find seventy-three times in Matthew, but only forty-six times in Mark and thirty-seven times in Luke. It also is no accident that, in Matthew, discipleship is defined as keeping Jesus' commands or words (19:17; 28:18–20). It is obvious that Matthew's Gospel focuses on instructions for disciples. Notice too how it ends with stories about how the disciples both doubt and believe even after Jesus is raised from the dead (28:17).

Becoming Teachers

Matthew focuses on Jesus as a Jewish sage and concentrates on his public forms of wisdom teaching—parables, aphorisms, riddles, and beatitudes. Matthew, like other Jewish wisdom literature, highlights the use of Father and Father-Son language. In Matthew, "Father" is used of God some forty-two times, compared to only five times in Mark (none of which occur before 8:38) and only fifteen times in Luke. This usage is closely tied not only with an understanding of Jesus as *the* Son of God, but also of disciples as sons and daughters of God. Theology, Christology, and discipleship are linked in this Gospel through the use of Father language. When we believe Jesus is God's Son, we can come to relate to God as Father, as Jesus did. Matthew stresses this in texts like 11:27, where it is made clear that we can only come to know the Father truly through the Son.

The first Evangelist carefully constructs his Gospel as a word to the wise (or at least to some Jewish Christians, who probably were already teachers). Matthew sees himself as being in the mold of the scribe described in Sir 39:1–3: "He seeks out the wisdom of all the ancients, and is concerned with prophecies; he preserves the sayings of the famous and penetrates the subtleties of parables; he seeks out the hidden meanings of proverbs." The Evangelist does not allude to himself and his audience as sages, but rather as scribes. This distinction is important to the first Evangelist, because he wants to portray Jesus as the great sage and master teacher, but himself and his audience as only recorders and passers down of the tradition. Scribes are not the originators of the tradition, but rather its transmitters, interpreters, and appliers.

It is no accident that Peter, the first key disciple of Jesus, is portrayed in 16:19 as the one given the authority to bind and loose, in the sense of making decisions and giving commandments about what one is bound to do and what one is free to do. In other words, Peter is portrayed as the disciple given the task of interpreting the Jesus tradition for the Church. There is a deliberate contrast between his teaching and that of the Pharisees, who, instead of using interpretive keys to open the gate to the kingdom as Peter does, do not allow people to go into the kingdom (23:13, 15). The commissioning of Peter in this role provides the climax of the first main part of Matthew's narrative. Of course, this parallels the climax of the whole work, 28:18–20, which declares that it is the duty of disciples to make other disciples and this task involves teaching them. In Matthew, but not in Mark, Jesus instructs his disciples on the dos and don'ts of being teachers (5:19). The whole point of mentioning the righteousness of the scribes and Pharisees in 5:20 is that they are rival teachers. Again, in 10:24–25, a passage not paralleled elsewhere, a disciple is said not to be above the master teacher (Jesus), but rather is called to be like the teacher.

More Than a Rabbi

Thus, Matthew edits and arranges his material in order to tell Jesus' story in a very Jewish way. Ancient biographies often portray their subjects indirectly, allowing words, deeds, and relationships to reveal the identity and character of the main figure. A close examination of the editorial work in Matthew's Gospel shows the type of teaching the author has in mind. Strikingly, the disciples repeatedly address Jesus as "Lord" (8:21, 25; 14:28; 16:22), but when a stranger or a Jewish leader addresses Jesus, it is as "Teacher," or in Hebrew "Rabbi" (8:19; 12:38; 19:16; 22:16, 24, 36). Notice that it is only the betrayer Judas among the disciples who calls Jesus "Rabbi" (26:25, 49). What this tells us immediately is that the first Evangelist does not consider a title or term of respect like "Teacher" or "Rabbi" adequate to describe Jesus. This is not to say that such a title is inaccurate, for texts like 23:8–10 make plain that Matthew does want to say Jesus is a sage or teacher—indeed, *the* teacher of the disciples. Thus, the disciples, who will in turn make disciples of others, should not seek to label themselves as "rabbi" or use the customary term of endearment *Abba*, "Father," sometimes used of Jewish teachers or sages.

Also, in 26:17–19, near the end of Jesus' earthly ministry, he calls himself "the Teacher" with the assumption the audience will know immediately who this is. The setting apart of Jesus from other potential teachers as sage, and more than sage, is also seen in the contrast found at the end of the Sermon on the Mount between Jesus, who teaches with independent authority, and the Jewish scribes (7:28–29). The point here is twofold—Jesus is no mere scribe, and the problem is not with scribes in general but with *these* scribes.

The image of Jesus as sage or teacher is so crucial for Matthew that, in editorial summary passages, he cites teaching ahead of preaching and healing as Jesus' chief task (4:23; 9:35; 11:1). (This is all the more striking when one compares the parallel summaries in Mark 1:39 and Luke 7:1, which do not mention the term "teaching.") The content of this teaching is seen repeatedly to be parables, aphorisms, and wisdom discourses. This image of Jesus as sage or teacher and his disciples as scribes or teachers gets at the heart of Matthew's contribution to the Christological discussion of who Jesus was. Matthew promoted this image by showing that (1) Jesus is a messianic son of David similar to but greater than Solomon, offering even greater wisdom; (2) he is Wisdom come in person and so embodies and conveys the very presence of God to his people (Immanuel); (3) he is Son of God whose characteristic intimacy with the Father is modeled in part on the relationship of Wisdom to God in Jewish sapiential literature; and (4) he is the great eschatological sage, offering God's final teaching for salvation.

In the Jewish tradition, ultimately Wisdom was *the* teacher of God's people (Prov 1:20–33; 8:10–16; Sir 4:24; Wisd of Sol 6:12–16; 8:4). Matthew assigns this role of Wisdom as *the* teacher to Jesus himself, which explains how Matthew can portray Jesus as both sage and Wisdom. This has profound implications for our spiritual formation.

In his resurrection Jesus becomes *the* Teacher who continues teaching and guiding his people how to live. Indeed, Jesus becomes the fulfillment of the Jewish expectation of the prophet like Moses who would teach his people himself; "The LORD your God will raise up for you a prophet like me from among your own people; you shall heed such a prophet. . . . I will put my words in the mouth of the prophet, who shall speak to them everything that I command" (Deut 18:15, 18). The task of this prophet is to teach his disciples (his students, us) how to live; the task of his disciples (his students, us) is to hear and to obey.

Matthew's Gospel is a masterful presentation of a Jesus who instructs, inspires, and transforms others. The Evangelist has carefully constructed a narrative that includes birth stories and then alternates between blocks of teaching material topically arranged and stories about miracles and other deeds of Jesus. This leads up to a passion narrative in which Jesus continues to be presented as the Teacher who is crucified, is raised, appears to various of his followers, and then commissions them to carry on the work of making disciples, a task that involves teaching them to obey everything that Jesus has commanded (28:20).

—*Ben Witherington III and Darlene Hyatt*

The Genealogy of Jesus the Messiah

1 An account of the genealogy[a] of Jesus the Messiah,[b] the son of David, the son of Abraham.

2 Abraham was the father of Isaac, and Isaac the father of Jacob, and Jacob the father of Judah and his brothers, 3 and Judah the father of Perez and Zerah by Tamar, and Perez the father of Hezron, and Hezron the father of Aram, 4 and Aram the father of Aminadab,

a Or *birth*   b Or *Jesus Christ*

1:1 *An account of the genealogy of Jesus.* The Evangelist presents Jesus as a Jewish royal figure, not merely son of Abraham, but also son of David. The genealogy commends Jesus as the perfect one, who has been preceded by seven times six generations and who thus begins the seventh seven of generations. *The* son of David before Jesus was Solomon, and the Evangelist will draw comparisons with Solomon and his wisdom throughout the text by presenting Jesus as both a sage, who speaks in parables, riddles, and aphorisms, and the Wisdom of God come in

and Aminadab the father of Nahshon, and Nahshon the father of Salmon, 5and Salmon the father of Boaz by Rahab, and Boaz the father of Obed by Ruth, and Obed the father of Jesse, 6and Jesse the father of King David.

And David was the father of Solomon by the wife of Uriah, 7and Solomon the father of Rehoboam, and Rehoboam the father of Abijah, and Abijah the father of Asaph,*a* 8and Asaph*a* the father of Jehoshaphat, and Jehoshaphat the father of Joram, and Joram the father of Uzziah, 9and Uzziah the father of Jotham, and Jotham the father of Ahaz, and Ahaz the father of Hezekiah, 10and Hezekiah the father of Manasseh, and Manasseh the father of Amos,*b* and Amos*b* the father of Josiah, 11and Josiah the father of Jechoniah and his brothers, at the time of the deportation to Babylon.

12 And after the deportation to Babylon: Jechoniah was the father of Salathiel, and Salathiel the father of Zerubbabel, 13and Zerubbabel the father of Abiud, and Abiud the father of Eliakim, and Eliakim the father of Azor, 14and Azor the father of Zadok, and Zadok the father of Achim, and Achim the father of Eliud, 15and Eliud the father of

Eleazar, and Eleazar the father of Matthan, and Matthan the father of Jacob, 16and Jacob the father of Joseph the husband of Mary, of whom Jesus was born, who is called the Messiah.*c*

17 So all the generations from Abraham to David are fourteen generations; and from David to the deportation to Babylon, fourteen generations; and from the deportation to Babylon to the Messiah,*c* fourteen generations.

The Birth of Jesus the Messiah

18 Now the birth of Jesus the Messiah*d* took place in this way. When his mother Mary had been engaged to Joseph, but before they lived together, she was found to be with child from the Holy Spirit. 19Her husband Joseph, being a righteous man and unwilling to expose her to public disgrace, planned to dismiss her quietly. 20But just when he had resolved to do this, an angel of the Lord appeared to him in a dream and said, "Joseph, son of David, do not be afraid

a Other ancient authorities read *Asa* *b* Other ancient authorities read *Amon* *c* Or *the Christ* *d* Or *Jesus Christ*

---

the flesh. The term "Son of David," applied to Jesus throughout the text, reminds the audience of his royalty (1:1; 9:27; 12:23; 15:22; 20:30–31; 21:9,15; 22:42,45). Most of this emphasis occurs at the end of the Gospel to stress Jesus was king of the Jews, even though paradoxically he was crucified.

1:18–25 *the birth of Jesus the Messiah took place in this way.* In antiquity, kings often were said to have had miraculous births, and Jesus is no different. Not only is Jesus born by means of virginal conception, but the Messiah will bear a divine throne name—Immanuel, meaning "God is with us" (v 23; Isa 7:14). God is personally present with his people in and through Jesus—Wisdom in the flesh and so a greater royal figure than even the earlier ultimate Jewish sage, Solomon (12:42). The concept of the virginal conception has no exact parallels in other prodigious birth narratives, either Jewish or Greco-Roman. The story of Jesus' birth told by early Christians led to the reading of Isa 7:14 in a new light, not the other way around. The virginal

conception signifies: (1) the holiness of the child, for he was conceived through the agency of the Holy Spirit; (2) the uniqueness of the child, for such a means of conception was unprecedented; and (3) the divinity of the child, because by this means it was made clear he was also Son of God.
1:20 *an angel of the Lord appeared to him in a dream.* The portrayal of Joseph as a righteous and law-abiding man, bound in marital contract to Mary and not wishing to disgrace her through public divorce proceedings, is important. Clearly he did not understand that Mary's pregnancy was the consequence of a virginal conception, and he feared she would be subject to public disgrace, perhaps even stoning, for immoral sexual activity. The Evangelist portrays Joseph as a person open to spiritual direction, even when it comes in the form of a dream. Spiritual guidance can take many forms, but here and elsewhere in the birth narratives (2:13,19) direction comes in the form of a dream. Joseph is obedient to the angelic message and weds Mary.

to take Mary as your wife, for the child conceived in her is from the Holy Spirit. [21]She will bear a son, and you are to name him Jesus, for he will save his people from their sins." [22]All this took place to fulfill what had been spoken by the Lord through the prophet:

[23] "Look, the virgin shall conceive and
bear a son,
and they shall name him
Emmanuel,"

which means, "God is with us." [24]When Joseph awoke from sleep, he did as the angel of the Lord commanded him; he took her as his wife, [25]but had no marital relations with her until she had borne a son;[a] and he named him Jesus.

The Visit of the Wise Men

2 In the time of King Herod, after Jesus was born in Bethlehem of Judea, wise men[b] from the East came to Jerusalem, [2]asking, "Where is the child who has been born king of the Jews? For we observed his star at its rising,[c] and have come to pay him homage." [3]When King Herod heard this, he was frightened, and all Jerusalem with him; [4]and calling together all the chief priests and scribes of the people, he inquired of them where the Messiah[d] was to be born. [5]They told him, "In Bethlehem of Judea; for so it has been written by the prophet:

[6] 'And you, Bethlehem, in the land of
Judah,
are by no means least among the
rulers of Judah;
for from you shall come a ruler
who is to shepherd[e] my people
Israel.' "

[7] Then Herod secretly called for the wise men[b] and learned from them the exact time when the star had appeared. [8]Then he sent them to Bethlehem, saying, "Go and search diligently for the child; and when you have found him, bring me word so that I may also go and pay him homage." [9]When they had heard the king, they set out; and there, ahead of them, went the star that they had seen at its rising,[c] until it stopped over the place where the child was. [10]When they saw that the star had stopped,[f] they were overwhelmed with joy. [11]On entering the house, they saw the child with Mary his mother; and they knelt down and paid him homage. Then, opening their treasure chests, they offered him gifts of gold, frankincense, and myrrh. [12]And having been warned in a dream not to return to Herod, they left for their own country by another road.

The Escape to Egypt

13 Now after they had left, an angel of the Lord appeared to Joseph in a dream and said, "Get up, take the child and his mother, and flee to Egypt, and remain there until I tell you; for Herod is about to search for the child, to destroy him." [14]Then Joseph[g] got up, took the child and his mother by night, and went to Egypt, [15]and remained there until the death of Herod. This was to fulfill what had been spoken by the Lord through the prophet, "Out of Egypt I have called my son."

a Other ancient authorities read *her firstborn son*
b Or *astrologers*; Gk *magi*   c Or *in the East*
d Or *the Christ*   e Or *rule*   f Gk *saw the star*
g Gk *he*

Responding

1:23 THE WITH-GOD LIFE. Finally, the ultimate with-God event is announced to Joseph. God had been present with individuals, with a family, with a tribe, then with a people. Now God announces that he will be with us personally and will experience all of the limitations, humiliations, and sufferings that are our fate as humans (Heb 5:1-8). How has the reality that God took on human flesh and lived among us changed your life? What can you

do to make it more real? *See also* Spiritual Disciplines Index.

2:15 *Out of Egypt I have called my son.* Jesus was to be seen as recapitulating the story of Israel, being called out of Egypt as God's son (quoting Hos 11:1). Only Jesus will be Israel gone right, not wandering grumbling in the wilderness for forty years. Jesus will pass the wilderness test in only forty days and go on not merely to dwell in the Land of Promise, but to teach and heal those who inhabit the land. He

The Massacre of the Infants

16 When Herod saw that he had been tricked by the wise men, *a* he was infuriated, and he sent and killed all the children in and around Bethlehem who were two years old or under, according to the time that he had learned from the wise men. *a* 17Then was fulfilled what had been spoken through the prophet Jeremiah:

18 "A voice was heard in Ramah,
　　wailing and loud lamentation,
　　Rachel weeping for her children;
　　she refused to be consoled, because
　　　they are no more."

The Return from Egypt

19 When Herod died, an angel of the Lord suddenly appeared in a dream to Joseph in Egypt and said, 20"Get up, take the child and his mother, and go to the land of Israel, for those who were seeking the child's life are dead." 21Then Joseph *b* got up, took the child and his mother, and went to the land of Israel. 22But when he heard that Archelaus was ruling over Judea in place of his father Herod, he was afraid to go there. And after being warned in a dream, he went away to the district of Galilee. 23There he made his home in a town called Nazareth, so that what had been spoken through the prophets might be fulfilled, "He will be called a Nazorean."

The Proclamation of John the Baptist

3 In those days John the Baptist appeared in the wilderness of Judea, proclaiming, 2"Repent, for the kingdom of heaven has come near." *c* 3This is the one of whom the prophet Isaiah spoke when he said,

"The voice of one crying out in the
　　wilderness:
'Prepare the way of the Lord,
　　make his paths straight.'"

4Now John wore clothing of camel's hair with a leather belt around his waist, and his food was locusts and wild honey. 5Then the people of Jerusalem and all Judea were going out to him, and all the region along the Jordan, 6and they were baptized by him in the river Jordan, confessing their sins.

7 But when he saw many Pharisees and Sadducees coming for baptism, he said to them, "You brood of vipers! Who warned you to flee from the wrath to come? 8Bear fruit worthy of repentance. 9Do not presume to say to yourselves, 'We have Abraham as our ancestor'; for I tell you, God is able from these stones to raise up children to Abraham. 10Even now the ax is lying at the root of the trees; every tree therefore that does not bear good fruit is cut down and thrown into the fire.

11 "I baptize you with *d* water for repentance, but one who is more powerful than I is coming after me; I am not worthy to carry his sandals. He will baptize you with *d* the Holy Spirit and fire. 12His winnowing fork is in his hand, and he will clear his threshing floor and will gather his wheat into the granary; but the chaff he will burn with unquenchable fire."

The Baptism of Jesus

13 Then Jesus came from Galilee to John at the Jordan, to be baptized by him. 14John would have prevented him, saying, "I need to

a Or *astrologers*; Gk *magi*　　*b* Gk *he*　　*c* Or *is at hand*　　*d* Or *in*

---

will save his people from their ills and sins, rather than sinning himself, as Israel had done. Jesus, like Joseph (vv 14, 21), will be obedient to Scripture and the direct guidance of God through various other means.

3:6 CONFESSION—*See* Spiritual Disciplines Index.

3:13–17 *Then Jesus came from Galilee to John at the Jordan.* Like other ancient kings, Jewish monarchs had to be anointed before they could speak or act as royal figures. Accordingly, Jesus' ceremony of anointing is recounted here. First is

the ritual of purification (baptism) and then the anointing by God's own Spirit. This story has direct echoes of the presentation of the king in the Wisdom of Solomon. It was the duty of the king to fulfill all righteousness: "Love righteousness, you rulers of the earth, think of the Lord in goodness and seek him with sincerity of heart; because he is found by those who do not put him to the test, and manifests himself to those who do not distrust him" (Wisd of Sol 1:1–2). In that earlier Jewish text, receiving the Spirit is the key to gaining wisdom, which then is used in

be baptized by you, and do you come to me?" [15]But Jesus answered him, "Let it be so now; for it is proper for us in this way to fulfill all righteousness." Then he consented. [16]And when Jesus had been baptized, just as he came up from the water, suddenly the heavens were opened to him and he saw the Spirit of God descending like a dove and alighting on him. [17]And a voice from heaven said, "This is my Son, the Beloved, *a* with whom I am well pleased."

The Temptation of Jesus

4 Then Jesus was led up by the Spirit into the wilderness to be tempted by the devil. [2]He fasted forty days and forty nights, and afterwards he was famished. [3]The tempter came and said to him, "If you are the Son of God, command these stones to become loaves of bread." [4]But he answered, "It is written,

a Or *my beloved Son*

performance of one's royal duties. In order to be seen as a righteous king, Jesus submits to the rite of purification, is publicly anointed by God for the office, and then is publicly proclaimed to be God's royal Son. Contrast the more private and visionary nature of anointing and announcement in Mark 1, and see that Matthew's anointing is a deliberate emphasis in this book. The announcement here must be compared to the one made to the inner circle of disciples in 17:5. Jesus is the one with whom God is well pleased. The description of Jesus on the mountain during the transfiguration as gleaming and shining like the sun (17:2) simply echoes the description of Wisdom in Wisd of Sol 7:26–29. Throughout this Gospel, Jesus is presented as God's Wisdom made manifest and as the royal figure who exercises and promulgates wisdom.

4:1–11 *Jesus was led up by the Spirit into the wilderness.* In the Wisdom of Solomon, after the discussion about the king's anointing and his righteousness, we have the tale of the king immediately being put to the test. Some ungodly ones say, "Let us lie in wait for the righteous man. . . . He professes to have knowledge of God, and calls himself a child of the Lord. . . . and boasts that God is his father. Let us see if his words are true, and let us test what will happen at the end of his life; for if the righteous man is God's child, he will help him, and will deliver him from . . . his adversaries" (2:12–18). The account advises that these ungodly ones were led astray through the devil's envy. In Matthew, however, Jesus is tempted directly by the devil, but also led to that testing by the Spirit. In all the synoptic Gospels, there are two tests of Jesus, one just before his ministry begins and one as it draws to a close in Gethsemane. The final test is not over until he dies. The first part of the above quote from the

Wisdom of Solomon illuminates Matthew 4 and the latter part illuminates Matthew 26–27— Jesus, the righteous king, being tested not only in his own spirit in the garden, but also being tried by ungodly men. Matt 4:1 says it is the Spirit that led Jesus out into the wilderness to be tested. By definition God tests (intending to strengthen the believer's moral character) and the devil tempts (intending to destroy that selfsame character). Paradoxically, the same set of circumstances can be taken either as a test or a temptation depending on the response. Jesus responds as a believer, indeed, a believing king, ought to respond—by relying on Scripture. The temptations Jesus faces are those that only the Son of God might or could face—temptations to misuse the miraculous power God had given him in various selfish and self-protective ways. But if Jesus had turned stones into bread, thrown himself down from the pinnacle of the Temple, or worshiped the devil (an ascending scale of severity of temptations) in order to feed himself, prove himself to the crowds, or gain his kingdom without dying for it, he would no longer have been the obedient Son of God worthy of emulation. Jesus is portrayed here as not taking shortcuts to glory, but rather following the hard and long path of obedience, living by God's word, and resisting temptation by relying on that word. Notice that the devil can cite Scripture (4:6 is a citation of Ps 91:11–12), but only Jesus fleshes it out and obeys it. Wisdom amounts not just to knowing the truth, but obeying it. When Jesus the King passes the test, the devil departs, leaving angels to attend to Jesus. Jesus' victory over temptation has stood throughout the centuries as a model for our resistance to the Evil One.

4:2 FASTING—*See* Spiritual Disciplines Index.

'One does not live by bread alone,
  but by every word that comes from
    the mouth of God.' "

5 Then the devil took him to the holy city and placed him on the pinnacle of the temple, 6saying to him, "If you are the Son of God, throw yourself down; for it is written,

'He will command his angels
    concerning you,'
  and 'On their hands they will bear
    you up,
so that you will not dash your foot
    against a stone.' "

7Jesus said to him, "Again it is written, 'Do not put the Lord your God to the test.' "

8 Again, the devil took him to a very high mountain and showed him all the kingdoms of the world and their splendor; 9and he said to him, "All these I will give you, if you will fall down and worship me." 10Jesus said to him, "Away with you, Satan! for it is written,

'Worship the Lord your God,
  and serve only him.' "

11Then the devil left him, and suddenly angels came and waited on him.

Jesus Begins His Ministry in Galilee

12 Now when Jesus[a] heard that John had been arrested, he withdrew to Galilee. 13He left Nazareth and made his home in Capernaum by the sea, in the territory of Zebulun and Naphtali, 14so that what had been spoken through the prophet Isaiah might be fulfilled:

15 "Land of Zebulun, land of Naphtali,
  on the road by the sea, across the
    Jordan, Galilee of the Gentiles—
16 the people who sat in darkness
    have seen a great light,
  and for those who sat in the region and
    shadow of death
  light has dawned."

17From that time Jesus began to proclaim, "Repent, for the kingdom of heaven has come near."[b]

Jesus Calls the First Disciples

18 As he walked by the Sea of Galilee, he saw two brothers, Simon, who is called Peter, and Andrew his brother, casting a net into the sea—for they were fishermen. 19And he said to them, "Follow me, and I will make you fish for people." 20Immediately they left their nets and followed him. 21As he went from there, he saw two other brothers, James son of Zebedee and his brother John, in the boat with their father Zebedee, mending their nets, and he called them. 22Immediately they left the boat and their father, and followed him.

Jesus Ministers to Crowds of People

23 Jesus[c] went throughout Galilee, teaching in their synagogues and proclaiming the good news[d] of the kingdom and curing every disease and every sickness among the people.

a Gk he   b Or is at hand   c Gk He
d Gk gospel

Responding

4:10 WORSHIP. This reiteration of Deut 6:13 is in response to the devil's attempt to bribe Jesus to worship him. How important is it for us to worship God with a heart free from the desire to get special power or particular favors or great wealth? As you are able, try to erase all of these kinds of desires from your mind and heart as you attend worship this week. Focus only on God and how to serve him. See also Spiritual Disciplines Index.

4:17 *Repent, for the kingdom of heaven has come near.* Jesus' ministry begins in earnest after John is imprisoned. He is said to go and live in Capernaum, and so yet another Scripture is fulfilled (Isa 9:1–2). With these words, Jesus

takes up the cry of John, whose voice has been silenced by imprisonment. This is a call not merely for us to feel sorry for our sins or even just to accept forgiveness for them, but to choose a different and wiser course of living.

4:23 *teaching . . . and proclaiming . . . and curing every disease.* Jesus traveled all over Galilee proclaiming God's wisdom in synagogues as well as preaching the good news. A distinction is made between his teaching and his preaching; the latter entails the call to repent and the announcement of the coming reign of God. He also is said to heal, attracting enormous crowds even from far-off Syria. In early Judaism, part of Solomon's wisdom involved the knowledge of the healing arts. Jesus not only proclaimed the presence of the

REVELATORY WISDOM

24So his fame spread throughout all Syria, and they brought to him all the sick, those who were afflicted with various diseases and pains, demoniacs, epileptics, and paralytics, and he cured them. 25And great crowds followed him from Galilee, the Decapolis, Jerusalem, Judea, and from beyond the Jordan.

The Beatitudes

5 When Jesus*a* saw the crowds, he went up the mountain; and after he sat down,

his disciples came to him. 2Then he began to speak, and taught them, saying:

3 "Blessed are the poor in spirit, for theirs is the kingdom of heaven.

4 "Blessed are those who mourn, for they will be comforted.

5 "Blessed are the meek, for they will inherit the earth.

6 "Blessed are those who hunger and thirst for righteousness, for they will be filled.

a Gk *he*

---

kingdom; he demonstrated the reality of its presence by works of healing.

5:1–7:29 *When Jesus saw the crowds, he went up the mountain.* The so-called Sermon on the Mount would be better called the "Teaching, or Wisdom, from the Mount." This first long discourse is a large collection of some of Jesus' most memorable wisdom sayings. Here we have the Beatitudes; metaphors inculcating good works (5:16); the upholding of Torah as an expression of wisdom and righteousness (see Sir 24); practical teaching on self-control, anger, sexual expression, oaths, loving enemies, almsgiving, prayer, and fasting; instructions regarding wealth, health, and loyalties; an appeal to wisdom from nature to reduce anxiety; a prohibition against judging others and against profanity; an insistence on following the Golden Rule and the narrow path; and advice to maintain integrity in word and deed and avoid false teachers—a virtual compendium of the usual standing topics for sages, as a comparison with Proverbs 1–6 or Sirach will show. The difference here is that Jesus offers both traditional and counterorder wisdom, and all of the teaching is served up with the understanding that God's eschatological reign is breaking in, and so new occasions teach some new duties as well as reaffirming some of the old ones. The new teachings, which involve counterorder and counterintuitive wisdom, include the teachings against the accumulation of wealth, oath taking, and divorce and in favor of nonretaliation and nonresistance, loving enemies, and the last being first and vice versa. Traditional Jewish wisdom sought to show people how to live practically, so they could be healthy, wealthy, and wise. Jesus' teaching does not simply baptize these agendas and call them good. In some cases, he

substitutes a very different sort of wisdom. The end of this first wisdom discourse focuses on the parable of the wise man (7:24–27). The one who hears and heeds all the teaching in this discourse Jesus names a wise person. The Evangelist stresses that much of this is revelatory wisdom, not wisdom deduced by evaluating human experience or nature. Thus, he presents Jesus as a sage teaching out of divine revelation; and, implicitly, he presents himself as a prophetic sage, like Jesus, who uses Scripture in sapiential ways and believes in the revelatory wisdom given from God to Jesus and through Jesus to disciples like himself. With this orientation, we can better comprehend all the wisdom discourses in Matthew.

5:1–12 *Then he . . . taught them, saying: "Blessed."* Jesus' teaching begins with what we have come to call the Beatitudes, *makarioi*, "the blessings." Jesus is here contrasting the two ways to blessedness: the kingdom way of pure gift from God (*makarios*) and the fleshly way of human attainment (*adimonia*). The Beatitudes give us a radical inversion of blessedness in God's order. Jesus takes those people ordinarily thought to be unblessed and unblessable and shows that there is something about life in the kingdom of God that makes them blessed. Many people simply cannot wrap their minds around Jesus' radical inversion here. For example, in the first Beatitude ("Blessed are the poor in spirit"), the phrase "poor in spirit" (*hoi ptokoi to pneumati*) simply means "the poverty-stricken in spiritual things"—the simpleminded, the untalented, the religiously unsophisticated. This is so contrary to our human way of thinking about what makes people well off that many English translators of the Bible cannot bring themselves to translate it directly. They will often add something about

7 "Blessed are the merciful, for they will receive mercy.

8 "Blessed are the pure in heart, for they will see God.

9 "Blessed are the peacemakers, for they will be called children of God.

10 "Blessed are those who are persecuted for righteousness' sake, for theirs is the kingdom of heaven.

11 "Blessed are you when people revile you and persecute you and utter all kinds of evil against you falsely [a] on my account. 12Rejoice and be glad, for your reward is great in heaven, for in the same way they persecuted the prophets who were before you.

Salt and Light

13 "You are the salt of the earth; but if salt has lost its taste, how can its saltiness be restored? It is no longer good for anything, but is thrown out and trampled under foot.

14 "You are the light of the world. A city built on a hill cannot be hid. 15No one after lighting a lamp puts it under the bushel basket, but on the lampstand, and it gives light to all in the house. 16In the same way, let your light shine before others, so that they may see your good works and give glory to your Father in heaven.

The Law and the Prophets

17 "Do not think that I have come to abolish the law or the prophets; I have come not to abolish but to fulfill. 18For truly I tell you, until heaven and earth pass away, not one letter, [b] not one stroke of a letter, will pass from the law until all is accomplished. 19Therefore, whoever breaks [c] one of the least of these commandments, and teaches others to do the same, will be called least in the kingdom of heaven; but whoever does them and teaches them will be called great in the kingdom of heaven. 20For I tell you, unless your righteousness exceeds that of the scribes and Pharisees, you will never enter the kingdom of heaven.

a Other ancient authorities lack *falsely*
b Gk *one iota*   c Or *annuls*

"consciousness" of spiritual poverty, which, of course, draws the sting from the teaching. And what is it about life in the kingdom of God that makes these unblessed and unblessable people well off? It is the loving, accepting, affirming presence of Jesus Christ, who freely welcomes and receives "the sat upon, spat upon, ratted on," to use the words of singers Simon and Garfunkel. Now, the teaching of the Sermon on the Mount has actually changed our minds on a number of these categories today, such as "the merciful" or "the pure in heart" or "the peacemakers," but they were not thought to be blessed in Jesus' day. And, frankly, even today when the priorities of life are set, these categories stand pretty low.

5:8 SIMPLICITY/FRUGALITY—*See* Spiritual Disciplines Index.

5:17–20 *Do not think that I have come to abolish the law.* In this famous passage, Jesus presents himself as a sage with independent and personal authority, without a need to cite the traditions or teachings of other rabbis. The formula "You have heard that it was said . . . but I say to you" sometimes finds Jesus contrasting his teaching with Moses', sometimes with other Jewish traditions. The famous aphorism in

verse 17 speaks of the fact that Jesus has come to fulfill the Torah, God's previous instructions to his people. But once something is fulfilled, whether a prophecy, a promise, or a teaching, then it is completed. Jesus says that not the smallest portion of the law will disappear until everything is accomplished, by which is meant the kingdom of God's saving reign fully come on earth. Remember, Jesus is addressing Jewish followers already under the Mosaic law, not Gentiles, and it is doubtful the author of Matthew has a different audience in mind. What is clear from verse 20 is that the inbreaking dominion of God does not mean a lessening of the requirements God places on his people—rather, the demands are intensified. From those to whom more grace is given, more is required.

5:20 *unless your righteousness exceeds that of the scribes and Pharisees.* The righteousness of the scribes and Pharisees consisted in externalism, or control over externals, often involving manipulative control over other people. This is contrasted with the internal righteousness of the kingdom of God. This is one of the most critical points for our spiritual formation. It is also the interpretive key to the Sermon on the Mount, for Jesus continually contrasts the internal

Concerning Anger

21 "You have heard that it was said to those of ancient times, 'You shall not murder'; and 'whoever murders shall be liable to judgment.' 22But I say to you that if you are angry with a brother or sister,*a* you will be liable to judgment; and if you insult*b* a brother or sister,*c* you will be liable to the council; and if you say, 'You fool,' you will be liable to the hell*d* of fire. 23So when you are offering your gift at the altar, if you remember that your brother or sister*e* has something against you, 24leave your gift there before the altar and go; first be reconciled to your brother or sister,*e* and then come and offer your gift. 25Come to terms quickly with your accuser while you are on the way to court*f* with him, or your accuser may hand you over to the judge, and the judge to the guard, and you will be thrown into prison. 26Truly I tell you, you will never get out until you have paid the last penny.

Concerning Adultery

27 "You have heard that it was said, 'You shall not commit adultery.' 28But I say to you

that everyone who looks at a woman with lust has already committed adultery with her in his heart. 29If your right eye causes you to sin, tear it out and throw it away; it is better for you to lose one of your members than for your whole body to be thrown into hell.*g* 30And if your right hand causes you to sin, cut it off and throw it away; it is better for you to lose one of your members than for your whole body to go into hell.*g*

Concerning Divorce

31 "It was also said, 'Whoever divorces his wife, let him give her a certificate of divorce.' 32But I say to you that anyone who divorces his wife, except on the ground of unchastity, causes her to commit adultery; and whoever marries a divorced woman commits adultery.

Concerning Oaths

33 "Again, you have heard that it was said to those of ancient times, 'You shall not swear

a Gk *a brother*; other ancient authorities add *without cause*   *b* Gk *say Raca to* (an obscure term of abuse)   *c* Gk *a brother*   *d* Gk *Gehenna*
e Gk *your brother*   *f* Gk lacks *to court*
g Gk *Gehenna*

---

righteousness of the kingdom with the external righteousness of the scribes and Pharisees. The scribes and Pharisees say, "Don't kill"; Jesus says, "Learn freedom from hate"; the scribes and Pharisees say, "Don't have extramarital sex"; Jesus says, "Learn freedom from lustful stewing"; the scribes and Pharisees say, "Be sure to tell the truth when under oath"; Jesus says, "Always tell the truth"; and so forth to the end of the sermon.

5:21–26 *You have heard that it was said.* The intensification of demands is made clear in this section. Jesus is by no means to be seen as merely a second Moses. He goes well beyond Moses. For example, the "Do not murder" commandment of Moses is extended to include an injunction against being angry with fellow believers or calling them fools; before we continue religious duties, including offerings, we need to be reconciled with those from whom we have become estranged.

5:27–32 CHASTITY—*See* Spiritual Disciplines Index.

5:29–30 *If your right eye causes you to sin.*

Note that Jesus says, "If the eye or hand offends." He never says *that* those external members offend. In fact, he taught just the opposite. He said that it is not what goes into the body that offends, but what is in the heart (15:11). It was the scribes and Pharisees who said external matters are what count. In fact, there was one exceedingly strict group, called "the bruised and battered Pharisees," who would shut their eyes upon merely seeing a woman, therefore earning their nickname by bumping into walls and posts. Jesus, as the master Teacher, simply uses a *reductio ad absurdum;* he takes their own teaching on externals and pushes it to the point of absurdity. "If the eyes offend, don't just close them, dig them out; cut off your arms and legs and roll into heaven a mutilated stump!" That is the logic of the external righteousness of the scribes and Pharisees. Gehenna (see NRSV text notes *d* and *g*) was a Jewish notion of hell; it was viewed as a stinking garbage dump where the fire never goes out and the worm eating the garbage never dies.

falsely, but carry out the vows you have made to the Lord.' 34But I say to you, Do not swear at all, either by heaven, for it is the throne of God, 35or by the earth, for it is his footstool, or by Jerusalem, for it is the city of the great King. 36And do not swear by your head, for you cannot make one hair white or black. 37Let your word be 'Yes, Yes' or 'No, No'; anything more than this comes from the evil one.

Concerning Retaliation

38 "You have heard that it was said, 'An eye for an eye and a tooth for a tooth.' 39But I say to you, Do not resist an evildoer. But if anyone strikes you on the right cheek, turn the other also; 40and if anyone wants to sue you and take your coat, give your cloak as well; 41and if anyone forces you to go one mile, go also the second mile. 42Give to everyone who begs from you, and do not refuse anyone who wants to borrow from you.

Love for Enemies

43 "You have heard that it was said, 'You shall love your neighbor and hate your enemy.' 44But I say to you, Love your enemies and pray for those who persecute you, 45so that you may be children of your Father in heaven; for he makes his sun rise on the evil and on the good, and sends rain on the righteous and on the unrighteous. 46For if you love those who love you, what reward do you have? Do not even the tax collectors do the same? 47And if you greet only your brothers and sisters,b what more are you doing than others? Do not even the Gentiles do the same? 48Be perfect, therefore, as your heavenly Father is perfect.

Concerning Almsgiving

6 "Beware of practicing your piety before others in order to be seen by them; for then you have no reward from your Father in heaven.

2 "So whenever you give alms, do not sound a trumpet before you, as the hypocrites do in the synagogues and in the streets, so that they may be praised by others. Truly I tell you, they have received their reward. 3But when you give alms, do not let your left hand know what your right hand is doing, 4so that your alms may be done in secret; and your Father who sees in secret will reward you.a

a Or evil   b Gk your brothers

5:43–48 *Love your enemies.* Jesus' higher standard for his disciples is made clear—we are to perfectly manifest the love God has for all persons. This call to love extends even to our enemies. The love demanded here has nothing to do with reciprocal relationships; rather, it is a matter of giving with no thought of return. God the Father is characterized as an indiscriminate lover and blesser of both the evil and the good, giving to both the sun and the rain needed for crops and sustenance.

5:44 **PRAYER**—*See* Spiritual Disciplines Index.

6:1–18 *Beware of practicing your piety.* In these verses, we have Jesus' own interpretation of the traditional Jewish duties of almsgiving, prayer, and fasting. Performing such tasks for human approbation precludes any reward from the heavenly Father. Giving, praying, and fasting are even to be done in secret, removing the motivation to show off or display piety before others. Instead of wordy prayers, Jesus provides his disciples with a simple prayer paradigm, which would be better called the Disciples' Prayer than the Lord's Prayer. God is addressed as Father, allowing the disciple the same privilege as Jesus and connoting an intimate relationship with the creator of the universe. The prayer for the kingdom to come and God's will to be done makes it clear that these things were not complete or fully done yet on earth. Hallowing God's name precedes the petitions for daily bread and forgiveness of sins. The linking of forgiveness received with the offering of forgiveness to others is crucial. If we are unforgiving, an impediment is placed in our own life, preventing the receiving of divine forgiveness (vv 14–15). Verse 13 is addressed to God, but since God tempts no one to do any evil thing, a better translation would be "Put us not to the test; rather, deliver us from the evil one." We pray to be delivered from temptation and any testing that we are ill-equipped to bear.

6:4 **SECRECY**—*See* Spiritual Disciplines Index.

RELATION BTWS
X's WORDS

Concerning Prayer

5 "And whenever you pray, do not be like the hypocrites; for they love to stand and pray in the synagogues and at the street corners, so that they may be seen by others. Truly I tell you, they have received their reward. 6But whenever you pray, go into your room and shut the door and pray to your Father who is in secret; and your Father who sees in secret will reward you. *a*

7 "When you are praying, do not heap up empty phrases as the Gentiles do; for they think that they will be heard because of their many words. 8Do not be like them, for your Father knows what you need before you ask him.

9 "Pray then in this way:
  Our Father in heaven,
    hallowed be your name.
10   Your kingdom come.
   Your will be done,
    on earth as it is in heaven.
11   Give us this day our daily bread. *b*
12   And forgive us our debts,
    as we also have forgiven our debtors.
13   And do not bring us to the time of
      trial, *c*
    but rescue us from the evil one. *d*
14For if you forgive others their trespasses, your heavenly Father will also forgive you; 15but if you do not forgive others, neither will your Father forgive your trespasses.

Concerning Fasting

16 "And whenever you fast, do not look dismal, like the hypocrites, for they disfigure their faces so as to show others that they are fasting. Truly I tell you, they have received their reward. 17But when you fast, put oil on your head and wash your face, 18so that your fasting may be seen not by others but by your Father who is in secret; and your Father who sees in secret will reward you. *a*

Concerning Treasures

19 "Do not store up for yourselves treasures on earth, where moth and rust *e* consume and where thieves break in and steal; 20but store up for yourselves treasures in heaven, where neither moth nor rust *e* consumes and where thieves do not break in and steal. 21For where your treasure is, there your heart will be also.

The Sound Eye

22 "The eye is the lamp of the body. So, if your eye is healthy, your whole body will be full of light; 23but if your eye is unhealthy, your whole body will be full of darkness. If then the light in you is darkness, how great is the darkness!

Serving Two Masters

24 "No one can serve two masters; for a slave will either hate the one and love the other, or be devoted to the one and despise the other. You cannot serve God and wealth. *f*

Do Not Worry

25 "Therefore I tell you, do not worry about your life, what you will eat or what you will drink, *g* or about your body, what

a Other ancient authorities add *openly*   *b* Or *our bread for tomorrow*   *c* Or *us into temptation*   *d* Or *from evil.* Other ancient authorities add, in some form, *For the kingdom and the power and the glory are yours forever. Amen.*   *e* Gk *eating*   *f* Gk *mammon*   *g* Other ancient authorities lack *or what you will drink*

6:19–24 *Do not store up for yourselves treasures on earth.* Jesus urges the disciples not to store up resources on earth, but rather in heaven. His point relates to what we place our trust in and where our security lies. Jesus stresses that two masters, God and money, cannot both be served. In light of this passage, it is ironic that U.S. currency says, "In God we trust."

you will wear. Is not life more than food, and the body more than clothing? 26Look at the birds of the air; they neither sow nor reap nor gather into barns, and yet your heavenly Father feeds them. Are you not of more value than they? 27And can any of you by worrying add a single hour to your span of life?[a] 28And why do you worry about clothing? Consider the lilies of the field, how they grow; they neither toil nor spin, 29yet I tell you, even Solomon in all his glory was not clothed like one of these. 30But if God so clothes the grass of the field, which is alive today and tomorrow is thrown into the oven, will he not much more clothe you—you of little faith? 31Therefore do not worry, saying, 'What will we eat?' or 'What will we drink?' or 'What will we wear?' 32For it is the Gentiles who strive for all these things; and indeed your heavenly Father knows that you need all these things. 33But strive first for the kingdom of God[b] and his[c] righteousness, and all these things will be given to you as well.

34 "So do not worry about tomorrow, for tomorrow will bring worries of its own. Today's trouble is enough for today.

Judging Others

7 "Do not judge, so that you may not be judged. 2For with the judgment you make you will be judged, and the measure you give will be the measure you get. 3Why do you see the speck in your neighbor's[d] eye, but do not notice the log in your own eye? 4Or how can you say to your neighbor,[e] 'Let me take the speck out of your eye,' while the log is in your own eye? 5You hypocrite, first take the log out of your own eye, and then you will see clearly to take the speck out of your neighbor's[d] eye.

Profaning the Holy

6 "Do not give what is holy to dogs; and do not throw your pearls before swine, or they will trample them under foot and turn and maul you.

Ask, Search, Knock

7 "Ask, and it will be given you; search, and you will find; knock, and the door will be opened for you. 8For everyone who asks receives, and everyone who searches finds, and for everyone who knocks, the door will be opened. 9Is there anyone among you who, if your child asks for bread, will give a stone? 10Or if the child asks for a fish, will give a snake? 11If you then, who are evil, know how

a Or add one cubit to your height   b Other ancient authorities lack of God   c Or its   d Gk brother's   e Gk brother

---

6:25–34 Therefore I tell you, do not worry. Although many things seem worrisome, Jesus reminds his disciples that God is greater than all human circumstances. The reference to Solomon in all his splendor (v 29) is Jesus' enunciation of a wisdom teaching that supersedes the teaching and the blessings of Solomon. Solomon was a collector of resources, but Jesus says his disciples should not live like that, but rather trust God and rely on his blessings. He can take care of humans as well as he can take care of other creatures. In verse 30, the Evangelist uses his characteristic Matthean descriptor of disciples, "you of little faith." The audience is not said to utterly lack faith, but this wisdom is meant to bolster, increase, and stretch that faith. We are to seek first the dominion of God and trust him to take care of our other needs. Ultimately, our greatest need is to be among the saved under the reign of God, which we call his kingdom or dominion. The term "dominion" is to be preferred, because it can refer to a reign or a realm, like the Hebrew and Greek concepts, while, to us, "kingdom" always connotes a place.

7:1–6 Do not judge, so that you may not be judged. This text calls for self-examination, rather than merely maintaining a nonjudgmental attitude toward others. The issue here is not the abandonment of critical judgment about human behavior. Rather, we are to abandon judging other persons even if and when they sin, for we are not omniscient and cannot take all things into account. Instead, we are to concentrate on our own foibles and the flaws in our own vision that prevent us from seeing ourselves accurately. Notice that Jesus focuses on how we view others with rigorous scrutiny, while overlooking or minimizing our own shortcomings and sins.

to give good gifts to your children, how much more will your Father in heaven give good things to those who ask him!

The Golden Rule

12 "In everything do to others as you would have them do to you; for this is the law and the prophets.

The Narrow Gate

13 "Enter through the narrow gate; for the gate is wide and the road is easy[a] that leads to destruction, and there are many who take it. 14For the gate is narrow and the road is hard that leads to life, and there are few who find it.

A Tree and Its Fruit

15 "Beware of false prophets, who come to you in sheep's clothing but inwardly are ravenous wolves. 16You will know them by their fruits. Are grapes gathered from thorns, or figs from thistles? 17In the same way, every good tree bears good fruit, but the bad tree bears bad fruit. 18A good tree cannot bear bad fruit, nor can a bad tree bear good fruit. 19Every tree that does not bear good fruit is cut down and thrown into the fire. 20Thus you will know them by their fruits.

Concerning Self-Deception

21 "Not everyone who says to me, 'Lord, Lord,' will enter the kingdom of heaven, but only the one who does the will of my Father in heaven. 22On that day many will say to me, 'Lord, Lord, did we not prophesy in your name, and cast out demons in your name, and do many deeds of power in your name?' 23Then I will declare to them, 'I never knew you; go away from me, you evildoers.'

Hearers and Doers

24 "Everyone then who hears these words of mine and acts on them will be like a wise man who built his house on rock. 25The rain fell, the floods came, and the winds blew and beat on that house, but it did not fall, because it had been founded on rock. 26And everyone who hears these words of mine and does not act on them will be like a foolish man who built his house on sand. 27The rain fell, and the floods came, and the winds blew and beat against that house, and it fell—and great was its fall!"

28 Now when Jesus had finished saying these things, the crowds were astounded at his teaching, 29for he taught them as one having authority, and not as their scribes.

a Other ancient authorities read *for the road is wide and easy*

7:15–20 *Beware of false prophets.* The warning against false prophets provides with it a test—if their teaching, or fruit, is good, then they also are good. On the other hand, if what they say bears "bad fruit," they themselves are likewise false. The tree is to be judged by its fruit.

7:21–23 *Not everyone who says . . . , "Lord."* Verse 21 is not talking about people who say that Jesus is Lord, but do not in fact believe he is the Savior; the contrast is not between words and belief. Rather, at issue here are words and action. Some call Jesus good teacher, master, sage, or rabbi in an ingratiating manner, but do not do the will of the Father in heaven. Even if such people perform miracles and exorcisms using Jesus' name, if they have not lived a wise life according to godly teaching, they will not enter the dominion of God. Nor will we.

7:24–29 *a wise man who built his house on*

rock. The concluding parable makes clear that Jesus has been offering the disciples a solid foundation of teaching on which to build their lives and ministry. But it is up to them to put his words into practice. Otherwise, they are like the fool described so often in Proverbs, who is not the intellectually challenged person, but rather the person who lacks good moral judgment. It is not common sense that Jesus' wisdom calls us to, but rather a Christian sense, which only makes sense in the context of a Christian vision of the world, a belief system attested to by ethical commitments and behavior.

7:28 *the crowds were astounded.* The crowds were amazed because Jesus taught as one who had independent authority, unlike a normal teacher of the law. But we must not confuse amazement with commitment or discipleship, then or now.

Jesus Cleanses a Leper

8 When Jesus[a] had come down from the mountain, great crowds followed him; [2]and there was a leper[b] who came to him and knelt before him, saying, "Lord, if you choose, you can make me clean." [3]He stretched out his hand and touched him, saying, "I do choose. Be made clean!" Immediately his leprosy[b] was cleansed. [4]Then Jesus said to him, "See that you say nothing to anyone; but go, show yourself to the priest, and offer the gift that Moses commanded, as a testimony to them."

Jesus Heals a Centurion's Servant

5 When he entered Capernaum, a centurion came to him, appealing to him [6]and saying, "Lord, my servant is lying at home paralyzed, in terrible distress." [7]And he said to him, "I will come and cure him." [8]The centurion answered, "Lord, I am not worthy to have you come under my roof; but only speak the word, and my servant will be healed. [9]For I also am a man under authority, with soldiers under me; and I say to one, 'Go,' and he goes, and to another, 'Come,' and he comes, and to my slave, 'Do this,' and the slave does it." [10]When Jesus heard him, he was amazed and said to those who followed him, "Truly I tell you, in no one[c] in Israel have I found such faith. [11]I tell you, many will come from east and west and will eat with Abraham and Isaac and Jacob in the kingdom of heaven, [12]while the heirs of the kingdom will be thrown into the outer darkness, where there will be weeping and gnashing of teeth." [13]And to the centurion Jesus said, "Go; let it be done for you according to your faith." And the servant was healed in that hour.

Jesus Heals Many at Peter's House

14 When Jesus entered Peter's house, he saw his mother-in-law lying in bed with a fever; [15]he touched her hand, and the fever left her, and she got up and began to serve him. [16]That evening they brought to him many who were possessed with demons; and he cast out the spirits with a word, and cured all who were sick. [17]This was to fulfill what had been spoken through the prophet Isaiah, "He took our infirmities and bore our diseases."

Would-Be Followers of Jesus

18 Now when Jesus saw great crowds around him, he gave orders to go over to the other side. [19]A scribe then approached and

a Gk he   b The terms *leper* and *leprosy* can refer to several diseases   c Other ancient authorities read *Truly I tell you, not even*

8:1–4 *a leper . . . knelt before him.* Jesus reaches out and touches a man with a dreaded skin disease in order to heal him. Being unclean in a culture that focused on ritual impurity made one an outcast, literally an untouchable. Since the dominion of God was breaking in, Jesus considered issues of ritual impurity moot and such restrictions needed no longer to be maintained. Jesus will advocate that only moral impurity defiles a person, which shows Jesus was greater than Moses, for he could even indicate when the law of Moses had been superseded. The leper participates in his own healing and realizes that Jesus has a choice about whether to heal or not. The man is to go and show himself to the priest so he can be reintegrated into the community, but Jesus sees no need to do this himself, because he did not consider touching the man to constitute defilement for him.

8:5–17 *a centurion came to him.* This may be a story about the healing of a gentile centurion's servant, but the centurion might also have been a Semite (e.g., an Edomite), since most Roman troops in the region were locally enlisted persons. In any case, this man is one of two figures in this Gospel who are said to have great faith, in contrast to the disciples, who are regularly castigated for their little faith. Verse 11 suggests the centurion will sit at the eschatological table with the patriarchs, while some Jews will lose their dinner invitations. The theme of reversal is a common one in the Jesus tradition, and it shows Jesus' wisdom was of a counterorder sort. The healing of Peter's mother-in-law is only mentioned in passing. Isa 53:4 is said to be fulfilled by Jesus' healings, making Jesus not only a figure like Solomon, but the ultimate Isaianic kingly figure—the suffering servant, who carried the diseases of his people and bore their infirmities.

said, "Teacher, I will follow you wherever you go." 20And Jesus said to him, "Foxes have holes, and birds of the air have nests; but the Son of Man has nowhere to lay his head." 21Another of his disciples said to him, "Lord, first let me go and bury my father." 22But Jesus said to him, "Follow me, and let the dead bury their own dead."

Jesus Stills the Storm

23 And when he got into the boat, his disciples followed him. 24A windstorm arose on the sea, so great that the boat was being swamped by the waves; but he was asleep. 25And they went and woke him up, saying, "Lord, save us! We are perishing!" 26And he said to them, "Why are you afraid, you of little faith?" Then he got up and rebuked the winds and the sea; and there was a dead calm. 27They were amazed, saying, "What sort of man is this, that even the winds and the sea obey him?"

Jesus Heals the Gadarene Demoniacs

28 When he came to the other side, to the country of the Gadarenes,ᵃ two demoniacs coming out of the tombs met him. They were so fierce that no one could pass that way. 29Suddenly they shouted, "What have you to do with us, Son of God? Have you come here to torment us before the time?" 30Now a large herd of swine was feeding at some distance from them. 31The demons begged him, "If you cast us out, send us into the herd of swine." 32And he said to them, "Go!" So they came out and entered the swine; and sud-

denly, the whole herd rushed down the steep bank into the sea and perished in the water. 33The swineherds ran off, and on going into the town, they told the whole story about what had happened to the demoniacs. 34Then the whole town came out to meet Jesus; and when they saw him, they begged him to leave their neighborhood. 1And after getting into a boat he crossed the sea and came to his own town.

9

Jesus Heals a Paralytic

2 And just then some people were carrying a paralyzed man lying on a bed. When Jesus saw their faith, he said to the paralytic, "Take heart, son; your sins are forgiven." 3Then some of the scribes said to themselves, "This man is blaspheming." 4But Jesus, perceiving their thoughts, said, "Why do you think evil in your hearts? 5For which is easier, to say, 'Your sins are forgiven,' or to say, 'Stand up and walk'? 6But so that you may know that the Son of Man has authority on earth to forgive sins"—he then said to the paralytic— "Stand up, take your bed and go to your home." 7And he stood up and went to his home. 8When the crowds saw it, they were filled with awe, and they glorified God, who had given such authority to human beings.

The Call of Matthew

9 As Jesus was walking along, he saw a man called Matthew sitting at the tax booth;

ᵃ Other ancient authorities read *Gergesenes*; others, *Gerasenes*

9:2–8 *a paralyzed man lying on a bed.* The story of the healing of the paralytic raises the important issue of the relationship of sickness to sin as well as the issue of what authority Jesus has to pronounce sins forgiven. On the former matter, Jesus suggests that sin is the more serious issue and can indeed have physiological effects. In this case, the physical healing is to be taken as an indicator that Jesus also has the power to deal with our deeper sickness, sin sickness. The text is not suggesting a one-to-one correspondence between sickness and sin such that noticeable sickness indicates notable sinners. Rather, Jesus has been authorized to forgive sins, not least

because he is the human expression of the mind and will of God—God's Wisdom in the flesh.

9:9–13 *a man called Matthew sitting at the tax booth.* The calling of Matthew is "Exhibit A" of the calling of outcasts and despised sinners, for tax collectors were collaborators with Rome and their client kings and bilked the people of their resources. The Pharisees, with their concern for both ritual and moral purity, could not understand why Jesus banqueted with the bad. Jesus' response is that of a healer— because it is precisely such people that most need the Great Physician. The call to the sinner is like the call of Wisdom to the simple

and he said to him, "Follow me." And he got up and followed him.

10 And as he sat at dinner*a* in the house, many tax collectors and sinners came and were sitting*b* with him and his disciples. ¹¹When the Pharisees saw this, they said to his disciples, "Why does your teacher eat with tax collectors and sinners?" ¹²But when he heard this, he said, "Those who are well have no need of a physician, but those who are sick. ¹³Go and learn what this means, 'I desire mercy, not sacrifice.' For I have come to call not the righteous but sinners."

The Question about Fasting

14 Then the disciples of John came to him, saying, "Why do we and the Pharisees fast often,*c* but your disciples do not fast?" ¹⁵And Jesus said to them, "The wedding guests cannot mourn as long as the bridegroom is with them, can they? The days will come when the bridegroom is taken away from them, and then they will fast. ¹⁶No one sews a piece of unshrunk cloth on an old cloak, for the patch pulls away from the cloak, and a worse tear is made. ¹⁷Neither is new wine put into old wineskins; otherwise, the skins burst, and the wine is spilled, and the skins are destroyed; but new wine is put into fresh wineskins, and so both are preserved."

A Girl Restored to Life and a Woman Healed

18 While he was saying these things to them, suddenly a leader of the synagogue*d* came in and knelt before him, saying, "My daughter has just died; but come and lay your hand on her, and she will live." ¹⁹And Jesus got up and followed him, with his disciples. ²⁰Then suddenly a woman who had been suffering from hemorrhages for twelve years

came up behind him and touched the fringe of his cloak, ²¹for she said to herself, "If I only touch his cloak, I will be made well." ²²Jesus turned, and seeing her he said, "Take heart, daughter; your faith has made you well." And instantly the woman was made well. ²³When Jesus came to the leader's house and saw the flute players and the crowd making a commotion, ²⁴he said, "Go away; for the girl is not dead but sleeping." And they laughed at him. ²⁵But when the crowd had been put outside, he went in and took her by the hand, and the girl got up. ²⁶And the report of this spread throughout that district.

Jesus Heals Two Blind Men

27 As Jesus went on from there, two blind men followed him, crying loudly, "Have mercy on us, Son of David!" ²⁸When he entered the house, the blind men came to him; and Jesus said to them, "Do you believe that I am able to do this?" They said to him, "Yes, Lord." ²⁹Then he touched their eyes and said, "According to your faith let it be done to you." ³⁰And their eyes were opened. Then Jesus sternly ordered them, "See that no one knows of this." ³¹But they went away and spread the news about him throughout that district.

Jesus Heals One Who Was Mute

32 After they had gone away, a demoniac who was mute was brought to him. ³³And when the demon had been cast out, the one who had been mute spoke; and the crowds were amazed and said, "Never has anything like this been seen in Israel." ³⁴But the Phar-

a Gk *reclined*   *b* Gk *were reclining*   *c* Other ancient authorities lack *often*   *d* Gk lacks *of the synagogue*

---

in Proverbs 9, but with this difference—Jesus actually believes that the wayward will listen and respond, especially since the heart of his approach is mercy.

Responding
9:13 SACRIFICE. Jesus is quoting Hos 6:6, "For I desire steadfast love and not sacrifice." Why does God desire steadfast love

or mercy instead of sacrifice? Could it be because love and mercy reveal that we have a transformed heart, while sacrifice is an outward act that can be done regardless of the condition of our heart (e.g., 15:18–19)? Discuss. *See also* Spiritual Disciplines Index.

9:14–15 FASTING—*See* Spiritual Disciplines Index.

isees said, "By the ruler of the demons he casts out the demons." *a*

The Harvest Is Great, the Laborers Few

35 Then Jesus went about all the cities and villages, teaching in their synagogues, and proclaiming the good news of the kingdom, and curing every disease and every sickness. 36When he saw the crowds, he had compassion for them, because they were harassed and helpless, like sheep without a shepherd. 37Then he said to his disciples, "The harvest is plentiful, but the laborers are few; 38therefore ask the Lord of the harvest to send out laborers into his harvest."

The Twelve Apostles

10 Then Jesus *b* summoned his twelve disciples and gave them authority over unclean spirits, to cast them out, and to cure every disease and every sickness. 2These are the names of the twelve apostles: first, Simon, also known as Peter, and his brother Andrew; James son of Zebedee, and his brother John; 3Philip and Bartholomew;

Thomas and Matthew the tax collector; James son of Alphaeus, and Thaddaeus; *c* 4Simon the Cananaean, and Judas Iscariot, the one who betrayed him.

The Mission of the Twelve

5 These twelve Jesus sent out with the following instructions: "Go nowhere among the Gentiles, and enter no town of the Samaritans, 6but go rather to the lost sheep of the house of Israel. 7As you go, proclaim the good news, 'The kingdom of heaven has come near.' *d* 8Cure the sick, raise the dead, cleanse the lepers, *e* cast out demons. You received without payment; give without payment. 9Take no gold, or silver, or copper in your belts, 10no bag for your journey, or two tunics, or sandals, or a staff; for laborers deserve their food. 11Whatever town or village you enter, find out who in it is worthy, and stay there

a Other ancient authorities lack this verse
b Gk *he*   *c* Other ancient authorities read *Lebbaeus*, or *Lebbaeus called Thaddaeus*   *d* Or *is at hand*   *e* The terms *leper* and *leprosy* can refer to several diseases

---

9:35–38 *he had compassion for them.* Jesus has compassion for the harassed and helpless and those without able leadership (v 36). Later, Jesus will send his disciples out to lead the lost into a relationship with the One who can lead them and provide them with wisdom, just as he calls us to make disciples.

10:1–42 *Then Jesus summoned his twelve disciples.* This long continuous discourse is the beginning of the second collection of wisdom material in this Gospel. Its emphasis on the mission of the disciples recommends calling this section "Rules for the Road." Jesus authorizes the disciples to do the same things he is doing, but notice it is only the inner circle he empowers and sends out, two by two. This pairing likely stems from the Jewish belief that the truth of anything must be confirmed by the testimony of two witnesses (Deut 17:6; 19:15). For the first time, we are given the names of the Twelve (vv 2–3). The disciples are to go only to the lost sheep of Israel, for the gospel is first of all for them (v 6). It is unclear whether this means all of Israel is lost, or they are to go to the lost among Israel. The disciples are to take no resources with them, but rather to rely on the

system of Jewish hospitality in each town (vv 9–11). The disciples are exhorted to act as sages—to be as wise as serpents but innocent as doves (v 16), aware of the potential for harm or evil from some people. They do not speak for themselves or of themselves, but the Spirit of the Father speaks through them, as is the case with Jesus (v 20). They must expect persecution, rejection, and to be a cause of division and turmoil. Jesus did not come to bring peace, but rather the hour of decision, the division of the righteous and the unrighteous, the wise and the foolish (vv 34–36). When persecuted, they are to flee to the next city, for there are more than enough such cities in Israel to last until the Son of Man returns (v 23). Verse 24 is crucial, as it shows again the context of this Gospel. It is for those who are already sages in training, apprentices in the school of Jesus, who is Wisdom. They may expect the same kind of rejection and treatment that the supreme Sage received. The advice about anxiety from the first discourse is recapitulated here (vv 28–31). Verse 40 indicates that the disciples are agents and extensions of their Master; those who reject the agents have rejected the Master.

until you leave. 12As you enter the house, greet it. 13If the house is worthy, let your peace come upon it; but if it is not worthy, let your peace return to you. 14If anyone will not welcome you or listen to your words, shake off the dust from your feet as you leave that house or town. 15Truly I tell you, it will be more tolerable for the land of Sodom and Gomorrah on the day of judgment than for that town.

Coming Persecutions

16 "See, I am sending you out like sheep into the midst of wolves; so be wise as serpents and innocent as doves. 17Beware of them, for they will hand you over to councils and flog you in their synagogues; 18and you will be dragged before governors and kings because of me, as a testimony to them and the Gentiles. 19When they hand you over, do not worry about how you are to speak or what you are to say; for what you are to say will be given to you at that time; 20for it is not you who speak, but the Spirit of your Father speaking through you. 21Brother will betray brother to death, and a father his child, and children will rise against parents and have them put to death; 22and you will be hated by all because of my name. But the one who endures to the end will be saved. 23When they persecute you in one town, flee to the next; for truly I tell you, you will not have gone through all the towns of Israel before the Son of Man comes.

24 "A disciple is not above the teacher, nor a slave above the master; 25it is enough for the disciple to be like the teacher, and the slave like the master. If they have called the master of the house Beelzebul, how much more will they malign those of his household!

Whom to Fear

26 "So have no fear of them; for nothing is covered up that will not be uncovered, and nothing secret that will not become known. 27What I say to you in the dark, tell in the light; and what you hear whispered, proclaim from the housetops. 28Do not fear those who kill the body but cannot kill the soul; rather fear him who can destroy both soul and body in hell. a 29Are not two sparrows sold for a penny? Yet not one of them will fall to the ground apart from your Father. 30And even the hairs of your head are all counted. 31So do not be afraid; you are of more value than many sparrows.

32 "Everyone therefore who acknowledges me before others, I also will acknowledge before my Father in heaven; 33but whoever denies me before others, I also will deny before my Father in heaven.

Not Peace, but a Sword

34 "Do not think that I have come to bring peace to the earth; I have not come to bring peace, but a sword.
35 For I have come to set a man against his
            father,
    and a daughter against her mother,
    and a daughter-in-law against her
            mother-in-law;
36 and one's foes will be members of one's
            own household.
37Whoever loves father or mother more than me is not worthy of me; and whoever loves son or daughter more than me is not worthy of me; 38and whoever does not take up the cross and follow me is not worthy of me. 39Those who find their life will lose it, and those who lose their life for my sake will find it.

Rewards

40 "Whoever welcomes you welcomes me, and whoever welcomes me welcomes the one who sent me. 41Whoever welcomes a prophet in the name of a prophet will receive a prophet's reward; and whoever welcomes a righteous person in the name of a righteous person will receive the reward of the righteous; 42and whoever gives even a cup of cold water to one of these little ones in the name of a disciple—truly I tell you, none of these will lose their reward."

a Gk Gehenna

10:26 SECRECY—See Spiritual Disciplines Index.

11 Now when Jesus had finished instructing his twelve disciples, he went on from there to teach and proclaim his message in their cities.

Messengers from John the Baptist

2 When John heard in prison what the Messiah*a* was doing, he sent word by his*b* disciples 3and said to him, "Are you the one who is to come, or are we to wait for another?" 4Jesus answered them, "Go and tell John what you hear and see: 5the blind receive their sight, the lame walk, the lepers*c* are cleansed, the deaf hear, the dead are raised, and the poor have good news brought to them. 6And blessed is anyone who takes no offense at me."

Jesus Praises John the Baptist

7 As they went away, Jesus began to speak to the crowds about John: "What did you go out into the wilderness to look at? A reed shaken by the wind? 8What then did you go out to see? Someone*d* dressed in soft robes? Look, those who wear soft robes are in royal palaces. 9What then did you go out to see? A prophet?*e* Yes, I tell you, and more than a prophet. 10This is the one about whom it is written,

'See, I am sending my messenger ahead
of you,
who will prepare your way before
you.'

11Truly I tell you, among those born of women no one has arisen greater than John the Baptist; yet the least in the kingdom of heaven is greater than he. 12From the days of John the Baptist until now the kingdom of heaven has suffered violence,*f* and the violent take it by force. 13For all the prophets and the law prophesied until John came; 14and if you are willing to accept it, he is Elijah who is to come. 15Let anyone with ears*g* listen!

16 "But to what will I compare this generation? It is like children sitting in the marketplaces and calling to one another,

17 'We played the flute for you, and you
did not dance;
we wailed, and you did not mourn.'

18For John came neither eating nor drinking, and they say, 'He has a demon'; 19the Son of Man came eating and drinking, and they say, 'Look, a glutton and a drunkard, a friend of tax collectors and sinners!' Yet wisdom is vindicated by her deeds."*h*

Woes to Unrepentant Cities

20 Then he began to reproach the cities in which most of his deeds of power had been done, because they did not repent. 21"Woe to you, Chorazin! Woe to you, Bethsaida! For if the deeds of power done in you had been done in Tyre and Sidon, they would have repented long ago in sackcloth and ashes. 22But I tell you, on the day of judgment it will be more tolerable for Tyre and Sidon than for you. 23And you, Capernaum,

will you be exalted to heaven?
No, you will be brought down to
Hades.

For if the deeds of power done in you had been done in Sodom, it would have remained until this day. 24But I tell you that on the day of judgment it will be more tolerable for the land of Sodom than for you."

Jesus Thanks His Father

25 At that time Jesus said, "I thank*i* you, Father, Lord of heaven and earth, because you have hidden these things from the wise

a Or *the Christ*   *b* Other ancient authorities read
two of his   *c* The terms *leper* and *leprosy* can refer
to several diseases   *d* Or *Why then did you go out?*
To see someone   *e* Other ancient authorities read
Why then did you go out? To see a prophet?
f Or *has been coming violently*   *g* Other ancient
authorities add *to hear*   *h* Other ancient
authorities read *children*   *i* Or *praise*

11:25–27 *you have hidden these things from the wise.* This is one of the most crucial passages for understanding the character of this Gospel and its presentation of Jesus as both sage and Wisdom incarnate. Jesus offers revelatory wisdom that is hidden from the conventionally

wise and intelligent and yet revealed even to infants. This passage is a deliberate echo of Dan 2:19–23, where another prophetic sage, Daniel himself, thanks God for the wisdom revealed to him. Here the royal Son, who is the true sage, is the only one who can truly reveal the heavenly

and the intelligent and have revealed them to infants; 26yes, Father, for such was your gracious will. *a* 27All things have been handed over to me by my Father; and no one knows the Son except the Father, and no one knows the Father except the Son and anyone to whom the Son chooses to reveal him.

28 "Come to me, all you that are weary and are carrying heavy burdens, and I will give you rest. 29Take my yoke upon you, and learn from me; for I am gentle and humble in heart, and you will find rest for your souls. 30For my yoke is easy, and my burden is light."

Plucking Grain on the Sabbath

12 At that time Jesus went through the grainfields on the sabbath; his disciples were hungry, and they began to pluck heads of grain and to eat. 2When the Pharisees saw it, they said to him, "Look, your disciples are doing what is not lawful to do on the sabbath." 3He said to them, "Have you not read what David did when he and his companions were hungry? 4He entered the house of God and ate the bread of the Presence, which it was not lawful for him or his companions to eat, but only for the priests. 5Or have you not read in the law that on the sabbath the priests in the temple break the sabbath and yet are guiltless? 6I tell you, something greater than the temple is here. 7But if you had known what this means, 'I desire mercy and not sacrifice,' you would not have condemned the guiltless. 8For the Son of Man is lord of the sabbath."

The Man with a Withered Hand

9 He left that place and entered their synagogue; 10a man was there with a withered hand, and they asked him, "Is it lawful to cure on the sabbath?" so that they might accuse him. 11He said to them, "Suppose one of you has only one sheep and it falls into a pit on the sabbath; will you not lay hold of it and lift it out? 12How much more valuable is a human being than a sheep! So it is lawful to do good on the sabbath." 13Then he said to the man, "Stretch out your hand." He stretched it out, and it was restored, as sound as the other. 14But the Pharisees went out and conspired against him, how to destroy him.

a Or *for so it was well-pleasing in your sight*

Father. The Father language, which is adopted from earlier Jewish wisdom literature, reiterates that Jesus is so intimate with the Father that he is the very expression of the mind of God on earth. The wisdom Jesus is referring to can be bestowed upon anyone and cannot be acquired by conventional learning or the study of nature or human nature. This is very similar to what we find in the other wisdom Gospel, John (5:20; 14:7).

11:28–30 *Come to me, all you that are weary.* Here the words of Wisdom about her yoke (spoken in Sir 6:23–26; 51:26) become the words of Jesus himself. Jesus is offering his own yoke, which involves both old and new teachings, not simply the yoke of the Mosaic law. Torah is seen as but one expression of God's larger wisdom, and not the final or definitive one. Jesus' person, life, and teaching are the climactic expression of God's wisdom and will. Jesus and his disciples are like the scribes described in 13:52, drawing on both old and new in presenting the gospel. Jesus' adaptation of Torah and his new teaching, which goes beyond and in some cases replaces Torah, can both be described as wisdom. Jesus' yoke, however, is light and his burden easy, even though disciples still must assume that yoke and burden.

12:1–50 *At that time Jesus went through the grainfields.* What happens when counterorder wisdom meets resistance? Chapter 12 presents a series of controversy dialogues and narratives—controversies over the plucking of grain, healing on the Sabbath, exorcisms, and the lack of a validating miracle or sign that Jesus possessed divine authority. The first half of the chapter concludes with the dramatic statement about who Jesus is—the humble servant spoken of by Isaiah (vv 18–21; cf. Isa 42:1–4), and the second half concludes with a dramatic statement as to who Jesus' true family is (vv 46–50). In both sections of the chapter, the issue of demons and exorcism is addressed (vv 22–32, 43–45). This suggests Jesus stirred up the most controversy because of the exorcisms, when he acted as the son of David, like Solomon, in knowledge of the spirit world and how to deal with it.

God's Chosen Servant

15　When Jesus became aware of this, he departed. Many crowds*a* followed him, and he cured all of them, 16and he ordered them not to make him known. 17This was to fulfill what had been spoken through the prophet Isaiah:

18 "Here is my servant, whom I have chosen,
　　my beloved, with whom my soul is
　　　well pleased.
I will put my Spirit upon him,
　　and he will proclaim justice to the
　　　Gentiles.
19 He will not wrangle or cry aloud,
　　nor will anyone hear his voice in the
　　　streets.
20 He will not break a bruised reed
　　or quench a smoldering wick
until he brings justice to victory.
21　And in his name the Gentiles will
　　hope."

Jesus and Beelzebul

22　Then they brought to him a demoniac who was blind and mute; and he cured him, so that the one who had been mute could speak and see. 23All the crowds were amazed and said, "Can this be the Son of David?" 24But when the Pharisees heard it, they said, "It is only by Beelzebul, the ruler of the demons, that this fellow casts out the demons." 25He knew what they were thinking and said to them, "Every kingdom divided against itself is laid waste, and no city or house divided against itself will stand. 26If Satan casts out Satan, he is divided against himself; how then will his kingdom stand? 27If I cast out demons by Beelzebul, by whom do your own exorcists*b* cast them out? Therefore they will be your judges. 28But if it is by the Spirit of God that I cast out demons, then the kingdom of God has come to you. 29Or how can one enter a strong man's house and plunder his property, without first tying up the strong man? Then indeed the house can be plundered. 30Whoever is not with me is against me, and whoever does not gather with me scatters. 31Therefore I tell you, people will be forgiven for every sin and blasphemy, but blasphemy against the Spirit will not be forgiven. 32Whoever speaks a word against the Son of Man will be forgiven, but whoever speaks against the Holy Spirit will not be forgiven, either in this age or in the age to come.

A Tree and Its Fruit

33　"Either make the tree good, and its fruit good; or make the tree bad, and its fruit bad; for the tree is known by its fruit. 34You brood of vipers! How can you speak good things, when you are evil? For out of the abundance of the heart the mouth speaks. 35The good person brings good things out of a good treasure, and the evil person brings evil things out of an evil treasure. 36I tell you, on the day of judgment you will have to give an account for every careless word you utter; 37for by your words you will be justified, and by your words you will be condemned."

The Sign of Jonah

38　Then some of the scribes and Pharisees said to him, "Teacher, we wish to see a sign from you." 39But he answered them, "An evil and adulterous generation asks for a sign, but no sign will be given to it except the sign of the prophet Jonah. 40For just as Jonah was three days and three nights in the belly of the sea monster, so for three days and three nights the Son of Man will be in the heart of the earth. 41The people of Nineveh will rise up at the judgment with this generation and condemn it, because they repented at the proclamation of Jonah, and see, something greater than Jonah is here! 42The queen of the South will rise up at the judgment with this generation and condemn it, because she came from the ends of the earth to listen to the wisdom of Solomon, and see, something greater than Solomon is here!

a Other ancient authorities lack *crowds*
b Gk *sons*

12:18 SERVICE—*See* Spiritual Disciplines Index.

The Return of the Unclean Spirit

43 "When the unclean spirit has gone out of a person, it wanders through waterless regions looking for a resting place, but it finds none. 44Then it says, 'I will return to my house from which I came.' When it comes, it finds it empty, swept, and put in order. 45Then it goes and brings along seven other spirits more evil than itself, and they enter and live there; and the last state of that person is worse than the first. So will it be also with this evil generation."

The True Kindred of Jesus

46 While he was still speaking to the crowds, his mother and his brothers were standing outside, wanting to speak to him. 47Someone told him, "Look, your mother and your brothers are standing outside, wanting to speak to you."[a] 48But to the one who had told him this, Jesus[b] replied, "Who is my mother, and who are my brothers?" 49And pointing to his disciples, he said, "Here are my mother and my brothers! 50For whoever does the will of my Father in heaven is my brother and sister and mother."

The Parable of the Sower

13 That same day Jesus went out of the house and sat beside the sea. 2Such great crowds gathered around him that he got into a boat and sat there, while the whole crowd stood on the beach. 3And he told them many things in parables, saying: "Listen! A sower went out to sow. 4And as he sowed, some seeds fell on the path, and the birds came and ate them up. 5Other seeds fell on rocky ground, where they did not have much soil, and they sprang up quickly, since they had no depth of soil. 6But when the sun rose, they were scorched; and since they had no root, they withered away. 7Other seeds fell among thorns, and the thorns grew up and choked them. 8Other seeds fell on good soil and brought forth grain, some a hundredfold, some sixty, some thirty. 9Let anyone with ears[c] listen!"

a Other ancient authorities lack verse 47
b Gk he   c Other ancient authorities add to hear

12:46–50 *his mother and his brothers were standing outside.* The important saying in verse 50 makes clear that Jesus' true family is his disciples; whoever does the will of God is Jesus' mother and brothers.

13:1–53 *That same day Jesus . . . sat beside the sea.* Chapter 13 contains the third of the Matthean discourses, focusing on parables, the form of wisdom speech whose most famous and frequent user was Jesus. The term we translate "parable" refers to a metaphorical form of speech meant to tease the mind into active thought. The term could refer to anything from a metaphorical one-liner (e.g., "Physician, heal yourself") to a riddle, proverb, or brief narrative. What distinguishes Jesus' use of this form of wisdom speech is that Jesus' parables talk about the inbreaking reign or divine saving activity of God in and through his ministry. In terms of pedagogy, the disciples are depicted as being capable of learning and understanding (vv 51–52), even though they have little faith. In other words, they are portrayed as being like the "simple" in earlier wisdom literature (Prov 1–9). Growth in wisdom is possible for such persons, but it may require revelation from Wisdom itself from time to time. Peter then is portrayed as having received and expressed such wisdom about who Jesus is in 16:16–17.

13:3–23 *A sower went out to sow.* The parable of the sower makes clear that reception of the gospel depends on the soil, that is, the condition of the recipient. In this parable, the seed and the sower are the same in each case, but the soil varies. The story could be a realistic representation of the response to Jesus' ministry. There were many who did not respond favorably to his message; but the few who did produced remarkable fruit. The quotation of Isa 6:9–10 suggests that reception of the message is not really possible unless one repents and becomes spiritually open to the message (vv 14–15). It also suggests that Jesus deliberately spoke in this indirect or veiled metaphorical manner precisely because many were unprepared to hear and heed the message. The explanation (vv 18–23) makes clear that there are a variety of factors hindering hearing— Satan, the lure of wealth, trouble, persecution, worries.

The Purpose of the Parables

10 Then the disciples came and asked him, "Why do you speak to them in parables?" [11]He answered, "To you it has been given to know the secrets[a] of the kingdom of heaven, but to them it has not been given. [12]For to those who have, more will be given, and they will have an abundance; but from those who have nothing, even what they have will be taken away. [13]The reason I speak to them in parables is that 'seeing they do not perceive, and hearing they do not listen, nor do they understand.' [14]With them indeed is fulfilled the prophecy of Isaiah that says:

'You will indeed listen, but never
    understand,
  and you will indeed look, but never
    perceive.
15 For this people's heart has grown dull,
  and their ears are hard of hearing,
    and they have shut their eyes;
      so that they might not look with
        their eyes,
  and listen with their ears,
and understand with their heart and
    turn—
  and I would heal them.'

[16]But blessed are your eyes, for they see, and your ears, for they hear. [17]Truly I tell you, many prophets and righteous people longed to see what you see, but did not see it, and to hear what you hear, but did not hear it.

The Parable of the Sower Explained

18 "Hear then the parable of the sower. [19]When anyone hears the word of the kingdom and does not understand it, the evil one comes and snatches away what is sown in the heart; this is what was sown on the path. [20]As for what was sown on rocky ground, this is the one who hears the word and immediately receives it with joy; [21]yet such a person has no root, but endures only for a while, and when trouble or persecution arises on account of the word, that person immediately falls away.[b] [22]As for what was sown among thorns, this is the one who hears the word, but the cares of the world and the lure of wealth choke the word, and it yields nothing. [23]But as for what was sown on good soil, this is the one who hears the word and un-

derstands it, who indeed bears fruit and yields, in one case a hundredfold, in another sixty, and in another thirty."

The Parable of Weeds among the Wheat

24 He put before them another parable: "The kingdom of heaven may be compared to someone who sowed good seed in his field; [25]but while everybody was asleep, an enemy came and sowed weeds among the wheat, and then went away. [26]So when the plants came up and bore grain, then the weeds appeared as well. [27]And the slaves of the householder came and said to him, 'Master, did you not sow good seed in your field? Where, then, did these weeds come from?' [28]He answered, 'An enemy has done this.' The slaves said to him, 'Then do you want us to go and gather them?' [29]But he replied, 'No; for in gathering the weeds you would uproot the wheat along with them. [30]Let both of them grow together until the harvest; and at harvest time I will tell the reapers, Collect the weeds first and bind them in bundles to be burned, but gather the wheat into my barn.' "

The Parable of the Mustard Seed

31 He put before them another parable: "The kingdom of heaven is like a mustard seed that someone took and sowed in his field; [32]it is the smallest of all the seeds, but when it has grown it is the greatest of shrubs and becomes a tree, so that the birds of the air come and make nests in its branches."

The Parable of the Yeast

33 He told them another parable: "The kingdom of heaven is like yeast that a woman took and mixed in with[c] three measures of flour until all of it was leavened."

The Use of Parables

34 Jesus told the crowds all these things in parables; without a parable he told them nothing. [35]This was to fulfill what had been spoken through the prophet:[d]

"I will open my mouth to speak in
    parables;

a Or *mysteries*   b Gk *stumbles*   c Gk *hid in*
d Other ancient authorities read *the prophet Isaiah*

I will proclaim what has been hidden from the foundation of the world." *a*

Jesus Explains the Parable of the Weeds

36 Then he left the crowds and went into the house. And his disciples approached him, saying, "Explain to us the parable of the weeds of the field." 37 He answered, "The one who sows the good seed is the Son of Man; 38 the field is the world, and the good seed are the children of the kingdom; the weeds are the children of the evil one, 39 and the enemy who sowed them is the devil; the harvest is the end of the age, and the reapers are angels. 40 Just as the weeds are collected and burned up with fire, so will it be at the end of the age. 41 The Son of Man will send his angels, and they will collect out of his kingdom all causes of sin and all evildoers, 42 and they will throw them into the furnace of fire, where there will be weeping and gnashing of teeth. 43 Then the righteous will shine like the sun in the kingdom of their Father. Let anyone with ears *b* listen!

Three Parables

44 "The kingdom of heaven is like treasure hidden in a field, which someone found and hid; then in his joy he goes and sells all that he has and buys that field.

45 "Again, the kingdom of heaven is like a merchant in search of fine pearls; 46 on finding one pearl of great value, he went and sold all that he had and bought it.

47 "Again, the kingdom of heaven is like a net that was thrown into the sea and caught fish of every kind; 48 when it was full, they drew it ashore, sat down, and put the good

into baskets but threw out the bad. 49 So it will be at the end of the age. The angels will come out and separate the evil from the righteous 50 and throw them into the furnace of fire, where there will be weeping and gnashing of teeth.

Treasures New and Old

51 "Have you understood all this?" They answered, "Yes." 52 And he said to them, "Therefore every scribe who has been trained for the kingdom of heaven is like the master of a household who brings out of his treasure what is new and what is old." 53 When Jesus had finished these parables, he left that place.

The Rejection of Jesus at Nazareth

54 He came to his hometown and began to teach the people *c* in their synagogue, so that they were astounded and said, "Where did this man get this wisdom and these deeds of power? 55 Is not this the carpenter's son? Is not his mother called Mary? And are not his brothers James and Joseph and Simon and Judas? 56 And are not all his sisters with us? Where then did this man get all this?" 57 And they took offense at him. But Jesus said to them, "Prophets are not without honor except in their own country and in their own house." 58 And he did not do many deeds of power there, because of their unbelief.

The Death of John the Baptist

14 At that time Herod the ruler *d* heard reports about Jesus; 2 and he said to his

---

a Other ancient authorities lack *of the world*
b Other ancient authorities add *to hear*
c Gk *them*   *d* Gk *tetrarch*

13:51–52 *who brings out of his treasure what is new and what is old.* Jesus is described as a sage who uses both conventional and counter-order wisdom in his parables.

13:54–58 *He came to his hometown.* Jesus' rejection at Nazareth is recounted. The crowd asks, "Where did this man get this wisdom?" The answer is, as a revelation from God, not from studying nature or human nature. Jesus is called "the carpenter's son" (in Mark 6 he is called "the carpenter"), which comports with the emphasis in Matthew 1 about his being

grafted into Joseph's genealogy. The hometown folk fulfill the sadder part of the parable of the sower. Jesus offers the aphorism that a prophet is only without honor in his own region, among his wider kinship circle, and within his own home. He is speaking of how his own family did not understand or accept him as a prophetic sage sent from God.

14:1–17:27 *At that time Herod the ruler heard reports about Jesus.* The stories found in chapters 14–17 further substantiate that Jesus was a healer and was involved in controversial dialogues with

servants, "This is John the Baptist; he has been raised from the dead, and for this reason these powers are at work in him." [3]For Herod had arrested John, bound him, and put him in prison on account of Herodias, his brother Philip's wife,[a] [4]because John had been telling him, "It is not lawful for you to have her." [5]Though Herod[b] wanted to put him to death, he feared the crowd, because they regarded him as a prophet. [6]But when Herod's birthday came, the daughter of Herodias danced before the company, and she pleased Herod [7]so much that he promised on oath to grant her whatever she might ask. [8]Prompted by her mother, she said, "Give me the head of John the Baptist here on a platter." [9]The king was grieved, yet out of regard for his oaths and for the guests, he commanded it to be given; [10]he sent and had John beheaded in the prison. [11]The head was brought on a platter and given to the girl, who brought it to her mother. [12]His disciples came and took the body and buried it; then they went and told Jesus.

Feeding the Five Thousand

13 Now when Jesus heard this, he withdrew from there in a boat to a deserted place by himself. But when the crowds heard it, they followed him on foot from the towns.

[14]When he went ashore, he saw a great crowd; and he had compassion for them and cured their sick. [15]When it was evening, the disciples came to him and said, "This is a deserted place, and the hour is now late; send the crowds away so that they may go into the villages and buy food for themselves." [16]Jesus said to them, "They need not go away; you give them something to eat." [17]They replied, "We have nothing here but five loaves and two fish." [18]And he said, "Bring them here to me." [19]Then he ordered the crowds to sit down on the grass. Taking the five loaves and the two fish, he looked up to heaven, and blessed and broke the loaves, and gave them to the disciples, and the disciples gave them to the crowds. [20]And all ate and were filled; and they took up what was left over of the broken pieces, twelve baskets full. [21]And those who ate were about five thousand men, besides women and children.

Jesus Walks on the Water

22 Immediately he made the disciples get into the boat and go on ahead to the other side, while he dismissed the crowds. [23]And after he had dismissed the crowds, he went up the mountain by himself to pray. When

a Other ancient authorities read his brother's wife
b Gk he

Pharisees and others. Indeed, we are meant to see Jesus as a teacher increasingly at odds with other sages of the day. In chapters 14–16, both the deeds and the controversies of the sage come to the fore, rather than just the teachings, though they are not entirely absent. The section is framed by the discussions of the death of John the Baptist (14:1–12), whom Jesus is mistaken for at the outset of this section, and the death and resurrection of Jesus at the other (16:21–27). In the middle of the section, we have two feeding miracles (14:13–21; 15:32–39), which make clear that Jesus is one who is somewhat like, but greater than, Moses. Chapter 17 adds the transfiguration narrative, another exorcism, and the Temple tax controversy on the way to the fourth discourse in chapter 18 (chaps 24–25 constitute the fifth discourse). The death of John the Baptist at the hands of Herod Antipas foreshadows what will happen to Jesus.

It also is presented as a flashback, for Herod is heard to comment that the powers that are at work in Jesus demonstrate he is John come back from the dead (14:2).

14:22–33 *Immediately he made the disciples get into the boat.* The miracle story of walking on the water is taken from Mark, but Matthew adds the element of Peter's attempt to walk on the water (vv 28–31). Jesus initially is mistaken for a ghost, since Jews viewed bodies of water as the dwelling place of spirits and demons. Only Peter attempts to step out in faith and walk toward Jesus, until the elements of wind and wave frighten him. It is a story of walking by faith, rather than in fear. Peter is called "you of little faith" (v 31), but the end result of the story is that all those in the boat, including Peter, venerate or worship Jesus as the divine Son of God.

14:23 PRAYER—*See* Spiritual Disciplines Index.

evening came, he was there alone, 24but by this time the boat, battered by the waves, was far from the land,*a* for the wind was against them. 25And early in the morning he came walking toward them on the sea. 26But when the disciples saw him walking on the sea, they were terrified, saying, "It is a ghost!" And they cried out in fear. 27But immediately Jesus spoke to them and said, "Take heart, it is I; do not be afraid."

28 Peter answered him, "Lord, if it is you, command me to come to you on the water." 29He said, "Come." So Peter got out of the boat, started walking on the water, and came toward Jesus. 30But when he noticed the strong wind,*b* he became frightened, and beginning to sink, he cried out, "Lord, save me!" 31Jesus immediately reached out his hand and caught him, saying to him, "You of little faith, why did you doubt?" 32When they got into the boat, the wind ceased. 33And those in the boat worshiped him, saying, "Truly you are the Son of God."

Jesus Heals the Sick in Gennesaret

34 When they had crossed over, they came to land at Gennesaret. 35After the people of that place recognized him, they sent word throughout the region and brought all who were sick to him, 36and begged him that they might touch even the fringe of his cloak; and all who touched it were healed.

The Tradition of the Elders

15 Then Pharisees and scribes came to Jesus from Jerusalem and said, 2"Why do your disciples break the tradition of the elders? For they do not wash their hands before they eat." 3He answered them, "And why do you break the commandment of God for the sake of your tradition? 4For God said,*c* 'Honor your father and your mother,' and, 'Whoever speaks evil of father or mother must surely die.' 5But you say that whoever tells father or mother, 'Whatever support you might have had from me is given to God,'*d* then that person need not honor the father.*e* 6So, for the sake of your tradition, you make void the word*f* of God. 7You hypocrites! Isaiah prophesied rightly about you when he said:

8 'This people honors me with their lips,
     but their hearts are far from me;
9 in vain do they worship me,
     teaching human precepts as
         doctrines.' "

Things That Defile

10 Then he called the crowd to him and said to them, "Listen and understand: 11it is not what goes into the mouth that defiles a

a Other ancient authorities read *was out on the sea*
b Other ancient authorities read *the wind*
c Other ancient authorities read *commanded, saying*
d Or *is an offering*   *e* Other ancient authorities add *or the mother*   *f* Other ancient authorities read *law*; others, *commandment*

Responding

14:23 SOLITUDE. Most of us probably live too far from mountains to climb one regularly to pray, but we have other ways to be alone with God. Consider taking a one-day silent retreat at a center or just find a place isolated from the hustle and bustle of everyday life. As you are on retreat, keep a notebook handy and write down what you hear and the impressions you receive from God. What did you learn? *See also* Spiritual Disciplines Index.

14:33 WORSHIP—*See* Spiritual Disciplines Index.

15:10–20 *it is not what goes into the mouth that defiles a person.* Here Jesus enunciates a fundamental principle showing that he relates to Mosaic law with sovereign freedom. He says that it is not what enters a person that defiles. Rather, it is what comes out of the mouth— words revealing what is in the heart—that defiles a person. The Pharisees are characterized as the blind leading the blind (this motif is absent from Mark's account). Jesus declares that the laws regarding ritual impurity no longer apply, since the dominion of God is breaking in. But the moral law has been intensified. Jesus displays his wisdom by indicating what is binding on believers in the new eschatological situation. Jesus offers a counterorder wisdom at odds with both Jewish tradition and Mosaic law.

person, but it is what comes out of the mouth that defiles." 12Then the disciples approached and said to him, "Do you know that the Pharisees took offense when they heard what you said?" 13He answered, "Every plant that my heavenly Father has not planted will be uprooted. 14Let them alone; they are blind guides of the blind.*a* And if one blind person guides another, both will fall into a pit." 15But Peter said to him, "Explain this parable to us." 16Then he said, "Are you also still without understanding? 17Do you not see that whatever goes into the mouth enters the stomach, and goes out into the sewer? 18But what comes out of the mouth proceeds from the heart, and this is what defiles. 19For out of the heart come evil intentions, murder, adultery, fornication, theft, false witness, slander. 20These are what defile a person, but to eat with unwashed hands does not defile."

The Canaanite Woman's Faith

21 Jesus left that place and went away to the district of Tyre and Sidon. 22Just then a Canaanite woman from that region came out and started shouting, "Have mercy on me, Lord, Son of David; my daughter is tormented by a demon." 23But he did not answer her at all. And his disciples came and urged him, saying, "Send her away, for she keeps shouting after us." 24He answered, "I was sent only to the lost sheep of the house of Israel." 25But she came and knelt before him, saying, "Lord, help me." 26He answered, "It is not fair to take the children's food and throw it to the dogs." 27She said, "Yes, Lord, yet even the dogs eat the crumbs that fall from their masters' table." 28Then Jesus answered her, "Woman, great is your faith! Let it be done for you as you wish." And her daughter was healed instantly.

Jesus Cures Many People

29 After Jesus had left that place, he passed along the Sea of Galilee, and he went up the mountain, where he sat down. 30Great crowds came to him, bringing with them the lame, the maimed, the blind, the mute, and many others. They put them at his feet, and he cured them, 31so that the crowd was amazed when they saw the mute speaking, the maimed whole, the lame walking, and the blind seeing. And they praised the God of Israel.

Feeding the Four Thousand

32 Then Jesus called his disciples to him and said, "I have compassion for the crowd, because they have been with me now for three days and have nothing to eat; and I do not want to send them away hungry, for they might faint on the way." 33The disciples said to him, "Where are we to get enough bread in the desert to feed so great a crowd?" 34Jesus asked them, "How many loaves have you?" They said, "Seven, and a few small fish." 35Then ordering the crowd to sit down on the ground, 36he took the seven loaves and the fish; and after giving thanks he broke them and gave them to the disciples, and the disciples gave them to the crowds. 37And all of them ate and were filled; and they took up the broken pieces left over, seven baskets full. 38Those who had eaten were four thousand men, besides women and children. 39After sending away the crowds, he got into the boat and went to the region of Magadan.*b*

The Demand for a Sign

16 The Pharisees and Sadducees came, and to test Jesus*c* they asked him to show them a sign from heaven. 2He answered them, "When it is evening, you say, 'It will be fair weather, for the sky is red.' 3And in the morning, 'It will be stormy today, for the sky is red and threatening.' You know how to interpret the appearance of the sky, but you cannot interpret the signs of the times.*d* 4An evil and adulterous generation asks for a sign, but no sign will be given to it except the sign of Jonah." Then he left them and went away.

The Yeast of the Pharisees and Sadducees

5 When the disciples reached the other side, they had forgotten to bring any bread. 6Jesus said to them, "Watch out, and beware of the yeast of the Pharisees and Sadducees." 7They said to one another, "It is because we

a Other ancient authorities lack *of the blind*
b Other ancient authorities read *Magdala* or
Magdalan   *c* Gk *him*   *d* Other ancient
authorities lack 2*When it is . . . of the times*

have brought no bread." [8]And becoming aware of it, Jesus said, "You of little faith, why are you talking about having no bread? [9]Do you still not perceive? Do you not remember the five loaves for the five thousand, and how many baskets you gathered? [10]Or the seven loaves for the four thousand, and how many baskets you gathered? [11]How could you fail to perceive that I was not speaking about bread? Beware of the yeast of the Pharisees and Sadducees!" [12]Then they understood that he had not told them to beware of the yeast of bread, but of the teaching of the Pharisees and Sadducees.

Peter's Declaration about Jesus

13 Now when Jesus came into the district of Caesarea Philippi, he asked his disciples, "Who do people say that the Son of Man is?" [14]And they said, "Some say John the Baptist, but others Elijah, and still others Jeremiah or one of the prophets." [15]He said to them, "But who do you say that I am?" [16]Simon Peter answered, "You are the Messiah,[a] the Son of the living God." [17]And Jesus answered him, "Blessed are you, Simon son of Jonah! For flesh and blood has not revealed this to you, but my Father in heaven. [18]And I tell you, you are

Peter,[b] and on this rock[c] I will build my church, and the gates of Hades will not prevail against it. [19]I will give you the keys of the kingdom of heaven, and whatever you bind on earth will be bound in heaven, and whatever you loose on earth will be loosed in heaven." [20]Then he sternly ordered the disciples not to tell anyone that he was[d] the Messiah.[a]

Jesus Foretells His Death and Resurrection

21 From that time on, Jesus began to show his disciples that he must go to Jerusalem and undergo great suffering at the hands of the elders and chief priests and scribes, and be killed, and on the third day be raised. [22]And Peter took him aside and began to rebuke him, saying, "God forbid it, Lord! This must never happen to you." [23]But he turned and said to Peter, "Get behind me, Satan! You are a stumbling block to me; for you are setting your mind not on divine things but on human things."

The Cross and Self-Denial

24 Then Jesus told his disciples, "If any want to become my followers, let them deny

a Or the Christ   b Gk Petros   c Gk petra
d Other ancient authorities add Jesus

16:13–28 *Now when Jesus came into the district.* The great confession of Peter (v 16) is followed by a promise from Jesus to Peter (vv 18–19). This, in turn, is followed by the first passion prediction (v 21) and a call to the disciples to take up their own crosses and follow Jesus (v 24). That the confession is in Caesarea Philippi is noteworthy, as that city was full of pagan shrines. Yet in the midst of that idolatry, Jesus is confessed. It also is noteworthy because the city had a river flowing from an underground spring, which was seen as an opening into Hades, the underworld, and the river Styx. Thus, when Jesus says the gates of Hades will not prevail against his community (v 18), he is proclaiming that his community will never die out. The blessing of Peter (vv 17–18) is important, since Jesus promises to build his community on people like Peter, that is, those who make such a confession. He reminds Peter that he came to this conclusion about Jesus due to a revelation from God, not from human

testimony. The play on words in verse 18 is between Peter, called "Rock," and the Greek term for a shelf of rocks, which would include Peter but not refer solely to him. The binding and loosing (v 19) refer to binding some rulings on community members and setting them free from other ones, which is precisely what Jesus has been doing—setting them free from some of the Mosaic requirements and binding on them other ones. Following this, Jesus requires self-denial and then the taking up of our own crosses (not Jesus'). Verse 28 refers to Jesus appearing in glory, which is depicted in chapter 17. Jesus is Wisdom incognito unless he reveals himself. Even when he does so, revelation is not enough—additional teaching is required. In the wake of the rising tide of opposition to Jesus' teaching, Jesus finally reveals the inside knowledge that he is destined to die.

16:19 THE WITH-GOD LIFE—*See* Spiritual Disciplines Index.

themselves and take up their cross and follow me. 25For those who want to save their life will lose it, and those who lose their life for my sake will find it. 26For what will it profit them if they gain the whole world but forfeit their life? Or what will they give in return for their life?

27 "For the Son of Man is to come with his angels in the glory of his Father, and then he will repay everyone for what has been done. 28Truly I tell you, there are some standing here who will not taste death before they see the Son of Man coming in his kingdom."

The Transfiguration

17 Six days later, Jesus took with him Peter and James and his brother John and led them up a high mountain, by themselves. 2And he was transfigured before them, and his face shone like the sun, and his clothes became dazzling white. 3Suddenly there appeared to them Moses and Elijah, talking with him. 4Then Peter said to Jesus, "Lord, it is good for us to be here; if you wish, I a will make three dwellings b here, one for you, one for Moses, and one for Elijah." 5While he was still speaking, suddenly a bright cloud overshadowed them, and from the cloud a voice said, "This is my Son, the Beloved; c with him I am well pleased; listen to him!" 6When the disciples heard this, they fell to the ground and were overcome by fear. 7But Jesus came and touched them, saying, "Get up and do not be afraid." 8And when they looked up, they saw no one except Jesus himself alone.

9 As they were coming down the mountain, Jesus ordered them, "Tell no one about the vision until after the Son of Man has been raised from the dead." 10And the disciples asked him, "Why, then, do the scribes say that Elijah must come first?" 11He replied, "Elijah is indeed coming and will restore all things; 12but I tell you that Elijah has already come, and they did not recognize him, but they did to him whatever they pleased. So also the Son of Man is about to suffer at their hands." 13Then the disciples understood that he was speaking to them about John the Baptist.

Jesus Cures a Boy with a Demon

14 When they came to the crowd, a man came to him, knelt before him, 15and said, "Lord, have mercy on my son, for he is an epileptic and he suffers terribly; he often falls into the fire and often into the water. 16And I brought him to your disciples, but they could not cure him." 17Jesus answered, "You faithless and perverse generation, how much longer must I be with you? How much longer must I put up with you? Bring him here to me." 18And Jesus rebuked the demon, d and it e came out of him, and the boy was cured instantly. 19Then the disciples came to Jesus privately and said, "Why could we not cast it

a Other ancient authorities read *we*   b Or *tents*
c Or *my beloved Son*   d Gk *it* or *him*   e Gk *the demon*

17:1–13 *Six days later, Jesus took with him.* The transfiguration narrative involves only Jesus and the inner circle of the three: Peter, James, and John. Jesus has a dialogue with Moses and Elijah, the two great prophetic figures of the Old Testament. The numinous quality of the story is greater in Matthew than in Mark (chap 9). In Matthew alone, we hear that Jesus' face shone like the sun, that the cloud that overshadowed the three was bright, and that the voice from the cloud said he was well pleased with his Son (directly echoing 3:17), that the disciples fell to the ground when they heard the divine voice, that Jesus came and touched them and told them to get up and not be afraid, and that they were told to tell no one about the "vision" until

"after the Son of Man has been raised from the dead" (v 9). The disciples are commanded to listen to the Son. Absent from this account is the Markan comment that Peter did not know what he was saying when he made the comment about building booths. Present is the comment that the disciples finally did understand that by Elijah Jesus was referring to John the Baptist, whose fate foreshadowed Jesus'. Peter is presented in a more favorable light here than in Mark. The transfiguration provides additional information for the inner circle of the disciples about Jesus' full identity—the glorious manifestation of God himself on earth, God's divine Son.

out?" 20He said to them, "Because of your little faith. For truly I tell you, if you have faith the size of a *a* mustard seed, you will say to this mountain, 'Move from here to there,' and it will move; and nothing will be impossible for you." *b*

Jesus Again Foretells His Death and Resurrection

22 As they were gathering *c* in Galilee, Jesus said to them, "The Son of Man is going to be betrayed into human hands, 23and they will kill him, and on the third day he will be raised." And they were greatly distressed.

Jesus and the Temple Tax

24 When they reached Capernaum, the collectors of the temple tax *d* came to Peter and said, "Does your teacher not pay the temple tax?" *d* 25He said, "Yes, he does." And when he came home, Jesus spoke of it first, asking, "What do you think, Simon? From whom do kings of the earth take toll or tribute? From their children or from others?" 26When Peter *e* said, "From others," Jesus said to him, "Then the children are free. 27However, so that we do not give offense to them, go to the sea and cast a hook; take the first fish that comes up; and when you open its mouth, you will find a coin; *f* take that and give it to them for you and me."

True Greatness

18 At that time the disciples came to Jesus and asked, "Who is the greatest in the kingdom of heaven?" 2He called a child, whom he put among them, 3and said, "Truly I tell you, unless you change and become like children, you will never enter the kingdom of heaven. 4Whoever becomes humble like this child is the greatest in the kingdom of heaven. 5Whoever welcomes one such child in my name welcomes me.

Temptations to Sin

6 "If any of you put a stumbling block before one of these little ones who believe in me, it would be better for you if a great millstone were fastened around your neck and you were drowned in the depth of the sea. 7Woe to the world because of stumbling blocks! Occasions for stumbling are bound to come, but woe to the one by whom the stumbling block comes!

8 "If your hand or your foot causes you to stumble, cut it off and throw it away; it is better for you to enter life maimed or lame than to have two hands or two feet and to be thrown into the eternal fire. 9And if your eye causes you to stumble, tear it out and throw it away; it is better for you to enter life with one eye than to have two eyes and to be thrown into the hell *g* of fire.

The Parable of the Lost Sheep

10 "Take care that you do not despise one of these little ones; for, I tell you, in heaven their angels continually see the face of my Father in heaven. *h* 12What do you think? If a shepherd has a hundred sheep, and one of them has gone astray, does he not leave the ninety-nine on the mountains and go in search of the one that went astray? 13And if he finds it, truly I tell you, he rejoices over it more than over the ninety-nine that never went astray. 14So it is not the will of your *i* Father in heaven that one of these little ones should be lost.

---

a Gk *faith as a grain of*　*b* Other ancient authorities add verse 21, *But this kind does not come out except by prayer and fasting*　*c* Other ancient authorities read *living*　*d* Gk *didrachma*　*e* Gk *he*　*f* Gk *stater;* the stater was worth two didrachmas　*g* Gk *Gehenna*　*h* Other ancient authorities add verse 11, *For the Son of Man came to save the lost*　*i* Other ancient authorities read *my*

18:1–10 *unless you . . . become like children.* The teaching about childlikeness, welcoming children, and avoiding the converse (causing them to stumble) presupposes a context in which the disciples must humble themselves and be teachable like children and in which they can even consider children as followers of Jesus. The woes in verses 7–9 are reserved for those who mislead and teach children in a false way. The little ones could include not only those who are actually children, but also neophytes in the faith. They are said to have guardian angels in heaven.

Reproving Another Who Sins

15 "If another member of the church[a] sins against you,[b] go and point out the fault when the two of you are alone. If the member listens to you, you have regained that one.[c] 16But if you are not listened to, take one or two others along with you, so that every word may be confirmed by the evidence of two or three witnesses. 17If the member refuses to listen to them, tell it to the church; and if the offender refuses to listen even to the church, let such a one be to you as a Gentile and a tax collector. 18Truly I tell you, whatever you bind on earth will be bound in heaven, and whatever you loose on earth will be loosed in heaven. 19Again, truly I tell you, if two of you agree on earth about anything you ask, it will be done for you by my Father in heaven. 20For where two or three are gathered in my name, I am there among them."

Forgiveness

21 Then Peter came and said to him, "Lord, if another member of the church[d] sins against me, how often should I forgive? As many as seven times?" 22Jesus said to him, "Not seven times, but, I tell you, seventy-seven[e] times.

The Parable of the Unforgiving Servant

23 "For this reason the kingdom of heaven may be compared to a king who wished to settle accounts with his slaves. 24When he began the reckoning, one who owed him ten thousand talents[f] was brought to him; 25and, as he could not pay, his lord ordered him to be sold, together with his wife and children and all his possessions, and payment to be made. 26So the slave fell on his knees before him, saying, 'Have patience with me, and I will pay you everything.' 27And out of pity for him, the lord of that slave released him and forgave him the debt. 28But that same slave, as he went out, came upon one of his fellow slaves who owed him a hundred denarii;[g] and seizing him by the throat, he said, 'Pay what you owe.' 29Then his fellow slave fell down and pleaded with him, 'Have patience with me, and I will pay you.' 30But he refused; then he went and threw him into prison until he would pay the debt. 31When his fellow slaves saw what had happened, they were greatly distressed, and they went and reported to their lord all that had taken place. 32Then his lord summoned him and said to him, 'You wicked slave! I forgave you all that debt because you pleaded with me. 33Should you not have had mercy on your fellow slave, as I had mercy on you?' 34And in anger his lord handed him over to be tortured until he would pay his entire debt. 35So my heavenly Father will also do to every one of you, if you do not forgive your brother or sister[h] from your heart."

a Gk If your brother   b Other ancient authorities lack against you   c Gk the brother   d Gk if my brother   e Or seventy times seven   f A talent was worth more than fifteen years' wages of a laborer   g The denarius was the usual day's wage for a laborer   h Gk brother

---

Responding

18:20 FELLOWSHIP and THE WITH-GOD LIFE. We don't normally think that a gathering of two or three people constitutes a fellowship and that Jesus could be in our midst there as much as he is present at our large gatherings. Why did Jesus give this teaching? The next time you meet with two or three Christian friends, ask them to make a special effort to be aware of the Spirit of Jesus moving among you and within you. Did you sense that Jesus' presence was stronger when there were several of you together? See also Spiritual Disciplines Index.

18:21–35 *how often should I forgive?* The parable of the unmerciful servant is told in response to a question raised by Peter about forgiveness. Jesus the sage goes well beyond conventional wisdom by offering the counterintuitive answer that one must completely forgive—forgive as many times as it takes—in order to be like Jesus himself. Peter likely thought he was being quite generous when he said he would forgive someone seven times. The parable illustrates the line in the Lord's Prayer that we need to be forgiving if we expect to receive divine forgiveness (6:12). And not just a grudging forgiveness, but forgiveness from our heart is expected (v 35), lest we incur judgment for being un-Christlike.

Teaching about Divorce

19 When Jesus had finished saying these things, he left Galilee and went to the region of Judea beyond the Jordan. ²Large crowds followed him, and he cured them there.

3 Some Pharisees came to him, and to test him they asked, "Is it lawful for a man to divorce his wife for any cause?" ⁴He answered, "Have you not read that the one who made them at the beginning 'made them male and female,' ⁵and said, 'For this reason a man shall leave his father and mother and be joined to his wife, and the two shall become one flesh'? ⁶So they are no longer two, but one flesh. Therefore what God has joined together, let no one separate." ⁷They said to him, "Why then did Moses command us to give a certificate of dismissal and to divorce her?" ⁸He said to them, "It was because you were so hard-hearted that Moses allowed you to divorce your wives, but from the beginning it was not so. ⁹And I say to you, whoever divorces his wife, except for unchastity, and marries another commits adultery." ᵃ

10 His disciples said to him, "If such is the case of a man with his wife, it is better not to marry." ¹¹But he said to them, "Not everyone can accept this teaching, but only those to whom it is given. ¹²For there are eunuchs who have been so from birth, and there are eunuchs who have been made eunuchs by others, and there are eunuchs who have made themselves eunuchs for the sake of the kingdom of heaven. Let anyone accept this who can."

Jesus Blesses Little Children

13 Then little children were being brought to him in order that he might lay his hands on them and pray. The disciples spoke sternly to those who brought them; ¹⁴but Jesus said, "Let the little children come to me, and do not stop them; for it is to such as these that the kingdom of heaven belongs." ¹⁵And he laid his hands on them and went on his way.

The Rich Young Man

16 Then someone came to him and said, "Teacher, what good deed must I do to have eternal life?" ¹⁷And he said to him, "Why do you ask me about what is good? There is only one who is good. If you wish to enter into life, keep the commandments." ¹⁸He said to him, "Which ones?" And Jesus said, "You shall not murder; You shall not commit adultery; You shall not steal; You shall not bear false witness; ¹⁹Honor your father and mother; also, You shall love your neighbor as yourself." ²⁰The young man said to him, "I have kept all these; ᵇ what do I still lack?" ²¹Jesus said to him, "If you wish to be perfect, go, sell your possessions, and give the money ᶜ to the poor, and you will have treasure in heaven; then come, follow me." ²²When the young man heard this word, he went away grieving, for he had many possessions.

23 Then Jesus said to his disciples, "Truly

ᵃ Other ancient authorities read *except on the ground of unchastity, causes her to commit adultery*; others add at the end of the verse *and he who marries a divorced woman commits adultery*
ᵇ Other ancient authorities add *from my youth*
ᶜ Gk lacks *the money*

19:16–30 *what . . . must I do to have eternal life?* Although youth is not an encumbrance to discipleship, wealth is clearly seen as such in this story. Wealth was a traditional topic for sages, as the book of Proverbs shows, but here Jesus' counterorder wisdom suggests that, rather than being a sign of blessing, wealth can actually be a hindrance to proper discipleship. The command is to sell all possessions, give the proceeds to the poor, and then follow Jesus (v 21). Liquidation of assets permits greater mobility and the ability to join the traveling fellowship of disciples (Luke 8:1–3). A rich person is said to be able to enter God's realm or eternal life only by God's grace. In all cases, salvation is a divine action, not a human one. The theme of heavenly, or eschatological, reward also is a regular one in wisdom literature. Jesus assures Peter that there are such rewards in the kingdom for those who have made sacrifices here (vv 28–30). Jesus the sage foresees a day of remarkable reversal of fortunes when the last, least, and lost will become the first, most, and found. Those who are among the elite in this world will also suffer a reversal of fortune.

I tell you, it will be hard for a rich person to enter the kingdom of heaven. 24Again I tell you, it is easier for a camel to go through the eye of a needle than for someone who is rich to enter the kingdom of God." 25When the disciples heard this, they were greatly astounded and said, "Then who can be saved?" 26But Jesus looked at them and said, "For mortals it is impossible, but for God all things are possible."

27 Then Peter said in reply, "Look, we have left everything and followed you. What then will we have?" 28Jesus said to them, "Truly I tell you, at the renewal of all things, when the Son of Man is seated on the throne of his glory, you who have followed me will also sit on twelve thrones, judging the twelve tribes of Israel. 29And everyone who has left houses or brothers or sisters or father or mother or children or fields, for my name's sake, will receive a hundredfold, *a* and will inherit eternal life. 30But many who are first will be last, and the last will be first.

The Laborers in the Vineyard

20 "For the kingdom of heaven is like a landowner who went out early in the morning to hire laborers for his vineyard. 2After agreeing with the laborers for the usual daily wage, *b* he sent them into his vineyard. 3When he went out about nine o'clock, he saw others standing idle in the marketplace; 4and he said to them, 'You also go into the vineyard, and I will pay you whatever is right.' So they went. 5When he went out again about noon and about three o'clock, he did the same. 6And about five o'clock he went out and found others standing around; and he said to them, 'Why are you standing here idle all day?' 7They said to him, 'Because no one has hired us.' He said to them, 'You also go into the vineyard.' 8When evening came, the owner of the vineyard said to his manager, 'Call the laborers and give them their pay, beginning with the last and then going to the first.' 9When those hired about five o'clock came, each of them received the usual daily wage. *b* 10Now when the first came, they thought they would receive more; but each of them also received the usual daily wage. *b* 11And when they received it, they

grumbled against the landowner, 12saying, 'These last worked only one hour, and you have made them equal to us who have borne the burden of the day and the scorching heat.' 13But he replied to one of them, 'Friend, I am doing you no wrong; did you not agree with me for the usual daily wage? *b* 14Take what belongs to you and go; I choose to give to this last the same as I give to you. 15Am I not allowed to do what I choose with what belongs to me? Or are you envious because I am generous?' *c* 16So the last will be first, and the first will be last." *d*

A Third Time Jesus Foretells His Death and Resurrection

17 While Jesus was going up to Jerusalem, he took the twelve disciples aside by themselves, and said to them on the way, 18"See, we are going up to Jerusalem, and the Son of Man will be handed over to the chief priests and scribes, and they will condemn him to death; 19then they will hand him over to the Gentiles to be mocked and flogged and crucified; and on the third day he will be raised."

The Request of the Mother of James and John

20 Then the mother of the sons of Zebedee came to him with her sons, and kneeling before him, she asked a favor of him. 21And he said to her, "What do you want?" She said to him, "Declare that these two sons of mine will sit, one at your right hand and one at your left, in your kingdom." 22But Jesus answered, "You do not know what you are asking. Are you able to drink the cup that I am about to drink?" *e* They said to him, "We are able." 23He said to them, "You will indeed drink my cup, but to sit at my right hand and at my left, this is not mine to grant, but it is for those for whom it has been prepared by my Father."

24 When the ten heard it, they were angry with the two brothers. 25But Jesus called them to him and said, "You know that the rulers of the Gentiles lord it over them, and their great

a Other ancient authorities read *manifold*
b Gk *a denarius*   *c* Gk *is your eye evil because I am good?*   *d* Other ancient authorities add *for many are called but few are chosen*   *e* Other ancient authorities add *or to be baptized with the baptism that I am baptized with?*

ones are tyrants over them. 26It will not be so among you; but whoever wishes to be great among you must be your servant, 27and whoever wishes to be first among you must be your slave; 28just as the Son of Man came not to be served but to serve, and to give his life a ransom for many."

Jesus Heals Two Blind Men

29 As they were leaving Jericho, a large crowd followed him. 30There were two blind men sitting by the roadside. When they heard that Jesus was passing by, they shouted, "Lord,*a* have mercy on us, Son of David!" 31The crowd sternly ordered them to be quiet; but they shouted even more loudly, "Have mercy on us, Lord, Son of David!" 32Jesus stood still and called them, saying, "What do you want me to do for you?" 33They said to him, "Lord, let our eyes be opened." 34Moved with compassion, Jesus touched their eyes. Immediately they regained their sight and followed him.

Jesus' Triumphal Entry into Jerusalem

21 When they had come near Jerusalem and had reached Bethphage, at the Mount of Olives, Jesus sent two disciples, 2saying to them, "Go into the village ahead of you, and immediately you will find a donkey tied, and a colt with her; untie them and bring them to me. 3If anyone says anything to you, just say this, 'The Lord needs them.' And he will send them immediately.*b*" 4This took place to fulfill what had been spoken through the prophet, saying,

5 "Tell the daughter of Zion,
   Look, your king is coming to you,
      humble, and mounted on a donkey,
         and on a colt, the foal of a donkey."

6The disciples went and did as Jesus had directed them; 7they brought the donkey and the colt, and put their cloaks on them, and he sat on them. 8A very large crowd*c* spread their cloaks on the road, and others cut branches from the trees and spread them on the road. 9The crowds that went ahead of him and that followed were shouting,

   "Hosanna to the Son of David!
      Blessed is the one who comes in the
         name of the Lord!
   Hosanna in the highest heaven!"

10When he entered Jerusalem, the whole city was in turmoil, asking, "Who is this?" 11The crowds were saying, "This is the prophet Jesus from Nazareth in Galilee."

Jesus Cleanses the Temple

12 Then Jesus entered the temple*d* and drove out all who were selling and buying in the temple, and he overturned the tables of the money changers and the seats of those who sold doves. 13He said to them, "It is written,

   'My house shall be called a house of
      prayer';
   but you are making it a den of
      robbers.'"

14 The blind and the lame came to him in the temple, and he cured them. 15But when the chief priests and the scribes saw the amazing things that he did, and heard*e* the children crying out in the temple, "Hosanna to the Son of David," they became angry 16and said to him, "Do you hear what these are saying?" Jesus said to them, "Yes; have you never read,

a Other ancient authorities lack *Lord*   *b* Or 'The Lord needs them and will send them back immediately.'   *c* Or *Most of the crowd*   *d* Other ancient authorities add *of God*   *e* Gk lacks *heard*

20:26 SERVICE—*See* Spiritual Disciplines Index.

Responding
20:28 SERVICE. In this push, shove, grab world we find it a hard saying that Jesus, God in the flesh, came to serve human beings. In what ways did Jesus serve human beings? What hints can we get from his service for the ways we can serve other people? *See also* Spiritual Disciplines Index.

21:1–11 *When they had come near Jerusalem.* In this triumphal entry, Jesus comes as Zechariah's king of peace on a donkey, a humble form of exaltation (Zech 9:9). Jesus is portrayed as a king and is praised as Son of David (cf. Mark 11:10). As verse 11 shows, the crowds do not quite get the picture, for they only identify him as a prophet from Nazareth, not as the all-wise king from the lineage of David.

21:13 PRAYER—*See* Spiritual Disciplines Index.

'Out of the mouths of infants and
    nursing babies
  you have prepared praise for yourself'?"
17 He left them, went out of the city to Bethany, and spent the night there.

Jesus Curses the Fig Tree

18 In the morning, when he returned to the city, he was hungry. 19 And seeing a fig tree by the side of the road, he went to it and found nothing at all on it but leaves. Then he said to it, "May no fruit ever come from you again!" And the fig tree withered at once. 20 When the disciples saw it, they were amazed, saying, "How did the fig tree wither at once?" 21 Jesus answered them, "Truly I tell you, if you have faith and do not doubt, not only will you do what has been done to the fig tree, but even if you say to this mountain, 'Be lifted up and thrown into the sea,' it will be done. 22 Whatever you ask for in prayer with faith, you will receive."

The Authority of Jesus Questioned

23 When he entered the temple, the chief priests and the elders of the people came to him as he was teaching, and said, "By what authority are you doing these things, and who gave you this authority?" 24 Jesus said to them, "I will also ask you one question; if you tell me the answer, then I will also tell you by what authority I do these things. 25 Did the baptism of John come from heaven, or was it of human origin?" And they argued with one another, "If we say, 'From heaven,' he will say to us, 'Why then did you not believe him?' 26 But if we say, 'Of human origin,' we are afraid of the crowd; for all regard John as a prophet." 27 So they answered Jesus, "We do not know." And he said to them, "Neither will I tell you by what authority I am doing these things.

The Parable of the Two Sons

28 "What do you think? A man had two sons; he went to the first and said, 'Son, go and work in the vineyard today.' 29 He answered, 'I will not'; but later he changed his mind and went. 30 The father[a] went to the second and said the same; and he answered,

'I go, sir'; but he did not go. 31 Which of the two did the will of his father?" They said, "The first." Jesus said to them, "Truly I tell you, the tax collectors and the prostitutes are going into the kingdom of God ahead of you. 32 For John came to you in the way of righteousness and you did not believe him, but the tax collectors and the prostitutes believed him; and even after you saw it, you did not change your minds and believe him.

The Parable of the Wicked Tenants

33 "Listen to another parable. There was a landowner who planted a vineyard, put a fence around it, dug a wine press in it, and built a watchtower. Then he leased it to tenants and went to another country. 34 When the harvest time had come, he sent his slaves to the tenants to collect his produce. 35 But the tenants seized his slaves and beat one, killed another, and stoned another. 36 Again he sent other slaves, more than the first; and they treated them in the same way. 37 Finally he sent his son to them, saying, 'They will respect my son.' 38 But when the tenants saw the son, they said to themselves, 'This is the heir; come, let us kill him and get his inheritance.' 39 So they seized him, threw him out of the vineyard, and killed him. 40 Now when the owner of the vineyard comes, what will he do to those tenants?" 41 They said to him, "He will put those wretches to a miserable death, and lease the vineyard to other tenants who will give him the produce at the harvest time."

42 Jesus said to them, "Have you never read in the scriptures:

'The stone that the builders rejected
  has become the cornerstone;[b]
this was the Lord's doing,
  and it is amazing in our eyes'?

43 Therefore I tell you, the kingdom of God will be taken away from you and given to a people that produces the fruits of the kingdom.[c] 44 The one who falls on this stone will be broken to pieces; and it will crush anyone on whom it falls."[d]

---

a Gk He   b Or keystone   c Gk the fruits of it
d Other ancient authorities lack verse 44

21:22 PRAYER—See Spiritual Disciplines Index.

45 When the chief priests and the Pharisees heard his parables, they realized that he was speaking about them. 46They wanted to arrest him, but they feared the crowds, because they regarded him as a prophet.

The Parable of the Wedding Banquet

22 Once more Jesus spoke to them in parables, saying: 2"The kingdom of heaven may be compared to a king who gave a wedding banquet for his son. 3He sent his slaves to call those who had been invited to the wedding banquet, but they would not come. 4Again he sent other slaves, saying, 'Tell those who have been invited: Look, I have prepared my dinner, my oxen and my fat calves have been slaughtered, and everything is ready; come to the wedding banquet.' 5But they made light of it and went away, one to his farm, another to his business, 6while the rest seized his slaves, mistreated them, and killed them. 7The king was enraged. He sent his troops, destroyed those murderers, and burned their city. 8Then he said to his slaves, 'The wedding is ready, but those invited were not worthy. 9Go therefore into the main streets, and invite everyone you find to the wedding banquet.' 10Those slaves went out into the streets and gathered all whom they found, both good and bad; so the wedding hall was filled with guests.

11 "But when the king came in to see the guests, he noticed a man there who was not wearing a wedding robe, 12and he said to him, 'Friend, how did you get in here without a wedding robe?' And he was speechless. 13Then the king said to the attendants, 'Bind him hand and foot, and throw him into the outer darkness, where there will be weeping and gnashing of teeth.' 14For many are called, but few are chosen."

The Question about Paying Taxes

15 Then the Pharisees went and plotted to entrap him in what he said. 16So they sent their disciples to him, along with the Herodians, saying, "Teacher, we know that you are sincere, and teach the way of God in accordance with truth, and show deference to no one; for you do not regard people with partiality. 17Tell us, then, what you think. Is it lawful to pay taxes to the emperor, or not?" 18But Jesus, aware of their malice, said, "Why are you putting me to the test, you hypocrites? 19Show me the coin used for the tax." And they brought him a denarius. 20Then he said to them, "Whose head is this, and whose title?" 21They answered, "The emperor's." Then he said to them, "Give therefore to the emperor the things that are the emperor's, and to God the things that are God's." 22When they heard this, they were amazed; and they left him and went away.

The Question about the Resurrection

23 The same day some Sadducees came to him, saying there is no resurrection;*a* and they asked him a question, saying, 24"Teacher, Moses said, 'If a man dies childless, his brother shall marry the widow, and raise up children for his brother.' 25Now there were seven brothers among us; the first married, and died childless, leaving the widow to his brother. 26The second did the same, so also the third, down to the seventh. 27Last of all, the woman herself died. 28In the resurrection, then, whose wife of the seven will she be? For all of them had married her."

29 Jesus answered them, "You are wrong, because you know neither the scriptures nor the power of God. 30For in the resurrection they neither marry nor are given in marriage, but are like angels*b* in heaven. 31And as for the resurrection of the dead, have you not read what was said to you by God, 32'I am the God of Abraham, the God of Isaac, and the God of Jacob'? He is God not of the dead, but of the living." 33And when the crowd heard it, they were astounded at his teaching.

The Greatest Commandment

34 When the Pharisees heard that he had silenced the Sadducees, they gathered together, 35and one of them, a lawyer, asked him a question to test him. 36"Teacher, which commandment in the law is the greatest?"

a Other ancient authorities read *who say that there is no resurrection*　*b* Other ancient authorities add *of God*

22:34–40 *which commandment in the law is the greatest?* Jesus' interpretation of the law is unveiled here. The entire law hinges on its central commands to love God and neighbor.

37He said to him, " 'You shall love the Lord your God with all your heart, and with all your soul, and with all your mind.' 38This is the greatest and first commandment. 39And a second is like it: 'You shall love your neighbor as yourself.' 40On these two commandments hang all the law and the prophets."

The Question about David's Son

41 Now while the Pharisees were gathered together, Jesus asked them this question: 42"What do you think of the Messiah?*a* Whose son is he?" They said to him, "The son of David." 43He said to them, "How is it then that David by the Spirit*b* calls him Lord, saying,

44 'The Lord said to my Lord,
   "Sit at my right hand,
      until I put your enemies under your feet" '?

45If David thus calls him Lord, how can he be his son?" 46No one was able to give him an answer, nor from that day did anyone dare to ask him any more questions.

Jesus Denounces Scribes and Pharisees

23 Then Jesus said to the crowds and to his disciples, 2"The scribes and the Pharisees sit on Moses' seat; 3therefore, do whatever they teach you and follow it; but do not do as they do, for they do not practice what they teach. 4They tie up heavy burdens, hard to bear,*c* and lay them on the shoulders of others; but they themselves are unwilling to lift a finger to move them. 5They do all their deeds to be seen by others; for they make their phylacteries broad and their fringes long. 6They love to have the place of honor at banquets and the best seats in the synagogues, 7and to be greeted with respect in the marketplaces, and to have people call them rabbi. 8But you are not to be called rabbi, for you have one teacher, and you are all students.*d* 9And call no one your father on earth, for you have one Father—the one in heaven. 10Nor are you to be called instruc-

a Or *Christ*   *b* Gk *in spirit*   *c* Other ancient authorities lack *hard to bear*   *d* Gk *brothers*

God is to be loved wholeheartedly, which is the greatest commandment. But this is impossible without the aid of God; hence the words of Augustine of Hippo, "Give what you command, Lord, and then command whatever you will." Once again, Jesus, as the incarnate expression of the mind of God, knows exactly what the heart of the matter is and how God sees things.

23:1–39 *Then Jesus said to the crowds.* This discourse is given in the Temple, and Jesus offers the divine wisdom. Teachers or rabbis are especially castigated at the outset of this material. Jesus' disciples are commanded not to accept the title rabbi, father, or teacher, for there is only one final and authoritative teacher—not Moses or Solomon, but the Christ (v 10). Thus, Jesus' followers must always remain learners. Those who exalt themselves will be humbled and vice versa (v 12). Jesus repeatedly condemns playacting, which is what the word we translate "hypocrite" actually means. The dichotomy between appearance and reality, between word and deed, draws Jesus' most profound criticism (vv 13–33). Jesus, as God's presence on earth, is said to be sending prophets, sages, and teachers to Israel (v 34). But they are rejected and in some cases executed. A choice must be made between

two sorts of teachers. Verses 37–39 portray Jesus as Wisdom, who, like a mother bird, gathers her chicks. Matt 17:2 has prepared for the conclusion of this discourse (vv 38–39). Jesus promises to leave the house desolate because, if he leaves, the presence of God has been removed from the people's midst. Although Solomon did build a house for God, Jesus is the presence that must fill that house or else it is left desolate. Henceforth, the presence of God is to be found in the midst of the community of Jesus' followers (28:20). In chapters 21–23, the Evangelist has masterfully tied together his chief ideas about Jesus. Solomon's greater son is not merely son of David, he is David's Lord, the very presence of God in his Temple, and like Wisdom in Sir 24:8–12.

Responding
23:1–39 STUDY. The scribes and Pharisees were the professors of their time. They studied Scripture in minute detail and memorized huge chunks of it. Yet all of their study and memorization didn't keep them from doing things contrary to what they were studying. How can we keep from being hypocrites: teaching one thing and doing another? *See also* Spiritual Disciplines Index.

tors, for you have one instructor, the Messiah.[a] 11The greatest among you will be your servant. 12All who exalt themselves will be humbled, and all who humble themselves will be exalted.

13 "But woe to you, scribes and Pharisees, hypocrites! For you lock people out of the kingdom of heaven. For you do not go in yourselves, and when others are going in, you stop them.[b] 15Woe to you, scribes and Pharisees, hypocrites! For you cross sea and land to make a single convert, and you make the new convert twice as much a child of hell[c] as yourselves.

16 "Woe to you, blind guides, who say, 'Whoever swears by the sanctuary is bound by nothing, but whoever swears by the gold of the sanctuary is bound by the oath.' 17You blind fools! For which is greater, the gold or the sanctuary that has made the gold sacred? 18And you say, 'Whoever swears by the altar is bound by nothing, but whoever swears by the gift that is on the altar is bound by the oath.' 19How blind you are! For which is greater, the gift or the altar that makes the gift sacred? 20So whoever swears by the altar, swears by it and by everything on it; 21and whoever swears by the sanctuary, swears by it and by the one who dwells in it; 22and whoever swears by heaven, swears by the throne of God and by the one who is seated upon it.

23 "Woe to you, scribes and Pharisees, hypocrites! For you tithe mint, dill, and cummin, and have neglected the weightier matters of the law: justice and mercy and faith. It is these you ought to have practiced without neglecting the others. 24You blind guides! You strain out a gnat but swallow a camel!

25 "Woe to you, scribes and Pharisees, hypocrites! For you clean the outside of the cup and of the plate, but inside they are full of greed and self-indulgence. 26You blind Pharisee! First clean the inside of the cup,[d] so that the outside also may become clean.

27 "Woe to you, scribes and Pharisees, hypocrites! For you are like whitewashed tombs, which on the outside look beautiful, but inside they are full of the bones of the dead and of all kinds of filth. 28So you also on the outside look righteous to others, but inside you are full of hypocrisy and lawlessness.

29 "Woe to you, scribes and Pharisees, hypocrites! For you build the tombs of the prophets and decorate the graves of the righteous, 30and you say, 'If we had lived in the days of our ancestors, we would not have taken part with them in shedding the blood of the prophets.' 31Thus you testify against yourselves that you are descendants of those who murdered the prophets. 32Fill up, then, the measure of your ancestors. 33You snakes, you brood of vipers! How can you escape being sentenced to hell?[c] 34Therefore I send you prophets, sages, and scribes, some of whom you will kill and crucify, and some you will flog in your synagogues and pursue from town to town, 35so that upon you may come all the righteous blood shed on earth, from the blood of righteous Abel to the blood of Zechariah son of Barachiah, whom you murdered between the sanctuary and the altar. 36Truly I tell you, all this will come upon this generation.

The Lament over Jerusalem

37 "Jerusalem, Jerusalem, the city that kills the prophets and stones those who are sent to it! How often have I desired to gather your children together as a hen gathers her brood under her wings, and you were not willing! 38See, your house is left to you, desolate.[e] 39For I tell you, you will not see me again until you say, 'Blessed is the one who comes in the name of the Lord.' "

a Or the Christ   b Other authorities add here (or after verse 12) verse 14, Woe to you, scribes and Pharisees, hypocrites! For you devour widows' houses and for the sake of appearance you make long prayers; therefore you will receive the greater condemnation
c Gk Gehenna   d Other ancient authorities add and of the plate   e Other ancient authorities lack desolate

---

23:11 SERVICE—See Spiritual Disciplines Index.

23:16 GUIDANCE—See Spiritual Disciplines Index.

The Destruction of the Temple Foretold

24 As Jesus came out of the temple and was going away, his disciples came to point out to him the buildings of the temple. [2]Then he asked them, "You see all these, do you not? Truly I tell you, not one stone will be left here upon another; all will be thrown down."

Signs of the End of the Age

3 When he was sitting on the Mount of Olives, the disciples came to him privately, saying, "Tell us, when will this be, and what will be the sign of your coming and of the end of the age?" [4]Jesus answered them, "Beware that no one leads you astray. [5]For many will come in my name, saying, 'I am the Messiah!'[a] and they will lead many astray. [6]And you will hear of wars and rumors of wars; see that you are not alarmed; for this must take place, but the end is not yet. [7]For nation will rise against nation, and kingdom against kingdom, and there will be famines[b] and earthquakes in various places: [8]all this is but the beginning of the birth pangs.

Persecutions Foretold

9 "Then they will hand you over to be tortured and will put you to death, and you will be hated by all nations because of my name. [10]Then many will fall away,[c] and they will betray one another and hate one another. [11]And many false prophets will arise and lead many astray. [12]And because of the increase of lawlessness, the love of many will grow cold. [13]But the one who endures to the end will be saved. [14]And this good news[d] of the kingdom will be proclaimed throughout the world, as a testimony to all the nations; and then the end will come.

The Desolating Sacrilege

15 "So when you see the desolating sacrilege standing in the holy place, as was spoken of by the prophet Daniel (let the reader understand), [16]then those in Judea must flee to the mountains; [17]the one on the housetop must not go down to take what is in the house; [18]the one in the field must not turn back to get a coat. [19]Woe to those who are pregnant and to those who are nursing infants in those days! [20]Pray that your flight may not be in winter or on a sabbath. [21]For at that time there will be great suffering, such as has not been from the beginning of the world until now, no, and never will be. [22]And if those days had not been cut short, no one would be saved; but for the sake of the elect those days will be cut short. [23]Then if anyone says to you, 'Look! Here is the Messiah!'[e] or 'There he is!'—do not believe it. [24]For false messiahs[f] and false prophets will appear and produce great signs and omens, to lead astray, if possible, even the elect. [25]Take note, I have told you beforehand. [26]So, if they say to you, 'Look! He is in the wilderness,' do not go out. If they say, 'Look! He is in the inner rooms,' do not believe it. [27]For as the lightning comes from the east and flashes as far as the west, so will be the coming of the Son of Man. [28]Wherever the corpse is, there the vultures will gather.

The Coming of the Son of Man

29 "Immediately after the suffering of those days

the sun will be darkened,
    and the moon will not give its light;
the stars will fall from heaven,
    and the powers of heaven will be
        shaken.

[30]Then the sign of the Son of Man will appear in heaven, and then all the tribes of the earth will mourn, and they will see 'the Son of Man coming on the clouds of heaven' with power and great glory. [31]And he will send out his angels with a loud trumpet call, and they will gather his elect from the four winds, from one end of heaven to the other.

The Lesson of the Fig Tree

32 "From the fig tree learn its lesson: as soon as its branch becomes tender and puts forth its leaves, you know that summer is near. [33]So also, when you see all these things, you know that he[g] is near, at the very gates. [34]Truly I tell you, this generation will not pass away until all these things have taken place. [35]Heaven and earth will pass away, but my words will not pass away.

a Or *the Christ*   *b* Other ancient authorities add *and pestilences*   *c* Or *stumble*   *d* Or *gospel*   *e* Or *the Christ*   *f* Or *christs*   *g* Or *it*

The Necessity for Watchfulness

36 "But about that day and hour no one knows, neither the angels of heaven, nor the Son, *a* but only the Father. 37For as the days of Noah were, so will be the coming of the Son of Man. 38For as in those days before the flood they were eating and drinking, marrying and giving in marriage, until the day Noah entered the ark, 39and they knew nothing until the flood came and swept them all away, so too will be the coming of the Son of Man, 40Then two will be in the field; one will be taken and one will be left. 41Two women will be grinding meal together; one will be taken and one will be left. 42Keep awake therefore, for you do not know on what day *b* your Lord is coming. 43But understand this: if the owner of the house had known in what part of the night the thief was coming, he would have stayed awake and would not have let his house be broken into. 44Therefore you also must be ready, for the Son of Man is coming at an unexpected hour.

The Faithful or the Unfaithful Slave

45 "Who then is the faithful and wise slave, whom his master has put in charge of his household, to give the other slaves *c* their allowance of food at the proper time? 46Blessed is that slave whom his master will find at work when he arrives. 47Truly I tell you, he will put that one in charge of all his possessions. 48But if that wicked slave says to himself, 'My master is delayed,' 49and he begins to beat his fellow slaves, and eats and drinks with drunkards, 50the master of that slave will come on a day when he does not expect him and at an hour that he does not know. 51He will cut him in pieces *d* and put him with the hypocrites, where there will be weeping and gnashing of teeth.

The Parable of the Ten Bridesmaids

25 "Then the kingdom of heaven will be like this. Ten bridesmaids *e* took their lamps and went to meet the bridegroom. *f* 2Five of them were foolish, and five were wise. 3When the foolish took their lamps, they took no oil with them; 4but the wise took flasks of oil with their lamps. 5As the bridegroom was delayed, all of them became drowsy and slept. 6But at midnight there was a shout, 'Look! Here is the bridegroom! Come out to meet him.' 7Then all those bridesmaids *e* got up and trimmed their lamps. 8The foolish said to the wise, 'Give us some of your oil, for our lamps are going out.' 9But the wise replied, 'No! there will not be enough for you and for us; you had better go to the dealers and buy some for yourselves.' 10And while they went to buy it, the bridegroom came, and those who were ready went with him into the wedding banquet; and the door was shut. 11Later the other bridesmaids *e* came also, saying, 'Lord, lord, open to us.' 12But he replied, 'Truly I tell you, I do not know you.' 13Keep awake therefore, for you know neither the day nor the hour. *g*

The Parable of the Talents

14 "For it is as if a man, going on a journey, summoned his slaves and entrusted his property to them; 15to one he gave five talents, *h* to another two, to another one, to each according to his ability. Then he went away. 16The one who had received the five talents went off at once and traded with them, and made five more talents. 17In the same way, the one who had the two talents made two more talents. 18But the one who had received the one talent went off and dug a hole in the ground and hid his master's money. 19After a long time the master of those slaves came and settled accounts with them. 20Then the one who had received the five talents came forward, bringing five more talents, saying, 'Master, you handed over to me five talents; see, I have made five more talents.' 21His master said to him, 'Well done, good and trustworthy slave; you have been trustworthy in a few things, I will put you in charge of many things; enter into the joy of your master.' 22And the one with the two talents also came forward, saying, 'Master, you handed over to me two talents; see, I have made two more talents.' 23His master said to him, 'Well done,

---

a Other ancient authorities lack *nor the Son*
b Other ancient authorities read *at what hour*
c Gk *to give them*　　*d* Or *cut him off*
e Gk *virgins*　　*f* Other ancient authorities add *and the bride*　　*g* Other ancient authorities add *in which the Son of Man is coming*　　*h* A talent was worth more than fifteen years' wages of a laborer

good and trustworthy slave; you have been trustworthy in a few things, I will put you in charge of many things; enter into the joy of your master.' 24Then the one who had received the one talent also came forward, saying, 'Master, I knew that you were a harsh man, reaping where you did not sow, and gathering where you did not scatter seed; 25so I was afraid, and I went and hid your talent in the ground. Here you have what is yours.' 26But his master replied, 'You wicked and lazy slave! You knew, did you, that I reap where I did not sow, and gather where I did not scatter? 27Then you ought to have invested my money with the bankers, and on my return I would have received what was my own with interest. 28So take the talent from him, and give it to the one with the ten talents. 29For to all those who have, more will be given, and they will have an abundance; but from those who have nothing, even what they have will be taken away. 30As for this worthless slave, throw him into the outer darkness, where there will be weeping and gnashing of teeth.'

The Judgment of the Nations

31 "When the Son of Man comes in his glory, and all the angels with him, then he will sit on the throne of his glory. 32All the nations will be gathered before him, and he will separate people one from another as a shepherd separates the sheep from the goats, 33and he will put the sheep at his right hand and the goats at the left. 34Then the king will say to those at his right hand, 'Come, you that are blessed by my Father, inherit the kingdom prepared for you from the foundation of the world; 35for I was hungry and you gave me food, I was thirsty and you gave me something to drink, I was a stranger and you welcomed me, 36I was naked and you gave me clothing, I was sick and you took care of me, I was in prison and you visited me.' 37Then the righteous will answer him, 'Lord, when was it that we saw you hungry and gave you food, or thirsty and gave you something to drink? 38And when was it that we saw you a stranger and welcomed you, or naked and gave you clothing? 39And when was it that we saw you sick or in prison and visited you?' 40And the king will answer them, 'Truly I tell you, just as you did it to one of the least of these who are members of my family,a you did it to me.' 41Then he will say to those at his left hand, 'You that are accursed, depart from me into the eternal fire prepared for the devil and his angels; 42for I was hungry and you gave me no food, I was thirsty and you gave me nothing to drink, 43I was a stranger and you did not welcome me, naked and you did not give me clothing, sick and in prison and you did not visit me.' 44Then they also will answer, 'Lord, when was it that we saw you hungry or thirsty or a stranger or naked or sick or in prison, and did not take care of you?' 45Then he will answer them, 'Truly I tell you, just as you did not do it to one of the least of these, you did not do it to me.' 46And these will go away into eternal punishment, but the righteous into eternal life."

The Plot to Kill Jesus

26 When Jesus had finished saying all these things, he said to his disciples, 2"You know that after two days the Passover is coming, and the Son of Man will be handed over to be crucified."

a Gk these my brothers

26:1–28:20 *When Jesus had finished saying all these things.* Chapters 26–28 make clear how Jesus' pronouncements about himself were wise and came true. Certainly, he was rejected but also vindicated by God. He was worshiped by both female and male disciples (28:9, 17), and he promised to go on being their Wisdom, God's presence and guidance in their midst (28:20). For Matthew, Jesus was the sage and teacher without parallel, and he would continue to fulfill

the role of their teacher (23:10). The yoke that Matthew beckons his scribes to take up is simultaneously the yoke of Jesus' wisdom and the yoke of Jesus as Wisdom (see note on 11:28–30).

26:2–5 *the Son of Man will . . . be crucified.* The victim himself is the first to announce the plot. Although Caiaphas planned to wait until after the Passover festival, Jesus knew better than Caiaphas what would transpire.

3 Then the chief priests and the elders of the people gathered in the palace of the high priest, who was called Caiaphas, 4and they conspired to arrest Jesus by stealth and kill him. 5But they said, "Not during the festival, or there may be a riot among the people."

The Anointing at Bethany

6 Now while Jesus was at Bethany in the house of Simon the leper,*a* 7a woman came to him with an alabaster jar of very costly ointment, and she poured it on his head as he sat at the table. 8But when the disciples saw it, they were angry and said, "Why this waste? 9For this ointment could have been sold for a large sum, and the money given to the poor." 10But Jesus, aware of this, said to them, "Why do you trouble the woman? She has performed a good service for me. 11For you always have the poor with you, but you will not always have me. 12By pouring this ointment on my body she has prepared me for burial. 13Truly I tell you, wherever this good news*b* is proclaimed in the whole world, what she has done will be told in remembrance of her."

Judas Agrees to Betray Jesus

14 Then one of the twelve, who was called Judas Iscariot, went to the chief priests 15and said, "What will you give me if I betray him to you?" They paid him thirty pieces of silver. 16And from that moment he began to look for an opportunity to betray him.

The Passover with the Disciples

17 On the first day of Unleavened Bread the disciples came to Jesus, saying, "Where do you want us to make the preparations for you to eat the Passover?" 18He said, "Go into the city to a certain man, and say to him, 'The Teacher says, My time is near; I will keep the Passover at your house with my disciples.' " 19So the disciples did as Jesus had directed them, and they prepared the Passover meal.

20 When it was evening, he took his place with the twelve;*c* 21and while they were eating, he said, "Truly I tell you, one of you will betray me." 22And they became greatly distressed and began to say to him one after another, "Surely not I, Lord?" 23He answered, "The one who has dipped his hand into the bowl with me will betray me. 24The Son of Man goes as it is written of him, but woe to that one by whom the Son of Man is betrayed! It would have been better for that one not to have been born." 25Judas, who betrayed him, said, "Surely not I, Rabbi?" He replied, "You have said so."

The Institution of the Lord's Supper

26 While they were eating, Jesus took a loaf of bread, and after blessing it he broke it, gave it to the disciples, and said, "Take, eat; this is my body." 27Then he took a cup, and after giving thanks he gave it to them, saying, "Drink from it, all of you; 28for this is my blood of the*d* covenant, which is poured out for many for the forgiveness of sins. 29I tell you, I will never again drink of this fruit of the vine until that day when I drink it new with you in my Father's kingdom."

30 When they had sung the hymn, they went out to the Mount of Olives.

Peter's Denial Foretold

31 Then Jesus said to them, "You will all become deserters because of me this night; for it is written,

'I will strike the shepherd,
     and the sheep of the flock will be
         scattered.'

32But after I am raised up, I will go ahead of you to Galilee." 33Peter said to him, "Though all become deserters because of you, I will never desert you." 34Jesus said to him, "Truly I tell you, this very night, before the cock crows, you will deny me three times." 35Peter said to him, "Even though I must die with you, I will not deny you." And so said all the disciples.

Jesus Prays in Gethsemane

36 Then Jesus went with them to a place called Gethsemane; and he said to his disci-

---

a The terms *leper* and *leprosy* can refer to several diseases   *b* Or *gospel*   *c* Other ancient authorities add *disciples*   *d* Other ancient authorities add *new*

ples, "Sit here while I go over there and pray." [37]He took with him Peter and the two sons of Zebedee, and began to be grieved and agitated. [38]Then he said to them, "I am deeply grieved, even to death; remain here, and stay awake with me." [39]And going a little farther, he threw himself on the ground and prayed, "My Father, if it is possible, let this cup pass from me; yet not what I want but what you want." [40]Then he came to the disciples and found them sleeping; and he said to Peter, "So, could you not stay awake with me one hour? [41]Stay awake and pray that you may not come into the time of trial;[a] the spirit indeed is willing, but the flesh is weak." [42]Again he went away for the second time and prayed, "My Father, if this cannot pass unless I drink it, your will be done." [43]Again he came and found them sleeping, for their eyes were heavy. [44]So leaving them again, he went away and prayed for the third time, saying the same words. [45]Then he came to the disciples and said to them, "Are you still sleeping and taking your rest? See, the hour is at hand, and the Son of Man is betrayed into the hands of sinners. [46]Get up, let us be going. See, my betrayer is at hand."

The Betrayal and Arrest of Jesus

47 While he was still speaking, Judas, one of the twelve, arrived; with him was a large crowd with swords and clubs, from the chief priests and the elders of the people. [48]Now the betrayer had given them a sign, saying, "The one I will kiss is the man; arrest him." [49]At once he came up to Jesus and said, "Greetings, Rabbi!" and kissed him. [50]Jesus said to him, "Friend, do what you are here to do." Then they came and laid hands on Jesus

and arrested him. [51]Suddenly, one of those with Jesus put his hand on his sword, drew it, and struck the slave of the high priest, cutting off his ear. [52]Then Jesus said to him, "Put your sword back into its place; for all who take the sword will perish by the sword. [53]Do you think that I cannot appeal to my Father, and he will at once send me more than twelve legions of angels? [54]But how then would the scriptures be fulfilled, which say it must happen in this way?" [55]At that hour Jesus said to the crowds, "Have you come out with swords and clubs to arrest me as though I were a bandit? Day after day I sat in the temple teaching, and you did not arrest me. [56]But all this has taken place, so that the scriptures of the prophets may be fulfilled." Then all the disciples deserted him and fled.

Jesus before the High Priest

57 Those who had arrested Jesus took him to Caiaphas the high priest, in whose house the scribes and the elders had gathered. [58]But Peter was following him at a distance, as far as the courtyard of the high priest; and going inside, he sat with the guards in order to see how this would end. [59]Now the chief priests and the whole council were looking for false testimony against Jesus so that they might put him to death, [60]but they found none, though many false witnesses came forward. At last two came forward [61]and said, "This fellow said, 'I am able to destroy the temple of God and to build it in three days.' " [62]The high priest stood up and said, "Have you no answer? What is it that they testify against you?" [63]But Jesus was silent. Then the high

a Or into temptation

26:36–46 *Then Jesus went with them to . . . Gethsemane.* The Matthean Gethsemane story is a dramatic portrayal of Jesus wrestling with God's will and then finally accepting it. In Mark, readers are not told what Jesus said to God the second time he went away to pray. Here Jesus, on the first occasion, asks if it is possible for the cup (referring to the expression of God's judgment in and by the cross) to be removed from him, yet not as he wills, but as God wills. But on the second occasion he says, "If this cannot pass

unless I drink it, your will be done" (v 42). In both cases, Jesus addresses God in the most intimate terms as "my Father" (vv 39, 42). During his third prayer, Jesus repeats the words of his second petition. The disciples, including even Peter, were unable to watch and pray with him. They had failed to do as he asked and show how far they were from being devoted disciples.

26:39 SUBMISSION—*See* Spiritual Disciplines Index.

HOT GOOD CONFESSIONS

priest said to him, "I put you under oath before the living God, tell us if you are the Messiah,[a] the Son of God." [64]Jesus said to him, "You have said so. But I tell you,

From now on you will see the Son of Man
       seated at the right hand of Power
       and coming on the clouds of heaven."

[65]Then the high priest tore his clothes and said, "He has blasphemed! Why do we still need witnesses? You have now heard his blasphemy. [66]What is your verdict?" They answered, "He deserves death." [67]Then they spat in his face and struck him; and some slapped him, [68]saying, "Prophesy to us, you Messiah![a] Who is it that struck you?"

Peter's Denial of Jesus

69 Now Peter was sitting outside in the courtyard. A servant-girl came to him and said, "You also were with Jesus the Galilean." [70]But he denied it before all of them, saying, "I do not know what you are talking about." [71]When he went out to the porch, another servant-girl saw him, and she said to the bystanders, "This man was with Jesus of Nazareth."[b] [72]Again he denied it with an oath, "I do not know the man." [73]After a little while the bystanders came up and said to Peter, "Certainly you are also one of them, for your accent betrays you." [74]Then he began to curse, and he swore an oath, "I do not know the man!" At that moment the cock crowed. [75]Then Peter remembered what Jesus had said: "Before the cock crows, you will deny me three times." And he went out and wept bitterly.

Jesus Brought before Pilate

27 When morning came, all the chief priests and the elders of the people conferred together against Jesus in order to bring about his death. [2]They bound him, led him away, and handed him over to Pilate the governor.

The Suicide of Judas

3 When Judas, his betrayer, saw that Jesus[c] was condemned, he repented and brought back the thirty pieces of silver to the chief priests and the elders. [4]He said, "I have sinned

by betraying innocent[d] blood." But they said, "What is that to us? See to it yourself." [5]Throwing down the pieces of silver in the temple, he departed; and he went and hanged himself. [6]But the chief priests, taking the pieces of silver, said, "It is not lawful to put them into the treasury, since they are blood money." [7]After conferring together, they used them to buy the potter's field as a place to bury foreigners. [8]For this reason that field has been called the Field of Blood to this day. [9]Then was fulfilled what had been spoken through the prophet Jeremiah,[e] "And they took[f] the thirty pieces of silver, the price of the one on whom a price had been set,[g] on whom some of the people of Israel had set a price, [10]and they gave[h] them for the potter's field, as the Lord commanded me."

Pilate Questions Jesus

11 Now Jesus stood before the governor; and the governor asked him, "Are you the King of the Jews?" Jesus said, "You say so." [12]But when he was accused by the chief priests and elders, he did not answer. [13]Then Pilate said to him, "Do you not hear how many accusations they make against you?" [14]But he gave him no answer, not even to a single charge, so that the governor was greatly amazed.

Barabbas or Jesus?

15 Now at the festival the governor was accustomed to release a prisoner for the crowd, anyone whom they wanted. [16]At that time they had a notorious prisoner, called Jesus[i] Barabbas. [17]So after they had gathered, Pilate said to them, "Whom do you want me to release for you, Jesus[i] Barabbas or Jesus who is called the Messiah?"[j] [18]For he realized that it was out of jealousy that they had handed him over. [19]While he was sitting on the judgment seat, his wife sent word to him, "Have nothing to do with that innocent man, for today I have suffered a great deal because of a dream about him." [20]Now the chief

a Or *Christ*   b Gk *the Nazorean*   c Gk *he*
d Other ancient authorities read *righteous*
e Other ancient authorities read *Zechariah* or *Isaiah*
f Or *I took*   g Or *the price of the precious One*
h Other ancient authorities read *I gave*   i Other
ancient authorities lack *Jesus*   j Or *the Christ*

priests and the elders persuaded the crowds to ask for Barabbas and to have Jesus killed. 21The governor again said to them, "Which of the two do you want me to release for you?" And they said, "Barabbas." 22Pilate said to them, "Then what should I do with Jesus who is called the Messiah?" *a* All of them said, "Let him be crucified!" 23Then he asked, "Why, what evil has he done?" But they shouted all the more, "Let him be crucified!"

Pilate Hands Jesus over to Be Crucified

24 So when Pilate saw that he could do nothing, but rather that a riot was beginning, he took some water and washed his hands before the crowd, saying, "I am innocent of this man's blood; *b* see to it yourselves." 25Then the people as a whole answered, "His blood be on us and on our children!" 26So he released Barabbas for them; and after flogging Jesus, he handed him over to be crucified.

The Soldiers Mock Jesus

27 Then the soldiers of the governor took Jesus into the governor's headquarters, *c* and they gathered the whole cohort around him. 28They stripped him and put a scarlet robe on him, 29and after twisting some thorns into a crown, they put it on his head. They put a reed in his right hand and knelt before him and mocked him, saying, "Hail, King of the Jews!" 30They spat on him, and took the reed and struck him on the head. 31After mocking him, they stripped him of the robe and put his own clothes on him. Then they led him away to crucify him.

The Crucifixion of Jesus

32 As they went out, they came upon a man from Cyrene named Simon; they compelled this man to carry his cross. 33And when they came to a place called Golgotha (which means Place of a Skull), 34they offered him wine to drink, mixed with gall; but when he tasted it, he would not drink it. 35And when they had crucified him, they divided his clothes among themselves by casting lots; *d* 36then they sat down there and kept watch over him. 37Over his head they put the charge against him, which read, "This is Jesus, the King of the Jews."

38 Then two bandits were crucified with him, one on his right and one on his left. 39Those who passed by derided *e* him, shaking their heads 40and saying, "You who would destroy the temple and build it in three days, save yourself! If you are the Son of God, come down from the cross." 41In the same way the chief priests also, along with the scribes and elders, were mocking him, saying, 42"He saved others; he cannot save himself. *f* He is the King of Israel; let him come down from the cross now, and we will believe in him.

---

a Or *the Christ*   *b* Other ancient authorities read *this righteous blood*, or *this righteous man's blood*   *c* Gk *the praetorium*   *d* Other ancient authorities add *in order that what had been spoken through the prophet might be fulfilled, "They divided my clothes among themselves, and for my clothing they cast lots."*   *e* Or *blasphemed*   *f* Or *is he unable to save himself?*

27:32–56 *they came to place called Golgotha.* In the Matthean portrayal of the crucifixion, Jesus is called not only the King of the Jews (v 37), but also the King of Israel (v 42; not in Mark). Matthew stresses that Jesus dies as true royalty. There is only one word from the cross in Matthew (as in Mark), the cry of desolation (v 46), quoting from the beginning of Psalm 22. But Jesus' death leads to an earthquake, which breaks open tombs. Many arise from the dead, signaling that the death of Jesus is the eschatological event known as the last judgment on sin. Paradoxically, this also is the event that will cause many to be made alive again. They do not appear to anyone until after the resurrection of Jesus, suggesting his resurrection triggers the resurrection of the saints (v 53). The witnesses to Jesus' death at the cross are the centurion and then finally the female disciples mentioned in this Gospel (vv 55–56). They were last at the cross, first at the tomb on Easter, and first to see the risen Jesus. They are portrayed as more faithful and spiritually perceptive than the male disciples, some of whom after the resurrection and Jesus' appearance to them in Galilee are still said to doubt (28:17). The story shows that Jesus must be viewed through the eyes of faith; even the resurrection appearances could not force someone to believe.

43He trusts in God; let God deliver him now, if he wants to; for he said, 'I am God's Son.' " 44The bandits who were crucified with him also taunted him in the same way.

The Death of Jesus

45 From noon on, darkness came over the whole land*a* until three in the afternoon. 46And about three o'clock Jesus cried with a loud voice, "Eli, Eli, lema sabachthani?" that is, "My God, my God, why have you forsaken me?" 47When some of the bystanders heard it, they said, "This man is calling for Elijah." 48At once one of them ran and got a sponge, filled it with sour wine, put it on a stick, and gave it to him to drink. 49But the others said, "Wait, let us see whether Elijah will come to save him."*b* 50Then Jesus cried again with a loud voice and breathed his last.*c* 51At that moment the curtain of the temple was torn in two, from top to bottom. The earth shook, and the rocks were split. 52The tombs also were opened, and many bodies of the saints who had fallen asleep were raised. 53After his resurrection they came out of the tombs and entered the holy city and appeared to many. 54Now when the centurion and those with him, who were keeping watch over Jesus, saw the earthquake and what took place, they were terrified and said, "Truly this man was God's Son!"*d*

55 Many women were also there, looking on from a distance; they had followed Jesus from Galilee and had provided for him. 56Among them were Mary Magdalene, and Mary the mother of James and Joseph, and the mother of the sons of Zebedee.

The Burial of Jesus

57 When it was evening, there came a rich man from Arimathea, named Joseph, who was also a disciple of Jesus. 58He went to Pilate and asked for the body of Jesus; then Pilate ordered it to be given to him. 59So Joseph took the body and wrapped it in a clean linen cloth 60and laid it in his own new tomb, which he had hewn in the rock. He then rolled a great stone to the door of the tomb and went away. 61Mary Magdalene and the other Mary were there, sitting opposite the tomb.

The Guard at the Tomb

62 The next day, that is, after the day of Preparation, the chief priests and the Pharisees gathered before Pilate 63and said, "Sir, we remember what that impostor said while he was still alive, 'After three days I will rise again.' 64Therefore command the tomb to be made secure until the third day; otherwise his disciples may go and steal him away, and tell the people, 'He has been raised from the dead,' and the last deception would be worse than the first." 65Pilate said to them, "You have a guard*e* of soldiers; go, make it as secure as you can."*f* 66So they went with the guard and made the tomb secure by sealing the stone.

The Resurrection of Jesus

28 After the sabbath, as the first day of the week was dawning, Mary Magdalene and the other Mary went to see the tomb. 2And suddenly there was a great earthquake; for an angel of the Lord, descending from heaven, came and rolled back the stone and sat on it. 3His appearance was like lightning, and his clothing white as snow. 4For fear of him the guards shook and became like

---

a Or *earth*   *b* Other ancient authorities add *And another took a spear and pierced his side, and out came water and blood*   *c* Or *gave up his spirit*   *d* Or *a son of God*   *e* Or *Take a guard*   *f* Gk *you know how*

28:1–10 *Mary Magdalene and the other Mary went to see the tomb.* Jesus appears to the women, who are the first to see both the empty tomb and the risen Christ. They are to tell the male disciples to get moving to Galilee, where they will see Jesus. Unlike in Mark, where the women simply flee in fear, here they are said to flee "with fear and great joy" (v 8) at the announcement that he is not in the tomb, but rather risen (the empty tomb being the negative counterpart to the bodily resurrection). The women also are the first to worship the risen Lord (v 9), and they are encouraged by him to witness to their brothers. Bearing witness is one of the essential tasks of the true disciple.

JUST FIND THE BODY

dead men. 5But the angel said to the women, "Do not be afraid; I know that you are looking for Jesus who was crucified. 6He is not here; for he has been raised, as he said. Come, see the place where he *a* lay. 7Then go quickly and tell his disciples, 'He has been raised from the dead, *b* and indeed he is going ahead of you to Galilee; there you will see him.' This is my message for you." 8So they left the tomb quickly with fear and great joy, and ran to tell his disciples. 9Suddenly Jesus met them and said, "Greetings!" And they came to him, took hold of his feet, and worshiped him. 10Then Jesus said to them, "Do not be afraid; go and tell my brothers to go to Galilee; there they will see me."

The Report of the Guard

11 While they were going, some of the guard went into the city and told the chief priests everything that had happened. 12After the priests *c* had assembled with the elders, they devised a plan to give a large sum of money to the soldiers, 13telling them, "You

must say, 'His disciples came by night and stole him away while we were asleep.' 14If this comes to the governor's ears, we will satisfy him and keep you out of trouble." 15So they took the money and did as they were directed. And this story is still told among the Jews to this day.

The Commissioning of the Disciples

16 Now the eleven disciples went to Galilee, to the mountain to which Jesus had directed them. 17When they saw him, they worshiped him; but some doubted. 18And Jesus came and said to them, "All authority in heaven and on earth has been given to me. 19Go therefore and make disciples of all nations, baptizing them in the name of the Father and of the Son and of the Holy Spirit, 20and teaching them to obey everything that I have commanded you. And remember, I am with you always, to the end of the age." *d*

a Other ancient authorities read *the Lord*
b Other ancient authorities lack *from the dead*
c Gk *they*   *d* Other ancient authorities add *Amen*

28:16–20 *Now the eleven disciples went to Galilee.* The eleven do go to Galilee, and Jesus appears as promised. Jesus says he has been given all authority, and then he authorizes his disciples to make disciples of all nations, which is said to involve baptizing in the trinitarian name and teaching the converts to obey all that Jesus commanded. But Jesus does far more than just authorize and empower his "learners." He promises to be with them (Immanuel) as the divine power, presence, and Wisdom of God until the close of the age. Never again will they be bereft of him. Thus, the Gospel closes with a presentation of Jesus as God's Wisdom, his wise presence, who dwells within the People of God and guards and guides them. As God's people we are called to live and call others to live

according to the counterorder wisdom of Jesus the sage. The Gospel for learners is also the Gospel for teachers. Ultimately, there is only one teacher, one sage, one Wisdom—Jesus himself.

28:17 WORSHIP—*See* Spiritual Disciplines Index.

Responding
28:18–20 THE WITH-GOD LIFE. Why did Jesus tell the disciples that he would be with them to the end of the age? In what ways is Jesus Christ with us today? Consider choosing one of those ways and attempting to be especially sensitive to Jesus' presence with you this week. *See also* Spiritual Disciplines Index.

THE GOSPEL ACCORDING TO

MARK

Matthew eases us into the good news of Jesus Christ with a genealogical history lesson. Luke starts off with a dedication to "Theophilus" and informs us he intends to offer us "an orderly account." Both of these Gospel writers start with background materials preparing us for the birth of Jesus. The Gospel According to John also begins gently too. The poetry of the Fourth Gospel starts with a whisper and then builds into the full-throated declaration of the Word, full of grace and truth.

Mark doesn't have time for any of that. Mark doesn't bother with shepherds or angels or baby pictures. Instead, this Gospel begins like a block of ice dropped from the balcony into the deep end of the pool: "The beginning of the good news of Jesus Christ, the Son of God." The impact of this startlingly good news arcs in all directions. By verse 5 we are all drenched—standing face to face with one of the wildest people in the entire New Testament: John the Baptist.

John's opening message and medium, "Repent [turn around, have a change of heart and mind], and receive forgiveness of sins" through baptism, introduce Jesus' own message and medium, "Repent, and believe in the good news" through the baptism of water and the Holy Spirit. With words from the prophet Isaiah at the beginning of the Gospel of Mark, we are reminded that as startling as Jesus' coming into the world is, God has intended it and has been preparing us for this new reality for centuries. Now "the time is fulfilled, and the kingdom of God has come near" (1:15). This announcement is not simply a news flash; it calls for a response from all who hear it.

The coming of Jesus, and with him God's reign, into the world and into our lives is decisive and dramatic. Whether we come to faith in Jesus suddenly, able to name the precise day and even moment he came into our heart and life, or whether Jesus has been a constant presence with us since birth, his claim upon us impacts the

See also "The With-God Life" essay for this section of the Bible,
"The People of God with Immanuel," pp. 1785–89.

decisions we make. His life dramatically affects who we understand God to be and who God is calling us to be in Christian discipleship.

The Movement of the Gospel

The Gospel of Mark moves at a breathless pace as though in a hurry to get the whole story out. We notice the frequent use of words such as "And," "And then," "Immediately," and "As soon as." People enter and exit the text with great frequency. Place-names pile upon place-names as we journey along with Jesus "on the way."

Similarly, we live in a hurried, harried world, as we rush about from task to task and place to place and person to person. We overlook how each task, place, and person contributes to the whole of our lives, to God's whole story that is taking shape within us, around us, and even beyond us. It should be noted, then, as we make our way through this Gospel, that although it moves along rapidly, it is worth pausing at each point along the way to see what new thing we may discover about Jesus, about others, or about ourselves.

Mark intends for us to notice everything, even the smallest of things, by tucking in a surprise detail here and there in the Gospel. Simon and Andrew were casting nets while James and John were mending theirs (1:16–20). Jesus, asleep in the boat during a storm, rests on a cushion (4:38). The woman with the hemorrhage had been sick for twelve years (5:25). And the five thousand people who were fed sat on the green grass in groups of hundreds and fifties (6:39–40). Mark also notices details of emotions. Jesus is moved with pity, warns sternly, looks around with anger, and is grieved. Jesus feels compassion, indignation, love, and distress. On a couple of occasions Jesus sighs. These details remind us that faith is made up of the real stuff of life and that living the faith will produce many kinds of feelings and reactions in us— and in God. We do well to pay attention to things great and small as we both receive and give ourselves to the transcendent yet incarnate God-with-us.

Date and Authorship of Mark

Mark's Gospel is considered the earliest of the four Gospels. Though an exact date for its writing cannot be certain, most scholars date it between 60 and 70. Matthew and Luke seem to have gotten their basic structure from Mark, though they may also have had access to another early document. This other document, now lost to us, has been designated as the "Q" source. It is thought to have contained more of the sayings and teachings of Jesus than Mark includes. Together Mark, Matthew, and Luke are known as the "synoptic" Gospels because of the similarities between them.

We cannot know for certain who "Mark" was. Some scholars believe that Mark knew Peter and wrote down accurately (though not necessarily "in order") the stories he heard from this eyewitness disciple. A fourth-century document written by Eusebius quotes Papias from the second-century as saying that Mark was the "interpreter" of Peter. In various letters in the New Testament, a person named Mark is mentioned, but we don't know if each "Mark" is the same person or is the author of our Gospel. Some find evidence that Mark was a Jewish Christian, because he explains

Jewish customs and translates Semitic words in this Greek text. Others use the same evidence to conclude that Mark was a gentile Christian, noting that some of Mark's explanations of Jewish practices seem awkward. Perhaps Mark does not mind such anonymity, because his focus is solely on one person: Jesus Christ, the Son of God.

Just as we cannot determine the identity of the author, neither can we determine with confidence the community for whom this Gospel was first intended. Perhaps Mark was writing to gentile Christians. Some believe Mark wrote this Gospel in Rome for Christians who were being persecuted under Nero shortly before or after Peter's death. Others argue that the Gospel is directed to gentile communities in the area of Palestine or Syria. Many early churches were made up of both Jewish and gentile Christians. Although the identity of the author and the "audience" may never be known, this much can be said: Mark did a new thing when he wrote about Jesus in this literary genre and called it a "Gospel."

Structure

The structure of Mark may be divided in any number of ways, just as later editors divided the Gospel into chapters and verses. The clearest way of presenting the Gospel is to divide it into two major parts right down the middle. Mark has sixteen chapters. The first eight chapters largely constitute the Galilean ministry of Jesus. In these chapters, Jesus travels extensively. He calls twelve disciples; he heals, casts out evil spirits, preaches and teaches, works miracles, and confronts opposition. In these chapters we are learning who Jesus is and what he has come to do as the kingdom of God breaks into the world.

Then, at 8:27, Jesus asks the question this Gospel has been building toward task after task, place after place, person after person. Jesus asks, "Who do people say that I am?" The disciples offer the popular culture's answers: "John the Baptist, Elijah, one of the prophets." Then Jesus hones in on the central question the disciples must each answer for themselves: "But who do you say that I am?"

It is Peter who answers first: "You are the Messiah" (8:29). What follows from this point is an unfolding of just what kind of Messiah Jesus intends to be and the nature of the kingdom he is bringing. From this turning point, the action moves out of Galilee and into Jerusalem to the cross. If we are to understand Jesus as Messiah, we will have to move to this new place. From chapter 9 on, we are preparing for the Passion.

Three times (8:31; 9:31; 10:33–34) Jesus explains to the disciples that the Messiah, "the Son of Man," will suffer, be rejected and killed, and after three days rise again. Jesus carefully makes the full and discomforting connection between his messiahship and their discipleship when he says: "If any want to become my followers, let them deny themselves and take up their cross and follow me" (8:34). Each of the three passion predictions is followed by a story illustrating that the disciples do not understand what Jesus is saying about himself or asking of them. They are blind to the full and discomforting connection between Jesus' messiahship and their discipleship. Mark emphasizes their blindness by bracketing the three passion predictions between two stories of Jesus healing a blind person. Jesus heals the blind man at Bethsaida (8:22–26) and then Jesus heals blind Bartimaeus (10:46–52) on the outskirts of Jericho. This last story is offered immediately before Jesus enters Jerusalem for the only (in Mark) and last time.

Headings for the major divisions of Mark, then, can be designated this way: 1:1–8:26: Jesus teaches, heals, and works miracles with power and authority; 8:27–29: the turning point; 8:30–16:8: the Passion—true messiahship and true discipleship.

A Dual Emphasis

The Gospel of Mark has a dual emphasis. The first and most important emphasis is on Jesus. On the way, we are invited to believe that Jesus is the Christ, the Son of God. Jesus teaches and preaches, heals and works miracles, and confronts authorities. We watch Jesus challenge and overturn customs and practices that put law above love. He extends and expands love by welcoming and including all people in discipleship and in the kingdom of God, refusing to accept the world's designations of some people as "unclean" and "outcasts and sinners" and therefore unworthy. In all of these ways, Jesus embodies divine power and authority. He suffers and dies at the hands of the authorities of this world, whose understanding of power and authority causes them to maintain a tight grip on people rather than responding with the Messiah's open-armed grace and mercy and all-inclusive love. They did the worst they could do by crucifying him. But death was no match for God, and the crucifixion is not the end of this story any more than it was the end of Jesus Christ, the Son of God.

The second emphasis in Mark is on the disciples. In the beginning, they seem to be models of faithfulness as they drop everything, literally, in order to follow Jesus. But time after time, the disciples are portrayed as followers who just don't "get it." They misunderstand Jesus at many points. They doubt and are afraid. He speaks of suffering and of being last and least, yet they want to know which of them is the greatest and if they can sit on his right and left side "in glory." They fall asleep when he needs them most. By the end of the Gospel, one of them has betrayed Jesus, one has denied him, and all have fallen away.

Oddly, we may find this comforting. If the life and faithfulness of Jesus were the only measure for our own discipleship, we would come up short every time. Jesus is our model, of course, but we are not perfect as he is perfect. We are like the slow, faltering disciples Mark dares to describe. We misunderstand. We doubt and are afraid to take up our cross. We prefer glory to suffering and shame. We fall asleep when we ought to be praying and watching. At times, we betray and deny and fall away from Jesus. And yet it is precisely to such disciples, to us, that Jesus makes a resurrection promise he will keep: he is going ahead of us. We will see him. We are still included! Jesus does not give up on us, but urges us to keep going, to meet him in Galilee and everywhere else he appears in the world.

An Abrupt Ending

Mark's Gospel ends as abruptly as it begins. Mark 16:8 is widely considered to be the original end of this Gospel: "So they went out and fled from the tomb, for terror and amazement had seized them; and they said nothing to anyone, for they were afraid." Perhaps such an abrupt, muted ending was so uncomfortable and so incomplete that two additional endings were added later. In reading these later endings, it is easy to see how different they are in style and tone from the rest of this Gospel. Some have suggested that additional verses were lost from the original manuscript. Surely Mark would never have ended the "good news" like this!

However, there is another way to look at this "incomplete" ending. What if Mark's whole Gospel is "the beginning of the good news of Jesus Christ, the Son of God"? What if all sixteen chapters are meant to be only the beginning? Then Mark's incomplete ending is not a mistake, but exactly right. Marks leaves us to continue and "complete" this story. We too will need to get over our fear and find our voices. We continue the story when we share with others the good news of this man Jesus, whom we have discovered to be the Christ, the Son of God. We continue the story when we have "turned around," had a change of heart and mind, and know ourselves to be forgiven and loved and included in the kingdom of God. We embody the truth of this story when we work for healing and wholeness and overturn legalisms that limit God's grace and mercy. The Gospel is continued among us as we practice Jesus' inclusive love so that no one is treated as unclean, an outcast or sinner, but all are welcomed into discipleship and into the coming reign of God.

Mark's Gospel is committed to our spiritual formation. It breaks into our lives with the invitation to believe in Jesus Christ, the Son of God, and to take up our cross and follow him. But this Gospel will not provide an easy, tidy end to our spiritual formation. No, in Mark we are on a continuing journey, as we too encounter the empty tomb and must decide where we will go and what we will say and do from here on.

—*Kimberly Clayton Richter*

The Proclamation of John the Baptist

1 The beginning of the good news[a] of Jesus Christ, the Son of God.[b]
2 As it is written in the prophet Isaiah,[c]
"See, I am sending my messenger ahead of you,[d]
who will prepare your way;

3 the voice of one crying out in the wilderness:
'Prepare the way of the Lord,
make his paths straight,' "

---

a Or gospel   b Other ancient authorities lack *the Son of God*   c Other ancient authorities read *in the prophets*   d Gk *before your face*

1:1 *the Son of God.* This is the beginning of more than a Gospel; it is the beginning of God's plan of salvation in a specific person, Jesus Christ, the Son of God. When we first profess our faith that "Jesus is my Lord and Savior," it is only the beginning of our discipleship. The rest of the Gospel, like the rest of our lives, is the journey of seeing and hearing, of knowing and sharing more deeply and fully this good news in the world.

1:2–3 *make his paths straight.* Mark immediately connects this "beginning" with the past by quoting from the Hebrew Scriptures. He combines quotes from Mal 3:1 and Isa 40:3 to introduce us to John the Baptist. Our Christian faith does not begin in isolation, but is rooted in our Jewish heritage. The promises God made to Israel through the voices of prophets like Malachi and Isaiah are being fulfilled in Jesus Christ.

4John the baptizer appeared*a* in the wilderness, proclaiming a baptism of repentance for the forgiveness of sins. 5And people from the whole Judean countryside and all the people of Jerusalem were going out to him, and were baptized by him in the river Jordan, confessing their sins. 6Now John was clothed with camel's hair, with a leather belt around his waist, and he ate locusts and wild honey. 7He proclaimed, "The one who is more powerful than I is coming after me; I am not worthy to stoop down and untie the thong of his sandals. 8I have baptized you with*b* water; but he will baptize you with*b* the Holy Spirit."

The Baptism of Jesus

9 In those days Jesus came from Nazareth of Galilee and was baptized by John in the Jordan. 10And just as he was coming up out of the water, he saw the heavens torn apart and the Spirit descending like a dove on him. 11And a voice came from heaven, "You are my Son, the Beloved;*c* with you I am well pleased."

The Temptation of Jesus

12 And the Spirit immediately drove him out into the wilderness. 13He was in the wilderness forty days, tempted by Satan; and he was with the wild beasts; and the angels waited on him.

The Beginning of the Galilean Ministry

14 Now after John was arrested, Jesus came to Galilee, proclaiming the good news*d* of God,*e* 15and saying, "The time is fulfilled, and the kingdom of God has come near;*f* repent, and believe in the good news."*d*

Jesus Calls the First Disciples

16 As Jesus passed along the Sea of Galilee, he saw Simon and his brother Andrew casting a net into the sea—for they were fishermen. 17And Jesus said to them, "Follow me and I will make you fish for people." 18And immediately they left their nets and followed him. 19As he went a little farther, he saw James son of Zebedee and his brother John, who were in their boat mending the nets. 20Immediately he called them; and they left their father Zebedee in the boat with the hired men, and followed him.

a Other ancient authorities read *John was baptizing* *b* Or *in* *c* Or *my beloved Son* *d* Or *gospel* *e* Other ancient authorities read *of the kingdom* *f* Or *is at hand*

1:4–8 *a baptism of repentance.* John the Baptist appears in the wilderness (another important Old Testament location). His dress and diet remind us of Elijah and other prophets. His baptism prepares people for baptism into Jesus. Repentance prepares us to receive the good news Jesus brings. A change of heart and mind that allows us to let go of old ways of life, old burdens and wrongs, and to know we are forgiven and loved makes us more ready to hear and believe that Jesus can bring us new life!

Responding
1:5 CONFESSION. In *Celebration of Discipline* Richard Foster writes that his confession of sin to a trusted friend set him free in ways he had never known before. As you are able, come before God and write down all of the sins you can recall. Then ask a trusted friend to hear your confession. One caution: don't be too hard on yourself. This is a time for confession, not self-flagellation. Did any new doors of understanding and ministry open to you? If so, what are they? *See also* Spiritual Disciplines Index.

1:9–13 *Jesus . . . was baptized by John.* All three synoptic Gospels mention Jesus' baptism by John, and Matthew adds that it was to "fulfill all righteousness" (3:15). All four Gospels make specific mention of the descent of the Spirit upon Jesus "like a dove." And it is this same Spirit that also drives Jesus into the wilderness, where he encounters both wild beasts and angels. In our own spiritual formation, we will experience blessings as well as temptations and hardships, both "wild beasts" and "angels." God is with us in all circumstances, blessing us, challenging us, giving us what we need to persevere.

1:16–20 *Jesus said, . . . "Follow me."* Jesus' call and claim disrupt our former allegiances and way of life. He gives us a new vocation, "to fish for people," as we share in his mission to proclaim the good news to all people.

JOHN THE BAPTIST
Sacrificially Submitted

Selected Scriptures: *Luke 1; 3:1–22; Mark 1:1–11; 6:14–29; Matthew 3:1–12; 11:1–19; 14:1–12; John 1:6–9, 19–34; 3:22–36; Philippians 2:1–11*

After waiting four hundred years with no word from God, Israel finally received a messenger from God. John the Baptist was born to a barren, elderly couple, heralding life and a new miracle not only for Elizabeth and Zechariah, but for the Jewish people.

From the time John was in Elizabeth's womb, God's hand was with him, forming and guiding him. As he grew, John "became strong in spirit" (Luke 1:80). He had an important job to do, and from all we're told it seems John stayed focused throughout his life. "Repent, for the kingdom of heaven has come near" (Matt 3:2), he began preaching to the people. They had long lived as if in darkness, and now John "came to testify to the light" (John 1:8).

His preaching stirred the people, who were accustomed to hearing of a detailed set of laws they had to keep in order to achieve a faraway hope of a better day. Their teachers sat ensconced in the Temple and synagogues, wearing flowing robes and boasting of their own righteousness. John preached in the desert, wearing the skin of a camel and eating insects and wild honey. He spoke of God's kingdom at hand and stressed repentance rather than laws. John differed from the scribes and Pharisees of his day in almost every respect.

Most of all, John sought no prominent place for himself in the eyes of the people. Although he acquired a following over time and even had some "disciples," John quickly turned them toward the coming Messiah, claiming, "He must increase, but I must decrease" (John 3:30). He did so with a sincere joy.

What can we learn from this strange man of extremes? Surely none of us will ever carry a message quite like John's. The wearing of animal skins today would often signify either great (and possibly inhumane) wealth or insanity. A sojourn in the desert would in many parts of the world leave us solitary and unheard, while John's diet might leave us malnourished. Still, apart from the specifics, John's choices point us toward a way of life we must embrace if we are ever to point, as he did, to the Savior, Jesus.

Theologian Dietrich Bonhoeffer has said, "If there is no element of asceticism in our lives, if we give free rein to the desires of the flesh . . . we shall find it hard to train for the service of Christ." John gave up life in a comfortable home, a conventional diet and clothing, and the accepted form of preaching for his day in order to announce the person of Jesus, who would also defy the expectations of the people. John sacrificed his comfort and his image for the service of Christ. He eventually sacrificed his life.

PROFILE

In one way or another, we too will need to make sacrifices of our comfort and our image to serve Christ in the way he has created us to serve him. These offerings need not, and should not, consume us by being approached as unbending legalism. Still, we can expect some discomfort as we seek to be faithful. We can be sure that as we carry on in God's call, a passion for him will increasingly beat stronger than our dismay at what we have given up, until giving even our life will not seem too much to offer for Christ.

Francis of Assisi wrote, "Blessed is the servant who esteems himself no better when he is praised and exalted by people than when he is considered worthless, simple, and despicable; for what a man is before God, that he is and nothing more."

John's strength of spirit allowed him to see himself not through the eyes of people, but through the eyes of God. His strength of spirit also helped him to live not seeking position, but seeking service. May we practice self-sacrifice well and appropriately as we train in Christ's service, and may God give strength to us as he did to John the Baptist.

Personal Reflection

- Can you identify the main work God has created for you to offer in your lifetime? What is it? If you aren't sure, what are some ways you could begin to identify God's overarching intention for your life?
- John the Baptist remained single-minded in carrying out his work of proclaiming the coming of Christ. He didn't fall into seeking the approval of those around him, and he readily humbled himself in order to lift up Jesus. Do you struggle either in seeking the approval of others or in wanting a high position? Or do you feel attached to certain comforts that might hinder your service to Christ? What Spiritual Disciplines or types of self-sacrifice might help you as you train to more naturally express Christ's attitude in these areas?
- Despite his fervent preaching on Christ and his life devoted to the service of Christ, John didn't fully understand who Jesus was or how he would offer salvation. How does John's life speak to you when you encounter doubts in your life of faith or when you struggle with questions about God you cannot answer?

PROFILE

Satan tries Two

The Man with an Unclean Spirit

21 They went to Capernaum; and when the sabbath came, he entered the synagogue and taught. 22 They were astounded at his teaching, for he taught them as one having authority, and not as the scribes. 23 Just then there was in their synagogue a man with an unclean spirit, 24 and he cried out, "What have you to do with us, Jesus of Nazareth? Have you come to destroy us? I know who you are, the Holy One of God." 25 But Jesus rebuked him, saying, "Be silent, and come out of him!" 26 And the unclean spirit, convulsing him and crying with a loud voice, came out of him. 27 They were all amazed, and they kept on asking one another, "What is this? A new teaching—with authority! He*a* commands even the unclean spirits, and they obey him." 28 At once his fame began to spread throughout the surrounding region of Galilee.

Jesus Heals Many at Simon's House

29 As soon as they*b* left the synagogue, they entered the house of Simon and Andrew, with James and John. 30 Now Simon's mother-in-law was in bed with a fever, and they told him about her at once. 31 He came and took her by the hand and lifted her up. Then the fever left her, and she began to serve them.

32 That evening, at sunset, they brought to him all who were sick or possessed with demons. 33 And the whole city was gathered around the door. 34 And he cured many who were sick with various diseases, and cast out many demons; and he would not permit the demons to speak, because they knew him.

A Preaching Tour in Galilee

35 In the morning, while it was still very dark, he got up and went out to a deserted place, and there he prayed. 36 And Simon and his companions hunted for him. 37 When they found him, they said to him, "Everyone is searching for you." 38 He answered, "Let us go on to the neighboring towns, so that I may proclaim the message there also; for that is what I came out to do." 39 And he went throughout Galilee, proclaiming the message in their synagogues and casting out demons.

Jesus Cleanses a Leper

Eternity Dreams

40 A leper*c* came to him begging him, and kneeling*d* he said to him, "If you choose, you can make me clean." 41 Moved with pity,*e* Jesus*f* stretched out his hand and touched

---

a Or *A new teaching! With authority he*   *b* Other ancient authorities read *he*   *c* The terms *leper* and *leprosy* can refer to several diseases   *d* Other ancient authorities lack *kneeling*   *e* Other ancient authorities read *anger*   *f* Gk *he*

1:23–27 *the unclean spirit . . . came out of him.* Jesus came not only to teach us about a new way of life, but to give us new life by healing us physically, emotionally, mentally, and spiritually. There are many stories in Mark about unclean spirits and demons being cast out. The evil spirits often recognize who Jesus is and ask him to leave them alone. The power of evil wants to avoid the greater power of God's truth and wholeness. These stories continue to teach us something important: we must take evil seriously, but we must never take evil more seriously than we take God. God has authority over all things.

1:35 *went out to a deserted place, and . . . prayed.* Several times Mark mentions that Jesus and the disciples go to a deserted place to rest and pray. Our own spiritual formation will be strengthened if, in our busy, crowded, and noisy lives, we find regular times and places for quiet,

for prayer, for listening to God. Time alone with God gives us renewed energy to live fully engaged with the world again.

1:35 SOLITUDE and PRAYER—See Spiritual Disciplines Index.

1:40–42 *If you choose, you can make me clean.* Part of our spiritual growth in the Christian life is to reach out to all people with healing and compassion and community. In Jesus' day, lepers were not permitted to come near others, but were isolated, stigmatized, and feared. Above all lepers were never to be touched. But Jesus reaches out and touches this man to heal and restore him. The leper teaches us all how to pray when he says, "If you choose, you can make me clean." God has the power to heal and to answer our prayers, yet our desired outcome in prayer always needs to be placed within God's larger plan and purposes.

him, and said to him, "I do choose. Be made clean!" [42]Immediately the leprosy left him, and he was made clean. [43]After sternly warning him he sent him away at once, [44]saying to him, "See that you say nothing to anyone; but go, show yourself to the priest, and offer for your cleansing what Moses commanded, as a testimony to them." [45]But he went out and began to proclaim it freely, and to spread the word, so that Jesus [b] could no longer go into a town openly, but stayed out in the country; and people came to him from every quarter.

Jesus Heals a Paralytic

2 When he returned to Capernaum after some days, it was reported that he was at home. [2]So many gathered around that there was no longer room for them, not even in front of the door; and he was speaking the word to them. [3]Then some people [c] came, bringing to him a paralyzed man, carried by four of them. [4]And when they could not bring him to Jesus because of the crowd, they removed the roof above him; and after having dug through it, they let down the mat on which the paralytic lay. [5]When Jesus saw their faith, he said to the paralytic, "Son, your sins are forgiven." [6]Now some of the scribes were sitting there, questioning in their hearts, [7]"Why does this fellow speak in this way? It is blasphemy! Who can forgive sins but God alone?" [8]At once Jesus perceived in his spirit that they were discussing these questions among themselves; and he said to them, "Why do you raise such questions in your hearts? [9]Which is easier, to say to the paralytic, 'Your sins are forgiven,' or to say, 'Stand up and take your mat and walk'? [10]But so

that you may know that the Son of Man has authority on earth to forgive sins"—he said to the paralytic— [11]"I say to you, stand up, take your mat and go to your home." [12]And he stood up, and immediately took the mat and went out before all of them; so that they were all amazed and glorified God, saying, "We have never seen anything like this!"

Jesus Calls Levi

13 Jesus [d] went out again beside the sea; the whole crowd gathered around him, and he taught them. [14]As he was walking along, he saw Levi son of Alphaeus sitting at the tax booth, and he said to him, "Follow me." And he got up and followed him.

15 And as he sat at dinner [e] in Levi's [f] house, many tax collectors and sinners were also sitting [g] with Jesus and his disciples—for there were many who followed him. [16]When the scribes of [h] the Pharisees saw that he was eating with sinners and tax collectors, they said to his disciples, "Why does he eat [i] with tax collectors and sinners?" [17]When Jesus heard this, he said to them, "Those who are well have no need of a physician, but those who are sick; I have come to call not the righteous but sinners."

The Question about Fasting

18 Now John's disciples and the Pharisees were fasting; and people [c] came and said to him, "Why do John's disciples and the disci-

---

a The terms *leper* and *leprosy* can refer to several diseases   b Gk *he*   c Gk *they*   d Gk *He*
e Gk *reclined*   f Gk *his*   g Gk *reclining*
h Other ancient authorities read *and*   i Other ancient authorities add *and drink*

2:2–5 *Son, your sins are forgiven.* God has called us not only to individual spiritual formation, but to be formed into communities of faith too. We pray for one another and work for the healing and wholeness of others, just as this paralytic's four friends help him receive the healing he needs. Jesus connects healing and forgiveness, recognizing that guilt or self-hatred can paralyze our spirit as much as a physical illness or injury can paralyze our limbs.

2:13–15 *there were many who followed him.* Jesus calls all sorts of people to be his disciples.

Tax collectors were not held in high esteem by society, yet Jesus called Levi to follow him. Jesus ate with "tax collectors and sinners," scandalizing those who sincerely tried to follow the law and serve God. Everyone is welcome at God's table. In our practice of the Christian life, we need the company of diverse people at our dinner tables and at the Lord's Table. People who are different from us help us experience the Lord's presence in new ways.

2:18–19 **FASTING**—*See* Spiritual Disciplines Index.

ples of the Pharisees fast, but your disciples do not fast?" [19]Jesus said to them, "The wedding guests cannot fast while the bridegroom is with them, can they? As long as they have the bridegroom with them, they cannot fast. [20]The days will come when the bridegroom is taken away from them, and then they will fast on that day.

[21] "No one sews a piece of unshrunk cloth on an old cloak; otherwise, the patch pulls away from it, the new from the old, and a worse tear is made. [22]And no one puts new wine into old wineskins; otherwise, the wine will burst the skins, and the wine is lost, and so are the skins; but one puts new wine into fresh wineskins." [a]

Pronouncement about the Sabbath

[23] One sabbath he was going through the grainfields; and as they made their way his disciples began to pluck heads of grain. [24]The Pharisees said to him, "Look, why are they doing what is not lawful on the sabbath?" [25]And he said to them, "Have you never read what David did when he and his companions were hungry and in need of food? [26]He entered the house of God, when Abiathar was high priest, and ate the bread of the Presence, which it is not lawful for any but the priests to eat, and he gave some to his companions." [27]Then he said to them, "The sabbath was made for humankind, and not humankind for the sabbath; [28]so the Son of Man is lord even of the sabbath."

The Man with a Withered Hand

3 Again he entered the synagogue, and a man was there who had a withered hand. [2]They watched him to see whether he would cure him on the sabbath, so that they might accuse him. [3]And he said to the man who had the withered hand, "Come for-

ward." [4]Then he said to them, "Is it lawful to do good or to do harm on the sabbath, to save life or to kill?" But they were silent. [5]He looked around at them with anger; he was grieved at their hardness of heart and said to the man, "Stretch out your hand." He stretched it out, and his hand was restored. [6]The Pharisees went out and immediately conspired with the Herodians against him, how to destroy him.

A Multitude at the Seaside

[7] Jesus departed with his disciples to the sea, and a great multitude from Galilee followed him; [8]hearing all that he was doing, they came to him in great numbers from Judea, Jerusalem, Idumea, beyond the Jordan, and the region around Tyre and Sidon. [9]He told his disciples to have a boat ready for him because of the crowd, so that they would not crush him; [10]for he had cured many, so that all who had diseases pressed upon him to touch him. [11]Whenever the unclean spirits saw him, they fell down before him and shouted, "You are the Son of God!" [12]But he sternly ordered them not to make him known.

Jesus Appoints the Twelve

[13] He went up the mountain and called to him those whom he wanted, and they came to him. [14]And he appointed twelve, whom he also named apostles, [b] to be with him, and to be sent out to proclaim the message, [15]and to have authority to cast out demons. [16]So he appointed the twelve: [c] Simon (to whom he gave the name Peter); [17]James son of Zebedee and John the brother of James (to whom he

a Other ancient authorities lack *but one puts new wine into fresh wineskins*   b Other ancient authorities lack *whom he also named apostles*   c Other ancient authorities lack *So he appointed the twelve*

2:27 *and not humankind for the sabbath.* There are no longer laws that close businesses (or prohibit children's sports!) on Sundays. Our culture has largely lost the concept of "Sabbath rest." Yet observing a Sabbath day of rest was meant to give freedom from labor not only to humans, but also to animals (beasts of burden) and to the earth itself. If we constantly work, or

ask others to work constantly on our behalf, then we become enslaved to our economy and our own efforts. We come to believe everything depends on what we can provide for ourselves. To keep a rhythm of Sabbath rest is to remember that God is the maker and giver of all good things; it tempers our everlasting itch to get ahead.

gave the name Boanerges, that is, Sons of Thunder); [18]and Andrew, and Philip, and Bartholomew, and Matthew, and Thomas, and James son of Alphaeus, and Thaddaeus, and Simon the Cananaean, [19]and Judas Iscariot, who betrayed him.

Jesus and Beelzebul

Then he went home; [20]and the crowd came together again, so that they could not even eat. [21]When his family heard it, they went out to restrain him, for people were saying, "He has gone out of his mind." [22]And the scribes who came down from Jerusalem said, "He has Beelzebul, and by the ruler of the demons he casts out demons." [23]And he called them to him, and spoke to them in parables, "How can Satan cast out Satan? [24]If a kingdom is divided against itself, that kingdom cannot stand. [25]And if a house is divided against itself, that house will not be able to stand. [26]And if Satan has risen up against himself and is divided, he cannot stand, but his end has come. [27]But no one can enter a strong man's house and plunder his property without first tying up the strong man; then indeed the house can be plundered.

[28] "Truly I tell you, people will be forgiven for their sins and whatever blasphemies they utter; [29]but whoever blasphemes against the Holy Spirit can never have forgiveness, but is guilty of an eternal sin"— [30]for they had said, "He has an unclean spirit."

The True Kindred of Jesus

[31] Then his mother and his brothers came; and standing outside, they sent to him and called him. [32]A crowd was sitting around him; and they said to him, "Your mother and your brothers and sisters[a] are outside, asking for you." [33]And he replied, "Who are my mother and my brothers?" [34]And looking at those who sat around him, he said, "Here are my mother and my brothers! [35]Whoever does the will of God is my brother and sister and mother."

The Parable of the Sower

4 Again he began to teach beside the sea. Such a very large crowd gathered around

a Other ancient authorities lack and sisters

3:16–19 *and Thaddeus, and Simon the Cananaean.* We know a few of the more famous (and infamous) disciples, but there are many in this list we know nothing about at all. In our own discipleship, we may be asked to do some work or to take a stand that gets noticed by others. But often discipleship consists of faithfulness in the small, even mundane acts of Christian service perhaps unnoticed by all except God.

3:22, 29 *whoever blasphemes . . . can never have forgiveness.* We certainly must be careful about our language and how we speak of God. But these verses are not simply about "taking the Lord's name in vain." The blasphemy is much more serious than that. Those who opposed Jesus claimed that his power to cast out demons came from the chief demonic power, Beelzebul. This serious charge, that power of the Holy Spirit was really a demonic power, is identified as blasphemy. The radical change and healing God brings through Jesus never have as their purpose to destroy or tear down; they are always for our building up and wholeness.

3:31–35 *Whoever does the will of God.* The family in Jewish life was extremely important and valued. Genealogies in the Bible attest to its importance. Religious instruction, economic viability, and claims to the land all were tied to family life. Families represented multiple generations and were also linked to specific tribes within Israel. Family loyalty, respect, and obedience were hallmarks of Jewish family life. In several places, the gospel begins to expand the definition of family in radical ways (e.g., sons leave their family fishing business to follow Jesus). Here Jesus offers a definition of family that must have shocked his hearers by subjecting kinship not to matters of biology or human loyalty, but to loyalty, respect, and obedience to God's will. The concept of an "extended family" has suddenly taken on very wide proportions indeed. Jesus is not advocating hostility toward one's family. Jesus is making it clear, however, that loving and following God binds us together more deeply than any ties of human kinship. Learning to love and care for those to whom we are bound in faith as deeply as we care for members of our family reorders our priorities and resources.

him that he got into a boat on the sea and sat there, while the whole crowd was beside the sea on the land. 2He began to teach them many things in parables, and in his teaching he said to them: 3"Listen! A sower went out to sow. 4And as he sowed, some seed fell on the path, and the birds came and ate it up. 5Other seed fell on rocky ground, where it did not have much soil, and it sprang up quickly, since it had no depth of soil. 6And when the sun rose, it was scorched; and since it had no root, it withered away. 7Other seed fell among thorns, and the thorns grew up and choked it, and it yielded no grain. 8Other seed fell into good soil and brought forth grain, growing up and increasing and yielding thirty and sixty and a hundredfold." 9And he said, "Let anyone with ears to hear listen!"

The Purpose of the Parables

10 When he was alone, those who were around him along with the twelve asked him about the parables. 11And he said to them, "To you has been given the secret a of the kingdom of God, but for those outside, everything comes in parables; 12in order that

'they may indeed look, but not
    perceive,
and may indeed listen, but not
    understand;

so that they may not turn again and be forgiven.' "

13 And he said to them, "Do you not understand this parable? Then how will you understand all the parables? 14The sower sows the word. 15These are the ones on the path where the word is sown: when they hear, Satan immediately comes and takes away the word that is sown in them. 16And these are the ones sown on rocky ground: when they hear the word, they immediately receive it with joy. 17But they have no root, and endure only for a while; then, when trouble or persecution arises on account of the word, immediately they fall away. b 18And others are those sown among the thorns: these are the ones who hear the word, 19but the cares of the world, and the lure of wealth, and the desire for other things come in and choke the word, and it yields nothing. 20And these are the ones sown on the good soil: they hear the word and accept it and bear fruit, thirty and sixty and a hundredfold."

A Lamp under a Bushel Basket

21 He said to them, "Is a lamp brought in to be put under the bushel basket, or under the bed, and not on the lampstand? 22For there is nothing hidden, except to be dis-

a Or mystery   b Or stumble

4:2 *He began to teach them many things in parables.* Jesus often used parables in order to teach and to invite new insights and discoveries in his hearers. The Greek word *parabole* comes from two smaller words put together that mean something like "tossed near" or "put beside" as in "compare." So Jesus will say, "The kingdom of God is like . . ." Jesus' parables use elements from ordinary, everyday life. The plot is at once interesting and accessible. Often there is an element of surprise. We used to think each element or character in a parable "stood for" something very specific, as in an allegory. Today there is an appreciation for the open-ended invitation many of these parables offer. They invite us into the story and offer us the opportunity to see things from various perspectives. Parables mostly do not "beat us over the head" with one obvious lesson to be learned or point to be made. Parables ask us to place ourselves

within the story and explore its meaning as we seek to live faithfully in God's realm.

4:3–9 *Listen! A sower went out to sow.* Parables are often not immediately clear, but require some thinking to penetrate their meaning. Jesus begins and ends this parable of the sower with the word "Listen!" That is the key to understanding it. God's word requires careful listening if we are to cultivate a healthy environment in which God's word can grow and flourish in us for the sake of the world. This parable reminds us that there are many challenges to our growth in faith. It cannot be taken for granted.

Responding
4:22 SECRECY. Dallas Willard in *The Spirit of the Disciplines* defines secrecy as abstaining "from causing our good deeds and qualities to be known," but this verse and its companions in Matthew and Luke are talking

closed; nor is anything secret, except to come to light. 23Let anyone with ears to hear listen!" 24And he said to them, "Pay attention to what you hear; the measure you give will be the measure you get, and still more will be given you. 25For to those who have, more will be given; and from those who have nothing, even what they have will be taken away."

The Parable of the Growing Seed

26 He also said, "The kingdom of God is as if someone would scatter seed on the ground, 27and would sleep and rise night and day, and the seed would sprout and grow, he does not know how. 28The earth produces of itself, first the stalk, then the head, then the full grain in the head. 29But when the grain is ripe, at once he goes in with his sickle, because the harvest has come."

The Parable of the Mustard Seed

30 He also said, "With what can we compare the kingdom of God, or what parable will we use for it? 31It is like a mustard seed, which, when sown upon the ground, is the smallest of all the seeds on earth; 32yet when it is sown it grows up and becomes the greatest of all shrubs, and puts forth large branches, so that the birds of the air can make nests in its shade."

The Use of Parables

33 With many such parables he spoke the word to them, as they were able to hear it; 34he did not speak to them except in parables, but he explained everything in private to his disciples.

Jesus Stills a Storm

35 On that day, when evening had come, he said to them, "Let us go across to the other side." 36And leaving the crowd behind, they took him with them in the boat, just as he was. Other boats were with him. 37A great windstorm arose, and the waves beat into the boat, so that the boat was already being swamped. 38But he was in the stern, asleep on the cushion; and they woke him up and said to him, "Teacher, do you not care that we are perishing?" 39He woke up and rebuked the wind, and said to the sea, "Peace! Be still!" Then the wind ceased, and there was a dead calm. 40He said to

---

about all of our secrets—good and bad—being revealed (10:26; 12:2). What is the connection between keeping good deeds and qualities secret and having all of our secrets revealed? Does this provide extra motivation to be quiet about the good works that we do? *See also* Spiritual Disciplines Index.

4:30–32 *the kingdom of God . . . is like a mustard seed.* Disciples of Jesus learn to look for signs, even the tiniest of signs, of the kingdom of God. God's kingdom is not only—or even primarily—found in people or places of might and wealth and great power. Like the tiny mustard seed, which, when it grows to its fullest, is still only a shrub (unlike the cedars of Lebanon!), the kingdom may not be towering or overpowering. Yet the kingdom is strong enough for birds to nest in its shade, for hope to have room to grow, for freedom to take root, and for the faith of a few to influence the many toward justice and peace.

4:35–41 *the waves beat into the boat.* This scene depicts chaos without (the storm at sea) and chaos and panic within (the disciples fear).

At least four disciples were experienced fishermen, so this storm must be very fierce to cause them to be afraid. Even experienced fishermen— or committed disciples of Jesus—can become afraid in times of terror or uncertainty. In the midst of this storm, Jesus sleeps. This story offers meaning on literal and figurative levels. The world of nature can and does bring terrible storms, and we must take necessary precautions. On a figurative level, there are many "storms" in life that cause us to feel swamped indeed, physically, emotionally, and spiritually. Often one of the first casualties when we are afraid or uncertain is our ability to sleep peacefully and restfully. Yet here Jesus sleeps in a storm of wind and waves at peace and unafraid. Jesus sleeps in trust and confidence, because he knows that in life and in death, he belongs to God. God has power over everything, including nature itself. Jesus' word to the wind and waves is also his word to disciples then and now, "Peace! Be still!" Believing that Jesus is the Son of God and has the power to save us replaces fear with trusting confidence, allowing us to sleep in peace.

them, "Why are you afraid? Have you still no faith?" 41And they were filled with great awe and said to one another, "Who then is this, that even the wind and the sea obey him?"

Jesus Heals the Gerasene Demoniac

5 They came to the other side of the sea, to the country of the Gerasenes.ᵃ 2And when he had stepped out of the boat, immediately a man out of the tombs with an unclean spirit met him. 3He lived among the tombs; and no one could restrain him any more, even with a chain; 4for he had often been restrained with shackles and chains, but the chains he wrenched apart, and the shackles he broke in pieces; and no one had the strength to subdue him. 5Night and day among the tombs and on the mountains he was always howling and bruising himself with stones. 6When he saw Jesus from a distance, he ran and bowed down before him; 7and he shouted at the top of his voice, "What have you to do with me, Jesus, Son of the Most High God? I adjure you by God, do not torment me." 8For he had said to him, "Come out of the man, you unclean spirit!" 9Then Jesusᵇ asked him, "What is your name?" He replied, "My name is Legion; for we are many." 10He begged him earnestly not to send them out of the country. 11Now there on the hillside a great herd of swine was feeding; 12and the unclean spiritsᶜ begged him, "Send us into the swine; let us enter them." 13So he gave them permission. And the unclean spirits came out and entered the swine; and the herd, numbering about two thousand, rushed down the steep bank into the sea, and were drowned in the sea.

14 The swineherds ran off and told it in the city and in the country. Then people came to see what it was that had happened. 15They came to Jesus and saw the demoniac sitting there, clothed and in his right mind, the very man who had had the legion; and they were afraid. 16Those who had seen what had happened to the demoniac and to the swine reported it. 17Then they began to beg Jesusᵈ to leave their neighborhood. 18As he was getting into the boat, the man who had been possessed by demons begged him that he might be with him. 19But Jesusᵇ refused, and said to him, "Go home to your friends, and tell them how much the Lord has done for you, and what mercy he has shown you." 20And he went away and began to proclaim in the Decapolis how much Jesus had done for him; and everyone was amazed.

A Girl Restored to Life and a Woman Healed

21 When Jesus had crossed again in the boatᵉ to the other side, a great crowd gathered around him; and he was by the sea. 22Then one of the leaders of the synagogue named Jairus came and, when he saw him, fell at his feet 23and begged him repeatedly, "My little daughter is at the point of death. Come and lay your hands on her, so that she may be made well, and live." 24So he went with him.

And a large crowd followed him and pressed in on him. 25Now there was a woman who had been suffering from hemorrhages for twelve years. 26She had endured much under many physicians, and had spent all that she

---

a Other ancient authorities read Gergesenes; others, Gadarenes   b Gk he   c Gk they   d Gk him
e Other ancient authorities lack in the boat

5:1–20 *a man . . . with an unclean spirit met him.* Jesus moves into a gentile region, breaking the barrier between Jew and Gentile. Encountering the demoniac, Jesus breaks down the barrier between things thought to be clean and unclean according to Jewish tradition: the man is possessed by a spirit and lives among tombs and near a herd of swine (all considered unclean). All of the settled divisions become unsettled and rearranged with Jesus. We could well consider what this might mean for our own encounters with "strangers." After he is healed,

this man wants to follow Jesus as he goes to new places to proclaim the gospel, but Jesus tells him to stay where he is (v 19). Not all of us are called to work far away or in some new place. We may serve God best right in our own neighborhood, community, or church, as we tell others how much God has done for us and what mercy he has shown us (v 19).

5:21–43 *one of the leaders of the synagogue. . . . a woman who had been suffering.* In this section we have two very different people who each come to Jesus with a desperate need. A

had; and she was no better, but rather grew worse. 27She had heard about Jesus, and came up behind him in the crowd and touched his cloak, 28for she said, "If I but touch his clothes, I will be made well." 29Immediately her hemorrhage stopped; and she felt in her body that she was healed of her disease. 30Immediately aware that power had gone forth from him, Jesus turned about in the crowd and said, "Who touched my clothes?" 31And his disciples said to him, "You see the crowd pressing in on you; how can you say, 'Who touched me?'" 32He looked all around to see who had done it. 33But the woman, knowing what had happened to her, came in fear and trembling, fell down before him, and told him the whole truth. 34He said to her, "Daughter, your faith has made you well; go in peace, and be healed of your disease."

35 While he was still speaking, some people came from the leader's house to say, "Your daughter is dead. Why trouble the teacher any further?" 36But overhearing[a] what they said, Jesus said to the leader of the synagogue, "Do not fear, only believe." 37He allowed no one to follow him except Peter, James, and John, the brother of James. 38When they came to the house of the leader of the synagogue, he saw a commotion, people weeping and wailing loudly. 39When he had entered, he said to them, "Why do you make a commotion and weep? The child is not dead but sleeping." 40And they laughed at him. Then he put them all outside, and took the child's father and mother and those who were with him, and went in where the child was. 41He took her by the hand and said to her, "Talitha cum," which means, "Little girl, get up!" 42And immediately the girl got up and began to walk about (she was twelve years of age). At this they were overcome with amazement. 43He strictly ordered them that no one should know this, and told them to give her something to eat.

The Rejection of Jesus at Nazareth

6 He left that place and came to his hometown, and his disciples followed him. 2On the sabbath he began to teach in the synagogue, and many who heard him were astounded. They said, "Where did this man get all this? What is this wisdom that has been given to him? What deeds of power are being done by his hands! 3Is not this the carpenter, the son of Mary[b] and brother of James and Joses and Judas and Simon, and are not his sisters here with us?" And they took offense[c] at him. 4Then Jesus said to them, "Prophets are not without honor, except in their hometown, and among their own kin, and in their own house." 5And he could do no deed of power there, except that he laid his hands on a few sick people and cured them. 6And he was amazed at their unbelief.

The Mission of the Twelve

Then he went about among the villages teaching. 7He called the twelve and began to send them out two by two, and gave them authority over the unclean spirits. 8He ordered

a Or ignoring; other ancient authorities read hearing   b Other ancient authorities read son of the carpenter and of Mary   c Or stumbled

---

nameless, outcast woman needs to be healed of bleeding. A named, respected leader of the synagogue comes because his daughter is dying, in fact, has died. The woman finds healing in even the fringes of Jesus' presence and is restored to community as Jesus calls her "daughter" (v 34). The little girl is restored to life and to her family as Jesus takes her hand (vv 41–42). No matter who we are, we may come to God with our deepest needs, knowing that God has the power to restore us. For some of us, God's restoration will come in physical healing in this life. For others, full restoration will come only in the life to come. One of our strongest affirmations of faith is that in life and in death we belong to God.

6:7–13 *He . . . began to send them out two by two.* The way of training disciples in Jesus' day was deceptively simple: disciples were to listen to the teacher's words and watch his actions and then try to say and do what he did. We can learn in the same way today. As we mature spiritually, we give ourselves more and more fully to God's care and keeping. Our security is not found in possessions, but in belonging to God. We find courage to take risks for the sake of the gospel, as we reach out to others with hospitality and healing and hope. We continue

them to take nothing for their journey except a staff; no bread, no bag, no money in their belts; [9]but to wear sandals and not to put on two tunics. [10]He said to them, "Wherever you enter a house, stay there until you leave the place. [11]If any place will not welcome you and they refuse to hear you, as you leave, shake off the dust that is on your feet as a testimony against them." [12]So they went out and proclaimed that all should repent. [13]They cast out many demons, and anointed with oil many who were sick and cured them.

The Death of John the Baptist

14   King Herod heard of it, for Jesus'[a] name had become known. Some were[b] saying, "John the baptizer has been raised from the dead; and for this reason these powers are at work in him." [15]But others said, "It is Elijah." And others said, "It is a prophet, like one of the prophets of old." [16]But when Herod heard of it, he said, "John, whom I beheaded, has been raised."

17   For Herod himself had sent men who arrested John, bound him, and put him in prison on account of Herodias, his brother Philip's wife, because Herod[c] had married her. [18]For John had been telling Herod, "It is not lawful for you to have your brother's wife." [19]And Herodias had a grudge against him, and wanted to kill him. But she could not, [20]for Herod feared John, knowing that he was a righteous and holy man, and he protected him. When he heard him, he was greatly perplexed;[d] and yet he liked to listen to him. [21]But an opportunity came when Herod on his birthday gave a banquet for his courtiers and officers and for the leaders of Galilee. [22]When his daughter Herodias[e] came in and danced, she pleased Herod and his guests; and the king said to the girl, "Ask me for whatever you wish, and I will give it." [23]And he solemnly swore to her, "Whatever you ask me, I will give you, even half of my kingdom." [24]She went out and said to her mother, "What should I ask for?" She replied, "The head of John the baptizer." [25]Immediately she rushed back to the king and requested, "I want you to give me at once the head of John the Baptist on a platter." [26]The king was deeply grieved; yet out of regard for his oaths and for the guests, he did not want to refuse her. [27]Immediately the king sent a soldier of the guard with orders to bring John's[a] head. He went and beheaded him in the prison, [28]brought his head on a platter, and gave it to the girl. Then the girl gave it to her mother. [29]When his disciples heard about it, they came and took his body, and laid it in a tomb.

a Gk his   b Other ancient authorities read He was   c Gk he   d Other ancient authorities read he did many things   e Other ancient authorities read the daughter of Herodias herself

---

the mission of the first disciples as we proclaim the good news of Jesus and work for healing and wholeness in individuals and groups. Disciples travel light, realizing their interdependence with others and, most of all, their dependence upon God.

6:14–29 *Herod . . . arrested John.* The Gospel of Mark is so focused on Jesus that we have not heard much about John the Baptist since the opening scene. Here we are told of John's gruesome fate. The Herod mentioned in this story is Herod Antipas. His father, Herod the Great, had ruled at the time of Jesus' birth and ordered the death of all male children under three in an attempt to remove any threat to the throne. This family was notoriously violent and ruthless. John, who had been preaching repentance, had included Herod Antipas in his list of those needing to repent of sin. Herod had divorced his own wife in order to marry his brother's wife, Herodias. Herod Antipas appears to have been both compelled and repelled by John's preaching (v 20). However, according to Mark, a deadly combination of political fear of John's popularity, family pressure, and public face-saving caused Herod first to imprison John and then to order his death.

6:27 *He . . . beheaded him in the prison.* What happened to John the Baptist has happened to other people of faith who have tried to speak truth to power. We are reminded here that following God and proclaiming God's word to others is not always an easy road and may not be heard by everyone as "good news." God's powerful word often threatens human power. Our spiritual formation requires strong conditioning and great courage in the face of real and fierce opposition.

Feeding the Five Thousand

30 The apostles gathered around Jesus, and told him all that they had done and taught. [31]He said to them, "Come away to a deserted place all by yourselves and rest a while." For many were coming and going, and they had no leisure even to eat. [32]And they went away in the boat to a deserted place by themselves. [33]Now many saw them going and recognized them, and they hurried there on foot from all the towns and arrived ahead of them. [34]As he went ashore, he saw a great crowd; and he had compassion for them, because they were like sheep without a shepherd; and he began to teach them many things. [35]When it grew late, his disciples came to him and said, "This is a deserted place, and the hour is now very late; [36]send them away so that they may go into the surrounding country and villages and buy something for themselves to eat." [37]But he answered them, "You give them something to eat." They said to him, "Are we to go and buy two hundred denarii[a] worth of bread, and give it to them to eat?" [38]And he said to them, "How many loaves have you? Go and see." When they had found out, they said, "Five, and two fish." [39]Then he ordered them to get all the people to sit down in groups on the green grass. [40]So they sat down in groups of hundreds and of fifties. [41]Taking the five loaves and the two fish, he looked up to heaven, and blessed and broke the loaves, and gave them to his disciples to set before the people; and he divided the two fish among them all. [42]And all ate and were filled; [43]and they took up twelve baskets full of broken pieces and of the fish. [44]Those who had eaten the loaves numbered five thousand men.

Jesus Walks on the Water

45 Immediately he made his disciples get into the boat and go on ahead to the other side, to Bethsaida, while he dismissed the crowd. [46]After saying farewell to them, he went up on the mountain to pray.

47 When evening came, the boat was out on the sea, and he was alone on the land. [48]When he saw that they were straining at the oars against an adverse wind, he came towards them early in the morning, walking on the sea. He intended to pass them by. [49]But when they saw him walking on the sea, they thought it was a ghost and cried out; [50]for they all saw him and were terrified. But immediately he spoke to them and said, "Take heart, it is I; do not be afraid." [51]Then he got into the boat with them and the wind ceased. And they were utterly astounded, [52]for they did not understand about the loaves, but their hearts were hardened.

Healing the Sick in Gennesaret

53 When they had crossed over, they came to land at Gennesaret and moored the boat. [54]When they got out of the boat, people at once recognized him, [55]and rushed about that whole region and began to bring

a The denarius was the usual day's wage for a laborer

6:31 SOLITUDE—See Spiritual Disciplines Index.

6:31–32 *Come away to a deserted place.* Jesus craves solitude and rest not for selfish reasons, but because this is where the spiritual resources for ministry are found. Solitude is a Spiritual Discipline we neglect to our detriment.

6:34–44 *You give them something to eat.* This is the first of two miraculous feedings. Jesus' actions remind us of the way the Lord's Supper is observed in many churches. Here Jesus' disciples are called upon to do more than they think it is possible for them to do. They only have five loaves of bread and two fish, yet there are five thousand men to be fed, plus women and children. We often feel daunted by the great needs of the world, when we seem to be only one person or only a small community of disciples facing them. However, when we take what we have, no matter how small, and ask God to bless our efforts and resources, together we can do more than what we imagined was possible on our own. Healthy spiritual development includes a Christian imagination that believes with God that all things are possible.

6:46 PRAYER—See Spiritual Disciplines Index.

6:47 SOLITUDE—See Spiritual Disciplines Index.

the sick on mats to wherever they heard he was. 56And wherever he went, into villages or cities or farms, they laid the sick in the marketplaces, and begged him that they might touch even the fringe of his cloak; and all who touched it were healed.

The Tradition of the Elders

7 Now when the Pharisees and some of the scribes who had come from Jerusalem gathered around him, 2they noticed that some of his disciples were eating with defiled hands, that is, without washing them. 3(For the Pharisees, and all the Jews, do not eat unless they thoroughly wash their hands,a thus observing the tradition of the elders; 4and they do not eat anything from the market unless they wash it;b and there are also many other traditions that they observe, the washing of cups, pots, and bronze kettles.c) 5So the Pharisees and the scribes asked him, "Why do your disciples not lived according to the tradition of the elders, but eat with defiled hands?" 6He said to them, "Isaiah prophesied rightly about you hypocrites, as it is written,

'This people honors me with their lips,
    but their hearts are far from me;
7 in vain do they worship me,
    teaching human precepts as
        doctrines.'

8You abandon the commandment of God and hold to human tradition."

9 Then he said to them, "You have a fine way of rejecting the commandment of God in order to keep your tradition! 10For Moses said, 'Honor your father and your mother'; and,

'Whoever speaks evil of father or mother must surely die.' 11But you say that if anyone tells father or mother, 'Whatever support you might have had from me is Corban' (that is, an offering to Gode)— 12then you no longer permit doing anything for a father or mother, 13thus making void the word of God through your tradition that you have handed on. And you do many things like this."

14 Then he called the crowd again and said to them, "Listen to me, all of you, and understand: 15there is nothing outside a person that by going in can defile, but the things that come out are what defile."f

17 When he had left the crowd and entered the house, his disciples asked him about the parable. 18He said to them, "Then do you also fail to understand? Do you not see that whatever goes into a person from outside cannot defile, 19since it enters, not the heart but the stomach, and goes out into the sewer?" (Thus he declared all foods clean.) 20And he said, "It is what comes out of a person that defiles. 21For it is from within, from the human heart, that evil intentions come: fornication, theft, murder, 22adultery, avarice, wickedness, deceit, licentiousness, envy, slander, pride, folly. 23All these evil things come from within, and they defile a person."

a Meaning of Gk uncertain   b Other ancient authorities read and when they come from the marketplace, they do not eat unless they purify themselves   c Other ancient authorities add and beds   d Gk walk   e Gk lacks to God   f Other ancient authorities add verse 16, "Let anyone with ears to hear listen"

Responding
7:6–7 WORSHIP. This quotation from Isa 29:13 is nested between segments of Jesus' confrontation with the scribes and Pharisees over their hypocrisy in fastidiously following the law of Moses, but neglecting its spirit. Can you name a time when human traditions hampered your worship of God? Explain. What did you do to overcome the hold they had on you? See also Spiritual Disciplines Index.

7:14–15 there is nothing outside . . . that by going in can defile. Jewish tradition declared

some foods clean and some unclean. Eating practices, then, helped to remind Israel that it was different from other nations. This in itself is not a bad thing. However, human tradition and custom can come to be regarded as divinely revealed and required. This still happens in religious circles today, as in "But we've always done it this way!" When such outward legalism takes over, basic internal Christian practices such as love, reconciliation, and hospitality can be lost. The gentile woman in the next story (vv 24–30) seems to make this same point to Jesus himself.

The Syrophoenician Woman's Faith

24 From there he set out and went away to the region of Tyre. *a* He entered a house and did not want anyone to know he was there. Yet he could not escape notice, 25but a woman whose little daughter had an unclean spirit immediately heard about him, and she came and bowed down at his feet. 26Now the woman was a Gentile, of Syrophoenician origin. She begged him to cast the demon out of her daughter. 27He said to her, "Let the children be fed first, for it is not fair to take the children's food and throw it to the dogs." 28But she answered him, "Sir, *b* even the dogs under the table eat the children's crumbs." 29Then he said to her, "For saying that, you may go—the demon has left your daughter." 30So she went home, found the child lying on the bed, and the demon gone.

Jesus Cures a Deaf Man

31 Then he returned from the region of Tyre, and went by way of Sidon towards the Sea of Galilee, in the region of the Decapolis. 32They brought to him a deaf man who had an impediment in his speech; and they begged him to lay his hand on him. 33He took him aside in private, away from the crowd, and put his fingers into his ears, and he spat and touched his tongue. 34Then looking up to heaven, he sighed and said to him, "Ephphatha," that is, "Be opened." 35And immediately his ears were opened, his tongue was released, and he spoke plainly. 36Then Jesus *c* ordered them to tell no one; but the more he ordered them, the more zealously they proclaimed it. 37They were astounded beyond measure, saying, "He has done everything well; he even makes the deaf to hear and the mute to speak."

Feeding the Four Thousand

8 In those days when there was again a great crowd without anything to eat, he called his disciples and said to them, 2"I have compassion for the crowd, because they have been with me now for three days and have nothing to eat. 3If I send them away hungry to their homes, they will faint on the way—and some of them have come from a great distance." 4His disciples replied, "How can one feed these people with bread here in the desert?" 5He asked them, "How many loaves do you have?" They said, "Seven." 6Then he ordered the crowd to sit down on the ground; and he took the seven loaves, and after giving thanks he broke them and gave them to his disciples to distribute; and they distributed them to the crowd. 7They had also a few small fish; and after blessing them, he ordered that these too should be distributed. 8They ate and were filled; and they took up the broken pieces left over, seven baskets full. 9Now there were about four thousand people. And he sent them away. 10And immediately he got into the boat with his disciples and went to the district of Dalmanutha. *d*

The Demand for a Sign

11 The Pharisees came and began to argue with him, asking him for a sign from heaven, to test him. 12And he sighed deeply in his spirit and said, "Why does this generation ask for a sign? Truly I tell you, no sign will be given to this generation." 13And he left them, and getting into the boat again, he went across to the other side.

a Other ancient authorities add *and Sidon*
b Or *Lord*; other ancient authorities prefix *Yes*
c Gk *he*   d Other ancient authorities read *Mageda* or *Magdala*

8:1–38 *there was again a great crowd.* In this chapter, we are presented with disciples and Pharisees alike who still do not see who Jesus is or hear his message. The disciples doubt they can feed four thousand people (v 4) when they have recently fed five thousand! The Pharisees demand a sign (v 11) when Jesus has been offering "neon-bright" signs like healing and teaching and casting out demons. How often are we shown the love and mercy and power of God, but miss it altogether? These stories culminate in Jesus healing a blind man whose sight is so deteriorated that it takes two attempts to restore his sight completely (vv 23–25). Part of our work in spiritual formation is to open our eyes and ears to everything and everyone around us for signs of the presence of God and glimpses of God's coming kingdom.

The Yeast of the Pharisees and of Herod

14 Now the disciples[a] had forgotten to bring any bread; and they had only one loaf with them in the boat. 15And he cautioned them, saying, "Watch out—beware of the yeast of the Pharisees and the yeast of Herod."[b] 16They said to one another, "It is because we have no bread." 17And becoming aware of it, Jesus said to them, "Why are you talking about having no bread? Do you still not perceive or understand? Are your hearts hardened? 18Do you have eyes, and fail to see? Do you have ears, and fail to hear? And do you not remember? 19When I broke the five loaves for the five thousand, how many baskets full of broken pieces did you collect?" They said to him, "Twelve." 20"And the seven for the four thousand, how many baskets full of broken pieces did you collect?" And they said to him, "Seven." 21Then he said to them, "Do you not yet understand?"

Jesus Cures a Blind Man at Bethsaida

22 They came to Bethsaida. Some people[c] brought a blind man to him and begged him to touch him. 23He took the blind man by the hand and led him out of the village; and when he had put saliva on his eyes and laid his hands on him, he asked him, "Can you see anything?" 24And the man[d] looked up and said, "I can see people, but they look like trees, walking." 25Then Jesus[d] laid his hands on his eyes again; and he looked intently and his sight was restored, and he saw everything clearly. 26Then he sent him away to his home, saying, "Do not even go into the village."[e]

Peter's Declaration about Jesus

27 Jesus went on with his disciples to the villages of Caesarea Philippi; and on the way he asked his disciples, "Who do people say that I am?" 28And they answered him, "John the Baptist; and others, Elijah; and still others, one of the prophets." 29He asked them, "But who do you say that I am?" Peter answered him, "You are the Messiah."[f] 30And he sternly ordered them not to tell anyone about him.

Jesus Foretells His Death and Resurrection

31 Then he began to teach them that the Son of Man must undergo great suffering, and be rejected by the elders, the chief priests, and the scribes, and be killed, and after three days rise again. 32He said all this quite openly. And Peter took him aside and began to rebuke him. 33But turning and looking at his disciples, he rebuked Peter and said, "Get behind me, Satan! For you are setting your mind not on divine things but on human things."

34 He called the crowd with his disciples, and said to them, "If any want to become my followers, let them deny themselves and take up their cross and follow me. 35For those who want to save their life will lose it, and those who lose their life for my sake, and for the sake of the gospel,[g] will save it. 36For what will it profit them to gain the whole world and forfeit their life? 37Indeed, what can they give in return for their life? 38Those who are ashamed of me and of my words in this adulterous and sinful generation, of them the Son of Man will also be ashamed when he comes in the glory of his Father with the holy 9 angels." 1And he said to them, "Truly I tell you, there are some standing here who will not taste death until they see that the kingdom of God has come with[i] power."

a Gk they   b Other ancient authorities read the Herodians   c Gk They   d Gk he   e Other ancient authorities add or tell anyone in the village   f Or the Christ   g Other ancient authorities read lose their life for the sake of the gospel   h Other ancient authorities read and of mine   i Or in

8:27–34 who do you say that I am? This question of Jesus to the disciples marks the theological turning point of Mark's Gospel and is the question every one of us must answer. Once we, like Peter, have made our confession of faith, we have only taken the first step. The second step is the lifelong journey of living our confession fully and authentically. Jesus tells us what kind of Messiah he has come to be and therefore what kind of life we are called to live: a life of service and sacrifice. Discipleship is not for the faint-hearted! Here also is the first of three passion predictions by Jesus (v 31). Each prediction is followed by a story that shows how reluctant the disciples are to take up the cross and follow Jesus in his way (v 34).

[handwritten: How Shall we at II Jesus]
[handwritten: Suffering & pain makes us know how much we need Jesus]

The Transfiguration

[handwritten: wow!]

2 Six days later, Jesus took with him Peter and James and John, and led them up a high mountain apart, by themselves. And he was transfigured before them, [3] and his clothes became dazzling white, such as no one[a] on earth could bleach them. [4] And there appeared to them Elijah with Moses, who were talking with Jesus. [5] Then Peter said to Jesus, "Rabbi, it is good for us to be here; let us make three dwellings,[b] one for you, one for Moses, and one for Elijah." [6] He did not know what to say, for they were terrified. [7] Then a cloud overshadowed them, and from the cloud there came a voice, "This is my Son, the Beloved;[c] listen to him!" [8] Suddenly when they looked around, they saw no one with them any more, but only Jesus.

The Coming of Elijah

9 As they were coming down the mountain, he ordered them to tell no one about what they had seen, until after the Son of Man had risen from the dead. [10] So they kept the matter to themselves, questioning what this rising from the dead could mean. [11] Then they asked him, "Why do the scribes say that Elijah must come first?" [12] He said to them, "Elijah is indeed coming first to restore all things. How then is it written about the Son of Man, that he is to go through many sufferings and be treated with contempt? *[handwritten: HUH?]* [13] But I tell you that Elijah has come, and they did to him whatever they pleased, as it is written about him."

The Healing of a Boy with a Spirit

14 When they came to the disciples, they saw a great crowd around them, and some scribes arguing with them. [15] When the whole crowd saw him, they were immediately overcome with awe, and they ran forward to greet him. [16] He asked them, "What are you arguing about with them?" [17] Someone from the crowd answered him, "Teacher, I brought you my son; he has a spirit that makes him unable to speak; [18] and whenever it seizes him, it dashes him down; and he foams and grinds his teeth and becomes rigid; and I asked your disciples to cast it out, but they could not do so." [19] He answered them, "You faithless generation, how much longer must I be among you? How much longer must I put up with you? Bring him to me." [20] And they brought the boy[d] to him. When the spirit saw him, immediately it convulsed the boy,[d] and he fell on the ground and rolled about, foaming at the mouth. [21] Jesus[e] asked the father, "How long has this been happening to him?" And he said, "From childhood. [22] It has often cast him into the fire and into the water, to destroy him; but if you are able to do anything, have pity on us and help us." [23] Jesus said to him, "If you are able!—All things can be done for the one who believes." [24] Immediately the father of the child cried out,[f] "I believe; help my unbelief!" [25] When Jesus saw that a crowd came running together, he rebuked the unclean spirit, saying to it, "You spirit that keeps this boy from speaking and hearing, I command you, come out of him, and never enter him again!" [26] After crying out and convulsing him terribly, it came out, and the boy was like a corpse, so that most of them said, "He is dead." [27] But

a Gk *no fuller*   b Or *tents*   c Or *my beloved Son*
d Gk *him*   e Gk *He*   f Other ancient
authorities add *with tears*

9:2 SOLITUDE—*See* Spiritual Disciplines Index.

9:9 *As they were coming down the mountain.* Jesus and his inner circle, Peter, James, and John, have had a "mountaintop experience" (vv 2–8) in which everything seemed so clear and perfect and close to God. They cannot stay up there forever, however. Jesus leads them down to the challenges and opportunities of the daily life of faith. We can be grateful when we have such soaring experiences of closeness to God too. Yet our lives are lived in the daily pains and pleasures of the world.

9:24 *I believe; help my unbelief!* This is one of the most honest cries in all of Scripture. We believe in God's power to heal and to save. We want to believe in God's power to heal and to save. But even faithful people doubt. Jesus encourages this father to believe that all things are possible with God. His cry to Jesus is our own plea too.

Jesus took him by the hand and lifted him up, and he was able to stand. 28When he had entered the house, his disciples asked him privately, "Why could we not cast it out?" 29He said to them, "This kind can come out only through prayer." [a]

Jesus Again Foretells His Death and Resurrection

30 They went on from there and passed through Galilee. He did not want anyone to know it; 31for he was teaching his disciples, saying to them, "The Son of Man is to be betrayed into human hands, and they will kill him, and three days after being killed, he will rise again." 32But they did not understand what he was saying and were afraid to ask him.

Who Is the Greatest?

33 Then they came to Capernaum; and when he was in the house he asked them, "What were you arguing about on the way?" 34But they were silent, for on the way they had argued with one another who was the greatest. 35He sat down, called the twelve, and said to them, "Whoever wants to be first must be last of all and servant of all." 36Then he took a little child and put it among them; and taking it in his arms, he said to them, 37"Whoever welcomes one such child in my name welcomes me, and whoever welcomes me welcomes not me but the one who sent me."

Another Exorcist

38 John said to him, "Teacher, we saw someone [b] casting out demons in your name, and we tried to stop him, because he was not following us." 39But Jesus said, "Do not stop him; for no one who does a deed of power in my name will be able soon afterward to speak evil of me. 40Whoever is not against us is for us. 41For truly I tell you, whoever gives you a cup of water to drink because you bear the name of Christ will by no means lose the reward.

Temptations to Sin

42 "If any of you put a stumbling block before one of these little ones who believe in me, [c] it would be better for you if a great millstone were hung around your neck and you were thrown into the sea. 43If your hand causes you to stumble, cut it off; it is better for you to enter life maimed than to have two hands and to go to hell, [d] to the unquenchable fire. [e] 45And if your foot causes you to stumble, cut it off; it is better for you to enter life lame than to have two feet and to be thrown into hell. [d,e] 47And if your eye causes you to stumble, tear it out; it is better for you to enter the kingdom of God with one eye than to have two eyes and to be thrown into hell, [d] 48where their worm never dies, and the fire is never quenched.

a Other ancient authorities add and fasting
b Other ancient authorities add who does not follow us   c Other ancient authorities lack in me
d Gk Gehenna   e Verses 44 and 46 (which are identical with verse 48) are lacking in the best ancient authorities

---

9:29 PRAYER—See Spiritual Disciplines Index.

Responding
9:35 SERVICE. In spite of this teaching, two thousand years later we still cater to the richest, fairest, and most powerful by setting aside the best seats, the choicest food, and the finest amenities for them, while barely paying attention to those at the bottom of the social and political ladders. What drives this tendency to reward the successful and ignore the servant? As you go about your errands this week, make a special effort to treat present-day "servants"—checkers, janitors, waiters—in the same manner as you would a millionaire. What effect did this small action have on your soul? See also Spiritual Disciplines Index.

9:42–48 If any of you put a stumbling block. The sayings in this passage are harsh and hard to hear. However, Jesus is reminding us that we have a serious responsibility for the well-being and spiritual formation of others. Our own behavior and manner of life should be a demonstration of the gospel that does not lead people astray, but leads people to wholeness of life in Christ.

49 "For everyone will be salted with fire. *a*
50Salt is good; but if salt has lost its saltiness,
how can you season it?*b* Have salt in yourselves, and be at peace with one another."

Teaching about Divorce

10 He left that place and went to the region of Judea and*c* beyond the Jordan. And crowds again gathered around him;
and, as was his custom, he again taught them.

2 Some Pharisees came, and to test him
they asked, "Is it lawful for a man to divorce
his wife?" 3He answered them, "What did
Moses command you?" 4They said, "Moses
allowed a man to write a certificate of dismissal and to divorce her." 5But Jesus said to
them, "Because of your hardness of heart he
wrote this commandment for you. 6But from
the beginning of creation, 'God made them
male and female.' 7'For this reason a man
shall leave his father and mother and be
joined to his wife,*d* 8and the two shall become one flesh.' So they are no longer two,
but one flesh. 9Therefore what God has
joined together, let no one separate."

10 Then in the house the disciples asked
him again about this matter. 11He said to
them, "Whoever divorces his wife and marries another commits adultery against her;

12and if she divorces her husband and marries
another, she commits adultery."

Jesus Blesses Little Children

13 People were bringing little children to
him in order that he might touch them; and
the disciples spoke sternly to them. 14But
when Jesus saw this, he was indignant and
said to them, "Let the little children come to
me; do not stop them; for it is to such as these
that the kingdom of God belongs. 15Truly I tell
you, whoever does not receive the kingdom of
God as a little child will never enter it." 16And
he took them up in his arms, laid his hands on
them, and blessed them.

The Rich Man

17 As he was setting out on a journey, a
man ran up and knelt before him, and asked
him, "Good Teacher, what must I do to inherit eternal life?" 18Jesus said to him, "Why
do you call me good? No one is good but God
alone. 19You know the commandments: 'You
shall not murder; You shall not commit adul-

a Other ancient authorities either add or substitute
and every sacrifice will be salted with salt   *b* Or *how
can you restore its saltiness?*   *c* Other ancient
authorities lack *and*   *d* Other ancient authorities
lack *and be joined to his wife*

10:2–9 *Is it lawful for a man to divorce his wife?*
This question posed to Jesus is controversial—
and politically dangerous (see note on 6:14–29).
The issue of divorce was controversial because
there were several schools of thought with accompanying interpretations in Jesus' day. The
schools of Shammai, Hillel, and Akiba differed
from one another in what constituted grounds
for divorce. The Shammai interpretation did not
allow a man to divorce his wife unless he found
something "shameful" in her. The Pharisees
want to trap Jesus into taking sides with one
school of thought or another. Jesus avoids this
by offering a radically deeper understanding of
marriage. He asks them to quote the law (Deut
24:1–4) and then recalls God's intention for
marriage in creation from Genesis. Marriage is
not a legal contract that can be broken; it is
meant to be a gift of grace in which lives are
lived mutually in compassion and grace. Lives
joined in this way cannot be separated by

appealing to loopholes and legalities. Jesus
reminds them (and us) that laws allowing for
divorce were given to help us because of our
own human failing to live faithfully and fully
in covenantal love and commitment to each
other. Jesus pushes beyond the view of marriage as a "contract" that can easily be nullified.
He pushes people to understand marriage as a
loving commitment and mutual covenant. This
passage is not meant to hold us hostage to a
damaging, dangerous relationship, but encourages us to honor and uphold mutually loving
and respectful committed relationships.

10:14–15 *to such as these . . . the kingdom of
God belongs.* Jesus' all-inclusive love reaches out
not only to adult "tax collectors and sinners,"
but to little children, who are often neglected,
abused, or ignored by "grown-up" society. To
fully participate in the kingdom of God, we will
need to teach—and learn from—the children
and youth in our midst.

(handwritten margin note: HE WAS GALLED BY TIGHT LIVING BUT WAS NOT COMMENSURATE OR GENEROUS)

tery; You shall not steal; You shall not bear false witness; You shall not defraud; Honor your father and mother.' " 20He said to him, "Teacher, I have kept all these since my youth." 21Jesus, looking at him, loved him and said, "You lack one thing; go, sell what you own, and give the money *a* to the poor, and you will have treasure in heaven; then come, follow me." 22When he heard this, he was shocked and went away grieving, for he had many possessions.

23 Then Jesus looked around and said to his disciples, "How hard it will be for those who have wealth to enter the kingdom of God!" 24And the disciples were perplexed at these words. But Jesus said to them again, "Children, how hard it is *b* to enter the kingdom of God! 25It is easier for a camel to go through the eye of a needle than for someone who is rich to enter the kingdom of God." 26They were greatly astounded and said to one another, *c* "Then who can be saved?" 27Jesus looked at them and said, "For mortals it is impossible, but not for God; for God all things are possible."

(handwritten: Amen!!!)

28 Peter began to say to him, "Look, we have left everything and followed you." 29Jesus said, "Truly I tell you, there is no one who has left house or brothers or sisters or mother or father or children or fields, for my sake and for the sake of the good news, *d* 30who will not receive a hundredfold now in this age—houses, brothers and sisters, mothers and children, and fields, with persecutions—and in the age to come eternal life. 31But many who are first will be last, and the last will be first."

A Third Time Jesus Foretells His Death and Resurrection

32 They were on the road, going up to Jerusalem, and Jesus was walking ahead of them; they were amazed, and those who fol-

lowed were afraid. He took the twelve aside again and began to tell them what was to happen to him, 33saying, "See, we are going up to Jerusalem, and the Son of Man will be handed over to the chief priests and the scribes, and they will condemn him to death; then they will hand him over to the Gentiles; 34they will mock him, and spit upon him, and flog him, and kill him; and after three days he will rise again."

The Request of James and John

(handwritten: TOO MUCH FOR THEM TO TAKE IN)

35 James and John, the sons of Zebedee, came forward to him and said to him, "Teacher, we want you to do for us whatever we ask of you." 36And he said to them, "What is it you want me to do for you?" 37And they said to him, "Grant us to sit, one at your right hand and one at your left, in your glory." 38But Jesus said to them, "You do not know what you are asking. Are you able to drink the cup that I drink, or be baptized with the baptism that I am baptized with?" 39They replied, "We are able." Then Jesus said to them, "The cup that I drink you will drink; and with the baptism with which I am baptized, you will be baptized; 40but to sit at my right hand or at my left is not mine to grant, but it is for those for whom it has been prepared."

41 When the ten heard this, they began to be angry with James and John. 42So Jesus called them and said to them, "You know that among the Gentiles those whom they recognize as their rulers lord it over them, and their great ones are tyrants over them. 43But it is not so among you; but whoever wishes to become great among you must be your servant, 44and whoever wishes to be first among you must be slave of all. 45For the Son of Man came

a Gk lacks *the money*   *b* Other ancient authorities add *for those who trust in riches*   *c* Other ancient authorities read *to him*   *d* Or *gospel*

10:17–27 *go, sell what you own, and give the money to the poor.* This story unsettles those of us who have many possessions. Do we have to give away all of our possessions? We ought not to dismiss this demand simply because it is uncomfortable. Perhaps another point Jesus is making is that we can never earn enough—or

give away enough—to merit eternal life. It is impossible for us to "earn" eternal life, but what is impossible for us turns out to be God's free gift to each of us (v 27).

10:45 SERVICE—*See* Spiritual Disciplines Index.

not to be served but to serve, and to give his life a ransom for many."

The Healing of Blind Bartimaeus

46 They came to Jericho. As he and his disciples and a large crowd were leaving Jericho, Bartimaeus son of Timaeus, a blind beggar, was sitting by the roadside. [47]When he heard that it was Jesus of Nazareth, he began to shout out and say, "Jesus, Son of David, have mercy on me!" [48]Many sternly ordered him to be quiet, but he cried out even more loudly, "Son of David, have mercy on me!" [49]Jesus stood still and said, "Call him here." And they called the blind man, saying to him, "Take heart; get up, he is calling you." [50]So throwing off his cloak, he sprang up and came to Jesus. [51]Then Jesus said to him, "What do you want me to do for you?" The blind man said to him, "My teacher,[a] let me see again." [52]Jesus said to him, "Go; your faith has made you well." Immediately he regained his sight and followed him on the way.

Jesus' Triumphal Entry into Jerusalem

11 When they were approaching Jerusalem, at Bethphage and Bethany, near the Mount of Olives, he sent two of his disciples [2]and said to them, "Go into the village ahead of you, and immediately as you enter it, you will find tied there a colt that has never been ridden; untie it and bring it. [3]If anyone says to you, 'Why are you doing this?' just say this, 'The Lord needs it and will send it back here immediately.' " [4]They went away and found a colt tied near a door, outside in the street. As they were untying it, [5]some of the bystanders said to them, "What are you doing, untying the colt?" [6]They told them

what Jesus had said; and they allowed them to take it. [7]Then they brought the colt to Jesus and threw their cloaks on it; and he sat on it. [8]Many people spread their cloaks on the road, and others spread leafy branches that they had cut in the fields. [9]Then those who went ahead and those who followed were shouting,

"Hosanna!
   Blessed is the one who comes in the
      name of the Lord!
10   Blessed is the coming kingdom of our
      ancestor David!
   Hosanna in the highest heaven!"

11 Then he entered Jerusalem and went into the temple; and when he had looked around at everything, as it was already late, he went out to Bethany with the twelve.

Jesus Curses the Fig Tree

12 On the following day, when they came from Bethany, he was hungry. [13]Seeing in the distance a fig tree in leaf, he went to see whether perhaps he would find anything on it. When he came to it, he found nothing but leaves, for it was not the season for figs. [14]He said to it, "May no one ever eat fruit from you again." And his disciples heard it.

Jesus Cleanses the Temple

15 Then they came to Jerusalem. And he entered the temple and began to drive out those who were selling and those who were buying in the temple, and he overturned the tables of the money changers and the seats of those who sold doves; [16]and he would not allow anyone to carry anything through the

a Aramaic Rabbouni

10:46–52 *Bartimaeus, . . . a blind beggar, was sitting by the roadside.* This section of passion predictions (8:31; 9:31; 10:33–34) and teaching about the cost of discipleship began with the healing of a blind man (8:22–26) and now ends with the healing of blind Bartimaeus (see Introduction). After this, Jesus and the disciples enter Jerusalem and move toward the cross. This story reminds us that it is the Passion, death, and resurrection of Jesus that we need

to see most clearly if we are to truly understand who Jesus Christ is.

11:10 *Hosanna in the highest heaven!* It is easier to follow and praise God when everything seems to be going well, when God is meeting our expectations, and when faith is supported by those all around us. The strength of our faith is tested when all of these supports and assumptions begin to fall away.

temple. [17]He was teaching and saying, "Is it not written,

'My house shall be called a house of
prayer for all the nations'?
But you have made it a den of
robbers."

[18]And when the chief priests and the scribes heard it, they kept looking for a way to kill him; for they were afraid of him, because the whole crowd was spellbound by his teaching. [19]And when evening came, Jesus and his disciples[a] went out of the city.

The Lesson from the Withered Fig Tree

20 In the morning as they passed by, they saw the fig tree withered away to its roots. [21]Then Peter remembered and said to him, "Rabbi, look! The fig tree that you cursed has withered." [22]Jesus answered them, "Have[b] faith in God. [23]Truly I tell you, if you say to this mountain, 'Be taken up and thrown into the sea,' and if you do not doubt in your heart, but believe that what you say will come to pass, it will be done for you. [24]So I tell you, whatever you ask for in prayer, believe that you have received[c] it, and it will be yours.

25 "Whenever you stand praying, forgive, if you have anything against anyone; so that your Father in heaven may also forgive you your trespasses."[d]

Jesus' Authority Is Questioned

27 Again they came to Jerusalem. As he was walking in the temple, the chief priests, the scribes, and the elders came to him [28]and said, "By what authority are you doing these things? Who gave you this authority to do them?" [29]Jesus said to them, "I will ask you one question; answer me, and I will tell you by what authority I do these things. [30]Did the baptism of John come from heaven, or was it of human origin? Answer me." [31]They argued with one another, "If we say, 'From heaven,' he will say, 'Why then did you not believe him?' [32]But shall we say, 'Of human origin'?"—they were afraid of the crowd, for all regarded John as truly a prophet. [33]So they answered Jesus, "We do not know." And Jesus

said to them, "Neither will I tell you by what authority I am doing these things."

The Parable of the Wicked Tenants

12 Then he began to speak to them in parables. "A man planted a vineyard, put a fence around it, dug a pit for the wine press, and built a watchtower; then he leased it to tenants and went to another country. [2]When the season came, he sent a slave to the tenants to collect from them his share of the produce of the vineyard. [3]But they seized him, and beat him, and sent him away empty-handed. [4]And again he sent another slave to them; this one they beat over the head and insulted. [5]Then he sent another, and that one they killed. And so it was with many others; some they beat, and others they killed. [6]He had still one other, a beloved son. Finally he sent him to them, saying, 'They will respect my son.' [7]But those tenants said to one another, 'This is the heir; come, let us kill him, and the inheritance will be ours.' [8]So they seized him, killed him, and threw him out of the vineyard. [9]What then will the owner of the vineyard do? He will come and destroy the tenants and give the vineyard to others. [10]Have you not read this scripture:

'The stone that the builders rejected
has become the cornerstone;[e]
[11] this was the Lord's doing,
and it is amazing in our eyes'?"

12 When they realized that he had told this parable against them, they wanted to arrest him, but they feared the crowd. So they left him and went away.

The Question about Paying Taxes

13 Then they sent to him some Pharisees and some Herodians to trap him in what he said. [14]And they came and said to him, "Teacher, we know that you are sincere, and show deference to no one; for you do not re-

a Gk they: other ancient authorities read he
b Other ancient authorities read "If you have
c Other ancient authorities read are receiving
d Other ancient authorities add verse 26, "But if you do not forgive, neither will your Father in heaven forgive your trespasses." e Or keystone

---

11:17, 24, 25 PRAYER—See Spiritual Disciplines Index.

gard people with partiality, but teach the way of God in accordance with truth. Is it lawful to pay taxes to the emperor, or not? 15Should we pay them, or should we not?" But knowing their hypocrisy, he said to them, "Why are you putting me to the test? Bring me a denarius and let me see it." 16And they brought one. Then he said to them, "Whose head is this, and whose title?" They answered, "The emperor's." 17Jesus said to them, "Give to the emperor the things that are the emperor's, and to God the things that are God's." And they were utterly amazed at him.

The Question about the Resurrection

18 Some Sadducees, who say there is no resurrection, came to him and asked him a question, saying, 19"Teacher, Moses wrote for us that if a man's brother dies, leaving a wife but no child, the man*a* shall marry the widow and raise up children for his brother. 20There were seven brothers; the first married and, when he died, left no children; 21and the second married the widow*b* and died, leaving no children; and the third likewise; 22none of the seven left children. Last of all the woman herself died. 23In the resurrection*c* whose

wife will she be? For the seven had married her."

24 Jesus said to them, "Is not this the reason you are wrong, that you know neither the scriptures nor the power of God? 25For when they rise from the dead, they neither marry nor are given in marriage, but are like angels in heaven. 26And as for the dead being raised, have you not read in the book of Moses, in the story about the bush, how God said to him, 'I am the God of Abraham, the God of Isaac, and the God of Jacob'? 27He is God not of the dead, but of the living; you are quite wrong."

The First Commandment

28 One of the scribes came near and heard them disputing with one another, and seeing that he answered them well, he asked him, "Which commandment is the first of all?" 29Jesus answered, "The first is, 'Hear, O Israel: the Lord our God, the Lord is one; 30you shall love the Lord your God with all your heart, and with all your soul, and with all your mind, and with all your strength.' 31The

a Gk *his brother*   *b* Gk *her*   *c* Other ancient authorities add *when they rise*

12:13–17 *Is it lawful to pay taxes to the emperor?* This is yet another question asked in order to trap Jesus. The Pharisees and Herodians think that Jesus will either make himself unpopular with the crowds by supporting Roman rule and its imposition of taxes or make himself a political target by rejecting the payment of the required Roman tribute. Jesus does not get caught in the trap. His answer is not political, but theological; it focuses not on what belongs to the emperor, but on what belongs to God. How are Christians, whose citizenship is in the kingdom of God, to be citizens of a particular country here on earth? Jesus shows in this lesson that the political and the religious are not always in conflict. Some things rightly belong to the state, but other things belong to God alone. Christians have had to decide, in times of conflict and oppression and injustice, to honor God above unjust laws and unfaithful practices. Our highest loyalty belongs to God and to the way of life that has been made known to us in Jesus Christ. Jesus exposes his questioners'

hypocrisy by asking them to produce for him a Roman coin, which Jews were not supposed to possess because it bore the image of the emperor and proclaimed him divine. Jesus' questioners apparently were able to pull the coin easily from their own pockets!

12:28–34 *Which commandment is the first?* In the midst of entrapments and hard questions, in the face of enemies and threats, Jesus speaks of the commandments to love God and neighbor. These foundational commandments are at the center of Jewish theology and life (Deut 6:4–9; Lev 19:18). They make it clear that to love God and to practice justice by loving neighbor are much more important than performing religious rituals or cultic sacrifices. This is hard spiritual work for even the most mature Christians among us, but by loving God and neighbor we most faithfully fulfill the whole law of God. In a section that contains one hostile question after another for Jesus, the scribe who asks this question opens the door for a welcome affirmation of Jesus' teaching.

second is this, 'You shall love your neighbor as yourself.' There is no other commandment greater than these." 32Then the scribe said to him, "You are right, Teacher; you have truly said that 'he is one, and besides him there is no other'; 33and 'to love him with all the heart, and with all the understanding, and with all the strength,' and 'to love one's neighbor as oneself,'—this is much more important than all whole burnt offerings and sacrifices." 34When Jesus saw that he answered wisely, he said to him, "You are not far from the kingdom of God." After that no one dared to ask him any question.

The Question about David's Son

35 While Jesus was teaching in the temple, he said, "How can the scribes say that the Messiah*a* is the son of David? 36David himself, by the Holy Spirit, declared,

'The Lord said to my Lord,
"Sit at my right hand,
    until I put your enemies under your
        feet." '

37David himself calls him Lord; so how can he be his son?" And the large crowd was listening to him with delight.

Jesus Denounces the Scribes

38 As he taught, he said, "Beware of the scribes, who like to walk around in long robes, and to be greeted with respect in the marketplaces, 39and to have the best seats in the synagogues and places of honor at banquets! 40They devour widows' houses and for the sake of appearance say long prayers. They will receive the greater condemnation."

The Widow's Offering

41 He sat down opposite the treasury, and watched the crowd putting money into the treasury. Many rich people put in large sums. 42A poor widow came and put in two small copper coins, which are worth a penny. 43Then he called his disciples and said to them, "Truly I tell you, this poor widow has put in more than all those who are contributing to the treasury. 44For all of them have contributed out of their abundance; but she out of her poverty has put in everything she had, all she had to live on."

The Destruction of the Temple Foretold

13 As he came out of the temple, one of his disciples said to him, "Look, Teacher, what large stones and what large buildings!" 2Then Jesus asked him, "Do you see these great buildings? Not one stone will be left here upon another; all will be thrown down."

3 When he was sitting on the Mount of Olives opposite the temple, Peter, James, John, and Andrew asked him privately, 4"Tell us, when will this be, and what will be the sign that all these things are about to be accomplished?" 5Then Jesus began to say to them, "Beware that no one leads you astray. 6Many will come in my name and say, 'I am he!'*b* and they will lead many astray. 7When you hear of wars and rumors of wars, do not be alarmed; this must take place, but the end is still to come. 8For nation will rise against nation, and kingdom against kingdom; there will be earthquakes in various places; there will be famines. This is but the beginning of the birth pangs.

Persecution Foretold

9 "As for yourselves, beware; for they will hand you over to councils; and you will be beaten in synagogues; and you will stand before governors and kings because of me, as a testimony to them. 10And the good news*c* must first be proclaimed to all nations.

a Or *the Christ*   *b* Gk *I am*   *c* Gk *gospel*

12:33 SACRIFICE—*See* Spiritual Disciplines Index.

12:41–44 *A poor widow . . . put in two small copper coins.* In the midst of religious and political power brokers, surrounded by the large, impressive buildings of Jerusalem, a lone, poor widow makes her quiet way into the Temple and gives her two small coins. She is the towering example of faithfulness and generosity. This widow, who has so little materially, has great faith. She knows that her welfare depends on God and her neighbors, not her own resources. Sacrifice is an essential part of spiritual formation.

11 When they bring you to trial and hand you over, do not worry beforehand about what you are to say; but say whatever is given you at that time, for it is not you who speak, but the Holy Spirit. 12 Brother will betray brother to death, and a father his child, and children will rise against parents and have them put to death; 13 and you will be hated by all because of my name. But the one who endures to the end will be saved.

The Desolating Sacrilege

14 "But when you see the desolating sacrilege set up where it ought not to be (let the reader understand), then those in Judea must flee to the mountains; 15 the one on the housetop must not go down or enter the house to take anything away; 16 the one in the field must not turn back to get a coat. 17 Woe to those who are pregnant and to those who are nursing infants in those days! 18 Pray that it may not be in winter. 19 For in those days there will be suffering, such as has not been from the beginning of the creation that God created until now, no, and never will be. 20 And if the Lord had not cut short those days, no one would be saved; but for the sake of the elect, whom he chose, he has cut short those days. 21 And if anyone says to you at that time, 'Look! Here is the Messiah!'a or 'Look! There he is!'—do not believe it. 22 False messiahs b and false prophets will appear and produce signs and omens, to lead astray, if

possible, the elect. 23 But be alert; I have already told you everything.

The Coming of the Son of Man

24 "But in those days, after that suffering,
   the sun will be darkened,
      and the moon will not give its light,
25 and the stars will be falling from heaven,
      and the powers in the heavens will be
         shaken.
26 Then they will see 'the Son of Man coming in clouds' with great power and glory. 27 Then he will send out the angels, and gather his elect from the four winds, from the ends of the earth to the ends of heaven.

The Lesson of the Fig Tree

28 "From the fig tree learn its lesson: as soon as its branch becomes tender and puts forth its leaves, you know that summer is near. 29 So also, when you see these things taking place, you know that he c is near, at the very gates. 30 Truly I tell you, this generation will not pass away until all these things have taken place. 31 Heaven and earth will pass away, but my words will not pass away.

The Necessity for Watchfulness

32 "But about that day or hour no one knows, neither the angels in heaven, nor the Son, but only the Father. 33 Beware, keep alert; d for you do not know when the time

a Or the Christ   b Or christs   c Or it
d Other ancient authorities add and pray

13:24–27 *the Son of Man.* In Mark, in addition to "Christ," the "son of David," and the "Son of God," Jesus is also called "Son of Man," which seems to have been Jesus' favorite way of designating who he is and what he has come to do. An Old Testament term, "son of man" appears in Psalms (referring to humankind in general, see NRSV note to 8:4) and in such texts as Daniel 7, *1 Enoch* 37–71, and 2 Esdras 13. It is used in Ezekiel as the term for the prophet. The other titles listed above for Jesus are associated with civil kingship, but the "Son of Man" has strictly religious meanings. Jesus uses it of himself at particularly meaningful moments, for example, in his three passion predictions (8:31; 9:31; 10:33–34), when he speaks of giving his life

as a ransom for many (10:45), and here when he talks about the fulfillment of the end of time. Other significant uses are in 2:10; 2:28; and 9:9. His coming again will bring both judgment and mercy. This is the term that describes so well God's work in Jesus on our behalf.

13:33 *for you do not know when the time will come.* Over the centuries, people have looked for signs and made predictions about the end of the world. Jesus is much more concerned about how we live our lives each day. Teaching, proclaiming, healing, feeding—these are our daily acts of discipleship. The important message is, "Keep alert." No one knows when the end will come except God. We keep alert when we live each day faithfully loving God and neighbor.

will come. [34]It is like a man going on a journey, when he leaves home and puts his slaves in charge, each with his work, and commands the doorkeeper to be on the watch. [35]Therefore, keep awake—for you do not know when the master of the house will come, in the evening, or at midnight, or at cockcrow, or at dawn, [36]or else he may find you asleep when he comes suddenly. [37]And what I say to you I say to all: Keep awake.'

The Plot to Kill Jesus

14 It was two days before the Passover and the festival of Unleavened Bread. The chief priests and the scribes were looking for a way to arrest Jesus[a] by stealth and kill him; [2]for they said, "Not during the festival, or there may be a riot among the people."

The Anointing at Bethany

3 While he was at Bethany in the house of Simon the leper,[b] as he sat at the table, a woman came with an alabaster jar of very costly ointment of nard, and she broke open the jar and poured the ointment on his head. [4]But some were there who said to one another in anger, "Why was the ointment wasted in this way? [5]For this ointment could have been sold for more than three hundred denarii,[c] and the money given to the poor." And they scolded her. [6]But Jesus said, "Let her alone; why do you trouble her? She has performed a good service for me. [7]For you always have the poor with you, and you can show kindness to them whenever you wish; but you will not always have me. [8]She has done what she could; she has anointed my body beforehand for its burial. [9]Truly I tell you, wherever the good news[d] is proclaimed in the whole world, what she has done will be told in remembrance of her."

Judas Agrees to Betray Jesus

10 Then Judas Iscariot, who was one of the twelve, went to the chief priests in order to betray him to them. [11]When they heard it, they were greatly pleased, and promised to give him money. So he began to look for an opportunity to betray him.

The Passover with the Disciples

12 On the first day of Unleavened Bread, when the Passover lamb is sacrificed, his disciples said to him, "Where do you want us to go and make the preparations for you to eat the Passover?" [13]So he sent two of his disciples, saying to them, "Go into the city, and a man carrying a jar of water will meet you; follow him, [14]and wherever he enters, say to the owner of the house, 'The Teacher asks, Where is my guest room where I may eat the Passover with my disciples?' [15]He will show you a large room upstairs, furnished and ready. Make preparations for us there." [16]So the disciples set out and went to the city, and

---

a Gk *him*   *b* The terms *leper* and *leprosy* can refer to several diseases   *c* The denarius was the usual day's wage for a laborer   *d* Or *gospel*

14:3–9 *she . . . poured the ointment on his head.* In Israel, kings were designated by anointing their heads with oil (see 1 Sam 10:1; 2 Kings 9:6). In this extravagant gesture, the woman pours the whole vial, not just a few drops, onto Jesus' head. Some see in this the symbolism that Jesus is indeed king of Israel. However, Jesus uses her act not to point to his kingship, but to his death. After all their instruction, the disciples still cannot see what this woman of faith is able to see. By saying her act will be remembered and told (v 9), Jesus indicates that the gospel will indeed be preached to the whole world. This story invites us to consider how fully we offer our own actions and resources to God in Christ, and how easy it is for us to misjudge the faithfulness of others. Jesus does not ask us to judge the worth of another person's gift. Every gift given in love and service to God is to be received with gratitude. Feeding the poor and showing kindness in a troubled time are both acceptable ways of loving God.

Responding
14:3–9 SACRIFICE. In *The Spirit of the Disciples* Dallas Willard defines sacrifice as "total abandonment to God." Does this definition fit the woman's lavish gift to Jesus? What could you do that would be as lavish? Are there things that keep you from doing it? *See also* Spiritual Disciplines Index.

found everything as he had told them; and they prepared the Passover meal.

17 When it was evening, he came with the twelve. 18 And when they had taken their places and were eating, Jesus said, "Truly I tell you, one of you will betray me, one who is eating with me." 19 They began to be distressed and to say to him one after another, "Surely, not I?" 20 He said to them, "It is one of the twelve, one who is dipping bread[a] into the bowl[b] with me. 21 For the Son of Man goes as it is written of him, but woe to that one by whom the Son of Man is betrayed! It would have been better for that one not to have been born."

The Institution of the Lord's Supper

22 While they were eating, he took a loaf of bread, and after blessing it he broke it, gave it to them, and said, "Take; this is my body." 23 Then he took a cup, and after giving thanks he gave it to them, and all of them drank from it. 24 He said to them, "This is my blood of the[c] covenant, which is poured out for many. 25 Truly I tell you, I will never again drink of the fruit of the vine until that day when I drink it new in the kingdom of God."

Peter's Denial Foretold

26 When they had sung the hymn, they went out to the Mount of Olives. 27 And Jesus said to them, "You will all become deserters; for it is written,

'I will strike the shepherd,
    and the sheep will be scattered.'

28 But after I am raised up, I will go before you to Galilee." 29 Peter said to him, "Even though all become deserters, I will not." 30 Jesus said to

him, "Truly I tell you, this day, this very night, before the cock crows twice, you will deny me three times." 31 But he said vehemently, "Even though I must die with you, I will not deny you." And all of them said the same.

Jesus Prays in Gethsemane

32 They went to a place called Gethsemane; and he said to his disciples, "Sit here while I pray." 33 He took with him Peter and James and John, and began to be distressed and agitated. 34 And he said to them, "I am deeply grieved, even to death; remain here, and keep awake." 35 And going a little farther, he threw himself on the ground and prayed that, if it were possible, the hour might pass from him. 36 He said, "Abba,[d] Father, for you all things are possible; remove this cup from me; yet, not what I want, but what you want." 37 He came and found them sleeping; and he said to Peter, "Simon, are you asleep? Could you not keep awake one hour? 38 Keep awake and pray that you may not come into the time of trial;[e] the spirit indeed is willing, but the flesh is weak." 39 And again he went away and prayed, saying the same words. 40 And once more he came and found them sleeping, for their eyes were very heavy; and they did not know what to say to him. 41 He came a third time and said to them, "Are you still sleeping and taking your rest? Enough! The hour has come; the Son of Man is betrayed into the hands of sinners. 42 Get up, let us be going. See, my betrayer is at hand."

---

a Gk lacks *bread*   b Other ancient authorities read *same bowl*   c Other ancient authorities add *new*   d Aramaic for *Father*   e Or *into temptation*

14:17–21, 26–42 *one of you will betray me.* In these passages, the disciples fail again and again. When Jesus says one will betray him, they all say, "Surely not I?" (vv 18–19). When Jesus tells Peter he will deny Jesus, Peter is sure he could never do such a thing (vv 30–31). And Peter, James, and John keep falling asleep just when Jesus needs them most (vv 32–42). We may find here an odd comfort because we too betray, deny, and practice a drowsy discipleship. The very first disciples shared our human weaknesses.

14:32–39 PRAYER—*See* Spiritual Disciplines Index.

14:35–36 *he . . . prayed.* Jesus shared our humanity and sympathizes with our weaknesses. In this prayer Jesus is distressed before God. He asks God to let the hour pass by him, to remove the cup from him. Jesus, though, ends his prayer by giving us a model for all our prayers: "Yet, not what I want, but what you want." Jesus does not fall into our sin of expecting God to give us what we want, but is obedient to God even to the point of death (Heb 4:15). This is a prayer that comes from a lifetime of spiritual formation.

The Betrayal and Arrest of Jesus

43 Immediately, while he was still speaking, Judas, one of the twelve, arrived; and with him there was a crowd with swords and clubs, from the chief priests, the scribes, and the elders. 44Now the betrayer had given them a sign, saying, "The one I will kiss is the man; arrest him and lead him away under guard." 45So when he came, he went up to him at once and said, "Rabbi!" and kissed him. 46Then they laid hands on him and arrested him. 47But one of those who stood near drew his sword and struck the slave of the high priest, cutting off his ear. 48Then Jesus said to them, "Have you come out with swords and clubs to arrest me as though I were a bandit? 49Day after day I was with you in the temple teaching, and you did not arrest me. But let the scriptures be fulfilled." 50All of them deserted him and fled.

51 A certain young man was following him, wearing nothing but a linen cloth. They caught hold of him, 52but he left the linen cloth and ran off naked.

Jesus before the Council

53 They took Jesus to the high priest; and all the chief priests, the elders, and the scribes were assembled. 54Peter had followed him at a distance, right into the courtyard of the high priest; and he was sitting with the guards, warming himself at the fire. 55Now the chief priests and the whole council were looking for testimony against Jesus to put him to death; but they found none. 56For many gave false testimony against him, and their testimony did not agree. 57Some stood up and gave false testimony against him, saying, 58"We heard him say, 'I will destroy this temple that is made with hands, and in three days I will build another, not made with hands.' " 59But even on this point their testimony did not agree. 60Then the high priest stood up before them and asked Jesus, "Have you no answer? What is it that they testify against you?" 61But he was silent and did not answer. Again the high priest asked him, "Are you the Messiah,[a] the Son of the Blessed One?" 62Jesus said, "I am; and

'you will see the Son of Man
    seated at the right hand of the Power,'
    and 'coming with the clouds of
        heaven.' "

63Then the high priest tore his clothes and said, "Why do we still need witnesses? 64You have heard his blasphemy! What is your decision?" All of them condemned him as deserving death. 65Some began to spit on him, to blindfold him, and to strike him, saying to him, "Prophesy!" The guards also took him over and beat him.

Peter Denies Jesus

66 While Peter was below in the courtyard, one of the servant-girls of the high priest came by. 67When she saw Peter warming himself, she stared at him and said, "You also were with Jesus, the man from Nazareth." 68But he denied it, saying, "I do not know or understand what you are talking about." And he went out into the forecourt.[b] Then the cock crowed.[c] 69And the servant-girl, on seeing him, began again to say to the bystanders, "This man is one of them." 70But again he denied it. Then after a little while the bystanders again said to Peter, "Certainly you are one of them; for you are a Galilean." 71But he began to curse, and he swore an oath, "I do not know this man you are talking about." 72At that moment the cock crowed for the second time. Then Peter remembered that Jesus had said to him, "Before the cock crows twice, you will deny me three times." And he broke down and wept.

Jesus before Pilate

15 As soon as it was morning, the chief priests held a consultation with the elders and scribes and the whole council. They bound Jesus, led him away, and hand-

a Or the Christ   b Or gateway   c Other ancient authorities lack Then the cock crowed

---

15:1–32 *They bound Jesus . . . and handed him over to Pilate.* In these passages on the conviction, torture, and mocking of Jesus leading up to his death, we must be careful not to look on at a distance at those mentioned in the story. Instead, we may consider how we are like the

ed him over to Pilate. [2]Pilate asked him, "Are you the King of the Jews?" He answered him, "You say so." [3]Then the chief priests accused him of many things. [4]Pilate asked him again, "Have you no answer? See how many charges they bring against you." [5]But Jesus made no further reply, so that Pilate was amazed.

Pilate Hands Jesus over to Be Crucified

6 Now at the festival he used to release a prisoner for them, anyone for whom they asked. [7]Now a man called Barabbas was in prison with the rebels who had committed murder during the insurrection. [8]So the crowd came and began to ask Pilate to do for them according to his custom. [9]Then he answered them, "Do you want me to release for you the King of the Jews?" [10]For he realized that it was out of jealousy that the chief priests had handed him over. [11]But the chief priests stirred up the crowd to have him release Barabbas for them instead. [12]Pilate spoke to them again, "Then what do you wish me to do[a] with the man you call[b] the King of the Jews?" [13]They shouted back, "Crucify him!" [14]Pilate asked them, "Why, what evil has he done?" But they shouted all the more, "Crucify him!" [15]So Pilate, wishing to satisfy the crowd, released Barabbas for them; and after flogging Jesus, he handed him over to be crucified.

The Soldiers Mock Jesus

16 Then the soldiers led him into the courtyard of the palace (that is, the governor's headquarters[c]); and they called together the whole cohort. [17]And they clothed him in a purple cloak; and after twisting some thorns into a crown, they put it on him. [18]And they began saluting him, "Hail, King of the Jews!" [19]They struck his head with a reed, spat upon him, and knelt down in homage to him. [20]After mocking him, they stripped him of the purple cloak and put his own clothes on him. Then they led him out to crucify him.

The Crucifixion of Jesus

21 They compelled a passer-by, who was coming in from the country, to carry his cross; it was Simon of Cyrene, the father of Alexander and Rufus. [22]Then they brought Jesus[d] to the place called Golgotha (which means the place of a skull). [23]And they offered him wine mixed with myrrh; but he did not take it. [24]And they crucified him, and divided his clothes among them, casting lots to decide what each should take.

25 It was nine o'clock in the morning when they crucified him. [26]The inscription of the charge against him read, "The King of the Jews." [27]And with him they crucified two bandits, one on his right and one on his left.[e] [29]Those who passed by derided[f] him, shaking their heads and saying, "Aha! You who would destroy the temple and build it in three days, [30]save yourself, and come down from the cross!" [31]In the same way the chief priests, along with the scribes, were also mocking him among themselves and saying, "He saved others; he cannot save himself. [32]Let the Messiah,[g] the King of Israel, come down from the cross now, so that we may see and believe." Those who were crucified with him also taunted him.

The Death of Jesus

33 When it was noon, darkness came over the whole land[h] until three in the afternoon. [34]At three o'clock Jesus cried out with a loud voice, "Eloi, Eloi, lema sabachthani?" which means, "My God, my God, why have you forsaken me?"[i] [35]When some of the bystanders heard it, they said, "Listen, he is calling for

a Other ancient authorities read what should I do
b Other ancient authorities lack the man you call
c Gk the praetorium   d Gk him   e Other
ancient authorities add verse 28, And the scripture
was fulfilled that says, "And he was counted among the
lawless."   f Or blasphemed   g Or the Christ
h Or earth   i Other ancient authorities read
made me a reproach

people who played a part in Jesus' crucifixion. As we enter the story and find ourselves at the cross, our task is to establish common ground with the chief priests and scribes, Pilate, the soldiers, Simon of Cyrene, the two bandits. The

chances are high that we will recognize ways in which we have mocked, contributed to suffering, or been a mere bystander in the way of Jesus and in our relationship with those whom Christ loves and comes to save.

Elijah." 36And someone ran, filled a sponge with sour wine, put it on a stick, and gave it to him to drink, saying, "Wait, let us see whether Elijah will come to take him down." 37Then Jesus gave a loud cry and breathed his last. 38And the curtain of the temple was torn in two, from top to bottom. 39Now when the centurion, who stood facing him, saw that in this way he*a* breathed his last, he said, "Truly this man was God's Son!"*b*

40 There were also women looking on from a distance; among them were Mary Magdalene, and Mary the mother of James the younger and of Joses, and Salome. 41These used to follow him and provided for him when he was in Galilee; and there were many other women who had come up with him to Jerusalem.

The Burial of Jesus

42 When evening had come, and since it was the day of Preparation, that is, the day before the sabbath, 43Joseph of Arimathea, a respected member of the council, who was also himself waiting expectantly for the kingdom of God, went boldly to Pilate and asked for the body of Jesus. 44Then Pilate wondered if he were already dead; and summoning the centurion, he asked him whether he had been dead for some time. 45When he learned from the centurion that he was dead, he granted the body to Joseph. 46Then Joseph*c* bought a linen cloth, and taking down the body,*d* wrapped it in the linen cloth, and laid it in a tomb that had been hewn out of the rock. He then rolled a stone against the door of the tomb. 47Mary Magdalene and Mary the mother of Joses saw where the body*d* was laid.

The Resurrection of Jesus

16 When the sabbath was over, Mary Magdalene, and Mary the mother of James, and Salome bought spices, so that they might go and anoint him. 2And very early on the first day of the week, when the sun had risen, they went to the tomb. 3They had been saying to one another, "Who will roll away the stone for us from the entrance to the tomb?" 4When they looked up, they saw that the stone, which was very large, had already been rolled back. 5As they entered the tomb, they saw a young man, dressed in a white robe, sitting on the right side; and they were alarmed. 6But he said to them, "Do not be alarmed; you are looking for Jesus of Nazareth, who was crucified. He has been raised; he is not here. Look, there is the place they laid him. 7But go, tell his disciples and Peter that he is going ahead of you to Galilee; there you will see him, just as he told you." 8So they went out and fled from the tomb, for terror and amazement had seized them; and they said nothing to anyone, for they were afraid.*e*

a Other ancient authorities add *cried out and*
b Or *a son of God*   c Gk *he*   d Gk *it*   e Some of the most ancient authorities bring the book to a close at the end of verse 8. One authority concludes the book with the shorter ending; others include the shorter ending and then continue with verses 9-20. In most authorities verses 9-20 follow immediately after verse 8, though in some of these authorities the passage is marked as being doubtful.

15:38–39 *Truly this man was God's Son!* True to the rest of his Gospel, Mark places this dramatic confession of faith in the words of an "outsider." At the cross, a Roman soldier recognizes who Jesus is. The barriers we put up between people of different races, nationalities, economic conditions, and other external distinctions are torn apart, rendered useless, in Jesus Christ, as surely as the curtain in the Temple was torn from top to bottom. The whole Gospel of Mark has been inviting and encouraging this confession of faith in Jesus Christ, the Son of God. A diverse "congregation" has gathered around him along the way.

16:8 *they said nothing to anyone, for they were afraid.* See the Introduction for more on this ending of the Gospel. This ending leaves us wanting, needing to say more. Mark would be pleased, for proclaiming the good news of Jesus Christ, the Son of God, is exactly what the whole Gospel has been encouraging and challenging us to do. The two additional endings show that we continue the gospel as we tell the good news of Jesus Christ, the Son of God, with our own lives and words and actions.

THE SHORTER ENDING OF MARK

⟦And all that had been commanded them they told briefly to those around Peter. And afterward Jesus himself sent out through them, from east to west, the sacred and imperishable proclamation of eternal salvation. *a*⟧

THE LONGER ENDING OF MARK

Jesus Appears to Mary Magdalene

9 ⟦Now after he rose early on the first day of the week, he appeared first to Mary Magdalene, from whom he had cast out seven demons. 10She went out and told those who had been with him, while they were mourning and weeping. 11But when they heard that he was alive and had been seen by her, they would not believe it.

Jesus Appears to Two Disciples

12 After this he appeared in another form to two of them, as they were walking into the country. 13And they went back and told the rest, but they did not believe them.

Jesus Commissions the Disciples

14 Later he appeared to the eleven themselves as they were sitting at the table; and he upbraided them for their lack of faith and stubbornness, because they had not believed those who saw him after he had risen. *b* 15And he said to them, "Go into all the world and proclaim the good news *c* to the whole creation. 16The one who believes and is baptized will be saved; but the one who does not believe will be condemned. 17And these signs will accompany those who believe: by using my name they will cast out demons; they will speak in new tongues; 18they will pick up snakes in their hands, *d* and if they drink any deadly thing, it will not hurt them; they will lay their hands on the sick, and they will recover."

The Ascension of Jesus

19 So then the Lord Jesus, after he had spoken to them, was taken up into heaven and sat down at the right hand of God. 20And they went out and proclaimed the good news everywhere, while the Lord worked with them and confirmed the message by the signs that accompanied it. *e*⟧

a Other ancient authorities add *Amen*   *b* Other ancient authorities add, in whole or in part, *And they excused themselves, saying, "This age of lawlessness and unbelief is under Satan, who does not allow the truth and power of God to prevail over the unclean things of the spirits. Therefore reveal your righteousness now"—thus they spoke to Christ. And Christ replied to them, "The term of years of Satan's power has been fulfilled, but other terrible things draw near. And for those who have sinned I was handed over to death, that they may return to the truth and sin no more, that they may inherit the spiritual and imperishable glory of righteousness that is in heaven."*   *c* Or *gospel*   *d* Other ancient authorities lack *in their hands*   *e* Other ancient authorities add *Amen*

Responding
16:20 THE WITH-GOD LIFE. "The Lord worked with them and confirmed the message by the signs that accompanied it." The Lord was the disciples' co-worker! This week as you serve in an office you hold in your church, in Sunday school, on an evangelism team, or during a call on the sick, try to hold in your mind that you are not alone, that the Lord is your co-worker in bringing the kingdom of God upon the earth. See how this affects your service. *See also* Spiritual Disciplines Index.

THE GOSPEL ACCORDING TO

LUKE

Luke gives us a Gospel with many episodes from Christ's life found in no other Gospel. Much of this uniqueness relies on Luke's inclusion of parables and events that have as the central characters women, the poor, or those tagged as the trash of society. People who are placed on the margins because they are considered inferior due to race, gender, age, economics, or politics find a significant place in Luke's portrayal of the life of Jesus. Part of this emphasis is due to Luke's ability to see the crucifixion and resurrection as ushering in a second exodus comparable to the first exodus that took place under Moses.

The key verse in Luke's perception of this second exodus is given in his account of the transfiguration, in which Moses and Elijah talk with Christ about the exodus, or departure, he is about to complete in Jerusalem (9:31). The Greek word used here is the same one used to give the second book of the Bible its name, the book that tells us the story of Moses, the freeing of the Hebrew slaves in Egypt, and the creation of Israel. No other Gospel writer uses this term, only Luke. It is clear that he envisions Christ's Passion as sparking another exodus, a greater exodus than the first, because this exodus will be led not by Moses, but by the Messiah, and this Messiah will liberate from slavery not only the Hebrew people, the Jews, but all people of all races, female, male, poor, rich, old, young—all generations who choose to believe in Jesus as Messiah, Savior, and Lord.

Nor is the freedom offered limited to a breaking of the physical chains of slavery. It is extended to all the forms of slavery that sin and evil use to bind the human spirit. It brings the promise of unending life and love and liberty as well as an unfettered relationship with God. No wonder this vision of Christ's exodus excites Luke and inspires him to include personalities, events, and stories that portray in primary colors the diverse humanity that Christ will set free when he dies on Golgotha.

See also "The With-God Life" essay for this section of the Bible,
"The People of God with Immanuel," pp. 1785–89.

The Stories of Jesus

It is Luke's desire to show us the strong love of Christ reaching across all borders and boundaries to create the essential exodus. This compels him to draw together strands of Jesus' life that others did not know or did not include in their Gospel versions. Can you imagine a life of Christ that did not tell the parable of the good Samaritan? Only Luke gives us that story. What if the parable of the lost or prodigal son were excluded from the Bible? Again, only Luke gives us that story. In fact, Luke presents us with sixteen parables that do not exist in any other Gospel account. Imagine never once hearing the story about the Pharisee and the tax collector at prayer, or the rich man and Lazarus. What if we were deprived of the story of the wicked judge and the widow who won't give up on justice, or the rich fool who pulls down his barns in order to put up larger ones, or the friend who comes for bread at midnight, or the great banquet to which are invited the crippled and the poor after the healthy and wealthy refuse to come? How would our understanding of the depth and comprehensiveness and recklessness of God's unstoppable love be sufficient without these incredible fictions and entertainments that brim fresh and bold and catastrophic with truth from Jesus' kaleidoscopic imagination?

Lost Images of Christ's Life

Only Luke and Matthew tell us the Christmas story. Think of how differently European and North American art and culture would have developed without knowledge of those events. How differently would Christian spirituality have developed without the account of the angel Gabriel coming to Mary at Nazareth, of Mary's cousin Elizabeth giving birth to John the Baptist, of Mary's immortal song of joy, the Magnificat? What if we knew nothing of a baby being wrapped up in blankets and placed in a manger to sleep, of a night sky exploding over shepherds' heads, of an angelic chant of "Glory to God in the highest"? How impoverished we would be if no one had related anything about a lost boy winding up in the Temple and engaging in a question-and-answer, if there were no Zaccheus, no "If these were silent, the stones would shout out" (19:40), no weeping over Jerusalem, no sweat like blood in Gethsemane, no startled Simon of Cyrene staggering under the cross, no thief suddenly in paradise? What if we never took the road to Emmaus, if we never recognized Christ's face in the flare of the lamp and the sudden crack of the breaking of the bread? We might even have lost the most poignant words from the cross: "Father, forgive them; for they do not know what they are doing" (23:34). If it were not for Luke, a paler Christ would stand in greater stillness among the arches and chambers of our minds and spirits.

The Spirit of God

It is important to remember as we read Luke's Gospel that it is the first part of a two-part story. The author of Luke also wrote Acts of the Apostles. But some like to rename that book the "Acts of the Holy Spirit," because the Spirit of God is ever-present and all-powerful in the history of the early Church that Luke recounts. The truth is that Luke's emphasis on the Holy Spirit has already begun in the first part. The first four chapters are rife with it.

The Christmas story has Gabriel telling a doubtful Zechariah that his son will be filled with the Holy Spirit immediately from his mother's womb. Then the angel tells Mary the Holy Spirit will come upon her and the power of the Most High will hover or swoop over her—exactly as the Spirit did at the creation of the earth. Before Luke's Christmas is completed, the Spirit of God will fill Zechariah, fill his wife Elizabeth, and come upon Simeon and cause him to prophesy the Nunc Dimittis, "Master, now you are dismissing your servant in peace" (2:29), as well as all the rest that is called the Canticle of Simeon. Luke insists on the startling presence of the Holy Spirit within a woman who cannot have children, a young virgin, a priest who is a skeptic, and an old man well out of the mainstream—people on the margins.

The work of the Spirit does not end with the birth of Jesus. The Spirit perches on Jesus at his baptism like a dove, fills him, leads him into the wilderness so that he can be tested by the devil, and fills him again so that he stands in the synagogue in Nazareth and tells his family and neighbors, quoting Isaiah, that the Spirit of the Lord is upon him, the son of Mary and Joseph. Luke spends the rest of his Gospel fleshing out that anointing of the Spirit in Jesus' actions and words. Continuing on into Acts, with the absence of Christ incarnate, the Holy Spirit moves even more into the forefront, just as in the first few chapters of the Gospel.

The Formation of Souls

Luke has other important emphases too, ones that also carry over into Acts. Angels is an obvious one. No other New Testament writer mentions them more than Luke in his two-part epic. The story of Christ's birth and the story of the Church's birth would scarcely be recognizable without the work of God's messengers. Not only do they bring important news, they warn, they encourage, they set people free. It seems today that either too much attention is paid to angels or too little; they are practically worshiped or they are practically ignored. Neither is healthy. Angels hold a rightful place in our spiritual development, though it may not be common experience to see or speak with them, and Luke is adamant not only about their presence in the life of believers, but their necessity as well.

Two other significant emphases in Luke are prayer and solitude, and once again these carry over from the story of Christ to the story of the Church. All the Gospel writers mention prayer, of course, but Luke gives us such wonderful tidbits as: "[Jesus] would withdraw to deserted places and pray" (5:16); "At daybreak he departed and went into a deserted place" (4:42); "He went out to the mountain to pray; and he spent the night in prayer to God" (6:12); and "Jesus was praying alone, with only the disciples near him" (9:18). Other Gospel writers mention his calling of the twelve apostles, but they don't tell us Jesus prayed all night about it (6:12). They relate his challenge to the disciples, "Who do the crowds say that I am?" (9:18), but not that he was praying before he put the question. Only Luke takes care to point this out. This is also true when he introduces the Lord's Prayer. Matthew drops it into the Sermon on the Mount without preamble. But Luke characteristically brings out the omnipresence of Jesus' life of prayer beforehand: "[Jesus] was praying in a certain place, and after he had finished, one of his disciples said to him, 'Lord, teach us to pray . . .'" (11:1). Matthew and Mark mention Jesus at Gethsemane, but they do not give us the great prayer of forgiveness Jesus utters from the cross.

Luke takes great pains to make Christ's life of prayer an example to us. He also highlights the interludes of quiet and solitude that Christ secures in the middle of a strenuous preaching and healing ministry. Even a cursory reading of Acts indicates that the same care is taken to show that prayer and personal worship have a prominent place in the lives of the first Christians. Whether they are apostles or new believers, women or men, Jews or Greeks or Romans, they pray, seek solitude, and worship. Of course, the prayer and worship of many is also part of Luke's view of spiritual devotion. Indeed, that is how his Gospel concludes, with a vivid glimpse of the promised land of the great community of faith: "They worshiped him, and returned to Jerusalem with great joy; and they were continually in the temple blessing God" (24:52–53).

The exodus of which Christ is not only the leader and catalyst but also the sacrifice brings about the creation of the Church, a community comprised of an eclectic mix of persons that proves the inclusiveness of God's love and justice. Luke uses thousands of words to drive this expansiveness home. How are they brought into the great community? How are their spirits formed once they are part of this great community, body and soul? Prayer matters; worship matters. But so does picking up the cross and following Christ. Ultimately, as we see when we pore over the Gospel of Luke and let that Gospel in turn pour over us, everything shapes our spirituality. All events and all words that impact us alter us. A touch by a hand. A nail driven through a hand. A blow to the face from a hand. All of it, midnight and noonday sun, turns us into what we become in Christ. Every scripture contributes to our reality, some more so or less so depending upon where we are situated on the great road. The whole perspective is rarely, if ever, given.

What we see and understand is limited. What we desire is grace to say what Mary says during one high among all the highs and lows of her frequently confusing and exhausting and hazardous experience of birthing the one who would give birth to her: "The Mighty One has done great things for me, and holy is his name" (1:49).

—Murray Andrew Pura

Dedication to Theophilus

1 Since many have undertaken to set down an orderly account of the events that have been fulfilled among us, ²just as they were handed on to us by those who from the beginning were eyewitnesses and servants of the word, ³I too decided, after investigating everything carefully from the very first,ᵃ to write an orderly account for you, most ex-

cellent Theophilus, ⁴so that you may know the truth concerning the things about which you have been instructed.

The Birth of John the Baptist Foretold

5 In the days of King Herod of Judea, there was a priest named Zechariah, who belonged to the priestly order of Abijah. His wife was a

a Or for a long time

ELIZABETH

Worth the Wait

Selected Scriptures: *Luke 1:5–80; 3:1–6*

Elizabeth was well acquainted with waiting. She and her husband, Zechariah, were "righteous before God, living blamelessly" (Luke 1:6), and yet they were childless, a condition that was often considered a disgrace and sign of God's displeasure. As the years passed, Elizabeth could no longer hope to conceive. Yet as he did with Abraham and Sarah, God surprised these faithful followers late in life, reversing barrenness and bringing forth a child he would use in a great way, a child who would come to be known as John the Baptist.

The message of this miracle was first delivered to Zechariah. An angel appeared to him in the Temple and announced that Elizabeth would bear a son who would "make ready a people prepared for the Lord" (Luke 1:17). In disbelief, Zechariah questioned the message and in return became mute until the time of John's birth. Elizabeth, upon learning of her pregnancy, remained in seclusion for five months, marveling at God's favor toward her in removing the disgrace she'd suffered as a barren woman.

While pregnant, Elizabeth received a visitor—her relative Mary, also with child in a miraculous way. As the angel had foretold in his time with Zechariah, John was filled with the Holy Spirit even before his birth (1:15), and as Mary walked into the room with the Savior in her womb, Elizabeth's baby leapt with joy (1:41). Elizabeth, herself overcome with the Spirit, proclaimed, "Blessed are you among women, and blessed is the fruit of your womb. And why has this happened to me, that the mother of my Lord comes to me?" (1:42–43). Although this visit greatly affected Elizabeth, it can be assumed that it was also deeply significant for Mary, because for the first time someone validated and recognized her private sacrifice to the Lord.

In Elizabeth we glimpse a woman required to do much waiting. And yet, Elizabeth remained faithful. Upon finally becoming pregnant, after her hopes had long since gone, she spent five months alone, hushed and marveling at the miracle under way. As many a pregnant woman has done, she closed out the world and sat with God as he performed his great work of preparation. Truly, all waiting involves such deep work of preparation. In quiet solitude we can best open ourselves to this work of God in us.

A present-day writer, Debra Rienstra, reflects on the period of pregnancy and waiting, likening it to the spiritual life in her book *Great with Child:* "Perhaps we should consider the special, holy work of pregnancy as the truer picture of all that human beings do, all our actions in this world. We fuss and flurry about anxiously to build and achieve and secure, thinking that the successful results redound credit to us. But

PROFILE: ELIZABETH

all that we are and are capable of is a gift, ultimately. . . . We simply watch in wonder for God's work to unfold into its vast and intricate completion."

"Prepare the way of the Lord," Elizabeth's child would one day call out. His mother also teaches us much about preparation, God's faithfulness, and how sometimes waiting can lead to the greatest blessings.

Personal Reflection

- How would you describe yourself when required to wait? On pins and needles, itching to change your situation? Resigned to what may be a long trial? Eager, yet willing to wait? What does your response to waiting reveal about your relationship with God?
- Waiting doesn't mean we are doing something wrong. Looking back, when has God done a major work of preparation within you as he asked you to wait?
- What is one thing you are waiting for? What value have you found, or might you find, in seeking solitude as you endure a period of waiting? Consider now a way you might seek times of solitude to sit with God as you wait.

descendant of Aaron, and her name was Elizabeth. 6Both of them were righteous before God, living blamelessly according to all the commandments and regulations of the Lord. 7But they had no children, because Elizabeth was barren, and both were getting on in years.

8 Once when he was serving as priest before God and his section was on duty, 9he was chosen by lot, according to the custom of the priesthood, to enter the sanctuary of the Lord and offer incense. 10Now at the time of the incense offering, the whole assembly of the people was praying outside. 11Then there appeared to him an angel of the Lord, standing at the right side of the altar of incense. 12When Zechariah saw him, he was terrified; and fear overwhelmed him. 13But the angel said to him, "Do not be afraid, Zechariah, for your prayer has been heard. Your wife Elizabeth will bear you a son, and you will name him John. 14You will have joy and gladness, and many will rejoice at his birth, 15for he will be great in the sight of the Lord. He must never drink wine or strong drink; even before his birth he will be filled with the Holy Spirit. 16He will turn many of the people of

1:11–20 *there appeared to [Zechariah] an angel of the Lord.* We call the apostle Thomas "Doubting Thomas" because of his skepticism about Christ's resurrection. We could just as easily apply the same title to Zechariah. Perhaps he deserves it even more, since Thomas never had Gabriel stand in front of him and tell him what to believe. Honest doubt and the all too human inability to trust in the miraculous without hard evidence land both these individuals in some difficulty. (Zechariah is scolded by Gabriel and loses his voice; Thomas is scolded by Jesus and loses his pride.) Yet what was the outcome of both their seasons of struggle and doubt? Thomas shouts an exclamation better than anything the other disciples have yet expressed: "My Lord and my God!" (John 20:28). Zechariah is filled with the Holy Spirit and exclaims, "The dawn from on high will break upon us, to give light to those who sit in darkness and in the shadow of death" (vv 78–79), joining the select company of Mary and Simeon in giving us not only one of the great bursts of praise of the Christmas story, but also of the entire Bible.

Israel to the Lord their God. 17With the spirit and power of Elijah he will go before him, to turn the hearts of parents to their children, and the disobedient to the wisdom of the righteous, to make ready a people prepared for the Lord." 18Zechariah said to the angel, "How will I know that this is so? For I am an old man, and my wife is getting on in years." 19The angel replied, "I am Gabriel. I stand in the presence of God, and I have been sent to speak to you and to bring you this good news. 20But now, because you did not believe my words, which will be fulfilled in their time, you will become mute, unable to speak, until the day these things occur."

21 Meanwhile the people were waiting for Zechariah, and wondered at his delay in the sanctuary. 22When he did come out, he could not speak to them, and they realized that he had seen a vision in the sanctuary. He kept motioning to them and remained unable to speak. 23When his time of service was ended, he went to his home.

24 After those days his wife Elizabeth conceived, and for five months she remained in seclusion. She said, 25"This is what the Lord has done for me when he looked favorably on me and took away the disgrace I have endured among my people."

The Birth of Jesus Foretold

26 In the sixth month the angel Gabriel was sent by God to a town in Galilee called Nazareth, 27to a virgin engaged to a man whose name was Joseph, of the house of David. The virgin's name was Mary. 28And he came to her and said, "Greetings, favored one! The Lord is with you."a 29But she was much perplexed by his words and pondered what sort of greeting this might be. 30The angel said to her, "Do not be afraid, Mary, for you have found favor with God. 31And now, you will conceive in your womb and bear a son, and you will name him Jesus. 32He will be great, and will be called the Son of

the Most High, and the Lord God will give to him the throne of his ancestor David. 33He will reign over the house of Jacob forever, and of his kingdom there will be no end." 34Mary said to the angel, "How can this be, since I am a virgin?"b 35The angel said to her, "The Holy Spirit will come upon you, and the power of the Most High will overshadow you; therefore the child to be bornc will be holy; he will be called Son of God. 36And now, your relative Elizabeth in her old age has also conceived a son; and this is the sixth month for her who was said to be barren. 37For nothing will be impossible with God." 38Then Mary said, "Here am I, the servant of the Lord; let it be with me according to your word." Then the angel departed from her.

Mary Visits Elizabeth

39 In those days Mary set out and went with haste to a Judean town in the hill country, 40where she entered the house of Zechariah and greeted Elizabeth. 41When Elizabeth heard Mary's greeting, the child leaped in her womb. And Elizabeth was filled with the Holy Spirit 42and exclaimed with a loud cry, "Blessed are you among women, and blessed is the fruit of your womb. 43And why has this happened to me, that the mother of my Lord comes to me? 44For as soon as I heard the sound of your greeting, the child in my womb leaped for joy. 45And blessed is she who believed that there would bed a fulfillment of what was spoken to her by the Lord."

Mary's Song of Praise

46 And Marye said,
    "My soul magnifies the Lord,
47   and my spirit rejoices in God my
        Savior,

a Other ancient authorities add Blessed are you among women   b Gk I do not know a man   c Other ancient authorities add of you   d Or believed, for there will be   e Other ancient authorities read Elizabeth

Responding
1:38 SUBMISSION. Try to place yourself in Mary's shoes. You are young and engaged. Gabriel appears. You become afraid, then ask Gabriel a question. Finally, you submit to the Lord. Try to recall a time in your life when you felt the Lord asking you to do something that was outrageous by all the world's standards. Did you submit to his call? How hard was it to submit? See also Spiritual Disciplines Index.

48 for he has looked with favor on the
     lowliness of his servant.
  Surely, from now on all generations
     will call me blessed;
49 for the Mighty One has done great
     things for me,
  and holy is his name.
50 His mercy is for those who fear him
     from generation to generation.
51 He has shown strength with his arm;
  he has scattered the proud in the
     thoughts of their hearts.
52 He has brought down the powerful
     from their thrones,
  and lifted up the lowly;
53 he has filled the hungry with good
     things,
  and sent the rich away empty.
54 He has helped his servant Israel,
  in remembrance of his mercy,
55 according to the promise he made to
     our ancestors,
  to Abraham and to his descendants
     forever."

56 And Mary remained with her about three months and then returned to her home.

The Birth of John the Baptist

57 Now the time came for Elizabeth to give birth, and she bore a son. 58Her neighbors and relatives heard that the Lord had shown his great mercy to her, and they rejoiced with her.

59 On the eighth day they came to circumcise the child, and they were going to name him Zechariah after his father. 60But his mother said, "No; he is to be called John." 61They said to her, "None of your relatives has this name." 62Then they began motioning to his father to find out what name he wanted to give him. 63He asked for a writing tablet and wrote, "His name is John." And all of them were amazed. 64Immediately his mouth was opened and his tongue freed, and he began to speak, praising God. 65Fear came over all their neighbors, and all these things were talked about throughout the entire hill country of Judea. 66All who heard them pondered them and said, "What then will this child become?" For, indeed, the hand of the Lord was with him.

Zechariah's Prophecy

67 Then his father Zechariah was filled with the Holy Spirit and spoke this prophecy:

68 "Blessed be the Lord God of Israel,
     for he has looked favorably on his
     people and redeemed them.
69 He has raised up a mighty savior[a]
     for us
  in the house of his servant David,
70 as he spoke through the mouth of his
     holy prophets from of old,
71   that we would be saved from our
     enemies and from the hand of all
     who hate us.
72 Thus he has shown the mercy promised
     to our ancestors,
  and has remembered his holy
     covenant,
73 the oath that he swore to our ancestor
     Abraham,
  to grant us 74that we, being rescued
     from the hands of our
     enemies,
  might serve him without fear, 75in
     holiness and righteousness
  before him all our days.
76 And you, child, will be called the
     prophet of the Most High;
  for you will go before the Lord to
     prepare his ways,
77 to give knowledge of salvation to his
     people
  by the forgiveness of their sins.
78 By the tender mercy of our God,
     the dawn from on high will break
     upon[b] us,

a Gk a horn of salvation   b Other ancient authorities read has broken upon

---

1:46–55 WORSHIP—See Spiritual Disciplines Index.

1:46–56 SUBMISSION—See Spiritual Disciplines Index.
  1:48 SERVICE—See Spiritual Disciplines Index.

MARY

Bearing Christ

Selected Scriptures: *Luke 1–2; Matthew 1–2; John 2:1–11, 19:25–27;*
Mark 3:31–35; Luke 11:27–28; Acts 1:14

Surely no one experienced Immanuel, "God with us," as did Mary, Jesus' mother.
She who watched the Son of God expand her belly and shift his form inside her; who
cradled in her arms a newly born, yet infinite, suckling babe; who taught a boy to
walk and talk while sitting before him, her Teacher; who let go her grown offspring
to see him embrace and die for a much larger family—this Mary lived as mama to
God-made-flesh, while bowing in her heart to the King of kings and Lord of lords.

Her role nearly unthinkable, Mary approached it with great emotion, with awe.
At first she simply stood perplexed at what would be, then sat amazed at the Child's
coming and the confirmation from hosts of heaven as well as shepherds and learned
foreigners. She pondered the words of the angel and the testimony of the shepherds,
and as the story of Jesus unfolded before her she treasured each piece in her heart
(Luke 2:19). Mary knew she had been the site of holy Miracle, the habitation of divinity.

"I am only the workshop in which God operates," Martin Luther has Mary say
in his writing on the Magnificat, Mary's song in Luke 1. His metaphor helps us envision Mary's utter faith in God as her Creator and Savior. Lifting God high, she offered herself as his servant.

Contemporary scholar Timothy George, in an essay on Mary, reflects: "Mary was
a disciple of Christ before she was his mother, for had she not believed, she would
not have conceived. Mary's faith too is not the achievement of merit, but the gift
of divine grace."

Perhaps more than anyone in the Bible Mary embodies this paradox of faith and
grace. Her faith made her *theotokos,* "God-bearer" or "mother of God," and yet she
first believed by the act of God's grace within her. Truly, Mary had been invaded by
Immanuel, "God with us," long before the Holy Spirit came upon her womb. And
we too, though not God-bearers in a physical sense, share Mary's God-invaded status. In his grace Immanuel has been at work in us long before we knew him. Now
God offers us the chance to respond, "I am only the workshop in which you operate, God. Let it be with me according to your word." Can we offer ourselves as Mary
did and let God form Christ in us?

Personal Reflection

- Mary knew little of childbirth, marriage, or parenting when she learned
  that she would give birth to God's Son. She did understand the disgrace

PROFILE

PROFILE: MARY

she would probably suffer and was told early on, "a sword will pierce your own soul too" (Luke 2:35). The glorious prospect of becoming Jesus' mother held the promise of untold pain. How similar to Mary's has your response been to living as a "carrier of Christ"?

- Mary spent her whole life pondering the coming of Jesus into her life and treasuring the words she received about him and from him. Our last glimpse of Mary in the Bible finds her in constant prayer with Jesus' disciples, his brothers, and other women (Acts 1:14). Mary lived as both contemplative and evangelical. How much is the contemplation, or pondering, of Jesus in your life a regular practice? How actively do you treasure the words of Scripture about Jesus and the words he has spoken to your spirit?

- Spend some moments pondering God's work of grace in your life, his Immanuel presence before you knew that you knew him. Let today be filled with a constant prayer of thanks for Jesus' coming in grace into your life.

79 to give light to those who sit in darkness
    and in the shadow of death,
to guide our feet into the way of
    peace."

80 The child grew and became strong in spirit, and he was in the wilderness until the day he appeared publicly to Israel.

The Birth of Jesus

2 In those days a decree went out from Emperor Augustus that all the world should be registered. ²This was the first registration and was taken while Quirinius was governor of Syria. ³All went to their own towns to be registered. ⁴Joseph also went from the town of Nazareth in Galilee to Judea, to the city of David called Bethlehem, because he was descended from the house and family of David. ⁵He went to be registered with Mary, to whom he was engaged and who was expecting a child. ⁶While they were there, the time came for her to deliver her child. ⁷And she gave birth to her firstborn son and wrapped him in bands of cloth, and laid him

---

2:1–20 *She gave birth to her firstborn.* The Christmas story is familiar to everyone. Christmas cards and other modern renditions give us glimpses of a flawless Mary in pristine wrinkle-free clothing, a steady and unperturbed Joseph in an equally immaculate robe, a cheerful stable with clean straw and friendly animals, and the arrival of shepherds in newly laundered snow-white tunics with dirt-free sandals on their feet. It is a romanticized version, of course, and can cause problems for our own spiritual growth if we take it too seriously. Luke's version is different: Mary isn't even officially married to Joseph yet she's pregnant; they have to travel from Nazareth to Bethlehem, a distance of forty miles through the Samaritan and Judean hills; Mary goes into labor in Bethlehem, but there is no proper room or bed for her; she gives birth—never an easy process under the best of circumstances—and has to lay her firstborn infant not in a cradle, but a feeding trough; in the middle of the night shepherds burst in upon them, shepherds who smell of woodsmoke and sweat and sheep, still shocked over what they have seen in the sky (not likely welcome intruders considering that shepherds were considered rough and dangerous). The true Christmas story

in a manger, because there was no place for them in the inn.

The Shepherds and the Angels

8 In that region there were shepherds living in the fields, keeping watch over their flock by night. 9 Then an angel of the Lord stood before them, and the glory of the Lord shone around them, and they were terrified. 10 But the angel said to them, "Do not be afraid; for see—I am bringing you good news of great joy for all the people: 11 to you is born this day in the city of David a Savior, who is the Messiah,[a] the Lord. 12 This will be a sign for you: you will find a child wrapped in bands of cloth and lying in a manger." 13 And suddenly there was with the angel a multitude of the heavenly host,[b] praising God and saying,

14 "Glory to God in the highest heaven,
    and on earth peace among those
        whom he favors!"[c]

15 When the angels had left them and gone into heaven, the shepherds said to one another, "Let us go now to Bethlehem and see this thing that has taken place, which the Lord has made known to us." 16 So they went with haste and found Mary and Joseph, and the child lying in the manger. 17 When they saw this, they made known what had been told them about this child; 18 and all who heard it were amazed at what the shepherds told them. 19 But Mary treasured all these words and pondered them in her heart. 20 The shepherds returned, glorifying and praising God for all they had heard and seen, as it had been told them.

Jesus Is Named

21 After eight days had passed, it was time to circumcise the child; and he was called Jesus, the name given by the angel before he was conceived in the womb.

Jesus Is Presented in the Temple

22 When the time came for their purification according to the law of Moses, they brought him up to Jerusalem to present him to the Lord 23 (as it is written in the law of the Lord, "Every firstborn male shall be designated as holy to the Lord"), 24 and they offered a sacrifice according to what is stated in the law of the Lord, "a pair of turtledoves or two young pigeons."

25 Now there was a man in Jerusalem whose name was Simeon;[d] this man was righ-

a Or the Christ   b Gk army   c Other ancient authorities read peace, goodwill among people   d Gk Symeon

AMEN!

---

seems like something of a mess. If we put ourselves into this situation, we sense pretty quickly it is no glittering Christmas card. It is real life. In our lives things, even important things, do not always or even usually happen exactly when and where we want them to. There can be a tendency, when things do not come together smoothly, to wonder what has gone wrong with our prayers or our relationship with God. This is why the true story of Christ's birth is far more helpful to us than the parody we immerse ourselves in every December 25. This account in Luke is indeed the birth of God's Son, a birth anticipated for thousands of years, a birth announced by angels in a blaze of light, a birth unquestionably superintended by God himself. And what do we find? A child born out of wedlock. A rough journey. No room to breathe. Noise. Confusion. The pain of childbirth unalleviated, but for Joseph, by familiar faces. Strangers breaking in out of the night. Yet God's will is done. If God brings about his Son's birth in such a dark and convoluted fashion—or so it appears to our eyes—may we not expect his will to be worked out in our lives, from time to time if not frequently, in a similar fashion?

2:25–38 a man . . . whose name was Simeon; . . . also a prophet, Anna. In modern society the elderly are rarely held in high esteem. They are shunted off to senior citizens' homes where they are cared for by professional staff rather than their own families. We seem to be saying their usefulness is past, and the increasing tolerance of euthanasia underscores that belief. This is not God's attitude. Simeon and Anna are the senior citizens of Luke's version of Jesus' birth, and they know and understand more than anyone else. Of all the people that Jerusalem's streets were teeming with the day that Jesus was named— the rich, the powerful, the young, the holy— only Simeon and Anna are given insight into who is being carried into the Temple courts in his

teous and devout, looking forward to the consolation of Israel, and the Holy Spirit rested on him. [26]It had been revealed to him by the Holy Spirit that he would not see death before he had seen the Lord's Messiah. [a] [27]Guided by the Spirit, Simeon[b] came into the temple; and when the parents brought in the child Jesus, to do for him what was customary under the law, [28]Simeon[c] took him in his arms and praised God, saying,

> [29]"Master, now you are dismissing your
>   servant[d] in peace,
>   according to your word;
> [30]for my eyes have seen your salvation,
> [31] which you have prepared in the
>   presence of all peoples,
> [32]a light for revelation to the Gentiles
>   and for glory to your people Israel."

[33] And the child's father and mother were amazed at what was being said about him. [34]Then Simeon[e] blessed them and said to his mother Mary, "This child is destined for the falling and the rising of many in Israel, and to be a sign that will be opposed [35]so that the inner thoughts of many will be revealed— and a sword will pierce your own soul too."

[36] There was also a prophet, Anna[f] the daughter of Phanuel, of the tribe of Asher. She was of a great age, having lived with her husband seven years after her marriage, [37]then as a widow to the age of eighty-four. She never left the temple but worshiped there with fasting and prayer night and day. [38]At that moment she came, and began to praise God and to speak about the child[g] to all who were looking for the redemption of Jerusalem.

The Return to Nazareth

[39] When they had finished everything required by the law of the Lord, they returned to Galilee, to their own town of Nazareth. [40]The child grew and became strong, filled with wisdom; and the favor of God was upon him.

The Boy Jesus in the Temple

[41] Now every year his parents went to Jerusalem for the festival of the Passover. [42]And when he was twelve years old, they went up as usual for the festival. [43]When the festival was ended and they started to return, the boy Jesus stayed behind in Jerusalem, but his parents did not know it. [44]Assuming that he was in the group of travelers, they went a day's journey. Then they started to look for him among their relatives and friends. [45]When they did not find him, they returned to Jerusalem to search for him. [46]After three days they found him in the temple, sitting among the teachers, listening to them and asking them questions. [47]And all who heard him were amazed at his understanding and his answers. [48]When his parents[h] saw him they were astonished; and his mother said to him, "Child, why have you treated us like this? Look, your father and I have been searching for you in great anxiety." [49]He said to them, "Why were you searching for me? Did you not know that I must be in my Father's house?"[i] [50]But they did not understand what he said to them. [51]Then he went down with them and came to Nazareth, and was obedient to them. His mother treasured all these things in her heart.

[52] And Jesus increased in wisdom and in years,[j] and in divine and human favor.

The Proclamation of John the Baptist

3 In the fifteenth year of the reign of Emperor Tiberius, when Pontius Pilate was governor of Judea, and Herod was ruler[k] of Galilee, and his brother Philip ruler[k] of the region of Ituraea and Trachonitis, and Lysanias ruler[k] of Abilene, [2]during the high priesthood of Annas and Caiaphas, the word of God came to John son of Zechariah in the wilderness.

---

a Or *the Lord's Christ*   b Gk *In the Spirit, he*   c Gk *he*   d Gk *slave*   e Gk *Symeon*   f Gk *Hanna*   g Gk *him*   h Gk *they*   i Or *be about my Father's interests?*   j Or *in stature* k Gk *tetrarch*

---

parents' arms. In fact, they know more than Mary or Joseph, who are astonished at what Simeon says about Jesus. It is clear that God has placed great value on Anna and Simeon and that he does not think he is wasting the Holy Spirit on

two seniors who have passed the prime of life.

  2:27 GUIDANCE—*See* Spiritual Disciplines Index.

  2:37 PRAYER and WORSHIP—*See* Spiritual Disciplines Index.

ANNA

Becoming God's Dwelling Place

Selected Scripture: *Luke 2:21–40*

She appears in only three verses of Scripture, yet the glimpse we get into Anna's life reveals a woman dedicated to living the with-God life. Spending all her time in God's earthly dwelling place, the Temple, she herself became a dwelling place of God and late in her life helped welcome Immanuel Jesus, the babe who embodied the promise "God with us."

Anna, a prophet of the tribe of Asher, had married and lived with her husband seven years before becoming a widow. She never remarried, choosing instead to take up residence in the Temple. Luke tells us she "worshiped there with fasting and prayer night and day" (2:37). Her love for God and worship of him filled all her waking moments. When Mary and Joseph came to present Jesus, eighty-four-year-old Anna gave thanks to God and spoke to them about their miraculous baby, the promised Redeemer.

We may not identify with Anna's call to prophecy or her living situation, yet her commitment to the Spiritual Disciplines of prayer, fasting, and worship—a life focused in mind, body, and activity on engaging with God—is a commitment we all can pursue. Brother Lawrence, a seventeenth-century monk, informs us in his writings that we can pray and worship both in times of focused quiet and spiritual activity and in times of work and routine daily life. Brother Lawrence served in the monastery's kitchen, performing mundane work familiar to most of us, yet he developed a way of focusing on God's presence throughout all of his days. In his timeless work *Practicing the Presence of God,* he reveals his focused perspective: "Applying my mind to these thoughts in the morning and then spending the rest of the day, even in the midst of all my work, in the presence of God, I considered that he was always with me, that he was even within me."

The disciplines of prayer, fasting, and worship are powerful tools that allow us to practice God's presence through all facets of our being, to live daily and hourly as a dwelling place of God. As Anna rejoiced at the coming of Jesus, our Immanuel, we too can experience the thrill of Jesus, "God with us," in increasing measure as we make prayer, fasting, and worship central in our lives.

Personal Reflection

- How often during the course of a typical day are you attentive to God's presence with you? Is your prayer limited to mealtimes and formal devotional times, or do you often turn to God in the activity of your day?
- Have you tried fasting, either from food or from some other habitual activity in your life (television, radio, newspaper, e-mail, Internet), in order to engage in greater worship of God? What kind of difference could, or does, the practice of fasting make in your life with God?
- Choose the most mundane activity of your daily life and think of a way you could practice the presence of God while doing it.

PROFILE

3He went into all the region around the Jordan, proclaiming a baptism of repentance for the forgiveness of sins, 4as it is written in the book of the words of the prophet Isaiah,

> "The voice of one crying out in the
> wilderness:
> 'Prepare the way of the Lord,
>   make his paths straight.
> 5 Every valley shall be filled,
>   and every mountain and hill shall be
>   made low,
> and the crooked shall be made straight,
>   and the rough ways made smooth;
> 6 and all flesh shall see the salvation of
>   God.'"

7 John said to the crowds that came out to be baptized by him, "You brood of vipers! Who warned you to flee from the wrath to come? 8Bear fruits worthy of repentance. Do not begin to say to yourselves, 'We have Abraham as our ancestor'; for I tell you, God is able from these stones to raise up children to Abraham. 9Even now the ax is lying at the root of the trees; every tree therefore that does not bear good fruit is cut down and thrown into the fire."

10 And the crowds asked him, "What then should we do?" 11In reply he said to them, "Whoever has two coats must share with anyone who has none; and whoever has food must do likewise." 12Even tax collectors came to be baptized, and they asked him, "Teacher, what should we do?" 13He said to them, "Collect no more than the amount prescribed for you." 14Soldiers also asked him, "And we, what should we do?" He said to them, "Do not extort money from anyone by threats or false accusation, and be satisfied with your wages."

15 As the people were filled with expectation, and all were questioning in their hearts concerning John, whether he might be the Messiah,ᵃ 16John answered all of them by saying, "I baptize you with water; but one who is more powerful than I is coming; I am not worthy to untie the thong of his sandals. He will baptize you withᵇ the Holy Spirit and fire. 17His winnowing fork is in his hand, to clear his threshing floor and to gather the wheat into his granary; but the chaff he will burn with unquenchable fire."

18 So, with many other exhortations, he proclaimed the good news to the people. 19But Herod the ruler,ᶜ who had been rebuked by him because of Herodias, his brother's wife, and because of all the evil things that Herod had done, 20added to them all by shutting up John in prison.

The Baptism of Jesus

21 Now when all the people were baptized, and when Jesus also had been baptized and was praying, the heaven was opened, 22and the Holy Spirit descended upon him in bodily form like a dove. And a voice came from heaven, "You are my Son, the Beloved;ᵈ with you I am well pleased."ᵉ

The Ancestors of Jesus

23 Jesus was about thirty years old when he began his work. He was the son (as was thought) of Joseph son of Heli, 24son of

a Or the Christ   b Or in   c Gk tetrarch
d Or my beloved Son   e Other ancient authorities
read You are my Son, today I have begotten you

3:21 PRAYER—See Spiritual Disciplines Index.

3:22 the Holy Spirit descended upon him in bodily form like a dove. Why a dove? Why not a butterfly or a sparrow or a ray of sunshine? Perhaps because of the bird's connection with the sacred. It returns to Noah with an olive leaf in its beak (Gen 8:8–12). David cries out for "wings like a dove" so he can fly away from danger and find a place of peace (Ps 55:6). It may well have been a pair of doves Joseph and Mary offered as a sacrifice when Jesus was consecrated. One of the doves would have been for a sin offering

(Luke 2:24; Lev 12:8). So when the bird lights on Jesus after his baptism, it carries with it not only a reputation for being gentle and harmless in and of itself. It also comes as a metaphor for new life and forgiveness (Noah); for freedom and sanctuary and peace (David); and for sacrifice, cleansing from sin, mercy, consecration, and holiness (Joseph and Mary).

3:23–38 He was the son (as was thought) of Joseph son of Heli, son of Matthat. Matthew's genealogy is grounded in Abraham (1:1), who carried in him the promise of the Jewish people and their Messiah. Luke's genealogy is grounded

Matthat, son of Levi, son of Melchi, son of Jannai, son of Joseph, 25son of Mattathias, son of Amos, son of Nahum, son of Esli, son of Naggai, 26son of Maath, son of Mattathias, son of Semein, son of Josech, son of Joda, 27son of Joanan, son of Rhesa, son of Zerubbabel, son of Shealtiel,*a* son of Neri, 28son of Melchi, son of Addi, son of Cosam, son of Elmadam, son of Er, 29son of Joshua, son of Eliezer, son of Jorim, son of Matthat, son of Levi, 30son of Simeon, son of Judah, son of Joseph, son of Jonam, son of Eliakim, 31son of Melea, son of Menna, son of Mattatha, son of Nathan, son of David, 32son of Jesse, son of Obed, son of Boaz, son of Sala,*b* son of Nahshon, 33son of Amminadab, son of Admin, son of Arni,*c* son of Hezron, son of Perez, son of Judah, 34son of Jacob, son of Isaac, son of Abraham, son of Terah, son of Nahor, 35son of Serug, son of Reu, son of Peleg, son of Eber, son of Shelah, 36son of Cainan, son of Arphaxad, son of Shem, son of Noah, son of Lamech, 37son of Methuselah, son of Enoch, son of Jared, son of Mahalaleel, son of Cainan, 38son of Enos, son of Seth, son of Adam, son of God.

The Temptation of Jesus

4 Jesus, full of the Holy Spirit, returned from the Jordan and was led by the Spirit in the wilderness, 2where for forty days he was tempted by the devil. He ate nothing at all during those days, and when they were over, he was famished. 3The devil said to him, "If you are the Son of God, command this stone to become a loaf of bread." 4Jesus answered him, "It is written, 'One does not live by bread alone.' "

5 Then the devil*d* led him up and showed him in an instant all the kingdoms of the world. 6And the devil*d* said to him, "To you I will give their glory and all this authority; for it has been given over to me, and I give it to anyone I please. 7If you, then, will worship me, it will all be yours." 8Jesus answered him, "It is written,

'Worship the Lord your God,
    and serve only him.' "

9 Then the devil*d* took him to Jerusalem, and placed him on the pinnacle of the temple, saying to him, "If you are the Son of God, throw yourself down from here, 10for it is written,

'He will command his angels
        concerning you,
    to protect you,'
11and

'On their hands they will bear you up,

a Gk *Salathiel*   *b* Other ancient authorities read *Salmon*   *c* Other ancient authorities read *Amminadab, son of Aram*; others vary widely   *d* Gk *he*

---

in Adam and God (v 38). As a non-Jew who is concerned that other non-Jews embrace Jesus as Savior and Lord, he wishes to show that Jesus is linked not only to Abraham and the Jews but, in Adam, to the entire human race. He is the Son of God and the Son of Humanity. He is for everyone. The genealogy also presents quite the family tree as far as Jesus' ancestry goes. Enoch may be famous for having walked with God, but it didn't take Noah long to get drunk after the ark came to rest. David is famous for his songs and his faith, but he is infamous for his adultery with Bathsheba and his murder of her husband. Boaz's mother was Rahab, a prostitute. The people who went into the creation of Jesus, whether we consider Mary's bloodline or Joseph's, were not a crowd of saints. The Son of God came to be out of a mix of the ungodly and the godly. The faceless also figure in Jesus' genetic code. Many of his ancestors are complete unknowns, ordinary people who would have vanished from history except that they form links in the chain that culminates in Christ. Our own genealogies are likewise a blend of the good, the bad, and the unknown. This is how God chose to create all of us. Our spiritual genealogies are no different. God uses saints and villains, persons we love and persons we have struggled not to hate to develop our spiritual natures.

4:1 *Jesus . . . was led by the Spirit in the wilderness.* The wilderness gives Jesus strength. It is not simply a place of negation or temptation. It is also a place of preparation and perception, absent of human power structures and controls, a wild place where supernatural forces move unfettered—a place that can empower, depending upon how the experience is handled. Our wildernesses and deserts are not our endings. It is the Spirit of God who leads us about in them. They are our opportunities.

so that you will not dash your foot against a stone.' "

12Jesus answered him, "It is said, 'Do not put the Lord your God to the test.' " 13When the devil had finished every test, he departed from him until an opportune time.

The Beginning of the Galilean Ministry

14 Then Jesus, filled with the power of the Spirit, returned to Galilee, and a report about him spread through all the surrounding country. 15He began to teach in their synagogues and was praised by everyone.

The Rejection of Jesus at Nazareth

16 When he came to Nazareth, where he had been brought up, he went to the synagogue on the sabbath day, as was his custom. He stood up to read, 17and the scroll of the prophet Isaiah was given to him. He unrolled the scroll and found the place where it was written:

18 "The Spirit of the Lord is upon me,
    because he has anointed me
       to bring good news to the poor.
He has sent me to proclaim release to
       the captives
    and recovery of sight to the blind,
       to let the oppressed go free,
19 to proclaim the year of the Lord's
       favor."

20And he rolled up the scroll, gave it back to the attendant, and sat down. The eyes of all in the synagogue were fixed on him. 21Then he began to say to them, "Today this scripture has been fulfilled in your hearing." 22All spoke well of him and were amazed at the gracious words that came from his mouth. They said, "Is not this Joseph's son?" 23He said to them, "Doubtless you will quote to me this proverb, 'Doctor, cure yourself!' And you will say, 'Do here also in your hometown the things that we have heard you did at Capernaum.' " 24And he said, "Truly I tell you, no

prophet is accepted in the prophet's hometown. 25But the truth is, there were many widows in Israel in the time of Elijah, when the heaven was shut up three years and six months, and there was a severe famine over all the land; 26yet Elijah was sent to none of them except to a widow at Zarephath in Sidon. 27There were also many lepers[a] in Israel in the time of the prophet Elisha, and none of them was cleansed except Naaman the Syrian." 28When they heard this, all in the synagogue were filled with rage. 29They got up, drove him out of the town, and led him to the brow of the hill on which their town was built, so that they might hurl him off the cliff. 30But he passed through the midst of them and went on his way.

The Man with an Unclean Spirit

31 He went down to Capernaum, a city in Galilee, and was teaching them on the sabbath. 32They were astounded at his teaching, because he spoke with authority. 33In the synagogue there was a man who had the spirit of an unclean demon, and he cried out with a loud voice, 34"Let us alone! What have you to do with us, Jesus of Nazareth? Have you come to destroy us? I know who you are, the Holy One of God." 35But Jesus rebuked him, saying, "Be silent, and come out of him!" When the demon had thrown him down before them, he came out of him without having done him any harm. 36They were all amazed and kept saying to one another, "What kind of utterance is this? For with authority and power he commands the unclean spirits, and out they come!" 37And a report about him began to reach every place in the region.

a The terms leper and leprosy can refer to several diseases

Responding

4:42 SOLITUDE. A primary hazard of ministry is attending to the needs of others and neglecting our need to be alone to "recharge" our inner lives. Take a moment now to sit down with a calendar and mark off two

days every three months during which you will "recharge" your soul. This can take any number of expressions: going to a retreat center, staying home by yourself, taking a short overnight trip, going hiking or snowshoeing. See also Spiritual Disciplines Index.

*I AM CONVICTED
BY MY LACK OF
WITHOUT HEARTWORK
CONVICTED*

Healings at Simon's House

38 After leaving the synagogue he entered Simon's house. Now Simon's mother-in-law was suffering from a high fever, and they asked him about her. 39 Then he stood over her and rebuked the fever, and it left her. Immediately she got up and began to serve them.

40 As the sun was setting, all those who had any who were sick with various kinds of diseases brought them to him; and he laid his hands on each of them and cured them. 41 Demons also came out of many, shouting, "You are the Son of God!" But he rebuked them and would not allow them to speak, because they knew that he was the Messiah. *a*

Jesus Preaches in the Synagogues

42 At daybreak he departed and went into a deserted place. And the crowds were looking for him; and when they reached him, they wanted to prevent him from leaving them. 43 But he said to them, "I must proclaim the good news of the kingdom of God to the other cities also; for I was sent for this purpose." 44 So he continued proclaiming the message in the synagogues of Judea. *b*

Jesus Calls the First Disciples

5 Once while Jesus *c* was standing beside the lake of Gennesaret, and the crowd was pressing in on him to hear the word of God, 2 he saw two boats there at the shore of the lake; the fishermen had gone out of them and were washing their nets. 3 He got into one of the boats, the one belonging to Simon, and asked him to put out a little way from the shore. Then he sat down and taught the crowds from the boat. 4 When he had finished speaking, he said to Simon, "Put out into the deep water and let down your nets for a catch." 5 Simon answered, "Master, we have worked all night long but have caught nothing. Yet if you say so, I will let down the nets." 6 When they had done this, they caught so many fish that their nets were beginning to break. 7 So they signaled their partners in the other boat to come and help them. And they came and filled both boats, so that they be-

gan to sink. 8 But when Simon Peter saw it, he fell down at Jesus' knees, saying, "Go away from me, Lord, for I am a sinful man!" 9 For he and all who were with him were amazed at the catch of fish that they had taken; 10 and so also were James and John, sons of Zebedee, who were partners with Simon. Then Jesus said to Simon, "Do not be afraid; from now on you will be catching people." 11 When they had brought their boats to shore, they left everything and followed him.

Jesus Cleanses a Leper

12 Once, when he was in one of the cities, there was a man covered with leprosy. *d* When he saw Jesus, he bowed with his face to the ground and begged him, "Lord, if you choose, you can make me clean." 13 Then Jesus *c* stretched out his hand, touched him, and said, "I do choose. Be made clean." Immediately the leprosy *d* left him. 14 And he ordered him to tell no one. "Go," he said, "and show yourself to the priest, and, as Moses commanded, make an offering for your cleansing, for a testimony to them." 15 But now more than ever the word about Jesus *e* spread abroad; many crowds would gather to hear him and to be cured of their diseases. 16 But he would withdraw to deserted places and pray.

Jesus Heals a Paralytic

17 One day, while he was teaching, Pharisees and teachers of the law were sitting near by (they had come from every village of Galilee and Judea and from Jerusalem); and the power of the Lord was with him to heal. *f* 18 Just then some men came, carrying a paralyzed man on a bed. They were trying to bring him in and lay him before Jesus; *e* 19 but finding no way to bring him in because of the crowd, they went up on the roof and let him down with his bed through the tiles into the middle of the crowd *g* in front of Jesus. 20 When he saw their faith, he said,

a Or *the Christ*   *b* Other ancient authorities read *Galilee*   *c* Gk *he*   *d* The terms *leper* and *leprosy* can refer to several diseases   *e* Gk *him* *f* Other ancient authorities read *was present to heal them*   *g* Gk *into the midst*

5:16 PRAYER and SOLITUDE—*See* Spiritual Disciplines Index.

"Friend,[a] your sins are forgiven you." [21]Then the scribes and the Pharisees began to question, "Who is this who is speaking blasphemies? Who can forgive sins but God alone?" [22]When Jesus perceived their questionings, he answered them, "Why do you raise such questions in your hearts? [23]Which is easier, to say, 'Your sins are forgiven you,' or to say, 'Stand up and walk'? [24]But so that you may know that the Son of Man has authority on earth to forgive sins"—he said to the one who was paralyzed—"I say to you, stand up and take your bed and go to your home." [25]Immediately he stood up before them, took what he had been lying on, and went to his home, glorifying God. [26]Amazement seized all of them, and they glorified God and were filled with awe, saying, "We have seen strange things today."

Jesus Calls Levi

27 After this he went out and saw a tax collector named Levi, sitting at the tax booth; and he said to him, "Follow me." [28]And he got up, left everything, and followed him.

29 Then Levi gave a great banquet for him in his house; and there was a large crowd of tax collectors and others sitting at the table[b] with them. [30]The Pharisees and their scribes were complaining to his disciples, saying, "Why do you eat and drink with tax collectors and sinners?" [31]Jesus answered, "Those who are well have no need of a physician, but those who are sick; [32]I have come to call not the righteous but sinners to repentance."

The Question about Fasting

33 Then they said to him, "John's disciples, like the disciples of the Pharisees, frequently fast and pray, but your disciples eat and drink." [34]Jesus said to them, "You cannot make wedding guests fast while the bridegroom is with them, can you? [35]The days will come when the bridegroom will be taken away from them, and then they will fast in those days." [36]He also told them a parable: "No one tears a piece from a new garment and sews it on an old garment; otherwise the new will be torn, and the piece from the new will not match the old. [37]And no one puts new wine into old wineskins; otherwise the new wine will burst the skins and will be spilled, and the skins will be destroyed. [38]But new wine must be put into fresh wineskins. [39]And no one after drinking old wine desires new wine, but says, 'The old is good.' "[c]

The Question about the Sabbath

6 One sabbath[d] while Jesus[e] was going through the grainfields, his disciples plucked some heads of grain, rubbed them in their hands, and ate them. [2]But some of the Pharisees said, "Why are you doing what is not lawful[f] on the sabbath?" [3]Jesus answered, "Have you not read what David did when he and his companions were hungry? [4]He entered the house of God and took and ate the bread of the Presence, which it is not lawful for any but the priests to eat, and gave some to his companions?" [5]Then he said to them, "The Son of Man is lord of the sabbath."

a Gk Man   b Gk reclining   c Other ancient authorities read better; others lack verse 39
d Other ancient authorities read On the second first sabbath   e Gk he   f Other ancient authorities add to do

---

5:18–20 *Friend, your sins are forgiven you.* A man's friends knock a hole in a roof and lower him down on his mat so that he is face-to-face with Jesus. The paralyzed man makes no declaration of faith, prays no sinner's prayer. But Jesus tells him his sins are forgiven. A few moments later his body is healed, and he is heading for home. It is all over in minutes, yet no standard procedure that we have come to recognize in our day regarding evangelism or healing has been followed. Clearly the same faith that Jesus could do something for the broken body, faith desperate enough to break open a roof to get to Jesus, is faith enough also to do something for the broken soul. Jesus recognizes no distinction. Nor does he require a certain protocol or precise verbalization. He knows whether we have staked everything on him or not. It is that, and not trusting to boxes others have packaged with directions on how God saves or heals, that makes all the difference in the world.

5:33–35 FASTING—*See* Spiritual Disciplines Index.

The Man with a Withered Hand

6 On another sabbath he entered the synagogue and taught, and there was a man there whose right hand was withered. [7]The scribes and the Pharisees watched him to see whether he would cure on the sabbath, so that they might find an accusation against him. [8]Even though he knew what they were thinking, he said to the man who had the withered hand, "Come and stand here." He got up and stood there. [9]Then Jesus said to them, "I ask you, is it lawful to do good or to do harm on the sabbath, to save life or to destroy it?" [10]After looking around at all of them, he said to him, "Stretch out your hand." He did so, and his hand was restored. [11]But they were filled with fury and discussed with one another what they might do to Jesus.

Jesus Chooses the Twelve Apostles

12 Now during those days he went out to the mountain to pray; and he spent the night in prayer to God. [13]And when day came, he called his disciples and chose twelve of them, whom he also named apostles: [14]Simon, whom he named Peter, and his brother Andrew, and James, and John, and Philip, and Bartholomew, [15]and Matthew, and Thomas, and James son of Alphaeus, and Simon, who was called the Zealot, [16]and Judas son of James, and Judas Iscariot, who became a traitor.

Jesus Teaches and Heals

17 He came down with them and stood on a level place, with a great crowd of his disciples and a great multitude of people from all Judea, Jerusalem, and the coast of Tyre and Si-

don. [18]They had come to hear him and to be healed of their diseases; and those who were troubled with unclean spirits were cured. [19]And all in the crowd were trying to touch him, for power came out from him and healed all of them.

Blessings and Woes

20 Then he looked up at his disciples and said:

"Blessed are you who are poor,
for yours is the kingdom of God.
21 "Blessed are you who are hungry now,
for you will be filled.
"Blessed are you who weep now,
for you will laugh.
22 "Blessed are you when people hate you, and when they exclude you, revile you, and defame you[a] on account of the Son of Man. [23]Rejoice in that day and leap for joy, for surely your reward is great in heaven; for that is what their ancestors did to the prophets.
24 "But woe to you who are rich,
for you have received your
consolation.
25 "Woe to you who are full now,
for you will be hungry.
"Woe to you who are laughing now,
for you will mourn and weep.
26 "Woe to you when all speak well of you, for that is what their ancestors did to the false prophets.

Love for Enemies

27 "But I say to you that listen, Love your enemies, do good to those who hate you,

a Gk *cast out your name as evil*

6:12 PRAYER and SOLITUDE—*See* Spiritual Disciplines Index.

6:20 *Blessed are you who are poor.* The blessings Jesus offers are for the have-nots of the earth, people who are deprived and impoverished spiritually or physically or both. They are starving for bread; they are starving for spirit. They miss God. They miss his love and his truth. They are homesick, their hearts broken in a world captivated by fossil fuels and plastic and trophies and violence and celebrities. But their anguish will not be endless. There will be a day

of peace when their stomachs and spirits will be filled, when the tears will dry on their skin.

6:27 *Love your enemies.* It is one thing to love a friend or a stranger or the virtually anonymous mass of humanity and another to love and forgive an enemy who hurts us and hates us. Such love would transform our world but, as G. K. Chesterton said, the trouble is that this kind of Christianity has never been tried. When Jesus tells us to love, bless, and pray for our enemies and turn the other cheek, he's emphasizing he doesn't want us to be

28bless those who curse you, pray for those who abuse you. 29If anyone strikes you on the cheek, offer the other also; and from anyone who takes away your coat do not withhold even your shirt. 30Give to everyone who begs from you; and if anyone takes away your goods, do not ask for them again. 31Do to others as you would have them do to you.

32 "If you love those who love you, what credit is that to you? For even sinners love those who love them. 33If you do good to those who do good to you, what credit is that to you? For even sinners do the same. 34If you lend to those from whom you hope to receive, what credit is that to you? Even sinners lend to sinners, to receive as much again. 35But love your enemies, do good, and lend, expecting nothing in return.a Your reward will be great, and you will be children of the Most High; for he is kind to the ungrateful and the wicked. 36Be merciful, just as your Father is merciful.

Judging Others

37 "Do not judge, and you will not be judged; do not condemn, and you will not be condemned. Forgive, and you will be forgiven; 38give, and it will be given to you. A good measure, pressed down, shaken together, running over, will be put into your lap; for the measure you give will be the measure you get back."

39 He also told them a parable: "Can a blind person guide a blind person? Will not both fall into a pit? 40A disciple is not above the teacher, but everyone who is fully qualified will be like the teacher. 41Why do you see the speck in your neighbor'sb eye, but do not notice the log in your own eye? 42Or how can you say to your neighbor,c 'Friend,c let me take out the speck in your eye,' when you yourself do not see the log in your own eye? You hypocrite, first take the log out of your own eye, and then you will see clearly to take the speck out of your neighbor'sb eye.

A Tree and Its Fruit

43 "No good tree bears bad fruit, nor again does a bad tree bear good fruit; 44for each tree is known by its own fruit. Figs are not gathered from thorns, nor are grapes picked from a bramble bush. 45The good person out of the good treasure of the heart produces good, and the evil person out of evil treasure produces evil; for it is out of the abundance of the heart that the mouth speaks.

The Two Foundations

46 "Why do you call me 'Lord, Lord,' and do not do what I tell you? 47I will show you what someone is like who comes to me, hears my words, and acts on them. 48That one is

a Other ancient authorities read despairing of no one   b Gk brother's   c Gk brother

---

people who thrive on aggression and retaliation, who return blow for blow, curse for curse, grudge for grudge, eye for eye, tooth for tooth. He doesn't want us walking around looking for a fight, brooding about how we can get even, planning an act of vengeance. He wants us to break the cycle of hostility. Protecting a woman or man or child who is being abused by physically restraining the perpetrator is one thing. But getting to the point of praying for the abusers, having mercy on them, visiting them in prison, or bringing them a gift to express your love and forgiveness is something else. This is where Jesus is telling us to go. This is loving an enemy. This is turning the other cheek. This is Christianity. It is not an easy thing to do. But following Christ has never been an easy thing to do. It makes us free. But

as Martin Luther King, Jr., stressed, "Freedom has always been an expensive thing."

Responding
6:28 PRAYER. The command to "pray for those who abuse you" reminds us of Corrie ten Boom's story about meeting the Nazi SS guard who stood at the shower room door in the processing center at Ravensbruck, the German concentration camp where she and her sister were imprisoned during World War II. When she recognized him at a church service, she could not bring herself to shake his hand until she breathed a silent prayer: "Jesus, . . . I cannot forgive him. Give me Your forgiveness" (The Hiding Place). Name one person who has abused you, and ask Jesus to give you his forgiveness for that person. See also Spiritual Disciplines Index.

like a man building a house, who dug deeply and laid the foundation on rock; when a flood arose, the river burst against that house but could not shake it, because it had been well built. *a* 49But the one who hears and does not act is like a man who built a house on the ground without a foundation. When the river burst against it, immediately it fell, and great was the ruin of that house."

Jesus Heals a Centurion's Servant

7 After Jesus *b* had finished all his sayings in the hearing of the people, he entered Capernaum. 2A centurion there had a slave whom he valued highly, and who was ill and close to death. 3When he heard about Jesus, he sent some Jewish elders to him, asking him to come and heal his slave. 4When they came to Jesus, they appealed to him earnestly, saying, "He is worthy of having you do this for him, 5for he loves our people, and it is he who built our synagogue for us." 6And Jesus went with them, but when he was not far from the house, the centurion sent friends to say to him, "Lord, do not trouble yourself, for I am not worthy to have you come under my roof; 7therefore I did not presume to come to you. But only speak the word, and let my servant be healed. 8For I also am a man set under authority, with soldiers under me; and I say to one, 'Go,' and he goes, and to another, 'Come,' and he comes, and to my slave, 'Do this,' and the slave does it." 9When Jesus heard this he was amazed at him, and turning to the crowd that followed him, he said, "I tell you, not even in Israel have I found such faith." 10When those who had been sent returned to the house, they found the slave in good health.

Jesus Raises the Widow's Son at Nain

11 Soon afterwards *c* he went to a town called Nain, and his disciples and a large

a Other ancient authorities read *founded upon the rock*   *b* Gk *he*   *c* Other ancient authorities read *Next day*

7:2–10 *not even in Israel have I found such faith.* The centurion, an officer in the hated Roman occupation force, asks Jesus to heal his dying servant and has no problem believing Jesus can do it, even from a distance. He is not a Jew, not one of the chosen people, yet his faith goes beyond what Jesus has experienced among the people of Israel. Jewish elders ask Jesus to perform the healing because of the centurion's kindness to the citizens of Capernaum, but there must have been those who detested the centurion just for being a Roman soldier. Such barriers, here as elsewhere in the Gospels, do not deter Jesus from acting with mercy and compassion. We may be surprised when God heals people we do not like, people who do not belong to our church or our religion, people who perform tasks we do not care for, who may indeed, now as then, be officers and soldiers in an occupying army whose role we despise. Yet such people may have a faith in God far beyond what we experience in ourselves or our church. They do not hold to our theology or our politics, but they experience a miracle just the same. It may not make sense to us, but we recognize, often to our annoyance and astonishment, that it makes sense to God. Blessings that fall upon those who are different from us are an invitation to humility on our part. They are also windows that permit us to see God not as we wish him to be, but as he is.

7:11–17 *he went to a town called Nain.* Just as John gives an account of Jesus' compassion in the face of death—in John's case, when Jesus weeps at Lazarus's grave (11:35)—so in this passage about the death of an only son Luke tells us that Jesus truly feels it. He is not cold and aloof to human suffering, but he has immersed himself in the entire human condition, for better or worse. This woman's husband is gone, and now she has lost her son as well. Jesus will raise him from the dead. But note how he does it. He could have just called out, as he did with Lazarus, and the young man would have sat up. But Jesus does more than that—he touches the coffin. By doing so he makes himself unclean, ritually impure, according to Jewish law. Until one was ritually cleansed from such a touch one was not allowed to mingle in society. Not for the last time—in chapter 8 Jesus will bring Jairus's daughter back to life—will Jesus touch death and in so doing reverse it, bringing life out of what is dead, making pure what is impure. Again and again during his ministry, Jesus will touch those who are dead to touch, whether they are corpses or the walking dead, the lepers. For

crowd went with him. 12As he approached the gate of the town, a man who had died was being carried out. He was his mother's only son, and she was a widow; and with her was a large crowd from the town. 13When the Lord saw her, he had compassion for her and said to her, "Do not weep." 14Then he came forward and touched the bier, and the bearers stood still. And he said, "Young man, I say to you, rise!" 15The dead man sat up and began to speak, and Jesus*a* gave him to his mother. 16Fear seized all of them; and they glorified God, saying, "A great prophet has risen among us!" and "God has looked favorably on his people!" 17This word about him spread throughout Judea and all the surrounding country.

Messengers from John the Baptist

18 The disciples of John reported all these things to him. So John summoned two of his disciples 19and sent them to the Lord to ask, "Are you the one who is to come, or are we to wait for another?" 20When the men had come to him, they said, "John the Baptist has sent us to you to ask, 'Are you the one who is to come, or are we to wait for another?' " 21Jesus*b* had just then cured many people of diseases, plagues, and evil spirits, and had given sight to many who were blind. 22And he answered them, "Go and tell John what you have seen and heard: the blind receive their sight, the lame walk, the lepers*c* are cleansed, the deaf hear, the dead are raised, the poor have good news brought to them. 23And blessed is anyone who takes no offense at me."

24 When John's messengers had gone, Jesus*a* began to speak to the crowds about John: "What did you go out into the wilderness to look at? A reed shaken by the wind? 25What then did you go out to see? Someone*e* dressed in soft robes? Look, those who put on fine clothing and live in luxury are in royal palaces. 26What then did you go out to

see? A prophet? Yes, I tell you, and more than a prophet. 27This is the one about whom it is written,

'See, I am sending my messenger ahead of you,
    who will prepare your way before you.'

28I tell you, among those born of women no one is greater than John; yet the least in the kingdom of God is greater than he." 29(And all the people who heard this, including the tax collectors, acknowledged the justice of God,*f* because they had been baptized with John's baptism. 30But by refusing to be baptized by him, the Pharisees and the lawyers rejected God's purpose for themselves.)

31 "To what then will I compare the people of this generation, and what are they like? 32They are like children sitting in the marketplace and calling to one another,

'We played the flute for you, and you did not dance;
    we wailed, and you did not weep.'

33For John the Baptist has come eating no bread and drinking no wine, and you say, 'He has a demon'; 34the Son of Man has come eating and drinking, and you say, 'Look, a glutton and a drunkard, a friend of tax collectors and sinners!' 35Nevertheless, wisdom is vindicated by all her children."

A Sinful Woman Forgiven

36 One of the Pharisees asked Jesus*d* to eat with him, and he went into the Pharisee's house and took his place at the table. 37And a woman in the city, who was a sinner, having learned that he was eating in the Pharisee's house, brought an alabaster jar of ointment. 38She stood behind him at his feet, weeping, and began to bathe his feet with her tears and to dry them with her hair. Then

a Gk *he*   *b* Gk *He*   *c* The terms *leper* and *leprosy* can refer to several diseases   *d* Gk *him*   *e* Or *Why then did you go out? To see someone*   *f* Or *praised God*

---

some it will be the first time they have been touched by a healthy person in years, in decades. Imagine how much Christ communicated to the untouchables by placing his hand on their diseased flesh; imagine what taking that kind of

risk out of love meant to those who had been thrust out of society, away from children and synagogues and markets, away from laughter and handshakes and hugging.

she continued kissing his feet and anointing them with the ointment. [39]Now when the Pharisee who had invited him saw it, he said to himself, "If this man were a prophet, he would have known who and what kind of woman this is who is touching him—that she is a sinner." [40]Jesus spoke up and said to him, "Simon, I have something to say to you." "Teacher," he replied, "speak." [41]"A certain creditor had two debtors; one owed five hundred denarii, [a] and the other fifty. [42]When they could not pay, he canceled the debts for both of them. Now which of them will love him more?" [43]Simon answered, "I suppose the one for whom he canceled the greater debt." And Jesus [b] said to him, "You have judged rightly." [44]Then turning toward the woman, he said to Simon, "Do you see this woman? I entered your house; you gave me no water for my feet, but she has bathed my feet with her tears and dried them with her hair. [45]You gave me no kiss, but from the time I came in she has not stopped kissing my feet. [46]You did not anoint my head with oil, but she has anointed my feet with ointment. [47]Therefore, I tell you, her sins, which were many, have been forgiven; hence she has shown great love. But the one to whom little is forgiven, loves little." [48]Then he said to her, "Your sins are forgiven." [49]But those who were at the table with him began to say among themselves, "Who is this who even forgives sins?" [50]And he said to the woman, "Your faith has saved you; go in peace."

Some Women Accompany Jesus

8 Soon afterwards he went on through cities and villages, proclaiming and bringing the good news of the kingdom of God. The twelve were with him, [2]as well as some women who had been cured of evil spirits and infirmities: Mary, called Magdalene, from whom seven demons had gone out, [3]and Joanna, the wife of Herod's steward Chuza, and Susanna, and many others, who provided for them [c] out of their resources.

The Parable of the Sower

4 When a great crowd gathered and people from town after town came to him, he said in a parable: [5]"A sower went out to sow his seed; and as he sowed, some fell on the path and was trampled on, and the birds of the air ate it up. [6]Some fell on the rock; and as it grew up, it withered for lack of moisture. [7]Some fell among thorns, and the thorns grew with it and choked it. [8]Some fell into good soil, and when it grew, it produced a hundredfold." As he said this, he called out, "Let anyone with ears to hear listen!"

The Purpose of the Parables

9 Then his disciples asked him what this parable meant. [10]He said, "To you it has been given to know the secrets [d] of the kingdom of God; but to others I speak [e] in parables, so that

'looking they may not perceive,
  and listening they may not
    understand.'

The Parable of the Sower Explained

11 "Now the parable is this: The seed is the word of God. [12]The ones on the path are those who have heard; then the devil comes and takes away the word from their hearts, so that they may not believe and be saved. [13]The ones on the rock are those who, when they hear the word, receive it with joy. But these have no root; they believe only for a while and in a time of testing fall away. [14]As for

a The denarius was the usual day's wage for a laborer   b Gk he   c Other ancient authorities read him   d Or mysteries   e Gk lacks I speak

---

7:37–39, 44–50 *Do you see this woman?* A woman washes Jesus' feet with her tears and wipes them with her hair. She kisses them and pours perfume over them. Not for the first time a religious leader considers that Jesus has soiled himself by touching or being touched by someone others consider morally, spiritually, or physically filthy. But Jesus asks Simon if he truly sees this woman—not an object, not a sinner, but a person, a woman, someone forgiven by God, a human who is weeping with gratitude and relief, a child who is loving as much as she can, a child of God who is saved by her faith and who is free to go in peace.

8:10 SECRECY—*See* Spiritual Disciplines Index.

what fell among the thorns, these are the ones who hear; but as they go on their way, they are choked by the cares and riches and pleasures of life, and their fruit does not mature. [15]But as for that in the good soil, these are the ones who, when they hear the word, hold it fast in an honest and good heart, and bear fruit with patient endurance.

A Lamp under a Jar

[16] "No one after lighting a lamp hides it under a jar, or puts it under a bed, but puts it on a lampstand, so that those who enter may see the light. [17]For nothing is hidden that will not be disclosed, nor is anything secret that will not become known and come to light. [18]Then pay attention to how you listen; for to those who have, more will be given; and from those who do not have, even what they seem to have will be taken away."

The True Kindred of Jesus

[19] Then his mother and his brothers came to him, but they could not reach him because of the crowd. [20]And he was told, "Your mother and your brothers are standing outside, wanting to see you." [21]But he said to them, "My mother and my brothers are those who hear the word of God and do it."

Jesus Calms a Storm

[22] One day he got into a boat with his disciples, and he said to them, "Let us go across to the other side of the lake." So they put out, [23]and while they were sailing he fell asleep. A windstorm swept down on the lake, and the boat was filling with water, and they were in danger. [24]They went to him and woke him up, shouting, "Master, Master, we are perishing!" And he woke up and rebuked the wind and the raging waves; they ceased, and there was a calm. [25]He said to them, "Where is your faith?" They were afraid and amazed, and said to one another, "Who then is this, that he commands even the winds and the water, and they obey him?"

Jesus Heals the Gerasene Demoniac

[26] Then they arrived at the country of the Gerasenes,[a] which is opposite Galilee. [27]As he stepped out on land, a man of the city who had demons met him. For a long time he had worn[b] no clothes, and he did not live in a house but in the tombs. [28]When he saw Jesus, he fell down before him and shouted at the top of his voice, "What have you to do with me, Jesus, Son of the Most High God? I beg you, do not torment me"— [29]for Jesus[c] had commanded the unclean spirit to come out of the man. (For many times it had seized him; he was kept under guard and bound with chains and shackles, but he would break the bonds and be driven by the demon into the wilds.) [30]Jesus then asked him, "What is your name?" He said, "Legion"; for many demons had entered him. [31]They begged him not to order them to go back into the abyss.

[32] Now there on the hillside a large herd of swine was feeding; and the demons[d] begged Jesus[e] to let them enter these. So he gave them permission. [33]Then the demons came out of the man and entered the swine, and the herd rushed down the steep bank into the lake and was drowned.

[34] When the swineherds saw what had happened, they ran off and told it in the city and in the country. [35]Then people came out to see what had happened, and when they came to Jesus, they found the man from whom the demons had gone sitting at the feet of Jesus, clothed and in his right mind. And they were afraid. [36]Those who had seen it told them how the one who had been possessed by demons had been healed. [37]Then all the people of the surrounding country of the Gerasenes[a] asked Jesus[e] to leave them; for they were seized with great fear. So he got into the boat and returned. [38]The man from whom the demons had gone begged that he might be with him; but Jesus[c] sent him away, saying, [39]"Return to your home, and declare how much God has done for you." So he went away, proclaiming throughout the city how much Jesus had done for him.

a Other ancient authorities read *Gadarenes*; others, *Gergesenes*   b Other ancient authorities read *a man of the city who had had demons for a long time met him. He wore*   c Gk *he*   d Gk *they*   e Gk *him*

A Girl Restored to Life and a Woman Healed

40 Now when Jesus returned, the crowd welcomed him, for they were all waiting for him. 41Just then there came a man named Jairus, a leader of the synagogue. He fell at Jesus' feet and begged him to come to his house, 42for he had an only daughter, about twelve years old, who was dying.

As he went, the crowds pressed in on him. 43Now there was a woman who had been suffering from hemorrhages for twelve years; and though she had spent all she had on physicians,[a] no one could cure her. 44She came up behind him and touched the fringe of his clothes, and immediately her hemorrhage stopped. 45Then Jesus asked, "Who touched me?" When all denied it, Peter[b] said, "Master, the crowds surround you and press in on you." 46But Jesus said, "Someone touched me; for I noticed that power had gone out from me." 47When the woman saw that she could not remain hidden, she came trembling; and falling down before him, she declared in the presence of all the people why she had touched him, and how she had been immediately healed. 48He said to her, "Daughter, your faith has made you well; go in peace."

49 While he was still speaking, someone came from the leader's house to say, "Your daughter is dead; do not trouble the teacher any longer." 50When Jesus heard this, he replied, "Do not fear. Only believe, and she will be saved." 51When he came to the house, he did not allow anyone to enter with him,

except Peter, John, and James, and the child's father and mother. 52They were all weeping and wailing for her; but he said, "Do not weep; for she is not dead but sleeping." 53And they laughed at him, knowing that she was dead. 54But he took her by the hand and called out, "Child, get up!" 55Her spirit returned, and she got up at once. Then he directed them to give her something to eat. 56Her parents were astounded; but he ordered them to tell no one what had happened.

The Mission of the Twelve

9 Then Jesus[c] called the twelve together and gave them power and authority over all demons and to cure diseases, 2and he sent them out to proclaim the kingdom of God and to heal. 3He said to them, "Take nothing for your journey, no staff, nor bag, nor bread, nor money—not even an extra tunic. 4Whatever house you enter, stay there, and leave from there. 5Wherever they do not welcome you, as you are leaving that town shake the dust off your feet as a testimony against them." 6They departed and went through the villages, bringing the good news and curing diseases everywhere.

Herod's Perplexity

7 Now Herod the ruler[d] heard about all that had taken place, and he was perplexed,

a Other ancient authorities lack *and though she had spent all she had on physicians* b Other ancient authorities add *and those who were with him* c Gk *he* d Gk *tetrarch*

8:43–48 *She . . . touched the fringe of his clothes.* It is not hard for us to identify with this woman. We may suffer from a chronic illness, or know those who do, and may have spent all our savings and traveled the world searching for a cure. Now a faith healer comes along. Should we risk it? Why not? We have risked everything else. Yet we may not feel important or brave enough to ask this person to help us. Long-term illness can destroy a person's sense of self-worth and significance. So we, like this woman, try to sneak up from behind and just touch the healer or a piece of his clothing. We hope to God it will be enough. Often we are taught that when we are in desperate need of something from God—

in a crisis caused by, say, cancer, bankruptcy, chronic depression, inescapable grief, or loss of faith—we must come boldly and without fear into God's presence if we expect him to answer our prayer. Yet this woman came in fear and trembling, having no idea what might happen, but thinking, "If I can just touch the edge of his cloak, who knows?" Sometimes all we can do is struggle toward God from behind and stretch with what little we have left in us to touch the edge of him, hoping he will not be angry with us or ignore us, hoping something will happen that we are almost beyond believing can happen. We discover, to our astonishment, that nothing more than this is required, and we live.

because it was said by some that John had been raised from the dead, [8]by some that Elijah had appeared, and by others that one of the ancient prophets had arisen. [9]Herod said, "John I beheaded; but who is this about whom I hear such things?" And he tried to see him.

Feeding the Five Thousand

10 On their return the apostles told Jesus[a] all they had done. He took them with him and withdrew privately to a city called Bethsaida. [11]When the crowds found out about it, they followed him; and he welcomed them, and spoke to them about the kingdom of God, and healed those who needed to be cured.

12 The day was drawing to a close, and the twelve came to him and said, "Send the crowd away, so that they may go into the surrounding villages and countryside, to lodge and get provisions; for we are here in a deserted place." [13]But he said to them, "You give them something to eat." They said, "We have no more than five loaves and two fish—unless we are to go and buy food for all these people." [14]For there were about five thousand men. And he said to his disciples, "Make them sit down in groups of about fifty each." [15]They did so and made them all sit down. [16]And taking the five loaves and the two fish, he looked up to heaven, and blessed and broke them, and gave them to the disciples to set before the crowd. [17]And all ate and were filled. What was left over was gathered up, twelve baskets of broken pieces.

Peter's Declaration about Jesus

18 Once when Jesus[b] was praying alone, with only the disciples near him, he asked them, "Who do the crowds say that I am?" [19]They answered, "John the Baptist; but others, Elijah; and still others, that one of the ancient prophets has arisen." [20]He said to them, "But who do you say that I am?" Peter answered, "The Messiah[c] of God."

Jesus Foretells His Death and Resurrection

21 He sternly ordered and commanded them not to tell anyone, [22]saying, "The Son of Man must undergo great suffering, and be rejected by the elders, chief priests, and scribes, and be killed, and on the third day be raised."

23 Then he said to them all, "If any want to become my followers, let them deny themselves and take up their cross daily and follow me. [24]For those who want to save their life will lose it, and those who lose their life for my sake will save it. [25]What does it profit them if they gain the whole world, but lose or forfeit themselves? [26]Those who are ashamed of me and of my words, of them the Son of Man will be ashamed when he comes in his glory and the glory of the Father and of the holy angels. [27]But truly I tell you, there are some standing here who will not taste death before they see the kingdom of God."

a Gk him   b Gk he   c Or The Christ

9:18 SOLITUDE—*See* Spiritual Disciplines Index.

9:20 *who do you say that I am?* As great a figure as Peter cuts in the history of the early Church, we know he, like the rest of us, had feet of clay. At the arrest of Christ he will deny three times he knew him. Nevertheless God revealed to him that Jesus was the Messiah, as we see in this verse. He also called Peter to be one of the great leaders of the infant Church, naming him the Rock. So despite Peter's flaws God still poured great life and light out of him in order to bless and transform others. The same is true for us. We are only too well aware of our own imperfections and may believe that, until we get

completely free of them, God cannot accomplish anything beneficial through our words and actions. But the example of Peter proves that this is not the case. If we are willing to respond to the opportunities God places in our path, instead of saying we are not good enough; if we are able to respond to the nudges from God's Word and Spirit, rather than make excuses based on our negative self-evaluation; if we are stubborn enough to persevere in following Christ despite our mistakes—then God, through us, can carve a furrow through this earth's murky waters and leave a shimmering residue of hope and faith in our wake.

The Transfiguration

28 Now about eight days after these sayings Jesus[a] took with him Peter and John and James, and went up on the mountain to pray. [29]And while he was praying, the appearance of his face changed, and his clothes became dazzling white. [30]Suddenly they saw two men, Moses and Elijah, talking to him. [31]They appeared in glory and were speaking of his departure, which he was about to accomplish at Jerusalem. [32]Now Peter and his companions were weighed down with sleep; but since they had stayed awake,[b] they saw his glory and the two men who stood with him. [33]Just as they were leaving him, Peter said to Jesus, "Master, it is good for us to be here; let us make three dwellings,[c] one for you, one for Moses, and one for Elijah"—not knowing what he said. [34]While he was saying this, a cloud came and overshadowed them; and they were terrified as they entered the cloud. [35]Then from the cloud came a voice that said, "This is my Son, my Chosen;[d] listen to him!" [36]When the voice had spoken, Jesus was found alone. And they kept silent and in those days told no one any of the things they had seen.

Jesus Heals a Boy with a Demon

37 On the next day, when they had come down from the mountain, a great crowd met him. [38]Just then a man from the crowd shouted, "Teacher, I beg you to look at my son; he is my only child. [39]Suddenly a spirit seizes him, and all at once he[e] shrieks. It convulses him until he foams at the mouth; it mauls him and will scarcely leave him. [40]I begged your disciples to cast it out, but they could not." [41]Jesus answered, "You faithless and perverse generation, how much longer must I be with you and bear with you? Bring your son here." [42]While he was coming, the demon dashed him to the ground in convulsions. But Jesus rebuked the unclean spirit, healed the boy, and gave him back to his father. [43]And all were astounded at the greatness of God.

Jesus Again Foretells His Death

While everyone was amazed at all that he was doing, he said to his disciples, [44]"Let these words sink into your ears: The Son of Man is going to be betrayed into human hands." [45]But they did not understand this saying; its meaning was concealed from them, so that they could not perceive it. And they were afraid to ask him about this saying.

True Greatness

46 An argument arose among them as to which one of them was the greatest. [47]But Jesus, aware of their inner thoughts, took a little child and put it by his side, [48]and said to them, "Whoever welcomes this child in my name welcomes me, and whoever welcomes me welcomes the one who sent me; for the least among all of you is the greatest."

Another Exorcist

49 John answered, "Master, we saw someone casting out demons in your name, and we tried to stop him, because he does not follow with us." [50]But Jesus said to him, "Do not stop him; for whoever is not against you is for you."

A Samaritan Village Refuses to Receive Jesus

51 When the days drew near for him to be taken up, he set his face to go to Jerusalem. [52]And he sent messengers ahead of him. On their way they entered a village of the Samaritans to make ready for him; [53]but they did not receive him, because his face was set toward Jerusalem. [54]When his disciples James and John saw it, they said, "Lord, do you want us to command fire to come down from heaven and consume them?"[f] [55]But he turned and rebuked them. [56]Then[g] they went on to another village.

a Gk *he*   *b* Or *but when they were fully awake*
c Or *tents*   *d* Other ancient authorities read *my Beloved*   *e* Or *it*   *f* Other ancient authorities add *as Elijah did*   *g* Other ancient authorities read *rebuked them, and said, "You do not know what spirit you are of,* [56]*for the Son of Man has not come to destroy the lives of human beings but to save them."* Then

---

9:28–29 PRAYER—*See* Spiritual Disciplines Index.

Would-Be Followers of Jesus

57 As they were going along the road, someone said to him, "I will follow you wherever you go." 58 And Jesus said to him, "Foxes have holes, and birds of the air have nests; but the Son of Man has nowhere to lay his head." 59 To another he said, "Follow me." But he said, "Lord, first let me go and bury my father." 60 But Jesus *a* said to him, "Let the dead bury their own dead; but as for you, go and proclaim the kingdom of God." 61 Another said, "I will follow you, Lord; but let me first say farewell to those at my home." 62 Jesus said to him, "No one who puts a hand to the plow and looks back is fit for the kingdom of God."

The Mission of the Seventy

10 After this the Lord appointed seventy *b* others and sent them on ahead of him in pairs to every town and place where he himself intended to go. 2 He said to them, "The harvest is plentiful, but the laborers are few; therefore ask the Lord of the harvest to send out laborers into his harvest. 3 Go on your way. See, I am sending you out like lambs into the midst of wolves. 4 Carry no purse, no bag, no sandals; and greet no one on the road. 5 Whatever house you enter, first say, 'Peace to this house!' 6 And if anyone is there who shares in peace, your peace will rest on that person; but if not, it will return to you. 7 Remain in the same house, eating and drinking whatever they provide, for the laborer deserves to be paid. Do not move about from house to house. 8 Whenever you enter a town and its people welcome you, eat what is set before you; 9 cure the sick who are there, and say to them, 'The kingdom of God has come near to you.' *c* 10 But whenever you enter a town and they do not welcome you, go out into its streets and say, 11 'Even the dust of your town that clings to our feet, we wipe off in protest against you. Yet know this: the kingdom of God has come near.' *d* 12 I tell you, on that day it will be more tolerable for Sodom than for that town.

Woes to Unrepentant Cities

13 "Woe to you, Chorazin! Woe to you, Bethsaida! For if the deeds of power done in you had been done in Tyre and Sidon, they would have repented long ago, sitting in sackcloth and ashes. 14 But at the judgment it will be more tolerable for Tyre and Sidon than for you. 15 And you, Capernaum,

will you be exalted to heaven?

No, you will be brought down to
Hades.

16 "Whoever listens to you listens to me, and whoever rejects you rejects me, and whoever rejects me rejects the one who sent me."

The Return of the Seventy

17 The seventy *e* returned with joy, saying, "Lord, in your name even the demons submit to us!" 18 He said to them, "I watched Satan fall from heaven like a flash of lightning. 19 See, I have given you authority to tread on snakes and scorpions, and over all the power of the enemy; and nothing will hurt you. 20 Nevertheless, do not rejoice at this, that the spirits submit to you, but rejoice that your names are written in heaven."

Jesus Rejoices

21 At that same hour Jesus *a* rejoiced in the Holy Spirit *f* and said, "I thank *g* you, Father, Lord of heaven and earth, because you have hidden these things from the wise and the intelligent and have revealed them to infants; yes, Father, for such was your gracious will. *h* 22 All things have been handed over to me by my Father; and no one knows who the Son is except the Father, or who the Father is except the Son and anyone to whom the Son chooses to reveal him."

23 Then turning to the disciples, Jesus *a* said to them privately, "Blessed are the eyes that see what you see! 24 For I tell you that many prophets and kings desired to see what

a Gk *he*   *b* Other ancient authorities read *seventy-two*   *c* Or *is at hand for you*   *d* Or *is at hand*
e Other ancient authorities read *seventy-two*
f Other authorities read *in the spirit*   *g* Or *praise*
h Or *for so it was well-pleasing in your sight*

10:11 THE WITH-GOD LIFE—*See* Spiritual Disciplines Index.

you see, but did not see it, and to hear what you hear, but did not hear it."

The Parable of the Good Samaritan

25 Just then a lawyer stood up to test Jesus. [a] "Teacher," he said, "what must I do to inherit eternal life?" 26 He said to him, "What is written in the law? What do you read there?" 27 He answered, "You shall love the Lord your God with all your heart, and with all your soul, and with all your strength, and with all your mind; and your neighbor as yourself." 28 And he said to him, "You have given the right answer; do this, and you will live."

29 But wanting to justify himself, he asked Jesus, "And who is my neighbor?" 30 Jesus replied, "A man was going down from Jerusalem to Jericho, and fell into the hands of robbers, who stripped him, beat him, and went away, leaving him half dead. 31 Now by chance a priest was going down that road; and when he saw him, he passed by on the other side. 32 So likewise a Levite, when he came to the place and saw him, passed by on the other side. 33 But a Samaritan while traveling came near him; and when he saw him, he was moved with pity. 34 He went to him and bandaged his wounds, having poured oil and wine on them. Then he put him on his own animal, brought him to an inn, and took care of him. 35 The next day he took out two denarii, [b] gave them to the innkeeper, and said, 'Take care of him; and when I come back, I will repay you whatever more you spend.' 36 Which of these three, do you think, was a neighbor to the man who fell into the hands of the robbers?" 37 He said, "The one who showed him mercy." Jesus said to him, "Go and do likewise."

Jesus Visits Martha and Mary

38 Now as they went on their way, he entered a certain village, where a woman named Martha welcomed him into her home. 39 She had a sister named Mary, who sat at the Lord's feet and listened to what he was saying. 40 But Martha was distracted by her many tasks; so

a Gk him b The denarius was the usual day's wage for a laborer

10:30–37 *A man was going down from Jerusalem to Jericho.* The parable of the good Samaritan is the most well known of all Jesus' stories (the only competitor is the story of the lost or prodigal son, 15:11–32). In it, the person you least expect to help the robbed and beaten man stops and saves him, while the ones you'd think would be the first to help him go right on by. For those listening to Jesus tell this story for the first time, it would have been very difficult to take. The hero is not a priest, but an enemy of the Jews. The enmity between Jews and Samaritans went back hundreds of years. It would have been inconceivable for Jews to have identified with the Samaritan. Not wanting to identify with the priest or Levite, who both erred on the side of caution rather than compassion (touching a possible corpse would have rendered them unclean and made social interaction temporarily impossible), their only choice would have been to put themselves in the place of the victim, bleeding and helpless in the dirt, beset by flies under the killing sun. Imagine then their mixture of horror and relief when the one who saves them is the one they hate. This story

is not only about stopping to help those whom we have been taught to mistrust or have had bitter conflict with. It is also about putting ourselves in the skin of the half-dead, the destitute, the despairing—sometimes a place where we can indeed find ourselves at one or more points on our own journey between Jericho and Jerusalem. It is about realizing our neighbor is the one who is kind to us, regardless of skin color, religion, politics, or personal past history. This may be much more difficult than finding the inner strength and grace to stop and give aid and comfort to our enemy. To comprehend our utter inability to help ourselves, swallow our pride, and permit those we dislike or detest to save us is to come to the point of calling them friends. It is the crossing of an enormous barrier on this earth, certainly one of the most unspannable for human nature. It is perhaps as difficult as the gap experienced by people who have always considered God false or, if he exists, a monster and then who discover, in fear and disgust and awe, that God is the only one stretching out to bring them back from the brink of death.

she came to him and asked, "Lord, do you not care that my sister has left me to do all the work by myself? Tell her then to help me." ⁴¹But the Lord answered her, "Martha, Martha, you are worried and distracted by many things; ⁴²there is need of only one thing.ᵃ Mary has chosen the better part, which will not be taken away from her."

The Lord's Prayer

11 He was praying in a certain place, and after he had finished, one of his disciples said to him, "Lord, teach us to pray, as John taught his disciples." ²He said to them, "When you pray, say:

Father,ᵇ hallowed be your name.
Your kingdom come.ᶜ
3   Give us each day our daily bread.ᵈ

a Other ancient authorities read *few things are necessary, or only one*   *b* Other ancient authorities read *Our Father in heaven*   *c* A few ancient authorities read *Your Holy Spirit come upon us and cleanse us.* Other ancient authorities add *Your will be done, on earth as in heaven*   *d* Or *our bread for tomorrow*

10:38–42 *Mary has chosen the better part.* Some think this passage gives a green light to contemplative spirituality and a red light to a spirituality of action and deeds. But this is impossible to reconcile with Jesus' own life. As we read Luke's Gospel, we find Jesus praying in solitude and then taking the strength he has gained from that encounter with the divine to preach the good news to thousands and heal them of all their infirmities. This passage is about something else. We know that Jesus became close friends with Mary and Martha and their brother Lazarus and often stayed and ate at their home (this is particularly brought out in John's Gospel). He obviously enjoyed their hospitality, which would have included Martha's home cooking. Jesus himself, after all, could not have despised cooks and cooking; he was one himself. He is the chef who, in John 21, is grilling fish and baking bread on the beach and telling the stunned apostles—who had gone back to fishing after Jesus' death—"Come and have breakfast!" So why is Martha reprimanded just for asking for a little help? No doubt part of the problem is Martha's attitude. If she had been happy offering her culinary gifts of hospitality to Jesus, she wouldn't have minded where her sister was. But on this occasion she wasn't able, like Brother Lawrence, a Carmelite who ran a monastery kitchen sixteen hundred years later, to cheerfully pray, "Oh, Lord of pots and pans," while she clattered about cooking her meal. It is not that Martha is a woman without faith. She is the one who will first come out to see Jesus when he arrives after Lazarus's death in John 11. She is the one who will share with Peter the honor (though not yet the fame) of boldly declaring Christ's messiahship minutes before Lazarus returns to life: "I believe that you are the Messiah, the Son of God, the one coming into the world" (John 11:27). Peter's confession, which Luke records in response to Jesus' query, is much the same, "The Messiah of God" (9:20). So Martha is a person whose seed of faith will grow into a tree. Jesus is not chiding her for cooking or being hospitable or because he knows there is no faith in her heart equal to Mary's. He is pointing out to her that the service she is rendering is coming out of frustration, anxiety, and anger and that it isn't necessary for her to be in such a state. If she's not happy doing the cooking, if she's not finding God there (as she could and Brother Lawrence will), why not join Mary and talk with him a while? There is a place for physical food, certainly, but it is never more important than taking in spiritual vitality, the robust kind that affects in the most positive fashion everything we do. Jesus is emphasizing, as he will on other occasions—notably when he won't eat the food his disciples urge on him: "I have food to eat that you do not know about" (John 4:32)—that drawing close to his words and Spirit are essential. Everything else, no matter how important it is, is secondary. Instead of agreeing to send Mary off to the kitchen, Jesus indicates that her choice to drink in his words is critical and uncensurable. Jesus appears to be offering the same choice to Martha, which, considering the tremendous growth in her spirituality by the time of Lazarus's death, we might conclude she accepts.

11:1 PRAYER—*See* Spiritual Disciplines Index.

11:1–4 *Lord, teach us to pray.* The pattern for prayer that Jesus gives his disciples is short on our wants and big on God's wants. Half of what Jesus tells us to do in prayer is worship God, keep him holy, and ask that his kingdom and his

4   And forgive us our sins,
          for we ourselves forgive everyone
               indebted to us.
          And do not bring us to the time of
               trial." [a]

Perseverance in Prayer

5 And he said to them, "Suppose one of you has a friend, and you go to him at midnight and say to him, 'Friend, lend me three loaves of bread; [6]for a friend of mine has arrived, and I have nothing to set before him.' [7]And he answers from within, 'Do not bother me; the door has already been locked, and my children are with me in bed; I cannot get up and give you anything.' [8]I tell you, even though he will not get up and give him anything because he is his friend, at least because of his persistence he will get up and give him whatever he needs.

9 "So I say to you, Ask, and it will be given you; search, and you will find; knock, and the door will be opened for you. [10]For everyone who asks receives, and everyone who searches finds, and for everyone who knocks, the door will be opened. [11]Is there anyone among you who, if your child asks for [b] a fish, will give a snake instead of a fish? [12]Or if the child asks for an egg, will give a scorpion? [13]If you then, who are evil, know how to give good gifts to your children, how much more will the heavenly Father give the Holy Spirit [c] to those who ask him!"

Jesus and Beelzebul

14 Now he was casting out a demon that was mute; when the demon had gone out, the one who had been mute spoke, and the crowds were amazed. [15]But some of them said, "He casts out demons by Beelzebul, the ruler of the demons." [16]Others, to test him, kept demanding from him a sign from heaven. [17]But he knew what they were thinking and said to them, "Every kingdom divided against itself becomes a desert, and house falls on house. [18]If Satan also is divided against himself, how will his kingdom stand? —for you say that I cast out the demons by Beelzebul. [19]Now if I cast out the demons by Beelzebul, by whom do your exorcists [d] cast them out? Therefore they will be your judges. [20]But if it is by the finger of God that I cast out the demons, then the kingdom of God has come to you. [21]When a strong man, fully armed, guards his castle, his property is safe. [22]But when one stronger than he attacks him and overpowers him, he takes away his armor in which he trusted and divides his plunder. [23]Whoever is not with me is against me, and whoever does not gather with me scatters.

The Return of the Unclean Spirit

24 "When the unclean spirit has gone out of a person, it wanders through waterless regions looking for a resting place, but not finding any, it says, 'I will return to my house from which I came.' [25]When it comes, it finds it swept and put in order. [26]Then it goes and brings seven other spirits more evil than itself, and they enter and live there; and the last state of that person is worse than the first."

a Or us into temptation. Other ancient authorities add but rescue us from the evil one (or from evil)
b Other ancient authorities add bread, will give a stone; or if your child asks for   c Other ancient authorities read the Father give the Holy Spirit from heaven   d Gk sons

---

will take shape, not ours. God the Father looms large. For us, it is enough that we get what we need for spiritual and physical sustenance, and that we ground our days in asking for and receiving forgiveness, as well as calling for freedom from evil and all that pulls us toward wrong. It is a very bare-bones sort of prayer compared to many of the ways we pray today. Jesus does back it up with a parable and some picturesque language that encourages us to persist in prayer, so that we may receive what we need (vv 5–13). If we know how to give good gifts, God knows even more so how to give the Holy Spirit. But it is still a very basic and elemental affair. There is nothing here about material wealth or perfect health or things that get me more of me. Instead, it is about there being more of God.

11:2–13 PRAYER—See Spiritual Disciplines Index.

True Blessedness

27 While he was saying this, a woman in the crowd raised her voice and said to him, "Blessed is the womb that bore you and the breasts that nursed you!" 28 But he said, "Blessed rather are those who hear the word of God and obey it!"

The Sign of Jonah

29 When the crowds were increasing, he began to say, "This generation is an evil generation; it asks for a sign, but no sign will be given to it except the sign of Jonah. 30 For just as Jonah became a sign to the people of Nineveh, so the Son of Man will be to this generation. 31 The queen of the South will rise at the judgment with the people of this generation and condemn them, because she came from the ends of the earth to listen to the wisdom of Solomon, and see, something greater than Solomon is here! 32 The people of Nineveh will rise up at the judgment with this generation and condemn it, because they repented at the proclamation of Jonah, and see, something greater than Jonah is here!

The Light of the Body

33 "No one after lighting a lamp puts it in a cellar, a but on the lampstand so that those who enter may see the light. 34 Your eye is the lamp of your body. If your eye is healthy, your whole body is full of light; but if it is not healthy, your body is full of darkness. 35 Therefore consider whether the light in you is not darkness. 36 If then your whole body is full of light, with no part of it in darkness, it will be as full of light as when a lamp gives you light with its rays."

Jesus Denounces Pharisees and Lawyers

37 While he was speaking, a Pharisee invited him to dine with him; so he went in and took his place at the table. 38 The Pharisee was amazed to see that he did not first wash before dinner. 39 Then the Lord said to him, "Now you Pharisees clean the outside of the cup and of the dish, but inside you are full of greed and wickedness. 40 You fools! Did not the one who made the outside make the inside also? 41 So give for alms those things that are within; and see, everything will be clean for you.

42 "But woe to you Pharisees! For you tithe mint and rue and herbs of all kinds, and neglect justice and the love of God; it is these you ought to have practiced, without neglecting the others. 43 Woe to you Pharisees! For you love to have the seat of honor in the synagogues and to be greeted with respect in the marketplaces. 44 Woe to you! For you are like unmarked graves, and people walk over them without realizing it."

45 One of the lawyers answered him, "Teacher, when you say these things, you insult us too." 46 And he said, "Woe also to you lawyers! For you load people with burdens hard to bear, and you yourselves do not lift a finger to ease them. 47 Woe to you! For you build the tombs of the prophets whom your ancestors killed. 48 So you are witnesses and approve of the deeds of your ancestors; for they killed them, and you build their tombs. 49 Therefore also the Wisdom of God said, 'I will send them prophets and apostles, some of whom they will kill and persecute,' 50 so that this generation may be charged with the blood of all the prophets shed since the foundation of the world, 51 from the blood of Abel to the blood of Zechariah, who perished between the altar and the sanctuary. Yes, I tell you, it will be charged against this generation. 52 Woe to you lawyers! For you have taken away the key of knowledge; you did not enter yourselves, and you hindered those who were entering."

53 When he went outside, the scribes and the Pharisees began to be very hostile toward

a Other ancient authorities add *or under the bushel basket*

11:29 THE WITH-GOD LIFE—*See* Spiritual Disciplines Index.

11:42–52 *woe to you Pharisees!* A prevalent idea in Christian spirituality, which crops up in every generation, teaches that a true spirituality is practically devoid of human emotion, especially anger of any kind. Along with this usually comes the assertion that gentle Jesus, meek and mild, never lost his temper. This passage pricks the balloon of that myth.

him and to cross-examine him about many things, [54] lying in wait for him, to catch him in something he might say.

A Warning against Hypocrisy

12 Meanwhile, when the crowd gathered by the thousands, so that they trampled on one another, he began to speak first to his disciples, "Beware of the yeast of the Pharisees, that is, their hypocrisy. [2] Nothing is covered up that will not be uncovered, and nothing secret that will not become known. [3] Therefore whatever you have said in the dark will be heard in the light, and what you have whispered behind closed doors will be proclaimed from the housetops.

Exhortation to Fearless Confession

[4] "I tell you, my friends, do not fear those who kill the body, and after that can do nothing more. [5] But I will warn you whom to fear: fear him who, after he has killed, has authority[a] to cast into hell.[b] Yes, I tell you, fear him! [6] Are not five sparrows sold for two pennies? Yet not one of them is forgotten in God's sight. [7] But even the hairs of your head are all counted. Do not be afraid; you are of more value than many sparrows.

[8] "And I tell you, everyone who acknowledges me before others, the Son of Man also will acknowledge before the angels of God;

[9] but whoever denies me before others will be denied before the angels of God. [10] And everyone who speaks a word against the Son of Man will be forgiven; but whoever blasphemes against the Holy Spirit will not be forgiven. [11] When they bring you before the synagogues, the rulers, and the authorities, do not worry about how[c] you are to defend yourselves or what you are to say; [12] for the Holy Spirit will teach you at that very hour what you ought to say."

The Parable of the Rich Fool

[13] Someone in the crowd said to him, "Teacher, tell my brother to divide the family inheritance with me." [14] But he said to him, "Friend, who set me to be a judge or arbitrator over you?" [15] And he said to them, "Take care! Be on your guard against all kinds of greed; for one's life does not consist in the abundance of possessions." [16] Then he told them a parable: "The land of a rich man produced abundantly. [17] And he thought to himself, 'What should I do, for I have no place to store my crops?' [18] Then he said, 'I will do this: I will pull down my barns and build larger ones, and there I will store all my grain and my goods. [19] And I will say to my soul, Soul, you have ample goods laid up for many

---

12:1–5 CONFESSION—*See* Spiritual Disciplines Index.

Responding
12:8–9 CONFESSION. We normally think of confession as admitting our sins before a priest or a trusted friend so that we can be freed for greater ministry. However, these verses speak of acknowledging or denying Jesus Christ before others. Try to recall a time in your life when you should have acknowledged Jesus before others, but didn't. Now lovingly give this failure to the Lord and trust him to forgive you and to heal the wound in your heart. *See also* Spiritual Disciplines Index.

12:13–21 *Soul, you have ample goods . . . relax, eat, drink, be merry.* We often consider this story in the light of material possessions—

too many cars, too many TVs, too many clothes, too big a house, too much in the bank—since that was certainly the rich man's problem: "I will pull down my barns and build larger ones, and there I will store all my grain and my goods." But Jesus' comment at the end does not specify money or possessions: "So it is with those who store up treasures for themselves but are not rich toward God." We might consider friendships or children or physical health to be our greatest possessions. We might even store up spiritual treasure after spiritual treasure, taking in as many as possible, living for the sense of God's presence to the exclusion of all else. We could say, "Soul, you have had ample religious experiences and picked up spiritual insights and wisdom to last a lifetime. Relax." And God could just as easily respond, "You fool! This very night your life is being demanded of you. And the

years; relax, eat, drink, be merry.' ²⁰But God said to him, 'You fool! This very night your life is being demanded of you. And the things you have prepared, whose will they be?' ²¹So it is with those who store up treasures for themselves but are not rich toward God."

Do Not Worry

22 He said to his disciples, "Therefore I tell you, do not worry about your life, what you will eat, or about your body, what you will wear. ²³For life is more than food, and the body more than clothing. ²⁴Consider the ravens: they neither sow nor reap, they have neither storehouse nor barn, and yet God feeds them. Of how much more value are you than the birds! ²⁵And can any of you by worrying add a single hour to your span of life?ᵃ ²⁶If then you are not able to do so small a thing as that, why do you worry about the rest? ²⁷Consider the lilies, how they grow: they neither toil nor spin;ᵇ yet I tell you, even Solomon in all his glory was not clothed like one of these. ²⁸But if God so clothes the grass of the field, which is alive today and tomorrow is thrown into the oven, how much more will he clothe you—you of little faith! ²⁹And do not keep striving for what you are to eat and what you are to drink, and do not keep worrying. ³⁰For it is the nations of the world that strive after all these things, and your Father knows that you need them. ³¹Instead, strive for hisᶜ kingdom, and these things will be given to you as well.

32 "Do not be afraid, little flock, for it is your Father's good pleasure to give you the kingdom. ³³Sell your possessions, and give alms. Make purses for yourselves that do not wear out, an unfailing treasure in heaven, where no thief comes near and no moth destroys. ³⁴For where your treasure is, there your heart will be also.

Watchful Slaves

35 "Be dressed for action and have your lamps lit; ³⁶be like those who are waiting for their master to return from the wedding banquet, so that they may open the door for him as soon as he comes and knocks. ³⁷Blessed are those slaves whom the master finds alert when he comes; truly I tell you, he will fasten his belt and have them sit down to eat, and he will come and serve them. ³⁸If he comes during the middle of the night, or near dawn, and finds them so, blessed are those slaves.

39 "But know this: if the owner of the house had known at what hour the thief was coming, heᵈ would not have let his house be broken into. ⁴⁰You also must be ready, for the Son of Man is coming at an unexpected hour."

The Faithful or the Unfaithful Slave

41 Peter said, "Lord, are you telling this parable for us or for everyone?" ⁴²And the Lord said, "Who then is the faithful and prudent manager whom his master will put in charge of his slaves, to give them their allowance of food at the proper time? ⁴³Blessed is that slave whom his master will find at work when he arrives. ⁴⁴Truly I tell you, he will put that one in charge of all his possessions. ⁴⁵But if that slave says to himself, 'My master is delayed in coming,' and if he begins to beat the other slaves, men and women, and to eat and drink and get drunk, ⁴⁶the master of that slave will come on a day when he does not expect him and at an hour that he does not know, and will cut him in pieces,ᵉ and put him with the unfaithful. ⁴⁷That slave who knew what his master wanted, but did not prepare himself or do what was wanted,

---

a Or *add a cubit to your stature*   *b* Other ancient authorities read *Consider the lilies; they neither spin nor weave   c* Other ancient authorities read *God's   d* Other ancient authorities add *would have watched and   e* Or *cut him off*

---

spirituality you have hidden away for yourself alone, who will benefit from it now?" We can make a god out of prayer and spiritual formation and solitude. We can live for our experiences rather than the God who is the source of them. We can hoard what we have learned and never share with others who are struggling. Our richness should be in God himself, not in the ways we enjoy worshiping him.

12:37 SERVICE—*See* Spiritual Disciplines Index.

will receive a severe beating. ⁴⁸But the one who did not know and did what deserved a beating will receive a light beating. From everyone to whom much has been given, much will be required; and from the one to whom much has been entrusted, even more will be demanded.

Jesus the Cause of Division

49 "I came to bring fire to the earth, and how I wish it were already kindled! ⁵⁰I have a baptism with which to be baptized, and what stress I am under until it is completed! ⁵¹Do you think that I have come to bring peace to the earth? No, I tell you, but rather division! ⁵²From now on five in one household will be divided, three against two and two against three; ⁵³they will be divided:

father against son
and son against father,
mother against daughter
and daughter against mother,
mother-in-law against her daughter-in-
law
and daughter-in-law against mother-
in-law."

Interpreting the Time

54 He also said to the crowds, "When you see a cloud rising in the west, you immediately say, 'It is going to rain'; and so it happens. ⁵⁵And when you see the south wind

blowing, you say, 'There will be scorching heat'; and it happens. ⁵⁶You hypocrites! You know how to interpret the appearance of earth and sky, but why do you not know how to interpret the present time?

Settling with Your Opponent

57 "And why do you not judge for yourselves what is right? ⁵⁸Thus, when you go with your accuser before a magistrate, on the way make an effort to settle the case,ᵃ or you may be dragged before the judge, and the judge hand you over to the officer, and the officer throw you in prison. ⁵⁹I tell you, you will never get out until you have paid the very last penny."

Repent or Perish

13 At that very time there were some present who told him about the Galileans whose blood Pilate had mingled with their sacrifices. ²He asked them, "Do you think that because these Galileans suffered in this way they were worse sinners than all other Galileans? ³No, I tell you; but unless you repent, you will all perish as they did. ⁴Or those eighteen who were killed when the tower of Siloam fell on them—do you think that they were worse offenders than all the others living in Jerusalem? ⁵No, I tell you;

a Gk settle with him

13:1–9 *do you think that they were worse offenders than all the others?* It is human nature to speculate that if bad things happen to people, it is because they have done something wrong and are being punished for it. Jesus discusses tragedy that is caused by humans and tragedy that occurs naturally or accidentally—what insurance agencies might call an "act of God"— and he swiftly dismisses this whole way of thinking. The Galileans Pilate murdered were not more terrible people than other Galileans. The eighteen who died when the tower of Siloam collapsed were not more guilty than the other citizens of Jerusalem. God had not cooked up any special plans to wipe out all these people. What is true, according to Jesus, is that anything can happen to anyone at any time, not because they are selected, but because that is

the nature of the world we live in. It may happen from an intruder's gun or a hurricane or the growth of a tumor. People die on this planet precisely because they are people and that is how the planet works. Given this, it is better to get things right with God and others sooner rather than later. Jesus softens this harsh reality with a parable about a fig tree. It has never produced any fruit, so its owner wants to destroy it. But the man who works the vineyard insists on giving the tree another chance. He will continue to help it live and grow and be what it was meant to be. God is a God of grace. He does not give up on anyone's life. He keeps working to make people whole. We may die at any moment. In the meantime, God keeps at it, giving us more time, more chances, offering us years of opportunities, lavishing his Spirit and

but unless you repent, you will all perish just as they did."

The Parable of the Barren Fig Tree

6 Then he told this parable: "A man had a fig tree planted in his vineyard; and he came looking for fruit on it and found none. 7So he said to the gardener, 'See here! For three years I have come looking for fruit on this fig tree, and still I find none. Cut it down! Why should it be wasting the soil?' 8He replied, 'Sir, let it alone for one more year, until I dig around it and put manure on it. 9If it bears fruit next year, well and good; but if not, you can cut it down.' "

Jesus Heals a Crippled Woman

10 Now he was teaching in one of the synagogues on the sabbath. 11And just then there appeared a woman with a spirit that had crippled her for eighteen years. She was bent over and was quite unable to stand up straight. 12When Jesus saw her, he called her over and said, "Woman, you are set free from your ailment." 13When he laid his hands on her, immediately she stood up straight and began praising God. 14But the leader of the synagogue, indignant because Jesus had cured on the sabbath, kept saying to the crowd, "There are six days on which work ought to be done; come on those days and be cured, and not on the sabbath day." 15But the Lord answered him and said, "You hypocrites! Does not each of you on the sabbath untie his ox or his donkey from the manger, and lead it away to give it water? 16And ought not this woman, a daughter of Abraham whom Satan bound for eighteen long years, be set free from this bondage on the sabbath day?" 17When he said this, all his opponents were put to shame; and the entire crowd was rejoicing at all the wonderful things that he was doing.

The Parable of the Mustard Seed

18 He said therefore, "What is the kingdom of God like? And to what should I compare it? 19It is like a mustard seed that someone took and sowed in the garden; it grew and became a tree, and the birds of the air made nests in its branches."

The Parable of the Yeast

20 And again he said, "To what should I compare the kingdom of God? 21It is like yeast that a woman took and mixed in with[a] three measures of flour until all of it was leavened."

The Narrow Door

22 Jesus[b] went through one town and village after another, teaching as he made his way to Jerusalem. 23Someone asked him, "Lord, will only a few be saved?" He said to them, 24"Strive to enter through the narrow door; for many, I tell you, will try to enter and will not be able. 25When once the owner of the house has got up and shut the door, and you begin to stand outside and to knock at the door, saying, 'Lord, open to us,' then in reply he will say to you, 'I do not know where you come from.' 26Then you will begin to say, 'We ate and drank with you, and you taught in our streets.' 27But he will say, 'I do not know where you come from; go away from me, all you evildoers!' 28There will be weeping and gnashing of teeth when you see Abraham and Isaac and Jacob and all the prophets in the kingdom of God, and you yourselves thrown out. 29Then people will come from east and west, from north and south, and will eat in the kingdom of God. 30Indeed, some are last who will be first, and some are first who will be last."

The Lament over Jerusalem

31 At that very hour some Pharisees came and said to him, "Get away from here, for Herod wants to kill you." 32He said to them, "Go and tell that fox for me,[c] 'Listen, I am casting out demons and performing cures today and tomorrow, and on the third day I finish my work. 33Yet today, tomorrow, and

a Gk hid in   b Gk He   c Gk lacks for me

---

his love upon us. After all, it is not this world that is the God we worship, nor is death the God we worship. It is the Lord of heaven and earth who is God and it is to him alone that we bend the knee and give the worship we offer no one and nothing else.

the next day I must be on my way, because it is impossible for a prophet to be killed outside of Jerusalem.' 34Jerusalem, Jerusalem, the city that kills the prophets and stones those who are sent to it! How often have I desired to gather your children together as a hen gathers her brood under her wings, and you were not willing! 35See, your house is left to you. And I tell you, you will not see me until the time comes when *a* you say, 'Blessed is the one who comes in the name of the Lord.' "

Jesus Heals the Man with Dropsy

14 On one occasion when Jesus *b* was going to the house of a leader of the Pharisees to eat a meal on the sabbath, they were watching him closely. 2Just then, in front of him, there was a man who had dropsy. 3And Jesus asked the lawyers and Pharisees, "Is it lawful to cure people on the sabbath, or not?" 4But they were silent. So Jesus *b* took him and healed him, and sent him away. 5Then he said to them, "If one of you has a child *c* or an ox that has fallen into a well, will you not immediately pull it out on a sabbath day?" 6And they could not reply to this.

Humility and Hospitality

7 When he noticed how the guests chose the places of honor, he told them a parable. 8"When you are invited by someone to a wedding banquet, do not sit down at the place of honor, in case someone more distinguished than you has been invited by your host; 9and the host who invited both of you may come and say to you, 'Give this person your place,' and then in disgrace you would start to take the lowest place. 10But when you are invited, go and sit down at the lowest place, so that when your host comes, he may say to you, 'Friend, move up higher'; then you will be honored in the presence of all who sit at the table with you. 11For all who exalt themselves will be humbled, and those who humble themselves will be exalted."

12 He said also to the one who had invited him, "When you give a luncheon or a dinner, do not invite your friends or your brothers or your relatives or rich neighbors, in case they may invite you in return, and you would be repaid. 13But when you give a banquet, invite the poor, the crippled, the lame, and the blind. 14And you will be blessed, because they cannot repay you, for you will be repaid at the resurrection of the righteous."

The Parable of the Great Dinner

15 One of the dinner guests, on hearing this, said to him, "Blessed is anyone who will eat bread in the kingdom of God!" 16Then Jesus *b* said to him, "Someone gave a great dinner and invited many. 17At the time for

a Other ancient authorities lack *the time comes when*   *b* Gk *he*   *c* Other ancient authorities read *a donkey*

14:16–24 *Someone gave a great dinner and invited many.* This parable makes cinema of what was only a snapshot when Jesus called Levi to be his disciple. At that point, Luke tells us, "Levi gave a great banquet for [Jesus] in his house; and there was a large crowd of tax collectors and others sitting at the table with them. The Pharisees and their scribes were complaining to his disciples, saying, 'Why do you eat and drink with tax collectors and sinners?'" (5:29–30). Now it is not only tax collectors and prostitutes who are entering the kingdom of God ahead of the religiously flawless (Matt 21:31), but the poor, the crippled, the blind, and the lame. This is the great supper of the Son of God, the Messianic Banquet, the Feast of Heaven, which Levi's banquet foreshadows, and the heavenly ones are not those we might expect to be the guests at such an immortal gathering. The first ones to be invited did not come, opening the way for those considered second-rate and inferior. We have often been told that we will be surprised by the sort of people who will populate the kingdom of heaven. It is actually easier to imagine all sorts of street people being there than some of the world's great villains or our own personal enemies, people who slandered, assaulted, or crushed us. Yet the God of Surprises will undoubtedly baffle us tomorrow even as he baffles us today by the sheer extravagance and inclusiveness of his grace. No sooner do we write an individual off than we can be sure God is working light and spirit into all the crevices and fissures of that person's soul.

the dinner he sent his slave to say to those who had been invited, 'Come; for everything is ready now.' 18But they all alike began to make excuses. The first said to him, 'I have bought a piece of land, and I must go out and see it; please accept my regrets.' 19Another said, 'I have bought five yoke of oxen, and I am going to try them out; please accept my regrets.' 20Another said, 'I have just been married, and therefore I cannot come.' 21So the slave returned and reported this to his master. Then the owner of the house became angry and said to his slave, 'Go out at once into the streets and lanes of the town and bring in the poor, the crippled, the blind, and the lame.' 22And the slave said, 'Sir, what you ordered has been done, and there is still room.' 23Then the master said to the slave, 'Go out into the roads and lanes, and compel people to come in, so that my house may be filled. 24For I tell you,a none of those who were invited will taste my dinner.' "

The Cost of Discipleship

25 Now large crowds were traveling with him; and he turned and said to them, 26"Whoever comes to me and does not hate father and mother, wife and children, brothers and sisters, yes, and even life itself, cannot be my disciple. 27Whoever does not carry the cross and follow me cannot be my disciple. 28For which of you, intending to build a tower, does not first sit down and estimate the cost, to see whether he has enough to complete it? 29Otherwise, when he has laid a foundation and is not able to finish, all who see it will begin to ridicule him, 30saying, 'This fellow began to build and was not able to finish.' 31Or what king, going out to wage war against another king, will not sit down first and consider whether he is able with ten thousand to oppose the one who comes against him with twenty thousand? 32If he cannot, then, while the other is still far away, he sends a delegation and asks for the terms of peace. 33So therefore, none of you can become my disciple if you do not give up all your possessions.

About Salt

34 "Salt is good; but if salt has lost its taste, how can its saltiness be restored?b 35It is fit neither for the soil nor for the manure pile; they throw it away. Let anyone with ears to hear listen!"

The Parable of the Lost Sheep

15 Now all the tax collectors and sinners were coming near to listen to him. 2And the Pharisees and the scribes were grumbling and saying, "This fellow welcomes sinners and eats with them."

3 So he told them this parable: 4"Which one of you, having a hundred sheep and losing one of them, does not leave the ninety-nine in the wilderness and go after the one that is lost until he finds it? 5When he has found it, he lays it on his shoulders and rejoices. 6And when he comes home, he calls together his friends and neighbors, saying to them, 'Rejoice with me, for I have found my sheep that was lost.' 7Just so, I tell you, there will be more joy in heaven over one sinner who repents than over ninety-nine righteous persons who need no repentance.

The Parable of the Lost Coin

8 "Or what woman having ten silver coins,c if she loses one of them, does not light a lamp, sweep the house, and search carefully until she finds it? 9When she has found it, she calls together her friends and neighbors, saying, 'Rejoice with me, for I have found the coin that I had lost.' 10Just so, I tell you, there is joy in the presence of the angels of God over one sinner who repents."

The Parable of the Prodigal and His Brother

11 Then Jesusd said, "There was a man who had two sons. 12The younger of them said to his father, 'Father, give me the share

a The Greek word for you here is plural   b Or how can it be used for seasoning?   c Gk drachmas, each worth about a day's wage for a laborer   d Gk he

15:11–32 *There was a man who had two sons.* In the parable of the prodigal son, neither of the two sons can do anything to save himself. The

younger, having thrown away his inheritance, cannot force his father to take him back, even as a hired man. The older brother, crippled by

of the property that will belong to me.' So he divided his property between them. 13A few days later the younger son gathered all he had and traveled to a distant country, and there he squandered his property in dissolute living. 14When he had spent everything, a severe famine took place throughout that country, and he began to be in need. 15So he went and hired himself out to one of the citizens of that country, who sent him to his fields to feed the pigs. 16He would gladly have filled himself with*a* the pods that the pigs were eating; and no one gave him anything. 17But when he came to himself he said, 'How many of my father's hired hands have bread enough and to spare, but here I am dying of hunger! 18I will get up and go to my father, and I will say to him, "Father, I have sinned against heaven and before you; 19I am no longer worthy to be called your son; treat me like one of your hired hands." ' 20So he set off and went to his father. But while he was still far off, his father saw him and was filled with compassion; he ran and put his arms around him and kissed him. 21Then the son said to him, 'Father, I have sinned against heaven and before you; I am no longer worthy to be called your son.'*b* 22But the father said to his slaves, 'Quickly, bring out a robe—the best one—and put it on him; put a ring on his finger and sandals on his feet. 23And get the fatted calf and kill it, and let us eat and celebrate; 24for this son of mine was dead and is

alive again; he was lost and is found!' And they began to celebrate.

25 "Now his elder son was in the field; and when he came and approached the house, he heard music and dancing. 26He called one of the slaves and asked what was going on. 27He replied, 'Your brother has come, and your father has killed the fatted calf, because he has got him back safe and sound.' 28Then he became angry and refused to go in. His father came out and began to plead with him. 29But he answered his father, 'Listen! For all these years I have been working like a slave for you, and I have never disobeyed your command; yet you have never given me even a young goat so that I might celebrate with my friends. 30But when this son of yours came back, who has devoured your property with prostitutes, you killed the fatted calf for him!' 31Then the father*c* said to him, 'Son, you are always with me, and all that is mine is yours. 32But we had to celebrate and rejoice, because this brother of yours was dead and has come to life; he was lost and has been found.' "

The Parable of the Dishonest Manager

16 Then Jesus*c* said to the disciples, "There was a rich man who had a manager, and charges were brought to him

a Other ancient authorities read *filled his stomach with*   *b* Other ancient authorities add *Treat me like one of your hired servants*   *c* Gk *he*

---

jealousy and bitterness, cannot force himself over the threshold to welcome his brother back to life. Only the father can be the catalyst of resurrection for them both—if he is willing to humble himself and fling himself at their feet and beg them to come into the house. But why should he? The younger son only returned home because he is starving, not because he is truly sorry for what he has done. The older brother is used to having everything and now is acting like a spoiled brat, humiliating his father by refusing to obey his summons to join the feast. Yet the father goes out to both of them. He is not concerned about how it looks, the great patriarch kissing the younger renegade, who has dishonored him, and pleading with the older renegade, who has also dishonored him. Love does not

care if it looks foolish. Love only asks that it be allowed to love at whatever cost. The sons do not have it in them to save themselves. So the love of the father does it for them. This parable is a watershed of the Bible. Either God loves like this or he doesn't. Jesus is adamant in this incredible fiction he has created: God's love for us is indeed spectacular—"Let's have a feast and celebrate!"—so our love must mesh with his and be equally spectacular. "We had to celebrate and rejoice, because this brother of yours was dead and has come to life; he was lost and has been found!" (v 32). In this one story, fashioned from the mind of Christ, we find the very essence of the gospel.

15:23–32 CELEBRATION—*See* Spiritual Disciplines Index.

that this man was squandering his property. 2So he summoned him and said to him, 'What is this that I hear about you? Give me an accounting of your management, because you cannot be my manager any longer.' 3Then the manager said to himself, 'What will I do, now that my master is taking the position away from me? I am not strong enough to dig, and I am ashamed to beg. 4I have decided what to do so that, when I am dismissed as manager, people may welcome me into their homes.' 5So, summoning his master's debtors one by one, he asked the first, 'How much do you owe my master?' 6He answered, 'A hundred jugs of olive oil.' He said to him, 'Take your bill, sit down quickly, and make it fifty.' 7Then he asked another, 'And how much do you owe?' He replied, 'A hundred containers of wheat.' He said to him, 'Take your bill and make it eighty.' 8And his master commended the dishonest manager because he had acted shrewdly; for the children of this age are more shrewd in dealing with their own generation than are the children of light. 9And I tell you, make friends for yourselves by means of dishonest wealth *a* so that when it is gone, they may welcome you into the eternal homes. *b*

10 "Whoever is faithful in a very little is faithful also in much; and whoever is dishonest in a very little is dishonest also in much. 11If then you have not been faithful with the dishonest wealth, *a* who will entrust to you the true riches? 12And if you have not been faithful with what belongs to another, who will give you what is your own? 13No slave can serve two masters; for a slave will either hate the one and love the other, or be devoted to the one and despise the other. You cannot serve God and wealth." *a*

The Law and the Kingdom of God

14 The Pharisees, who were lovers of money, heard all this, and they ridiculed him. 15So he said to them, "You are those who justify yourselves in the sight of others; but God knows your hearts; for what is prized by human beings is an abomination in the sight of God.

16 "The law and the prophets were in effect until John came; since then the good news of the kingdom of God is proclaimed, and everyone tries to enter it by force. *c* 17But it is easier for heaven and earth to pass away, than for one stroke of a letter in the law to be dropped.

18 "Anyone who divorces his wife and marries another commits adultery, and whoever marries a woman divorced from her husband commits adultery.

The Rich Man and Lazarus

19 "There was a rich man who was dressed in purple and fine linen and who feasted sumptuously every day. 20And at his gate lay a poor man named Lazarus, covered with sores, 21who longed to satisfy his hunger with what fell from the rich man's table; even the dogs would come and lick his sores. 22The poor man died and was carried away by the angels to be with Abraham. *d* The rich man also died and was buried. 23In Hades, where he was being tormented, he looked up and saw Abraham far away with Lazarus by his side. *e* 24He called out, 'Father Abraham, have mercy on me, and send Lazarus to dip the tip of his finger in water and cool my tongue; for I am in agony in these flames.' 25But Abraham said, 'Child, remember that during your lifetime you received your good things, and Lazarus in like manner evil things; but now he is comforted here, and you are in agony. 26Besides all this, between you and us a great chasm has been fixed, so that those who might want to pass from here to you cannot do so, and no one can cross from there to us.' 27He said, 'Then, father, I beg you to send him to my father's house— 28for I have five brothers—that he may warn them, so that they will not also come into this place of torment.' 29Abraham replied, 'They have Moses and the prophets; they should listen to

a Gk *mammon*   *b* Gk *tents*   *c* Or *everyone is strongly urged to enter it*   *d* Gk *to Abraham's bosom*   *e* Gk *in his bosom*

16:13 SERVICE—*See* Spiritual Disciplines Index.

them.' 30He said, 'No, father Abraham; but if someone goes to them from the dead, they will repent.' 31He said to him, 'If they do not listen to Moses and the prophets, neither will they be convinced even if someone rises from the dead.' "

Some Sayings of Jesus

17 Jesus[a] said to his disciples, "Occasions for stumbling are bound to come, but woe to anyone by whom they come! 2It would be better for you if a millstone were hung around your neck and you were thrown into the sea than for you to cause one of these little ones to stumble. 3Be on your guard! If another disciple[b] sins, you must rebuke the offender, and if there is repentance, you must forgive. 4And if the same person sins against you seven times a day, and turns back to you seven times and says, 'I repent,' you must forgive."

5 The apostles said to the Lord, "Increase our faith!" 6The Lord replied, "If you had faith the size of a[c] mustard seed, you could say to this mulberry tree, 'Be uprooted and planted in the sea,' and it would obey you.

7 "Who among you would say to your slave who has just come in from plowing or tending sheep in the field, 'Come here at once and take your place at the table'? 8Would you not rather say to him, 'Prepare supper for me, put on your apron and serve me while I eat and drink; later you may eat and drink'? 9Do you thank the slave for doing what was commanded? 10So you also, when you have done all that you were ordered to do, say, 'We are worthless slaves; we have done only what we ought to have done!' "

Jesus Cleanses Ten Lepers

11 On the way to Jerusalem Jesus[d] was going through the region between Samaria and Galilee. 12As he entered a village, ten lepers[e] approached him. Keeping their distance, 13they called out, saying, "Jesus, Master, have mercy on us!" 14When he saw them, he said to them, "Go and show yourselves to the priests." And as they went, they were made clean. 15Then one of them, when he saw that he was healed, turned back, praising God with a loud voice. 16He prostrated himself at Jesus'[f] feet and thanked him. And he was a Samaritan. 17Then Jesus asked, "Were not ten made clean? But the other nine, where are they? 18Was none of them found to return and give praise to God except this foreigner?" 19Then he said to him, "Get up and go on your way; your faith has made you well."

The Coming of the Kingdom

20 Once Jesus[d] was asked by the Pharisees when the kingdom of God was coming, and he answered, "The kingdom of God is not coming with things that can be observed; 21nor will they say, 'Look, here it is!' or 'There it is!' For, in fact, the kingdom of God is among[g] you."

22 Then he said to the disciples, "The days are coming when you will long to see one of the days of the Son of Man, and you will not see it. 23They will say to you, 'Look there!' or 'Look here!' Do not go, do not set off in pursuit. 24For as the lightning flashes and lights up the sky from one side to the other, so will the Son of Man be in his day.[h] 25But first he must endure much suffering and be rejected by this generation. 26Just as it was in the days of Noah, so too it will be in the days of the Son of Man. 27They were eating and drinking, and marrying and being given in marriage,

a Gk He   b Gk *your brother*   c Gk *faith as a grain of*   d Gk *he*   e The terms *leper* and *leprosy* can refer to several diseases   f Gk *his* g Or *within*   h Other ancient authorities lack *in his day*

Responding
17:7–10 SERVICE. In this passage Jesus first challenges the disciples, then tells them that their service should be in response to what they have been commanded to do. What have we been commanded to do? Why do we do it? Because it is what we ought

to do or because we love the Lord? Try to explain as best you can. *See also* Spiritual Disciplines Index.

17:21 THE WITH-GOD LIFE—*See* Spiritual Disciplines Index.

until the day Noah entered the ark, and the flood came and destroyed all of them. 28Likewise, just as it was in the days of Lot: they were eating and drinking, buying and selling, planting and building, 29but on the day that Lot left Sodom, it rained fire and sulfur from heaven and destroyed all of them 30—it will be like that on the day that the Son of Man is revealed. 31On that day, anyone on the housetop who has belongings in the house must not come down to take them away; and likewise anyone in the field must not turn back. 32Remember Lot's wife. 33Those who try to make their life secure will lose it, but those who lose their life will keep it. 34I tell you, on that night there will be two in one bed; one will be taken and the other left. 35There will be two women grinding meal together; one will be taken and the other left." [a] 37Then they asked him, "Where, Lord?" He said to them, "Where the corpse is, there the vultures will gather."

The Parable of the Widow and the Unjust Judge

18 Then Jesus [b] told them a parable about their need to pray always and not to lose heart. 2He said, "In a certain city there was a judge who neither feared God nor had respect for people. 3In that city there was a widow who kept coming to him and saying, 'Grant me justice against my opponent.' 4For a while he refused; but later he said to himself, 'Though I have no fear of God and no respect for anyone, 5yet because this widow keeps bothering me, I will grant her justice, so that she may not wear me out by continually coming.' " [c] 6And the Lord said, "Listen to what the unjust judge says. 7And will not God grant justice to his chosen ones who cry to him day and night? Will he delay long in helping them? 8I tell you, he will quickly grant justice to them. And yet, when the Son of Man comes, will he find faith on earth?"

The Parable of the Pharisee and the Tax Collector

9 He also told this parable to some who trusted in themselves that they were righteous and regarded others with contempt: 10"Two men went up to the temple to pray, one a Pharisee and the other a tax collector. 11The Pharisee, standing by himself, was praying thus, 'God, I thank you that I am not like other people: thieves, rogues, adulterers, or even like this tax collector. 12I fast twice a week; I give a tenth of all my income.' 13But the tax collector, standing far off, would not even look up to heaven, but was beating his breast and saying, 'God, be merciful to me, a sinner!' 14I tell you, this man went down to his home justified rather than the other; for all who exalt themselves will be humbled, but all who humble themselves will be exalted."

Jesus Blesses Little Children

15 People were bringing even infants to him that he might touch them; and when the disciples saw it, they sternly ordered them not to do it. 16But Jesus called for them and said, "Let the little children come to me, and do not stop them; for it is to such as these that the kingdom of God belongs. 17Truly I tell you, whoever does not receive the kingdom of God as a little child will never enter it."

The Rich Ruler

18 A certain ruler asked him, "Good Teacher, what must I do to inherit eternal life?" 19Jesus said to him, "Why do you call me good? No one is good but God alone. 20You know the commandments: 'You shall not commit adultery; You shall not murder; You shall not steal; You shall not bear false witness; Honor your father and mother.' " 21He replied, "I have kept all these since my youth." 22When Jesus heard this, he said to him, "There is still one thing lacking. Sell all that you own and distribute the money [d] to the poor, and you will have treasure in heaven; then come, follow me." 23But when

a Other ancient authorities add verse 36, *"Two will be in the field; one will be taken and the other left."*
b Gk *he*   c Or *so that she may not finally come and slap me in the face*   d Gk lacks *the money*

18:1-8, 10–14 PRAYER—*See* Spiritual Disciplines Index.

18:16–17 THE WITH-GOD LIFE—*See* Spiritual Disciplines Index.

he heard this, he became sad; for he was very rich. 24Jesus looked at him and said, "How hard it is for those who have wealth to enter the kingdom of God! 25Indeed, it is easier for a camel to go through the eye of a needle than for someone who is rich to enter the kingdom of God."

26 Those who heard it said, "Then who can be saved?" 27He replied, "What is impossible for mortals is possible for God."

28 Then Peter said, "Look, we have left our homes and followed you." 29And he said to them, "Truly I tell you, there is no one who has left house or wife or brothers or parents or children, for the sake of the kingdom of God, 30who will not get back very much more in this age, and in the age to come eternal life."

A Third Time Jesus Foretells His Death and Resurrection

31 Then he took the twelve aside and said to them, "See, we are going up to Jerusalem, and everything that is written about the Son of Man by the prophets will be accomplished. 32For he will be handed over to the Gentiles; and he will be mocked and insulted and spat upon. 33After they have flogged him, they will kill him, and on the third day he will rise again." 34But they understood nothing about all these things; in fact, what he said was hidden from them, and they did not grasp what was said.

Jesus Heals a Blind Beggar Near Jericho

35 As he approached Jericho, a blind man was sitting by the roadside begging. 36When he heard a crowd going by, he asked what was happening. 37They told him, "Jesus of Nazareth[a] is passing by." 38Then he shouted, "Jesus, Son of David, have mercy on me!" 39Those who were in front sternly ordered him to be quiet; but he shouted even more loudly, "Son of David, have mercy on me!" 40Jesus stood still and ordered the man to be brought to him; and when he came near, he asked him, 41"What do you want me to do for you?" He said, "Lord, let me see again." 42Jesus said to him, "Receive your sight; your faith has saved you." 43Immediately he regained his sight and followed him, glorifying God; and all the people, when they saw it, praised God.

Jesus and Zacchaeus

19 He entered Jericho and was passing through it. 2A man was there named Zacchaeus; he was a chief tax collector and was rich. 3He was trying to see who Jesus was, but on account of the crowd he could not, because he was short in stature. 4So he ran ahead and climbed a sycamore tree to see him, because he was going to pass that way. 5When Jesus came to the place, he looked up and said to him, "Zacchaeus, hurry and come down; for I must stay at your house today." 6So he hurried down and was happy to welcome him. 7All who saw it began to grumble and said, "He has gone to be the guest of one who is a sinner." 8Zacchaeus stood there and said to the Lord, "Look, half of my possessions, Lord, I will give to the poor; and if I have defrauded anyone of anything, I will pay back four times as much." 9Then Jesus said to him,

a Gk the Nazorean

19:2–10 *A man was there named Zacchaeus.* Our Christian spirituality sometimes seems saturated with formulas. Convention dictates we use certain words when we converse with others about spiritual matters—a kind of "Christianese" that varies from denomination to denomination and affects not only conversation, but worship, prayer, and evangelism. It is not, however, Jesus' way. With Jesus, no two prayers are the same. No two people are spoken to in the same way. Zacchaeus is not told he must be born a second time, or that he can have living water, or to give all he has to the poor and follow Jesus. Christ only calls to Zacchaeus that he is going to pay a visit to his house. No sermon. No altar call. In fact, nothing remotely spiritual at all is verbalized. Yet despite the lack of any spiritual alphabet, Zacchaeus is suddenly exploding into a conversion experience that has him giving half his wealth to the poor and paying back four times what he owes to the people he has cheated. Salvation has come to his house—without any pat phrases, religious patter, or formulaic vocabulary.

"Today salvation has come to this house, because he too is a son of Abraham. [10]For the Son of Man came to seek out and to save the lost."

The Parable of the Ten Pounds

11 As they were listening to this, he went on to tell a parable, because he was near Jerusalem, and because they supposed that the kingdom of God was to appear immediately. [12]So he said, "A nobleman went to a distant country to get royal power for himself and then return. [13]He summoned ten of his slaves, and gave them ten pounds,[a] and said to them, 'Do business with these until I come back.' [14]But the citizens of his country hated him and sent a delegation after him, saying, 'We do not want this man to rule over us.' [15]When he returned, having received royal power, he ordered these slaves, to whom he had given the money, to be summoned so that he might find out what they had gained by trading. [16]The first came forward and said, 'Lord, your pound has made ten more pounds.' [17]He said to him, 'Well done, good slave! Because you have been trustworthy in a very small thing, take charge of ten cities.' [18]Then the second came, saying, 'Lord, your pound has made five pounds.' [19]He said to him, 'And you, rule over five cities.' [20]Then the other came, saying, 'Lord, here is your pound. I wrapped it up in a piece of cloth, [21]for I was afraid of you, because you are a harsh man; you take what you did not deposit, and reap what you did not sow.' [22]He said to him, 'I will judge you by your own words, you wicked slave! You knew, did you, that I was a harsh man, taking what I did not deposit and reaping what I did not sow? [23]Why then did you not put my money into the bank? Then when I returned, I could have collected it with interest.' [24]He said to the bystanders, 'Take the pound from him and give it to the one who has ten pounds.' [25](And they said to him, 'Lord, he has ten pounds!') [26]'I tell you, to all those who have, more will be given; but from those who have nothing, even what they have will be taken away. [27]But as for these enemies of mine who did not want me to be king over them—bring them here and slaughter them in my presence.' "

Jesus' Triumphal Entry into Jerusalem

28 After he had said this, he went on ahead, going up to Jerusalem.

29 When he had come near Bethphage and Bethany, at the place called the Mount of Olives, he sent two of the disciples, [30]saying, "Go into the village ahead of you, and as you enter it you will find tied there a colt that has never been ridden. Untie it and bring it here. [31]If anyone asks you, 'Why are you untying it?' just say this, 'The Lord needs it.' " [32]So those who were sent departed and found it as he had told them. [33]As they were untying the colt, its owners asked them, "Why are you untying the colt?" [34]They said, "The Lord needs it." [35]Then they brought it to Jesus; and after throwing their cloaks on the colt, they set Jesus on it. [36]As he rode along, people kept spreading their cloaks on the road. [37]As he was now approaching the path down from the Mount of Olives, the whole multitude of the disciples began to praise God joyfully with a loud voice for all the deeds of power that they had seen, [38]saying,

"Blessed is the king
　who comes in the name of the Lord!
Peace in heaven,
　and glory in the highest heaven!"
[39]Some of the Pharisees in the crowd said to him, "Teacher, order your disciples to stop." [40]He answered, "I tell you, if these were silent, the stones would shout out."

Jesus Weeps over Jerusalem

41 As he came near and saw the city, he wept over it, [42]saying, "If you, even you, had

a The mina, rendered here by *pound,* was about three months' wages for a laborer

---

19:41 *As he came near and saw the city, he wept over it.* Frequently we are told that Jesus wept over Lazarus's grave as if that were the only time he ever shed tears. But Jesus loved Jerusalem and the entire nation and people of which it was the heart. He saw the rebellion against Rome forming in their spirits, and he knew it would result in a military retaliation that would crush them. He spoke the pain through his tears and the tightness in his throat. There

only recognized on this day the things that make for peace! But now they are hidden from your eyes. 43Indeed, the days will come upon you, when your enemies will set up ramparts around you and surround you, and hem you in on every side. 44They will crush you to the ground, you and your children within you, and they will not leave within you one stone upon another; because you did not recognize the time of your visitation from God."a

Jesus Cleanses the Temple

45 Then he entered the temple and began to drive out those who were selling things there; 46and he said, "It is written,

'My house shall be a house of prayer';
    but you have made it a den of
        robbers."

47 Every day he was teaching in the temple. The chief priests, the scribes, and the leaders of the people kept looking for a way to kill him; 48but they did not find anything they could do, for all the people were spellbound by what they heard.

The Authority of Jesus Questioned

20 One day, as he was teaching the people in the temple and telling the good news, the chief priests and the scribes came with the elders 2and said to him, "Tell us, by what authority are you doing these things? Who is it who gave you this authority?" 3He

answered them, "I will also ask you a question, and you tell me: 4Did the baptism of John come from heaven, or was it of human origin?" 5They discussed it with one another, saying, "If we say, 'From heaven,' he will say, 'Why did you not believe him?' 6But if we say, 'Of human origin,' all the people will stone us; for they are convinced that John was a prophet." 7So they answered that they did not know where it came from. 8Then Jesus said to them, "Neither will I tell you by what authority I am doing these things."

The Parable of the Wicked Tenants

9 He began to tell the people this parable: "A man planted a vineyard, and leased it to tenants, and went to another country for a long time. 10When the season came, he sent a slave to the tenants in order that they might give him his share of the produce of the vineyard; but the tenants beat him and sent him away empty-handed. 11Next he sent another slave; that one also they beat and insulted and sent away empty-handed. 12And he sent still a third; this one also they wounded and threw out. 13Then the owner of the vineyard said, 'What shall I do? I will send my beloved son; perhaps they will respect him.' 14But when the tenants saw him, they discussed it among themselves and said, 'This is the heir; let us kill him so that the inheritance may be ours.' 15So they threw him out of the vineyard

a Gk lacks from God

---

are cities and peoples and nations whose predicaments are so dire and hopeless that sometimes we can do nothing for them except weep out of our shattered hearts. It may not seem like much. But that pain has its place in the spirit of Jesus, and that is spirit enough.

19:45–46 *My house shall be a house of prayer.* Our churches are centers for many good things, but is prayer an overriding concern within our walls or simply a nice extra? Is it the heart and soul of the body of believers who meet under one roof? It is the people who are the temple of God in the New Testament; it is you and I who are the house of prayer. But how much of a house of prayer are we? Are we full of buying and selling? Are we a place where spiritual greed, theft, and religious sleight of hand are

firmly lodged? Jesus thought it was so important that his Father's house be a place of praying instead of preying that he acted with an aggression that was uncharacteristic of him; he went wild, knocking over tables and chairs, scattering stacks of coins, driving cattle and sheep from their stalls, getting in people's faces: "Take these things out of here!" He even made a whip (John 2:15–16). Perhaps he felt without that communion with God the Father nothing else would ever fit into place, nothing else would ever make any difference, the lost would never be found, those enslaved would never be freed. Do we share that same passion for prayer in our houses of bone and skin and blood? Do we believe it is so critical, so essential that everything else is at risk without it?

and killed him. What then will the owner of the vineyard do to them? 16He will come and destroy those tenants and give the vineyard to others." When they heard this, they said, "Heaven forbid!" 17But he looked at them and said, "What then does this text mean:

'The stone that the builders rejected
    has become the cornerstone'?*a*

18Everyone who falls on that stone will be broken to pieces; and it will crush anyone on whom it falls." 19When the scribes and chief priests realized that he had told this parable against them, they wanted to lay hands on him at that very hour, but they feared the people.

The Question about Paying Taxes

20 So they watched him and sent spies who pretended to be honest, in order to trap him by what he said, so as to hand him over to the jurisdiction and authority of the governor. 21So they asked him, "Teacher, we know that you are right in what you say and teach, and you show deference to no one, but teach the way of God in accordance with truth. 22Is it lawful for us to pay taxes to the emperor, or not?" 23But he perceived their craftiness and said to them, 24"Show me a denarius. Whose head and whose title does it bear?" They said, "The emperor's." 25He said to them, "Then give to the emperor the things that are the emperor's, and to God the things that are God's." 26And they were not able in the presence of the people to trap him by what he said; and being amazed by his answer, they became silent.

The Question about the Resurrection

27 Some Sadducees, those who say there is no resurrection, came to him 28and asked him a question, "Teacher, Moses wrote for us that if a man's brother dies, leaving a wife but no children, the man*b* shall marry the widow and raise up children for his brother. 29Now there were seven brothers; the first married, and died childless; 30then the second 31and the third married her, and so in the same way all seven died childless. 32Finally the woman also died. 33In the resurrection, therefore, whose wife will the woman be? For the seven had married her."

34 Jesus said to them, "Those who belong to this age marry and are given in marriage; 35but those who are considered worthy of a place in that age and in the resurrection from the dead neither marry nor are given in marriage. 36Indeed they cannot die anymore, because they are like angels and are children of God, being children of the resurrection. 37And the fact that the dead are raised Moses himself showed, in the story about the bush, where he speaks of the Lord as the God of Abraham, the God of Isaac, and the God of Jacob. 38Now he is God not of the dead, but of the living; for to him all of them are alive." 39Then some of the scribes answered, "Teacher, you have spoken well." 40For they no longer dared to ask him another question.

The Question about David's Son

41 Then he said to them, "How can they say that the Messiah*c* is David's son? 42For David himself says in the book of Psalms,

a Or *keystone*   *b* Gk *his brother*   *c* Or *the Christ*

20:22–25 *give to the emperor the things that are the emperor's.* Christians invariably quote Romans 13 when it comes to discussions about the relationship between followers of Christ and the government. The implication often is that, when issues arise, good Christians will obey the authorities God has placed over them. Jesus makes a distinction. The demands of the state and the demands of God are not the same. He suggests it is possible to meet both at the same time, but he never suggests that obeying one is exactly the same as obeying the other. He does not say, "Give to Caesar what is Caesar's, and also give to Caesar what is God's." As Luke well knew, the time would come when obedience to God would mean disobedience to the emperor. Even before the clash between Rome and Christ, the early Church would defy the Jewish authorities: "We must obey God rather than any human authority" (Acts 5:29). The separation Jesus established between church and state is a distinction many Christians in the twenty-first century have yet to come to grips with.

'The Lord said to my Lord,
  "Sit at my right hand,
43 until I make your enemies your
    footstool." '
44David thus calls him Lord; so how can he be his son?"

Jesus Denounces the Scribes

45 In the hearing of all the people he said to the*a* disciples, 46"Beware of the scribes, who like to walk around in long robes, and love to be greeted with respect in the marketplaces, and to have the best seats in the synagogues and places of honor at banquets. 47They devour widows' houses and for the sake of appearance say long prayers. They will receive the greater condemnation."

The Widow's Offering

21 He looked up and saw rich people putting their gifts into the treasury; 2he also saw a poor widow put in two small copper coins. 3He said, "Truly I tell you, this poor widow has put in more than all of them; 4for all of them have contributed out of their abundance, but she out of her poverty has put in all she had to live on."

The Destruction of the Temple Foretold

5 When some were speaking about the temple, how it was adorned with beautiful stones and gifts dedicated to God, he said, 6"As for these things that you see, the days will come when not one stone will be left upon another; all will be thrown down."

Signs and Persecutions

7 They asked him, "Teacher, when will this be, and what will be the sign that this is about to take place?" 8And he said, "Beware that you are not led astray; for many will come in my name and say, 'I am he!'*b* and, 'The time is near!'*c* Do not go after them. 9 "When you hear of wars and insurrections, do not be terrified; for these things must take place first, but the end will not follow immediately." 10Then he said to them, "Nation will rise against nation, and kingdom against kingdom; 11there will be great earthquakes, and in various places famines

and plagues; and there will be dreadful portents and great signs from heaven.

12 "But before all this occurs, they will arrest you and persecute you; they will hand you over to synagogues and prisons, and you will be brought before kings and governors because of my name. 13This will give you an opportunity to testify. 14So make up your minds not to prepare your defense in advance; 15for I will give you words*d* and a wisdom that none of your opponents will be able to withstand or contradict. 16You will be betrayed even by parents and brothers, by relatives and friends; and they will put some of you to death. 17You will be hated by all because of my name. 18But not a hair of your head will perish. 19By your endurance you will gain your souls.

The Destruction of Jerusalem Foretold

20 "When you see Jerusalem surrounded by armies, then know that its desolation has come near.*e* 21Then those in Judea must flee to the mountains, and those inside the city must leave it, and those out in the country must not enter it; 22for these are days of vengeance, as a fulfillment of all that is written. 23Woe to those who are pregnant and to those who are nursing infants in those days! For there will be great distress on the earth and wrath against this people; 24they will fall by the edge of the sword and be taken away as captives among all nations; and Jerusalem will be trampled on by the Gentiles, until the times of the Gentiles are fulfilled.

The Coming of the Son of Man

25 "There will be signs in the sun, the moon, and the stars, and on the earth distress among nations confused by the roaring of the sea and the waves. 26People will faint from fear and foreboding of what is coming upon the world, for the powers of the heavens will be shaken. 27Then they will see 'the Son of Man coming in a cloud' with power and great glory. 28Now when these things begin to take place, stand up and raise your heads, because your redemption is drawing near."

a Other ancient authorities read *his*   *b* Gk *I am*
c Or *at hand*   *d* Gk *a mouth*   *e* Or *is at hand*

The Lesson of the Fig Tree

29 Then he told them a parable: "Look at the fig tree and all the trees; 30as soon as they sprout leaves you can see for yourselves and know that summer is already near. 31So also, when you see these things taking place, you know that the kingdom of God is near. 32Truly I tell you, this generation will not pass away until all things have taken place. 33Heaven and earth will pass away, but my words will not pass away.

Exhortation to Watch

34 "Be on guard so that your hearts are not weighed down with dissipation and drunkenness and the worries of this life, and that day does not catch you unexpectedly, 35like a trap. For it will come upon all who live on the face of the whole earth. 36Be alert at all times, praying that you may have the strength to escape all these things that will take place, and to stand before the Son of Man."

37 Every day he was teaching in the temple, and at night he would go out and spend the night on the Mount of Olives, as it was called. 38And all the people would get up early in the morning to listen to him in the temple.

The Plot to Kill Jesus

22 Now the festival of Unleavened Bread, which is called the Passover, was near. 2The chief priests and the scribes were looking for a way to put Jesus[a] to death, for they were afraid of the people.

3 Then Satan entered into Judas called Iscariot, who was one of the twelve; 4he went away and conferred with the chief priests and officers of the temple police about how he might betray him to them. 5They were greatly pleased and agreed to give him money. 6So he consented and began to look for an opportunity to betray him to them when no crowd was present.

The Preparation of the Passover

7 Then came the day of Unleavened Bread, on which the Passover lamb had to be sacrificed. 8So Jesus[b] sent Peter and John, saying, "Go and prepare the Passover meal for us that we may eat it." 9They asked him, "Where do you want us to make preparations for it?" 10"Listen," he said to them, "when you have entered the city, a man carrying a jar of water will meet you; follow him into the house he enters 11and say to the owner of the house, 'The teacher asks you, "Where is the guest room, where I may eat the Passover with my disciples?" ' 12He will show you a large room upstairs, already furnished. Make preparations for us there." 13So they went and found everything as he had told them; and they prepared the Passover meal.

The Institution of the Lord's Supper

14 When the hour came, he took his place at the table, and the apostles with him. 15He said to them, "I have eagerly desired to eat this Passover with you before I suffer; 16for I tell you, I will not eat it[c] until it is fulfilled in the kingdom of God." 17Then he took a cup, and after giving thanks he said, "Take this and divide it among yourselves; 18for I tell you that from now on I will not drink of the fruit of the vine until the kingdom of God comes." 19Then he took a loaf of bread, and when he had given thanks, he broke it and gave it to them, saying, "This is my body, which is given for you. Do this in remembrance of me." 20And he did the same with the cup after supper, saying, "This cup that is poured out for you is the new covenant in my blood.[d] 21But see, the one who betrays me is with me, and his hand is on the table. 22For the Son of Man is going as it has been determined, but woe to that one by whom he is betrayed!" 23Then they began to ask one another which one of them it could be who would do this.

The Dispute about Greatness

24 A dispute also arose among them as to which one of them was to be regarded as the greatest. 25But he said to them, "The kings of the Gentiles lord it over them; and those in authority over them are called benefactors.

a Gk him   b Gk he   c Other ancient authorities read never eat it again   d Other ancient authorities lack, in whole or in part, verses 19b-20 (which is given . . . in my blood)

26But not so with you; rather the greatest among you must become like the youngest, and the leader like one who serves. 27For who is greater, the one who is at the table or the one who serves? Is it not the one at the table? But I am among you as one who serves.

28 "You are those who have stood by me in my trials; 29and I confer on you, just as my Father has conferred on me, a kingdom, 30so that you may eat and drink at my table in my kingdom, and you will sit on thrones judging the twelve tribes of Israel.

Jesus Predicts Peter's Denial

31 "Simon, Simon, listen! Satan has demanded *a* to sift all of you like wheat, 32but I have prayed for you that your own faith may not fail; and you, when once you have turned back, strengthen your brothers." 33And he said to him, "Lord, I am ready to go with you to prison and to death!" 34Jesus *b* said, "I tell you, Peter, the cock will not crow this day, until you have denied three times that you know me."

Purse, Bag, and Sword

35 He said to them, "When I sent you out without a purse, bag, or sandals, did you lack anything?" They said, "No, not a thing." 36He said to them, "But now, the one who has a purse must take it, and likewise a bag. And the one who has no sword must sell his cloak and buy one. 37For I tell you, this scripture must be fulfilled in me, 'And he was counted among the lawless'; and indeed what is writ-

ten about me is being fulfilled." 38They said, "Lord, look, here are two swords." He replied, "It is enough."

Jesus Prays on the Mount of Olives

39 He came out and went, as was his custom, to the Mount of Olives; and the disciples followed him. 40When he reached the place, he said to them, "Pray that you may not come into the time of trial." *c* 41Then he withdrew from them about a stone's throw, knelt down, and prayed, 42"Father, if you are willing, remove this cup from me; yet, not my will but yours be done." ⟦ 43Then an angel from heaven appeared to him and gave him strength. 44In his anguish he prayed more earnestly, and his sweat became like great drops of blood falling down on the ground.⟧ *d* 45When he got up from prayer, he came to the disciples and found them sleeping because of grief, 46and he said to them, "Why are you sleeping? Get up and pray that you may not come into the time of trial." *e*

The Betrayal and Arrest of Jesus

47 While he was still speaking, suddenly a crowd came, and the one called Judas, one of the twelve, was leading them. He approached Jesus to kiss him; 48but Jesus said to him, "Judas, is it with a kiss that you are betraying the Son of Man?" 49When those who were around him saw what was coming, they

a Or *has obtained permission*   *b* Gk *He*
c Or *into temptation*   *d* Other ancient authorities lack verses 43 and 44   *e* Or *into temptation*

22:26–27 SERVICE—*See* Spiritual Disciplines Index.

Responding
22:32 PRAYER. During the time of Simon Peter's greatest testing, Jesus prayed for him. Do you know someone who is undergoing great testing? If you do, come alongside them in prayer, asking that their faith in Jesus Christ will not fail. *See also* Spiritual Disciplines Index.

22:40–46 PRAYER—*See* Spiritual Disciplines Index.
22:41–42 *remove this cup from me.* The idea

that our spirituality must stoically and triumphantly face all suffering is extinguished by Jesus' struggles in Gethsemane. He knows what he should do, but he desperately hopes there is another way to do it. He is looking for a way out of the agony and the darkness. Many consider this verse an important affirmation of the humanness of the divine Son of God. But it is just as much an affirmation that our spirituality can express weakness and pain and fear and reluctance and still be an honest-to-God spirituality. In fact, a spirituality that suppresses what we truly feel and substitutes for it what we think we ought to feel is no spirituality at all. It is a mask that bears no resemblance to Christ.

asked, "Lord, should we strike with the sword?" ⁵⁰Then one of them struck the slave of the high priest and cut off his right ear. ⁵¹But Jesus said, "No more of this!" And he touched his ear and healed him. ⁵²Then Jesus said to the chief priests, the officers of the temple police, and the elders who had come for him, "Have you come out with swords and clubs as if I were a bandit? ⁵³When I was with you day after day in the temple, you did not lay hands on me. But this is your hour, and the power of darkness!"

Peter Denies Jesus

54 Then they seized him and led him away, bringing him into the high priest's house. But Peter was following at a distance. ⁵⁵When they had kindled a fire in the middle of the courtyard and sat down together, Peter sat among them. ⁵⁶Then a servant-girl, seeing him in the firelight, stared at him and said, "This man also was with him." ⁵⁷But he denied it, saying, "Woman, I do not know him." ⁵⁸A little later someone else, on seeing him, said, "You also are one of them." But Peter said, "Man, I am not!" ⁵⁹Then about an hour later still another kept insisting, "Surely this man also was with him; for he is a Galilean." ⁶⁰But Peter said, "Man, I do not know what you are talking about!" At that moment, while he was still speaking, the cock crowed. ⁶¹The Lord turned and looked at Peter. Then Peter remembered the word of the Lord, how he had said to him, "Before the cock crows today, you will deny me three times." ⁶²And he went out and wept bitterly.

The Mocking and Beating of Jesus

63 Now the men who were holding Jesus began to mock him and beat him; ⁶⁴they also blindfolded him and kept asking him, "Prophesy! Who is it that struck you?" ⁶⁵They kept heaping many other insults on him.

Jesus before the Council

66 When day came, the assembly of the elders of the people, both chief priests and scribes, gathered together, and they brought him to their council. ⁶⁷They said, "If you are the Messiah,ᵃ tell us." He replied, "If I tell you, you will not believe; ⁶⁸and if I question you, you will not answer. ⁶⁹But from now on the Son of Man will be seated at the right hand of the power of God." ⁷⁰All of them asked, "Are you, then, the Son of God?" He said to them, "You say that I am." ⁷¹Then they said, "What further testimony do we need? We have heard it ourselves from his own lips!"

Jesus before Pilate

23 Then the assembly rose as a body and brought Jesusᵇ before Pilate. ²They began to accuse him, saying, "We found this man perverting our nation, forbidding us to pay taxes to the emperor, and saying that he himself is the Messiah, a king."ᶜ ³Then Pilate asked him, "Are you the king of the Jews?" He answered, "You say so." ⁴Then Pilate said to the chief priests and the crowds, "I find no basis for an accusation against this man." ⁵But they were insistent and said, "He stirs up the people by teaching throughout all Judea, from Galilee where he began even to this place."

Jesus before Herod

6 When Pilate heard this, he asked whether the man was a Galilean. ⁷And when

---

a Or *the Christ*   *b* Gk *him*   *c* Or *is an anointed king*

22:66–23:12 *the assembly . . . brought him to their council.* Jesus is put on trial before religious authorities (the Sanhedrin), local and national authorities (King Herod), and international and global authorities (Pontius Pilate, who speaks with the authority of Caesar and the Roman Empire). He is condemned by all these earthly powers. Even the people condemn him (23:18). Given this antipathy between earthly powers, including the will of the people,

and the rule of Jesus and the kingdom of God, is it likely that Christianity can ever be embraced by all governments and all peoples? Is it ever an authentic Christianity once it becomes a popular movement? Or is something lost when it becomes so dominant a force it emerges as an earthly authority like all the rest? It may be that the Christian faith is most true to its founder and his spirituality when it is in the minority and has nothing to gain but the cross.

he learned that he was under Herod's jurisdiction, he sent him off to Herod, who was himself in Jerusalem at that time. [8]When Herod saw Jesus, he was very glad, for he had been wanting to see him for a long time, because he had heard about him and was hoping to see him perform some sign. [9]He questioned him at some length, but Jesus[a] gave him no answer. [10]The chief priests and the scribes stood by, vehemently accusing him. [11]Even Herod with his soldiers treated him with contempt and mocked him; then he put an elegant robe on him, and sent him back to Pilate. [12]That same day Herod and Pilate became friends with each other; before this they had been enemies.

Jesus Sentenced to Death

13 Pilate then called together the chief priests, the leaders, and the people, [14]and said to them, "You brought me this man as one who was perverting the people; and here I have examined him in your presence and have not found this man guilty of any of your charges against him. [15]Neither has Herod, for he sent him back to us. Indeed, he has done nothing to deserve death. [16]I will therefore have him flogged and release him."[b]

18 Then they all shouted out together, "Away with this fellow! Release Barabbas for us!" [19](This was a man who had been put in prison for an insurrection that had taken place in the city, and for murder.) [20]Pilate, wanting to release Jesus, addressed them again; [21]but they kept shouting, "Crucify, crucify him!" [22]A third time he said to them, "Why, what evil has he done? I have found in him no ground for the sentence of death; I will therefore have him flogged and then release him." [23]But they kept urgently demanding with loud shouts that he should be crucified; and their voices prevailed. [24]So Pilate gave his verdict that their demand should be granted. [25]He released the man they asked for, the one who had been put in prison for insurrection and murder, and he handed Jesus over as they wished.

The Crucifixion of Jesus

26 As they led him away, they seized a man, Simon of Cyrene, who was coming from the country, and they laid the cross on him, and made him carry it behind Jesus. [27]A great number of the people followed him, and among them were women who were beating their breasts and wailing for him. [28]But Jesus turned to them and said, "Daughters of Jerusalem, do not weep for me, but weep for yourselves and for your children. [29]For the days are surely coming when they will say, 'Blessed are the barren, and the wombs that never bore, and the breasts that never nursed.' [30]Then they will begin to say to the mountains, 'Fall on us'; and to the hills, 'Cover us.' [31]For if they do this when the wood is green, what will happen when it is dry?"

32 Two others also, who were criminals, were led away to be put to death with him. [33]When they came to the place that is called The Skull, they crucified Jesus[c] there with the criminals, one on his right and one on his left. [34]Then Jesus said, "Father, forgive them; for they do not know what they are doing."[d]

---

a Gk he   b Here, or after verse 19, other ancient authorities add verse 17, *Now he was obliged to release someone for them at the festival*   c Gk *him*
d Other ancient authorities lack the sentence *Then Jesus . . . what they are doing*

23:26 *they seized a man, Simon of Cyrene, . . . and they laid the cross on him.* Jesus does not carry the cross alone, nor does he die alone. Two men will perish beside him on Calvary, and another carries the wood upon which he will die to the place of execution. Humanity is intertwined with divinity not only in Jesus' own flesh and spirit, but during the entire process of redemption. The cross that brings life out of death does not exist unless fashioned by human hands. It does not stand upon The Skull (Golgotha) unless carried there by human hands. God may have placed iron in the earth, but human hands have forged it into the killing nails. So it is fitting that Simon share in the terrible beauty of human salvation, just as it is fitting that the good thief be the first to believe in the cross Simon carried and receive the life it has to offer. The crucifixion makes us one with Christ and with the human race.

23:34 *Father, forgive them; for they do not know what they are doing.* Though warfare will

And they cast lots to divide his clothing. [35]And the people stood by, watching; but the leaders scoffed at him, saying, "He saved others; let him save himself if he is the Messiah[a] of God, his chosen one!" [36]The soldiers also mocked him, coming up and offering him sour wine, [37]and saying, "If you are the King of the Jews, save yourself!" [38]There was also an inscription over him,[b] "This is the King of the Jews."

[39] One of the criminals who were hanged there kept deriding[c] him and saying, "Are you not the Messiah?[a] Save yourself and us!" [40]But the other rebuked him, saying, "Do you not fear God, since you are under the same sentence of condemnation? [41]And we indeed have been condemned justly, for we are getting what we deserve for our deeds, but this man has done nothing wrong." [42]Then he said, "Jesus, remember me when you come into[d] your kingdom." [43]He replied, "Truly I tell you, today you will be with me in Paradise."

The Death of Jesus

[44] It was now about noon, and darkness came over the whole land[e] until three in the afternoon, [45]while the sun's light failed;[f] and the curtain of the temple was torn in two. [46]Then Jesus, crying with a loud voice, said, "Father, into your hands I commend my spirit." Having said this, he breathed his last. [47]When the centurion saw what had taken place, he praised God and said, "Certainly this man was innocent."[g] [48]And when all the crowds who had gathered there for this spectacle saw what had taken place, they returned home, beating their breasts. [49]But all his acquaintances, including the women who had followed him from Galilee, stood at a distance, watching these things.

The Burial of Jesus

[50] Now there was a good and righteous man named Joseph, who, though a member of the council, [51]had not agreed to their plan and action. He came from the Jewish town of Arimathea, and he was waiting expectantly for the kingdom of God. [52]This man went to Pilate and asked for the body of Jesus. [53]Then he took it down, wrapped it in a linen cloth, and laid it in a rock-hewn tomb where no one had ever been laid. [54]It was the day of Preparation, and the sabbath was beginning.[h] [55]The women who had come with him from Galilee followed, and they saw the tomb and how his body was laid. [56]Then they returned, and prepared spices and ointments.

On the sabbath they rested according to the commandment.

The Resurrection of Jesus

24 But on the first day of the week, at early dawn, they came to the tomb, taking the spices that they had prepared. [2]They found the stone rolled away from the tomb, [3]but when they went in, they did not find the body.[i] [4]While they were perplexed about this, suddenly two men in dazzling clothes stood beside them. [5]The women[j] were terrified and bowed their faces to the ground, but the men[k] said to them, "Why do you look for the living among the dead? He is not here, but has risen.[l] [6]Remember how he told you,

a Or the Christ   b Other ancient authorities add written in Greek and Latin and Hebrew (that is, Aramaic)   c Or blaspheming   d Other ancient authorities read in   e Or earth   f Or the sun was eclipsed. Other ancient authorities read the sun was darkened   g Or righteous   h Gk was dawning   i Other ancient authorities add of the Lord Jesus   j Gk They   k Gk but they   l Other ancient authorities lack He is not here, but has risen

come to Jerusalem and the Temple fall a second time, this prayer lifts any curse thought to apply to those who crucified the Messiah. The cross is all about forgiveness: sin is judged, but people are freed. It is the second exodus, the great exodus of the human race, the ultimate liberation of any who believe in Christ. The prayer is a necessary redemption for persons far beyond the foot of the cross. Many times, in each generation, Jesus is mocked, detested, and cursed, and even his disciples ignore his words, disobey his commands, and remain indifferent to his fate as they take the cup and break the bread. There are days and nights in a lifetime when nails jingle in our pockets and a mallet swings from our belt. This prayer is not only about Jews or Romans. It is about us.

while he was still in Galilee, [7]that the Son of Man must <u>be handed over to sinners</u>, and be <u>crucified, and on the third day rise again.</u>" [8]Then th<u>ey remembered his words</u>, [9]and returning from the tomb, they told all this to the eleven and to all the rest. [10]Now it was Mary Magdalene, Joanna, Mary the mother of James, and the other women with them who told this to the apostles. [11]<u>But these</u> words seem<u>ed to them an idle tale, and they</u> did not belie<u>ve them. [12]But Peter got up and ran to the</u> tomb; stooping and looking in, he saw the <u>linen cloths by themselves; then he went</u> home, amazed at what had happened. *a*

The Walk to Emmaus

13 Now on that same day two of them were going to a village called Emmaus, about seven miles *b* from Jerusalem, [14]and talking

a Other ancient authorities lack verse 12
b Gk *sixty stadia;* other ancient authorities read *a hundred sixty stadia*

24:11 *they did not believe [the women].* The story of Jesus begins with angels and ends with angels. But at the resurrection it is not a cluster of shepherds who see them, but a cluster of women—Mary Magdalene, Joanna, Mary the mother of James, and several unnamed others. No angels appear to the apostles or the other men. There is something wonderful about the Son of God, who came to life born of a woman—a blessing that unravels the Genesis curse of childbirth, if ever there was one—coming to life a second time and the news first being given to women. Indeed, the very first to see him, according to John, was Mary Magdalene (20:16). There is also something in the fact that people had little trouble believing that the rough and ready shepherds really had seen something extraordinary ("All who heard it were amazed at what the shepherds told them," Luke 2:18), but when it comes to the women spreading the word about what had been told them, also by angels, about the same child who has become a man, no one is amazed—except perhaps amazed that such a fantastic tale could have emerged full-blown from apparently overactive or grief-shattered imaginations. Stereotypes about people, whether based on gender, race, language, or religion, always blind us to what God is actually doing in our world. They prevent him from showing us, at least for a time, what he is anxious for us to see.

24:13–35 *two of them were going to . . . Emmaus.* How many times on our network of roads have we lurched with broken spirits because the unexpected seized the place of the expected and that with a wrenching disappointment? In such moods even if what was expected then comes to us, we cannot see it. It is unrecognizable to our pain and our splintered hopes and wishes, all of which had taken on a certain shape. What should have been familiar, because it was what we longed to see and consistently prayed for, is unfamiliar to us, a stranger. Two disciples, likely a married couple named Cleopas (or Clopas) and Mary, who is mentioned by John (19:25), are walking the seven miles between Jerusalem and Emmaus. They are despondent due to Christ's death. A stranger joins them who, instead of being sympathetic, bursts with impatience at their grief and hotly argues that the crucifixion of Jesus is a necessary good—if only they could see it—and something to celebrate along with a resurrection promised for centuries. No doubt the miles peel away. The couple ask the stranger to stay at their house when they reach the village. One gets the image of a hooded man stooping through the doorway to sit at the table. There have always been hooded men who were more than they seemed—Henry V slipping among his troops before the battle of Agincourt in Shakespeare's play, Richard the Lionhearted returning to England from the Crusades in the guise of a beggar, or Eowyn, princess and heroine in J. R. R. Tolkien's *Return of the King,* hooded and helmed to the glare of the monster Nazgul, who thinks she is something less than what she is. The stranger is asked to give the blessing. He picks up the bread, breaks it, passes it to Cleopas and Mary, and in that glimpse of the way a friend always blessed and broke the bread, in that interstice of human and divine, a crack between heaven and earth, they see God. But it is only a glimpse. Then God is gone—but not gone. "Were not our hearts burning within us while he was talking to us?" they whisper (v 32). The broken hearts become the hearts that burn. So we too can be surprised and blessed by the God who is expected, but rarely appears where and when

with each other about all these things that had happened. 15While they were talking and discussing, Jesus himself came near and went with them, 16but their eyes were kept from recognizing him. 17And he said to them, "What are you discussing with each other while you walk along?" They stood still, looking sad.*a* 18Then one of them, whose name was Cleopas, answered him, "Are you the only stranger in Jerusalem who does not know the things that have taken place there in these days?" 19He asked them, "What things?" They replied, "The things about Jesus of Nazareth,*b* who was a prophet mighty in deed and word before God and all the people, 20and how our chief priests and leaders handed him over to be condemned to death and crucified him. 21But we had hoped that he was the one to redeem Israel.*c* Yes, and besides all this, it is now the third day since these things took place. 22Moreover, some women of our group astounded us. They were at the tomb early this morning, 23and when they did not find his body there, they came back and told us that they had indeed seen a vision of angels who said that he was alive. 24Some of those who were with us went to the tomb and found it just as the women had said; but they did not see him." 25Then he said to them, "Oh, how foolish you are, and how slow of heart to believe all that the prophets have declared! 26Was it not necessary that the Messiah*d* should suffer these things and then enter into his glory?" 27Then beginning with Moses and all the prophets, he interpreted to them the things about himself in all the scriptures.

28 As they came near the village to which they were going, he walked ahead as if he were going on. 29But they urged him strongly, saying, "Stay with us, because it is almost evening and the day is now nearly over." So he went in to stay with them. 30When he was at the table with them, he took bread, blessed and broke it, and gave it to them. 31Then their eyes were opened, and they recognized him; and he vanished from their sight. 32They said to each other, "Were not our hearts burning within us*e* while he was talking to us on the road, while he was opening the scriptures to us?" 33That same hour they got up and returned to Jerusalem; and they found the eleven and their companions gathered together. 34They were saying, "The Lord has risen indeed, and he has appeared to Simon!" 35Then they told what had happened on the road, and how he had been made known to them in the breaking of the bread.

Jesus Appears to His Disciples

36 While they were talking about this, Jesus himself stood among them and said to them, "Peace be with you."*f* 37They were startled and terrified, and thought that they were seeing a ghost. 38He said to them, "Why are you frightened, and why do doubts arise in your hearts? 39Look at my hands and my feet; see that it is I myself. Touch me and see; for a ghost does not have flesh and bones as you

a Other ancient authorities read *walk along, looking sad?"*   b Other ancient authorities read *Jesus the Nazorean*   c Or *to set Israel free*   d Or *the Christ*   e Other ancient authorities lack *within us*   f Other ancient authorities lack *and said to them, "Peace be with you."*

and how we imagine. It is God's way to come cloaked, and also for his greatest promises to come cloaked. It is his way to come when the storm is peaking or fear deepest or when hope is almost gone or, if we are honest, utterly gone. It has always been his way. No resurrection without Golgotha. No freedom without Gethsemane. No Christmas Eve without a Good Friday. It is stitched into the fabric of thousands of years of the human race. But the other truth is that the world is interstitial—he will fling back his hood, he will throw off his robe to make obvious his heraldry, he will reveal his glory in those flashes of light between mortal and immortal, between the now and the forever, he will incarnate his power and love in the Son of God when we least expect it. Our task is not to figure everything out or imagine every angle God might come at us from, but to stay on the roads of our years, plodding on, encouraging one another with the voices and the mysteries of heaven. It is only that. To stay on the road until God in Disguise joins us and eventually comes to sit at our table. Or we at his.

see that I have." [40]And when he had said this, he showed them his hands and his feet. [a] [41]While in their joy they were disbelieving and still wondering, he said to them, "Have you anything here to eat?" [42]They gave him a piece of broiled fish, [43]and he took it and ate in their presence.

44 Then he said to them, "These are my words that I spoke to you while I was still with you—that everything written about me in the law of Moses, the prophets, and the psalms must be fulfilled." [45]Then he opened their minds to understand the scriptures, [46]and he said to them, "Thus it is written, that the Messiah [b] is to suffer and to rise from the dead on the third day, [47]and that repentance and forgiveness of sins is to be proclaimed in his name to all nations, beginning from Jerusalem. [48]You are witnesses [c]

of these things. [49]And see, I am sending upon you what my Father promised; so stay here in the city until you have been clothed with power from on high."

The Ascension of Jesus

50 Then he led them out as far as Bethany, and, lifting up his hands, he blessed them. [51]While he was blessing them, he withdrew from them and was carried up into heaven. [d] [52]And they worshiped him, and [e] returned to Jerusalem with great joy; [53]and they were continually in the temple blessing God. [f]

[a] Other ancient authorities lack verse 40
[b] Or *the Christ*   [c] Or *nations. Beginning from Jerusalem* [48]*you are witnesses*   [d] Other ancient authorities lack *and was carried up into heaven*
[e] Other ancient authorities lack *worshiped him, and*
[f] Other ancient authorities add *Amen*

24:49 THE WITH-GOD LIFE—*See* Spiritual Disciplines Index.

24:52 WORSHIP—*See* Spiritual Disciplines Index.

THE GOSPEL ACCORDING TO

JOHN

Reading the Gospel of John is like entering a whirlpool, a vortex, a funnel, that sweeps us into a compelling embrace of alluring, gracious lines—all interconnected and propelling us toward the center. That focal point is clearly announced at the beginning (1:1) and repeated near the end (20:28): God! Everything in the Gospel propels us toward that heart (double meaning intended). We can't take anything lightly.

We know that the whirlpool is plunging us toward its focal point, God, but we also recognize that every major line emanates from the center. Moreover, as in a spider's web, those lines spiral into more spacious and extensive arrays through their constantly varying connections with other strands.

Lines to Ponder

John parades several of his strands promptly in the first five verses: Word, Light, Life. Soon these strands are reinforced with the addition of new ones: Believe, Glory, Truth. All these names flow out along the lines from the central focus and, at the same time, graciously carry us back to their Source: God. En route, they are elaborated: "words," "true light," "eternal life," "love," "works," "signs," "one." Complex metaphors expound them: "bread," "good shepherd," "vine."

John is perhaps best known for these compelling, comforting sketches. But his webbing frequently runs into snags: "world," "darkness," "did not know," "chief priests," "Pharisees," "did not accept." There are numerous terms of conflict: "stone," "hide," "arrest," "kill." If we pay close attention to the conversations in John's Gospel, we will find them often spiraling deeper into danger.

For the Word to come from the One True Source obviously was not easy, and the line that carries us back could give us a rough ride too. John, the "beloved disciple,"

See also *"The With-God Life" essay for this section of the Bible,*
"The People of God with Immanuel," pp. 1785–89.

knew Jesus' sufferings intimately and no doubt himself experienced many conflicts about the faith. His Gospel encourages believers to be diligently attentive and hang on tightly to Jesus. We can trust the Word and words that uphold us; the Gospel writer's testimony is true, no matter what our accusers contend.

The Gospel's conflicts stir us to ponder each spiral to notice the progressions of the arguments, which reveal not only various negative attributes in the enemies' character (and our own?), but also more and more of Jesus and often of his relationship to his Father. Dense arguments challenge us to separate confusions to find the basic issues at stake and to ask how each issue impacts our own discipleship. Christ's steadfastness in the face of danger motivates and empowers our own.

Positive lines invite us to notice how various gifts from God reinforce and develop each other, how the words and works of Jesus intertwine, how we cannot know the life Jesus promises unless we live God's truth Christ's way (14:6). John's strands are not mere doctrinal words; they show us the means by which God achieves—in the appropriate "hour"—the fullness of salvation. John's web urges us to trace words throughout the Gospel and learn their many dimensions and connections, so that Christ's Spirit can form those very traits in our own character.

Irony and Ambiguity Call for Contemplation

John ought not to be read quickly. It is full of double and triple meanings, endlessly suggestive images, "signs" that seem obvious on the surface but yield much deeper truth if we are willing to dig contemplatively, and terms that can have positive, neutral, or negative connotations in different settings. For example, the "world" is unquestionably the recipient of God's love (3:16), salvation (3:17; 4:42), life (6:33, 51), and light (3:19; 8:12; 9:5; 11:9), and, in response, "the world has gone after" Jesus (12:19). In contrast, the "world" did not know Jesus, needs its sin taken away (1:29), and is the place of those who reject him (8:23). Even "love," which seems unambiguous, is sometimes negative (3:19; 12:43) and a source of mortification for Peter (21:15–17).

John uses the names "chief priests" and "Pharisees" always with negative connotations. On the other hand, he uses the singular "Pharisee" only once and then for Nicodemus, who is searching for the truth about Jesus. This leads to one of John's subtle jokes, for in 7:45–49 the Pharisees confront the Temple police for not arresting Jesus and ask, "Has any one of the authorities or of the Pharisees believed in him?" To make sure we get the irony John quotes Nicodemus indirectly defending Jesus by insisting he should first be given a hearing. A similar irony arises when the high priest Caiaphas insults the council in 11:49–50 concerning how much better it is for one person to die for the people (see also 18:14).

John records both of these situations in a way that makes the irony perfectly clear. But we dare not think we have received all that the text has to offer when we have understood what has been made so apparent. The irony goes deeper into our own discipleship. Like Nicodemus, do we come to Jesus in the hiddenness of night and defend him only indirectly? Like Caiaphas, do we misunderstand what God is doing in and through our lives and think that it applies only to us?

Contemplation of ironies and ambiguities in terms might often lead to repentance, to a deeper desire to welcome God's action through us in witness, and to a greater openness to see wider implications for what God is doing. It can also lead to less judgmentalism on our part—as, for example, if we notice the widely divergent ways in which John uses the term "Jews."

Some accuse John's Gospel of being anti-Semitic, but a closer inspection of the word "Jews" in its many contexts rebuts that false deduction. John, the writer, was a Jew; so was Jesus (4:9); Nicodemus was a Jewish leader (3:1). Jesus favorably participated in the Jewish festivals (2:13; 5:1; 6:4; 11:55). Salvation is from the Jews (4:22). Some Jews were astonished by Jesus' teaching (7:15), and others believed (8:31; 12:9–11), including those who came to console Mary and then witnessed the raising of Lazarus (11:31, 33, 36, 45). Sometimes the group was divided (7:12, 40–41; 9:16; 10:19–21).

Pilate's oscillating relationship with both Jesus and the Jews leads to the dramatic irony of the inscription "King of the Jews," titling Jesus on the cross (18:33, 39; 19:19, 21). That irony requires Jesus' followers to acclaim his lordship for the Jews too, and the presence of so many positive uses of the term "Jews" demands that we approach the word with more openness to positive possibilities.

Such openness is a crucial Spiritual Discipline in our violent age. Do we wholeheartedly accept all groups of people as communities for whom Jesus also came, as other folds under his shepherding (10:16)?

Sevens

Both near the beginning and at the end of the Gospel, John sets up a series of seven scenes to underscore development (see notes on 1:19–2:25; 18:28–19:16). Other sets of sevens in the Gospel include seven "signs" (2:1–11; 4:43–54; 5:1–9; 6:1–14; 9:1–7; 11:1–45; 21:1–14) and seven major types of "I am" statements (see below).

Each of these sets spirals into deeper understanding of who Jesus is in all the fullness of God's power. The progressions also expand our insight into the intensifying of his enemies' anger and designs. Both of these heightenings are important for our discipleship.

How can our own understanding of Jesus grow? What signs do we see that teach us more of his divinity? In what ways do we ask wrongly for signs? How do the biblical signs and the true signs we see now deepen our belief?

What escalations of enmity against God do we observe in the world around us? How does Jesus counter his enemies' attacks? How might we?

"I Am" Statements Advance Adoration

John's Gospel cites the phrase "I am" together with seven sets of names to record metaphors for Christ. Jesus says, "I am the bread of life" (6:35, 48), "the light of the world" (8:12; 9:5), "the gate" (10:7, 9), "the good shepherd" (10:11, 14), "the resurrection and the life" (11:25), "the way, and the truth, and the life" (14:6), and "the vine" (15:1, 5). All these pictures are expanded in ways that teach us more thoroughly about the triune Grace that rescues, restores, establishes, nourishes, indwells, enlightens, guides, protects, saves, and raises us. Yet almost all of the portraits also lead to conflict with enemies who misunderstand what Jesus is saying and who he is.

John reveals several divisions of the people over who Jesus is. The same is still true today. Some want to make him simply a good man, model, teacher, prophet, or preacher. But the "I am" statements continually force us to ask, "Is Jesus who he says he is?" Is he the Bread of *my* life? Do I live by *his* Light? Do I enter through him as the Gate to salvation, or do I keep trying to rescue myself? Do I trust him to Shepherd me? Do I depend on his Resurrection, or do I keep trying to lift myself up? Do I let him be the Way for me or do I keep asking for directions? Is he the Truth by which I judge all other lesser truths? Is he my Life, or do I employ entertainments to bring me life? Do I abide in him, cling to him as a branch to a Vine, and draw all my spiritual nourishment from him?

Several times in the original Greek John records Jesus' words with the simple phrase "I am" without subsequent nouns or pronouns. In response to Moses at the burning bush God had named himself "I am" (Exod 3:14), and the Hebrew word for which we substitute "LORD" means "I am." Since this is God's name, Jesus is stating his divinity clearly whenever he says "I am." He says it to the woman at the well (4:26), to the frightened disciples in a storm (6:20), to Pharisees in reply to their challenge, "Who are you?" (8:24, 28), to Jewish opponents in response to their cynicism, "Have you seen Abraham?" (8:58), to the disciples so they might derive comfort from his divinity when they see his prophecy of betrayal fulfilled (13:19), and to those who arrested him to inform them that he was indeed the one for whom they searched (18:5, 8).

The last two instances especially hint at John's purposes in recording Jesus' answer, "I am." Anyone reading the Gospel in the original language would be struck by the irony that those who think they are looking merely for "Jesus of Nazareth" are actually finding God himself. The irony is made more poignant by the fact that in the same chapter Peter denies Jesus by saying "I am not" one of his followers (18:17, 25).

Like the Samaritan woman, do we let ourselves be set free by the fullness of Jesus' divinity? Wouldn't it calm our fears more thoroughly in the storms of our lives if we thought about the profound union of Jesus our friend with all the power of the Godhead? Do we sometimes look for much less, and yet God appears to us?

Life With God as Trinity

More than the other Gospels, John includes many statements from Jesus regarding his relationship with the triune Godhead, not only in naming what the Father does, but also when Jesus repeatedly uses such phrases as "I am in the Father and the Father is in me," "I have come from the Father," or "I am going to the Father." A comparison with the other Gospels is powerful: in John Jesus names his Father 104 times, including 8 times (6 in the high-priestly prayer of chap 17) when he invokes his Father directly. In contrast, Matthew cites 34 instances when Jesus names his

Father, including 4 times in prayer. Mark inserts only 3 cases, once in prayer, while Luke quotes Jesus addressing the Father 6 times in prayer and adds only 3 other instances in which he names the Father.

Surely John, the beloved disciple, recognized more deeply than the other Gospel writers the intense intimacy of Jesus with his Father. Consequently, John records much more thoroughly Jesus' invitation through himself into the triune fellowship, for just as he is one with his Father, so we too can be one in him with the Trinity.

Though Luke's Gospel is usually associated with the Spirit (as narrator he mentions the Holy Spirit ten times), Luke includes only three times that Jesus himself names the Spirit. John, as a result of his remarkable friendship with Jesus, is more alert to the Trinity's fellowship, for he records eight times that Jesus names the Spirit and four times that he uses the word "Advocate" for the Spirit. Also, perhaps in as many as five other instances of the word "spirit" Jesus might be referring to the Holy Spirit, rather than a human one.

Why does all this matter? These days when churches seem to specialize in only one or two of the three Persons in the Godhead, John's Gospel is crucial for reminding us how integrally connected the Persons of the Trinity are and how thoroughly involved the entire Tri-unity is in all dimensions of our creation, redemption, and sanctification. Furthermore, in these days when some individuals refuse to name the First Person of the Trinity "Father" because some people find that word "oppressive," it is essential that we recapture the love and grace of that name and recognize how profoundly Jesus carries us into his own intimacy with his Father by the power of their Spirit. Indeed, the "Father" language of John (and Jesus) actually describes inclusive relationships, revealing the First Person of the Trinity's sovereign strength and abundant provision, as well as tender intimacy and compassionate embrace.

The Trinity is not simply an abstract doctrine made up by the Church. It is the way God is and works. The triune fellowship of God invites our participation; we are embraced in the coinherence of the three Persons of the Godhead. By the intercession and redeeming work of Jesus and by the Advocate's witness, we can know the Father.

The webbed lines of John's Gospel disclose to us the Trinity's intertwining relationships and invite us to keep asking what all this means for us. Exploring those lines diligently will increase our celebration of, and participation in, the divine mystery.

Examples in the Notes

As this Introduction reveals, John's Gospel is much too complex to be thoroughly examined in the notes that follow. Instead, the notes will give hints of how we might ponder and explore some of the themes above—one of John's lines, one of Jesus' "signs," a series of seven scenes. Let the whirlpool pull us in more deeply to God. As we are swept toward enraptured adoration, we will discover ever afresh how thoroughly the Father will form us into Christ's image, from one degree of glory to another, by the power and in the freedom of the Spirit (2 Cor 3:18).

—*Marva J. Dawn*

The Word Became Flesh

1 In the beginning was the Word, and the Word was with God, and the Word was God. ²He was in the beginning with God. ³All things came into being through him, and without him not one thing came into being. What has come into being ⁴in him was life, ª and the life was the light of all people. ⁵The light shines in the darkness, and the darkness did not overcome it.

6 There was a man sent from God, whose name was John. ⁷He came as a witness to testify to the light, so that all might believe

through him. ⁸He himself was not the light, but he came to testify to the light. ⁹The true light, which enlightens everyone, was coming into the world. ᵇ

10 He was in the world, and the world came into being through him; yet the world did not know him. ¹¹He came to what was his own, ᶜ and his own people did not accept

a Or ³through him. And without him not one thing came into being that has come into being. ⁴In him was life   b Or He was the true light that enlightens everyone coming into the world   c Or to his own home

---

1:1–18 *In the beginning.* With endlessly suggestive images, John's beginning hymn of praise calls us to contemplation. The following individual notes on the passage display questions we might ask of ourselves, so that the poem's themes might work more deeply into our character.

1:1 *In the beginning was the Word.* John's Gospel begins with the Word and ends with the need for so many words that the world could not contain all the necessary books (21:24–25). The whole Gospel pays close attention to the Word and his words and thereby invites our careful observation of Christ and his speech. In doing so, we are invited to be attentive to our own words, that they might constantly express obedience, witness, and worship. *the Word was God.* John immediately asserts Christ's divinity. Ponder how that divinity is revealed throughout the Gospel. In this age when many reject Jesus' divinity, why is it crucial for our discipleship? What Spiritual Disciplines help us keep his humanity and divinity in appropriate balance?

1:2 *He was in the beginning with God.* Glorious mystery: the Word is both God and with God! How can we help but adore the divine Word, who *is* inseparably God with the Father and Spirit and yet uniquely *with* God as Person! The Word's divinity enables us to learn true humanity as the Word exhibits the with-God life.

1:3 *All things came into being through him.* How does it impact the way we live out our creation to recognize it as the work not only of the Father, but of the entire Trinity?

1:4 *in him was life.* Trace throughout the Gospel how John develops the themes of both light and life. (Notice 8:12, where they cross

again.) Because the life of the Word is the light of all people, we are spurred to witness. We long for everyone to know the One True Light's genuine life.

Responding

1:4 THE WITH-GOD LIFE. What are the characteristics of real life? What phony imitations hinder our discipleship? *See also* Spiritual Disciplines Index.

1:5 *The light shines in the darkness.* What darknesses in our lives hide God's light? How have we experienced the gift of light shining in our personal darknesses? Especially in seasons of repentance like Advent and Lent, it is good for us to ponder the depth of the world's darkness and to watch for the gift of light—learning to wait until it dawns. What Spiritual Disciplines can increase our confidence that the darkness will never be able to overcome God's light?

1:6 *There was a man sent from God.* Ponder how each of us has been sent by God—to various occupations, people, places.

1:7 *He came as a witness.* We each are sent by God into the vocation of "witness"—which frees us from burden because nothing depends on us. Like the Baptizer, we merely tell others what we see and know; we testify to the light. We don't need to "succeed," if all "believe through him," not through us.

1:8 *He himself was not the light.* How might it strip from us our false sense of importance to be regularly reminded that we are not the light, but merely testify to it?

1:9–10 THE WITH-GOD LIFE—*See* Spiritual Disciplines Index.

him. [12]But to all who received him, who believed in his name, he gave power to become children of God, [13]who were born, not of blood or of the will of the flesh or of the will of man, but of God.

14 And the Word became flesh and lived among us, and we have seen his glory, the glory as of a father's only son, [a] full of grace and truth. [15](John testified to him and cried out, "This was he of whom I said, 'He who comes after me ranks ahead of me because he was before me.' ") [16]From his fullness we have all received, grace upon grace. [17]The law in-

deed was given through Moses; grace and truth came through Jesus Christ. [18]No one has ever seen God. It is God the only Son, [b] who is close to the Father's heart, [c] who has made him known.

The Testimony of John the Baptist

19 This is the testimony given by John when the Jews sent priests and Levites from Jerusalem to ask him, "Who are you?" [20]He

a Or *the Father's only Son*   *b* Other ancient authorities read *It is an only Son, God,* or *It is the only Son*   *c* Gk *bosom*

1:9–11 *The true light, which enlightens everyone.* Though not everyone chooses to receive the true light (see 3:19), consider how it affects our witness to remember that the Word's enlightenment is for everyone. What kinds of stubbornness in our own life keep us from knowing and accepting all that the Word wants to teach us about himself? What practices open us to grace and free us to know and accept it?

1:12–13 *But to all who received him.* Becoming God's children is entirely by God's power. We can't will what is a gracious gift. Trace the ways that John elaborates the nature of our relationship with the Trinity throughout his Gospel. How does it change the way we live out our discipleship to keep remembering that our ability to follow Jesus is sheer gift?

1:14 *the Word became flesh and lived among us.* Glorious mystery again: that God should become human! Imagine if a shoemaker would become a shoe! The Greek word translated "lived" more literally says "pitched his tent" or "tabernacled," which invites us to ponder all the biblical passages about God's glory descending upon the Israelites' tabernacle in the wilderness to signify his presence among them. Compare Rev 21:3, which extends the hope that someday we will know God again as intimately, face-to-face, as the disciples did being with Jesus. How can we learn to live that hope more deeply now?

1:14–17 *his glory . . . full of grace and truth.* Three of the lines from John's webbing (see Introduction) here converge. Though the word "grace" occurs only in verses 14 and 16–17, this theme underlies the entire Gospel. "Glory" and "truth" both occur in many contexts; each time the words invite us to notice connections, to expand our understanding of how God's glory is

revealed and of how his truth undergirds all of life, and to learn skills for recognizing untruthful glories in order to become more devoted to the only glorious truth. Reflect on how the truth of God's Word enables us to sort and judge all the other truths the world offers. How does seeing more of the fullness of God's glory form us for deeper discipleship?

1:18 *No one has ever seen God.* The theme that the Son makes the Father known is fleshed out throughout John. As we constantly ponder each Gospel segment, what do we learn about God from what Jesus does and says, from how he treats people, from his humanity and divinity together? What difference will each insight make in how we respond to our own life situations?

1:19–2:25 *This is the testimony.* Chapters 1–2 present a series of short, positive interchanges with various members of Jesus' new "crew." Notice that these first disciples are on a voyage of discovery, as indicated by the escalation in experiences and by the names with which they speak of or to Jesus. John hints at this growing awareness of who Jesus is by his notation of seven days (see 1:19, 29, 35, 43; 2:1), culminating in the first "sign" and the disciples' full belief (2:11). How has our own understanding of Jesus grown since we first met him? The awareness that people are at various stages of comprehension frees us to be agents drawing them ever toward new visions and names that lead to belief.

1:19, 22, 24 *Who are you?* These verses give the first hint of opposition to those who testify to Jesus. How does John demonstrate the power of humility and telling the truth to free us from our fear of enemies?

confessed and did not deny it, but confessed, "I am not the Messiah." [a] 21And they asked him, "What then? Are you Elijah?" He said, "I am not." "Are you the prophet?" He answered, "No." 22Then they said to him, "Who are you? Let us have an answer for those who sent us. What do you say about yourself?" 23He said,

"I am the voice of one crying out in the wilderness,
'Make straight the way of the Lord,' "

as the prophet Isaiah said.

24 Now they had been sent from the Pharisees. 25They asked him, "Why then are you baptizing if you are neither the Messiah, [a] nor Elijah, nor the prophet?" 26John answered them, "I baptize with water. Among you stands one whom you do not know, 27the one who is coming after me; I am not worthy to untie the thong of his sandal." 28This took place in Bethany across the Jordan where John was baptizing.

The Lamb of God

29 The next day he saw Jesus coming toward him and declared, "Here is the Lamb of God who takes away the sin of the world! 30This is he of whom I said, 'After me comes a man who ranks ahead of me because he was before me.' 31I myself did not know him; but I came baptizing with water for this reason, that he might be revealed to Israel." 32And John testified, "I saw the Spirit descending from heaven like a dove, and it remained on him. 33I myself did not know him, but the one who sent me to baptize with water said to me, 'He on whom you see the Spirit descend and remain is the one who baptizes with the Holy Spirit.' 34And I myself have seen and have testified that this is the Son of God." [b]

The First Disciples of Jesus

35 The next day John again was standing with two of his disciples, 36and as he watched Jesus walk by, he exclaimed, "Look, here is the Lamb of God!" 37The two disciples heard him say this, and they followed Jesus. 38When Jesus turned and saw them following, he said to them, "What are you looking for?" They said to him, "Rabbi" (which translated means Teacher), "where are you staying?" 39He said to them, "Come and see." They came and saw where he was staying, and they remained with him that day. It was about four o'clock in the afternoon. 40One of the two who heard John speak and followed him was Andrew, Simon Peter's brother. 41He first found his brother Simon and said to him, "We have found the Messiah" (which is translated Anointed [c]). 42He brought Simon [d] to Jesus, who looked at him and said, "You are Simon son of John. You are to be called Cephas" (which is translated Peter [e]).

Jesus Calls Philip and Nathanael

43 The next day Jesus decided to go to Galilee. He found Philip and said to him, "Follow me." 44Now Philip was from Bethsaida, the city of Andrew and Peter. 45Philip found Nathanael and said to him, "We have found him about whom Moses in the law and also the prophets wrote, Jesus son of Joseph from Nazareth." 46Nathanael said to him, "Can anything good come out of Nazareth?" Philip said to him, "Come and see." 47When Jesus saw Nathanael coming toward him, he said of him, "Here is truly an Israelite in whom there is no deceit!" 48Nathanael asked him, "Where did you get to know me?"

a Or the Christ   b Other ancient authorities read is God's chosen one   c Or Christ   d Gk him   e From the word for rock in Aramaic (kepha) and Greek (petra), respectively

---

1:20–21 *I am not the Messiah.* Perhaps we all sometimes fall into the trap of thinking that we're the Messiah. What can foster the sort of humility we need to let God work through us instead?

1:25–27 *I am not worthy.* Still today people wonder what right Christians have to do what we do or say what we say if we're not big shots. What opportunities does God give us simply to

point to Jesus? (See also 1:29–34.)

1:38–39 *they remained with him that day.* These verses introduce the theme of abiding or remaining, elaborated in chapter 15.

1:46 *Come and see.* We do not need to defend Jesus against his scoffers. We need only to follow (vv 37, 43) and to repeat his invitation (v 39), "Come and see."

Jesus answered, "I saw you under the fig tree before Philip called you." ⁴⁹Nathanael replied, "Rabbi, you are the Son of God! You are the King of Israel!" ⁵⁰Jesus answered, "Do you believe because I told you that I saw you under the fig tree? You will see greater things than these." ⁵¹And he said to him, "Very truly, I tell you,ᵃ you will see heaven opened and the angels of God ascending and descending upon the Son of Man."

The Wedding at Cana

2 On the third day there was a wedding in Cana of Galilee, and the mother of Jesus was there. ²Jesus and his disciples had also been invited to the wedding. ³When the wine gave out, the mother of Jesus said to him, "They have no wine." ⁴And Jesus said to her, "Woman, what concern is that to you and to me? My hour has not yet come." ⁵His mother said to the servants, "Do whatever he tells you." ⁶Now standing there were six stone water jars for the Jewish rites of purification, each holding twenty or thirty gallons. ⁷Jesus said to them, "Fill the jars with water." And they filled them up to the brim. ⁸He said to them, "Now draw some out, and take it to the chief steward." So they took it. ⁹When the steward tasted the water that had become wine, and did not know where it came from (though the servants who had drawn the water knew), the steward called the bridegroom ¹⁰and said to him, "Everyone serves the good wine first, and then the inferior wine after the guests have become drunk. But you have kept the good wine until now." ¹¹Jesus did this, the first of his signs, in Cana of Galilee, and revealed his glory; and his disciples believed in him.

12 After this he went down to Capernaum with his mother, his brothers, and his disciples; and they remained there a few days.

Jesus Cleanses the Temple

13 The Passover of the Jews was near, and Jesus went up to Jerusalem. ¹⁴In the temple he found people selling cattle, sheep, and doves, and the money changers seated at their tables. ¹⁵Making a whip of cords, he drove all of them out of the temple, both the sheep and the cattle. He also poured out the coins of the money changers and overturned their

ᵃ Both instances of the Greek word for *you* in this verse are plural

---

1:48 *I saw you under the fig tree.* People familiar with the Sea of Galilee suggest that the "fig tree" might have been the seafarers' name for a good fishing spot. Perhaps Jesus had watched Nathanael at his occupation and thereby knew his character.

Responding
1:48 SERVICE. In which places does Jesus watch us? What kind of work are we doing, and what is revealed in our character by the way we work? How is that a witness to others? What gifts do we contribute to Jesus' "crew" for present-day "fishing for people"? *See also* Spiritual Disciplines Index.

1:51 *you will see heaven opened.* This reference to Gen 28:12, 17 presents Jesus as the incarnate "house of God" (the meaning of Bethel) and ends chapter 1 as it began—with the Word's divinity.

2:1–10 CELEBRATION—*See* Spiritual Disciplines Index.

2:1–11 *On the third day there was a wedding in Cana of Galilee.* The details surrounding Jesus' performance of a "sign" (not called "miracles" as in the synoptic Gospels) necessitate careful pondering. John includes only seven signs, but stresses that they symbolize many others (20:30). Signs aren't valued primarily for their own sake (though they miraculously impart great gifts), but as pointers to God's glory and entries to belief (2:23). How might this "sign" theology transform our attitudes about, and understanding of, healing and God's provision?

2:3–5 *the mother of Jesus said to him.* Jesus' mother is a model of discipleship—teaching us compassion for those who lack what they need and awareness that all is well if we do whatever Jesus tells us.

2:6–7 *six stone water jars for the Jewish rites of purification.* John's Gospel is filled with rich symbolism to contemplate. This narrative of the seventh day (see note on 1:19–2:25) replaces Jewish purification rites with Communion wine.

tables. [16]He told those who were selling the doves, "Take these things out of here! Stop making my Father's house a marketplace!" [17]His disciples remembered that it was written, "Zeal for your house will consume me." [18]The Jews then said to him, "What sign can you show us for doing this?" [19]Jesus answered them, "Destroy this temple, and in three days I will raise it up." [20]The Jews then said, "This temple has been under construction for forty-six years, and will you raise it up in three days?" [21]But he was speaking of the temple of his body. [22]After he was raised from the dead, his disciples remembered that he had said this; and they believed the scripture and the word that Jesus had spoken.

23 When he was in Jerusalem during the Passover festival, many believed in his name because they saw the signs that he was doing. [24]But Jesus on his part would not entrust himself to them, because he knew all people [25]and needed no one to testify about anyone; for he himself knew what was in everyone.

Nicodemus Visits Jesus

3 Now there was a Pharisee named Nicodemus, a leader of the Jews. [2]He came to Jesus[a] by night and said to him, "Rabbi, we know that you are a teacher who has come from God; for no one can do these signs that you do apart from the presence of God." [3]Jesus answered him, "Very truly, I tell you, no one can see the kingdom of God without being born from above."[b] [4]Nicodemus said to him, "How can anyone be born after having grown old? Can one enter a second time into the mother's womb and be born?" [5]Jesus answered, "Very truly, I tell you, no one can enter the kingdom of God without being born of water and Spirit. [6]What is born of the flesh

is flesh, and what is born of the Spirit is spirit.[c] [7]Do not be astonished that I said to you, 'You[d] must be born from above.'[e] [8]The wind[c] blows where it chooses, and you hear the sound of it, but you do not know where it comes from or where it goes. So it is with everyone who is born of the Spirit." [9]Nicodemus said to him, "How can these things be?" [10]Jesus answered him, "Are you a teacher of Israel, and yet you do not understand these things?

11 "Very truly, I tell you, we speak of what we know and testify to what we have seen; yet you[f] do not receive our testimony. [12]If I have told you about earthly things and you do not believe, how can you believe if I tell you about heavenly things? [13]No one has ascended into heaven except the one who descended from heaven, the Son of Man.[g] [14]And just as Moses lifted up the serpent in the wilderness, so must the Son of Man be lifted up, [15]that whoever believes in him may have eternal life.[h]

16 "For God so loved the world that he gave his only Son, so that everyone who believes in him may not perish but may have eternal life.

17 "Indeed, God did not send the Son into the world to condemn the world, but in order that the world might be saved through him. [18]Those who believe in him are not condemned; but those who do not believe are condemned already, because they have not believed in the name of the only Son of God. [19]And this is the judgment, that the light has

a Gk *him*   b Or *born anew*   c The same Greek word means both *wind* and *spirit*   d The Greek word for *you* here is plural   e Or *anew* f The Greek word for *you* here and in verse 12 is plural   g Other ancient authorities add *who is in heaven*   h Some interpreters hold that the quotation concludes with verse 15

2:22 *After he was raised from the dead.* Events lead to belief when Jesus' word is fulfilled.

3:1–21 *Now there was a Pharisee named Nicodemus.* In what ways are we like Nicodemus—afraid to come into the light (vv 2, 19–20), missing the double meanings (vv 3–8), not familiar with our own faith heritage (vv 10–12), not open to God's way of doing things (vv 12–14)?

3:15–16, 36 *that whoever believes in him may have eternal life.* Throughout John, having "eternal life" is in the present tense. Too often we imagine eternal life only in the future. How does it change our discipleship if we live eternal life now?

3:17–21 *the light has come into the world.* See note on 1:9–11.

NICODEMUS

Meeting Jesus in the Dark

Selected Scriptures: *John 3:1–21; 7:45–52; 19:38–42*

Nicodemus came to Jesus in the night. Perhaps this was the time he could find Jesus away from the crowds. Maybe evenings were the proper time to pay a visit. Or maybe Nicodemus needed the cover of darkness to hide his interest in Jesus from fellow Pharisees. Whatever his reason, John made note of the darkness surrounding this visit, and Jesus himself used the images of darkness and light as he spoke with his visitor.

Surely Nicodemus was "in the dark" when it came to his understanding of Jesus. He saw that Jesus must be from God, but he could see no farther. Jesus' words to him about being born from above, about the wind and the serpent and the light and the darkness (3:3–21) didn't help illumine much. After hearing words of Jesus that would become some of his most foundational and often quoted teachings ever, it's likely Nicodemus went away still bewildered, still uncertain about this man who had drawn him away in the night.

A leader of the Pharisees, this man had a spiritual life that was shaped around avoiding, to the greatest degree possible, condemnation. Now Jesus announced he had come not to condemn, but to save (v 17). As Nicodemus began to lay hold of this truth, light began to seep in and understanding slowly gathered momentum.

It happened when Nicodemus stepped out, even in the dark, to question Jesus. He was willing to approach Jesus at night and, because of it, in time Christ would help his visitor to live in the light.

We too, like Nicodemus, know the darkness of doubt, ignorance, and fear. We know the night of desperation and despair. We know the dark of confusion and even disobedience, and as with Nicodemus's later halfhearted defense of Jesus before the Pharisees, we know the ambivalence of belief. For us too Jesus' word is, "I have come not to condemn, but to save."

Another man met Jesus in the night. For Dag Hammarskjöld the night lasted many years—three years of intense darkness and many years before that without the light. This respected diplomat, who eventually became head of the United Nations, lived in anguished, silent inner turmoil, until at last, "at some moment I did answer Yes to Someone—or Something—and from that hour I was certain that existence is meaningful and that, therefore, my life, in self-surrender, had a goal." Light, for Hammarskjöld, began to seep in.

He wrote in one of his first responses to the light: "For all that has been— Thanks! For all that shall be—Yes!" He had walked a long time in the night, and yet God had used that cover of darkness to meet with Hammarskjöld and prepare him for the light. "Night is drawing nigh," he wrote along the way. "How long the road

PROFILE: NICODEMUS

is. But for all the time the journey has already taken, how you have needed every second of it."

Both men faced a dark night. Nicodemus battled new birth within and watched Jesus suffer and die, coming to belief somewhere along the way. He had missed the chance of anointing Jesus' body in life, but he heaped spices on Christ after his death, risking his own life to finally let loose the overpowering fragrance of belief. Because Nicodemus had approached Jesus, even in the night, God brought a slow, steady wind of understanding, of new life, of light.

Personal Reflection

- When have you needed to come to Jesus in the night? What kind of understanding did God begin to stir in you? Can you explain how God brought you from the darkness into the light?

- People like Nicodemus and Hammarskjöld may have looked back with regret at the time they had spent living without belief in Christ. Yet, as Hammarskjöld wrote, he had needed all of his journey. In *Amazing Grace,* contemporary poet and author Kathleen Norris writes in a similar vein: "I came to understand that God hadn't lost me, even if I seemed for years to have misplaced God." How do you view the time you have spent wandering in darkness, maybe struggling against new birth?

come into the world, and people loved darkness rather than light because their deeds were evil. ²⁰For all who do evil hate the light and do not come to the light, so that their deeds may not be exposed. ²¹But those who do what is true come to the light, so that it may be clearly seen that their deeds have been done in God."ᵃ

Jesus and John the Baptist

22 After this Jesus and his disciples went into the Judean countryside, and he spent some time there with them and baptized. ²³John also was baptizing at Aenon near Salim because water was abundant there; and people kept coming and were being baptized ²⁴—John, of course, had not yet been thrown into prison.

25 Now a discussion about purification arose between John's disciples and a Jew.ᵇ ²⁶They came to John and said to him, "Rabbi, the one who was with you across the Jordan, to whom you testified, here he is baptizing, and all are going to him." ²⁷John answered, "No one can receive anything except what has been given from heaven. ²⁸You yourselves are my witnesses that I said, 'I am not the Messiah,ᶜ but I have been sent ahead of him.' ²⁹He who has the bride is the bridegroom. The friend of the bridegroom, who stands and hears him, rejoices greatly at the bridegroom's voice. For this reason my joy has been fulfilled. ³⁰He must increase, but I must decrease."ᵈ

The One Who Comes from Heaven

31 The one who comes from above is above all; the one who is of the earth belongs to the earth and speaks about earthly things. The one who comes from heaven is above

---

a Some interpreters hold that the quotation concludes with verse 15   b Other ancient authorities read *the Jews*   c Or *the Christ*
d Some interpreters hold that the quotation continues through verse 36

3:29–30 *He who has the bride is the bridegroom.* The Jewish custom of the bridegroom's friend watching over the bride until the groom comes offers a superb image for our ministries: we serve best by becoming less so that Christ becomes more in others' lives.

all. 32He testifies to what he has seen and heard, yet no one accepts his testimony. 33Whoever has accepted his testimony has certified[a] this, that God is true. 34He whom God has sent speaks the words of God, for he gives the Spirit without measure. 35The Father loves the Son and has placed all things in his hands. 36Whoever believes in the Son has eternal life; whoever disobeys the Son will not see life, but must endure God's wrath.

Jesus and the Woman of Samaria

4 Now when Jesus[b] learned that the Pharisees had heard, "Jesus is making and baptizing more disciples than John" 2—although it was not Jesus himself but his disciples who baptized— 3he left Judea and started back to Galilee. 4But he had to go through Samaria. 5So he came to a Samaritan city called Sychar, near the plot of ground that Jacob had given to his son Joseph. 6Jacob's well was there, and Jesus, tired out by his journey, was sitting by the well. It was about noon.

7 A Samaritan woman came to draw water, and Jesus said to her, "Give me a drink." 8(His disciples had gone to the city to buy food.) 9The Samaritan woman said to him, "How is it that you, a Jew, ask a drink of me, a woman of Samaria?" (Jews do not share things in common with Samaritans.)[c] 10Jesus answered her, "If you knew the gift of God, and who it is that is saying to you, 'Give me a drink,' you would have asked him, and he would have given you living water." 11The woman said to him, "Sir, you have no bucket, and the well is deep. Where do you get that living water? 12Are you greater than our ancestor Jacob, who gave us the well, and with his sons and his flocks drank from it?" 13Jesus said to her, "Everyone who drinks of this water will be thirsty again,

14but those who drink of the water that I will give them will never be thirsty. The water that I will give will become in them a spring of water gushing up to eternal life." 15The woman said to him, "Sir, give me this water, so that I may never be thirsty or have to keep coming here to draw water."

16 Jesus said to her, "Go, call your husband, and come back." 17The woman answered him, "I have no husband." Jesus said to her, "You are right in saying, 'I have no husband'; 18for you have had five husbands, and the one you have now is not your husband. What you have said is true!" 19The woman said to him, "Sir, I see that you are a prophet. 20Our ancestors worshiped on this mountain, but you[d] say that the place where people must worship is in Jerusalem." 21Jesus said to her, "Woman, believe me, the hour is coming when you will worship the Father neither on this mountain nor in Jerusalem. 22You worship what you do not know; we worship what we know, for salvation is from the Jews. 23But the hour is coming, and is now here, when the true worshipers will worship the Father in spirit and truth, for the Father seeks such as these to worship him. 24God is spirit, and those who worship him must worship in spirit and truth." 25The woman said to him, "I know that Messiah is coming" (who is called Christ). "When he comes, he will proclaim all things to us." 26Jesus said to her, "I am he,[e] the one who is speaking to you."

27 Just then his disciples came. They were astonished that he was speaking with a woman, but no one said, "What do you

---

3:34–35 *He whom God has sent.* See the Introduction on the Trinity.

4:1–4 *Now when Jesus learned that the Pharisees had heard.* We might be tempted to ignore verses such as these, but John has no throwaway remarks. Details enable us to find our place in biblical narratives more applicably. Here we see hints of opposition, of the disciples' participation in Jesus' work, of cultural animosities.

4:5–26 *So he came to a Samaritan city.* Notice how Jesus' conversation with the woman spirals into successive insights into who he is. It is the same when we read the Scriptures—each reading adds new insights that also clarify previous ones.

4:20–24 **WORSHIP**—*See* Spiritual Disciplines Index.

4:26 *I am he.* See the Introduction on "I am" statements.

want?" or, "Why are you speaking with her?" 28Then the woman left her water jar and went back to the city. She said to the people, 29"Come and see a man who told me everything I have ever done! He cannot be the Messiah, *a* can he?" 30They left the city and were on their way to him.

31 Meanwhile the disciples were urging him, "Rabbi, eat something." 32But he said to them, "I have food to eat that you do not know about." 33So the disciples said to one another, "Surely no one has brought him something to eat?" 34Jesus said to them, "My food is to do the will of him who sent me and to complete his work. 35Do you not say, 'Four months more, then comes the harvest'? But I tell you, look around you, and see how the fields are ripe for harvesting. 36The reaper is already receiving*b* wages and is gathering fruit for eternal life, so that sower and reaper may rejoice together. 37For here the saying holds true, 'One sows and another reaps.' 38I sent you to reap that for which you did not labor. Others have labored, and you have entered into their labor."

39 Many Samaritans from that city believed in him because of the woman's testimony, "He told me everything I have ever done." 40So when the Samaritans came to him, they asked him to stay with them; and he stayed there two days. 41And many more believed because of his word. 42They said to the woman, "It is no longer because of what you said that we believe, for we have heard for ourselves, and we know that this is truly the Savior of the world."

Jesus Returns to Galilee

43 When the two days were over, he went from that place to Galilee 44(for Jesus himself had testified that a prophet has no honor in the prophet's own country). 45When he came to Galilee, the Galileans welcomed him, since they had seen all that he had done in Jerusalem at the festival; for they too had gone to the festival.

Jesus Heals an Official's Son

46 Then he came again to Cana in Galilee where he had changed the water into wine. Now there was a royal official whose son lay ill in Capernaum. 47When he heard that Jesus had come from Judea to Galilee, he went and begged him to come down and heal his son, for he was at the point of death. 48Then Jesus said to him, "Unless you*c* see signs and wonders you will not believe." 49The official said to him, "Sir, come down before my little boy dies." 50Jesus said to him, "Go; your son will live." The man believed the word that Jesus spoke to him and started on his way. 51As he was going down, his slaves met him and told him that his child was alive. 52So he asked them the hour when he began to recover, and they said to him, "Yesterday at one in the afternoon the fever left him." 53The father realized that this was the hour when Jesus had said to him, "Your son will live." So he himself believed, along with his whole household. 54Now this was the second sign that Jesus did after coming from Judea to Galilee.

Jesus Heals on the Sabbath

5 After this there was a festival of the Jews, and Jesus went up to Jerusalem.

2 Now in Jerusalem by the Sheep Gate there is a pool, called in Hebrew*d* Beth-za-tha,*e* which has five porticoes. 3In these lay many invalids—blind, lame, and paralyzed.*f* 5One man was there who had been ill for thirty-eight years. 6When Jesus saw him lying

a Or *the Christ*   *b* Or *35. . . . the fields are already ripe for harvesting. 36The reaper is receiving*   *c* Both instances of the Greek word for *you* in this verse are plural   *d* That is, *Aramaic*   *e* Other ancient authorities read *Bethesda*, others *Bethsaida*   *f* Other ancient authorities add, wholly or in part, *waiting for the stirring of the water; 4for an angel of the Lord went down at certain seasons into the pool, and stirred up the water; whoever stepped in first after the stirring of the water was made well from whatever disease that person had.*

4:27–42 *Many . . . believed . . . because of the woman's testimony.* See note on 1:7.

4:43–45 *When the two days were over.* See note on 4:1–4.

4:48 *Unless you see signs and wonders.* In the midst of his second sign (see note on 2:1–11),

Jesus admonishes those who wrongly crave signs (he is not admonishing the official; see NRSV text note). How can we distinguish between a righteous reception of signs and a sinful craving for them? Other uses of the words "sign" and "signs" in John's Gospel will help us discern.

there and knew that he had been there a long time, he said to him, "Do you want to be made well?" 7The sick man answered him, "Sir, I have no one to put me into the pool when the water is stirred up; and while I am making my way, someone else steps down ahead of me." 8Jesus said to him, "Stand up, take your mat and walk." 9At once the man was made well, and he took up his mat and began to walk.

Now that day was a sabbath. 10So the Jews said to the man who had been cured, "It is the sabbath; it is not lawful for you to carry your mat." 11But he answered them, "The man who made me well said to me, 'Take up your mat and walk.' " 12They asked him, "Who is the man who said to you, 'Take it up and walk'?" 13Now the man who had been healed did not know who it was, for Jesus had disappeared in*a* the crowd that was there. 14Later Jesus found him in the temple and said to him, "See, you have been made well! Do not sin any more, so that nothing worse happens to you." 15The man went away and told the Jews that it was Jesus who had made him well. 16Therefore the Jews started persecuting Jesus, because he was doing such things on the sabbath. 17But Jesus answered them, "My Father is still working, and I also am working." 18For this reason the Jews were seeking all the more to kill him, because he was not only breaking the sabbath, but was also calling God his own Father, thereby making himself equal to God.

The Authority of the Son

19 Jesus said to them, "Very truly, I tell you, the Son can do nothing on his own, but only what he sees the Father doing; for whatever the Father *b* does, the Son does likewise. 20The Father loves the Son and shows him all that he himself is doing; and he will show him greater works than these, so that you will be astonished. 21Indeed, just as the Father raises the dead and gives them life, so also the Son gives life to whomever he wishes. 22The Father judges no one but has given all judgment to the Son, 23so that all may honor the Son just as they honor the Father. Anyone who does not honor the Son does not honor the Father who sent him. 24Very truly, I tell you, anyone who hears my word and believes him who sent me has eternal life, and does not come under judgment, but has passed from death to life.

25 "Very truly, I tell you, the hour is coming, and is now here, when the dead will hear the voice of the Son of God, and those who hear will live. 26For just as the Father has life in himself, so he has granted the Son also to have life in himself; 27and he has given him authority to execute judgment, because he is the Son of Man. 28Do not be astonished at this; for the hour is coming when all who are in their graves will hear his voice 29and will come out—those who have done good, to the resurrection of life, and those who have done evil, to the resurrection of condemnation.

Witnesses to Jesus

30 "I can do nothing on my own. As I hear, I judge; and my judgment is just, be-

a Or *had left because of*   b Gk *that one*

5:7 *I have no one to put me into the pool.* This narrative of Jesus' third sign exhibits another obstacle to Christ's healing and our belief—our excuses. What rationalizations keep us from receiving whatever God wants to do for, in, or through us?

5:14–18 *The man went away and told the Jews.* John's cryptic summary of the healed man's encounters with Jesus and the Jewish leaders raises many questions. Was the man blind to his own betrayal in reporting Jesus to the leaders? Why does Jesus' divinity make people so angry—then and now? How can our practice of Sabbath keeping be a source of healing to others?

5:19–47 *the Son can do nothing on his own.* Consider what we learn about Jesus and about the Trinity in each phrase of this extended discourse and in the spiraling elaborations of phrases. How do these phrases form our own receptivity to the Father's working through us? Let us pray that our own testimony might be characterized by such integrity of words and works.

[handwritten note at top: THIS IS A HUGE CROWD FOR THAT DAY IN MINUTE AREA ONLY TWO CITY 20,000 or]

cause I seek to do not my own will but the will of him who sent me.

31 "If I testify about myself, my testimony is not true. [32]There is another who testifies on my behalf, and I know that his testimony to me is true. [33]You sent messengers to John, and he testified to the truth. [34]Not that I accept such human testimony, but I say these things so that you may be saved. [35]He was a burning and shining lamp, and you were willing to rejoice for a while in his light. [36]But I have a testimony greater than John's. The works that the Father has given me to complete, the very works that I am doing, testify on my behalf that the Father has sent me. [37]And the Father who sent me has himself testified on my behalf. You have never heard his voice or seen his form, [38]and you do not have his word abiding in you, because you do not believe him whom he has sent.

39 "You search the scriptures because you think that in them you have eternal life; and it is they that testify on my behalf. [40]Yet you refuse to come to me to have life. [41]I do not accept glory from human beings. [42]But I know that you do not have the love of God in[a] you. [43]I have come in my Father's name, and you do not accept me; if another comes in his own name, you will accept him. [44]How can you believe when you accept glory from one another and do not seek the glory that comes from the one who alone is God? [45]Do not think that I will accuse you before the Father; your accuser is Moses, on whom you have set your hope. [46]If you believed Moses, you would believe me, for he wrote about me. [47]But if you do not believe what he wrote, how will you believe what I say?"

Feeding the Five Thousand

6 After this Jesus went to the other side of the Sea of Galilee, also called the Sea of Tiberias.[b] [2]A large crowd kept following him, because they saw the signs that he was doing for the sick. [3]Jesus went up the mountain and sat down there with his disciples. [4]Now the Passover, the festival of the Jews, was near. [5]When he looked up and saw a large crowd coming toward him, Jesus said to Philip, "Where are we to buy bread for these people to eat?" [6]He said this to test him, for he himself knew what he was going to do. [7]Philip answered him, "Six months' wages[c] would not buy enough bread for each of them to get a little." [8]One of his disciples, Andrew, Simon Peter's brother, said to him, [9]"There is a boy here who has five barley loaves and two fish. But what are they among so many people?" [10]Jesus said, "Make the people sit down." Now there was a great deal of grass in the place; so they[d] sat down, about five thousand in all. [11]Then Jesus took the loaves, and when he had given thanks, he distributed them to those who were seated; so also the fish, as much as they wanted. [12]When they were satisfied, he told his disciples, "Gather up the fragments left over, so that nothing may be lost." [13]So they gathered them up, and from the fragments of the five barley loaves, left by those who had eaten, they filled twelve baskets. [14]When the people saw the sign that he had done, they began to say, "This is indeed the prophet who is to come into the world."

15 When Jesus realized that they were about to come and take him by force to make him king, he withdrew again to the mountain by himself.

Jesus Walks on the Water

16 When evening came, his disciples went down to the sea, [17]got into a boat, and started across the sea to Capernaum. It was now dark, and Jesus had not yet come to them. [18]The sea became rough because a strong wind was blowing. [19]When they had rowed about three or four miles,[e] they saw Jesus walking on the sea and coming near the boat, and they were

a Or *among*   b Gk *of Galilee of Tiberias*
c Gk *Two hundred denarii*; the denarius was the usual day's wage for a laborer   d Gk *the men*
e Gk *about twenty-five or thirty stadia*

5:39–40 *You search the scriptures.* How *do* we search the Scriptures—just for information or for life? How we need more often to confess and repent for our misreadings and to celebrate the gifts of biblical contemplation!

6:1–14 *When the people saw the sign.* See note on 2:1–11.

terrified. 20But he said to them, "It is I;[a] do not be afraid." 21Then they wanted to take him into the boat, and immediately the boat reached the land toward which they were going.

The Bread from Heaven

22 The next day the crowd that had stayed on the other side of the sea saw that there had been only one boat there. They also saw that Jesus had not got into the boat with his disciples, but that his disciples had gone away alone. 23Then some boats from Tiberias came near the place where they had eaten the bread after the Lord had given thanks.[b] 24So when the crowd saw that neither Jesus nor his disciples were there, they themselves got into the boats and went to Capernaum looking for Jesus.

25 When they found him on the other side of the sea, they said to him, "Rabbi, when did you come here?" 26Jesus answered them, "Very truly, I tell you, you are looking for me, not because you saw signs, but because you ate your fill of the loaves. 27Do not work for the food that perishes, but for the food that endures for eternal life, which the Son of Man will give you. For it is on him that God the Father has set his seal." 28Then they said to him, "What must we do to perform the works of God?" 29Jesus answered them, "This is the work of God, that you believe in him whom he has sent." 30So they said to him, "What sign are you going to give us then, so that we may see it and believe you? What work are you performing? 31Our ancestors ate the manna in the wilderness; as it is written, 'He gave them bread from heaven to

eat.' " 32Then Jesus said to them, "Very truly, I tell you, it was not Moses who gave you bread from heaven, but it is my Father who gives you the true bread from heaven. 33For the bread of God is that which[c] comes down from heaven and gives life to the world." 34They said to him, "Sir, give us this bread always."

35 Jesus said to them, "I am the bread of life. Whoever comes to me will never be hungry, and whoever believes in me will never be thirsty. 36But I said to you that you have seen me and yet do not believe. 37Everything that the Father gives me will come to me, and anyone who comes to me I will never drive away; 38for I have come down from heaven, not to do my own will, but the will of him who sent me. 39And this is the will of him who sent me, that I should lose nothing of all that he has given me, but raise it up on the last day. 40This is indeed the will of my Father, that all who see the Son and believe in him may have eternal life; and I will raise them up on the last day."

41 Then the Jews began to complain about him because he said, "I am the bread that came down from heaven." 42They were saying, "Is not this Jesus, the son of Joseph, whose father and mother we know? How can he now say, 'I have come down from heaven'?" 43Jesus answered them, "Do not complain among yourselves. 44No one can come to me unless drawn by the Father who sent me; and I will raise that person up on the last day. 45It is written in the prophets, 'And they shall all be

a Gk I am   b Other ancient authorities lack after the Lord had given thanks   c Or he who

---

6:20 It is I. See Introduction on "I am" statements.

6:25–34 When they found him on the other side of the sea. John quickly summarizes Jesus' walking on the sea in order to move directly to the crowd's failure to respond with belief to the "sign" of the bread. Their attention remains on the material level. Let us confess how often we too seek physical rather than divine blessings.

6:35–59 I am the bread of life. Review the Introduction on "I am" statements; then ponder this passage's metaphor by questioning each

phrase. What do we learn about who Jesus is for us? How do our insights deepen as images are elaborated and combined? If the crowd or disciples protest, are there analogies to our own objections? Why do we sometimes reject Christ's gifts of himself? What promises does the discourse include?

Responding
6:35–59 STUDY. How might we grow in living the metaphor of Jesus as the bread of life? See also Spiritual Disciplines Index.

taught by God.' Everyone who has heard and learned from the Father comes to me. 46Not that anyone has seen the Father except the one who is from God; he has seen the Father. 47Very truly, I tell you, whoever believes has eternal life. 48I am the bread of life. 49Your ancestors ate the manna in the wilderness, and they died. 50This is the bread that comes down from heaven, so that one may eat of it and not die. 51I am the living bread that came down from heaven. Whoever eats of this bread will live forever; and the bread that I will give for the life of the world is my flesh."

52 The Jews then disputed among themselves, saying, "How can this man give us his flesh to eat?" 53So Jesus said to them, "Very truly, I tell you, unless you eat the flesh of the Son of Man and drink his blood, you have no life in you. 54Those who eat my flesh and drink my blood have eternal life, and I will raise them up on the last day; 55for my flesh is true food and my blood is true drink. 56Those who eat my flesh and drink my blood abide in me, and I in them. 57Just as the living Father sent me, and I live because of the Father, so whoever eats me will live because of me. 58This is the bread that came down from heaven, not like that which your ancestors ate, and they died. But the one who eats this bread will live forever." 59He said these things while he was teaching in the synagogue at Capernaum.

The Words of Eternal Life

60 When many of his disciples heard it, they said, "This teaching is difficult; who can accept it?" 61But Jesus, being aware that his disciples were complaining about it, said to them, "Does this offend you? 62Then what if you were to see the Son of Man ascending to where he was before? 63It is the spirit that gives life; the flesh is useless. The words that I have spoken to you are spirit and life. 64But among you there are some who do not believe." For Jesus knew from the first who were the ones that did not believe, and who was the one that would betray him. 65And he said, "For this reason I have told you that no one can come to me unless it is granted by the Father."

66 Because of this many of his disciples turned back and no longer went about with him. 67So Jesus asked the twelve, "Do you also wish to go away?" 68Simon Peter answered him, "Lord, to whom can we go? You have the words of eternal life. 69We have come to believe and know that you are the Holy One of God." a 70Jesus answered them, "Did I not choose you, the twelve? Yet one of you is a devil." 71He was speaking of Judas son of Simon Iscariot, b for he, though one of the twelve, was going to betray him.

The Unbelief of Jesus' Brothers

7 After this Jesus went about in Galilee. He did not wish c to go about in Judea because the Jews were looking for an opportunity to kill him. 2Now the Jewish festival of Booths d was near. 3So his brothers said to

a Other ancient authorities read *the Christ, the Son of the living God*   b Other ancient authorities read *Judas Iscariot son of Simon;* others, *Judas son of Simon from Karyot* (Kerioth)   c Other ancient authorities read *was not at liberty*
d Or *Tabernacles*

6:51–58 *I am the living bread.* Consider what we can learn about the Lord's Supper (Eucharist) through this sacramental discourse. How will that affect our participation?

6:56–58 THE WITH-GOD LIFE—*See* Spiritual Disciplines Index.

6:60–71 *This teaching is difficult.* Following Jesus is difficult. How does Peter's response (vv 68–69) change our attitudes about the struggles?

7:1–52 *After this Jesus went about in Galilee.* There are numerous conflict narratives in the Gospel of John. Each of these narratives propels us to ask different sorts of questions to gain insights into Jesus, his life for us, and how to respond to our faith opponents. What are the reasons for antagonism? What do we learn about Jesus from his rejoinder to each issue? What extra insights do we gain from rejoinders with multiple meanings? If the narrative names a festival, what might be the relationship of the Jewish observance to what we learn about Jesus? What crowd reactions do we recognize in ourselves, and why? Which assertions divide the crowd, and why? What promises does Jesus give? How might our answers to these questions change the way we pray and live?

him, "Leave here and go to Judea so that your disciples also may see the works you are doing; [4]for no one who wants[a] to be widely known acts in secret. If you do these things, show yourself to the world." [5](For not even his brothers believed in him.) [6]Jesus said to them, "My time has not yet come, but your time is always here. [7]The world cannot hate you, but it hates me because I testify against it that its works are evil. [8]Go to the festival yourselves. I am not[b] going to this festival, for my time has not yet fully come." [9]After saying this, he remained in Galilee.

Jesus at the Festival of Booths

10 But after his brothers had gone to the festival, then he also went, not publicly but as it were[c] in secret. [11]The Jews were looking for him at the festival and saying, "Where is he?" [12]And there was considerable complaining about him among the crowds. While some were saying, "He is a good man," others were saying, "No, he is deceiving the crowd." [13]Yet no one would speak openly about him for fear of the Jews.

14 About the middle of the festival Jesus went up into the temple and began to teach. [15]The Jews were astonished at it, saying, "How does this man have such learning,[d] when he has never been taught?" [16]Then Jesus answered them, "My teaching is not mine but his who sent me. [17]Anyone who resolves to do the will of God will know whether the teaching is from God or whether I am speaking on my own. [18]Those who speak on their own seek their own glory; but the one who seeks the glory of him who sent him is true, and there is nothing false in him.

19 "Did not Moses give you the law? Yet none of you keeps the law. Why are you looking for an opportunity to kill me?" [20]The crowd answered, "You have a demon! Who is trying to kill you?" [21]Jesus answered them, "I performed one work, and all of you are astonished. [22]Moses gave you circumcision (it is, of course, not from Moses, but from the patriarchs), and you circumcise a man on the sabbath. [23]If a man receives circumcision on the sabbath in order that the law of Moses may not be broken, are you angry with me because I healed a man's whole body on the

sabbath? [24]Do not judge by appearances, but judge with right judgment."

Is This the Christ?

25 Now some of the people of Jerusalem were saying, "Is not this the man whom they are trying to kill? [26]And here he is, speaking openly, but they say nothing to him! Can it be that the authorities really know that this is the Messiah?[e] [27]Yet we know where this man is from; but when the Messiah[e] comes, no one will know where he is from." [28]Then Jesus cried out as he was teaching in the temple, "You know me, and you know where I am from. I have not come on my own. But the one who sent me is true, and you do not know him. [29]I know him, because I am from him, and he sent me." [30]Then they tried to arrest him, but no one laid hands on him, because his hour had not yet come. [31]Yet many in the crowd believed in him and were saying, "When the Messiah[e] comes, will he do more signs than this man has done?"[f]

Officers Are Sent to Arrest Jesus

32 The Pharisees heard the crowd muttering such things about him, and the chief priests and Pharisees sent temple police to arrest him. [33]Jesus then said, "I will be with you a little while longer, and then I am going to him who sent me. [34]You will search for me, but you will not find me; and where I am, you cannot come." [35]The Jews said to one another, "Where does this man intend to go that we will not find him? Does he intend to go to the Dispersion among the Greeks and teach the Greeks? [36]What does he mean by saying, 'You will search for me and you will not find me' and 'Where I am, you cannot come'?"

Rivers of Living Water

37 On the last day of the festival, the great day, while Jesus was standing there, he cried out, "Let anyone who is thirsty come to me, [38]and let the one who believes in me drink.

a Other ancient authorities read *wants it*
b Other ancient authorities add *yet*   c Other ancient authorities lack *as it were*   d Or *this man know his letters*   e Or *the Christ*   f Other ancient authorities read *is doing*

As*a* the scripture has said, 'Out of the believer's heart*b* shall flow rivers of living water.'" ³⁹Now he said this about the Spirit, which believers in him were to receive; for as yet there was no Spirit,*c* because Jesus was not yet glorified.

Division among the People

40 When they heard these words, some in the crowd said, "This is really the prophet." ⁴¹Others said, "This is the Messiah."*d* But some asked, "Surely the Messiah*d* does not come from Galilee, does he? ⁴²Has not the scripture said that the Messiah*d* is descended from David and comes from Bethlehem, the village where David lived?" ⁴³So there was a division in the crowd because of him. ⁴⁴Some of them wanted to arrest him, but no one laid hands on him.

The Unbelief of Those in Authority

45 Then the temple police went back to the chief priests and Pharisees, who asked them, "Why did you not arrest him?" ⁴⁶The police answered, "Never has anyone spoken like this!" ⁴⁷Then the Pharisees replied, "Surely you have not been deceived too, have you? ⁴⁸Has any one of the authorities or of the Pharisees believed in him? ⁴⁹But this crowd, which does not know the law—they are accursed." ⁵⁰Nicodemus, who had gone to Jesus*e* before, and who was one of them, asked, ⁵¹"Our law does not judge people without first giving them a hearing to find out what they are doing, does it?" ⁵²They replied, "Surely you are not also from Galilee, are you? Search and you will see that no prophet is to arise from Galilee."

The Woman Caught in Adultery

8 ⟦⁵³Then each of them went home, ¹while Jesus went to the Mount of Olives.

²Early in the morning he came again to the temple. All the people came to him and he sat down and began to teach them. ³The scribes and the Pharisees brought a woman who had been caught in adultery; and making her stand before all of them, ⁴they said to him, "Teacher, this woman was caught in the very act of committing adultery. ⁵Now in the law Moses commanded us to stone such women. Now what do you say?" ⁶They said this to test him, so that they might have some charge to bring against him. Jesus bent down and wrote with his finger on the ground. ⁷When they kept on questioning him, he straightened up and said to them, "Let anyone among you who is without sin be the first to throw a stone at her." ⁸And once again he bent down and wrote on the ground.*f* ⁹When they heard it, they went away, one by one, beginning with the elders; and Jesus was left alone with the woman standing before him. ¹⁰Jesus straightened up and said to her, "Woman, where are they? Has no one condemned you?" ¹¹She said, "No one, sir."*g* And Jesus said, "Neither do I condemn you. Go your way, and from now on do not sin again."⟧*h*

Jesus the Light of the World

12 Again Jesus spoke to them, saying, "I am the light of the world. Whoever follows me will never walk in darkness but will have the light of life." ¹³Then the Pharisees said to

a Or *come to me and drink.* ³⁸*The one who believes in me, as*   *b* Gk *out of his belly*   *c* Other ancient authorities read *for as yet the Spirit* (others, *Holy Spirit*) *had not been given*   *d* Or *the Christ*   *e* Gk *him*   *f* Other ancient authorities add *the sins of each of them*   *g* Or *Lord*   *h* The most ancient authorities lack 7.53—8.11; other authorities add the passage here or after 7.36 or after 21.25 or after Luke 21.38, with variations of text; some mark the passage as doubtful.

7:37–39 *Let anyone who is thirsty come to me.* What great gifts this passage promises! The multiple meanings in these verses are amplified by their connections to such texts as Isaiah 55; John 19:34; and Rev 7:17.

7:45–49 *Has any one of the authorities . . . believed?* See the Introduction on irony.

8:1–11 *a woman who had been caught in adultery.* What does Jesus' treatment of the woman teach us about dealing with the sins of others?

8:12 *I am the light of the world.* (See also 9:5.) See note on 6:35–59.

8:12–59 *Again Jesus spoke to them.* See note on 7:1–52.

him, "You are testifying on your own behalf; your testimony is not valid." [14]Jesus answered, "Even if I testify on my own behalf, my testimony is valid because I know where I have come from and where I am going, but you do not know where I come from or where I am going. [15]You judge by human standards;[a] I judge no one. [16]Yet even if I do judge, my judgment is valid; for it is not I alone who judge, but I and the Father[b] who sent me. [17]In your law it is written that the testimony of two witnesses is valid. [18]I testify on my own behalf, and the Father who sent me testifies on my behalf." [19]Then they said to him, "Where is your Father?" Jesus answered, "You know neither me nor my Father. If you knew me, you would know my Father also." [20]He spoke these words while he was teaching in the treasury of the temple, but no one arrested him, because his hour had not yet come.

Jesus Foretells His Death

21 Again he said to them, "I am going away, and you will search for me, but you will die in your sin. Where I am going, you cannot come." [22]Then the Jews said, "Is he going to kill himself? Is that what he means by saying, 'Where I am going, you cannot come'?" [23]He said to them, "You are from below, I am from above; you are of this world, I am not of this world. [24]I told you that you would die in your sins, for you will die in

your sins unless you believe that I am he."[c] [25]They said to him, "Who are you?" Jesus said to them, "Why do I speak to you at all?[d] [26]I have much to say about you and much to condemn; but the one who sent me is true, and I declare to the world what I have heard from him." [27]They did not understand that he was speaking to them about the Father. [28]So Jesus said, "When you have lifted up the Son of Man, then you will realize that I am he,[c] and that I do nothing on my own, but I speak these things as the Father instructed me. [29]And the one who sent me is with me; he has not left me alone, for I always do what is pleasing to him." [30]As he was saying these things, many believed in him.

True Disciples

31 Then Jesus said to the Jews who had believed in him, "If you continue in my word, you are truly my disciples; [32]and you will know the truth, and the truth will make you free." [33]They answered him, "We are descendants of Abraham and have never been slaves to anyone. What do you mean by saying, 'You will be made free'?"

34 Jesus answered them, "Very truly, I tell you, everyone who commits sin is a slave to sin. [35]The slave does not have a permanent place in the household; the son has a place there for-

a Gk *according to the flesh*   *b* Other ancient authorities read *he*   *c* Gk *I am*   *d* Or *What I have told you from the beginning*

8:24, 28, 58 *I am he.* See the Introduction on "I am" statements.

Responding
8:29 SOLITUDE. The Father was with the Son in every situation, and Jesus promises that the Advocate, the Holy Spirit, will be with us forever (John 14:16). Why does solitude make us more aware of the indwelling Holy Spirit's sustaining presence? What can we do to nurture solitude in the midst of our everyday lives? *See also* Spiritual Disciplines Index.

8:31 *If you continue in my word.* Jesus continually calls us to deepen our belief with

steadfast study of his Word. When we abide in Scripture, its language forms our life.

8:32 *you will know the truth.* Postmodern thought rejects any universal "truth"; Christians believe that all truth comes from the Trinity. Jesus manifests the truth about God. His Word teaches us the truth about our lives, about the world.

8:33 *We . . . have never been slaves to anyone.* These people seem to have forgotten their own history. What can we learn from our heritage about the way the world works and ways that God works in the world?

8:34 *everyone who commits sin is a slave to sin.* Most of our slaveries are from inside us, not outside us. To what are we enslaved? How does God free us?

ever. 36So if the Son makes you free, you will be free indeed. 37I know that you are descendants of Abraham; yet you look for an opportunity to kill me, because there is no place in you for my word. 38I declare what I have seen in the Father's presence; as for you, you should do what you have heard from the Father." a

Jesus and Abraham

39 They answered him, "Abraham is our father." Jesus said to them, "If you were Abraham's children, you would be doing b what Abraham did, 40but now you are trying to kill me, a man who has told you the truth that I heard from God. This is not what Abraham did. 41You are indeed doing what your father does." They said to him, "We are not illegitimate children; we have one father, God himself." 42Jesus said to them, "If God were your Father, you would love me, for I came from God and now I am here. I did not come on my own, but he sent me. 43Why do you not understand what I say? It is because you cannot accept my word. 44You are from your father the devil, and you choose to do your father's desires. He was a murderer from the beginning and does not stand in the truth, because there is no truth in him. When he lies, he speaks according to his own nature, for he is a liar and the father of lies. 45But because I tell the truth, you do not believe me. 46Which of you convicts me of sin? If I tell the truth, why do you not believe me? 47Whoever is from God hears the words of God. The reason you do not hear them is that you are not from God."

48 The Jews answered him, "Are we not right in saying that you are a Samaritan and have a demon?" 49Jesus answered, "I do not have a demon; but I honor my Father, and you dishonor me. 50Yet I do not seek my own glory; there is one who seeks it and he is the judge. 51Very truly, I tell you, whoever keeps

my word will never see death." 52The Jews said to him, "Now we know that you have a demon. Abraham died, and so did the prophets; yet you say, 'Whoever keeps my word will never taste death.' 53Are you greater than our father Abraham, who died? The prophets also died. Who do you claim to be?" 54Jesus answered, "If I glorify myself, my glory is nothing. It is my Father who glorifies me, he of whom you say, 'He is our God,' 55though you do not know him. But I know him; if I would say that I do not know him, I would be a liar like you. But I do know him and I keep his word. 56Your ancestor Abraham rejoiced that he would see my day; he saw it and was glad." 57Then the Jews said to him, "You are not yet fifty years old, and have you seen Abraham?" c 58Jesus said to them, "Very truly, I tell you, before Abraham was, I am." 59So they picked up stones to throw at him, but Jesus hid himself and went out of the temple.

A Man Born Blind Receives Sight

9 As he walked along, he saw a man blind from birth. 2His disciples asked him, "Rabbi, who sinned, this man or his parents, that he was born blind?" 3Jesus answered, "Neither this man nor his parents sinned; he was born blind so that God's works might be revealed in him. 4We d must work the works of him who sent me e while it is day; night is coming when no one can work. 5As long as I am in the world, I am the light of the world." 6When he had said this, he spat on the ground and made mud with the saliva and spread the mud on the man's eyes, 7saying to him, "Go, wash

a Other ancient authorities read *you do what you have heard from your father* b Other ancient authorities read *If you are Abraham's children, then do* c Other ancient authorities read *has Abraham seen you?* d Other ancient authorities read *I* e Other ancient authorities read *us*

8:36 *So if the Son makes you free.* True freedom is not libertinism, but the liberation that delivers us from ourselves.

9:3 *Neither this man nor his parents sinned.* Subconsciously, many people still treat those who suffer as if handicaps were the result of sin or inadequate prayer. Jesus sternly rejects any notion that illness is a direct punishment for sin

(though sins often do reap their own consequences).

Responding
9:3 SERVICE. How might Jesus' response change the way we deal with others' or our own physical sufferings? *See also* Spiritual Disciplines Index.

CHRONIC UNBELIEF

I LOVE THIS MANS SPUNK ↓

in the pool of Siloam" (which means Sent). Then he went and washed and came back able to see. 8 The neighbors and those who had seen him before as a beggar began to ask, "Is this not the man who used to sit and beg?" 9 Some were saying, "It is he." Others were saying, "No, but it is someone like him." He kept saying, "I am the man." 10 But they kept asking him, "Then how were your eyes opened?" 11 He answered, "The man called Jesus made mud, spread it on my eyes, and said to me, 'Go to Siloam and wash.' Then I went and washed and received my sight." 12 They said to him, "Where is he?" He said, "I do not know."

The Pharisees Investigate the Healing

13 They brought to the Pharisees the man who had formerly been blind. 14 Now it was a sabbath day when Jesus made the mud and opened his eyes. 15 Then the Pharisees also began to ask him how he had received his sight. He said to them, "He put mud on my eyes. Then I washed, and now I see." 16 Some of the Pharisees said, "This man is not from God, for he does not observe the sabbath." But others said, "How can a man who is a sinner perform such signs?" And they were divided. 17 So they said again to the blind man, "What do you say about him? It was your eyes he opened." He said, "He is a prophet."

18 The Jews did not believe that he had been blind and had received his sight until they called the parents of the man who had received his sight 19 and asked them, "Is this your son, who you say was born blind? How then does he now see?" 20 His parents answered, "We know that this is our son, and that he was born blind; 21 but we do not know how it is that now he sees, nor do we know who opened his eyes. Ask him; he is of age. He will speak for himself." 22 His parents said this because they were afraid of the Jews; for the Jews had already agreed that anyone who confessed Jesus[a] to be the Messiah[b] would

be put out of the synagogue. 23 Therefore his parents said, "He is of age; ask him."

24 So for the second time they called the man who had been blind, and they said to him, "Give glory to God! We know that this man is a sinner." 25 He answered, "I do not know whether he is a sinner. One thing I do know, that though I was blind, now I see." 26 They said to him, "What did he do to you? How did he open your eyes?" 27 He answered them, "I have told you already, and you would not listen. Why do you want to hear it again? Do you also want to become his disciples?" 28 Then they reviled him, saying, "You are his disciple, but we are disciples of Moses. 29 We know that God has spoken to Moses, but as for this man, we do not know where he comes from." 30 The man answered, "Here is an astonishing thing! You do not know where he comes from, and yet he opened my eyes. 31 We know that God does not listen to sinners, but he does listen to one who worships him and obeys his will. 32 Never since the world began has it been heard that anyone opened the eyes of a person born blind. 33 If this man were not from God, he could do nothing." 34 They answered him, "You were born entirely in sins, and are you trying to teach us?" And they drove him out.

Spiritual Blindness

35 Jesus heard that they had driven him out, and when he found him, he said, "Do you believe in the Son of Man?"[c] 36 He answered, "And who is he, sir?[d] Tell me, so that I may believe in him." 37 Jesus said to him, "You have seen him, and the one speaking with you is he." 38 He said, "Lord,[d] I believe." And he worshiped him. 39 Jesus said, "I came into this world for judgment so that those who do not see may see, and those who do see

a Gk *him*   b Or *the Christ*   c Other ancient authorities read *the Son of God*   d *Sir* and *Lord* translate the same Greek word

9:8–41 *Then how were your eyes opened?* Since John includes the unique participation of the one healed in the conflict following Jesus' fifth "sign," consider these questions besides those in the note on 7:1–52: How does the faith

and witness of the healed man develop? What can we learn from his responses? What prejudices blind us to God's works?

9:31 WORSHIP—*See* Spiritual Disciplines Index.

may become blind." 40Some of the Pharisees near him heard this and said to him, "Surely we are not blind, are we?" 41Jesus said to them, "If you were blind, you would not have sin. But now that you say, 'We see,' your sin remains.

Jesus the Good Shepherd

10 "Very truly, I tell you, anyone who does not enter the sheepfold by the gate but climbs in by another way is a thief and a bandit. 2The one who enters by the gate is the shepherd of the sheep. 3The gatekeeper opens the gate for him, and the sheep hear his voice. He calls his own sheep by name and leads them out. 4When he has brought out all his own, he goes ahead of them, and the sheep follow him because they know his voice. 5They will not follow a stranger, but they will run from him because they do not know the voice of strangers." 6Jesus used this figure of speech with them, but they did not understand what he was saying to them.

7 So again Jesus said to them, "Very truly, I tell you, I am the gate for the sheep. 8All who came before me are thieves and bandits; but the sheep did not listen to them. 9I am the gate. Whoever enters by me will be saved, and will come in and go out and find pasture. 10The thief comes only to steal and kill and destroy. I came that they may have life, and have it abundantly.

11 "I am the good shepherd. The good shepherd lays down his life for the sheep. 12The hired hand, who is not the shepherd and does not own the sheep, sees the wolf coming and leaves the sheep and runs away— and the wolf snatches them and scatters them. 13The hired hand runs away because a hired hand does not care for the sheep. 14I am the good shepherd. I know my own and my own know me, 15just as the Father knows me and I know the Father. And I lay down my life for the sheep. 16I have other sheep that do not belong to this fold. I must bring them also,

and they will listen to my voice. So there will be one flock, one shepherd. 17For this reason the Father loves me, because I lay down my life in order to take it up again. 18No one takes[a] it from me, but I lay it down of my own accord. I have power to lay it down, and I have power to take it up again. I have received this command from my Father."

19 Again the Jews were divided because of these words. 20Many of them were saying, "He has a demon and is out of his mind. Why listen to him?" 21Others were saying, "These are not the words of one who has a demon. Can a demon open the eyes of the blind?"

Jesus Is Rejected by the Jews

22 At that time the festival of the Dedication took place in Jerusalem. It was winter, 23and Jesus was walking in the temple, in the portico of Solomon. 24So the Jews gathered around him and said to him, "How long will you keep us in suspense? If you are the Messiah,[b] tell us plainly." 25Jesus answered, "I have told you, and you do not believe. The works that I do in my Father's name testify to me; 26but you do not believe, because you do not belong to my sheep. 27My sheep hear my voice. I know them, and they follow me. 28I give them eternal life, and they will never perish. No one will snatch them out of my hand. 29What my Father has given me is greater than all else, and no one can snatch it out of the Father's hand.[c] 30The Father and I are one."

31 The Jews took up stones again to stone him. 32Jesus replied, "I have shown you many good works from the Father. For which of these are you going to stone me?" 33The Jews answered, "It is not for a good work that we are going to stone you, but for blasphemy, because you, though only a human being, are

a Other ancient authorities read *has taken*
b Or *the Christ*   c Other ancient authorities read *My Father who has given them to me is greater than all, and no one can snatch them out of the Father's hand*

10:1–10 *I am the gate.* See note on 6:35–59.
10:11–18 *I am the good shepherd.* See note on 6:35–59.
10:15 *I lay down my life for the sheep.* Jesus' foretellings of his death are less direct in but many passages on conflicts, threats,

and dangers are included. What subtle threats to faith characterize our times?
10:16 *other sheep that do not belong to this fold.* See the Introduction on irony.
10:19–39 *the Jews were divided.* See note on 7:1–52.

making yourself God." 34Jesus answered, "Is it not written in your law,*a* 'I said, you are gods'? 35If those to whom the word of God came were called 'gods'—and the scripture cannot be annulled— 36can you say that the one whom the Father has sanctified and sent into the world is blaspheming because I said, 'I am God's Son'? 37If I am not doing the works of my Father, then do not believe me. 38But if I do them, even though you do not believe me, believe the works, so that you may know and understand*b* that the Father is in me and I am in the Father." 39Then they tried to arrest him again, but he escaped from their hands.

40 He went away again across the Jordan to the place where John had been baptizing earlier, and he remained there. 41Many came to him, and they were saying, "John performed no sign, but everything that John said about this man was true." 42And many believed in him there.

The Death of Lazarus

11 Now a certain man was ill, Lazarus of Bethany, the village of Mary and her sister Martha. 2Mary was the one who anointed the Lord with perfume and wiped his feet with her hair; her brother Lazarus was ill. 3So the sisters sent a message to Jesus,*c* "Lord, he whom you love is ill." 4But when Jesus heard it, he said, "This illness does not lead to death; rather it is for God's glory, so that the Son of God may be glorified through it." 5Accordingly, though Jesus loved Martha and her sister and Lazarus, 6after having heard that Lazarus*d* was ill, he stayed two days longer in the place where he was.

7 Then after this he said to the disciples, "Let us go to Judea again." 8The disciples said to him, "Rabbi, the Jews were just now trying to stone you, and are you going there again?" 9Jesus answered, "Are there not twelve hours of daylight? Those who walk during the day

do not stumble, because they see the light of this world. 10But those who walk at night stumble, because the light is not in them." 11After saying this, he told them, "Our friend Lazarus has fallen asleep, but I am going there to awaken him." 12The disciples said to him, "Lord, if he has fallen asleep, he will be all right." 13Jesus, however, had been speaking about his death, but they thought that he was referring merely to sleep. 14Then Jesus told them plainly, "Lazarus is dead. 15For your sake I am glad I was not there, so that you may believe. But let us go to him." 16Thomas, who was called the Twin,*e* said to his fellow disciples, "Let us also go, that we may die with him."

Jesus the Resurrection and the Life

17 When Jesus arrived, he found that Lazarus*d* had already been in the tomb four days. 18Now Bethany was near Jerusalem, some two miles*f* away, 19and many of the Jews had come to Martha and Mary to console them about their brother. 20When Martha heard that Jesus was coming, she went and met him, while Mary stayed at home. 21Martha said to Jesus, "Lord, if you had been here, my brother would not have died. 22But even now I know that God will give you whatever you ask of him." 23Jesus said to her, "Your brother will rise again." 24Martha said to him, "I know that he will rise again in the resurrection on the last day." 25Jesus said to her, "I am the resurrection and the life.*g* Those who believe in me, even though they die, will live, 26and everyone who lives and believes in me will never die. Do you believe this?" 27She said to him, "Yes, Lord, I believe that you are

a Other ancient authorities read *in the law*
b Other ancient authorities lack *and understand*; others read *and believe*   *c* Gk *him*   *d* Gk *he*
e Gk *Didymus*   *f* Gk *fifteen stadia*   *g* Other ancient authorities lack *and the life*

10:40–42 *everything that John said about this man was true.* See note on 2:1–11.

11:1–45 *a certain man was ill, Lazarus of Bethany.* This "sign" gathers in this Gospel's themes of light and life and stands in stark contrast to the darkness and death soon to follow. What do the diverse conversations in

John's longest healing narrative teach us about ourselves and about Jesus? What do his responses show us about God? What does this narrative teach us about suffering and glory, about love?

11:21–27 *I am the resurrection and the life.* See note on 6:35–59.

the Messiah, *a* the Son of God, the one coming into the world."

Jesus Weeps

28 When she had said this, she went back and called her sister Mary, and told her privately, "The Teacher is here and is calling for you." 29And when she heard it, she got up quickly and went to him. 30Now Jesus had not yet come to the village, but was still at the place where Martha had met him. 31The Jews who were with her in the house, consoling her, saw Mary get up quickly and go out. They followed her because they thought that she was going to the tomb to weep there. 32When Mary came where Jesus was and saw him, she knelt at his feet and said to him, "Lord, if you had been here, my brother would not have died." 33When Jesus saw her weeping, and the Jews who came with her also weeping, he was greatly disturbed in spirit and deeply moved. 34He said, "Where have you laid him?" They said to him, "Lord, come and see." 35Jesus began to weep. 36So the Jews said, "See how he loved him!" 37But some of them said, "Could not he who opened the eyes of the blind man have kept this man from dying?"

Jesus Raises Lazarus to Life

38 Then Jesus, again greatly disturbed, came to the tomb. It was a cave, and a stone was lying against it. 39Jesus said, "Take away the stone." Martha, the sister of the dead man, said to him, "Lord, already there is a stench because he has been dead four days." 40Jesus said to her, "Did I not tell you that if you believed, you would see the glory of God?" 41So they took away the stone. And Jesus looked upward and said, "Father, I thank you for having heard me. 42I knew that you always hear me, but I have said this for the sake of the crowd standing here, so that they may believe that you sent me." 43When he had said this, he cried with a loud voice, "Lazarus, come out!" 44The dead man came out, his hands and feet bound with strips of cloth, and his face wrapped in a cloth. Jesus said to them, "Unbind him, and let him go."

The Plot to Kill Jesus

45 Many of the Jews therefore, who had come with Mary and had seen what Jesus did, believed in him. 46But some of them went to the Pharisees and told them what he had done. 47So the chief priests and the Pharisees called a meeting of the council, and said, "What are we to do? This man is performing many signs. 48If we let him go on like this, everyone will believe in him, and the Romans will come and destroy both our holy place *b* and our nation." 49But one of them, Caiaphas, who was high priest that year, said to them, "You know nothing at all! 50You do not understand that it is better for you to have one man die for the people than to have the whole nation destroyed." 51He did not say this on his own, but being high priest that year he prophesied that Jesus was about to die for the nation, 52and not for the nation only, but to gather into one the dispersed children of God. 53So from that day on they planned to put him to death.

54 Jesus therefore no longer walked about openly among the Jews, but went from there to a town called Ephraim in the region near the wilderness; and he remained there with the disciples.

55 Now the Passover of the Jews was near, and many went up from the country to Jerusalem before the Passover to purify themselves. 56They were looking for Jesus and were

a Or *the Christ*   *b* Or *our temple*; Greek *our place*

11:40 *Did I not tell you that if you believed, you would see the glory of God?* Note the ordering of belief and glory. How often we reverse these two and demand to see glory in order to believe! God's glory is always more deeply revealed to those whose faith opens their eyes.

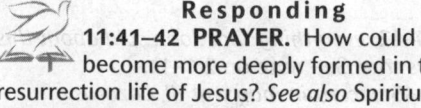

Responding
11:41–42 PRAYER. How could we become more deeply formed in the resurrection life of Jesus? *See also* Spiritual Disciplines Index.

11:45–48 *This man is performing many signs.* See note on 2:1–11.

asking one another as they stood in the temple, "What do you think? Surely he will not come to the festival, will he?" [57]Now the chief priests and the Pharisees had given orders that anyone who knew where Jesus[a] was should let them know, so that they might arrest him.

Mary Anoints Jesus

12 Six days before the Passover Jesus came to Bethany, the home of Lazarus, whom he had raised from the dead. [2]There they gave a dinner for him. Martha served, and Lazarus was one of those at the table with him. [3]Mary took a pound of costly perfume made of pure nard, anointed Jesus' feet, and wiped them[b] with her hair. The house was filled with the fragrance of the perfume. [4]But Judas Iscariot, one of his disciples (the one who was about to betray him), said, [5]"Why was this perfume not sold for three hundred denarii[c] and the money given to the poor?" [6](He said this not because he cared about the poor, but because he was a thief; he kept the common purse and used to steal what was put into it.) [7]Jesus said, "Leave her alone. She bought it[d] so that she might keep it for the day of my burial. [8]You always have the poor with you, but you do not always have me."

The Plot to Kill Lazarus

9 When the great crowd of the Jews learned that he was there, they came not only because of Jesus but also to see Lazarus, whom he had raised from the dead. [10]So the chief priests planned to put Lazarus to death as well, [11]since it was on account of him that many of the Jews were deserting and were believing in Jesus.

Jesus' Triumphal Entry into Jerusalem

12 The next day the great crowd that had come to the festival heard that Jesus was coming to Jerusalem. [13]So they took branches of palm trees and went out to meet him, shouting,
"Hosanna!
Blessed is the one who comes in the
name of the Lord—
the King of Israel!"
[14]Jesus found a young donkey and sat on it; as it is written:
[15] "Do not be afraid, daughter of Zion.
Look, your king is coming,
sitting on a donkey's colt!"
[16]His disciples did not understand these things at first; but when Jesus was glorified, then they remembered that these things had been written of him and had been done to him. [17]So the crowd that had been with him when he called Lazarus out of the tomb and raised him from the dead continued to testify.[e] [18]It was also because they heard that he had performed this sign that the crowd went to meet him. [19]The Pharisees then said to one another, "You see, you can do nothing. Look, the world has gone after him!"

Some Greeks Wish to See Jesus

20 Now among those who went up to worship at the festival were some Greeks. [21]They came to Philip, who was from Bethsaida in Galilee, and said to him, "Sir, we wish to see Jesus." [22]Philip went and told Andrew; then Andrew and Philip went and told Jesus. [23]Jesus answered them, "The hour has come for the

a Gk he   b Gk his feet   c Three hundred denarii would be nearly a year's wages for a laborer   d Gk lacks She bought it   e Other ancient authorities read with him began to testify that he had called . . . from the dead

---

11:48–53 *to have one man die for the people.* See the Introduction on irony.

12:1–19 *Six days before the Passover Jesus came to Bethany.* We forget too easily the tension and danger under which Jesus fulfilled his ministry and thereby misunderstand the extent of his sufferings for us. His recognition in verses 7–8 of his imminent burial (notice the forewarnings in 11:2, 8–16) is substantiated by the escalating animosity of the religious

leaders in verses 9–19.

12:20–50 *The hour has come for the Son of Man to be glorified.* This summary of Jesus' final days is an extraordinary mixture of anguish, promise, revelation, and threat. Many strands (see Introduction) come together here—"glory," "hour," "eternal life," "world," "light," "darkness," "belief," "words," "the Father." How do the interminglings of these themes enlarge our gratitude for all that Christ has done for us?

Son of Man to be glorified. 24Very truly, I tell you, unless a grain of wheat falls into the earth and dies, it remains just a single grain; but if it dies, it bears much fruit. 25Those who love their life lose it, and those who hate their life in this world will keep it for eternal life. 26Whoever serves me must follow me, and where I am, there will my servant be also. Whoever serves me, the Father will honor.

Jesus Speaks about His Death

27 "Now my soul is troubled. And what should I say—'Father, save me from this hour'? No, it is for this reason that I have come to this hour. 28Father, glorify your name." Then a voice came from heaven, "I have glorified it, and I will glorify it again." 29The crowd standing there heard it and said that it was thunder. Others said, "An angel has spoken to him." 30Jesus answered, "This voice has come for your sake, not for mine. 31Now is the judgment of this world; now the ruler of this world will be driven out. 32And I, when I am lifted up from the earth, will draw all people[a] to myself." 33He said this to indicate the kind of death he was to die. 34The crowd answered him, "We have heard from the law that the Messiah[b] remains forever. How can you say that the Son of Man must be lifted up? Who is this Son of Man?" 35Jesus said to them, "The light is with you for a little longer. Walk while you have the light, so that the darkness may not overtake you. If you walk in the darkness, you do not know where you are going. 36While you have the light, believe in the light, so that you may become children of light."

The Unbelief of the People

After Jesus had said this, he departed and hid from them. 37Although he had performed so many signs in their presence, they did not believe in him. 38This was to fulfill the word spoken by the prophet Isaiah:

"Lord, who has believed our message,
     and to whom has the arm of the Lord
          been revealed?"

39And so they could not believe, because Isaiah also said,

40 "He has blinded their eyes
     and hardened their heart,
so that they might not look with their
     eyes,
     and understand with their heart and
          turn—
     and I would heal them."

41Isaiah said this because[c] he saw his glory and spoke about him. 42Nevertheless many, even of the authorities, believed in him. But because of the Pharisees they did not confess it, for fear that they would be put out of the synagogue; 43for they loved human glory more than the glory that comes from God.

Summary of Jesus' Teaching

44 Then Jesus cried aloud: "Whoever believes in me believes not in me but in him who sent me. 45And whoever sees me sees him who sent me. 46I have come as light into the world, so that everyone who believes in me should not remain in the darkness. 47I do not judge anyone who hears my words and does not keep them, for I came not to judge the world, but to save the world. 48The one who rejects me and does not receive my word has a judge; on the last day the word that I have spoken will serve as judge, 49for I have not spoken on my own, but the Father who sent me has himself given me a commandment about what to say and what to speak. 50And I know that his commandment is eternal life. What I speak, therefore, I speak just as the Father has told me."

Jesus Washes the Disciples' Feet

13 Now before the festival of the Passover, Jesus knew that his hour had come to depart from this world and go to the Father. Having loved his own who were in the world, he loved them to the end. 2The devil had already put it into the heart of

a Other ancient authorities read *all things*
b Or *the Christ*   c Other ancient witnesses read
when

12:26 SERVICE—*See* Spiritual Disciplines Index.

12:42–43 *because of the Pharisees they did not confess it.* Still today similar situations persist. Is it ever the case in our lives?

Judas son of Simon Iscariot to betray him. And during supper [3]Jesus, knowing that the Father had given all things into his hands, and that he had come from God and was going to God, [4]got up from the table, [a] took off his outer robe, and tied a towel around himself. [5]Then he poured water into a basin and began to wash the disciples' feet and to wipe them with the towel that was tied around him. [6]He came to Simon Peter, who said to him, "Lord, are you going to wash my feet?" [7]Jesus answered, "You do not know now what I am doing, but later you will understand." [8]Peter said to him, "You will never wash my feet." Jesus answered, "Unless I wash you, you have no share with me." [9]Simon Peter said to him, "Lord, not my feet only but also my hands and my head!" [10]Jesus said to him, "One who has bathed does not need to wash, except for the feet, [b] but is entirely clean. And you [c] are clean, though not all of you." [11]For he knew who was to betray him; for this reason he said, "Not all of you are clean."

12 After he had washed their feet, had put on his robe, and had returned to the table, he said to them, "Do you know what I have done to you? [13]You call me Teacher and Lord—and you are right, for that is what I am. [14]So if I, your Lord and Teacher, have washed your feet, you also ought to wash one another's feet. [15]For I have set you an example, that you also should do as I have done to you. [16]Very truly, I tell you, servants [d] are not greater than their master, nor are messengers greater than the one who sent them. [17]If you know these things, you are blessed if you do them. [18]I am not speaking of all of you; I know whom I have chosen. But it is to fulfill the scripture, 'The one who ate my bread [e] has lifted his heel against me.' [19]I tell you

this now, before it occurs, so that when it does occur, you may believe that I am he. [f] [20]Very truly, I tell you, whoever receives one whom I send receives me; and whoever receives me receives him who sent me."

Jesus Foretells His Betrayal

21 After saying this Jesus was troubled in spirit, and declared, "Very truly, I tell you, one of you will betray me." [22]The disciples looked at one another, uncertain of whom he was speaking. [23]One of his disciples—the one whom Jesus loved—was reclining next to him; [24]Simon Peter therefore motioned to him to ask Jesus of whom he was speaking. [25]So while reclining next to Jesus, he asked him, "Lord, who is it?" [26]Jesus answered, "It is the one to whom I give this piece of bread when I have dipped it in the dish." [g] So when he had dipped the piece of bread, he gave it to Judas son of Simon Iscariot. [h] [27]After he received the piece of bread, [i] Satan entered into him. Jesus said to him, "Do quickly what you are going to do." [28]Now no one at the table knew why he said this to him. [29]Some thought that, because Judas had the common purse, Jesus was telling him, "Buy what we need for the festival"; or, that he should give something to the poor. [30]So, after receiving the piece of bread, he immediately went out. And it was night.

The New Commandment

31 When he had gone out, Jesus said, "Now the Son of Man has been glorified, and

---

a Gk *from supper*   *b* Other ancient authorities lack *except for the feet*   *c* The Greek word for *you* here is plural   *d* Gk *slaves*   *e* Other ancient authorities read *ate bread with me*   *f* Gk *I am*   *g* Gk *dipped it*   *h* Other ancient authorities read *Judas Iscariot son of Simon*; others, *Judas son of Simon from Karyot* (Kerioth)   *i* Gk *After the piece of bread*

13:1–17 *Jesus knew that his hour had come.* Jesus' Last Supper begins with profound lessons in humility and baptism. Notice the incredible extent of Jesus' love, the ignorance of human responses, and the immensity of Christ's servanthood.

Responding
13:1–17 SERVICE. What Spiritual Disciplines might God use to form the

humble, baptized life more deeply in us? *See also* Spiritual Disciplines Index.

13:18–30 *The one who ate my bread has lifted his heel against me.* Judas' betrayal (alluded to in vv 10–11) compels us to confess our own betrayals.

13:31–38 *Now the Son of Man has been glorified.* What a contrast between Christ's glorification and human denial! (Cf. also v 37

God has been glorified in him. 32If God has been glorified in him,*a* God will also glorify him in himself and will glorify him at once. 33Little children, I am with you only a little longer. You will look for me; and as I said to the Jews so now I say to you, 'Where I am going, you cannot come.' 34I give you a new commandment, that you love one another. Just as I have loved you, you also should love one another. 35By this everyone will know that you are my disciples, if you have love for one another."

Jesus Foretells Peter's Denial

36 Simon Peter said to him, "Lord, where are you going?" Jesus answered, "Where I am going, you cannot follow me now; but you will follow afterward." 37Peter said to him, "Lord, why can I not follow you now? I will lay down my life for you." 38Jesus answered, "Will you lay down your life for me? Very truly, I tell you, before the cock crows, you will have denied me three times.

Jesus the Way to the Father

14 "Do not let your hearts be troubled. Believe*b* in God, believe also in me. 2In my Father's house there are many dwelling places. If it were not so, would I have told you that I go to prepare a place for you?*c* 3And if I go and prepare a place for you, I will come again and will take you to myself, so that where I am, there you may be also. 4And you know the way to the place where I am going." *d* 5Thomas said to him, "Lord, we do not know where you are going. How can we know the way?" 6Jesus said to him, "I am the way, and the truth, and the life. No one comes to the Father except through me. 7If you know me, you will know*e* my Father also. From now on you do know him and have seen him."

8 Philip said to him, "Lord, show us the Father, and we will be satisfied." 9Jesus said to him, "Have I been with you all this time, Philip, and you still do not know me? Whoever has seen me has seen the Father. How can you say, 'Show us the Father'? 10Do you not believe that I am in the Father and the Father is in me? The words that I say to you I do not speak on my own; but the Father who dwells in me does his works. 11Believe me that I am in the Father and the Father is in me; but if you do not, then believe me because of the works themselves. 12Very truly, I tell you, the one who believes in me will also do the works that I do and, in fact, will do greater works than these, because I am going to the Father. 13I will do whatever you ask in my name, so that the Father may be glorified in the Son. 14If in my name you ask me*f* for anything, I will do it.

The Promise of the Holy Spirit

15 "If you love me, you will keep*g* my commandments. 16And I will ask the Father, and he will give you another Advocate,*h* to be with you forever. 17This is the Spirit of truth,

a Other ancient authorities lack *If God has been glorified in him*   *b* Or *You believe*   *c* Or *If it were not so, I would have told you; for I go to prepare a place for you*   *d* Other ancient authorities read *Where I am going you know, and the way you know*   *e* Other ancient authorities read *If you had known me, you would have known*   *f* Other ancient authorities lack *me*   *g* Other ancient authorities read *me, keep*   *h* Or *Helper*

---

with 10:11.) Today is Jesus being glorified in us or in spite of us?

14:1–31 *Do not let your hearts be troubled.* This last discourse of Jesus is thoroughly trinitarian (see the Introduction on the Trinity). Contemplate deeply what this chapter teaches about the Godhead's interrelationships and our relationship with the Trinity. Meditate on how we are immersed in themes of belief, words, works, love, peace, the world and its troubles or persecutions, and glory. Do we share the disciples' misunderstandings? What commandments are we given? What promises?

Responding
14:1–31 GUIDANCE. How does the imminence of Jesus' death heighten the impact of the topics in this passage? *See also* Spiritual Disciplines Index.

14:6 *I am the way, and the truth, and the life.* See notes on 6:35–59; 8:32. What are the interconnections of this text's three metaphors?

whom the world cannot receive, because it neither sees him nor knows him. You know him, because he abides with you, and he will be in*a* you.

18 "I will not leave you orphaned; I am coming to you. ¹⁹In a little while the world will no longer see me, but you will see me; because I live, you also will live. ²⁰On that day you will know that I am in my Father, and you in me, and I in you. ²¹They who have my commandments and keep them are those who love me; and those who love me will be loved by my Father, and I will love them and reveal myself to them." ²²Judas (not Iscariot) said to him, "Lord, how is it that you will reveal yourself to us, and not to the world?" ²³Jesus answered him, "Those who love me will keep my word, and my Father will love them, and we will come to them and make our home with them. ²⁴Whoever does not love me does not keep my words; and the word that you hear is not mine, but is from the Father who sent me.

25 "I have said these things to you while I am still with you. ²⁶But the Advocate,*b* the Holy Spirit, whom the Father will send in my name, will teach you everything, and remind you of all that I have said to you. ²⁷Peace I leave with you; my peace I give to you. I do not give to you as the world gives. Do not let your hearts be troubled, and do not let them be afraid. ²⁸You heard me say to you, 'I am going away, and I am coming to you.' If you loved me, you would rejoice that I am going to the Father, because the Father is greater than I. ²⁹And now I have told you this before it occurs, so that when it does occur, you may believe. ³⁰I will no longer talk much with you, for the ruler of this world is coming. He has no power over me; ³¹but I do as the Father has commanded me, so that the world

may know that I love the Father. Rise, let us be on our way.

Jesus the True Vine

15 "I am the true vine, and my Father is the vinegrower. ²He removes every branch in me that bears no fruit. Every branch that bears fruit he prunes*c* to make it bear more fruit. ³You have already been cleansed*c* by the word that I have spoken to you. ⁴Abide in me as I abide in you. Just as the branch cannot bear fruit by itself unless it abides in the vine, neither can you unless you abide in me. ⁵I am the vine, you are the branches. Those who abide in me and I in them bear much fruit, because apart from me you can do nothing. ⁶Whoever does not abide in me is thrown away like a branch and withers; such branches are gathered, thrown into the fire, and burned. ⁷If you abide in me, and my words abide in you, ask for whatever you wish, and it will be done for you. ⁸My Father is glorified by this, that you bear much fruit and become*d* my disciples. ⁹As the Father has loved me, so I have loved you; abide in my love. ¹⁰If you keep my commandments, you will abide in my love, just as I have kept my Father's commandments and abide in his love. ¹¹I have said these things to you so that my joy may be in you, and that your joy may be complete.

12 "This is my commandment, that you love one another as I have loved you. ¹³No one has greater love than this, to lay down one's life for one's friends. ¹⁴You are my friends if you do what I command you. ¹⁵I do not call you servants*e* any longer, because the servant*f* does not know what the master

a Or *among*   *b* Or *Helper*   *c* The same Greek root refers to pruning and cleansing   *d* Or *be*   *e* Gk *slaves*   *f* Gk *slave*

15:1–27 *I am the true vine, and my Father is the vinegrower.* See note on 14:1–31.
15:1–5 **THE WITH-GOD LIFE—***See* Spiritual Disciplines Index.
15:1–11 *I am the true vine.* The metaphor of Vine and Branches reminds us that our spiritual life is entirely dependent upon God's grace. See note on 6:35–59.
15:10 *If you keep my commandments.* Because

Jesus has perfectly kept the commandments, our abiding in God's commands helps us to understand how full is his love.
15:12–17 *This is my commandment.* Christ loved us to his death because that is his character (see also 13:1). This assurance frees us to love.
15:15 **SERVICE—***See* Spiritual Disciplines Index.

is doing; but I have called you friends, because I have made known to you everything that I have heard from my Father. 16You did not choose me but I chose you. And I appointed you to go and bear fruit, fruit that will last, so that the Father will give you whatever you ask him in my name. 17I am giving you these commands so that you may love one another.

The World's Hatred

18 "If the world hates you, be aware that it hated me before it hated you. 19If you belonged to the world,*a* the world would love you as its own. Because you do not belong to the world, but I have chosen you out of the world—therefore the world hates you. 20Remember the word that I said to you, 'Servants*b* are not greater than their master.' If they persecuted me, they will persecute you; if they kept my word, they will keep yours also. 21But they will do all these things to you on account of my name, because they do not know him who sent me. 22If I had not come and spoken to them, they would not have sin; but now they have no excuse for their sin. 23Whoever hates me hates my Father also. 24If I had not done among them the works that no one else did, they would not have sin. But now they have seen and hated both me and my Father. 25It was to fulfill the word that is written in their law, 'They hated me without a cause.'

26 "When the Advocate*c* comes, whom I will send to you from the Father, the Spirit of truth who comes from the Father, he will testify on my behalf. 27You also are to testify because you have been with me from the beginning.

16 "I have said these things to you to keep you from stumbling. 2They will put you out of the synagogues. Indeed, an hour is coming when those who kill you will think that by doing so they are offering worship to God. 3And they will do this because they have not known the Father or me. 4But I have said these things to you so that when

their hour comes you may remember that I told you about them.

The Work of the Spirit

"I did not say these things to you from the beginning, because I was with you. 5But now I am going to him who sent me; yet none of you asks me, 'Where are you going?' 6But because I have said these things to you, sorrow has filled your hearts. 7Nevertheless I tell you the truth: it is to your advantage that I go away, for if I do not go away, the Advocate*c* will not come to you; but if I go, I will send him to you. 8And when he comes, he will prove the world wrong about*d* sin and righteousness and judgment: 9about sin, because they do not believe in me; 10about righteousness, because I am going to the Father and you will see me no longer; 11about judgment, because the ruler of this world has been condemned.

12 "I still have many things to say to you, but you cannot bear them now. 13When the Spirit of truth comes, he will guide you into all the truth; for he will not speak on his own, but will speak whatever he hears, and he will declare to you the things that are to come. 14He will glorify me, because he will take what is mine and declare it to you. 15All that the Father has is mine. For this reason I said that he will take what is mine and declare it to you.

Sorrow Will Turn into Joy

16 "A little while, and you will no longer see me, and again a little while, and you will see me." 17Then some of his disciples said to one another, "What does he mean by saying to us, 'A little while, and you will no longer see me, and again a little while, and you will see me'; and 'Because I am going to the Father'?" 18They said, "What does he mean by this 'a little while'? We do not know what he is talking about." 19Jesus knew that they wanted to ask him, so he said to them, "Are you discussing among yourselves what I meant when I said,

---

a Gk *were of the world*   *b* Gk *Slaves*
c Or *Helper*   *d* Or *convict the world of*

15:20 SERVICE—*See* Spiritual Disciplines Index.

16:1–33 *I have said these things to you.* See

note on 14:1–31.

16:13 GUIDANCE—*See* Spiritual Disciplines Index.

'A little while, and you will no longer see me, and again a little while, and you will see me'? 20Very truly, I tell you, you will weep and mourn, but the world will rejoice; you will have pain, but your pain will turn into joy. 21When a woman is in labor, she has pain, because her hour has come. But when her child is born, she no longer remembers the anguish because of the joy of having brought a human being into the world. 22So you have pain now; but I will see you again, and your hearts will rejoice, and no one will take your joy from you. 23On that day you will ask nothing of me. *a* Very truly, I tell you, if you ask anything of the Father in my name, he will give it to you. *b* 24Until now you have not asked for anything in my name. Ask and you will receive, so that your joy may be complete.

Peace for the Disciples

25 "I have said these things to you in figures of speech. The hour is coming when I will no longer speak to you in figures, but will tell you plainly of the Father. 26On that day you will ask in my name. I do not say to you that I will ask the Father on your behalf; 27for the Father himself loves you, because you have loved me and have believed that I came from God. *c* 28I came from the Father and have come into the world; again, I am leaving the world and am going to the Father."

29 His disciples said, "Yes, now you are speaking plainly, not in any figure of speech! 30Now we know that you know all things, and do not need to have anyone question you; by this we believe that you came from God." 31Jesus answered them, "Do you now believe? 32The hour is coming, indeed it has come, when you will be scattered, each one to his home, and you will leave me alone. Yet I am not alone because the Father is with me. 33I have said this to you, so that in me you may have peace. In the world you face persecution. But take courage; I have conquered the world!"

Jesus Prays for His Disciples

17 After Jesus had spoken these words, he looked up to heaven and said, "Father, the hour has come; glorify your Son so that the Son may glorify you, 2since you have given him authority over all people, *d* to give eternal life to all whom you have given him. 3And this is eternal life, that they may know you, the only true God, and Jesus Christ whom you have sent. 4I glorified you on earth by finishing the work that you gave me to do. 5So now, Father, glorify me in your own presence with the glory that I had in your presence before the world existed.

6 "I have made your name known to those whom you gave me from the world. They were yours, and you gave them to me, and they have kept your word. 7Now they know that everything you have given me is from you;

a Or *will ask me no question*   *b* Other ancient authorities read *Father, he will give it to you in my name*   *c* Other ancient authorities read *the Father*   *d* Gk *flesh*

Responding

16:32 SOLITUDE. History is replete with stories of Christians who have been alone for extended periods of time— voluntarily in deserts or involuntarily in prison— but who came through the experience knowing that God was with them. If you have not already done so, read a book about the desert fathers and mothers. You might want to start with John Chryssavgis's *In the Heart of the Desert: The Spirituality of the Desert Fathers and Mothers*, a compilation of their sayings accompanied by original commentary by Chryssavgis. *See also* Spiritual Disciplines Index.

17:1–8 *Father, the hour has come.* What do we learn about the Trinity from Jesus' request to be glorified and his description to his Father of his work? What do we learn of our own ministries in the world? See also note on 14:1–31.

17:3 *And this is eternal life.* In this verse, the only biblical definition of eternal life, it is not "pie in the sky in the bye and bye when you die," but genuinely *knowing* the only true God through Jesus Christ *now!*

17:6 *I have made your name known.* In the Scriptures, one's "name" implies one's character. To learn God's name is to become God's and to be formed in the Trinity's character.

17:7–8 *they know that everything you have given me is from you.* Jesus' total dependence on his Father teaches us the same. By what

8for the words that you gave to me I have given to them, and they have received them and know in truth that I came from you; and they have believed that you sent me. 9I am asking on their behalf; I am not asking on behalf of the world, but on behalf of those whom you gave me, because they are yours. 10All mine are yours, and yours are mine; and I have been glorified in them. 11And now I am no longer in the world, but they are in the world, and I am coming to you. Holy Father, protect them in your name that you have given me, so that they may be one, as we are one. 12While I was with them, I protected them in your name that*a* you have given me. I guarded them, and not one of them was lost except the one destined to be lost,*b* so that the scripture might be fulfilled. 13But now I am coming to you, and I speak these things in the world so that they may have my joy made complete in themselves.*c* 14I have given them your word, and the world has hated them because they do not belong to the world, just as I do not belong to the world. 15I am not asking you to take them out of the world, but I ask you to protect them from the evil one.*d* 16They do not belong to the world, just as I do not belong to the world. 17Sanctify them in the truth; your word is truth. 18As you have sent me into the world, so I have sent them into the world. 19And for their sakes I sanctify myself, so that they also may be sanctified in truth.

20 "I ask not only on behalf of these, but also on behalf of those who will believe in me through their word, 21that they may all be one. As you, Father, are in me and I am in you, may they also be in us,*e* so that the world may believe that you have sent me. 22The glory that you have given me I have given them, so that they may be one, as we are one, 23I in them and you in me, that they may become completely one, so that the world may know that you have sent me and have loved them even as you have loved me. 24Father, I desire that those also, whom you have given me, may be with me where I am, to see my glory, which you have given me because you loved me before the foundation of the world.

25 "Righteous Father, the world does not know you, but I know you; and these know that you have sent me. 26I made your name known to them, and I will make it known, so that the love with which you have loved me may be in them, and I in them."

The Betrayal and Arrest of Jesus

18 After Jesus had spoken these words, he went out with his disciples across the Kidron valley to a place where there was a garden, which he and his disciples entered. 2Now Judas, who betrayed him, also knew the place, because Jesus often met there with his disciples. 3So Judas brought a detachment of soldiers together with police from the chief priests and the Pharisees, and they came there with lanterns and torches and weapons. 4Then Jesus, knowing all that was to happen to him, came forward and asked them, "Whom are you looking for?" 5They answered, "Jesus of Nazareth."*f* Jesus replied, "I am he."*g* Judas, who betrayed him, was

a Other ancient authorities read *protected in your name those whom*   *b* Gk *except the son of destruction*   *c* Or *among themselves*   *d* Or *from evil*   *e* Other ancient authorities read *be one in us*   *f* Gk *the Nazorean*   *g* Gk *I am*

---

practices could we grow in such total reliance on the Spirit's working through us?

17:9–19 *I am asking on their behalf.* Ponder all that we learn of the Trinity's work and our own as Jesus prays for his disciples. Too often we fail to realize how much God wants the Christian community to be one as part of the triune character. The community follows Jesus in abiding in the Father's word; how much more of an impact the Church would have on the world if we didn't belong to it so much! Are we willing to die for the world? To live for its sake?

To give our all at great cost?

17:20–26 *I ask not only on behalf of these.* Throughout chapter 17 and especially when Jesus prays for us, we join the beloved disciple in eavesdropping on the conversation of the Trinity. Let us rejoice in the immense privilege given to us to be part of that fellowship by Jesus' invitation and mediation.

17:21–23 **THE WITH-GOD LIFE**—*See* Spiritual Disciplines Index.

18:4–9 *I am he.* See the Introduction on "I am" statements.

standing with them. [6]When Jesus[a] said to them, "I am he,"[b] they stepped back and fell to the ground. [7]Again he asked them, "Whom are you looking for?" And they said, "Jesus of Nazareth."[c] [8]Jesus answered, "I told you that I am he.[b] So if you are looking for me, let these men go." [9]This was to fulfill the word that he had spoken, "I did not lose a single one of those whom you gave me." [10]Then Simon Peter, who had a sword, drew it, struck the high priest's slave, and cut off his right ear. The slave's name was Malchus. [11]Jesus said to Peter, "Put your sword back into its sheath. Am I not to drink the cup that the Father has given me?"

Jesus before the High Priest

12 So the soldiers, their officer, and the Jewish police arrested Jesus and bound him. [13]First they took him to Annas, who was the father-in-law of Caiaphas, the high priest that year. [14]Caiaphas was the one who had advised the Jews that it was better to have one person die for the people.

Peter Denies Jesus

15 Simon Peter and another disciple followed Jesus. Since that disciple was known to the high priest, he went with Jesus into the courtyard of the high priest, [16]but Peter was standing outside at the gate. So the other disciple, who was known to the high priest, went out, spoke to the woman who guarded the gate, and brought Peter in. [17]The woman said to Peter, "You are not also one of this man's disciples, are you?" He said, "I am not." [18]Now the slaves and the police had made a charcoal fire because it was cold, and they were standing around it and warming themselves. Peter also was standing with them and warming himself.

The High Priest Questions Jesus

19 Then the high priest questioned Jesus about his disciples and about his teaching. [20]Jesus answered, "I have spoken openly to the world; I have always taught in synagogues and in the temple, where all the Jews come together. I have said nothing in secret. [21]Why do you ask me? Ask those who heard what I said to them; they know what I said." [22]When he had said this, one of the police standing nearby struck Jesus on the face, saying, "Is that how you answer the high priest?" [23]Jesus answered, "If I have spoken wrongly, testify to the wrong. But if I have spoken rightly, why do you strike me?" [24]Then Annas sent him bound to Caiaphas the high priest.

Peter Denies Jesus Again

25 Now Simon Peter was standing and warming himself. They asked him, "You are not also one of his disciples, are you?" He denied it and said, "I am not." [26]One of the slaves of the high priest, a relative of the man whose ear Peter had cut off, asked, "Did I not see you in the garden with him?" [27]Again Peter denied it, and at that moment the cock crowed.

Jesus before Pilate

28 Then they took Jesus from Caiaphas to Pilate's headquarters.[d] It was early in the morning. They themselves did not enter the headquarters,[d] so as to avoid ritual defilement and to be able to eat the Passover. [29]So Pilate went out to them and said, "What ac-

a Gk he   b Gk I am   c Gk the Nazorean
d Gk the praetorium

18:10–27 *Then Simon Peter, who had a sword, drew it.* John alternates scenes about Peter (vv 10–11, 15–18, 25–27) and Annas (vv 13–14, 19–24) to heighten the difference between Peter's denial and Jesus' truth telling. We don't serve God's kingdom with violence and falsehood.

18:14 *it was better to have one person die for the people.* See the Introduction on irony.

18:28–19:16 *Then they took Jesus from*

Caiaphas to Pilate's headquarters. John's seven scenes between Jesus and Pilate (18:28–32, 33–38a, 38b–40; 19:1–3, 4–8, 9–12a, 12b–16) alternate between "outside" and "inside," symbolic and ironic because entering a Gentile's domain would render Jews impure for the Passover. Notice how the leaders' accusations against Jesus change over time and consider why. How does Pilate change? In contrast, what do we learn from Jesus' steadfastness?

cusation do you bring against this man?" [30]They answered, "If this man were not a criminal, we would not have handed him over to you." [31]Pilate said to them, "Take him yourselves and judge him according to your law." The Jews replied, "We are not permitted to put anyone to death." [32](This was to fulfill what Jesus had said when he indicated the kind of death he was to die.)

33 Then Pilate entered the headquarters[a] again, summoned Jesus, and asked him, "Are you the King of the Jews?" [34]Jesus answered, "Do you ask this on your own, or did others tell you about me?" [35]Pilate replied, "I am not a Jew, am I? Your own nation and the chief priests have handed you over to me. What have you done?" [36]Jesus answered, "My kingdom is not from this world. If my kingdom were from this world, my followers would be fighting to keep me from being handed over to the Jews. But as it is, my kingdom is not from here." [37]Pilate asked him, "So you are a king?" Jesus answered, "You say that I am a king. For this I was born, and for this I came into the world, to testify to the truth. Everyone who belongs to the truth listens to my voice." [38]Pilate asked him, "What is truth?"

Jesus Sentenced to Death

After he had said this, he went out to the Jews again and told them, "I find no case against him. [39]But you have a custom that I release someone for you at the Passover. Do you want me to release for you the King of the Jews?" [40]They shouted in reply, "Not this man, but Barabbas!" Now Barabbas was a bandit.

19 Then Pilate took Jesus and had him flogged. [2]And the soldiers wove a crown of thorns and put it on his head, and they dressed him in a purple robe. [3]They kept coming up to him, saying, "Hail, King of the Jews!" and striking him on the face. [4]Pilate went out again and said to them, "Look, I am bringing him out to you to let you know that I find no case against him." [5]So Jesus came out, wearing the crown of thorns and the pur-

ple robe. Pilate said to them, "Here is the man!" [6]When the chief priests and the police saw him, they shouted, "Crucify him! Crucify him!" Pilate said to them, "Take him yourselves and crucify him; I find no case against him." [7]The Jews answered him, "We have a law, and according to that law he ought to die because he has claimed to be the Son of God."

8 Now when Pilate heard this, he was more afraid than ever. [9]He entered his headquarters[a] again and asked Jesus, "Where are you from?" But Jesus gave him no answer. [10]Pilate therefore said to him, "Do you refuse to speak to me? Do you not know that I have power to release you, and power to crucify you?" [11]Jesus answered him, "You would have no power over me unless it had been given you from above; therefore the one who handed me over to you is guilty of a greater sin." [12]From then on Pilate tried to release him, but the Jews cried out, "If you release this man, you are no friend of the emperor. Everyone who claims to be a king sets himself against the emperor."

13 When Pilate heard these words, he brought Jesus outside and sat[b] on the judge's bench at a place called The Stone Pavement, or in Hebrew[c] Gabbatha. [14]Now it was the day of Preparation for the Passover; and it was about noon. He said to the Jews, "Here is your King!" [15]They cried out, "Away with him! Away with him! Crucify him!" Pilate asked them, "Shall I crucify your King?" The chief priests answered, "We have no king but the emperor." [16]Then he handed him over to them to be crucified.

The Crucifixion of Jesus

So they took Jesus; [17]and carrying the cross by himself, he went out to what is called The Place of the Skull, which in Hebrew[c] is called Golgotha. [18]There they crucified him, and with him two others, one on either side, with Jesus between them. [19]Pilate also had an inscription written and put on the cross. It read, "Jesus of Nazareth,[d] the King of the Jews." [20]Many of the Jews read this inscription, because the place

a Gk *the praetorium*   b Or *seated him*   c That is, *Aramaic*   d Gk *the Nazorean*

19:13–16, 19–22 *Here is your King!* Note the profound ironies of Pilate's proclamation of Jesus' kingship (cf. vv 1–3).

where Jesus was crucified was near the city; and it was written in Hebrew, *a* in Latin, and in Greek. 21Then the chief priests of the Jews said to Pilate, "Do not write, 'The King of the Jews,' but, 'This man said, I am King of the Jews.' " 22Pilate answered, "What I have written I have written." 23When the soldiers had crucified Jesus, they took his clothes and divided them into four parts, one for each soldier. They also took his tunic; now the tunic was seamless, woven in one piece from the top. 24So they said to one another, "Let us not tear it, but cast lots for it to see who will get it." This was to fulfill what the scripture says,

"They divided my clothes among
themselves,
and for my clothing they cast lots."
25And that is what the soldiers did.

Meanwhile, standing near the cross of Jesus were his mother, and his mother's sister, Mary the wife of Clopas, and Mary Magdalene. 26When Jesus saw his mother and the disciple whom he loved standing beside her, he said to his mother, "Woman, here is your son." 27Then he said to the disciple, "Here is your mother." And from that hour the disciple took her into his own home.

28 After this, when Jesus knew that all was now finished, he said (in order to fulfill the scripture), "I am thirsty." 29A jar full of sour wine was standing there. So they put a sponge full of the wine on a branch of hyssop and held it to his mouth. 30When Jesus had received the wine, he said, "It is finished." Then he bowed his head and gave up his spirit.

Jesus' Side Is Pierced

31 Since it was the day of Preparation, the Jews did not want the bodies left on the cross during the sabbath, especially because that sabbath was a day of great solemnity. So they asked Pilate to have the legs of the crucified men broken and the bodies removed. 32Then the soldiers came and broke the legs of the first and of the other who had been crucified with him. 33But when they came to Jesus and saw that he was already dead, they did not break his legs. 34Instead, one of the soldiers pierced his side with a spear, and at once blood and water came out. 35(He who saw this has testified so that you also may believe. His testimony is true, and he knows *b* that he tells the truth.) 36These things occurred so that the scripture might be fulfilled, "None of his bones shall be broken." 37And again another passage of scripture says, "They will look on the one whom they have pierced."

The Burial of Jesus

38 After these things, Joseph of Arimathea, who was a disciple of Jesus, though a secret one because of his fear of the Jews, asked Pilate to let him take away the body of Jesus. Pilate gave him permission; so he came and

---

a That is, *Aramaic*　　*b* Or *there is one who knows*

19:23–24 *the tunic was seamless.* John may include the detail of Jesus' seamless robe (like a priest's!) to symbolize his high-priesthood as well as kingship, besides his fulfillment of prophecy.

19:25–27 *Woman, here is your son.* John includes few details of Jesus' horrible death, yet these verses express above all the vast theological significance of Jesus' immense love—his incredible care for his mother in the midst of his own pain and his special friendship with the beloved disciple that allows this solemn commission. Does our discipleship follow Jesus' lead with similar compassion and hospitality?

19:28–37 *in order to fulfill the scripture.* We can trust the truth of Scripture; Christ keeps all God's promises. Throughout John's Gospel details underscore Jesus' fulfillment of Jewish practices and festivals. In the exodus, hyssop branches (v 29) painted the paschal lamb's blood on doorposts (Exod 12:22), and no bones of the paschal lamb were broken (vv 33, 36; Exod 12:46). What does it mean for daily life that Jesus is the Lamb of God (see 1:29–34)?

19:30 *It is finished.* The tense of the Greek word translated "It is finished" suggests a debt fully paid. If we don't admit the depths of our sin, such a complete atonement at such an appalling cost is an outrageous stumbling block. Jesus "handed over his spirit" (the literal Greek of v 30b) and thus begins to communicate the Spirit in his glorification (see also 20:22). We can live the Scriptures only because Jesus did—and gives us his Spirit.

removed his body. 39Nicodemus, who had at first come to Jesus by night, also came, bringing a mixture of myrrh and aloes, weighing about a hundred pounds. 40They took the body of Jesus and wrapped it with the spices in linen cloths, according to the burial custom of the Jews. 41Now there was a garden in the place where he was crucified, and in the garden there was a new tomb in which no one had ever been laid. 42And so, because it was the Jewish day of Preparation, and the tomb was nearby, they laid Jesus there.

The Resurrection of Jesus

20 Early on the first day of the week, while it was still dark, Mary Magdalene came to the tomb and saw that the stone had been removed from the tomb. 2So she ran and went to Simon Peter and the other disciple, the one whom Jesus loved, and said to them, "They have taken the Lord out of the tomb, and we do not know where they have laid him." 3Then Peter and the other disciple set out and went toward the tomb. 4The two were running together, but the other disciple outran Peter and reached the tomb first. 5He bent down to look in and saw the linen wrappings lying there, but he did not go in. 6Then Simon Peter came, following him, and went into the tomb. He saw the linen wrappings lying there, 7and the cloth that had been on Jesus' head, not lying with the linen wrappings but rolled up in a place by itself. 8Then the other disciple, who reached the tomb first, also went in, and he saw and believed; 9for as yet they did not understand the scripture, that he must rise from the dead. 10Then the disciples returned to their homes.

Jesus Appears to Mary Magdalene

11 But Mary stood weeping outside the tomb. As she wept, she bent over to look[a] into the tomb; 12and she saw two angels in white, sitting where the body of Jesus had been lying, one at the head and the other at the feet. 13They said to her, "Woman, why are you weeping?" She said to them, "They have taken away my Lord, and I do not know where they have laid him." 14When she had said this, she turned around and saw Jesus standing there, but she did not know that it was Jesus. 15Jesus said to her, "Woman, why are you weeping? Whom are you looking for?" Supposing him to be the gardener, she said to him, "Sir, if you have carried him away, tell me where you have laid him, and I will take him away." 16Jesus said to her, "Mary!" She turned and said to him in Hebrew, "Rabbouni!" (which means Teacher). 17Jesus said to her, "Do not hold on to me, because I have not yet ascended to the Father. But go to my brothers and say to them, 'I am ascending to my Father and your Father, to my God and your God.' " 18Mary Magdalene went and announced to the disciples, "I have seen the Lord"; and she told them that he had said these things to her.

Jesus Appears to the Disciples

19 When it was evening on that day, the first day of the week, and the doors of the house where the disciples had met were locked for fear of the Jews, Jesus came and stood among them and said, "Peace be with you." 20After he said this, he showed them his hands and his side. Then the disciples rejoiced when they saw the Lord. 21Jesus said to them again, "Peace be with you. As the Father has sent me, so I send you." 22When he had said this, he breathed on them and said to

a Gk lacks to look   b That is, Aramaic

20:1–18 *Mary Magdalene came to the tomb.* Contemplating the characters in John's resurrection accounts forms our own. Why did the beloved disciple's "observations" (v 8 has a different Greek word for "saw" than does v 6) enable him to believe (see vv 6–7)? Notice the depth of devotion revealed by Mary's answer to the "gardener." Why does Mary's name (v 16) quicken her (see 10:3; Isa 43:1)?

20:19–29 *Jesus came and stood among them.* Thomas is no more frightened or "doubtful" than the others (v 19). Without Thomas's realism about Jesus' death (see 11:16) and suffering (v 25), we perhaps take too lightly the price Jesus paid for us. Jesus doesn't rebuke him (v 27), and Thomas responds with the strongest witness in the Gospel (v 28).

them, "Receive the Holy Spirit. 23If you forgive the sins of any, they are forgiven them; if you retain the sins of any, they are retained."

Jesus and Thomas

24 But Thomas (who was called the Twin*a*), one of the twelve, was not with them when Jesus came. 25So the other disciples told him, "We have seen the Lord." But he said to them, "Unless I see the mark of the nails in his hands, and put my finger in the mark of the nails and my hand in his side, I will not believe."

26 A week later his disciples were again in the house, and Thomas was with them. Although the doors were shut, Jesus came and stood among them and said, "Peace be with you." 27Then he said to Thomas, "Put your finger here and see my hands. Reach out your hand and put it in my side. Do not doubt but believe." 28Thomas answered him, "My Lord and my God!" 29Jesus said to him, "Have you believed because you have seen me? Blessed are those who have not seen and yet have come to believe."

The Purpose of This Book

30 Now Jesus did many other signs in the presence of his disciples, which are not written in this book. 31But these are written so that you may come to believe*b* that Jesus is the Messiah,*c* the Son of God, and that through believing you may have life in his name.

Jesus Appears to Seven Disciples

21 After these things Jesus showed himself again to the disciples by the Sea of Tiberias; and he showed himself in this way. 2Gathered there together were Simon Peter, Thomas called the Twin,*a* Nathanael of Cana in Galilee, the sons of Zebedee, and two others of his disciples. 3Simon Peter said to them, "I am going fishing." They said to him, "We will go with you." They went out and got

into the boat, but that night they caught nothing.

4 Just after daybreak, Jesus stood on the beach; but the disciples did not know that it was Jesus. 5Jesus said to them, "Children, you have no fish, have you?" They answered him, "No." 6He said to them, "Cast the net to the right side of the boat, and you will find some." So they cast it, and now they were not able to haul it in because there were so many fish. 7That disciple whom Jesus loved said to Peter, "It is the Lord!" When Simon Peter heard that it was the Lord, he put on some clothes, for he was naked, and jumped into the sea. 8But the other disciples came in the boat, dragging the net full of fish, for they were not far from the land, only about a hundred yards*d* off.

9 When they had gone ashore, they saw a charcoal fire there, with fish on it, and bread. 10Jesus said to them, "Bring some of the fish that you have just caught." 11So Simon Peter went aboard and hauled the net ashore, full of large fish, a hundred fifty-three of them; and though there were so many, the net was not torn. 12Jesus said to them, "Come and have breakfast." Now none of the disciples dared to ask him, "Who are you?" because they knew it was the Lord. 13Jesus came and took the bread and gave it to them, and did the same with the fish. 14This was now the third time that Jesus appeared to the disciples after he was raised from the dead.

Jesus and Peter

15 When they had finished breakfast, Jesus said to Simon Peter, "Simon son of John, do you love me more than these?" He said to him, "Yes, Lord; you know that I love you." Jesus said to him, "Feed my lambs." 16A second time he said to him, "Simon son of John,

a Gk *Didymus*   *b* Other ancient authorities read *may continue to believe*   *c* Or *the Christ*   *d* Gk *two hundred cubits*

20:29–31 *Have you believed because you have seen me?* Realism, however, must be paired with hope. Today we can't prove the resurrection, but nothing disproves it either, and John's testimony is enough (see also 21:24–25). Signs foster

belief, and Jesus' divinity and "name" (character) confer life.

21:1–14 *Jesus showed himself again to the disciples.* See note on 2:1–11.

do you love me?" He said to him, "Yes, Lord; you know that I love you." Jesus said to him, "Tend my sheep." 17He said to him the third time, "Simon son of John, do you love me?" Peter felt hurt because he said to him the third time, "Do you love me?" And he said to him, "Lord, you know everything; you know that I love you." Jesus said to him, "Feed my sheep. 18Very truly, I tell you, when you were younger, you used to fasten your own belt and to go wherever you wished. But when you grow old, you will stretch out your hands, and someone else will fasten a belt around you and take you where you do not wish to go." 19(He said this to indicate the kind of death by which he would glorify God.) After this he said to him, "Follow me."

Jesus and the Beloved Disciple

20 Peter turned and saw the disciple whom Jesus loved following them; he was the one who had reclined next to Jesus at the supper and had said, "Lord, who is it that is going to betray you?" 21When Peter saw him, he said to Jesus, "Lord, what about him?" 22Jesus said to him, "If it is my will that he remain until I come, what is that to you? Follow me!" 23So the rumor spread in the community*a* that this disciple would not die. Yet Jesus did not say to him that he would not die, but, "If it is my will that he remain until I come, what is that to you?"*b*

24 This is the disciple who is testifying to these things and has written them, and we know that his testimony is true. 25But there are also many other things that Jesus did; if every one of them were written down, I suppose that the world itself could not contain the books that would be written.

a Gk *among the brothers*   *b* Other ancient authorities lack *what is that to you*

21:15–19 *do you love me?* This narrative's many themes challenge us—genuine love, laying down one's life (see esp. 10:11–18; 13:36–38; 21:18), shepherding (10:11–18; 21:15–17). What a wonder that Jesus commissions us to do his work even though we love so inadequately!

Responding
21:18 SACRIFICE. In other verses in John, Jesus talks about laying down his life (10:11), Peter says he is willing to lay down his life for Jesus (13:37), and Jesus says, "No one has greater love than this, to lay down one's life for one's friends" (15:13). If you haven't done so before, take a few moments to contemplate if you would be able to die physically in order to save a friend's life. Write down your thoughts and feelings. *See also* Spiritual Disciplines Index.

XIII. THE PEOPLE OF GOD IN MISSION

Scriptures: *Acts*

> *The aim of God in history is the creation of an all-inclusive community of loving persons with God himself at the very center of this community as its prime Sustainer and most glorious Inhabitant (Eph 2:19–22; 3:10). The Bible traces the formation of this community from the creation in the Garden of Eden all the way to the new heaven and the new earth. Come, join us as we explore the many dimensions of this with-God history—from individual to family to tribe to people to nation to all humanity—and apply what we learn to our own spiritual formation.*

Previously we discovered how God acted to bring Immanuel, "God with us," as the supreme expression of his mediating work for the formation of an all-inclusive community of loving persons. In Acts, we discover God, in the person of the Holy Spirit, inhabiting his people and empowering them to proclaim the Gospel of the kingdom.

God's Action

The central theme of the book of Acts is the forward thrust of God's activity in history. Here, in more profound depth and detail than in any other book in the New Testament, Luke offers a historical interpretation of our life with God. It is here that we see God's aim of forming an all-inclusive community of loving persons with God himself at its very center.

Although the twelve disciples had been apprentices of Jesus for some years, learning from the master Teacher how to live in the kingdom of God, they simply were not prepared for Jesus' death. It is predictable, then, that the confusion surrounding his crucifixion and the exhilaration surrounding his subsequent resurrection would elicit a broad range of contrasting emotions. After days of being on such an emotional roller coaster and their seeing Jesus ascend into heaven, an angel instructs them to stay in Jerusalem until they are "clothed with power from on high" (Luke 24:49). Finally, God had found a people who, when he said "wait," would wait.

The Twelve gather in an upstairs room with other disciples to wait for God. As they were gathered, the Spirit of God descends like the downdraft of a mighty thunderstorm (Acts 2:2). And suddenly and unexpectedly this ragtag bunch of first disciples is galvanized into an unstoppable force that will change the world.

For centuries God had been present with individuals like Abraham and Sarah; with the twelve tribes as they left Egypt; with the People of God as they occupied Canaan; with the nation of Israel in its glory, exile, and restoration; but this was different, utterly different. The disciples *hear* the Holy Spirit's presence in the roaring wind and *see* tongues with the appearance of fire resting on the heads of those gathered. Each person receives from the Spirit the knowledge and power that connect the enduring memories of God's action in history with Jesus of Nazareth. Now, for the first time, the life and teachings of Jesus make sense. This man, this teacher whom they had followed for these many long, trying months was—is—the long-promised Messiah, the Anointed One of God!

The transformation of the disciples' mood is as dramatic as it is sudden. God himself is inhabiting and living in them, giving them power to proclaim fearlessly the message of Jesus' resurrection to everyone they meet. Astonished masses hear and understand the gospel of the kingdom in their own tongue. The confusion reigning on earth since the Tower of Babel (Gen 11:1–9) is reversed as God's Spirit brings order and understanding.

With the outpouring of the Holy Spirit on Pentecost, it now becomes clear that God is breaking down the ethnic walls that have circumscribed the gospel message. A divine vision enables the apostle Peter to take the message of Jesus Christ to a household of Gentiles. While Peter is still speaking, the Holy Spirit falls on the whole family and their servants, confirming that all races, all social classes, all nations are to be included in the People of God (Acts 10). From its womb in Jerusalem, the ever expanding company of Spirit-empowered disciples responds to the call of Jesus to be his "witnesses in Jerusalem, in all Judea and Samaria, and to the ends of the earth," a call that continues right up to the present day (1:8).

Human Reaction

From the outset, it is evident that there will be a multiplicity of reactions to the dramatic works of the Holy Spirit. On the day of Pentecost, scoffers accuse the disciples of being drunk (Acts 2:13). But the crowd becomes silent when Peter's Spirit-empowered preaching reveals God's presence and explains his worldwide plan for the salvation of all peoples. Such preaching, recorded throughout Acts, forms a common core to the gospel presentations. As we read them now some two thousand years later, we marvel at the way each successive sermon broadens our understanding of God's purposes for all humanity.

Wherever the gospel spreads, new disciples of Jesus gather into groups. Preaching is the primary means of publicly declaring the person and work of Jesus to nonbelievers, but conversational speech in private gatherings reinforces and expands the public message to believers. Careful attention is given to the life and teachings of Jesus in both settings. Public sermons powerfully communicate the essential truths needed to activate the drawing of the Holy Spirit into the hearts of the people to bring them to saving faith. More in-depth teaching takes place in private households, enabling the followers of Jesus to grow in their own love and understanding.

The With-God Life

In these homes, "They devoted themselves to the apostles' teaching and fellowship, to the breaking of bread and the prayers" (Acts 2:42).

Once again, Luke records that groups respond quite differently to the disciples' messages. When Paul summarizes the person and work of Jesus, some scoff, some believe, and some want to hear more (Acts 17:32–34). From this and other similar passages we see that only the work of the Holy Spirit is able to generate the understanding necessary to sustain the with-God life.

Not long after Jesus' ascension we find the disciples forming new communities of faith based on prayer and worship and taking up new rituals or sacraments—most prominently baptism and the Lord's Supper. Prayer is the centerpiece of communal life. It is also the most prominent individual discipline. Repeatedly, we find Peter, John, then Barnabas, and eventually Paul waiting for God in prayer and then exploding in action as God's spirit propels them into the world. Vigorous petition, profound intercession, and pleas for guidance pour forth from the hearts of these early disciples. And heaven answers: "When they had prayed, the place in which they were gathered together was shaken; and they were all filled with the Holy Spirit and spoke the word of God with boldness" (Acts 4:31).

Acts is also saturated with the spirit of worship. In worship these valiant disciples of Jesus move beyond the narrow experiences of personal faith into the reality of God's presence in community. Later, it will lead to the full manifestation of God across time and history, and into eternity. Here, worship demonstrates the way in which God leads the first Christians beyond their narrow ethnic religion to embrace a universal call to all the peoples of the earth.

Likewise, the rituals of baptism and the Lord's Supper strengthen the first disciples. These new sacraments are not a recovery of Old Testament practices, but entirely new activities generated by the active presence of the Holy Spirit. Baptism and Communion become historic landmarks in the life of the Church. Baptism evolves into many forms and practices, but always it inaugurates a sustained awareness of the disciple's ongoing fellowship with Christ.

Likewise, the Lord's Supper, or Eucharist, becomes a part of the gathered community's life. While eating the bread and drinking from the cup, these new apprentices to Jesus rehearse his birth, life, death, and resurrection, seek the power to remain faithful to him, and look forward to his coming again. The sacraments and communal celebrations featured in Acts manifest new ways in which we are to live and practice our faith in God.

Blessings and Benefits for Our Formation

In Acts, the Holy Spirit acts with and through the apostles, spreading God's ways throughout the world and creating an all-inclusive community that leads the Jewish people beyond their ethnic identity to full identity as the universal People of God. Nothing can stop this forward movement of God through time. As God's way is unleashed in the world, it transcends every race, every creed, every culture and brings to bear on humanity the with-God life people so desire.

The With-God Life

This unstoppable movement of the Holy Spirit reaches its pinnacle at the Jerusalem council (Acts 15). Some in the early community had been insisting that circumcision was essential for salvation. Paul, understanding that this would be tantamount to a Jewish cultural captivity of the gospel message, brings the issue to the apostles and elders based in Jerusalem for a decision. In Acts 15, the core meaning of the entire book becomes clear, demonstrating the way in which God's love reaches beyond the bounds of its native Judaism to touch the whole world. With a few simple prescriptions the leaders of the early Christian community establish the grounds upon which God's all-encompassing gospel will be carried to the entire world (15:22–29; cf. Gal 2:9–10).

No limits are placed on this liberating message with regard to bloodline, gender, social status, or national identity. This one book becomes the Magna Carta of the Christian faith, releasing it from the bonds of its native Judaism, breaking the clay pot of its cultural captivity. The Word of God is set free to transform all who respond to the new humanity in Jesus Christ. The transformation of human character by the power of the Holy Spirit can now be fully realized.

With the advent of this new order, the Church is established. Drawing on the practices of the Jewish synagogue, the infant Church continues the tradition of reading Scripture, singing psalms, and instructing the faithful during worship and informal gatherings. Those gifted in evangelism are sent out to spread the good news of the kingdom of God into new regions and to establish new fellowships. The cycle then repeats itself, as Jesus' self-replicating society of God-inhabited people spreads throughout the world. In the process of declaring God's love to all humanity, the Church becomes a blessing without equal.

Limits and Liabilities for Our Formation

For all the wonder and power we see in Acts, limitations are still evident. The Jerusalem council of Acts 15 reminds us that legalism was a problem in the early Church, and it continues so in our day. Any transforming experience with God can sorely tempt us to set up some mandatory "system" to help others have the same encounter. By doing this we substitute our freedom in Christ for slavery to a human-imposed law.

The opposite danger exists as well: believing that since faith in Jesus Christ alone saves us, we do not have to abide by any moral law and are thus free to do whatever we want. Historically this is called antinomianism. Our freedom in Christ does allow us to throw off the shackles of legalism, but we abuse our freedom at our own risk. This is where the disciplines of the spiritual life train us to become like Christ in our thoughts, speech, and actions. In the power of the Holy Sprit we become capable of doing what we can to promote the kingdom of God on earth—*Credo ergo ago:* "I believe, therefore I do."

Another limitation: the indwelling of the Holy Spirit did not automatically produce unity in the early Christian community, nor does it in our church gatherings today. Think of Ananias and Sapphira: "But a man named Ananias, with the con-

The With-God Life

sent of his wife Sapphira, sold a piece of property; with his wife's knowledge, he kept back some of the proceeds, and brought only a part and laid it at the apostles' feet" (Acts 5:1–2). Or consider Paul and Barnabas who, after their glorious victory at the Jerusalem Council, fall into such a sharp dispute that they never again work together in the spread of the gospel (15:36–40). These and other notable examples illustrate the fact that the work of spiritual formation is always ongoing.

Insights and Instructions for Our Formation

A lifetime of study could not exhaust the lessons from Acts for our own growth in Christ. First of all, the most profound teaching from Acts is the universal nature of God's love. God is the God of all people for all time. God continues to love his chosen people, the Jews, but he equally loves all the peoples of the earth. God's universal love and acceptance reverberates throughout the many stories in Acts. It is a reality that can strengthen us in times of loneliness and despair.

Second, the Holy Spirit is the Spirit of courage and boldness who gives us the strength to follow Jesus Christ and to learn from him to do the kinds of things he did. Across the pages of Acts stride many ordinary people who did extraordinary things through the power of the Holy Spirit. Signs and wonders, casting out demons, healings of every kind, even raising the dead—all are seen in Acts. The same Spirit of courage and boldness is available to us today.

Finally, we can rejoice in suffering because truly God is with us. Recall the apos- tles being flogged and then rejoicing "that they were considered worthy to suffer dishonor for the sake of the name" (Acts 5:41). Recall the stoning of Stephen and his grace-filled words: "Lord, do not hold this sin against them" (7:60). Recall Paul and Silas locked in prison, "praying and singing hymns to God" (16:25). The Christian life is one of strength and endurance in the face of suffering. We learn by the power of the Holy Spirit to walk cheerfully on the earth. And when we do, God strengthens our resolve and empowers us to engage life without compromise. In so doing, we participate in God's plan for transforming the world and ourselves.

As you read this majestic book of Acts, note the tremendous force of God's Spirit in the world and open yourself to it. Observe the life-changing conversations that occur between established disciples and new converts. Notice how the Holy Spirit repeatedly brings fresh insights and new life. Finally, experience a whole new appreciation for the way in which God continually draws people to himself, transforming their lives and redirecting their eternal destiny.

The With-God Life

THE ACTS
OF THE APOSTLES

The book of Acts shows how the center of gravity of early Christianity shifted from Jerusalem to Rome and how, as Paul wrote in Gal 6:15, God brought about a "new creation," the Church.

As the first phrase of chapter 1 suggests, Acts is the second of a two-part work. The Acts of the Apostles continues the narrative of Luke's Gospel and is written by its author (see also the Introduction to the Gospel of Luke). In Acts 1:1–5 Luke summarizes the events in his first book, the story of Jesus' ministry to Israel. Now he turns to the story of the early believers and their task of spreading the good news of Jesus Christ to Gentiles. Acts is the fulfillment of Simeon's prophecy that Jesus would be "a light for revelation to the Gentiles and for glory to [God's] people Israel" (Luke 2:32).

Background and Sources

Some scholars suggest there is no tradition behind Acts like those behind the Gospels. Others suggest a Jerusalem source for chapters 2–5, an Antiochene one for 6–15, and a Pauline one for 13–28. Traditionally the "we" material beginning in chapter 16 is attributed to Luke who, throughout, writes elegant Greek using the Septuagint as a model. A careful writer, Luke apparently sketched out the Gospel and Acts before writing either. Attentive readers notice that events in the life of Jesus have parallels in the life of the early Church. For example, Jesus' public ministry begins with his baptism (Luke 3:21–22), and the public life of the Church begins with a great baptismal event (Acts 2:1–41). Luke quickly establishes Jesus as a healer in the Gospel (e.g., 4:31–44), and the apostles have the gift of healing in Acts (Acts 3:1–10). The Holy Spirit figures prominently in both books. Jesus' origin is with the Holy Spirit (Luke 1:35); his ministry begins when it falls on him (3:22); and he dies at

---

See also the "The With-God Life" essay for this section of the Bible,
"The People of God in Mission," pp. 1973–77.

its departure (23:46). Similarly the first disciples are commanded to await the Spirit's direction (Acts 1:4, 8); the Church commences when it arrives (2:1–4); and its mission is under its direction (e.g., 4:31; 5:32; 8:15, 39; 9:17; 10:44–48; 13:2, 16:6).

By genre, Acts is history, but Hellenistic and not modern history. Of the New Testament writers, Luke is most likely to refer to contemporary events and persons (see, e.g., Luke 2:1–3; Acts 12:1, 20–23; 18:2–3, 12). Luke wants us to know God is at work with real people living in this world. His focus on "secular history" is important to his theological agenda, which is to demonstrate that the gospel is for all nations and that God's concern for human beings is limitless. Luke models his work on that of classical historians like Thucydides and uses Greek literary conventions, for example, prologues and travel narratives. Greek historians wrote speeches for their main characters. The twenty-four speeches in Acts make up roughly one-third of Luke's narrative. They convey insights about the narrative, the meaning of events, the character of the speakers, and general ideas that explain the surrounding story. Luke uses speeches to highlight the meaning of the events he narrates. These, and the other Greek literary features, appealed to the gentile Christians for whom Luke was writing. It provided them easier access to the gospel.

Luke and Acts are so closely linked that Acts must have been written about the same time as the Gospel. Estimates vary from the early AD 60s (after Festus's procuratorship) to AD 100, but the general consensus is about AD 85.

The purpose of Luke's writing is clear: to continue the story of what God was doing in Jesus Christ. Luke understands the spread of the gospel to be the work of God and not human beings. At crucial points in the story angels intervene to direct the action (8:26; 12:7) or the characters have heavenly visions like those experienced by Zechariah and Mary in Luke 1–2 that direct their actions (Acts 10:1–6; 16:9–10). Luke is thereby telling us that God directs the course of Christian history.

The Coming Together of Jew and Gentile

Both Luke's Gospel and Acts are dedicated to the Greek Theophilus (or to "God lovers" in general) and thus commend Christianity to a non-Jew. Acts has as a subtext Luke's belief that Christianity and the Roman state can coexist peacefully. Another purpose of Acts, then, is to convince Greeks and Romans that Christianity is not a subversive movement, but a religion that transcends racial and national boundaries. It shows the God of Abraham and Sarah reaching out to embrace the gentile world by means of Jesus. Indeed, God's aim in history for the creation of an all-inclusive community of loving persons comes to pass in the course of the book of Acts.

This coming together of Jew and Gentile was of particular practical concern to Luke. The cultural divide between the two was a gaping chasm. We see Luke's concern as he narrates Peter's struggle with Jewish dietary laws and table fellowship. Also of concern are circumcision and Jewish cultic and ritual life. At the center of Acts is the Jerusalem council (chap 15), at which the whole Church gathers to work out a compromise so that Jew and Gentile can be in full Christian fellowship. There we see the Church interpreting Christianity's root tradition in new circumstances and for a new day. Luke's point is that Christianity is not a static tradition; he both shows the continuity of early Christianity with its Jewish origins and depicts how it moved into and was changed by new cultural contexts. Indeed, throughout Acts we see the explosive power of the gospel being welcomed and received into differing cultural settings.

Structure

As a historical book with a theological agenda, Acts has a clear narrative structure. First, the words of Jesus in 1:8 provide an outline of the book: "You will be my witnesses in Jerusalem [1:15–8:3, the work primarily of Peter and Stephen], in all Judea and Samaria [8:4–11:18, the work of Philip and Peter], and to the ends of the earth [11:19–28:31, the ministry of Paul and his associates]." Second, Acts reflects two periods of apostolic authority. The first focuses on the authority of the Jerusalem church and the authority of Peter and James, and the second on the gentile mission under Paul's authority. Third, the geographic and cultural center of gravity of Christianity shifts in the narrative from Jerusalem and the Temple (the center of Judaism) to Rome (the center of the gentile world).

In reading Acts we share the adventures of travel from Jerusalem to Rome and remember that a journey theme was also prominent in Luke's Gospel. According to Luke, discipleship is learned "on the way." The Acts journey depicts the effect of Jesus on those who encountered him as the risen Christ who operates through the Holy Spirit, clearly a major character in the book. The labors of Peter and the Twelve among the Jews and Paul and his associates among the Gentiles dramatizes the progress of faith in Jesus from Jerusalem to Rome. Thus, Acts forms the bridge between the Gospels as Jesus' story and the Letters as the Church's story.

Saul of Tarsus

Acts is of particular importance in understanding the life, ministry, and Letters of Saul of Tarsus, the apostle Paul, author of a major portion of the New Testament. His conversion is narrated in Acts 9 (and retold in 22:1–21 and 26:1–23, which, with Gal 1:11–24 and 1 Corinthians 9 and 15, make Paul's the best documented conversion experience in Scripture); Acts 13–28 records his ministry. The following references in Acts make dating events in Paul's life possible: a famine in Palestine under the emperor Claudius (11:28; AD 46); the death of Herod Agrippa I (12:23; AD 44); the banning of Jews from Rome by Claudius (18:2; AD 49/50); the arrival of Gallio in Corinth (18:12; AD 51); and the arrival of Festus in Caesarea (24:27; AD 56 or 59). Although scholars take the material in Paul's Letters as primary for biographical purposes, none ignore Acts in their reconstruction of Paul's apostolic work.

Thus Acts contributes to one of the most interesting spiritual biographies in Christian history. Readers of Acts observe as the Pharisee (Phil 3:5) and Sanhedrin member (Acts 26:10) Saul grows in his understanding of the One he met on the Damascus road (Acts 9). Luke depicts him both as a pious Jew and as a Hellenist, a Greek whose education in that language and tradition is everywhere apparent in his

Letters as he "translates" the theological and spiritual riches of Israel into terms Gentiles will understand. Paul's Areopagus speech in Athens in 17:22–31 is an example of his genius. As the Jewish Christian Paul preaches Jesus in the Greco-Roman world, we are shown that Christian spirituality is not the possession of any one culture, language, or people, but is universal in its scope and appeal. In Paul's life we see how a Christian faces all manner of challenge, from problems with fellow missionaries, to difficult travel, to theological debate, to imprisonment. Acts 9–28 can be read as the story of Paul's spiritual growth under that greatest of spiritual directors, the Holy Spirit.

Of course, the "body" that is in formation in Acts is that of the Church itself. In Acts the Church engages in the same activities that characterized the life and ministry of Jesus. Foremost among them is prayer. Just as Luke's Gospel includes material on prayer that does not appear elsewhere and depicts Jesus in prayer at crucial junctures in his life, the focus on prayer continues in Acts (see, e.g., 4:23–31; 8:15; 9:40; 13:3; 14:23; 16:25; 20:36). Prayer characterizes both the communal life of the early Church and its individual spiritual leaders. For Luke, prayer is the means by which the power that filled Jesus is transmitted to his followers. Thus the members of the Jerusalem congregation "were constantly devoting themselves to prayer" (1:14; 2:42). The Church prayed to choose leaders (1:15–26; 6:1–7) and to commission those leaders (6:6; 13:1–3). Christians prayed at the Temple at the Jewish hours of prayer (3:1) and in all times of crisis (4:23–31). The energetic growth of the Church in Jerusalem derived not from its proximity to the scenes of Jesus' Passion, but from constant openness in prayer to the Power who raised him from the dead.

Luke understands prayer as the foundation of the Church's life and growth. And if that is so for the Body, it is so for any individual member of it. But unlike our individualistic culture, the ethos of the first century was communal. In Acts, Luke depicts the Christian community as the locus of divine activity. His understanding of the Church is charismatic; that is, through the Holy Spirit, God directs the Church. The events in Acts are, finally, the work of God and not the product of the individual human ingenuity of Peter or Tabitha or Paul or Lydia or Priscilla and Aquila.

A theological historian, Luke, under the direction and empowerment of the Holy Spirit, shows how the gospel was carried from Jerusalem to Rome, how its cultural center of gravity shifted. But Luke is also a spiritual director. He wants us to understand and act as members who are in unity with one another, charitable to all, and held in high esteem (2:47; 5:13). He describes a community in which fellowship includes economic responsibility for one another. He shows us how early Christians gathered to hear the word, break bread and pray, and how they went out from their meetings to bring others into the Christian community. And he expects us to "go and do likewise."

—*Bonnie Thurston*

Jesus + the Mother Church
First Xians in Israel (handwritten)

The Promise of the Holy Spirit

1 In the first book, Theophilus, I wrote about all that Jesus did and taught from the beginning 2until the day when he was taken up to heaven, after giving instructions through the Holy Spirit to the apostles whom he had chosen. 3After his suffering he presented himself alive to them by many convincing proofs, appearing to them during forty days and speaking about the kingdom of God. 4While staying*a* with them, he ordered them not to leave Jerusalem, but to wait there for the promise of the Father. "This," he said, "is what you have heard from me; 5for John baptized with water, but you will be baptized with*b* the Holy Spirit not many days from now."

The Ascension of Jesus

6 So when they had come together, they asked him, "Lord, is this the time when you will restore the kingdom to Israel?" 7He replied, "It is not for you to know the times or periods that the Father has set by his own authority. 8But you will receive power when the Holy Spirit has come upon you; and you will be my witnesses in Jerusalem, in all Judea and Samaria, and to the ends of the earth." 9When he had said this, as they were watch-ing, he was lifted up, and a cloud took him out of their sight. 10While he was going and they were gazing up toward heaven, suddenly two men in white robes stood by them. 11They said, "Men of Galilee, why do you stand looking up toward heaven? This Jesus, who has been taken up from you into heaven, will come in the same way as you saw him go into heaven."

Matthias Chosen to Replace Judas

12 Then they returned to Jerusalem from the mount called Olivet, which is near Jerusalem, a sabbath day's journey away. 13When they had entered the city, they went to the room upstairs where they were staying, Peter, and John, and James, and Andrew, Philip and Thomas, Bartholomew and Matthew, James son of Alphaeus, and Simon the Zealot, and Judas son of*c* James. 14All these were constantly devoting themselves to prayer, together with certain women, including Mary the mother of Jesus, as well as his brothers.

15 In those days Peter stood up among the believers*d* (together the crowd numbered about one hundred twenty persons) and said, 16"Friends,*e* the scripture had to be fulfilled,

a Or *eating*   *b* Or *by*   *c* Or *the brother of*
d Gk *brothers*   *e* Gk *Men, brothers*

1:2 *the day when he was taken up to heaven.* This verse echoes Luke 24:44–53, which also promises "power from on high" (24:49). This promise is fulfilled; the Holy Spirit guides the action, functioning as the "spiritual director" of the early Church.

1:4 *he ordered them . . . to wait there for the promise of the Father.* God finally found a people who, when he said, "Wait!" would wait. What might it mean for us to wait today?

1:6 *Lord, . . . when you will restore the kingdom to Israel?* The disciples were looking for a "kingdom" in which they could exercise power. Jesus said they would receive power from the Holy Spirit without any human kingdom. Throughout Acts we will see this clash between the "kingdomless power" of the People of God and the "powerless kingdoms" of this world.

1:8 **THE WITH-GOD LIFE**—*See* Spiritual Disciplines Index.

1:11 *This Jesus . . . will come in the same way.* See Luke 24:50–53. The promise of Christ's return is a source of hope and spiritual formation for Christians even if, as verse 7 indicates, we cannot know when his return will occur.

1:14 **PRAYER**—*See* Spiritual Disciplines Index.

1:14 *constantly devoting themselves to prayer, together with certain women.* The first of many references indicating the primary activity of the early Christians was prayer and that both men and women participated equally in the Church's spiritual life. When the community gathered to worship or make important decisions, both participated. The early Church's spirituality was communal; important decisions were made when the Body gathered (cf. chap 15).

1:16 *Friends, the scripture had to be fulfilled.* The early Church studied Scripture, the Septuagint (the Old Testament in Greek), to understand events. Prayerful consideration of God's word was crucial.

which the Holy Spirit through David foretold concerning Judas, who became a guide for those who arrested Jesus— [17]for he was numbered among us and was allotted his share in this ministry." [18](Now this man acquired a field with the reward of his wickedness; and falling headlong, [a] he burst open in the middle and all his bowels gushed out. [19]This became known to all the residents of Jerusalem, so that the field was called in their language Hakeldama, that is, Field of Blood.) [20]"For it is written in the book of Psalms,

'Let his homestead become desolate,
     and let there be no one to live in it';
and
'Let another take his position of
     overseer.'

[21]So one of the men who have accompanied us during all the time that the Lord Jesus went in and out among us, [22]beginning from the baptism of John until the day when he was taken up from us—one of these must become a witness with us to his resurrection." [23]So they proposed two, Joseph called Barsabbas, who was also known as Justus, and Matthias. [24]Then they prayed and said, "Lord, you know everyone's heart. Show us which one of these two you have chosen [25]to take the place[b] in this ministry and apostleship from which Judas turned aside to go to his own place." [26]And they cast lots for them, and the lot fell on Matthias; and he was added to the eleven apostles.

The Coming of the Holy Spirit

2 When the day of Pentecost had come, they were all together in one place. [2]And suddenly from heaven there came a sound like the rush of a violent wind, and it filled the entire house where they were sitting. [3]Divided tongues, as of fire, appeared among them, and a tongue rested on each of them. [4]All of them were filled with the Holy Spirit and began to speak in other languages, as the Spirit gave them ability.

[5] Now there were devout Jews from every nation under heaven living in Jerusalem. [6]And at this sound the crowd gathered and was bewildered, because each one heard them speaking in the native language of each. [7]Amazed and astonished, they asked, "Are not all these who are speaking Galileans? [8]And how is it that we hear, each of us, in our own native language? [9]Parthians, Medes, Elamites, and residents of Mesopotamia, Judea and Cappadocia, Pontus and Asia, [10]Phrygia and Pamphylia, Egypt and the parts of Libya belonging to Cyrene, and visitors from Rome, both Jews and proselytes, [11]Cretans and Arabs—in our own languages we hear them speaking about God's deeds of power." [12]All were amazed and perplexed, saying to one another, "What does this mean?" [13]But others sneered and said, "They are filled with new wine."

a Or *swelling up*   *b* Other ancient authorities read *the share*

1:21–22 *one of these must become a witness with us.* Peter suggests the believers must "elect" a twelfth apostle—someone who had been with them from the beginning of Jesus' ministry in Galilee and who had experienced Jesus' resurrection and ascension, the central message in the early preaching.

1:26 *they cast lots for them.* Deciding an issue by means of casting lots mimicked the use of Urim and Thummin in the Temple. It was understood that God directed the outcome (see Prov 16:9). Matthias is chosen, but that is the last we hear of him.

2:1–13 *When the day of Pentecost had come.* Pentecost was the Jewish feast day, fifty days

after Passover, commemorating the giving of the law on Mt. Sinai (see Lev 23:15–21). This passage exhibits rich associations with that event (Exod 19–20). Again, when important things happen, the community is "all together."

2:4–11 *began to speak in other languages.* Scholars are divided over whether this is glossolalia (ecstatic utterance like Paul describes in 1 Corinthians 14) or xenologia (speaking in a foreign tongue, i.e., in a language not one's own). Here the curse of Babel is reversed; God allows people of different languages (tongues) to understand one another. The first miracle in Acts is auditory, a miracle of understanding.

Peter Addresses the Crowd

14 But Peter, standing with the eleven, raised his voice and addressed them, "Men of Judea and all who live in Jerusalem, let this be known to you, and listen to what I say. 15 Indeed, these are not drunk, as you suppose, for it is only nine o'clock in the morning. 16 No, this is what was spoken through the prophet Joel:

17 'In the last days it will be, God declares, that I will pour out my Spirit upon all flesh,
  and your sons and your daughters shall prophesy,
and your young men shall see visions, and your old men shall dream dreams.
18 Even upon my slaves, both men and women,
  in those days I will pour out my Spirit;
  and they shall prophesy.
19 And I will show portents in the heaven above
  and signs on the earth below,
  blood, and fire, and smoky mist.
20 The sun shall be turned to darkness
  and the moon to blood,
    before the coming of the Lord's great and glorious day.
21 Then everyone who calls on the name of the Lord shall be saved.'

22 "You that are Israelites,[a] listen to what I have to say: Jesus of Nazareth,[b] a man attested to you by God with deeds of power, wonders, and signs that God did through him among you, as you yourselves know— 23 this man, handed over to you according to the definite plan and foreknowledge of God, you crucified and killed by the hands of those outside the law. 24 But God raised him up, having freed him from death,[c] because it was impossible for him to be held in its power. 25 For David says concerning him,

'I saw the Lord always before me,
  for he is at my right hand so that I will not be shaken;
26 therefore my heart was glad, and my tongue rejoiced;
  moreover my flesh will live in hope.
27 For you will not abandon my soul to Hades,
  or let your Holy One experience corruption.
28 You have made known to me the ways of life;
  you will make me full of gladness with your presence.'

29 "Fellow Israelites,[d] I may say to you confidently of our ancestor David that he both died and was buried, and his tomb is with us to this day. 30 Since he was a prophet, he knew that God had sworn with an oath to him that he would put one of his descendants on his throne. 31 Foreseeing this, David[e] spoke of the resurrection of the Messiah,[f] saying,

'He was not abandoned to Hades,
  nor did his flesh experience corruption.'

32 This Jesus God raised up, and of that all of us are witnesses. 33 Being therefore exalted at[g] the right hand of God, and having received from the Father the promise of the Holy Spirit, he has poured out this that you both see and hear. 34 For David did not ascend into the heavens, but he himself says,

'The Lord said to my Lord,
  "Sit at my right hand,
35   until I make your enemies your footstool." '

36 Therefore let the entire house of Israel know with certainty that God has made him both

a Gk Men, Israelites   b Gk the Nazorean
c Gk the pains of death   d Gk Men, brothers
e Gk he   f Or the Christ   g Or by

2:13 *But others sneered.* There are two responses to manifestations of God's power: some marvel and seriously inquire; others scoff. Acts closes with the same observation about preaching (28:24).

2:14–36 *Peter . . . addressed them.* Peter is the representative disciple and spokesman. His sermon explains that what is happening fulfills Joel 2:28–32. It summarizes the Church's proclamation that (1) the Old Testament predicts Jesus; (2) Jesus is the Messiah who is exalted by God; and (3) God sends the empowering Holy Spirit. The basic principle of preaching in Acts is to show how Jesus fulfills Scripture.

Lord and Messiah, *a* this Jesus whom you crucified."

The First Converts

37 Now when they heard this, they were cut to the heart and said to Peter and to the other apostles, "Brothers, *b* what should we do?" 38Peter said to them, "Repent, and be baptized every one of you in the name of Jesus Christ so that your sins may be forgiven; and you will receive the gift of the Holy Spirit. 39For the promise is for you, for your children, and for all who are far away, everyone whom the Lord our God calls to him." 40And he testified with many other arguments and exhorted them, saying, "Save yourselves from this corrupt generation." 41So those who welcomed his message were baptized, and that day about three thousand persons were added. 42They devoted themselves to the apostles' teaching and fellowship, to the breaking of bread and the prayers.

Life among the Believers

43 Awe came upon everyone, because many wonders and signs were being done by the apostles. 44All who believed were together and had all things in common; 45they would sell their possessions and goods and distribute the proceeds *c* to all, as any had need. 46Day by day, as they spent much time together in the temple, they broke bread at home *d* and ate their food with glad and generous *e* hearts, 47praising God and having the goodwill of all the people. And day by day the Lord added to their number those who were being saved.

Peter Heals a Crippled Beggar

3 One day Peter and John were going up to the temple at the hour of prayer, at three o'clock in the afternoon. 2And a man lame

a Or *Christ*   *b* Gk *Men, brothers*   *c* Gk *them*
d Or *from house to house*   *e* Or *sincere*

2:37–38 *Brothers, what should we do?* Good preaching is convicting. Peter's hearers want to know what to do. Peter suggests two demands and two promises. They must repent and be baptized, giving public evidence of allegiance to the Christian community. They are promised both release from sins and the same Holy Spirit who has participated in this event.

2:42 *the apostles' teaching and fellowship . . . the breaking of bread and the prayers.* This verse summarizes the Church's inner life. Each activity reappears in chapters 3–6. The apostles' teaching was of Jesus. Fellowship was the "common life" or partnership, which included not only meeting together, but attending to each other's needs. The "breaking of bread" was likely the Lord's Supper. Prayer characterized the community's life.

2:42 PRAYER—*See* Spiritual Disciplines Index.

Responding
2:42 FELLOWSHIP. A statement by Dallas Willard in *The Spirit of the Disciplines,* "In fellowship we engage in common activities of worship, study, prayer, celebration, and service," perfectly describes the activities of the disciples and new believers. In spite of this clear teaching, many people feel that they do not need to be part of a Christian fellowship.

What does this attitude ignore? How can it be overcome either in your own life or the lives of people you know? *See also* Spiritual Disciplines Index.

2:43–47 *many wonders and signs were being done.* A summary passage. "Wonders and signs" are evidence of God's power and appear with all missionary advances in Acts (4:30; 5:12,19; 19:10–12).

2:44–45 *All who believed . . . had all things in common.* Christian community implies economic responsibility and commitment. The idea is exemplified in 4:32–5:11 and discussed by Paul in 2 Corinthians 8–9.

2:46 *they broke bread at home.* The early Church continued to be closely connected with Judaism (of which it was thought to be a "sect," 28:22), but members also met in private homes for Christian celebration of the Lord's Supper. Gratitude ("glad and generous hearts") is the hallmark of true Christian spirituality.

2:47 *day by day the Lord added to their number.* Christian commitment led believers to live exemplary lives, but the increase in their numbers was God's work.

3:1 *Peter and John were going up to the temple at the hour of prayer.* The apostles continued Jewish practice and Temple piety.

from birth was being carried in. People would lay him daily at the gate of the temple called the Beautiful Gate so that he could ask for alms from those entering the temple. 3When he saw Peter and John about to go into the temple, he asked them for alms. 4Peter looked intently at him, as did John, and said, "Look at us." 5And he fixed his attention on them, expecting to receive something from them. 6But Peter said, "I have no silver or gold, but what I have I give you; in the name of Jesus Christ of Nazareth, a stand up and walk." 7And he took him by the right hand and raised him up; and immediately his feet and ankles were made strong. 8Jumping up, he stood and began to walk, and he entered the temple with them, walking and leaping and praising God. 9All the people saw him walking and praising God, 10and they recognized him as the one who used to sit and ask for alms at the Beautiful Gate of the temple; and they were filled with wonder and amazement at what had happened to him.

Peter Speaks in Solomon's Portico

11 While he clung to Peter and John, all the people ran together to them in the portico called Solomon's Portico, utterly astonished. 12When Peter saw it, he addressed the people, "You Israelites, b why do you wonder at this, or why do you stare at us, as though by our own power or piety we had made him walk? 13The God of Abraham, the God of Isaac, and the God of Jacob, the God of our ancestors has glorified his servant c Jesus, whom you handed over and rejected in the presence of Pilate, though he had decided to release him. 14But you rejected the Holy and Righteous One and asked to have a murderer given to you, 15and you killed the Author of life, whom God raised from the dead. To this we

are witnesses. 16And by faith in his name, his name itself has made this man strong, whom you see and know; and the faith that is through Jesus d has given him this perfect health in the presence of all of you.

17 "And now, friends, e I know that you acted in ignorance, as did also your rulers. 18In this way God fulfilled what he had foretold through all the prophets, that his Messiah f would suffer. 19Repent therefore, and turn to God so that your sins may be wiped out, 20so that times of refreshing may come from the presence of the Lord, and that he may send the Messiah g appointed for you, that is, Jesus, 21who must remain in heaven until the time of universal restoration that God announced long ago through his holy prophets. 22Moses said, 'The Lord your God will raise up for you from your own people e a prophet like me. You must listen to whatever he tells you. 23And it will be that everyone who does not listen to that prophet will be utterly rooted out of the people.' 24And all the prophets, as many as have spoken, from Samuel and those after him, also predicted these days. 25You are the descendants of the prophets and of the covenant that God gave to your ancestors, saying to Abraham, 'And in your descendants all the families of the earth shall be blessed.' 26When God raised up his servant, c he sent him first to you, to bless you by turning each of you from your wicked ways."

Peter and John before the Council

4 While Peter and John h were speaking to the people, the priests, the captain of the temple, and the Sadducees came to them,

a Gk the Nazorean   b Gk Men, Israelites
c Or child   d Gk him   e Gk brothers
f Or his Christ   g Or the Christ   h Gk While they

3:2 a man lame from birth was being carried in. Beggars gathered at places of worship expecting people to be more generous after prayer.

3:6–26 stand up and walk. The "kingdomless power" of the gospel heals a man lame from birth. Peter uses the event to bring the good news of the kingdom of God. First, Peter disclaims any power or piety of his own did the healing (v 12). Next, he ascribes this miracle to Jesus, the murdered One (vv 13–16). Then he

acknowledges that God's plan was fulfilled in the events of Jesus' death and that the Jews acted in ignorance (vv 17–18). Finally, he tells how Jews may yet receive the Messiah (vv 19–26).

4:1–2 the Sadducees came to them, much annoyed. The Sadducees did not believe in the resurrection of the dead; Peter and John are arrested not for healing, but for preaching the resurrection (cf. 23:6–10).

2much annoyed because they were teaching the people and proclaiming that in Jesus there is the resurrection of the dead. 3So they arrested them and put them in custody until the next day, for it was already evening. 4But many of those who heard the word believed; and they numbered about five thousand.

5 The next day their rulers, elders, and scribes assembled in Jerusalem, 6with Annas the high priest, Caiaphas, John,a and Alexander, and all who were of the high-priestly family. 7When they had made the prisonersb stand in their midst, they inquired, "By what power or by what name did you do this?" 8Then Peter, filled with the Holy Spirit, said to them, "Rulers of the people and elders, 9if we are questioned today because of a good deed done to someone who was sick and are asked how this man has been healed, 10let it be known to all of you, and to all the people of Israel, that this man is standing before you in good health by the name of Jesus Christ of Nazareth,c whom you crucified, whom God raised from the dead. 11This Jesusd is

'the stone that was rejected by you, the builders;
it has become the cornerstone.'e

12There is salvation in no one else, for there is no other name under heaven given among mortals by which we must be saved."

13 Now when they saw the boldness of Peter and John and realized that they were uneducated and ordinary men, they were amazed and recognized them as companions of Jesus. 14When they saw the man who had been cured standing beside them, they had nothing to say in opposition. 15So they ordered them to leave the council while they discussed the matter with one another. 16They said, "What will we do with them? For it is obvious to all who live in Jerusalem that a notable sign has been done through them; we cannot deny it. 17But to keep it from spreading further among the people, let us warn them to speak no more to anyone in this name." 18So they called them and ordered them not to speak or teach at all in the name of Jesus. 19But Peter and John answered them, "Whether it is right in God's sight to listen to you rather than to God, you must judge; 20for we cannot keep from speaking about what we have seen and heard." 21After threatening them again, they let them go, finding no way to punish them because of the people, for all of them praised God for what had happened. 22For the man on whom this sign of healing had been performed was more than forty years old.

The Believers Pray for Boldness

23 After they were released, they went to their friendsf and reported what the chief priests and the elders had said to them. 24When they heard it, they raised their voices together to God and said, "Sovereign Lord, who made the heaven and the earth, the sea, and everything in them, 25it is you who said

a Other ancient authorities read *Jonathan*
b Gk *them*   c Gk *the Nazorean*   d Gk *This*
e Or *keystone*   f Gk *their own*

4:4 *many . . . who heard the word believed.* Although preaching draws official opposition, it is embraced by many people. Historically, the Church and individual Christians have grown through persecution. Throughout Acts, persecution leads to advances for the gospel.

4:8 *Peter, filled with the Holy Spirit, said to them.* Peter's eloquence results from the Spirit and fulfills Jesus' words in Matt 10:17–20.

4:12 *There is salvation in no one else.* In a religiously plural world, Peter stresses the exclusive claims of Christianity. That salvation is only in the name of Jesus is the position of Paul, John, and the writer of Hebrews.

4:13 *they saw the boldness of Peter and John.*

Peter and John's authority and eloquence come from Jesus. "Uneducated and ordinary," they were vehicles of enormous power. As verse 14 indicates, the proof of their claims was standing right there.

4:19–20 *Whether it is right . . . to listen to you rather than to God.* Peter and John articulate the principle of supremacy of conscience over even religious institutions. The ancients felt it necessary to obey divine commissions. The apostles have a holy compulsion to speak of their experiences.

4:23–30 *they raised their voices together to God.* Peter and John seek out the community to report what happened; naturally, they pray. This

by the Holy Spirit through our ancestor David, your servant:[a]

'Why did the Gentiles rage,
        and the peoples imagine vain things?
26 The kings of the earth took their stand,
        and the rulers have gathered together
            against the Lord and against his
                Messiah.'[b]

27 For in this city, in fact, both Herod and Pontius Pilate, with the Gentiles and the peoples of Israel, gathered together against your holy servant[a] Jesus, whom you anointed, 28 to do whatever your hand and your plan had predestined to take place. 29 And now, Lord, look at their threats, and grant to your servants[c] to speak your word with all boldness, 30 while you stretch out your hand to heal, and signs and wonders are performed through the name of your holy servant[a] Jesus." 31 When they had prayed, the place in which they were gathered together was shaken; and they were all filled with the Holy Spirit and spoke the word of God with boldness.

The Believers Share Their Possessions

32 Now the whole group of those who believed were of one heart and soul, and no one claimed private ownership of any possessions, but everything they owned was held in common. 33 With great power the apostles gave their testimony to the resurrection of the Lord Jesus, and great grace was upon them all. 34 There was not a needy person among them, for as many as owned lands or houses sold them and brought the proceeds of what was sold. 35 They laid it at the apostles' feet, and it was distributed to each as any had need. 36 There was a Levite, a native of Cyprus, Joseph, to whom the apostles gave the name Barnabas (which means "son of encouragement"). 37 He sold a field that belonged to him, then brought the money, and laid it at the apostles' feet.

Ananias and Sapphira

5 But a man named Ananias, with the consent of his wife Sapphira, sold a piece of property; 2 with his wife's knowledge, he kept back some of the proceeds, and brought only a part and laid it at the apostles' feet. 3 "Ananias," Peter asked, "why has Satan filled your heart to lie to the Holy Spirit and to keep back part of the proceeds of the land? 4 While it remained unsold, did it not remain your own? And after it was sold, were not the proceeds at your disposal? How is it that you have contrived this deed in your heart? You did not lie to us[d] but to God!" 5 Now when Ananias heard these words, he fell down and died. And great fear seized all who heard of it.

a Or child   b Or his Christ   c Gk slaves
d Gk to men

---

is one of the few complete prayer texts from the early Church. In form it is very Jewish. It praises God as the creator of the universe (v 24) and the director of history (vv 25–28) and asks not for release from persecution, but for boldness to speak the word (vv 29–30).

4:31 *they were all filled with the Holy Spirit.* This "second Pentecost" is the immediate answer to the community' prayer (vv 24–30).

4:32–35 *those who believed were of one heart and soul.* A second summary focusing on the ownership of property and the Church's response to need. Classical writers like Plato and Aristotle wrote of the ideal of holding possessions in common and sharing to meet need. Luke understands the Church's economic arrangements as "testimony to the resurrection." The principle of sharing resources

(vv 34–35) is followed by the positive example of Joseph/Barnabas (4:36–37) and the negative example of Ananias and Sapphira (5:1–11). Luke highlights the profound responsibility the Christians felt for each other. Compassion is a hallmark of Christian spirituality.

5:1–11 *he kept back some of the proceeds.* The attack from without is now matched by an attack from within the community, which comes in the form of lying. Distribution of private property for communal need was voluntary. Ananias's sin was, with Sapphira's knowledge, lying to Peter, whose challenge (v 3) suggests the event is part of a struggle with Satan. The early Christians experienced a personification of evil (Satan) who tempted them to sin, and they took it seriously. The effect of the truth upon Ananias and Sapphira was death.

6The young men came and wrapped up his body,*a* then carried him out and buried him.

7 After an interval of about three hours his wife came in, not knowing what had happened. 8Peter said to her, "Tell me whether you and your husband sold the land for such and such a price." And she said, "Yes, that was the price." 9Then Peter said to her, "How is it that you have agreed together to put the Spirit of the Lord to the test? Look, the feet of those who have buried your husband are at the door, and they will carry you out." 10Immediately she fell down at his feet and died. When the young men came in they found her dead, so they carried her out and buried her beside her husband. 11And great fear seized the whole church and all who heard of these things.

The Apostles Heal Many

12 Now many signs and wonders were done among the people through the apostles. And they were all together in Solomon's Portico. 13None of the rest dared to join them, but the people held them in high esteem. 14Yet more than ever believers were added to the Lord, great numbers of both men and women, 15so that they even carried out the sick into the streets, and laid them on cots and mats, in order that Peter's shadow might fall on some of them as he came by. 16A great number of people would also gather from the towns around Jerusalem, bringing the sick and those tormented by unclean spirits, and they were all cured.

The Apostles Are Persecuted

17 Then the high priest took action; he and all who were with him (that is, the sect of the Sadducees), being filled with jealousy, 18arrested the apostles and put them in the public prison. 19But during the night an angel of the Lord opened the prison doors, brought them out, and said, 20"Go, stand in the temple and tell the people the whole message about this life." 21When they heard this, they entered the temple at daybreak and went on with their teaching.

When the high priest and those with him arrived, they called together the council and the whole body of the elders of Israel, and sent to the prison to have them brought. 22But when the temple police went there, they did not find them in the prison; so they returned and reported, 23"We found the prison securely locked and the guards standing at the doors, but when we opened them, we found no one inside." 24Now when the captain of the temple and the chief priests heard these words, they were perplexed about them, wondering what might be going on. 25Then someone arrived and announced, "Look, the men whom you put in prison are standing in the temple and teaching the people!" 26Then the captain went with the temple police and brought them, but without violence, for they were afraid of being stoned by the people.

27 When they had brought them, they had them stand before the council. The high priest questioned them, 28saying, "We gave you strict orders not to teach in this name,*b* yet here you have filled Jerusalem with your teaching and you are determined to bring this man's blood on us." 29But Peter and the apostles answered, "We must obey God rather than any human authority.*c* 30The God of

a Meaning of Gk uncertain *b* Other ancient authorities read *Did we not give you strict orders not to teach in this name?* *c* Gk *than men*

5:11 *And great fear seized the whole church.* This is the first use of the word "church" in Acts.

5:12–16 *many signs and wonders were done.* The third summary passage focuses on healing, which Luke stresses is "through" the apostles. Healing comes from God. The apostles' popularity as healers draws the attention of the Sadducees (4:1) and leads to their arrest.

5:19–20 *an angel of the Lord opened the prison doors.* The first of three miraculous releases in Acts (12:6–19; 16:25–34). Angelic messengers indicate God's direction. Nothing, not even the opposition of religious officials, can stop the work of God.

5:29–32 *We must obey God rather than any human authority.* Peter reiterates 4:19–20 and delivers his third sermon in Acts. It is highly Christological, focusing on the fact that God vindicated Jesus, whom Peter calls "Leader and Savior."

ANANIAS AND SAPPHIRA

Lying to God

Selected Scriptures: *Acts 5:1–11*

The early Christians spent much time in prayer and worship together. They also ate together, fellowshiped, and listened to the apostles' teaching. And out of their devotion to the life of God came a willing, even joyful surrender of their possessions to care for the needs of others. For all those who had abandoned themselves to God and his new movement in the Church, it proved an idyllic time, corporately speaking.

But not all Christians in the early Church had abandoned themselves to God. Ananias and Sapphira, husband and wife, appeared to be believers, but their sin brought about dire consequences—the loss of their lives.

Others were selling fields and giving the money to the apostles for charitable use; this couple decided to do the same. They sold a piece of land, but rather than offering all the proceeds to the Church, they kept some. Ananias brought the remainder to the apostles, claiming he was giving the entire price for the land. Peter confronted him about his lie, and immediately Ananias fell down and died. Later, when Peter questioned Sapphira, she too lied about the price and suffered the same result.

The consequence of their sin is jarring. What believer possesses unfailing honesty? Can any Christian claim never to have lied? Yet this sin brought death to two members of the early Church. Peter made it clear that their sin was not in keeping part of the proceeds, but in lying to God, for when they lied to the apostles, they were lying to God.

Here Acts provides an early lesson on how the Spirit of Christ became incarnate in all believers. Just as Jesus taught people that in caring for others they were caring for him, so in sinning against others they were sinning against him. God took such sin seriously. The with-God life is serious business, and the Holy Spirit had come to enliven only those who would act in honesty when it came to the Spirit's life in them.

It seems Ananias and Sapphira were bound by their desire for approval or acclaim. They couldn't give in freedom and honesty as led by the Holy Spirit, but rather needed to use their giving to increase their reputation. God could not allow such motives to pollute the powerful work of his Spirit in this first body of Christians.

Richard Foster writes in *Freedom of Simplicity:* "The person who is still bound to sin and enslaved to others is not free to truly love his neighbor. . . . If we are still in bondage to sin, our serving will flow out of that center. We will not have the single eye that gives light to all we do. Pride and fear and manipulation will control our actions. We will not be free to serve our neighbor in simplicity."

PROFILE

PROFILE: ANANIAS AND SAPPHIRA

In the early Church we see a picture not only of what the Holy Spirit may bring about in a group abandoned to him, but of how this life can be skewed by those whose loyalties are divided. May we pursue a simple, single-minded devotion to our Lord, entrusting ourselves and our reputations to him alone.

Personal Reflection

- Simplicity can be defined as the state of being simple, uncomplicated, or uncompounded, but it can also mean directness of expression. How much does your speech benefit from the discipline of simplicity? How honest and open are you with others? How often do you hide by means of controlled speech? When do you craft your words to make yourself look good? How often do you employ the use of "white lies"?

- Ananias and Sapphira lacked simplicity in their attitude toward the opinions of others and possibly in their attitude toward material things and money. Where do you find it most difficult to practice simplicity? In your reputation? Your desire for material things? Your need for security? Your drive to seek entertainment?

our ancestors raised up Jesus, whom you had killed by hanging him on a tree. [31]God exalted him at his right hand as Leader and Savior that he might give repentance to Israel and forgiveness of sins. [32]And we are witnesses to these things, and so is the Holy Spirit whom God has given to those who obey him."

33 When they heard this, they were enraged and wanted to kill them. [34]But a Pharisee in the council named Gamaliel, a teacher of the law, respected by all the people, stood up and ordered the men to be put outside for a short time. [35]Then he said to them, "Fellow Israelites,[a] consider carefully what you propose to do to these men. [36]For some time ago Theudas rose up, claiming to be somebody, and a number of men, about four hundred, joined him; but he was killed, and all who followed him were dispersed and disappeared. [37]After him Judas the Galilean rose up at the time of the census and got people to follow him; he also perished, and all who followed him were scattered. [38]So in the present case, I tell you, keep away from these men and let them alone; because if this plan or this undertaking is of human origin, it will fail; [39]but if it is of God, you will not be able to overthrow them—in that case you may even be found fighting against God!"

They were convinced by him, [40]and when they had called in the apostles, they had them flogged. Then they ordered them not to speak in the name of Jesus, and let them go. [41]As they left the council, they rejoiced that they were considered worthy to suffer dishonor for the sake of the name. [42]And every day in the temple and at home[b] they did not cease to teach and proclaim Jesus as the Messiah.[c]

a Gk Men, Israelites   b Or from house to house
c Or the Christ

5:40 *they had them flogged.* Opposition to the apostles increases. Previously they were warned; now they are flogged.

5:41–42 *worthy to suffer dishonor for the sake of the name.* The apostles are honored to be "shamed for the Name" and continue their proclamation (cf. 4:19–20).

Seven Chosen to Serve

6 Now during those days, when the disciples were increasing in number, the Hellenists complained against the Hebrews because their widows were being neglected in the daily distribution of food. [2]And the twelve called together the whole community of the disciples and said, "It is not right that we should neglect the word of God in order to wait on tables.[a] [3]Therefore, friends,[b] select from among yourselves seven men of good standing, full of the Spirit and of wisdom, whom we may appoint to this task, [4]while we, for our part, will devote ourselves to prayer and to serving the word." [5]What they said pleased the whole community, and they chose Stephen, a man full of faith and the Holy Spirit, together with Philip, Prochorus, Nicanor, Timon, Parmenas, and Nicolaus, a proselyte of Antioch. [6]They had these men stand before the apostles, who prayed and laid their hands on them.

[7]The word of God continued to spread; the number of the disciples increased greatly in Jerusalem, and a great many of the priests became obedient to the faith.

The Arrest of Stephen

[8]Stephen, full of grace and power, did great wonders and signs among the people. [9]Then some of those who belonged to the synagogue of the Freedmen (as it was called), Cyrenians, Alexandrians, and others of those from Cilicia and Asia, stood up and argued with Stephen. [10]But they could not withstand the wisdom and the Spirit[c] with which he spoke. [11]Then they secretly instigated some men to say, "We have heard him speak blasphemous words against Moses and God." [12]They stirred up the people as well as the elders and the scribes; then they suddenly confronted him, seized him, and brought him before the council. [13]They set up false

a Or *keep accounts*   *b* Gk *brothers*   *c* Or *spirit*

6:1–5 *the Hellenists complained against the Hebrews because their widows were being neglected.* When poor Jews became Christian, they lost Jewish public support. Increasing numbers of Christians meant more needy people, which necessitated greater church organization. The issue is related to 2:44–45 and 4:32–35. The culturally Greek Jews (Hellenists) felt the culturally Semitic Jews (Hebrews) were not providing equally for their widows. The passage reflects incipient racial tensions.

Responding
6:1–6 SERVICE. The early disciples chosen to make even distributions of food to the widows in their fellowship had to be reputable, Spirit filled, and wise. Why are these qualities important in people who are enlisted to serve the needs of others? Can you describe what happens if these qualities are ignored? What can you do to ensure that the people in positions of service in your fellowship meet these qualifications? *See also* Spiritual Disciplines Index.

6:2 *the twelve called together the whole community.* In a new situation, Christian leaders call the whole community together to seek a solution. God uses administrative means to solve a spiritual problem. Structural change results.

6:3–4 *select . . . seven men of good standing, full of the Spirit and of wisdom.* Requirements for ministry and a "job description" are clarified. The new ministry is for those who are of good reputation, full of the Spirit, and wise. Ministry is now divided between "prayer and serving the word" (worship and preaching) and "waiting on tables" (benevolent work). From the outset, the Church has needed various ministries (cf. Num 11).

6:4 PRAYER—*See* Spiritual Disciplines Index.

6:5 *Stephen, . . . Philip, Prochorus, Nicanor, Timon, Parmenas, and Nicolaus.* Note that the seven men all have Greek names. Those chosen for this ministry were from the aggrieved party.

6:6 PRAYER—*See* Spiritual Disciplines Index.

6:8–8:3 *Stephen . . . did great wonders and signs.* These chapters represent another cycle of confrontation in Jerusalem. Stephen, first named of the "social servants" (6:5), "witnesses" (1:8; 2:32; 3:15; 5:32) to Jews who bring him before the Sanhedrin. His "sermon," 7:2–53, contains the same points as Peter's Pentecost sermon (see note on 2:14–36). The Greek word meaning "witness" is the same root from which we get the term "martyr." It "costs" to proclaim Jesus.

witnesses who said, "This man never stops saying things against this holy place and the law; 14for we have heard him say that this Jesus of Nazareth*a* will destroy this place and will change the customs that Moses handed on to us." 15And all who sat in the council looked intently at him, and they saw that his face was like the face of an angel.

Stephen's Speech to the Council

7 Then the high priest asked him, "Are these things so?" 2And Stephen replied: "Brothers*b* and fathers, listen to me. The God of glory appeared to our ancestor Abraham when he was in Mesopotamia, before he lived in Haran, 3and said to him, 'Leave your country and your relatives and go to the land that I will show you.' 4Then he left the country of the Chaldeans and settled in Haran. After his father died, God had him move from there to this country in which you are now living. 5He did not give him any of it as a heritage, not even a foot's length, but promised to give it to him as his possession and to his descendants after him, even though he had no child. 6And God spoke in these terms, that his descendants would be resident aliens in a country belonging to others, who would enslave them and mistreat them during four hundred years. 7'But I will judge the nation that they serve,' said God, 'and after that they shall come out and worship me in this place.' 8Then he gave him the covenant of circumcision. And so Abraham*c* became the father of Isaac and circumcised him on the eighth day; and Isaac became the father of Jacob, and Jacob of the twelve patriarchs.

9 "The patriarchs, jealous of Joseph, sold him into Egypt; but God was with him, 10and rescued him from all his afflictions, and enabled him to win favor and to show wisdom when he stood before Pharaoh, king of Egypt, who appointed him ruler over Egypt and over all his household. 11Now there came a famine throughout Egypt and Canaan, and great suffering, and our ancestors could find no food. 12But when Jacob heard that there was grain in Egypt, he sent our ancestors there on their first visit. 13On the second visit Joseph made himself known to his brothers, and Joseph's family became known to Pharaoh. 14Then Joseph sent and invited his father Jacob and all his relatives to come to him, seventy-five in all; 15so Jacob went down to Egypt. He himself died there as well as our ancestors, 16and their bodies*d* were brought back to Shechem and laid in the tomb that Abraham had bought for a sum of silver from the sons of Hamor in Shechem.

17 "But as the time drew near for the fulfillment of the promise that God had made to Abraham, our people in Egypt increased and multiplied 18until another king who had not known Joseph ruled over Egypt. 19He dealt craftily with our race and forced our ancestors to abandon their infants so that they would die. 20At this time Moses was born, and he was beautiful before God. For three months he was brought up in his father's house; 21and when he was abandoned, Pharaoh's daughter adopted him and brought him up as her own son. 22So Moses was instructed in all the wisdom of the Egyptians and was powerful in his words and deeds.

23 "When he was forty years old, it came into his heart to visit his relatives, the Israelites.*e* 24When he saw one of them being wronged, he defended the oppressed man and avenged him by striking down the Egyptian. 25He supposed that his kinsfolk would understand that God through him was rescuing them, but they did not understand. 26The next day he came to some of them as they were quarreling and tried to reconcile them, saying, 'Men, you are brothers; why do you wrong each other?' 27But the man who was wronging his neighbor pushed Moses*f* aside, saying, 'Who made you a ruler and a judge over us? 28Do you want to kill me as you killed the Egyptian yesterday?' 29When he heard this, Moses fled and became a resident alien in the land of Midian. There he became the father of two sons.

30 "Now when forty years had passed, an angel appeared to him in the wilderness of Mount Sinai, in the flame of a burning bush. 31When Moses saw it, he was amazed at the

a Gk *the Nazorean*   *b* Gk *Men, brothers*
c Gk *he*   *d* Gk *they*   *e* Gk *his brothers, the sons of Israel*   *f* Gk *him*

STEPHEN

Full Surrender

Selected Scriptures: *Acts 6–7*

Stephen stood out as "a man full of faith and the Holy Spirit," we're told in Acts (6:5). He was chosen along with six others to carry on the ministry of daily distribution of food to widows. Every day he worked to get food out to single women in need, operating a kind of first-century food bank or Meals on Wheels. Surely this work didn't feel glamorous, and it wasn't done before the crowds or the influential people of Jerusalem. Rather, it remained a simple work of love and compassion offered to meet real needs.

Stephen and the others were appointed because they were filled with the Holy Spirit and wisdom—the apostles understood that the Spirit of God needed to be just as present in "unseen" works of compassion as in public ministries of preaching and evangelism. Stephen and his team, in their wisdom, understood their work as essential within the scope of all the Church was and is called to be as an extension of Jesus' love to the world.

Stephen also performed great wonders and signs for the people, causing some of the leaders of the synagogue to question him. However, no matter how hard they argued, "they could not withstand the wisdom and the Spirit with which he spoke" (6:10). Stephen's faith became more public when through the Spirit he spoke with wisdom. Early on, even before his death, we get a picture of Stephen as one of the greats of the early Church.

A closer look at Stephen tells us more. The leaders opposed to him stirred up controversy, turning people against Stephen and bringing false witnesses against him. They brought Stephen before the council, charging him with threatening the Temple and Mosaic law.

Stephen calmly replied to their accusations with a riveting account of God's presence and guidance throughout history from Abraham to present day. Yet his passion that people recognize God enflamed his narrative into an accusation: "You stiffnecked people, uncircumcised in heart and ears, you are forever opposing the Holy Spirit" (7:51). The assembly rose in anger and stoned Stephen to death for his words, making him the first martyr in the Christian community.

Like Stephen, others have surrendered to God in similar ways, only to see God do exceedingly great things in and through their acts of surrender. One man, Rees Howells, came to Christ during the Welsh revivals of the early twentieth century. When the Holy Spirit led him to turn over leadership of an early mission he had put all his time and money into for three years, he struggled to obey. God told him, nonetheless, to intercede for the new leader and ask that he might have even greater ministry success. Howells responded by entering into a time of hidden prayer and

PROFILE: STEPHEN

encouragement and discovered there was "as much joy in a hidden life of service as in an open and successful one." Later he founded a Bible college and led hundreds of students in the life of deep intercession for individuals and world situations.

Stephen also had prayed, "Send me! Use me!" surrendering even his life to proclaim Christ. When he died, persecution of Christians began in earnest, and the Church scattered from Jerusalem throughout Judea and Samaria. Stephen's death became his final act of service, moving believers to new areas to spread the gospel. Today his legacy as Christianity's first martyr lives on. Even in facing death he knew the joy of remaining surrendered to Jesus. He modeled for us not only how to die for Christ, but how to live for him, surrendered and willing to serve wherever and however he asks, open to the Spirit's leading, and always seeking growth in God's wisdom and grace.

Personal Reflection

- When have you felt God calling you to serve in an unseen way? What did you learn in being obedient?
- Have you ever experienced God's Spirit moving through you in a powerful way after a period of simple, obedient service to him? If so, how has God helped you grow in wisdom and grace through these experiences?
- How fully have you surrendered yourself, your time, and your concept of your own importance to God? Sit with God now and in the coming days, listening to what he may be asking you to do in service to him.

sight; and as he approached to look, there came the voice of the Lord: [32]'I am the God of your ancestors, the God of Abraham, Isaac, and Jacob.' Moses began to tremble and did not dare to look. [33]Then the Lord said to him, 'Take off the sandals from your feet, for the place where you are standing is holy ground. [34]I have surely seen the mistreatment of my people who are in Egypt and have heard their groaning, and I have come down to rescue them. Come now, I will send you to Egypt.'

35 "It was this Moses whom they rejected when they said, 'Who made you a ruler and a judge?' and whom God now sent as both ruler and liberator through the angel who appeared to him in the bush. [36]He led them out, having performed wonders and signs in Egypt, at the Red Sea, and in the wilderness for forty years. [37]This is the Moses who said to the Israelites, 'God will raise up a prophet for you from your own people[a] as he raised me up.' [38]He is the one who was in the congregation in the wilderness with the angel who spoke to him at Mount Sinai, and with our ancestors; and he received living oracles to give to us. [39]Our ancestors were unwilling to obey him; instead, they pushed him aside, and in their hearts they turned back to Egypt, [40]saying to Aaron, 'Make gods for us who will lead the way for us; as for this Moses who led us out from the land of Egypt, we do not know what has happened to him.' [41]At that time they made a calf, offered a sacrifice to the idol, and reveled in the works of their hands. [42]But God turned away from them and handed them over to worship the host of heaven, as it is written in the book of the prophets:

'Did you offer to me slain victims and
    sacrifices
forty years in the wilderness, O house
    of Israel?
[43] No; you took along the tent of Moloch,
    and the star of your god Rephan,
      the images that you made to
        worship;
so I will remove you beyond Babylon.'

44 "Our ancestors had the tent of testimony in the wilderness, as God[b] directed when he spoke to Moses, ordering him to

make it according to the pattern he had seen. ⁴⁵Our ancestors in turn brought it in with Joshua when they dispossessed the nations that God drove out before our ancestors. And it was there until the time of David, ⁴⁶who found favor with God and asked that he might find a dwelling place for the house of Jacob. *a* ⁴⁷But it was Solomon who built a house for him. ⁴⁸Yet the Most High does not dwell in houses made with human hands; *b* as the prophet says,

⁴⁹ 'Heaven is my throne,
    and the earth is my footstool.
What kind of house will you build for
        me, says the Lord,
    or what is the place of my rest?
⁵⁰ Did not my hand make all these
        things?'

51 "You stiff-necked people, uncircumcised in heart and ears, you are forever opposing the Holy Spirit, just as your ancestors used to do. ⁵²Which of the prophets did your ancestors not persecute? They killed those who foretold the coming of the Righteous One, and now you have become his betrayers and murderers. ⁵³You are the ones that received the law as ordained by angels, and yet you have not kept it."

The Stoning of Stephen

54 When they heard these things, they became enraged and ground their teeth at Stephen. *c* ⁵⁵But filled with the Holy Spirit, he gazed into heaven and saw the glory of God and Jesus standing at the right hand of God. ⁵⁶"Look," he said, "I see the heavens opened and the Son of Man standing at the right hand of God!" ⁵⁷But they covered their ears, and with a loud shout all rushed together against him. ⁵⁸Then they dragged him out of the city and began to stone him; and the witnesses laid their coats at the feet of a young man named Saul. ⁵⁹While they were stoning Stephen, he prayed, "Lord Jesus, receive my spirit." ⁶⁰Then he knelt down and cried out in a loud voice, "Lord, do not hold this sin against them." When he had said this,

8 he died. *d* ¹And Saul approved of their killing him.

Saul Persecutes the Church

That day a severe persecution began against the church in Jerusalem, and all except the apostles were scattered throughout the countryside of Judea and Samaria. ²Devout men buried Stephen and made loud lamentation over him. ³But Saul was ravaging the church by entering house after house; dragging off both men and women, he committed them to prison.

Philip Preaches in Samaria

4 Now those who were scattered went from place to place, proclaiming the word. ⁵Philip went down to the city *e* of Samaria and proclaimed the Messiah *f* to them. ⁶The crowds with one accord listened eagerly to what was said by Philip, hearing and seeing the signs that he did, ⁷for unclean spirits, crying with loud shrieks, came out of many

---

a Other ancient authorities read *for the God of Jacob*
b Gk *with hands*   *c* Gk *him*   *d* Gk *fell asleep*
e Other ancient authorities read *a city*   *f* Or *the Christ*

7:58; 8:1 *a young man named Saul.* Luke introduces Saul of Tarsus, persecutor of Christians.

7:59–60 *While they were stoning Stephen, he prayed.* Luke highlights parallels between Stephen and Jesus. Stephen was accused of the same things as Jesus, blasphemy and speaking against the law and the Temple (6:11–14). His response to martyrdom mirrors Jesus' (Luke 23:34). As Jesus was, so are Christians to be. Opposition to the gospel intensified from warning (4:17, 21) to flogging (5:40) to martyrdom (7:60). Stephen's death introduces a general persecution (8:1–3).

8:4 *those who were scattered went from place to place.* In response to persecution, the gospel spreads. Physical violence cannot kill ideology and often encourages those who are persecuted.

8:5 *Philip went down to the city of Samaria.* Preaching in Samaria is remarkable; deep enmity existed between Samaritans and Jews; the latter regarded the former as racially impure heretics. If Christian fellowship could include Samaritans, it could include anyone. As in chapter 4, a demonstration of power (vv 6–7) is the catalyst for preaching.

who were possessed; and many others who were paralyzed or lame were cured. 8So there was great joy in that city.

9 Now a certain man named Simon had previously practiced magic in the city and amazed the people of Samaria, saying that he was someone great. 10All of them, from the least to the greatest, listened to him eagerly, saying, "This man is the power of God that is called Great." 11And they listened eagerly to him because for a long time he had amazed them with his magic. 12But when they believed Philip, who was proclaiming the good news about the kingdom of God and the name of Jesus Christ, they were baptized, both men and women. 13Even Simon himself believed. After being baptized, he stayed constantly with Philip and was amazed when he saw the signs and great miracles that took place.

14 Now when the apostles at Jerusalem heard that Samaria had accepted the word of God, they sent Peter and John to them. 15The two went down and prayed for them that they might receive the Holy Spirit 16(for as yet the Spirit had not come a upon any of them; they had only been baptized in the name of the Lord Jesus). 17Then Peter and John b laid their hands on them, and they received the Holy Spirit. 18Now when Simon saw that the Spirit was given through the laying on of the apostles' hands, he offered them money, 19saying, "Give me also this power so that anyone on

whom I lay my hands may receive the Holy Spirit." 20But Peter said to him, "May your silver perish with you, because you thought you could obtain God's gift with money! 21You have no part or share in this, for your heart is not right before God. 22Repent therefore of this wickedness of yours, and pray to the Lord that, if possible, the intent of your heart may be forgiven you. 23For I see that you are in the gall of bitterness and the chains of wickedness." 24Simon answered, "Pray for me to the Lord, that nothing of what you c have said may happen to me."

25 Now after Peter and John d had testified and spoken the word of the Lord, they returned to Jerusalem, proclaiming the good news to many villages of the Samaritans.

Philip and the Ethiopian Eunuch

26 Then an angel of the Lord said to Philip, "Get up and go toward the south e to the road that goes down from Jerusalem to Gaza." (This is a wilderness road.) 27So he got up and went. Now there was an Ethiopian eunuch, a court official of the Candace, queen of the Ethiopians, in charge of her entire treasury. He had come to Jerusalem to worship 28and was returning home; seated in his chariot, he was reading the prophet

a Gk fallen   b Gk they   c The Greek word for you and the verb pray are plural   d Gk after they
e Or go at noon

8:9–13 *Simon had previously practiced magic in the city.* Philip's (see 6:1–6, esp. v 5) experience with Simon contrasts magical arts and gifts of the Spirit. Sorcery was common in the Roman Empire. Jews assumed Samaritans were involved with magic. Authentic spiritual power comes from the Holy Spirit for the building up of the community (cf. 1 Cor 12:7).

8:14–17 *that they might receive the Holy Spirit.* As headquarters and locus of Christian authority, the Jerusalem church sends Peter and John to ratify Philip's work. This results in a "Samaritan Pentecost" and official sanction of the mission (see v 25). The Holy Spirit has fallen on non-Jews, a major turning point. The despised Samaritans are saved and brought into God's new community without becoming Jewish proselytes.

8:15 PRAYER—*See* Spiritual Disciplines Index.

8:18–24 *he offered them money.* Simon Magus misunderstands the conditions of transmittal of the Holy Spirit. Peter makes it clear that the Spirit is not to be sold as merchandise. The sin of Simon Magus was to attempt to take the power of God and use it for his own ends. Simon represents a completely materialistic view of the gifts of the Spirit. Peter shows him the error of his ways, and he immediately repents.

8:26 *Then an angel of the Lord said.* God continues to direct the Church with angelic messengers. Christians cannot chart an accurate course without God's direction.

8:27–35 *he was reading the prophet Isaiah.* A politically powerful African (v 27) reads Isaiah 53, which early Christians understood as prophecy of the Messiah. Philip explains the text. Note here the ease of the guided, unforced witness.

PHILIP

The Evangelist

Selected Scriptures: *Acts 6:1–6; 8; 21:7–9*

We call him "Philip the evangelist," and for good reason. Philip proved faithful in communicating the profound yet simple truths of the good news of Christ.

After Stephen was martyred, persecution of the Church increased and Christian believers scattered from Jerusalem. As they moved out of the city and into surrounding areas, they spread the gospel wherever they went. Philip went north to Samaria, where the people had long been despised by Jews.

Seven hundred years earlier, Assyria had overtaken the Northern Kingdom, Israel, including Samaria; and many Jews were deported. People of other nationalities were brought in, and these people both adopted some Jewish beliefs and practices over time and continued to worship the gods of their home cultures. The Samaritans' religion had become a sort of mixed bag.

When Philip arrived in Samaria, the city buzzed with excitement over Simon the magician. Yet when Philip began to speak of Jesus Christ, people believed quickly and many were baptized. Lacking a unified faith, these people seemed eager to jump at any message that looked to be from God, whoever he might be.

Later, when the Spirit told Philip to approach the chariot of the Ethiopian eunuch, he found another person seeking God who was without any understanding of Jesus or salvation. The eunuch too believed quickly after hearing Philip speak and wanted to be baptized immediately.

In both instances, people clearly were seeking God. They didn't know about Jesus and did not yet understand much of what it would mean to become a disciple of Jesus. They simply wanted to meet God, and Philip helped them by telling them plainly of Christ.

The Samaritans may have been eager to accept any teaching that came along. The Ethiopian may have been returning to a home where no Christians were present to teach him how to follow Christ. Yet he and the Samaritans had approached God with an honest heart. And the Holy Spirit, which had been poured out on them, brought Philip to proclaim Christ and remained present to make a way for their future needs.

Philip's life reminds us of what it really means to proclaim Christ. We come in the love of the Holy Spirit to those who honestly seek God, trusting that the Spirit began the work before we did and will carry it on after us. We can all, at some level, live as Philip did, speaking Jesus to those who seek God, trusting that in even the simplest offering of Jesus the Spirit can draw souls to salvation.

PROFILE: PHILIP

Personal Reflection

- The mixed-bag religion of the Samaritans may remind us of how many in our culture approach their spiritual lives. Philip was full of the Spirit and of wisdom. He brought demons out of many Samaritans who were possessed and cured others who were lame or paralyzed. How might the Spirit work through us today to meet the needs around us and point to the truth of our words about Christ?

- The Word of God became a springboard for Philip to use to share with the Ethiopian. What are some ways of letting the Bible open doors for further discussion about Jesus?

- Are people of our day hungry for God and his kingdom, as the Samaritans and the Ethiopian were? Why or why not? In what ways has God led you to speak to spiritual hunger that is already there?

- How does Philip's life encourage you as you speak of Jesus?

- The Ethiopian "invited Philip to get in and sit beside him" (8:31). Are you so inviting to those who seek to better your understanding, especially those who are different from you? How can you be more receptive to those in your life who would teach you?

Isaiah. [29]Then the Spirit said to Philip, "Go over to this chariot and join it." [30]So Philip ran up to it and heard him reading the prophet Isaiah. He asked, "Do you understand what you are reading?" [31]He replied, "How can I, unless someone guides me?" And he invited Philip to get in and sit beside him. [32]Now the passage of the scripture that he was reading was this:

> "Like a sheep he was led to the slaughter,
>   and like a lamb silent before its
>   shearer,
>   so he does not open his mouth.
> [33] In his humiliation justice was denied
>   him.
>   Who can describe his generation?
>   For his life is taken away from the
>   earth."

[34]The eunuch asked Philip, "About whom, may I ask you, does the prophet say this, about himself or about someone else?" [35]Then Philip began to speak, and starting with this scripture, he proclaimed to him the good news about Jesus. [36]As they were going along the road, they came to some water; and the eunuch said, "Look, here is water! What is to prevent me from being baptized?"[a] [38]He commanded the chariot to stop, and both of them, Philip and the eunuch, went down into the water, and Philip[b] baptized him. [39]When they came up out of the water, the Spirit of the Lord snatched Philip away; the eunuch saw him no more, and went on his way rejoicing. [40]But Philip found himself at Azotus, and as

a Other ancient authorities add all or most of verse 37, *And Philip said, "If you believe with all your heart, you may." And he replied, "I believe that Jesus Christ is the Son of God."*   *b* Gk *he*

8:36–39 *What is to prevent me from being baptized?* Like Jews who heard Peter's preaching (2:37), the Ethiopian responds and is baptized by immersion. Philip is "missionary to outcasts," as the Ethiopian was both a Gentile and excluded from Israel by his physical condition (Deut 23:1). But the gospel excludes nobody.

8:40 *Philip found himself at Azotus.* Philip preaches to yet another ethnic group—descendants of the Philistines—at Azotus and on his way north to Caesarea.

he was passing through the region, he proclaimed the good news to all the towns until he came to Caesarea.

The Conversion of Saul

9 Meanwhile Saul, still breathing threats and murder against the disciples of the Lord, went to the high priest 2and asked him for letters to the synagogues at Damascus, so that if he found any who belonged to the Way, men or women, he might bring them bound to Jerusalem. 3Now as he was going along and approaching Damascus, suddenly a light from heaven flashed around him. 4He fell to the ground and heard a voice saying to him, "Saul, Saul, why do you persecute me?" 5He asked, "Who are you, Lord?" The reply came, "I am Jesus, whom you are persecuting. 6But get up and enter the city, and you will be told what you are to do." 7The men who were traveling with him stood speechless because they heard the voice but saw no one. 8Saul got up from the ground, and though his eyes were open, he could see nothing; so they led him by the hand and brought him into Damascus. 9For three days he was without sight, and neither ate nor drank.

10 Now there was a disciple in Damascus named Ananias. The Lord said to him in a vision, "Ananias." He answered, "Here I am, Lord." 11The Lord said to him, "Get up and go to the street called Straight, and at the house of Judas look for a man of Tarsus named Saul. At this moment he is praying, 12and he has seen in a vision *a* a man named Ananias come in and lay his hands on him so that he might regain his sight." 13But Ananias answered,

"Lord, I have heard from many about this man, how much evil he has done to your saints in Jerusalem; 14and here he has authority from the chief priests to bind all who invoke your name." 15But the Lord said to him, "Go, for he is an instrument whom I have chosen to bring my name before Gentiles and kings and before the people of Israel; 16I myself will show him how much he must suffer for the sake of my name." 17So Ananias went and entered the house. He laid his hands on Saul *b* and said, "Brother Saul, the Lord Jesus, who appeared to you on your way here, has sent me so that you may regain your sight and be filled with the Holy Spirit." 18And immediately something like scales fell from his eyes, and his sight was restored. Then he got up and was baptized, 19and after taking some food, he regained his strength.

Saul Preaches in Damascus

For several days he was with the disciples in Damascus, 20and immediately he began to proclaim Jesus in the synagogues, saying, "He is the Son of God." 21All who heard him were amazed and said, "Is not this the man who made havoc in Jerusalem among those who invoked this name? And has he not come here for the purpose of bringing them bound before the chief priests?" 22Saul became increasingly more powerful and confounded the Jews who lived in Damascus by proving that Jesus *c* was the Messiah. *d*

a Other ancient authorities lack *in a vision*
b Gk *him*   *c* Gk *that this*   *d* Or *the Christ*

9:1–22 *suddenly a light from heaven flashed around him.* Saul's conversion (see also 22:4–16; 26:9–18) exhibits the five parts of a Hellenistic conversion story: context (vv 1–2), catalysts (vv 3–6), counterforces (vv 7–9), conversion (vv 18–19), and confirmation of genuineness (vv 19–22). Ancients thought religious vocation was based on divine manifestation, here the risen Christ to Saul. The movement away from Jewish Christianity that began with Philip's ministry will be brought to completion by Paul. This passage is the first revelation of Christ outside Roman Palestine.

9:10–17 *a disciple in Damascus named Ananias.* Saul's conversion depends upon Ananias's obedience to his own vision: to help a great persecutor of Christians (vv 13–14). Ananias's faithfulness is highlighted in his first word to Saul: "Brother" (v 17). It is instructive to see how God directs and blesses through his people.

9:11 PRAYER—*See* Spiritual Disciplines Index.

9:18 *Then he got up and was baptized.* Baptism confirms reception of the gospel (cf. 2:41; 8:36).

Saul Escapes from the Jews

23 After some time had passed, the Jews plotted to kill him, 24but their plot became known to Saul. They were watching the gates day and night so that they might kill him; 25but his disciples took him by night and let him down through an opening in the wall,*a* lowering him in a basket.

Saul in Jerusalem

26 When he had come to Jerusalem, he attempted to join the disciples; and they were all afraid of him, for they did not believe that he was a disciple. 27But Barnabas took him, brought him to the apostles, and described for them how on the road he had seen the Lord, who had spoken to him, and how in Damascus he had spoken boldly in the name of Jesus. 28So he went in and out among them in Jerusalem, speaking boldly in the name of the Lord. 29He spoke and argued with the Hellenists; but they were attempting to kill him. 30When the believers*b* learned of it, they brought him down to Caesarea and sent him off to Tarsus.

31 Meanwhile the church throughout Judea, Galilee, and Samaria had peace and was built up. Living in the fear of the Lord and in the comfort of the Holy Spirit, it increased in numbers.

The Healing of Aeneas

32 Now as Peter went here and there among all the believers,*c* he came down also to the saints living in Lydda. 33There he found a man named Aeneas, who had been bedridden for eight years, for he was paralyzed. 34Peter said to him, "Aeneas, Jesus Christ heals you; get up and make your bed!" And immediately he got up. 35And all the residents of Lydda and Sharon saw him and turned to the Lord.

Peter in Lydda and Joppa

36 Now in Joppa there was a disciple whose name was Tabitha, which in Greek is Dorcas.*d* She was devoted to good works and acts of charity. 37At that time she became ill and died. When they had washed her, they laid her in a room upstairs. 38Since Lydda was near Joppa, the disciples, who heard that Peter was there, sent two men to him with the request, "Please come to us without delay." 39So Peter got up and went with them; and when he arrived, they took him to the room upstairs. All the widows stood beside him, weeping and showing tunics and other clothing that Dorcas had made while she was with them. 40Peter put all of them outside, and then he knelt down and prayed. He turned to

a Gk *through the wall*   *b* Gk *brothers*   *c* Gk *all of them*   *d* The name Tabitha in Aramaic and the name Dorcas in Greek mean *a gazelle*

9:26–27 *they were all afraid of him.* Saul goes to Jerusalem, to the "mother church," and is, justifiably, feared (see vv 1–2). Now it requires the courage and faithfulness of Barnabas to bring Saul into the fellowship.

9:29 *He spoke and argued with the Hellenists.* Educated in the Hellenistic city of Tarsus, Saul is well positioned to argue the gospel with Greek-speaking Jews. This prefigures his ministry in Greek cities of Asia Minor and Europe and reminds us that, although the gospel is not "culture bound," it must be presented in a way that people can understand.

9:30 *they . . . sent him off to Tarsus.* From Gal 1:15–18 we learn that Saul spends three years in Arabia, and here we learn that he flees to his old hometown of Tarsus for a number of years. It is approximately thirteen years from the time

of Saul's conversion until he reappears at Antioch (13:1). This is the hidden preparation through which God puts his ministers.

9:31 *the church . . . had peace and was built up.* A summary verse demonstrating fulfillment of Jesus' words in 1:8.

9:36 *there was a disciple whose name was Tabitha.* Tabitha/Dorcas and her friends represent early Christian women's communities. Perhaps she was leader of a group of widows (v 39; 1 Tim 5) for whom she took financial responsibility (Acts 2:44–45; 4:32–34). It is worth meditating on this woman Dorcas, who is described as a person "devoted to good works and acts of charity." She shows us the importance of the life of simple goodness in the kingdom of God.

the body and said, "Tabitha, get up." Then she opened her eyes, and seeing Peter, she sat up. 41He gave her his hand and helped her up. Then calling the saints and widows, he showed her to be alive. 42This became known throughout Joppa, and many believed in the Lord. 43Meanwhile he stayed in Joppa for some time with a certain Simon, a tanner.

Peter and Cornelius

10 In Caesarea there was a man named Cornelius, a centurion of the Italian Cohort, as it was called. 2He was a devout man who feared God with all his household; he gave alms generously to the people and prayed constantly to God. 3One afternoon at about three o'clock he had a vision in which he clearly saw an angel of God coming in and saying to him, "Cornelius." 4He stared at him in terror and said, "What is it, Lord?" He answered, "Your prayers and your alms have ascended as a memorial before God. 5Now send men to Joppa for a certain Simon who is called Peter; 6he is lodging with Simon, a tanner, whose house is by the sea-

side." 7When the angel who spoke to him had left, he called two of his slaves and a devout soldier from the ranks of those who served him, 8and after telling them everything, he sent them to Joppa.

9 About noon the next day, as they were on their journey and approaching the city, Peter went up on the roof to pray. 10He became hungry and wanted something to eat; and while it was being prepared, he fell into a trance. 11He saw the heaven opened and something like a large sheet coming down, being lowered to the ground by its four corners. 12In it were all kinds of four-footed creatures and reptiles and birds of the air. 13Then he heard a voice saying, "Get up, Peter; kill and eat." 14But Peter said, "By no means, Lord; for I have never eaten anything that is profane or unclean." 15The voice said to him again, a second time, "What God has made clean, you must not call profane." 16This happened three times, and the thing was suddenly taken up to heaven.

17 Now while Peter was greatly puzzled about what to make of the vision that he had

---

9:40 *Then she opened her eyes.* Jesus healed the sick and lame; the disciples heal the sick and lame by his Spirit. Just as Jesus raised the dead (Luke 7:11–17; 8:40–56), the disciples, of whom Peter is representative, raise the dead (see 1 Kings 17:17–24; 2 Kings 4:8–37). The power of Jesus continues in his Church.

9:43 *he stayed . . . with a certain Simon, a tanner.* Peter resided with a tanner, someone Jewish law regarded as ritually unclean because of his work with dead animals. Peter here is already breaking boundaries, a preparation for what is to come in chapter 10.

10:1–2 *a man named Cornelius.* Cornelius, a low-ranking Roman military officer, is a God-fearer whose spirituality (prayer and almsgiving) reflects Jewish practice.

Responding
10:2 PRAYER. Taking a cue from this verse and the apostle Paul to "pray without ceasing" (1 Thess 5:17), missionary to the Philippines Frank Laubach tried to think of God for at least a second of every minute, a practice he called "Game with Minutes." Today

try to call God to mind for at least a second of every minute. How successful were you? Did this experiment motivate you to think of God and his presence more often? *See also* Spiritual Disciplines Index.

10:3 *he had a vision.* An angelic vision is granted to a Gentile whose obedience (vv 7–8) leads to a "gentile Pentecost" (vv 44–48).

10:4 PRAYER—*See* Spiritual Disciplines Index.

10:9 *Peter went up on the roof to pray.* For the Church and for individuals, great turning points begin with prayer (e.g., 1:24; 6:6).

10:10–16 *He became hungry and . . . fell into a trance.* Fasting and prayer (v 9) are frequently associated with visions. Although hungry, Peter, an observant Jew, will not touch unclean foods. Peter explains his vision in 11:4–17.

10:17–23 *Peter was greatly puzzled about what to make of the vision.* This section unites the visions of Cornelius and Peter. Peter enters a Gentile's house, considered a defilement by Jews (see v 28). Advancement of the gospel sometimes requires Christians to step out of their "comfort zone."

seen, suddenly the men sent by Cornelius appeared. They were asking for Simon's house and were standing by the gate. [18]They called out to ask whether Simon, who was called Peter, was staying there. [19]While Peter was still thinking about the vision, the Spirit said to him, "Look, three men are searching for you. [20]Now get up, go down, and go with them without hesitation; for I have sent them." [21]So Peter went down to the men and said, "I am the one you are looking for; what is the reason for your coming?" [22]They answered, "Cornelius, a centurion, an upright and God-fearing man, who is well spoken of by the whole Jewish nation, was directed by a holy angel to send for you to come to his house and to hear what you have to say." [23]So Peter[b] invited them in and gave them lodging.

The next day he got up and went with them, and some of the believers[c] from Joppa accompanied him. [24]The following day they came to Caesarea. Cornelius was expecting them and had called together his relatives and close friends. [25]On Peter's arrival Cornelius met him, and falling at his feet, worshiped him. [26]But Peter made him get up, saying, "Stand up; I am only a mortal." [27]And as he talked with him, he went in and found that many had assembled; [28]and he said to them, "You yourselves know that it is unlawful for a Jew to associate with or to visit a Gentile; but God has shown me that I should not call anyone profane or unclean. [29]So when I was sent for, I came without objection. Now may I ask why you sent for me?"

30 Cornelius replied, "Four days ago at this very hour, at three o'clock, I was praying in my house when suddenly a man in dazzling clothes stood before me. [31]He said, 'Cornelius, your prayer has been heard and your alms have been remembered before God. [32]Send therefore to Joppa and ask for Simon, who is called Peter; he is staying in the home of Simon, a tanner, by the sea.' [33]Therefore I sent for you immediately, and you have been kind enough to come. So now all of us are here in the presence of God to listen to all that the Lord has commanded you to say."

Gentiles Hear the Good News

34 Then Peter began to speak to them: "I truly understand that God shows no partiality, [35]but in every nation anyone who fears him and does what is right is acceptable to him. [36]You know the message he sent to the people of Israel, preaching peace by Jesus Christ—he is Lord of all. [37]That message spread throughout Judea, beginning in Galilee after the baptism that John announced: [38]how God anointed Jesus of Nazareth with the Holy Spirit and with power; how he went about doing good and healing all who were oppressed by the devil, for God was with him. [39]We are witnesses to all that he did both in Judea and in Jerusalem. They put him to death by hanging him on a tree; [40]but God raised him on the third day and allowed him to appear, [41]not to all the people but to us who were chosen by God as witnesses, and who ate and drank with him after he rose from the dead. [42]He commanded us to preach to the people and to testify that he is the one ordained by God as judge of the living and the dead. [43]All the prophets testify about him that everyone who believes in him receives forgiveness of sins through his name."

Gentiles Receive the Holy Spirit

44 While Peter was still speaking, the Holy Spirit fell upon all who heard the word. [45]The circumcised believers who had come with Peter were astounded that the gift of the Holy

a One ancient authority reads *two*; others lack the word   *b* Gk *he*   *c* Gk *brothers*

10:34–43 *I truly understand that God shows no partiality.* This first line of Peter's sermon is one of Acts' great programmatic statements. God's heart is turned toward whoever rightly honors God and acts justly. The sermon goes on to summarize what Jesus did (vv 36–38), what

was done to Jesus (vv 39–40), and what Jesus wanted done (vv 41–43).

10:44–48 *the Holy Spirit fell upon all who heard the word.* A "gentile Pentecost" follows the Jewish (2:1–4) and Samaritan (8:17) ones. Symbolically, the Spirit has been given to all people.

Spirit had been poured out even on the Gentiles, [46]for they heard them speaking in tongues and extolling God. Then Peter said, [47]"Can anyone withhold the water for baptizing these people who have received the Holy Spirit just as we have?" [48]So he ordered them to be baptized in the name of Jesus Christ. Then they invited him to stay for several days.

Peter's Report to the Church at Jerusalem

11 Now the apostles and the believers[a] who were in Judea heard that the Gentiles had also accepted the word of God. [2]So when Peter went up to Jerusalem, the circumcised believers[b] criticized him, [3]saying, "Why did you go to uncircumcised men and eat with them?" [4]Then Peter began to explain it to them, step by step, saying, [5]"I was in the city of Joppa praying, and in a trance I saw a vision. There was something like a large sheet coming down from heaven, being lowered by its four corners; and it came close to me. [6]As I looked at it closely I saw four-footed animals, beasts of prey, reptiles, and birds of the air. [7]I also heard a voice saying to me, 'Get up, Peter; kill and eat.' [8]But I replied, 'By no means, Lord; for nothing profane or unclean has ever entered my mouth.' [9]But a second time the voice answered from heaven, 'What God has made clean, you must not call profane.' [10]This happened three times; then everything was pulled

up again to heaven. [11]At that very moment three men, sent to me from Caesarea, arrived at the house where we were. [12]The Spirit told me to go with them and not to make a distinction between them and us.[c] These six brothers also accompanied me, and we entered the man's house. [13]He told us how he had seen the angel standing in his house and saying, 'Send to Joppa and bring Simon, who is called Peter; [14]he will give you a message by which you and your entire household will be saved.' [15]And as I began to speak, the Holy Spirit fell upon them just as it had upon us at the beginning. [16]And I remembered the word of the Lord, how he had said, 'John baptized with water, but you will be baptized with the Holy Spirit.' [17]If then God gave them the same gift that he gave us when we believed in the Lord Jesus Christ, who was I that I could hinder God?" [18]When they heard this, they were silenced. And they praised God, saying, "Then God has given even to the Gentiles the repentance that leads to life."

The Church in Antioch

[19] Now those who were scattered because of the persecution that took place over Stephen traveled as far as Phoenicia, Cyprus, and Antioch, and they spoke the word to no one except Jews. [20]But among them were

a Gk brothers   b Gk lacks believers.   c Or not to hesitate

11:2 *Peter went up to Jerusalem.* Jerusalem is the locus of church authority. Peter returns there to justify his mission in Caesarea, just as he had gone to Samaria to legitimate Philip's work (8:14).

11:3 *Why did you go to uncircumcised men and eat with them?* When God moves in new and unfamiliar ways, not everyone is overjoyed. As we sometimes do, early Christians struggled to understand the new things God was doing.

11:5 PRAYER—See Spiritual Disciplines Index.

11:17 THE WITH-GOD LIFE—See Spiritual Disciplines Index.

11:17 *If then God gave them the same gift that he gave us.* Peter realizes his vision (10:9–16) is not about food, but people. The full import of his original experience needed time to develop and be understood. Often we understand the

spiritual meaning of events in retrospect.

11:18 *God has given even to the Gentiles the repentance that leads to life.* The stress falls on "even." Peter convinces the Jerusalem church of the truth of 10:34, that God truly shows no partiality. What appeared to be an "exception" charts the Church's future. An example of similar inclusivity follows in 11:19–24.

11:19–26 *those who were scattered because of the persecution . . . traveled as far as Phoenicia.* Persecution again spreads the gospel, which is still preached only to Jews. But some non-Judean Jews spoke to Greeks, who caught fire at the word of God. Barnabas is sent from Jerusalem to check this out; he sees that this is God's work and that brother Saul is just the man needed here, and he brings him in.

some men of Cyprus and Cyrene who, on coming to Antioch, spoke to the Hellenists *a* also, proclaiming the Lord Jesus. ²¹The hand of the Lord was with them, and a great number became believers and turned to the Lord. ²²News of this came to the ears of the church in Jerusalem, and they sent Barnabas to Antioch. ²³When he came and saw the grace of God, he rejoiced, and he exhorted them all to remain faithful to the Lord with steadfast devotion; ²⁴for he was a good man, full of the Holy Spirit and of faith. And a great many people were brought to the Lord. ²⁵Then Barnabas went to Tarsus to look for Saul, ²⁶and when he had found him, he brought him to Antioch. So it was that for an entire year they met with *b* the church and taught a great many people, and it was in Antioch that the disciples were first called "Christians."

27 At that time prophets came down from Jerusalem to Antioch. ²⁸One of them named Agabus stood up and predicted by the Spirit that there would be a severe famine over all the world; and this took place during the reign of Claudius. ²⁹The disciples determined that according to their ability, each would send relief to the believers *c* living in Judea; ³⁰this they did, sending it to the elders by Barnabas and Saul.

James Killed and Peter Imprisoned

12 About that time King Herod laid violent hands upon some who belonged to the church. ²He had James, the brother of John, killed with the sword. ³After he saw that it pleased the Jews, he proceeded to arrest Peter also. (This was during the festival of Unleavened Bread.) ⁴When he had seized him, he put him in prison and handed him over to four squads of soldiers to guard him, intending to bring him out to the people after the Passover. ⁵While Peter was kept in prison, the church prayed fervently to God for him.

Peter Delivered from Prison

6 The very night before Herod was going to bring him out, Peter, bound with two chains, was sleeping between two soldiers, while guards in front of the door were keeping watch over the prison. ⁷Suddenly an angel of the Lord appeared and a light shone in the cell. He tapped Peter on the side and woke him, saying, "Get up quickly." And the chains fell off his wrists. ⁸The angel said to him, "Fasten your belt and put on your sandals." He did so. Then he said to him, "Wrap your cloak around you and follow me." ⁹Peter *d* went out and followed him; he did not realize that what was happening with the angel's help was real; he thought he was seeing a vision. ¹⁰After they had passed the first and the second guard, they came before the iron gate leading into the city. It opened for them of its own accord, and they went outside and walked along a lane, when suddenly the

a Other ancient authorities read *Greeks*
b Or *were guests of*   *c* Gk *brothers*   *d* Gk *He*

11:21 THE WITH-GOD LIFE—*See* Spiritual Disciplines Index.

11:26 *in Antioch . . . the disciples were first called "Christians."* In a gentile city, the third largest in the empire and one known for the worship of Artemis and Apollo, the followers of Jesus are first called Christians.

11:28 *predicted by the Spirit.* The first mention of the gift of prophecy in Acts (cf. 21:8–10; 3:1; 15:32; Rom 12:6; 1 Cor 12:10). Some Christians could see and speak from God's point of view.

11:29–30 *each would send relief to the believers living in Judea.* Another example of Christians' mutual responsibility. The verses introduce the "collection," a benevolence dear to Paul, who exhorted gentile Christians to send financial support to their poorer brethren in Judea, who, in their spiritual riches, had offered *them* the heritage of Israel and the gospel. The image is of reciprocity (see 2 Cor 8–9).

12:1–3 *King Herod laid violent hands upon some who belonged to the church.* New persecution under Herod Agrippa I (AD 41–44) is aimed at Christian leaders in Jerusalem. James is the first of the Twelve to be martyred. The Church makes no attempt to reconstitute the Twelve (cf. 1:12–26). Christians leaders must accept what comes as the result of their public role.

12:5 PRAYER—*See* Spiritual Disciplines Index.

BARNABAS

The Encourager

Selected Scriptures: *Acts 4:36–37; 9:26–27; 11:19–30; 13:1–14; 13:42–15:41; Colossians 4:10*

We don't learn a lot about Barnabas, and initially he appears as a fairly minor New Testament character, taking a backseat to Paul and disappearing from mention once he and Paul separate. Yet when we take a closer look, we see a man whose quiet focus on others must have elevated him greatly in God's eyes, someone who serves us still as a model for selfless, humble servanthood.

The apostles nicknamed him "Barnabas," or "son of encouragement." We first see Barnabas selling a field and bringing the money to the apostles to be used for others in need (Acts 4:37). Later we see him encouraging the believers in Jerusalem to accept Paul into their fellowship, despite Paul's history of persecuting followers of Christ (9:27). Both Paul and Barnabas then travel to Antioch, encouraging the new gentile believers to remain faithful. The pair spend a year teaching and caring for the Christians of this new church, and Barnabas is described as "a good man, full of the Holy Spirit and of faith" (11:24).

The church in Antioch then commissions Barnabas and Paul at the Lord's command to travel, proclaiming Jesus throughout the region: "Set apart for me Barnabas and Saul for the work to which I have called them" (Acts 13:2). John Mark, a young member of the church and probably the writer of the second Gospel, joins them for a short time. Paul and Barnabas preach boldly and experience success as well as persecution. They return to Antioch, where they "strengthened the souls of the disciples and encouraged them to continue in the faith" (14:22).

The last time Barnabas and Paul minister together, they bring a letter of instruction concerning circumcision from Jerusalem to Antioch (Acts 15:30). However, as they prepare to leave, they disagree over whether to take John Mark with them in their continuing travels (he previously deserted them), and so they separate, with Paul taking Silas and Barnabas taking John Mark. We don't hear of Barnabas again.

As quietly as he enters Acts, he disappears, and we don't learn anything more about his service. Yet even in this aspect we hear echoes of Jesus: "Whoever wishes to be great among you must be your servant" (Matt 20:26). We never hear from Barnabas, but we do discover that his confidence in John Mark was well founded. Besides traditionally being identified as the author of the second Gospel, Mark is likely the one later positively commended by Paul himself in one of his final Letters, "Get Mark and bring him with you, for he is useful in my ministry" (2 Tim 4:11).

Barnabas stood up for those, like Paul and Mark, who lacked the support of others. He faithfully opened his arms to gentile churches despite the difficulty for a Jew

PROFILE: BARNABAS

in this period of great change. And he willingly moved on in service to God when it meant leaving a good friend and ministry partner to support another whom he felt God desired to use.

When we think of those in our life who have impacted us most deeply, isn't it often a person like Barnabas who has believed in us and supported us when we sorely needed it? Isn't it often one who, as Barnabas did, "strengthened [our] souls . . . and encouraged [us] to continue in the faith" (Acts 14:22)? We also can follow the example that Barnabas left, encouraging others as a way of life, becoming a servant to all people, an advocate for God's redemption and love.

John Sloan writes in *The Barnabas Way:* "Jesus made it clear that one who is pure in heart and one who is merciful will see and experience God—like Barnabas. . . . The best way to receive from God may just be to give to those who need help—as Barnabas did."

Personal Reflection

- If your friends were to give you a nickname, what would it be? What would you like it to be?
- In a society that is largely self-focused, what helps you focus on the needs of others rather than dwelling on your own needs? How have you met God in a new way through your service to others?
- Barnabas could be characterized as a giver—he gave of his money, his time, his energy, and his position. Which of these types of giving is most difficult for you? In what way might God be asking you to give right now?

angel left him. [11] Then Peter came to himself and said, "Now I am sure that the Lord has sent his angel and rescued me from the hands of Herod and from all that the Jewish people were expecting."

12 As soon as he realized this, he went to the house of Mary, the mother of John whose other name was Mark, where many had gathered and were praying. [13] When he knocked at the outer gate, a maid named Rhoda came to answer. [14] On recognizing Peter's voice, she was so overjoyed that, instead of opening the gate, she ran in and announced that Peter was standing at the gate. [15] They said to her, "You are out of your mind!" But she insisted that it was so. They said, "It is his angel." [16] Meanwhile Peter continued knocking; and when they opened the gate, they saw him and were amazed. [17] He motioned to them with his hand to be silent, and described for them how the Lord had brought him out of the prison. And he added, "Tell this to James and to the believers." [a] Then he left and went to another place.

18 When morning came, there was no small commotion among the soldiers over what had become of Peter. [19] When Herod had searched for him and could not find him, he examined the guards and ordered them to be put to death. Then he went down from Judea to Caesarea and stayed there.

The Death of Herod

20 Now Herod [b] was angry with the people of Tyre and Sidon. So they came to him in a body; and after winning over Blastus, the king's chamberlain, they asked for a reconciliation, because their country depended on the king's country for food. [21] On an appointed day Herod put on his royal robes, took his seat on the platform, and delivered a public address to them. [22] The people kept

a Gk *brothers*   *b* Gk *he*

12:11–12 *Then Peter came to himself.* As with his vision, Peter does not immediately understand what is happening. After his miraculous release, he immediately seeks Christian community, a frequent pattern in Acts pointing to the necessity of Christian fellowship.

shouting, "The voice of a god, and not of a mortal!" 23And immediately, because he had not given the glory to God, an angel of the Lord struck him down, and he was eaten by worms and died.

24 But the word of God continued to advance and gain adherents. 25Then after completing their mission Barnabas and Saul returned to*a* Jerusalem and brought with them John, whose other name was Mark.

Barnabas and Saul Commissioned

13 Now in the church at Antioch there were prophets and teachers: Barnabas, Simeon who was called Niger, Lucius of Cyrene, Manaen a member of the court of Herod the ruler,*b* and Saul. 2While they were worshiping the Lord and fasting, the Holy Spirit said, "Set apart for me Barnabas and Saul for the work to which I have called them." 3Then after fasting and praying they laid their hands on them and sent them off.

The Apostles Preach in Cyprus

4 So, being sent out by the Holy Spirit, they went down to Seleucia; and from there they sailed to Cyprus. 5When they arrived at Salamis, they proclaimed the word of God in the synagogues of the Jews. And they had John also to assist them. 6When they had gone through the whole island as far as Paphos, they met a certain magician, a Jewish false prophet, named Bar-Jesus. 7He was with the proconsul, Sergius Paulus, an intelligent man, who summoned Barnabas and Saul and wanted to hear the word of God. 8But the magician Elymas (for that is the translation of his name) opposed them and tried to turn the proconsul away from the faith. 9But Saul, also known as Paul, filled with the Holy Spirit, looked intently at him 10and said, "You son of the devil, you enemy of all righteousness, full of all deceit and villainy, will you not

a Other ancient authorities read *from*
b Gk *tetrarch*

12:20–23 *an angel of the Lord struck him down.* Herod's death (AD 44) exemplifies Luke's concern with "secular" history. Herod accepts acclaim proper only to God and suffers the consequences.

13:1–3 *in the church at Antioch there were prophets and teachers.* This marks the great turn of the Church to missions. It is worth pondering why at this point the new community is able to reach out with conscious, voluntary effort—not just as a result of being scattered by persecution as in 8:4—in an attempt to reach all people according to Matt 28:19–20? It is because only now do the disciples of Jesus understand that all peoples are equally precious to God and are welcome to enter into this all-inclusive community. In the Antiochene church a number of people ("prophets and teachers") have been constantly working together over a lengthy period of time. During periods of "worshiping and fasting" an impression grows that Barnabas and Saul have a special work to do. And the group response to this impression is fasting, prayer, and the laying on of hands.

Responding
13:1–3 WORSHIP. In this passage we see worship, prayer, and fasting as integral to the selection and installation of Barnabas and Saul as missionaries. Today worship and prayer are common in the ordination of pastors and installation of missionaries, but fasting is not. Why do you think fasting has been dropped from the preparation for these times of consecration? How possible would it be for you to suggest that fasting be part of the next ordination or installation service in your fellowship? *See also* Spiritual Disciplines Index.

13:3 PRAYER—*See* Spiritual Disciplines Index.

13:4 *they went down to Seleucia.* The beginning of Paul's first missionary journey (13:4–14:28), which lasts two years and covers about fourteen hundred miles through Cyprus and Asia Minor. Paul, demonstrating his authority, heals by the power of the Spirit and first preaches in synagogues (13:14, 44), turning elsewhere when rejected there (13:46, 51; 19:8–9).

13:6–12 *But the magician Elymas . . . opposed them.* Paul's encounter with Elymas parallels Philip's with Simon (8:9–13). There are many spiritual powers, some malign. Paul's (and the Christians') power is from the Spirit.

stop making crooked the straight paths of the Lord? [11]And now listen—the hand of the Lord is against you, and you will be blind for a while, unable to see the sun." Immediately mist and darkness came over him, and he went about groping for someone to lead him by the hand. [12]When the proconsul saw what had happened, he believed, for he was astonished at the teaching about the Lord.

Paul and Barnabas in Antioch of Pisidia

[13] Then Paul and his companions set sail from Paphos and came to Perga in Pamphylia. John, however, left them and returned to Jerusalem; [14]but they went on from Perga and came to Antioch in Pisidia. And on the sabbath day they went into the synagogue and sat down. [15]After the reading of the law and the prophets, the officials of the synagogue sent them a message, saying, "Brothers, if you have any word of exhortation for the people, give it." [16]So Paul stood up and with a gesture began to speak:

"You Israelites, [a] and others who fear God, listen. [17]The God of this people Israel chose our ancestors and made the people great during their stay in the land of Egypt, and with uplifted arm he led them out of it. [18]For about forty years he put up with [b] them in the wilderness. [19]After he had destroyed seven nations in the land of Canaan, he gave them their land as an inheritance [20]for about four hundred fifty years. After that he gave them judges until the time of the prophet Samuel. [21]Then they asked for a king; and God gave them Saul son of Kish, a man of the tribe of Benjamin, who reigned for forty years. [22]When he had removed him, he made David their king. In his testimony about him he said, 'I have found David, son of Jesse, to be a man after my heart, who will carry out all my wishes.' [23]Of this man's posterity God has brought to Israel a Savior, Jesus, as he promised; [24]before his coming John had already proclaimed a baptism of repentance to all the people of Israel. [25]And as John was finishing his work, he said, 'What do you suppose that I am? I am not he. No, but one is coming after me; I am not worthy to untie the thong of the sandals [c] on his feet.'

[26] "My brothers, you descendants of Abraham's family, and others who fear God, to us [d] the message of this salvation has been sent. [27]Because the residents of Jerusalem and their leaders did not recognize him or understand the words of the prophets that are read every sabbath, they fulfilled those words by condemning him. [28]Even though they found no cause for a sentence of death, they asked Pilate to have him killed. [29]When they had carried out everything that was written about him, they took him down from the tree and laid him in a tomb. [30]But God raised him from the dead; [31]and for many days he appeared to those who came up with him from Galilee to Jerusalem, and they are now his witnesses to the people. [32]And we bring you the good news that what God promised to our ancestors [33]he has fulfilled for us, their children, by raising Jesus; as also it is written in the second psalm,

'You are my Son;
    today I have begotten you.'

[34]As to his raising him from the dead, no more to return to corruption, he has spoken in this way,

'I will give you the holy promises made
    to David.'

[35]Therefore he has also said in another psalm,

'You will not let your Holy One
    experience corruption.'

[36]For David, after he had served the purpose of God in his own generation, died, [e] was laid beside his ancestors, and experienced corruption; [37]but he whom God raised up experienced no corruption. [38]Let it be known to

a Gk Men, Israelites   b Other ancient authorities read cared for   c Gk untie the sandals   d Other ancient authorities read you   e Gk fell asleep

---

13:11 THE WITH-GOD LIFE—See Spiritual Disciplines Index.

13:14–15 on the sabbath day they went into the synagogue. Paul's mission is in continuity with his Jewish roots. These verses reflect contemporary synagogue practice. In his sermon, Paul explains how Israel's history prepared for Jesus (vv 16–41). Paul's own life had prepared him for this mission.

Words of Encouragement (handwritten)

you therefore, my brothers, that through this man forgiveness of sins is proclaimed to you; [39]by this Jesus[a] everyone who believes is set free from all those sins[b] from which you could not be freed by the law of Moses. [40]Beware, therefore, that what the prophets said does not happen to you:

[41] 'Look, you scoffers!
　　Be amazed and perish,
　for in your days I am doing a work,
　　a work that you will never believe,
　　　even if someone tells you.' "

42　As Paul and Barnabas[c] were going out, the people urged them to speak about these things again the next sabbath. [43]When the meeting of the synagogue broke up, many Jews and devout converts to Judaism followed Paul and Barnabas, who spoke to them and urged them to continue in the grace of God.

44　The next sabbath almost the whole city gathered to hear the word of the Lord.[d] [45]But when the Jews saw the crowds, they were filled with jealousy; and blaspheming, they contradicted what was spoken by Paul. [46]Then both Paul and Barnabas spoke out boldly, saying, "It was necessary that the word of God should be spoken first to you. Since you reject it and judge yourselves to be unworthy of eternal life, we are now turning to the Gentiles. [47]For so the Lord has commanded us, saying,

　'I have set you to be a light for the
　　Gentiles,
　so that you may bring salvation to the
　　ends of the earth.' "

48　When the Gentiles heard this, they were glad and praised the word of the Lord; and as many as had been destined for eternal life became believers. [49]Thus the word of the Lord spread throughout the region. [50]But the Jews incited the devout women of high standing and the leading men of the city, and stirred up persecution against Paul and Barnabas, and drove them out of their region. [51]So they shook the dust off their feet in protest against them, and went to Iconium. [52]And the disciples were filled with joy and with the Holy Spirit.

Paul and Barnabas in Iconium

14 The same thing occurred in Iconium, where Paul and Barnabas[c] went into the Jewish synagogue and spoke in such a way that a great number of both Jews and Greeks became believers. [2]But the unbelieving Jews stirred up the Gentiles and poisoned their minds against the brothers. [3]So they remained for a long time, speaking boldly for the Lord, who testified to the word of his grace by granting signs and wonders to be done through them. [4]But the residents of the city were divided; some sided with the Jews, and some with the apostles. [5]And when an attempt was made by both Gentiles and Jews, with their rulers, to mistreat them and to stone them, [6]the apostles[c] learned of it and fled to Lystra and Derbe, cities of Lycaonia, and to the surrounding country; [7]and there they continued proclaiming the good news.

Paul and Barnabas in Lystra and Derbe

8　In Lystra there was a man sitting who could not use his feet and had never walked, for he had been crippled from birth. [9]He listened to Paul as he was speaking. And Paul, looking at him intently and seeing that he had faith to be healed, [10]said in a loud voice, "Stand upright on your feet." And the man[e] sprang up and began to walk. [11]When the crowds saw what Paul had done, they shouted in the Lycaonian language, "The gods have come down

a Gk this　　b Gk all　　c Gk they　　d Other ancient authorities read God　　e Gk he

---

13:38—39 *by this Jesus everyone who believes is set free.* The Pauline gospel in miniature (expanded in Galatians and Romans). The law makes one aware of sin; only Jesus liberates from it.

13:46 *we are now turning to the Gentiles.* A programmatic verse indicating the direction of Paul's future ministry (cf. 18:6).

14:1 *both Jews and Greeks became believers.* As in Pisidian Antioch, Paul's ministry in Iconium was successful until unbelieving Jews embittered Gentiles against him (cf. 14:19). Luke often depicts Jews as Paul's opponents and Gentiles as his protectors (see the Introduction).

14:3 *granting signs and wonders.* Preaching is confirmed by miracles.

to us in human form!" [12]Barnabas they called Zeus, and Paul they called Hermes, because he was the chief speaker. [13]The priest of Zeus, whose temple was just outside the city,[a] brought oxen and garlands to the gates; he and the crowds wanted to offer sacrifice. [14]When the apostles Barnabas and Paul heard of it, they tore their clothes and rushed out into the crowd, shouting, [15]"Friends,[b] why are you doing this? We are mortals just like you, and we bring you good news, that you should turn from these worthless things to the living God, who made the heaven and the earth and the sea and all that is in them. [16]In past generations he allowed all the nations to follow their own ways; [17]yet he has not left himself without a witness in doing good—giving you rains from heaven and fruitful seasons, and filling you with food and your hearts with joy." [18]Even with these words, they scarcely restrained the crowds from offering sacrifice to them.

19 But Jews came there from Antioch and Iconium and won over the crowds. Then they stoned Paul and dragged him out of the city, supposing that he was dead. [20]But when the disciples surrounded him, he got up and went into the city. The next day he went on with Barnabas to Derbe.

The Return to Antioch in Syria

21 After they had proclaimed the good news to that city and had made many disciples, they returned to Lystra, then on to Iconium and Antioch. [22]There they strengthened the souls of the disciples and encouraged them to continue in the faith, saying, "It is through many persecutions that we must enter the kingdom of God." [23]And after they had appointed elders for them in each church, with prayer and fasting they entrusted them to the Lord in whom they had come to believe.

24 Then they passed through Pisidia and came to Pamphylia. [25]When they had spoken the word in Perga, they went down to Attalia. [26]From there they sailed back to Antioch, where they had been commended to the grace of God for the work[c] that they had completed. [27]When they arrived, they called the church together and related all that God had done with them, and how he had opened a door of faith for the Gentiles. [28]And they stayed there with the disciples for some time.

The Council at Jerusalem

15 Then certain individuals came down from Judea and were teaching the brothers, "Unless you are circumcised according to the custom of Moses, you cannot be saved." [2]And after Paul and Barnabas had

a Or *The priest of Zeus-Outside-the-City*
b Gk *Men*   c Or *committed in the grace of God to the work*

14:8–20 *The gods have come down to us in human form!* This passage parallels the experience of Peter and John (3:1–4:31). The story accurately reflects the Hellenistic religious environment (vv 11–13). As today, religious culture was pluralistic and many spiritual "choices" were available, so clear presentation of the gospel was crucial.

14:22 *they strengthened the souls of the disciples.* Paul supposed that the purpose of ministry was to "equip the saints" (Eph 4:12–13). We are commanded not only to make disciples, but also to teach them to obey everything that Jesus commanded (Matt 28:20). This is today the "Great Omission from the Great Commission" in many churches.

14:23 PRAYER—*See* Spiritual Disciplines Index.

14:27 THE WITH-GOD LIFE—*See* Spiritual Disciplines Index.

14:27 *they called the church together.* The early Church's missionaries are eager to maintain contact with and report to their "sending church." Paul understands God has opened the way for Gentiles to come to faith.

15:1–31 *Unless you are circumcised.* In this report of the critical Jerusalem council, the surface issue is whether one must first be a Jew in order to be Christian. The deeper issue is how Jewish and gentile believers can share fellowship. Jews maintained a strict lifestyle and were generally suspicious of Gentiles, as Gentiles were of them. Now both groups have been baptized into Christ. Characteristically, the church gathers (v 22); representatives of different viewpoints speak (vv 5, 7, 12); and a compromise is found

no small dissension and debate with them, Paul and Barnabas and some of the others were appointed to go up to Jerusalem to discuss this question with the apostles and the elders. ³So they were sent on their way by the church, and as they passed through both Phoenicia and Samaria, they reported the conversion of the Gentiles, and brought great joy to all the believers. ᵃ ⁴When they came to Jerusalem, they were welcomed by the church and the apostles and the elders, and they reported all that God had done with them. ⁵But some believers who belonged to the sect of the Pharisees stood up and said, "It is necessary for them to be circumcised and ordered to keep the law of Moses."

6 The apostles and the elders met together to consider this matter. ⁷After there had been much debate, Peter stood up and said to them, "My brothers, ᵇ you know that in the early days God made a choice among you, that I should be the one through whom the Gentiles would hear the message of the good news and become believers. ⁸And God, who knows the human heart, testified to them by giving them the Holy Spirit, just as he did to us; ⁹and in cleansing their hearts by faith he has made no distinction between them and us. ¹⁰Now therefore why are you putting God to the test by placing on the neck of the disciples a yoke that neither our ancestors nor we have been able to bear? ¹¹On the contrary, we believe that we will be saved through the grace of the Lord Jesus, just as they will."

12 The whole assembly kept silence, and listened to Barnabas and Paul as they told of all the signs and wonders that God had done through them among the Gentiles. ¹³After they finished speaking, James replied, "My brothers, ᵇ listen to me. ¹⁴Simeon has related how God first looked favorably on the Gentiles, to take from among them a people for his name. ¹⁵This agrees with the words of the prophets, as it is written,

¹⁶ 'After this I will return,
    and I will rebuild the dwelling of David,
        which has fallen;
    from its ruins I will rebuild it,
        and I will set it up,
¹⁷ so that all other peoples may seek the
        Lord—
    even all the Gentiles over whom my
        name has been called.
    Thus says the Lord, who has been
        making these things ¹⁸known
    from long ago.' ᶜ

¹⁹Therefore I have reached the decision that we should not trouble those Gentiles who are turning to God, ²⁰but we should write to them to abstain only from things polluted by idols and from fornication and from whatever has been strangled ᵈ and from blood. ²¹For in every city, for generations past, Moses has had those who proclaim him, for he has been read aloud every sabbath in the synagogues."

The Council's Letter to Gentile Believers

22 Then the apostles and the elders, with the consent of the whole church, decided to choose men from among their members ᵉ

a Gk brothers   b Gk Men, brothers   c Other ancient authorities read things. ¹⁸Known to God from of old are all his works.'   d Other ancient authorities lack and from whatever has been strangled   e Gk from among them

---

in which Gentiles do not have to be circumcised, but they must avoid idolatry and unchastity and not eat strangled animals or those with blood (v 20). The Gentiles must observe two moral and two ritual rules that will make fellowship with Jews possible. Church unity is maintained across a great cultural divide in a wonderful example of compromise.

Responding
15:12 THE WITH-GOD LIFE. It is interesting that the author of Acts reports that Barnabas and Paul didn't take credit for the signs and wonders, but rather gave credit to God. It would have been easy for them to have taken the credit, because none of those on the council were present when people were cured of diseases and demons were cast out. Why did Barnabas and Paul report that God worked through them to perform the signs and wonders? How tempted would you be to claim credit if God suddenly used you to perform miracles? *See also* Spiritual Disciplines Index.

and to send them to Antioch with Paul and Barnabas. They sent Judas called Barsabbas, and Silas, leaders among the brothers, 23with the following letter: "The brothers, both the apostles and the elders, to the believers*a* of Gentile origin in Antioch and Syria and Cilicia, greetings. 24Since we have heard that certain persons who have gone out from us, though with no instructions from us, have said things to disturb you and have unsettled your minds,*b* 25we have decided unanimously to choose representatives*c* and send them to you, along with our beloved Barnabas and Paul, 26who have risked their lives for the sake of our Lord Jesus Christ. 27We have therefore sent Judas and Silas, who themselves will tell you the same things by word of mouth. 28For it has seemed good to the Holy Spirit and to us to impose on you no further burden than these essentials: 29that you abstain from what has been sacrificed to idols and from blood and from what is strangled*d* and from fornication. If you keep yourselves from these, you will do well. Farewell."

30 So they were sent off and went down to Antioch. When they gathered the congregation together, they delivered the letter. 31When its members*e* read it, they rejoiced at the exhortation. 32Judas and Silas, who were themselves prophets, said much to encourage and strengthen the believers.*a* 33After they had been there for some time, they were sent off in peace by the believers*a* to those who had sent them.*f* 35But Paul and Barnabas remained in Antioch, and there, with many others, they taught and proclaimed the word of the Lord.

Paul and Barnabas Separate

36 After some days Paul said to Barnabas, "Come, let us return and visit the believers*a* in every city where we proclaimed the word of the Lord and see how they are doing." 37Barnabas wanted to take with them John called Mark. 38But Paul decided not to take with them one who had deserted them in Pamphylia and had not accompanied them in the work. 39The disagreement became so sharp that they parted company; Barnabas took Mark with him and sailed away to Cyprus. 40But Paul chose Silas and set out, the believers*a* commending him to the grace of the Lord. 41He went through Syria and Cilicia, strengthening the churches.

Timothy Joins Paul and Silas

16 Paul*g* went on also to Derbe and to Lystra, where there was a disciple named Timothy, the son of a Jewish woman who was a believer; but his father was a Greek. 2He was well spoken of by the believers*a* in Lystra and Iconium. 3Paul wanted Timothy to accompany him; and he took him and had him circumcised because of the Jews who were in those places, for they all knew that his father was a Greek. 4As they went from town to town, they delivered to them for observance the decisions that had been reached by the apostles and elders who were in Jerusalem. 5So the churches were strengthened in the faith and increased in numbers daily.

Paul's Vision of the Man of Macedonia

6 They went through the region of Phrygia and Galatia, having been forbidden by

a Gk *brothers*   *b* Other ancient authorities add saying, 'You must be circumcised and keep the law,' *c* Gk *men*   *d* Other ancient authorities lack *and from what is strangled*   *e* Gk *When they* *f* Other ancient authorities add verse 34, *But it seemed good to Silas to remain there*   *g* Gk *He*

15:39 *The disagreement became so sharp that they parted company.* Apostles disagreed, sometimes strongly. Because John Mark had abandoned the mission in Perga (13:13), Paul refused to take him on a second journey; thus the split with Barnabas. Happily Col 4:10 suggests this rift was healed. A divine call does not exclude human friction and difficulty with other believers, or the responsibility to address both.

16:1–3 *Timothy, the son of a Jewish woman; . . . his father was a Greek.* Timothy, one of Paul's most important associates (Phil 2:19–24), is coauthor of several Letters (2 Cor 1:1; Phil 1:1; Col 1:1; 1 Thess 1:1; 2 Thess 1:1) and apparent recipient of two (1 & 2 Timothy). His own culturally mixed family prepared him for work in the Greek cities. Like Paul, Timothy exemplifies God's economy, in which no experience is wasted.

the Holy Spirit to speak the word in Asia. [7]When they had come opposite Mysia, they attempted to go into Bithynia, but the Spirit of Jesus did not allow them; [8]so, passing by Mysia, they went down to Troas. [9]During the night Paul had a vision: there stood a man of Macedonia pleading with him and saying, "Come over to Macedonia and help us." [10]When he had seen the vision, we immediately tried to cross over to Macedonia, being convinced that God had called us to proclaim the good news to them.

The Conversion of Lydia

11 We set sail from Troas and took a straight course to Samothrace, the following day to Neapolis, [12]and from there to Philippi, which is a leading city of the district[a] of Macedonia and a Roman colony. We remained in this city for some days. [13]On the sabbath day we went outside the gate by the river, where we supposed there was a place of prayer; and we sat down and spoke to the women who had gathered there. [14]A certain woman named Lydia, a worshiper of God, was listening to us; she was from the city of Thyatira and a dealer in purple cloth. The Lord opened her heart to listen eagerly to what was said by Paul. [15]When she and her household were baptized, she urged us, saying, "If you have judged me to be faithful to the Lord, come and stay at my home." And she prevailed upon us.

Paul and Silas in Prison

16 One day, as we were going to the place of prayer, we met a slave-girl who had a spirit of divination and brought her owners a great deal of money by fortune-telling. [17]While she followed Paul and us, she would cry out, "These men are slaves of the Most High God, who proclaim to you[b] a way of salvation." [18]She kept doing this for many days. But Paul, very much annoyed, turned and said to the spirit, "I order you in the name of Jesus Christ to come out of her." And it came out that very hour.

19 But when her owners saw that their hope of making money was gone, they seized Paul and Silas and dragged them into the marketplace before the authorities. [20]When they had brought them before the magistrates, they said, "These men are disturbing our city; they are Jews [21]and are advocating

---

a Other authorities read *a city of the first district*
b Other ancient authorities read *to us*

16:6–8 *They went through the region of Phrygia and Galatia.* These verses subtly suggest that the disruptions of 15:36–41 caused difficulties in the mission. Human frailty impedes God's work.

16:9–10 *Paul had a vision.* Paul's vision indicates God directed the missionary advance into Europe. Verse 10 begins the "we source" (see the Introduction) some scholars think reflects Luke's travel notes.

16:11 *We set sail from Troas.* The beginning of Paul's second missionary journey (16:11–18:22), which lasted three years and covered about two thousand miles. Paul visits Greek cities to which he addressed letters: Philippi, Thessalonica, Corinth, Ephesus.

16:13 PRAYER—*See* Spiritual Disciplines Index.

16:13 *On the sabbath day . . . we sat down and spoke to the women.* Paul preached on the Sabbath (13:14, 44; 17:2). Greeks experienced places of "living water" as holy. Philippi must not have had ten Jewish males to make a synagogue.

By preaching to women in this context, Paul transcended his own cultural barriers and founded the first European church among women. Its leader was clearly Lydia (16:14–15, 40), to whose house church the Philippian Letter may have been sent.

16:14 WORSHIP—*See* Spiritual Disciplines Index.

16:14 *The Lord opened her heart.* Conversions are God's work. Paul preached, but God opened Lydia's heart. A God-fearer like Cornelius, she was an independent businesswoman, a dealer in the purple cloth worn by Roman nobility.

16:16 *we met a slave-girl who had a spirit of divination.* Christians encountered "spiritual powers" (see 8:9; 13:8). Paul and associates meet a slave with a "Pythian spirit." (The Greek text is literally "pneuma pythona." The Python was the symbol of the Delphic oracle.) Her owner uses her "gift" for profit. When Paul exorcises her, the owner loses money and for this reason has the Christians arrested (v 19).

customs that are not lawful for us as Romans to adopt or observe." [22]The crowd joined in attacking them, and the magistrates had them stripped of their clothing and ordered them to be beaten with rods. [23]After they had given them a severe flogging, they threw them into prison and ordered the jailer to keep them securely. [24]Following these instructions, he put them in the innermost cell and fastened their feet in the stocks.

[25] About midnight Paul and Silas were praying and singing hymns to God, and the prisoners were listening to them. [26]Suddenly there was an earthquake, so violent that the foundations of the prison were shaken; and immediately all the doors were opened and everyone's chains were unfastened. [27]When the jailer woke up and saw the prison doors wide open, he drew his sword and was about to kill himself, since he supposed that the prisoners had escaped. [28]But Paul shouted in a loud voice, "Do not harm yourself, for we are all here." [29]The jailer[a] called for lights, and rushing in, he fell down trembling before Paul and Silas. [30]Then he brought them outside and said, "Sirs, what must I do to be saved?" [31]They answered, "Believe on the Lord Jesus, and you will be saved, you and your household." [32]They spoke the word of the Lord[b] to him and to all who were in his house. [33]At the same hour of the night he took them and washed their wounds; then he and his entire family were baptized without delay. [34]He brought them up into the house and set food before them; and he and his entire household rejoiced that he had become a believer in God.

[35] When morning came, the magistrates sent the police, saying, "Let those men go." [36]And the jailer reported the message to Paul, saying, "The magistrates sent word to let you go; therefore come out now and go in peace." [37]But Paul replied, "They have beaten us in public, uncondemned, men who are Roman citizens, and have thrown us into prison; and now are they going to discharge us in secret? Certainly not! Let them come and take us out themselves." [38]The police reported these words to the magistrates, and they were afraid when they heard that they were Roman citizens; [39]so they came and apologized to them. And they took them out and asked them to leave the city. [40]After leaving the prison they went to Lydia's home; and when they had seen and encouraged the brothers and sisters[a] there, they departed.

The Uproar in Thessalonica

17 After Paul and Silas[d] had passed through Amphipolis and Apollonia,

---

a Gk *He*   *b* Other ancient authorities read *word of God*   *c* Gk *brothers*   *d* Gk *they*

16:21 *customs that are not lawful for us as Romans.* Religions were either legal or illegal under Roman law. Judaism was legal; Christianity was not (cf. 18:13).

16:25 PRAYER—*See* Spiritual Disciplines Index.

16:25 *Paul and Silas were praying and singing hymns to God.* Paul and Silas's response to beating and arrest is prayer and praise, a powerful witness to the other prisoners. How Christians respond to vicissitude reveals their real faith.

16:26 *all the doors were opened.* Another miraculous prison escape demonstrates that the gospel cannot be imprisoned.

16:30 *Sirs, what must I do to be saved?* Compare 2:37.

16:33 *he and his entire family were baptized without delay.* The jailer's is the second household in Philippi to come to Christ. Greco-

Roman households were extended families and small economic units. The members followed the religion of its *pater familias*, father or head of the household. Although an imperfect parallel, the verse suggests the importance of the spiritual witness of the head of a family.

16:37 *They have beaten us in public.* Paul claims his rights as a Roman citizen. He has been unlawfully beaten and imprisoned and will not be summarily dismissed; he demands a public apology, probably for the sake of the reputation of the Philippian church. Christians are not society's scapegoats, and Paul demonstrates the communal importance of an individual's healthy self-concept.

16:40 *After leaving the prison they went to Lydia's home.* As did Peter, when Paul is released from prison, he seeks the fellowship of believers.

they came to Thessalonica, where there was a synagogue of the Jews. [2] And Paul went in, as was his custom, and on three sabbath days argued with them from the scriptures, [3] explaining and proving that it was necessary for the Messiah[a] to suffer and to rise from the dead, and saying, "This is the Messiah,[a] Jesus whom I am proclaiming to you." [4] Some of them were persuaded and joined Paul and Silas, as did a great many of the devout Greeks and not a few of the leading women. [5] But the Jews became jealous, and with the help of some ruffians in the marketplaces they formed a mob and set the city in an uproar. While they were searching for Paul and Silas to bring them out to the assembly, they attacked Jason's house. [6] When they could not find them, they dragged Jason and some believers[b] before the city authorities,[c] shouting, "These people who have been turning the world upside down have come here also, [7] and Jason has entertained them as guests. They are all acting contrary to the decrees of the emperor, saying that there is another king named Jesus." [8] The people and the city officials were disturbed when they heard this, [9] and after they had taken bail from Jason and the others, they let them go.

Paul and Silas in Beroea

[10] That very night the believers[b] sent Paul and Silas off to Beroea; and when they arrived, they went to the Jewish synagogue. [11] These Jews were more receptive than those in Thessalonica, for they welcomed the message very eagerly and examined the scriptures every day to see whether these things were so. [12] Many of them therefore believed, including not a few Greek women and men

of high standing. [13] But when the Jews of Thessalonica learned that the word of God had been proclaimed by Paul in Beroea as well, they came there too, to stir up and incite the crowds. [14] Then the believers[b] immediately sent Paul away to the coast, but Silas and Timothy remained behind. [15] Those who conducted Paul brought him as far as Athens; and after receiving instructions to have Silas and Timothy join him as soon as possible, they left him.

Paul in Athens

[16] While Paul was waiting for them in Athens, he was deeply distressed to see that the city was full of idols. [17] So he argued in the synagogue with the Jews and the devout persons, and also in the marketplace[d] every day with those who happened to be there. [18] Also some Epicurean and Stoic philosophers debated with him. Some said, "What does this babbler want to say?" Others said, "He seems to be a proclaimer of foreign divinities." (This was because he was telling the good news about Jesus and the resurrection.) [19] So they took him and brought him to the Areopagus and asked him, "May we know what this new teaching is that you are presenting? [20] It sounds rather strange to us, so we would like to know what it means." [21] Now all the Athenians and the foreigners living there would spend their time in nothing but telling or hearing something new.

[22] Then Paul stood in front of the Areopagus and said, "Athenians, I see how extremely religious you are in every way. [23] For

a Or *the Christ*   *b* Gk *brothers*   *c* Gk *politarchs*
d Or *civic center;* Gk *agora*

17:6–7 *Jason has entertained them as guests.* It can be dangerous to be associated with the Christian mission. For having been hospitable, Jason is implicated in the jealousy against Paul.

17:11 *examined the scriptures . . . to see whether these things were so.* Confirmation of God's action is sought in Scripture. The litmus test of any idea or practice is whether it accords with God's word.

17:16–21 *Paul was waiting for them in Athens.* Athens was a center of intellectual

inquiry. Paul's training prepared him to engage Greek intellectuals on their terms. Interestingly, he experiences no persecution in Athens and little evangelistic success.

17:22–31 *Athenians, I see how extremely religious you are.* Paul's Areopagus sermon departs from the pattern established by Peter, Stephen, and Philip (see note on 2:14–36). His point of reference is not Hebrew Scripture, but Greek philosophy. With precision and delicacy, Paul refutes idolatry and introduces the One

as I went through the city and looked carefully at the objects of your worship, I found among them an altar with the inscription, 'To an unknown god.' What therefore you worship as unknown, this I proclaim to you. 24The God who made the world and everything in it, he who is Lord of heaven and earth, does not live in shrines made by human hands, 25nor is he served by human hands, as though he needed anything, since he himself gives to all mortals life and breath and all things. 26From one ancestor*a* he made all nations to inhabit the whole earth, and he allotted the times of their existence and the boundaries of the places where they would live, 27so that they would search for God*b* and perhaps grope for him and find him— though indeed he is not far from each one of us. 28For 'In him we live and move and have our being'; as even some of your own poets have said,

'For we too are his offspring.'

29Since we are God's offspring, we ought not to think that the deity is like gold, or silver, or stone, an image formed by the art and imagination of mortals. 30While God has overlooked the times of human ignorance, now he commands all people everywhere to repent, 31because he has fixed a day on which he will have the world judged in righteousness by a man whom he has appointed, and of this he has given assurance to all by raising him from the dead."

32 When they heard of the resurrection of the dead, some scoffed; but others said, "We will hear you again about this." 33At that point Paul left them. 34But some of them joined him and became believers, including Dionysius the Areopagite and a woman named Damaris, and others with them.

Paul in Corinth

18 After this Paul*c* left Athens and went to Corinth. 2There he found a Jew named Aquila, a native of Pontus, who had recently come from Italy with his wife Priscilla, because Claudius had ordered all Jews to leave Rome. Paul*d* went to see them, 3and, because he was of the same trade, he stayed with them, and they worked together—by trade they were tentmakers. 4Every sabbath he would argue in the synagogue and would try to convince Jews and Greeks.

5 When Silas and Timothy arrived from Macedonia, Paul was occupied with proclaiming the word,*e* testifying to the Jews that the Messiah*f* was Jesus. 6When they opposed and reviled him, in protest he shook the dust from his clothes*g* and said to them, "Your blood be on your own heads! I am innocent. From now on I will go to the Gentiles." 7Then he left the synagogue*h* and went to the house of a man named Titius*i* Justus, a worshiper of God; his house was next door to the synagogue. 8Crispus, the official of the synagogue, became a believer in the Lord, together with all his household; and many of the Corinthians who heard Paul became be-

a Gk *From one*; other ancient authorities read *From one blood*   b Other ancient authorities read *the Lord*   c Gk *he*   d Gk *He*   e Gk *with the word*   f Or *the Christ*   g Gk *reviled him; he shook out his clothes*   h Gk *left there*   i Other ancient authorities read *Titus*

God. The gospel is most persuasive when presented in terms its hearers understand.

17:23 WORSHIP—*See* Spiritual Disciplines Index.

17:27 *indeed he is not far from each one of us.* Scripture affirms God's imminence. Jesus, Immanuel, incarnates it (cf. John 1:12).

17:32 *When they heard of the resurrection of the dead, some scoffed.* Greeks were familiar with the concept of an eternal spirit, but resurrection was a startling idea (see 1 Cor 15:12).

18:1–3 *Paul left Athens and went to Corinth.* The journey from Athens to Corinth is like going from Oxford to London, from an academic to a commercial city. Wherever he goes, Paul seeks out Christians. Paul was not a "Lone Ranger," but worked in association with others. Priscilla and Aquila, who became Christians in Rome, will travel with Paul (v 18) and become important in the Ephesian church (see Rom 16:3–4; 1 Cor 16:19; 2 Tim 4:19). Especially when Christian work is demanding, we need the support of other believers.

18:6 *I am innocent. From now on I will go to the Gentiles.* With 13:46, an important statement of Paul's understanding of his ministry.

lievers and were baptized. ⁹One night the Lord said to Paul in a vision, "Do not be afraid, but speak and do not be silent; ¹⁰for I am with you, and no one will lay a hand on you to harm you, for there are many in this city who are my people." ¹¹He stayed there a year and six months, teaching the word of God among them.

12 But when Gallio was proconsul of Achaia, the Jews made a united attack on Paul and brought him before the tribunal. ¹³They said, "This man is persuading people to worship God in ways that are contrary to the law." ¹⁴Just as Paul was about to speak, Gallio said to the Jews, "If it were a matter of crime or serious villainy, I would be justified in accepting the complaint of you Jews; ¹⁵but since it is a matter of questions about words and names and your own law, see to it yourselves; I do not wish to be a judge of these matters." ¹⁶And he dismissed them from the tribunal. ¹⁷Then all of them[a] seized Sosthenes, the official of the synagogue, and beat him in front of the tribunal. But Gallio paid no attention to any of these things.

Paul's Return to Antioch

18 After staying there for a considerable time, Paul said farewell to the believers[b] and sailed for Syria, accompanied by Priscilla and Aquila. At Cenchreae he had his hair cut, for he was under a vow. ¹⁹When they reached Ephesus, he left them there, but first he himself went into the synagogue and had a discussion with the Jews. ²⁰When they asked him to stay longer, he declined; ²¹but on taking leave of them, he said, "I[c] will return to you, if God wills." Then he set sail from Ephesus.

22 When he had landed at Caesarea, he went up to Jerusalem[d] and greeted the church, and then went down to Antioch. ²³After spending some time there he departed and went from place to place through the region of Galatia[e] and Phrygia, strengthening all the disciples.

Ministry of Apollos

24 Now there came to Ephesus a Jew named Apollos, a native of Alexandria. He was an eloquent man, well-versed in the scriptures. ²⁵He had been instructed in the Way of the Lord; and he spoke with burning enthusiasm and taught accurately the things concerning Jesus, though he knew only the baptism of John. ²⁶He began to speak boldly in the synagogue; but when Priscilla and Aquila heard him, they took him aside and explained the Way of God to him more accurately. ²⁷And when he wished to cross over to Achaia, the believers[b] encouraged him and wrote to the disciples to welcome him. On his arrival he greatly helped those who through grace had become believers, ²⁸for

a Other ancient authorities read *all the Greeks*
b Gk *brothers*   c Other ancient authorities read *I must at all costs keep the approaching festival in Jerusalem, but I*   d Gk *went up*   e Gk *the Galatian region*

18:9 *the Lord said to Paul in a vision.* As Paul's venture into Europe began with a vision (16:9), it is confirmed and encouraged by a vision of Jesus.

18:13 *to worship God in ways that are contrary to the law.* Compare 16:21.

18:18 *he had his hair cut, for he was under a vow.* Perhaps Paul had taken a Nazirite vow (Num 6:1–21). Vows were taken in gratitude for deliverance from danger. Shaving one's head marked the end of the vow (see Acts 21:24).

18:22 *he went up to Jerusalem . . . and then went down to Antioch.* At the end of the second missionary journey, Paul stops in Jerusalem, center of Jewish Christianity, and then returns to Antioch, his "home base" and center of the gentile mission.

18:23 *he . . . went from place to place.* Paul begins his third missionary journey (18:23–21:26) by revisiting established churches. The journey lasted more than three years (19:10), much of it in Ephesian imprisonment, where Paul wrote letters to Greek churches. Imprisonment became opportunity.

18:24–26 *Apollos, a native of Alexandria.* Alexandria, with its famous library, was a great intellectual center. Apollos is characterized positively for knowledge of Scripture, eloquence, and spirit, but he is not too proud to learn from tentmakers Priscilla and Aquila. A truly wise Christian is always ready to learn, knowing the mystery of Christ is never exhausted.

he powerfully refuted the Jews in public, showing by the scriptures that the Messiah[a] is Jesus.

Paul in Ephesus

19 While Apollos was in Corinth, Paul passed through the interior regions and came to Ephesus, where he found some disciples. [2]He said to them, "Did you receive the Holy Spirit when you became believers?" They replied, "No, we have not even heard that there is a Holy Spirit." [3]Then he said, "Into what then were you baptized?" They answered, "Into John's baptism." [4]Paul said, "John baptized with the baptism of repentance, telling the people to believe in the one who was to come after him, that is, in Jesus." [5]On hearing this, they were baptized in the name of the Lord Jesus. [6]When Paul had laid his hands on them, the Holy Spirit came upon them, and they spoke in tongues and prophesied— [7]altogether there were about twelve of them.

[8] He entered the synagogue and for three months spoke out boldly, and argued persuasively about the kingdom of God. [9]When some stubbornly refused to believe and spoke evil of the Way before the congregation, he left them, taking the disciples with him, and argued daily in the lecture hall of Tyrannus.[b] [10]This continued for two years, so that all the residents of Asia, both Jews and Greeks, heard the word of the Lord.

The Sons of Sceva

[11] God did extraordinary miracles through Paul, [12]so that when the handkerchiefs or aprons that had touched his skin were brought to the sick, their diseases left them, and the evil spirits came out of them. [13]Then some itinerant Jewish exorcists tried to use the name of the Lord Jesus over those who had evil spirits, saying, "I adjure you by the Jesus whom Paul proclaims." [14]Seven sons of a Jewish high priest named Sceva were doing this. [15]But the evil spirit said to them in reply, "Jesus I know, and Paul I know; but who are you?" [16]Then the man with the evil spirit leaped on them, mastered them all, and so overpowered them that they fled out of the house naked and wounded. [17]When this became known to all residents of Ephesus, both Jews and Greeks, everyone was awestruck; and the name of the Lord Jesus was praised. [18]Also many of those who became believers confessed and disclosed their practices. [19]A number of those who practiced magic collected their books and burned them publicly; when the value of these books[c] was calculated, it was found to come to fifty thousand silver coins. [20]So the word of the Lord grew mightily and prevailed.

The Riot in Ephesus

[21] Now after these things had been accomplished, Paul resolved in the Spirit to go

a Or *the Christ*   b Other ancient authorities read *of a certain Tyrannus, from eleven o'clock in the morning to four in the afternoon*   c Gk *them*

19:3–5 *Into what then were you baptized?* Both Luke and John indicate that followers of John the Baptist continued to be numerous and clarify that Jesus is superior to John (cf. John 1:29–42). Partial religious understanding is always subject to correction. We must be open to new information in order to grow in the Spirit.

19:6 *the Holy Spirit came upon them, and they spoke in tongues.* Another "gentile Pentecost" (cf. 10:44–48). The Holy Spirit shows no "partiality"; those who confess Jesus and are baptized receive it.

19:8–9 *He entered the synagogue.* Paul's missionary procedure in miniature.

19:11 *God did extraordinary miracles through Paul.* Miracles are done *through* a human agent; God is the doer.

19:19 *those who practiced magic collected their books and burned them.* Throughout the Hellenistic world Christianity encountered magic and malign spirits (see Eph 6:12). Christ triumphed over them (cf. Phil 2:9–11; Col 1:15–20). C. S. Lewis wisely remarked we make two mistakes with regard to evil spirits: we assume they don't exist, or we have an unhealthy interest in them.

19:20 **THE WITH-GOD LIFE**—*See* Spiritual Disciplines Index.

19:21 *Paul resolved in the Spirit to go through Macedonia.* Paul's "plan" foreshadows the remainder of Acts.

through Macedonia and Achaia, and then to go on to Jerusalem. He said, "After I have gone there, I must also see Rome." 22So he sent two of his helpers, Timothy and Erastus, to Macedonia, while he himself stayed for some time longer in Asia.

23 About that time no little disturbance broke out concerning the Way. 24A man named Demetrius, a silversmith who made silver shrines of Artemis, brought no little business to the artisans. 25These he gathered together, with the workers of the same trade, and said, "Men, you know that we get our wealth from this business. 26You also see and hear that not only in Ephesus but in almost the whole of Asia this Paul has persuaded and drawn away a considerable number of people by saying that gods made with hands are not gods. 27And there is danger not only that this trade of ours may come into disrepute but also that the temple of the great goddess Artemis will be scorned, and she will be deprived of her majesty that brought all Asia and the world to worship her."

28 When they heard this, they were enraged and shouted, "Great is Artemis of the Ephesians!" 29The city was filled with the confusion; and people*a* rushed together to the theater, dragging with them Gaius and Aristarchus, Macedonians who were Paul's travel companions. 30Paul wished to go into the crowd, but the disciples would not let him; 31even some officials of the province of Asia,*b* who were friendly to him, sent him a message urging him not to venture into the theater. 32Meanwhile, some were shouting one thing, some another; for the assembly was in confusion, and most of them did not know why they had come together. 33Some of the crowd

gave instructions to Alexander, whom the Jews had pushed forward. And Alexander motioned for silence and tried to make a defense before the people. 34But when they recognized that he was a Jew, for about two hours all of them shouted in unison, "Great is Artemis of the Ephesians!" 35But when the town clerk had quieted the crowd, he said, "Citizens of Ephesus, who is there that does not know that the city of the Ephesians is the temple keeper of the great Artemis and of the statue that fell from heaven?*c* 36Since these things cannot be denied, you ought to be quiet and do nothing rash. 37You have brought these men here who are neither temple robbers nor blasphemers of our*d* goddess. 38If therefore Demetrius and the artisans with him have a complaint against anyone, the courts are open, and there are proconsuls; let them bring charges there against one another. 39If there is anything further*e* you want to know, it must be settled in the regular assembly. 40For we are in danger of being charged with rioting today, since there is no cause that we can give to justify this commotion." 41When he had said this, he dismissed the assembly.

Paul Goes to Macedonia and Greece

20 After the uproar had ceased, Paul sent for the disciples; and after encouraging them and saying farewell, he left for Macedonia. 2When he had gone through those regions and had given the believers*f*

a Gk *they*   *b* Gk *some of the Asiarchs*
c Meaning of Gk uncertain   *d* Other ancient authorities read *your*   *e* Other ancient authorities read *about other matters*   *f* Gk *given them*

19:24–27 *Demetrius . . . brought no little business to the artisans.* As in Philippi (16:16–24) public objection to Paul is rooted in finances. Demetrius argues that so many people have become Christian that the votive industry in Ephesus is in jeopardy. Pilgrims who bought small silver idols had stopped doing so. The extended passage (vv 23–41) is an example of 1 Tim 6:10—"the love of money is a root of all kinds of evil."

19:28 *Great is Artemis of the Ephesians!* Artemis (Roman Diana) was worshiped in

Ephesus as Cybele, a mother goddess. Ephesians who felt she was being insulted rioted (vv 28–41). People feel strongly about their religious beliefs. The center of this fertility cult, the Ephesian Temple of Artemis, was one of the seven wonders of the ancient world. Today all that remains is a few pillars in a swamp.

20:1–2 *had given the believers much encouragement.* Paul revisits previously established churches to encourage them, underlining the importance of fellowship among churches and "reinforcement" of teachings.

much encouragement, he came to Greece, [3]where he stayed for three months. He was about to set sail for Syria when a plot was made against him by the Jews, and so he decided to return through Macedonia. [4]He was accompanied by Sopater son of Pyrrhus from Beroea, by Aristarchus and Secundus from Thessalonica, by Gaius from Derbe, and by Timothy, as well as by Tychicus and Trophimus from Asia. [5]They went ahead and were waiting for us in Troas; [6]but we sailed from Philippi after the days of Unleavened Bread, and in five days we joined them in Troas, where we stayed for seven days.

Paul's Farewell Visit to Troas

[7] On the first day of the week, when we met to break bread, Paul was holding a discussion with them; since he intended to leave the next day, he continued speaking until midnight. [8]There were many lamps in the room upstairs where we were meeting. [9]A young man named Eutychus, who was sitting in the window, began to sink off into a deep sleep while Paul talked still longer. Overcome by sleep, he fell to the ground three floors below and was picked up dead. [10]But Paul went down, and bending over him took him in his arms, and said, "Do not be alarmed, for his life is in him." [11]Then Paul went upstairs, and after he had broken bread and eaten, he continued to converse with them until dawn; then he left. [12]Meanwhile they had taken the boy away alive and were not a little comforted.

The Voyage from Troas to Miletus

[13] We went ahead to the ship and set sail for Assos, intending to take Paul on board there; for he had made this arrangement, intending to go by land himself. [14]When he met us in Assos, we took him on board and went to Mitylene. [15]We sailed from there, and on the following day we arrived opposite Chios. The next day we touched at Samos, and [a] the day after that we came to Miletus. [16]For Paul had decided to sail past Ephesus, so that he might not have to spend time in Asia; he was eager to be in Jerusalem, if possible, on the day of Pentecost.

Paul Speaks to the Ephesian Elders

[17] From Miletus he sent a message to Ephesus, asking the elders of the church to meet him. [18]When they came to him, he said to them:

"You yourselves know how I lived among you the entire time from the first day that I set foot in Asia, [19]serving the Lord with all humility and with tears, enduring the trials that

a Other ancient authorities add *after remaining at Trogyllium*

20:6 *we sailed from Philippi.* The "we source" (see 20:13–16; 21:1–6).

20:7 *when we met to break bread.* Paul's mission churches follow Jerusalem's practice of the Lord's Supper on the first day of the week. The Church is nourished by its sacraments.

20:9–10 *Paul, . . . bending over him took him in his arms.* Even Paul put some people to sleep! As Jesus (Luke 7:11–17; 8:49–56; John 11) and Peter (Acts 9:36–43) had raised the dead, so Paul also manifests that power of God.

20:16 *he was eager to be in Jerusalem . . . on the day of Pentecost.* Does Paul's eagerness to be in Jerusalem on Pentecost reflect his Jewish heritage or was Pentecost already a Christian commemoration?

20:18–35 *You yourselves know how I lived among you.* The Hellenistic genre of "farewell address" is reflected here. Paul recollects what he has done and introduces his future work, indicating possible difficulty in Jerusalem (v 22). Included are a powerful charge to church leaders (vv 28–31) and a suggestion Paul knew Jesus' teaching (v 35).

Responding
20:19 SERVICE. In his farewell to the elders of Ephesus, Paul describes himself as "serving the Lord with all humility and with tears." Richard Foster writes in *Celebration of Discipline:* "Service enables us to say 'no!' to the world's games of promotion and authority." Try to name contemporary people who are models of service to the Lord and the ways they serve. Choose one of these ways and consider doing it within the next month. *See also* Spiritual Disciplines Index.

came to me through the plots of the Jews. 20I did not shrink from doing anything helpful, proclaiming the message to you and teaching you publicly and from house to house, 21as I testified to both Jews and Greeks about repentance toward God and faith toward our Lord Jesus. 22And now, as a captive to the Spirit,a I am on my way to Jerusalem, not knowing what will happen to me there, 23except that the Holy Spirit testifies to me in every city that imprisonment and persecutions are waiting for me. 24But I do not count my life of any value to myself, if only I may finish my course and the ministry that I received from the Lord Jesus, to testify to the good news of God's grace.

25 "And now I know that none of you, among whom I have gone about proclaiming the kingdom, will ever see my face again. 26Therefore I declare to you this day that I am not responsible for the blood of any of you, 27for I did not shrink from declaring to you the whole purpose of God. 28Keep watch over yourselves and over all the flock, of which the Holy Spirit has made you overseers, to shepherd the church of Godb that he obtained with the blood of his own Son.c 29I know that after I have gone, savage wolves will come in among you, not sparing the flock. 30Some even from your own group will come distorting the truth in order to entice the disciples to follow them. 31Therefore be alert, remembering that for three years I did not cease night or day to warn everyone with tears. 32And now I commend you to God and to the message of his grace, a message that is able to build you up and to give you the inheritance among all who are sanctified. 33I coveted no one's silver or gold or clothing. 34You know for yourselves that I worked with my own hands to support myself and my companions. 35In all this I have given you an example that by such work we must support the weak, remembering the

words of the Lord Jesus, for he himself said, 'It is more blessed to give than to receive.' "

36 When he had finished speaking, he knelt down with them all and prayed. 37There was much weeping among them all; they embraced Paul and kissed him, 38grieving especially because of what he had said, that they would not see him again. Then they brought him to the ship.

Paul's Journey to Jerusalem

21 When we had parted from them and set sail, we came by a straight course to Cos, and the next day to Rhodes, and from there to Patara.d 2When we found a ship bound for Phoenicia, we went on board and set sail. 3We came in sight of Cyprus; and leaving it on our left, we sailed to Syria and landed at Tyre, because the ship was to unload its cargo there. 4We looked up the disciples and stayed there for seven days. Through the Spirit they told Paul not to go on to Jerusalem. 5When our days there were ended, we left and proceeded on our journey; and all of them, with wives and children, escorted us outside the city. There we knelt down on the beach and prayed 6and said farewell to one another. Then we went on board the ship, and they returned home.

7 When we had finishede the voyage from Tyre, we arrived at Ptolemais; and we greeted the believersf and stayed with them for one day. 8The next day we left and came to Caesarea; and we went into the house of Philip the evangelist, one of the seven, and stayed with him. 9He had four unmarried daughtersg who had the gift of prophecy. 10While we were staying there for several days, a prophet

a Or And now, bound in the spirit   b Other ancient authorities read of the Lord   c Or with his own blood; Gk with the blood of his Own   d Other ancient authorities add and Myra   e Or continued f Gk brothers   g Gk four daughters, virgins,

---

20:36 *he knelt down with them all and prayed.* Prayer opens and closes Paul's journeys (see 21:5–6).

20:37–38 *There was much weeping among them all.* The sentiment here counters the misconception of Paul as unlikable. In Ephesus he was obviously much loved.

21:7 *we greeted the believers and stayed with them for one day.* Itinerant Christians depended upon fellow Christians for hospitality, an important Christian virtue (cf. 21:8,16).

21:9 *four unmarried daughters who had the gift of prophecy.* Acts 8 recounts Philip's work. He was married, with daughters who had the

named Agabus came down from Judea. [11] He came to us and took Paul's belt, bound his own feet and hands with it, and said, "Thus says the Holy Spirit, 'This is the way the Jews in Jerusalem will bind the man who owns this belt and will hand him over to the Gentiles.' " [12] When we heard this, we and the people there urged him not to go up to Jerusalem. [13] Then Paul answered, "What are you doing, weeping and breaking my heart? For I am ready not only to be bound but even to die in Jerusalem for the name of the Lord Jesus." [14] Since he would not be persuaded, we remained silent except to say, "The Lord's will be done."

15 After these days we got ready and started to go up to Jerusalem. [16] Some of the disciples from Caesarea also came along and brought us to the house of Mnason of Cyprus, an early disciple, with whom we were to stay.

Paul Visits James at Jerusalem

17 When we arrived in Jerusalem, the brothers welcomed us warmly. [18] The next day Paul went with us to visit James; and all the elders were present. [19] After greeting them, he related one by one the things that God had done among the Gentiles through his ministry. [20] When they heard it, they praised God. Then they said to him, "You see, brother, how many thousands of believers there are among the Jews, and they are all zealous for the law. [21] They have been told about you that you teach all the Jews living among the Gentiles to forsake Moses, and that you tell them not to circumcise their children or observe the customs. [22] What then is to be done? They will certainly hear that you have come. [23] So do what we tell you. We have four men who are under a vow. [24] Join these men, go through the rite of purification with them, and pay for the shaving of their heads. Thus all will know that there is nothing in what they have been told about you, but that you yourself observe and guard the law. [25] But as for the Gentiles who have become believers, we have sent a letter with our judgment that they should abstain from what has been sacrificed to idols and from blood and from what is strangled[a] and from fornication." [26] Then Paul took the men, and the next day, having purified himself, he entered the temple with them, making public the completion of the days of purification when the sacrifice would be made for each of them.

Paul Arrested in the Temple

27 When the seven days were almost completed, the Jews from Asia, who had seen him in the temple, stirred up the whole crowd. They seized him, [28] shouting, "Fellow Israelites, help! This is the man who is teaching everyone everywhere against our people, our law, and this place; more than that, he has actually brought Greeks into the temple and has defiled this holy place." [29] For they had

a Other ancient authorities lack *and from what is strangled*

---

gift of prophecy (see 1 Cor 12:28; Rom 12:6). Philip's life suggests that important Christian work is not reserved for singles.

21:10–11 *a prophet named Agabus.* In 11:28 Agabus predicted a famine that occurred. Here he predicts Paul's troubles in Jerusalem. Through these verses and 20:22, Luke builds suspense as Paul approaches Jerusalem.

21:14 *The Lord's will be done.* God disposes the life of every person. Christian maturity concedes to God's will in everything.

21:17–26 *When we arrived in Jerusalem.* Paul returns to Jerusalem and immediately reports to James, the leader of the Church, who is concerned that Paul's work among Gentiles will cause trouble. James prescribes a public act of solidarity with Jews (vv 20–25), with which Paul complies (v 26).

21:25 *But as for the Gentiles.* Compare Acts 15 and Galatians 2.

21:27 *the Jews from Asia . . . stirred up the whole crowd.* Jews from Asia who knew of Paul's association with Gentiles there precipitate his arrest. This verse and verse 29 comprise an object lesson in the dangers of acting on appearances and partial knowledge. Paul is charged with bringing Gentiles into the inner Temple courts. From this verse on, the narrative focuses on Paul's treatment by the Roman system. Luke depicts the Jews as against Paul and the Romans as benign. Paul uses his imprisonment and trials as opportunities to preach. Like

previously seen Trophimus the Ephesian with him in the city, and they supposed that Paul had brought him into the temple. ³⁰Then all the city was aroused, and the people rushed together. They seized Paul and dragged him out of the temple, and immediately the doors were shut. ³¹While they were trying to kill him, word came to the tribune of the cohort that all Jerusalem was in an uproar. ³²Immediately he took soldiers and centurions and ran down to them. When they saw the tribune and the soldiers, they stopped beating Paul. ³³Then the tribune came, arrested him, and ordered him to be bound with two chains; he inquired who he was and what he had done. ³⁴Some in the crowd shouted one thing, some another; and as he could not learn the facts because of the uproar, he ordered him to be brought into the barracks. ³⁵When Paul*ᵃ* came to the steps, the violence of the mob was so great that he had to be carried by the soldiers. ³⁶The crowd that followed kept shouting, "Away with him!"

Paul Defends Himself

37 Just as Paul was about to be brought into the barracks, he said to the tribune, "May I say something to you?" The tribune*ᵇ* replied, "Do you know Greek? ³⁸Then you are not the Egyptian who recently stirred up a revolt and led the four thousand assassins out into the wilderness?" ³⁹Paul replied, "I am a Jew, from Tarsus in Cilicia, a citizen of an important city; I beg you, let me speak to the people." ⁴⁰When he had given him permission, Paul stood on the steps and motioned to the people for silence; and when there was a great hush, he addressed them in the Hebrew*ᶜ* language, saying:

22 "Brothers and fathers, listen to the defense that I now make before you."

2 When they heard him addressing them

in Hebrew,*ᶜ* they became even more quiet. Then he said:

3 "I am a Jew, born in Tarsus in Cilicia, but brought up in this city at the feet of Gamaliel, educated strictly according to our ancestral law, being zealous for God, just as all of you are today. ⁴I persecuted this Way up to the point of death by binding both men and women and putting them in prison, ⁵as the high priest and the whole council of elders can testify about me. From them I also received letters to the brothers in Damascus, and I went there in order to bind those who were there and to bring them back to Jerusalem for punishment.

Paul Tells of His Conversion

6 "While I was on my way and approaching Damascus, about noon a great light from heaven suddenly shone about me. ⁷I fell to the ground and heard a voice saying to me, 'Saul, Saul, why are you persecuting me?' ⁸I answered, 'Who are you, Lord?' Then he said to me, 'I am Jesus of Nazareth*ᵈ* whom you are persecuting.' ⁹Now those who were with me saw the light but did not hear the voice of the one who was speaking to me. ¹⁰I asked, 'What am I to do, Lord?' The Lord said to me, 'Get up and go to Damascus; there you will be told everything that has been assigned to you to do.' ¹¹Since I could not see because of the brightness of that light, those who were with me took my hand and led me to Damascus.

12 "A certain Ananias, who was a devout man according to the law and well spoken of by all the Jews living there, ¹³came to me; and standing beside me, he said, 'Brother Saul, regain your sight!' In that very hour I regained my sight and saw him. ¹⁴Then he said,

---

a Gk *he*   *b* Gk *He*   *c* That is, *Aramaic*
d Gk *the Nazorean*

John the Baptist, he points away from himself and toward the Christ.

21:30–36 *Then all the city was aroused.* Compare the crowd scene here to that in Ephesus (19:23–41), noting the energy with which Luke renders such scenes.

21:37 *May I say something to you?* Paul speaks Greek to the Roman tribune and Aramaic ("He-

brew") to Jerusalem Jews (v 40; 22:2). He articulates the gospel clearly to both cultures.

22:3–21 *I am a Jew.* Paul's speech recounts his Jewish background (vv 3–5) and conversion (vv 6–16, cf. 9:1–22). He reveals a vision of Jesus during his first Jerusalem visit (vv 17–21; cf. 7:58; 8:1; 9:26–30) that sent him to the Gentiles. This turns the crowd against him (v 22).

The God of our ancestors has chosen you to know his will, to see the Righteous One and to hear his own voice; 15for you will be his witness to all the world of what you have seen and heard. 16And now—why do you delay? Get up, be baptized, and have your sins washed away, calling on his name.'

Paul Sent to the Gentiles

17 "After I had returned to Jerusalem and while I was praying in the temple, I fell into a trance 18and saw Jesus[a] saying to me, 'Hurry and get out of Jerusalem quickly, because they will not accept your testimony about me.' 19And I said, 'Lord, they themselves know that in every synagogue I imprisoned and beat those who believed in you. 20And while the blood of your witness Stephen was shed, I myself was standing by, approving and keeping the coats of those who killed him.' 21Then he said to me, 'Go, for I will send you far away to the Gentiles.' "

Paul and the Roman Tribune

22 Up to this point they listened to him, but then they shouted, "Away with such a fellow from the earth! For he should not be allowed to live." 23And while they were shouting, throwing off their cloaks, and tossing dust into the air, 24the tribune directed that he was to be brought into the barracks, and ordered him to be examined by flogging, to find out the reason for this outcry against him. 25But when they had tied him up with thongs,[b] Paul said to the centurion who was standing by, "Is it legal for you to flog a Roman citizen who is uncondemned?" 26When the centurion heard that, he went to the tribune and said to him, "What are you about to

do? This man is a Roman citizen." 27The tribune came and asked Paul,[a] "Tell me, are you a Roman citizen?" And he said, "Yes." 28The tribune answered, "It cost me a large sum of money to get my citizenship." Paul said, "But I was born a citizen." 29Immediately those who were about to examine him drew back from him; and the tribune also was afraid, for he realized that Paul was a Roman citizen and that he had bound him.

Paul before the Council

30 Since he wanted to find out what Paul[c] was being accused of by the Jews, the next day he released him and ordered the chief priests and the entire council to meet. He brought Paul down and had him stand before them.

23 While Paul was looking intently at the council he said, "Brothers,[d] up to this day I have lived my life with a clear conscience before God." 2Then the high priest Ananias ordered those standing near him to strike him on the mouth. 3At this Paul said to him, "God will strike you, you whitewashed wall! Are you sitting there to judge me according to the law, and yet in violation of the law you order me to be struck?" 4Those standing nearby said, "Do you dare to insult God's high priest?" 5And Paul said, "I did not realize, brothers, that he was high priest; for it is written, 'You shall not speak evil of a leader of your people.' "

6 When Paul noticed that some were Sadducees and others were Pharisees, he called out in the council, "Brothers, I am a Pharisee, a son of Pharisees. I am on trial concerning the

a Gk *him*　　*b* Or *up for the lashes*　　*c* Gk *he*
d Gk *Men, brothers*

22:17 PRAYER—*See* Spiritual Disciplines Index.

22:25–29 *Is it legal for you to flog a Roman citizen?* As in Philippi (16:37), Paul insists on his rights as a Roman citizen.

22:30 *ordered the chief priests and the entire council to meet.* The Roman tribune orders the Sanhedrin to meet, a clear picture of the political reality. Like first-century Judaism, the Church has often been in political captivity.

23:1 *I have lived my life with a clear conscience*

before God. A startling admission, repeated in Phil 3:6.

23:5 *I did not realize . . . that he was high priest.* Even under duress, Paul attempts to be conciliatory and observe proper Jewish conventions.

23:6–10 *Paul noticed that some were Sadducees and others were Pharisees.* Sadducees did not believe in resurrection; Pharisees did. Paul cleverly shifts the focus from himself to theological issues.

hope of the resurrection[a] of the dead." 7When he said this, a dissension began between the Pharisees and the Sadducees, and the assembly was divided. 8(The Sadducees say that there is no resurrection, or angel, or spirit; but the Pharisees acknowledge all three.) 9Then a great clamor arose, and certain scribes of the Pharisees' group stood up and contended, "We find nothing wrong with this man. What if a spirit or an angel has spoken to him?" 10When the dissension became violent, the tribune, fearing that they would tear Paul to pieces, ordered the soldiers to go down, take him by force, and bring him into the barracks.

11 That night the Lord stood near him and said, "Keep up your courage! For just as you have testified for me in Jerusalem, so you must bear witness also in Rome."

The Plot to Kill Paul

12 In the morning the Jews joined in a conspiracy and bound themselves by an oath neither to eat nor drink until they had killed Paul. 13There were more than forty who joined in this conspiracy. 14They went to the chief priests and elders and said, "We have strictly bound ourselves by an oath to taste no food until we have killed Paul. 15Now then, you and the council must notify the tribune to bring him down to you, on the pretext that you want to make a more thorough examination of his case. And we are ready to do away with him before he arrives."

16 Now the son of Paul's sister heard about the ambush; so he went and gained entrance to the barracks and told Paul. 17Paul called one of the centurions and said, "Take this young man to the tribune, for he has something to report to him." 18So he took him, brought him to the tribune, and said, "The prisoner Paul called me and asked me to bring this young man to you; he has something to tell you." 19The tribune took him by the hand, drew him aside privately, and asked, "What is it that you have to report to me?" 20He answered, "The Jews have agreed to ask you to bring Paul down to the council tomorrow, as though they were going to inquire more thoroughly into his case. 21But do not be persuaded by them, for more than forty of their men are lying in ambush for him. They have bound themselves by an oath neither to eat nor drink until they kill him. They are ready now and are waiting for your consent." 22So the tribune dismissed the young man, ordering him, "Tell no one that you have informed me of this."

Paul Sent to Felix the Governor

23 Then he summoned two of the centurions and said, "Get ready to leave by nine o'clock tonight for Caesarea with two hundred soldiers, seventy horsemen, and two hundred spearmen. 24Also provide mounts for Paul to ride, and take him safely to Felix the governor." 25He wrote a letter to this effect:

26 "Claudius Lysias to his Excellency the governor Felix, greetings. 27This man was seized by the Jews and was about to be killed by them, but when I had learned that he was a Roman citizen, I came with the guard and rescued him. 28Since I wanted to know the charge for which they accused him, I had him brought to their council. 29I found that he was accused concerning questions of their law, but was charged with nothing deserving death or imprisonment. 30When I was informed that there would be a plot against the man, I sent him to you at

a Gk concerning hope and resurrection

23:11 *the Lord stood near him.* Paul is frequently directed and encouraged by visions and dreams (9:3; 16:9; 22:17–21), which Luke's readers understood as divine directives.

Responding
23:11 THE WITH-GOD LIFE.
Describe a time when you felt the Lord especially near to you. What circumstances caused this sense of the Lord's presence? What were the results? *See also* Spiritual Disciplines Index.

23:18–22 *So he took him, brought him to the tribune.* As in 22:25–29 Luke focuses on the Roman tribune's willingness to protect Paul. The extended passage (vv 16–35) accurately reflects the Roman administration's concern for the proper jurisdiction of disputes.

once, ordering his accusers also to state before you what they have against him. *a*"

31 So the soldiers, according to their instructions, took Paul and brought him during the night to Antipatris. 32The next day they let the horsemen go on with him, while they returned to the barracks. 33When they came to Caesarea and delivered the letter to the governor, they presented Paul also before him. 34On reading the letter, he asked what province he belonged to, and when he learned that he was from Cilicia, 35he said, "I will give you a hearing when your accusers arrive." Then he ordered that he be kept under guard in Herod's headquarters. *b*

Paul before Felix at Caesarea

24 Five days later the high priest Ananias came down with some elders and an attorney, a certain Tertullus, and they reported their case against Paul to the governor. 2When Paul *c* had been summoned, Tertullus began to accuse him, saying:

"Your Excellency, *d* because of you we have long enjoyed peace, and reforms have been made for this people because of your foresight. 3We welcome this in every way and everywhere with utmost gratitude. 4But, to detain you no further, I beg you to hear us briefly with your customary graciousness. 5We have, in fact, found this man a pestilent fellow, an agitator among all the Jews throughout the world, and a ringleader of the sect of the Nazarenes. *e* 6He even tried to profane the temple, and so we seized him. *f* 8By examining him yourself you will be able to learn from him concerning everything of which we accuse him."

9 The Jews also joined in the charge by asserting that all this was true.

Paul's Defense before Felix

10 When the governor motioned to him to speak, Paul replied:

"I cheerfully make my defense, knowing that for many years you have been a judge over this nation. 11As you can find out, it is not more than twelve days since I went up to worship in Jerusalem. 12They did not find me disputing with anyone in the temple or stirring up a crowd either in the synagogues or throughout the city. 13Neither can they prove to you the charge that they now bring against me. 14But this I admit to you, that according to the Way, which they call a sect, I worship the God of our ancestors, believing everything laid down according to the law or written in the prophets. *g* 15I have a hope in God—a hope that they themselves also accept—that there will be a resurrection of both *g* the righteous and the unrighteous. 16Therefore I do my best always to have a clear conscience toward God and all people. 17Now after some years I came to bring alms to my nation and to offer sacrifices. 18While I was doing this, they found me in the temple, completing the rite of purification, without any crowd or disturbance. 19But there were some Jews from Asia—they ought to be here before you to make an accusation, if they have anything against me. 20Or let these men here tell what crime they had found when I stood before the council, 21unless it was this one sentence that I called out while standing before them, 'It is about the resurrection of the dead that I am on trial before you today.'"

22 But Felix, who was rather well informed about the Way, adjourned the hearing with

---

a Other ancient authorities add *Farewell*
b Gk *praetorium*   *c* Gk *he*   *d* Gk lacks *Your Excellency*   *e* Gk *Nazoreans*   *f* Other ancient authorities add *and we would have judged him according to our law.* 7*But the chief captain Lysias came and with great violence took him out of our hands,* 8*commanding his accusers to come before you.*
g Other ancient authorities read *of the dead, both of*

24:1–8 *the high priest Ananias came down.* Under Roman occupation, even the high priest had to appeal cases to the Roman governor. "Attorney" is literally "orator," someone trained in forensic rhetoric, perhaps a Hellenistic Jew who knew Roman legal procedures; he accuses Paul of being an "agitator" (vv 2–8).

24:10–21 *I cheerfully make my defense.* Paul dismisses the charge (vv 10–13) and uses the proceeding as an opportunity to share the gospel (vv 14–21). Paul still considers himself a good Jew (vv 14, 17–18) and, as in verses 6–8, maintains that the issue is resurrection (v 21).

the comment, "When Lysias the tribune comes down, I will decide your case." 23Then he ordered the centurion to keep him in custody, but to let him have some liberty and not to prevent any of his friends from taking care of his needs.

Paul Held in Custody

24 Some days later when Felix came with his wife Drusilla, who was Jewish, he sent for Paul and heard him speak concerning faith in Christ Jesus. 25And as he discussed justice, self-control, and the coming judgment, Felix became frightened and said, "Go away for the present; when I have an opportunity, I will send for you." 26At the same time he hoped that money would be given him by Paul, and for that reason he used to send for him very often and converse with him.

27 After two years had passed, Felix was succeeded by Porcius Festus; and since he wanted to grant the Jews a favor, Felix left Paul in prison.

Paul Appeals to the Emperor

25 Three days after Festus had arrived in the province, he went up from Caesarea to Jerusalem 2where the chief priests and the leaders of the Jews gave him a report against Paul. They appealed to him 3and requested, as a favor to them against Paul, *a* to have him transferred to Jerusalem. They were, in fact, planning an ambush to kill him along the way. 4Festus replied that Paul was being kept at Caesarea, and that he himself intended to go there shortly. 5"So," he said, "let those of you who have the authority

come down with me, and if there is anything wrong about the man, let them accuse him."

6 After he had stayed among them not more than eight or ten days, he went down to Caesarea; the next day he took his seat on the tribunal and ordered Paul to be brought. 7When he arrived, the Jews who had gone down from Jerusalem surrounded him, bringing many serious charges against him, which they could not prove. 8Paul said in his defense, "I have in no way committed an offense against the law of the Jews, or against the temple, or against the emperor." 9But Festus, wishing to do the Jews a favor, asked Paul, "Do you wish to go up to Jerusalem and be tried there before me on these charges?" 10Paul said, "I am appealing to the emperor's tribunal; this is where I should be tried. I have done no wrong to the Jews, as you very well know. 11Now if I am in the wrong and have committed something for which I deserve to die, I am not trying to escape death; but if there is nothing to their charges against me, no one can turn me over to them. I appeal to the emperor." 12Then Festus, after he had conferred with his council, replied, "You have appealed to the emperor; to the emperor you will go."

Festus Consults King Agrippa

13 After several days had passed, King Agrippa and Bernice arrived at Caesarea to welcome Festus. 14Since they were staying there several days, Festus laid Paul's case before the king, saying, "There is a man here

a Gk *him*

24:22–23 *Felix . . . was rather well informed about the Way.* Felix already knows about Christianity, "the Way." Here again Luke depicts a Roman protecting Paul.

24:24–26 *he sent for Paul.* Paul's Caesarean imprisonment allows him to speak to highborn Romans at length about Jesus. Felix apparently hoped for a bribe from Paul.

25:1–5 *the chief priests and the leaders of the Jews gave . . . a report against Paul.* Another example of the Jewish leaders' antagonism toward Paul and Rome's protection of him.

25:11 *I appeal to the emperor.* Roman citizens could have their cases heard before the highest court, the emperor. Winning his case there would, in effect, legitimize Christianity. As in Philippi, Paul exercises his political rights as a citizen for the good of the Church.

25:13–27 *King Agrippa and Bernice arrived at Caesarea.* Agrippa II became king in AD 44. His consort, Bernice, was of dubious reputation. They make a "courtesy call" on Festus, who became governor in 59 or 60. Festus rehearses the particulars of Paul's imprisonment twice (vv 13–21, 24–27).

who was left in prison by Felix. 15When I was in Jerusalem, the chief priests and the elders of the Jews informed me about him and asked for a sentence against him. 16I told them that it was not the custom of the Romans to hand over anyone before the accused had met the accusers face to face and had been given an opportunity to make a defense against the charge. 17So when they met here, I lost no time, but on the next day took my seat on the tribunal and ordered the man to be brought. 18When the accusers stood up, they did not charge him with any of the crimes*a* that I was expecting. 19Instead they had certain points of disagreement with him about their own religion and about a certain Jesus, who had died, but whom Paul asserted to be alive. 20Since I was at a loss how to investigate these questions, I asked whether he wished to go to Jerusalem and be tried there on these charges.*b* 21But when Paul had appealed to be kept in custody for the decision of his Imperial Majesty, I ordered him to be held until I could send him to the emperor." 22Agrippa said to Festus, "I would like to hear the man myself." "Tomorrow," he said, "you will hear him."

Paul Brought before Agrippa

23 So on the next day Agrippa and Bernice came with great pomp, and they entered the audience hall with the military tribunes and the prominent men of the city. Then Festus gave the order and Paul was brought in. 24And Festus said, "King Agrippa and all here present with us, you see this man about whom the whole Jewish community petitioned me, both in Jerusalem and here, shouting that he ought not to live any longer. 25But I found that he had done nothing deserving death; and when he appealed to his Imperial Majesty, I decided to send him. 26But I have

nothing definite to write to our sovereign about him. Therefore I have brought him before all of you, and especially before you, King Agrippa, so that, after we have examined him, I may have something to write— 27for it seems to me unreasonable to send a prisoner without indicating the charges against him."

Paul Defends Himself before Agrippa

26 Agrippa said to Paul, "You have permission to speak for yourself." Then Paul stretched out his hand and began to defend himself:

2 "I consider myself fortunate that it is before you, King Agrippa, I am to make my defense today against all the accusations of the Jews, 3because you are especially familiar with all the customs and controversies of the Jews; therefore I beg of you to listen to me patiently.

4 "All the Jews know my way of life from my youth, a life spent from the beginning among my own people and in Jerusalem. 5They have known for a long time, if they are willing to testify, that I have belonged to the strictest sect of our religion and lived as a Pharisee. 6And now I stand here on trial on account of my hope in the promise made by God to our ancestors, 7a promise that our twelve tribes hope to attain, as they earnestly worship day and night. It is for this hope, your Excellency,*c* that I am accused by Jews! 8Why is it thought incredible by any of you that God raises the dead?

9 "Indeed, I myself was convinced that I ought to do many things against the name of Jesus of Nazareth.*d* 10And that is what I did in Jerusalem; with authority received from

a Other ancient authorities read *with anything*
b Gk *on them*   *c* Gk *O king*   *d* Gk *the Nazorean*

26:2–29 *I am to make my defense today.* Agrippa's visit provides Paul with an opportunity to share the gospel with Roman Palestine's rulers. This is his witness.

26:3 *you are especially familiar with all the customs . . . of the Jews.* Paul secures Agrippa's favor by praising his knowledge of Judaism, high irony considering his morals.

26:4–23 *All the Jews know my way of life.* Paul recounts his autobiography, stressing his strict Pharisaic roots (vv 4–8), his persecution of Christians (vv 9–11), and his conversion experience (vv 12–18) and subsequent ministry (vv 19–23). As in 23:6–10, he suggests the real issue is resurrection (vv 6–8).

the chief priests, I not only locked up many of the saints in prison, but I also cast my vote against them when they were being condemned to death. [11]By punishing them often in all the synagogues I tried to force them to blaspheme; and since I was so furiously enraged at them, I pursued them even to foreign cities.

Paul Tells of His Conversion

12 "With this in mind, I was traveling to Damascus with the authority and commission of the chief priests, [13]when at midday along the road, your Excellency,[a] I saw a light from heaven, brighter than the sun, shining around me and my companions. [14]When we had all fallen to the ground, I heard a voice saying to me in the Hebrew[b] language, 'Saul, Saul, why are you persecuting me? It hurts you to kick against the goads.' [15]I asked, 'Who are you, Lord?' The Lord answered, 'I am Jesus whom you are persecuting. [16]But get up and stand on your feet; for I have appeared to you for this purpose, to appoint you to serve and testify to the things in which you have seen me[c] and to those in which I will appear to you. [17]I will rescue you from your people and from the Gentiles—to whom I am sending you [18]to open their eyes so that they may turn from darkness to light and from the power of Satan to God, so that they may receive forgiveness of sins and a place among those who are sanctified by faith in me.'

Paul Tells of His Preaching

19 "After that, King Agrippa, I was not disobedient to the heavenly vision, [20]but declared first to those in Damascus, then in Jerusalem and throughout the countryside of Judea, and also to the Gentiles, that they should repent and turn to God and do deeds consistent with repentance. [21]For this reason the Jews seized me in the temple and tried to kill me. [22]To this day I have had help from God, and so I stand here, testifying to both small and great, saying nothing but what the prophets and Moses said would take place: [23]that the Messiah[d] must suffer, and that, by being the first to rise from the dead, he would proclaim light both to our people and to the Gentiles."

Paul Appeals to Agrippa to Believe

24 While he was making this defense, Festus exclaimed, "You are out of your mind, Paul! Too much learning is driving you insane!" [25]But Paul said, "I am not out of my mind, most excellent Festus, but I am speaking the sober truth. [26]Indeed the king knows about these things, and to him I speak freely; for I am certain that none of these things has escaped his notice, for this was not done in a corner. [27]King Agrippa, do you believe the prophets? I know that you believe." [28]Agrippa said to Paul, "Are you so quickly persuading me to become a Christian?"[e] [29]Paul replied, "Whether quickly or not, I pray to God that not only you but also all who are listening to me today might become such as I am—except for these chains."

30 Then the king got up, and with him the governor and Bernice and those who had been seated with them; [31]and as they were leaving, they said to one another, "This man is doing nothing to deserve death or imprisonment." [32]Agrippa said to Festus, "This man

a Gk O king   b That is, Aramaic   c Other ancient authorities read the things that you have seen   d Or the Christ   e Or Quickly you will persuade me to play the Christian

26:17–18 I will rescue you from your people and from the Gentiles. Paul recounts Jesus' words promising him deliverance from his people (Agrippa) and the Gentiles (Festus). They highlight his ministry to Gentiles, which has led to his imprisonment (vv 20–21).

26:22–23 saying nothing but what the prophets and Moses said. Paul stresses continuity of Jewish tradition with what God is doing in Jesus the Messiah. His Christology is rooted in Isaiah's thought. The claim that the Messiah must suffer is one of Paul's key points (cf., e.g., 17:3) and a difficult one for Jews (cf. 1 Cor 1:23).

26:24 Too much learning is driving you insane! Scholarly pursuit is often misunderstood.

26:29 I pray . . . all who are listening . . . might become such as I am. Paul's hearers understand that he wants to convert them to Christianity. Paul agrees, hoping everyone will come to faith in Jesus.

could have been set free if he had not appealed to the emperor."

Paul Sails for Rome

27 When it was decided that we were to sail for Italy, they transferred Paul and some other prisoners to a centurion of the Augustan Cohort, named Julius. [2]Embarking on a ship of Adramyttium that was about to set sail to the ports along the coast of Asia, we put to sea, accompanied by Aristarchus, a Macedonian from Thessalonica. [3]The next day we put in at Sidon; and Julius treated Paul kindly, and allowed him to go to his friends to be cared for. [4]Putting out to sea from there, we sailed under the lee of Cyprus, because the winds were against us. [5]After we had sailed across the sea that is off Cilicia and Pamphylia, we came to Myra in Lycia. [6]There the centurion found an Alexandrian ship bound for Italy and put us on board. [7]We sailed slowly for a number of days and arrived with difficulty off Cnidus, and as the wind was against us, we sailed under the lee of Crete off Salmone. [8]Sailing past it with difficulty, we came to a place called Fair Havens, near the city of Lasea.

[9] Since much time had been lost and sailing was now dangerous, because even the Fast had already gone by, Paul advised them, [10]saying, "Sirs, I can see that the voyage will be with danger and much heavy loss, not only of the cargo and the ship, but also of our lives." [11]But the centurion paid more attention to the pilot and to the owner of the ship than to what Paul said. [12]Since the harbor was not suitable for spending the winter, the majority was in favor of putting to sea from there, on the chance that somehow they could reach Phoenix, where they could spend the winter. It was a harbor of Crete, facing southwest and northwest.

The Storm at Sea

[13] When a moderate south wind began to blow, they thought they could achieve their purpose; so they weighed anchor and began to sail past Crete, close to the shore. [14]But soon a violent wind, called the northeaster, rushed down from Crete.[a] [15]Since the ship was caught and could not be turned head-on into the wind, we gave way to it and were driven. [16]By running under the lee of a small island called Cauda[b] we were scarcely able to get the ship's boat under control. [17]After hoisting it up they took measures[c] to undergird the ship; then, fearing that they would run on the Syrtis, they lowered the sea anchor and so were driven. [18]We were being pounded by the storm so violently that on the next day they began to throw the cargo overboard, [19]and on the third day with their own hands they threw the ship's tackle overboard. [20]When neither sun nor stars appeared for many days, and no small tempest raged, all hope of our being saved was at last abandoned.

[21] Since they had been without food for a long time, Paul then stood up among them and said, "Men, you should have listened to me and not have set sail from Crete and thereby avoided this damage and loss. [22]I urge you now to keep up your courage, for there will be no loss of life among you, but only of the ship. [23]For last night there stood by me an angel of the God to whom I belong and whom I worship, [24]and he said, 'Do not

a Gk it   b Other ancient authorities read *Clauda*
c Gk *helps*

26:30–32 *This man is doing nothing.* Paul is not guilty under either Jewish or Roman law. But having appealed to the emperor, he must be tried.

27:1–44 *we were to sail to Italy.* The "we source" is picked up again. Although this chapter follows the literary conventions of Hellenistic sea voyage narratives, it exhibits geographic accuracy and is one of the most exciting in Acts.

27:10 *I can see that the voyage will be with danger.* Paul has the gift of prophecy. Compare verses 22–26, 31, 33–34, which show Paul the prisoner to be protector of his captors.

27:21–26 *you should have listened to me.* Paul has an angelic visitation assuring him of the crew's ultimate safety. Such visions charted Paul's travels; he continues to be obedient to them.

27:23 WORSHIP—*See* Spiritual Disciplines Index.

be afraid, Paul; you must stand before the emperor; and indeed, God has granted safety to all those who are sailing with you.' ²⁵So keep up your courage, men, for I have faith in God that it will be exactly as I have been told. ²⁶But we will have to run aground on some island."

27 When the fourteenth night had come, as we were drifting across the sea of Adria, about midnight the sailors suspected that they were nearing land. ²⁸So they took soundings and found twenty fathoms; a little farther on they took soundings again and found fifteen fathoms. ²⁹Fearing that we might run on the rocks, they let down four anchors from the stern and prayed for day to come. ³⁰But when the sailors tried to escape from the ship and had lowered the boat into the sea, on the pretext of putting out anchors from the bow, ³¹Paul said to the centurion and the soldiers, "Unless these men stay in the ship, you cannot be saved." ³²Then the soldiers cut away the ropes of the boat and set it adrift.

33 Just before daybreak, Paul urged all of them to take some food, saying, "Today is the fourteenth day that you have been in suspense and remaining without food, having eaten nothing. ³⁴Therefore I urge you to take some food, for it will help you survive; for none of you will lose a hair from your heads." ³⁵After he had said this, he took bread; and giving thanks to God in the presence of all, he broke it and began to eat. ³⁶Then all of them were encouraged and took food for themselves. ³⁷(We were in all two hundred seventy-six ᵃ persons in the ship.) ³⁸After they had satisfied their hunger, they lightened the ship by throwing the wheat into the sea.

The Shipwreck

39 In the morning they did not recognize the land, but they noticed a bay with a beach, on which they planned to run the ship ashore, if they could. ⁴⁰So they cast off the anchors and left them in the sea. At the same time they loosened the ropes that tied the steering-oars; then hoisting the foresail to the wind, they made for the beach. ⁴¹But striking a reef, ᵇ they ran the ship aground; the bow stuck and remained immovable, but the stern was being broken up by the force of the waves. ⁴²The soldiers' plan was to kill the prisoners, so that none might swim away and escape; ⁴³but the centurion, wishing to save Paul, kept them from carrying out their plan. He ordered those who could swim to jump overboard first and make for the land, ⁴⁴and the rest to follow, some on planks and others on pieces of the ship. And so it was that all were brought safely to land.

Paul on the Island of Malta

28 After we had reached safety, we then learned that the island was called Malta. ²The natives showed us unusual kindness. Since it had begun to rain and was cold, they kindled a fire and welcomed all of us around it. ³Paul had gathered a bundle of brushwood and was putting it on the fire, when a viper, driven out by the heat, fastened itself on his hand. ⁴When the natives saw the creature hanging from his hand, they said to one another, "This man must be a murderer; though he has escaped from the sea, justice has not allowed him to live." ⁵He, however, shook off the creature into the fire and suffered no harm. ⁶They were expecting him to swell up or drop dead, but after they had waited a long time and saw that nothing unusual had happened to him, they changed their minds and began to say that he was a god.

7 Now in the neighborhood of that place were lands belonging to the leading man of the island, named Publius, who received us

---

a Other ancient authorities read *seventy-six*; others, *about seventy-six*   *b* Gk *place of two seas*

27:44 *all were brought safely to land.* The proof of a true prophet is that his predictions come true (see 11:28).

28:3–6 *a viper . . . fastened itself on his hand.* The narrative of Paul and the viper reflects the common belief that the guilty could not escape the wrath of the gods and is parallel to 14:11–18.

28:3–10 **THE WITH-GOD LIFE**—*See* Spiritual Disciplines Index.

and entertained us hospitably for three days. [8]It so happened that the father of Publius lay sick in bed with fever and dysentery. Paul visited him and cured him by praying and putting his hands on him. [9]After this happened, the rest of the people on the island who had diseases also came and were cured. [10]They bestowed many honors on us, and when we were about to sail, they put on board all the provisions we needed.

Paul Arrives at Rome

11 Three months later we set sail on a ship that had wintered at the island, an Alexandrian ship with the Twin Brothers as its figurehead. [12]We put in at Syracuse and stayed there for three days; [13]then we weighed anchor and came to Rhegium. After one day there a south wind sprang up, and on the second day we came to Puteoli. [14]There we found believers[a] and were invited to stay with them for seven days. And so we came to Rome. [15]The believers[a] from there, when they heard of us, came as far as the Forum of Appius and Three Taverns to meet us. On seeing them, Paul thanked God and took courage.

16 When we came into Rome, Paul was allowed to live by himself, with the soldier who was guarding him.

Paul and Jewish Leaders in Rome

17 Three days later he called together the local leaders of the Jews. When they had assembled, he said to them, "Brothers, though I had done nothing against our people or the customs of our ancestors, yet I was arrested in Jerusalem and handed over to the Romans. [18]When they had examined me, the Romans[b] wanted to release me, because there was no reason for the death penalty in my case. [19]But when the Jews objected, I was compelled to appeal to the emperor—even though I had no charge to bring against my nation. [20]For this reason therefore I have asked to see you and speak with you,[c] since it is for the sake of the hope of Israel that I am bound with this chain." [21]They replied, "We have received no letters from Judea about you, and none of the brothers coming here has reported or spoken anything evil about you. [22]But we would like to hear from you what you think, for with regard to this sect we know that everywhere it is spoken against."

Paul Preaches in Rome

23 After they had set a day to meet with him, they came to him at his lodgings in great numbers. From morning until evening he explained the matter to them, testifying to the kingdom of God and trying to convince them about Jesus both from the law of Moses and from the prophets. [24]Some were con-

a Gk brothers   *b* Gk they   *c* Or *I have asked you to see me and speak with me*

Responding
28:8 PRAYER. Try to imagine Paul praying for and putting his hands on the father of Publius. How does the simple act of touching someone with your hands as you pray increase the power of the prayer? When you feel comfortable enough to do so, pray for and lay your hands on someone who has a simple illness like a cold or fever. This can be a person in your family, a good friend, or a co-worker, but be sure to first ask permission. Did you have the sense that God was working through you to help the person become well? *See also* Spiritual Disciplines Index.

28:8–9 *Paul . . . cured.* Paul's ability to heal, here Publius's father and others, parallels that of Peter. Luke depicts the powers of Jesus con-

tinuing to be manifested in his Church. The power of God among us is limited only according to our degree of openness to it.

28:14 *There we found believers.* Christians depended upon fellow believers for hospitality, that important, practical virtue.

28:16 *Paul was allowed to live by himself.* Paul was under "house arrest," which allowed him to receive visitors and to preach (cf. vv 17, 23, 30–31).

28:17 *he called together the local leaders of the Jews.* As usual, Paul preached first to the Jews wishing to hear more about his "sect" (28:22).

28:23 *both from the law of Moses and from the prophets.* Paul presents Jesus in terms of Judaism's Scriptures. His thinking is shaped by Isaiah's (vv 26–28; 13:47; 26:23).

vinced by what he had said, while others refused to believe. 25So they disagreed with each other; and as they were leaving, Paul made one further statement: "The Holy Spirit was right in saying to your ancestors through the prophet Isaiah,

26 'Go to this people and say,
   You will indeed listen, but never
      understand,
   and you will indeed look, but never
      perceive.
27 For this people's heart has grown dull,
   and their ears are hard of hearing,
      and they have shut their eyes;
         so that they might not look with
            their eyes,

and listen with their ears,
   and understand with their heart and
      turn—
   and I would heal them.'

28Let it be known to you then that this salvation of God has been sent to the Gentiles; they will listen."*a*

` 30 He lived there two whole years at his own expense*b* and welcomed all who came to him, 31 proclaiming the kingdom of God and teaching about the Lord Jesus Christ with all boldness and without hindrance.

a Other ancient authorities add verse 29, *And when he had said these words, the Jews departed, arguing vigorously among themselves*   *b* Or *in his own hired dwelling*

28:28 *this salvation of God has been sent to the Gentiles.* The focus at the close of Acts is on Paul's mission to the Gentiles. His own story is left unfinished.

28:30 *welcomed all who came to him.* Paul preaches to all comers without distinction. As he has received hospitality, he offers it to "all who came to him." As "God shows no partiality"

(10:34), God's messengers must be similarly inclusive.

28:31 *proclaiming the kingdom of God and teaching about the Lord Jesus Christ.* Paul's basic message is Jesus, that he is "Lord" and "Christ," both heavy with association for Gentiles and Jews, respectively. The verse shows prayers of the early Christians being answered (see 4:29–30).

XIV. The People of God in Community

Scriptures: *Romans, 1 & 2 Corinthians, Galatians, Ephesians, Philippians, Colossians, 1 & 2 Thessalonians, 1 & 2 Timothy, Titus, Philemon, Hebrews, James, 1 & 2 Peter, 1, 2, & 3 John, Jude*

> *The aim of God in history is the creation of an all-inclusive community of loving persons with God himself at the very center of this community as its prime Sustainer and most glorious Inhabitant (Eph 2:19–22; 3:10). The Bible traces the formation of this community from the creation in the Garden of Eden all the way to the new heaven and the new earth. Come, join us as we explore the many dimensions of this with-God history—from individual to family to tribe to people to nation to all humanity—and apply what we learn to our own spiritual formation.*

In the book of Acts we saw how the People of God took their first great leaps as an all-inclusive community of loving persons through the empowerment of the indwelling Holy Spirit. In these Scriptures, we will see how the early communities of faith based on discipleship to Jesus Christ are established and nurture living communion with God and abiding fellowship with one another.

God's Action

In the Letters of the New Testament we find the continuing incarnation of Jesus Christ in "gathered communities." This context for God's people is meant to set them free from the constraints of ethnicity, gender, nationality, race, and religion. These communities of faith—the Body of Christ in the world—literally become a new substance, a new organism, in which people become part of one another and, through the power of the Holy Spirit, help one another begin, nurture, and sustain their relationship with God. The world had seen countless humanly contrived religions with their innumerable laws and rituals, but they all failed to bring people into constant, living communion with the Creator of the universe. But now, in these called-out communities established by the sovereign hand of God, we witness people from every walk of life gathering in the name of Jesus Christ.

These gathered communities of faith become hubs of life and spiritual vitality. As we saw in Acts, they are the birthplace of proclamation that initiates belief in Jesus as the Christ. Beyond this, they become centers of intense instruction in this new life with God in Christ (Col 3). They help new disciples discover and cultivate their own spiritual gifts while teaching them to celebrate the gifts of others (Eph 4). Ultimately, these early gathered communities help disciples maintain loving contact with God and give them a deeper understanding of the with-God life, which is to permeate every aspect of human existence (1 John). "And let us consider," instructs the writer of Hebrews, "how to provoke one another to love and good deeds, not neglecting to meet together, as is the habit of some, but encouraging one another" (10:24–25).

Earlier, we described the Church as Jesus' self-replicating society of God-inhabited people. In contrast to all earthbound institutions, the Church originates with God on a foundation of love, truth, and power. It is the place where all people can gather as Christ's apprentices in order to be formed, conformed, and transformed into his image. Christ is ever in the midst of the gathered community to teach his people himself. Ultimately, the Church is the place where all who "confess that Jesus Christ is Lord" are to be brought to such a level of God-awareness that they can respond to all of life's demands as Christ himself would (Phil 2:11; Gal 5:22–26).

Human Reaction

The Greek word we translate "church"—*ekklesia*—points to the fundamental nature of the Christian community: assembly. Early believers gathered in assembly as the followers of Jesus, and we continue to so gather to this day. Various images of the "assembly" dominate Scripture, but especially prominent in the Letters are the People of God, the Body of Christ, the Bride of Christ, the Community of the Holy Spirit, and the Family of God. The assembly becomes a primary place where followers of "the Way" participate in Christ's life, death, and resurrection.

This early self-understanding of the Christian community, established and sustained by God, led to a variety of functions that define its core life. These functions include coming to belief, entering into fellowship, accepting corrective discipline, embracing wise guidance, shaping Christian liberty, discovering appropriate behavior, and practicing corporate unity. These functions define and reflect the nature of the early Church and have as their ultimate goal bringing each person into a dynamic relationship with Jesus Christ.

But, true to human nature, along with these functions come questions and problems. All of the Letters, from Romans through the short letter to Jude, address particular community needs or specific individual concerns. Written as occasional letters, just as we might write letters of counsel today, the Letters provide guidance and insight into the with-God life. For example, Paul writes to those in the gathered community in Galatia about their relationship to Jesus Christ and to each other: "in Christ Jesus you are all children of God through faith. . . . There is no longer Jew or Greek, there is no longer slave or free, there is no longer male and female; for all of you are one in Christ Jesus" (Gal 3:26, 28). In Ephesians, he emphasizes that God reveals his ultimate purposes through Jesus Christ and establishes the nature of their unity and new life in him: "But now in Christ Jesus you who once were far off have been brought near. . . . For he is our peace; in his flesh he has made both groups into one and has broken down the dividing wall, that is, the hostility between us" (2:13–14).

Individuals too had problems to resolve and questions to ask, so they receive instruction in practical matters as well as theological training. Paul writes to Timothy, "Remain in Ephesus so that you may instruct certain people not to teach any different doctrine" (1 Tim 1:3), and then he goes on to explain the different doctrines. In many ways, the Letters functioned as the wisdom literature of the early Church, providing both telescopic and microscopic guidance for life. They contain wisdom sayings reminiscent of the Old Testament as well as theological implications of the Gospels in order to provide a broader understanding: "Now we command you, beloved . . . to keep away from believers who are living in idleness. . . . Brothers and sisters, do not be weary in doing what is right" (2 Thess 3:6, 13).

Although each of the Letters offers a unique understanding of its community's with-God life, particularly significant is the Letter to the Romans. Of all Paul's Letters, Romans has had the most measurable, long-lasting impact. As a result of reading Romans Augustine became a Christian, Martin Luther started the Reformation, John Wesley experienced the reality of God's grace, and Karl Barth recovered the centrality of Christ for Christian living. Originally written for a particular gathered community during a specific time, Romans has captivated the minds and imaginations of people throughout history.

The central theme in this seminal work is the person and work of Jesus Christ. "There is therefore now no condemnation for those who are in Christ Jesus. For the law of the Spirit of life in Christ Jesus has set you free from the law of sin and death" (Rom 8:1–2). Under the inspiration of the Holy Sprit, Paul identifies the secret of our life hidden with Christ in God: *zōē,* the eternal, uncreated life that originates in God alone.

Scripture identifies two types of life: *bios,* the physical, created life; and *zōē,* the spiritual, eternal life. Likewise, there are two types of death: *teleute,* physical death; and *thanatos,* spiritual death. Thus, the challenge with which we must contend is the very real fact that a person can be physically alive (*bios*) while spiritually dead (*thanatos*). Failure to understand this is the very source of so much present-day alienation and despair. Mistaking *bios* for *zōē* always causes misguided spiritual formation. This problem, massive today, is seen in the proliferation of spiritual practices that are little more than self-help techniques. We must discover again the hidden reservoir of God's love and power (*zōē*) if we are to be formed into disciples of Jesus, expressing his love and teachings through our own lives.

Blessings and Benefits for Our Formation

Because God has created us with a need for community, the community of faith (the Church) is necessary. But it also fundamentally shapes what we know, how we believe, and who we are. In community we learn of our individual responsibilities to God and our corporate responsibilities to one another. There are exceptions, to be sure, but sustaining a life with God without an active, living connection to a visible expression of the Body of Christ is virtually impossible and is not a goal to be sought after.

The With-God Life

We now find the Abrahamic covenant of blessing to all peoples fulfilled in this living community, the Church, as the whole earth is blessed in a new way with the possibility that God—in the person of Jesus and through his Holy Spirit—can be present and available to every human being. In faith, Jesus' disciples become a self-replicating fellowship, and, as was promised to Abraham's spiritual descendants, they become "as numerous as the stars of heaven and as the sand that is on the seashore" (Gen 22:17). And so the People of God form a living community of disciples who spread the gospel of the kingdom throughout the world and provide mutual support as they ever learn to walk in the way of Jesus Christ.

In the new community formed by God the barriers introduced in Genesis 3 that separate human beings from each other are torn down as the Holy Spirit unites all peoples in the community of faith: "There is no longer Greek and Jew, circumcised and uncircumcised, barbarian, Scythian, slave and free; but Christ is all and in all!" (Col 3:11). God's will for the world—an all-inclusive community of loving persons—is fully disclosed, which brings an end to merely human techniques for understanding life.

Limits and Liabilities for Our Formation

Nevertheless, we all know that there are limitations to being spiritually formed in a community of like-minded, though extremely different (and perhaps difficult), people. Doctrinal disputes, for example, can at times sorely strain the unity of the community. Sometimes issues of genuine substance are at stake, and when this is the case we need to wrestle together over the matter until gospel truth prevails. But at other times it seems that people are majoring on minors, when they believe they know, for example, the will of God for the color of the church nursery. At such times we come face-to-face with the limits and liabilities of our life together. Divisions over such trivia—and their number is legion—injure the work of spiritual formation.

If sin is allowed to fester in the community without loving, firm discipline, it hinders the work of spiritual formation and brings disrepute upon the entire Christian community. If loving, Spirit-led pastoral care is missing, the lack is felt throughout the community. If a congregation is prone to run after religious fads and in doing so neglects its calling to help people grow in Christlikeness, the loss is immeasurable. The list could go on and on. We are all painfully aware of the limits and liabilities of the local expressions of the Body of Christ.

But it is precisely here that the Letters give us hope. They describe the real struggles of real churches and how they can be increasingly transformed into vital communities of faith "for building up the body of Christ, until all of us come to the unity of the faith and of the knowledge of the Son of God, to maturity, to the measure of the full stature of Christ" (Eph 4:12–13).

Individual faith joined to a community of faith is meant to strengthen our relationship with God. God never intended that being part of a church should stifle our faith. In fact, God gives us a clear measure of a false church cultivating a false faith: anything that stifles the life-giving power of Christ's love is against God. It is really that basic.

Insights and Instructions for Our Formation

The insights for our own formation are considerable. Primarily, we learn that the community of faith has been established to bring us into living communion with God and abiding fellowship with one another. We seek God and find him most often through the ministry of a local church. Here we experience, in real and concrete ways, the love of Christ and learn how we are to love one another despite disagreements and imperfections. This love, witnessed by those outside the community and proclaimed by word and sacrament, draws the world to God. This *is* the community of loving persons intended from the beginning of time.

Second, every community of faith in its own unique way is a real, if imperfect, reflection of the kingdom of God. Each church, and each Letter that represents the life of a local church, reminds us that life on earth is filled with challenges to genuine faith. Each faith community, while existing in a unique culture and generating a unique understanding of Christ for a particular time, ultimately exists to preserve a living witness to the life of love, power, and peace that comes from God alone.

Third, under the discipline of guidance, by the spiritually mature in the local community of faith, we learn the secret of spiritual formation as we put off the old nature and "put on Jesus Christ." When we "put on Christ" we do so in the spirit of love that forms the foundation of the universal community in which we encounter the reality of the risen Christ. As a result, we fall deeper and deeper in love with God and "love one another . . . in truth and action" (1 John 3:11, 18).

Fourth, in the gathered community we witness the reality of a God-given power that transcends human conventions. We come to realize that true power resides not in human structures—corporations or governments or institutions or nations—but rather in divine gifts that are used to benefit others. We exercise these spiritual gifts in the context of an unshakable kingdom that is invisible and without boundaries or limit.

Finally, in our life together we experience the risen Christ, from whom we learn the reality of true life followed by meaningful death. Life finds its truest, fullest expression in pouring ourselves out as a sacrifice to God, working with him to bring his kingdom to earth. Death then becomes meaningful when we can say, with Paul, that we have pressed on "toward the goal for the prize of the heavenly call of God in Christ Jesus" (Phil 3:14). When our life is immersed in the love and service of God, death becomes a transition moment rather than the dreaded end; it is, as Paul says, "swallowed up in victory" (1 Cor 15:54).

So, as you read these Letters reflect again on God's desire that you have a deeper, fuller life with him. Watch as Paul works with Peter in Galatians to overcome his own deep prejudice, and consider your own battles with prejudice as well. Discover again, or even for the first time, your hidden life in Christ that gains its strength from God's reservoir of love for the world (Colossians). Celebrate with Timothy his

The With-God Life

successful transition to leadership in the Church, and then consider what God may be calling you to do. Squirm with the Corinthians as Paul chastises them for their wayward behavior, and then pause to reflect on your own moral lapses. Savor the uniqueness of Ephesians as Paul first shows us how to come to saving faith (chaps 1–3) and then teaches us how to grow in it (chaps 4–6); then reflect on the way in which God is building a bulwark of faith within you. Enjoy the majesty of Romans as Paul lays out his last and most comprehensive theology of the Christian faith and captures the spirit of eternal life that is life indeed. As you work your way through these and the other Letters, remember that God's intention is that we each come to a fuller knowledge of him as we deepen our personal fellowship with one another.

The With-God Life

THE LETTER OF PAUL TO THE

ROMANS

Paul's Letter to the Romans was written to encourage and guide Christians in living their lives Christianly, that is, living lives formed by the Spirit in Jesus Christ. As are all the documents of Holy Scripture, it is primarily a text directed toward daily, ordinary living. There are no generalities here, nothing programmatic. Paul works entirely in the context of a congregation of souls, men and women who are called upon to repent and believe, obey and love, pray and forgive as they go about their daily lives of preparing meals, raising children, and going to work.

This needs saying up front, for perhaps more than any other book in the Bible Romans has been turned over to the experts. In one sense this is understandable. Scholars and theologians have spent their lives probing its depths and writing learned books on its theological content—it is clearly a book that challenges the best minds in the community. All of us would be the poorer without their devout and disciplined work. What is unfortunate, however, is when the rest of us disqualify ourselves from reading it firsthand. The scholars are here to help us read it, not read it for us.

The first thing we must do is simply start reading Romans on our own. Everyone who comes to this book needs to be reminded that Romans is primarily a work of spiritual formation in a community of souls. It is a personal address to a mixed congregation of Gentiles and Jews, many of whom were slaves and most of whom could not read. Paul's intellect is totally in the service of men and women like us who are being formed by the Spirit in the life of Christ. Prepare to be impressed by Romans, but don't be intimidated by Romans.

Integrated into the text are four aspects of spiritual formation that were formative in Paul's life and are intended for the formation of our lives: his submission to Scripture, his embrace of mystery, his particular use of language, and his insistence on community.

See also "The With-God Life" essay for this section of the Bible,
"The People of God in Community," pp. 2037–42.

Submission to Scripture

In reading Romans it becomes clear that Paul is not an independent thinker figuring things out on his own. Nor is he a speculative thinker playing with ideas, searching for some ultimate truth. His thinking is subordinated to all that God has revealed of himself and his purposes in Holy Scripture. Scripture for Paul was the Jewish Bible that we now designate the Old Testament. As he writes to the Roman congregation, Paul's mind is entirely harnessed to Scripture.

Prideful condescension is often a by-product of superior minds. It is easy to assume that a man who writes excellent books ranks higher than a migrant worker picking fruit; that a woman who manages the financial affairs of a large corporation is worth more than the woman who cleans the toilets in a public restroom. But Paul, one of the most competent minds in history, shows no such arrogance. All his mental processes are subdued and submissive to what has been handed to him by revelation in Scripture. The words of scriptural revelation are the means by which he thinks and prays.

Paul's relation to Scripture was not that of a student boning up for an exam, but that of a disciple of Jesus living the text. He spent the first part of his life as a Pharisee, using the Scriptures zealously but wrongly. He spent the second part of his life as a Christian, living these same Scriptures just as zealously, but in a very different way. The difference was this: as an activist Pharisee he used the Scriptures to support an angry crusade; as a believing Christian he let the Spirit use the Scriptures to form Christ in him. The Scriptures furnish his vocabulary, shape his imagination, form his life. They are vast presences, suggesting the immense horizons within which he writes.

Laced through the letter are sixty-five quotations from sixteen of the thirty-nine Old Testament books available to Paul. He cites his favorites, Isaiah and Psalms, eighteen and thirteen times, respectively, but he ranges widely, covering most of the territory from Genesis to Malachi. But it is not only that Paul quotes Scripture; he *inhabits* the story of Scripture. He gives the impression of being on familiar terms with everything written by his prophet ancestors, totally at ease in this richly expansive narrative of God's Word. To use a phrase from Scottish pastor Alexander Whyte, the Scriptures had become "all over autobiographic" for Paul.

Embrace of Mystery

Another aspect of spiritual formation embedded in Paul's Letter to the Romans is his extravagant embrace of mystery. He accepts mystery, is comfortable with mystery, even delights in mystery. His celebrated outburst in 11:33–36 is characteristic: "O the depth of the riches and wisdom and knowledge of God! How unsearchable are his judgments and how inscrutable his ways! 'For who has known the mind of the Lord? Or who has been his counselor?' [Isa 40:13–14]. 'Or who has given a gift to him, to receive a gift in return?' [Job 35:7; 41:11]. For from him and through him and to him are all things. To him be the glory forever. Amen." It is significant that this reverent but exuberant stance before the God who cannot be figured out or diagrammed comes in the context of some of Paul's most vigorous reasoning (chaps 9–11). Mystery, for Paul, is not what is left over after we have done our best to reason things out on our own. No, it is inherent in the very nature of who God is and how he works.

As the Spirit forms the life of Christ in us we necessarily encounter in God more than we can grasp, more than we are capable of explaining or understanding. But the "more" we encounter is not some secret kept hidden from us; it is not "classified" information from which we common people are excluded. Far from it. It is, rather, an open invitation for us to live in a world larger than our own sin-cramped selves.

There is a mind-set, too common among us, that is impatient with mystery— we want to know what is going on. But such impatience short-circuits our spiritual formation. The ability of the human intellect to penetrate areas of ignorance and to map reality is, of course, formidable. Aggressive intellectual activity produces results that stagger the imagination. It is understandable that the modern mind, accustomed to seeing the tangled undergrowth of "mystery" cleared out by the "knowledge" bulldozers, may little appreciate the kind of mystery that Paul wrestles with, a mystery that deepens even as our knowledge increases.

The mystery that Paul embraces is not the mystery of darkness that must be dispelled, but the mystery of light that may be entered. God and his operations cannot be reduced to what we are capable of explaining and then reproducing. It takes considerable humility to embrace this mystery, for in the presence of mystery we are not in a position to control anything, predict outcomes, manage people, or pose as authorities.

Use of Metaphorical Language

The way we use language is critical in spiritual formation. This should come as no surprise to us, since language is primary to the gospel message itself: "The word is near you, on your lips and in your heart" (Rom 10:8, quoting Deut 30:14). And Jesus, of course, is *the* Word. Language, one of the defining characteristics of being human, is integral to the way God reveals and works. It follows that the *way* we use language, not simply *that* we use it, is significant.

The way Paul uses language in Romans is to load it with metaphor, a practice he learned from the Hebrew prophets before him. There is hardly a paragraph in this letter without a metaphor.

Metaphor is not a precise use of language, but quite the opposite. Instead of pinning meaning down, metaphor lets it loose. Metaphor does not so much define or label; it expands, forcing the mind into participating action. When we use "rock" as a metaphor for God, as in "The Lord is my rock" (Ps 18:2), "rock" does not define God. Taken literally, the statement is absurd. What metaphor does is force our mind into action to find meaning at another level, engaging the imagination to look for relationships and resonances that tell us more than any literal description ever could. We cannot be passive before a metaphor. We must imagine and enter into it. Metaphor enlists us in a believing, obeying, living participation.

Do we like things tidy and neat, without loose ends and devoid of ambiguity? Are we rubber-hits-the-road pragmatists who like things organized and orderly?

That is not the kind of language we find in Romans. Paul uses words not to define, but to evoke. He doesn't serve up God's truth depersonalized, like a specimen under a microscope. He doesn't take sentences apart, prying the truth out of them. He doesn't, in the words of Wordsworth, "murder to dissect."

Paul's language is a living energy field. He doesn't develop a technical jargon for the sake of being precise about God. Rather, he takes the language of common discourse, redolent with metaphor—common things, common actions—and uses it freely, at ease with the ambiguities necessarily inherent in it. This is language alive, expressing and forming our lives from the inside out. Spiritual formation requires this lively, participatory language.

Insistence on Community

Finally, Paul comes to community. Spiritual formation can never take place in isolation or develop in impersonal or functional ways. Spiritual formation is never just between me and God. Persons, persons-in-relationship, are necessarily involved. On the opening page of the letter Paul signals this reality when he addresses the congregation as "all God's beloved in Rome" (1:7), expresses his personal feeling toward them in the phrase "I am longing to see you" (1:11), and notes how he has often looked forward to being with them so that he "may reap some harvest among [them]" (1:13). This is not generalized spirituality; it is personally written to a specific congregation of Christians living in a particular place. Even though Paul had not yet been to Rome, he knows the names of many people there. Before the letter ends, we will read some of their names (chap 16).

But it is easy for us to lose touch with this personal context once Paul launches into the main body of his text at 1:16. Here the rich interpersonal context seems to recede into the shadows as Paul deals with the pressing issue of relations between Jews and Gentiles. But it really only "seems to," for Paul is dealing with a disintegrating community, the "communion (or rather lack thereof) of saints." In the Roman congregation Jews are feeling superior to Gentiles, and Gentiles are feeling superior to Jews. Substantive spiritual formation cannot take place under such conditions, and so Paul tackles the issue of community head-on.

In chapters 1–8 Paul deals with Jews, insiders to the historic revelation to Israel, but ones who are here using their ethnic distinction as a mark of privilege over Gentiles. Paul argues vigorously that there is no difference, "no distinction" (3:22). In chapters 9–11 he turns the tables: "Now I am speaking to you Gentiles" (11:13). Gentiles are warned against looking down on Israel. They are the ones now assuming the place of privilege as insiders to God's grace. In chapters 1–8 Paul prevents Jews from excluding Gentiles by insisting Jews are sinners to the same degree as Gentiles; in chapters 9–11 Paul prevents Gentiles from excluding Jews by reminding them that they themselves are "in" only by God's miracle of "grafting" them onto the salvation tree. Gentiles are in because of God's miracle; Jews will also get in by means of miracle. Neither group has anything to be proud of. Paul approaches Jew and Gentile differently, but the effect is the same. The sin argument ("all have sinned,"

3:23) directed to the Jews in chapters 1–8 is matched by the miracle argument ("life from the dead," 11:15) in chapters 9–11. We are all first-class sinners; we are all miraculously "grafted" into God's olive tree Church.

In chapter 12, having gotten the members of the Roman congregation truly thinking about one another, their minds scrubbed clean of distorting class assumptions, Paul addresses them as a community, Jews and Gentiles standing on level ground, brothers and sisters in the same family. There is neither motive nor excuse now for Jews to push Gentiles into the background or for Gentiles to elbow Jews to the sidelines. Class separations of any sort (Jew/Gentile, capitalist/worker, native/immigrant, rich/poor, young/old, literate/illiterate) are death to community. In the final chapters (12–16) Paul instructs them in the formation of community ("I appeal to you therefore, brothers and sisters," 12:1). He brings the letter to a conclusion in a flourish of personal names, thirty-five of them, Jews and Gentiles together, truly the "communion of saints."

As we read Paul's Letter to the Romans we find ourselves immersed in a classic work of spiritual formation. We note the absence of large abstract truths, on the one hand, and individual anecdotes, on the other. What we find, instead, is a working model of what continues to aid in the formation of our souls by the power of the Spirit: submission to Scripture, embrace of mystery, metaphorical language, and insistence on community.

—*Eugene H. Peterson*

Salutation

1 Paul, a servant[a] of Jesus Christ, called to be an apostle, set apart for the gospel of God, [2]which he promised beforehand through his prophets in the holy scriptures, [3]the gospel concerning his Son, who was descended from David according to the flesh [4]and was declared to be Son of God with power according to the spirit[b] of holiness by resurrection from the dead, Jesus Christ our Lord, [5]through whom we have received grace and apostleship to bring about the obedience of faith among all the Gentiles for the sake of his name, [6]including yourselves who are called to belong to Jesus Christ,

7 To all God's beloved in Rome, who are called to be saints:

Grace to you and peace from God our Father and the Lord Jesus Christ.

Prayer of Thanksgiving

8 First, I thank my God through Jesus Christ for all of you, because your faith is proclaimed throughout the world. [9]For God, whom I serve with my spirit by announcing the gospel[c] of his Son, is my witness that without ceasing I remember you always in my prayers, [10]asking that by God's will I may somehow at last succeed in coming to you. [11]For I am longing to see you so that I may share with you some spiritual gift to strengthen you—[12]or rather so that we may be

a Gk *slave*   *b* Or *Spirit*   *c* Gk *my spirit in the gospel*

1:8 *First, I thank my God.* Paul, mature in all matters of spiritual formation, begins, as life itself begins, with gratitude for lives placed in his care. Life in itself—sheer, raw, unadorned life—is pure gift. Spontaneous, grateful thanksgiving establishes the working conditions for all growth and development in Christ.

mutually encouraged by each other's faith, both yours and mine. [13]I want you to know, brothers and sisters,[a] that I have often intended to come to you (but thus far have been prevented), in order that I may reap some harvest among you as I have among the rest of the Gentiles. [14]I am a debtor both to Greeks and to barbarians, both to the wise and to the foolish [15]—hence my eagerness to proclaim the gospel to you also who are in Rome.

The Power of the Gospel

[16] For I am not ashamed of the gospel; it is the power of God for salvation to everyone who has faith, to the Jew first and also to the Greek. [17]For in it the righteousness of God is revealed through faith for faith; as it is written, "The one who is righteous will live by faith."[b]

The Guilt of Humankind

[18] For the wrath of God is revealed from heaven against all ungodliness and wickedness of those who by their wickedness suppress the truth. [19]For what can be known about God is plain to them, because God has shown it to them. [20]Ever since the creation of the world his eternal power and divine nature, invisible though they are, have been understood and seen through the things he has made. So they are without excuse; [21]for though they knew God, they did not honor him as God or give thanks to him, but they became futile in their thinking, and their senseless minds were darkened. [22]Claiming to be wise, they became fools; [23]and they exchanged the glory of the immortal God for images resembling a mortal human being or birds or four-footed animals or reptiles.

[24] Therefore God gave them up in the lusts of their hearts to impurity, to the degrading of their bodies among themselves, [25]because they exchanged the truth about God for a lie and worshiped and served the creature rather than the Creator, who is blessed forever! Amen.

[26] For this reason God gave them up to degrading passions. Their women exchanged natural intercourse for unnatural, [27]and in the same way also the men, giving up natural intercourse with women, were consumed with passion for one another. Men committed shameless acts with men and received in their own persons the due penalty for their error.

[28] And since they did not see fit to acknowledge God, God gave them up to a debased mind and to things that should not be done. [29]They were filled with every kind of wickedness, evil, covetousness, malice. Full of envy, murder, strife, deceit, craftiness, they are gossips, [30]slanderers, God-haters,[c] insolent, haughty, boastful, inventors of evil, rebellious toward parents, [31]foolish, faithless, heartless, ruthless. [32]They know God's decree, that those who practice such things deserve to die—yet they not only do them but even applaud others who practice them.

a Gk brothers   *b* Or *The one who is righteous through faith will live*   *c* Or *God-hated*

1:12 *that we may be mutually encouraged.* There are no "masters" in the spiritual life. Mature and wise teachers, yes. But fundamentally we are all beginners receiving and giving on our knees before God and with open hands before one another. In this business no one "lords it over" another.

1:17 *the righteousness of God.* Who God is and what he does, summed up in this term, are foundational to who we are and what we do. The Christian life derives entirely from God's righteousness, his will, enacted in Christ, to "set us right" with him. Everything of God is put to the work of setting us and our world right. The term is comprehensive of both God and our relation with God. The meaning gets richer each time Paul uses it (3:5 [translated "justice" in the NRSV], 21, 22, 25, 26; 10:3 [twice]). *revealed through faith for faith.* Faith is not "believing in something without proof," but trusting in someone in a participating way. It is not just thinking with our minds; it is assenting with our lives. It is how we get in on the righteousness of God.

1:18–32 *all ungodliness and wickedness.* When we do wrong, we are not "just being human." The many synonyms for "sin" that pile up here are evidence, not of our humanity, but of our loss of it. The spiritual life is a radical recovery of our true God-created selves, our souls.

The Righteous Judgment of God

2 Therefore you have no excuse, whoever you are, when you judge others; for in passing judgment on another you condemn yourself, because you, the judge, are doing the very same things. [2]You say,[a] "We know that God's judgment on those who do such things is in accordance with truth." [3]Do you imagine, whoever you are, that when you judge those who do such things and yet do them yourself, you will escape the judgment of God? [4]Or do you despise the riches of his kindness and forbearance and patience? Do you not realize that God's kindness is meant to lead you to repentance? [5]But by your hard and impenitent heart you are storing up wrath for yourself on the day of wrath, when God's righteous judgment will be revealed. [6]For he will repay according to each one's deeds: [7]to those who by patiently doing good seek for glory and honor and immortality, he will give eternal life; [8]while for those who are self-seeking and who obey not the truth but wickedness, there will be wrath and fury. [9]There will be anguish and distress for everyone who does evil, the Jew first and also the Greek, [10]but glory and honor and peace for everyone who does good, the Jew first and also the Greek. [11]For God shows no partiality.

[12] All who have sinned apart from the law will also perish apart from the law, and all who have sinned under the law will be judged by the law. [13]For it is not the hearers of the law who are righteous in God's sight, but the doers of the law who will be justified. [14]When Gentiles, who do not possess the law, do instinctively what the law requires, these, though not having the law, are a law to themselves. [15]They show that what the law requires is written on their hearts, to which their own conscience also bears witness; and their conflicting thoughts will accuse or perhaps excuse them [16]on the day when, according to my gospel, God, through Jesus Christ, will judge the secret thoughts of all.

The Jews and the Law

17 But if you call yourself a Jew and rely on the law and boast of your relation to God [18]and know his will and determine what is best because you are instructed in the law, [19]and if you are sure that you are a guide to the blind, a light to those who are in darkness, [20]a corrector of the foolish, a teacher of children, having in the law the embodiment of knowledge and truth, [21]you, then, that teach others, will you not teach yourself? While you preach against stealing, do you steal? [22]You that forbid adultery, do you com-

---

a Gk lacks *You say*

2:1 *when you judge others.* Looking around and clucking with disapproval at what others do wrong is a time-honored way of averting detection of our own wrongs. Cataloguing wrongs, whether in our family, our neighborhood, or the world, does not qualify as a spiritual life, and God has no patience with it.

2:9 *Jew first and also the Greek.* Jews are insiders to the law revealed to Moses; Greeks are outsiders. Paul, knowing how we love to put people into categories that give us a vocabulary for treating them impersonally and giving us an edge over them, puts a stop to it from the start. God does not deal with us in categories. This habit of making distinctions and assuming superiorities is deadly to spiritual formation; Paul is relentless in exposing and rooting it out.

2:16 **SECRECY**—*See* Spiritual Disciplines Index.

2:21 *you, then, that teach others.* Teaching is so much easier than learning. It is also more dangerous. In the act of teaching, especially when we know what we are saying is right, we inevitably sense that we embody what we teach. The admiration and appreciation of others reinforce the feeling. Meanwhile, a huge gap gradually widens between what we say and the way we live. It happens a lot in life, but nowhere with more deadly consequences than among those who teach about God and his ways with us.

Responding

2:21 STUDY. As children, most of us looked forward to going to school to study and learn, but as we grow older, we often become jaded and disinterested. What actions can we take so that we stay continuously energized and interested in studying and learning about the with-God life? *See also* Spiritual Disciplines Index.

mit adultery? You that abhor idols, do you rob temples? 23 You that boast in the law, do you dishonor God by breaking the law? 24 For, as it is written, "The name of God is blasphemed among the Gentiles because of you."

25 Circumcision indeed is of value if you obey the law; but if you break the law, your circumcision has become uncircumcision. 26 So, if those who are uncircumcised keep the requirements of the law, will not their uncircumcision be regarded as circumcision? 27 Then those who are physically uncircumcised but keep the law will condemn you that have the written code and circumcision but break the law. 28 For a person is not a Jew who is one outwardly, nor is true circumcision something external and physical. 29 Rather, a person is a Jew who is one inwardly, and real circumcision is a matter of the heart—it is spiritual and not literal. Such a person receives praise not from others but from God.

3 Then what advantage has the Jew? Or what is the value of circumcision? 2 Much, in every way. For in the first place the Jews*a* were entrusted with the oracles of God. 3 What if some were unfaithful? Will their faithlessness nullify the faithfulness of God? 4 By no means! Although everyone is a liar, let God be proved true, as it is written,

"So that you may be justified in your words,
      and prevail in your judging."*b*

5 But if our injustice serves to confirm the justice of God, what should we say? That God is unjust to inflict wrath on us? (I speak in a human way.) 6 By no means! For then how could God judge the world? 7 But if through my falsehood God's truthfulness abounds to his glory, why am I still being condemned as a sinner? 8 And why not say (as some people slander us by saying that we say), "Let us do evil so that good may come"? Their condemnation is deserved!

None Is Righteous

9 What then? Are we any better off?*c* No, not at all; for we have already charged that all, both Jews and Greeks, are under the power of sin, 10 as it is written:

"There is no one who is righteous, not even one;
11   there is no one who has understanding,
      there is no one who seeks God.
12 All have turned aside, together they have become worthless;
      there is no one who shows kindness,
      there is not even one."
13 "Their throats are opened graves;
      they use their tongues to deceive."
"The venom of vipers is under their lips."
14   "Their mouths are full of cursing and bitterness."
15 "Their feet are swift to shed blood;
16   ruin and misery are in their paths,
17 and the way of peace they have not known."
18   "There is no fear of God before their eyes."

19 Now we know that whatever the law says, it speaks to those who are under the law, so that every mouth may be silenced, and the whole world may be held accountable to God. 20 For "no human being will be justified in his sight" by deeds prescribed by the law, for through the law comes the knowledge of sin.

Righteousness through Faith

21 But now, apart from law, the righteousness of God has been disclosed, and is attested by the law and the prophets, 22 the righteousness of God through faith in Jesus Christ*d* for all who believe. For there is no

a Gk *they*   b Gk *when you are being judged*
c Or *at any disadvantage?*   d Or *through the faith of Jesus Christ*

3:1 *what advantage has the Jew?* Jews and Gentiles, insiders and outsiders (to Mosaic law), are in the same boat regarding sin and judgment. But insider Jews have been honored with the responsibility of preserving and teaching the

Holy Scriptures, a privileged responsibility but by no means one that makes them "better off" (v 9).

3:19 SILENCE—*See* Spiritual Disciplines Index.

distinction, 23since all have sinned and fall short of the glory of God; 24they are now justified by his grace as a gift, through the redemption that is in Christ Jesus, 25whom God put forward as a sacrifice of atonement*a* by his blood, effective through faith. He did this to show his righteousness, because in his divine forbearance he had passed over the sins previously committed; 26it was to prove at the present time that he himself is righteous and that he justifies the one who has faith in Jesus.*b*

27 Then what becomes of boasting? It is excluded. By what law? By that of works? No, but by the law of faith. 28For we hold that a person is justified by faith apart from works prescribed by the law. 29Or is God the God of Jews only? Is he not the God of Gentiles also? Yes, of Gentiles also, 30since God is one; and he will justify the circumcised on the ground of faith and the uncircumcised through that same faith. 31Do we then overthrow the law by this faith? By no means! On the contrary, we uphold the law.

The Example of Abraham

4 What then are we to say was gained by*c* Abraham, our ancestor according to the flesh? 2For if Abraham was justified by works, he has something to boast about, but not before God. 3For what does the scripture say? "Abraham believed God, and it was reckoned to him as righteousness." 4Now to one who works, wages are not reckoned as a gift but as something due. 5But to one who without works trusts him who justifies the ungodly, such faith is reckoned as righteousness. 6So also David speaks of the blessedness of those to whom God reckons righteousness apart from works:

7 "Blessed are those whose iniquities are
            forgiven,
        and whose sins are covered;
8 blessed is the one against whom the
        Lord will not reckon sin."

9 Is this blessedness, then, pronounced only on the circumcised, or also on the un-

---

a Or *a place of atonement*   *b* Or *who has the faith of Jesus*   *c* Other ancient authorities read *say about*

3:23 *all have sinned.* The relentless insistence that we all have sinned is not a blanket condemnation telling us how bad we are; it simply clears away any assumption that we have it within ourselves to form our own spirituality. We don't. Not even a little bit. Once we get this through our heads, we will be saved from a lot of false starts.

3:24–25 *redemption . . . atonement.* All the energy and action of the Christian life come from Jesus: God in Christ sets us right with himself. "Redemption" and "atonement" are gateway words into vast mysteries, words we cannot hope to completely comprehend, but ones we can spend the rest of our lives entering into and letting continuously expand our living space. The beyond-our-comprehension reality at the heart of the universe is that God in Christ on the cross has forgiven all our sins, set us right with him, and gathered us into his righteousness. We cannot comprehend it, but we can most certainly live it—a way of life in which everything about us is and continues to be formed in the likeness of Christ.

3:25 SACRIFICE—*See* Spiritual Disciplines Index.

4:1–25 *Abraham.* The story of Abraham makes it plain that all matters of salvation and righteousness are God's business; if we want to be involved with God and his ways, we have to let God do it his way. Abraham didn't get any say in the matter, and neither do we. Nothing in the Abraham story suggests he did anything to become righteous. Abraham's getting circumcised is disallowed as having anything to do with his living in right relationship with God, as is also the keeping of the law by his ancestors. The verbs used of Abraham, "believe" (five times), "trust" (once), and "have faith" (eleven times) signify acts that get all their content from the person and action of God. All three verbs indicate a trusting readiness to let God work his will in Abraham without any well-intentioned assistance from Abraham. This may be the hardest thing to understand and practice in the Christian life, this "not doing," this letting God initiate by command and promise, this trusting in a participating way, not just at the beginning but continuously all our lives. Too often, once we get a little experience and confidence, we want to "take over." And then the trouble starts.

FULLY CONVINCED THAT GOD WAS ABLE

circumcised? We say, "Faith was reckoned to Abraham as righteousness." 10How then was it reckoned to him? Was it before or after he had been circumcised? It was not after, but before he was circumcised. 11He received the sign of circumcision as a seal of the righteousness that he had by faith while he was still uncircumcised. The purpose was to make him the ancestor of all who believe without being circumcised and who thus have righteousness reckoned to them, 12and likewise the ancestor of the circumcised who are not only circumcised but who also follow the example of the faith that our ancestor Abraham had before he was circumcised.

God's Promise Realized through Faith

13 For the promise that he would inherit the world did not come to Abraham or to his descendants through the law but through the righteousness of faith. 14If it is the adherents of the law who are to be the heirs, faith is null and the promise is void. 15For the law brings wrath; but where there is no law, neither is there violation.

16 For this reason it depends on faith, in order that the promise may rest on grace and be guaranteed to all his descendants, not only to the adherents of the law but also to those who share the faith of Abraham (for he is the father of all of us, 17as it is written, "I have made you the father of many nations")—in the presence of the God in whom he believed, who gives life to the dead and calls into existence the things that do not exist. 18Hoping against hope, he believed that he would become "the father of many nations," according to what was said, "So numerous shall your descendants be." 19He did not weaken in faith when he considered his own body, which was already*a* as good as dead (for he was about a hundred years old), or when he considered the barrenness of Sarah's womb. 20No distrust made him waver concerning the promise of God, but he grew strong in

his faith as he gave glory to God, 21being fully convinced that God was able to do what he had promised. 22Therefore his faith*b* "was reckoned to him as righteousness." 23Now the words, "it was reckoned to him," were written not for his sake alone, 24but for ours also. It will be reckoned to us who believe in him who raised Jesus our Lord from the dead, 25who was handed over to death for our trespasses and was raised for our justification.

Results of Justification

5 Therefore, since we are justified by faith, we*c* have peace with God through our Lord Jesus Christ, 2through whom we have obtained access*d* to this grace in which we stand; and we*e* boast in our hope of sharing the glory of God. 3And not only that, but we*e* also boast in our sufferings, knowing that suffering produces endurance, 4and endurance produces character, and character produces hope, 5and hope does not disappoint us, because God's love has been poured into our hearts through the Holy Spirit that has been given to us.

6 For while we were still weak, at the right time Christ died for the ungodly. 7Indeed, rarely will anyone die for a righteous person—though perhaps for a good person someone might actually dare to die. 8But God proves his love for us in that while we still were sinners Christ died for us. 9Much more surely then, now that we have been justified by his blood, will we be saved through him from the wrath of God.*f* 10For if while we were enemies, we were reconciled to God through the death of his Son, much more surely, having been reconciled, will we be saved by his life. 11But more than that, we even boast in God through our Lord Jesus Christ, through whom we have now received reconciliation.

a Other ancient authorities lack *already*
b Gk *Therefore it* *c* Other ancient authorities read *let us* *d* Other ancient authorities add *by faith* *e* Or *let us* *f* Gk *the wrath*

5:1–11 *we boast.* Now Paul becomes exuberant. Careful arguments give way to artesian praise. This justified-by-faith life, this life in which we live out of the abundance of God's grace instead of our own meager sin resources,

is explosive with energetic thanksgiving. Paul uses the noisiest word he can find, "boast," to express the robust quality of this life; he uses it three times (vv 2, 3, 11).

Adam and Christ

12 Therefore, just as sin came into the world through one man, and death came through sin, and so death spread to all because all have sinned— [13] sin was indeed in the world before the law, but sin is not reckoned when there is no law. [14] Yet death exercised dominion from Adam to Moses, even over those whose sins were not like the transgression of Adam, who is a type of the one who was to come.

15 But the free gift is not like the trespass. For if the many died through the one man's trespass, much more surely have the grace of God and the free gift in the grace of the one man, Jesus Christ, abounded for the many. [16] And the free gift is not like the effect of the one man's sin. For the judgment following one trespass brought condemnation, but the free gift following many trespasses brings justification. [17] If, because of the one man's trespass, death exercised dominion through that one, much more surely will those who receive the abundance of grace and the free gift of righteousness exercise dominion in life through the one man, Jesus Christ.

18 Therefore just as one man's trespass led to condemnation for all, so one man's act of righteousness leads to justification and life for all. [19] For just as by the one man's disobedience the many were made sinners, so by the one man's obedience the many will be made righteous. [20] But law came in, with the result that the trespass multiplied; but where sin increased, grace abounded all the more, [21] so that, just as sin exercised dominion in death, so grace might also exercise dominion through justification[a] leading to eternal life through Jesus Christ our Lord.

Dying and Rising with Christ

6 What then are we to say? Should we continue in sin in order that grace may abound? [2] By no means! How can we who died to sin go on living in it? [3] Do you not know that all of us who have been baptized into Christ Jesus were baptized into his death? [4] Therefore we have been buried with him by baptism into death, so that, just as Christ was raised from the dead by the glory of the Father, so we too might walk in newness of life.

5 For if we have been united with him in a death like his, we will certainly be united with him in a resurrection like his. [6] We know that our old self was crucified with him so that the body of sin might be destroyed, and we might no longer be enslaved to sin. [7] For whoever has died is freed from sin. [8] But if we have died with Christ, we believe that we will also live with him. [9] We know that Christ, being raised from the dead, will never die again; death no longer has dominion over him. [10] The death he died, he died to sin, once for all; but the life he lives, he lives to God. [11] So you also must consider yourselves dead to sin and alive to God in Christ Jesus.

12 Therefore, do not let sin exercise do-

a Or righteousness

5:15–21 *grace . . . abounded.* The exuberance is followed by extravagance: grace abounded (vv 15, 20). Sin and death, introduced by Adam, as extensive and terrible as they are, turn out to be a puny business compared to the free gift of life accomplished by Jesus Christ. When it's sin versus grace, grace wins hands down. There is nothing stingy or pinched about this Christ life. The deeper we live into the free gift, the larger and more interesting our world becomes.

6:1–7:13 *By no means!* Why make such a big deal about sin? God has solved the sin problem—why do we have to bother with it? Didn't we just read (5:20) that the more sin, the more grace? Eleven variations on such questions are anticipated (6:1–3, 15–16; 7:1, 7, 13).

Anticipated—but immediately squashed with the indignant "by no means" (6:2, 15; 7:7, 13). There is no "wiggle room" for chosen or rationalized sin.

6:3 *baptized.* Baptism defines the Christian life. It marks a dramatic and decisive death to a sin-dominated existence; it marks a dramatic and glorious resurrection into a Christ-animated way of life. Meditating on our baptism is a prayerful and time-honored way of maintaining awareness of the radical before-and-after reality of our new identity.

6:6–11 *dead to sin.* Sin is a multilayered accumulation of attitudes, actions, habits, emotional assumptions, and wrongheaded ideas that puts us at odds with God. Sometimes it

minion in your mortal bodies, to make you obey their passions. [13]No longer present your members to sin as instruments[a] of wickedness, but present yourselves to God as those who have been brought from death to life, and present your members to God as instruments[a] of righteousness. [14]For sin will have no dominion over you, since you are not under law but under grace.

Slaves of Righteousness

15 What then? Should we sin because we are not under law but under grace? By no means! [16]Do you not know that if you present yourselves to anyone as obedient slaves, you are slaves of the one whom you obey, either of sin, which leads to death, or of obedience, which leads to righteousness? [17]But thanks be to God that you, having once been slaves of sin, have become obedient from the heart to the form of teaching to which you were entrusted, [18]and that you, having been set free from sin, have become slaves of righteousness. [19]I am speaking in human terms because of your natural limitations.[b] For just as you once presented your members as slaves to impurity and to greater and greater iniquity, so now present your members as slaves to righteousness for sanctification.

20 When you were slaves of sin, you were free in regard to righteousness. [21]So what advantage did you then get from the things of which you now are ashamed? The end of those things is death. [22]But now that you have been freed from sin and enslaved to God, the advantage you get is sanctification. The end is eternal life. [23]For the wages of sin is death, but the free gift of God is eternal life in Christ Jesus our Lord.

An Analogy from Marriage

7 Do you not know, brothers and sisters[c]— for I am speaking to those who know the law—that the law is binding on a person only during that person's lifetime? [2]Thus a married woman is bound by the law to her husband as long as he lives; but if her husband dies, she is discharged from the law concerning the husband. [3]Accordingly, she will be called an adulteress if she lives with another man while her husband is alive. But if her husband dies, she is free from that law, and if she marries another man, she is not an adulteress.

4 In the same way, my friends,[c] you have died to the law through the body of Christ, so that you may belong to another, to him who has been raised from the dead in order that we may bear fruit for God. [5]While we were living in the flesh, our sinful passions, aroused by the law, were at work in our members to bear fruit for death. [6]But now we are discharged from the law, dead to that which held us captive, so that we are slaves not under the old written code but in the new life of the Spirit.

---

a Or *weapons* b Gk *the weakness of your flesh*
c Gk *brothers*

---

breaks out in open rebellion; more often it works in silence and subtlety. Living the spiritual life requires perpetual vigilance regarding all this sin baggage. None of us is exempt. Ever. Paul devotes most of chapters 6 and 7 to training us in sin awareness in the gospel context of Christ's resurrection.

Responding
6:13 THE WITH-GOD LIFE. This verse gives a picture of a people presenting their "members" to God so that they can be used to bring goodness into the world. During your next time alone with God, dedicate your limbs and body to God's service. You might want to paraphrase the 4-H pledge: "I dedicate

my head to clearer thinking, my heart to greater love, my hands to larger service, and my health to righteous living, for my family, my worship community, my God, and his kingdom." *See also* Spiritual Disciplines Index.

6:22 *enslaved to God.* A significant aspect of Christian spiritual formation involves acquiring a vocabulary and imagination adequate to the new reality in which we live, terms and concepts that give us access to grand, expansive, all-life-involving phrases like "enslaved to God." *Enslaved?*—the imagination somersaults!

6:23 THE WITH-GOD LIFE—*See* Spiritual Disciplines Index.

The Law and Sin

7 What then should we say? That the law is sin? By no means! Yet, if it had not been for the law, I would not have known sin. I would not have known what it is to covet if the law had not said, "You shall not covet." 8 But sin, seizing an opportunity in the commandment, produced in me all kinds of covetousness. Apart from the law sin lies dead. 9 I was once alive apart from the law, but when the commandment came, sin revived 10 and I died, and the very commandment that promised life proved to be death to me. 11 For sin, seizing an opportunity in the commandment, deceived me and through it killed me. 12 So the law is holy, and the commandment is holy and just and good.

13 Did what is good, then, bring death to me? By no means! It was sin, working death in me through what is good, in order that sin might be shown to be sin, and through the commandment might become sinful beyond measure.

The Inner Conflict

14 For we know that the law is spiritual; but I am of the flesh, sold into slavery under sin. *a* 15 I do not understand my own actions. For I do not do what I want, but I do the very thing I hate. 16 Now if I do what I do not want, I agree that the law is good. 17 But in fact it is no longer I that do it, but sin that dwells within me. 18 For I know that nothing good dwells within me, that is, in my flesh. I can

will what is right, but I cannot do it. 19 For I do not do the good I want, but the evil I do not want is what I do. 20 Now if I do what I do not want, it is no longer I that do it, but sin that dwells within me.

21 So I find it to be a law that when I want to do what is good, evil lies close at hand. 22 For I delight in the law of God in my inmost self, 23 but I see in my members another law at war with the law of my mind, making me captive to the law of sin that dwells in my members. 24 Wretched man that I am! Who will rescue me from this body of death? 25 Thanks be to God through Jesus Christ our Lord!

So then, with my mind I am a slave to the law of God, but with my flesh I am a slave to the law of sin.

Life in the Spirit

8 There is therefore now no condemnation for those who are in Christ Jesus. 2 For the law of the Spirit *b* of life in Christ Jesus has set you *c* free from the law of sin and of death. 3 For God has done what the law, weakened by the flesh, could not do: by sending his own Son in the likeness of sinful flesh, and to deal with sin, *d* he condemned sin in the flesh, 4 so that the just requirement of the law might be fulfilled in us, who walk not according to the flesh

a Gk *sold under sin*   *b* Or *spirit*   *c* Here the Greek word *you* is singular number; other ancient authorities read *me* or *us*   *d* Or *and as a sin offering*

7:14–25 *I am of the flesh.* There is no use looking for a "secret" to the spiritual life that exempts us from trouble and conflict, defeat and doubt, despair and inadequacy. If there ever was such a secret, it is odd that it was withheld from Job, David, Jeremiah, Elijah, Paul, and even Jesus. We are at war (v 23). There is no clear consensus among Christians about this much-discussed passage, but at least this is clear: there are fierce difficulties involved in this resurrection life and Paul faces them. He does not smooth them over or deny them.

8:1 *no condemnation.* Guilt is the crudest of blunt instruments for forming Christian identity and conduct. Its effects, though sometimes immediately dramatic, are short-lived. It is no

part of the Gospel to reduce us to the cowering, frightened condition of trapped animals. Whatever "sentence" has been laid on us by another person, our conscience, or the world in general is commuted by Christ. No condemnation—what a verdict!

8:2 *the law of the Spirit of life . . . the law of sin and of death.* The words chosen for "life" and "death" dramatize the power of the Greek language. Here, "life" (*zōē*) means the eternal, uncreated life that originates in God alone. "Death" (*thanatos*) is not simply physical death, but spiritual death. In essence, Paul says that while we are physically alive, we can experience eternal life or spiritual death.

but according to the Spirit.ᵃ ⁵For those who live according to the flesh set their minds on the things of the flesh, but those who live according to the Spiritᵃ set their minds on the things of the Spirit.ᵃ ⁶To set the mind on the flesh is death, but to set the mind on the Spiritᵃ is life and peace. ⁷For this reason the mind that is set on the flesh is hostile to God; it does not submit to God's law—indeed it cannot, ⁸and those who are in the flesh cannot please God.

9 But you are not in the flesh; you are in the Spirit,ᵃ since the Spirit of God dwells in you. Anyone who does not have the Spirit of Christ does not belong to him. ¹⁰But if Christ is in you, though the body is dead because of sin, the Spiritᵃ is life because of righteousness. ¹¹If the Spirit of him who raised Jesus from the dead dwells in you, he who raised Christᵇ from the dead will give life to your mortal bodies also throughᶜ his Spirit that dwells in you.

12 So then, brothers and sisters,ᵈ we are debtors, not to the flesh, to live according to the flesh— ¹³for if you live according to the flesh, you will die; but if by the Spirit you put to death the deeds of the body, you will live. ¹⁴For all who are led by the Spirit of God are children of God. ¹⁵For you did not receive a spirit of slavery to fall back into fear, but you have received a spirit of adoption. When we cry, "Abba!ᵉ Father!" ¹⁶it is that very Spirit bearing witnessᶠ with our spirit that we are children of God, ¹⁷and if children, then heirs,

heirs of God and joint heirs with Christ—if, in fact, we suffer with him so that we may also be glorified with him.

Future Glory

18 I consider that the sufferings of this present time are not worth comparing with the glory about to be revealed to us. ¹⁹For the creation waits with eager longing for the revealing of the children of God; ²⁰for the creation was subjected to futility, not of its own will but by the will of the one who subjected it, in hope ²¹that the creation itself will be set free from its bondage to decay and will obtain the freedom of the glory of the children of God. ²²We know that the whole creation has been groaning in labor pains until now; ²³and not only the creation, but we ourselves, who have the first fruits of the Spirit, groan inwardly while we wait for adoption, the redemption of our bodies. ²⁴For inᵍ hope we were saved. Now hope that is seen is not hope. For who hopesʰ for what is seen? ²⁵But if we hope for what we do not see, we wait for it with patience.

26 Likewise the Spirit helps us in our weakness; for we do not know how to pray as we

a Or spirit   b Other ancient authorities read the Christ or Christ Jesus or Jesus Christ   c Other ancient authorities read on account of   d Gk brothers   e Aramaic for Father   f Or ¹⁵a spirit of adoption, by which we cry, "Abba! Father!" ¹⁶The Spirit itself bears witness   g Or by   h Other ancient authorities read awaits

---

8:7 SUBMISSION—See Spiritual Disciplines Index.

8:11 the Spirit of him who raised Jesus. Resurrection is the biggest thing about Jesus. It is also the biggest thing about us. The very same Spirit who raised Jesus from the tomb raises us from a dead life. Paul works every variation he can come up with to get us to understand, and to get it deep into our imaginations, that the same resurrection miracle that brought Jesus alive brings us alive. Resurrection is the most unnoticed and underappreciated miracle that takes place in our common lives. But, of course, that's the way it was also with Jesus, hardly noticed at the time and certainly by nobody in authority or of "importance."

8:11–13 THE WITH-GOD LIFE—See Spiritual Disciplines Index.

8:22–23 the whole creation has been groaning in labor pains. This is a bold metaphor: the very creation pregnant! Labor pains, birth pangs, are signs of an imminent and glorious birth, the "redemption of our bodies." This is certainly a different way of understanding groans and suffering. And it makes it impossible to understand Christian growth as something private, isolated from everything that is going on in creation and history.

Responding

8:26 PRAYER. What do you think it means that the "Spirit intercedes with sighs too deep for words"? Can you recall any similar experience? What did you learn from it? See also Spiritual Disciplines Index.

ought, but that very Spirit intercedes *a* with sighs too deep for words. 27And God, *b* who searches the heart, knows what is the mind of the Spirit, because the Spirit *c* intercedes for the saints according to the will of God. *d*

28 We know that all things work together for good *e* for those who love God, who are called according to his purpose. 29For those whom he foreknew he also predestined to be conformed to the image of his Son, in order that he might be the firstborn within a large family. *f* 30And those whom he predestined he also called; and those whom he called he also justified; and those whom he justified he also glorified.

God's Love in Christ Jesus

31 What then are we to say about these things? If God is for us, who is against us? 32He who did not withhold his own Son, but gave him up for all of us, will he not with him also give us everything else? 33Who will bring any charge against God's elect? It is God who justifies. 34Who is to condemn? It is Christ Jesus, who died, yes, who was raised, who is at the right hand of God, who indeed intercedes for us. *g* 35Who will separate us from the love of Christ? Will hardship, or distress, or persecution, or famine, or nakedness, or peril, or sword? 36As it is written,

"For your sake we are being killed all day long;
  we are accounted as sheep to be slaughtered."

37No, in all these things we are more than conquerors through him who loved us. 38For I am convinced that neither death, nor life, nor angels, nor rulers, nor things present, nor things to come, nor powers, 39nor height, nor depth, nor anything else in all creation, will be able to separate us from the love of God in Christ Jesus our Lord.

God's Election of Israel

9 I am speaking the truth in Christ—I am not lying; my conscience confirms it by the Holy Spirit— 2I have great sorrow and unceasing anguish in my heart. 3For I could wish that I myself were accursed and cut off from Christ for the sake of my own people, *h* my kindred according to the flesh. 4They are Israelites, and to them belong the adoption, the glory, the covenants, the giving of the law, the worship, and the promises; 5to them belong the patriarchs, and from them, ac-

a Other ancient authorities add *for us*   *b* Gk *the one*   *c* Gk *he* or *it*   *d* Gk *according to God*   *e* Other ancient authorities read *God makes all things work together for good*, or *in all things God works for good*   *f* Gk *among many brothers*   *g* Or *Is it Christ Jesus . . . for us?*   *h* Gk *my brothers*

8:27 *the Spirit intercedes.* When we pray, we are never "on our own." The Spirit at all times is praying in and for us. This means that the primary energy and influence in our spiritual formation are not our will or knowledge, not our determination or stamina, but the ever-present and active Spirit. Prayer involves far more than God's listening to us; the greater part of prayer, as in so much else, is the active intercessory Presence of the Spirit of God in our lives.

8:31–35 *What then are we to say?* Seven questions bring the whole field of spiritual formation into sharp focus: this is about God at work on an inconceivably vast scale embracing all of creation, all of history; it is not about being fussy with our souls. The questions thrust us into recognizing a resurrection-defined life, the whole world robust with God's eternal, embracing love. Hard as it is for minds flattened by secularism to imagine, this is the resurrection

world in which the followers of Jesus live.

9:1–11:36 *I have great sorrow and unceasing anguish.* Chapters 9–11 deal with the fact that the Jewish people as a nation have not embraced the Christian way. What are gentile Christians to make of this? This is a painful and puzzling subject. What is striking at the outset is Paul's tone, his attitude. Paul is about as Jewish as it is possible to be and never apologizes, depreciates, or hedges that identity. He is openly Jewish through and through. But he has been treated very badly by Jews: persecuted, beaten, accused, rejected, and treated as an enemy. When, though, he brings up the subject of Jews, there is not a trace of animosity in what he says or the way he says it. Given the amount and frequency of religious hate in our world, this is a most remarkable "love your enemies" exhibit. No self-pity, no rancor. Paul will not for a moment hate in Jesus' name.

cording to the flesh, comes the Messiah,[a] who is over all, God blessed forever.[b] Amen.

6 It is not as though the word of God had failed. For not all Israelites truly belong to Israel, [7]and not all of Abraham's children are his true descendants; but "It is through Isaac that descendants shall be named for you." [8]This means that it is not the children of the flesh who are the children of God, but the children of the promise are counted as descendants. [9]For this is what the promise said, "About this time I will return and Sarah shall have a son." [10]Nor is that all; something similar happened to Rebecca when she had conceived children by one husband, our ancestor Isaac. [11]Even before they had been born or had done anything good or bad (so that God's purpose of election might continue, [12]not by works but by his call) she was told, "The elder shall serve the younger." [13]As it is written,

"I have loved Jacob,
    but I have hated Esau."

14 What then are we to say? Is there injustice on God's part? By no means! [15]For he says to Moses,

"I will have mercy on whom I have
    mercy,
and I will have compassion on whom
    I have compassion."

[16]So it depends not on human will or exertion, but on God who shows mercy. [17]For the scripture says to Pharaoh, "I have raised you up for the very purpose of showing my power in you, so that my name may be proclaimed in all the earth." [18]So then he has mercy on whomever he chooses, and he hardens the heart of whomever he chooses.

God's Wrath and Mercy

19 You will say to me then, "Why then does he still find fault? For who can resist his will?" [20]But who indeed are you, a human being, to argue with God? Will what is molded say to the one who molds it, "Why have you made me like this?" [21]Has the potter no right over the clay, to make out of the same lump one object for special use and another for ordinary use? [22]What if God, desiring to show his wrath and to make known his power, has endured with much patience the objects of wrath that are made for destruction; [23]and what if he has done so in order to make known the riches of his glory for the objects of mercy, which he has prepared beforehand for glory— [24]including us whom he has called, not from the Jews only but also from the Gentiles? [25]As indeed he says in Hosea,

"Those who were not my people I will
    call 'my people,'
and her who was not beloved I will
    call 'beloved.' "

[26] "And in the very place where it was said
        to them, 'You are not my people,'
    there they shall be called children of
        the living God."

27 And Isaiah cries out concerning Israel, "Though the number of the children of Israel were like the sand of the sea, only a remnant of them will be saved; [28]for the Lord will execute his sentence on the earth quickly and decisively."[c] [29]And as Isaiah predicted,

"If the Lord of hosts had not left
        survivors[d] to us,
    we would have fared like Sodom
        and been made like Gomorrah."

a Or the Christ   b Or Messiah, who is God over all, blessed forever; or Messiah. May he who is God over all be blessed forever   c Other ancient authorities read for he will finish his work and cut it short in righteousness, because the Lord will make the sentence shortened on the earth   d Or descendants; Gk seed

---

9:11 *God's purpose of election.* God's purposes work at a deeper level than can be observed by adding up human motives and actions. God's willing and acting, often hidden to our eyes, work salvation beyond our figuring out. There is more here than meets the eye, and "election," God's action in all this, is the term for it. But it is no less a mystery for all that.

9:19–24 *Has the potter no right over the clay?*

When Job questioned God about his suffering, he got sixty-one questions back, none of which he could answer (see Job 38–41). Paul is considerably more restrained, responding to the issue of the status of the Jews with only seven questions, also unanswerable. There are some things we cannot know because we are not ready for them. God does not work within the limits of our capacity for understanding.

Israel's Unbelief

30 What then are we to say? Gentiles, who did not strive for righteousness, have attained it, that is, righteousness through faith; 31but Israel, who did strive for the righteousness that is based on the law, did not succeed in fulfilling that law. 32Why not? Because they did not strive for it on the basis of faith, but as if it were based on works. They have stumbled over the stumbling stone, 33as it is written,

"See, I am laying in Zion a stone that
 will make people stumble, a rock
  that will make them fall,
and whoever believes in him*a* will not
 be put to shame."

10 Brothers and sisters,*b* my heart's desire and prayer to God for them is that they may be saved. 2I can testify that they have a zeal for God, but it is not enlightened. 3For, being ignorant of the righteousness that comes from God, and seeking to establish their own, they have not submitted to God's righteousness. 4For Christ is the end of the law so that there may be righteousness for everyone who believes.

Salvation Is for All

5 Moses writes concerning the righteousness that comes from the law, that "the person who does these things will live by them." 6But the righteousness that comes from faith says, "Do not say in your heart, 'Who will ascend into heaven?'" (that is, to bring Christ down) 7"or 'Who will descend into the abyss?'" (that is, to bring Christ up from the dead). 8But what does it say?

"The word is near you,
 on your lips and in your heart"
(that is, the word of faith that we proclaim); 9because*c* if you confess with your lips that Jesus is Lord and believe in your heart that God raised him from the dead, you will be saved. 10For one believes with the heart and so is justified, and one confesses with the mouth and so is saved. 11The scripture says, "No one who believes in him will be put to shame." 12For there is no distinction between Jew and Greek; the same Lord is Lord of all and is generous to all who call on him. 13For, "Everyone who calls on the name of the Lord shall be saved."

14 But how are they to call on one in whom they have not believed? And how are they to believe in one of whom they have never heard? And how are they to hear without someone to proclaim him? 15And how are they to proclaim him unless they are sent? As it is written, "How beautiful are the feet of those who bring good news!" 16But not all have obeyed the good news;*d* for Isaiah says, "Lord, who has believed our message?" 17So faith comes from what is heard, and what is heard comes through the word of Christ.*e*

a Or *trusts in it* *b* Gk *Brothers* *c* Or *namely, that* *d* Or *gospel* *e* Or *about Christ*; other ancient authorities read *of God*

9:30–33 *What then are we to say?* Then Paul asks two more questions (vv 30, 32) that he does answer by using lines from Isaiah (8:14; 28:16) that both Jews and Christians identify as messianic. The "stone" (messiah) can be either a cornerstone that provides a firm foothold for a life of faith or a rock that gets in the way of getting our own way. We cannot use God to get our way; God, revealed in Jesus, gets his salvation way in us.

10:8 *The word is near you.* Now Paul quotes from Moses' great farewell address on the plains of Moab (Deut 30:14), the sermon that gathers up the immense salvation experience of Egypt and the wilderness and makes it a matter of present faith and obedience. Jews and Christians read the same Scripture. For all their differences, Paul patiently, detail by scriptural detail, establishes common ground between them. He guards against any Christian escalation of their differences into conflict. Jews and Gentiles are both subject to the same word of God, subject to the same sovereignty of God.

Responding
10:9–10 CONFESSION. Beyond the fact that we will be saved, why is it important for us to confess with our lips that Jesus is Lord and believe that God raised him from the dead? As a short exercise today, say aloud twenty times, "Jesus, whom God raised from the dead, is Lord." How did it affect your heart? *See also* Spiritual Disciplines Index.

18 But I ask, have they not heard? Indeed they have; for

"Their voice has gone out to all the earth,
and their words to the ends of the world."

19 Again I ask, did Israel not understand? First Moses says,

"I will make you jealous of those who are not a nation;
with a foolish nation I will make you angry."

20 Then Isaiah is so bold as to say,

"I have been found by those who did not seek me;
I have shown myself to those who did not ask for me."

21 But of Israel he says, "All day long I have held out my hands to a disobedient and contrary people."

Israel's Rejection Is Not Final

11 I ask, then, has God rejected his people? By no means! I myself am an Israelite, a descendant of Abraham, a member of the tribe of Benjamin. 2God has not rejected his people whom he foreknew. Do you not know what the scripture says of Elijah, how he pleads with God against Israel? 3"Lord, they have killed your prophets, they have demolished your altars; I alone am left, and they are seeking my life." 4But what is the divine reply to him? "I have kept for myself seven thousand who have not bowed the knee to Baal." 5So too at the present time there is a remnant, chosen by grace. 6But if it is by grace, it is no longer on the basis of works, otherwise grace would no longer be grace.a

7 What then? Israel failed to obtain what it was seeking. The elect obtained it, but the rest were hardened, 8as it is written,

"God gave them a sluggish spirit,

eyes that would not see
and ears that would not hear,
down to this very day."

9And David says,

"Let their table become a snare and a trap,
a stumbling block and a retribution for them;

10 let their eyes be darkened so that they cannot see,
and keep their backs forever bent."

The Salvation of the Gentiles

11 So I ask, have they stumbled so as to fall? By no means! But through their stumblingb salvation has come to the Gentiles, so as to make Israelc jealous. 12Now if their stumblingb means riches for the world, and if their defeat means riches for Gentiles, how much more will their full inclusion mean!

13 Now I am speaking to you Gentiles. Inasmuch then as I am an apostle to the Gentiles, I glorify my ministry 14in order to make my own peopled jealous, and thus save some of them. 15For if their rejection is the reconciliation of the world, what will their acceptance be but life from the dead! 16If the part of the dough offered as first fruits is holy, then the whole batch is holy; and if the root is holy, then the branches also are holy.

17 But if some of the branches were broken off, and you, a wild olive shoot, were grafted in their place to share the rich roote of the olive tree, 18do not boast over the branches. If you do boast, remember that it is not you that support the root, but the root that supports you. 19You will say, "Branches were broken off so that I might be grafted in." 20That

a Other ancient authorities add *But if it is by works, it is no longer on the basis of grace, otherwise work would no longer be work*   b Gk *transgression*   c Gk *them*   d Gk *my flesh*   e Other ancient authorities read *the richness*

11:13–24 *grafted in . . . to share the rich root of the olive tree.* Gentile Christians are now directly addressed (v 13) and warned against developing any airs of superiority over Jews. Gentiles are "in" only by virtue of a miracle, God's miracle of "grafting" them into the salvation tree. The natural branches (the Jews),

which have been broken off, can be put back in again (v 23). Gentiles are not privileged because of their miraculous grafting in; Jews will also get in by means of miracle. There are no categories in the Christian community; we are all miraculously "grafted" into God's olive tree.

is true. They were broken off because of their unbelief, but you stand only through faith. So do not become proud, but stand in awe. 21For if God did not spare the natural branches, perhaps he will not spare you. *a* 22Note then the kindness and the severity of God: severity toward those who have fallen, but God's kindness toward you, provided you continue in his kindness; otherwise you also will be cut off. 23And even those of Israel, *b* if they do not persist in unbelief, will be grafted in, for God has the power to graft them in again. 24For if you have been cut from what is by nature a wild olive tree and grafted, contrary to nature, into a cultivated olive tree, how much more will these natural branches be grafted back into their own olive tree.

All Israel Will Be Saved

25 So that you may not claim to be wiser than you are, brothers and sisters, *c* I want you to understand this mystery: a hardening has come upon part of Israel, until the full number of the Gentiles has come in. 26And so all Israel will be saved; as it is written,

"Out of Zion will come the Deliverer;
  he will banish ungodliness from
    Jacob."
27 "And this is my covenant with them,
  when I take away their sins."

28As regards the gospel they are enemies of God *d* for your sake; but as regards election they are beloved, for the sake of their ancestors; 29for the gifts and the calling of God are irrevocable. 30Just as you were once disobedient to God but have now received mercy because of their disobedience, 31so they have now been disobedient in order that, by the mercy shown to you, they too may now *e* receive mercy. 32For God has imprisoned all in disobedience so that he may be merciful to all.

33 O the depth of the riches and wisdom and knowledge of God! How unsearchable are his judgments and how inscrutable his ways!
34 "For who has known the mind of the
    Lord?
  Or who has been his counselor?"
35 "Or who has given a gift to him,
    to receive a gift in return?"
36For from him and through him and to him are all things. To him be the glory forever. Amen.

The New Life in Christ

12
I appeal to you therefore, brothers and sisters, *c* by the mercies of God, to

a Other ancient authorities read *neither will he spare you*   *b* Gk lacks *of Israel*   *c* Gk *brothers*
d Gk lacks *of God*   *e* Other ancient authorities lack *now*

11:33–36 *how inscrutable his ways!* Paul has been dealing with complex matters; he has done his best by vigorous reasoning and devout meditation on Scripture to bring Gentiles and Jews into a mutual awareness of community. But there is more: there is mystery. Mystery is not what is left over after we have done our best to figure things out on our own; it is inherent in the very nature of God and his works. It is the "more" that we consistently encounter in God— more than we ever expected, more than we can ever grasp, more than we are capable of explaining. "Glory" is Paul's word for the "more."

12:1 WORSHIP—*See* Spiritual Disciplines Index.

12:1 *therefore . . . present your bodies as a living sacrifice.* The "therefore" signals a shift of emphasis. Are we, Jews and Gentiles, now on common ground? Are we, sinners all, brothers and sisters in Christ? Do we understand that

Jesus is our Savior? Do we realize that we are all, every one of us, new creatures, resurrection men and women through the work of the Holy Spirit? Well, then—therefore!—let us live this new life to the hilt, placing our bodies simply, wholly, believingly on the altar, a daily offering so that God can work his will in us.

Responding

12:1 SACRIFICE. In commenting on this verse, Richard Foster says that the problem with a "living" sacrifice is that it always wants to get off the altar. On a scale of 1 to 10 ("easy" to "hard"), rank the difficulty you think you would have in giving your entire being— thoughts, words, and actions—to God. As you go about your work this week, make every effort to dedicate everything you think, say, or do to God. How often did you want to get off the altar? *See also* Spiritual Disciplines Index.

present your bodies as a living sacrifice, holy and acceptable to God, which is your spiritual[a] worship. 2Do not be conformed to this world,[b] but be transformed by the renewing of your minds, so that you may discern what is the will of God—what is good and acceptable and perfect.[c]

3 For by the grace given to me I say to everyone among you not to think of yourself more highly than you ought to think, but to think with sober judgment, each according to the measure of faith that God has assigned. 4For as in one body we have many members, and not all the members have the same function, 5so we, who are many, are one body in Christ, and individually we are members one of another. 6We have gifts that differ according to the grace given to us: prophecy, in proportion to faith; 7ministry, in ministering; the teacher, in teaching; 8the exhorter, in exhortation; the giver, in generosity; the leader, in diligence; the compassionate, in cheerfulness.

Marks of the True Christian

9 Let love be genuine; hate what is evil, hold fast to what is good; 10love one another with mutual affection; outdo one another in showing honor. 11Do not lag in zeal, be ardent in spirit, serve the Lord.[d] 12Rejoice in hope, be patient in suffering, persevere in prayer. 13Contribute to the needs of the saints; extend hospitality to strangers.

14 Bless those who persecute you; bless and do not curse them. 15Rejoice with those who rejoice, weep with those who weep. 16Live in harmony with one another; do not be haughty, but associate with the lowly;[e] do not claim to be wiser than you are. 17Do not repay anyone evil for evil, but take thought for what is noble in the sight of all. 18If it is possible, so far as it depends on you, live peaceably with all. 19Beloved, never avenge yourselves, but leave room for the wrath of God;[f] for it is written, "Vengeance is mine, I will repay, says the Lord." 20No, "if your enemies are hungry, feed them; if they are thirsty, give them something to drink; for by doing this you will heap burning coals on their heads." 21Do not be overcome by evil, but overcome evil with good.

Being Subject to Authorities

13 Let every person be subject to the governing authorities; for there is no authority except from God, and those authorities that exist have been instituted by God. 2Therefore whoever resists authority resists what God has appointed, and those who resist will incur judgment. 3For rulers are not a terror to good conduct, but to bad. Do you

a Or reasonable   b Gk age   c Or what is the good and acceptable and perfect will of God
d Other ancient authorities read serve the opportune time   e Or give yourselves to humble tasks
f Gk the wrath

12:4–17 FELLOWSHIP—See Spiritual Disciplines Index.

12:6 THE WITH-GOD LIFE—See Spiritual Disciplines Index.

12:6 *gifts that differ.* The Christian life is not monochrome. Yes, we are all the same, sharing a common Christ identity, yet we are all different; each of us is uniquely gifted to live out this endlessly creative identity in fresh and particular ways.

12:9–21 *Let love be genuine.* An arpeggio of twenty-nine imperatives runs up and down the scale of love. We will never run out of ways to love; we will never lack for occasions to love; we will never come up short of people to love.

12:11 SERVICE—See Spiritual Disciplines Index.

12:12 PRAYER—See Spiritual Disciplines Index.

13:1–7 *the governing authorities.* This is a most difficult passage. This much is clear: the freedom we have in Christ is not a freedom to do whatever we wish against whomever we disapprove of. Christians are not absolved from lives of courtesy, civility, and law-keeping in the community. But, by and large, Christians have struggled mightily to find ways to be faithful to Christ while living under evil and unjust rulers who command disobedience to Christ. Although there don't seem to be any black-and-white answers regarding the extent to which we need to obey unjust "authorities," it is clear that we are to obey to the fullest extent that our Christian consciences allow.

wish to have no fear of the authority? Then do what is good, and you will receive its approval; [4]for it is God's servant for your good. But if you do what is wrong, you should be afraid, for the authority[a] does not bear the sword in vain! It is the servant of God to execute wrath on the wrongdoer. [5]Therefore one must be subject, not only because of wrath but also because of conscience. [6]For the same reason you also pay taxes, for the authorities are God's servants, busy with this very thing. [7]Pay to all what is due them—taxes to whom taxes are due, revenue to whom revenue is due, respect to whom respect is due, honor to whom honor is due.

Love for One Another

[8]Owe no one anything, except to love one another; for the one who loves another has fulfilled the law. [9]The commandments, "You shall not commit adultery; You shall not murder; You shall not steal; You shall not covet"; and any other commandment, are summed up in this word, "Love your neighbor as yourself." [10]Love does no wrong to a neighbor; therefore, love is the fulfilling of the law.

An Urgent Appeal

[11]Besides this, you know what time it is, how it is now the moment for you to wake from sleep. For salvation is nearer to us now than when we became believers; [12]the night is far gone, the day is near. Let us then lay aside the works of darkness and put on the armor of light; [13]let us live honorably as in the day, not in reveling and drunkenness, not in debauchery and licentiousness, not in quar-

reling and jealousy. [14]Instead, put on the Lord Jesus Christ, and make no provision for the flesh, to gratify its desires.

Do Not Judge Another

14 Welcome those who are weak in faith,[b] but not for the purpose of quarreling over opinions. [2]Some believe in eating anything, while the weak eat only vegetables. [3]Those who eat must not despise those who abstain, and those who abstain must not pass judgment on those who eat; for God has welcomed them. [4]Who are you to pass judgment on servants of another? It is before their own lord that they stand or fall. And they will be upheld, for the Lord[c] is able to make them stand.

5 Some judge one day to be better than another, while others judge all days to be alike. Let all be fully convinced in their own minds. [6]Those who observe the day, observe it in honor of the Lord. Also those who eat, eat in honor of the Lord, since they give thanks to God; while those who abstain, abstain in honor of the Lord and give thanks to God.

7 We do not live to ourselves, and we do not die to ourselves. [8]If we live, we live to the Lord, and if we die, we die to the Lord; so then, whether we live or whether we die, we are the Lord's. [9]For to this end Christ died and lived again, so that he might be Lord of both the dead and the living.

10 Why do you pass judgment on your brother or sister?[d] Or you, why do you despise your brother or sister?[d] For we will all

a Gk it   b Or *conviction*   c Other ancient authorities read *for God*   d Gk *brother*

13:6 SERVICE—*See* Spiritual Disciplines Index.

13:11 *what time it is.* The present moment is the only time available to us for living in the Spirit, for following Jesus, for obeying his commands, for receiving the Father's love. We do not live the gospel in nostalgia, savoring past blessings; and we do not live in fantasy, anticipating a more convenient time. The time is now—sink into this present, this Presence.

14:10 *Why do you pass judgment?* For a community that lives, every last one of us, solely by forgiveness and grace, keeping up a running

commentary on what we disapprove of or dislike in one another is outrageous. Critical barbs and gossipy asides are corrosive and corrupting. Every judgmental word out of our mouths violates an eternal soul for whom Christ died.

Responding
14:10 FELLOWSHIP. Where have you seen fellowship destroyed by judgmental criticisms and gossip? Try this month to speak words of encouragement and hope that build community at every possible opportunity. *See also* Spiritual Disciplines Index.

stand before the judgment seat of God. *a* [11]For it is written,

> "As I live, says the Lord, every knee shall
>   bow to me,
>   and every tongue shall give praise to *b*
>   God."

[12]So then, each of us will be accountable to God. *c*

Do Not Make Another Stumble

13 Let us therefore no longer pass judgment on one another, but resolve instead never to put a stumbling block or hindrance in the way of another. *d* [14]I know and am persuaded in the Lord Jesus that nothing is unclean in itself; but it is unclean for anyone who thinks it unclean. [15]If your brother or sister *e* is being injured by what you eat, you are no longer walking in love. Do not let what you eat cause the ruin of one for whom Christ died. [16]So do not let your good be spoken of as evil. [17]For the kingdom of God is not food and drink but righteousness and peace and joy in the Holy Spirit. [18]The one who thus serves Christ is acceptable to God and has human approval. [19]Let us then pursue what makes for peace and for mutual upbuilding. [20]Do not, for the sake of food, destroy the work of God. Everything is indeed clean, but it is wrong for you to make others fall by what you eat; [21]it is good not to eat meat or drink wine or do anything that makes your brother or sister *e* stumble. *f* [22]The faith that you have, have as your own conviction before God. Blessed are those who have no reason to condemn themselves because of what they approve. [23]But those who have doubts are condemned if they eat, because they do not act from faith; *g* for whatever does not proceed from faith *g* is sin. *h*

Please Others, Not Yourselves

15 We who are strong ought to put up with the failings of the weak, and not to please ourselves. [2]Each of us must please our neighbor for the good purpose of building up the neighbor. [3]For Christ did not please himself; but, as it is written, "The insults of those who insult you have fallen on me." [4]For whatever was written in former days was written for our instruction, so that by steadfastness and by the encouragement of the scriptures we might have hope. [5]May the God of steadfastness and encouragement grant you to live in harmony with one another, in accordance with Christ Jesus, [6]so that together you may with one voice glorify the God and Father of our Lord Jesus Christ.

The Gospel for Jews and Gentiles Alike

7 Welcome one another, therefore, just as Christ has welcomed you, for the glory of God. [8]For I tell you that Christ has become a servant of the circumcised on behalf of the truth of God in order that he might confirm the promises given to the patriarchs, [9]and in order that the Gentiles might glorify God for his mercy. As it is written,

> "Therefore I will confess *i* you among
>   the Gentiles,
>   and sing praises to your name";

[10]and again he says,

> "Rejoice, O Gentiles, with his people";

[11]and again,

> "Praise the Lord, all you Gentiles,
>   and let all the peoples praise him";

[12]and again Isaiah says,

> "The root of Jesse shall come,
>   the one who rises to rule the Gentiles;
>   in him the Gentiles shall hope."

a Other ancient authorities read *of Christ*
b Or *confess*   *c* Other ancient authorities lack *to God*   *d* Gk *of a brother*   *e* Gk *brother*
f Other ancient authorities add *or be upset or be weakened*   *g* Or *conviction*   *h* Other authorities, some ancient, add here 16.25–27
i Or *thank*

14:17 THE WITH-GOD LIFE—See Spiritual Disciplines Index.

15:1–3 *Christ did not please himself.* Do we think that the people with whom we worship should be "our kind"—affable and congenial fellow Christians who think well of us and make us feel at home? And if they do not please us, do we go off looking for others who will? This is a weak view of the Church, and certainly not what Christ experienced. Paul puts the shoe on the other foot: *we* are to be the ones out to please others. We come to church not to get our needs met, but to meet the needs of our neighbors.

[13]May the God of hope fill you with all joy and peace in believing, so that you may abound in hope by the power of the Holy Spirit.

Paul's Reason for Writing So Boldly

14 I myself feel confident about you, my brothers and sisters,[a] that you yourselves are full of goodness, filled with all knowledge, and able to instruct one another. [15]Nevertheless on some points I have written to you rather boldly by way of reminder, because of the grace given me by God [16]to be a minister of Christ Jesus to the Gentiles in the priestly service of the gospel of God, so that the offering of the Gentiles may be acceptable, sanctified by the Holy Spirit. [17]In Christ Jesus, then, I have reason to boast of my work for God. [18]For I will not venture to speak of anything except what Christ has accomplished[b] through me to win obedience from the Gentiles, by word and deed, [19]by the power of signs and wonders, by the power of the Spirit of God,[c] so that from Jerusalem and as far around as Illyricum I have fully proclaimed the good news[d] of Christ. [20]Thus I make it my ambition to proclaim the good news,[d] not where Christ has already been named, so that I do not build on someone else's foundation, [21]but as it is written,

"Those who have never been told of
       him shall see,
   and those who have never heard of
       him shall understand."

Paul's Plan to Visit Rome

22 This is the reason that I have so often been hindered from coming to you. [23]But now, with no further place for me in these regions, I desire, as I have for many years, to come to you

[24]when I go to Spain. For I do hope to see you on my journey and to be sent on by you, once I have enjoyed your company for a little while. [25]At present, however, I am going to Jerusalem in a ministry to the saints; [26]for Macedonia and Achaia have been pleased to share their resources with the poor among the saints at Jerusalem. [27]They were pleased to do this, and indeed they owe it to them; for if the Gentiles have come to share in their spiritual blessings, they ought also to be of service to them in material things. [28]So, when I have completed this, and have delivered to them what has been collected,[e] I will set out by way of you to Spain; [29]and I know that when I come to you, I will come in the fullness of the blessing[f] of Christ.

30 I appeal to you, brothers and sisters,[a] by our Lord Jesus Christ and by the love of the Spirit, to join me in earnest prayer to God on my behalf, [31]that I may be rescued from the unbelievers in Judea, and that my ministry[g] to Jerusalem may be acceptable to the saints, [32]so that by God's will I may come to you with joy and be refreshed in your company. [33]The God of peace be with all of you.[h] Amen.

Personal Greetings

16 I commend to you our sister Phoebe, a deacon[i] of the church at Cenchreae, [2]so that you may welcome her in the Lord as is fitting for the saints, and help her in what-

a Gk brothers   b Gk speak of those things that Christ has not accomplished   c Other ancient authorities read of the Spirit or of the Holy Spirit
d Or gospel   e Gk have sealed to them this fruit
f Other ancient authorities add of the gospel
g Other ancient authorities read my bringing of a gift   h One ancient authority adds 16.25–27 here
i Or minister

15:16 SERVICE—See Spiritual Disciplines Index.

15:22–33 when I go to Spain. Every moment of this Christian life is lived out on the ground, in some physical place. Geography is as much a part of the spiritual life as theology. The more or less offhand mention of Spain brings the immediate conditions of this letter, this extravagant immersion in the work of God in Christ among us, to the fore: Paul is planning to travel to Jerusalem by way of Macedonia and Achaia, booking passage on a ship, and then anticipa-

ting a good visit in Rome and going on to Spain. Our conditions—our present street address and where we expect to be next week—are likewise the stuff of spiritual formation.

16:1–16 our sister Phoebe. Just as the gospel lodges in places, it affects named individuals. It is never unplaced, never impersonal. Every detail finds root in some place and embodiment in some one—Phoebe and her twenty-six personally named brothers and sisters in the church at Rome for a start.

ever she may require from you, for she has been a benefactor of many and of myself as well.

3 Greet Prisca and Aquila, who work with me in Christ Jesus, [4]and who risked their necks for my life, to whom not only I give thanks, but also all the churches of the Gentiles. [5]Greet also the church in their house. Greet my beloved Epaenetus, who was the first convert[a] in Asia for Christ. [6]Greet Mary, who has worked very hard among you. [7]Greet Andronicus and Junia,[b] my relatives[c] who were in prison with me; they are prominent among the apostles, and they were in Christ before I was. [8]Greet Ampliatus, my beloved in the Lord. [9]Greet Urbanus, our co-worker in Christ, and my beloved Stachys. [10]Greet Apelles, who is approved in Christ. Greet those who belong to the family of Aristobulus. [11]Greet my relative[d] Herodion. Greet those in the Lord who belong to the family of Narcissus. [12]Greet those workers in the Lord, Tryphaena and Tryphosa. Greet the beloved Persis, who has worked hard in the Lord. [13]Greet Rufus, chosen in the Lord; and greet his mother—a mother to me also. [14]Greet Asyncritus, Phlegon, Hermes, Patrobas, Hermas, and the brothers and sisters[e] who are with them. [15]Greet Philologus, Julia, Nereus and his sister, and Olympas, and all the saints who are with them. [16]Greet one another with a holy kiss. All the churches of Christ greet you.

Final Instructions

17 I urge you, brothers and sisters,[e] to keep an eye on those who cause dissensions and offenses, in opposition to the teaching that you have learned; avoid them. [18]For such people do not serve our Lord Christ, but their own appetites,[f] and by smooth talk and flattery they deceive the hearts of the simpleminded. [19]For while your obedience is known to all, so that I rejoice over you, I want you to be wise in what is good and guileless in what is evil. [20]The God of peace will shortly crush Satan under your feet. The grace of our Lord Jesus Christ be with you.[g]

21 Timothy, my co-worker, greets you; so do Lucius and Jason and Sosipater, my relatives.[c]

22 I Tertius, the writer of this letter, greet you in the Lord.[h]

23 Gaius, who is host to me and to the whole church, greets you. Erastus, the city treasurer, and our brother Quartus, greet you.[i]

Final Doxology

25 Now to God[j] who is able to strengthen you according to my gospel and the proclamation of Jesus Christ, according to the revelation of the mystery that was kept secret for long ages [26]but is now disclosed, and through the prophetic writings is made known to all the Gentiles, according to the command of the eternal God, to bring about the obedience of faith— [27]to the only wise God, through Jesus Christ, to whom[k] be the glory forever! Amen.[l]

a Gk *first fruits*   b Or *Junias*; other ancient authorities read *Julia*   c Or *compatriots*
d Or *compatriot*   e Gk *brothers*   f Gk *their own belly*   g Other ancient authorities lack this sentence   h Or *I Tertius, writing this letter in the Lord, greet you*   i Other ancient authorities add verse 24, *The grace of our Lord Jesus Christ be with all of you. Amen.*   j Gk *the one*   k Other ancient authorities lack *to whom*. The verse then reads, *to the only wise God be the glory through Jesus Christ forever. Amen.*   l Other ancient authorities lack 16.25-27 or include it after 14.23 or 15.33; others put verse 24 after verse 27

16:25–27 *Amen.* Paul's final words are a prayer. And the last word of his prayer is "Amen"—the great Hebrew word that resonates throughout Scripture and life, affirming the solid, foundational underpinnings of God in all that we are and do in Jesus' name.

THE FIRST LETTER OF PAUL TO THE

CORINTHIANS

P aul's First Letter to the Corinthians directly addresses the spiritual formation
of a particular church community. Paul urges the members of this congregation, which he founded and loves, to lead their communal life in keeping with the
gospel of the crucified Christ. Again and again on specific points he enjoins the Corinthians to change their behavior in a spirit of unity, mutual upbuilding, and love.
His ideas are often at odds with those of his listeners, at least some of whom are flush
with a sense that they are already spiritually mature.

As Paul argues, urges, and at times commands the church to align its behavior
with the gospel, glimpses of Paul's own spiritual maturity are revealed. First Corinthians is an intimate window into the mind and heart of an apostle as well as the
struggles of a proud and youthful church. Here are believers in tension with one another and their founding missionary about practical issues the Church struggles with
still: divisions caused when people choose to follow this or that spiritual leader; problems that stem from arrogant certitude; and thorny disagreements about right sexual behavior, equal access to power, what makes for worshipful Communion, the
proper use of spiritual gifts, even the need for order in worship. The letter is a nitty-
gritty document written to a church struggling to discover the boundaries and fullness of its life with God.

Reading 1 Corinthians

Because Paul addresses so many specifics, it is all too easy to read 1 Corinthians as
a list of "right answers" proffered by a bona fide apostle to help his former congregation. But those who read 1 Corinthians as an apostolic answer sheet will miss many
of its deepest implications for spiritual formation. Paul himself urges those who are
unsure about how to proceed on the question of eating meat put before idols, for

---

*See also "The With-God Life" essay for this section of the Bible,
"The People of God in Community," pp. 2037–42.*

example, to put the needs of others before their own comfortable certitudes. Neither is the letter a good source of advice for individual Christians, for here Paul is addressing the whole church. In several instances he resists giving pat answers and urges listeners to make up their own minds while tolerating differences in the community (7:28, 36–38; 10:31). Not only does he frequently allow the Corinthians a say, but some of the advice Paul offers here will be rejected by the Corinthian congregation. There is evidence in 2 Corinthians that in at least one instance Paul reverses his previous position (2 Cor 2:5–11).

Paul's own responsiveness to his congregation implies that putting faith into practice requires an ongoing conversation between church leaders and members, and among the members themselves. In earnest and at times testy conversation, pastor and people together work toward what it means to live the with-God life as members of a faith community. They do not finish their task; and neither will we. In the meantime this intimate letter gives us a good look at the effort—and at times the sacrifice of certitudes—involved in the journey. Overzealous attempts to apply Paul's teaching on particular issues in the Corinthian church to situations in our time are misguided and, at worst, might lead to the denial of basic freedoms affirmed by the gospel and by Paul himself.

Themes for Spiritual Formation

Several themes are available to those who turn to 1 Corinthians for help with the task of spiritual formation today.

The first and most prominent is that God alone is the source of the Spirit-lived life. From the letter's first words of thanksgiving, Paul attributes all the benefits of the life of faith to God's saving initiative. It is God who calls, graces, strengthens, and sustains the with-God life, and Christ and the Spirit who are the agents of such gifts (1:1–9; 2:4, 10; 6:14; 8:6; 12:4–7). Each time the Corinthians want to take credit for their own wisdom, insight, or spiritual abilities, Paul reminds them of the divine source of their blessings, "so that no one might boast in the presence of God" (1:29).

God is seen most clearly in the scandal of the cross, whose saving message is the "power of God" (1:18). It is God who is the source of life in Christ (1:30) and who determines what is wise in opposition to the wisdom of the world (1:21–25). God gives the church growth (3:6–7), judges those outside the church (5:13), and activates all spiritual gifts (12:6). When Paul addresses those in the church who do not accept believers' resurrection, he reminds them that to deny resurrection is to misrepresent God, who raised Christ from the dead (15:15). It is God who abides at the beginning and end of life as its Creator and goal. Indeed, much of Paul's distress with the Corinthians' behavior stems from his awareness that by their indulgent and misguided actions they are keeping others from discerning the true nature of God.

Second, although rare individuals have managed to be Christians in isolation, Christian life is most fully expressed within a faith community. A church ought never to be a collection of individuals; its entire integrity lies in the quality of its community life. A great many of the admonitions in 1 Corinthians that can be read as critiques of individual behavior are, rather, Paul's attempt to lead the whole church community to act in ways that reveal how the gospel transforms human relationships. An important example is Paul's admonition not to come to the table in "an unworthy manner" (11:27). Through the centuries many individual readers have taken those words to heart and wrongly denied themselves Communion. A quick look at the context, however, reveals that it is the *church* that must be worthy by giving up arrangements that highlight social divisions.

In a similar example, Paul's distress about the man who is in violation of Jewish incest laws is not based on personal moral outrage. His concern is for the sake of the *church,* which seems not to care enough about the man to be deeply saddened by his living arrangements (5:1–2). A community that does not bother to mourn openly when members put themselves at risk is not a community at all, much less a reflection of a new reality let loose in the world by the cross.

Third, for all their sinfulness, churches must strive to be communities that reflect the transforming power of the gospel. Success will be most evident first in the way individuals are treated within the community, and then in the way the community interacts with outsiders. For Paul, life in Christ means that previous social arrangements must be thoroughly transformed. He wants the actions of the Corinthian community to reflect the new reality brought about by the gospel. That means opposing at least some standing features of Greco-Roman society, which was tightly organized around patriarchal households that functioned as centers of both family life and economic activity. In ancient Mediterranean culture the needs of the group were always paramount over the needs of individual household members, an arrangement Paul readily embraced. Old structures of domination, however, have no place in the new church community (7:15, 22; 9:19; 11:11–12).

Paul's Social Views

Many of Paul's comments in the letter about men and women reveal his awareness that life lived according to the gospel means new social arrangements. A few of his comments about marriage are astonishingly fair-minded for his era. For example, some in the church seem to have concluded that sexual abstinence ought to be the norm for all members, married and unmarried. Paul disagrees in the interest of preventing immoral behavior, then adds, "For the wife does not have authority over her own body, but the husband does; likewise the husband does not have authority over his own body, but the wife does. Do not deprive one another except perhaps by agreement for a set time" (7:4–5). Although Paul quibbles about what women ought to wear when prophesying, he is careful to protect their right to prophesy (11:5). (For comment on the controversial admonition that "women should be silent in the churches," see the note on 14:33–35.)

By the same token, rigid patterns for recognizing wealth or social standing such as sitting in rank order at table are unacceptable in the new family that is the

Church. That is why Paul argues so strongly against the Corinthians' continuation of old social patterns. When the church gathered for Communion, wealthier members were eating sumptuously in the dining room, and some were even getting drunk on wine, while poorer members were eating little or nothing at all, a situation that would have been standard procedure for secular gatherings in that day (11:21). But the Church is the gathering of Christ's Body, and Paul is adamant that members act differently, so that the Body of Christ might be discernible to all.

An insight not to be overlooked in any close reading of 1 Corinthians is Paul's joy in his own relationship with and absolute reliance on God. There is enormous energy as well as concern in his correspondence with the Corinthian church. Such energy is not generated by anxiety. His energy and passion come from a longing to share the joy found in the life of faith. Joy is not a superficial emotion, nor one that can be experienced on command. True joy emerges when we have had experience with both suffering and love. It is impossible not to be moved by the joyful surrender that lies behind such statements as: "I have become all things to all people, that I might by all means save some. I do it all for the sake of the gospel, so that I may share in its blessings" (9:22–23); and "For now we see in a mirror, dimly, but then we will see face to face" (13:12). Most telling perhaps, here as in other letters, Paul at times breaks the flow of his own argument with sheer doxology: "The sting of death is sin, and the power of sin is the law. But thanks be to God, who gives us the victory through our Lord Jesus Christ" (15:56–57).

Finally, 1 Corinthians is an excellent document for those seeking to deepen what it means to read the whole Word of God. Here are statements so foundational to liturgical worship that many people can repeat them by heart: "For I received from the Lord what I also handed on to you, that the Lord Jesus on the night when he was betrayed took a loaf of bread, and when he had given thanks, he broke it and said, 'This is my body that is for you. Do this in remembrance of me.' In the same way he took the cup also, after supper, saying, 'This cup is the new covenant in my blood. Do this, as often as you drink it, in remembrance of me.' For as often as you eat this bread and drink the cup, you proclaim the Lord's death until he comes"(11:23–26); "And now faith, hope, and love abide, these three; and the greatest of these is love" (13:13). Beside these words are others so contentious some prefer not to read them at all: angry commands to expel people from church fellowship, lists of behaviors that preclude entry into the kingdom of God, and the infamous comment that "women should be silent in the churches" (14:34). The ability to hold in tension Scripture that we love with Scripture that makes us uncomfortable or even angry is a skill to be sought by those who would be spiritually mature. Just as Paul makes no attempt to reconcile his disparate moods and statements, we must not seek to domesticate his writing through rationalization or avoidance. Rather, we stand before this writer as his first readers did, willing to learn, argue, listen, and respond with a passion equal to Paul's own.

—*Catherine Taylor*

Salutation

1 Paul, called to be an apostle of Christ Jesus by the will of God, and our brother Sosthenes,

2 To the church of God that is in Corinth, to those who are sanctified in Christ Jesus, called to be saints, together with all those who in every place call on the name of our Lord Jesus Christ, both their Lord[a] and ours:

3 Grace to you and peace from God our Father and the Lord Jesus Christ.

4 I give thanks to my[b] God always for you because of the grace of God that has been given you in Christ Jesus, 5for in every way you have been enriched in him, in speech and knowledge of every kind— 6just as the testimony of[c] Christ has been strengthened among you— 7so that you are not lacking in any spiritual gift as you wait for the revealing of our Lord Jesus Christ. 8He will also strengthen you to the end, so that you may be blameless on the day of our Lord Jesus Christ. 9God is faithful; by him you were called into the fellowship of his Son, Jesus Christ our Lord.

Divisions in the Church

10 Now I appeal to you, brothers and sisters,[d] by the name of our Lord Jesus Christ, that all of you be in agreement and that there be no divisions among you, but that you be united in the same mind and the same purpose. 11For it has been reported to me by Chloe's people that there are quarrels among you, my brothers and sisters.[e] 12What I mean is that each of you says, "I belong to Paul," or "I belong to Apollos," or "I belong to Cephas," or "I belong to Christ." 13Has Christ been divided? Was Paul crucified for you? Or were you baptized in the name of Paul? 14I

a Gk theirs   b Other ancient authorities lack my
c Or to   d Gk brothers   e Gk my brothers

1:1 *by the will of God.* With his first words Paul names God as the source of his vocation, a signal that throughout the letter God will be recognized as the originator of all faith, grace, and spiritual gifts. From first to last God's sovereign power and presence with the Corinthian church and us are affirmed.

1:2 *called to be saints.* Just as Paul is called by the will of God, so are the Corinthians. Paul uses the word "saints" for all church members, meaning those whom God has set apart as God's holy people (Lev 11:44–45). Efforts to earn or deserve this designation will always fall short (vv 26–30). Our holy status is a gift of God's grace.

1:4 *I give thanks to my God always for you.* Thanksgiving for the gift of human relationships is the first and most necessary response of those who belong to God.

Responding

1:4 PRAYER. The Greek word translated "thanks" in this verse is *eucharistio,* which is the root for the English word "Eucharist," and the "you" is plural. In other words, Paul thanks God for the people who are part of the gathering of Christians in Corinth. The next time you participate in the Eucharist or Communion, pay special attention to giving thanks for the congregation of which you are a part. Were you able to give wholehearted thanks, or did something hold you back? Try to explain. *See also* Spiritual Disciplines Index.

1:10 *Now I appeal to you.* Here begins Paul's primary purpose for writing the letter at this time. The phrase is repeated in 4:16. Between the two appearances of this phrase lies the whole of Paul's argument against divisions in the church, which takes up a full fourth of the letter. Although the Corinthians boast about their spiritual attainments, divisions in the community indicate to Paul that they are spiritually immature.

1:11 *Chloe's people.* Paul has received either a letter or a verbal report from relatives or associates of Chloe's household. (For a discussion of ancient Mediterranean households, see the Introduction.)

1:12 *I belong to Apollos.* Paul sent Apollos, a Jewish Christian from Alexandria, to Corinth. He is described in Acts 18:24–28 in appealing terms as a bold and charismatic leader. Note that Paul in no way criticizes Apollos. Rather, he focuses his argument on the destructiveness that results when believers value the proclaimer more than the proclamation.

thank God[a] that I baptized none of you except Crispus and Gaius, [15]so that no one can say that you were baptized in my name. [16](I did baptize also the household of Stephanas; beyond that, I do not know whether I baptized anyone else.) [17]For Christ did not send me to baptize but to proclaim the gospel, and not with eloquent wisdom, so that the cross of Christ might not be emptied of its power.

Christ the Power and Wisdom of God

18 For the message about the cross is foolishness to those who are perishing, but to us who are being saved it is the power of God. [19]For it is written,

"I will destroy the wisdom of the wise,
    and the discernment of the
        discerning I will thwart."

[20]Where is the one who is wise? Where is the scribe? Where is the debater of this age? Has not God made foolish the wisdom of the world? [21]For since, in the wisdom of God, the world did not know God through wisdom, God decided, through the foolishness of our proclamation, to save those who believe. [22]For Jews demand signs and Greeks desire wisdom, [23]but we proclaim Christ crucified, a stumbling block to Jews and foolishness to Gentiles, [24]but to those who are the called, both Jews and Greeks, Christ the power of God and the wisdom of God. [25]For God's foolishness is wiser than human wisdom, and God's weakness is stronger than human strength.

26 Consider your own call, brothers and sisters:[b] not many of you were wise by human standards,[c] not many were powerful, not many were of noble birth. [27]But God chose what is foolish in the world to shame the wise; God chose what is weak in the world to shame the strong; [28]God chose what is low and despised in the world, things that are not, to reduce to nothing things that are, [29]so that no one[d] might boast in the presence of God. [30]He is the source of your life in Christ Jesus, who became for us wisdom from God, and righteousness and sanctification and redemption, [31]in order that, as it is written, "Let the one who boasts, boast in[e] the Lord."

Proclaiming Christ Crucified

2 When I came to you, brothers and sisters,[b] I did not come proclaiming the mystery[f] of God to you in lofty words or wisdom. [2]For I decided to know nothing among you except Jesus Christ, and him crucified. [3]And I came to you in weakness and in fear and in much trembling. [4]My speech and my proclamation were not with plausible words of wisdom,[g] but with a demonstration of the Spirit and of power, [5]so that your faith might rest not on human wisdom but on the power of God.

The True Wisdom of God

6 Yet among the mature we do speak wisdom, though it is not a wisdom of this age or of the rulers of this age, who are doomed to perish. [7]But we speak God's wisdom, secret and hidden, which God decreed before the

---

a Other ancient authorities read *I am thankful*
b Gk *brothers*   c Gk *according to the flesh*
d Gk *no flesh*   e Or *of*   f Other ancient authorities read *testimony*   g Other ancient authorities read *the persuasiveness of wisdom*

1:18 *it is the power of God.* The goal of all spiritual wisdom is the awareness that God alone saves; God alone transforms life now and in the future. Thus true spiritual wisdom looks beyond itself to its source in God.

2:2 *and him crucified.* Paul fears the Corinthians have completely misunderstood the gospel. Full of their own gifts and accomplishments, they are behaving like people who think they can save themselves by their own efforts. Paul insists they remember that salvation is accomplished by nothing less—and nothing more—than Jesus' death on the cross, a defeat according to worldly standards. From this seeming defeat comes the complete transformation of reality and history. No effort to live the spiritual life that does not have the cross at its center can lead to anything other than illusion.

2:6 *we do speak wisdom.* Spiritual wisdom comes from giving up competitive striving after human attainment and relying on the hidden wisdom of the cross.

ages for our glory. 8None of the rulers of this age understood this; for if they had, they would not have crucified the Lord of glory. 9But, as it is written,

"What no eye has seen, nor ear heard,
    nor the human heart conceived,
  what God has prepared for those who
        love him"—

10these things God has revealed to us through the Spirit; for the Spirit searches everything, even the depths of God. 11For what human being knows what is truly human except the human spirit that is within? So also no one comprehends what is truly God's except the Spirit of God. 12Now we have received not the spirit of the world, but the Spirit that is from God, so that we may understand the gifts bestowed on us by God. 13And we speak of these things in words not taught by human wisdom but taught by the Spirit, interpreting spiritual things to those who are spiritual. *a*

14 Those who are unspiritual *b* do not receive the gifts of God's Spirit, for they are foolishness to them, and they are unable to understand them because they are spiritually discerned. 15Those who are spiritual discern all things, and they are themselves subject to no one else's scrutiny.

16 "For who has known the mind of the
        Lord
    so as to instruct him?"
But we have the mind of Christ.

On Divisions in the Corinthian Church

3 And so, brothers and sisters, *c* I could not speak to you as spiritual people, but rather as people of the flesh, as infants in Christ. 2I fed you with milk, not solid food, for you were not ready for solid food. Even

now you are still not ready, 3for you are still of the flesh. For as long as there is jealousy and quarreling among you, are you not of the flesh, and behaving according to human inclinations? 4For when one says, "I belong to Paul," and another, "I belong to Apollos," are you not merely human?

5 What then is Apollos? What is Paul? Servants through whom you came to believe, as the Lord assigned to each. 6I planted, Apollos watered, but God gave the growth. 7So neither the one who plants nor the one who waters is anything, but only God who gives the growth. 8The one who plants and the one who waters have a common purpose, and each will receive wages according to the labor of each. 9For we are God's servants, working together; you are God's field, God's building.

10 According to the grace of God given to me, like a skilled master builder I laid a foundation, and someone else is building on it. Each builder must choose with care how to build on it. 11For no one can lay any foundation other than the one that has been laid; that foundation is Jesus Christ. 12Now if anyone builds on the foundation with gold, silver, precious stones, wood, hay, straw— 13the work of each builder will become visible, for the Day will disclose it, because it will be revealed with fire, and the fire will test what sort of work each has done. 14If what has been built on the foundation survives, the builder will receive a reward. 15If the work is burned up, the builder will suffer loss; the

a Or *interpreting spiritual things in spiritual language,* or *comparing spiritual things with spiritual*
b Or *natural*   *c* Gk *brothers*

2:13 *interpreting spiritual things to those who are spiritual.* Paul is not going back on his previous argument that there is no such thing as wisdom apart from the cross. Rather, he is using irony to chide boastful church members. The quality of all spirituality rests in humble reliance on the Spirit.

3:4 *are you not merely human?* Divisiveness in the church community is clear evidence that the Corinthians are little more than spiritual beginners. We cannot have much hope for

deepening our relationship with God if we are incapable of living harmoniously with those around us. Such harmony is not a superficial "getting along with" everybody. Paul is profoundly aware that it takes hard work, commitment, and even sacrifice to respect the very real differences between people. Chapters 8–10 repeatedly address the restraint and self-control required by life in the new community of God's people.

builder will be saved, but only as through fire.

16 Do you not know that you are God's temple and that God's Spirit dwells in you?[a] 17If anyone destroys God's temple, God will destroy that person. For God's temple is holy, and you are that temple.

18 Do not deceive yourselves. If you think that you are wise in this age, you should become fools so that you may become wise. 19For the wisdom of this world is foolishness with God. For it is written,

"He catches the wise in their
        craftiness,"

20and again,

"The Lord knows the thoughts of the
        wise,
    that they are futile."

21So let no one boast about human leaders. For all things are yours, 22whether Paul or Apollos or Cephas or the world or life or death or the present or the future—all belong to you, 23and you belong to Christ, and Christ belongs to God.

The Ministry of the Apostles

4 Think of us in this way, as servants of Christ and stewards of God's mysteries. 2Moreover, it is required of stewards that they be found trustworthy. 3But with me it is a very small thing that I should be judged by you or by any human court. I do not even judge myself. 4I am not aware of anything

against myself, but I am not thereby acquitted. It is the Lord who judges me. 5Therefore do not pronounce judgment before the time, before the Lord comes, who will bring to light the things now hidden in darkness and will disclose the purposes of the heart. Then each one will receive commendation from God.

6 I have applied all this to Apollos and myself for your benefit, brothers and sisters,[b] so that you may learn through us the meaning of the saying, "Nothing beyond what is written," so that none of you will be puffed up in favor of one against another. 7For who sees anything different in you?[c] What do you have that you did not receive? And if you received it, why do you boast as if it were not a gift?

8 Already you have all you want! Already you have become rich! Quite apart from us you have become kings! Indeed, I wish that you had become kings, so that we might be kings with you! 9For I think that God has exhibited us apostles as last of all, as though sentenced to death, because we have become a spectacle to the world, to angels and to mortals. 10We are fools for the sake of Christ, but you are wise in Christ. We are weak, but you are strong. You are held in honor, but we in disrepute. 11To the present hour we are hungry and thirsty, we are poorly clothed and

---

a In verses 16 and 17 the Greek word for *you* is plural   *b* Gk *brothers*   *c* Or *Who makes you different from another?*

3:15 *but only as through fire.* Those who teach or share leadership in the church should take care to build on Christ in ways that will endure extreme hardship and strain, even cataclysm. Spiritual leadership that is self-serving or not based on the gospel of Christ crucified will not survive such tests. Yet God in grace may still save wrongheaded spiritual leaders in spite of themselves!

3:21 *For all things are yours.* The proofs of spiritual attainment the Corinthians want so much to claim for themselves are not only illusions; they are altogether unnecessary. What is valuable and uplifting in life cannot be "attained" at all, only enjoyed freely through God's grace in the fellowship of Christ. One can almost hear Paul's relief and delight as he shares

this liberating truth with his distant congregation.

4:8–13 *Already you have all you want!* Using what may be quotes from a previous letter to him from the Corinthian church, Paul mocks the Corinthians' claim to have achieved spiritual perfection by contrasting their condition with his own suffering for the gospel. Spiritual certitude is almost always an indication that we are either insecure or afraid of life's uncontrollable ambiguities. Mastery of spiritual practices or gifts is not the goal of the Spirit-lived life. Trust in God's absolute reliability is the goal. This trust has no basis in our own condition; it is based on God's faithfulness. Such trust will aid in times of sorrow and serve as a guide when all is well. Paul would have the Corinthians know the value of trust in God by imitating his own trust.

beaten and homeless, [12]and we grow weary from the work of our own hands. When reviled, we bless; when persecuted, we endure; [13]when slandered, we speak kindly. We have become like the rubbish of the world, the dregs of all things, to this very day.

Fatherly Admonition

14 I am not writing this to make you ashamed, but to admonish you as my beloved children. [15]For though you might have ten thousand guardians in Christ, you do not have many fathers. Indeed, in Christ Jesus I became your father through the gospel. [16]I appeal to you, then, be imitators of me. [17]For this reason I sent[a] you Timothy, who is my beloved and faithful child in the Lord, to remind you of my ways in Christ Jesus, as I teach them everywhere in every church. [18]But some of you, thinking that I am not coming to you, have become arrogant. [19]But I will come to you soon, if the Lord wills, and I will find out not the talk of these arrogant people but their power. [20]For the kingdom of God depends not on talk but on power. [21]What would you prefer? Am I to come to you with a stick, or with love in a spirit of gentleness?

Sexual Immorality Defiles the Church

5 It is actually reported that there is sexual immorality among you, and of a kind that is not found even among pagans; for a man is living with his father's wife. [2]And you are arrogant! Should you not rather have mourned, so that he who has done this would have been removed from among you?

3 For though absent in body, I am present in spirit; and as if present I have already pronounced judgment [4]in the name of the Lord Jesus on the man who has done such a thing.[b] When you are assembled, and my spirit is present with the power of our Lord Jesus, [5]you are to hand this man over to Satan for the destruction of the flesh, so that his spirit may be saved in the day of the Lord.[c]

6 Your boasting is not a good thing. Do you not know that a little yeast leavens the whole batch of dough? [7]Clean out the old yeast so that you may be a new batch, as you really are unleavened. For our paschal lamb, Christ, has been sacrificed. [8]Therefore, let us celebrate the festival, not with the old yeast, the yeast of malice and evil, but with the unleavened bread of sincerity and truth.

Sexual Immorality Must Be Judged

9 I wrote to you in my letter not to associate with sexually immoral persons— [10]not at all meaning the immoral of this world, or the

a Or *am sending*   b Or *on the man who has done such a thing in the name of the Lord Jesus*   c Other ancient authorities add *Jesus*

4:20 THE WITH-GOD LIFE—*See* Spiritual Disciplines Index.

5:1–2 *for a man is living with his father's wife.* Paul is deeply critical of the church for boasting about its accomplishments while ignoring the spiritual state of individual members, some of whom may think themselves above human laws by virtue of church fellowship. The man in question is breaking the incest laws of his day (see also Deut 22:30). Refraining from sexual sin is not the critical issue here. The issue is how the community of the faithful should respond to the man. Paul makes clear that they should be as sad as if their brother has died, a response remarkable for the degree of love implied, rather than condemnation. When he does go so far as to command expulsion, it is so the man might ultimately be saved. Fighting within the Church about what constitutes sexual sin today often falls far short of this level of communal concern and love.

Responding
5:7 SACRIFICE. In this verse Paul refers to "Christ," the Greek term for the Hebrew word "Messiah" and the divine name for the resurrected Jesus, as our paschal lamb. In a theological dictionary or on the Internet, look up the term "paschal lamb." What did you learn? As you can, read and prayerfully consider all of chapter 5. In what ways does Paul's teaching affect your understanding of and relationship with Jesus Christ? *See also* Spiritual Disciplines Index.

5:8 CELEBRATION—*See* Spiritual Disciplines Index.

greedy and robbers, or idolaters, since you would then need to go out of the world. [11]But now I am writing to you not to associate with anyone who bears the name of brother or sister[a] who is sexually immoral or greedy, or is an idolater, reviler, drunkard, or robber. Do not even eat with such a one. [12]For what have I to do with judging those outside? Is it not those who are inside that you are to judge? [13]God will judge those outside. "Drive out the wicked person from among you."

Lawsuits among Believers

6 When any of you has a grievance against another, do you dare to take it to court before the unrighteous, instead of taking it before the saints? [2]Do you not know that the saints will judge the world? And if the world is to be judged by you, are you incompetent to try trivial cases? [3]Do you not know that we are to judge angels—to say nothing of ordinary matters? [4]If you have ordinary cases, then, do you appoint as judges those who have no standing in the church? [5]I say this to your shame. Can it be that there is no one among you wise enough to decide between one believer[a] and another, [6]but a believer[a] goes to court against a believer[a]—and before unbelievers at that?

7 In fact, to have lawsuits at all with one another is already a defeat for you. Why not rather be wronged? Why not rather be defrauded? [8]But you yourselves wrong and defraud—and believers[b] at that.

9 Do you not know that wrongdoers will not inherit the kingdom of God? Do not be deceived! Fornicators, idolaters, adulterers, male prostitutes, sodomites, [10]thieves, the greedy, drunkards, revilers, robbers—none of these will inherit the kingdom of God. [11]And this is what some of you used to be. But you were washed, you were sanctified, you were justified in the name of the Lord Jesus Christ and in the Spirit of our God.

Glorify God in Body and Spirit

12 "All things are lawful for me," but not all things are beneficial. "All things are lawful for me," but I will not be dominated by anything. [13]"Food is meant for the stomach and the stomach for food,"[c] and God will destroy both one and the other. The body is meant not for fornication but for the Lord, and the Lord for the body. [14]And God raised the Lord and will also raise us by his power. [15]Do you not know that your bodies are members of Christ? Should I therefore take the members of Christ and make them members of a prostitute? Never! [16]Do you not know that whoever is united to a prostitute becomes one body with her? For it is said, "The two shall be one flesh." [17]But anyone united to the Lord becomes one spirit with him. [18]Shun fornication! Every sin that a person commits is outside the body; but the fornicator sins against the body itself. [19]Or do you not know that your body is a temple[d] of the Holy Spirit within you, which you have from God, and that you are not your own? [20]For you were bought with a price; therefore glorify God in your body.

a Gk *brother*   *b* Gk *brothers*   *c* The quotation may extend to the word *other*   *d* Or *sanctuary*

5:11 *Do not even eat with such a one.* The six behaviors by church members that Paul names here are very similar to actions that warrant capital punishment in Deuteronomy (13:1–5; 17:2–7; 21:18–21; 22:21–22, 30; 24:7; 19:16–19 [if a false witness testifies in a capital case]). In each instance harm is deemed to have been done to other people or to the whole community. Paul settles for excluding culpable church members. If 2 Cor 2:5–11 is a reference to this portion of the letter ("Anyone whom you forgive, I also forgive"), his call for excommunication may have been rejected outright by the Corinthians as too harsh. Note that Paul's primary intention is to protect the church, not mete out punishment or sort people into categories. As far as people outside the church are concerned, only God should be the judge (v 13).

6:9–10 *none of these will inherit the kingdom of God.* Paul shares the ancient Jewish condemnation of homosexuality. He bases his argument on God's will in creation (v 16; Gen 1:27; Rom 1:26–27). How binding his opinion should be today has been the source of much contemporary debate, as efforts to determine the nature and cause of sexual orientation and their role in God's creative will have been considered.

Directions concerning Marriage

7 Now concerning the matters about which you wrote: "It is well for a man not to touch a woman." ²But because of cases of sexual immorality, each man should have his own wife and each woman her own husband. ³The husband should give to his wife her conjugal rights, and likewise the wife to her husband. ⁴For the wife does not have authority over her own body, but the husband does; likewise the husband does not have authority over his own body, but the wife does. ⁵Do not deprive one another except perhaps by agreement for a set time, to devote yourselves to prayer, and then come together again, so that Satan may not tempt you because of your lack of self-control. ⁶This I say by way of concession, not of command. ⁷I wish that all were as I myself am. But each has a particular gift from God, one having one kind and another a different kind.

8 To the unmarried and the widows I say that it is well for them to remain unmarried as I am. ⁹But if they are not practicing self-control, they should marry. For it is better to marry than to be aflame with passion.

10 To the married I give this command—not I but the Lord—that the wife should not separate from her husband ¹¹(but if she does separate, let her remain unmarried or else be reconciled to her husband), and that the husband should not divorce his wife.

12 To the rest I say—I and not the Lord—that if any believer*a* has a wife who is an unbeliever, and she consents to live with him, he should not divorce her. ¹³And if any woman has a husband who is an unbeliever, and he consents to live with her, she should not divorce him. ¹⁴For the unbelieving husband is made holy through his wife, and the unbelieving wife is made holy through her husband. Otherwise, your children would be unclean, but as it is, they are holy. ¹⁵But if the unbelieving partner separates, let it be so; in such a case the brother or sister is not bound. It is to peace that God has called you.*b* ¹⁶Wife, for all you know, you might save your husband. Husband, for all you know, you might save your wife.

The Life That the Lord Has Assigned

17 However that may be, let each of you lead the life that the Lord has assigned, to which God called you. This is my rule in all the churches. ¹⁸Was anyone at the time of his call already circumcised? Let him not seek to remove the marks of circumcision. Was anyone at the time of his call uncircumcised? Let him not seek circumcision. ¹⁹Circumcision is nothing, and uncircumcision is nothing; but obeying the commandments of God is everything. ²⁰Let each of you remain in the condition in which you were called.

21 Were you a slave when called? Do not be concerned about it. Even if you can gain your freedom, make use of your present condition now more than ever.*c* ²²For whoever was called in the Lord as a slave is a freed person belonging to the Lord, just as whoever was free when called is a slave of Christ. ²³You

a Gk *brother*   *b* Other ancient authorities read *us*   *c* Or *avail yourself of the opportunity*

7:1 *Now concerning the matters about which you wrote.* Paul now turns to topics raised by the Corinthians themselves in a previous letter. The opening phrase, "Now concerning," will appear five more times in the letter (7:25; 8:1; 12:1; 16:1; 16:12), each time signaling a shift to a new topic. *It is well for a man not to touch a woman.* Someone in the community is asserting that sexual abstinence should be the norm for all church members, married and unmarried. Paul disagrees. Not only does sexual intercourse prevent immorality; marriage partners have an equal right to sexual fulfillment.

Responding
7:5 PRAYER and CHASTITY. In the midst of instruction about Christian marriage, Paul advises husbands and wives to abstain from conjugal relations for only a "set time, to devote [themselves] to prayer." Is this possible in today's sex-saturated society? Can you name advantages to this practice? Disadvantages? According to the last part of verse 5, what are the dangers of going beyond that set time? *See also* Spiritual Disciplines Index.

7:7 *each has a particular gift from God.* Here Paul names celibacy as a gift of God, not a

were bought with a price; do not become slaves of human masters. 24In whatever condition you were called, brothers and sisters,*a* there remain with God.

The Unmarried and the Widows

25 Now concerning virgins, I have no command of the Lord, but I give my opinion as one who by the Lord's mercy is trustworthy. 26I think that, in view of the impending*b* crisis, it is well for you to remain as you are. 27Are you bound to a wife? Do not seek to be free. Are you free from a wife? Do not seek a wife. 28But if you marry, you do not sin, and if a virgin marries, she does not sin. Yet those who marry will experience distress in this life,*c* and I would spare you that. 29I mean, brothers and sisters,*a* the appointed time has grown short; from now on, let even those who have wives be as though they had none, 30and those who mourn as though they were not mourning, and those who rejoice as though they were not rejoicing, and those who buy as though they had no possessions, 31and those who deal with the world as though they had no dealings with it. For the present form of this world is passing away.

32 I want you to be free from anxieties. The unmarried man is anxious about the affairs of the Lord, how to please the Lord; 33but the married man is anxious about the affairs of the world, how to please his wife, 34and his interests are divided. And the unmarried woman and the virgin are anxious about the affairs of the Lord, so that they may be holy in body and spirit; but the married woman is anxious about the affairs of the world, how to please her husband. 35I say this for your own benefit, not to put any restraint upon you, but to promote good order and unhindered devotion to the Lord.

36 If anyone thinks that he is not behaving properly toward his fiancée,*d* if his passions are strong, and so it has to be, let him marry as he wishes; it is no sin. Let them marry. 37But if someone stands firm in his resolve, being under no necessity but having his own desire under control, and has determined in his own mind to keep her as his fiancée,*d* he will do well. 38So then, he who marries his fiancée*d* does well; and he who refrains from marriage will do better.

39 A wife is bound as long as her husband lives. But if the husband dies,*e* she is free to marry anyone she wishes, only in the Lord. 40But in my judgment she is more blessed if she remains as she is. And I think that I too have the Spirit of God.

Food Offered to Idols

8 Now concerning food sacrificed to idols: we know that "all of us possess knowledge." Knowledge puffs up, but love builds up. 2Anyone who claims to know something does not yet have the necessary knowledge; 3but anyone who loves God is known by him.

4 Hence, as to the eating of food offered to idols, we know that "no idol in the world really exists," and that "there is no God but one." 5Indeed, even though there may be so-called gods in heaven or on earth—as in fact there are many gods and many lords— 6yet for us there is one God, the Father, from whom are all things and for whom we exist, and one Lord, Jesus Christ, through whom are all things and through whom we exist.

a Gk *brothers*   *b* Or *present*   *c* Gk *in the flesh*
d Gk *virgin*   *e* Gk *falls asleep*

---

condition to be sought or imitated. Again, differences between members of the community are affirmed.

7:28 *and I would spare you that.* Paul has a very high view of marriage and worries that those who are married when Christ returns may experience distress, perhaps as a result of conflicting devotion. Even so, he does not command one response with regard to marriage. Instead, he encourages people to make up their own minds. Having the flexibility to allow others to make choices different from our own is an important aspect of spiritual life (see also vv 36–38).

7:31 *For the present form of this world is passing away.* This statement may refer not only to Paul's expectation of the imminent return of Christ but also to the transformation of the world that takes place in the Body of Christ, the Church. Paul's insistence that the Corinthians conform to loving standards of behavior is part of the passing away of the former world.

7 It is not everyone, however, who has this knowledge. Since some have become so accustomed to idols until now, they still think of the food they eat as food offered to an idol; and their conscience, being weak, is defiled. 8 "Food will not bring us close to God." *a* We are no worse off if we do not eat, and no better off if we do. 9 But take care that this liberty of yours does not somehow become a stumbling block to the weak. 10 For if others see you, who possess knowledge, eating in the temple of an idol, might they not, since their conscience is weak, be encouraged to the point of eating food sacrificed to idols? 11 So by your knowledge those weak believers for whom Christ died are destroyed. *b* 12 But when you thus sin against members of your family, *c* and wound their conscience when it is weak, you sin against Christ. 13 Therefore, if food is a cause of their falling, *d* I will never eat meat, so that I may not cause one of them *e* to fall.

The Rights of an Apostle

9 Am I not free? Am I not an apostle? Have I not seen Jesus our Lord? Are you not my work in the Lord? 2 If I am not an apostle to others, at least I am to you; for you are the seal of my apostleship in the Lord.

3 This is my defense to those who would examine me. 4 Do we not have the right to our food and drink? 5 Do we not have the right to be accompanied by a believing wife, *f* as do the other apostles and the brothers of the Lord and Cephas? 6 Or is it only Barnabas and I who have no right to refrain from working for a living? 7 Who at any time pays the expenses for doing military service? Who plants a vineyard and does not eat any of its fruit? Or who tends a flock and does not get any of its milk?

8 Do I say this on human authority? Does not the law also say the same? 9 For it is written in the law of Moses, "You shall not muzzle an ox while it is treading out the grain." Is it for oxen that God is concerned? 10 Or does he not speak entirely for our sake? It was indeed written for our sake, for whoever plows should plow in hope and whoever threshes should thresh in hope of a share in the crop. 11 If we have sown spiritual good among you, is it too much if we reap your material benefits? 12 If others share this rightful claim on you, do not we still more?

Nevertheless, we have not made use of this right, but we endure anything rather than put an obstacle in the way of the gospel of Christ. 13 Do you not know that those who are employed in the temple service get their food from the temple, and those who serve at the altar share in what is sacrificed on the altar? 14 In the same way, the Lord commanded that those who proclaim the gospel should get their living by the gospel.

15 But I have made no use of any of these rights, nor am I writing this so that they may be applied in my case. Indeed, I would rather die than that—no one will deprive me of my ground for boasting! 16 If I proclaim the gospel, this gives me no ground for boasting, for an obligation is laid on me, and woe to me if I do not proclaim the gospel! 17 For if I do this of my own will, I have a reward; but if not of my own will, I am entrusted with a commission. 18 What then is my reward? Just this: that in my proclamation I may make the gospel free of charge, so as not to make full use of my rights in the gospel.

19 For though I am free with respect to all, I have made myself a slave to all, so that I might win more of them. 20 To the Jews I became as a Jew, in order to win Jews. To those under the law I became as one under the law (though I myself am not under the law) so that I might win those under the law. 21 To those outside the law I became as one outside the law (though I am not free from God's law but am under Christ's law) so that I might win those outside the law. 22 To the weak I became weak, so that I might win the weak. I have become all things to all people, that I might by all means save some. 23 I do it all for the sake of the gospel, so that I may share in its blessings.

24 Do you not know that in a race the runners all compete, but only one receives the prize? Run in such a way that you may win it. 25 Athletes exercise self-control in all

a The quotation may extend to the end of the verse
b Gk *the weak brother . . . is destroyed*   *c* Gk *against the brothers*   *d* Gk *my brother's falling*
e Gk *cause my brother*   *f* Gk *a sister as wife*

things; they do it to receive a perishable wreath, but we an imperishable one. [26] So I do not run aimlessly, nor do I box as though beating the air; [27] but I punish my body and enslave it, so that after proclaiming to others I myself should not be disqualified.

Warnings from Israel's History

10 I do not want you to be unaware, brothers and sisters, *a* that our ancestors were all under the cloud, and all passed through the sea, [2] and all were baptized into Moses in the cloud and in the sea, [3] and all ate the same spiritual food, [4] and all drank the same spiritual drink. For they drank from the spiritual rock that followed them, and the rock was Christ. [5] Nevertheless, God was not pleased with most of them, and they were struck down in the wilderness.

[6] Now these things occurred as examples for us, so that we might not desire evil as they did. [7] Do not become idolaters as some of them did; as it is written, "The people sat down to eat and drink, and they rose up to play." [8] We must not indulge in sexual immorality as some of them did, and twenty-three thousand fell in a single day. [9] We must not put Christ *b* to the test, as some of them did, and were destroyed by serpents. [10] And do not complain as some of them did, and were destroyed by the destroyer. [11] These things happened to them to serve as an example, and they were written down to instruct us, on whom the ends of the ages have come. [12] So if you think you are standing, watch out that you do not fall. [13] No testing has overtaken you that is not common to everyone. God is faithful, and he will not let you be tested beyond your strength, but with the testing he will also provide the way out so that you may be able to endure it.

[14] Therefore, my dear friends, *c* flee from the worship of idols. [15] I speak as to sensible people; judge for yourselves what I say. [16] The cup of blessing that we bless, is it not a shar-

ing in the blood of Christ? The bread that we break, is it not a sharing in the body of Christ? [17] Because there is one bread, we who are many are one body, for we all partake of the one bread. [18] Consider the people of Israel; *d* are not those who eat the sacrifices partners in the altar? [19] What do I imply then? That food sacrificed to idols is anything, or that an idol is anything? [20] No, I imply that what pagans sacrifice, they sacrifice to demons and not to God. I do not want you to be partners with demons. [21] You cannot drink the cup of the Lord and the cup of demons. You cannot partake of the table of the Lord and the table of demons. [22] Or are we provoking the Lord to jealousy? Are we stronger than he?

Do All to the Glory of God

[23] "All things are lawful," but not all things are beneficial. "All things are lawful," but not all things build up. [24] Do not seek your own advantage, but that of the other. [25] Eat whatever is sold in the meat market without raising any question on the ground of conscience, [26] for "the earth and its fullness are the Lord's." [27] If an unbeliever invites you to a meal and you are disposed to go, eat whatever is set before you without raising any question on the ground of conscience. [28] But if someone says to you, "This has been offered in sacrifice," then do not eat it, out of consideration for the one who informed you, and for the sake of conscience— [29] I mean the other's conscience, not your own. For why should my liberty be subject to the judgment of someone else's conscience? [30] If I partake with thankfulness, why should I be denounced because of that for which I give thanks?

[31] So, whether you eat or drink, or whatever you do, do everything for the glory of

a Gk *brothers*   *b* Other ancient authorities read *the Lord*   *c* Gk *my beloved*   *d* Gk *Israel according to the flesh*

9:27 SACRIFICE—*See* Spiritual Disciplines Index.

10:31 *or whatever you do.* Again, Paul here gives the Corinthians leeway to make their own decisions. Being able to judge situations and

make decisions that allow the gospel to have an impact on others is more important, and more faithful to the pattern of Christ (see 11:1), than following a rigid, preset plan.

God. 32Give no offense to Jews or to Greeks or to the church of God, 33just as I try to please everyone in everything I do, not seeking my own advantage, but that of many, so that 11 they may be saved. 1Be imitators of me, as I am of Christ.

Head Coverings

2 I commend you because you remember me in everything and maintain the traditions just as I handed them on to you. 3But I want you to understand that Christ is the head of every man, and the husband*a* is the head of his wife,*b* and God is the head of Christ. 4Any man who prays or prophesies with something on his head disgraces his head, 5but any woman who prays or prophesies with her head unveiled disgraces her head—it is one and the same thing as having her head shaved. 6For if a woman will not veil herself, then she should cut off her hair; but if it is disgraceful for a woman to have her hair cut off or to be shaved, she should wear a veil. 7For a man ought not to have his head veiled, since he is the image and reflection*c* of God; but woman is the reflection*c* of man. 8Indeed, man was not made from woman, but woman from man. 9Neither was man created for the sake of woman, but woman for the sake of man. 10For this reason a woman ought to have a symbol of*d* authority on her head,*e* because of the angels. 11Nevertheless, in the Lord woman is not independent of man or man independent of woman. 12For just as woman came from man, so man comes through woman; but all things come from God. 13Judge for yourselves: is it proper for a woman to pray to God with her head unveiled? 14Does not nature itself teach you that

if a man wears long hair, it is degrading to him, 15but if a woman has long hair, it is her glory? For her hair is given to her for a covering. 16But if anyone is disposed to be contentious—we have no such custom, nor do the churches of God.

Abuses at the Lord's Supper

17 Now in the following instructions I do not commend you, because when you come together it is not for the better but for the worse. 18For, to begin with, when you come together as a church, I hear that there are divisions among you; and to some extent I believe it. 19Indeed, there have to be factions among you, for only so will it become clear who among you are genuine. 20When you come together, it is not really to eat the Lord's supper. 21For when the time comes to eat, each of you goes ahead with your own supper, and one goes hungry and another becomes drunk. 22What! Do you not have homes to eat and drink in? Or do you show contempt for the church of God and humiliate those who have nothing? What should I say to you? Should I commend you? In this matter I do not commend you!

The Institution of the Lord's Supper

23 For I received from the Lord what I also handed on to you, that the Lord Jesus on the night when he was betrayed took a loaf of bread, 24and when he had given thanks, he broke it and said, "This is my body that is for*f* you. Do this in remembrance of me."

a The same Greek word means *man* or *husband*
b Or *head of the woman*   *c* Or *glory*   *d* Gk lacks *a symbol of*   *e* Or *have freedom of choice regarding her head*   *f* Other ancient authorities read *is broken for*

11:2 *just as I handed them on to you.* Apparently one of the traditions Paul handed on was the right of women to prophesy, albeit while wearing a veil (v 5).

11:10 *a symbol of authority on her head.* Note that in this difficult passage the veil is not a sign of lesser status, but a symbol of authority.

11:23–26 *what I also handed on to you.* Just as Jesus allowed himself to be handed over to those who would try to execute him, Paul now hands over the tradition of Jesus, who

repeatedly established community for people who were denied community or cast in the position of outsiders. Paul refers to the tradition of Jesus in order to insist that the Corinthian church eat the Lord's Supper in a manner that eliminates all false social divisions (see the Introduction).

11:23 *on the night when he was betrayed.* There is a moving play on words here. The word translated "betrayed" can also be translated "handed over."

25In the same way he took the cup also, after supper, saying, "This cup is the new covenant in my blood. Do this, as often as you drink it, in remembrance of me." 26For as often as you eat this bread and drink the cup, you proclaim the Lord's death until he comes.

Partaking of the Supper Unworthily

27 Whoever, therefore, eats the bread or drinks the cup of the Lord in an unworthy manner will be answerable for the body and blood of the Lord. 28Examine yourselves, and only then eat of the bread and drink of the cup. 29For all who eat and drink*a* without discerning the body,*b* eat and drink judgment against themselves. 30For this reason many of you are weak and ill, and some have died.*c* 31But if we judged ourselves, we would not be judged. 32But when we are judged by the Lord, we are disciplined*d* so that we may not be condemned along with the world.

33 So then, my brothers and sisters,*e* when you come together to eat, wait for one another. 34If you are hungry, eat at home, so that when you come together, it will not be for your condemnation. About the other things I will give instructions when I come.

Spiritual Gifts

12 Now concerning spiritual gifts,*f* brothers and sisters,*e* I do not want you to be uninformed. 2You know that when you were pagans, you were enticed and led astray to idols that could not speak. 3Therefore I want you to understand that no one speaking by the Spirit of God ever says "Let Jesus be cursed!" and no one can say "Jesus is Lord" except by the Holy Spirit.

4 Now there are varieties of gifts, but the same Spirit; 5and there are varieties of services, but the same Lord; 6and there are varieties of activities, but it is the same God who activates all of them in everyone. 7To each is given the manifestation of the Spirit for the common good. 8To one is given through the Spirit the utterance of wisdom, and to another the utterance of knowledge according to the same Spirit, 9to another faith by the same Spirit, to another gifts of healing by the one Spirit, 10to another the working of miracles, to another prophecy, to another the discernment of spirits, to another various kinds of tongues, to another the interpretation of tongues. 11All these are activated by one and the same Spirit, who allots to each one individually just as the Spirit chooses.

One Body with Many Members

12 For just as the body is one and has many members, and all the members of the body, though many, are one body, so it is

a Other ancient authorities add *in an unworthy manner,* *b* Other ancient authorities read *the Lord's body* *c* Gk *fallen asleep* *d* Or *When we are judged, we are being disciplined by the Lord* *e* Gk *brothers* *f* Or *spiritual persons*

11:26 *proclaim the Lord's death until he comes.* The actions of the Lord's Supper— taking, giving thanks, breaking, and giving—are actions that those who eat the meal receive from the Lord as gifts of grace. The Church receives the gift of the meal, has its brokenness restored, and is then enabled to pass the thanksgiving, breaking, and giving on in mission. All creative power for restoration and mission lies with God in Jesus. This process is a crucial element in our formation into Christlikeness.

11:27 *in an unworthy manner.* This statement is addressed to the Church, not to individual members (see the Introduction).

12:9 *to another faith by the same Spirit.* Faith itself is a gift of the Spirit. Some may enjoy other gifts as well, but that does not make them better

Christians than those whose primary gift is faith.

Responding
12:11 THE WITH-GOD LIFE. In his discussion of the gifts of the Spirit, Paul writes that the Spirit chooses the gifts that are allotted each person. To the contemporary mind, this seems awfully arbitrary, but it seems perfectly normal in the economy of God, who knows us better than we even know ourselves (Luke 12:7). If you have never done it before, make a special study of the gifts of the Spirit listed in verses 4–11, 28–30; Rom 12:6–8; and Eph 4:11–13. How does the fact that the Spirit knows you well enough to give you the gifts best suited to you affect your view of those gifts? *See also* Spiritual Disciplines Index.

with Christ. 13For in the one Spirit we were all baptized into one body—Jews or Greeks, slaves or free—and we were all made to drink of one Spirit.

14 Indeed, the body does not consist of one member but of many. 15If the foot would say, "Because I am not a hand, I do not belong to the body," that would not make it any less a part of the body. 16And if the ear would say, "Because I am not an eye, I do not belong to the body," that would not make it any less a part of the body. 17If the whole body were an eye, where would the hearing be? If the whole body were hearing, where would the sense of smell be? 18But as it is, God arranged the members in the body, each one of them, as he chose. 19If all were a single member, where would the body be? 20As it is, there are many members, yet one body. 21The eye cannot say to the hand, "I have no need of you," nor again the head to the feet, "I have no need of you." 22On the contrary, the members of the body that seem to be weaker are indispensable, 23and those members of the body that we think less honorable we clothe with greater honor, and our less respectable members are treated with greater respect; 24whereas our more respectable members do not need this. But God has so arranged the body, giving the greater honor to the inferior member, 25that there may be no dissension within the body, but the members may have the same care for one another. 26If one member suffers, all suffer together with it; if one member is honored, all rejoice together with it.

27 Now you are the body of Christ and individually members of it. 28And God has appointed in the church first apostles, second prophets, third teachers; then deeds of power, then gifts of healing, forms of assistance, forms of leadership, various kinds of tongues. 29Are all apostles? Are all prophets? Are all teachers? Do all work miracles? 30Do all possess gifts of healing? Do all speak in tongues? Do all interpret? 31But strive for the greater gifts. And I will show you a still more excellent way.

The Gift of Love

13 If I speak in the tongues of mortals and of angels, but do not have love, I am a noisy gong or a clanging cymbal. 2And if I have prophetic powers, and understand all mysteries and all knowledge, and if I have all faith, so as to remove mountains, but do not have love, I am nothing. 3If I give away all my possessions, and if I hand over my body so that I may boast,a but do not have love, I gain nothing.

4 Love is patient; love is kind; love is not envious or boastful or arrogant 5or rude. It does not insist on its own way; it is not irritable or resentful; 6it does not rejoice in wrongdoing, but rejoices in the truth. 7It bears all things, believes all things, hopes all things, endures all things.

8 Love never ends. But as for prophecies, they will come to an end; as for tongues, they will cease; as for knowledge, it will come to an end. 9For we know only in part, and we prophesy only in part; 10but when the complete comes, the partial will come to an end. 11When I was a child, I spoke like a child, I thought like a child, I reasoned like a child; when I became an adult, I put an end to childish ways. 12For now we see in a mirror, dimly,b but then we will see face to face. Now I know only in part; then I will know fully, even as I have been fully known. 13And now faith, hope, and love abide, these three; and the greatest of these is love.

a Other ancient authorities read body to be burned
b Gk in a riddle

13:4–6 CHASTITY—See Spiritual Disciplines Index.

13:13 and the greatest of these is love. As a pastor speaking to a specific situation in his former congregation, Paul here offers a statement on love unequaled in spiritual writing. Though he presents an ideal seldom attained by any community, his very words uplift and inspire. The love outlined here is what Paul wants the Corinthians to show toward one another in all their behavior, that they might experience such love themselves. We too experience and are sustained by the love we are able to show others.

Gifts of Prophecy and Tongues

14 Pursue love and strive for the spiritual gifts, and especially that you may prophesy. 2For those who speak in a tongue do not speak to other people but to God; for nobody understands them, since they are speaking mysteries in the Spirit. 3On the other hand, those who prophesy speak to other people for their upbuilding and encouragement and consolation. 4Those who speak in a tongue build up themselves, but those who prophesy build up the church. 5Now I would like all of you to speak in tongues, but even more to prophesy. One who prophesies is greater than one who speaks in tongues, unless someone interprets, so that the church may be built up.

6 Now, brothers and sisters,*a* if I come to you speaking in tongues, how will I benefit you unless I speak to you in some revelation or knowledge or prophecy or teaching? 7It is the same way with lifeless instruments that produce sound, such as the flute or the harp. If they do not give distinct notes, how will anyone know what is being played? 8And if the bugle gives an indistinct sound, who will get ready for battle? 9So with yourselves; if in a tongue you utter speech that is not intelligible, how will anyone know what is being said? For you will be speaking into the air. 10There are doubtless many different kinds of sounds in the world, and nothing is without sound. 11If then I do not know the meaning of a sound, I will be a foreigner to the speaker and the speaker a foreigner to me. 12So with yourselves; since you are eager for spiritual gifts, strive to excel in them for building up the church.

13 Therefore, one who speaks in a tongue should pray for the power to interpret. 14For if I pray in a tongue, my spirit prays but my mind is unproductive. 15What should I do

then? I will pray with the spirit, but I will pray with the mind also; I will sing praise with the spirit, but I will sing praise with the mind also. 16Otherwise, if you say a blessing with the spirit, how can anyone in the position of an outsider say the "Amen" to your thanksgiving, since the outsider does not know what you are saying? 17For you may give thanks well enough, but the other person is not built up. 18I thank God that I speak in tongues more than all of you; 19nevertheless, in church I would rather speak five words with my mind, in order to instruct others also, than ten thousand words in a tongue.

20 Brothers and sisters,*a* do not be children in your thinking; rather, be infants in evil, but in thinking be adults. 21In the law it is written,

"By people of strange tongues
    and by the lips of foreigners
I will speak to this people;
    yet even then they will not listen to
    me,"

says the Lord. 22Tongues, then, are a sign not for believers but for unbelievers, while prophecy is not for unbelievers but for believers. 23If, therefore, the whole church comes together and all speak in tongues, and outsiders or unbelievers enter, will they not say that you are out of your mind? 24But if all prophesy, an unbeliever or outsider who enters is reproved by all and called to account by all. 25After the secrets of the unbeliever's heart are disclosed, that person will bow down before God and worship him, declaring, "God is really among you."

Orderly Worship

26 What should be done then, my friends?*a* When you come together, each one has a hymn, a lesson, a revelation, a tongue,

a Gk *brothers*

14:13–15 PRAYER—*See* Spiritual Disciplines Index.

14:15 *but I will pray with the mind also.* Spiritual gifts are not given for the benefit of the possessor. The purpose of all spiritual gifts is to build up the whole Body of Christ and those the Body serves. Paul accepts ecstatic spiritual

experience as a reality, but insists that it never remain private or exclusive. His emphasis on the mind as well as the heart is not a preference for intellectual faith. Rather, Paul values wholeness in spiritual experience and pushes for both practitioner and witnesses to seek the greatest degree of participation and understanding.

or an interpretation. Let all things be done for building up. 27If anyone speaks in a tongue, let there be only two or at most three, and each in turn; and let one interpret. 28But if there is no one to interpret, let them be silent in church and speak to themselves and to God. 29Let two or three prophets speak, and let the others weigh what is said. 30If a revelation is made to someone else sitting nearby, let the first person be silent. 31For you can all prophesy one by one, so that all may learn and all be encouraged. 32And the spirits of prophets are subject to the prophets, 33for God is a God not of disorder but of peace.

(As in all the churches of the saints, 34women should be silent in the churches. For they are not permitted to speak, but should be subordinate, as the law also says. 35If there is anything they desire to know, let them ask their husbands at home. For it is shameful for a woman to speak in church.*a* 36Or did the word of God originate with you? Or are you the only ones it has reached?)

37 Anyone who claims to be a prophet, or to have spiritual powers, must acknowledge that what I am writing to you is a command of the Lord. 38Anyone who does not recognize this is not to be recognized. 39So, my friends,*b* be eager to prophesy, and do not forbid speaking in tongues; 40but all things should be done decently and in order.

The Resurrection of Christ

15 Now I would remind you, brothers and sisters,*c* of the good news*d* that I proclaimed to you, which you in turn received, in which also you stand, 2through which also you are being saved, if you hold firmly to the message that I proclaimed to you—unless you have come to believe in vain.

3 For I handed on to you as of first importance what I in turn had received: that Christ died for our sins in accordance with the scriptures, 4and that he was buried, and that he was raised on the third day in accordance with the scriptures, 5and that he appeared to Cephas, then to the twelve. 6Then he appeared to more than five hundred brothers and sisters*c* at one time, most of whom are still alive, though some have died.*e* 7Then he appeared to James, then to all the apostles. 8Last of all, as to one untimely born, he appeared also to me. 9For I am the least of the apostles, unfit to be called an apostle, because I persecuted the church of God. 10But by the grace of God I am what I

a Other ancient authorities put verses 34–35 after verse 40   *b* Gk *my brothers*   *c* Gk *brothers*
d Or *gospel*   *e* Gk *fallen asleep*

14:26 *Let all things be done for building up.* Again, for Paul orderly worship increases understanding and the building up of the Body of Christ. He encourages an array of forms—prophecy, prayers, speaking in tongues—but nothing to excess, and everything is to be done with the sole purpose of uplifting and enlightening the people.

14:33–35 *women should be silent in the churches.* These words are jarring after what has come before. Paul was addressing one church in 1 Corinthians, not "the churches." The statement is also in direct conflict with Paul's defense of women prophesying (11:2–12) and his insistence that "the present form of this world is passing away" (7:31), including at least some of the limitations imposed on the leadership of women. This teaching is so startling compared to what Paul says elsewhere that some scholars have argued that this statement was inserted into 1 Corinthians at an early stage by another writer.

Other scholars have suggested that, far from expressing his own views, Paul was here quoting from a letter that the Corinthians had sent to him.

15:1–58 *unless you have come to believe in vain.* Christ's resurrection is not a separate event unlinked with believers' resurrection, as some in the Corinthian church apparently believed. Although we do not know why some in the church did not think they would be resurrected, some insight lies in the way believers today seem to want to overlook the reality of death. Many cling to the non-Christian idea of a disembodied "soul," an inner spark that does not go out with death, but somehow passes over into union with God. Paul will have none of it. In this powerful chapter he insists that death is real and that the power to bring life out of death lies with God alone. What God has done for Jesus God will do for those who trust in him.

15:10 THE WITH-GOD LIFE—*See* Spiritual Disciplines Index.

am, and his grace toward me has not been in vain. On the contrary, I worked harder than any of them—though it was not I, but the grace of God that is with me. [11]Whether then it was I or they, so we proclaim and so you have come to believe.

The Resurrection of the Dead

12 Now if Christ is proclaimed as raised from the dead, how can some of you say there is no resurrection of the dead? [13]If there is no resurrection of the dead, then Christ has not been raised; [14]and if Christ has not been raised, then our proclamation has been in vain and your faith has been in vain. [15]We are even found to be misrepresenting God, because we testified of God that he raised Christ—whom he did not raise if it is true that the dead are not raised. [16]For if the dead are not raised, then Christ has not been raised. [17]If Christ has not been raised, your faith is futile and you are still in your sins. [18]Then those also who have died[a] in Christ have perished. [19]If for this life only we have hoped in Christ, we are of all people most to be pitied.

20 But in fact Christ has been raised from the dead, the first fruits of those who have died. [a] [21]For since death came through a human being, the resurrection of the dead has also come through a human being; [22]for as all die in Adam, so all will be made alive in Christ. [23]But each in his own order: Christ the first fruits, then at his coming those who belong to Christ. [24]Then comes the end, [b] when he hands over the kingdom to God the Father, after he has destroyed every ruler and every authority and power. [25]For he must reign until he has put all his enemies under his feet. [26]The last enemy to be destroyed is death. [27]For "God[c] has put all things in subjection under his feet." But when it says, "All things are put in subjection," it is plain that this does not include the one who put all things in subjection under him. [28]When all things are subjected to him, then the Son himself will also be subjected to the one who put all things in subjection under him, so that God may be all in all.

29 Otherwise, what will those people do who receive baptism on behalf of the dead? If the dead are not raised at all, why are people baptized on their behalf?

30 And why are we putting ourselves in danger every hour? [31]I die every day! That is as certain, brothers and sisters,[d] as my boasting of you—a boast that I make in Christ Jesus our Lord. [32]If with merely human hopes I fought with wild animals at Ephesus, what would I have gained by it? If the dead are not raised,

"Let us eat and drink,
for tomorrow we die."

[33]Do not be deceived:

"Bad company ruins good morals."

[34]Come to a sober and right mind, and sin no more; for some people have no knowledge of God. I say this to your shame.

The Resurrection Body

35 But someone will ask, "How are the dead raised? With what kind of body do they come?" [36]Fool! What you sow does not come to life unless it dies. [37]And as for what you sow, you do not sow the body that is to be, but a bare seed, perhaps of wheat or of some other grain. [38]But God gives it a body as he has chosen, and to each kind of seed its own body. [39]Not all flesh is alike, but there is one flesh for human beings, another for animals, another for birds, and another for fish. [40]There are both heavenly bodies and earthly bodies, but the glory of the heavenly is one thing, and that of the earthly is another. [41]There is one glory of the sun, and another

a Gk *fallen asleep*   b Or *Then come the rest*
c Gk *he*   d Gk *brothers*

15:35 *With what kind of body do they come?* With metaphors taken from gardens and fields, Paul describes the reality of bodily resurrection without negating its deep mystery. Like a plant in seed, what would live must die. A spiritual body will be given by God, one that reflects even more fully the identity of the individual than the body known in this life. A capacity to engage mystery is necessary for the life of faith, and it is enormously comforting for those who have made the journey from small certitudes to the embrace of the unknown.

glory of the moon, and another glory of the stars; indeed, star differs from star in glory.

42 So it is with the resurrection of the dead. What is sown is perishable, what is raised is imperishable. 43It is sown in dishonor, it is raised in glory. It is sown in weakness, it is raised in power. 44It is sown a physical body, it is raised a spiritual body. If there is a physical body, there is also a spiritual body. 45Thus it is written, "The first man, Adam, became a living being"; the last Adam became a life-giving spirit. 46But it is not the spiritual that is first, but the physical, and then the spiritual. 47The first man was from the earth, a man of dust; the second man is*a* from heaven. 48As was the man of dust, so are those who are of the dust; and as is the man of heaven, so are those who are of heaven. 49Just as we have borne the image of the man of dust, we will*b* also bear the image of the man of heaven.

50 What I am saying, brothers and sisters,*c* is this: flesh and blood cannot inherit the kingdom of God, nor does the perishable inherit the imperishable. 51Listen, I will tell you a mystery! We will not all die,*d* but we will all be changed, 52in a moment, in the twinkling of an eye, at the last trumpet. For the trumpet will sound, and the dead will be raised imperishable, and we will be changed. 53For this perishable body must put on imperishability, and this mortal body must put on immortality. 54When this perishable body puts on imperishability, and this mortal body puts on immortality, then the saying that is written will be fulfilled:

"Death has been swallowed up in
      victory."
55 "Where, O death, is your victory?
      Where, O death, is your sting?"
56The sting of death is sin, and the power of sin is the law. 57But thanks be to God, who gives us the victory through our Lord Jesus Christ. 58 Therefore, my beloved,*e* be steadfast, immovable, always excelling in the work of the Lord, because you know that in the Lord your labor is not in vain.

The Collection for the Saints

16 Now concerning the collection for the saints: you should follow the directions I gave to the churches of Galatia. 2On the first day of every week, each of you is to put aside and save whatever extra you earn, so that collections need not be taken when I come. 3And when I arrive, I will send any whom you approve with letters to take your gift to Jerusalem. 4If it seems advisable that I should go also, they will accompany me.

Plans for Travel

5 I will visit you after passing through Macedonia—for I intend to pass through Macedonia— 6and perhaps I will stay with you or even spend the winter, so that you may send me on my way, wherever I go. 7I do not want to see you now just in passing, for I hope to spend some time with you, if the Lord permits. 8But I will stay in Ephesus until Pentecost, 9for a wide door for effective work has opened to me, and there are many adversaries.

10 If Timothy comes, see that he has nothing to fear among you, for he is doing the work of the Lord just as I am; 11therefore let no one despise him. Send him on his way in peace, so that he may come to me; for I am expecting him with the brothers.

12 Now concerning our brother Apollos, I strongly urged him to visit you with the other brothers, but he was not at all willing*f* to come now. He will come when he has the opportunity.

Final Messages and Greetings

13 Keep alert, stand firm in your faith, be courageous, be strong. 14Let all that you do be done in love.

a Other ancient authorities add *the Lord*
b Other ancient authorities read *let us*
c Gk *brothers*   *d* Gk *fall asleep*   *e* Gk *beloved brothers*   *f* Or *it was not at all God's will for him*

16:14 *Let all that you do be done in love.* With these words Paul summarizes the thrust of a letter intended to bring a stubborn church back into a practice of the gospel consistent with a crucified Lord. Undertaking our own spiritual development in love means forgiving ourselves for our own frailty in the endeavor, persisting, forgiving, enduring, and being patient with

15 Now, brothers and sisters,[a] you know that members of the household of Stephanas were the first converts in Achaia, and they have devoted themselves to the service of the saints; [16]I urge you to put yourselves at the service of such people, and of everyone who works and toils with them. [17]I rejoice at the coming of Stephanas and Fortunatus and Achaicus, because they have made up for your absence; [18]for they refreshed my spirit as well as yours. So give recognition to such persons.

19 The churches of Asia send greetings. Aquila and Prisca, together with the church in their house, greet you warmly in the Lord. [20]All the brothers and sisters[a] send greetings. Greet one another with a holy kiss.

21 I, Paul, write this greeting with my own hand. [22]Let anyone be accursed who has no love for the Lord. Our Lord, come![b] [23]The grace of the Lord Jesus be with you. [24]My love be with all of you in Christ Jesus.[c]

a Gk brothers   b Gk Marana tha. These Aramaic words can also be read Maran atha, meaning Our Lord has come   c Other ancient authorities add Amen

---

ourselves while learning and growing in faith. The statement has no time frame, and we do not need to keep lists of what we have managed, remarkably, to do in love from day to day. Rather, we can let all that we do be done in love, and love ourselves throughout the process.

Responding

16:16 SERVICE. In these final instructions to the Christians at Corinth, Paul first charges them to let all that they do "be done in love" (v 14) and then to put themselves "at the service" of such people as the household of Stephanas. Loving service to the saints seems to be the norm, not the exception. In what ways have you "served the saints" during the past year? In what ways can you serve them in the future? See also Spiritual Disciplines Index.

THE SECOND LETTER OF PAUL TO THE

CORINTHIANS

The Second Letter of Paul to the Corinthians gives us the best picture of the spiritual struggle of an apostle in the New Testament. Paul is an evangelist and an apostle, but in the Corinthian correspondence we see what happens after evangelization. We see Paul, in his role as spiritual father of the community, burdened with the weight of leadership. Between the lines of this letter, written to instruct and admonish the immature Christians of Corinth, we see Paul careworn yet working to live out a theology of reconciliation and transformation in the image of Christ.

The Situation

This letter picks up amid a stressful relationship between Paul and the local church he founded. He and the Corinthians have issues to work out before they can continue in ministry together. That work is the crucible that tests their Christian strength and ingenuity. We have the Corinthians' side of the story only through Paul's version of it, and he was writing not to us but to people who knew that history. Still, we can see the outlines of what has happened.

We know from 1 Corinthians that these Christians were fumbling as they sought to work out Christian discipline regarding food, sex, marriage, and lawsuits. It would appear that Paul visited the church a second time after he wrote that letter, either to follow up on the charge of incest (1 Cor 5:1) or in response to some other weighty matter. For whatever reasons, the meeting did not go well. There must have been an unpleasant scene, because Paul left early, leaving sour feelings all around. Perhaps this gave some members of the church the impetus to listen to other gospel preachers and to question Paul's authority.

From this letter, as well as from the letter to the Galatian churches, we know that many people evangelized and that some of them were apparently unscrupulous.

See also "The With-God Life" essay for this section of the Bible,
"The People of God in Community," pp. 2037–42.

2089

Whatever it was, one crisis seems to have led to another. After leaving Corinth for the second time, Paul may have written an angry letter to the congregation (which we do not have) instructing them to discipline an offending member. The offender could have been the man guilty of incest reported in 1 Corinthians, or it could have been someone from a completely unrelated incident in which Paul or his authority was called into question during his second visit. Some think that we see parts of such a letter in the last four chapters of 2 Corinthians. Whatever happened, everyone was so distressed that Paul decided not to return to Corinth himself, for fear of having another problematic confrontation that would upset everyone again. Instead, he sent Titus to see what had happened and to try to patch things up. Paul was apparently distressed that he might lose this congregation to his apostolic competitors.

As it turned out, the Corinthians decided to obey Paul's order. They disciplined their offending member, so harshly, in fact, that Paul had to admonish them (in his next letter, 2 Corinthians) to rehabilitate him back into the church after his punishment. We can see from this incident how difficult it is for congregations to discipline members when they step out of line. It is easier to gossip behind someone's back than to administer weighty pastoral care. The question of intentional rehabilitation is just as important.

These Christians eventually faced up to their responsibility and reaffirmed their obedience to Paul's authority. This encouraged him to resume his leadership of them and to exhort them (in 2 Corinthians) to pay the pledge of support for the church at Jerusalem that they had made the previous year (made perhaps during Paul's second stay in Corinth). Instructively, Paul is at pains to try to patch up his relationship with them in writing before raising the always delicate subject of money.

The Tensions

It is easier to conceive of a Christlike life than to live one. In 2 Cor 3:18, Paul teaches that Christians, beholding the beauty of the Lord, are being transformed into his image one splendorous step at a time. Spiritual transformation is a gradual process, and Paul knows that we have this treasure in what he calls clay jars (4:7), meaning our fragile selves, perhaps referring to himself.

Indeed, reading between the lines, we can see what seems to have gotten him in hot water with his converts. The Corinthian Christians complained that Paul was egocentric, and we do see evidence of this throughout the letter. He boasts of how strong he is in affliction, and he takes comfort in his suffering because it is for the sake of the very persons who are now quite unhappy with him. This may have fallen as badly on people's ears then as it would now.

Further, having been persuaded to give up what was considered a normal way of life to embrace the beliefs of an unproven sect that brought with it hardships, calamities, insults, and so on was tough stuff. Paul constantly told them of all his suffering on their behalf as a sign of his love. His cry for sympathy simply did not sit well with people, but appeared boastful. As a strategy, it appears to have backfired.

The Corinthians also accused him of misleading them financially. When he first evangelized them, he would not take any money from them—he lived on funds he had raised in another local church—but later he asked for money for the church in Jerusalem. They agreed, but after he left, some church members felt that he had manipulated them, beguiling them into thinking that becoming Christians would not cost them anything and then slapping a tax on them after they had signed up. Perhaps their ardor cooled somewhat after he left. It all may have become more than the Corinthians bargained for when they were first captivated by Paul's teaching. At least to some of them, Paul had become a nuisance.

This letter contains Paul's spirited defense of himself. In the last three chapters, we see his anger seep out. He is grappling with his fear that the troubles in this congregation could harm his ministry elsewhere, because they could damage his reputation. Yet he is doing more than venting his frustration here. It is no accident that the teaching on reconciliation that is the heart of the meaning of Christ's death finds its most beautiful expression here. Paul is giving the Corinthians the theology that can get them all through this and help them come out as one community on the other side. It is not enough, then, to work out the misunderstandings and vent the anger that have accrued between visits and letters. There must be a theological context that calls both Paul and his new Christians into a higher spiritual space, above their petty quarrels. Reconciliation must be the result of the maturity they acquire in Christ.

As their spiritual leader, even under pressure Paul assures those who find him bothersome that he loves them. And, perhaps more poignantly, he pledges his trust that, despite the conflicts that beset their relationship, they will come through these trials and be strengthened by them. The situation of conflict spurs him to articulate the meat of the gospel—reconciliation—amid his own anger and frustration.

Theology and Ministry

Theology is not an armchair discipline, but arises from particular needs we face in life. Often those needs become apparent only in the midst of a crisis of some sort, in this case a pastoral one. Second Corinthians shows us that professional Christian ministry is spiritually stressful, even spiritually dangerous. We see Paul struggling to put on the "weapons of righteousness for the right hand and for the left": "purity, knowledge, patience, kindness, holiness of spirit, genuine love, truthful speech, and the power of God" (2 Cor 6:6–7).

Paul grounds his ministry in Christian theology, although the latter is often difficult to grasp and even more difficult to live. He is big enough to see his own weaknesses and mistakes in judgment, sure enough of his call not to back down, and strong enough to take the heat. We see him here in a defensive posture and so perhaps not in the best light, yet the theology flows like honey from a comb—thick and sweet. He is interpreting Jesus Christ as much for himself as for the Corinthian Christians. Each letter he writes, shaped by its different circumstances, enables Paul to articulate the gospel in a slightly different way, so that it will guide his readers in their present situation. The good news of God's work with us cannot be cramped into a single articulation.

The meaning of Christ Jesus, especially in his death and resurrection, does not have one precise expression, for these are events pregnant with limitlessly rich ramifications. Paul's point is that the various articulations are guideposts toward the full stature of Christ amid the friction and resentments that inevitably come in the course of our common life, so that we may be transformed into the splendor of God.

—Ellen T. Charry

Salutation

1 Paul, an apostle of Christ Jesus by the will of God, and Timothy our brother,

To the church of God that is in Corinth, including all the saints throughout Achaia:

2 Grace to you and peace from God our Father and the Lord Jesus Christ.

Paul's Thanksgiving after Affliction

3 Blessed be the God and Father of our Lord Jesus Christ, the Father of mercies and the God of all consolation, [4]who consoles us in all our affliction, so that we may be able to console those who are in any affliction with the consolation with which we ourselves are consoled by God. [5]For just as the sufferings of Christ are abundant for us, so also our consolation is abundant through Christ. [6]If we are being afflicted, it is for your consolation and salvation; if we are being consoled, it is for your consolation, which you experience when you patiently endure the same sufferings that we are also suffering. [7]Our hope for you is unshaken; for we know that as you share in our sufferings, so also you share in our consolation.

8 We do not want you to be unaware, brothers and sisters,[a] of the affliction we experienced in Asia; for we were so utterly, unbearably crushed that we despaired of life itself. [9]Indeed, we felt that we had received the sentence of death so that we would rely not on ourselves but on God who raises the dead. [10]He who rescued us from so deadly a peril will continue to rescue us; on him we have set our hope that he will rescue us again, [11]as you also join in helping us by your prayers, so that many will give thanks on our[b] behalf for the blessing granted us through the prayers of many.

The Postponement of Paul's Visit

12 Indeed, this is our boast, the testimony of our conscience: we have behaved in the world with frankness[c] and godly sincerity, not by earthly wisdom but by the grace of God—and all the more toward you. [13]For we write you nothing other than what you can read and also understand; I hope you will understand until the end— [14]as you have already understood us in part—that on the day of the Lord Jesus we are your boast even as you are our boast.

15 Since I was sure of this, I wanted to come to you first, so that you might have a double favor;[d] [16]I wanted to visit you on my way to Macedonia, and to come back to you from

a Gk *brothers*   b Other ancient authorities read *your*   c Other ancient authorities read *holiness*   d Other ancient authorities read *pleasure*

1:1 *an apostle . . . by the will of God.* Paul does not undertake his ministry of his own accord; he is pressed into it by God. Difficult undertakings can be like that. Projects come to us from which we cannot turn aside. They may complicate our life, but we have no choice but to follow their lead.

1:4 *so that we may be able to console those . . . in any affliction.* Here Paul is speaking specifically about Christian rather than economic or social affliction. He suffers because he responds to God's hand on his life. This gives him credibility. Acting out the reconciliation that God has accomplished may bring suffering, but it is a suffering filled with joy because of its purpose, regardless of what is accomplished on the surface.

1:11 PRAYER—*See* Spiritual Disciplines Index.

Macedonia and have you send me on to Judea. [17]Was I vacillating when I wanted to do this? Do I make my plans according to ordinary human standards,[a] ready to say "Yes, yes" and "No, no" at the same time? [18]As surely as God is faithful, our word to you has not been "Yes and No." [19]For the Son of God, Jesus Christ, whom we proclaimed among you, Silvanus and Timothy and I, was not "Yes and No"; but in him it is always "Yes." [20]For in him every one of God's promises is a "Yes." For this reason it is through him that we say the "Amen," to the glory of God. [21]But it is God who establishes us with you in Christ and has anointed us, [22]by putting his seal on us and giving us his Spirit in our hearts as a first installment.

23 But I call on God as witness against me: it was to spare you that I did not come again to Corinth. [24]I do not mean to imply that we lord it over your faith; rather, we are workers with you for your joy, because you stand firm

2 in the faith. [1]So I made up my mind not to make you another painful visit. [2]For if I cause you pain, who is there to make me glad but the one whom I have pained? [3]And I wrote as I did, so that when I came, I might not suffer pain from those who should have made me rejoice; for I am confident about all of you, that my joy would be the joy of all of you. [4]For I wrote you out of much distress and anguish of heart and with many tears,

not to cause you pain, but to let you know the abundant love that I have for you.

Forgiveness for the Offender

5 But if anyone has caused pain, he has caused it not to me, but to some extent—not to exaggerate it—to all of you. [6]This punishment by the majority is enough for such a person; [7]so now instead you should forgive and console him, so that he may not be overwhelmed by excessive sorrow. [8]So I urge you to reaffirm your love for him. [9]I wrote for this reason: to test you and to know whether you are obedient in everything. [10]Anyone whom you forgive, I also forgive. What I have forgiven, if I have forgiven anything, has been for your sake in the presence of Christ. [11]And we do this so that we may not be outwitted by Satan; for we are not ignorant of his designs.

Paul's Anxiety in Troas

12 When I came to Troas to proclaim the good news of Christ, a door was opened for me in the Lord; [13]but my mind could not rest because I did not find my brother Titus there. So I said farewell to them and went on to Macedonia.

14 But thanks be to God, who in Christ always leads us in triumphal procession, and through us spreads in every place the fragrance

a Gk *according to the flesh*

1:21 *it is God who establishes us with you in Christ.* The ability to respond to the call of Christ does not rest with us, but is wholly the work of God. It cannot be forced on anyone, nor can we force it on ourselves in order to please others. Being established in Christ is a divine gift.

1:22 *putting his seal on us.* Baptism seals us with the Holy Spirit and marks us as Christ's own forever. No matter how far we roam, like the prodigal son, this holy seal can never be taken from us, even if we think we have lost it. Our fundamental identity is that we belong to God in Christ, and that trumps other aspects of our identity. We may return to this identity after each mistake and cling to it when challenged.

2:7 *forgive and console him.* Paul is admonishing the Corinthians to rehabilitate a sinner in their midst. The community's disapproval of him has gone on long enough. There comes a

time when shaming eats the soul, and Paul wisely does not want discouragement to set in. Communities must tend to comforting those who have fallen, lest they despair. Trying to discern when punishment is helpful and when forgiveness and love are what are needed is a delicate matter. Those bound together by baptism in the Body of Christ are called to this ministry for one another.

2:14 *the fragrance that comes from knowing him.* The word "fragrance" recalls the pleasing odor of Israel's sacrifices offered to God. Through his death, Christ now spreads fragrant knowledge of God throughout the world. This knowledge is fragrant because it expands us, filling us with the wisdom revealed in the cross that equips us to live into the uplifted life sealed in our bodies at baptism. Knowing God, then, makes us fragrant.

that comes from knowing him. 15For we are the aroma of Christ to God among those who are being saved and among those who are perishing; 16to the one a fragrance from death to death, to the other a fragrance from life to life. Who is sufficient for these things? 17For we are not peddlers of God's word like so many;*a* but in Christ we speak as persons of sincerity, as persons sent from God and standing in his presence.

Ministers of the New Covenant

3 Are we beginning to commend ourselves again? Surely we do not need, as some do, letters of recommendation to you or from you, do we? 2You yourselves are our letter, written on our*b* hearts, to be known and read by all; 3and you show that you are a letter of Christ, prepared by us, written not with ink but with the Spirit of the living God, not on tablets of stone but on tablets of human hearts.

4 Such is the confidence that we have through Christ toward God. 5Not that we are competent of ourselves to claim anything as coming from us; our competence is from God, 6who has made us competent to be ministers of a new covenant, not of letter but of spirit; for the letter kills, but the Spirit gives life.

7 Now if the ministry of death, chiseled in letters on stone tablets,*c* came in glory so that the people of Israel could not gaze at Moses' face because of the glory of his face, a glory now set aside, 8how much more will the ministry of the Spirit come in glory? 9For if there was glory in the ministry of condemnation, much more does the ministry of justification abound in glory! 10Indeed, what once had glory has lost its glory because of the greater glory; 11for if what was set

aside came through glory, much more has the permanent come in glory!

12 Since, then, we have such a hope, we act with great boldness, 13not like Moses, who put a veil over his face to keep the people of Israel from gazing at the end of the glory that*d* was being set aside. 14But their minds were hardened. Indeed, to this very day, when they hear the reading of the old covenant, that same veil is still there, since only in Christ is it set aside. 15Indeed, to this very day whenever Moses is read, a veil lies over their minds; 16but when one turns to the Lord, the veil is removed. 17Now the Lord is the Spirit, and where the Spirit of the Lord is, there is freedom. 18And all of us, with unveiled faces, seeing the glory of the Lord as though reflected in a mirror, are being transformed into the same image from one degree of glory to another; for this comes from the Lord, the Spirit.

Treasure in Clay Jars

4 Therefore, since it is by God's mercy that we are engaged in this ministry, we do not lose heart. 2We have renounced the shameful things that one hides; we refuse to practice cunning or to falsify God's word; but by the open statement of the truth we commend ourselves to the conscience of everyone in the sight of God. 3And even if our gospel is veiled, it is veiled to those who are perishing. 4In their case the god of this world has blinded the minds of the unbelievers, to keep them from seeing the light of the gospel of the glory of Christ, who is the image of God. 5For we do not proclaim ourselves; we proclaim Jesus Christ as Lord and ourselves as your slaves for

a Other ancient authorities read *like the others*
b Other ancient authorities read *your*   *c* Gk *on stones*   *d* Gk *of what*

3:18 *transformed into the same image.* When we rest in the splendor of God revealed by Christ, we find ourselves changed by it. Gradually, by degrees, Paul says, we incline toward the divine glory and it begins to overtake us. This is by the power of the Spirit, which prepared us for such growth beginning at baptism. We are transformed into his likeness, becoming splendid and glorious, to the glory of God.

Responding
3:18 STUDY. How does study help transform us into the image of Jesus Christ? To help you understand how we can be changed gradually into Christ's likeness, read *The Imitation of Christ* by Thomas à Kempis. What did you learn? *See also* Spiritual Disciplines Index.

Jesus' sake. 6For it is the God who said, "Let light shine out of darkness," who has shone in our hearts to give the light of the knowledge of the glory of God in the face of Jesus Christ.

7 But we have this treasure in clay jars, so that it may be made clear that this extraordinary power belongs to God and does not come from us. 8We are afflicted in every way, but not crushed; perplexed, but not driven to despair; 9persecuted, but not forsaken; struck down, but not destroyed; 10always carrying in the body the death of Jesus, so that the life of Jesus may also be made visible in our bodies. 11For while we live, we are always being given up to death for Jesus' sake, so that the life of Jesus may be made visible in our mortal flesh. 12So death is at work in us, but life in you.

13 But just as we have the same spirit of faith that is in accordance with scripture—"I believed, and so I spoke"—we also believe, and so we speak, 14because we know that the one who raised the Lord Jesus will raise us also with Jesus, and will bring us with you into his presence. 15Yes, everything is for your sake, so that grace, as it extends to more and more people, may increase thanksgiving, to the glory of God.

Living by Faith

16 So we do not lose heart. Even though our outer nature is wasting away, our inner nature is being renewed day by day. 17For this slight momentary affliction is preparing us for an eternal weight of glory beyond all measure, 18because we look not at what can be seen but at what cannot be seen; for what can be seen is temporary, but what cannot be seen is eternal.

5 For we know that if the earthly tent we live in is destroyed, we have a building from God, a house not made with hands, eternal in the heavens. 2For in this tent we groan, longing to be clothed with our heavenly dwelling— 3if indeed, when we have taken it off a we will not be found naked. 4For while we are still in this tent, we groan under our burden, because we wish not to be unclothed but to be further clothed, so that what is mortal may be swallowed up by life. 5He who has prepared us for this very thing is God, who has given us the Spirit as a guarantee.

6 So we are always confident; even though we know that while we are at home in the body we are away from the Lord— 7for we walk by faith, not by sight. 8Yes, we do have confidence,

a Other ancient authorities read put it on

4:10 *so that the life of Jesus may also be made visible.* Paul rarely refers to Jesus' life. In doing so here, he connects Jesus' life—that is, his death—to our way of life; it takes effect in our bodies. His death is reenacted in our bodies in baptism, that we might rise with him to new life. This reminds us of Paul's teaching about the cross in his earlier letter to the Corinthian church. Christ's submission to death—which looks to the world like humiliation and weakness—is really the revelation of the fragrant wisdom of God. It is a fresh vision of nobility and strength undertaken to reconcile the world to God and people to one another. There can be no greater dignity than this, and it is this that is now to be made visible in our bodies.

4:16–18 *we do not lose heart.* Endurance is one of the great and most strenuous of Christian virtues. We fall short of Paul's call to live Jesus' life in our bodies. Further, if we urge institutional structures to carry Jesus' life and death in their bodies, we open ourselves to ridicule, affliction, and recrimination. How are we to remain hopeful when the world supports empires propelled by violence, enmity, and worldly power? Paul's answer is that living with Jesus made visible in our bodies is its own reward. It strengthens us against affliction and sings of eternal life.

4:18 STUDY—*See* Spiritual Disciplines Index.

5:1–10 *we have a building from God.* Courage to endure the radical call of the Christian claim on our lives comes from the belief that the eventual reward will outweigh the temporary suffering we incur by challenging the world's values as Jesus and Paul did. When our valiant struggle for God's better way goes unappreciated and misunderstood, we have the hope of what later theologians would call the vision of God, utter delight at being in the divine presence. But we also might add that we have the happiness of experiencing our own growth into the splendor of divine wisdom, so that our groaning here for the redemption of our bodies is not without reward in its own right.

and we would rather be away from the body and at home with the Lord. 9So whether we are at home or away, we make it our aim to please him. 10For all of us must appear before the judgment seat of Christ, so that each may receive recompense for what has been done in the body, whether good or evil.

The Ministry of Reconciliation

11 Therefore, knowing the fear of the Lord, we try to persuade others; but we ourselves are well known to God, and I hope that we are also well known to your consciences. 12We are not commending ourselves to you again, but giving you an opportunity to boast about us, so that you may be able to answer those who boast in outward appearance and not in the heart. 13For if we are beside ourselves, it is for God; if we are in our right mind, it is for you. 14For the love of Christ urges us on, because we are convinced that one has died for all; therefore all have died. 15And he died for all, so that those who live might live no longer for themselves, but for him who died and was raised for them.

16 From now on, therefore, we regard no one from a human point of view;a even though we once knew Christ from a human point of view,a we know him no longer in that way. 17So if anyone is in Christ, there is a new creation: everything old has passed

away; see, everything has become new! 18All this is from God, who reconciled us to himself through Christ, and has given us the ministry of reconciliation; 19that is, in Christ God was reconciling the world to himself,b not counting their trespasses against them, and entrusting the message of reconciliation to us. 20So we are ambassadors for Christ, since God is making his appeal through us; we entreat you on behalf of Christ, be reconciled to God. 21For our sake he made him to be sin who knew no sin, so that in him we might become the righteousness of God.

6 As we work together with him,c we urge you also not to accept the grace of God in vain. 2For he says,

"At an acceptable time I have listened to you,
    and on a day of salvation I have helped you."

See, now is the acceptable time; see, now is the day of salvation! 3We are putting no obstacle in anyone's way, so that no fault may be found with our ministry, 4but as servants of God we have commended ourselves in every way: through great endurance, in afflictions, hardships, calamities, 5beatings, imprisonments, riots, labors, sleepless nights,

a Gk *according to the flesh*   *b* Or *God was in Christ reconciling the world to himself* . *c* Gk *As we work together*

5:14 *the love of Christ controls us* (NASB). This is one of the most powerful phrases in Scripture. It vividly amplifies Paul's opening phrase, that he is an apostle not of his own accord, but by the will of God. This is true of all Christian vocation; we do not seek but discern it and then follow as the way opens to us. This phrase is the key to a great secret that Christians discovered and that the Roman world had no access to: love, not military occupation, compels allegiance. The use of force or the threat of punishment seeks to break the spirit, while love nourishes it. Christians themselves have often forgotten this crucial point, and parents know that sometimes tough love is necessary. Yet Christians' responsibility is to teach the world that love, not might, transforms.
5:19 *entrusting the message of reconciliation to us.* The message of the cross—that love captures minds better than might does, and that

Christ's love revealed by his death, rather than threat of punishment, brings us to know God and to see one another afresh—cannot be kept to ourselves. Its point is to transform the world. And so Christians are—willy-nilly—ambassadors of this message for Christ; God makes his appeal to the world through us.

Responding
6:4–7 SERVICE. Paul lists the ways he has been a servant of God in spite of numerous barriers. When we read this list many of us think, "But that was Paul! There is no way I can be like him." What does this attitude reveal about us? Take a moment to ask God for the insight and humility to become full of "purity, knowledge, patience, kindness, holiness of spirit, genuine love, truthful speech, and the power of God." *See also* Spiritual Disciplines Index.

hunger; [6]by purity, knowledge, patience, kindness, holiness of spirit, genuine love, [7]truthful speech, and the power of God; with the weapons of righteousness for the right hand and for the left; [8]in honor and dishonor, in ill repute and good repute. We are treated as impostors, and yet are true; [9]as unknown, and yet are well known; as dying, and see—we are alive; as punished, and yet not killed; [10]as sorrowful, yet always rejoicing; as poor, yet making many rich; as having nothing, and yet possessing everything.

11 We have spoken frankly to you Corinthians; our heart is wide open to you. [12]There is no restriction in our affections, but only in yours. [13]In return—I speak as to children—open wide your hearts also.

The Temple of the Living God

14 Do not be mismatched with unbelievers. For what partnership is there between righteousness and lawlessness? Or what fellowship is there between light and darkness? [15]What agreement does Christ have with Beliar? Or what does a believer share with an unbeliever? [16]What agreement has the temple of God with idols? For we[a] are the temple of the living God; as God said,

> "I will live in them and walk among them,
> and I will be their God,
> and they shall be my people.
> [17] Therefore come out from them,
> and be separate from them, says the Lord,
> and touch nothing unclean;
> then I will welcome you,
> [18] and I will be your father,
> and you shall be my sons and daughters,
> says the Lord Almighty."

7 Since we have these promises, beloved, let us cleanse ourselves from every defilement of body and of spirit, making holiness perfect in the fear of God.

Paul's Joy at the Church's Repentance

2 Make room in your hearts[b] for us; we have wronged no one, we have corrupted no one, we have taken advantage of no one. [3]I do

---

a Other ancient authorities read *you*   *b* Gk lacks *in your hearts*

6:10 *as having nothing, and yet possessing everything.* Here is a further elaboration of Paul's basic point about the Christian vocation: for Christians, joy is independent of our circumstances. Happiness is counterintuitive. It does not lie where we instinctively look for it: in a fine reputation, a successful career, fame, being honored for our accomplishments, or being blessed with a comfortable life that comes along with success. Rather, Christians possess everything even amid sorrow and suffering, because we are emotionally dependent not on these goods, but rather on the wisdom and beauty of the compelling love of Christ, with which we are entrusted.

6:16 *we are the temple of the living God.* In its context, this is an outrageous statement. The Romans all knew about temples dedicated to the worship of various gods, who protected their cities and directed people's lives, and to the emperor, who maintained peace and order throughout the empire. The Jews too knew about the Temple, but for them there was only one—in Jerusalem—where the nation's worship

was centered. It was still operating at the time Paul wrote this line. Paul here is scoffing at both ancient and venerable communities. Christians, perhaps as individuals, but perhaps as a new collective body, have now become the temple of the living God! Paul could easily have been strung up by either community for such audacity. Do Christians today feel the power of this statement? God is located in the Christian Body!

7:1 *making holiness perfect.* With such a weighty identity and awesome responsibility laid upon them, it is not surprising that Paul immediately urges his readers to purify their bodies and minds and make holiness perfect. He proceeds to regale them with his own accomplishment in this area. Indeed, he frequently presents himself for imitation in other letters too. He suggests discipleship by apprenticeship to a master. Today, the media encourage us to apprentice ourselves to rock stars, sports figures, and corporate giants to reach perfection as the world knows it. Paul's way may never be very popular, but it is always the most effective and enduring.

not say this to condemn you, for I said before that you are in our hearts, to die together and to live together. [4]I often boast about you; I have great pride in you; I am filled with consolation; I am overjoyed in all our affliction.

5 For even when we came into Macedonia, our bodies had no rest, but we were afflicted in every way—disputes without and fears within. [6]But God, who consoles the downcast, consoled us by the arrival of Titus, [7]and not only by his coming, but also by the consolation with which he was consoled about you, as he told us of your longing, your mourning, your zeal for me, so that I rejoiced still more. [8]For even if I made you sorry with my letter, I do not regret it (though I did regret it, for I see that I grieved you with that letter, though only briefly). [9]Now I rejoice, not because you were grieved, but because your grief led to repentance; for you felt a godly grief, so that you were not harmed in any way by us. [10]For godly grief produces a repentance that leads to salvation and brings no regret, but worldly grief produces death. [11]For see what earnestness this godly grief has produced in you, what eagerness to clear yourselves, what indignation, what alarm, what longing, what zeal, what punishment! At every point you have proved yourselves guiltless in the matter. [12]So although I wrote to you, it was not on account of the one who did the wrong, nor on account of the one who was wronged, but in order that your zeal for us might be made known to you before God. [13]In this we find comfort.

In addition to our own consolation, we rejoiced still more at the joy of Titus, because his mind has been set at rest by all of you. [14]For if I have been somewhat boastful about you to him, I was not disgraced; but just as everything we said to you was true, so our boasting to Titus has proved true as well. [15]And his heart goes out all the more to you, as he remembers the obedience of all of you, and how you welcomed him with fear and trembling. [16]I rejoice, because I have complete confidence in you.

Encouragement to Be Generous

8 We want you to know, brothers and sisters,[a] about the grace of God that has been granted to the churches of Macedonia; [2]for during a severe ordeal of affliction, their abundant joy and their extreme poverty have overflowed in a wealth of generosity on their part. [3]For, as I can testify, they voluntarily gave according to their means, and even beyond their means, [4]begging us earnestly for the privilege[b] of sharing in this ministry to the saints— [5]and this, not merely as we expected; they gave themselves first to the Lord and, by the will of God, to us, [6]so that we might urge Titus that, as he had already made a beginning, so he should also complete this generous undertaking[c] among you. [7]Now as you excel in everything—in faith, in speech, in knowledge, in utmost eagerness, and in our love for you[d]—so we want you to excel also in this generous undertaking.[c]

8 I do not say this as a command, but I am testing the genuineness of your love against the earnestness of others. [9]For you know the generous act[c] of our Lord Jesus Christ, that though he was rich, yet for your sakes he became poor, so that by his poverty you might become rich. [10]And in this matter I am giving my advice: it is appropriate for you who began last year not only to do something but even to desire to do something— [11]now finish doing it, so that your eagerness may be matched by completing it according to your means. [12]For if the eagerness is there, the gift is acceptable according to what one has—not according to what one does not have. [13]I do not mean that there should be relief for others and pressure on you, but it is a question of a fair balance between [14]your present abundance and their need, so that their abundance may be for your need, in order that there may be a fair balance. [15]As it is written,

a Gk brothers   b Gk grace   c Gk this grace
d Other ancient authorities read your love for us

7:9 *a godly grief.* Godly grief produces repentance, and with it come spiritual insight and thus maturity. It should be welcomed.

8:1–9 SACRIFICE—*See* Spiritual Disciplines Index.

"The one who had much did not have
    too much,
and the one who had little did not
    have too little."

Commendation of Titus

16 But thanks be to God who put in the
heart of Titus the same eagerness for you that
I myself have. [17]For he not only accepted our
appeal, but since he is more eager than ever, he
is going to you of his own accord. [18]With him
we are sending the brother who is famous
among all the churches for his proclaiming
the good news;[a] [19]and not only that, but he
has also been appointed by the churches to
travel with us while we are administering this
generous undertaking[b] for the glory of the
Lord himself[c] and to show our goodwill. [20]We
intend that no one should blame us about
this generous gift that we are administering,
[21]for we intend to do what is right not only in
the Lord's sight but also in the sight of others.
[22]And with them we are sending our brother
whom we have often tested and found eager in
many matters, but who is now more eager
than ever because of his great confidence in
you. [23]As for Titus, he is my partner and co-
worker in your service; as for our brothers,
they are messengers[d] of the churches, the glory of Christ. [24]Therefore openly before the
churches, show them the proof of your love
and of our reason for boasting about you.

The Collection for Christians at Jerusalem

9 Now it is not necessary for me to write
you about the ministry to the saints, [2]for

I know your eagerness, which is the subject of
my boasting about you to the people of Macedonia, saying that Achaia has been ready since
last year; and your zeal has stirred up most of
them. [3]But I am sending the brothers in order
that our boasting about you may not prove to
have been empty in this case, so that you may
be ready, as I said you would be; [4]otherwise, if
some Macedonians come with me and find
that you are not ready, we would be humiliated—to say nothing of you—in this undertaking.[e] [5]So I thought it necessary to urge the
brothers to go on ahead to you, and arrange
in advance for this bountiful gift that you
have promised, so that it may be ready as a voluntary gift and not as an extortion.

6 The point is this: the one who sows sparingly will also reap sparingly, and the one
who sows bountifully will also reap bountifully. [7]Each of you must give as you have made
up your mind, not reluctantly or under compulsion, for God loves a cheerful giver. [8]And
God is able to provide you with every blessing
in abundance, so that by always having
enough of everything, you may share abundantly in every good work. [9]As it is written,

"He scatters abroad, he gives to the poor;
    his righteousness[f] endures forever."
[10]He who supplies seed to the sower and
bread for food will supply and multiply your
seed for sowing and increase the harvest of
your righteousness.[f] [11]You will be enriched in

a Or *the gospel*   b Gk *this grace*   c Other
ancient authorities lack *himself*   d Gk *apostles*
e Other ancient authorities add *of boasting*
f Or *benevolence*

9:6 *the one who sows bountifully will also
reap bountifully.* The demands of the Christian
enterprise are great, but it is only when they are
met that its rewards make one flush with joy.
Perhaps this is true of most things in life. With
things that come easily we do not have the time
to spend on the attention to detail that enables
deep appreciation.

Responding
9:6–7 SACRIFICE. Examine your
attitudes as you give to charity or your
church. Do you give generously and cheerfully
or reluctantly and under compulsion? Why do

you give? Guilt? Hoping to increase your favorable rating with God? Trying to make an impression on your friends? Why should we give
sacrificially? *See also* Spiritual Disciplines Index.

9:8 THE WITH-GOD LIFE—*See* Spiritual
Disciplines Index.

9:11 *You will be enriched in every way for your
great generosity.* This is the forerunner of the
line in the prayer attributed to St. Francis: it
is in giving that we receive. Giving outstrips
receiving, because it strengthens and expands
us, enabling us to experience the true scope
of our power. Paul here is talking about

every way for your great generosity, which will produce thanksgiving to God through us; 12for the rendering of this ministry not only supplies the needs of the saints but also overflows with many thanksgivings to God. 13Through the testing of this ministry you glorify God by your obedience to the confession of the gospel of Christ and by the generosity of your sharing with them and with all others, 14while they long for you and pray for you because of the surpassing grace of God that he has given you. 15Thanks be to God for his indescribable gift!

Paul Defends His Ministry

10 I myself, Paul, appeal to you by the meekness and gentleness of Christ— I who am humble when face to face with you, but bold toward you when I am away!—2I ask that when I am present I need not show boldness by daring to oppose those who think we are acting according to human standards.a 3Indeed, we live as human beings,b but we do not wage war according to human standards;a 4for the weapons of our warfare are not merely human,c but they have divine power to destroy strongholds. We destroy arguments 5and every proud obstacle raised up against the knowledge of God, and we take every thought captive to obey Christ. 6We are ready to punish every disobedience when your obedience is complete.

7 Look at what is before your eyes. If you are confident that you belong to Christ, remind yourself of this, that just as you belong to Christ, so also do we. 8Now, even if I boast a little too much of our authority, which the Lord gave for building you up and not for tearing you down, I will not be ashamed of it. 9I do not want to seem as though I am trying to frighten you with my letters. 10For they say, "His letters are weighty and strong, but his bodily presence is weak, and his speech contemptible." 11Let such people understand that what we say by letter when absent, we will also do when present.

12 We do not dare to classify or compare ourselves with some of those who commend themselves. But when they measure themselves by one another, and compare themselves with one another, they do not show good sense. 13We, however, will not boast beyond limits, but will keep within the field that God has assigned to us, to reach out even as far as you. 14For we were not overstepping our limits when we reached you; we were the first to come all the way to you with the good newsd of Christ. 15We do not boast beyond limits, that is, in the labors of others; but our hope is that, as your faith increases, our sphere of action among you may be greatly enlarged, 16so that we may proclaim the good newsd in lands beyond you, without boasting of work already done in someone else's sphere of action. 17"Let the one who boasts, boast in the Lord." 18For it is not those who commend themselves that are approved, but those whom the Lord commends.

Paul and the False Apostles

11 I wish you would bear with me in a little foolishness. Do bear with me! 2I feel a divine jealousy for you, for I promised

a Gk according to the flesh   b Gk in the flesh
c Gk fleshly   d Or the gospel

---

philanthropy, but the point applies to other forms of giving as well. Those who are often on the receiving end of things eventually must reclaim their dignity by turning to giving themselves. Since what we have to give and what is needed constantly vary, there is little doubt that all can do it if they train their eyes to see. The trick in giving is to give what is needed, not simply what one has in excess, be it money, advice, or even one's presence.

10:3–5 THE WITH-GOD LIFE—See Spiritual Disciplines Index.

11:2 *I promised you in marriage . . . to Christ.* Paul here puts himself in the place of the dramatically flamboyant prophet Hosea, who promises to take a woman mired in prostitution as his wife forever, in righteousness and faithfulness (Hos 2:19–20). Paul is thus making a powerful commitment to the Corinthians with this statement. Just as Hosea did with Gomer, Paul transforms the identity of those he betroths to Christ. Being married to Christ became a powerful expression of the desire for union with God in the Middle Ages.

you in marriage to one husband, to present you as a chaste virgin to Christ. 3But I am afraid that as the serpent deceived Eve by its cunning, your thoughts will be led astray from a sincere and pure *a* devotion to Christ. 4For if someone comes and proclaims another Jesus than the one we proclaimed, or if you receive a different spirit from the one you received, or a different gospel from the one you accepted, you submit to it readily enough. 5I think that I am not in the least inferior to these super-apostles. 6I may be untrained in speech, but not in knowledge; certainly in every way and in all things we have made this evident to you.

7 Did I commit a sin by humbling myself so that you might be exalted, because I proclaimed God's good news *b* to you free of charge? 8I robbed other churches by accepting support from them in order to serve you. 9And when I was with you and was in need, I did not burden anyone, for my needs were supplied by the friends *c* who came from Macedonia. So I refrained and will continue to refrain from burdening you in any way. 10As the truth of Christ is in me, this boast of mine will not be silenced in the regions of Achaia. 11And why? Because I do not love you? God knows I do!

12 And what I do I will also continue to do, in order to deny an opportunity to those who want an opportunity to be recognized as our equals in what they boast about. 13For such boasters are false apostles, deceitful workers, disguising themselves as apostles of Christ. 14And no wonder! Even Satan disguises himself as an angel of light. 15So it is not strange if his ministers also disguise themselves as ministers of righteousness. Their end will match their deeds.

Paul's Sufferings as an Apostle

16 I repeat, let no one think that I am a fool; but if you do, then accept me as a fool, so that I too may boast a little. 17What I am saying in regard to this boastful confidence, I am saying not with the Lord's authority, but as a fool; 18since many boast according to human standards, *d* I will also boast. 19For you gladly put up with fools, being wise yourselves! 20For you put up with it when someone makes slaves of you, or preys upon you, or takes advantage of you, or puts on airs, or gives you a slap in the face. 21To my shame, I must say, we were too weak for that!

But whatever anyone dares to boast of—I am speaking as a fool—I also dare to boast of that. 22Are they Hebrews? So am I. Are they Israelites? So am I. Are they descendants of Abraham? So am I. 23Are they ministers of Christ? I am talking like a madman—I am a better one: with far greater labors, far more imprisonments, with countless floggings, and often near death. 24Five times I have received from the Jews the forty lashes minus one. 25Three times I was beaten with rods. Once I received a stoning. Three times I was shipwrecked; for a night and a day I was adrift at sea; 26on frequent journeys, in danger from

a Other ancient authorities lack *and pure*
b Gk *the gospel of God*   *c* Gk *brothers*
d Gk *according to the flesh*

Responding
11:2 CHASTITY. In *The Spirit of the Disciplines* Dallas Willard writes, "The main effect we seek through [chastity] is the proper disposal of sexual acts, feelings, thoughts, and attitudes within our life as a whole, inside of marriage and out." What are some of the "proper disposals" of sexual acts, feelings, thoughts, and attitudes? Improper disposals? How does immersing ourselves in a life with God help us keep our sexuality in proper perspective? *See also* Spiritual Disciplines Index.

11:3 SIMPLICITY/FRUGALITY—*See* Spiritual Disciplines Index.

11:14 *Even Satan disguises himself as an angel of light.* Discerning sincere desire from strategically organized self-interest is not easy when sizing up the motives of those who make overtures toward us. Perhaps people we would judge as evil do not account themselves so, but have a mission they are intent on fulfilling at all costs. More bitingly, self-deception is one of Satan's great ploys in luring us to himself. Submitting one's passionate convictions to the judgment of the community is one opportunity for church members to check out self-distortion.

rivers, danger from bandits, danger from my own people, danger from Gentiles, danger in the city, danger in the wilderness, danger at sea, danger from false brothers and sisters;[a] [27]in toil and hardship, through many a sleepless night, hungry and thirsty, often without food, cold and naked. [28]And, besides other things, I am under daily pressure because of my anxiety for all the churches. [29]Who is weak, and I am not weak? Who is made to stumble, and I am not indignant?

[30] If I must boast, I will boast of the things that show my weakness. [31]The God and Father of the Lord Jesus (blessed be he forever!) knows that I do not lie. [32]In Damascus, the governor[b] under King Aretas guarded the city of Damascus in order to[c] seize me, [33]but I was let down in a basket through a window in the wall,[d] and escaped from his hands.

Paul's Visions and Revelations

12 It is necessary to boast; nothing is to be gained by it, but I will go on to visions and revelations of the Lord. [2]I know a person in Christ who fourteen years ago was caught up to the third heaven—whether in the body or out of the body I do not know; God knows. [3]And I know that such a person—whether in the body or out of the body I do not know; God knows— [4]was caught up into Paradise and heard things that are not to be told, that no mortal is permitted to repeat. [5]On behalf of such a one I will boast, but on my own behalf I will not boast, except of

my weaknesses. [6]But if I wish to boast, I will not be a fool, for I will be speaking the truth. But I refrain from it, so that no one may think better of me than what is seen in me or heard from me, [7]even considering the exceptional character of the revelations. Therefore, to keep[e] me from being too elated, a thorn was given me in the flesh, a messenger of Satan to torment me, to keep me from being too elated.[f] [8]Three times I appealed to the Lord about this, that it would leave me, [9]but he said to me, "My grace is sufficient for you, for power[g] is made perfect in weakness." So, I will boast all the more gladly of my weaknesses, so that the power of Christ may dwell in me. [10]Therefore I am content with weaknesses, insults, hardships, persecutions, and calamities for the sake of Christ; for whenever I am weak, then I am strong.

Paul's Concern for the Corinthian Church

11 I have been a fool! You forced me to it. Indeed you should have been the ones commending me, for I am not at all inferior to these super-apostles, even though I am nothing. [12]The signs of a true apostle were performed among you with utmost patience, signs and wonders and mighty works. [13]How

a Gk brothers　　b Gk ethnarch　　c Other ancient authorities read and wanted to　　d Gk through the wall　　e Other ancient authorities read To keep　f Other ancient authorities lack to keep me from being too elated　　g Other ancient authorities read my power

---

11:26 danger. Paul notes that danger lurks along the Christian path. Paul experienced physical danger, but spiritual dangers also lurk, perhaps especially for Christian leaders. They include the danger of self-assurance, which keeps us from seeing others or other ways of doing things, the danger of succumbing to flattery, and the danger of enjoying power over those who benefit from our work.

12:4 Paradise. "Paradise" is a synonym for "happiness." It is the promise of Christian faith, yet so remote from our grasp. Christian piety has usually not drawn a sharp distinction between enjoying God in this life and perfect enjoyment in the next. The glimpses and tastes

of God in this life whet our appetite for the feast that is to come.

12:9–10 THE WITH-GOD LIFE—See Spiritual Disciplines Index.

12:9–10 whenever I am weak, then I am strong. Paul is so consistently counterintuitive! His insistence on the inversion of power and weakness is central to his teaching. Human glory is revealed in what the world misconstrues as weakness, for example, failing to take advantage of one's opponents or standing aside so that one's own will does not impede true obedience to God. Paul is especially proud that the "thorn . . . in the flesh" (v 7) has not deterred his ministry, which has thrived in spite of it. Overcoming adversity enables one to glorify God all the more.

have you been worse off than the other churches, except that I myself did not burden you? Forgive me this wrong!

14 Here I am, ready to come to you this third time. And I will not be a burden, because I do not want what is yours but you; for children ought not to lay up for their parents, but parents for their children. 15I will most gladly spend and be spent for you. If I love you more, am I to be loved less? 16Let it be assumed that I did not burden you. Nevertheless (you say) since I was crafty, I took you in by deceit. 17Did I take advantage of you through any of those whom I sent to you? 18I urged Titus to go, and sent the brother with him. Titus did not take advantage of you, did he? Did we not conduct ourselves with the same spirit? Did we not take the same steps?

19 Have you been thinking all along that we have been defending ourselves before you? We are speaking in Christ before God. Everything we do, beloved, is for the sake of building you up. 20For I fear that when I come, I may find you not as I wish, and that you may find me not as you wish; I fear that there may perhaps be quarreling, jealousy, anger, selfishness, slander, gossip, conceit, and disorder. 21I fear that when I come again, my God may humble me before you, and that I may have to mourn over many who previously sinned and have not repented of the impurity, sexual immorality, and licentiousness that they have practiced.

Further Warning

13 This is the third time I am coming to you. "Any charge must be sustained by the evidence of two or three witnesses." 2I warned those who sinned previously and all the others, and I warn them now while absent, as I did when present on my second visit, that if I come again, I will not be lenient— 3since you desire proof that Christ is speaking in me. He is not weak in dealing with you, but is powerful in you. 4For he was crucified in weakness, but lives by the power of God. For we are weak in him, *a* but in dealing with you we will live with him by the power of God.

5 Examine yourselves to see whether you are living in the faith. Test yourselves. Do you not realize that Jesus Christ is in you?—unless, indeed, you fail to meet the test! 6I hope you will find out that we have not failed. 7But we pray to God that you may not do anything wrong—not that we may appear to have met the test, but that you may do what is right, though we may seem to have failed. 8For we cannot do anything against the truth, but only for the truth. 9For we rejoice when we are weak and you are strong. This is what we pray for, that you may become perfect. 10So I write these things while I am away from you, so that when I come, I may not have to be severe in using the authority that the Lord has given me for building up and not for tearing down.

Final Greetings and Benediction

11 Finally, brothers and sisters, *b* farewell. *c* Put things in order, listen to my appeal, *d* agree with one another, live in peace; and the God of love and peace will be with you. 12Greet one another with a holy kiss. All the saints greet you.

13 The grace of the Lord Jesus Christ, the love of God, and the communion of *e* the Holy Spirit be with all of you.

a Other ancient authorities read *with him*
b Gk *brothers*   *c* Or *rejoice*   *d* Or *encourage one another*   *e* Or *and the sharing in*

12:20 *you may find me not as you wish.* Paul seems to be aware that he is more impressive in print than in person. Perhaps the "thorn . . . in the flesh" (v 7) is better hidden from afar. Yet this does not deter him from making claims on those he has evangelized. The absence of commanding stature does not deter him. His mission is too important for him to be intimidated by his personal limitations. Christian ministry is for the stouthearted, those able to endure rejection, misunderstanding, and discord. Thus, being weak in one way enables true strength of character to be manifest.

13:5 *Do you not realize that Jesus Christ is in you?* Understanding ourselves to be indwelt by Christ suffices against formidable odds and temptations. Christians extend the incarnation throughout time and space. Paul prays that he might not be found wanting.

THE LETTER OF PAUL TO THE

GALATIANS

Freedom is one of the deepest longings of the human soul. Poems have been written, songs sung, philosophies developed, and wars fought—all for the cause of freedom. So it is not surprising that when Jesus stepped onto the stage of human history some of his earliest public words were, "The Spirit of the Lord is upon me . . . to proclaim release to the captives . . . to let the oppressed go free" (Luke 4:18). Echoing the words of his Master, the apostle Paul writes, "For freedom Christ has set us free" (Gal 5:1)—Christ has set us free to become the persons God has created and redeemed us to be.

For some this freedom is too wild, too unpredictable, and too available. Surely, they say, God never intended to include anyone and everyone. We must have standards and controls. People have to do or know the right things in order to please God. Thus the perversions, distortions, and substitutes for Jesus' original offer are born.

So now the authentic free life in Christ needs a warning label to keep us alert to this danger. Paul's Letter to the Galatians serves us well in this capacity. The poison to avoid is "a different gospel" (1:6). The Galatians were in danger of ingesting a toxic mix of self-help, outward religious observance, and lies about God. This was the first in a long line of different gospels that continue even now to raise their ugly heads. The warning sounded by Paul in his letter has largely gone unheeded. However, those willing to listen to its message will preserve and deepen the life of freedom that Jesus came to give. And what a glorious freedom it is! We have been set free from "the present evil age" (1:4), the "works of the law" (2:16), and the "works of the flesh" (5:19).

Paul, astonished and outraged, is not content to warn. In Galatians he provides the antidote for each virus that has infected these churches. For the false human gospel he offers the "revelation of Jesus Christ" (1:12). Rather than the works of the law he prescribes simple faith in the grace of God. Instead of "trying harder" to gain God's approval he directs us to life in the Spirit.

See also *"The With-God Life" essay for this section of the Bible,*
"The People of God in Community," pp. 2037–42.

Two Controlling Passions

As we read Galatians, Paul's two controlling passions stand out. The first is his zeal for the gospel of freedom. Second is his parental love ("my little children") for the Galatians. The two come together in Paul's painful labor to see Christ formed in them (4:19). The pain accompanied the difficult work of addressing the deforming effects of the different gospel to which they had begun to turn.

A hallmark verse for spiritual formation, Gal 4:19 provides an image of the process of growth for Christians. In this picture it is Christ who is growing in us, rather than we who are growing in Christ. Christ is formed in us by the power of the Holy Spirit as we respond to his ever-present grace in our lives. This occurs in daily, ordinary life as we "practice the presence of God" in our work, our play, our relationships, and all of life. By the Spirit in our hearts we cry out to God "Abba! Father!" (4:6) many times throughout the course of a day, acknowledging who we are and whose we are. Christ is also formed in us as we present ourselves as living sacrifices to him through the Spiritual Disciplines, which, far from being the binding legalism Paul condemns in this letter, are the loving response of disciples to God's grace.

Steadily, gradually, Christ looms larger and larger within us. We find ourselves thinking, feeling, believing, serving, and living more like him. Not only are we becoming more like Jesus; we are becoming more human, more ourselves.

This work of spiritual formation is the subject of this letter. That the Galatians were submitting again to a yoke of slavery—the opposite of spiritual formation—prompted Paul to couch his communication in the vocabulary of freedom. Spiritual formation and freedom have a dynamic relationship. Curtail one, and the other is stifled. Grow in one, and the other flourishes. Five dimensions of spiritual formation emerge from the text as a result of Paul's emphasis on freedom. These are not simple cosmetic enhancements. These are seismic shifts in the core of his being as Christ is formed in him, in the Galatians, and in us.

Centered in the Gospel (1:1–12)

Christian spiritual formation begins with the good news of grace. It is where Paul begins his letter to the Galatians, because he needed to take them back to the starting line. The trajectory of their spiritual journey was skewed, because they had deserted their gospel beginning. The simple yet powerful good news is that forgiveness, freedom, love, and joy in the kingdom of God can be had by faith alone. We rely upon the sufficiency of Christ's death and resurrection to give us life with God now and for eternity.

The Galatians started in grace by the Spirit, but then turned back to performing for God (3:3). This is a common detour in spiritual formation. Having been forgiven, given the Spirit, and baptized into Christ, we think we are now capable of living this life by our own independent effort. We lose the center, deny the gospel, and nullify the grace of God, and as a result spiritual formation is arrested. Paul energetically guides us back to experience afresh the gospel of grace. We regain the center with the realization that, no matter how far we go on this journey, we never outgrow our need for the good news that got us started.

⟲ Lived as Story (1:13–2:14)

Paul could write about freedom because he had experienced the transformation from slavery under the law to freedom in Christ. The Galatians had experienced freedom through the gospel, but were submitting again to the yoke of slavery to the law. Two stories moving in opposite directions provide a plot that draws us in because we see ourselves in both dramas.

Paul, aware of his own story, was free to enter into the Galatians' story with a bold presence. He had been where they were headed and used his own story as the strongest argument for the life of Spirit and grace. This was because his story was part of The Story—God creating a loving community of freedom called the Church. It included Titus, Phoebe, Barnabas, Peter, James, John, Lydia, and Jews and Gentiles, to name just a few.

Like the Galatians, we are tempted to turn spiritual formation into formulas, rule keeping, a series of steps, or a to-do list. But the Christ-in-us life is a one-of-a-kind story. Rules, steps, and lists can be copied without limit, but as Catholic lay theologian and spiritual director Friedrich von Hügel said, "There are no dittos among souls" or, we might add, among their stories.

⟲ Realized through Faith (2:15–4:31)

Participation in the gospel, in God's grand story, is our being made right with God as Christ is formed in us by faith. Five times in this section and once in 5:5 the phrase "by faith" occurs. Three times it refers to justification with God in the past (2:16; 3:8; 3:24). Twice it speaks of living by faith in the present moment (2:20; 3:11), and once it looks to the future hope of the believer (5:5). Past, present, and future are comprehended by faith, which leaves no room for earning by performance. The life of faith is dominated by being rather than doing—being present to God, being aware of his presence in and with us, being grateful for his care, and being responsive to his love. In this posture of faith we are clay in the Potter's hands, to be shaped into the image of Jesus.

⟲ Accomplished by the Spirit (5:1–26)

Spiritual formation is being formed by the Spirit into the image of Christ. It is the Spirit's work, in the Spirit's way, and in the Spirit's time. The Spirit keeps us free and fruitful. When we draw our life and strength from the Spirit, we are freed from the sinful desires that arise from human weakness (5:16). When we are led by the Spirit, we are freed from the need to earn and perform (5:18). We are even freed from trying to be virtuous by the guarantee of fruitfulness (5:22 and note; John 15).

⟲ Experienced in Community (6:1–18)

It is in the all-inclusive, God-created loving community that the gospel is experienced, stories are shared, faith is developed, and the Spirit works. Spiritual formation is always in the context of community. God's forming work in an individual is extremely personal, but not private. Our freedom and formation stories are to be shared for the enriching of our brothers and sisters. In so doing we both challenge (6:1) and encourage (6:2) one another. Paul, in the Letter to the Galatians, speaks powerfully, yet lovingly, into the lives of his fellow Christians in order to build a community without distinctions and hierarchies in which all are one in Christ Jesus (3:28).

—*Howard Baker*

Salutation

1 Paul an apostle—sent neither by human commission nor from human authorities, but through Jesus Christ and God the Father, who raised him from the dead—²and all the members of God's family*a* who are with me,

To the churches of Galatia:

3 Grace to you and peace from God our Father and the Lord Jesus Christ, ⁴who gave himself for our sins to set us free from the present evil age, according to the will of our God and Father, ⁵to whom be the glory forever and ever. Amen.

There Is No Other Gospel

6 I am astonished that you are so quickly deserting the one who called you in the grace of Christ and are turning to a different gospel—⁷not that there is another gospel, but there are some who are confusing you and want to pervert the gospel of Christ. ⁸But even if we or an angel*b* from heaven should proclaim to you a gospel contrary to what we proclaimed to you, let that one be accursed! ⁹As we have said before, so now I repeat, if anyone proclaims to you a gospel contrary to what you received, let that one be accursed!

10 Am I now seeking human approval, or God's approval? Or am I trying to please people? If I were still pleasing people, I would not be a servant*c* of Christ.

Paul's Vindication of His Apostleship

11 For I want you to know, brothers and sisters, *d* that the gospel that was proclaimed by me is not of human origin; ¹²for I did not receive it from a human source, nor was I taught it, but I received it through a revelation of Jesus Christ.

13 You have heard, no doubt, of my earlier life in Judaism. I was violently persecuting the church of God and was trying to destroy it. ¹⁴I advanced in Judaism beyond many among my people of the same age, for I was far more zealous for the traditions of my ancestors. ¹⁵But when God, who had set me apart before I was born and called me through his grace, was pleased ¹⁶to reveal his Son to me, *e* so that I might proclaim him among the Gentiles, I did not confer with any human being, ¹⁷nor did I go up to Jerusalem to those who were already apostles

a Gk *all the brothers*   *b* Or *a messenger*
c Gk *slave*   *d* Gk *brothers*   *e* Gk *in me*

1:4 *to set us free.* Paul, brimming with holy outrage, calmly proclaims freedom as the purpose of the gospel, the intended experience of the followers of Jesus and the theme of his letter. Spiritual formation both needs and feeds the free life. Paul is keenly aware that bondage to sin, bondage to "the present evil age," bondage to the law, or bondage to the flesh destroys this necessary freedom. So he responds with the urgency of a woman "in the pain of childbirth," calling the Galatians back to freedom "until Christ is formed" in them (4:19). Anything that limits our freedom in Christ limits his formation in us as well.

1:6–9 *I am astonished.* Where we would expect thanksgiving (in all of Paul's other letters the greeting is followed by an expression of gratitude for the recipient) there is astonishment. Where we would expect blessing there is a curse. The Galatians' unexpected desertion to a "different gospel" prompts this unexpected response from Paul.

1:8 *a gospel contrary to what we proclaimed!* The good news of Jesus is that through his death and resurrection the rule and life of God are available to all by faith. This gospel is the huge center out of which a free life is lived and formed. Any distortion or perversion of that good news is not simply a doctrinal misstep, but a denial of the revelation of God that forms our lives in every detail. So Paul is willing to fight to maintain the purity and centrality of the gospel of grace.

1:13–2:10 *my earlier life.* Far from a decision or formula, transformation of life is a process and a story. Here, for the fourth time (see Acts 9:1–30; 22:1–21; 26:1–23), is Paul's freedom story. The elements in it are common to every spiritual journey toward freedom in Christ: life without Christ (1:13–14); encounter with Christ (1:15–16); formation through solitude (1:17); sharing the story (1:18–20); mission in the world (1:21–24); and transformed relationships with friends and enemies (2:1–10).

PAUL

The Way of Christlikeness

Selected Scriptures: *Acts 8:1–3; 9; 13–28; Romans 1; 5–8; 12; 16;*
1 Corinthians 2–4; 9; 11–12; Galatians 1–2; Ephesians 3; Philippians 1; 3–4;
1 Thessalonians 2; 1 Timothy 1; 2 Timothy 1; 4; Philemon

Paul's message defies any quick summary, for his words are the very words of God to us on many issues. Yet Paul the man remains an enigma largely because, although we laud him, we fail to imitate his way of living by practicing the many and varied Spiritual Disciplines he practiced throughout his life.

Paul reminds us that even before his conversion he was "far more zealous [than other Jews] for the traditions of [his] ancestors," traditions that included fasting, tithing, study, and more (Gal 1:14). He knew a lifetime of committed discipline, and upon coming to Jesus his discipline took on new meaning and purpose.

How did he live? After meeting Christ on the Damascus road Paul prayed and fasted for three days. Shortly after his conversion he spent a long period of time, thought to be three years, in solitude in the Arabian desert. Throughout his years of ministry and travel Paul spent time in fasting and prayer, both alone and with his ministry partners. He modeled continual self-sacrifice, simplicity, frugality, and service. He worked to support his ministry life and gracefully endured imprisonment and beatings. He often went without food, sleep, or adequate clothes, and he dealt in love and perseverance with those who took him for granted.

Paul asked his fellow Christians to imitate him and "train . . . in godliness" (1 Tim 4:7), as he was doing, in a way similar to physical training. "Just as with the physical, there is a specific round of activities we must do to establish, maintain, and enhance our spiritual powers. One must *train* as well as *try*," writes Dallas Willard in *The Spirit of the Disciplines.* "The key to understanding Paul is to know that, with all his 'weaknesses' and failures and personality deficiencies, he gave himself solely to being like his Lord. He lived and practiced daily the things his Lord taught and practiced. He lived a life of abandonment; and it was his confidence in this path, and in the power that derived from the rich union with Christ it created, that enabled him to call others to do the same. His actions, his character, his motivations—and the astonishing world-changing power derived from his lowly lifestyle—can only be understood by keeping this fact in mind: *Paul followed Jesus by living as he lived.* And how did he do that? Through activities and ways of living that would train his whole personality to depend upon the risen Christ as Christ trained himself to depend upon the Father.

"In other words," Willard continues, "Paul and his Lord were people of immense power, who saw clearly the wayward ways the world considered natural. With calm premeditation and clear vision of a deeper order, they took their stand always among those 'last who shall be first' mentioned repeatedly in the Gospels. With their feet planted in the deeper order of God, they lived lives of utter self-sacrifice and abandonment, seeing in such a life the highest possible personal attainment."

We may be familiar with the phrases Paul used frequently throughout his Letters, yet can we truly seek to share in what he writes without living as he did? Where do we begin, or how can we continue growing in our realistic attempts to live as Paul did and taught? "This will come down to what you do on Sunday, Monday, Tuesday, Wednesday, Thursday, Friday, and Saturday," writes Willard. "More importantly, at the outset, it will come down to what you do *not* do, to how you will manage to step out of the everlasting busyness that curses our lives."

By making space in our lives to practice some of the disciplines Paul practiced, we can begin to share in the life Paul led—and more, in the life of Christ our Lord. Dallas Willard writes, "People we admit to be far greater than we are—and in the case of Jesus himself, even divine—found it necessary to practice disciplines and engage in activities with which we blithely dispense." Spiritual Disciplines are merely activities we do to enable us to receive more of Jesus' life and power. As we put them into practice, we will see our mind turning more continually to Christ, our spirit resting more in peace, and our passions being shaped more like God's. Indeed, by training in godliness we will begin to live daily in Christ as a new creation.

Personal Reflection

- If you have practiced any of the Spiritual Disciplines, how has God met you, changed you, and moved in your life as a result?
- What do you think of Paul's idea of "training in godliness"?
- What is it that hinders you from making Spiritual Disciplines a more committed part of your life? In *Celebration of Discipline* Richard Foster teaches: "Every discipline has its corresponding freedom. If I have schooled myself in the art of rhetoric, I am free to deliver a moving speech when the occasion requires it. . . . The purpose of the Disciplines is freedom. Our aim is the freedom, not the Discipline. The moment we make the Discipline our central focus, we turn it into law and lose the corresponding freedom." Consider a couple of the disciplines you have practiced or would like to practice. In what way might you turn these into law if you are not cautious?
- Consider the following Spiritual Disciplines: meditation, prayer, fasting, study, simplicity, solitude, submission, service, confession, worship, guidance, and celebration. Spend a few days holding these before God, asking which of them he would have you begin practicing. If you need to, do some reading to learn more about them. Pray that through a commitment to training in godliness you will draw closer to the heart of Christ.

PROFILE

Freedom for order

before me, but I went away at once into Arabia, and afterwards I returned to Damascus.

18 Then after three years I did go up to Jerusalem to visit Cephas and stayed with him fifteen days; 19but I did not see any other apostle except James the Lord's brother. 20In what I am writing to you, before God, I do not lie! 21Then I went into the regions of Syria and Cilicia, 22and I was still unknown by sight to the churches of Judea that are in Christ; 23they only heard it said, "The one who formerly was persecuting us is now proclaiming the faith he once tried to destroy." 24And they glorified God because of me.

Paul and the Other Apostles

2 Then after fourteen years I went up again to Jerusalem with Barnabas, taking Titus along with me. 2I went up in response to a revelation. Then I laid before them (though only in a private meeting with the acknowledged leaders) the gospel that I proclaim among the Gentiles, in order to make sure that I was not running, or had not run, in vain. 3But even Titus, who was with me, was not compelled to be circumcised, though he was a Greek. 4But

because of false believers a secretly brought in, who slipped in to spy on the freedom we have in Christ Jesus, so that they might enslave us—5we did not submit to them even for a moment, so that the truth of the gospel might always remain with you. 6And from those who were supposed to be acknowledged leaders (what they actually were makes no difference to me; God shows no partiality)—those leaders contributed nothing to me. 7On the contrary, when they saw that I had been entrusted with the gospel for the uncircumcised, just as Peter had been entrusted with the gospel for the circumcised 8(for he who worked through Peter making him an apostle to the circumcised also worked through me in sending me to the Gentiles), 9and when James and Cephas and John, who were acknowledged pillars, recognized the grace that had been given to me, they gave to Barnabas and me the right hand of fellowship, agreeing that we should go to the Gentiles and they to the circumcised. 10They asked only one thing, that we remember the poor, which was actually what I was b eager to do.

a Gk false brothers   b Or had been

1:17 *Arabia.* Paul "at once" retreated to Arabia to begin the process of learning from Jesus how to live this new life of grace and freedom. Through intentional withdrawal into silence and solitude we process and assimilate what God is doing in our lives. Solitude is both a "vacation with God" and a "furnace of transformation." No doubt Paul experienced both in Arabia.

Responding
1:17–22 SOLITUDE. Paul recounts that after his conversion he went to Arabia, an area in present-day Jordan east of the Jordan River and south of the city of Damascus. Because of Arabia's remote location and desert climate, he most likely went there to ponder what had happened—just as Jesus did after his baptism—and to prepare for his new life as a disciple of Christ. How do remote places prompt us to pray and concentrate on our relationship with God? Why do noisy, crowded places work against our life with God? *See also* Spiritual Disciplines Index.

Responding
2:5 SUBMISSION. In this verse Paul cautions against submitting to false believers who try to take away our freedom in Christ. Has there been a time in your life when you submitted to a teaching that later turned out to be false? Which Spiritual Disciplines help us avoid being misled? *See also* Spiritual Disciplines Index.

2:7 *entrusted.* Noticing how our companions in Christ have been "entrusted" with the gospel in a unique way allows our differences to unite rather than divide us.

2:10 *remember the poor.* We are free to live out our own unique stories of transformation. We are free to follow the Spirit's leading into unique ministries. However, we are not free to do so in ways that cause the weakest among us to be neglected. Our heart toward the poor is among the surest tests of whether Christ is being formed within us. To "remember the poor" is a primary way to practice simplicity, giving, and service, practices fundamental to spiritual formation.

Paul Rebukes Peter at Antioch

11 But when Cephas came to Antioch, I opposed him to his face, because he stood self-condemned; 12for until certain people came from James, he used to eat with the Gentiles. But after they came, he drew back and kept himself separate for fear of the circumcision faction. 13And the other Jews joined him in this hypocrisy, so that even Barnabas was led astray by their hypocrisy. 14But when I saw that they were not acting consistently with the truth of the gospel, I said to Cephas before them all, "If you, though a Jew, live like a Gentile and not like a Jew, how can you compel the Gentiles to live like Jews?" a

Jews and Gentiles Are Saved by Faith

15 We ourselves are Jews by birth and not Gentile sinners; 16yet we know that a person is justified b not by the works of the law but through faith in Jesus Christ. c And we have come to believe in Christ Jesus, so that we might be justified by faith in Christ, d and not by doing the works of the law, because no one will be justified by the works of the law. 17But if, in our effort to be justified in Christ, we ourselves have been found to be sinners, is Christ then a servant of sin? Certainly not! 18But if I build up again the very things that I once tore down, then I demonstrate that I am a transgressor. 19For through the law I died to the law, so that I might live to God. I have been crucified with Christ; 20and it is no longer I who live, but it is Christ who lives in me. And the life I now live in the flesh I live by faith in the Son of God, e who loved me and gave himself for me. 21I do not nullify the grace of God; for if justification f comes through the law, then Christ died for nothing.

Law or Faith

3 You foolish Galatians! Who has bewitched you? It was before your eyes that Jesus Christ was publicly exhibited as crucified! 2The only thing I want to learn from you is this: Did you receive the Spirit by doing the works of the law or by believing what you heard? 3Are you so foolish? Having started with the Spirit, are you now ending with the flesh? 4Did you experience so much for nothing?—if it really was for nothing. 5Well then, does God g supply you with the Spirit and work miracles among you by your doing the works of the law, or by your believing what you heard?

6 Just as Abraham "believed God, and it was reckoned to him as righteousness," 7so,

a Some interpreters hold that the quotation extends into the following paragraph   b Or reckoned as righteous; and so elsewhere   c Or the faith of Jesus Christ   d Or the faith of Christ   e Or by the faith of the Son of God   f Or righteousness   g Gk he

---

2:14 *But when I saw.* The act of noticing and naming according to "the truth of the gospel" is referred to as "discernment" in Christian spirituality. Never are we to judge or condemn, but always to be on the alert for antigospel words and actions—a discerning life.

2:16 *by faith . . . not by doing the works of the law.* The gospel life of freedom is entered into and sustained by faith, trusting in what God has done and is doing rather than in what we can do. Three times in this verse Paul refers to "the works of the law," the polar opposite of the faith life. Through our faith in Christ we are set free from earning God's approval, from moral and religious performance, from externalism, and from legalism. We are freed by faith to be transformed from the inside out.

2:19–20 *crucified with Christ.* Another translation of the verb would be "cocrucified," which captures the stunning boldness of our union with Christ. This word is used of the two thieves who were crucified at the same time as Jesus (Matt 27:44; Mark 15:32; John 19:32). Paul thrusts us into full and immediate participation with Christ. The old life is over and the new Christ-in-us life has begun. We live this life as we started it—by faith in Jesus. This inward reality will, over time, produce outward evidences (see 5:22–24).

3:1–5 *Who has bewitched you?* Six times in these five verses Paul, in rapid-fire succession, asks incisive, pointed, and personal questions. The life of freedom and faith flourishes through rigorous thinking as well as through heartfelt believing. Questions allow us to pause and reflect, leading us into the formative practice of meditation. They challenge us to be aware of God, our personal experience, and our growth in Christ.

you see, those who believe are the descendants of Abraham. 8And the scripture, foreseeing that God would justify the Gentiles by faith, declared the gospel beforehand to Abraham, saying, "All the Gentiles shall be blessed in you." 9For this reason, those who believe are blessed with Abraham who believed.

10 For all who rely on the works of the law are under a curse; for it is written, "Cursed is everyone who does not observe and obey all the things written in the book of the law." 11Now it is evident that no one is justified before God by the law; for "The one who is righteous will live by faith."a 12But the law does not rest on faith; on the contrary, "Whoever does the works of the lawb will live by them." 13Christ redeemed us from the curse of the law by becoming a curse for us—for it is written, "Cursed is everyone who hangs on a tree"—14in order that in Christ Jesus the blessing of Abraham might come to the Gentiles, so that we might receive the promise of the Spirit through faith.

The Promise to Abraham

15 Brothers and sisters,c I give an example from daily life: once a person's willd has been ratified, no one adds to it or annuls it. 16Now the promises were made to Abraham and to his offspring;e it does not say, "And to offsprings,"f as of many; but it says, "And to your offspring,"e that is, to one person, who is Christ. 17My point is this: the law, which came four hundred thirty years later, does not annul a covenant previously ratified by God, so as to nullify the promise. 18For if the inheritance comes from the law, it no longer comes from the promise; but God granted it to Abraham through the promise.

The Purpose of the Law

19 Why then the law? It was added be-

cause of transgressions, until the offspringe would come to whom the promise had been made; and it was ordained through angels by a mediator. 20Now a mediator involves more than one party; but God is one.

21 Is the law then opposed to the promises of God? Certainly not! For if a law had been given that could make alive, then righteousness would indeed come through the law. 22But the scripture has imprisoned all things under the power of sin, so that what was promised through faith in Jesus Christg might be given to those who believe.

23 Now before faith came, we were imprisoned and guarded under the law until faith would be revealed. 24Therefore the law was our disciplinarian until Christ came, so that we might be justified by faith. 25But now that faith has come, we are no longer subject to a disciplinarian, 26for in Christ Jesus you are all children of God through faith. 27As many of you as were baptized into Christ have clothed yourselves with Christ. 28There is no longer Jew or Greek, there is no longer slave or free, there is no longer male and female; for all of you are one in Christ Jesus. 29And if you belong to Christ, then you are Abraham's offspring,e heirs according to the promise.

4 My point is this: heirs, as long as they are minors, are no better than slaves, though they are the owners of all the property; 2but they remain under guardians and trustees until the date set by the father. 3So with us; while we were minors, we were enslaved to the elemental spiritsh of the world. 4But

a Or The one who is righteous through faith will live
b Gk does them   c Gk Brothers   d Or covenant
(as in verse 17)   e Gk seed   f Gk seeds
g Or through the faith of Jesus Christ   h Or the
rudiments

3:14 *Abraham.* See note on Rom 4:1–25.
3:24 *the law was our disciplinarian.* In the Greek world a disciplinarian or guardian would escort a child from home to school, providing protection and guidance. So, then, the purpose of the law was to escort the People of God from the promise given to Abraham to its fulfillment in Christ. Prayerful Scripture reading serves us in a similar way, continuing to guide us on this

long journey of apprenticeship to Jesus.
3:28 *one in Christ Jesus.* Jewish men, possibly Saul himself, as part of their regular morning prayers thanked God that they were not born a Gentile, a slave, or a female. Baptism into Christ obliterates all distinctions and creates an all-inclusive loving community. Paul, the new creation in Christ, is its chief ambassador.

when the fullness of time had come, God sent his Son, born of a woman, born under the law, [5]in order to redeem those who were under the law, so that we might receive adoption as children. [6]And because you are children, God has sent the Spirit of his Son into our[a] hearts, crying, "Abba![b] Father!" [7]So you are no longer a slave but a child, and if a child then also an heir, through God.[c]

Paul Reproves the Galatians

8 Formerly, when you did not know God, you were enslaved to beings that by nature are not gods. [9]Now, however, that you have come to know God, or rather to be known by God, how can you turn back again to the weak and beggarly elemental spirits?[d] How can you want to be enslaved to them again? [10]You are observing special days, and months, and seasons, and years. [11]I am afraid that my work for you may have been wasted.

12 Friends,[e] I beg you, become as I am, for I also have become as you are. You have done me no wrong. [13]You know that it was because of a physical infirmity that I first announced the gospel to you; [14]though my condition put you to the test, you did not scorn or despise me, but welcomed me as an angel of God, as Christ Jesus. [15]What has become of the goodwill you felt? For I testify that, had it been possible, you would have torn out your eyes and given them to me. [16]Have I now become your enemy by telling you the truth? [17]They make much of you, but for no good purpose; they want to exclude you, so that you may make much of them. [18]It is good to be made much of for a good purpose at all times, and not only when I am present with you. [19]My little children, for whom I am again in the pain of childbirth until Christ is formed in you, [20]I wish I were present with you now and could change my tone, for I am perplexed about you.

The Allegory of Hagar and Sarah

21 Tell me, you who desire to be subject to the law, will you not listen to the law? [22]For it is written that Abraham had two sons, one by a slave woman and the other by a free woman. [23]One, the child of the slave, was born according to the flesh; the other, the child of the free woman, was born through the promise. [24]Now this is an allegory: these women are two covenants. One woman, in fact, is Hagar, from Mount Sinai, bearing children for slavery. [25]Now Hagar is Mount Sinai in Arabia[f] and corresponds to the present Jerusalem, for she is in slavery with her children. [26]But the other woman corresponds to the Jerusalem above; she is free, and she is our mother. [27]For it is written,

"Rejoice, you childless one, you who
        bear no children,
    burst into song and shout, you who
        endure no birth pangs;
    for the children of the desolate woman
        are more numerous
    than the children of the one who is
        married."

[28]Now you,[g] my friends,[h] are children of the promise, like Isaac. [29]But just as at that time the child who was born according to the flesh

a Other ancient authorities read *your*   b Aramaic for *Father*   c Other ancient authorities read *an heir of God through Christ*   d Or *beggarly rudiments*   e Gk *Brothers*   f Other ancient authorities read *For Sinai is a mountain in Arabia*   g Other ancient authorities read *we*   h Gk *brothers*

4:4–7 *the fullness of time . . . God.* Roman government, Greek culture, and Jewish faith converge to create the "fullness of time." The kingdom of God is at hand (Mark 1:15). God acts, God initiates, God saves, God sends his Son. Slaves are set free and are adopted into God's own family as children. The present moment is now the "fullness of time" in which God redeems, blesses, and loves. God, now as then, always makes the first move toward us in love (v 9).

4:19 *Christ is formed in you.* The alternative to the deathly strain of self-improvement under the law is the life-giving formation of Christ in us by the Spirit. This is God's purposeful work in us, using all the raw material of our lives—circumstances, family, personality, successes, and failures—to conform us to the image of Christ (Rom 8:28–29). We participate passively by trusting God's love and wisdom in the process. We participate actively through the practice of the Spiritual Disciplines, which, far from being the binding legalism Paul condemns in this letter, are the liberating pathways to God's grace.

persecuted the child who was born according to the Spirit, so it is now also. ³⁰But what does the scripture say? "Drive out the slave and her child; for the child of the slave will not share the inheritance with the child of the free woman." ³¹So then, friends,ᵃ we are children, not of the slave but of the free woman.

5 ¹For freedom Christ has set us free. Stand firm, therefore, and do not submit again to a yoke of slavery.

The Nature of Christian Freedom

2 Listen! I, Paul, am telling you that if you let yourselves be circumcised, Christ will be of no benefit to you. ³Once again I testify to every man who lets himself be circumcised that he is obliged to obey the entire law. ⁴You who want to be justified by the law have cut yourselves off from Christ; you have fallen away from grace. ⁵For through the Spirit, by faith, we eagerly wait for the hope of righteousness. ⁶For in Christ Jesus neither circumcision nor uncircumcision counts for anything; the only thing that counts is faith workingᵇ through love.

7 You were running well; who prevented you from obeying the truth? ⁸Such persuasion does not come from the one who calls you. ⁹A little yeast leavens the whole batch of dough. ¹⁰I am confident about you in the Lord that you will not think otherwise. But whoever it is that is confusing you will pay the penalty. ¹¹But my friends,ᵃ why am I still being persecuted if I am still preaching circumcision? In that case the offense of the cross has been removed. ¹²I wish those who unsettle you would castrate themselves!

13 For you were called to freedom, brothers and sisters;ᵃ only do not use your freedom as an opportunity for self-indulgence,ᶜ but through love become slaves to one another. ¹⁴For the whole law is summed up in a single commandment, "You shall love your neighbor as yourself." ¹⁵If, however, you bite and devour one another, take care that you are not consumed by one another.

The Works of the Flesh

16 Live by the Spirit, I say, and do not gratify the desires of the flesh. ¹⁷For what the flesh desires is opposed to the Spirit, and what the Spirit desires is opposed to the flesh; for these are opposed to each other, to prevent you from doing what you want. ¹⁸But if you are led by the Spirit, you are not subject to the law. ¹⁹Now the works of the flesh are obvious: fornication, impurity, licentiousness, ²⁰idolatry, sorcery, enmities, strife, jealousy, anger, quarrels, dissensions, factions, ²¹envy,ᵈ drunkenness, carousing, and things like these. I am warning you, as I warned you before: those who do such things will not inherit the kingdom of God.

The Fruit of the Spirit

22 By contrast, the fruit of the Spirit is love, joy, peace, patience, kindness, generosity, faith-

---

ᵃ Gk brothers   ᵇ Or made effective   ᶜ Gk the flesh   ᵈ Other ancient authorities add murder

---

5:1 *freedom.* The bright, shining star of Paul's message to the Galatians, freedom, is actually a constellation made up of Spirit, grace, and faith. Those stars dispel the darkness of the flesh, the law, and works and set us free from their enslaving yokes.

5:4 *fallen away from grace.* Having walked in the bright light of grace, the Galatians "nullify" (2:21) that grace when they "turn back" (4:9) and "submit again to a yoke of slavery" (5:1). Far from being a deficiency of works, falling from grace is a dependency on works—the result of a "contrary" gospel, which sends Paul into fits of holy rage (see 5:12; 1:6–9).

5:16 *Live by the Spirit.* The life of discipleship, of following Jesus, and of holiness is not defined by what we avoid doing. It is characterized by vibrant, robust, and adventurous living "by the Spirit." Allowing ourselves to be "led by the Spirit" (v 18), we are free to say no to the "desires of the flesh."

5:19–21 *the works of the flesh.* Paul, concerned with the spiritually deforming effect of the works of the law, now addresses the opposite error, the works of the flesh, which can be equally destructive to spiritual formation. Veering from the narrow way of Jesus leads to the ditch of duty—the works of the law—or to the ditch of indulgence—the works of the flesh. Either way we are stuck in the ditch.

5:22 *the fruit of the Spirit.* As Jesus pointed out, "The tree is known by its fruit" (Matt

fulness, 23gentleness, and self-control. There is no law against such things. 24And those who belong to Christ Jesus have crucified the flesh with its passions and desires. 25If we live by the Spirit, let us also be guided by the Spirit. 26Let us not become conceited, competing against one another, envying one another.

Bear One Another's Burdens

6 My friends,*a* if anyone is detected in a transgression, you who have received the Spirit should restore such a one in a spirit of gentleness. Take care that you yourselves are not tempted. 2Bear one another's burdens, and in this way you will fulfill*b* the law of Christ. 3For if those who are nothing think they are something, they deceive themselves. 4All must test their own work; then that work, rather than their neighbor's work, will become a cause for pride. 5For all must carry their own loads.

6 Those who are taught the word must share in all good things with their teacher.

7 Do not be deceived; God is not mocked, for you reap whatever you sow. 8If you sow to your own flesh, you will reap corruption from the flesh; but if you sow to the Spirit, you will reap eternal life from the Spirit. 9So let us not grow weary in doing what is right, for we will reap at harvest time, if we do not give

up. 10So then, whenever we have an opportunity, let us work for the good of all, and especially for those of the family of faith.

Final Admonitions and Benediction

11 See what large letters I make when I am writing in my own hand! 12It is those who want to make a good showing in the flesh that try to compel you to be circumcised— only that they may not be persecuted for the cross of Christ. 13Even the circumcised do not themselves obey the law, but they want you to be circumcised so that they may boast about your flesh. 14May I never boast of anything except the cross of our Lord Jesus Christ, by which*c* the world has been crucified to me, and I to the world. 15For*d* neither circumcision nor uncircumcision is anything; but a new creation is everything! 16As for those who will follow this rule—peace be upon them, and mercy, and upon the Israel of God.

17 From now on, let no one make trouble for me; for I carry the marks of Jesus branded on my body.

18 May the grace of our Lord Jesus Christ be with your spirit, brothers and sisters.*e* Amen.

a Gk *Brothers*   *b* Other ancient authorities read *in this way fulfill*   *c* Or *through whom*   *d* Other ancient authorities add *in Christ Jesus*   *e* Gk *brothers*

12:33). Here Paul echoes the reality that fruit is a result of the nature of the tree, and for him that nature is the "new creation" (6:15). This metaphor of fruit is basic to spiritual formation. The fruit of the Spirit is the outward evidence of the inward reality of a heart "abiding" in Christ. In John 15 Jesus uses this metaphor to show that fruit is born as a result of relationship to the Vine. Therefore, we give our total energy and attention to grace-filled "training hard" by practicing the disciplines of being present to Jesus rather than in misguided "trying hard" to bear fruit. Through "abiding" (John 8:31–32, NKJV) we are set free to release the fruit of the Spirit.

Responding
5:25 GUIDANCE. Have you ever asked the Holy Spirit for guidance when facing a problem? What happened? If you haven't ever asked, try it today. Watch how it

changes your perception of the problem. *See also* Spiritual Disciplines Index.

6:1 *My friends.* The abrupt change of tone from astonished rebuke to gentle care reflects Paul's dual concern for the truth of the gospel of freedom and for the Galatians themselves. The remainder of his letter is "family business," revealing that the life of freedom is developed and demonstrated in community—in relationships of truth, trust, and grace.

6:17 *the marks of Jesus.* Because Paul is set free from sin and self, his only claim to fame is his union with Christ on the cross (v 14). The marks on his body would have identified him in that culture as a slave, and a willing slave he was to Jesus. But for Paul those scars were a symbol of his transformation from persecutor to lover, from performer to believer, and from slave to one freed in Christ.

THE LETTER OF PAUL TO THE

EPHESIANS

T wentieth-century archaeology has uncovered several curious things about the ancient Temple Mount in Jerusalem. Among them is the random design of the southern stairs, which carried weary pilgrims from the Tyropoean Valley several hundred feet up to the Temple itself. It was discovered that the steps were an engineering nightmare. The rise of the steps varied in some instances by several inches, while the stretch often varied by several feet. The conclusion was as painful as it was obvious: either the design engineers were incompetent or intoxicated! The ancient rabbis, our primary teachers in spiritual formation, however, had a different take. They thought theologically about this matter as well as every other. In their view, the engineers of the ancient Temple Mount knew that to ascend the hill of the Lord hurriedly and without thought would be spiritually ill-advised. You must approach the Temple as you would approach God, cautiously and with measured steps. These uneven steps to the presence of God are a metaphor for reading Ephesians, and indeed the entire Bible, with a view toward spiritual formation. Read it slowly and cautiously or else you fall!

The Saints of Ephesus

The Letter to the Ephesians begins, as most other ancient letters do, with a traditional greeting that identifies both sender and recipient. In this instance "Paul, an apostle of Christ Jesus by the will of God," is the sender, and "the saints who are in Ephesus and are faithful in Christ Jesus" are the recipients (1:1). Four specific things said about the recipients of this magnificent ancient letter indicate how we ought to read it as a tool for spiritual formation. They are identified as "saints," "in Ephesus," "faithful," and "in Christ Jesus."

First, we ought to read the Letter to the Ephesians as "saints." The New Testament

---

*See also "The With-God Life" essay for this section of the Bible,
"The People of God in Community," pp. 2037–42.*

term "saints" (*hagioi*) refers not to those with particular moral or spiritual qualities, but to those in a particular spiritual location. "Saints" are people set apart for the purposes of God. The backdrop to this basic biblical designation is the relationship between the nation of Israel and God. Israel was chosen by God to be an instrument of righteousness in the world. Just as God had chosen Abraham to be the means through whom "all the families of the earth" would be blessed (Gen 12:3), God created the Church to be a blessing to the world. Jesus surely must have been thinking along these lines when he said to his gathered disciples, "You are the salt of the earth, . . . the light of the world" (Matt 5:13–14). To read Ephesians with a view toward discovering the rugged and redemptive purposes of God while living them out in a hard-labor existence of radical obedience is to read it rightly.

Second, we ought to read the letter as though we were "in Ephesus." Many ancient manuscripts do not include the geographical location of the original recipients of this letter; in fact, the most ancient ones do not. The NRSV, however, includes it for a list of reasons appropriate to scholarly consideration, and we ought to consider it for a list of reasons appropriate to spiritual formation. All of the issues that surface in this book, whether they have to do with the efficacy of prayer, the uniqueness of Christ, the nature of Christian calling, the power and work of the Holy Spirit, the theological basis for social relationships, or the wild and chaotic nature of spiritual warfare, have to be worked out in a particular locale. For the first readers of this letter, it was finding a way to live out a particular truth in a pluralist culture, to live a creative new life in the context of old, repressive ways. Ephesus was the jewel of ancient Asia Minor. Its popular seaport, thriving economy, strategic military location, and natural "melting pot" culture made it a model city to display the prowess of Roman citizenry.

The stark problem for the early Christians was that their allegiance was not to Rome and its Caesar, but to the kingdom of heaven and its God. If the gospel were going to mean anything at all, it had to mean something in Ephesus. Christian believers are always called to live locally—in Los Angeles or London, in Beijing or the Bronx. Spiritual formation is a geographical as well as a theological phenomenon.

A Call to Spiritual Athleticism

Third, we ought to read Ephesians as the "faithful" always do—on bended knees wearing blue jeans. The adjective *pistis* can have either an active meaning ("trusting," "having faith") or a passive meaning ("trustworthy," "being faithful"). A faithful reading of this letter will be marked by both a penchant for prayer and a bias toward action. Among the distinctive features of Ephesians is the way that prose and prayer are mixed with gospel instruction. Prayer is the pen that wrote this letter, and prayer is the lens required for reading it. Blessings, supplications, and calls to prayer are the harnesses and ropes used to ascend the rocky slope of the spiritual life. And, similarly, a faithful reading of this letter will also be marked by a bias toward action. In the ancient Jewish tradition of *haggadah* (meditation) and *halakah* (walking in the truth), Paul's spirituality shifts effortlessly from theory to practice. "I therefore, the prisoner in the Lord, beg you to lead a life worthy of the calling to which you have been called" (Eph 4:1). Ephesians is not a vapid call for spiritual detachment; it is an urgent call for spiritual athleticism. If we do not read it ready to pray and eager to rise up, we will be left wondering.

Fourth, we ought to read Ephesians "in Christ Jesus." Everything in Paul's life and theology hinged on the resurrection of Jesus Christ and his mysterious inclusion in it. It was no longer possible for him to even imagine a life independent of the Christ. The overwhelming glory of the Risen One had finally and completely consumed him. A faithful reading of this letter will necessarily require us to wear a "Christ lens." Our destiny is kept secretly in Christ (1:11); our lives are gathered up with Christ (2:4–5); our access to grace is predicated on the work of Christ (3:12); our gifts for ministry flow from the ascension of Christ (4:8); the agency for social transformation is lodged in the imitation of Christ (5:1); and the hardware needed to enter the cosmic conflict around us is bequeathed by Christ (6:24). This is why John Calvin writes in the *Institutes of the Christian Religion,* "Since so great a storehouse of every good thing is found in him, let us drink our fill from this fountain and no other." Without this commitment to viewing Paul's words "in Christ Jesus," we will end with nothing more than a sleepy-eyed reading of this spine-tingling letter!

Tolle lege! Take and read!

—*Timothy Brown*

Salutation

1 Paul, an apostle of Christ Jesus by the will of God,

To the saints who are in Ephesus and are faithful[a] in Christ Jesus:

2 Grace to you and peace from God our Father and the Lord Jesus Christ.

Spiritual Blessings in Christ

3 Blessed be the God and Father of our Lord Jesus Christ, who has blessed us in Christ with every spiritual blessing in the heavenly places, 4just as he chose us in Christ[b] before the foundation of the world to be holy and blameless before him in love. 5He destined us for adoption as his children through Jesus Christ, according to the good

a Other ancient authorities lack *in Ephesus,* reading *saints who are also faithful*   b Gk *in him*

1:1 *Paul, an apostle of Christ Jesus by the will of God.* Paul begins where all spiritual formation begins, by deliberately placing himself and his Ephesian readers in a Christ frame. He chose to see himself as God saw him, inextricably bound to the One who loved him and gave himself for him. Genes and social location have neither the first nor the last word in spiritual formation.

1:3 *Blessed be the God and Father of our Lord Jesus Christ.* Echoing loudly through this exuberant blessing of God are the synagogue prayers of Paul's Jewish past. The Berachot portion of the Amidah, the central prayer of the synagogue liturgy, turned on the blessing of God for all good gifts. It would also have been customary in some Jewish communities to offer these blessings thrice daily, giving insight into the notion of praying constantly. This practice was clearly continued by the earliest Christians.

1:4–5 *he chose us in Christ, . . . destined us for adoption.* Paul speaks some of the Bible's best words—"chose" and "destined." They contain volumes about God's meticulous care for us. Some Christians construe the "choosing" and "destining" of God as equivalents to "fate" or "inevitability." This is an enormous mistake. The images behind the latter are bloodless clones of the former. Behind Paul's living vision is a loving God forming an adoptive family.

pleasure of his will, 6to the praise of his glorious grace that he freely bestowed on us in the Beloved. 7In him we have redemption through his blood, the forgiveness of our trespasses, according to the riches of his grace 8that he lavished on us. With all wisdom and insight 9he has made known to us the mystery of his will, according to his good pleasure that he set forth in Christ, 10as a plan for the fullness of time, to gather up all things in him, things in heaven and things on earth. 11In Christ we have also obtained an inheritance,*a* having been destined according to the purpose of him who accomplishes all things according to his counsel and will, 12so that we, who were the first to set our hope on Christ, might live for the praise of his glory. 13In him you also, when you had heard the word of truth, the gospel of your salvation, and had believed in him, were marked with the seal of the promised Holy Spirit; 14this*b* is the pledge of our inheritance toward redemption as God's own people, to the praise of his glory.

Paul's Prayer

15 I have heard of your faith in the Lord Jesus and your love*c* toward all the saints, and for this reason 16I do not cease to give thanks for you as I remember you in my prayers. 17I pray that the God of our Lord Jesus Christ, the Father of glory, may give you a spirit of wisdom and revelation as you come to know him, 18so that, with the eyes of your heart enlightened, you may know what is the hope to which he has called you, what are the riches of his glorious inheritance among the saints, 19and what is the immeasurable greatness of his power for us who believe, according to the working of his great power. 20God*d* put this power to work in Christ when he raised him from the dead and seated him at his right hand in the heavenly places, 21far above all rule and authority and power and dominion, and above every name that is named, not only in this age but also in the age to come. 22And

a Or *been made a heritage*   *b* Other ancient authorities read *who*   *c* Other ancient authorities lack *and your love*   *d* Gk *He*

1:13 *when you had heard the word of truth . . . and had believed in him.* Spiritual formation requires a peculiar way of interpreting Scripture. The scholarly world suggests using a "suspicious" reading of texts—doubting and questioning what we find—which may be appropriate for some bodies of literature. Although a certain level of questioning is appropriate in the spiritual life, it is never the primary way we should read Scripture. We are believers first, before we are doubters.

1:14 *to the praise of his glory.* These words bring to a conclusion the Bible's longest and most complex sentence. A single sentence in the Greek text extends from verse 3 to 14. To make it more manageable and understandable to average readers, most English translations make it several sentences. This is a mistake. The length and complexity of this sentence are a fitting reflection of the length and complexity of our redemption in Christ. Being formed into the Christ life is not a simple procedure. It will require our hearts, souls, and minds for a lifetime.

1:15 *I have heard of your faith . . . and your love.* The careful reader will hear a Christ echo in these words. Jesus interpreted the main

teachings of the Torah as love for God and neighbor (see Matt 22:34–40; Mark 12:28–34; Luke 10:25–28). This was his teaching "yoke" (Matt 11:29–30). Faith in Christ and love for neighbor are the two sides of the spiritual formation coin. With Jesus' yoke squarely before our eyes, all of our actions can be judged by their capacity to honor God and provide care for others. The first-century document known as the *Didache,* or "The Teaching of the Twelve Apostles," includes this provocative hope: "If you are able to bear the Lord's yoke in its entirety, you will be perfect."

Responding

1:16 PRAYER. Paul gives thanks for the Christians in Ephesus because of their faith in Jesus Christ and their love for one another. When the time is appropriate, give thanks for the people in your family or circle of friends for their faith in Jesus Christ and ask God to help you love each one more. *See also* Spiritual Disciplines Index.

1:17–19 THE WITH-GOD LIFE—*See* Spiritual Disciplines Index.

he has put all things under his feet and has made him the head over all things for the church, 23which is his body, the fullness of him who fills all in all.

From Death to Life

2 You were dead through the trespasses and sins 2in which you once lived, following the course of this world, following the ruler of the power of the air, the spirit that is now at work among those who are disobedient. 3All of us once lived among them in the passions of our flesh, following the desires of flesh and senses, and we were by nature children of wrath, like everyone else. 4But God, who is rich in mercy, out of the great love with which he loved us 5even when we were dead through our trespasses, made us alive together with Christ*a*—by grace you have been saved— 6and raised us up with him and seated us with him in the heavenly places in Christ Jesus, 7so that in the ages to come he might show the immeasurable riches of his grace in kindness toward us in Christ Jesus. 8For by grace you have been

saved through faith, and this is not your own doing; it is the gift of God— 9not the result of works, so that no one may boast. 10For we are what he has made us, created in Christ Jesus for good works, which God prepared beforehand to be our way of life.

One in Christ

11 So then, remember that at one time you Gentiles by birth,*b* called "the uncircumcision" by those who are called "the circumcision"—a physical circumcision made in the flesh by human hands— 12remember that you were at that time without Christ, being aliens from the commonwealth of Israel, and strangers to the covenants of promise, having no hope and without God in the world. 13But now in Christ Jesus you who once were far off have been brought near by the blood of Christ. 14For he is our peace; in his flesh he has made both groups into one and has broken down the dividing wall, that is, the hostility

a Other ancient authorities read *in Christ*
b Gk *in the flesh*

1:22 *he has put all things under his feet.* Two things are striking about this reference. The first is the effortless way that Paul refers to Psalm 110 and applies it to the life of faith. Here he is modeling the borrowed nature of spirituality. Spiritual formation does not require innovation, just faithfulness. The second striking thing is its implied political subversiveness. "Under his feet" is also the language of the Caesars, who required their subjects to acknowledge their lordship. The early followers of Jesus bracketed all earthly powers and unbridled heavenly ones.

2:1–6 *You were dead. . . . But God . . . made us alive.* Technically the little word "but" is an adversative conjunction. It joins two things together in an adversarial way. It certainly does here. We were dead, but God "made us alive together with Christ." The same resurrection life that coursed through Jesus' body on the morning of "First Fruits" now, by a kind of spiritual capillary fashion, courses through our bodies also!

2:8 *by grace you have been saved through faith.* Like a portrait beautifully framed, in a single sentence our best nouns are put on full display: "grace," "save," "faith." Take these

words out of the Christian vocabulary, and our holidays have no celebration and the Blessed Sacrament itself is a child's tea party. The big realities of the Christian life are not things we wrestle from the hand of a parsimonious God; they are things God gives gladly with all the joy of a parent on Christmas morning.

2:10 *created in Christ Jesus for good works.* Works are to faith as exhaling is to inhaling. They complete the gift of salvation. Good works are not what we do to win salvation; they are what we do to demonstrate and enjoy it. Followers of Jesus have for the longest time been perplexed by the relationship between faith and works. The One whom we follow is not. Jesus said, "If you know these things, you are blessed if you do them" (John 13:17).

2:14 *the dividing wall, that is, the hostility between us.* On the Temple Mount, dividing the inner courts of Israel from the Court of the Gentiles, was a three-meter barrier keeping the chosen people of God separate from the Gentiles. Now in Christ Jesus all such barriers are gone. The staggering claim this makes on followers of this Jesus is clear. In a world of walls—walls between the East and West (great

between us. 15He has abolished the law with its commandments and ordinances, that he might create in himself one new humanity in place of the two, thus making peace, 16and might reconcile both groups to God in one body[a] through the cross, thus putting to death that hostility through it.[b] 17So he came and proclaimed peace to you who were far off and peace to those who were near; 18for through him both of us have access in one Spirit to the Father. 19So then you are no longer strangers and aliens, but you are citizens with the saints and also members of the household of God, 20built upon the foundation of the apostles and prophets, with Christ Jesus himself as the cornerstone.[c] 21In him the whole structure is joined together and grows into a holy temple in the Lord; 22in whom you also are built together spiritually[d] into a dwelling place for God.

Paul's Ministry to the Gentiles

3 This is the reason that I Paul am a prisoner for[e] Christ Jesus for the sake of you Gentiles— 2for surely you have already heard of the commission of God's grace that was given me for you, 3and how the mystery was made known to me by revelation, as I wrote above in a few words, 4a reading of which will enable you to perceive my understanding of the mystery of Christ. 5In former generations this mystery[f] was not made known to humankind, as it has now been revealed to his holy apostles and prophets by the Spirit: 6that is, the Gentiles have become fellow heirs, members of the same body, and sharers in the promise in Christ Jesus through the gospel.

7 Of this gospel I have become a servant according to the gift of God's grace that was given me by the working of his power. 8Although I am the very least of all the saints, this grace was given to me to bring to the Gentiles the news of the boundless riches of Christ, 9and to make everyone see[g] what is the plan of the mystery hidden for ages in[h] God who created all things; 10so that through the church the wisdom of God in its rich variety might now be made known to the rulers and authorities in the heavenly places. 11This was in accordance with the eternal purpose that he has carried out in Christ Jesus our Lord, 12in whom we have access to God in boldness and confidence through faith in him.[i] 13I pray therefore that you[j] may not lose heart over my sufferings for you; they are your glory.

a Or reconcile both of us in one body for God
b Or in him, or in himself   c Or keystone
d Gk in the Spirit   e Or of   f Gk it   g Other ancient authorities read to bring to light   h Or by
i Or the faith of him   j Or I

---

religious divides) and walls between North and South (great economic divides)—we are to join him in the work by so living a radically alternative gospel life that it brings walls crashing down.

2:22 *built together spiritually into a dwelling place for God.* The landscape of Ephesus was dominated by the Temple of Artemis with its many-breasted statue of the goddess. This chief figure in an ancient fertility cult defiantly stood as an imposing and enticing symbol of humankind's desire to both placate and manipulate the gods. Our being built together as a "dwelling place for God" echoes a vision of Ezekiel's (37:27) and reminds us again that we are caught up in a vast and sprawling salvation story.

3:5 *In former generations this mystery was not made known.* Theologians distinguish between problems, puzzles, and mystery. Problems can e solved if new data can be found. Puzzles can be put together if new techniques can be employed. Mystery defies either resolution or manipulation and invites only embrace. The mystery "hidden for ages" is "the breadth and length and height and depth" of the living Christ (vv 9, 18). Spiritual formation requires a capacity to lose oneself in the cosmic enormity gathered together by the particularity of the incarnation.

3:7 THE WITH-GOD LIFE—*See* Spiritual Disciplines Index.

Responding
3:7 SERVICE. We normally think of a servant as being in the employment of another person, but Paul states he is a servant of the gospel. What does he mean? Can we be a servant of the gospel without serving other people? Why or why not? *See also* Spiritual Disciplines Index.

Prayer for the Readers

14 For this reason I bow my knees before the Father,[a] 15from whom every family[b] in heaven and on earth takes its name. 16I pray that, according to the riches of his glory, he may grant that you may be strengthened in your inner being with power through his Spirit, 17and that Christ may dwell in your hearts through faith, as you are being rooted and grounded in love. 18I pray that you may have the power to comprehend, with all the saints, what is the breadth and length and height and depth, 19and to know the love of Christ that surpasses knowledge, so that you may be filled with all the fullness of God.

20 Now to him who by the power at work within us is able to accomplish abundantly far more than all we can ask or imagine, 21to him be glory in the church and in Christ Jesus to all generations, forever and ever. Amen.

Unity in the Body of Christ

4 I therefore, the prisoner in the Lord, beg you to lead a life worthy of the calling to which you have been called, 2with all humility and gentleness, with patience, bearing with one another in love, 3making every effort to maintain the unity of the Spirit in the bond of peace. 4There is one body and one Spirit, just as you were called to the one hope of your calling, 5one Lord, one faith, one baptism, 6one God and Father of all, who is above all and through all and in all.

7 But each of us was given grace according to the measure of Christ's gift. 8Therefore it is said,

"When he ascended on high he made
captivity itself a captive;
he gave gifts to his people."

9(When it says, "He ascended," what does it mean but that he had also descended[c] into the lower parts of the earth? 10He who descended is the same one who ascended far above all the heavens, so that he might fill all things.) 11The gifts he gave were that some would be apostles, some prophets, some evangelists, some pastors and teachers, 12to equip the saints for the work of ministry, for building up the body of Christ, 13until all of us come to the unity of the faith and of the knowledge of the Son of God, to maturity, to the measure of the full stature of Christ. 14We must no longer be children, tossed to and fro and blown about by every wind of doctrine, by people's trickery, by their craftiness in deceitful scheming. 15But

a Other ancient authorities add *of our Lord Jesus Christ* b Gk *fatherhood* c Other ancient authorities add *first*

3:14 *For this reason I bow my knees.* Prayer is the practice most congruent with the accomplishment of God's eternal purposes. The best of practitioners in the spiritual life have all affirmed, to borrow an image of one of them, that God has conferred on his children the "dignity of causality"! Ancient rabbis debated at some length the proper position for prayer. The result of their debate was the Jewish notion of *kavanah,* which means "single-mindedness." Standing upright, lifting the hands, and bowing the knees are all physical responses to the quest for spiritual focus.

3:16, 20 THE WITH-GOD LIFE—See Spiritual Disciplines Index.

4:1 *the calling to which you have been called.* Spiritual formation is largely dependent on our capacity to live a called life. Calling presupposes a God who graciously speaks (the doctrine of revelation) and a people who willingly listen (the doctrine of sanctification). In Revelation, the letter sent to the church in Ephesus ends this way: "Let anyone who has an ear listen to what the Spirit is saying to the churches" (2:7). Listening is a primary spiritual formation practice.

4:8 *When he ascended on high . . . he gave gifts.* The end toward which the colossal gift giving of the risen Christ moves is the equipping of the saints for the work of ministry. Christians show themselves to be what they are when they do "the work of ministry" (v 12). The spiritually formed need not cast about for a purpose in life. It is given to them as a gift!

Responding
4:15–16 FELLOWSHIP. Why does Paul use the metaphor of a body when trying to describe the relationship of Christians to one another? In examining your role in the Body of Christ, what have you done to help it work properly and to promote love? What else could you do? *See also* Spiritual Disciplines Index.

speaking the truth in love, we must grow up in every way into him who is the head, into Christ, 16from whom the whole body, joined and knit together by every ligament with which it is equipped, as each part is working properly, promotes the body's growth in building itself up in love.

The Old Life and the New

17 Now this I affirm and insist on in the Lord: you must no longer live as the Gentiles live, in the futility of their minds. 18They are darkened in their understanding, alienated from the life of God because of their ignorance and hardness of heart. 19They have lost all sensitivity and have abandoned themselves to licentiousness, greedy to practice every kind of impurity. 20That is not the way you learned Christ! 21For surely you have heard about him and were taught in him, as truth is in Jesus. 22You were taught to put away your former way of life, your old self, corrupt and deluded by its lusts, 23and to be renewed in the spirit of your minds, 24and to clothe yourselves with the new self, created according to the likeness of God in true righteousness and holiness.

Rules for the New Life

25 So then, putting away falsehood, let all of us speak the truth to our neighbors, for we are members of one another. 26Be angry but do not sin; do not let the sun go down on your anger, 27and do not make room for the devil. 28Thieves must give up stealing; rather let them labor and work honestly with their own hands, so as to have something to share with the needy. 29Let no evil talk come out of your mouths, but only what is useful for building up,*a* as there is need, so that your words may give grace to those who hear. 30And do not grieve the Holy Spirit of God, with which you were marked with a seal for the day of redemption. 31Put away from you all bitterness and wrath and anger and wrangling and slander, together with all malice, 32and be kind to one another, tenderhearted, forgiving one another, as God in Christ has

5 forgiven you.*b* 1Therefore be imitators of God, as beloved children, 2and live in love, as Christ loved us*c* and gave himself up for us, a fragrant offering and sacrifice to God.

Renounce Pagan Ways

3 But fornication and impurity of any kind, or greed, must not even be mentioned among you, as is proper among saints. 4Entirely out of place is obscene, silly, and vulgar talk; but instead, let there be thanksgiving. 5Be sure of this, that no fornicator or impure person, or one who is greedy (that is, an idolater), has any inheritance in the kingdom of Christ and of God.

6 Let no one deceive you with empty words, for because of these things the wrath of God comes on those who are disobedient. 7Therefore do not be associated with them.

a Other ancient authorities read *building up faith*
b Other ancient authorities read *us*   *c* Other ancient authorities read *you*

4:20–21 *the way you learned Christ!* The language of learning stands in stark contrast to the cultic manipulation of the gods. This passage suggests that Jesus Christ is the substance of that learning, is himself the teacher, and is the context in which this teaching takes place. Jesus Christ is the source, the substance, and the goal toward which spiritual formation moves.

4:25 *So then, putting away falsehood.* Spiritual formation requires a willful intentionality. It is not for the faint of heart. This "putting away" is reminiscent of more graphic language in other Letters (e.g., "put to death," Col 3:5) and of Jesus' strident teaching about plucking out a wandering eye or cutting off a wayward hand in the Sermon on the Mount (Matt 5:29–30), but it carries the same weight. To be formed into Christ will require us to jettison things cherished by us but abhorrent to God.

5:1 *be imitators of God.* No spiritual practice is as fundamental to our being formed into the Christ life than imitation. The whole of Jesus' ministry with his disciples turned on this practice. When we pretend to be what we are not naturally, Jesus Christ mysteriously "injects" his kind of life into ours. And here is the most unthinkable of all—we can imitate God!

5:2 SACRIFICE—*See* Spiritual Disciplines Index.

8For once you were darkness, but now in the Lord you are light. Live as children of light— 9for the fruit of the light is found in all that is good and right and true. 10Try to find out what is pleasing to the Lord. 11Take no part in the unfruitful works of darkness, but instead expose them. 12For it is shameful even to mention what such people do secretly; 13but everything exposed by the light becomes visible, 14for everything that becomes visible is light. Therefore it says,

"Sleeper, awake!
    Rise from the dead,
    and Christ will shine on you."

15 Be careful then how you live, not as unwise people but as wise, 16making the most of the time, because the days are evil. 17So do not be foolish, but understand what the will of the Lord is. 18Do not get drunk with wine, for that is debauchery; but be filled with the Spirit, 19as you sing psalms and hymns and spiritual songs among yourselves, singing and making melody to the Lord in your hearts, 20giving thanks to God the Father at all times and for everything in the name of our Lord Jesus Christ.

The Christian Household

21 Be subject to one another out of reverence for Christ.
22 Wives, be subject to your husbands as you are to the Lord. 23For the husband is the head of the wife just as Christ is the head of the church, the body of which he is the Savior. 24Just as the church is subject to Christ,

so also wives ought to be, in everything, to their husbands.

25 Husbands, love your wives, just as Christ loved the church and gave himself up for her, 26in order to make her holy by cleansing her with the washing of water by the word, 27so as to present the church to himself in splendor, without a spot or wrinkle or anything of the kind—yes, so that she may be holy and without blemish. 28In the same way, husbands should love their wives as they do their own bodies. He who loves his wife loves himself. 29For no one ever hates his own body, but he nourishes and tenderly cares for it, just as Christ does for the church, 30because we are members of his body.a 31"For this reason a man will leave his father and mother and be joined to his wife, and the two will become one flesh." 32This is a great mystery, and I am applying it to Christ and the church. 33Each of you, however, should love his wife as himself, and a wife should respect her husband.

Children and Parents

6 Children, obey your parents in the Lord,b for this is right. 2"Honor your father and mother"—this is the first commandment with a promise: 3"so that it may be well with you and you may live long on the earth."
4 And, fathers, do not provoke your children to anger, but bring them up in the discipline and instruction of the Lord.

a Other ancient authorities add *of his flesh and of his bones*   b Other ancient authorities lack *in the Lord*

5:14 *Sleeper, awake! Rise from the dead.* The reference here is unclear. It could be to a vision of Isaiah's (see 60:1) or, as some scholars think, to an ancient Easter or baptismal liturgy. In either case it reveals Paul's inclination to borrow from a deep, wide, and long tradition in the task of spiritual formation.
5:21–6:9 SUBMISSION—*See* Spiritual Disciplines Index.
5:21–6:9 *Be subject to one another.* Serious seekers of the Christ life will take these countercultural instructions seriously. Paul's comparison of the spousal relationship with that between Christ and the Church and his abiding concern for the relationship between the gospel

and culture require it. Spiritual formation requires that every part of our lives be under a Christ scrutiny.

Responding
5:22–33 CHASTITY. Instead of telling couples they should not commit adultery, Paul gives positive guidance that, if followed, will overcome the temptation to be unfaithful. Why is positive instruction more effective than a negative command? Examine your relationship with your spouse. What will staying faithful nurture in your relationship? *See also* Spiritual Disciplines Index.

Slaves and Masters

5 Slaves, obey your earthly masters with fear and trembling, in singleness of heart, as you obey Christ; [6]not only while being watched, and in order to please them, but as slaves of Christ, doing the will of God from the heart. [7]Render service with enthusiasm, as to the Lord and not to men and women, [8]knowing that whatever good we do, we will receive the same again from the Lord, whether we are slaves or free.

9 And, masters, do the same to them. Stop threatening them, for you know that both of you have the same Master in heaven, and with him there is no partiality.

The Whole Armor of God

10 Finally, be strong in the Lord and in the strength of his power. [11]Put on the whole armor of God, so that you may be able to stand against the wiles of the devil. [12]For our[a] struggle is not against enemies of blood and flesh, but against the rulers, against the authorities, against the cosmic powers of this present darkness, against the spiritual forces of evil in the heavenly places. [13]Therefore take up the whole armor of God, so that you may be able to withstand on that evil day, and having done everything, to stand firm. [14]Stand therefore, and fasten the belt of truth around your waist, and put on the breastplate of righteousness. [15]As shoes for your feet put on whatever will make you ready to proclaim the gospel of peace. [16]With all of these,[b] take the shield of faith, with which you will be able to quench all the flaming arrows of the evil one. [17]Take the helmet of salvation, and the sword of the Spirit, which is the word of God.

18 Pray in the Spirit at all times in every prayer and supplication. To that end keep alert and always persevere in supplication for all the saints. [19]Pray also for me, so that when I speak, a message may be given to me to make known with boldness the mystery of the gospel,[c] [20]for which I am an ambassador in chains. Pray that I may declare it boldly, as I must speak.

Personal Matters and Benediction

21 So that you also may know how I am and what I am doing, Tychicus will tell you

a Other ancient authorities read *your*   b Or *In all circumstances*   c Other ancient authorities lack *of the gospel*

6:7 SERVICE—*See* Spiritual Disciplines Index.
6:10 THE WITH-GOD LIFE—*See* Spiritual Disciplines Index.

6:10 *strong . . . strength . . . power.* These three words emboldening Christian believers— *dynamis, kratos,* and *ischus*—are, interestingly enough, also used in 1:19 to describe God's enormous power in raising Jesus from the dead. The apostle is reminding us that spiritual formation is God's doing from start to finish. The spiritual life begins, is sustained, and ends by the power of God.

6:13–17 *take up the whole armor of God.* Although our modern sensibilities may recoil from such graphic military imagery, this passage signals two very important dynamics of the spiritual life: the malevolent intent of our adversary and the necessity of a radical rearrangement of the world's settled order. There is a greater power afoot in the universe than Rome with its military prowess. The truth, righteousness, peace, faith, salvation, and word of God trump Rome every time!

6:18 *Pray in the Spirit at all times.* To thrive in the land of spiritual formation we must grow deep into the soil of prayer. The expansive life of prayer is underscored by the fourfold repetition of "all" in the Greek of this verse— "all times," "all prayer," "all perseverance," and "all the saints." This kind of expansiveness far surpasses the inclinations of any individual believer's heart and points to a Word-centered, communally framed prayer life.

Responding
6:18 PRAYER. Today, as you are praying, make a special effort to "pray in the Spirit." What did you learn about the Spirit? About yourself? *See also* Spiritual Disciplines Index.

6:21 *Tychicus will tell you everything.* Ephesians is surprisingly bereft of personal references. The inclusion of Tychicus at the end reminds us of a long list of other gospel co-workers for whom Paul was deeply grateful (see

everything. He is a dear brother and a faithful minister in the Lord. ²²I am sending him to you for this very purpose, to let you know how we are, and to encourage your hearts.

23 Peace be to the whole community, *a* and love with faith, from God the Father and the Lord Jesus Christ. ²⁴Grace be with all who have an undying love for our Lord Jesus Christ. *b*

a Gk *to the brothers*   *b* Other ancient authorities add *Amen*

Rom 16:1–15). (For more on Tychicus, see Acts 20:4; Col 4:7; 2 Tim 4:12; Titus 3:12.) All of this points to the communal nature of spiritual formation.

6:24 *Grace be with all.* Ephesians, and the Christian life itself, ends where it began—with grace! Ancient benedictions were a good deal more than a social convention. They accomplished the very thing they pronounced.

THE LETTER OF PAUL TO THE

PHILIPPIANS

P hilippians is one of Paul's most personal letters. Paul was actively involved in founding the church at Philippi, even enduring mistreatment by the civil authorities (see Acts 16:11–40). The Philippians, in turn, "shared" with Paul from the very beginning (Phil 1:5), providing regular financial support. Given such intimacy, Paul and his co-workers long for the Philippians (1:8; 2:26), just as the Philippians "hold" Paul in their "heart" (1:7–8). Paul has no need to defend his apostleship in this letter. He knows he is welcomed and revered. For this reason he can appeal to the Philippians' tenderness toward him in order to urge them to self-sacrificing love for one another (2:1–2). He can open his own life, revealing his own experience of God and his own formation in Christ (1:12–26; 3:4–16; 4:10–20).

Paul wrote this letter while in prison, late in his missionary career. The Philippian church, out of concern for him, had sent support through a brother named Epaphroditus (4:18). While staying with Paul, Epaphroditus had suffered a serious illness, delaying his return to Philippi (2:25–27). But now that he had recovered, Paul was eager to send Epaphroditus home with expressions of Paul's gratitude and the latest news of his imprisonment (2:28).

Joy: The Fruit of Life in Christ

In response to the Philippians' concern and kindnesses, Paul sends them a letter full of joy. Paul not only remembers them joyfully in prayer (1:4), but rejoices at the proclamation of the gospel, whatever the motive (1:18). Paul identifies the aim of his ministry as their "progress and joy in faith" (1:25). He appeals to their tenderheartedness, essentially telling them that if they really want him to be fully joyful, then they must get along with each other (2:2). He is grateful for, and rejoices at, their concern for him (4:10). Paul encourages them to rejoice over each other (2:17–18, 28–29; 4:10) and even to rejoice for no particular reason at all (3:1; 4:4). Late in his

---

See also "The With-God Life" essay for this section of the Bible,
"The People of God in Community," pp. 2037–42.

---

ministry—having endured hardships and opposition from all sides—Paul expresses joy. Here is spiritual maturity: when Paul had every reason to be tired and bitter, he responded to life with joy. This is the fruit of a life lived in close relationship with God, the fruit of a life formed in Christ.

A Single-Minded Focus on Christ

What lies behind this theme of joy expressed in Philippians is Paul's complete identification with the concerns of the gospel. Paul's appraisal of situations, which shapes the character of his emotions, is made wholeheartedly in light of the cause of Christ. His entire life—heart, mind, will—is caught up in knowing (3:8-10) and communicating (1:18-20) Christ. This is spiritual formation, Pauline style. It is about becoming so single-mindedly focused on following Christ that one can't help thinking like Christ, acting like Christ, feeling like Christ. Of course this kind of identification with Christ will look different for different people, but a study of Paul's life and his encouragement to others gives us a taste of what a life formed around Christ (a God-inhabited life) can look like: it is joyful (1:4), unselfish (1:20-26), humble (2:3), and passionate for the true gospel and against falsehood (3:1-3); it strains toward full maturity (3:12-14) and is content in poverty or riches (4:11-13). Paul desires his whole life to be a life lived "in Christ."

Why did Paul send Timothy, of all his followers, to Philippi (2:19)? He chose Timothy because the others were "seeking their own interests, not those of Jesus Christ" (2:21). He writes also that the Philippians should honor people such as Epaphroditus, because he came close to death for the "work of Christ" (2:30). For such laborers, and for us, the riches of God's glory are found in Christ Jesus (4:19).

This attention to modeling our lives in imitation of Christ's life is seen most clearly in a passage (2:2-15) in which Paul makes use of an early Christian hymn (2:6-11). Paul begins by urging the Philippians toward unity, formed through the practice of humility (2:2-4). Where does Paul find a model of humility for us to imitate? In the person of Jesus (2:5). Jesus did not exploit his equality with God. Rather, he identified with humankind and lived a life of obedient service, even to the point of death (2:6-8). In consequence of this self-sacrificing obedience, Christ is exalted to the highest place (2:9-11). Paul then applies this summary of the gospel to the Philippians' obedience (2:12), urging them to service and humility (2:14) and identifying their "exalted" position in this kind of life as a call to shine like "stars in the world" (2:9,15). A spiritually formed life is one formed in Christ; it is a life that embodies, in the concrete realities of everyday life, the obedience of the crucified and exalted Son.

Spiritual Maturity as a Community Effort

The realities of everyday life for the Christians in Philippi include the limits and liabilities of church life. Although the community of faith is established to bring believers into communion with God and abiding fellowship with one another, tensions in the Philippian church have led some to experience estrangement from God and dissension with each other. Paul prays that their love would overflow more and more (1:9), emphasizing his own disinterestedness in his reputation (1:15-18). He encourages them to be united in heart and mind (2:2), "without murmuring and arguing" (2:14). Paul praises genuine concern for the welfare of others (2:3–4, 20). At the same time, he uses some of the harshest language found in his writings for those who would divide the church by imposing unnecessary demands on the believers (3:2, 18–19). He pleads with Euodia and Syntyche, two women who had struggled alongside Paul in the work of the gospel, to be reconciled, and he asks for the help of a third party (4:2–3).

When community works, it is Paul's support and his joy. When it doesn't work, it is the bane of Paul's life—and ours as well. Spiritual formation involves not only individuals, but also groups. Paul's letters are letters of formation written to *communities*. He advertises a new citizenship (3:20). It is one thing to aim toward personal spiritual growth. It is another to strive as a community toward spiritual maturity.

When we open and read the book of Philippians, we get a privileged look into Paul's own relationship with God. We hear Paul's invitation to the kind of spiritual formation that a life centered on Christ can bring. It is to discover habits of thought, feeling, and life that form us in Christ, both individually and as communities. And finally, we learn something of the riches of a life filled with Christ in any circumstance.

—Evan B. Howard

Salutation

1 Paul and Timothy, servants[a] of Christ Jesus,

To all the saints in Christ Jesus who are in Philippi, with the bishops[b] and deacons:[c]

2 Grace to you and peace from God our Father and the Lord Jesus Christ.

Paul's Prayer for the Philippians

3 I thank my God every time I remember you, [4]constantly praying with joy in every one of my prayers for all of you, [5]because of your sharing in the gospel from the first day until now. [6]I am confident of this, that the one who began a good work among you will bring it to completion by the day of Jesus Christ. [7]It is right for me to think this way about all of you, because you hold me in your heart,[d] for all of you share in God's grace[e] with me, both in my imprisonment and in the defense and confirmation of the gospel. [8]For God is my witness, how I long for all of you with the compassion of Christ Jesus. [9]And this is my prayer, that your love may overflow more and more with knowledge and full insight [10]to help you to determine what is best, so that in the day of Christ you may be pure and blameless, [11]having produced the harvest of righteousness that comes through Jesus Christ for the glory and praise of God.

Paul's Present Circumstances

12 I want you to know, beloved,[f] that what has happened to me has actually helped to spread the gospel, [13]so that it has become

---

a Gk *slaves*   b Or *overseers*   c Or *overseers and helpers*   d Or *because I hold you in my heart*   e Gk *in grace*   f Gk *brothers*

1:3–4 PRAYER—*See* Spiritual Disciplines Index.

1:6 *the one who began a good work among you.* Paul reveals here his understanding of spiritual formation. First, God begins a good work. Next, there is progress in the work, measured by love, ever flowing "more and more" (v 9). Finally, God's work is brought to completion. God's work in us—as individuals and as communities of believers—is a cumulative process.

known throughout the whole imperial guard[a] and to everyone else that my imprisonment is for Christ; [14]and most of the brothers and sisters,[b] having been made confident in the Lord by my imprisonment, dare to speak the word[c] with greater boldness and without fear.

15 Some proclaim Christ from envy and rivalry, but others from goodwill. [16]These proclaim Christ out of love, knowing that I have been put here for the defense of the gospel; [17]the others proclaim Christ out of selfish ambition, not sincerely but intending to increase my suffering in my imprisonment. [18]What does it matter? Just this, that Christ is proclaimed in every way, whether out of false motives or true; and in that I rejoice.

Yes, and I will continue to rejoice, [19]for I know that through your prayers and the help of the Spirit of Jesus Christ this will turn out for my deliverance. [20]It is my eager expectation and hope that I will not be put to shame in any way, but that by my speaking with all boldness, Christ will be exalted now as always in my body, whether by life or by death. [21]For to me, living is Christ and dying is gain. [22]If I am to live in the flesh, that means fruitful labor for me; and I do not know which I prefer. [23]I am hard pressed between the two: my desire is to depart and be with Christ, for

that is far better; [24]but to remain in the flesh is more necessary for you. [25]Since I am convinced of this, I know that I will remain and continue with all of you for your progress and joy in faith, [26]so that I may share abundantly in your boasting in Christ Jesus when I come to you again.

27 Only, live your life in a manner worthy of the gospel of Christ, so that, whether I come and see you or am absent and hear about you, I will know that you are standing firm in one spirit, striving side by side with one mind for the faith of the gospel, [28]and are in no way intimidated by your opponents. For them this is evidence of their destruction, but of your salvation. And this is God's doing. [29]For he has graciously granted you the privilege not only of believing in Christ, but of suffering for him as well— [30]since you are having the same struggle that you saw I had and now hear that I still have.

Imitating Christ's Humility

2 If then there is any encouragement in Christ, any consolation from love, any sharing in the Spirit, any compassion and sympathy, [2]make my joy complete: be of the same mind, having the same love, being in

a Gk whole praetorium   b Gk brothers   c Other ancient authorities read word of God

---

1:12–26 *What does it matter?* What does it matter if Paul is in prison, so long as Christ is made known (vv 12–14)? What does it matter if others preach out of a desire to hurt Paul, so long as the gospel is proclaimed (vv 15–18)? What does it matter whether Paul lives or dies, so long as Christ is exalted (vv 20–24)? Paul is a model of the mature believer. His joys, pains, and concerns have been informed by his intimacy with the heart of God. As we, like Paul, grow in ever deepening communion with Christ, we will find that our needs for comfort, approval, even life itself will diminish in light of our much deeper need to see Christ exalted.

1:27–28 *Only, live your life in a manner worthy of the gospel.* What Paul models by his life he now exhorts with his words. Our life is to be lived (and formed) with the gospel in mind. It is not about self-fulfillment or self-improvement. It is about gospel fulfillment. Paul, who accepted

injury from friend and foe alike for the sake of the gospel (1:12–18), now urges his readers to strive "side by side" for the gospel and not to be intimidated by their opponents.

1:29 *granted you the privilege . . . of suffering.* Paul says later that his desire was to know the "sharing of [Jesus'] sufferings" (3:10), an honor that was granted to the Philippians as well. A rich knowledge of God comes from sharing the kinds of suffering Christ experienced. The value of this suffering is affirmed not only by the apostles (1 Pet 4:12–16), but also by mature believers throughout the history of the Church.

2:2 *be of the same mind, having the same love.* Paul pleads with his readers, appealing to their own tender care for him (v 1), to live in unity and humility. Paul's joy (and God's) is made complete when the Church is united in both head and heart. This unity is experienced through the practice of the discipline of

full accord and of one mind. ³Do nothing from selfish ambition or conceit, but in humility regard others as better than yourselves. ⁴Let each of you look not to your own interests, but to the interests of others. ⁵Let the same mind be in you that was*ᵃ* in Christ Jesus,

6 who, though he was in the form of God,
    did not regard equality with God
    as something to be exploited,
7 but emptied himself,
    taking the form of a slave,
    being born in human likeness.
   And being found in human form,
8   he humbled himself
    and became obedient to the point of
        death—
    even death on a cross.

9 Therefore God also highly exalted him
    and gave him the name
    that is above every name,
10 so that at the name of Jesus
    every knee should bend,
    in heaven and on earth and under the
        earth,

11 and every tongue should confess
    that Jesus Christ is Lord,
    to the glory of God the Father.

Shining as Lights in the World

12 Therefore, my beloved, just as you have always obeyed me, not only in my presence, but much more now in my absence, work out your own salvation with fear and trembling; ¹³for it is God who is at work in you, enabling you both to will and to work for his good pleasure.

14 Do all things without murmuring and arguing, ¹⁵so that you may be blameless and innocent, children of God without blemish in the midst of a crooked and perverse generation, in which you shine like stars in the world. ¹⁶It is by your holding fast to the word of life that I can boast on the day of Christ that I did not run in vain or labor in vain. ¹⁷But even if I am being poured out as a libation over the sacrifice and the offering of your faith, I am glad and rejoice with all of you— ¹⁸and in the same way you also must be glad and rejoice with me.

a Or that you have

---

humility: renouncing self-centered pursuits, actively regarding others in the best light possible, paying attention to the concerns and interests of others (1:3–4). As our hearts and minds are directed away from self and toward others in the practice of attentive, humble service, we begin to identify with one another; and before we know it, we find ourselves sharing the "same mind" with them.

2:5–11 *Let the same mind be in you that was in Christ Jesus.* Paul here, using the words of an early Christian hymn, singles out Jesus' own spirituality as the premier example of Christian life. Christian spiritual formation is growing in con-*form*-ity to Christ. Jesus had it all. Before becoming human, he was equal with God. Nonetheless, Jesus did not "exploit" his status. He did not take advantage of his supreme authority for selfish ends. Instead, he "emptied himself," giving himself to others in life and in death (vv 7–8). Jesus' spirituality was a spirituality of humble obedience. And God recognized this life of obedience by exalting Jesus above all others (vv 9–11). This Jesus is our model of spir-

itual formation, for status is gained not through "looking out for number one," but rather by humbly sacrificing ourselves for others.

2:12–13 *work out your own salvation . . . for it is God who is at work in you.* Our relationship with God, our "salvation," is a cooperative venture. God works salvation in, and we work salvation out. God initiates transformation by stimulating our desire to follow him, inspiring acts expressing that desire, providing strength to persevere, and so on. We, in turn, respond by deciding to follow, acting on God's inspiration, and choosing to persevere.

Responding
2:17 SACRIFICE. It seems strange to refer to our faith as a sacrifice and offering, but in *The Spirit of the Disciplines* Dallas Willard writes, "Our need to give is greater than God's need to receive." How long has it been since you freely offered your faith in Jesus Christ to God? Try to make this part of your with-God life during the next month and see what you learn. *See also* Spiritual Disciplines Index.

Timothy and Epaphroditus

19 I hope in the Lord Jesus to send Timothy to you soon, so that I may be cheered by news of you. 20I have no one like him who will be genuinely concerned for your welfare. 21All of them are seeking their own interests, not those of Jesus Christ. 22But Timothy's*a* worth you know, how like a son with a father he has served with me in the work of the gospel. 23I hope therefore to send him as soon as I see how things go with me; 24and I trust in the Lord that I will also come soon.

25 Still, I think it necessary to send to you Epaphroditus—my brother and co-worker and fellow soldier, your messenger*b* and minister to my need; 26for he has been longing for*c* all of you, and has been distressed because you heard that he was ill. 27He was indeed so ill that he nearly died. But God had mercy on him, and not only on him but on me also, so that I would not have one sorrow after another. 28I am the more eager to send him, therefore, in order that you may rejoice at seeing him again, and that I may be less anxious. 29Welcome him then in the Lord with all joy, and honor such people, 30because he came close to death for the work of Christ,*d* risking his life to make up for those services that you could not give me.

3 Finally, my brothers and sisters,*e* rejoice*f* in the Lord.

Breaking with the Past

To write the same things to you is not troublesome to me, and for you it is a safeguard.

2 Beware of the dogs, beware of the evil workers, beware of those who mutilate the flesh!*g* 3For it is we who are the circumcision, who worship in the Spirit of God*h* and boast in Christ Jesus and have no confidence in the flesh— 4even though I, too, have reason for confidence in the flesh.

If anyone else has reason to be confident in the flesh, I have more: 5circumcised on the eighth day, a member of the people of Israel, of the tribe of Benjamin, a Hebrew born of Hebrews; as to the law, a Pharisee; 6as to zeal, a persecutor of the church; as to righteousness under the law, blameless.

7 Yet whatever gains I had, these I have come to regard as loss because of Christ. 8More than that, I regard everything as loss because of the surpassing value of knowing Christ Jesus my Lord. For his sake I have suffered the loss of all things, and I regard them as rubbish, in order that I may gain Christ 9and be found in him, not having a righteousness of my own that comes from the law, but one that comes through faith in Christ,*i* the righteousness from God based on faith. 10I want to know Christ*j* and the power of his resurrection and the sharing of his sufferings by becoming like him in his death, 11if somehow I may attain the resurrection from the dead.

a Gk *his*   *b* Gk *apostle*   *c* Other ancient authorities read *longing to see*   *d* Other ancient authorities read *of the Lord*   *e* Gk *my brothers*   *f* Or *farewell*   *g* Gk *the mutilation*   *h* Other ancient authorities read *worship God in spirit*   *i* Or *through the faith of Christ*   *j* Gk *him*

2:30 SERVICE—*See* Spiritual Disciplines Index.

3:3 WORSHIP—*See* Spiritual Disciplines Index.

3:3 *who worship in the Spirit of God and boast in Christ Jesus.* The Christian life is not about "confidence in the flesh," Paul insists. Rather, it is about boasting in Christ Jesus. It is not about "having a righteousness of my own that comes from the law"; rather, it is about "faith in Christ" (v 9). The source and the strength of the Christian life are found in the Spirit of God, not in our religious performance.

3:8 *I have suffered the loss of all things . . . in order that I may gain Christ.* Paul certainly had

credentials. His family heritage, training, and zeal would have secured him a place as one of the up-and-coming Jewish leaders. But Paul's encounter with Christ radically changed his appraisal of those credentials. When Paul stood face-to-face with the risen Christ, his résumé did nothing for him. And all that Paul had once considered assets he now counted as losses. What mattered now was relationship with God: knowing Christ (also v 10) and gaining Christ. Spiritual formation is learning to recognize and abandon those things that must be counted as losses in light of our encounter with Christ (possessions, credentials, attitudes, etc.), so that we might focus on the "gain" of relationship with Christ.

Pressing toward the Goal

12 Not that I have already obtained this or have already reached the goal;[a] but I press on to make it my own, because Christ Jesus has made me his own. 13Beloved,[b] I do not consider that I have made it my own;[c] but this one thing I do: forgetting what lies behind and straining forward to what lies ahead, 14I press on toward the goal for the prize of the heavenly[d] call of God in Christ Jesus. 15Let those of us then who are mature be of the same mind; and if you think differently about anything, this too God will reveal to you. 16Only let us hold fast to what we have attained.

17 Brothers and sisters,[b] join in imitating me, and observe those who live according to the example you have in us. 18For many live as enemies of the cross of Christ; I have often told you of them, and now I tell you even with tears. 19Their end is destruction; their god is the belly; and their glory is in their shame; their minds are set on earthly things. 20But our citizenship[e] is in heaven, and it is from there that we are expecting a Savior, the Lord Jesus Christ. 21He will transform the body of our humiliation[f] that it may be conformed to the body of his glory,[g] by the power that also enables him to make all things subject to himself. 1Therefore, my brothers and sisters,[h] whom I love and long

4

for, my joy and crown, stand firm in the Lord in this way, my beloved.

Exhortations

2 I urge Euodia and I urge Syntyche to be of the same mind in the Lord. 3Yes, and I ask you also, my loyal companion,[i] help these women, for they have struggled beside me in the work of the gospel, together with Clement and the rest of my co-workers, whose names are in the book of life.

4 Rejoice[j] in the Lord always; again I will say, Rejoice.[j] 5Let your gentleness be known to everyone. The Lord is near. 6Do not worry about anything, but in everything by prayer and supplication with thanksgiving let your requests be made known to God. 7And the peace of God, which surpasses all understanding, will guard your hearts and your minds in Christ Jesus.

8 Finally, beloved,[k] whatever is true, whatever is honorable, whatever is just, whatever is pure, whatever is pleasing, whatever is commendable, if there is any excellence and if there is anything worthy of praise, think about[l] these things. 9Keep on doing the

a Or have already been made perfect   b Gk Brothers
c Other ancient authorities read my own yet
d Gk upward   e Or commonwealth   f Or our
humble bodies   g Or his glorious body   h Gk my
brothers   i Or loyal Syzygus   j Or Farewell
k Gk brothers   l Gk take account of

3:12–14 *straining forward . . . I press on.* Although spiritual formation is not a matter of religious performance, neither is it a passive, "couch potato" contentment in God. God, in his grace, has taken hold of us. Our response is to take hold of God in hope. There is a kind of aggressiveness about authentic Christian spirituality. Paul, knowing that his encounter with Christ has brought him only to the doorway of everything that God has for him, communicates this aggressiveness with powerful imagery. He presses on—he intently pursues—making the goal of the Christian life his own. He strains forward to what lies ahead. Spiritual formation involves the aggressive pursuit of complete identification with Christ.

3:13 **SIMPLICITY/FRUGALITY**—*See* Spiritual Disciplines Index.

4:4–6 *Rejoice . . . prayer and supplication.* Paul here encourages the Philippians to take on the disciplines of rejoicing and prayer. This is the third time Paul tells this community to rejoice (2:18; 3:1; see also the Introduction). Their concerns (and ours) are to be addressed not by worrying about them, but by developing habits of prayer and rejoicing.

4:4–13 **CELEBRATION**—*See* Spiritual Disciplines Index.

4:6 **PRAYER**—*See* Spiritual Disciplines Index.

4:8 **MEDITATION**—*See* Spiritual Disciplines Index.

4:8–9 **STUDY**—*See* Spiritual Disciplines Index.

4:8–9 *think about these things. Keep on doing the things.* The spiritual life is a cooperative transformation of thought and action. First, God

things that you have learned and received and heard and seen in me, and the God of peace will be with you.

Acknowledgment of the Philippians' Gift

10 I rejoice*a* in the Lord greatly that now at last you have revived your concern for me; indeed, you were concerned for me, but had no opportunity to show it.*b* 11Not that I am referring to being in need; for I have learned to be content with whatever I have. 12I know what it is to have little, and I know what it is to have plenty. In any and all circumstances I have learned the secret of being well-fed and of going hungry, of having plenty and of being in need. 13I can do all things through him who strengthens me. 14In any case, it was kind of you to share my distress.

15 You Philippians indeed know that in the early days of the gospel, when I left Macedonia, no church shared with me in the matter of giving and receiving, except you alone. 16For even when I was in Thessalonica, you sent me help for my needs more than once. 17Not that I seek the gift, but I seek the profit that accumulates to your account. 18I have been paid in full and have more than enough; I am fully satisfied, now that I have received from Epaphroditus the gifts you sent, a fragrant offering, a sacrifice acceptable and pleasing to God. 19And my God will fully satisfy every need of yours according to his riches in glory in Christ Jesus. 20To our God and Father be glory forever and ever. Amen.

Final Greetings and Benediction

21 Greet every saint in Christ Jesus. The friends*c* who are with me greet you. 22All the saints greet you, especially those of the emperor's household.

23 The grace of the Lord Jesus Christ be with your spirit.*d*

---

a Gk *I rejoiced*   *b* Gk lacks *to show it*
c Gk *brothers*   *d* Other ancient authorities add *Amen*

---

is at work in us, enabling us "both to will and to work for his good pleasure" (2:13). Yet we also have a part to play. As Paul urges, we must choose to *think* of the things of God and choose to *do* the things of God. As we model our thoughts after the highest of standards and model our lives after the life and message of Paul himself, we will find that the "God of peace" himself accompanies us on our transforming journey.

Responding
4:11–13 SIMPLICITY/FRUGALITY. In defining simplicity, Richard Foster writes that it is "an inward reality that results in an outward lifestyle" (*Celebration of Discipline*). According to Paul, what is the inward reality? How close are you to experiencing this in your life? What can you do to encourage it? *See also* Spiritual Disciplines Index.

4:12 *I have learned the secret . . . of having plenty and of being in need.* One of the lessons of spiritual maturity is the secret of living well whatever our means. Paul shares this lesson as he thanks the Philippians for their financial support. Although he is grateful for their generosity, Paul wants the Church to know that in Christ he can be satisfied with any standard of living, even in prison.

THE LETTER OF PAUL TO THE

COLOSSIANS

Paul's Letter to the Colossians deals with several themes that aid us in our practical attempts to know God in order to grow in our relationship with him.

The Word of Truth

Colossians is first of all concerned with "the word of the truth" (Col 1:5), the gospel as it was taught to the Colossians (1:7; 2:7). Some teachers have come into the congregation with new ideas espousing ascetic practices that lead to a special knowledge necessary for the proper worship of God. Paul goes to considerable effort to decry this "philosophy and empty deceit" (2:8). Special observances and pious practices have no merit.

Christ alone is sufficient! He is the true and only mediator, who takes us to the Father. He is the image of the invisible God and the firstborn of creation (1:15). "All things" (a choruslike phrase that repeats throughout the Christ hymn, 1:15–20) have been created through and for him (1:16). "In him all the fullness of God was pleased to dwell" (1:19). And through him God reconciled all things on earth and in heaven (1:20). Thus Colossians rightly gives pride of place to the all-sufficient Lord Christ. He is Lord of all, Lord of the cosmos. In this way, Colossians has the "highest" doctrine concerning Jesus Christ in the New Testament.

The idea of an ultimate truth is a difficult concept today, because many assert the legitimacy of a diversity of approaches to knowing God. Furthermore, what we can claim to know is lodged primarily in personal experience. The teaching of Colossians, then, comes as an alien word into such a worldview.

The word of truth is made specific in three ways. First, Paul insists that Christ is all-sufficient for knowledge of God and our relationship to him. Nothing and no one else is required. Second, what has separated us from God, the debt of our trespasses, has been paid off in full, nailed to the cross (2:14). Third, any alien powers—

See also "The With-God Life" essay for this section of the Bible,
"The People of God in Community," pp. 2037–42.

spiritual forces at war with God—have been disarmed and their shame paraded in public (2:15). In Christ, and in Christ alone, is the fullness of salvation. Believers can thus be presented to God as holy, blameless, and free from accusation (1:22).

A Universal Faith

At the beginning of the letter, and throughout, Paul makes reference to the universal aspect of faith in Christ. The word of truth is bearing fruit and growing in the whole world (1:6). It has been proclaimed to every creature under heaven (1:23). The goal is to "present everyone mature in Christ" (1:28). Because believers are in relationship with Jesus Christ, their fullness or perfection is the goal of Paul's teaching and preaching. And people of nations far away—even barbarians and Scythians—are included (3:11).

Faith in God and true knowledge of God through Christ have broken the boundaries of racial, national, and religious exclusivism. The gospel is for everybody! It is not the preserve of a few. Christianity is an international religion, not simply the "official" religion of the West. It comes to faithful expression in every language under heaven. It has many cultural expressions, as it has become embedded in every nation and people.

Believers today worship and pray and serve in company with a vast array of people. No one worships, prays, or serves alone. Christians are a worldwide community of believers who transcend historical boundaries as the communion of saints. When we sit in a quiet place to pray and reflect upon the Scriptures (Matt 6:6), we do so participating in a wonderful spiritual dialectic: at once alone, yet joined to the great throng of the faithful across the world and throughout history.

Filled with Knowledge of God's Will

Wrong knowledge of God—getting God "wrong," being "hostile in mind" (Col 1:21)—leads to broken and misshapen lives. This is a major theme in the letter. So often today an antitheological bent is allowed to take over our spirituality. It is enough apparently to feel or experience something that we take to be the presence of God. The author of Colossians is wiser. He understands that theology—knowledge of God—and experience belong together, for without a true knowledge of God our piety will go astray. We will have no basis for interpreting our piety and our spiritual experience. We will be in danger of being taken captive by plausible arguments (2:4) that will lead us into error. Thus Paul insists that we are to grow "in the knowledge of God" (1:10). In this sense, every Christian is a theologian.

This knowledge, of course, is of a mystery (1:26–27; 2:2). It has been hidden throughout the ages, but is now revealed. This mystery is also understood to be the life of Christ within believers. Thus this is not a generalized mystery or a vague sense of the numinous. It is Christ himself, who is the treasure of wisdom and knowledge. It is a truth not reducible to our categories of thought. And even though we see as in a mirror dimly (1 Cor 13:12), nonetheless we do actually see something of the truth, enough for knowing the love and salvation of God.

Living in Christ

Colossians teaches that we must be rooted and grounded in Christ (Col 2:7). Only in that way will we come to the fullness of our relationship with God and service to him. Col 2:6–7 offers a pithy summary of the Christian life. These verses immediately recall Ps 1:1–3, in which the exiles in Babylon have placed before them the two ways, scoffing at God or being rooted in the soil of the word of God. Those who chose the latter are like trees blooming in the desert, full of a fruitfulness that does not decline (see Jer 17:8).

Likewise, Christians are to be rooted and built up in the Word, who is Christ. "In Christ" is one of Paul's favorite designations for being Christian (some form of this is used 164 times in the Pauline and deutero-Pauline Letters), implying an intimate relationship with the Lord. Rooted and grounded in Christ, Christians are a maturing people (Col 1:28) who grow into the fullness of being pleasing to the Lord (1:10). This growth is guided by faithfulness to the teaching of the apostles, which acts like a trellis guiding the growth of a fragile flower. Christians' growth is protected and nurtured by the apostolic teaching that has been given to them.

The result is spectacular! They abound in thanksgiving (2:7). Often the Christian life has been cast in terms of guilt and duty. This leads to joyless and gloomy faith and vocation stripped of energy. Colossians holds out a different prospect. The driving energy force behind the Christian life is gratitude or thanksgiving. Grace and gratitude make up the rhythm of Christian identity and practice. "To abound" (in the Greek text) means "to overflow." The Christian's response is not a trickle, but a gushing forth of joyous gratitude.

Rejoicing in Suffering

The Pauline tradition makes much of the apostle's suffering and weakness, on the one hand, and even more of God's or Christ's strength, on the other. The gospel is not about Paul, but about Jesus Christ. Paul, a servant of the gospel (1:23), labors tirelessly for the spreading of the word of God (1:29). Serving his Lord, he shares also in his Lord's burden. In effect, he shares in his Lord's cross. In general, we might say that through the selfless sacrifice of believers, the reality and power of the cross of Christ extend through history in a real way.

Paul rejoices in his suffering (1:24). There is something counterintuitive about this. What Paul means is that in his suffering as a result of his ministry he has entered more fully into communion with the Lord of the cross. He shares in the life and death of Christ, and thus also in his resurrection. This, for Paul, is living out of his baptism, a theme that is just below the surface throughout Colossians.

Christians live between the times; the kingdom is announced, yet not fully present. They also live between the cross and the resurrection. Death is defeated, yet that defeat is still to be fully present. They will rise again, but at the end of the age when Christ comes again. In this present age, in union with Christ, Christians pick up their crosses daily, sharing thereby in Christ's ministry, but in joyful obedience and hopeful expectation of the fullness of Christ's redemption. It is in this context that we may rejoice in suffering.

It is important to note that Paul rejoices in his suffering for the sake of the Colossians. This is not a masochistic delight in self-degradation. It is suffering that comes from ministry, from Paul's conviction that his commission is "to make the word of God fully known" (1:25).

Clothed in Love

Knowing God rightly in, through, and as Jesus Christ, believers can confidently "seek the things that are above" (3:1). Knowing the good news of salvation (indicative mode), believers are to live a life clothed with love (imperative mode; 3:14). The command follows the proclamation of the good news as a consequence and never as a condition. This order is not reversible. Reverse it, and the gospel is turned into a new law.

—Andrew Purves

Salutation

1 Paul, an apostle of Christ Jesus by the will of God, and Timothy our brother,

2 To the saints and faithful brothers and sisters*a* in Christ in Colossae:

Grace to you and peace from God our Father.

Paul Thanks God for the Colossians

3 In our prayers for you we always thank God, the Father of our Lord Jesus Christ, 4for we have heard of your faith in Christ Jesus and of the love that you have for all the saints, 5because of the hope laid up for you in heaven. You have heard of this hope before in the word of the truth, the gospel 6that has come to you. Just as it is bearing fruit and growing in the whole world, so it has been bearing fruit among yourselves from the day you heard it and truly comprehended the grace of God. 7This you learned from Epaphras, our beloved fellow servant.*b* He is a faithful minister of Christ on your*c* behalf, 8and he has made known to us your love in the Spirit.

9 For this reason, since the day we heard it, we have not ceased praying for you and asking that you may be filled with the knowledge of God's*d* will in all spiritual wisdom and understanding, 10so that you may lead lives wor-

a Gk *brothers*   *b* Gk *slave*   *c* Other ancient authorities read *our*   *d* Gk *his*

1:3 *we always thank God.* Too often Christian life is thought of as being energized by guilt and duty. When that is the case, so easily we become exhausted and dispirited. Grounding our lives in thankfulness for what God has given to us comes as surprising good news. In 2:7, thankfulness is to abound. This is the energy source for discipleship. Everything in the practice of the faith begins here.

1:5 *the word of the truth.* Over and against false teaching (2:8–23), the word of the gospel that Paul teaches is the truth. This is an objective and personal reality. This Word is Jesus Christ. This word is the gospel, good news to live by. Paul spends much of the letter developing this theme.

1:9 *filled with the knowledge of God's will.* The truth of faith is not "library" knowledge, a kind of abstract and impractical knowing. Knowledge of God is not neutral knowledge. Rather, it is knowledge of the God who acts purposely in history to bring people to live lives fully pleasing to God through the person and ministry of Jesus Christ. Christians are expected to grow in this knowledge and conform their lives to it. In this way it is the anchor and source of the kind of living that God empowers within and among us.

thy of the Lord, fully pleasing to him, as you bear fruit in every good work and as you grow in the knowledge of God. [11] May you be made strong with all the strength that comes from his glorious power, and may you be prepared to endure everything with patience, while joyfully [12] giving thanks to the Father, who has enabled[a] you[b] to share in the inheritance of the saints in the light. [13] He has rescued us from the power of darkness and transferred us into the kingdom of his beloved Son, [14] in whom we have redemption, the forgiveness of sins.[c]

The Supremacy of Christ

[15] He is the image of the invisible God, the firstborn of all creation; [16] for in[d] him all things in heaven and on earth were created, things visible and invisible, whether thrones or dominions or rulers or powers—all things have been created through him and for him. [17] He himself is before all things, and in[d] him all things hold together. [18] He is the head of the body, the church; he is the beginning, the firstborn from the dead, so that he might come to have first place in everything. [19] For in him all the fullness of God was pleased to dwell, [20] and through him God was pleased to reconcile to himself all things, whether on earth or in heaven, by making peace through the blood of his cross.

[21] And you who were once estranged and hostile in mind, doing evil deeds, [22] he has now reconciled[e] in his fleshly body[f] through death, so as to present you holy and blameless and irreproachable before him— [23] provided that you continue securely established and steadfast in the faith, without shifting from the hope promised by the gospel that you heard, which has been proclaimed to every creature under heaven. I, Paul, became a servant of this gospel.

Paul's Interest in the Colossians

[24] I am now rejoicing in my sufferings for your sake, and in my flesh I am completing what is lacking in Christ's afflictions for the sake of his body, that is, the church. [25] I became its servant according to God's commission that was given to me for you, to make the word of God fully known, [26] the mystery that has been hidden throughout the ages and generations but has now been revealed to his saints. [27] To them God chose to make known how great among the Gentiles are the riches of the glory of this mystery, which is Christ in you, the hope of glory. [28] It is he whom we proclaim, warning everyone and teaching everyone in all wis-

a Other ancient authorities read *called*   *b* Other ancient authorities read *us*   *c* Other ancient authorities add *through his blood*   *d* Or *by*   *e* Other ancient authorities read *you have now been reconciled*   *f* Gk *in the body of his flesh*

1:13 *He has rescued us from the power of darkness.* This is strong language! It is also challengingly countercultural, for it is assumed today by many that we really are good people. The fact is, however, that humanity in its "natural" state lives in separation from God manifested by incessant self-centeredness. Colossians refers to an estrangement and a hostility of mind (1:21). This is deadly—it is thralldom to the power of darkness. God, however, has dealt with this through the person and work of Jesus Christ. He erased the record that stood against us, nailing it to the cross, and disarmed the powers that would hold us captive (2:14–15). Christianity is a religion of liberation, of salvation. As the letter progresses, we find that knowing this freedom is also to live in this freedom.

1:15–20 *He is.* Christ is Lord over all creation and is the reconciler between God and this creation. This great hymn of acclamation expresses this central truth of Christian faith. Our lives are built upon it, shaped in every way by it, so that now through Christ's reconciliation we may be given back to God as persons who are holy, blameless, and irreproachable. This describes the transformation at the heart of Christian faith. Once we were hostile toward God and acting wrongly. Now, through Christ's death, we are a new people, acting rightly. Thus, we are to remain steadfast in this new reality of life and not shift from the hope that it promises.

1:23 SERVICE—*See* Spiritual Disciplines Index.

dom, so that we may present everyone mature in Christ. [29]For this I toil and struggle with all the energy that he powerfully inspires within me.

2 For I want you to know how much I am struggling for you, and for those in Laodicea, and for all who have not seen me face to face. [2]I want their hearts to be encouraged and united in love, so that they may have all the riches of assured understanding and have the knowledge of God's mystery, that is, Christ himself,[a] [3]in whom are hidden all the treasures of wisdom and knowledge. [4]I am saying this so that no one may deceive you with plausible arguments. [5]For though I am absent in body, yet I am with you in spirit, and I rejoice to see your morale and the firmness of your faith in Christ.

Fullness of Life in Christ

6 As you therefore have received Christ Jesus the Lord, continue to live your lives[b] in him, [7]rooted and built up in him and established in the faith, just as you were taught, abounding in thanksgiving.

8 See to it that no one takes you captive through philosophy and empty deceit, according to human tradition, according to the elemental spirits of the universe,[c] and not according to Christ. [9]For in him the whole fullness of deity dwells bodily, [10]and you have come to fullness in him, who is the head of every ruler and authority. [11]In him also you were circumcised with a spiritual circumcision,[d] by putting off the body of the flesh in the circumcision of Christ; [12]when you were buried with him in baptism, you were also raised with him through faith in the power of God, who raised him from the dead. [13]And when you were dead in trespasses and the uncircumcision of your flesh, God[e] made you[f] alive together with him, when he forgave us all our trespasses, [14]erasing the record that stood against us with its legal demands. He set this aside, nailing it to the cross. [15]He disarmed[g] the rulers and authorities and made a public example of them, triumphing over them in it.

16 Therefore do not let anyone condemn you in matters of food and drink or of observing festivals, new moons, or sabbaths. [17]These are only a shadow of what is to come, but the substance belongs to Christ. [18]Do not let anyone disqualify you, insisting on self-abasement and worship of angels, dwelling[h] on visions,[i] puffed up without cause by a human way of thinking,[j] [19]and not holding fast to the head, from whom the whole body, nourished and held together by its ligaments and sinews, grows with a growth that is from God.

a Other ancient authorities read *of the mystery of God, both of the Father and of Christ*   b Gk *to walk*   c Or *the rudiments of the world*   d Gk *a circumcision made without hands*   e Gk *he*   f Other ancient authorities read *made us*; others, *made*   g Or *divested himself of*   h Other ancient authorities read *not dwelling*   i Meaning of Gk uncertain   j Gk *by the mind of his flesh*

2:2 *I want their hearts to be encouraged and united in love.* This is Paul's pastoral goal, but it is not merely a wish for good feelings. What encourages and unites us in love is a relationship with Jesus Christ. Outside of Christ, we remain in darkness.

2:8 *See to it that no one takes you captive through philosophy.* This verse introduces the main purpose for the letter, and a controversial subject, namely, Paul's insistence on the singular nature of truth. Christ alone is adequate for knowledge of God and salvation. There is no need for special experiences, disciplines, or teachings that augment the gospel he taught. The remainder of chapter 2 deals with the nature of the false teaching and insists on the need to rely only on the all-sufficiency of Christ. The religious world today is suffused with claims of special teachings and practices necessary for a full experience of salvation, from Mormonism to New Age spirituality. Add to this the common assumptions that God has many names and that many paths lead to the one Divinity, and the singularity and all-sufficiency of Jesus Christ becomes a matter of serious, even acrimonious, debate. Remember, says Paul, you have died with Christ, so pay no attention to these other teachings. This is the teaching also of Heb 12:1–2—run the race of faith looking to Jesus.

Warnings against False Teachers

20 If with Christ you died to the elemental spirits of the universe, *a* why do you live as if you still belonged to the world? Why do you submit to regulations, 21"Do not handle, Do not taste, Do not touch"? 22All these regulations refer to things that perish with use; they are simply human commands and teachings. 23These have indeed an appearance of wisdom in promoting self-imposed piety, humility, and severe treatment of the body, but they are of no value in checking self-indulgence. *b*

The New Life in Christ

3 So if you have been raised with Christ, seek the things that are above, where Christ is, seated at the right hand of God. 2Set your minds on things that are above, not on things that are on earth, 3for you have died, and your life is hidden with Christ in God. 4When Christ who is your *c* life is revealed, then you also will be revealed with him in glory.

5 Put to death, therefore, whatever in you is earthly: fornication, impurity, passion, evil desire, and greed (which is idolatry). 6On account of these the wrath of God is coming on those who are disobedient. *d* 7These are the ways you also once followed, when you were living that life. *e* 8But now you must get rid of all such things—anger, wrath, malice, slander, and abusive *f* language from your mouth. 9Do not lie to one another, seeing that you

have stripped off the old self with its practices 10and have clothed yourselves with the new self, which is being renewed in knowledge according to the image of its creator. 11In that renewal *g* there is no longer Greek and Jew, circumcised and uncircumcised, barbarian, Scythian, slave and free; but Christ is all and in all!

12 As God's chosen ones, holy and beloved, clothe yourselves with compassion, kindness, humility, meekness, and patience. 13Bear with one another and, if anyone has a complaint against another, forgive each other; just as the Lord *h* has forgiven you, so you also must forgive. 14Above all, clothe yourselves with love, which binds everything together in perfect harmony. 15And let the peace of Christ rule in your hearts, to which indeed you were called in the one body. And be thankful. 16Let the word of Christ *i* dwell in you richly; teach and admonish one another in all wisdom; and with gratitude in your hearts sing psalms, hymns, and spiritual songs to God. *j* 17And whatever you do, in word or deed, do everything in the name of

a Or *the rudiments of the world*   *b* Or *are of no value, serving only to indulge the flesh*   *c* Other authorities read *our*   *d* Other ancient authorities lack *on those who are disobedient* (Gk *the children of disobedience*)   *e* Or *living among such people*   *f* Or *filthy*   *g* Gk *its creator,* 11*where*   *h* Other ancient authorities read *just as Christ*   *i* Other ancient authorities read *of God,* or *of the Lord*   *j* Other ancient authorities read *to the Lord*

2:20–23 SIMPLICITY/FRUGALITY—*See* Spiritual Disciplines Index.

3:1–17 *seek the things that are above.* Paul's response to false teaching is not only to lecture on true and false doctrine. The truth of life in Christ must be lived out in the routines and rhythms of life. He is concerned with truth in actions as well as in teaching. To confess Jesus Christ means a way of living. Here begins the move from the indicative to the imperative, from the content of the gospel proclaimed to the demands of living the Christian life. Paul lists two five-topic sets of vices. The first largely has to do with sexual sins (v 5); the second with vices of speech (vv 8–9). Then, Paul follows with one five-topic list of virtues (v 12). There is an

expected way to live that bears witness to the truth of the gospel within a person.

3:1–2 SIMPLICITY/FRUGALITY—*See* Spiritual Disciplines Index.

3:1–4 THE WITH-GOD LIFE—*See* Spiritual Disciplines Index.

Responding
3:2 MEDITATION. What are "things that are above"? Try to make a list. How can meditating on them bring us more fully into a life with God? Attempt to set aside an hour this week to meditate on "things that are above." *See also* Spiritual Disciplines Index.

3:8–17 FELLOWSHIP—*See* Spiritual Disciplines Index.

the Lord Jesus, giving thanks to God the Father through him.

Rules for Christian Households

18 Wives, be subject to your husbands, as is fitting in the Lord. [19]Husbands, love your wives and never treat them harshly.

20 Children, obey your parents in everything, for this is your acceptable duty in the Lord. [21]Fathers, do not provoke your children, or they may lose heart. [22]Slaves, obey your earthly masters[a] in everything, not only while being watched and in order to please them, but wholeheartedly, fearing the Lord.[a] [23]Whatever your task, put yourselves into it, as done for the Lord and not for your masters,[b] [24]since you know that from the Lord you will receive the inheritance as your reward; you serve[c] the Lord Christ. [25]For the wrongdoer will be paid back for whatever wrong has been done, and there is no partiality. 4 [1]Masters, treat your slaves justly and fairly, for you know that you also have a Master in heaven.

Further Instructions

2 Devote yourselves to prayer, keeping alert in it with thanksgiving. [3]At the same time pray for us as well that God will open to us a door for the word, that we may declare the mystery of Christ, for which I am in prison, [4]so that I may reveal it clearly, as I should.

5 Conduct yourselves wisely toward outsiders, making the most of the time.[d] [6]Let your speech always be gracious, seasoned with salt, so that you may know how you ought to answer everyone.

Final Greetings and Benediction

7 Tychicus will tell you all the news about me; he is a beloved brother, a faithful minister, and a fellow servant[e] in the Lord. [8]I have sent him to you for this very purpose, so that you may know how we are[f] and that he may encourage your hearts; [9]he is coming with Onesimus, the faithful and beloved brother, who is one of you. They will tell you about everything here.

10 Aristarchus my fellow prisoner greets you, as does Mark the cousin of Barnabas, concerning whom you have received instructions—if he comes to you, welcome him. [11]And Jesus who is called Justus greets you.

a In Greek the same word is used for *master* and *Lord*   b Gk *not for men*   c Or *you are slaves of,* or *be slaves of*   d Or *opportunity*   e Gk *slave*   f Other authorities read *that I may know how you are*

3:18–4:1 *Wives, be subject to your husbands.* The ethical portion of the letter contains the so-called household code, rules for Christian households concerning husbands and wives, fathers and children, and masters and slaves. This is very controversial today mainly because of the implied patriarchy and the assumption of legitimacy given to slavery. Concern to find in the text an especially Christian significance remains difficult, although its enduring emphasis on the reciprocity of relationship illustrates that relationships always have the components of mutual commitment and mutual responsibility. However, the ethic of life together is not to be dismissed. Family and personal relations are not neutral, but must reflect the gospel ethic of love and forbearance. What does it mean for us today, for husbands and wives, for parents and children, for employer and employee, and so on, that the word of Christ must dwell in us richly (3:16)? What does being God's chosen ones (3:12) mean for economic and political responsibility? With just a little imagination these core ethical demands, written in their context two thousand years ago, burst from the page with surprising and perhaps disturbing relevance.

3:18–24 SUBMISSION—*See* Spiritual Disciplines Index.

3:24 SERVICE—*See* Spiritual Disciplines Index.

4:2 PRAYER—*See* Spiritual Disciplines Index.

4:2 *Devote yourselves to prayer.* The ethical section ends with an *inclusio*, a kind of bookend. The letter began with giving thanks; it ends with the encouragement to be devoted to prayer, keeping alert in it by giving thanks. This is a timely reminder that we must pay attention to those things that keep us focused on God. Prayer is not an elective in the Christian's life, but functions to keep us before God in a disciplined and attentive way.

These are the only ones of the circumcision among my co-workers for the kingdom of God, and they have been a comfort to me. [12]Epaphras, who is one of you, a servant[a] of Christ Jesus, greets you. He is always wrestling in his prayers on your behalf, so that you may stand mature and fully assured in everything that God wills. [13]For I testify for him that he has worked hard for you and for those in Laodicea and in Hierapolis. [14]Luke, the beloved physician, and Demas greet you. [15]Give my greetings to the brothers and sisters[b] in Laodicea, and to Nympha and the church in her house. [16]And when this letter has been read among you, have it read also in the church of the Laodiceans; and see that you read also the letter from Laodicea. [17]And say to Archippus, "See that you complete the task that you have received in the Lord."

18 I, Paul, write this greeting with my own hand. Remember my chains. Grace be with you.[c]

a Gk *slave*   *b* Gk *brothers*   *c* Other ancient authorities add *Amen*

Responding
4:12 PRAYER. Although it may not be so obvious how intercessory prayer changes the person being prayed for, how does it change the person engaging in prayer? As you are able, pray for one person or situation for an entire month. How did this experiment change you? *See also* Spiritual Disciplines Index.

THE FIRST LETTER OF PAUL TO THE

THESSALONIANS

The year is AD 51, and a man named Paul and his friends Silas, Luke, and Timothy have arrived in Corinth. Paul decides to write a letter to a group of young Christians in Thessalonica, the capital city of the Roman province of Macedonia.

The two brief letters he then wrote have been preserved, and we are able to read them almost two millennia later. What Paul has to say is still fresh and challenging, because the problems that were the concerns of the Thessalonian Christians are still active issues today. But more important than the issues, it is the faith of Paul that is as relevant now as it was in the first century. What Paul believed continues to be as startling and as good when we meet it in the twenty-first century as it was in the first century, in the world of Claudius, Seneca, Gallio, and the rapidly growing bands of Christians that were scattered throughout the cities of the Roman Empire.

These letters are teaching letters written from a teacher-pastor to an urban congregation of Christians. They are also personal letters written from a friend to friends. The letters are warm and human, clear-headed and salty.

The Christians in Thessalonica, to whom the letters are addressed, lived in an old city. In its earliest years it was called Therma. Its location was strategic, on the Via Egnatia, the major overland route from Italy to the East, and at the northeast corner of the Thermaic Gulf (the Gulf of Salonika). In 315 BC the city was renamed Thessalonica in honor of the half sister of Alexander the Great. In the year 146 BC, after the Roman takeover of ancient Greece, this city was made capital of the Roman province of Macedonia. In 42 BC the city was further honored by being recognized by Rome as a "free city," a status allowing more self-rule. In Rome's attempt to win Greek support, several cities of ancient Greece held this distinction (e.g., Athens and Sparta).

See also "The With-God Life" essay for this section of the Bible,
"The People of God in Community," pp. 2037–42.

Paul's Ministry in Thessalonica

Luke gives a brief but very interesting narrative of the establishment of the Christian church in Thessalonica in the book of Acts. He tells us that following Paul and Silas's imprisonment and release at Philippi (Acts 16:16–40), they left for Thessalonica: "After Paul and Silas had passed through Amphipolis and Apollonia, they came to Thessalonica, where there was a synagogue of the Jews" (17:1).

Luke tells us that Paul's practice was to attend the local synagogue and share his faith in Jesus Christ as Messiah from within that setting: "And Paul went in, as was his custom, and on three sabbath days argued with them from the scriptures, explaining and proving that it was necessary for the Messiah to suffer and to rise from the dead, and saying, 'This is the Messiah, Jesus whom I am proclaiming to you,'" (17:2–3). Paul's message, according to Luke, is that the Messiah must suffer and that this suffering Messiah is in fact Jesus.

Paul has surprising good news to announce: the Messiah has conquered evil and death by taking upon himself the fury of evil and the suffering and loneliness of death. Jesus disarms these foes by absorbing their full intensity. Not only does the Messiah suffer real brokenness, but he conquers death with the real victory of resurrection. As for the enemies of righteousness, the Messiah identifies with their loneliness too and takes their place as well. This is Paul's message to the people in Thessalonica.

Luke tells of their mixed response: "Some of them were persuaded and joined Paul and Silas, as did a great many of the devout Greeks and not a few of the leading women. But the Jews became jealous, and with the help of some ruffians in the marketplaces they formed a mob" (17:4–5). Of those who responded to Paul's message, including both Jews and Gentiles, Luke makes a special point of mentioning the fact that some of the city's prominent women accepted the message of Paul and Silas. Women played a vital role in the New Testament Church, and this reference is one specific marker of that fact.

Those who opposed Paul's message "set the city in an uproar. While they were searching for Paul and Silas to bring them out to the assembly, they attacked Jason's house. When they could not find them, they dragged Jason and some believers before the city authorities" (17: 5–6). Luke also tells us of the charges made against Paul and Silas and the new church at Thessalonica. Note the unintentional but unmistakable compliment paid to the early Christians and to their Lord: " 'These people who have been turning the world upside down have come here also, and Jason has entertained them as guests. They are all acting contrary to the decrees of the emperor, saying that there is another king named Jesus' " (17:6–7).

Continuing Relevance

It is likely that the First Letter of Paul to the Thessalonians is the earliest letter of the New Testament. This means that, for us as readers of the New Testament, we find in 1 Thessalonians what was first on the mind of Paul and what troubling issues first confronted the early Church.

Three issues become clear. One concerns the timing of the return of Jesus Christ in fulfillment of his promise following his victory over death. The second issue has to do with the ethical behavior of Christians, especially in regard to marriage. The third concerns the role of Christians in the world today. Three issues of critical concern then—and now. What is our task as disciples of Jesus Christ here and now? As we read its pages and watch the book unfold, Paul will clear the air for us today just as he did for his first-century friends.

—*Earl F. Palmer*

Salutation

1 Paul, Silvanus, and Timothy,
To the church of the Thessalonians in God the Father and the Lord Jesus Christ:
Grace to you and peace.

The Thessalonians' Faith and Example

2 We always give thanks to God for all of you and mention you in our prayers, constantly [3]remembering before our God and Father your work of faith and labor of love and steadfastness of hope in our Lord Jesus Christ. [4]For we know, brothers and sisters[a] beloved by God, that he has chosen you, [5]because our message of the gospel came to you not in word only, but also in power and in the Holy Spirit and with full conviction; just as you know what kind of persons we proved to be among you for your sake. [6]And you became imitators of us and of the Lord, for in spite of persecution you received the word with joy inspired by the Holy Spirit, [7]so that you became an example to all the believers in Macedonia and in Achaia. [8]For the word of the Lord has sounded forth from you not only in Macedonia and Achaia, but in every place your faith in God has become known, so that we have no need to speak about it. [9]For the people of those regions[b] report about us what kind of welcome we had among you, and how you turned to God from idols, to serve a living and true God, [10]and to wait for his Son from heaven, whom he raised from the dead—Jesus, who rescues us from the wrath that is coming.

Paul's Ministry in Thessalonica

2 You yourselves know, brothers and sisters,[a] that our coming to you was not in vain, [2]but though we had already suffered and been shamefully mistreated at Philippi, as you know, we had courage in our God to declare to you the gospel of God in spite of great opposition. [3]For our appeal does not spring from deceit or impure motives or trickery, [4]but just as we have been approved by

a Gk *brothers*   *b* Gk *For they*

1:2–3 *We always give thanks.* Paul begins his letter with a prayer for his friends. He prays that their faith will have "work" in it; he means faith as an event that happens. He prays for love in their lives that toils. He prays for hope that stays and holds out and endures. All of this prayer is possible because of God's love, which made us his own before we loved or hoped or believed. This is the theme of grace that dominates the opening of the letter.

Responding
1:5 THE WITH-GOD LIFE. In addition to his teaching, Paul names three ways the gospel came to the Thessalonians: through power, the Holy Spirit, and conviction. Recall when you became convinced of the truth of the gospel, that is, that Jesus was born, lived, died, rose from the dead, and lives among his people today through the presence of his Spirit to guide and teach them. As a way to reinforce this teaching, read and memorize Rom 8:9–11, a wonderful passage that describes the Holy Spirit's relationship with the People of God. *See also* Spiritual Disciplines Index.

1:6 *And you became imitators of us and of the Lord.* Imitation is how human beings learn and grow. Everything depends on whom or what we choose to imitate. The disciples at Thessalonica had it exactly right: they imitated Paul and his company and the Lord.
1:9–10 *you turned to God.* It is because of God's truth and grace that people such as the Thessalonians have turned away from the idols, because the better hope met them in God's truth.

God to be entrusted with the message of the gospel, even so we speak, not to please mortals, but to please God who tests our hearts. [5] As you know and as God is our witness, we never came with words of flattery or with a pretext for greed; [6] nor did we seek praise from mortals, whether from you or from others, [7] though we might have made demands as apostles of Christ. But we were gentle[a] among you, like a nurse tenderly caring for her own children. [8] So deeply do we care for you that we are determined to share with you not only the gospel of God but also our own selves, because you have become very dear to us.

[9] You remember our labor and toil, brothers and sisters;[b] we worked night and day, so that we might not burden any of you while we proclaimed to you the gospel of God. [10] You are witnesses, and God also, how pure, upright, and blameless our conduct was toward you believers. [11] As you know, we dealt with each one of you like a father with his children, [12] urging and encouraging you and pleading that you lead a life worthy of God, who calls you into his own kingdom and glory.

[13] We also constantly give thanks to God for this, that when you received the word of God that you heard from us, you accepted it not as a human word but as what it really is, God's word, which is also at work in you believers. [14] For you, brothers and sisters,[b] became imitators of the churches of God in Christ Jesus that are in Judea, for you suffered the same things from your own compatriots as they did from the Jews, [15] who killed both the Lord Jesus and the prophets,[c] and drove us out; they displease God and oppose everyone [16] by hindering us from speaking to the Gentiles so that they may be saved. Thus they have constantly been filling up the measure of their sins; but God's wrath has overtaken them at last.[d]

Paul's Desire to Visit the Thessalonians Again

[17] As for us, brothers and sisters,[b] when, for a short time, we were made orphans by being separated from you—in person, not in heart—we longed with great eagerness to see you face to face. [18] For we wanted to come to you—certainly I, Paul, wanted to again and again—but Satan blocked our way. [19] For what is our hope or joy or crown of boasting before our Lord Jesus at his coming? Is it not you? [20] Yes, you are our glory and joy!

3 Therefore when we could bear it no longer, we decided to be left alone in Athens; [2] and we sent Timothy, our brother and co-worker for God in proclaiming[e] the gospel of Christ, to strengthen and encourage you for the sake of your faith, [3] so that no one would be shaken by these persecutions. Indeed, you yourselves know that this is what we are destined for. [4] In fact, when we were with you, we told you beforehand that we were to suffer persecution; so it turned out, as you know. [5] For this reason, when I could bear it no longer, I sent to find out about your faith; I was afraid that somehow the tempter had tempted you and that our labor had been in vain.

Timothy's Encouraging Report

[6] But Timothy has just now come to us from you, and has brought us the good news of your faith and love. He has told us also that you always remember us kindly and long to see us—just as we long to see you. [7] For this reason, brothers and sisters,[b] during all our distress and persecution we have been encouraged about you through your faith. [8] For we now live, if you continue to stand firm in

a Other ancient authorities read *infants*
b Gk *brothers*   c Other ancient authorities read *their own prophets*   d Or *completely* or *forever*
e Gk lacks *proclaiming*

2:1–20 *share with you not only the gospel of God but also our own selves.* In chapter 2 Paul affirms his own relationship as teacher and friend with the young Christians at Thessalonica. This demonstrates the pastoral task of spiritual formation in all its tenderness. Paul even uses the image of a nurse caring for helpless infants (v 7).

2:14 *you . . . became imitators of the churches of God . . . in Judea.* The circle of imitation now expands to others. Imitation is a humble action, and children, for example, are always eager to do it.

the Lord. [9]How can we thank God enough for you in return for all the joy that we feel before our God because of you? [10]Night and day we pray most earnestly that we may see you face to face and restore whatever is lacking in your faith.

[11] Now may our God and Father himself and our Lord Jesus direct our way to you. [12]And may the Lord make you increase and abound in love for one another and for all, just as we abound in love for you. [13]And may he so strengthen your hearts in holiness that you may be blameless before our God and Father at the coming of our Lord Jesus with all his saints.

A Life Pleasing to God

4 Finally, brothers and sisters,[a] we ask and urge you in the Lord Jesus that, as you learned from us how you ought to live and to please God (as, in fact, you are doing), you should do so more and more. [2]For you know what instructions we gave you through the Lord Jesus. [3]For this is the will of God, your sanctification: that you abstain from fornication; [4]that each one of you know how to control your own body[b] in holiness and honor, [5]not with lustful passion, like the Gentiles who do not know God; [6]that no one wrong or exploit a brother or sister[c] in this matter, because the Lord is an avenger in all these things, just as we have already told you beforehand and solemnly warned you. [7]For

God did not call us to impurity but in holiness. [8]Therefore whoever rejects this rejects not human authority but God, who also gives his Holy Spirit to you.

[9] Now concerning love of the brothers and sisters,[a] you do not need to have anyone write to you, for you yourselves have been taught by God to love one another; [10]and indeed you do love all the brothers and sisters[a] throughout Macedonia. But we urge you, beloved,[a] to do so more and more, [11]to aspire to live quietly, to mind your own affairs, and to work with your hands, as we directed you, [12]so that you may behave properly toward outsiders and be dependent on no one.

The Coming of the Lord

[13] But we do not want you to be uninformed, brothers and sisters,[a] about those who have died,[d] so that you may not grieve as others do who have no hope. [14]For since we believe that Jesus died and rose again, even so, through Jesus, God will bring with him those who have died.[d] [15]For this we declare to you by the word of the Lord, that we who are alive, who are left until the coming of the Lord, will by no means precede those who have died.[d] [16]For the Lord himself, with a cry of command, with the archangel's call and with the sound of God's trumpet, will de-

a Gk brothers   b Or how to take a wife for himself
c Gk brother   d Gk fallen asleep

3:12 *increase and abound in love for one another.* Paul urges the Thessalonians to live here and now as men and women and as married folk in a way that honors God because Jesus Christ has given them his grace.

4:1–18 *Finally, brothers and sisters.* In chapter 4, Paul urges the Christians to live in marriage with tenderness and honor. The health of marriages is a major pastoral concern for Paul. For us too.

4:3 *For this is the will of God, your sanctification.* Sanctification, that is, our growth in grace, is here directly applied to sexual purity, and specifically to the problem of fornication— sexual intercourse between people who are not married to each other. And we thought times had changed!

Responding
4:11 STUDY. The King James Version translates the beginning of this verse "study to be quiet," while the NRSV translates it "aspire to live quietly." What qualities are needed to "study to be quiet"? During the next three weeks do things that will encourage these qualities in your life: driving the speed limit, perhaps, or visiting with your neighbors, or reading a book to your spouse, child, or friend. *See also* Spiritual Disciplines Index.

4:13–18 *But we do not want you to be uninformed.* The apostle assures believers of the hope they have as those who belong to Christ. Paul faces up to false teachers who are arguing that select, and therefore superior, believers

scend from heaven, and the dead in Christ will rise first. [17]Then we who are alive, who are left, will be caught up in the clouds together with them to meet the Lord in the air; and so we will be with the Lord forever. [18]Therefore encourage one another with these words.

5 Now concerning the times and the seasons, brothers and sisters,[a] you do not need to have anything written to you. [2]For you yourselves know very well that the day of the Lord will come like a thief in the night. [3]When they say, "There is peace and security," then sudden destruction will come upon them, as labor pains come upon a pregnant woman, and there will be no escape! [4]But you, beloved,[a] are not in darkness, for that day to surprise you like a thief; [5]for you are all children of light and children of the day; we are not of the night or of darkness. [6]So then let us not fall asleep as others do, but let us keep awake and be sober; [7]for those who sleep sleep at night, and those who are drunk get drunk at night. [8]But since we belong to the day, let us be sober, and put on the breastplate of faith and love, and for a helmet the hope of salvation. [9]For God has destined us not for wrath but for obtaining salvation through our Lord Jesus Christ, [10]who died for us, so that whether we are awake or asleep we may live with him. [11]Therefore encourage one an-

other and build up each other, as indeed you are doing.

Final Exhortations, Greetings, and Benediction

12 But we appeal to you, brothers and sisters,[a] to respect those who labor among you, and have charge of you in the Lord and admonish you; [13]esteem them very highly in love because of their work. Be at peace among yourselves. [14]And we urge you, beloved,[a] to admonish the idlers, encourage the fainthearted, help the weak, be patient with all of them. [15]See that none of you repays evil for evil, but always seek to do good to one another and to all. [16]Rejoice always, [17]pray without ceasing, [18]give thanks in all circumstances; for this is the will of God in Christ Jesus for you. [19]Do not quench the Spirit. [20]Do not despise the words of prophets,[b] [21]but test everything; hold fast to what is good; [22]abstain from every form of evil.

23 May the God of peace himself sanctify you entirely; and may your spirit and soul and body be kept sound[c] and blameless at the coming of our Lord Jesus Christ. [24]The one who calls you is faithful, and he will do this.

25 Beloved,[d] pray for us.

a Gk brothers   b Gk despise prophecies
c Or complete   d Gk Brothers

---

have already won ultimate victory and that other ordinary believers are left behind. Paul is here challenging the early development of a false Gnostic ideology that the early Church will confront in full force in the second and third centuries.

5:1–22 *Now concerning the times and the seasons.* Paul's major point in this passage is that Christ will come again like a thief in the night; therefore Christians should not be terrorized by the false teachers who have timetables with which they have frightened many at Thessalonica. Instead, Paul urges each of us who are believers to stay faithfully at our post. His word "idlers" in verse 14 is *ataktos,* which means literally "to be away from one's post." We are to live our lives in faith, hope, and love, as he prayed in the beginning of the letter, and to trust God with the timing of our lives and of history.

5:12–22 *But we appeal to you.* This final laundry list of counsels is pregnant with spiritual formation implications. It describes the effective functioning of community life. Note how counsels for ordinary tasks mingle with counsels on matters of deep spiritual import. In the community of disciplined grace, respecting co-workers and helping the weak are just as essential as praying without ceasing and not quenching the Spirit.

5:17 PRAYER—*See* Spiritual Disciplines Index.

5:24 *The one who calls you is faithful.* If we believe in this Lord, there will be a change in our life. Paul teaches that the Holy Spirit, who confirms the reality of Christ to us, also changes our motivation and our self-understanding. The Holy Spirit does not cancel out our freedom—in fact, our freedom is intensified—but the Holy Spirit fills us with the living companionship of

26 Greet all the brothers and sisters*a* with a holy kiss. 27I solemnly command you by the Lord that this letter be read to all of them.*b*

28 The grace of our Lord Jesus Christ be with you.*c*

a Gk *brothers*   *b* Gk *to all the brothers*   *c* Other ancient authorities add *Amen*

Christ (1:2–10). In Paul's way of looking at this, the results are far-reaching and demanding. Christ as our Shepherd-Lord calls us to the way of righteousness. This call has direct implications in our marriage, work, and personal relationships. Another discovery we make in this letter is that the Christian Church itself is in continual need of renewal and correction. The Church as a fellowship is not within itself absolute; in fact, it often goes astray, so that it must be repeatedly called back to its good center, Jesus Christ himself.

THE SECOND LETTER OF PAUL TO THE

THESSALONIANS

Paul's second letter to his friends at Thessalonica likely was written very soon after the first (see the Introduction to 1 Thessalonians). Paul has heard additional reports of the situation in the church; he now has available to him more details about the false teaching the church is confronting, including the news that the false prophets purport to have a letter from Paul himself, which they claim gives support to their special theories (2 Thess 2:2). Therefore Paul quickly responds with this second letter. Second Thessalonians repeats themes that have been stated in the first letter, but it expands upon the doctrinal question that continues to trouble the church, namely, the teaching concerning the second coming of Jesus Christ.

We should not be surprised by the atmosphere of argument and dispute in the early Church concerning such vital doctrines as the second coming of Christ, especially with reference to the chronology of future expectations. Christians argue because they care and also because the Christian fellowship has always faced the problem of false or confused teaching. It was the theologian Karl Barth who noted, "There are no New Testament letters that are written apart from the problems of the church."

Paul's pastoral approach to the problems of the church is to teach his way through error. Second Thessalonians gives us the continuation of this pastoral teaching approach.

Paul did not try to convert anyone to Christianity in the two letters to the Thessalonians, yet there is a persuasive quality to these letters. If you are a non-Christian who is watching this young church in action, you will make some very significant discoveries that will help you in making up your mind about the credibility of the Christian faith.

First of all, Paul's letters to the Thessalonians establish the fact that, whatever else Christianity is, it has to do with real people in real places. They live their lives in the time and culture in which they find themselves, just like all other human beings in

See also *"The With-God Life"* essay for this section of the Bible,
"The People of God in Community," pp. 2037–42.

2155

the human story. Christian faith is historical and concrete. Believers in Christ are not disconnected from historical life, with its daily cycle of work and play, of suffering and joy, of life beginning and life ending.

The second great discovery that readers make in these two letters is that there is no mistaking what the center of Paul's faith is. Paul is a man in Christ; it is Jesus Christ who has won Paul's respect and faith. We learn from Paul in these letters that the Christ of his faith is the Jesus of history: "We believe that Jesus died and rose again" (1 Thess 4:14). Paul's faith and hope are not directed toward a phantom redeemer or an inhabitant of the spirit world, but toward the concrete Jesus of Nazareth, who identified totally with humanity in the companionship of the road and even in the loneliness of death, and who shares his triumph over death with us as well.

—Earl F. Palmer

Salutation

1 Paul, Silvanus, and Timothy,
To the church of the Thessalonians in God our Father and the Lord Jesus Christ:

2 Grace to you and peace from God our *a* Father and the Lord Jesus Christ.

Thanksgiving

3 We must always give thanks to God for you, brothers and sisters, *b* as is right, because your faith is growing abundantly, and the love of every one of you for one another is increasing. 4Therefore we ourselves boast of you among the churches of God for your steadfastness and faith during all your persecutions and the afflictions that you are enduring.

The Judgment at Christ's Coming

5 This is evidence of the righteous judgment of God, and is intended to make you worthy of the kingdom of God, for which

you are also suffering. 6For it is indeed just of God to repay with affliction those who afflict you, 7and to give relief to the afflicted as well as to us, when the Lord Jesus is revealed from heaven with his mighty angels 8in flaming fire, inflicting vengeance on those who do not know God and on those who do not obey the gospel of our Lord Jesus. 9These will suffer the punishment of eternal destruction, separated from the presence of the Lord and from the glory of his might, 10when he comes to be glorified by his saints and to be marveled at on that day among all who have believed, because our testimony to you was believed. 11To this end we always pray for you, asking that our God will make you worthy of his call and will fulfill by his power every good resolve and work of faith, 12so that the name of our Lord Jesus may be glorified in

a Other ancient authorities read *the*
b Gk *brothers*

1:11–12 *To this end we always pray for you.* Paul's opening prayer in 2 Thessalonians asks for God's grace that the believers in Thessalonica will continue in their work of faith so that their lives will be congruent with God's intention. The word *axios*, translated "worthy," means the true balance that comes from congruence. This is a model prayer for any spiritual director. Although the Thessalonian believers (and we) have work to do in loving one another (v 3) and in remaining steadfast and enduring persecution (v 4), it is God who is making them (and us) "worthy of his call," and it is God's power that accomplishes the transforming work of congruence in their lives (and ours). The result of this formation process is that the name of the Lord Jesus is glorified; and since the Messiah is most generous, his glory spills over upon them (and us). And all of this marvelous fruit is accomplished by divine grace.

you, and you in him, according to the grace of our God and the Lord Jesus Christ.

The Man of Lawlessness

2 As to the coming of our Lord Jesus Christ and our being gathered together to him, we beg you, brothers and sisters, [a] [2]not to be quickly shaken in mind or alarmed, either by spirit or by word or by letter, as though from us, to the effect that the day of the Lord is already here. [3]Let no one deceive you in any way; for that day will not come unless the rebellion comes first and the lawless one [b] is revealed, the one destined for destruction. [c] [4]He opposes and exalts himself above every so-called god or object of worship, so that he takes his seat in the temple of God, declaring himself to be God. [5]Do you not remember that I told you these things when I was still with you? [6]And you know what is now restraining him, so that he may be revealed when his time comes. [7]For the mystery of lawlessness is already at work, but only until the one who now restrains it is removed. [8]And then the lawless one will be revealed, whom the Lord Jesus [d] will destroy [e] with the breath of his mouth, annihilating him by the manifestation of his coming. [9]The coming of the lawless one is apparent in the working of Satan, who uses all power, signs, lying wonders, [10]and every kind of wicked deception for those who are perishing, because they refused to love the truth and so be saved. [11]For this reason God sends them a powerful delusion, leading them to believe what is false, [12]so that all who have not believed the truth but took pleasure in unrighteousness will be condemned.

Chosen for Salvation

13 But we must always give thanks to God for you, brothers and sisters [a] beloved by the Lord, because God chose you as the first fruits [f] for salvation through sanctification by the Spirit and through belief in the truth. [14]For this purpose he called you through our proclamation of the good news, [g] so that you may obtain the glory of our Lord Jesus Christ. [15]So then, brothers and sisters, [a] stand firm and hold fast to the traditions that you were taught by us, either by word of mouth or by our letter.

16 Now may our Lord Jesus Christ himself and God our Father, who loved us and through grace gave us eternal comfort and good hope, [17]comfort your hearts and strengthen them in every good work and word.

Request for Prayer

3 Finally, brothers and sisters, [a] pray for us, so that the word of the Lord may spread rapidly and be glorified everywhere, just as it is among you, [2]and that we may be rescued from wicked and evil people; for not all have faith. [3]But the Lord is faithful; he will strengthen you and guard you from the

a Gk brothers   b Gk the man of lawlessness; other ancient authorities read the man of sin   c Gk the son of destruction   d Other ancient authorities lack Jesus   e Other ancient authorities read consume   f Other ancient authorities read from the beginning   g Or through our gospel

---

2:1–12 *As to the coming of our Lord.* In chapter 2 Paul again speaks to the question of the return of Jesus Christ. He notes that some religious leaders are teaching that the day of the Lord has already come and this false teaching has troubled believers. He challenges this untruth and encourages believers to trust in the faithfulness of God to keep those who trust him safely in his hands. Paul's solid, steady teaching here is crucial for us today with so many end-time speculations polluting the atmosphere. Our hope is not in a theory of the future, but in the Lord who holds the future in his hands.

2:15–17 *So then, brothers and sisters, stand firm.* Paul assures his friends, "May our Lord Jesus Christ himself . . . strengthen [you] in every good work and word." With this confidence in God's faithfulness ringing in their ears, Paul calls them to be at work here and now and stay faithfully at their posts.

Responding
2:17 SERVICE. Try to name good works and words that will strengthen our hearts. What kind of strength do they give us and why? *See also* Spiritual Disciplines Index.

evil one.*a* *4*And we have confidence in the Lord concerning you, that you are doing and will go on doing the things that we command. *5*May the Lord direct your hearts to the love of God and to the steadfastness of Christ.

Warning against Idleness

6 Now we command you, beloved,*b* in the name of our Lord Jesus Christ, to keep away from believers who are*c* living in idleness and not according to the tradition that they*d* received from us. *7*For you yourselves know how you ought to imitate us; we were not idle when we were with you, *8*and we did not eat anyone's bread without paying for it; but with toil and labor we worked night and day, so that we might not burden any of you. *9*This was not because we do not have that right, but in order to give you an example to imitate. *10*For even when we were with you, we gave you this command: Anyone unwilling to work should not eat. *11*For we hear that some of you are living in idleness, mere busybodies,

not doing any work. *12*Now such persons we command and exhort in the Lord Jesus Christ to do their work quietly and to earn their own living. *13*Brothers and sisters,*e* do not be weary in doing what is right.

14 Take note of those who do not obey what we say in this letter; have nothing to do with them, so that they may be ashamed. *15*Do not regard them as enemies, but warn them as believers.*f*

Final Greetings and Benediction

16 Now may the Lord of peace himself give you peace at all times in all ways. The Lord be with all of you.

17 I, Paul, write this greeting with my own hand. This is the mark in every letter of mine; it is the way I write. *18*The grace of our Lord Jesus Christ be with all of you.*g*

a Or *from evil*   *b* Gk *brothers*   *c* Gk *from every brother who is*   *d* Other ancient authorities read *you*   *e* Gk *Brothers*   *f* Gk *a brother*   *g* Other ancient authorities add *Amen*

3:7–9 *you ought to imitate us.* Paul unabashedly uses the principle of imitation repeatedly in his writings, because he knows that on its most fundamental level this is how spiritual formation works. The formation of habits (even holy habits) comes only by imitation until they become our own. This is why the formation of the leader into Christlikeness is so essential to leading. In this case the issue at hand is idleness, and Paul and his co-workers have modeled how believers are to "work quietly and to earn their own living" (v 12). Even here, in the most basic and ordinary of matters, spiritual formation pertains to our lives.

3:13 *do not be weary in doing what is right.* Paul is confident that Jesus has conquered death with the same realism and actuality that he endured death with. The death and the resurrection of Jesus Christ is for Paul "total

help for total need" (Karl Barth). Just as we are real and live our lives in a real world, so the Lord Jesus Christ is real. All escapism from this reality of history is foreign to Paul in both his theology and his discipleship ethics. Paul also affirms throughout these letters that this same Jesus Christ of history is alive and reigns and will come again. He is the boundary of history at its end, as he is at its beginning and as he has radically entered at its center. The best part of Paul's letters are his sentences about the love and faithfulness of Jesus Christ. Paul believes that Christ's love and faithfulness are real and practical and therefore knowable by ordinary men and women. Though Paul did not set out in his letters to win over skeptics and non-Christians, his books do so because he was good enough to point on every page to Jesus Christ, the Lord of the center and the friend of the way.

THE FIRST LETTER OF PAUL TO

TIMOTHY

The First and Second Letters to Timothy and the Letter to Titus have traditionally been called "the Pastorals"—not because they are only for pastors, though they have some of the most explicitly clergy-related material in the New Testament, but because they are concerned with the ongoing health of congregations. Short on theoretical doctrine and long on practical, congregational wisdom, the Pastorals are a wonderful resource for the continuing spiritual formation of Christians in the Church.

Anyone who thinks the Christian life is mainly a matter of high-flown, ethereal thoughts and feelings will be rightly challenged by these writings. Here is real life among a particular people formed by the incarnation in the day-to-day concerns of life in the Body of Christ. Here spiritual formation occurs as actual, specific tensions within the congregation collide with the soaring ideals of the Christian faith. Having affirmed together that we are attempting to follow "Christ Jesus our hope" (1 Tim 1:1), what does that mean when we must live out our faith among ordinary people in the ordinary Church?

Church of the Nitty-Gritty

Contemporary Christians who think the Church ought to be more "spiritual"—that is, above the mundane, nitty-gritty problems of living in community with other Christians (who can often be a pain in the neck)—will not care for the Pastorals. Here are writings that take seriously the mundane but utterly necessary tasks of church administration among folk who don't always want to be led, teaching among people who don't always want to know, and discipline among disciples who would rather do their own thing than follow the apostolic faith. On the other hand, if you expend much time and energy helping the Church to be the Body of Christ rather than just another helpful volunteer organization, you will find much encouragement here.

See also "The With-God Life" essay for this section of the Bible,
"The People of God in Community," pp. 2037–42.

Contemporary Christians who think that Christian ethics is mainly about global, systemic issues such as world poverty, war, and global warming may, at first reading, consider the ethics of the Pastorals too parochial, too limited and domestic, with their concerns about the role of women in the congregation, the behavior of pastors, and issues of church authority. Here are writings of a Church attempting to move out in mission into a pagan world (Timothy was a leader in the Pauline push out of Asia into Europe), while at the same time maintaining its unique identity as the Body of Christ. At a time when the Church was fighting for its life, it fought not by throwing open its doors to all opinions and lifestyles, but by patient, intentional formation of Christians who were willing to be part of a community that looked different. Today our Church struggles with how to reach out to the world without falling face down, with how to be a body of believers who live for the sake of Christ's salvation of the world without degenerating into just one more worldly organization indistinguishable from all the rest. The Pastorals can be a veritable handbook for would-be Jesus revolutionaries.

Five areas of spiritual formation concern the Pastorals: spiritual elitism, rejection of the bodily resurrection, spiritual asceticism in regard to special food and sexual practices, spiritual license, and fruitless spiritual speculation in regard to doctrine and practices.

Spiritual Elitism

From the beginning, the early Church had to struggle with the Gnostic tendencies of some believers ("Gnostic" is derived from the Greek word for "knowledge"). Gnostics thought that being a faithful Christian meant having superior, secret, elite spiritual insights that ordinary folk were not given. Paul combats this with his frequent use of "all" or "everyone" (1 Tim 2:4; Titus 2:11). Paul tells Timothy to tell these spiritual know-it-alls that our hope is not in what we know, but rather in the God who knows us and "who is the Savior of all people" (1 Tim 4:10).

Rejection of the Bodily Resurrection

Paul had consistently preached, and the Church had believed, that just as God raised Jesus from the dead in a bodily resurrected form, so we would be raised. The idea of a corporeal resurrection, rather than some spiritualized, disembodied immortality, was a real reach for most pagan minds. Much classical Greek and Roman thought held that the body is evil and that the purpose of spirituality is to rise above the creaturely confines of the body into some disembodied spiritual existence. Paul condemns those not completely converted pagans such as Hymenaeus and Alexander who "have suffered shipwreck in the faith" (1:19–20).

Spiritual Asceticism with Regard to Food and Sex

We are reminded in 1 Timothy that the term "spiritual" must be used in a formative, incarnational, specifically congregational context; otherwise, it can be a real problem. Some in the early communities had apparently decided that Christians must reject all former attachments to the world and human culture. They labeled some foods forbidden, despite the fact that the God who created all things called them good (4:3–5; Titus 1:15). Some even denigrated sex and marriage (1 Tim 4:3), urging new Christians to repudiate their marriages because bodily activity was evil.

Spiritual License

Misunderstanding of "spirituality" can also move in the opposite direction. There appear to have been some in the community who thought that, since Jesus was resurrected, they were resurrected, and since they were now among the spiritually elite, none of the old rules applied. So they lived licentiously (2 Tim 3:6), taught doctrine for profit (1 Tim 6:5), and engaged in other activity that showed a disconnect between their profession of faith and their lifestyle. So Paul tells Timothy to keep himself "pure" (5:22) and combat bad doctrine with good living.

Fruitless Spiritual Speculation

Communities found themselves torn asunder by fruitless speculation on various myths and esoteric practices (1:4; 4:7). Paul had had it with these "stupid and senseless controversies" that merely "breed quarrels" (2 Tim 2:23). Healthy spiritual formation requires a discernment of the essential from the nonessential, the core of the faith from the superficialities. It is spiritual wisdom to keep forming one's community on the basis of the chief affirmations of the faith and leave peripheral concerns at the margins.

The Reality of Messy Churches

First Timothy gives us a real-life peek at an early Christian congregation or gathering of congregations that was having trouble embodying the fullness of the good news in Christ. (Do you know any church like that?) For many contemporary believers, the toughest thing about being a Christian is the Christian Church. Being in the Body of Christ can be a real challenge, considering the sad state of much of the Body. It is easy to lose heart when we witness the great gap between the soaring vision of the Church and the grubby sociological reality of it.

"Oh, if we could only be more like the early Church," some romantics may exclaim. First Timothy assures us, "You already do look like the early Church—difficult, contentious, fractured, and confused."

There is hope in that insight, however. A close reading of 1 Timothy reminds us that the Church is a mess—and always has been. The good news for churches is that we are, with all our faults, the very Body of Christ, the visible form of Christ in the world, God's answer to what's wrong with the world (1 Cor 12:27). Christ does not leave us to our own miserable devices, does not abandon us because of our failures at faith. God keeps working with us, correcting us, teaching us, patiently guiding us, reaching out to us through two thousand years of Church in encouraging Scripture such as 1 Timothy.

—*William H. Willimon*

Salutation

1 Paul, an apostle of Christ Jesus by the command of God our Savior and of Christ Jesus our hope,

2 To Timothy, my loyal child in the faith: Grace, mercy, and peace from God the Father and Christ Jesus our Lord.

Warning against False Teachers

3 I urge you, as I did when I was on my way to Macedonia, to remain in Ephesus so that you may instruct certain people not to teach any different doctrine, 4 and not to occupy themselves with myths and endless genealogies that promote speculations rather than the divine training*a* that is known by faith. 5 But the aim of such instruction is love that comes from a pure heart, a good conscience, and sincere faith. 6 Some people have deviated from these and turned to meaningless talk, 7 desiring to be teachers of the law, without understanding either what they are saying or the things about which they make assertions.

8 Now we know that the law is good, if one uses it legitimately. 9 This means understanding that the law is laid down not for the innocent but for the lawless and disobedient, for the godless and sinful, for the unholy and profane, for those who kill their father or mother, for murderers, 10 fornicators, sodomites, slave traders, liars, perjurers, and

whatever else is contrary to the sound teaching 11 that conforms to the glorious gospel of the blessed God, which he entrusted to me.

Gratitude for Mercy

12 I am grateful to Christ Jesus our Lord, who has strengthened me, because he judged me faithful and appointed me to his service, 13 even though I was formerly a blasphemer, a persecutor, and a man of violence. But I received mercy because I had acted ignorantly in unbelief, 14 and the grace of our Lord overflowed for me with the faith and love that are in Christ Jesus. 15 The saying is sure and worthy of full acceptance, that Christ Jesus came into the world to save sinners—of whom I am the foremost. 16 But for that very reason I received mercy, so that in me, as the foremost, Jesus Christ might display the utmost patience, making me an example to those who would come to believe in him for eternal life. 17 To the King of the ages, immortal, invisible, the only God, be honor and glory forever and ever.*b* Amen.

18 I am giving you these instructions, Timothy, my child, in accordance with the prophecies made earlier about you, so that by following them you may fight the good fight, 19 having faith and a good conscience. By rejecting conscience, certain persons have suffered shipwreck in the faith; 20 among them

a Or *plan*   *b* Gk *to the ages of the ages*

1:4 *not to occupy themselves with . . . speculations.* The Christian faith, compared with some other religions, is wonderfully basic, simple. We must stick close to the basics of the faith, contenting ourselves with the grand revelation we have without venturing out into less certain speculation. Here the test for our doctrinal wrangling is "divine training." When debating an issue, we need to ask ourselves: How well does this particular belief form disciples whose lives embody their beliefs?

1:15 *to save sinners.* Here is the basis of our spiritual formation—a God who came among sinners to seek and save the lost. The mention of sin is not meant as some sort of put-down of early Christians, but rather as a humility-generating confession that in all our doctrinal disputes and church controversies, we are

sinners—we are being saved, true, but we are still sinners. The apostle Paul, the preacher, pastor, and leader, is the biggest sinner—a confession that all Christian leaders ought to make on a regular basis. Paul is able to talk to these Christians about their sin, because he never forgets that he is the "foremost" sinner.

1:19 *suffered shipwreck in the faith.* Those who are weaker or less secure in their faith can become "shipwrecked" because of bad doctrine. Bad theology, stupid ideas, or strange notions are not just an intellectual problem, but also a pastoral-care problem. People can be hurt by bad thinking. False doctrine harms. With "sound teaching" (v 10) the Church is not just engaging in an intellectual discussion; it is caring for people in their need for truth and light.

are Hymenaeus and Alexander, whom I have turned over to Satan, so that they may learn not to blaspheme.

Instructions concerning Prayer

2 First of all, then, I urge that supplications, prayers, intercessions, and thanksgivings be made for everyone, [2]for kings and all who are in high positions, so that we may lead a quiet and peaceable life in all godliness and dignity. [3]This is right and is acceptable in the sight of God our Savior, [4]who desires everyone to be saved and to come to the knowledge of the truth. [5]For

there is one God;
there is also one mediator between
God and humankind,
Christ Jesus, himself human,
[6] who gave himself a ransom for all

—this was attested at the right time. [7]For this I was appointed a herald and an apostle (I am telling the truth,[a] I am not lying), a teacher of the Gentiles in faith and truth.

[8] I desire, then, that in every place the men should pray, lifting up holy hands without anger or argument; [9]also that the women should dress themselves modestly and decently in suitable clothing, not with their hair braided, or with gold, pearls, or expensive clothes, [10]but with good works, as is proper for women who profess reverence for God.

[11]Let a woman[b] learn in silence with full submission. [12]I permit no woman[b] to teach or to have authority over a man;[c] she is to keep silent. [13]For Adam was formed first, then Eve; [14]and Adam was not deceived, but the woman was deceived and became a transgressor. [15]Yet she will be saved through childbearing, provided they continue in faith and love and holiness, with modesty.

Qualifications of Bishops

3 The saying is sure:[d] whoever aspires to the office of bishop[e] desires a noble task. [2]Now a bishop[f] must be above reproach, married only once,[g] temperate, sensible, respectable, hospitable, an apt teacher, [3]not a drunkard, not violent but gentle, not quarrelsome, and not a lover of money. [4]He must manage his own household well, keeping his children submissive and respectful in every way— [5]for if someone does not know how to manage his own household, how can he take care of God's church? [6]He must not be a recent convert, or he may be puffed up with conceit and fall into the condemnation of the devil. [7]Moreover, he must be well thought

a Other ancient authorities add in Christ
b Or wife   c Or her husband   d Some interpreters place these words at the end of the previous paragraph. Other ancient authorities read The saying is commonly accepted   e Or overseer
f Or an overseer   g Gk the husband of one wife

2:1 *prayers . . . be made for everyone.* Prayer is the serious business of the Church, the first and best service it renders for the world. The community's prayers are not limited to the confines of the community, but stretch forth even to those who are not part of or who may even be in opposition to the community. We are to be the sort of people who can pray for our enemies.

2:8 **PRAYER**—*See* Spiritual Disciplines Index.

3:1–7 *above reproach.* The Church is dependent upon God's raising up, in every age, the right sort of leaders. Furthermore, leaders such as bishops and deacons are expected to be moral exemplars to the community. Our leaders may struggle under the burden of having to lead morally exemplary lives; nevertheless, this is a function of church leadership. Sometimes, when a Christian leader commits some moral lapse,

there is always someone to say, "Well, our pastors are only human." True. But 1 Timothy boldly asserts that the leaders of the Church are more interesting than merely "human." They are those human beings who are called to lead, to teach, and to care for the Body of Christ and therefore they are those whom we are justified in expecting to embody the highest Christian lifestyle.

Responding
3:4 **SUBMISSION.** Consider the best way to train children to be submissive and respectful. Why was this important in Paul's time? Why is it important today? What are some of the things we can do to encourage this trait in children? Seek to deliberately treat children respectfully this week. *See also* Spiritual Disciplines Index.

of by outsiders, so that he may not fall into disgrace and the snare of the devil.

Qualifications of Deacons

8 Deacons likewise must be serious, not double-tongued, not indulging in much wine, not greedy for money; [9]they must hold fast to the mystery of the faith with a clear conscience. [10]And let them first be tested; then, if they prove themselves blameless, let them serve as deacons. [11]Women[a] likewise must be serious, not slanderers, but temperate, faithful in all things. [12]Let deacons be married only once,[b] and let them manage their children and their households well; [13]for those who serve well as deacons gain a good standing for themselves and great boldness in the faith that is in Christ Jesus.

The Mystery of Our Religion

14 I hope to come to you soon, but I am writing these instructions to you so that, [15]if I am delayed, you may know how one ought to behave in the household of God, which is the church of the living God, the pillar and bulwark of the truth. [16]Without any doubt, the mystery of our religion is great:

He[c] was revealed in flesh,
    vindicated[d] in spirit,[e]
        seen by angels,
    proclaimed among Gentiles,
        believed in throughout the world,
            taken up in glory.

False Asceticism

4 Now the Spirit expressly says that in later[f] times some will renounce the faith by paying attention to deceitful spirits and teachings of demons, [2]through the hypocrisy of liars whose consciences are seared with a hot iron; [3]They forbid marriage and demand abstinence from foods, which God created to be received with thanksgiving by

those who believe and know the truth. [4]For everything created by God is good, and nothing is to be rejected, provided it is received with thanksgiving; [5]for it is sanctified by God's word and by prayer.

A Good Minister of Jesus Christ

6 If you put these instructions before the brothers and sisters,[g] you will be a good servant[h] of Christ Jesus, nourished on the words of the faith and of the sound teaching that you have followed. [7]Have nothing to do with profane myths and old wives' tales. Train yourself in godliness, [8]for, while physical training is of some value, godliness is valuable in every way, holding promise for both the present life and the life to come. [9]The saying is sure and worthy of full acceptance. [10]For to this end we toil and struggle,[i] because we have our hope set on the living God, who is the Savior of all people, especially of those who believe.

11 These are the things you must insist on and teach. [12]Let no one despise your youth, but set the believers an example in speech and conduct, in love, in faith, in purity. [13]Until I arrive, give attention to the public reading of scripture,[j] to exhorting, to teaching. [14]Do not neglect the gift that is in you, which was given to you through prophecy with the laying on of hands by the council of elders.[k] [15]Put these things into practice, devote yourself to them, so that all may see your progress. [16]Pay close attention to yourself and to your teaching; continue in these things, for in doing this you will save both yourself and your hearers.

a Or *Their wives,* or *Women deacons*   b Gk *be husbands of one wife*   c Gk *Who;* other ancient authorities read *God;* others, *Which*   d Or *justified*   e Or *by the Spirit*   f Or *the last*   g Gk *brothers*   h Or *deacon*   i Other ancient authorities read *suffer reproach*   j Gk *to the reading*   k Gk *by the presbytery*

3:13 SERVICE—*See* Spiritual Disciplines Index.

4:3 *They forbid marriage and demand abstinence from foods.* Spiritual formation is not a matter of utter detachment from life in this world. Jesus brought God's love *into* the world, not set apart from it. Though Christians follow

the upward path demanded by the Spirit of God, they must live their lives in the tangle of commitments and responsibilities incurred through service to one another in this world.

4:5 PRAYER—*See* Spiritual Disciplines Index.
4:15 MEDITATION—*See* Spiritual Disciplines Index.

TIMOTHY

Humility in Action

Selected Scriptures: *Acts 16:1–5; Philippians 2:19–23; 1 & 2 Timothy*

Oh, that we might all have a partner in the faith like the apostle Paul had in Timothy. They met during Paul's second missionary journey and worked together for some seventeen years. It is hard to imagine Paul's ministry without the presence of his faithful partner, Timothy.

Although Timothy was young and probably fairly new to the Christian faith, he possessed a spiritual maturity beyond his years. Raised by a devout Jewish mother and grandmother, Timothy likely had a strong commitment to God and a good knowledge of Old Testament Scriptures before meeting Christ. After he became a Christian, his community soon realized his leadership potential, and Paul took him on as a companion, acting as a spiritual father to the young man.

Paul refers often to Timothy as "my child" and calls him "loyal," "beloved," and "my co-worker." He had good reason to care so deeply for his partner; Timothy traveled with Paul to nearly every city on his journeys and sometimes stayed behind to lead a church after Paul's departure. He was with Paul at the writing of six of the Letters and often took these and other messages to the congregations. Few were as loyal in supporting and assisting Paul's work.

Paul wrote to the Philippians: "I hope in the Lord Jesus to send Timothy to you soon, so that I may be cheered by news of you. I have no one like him who will be genuinely concerned for your welfare. All of them are seeking their own interests, not those of Jesus Christ. But Timothy's worth you know, how like a son with a father he has served with me in the work of the gospel" (Phil 2:19–22). Here we find the core of Paul's love for Timothy. Although many had joined Paul in his ministry, some were ultimately more concerned with themselves and their own lives than they were with the welfare of the churches and the work of the gospel—the interests of Jesus Christ. Timothy demonstrated again and again that truly he did love those he served with the love of Christ. He loved Paul and shared Paul's sense of commitment to serving God. Even in Paul's days while in prison in Rome, Timothy was among the few who remained loyal, not deserting Paul as the others did when their connection with him became risky.

As we consider Timothy's unfailing devotion, what can we take from him to help us grow in a devoted and selfless spirit? Three attitudes stand out. First, Timothy had a humble spirit. So humble was he that he often appeared reserved and timid, prompting Paul to encourage boldness in his leadership. "I remind you to rekindle the gift of God that is within you through the laying on of my hands; for God did not give us a spirit of cowardice, but rather a spirit of power and of love and of self-discipline" (2 Tim 1:6–7). Spirit-empowered leadership never loses its humility, Paul seemed to remind, for it remains loving and disciplined.

Madame Jeanne Guyon, in her seventeenth-century classic *Experiencing the Depths of Jesus Christ,* explained an important outgrowth of humility: "If the Lord should be so merciful as to give you a true spirit of His humility, you will not be surprised at your faults, or even your own basic nature. The more clearly you see your true self, the clearer you also see how miserable your self-nature really is; and the more you will abandon your whole being to God. Seeing that you have such a desperate need of Him, you will press toward a more intimate relationship with Him."

This desire for an intimate relationship with Christ was Timothy's second attitude. He had been transformed through the coming of Jesus into his life. Although he was a longtime worshiper of God, his meeting Christ had made him new, forming in him the mind and heart of Jesus. No longer caring primarily for his own interests, Timothy began to care most for the concerns of God.

William Temple, a leader of modern Protestantism, wrote: "The only way to deliver me from my self-centeredness is by winning my entire heart's devotion, the total allegiance of my will to God—and this can only be done by the Divine Love of God disclosed by Christ in his life and death." This love for God in Christ sparked an undying passion in Timothy.

His passion, along with his humility, engendered a third attitude. Timothy sensed his own need for guidance. In Paul he found someone who could train him in his faith, someone who could love him and guide his growth while modeling for him a life lived in wholehearted service to Christ. We might call it mentoring or spiritual direction or holy friendship—whichever term we use, Timothy submitted to the discipline of guidance by opening his life to Paul and seeking growth through Paul's influence as they worked together.

Richard Foster writes: "If we have the humility to believe that we can learn from our brothers and sisters and the understanding that some have gone further into the divine Center than others, then we can see the necessity of spiritual direction. As Virgil Vogt of Reba Place Fellowship says, 'If you cannot listen to your brother, you cannot listen to the Holy Spirit.'"

Timothy viewed himself rightly, and because he didn't focus on himself, demanding comfort and control of his life, God used him to do great works of ministry. The fourth-century historian Eusebius records Timothy's appointment as the first bishop of Ephesus. Another writing from the same period details his martyrdom in Ephesus some thirty years after Paul's death. Timothy remained devoted to the cause of Christ until his death. Oh, that we might show the same devotion to our Lord.

Personal Reflection

- Timothy's humility made it possible for him to work so well alongside Paul. Whom do you work alongside? Do you struggle in remaining humble? What part of your relationship or work might be helped by greater humility on your part?
- Have you ever practiced the Spiritual Discipline of guidance on a one-on-one basis? Who has served as a guide (or mentor or spiritual director) for you? Do you see ways God might use such a person in your life now? Ask God to lead you to an individual who could serve you in this way.

PROFILE

Duties toward Believers

5 Do not speak harshly to an older man,[a] but speak to him as to a father, to younger men as brothers, [2]to older women as mothers, to younger women as sisters—with absolute purity.

3 Honor widows who are really widows. [4]If a widow has children or grandchildren, they should first learn their religious duty to their own family and make some repayment to their parents; for this is pleasing in God's sight. [5]The real widow, left alone, has set her hope on God and continues in supplications and prayers night and day; [6]but the widow[b] who lives for pleasure is dead even while she lives. [7]Give these commands as well, so that they may be above reproach. [8]And whoever does not provide for relatives, and especially for family members, has denied the faith and is worse than an unbeliever.

9 Let a widow be put on the list if she is not less than sixty years old and has been married only once;[c] [10]she must be well attested for her good works, as one who has brought up children, shown hospitality, washed the saints' feet, helped the afflicted, and devoted herself to doing good in every way. [11]But refuse to put younger widows on the list; for when their sensual desires alienate them from Christ, they want to marry, [12]and so they incur condemnation for having violated their first pledge. [13]Besides that, they learn to be idle, gadding about from house to house; and they are not merely idle, but also gossips and busybodies, saying what they should not say. [14]So I would have younger widows marry, bear children, and manage their households, so as to give the adversary no occasion to revile us. [15]For some have already turned away to follow Satan. [16]If any believing woman[d] has relatives who are really widows, let her assist them; let the church not be burdened, so that it can assist those who are real widows.

17 Let the elders who rule well be considered worthy of double honor,[e] especially those who labor in preaching and teaching; [18]for the scripture says, "You shall not muzzle an ox while it is treading out the grain," and, "The laborer deserves to be paid." [19]Never accept any accusation against an elder except on the evidence of two or three witnesses. [20]As for those who persist in sin, rebuke them in the presence of all, so that the rest also may stand in fear. [21]In the presence of God and of Christ Jesus and of the elect angels, I warn you to keep these instructions without prejudice, doing nothing on the basis of partiality. [22]Do not ordain[f] anyone hastily, and do not participate in the sins of others; keep yourself pure.

23 No longer drink only water, but take a little wine for the sake of your stomach and your frequent ailments.

24 The sins of some people are conspicuous and precede them to judgment, while the sins of others follow them there. [25]So also good works are conspicuous; and even when they are not, they cannot remain hidden.

6 Let all who are under the yoke of slavery regard their masters as worthy of all honor, so that the name of God and the teaching may not be blasphemed. [2]Those who have believing masters must not be disrespectful to

a Or *an elder,* or *a presbyter*   b Gk *she*   c Gk *the wife of one husband*   d Other ancient authorities read *believing man or woman*; others, *believing man*   e Or *compensation*   f Gk *Do not lay hands on*

Responding

5:2 CHASTITY. Because Paul cautions Timothy to treat the younger women in his congregation as sisters, we know that he was young. Are the sexual temptations that pastors today face in ministering to their congregations significantly different from the temptations Timothy had to face? *See also* Spiritual Disciplines Index.

5:3–16 *Honor widows.* A church is judged by its care of its most vulnerable. At the time the letter was written, widows were the epitome of need and dependency; therefore, 1 Timothy expends much text dealing in detail with the community's responsibility for them. As Christians we are obligated to cultivate those Spiritual Disciplines that constantly call to mind the needs of the most vulnerable and form our lives in service to those needs.

5:5 PRAYER and SOLITUDE—*See* Spiritual Disciplines Index.

5:9–14 CHASTITY—*See* Spiritual Disciplines Index.

them on the ground that they are members of the church;*a* rather they must serve them all the more, since those who benefit by their service are believers and beloved.*b*

False Teaching and True Riches

Teach and urge these duties. 3Whoever teaches otherwise and does not agree with the sound words of our Lord Jesus Christ and the teaching that is in accordance with godliness, 4is conceited, understanding nothing, and has a morbid craving for controversy and for disputes about words. From these come envy, dissension, slander, base suspicions, 5and wrangling among those who are depraved in mind and bereft of the truth, imagining that godliness is a means of gain.*c* 6Of course, there is great gain in godliness combined with contentment; 7for we brought nothing into the world, so that*d* we can take nothing out of it; 8but if we have food and clothing, we will be content with these. 9But those who want to be rich fall into temptation and are trapped by many senseless and harmful desires that plunge people into ruin and destruction. 10For the love of money is a root of all kinds of evil, and in their eagerness to be rich some have wandered away from the faith and pierced themselves with many pains.

The Good Fight of Faith

11 But as for you, man of God, shun all this; pursue righteousness, godliness, faith, love, endurance, gentleness. 12Fight the good fight of the faith; take hold of the eternal life, to which you were called and for which you made*e* the good confession in the pres-ence of many witnesses. 13In the presence of God, who gives life to all things, and of Christ Jesus, who in his testimony before Pontius Pilate made the good confession, I charge you 14to keep the commandment without spot or blame until the manifestation of our Lord Jesus Christ, 15which he will bring about at the right time—he who is the blessed and only Sovereign, the King of kings and Lord of lords. 16It is he alone who has immortality and dwells in unapproachable light, whom no one has ever seen or can see; to him be honor and eternal dominion. Amen.

17 As for those who in the present age are rich, command them not to be haughty, or to set their hopes on the uncertainty of riches, but rather on God who richly provides us with everything for our enjoyment. 18They are to do good, to be rich in good works, generous, and ready to share, 19thus storing up for themselves the treasure of a good foundation for the future, so that they may take hold of the life that really is life.

Personal Instructions and Benediction

20 Timothy, guard what has been entrusted to you. Avoid the profane chatter and contradictions of what is falsely called knowledge; 21by professing it some have missed the mark as regards the faith.

Grace be with you.*f*

a Gk *are brothers*   *b* Or *since they are believers and beloved, who devote themselves to good deeds*   *c* Other ancient authorities add *Withdraw yourself from such people*   *d* Other ancient authorities read *world—it is certain that*   *e* Gk *confessed*   *f* The Greek word for *you* here is plural; in other ancient authorities it is singular. Other ancient authorities add *Amen*

6:2 SERVICE—*See* Spiritual Disciplines Index.

6:2 *Teach and urge these duties.* This letter emphasizes the central role of teaching in the life of the community. The Christian life does not come naturally. Only through education, formation, and transformation do we become faithful followers of Christ. Ethical chaos results from bad teaching. This is quite a claim for the importance of education.

6:17–19 *those who . . . are rich.* Not all of the earliest Christians were poor. Note that the rich are instructed last, after more pressing concerns for the most vulnerable are addressed—the first shall be last (Matt 20:16). From those to whom much has been given much will be required (Luke 12:48). Our full, affluent churches must admit that riches are not spiritually neutral. Scripture is clear that those with riches are in a vulnerable situation as far as their souls are concerned (Matt 19:24). Money is a spiritual issue. Spiritual formation and renovation for those who have material goods means quite specific responsibility—"They are to do good, to be rich in good works, generous, and ready to share."

THE SECOND LETTER OF PAUL TO
TIMOTHY

Paul gets personal in the Second Letter to Timothy. Here is a wise, seasoned Christian leader giving counsel to a younger Christian minister. In a number of places in his letters, Paul mentions Timothy (e.g., Rom 16:21; 1 Cor 4:17), indicating that Paul had not only close ties to Timothy, but to his extended family as well. Timothy appears to be a younger colleague who is responsible for a group of churches; therefore, this letter is particularly appropriate for those who have been given leadership, teaching, and pastoral roles in the Christian community. Whereas the concerns of 1 Timothy and Titus are sometimes general, here Paul gets quite specific. Here are real-life concerns of a specific church attempting to make its way in the world.

Endurance

Although Paul does mention the challenges of living in "the last days" (2 Tim 3:1), there is a marked concern for the maintenance of continuity with the apostolic tradition for a church that knows how to keep on "keeping on." When endurance is listed as an important characteristic for Christian leaders, you know that the church is in this for the long haul.

Young Timothy is urged to "rekindle" the gift that was given him (1:3–7), to endure suffering as a good soldier for Christ (2:1–13), and to handle the word of God like a careful, skilled worker (2:14–19). Therefore, in this matter of spiritual formation, 2 Timothy is a wonderful resource for those of us who struggle with how to endure, to keep on keeping on in our faith, to stay Christian even though we must put up with the church, to keep close to the community of faith even though it disappoints us greatly from time to time.

Leadership by Example

In enduring and triumphing in the faith, Timothy is to profit by the good example

---

See also *"The With-God Life"* essay for this section of the Bible,
"The People of God in Community," pp. 2037–42.

of his mentor, Paul. Paul dares to offer himself as a worthy example of spiritual depth (3:10–17). Having urged Christian leaders to be examples to the flock in 1 Timothy, here Paul does not shrink from telling Timothy to observe Paul's own "teaching," "conduct," "aim in life," "faith," "patience," "love," and "steadfastness" (3:10).

To our ears this may sound like apostolic pride at its worst. But we have been conditioned to tolerate a disconnect between people's profession of faith and their actual practice of it. Paul was part of the spiritual tradition that taught that faith is proved by its embodiment. Our spiritual feelings and affirmations are meant to be put into practice. Therefore Paul dared to offer himself as an example to young Timothy.

That call to observe and imitate may be for us the most scandalous and demanding aspect of this sort of letter. Paul would not understand the disjunction that many of us make between our beliefs and our practice, the life of the spirit and the life of the flesh.

Who are our mentors and examples of the faith? The Christian faith is too difficult to be done alone; we must have worthy models. Are we living a life that might be an example to others? Can others find in our Spiritual Disciplines and practices a healthy congruence between the way we talk and the way we walk? These are among the spiritual formation questions that make 2 Timothy valuable for evaluation and improvement of our spiritual life.

—William H. Willimon

Salutation

1 Paul, an apostle of Christ Jesus by the will of God, for the sake of the promise of life that is in Christ Jesus,

2 To Timothy, my beloved child:

Grace, mercy, and peace from God the Father and Christ Jesus our Lord.

Thanksgiving and Encouragement

3 I am grateful to God—whom I worship with a clear conscience, as my ancestors did—when I remember you constantly in my prayers night and day. 4Recalling your tears, I long to see you so that I may be filled with joy. 5I am reminded of your sincere faith, a faith that lived first in your grandmother Lois and your mother Eunice and now, I am

sure, lives in you. 6For this reason I remind you to rekindle the gift of God that is within you through the laying on of my hands; 7for God did not give us a spirit of cowardice, but rather a spirit of power and of love and of self-discipline.

8 Do not be ashamed, then, of the testimony about our Lord or of me his prisoner, but join with me in suffering for the gospel, relying on the power of God, 9who saved us and called us with a holy calling, not according to our works but according to his own purpose and grace. This grace was given to us in Christ Jesus before the ages began, 10but it has now been revealed through the appearing of our Savior Christ Jesus, who abolished death and brought life and immortality to

---

1:8 *join with me in suffering.* What a curious invitation this is. In our day, too many think that Jesus is the end of all suffering, the way to get life fixed, the way to ensure that life will never be in great difficulty. Paul invites Timothy toward the gospel, which is for many not the ending of all their problems, but the beginning of problems they would never have had if they had not met Jesus! Note that he is talking about suffering "for the gospel," not sickness, aging, and death that afflict humanity in general. Our times of suffering become spiritually significant when they are induced by faithful discipleship and when we see them as opportunities to rely on the power of God.

light through the gospel. [11]For this gospel I was appointed a herald and an apostle and a teacher,[a] [12]and for this reason I suffer as I do. But I am not ashamed, for I know the one in whom I have put my trust, and I am sure that he is able to guard until that day what I have entrusted to him.[b] [13]Hold to the standard of sound teaching that you have heard from me, in the faith and love that are in Christ Jesus. [14]Guard the good treasure entrusted to you, with the help of the Holy Spirit living in us.

15 You are aware that all who are in Asia have turned away from me, including Phygelus and Hermogenes. [16]May the Lord grant mercy to the household of Onesiphorus, because he often refreshed me and was not ashamed of my chain; [17]when he arrived in Rome, he eagerly[c] searched for me and found me [18]—may the Lord grant that he will find mercy from the Lord on that day! And you know very well how much service he rendered in Ephesus.

A Good Soldier of Christ Jesus

2 You then, my child, be strong in the grace that is in Christ Jesus; [2]and what you have heard from me through many witnesses entrust to faithful people who will be able to teach others as well. [3]Share in suffering like a good soldier of Christ Jesus. [4]No one serving in the army gets entangled in everyday affairs; the soldier's aim is to please the enlisting officer. [5]And in the case of an athlete, no one is crowned without competing according to the rules. [6]It is the farmer who does the work who ought to have the first share of the crops. [7]Think over what I say, for the Lord will give you understanding in all things.

8 Remember Jesus Christ, raised from the dead, a descendant of David—that is my gospel, [9]for which I suffer hardship, even to the point of being chained like a criminal. But the word of God is not chained. [10]Therefore I endure everything for the sake of the elect, so that they may also obtain the salvation that is in Christ Jesus, with eternal glory. [11]The saying is sure:

If we have died with him, we will also
        live with him;

a Other ancient authorities add *of the Gentiles*
b Or *what has been entrusted to me*   c Or *promptly*

1:12 *for this reason I suffer as I do.* Jesus came to us, preached words of life, and showed us the way, and we crucified him for it. His way is that narrow way that seems, no matter how charmingly and beguilingly we try to put the gospel, to involve suffering. Few of us North American Christians find ourselves in circumstances where we are persecuted for our faith, yet millions of Christians are persecuted and martyred still because of their commitment to Christ. It cannot be that we have at last found a society in which no one can be hurt following Jesus. More likely, our Church has settled in comfortably with the powers; we have scaled the gospel down to some message that never offends; we have practiced the faith in ways that never present a rebuke to the ways of the world.

Responding
2:4 SERVICE and SIMPLICITY/ FRUGALITY. Soldiers' lives are the epitome of simplicity. Their possessions are limited to personal effects and clothes, since all of their energies must be focused on their job.

Try to imagine a life pared down to such bare essentials. How does ridding ourselves of possessions make it easier to seek first God's kingdom and its righteousness, the "only thing central to the Spiritual Discipline of simplicity," as Richard Foster writes in *Celebration of Discipline*? *See also* Spiritual Disciplines Index.

2:8–9 *Remember Jesus Christ.* The Christian faith is distinctly traditionalist. Much of our worship on Sunday is consumed with the loving reiteration and joyful celebration of tradition— remembering Jesus Christ. Here you are, studying a two-thousand-year-old letter. That's the way we Christians continue as Christians. Our remembering of the tradition is our revolutionary act of defiance against the lures of the present age, one of our most significant practices of the faith. Through such remembering, we are freed from the merely contemporary. In our reading and studying the Word of God, that Word speaks anew, lives among us. The Word of God is not, thank God, chained!

12 if we endure, we will also reign with
    him;
   if we deny him, he will also deny us;
13 if we are faithless, he remains faithful—
    for he cannot deny himself.

A Worker Approved by God

14 Remind them of this, and warn them
before God*a* that they are to avoid wrangling
over words, which does no good but only ruins those who are listening. 15 Do your best to
present yourself to God as one approved by
him, a worker who has no need to be
ashamed, rightly explaining the word of
truth. 16 Avoid profane chatter, for it will lead
people into more and more impiety, 17 and
their talk will spread like gangrene. Among
them are Hymenaeus and Philetus, 18 who
have swerved from the truth by claiming that
the resurrection has already taken place. They
are upsetting the faith of some. 19 But God's
firm foundation stands, bearing this inscription: "The Lord knows those who are
his," and, "Let everyone who calls on the
name of the Lord turn away from wickedness."

20 In a large house there are utensils not
only of gold and silver but also of wood and
clay, some for special use, some for ordinary.
21 All who cleanse themselves of the things I
have mentioned*b* will become special utensils, dedicated and useful to the owner of the
house, ready for every good work. 22 Shun
youthful passions and pursue righteousness,
faith, love, and peace, along with those who
call on the Lord from a pure heart. 23 Have

nothing to do with stupid and senseless controversies; you know that they breed quarrels. 24 And the Lord's servant*c* must not be
quarrelsome but kindly to everyone, an apt
teacher, patient, 25 correcting opponents with
gentleness. God may perhaps grant that they
will repent and come to know the truth,
26 and that they may escape from the snare of
the devil, having been held captive by him to
do his will.*d*

Godlessness in the Last Days

3 You must understand this, that in the
  last days distressing times will come. 2 For
people will be lovers of themselves, lovers of
money, boasters, arrogant, abusive, disobedient to their parents, ungrateful, unholy,
3 inhuman, implacable, slanderers, profli-
gates, brutes, haters of good, 4 treacherous,
reckless, swollen with conceit, lovers of pleasure rather than lovers of God, 5 holding to
the outward form of godliness but denying its
power. Avoid them! 6 For among them are
those who make their way into households
and captivate silly women, overwhelmed by
their sins and swayed by all kinds of desires,
7 who are always being instructed and can
never arrive at a knowledge of the truth. 8 As
Jannes and Jambres opposed Moses, so these
people, of corrupt mind and counterfeit faith,
also oppose the truth. 9 But they will not
make much progress, because, as in the case

a Other ancient authorities read *the Lord*
b Gk *of these things*   *c* Gk *slave*   *d* Or *by him,
to do his* (that is, God's) *will*

2:14 *Remind them of this.* Do our worship,
our church life, our study together have enough
biblical content ("Jesus Christ, raised from the
dead . . . ," v 8) to keep contemporary Christians
going? When, in some congregations, we crank
the Christian faith down to the lowest common
denominator, when we reduce the good news
to a set of slogans and platitudes, we risk
jettisoning our greatest comfort and strength.
Second Timothy is clear that we have a distinct,
demanding body of doctrine that needs to be
taught, a message that requires reiteration
every Sunday if we, as the Church, are to be
who we are called to be.

2:15 **STUDY**—*See* Spiritual Disciplines Index.
2:22 **CHASTITY**—*See* Spiritual Disciplines
Index.

3:1 *distressing times will come.* No false
advertising here! Discipleship may be a great
blessing, but it can also be very difficult and
demanding. Too often the gospel is presented
today as the best deal a person ever had, a
technique for making successful, contented
people even more successful and contented.
Paul tells Timothy the truth: suffering comes
with the territory. Therefore we must develop
those spiritual practices that enable us to
endure in a sometimes hostile world.

of those two men,[a] their folly will become plain to everyone.

Paul's Charge to Timothy

10 Now you have observed my teaching, my conduct, my aim in life, my faith, my patience, my love, my steadfastness, [11]my persecutions, and my suffering the things that happened to me in Antioch, Iconium, and Lystra. What persecutions I endured! Yet the Lord rescued me from all of them. [12]Indeed, all who want to live a godly life in Christ Jesus will be persecuted. [13]But wicked people and impostors will go from bad to worse, deceiving others and being deceived. [14]But as for you, continue in what you have learned and firmly believed, knowing from whom you learned it, [15]and how from childhood you have known the sacred writings that are able to instruct you for salvation through faith in Christ Jesus. [16]All scripture is inspired by God and is[b] useful for teaching, for reproof, for correction, and for training in righteousness, [17]so that everyone who belongs to God may be proficient, equipped for every good work.

4 In the presence of God and of Christ Jesus, who is to judge the living and the dead, and in view of his appearing and his kingdom, I solemnly urge you: [2]proclaim the message; be persistent whether the time is favorable or unfavorable; convince, rebuke,

and encourage, with the utmost patience in teaching. [3]For the time is coming when people will not put up with sound doctrine, but having itching ears, they will accumulate for themselves teachers to suit their own desires, [4]and will turn away from listening to the truth and wander away to myths. [5]As for you, always be sober, endure suffering, do the work of an evangelist, carry out your ministry fully.

6 As for me, I am already being poured out as a libation, and the time of my departure has come. [7]I have fought the good fight, I have finished the race, I have kept the faith. [8]From now on there is reserved for me the crown of righteousness, which the Lord, the righteous judge, will give me on that day, and not only to me but also to all who have longed for his appearing.

Personal Instructions

9 Do your best to come to me soon, [10]for Demas, in love with this present world, has deserted me and gone to Thessalonica; Crescens has gone to Galatia,[c] Titus to Dalmatia. [11]Only Luke is with me. Get Mark and bring him with you, for he is useful in my ministry. [12]I have sent Tychicus to Ephesus. [13]When you come, bring the cloak that I left with

a Gk lacks two men   b Or Every scripture inspired by God is also   c Other ancient authorities read Gaul

---

3:10 *you have observed my teaching, my conduct.* The Christian faith is contagious. If we are to endure as Christians, it must be through apprenticeship—observing more experienced and well-formed Christians, following their moves, taking up their way of life, inculcating their virtues. Through such observation and imitation, we take up the practices of the faith and come to embody those practices for ourselves. The Church must look for ample opportunities for its members to be observed by and to observe one another as we mature in the faith.

4:1–5 *be persistent.* There is a kind of relentlessness in the work of the early Christian teacher who wrote 2 Timothy. Using every literary means, the writer seeks to stir up in the rest of us a passion for teaching the good news

in a way that renovates lives. If one is called to be a teacher (Paul says, "I was appointed a herald and an apostle and a teacher," 1:11), then the two virtues that must constantly be cultivated are persistence and patience. Our students are afflicted with "itching ears" (v 3) and hanker after easy, simple, cost-free answers to their spiritual problems. The gospel's "sound doctrine" (v 3) is demanding upon those who would understand it and live it. What keeps us working at our teaching is not that our teaching is always received with gratitude, but rather the power of Christ in the gospel to make the kind of people he deserves. So, whether it's a good time for Christian formation and renovation or a bad time, favorable or unfavorable, we are to keep at it, confident that God's grace is sufficient to the task.

Carpus at Troas, also the books, and above all the parchments. [14]Alexander the coppersmith did me great harm; the Lord will pay him back for his deeds. [15]You also must beware of him, for he strongly opposed our message.

[16] At my first defense no one came to my support, but all deserted me. May it not be counted against them! [17]But the Lord stood by me and gave me strength, so that through me the message might be fully proclaimed and all the Gentiles might hear it. So I was rescued from the lion's mouth. [18]The Lord will rescue me from every evil attack and save me for his heavenly kingdom. To him be the glory forever and ever. Amen.

Final Greetings and Benediction

[19] Greet Prisca and Aquila, and the household of Onesiphorus. [20]Erastus remained in Corinth; Trophimus I left ill in Miletus. [21]Do your best to come before winter. Eubulus sends greetings to you, as do Pudens and Linus and Claudia and all the brothers and sisters. *a*

[22] The Lord be with your spirit. Grace be with you. *b*

a Gk *all the brothers*   *b* The Greek word for *you* here is plural. Other ancient authorities add *Amen*

THE LETTER OF PAUL TO

TITUS

P aul says that he left his colleague <u>Titus on the island of Crete</u>, so that he could "put in order what remained to be done" (Titus 1:5). Things seem to have been in great di<u>sorder in Crete. Crete</u> had a bad reputation as a cesspool of iniquity and moral chaos. "Cret<u>ans are always liars, vicious brutes, lazy gluttons</u>" (1:12), says Paul, repeating a common slur against them.

"That testimony is true," is Paul's laconic verdict upon the Cretans. "Rebuke them sharply, so that they may become sound in the faith" (1:13). If you think that spiritual formation is a pleasant, benign matter of making basically nice people just a bit nicer, then check out spiritual formation as it appears here: a rough-and-tumble series of confrontations between wayward congregations of the "detestable, disobedient, [and] unfit" (1:16) and strong moral leaders such as Paul and Titus, who love their people enough not to leave them in their sin.

Transformed, Down to the Smallest Details

The Letter of Paul to Titus is redundant with multiple characteristics of the transformed life, down to the smallest details. Especially valuable is the way the wise apostle tailors his pastoral formation guidance to the specific needs of the various groups under his care—"elders," "older men," "older women," "young women," "younger men," and "slaves." In each case he is describing a life that comes only as the result of deeply ingrained habits of love and joy and peace in the Holy Spirit.

For Christian leaders (elders, overseers, or bishops), for instance, the list of positive virtues describes a deep life indeed. Elders are to be blameless, hospitable, prudent, upright, devout, self-controlled, and lovers of goodness, with a firm grasp of the Word so that the teaching and preaching will be sound (1:6–9). The list of vices to avoid is equally extensive. They should not be arrogant, quick-tempered, addicted to wine, violent, or greedy for gain (1:7). The same kind of detailed specificity is seen in each

---

See also *"The With-God Life" essay for this section of the Bible,*
"The People of God in Community," pp. 2037–42.

group. Some of the ethical instruction is lofty: "Show yourself in all respects a model of good works" (2:7). At other times Paul deals with the hidden cracks and crevices of the moral life: people should not be "slanderers or slaves to drink" (2:3).

We today might find some of this instruction grating, for example, for young women to be submissive to their husbands, for slaves to be submissive to their masters, or for citizens to be subject to rulers and authorities. Then again, when we live in a culture that so elevates personal autonomy, the lack of accountability to anything but our own desires, and complete detachment from the community in favor of personal freedom, perhaps what sounds reactionary or old to our ears is, in the Christian community, true freedom.

Loving Accountability

We live in a time when many Christians seek to cultivate those disciplines and practices that enable them to live the Christian life more faithfully. Scripture such as Titus reminds us that the Christian faith is not only something we believe, but also something we practice. Our beliefs are meant to be embodied in our lives. In too many contemporary communities, there is reluctance to make moral judgments upon anyone's behavior.

Who am I to judge you? Your brother or sister in Christ, that's who. The Letter to Titus suffers no reservations in making specific moral demands upon these new Christians. The world is quite right in assuming that if the way of Christ is true and life-giving, it ought to be able to look at our lives and see that way personified in what we do and say. Titus helps guide us toward the personification of the way of Christ.

—*William H. Willimon*

Salutation

1 Paul, a servant[a] of God and an apostle of Jesus Christ, for the sake of the faith of God's elect and the knowledge of the truth that is in accordance with godliness, [2]in the hope of eternal life that God, who never lies, promised before the ages began— [3]in due time he revealed his word through the proclamation with which I have been entrusted by the command of God our Savior,

4 To Titus, my loyal child in the faith we share:

Grace[b] and peace from God the Father and Christ Jesus our Savior.

Titus in Crete

5 I left you behind in Crete for this reason, so that you should put in order what remained to be done, and should appoint elders in every town, as I directed you: [6]someone who is blameless, married only once,[c] whose children are believers, not accused of debauchery and not rebellious. [7]For a bishop,[d] as God's steward, must be blameless; he must not be arrogant or quick-tempered or addicted to wine or violent or greedy for gain; [8]but he must be hospitable, a lover of goodness, prudent, upright, devout, and self-controlled. [9]He must have a firm grasp of the word that is trustworthy in accordance with the teaching, so that he may be able both to preach with sound doctrine and to refute those who contradict it.

10 There are also many rebellious people, idle talkers and deceivers, especially those of the circumcision; [11]they must be silenced, since they are upsetting whole families by

a Gk *slave*   b Other ancient authorities read
Grace, mercy,   c Gk *husband of one wife*
d Or *an overseer*

teaching for sordid gain what it is not right to teach. [12]It was one of them, their very own prophet, who said,

"Cretans are always liars, vicious brutes, lazy gluttons."

[13]That testimony is true. For this reason rebuke them sharply, so that they may become sound in the faith, [14]not paying attention to Jewish myths or to commandments of those who reject the truth. [15]To the pure all things are pure, but to the corrupt and unbelieving nothing is pure. Their very minds and consciences are corrupted. [16]They profess to know God, but they deny him by their actions. They are detestable, disobedient, unfit for any good work.

Teach Sound Doctrine

2 But as for you, teach what is consistent with sound doctrine. [2]Tell the older men to be temperate, serious, prudent, and sound in faith, in love, and in endurance.

3 Likewise, tell the older women to be reverent in behavior, not to be slanderers or slaves to drink; they are to teach what is good, [4]so that they may encourage the young women to love their husbands, to love their children, [5]to be self-controlled, chaste, good managers of the household, kind, being submissive to their husbands, so that the word of God may not be discredited.

6 Likewise, urge the younger men to be self-controlled. [7]Show yourself in all respects a model of good works, and in your teaching show integrity, gravity, [8]and sound speech that cannot be censured; then any opponent will be put to shame, having nothing evil to say of us.

9 Tell slaves to be submissive to their masters and to give satisfaction in every respect; they are not to talk back, [10]not to pilfer, but to show complete and perfect fidelity, so that in everything they may be an ornament to the doctrine of God our Savior.

11 For the grace of God has appeared, bringing salvation to all,[a] [12]training us to renounce impiety and worldly passions, and in the present age to live lives that are self-controlled, upright, and godly, [13]while we wait for the blessed hope and the manifestation of the glory of our great God and Savior,[b] Jesus Christ. [14]He it is who gave himself for us that he might redeem us from all iniquity and purify for himself a people of his own who are zealous for good deeds.

15 Declare these things; exhort and reprove with all authority.[c] Let no one look down on you.

a Or *has appeared to all, bringing salvation*
b Or *of the great God and our Savior*
c Gk *commandment*

1:13 *rebuke them sharply.* Life in the community cannot always be sweetness and light. There is a time and a place for righteous rebuke. Leaders sometimes must take action for the sake of good order. Those whose idle and deceptive talk is "upsetting whole families" ought to be silenced (v 11). Those who are vulnerable must be protected, and sometimes that cannot happen without rebuke to the proud and the strong. We live in a permissive age when few of us are willing to confront or to judge. Better to ignore irresponsible, unfaithful behavior and just go along to get along. But that is the world's way of community, not that of the Church. Paul advises Titus to set for himself the way of truth telling and truth living. There can be no real renovation of the Christian community without the willingness to confront and to tell the truth about ourselves.

Responding

2:5 CHASTITY. Dallas Willard explains in *The Spirit of the Disciplines,* "To practice chastity, then we must first practice love." How does genuine love encourage chastity? As you contemplate your answer, ask God to show you the way to love him, your neighbor, and yourself more completely. *See also* Spiritual Disciplines Index.

2:9 SUBMISSION—*See* Spiritual Disciplines Index.

2:11 *For the grace of God has appeared.* Paul has a rather long string of exhortations, judgments, and condemnations for the flock under Titus's leadership. But now he places his rebuke in the context of the gospel. The hard admonitions of the preceding verses ought to be balanced with this affirmation of faith. Grace

Maintain Good Deeds

3 Remind them to be subject to rulers and authorities, to be obedient, to be ready for every good work, [2]to speak evil of no one, to avoid quarreling, to be gentle, and to show every courtesy to everyone. [3]For we ourselves were once foolish, disobedient, led astray, slaves to various passions and pleasures, passing our days in malice and envy, despicable, hating one another. [4]But when the goodness and loving kindness of God our Savior appeared, [5]he saved us, not because of any works of righteousness that we had done, but according to his mercy, through the water[a] of rebirth and renewal by the Holy Spirit. [6]This Spirit he poured out on us richly through Jesus Christ our Savior, [7]so that, having been justified by his grace, we might become heirs according to the hope of eternal life. [8]The saying is sure.

I desire that you insist on these things, so that those who have come to believe in God may be careful to devote themselves to good works; these things are excellent and profitable to everyone. [9]But avoid stupid controversies, genealogies, dissensions, and quarrels about the law, for they are unprofitable and worthless. [10]After a first and second admonition, have nothing more to do with anyone who causes divisions, [11]since you know that such a person is perverted and sinful, being self-condemned.

Final Messages and Benediction

12 When I send Artemas to you, or Tychicus, do your best to come to me at Nicopolis, for I have decided to spend the winter there. [13]Make every effort to send Zenas the lawyer and Apollos on their way, and see that they lack nothing. [14]And let people learn to devote themselves to good works in order to meet urgent needs, so that they may not be unproductive.

15 All who are with me send greetings to you. Greet those who love us in the faith.

Grace be with all of you.[b]

a Gk washing   b Other ancient authorities add Amen

---

comes to all. Yet salvation has an ethical component: renouncing and training, letting go of our old selves in order to embrace our new selves in Christ.

3:4-5 *not because of any works of righteousness.* In a letter so full of ethical admonition and moral exhortation, with so many calls to good works, Paul closes with a typical Pauline reminder that we do good works not in order to win the favor of God, but because, in Christ, God's favor has been graciously given to us. Therefore, we ought to live like it. What a wonderful theological reminder of the unmerited mercy of God, coming at the end of a rather moralistic list of ethical exhortations. We are to live disciplined, purified, spiritually committed lives—lives that put faith into practice—not in order to get somewhere with God but, rather, because of the mercy of God. "Grace be with all of you" (v 15).

THE LETTER OF PAUL TO

PHILEMON

A short, personal letter, the Letter to Philemon is almost a coda to the gathered Pauline corpus. Its brevity and personal nature allied to the issue of slavery might suggest that it has nothing to say to us today. The letter is of interest to us, however, because it is an appeal for action on the basis of love rather than law. Onesimus, for an unknown reason, has run away from his master, Philemon. Somehow or other he met up with Paul, through whom he was converted to Christianity, and he now shares with Paul in Christian ministry. Paul sends the letter commending Onesimus to Philemon "no longer as a slave but more than a slave, a beloved brother" (Philem v 16). He is returned as if Paul himself were the returnee (v 17).

"I Always Thank My God Because I Hear of Your Love"

Philemon was clearly a wealthy man who hosted a fledgling congregation in his house, probably in Colossae. He had been converted under Paul's ministry and had spent some time in his company. He owes Paul his Christian life. And a commendable Christian life it is. Paul goes out of his way to thank God for Philemon's love and faith (v 4)—an interesting order, suggesting an appeal to the practice of Christian living, perhaps. More than a church host, he is significantly involved in Christian ministry.

The appeal to love is very strongly asserted. Paul says that he could order Philemon to accept Onesimus back. But he makes his appeal on the basis of Philemon's love—for both Jesus Christ and his brothers and sisters in the faith. We are reminded of the teaching in 1 Cor 13:13: "Faith, hope and love abide, these three; and the greatest of these is love."

"I Am Appealing to You for My Child, Onesimus"

Paul writes as the spiritual father of the runaway slave (v 10). But his interest is more than simply returning Onesimus to his master. The deeper issue is Christian

See also *"The With-God Life" essay for this section of the Bible,*
"The People of God in Community," pp. 2037–42.

fellowship. In Christ, the slave owner and the slave are brothers. Although Paul does not attack the institution of slavery directly, he undermines its hierarchical structure with an appeal to Christian fellowship—his with Philemon (v 6, a difficult verse to translate), and Philemon's with the saints, who have been refreshed through him (v 7).

The broken relationship between Philemon and Onesimus is more than a legal problem (although it is also that). It is a Christian problem involving the need for forgiveness and restoration to fellowship. The Body is broken and needs to be healed. Paul even goes out of his way to say that any debts incurred should be charged to his account (v 18).

"I, Paul, Am Writing This with My Own Hand"

The appeal has apostolic authority behind it (v 19). Clearly, it is an irrefutable request made in love. Paul plays the "heavy" hand: "You owe me your very own self, so let me have my request. Go the extra mile; hold nothing back. And, by the way, sometime soon," says Paul, "I will be visiting you." This comes as both a promise of Christian fellowship and an indication of Paul's commitment to Philemon's ongoing Christian discipleship.

—Andrew Purves

Salutation

1 Paul, a prisoner of Christ Jesus, and Timothy our brother, *a*

To Philemon our dear friend and co-worker, 2to Apphia our sister, *b* to Archippus our fellow soldier, and to the church in your house: 3 Grace to you and peace from God our Father and the Lord Jesus Christ.

Philemon's Love and Faith

4 When I remember you *c* in my prayers, I always thank my God 5because I hear of your love for all the saints and your faith toward the Lord Jesus. 6I pray that the sharing of your faith may become effective when you perceive all the good that we *d* may do for Christ. 7I have indeed received much joy and encouragement from your love, because the hearts of the saints have been refreshed through you, my brother.

Paul's Plea for Onesimus

8 For this reason, though I am bold enough in Christ to command you to do your duty, 9yet I would rather appeal to you on the basis of love—and I, Paul, do this as an old man, and now also as a prisoner of Christ Jesus. *e* 10I am appealing to you for my child, Onesimus, whose father I have become during my imprisonment. 11Formerly he was useless to you, but now he is indeed useful *f*

a Gk *the brother*   *b* Gk *the sister*   *c* From verse 4 through verse 21, *you* is singular   *d* Other ancient authorities read *you* (plural)   *e* Or *as an ambassador of Christ Jesus, and now also his prisoner*   *f* The name Onesimus means *useful* or (compare verse 20) *beneficial*

---

4 *I remember you in my prayers.* The relationship between Paul and Philemon is one of prayerful gratitude. Paul remembers him before God with thanksgiving, in effect reminding us to pray for one another, and to do so with a right spirit. The ministry and life of Christian discipleship cannot move forward unless it is cradled in our common prayers in which we commend one another to God.

9 *I would rather appeal to you on the basis of love.* Certainly love is the ground for Christian community. Paul's appeal, however, is not to

you owe me one!!

both to you and to me. 12I am sending him, that is, my own heart, back to you. 13I wanted to keep him with me, so that he might be of service to me in your place during my imprisonment for the gospel; 14but I preferred to do nothing without your consent, in order that your good deed might be voluntary and not something forced. 15Perhaps this is the reason he was separated from you for a while, so that you might have him back forever, 16no longer as a slave but more than a slave, a beloved brother—especially to me but how much more to you, both in the flesh and in the Lord.

17 So if you consider me your partner, welcome him as you would welcome me. 18If he has wronged you in any way, or owes you anything, charge that to my account. 19I, Paul, am writing this with my own hand: I will repay it. I say nothing about your owing me even your own self. 20Yes, brother, let me have this benefit from you in the Lord. Refresh my heart in Christ. 21Confident of your obedience, I am writing to you, knowing that you will do even more than I say.

22 One thing more—prepare a guest room for me, for I am hoping through your prayers to be restored to you.

Final Greetings and Benediction

23 Epaphras, my fellow prisoner in Christ Jesus, sends greetings to you, *a* 24and so do Mark, Aristarchus, Demas, and Luke, my fellow workers.

25 The grace of the Lord Jesus Christ be with your spirit. *b*

a Here *you* is singular   *b* Other ancient authorities add *Amen*

---

sentimentality or good feelings; he wants Philemon to make a willed, disciplined response to Onesimus that is distinctly and identifiably Christian. It is a call for the sacrifice of self-interest in favor of restoration to relationship. In such a way Philemon, in his life together with Onesimus, reflects the nature of God. In making such an appeal for Onesimus, Paul is both claiming for himself and reminding his correspondent of the highest obligations of Christian discipleship. All Christians live within the framework of the appeal on the basis of love, which builds up Christian community by enabling and restoring relationships.

12 *I am sending him, that is, my own heart, back to you.* So close in Christian fraternity are Paul and Onesimus that Paul says that to receive the slave is to receive him. "Welcome him as you would welcome me," says Paul (v 17). This is the demand of love. The word of grace for our experiences of Christian community is also to look upon one another as we would look upon those we love, and especially as we would choose to look upon Jesus Christ. I am reminded of Mother Teresa of Calcutta, who used to teach that she could see the face of Jesus in the faces of the poor.

20 *Refresh my heart in Christ.* Paul tells Philemon that he will be blessed by his charitable act. Acting in love builds up; acting in self-interest tears down.

25 *The grace of the Lord Jesus Christ.* This is a conventional ending for Paul, but not one to take for granted. All is grace; all is from Jesus Christ. He is the ground of everything that Paul asserts, asks for, and expects.

THE LETTER TO THE
HEBREWS

The Letter to the Hebrews is a carefully argued theological treatise written to remind negligent believers of the greatness of their salvation and to rekindle their commitment to it. It reminds believers of the sublime revelation of God in Jesus Christ and of the thoroughgoing superiority of Christ to the Mosaic covenant. Because it addresses the problem of spiritual indifference and the danger of renouncing the Christian faith, Hebrews is an ideal letter for believers who have grown up in the Christian faith but have grown away from it, for those whose conversion experiences have become lackluster, or for those thinking of experimenting with non-Christian religions and spiritualities. Hebrews warns against theological drift (Heb 2:1), abandoning the promise of the gospel (4:1; 10:35), and falling away from the light of salvation (6:6). Through repeated references to texts and types in the old covenant, the author proves that Jesus, the author of the new covenant, is the consummate, all-sufficient Savior whose person and work are superior to anything Judaism or any other religion can offer.

Hebrews develops in a manner atypical of a New Testament Letter. It does not begin with a greeting and the identification of its author, as was customary in Hellenistic letters; nor does it name the people, place, and circumstances to which the letter was addressed. The letter was already referred to as "The Epistle to the Hebrews" by Church writers in the second century, presumably because of its extensive reliance upon Old Testament references, as well as indications within the letter that its recipients were converts to Christianity from Judaism. The author remains unnamed, identified only as a friend of "Timothy" who writes, presumably, from Italy (13:23–24). The vocabulary, style, and even theology of Hebrews differ noticeably from the letters of Paul. Although the King James Version entitles the book "The Epistle of Paul the Apostle to the Hebrews," it is very improbable that Paul was the

See also *"The With-God Life"* essay for this section of the Bible,
"The People of God in Community," pp. 2037–42.

2183

author of Hebrews. Over the centuries the names of Luke, Apollos, Clement, Priscilla, and Barnabas have been suggested as possible authors. Nevertheless, the conclusion of the third-century church father Origen, who considered the question thoroughly, is still apropos today: "Who wrote the letter [to the Hebrews], in truth God knows" (Eusebius *Ecclesiastical History* 6.25.14).

References within the body of the letter describe the good start that the recipients had made in "earlier days" (10:32). They had been zealous in showing solidarity with and compassion for prisoners and the needy. They had counted the cost of discipleship with cheerfulness, including suffering abuse, persecution, and the plundering of their possessions (10:32–39). Then their faith and fervor waned. They grew lax in gathering together (10:23–25) and rejected their leaders (13:7, 17). Evidently, the Jewish Christians to whom this letter was addressed were considering abandoning the Christian faith and reverting to a safer and less stressful life in Judaism.

From the Old Testament onward, pioneers of the spiritual life have wrestled with the problem of spiritual erosion and loss of zeal. Sometimes the soul "melts away for sorrow" (Ps 119:28) or withers to "a faint spirit" (Isa 61:3). Christian ascetics in the ancient Church called it *acedia* (from the Greek for "negligence" or "indifference"), a condition the Middle Ages counted among the seven deadly sins. Hebrews addresses this problem by launching a spiritual campaign of faith recovery. "Take care, brothers and sisters, that none of you may have an evil, unbelieving heart that turns away from the living God" (Heb 3:12). The Greek word for "turn away" is the word from which the English term "apostasy" is derived, meaning abandonment of the faith. Hebrews rekindles the faith of readers by reminding them of the incomparability of the person, high-priesthood, and sacrifice of Jesus Christ, God's Son and their Savior.

The Incomparable Christ

The author develops the case for the recovery of faith in three stages, all of which depend on the person and work of Jesus Christ. The first stage (1:1–4:13) stresses the incomparability of the *person* of Jesus to anything in heaven or on earth. In a powerful hymnic confession, the first four verses of Hebrews declare the unparalleled preeminence of Christ. As the Son of God, Jesus is "the reflection of God's glory and the exact imprint of God's very being, and he sustains all things by his powerful word" (1:3). He is the One through whom all things were created and also the One through whom all things are redeemed from sin (1:1–4). Because Jesus shares the very nature of God, he is superior to everything in creation.

This means that Jesus is superior to angels and spiritual beings. The first chapter of Hebrews offers a collage of Old Testament quotations demonstrating that God spoke of and to his Son in ways that God never spoke of or to angels. Hence, Jesus is empowered by God as no angel is empowered. We live in a day enamored with spiritual realities and forces, including angels. The author of Hebrews reminds readers not to transfer to spiritual and angelic powers the worship and obedience due to Christ alone. Do not "drift away . . . [and] neglect so great a salvation," the author warns (2:1, 3).

Jesus is incomparably greater than spiritual leaders and gurus as well. Jewish readers rightly took pride in being children of Moses, the great lawgiver. Moses was a servant in God's "house," that is, God's designated family of fellowship. But Jesus was far more than a servant. He was the builder of the house—indeed, he and his followers *are* the house. "Jesus is worthy of more glory than Moses" (3:3), declares the author. This is an important reminder in our day, lest we make idols of charismatic leaders, or demand of human community and personal intimacy the degree of fulfillment granted only by Jesus Christ. Believers are warned not to elevate the leaders of the community or the community itself above the "builder" of the house (3:3–4).

Finally, Jesus is not only greater than spiritual realities and spiritual leaders; he is incomparably greater than Spiritual Disciplines (4:1–13). Observance of the Sabbath was one of the two defining pillars (along with circumcision) of Judaism. Faithful observance of Sabbath was the chief way Jews demonstrated their love for God. Like all Spiritual Disciplines, however, the discipline itself might become a means of pride and security rather than an approach to God. The author of Hebrews reminds readers that the ultimate Sabbath "rest" is not a human achievement, but a gift of grace to those who obey the gospel of Jesus Christ (4:6).

The Incomparable High-Priesthood of Jesus

The second stage in the process of faith recovery (4:14–7:28) is related to the work of Jesus as *high priest.* Jewish high priests wore special vestments, interpreted oracles, and, most important, made representative offerings for the sins of the people. Hebrews shows this office to be fulfilled and perfected in Jesus. Jesus is the perfect high priest because of his unmatched compassion for people and complete obedience to God (4:14–5:10). Unlike those of the priesthood passed down through the line of Aaron, however, Jesus is "a great high priest who has passed through the heavens, . . . the Son of God" (4:14). The heavenly origin of Jesus' high-priesthood is illustrated by the obscure figure of Melchizedek in chapter 7, who is mentioned only twice in the Old Testament (Gen 14:18–20; Ps 110:4). Unlike that of Aaron, the priesthood of Melchizedek originated directly with God. Melchizedek was a priest forever, with no predecessors or successors, and therefore the true prototype of Jesus, the Son of God. Jesus was a high priest, "holy, blameless, [and] undefiled," who, unlike other high priests, did not need to offer sacrifices for his own sins. Rather, as "a Son who has been made perfect forever," Jesus devoted his self-sacrifice wholly for the benefit of others (7:26–28).

The incomparable high-priesthood of Jesus has important ramifications for Christian spirituality. "Spiritual formation" may suggest that the formation of our spiritual lives rests on our own shoulders. The office of high priest is significant in this regard, for a high priest does for others what they cannot do for themselves. Those who by their own efforts are unable to put themselves right with God are first, finally, and forever made right with God by Jesus the high priest. True spiritual existence is not initiated and sustained by our efforts. It is a gift of God made possible only by Jesus, "a high priest . . . who is seated at the right hand of the throne of the Majesty in the heavens" (8:1).

The Incomparable Sacrifice of Jesus

Jesus is not only the high priest of God, however. He is also the high-priestly *sacrifice* to God. The elaborate sacrifices prescribed in the Old Testament did not finally remove sin (9:9–10; 10:1–4). They were only preparatory and symbolic—"shadow[s]" (10:1)—of a future sacrifice that would remove sin "once for all" (10:10) and restore believers to full communion with God. That sacrifice occurred on the cross of Calvary, "when Christ had offered for all time a single sacrifice for sins" (10:12).

In the third stage of the argument for the recovery of faith (8:1–10:18), the author of Hebrews details the significance of the death of Jesus for believers. First, the self-sacrifice of Jesus was so perfect and effective that it rendered the first covenant "obsolete" (8:13), initiating the new and better covenant foreseen by the prophet Jeremiah (8:1–13). Likewise, the death of Jesus on the cross was fully sufficient, "once for all," rendering the levitical sacrifices, which needed to be continually repeated, redundant and void (9:25–10:7). Third, believers now meet God not in a special place, but in a relationship with Jesus, whose person and sacrifice fulfill and replace the tabernacle in the wilderness and the Temple in Jerusalem (9:1–14). The Old Testament "tent of meeting" has become, literally, a meeting and relationship of the believer with Jesus. Finally, the sacrifice of Jesus is meaningful in a way that the sacrifice of a passive and unknowing animal cannot be. Jesus' sacrifice was knowingly offered by a free moral agent and hence in full and willing conformity to the saving purpose of God (10:9–10).

Like the person and priesthood of Jesus, the sacrifice of Jesus is also of special significance for the spiritual life. The purpose of a sacrifice is to change the status of people before God. The essential element in spiritual formation, in other words, is always spiritual transformation, which is effected by the acceptance of the redeeming sacrifice of Jesus as high priest and faithful commitment, according to the example and inspiration of the "cloud of witnesses" (12:1), to the compassionate person of Jesus as high priest. Progress in the spiritual life is not an automatic evolutionary process. Spiritual progress is the result of deliberate and discerning choices. Like a marriage, it is entered into by conscious commitment. We are to "lay aside every weight and the sin that clings so closely, and . . . run with perseverance the race that is set before us, looking to Jesus the pioneer and perfecter of our faith" (12:1–2).

The Shaking of the Foundations and Fire

The incomparability of Christ's person, priesthood, and sacrifice produces within believers a spiritual life that will withstand the dissolution of the created order. Hebrews effectively ends with two images describing that dissolution: the shaking of earth's foundations and fire: "What cannot be shaken may remain, . . . for indeed our God is a consuming fire" (12:27–29). These are not intended as images of dread and terror, but as images of eternity. Like the wall of fire before heaven in Dante's *Divine Comedy* (*Purgatory,* canto 27), God is not a consuming fire in the sense of punishment or torment, but as the purifier of faith, burning away the dross of cowardice, double-mindedness, disbelief, and whatever would obstruct eternal fellowship with God, so that Sanctifier and sanctified shall be one forever (2:11).

—*James R. Edwards*

God Has Spoken by His Son

1 Long ago God spoke to our ancestors in many and various ways by the prophets, [2] but in these last days he has spoken to us by a Son, [a] whom he appointed heir of all things, through whom he also created the worlds. [3] He is the reflection of God's glory and the exact imprint of God's very being, and he sustains [b] all things by his powerful word. When he had made purification for sins, he sat down at the right hand of the Majesty on high, [4] having become as much superior to angels as the name he has inherited is more excellent than theirs.

The Son Is Superior to Angels

[5] For to which of the angels did God ever say,

"You are my Son;
     today I have begotten you"?

Or again,

"I will be his Father,
     and he will be my Son"?

[6] And again, when he brings the firstborn into the world, he says,

"Let all God's angels worship him."

[7] Of the angels he says,

"He makes his angels winds,
     and his servants flames of fire."

[8] But of the Son he says,

"Your throne, O God, is [c] forever and ever,
     and the righteous scepter is the
          scepter of your [d] kingdom.
[9] You have loved righteousness and hated
          wickedness;
     therefore God, your God, has anointed
          you
     with the oil of gladness beyond your
          companions."

[10] And,

"In the beginning, Lord, you founded
          the earth,
     and the heavens are the work of your
          hands;
[11] they will perish, but you remain;
     they will all wear out like clothing;
[12] like a cloak you will roll them up,
     and like clothing [e] they will be
          changed.
But you are the same,
     and your years will never end."

[13] But to which of the angels has he ever said,

"Sit at my right hand
     until I make your enemies a footstool
          for your feet"?

a Or *the Son*   b Or *bears along*   c Or *God is your throne*   d Other ancient authorities read *his* e Other ancient authorities lack *like clothing*

1:1–4 *the reflection of God's glory.* The prologue to Hebrews is an exalted hymn to Jesus, God's Son, who is the final revelation of God. The first four verses of the letter identify Jesus as the agent, the sustainer, and the redeemer of creation. Jesus is the mirror image of God, sharing his very nature and mission.

1:4–2:9 *having become as much superior to angels.* Hebrews begins by accentuating the difference between Jesus and angels. As the Son of God, Jesus is vastly superior to angels, indeed is worshiped by them (1:6). The Son sits at the right hand of God and is given all authority by God (1:13–14). The Son is like God, forever the same, whereas all else is transient (1:12). God has subjected both the present world (2:8) and the world to come (2:5–6) to the Son, not to angels. A salvo of scriptural quotations in chapter 1 demonstrates that spiritual creatures and spiritual experience are subordinate to Jesus Christ, the Son of God, and cannot be substituted for him. Making spiritual experience one's primary objective is like being in love with marriage instead of one's spouse. A good marriage results from loving and serving one's spouse; a healthy spiritual life results from glorifying Christ. Being in love with spiritual experience is not the same as loving and serving Christ and can even eclipse Christ.

Responding
1:6 WORSHIP. This verse reminds us of the scene in Luke in which the angels praised God in the fields outside Bethlehem at Jesus' birth (2:13–14) and the one in Revelation in which multitudes of angels worship the Lamb, Jesus Christ (5:11–12). When you attend church this Sunday, imagine that angels are watching and participating in the service as the congregation sings choruses of praise and hymns of worship. Note how your own worship was affected. *See also* Spiritual Disciplines Index.

[14]Are not all angels[a] spirits in the divine service, sent to serve for the sake of those who are to inherit salvation?

Warning to Pay Attention

2 Therefore we must pay greater attention to what we have heard, so that we do not drift away from it. [2]For if the message declared through angels was valid, and every transgression or disobedience received a just penalty, [3]how can we escape if we neglect so great a salvation? It was declared at first through the Lord, and it was attested to us by those who heard him, [4]while God added his testimony by signs and wonders and various miracles, and by gifts of the Holy Spirit, distributed according to his will.

Exaltation through Abasement

5 Now God[b] did not subject the coming world, about which we are speaking, to angels. [6]But someone has testified somewhere,

"What are human beings that you are
        mindful of them,[c]
    or mortals, that you care for them?[d]
7 You have made them for a little while
        lower[e] than the angels;
    you have crowned them with glory
        and honor,[f]
8   subjecting all things under their feet."

Now in subjecting all things to them, God[b] left nothing outside their control. As it is, we do not yet see everything in subjection to them, [9]but we do see Jesus, who for a little while was made lower[g] than the angels, now crowned with glory and honor because of

the suffering of death, so that by the grace of God[h] he might taste death for everyone.

10 It was fitting that God,[b] for whom and through whom all things exist, in bringing many children to glory, should make the pioneer of their salvation perfect through sufferings. [11]For the one who sanctifies and those who are sanctified all have one Father.[i] For this reason Jesus[b] is not ashamed to call them brothers and sisters,[j] [12]saying,

"I will proclaim your name to my
        brothers and sisters,[j]
    in the midst of the congregation I will
        praise you."

[13]And again,

"I will put my trust in him."

And again,

"Here am I and the children whom God
        has given me."

14 Since, therefore, the children share flesh and blood, he himself likewise shared the same things, so that through death he might destroy the one who has the power of death, that is, the devil, [15]and free those who all their lives were held in slavery by the fear of death. [16]For it is clear that he did not come to help angels, but the descendants of Abraham. [17]Therefore he had to become like his

a Gk all of them   b Gk he   c Gk What is man that you are mindful of him?   d Gk or the son of man that you care for him? In the Hebrew of Psalm 8.4-6 both man and son of man refer to all humankind   e Or them only a little lower   f Other ancient authorities add and set them over the works of your hands   g Or who was made a little lower   h Other ancient authorities read apart from God   i Gk are all of one   j Gk brothers

---

1:14 SERVICE and THE WITH-GOD LIFE— See Spiritual Disciplines Index.

2:1 *we must pay greater attention to what we have heard.* Spiritual maturity consists not simply in knowing the gospel, but in heeding it, that is, intentionally practicing it. Heeding the gospel sets an anchor from which believers will not drift away. Without the anchor, believers are buffeted by changing winds of doctrine. "How can we escape if we neglect so great a salvation?" (v 3).

2:9–10 *crowned with glory and honor because of the suffering of death.* Because of his willingness to relinquish his power and glory, suffer,

and die, Jesus has been justly crowned with all glory and honor. The one who tasted "death for everyone" (2:9) is the only one fully able to lead sons and daughters into glory, where he now reigns supreme over all things. Jesus is the Holy One who makes believers holy like himself and one with him as he is one with the Father.

2:14–18 *through death he might . . . free those . . . held in slavery.* In his radical identification with sinful humanity, Jesus has become "like his brothers and sisters in every respect." In so doing, Jesus showed himself a faithful high priest of God, whose "sacrifice of atonement" makes payment for all people's sins. Moreover,

brothers and sisters[a] in every respect, so that he might be a merciful and faithful high priest in the service of God, to make a sacrifice of atonement for the sins of the people. [18]Because he himself was tested by what he suffered, he is able to help those who are being tested.

Moses a Servant, Christ a Son

3 Therefore, brothers and sisters,[a] holy partners in a heavenly calling, consider that Jesus, the apostle and high priest of our confession, [2]was faithful to the one who appointed him, just as Moses also "was faithful in all[b] God's[c] house." [3]Yet Jesus[d] is worthy of more glory than Moses, just as the builder of a house has more honor than the house itself. [4](For every house is built by someone, but the builder of all things is God.) [5]Now Moses was faithful in all God's[c] house as a servant, to testify to the things that would be spoken later. [6]Christ, however, was faithful over God's[c] house as a son, and we are his house if we hold firm[e] the confidence and the pride that belong to hope.

Warning against Unbelief

7 Therefore, as the Holy Spirit says,
  "Today, if you hear his voice,
8 do not harden your hearts as in the
      rebellion,

as on the day of testing in the
      wilderness,
9 where your ancestors put me to the test,
      though they had seen my works [10]for
      forty years.
  Therefore I was angry with that
      generation,
  and I said, 'They always go astray in
      their hearts,
      and they have not known my ways.'
11 As in my anger I swore,
      'They will not enter my rest.' "

[12]Take care, brothers and sisters,[a] that none of you may have an evil, unbelieving heart that turns away from the living God. [13]But exhort one another every day, as long as it is called "today," so that none of you may be hardened by the deceitfulness of sin. [14]For we have become partners of Christ, if only we hold our first confidence firm to the end. [15]As it is said,

  "Today, if you hear his voice,
      do not harden your hearts as in the
          rebellion."

[16]Now who were they who heard and yet were rebellious? Was it not all those who left Egypt under the leadership of Moses? [17]But with whom was he angry forty years? Was it not those who sinned, whose bodies fell in

---

a Gk brothers   b Other ancient authorities lack all   c Gk his   d Gk this one   e Other ancient authorities add to the end

---

since Jesus has been tested as we have been, he is merciful to all those undergoing trials (see 4:14–16). The final result of Jesus' powerful sacrifice and great mercy is that he frees us from bondage to the devil and from the fear of death.

3:1–2 MEDITATION and STUDY—See Spiritual Disciplines Index.

3:6 *we are his house.* Spiritual existence is not isolated existence. The work of Jesus reconciles believers to God, but it also forms them into a new community, a "house" far greater than was possible through the law of Moses. Believers are urged to "consider . . . Jesus, the apostle and high priest of our confession" (v 1). The Greek word for "consider" means to think about Jesus in a careful and reflective manner. The relation of Jesus to his "house" is different than the relation of Moses to his "house." Jesus is the Son

and thus the true heir, whereas Moses was a servant. Moses "had" a house, that is, the law possessed believers; Christ and believers "are" a house, a new community of Sanctifier and sanctified (2:11), one with the Lord and with each other.

3:7–19 *do not harden your hearts.* These verses warn against two enemies of the spiritual life, hardness of heart and disbelief. Those who rebel against God find neither rest nor peace, whereas those who hear the voice of Christ and accept it in faith are granted rest and peace. The Church is truly Christ's community not when it is divided and embittered, but when we know ourselves as "partners of Christ" and "exhort one another every day" (3:13–14). The Greek word for "exhort" means to stand beside others with encouragement.

the wilderness? [18]And to whom did he swear that they would not enter his rest, if not to those who were disobedient? [19]So we see that they were unable to enter because of unbelief.

The Rest That God Promised

4 Therefore, while the promise of entering his rest is still open, let us take care that none of you should seem to have failed to reach it. [2]For indeed the good news came to us just as to them; but the message they heard did not benefit them, because they were not united by faith with those who listened.[a] [3]For we who have believed enter that rest, just as God[b] has said,

"As in my anger I swore,
'They shall not enter my rest,' "

though his works were finished at the foundation of the world. [4]For in one place it speaks about the seventh day as follows, "And God rested on the seventh day from all his works." [5]And again in this place it says, "They shall not enter my rest." [6]Since therefore it remains open for some to enter it, and those who formerly received the good news failed to enter because of disobedience, [7]again he sets a certain day—"today"—saying through David much later, in the words already quoted,

"Today, if you hear his voice,
do not harden your hearts."

[8]For if Joshua had given them rest, God[b] would not speak later about another day. [9]So then, a sabbath rest still remains for the people of God; [10]for those who enter God's rest also cease from their labors as God did from his. [11]Let us therefore make every effort to enter that rest, so that no one may fall through such disobedience as theirs.

12 Indeed, the word of God is living and active, sharper than any two-edged sword, piercing until it divides soul from spirit, joints from marrow; it is able to judge the thoughts and intentions of the heart. [13]And before him no creature is hidden, but all are naked and laid bare to the eyes of the one to whom we must render an account.

Jesus the Great High Priest

14 Since, then, we have a great high priest who has passed through the heavens, Jesus,

a Other ancient authorities read it did not meet with faith in those who listened   b Gk he

---

4:2 *they were not united by faith with those who listened.* Spiritual discontentment is not due to the ineffectiveness of the gospel, but to our disbelief, disobedience, and hardness of heart (vv 6–7). Warnings against spiritual laxity and laziness run like a refrain through Hebrews. When the good news of Christ is not heard and received with faith (see the alternate translation in the NRSV text note), spiritual indifference results, and we find no rest with God. The original Greek urges readers to "mix," "blend," or "weave" a response of faith to the gospel proclaimed. Then the gospel benefits us, and we find rest and peace.

4:12 *the word of God is living and active, sharper than any two-edged sword.* The "word of God" is the living voice of God in the gospel of Jesus Christ. It is like a sharp sword, discerning the intentions of the heart, which though hidden from human sight are naked and exposed before God. The decisive criterion for the spiritual life is thus not impulsive activism or emotional comfort, but the living word of God that clarifies our minds, incites our hearts, and quickens our wills.

Responding
4:12 THE WITH-GOD LIFE. Many times the living and active "word of God" is interpreted as the "written" word of God, the Bible, but the note on 4:12 says it is the "living voice of God in the gospel of Jesus Christ." Do these two interpretations contradict or complement each other? Could this verse be interpreted another way? What difference should the view that the word of God is living and active make in our relationship with God? *See also* Spiritual Disciplines Index.

4:14–5:2 *a great high priest who has passed through the heavens.* Unlike other high priests, Jesus comes not from the line of Aaron, but from heaven. Even though he is the Son of God, he has identified with our trials and weaknesses more closely than any human high priest, though without sinning. His power as Son of God and his solidarity with our weakness and temptation make his confession entirely trustworthy. Jesus understands our frailty and gives grace and mercy to those who need them.

the Son of God, let us hold fast to our confession. [15]For we do not have a high priest who is unable to sympathize with our weaknesses, but we have one who in every respect has been tested[a] as we are, yet without sin. [16]Let us therefore approach the throne of grace with boldness, so that we may receive mercy and find grace to help in time of need.

5 Every high priest chosen from among mortals is put in charge of things pertaining to God on their behalf, to offer gifts and sacrifices for sins. [2]He is able to deal gently with the ignorant and wayward, since he himself is subject to weakness; [3]and because of this he must offer sacrifice for his own sins as well as for those of the people. [4]And one does not presume to take this honor, but takes it only when called by God, just as Aaron was.

5 So also Christ did not glorify himself in becoming a high priest, but was appointed by the one who said to him,

"You are my Son,
    today I have begotten you";

[6]as he says also in another place,

"You are a priest forever,
    according to the order of
        Melchizedek."

7 In the days of his flesh, Jesus[b] offered up prayers and supplications, with loud cries and tears, to the one who was able to save him from death, and he was heard because of his reverent submission. [8]Although he was a

Son, he learned obedience through what he suffered; [9]and having been made perfect, he became the source of eternal salvation for all who obey him, [10]having been designated by God a high priest according to the order of Melchizedek.

Warning against Falling Away

11 About this[c] we have much to say that is hard to explain, since you have become dull in understanding. [12]For though by this time you ought to be teachers, you need someone to teach you again the basic elements of the oracles of God. You need milk, not solid food; [13]for everyone who lives on milk, being still an infant, is unskilled in the word of righteousness. [14]But solid food is for the mature, for those whose faculties have been trained by practice to distinguish good from evil.

The Peril of Falling Away

6 Therefore let us go on toward perfection,[d] leaving behind the basic teaching about Christ, and not laying again the foundation: repentance from dead works and faith toward God, [2]instruction about baptisms, laying on of hands, resurrection of the dead, and eternal judgment. [3]And we will do[e] this, if God permits. [4]For it is impossible

a Or tempted   b Gk he   c Or him
d Or toward maturity   e Other ancient
authorities read let us do

5:7 PRAYER and SUBMISSION—See Spiritual Disciplines Index.

5:7–9 he learned obedience through what he suffered. Jesus did not seek his own glory (v 5), but offered prayers and supplications to God. Like all humans, he had to learn obedience from what he suffered. But unlike the letter's intended recipients, and perhaps also unlike ourselves, Jesus did not become lax in faith, disbelieving, and hard-hearted. In all his trials and sufferings he reverently submitted to God and thus became both the model and means of salvation for us in our own trials and sufferings.

5:11–6:12 you need someone to teach you again. In this passage the theme changes from falling away from the faith to failing to grow in it. Despite time and opportunity, these believers did not mature beyond the inquirer stage. They

were "bottle-fed" believers whose primary interest was in getting their own needs met. Their faith, summarized in 6:1–2, consisted of those doctrines that overlapped with Judaism, but it lacked the distinctive and saving beliefs of the Christian gospel. The author urges the community "on toward perfection" (6:1), to push forward and "realize the full assurance of hope to the very end" (6:11). Mature Christians possess trained faculties to know the difference between right and wrong (5:14). Mature Christians also imitate those who have learned to wait patiently and faithfully for the final inheritance of salvation (6:12). These qualities do not come easily or naturally. Spiritual formation consists of training (the word in 5:12 connotes athletic training), steadfastness, and being knowledgeable in righteousness (5:13).

to restore again to repentance those who have once been enlightened, and have tasted the heavenly gift, and have shared in the Holy Spirit, 5and have tasted the goodness of the word of God and the powers of the age to come, 6and then have fallen away, since on their own they are crucifying again the Son of God and are holding him up to contempt. 7Ground that drinks up the rain falling on it repeatedly, and that produces a crop useful to those for whom it is cultivated, receives a blessing from God. 8But if it produces thorns and thistles, it is worthless and on the verge of being cursed; its end is to be burned over.

9 Even though we speak in this way, beloved, we are confident of better things in your case, things that belong to salvation. 10For God is not unjust; he will not overlook your work and the love that you showed for his sake*a* in serving the saints, as you still do. 11And we want each one of you to show the same diligence so as to realize the full assurance of hope to the very end, 12so that you may not become sluggish, but imitators of those who through faith and patience inherit the promises.

The Certainty of God's Promise

13 When God made a promise to Abra-

ham, because he had no one greater by whom to swear, he swore by himself, 14saying, "I will surely bless you and multiply you." 15And thus Abraham,*b* having patiently endured, obtained the promise. 16Human beings, of course, swear by someone greater than themselves, and an oath given as confirmation puts an end to all dispute. 17In the same way, when God desired to show even more clearly to the heirs of the promise the unchangeable character of his purpose, he guaranteed it by an oath, 18so that through two unchangeable things, in which it is impossible that God would prove false, we who have taken refuge might be strongly encouraged to seize the hope set before us. 19We have this hope, a sure and steadfast anchor of the soul, a hope that enters the inner shrine behind the curtain, 20where Jesus, a forerunner on our behalf, has entered, having become a high priest forever according to the order of Melchizedek.

The Priestly Order of Melchizedek

7 This "King Melchizedek of Salem, priest of the Most High God, met Abraham as

a Gk *for his name*   *b* Gk *he*

6:4–6 *it is impossible to restore.* This passage and 10:26 often trouble readers. The intent of these passages is to remind us, unambiguously but pastorally, that those who renounce the gospel can no longer be forgiven. Apostasy cuts us off from the cross, which is the only means by which sins can be forgiven. The intent of these passages is not to cause us to doubt our salvation, but to warn that spiritual apathy can lead to apostasy. As in mountain climbing, where the possibility of falling makes one a more diligent climber, so too in Christian faith the presence of genuine spiritual dangers should admonish us not to be indifferent to the costly grace of God in the cross of Christ.

Responding
6:10 SERVICE. In *Celebration of Discipline* Richard Foster makes a distinction between self-righteous service and true service. Self-righteous service flows out of human effort and goals; true service flows out of

God and love. As you are "serving the saints" this week, examine your motives. Is your service based on getting praise and accolades from others or done because you love the people you are serving? Or are your motives mixed? *See also* Spiritual Disciplines Index.

6:19 *hope, a sure and steadfast anchor of the soul.* The spiritual life is not overshadowed by anxiety or fear, but rather confident that it would be "impossible that God would prove false" (v 18). All spiritual formation is founded on the trustworthiness of God's character and the truth of God's revelation in the person of Jesus Christ. This conviction leads to life-sustaining hope, and hope is a "sure and steadfast anchor of the soul."

7:1–28 *Melchizedek . . . resembling the Son of God.* The comparison of Jesus to Melchizedek in chapter 7 is patterned after a rabbinic style of argumentation that would have been familiar to Jewish Christians. The author of Hebrews has

he was returning from defeating the kings and blessed him"; [2]and to him Abraham apportioned "one-tenth of everything." His name, in the first place, means "king of righteousness"; next he is also king of Salem, that is, "king of peace." [3]Without father, without mother, without genealogy, having neither beginning of days nor end of life, but resembling the Son of God, he remains a priest forever.

[4] See how great he is! Even[a] Abraham the patriarch gave him a tenth of the spoils. [5]And those descendants of Levi who receive the priestly office have a commandment in the law to collect tithes[b] from the people, that is, from their kindred,[c] though these also are descended from Abraham. [6]But this man, who does not belong to their ancestry, collected tithes[b] from Abraham and blessed him who had received the promises. [7]It is beyond dispute that the inferior is blessed by the superior. [8]In the one case, tithes are received by those who are mortal; in the other, by one of whom it is testified that he lives. [9]One might even say that Levi himself, who receives tithes, paid tithes through Abraham, [10]for he was still in the loins of his ancestor when Melchizedek met him.

Another Priest, Like Melchizedek

[11] Now if perfection had been attainable through the levitical priesthood—for the people received the law under this priesthood—what further need would there have been to speak of another priest arising according to the order of Melchizedek, rather than one according to the order of Aaron? [12]For when there is a change in the priesthood, there is necessarily a change in the law as well. [13]Now the one of whom these things are spoken belonged to another tribe, from which no one has ever served at the altar. [14]For it is evident that our Lord was descended from Judah, and in connection with that tribe Moses said nothing about priests.

[15] It is even more obvious when another priest arises, resembling Melchizedek, [16]one who has become a priest, not through a legal requirement concerning physical descent, but through the power of an indestructible life. [17]For it is attested of him,

"You are a priest forever,
    according to the order of
        Melchizedek."

[18]There is, on the one hand, the abrogation of an earlier commandment because it was weak and ineffectual [19](for the law made nothing perfect); there is, on the other hand, the introduction of a better hope, through which we approach God.

[20] This was confirmed with an oath; for others who became priests took their office without an oath, [21]but this one became a priest with an oath, because of the one who said to him,

"The Lord has sworn
    and will not change his mind,
'You are a priest forever' "—

[22]accordingly Jesus has also become the guarantee of a better covenant.

[23] Furthermore, the former priests were many in number, because they were prevented by death from continuing in office; [24]but he holds his priesthood permanently, because he continues forever. [25]Consequently he is able for all time to save[d] those who approach God through him, since he always lives to make intercession for them.

[26] For it was fitting that we should have

a Other ancient authorities lack Even   b Or a tenth   c Gk brothers   d Or able to save completely

already shown that Jesus was superior to the Jewish tradition, including Moses, the Sabbath, the law, and even angels. But Jesus was not without a prototype in the Old Testament. The one figure who foreshadowed Jesus' highpriesthood and divine sonship was Melchizedek, a mysterious figure who appears and disappears abruptly in Gen 14:18–20. The true approach to God would not be through the Aaronic priesthood and sacrifices, but by "a better hope, through which we approach God" (v 19). Melchizedek was an omen of Christ, the true "high priest, holy, blameless, undefiled, separated from sinners, and exalted above the heavens" (v 26).

7:25 THE WITH-GOD LIFE—See Spiritual Disciplines Index.

such a high priest, holy, blameless, undefiled, separated from sinners, and exalted
above the heavens. [27]Unlike the other[a] high
priests, he has no need to offer sacrifices day
after day, first for his own sins, and then for
those of the people; this he did once for all
when he offered himself. [28]For the law appoints as high priests those who are subject
to weakness, but the word of the oath, which
came later than the law, appoints a Son who
has been made perfect forever.

Mediator of a Better Covenant

8 Now the main point in what we are saying is this: we have such a high priest,
one who is seated at the right hand of the
throne of the Majesty in the heavens, [2]a minister in the sanctuary and the true tent[b] that
the Lord, and not any mortal, has set up. [3]For
every high priest is appointed to offer gifts
and sacrifices; hence it is necessary for this
priest also to have something to offer. [4]Now
if he were on earth, he would not be a priest
at all, since there are priests who offer gifts according to the law. [5]They offer worship in a
sanctuary that is a sketch and shadow of the
heavenly one; for Moses, when he was about
to erect the tent,[b] was warned, "See that you
make everything according to the pattern
that was shown you on the mountain." [6]But

Jesus[c] has now obtained a more excellent
ministry, and to that degree he is the mediator of a better covenant, which has been enacted through better promises. [7]For if that
first covenant had been faultless, there would
have been no need to look for a second one.
[8]God[d] finds fault with them when he
says:

"The days are surely coming, says the
Lord,
when I will establish a new covenant
with the house of Israel
and with the house of Judah;
[9] not like the covenant that I made with
their ancestors,
on the day when I took them by the
hand to lead them out of the land
of Egypt;
for they did not continue in my
covenant,
and so I had no concern for them,
says the Lord.
[10] This is the covenant that I will make
with the house of Israel
after those days, says the Lord:
I will put my laws in their minds,
and write them on their hearts,
and I will be their God,

a Gk lacks *other*   b Or *tabernacle*   c Gk *he*
d Gk *He*

8:1–10:18 *a more excellent ministry . . . the
mediator of a better covenant.* This section deals
with the theme of foreshadowings in the Old
Testament that are fulfilled in Jesus. Jesus
ministers not in a sanctuary made by human
hands, but in the true sanctuary in heaven (8:1–2;
9:24). Earthly priests repeatedly made imperfect
offerings that were sketches and shadows (8:5;
9:23). These offerings could never take away sin
(10:4,11), whereas the supreme self-sacrifice of
Christ is the fully sufficient sin offering, perfect,
"once for all" (9:26–28), and forever (10:12–14).
The conscience could not be cleansed by priestly
offerings (9:9), but only in the sacrifice of Christ
(9:14). Priests made offerings for their own sins
(9:7), but Jesus was without sin and therefore
the effective sin-bearer for all (9:28). The first
covenant has been rendered obsolete (8:13) by
Jesus' fulfillment of the long awaited promise of
Jer 31:31–34 (8:7–12), inaugurating the new and

perfect covenant of God. The theme of foreshadowing and fulfillment is captured in a
wordplay in the original Greek. The old covenant
required *latreia* ("ritual duties," 9:6), the payment
of regulations and rites; the new offers *lutrosis*
("eternal redemption," 9:12), the self-sacrifice
of Jesus Christ for eternal redemption. All the
regulations of the first covenant were provisional,
"until the time comes to set things right" in
Christ (9:10). Jesus is a better priest, who serves
in a better place, as the mediator of a better
covenant, based on better promises of God, who
renders a better conscience. Jesus is therefore
the perfect servant of believers on God's behalf
who purifies "our conscience from dead works to
worship the living God!" (9:14). Allowing this all-
sufficient Savior to perfect his will and way in our
lives is the supreme act of spiritual formation,
"for by a single offering he has perfected for all
time those who are sanctified" (10:14).

and they shall be my people.
11 And they shall not teach one another
    or say to each other, 'Know the Lord,'
  for they shall all know me,
    from the least of them to the greatest.
12 For I will be merciful toward their
    iniquities,
    and I will remember their sins no
    more."
13 In speaking of "a new covenant," he has made the first one obsolete. And what is obsolete and growing old will soon disappear.

The Earthly and the Heavenly Sanctuaries

9 Now even the first covenant had regulations for worship and an earthly sanctuary. [2]For a tent[a] was constructed, the first one, in which were the lampstand, the table, and the bread of the Presence;[b] this is called the Holy Place. [3]Behind the second curtain was a tent[a] called the Holy of Holies. [4]In it stood the golden altar of incense and the ark of the covenant overlaid on all sides with gold, in which there were a golden urn holding the manna, and Aaron's rod that budded, and the tablets of the covenant; [5]above it were the cherubim of glory overshadowing the mercy seat.[c] Of these things we cannot speak now in detail.

6 Such preparations having been made, the priests go continually into the first tent[a] to carry out their ritual duties; [7]but only the high priest goes into the second, and he but once a year, and not without taking the blood that he offers for himself and for the sins committed unintentionally by the people. [8]By this the Holy Spirit indicates that the way into the sanctuary has not yet been disclosed as long as the first tent[a] is still standing. [9]This is a symbol[d] of the present time, during which gifts and sacrifices are offered that cannot perfect the conscience of the worshiper, [10]but deal only with food and drink and various baptisms, regulations for the body imposed until the time comes to set things right.

11 But when Christ came as a high priest of the good things that have come,[e] then through the greater and perfect[f] tent[a] (not made with hands, that is, not of this creation), [12]he entered once for all into the Holy Place, not with the blood of goats and calves, but with his own blood, thus obtaining eternal redemption. [13]For if the blood of goats and bulls, with the sprinkling of the ashes of a heifer, sanctifies those who have been defiled so that their flesh is purified, [14]how much more will the blood of Christ, who through the eternal Spirit[g] offered himself without blemish to God, purify our[h] conscience from dead works to worship the living God!

15 For this reason he is the mediator of a new covenant, so that those who are called may receive the promised eternal inheritance, because a death has occurred that redeems them from the transgressions under the first covenant.[i] [16]Where a will[i] is involved, the death of the one who made it must be established. [17]For a will[i] takes effect only at death, since it is not in force as long as the one who made it is alive. [18]Hence not even the first covenant was inaugurated without blood. [19]For when every commandment had been told to all the people by Moses in accordance with the law, he took the blood of calves and goats,[j] with water and scarlet wool and hyssop, and sprinkled both the scroll itself and all the people, [20]saying, "This is the blood of the covenant that God has ordained for you." [21]And in the same way he sprinkled with the blood both the tent[a] and all the vessels used in worship. [22]Indeed, under the law almost everything is purified with blood, and without the shedding of blood there is no forgiveness of sins.

Christ's Sacrifice Takes Away Sin

23 Thus it was necessary for the sketches of the heavenly things to be purified with

a Or tabernacle   b Gk the presentation of the loaves   c Or the place of atonement
d Gk parable   e Other ancient authorities read good things to come   f Gk more perfect   g Other ancient authorities read Holy Spirit   h Other ancient authorities read your   i The Greek word used here means both covenant and will   j Other ancient authorities lack and goats

these rites, but the heavenly things themselves need better sacrifices than these. 24For Christ did not enter a sanctuary made by human hands, a mere copy of the true one, but he entered into heaven itself, now to appear in the presence of God on our behalf. 25Nor was it to offer himself again and again, as the high priest enters the Holy Place year after year with blood that is not his own; 26for then he would have had to suffer again and again since the foundation of the world. But as it is, he has appeared once for all at the end of the age to remove sin by the sacrifice of himself. 27And just as it is appointed for mortals to die once, and after that the judgment, 28so Christ, having been offered once to bear the sins of many, will appear a second time, not to deal with sin, but to save those who are eagerly waiting for him.

Christ's Sacrifice Once for All

10 Since the law has only a shadow of the good things to come and not the true form of these realities, it*a* can never, by the same sacrifices that are continually offered year after year, make perfect those who approach. 2Otherwise, would they not have ceased being offered, since the worshipers, cleansed once for all, would no longer have any consciousness of sin? 3But in these sacrifices there is a reminder of sin year after year. 4For it is impossible for the blood of bulls and goats to take away sins. 5Consequently, when Christ*b* came into the world, he said,

"Sacrifices and offerings you have not
desired,
but a body you have prepared for me;
6 in burnt offerings and sin offerings
you have taken no pleasure.
7 Then I said, 'See, God, I have come to do
your will, O God'
(in the scroll of the book*c* it is written
of me)."

8When he said above, "You have neither desired nor taken pleasure in sacrifices and offerings and burnt offerings and sin offerings" (these are offered according to the law), 9then he added, "See, I have come to do your will." He abolishes the first in order to establish the second. 10And it is by God's will*d* that we have been sanctified through the offering of the body of Jesus Christ once for all.

11 And every priest stands day after day at his service, offering again and again the same sacrifices that can never take away sins. 12But when Christ*e* had offered for all time a single sacrifice for sins, "he sat down at the right hand of God," 13and since then has been waiting "until his enemies would be made a footstool for his feet." 14For by a single offering he has perfected for all time those who are sanctified. 15And the Holy Spirit also testifies to us, for after saying,

16 "This is the covenant that I will make
with them
after those days, says the Lord:
I will put my laws in their hearts,
and I will write them on their minds,"
17he also adds,
"I will remember*f* their sins and their
lawless deeds no more."
18Where there is forgiveness of these, there is no longer any offering for sin.

A Call to Persevere

19 Therefore, my friends,*g* since we have confidence to enter the sanctuary by the blood of Jesus, 20by the new and living way that he opened for us through the curtain (that is, through his flesh), 21and since we have a great priest over the house of God, 22let us approach with a true heart in full assurance of faith, with our hearts sprinkled clean from an evil conscience and our bodies washed with pure water. 23Let us hold fast to the confession of our hope without wavering,

a Other ancient authorities read *they*   *b* Gk *he*
c Meaning of Gk uncertain   *d* Gk *by that will*
e Gk *this one*   *f* Gk *on their minds and I will*
remember   *g* Gk *Therefore, brothers*

9:23; 10:5; 10:12 SACRIFICE—*See* Spiritual Disciplines Index.

10:19–39 *Let us hold fast to the confession of our hope.* In verse 19 the subject of Hebrews changes from the all-sufficiency of Jesus' priesthood and sacrifice to the proper response believers should make to it. As believers we are exhorted to five spiritual practices. First, we may

for he who has promised is faithful. 24And let us consider how to provoke one another to love and good deeds, 25not neglecting to meet together, as is the habit of some, but encouraging one another, and all the more as you see the Day approaching.

26 For if we willfully persist in sin after having received the knowledge of the truth, there no longer remains a sacrifice for sins, 27but a fearful prospect of judgment, and a fury of fire that will consume the adversaries. 28Anyone who has violated the law of Moses dies without mercy "on the testimony of two or three witnesses." 29How much worse punishment do you think will be deserved by those who have spurned the Son of God, profaned the blood of the covenant by which they were sanctified, and outraged the Spirit of grace? 30For we know the one who said, "Vengeance is mine, I will repay." And again, "The Lord will judge his people." 31It is a fearful thing to fall into the hands of the living God.

32 But recall those earlier days when, after you had been enlightened, you endured a hard struggle with sufferings, 33sometimes being publicly exposed to abuse and persecution, and sometimes being partners with those so treated. 34For you had compassion for those who were in prison, and you cheerfully accepted the plundering of your possessions, knowing that you yourselves possessed something better and more lasting. 35Do not, therefore, abandon that confidence of yours; it brings a great reward. 36For you need endurance, so that when you have done the will of God, you may receive what was promised. 37For yet

"in a very little while,
        the one who is coming will come and
            will not delay;
38 but my righteous one will live by faith.
    My soul takes no pleasure in anyone
        who shrinks back."

39But we are not among those who shrink back and so are lost, but among those who have faith and so are saved.

The Meaning of Faith

11 Now faith is the assurance of things hoped for, the conviction of things not seen. 2Indeed, by faith a our ancestors received approval. 3By faith we understand that the worlds were prepared by the word of God,

a Gk by this

---

freely and confidently approach God in faith (v 22). Second, we are urged to be steadfast and not waver from the faithful promises of God (v 23). Third, we should constantly encourage one another in love and good works (v 24). Fourth, we should commit to gathering regularly in fellowship (v 25). Finally, we are warned not to reject the work of Christ, but recall how God has faithfully preserved us in the past (vv 26–35). Rejecting these exhortations leads to spiritual timidity and perdition, whereas following them results in spiritual endurance and the safekeeping of our souls (v 39).

Responding
10:23 CONFESSION. What is the "hope that is in you" (1 Pet 3:15)? (See also the note on Heb 6:19.) In Western civilizations most Christians feel pressure not to talk about their faith. When was the last time you felt free to express your faith in Jesus Christ and the hope that this gives you? If you have been feeling intimidated by others, take a moment to ask God for the strength to express your faith in all circumstances. *See also* Spiritual Disciplines Index.

10:23–25 FELLOWSHIP—*See* Spiritual Disciplines Index.

10:26 *there no longer remains a sacrifice for sins.* See note on 6:4–6.

11:1–40 *by faith our ancestors received approval.* We often think of the Christian faith as the intellectual content of belief. Chapter 11, however, defines faith in terms of trusting in the promises of God and growing in maturity by bearing witness to them in practical life choices. The roll call of Israelite heroes and heroines of faith portrays faith as a life pilgrimage that is pleasing to God. Faith, in other words, is something that is practiced, not simply believed. Spiritual formation, accordingly, consists in ensuring the practicability of our faith in everyday life.

so that what is seen was made from things that are not visible. *a*

The Examples of Abel, Enoch, and Noah

4 By faith Abel offered to God a more acceptable *b* sacrifice than Cain's. Through this he received approval as righteous, God himself giving approval to his gifts; he died, but through his faith *c* he still speaks. 5By faith Enoch was taken so that he did not experience death; and "he was not found, because God had taken him." For it was attested before he was taken away that "he had pleased God." 6And without faith it is impossible to please God, for whoever would approach him must believe that he exists and that he rewards those who seek him. 7By faith Noah, warned by God about events as yet unseen, respected the warning and built an ark to save his household; by this he condemned the world and became an heir to the righteousness that is in accordance with faith.

The Faith of Abraham

8 By faith Abraham obeyed when he was called to set out for a place that he was to receive as an inheritance; and he set out, not knowing where he was going. 9By faith he stayed for a time in the land he had been promised, as in a foreign land, living in tents, as did Isaac and Jacob, who were heirs with him of the same promise. 10For he looked forward to the city that has foundations, whose architect and builder is God. 11By faith he received power of procreation, even though he was too old—and Sarah herself was barren—because he considered him faithful who had promised. *d* 12Therefore from one person, and this one as good as dead, descendants were born, "as many as the stars of heaven and as the innumerable grains of sand by the seashore."

13 All of these died in faith without having received the promises, but from a distance they saw and greeted them. They confessed that they were strangers and foreigners on the earth, 14for people who speak in this way make it clear that they are seeking a homeland. 15If they had been thinking of the land that they had left behind, they would have had opportunity to return. 16But

as it is, they desire a better country, that is, a heavenly one. Therefore God is not ashamed to be called their God; indeed, he has prepared a city for them.

17 By faith Abraham, when put to the test, offered up Isaac. He who had received the promises was ready to offer up his only son, 18of whom he had been told, "It is through Isaac that descendants shall be named for you." 19He considered the fact that God is able even to raise someone from the dead— and figuratively speaking, he did receive him back. 20By faith Isaac invoked blessings for the future on Jacob and Esau. 21By faith Jacob, when dying, blessed each of the sons of Joseph, "bowing in worship over the top of his staff." 22By faith Joseph, at the end of his life, made mention of the exodus of the Israelites and gave instructions about his burial. *e*

The Faith of Moses

23 By faith Moses was hidden by his parents for three months after his birth, because they saw that the child was beautiful; and they were not afraid of the king's edict. *f* 24By faith Moses, when he was grown up, refused to be called a son of Pharaoh's daughter, 25choosing rather to share ill-treatment with the people of God than to enjoy the fleeting pleasures of sin. 26He considered abuse suffered for the Christ *g* to be greater wealth than the treasures of Egypt, for he was looking ahead to the reward. 27By faith he left Egypt, unafraid of the king's anger; for he persevered as though *h* he saw him who is invisible. 28By faith he kept the Passover and the sprinkling of blood, so that the destroyer of the firstborn would not touch the firstborn of Israel. *i*

The Faith of Other Israelite Heroes

29 By faith the people passed through the

a Or *was not made out of visible things*
b Gk *greater*   c Gk *through it*   d Or *By faith Sarah herself, though barren, received power to conceive, even when she was too old, because she considered him faithful who had promised.*   e Gk *his bones*
f Other ancient authorities add *By faith Moses, when he was grown up, killed the Egyptian, because he observed the humiliation of his people* (Gk *brothers*)
g Or *the Messiah*   h Or *because*   i Gk *would not touch them*

Red Sea as if it were dry land, but when the Egyptians attempted to do so they were drowned. [30]By faith the walls of Jericho fell after they had been encircled for seven days. [31]By faith Rahab the prostitute did not perish with those who were disobedient, [a] because she had received the spies in peace.

32 And what more should I say? For time would fail me to tell of Gideon, Barak, Samson, Jephthah, of David and Samuel and the prophets— [33]who through faith conquered kingdoms, administered justice, obtained promises, shut the mouths of lions, [34]quenched raging fire, escaped the edge of the sword, won strength out of weakness, became mighty in war, put foreign armies to flight. [35]Women received their dead by resurrection. Others were tortured, refusing to accept release, in order to obtain a better resurrection. [36]Others suffered mocking and flogging, and even chains and imprisonment. [37]They were stoned to death, they were sawn in two, [b] they were killed by the sword; they went about in skins of sheep and goats, destitute, persecuted, tormented— [38]of whom the world was not worthy. They wandered in deserts and mountains, and in caves and holes in the ground.

39 Yet all these, though they were commended for their faith, did not receive what was promised, [40]since God had provided something better so that they would not, apart from us, be made perfect.

The Example of Jesus

12 Therefore, since we are surrounded by so great a cloud of witnesses, let us also lay aside every weight and the sin that clings so closely, [c] and let us run with perseverance the race that is set before us, [2]looking to Jesus the pioneer and perfecter of our faith, who for the sake of [d] the joy that was set before him endured the cross, disregarding its shame, and has taken his seat at the right hand of the throne of God.

3 Consider him who endured such hostility against himself from sinners, [e] so that you may not grow weary or lose heart. [4]In your struggle against sin you have not yet resisted to the point of shedding your blood. [5]And you have forgotten the exhortation that addresses you as children—

"My child, do not regard lightly the
　　discipline of the Lord,
　or lose heart when you are punished
　　by him;

a Or *unbelieving*　　b Other ancient authorities add *they were tempted*　　c Other ancient authorities read *sin that easily distracts*　　d Or *who instead of*　　e Other ancient authorities read *such hostility from sinners against themselves*

11:39 *though they were commended for their faith.* Chapter 11 does not present the faith of the great figures of the Old Testament as a museum piece relegated to the past. The faith of those who have gone before is still alive today; we not only participate in it, we complete it. Spiritual formation is participation in a relay race of faith, receiving the baton from those who have gone before and handing it off to those who come after. The Church is thus not only united throughout space; it is also united throughout time. The faithfulness of our forebears is completed in our faithfulness, and our faithfulness is completed in the faithfulness of those yet to come.

12:1–2 *surrounded by so great a cloud of witnesses, . . . looking to Jesus the pioneer and perfecter of our faith.* The faith of other believers throughout space and time supports and encourages our own faith. We draw strength from the "great cloud of witnesses" that has gone faithfully before us. We do not concentrate on the faith per se, but we set our sights deliberately on "Jesus the pioneer and perfecter of our faith." Jesus pioneers a way for believers through the uncharted territory of this world, perfecting our faith as we follow him. We must, like pilgrims, travel light by laying "aside every weight and the sin that clings so closely," willingly enduring hardships until we joyfully reach "the heavenly Jerusalem, and . . . the assembly of the firstborn who are enrolled in heaven" (vv 22–23).

12:1–3 SIMPLICITY/FRUGALITY—*See* Spiritual Disciplines Index.

12:2–3 MEDITATION—*See* Spiritual Disciplines Index.

12:3 STUDY—*See* Spiritual Disciplines Index.

6 for the Lord disciplines those whom he
    loves,
    and chastises every child whom he
    accepts."
7 Endure trials for the sake of discipline. God
is treating you as children; for what child is
there whom a parent does not discipline? 8 If
you do not have that discipline in which all
children share, then you are illegitimate and
not his children. 9 Moreover, we had human
parents to discipline us, and we respected
them. Should we not be even more willing to
be subject to the Father of spirits and live?
10 For they disciplined us for a short time as
seemed best to them, but he disciplines us
for our good, in order that we may share his
holiness. 11 Now, discipline always seems
painful rather than pleasant at the time, but
later it yields the peaceful fruit of righteousness to those who have been trained by it.

12 Therefore lift your drooping hands and
strengthen your weak knees, 13 and make
straight paths for your feet, so that what is
lame may not be put out of joint, but rather
be healed.

Warnings against Rejecting God's Grace

14 Pursue peace with everyone, and the
holiness without which no one will see the
Lord. 15 See to it that no one fails to obtain the
grace of God; that no root of bitterness

springs up and causes trouble, and through
it many become defiled. 16 See to it that no
one becomes like Esau, an immoral and godless person, who sold his birthright for a single meal. 17 You know that later, when he
wanted to inherit the blessing, he was rejected, for he found no chance to repent,[a]
even though he sought the blessing[b] with
tears.

18 You have not come to something[c] that
can be touched, a blazing fire, and darkness,
and gloom, and a tempest, 19 and the sound
of a trumpet, and a voice whose words made
the hearers beg that not another word be spoken to them. 20 (For they could not endure
the order that was given, "If even an animal
touches the mountain, it shall be stoned to
death." 21 Indeed, so terrifying was the sight
that Moses said, "I tremble with fear.") 22 But
you have come to Mount Zion and to the
city of the living God, the heavenly Jerusalem, and to innumerable angels in festal gathering, 23 and to the assembly[d] of the firstborn
who are enrolled in heaven, and to God the
judge of all, and to the spirits of the righteous made perfect, 24 and to Jesus, the mediator of a new covenant, and to the sprinkled

a Or no chance to change his father's mind   b Gk it
c Other ancient authorities read a mountain
d Or angels, and to the festal gathering 23 and assembly

12:5–12 *the Lord disciplines those whom he
loves.* These verses remind followers of Christ
of the importance of discipline in their lives.
Discipline, however, is not punishment. Punishment is retribution for an offense committed.
That is not the sense of the Greek word *paideia*
("discipline"), which means to instruct and train
for responsible living. Punishment is a sign of
God's displeasure; discipline is a sign of God's
love. Discipline is likened to strength training
(v 12), so that our spiritual muscles may be
strong and healthy. Discipline is an act of training for our good (vv 6, 10), so that we may grow
in holiness, experience "the peaceful fruit of
righteousness" (v 11), and finish the race set
before us.
    12:18–29 *You have not come to . . . a blazing
fire, and darkness, and gloom, . . . But . . . to
Mount Zion.* Like the apostle Paul (Gal

4:21–5:1), the author of Hebrews contrasts a
spirituality of law with a spirituality of grace. A
spirituality of law, like Mt. Sinai, makes demands
that cannot be endured (v 20) and produces
fear (v 21). The gospel calls people away from
the forbidding "darkness and gloom" of Mt.
Sinai (v 18) to Mt. Zion, where a joyful gathering
of believers shares in the privileges of firstborn
children of God. A spirituality of grace does not
require our blood, as does a spirituality of law
(v 24). A spirituality of grace is participation in a
new covenant community where we are made
truly righteous and perfect because of the
shedding of Jesus' blood. The same "reverent
submission" (Greek, *eulabeia*) that characterized the life of Jesus (5:7) now characterizes
our lives (v 28).
    12:22–24 **THE WITH-GOD LIFE**—*See*
Spiritual Disciplines Index.

blood that speaks a better word than the blood of Abel.

25 See that you do not refuse the one who is speaking; for if they did not escape when they refused the one who warned them on earth, how much less will we escape if we reject the one who warns from heaven! 26At that time his voice shook the earth; but now he has promised, "Yet once more I will shake not only the earth but also the heaven." 27This phrase, "Yet once more," indicates the removal of what is shaken—that is, created things—so that what cannot be shaken may remain. 28Therefore, since we are receiving a kingdom that cannot be shaken, let us give thanks, by which we offer to God an acceptable worship with reverence and awe; 29for indeed our God is a consuming fire.

Service Well-Pleasing to God

13 Let mutual love continue. 2Do not neglect to show hospitality to strangers, for by doing that some have entertained angels without knowing it. 3Remember those who are in prison, as though you were in prison with them; those who are being tortured, as though you yourselves were being tortured. a 4Let marriage be held in honor by all, and let the marriage bed be kept undefiled; for God will judge fornicators and adulterers. 5Keep your lives free from the love

of money, and be content with what you have; for he has said, "I will never leave you or forsake you." 6So we can say with confidence,

"The Lord is my helper;
I will not be afraid.
What can anyone do to me?"

7 Remember your leaders, those who spoke the word of God to you; consider the outcome of their way of life, and imitate their faith. 8Jesus Christ is the same yesterday and today and forever. 9Do not be carried away by all kinds of strange teachings; for it is well for the heart to be strengthened by grace, not by regulations about food, b which have not benefited those who observe them. 10We have an altar from which those who officiate in the tent c have no right to eat. 11For the bodies of those animals whose blood is brought into the sanctuary by the high priest as a sacrifice for sin are burned outside the camp. 12Therefore Jesus also suffered outside the city gate in order to sanctify the people by his own blood. 13Let us then go to him outside the camp and bear the abuse he endured. 14For here we have no lasting city, but we are looking for the city that is to come. 15Through him, then, let us continually offer a sacrifice of praise to God, that is, the fruit of

a Gk were in the body   b Gk not by foods
c Or tabernacle

12:28 WORSHIP—See Spiritual Disciplines Index.

13:1–19 Let mutual love continue. Chapter 13 contains a checklist of seven spiritual exercises. The cardinal virtue of all is love of those inside the fellowship of faith (the sense of the Greek word philadelphia, "mutual love," in v 1), seconded by hospitality toward those outside it (v 2). A third behavior is remembering prisoners and victims of torture (v 3). Fourth, marriage must be honored, remembering that God will judge the sexually immoral, whether fornicators or adulterers (v 4). Fifth, believers should learn to be content with what they have and trust God, who provides, rather than pursue the love of money (vv 5–6). Sixth, believers should honor and imitate their spiritual leaders (vv 7, 17). And finally, believers should "not be carried away by all kinds of strange teachings" (v 9), but become

strong in the grace of the gospel.

13:5–6 THE WITH-GOD LIFE—See Spiritual Disciplines Index.

13:11 SACRIFICE—See Spiritual Disciplines Index.

13:13 Let us then go to him outside the camp. The tabernacle in the wilderness is a fitting metaphor of the spiritual life. In the first covenant, animals were sacrificed "outside the camp" (v 11). Jesus likewise was crucified "outside the city gate" (v 12). We, therefore, should also take our stand with Christ, bearing the abuse he endured, "outside the camp." The object of the spiritual life is not to make the gospel compatible with the camp, but to train us to live outside it, as resident aliens in the world. The true spiritual life is formed and lived outside the promises and security of this world, accepting Jesus' mission and participating in his sufferings.

lips that confess his name. 16Do not neglect to do good and to share what you have, for such sacrifices are pleasing to God.

17 Obey your leaders and submit to them, for they are keeping watch over your souls and will give an account. Let them do this with joy and not with sighing—for that would be harmful to you.

18 Pray for us; we are sure that we have a clear conscience, desiring to act honorably in all things. 19I urge you all the more to do this, so that I may be restored to you very soon.

Benediction

20 Now may the God of peace, who brought back from the dead our Lord Jesus, the great shepherd of the sheep, by the blood of the eternal covenant, 21make you com-plete in everything good so that you may do his will, working among us*a* that which is pleasing in his sight, through Jesus Christ, to whom be the glory forever and ever. Amen.

Final Exhortation and Greetings

22 I appeal to you, brothers and sisters,*b* bear with my word of exhortation, for I have written to you briefly. 23I want you to know that our brother Timothy has been set free; and if he comes in time, he will be with me when I see you. 24Greet all your leaders and all the saints. Those from Italy send you greet-ings. 25Grace be with all of you.*c*

a Other ancient authorities read *you*
b Gk *brothers*   c Other ancient authorities add *Amen*

13:15 SACRIFICE—*See* Spiritual Disciplines Index.

Responding
13:16 SACRIFICE. How do you view doing good and sharing what you have? Is it a burden? A sacrifice? An act of love? Take a moment to examine your motives. Do you do good and share with others grudgingly or out of love? *See also* Spiritual Disciplines Index.

13:17 SUBMISSION—*See* Spiritual Disciplines Index.

13:17 *your leaders . . . are keeping watch over your souls.* The goal of Christian leadership is to be vigilant over the spiritual welfare of believers.

13:20–21 *Now may the God of peace.* The closing benediction is both a perfect summary of Hebrews and a perfect prayer of spiritual formation.

THE LETTER OF

JAMES

T he book of James is often called a "catholic" Letter because of its lack of address or reference to any named congregation. Unlike the Pauline Letters, which mention specific audiences, James and the other catholic Letters are more general in application, and questions about their authorship, date, and first recipients have never been completely settled. These Letters were in use in many sectors of the Church from an early period; citations found in later writings point back clearly to them as earlier widely accepted and authoritative documents.

Who Was James?

The Letter of James opens with the words "James, a servant of God and of the Lord Jesus Christ" (James 1:1). That no further description is offered and no additional claim made by the writer for himself may mean that he was well known and possessed authority.

The Gospels mention four persons associated with Jesus named James. There was James, son of Zebedee and brother of John (Matt 10:2); James, son of Alphaeus (Matt 10:3); James the younger, one of the sons of Mary and Clopas (Mark 15:40; 16:1; John 19:25); and James, the brother of Jesus (Mark 6:3). The weight of church tradition has been crucial in linking this letter with James the brother of Jesus. Perhaps this explains the absence of additional personal claims on the author's part.

The Letter of James makes no reference to any specific events in the period of its creation. The letter contains few names, only the writer's own name, James; some revered Old Testament figures—Abraham (2:21, 23), Isaac (2:21), Rahab (2:25), Job (5:11), Elijah (5:17–18); and some unnamed "prophets who spoke in the name of the Lord" (5:10). Although explicit references to "Jesus Christ" are few (1:1; 2:1), the designation "Lord" is used again and again, sometimes with reference to God (4:10; 5:4,

See also *"The With-God Life" essay for this section of the Bible,*
"The People of God in Community," pp. 2037–42.

10–11) and sometimes with reference to Jesus (1:1, 12; 2:1; 5:7–8, 14). The letter is manifestly Jewish in background, but clearly Christian in substance, obviously intended to appeal both to Jews and Christians. Personal spiritual development and a vital congregational life are the writer's concerns.

The leadership position James held in the Jerusalem church could account for his authoritative manner in writing. Converted after the resurrection of Jesus (1 Cor 15:7 tells us that the resurrected Jesus appeared to James), James rose to a position of considerable responsibility, as the book of Acts shows (12:17; 15:13–21). Gal 2:9 mentions James, Peter, and John as "pillar" leaders. This James died in AD 62, the victim of a conspiracy by members of the Sanhedrin. The writer was a teacher (James 3:1) steeped in Old Testament thought, wisdom expressions, and the teaching tradition from Jesus. Many teachings in this letter directly parallel or allude to the teaching tradition from Jesus as found in the Sermon on the Mount (e.g., James 1:2 / Matt 5:11–12; Luke 6:22–23; James 1:4 / Matt 5:48; James 1:5 / Matt 7:7; James 1:17 / Matt 7:11; James 1:22 / Matt 7:24).

The writer calls for full adherence to the Christian faith and life. The thoroughgoing commitment being promoted is clearly voiced in his insistence that being Christian means being "doers of the word, and not merely hearers" (1:22), which is a lived "religion that is pure and undefiled before God" (1:27).

Rules for the Christian Life

Organized around what appear to have been three brief homilies (2:1–13; 2:14–26; 3:1–12), the Letter of James treats a seemingly disconnected series of topics that relate to "rules" for Christian life at its best. These topics include a proper understanding and prompt handling of temptation (1:2, 12–14), the indispensability of a working faith (1:3, 6; 2:14, 17–18, 20, 22, 24, 26; 5:15); dependence on godly wisdom (1:5; 3:13, 15, 17); the necessity for patience (5:7–8, 10–11); and prayer (5:13–18).

The rest of the letter is filled with wisdom statements, slogans, and admonitions. The many admonitions are forcefully stated as imperatives, but the letter is really a blend of stirring reminders and pastoral encouragement. The writer has placed emphasis on wholehearted righteous living, with the promised "coming of the Lord" (5:7–8) as the encouraging motivational incentive and expected gain.

The letter makes a strong appeal for all to avoid divisive distinctions between social classes in the fellowship (1:9–11; 2:1–9); all are reminded that class lines should not affect or determine the way believers relate to each other. The insistence is that the Christian faith levels all believers, allowing no authoritative pride of place by the rich over the poor.

The passage about prayer for the sick in 5:14–16 echoes Sir 38:9–15, which also links recovery with anointing with oil and prayer and in connection with open confession of sin and full obedience to the One who can assist recovery. The letter highlights "elders of the church" (v 14) as agents of help as they practice personal and congregational care. James is loaded with admonitions to live by the rules; it accents the need to internalize the teachings, offering instructive insights for believers for living the Christian faith. The following outline suggests the flow of the writer's message:

Though comparatively brief, the Letter of James is neither thin nor deficient; it is a call to action after hearing (i.e., learning what is to be known and done, 1:22–25). It binds believers to deal with the common issues of life as informed believers, and to do so with full regard for the wisdom by which this is best done. This letter is a clear statement to believers about personal religious integrity, spiritual maturity, unselfishness in relations, and how to live responsibly in the Church and the world.

—James Earl Massey

Salutation

1 James, a servant *a* of God and of the Lord Jesus Christ,
To the twelve tribes in the Dispersion:
Greetings.

Faith and Wisdom

2 My brothers and sisters, *b* whenever you face trials of any kind, consider it nothing but joy, 3because you know that the testing of your faith produces endurance; 4and let endurance have its full effect, so that you may be mature and complete, lacking in nothing.

5 If any of you is lacking in wisdom, ask God, who gives to all generously and un-

a Gk *slave*   *b* Gk *brothers*

1:1 *James, a servant of God and of the Lord Jesus Christ.* The bold but humble acceptance of his rightful place before God and Jesus speaks to the wisdom and humility of the writer and provides a sound reason why he should be heard and regarded by those to whom he writes—"the twelve tribes in the Dispersion," initially Jewish Christians living in areas beyond Jerusalem who looked to the Church leaders there for instruction and oversight. *the Lord Jesus Christ.* This description of Jesus is regal—and warranted.

The writer's Christology is in plain view. Jesus is also revered as "our glorious Lord Jesus Christ" (2:1), and his name is honored as "excellent" (2:7). His is the Name in which each community member was baptized upon accepting the faith and the Name in which the community prays (5:14). Our spiritual growth and steadiness take place through obedient submission and service to God and Jesus.

1:2–8 *whenever you face trials.* Life involves us in "trials" and "testings" of many kinds; some

grudgingly, and it will be given you. 6But ask in faith, never doubting, for the one who doubts is like a wave of the sea, driven and tossed by the wind; 7, 8for the doubter, being double-minded and unstable in every way, must not expect to receive anything from the Lord.

Poverty and Riches

9 Let the believer*a* who is lowly boast in being raised up, 10and the rich in being brought low, because the rich will disappear like a flower in the field. 11For the sun rises with its scorching heat and withers the field; its flower falls, and its beauty perishes. It is the same way with the rich; in the midst of a busy life, they will wither away.

Trial and Temptation

12 Blessed is anyone who endures temptation. Such a one has stood the test and will receive the crown of life that the Lord*b* has promised to those who love him. 13No one,

when tempted, should say, "I am being tempted by God"; for God cannot be tempted by evil and he himself tempts no one. 14But one is tempted by one's own desire, being lured and enticed by it; 15then, when that desire has conceived, it gives birth to sin, and that sin, when it is fully grown, gives birth to death. 16Do not be deceived, my beloved.*c*

17 Every generous act of giving, with every perfect gift, is from above, coming down from the Father of lights, with whom there is no variation or shadow due to change.*d* 18In fulfillment of his own purpose he gave us birth by the word of truth, so that we would become a kind of first fruits of his creatures.

Hearing and Doing the Word

19 You must understand this, my beloved:*c*

a Gk *brother*   *b* Gk *he*; other ancient authorities read *God*   *c* Gk *my beloved brothers*   *d* Other ancient authorities read *variation due to a shadow of turning*

---

happen because of our exposed humanity, and some because of our quest for holiness. Believing in God includes trusting God to produce meaning even from our miseries and to shape us through our struggles, since a tested "faith produces endurance" (v 3) whose effects contribute to our maturity and usefulness.

1:5 GUIDANCE—*See* Spiritual Disciplines Index.

1:8 SIMPLICITY/FRUGALITY—*See* Spiritual Disciplines Index.

1:9–11 *Let the believer who is lowly.* Wealth is a major preoccupation of the letter. If poor or disadvantaged, we are advised not to seek wealth as an ultimate good, and if rich, we are not to hoard wealth and enjoy privilege as if these can be possessed eternally. Although the "lowly" are lacking in relation to others who have much, there should be pride in having been "raised" higher in Christ; the "rich" are charged to remember how temporary the material side of life really is. In additional passages, James will address other issues connected to wealth and possessions (2:6–7; 4:13–16; 5:1–6).

1:12–13 *Blessed is anyone who endures temptation.* Temptation is a human problem that can be rightly managed with a disciplined will and an attitude of anticipated good. We can stand up to forces that converge to press us down; we can

indeed endure the pressure and win against it. Being "tried" or "tempted" can make us feel so terribly vulnerable, so individually exposed, but we can maintain stability by realizing that the outcome is not determined by what happens to us, but what happens within us. Trusting God's resourcefulness gets us through such extreme times, because faith determines the real outcome. For believers, faith affects everything, and this wisdom (v 5) must inform our consciousness and form our character. We mature through dealing with what faith must endure.

1:14 *But one is tempted by one's own desire.* The anatomy of sinning is in view here. The key to successfully handling a test or trial is to discipline our desires, purify our motives, and trust God's plan and timetable to meet our needs honorably. (See Matt 4:1–11; Luke 4:1–13 for the example Jesus set.)

Responding

1:19 SILENCE. Most of us are so intent on thinking about what we are going to say during a conversation that we fail to listen to the other person. For the next month concentrate on listening, really listening, to those with whom you are talking. What stirrings did you feel in your spirit? *See also* Spiritual Disciplines Index.

JAMES

Growing Up with Jesus

Selected Scriptures: *Mark 3:20–21, 31–32; 6:3; John 7:1–9; Acts 1:12–14; 15:12–21; 21:18; 1 Corinthians 15:3–7; Galatians 1:19; 2:7–9; James 1–5*

James grew up with Jesus. As brothers, they played together, were schooled together, and learned carpentry together. Along with their siblings, they probably spent more than twenty years sharing everyday life in the small town of Nazareth. Surely James knew Jesus as a living, breathing person as well as anyone on earth ever knew him. How fitting, then, that when writing to the early Church decades later James would focus on the everyday lives of believers. He had seen Jesus live his life and had, no doubt, heard Jesus teach the crowds. He knew his brother and understood that the love Jesus lived out in his day-to-day interactions remained inseparable from the salvation he had come to bring.

As the Scriptures above indicate, James didn't believe in Jesus as Messiah before the resurrection. We know Mary had been told by the angel that Jesus was the Son of God, and through the shepherds she knew Jesus was to be the Messiah. Joseph too learned from the angel that Jesus would "save his people from their sins" (Matt 1:21). We don't know how much Mary and Joseph told their children of Jesus' birth and the prophecy about him, yet it's clear that even they didn't understand how Jesus would live out his role as Messiah. Perhaps the family pondered it together once Jesus was grown and began his ministry. In any case, James and his brothers couldn't accept that their family member, Jesus, was God's Son and the Savior of all people.

The resurrection changed everything. Jesus appeared to James before he ascended, and James received the Holy Spirit at Pentecost along with the others. Now he saw Jesus in a new light. Not just the loving and eccentric elder child, Jesus was the Lover of souls and the Only Begotten of God. Jesus no longer walked alongside James or shared his meals, but Christ lived inside him. This once flesh-and-blood brother had now become a part of James, and the daily life Jesus had lived took on eternal significance.

We hear echoes of Jesus' example in James's Letter. James must have recalled the way Jesus had handled family and personal trials and the trial that ended in crucifixion. He recalled how Jesus had endured temptation and been slow to anger, how Jesus had cared for all people, rich and poor, and how Jesus had controlled his tongue. He remembered Jesus' gentleness and willingness to yield, his friendship with God, his humility. James remembered Jesus' patience and perseverance. And he recalled how Jesus prayed in faith and healed the sick, how he gave his followers the power to go from town to town doing the same. He remembered how Jesus forgave sins and how he cared desperately for finding the lone, lost sheep.

So James wrote on these same matters that make up daily life for us all. The other

PROFILE: JAMES

apostles were preaching and teaching on the heady matters of sin and salvation, grace and faith, for the Church needed a clear understanding of these doctrines on which their newfound faith was based. Still, James knew that none of the doctrine would matter if Jesus' followers didn't live out their faith in their minute-by-minute, day-by-day dealings in the world.

We might think of James as one of the world's first spiritual directors. He grew up with Jesus and went on to help Christians of the world also to grow up with Christ. What you *do* matters, he says. Your attitudes toward yourself matter, and so does the way you treat the stranger in your midst, the solicitor at your door, the co-worker at your job. Jesus is within you and his power is only a prayer away. Open the small parts, the ordinary goings-on of your life, to him and count these the measure of your faith.

Personal Reflection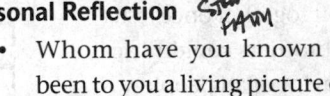

- Whom have you known who has been to you a living picture of Christ? How has this person changed the way you live?

- William Law, an eighteenth-century Anglican priest and spiritual director, wrote: "If we are to be new people in Christ, then we must show our newness to the world. If we are to follow Christ, it must be in the way we spend each day." How will you spend today? Ask Jesus to make you new today and to make his presence with you like that of a brother, walking alongside you and showing you how to live newly in each ordinary moment.

let everyone be quick to listen, slow to speak, slow to anger; [20]for your anger does not produce God's righteousness. [21]Therefore rid yourselves of all sordidness and rank growth of wickedness, and welcome with meekness the implanted word that has the power to save your souls.

22 But be doers of the word, and not merely hearers who deceive themselves. [23]For if any are hearers of the word and not doers, they are like those who look at themselves[a] in a mirror; [24]for they look at themselves and, on going away, immediately forget what they were like. [25]But those who look into the perfect law, the law of liberty, and persevere, being not hearers who forget but doers who act—they will be blessed in their doing.

26 If any think they are religious, and do not bridle their tongues but deceive their hearts, their religion is worthless. [27]Religion that is pure and undefiled before God, the Father, is this: to care for orphans and widows

a Gk *at the face of his birth*

1:21 *welcome with meekness the implanted word.* God is the giver of good (v 17), not evil, and the central "perfect gift" is his word of truth by which we are born anew (v 18). The gospel and spiritual regeneration are in view here, the gospel being the word of truth (also described in v 25 as "perfect law" and "law of liberty" and in 2:8 as "royal law"). We are urged to reject all moral evils and vices, which only serve wickedness, and to welcome with meekness a steady hearing and receiving of the word that connects us with salvation. (In this connection, see also 1 Pet 2:1–2.) James equates God's word and truth (as elsewhere in Scripture, e.g., John 17:17; 2 Tim 2:15; 4:2, 4), by which God's will is revealed to and executed in us. So he insists: "Be doers of the word, and not merely hearers" (v 22). This is the basis for a virtuous life that is "pure and undefiled before God" (v 27), allied with the corresponding need to care for the needy, especially those whose situation in life subjects them to exploitation by others. James here reminds us that Christian faith, rightly understood, not only connects us meaningfully to God in a life of virtue, but also connects us to needy persons in a life of sharing.

in their distress, and to keep oneself unstained by the world.

Warning against Partiality

2 My brothers and sisters,[a] do you with your acts of favoritism really believe in our glorious Lord Jesus Christ?[b] ²For if a person with gold rings and in fine clothes comes into your assembly, and if a poor person in dirty clothes also comes in, ³and if you take notice of the one wearing the fine clothes and say, "Have a seat here, please," while to the one who is poor you say, "Stand there," or, "Sit at my feet,"[c] ⁴have you not made distinctions among yourselves, and become judges with evil thoughts? ⁵Listen, my beloved brothers and sisters.[d] Has not God chosen the poor in the world to be rich in faith and to be heirs of the kingdom that he has promised to those who love him? ⁶But you have dishonored the poor. Is it not the rich who oppress you? Is it not they who drag you into court? ⁷Is it not they who blaspheme the excellent name that was invoked over you?

8 You do well if you really fulfill the royal law according to the scripture, "You shall love your neighbor as yourself." ⁹But if you show partiality, you commit sin and are convicted by the law as transgressors. ¹⁰For whoever keeps the whole law but fails in one point has become accountable for all of it. ¹¹For the one who said, "You shall not commit adultery," also said, "You shall not murder." Now if you do not commit adultery but if you murder, you have become a transgressor of the law. ¹²So speak and so act as those who are to be judged by the law of liberty. ¹³For judgment will be without mercy to anyone who has shown no mercy; mercy triumphs over judgment.

Faith without Works Is Dead

14 What good is it, my brothers and sisters,[d] if you say you have faith but do not have works? Can faith save you? ¹⁵If a brother or sister is naked and lacks daily food, ¹⁶and one of you says to them, "Go in peace; keep warm and eat your fill," and yet you do not supply their bodily needs, what is the good of that? ¹⁷So faith by itself, if it has no works, is dead.

a Gk My brothers   b Or hold the faith of our glorious Lord Jesus Christ without acts of favoritism   c Gk Sit under my footstool   d Gk brothers

2:1–13 *acts of favoritism.* Here James addresses the great issue of how we as believers are to regard each other and how our motives can build up or destroy a sense of true community. The communal model Jesus expects forbids all partisan concerns (see Matt 23:8, 10; Luke 22:24–27), just as advised in Lev 19:15, "You shall not be partial to the poor or defer to the great," the passage reflected here.

2:8 *You shall love your neighbor as yourself.* This verse echoes Lev 19:18. Social distinctions must not influence our choices and God-given relationship to fellow believers. The Christian faith levels all believers. It allows no authoritative pride of place by the rich over the poor. James rebukes selfish social distinctions as unwarranted and deadly, because favoritism breaks the "royal law" of communal love and blocks the good that should come through being part of an "assembly" of the faithful.

2:12–13 *So speak and so act as those who are to be judged.* These verses are a reminder that God will show mercy to those who honor the royal law, but will judge those who transgress it

(see Prov 21:13; Matt 5:7). Consistency in obeying all of the known will of God is stressed.

2:14–26 *if . . . you have faith but do not have works?* James stresses the importance of acting out our faith. This is no polemic against Paul's teaching that works are not the way to righteousness (see Rom 3:21–31; Gal 3:6–14, 23–26). Although James might have been trying to correct a misreading or misunderstanding of Paul, he is really arguing that a true belief leads us to action. Following the teaching tradition of Jesus, James reminds believers that *doing* "the will of [the] Father in heaven" (Matt 7:21) is the lifestyle of true believers.

2:15 *If a brother or sister . . . lacks daily food.* James illustrates the need to act charitably and to do what is in our power for others at their time of need. The true character of faith shows itself in what it incites us to do. Paul was warning against viewing deeds as meritorious for salvation, but James's appeal is to obey what faith demands when allied with love. Both stress faith as essential, but James speaks about faith's being evidenced in acts of love.

18 But someone will say, "You have faith and I have works." Show me your faith apart from your works, and I by my works will show you my faith. 19You believe that God is one; you do well. Even the demons believe—and shudder. 20Do you want to be shown, you senseless person, that faith apart from works is barren? 21Was not our ancestor Abraham justified by works when he offered his son Isaac on the altar? 22You see that faith was active along with his works, and faith was brought to completion by the works. 23Thus the scripture was fulfilled that says, "Abraham believed God, and it was reckoned to him as righteousness," and he was called the friend of God. 24You see that a person is justified by works and not by faith alone. 25Likewise, was not Rahab the prostitute also justified by works when she welcomed the messengers and sent them out by another road? 26For just as the body without the spirit is dead, so faith without works is also dead.

Taming the Tongue

3 Not many of you should become teachers, my brothers and sisters, a for you know that we who teach will be judged with greater strictness. 2For all of us make many mistakes. Anyone who makes no mistakes in speaking is perfect, able to keep the whole body in check with a bridle. 3If we put bits into the mouths of horses to make them obey

us, we guide their whole bodies. 4Or look at ships: though they are so large that it takes strong winds to drive them, yet they are guided by a very small rudder wherever the will of the pilot directs. 5So also the tongue is a small member, yet it boasts of great exploits.

How great a forest is set ablaze by a small fire! 6And the tongue is a fire. The tongue is placed among our members as a world of iniquity; it stains the whole body, sets on fire the cycle of nature, b and is itself set on fire by hell. c 7For every species of beast and bird, of reptile and sea creature, can be tamed and has been tamed by the human species, 8but no one can tame the tongue—a restless evil, full of deadly poison. 9With it we bless the Lord and Father, and with it we curse those who are made in the likeness of God. 10From the same mouth come blessing and cursing. My brothers and sisters, d this ought not to be so. 11Does a spring pour forth from the same opening both fresh and brackish water? 12Can a fig tree, my brothers and sisters, e yield olives, or a grapevine figs? No more can salt water yield fresh.

Two Kinds of Wisdom

13 Who is wise and understanding among you? Show by your good life that your works are done with gentleness born of wisdom.

a Gk brothers   b Or wheel of birth
c Gk Gehenna   d Gk My brothers   e Gk my brothers

3:1–12 SILENCE—See Spiritual Disciplines Index.

3:1–12 *Not many of you should become teachers.* Since sins of speech are so prevalent in human interaction, James offers wisdom to church leaders and members on how these can be avoided in their fellowship. Being a church official makes one prominent, but also exposed and vulnerable. Those who teach can become targets of jealousy, because they hold a position of authority to which others ambitiously aspire. Those who teach can also err by talking or using their role to selfish advantage and be guilty of "many mistakes" (v 2). Thus the warning: "We who teach will be judged with greater strictness." Those who teach must weigh their words with care, exercise their office with godly intent, and model behavior that nurtures community and

promotes peace. Earlier, in 1:19, James advises believers about the need to listen carefully, to speak considerately, and to be of a calm demeanor. Here he warns further about the use of the tongue. A Christian's speech should bless, not berate or abuse (v 10). Illustrative imagery and wisdom proverbs abound in this section, all advising the importance of a disciplined tongue. The tongue betrays the world that is in one's heart; it is a microcosm of the inner self.

3:2 *all of us make many mistakes.* According to this verse, a disciplined tongue indicates a mature believer, someone who, making "no mistakes in speaking is perfect, able to keep the whole body [self] in check with a bridle." This verse is akin to 1:4, where to be "mature and complete, lacking in nothing" is the proper quest for believers.

¹⁴But if you have bitter envy and selfish ambition in your hearts, do not be boastful and false to the truth. ¹⁵Such wisdom does not come down from above, but is earthly, unspiritual, devilish. ¹⁶For where there is envy and selfish ambition, there will also be disorder and wickedness of every kind. ¹⁷But the wisdom from above is first pure, then peaceable, gentle, willing to yield, full of mercy and good fruits, without a trace of partiality or hypocrisy. ¹⁸And a harvest of righteousness is sown in peace for*ᵃ* those who make peace.

Friendship with the World

4 Those conflicts and disputes among you, where do they come from? Do they not come from your cravings that are at war within you? ²You want something and do not have it; so you commit murder. And you covet*ᵇ* something and cannot obtain it; so you engage in disputes and conflicts. You do not have, because you do not ask. ³You ask and do not receive, because you ask wrongly, in order to spend what you get on your pleasures. ⁴Adulterers! Do you not know that friendship with the world is enmity with God? Therefore whoever wishes to be a friend of the world becomes an enemy of God. ⁵Or do you suppose that it is for nothing that the scripture says, "God*ᶜ* yearns jealously for the spirit that he has made to dwell in us"? ⁶But he gives all the more grace; therefore it says,

"God opposes the proud,
    but gives grace to the humble."

⁷Submit yourselves therefore to God. Resist the devil, and he will flee from you. ⁸Draw near to God, and he will draw near to you.

a Or *by*   *b* Or *you murder and you covet*
c Gk *He*

3:13–18 *Who is wise?* True teachers impart godly wisdom that informs our faith and forms our character. Thus the emphasis on "wisdom" and "understanding" in contrast to the "envy and selfish ambition" that reveal immaturity and ungodliness (vv 13–14). James advises about how to discern between so-called wisdoms. There is an earthly wisdom that is "unspiritual, devilish" and leads to "disorder and wickedness" because it seeks a selfish human end (vv 15–16); and there is a heavenly wisdom that makes one pure, peaceable, gentle, willing to yield, merciful, and fruitful and brings about godly results (vv 17–18). The qualities of a godly teacher are described here and, as well, the qualities engendered in believers who are properly nurtured in "the truth" (v 14).

3:15–18 GUIDANCE—*See* Spiritual Disciplines Index.

3:18 *a harvest of righteousness is sown in peace.* Godly teachers and mature believers seek a harvest of righteousness from what they say and do. The image here of "sowing peace" suggests that righteousness becomes visible in persons who work for peace and live by peaceful rules. This line recalls Jesus' Beatitude: "Blessed are the peacemakers" (Matt 5:9). Self-promoting leaders work against righteousness, lacking as they do what verse 13 mentions as a "good life" and the "gentleness born of wisdom [from above]." Just as true faith shows itself in good works, true wisdom shows itself in unselfish, godly conduct.

4:1–17 *conflicts and disputes among you.* "Conflicts and disputes" undermine and destroy congregational unity. Selfish and unsettling "cravings" result in warring attitudes and ambitions that reveal the spirit of worldliness. When these attitudes and ambitions show themselves in a church, a prophetic word is demanded to stem the tide and correct the offenders.

4:4 *friendship with the world.* Worldliness is the enemy of godliness, and only a complete submission to God and God's ways can defeat its pernicious spirit.

4:7 *Submit yourselves therefore to God.* Humbling ourselves before the Lord places us in the position to be freed from double-mindedness, a worldly and competitive spirit, and a judgmental attitude toward others. *Resist the devil.* See also 1 Pet 5:8–9.

Responding
4:7 SUBMISSION. Why do we resist submitting to God? *See also* Spiritual Disciplines Index.

4:8 SIMPLICITY/FRUGALITY—*See* Spiritual Disciplines Index.

4:8–12 *Draw near to God.* (See also 1 Pet 5:5b–6.) The act of "drawing near" is the proper

Cleanse your hands, you sinners, and purify your hearts, you double-minded. [9]Lament and mourn and weep. Let your laughter be turned into mourning and your joy into dejection. [10]Humble yourselves before the Lord, and he will exalt you.

Warning against Judging Another

11 Do not speak evil against one another, brothers and sisters.[a] Whoever speaks evil against another or judges another, speaks evil against the law and judges the law; but if you judge the law, you are not a doer of the law but a judge. [12]There is one lawgiver and judge who is able to save and to destroy. So who, then, are you to judge your neighbor?

Boasting about Tomorrow

13 Come now, you who say, "Today or tomorrow we will go to such and such a town and spend a year there, doing business and making money." [14]Yet you do not even know what tomorrow will bring. What is your life? For you are a mist that appears for a little while and then vanishes. [15]Instead you ought to say, "If the Lord wishes, we will live and do this or that." [16]As it is, you boast in your arrogance; all such boasting is evil. [17]Anyone, then, who knows the right thing to do and fails to do it, commits sin.

Warning to Rich Oppressors

5 Come now, you rich people, weep and wail for the miseries that are coming to you. [2]Your riches have rotted, and your clothes are moth-eaten. [3]Your gold and silver have rusted, and their rust will be evidence against you, and it will eat your flesh like fire. You have laid up treasure[b] for the last days. [4]Listen! The wages of the laborers who mowed your fields, which you kept back by fraud, cry out, and the cries of the harvesters have reached the ears of the Lord of hosts. [5]You have lived on the earth in luxury and in pleasure; you have fattened your hearts in a day of slaughter. [6]You have condemned and murdered the righteous one, who does not resist you.

Patience in Suffering

7 Be patient, therefore, beloved,[a] until the coming of the Lord. The farmer waits for the

a Gk brothers   b Or will eat your flesh, since you have stored up fire

---

response to God's invitation to receive the inner results of forgiveness, acceptance, restoration, renewal, and guidance. The outer result is peaceful relations with others, in which censorious and judgmental attitudes are cast aside in the interest of love and peace.

4:13–17 *you do no even know what tomorrow will bring.* Those who have a gift for projecting and planning in the world of business are warned against planning and acting independently of God's counsel. James warns that no human controls tomorrow and that life is dependent upon God. The look must always be beyond ourselves to God, with an appeal to God's graciousness and guidance: "If the Lord wishes, we will live and do this or that" (v 15). Requisite planning has its place; so do we have a place—humble before God, prudently seeking God's counsel for our lives. (See also Prov 3:5–6.)

5:1–6 *you rich people, weep and wail.* The problem of rich and poor is treated again, this time in a radical rebuke against those whose wealth and affluence, gained by unfairness,

oppression, and fraud, are arrogantly used. God's judgment against such sins is announced.

5:4 *The wages of the laborers.* This verse cautions employers against defrauding or treating those who work for them unfairly (see Lev 19:13; Deut 24:14–15; Mal 3:5; Luke 6:24–25; 1 Tim 5:18). Arrogant violation of the righteous invites divine judgment because their sure recourse is God's justice.

5:7–12 *Be patient . . . until the coming of the Lord.* Patience, like love, helps us to manage ourselves when pressured, provoked, or pained across a span of time. Periodic trials and temptations must be expected, but patient endurance of them will be rewarded in character development (1:4) and in receiving "the crown of life" (1:12) at the coming of the Lord. All that we suffer as Christians will be recompensed (see Matt 5:10–12). Love for God, gratitude for experienced compassions, and the expectation of the Lord's return motivate believers to be patient, steadied in a lively hope. (See also Titus 3:7; 1 Pet 1:3–9.)

precious crop from the earth, being patient with it until it receives the early and the late rains. 8You also must be patient. Strengthen your hearts, for the coming of the Lord is near. *a* 9Beloved, *b* do not grumble against one another, so that you may not be judged. See, the Judge is standing at the doors! 10As an example of suffering and patience, beloved, *c* take the prophets who spoke in the name of the Lord. 11Indeed we call blessed those who showed endurance. You have heard of the endurance of Job, and you have seen the purpose of the Lord, how the Lord is compassionate and merciful.

12 Above all, my beloved, *c* do not swear, either by heaven or by earth or by any other oath, but let your "Yes" be yes and your "No" be no, so that you may not fall under condemnation.

The Prayer of Faith

13 Are any among you suffering? They should pray. Are any cheerful? They should sing songs of praise. 14Are any among you sick? They should call for the elders of the church and have them pray over them, anointing them with oil in the name of the Lord. 15The prayer of faith will save the sick, and the Lord will raise them up; and anyone who has committed sins will be forgiven. 16Therefore confess your sins to one another, and pray for one another, so that you may be healed. The prayer of the righteous is powerful and effective. 17Elijah was a human being like us, and he prayed fervently that it might not rain, and for three years and six months it did not rain on the earth. 18Then he prayed again, and the heaven gave rain and the earth yielded its harvest.

19 My brothers and sisters, *d* if anyone among you wanders from the truth and is brought back by another, 20you should know that whoever brings back a sinner from wandering will save the sinner's *e* soul from death and will cover a multitude of sins.

a Or *is at hand*   *b* Gk *Brothers*   *c* Gk *brothers*
d Gk *My brothers*   *e* Gk *his*

5:13–16 PRAYER—*See* Spiritual Disciplines Index.

5:13–20 *Are any among you suffering?* James focuses on community life here, underscoring the importance of congregational care for each member. Those who are suffering distress or experiencing sickness are worthy of visitation, prayer, and the benefits of listening or conversing. The "elders of the church" take the lead in situations of distress and sickness, praying at the scene in "the name of the Lord." Just as "the Name" is called out in baptism (see Matt 28:19; Acts 2:38; 8:16; 10:48; 19:5), so it is called out at scenes of sickness. If sin has occasioned the sickness—or if the sickness has occasioned a sin (i.e., anger against God or questioning God; see 1:13)—confession and prayer aid healing.

Anointing with oil is a dedicatory action by which the person is presented to God as "a living sacrifice" (see Rom 12:1–2) to be renewed as a total self (body-mind-soul). Recovery, renewal, and reinstatement are the works of divine compassion and should be prime concerns within the fellowship "if anyone . . . wanders from the truth" (v 19). Corporate faith, steadfast living, fervent prayer, and corporate care are contagious evidences of spiritual health, and James writes to encourage Christians to cultivate these in the church.

5:16 CONFESSION—*See* Spiritual Disciplines Index.

5:17–18 PRAYER—*See* Spiritual Disciplines Index.

THE FIRST LETTER OF

PETER

The authorship of 1 & 2 Peter has been a subject of debate for many years. There is general consensus, though, among the church fathers and not a few modern New Testament scholars that the apostle Peter composed what is known as his first letter shortly before his martyrdom in Rome, around AD 64. Peter likely used Silvanus as his amanuensis, or secretary, and probably wrote from Rome (1 Pet 5:12–13). Early testimonies to Peter's authorship were made by Clement of Rome, Polycarp, and Papias.

Peter's salutation to "exiles of the Dispersion in Pontus, Galatia, Cappadocia, Asia, and Bithynia" points to an audience in northern Asia Minor (1:1). Romans living in this area viewed the burgeoning Christian movement with a high degree of suspicion, misunderstanding, and occasional intolerance and persecution. It is not surprising, then, that Peter finds it necessary to remind these early Christians that suffering on behalf of Christ is to be expected and, indeed, embraced (1:6–7; 2:20–23; 3:14–18). Peter is especially concerned to encourage believers in Christ, some of whom might be relatively new converts (2:2), to live a life that matches the wonder of the gospel and the gospel's Lord (1:13–16).

The recipients of the First Letter of Peter found themselves in the confusing and painful position of living in the Roman Empire while simultaneously living as faithful members of Christ's Body, the Church. How could one inhabit safely, sanely, and faithfully the world of Roman culture and the world of Christ's kingdom—domains and communities so radically different in outlook, allegiance, and king?

Peter had experienced firsthand the tensions and conflicts involved in living within more than one community. He had grown up in a Jewish environment surrounded by the political and military power of Rome. As Peter followed Christ, he soon found himself led by the Spirit into a significantly broader and more pluralistic world. The gospel itself forced Peter and the Christian community to move out into Roman culture, whose values clashed dramatically with those of Christ's

See also *"The With-God Life"* essay for this section of the Bible,
"The People of God in Community," pp. 2037–42.

kingdom. Christ's Spirit was forming a new and unique community composed of both Jews and Gentiles, "a chosen race, a royal priesthood, a holy nation, God's own people" (2:9). Hence, Peter devotes much of this pithy, direct letter to coaching his largely gentile Christian audience in the skills necessary for living faithful, wise lives in the midst of the watching Roman world.

In Peter's letter to Christian pilgrims three themes emerge that are especially relevant for spiritual formation: the Church as a pilgrim community presently in exile, the model of Christ's own suffering as an interpretive lens for the Church's experience of life in exile, and the skills and perspectives required of a pilgrim community.

The Church as a Community in Exile

Peter immediately reminds his readers that they are a pilgrim community, "aliens and exiles" journeying toward home, but still living before a watching world (1:1; 2:11). The wilderness faced by Peter's exiles was neither the barren desert experienced by Moses and the Israelites nor the cosmopolitan spiritual wilderness of Nineveh or Babylon. Rather, Christ's traveling companions lived in the midst of the power-hungry, sexually overheated, violent Roman Empire. Peter promises his readers that God will always be with them as they journey toward home. Even so, life with Christ in the Roman world will require a specific set of attitudes and skills. Mindless, undisciplined Christians will soon find themselves extruded into a foreign mold by the viselike pressure of Roman outlooks and practices.

The Pattern of Suffering

Life between the times is never easy. In the years to come, Peter's readers and their descendants would experience Roman misunderstanding and antagonism and periodic, intense persecution. Christ's own sufferings, Peter teaches, provide the fundamental lens for comprehending why his exiled Church continues to suffer during its earthly sojourn. He was misunderstood and suffered unjustly, but did not respond in kind (2:23). Likewise, Jesus' disciples must "arm" themselves "with the same intention," learning "to live . . . no longer by human desires but by the will of God" (4:1–2). Such is the inescapable privilege of those who have chosen to follow a new king and are heading home, but have yet to arrive at their destination.

In short, Peter has provided his original audience, and us his later readers, with a handbook for living between the times. We still find ourselves in the midst of an age that often misinterprets, denigrates, and opposes the values of a crucified, resurrected king. Often we feel out of place, aching for a home we have yet to reach, and the journey seems unbearably long. Yet we too are called to faithfulness, courage, perseverance, and love as we journey home. Best to admit that suffering, at times more or less intense, will mark our way. But should we be surprised? The same pattern is clearly identifiable in Christ's own life.

Skills and Perspectives for a Pilgrim Community

Peter highlights three skills and perspectives that will serve pilgrims well as they travel through a hazardous, alien environment. First, Peter exhorts his audience in exile to cultivate a disciplined mind. The ability to maintain one's bearings toward home and to withstand suffering and the wiles of the devil is linked to the clarity of a mind deeply shaped by the truth of the gospel. A war zone is no place for foggy, shoddy thinking. "Therefore prepare your minds for action; discipline yourselves" (1:13; 4:7; 5:8–9).

Second, Peter warns against foolishly and unnecessarily offending, confusing, or antagonizing the inhabitants of the land through which the Church in exile continues to pass (2:12; 3:14–16; 4:3–5). Peter's teaching on authority and submission occurs as a secondary theme in this context. To disrupt patterns of authority could offend Roman sensibilities and only create additional difficulties for a suffering community in exile (2:13–17; 5:5). This, of course, does not answer the question of when disciples of Jesus should, instead, respond with courageous countercultural Christian action, but it does help us to better understand culturally Peter's words regarding authority and submission.

Third, Christ calls his people to holiness and obedience, with love as purity's fruit (1:22; 4:8). Jesus himself has modeled the fundamental pattern for us: "As he who called you is holy, be holy yourselves in all your conduct; for it is written, 'You shall be holy, for I am holy'" (1:15–16). If we are to suffer, Peter exhorts, let it be because of the resemblance the Church bears to its king, a ruler whose authority the broader world refuses to accept or acknowledge. A clear conscience and purified faith will be the happy result (3:16; 1:6–7). Suffering resulting from rebellion, disobedience, or disrespect indeed hurts, but is radically dissimilar to the suffering patterned after Christ's willing submission to his Father's will (2:17–18; 4:15, 19).

—Christopher A. Hall

Salutation

1 Peter, an apostle of Jesus Christ,
To the exiles of the Dispersion in Pontus, Galatia, Cappadocia, Asia, and Bithynia, ²who have been chosen and destined by God the Father and sanctified by the Spirit to be obedient to Jesus Christ and to be sprinkled with his blood:

May grace and peace be yours in abundance.

1:1 *To the exiles of the Dispersion.* The readers of Peter's first letter were largely gentile Christians scattered throughout the Mediterranean basin. They frequently experienced the tension of living in two strikingly different worlds, the gentile world of the Roman Empire and the new community of the Church. As partakers in a new priesthood, new race, new covenant, and new nation (2:4–10), these Christians often found themselves at odds with the community in which they had grown up. The image of Christians as pilgrims traveling in a strange land continually reappears in ancient Christian literature, reflecting the early Church's awareness that it was a people on the move rather than a nation that had reached its destination. We, like Peter's original audience, are travelers heading toward home, a journey often marked by struggle, testing, and suffering. Best to travel light, always remembering that the lay of the land looks different to pilgrims than to settlers. Life for pilgrims is a fine balancing act. On the one hand, we are presently more exiles than permanent residents. On the other hand, we are called to be agents of healing, restoration, love, and justice. God's broken creation will one day be renewed. As pilgrims we travel light, yet we remain committed and engaged in the extension of Christ's reign here and now as we head toward home.

A Living Hope

3 Blessed be the God and Father of our Lord Jesus Christ! By his great mercy he has given us a new birth into a living hope through the resurrection of Jesus Christ from the dead, [4]and into an inheritance that is imperishable, undefiled, and unfading, kept in heaven for you, [5]who are being protected by the power of God through faith for a salvation ready to be revealed in the last time. [6]In this you rejoice,[a] even if now for a little while you have had to suffer various trials, [7]so that the genuineness of your faith—being more precious than gold that, though perishable, is tested by fire—may be found to result in praise and glory and honor when Jesus Christ is revealed. [8]Although you have not seen[b] him, you love him; and even though you do not see him now, you believe in him and rejoice with an indescribable and glorious joy, [9]for you are receiving the outcome of your faith, the salvation of your souls.

10 Concerning this salvation, the prophets who prophesied of the grace that was to be yours made careful search and inquiry, [11]inquiring about the person or time that the Spirit of Christ within them indicated when it testified in advance to the sufferings destined for Christ and the subsequent glory. [12]It was revealed to them that they were serving not themselves but you, in regard to the things that have now been announced to you through those who brought you good news by the Holy Spirit sent from heaven—things into which angels long to look!

A Call to Holy Living

13 Therefore prepare your minds for action;[c] discipline yourselves; set all your hope on the grace that Jesus Christ will bring you when he is revealed. [14]Like obedient children, do not be conformed to the desires that you formerly had in ignorance. [15]Instead, as he who called you is holy, be holy yourselves

a Or *Rejoice in this*   b Other ancient authorities read *known*   c Gk *gird up the loins of your mind*

1:6–7 *you have had to suffer various trials.* The movement from self-deception to self-awareness is a fundamental rhythm of spiritual growth. So often we are apt to lie about the true state of affairs in our lives. Peter reminds his letter's recipients that God's love is cleansing, fiery, astringent. At times God will place us in what seems to be a furnace—not to harm us, but to cleanse and refine our faith, so that only what is genuine remains.

1:13 *prepare your minds for action; discipline yourselves.* Peter is well aware that ideas have legs. Skewed thinking inevitably leads to a skewed life. Learning to think well as Christians, though, will not come easily, particularly as Christ's Church lives within a foreign, toxic environment. Peter warns that without disciplined thinking and its accompanying life, the surrounding world will quickly shape Christ's community into a foreign mold.

1:15 *be holy yourselves in all your conduct.* Peter's call to holiness can be confusing and intimidating if we misidentify what holiness actually is. One of the problems facing modern Christians is that few of us have encountered genuine holiness. Instead, we have been bombarded by "phantoms of devotion," as Francis

de Sales puts it. Too often in the media "holy" people have been portrayed as stiff, sexually repressed, boring, lifeless, self-righteous, judgmental, and deeply hypocritical. Yet to be holy is to be transformed into Christ's image. If so, holiness incarnated would look like Christ. What is particularly striking about Jesus is that sinful people flocked to him, while self-righteous folk tended to avoid an encounter. Peter himself had experienced firsthand Christ's penetrating, loving holiness, and even after his greatest mistakes he couldn't keep away from Jesus. Peter knew Jesus loved him and would know what to do with his great moral failures. To be holy in our conduct, then, is to embody Christ's love in whatever situation we find ourselves. Holiness can be astringent in the presence of sin, and its cleansing can burn deeply like fire. Holiness, though, will never harm us or others. Like Christ, the holy person will lovingly welcome fellow strugglers and know how to help them move beyond their sin. The characteristics of the pilgrim's life are clearly identifiable: hope in Christ, who for the moment is unseen; refusal by God's grace to be any longer conformed to desires grounded in ignorance and folly rather than truth and wisdom; holiness patterned on

in all your conduct; [16]for it is written, "You shall be holy, for I am holy."

17 If you invoke as Father the one who judges all people impartially according to their deeds, live in reverent fear during the time of your exile. [18]You know that you were ransomed from the futile ways inherited from your ancestors, not with perishable things like silver or gold, [19]but with the precious blood of Christ, like that of a lamb without defect or blemish. [20]He was destined before the foundation of the world, but was revealed at the end of the ages for your sake. [21]Through him you have come to trust in God, who raised him from the dead and gave him glory, so that your faith and hope are set on God.

22 Now that you have purified your souls by your obedience to the truth[a] so that you have genuine mutual love, love one another deeply[b] from the heart.[c] [23]You have been born anew, not of perishable but of imperishable seed, through the living and enduring word of God.[d] [24]For

"All flesh is like grass
  and all its glory like the flower of
    grass.
The grass withers,
  and the flower falls,

[25]but the word of the Lord endures
    forever."

That word is the good news that was announced to you.

The Living Stone and a Chosen People

2 Rid yourselves, therefore, of all malice, and all guile, insincerity, envy, and all slander. [2]Like newborn infants, long for the pure, spiritual milk, so that by it you may grow into salvation— [3]if indeed you have tasted that the Lord is good.

4 Come to him, a living stone, though rejected by mortals yet chosen and precious in God's sight, and [5]like living stones, let yourselves be built[e] into a spiritual house, to be a holy priesthood, to offer spiritual sacrifices acceptable to God through Jesus Christ. [6]For it stands in scripture:

"See, I am laying in Zion a stone,
  a cornerstone chosen and precious;
  and whoever believes in him[f] will not
    be put to shame."

[7]To you then who believe, he is precious; but for those who do not believe,

a Other ancient authorities add *through the Spirit*
b Or *constantly*　c Other ancient authorities read
a pure heart　d Or *through the word of the living and
enduring God*　e Or *you yourselves are being built*
f Or *it*

---

the life and power of the One who has called us into a relationship founded on life, not death; and reverent fear rather than chummy familiarity.

2:2 *long for the pure, spiritual milk.* Peter returns to the theme of the Christian community as a new Israel, one in continuity with "old" Israel, but new just the same. Peter's readers are both babies and exiles, in need of both milk and a road map. We must nurse deeply to grow to full maturity, longing for the milk Christ desires to give us.

2:5 *like living stones . . . built into a spiritual house.* At first glance, Peter's metaphor of "living stones" seems strange. How could stones live? Meditate carefully on the connection Peter draws between a nursing child (v 2) and a living stone. Consider, for instance, Abraham's relationship to his concubine, Hagar. Sarah asks Abraham to initiate a sexual relationship with Hagar so that Sarah might receive children through her hand-

maid. What is translated "that I shall obtain children by her" is in the Hebrew literally "so that I might be built through her" (Gen 16:2). From a Jewish perspective, then, to be blessed by God with children was to build a house of living stones. Peter takes this idea and expands it in light of Christ's death and resurrection (1:3). As we drink continually the milk the Word offers, like a child nursing at a mother's breast, we become "living stones" resting on Christ himself. Many in Israel rejected the foundation stone offered to them in Christ (Matt 21:42; Mark 12:10; Luke 20:17). Yet Christ's resurrection vividly demonstrates that he is indeed the living foundation stone of a new Israel. This "spiritual house" is no ordinary, humdrum affair. It is a temple inhabited by a new priesthood continually offering sacrifices of praise to God. Simultaneously, in a happily mixed metaphor, Peter views us as babies, stones, a temple, and priests offering "spiritual sacrifices acceptable to God through Jesus Christ."

"The stone that the builders rejected
has become the very head of the
corner,"
[8]and
"A stone that makes them stumble,
and a rock that makes them fall."
They stumble because they disobey the word,
as they were destined to do.

9 But you are a chosen race, a royal priesthood, a holy nation, God's own people, [a] in order that you may proclaim the mighty acts of him who called you out of darkness into his marvelous light.
[10] Once you were not a people,
but now you are God's people;
once you had not received mercy,
but now you have received mercy.

Live as Servants of God

11 Beloved, I urge you as aliens and exiles to abstain from the desires of the flesh that wage war against the soul. [12]Conduct yourselves honorably among the Gentiles, so that, though they malign you as evildoers, they may see your honorable deeds and glorify God when he comes to judge. [b]

13 For the Lord's sake accept the authority of every human institution, [c] whether of the emperor as supreme, [14]or of governors, as sent by him to punish those who do wrong and to praise those who do right. [15]For it is

a Gk *a people for his possession* — b Gk *God on the day of visitation* c Or *every institution ordained for human beings*

2:8 *A stone that makes them stumble.* Those who reject Christ, Peter insists, will still find him unavoidable. Sadly, it is possible to stumble over the "living stone" (v 4). How so? To "disobey the word" is to remain isolated from God's new work in Christ as he creates a new people. Inevitably, Peter warns, those who disobey Christ's word will stumble over him. And in their fall they will be broken into pieces. Such is the inescapable destiny of those who freely choose to reject God's redemptive story in Christ as irrelevant, far-fetched, unrealistic, exclusive, intolerant, naïve, or misguided. Peter unhesitatingly lays out stark alternatives: either be united to Christ and receive life in communion with him and the People of God, or disobey Christ and be broken as you stumble over his inescapable presence. Embrace or rejection, communion or isolation, obedience or disobedience, life or death—stark destinies freely chosen.

2:9 *a chosen race, a royal priesthood, a holy nation, God's own people.* What is God up to? God's plan and work in the narrative of Israel has not been nullified or rejected. Rather, in the ministry, death, resurrection, and ascension of Christ, Israel's story has been both expanded and fulfilled. The acts of God celebrated by Israel under the old covenant have reached their consummation in the most unlikely of places, a cross and an empty tomb. Initially, the idea of a suffering and dying Messiah had made little sense to Peter. In the light of Christ's resurrection, however, Peter realized that the cross and resurrection of the incarnate Word

were essential chapters in the story of Israel, which Peter had imbibed as a child growing up in Galilee. God's work included Israel, Peter's own race, but went beyond it in the creation of a new people, one whose life's blood was actually that of the Messiah himself. In Christ, the holy nation of Israel had become a much greater nation, the regenerated race of Adam, a people of light rather than darkness (cf. 1:14).

2:13 *accept the authority of every human institution.* In each instance in which Peter asks his "exiles" to submit to authority—here, 2:18 (slaves to masters), and 3:1 (wives to husbands)—he has a higher end in view than submission itself. If we submit to authorities, even to those who will occasionally harm us, a higher purpose will be accomplished, that of reflecting the life of our Savior, who himself suffered unjustly for the sake of his enemies. This having been said, there is also a time when "submission" is simply wrong. The same Peter who here counsels submission to "every human institution," also told the Sanhedrin, "Whether it is right in God's sight to listen to you rather than to God, you must judge; for we cannot keep from speaking about what we have seen and heard" (Acts 4:19–20). Later, speaking to the high priest, he said flatly, "We must obey God rather than any human authority" (Acts 5:29). We see the same dual approach in the apostle Paul. To Roman Christians he counsels, "Let every person be subject to the governing authorities" (Rom 13:1). When Paul, however, saw that the governing authorities were failing to fulfill their God-ordained function of providing

God's will that by doing right you should silence the ignorance of the foolish. 16As servants[a] of God, live as free people, yet do not use your freedom as a pretext for evil. 17Honor everyone. Love the family of believers.[b] Fear God. Honor the emperor.

The Example of Christ's Suffering

18 Slaves, accept the authority of your masters with all deference, not only those who are kind and gentle but also those who are harsh. 19For it is a credit to you if, being aware of God, you endure pain while suffering unjustly. 20If you endure when you are beaten for doing wrong, what credit is that? But if you endure when you do right and suffer for it, you have God's approval. 21For to this you have been called, because Christ also suffered for you, leaving you an example, so that you should follow in his steps.

22 "He committed no sin,
     and no deceit was found in his
         mouth."

23When he was abused, he did not return abuse; when he suffered, he did not threaten; but he entrusted himself to the one who

judges justly. 24He himself bore our sins in his body on the cross,[c] so that, free from sins, we might live for righteousness; by his wounds[d] you have been healed. 25For you were going astray like sheep, but now you have returned to the shepherd and guardian of your souls.

Wives and Husbands

3 Wives, in the same way, accept the authority of your husbands, so that, even if some of them do not obey the word, they may be won over without a word by their wives' conduct, 2when they see the purity and reverence of your lives. 3Do not adorn yourselves outwardly by braiding your hair, and by wearing gold ornaments or fine clothing; 4rather, let your adornment be the inner self with the lasting beauty of a gentle and quiet spirit, which is very precious in God's sight. 5It was in this way long ago that the holy women who hoped in God used to adorn themselves by accepting the authority of their husbands. 6Thus Sarah obeyed Abraham and called him lord. You have

a Gk slaves   b Gk Love the brotherhood
c Or carried up our sins in his body to the tree
d Gk bruise

---

justice for all, he called them to account and insisted that the wrong be righted (Acts 16:37). Were Peter and Paul opposing their own principle of submission? No. They simply understood that submission reaches its limit when it becomes destructive. When the Spiritual Discipline of submission becomes destructive, it then becomes a denial of the law of love as taught by Jesus and is an affront to genuine biblical submission (Matt 5–7, esp. 22:37–39). Indeed, we can and should applaud the sacrificial work done in Jesus' name to end injustice, violence, and oppression of all kinds.

2:16 SERVICE—*See* Spiritual Disciplines Index.

2:21 *because Christ also suffered for you, leaving you an example.* Peter did not always understand that Christ's disciples should expect to suffer unjustly. When Jesus first introduced his teaching that the Messiah must suffer and finally die unjustly in Jerusalem, Peter overstepped himself and attempted to correct Christ. The idea of a crucified Messiah seemed a contradiction in terms (Mark 8:31–32). How could the

anointed one of Israel suffer unjustly and then die on a Roman cross? Paul struggled with the same question (cf. Gal 3:13–14). Jesus' response to Peter's misguided effort to protect him from unjust suffering was abrupt and to the point: "You are speaking like the devil. Stop it" (Mark 8:33). The Peter we encounter in this letter now understands that unjust suffering could bear the most surprising fruit: redemption, the creation of a new Israel, death conquered, new life, triumph over the demonic realm, and the dispersion of sin's darkness. Hence, Peter teaches, those who would follow Christ are called to imitate the Master's willingness to embrace unjust suffering. Peter is not interested in Christian masochists. If we walk in Christ's steps, however, incarnating his concern for the outcasts of society and their unjust suffering, we can expect to suffer unjustly ourselves. Christ surely did. Did Christ ever turn a blind eye to the needy for the sake of his own comfort? Hardly. The manifestation of Christ's love to a fallen world is often cruciform. It was for Jesus and will often be so for Christ's disciples.

become her daughters as long as you do what is good and never let fears alarm you.

7 Husbands, in the same way, show consideration for your wives in your life together, paying honor to the woman as the weaker sex,[a] since they too are also heirs of the gracious gift of life—so that nothing may hinder your prayers.

Suffering for Doing Right

8 Finally, all of you, have unity of spirit, sympathy, love for one another, a tender heart, and a humble mind. 9Do not repay evil for evil or abuse for abuse; but, on the contrary, repay with a blessing. It is for this that you were called—that you might inherit a blessing. 10For

"Those who desire life
    and desire to see good days,
  let them keep their tongues from evil
    and their lips from speaking deceit;
11 let them turn away from evil and do
        good;
  let them seek peace and pursue it.
12 For the eyes of the Lord are on the
        righteous,
  and his ears are open to their prayer.
  But the face of the Lord is against those
        who do evil."

13 Now who will harm you if you are eager to do what is good? 14But even if you do suffer for doing what is right, you are blessed. Do not fear what they fear,[b] and do not be intimidated, 15but in your hearts sanctify Christ as Lord. Always be ready to make your defense to anyone who demands from you an accounting for the hope that is in you; 16yet do it with gentleness and reverence.[c] Keep your conscience clear, so that, when you are maligned, those who abuse you for your good conduct in Christ may be put to shame. 17For it is better to suffer for doing good, if suffering should be God's will, than to suffer for doing evil. 18For Christ also suffered[d] for sins once for all, the righteous for the unrighteous, in order to bring you[e] to God. He was put to death in the flesh, but made alive in the spirit, 19in which also he went and made a proclamation to the spirits in prison, 20who in former times did not obey, when God waited patiently in the days of Noah, during the building of the ark, in which a few, that is, eight persons, were saved through water. 21And baptism, which this prefigured, now saves you—not as a removal of dirt from the body, but as an appeal to God for[f] a good conscience, through the resurrection of Jesus Christ, 22who has gone into heaven and is

a Gk vessel   b Gk their fear   c Or respect
d Other ancient authorities read died   e Other
ancient authorities read us   f Or a pledge to God
from

Responding

3:7 PRAYER. Besides not honoring our spouses, what other things can hinder our prayers? Write them down. For the next few days, hold this list before God and ask him to help you overcome these hindrances to your prayer life. See also Spiritual Disciplines Index.

3:12 PRAYER—See Spiritual Disciplines Index.
3:12–13 THE WITH-GOD LIFE—See Spiritual Disciplines Index.
3:14–17 if you do suffer for doing what is right, you are blessed. The pilgrim's journey, Peter teaches, will inevitably entail suffering, yet he warns against the self-inflicted suffering that comes from sin. That is, is our suffering the result of faithfully following our new and greater Moses through the wilderness, or is it the result of attempting to set up permanent camp in terrain meant only to be a way station? Settlers fear many things: sickness, the loss of wealth or reputation, unjust suffering, death itself. Also, settlers' fear often fuels resentment against pilgrims, whose internal freedom and movement against the grain mark them as different, as willing to speak and act against the status quo. Jesus not only suffered at the time of his crucifixion, but he suffered daily as he challenged perceptions and structures within Israel that promoted and nourished injustice, insensitivity, and prejudice (cf. Luke 14). The crowd may well use intimidation against those who are unwilling to fit in and swallow whatever the current cultural consensus may be. "Do not fear what they fear," Peter advises. Rather, protect and preserve your internal moral compass. Keep it focused on Christ as your North Star. He will lead his pilgrims home safely.

PETER

The Discipleship of Failing and Learning

Selected Scriptures: *Matthew 14:22–33; 16:13–23; 17:1–13; 18:21–35; 26:31–75; Mark 10:17–31; Luke 4:38–5:11; 6:12–16; 22:31–62; 24:1–12; John 1:35–51; 6:60–71; 13:1–20; 18:1–27; 20:1–10; 21:1–25; Acts 1–5; 8:14–25; 9:32–11:18; 12:1–18; 15:1–21; Galatians 2:1–14; 1 & 2 Peter*

An "uneducated and ordinary" (Acts 4:13) man before he met Christ, Peter worked hard as a fisherman and knew success in his profession. When he met Jesus through his brother Andrew, he left his boat and nets to be with Jesus, and so began his life of discipleship. He may have understood fishing, but he didn't understand a lot about Jesus and, passionate as he was, he would grow in many areas as he began to live out Jesus' call for him to be a "fisher of people" (Matt 4:19).

Peter's parting words to the Church act as a fitting summary of his own journey of spiritual formation: "Grow in the grace and knowledge of our Lord and Savior Jesus Christ" (2 Pet 3:18). His words resonate deeply with his own life. Peter himself had been transformed through the grace and knowledge of Jesus.

Peter was the first disciple to identify Jesus as the Messiah, the Son of the living God (Matt 16:16). He had seen Jesus fill his nets with fish, heal his mother-in-law, walk on water, and even give him the power to walk on water. He had seen Jesus heal the blind and the lame, cast out evil spirits, feed thousands of people, and draw great crowds to listen to his teaching. He believed Jesus had the words of eternal life. Yet he didn't really understand those words. He didn't understand what the Messiah would be.

And so Jesus taught Peter. He taught him on the sea about having faith even when the winds were raging and he knew he might sink (Luke 8:22–25). He taught him that even at a point of greatest faith, when Peter first confessed Jesus as the Son of God, Peter could in the next breath utter words that Jesus had to rebuke by calling them the very words of the devil (Matt 16:23). Jesus taught him on the mount about keeping silent and submitting his understanding and his will to God (Matt 17:1–13). He taught him on the road about how God will bless those who leave everything to follow him and about God's "reversal" of greatness in eternity, where the first will be last and the last first (Matt 19:27–30). He taught Peter in the upper room about praying for the faith of those we see denying Christ and about serving as a leader (John 17:11–15; 13:1–20). Later, after his resurrection, Jesus taught Peter by the Sea of Galilee about caring for God's children and continuing to follow Christ even after Peter had failed him (John 21:15–19).

Then the Holy Spirit entered into Peter's spiritual formation. With Jesus ascended, the Spirit came upon Peter and brought an understanding of Christ that made sense of all Peter had learned from his Teacher. Now Peter understood Jesus' words and his coming as Messiah, and he became emboldened to preach and proclaim Christ as he had never done before. Now Peter himself would teach about submission to authorities and masters and family members as an act of submission to God. He would teach about serving through hospitality and accepting even persecution, for the sake of Christ, with joy. He would bring the message of God's gift of salvation opened to all people.

Peter had come a long way as a disciple of Christ. Yet even in his days as an apostle and leader of the early Church, Peter continued to learn. Losing confidence around Jewish Christians from Jerusalem, he stopped eating with Gentiles and was reprimanded by Paul for going back on his teaching. Peter's story reminds us that no matter where we may be on the path of spiritual formation, we need to stay humble and teachable. Our growth in grace will be necessary until we join the Author of grace, in eternity.

Once Peter had been a reputable fisherman. But God called him and shaped him to become a successful "fisher of people." Surely God's desire for us is the one he voiced through Peter's pen: "Grow in the grace and knowledge of our Lord and Savior Jesus Christ."

Personal Reflection

- Are all believers in Christ disciples of Christ? What would you say to the person who believes, but has no interest in actively pursuing discipleship to Jesus?
- When you consider Peter's life as a disciple of Jesus, would you say that you are serious in the same way he was about being taught by Christ? In *Renovation of the Heart* Dallas Willard says: "Disciples of Jesus are those who are with him learning to be like him. That is, they are learning to lead their life, their actual existence, as he would lead their life if he were they. . . . They are learning how to walk with Jesus and learn from him in every aspect of their individual lives." What aspect of your life has Jesus been focusing on recently? What is he teaching you?
- How has your knowledge of Jesus grown since you first came to believe in him? How has your interaction with him grown over time? How are you different?
- In what ways has the Holy Spirit helped to bring about "breakthroughs" in your spiritual formation? Pray now that God would guide and enable you in a close walk of discipleship with Jesus, that he would grow you in the grace and knowledge of our Lord and Savior, Jesus Christ.

PROFILE

at the right hand of God, with angels, authorities, and powers made subject to him.

Good Stewards of God's Grace

4 Since therefore Christ suffered in the flesh,[a] arm yourselves also with the same intention (for whoever has suffered in the flesh has finished with sin), [2]so as to live for the rest of your earthly life[b] no longer by human desires but by the will of God. [3]You have already spent enough time in doing what the Gentiles like to do, living in licentiousness, passions, drunkenness, revels, carousing, and lawless idolatry. [4]They are surprised that you no longer join them in the same excesses of dissipation, and so they blaspheme.[c] [5]But they will have to give an accounting to him who stands ready to judge the living and the dead. [6]For this is the reason the gospel was proclaimed even to the dead, so that, though they had been judged in the flesh as everyone is judged, they might live in the spirit as God does.

[7] The end of all things is near;[d] therefore be serious and discipline yourselves for the sake of your prayers. [8]Above all, maintain constant love for one another, for love covers a multitude of sins. [9]Be hospitable to one another without complaining. [10]Like good stewards of the manifold grace of God, serve one another with whatever gift each of you has received. [11]Whoever speaks must do so as one speaking the very words of God; whoever serves must do so with the strength that God supplies, so that God may be glorified in all things through Jesus Christ. To him belong the glory and the power forever and ever. Amen.

Suffering as a Christian

[12] Beloved, do not be surprised at the fiery ordeal that is taking place among you to test you, as though something strange were happening to you. [13]But rejoice insofar as you are sharing Christ's sufferings, so that you may also be glad and shout for joy when his glory is revealed. [14]If you are reviled for the name of Christ, you are blessed, because the spirit of glory,[e] which is the Spirit of God, is resting on you.[f] [15]But let none of you suffer as a murderer, a thief, a criminal, or even as a mischief maker. [16]Yet if any of you suffers as a Christian, do not consider it a disgrace, but glorify God because you bear this name. [17]For the time has come for judgment to begin with the household of God; if it begins with us, what will be the end for those who do not obey the gospel of God? [18]And

> "If it is hard for the righteous to be saved,
>   what will become of the ungodly and
>   the sinners?"

[19]Therefore, let those suffering in accordance with God's will entrust themselves to a faithful Creator, while continuing to do good.

Tending the Flock of God

5 Now as an elder myself and a witness of the sufferings of Christ, as well as one who shares in the glory to be revealed, I exhort

a Other ancient authorities add *for us*; others, *for you* *b* Gk *rest of the time in the flesh* *c* Or *they malign you* *d* Or *is at hand* *e* Other ancient authorities add *and of power* *f* Other ancient authorities add *On their part he is blasphemed, but on your part he is glorified*

4:3 *what the Gentiles like to do, living in licentiousness . . . and lawless idolatry.* Peter describes the Roman world of his day as a society that has lost its mind. Violence, oppression, cruelty, the abuse of power, and sexual insanity dominate the landscape. How, for instance, is it possible for Christians to maintain sexual sanity in a sexually overheated society? Is the inevitable result the distortion of spiritual formation into a "hot-tub" spirituality? Once again, Peter calls his exiles to a loving discipline marked by seriousness and compassion. To maintain our sense of direction under the leadership of God, who is with us, Christ's

fellow travelers must be willing to say yes and to say no, to embrace and to refrain from embracing, to love and to refuse to lust. Peter is convinced that the habitual cultivation of sympathy, humility, prayer, genuineness, courage, mercy, gentleness, and reverence will help Christ's pilgrim community maintain its bearings. The alternative is to lose sight of home as our culture blankets us in its fog. Purposeless wandering will quickly replace purposeful direction.

4:7 PRAYER—*See* Spiritual Disciplines Index.

4:10–11 SERVICE—*See* Spiritual Disciplines Index.

the elders among you [2]to tend the flock of God that is in your charge, exercising the oversight,[a] not under compulsion but willingly, as God would have you do it[b]—not for sordid gain but eagerly. [3]Do not lord it over those in your charge, but be examples to the flock. [4]And when the chief shepherd appears, you will win the crown of glory that never fades away. [5]In the same way, you who are younger must accept the authority of the elders.[c] And all of you must clothe yourselves with humility in your dealings with one another, for

"God opposes the proud,
   but gives grace to the humble."

6 Humble yourselves therefore under the mighty hand of God, so that he may exalt you in due time. [7]Cast all your anxiety on him, because he cares for you. [8]Discipline yourselves, keep alert.[d] Like a roaring lion your adversary the devil prowls around, looking for someone to devour. [9]Resist him, steadfast in your faith, for you know that your brothers

and sisters[e] in all the world are undergoing the same kinds of suffering. [10]And after you have suffered for a little while, the God of all grace, who has called you to his eternal glory in Christ, will himself restore, support, strengthen, and establish you. [11]To him be the power forever and ever. Amen.

Final Greetings and Benediction

12 Through Silvanus, whom I consider a faithful brother, I have written this short letter to encourage you and to testify that this is the true grace of God. Stand fast in it. [13]Your sister church[f] in Babylon, chosen together with you, sends you greetings; and so does my son Mark. [14]Greet one another with a kiss of love.

Peace to all of you who are in Christ.[g]

a Other ancient authorities lack *exercising the oversight*   *b* Other ancient authorities lack *as God would have you do it*   *c* Or *of those who are older*   *d* Or *be vigilant*   *e* Gk *your brotherhood*   *f* Gk *She who is*   *g* Other ancient authorities add *Amen*

5:5 *you who are younger must accept the authority of the elders.* Again, Peter raises the issue of authority (see note on 2:13), in this instance exhorting those who are younger to willingly submit to the authority of the elders in their local congregation. Submission to authority can be a difficult and dangerous business, particularly if the authorities in question are themselves self-deceived and inflated with a sense of their own importance, wisdom, and power. The safety net for submission and the safe exercise of authority is humility itself, a virtue Peter highlights throughout his letter. And what is humility? A realistic and honest self-appraisal in which we acknowledge our strengths and weaknesses, our abilities and inabilities, the gifts that God has given us and those gifts we can receive only from others. In the final analysis, those who embrace humility openly admit that they are not the center of the universe and stand in dire need of Christ and Christ's Body, the Church.

Responding
5:6–7 THE WITH-GOD LIFE. Try to recall times that you have been especially aware that God cares for you. Did you feel more free to "cast" your anxieties on God then or during other times when his love didn't seem so close? What do you think causes these differ-

ences in feeling? *See also* Spiritual Disciplines Index.

5:8–9 *your adversary the devil prowls around.* As Peter draws his letter to a close, he reminds his readers that reality is multifaceted. Indeed, both Peter and Jude warn that we can expect opposition not only from our broader cultural context, but also from powerful, personal forces of evil that seek to deflect and deface God's purposes for our lives. For the third time Peter exhorts us to discipline ourselves (see also 1:13; 4:7), in this case by keeping alert to the wiles of the devil. Just as Peter had earlier encouraged his readers to not be intimidated by the opposition of the world around them, so here he pictures the devil as a roaring lion bent on frightening his opponents into submission. Here, however, submission is never an option. Struggle and stiff resistance are called for as we stand against the machinations of the evil one. In reality, though, it is Christ himself who fights on our behalf as we place our faith in him. Indeed, he has already won the final victory in his death and resurrection. His pilgrim people are now engaged in a mopping-up operation. Costly sacrifices will be necessary, casualties suffered, and at times even resistance unto death required. In Christ, however, suffering and death are never the last word.

THE SECOND LETTER OF
PETER

The authorship of the Second Letter of Peter has long been a disputed topic. Eusebius, for instance, writing in the fourth century, lists 2 Peter among the "questioned" books of the New Testament canon, and Origen expressed doubts as to Petrine authorship. New Testament scholars have also had their reservations. For starters, the Greek literary style of 2 Peter is quite distinct from that of 1 Peter. Also, the striking similarities between 2 Peter and Jude have confused readers ancient and modern. Why such similarities between these two letters if the greatest of the apostles is the genuine author of 2 Peter?

Still, others argue that the difference in style may be the result of Peter's use of Silvanus as a secretary for his first letter and not for the second. Also, the fourth-century councils of Hippo, Laodicea, and Carthage attested the apostolic authority of the letter after a careful sifting of the evidence. Within 2 Peter itself are signs pointing to Peter as the author. The writer claims to have witnessed Christ's transfiguration (2 Pet 1:16–18) and predicts his approaching death (1:14–15). The early Church did not take a favorable view of pious imitations of apostolic letters, especially as heretics were more than willing to borrow the name of an apostle to pawn off their own idiosyncratic ideas on the Church. It seems highly implausible that a letter largely devoted to combating the danger of false teaching would undercut its own authority and integrity by employing pious falsehood. As for the similarities between 2 Peter and Jude, the relationship is quite complex and only points to that fact that either one borrowed from the other or Peter and Jude drew upon a common source for certain ideas.

No matter who we settle on as the author, though, it is important to remember that the Church has accepted this letter into the canon as a trustworthy guide for us who wish to follow Jesus as Lord.

See also *"The With-God Life" essay for this section of the Bible,
"The People of God in Community," pp. 2037–42.*

God Has Given Us All We Need

The second letter attributed to Peter focuses on two main themes relevant to issues of spiritual formation.

Peter first reminds his audience that Christians have been given gracefully by God "everything" they need to grow fully into the divine image and to live a life of integrity in which their words and actions fit together as one piece (1:3–9). We have been created to participate in the divine nature as we "escape from the corruption that is in the world because of lust" (1:4). Peter's second point, though, is that our participation in the divine nature is facilitated as we embrace God's "precious and very great promises" (1:4). Knowledge wedded to the cultivation of habitual patterns of "goodness," "self-control," "endurance," "godliness," "mutual affection," and "love" buttresses our faith (1:5–7). We have left past sins behind, and only the poorly disciplined, the "shortsighted and blind," foolishly forget or neglect the lessons our past sins can teach us (1:9–12).

False Words, False Lives

Peter's second theme hovers over his letter like a dark and foreboding shadow. False prophets have infiltrated the Christian community, supposedly inspired voices that blatantly undercut Peter's insistence that believers' lives must demonstrate the truthfulness of their words.

False teachers had invaded the Church and were promoting ideas and actions inimical to Christ's call to holiness, love, and obedience. These teachers claimed to possess freedom in Christ and yet were actually enslaved to licentiousness, self-indulgence, greed, and deep self-deception (2:1–5). Their licentious lives undercut their claim to speak genuinely on God's behalf.

Peter calls his readers to both speak and live the truth, but his deceptive opponents speak and live falsely. Consider the character traits and actions of the false prophets: deceptiveness (2:1), denial of God's redemptive acts in Christ (2:1), a rampantly licentious lifestyle (2:2), manipulative and deceptive language fomented by greed (2:3), unbridled sexual appetite (2:10, 13–14), and an inflated self-estimation characterized by arrogance and recklessness (2:10). Paradoxically, the false prophets have promised freedom to those who would embrace their teaching, while they themselves remain "slaves of corruption" (2:19). They have disregarded the promises of God emphasized by Peter at the beginning of his letter (1:4) and instead spout their own corrupt ideas; quickly the false teachers and those who listen to them spiral into inhuman, animalistic behaviors. As the false prophets reject the apostolic truth and wisdom offered by Peter, they become increasingly hollow, heedlessly unaware of the impending judgment of God. Most seriously, these false prophets will be harshly judged because they are rejecting truth they once understood and embraced (2:20–22).

Peter clearly lays out two possibilities for his readers. They can either embrace the promises offered to human beings by God in Christ, and in that very embrace discover that they have been created for ever increasing participation in the divine nature, or they can embrace the teaching of the false prophets and descend into irrationality, inhumanity, and finally judgment. If in a misguided quest for freedom people choose to act like animals, God will grant their request to return to the pig pen. The false sophistication of these teachers could not disguise the hollowness of their lives. They and their followers had descended to the level of irrational beasts directed only by base instinct (2:10–22).

The Danger of Spiritual Amnesia

Why were some among Peter's audience attracted to a false message that so patently contradicted the gospel Peter preached and modeled?

Some were falling away from the truth because of a short and selective memory. Caught up in the immediate pleasures and extravagant promises offered to them by the false teachers, these deeply deceived Christians had forgotten that Christ would indeed come again to judge the living and the dead. After all, they said to themselves, so many years had passed since Jesus had ascended into heaven. The false teachers' earlier neglect of God's promises fed the desire to set aside the great promise of Christ's return (3:1–7).

Hence, Peter works hard to revive his readers' memory. The false prophets and their disciples misinterpreted the delay in Christ's return as a sign that things would always remain the same (3:3–4). An awakened memory, Peter hopes, may deliver these deluded and self-indulgent Christians from their delirium: "I am trying to arouse your sincere intention by reminding you that you should remember the words spoken in the past by the holy prophets" (3:1–2). If they remain in the numbed state of spiritual amnesia, though, they may rest assured that God's judgment will come swiftly and unexpectedly as a cleansing, punishing, re-creating fire (3:8–13).

Peter's second letter, then, offers blessing and encouragement to those who, through the power of the Spirit, refuse to judge on the basis of appearances, and live in light of the surety of God's promises, though those promises may not be consummated for many years. Yet Peter is not hesitant to warn sharply those tempted by complacency, self-indulgence, and an inability to discern between truth and error. Decisions, perspectives, and behaviors cultivated in the present will not magically disappear into a moral black hole. Though God may seem absent and the coming of his Son delayed, the fabric of the universe is divine and moral and will be re-created in love and judgment. To forget the most important things in the present is to court disaster in the future.

—*Christopher A. Hall*

Salutation

1 Simeon[a] Peter, a servant[b] and apostle of Jesus Christ,

To those who have received a faith as precious as ours through the righteousness of our God and Savior Jesus Christ:[c]

2 May grace and peace be yours in abundance in the knowledge of God and of Jesus our Lord.

The Christian's Call and Election

3 His divine power has given us everything needed for life and godliness, through the knowledge of him who called us by[d] his own glory and goodness. 4Thus he has given us, through these things, his precious and very great promises, so that through them you may escape from the corruption that is in the world because of lust, and may become participants of the divine nature. 5For this very reason, you must make every effort to support your faith with goodness, and goodness with knowledge, 6and knowledge with self-control, and self-control with endurance, and endurance with godliness, 7and godliness with mutual[e] affection, and mutual[e] affection with love. 8For if these things are yours and are increasing among you, they keep you from being ineffective and unfruitful in the knowledge of our Lord Jesus Christ. 9For anyone who lacks these things is shortsighted and blind, and is forgetful of the cleansing of past sins. 10Therefore, brothers

and sisters,[f] be all the more eager to confirm your call and election, for if you do this, you will never stumble. 11For in this way, entry into the eternal kingdom of our Lord and Savior Jesus Christ will be richly provided for you.

12 Therefore I intend to keep on reminding you of these things, though you know them already and are established in the truth that has come to you. 13I think it right, as long as I am in this body,[g] to refresh your memory, 14since I know that my death[h] will come soon, as indeed our Lord Jesus Christ has made clear to me. 15And I will make every effort so that after my departure you may be able at any time to recall these things.

Eyewitnesses of Christ's Glory

16 For we did not follow cleverly devised myths when we made known to you the power and coming of our Lord Jesus Christ, but we had been eyewitnesses of his majesty. 17For he received honor and glory from God the Father when that voice was conveyed to him by the Majestic Glory, saying, "This is my Son, my Beloved,[i] with whom I am well pleased." 18We ourselves heard this voice come from

a Other ancient authorities read *Simon*
b Gk *slave*   *c* Or *of our God and the Savior Jesus Christ*   *d* Other ancient authorities read *through*
e Gk *brotherly*   *f* Gk *brothers*   *g* Gk *tent*
h Gk *the putting off of my tent*   *i* Other ancient authorities read *my beloved Son*

1:3–4 *everything needed for life and godliness.* Peter begins by reminding his readers that God has provided all that is needed, through both God's actions and promises, for full participation in God's divine nature. No, Christians will never become God, as though we could erase the distinction between Creator and creature. We can, though, increasingly take on the divine image, so that when the watching world views us, they see a reflection of our Creator and Redeemer. Peter insists that we cultivate the family image in a disciplined manner, and he has little time or tolerance for the teacher who would claim to speak for God while living a dehumanizing, degrading life.

1:5–9 *support your faith with goodness.* God has wired human beings for deep communion

with God and each other. As we grow in holiness, godliness, love, and self-control, we become simultaneously more human and more like God. Growing into the family resemblance, however, is not a passive affair. Peter exhorts us to "make every effort" to "support" our faith with the substructure of specific virtues grounded in the grace of the Holy Spirit. The order and progression of these virtues have important implications for our spiritual formation. Growth in goodness, for instance, supports and strengthens faith, while a licentious, self-absorbed lifestyle like that of the false teachers undercuts our willingness and ability to trust anyone but ourselves. The created order implodes when we place ourselves at its center.

TRANSFIGURATION

heaven, while we were with him on the holy mountain.

19 So we have the prophetic message more fully confirmed. You will do well to be attentive to this as to a lamp shining in a dark place, until the day dawns and the morning star rises in your hearts. 20First of all you must understand this, that no prophecy of scripture is a matter of one's own interpretation, 21because no prophecy ever came by human will, but men and women moved by the Holy Spirit spoke from God. *a*

False Prophets and Their Punishment

2 But false prophets also arose among the people, just as there will be false teachers among you, who will secretly bring in destructive opinions. They will even deny the Master who bought them—bringing swift destruction on themselves. 2Even so, many will follow their licentious ways, and because of these teachers *b* the way of truth will be maligned. 3And in their greed they will exploit you with deceptive words. Their condemnation, pronounced against them long ago, has not been idle, and their destruction is not asleep.

4 For if God did not spare the angels when they sinned, but cast them into hell *c* and committed them to chains *d* of deepest darkness to be kept until the judgment; 5and if he did not spare the ancient world, even though he saved Noah, a herald of righteousness, with seven others, when he brought a flood on a world of the ungodly; 6and if by turning the cities of Sodom and Gomorrah to ashes he condemned them to extinction *e* and made them an example of what is coming to the ungodly; *f* 7and if he rescued Lot, a righteous man greatly distressed by the licentiousness of the lawless 8(for that righteous man, living among them day after day, was tormented in his righteous soul by their lawless deeds that he saw and heard), 9then the Lord knows how to rescue the godly from

trial, and to keep the unrighteous under punishment until the day of judgment 10—especially those who indulge their flesh in depraved lust, and who despise authority.

Bold and willful, they are not afraid to slander the glorious ones, *g* 11whereas angels, though greater in might and power, do not bring against them a slanderous judgment from the Lord. *h* 12These people, however, are like irrational animals, mere creatures of instinct, born to be caught and killed. They slander what they do not understand, and when those creatures are destroyed, *i* they also will be destroyed, 13suffering *j* the penalty for doing wrong. They count it a pleasure to revel in the daytime. They are blots and blemishes, reveling in their dissipation *k* while they feast with you. 14They have eyes full of adultery, insatiable for sin. They entice unsteady souls. They have hearts trained in greed. Accursed children! 15They have left the straight road and have gone astray, following the road of Balaam son of Bosor, *l* who loved the wages of doing wrong, 16but was rebuked for his own transgression; a speechless donkey spoke with a human voice and restrained the prophet's madness.

17 These are waterless springs and mists driven by a storm; for them the deepest darkness has been reserved. 18For they speak bombastic nonsense, and with licentious desires of the flesh they entice people who have just *m* escaped from those who live in error. 19They

a Other ancient authorities read *but moved by the Holy Spirit saints of God spoke*   *b* Gk *because of them*   *c* Gk *Tartaros*   *d* Other ancient authorities read *pits*   *e* Other ancient authorities lack *to extinction*   *f* Other ancient authorities read *an example to those who were to be ungodly*   *g* Or *angels*; Gk *glories*   *h* Other ancient authorities read *before the Lord*; others lack the phrase   *i* Gk *in their destruction*   *j* Other ancient authorities read *receiving*   *k* Other ancient authorities read *love-feasts*   *l* Other ancient authorities read *Beor*   *m* Other ancient authorities read *actually*

Responding

2:1 STUDY. The primary means of avoiding being misled by false teachers is through study of the Bible. If you have not done so earlier, use the index in the back of this Bible or an exhaustive concordance to look up every reference to study. Don't be discouraged at the number of references; divide them into bite-size pieces and do a few a day. Record what you learn. *See also* Spiritual Disciplines Index.

promise them freedom, but they themselves are slaves of corruption; for people are slaves to whatever masters them. [20]For if, after they have escaped the defilements of the world through the knowledge of our Lord and Savior Jesus Christ, they are again entangled in them and overpowered, the last state has become worse for them than the first. [21]For it would have been better for them never to have known the way of righteousness than, after knowing it, to turn back from the holy commandment that was passed on to them. [22]It has happened to them according to the true proverb,

"The dog turns back to its own vomit,"

and,

"The sow is washed only to wallow in the mud."

The Promise of the Lord's Coming

3 This is now, beloved, the second letter I am writing to you; in them I am trying to arouse your sincere intention by reminding you [2]that you should remember the words spoken in the past by the holy prophets, and the commandment of the Lord and Savior

spoken through your apostles. [3]First of all you must understand this, that in the last days scoffers will come, scoffing and indulging their own lusts [4]and saying, "Where is the promise of his coming? For ever since our ancestors died,[a] all things continue as they were from the beginning of creation!" [5]They deliberately ignore this fact, that by the word of God heavens existed long ago and an earth was formed out of water and by means of water, [6]through which the world of that time was deluged with water and perished. [7]But by the same word the present heavens and earth have been reserved for fire, being kept until the day of judgment and destruction of the godless.

8 But do not ignore this one fact, beloved, that with the Lord one day is like a thousand years, and a thousand years are like one day. [9]The Lord is not slow about his promise, as some think of slowness, but is patient with you,[b] not wanting any to perish, but all to come to repentance. [10]But the day of the Lord will come like a thief, and then the heavens

a Gk *our fathers fell asleep*   b Other ancient authorities read *on your account*

2:18–19 *they themselves are slaves of corruption.* Genuine freedom, Peter insists, is found in willingly submitting to the rhyme and reason of life as God has ordered and arranged it. The false teachers declare, "We are free because we do whatever we please. We are free from all boundaries, restrictions, restraints." Exactly the opposite is true. We have been created for freedom, but we discover our freedom only by learning the steps to the dance God has orchestrated. False teachers ignore the score that God has composed for life's symphony, and hence can only limp when God has created them to waltz.

3:1–2 *remember the words spoken in the past.* Too often Christ's disciples suffer from a selective memory. At times we recall the pleasures that past sinful habits afforded, but easily forget the shame, disillusionment, disgrace, torment, and guilt that accompanied our willful acts of disobedience. We forget those things we should remember, and remember those things we should forget. Peter urges us to remember the most important things, specifically the promises declared by God through the prophets. Though

at times it may appear that God has forgotten his promises and seems strikingly absent from the universe, we shouldn't judge by appearances.

3:8 *with the Lord one day is like a thousand years.* Many in Peter's audience were concerned and dismayed that Christ's second coming had not yet occurred. Why the delay? Peter reminds his readers that a very long time for us is a very short time for God. As for the delay in Christ's coming, Peter comments that God's patience is responsible for the long wait. God has no desire for anyone to "perish" (v 9) and understands that some things simply can't be rushed. The patience we learn in waiting for Christ is a virtue relevant to wider issues of spiritual formation. Someone has commented that transformation into the image of Christ "is the slowest of all human movements." Too easily we become impatient with ourselves, confused, disappointed, and angered over how long it takes to change. Will I ever conquer this habit? Will I ever learn to love? Will I ever have the courage to speak out on behalf of the poor and oppressed? Will I ever be willing to leave my comfort zone? Will I always be so fearful? Or selfish? Or self-deceived? Peter's

will pass away with a loud noise, and the elements will be dissolved with fire, and the earth and everything that is done on it will be disclosed.*a*

11 Since all these things are to be dissolved in this way, what sort of persons ought you to be in leading lives of holiness and godliness, [12]waiting for and hastening*b* the coming of the day of God, because of which the heavens will be set ablaze and dissolved, and the elements will melt with fire? [13]But, in accordance with his promise, we wait for new heavens and a new earth, where righteousness is at home.

Final Exhortation and Doxology

14 Therefore, beloved, while you are waiting for these things, strive to be found by him at peace, without spot or blemish; [15]and regard the patience of our Lord as salvation. So also our beloved brother Paul wrote to you according to the wisdom given him, [16]speaking of this as he does in all his letters. There are some things in them hard to understand, which the ignorant and unstable twist to their own destruction, as they do the other scriptures. [17]You therefore, beloved, since you are forewarned, beware that you are not carried away with the error of the lawless and lose your own stability. [18]But grow in the grace and knowledge of our Lord and Savior Jesus Christ. To him be the glory both now and to the day of eternity. Amen.*c*

a Other ancient authorities read *will be burned up* *b* Or *earnestly desiring*   *c* Other ancient authorities lack *Amen*

---

words remind us that God is in no rush. He knows what we are made of. The spiritual life is more a marathon than a sprint, and God is more than willing to run alongside of us or to walk with us if we grow weary. The goal will be reached. It may take longer than we expected, but that is no surprise to God.

3:11–12 *what sort of persons ought you to be?* Peter counsels Christ's Church to live in the present in light of what God has promised for the future. Positively, Christ will come back for those who are his own. How will he determine who are truly his and who are his in name only? The catalog of vices that characterize the false teachers are clear marks of goats, not sheep (Matt 25:31–46): love for "cleverly devised myths" (2 Pet 1:16), secretive exploitation and deception of the naïve (2:1–3), rampant sexual promiscuity (2:2, 7, 10, 13–14, 18), greed (2:14), and an overblown claim to knowledge of supernatural realities (2:10; 2:12). These teachers have lived in an insane moral and spiritual vortex for so long that the abnormal, grotesque, and immoral appear moral and mundane. A false sophistication has warped their ability to distinguish good from evil, truth from falsehood. The sad result is a descent into habitual behaviors and perspectives Peter can only brand as irrational and beastly (2:12). Animal instinct rules the day. As the false teachers and their disciples have descended into sin, they have become less and less human.

3:14 *while you are waiting for these things.* At least twice Peter comments that those who are Christ's have learned to wait well (vv 12, 13). They have learned to avoid hasty or premature conclusions. They have judiciously avoided the trap of judging by appearances rather than by what God has promised. They have cultivated responses of obedience, holiness, godliness, and patience in the midst of perplexing and discouraging circumstances. They have honed the skills and virtues required for discerning truth from error: sincerity (3:1), remembrance (3:2; 1:9), self-control (1:6), minds and hearts saturated in the Scripture and the knowledge of Christ (1:3–4), stability (3:17), attentiveness (1:19), and endurance (1:6).

3:17–18 *beware that you are not carried away with the error of the lawless.* Finally, Peter reminds his readers of a fundamental principle in spiritual formation. The environment in which we live and those with whom we choose to associate will continually press against us and inevitably shape us, for good or for ill. Peter is particularly concerned that the skewed biblical interpretation and lifestyle of the false teachers, if heard and seen often enough by his readers, will eventually erode their ability to distinguish truth from error (vv 16–17) and will increasingly be viewed as acceptable in the eyes of the Church and of God. Repeat a bad idea or praise a sinful behavior often enough, and the entire cultural and moral landscape will eventually shift. Thus, Peter's strong exhortation to maintain "stability" in the midst of spiritual and moral chaos.

THE FIRST LETTER OF

JOHN

The First Letter of John was written to encourage believers to embrace the light of God's truth and love in a time of church conflict. Division within a church can create much confusion about what is central and nonnegotiable to the Christian faith. To bring clarity, hope, and joy, the author takes his readers back to the solid foundations of faith concerning the very "word of life" (1:1). Through reflection on this "word of life," which was with the Father and revealed in Jesus Christ, the letter urges believers to be discerning and to remain faithful to what they have experienced in Christ.

Historical Background

Early church tradition attributes the writing of 1, 2, & 3 John to the apostle John, son of Zebedee. Because there are both differences and similarities in themes and styles of writing between the Letters and the Gospel of John, recent scholarship has debated whether the idea of common authorship is legitimate. The Letters are actually anonymous, though "the Elder" is identified as the source of 2 & 3 John. There are enough similarities between the Letters and the Fourth Gospel to warrant the view among numerous scholars that John, the "beloved disciple," was the source for them all. Similarly, though recently debated, the Letters are believed by many to have been written before the end of the first century in Asia Minor. As one who has pastoral responsibility for the larger community, the author addresses problems in one of the smaller congregations and warns other churches accordingly. The problems revolve around differences in Christian belief, spirituality, and conduct.

The Way of the Cross

In times of disagreement it is natural to respond in one of two mistaken ways: the way of moral laxity and cheap grace, as if truth is not all that important or discernible;

See also *"The With-God Life" essay for this section of the Bible,*
"The People of God in Community," pp. 2037–42.

or the way of arrogance and self-justification, as if one can pridefully claim owner-ship of the truth. The letter pulls back the veil of discouragement leading one to be-lieve that discord allows only these options. Behind the veil the light of God radiates to reveal a third way, the way of the cross—radical condemnation and yet radical grace for all. Costly darkness confronted by everlasting light. With this exposure to the light, readers face the reality of the darkness that lurks within their own being, which can be penetrated and dispelled only by God, who is light. God's illuminating presence offers ongoing guidance, forgiveness, and strength to equip believers to live differently than the world around them. We see in this letter the challenge to take seriously both human brokenness, which must be addressed in an ongoing way, and believers' identity as children of God. We also see the way in which evil spreads if it is denied, minimized, or allowed to divide those whom God has cleansed and called.

God Is Light

Clarity comes in the midst of confusion and conflict by remembering first and foremost who God is. Thus, this letter offers rich reminders of God's nature and char-acter. "God is light and in him there is no darkness at all" (1:5). Nothing in God's character is shady, false, or sinister. God is completely righteous, loving, and just. In fact, "God is love" (4:8). Love is no vague concept, open to whatever definition one might fancy. Rather, God's love and utter faithfulness have been manifestly re-vealed in the sending of the Son of God, Jesus Christ. "We know love by this, that he laid down his life for us" (3:16). Love is self-giving. Christ's love leads to his death in order to cleanse us from all sin (1:7) that we might be born into new life through him. In this way we are drawn into fellowship with God and one another. This is our salvation. This is what transports us from death to life, from darkness to light, from alienation to loving communion, and from sin to righteousness.

Through Jesus' life, death, and resurrection, we have become God's own children, those who are "born of God" (3:9). As God's children, our lives will reflect the light and love of God's character. Though children do not reflect their parents' charac-ter fully, they show evidence that they are influenced by them in distinguishing ways. Even so, God's children, in intimate relationship with God, are in the process of be-ing transformed to love as God loves. God remains the source of light and love, but now allows and invites us to dwell in that light and love. Furthermore, God empowers us to share that radiant goodness with others, knowing Christ's death was an offering for the whole world.

Jesus Christ and the Way of Love

Christ's life and work are central to knowing and being saved by God. The letter points repeatedly to Jesus Christ as the unique Son of the Father who continues to inter-cede for us and mediate forgiveness to us. Those who confess Christ live in and through him. To confess Christ is to trust in his ongoing role as mediator with the Father (2:1). It also means to admit that we fail and thus need ongoing cleansing from sin and ever renewed commitment to become like Christ. Those who deny the Son do not have the Father, and thus they cut themselves off from light and life. Salvation is a dynamic relationship with the Father through the Son that will be made apparent by the way people live and love.

Even as Jesus Christ is God's love made tangible for the world, so believers are those who make God's love tangible to those around them. As Jesus laid down his life for others, so "we ought to lay down our lives for one another" (3:16). First John clarifies what this will involve. It will mean sharing one's possessions with those who are in need and loving others in truth and action, not in mere words. Such self-giving love will create unity rather than division among the community of believers. Seeking to follow God's commandments and to be like Christ will evoke among the children of God persistence, faithfulness, and commitment to one another.

Walking in the Light

It is not that believers have already arrived at some static state of perfection. "What we will be has not yet been revealed. What we do know is this: when he is revealed, we will be like him, for we will see him as he is" (3:2–3). Believers are thus called to dynamic responses to God's love as conveyed in the images of abiding and walking. The author emphasizes that the power to live as children born of God does not come from us. Rather, we are called to abide in the Son and in the Father and to walk in the light of God. God's children have received God's own Spirit, who reassures us that Christ is abiding in us, who empowers us to obey God's commandments, and who leads us into the truth. We are given understanding, so that we might stand "in him who is true, in his Son Jesus Christ" (5:20).

The letter reassures believers that they can be utterly confident that they are beloved children of God. With hearts and minds continually being shaped by God's life and commandments, we know God "hears us in whatever we ask" (5:15). We know that the "one who is in [us] is greater than the one who is in the world" (4:4). And we also know that, since our new life comes from God, we are called to humbly reflect God's goodness and love to those around us.

—*Kerry Dearborn*

The Word of Life

1 We declare to you what was from the beginning, what we have heard, what we have seen with our eyes, what we have looked at and touched with our hands, concerning the word of life— ²this life was revealed, and we have seen it and testify to it, and declare to you the eternal life that was with the Father and was revealed to us— ³we declare to you what we have seen and heard so that you also may have fellowship with us; and truly our fellowship is with the Father and with

---

1:1–4 *We declare to you . . . concerning the word of life.* The life that is in Jesus Christ is the solid foundation from which the confidence, concerns, and challenges of 1 John flow. This "word of life" is both eternal and has been made so tangible that the author refers four times to what he has seen and twice to what he has heard.

The goal of drawing attention to Jesus Christ is not to emphasize readers' religious experiences of him, but to draw them into fellowship with one another and God. This is what joy is all about, for eternal life can be experienced here and now.

1:3 FELLOWSHIP—*See* Spiritual Disciplines Index.

his Son Jesus Christ. ⁴We are writing these things so that our *a* joy may be complete.

God Is Light

5 This is the message we have heard from him and proclaim to you, that God is light and in him there is no darkness at all. ⁶If we say that we have fellowship with him while we are walking in darkness, we lie and do not do what is true; ⁷but if we walk in the light as he himself is in the light, we have fellowship with one another, and the blood of Jesus his Son cleanses us from all sin. ⁸If we say that we have no sin, we deceive ourselves, and the truth is not in us. ⁹If we confess our sins, he who is faithful and just will forgive us our sins and cleanse us from all unrighteousness. ¹⁰If we say that we have not sinned, we make him a liar, and his word is not in us.

Christ Our Advocate

2 My little children, I am writing these things to you so that you may not sin. But if anyone does sin, we have an advocate with the Father, Jesus Christ the righteous;

²and he is the atoning sacrifice for our sins, and not for ours only but also for the sins of the whole world.

3 Now by this we may be sure that we know him, if we obey his commandments. ⁴Whoever says, "I have come to know him," but does not obey his commandments, is a liar, and in such a person the truth does not exist; ⁵but whoever obeys his word, truly in this person the love of God has reached perfection. By this we may be sure that we are in him: ⁶whoever says, "I abide in him," ought to walk just as he walked.

A New Commandment

7 Beloved, I am writing you no new commandment, but an old commandment that you have had from the beginning; the old commandment is the word that you have heard. ⁸Yet I am writing you a new commandment that is true in him and in you, because *b* the darkness is passing away and the true light is already shining. ⁹Whoever says, "I am in the light," while hating a brother or

a Other ancient authorities read *your*   *b* Or *that*

1:5–7 *If we say that we have fellowship.* To be in fellowship with God, who is light, means we have entered into the light and live according to the light. In contrast to those who had left the fellowship claiming to be without sin, the faithful must admit that they sin. They must also acknowledge their need for Jesus, who alone is the light and who will forgive and cleanse them from sin that they may continue walking in the light.

Responding
1:5–7 FELLOWSHIP. This passage states that to have genuine fellowship with one another and with God, we must walk in the light of God "as he himself is in the light" (also see John 3:19–21; 8:12; 11:9–10; 12:35–36). Why does John use the metaphor of light in describing God and Christian fellowship? Pray that God will fill you with that light and help you walk in it. *See also* Spiritual Disciplines Index.

1:9 CONFESSION—*See* Spiritual Disciplines Index.

2:1–7 *My little children, I am writing.* The key to the Christian life is to know and love Christ, which is reflected both in our responsiveness to Jesus' guidance and in a readiness to confess times of failure. Jesus would keep the way clear for us to come to him. His death offers purification to the whole world, and now he prays to the Father for us, to keep us cleansed and filled with God's love. Jesus wants us close enough to actually live in him, and in this way we can walk with him and become more like him. We can live as we were created to live. Though this call to God's loving nature and ways has existed from the beginning, it has now assumed newness in its embodiment in Christ and in us as we abide in him. This is no theoretical belief system, but a dynamic and transforming embrace.

2:2 SACRIFICE—*See* Spiritual Disciplines Index.

2:9 *Whoever says, "I am in the light," while hating.* Hatred of one's brother or sister means one is in the darkness rather than in the light. Those who abandon the fellowship also walk without the light and thus stumble in blindness

sister,[a] is still in the darkness. [10]Whoever loves a brother or sister[b] lives in the light, and in such a person[c] there is no cause for stumbling. [11]But whoever hates another believer[d] is in the darkness, walks in the darkness, and does not know the way to go, because the darkness has brought on blindness.

[12] I am writing to you, little children,
because your sins are forgiven on
account of his name.
[13] I am writing to you, fathers,
because you know him who is from
the beginning.
I am writing to you, young people,
because you have conquered the evil
one.
[14] I write to you, children,
because you know the Father.
I write to you, fathers,
because you know him who is from
the beginning.
I write to you, young people,
because you are strong
and the word of God abides in you,
and you have overcome the evil one.
[15] Do not love the world or the things in the world. The love of the Father is not in those who love the world; [16]for all that is in the world—the desire of the flesh, the desire of the eyes, the pride in riches—comes not from the Father but from the world. [17]And the world and its desire[e] are passing away, but those who do the will of God live forever.

Warning against Antichrists

[18] Children, it is the last hour! As you have heard that antichrist is coming, so now many antichrists have come. From this we know that it is the last hour. [19]They went out from us, but they did not belong to us; for if they had belonged to us, they would have remained with us. But by going out they made it plain that none of them belongs to us. [20]But you have been anointed by the Holy One, and all of you have knowledge.[f] [21]I write to you, not because you do not know the truth, but because you know it, and you know that no lie comes from the truth. [22]Who is the liar but the one who denies that Jesus is the Christ?[g] This is the antichrist, the one

a Gk hating a brother   b Gk loves a brother
c Or in it   d Gk hates a brother   e Or the desire
for it   f Other ancient authorities read you know
all things   g Or the Messiah

and cause others to stumble. We must choose whether we will live in God's guiding light, and so love others, or dwell in the realm of darkness and reject our brothers and sisters. We cannot do both.

2:12–14 *I am writing to you, little children.* John is full of encouragement for believers at various stages in their walk with God. In contrast to those who have left, these faithful believers can be assured that they do indeed know God, are forgiven, and have overcome the evil one. They are on a pilgrimage walking in rhythm with God's word and need not fear.

2:15 *Do not love the world.* There is no place for complacency. It is easy to become self-centered and drawn away from God by the glamour of sensuality, status, and riches, even though these things will not last. In contrast, those who remain on pilgrimage with God will live forever. The author reminds us that we must choose; we can have only one master.

2:19–20 *They went out from us.* As evidence of what does not endure, John points to the false teachers who have left the fellowship. Gnosticism or pre-Gnostic ideas have been seen as influences on these secessionists. These ideas include claims to special knowledge of God, a divine spark within them, a sinless nature that precludes the need for atonement, and dualistic understandings of the spiritual and material realms. Also evident is a tendency toward docetism, the denial of the full incarnation and true suffering of Jesus Christ. The very fact that they have left the fellowship means they never fully belonged. They claimed true knowledge, but their separatist ways reveal they stood against what Christ lived and taught. In contrast, those who stayed are assured that they have been given true knowledge and the Spirit's enduring presence. As the author has made clear, these gifts of grace are for the service of God and one another, not for the exultation of oneself.

2:22–24 *denies that Jesus is the Christ.* John identifies the central fallacy of those who have left the community of faith—they deny that

who denies the Father and the Son. 23No one who denies the Son has the Father; everyone who confesses the Son has the Father also. 24Let what you heard from the beginning abide in you. If what you heard from the beginning abides in you, then you will abide in the Son and in the Father. 25And this is what he has promised us, *a* eternal life.

26 I write these things to you concerning those who would deceive you. 27As for you, the anointing that you received from him abides in you, and so you do not need anyone to teach you. But as his anointing teaches you about all things, and is true and is not a lie, and just as it has taught you, abide in him. *b*

28 And now, little children, abide in him, so that when he is revealed we may have confidence and not be put to shame before him at his coming.

Children of God

29 If you know that he is righteous, you may be sure that everyone who does right has been born of him. 1See what love the Father has given us, that we should

be called children of God; and that is what we are. The reason the world does not know us is that it did not know him. 2Beloved, we are God's children now; what we will be has not yet been revealed. What we do know is this: when he *b* is revealed, we will be like him, for we will see him as he is. 3And all who have this hope in him purify themselves, just as he is pure.

4 Everyone who commits sin is guilty of lawlessness; sin is lawlessness. 5You know that he was revealed to take away sins, and in him there is no sin. 6No one who abides in him sins; no one who sins has either seen him or known him. 7Little children, let no one deceive you. Everyone who does what is right is righteous, just as he is righteous. 8Everyone who commits sin is a child of the devil; for the devil has been sinning from the beginning. The Son of God was revealed for this purpose, to destroy the works of the devil. 9Those who have been born of God do not sin, because God's seed abides in them; *c* they

a Other ancient authorities read *you*   *b* Or *it*
c Or *because the children of God abide in him*

Jesus is the Christ. They do not affirm the truth that God the Father can be known through Jesus Christ the Son, who was fully human and died to cleanse us from sin. This explains their dismissal of the atonement and confession as ways through which one must be purified by Jesus. One encounters the term "antichrist" in the New Testament only in the Johannine Letters. The challenge is to be wary of false teachers, and to be careful that one's own beliefs, life, and teaching convey the truth of Jesus Christ and lead to confession of the Father as revealed through the Son. We dare not water down the wondrous message of the gospel through faulty teaching or lives that reflect cheap grace.

2:27–29 *the anointing . . . abides in you.* The author uses rich imagery to convey the theme of abiding—we let the ancient truths abide in us and thus abide in the Son and the Father. God's children do not need the false new teaching offered to them by those who had left. They can be confident that the Holy Spirit has been given to guide them into all truth. The life of discipleship is one of abiding in Christ, being confident that he is the source of all truth and

will enable us to do what is right.

3:1 *See what love the Father has given us.* So who are we? We are God's beloved children, and the letter now offers reminders of what this means. The author wants to prepare believers by reminding them of the promises to those born of God as well as the demands. We can rejoice that, because of God's initiative, one day we will see God and be like God, though we are not there yet. In the meantime we can stand fast as we abide in Christ, for it is through Christ that we can stay pure.

3:4–8 *Everyone who commits sin.* Here is a call to take sin very seriously. Sin is not to be tolerated, for it is everything that Christ is not. Sin mars the family resemblance, and thus Christ came to take sin away. If one makes a practice of sin, it will reflect a lack of fundamental connection to the One who is sinless. Continual sin makes one resemble the devil, who exists in rebellion against God. God has made us his children to give us the freedom of walking with him in the light, where God's love and empowerment liberate us from enslavement to the lord of darkness.

JOHN

Simple Love

Selected Scriptures: *Matthew 17:1–21; 20:20–28; Mark 1:16–22; 3:13–19; 5:21–43; 14:32–42; Luke 5:1–11; 6:12–16; 9:46–56; John 13:21–25, 33–35; 19:25–27; 20:1–10; 21:1–14, 20–25; Galatians 2:7–10; 1, 2, & 3 John; Revelation 1–5; 13–14; 18–22*

John is perhaps best known as the "disciple whom Jesus loved." He is also considered by many to be the "John" named at the opening of the fantastic vision that makes up Revelation. Yet early in John's career as a disciple, Jesus nicknamed John and his brother James the "Sons of Thunder" (Mark 3:17). We're told that one day John wanted to stop a man from driving out demons in Jesus' name because "he does not follow with us" (Luke 9:50). Another time, as they traveled through Samaria and the people refused to give shelter to Jesus and the disciples, John and James asked if they should command fire to come from heaven and consume the villagers (Luke 9:51–55). And later, the brothers had their mother ask Jesus to grant them special places of authority next to him in his coming kingdom (Matt 20:20–28).

John claimed great love for Jesus early on; yet these three scenes don't reflect a deep understanding of the kind of love Jesus taught and lived. John seemed to view Jesus as an earthly ruler. Yet when we jump ahead to John's leadership of the church at Ephesus, where he spent his final years, his perspective had changed greatly. Now he spoke mostly of love—simple and selfless Christlike love. An early tradition reports that in old age John eventually became too weak to walk and was carried to church meetings on a pallet, where he would whisper again and again, "Little children, love one another."

After John spent much time with Jesus on earth and many years as a leader of the early Church, with many issues to address in instructing the early Christians, his message became only more basic. "Love one another," he pleaded over and over. He had come to understand the essence of Jesus and of God the Father. He understood why Jesus came, why he died and rose, and why he promised a fantastic future for his own. Jesus possesses a love like no other, a love that only God can supply, and those who know Jesus can do nothing else but reflect that same love. Truly, the gospel message remains this simple: love God, and love your neighbor as yourself (Matt 22:37–40).

What brought about such transformation in John? Jesus' death and resurrection moved like thunder in John's spirit, changing his aggression and pride to a love for Christ and others. John was transformed through the power of the resurrected Christ, and as he grew old his yearning to point to Jesus only increased. The insights of a fourteenth-century Italian mystic and public servant may shed some light on how Christ transformed John and others like him.

Catherine of Siena writes, as if God were speaking, of the power of Jesus' love: "When my goodness saw that you could be drawn in no other way, I sent him to be lifted onto the wood of the cross. I made of that cross an anvil where this child of humankind could be hammered into an instrument to release humankind from death and restore it to the life of grace. In this way he drew everything to himself: for he proved his unspeakable love, and the human heart is always drawn by love. He could not have shown you greater love than by giving his life for you (John 15:13). . . .

"I said that, having been raised up, he would draw everything to himself. This is true in two ways: First, the human heart is drawn by love as I said, and with all its powers: memory, understanding, and will. If these three powers are harmoniously united in my name, everything else you do, in fact or intention, will be drawn to union with me in peace through the movement of love, because all will be lifted up in the pursuit of crucified love." (*Devotional Classics*)

Here Catherine breaks down the "powers" of the heart into memory, understanding, and will. In John's life we see that each of these components of his heart was drawn by Jesus' love. His memory of Christ changed him, and in writing the Gospel of John he shared many words and teachings of Jesus that were not included in any of the other Gospels. The word "believe" occurs ninety-eight times in his Gospel; John aimed to draw others to the Christ he knew.

John's understanding of Jesus began with his comprehension of Christ's love. His Letters keep circling back to that love and pleading with Christians to let the same love be true of them. "Believe," he had pressed in his Gospel. "Walk just as he walked" (2:6), he exhorts in his First Letter. "Those who love God must love their brothers and sisters also" (4:21). And at last John writes in Revelation, as he encounters the King of the ages and of all eternity, "Blessed are those who hear and who keep what is written" (1:3). John's will had been turned fully to Christ, and he cared only that he and his fellow believers followed faithfully in the way of Christ, the way of love toward God and one another.

Jesus may have had a special love for John, singling him out from the other disciples. Certainly John was a part, along with James and Peter, of an inner circle who shared some special experiences with Jesus. He was chosen, as well, to take Jesus' place as Mary's son after the crucifixion (John 19:25–27). Yet maybe Jesus simply loved John with the same holy love he had for each one of his followers and has for us. Could it be that John simply became so struck with the overpowering reality of Jesus' love that he christened himself the "disciple whom Jesus loved," just as each one of us might as we enter into a true understanding of this fantastic, unending love of our Savior for us?

Personal Reflection

- Does your love for God ever resemble John's early character—aggressive, quick to point a finger at others, concerned about your place in the spiritual pecking order? In what ways does Jesus set you apart as a "favorite" anyway?
- What in your memory of Jesus draws you to love him? What in your understanding of Jesus draws you to love him? How fully is your will drawn toward loving Jesus? How well are these three "powers" of your heart working to transform your character and saturate you with a love for God and others?

cannot sin, because they have been born of God. [10]The children of God and the children of the devil are revealed in this way: all who do not do what is right are not from God, nor are those who do not love their brothers and sisters. [a]

Love One Another

11 For this is the message you have heard from the beginning, that we should love one another. [12]We must not be like Cain who was from the evil one and murdered his brother. And why did he murder him? Because his own deeds were evil and his brother's righteous. [13]Do not be astonished, brothers and sisters, [b] that the world hates you. [14]We know that we have passed from death to life because we love one another. Whoever does not love abides in death. [15]All who hate a brother or sister [a] are murderers, and you know that murderers do not have eternal life abiding in them. [16]We know love by this, that he laid down his life for us—and we ought to lay down our lives for one another. [17]How does God's love abide in anyone who has the world's goods and sees a brother or sister [c] in need and yet refuses help?

18 Little children, let us love, not in word or speech, but in truth and action. [19]And by this we will know that we are from the truth and will reassure our hearts before him [20]whenever our hearts condemn us; for God is greater than our hearts, and he knows everything. [21]Beloved, if our hearts do not condemn us, we have boldness before God; [22]and we receive from him whatever we ask, because we obey his commandments and do what pleases him.

23 And this is his commandment, that we should believe in the name of his Son Jesus Christ and love one another, just as he has commanded us. [24]All who obey his commandments abide in him, and he abides in them. And by this we know that he abides in us, by the Spirit that he has given us.

Testing the Spirits

4 Beloved, do not believe every spirit, but test the spirits to see whether they are from God; for many false prophets have gone out into the world. [2]By this you know the Spirit of God: every spirit that confesses that Jesus Christ has come in the flesh is from God, [3]and every spirit that does not confess Jesus [d] is not from God. And this is the spirit of the antichrist, of which you have heard that it is coming; and now it is already in the world. [4]Little children, you are from God, and have conquered them; for the one who is in you is greater than the one who is in the world. [5]They are from the world; there-

a Gk his brother   b Gk brothers   c Gk brother
d Other ancient authorities read does away with Jesus (Gk dissolves Jesus)

3:13–18 *that the world hates you.* One of the challenges of being God's children is to continue to express God's love in the midst of the hostility of those who oppose God's ways. Real love will be conveyed tangibly and concretely to others' lives. It isn't enough to proclaim love to others. Love demands Christlike self-giving to others. Such love is possible and to be expected in those who believe, for they have crossed over from spiritual death (*thanatos*) to spiritual life (*zōē*). Cain is the archetype of those who hate and thus are spiritually dead (v 12). Christ exemplifies and is the source of eternal life, which begins for believers now and is manifested as love for one another.

3:21–22 *we have boldness before God.* God's children can run into their Father's presence with boldness. We can have confidence that God hears and responds to our requests, which will reflect the Father's good pleasure even as our lives are consistent with God's purposes. Our prayers and lives are shaped by intimacy with God, who loved us while we were yet sinners. They flow from, rather than qualify us for, a relationship with God.

4:2 *By this you know the Spirit of God.* What does it mean for us, as God's children, to be filled with God's own Spirit? The author has clarified two key signs. First, we know we are filled with God's Spirit when God's love flows from our lives. Second, with God's Spirit we will confess the truth that Jesus Christ is the Word made flesh who reveals God to us. One who hates others and denies the reality of God's work in Christ clearly cannot be filled with God's Spirit.

fore what they say is from the world, and the world listens to them. 6We are from God. Whoever knows God listens to us, and whoever is not from God does not listen to us. From this we know the spirit of truth and the spirit of error.

God Is Love

7 Beloved, let us love one another, because love is from God; everyone who loves is born of God and knows God. 8Whoever does not love does not know God, for God is love. 9God's love was revealed among us in this way: God sent his only Son into the world so that we might live through him. 10In this is love, not that we loved God but that he loved us and sent his Son to be the atoning sacrifice for our sins. 11Beloved, since God loved us so much, we also ought to love one another. 12No one has ever seen God; if we love one another, God lives in us, and his love is perfected in us.

13 By this we know that we abide in him and he in us, because he has given us of his Spirit. 14And we have seen and do testify that the Father has sent his Son as the Savior of the world. 15God abides in those who confess that Jesus is the Son of God, and they abide in God. 16So we have known and believe the love that God has for us.

God is love, and those who abide in love abide in God, and God abides in them. 17Love has been perfected among us in this: that we may have boldness on the day of judgment, because as he is, so are we in this world. 18There is no fear in love, but perfect love casts out fear; for fear has to do with punishment, and whoever fears has not reached perfection in love. 19We love*a* because he first loved us. 20Those who say, "I love God," and hate their brothers or sisters,*b* are liars; for those who do not love a brother or sister*c* whom they have seen, cannot love God whom they have not seen. 21The commandment we have from him is this: those who love God must love their brothers and sisters*b* also.

Faith Conquers the World

5 Everyone who believes that Jesus is the Christ*d* has been born of God, and everyone who loves the parent loves the child. 2By this we know that we love the children of God, when we love God and obey his commandments. 3For the love of God is this, that we obey his commandments. And his commandments are not burdensome, 4for whatever is born of God conquers the world. And this is the victory that conquers the world, our faith. 5Who is it that conquers the world but the one who believes that Jesus is the Son of God?

a Other ancient authorities add *him*; others add *God*   *b* Gk *brothers*   *c* Gk *brother*   *d* Or *the Messiah*

4:10 *In this is love.* Since God is both the source and initiator of love, we are called to look toward God for love. It is not because we are better than others that we love, but because God has poured his own love into us. The love we express is a way of pointing people to the wonder of who God is. It is also the way we know we are living in God's house of love and God is living in us.

Responding
4:15 CONFESSION. How long has it been since you confessed that Jesus is the Son of God? As the Spirit leads, say out loud, "Jesus is the Son of God," a number of times, then wait for his presence to "abide" with you. *See also* Spiritual Disciplines Index.

4:16–18 *God is love.* These verses are one of the clearest statements in all of Scripture that the nature of God is love. This is love as enfleshed by Jesus Christ. It is this love in which we are invited to dwell and to have dwell in us. Thus we need not fear judgment, for as God's children we are participants in God's own nature. God works with us to bring our love to perfection.

5:2–4 *when we love God and obey his commandments.* The notion of victory in 1 John challenges us to think of God's commandments as the way to freedom rather than a restriction of freedom. Thus obedience is not oppressive, but is the very route to triumph over all that is dark and crushing in the world.

Testimony concerning the Son of God

6 This is the one who came by water and blood, Jesus Christ, not with the water only but with the water and the blood. And the Spirit is the one that testifies, for the Spirit is the truth. [7]There are three that testify: [8]the Spirit and the water and the blood, and these three agree. [9]If we receive human testimony, the testimony of God is greater; for this is the testimony of God that he has testified to his Son. [10]Those who believe in the Son of God have the testimony in their hearts. Those who do not believe in God[b] have made him a liar by not believing in the testimony that God has given concerning his Son. [11]And this is the testimony: God gave us eternal life, and this life is in his Son. [12]Whoever has the Son has life; whoever does not have the Son of God does not have life.

Epilogue

13 I write these things to you who believe in the name of the Son of God, so that you may know that you have eternal life.

14 And this is the boldness we have in him, that if we ask anything according to his will, he hears us. [15]And if we know that he hears us in whatever we ask, we know that we have obtained the requests made of him. [16]If you see your brother or sister[c] committing what is not a mortal sin, you will ask, and God[d] will give life to such a one—to those whose sin is not mortal. There is sin that is mortal; I do not say that you should pray about that. [17]All wrongdoing is sin, but there is sin that is not mortal.

18 We know that those who are born of God do not sin, but the one who was born of God protects them, and the evil one does not touch them. [19]We know that we are God's children, and that the whole world lies under the power of the evil one. [20]And we know that the Son of God has come and has given us understanding so that we may know him who is true;[e] and we are in him who is true, in his Son Jesus Christ. He is the true God and eternal life.

21 Little children, keep yourselves from idols.[f]

---

a A few other authorities read (with variations) [7]There are three that testify in heaven, the Father, the Word, and the Holy Spirit, and these three are one. [8]And there are three that testify on earth: b Other ancient authorities read in the Son   c Gk your brother   d Gk he   e Other ancient authorities read know the true God   f Other ancient authorities add Amen

---

5:6–9 the one who came by water and blood. The guidance of God's Spirit, the word of faithful witnesses, and the historical reality of Jesus' bodily existence lead to true confession of Jesus Christ, which will be manifest through one's life and word. These are the sources of authority that can settle disputes over issues of faith. To affirm that Jesus came by the water and the blood is to acknowledge that God's salvation comes to the world through his life and his death.

5:16 If you see your brother or sister. As the letter comes to an end, the author urges believers to be in prayer for one another, that God might give life to those who have sinned, lest they be led astray like the false teachers who had left the church. Prayer about "mortal sin" is discouraged. Throughout the letter "mortal sin" is characterized as ongoing denial of Jesus Christ and rejection of fellow believers. People whose sin is "mortal" must come to repentance before they can be brought into life. The emphasis is on a call for believers to lay down their lives in love for one another through prayer so that no one in the community is lost to the utter darkness.

5:18–21 those who are born of God. Three certainties distinguish God's children. They are born of God and thus liberated from a life of sin; they are protected by Jesus Christ from the evil one; and they have been given understanding of God through his Son. Though as believers we do at times sin and need prayer and confession, our conduct is the ultimate test of whether we are born of God and thus in Christ, who is true. To follow any other beliefs is to pursue idols, which the author lovingly enjoins his readers to resist.

THE SECOND LETTER OF

JOHN

The Second Letter of John is similar in length to most other ancient letters, for, although brief in comparison with most New Testament Letters, it comprises about the amount of material that could be written on a single sheet of papyrus. Similar to 1 John, 2 John gives readers a glimpse into the challenges and practices of the early Church. It too was sent to strengthen believers in their core beliefs and identity and to warn them about those who would lead them astray. Furthermore, this letter includes a warning that calls for separation from false teachers who will lead believers away from the love of God. One senses that, as a good shepherd who loves his sheep, the author desires to both feed them solid food and protect them from what will poison their communion with God and one another. He is also determined that the Church not give any seal of approval to those who would distort the good news of God's love in Jesus Christ.

The Promise of God's Gifts

Writing to "the elect lady," either a woman who leads a house church or a metaphor for the congregation, "the Elder" expresses intimate affection for the members of this community (1:1). He shares with them the promise that God's gifts of grace, mercy, and peace will be with them. They share a common heritage of truth that will be theirs forever. Truth is not identified as a set of principles or propositions, as in knowledge we possess that will fade away. Rather, truth is identified with the eternal Father and Son and is thus a powerful shaping force that takes hold of us through the Spirit.

The author rejoices to have discovered that some of these believers' lives dynamically reflect the truth of God's ways. He urges them to remember what is central to their life together—that they love one another. Truth will manifest itself in

---

See also "The With-God Life" essay for this section of the Bible,
"The People of God in Community," pp. 2037–42.

love, which is expressed tangibly. Love does not consist of emotions that vacillate, but rather actions and relationships that flow from the eternal life that originates in God alone.

Living in God's Truth and Love

If love is to thrive, it must remain anchored in God's truth and God's ways. It cannot be adapted to the world around by adding to it or altering it. False teachers abound who would shape the truth to fit with the values and views of their time. Denials of Jesus' full humanity might make faith more attractive to some, but such a distortion means being cut off from God. If Jesus is not fully human, "God's love" for us becomes only a vague concept. It would mean that God did not fully identify with us, cleanse us from sin by Jesus' death on the cross, or fully reveal the divine Self to us. This in turn would result in a shrinking of our love for one another, for we would have no power to overcome the selfishness in our lives, no unveiling of what love means, no promise that sacrificial living would make any difference. Thus the Elder is very concerned that false teachers be given no encouragement to communicate such crippling falsehood. He does not want believers to lose all that they have gained—the grace, mercy, and peace of God, the freedom to walk in the light of love, and the gift of eternal life with Christ.

He commands them to refuse the false teachers entry into their house (or house church). Offering food and shelter to people in this context would give validation to their teaching and introduce darkness into the community. Truth and love are the highest calling and are meant to be inseparable. Love is not expressed by allowing people to spread the darkness or by welcoming that darkness into a community of faith.

The Elder clearly loves those to whom he writes and wants to be able to communicate more fully with them face-to-face. Being present to one another, rather than giving in to the efficiency of virtual communication and relationships, is integral to the growth of love. This is the complete joy for which we hunger, the expression of the loving nature that God has given us in Jesus Christ.

—*Kerry Dearborn*

Salutation

1 The elder to the elect lady and her children, whom I love in the truth, and not only I but also all who know the truth, 2because of the truth that abides in us and will be with us forever:

3 Grace, mercy, and peace will be with us from God the Father and from*a* Jesus Christ, the Father's Son, in truth and love.

Truth and Love

4 I was overjoyed to find some of your children walking in the truth, just as we have been commanded by the Father. 5But now, dear lady, I ask you, not as though I were writing you a new commandment, but one we have had from the beginning, let us love one another. 6And this is love, that we walk according to his commandments; this is the commandment just as you have heard it from the beginning—you must walk in it.

7 Many deceivers have gone out into the world, those who do not confess that Jesus Christ has come in the flesh; any such person is the deceiver and the antichrist! 8Be on your guard, so that you do not lose what we*b* have worked for, but may receive a full reward. 9Everyone who does not abide in the teaching of Christ, but goes beyond it, does not have God; whoever abides in the teaching has both the Father and the Son. 10Do not receive into the house or welcome anyone who comes to you and does not bring this teaching; 11for to welcome is to participate in the evil deeds of such a person.

Final Greetings

12 Although I have much to write to you, I would rather not use paper and ink; instead I hope to come to you and talk with you face to face, so that our joy may be complete.

13 The children of your elect sister send you their greetings.*c*

---

a Other ancient authorities add *the Lord*
b Other ancient authorities read *you*   *c* Other ancient authorities add *Amen*

1–3 *The elder to the elect lady.* It is significant that the letter is addressed to "the elect lady"; Greek *kyria,* "lady," is the feminine form of *kyrios,* "lord." Though some scholars view this as a metaphor for the congregation, nowhere else is a congregation or community addressed in this way. Others believe that the Elder may have had in mind a specific female leader with a house church under her care. Though unidentified in the letter, the Elder has traditionally been assumed to be John, the apostle of Jesus. The author begins and ends his letter with an expression of deep love for this congregation, modeling the central thrust of his teaching: that they love one another. In the first two verses he highlights important Johannine concepts for expressions of faith: love, truth, knowledge, and abiding. Worthy leaders will not only teach the truth of Jesus Christ; they will convey it through their lives.

4–6 *your children walking in the truth.* Walking in the truth, and thus according to God's commandments, can be summed up as "Let us love one another." The Christian life is a dynamic pilgrimage of self-giving love. It is not a comfortable resting place of self-indulgence.

8–9 *Be on your guard.* The author is addressing the problem of former church members who have become itinerant teachers in order to win over others to their false teaching. The call to vigilance is twofold. Believers must be on guard against those who distort the teaching of Christ by denying that Jesus took on human flesh to give his life for the world. And they must continue to abide in the truth that Jesus Christ is the Word made flesh. Those who alter this truth cut themselves off from God. Those who abide in this truth will be abiding in the Son and in the Father and will be rewarded with the fullness of life that comes from Jesus.

10 *Do not receive into the house.* Hospitality was central to early Christian mission work. To welcome itinerant teachers into one's home was to encourage and participate in their work. Christians are thus cautioned against becoming so tolerant that the radiant truth of Jesus Christ becomes veiled to the world.

Salutation

1 The elder to the elder lady and her children whom I love in the truth, and not only I but also all who know the truth, because of the truth that abides in us and will be with us forever.

3 Grace, mercy, and peace will be with us from God the Father and from Jesus Christ the Father's son, in truth and love.

Truth and Love

4 I was overjoyed to find some of your children walking in the truth, just as we have been commanded by the Father. 5But now, dear lady, I ask you, not as though I were writing you a new commandment, but the one we have had from the beginning: let us love one another. 6And this is love, that we walk according to his commandments; this is the commandment just as you have heard it from the beginning—you must walk in it.

7 Many deceivers have gone out into the world, those who do not confess that Jesus Christ has come in the flesh; any such person

THE THIRD LETTER OF

JOHN

The issues of integrity and love come into focus in the Third Letter of John, the shortest letter in the New Testament. The Elder, traditionally assumed to be the apostle John, is exuberant in affirming his beloved friend Gaius for walking in the truth. He also offers guidance about hospitality and urges him to welcome those who journey for the sake of Christ. His trouble is that another leader, Diotrephes, has rejected the Elder's authority, has refused to welcome his messengers, and excommunicates members who do welcome them.

Call for Discernment

Hospitality was crucial in mission work in the early Church, for inns were not readily available. Those who spread the gospel depended on the support of those who provided lodging and food, as is evident also when Jesus sent out his disciples to proclaim the good news (Mark 6:10–11; Matt 10). In 2 John the author warns believers not to welcome false teachers. In this letter he clarifies that fellow believers should be received with open arms. Discernment is necessary in knowing whether to welcome an itinerant teacher or bar the door.

Two important keys in such discernment are character and content. The author's own character is one of love and concern for the entire well-being of his friend Gaius, for his body and his soul. What brings the Elder joy is the good news that his "children" are living out their faith with integrity. His recommendations emerge from this basis of love and concern for the people of God. Gaius, to whom he writes, is a person of highest character, as confirmed by the testimony of others. He embodies the very message that has been presented in 1 & 2 John. Here is one who knows the truth and lives it out. Thus he is gracious in loving and welcoming fellow believers into his home, even those he does not know.

See also *"The With-God Life" essay for this section of the Bible,*
"The People of God in Community," pp. 2037–42.

The goal of hospitality is not mere entertainment. It is to further the message of Jesus Christ. We offer hospitality so those who bear that message, who "journey for the sake of Christ," receive hospitality and love (3 John 7). The Elder is overflowing with expressions of love and praise for his friend and is clearly a person who wants to build up the Church while protecting it from false teaching and action.

Concern About Character and Message

In contrast, Diotrephes seems to lack the character needed for such grace and wisdom. He is self-promoting and disrespectful of the Elder's authority. Not only does he spread lies about the Elder, but he refuses entry to his messengers and prevents others from receiving them. If they should welcome missionaries in opposition to his direction, he expels them from the church. It seems to matter little to him what character or content is conveyed by the travelers. He is centered on his own desire for power, and thus he fails to reflect the heart of the gospel, which is to love one another and to preserve the unity of the Church.

The Elder calls his friend Gaius to be discerning and to model good, not evil. Rather than being swayed by a powerful leader in his community, Gaius is urged to maintain wholehearted allegiance to the kind of goodness that is harmonious with God's character and ways. Thus he is urged to receive Demetrius, a person whose good character and teaching is attested by "everyone."

As in 2 John, the author is eager to see his friend face-to-face. He extends a blessing of peace to him and urges him to greet each of his friends there by name.

—*Kerry Dearborn*

Salutation

1 The elder to the beloved Gaius, whom I love in truth.

Gaius Commended for His Hospitality

2 Beloved, I pray that all may go well with you and that you may be in good health, just as it is well with your soul. [3]I was overjoyed when some of the friends[a] arrived and testified to your faithfulness to the truth, namely how you walk in the truth. [4]I have no greater joy than this, to hear that my children are walking in the truth.

5 Beloved, you do faithfully whatever you do for the friends,[a] even though they are strangers to you; [6]they have testified to your love before the church. You will do well to send them on in a manner worthy of God; [7]for they began their journey for the sake of Christ,[b] accepting no support from non-believers.[c] [8]Therefore we ought to support such people, so that we may become co-workers with the truth.

Diotrephes and Demetrius

9 I have written something to the church; but Diotrephes, who likes to put himself first, does not acknowledge our authority. [10]So if I come, I will call attention to what he is doing in spreading false charges against us. And not content with those charges, he refuses to welcome the friends,[a] and even prevents those who want to do so and expels them from the church.

11 Beloved, do not imitate what is evil but imitate what is good. Whoever does good is from God; whoever does evil has not seen God. [12]Everyone has testified favorably about Demetrius, and so has the truth itself. We also testify for him,[d] and you know that our testimony is true.

Final Greetings

13 I have much to write to you, but I would rather not write with pen and ink; [14]instead I hope to see you soon, and we will talk together face to face.

15 Peace to you. The friends send you their greetings. Greet the friends there, each by name.

a Gk brothers   b Gk for the sake of the name
c Gk the Gentiles   d Gk lacks for him

---

1 *The elder to the beloved Gaius, whom I love in truth.* The Johannine concern to hold love and truth together is evident from the outset of this letter. The Elder addresses this concern to his dear friend Gaius, who has been generous in extending hospitality to itinerant Christians.

2 *just as it is well with your soul.* "Soul" (*psyche*) should be understood holistically as referring to one's entire being, that which one can commit wholeheartedly to the service of others (as in John 10:11, 15, 17; 1 John 3:16). Gaius's soul is well because he extends himself in tangible love for others.

5–8 *Beloved, you do faithfully.* Hospitality is clear evidence of love. Missionaries were not to be a burden on unbelievers, but rather needed fellow believers to support and welcome them. With such generous hospitality, Gaius and others become co-workers with the missionaries and fellow workers in the truth.

9–11 *Diotrephes, who likes to put himself first.* To walk in the truth is to receive others as Jesus did, to serve rather than try to dominate and maintain first place. Diotrephes is described as asserting authority in the church that is self-serving and obstructs the Elder's initiatives. The Church is not well served by self-promoters who will not humbly acknowledge the authority of others.

12 *Everyone has testified favorably.* Letters of recommendation were increasingly necessary as the Church grew, so even though Demetrius is commended by his own life and others' testimonies, the Elder adds his own affirmation. Demetrius is most likely one of the traveling teachers who, because of his integrity and truthful witness, deserves hospitality. Issues of authority are pivotal within the Church and must be approached in a way that furthers unity rather than rivalry. The Elder claims truth as the basis of his authority: "You know that our testimony is true" (v 12). It is obvious that he desires to put the Church before his own interests, as he works to spread the news of Jesus Christ rather than to preserve his power.

THE LETTER OF

JUDE

Exactly who was Jude? Jude identifies himself as "brother of James" (Jude 1). In all likelihood, we should identify "James" as the brother of Jesus mentioned in Matt 13:55. No other James is mentioned in Scripture as the brother of Jude, although the father of Judas (not Iscariot) was also named James (Luke 6:16; Acts 1:13). Jude, then, would have been a member of Jesus' own family circle.

When did Jude write this letter? Evidence within the letter points to a date in the mid-first century. Jude's references to the Second Coming (Jude 1, 14, 21, 24) and the nature of the antinomian heresy (vv 4, 8, 10, 12–13, 16) that had invaded the church that Jude addresses fit the first century well. A more exact date is harder to pinpoint. The absence of the adjective "good" or "blessed" before James's name in verse 1 may indicate James's martyrdom in AD 62 had yet to occur, so a date in the late 50s is a possibility.

The purpose of the Letter of Jude is plain. Pseudosophisticates were parading disastrous behavior as the genuine demonstration of freedom in the Spirit. Jude will have none of this. He invites us to ponder what genuine spirituality is and isn't, warning his readers: "It is these worldly people, devoid of the Spirit, who are causing divisions" (v 19).

In short, Jude's short letter is a terse, direct warning against the preaching of the false teachers who have infiltrated Christ's Church. Though Jude had the immediate goal of "eagerly preparing to write . . . about the salvation we share," he found it necessary to write and appeal to his readers "to contend for the faith that was once for all entrusted to the saints" (v 3).

Jude's letter is remarkable on a number of counts. First, Jude has no doubt that the gospel has been faithfully handed on to his readers and fully expects that they are capable of both defending it and living it. Second, Jude is convinced that the ideas promulgated by these false teachers are designed to eviscerate the gospel by splitting

See also "The With-God Life" essay for this section of the Bible,
"The People of God in Community," pp. 2037–42.

apart the message of salvation from the ethic of love that genuine salvation always manifests.

What are the specific markers that characterize this false teaching? Like the false teachers in 2 Peter, these are claiming that what we do with our bodies is irrelevant for our spiritual growth and formation (v 8). They are behaving more like animals than humans, covering their barbarity with a veil of religiosity. They are hollow, shallow people, "waterless clouds carried along by the winds" (v 12).

Jude exhorts his readers, then and now, to remember that the virus of false teaching will occasionally invade the Church's bloodstream. So Jude's readers should not be caught off guard by the bombastic arrogance and exotic sensuality of these teachers. The apostles had predicted that such twisted thinking and living might occur (v 17). Jude counsels us to ground ourselves in the faith and love of God, to pray "in the Holy Spirit," and to "look forward" to the "mercy of our Lord Jesus Christ that leads to eternal life" (vv 20–21).

—*Christopher A. Hall*

Salutation

1 Jude,[a] a servant[b] of Jesus Christ and brother of James,

To those who are called, who are beloved[c] in[d] God the Father and kept safe for[d] Jesus Christ:

2 May mercy, peace, and love be yours in abundance.

Occasion of the Letter

3 Beloved, while eagerly preparing to write to you about the salvation we share, I find it necessary to write and appeal to you to contend for the faith that was once for all entrusted to the saints. 4For certain intruders have stolen in among you, people who long ago were designated for this condemnation as ungodly, who pervert the grace of our God into licentiousness and deny our only Master and Lord, Jesus Christ.[e]

Judgment on False Teachers

5 Now I desire to remind you, though you are fully informed, that the Lord, who once for all saved[f] a people out of the land of Egypt, afterward destroyed those who did not believe. 6And the angels who did not keep their

a Gk *Judas*   b Gk *slave*   c Other ancient authorities read *sanctified*   d Or *by*   e Or *the only Master and our Lord Jesus Christ*   f Other ancient authorities read *though you were once for all fully informed, that Jesus* (or *Joshua*) *who saved*

3–4 *certain intruders have stolen in among you.* Jude is fully convinced that disciples grounded in Christ will be able to discern goodness from evil and what is natural from what is perverted. A church's vision of the gospel and the inherent call within the gospel to goodness, holiness, and love may become blurred or twisted, however. The sad result is perspectives and behaviors that are perverted, that is, inverted or turned upside down. Jude understands this dynamic well, precisely because he had encountered Christians who had stood the grace of God on its head. Grace in the proper understanding enables repentance and genuine conversion; but now grace had become an excuse for hellish behaviors worthy of God's judgment and wrath.

5–7 *the Lord . . . destroyed those who did not believe.* God's judgment and wrath are the signposts that we live in a moral universe created and ruled by a compassionate, loving, holy Creator and Redeemer. God's wrath is not antithetical to God's love. Rather, love manifests its moral character as it responds to evil in judgment and wrath. God doesn't lose his temper whenever an evil thought or act erupts. If God's wrath caused him to do so, God would be continually wrestling with heated emotions. God's wrath and judgment

own position, but left their proper dwelling, he has kept in eternal chains in deepest darkness for the judgment of the great day. [7]Likewise, Sodom and Gomorrah and the surrounding cities, which, in the same manner as they, indulged in sexual immorality and pursued unnatural lust,[a] serve as an example by undergoing a punishment of eternal fire.

[8] Yet in the same way these dreamers also defile the flesh, reject authority, and slander the glorious ones.[b] [9]But when the archangel Michael contended with the devil and disputed about the body of Moses, he did not dare to bring a condemnation of slander[c] against him, but said, "The Lord rebuke you!" [10]But these people slander whatever they do not understand, and they are destroyed by those things that, like irrational animals, they know by instinct. [11]Woe to them! For they go the way of Cain, and abandon themselves to Balaam's error for the sake of gain, and perish in Korah's rebellion. [12]These are blemishes[d] on your love-feasts, while they feast with you without fear, feeding themselves.[e] They are waterless clouds carried along by the winds; autumn trees without fruit, twice dead, uprooted; [13]wild waves of the sea, casting up the foam of their own shame; wandering stars, for whom the deepest darkness has been reserved forever.

[14] It was also about these that Enoch, in the seventh generation from Adam, prophesied, saying, "See, the Lord is coming[f] with ten thousands of his holy ones, [15]to execute judgment on all, and to convict everyone of all the deeds of ungodliness that they have committed in such an ungodly way, and of all the harsh things that ungodly sinners have spoken against him." [16]These are grumblers and malcontents; they indulge their own lusts; they are bombastic in speech, flattering people to their own advantage.

Warnings and Exhortations

[17] But you, beloved, must remember the predictions of the apostles of our Lord Jesus Christ; [18]for they said to you, "In the last time there will be scoffers, indulging their own ungodly lusts." [19]It is these worldly people,

a Gk went after other flesh   b Or angels; Gk glories
c Or condemnation for blasphemy   d Or reefs
e Or without fear. They are shepherds who care only for themselves   f Gk came

---

are simply God's consistent "no" to evil, whether the sin under judgment is angelic or human. Hence, the insistent warnings Jude issues to his readers. "Change your perspective," he says, "change your behaviors, for it is impossible for God to change his." And, on our better days, we are glad that God cannot condone what we ourselves know to be wrong.

15–16 *grumblers and malcontents.* There are some things we should be afraid of. The perspectives of Jude's false teachers should be enough to frighten any sane Christian. Without proper caution, we can too quickly find ourselves doing the very things we hate in our sanest moments. Mercy is always to be extended, but with the recognition that the disease under treatment is highly infectious. Without proper precautions and protections, we too may find ourselves as sick as those we are attempting to treat. In Jesus' words, to be in the world and not of it requires carefully honed skills, perspectives, habits, and dispositions cultivated within us by the Spirit.

19 *these worldly people, devoid of the Spirit.*

The absence of the Spirit in the lives of the false teachers has resulted in a catalog of sin: sexual promiscuity on a grand scale (vv 7–8,16); a deep disdain for authority, human, angelic, or divine (vv 8–9, 15); the use of human speech to slander, flatter, grumble, scoff, and blaspheme (vv 8, 15–16, 18); and the perversion of the grace of God into an invitation to sin (v 4). They have denied Christ and divided his Body (vv 4, 19). Empty of the Spirit, the false teachers are the religious hawkers of a skewed gospel, eager to make a financial profit as they prey on the weaknesses of their audience. Much like his brother Jesus, Jude insists that the mark of the Spirit is a fruitful life. These teachers are hollow people, all talk, no substance. Rather than manifesting the glory the Spirit brings to human lives, these "wandering stars" (v 13) shed no light. Jude piles metaphor on metaphor to describe the horror and attendant judgment of a false spirituality. The false teachers have warped into mere animals, governed by instinct, "waterless clouds carried along by the winds; autumn trees without fruit, twice dead, uprooted" (v 12).

devoid of the Spirit, who are causing divisions. 20But you, beloved, build yourselves up on your most holy faith; pray in the Holy Spirit; 21keep yourselves in the love of God; look forward to the mercy of our Lord Jesus Christ that leads to*a* eternal life. 22And have mercy on some who are wavering; 23save others by snatching them out of the fire; and have mercy on still others with fear, hating even the tunic defiled by their bodies.*b*

Benediction

24 Now to him who is able to keep you from falling, and to make you stand without blemish in the presence of his glory with rejoicing, 25to the only God our Savior, through Jesus Christ our Lord, be glory, majesty, power, and authority, before all time and now and forever. Amen.

a Gk *Christ to*   *b* Gk *by the flesh.* The Greek text of verses 22-23 is uncertain at several points

---

20 PRAYER—*See* Spiritual Disciplines Index.
20–21 *build yourselves up on your most holy faith.* The false teachers' words and lives, because of the absence of the Spirit, dangerously imperiled the unity of the church (v 19). Jude issues a strong call to replace spiritual and moral chaos with a life grounded in the Spirit. Life in the Spirit, though, is not formed in a vacuum. Jude encourages us to ground ourselves in the same concrete means of grace his ancient

readers employed to nourish their spiritual lives. To them and us he says: "Build yourselves up on your most holy faith" (v 20), a construction project utilizing worship, meditation, and study; "pray in the Holy Spirit" (v 20), quite possibly a reference to tongues as well as to liturgical prayer; and "keep yourselves in the love of God" (v 21) through concrete acts of mercy rather than the self-centered, self-indulgent lifestyle of the false teachers (vv 21–22).

XV. The People of God into Eternity

Scripture: *Revelation*

> *The aim of God in history is the creation of an all-inclusive community of loving persons with God himself at the very center of this community as its prime Sustainer and most glorious Inhabitant (Eph 2:19–22; 3:10). The Bible traces the formation of this community from the creation in the Garden of Eden all the way to the new heaven and the new earth. Come, join us as we explore the many dimensions of this* with-God *history—from individual to family to tribe to people to nation to all humanity—and apply what we learn to our own spiritual formation.*

During the early years of the Church, we saw how the Christian community struggled with numerous issues of faith and life. In the book of Revelation we will see the ways God completes the process of forming an all-inclusive community as the Church remains faithful in tribulation and transitions into eternity.

God's Action

In the book of Revelation we see the completion of God's plan for humanity and the extension of human existence on into eternity. Revelation pulls aside the curtain veiling God's larger world from human eyes—a curtain that fell during the period recorded in Genesis 1–11. In Revelation we see a vision of the future from the perspective of the first generation of disciples to experience the world revolution set ablaze by Jesus. It shows us the cosmic character of Christ, who promises to be with us "always, to the end of the age" (Matt 28:20), and of the Lord God Almighty, who has always made human history his project. Revelation brings the reality of God-with-us to the fullness God always intended.

Revelation is the counterpart of Genesis, as both books locate humanity in an environment distinctly outside human history as we normally understand it. The breaking away of the Church from Judaism, a religion confined to a particular ethnic people, is described in the Gospels, Acts, and Letters; this separation is completed by the time Revelation opens. Accordingly, one of the most repeated references in Revelation is to all "peoples and tribes and languages and nations" (Rev 11:9) and similar variations (e.g., 13:7). This is the calling forth of that all-inclusive community of loving persons that God has been intent upon forming throughout all of history.

In the opening of Revelation Jesus Christ is described as "the ruler of the kings of the earth" and the beginning and the end of everything (1:5). The future Jesus presents through John has three clearly articulated sections with three distinct ways God is with his people.

The first section is a vision of the future of the *ekklesia*—the Church of Jesus Christ—on the world stage (1:9–3:22). It is a revelation of Christ over the worldwide Church until "the end of the age" (Matt 28:20). It is presented in the form of letters to the "seven churches that are in Asia" (1:4) and it is perhaps best understood as a vision of the typical ways—both good and bad—the people of Jesus gather together to be the continuing incarnation of Jesus Christ upon the earth for the period during which such churches will exist.

Although the Church is ideally free from ethnic bondage, peculiar legalisms, and cultural self-righteousness, the picture remains one of great struggle, temptation, and failure, of blood and death as well as faithfulness to God and triumphant life. Many similarities exist between the earlier dispersion of the Jewish people into exile and the worldwide dispersion of Christ's followers. Clearly the church age is not the ultimate end of God's plan. But it is the last stage of that plan within "ordinary" human history. God is not only present with his people through his Word and Spirit, but also through the accruing artifacts, traditions, and institutions of the Church.

In the second section a time of tremendous upheaval and calamity is foreseen upon earth, when human wickedness, in conjunction with both good and evil superhuman agencies, strides across the world stage (4:1–20:15). Massive battles between good and evil occur as well as immense public judgments upon humankind by God. The People of God who remain on earth suffer greatly from widespread persecution and martyrdom, but they bear it triumphantly with the full assurance that their faithfulness to Jesus will be vindicated.

The earth itself suffers such geological, biological, and human devastation in this transition period that it is scarcely habitable by the end of it. The human system of life ("Babylon") is rendered nonfunctional (18:1–19:3). God is with humankind in judgment and with his people in upholding and delivering them. Christ himself finally comes on the scene as cosmic ruler to end the history-long battle of good and evil through his unquestioned victory and overwhelming presence.

The last scene in this transition period is judgment, first of Satan and his helpers and then of human beings "great and small" (20:1–12). Accounts are settled. Justice is done. Evil is permanently put in its place and rendered powerless forever.

Finally, in the third section the People of God enter into the fullness of God's cosmos and the fullness of his presence (21:1–22:21). Jeremiah, the prophet of exile, had foreseen a time when "no longer shall they teach one another, or say to each other, 'Know the Lord,' for they shall all know me, from the least of them to the greatest." It would be a time when, finally, "I will put my law within them, and I will write it on their hearts; and I will be their God, and they shall be my people" (Jer 31:33–34).

We should not suppose that Jeremiah's words mean that God will, at some specific point, give up on his efforts to win humankind to himself and simply "rewire" them as one might do to a robot. If that was what God had wanted, he could have done the "rewiring" at creation, or after Adam and Eve fell, or at any other time along

The With-God Life

the way. No, the phrase "the law within them" refers to the inward identification of our character with God: "Let the same mind be in you that was in Christ Jesus" (Phil 2:5).

In eternity there will be no need for God to give us space to grow, for we will have grown into his very own character. We will not be innocents, as were Adam and Eve, but fully knowledgeable of evil and what it means. Therefore we will not be tempted by it, for we will see it for what it is and not as something in some sense "good" (Gen 3:6). We can now be fully trusted whether God is present or absent, and he is present with us always because we have his character and constantly do his work in union with him. Now God's intention for us is fulfilled, and we reign with him "forever and ever" (Rev 22:5).

This "reigning with" is the form the with-God life takes in ongoing eternity. There is no temple in the city, "for its temple is the Lord God the Almighty and the Lamb" (21:22). There are no religious jobs. The work of mediation is finally done, though its role in redemption and its results are an everlasting element of God's world, emblazoned in the identity of God's people. The Mediator—the "Lamb"—stands forever as a part of our being and as a revelation of who God is. This reality stabilizes our character in godliness beyond the slightest tremor. We are lost in goodness with God and in doing what God is doing.

Human Reaction

Multitudes of people were drawn to the incarnate Christ and became his apprentices in kingdom living. His followers out-loved, out-thought, and out-sacrificed the surrounding pagan world, and, by the force of Jesus' presence in them, the dominant culture in the Mediterranean world became identified with him. For centuries this continued to develop and expand, though not always in directions reflecting the clear nature and intentions of Jesus.

On the contemporary scene apprenticeship to Jesus remains a widespread ideal, but there is often little understanding of what it means for spiritual formation in Christlikeness. Now, only in the rarest of cases do we find in Christian churches purposeful, continuously progressive, and all-inclusive spiritual growth through discipleship to Jesus. Through the ages there have been many brilliant examples of what discipleship can be, but on the present scene what we generally face, and what the world sees, especially in the West, is a Christian culture without discipleship to Jesus.

It is yet to be seen what the future response will be to apprenticeship to Jesus and what the Church will mean for world society throughout the twenty-first century and beyond. What can it possibly mean to "accept" Jesus Christ, but not be his student? And what is the fate of a modern world that rejects him?

By contrast, the period of transition described in Revelation 4–20 will most certainly eliminate "lukewarm Christians," for those who face suffering and death on Jesus' behalf will without doubt be his intensely devoted apprentices. And, of course, in the new heaven and the new earth the People of God will be entirely given up to

God and his glorious reign throughout the universe: "God . . . will dwell with . . . his people, and . . . he will wipe away every tear from their eyes, and death shall be no more, neither shall there be mourning nor crying nor pain any more" (21:3–4, RSV). Evil and disappointment will utterly disappear in favor of good and perpetual progressive fulfillment of human destiny (chaps 21–22).

Blessings and Benefits for Our Formation

Apprenticeship to Jesus Christ, under the direction of the revealed Word of God and the administration of the Holy Spirit, is the single most powerful and beneficial transformational process known to humankind. It stands head and shoulders above all possible competitors—of which there have been and are many. This is because through Christ the fullness of God—who is powerful and intelligent love—breaks through to human beings as nowhere else.

All of the past ways God has been with human beings reach their fulfillment in Christ as he lives among his people. Grace and righteousness are dynamically combined in our faith in Christ and in our walk with Christ: "Steadfast love and faithfulness will meet; righteousness and peace will kiss each other" (Ps 85:10). The power of the Word and the Spirit in the people of Christ, past and present, transforms every essential dimension of the human self and liberates us from rebellion and alienation to such a degree that we routinely "reign in life by one, Christ Jesus" (Rom 5:17, KJV).

Looking beyond the time of the Church on earth, we are eternally living with the triune God in ever increasing competence, creativity, and responsibility under him. This is truly "the blessed life" that poets, artists, and prophets can only vaguely dream about.

Limits and Liabilities for Our Formation

In the final stage revealed in the book of Revelation there are no limitations whatsoever to this form of God-with-us: "There will be no more night . . . for the Lord God will be their light, and they will reign forever and ever" (Rev 22:5). In the transition stage the limitations are human weakness and appalling, external evil. During the church age, in which we now live, the limitations on spiritual formation lie in the power that evil—"the world, the flesh, and the devil"—continues to have in deflecting and hindering intense apprenticeship to Christ, even among those who know him and profess faith in him. Though we may clearly be born into the kingdom of God, we still have to deal with the other "kingdoms" that temporarily remain present on earth—government, finance, education, art, and culture—as well as the many individuals with whom we share the earth.

Ideas and systems are among the most pernicious enemies of apprenticeship to Jesus, and these are often within the Church itself. This can be seen today, for example, in the self-righteousness of denominationalism and sectarianism. It can also be seen in the subjugation of authoritative Christian teaching to the intellectual or social idols of the age. And it shows itself in the preaching of a "gospel" that has no essential connection with honest, practical, all-inclusive apprenticeship to Jesus in kingdom living now.

Also, the incarnate and therefore finite form of human existence continues. This means that movement forward in Christlikeness, for the individual or for society, is highly time-intensive. That, of course, is why God works through history instead of just waving a magic wand and transforming everything at once. Character is costly, and only choice and experience through time can produce it.

Insights and Instructions for Our Formation

Apprenticeship to Jesus in the fellowship of his people is the only assured path of life under God. On that path we move from faith to more faith, from grace to more grace, and are able to walk increasingly in holiness and power.

We will never escape our finitude in this life or find complete freedom from the presence of evil around us. Therefore we must not expect to escape some measure of suffering and failure. But God is always with us in Christ, and we can triumph over all trials. Moment by moment and day by day, we, by means of appropriate Spiritual Disciplines, keep ourselves constantly under the direction of Jesus through his Word and Spirit.

No matter how far we advance while in this life on earth, we know only in part and we prophesy only in part. We really do not have enough mind power, even under divine inspiration, to keep everything straight. But the complete is coming, and when it does the partial will come to an end. "For now we see in a mirror, dimly," but we *will* see clearly (1 Cor 13:12). Then we will dwell with God and God will dwell with us as he intended from the beginning of time. *Maranatha!*

The With-God Life

THE REVELATION
TO JOHN

The Revelation to John is a scary book. It may well be the least read and most feared book in the New Testament. Not only is it full of malicious monsters, but even the good guys strike us as bizarre creatures—a lion, an ox, a human face, and an eagle, each with six wings and covered all over with eyes (Rev 4:7–8). In addition, some of the settings—glassy seas, bottomless pits, rivers of blood—are like nothing we've seen before, nor are we sure we ever want to.

Not only are there monsters, but the action often seems incongruous, disjunctive. One moment we are listening to the heavenly choir sing praises around God's throne, and the next we hear angels pronounce terrible plagues upon the earth and its inhabitants.

Jesus himself, whom we are used to envisioning as a man in a simple peasant caftan, transmogrifies into strange shapes throughout this vision. Often we see him as a bloody, slaughtered lamb (e.g., 5:6); later, as a warrior with fiery eyes, arrayed in an equally bloody robe, with a sword protruding from his mouth (19:11–16).

But when you open yourself to a vision, as John did on that barren, volcanic prison island of Patmos, you don't get to choose its contents. It's not like going to the video store to pick out a movie that fits your taste and mood.

God's Timing

John's vision probably confuses Westerners more than it would either John's Asian churches or many non-Western cultures today. For one thing, we understand time as sequential, irreversible forward movement. We have trouble imagining earthly existence without that consecutively ticking clock.

Events in John's vision, however, are not strung like beads on a string, one scene

---

See also "The With-God Life" essay for this section of the Bible,
"The People of God into Eternity," pp. 2259–63.

---

following upon another. Instead, the scenes are arranged in a collage, with God on his throne at the center. To follow this concentric mode of telling what John saw in his visions requires a radical readjustment of our internal spiritual clock. Our tendency is to arrange a "time line" that we can then use to "solve" Revelation. This gives us a sense of control over what otherwise appears to us a surrealistic hodgepodge. Consequently, this last book of the Bible has become the private preserve of individuals or groups professing to have the key that unlocks the mysteries encased in its symbols. But control is not what Revelation is about. Indeed, it is just the opposite.

The people to whom John is writing have very little control over their situation. Their choices are simple—giving in or giving up. They desperately need to know that the One on whom they stake their lives, the Lord to whom they have pledged their allegiance, will keep his promise to return and overcome the wicked powers oppressing them.

God's timing is not governed by our clocks or calendars. The psalmist understood this when he said: "A thousand years in your sight are like yesterday when it is past, or like a watch in the night" (Ps 90:4). Second Peter affirms: "With the Lord one day is like a thousand years, and a thousand years are like one day" (3:8). In eternity, earthly time is dissolved in God's encompassing reality.

Surrendering Control

For John's seven Asian churches, surrending control meant the discipline of waiting. Their members yearned for the "last days," when the risen Messiah would come to defeat their oppressors. They, like John, were vulnerable to imprisonment—or worse. In fact, a member of the Pergamum Church has already been executed, probably for the crime of refusing to burn incense on the altar dedicated to Domitian, the Roman emperor (Rev 2:13). Christians were punished not so much for believing in Jesus as for not believing in the divinity of the emperor. This explains the puzzling references to Christians as "atheists" in official documents of the time.

The communities to whom John writes feel their powerlessness keenly and are tempted by spiritual compromise. Because of his own experience, John knows the questions that assail his fellow believers as they wait for the risen Messiah's inexplicably delayed return. They are the same questions that echo in the Psalms: "How long, O LORD? Will you forget me forever? How long will you hide your face from me?" (13:1). And the prophets: "Why does the way of the guilty prosper?" (Jer 12:1). And even from Jesus: "My God, my God, why have you forsaken me?" (Mark 15:34).

The people listening as one of their church leaders reads John's letter are worn down and disheartened. They are hanging on by their fingernails. Many wonder if they made a bad choice by throwing in their lot with a Jesus they have never seen and who doesn't seem to be doing much on their behalf.

John's vision of all creation worshiping in the heavenly court reassures them that, despite all outward appearances, God knows their suffering and stores up their cries for justice in golden bowls (Rev 5:8). Indeed, even as they worship on earth, they are already a part of that cosmic chorus.

Many times over the centuries John's letter to the churches of Asia has been used as a crystal ball to predict the end of time. But by now, many "last days" have come and gone, not only leaving the code breakers' coteries disillusioned, but undermining as well Revelation's true office as a pastoral letter, meant to sustain the suffering and hearten the weary faithful.

Surrendering control is no less difficult for us today. Indeed, our culture advocates "taking control of one's own life." For us, dissolving our time in God's eternity demands another kind of discipline. Pascal considered our inability to sit still in a room to be the root of "all human evil." That may be overstating the case, but it is certainly true that we must give God our rapt and undivided attention before we can catch a glimpse of his kingdom through the veil of earthly time. But if we can learn to sit still in a room—or on a stump—and wrest our attention from the thousand chattering voices without and within, we will find ourselves gradually living more of our lives in that kingdom.

Keeping still and silent gives us time-bound creatures access to the worship continually going on before God's eternal throne in heaven. It allows us to join our voices with those of angels and archangels and with all the company of heaven. Such worship not only restores our strength for the earthly journey; it reminds us of where that journey is taking us.

Judgment

But there is yet another reason Revelation makes us uneasy. It is a book about judgment, a subject about which our age and culture are deeply conflicted. Who has not felt a hot surge of anger rise within at some perceived injustice? A concept of justice seems bred into humankind. Even small children wail, "It's not fair!" as they appeal to a parent or teacher to restore the balance of justice. Few desires are so universal as the desire for justice, at least for ourselves. It is buried in the heart of every person on earth, regardless of age, gender, or culture.

When we suffer injustice and violence, we want to know just what God intends to do about it. All of us have uttered, if only under our breath, the psalmist's "How long, O Lord, how long?" Even nonbelievers have been known to cry out against a God they profess not to believe in.

Few of us expect to ever face martyrdom for our faith, as John's Asian flock did. Our own disasters are largely personal and come in the form of broken marriages, loss or lack of employment, devastating diseases, or children bent on throwing away their youthful, promising lives. And though our lives may lack the drama or heroism of martyrdom, our anguish is just as intense.

But John's vision doesn't start with the last liberating battle and the punishment of the wicked. Instead, it begins with a reckoning of the righteous. In John's opening vision (1:9–3:22), the glorified Christ judges not the Roman emperor or his minions, but the seven churches of Asia themselves. Their spiritual report cards begin by pointing out their assets—faithfulness, patience, endurance, love—as well as their deficits. Each of the seven churches receives its individual accounting, one that recognizes how each has responded to its precarious situation.

Taking such internal inventories lays a firm foundation on which to form our spirit. Honestly reviewing our present spiritual state, repenting for the breakdowns, and resolving to rectify them are the first steps. Unless we clear away the debris created by our neglect or self-deception, all subsequent steps are likely to lead us down false trails.

We still have this knot of judgmentalism to deal with, however. As creatures of our time, we yearn for justice (though not quite as much as we long for peace), while not wanting to be judgmental. That attitude has its good side. After all, Jesus teaches his disciples that they—we—are not to judge others (Matt 7:1). So we are rightly concerned about judgmentalism.

Nevertheless, the bleak and bloody scenes in chapters 6–18 can physically repel us and throw us morally off balance. What happened to loving your enemies? How can we sing praises to God while others are suffering torment? True, sometimes in the Psalms angry calls for vengeance are embedded in songs of surpassing praise. But the anger and vengeance we can accept in the Psalms as honest reflections of human experience we find hard to swallow in Revelation. We would like to skip over this grotesque midsection of Revelation and get to those last consoling chapters, the ones most often read at funerals. But how can we fully and unreservedly rejoice in John's final vision of a new heaven and new earth with the smell of brimstone still in our noses? What links the scenes of blood and judgment with those of rapturous worship? Always, it is the Lamb.

The Victory of the Lamb

We first see Christ portrayed as the bloody Lamb in chapter 5, where he is proclaimed worthy to be worshiped because of his sacrifice for "every tribe and language and people and nation" (5:9). In the ensuing chapters, natural disasters straight out of Exodus and scenes of cosmic warfare are interwoven with worship of the Lamb, for the bloody Lamb stands ever as the point of reversal. His sacrifice is the source of creation's redemption. Did we think that, once we were all safe in heaven, we'd get to forget that sacrifice as if it were a distant bad dream that never really happened? In God's eternal Now, that act stands forever. The Lamb's blood is irrevocably bound to beauty. The battle for the world was won at Calvary.

That victory continues to be won as we cling to faith in the Lamb today. John never sugarcoats the fact that we still must live in the world, contending with its principalities and powers, until the close of history. The Lamb gives our suffering in his name—and, indeed, the agony of all creation—its meaning (Rom 8:22–23). And the Lamb as Redeeming Judge affirms that judgment is not ours to make. That job belongs to the One worthy to divide the sheep from the goats (Matt 25:31–46), because he has paid their ransom.

John's vision reveals that, in God's eternity, the battle *has been* won, the battle *is* raging still, and the battle *will be* won. Not that our fears and burdens are magically whisked away, but we see our earthly life-in-time illuminated by the light falling through the crack in the door that opens to eternal life. That light transforms our perceptions and purifies our expectations. Our call is to remember, endure, and anticipate.

Whatever obsession formerly ruled our lives now looks like a shopworn sham when eternal light falls on it. Thus, over earthly time we move more and more of ourselves into the light streaming through the crack in the door. We root out the false hopes by which we live such desperate lives, and we bask in "the true light, which enlightens everyone" (John 1:9).

—*Virginia Stem Owens*

Introduction and Salutation

1 The revelation of Jesus Christ, which God gave him to show his servants[a] what must soon take place; he made[b] it known by sending his angel to his servant[c] John, 2who testified to the word of God and to the testimony of Jesus Christ, even to all that he saw.

3 Blessed is the one who reads aloud the words of the prophecy, and blessed are those who hear and who keep what is written in it; for the time is near.

4 John to the seven churches that are in Asia:

Grace to you and peace from him who is and who was and who is to come, and from the seven spirits who are before his throne, 5and from Jesus Christ, the faithful witness, the firstborn of the dead, and the ruler of the kings of the earth.

To him who loves us and freed[d] us from our sins by his blood, 6and made[e] us to be a kingdom, priests serving[f] his God and Father, to him be glory and dominion forever and ever. Amen.

7 Look! He is coming with the clouds;
  every eye will see him,
  even those who pierced him;
    and on his account all the tribes of
      the earth will wail.
So it is to be. Amen.

8 "I am the Alpha and the Omega," says the Lord God, who is and who was and who is to come, the Almighty.

A Vision of Christ

9 I, John, your brother who share with you in Jesus the persecution and the kingdom and the patient endurance, was on the island called Patmos because of the word of God and the testimony of Jesus.[g] 10I was in the spirit[h] on the Lord's day, and I heard behind me a loud voice like a trumpet 11saying, "Write in a book what you see and send it to the seven churches, to Ephesus, to Smyrna, to Pergamum, to Thyatira, to Sardis, to Philadelphia, and to Laodicea."

a Gk *slaves*   b Gk *and he made*   c Gk *slave*
d Other ancient authorities read *washed*
e Gk *and he made*   f Gk *priests to*
g Or *testimony to Jesus*   h Or *in the Spirit*

1:3 *for the time is near.* In the Gospels, Jesus repeatedly proclaims that the kingdom of God is "near" (Matt 3:2; 4:17; 10:7; Mark 1:15; Luke 21:31) or even "among you" (Luke 17:21). In God's kingdom, the time is always NOW!

1:4 *him who is and who was and who is to come.* To Moses, God revealed himself as "I AM" (Exod 3:14). We must learn to think in that present tense in order to discern God's kingdom, where our true identity lives.

1:6 SERVICE—*See* Spiritual Disciplines Index.

1:6 *made us to be a kingdom, priests serving his God and Father.* Our true identity includes not only who we are, but also whose we are. This identity is both exalting and frightening in its responsibilities.

1:9 *who share with you in Jesus.* Just as John avoids dramatizing himself or boasting of being a seer, we should keep Jesus, not ourselves, at the center of our message.

1:11 *Write in a book what you see.* John's commission is not to explain the vision, only to

12 Then I turned to see whose voice it was that spoke to me, and on turning I saw seven golden lampstands, 13and in the midst of the lampstands I saw one like the Son of Man, clothed with a long robe and with a golden sash across his chest. 14His head and his hair were white as white wool, white as snow; his eyes were like a flame of fire, 15his feet were like burnished bronze, refined as in a furnace, and his voice was like the sound of many waters. 16In his right hand he held seven stars, and from his mouth came a sharp, two-edged sword, and his face was like the sun shining with full force.

17 When I saw him, I fell at his feet as though dead. But he placed his right hand on me, saying, "Do not be afraid; I am the first and the last, 18and the living one. I was dead, and see, I am alive forever and ever; and I have the keys of Death and of Hades. 19Now write what you have seen, what is, and what is to take place after this. 20As for the mystery of the seven stars that you saw in my right hand, and the seven golden lampstands: the seven stars are the angels of the seven churches, and the seven lampstands are the seven churches.

The Message to Ephesus

2 "To the angel of the church in Ephesus write: These are the words of him who holds the seven stars in his right hand, who walks among the seven golden lampstands:

2 "I know your works, your toil and your patient endurance. I know that you cannot tolerate evildoers; you have tested those who claim to be apostles but are not, and have found them to be false. 3I also know that you are enduring patiently and bearing up for the sake of my name, and that you have not grown weary. 4But I have this against you, that you have abandoned the love you had at first. 5Remember then from what you have fallen; repent, and do the works you did at first. If not, I will come to you and remove your lampstand from its place, unless you repent. 6Yet this is to your credit: you hate the works of the Nicolaitans, which I also hate. 7Let anyone who has an ear listen to what the Spirit is saying to the churches. To everyone who conquers, I will give permission to eat from the tree of life that is in the paradise of God.

The Message to Smyrna

8 "And to the angel of the church in Smyrna write: These are the words of the first and the last, who was dead and came to life:

9 "I know your affliction and your poverty, even though you are rich. I know the slander on the part of those who say that they are Jews and are not, but are a synagogue of

---

report what he sees. Our mission is not theological debate about abstract ideas, but telling what we see the Lord doing in our lives.

1:17 *I fell at his feet as though dead.* John's first vision of Christ as the Son of Man literally bowls him over with its awesome glory. Because we are constantly fed with fantastic, technologically manipulated images, we rarely feel a sense of awe. Yet to worship, our spirits need the nourishment of wonder and astonishment. *Do not be afraid.* Awe is often accompanied by fear. Whenever heavenly visitors appear to anyone in the Bible, their first words are usually, "Don't be afraid." Jesus touches John and speaks those reassuring words. If fear overwhelms awe, our worship becomes a way of placating a terrifying divinity. Jesus taught his followers that "perfect love casts out fear" (1 John 4:18).

1:20 *seven stars . . . seven golden lampstands.*

The message to each Asian church is given to that particular church's angel to deliver to its congregation. The celestial light of stars represents the angels, while the earthly light of lampstands symbolizes the churches. This image echoes Jesus' admonition not to put our light under a bushel, but on a lampstand, so that it may give "light to all in the house" (Matt 5:15–16).

2:1 *who walks among the seven golden lampstands.* Christ, unseen but experienced, still moves among us when we gather.

2:7 *to eat from the tree of life.* Eating the forbidden fruit from the tree of the knowledge of good and evil in Eden separated us from God. But to those who stand fast in faith, Christ gives the promise of reunion with the very source of our being. Thus humanity comes full circle. At last we attain our true destiny and manifest God's purpose for us.

Satan. [10]Do not fear what you are about to suffer. Beware, the devil is about to throw some of you into prison so that you may be tested, and for ten days you will have affliction. Be faithful until death, and I will give you the crown of life. [11]Let anyone who has an ear listen to what the Spirit is saying to the churches. Whoever conquers will not be harmed by the second death.

The Message to Pergamum

12 "And to the angel of the church in Pergamum write: These are the words of him who has the sharp two-edged sword:

13 "I know where you are living, where Satan's throne is. Yet you are holding fast to my name, and you did not deny your faith in me [a] even in the days of Antipas my witness, my faithful one, who was killed among you, where Satan lives. [14]But I have a few things against you: you have some there who hold to the teaching of Balaam, who taught Balak to put a stumbling block before the people of Israel, so that they would eat food sacrificed to idols and practice fornication. [15]So you also have some who hold to the teaching of the Nicolaitans. [16]Repent then. If not, I will come to you soon and make war against them with the sword of my mouth. [17]Let anyone who has an ear listen to what the Spirit is saying to the churches. To everyone who conquers I will give some of the hidden manna, and I will give a white stone, and on the white stone is written a new name that no one knows except the one who receives it.

The Message to Thyatira

18 "And to the angel of the church in Thyatira write: These are the words of the Son of God, who has eyes like a flame of fire, and whose feet are like burnished bronze:

19 "I know your works—your love, faith, service, and patient endurance. I know that your last works are greater than the first. [20]But I have this against you: you tolerate that woman Jezebel, who calls herself a prophet and is teaching and beguiling my servants [b] to practice fornication and to eat food sacrificed to idols. [21]I gave her time to repent, but she refuses to repent of her fornication. [22]Beware, I am throwing her on a bed, and those who commit adultery with her I am throwing into great distress, unless they repent of her doings; [23]and I will strike her children dead. And all the churches will know that I am the one who searches minds and hearts, and I will give to each of you as your works deserve. [24]But to the rest of you in Thyatira, who do not hold this teaching, who have not learned what some call 'the deep things of Satan,' to you I say, I do not lay on you any other burden; [25]only hold fast to what you have until I come. [26]To everyone who conquers and continues to do my works to the end,

I will give authority over the nations;

a Or deny my faith   b Gk slaves

2:10 *what you are about to suffer.* Christ makes no bones about the suffering his followers will face in this world. Indeed, he tells the Smyrna congregation—the one church of the seven in whom he finds no fault—that it will soon face death.

2:11 *the second death.* Again we hear the echo of Jesus' teaching to his disciples: "Do not fear those who kill the body but cannot kill the soul; rather fear him who can destroy both soul and body in hell" (Matt 10:28).

2:17 *on the white stone is written a new name.* In this life, so full of imperfect understandings, we are sometimes uncertain even of our own identity. We often feel how feeble, futile, and insubstantial we are. Only the One who made us can supply the full answer to the question of who we are. In his hand we have weight and substance. When time is fulfilled, we will "know fully," even as we "have been fully known" (1 Cor 13:12).

2:23 *I am the one who searches minds and hearts.* God intends to bring us to fullness of being. We, on the other hand, invent ever-new ways to thwart that purpose. We settle for superficial and fleeting gratification, rather than hold out for true joy. Without the aid of the Spirit, we are stuck with self-deception, leading to self-destructive ways. Our job is to quit fooling ourselves and live up to our true identity, known only to God.

[27] to rule[a] them with an iron rod,

as when clay pots are shattered—
[28] even as I also received authority from my Father. To the one who conquers I will also give the morning star. [29] Let anyone who has an ear listen to what the Spirit is saying to the churches.

The Message to Sardis

3 "And to the angel of the church in Sardis write: These are the words of him who has the seven spirits of God and the seven stars:

"I know your works; you have a name of being alive, but you are dead. [2] Wake up, and strengthen what remains and is on the point of death, for I have not found your works perfect in the sight of my God. [3] Remember then what you received and heard; obey it, and repent. If you do not wake up, I will come like a thief, and you will not know at what hour I will come to you. [4] Yet you have still a few persons in Sardis who have not soiled their clothes; they will walk with me, dressed in white, for they are worthy. [5] If you conquer, you will be clothed like them in white robes, and I will not blot your name out of the book of life; I will confess your name before my Father and before his angels. [6] Let anyone who has an ear listen to what the Spirit is saying to the churches.

The Message to Philadelphia

7 "And to the angel of the church in Philadelphia write:

These are the words of the holy one, the true one,
who has the key of David,
who opens and no one will shut,
who shuts and no one opens:

[8] "I know your works. Look, I have set before you an open door, which no one is able to shut. I know that you have but little power, and yet you have kept my word and have not denied my name. [9] I will make those of the synagogue of Satan who say that they are Jews and are not, but are lying—I will make them come and bow down before your feet, and they will learn that I have loved you. [10] Because you have kept my word of patient endurance, I will keep you from the hour of trial that is coming on the whole world to test the inhabitants of the earth. [11] I am coming soon; hold fast to what you have, so that no one may seize your crown. [12] If you conquer, I will make you a pillar in the temple of my God; you will never go out of it. I will write on you the name of my God, and the name of the city of my God, the new Jerusalem that comes down from my God out of heaven, and my own new name. [13] Let anyone who has an ear listen to what the Spirit is saying to the churches.

The Message to Laodicea

14 "And to the angel of the church in Laodicea write: The words of the Amen, the faithful and true witness, the origin[b] of God's creation:

15 "I know your works; you are neither cold nor hot. I wish that you were either cold or hot. [16] So, because you are lukewarm, and neither cold nor hot, I am about to spit you out of my mouth. [17] For you say, 'I am rich, I have prospered, and I need nothing.' You do not realize that you are wretched, pitiable,

a Or *to shepherd*   *b* Or *beginning*

3:2 *strengthen what remains and is on the point of death.* The congregation in Sardis is like the seed that fell on rocky ground (Matt 13:5–6). It sprang up, but wilted in the sun's heat, because its roots were shallow. All faith communities are tested by adversity. We must be deeply rooted in the Word to sustain us when difficulties beset us.

3:4 *Yet you have still a few persons.* One cannot help but feel the chill of spiritual death when one's community is dying. Even so, the faithful remnant is given this special promise of Christ's presence.

3:10 *I will keep you from the hour of trial.* Jesus taught his disciples to pray, "Do not put us to the test" (Matt 6:13, Jerusalem Bible). But when our strength is exhausted, he makes a way for us, opens a door, "which no one is able to shut" (v 8).

3:17 *You do not realize that you are wretched.* Focusing on the superficial signs of wealth and health blocks our awareness of spiritual reality. We feel safe and secure as long as we have

poor, blind, and naked. [18]Therefore I counsel you to buy from me gold refined by fire so that you may be rich; and white robes to clothe you and to keep the shame of your nakedness from being seen; and salve to anoint your eyes so that you may see. [19]I reprove and discipline those whom I love. Be earnest, therefore, and repent. [20]Listen! I am standing at the door, knocking; if you hear my voice and open the door, I will come in to you and eat with you, and you with me. [21]To the one who conquers I will give a place with me on my throne, just as I myself conquered and sat down with my Father on his throne. [22]Let anyone who has an ear listen to what the Spirit is saying to the churches."

The Heavenly Worship

4 After this I looked, and there in heaven a door stood open! And the first voice, which I had heard speaking to me like a trumpet, said, "Come up here, and I will show you what must take place after this." [2]At once I was in the spirit,[a] and there in heaven stood a throne, with one seated on the throne! [3]And the one seated there looks like jasper and carnelian, and around the throne is a rainbow that looks like an emerald. [4]Around the throne are twenty-four thrones, and seated on the thrones are twenty-four elders, dressed

in white robes, with golden crowns on their heads. [5]Coming from the throne are flashes of lightning, and rumblings and peals of thunder, and in front of the throne burn seven flaming torches, which are the seven spirits of God; [6]and in front of the throne there is something like a sea of glass, like crystal.

Around the throne, and on each side of the throne, are four living creatures, full of eyes in front and behind: [7]the first living creature like a lion, the second living creature like an ox, the third living creature with a face like a human face, and the fourth living creature like a flying eagle. [8]And the four living creatures, each of them with six wings, are full of eyes all around and inside. Day and night without ceasing they sing,

> "Holy, holy, holy,
>   the Lord God the Almighty,
>   who was and is and is to come."

[9]And whenever the living creatures give glory and honor and thanks to the one who is seated on the throne, who lives forever and ever, [10]the twenty-four elders fall before the one who is seated on the throne and worship the one who lives forever and ever; they cast their crowns before the throne, singing,

> [11] "You are worthy, our Lord and God,
>   to receive glory and honor and power,

a Or *in the Spirit*

---

money in the bank, cars in the garage, and plenty of credit cards. But these do not feed the deepest longings of our spirit, which may be starving in the midst of apparent plenty.

Responding
3:17 SIMPLICITY/FRUGALITY. List ways that wealth can work against living a simple life, both inwardly and outwardly. Choose one problem in this area of your life, for example, trusting in money more than God for security. Hold it before God and quietly give it to God. See what you learn. *See also* Spiritual Disciplines Index.

3:19 *I reprove and discipline those whom I love.* Judgment exposes our hidden weaknesses. This does not mean, however, that the Judge does not love us (e.g., Heb 12:6). The healthy response to judgment is repentance and

reformation, not denial or defensiveness. God's discipline can open the door to closer communion with him (vv 20–21).

4:1–8 *in heaven a door stood open!* At this point, the revelation becomes richly visual. John describes the heavenly court in images of colored jewels, clear crystal, and gleaming gold. Strange, surreal creatures worship there. Lightning flashes and torchlight illumine the scene. The effect is dramatic, not sentimental. Our imaginations need this challenge in order to dislodge our culture's notion of the celestial realm as a pastel Disneyland for grown-ups.

4:8 *without ceasing they sing.* When we worship, we join with all the company of heaven in the praise that continually echoes throughout the cosmos. Their hymn hallows God as Creator of all realities.

4:10 WORSHIP—*See* Spiritual Disciplines Index.

for you created all things,
and by your will they existed and
were created."

The Scroll and the Lamb

5 Then I saw in the right hand of the one seated on the throne a scroll written on the inside and on the back, sealed[a] with seven seals; [2] and I saw a mighty angel proclaiming with a loud voice, "Who is worthy to open the scroll and break its seals?" [3] And no one in heaven or on earth or under the earth was able to open the scroll or to look into it. [4] And I began to weep bitterly because no one was found worthy to open the scroll or to look into it. [5] Then one of the elders said to me, "Do not weep. See, the Lion of the tribe of Judah, the Root of David, has conquered, so that he can open the scroll and its seven seals."

[6] Then I saw between the throne and the four living creatures and among the elders a Lamb standing as if it had been slaughtered, having seven horns and seven eyes, which are the seven spirits of God sent out into all the earth. [7] He went and took the scroll from the right hand of the one who was seated on the throne. [8] When he had taken the scroll, the four living creatures and the twenty-four elders fell before the Lamb, each holding a harp and golden bowls full of incense, which are the prayers of the saints. [9] They sing a new song:

"You are worthy to take the scroll
and to open its seals,
for you were slaughtered and by your
blood you ransomed for God
saints from[b] every tribe and language
and people and nation;
[10] you have made them to be a kingdom
and priests serving[c] our God,
and they will reign on earth."

[11] Then I looked, and I heard the voice of many angels surrounding the throne and the living creatures and the elders; they numbered myriads of myriads and thousands of thousands, [12] singing with full voice,

"Worthy is the Lamb that was
slaughtered
to receive power and wealth and
wisdom and might
and honor and glory and blessing!"

[13] Then I heard every creature in heaven and on earth and under the earth and in the sea, and all that is in them, singing,

"To the one seated on the throne and to
the Lamb
be blessing and honor and glory and
might
forever and ever!"

[14] And the four living creatures said, "Amen!" And the elders fell down and worshiped.

a Or written on the inside, and sealed on the back
b Gk ransomed for God from   c Gk priests to

5:4 *I began to weep bitterly because no one was found worthy.* Often we plunge into despair, overcome by our own inadequacy to right wrongs. Only the Lamb of God, who takes away the sin of this world, can embody the paradox of being both victim and vanquisher.

5:8 PRAYER—*See* Spiritual Disciplines Index.

5:8 *golden bowls of incense, which are the prayers of the saints.* Our prayers are honored beyond anything we imagine here on earth. They break through the time barrier to join the eternal worship. Angels bring them before God with reverence and tenderness.

5:9 *saints from every tribe and language and people and nation.* This universal embrace of Christ's sacrifice leaves no one out, a theme repeated many times throughout the vision (see 7:9; 10:11; 11:9; 13:7; 14:6; 17:15).

Responding

5:10 SERVICE. How does your spirit react to the possibility of serving and worshiping God for eternity and reigning with Jesus Christ forever and ever (see 22:5)? Are you indifferent? Happy? Rebellious? Complacent? Anxious? Examine your feelings and write down your reactions. If they are negative, ask God to show you why they are negative and how to change them into positive feelings. *See also* Spiritual Disciplines Index.

5:13 *every creature in heaven and on earth.* Indeed, Christ's sacrifice offers redemption to not only all the earth's people, but redeems all creation.

The Seven Seals

6 Then I saw the Lamb open one of the seven seals, and I heard one of the four living creatures call out, as with a voice of thunder, "Come!"[a] 2I looked, and there was a white horse! Its rider had a bow; a crown was given to him, and he came out conquering and to conquer.

3 When he opened the second seal, I heard the second living creature call out, "Come!"[a] 4And out came[b] another horse, bright red; its rider was permitted to take peace from the earth, so that people would slaughter one another; and he was given a great sword.

5 When he opened the third seal, I heard the third living creature call out, "Come!"[a] I looked, and there was a black horse! Its rider held a pair of scales in his hand, 6and I heard what seemed to be a voice in the midst of the four living creatures saying, "A quart of wheat for a day's pay,[c] and three quarts of barley for a day's pay,[c] but do not damage the olive oil and the wine!"

7 When he opened the fourth seal, I heard the voice of the fourth living creature call out, "Come!"[a] 8I looked and there was a pale green horse! Its rider's name was Death, and Hades followed with him; they were given authority over a fourth of the earth, to kill with sword, famine, and pestilence, and by the wild animals of the earth.

9 When he opened the fifth seal, I saw under the altar the souls of those who had been slaughtered for the word of God and for the testimony they had given; 10they cried out with a loud voice, "Sovereign Lord, holy and true, how long will it be before you judge and avenge our blood on the inhabitants of the earth?" 11They were each given a white robe and told to rest a little longer, until the number would be complete both of their fellow servants[d] and of their brothers and sisters,[e] who were soon to be killed as they themselves had been killed.

12 When he opened the sixth seal, I looked, and there came a great earthquake; the sun became black as sackcloth, the full moon became like blood, 13and the stars of the sky fell to the earth as the fig tree drops its winter fruit when shaken by a gale. 14The sky vanished like a scroll rolling itself up, and every mountain and island was removed from its place. 15Then the kings of the earth and the magnates and the generals and the rich and the powerful, and everyone, slave and free, hid in the caves and among the rocks of the mountains, 16calling to the mountains and rocks, "Fall on us and hide us from the face of the one seated on the throne and from the wrath of the Lamb; 17for the great day of their wrath has come, and who is able to stand?"

The 144,000 of Israel Sealed

7 After this I saw four angels standing at the four corners of the earth, holding back the four winds of the earth so that no

a Or "Go!"   b Or went   c Gk a denarius
d Gk slaves   e Gk brothers

6:1–8 *I saw the Lamb open one of the seven seals.* Breaking the first four seals brings forth the notorious "four horsemen of the apocalypse," which have been given various names, including conquest, violence, war, famine, corruption, pestilence, and death. These scourges have lost none of their power to afflict humankind today.

6:10 *how long will it be?* The cry of martyrs is a demand for God's justice, the other side of God's love for the world. The Lord shelters martyrs under the altar, symbolically linking their suffering and death to Christ's (Rom 6:5; Phil 3:10).

6:11 *rest a little longer.* Though none of us have died for the faith, we have all felt like demanding justice to redress the wrongs we have suffered. The heavenly counsel is not merely to wait, but to "rest," to let the Judge settle our case.

6:15–17 *Fall on us and hide us.* The natural disasters that attend the breaking of the sixth seal (vv 12–14) level all of society from king to slave. Earth's inhabitants, like Adam and Eve, try to hide rather than face their Creator and Savior. The urge to hide our flaws by defensiveness or denial can make us withdraw into our own internal caves.

7:1–3 *holding back the four winds.* Nevertheless, divine justice is delayed by mercy while the faithful are sealed as God's own forever. The faithful will not escape the common fate of humanity—suffering and death—but there is no "second death" for those sealed for Christ.

wind could blow on earth or sea or against any tree. [2]I saw another angel ascending from the rising of the sun, having the seal of the living God, and he called with a loud voice to the four angels who had been given power to damage earth and sea, [3]saying, "Do not damage the earth or the sea or the trees, until we have marked the servants[a] of our God with a seal on their foreheads."

4 And I heard the number of those who were sealed, one hundred forty-four thousand, sealed out of every tribe of the people of Israel:

5 From the tribe of Judah twelve thousand sealed,
   from the tribe of Reuben twelve thousand,
   from the tribe of Gad twelve thousand,
6 from the tribe of Asher twelve thousand,
   from the tribe of Naphtali twelve thousand,
   from the tribe of Manasseh twelve thousand,
7 from the tribe of Simeon twelve thousand,
   from the tribe of Levi twelve thousand,
   from the tribe of Issachar twelve thousand,
8 from the tribe of Zebulun twelve thousand,
   from the tribe of Joseph twelve thousand,
   from the tribe of Benjamin twelve thousand sealed.

The Multitude from Every Nation

9 After this I looked, and there was a great multitude that no one could count, from every nation, from all tribes and peoples and languages, standing before the throne and before the Lamb, robed in white, with palm branches in their hands. [10]They cried out in a loud voice, saying,

"Salvation belongs to our God who is
       seated on the throne, and to the
    Lamb!"

[11]And all the angels stood around the throne and around the elders and the four living creatures, and they fell on their faces before the throne and worshiped God, [12]singing,

"Amen! Blessing and glory and wisdom
   and thanksgiving and honor
   and power and might
be to our God forever and ever! Amen."

13 Then one of the elders addressed me, saying, "Who are these, robed in white, and where have they come from?" [14]I said to him, "Sir, you are the one that knows." Then he said to me, "These are they who have come out of the great ordeal; they have washed their robes and made them white in the blood of the Lamb.

[15] For this reason they are before the
       throne of God,
    and worship him day and night
       within his temple,
    and the one who is seated on the
       throne will shelter them.
[16] They will hunger no more, and thirst
       no more;
    the sun will not strike them,
    nor any scorching heat;
[17] for the Lamb at the center of the throne
       will be their shepherd,

a Gk slaves

7:3 *Do not damage the earth.* The earth remains humanity's home. God's concern is for all his creation.

7:9 *a great multitude that no one could count.* God's multicultural choir outstrips our own feeble attempts at inclusiveness.

7:11 WORSHIP—*See* Spiritual Disciplines Index.

7:14 *robes . . . made . . . white in the blood of the Lamb.* Adding to the heavenly worship are countless martyrs, their names and numbers known only to God. Again we are confronted with the paradox of salvation: washing in the Lamb's blood makes their garments white, their beings whole.

7:15 WORSHIP—*See* Spiritual Disciplines Index.

7:16 *They will hunger no more.* Not only are the martyrs rescued from death and torment, but their common needs are fulfilled by God. Like the lilies of the field, "they neither toil nor spin" (Matt 6:28; Luke 12:27), in effect reversing the burden laid upon Adam to earn his bread by the sweat of his brow (Gen 3:17–19).

and he will guide them to springs of
   the water of life,
and God will wipe away every tear from
   their eyes."

The Seventh Seal and the Golden Censer

8 When the Lamb opened the seventh
   seal, there was silence in heaven for
about half an hour. [2]And I saw the seven angels who stand before God, and seven trumpets were given to them.

3 Another angel with a golden censer
came and stood at the altar; he was given a
great quantity of incense to offer with the
prayers of all the saints on the golden altar
that is before the throne. [4]And the smoke of
the incense, with the prayers of the saints,
rose before God from the hand of the angel.
[5]Then the angel took the censer and filled it
with fire from the altar and threw it on the
earth; and there were peals of thunder, rumblings, flashes of lightning, and an earthquake.

The Seven Trumpets

6 Now the seven angels who had the sev-
en trumpets made ready to blow them.

7 The first angel blew his trumpet, and
there came hail and fire mixed with blood,
and they were hurled to the earth; and a third
of the earth was burned up, and a third of the
trees were burned up, and all green grass was
burned up.

8 The second angel blew his trumpet, and
something like a great mountain, burning
with fire, was thrown into the sea. [9]A third of
the sea became blood, a third of the living
creatures in the sea died, and a third of the
ships were destroyed.

10 The third angel blew his trumpet, and
a great star fell from heaven, blazing like a
torch, and it fell on a third of the rivers and
on the springs of water. [11]The name of the
star is Wormwood. A third of the waters became wormwood, and many died from the
water, because it was made bitter.

12 The fourth angel blew his trumpet, and
a third of the sun was struck, and a third of
the moon, and a third of the stars, so that a
third of their light was darkened; a third of
the day was kept from shining, and likewise
the night.

13 Then I looked, and I heard an eagle crying with a loud voice as it flew in midheaven,
"Woe, woe, woe to the inhabitants of the
earth, at the blasts of the other trumpets that
the three angels are about to blow!"

9 And the fifth angel blew his trumpet,
   and I saw a star that had fallen from
heaven to earth, and he was given the key to
the shaft of the bottomless pit; [2]he opened
the shaft of the bottomless pit, and from the
shaft rose smoke like the smoke of a great

7:17 GUIDANCE—*See* Spiritual Disciplines
Index.

8:1–13 *there was silence in heaven.* At the
beginning of chapter 8, we are at the moment
when, quite literally, all hell is about to break
loose. But heaven does not prepare for holy war
with bombastic speeches or missiles and bombs.
Instead, a hush falls over the heavenly court, the
calm before the storm. The prayers of the
faithful are placed upon the altar. At long last
those noiseless cries for justice are about to be
answered. In this chapter, the four trumpets
signal creation, which erupts and turns on its
human inhabitants, whose abuse has caused it
to groan (Rom 8:22). Because of Adam's fall, the
earth itself was cursed (Gen 3:17) and must be
redeemed.

Responding
8:1 SILENCE. Because we are
surrounded by noise—talking people,
barking dogs, blaring TVs, ringing telephones,
booming radios—most of us cannot imagine the
thick, profound silence described in this verse.
This Saturday get up early, find a quiet place,
and be still for half an hour. What does the
silence do for your spirit? *See also* Spiritual
Disciplines Index.

8:3–4 PRAYER—*See* Spiritual Disciplines
Index.

9:1–6 *the bottomless pit.* The fifth trumpet
heralds the dark forces of death and destruction.
Those who have used these forces to oppress
and persecute now find themselves the target of
their former weapons.

furnace, and the sun and the air were darkened with the smoke from the shaft. ³Then from the smoke came locusts on the earth, and they were given authority like the authority of scorpions of the earth. ⁴They were told not to damage the grass of the earth or any green growth or any tree, but only those people who do not have the seal of God on their foreheads. ⁵They were allowed to torture them for five months, but not to kill them, and their torture was like the torture of a scorpion when it stings someone. ⁶And in those days people will seek death but will not find it; they will long to die, but death will flee from them.

7 In appearance the locusts were like horses equipped for battle. On their heads were what looked like crowns of gold; their faces were like human faces, ⁸their hair like women's hair, and their teeth like lions' teeth; ⁹they had scales like iron breastplates, and the noise of their wings was like the noise of many chariots with horses rushing into battle. ¹⁰They have tails like scorpions, with stingers, and in their tails is their power to harm people for five months. ¹¹They have as king over them the angel of the bottomless pit; his name in Hebrew is Abaddon, ᵃ and in Greek he is called Apollyon. ᵇ

12 The first woe has passed. There are still two woes to come.

13 Then the sixth angel blew his trumpet, and I heard a voice from the four ᶜ horns of the golden altar before God, ¹⁴saying to the sixth angel who had the trumpet, "Release the four angels who are bound at the great river Euphrates." ¹⁵So the four angels were released, who had been held ready for the hour, the day, the month, and the year, to kill a third of humankind. ¹⁶The number of the troops of cavalry was two hundred million; I heard their number. ¹⁷And this was how I saw the horses in my vision: the riders wore breastplates the color of fire and of sapphire ᵈ and of sulfur; the heads of the horses were like

lions' heads, and fire and smoke and sulfur came out of their mouths. ¹⁸By these three plagues a third of humankind was killed, by the fire and smoke and sulfur coming out of their mouths. ¹⁹For the power of the horses is in their mouths and in their tails; their tails are like serpents, having heads; and with them they inflict harm.

20 The rest of humankind, who were not killed by these plagues, did not repent of the works of their hands or give up worshiping demons and idols of gold and silver and bronze and stone and wood, which cannot see or hear or walk. ²¹And they did not repent of their murders or their sorceries or their fornication or their thefts.

The Angel with the Little Scroll

10 And I saw another mighty angel coming down from heaven, wrapped in a cloud, with a rainbow over his head; his face was like the sun, and his legs like pillars of fire. ²He held a little scroll open in his hand. Setting his right foot on the sea and his left foot on the land, ³he gave a great shout, like a lion roaring. And when he shouted, the seven thunders sounded. ⁴And when the seven thunders had sounded, I was about to write, but I heard a voice from heaven saying, "Seal up what the seven thunders have said, and do not write it down." ⁵Then the angel whom I saw standing on the sea and the land

raised his right hand to heaven
6   and swore by him who lives forever
          and ever,

who created heaven and what is in it, the earth and what is in it, and the sea and what is in it: "There will be no more delay, ⁷but in the days when the seventh angel is to blow his trumpet, the mystery of God will be fulfilled, as he announced to his servants ᵉ the prophets."

a That is, *Destruction*   b That is, *Destroyer*
c Other ancient authorities lack *four*
d Gk *hyacinth*   e Gk *slaves*

9:20 *did not repent of the works of their hands.* Incredibly, despite the stark evidence that the works of their hands bring disease and death to the human race, many obstinately stick to "doing it their way."

10:4 *do not write it down.* John is forbidden to reveal the final stage of God's judgment, a point often overlooked by those who claim to have solved "the mystery of God" (v 7).

EAT IT

8 Then the voice that I had heard from heaven spoke to me again, saying, "Go, take the scroll that is open in the hand of the angel who is standing on the sea and on the land." 9So I went to the angel and told him to give me the little scroll; and he said to me, "Take it, and eat; it will be bitter to your stomach, but sweet as honey in your mouth." 10So I took the little scroll from the hand of the angel and ate it; it was sweet as honey in my mouth, but when I had eaten it, my stomach was made bitter.

11 Then they said to me, "You must prophesy again about many peoples and nations and languages and kings."

The Two Witnesses

11 Then I was given a measuring rod like a staff, and I was told, "Come and measure the temple of God and the altar and those who worship there, 2but do not measure the court outside the temple; leave that out, for it is given over to the nations, and they will trample over the holy city for forty-two months. 3And I will grant my two witnesses authority to prophesy for one thousand two hundred sixty days, wearing sackcloth."

4 These are the two olive trees and the two lampstands that stand before the Lord of the earth. 5And if anyone wants to harm them, fire pours from their mouth and consumes their foes; anyone who wants to harm them must be killed in this manner. 6They have authority to shut the sky, so that no rain may fall during the days of their prophesying, and they have authority over the waters to turn them into blood, and to strike the earth with every kind of plague, as often as they desire.

7 When they have finished their testimony, the beast that comes up from the bottomless pit will make war on them and conquer them and kill them, 8and their dead bodies will lie in the street of the great city that is prophetically[a] called Sodom and Egypt, where also their Lord was crucified. 9For three and a half days members of the peoples and tribes and languages and nations will gaze at their dead bodies and refuse to let them be placed in a tomb; 10and the inhabitants of the earth will gloat over them and celebrate and exchange presents, because these two prophets had been a torment to the inhabitants of the earth.

11 But after the three and a half days, the breath[b] of life from God entered them, and they stood on their feet, and those who saw them were terrified. 12Then they[c] heard a loud voice from heaven saying to them, "Come up here!" And they went up to heaven in a cloud while their enemies watched them. 13At that moment there was a great earthquake, and a tenth of the city fell; seven thousand people were killed in the earthquake, and the rest were terrified and gave glory to the God of heaven.

14 The second woe has passed. The third woe is coming very soon.

The Seventh Trumpet

15 Then the seventh angel blew his trumpet, and there were loud voices in heaven, saying,

　"The kingdom of the world has become
　　the kingdom of our Lord
　　and of his Messiah,[d]
　and he will reign forever and ever."

worship

a Or *allegorically*; Gk *spiritually*　　b Or *the spirit*
c Other ancient authorities read I　　d Gk *Christ*

10:9 *bitter to your stomach, but sweet . . . in your mouth.* Anyone who aspires to be a prophet should consider these lines. Giving vent to one's righteous indignation may taste sweet, but speaking for God, as the Hebrew prophets found, is not always a pleasant experience (e.g., Jer 15:16–18; Ezek 2:9–3:3).

11:8 *where also their Lord was crucified.* Having their deaths linked with Jesus' own honors the two witnesses, into whom God then breathes life again and invites into his heavenly court (vv 11–12).

11:15 *The kingdom of the world has become.* Handel breaks this verse into discrete parts in his *Messiah* in a way that perfectly expresses the darkness of the world's kingdom in the verse's initial words. The music swells with the transition "has become," and then bursts into the joy of the coming kingdom of heaven, an affirmation that later culminates in the "Hallelujah Chorus."

16 Then the twenty-four elders who sit on their thrones before God fell on their faces and worshiped God, [17]singing,

"We give you thanks, Lord God
        Almighty,
    who are and who were,
    for you have taken your great power
        and begun to reign.
[18] The nations raged,
    but your wrath has come,
    and the time for judging the dead,
    for rewarding your servants, [a] the
        prophets
    and saints and all who fear your
        name,
        both small and great,
    and for destroying those who destroy
        the earth."

19 Then God's temple in heaven was opened, and the ark of his covenant was seen within his temple; and there were flashes of lightning, rumblings, peals of thunder, an earthquake, and heavy hail.

The Woman and the Dragon

12 A great portent appeared in heaven: a woman clothed with the sun, with the moon under her feet, and on her head a crown of twelve stars. [2]She was pregnant and was crying out in birth pangs, in the agony of giving birth. [3]Then another portent appeared in heaven: a great red dragon, with seven heads and ten horns, and seven diadems on his heads. [4]His tail swept down a third of the stars of heaven and threw them to the earth. Then the dragon stood before the woman who was about to bear a child, so that he might devour her child as soon as it was born. [5]And she gave birth to a son, a male child, who is to rule [b] all the nations with a rod of iron. But her child was snatched away and taken to God and to his throne; [6]and the woman fled into the wilderness, where she has a place prepared by God, so that there she can be nourished for one thousand two hundred sixty days.

Michael Defeats the Dragon

7 And war broke out in heaven; Michael and his angels fought against the dragon. The dragon and his angels fought back, [8]but they were defeated, and there was no longer any place for them in heaven. [9]The great dragon was thrown down, that ancient serpent, who is called the Devil and Satan, the deceiver of the whole world—he was thrown down to the earth, and his angels were thrown down with him.

10 Then I heard a loud voice in heaven, proclaiming,

"Now have come the salvation and the
        power
    and the kingdom of our God
    and the authority of his Messiah, [c]
    for the accuser of our comrades [d] has
        been thrown down,
    who accuses them day and night
        before our God.
[11] But they have conquered him by the
        blood of the Lamb
    and by the word of their testimony,
    for they did not cling to life even in the
        face of death.
[12] Rejoice then, you heavens
    and those who dwell in them!
But woe to the earth and the sea,
    for the devil has come down to you
    with great wrath,
        because he knows that his time is
        short!"

The Dragon Fights Again on Earth

13 So when the dragon saw that he had been thrown down to the earth, he pursued [e] the woman who had given birth to the male

a Gk slaves   b Or to shepherd   c Gk Christ
d Gk brothers   e Or persecuted

11:19 *the ark of his covenant was seen within his temple.* God's bond with his people withstands even the worst betrayals they can invent.
12:5–6 *the woman fled into the wilderness.* The vision now incorporates a figure like Hagar,

who fled persecution and was, with her child, protected by God (Gen 21:8–19).
12:10 *the accuser of our comrades has been thrown down.* The martyrs in heaven vouch for the faithful on earth—another example of our partaking in the eternal community.

child. 14But the woman was given the two wings of the great eagle, so that she could fly from the serpent into the wilderness, to her place where she is nourished for a time, and times, and half a time. 15Then from his mouth the serpent poured water like a river after the woman, to sweep her away with the flood. 16But the earth came to the help of the woman; it opened its mouth and swallowed the river that the dragon had poured from his mouth. 17Then the dragon was angry with the woman, and went off to make war on the rest of her children, those who keep the commandments of God and hold the testimony of Jesus.

The First Beast

18 Then the dragon*a* took his stand on the sand of the seashore. 1And I saw a beast rising out of the sea, having ten horns and seven heads; and on its horns were ten diadems, and on its heads were blasphemous names. 2And the beast that I saw was like a leopard, its feet were like a bear's, and its mouth was like a lion's mouth. And the dragon gave it his power and his throne and great authority. 3One of its heads seemed to have received a death-blow, but its mortal wound*b* had been healed. In amazement the whole earth followed the beast. 4They worshiped the dragon, for he had given his authority to the beast, and they worshiped the beast, saying, "Who is like the beast, and who can fight against it?"

5 The beast was given a mouth uttering haughty and blasphemous words, and it was allowed to exercise authority for forty-two

months. 6It opened its mouth to utter blasphemies against God, blaspheming his name and his dwelling, that is, those who dwell in heaven. 7Also it was allowed to make war on the saints and to conquer them.*c* It was given authority over every tribe and people and language and nation, 8and all the inhabitants of the earth will worship it, everyone whose name has not been written from the foundation of the world in the book of life of the Lamb that was slaughtered.*d*

9 Let anyone who has an ear listen:
10 If you are to be taken captive,
　　into captivity you go;
　if you kill with the sword,
　　with the sword you must be killed.
Here is a call for the endurance and faith of the saints.

The Second Beast

11 Then I saw another beast that rose out of the earth; it had two horns like a lamb and it spoke like a dragon. 12It exercises all the authority of the first beast on its behalf, and it makes the earth and its inhabitants worship the first beast, whose mortal wound*e* had been healed. 13It performs great signs, even making fire come down from heaven to earth in the sight of all; 14and by the signs that it is allowed to perform on behalf of the beast, it deceives the inhabitants of earth, telling

a Gk *Then he*; other ancient authorities read *Then I stood* *b* Gk *the plague of its death* *c* Other ancient authorities lack this sentence *d* Or *written in the book of life of the Lamb that was slaughtered from the foundation of the world* *e* Gk *whose plague of its death*

13:10 *if you kill with the sword.* Our automatic response to attack is to fight back. Paul warns that the dark forces of evil cannot be defeated by violence, but by the armament of truth, righteousness, the gospel of peace, salvation, and the power of the Spirit (Eph 6:14–17).

Responding
13:10 FASTING. Though it is not mentioned here, one Spiritual Discipline, fasting, helps prepare us for enduring great hardship and builds our faith in God's provision. Unless you have a physical condition

that prohibits fasting from food, experiment with several types over the next few weeks; for example, skip lunch for a week, drink only fruit juices and water for thirty-six hours, or abstain from your favorite food for a month. Does your spirit feel stronger? *See also* Spiritual Disciplines Index.

13:14 *it deceives the inhabitants of earth.* The dark force tries to deceive us by disguising itself as the world's savior, the Lamb of God. Be on guard against God substitutes that claim to deliver health, wealth, and immortality.

them to make an image for the beast that had been wounded by the sword[a] and yet lived; [15]and it was allowed to give breath[b] to the image of the beast so that the image of the beast could even speak and cause those who would not worship the image of the beast to be killed. [16]Also it causes all, both small and great, both rich and poor, both free and slave, to be marked on the right hand or the forehead, [17]so that no one can buy or sell who does not have the mark, that is, the name of the beast or the number of its name. [18]This calls for wisdom; let anyone with understanding calculate the number of the beast, for it is the number of a person. Its number is six hundred sixty-six.[c]

The Lamb and the 144,000

14 Then I looked, and there was the Lamb, standing on Mount Zion! And with him were one hundred forty-four thousand who had his name and his Father's name written on their foreheads. [2]And I heard a voice from heaven like the sound of many waters and like the sound of loud thunder; the voice I heard was like the sound of harpists playing on their harps, [3]and they sing a new song before the throne and before the four living creatures and before the elders. No one could learn that song except the one hundred forty-four thousand who have been redeemed from the earth. [4]It is these who have not defiled themselves with women, for they are virgins; these follow the Lamb wherever he goes. They have been redeemed from humankind as first fruits for God and the Lamb, [5]and in their mouth no lie was found; they are blameless.

The Messages of the Three Angels

6 Then I saw another angel flying in midheaven, with an eternal gospel to proclaim to those who live[d] on the earth—to every nation and tribe and language and people. [7]He said in a loud voice, "Fear God and give him

glory, for the hour of his judgment has come; and worship him who made heaven and earth, the sea and the springs of water."

8 Then another angel, a second, followed, saying, "Fallen, fallen is Babylon the great! She has made all nations drink of the wine of the wrath of her fornication."

9 Then another angel, a third, followed them, crying with a loud voice, "Those who worship the beast and its image, and receive a mark on their foreheads or on their hands, [10]they will also drink the wine of God's wrath, poured unmixed into the cup of his anger, and they will be tormented with fire and sulfur in the presence of the holy angels and in the presence of the Lamb. [11]And the smoke of their torment goes up forever and ever. There is no rest day or night for those who worship the beast and its image and for anyone who receives the mark of its name."

12 Here is a call for the endurance of the saints, those who keep the commandments of God and hold fast to the faith of[e] Jesus.

13 And I heard a voice from heaven saying, "Write this: Blessed are the dead who from now on die in the Lord." "Yes," says the Spirit, "they will rest from their labors, for their deeds follow them."

Reaping the Earth's Harvest

14 Then I looked, and there was a white cloud, and seated on the cloud was one like the Son of Man, with a golden crown on his head, and a sharp sickle in his hand! [15]Another angel came out of the temple, calling with a loud voice to the one who sat on the cloud, "Use your sickle and reap, for the hour to reap has come, because the harvest of the earth is fully ripe." [16]So the one who sat on the cloud swung his sickle over the earth, and the earth was reaped.

a Or *that had received the plague of the sword* *b* Or *spirit* *c* Other ancient authorities read *six hundred sixteen* *d* Gk *sit* *e* Or *to their faith in*

14:12 *a call for the endurance of the saints.* Though we live in days of catastrophes, of greed and lust for power, our role in this cosmic drama is to hold out against the seductive appeals of a culture that glorifies violence and sensuality.

14:13 *Blessed are the dead who from now on die in the Lord.* John's message is not one of easy triumphalism. Death will come. But for the faithful, death is only a transition to closer communion with Christ.

17 Then another angel came out of the temple in heaven, and he too had a sharp sickle. [18]Then another angel came out from the altar, the angel who has authority over fire, and he called with a loud voice to him who had the sharp sickle, "Use your sharp sickle and gather the clusters of the vine of the earth, for its grapes are ripe." [19]So the angel swung his sickle over the earth and gathered the vintage of the earth, and he threw it into the great wine press of the wrath of God. [20]And the wine press was trodden outside the city, and blood flowed from the wine press, as high as a horse's bridle, for a distance of about two hundred miles. [a]

The Angels with the Seven Last Plagues

15 Then I saw another portent in heaven, great and amazing: seven angels with seven plagues, which are the last, for with them the wrath of God is ended.

2 And I saw what appeared to be a sea of glass mixed with fire, and those who had conquered the beast and its image and the number of its name, standing beside the sea of glass with harps of God in their hands. [3]And they sing the song of Moses, the servant [b] of God, and the song of the Lamb:

"Great and amazing are your deeds,
    Lord God the Almighty!
Just and true are your ways,
    King of the nations! [c]
4 Lord, who will not fear
    and glorify your name?
For you alone are holy.
    All nations will come
    and worship before you,
for your judgments have been revealed."

5 After this I looked, and the temple of the tent [d] of witness in heaven was opened, [6]and out of the temple came the seven angels with the seven plagues, robed in pure bright linen, [e] with golden sashes across their chests.

[7]Then one of the four living creatures gave the seven angels seven golden bowls full of the wrath of God, who lives forever and ever; [8]and the temple was filled with smoke from the glory of God and from his power, and no one could enter the temple until the seven plagues of the seven angels were ended.

The Bowls of God's Wrath

16 Then I heard a loud voice from the temple telling the seven angels, "Go and pour out on the earth the seven bowls of the wrath of God."

2 So the first angel went and poured his bowl on the earth, and a foul and painful sore came on those who had the mark of the beast and who worshiped its image.

3 The second angel poured his bowl into the sea, and it became like the blood of a corpse, and every living thing in the sea died.

4 The third angel poured his bowl into the rivers and the springs of water, and they became blood. [5]And I heard the angel of the waters say,

"You are just, O Holy One, who are and
    were,
for you have judged these things;
6 because they shed the blood of saints
        and prophets,
    you have given them blood to drink.
    It is what they deserve!"
[7]And I heard the altar respond,
"Yes, O Lord God, the Almighty,
    your judgments are true and just!"

8 The fourth angel poured his bowl on the sun, and it was allowed to scorch people with fire; [9]they were scorched by the fierce heat, but they cursed the name of God, who had authority over these plagues, and they did not repent and give him glory.

a Gk one thousand six hundred stadia   b Gk slave
c Other ancient authorities read the ages
d Or tabernacle   e Other ancient authorities read stone

15:3 they sing the song of Moses . . . and the song of the Lamb. Again, worship and spiritual warfare are necessarily intertwined. Praise and prayer are our powerful weapons.

16:1 pour out on the earth the seven bowls. The prayers of the persecuted are held in heavenly bowls against the day of judgment. They are not forgotten, but will be answered and do their work in God's good time.

16:9 and they did not repent. God's mercy is indeed everlasting, extended even during judgment. But it can only follow repentance.

10 The fifth angel poured his bowl on the throne of the beast, and its kingdom was plunged into darkness; people gnawed their tongues in agony, 11and cursed the God of heaven because of their pains and sores, and they did not repent of their deeds.

12 The sixth angel poured his bowl on the great river Euphrates, and its water was dried up in order to prepare the way for the kings from the east. 13And I saw three foul spirits like frogs coming from the mouth of the dragon, from the mouth of the beast, and from the mouth of the false prophet. 14These are demonic spirits, performing signs, who go abroad to the kings of the whole world, to assemble them for battle on the great day of God the Almighty. 15("See, I am coming like a thief! Blessed is the one who stays awake and is clothed, a not going about naked and exposed to shame.") 16And they assembled them at the place that in Hebrew is called Harmagedon.

17 The seventh angel poured his bowl into the air, and a loud voice came out of the temple, from the throne, saying, "It is done!" 18And there came flashes of lightning, rumblings, peals of thunder, and a violent earthquake, such as had not occurred since people were upon the earth, so violent was that earthquake. 19The great city was split into three parts, and the cities of the nations fell. God remembered great Babylon and gave her the wine-cup of the fury of his wrath. 20And every island fled away, and no mountains were to be found; 21and huge hailstones, each weighing about a hundred pounds, b dropped from heaven on people, until they cursed God for the plague of the hail, so fearful was that plague.

The Great Whore and the Beast

17 Then one of the seven angels who had the seven bowls came and said to me, "Come, I will show you the judgment of the great whore who is seated on many waters, 2with whom the kings of the earth have committed fornication, and with the wine of whose fornication the inhabitants of the earth have become drunk." 3So he carried me away in the spirit c into a wilderness, and I saw a woman sitting on a scarlet beast that was full of blasphemous names, and it had seven heads and ten horns. 4The woman was clothed in purple and scarlet, and adorned with gold and jewels and pearls, holding in her hand a golden cup full of abominations and the impurities of her fornication; 5and on her forehead was written a name, a mystery: "Babylon the great, mother of whores and of earth's abominations." 6And I saw that the woman was drunk with the blood of the saints and the blood of the witnesses to Jesus.

When I saw her, I was greatly amazed. 7But the angel said to me, "Why are you so amazed? I will tell you the mystery of the woman, and of the beast with seven heads and ten horns that carries her. 8The beast that you saw was, and is not, and is about to ascend from the bottomless pit and go to destruction. And the inhabitants of the earth, whose names have not been written in the book of life from the foundation of the world, will be amazed when they see the beast, because it was and is not and is to come.

9 "This calls for a mind that has wisdom: the seven heads are seven mountains on which the woman is seated; also, they are seven kings, 10of whom five have fallen, one is living, and the other has not yet come; and when he comes, he must remain only a little while. 11As for the beast that was and is not, it is an eighth but it belongs to the seven,

a Gk and keeps his robes   b Gk weighing about a talent   c Or in the Spirit

---

16:15 *See, I am coming like a thief!* Christ reaffirms his often repeated intention to come when he is least expected (Matt 24:43–44; Luke 12:39–40; 1 Thess 5:2; 2 Pet 3:10; Rev 3:3) as well as his command to stay awake and watchful.

16:17 *It is done!* The voice from the throne echoes Jesus' "It is finished" from the cross (John 19:30). Human history is telescoped into God's eternal Now.

17:4–6 *the woman was drunk with the blood of the saints and . . . the witnesses to Jesus.* This figure embodies those institutions that, across the ages, have sold themselves to the dark forces, doing their bidding in order to enjoy privilege and riches.

and it goes to destruction. 12And the ten horns that you saw are ten kings who have not yet received a kingdom, but they are to receive authority as kings for one hour, together with the beast. 13These are united in yielding their power and authority to the beast; 14they will make war on the Lamb, and the Lamb will conquer them, for he is Lord of lords and King of kings, and those with him are called and chosen and faithful."

15 And he said to me, "The waters that you saw, where the whore is seated, are peoples and multitudes and nations and languages. 16And the ten horns that you saw, they and the beast will hate the whore; they will make her desolate and naked; they will devour her flesh and burn her up with fire. 17For God has put it into their hearts to carry out his purpose by agreeing to give their kingdom to the beast, until the words of God will be fulfilled. 18The woman you saw is the great city that rules over the kings of the earth."

The Fall of Babylon

18 After this I saw another angel coming down from heaven, having great authority, and the earth was made bright with his splendor. 2He called out with a mighty voice,

"Fallen, fallen is Babylon the great!
    It has become a dwelling place of
        demons,
a haunt of every foul spirit,
    a haunt of every foul bird,
    a haunt of every foul and hateful
        beast. *a*
3 For all the nations have drunk *b*
    of the wine of the wrath of her
        fornication,
and the kings of the earth have
        committed fornication with her,
and the merchants of the earth have
    grown rich from the power *c* of
        her luxury."

4 Then I heard another voice from heaven saying,

"Come out of her, my people,
    so that you do not take part in her
        sins,
and so that you do not share in her
        plagues;
5 for her sins are heaped high as heaven,
    and God has remembered her
        iniquities.
6 Render to her as she herself has
        rendered,
    and repay her double for her deeds;
    mix a double draught for her in the
        cup she mixed.
7 As she glorified herself and lived
        luxuriously,
    so give her a like measure of torment
        and grief.
Since in her heart she says,
    'I rule as a queen;
I am no widow,
    and I will never see grief,'
8 therefore her plagues will come in a
        single day—
    pestilence and mourning and
        famine—
    and she will be burned with fire;
        for mighty is the Lord God who
            judges her."

9 And the kings of the earth, who committed fornication and lived in luxury with her, will weep and wail over her when they see the smoke of her burning; 10they will stand far off, in fear of her torment, and say,

"Alas, alas, the great city,
    Babylon, the mighty city!
For in one hour your judgment has
        come."

11 And the merchants of the earth weep

a Other ancient authorities lack the words *a haunt of every foul beast* and attach the words *and hateful* to the previous line so as to read *a haunt of every foul and hateful bird*   *b* Other ancient authorities read *She has made all nations drink*   *c* Or *resources*

17:17 *agreeing to give their kingdom to the beast.* Evil ultimately falls by turning on its own. Earthly rulers worship "Not-with-us," the opposite of Immanuel's "God-with-us."

18:1–24 *fallen is Babylon!* This chapter

pictures the ultimate collapse of all human institutions given over to the lust for power or greed. The more we entwine our identities with them, the more we will suffer at their disintegration.

and mourn for her, since no one buys their cargo anymore, 12cargo of gold, silver, jewels and pearls, fine linen, purple, silk and scarlet, all kinds of scented wood, all articles of ivory, all articles of costly wood, bronze, iron, and marble, 13cinnamon, spice, incense, myrrh, frankincense, wine, olive oil, choice flour and wheat, cattle and sheep, horses and chariots, slaves—and human lives. *a*

14 "The fruit for which your soul longed
    has gone from you,
  and all your dainties and your splendor
    are lost to you,
  never to be found again!"

15The merchants of these wares, who gained wealth from her, will stand far off, in fear of her torment, weeping and mourning aloud,

16 "Alas, alas, the great city,
    clothed in fine linen,
      in purple and scarlet,
    adorned with gold,
      with jewels, and with pearls!
17 For in one hour all this wealth has been
    laid waste!"

And all shipmasters and seafarers, sailors and all whose trade is on the sea, stood far off 18and cried out as they saw the smoke of her burning,

    "What city was like the great city?"

19And they threw dust on their heads, as they wept and mourned, crying out,

    "Alas, alas, the great city,
    where all who had ships at sea
      grew rich by her wealth!
    For in one hour she has been laid
      waste."

20 Rejoice over her, O heaven, you saints and apostles and prophets! For God has given judgment for you against her.

21 Then a mighty angel took up a stone like a great millstone and threw it into the sea, saying,

    "With such violence Babylon the great
      city
    will be thrown down,
    and will be found no more;
22 and the sound of harpists and minstrels
      and of flutists and trumpeters
    will be heard in you no more;
    and an artisan of any trade
    will be found in you no more;

and the sound of the millstone
    will be heard in you no more;
23 and the light of a lamp
    will shine in you no more;
  and the voice of bridegroom and bride
    will be heard in you no more;
  for your merchants were the magnates
    of the earth,
    and all nations were deceived by your
    sorcery.
24 And in you *b* was found the blood of
    prophets and of saints,
    and of all who have been slaughtered
    on earth."

The Rejoicing in Heaven

19 After this I heard what seemed to be the loud voice of a great multitude in heaven, saying,

  "Hallelujah!
  Salvation and glory and power to our
    God,
2   for his judgments are true and just;
  he has judged the great whore
    who corrupted the earth with her
    fornication,
  and he has avenged on her the blood of
    his servants." *c*

3Once more they said,
  "Hallelujah!
  The smoke goes up from her forever and
    ever."

4And the twenty-four elders and the four living creatures fell down and worshiped God who is seated on the throne, saying,

  "Amen. Hallelujah!"

5 And from the throne came a voice saying,

  "Praise our God,
    all you his servants, *c*
  and all who fear him,
    small and great."

6Then I heard what seemed to be the voice of a great multitude, like the sound of many waters and like the sound of mighty thunderpeals, crying out,

  "Hallelujah!
  For the Lord our God
    the Almighty reigns.

a Or *chariots, and human bodies and souls*
b Gk *her*   *c* Gk *slaves*

Handwritten annotations (top margin):
30:15 21:27 BLESSED (1) THOSE WHOSE NAMES WRITTEN IN LAMBS BOOK OF LIFE (2) THOSE INVITED TO THE MARRIAGE SUPPER (SUPPER) 1:3 OF THE LAMB (3) BLESSED AND THOSE WHO READ ALOUD THESE WORDS (4) THOSE WHO SHARE FIRST RESURRECTION 20:6

7 Let us rejoice and exult
   and give him the glory,
   for the marriage of the Lamb has come,
   and his bride has made herself ready;
8 to her it has been granted to be clothed
   with fine linen, bright and pure"—
for the fine linen is the righteous deeds of
the saints.

9 And the angel said[a] to me, "Write this:
Blessed are those who are invited to the marriage supper of the Lamb." And he said to
me, "These are true words of God." 10 Then I
fell down at his feet to worship him, but he
said to me, "You must not do that! I am a fellow servant[b] with you and your comrades[c]
who hold the testimony of Jesus.[d] Worship
God! For the testimony of Jesus[d] is the spirit
of prophecy."

Handwritten: WORSHIP

The Rider on the White Horse

11 Then I saw heaven opened, and there
was a white horse! Its rider is called Faithful
and True, and in righteousness he judges and
makes war. 12 His eyes are like a flame of fire,
and on his head are many diadems; and he
has a name inscribed that no one knows but
himself. 13 He is clothed in a robe dipped in[e]
blood, and his name is called The Word of
God. 14 And the armies of heaven, wearing
fine linen, white and pure, were following
him on white horses. 15 From his mouth
comes a sharp sword with which to strike
down the nations, and he will rule[f] them
with a rod of iron; he will tread the wine press
of the fury of the wrath of God the Almighty.
16 On his robe and on his thigh he has a name
inscribed, "King of kings and Lord of lords."

The Beast and Its Armies Defeated

17 Then I saw an angel standing in the sun,
and with a loud voice he called to all the birds
that fly in midheaven, "Come, gather for the
great supper of God, 18 to eat the flesh of kings,
the flesh of captains, the flesh of the mighty,
the flesh of horses and their riders—flesh of all,
both free and slave, both small and great."
19 Then I saw the beast and the kings of the
earth with their armies gathered to make war
against the rider on the horse and against his
army. 20 And the beast was captured, and with
it the false prophet who had performed in its
presence the signs by which he deceived those
who had received the mark of the beast and
those who worshiped its image. These two
were thrown alive into the lake of fire that
burns with sulfur. 21 And the rest were killed by
the sword of the rider on the horse, the sword
that came from his mouth; and all the birds
were gorged with their flesh.

Handwritten annotations (right margin):
(5) WHO HAVE HIS NAME ON FOREHEAD 22:4 (6) WHO KEEP WORDS OF THE BOOK 22:7 (7) WHO WASH THEIR ROBE 22:14

The Thousand Years

20 Then I saw an angel coming down
   from heaven, holding in his hand
the key to the bottomless pit and a great
chain. 2 He seized the dragon, that ancient
serpent, who is the Devil and Satan, and
bound him for a thousand years, 3 and threw
him into the pit, and locked and sealed it
over him, so that he would deceive the nations no more, until the thousand years were
ended. After that he must be let out for a little while.

a Gk he said   b Gk slave   c Gk brothers
d Or to Jesus   e Other ancient authorities read
sprinkled with   f Or will shepherd

Handwritten: YES YES!

19:9 *Blessed are those who are invited to the
marriage supper of the Lamb.* Recognizing how
empty are the promises of corrupt powers is
only the first step. Stopping there ends in disillusionment and despair. The vision of Christ's
true intimacy with his bride, the Faithful, fulfills
our joyful expectation.

Responding
19:9 CELEBRATION. In most cultures
weddings and the accompanying rituals
are times of great celebration. Consider the
many different celebrations that bring joy and
jubilation into your life. Why is celebrating
important to our spiritual formation? *See also*
Spiritual Disciplines Index.

19:10 SERVICE—*See* Spiritual Disciplines
Index.
19:13 *his name is called The Word of God.*
Again we hear an echo of the Gospel of John:
"In the beginning was the Word" (John 1:1).
Christ remains the Living Word.

4 Then I saw thrones, and those seated on them were given authority to judge. I also saw the souls of those who had been beheaded for their testimony to Jesus[a] and for the word of God. They had not worshiped the beast or its image and had not received its mark on their foreheads or their hands. They came to life and reigned with Christ a thousand years. 5 (The rest of the dead did not come to life until the thousand years were ended.) This is the first resurrection. 6 Blessed and holy are those who share in the first resurrection. Over these the second death has no power, but they will be priests of God and of Christ, and they will reign with him a thousand years.

Satan's Doom

7 When the thousand years are ended, Satan will be released from his prison 8 and will come out to deceive the nations at the four corners of the earth, Gog and Magog, in order to gather them for battle; they are as numerous as the sands of the sea. 9 They marched up over the breadth of the earth and surrounded the camp of the saints and the beloved city. And fire came down from heaven[b] and consumed them. 10 And the devil who had deceived them was thrown into the lake of fire and sulfur, where the beast and the false prophet were, and they will be tormented day and night forever and ever.

The Dead Are Judged

11 Then I saw a great white throne and the one who sat on it; the earth and the heaven fled from his presence, and no place was found for them. 12 And I saw the dead, great and small, standing before the throne, and books were opened. Also another book was opened, the book of life. And the dead were judged according to their works, as recorded in the books. 13 And the sea gave up the dead that were in it, Death and Hades gave up the dead that were in them, and all were judged according to what they had done. 14 Then Death and Hades were thrown into the lake of fire. This is the second death, the lake of fire; 15 and anyone whose name was not found written in the book of life was thrown into the lake of fire.

The New Heaven and the New Earth

21 Then I saw a new heaven and a new earth; for the first heaven and the first earth had passed away, and the sea was no more. 2 And I saw the holy city, the new Jerusalem, coming down out of heaven from God, prepared as a bride adorned for her husband. 3 And I heard a loud voice from the throne saying,

"See, the home[c] of God is among
        mortals.
He will dwell[d] with them;
they will be his peoples,[e]
and God himself will be with them;[f]

a Or for the testimony of Jesus   b Other ancient authorities read from God, out of heaven, or out of heaven from God   c Gk the tabernacle   d Gk will tabernacle   e Other ancient authorities read people   f Other ancient authorities add and be their God

---

20:9 They . . . surrounded the camp of the saints and the beloved city. Be clear about our earthly situation. As Israel did, we may delude ourselves that we are "at ease in Zion" (Amos 6:1), but armies of darkness surround us.

20:12 I saw the dead, great and small, standing before the throne. Every person stands equal before God, regardless of social position or power.

20:13 Death and Hades gave up the dead. Death truly has no dominion under God. Even this last enemy has been conquered by Christ and is subject to God's command.

21:1 a new heaven and a new earth. All creation, material and spiritual, God renews with his inexhaustible creative energy. Indeed, "his mercies never come to an end" (Lam 3:22).

21:2 prepared as a bride adorned for her husband. Jesus identified himself with the figure of the bridegroom in the three synoptic Gospels (Matt 25:1–10; Mark 2:19–20; Luke 5:34–35). Only John's Gospel speaks directly of the bride (3:29). Only this intimacy can convey how fully Christ embraces his faithful.

21:3 the home of God is among mortals. Simply being safe, free from persecution and oppression, is not enough for God-lovers. They must have God himself dwelling with them if this deepest hunger of the human heart is to be satisfied.

4 he will wipe every tear from their eyes.
Death will be no more;
mourning and crying and pain will be
    no more,
for the first things have passed away."

5 And the one who was seated on the throne said, "See, I am making all things new." Also he said, "Write this, for these words are trustworthy and true." 6Then he said to me, "It is done! I am the Alpha and the Omega, the beginning and the end. To the thirsty I will give water as a gift from the spring of the water of life. 7Those who conquer will inherit these things, and I will be their God and they will be my children. 8But as for the cowardly, the faithless,a the polluted, the murderers, the fornicators, the sorcerers, the idolaters, and all liars, their place will be in the lake that burns with fire and sulfur, which is the second death."

Vision of the New Jerusalem

9 Then one of the seven angels who had the seven bowls full of the seven last plagues came and said to me, "Come, I will show you the bride, the wife of the Lamb." 10And in the spiritb he carried me away to a great, high mountain and showed me the holy city Jerusalem coming down out of heaven from God. 11It has the glory of God and a radiance like a very rare jewel, like jasper, clear as crystal. 12It has a great, high wall with twelve gates, and at the gates twelve angels, and on the gates are inscribed the names of the twelve tribes of the Israelites; 13on the east three gates, on the north three gates, on the south three gates, and on the west three gates. 14And the wall of the city has twelve foundations, and on them are the twelve names of the twelve apostles of the Lamb.

15 The angelc who talked to me had a measuring rod of gold to measure the city and its gates and walls. 16The city lies foursquare, its length the same as its width; and he measured the city with his rod, fifteen hundred miles;d its length and width and height are equal. 17He also measured its wall, one hundred forty-four cubitse by human measurement, which the angel was using. 18The wall is built of jasper, while the city is pure gold, clear as glass. 19The foundations of the wall of the city are adorned with every jewel; the first was jasper, the second sapphire, the third agate, the fourth emerald, 20the fifth onyx, the sixth carnelian, the seventh chrysolite, the eighth beryl, the ninth topaz, the tenth chrysoprase, the eleventh jacinth, the twelfth amethyst. 21And the twelve gates are twelve pearls, each of the gates is a single pearl, and the street of the city is pure gold, transparent as glass.

22 I saw no temple in the city, for its temple is the Lord God the Almighty and the Lamb. 23And the city has no need of sun or moon to shine on it, for the glory of God is its light, and its lamp is the Lamb. 24The nations will walk by its light, and the kings of the earth will bring their glory into it. 25Its gates will never be shut by day—and there will be no night there. 26People will bring into it the glory and the honor of the nations. 27But nothing unclean will enter it, nor anyone who practices abomination or falsehood, but only those who are written in the Lamb's book of life.

The River of Life

22 Then the angelf showed me the river of the water of life, bright as crystal, flowing from the throne of God and of the Lamb 2through the middle of the street of the city. On either side of the river is the tree of lifeg with its twelve kinds of fruit, producing its fruit each month; and the leaves of the tree are for the healing of the nations. 3Nothing accursed will be found there any

a Or the unbelieving   b Or in the Spirit
c Gk He   d Gk twelve thousand stadia   e That is, almost seventy-five yards   f Gk he   g Or the Lamb. 2In the middle of the street of the city, and on either side of the river, is the tree of life

---

21:26 *People will bring into it the glory and the honor of the nations.* Note how expansive is this embrace of the holy city. As the heavenly chorus sang in 15:4, "All nations will come and worship before you."

22:3 *Nothing accursed will be found there any more.* Here, at last, the cycles of blame and shame that have governed all communities, from couples to civilizations, are broken. We are healed of the curse by the tree of life.

more. But the throne of God and of the Lamb will be in it, and his servants *will worship him; [4]they will see his face, and his name will be on their foreheads. [5]And there will be no more night; they need no light of lamp or sun, for the Lord God will be their light, and they will reign forever and ever.

6 And he said to me, "These words are trustworthy and true, for the Lord, the God of the spirits of the prophets, has sent his angel to show his servants[a] what must soon take place."

7 "See, I am coming soon! Blessed is the one who keeps the words of the prophecy of this book."

Epilogue and Benediction

8 I, John, am the one who heard and saw these things. And when I heard and saw them, I fell down to worship at the feet of the angel who showed them to me; [9]but he said to me, "You must not do that! I am a fellow servant[b] with you and your comrades[c] the prophets, and with those who keep the words of this book. Worship God!"

10 And he said to me, "Do not seal up the words of the prophecy of this book, for the time is near. [11]Let the evildoer still do evil, and the filthy still be filthy, and the righteous still do right, and the holy still be holy."

12 "See, I am coming soon; my reward is with me, to repay according to everyone's work. [13]I am the Alpha and the Omega, the first and the last, the beginning and the end."

14 Blessed are those who wash their robes,[d] so that they will have the right to the tree of life and may enter the city by the gates. [15]Outside are the dogs and sorcerers and fornicators and murderers and idolaters, and everyone who loves and practices falsehood.

16 "It is I, Jesus, who sent my angel to you with this testimony for the churches. I am the root and the descendant of David, the bright morning star."

17 The Spirit and the bride say, "Come."
 And let everyone who hears say,
       "Come."
 And let everyone who is thirsty come.
 Let anyone who wishes take the water
       of life as a gift.

18 I warn everyone who hears the words of the prophecy of this book: if anyone adds to them, God will add to that person the plagues described in this book; [19]if anyone takes away from the words of the book of this prophecy, God will take away that person's share in the tree of life and in the holy city, which are described in this book.

20 The one who testifies to these things says, "Surely I am coming soon."
 Amen. Come, Lord Jesus!

21 The grace of the Lord Jesus be with all the saints. Amen.[e]

---

a Gk slaves   b Gk slave   c Gk brothers
d Other ancient authorities read do his commandments   e Other ancient authorities lack all; others lack the saints; others lack Amen

---

Responding
22:3–5 THE WITH-GOD LIFE. We have come full circle. God walked with Adam and Eve in the garden; now the creation of an all-inclusive community of loving persons with God himself at the very center of this community as its prime Sustainer and most glorious Inhabitant is completed. How prepared are you to spend eternity in this community?

What do you need to do to better prepare yourself? See also Spiritual Disciplines Index.

22:9 WORSHIP—See Spiritual Disciplines Index.

22:17 And let everyone who hears say, "Come." Here again is our gospel commissioning: to offer spiritual hospitality to all who are thirsty for Life.

SPIRITUAL DISCIPLINES INDEX

This selective, topical index is designed to help readers get a picture of the with-God life presented in the Bible and the role of the Spiritual Disciplines in fostering that kind of life toward its fullness. The passages listed either contain a specific reference to a topic serving as a discipline (e.g., the word "meditation") or are about that topic without using the specific term. Because this index is selective, it does not list every passage in the Bible on each topic, and the entries are restricted to the topic's role as a Spiritual Discipline. Some of the entries are negative examples of the practice of a particular discipline.

The list of disciplines chosen for this index also does not include every practice or situation that could actually serve as a discipline in the process of spiritual formation. The disciplines under consideration here include celebration, chastity, confession, fasting, fellowship, guidance, meditation, prayer, sacrifice, secrecy, service, silence, simplicity/frugality, solitude, study, submission, and worship. Since the central focus of Christian spiritual formation is the with-God life, that topic begins the index. It is followed by sections containing scriptural references for the various disciplines, in alphabetical order. Those references for which there are spiritual formation exercises are designated by an asterisk.

No doubt some passages may have been omitted that might be very useful for understanding spiritual formation. What is given here is intended to provide only a substantial introduction to the presence and importance of Spiritual Disciplines in the Bible. For further study on disciplines and how they are to be practiced, please see Richard Foster, *Celebration of Discipline,* and Dallas Willard, *The Spirit of the Disciplines.*

THE WITH-GOD LIFE: The Bible is all about human life "with God" and how God has made this "with-God" life possible and will bring it to pass. The name Immanuel, meaning "God is with us," is the title given to the one and only Redeemer, because it refers to God's everlasting intent for human life—namely, that we should be in every aspect a dwelling place of God.

Gen 1:26–30 Let us make humankind in our image, according to our likeness; and let them have dominion.

Gen 2:7–8 Then the LORD God formed man from the dust of the ground, and breathed into his nostrils the breath of life.

*Gen 3:8 They heard the sound of the LORD God walking in the garden.

Gen 4:14–16 The LORD put a mark on Cain, so that no one who came upon him would kill him.

Gen 17:1–2 I am God Almighty; walk before me, and be blameless. And I will make my covenant between me and you.

Gen 24:7, 27 The LORD, God of heaven, . . . took me from my father's house and from the land of my birth, and . . . spoke to me.

Gen 26:24–28 Do not be afraid, for I am with you and will bless you.

*Gen 28:11–22 Know that I am with you and will keep you wherever you go, and will bring you back.

*Gen 39:2–5, 21–23 The LORD was with Joseph.

Exod 4:12–16 Now go, and I will be with your mouth and teach you what you are to speak.

*Exod 8:19 Pharaoh's heart was hardened, and he would not listen to them, just as the LORD had said.

Exod 14:13–16 Lift up your staff, and stretch out your hand over the sea and divide it, that the Israelites may go into the sea on dry ground.

Exod 19:3–6 If you obey my voice and keep my covenant, you shall be my treasured possession out of all the peoples.

*Exod 29:44–46 I will dwell among the Israelites, and I will be their God.

Exod 33:12–16 My presence will go with you, and I will give you rest.

Exod 34:9–10 O Lord, I pray, let the Lord go with us.

Exod 34:29–35 Whenever Moses went in before the LORD to speak with him, he would take the veil off.

*Exod 40:34–38 The cloud covered the tent of meeting, and the glory of the LORD filled the tabernacle.

*Lev 16:1–2 I appear in the cloud upon the mercy seat.

*Lev 25:18–22 I will order my blessing for you in the sixth year, so that it will yield a crop for three years.

Num 6:24–26 The LORD bless you and keep you; the LORD make his face to shine upon you.

*Num 7:89 When Moses went into the tent of meeting to speak with the LORD, he would hear the voice speaking to him.

Num 17:8 The staff of Aaron for the house of Levi had sprouted.

Deut 8:2–5 Remember the long way that the LORD your God has led you these forty years in the wilderness.

Deut 8:14–18 The LORD your God . . . brought you out of the land of Egypt, out of the house of slavery.

*Deut 28:1–14 All these blessings shall come upon you and overtake you, if you obey the LORD your God.

Deut 31:6 Have no fear or dread of them, because it is the LORD your God who goes with you.

Deut 33:26–29 There is none like God, O Jeshurun, who rides through the heavens to your help.

*Josh 1:5 As I was with Moses, so I will be with you; I will not fail you or forsake you.

*Judg 6:16 The LORD said to him, "But I will be with you."

*Judg 16:20 He did not know that the LORD had left him.

1 Sam 17:46–47 The battle is the LORD's and he will give you into our hand.

*1 Sam 18:12–15 Saul was afraid of David, because the LORD was with him but had departed from Saul.

2 Sam 5:24 Then the LORD has gone before you.

*2 Sam 22:17–51 He reached from on high, he took me, he drew me out of mighty waters.

*1 Kings 8:10–11 The glory of the LORD filled the house of the LORD.

*2 Kings 6:16–17 The LORD opened the eyes of the servant, and he saw.

*1 Chron 29:10–19 It is in your hand to make great and to give strength to all.

2 Chron 15:9 Great numbers had deserted to him from Israel when they saw that the LORD his God was with him.

*2 Chron 16:9 For the eyes of the LORD range throughout the entire earth, to strengthen those whose heart is true to him.

2 Chron 17:1–10 The LORD was with Jehoshaphat, because he walked in the earlier ways of his father.

*2 Chron 20:15–22, 29–30 This battle is not for you to fight; take your position, stand still, and see the victory of the LORD on your behalf.

2 Chron 32:7–8 With him is an arm of flesh; but with us is the LORD our God, to help us and to fight our battles.

*Neh 2:8, 18 The king granted me what I asked, for the gracious hand of my God was upon me.

*Ps 16:8–11 Because he is at my right hand, I shall not be moved.

*Ps 23:1–6 The LORD is my shepherd, I shall not want. He makes me lie down in green pastures; he leads me beside still waters.

Ps 33:13–22 The LORD looks down from heaven; he sees all humankind.

Ps 34:15–19 The eyes of the LORD are on the righteous, and his ears are open to their cry.

Ps 91:16 With long life I will satisfy them, and show them my salvation.

*Isa 7:14 The LORD himself will give you a sign. Look, the young woman is with child and shall bear a son, and shall name him Immanuel.

Isa 41:10 Do not fear, for I am with you, do not be afraid, for I am your God.

*Isa 43:1–5 When you pass through the waters, I will be with you.

Isa 45:14–15 God is with you alone, and there is no other; there is no god besides him.

Isa 63:11–13 Where is the one . . . who divided the waters before them to make for himself an everlasting name?

*Ezek 37:27–28 My dwelling place shall be with them; and I will be their God, and they shall be my people.

Dan 3:25 I see four men unbound, walking in the middle of the fire, and they are not hurt; and the fourth has the appearance of a god.

Dan 6:22–23 My God sent his angel and shut the lions' mouths so that they would not hurt me.

*Matt 1:23 "The virgin shall conceive and bear a son, and they shall name him Emmanuel," which means, "God is with us."

Matt 16:19 Whatever you bind on earth will be bound in heaven, and whatever you loose on earth will be loosed in heaven.

*Matt 18:20 Where two or three are gathered in my name, I am there among them.

*Matt 28:18–20 And remember, I am with you always, to the end of the age.

*Mark 16:20 The Lord worked with them and confirmed the message by the signs that accompanied it.

Luke 10:11 Yet know this: the kingdom of God has come near.

Luke 11:29 This generation is an evil generation; it asks for a sign, but no sign will be given.

Luke 17:21 The kingdom of God is among you.

Luke 18:16–17 Let the little children come to me, and do not stop them; for it is to such as these that the kingdom of God belongs.

Luke 24:49 I am sending upon you what my Father promised; so stay here in the city until you have been clothed with power from on high.

*John 1:4 In him was life, and the life was the light of all people.

John 1:9–10 He was in the world, and the world came into being through him; yet the world did not know him.

John 6:56–58 Those who eat my flesh and drink my blood abide in me, and I in them.

John 15:1–5 I am the vine, you are the branches. Those who abide in me and I in them bear much fruit, because apart from me you can do nothing.

John 17:21–23 As you, Father, are in me and I am in you, may they also be in us, so that the world may believe that you have sent me.

Acts 1:8 You will receive power when the Holy Spirit has come upon you; and you will be my witnesses.

Acts 11:17 God gave them the same gift that he gave us when we believed.

Acts 11:21 The hand of the Lord was with them, and a great number became believers and turned to the Lord.

Acts 13:11 "The hand of the Lord is against you, and you will be blind for a while, unable to see the sun." Immediately mist and darkness came over him.

Acts 14:27 They called the church together and related all that God had done with them, and how he had opened a door of faith for the Gentiles.

*Acts 15:12 They told of all the signs and wonders that God had done through them among the Gentiles.

Acts 19:20 So the word of the Lord grew mightily and prevailed.

*Acts 23:11 That night the Lord stood near him and said, "Keep up your courage!"

Acts 28:3–10 Paul visited him and cured him by praying and putting his hands on him.

*Rom 6:13 Present your members to God as instruments of righteousness.

Rom 6:23 The free gift of God is eternal life in Christ Jesus.

Rom 8:11–13 He who raised Christ from the dead will give life to your mortal bodies also through his Spirit that dwells in you.

Rom 12:6 We have gifts that differ according to the grace given to us.

Rom 14:17 For the kingdom of God is not food and drink but righteousness and peace and joy in the Holy Spirit.

1 Cor 4:20 For the kingdom of God depends not on talk but on power.

*1 Cor 12:11 All these are activated by one and the same Spirit, who allots to each one individually just as the Spirit chooses.

1 Cor 15:10 I worked harder than any of them—though it was not I, but the grace of God that is with me.

2 Cor 9:8 God is able to provide you with every blessing in abundance.

2 Cor 10:3–5 The weapons of our warfare are not merely human, but they have divine power to destroy strongholds.

2 Cor 12:9–10 I will boast all the more gladly of my weaknesses, so that the power of Christ may dwell in me.

Eph 1:17–19 I pray that . . . you may know . . . the immeasurable greatness of his power for us who believe, according to the working of his great power.

Eph 3:7 I have become a servant according to the gift of God's grace.

Eph 3:16 I pray that . . . you may be strengthened in your inner being with power through his Spirit.

Eph 3:20 Now to him who by the power at work within us is able to accomplish abundantly far more than all we can ask or imagine, to him be glory.

Eph 6:10 Be strong in the Lord and in the strength of his power.

Col 3:1–4 Set your mind on things that are above, not on things that are on earth, for you have died, and your life is hidden with Christ in God.

*1 Thess 1:5 Our message of the gospel came to you not in word only, but also in power and in the Holy Spirit and with full conviction.

Heb 1:14 Are not all angels spirits in the divine service, sent to serve for the sake of those who are to inherit salvation?

*Heb 4:12 Indeed, the word of God is living and active, sharper than any two-edged sword.

Heb 7:25 Consequently he is able for all time to save those who approach God through him, since he always lives to make intercession for them.

Heb 12:22–24 You have come to Mount Zion and to the city of the living God, the heavenly Jerusalem.

Heb 13:5–6 Be content with what you have; for he has said, "I will never leave you or forsake you."

1 Pet 3:12–13 For the eyes of the Lord are on the righteous, and his ears are open to their prayer.

*1 Pet 5:6–7 Cast all your anxiety on him, because he cares for you.

*Rev 22:3–5 Nothing accursed will be found there any more. But the throne of God and of the Lamb will be in it.

CELEBRATION: Utter delight and joy in ourselves, our life, and our world as a result of our faith and confidence in God's greatness, beauty, and goodness.

*Exod 5:1 Thus says the Lord, the God of Israel, "Let my people go, so that they may celebrate a festival to me in the wilderness."

*Exod 12:14 This day shall be a day of remembrance for you. You shall celebrate it as a festival to the Lord.

*Lev 23:4, 37 These are the appointed festivals of the Lord, the holy convocations, which you shall celebrate at the time appointed for them.

*Num 10:10 On your days of rejoicing, at your appointed festivals, and at the beginnings of your months, you shall blow the trumpets.

*Num 29:12 On the fifteenth day of the seventh month you shall have a holy convocation; you shall not work at your occupations. You shall celebrate a festival to the Lord seven days.

Deut 14:22–29 You shall eat there in the presence of the Lord your God, you and your household rejoicing together.

Deut 16:15 Seven days you shall keep the festival to the Lord your God at the place that the Lord will choose; for the Lord your God will bless you in all your produce and in all your undertakings, and you shall surely celebrate.

*2 Sam 6:14 David danced before the Lord with all his might.

*Ezra 6:22 With joy they celebrated the festival of unleavened bread seven days; for the LORD had made them joyful.

Neh 12:27 They sought out the Levites in all their places, to bring them to Jerusalem to celebrate the dedication with rejoicing, with thanksgivings and with singing, with cymbals, harps, and lyres.

*Esther 9:22 The month . . . had been turned for them from sorrow into gladness and from mourning into a holiday.

*Ps 45:1–17 My heart overflows with a goodly theme.

*Ps 126:2 Then our mouth was filled with laughter, and our tongue with shouts of joy.

*Ps 145:7 They shall celebrate the fame of your abundant goodness, and shall sing aloud of your righteousness.

*Song of Sol 1:4 We will exult and rejoice in you.

*Isa 51:11 So the ransomed of the LORD shall return, and come to Zion with singing; everlasting joy shall be upon their heads.

*Nah 1:15 Celebrate your festivals, O Judah, fulfill your vows.

*Jth 16:1–17 Begin a song to my God with tambourines, sing to my Lord with cymbals.

*1 Macc 4:54–58 All the people fell on their faces and worshiped and blessed Heaven, who had prospered them.

*Pr of Azar 65 Bless the Lord, you who are holy and humble in heart; sing praise to him and highly exalt him forever.

Luke 15:23–32 And get the fatted calf and kill it, and let us eat and celebrate; for this son of mine was dead and is alive again.

John 2:1–10 On the third day there was a wedding in Cana of Galilee.

1 Cor 5:8 Therefore, let us celebrate the festival, not with the old yeast, the yeast of malice and evil, but with the unleavened bread of sincerity and truth.

Phil 4:4–13 Rejoice in the Lord always; again I will say, Rejoice.

*Rev 19:9 Blessed are those who are invited to the marriage supper of the Lamb.

CHASTITY: Purposefully turning away for a time from dwelling upon or engaging in the sexual dimension of our relationship to others—even our husband or wife—and thus learning how not to be governed by this powerful aspect of our life.

*Job 31:7–10 If my step has turned aside from the way, and my heart has followed my eyes, and if any spot has clung to my hands; then let me sow, and another eat.

*Prov 5:15–22 Rejoice in the wife of your youth.

*Song of Sol 7:10 I am my beloved's, and his desire is for me.

*Hos 1:2 Go, take for yourself a wife of whoredom and have children of whoredom.

*4 Macc 2:1–3 The temperate Joseph is praised, because by mental effort he overcame sexual desire.

Sir 7:24 Do you have daughters? Be concerned for their chastity, and do not show yourself too indulgent with them.

*Sir 26:15 A modest wife adds charm to charm, and no scales can weigh the value of her chastity.

Matt 5:27–32 Everyone who looks at a woman with lust has already committed adultery with her in his heart.

*1 Cor 7:5 Do not deprive one another except perhaps by agreement for a set time, to devote yourselves to prayer.

1 Cor 13:4–6 Love is patient; love is kind; love is not envious or boastful or arrogant or rude.

*2 Cor 11:2 I feel a divine jealousy for you, for I promised you in marriage to one husband, to present you as a chaste virgin to Christ.

*Eph 5:22–33 Wives, be subject to your husbands as you are to the Lord.

1 Tim 5:2 [Speak] to older women as mothers, to younger women as sisters—with absolute purity.

1 Tim 5:9–14 Refuse to put younger widows on the list; for when their sensual desires alienate them from Christ, they want to marry.

2 Tim 2:22 Shun youthful passions and pursue righteousness, faith, love, and peace.

*Titus 2:5 Be self-controlled, chaste, good managers of the household, kind, . . . submissive to . . . husbands, so that the word of God may not be discredited.

CONFESSION: Sharing our deepest weaknesses and failures with God and trusted others, so that we may enter into God's grace and mercy and experience his ready forgiveness and healing.

*Gen 45:25–28 And they told him, "Joseph is still alive!"

*Lev 5:5 When you realize your guilt in any of these, you shall confess the sin that you have committed.

Num 5:7 Confess the sin that has been committed. . . . Make full restitution for the wrong, adding one fifth to it, and giving it to the one who was wronged.

1 Kings 8:33 Your people Israel, having sinned against you, are defeated before an enemy but turn again to you, confess your name, pray and plead with you in this house.

*2 Chron 6:26–27 They have sinned against you, and then they pray toward this place, confess your name, and turn from their sin, because you punish them.

*Ezra 10:1 Ezra prayed and made confession, weeping and throwing himself down before the house of God.

*Neh 1:6–7 Let your ear be attentive and your eyes open to hear the prayer of your servant that I now pray before you day and night for your servants, the people of Israel, confessing the sins of the people of Israel, which we have sinned against you.

Ps 32:5 Then I acknowledged my sin to you, and I did not hide my iniquity; I said, "I will confess my transgressions to the Lord," and you forgave the guilt of my sin.

Ps 38:18 I confess my iniquity; I am sorry for my sin.

*Prov 28:13 No one who conceals transgressions will prosper, but one who confesses and forsakes them will obtain mercy.

*Ezek 33:10 Our transgressions and our sins weigh upon us, and we waste away because of them; how then can we live?

*Dan 9:20 I was speaking, and was praying and confessing my sin and the sin of my people Israel, and presenting my supplication before the Lord my God on behalf of the holy mountain of my God.

*Hos 14:2 Take words with you and return to the Lord; say to him, "Take away all guilt; accept that which is good, and we will offer the fruit of our lips."

*1 Esd 8:91 Ezra was praying and making his confession, weeping and lying on the ground before the temple.

*Sir 4:26 Do not be ashamed to confess your sins.

*Bar 2:10 Yet we have not obeyed his voice, to walk in the statutes of the Lord that he set before us.

Pr of Man 8–15 For the sins I have committed are more in number than the sand of the sea.

Sus 14 When each pressed the other for the reason, they confessed their lust.

Matt 3:6 They were baptized by him in the river Jordan, confessing their sins.

*Mark 1:5 And people . . . were going out to him, and were baptized by him in the river Jordan, confessing their sins.

Luke 12:1–5 Nothing is covered up that will not be uncovered, and nothing secret that will not become known.

*Luke 12:8–9 Everyone who acknowledges me before others, the Son of Man also will acknowledge before the angels of God.

*Rom 10:9–10 If you confess with your lips that Jesus is Lord and believe in your heart that God raised him from the dead, you will be saved.

*Heb 10:23 Let us hold fast to the confession of our hope without wavering, for he who has promised is faithful.

James 5:16 Therefore confess your sins to one another, and pray for one another, so that you may be healed.

1 John 1:9 If we confess our sins, he who is faithful and just will forgive us our sins and cleanse us from all unrighteousness.

*1 John 4:15 God abides in those who confess that Jesus is the Son of God, and they abide in God.

FASTING: The voluntary abstention from an otherwise normal function—most often eating—for the sake of intense spiritual activity.

*Deut 8:3 One does not live by bread alone, but by every word that comes from the mouth of the LORD.

*1 Sam 7:6 They fasted that day, and said, "We have sinned against the LORD."

*1 Sam 31:13 Then they took their bones and buried them under the tamarisk tree in Jabesh, and fasted seven days.

*2 Sam 12:16, 21–23 David therefore pleaded with God for the child; David fasted, and went in and lay all night on the ground.

*1 Kings 21:27–29 When Ahab heard those words, he tore his clothes and put sackcloth over his bare flesh; he fasted, lay in the sackcloth, and went about dejectedly.

*2 Chron 20:3 Jehoshaphat was afraid; he set himself to seek the LORD, and proclaimed a fast throughout all Judah.

*Ezra 8:21–23 I proclaimed a fast there, at the river Ahava, that we might deny ourselves before our God.

Neh 1:4 When I heard these words I sat down and wept, and mourned for days, fasting and praying before the God of heaven.

*Neh 9:1 Now on the twenty-fourth day of this month the people of Israel were assembled with fasting and in sackcloth, and with earth on their heads.

*Esther 4:3 In every province, wherever the king's command and his decree came, there was great mourning among the Jews, with fasting and weeping and lamenting.

*Esther 4:16 Hold a fast on my behalf, and neither eat nor drink for three days, night or day. I and my maids will also fast as you do.

Esther 9:31 They had laid down for themselves and for their descendants regulations concerning their fasts and their lamentations.

*Ps 35:13 But as for me, when they were sick, I wore sackcloth; I afflicted myself with fasting.

Ps 69:10 When I humbled my soul with fasting, they insulted me for doing so.

*Ps 109:24 My knees are weak through fasting; my body has become gaunt.

*Isa 58:3–6 You fast only to quarrel and to fight and to strike with a wicked fist. Such fasting as you do today will not make your voice heard on high.

Jer 14:12 Although they fast, I do not hear their cry.

Dan 6:18 Then the king went to his palace and spent the night fasting; no food was brought to him, and sleep fled from him.

Dan 9:3 Then I turned to the Lord God, to seek an answer by prayer and supplication with fasting and sackcloth and ashes.

*Joel 2:12–13 Yet even now, says the LORD, return to me with all your heart, with fasting, with weeping, and with mourning.

Joel 2:15 Blow the trumpet in Zion; sanctify a fast; call a solemn assembly.

*Jon 3:5 And the people of Nineveh believed God; they proclaimed a fast, and everyone, great and small, put on sackcloth.

*Zech 7:5 When you fasted and lamented in the fifth month and in the seventh, for these seventy years, was it for me that you fasted?

*Zech 8:19 The fast of the fourth month, and the fast of the fifth, and the fast of the seventh, and the fast of the tenth, shall be seasons of joy and gladness, and cheerful festivals for the house of Judah.

*1 Esd 8:50 There I proclaimed a fast for the young men before our Lord, to seek from him a prosperous journey for ourselves.

*2 Esd 5:13, 20 If you pray again, and weep as you do now, and fast for seven days, you shall hear yet greater things than these.

2 Esd 6:31–35 If therefore you will pray again and fast again for seven days, I will again declare to you greater things than these.

*Jth 4:9–13 The Lord heard their prayers and had regard for their distress; for the people fasted many days . . . before the sanctuary of the Lord Almighty.

*Jth 8:6 She fasted all the days of her widowhood, except the day before the sabbath and the sabbath itself, the day before the new moon and the day of the new moon, and the festivals and days of rejoicing of the house of Israel.

*1 Macc 3:47 They fasted that day, put on sackcloth and sprinkled ashes on their heads, and tore their clothes.

2 Macc 13:12 They had all joined in the same petition and had implored the merciful Lord with weeping and fasting and lying prostrate for three days without ceasing.

Sir 34:31 So if one fasts for his sins, and goes again and does the same things, who will listen to his prayer?

Bar 1:5 Then they wept, and fasted, and prayed before the Lord.

*Tob 12:8 Prayer with fasting is good, but better than both is almsgiving with righteousness.

Matt 4:2 He fasted forty days and forty nights, and afterwards he was famished.

Matt 6:16–18 And whenever you fast, do not look dismal, like the hypocrites, for they disfigure their faces so as to show others that they are fasting.

Matt 9:14–15 The days will come when the bridegroom is taken away from them, and then they will fast.

Mark 2:18–19 The days will come when the bridegroom is taken away from them, and then they will fast on that day.

Luke 5:33–35 The days will come when the bridegroom will be taken away from them, and then they will fast in those days.

*Rev 13:10 Here is a call for the endurance and faith of the saints.

FELLOWSHIP: Engaging with other disciples in the common activities of worship, study, prayer, celebration, and service, which sustain our life together and enlarge our capacity to experience more of God.

*1 Kings 19:10 I alone am left, and they are seeking my life, to take it away.

*Ps 133:1–3 How very good and pleasant it is when kindred live together in unity!

*Mic 4:7 The lame I will make the remnant, and those who were cast off, a strong nation.

*3 Macc 2:25–26 He increased in his deeds of malice, abetted by the previously mentioned drinking companions and comrades, who were strangers to everything just.

*4 Macc 13:8–17 They constituted a holy chorus of religion and encouraged one another.

*Matt 18:20 Where two or three are gathered in my name, I am there among them.

*Acts 2:42 They devoted themselves to the apostles' teaching and fellowship, to the breaking of bread and the prayers.

Rom 12:4–17 So we, who are many, are one body in Christ, and individually we are members one of another.

*Rom 14:10 Why do you pass judgment on your brother or sister?

*Eph 4:15–16 The whole body, joined and knit together by every ligament with which it is equipped, as each part is working properly, promotes the body's growth in building itself up in love.

Col 3:8–17 As God's chosen ones, holy and beloved, clothe yourselves with compassion, kindness, humility, meekness, and patience.

Heb 10:23–25 Let us consider how to provoke one another to love and good deeds, not neglecting to meet together.

1 John 1:3 We declare to you what we have seen and heard so that you also may have fellowship with us; and truly our fellowship is with the Father and with his Son Jesus Christ.

*1 John 1:5–7 If we say that we have fellowship with him while we are walking in darkness, we lie and do not do what is true.

GUIDANCE: Experiencing an interactive friendship with God that gives direction and purpose to daily life.

*Exod 15:13 In your steadfast love you led the people whom you redeemed; you guided them by your strength to your holy abode.

*Num 12:8 With him I speak face to face—clearly, not in riddles; and he beholds the form of the LORD.

*Num 22:18–35 If the men have come to summon you, get up and go with them; but do only what I tell you to do.

*2 Sam 5:19 David inquired of the LORD, "Shall I go up against the Philistines?"

*2 Kings 22:14 So the priest Hilkiah, Ahikam, Achbor, Shaphan, and Asaiah went to the prophetess Huldah.

*1 Chron 10:13–14 He had consulted a medium, seeking guidance, and did not seek guidance from the LORD.

*Job 32:8–9 Truly it is the spirit in a mortal, the breath of the Almighty, that makes for understanding.

*Ps 31:3 You are indeed my rock and my fortress; for your name's sake lead me and guide me.

*Ps 67:4 Let the nations be glad and sing for joy, for you judge the peoples with equity and guide the nations upon earth.

Ps 73:24 You guide me with your counsel, and afterward you will receive me with honor.

*Isa 30:20–21 When you turn to the right or when you turn to the left, your ears shall hear a word behind you, saying "This is the way; walk in it."

Isa 42:16 I will lead the blind by a road they do not know, by paths they have not known I will guide them.

Isa 58:11 The LORD will guide you continually, and satisfy your needs in parched places, and make your bones strong.

*Jer 1:6–8 You shall speak whatever I command you.

*Obad 1 We have heard a report from the LORD, and a messenger has been sent among the nations.

*1 Macc 16:6 He saw that the soldiers were afraid to cross the stream, so he crossed over first.

*2 Macc 15:12–16 Onias . . . was praying with outstretched hands for the whole body of the Jews.

Wisd of Sol 7:15 May God grant me to speak with judgment; . . . for he is the guide even of wisdom and the corrector of the wise.

Wisd of Sol 10:10 She guided him on straight paths; she showed him the kingdom of God, and gave him knowledge of holy things.

*Wisd of Sol 12:2 Therefore you correct little by little those who trespass, and you remind and warn them of the things through which they sin.

Matt 23:16 Woe to you, blind guides.

Luke 2:27 Guided by the Spirit, Simeon came into the temple.

*John 14:1–31 And if I go and prepare a place for you, I will come again and will take you to myself, so that where I am, there you may be also.

John 16:13 When the Spirit of truth comes, he will guide you into all the truth.

*Gal 5:25 If we live by the Spirit, let us also be guided by the Spirit.

James 1:5 If any of you is lacking in wisdom, ask God, who gives to all generously and ungrudgingly, and it will be given you.

James 3:15–18 The wisdom from above is first pure, then peaceable, gentle, willing to yield, full of mercy and good fruits, without a trace of partiality or hypocrisy.

Rev 7:17 The Lamb at the center of the throne will be their shepherd, and he will guide them to springs of the water of life.

MEDITATION: Prayerful rumination upon God, his Word, and his world.

*Gen 24:63 Isaac went out in the evening to walk in the field.

*Josh 1:8 This book of the law shall not depart out of your mouth; you shall meditate on it day and night.

*Job 15:4 But you are doing away with the fear of God, and hindering meditation before God.

Ps 1:2 Their delight is in the law of the LORD, and on his law they meditate day and night.

*Ps 19:14 Let the words of my mouth and the meditation of my heart be acceptable to you.

Ps 63:6 I think of you on my bed, and meditate on you in the watches of the night.

Ps 77:6 I commune with my heart in the night; I meditate and search my spirit.

*Ps 77:12 I will meditate on all your work, and muse on your mighty deeds.

*Ps 119:15 I will meditate on your precepts, and fix my eyes on your ways.

*Ps 119:23 Even though princes sit plotting against me, your servant will meditate on your statutes.

*Ps 119:27 Make me understand the way of your precepts, and I will meditate on your wondrous works.

*Ps 119:97 Oh, how I love your law! It is my meditation all day long.

*Ps 119:99 I have more understanding than all my teachers, for your decrees are my meditation.

*Ps 119:148 My eyes are awake before each watch of the night, that I may meditate on your promise.

Ps 143:5 I think about all your deeds, I meditate on the works of your hands.

Ps 145:5 On the glorious splendor of your majesty, and on your wondrous works, I will meditate.

*Isa 1:26 And I will restore your judges as at the first, and your counselors as at the beginning.

*Wisd of Sol 12:22 When we judge, we may meditate upon your goodness, and when we are judged, we may expect mercy.

*Sir 6:37 Reflect on the statutes of the Lord, and meditate at all times on his commandments.

Sir 14:20 Happy is the person who meditates on wisdom and reasons intelligently.

*Sir 39:7 The Lord will direct his counsel and knowledge, as he meditates on his mysteries.

Phil 4:8 Whatever is true, whatever is honorable, . . . if there is any excellence and if there is anything worthy of praise, think about these things.

*Col 3:2 Set your minds on things that are above, not on things that are on earth.

1 Tim 4:15 Put these things into practice, devote yourself to them, so that all may see your progress.

Heb 3:1–2 Consider that Jesus, the apostle and high priest of our confession, was faithful to the one who appointed him.

Heb 12:2–3 Consider him who endured such hostility against himself from sinners, so that you may not grow weary or lose heart.

PRAYER: Interactive conversation with God about what we and God are thinking and doing together.

Gen 18:23–33 Let me take it upon myself to speak to the Lord.

*Gen 20:7 He will pray for you and you shall live.

Gen 25:21 Isaac prayed to the LORD for his wife, because she was barren; and the LORD granted his prayer.

Exod 33:18 Show me your glory, I pray.

*1 Sam 1:9–20 Hannah . . . was deeply distressed and prayed to the LORD, and wept bitterly.

1 Sam 7:8 Do not cease to cry out to the LORD our God for us, and pray that he may save us.

*1 Sam 12:23 Far be it from me that I should sin against the LORD by ceasing to pray for you; and I will instruct you in the good and the right way.

*1 Kings 8:28–53 Regard your servant's prayer and his plea, O LORD my God, heeding the cry and the prayer that your servant prays to you today.

1 Kings 9:3 I have heard your prayer and your plea, which you made before me.

2 Kings 6:17 Then Elisha prayed: "O LORD, please open his eyes that he may see."

*2 Kings 19:15–19 And Hezekiah prayed before the LORD.

*1 Chron 17:16–27 Then King David went in and sat before the LORD.

*1 Chron 21:17 Let your hand, I pray, O LORD my God, be against me and against my father's house; but do not let your people be plagued!

2 Chron 6:19 Regard your servant's prayer and his plea, O LORD my God, heeding the cry and the prayer that your servant prays to you.

2 Chron 7:14 If my people who are called by my name humble themselves, pray, seek my face, and turn from their wicked ways, then I will hear from heaven.

*2 Chron 30:18–19 Hezekiah prayed for them, saying, "The good LORD pardon all."

2 Chron 33:13 He prayed to him, and God received his entreaty, heard his plea, and restored him again to Jerusalem and to his kingdom.

Ezra 10:1 Ezra prayed and made confession, weeping and throwing himself down before the house of God.

*Neh 1:4–11 When I heard these words I sat down and wept, and mourned for days, fasting and praying before the God of heaven.

*Neh 2:4–5 So I prayed to the God of heaven.

Neh 4:9 So we prayed to our God, and set a guard as a protection against them day and night.

Neh 11:17 Mattaniah . . . who was the leader to begin the thanksgiving in prayer.

*Job 42:10 And the LORD restored the fortunes of Job when he had prayed for his friends.

Ps 17:1 Hear a just cause, O LORD; attend to my cry; give ear to my prayer from lips free of deceit.

Ps 32:6 Therefore let all who are faithful offer prayer to you.

Ps 39:12 Hear my prayer, O LORD, and give ear to my cry.

Ps 42:8 By day the LORD commands his steadfast love, and at night his song is with me, a prayer to the God of my life.

Ps 65:2 O you who answer prayer! To you all flesh shall come.

Ps 69:13 But as for me, my prayer is to you, O LORD.

Ps 72:15 May prayer be made for him continually, and blessings invoked for him all day long.

Ps 102:17 He will regard the prayer of the destitute, and will not despise their prayer.

Ps 109:4 In return for my love they accuse me, even while I make prayer for them.

*Ps 123:3 Have mercy upon us, O LORD.

*Ps 141:2 Let my prayer be counted as incense before you, and the lifting up of my hands as an evening sacrifice.

Ps 143:1 Hear my prayer, O LORD; give ear to my supplications in your faithfulness; answer me in your righteousness.

Prov 15:29 The LORD is far from the wicked, but he hears the prayer of the righteous.

*Prov 28:9 When one will not listen to the law, even one's prayers are an abomination.

*Isa 26:16 O LORD, in distress they sought you, they poured out a prayer when your chastening was on them.

*Isa 36:15 Do not let Hezekiah make you rely on the LORD by saying, The LORD will surely deliver us.

Isa 37:21–22 Because you have prayed to me . . . this is the word that the LORD has spoken.

*Isa 38:3–7 Remember now, O LORD, I implore you, how I have walked before you in faithfulness with a whole heart.

*Isa 56:7 My house shall be called a house of prayer for all peoples.

*Jer 12:1 You will be in the right, O LORD, when I lay charges against you; but let me put my case to you.

*Jer 29:7 But seek the welfare of the city where I have sent you into exile, and pray to the LORD on its behalf.

*Jer 29:11–13 Then when you call upon me and come and pray to me, I will hear you.

*Lam 3:44 You have wrapped yourself with a cloud so that no prayer can pass through.

*Dan 6:10 Daniel . . . continued to . . . get down on his knees three times a day to pray to his God and praise him, just as he had done previously.

*Dan 9:3–21 I prayed to the LORD my God and made confession.

*Jon 2:1–9 Then Jonah prayed to the LORD his God from the belly of the fish.

*Jon 4:2–3 He prayed to the LORD and said, "O LORD! Is not this what I said while I was still in my own country?"

*Add to Esther 14:1–3 She prayed to the Lord God of Israel, and said: "O my Lord, you only are our king; help me, who am alone and have no helper but you."

1 Esd 8:91 Ezra was praying and making his confession, weeping and lying on the ground before the temple.

2 Esd 7:110–12 So if now, when corruption has increased and unrighteousness has multiplied, the righteous have prayed for the ungodly, why will it not be so then as well?

*2 Esd 9:43–45 Every hour and every day during those thirty years I prayed to the Most High, night and day.

*1 Macc 12:11 We therefore remember you constantly . . . in our prayers, as it is right and proper to remember brothers.

*2 Macc 1:2–6 May God do good to you.

*2 Macc 13:10–12 He ordered the people to call upon the Lord day and night.

*3 Macc 5:7–9 With tears and a voice hard to silence they all called upon the Almighty God and Ruler of all power.

*Wisd of Sol 7:7 Therefore I prayed, and understanding was given me.

*Wisd of Sol 16:28 One must rise before the sun to give you thanks, and must pray to you at the dawning of the light.

*Sir 7:10 Do not grow weary when you pray.

*Sir 21:5 The prayer of the poor goes from their lips to the ears of God, and his judgment comes speedily.

Sir 34:31 So if one fasts for his sins, and goes again and does the same things, who will listen to his prayer?

Sir 35:20–22 The one whose service is pleasing to the Lord will be accepted, and his prayer will reach to the clouds.

*Sir 38:9–14 My child, when you are ill, do not delay, but pray to the Lord, and he will heal you.

*Sir 39:5–6 He sets his heart to rise early to seek the Lord who made him, and to petition the Most High.

Sir 51:13 While I was still young, before I went on my travels, I sought wisdom openly in my prayer.

Bar 2:14 Hear, O Lord, our prayer and our supplication, and for your own sake deliver us.

Tob 3:1 Then with much grief and anguish of heart I wept, and with groaning began to pray.

*Tob 3:11–16 At that same time, with hands outstretched toward the window, she prayed.

*Tob 7:16 Take courage, my daughter; the Lord of heaven grant you joy in place of your sorrow.

Matt 5:44 Love your enemies and pray for those who persecute you.

Matt 6:5–9 Whenever you pray, do not be like the hypocrites; for they love to stand and pray . . . so that they may be seen by others.

Matt 14:23 After he had dismissed the crowds, he went up the mountain by himself to pray.

Matt 21:13 It is written, "My house shall be called a house of prayer"; but you are making it a den of robbers.

Matt 21:22 Whatever you ask for in prayer with faith, you will receive.

Matt 26:36–44 Then Jesus went with them to a place called Gethsemane; and he said to his disciples, "Sit here while I go over there and pray."

Mark 1:35 In the morning, while it was still very dark, he got up and went out to a deserted place, and there he prayed.

Mark 6:46 After saying farewell to them, he went up on the mountain to pray.

Mark 9:29 This kind can come out only through prayer.

Mark 11:17 Is it not written, "My house shall be called a house of prayer for all the nations"? But you have made it a den of robbers.

Mark 11:24 Whatever you ask for in prayer, believe that you have received it, and it will be yours.

Mark 11:25 Whenever you stand praying, forgive, if you have anything against anyone; so that your Father in heaven may also forgive you your trespasses.

Mark 14:32–39 They went to a place called Gethsemane; and he said to his disciples, "Sit here while I pray."

Luke 2:37 She never left the temple but worshiped there with fasting and prayer night and day.

Luke 3:21 When Jesus also had been baptized and was praying, the heaven was opened.

Luke 5:16 He would withdraw to deserted places and pray.

Luke 6:12 Now during those days he went out to the mountain to pray; and he spent the night in prayer to God.

*Luke 6:28 Bless those who curse you, pray for those who abuse you.

Luke 9:28–29 Jesus took with him Peter and John and James, and went up on the mountain to pray.

Luke 11:1 He was praying in a certain place, and after he had finished, one of his disciples said to him, "Lord, teach us to pray, as John taught his disciples."

Luke 11:2–13 When you pray, say: "Father, hallowed be your name."

Luke 18:1–8 Then Jesus told them a parable about their need to pray always and not to lose heart.

Luke 18:10–14 Two men went up to the temple to pray, one a Pharisee and the other a tax collector.

*Luke 22:32 I have prayed for you that your own faith may not fail.

Luke 22:40–46 In his anguish he prayed more earnestly, and his sweat became like great drops of blood falling down on the ground.

*John 11:41–42 And Jesus looked upward and said, "Father, I thank you for having heard me."

Acts 1:14 All these were constantly devoting themselves to prayer.

Acts 2:42 They devoted themselves to the apostles' teaching and fellowship, to the breaking of bread and the prayers.

Acts 6:4 We, for our part, will devote ourselves to prayer and to serving the word.

Acts 6:6 They had these men stand before the apostles, who prayed and laid their hands on them.

Acts 8:15 The two went down and prayed for them that they might receive the Holy Spirit.

Acts 9:11 Get up and go . . . look for a man of Tarsus named Saul. At this moment he is praying.

*Acts 10:2 He was a devout man who feared God with all his household; he gave alms generously to the people and prayed constantly to God.

Acts 10:4 Your prayers and your alms have ascended as a memorial before God.

Acts 11:5 I was in the city of Joppa praying, and in a trance I saw a vision.

Acts 12:5 While Peter was kept in prison, the church prayed fervently to God for him.

Acts 13:3 Then after fasting and praying they laid their hands on them and sent them off.

Acts 14:23 With prayer and fasting they entrusted them to the Lord in whom they had come to believe.

Acts 16:13 There was a place of prayer; and we sat down and spoke to the women who had gathered there.

Acts 16:25 About midnight Paul and Silas were praying and singing hymns to God.

Acts 22:17 While I was praying in the temple, I fell into a trance.

*Acts 28:8 Paul visited him and cured him by praying and putting his hands on him.

*Rom 8:26 We do not know how to pray as we ought, but that very Spirit intercedes with sighs too deep for words.

Rom 12:12 Rejoice in hope, be patient in suffering, persevere in prayer.

*1 Cor 1:4 I give thanks to my God always for you.

*1 Cor 7:5 Do not deprive one another except perhaps by agreement for a set time, to devote yourselves to prayer.

1 Cor 14:13–15 Therefore, one who speaks in a tongue should pray for the power to interpret.

2 Cor 1:11 Many will give thanks on our behalf for the blessing granted us through the prayers of many.

*Eph 1:16 I do not cease to give thanks for you as I remember you in my prayers.

*Eph 6:18 Pray in the Spirit at all times in every prayer and supplication.

Phil 1:3–4 I thank my God every time I remember you, constantly praying with joy in every one of my prayers for all of you.

Phil 4:6 In everything by prayer and supplication with thanksgiving let your requests be made known to God.

Col 4:2 Devote yourselves to prayer, keeping alert in it with thanksgiving.

*Col 4:12 He is always wrestling in his prayers on your behalf, so that you may stand mature and fully assured in everything that God wills.

1 Thess 5:17 Pray without ceasing.

1 Tim 2:8 I desire, then, that in every place the men should pray, lifting up holy hands without anger or argument.

1 Tim 4:5 It is sanctified by God's word and by prayer.

1 Tim 5:5 The real widow, left alone, has set her hope on God and continues in supplications and prayers night and day.

Heb 5:7 In the days of his flesh, Jesus offered up prayers and supplications, with loud cries and tears.

James 5:13–16 Are any among you suffering? They should pray.

James 5:17–18 Elijah . . . prayed fervently that it might not rain, and for three years and six months it did not rain on the earth.

*1 Pet 3:7 Husbands, in the same way, show consideration for your wives . . . so that nothing may hinder your prayers.

1 Pet 3:12 For the eyes of the Lord are on the righteous, and his ears are open to their prayer.

1 Pet 4:7 Be serious and discipline yourselves for the sake of your prayers.

Jude 20 But you, beloved, build yourselves up on your most holy faith; pray in the Holy Spirit.

Rev 5:8 Each [held] a harp and golden bowls full of incense, which are the prayers of the saints.

Rev 8:3–4 He was given a great quantity of incense to offer with the prayers of all the saints on the golden altar that is before the throne.

SACRIFICE: Deliberately forsaking the security of satisfying our own needs with our resources in the faith and hope that God will sustain us.

*Gen 13:8–18 Separate yourself from me. If you take the left hand, then I will go to the right.

Gen 15:9–14 Your offspring shall be aliens in a land that is not theirs, and shall be slaves there . . . but I will bring judgment.

*Lev 9:7 Draw near to the altar and sacrifice your sin offering and your burnt offering, and make atonement for yourself and for the people.

Lev 23:37 You shall celebrate . . . times of holy convocation, for presenting to the LORD offerings by fire—burnt offerings and grain offerings, sacrifices and drink offerings, each on its proper day.

Num 10:10 You shall blow the trumpets over your burnt offerings and over your sacrifices of well-being; they shall serve as a reminder on your behalf before the LORD your God.

*Deut 15:21 If it has any defect—any serious defect, such as lameness or blindness—you shall not sacrifice it to the LORD your God.

Deut 18:1–2 They may eat the sacrifices that are the LORD's portion.

*Josh 8:31 They offered on it burnt offerings to the LORD, and sacrificed offerings of well-being.

*Ruth 4:5 The day you acquire the field from the hand of Naomi, you are also acquiring Ruth the Moabite.

1 Sam 15:22 Surely, to obey is better than sacrifice, and to heed than the fat of rams.

*2 Sam 24:24 I will not offer burnt offerings to the LORD my God that cost me nothing.

*2 Chron 7:1 When Solomon had ended his prayer, fire came down from heaven and consumed the burnt offering and the sacrifices; and the glory of the LORD filled the temple.

Ps 4:5 Offer right sacrifices, and put your trust in the LORD.

*Ps 40:6–8 Sacrifice and offering you do not desire, but you have given me an open ear.

Ps 50:23 Those who bring thanksgiving as their sacrifice honor me.

Ps 51:16–19 The sacrifice acceptable to God is a broken spirit; a broken and contrite heart, O God, you will not despise.

Prov 21:3 To do righteousness and justice is more acceptable to the LORD than sacrifice.

Hos 6:6 I desire steadfast love and not sacrifice, the knowledge of God rather than burnt offerings.

*Mic 6:6–8 What does the LORD require of you but to do justice, and to love kindness, and to walk humbly with your God?

*Mal 1:8, 14 When you offer blind animals in sacrifice, is that not wrong?

Sir 34:21–24 The Most High is not pleased with the offerings of the ungodly, nor for a multitude of sacrifices does he forgive sins.

Sir 35:4 One who gives alms sacrifices a thank offering.

Sir 35:9 The sacrifice of the righteous is acceptable, and it will never be forgotten.

*Pr of Azar 16–17 Yet with a contrite heart and a humble spirit may we be accepted, as though it were with burnt offerings.

*Matt 9:13 Go and learn what this means, "I desire mercy, not sacrifice."

Mark 12:33 "To love him with all the heart, and with all the understanding, and with all the strength," and "to love one's neighbor as oneself,"—this is much more important than all whole burnt offerings and sacrifices.

*Mark 14:3–9 A woman came with an alabaster jar of very costly ointment of nard, and she broke open the jar and poured the ointment on his head.

*John 21:18 When you grow old, you will stretch out your hands, and someone else will fasten a belt around you and take you where you do not wish to go.

Rom 3:25 God put forward [Christ Jesus] as a sacrifice of atonement by his blood, effective through faith.

*Rom 12:1 Present your bodies as a living sacrifice, holy and acceptable to God, which is your spiritual worship.

*1 Cor 5:7 For our paschal lamb, Christ, has been sacrificed.

1 Cor 9:27 I punish my body and enslave it, so that after proclaiming to others I myself should not be disqualified.

2 Cor 8:1–9 They voluntarily gave according to their means, and even beyond their means.

*2 Cor 9:6–7 Each of you must give as you have made up your mind, not reluctantly or under compulsion, for God loves a cheerful giver.

Eph 5:2 Live in love, as Christ loved us and gave himself up for us, a fragrant offering and sacrifice to God.

*Phil 2:17 Even if I am being poured out as a libation over the sacrifice and the offering of your faith, I am glad and rejoice with all of you.

Heb 9:23 Thus it was necessary for the sketches of the heavenly things to be purified with these rites, but the heavenly things themselves need better sacrifices than these.

Heb 10:5 Sacrifices and offerings you have not desired, but a body you have prepared for me.

Heb 10:12 When Christ had offered for all time a single sacrifice for sins, "he sat down at the right hand of God."

Heb 13:11 Those animals whose blood is brought into the sanctuary by the high priest as a sacrifice for sin are burned outside the camp.

Heb 13:15 Through him, then, let us continually offer a sacrifice of praise to God, that is, the fruit of lips that confess his name.

*Heb 13:16 Do not neglect to do good and to share what you have, for such sacrifices are pleasing to God.

1 John 2:2 He is the atoning sacrifice for our sins, and not for ours only but also for the sins of the whole world.

SECRECY: Consciously refraining from having our good deeds and qualities generally known, which, in turn, rightly disciplines our longing for recognition.

*Ps 51:6 You desire truth in the inward being; therefore teach me wisdom in my secret heart.

*Ps 91:1 You . . . live in the shelter of the Most High, . . . abide in the shadow of the Almighty.

Isa 45:3 I will give you the treasures of darkness and riches hidden in secret places, so that you may know that it is I, the LORD, the God of Israel, who call you by your name.

*Ezek 16:15 You . . . lavished your whorings on any passer-by.

Sir 42:18 He searches out the abyss and the human heart; he understands their innermost secrets. For the Most High knows all that may be known; he sees from of old the things that are to come.

Matt 6:4 [May] your alms . . . be done in secret; and your Father who sees in secret will reward you.

Matt 6:6 Whenever you pray, go into your room and shut the door and pray to your Father who is in secret; and your Father who sees in secret will reward you.

Matt 6:18 [May] your fasting . . . be seen not by others but by your Father who is in secret; and your Father who sees in secret will reward you.

Matt 10:26 Nothing is covered up that will not be uncovered, and nothing secret that will not become known.

*Mark 4:22 There is nothing hidden, except to be disclosed; nor is anything secret, except to come to light.

Luke 8:10 To you it has been given to know the secrets of the kingdom of God.

Rom 2:16 According to my gospel, God, through Jesus Christ, will judge the secret thoughts of all.

SERVICE: Loving, thoughtful, active promotion of the good of others and the causes of God in our world, through which we experience the many little deaths of going beyond ourselves.

*Gen 18:3–7 My lord, if I find favor with you, do not pass by your servant.

Gen 24:14 Let her be the one whom you have appointed for your servant Isaac.

Gen 29:20 So Jacob served seven years for Rachel, and they seemed to him but a few days because of the love he had for her.

Gen 32:10 I am not worthy of the least of all the steadfast love and all the faithfulness that you have shown to your servant.

*Exod 35:21, 29 And they came, everyone whose heart was stirred, and everyone whose spirit was willing, and brought the LORD's offering to be used for the tent of meeting.

*Num 4:24, 27 This is the service of the clans of the Gershonites, in serving and bearing burdens.

Num 8:11 Aaron shall present the Levites before the LORD as an elevation offering from the Israelites, that they may do the service of the LORD.

Num 12:7–8 Not so with my servant Moses; he is entrusted with all my house.

*Num 14:24 My servant Caleb, because he has a different spirit and has followed me wholeheartedly, I will bring into the land.

*Deut 3:24 O Lord GOD, you have only begun to show your servant your greatness and your might.

Josh 22:26–27 Let us now build an altar . . . to be a witness between us and you . . . that we do perform the service of the LORD in his presence.

*Josh 24:15 Choose this day whom you will serve, . . . but as for me and my household, we will serve the LORD.

*Ruth 2:11–16 May the LORD reward you for your deeds, and may you have a full reward from the LORD, the God of Israel.

1 Sam 1:11 O LORD of hosts, if only you will look on the misery of your servant, and remember me, and not forget your servant, but will give to your servant a male child.

1 Sam 2:11–26 Samuel was ministering before the LORD.

*1 Sam 3:9 Go, lie down; and if he calls you, you shall say, "Speak, LORD, for your servant is listening."

1 Sam 12:24 Only fear the LORD, and serve him faithfully with all your heart.

*1 Sam 16:16–22 And David came to Saul, and entered his service.

1 Sam 18:5 David went out and was successful wherever Saul sent him; as a result, Saul set him over the army.

1 Sam 22:14 Who among all your servants is so faithful as David? He is the king's son-in-law, and is quick to do your bidding, and is honored in your house.

*1 Sam 25:41 She rose and bowed down, with her face to the ground, and said, "Your servant is a slave to wash the feet of the servants of my lord."

2 Sam 7:8 Thus you shall say to my servant David: Thus says the LORD of hosts: I took you from the pasture, from following the sheep to be prince over my people Israel.

*2 Sam 7:21 Because of your promise, and according to your own heart, you have wrought all this greatness, so that your servant may know it.

*2 Sam 11:11 The ark and Israel and Judah remain in booths; . . . shall I then go to my house, to eat and to drink, and to lie with my wife? . . . I will not do such a thing.

*2 Sam 16:1 When David had passed a little beyond the summit, Ziba the servant of Mephibosheth met him.

1 Kings 3:9 Give your servant therefore an understanding mind to govern your people, able to discern between good and evil.

*Neh 5:15–16 The former governors who were before me laid heavy burdens on the people. . . . Even their servants lorded it over the people. But I did not do so, because of the fear of God.

*Ps 8:6–8 You have given them dominion over the works of your hands.

Ps 35:27 Great is the LORD, who delights in the welfare of his servant.

*Ps 113:1 Praise, O servants of the LORD.

Ps 134:1 Come, bless the LORD, all you servants of the LORD, who stand by night in the house of the LORD!

*Prov 3:27–28 Do not withhold good from those to whom it is due.

*Prov 31:15 She rises while it is still night and provides food for her household and tasks for her servant-girls.

*Isa 49:6 It is too light a thing that you should be my servant to raise up the tribes of Jacob and to restore the survivors of Israel; I will give you as a light to the nations.

Isa 58:3 You serve your own interest on your fast day, and oppress all your workers.

*Jer 29:7 Seek the welfare of the city where I have sent you into exile, and pray to the LORD on its behalf.

Jer 45:5 I am going to bring disaster upon all flesh, says the LORD; but I will give you your life as a prize of war in every place to which you may go.

*Dan 3:17–18 If our God whom we serve is able to deliver us from the furnace of blazing fire and out of your hand, O king, let him deliver us.

Dan 6:20 O Daniel, servant of the living God, has your God whom you faithfully serve been able to deliver you from the lions?

*Amos 2:6–8 They sell the righteous for silver, and the needy for a pair of sandals—they who trample the head of the poor into the dust.

Zech 3:8 I am going to bring my servant the Branch.

*Mal 3:17–18 Then once more you shall see the difference between the righteous and the wicked, between one who serves God and one who does not serve him.

*2 Macc 4:33 When Onias became fully aware of these acts, he publicly exposed them.

Wisd of Sol 10:9 Wisdom rescued from troubles those who served her.

Sir 35:20 The one whose service is pleasing to the Lord will be accepted, and his prayer will reach to the clouds.

Tob 4:14 Do not keep over until the next day the wages of those who work for you, but pay them at once. If you serve God you will receive payment.

Matt 6:24 No one can serve two masters. . . .You cannot serve God and wealth.

Matt 12:18 Here is my servant, whom I have chosen, my beloved, with whom my soul is well pleased.

Matt 20:26 Whoever wishes to be great among you must be your servant.

*Matt 20:28 The Son of Man came not to be served but to serve, and to give his life a ransom for many."

Matt 23:11 The greatest among you will be your servant.

*Mark 9:35 Whoever wants to be first must be last of all and servant of all.

Mark 10:45 The Son of Man came not to be served but to serve, and to give his life a ransom for many.

Luke 1:48 He has looked with favor on the lowliness of his servant.

Luke 12:37 Blessed are those slaves whom the master finds alert when he comes; . . . he will come and serve them.

Luke 16:13 No slave can serve two masters. . . . You cannot serve God and wealth.

*Luke 17:7–10 Do you thank the slave for doing what was commanded?

Luke 22:26–27 I am among you as one who serves.

*John 1:48 I saw you under the fig tree before Philip called you.

*John 9:3 Neither this man nor his parents sinned; he was born blind so that God's works might be revealed in him.

John 12:26 Whoever serves me must follow me, and where I am, there will my servant be also. Whoever serves me, the Father will honor.

*John 13:1–17 If I, your Lord and Teacher, have washed your feet, you also ought to wash one another's feet.

John 15:15, 20 I do not call you servants any longer, because the servant does not know what the master is doing; but I have called you friends.

*Acts 6:1–6 Select from among yourselves seven men of good standing, full of the Spirit and of wisdom, whom we may appoint to this task.

*Acts 20:19 [Serve] the Lord with all humility and with tears.

Rom 12:11 Do not lag in zeal, be ardent in spirit, serve the Lord.

Rom 13:6 For the same reason you also pay taxes, for the authorities are God's servants.

Rom 15:16 [God gave me the grace] to be a minister of Christ Jesus to the Gentiles in the priestly service of the gospel of God.

*1 Cor 16:16 I urge you to put yourselves at the service of such people, and of everyone who works and toils with them.

*2 Cor 6:4–7 As servants of God we have commended ourselves in every way: through great endurance, in afflictions, hardships, calamities.

*Eph 3:7 Of this gospel I have become a servant according to the gift of God's grace that was given me by the working of his power.

Eph 6:7 Render service with enthusiasm, as to the Lord and not to men and women.

Phil 2:30 He came close to death for the work of Christ, risking his life to make up for those services that you could not give me.

Col 1:23 I, Paul, became a servant of this gospel.

Col 3:24 You know that from the Lord you will receive the inheritance as your reward; you serve the Lord Christ.

*2 Thess 2:17 Comfort your hearts and strengthen them in every good work and word.

1 Tim 3:13 Those who serve well as deacons gain a good standing for themselves and great boldness in the faith that is in Christ Jesus.

1 Tim 6:2 Those who have believing masters must not be disrespectful to them on the ground that they are members of the church; rather they must serve them all the more.

*2 Tim 2:4 No one serving in the army gets entangled in everyday affairs; the soldier's aim is to please the enlisting officer.

Heb 1:14 Are not all angels spirits in the divine service, sent to serve for the sake of those who are to inherit salvation?

*Heb 6:10 God . . . will not overlook your work and the love that you showed for his sake in serving the saints.

1 Pet 2:16 As servants of God, live as free people, yet do not use your freedom as a pretext for evil.

1 Pet 4:10–11 Like good stewards of the manifold grace of God, serve one another with whatever gift each of you has received.

Rev 1:6 [Jesus Christ] made us to be a kingdom, priests serving his God and Father.

*Rev 5:10 You have made them to be a kingdom and priests serving our God, and they will reign on earth.

Rev 19:10 I am a fellow servant with you and your comrades who hold the testimony of Jesus.

SILENCE: Closing off our souls from "sounds," whether noise, music, or words, so that we may better still the inner chatter and clatter of our noisy hearts and be increasingly attentive to God.

Gen 24:21 The man gazed at her in silence to learn whether or not the LORD had made his journey successful.

1 Sam 1:13 Hannah was praying silently; only her lips moved, but her voice was not heard.

*1 Kings 19:12 After the earthquake [there was] a fire, but the LORD was not in the fire; and after the fire a sound of sheer silence.

*Job 6:24 Teach me, and I will be silent; make me understand how I have gone wrong.

*Job 13:5 If you would only keep silent, that would be your wisdom!

Ps 4:4 When you are disturbed, do not sin; ponder it on your beds, and be silent.

Ps 39:9 I am silent; I do not open my mouth, for it is you who have done it.

*Ps 62:1, 5 For God alone my soul waits in silence; from him comes my salvation.

*Ps 131:2 But I have calmed and quieted my soul, like a weaned child with its mother.

*Prov 11:12 Whoever belittles another lacks sense, but an intelligent person remains silent.

Isa 30:15 In returning and rest you shall be saved; in quietness and in trust shall be your strength.

*Isa 32:17 The effect of righteousness will be peace, and the result of righteousness, quietness and trust forever.

*Isa 53:7 Like a lamb that is led to the slaughter, and like a sheep that before its shearers is silent, so he did not open his mouth.

Lam 3:26 It is good that one should wait quietly for the salvation of the LORD.

*Hab 2:20 The LORD is in his holy temple; let all the earth keep silence before him!

*Zeph 1:7 Be silent before the Lord GOD! For the day of the LORD is at hand.

*Sir 20:1, 6 There is a rebuke that is untimely, and there is the person who is wise enough to keep silent.

Rom 3:19 We know that whatever the law says, it speaks to those who are under the law, so that every mouth may be silenced.

*James 1:19 Let everyone be quick to listen, slow to speak, slow to anger.

James 3:1–12 No one can tame the tongue— a restless evil, full of deadly poison.

*Rev 8:1 When the Lamb opened the seventh seal, there was silence in heaven for about half an hour.

SIMPLICITY/FRUGALITY: The inward reality of single-hearted focus upon God and his kingdom, which results in an outward lifestyle of modesty, openness, and unpretentiousness and which disciplines our hunger for status, glamour, and luxury.

*Deut 17:16–17 He must not acquire many horses for himself. . . . He must not acquire many wives; . . . also silver and gold he must not acquire in great quantity for himself.

*Eccl 5:10 The lover of money will not be satisfied with money; nor the lover of wealth, with gain.

*Dan 5:17 Let your gifts be for yourself, or give your rewards to someone else!

*Hag 1:2–11 You have sown much, and harvested little; you eat, but you never have enough; you drink, but you never have your fill.

*3 Macc 6:36 They instituted the observance of the aforesaid days as a festival, not for drinking and gluttony, but because of the deliverance that had come to them through God.

Matt 5:8 Blessed are the pure in heart, for they will see God.

Matt 6:22–24 You cannot serve God and wealth.

2 Cor 11:3 I am afraid that . . . your thoughts will be led astray from a sincere and pure devotion to Christ.

Phil 3:13 I do not consider that I have made it my own.

*Phil 4:11–13 I know what it is to have little, and I know what it is to have plenty. . . . I have learned the secret of being well-fed and of going hungry, of having plenty and of being in need.

Col 2:20–23 If with Christ you died to the elemental spirits of the universe, why do you live as if you still belonged to the world?

Col 3:1–2 Set your minds on things that are above, not on things that are on earth.

*2 Tim 2:4 No one serving in the army gets entangled in everyday affairs; the soldier's aim is to please the enlisting officer.

Heb 12:1–3 Let us also lay aside every weight and the sin that clings so closely, and let us run with perseverance the race that is set before us.

James 1:8 The doubter, being double-minded and unstable in every way, must not expect to receive anything from the Lord.

James 4:8 Cleanse your hands, you sinners, and purify your hearts, you double-minded.

*Rev 3:17 You say, "I am rich, I have prospered, and I need nothing." You do not realize that you are wretched, pitiable, poor, blind, and naked.

SOLITUDE: The creation of an open, empty space in our lives by purposefully abstaining from interaction with other human beings, so that, freed from competing loyalties, we can be found by God.

*Gen 32:24 Jacob was left alone; and a man wrestled with him until daybreak.

Num 23:9 Here is a people living alone, and not reckoning itself among the nations!

*1 Kings 17:4 I have commanded the ravens to feed you there.

Ps 62:5 For God alone my soul waits in silence, for my hope is from him.

*Isa 35:1 The wilderness and the dry land shall be glad, the desert shall rejoice and blossom.

*Jer 15:16–18 Under the weight of your hand I sat alone.

Jth 12:6–9 She went out each night to the valley of Bethulia, and bathed at the spring in the camp.

Matt 14:23 After he had dismissed the crowds, he went up the mountain by himself to pray. When evening came, he was there alone.

Mark 1:35 In the morning, while it was still very dark, he got up and went out to a deserted place, and there he prayed.

Mark 6:31 Come away to a deserted place all by yourselves and rest a while.

Mark 6:47 When evening came, the boat was out on the sea, and he was alone on the land.

Mark 9:2 Jesus took with him Peter and James and John, and led them up a high mountain apart, by themselves.

*Luke 4:42 At daybreak he departed and went into a deserted place.

Luke 5:16 He would withdraw to deserted places and pray.

Luke 6:12 He went out to the mountain to pray; and he spent the night in prayer to God.

Luke 9:18 Jesus was praying alone, with only the disciples near him.

*John 8:29 The one who sent me is with me; he has not left me alone.

*John 16:32 The hour is coming, indeed it has come, when . . . you will leave me alone. Yet I am not alone because the Father is with me.

*Gal 1:17–22 I went away at once into Arabia.

1 Tim 5:5 The real widow, left alone, has set her hope on God.

STUDY: The intentional process of engaging the mind with the written and spoken Word of God and the world God has created in such a way that the mind takes on an order conforming to the order upon which it concentrates.

Deut 17:19–20 It shall remain with him and he shall read in it all the days of his life, so that he may learn to fear the LORD his God.

*Deut 31:10–13 You shall read this law before all Israel in their hearing . . . so that they may hear and learn to fear the LORD your God.

*Josh 1:8 This book of the law shall not depart out of your mouth; you shall meditate on it day and night.

*Ezra 7:10 Ezra had set his heart to study the law of the LORD, and to do it, and to teach the statutes and ordinances in Israel.

*Ps 1:1–6 Their delight is in the law of the LORD, and on his law they meditate day and night.

Ps 19:1–14 The law of the LORD is perfect, reviving the soul; the decrees of the LORD are sure, making wise the simple.

*Ps 101:2 I will study the way that is blameless. When shall I attain it?

Ps 111:2 Great are the works of the LORD, studied by all who delight in them.

*Ps 119:1–176 I will meditate on your precepts, and fix my eyes on your ways.

*Eccl 12:9 Besides being wise, the Teacher also taught the people knowledge, weighing and studying and arranging many proverbs.

*Jer 51:50 Remember the LORD in a distant land, and let Jerusalem come into your mind.

*Ezek 3:1–3 Eat this scroll and go, speak to the house of Israel.

*1 Esd 9:40–41, 48 Ezra the chief priest brought the law, for all the multitude, men and women, and all the priests to hear the law.

*1 Macc 3:48 They opened the book of the law to inquire into those matters.

2 Macc 15:9 Encouraging them from the law and the prophets, . . . he made them the more eager.

3 Macc 2:2–20 Lord, Lord, king of the heavens, and sovereign of all creation, . . . give attention to us.

4 Macc 1:10 On this anniversary it is fitting for me to praise for their virtues those who . . . died for the sake of nobility and goodness.

Sir 38:34 How different the one who devotes himself to the study of the law of the Most High!

Bar 4:1 She is the book of the commandments of God. . . . All who hold her fast will live, and those who forsake her will die.

Matt 23:1–39 Do whatever they teach you and follow it; but do not do as they do, for they do not practice what they teach.

John 6:35–59 I am the bread of life.

Rom 2:21 You then, that teach others, will you not teach yourself?

2 Cor 3:18 All of us, . . . seeing the glory of the Lord, . . . are being transformed into the same image.

2 Cor 4:18 We look not at what can be seen but at what cannot be seen; for what can be seen is temporary, but what cannot be seen is eternal.

Phil 4:8–9 Whatever is true, whatever is honorable . . . if there is any excellence and if there is anything worthy of praise, think about these things.

*1 Thess 4:11 Aspire to live quietly, to mind your own affairs, and to work with your hands, as we directed you.

2 Tim 2:15 Present yourself to God as one approved by him, a worker who has no need to be ashamed, rightly explaining the word of truth.

*Heb 3:1–2 Consider that Jesus, the apostle and high priest of our confession, was faithful to the one who appointed him.

Heb 12:3 Consider him who endured such hostility against himself from sinners, so that you may not grow weary or lose heart.

*2 Pet 2:1 False prophets also arose among the people, just as there will be false teachers among you.

SUBMISSION: Subordination to the guidance of God; within the Christian fellowship, a constant mutual subordination out of reverence for Christ, which opens the way for particular subordination to those who are qualified to direct our efforts toward Christlikeness and who then add the weight of their wise authority on the side of our willing spirit to help us do the things we would like to do and refrain from doing the things we don't want to do.

*Gen 13:8–18 "Rise up, walk through the length and the breadth of the land, for I will give it to you." So Abram moved his tent, and came and settled.

Gen 15:9–14 "Bring me a heifer three years old, a female goat three years old, a ram. . . ." He brought him all these.

Gen 16:9 Return to your mistress, and submit to her.

*2 Kings 18:31–32 Do not listen to Hezekiah. . . . "Make your peace with me and come out to me."

*Esther 1:12 Queen Vashti refused to come at the king's command.

*Ps 81:11 My people did not listen to my voice; Israel would not submit to me.

*Prov 1:8–9 Hear, my child, your father's instruction.

*Prov 6:20–21 My child, keep your father's commandment, and do not forsake your mother's teaching.

*Eccl 8:8 No one has power over the wind to restrain the wind, or power over the day of death.

*Isa 28:15–18 I am laying in Zion a . . . sure foundation: "One who trusts will not panic."

*4 Macc 5:26 He has permitted us to eat what will be most suitable for our lives.

Matt 6:10 Your kingdom come. Your will be done, on earth as it is in heaven.

Matt 26:39 My Father, if it is possible, let this cup pass from me: yet not what I want but what you want.

*Luke 1:38 Here am I, the servant of the Lord; let it be with me according to your word.

Luke 1:46–56 My soul magnifies the Lord, and my spirit rejoices in God my Savior, for he has looked with favor on the lowliness of his servant.

Rom 8:7 The mind that is set on the flesh is hostile to God; it does not submit to God's law.

*Gal 2:5 We did not submit to them even for a moment, so that the truth of the gospel might always remain with you.

Eph 5:21–6:9 Be subject to one another out of reverence for Christ.

Col 3:18–24 Wives, be subject to your husbands. . . . Husbands, love your wives. . . . Children obey your parents.

*1 Tim 3:4 He must manage his own household well, keeping his children submissive and respectful in every way.

Titus 2:9 Tell slaves to be submissive to their masters and to give satisfaction in every respect.

Heb 5:7 Jesus offered up prayers and supplications . . . and he was heard because of his reverent submission.

Heb 13:17 Obey your leaders and submit to them, for they are keeping watch over your souls and will give an account.

*James 4:7 Submit yourselves therefore to God. Resist the devil, and he will flee from you.

WORSHIP: Expressing in words, music, rituals, and silent adoration the greatness, beauty, and goodness of God, by means of which we enter the supranatural reality of the *shekinah*, or glory, of God.

*Gen 22:5 We will worship, and then we will come back to you.

Gen 24:48 Then I bowed my head and worshiped the Lord, and blessed the Lord.

Exod 8:1; 9:13 Let my people go, so that they may worship me.

Exod 20:5 You shall not bow down to them or worship them; for I the Lord your God am a jealous God.

*Exod 23:25 You shall worship the Lord your God, and I will bless your bread and your water; and I will take sickness away from among you.

*Deut 12:4 You shall not worship the Lord your God in such ways.

*Josh 5:14 Joshua fell on his face to the earth and worshiped.

*Judg 7:15 When Gideon heard the telling of the dream and its interpretation, he worshiped.

*1 Kings 1:47 The king bowed in worship on the bed.

*1 Kings 6:1 He began to build the house of the Lord.

*1 Kings 12:32 He offered sacrifices on the altar . . . . sacrificing to the calves that he had made.

*2 Kings 5:18–19 When I do bow down in the house of Rimmon, may the Lord pardon your servant on this one count.

*2 Kings 17:24–41 So these nations worshiped the Lord, but also served their carved images.

*1 Chron 6:31–32 They ministered with song.

2 Chron 7:3 All the people of Israel . . . bowed down on the pavement with their faces to the ground, and worshiped and gave thanks to the Lord.

*Ezra 3:10–13 The priests in their vestments were stationed to praise the Lord with trumpets.

*Neh 8:6 All the people . . . bowed their heads and worshiped the Lord with their faces to the ground.

Neh 9:6 You are the Lord, you alone, . . . and the host of heaven worships you.

*Job 1:20 Then Job arose, tore his robe, shaved his head, and fell on the ground and worshiped.

*Job 19:25 For I know that my Redeemer lives, and that at the last he will stand upon the earth.

*Ps 96:9 Worship the Lord in holy splendor; tremble before him, all the earth.

Ps 99:5 Extol the Lord our God; worship at his footstool. Holy is he!

*Isa 19:23 On that day . . . the Egyptians will worship with the Assyrians.

*Isa 29:13 These people draw near with their mouths and honor me with their lips, while their hearts are far from me, and their worship of me is a human commandment learned by rote.

*Isa 66:23 All flesh shall come to worship before me, says the Lord.

*Ezek 1:28 This was the appearance of the likeness of the glory of the Lord. When I saw it, I fell on my face.

*Dan 3:12 Certain Jews . . . pay no heed to you, O King. They do not serve your gods and they do not worship the golden statue that you have set up.

*2 Esd 1:37 I call to witness the gratitude of the people that is to come, whose children rejoice with gladness.

Sir 35:10 Be generous when you worship the Lord, and do not stint the first fruits of your hands.

Sir 50:17 Then all the people together quickly fell to the ground on their faces to worship their Lord, the Almighty, God Most High.

Sir 50:21 They bowed down in worship a second time, to receive the blessing from the Most High.

*Ltr of Jer 6 It is you, O Lord, whom we must worship.

*Bel and Dragon 4 The king revered it and went every day to worship it. But Daniel worshiped his own God.

*Matt 4:10 Worship the Lord your God, and serve only him.

Matt 14:33 Those in the boat worshiped him, saying, "Truly you are the Son of God."

Matt 28:17 When they saw him, they worshiped him; but some doubted.

*Mark 7:6–7 In vain do they worship me, teaching human precepts as doctrines.

Luke 1:46–55 My soul magnifies the Lord, and my spirit rejoices in God my Savior.

Luke 2:37 She never left the temple but worshiped there with fasting and prayer night and day.

Luke 24:52 And they worshiped him, and returned to Jerusalem with great joy.

John 4:20–24 The hour is coming . . . when the true worshipers will worship the Father in spirit and truth, for the Father seeks such as these to worship him.

John 9:31 God does not listen to sinners, but he does listen to one who worships him and obeys his will.

*Acts 13:1–3 While they were worshiping the Lord and fasting, the Holy Spirit said, "Set apart for me Barnabas and Saul."

Acts 16:14 A certain woman named Lydia, a worshiper of God, was listening to us.

Acts 17:23 I found . . . an altar with the inscription, "To an unknown god." What therefore you worship as unknown, this I proclaim to you.

Acts 27:23 Last night there stood by me an angel of the God to whom I belong and whom I worship.

Rom 12:1 Present your bodies as a living sacrifice, holy and acceptable to God, which is your spiritual worship.

Phil 3:3 It is we who are the circumcision, who worship in the Spirit of God and boast in Christ Jesus and have no confidence in the flesh.

*Heb 1:6 Let all God's angels worship him.

Heb 9:14 How much more will the blood of Christ . . . purify our conscience from dead works to worship the living God!

Heb 12:28 Since we are receiving a kingdom that cannot be shaken, let us give thanks, by which we offer to God an acceptable worship with reverence and awe.

Rev 4:10 The twenty-four elders fall before the one who is seated on the throne and worship the one who lives forever and ever.

Rev 7:11 All the angels . . . fell on their faces before the throne and worshiped God.

Rev 7:15 For this reason they are before the throne of God, and worship him day and night within his temple.

Rev 22:9 I am a fellow servant with you and your comrades the prophets, and with those who keep the words of this book. Worship God!

PROFILES INDEX

SPIRITUAL FORMATION BIBLIOGRAPHY

Augustine. *The Confessions of St. Augustine.* Orleans, MA: Paraclete, 1986.

Bonhoeffer, Dietrich. *The Cost of Discipleship.* New York: Simon & Schuster, Touchstone, 1995.

Brother Lawrence. *The Practice of the Presence of God.* Translated by John J. Delaney. New York: Doubleday, 1977.

Bunyan, John. *Pilgrim's Progress.* Chicago: Moody, 1964.

Catherine of Siena. *The Dialogue.* Edited by Richard J. Payne. Classics of Western Spirituality. New York: Paulist, 1980.

Caussade, Jean-Pierre de. *The Sacrament of the Present Moment.* San Francisco: HarperSanFrancisco, 1982.

Devotional Classics. Edited by Richard J. Foster and James Bryan Smith. Rev. ed. San Francisco: HarperSanFrancisco, 2005.

Foster, Richard J. *Celebration of Discipline.* Rev. ed. San Francisco: HarperSanFrancisco, 1988.

———. *Freedom of Simplicity.* Rev. ed. San Francisco: HarperSanFrancisco, 2005.

———. *Prayer: Finding the Heart's True Home.* San Francisco: HarperSanFrancisco, 1992.

———. *Streams of Living Water.* San Francisco: HarperSanFrancisco, 1998.

Fox, George. *The Journal of George Fox.* Richmond, IN: Friends United Press, 1976.

Francis of Assisi. *Praying with St. Francis.* Translated by Regis J. Armstrong and Ignatius C. Brady. Grand Rapids, MI: Eerdmans, 1996.

Garlett, Mari Watson, and Valerie E. Hess. *Habits of a Child's Heart.* Colorado Springs, CO: NavPress, 2004. (For families with children.)

Gregory of Nyssa. *The Life of Moses.* Translated by Abraham J. Malherbe and Everett Ferguson. New York: Paulist, 1978.

Guyon, Madame Jeanne. *Experiencing the Depths of Jesus Christ.* Jacksonville, FL: Christian Books, Seedsowers, 1981.

Hammerskjöld, Dag. *Markings.* New York: Knopf, 1964.

John of the Cross. *Dark Night of the Soul.* New York: Doubleday, Image, 1959.

Jones, E. Stanley. *The Christ of Every Road.* New York: Abingdon, 1930.

Julian of Norwich. *Revelations of Divine Love.* New York: Penguin, 1999.

Kelley, Thomas. *A Testament of Devotion.* San Francisco: HarperSanFrancisco, 1996.

Laubach, Frank. *Letters by a Modern Mystic.* Heritage Collection. Syracuse, NY: New Readers Press, 1979.

Law, William. *A Serious Call to a Devout and Holy Life.* New York: Random House, Vintage, 2002.

Lewis, C. S. *Mere Christianity.* San Francisco: HarperSanFrancisco, 2001.

Loyola, Ignatius. *The Spiritual Exercises of St. Ignatius.* Edited by John F. Thornton. Translated by Louis J. Puhl. New York: Random House, Vintage, 2000.

Nee, Watchman. *The Normal Christian Life.* Carol Stream, IL: Tyndale, 1977.

Peterson, Eugene. *A Long Obedience in the Same Direction.* Westmont, IL: InterVarsity, 2000.

——. *Subversive Spirituality.* Grand Rapids, MI: Eerdmans, 1997.

Sanford, Agnes. *The Healing Light.* Westminster, MD: Ballantine, 1983.

Santa Maria, Brother Ugolino di Monte. *The Little Flowers of St. Francis.* Translated by Raphael Brown. New York: Doubleday, Image, 1971.

Schaeffer, Francis. *True Spirituality.* Carol Stream, IL: Tyndale, 1979.

Singh, Sadhu Sundar. *With and without Christ.* New York: Harper & Brothers, 1929; n.c.: Rhwymbooks, 2002.

Smith, Hannah Whitall. *The Christian's Secret of a Happy Life.* New Kensington, PA: Whitaker House, 1983.

Smith, James Bryan, with Lynda L. Graybeal. *A Spiritual Formation Workbook.* Rev. ed. San Francisco: HarperSanFrancisco, 1999. (For mature teenagers and adults.)

Spiritual Classics. Edited by Richard J. Foster and Emilie Griffin. San Francisco: HarperSanFrancisco, 1999.

Taylor, Jeremy. *The Rule and Exercises of Holy Living and the Rule and Exercises of Holy Dying.* Treasures from the Spiritual Classics. Wilton, CT: Morehouse Barlow, 1982.

Teresa of Avila. *The Interior Castle.* New York: Doubleday, Image, 1972.

Thomas à Kempis. *The Imitation of Christ.* Translated by William C. Creasy. Notre Dame, IN: Ave Maria, 1989.

Tozer, A. W. *The Pursuit of God.* Harrisburg, PA: Christian Publications, 1982.

Wallis, Arthur. *God's Chosen Fast.* Fort Washington, PA: Christian Literature Crusade, 1971.

Way to Live. Edited by Dorothy C. Bass and Don C. Richter. Nashville, TN: Upper Room, 2002. (For teenagers.)

Willard, Dallas. *The Divine Conspiracy.* San Francisco: HarperSanFrancisco, 1998.

——. *Hearing God.* Westmont, IL: InterVarsity, 1999.

——. *Renovation of the Heart.* Colorado Springs, CO: NavPress, 2000.

——. *The Spirit of the Disciplines.* San Francisco: HarperSanFrancisco, 1988.

Woolman, John. *The Journal and Major Essays of John Woolman.* Richmond, IN: Friends United Press, 1989.

Suggested Ways to Use This Bible for Spiritual Formation

SUGGESTED WAYS TO USE THIS BIBLE
FOR SPIRITUAL FORMATION

In the essay titled "The With-God Life," the general editors write that the two most common objectives people have for studying the Bible are "for information or knowledge alone" and "to find some formula that will solve the pressing need of the moment" (see pp. xix–xxx). In the *Renovaré Spiritual Formation Bible,* the editors and contributors have worked exceedingly hard to go beyond these two notions to write essays, notes, and exercises that will help you integrate the teachings of the Bible into your very heart and soul. To help you see how many ways this can be accomplished, below are several suggestions for using this Bible.

Individuals will find the suggestions listed under the headings of one day, one week, and one month helpful in their private devotional lives. The longer formats—three months and a year or more—could be used in Sunday school or church-school classes and in small groups or by individuals. Feel free to use the suggestions as they are written or to modify them as needs arise or change. Since the ideas are suggestive, not exhaustive, we encourage you to think of multiple other ways to use this Bible in both individual and group settings. We hope our suggestions will help you walk in the ways of Christ and increase your desire to become more like him.

Suggestions for One Day

- Pick a favorite chapter, for example, 1 Corinthians 13, Psalm 23, or Hebrews 11, and read it several times during the day. Then reflect on it before going to bed and answer the question: How did reading this passage several times in one day affect my spirit? Or expand this exercise to a week or more by reading other favorite passages of Scripture at various intervals.

- Read "The With-God Life" (pp. xxv–xxxvi) essay at least twice. After you have read it the second time, explain it to another person.

- Take a psalm (any psalm; Psalms is the prayer book of the Church) and read through it slowly and prayerfully. Now, go back for a second reading, and as you read highlight phrases or verses that especially speak to your present condition. Return for a third reading, this time reading only the

2323

highlighted passages. As you read, pray each phrase or verse, applying the words of the passage to your particular situation. You might want to write out some of these prayers in a journal. Perhaps you will want to kneel with the highlighted passages laid out before you on the floor. As you are praying through the passages, be attentive to the Spirit's touch and loving care upon you.

Suggestions for One Week

- Choose a book that contains five chapters (Micah, Baruch, 1 Thessalonians, James, 1 Peter, 1 John). On the first day, read the introduction to the book. On the second through sixth days, read one chapter and its notes per day, and try to do the exercises. Then on the seventh day reread everything, mentally noting as you go through the passages the difference reading them several times in one week has made in your spiritual life.

- Read "The With-God Life," "A Panoramic View of God's Purpose in History," and "A Brief Overview of the With-God Life" essays (pp. xxv–xxxvi, pp. xxxvii–xxxix, xli–xlv). Then, using "A Brief Overview of the With-God Life" chart as a guide (pp. xlvi–xlvii), read the essays that introduce each of the fifteen sections. When you are through reading, ask yourself these questions: What is unique about these essays? What themes do they introduce? How does the emphasis on these themes affect my approach to the Bible? How will emphasizing these themes as I study the Bible help me grow spiritually?

- Trace over "A Panoramic View of God's Purpose in History" (p. xxxix) once a day for the next six days. On the seventh day try to draw it from memory. If you find you have difficulty, do this exercise a second week.

Suggestions for One Month

- Without reading the notes or referring to the Spiritual Disciplines Index, read a book of the Bible and look for the Spiritual Disciplines that are being practiced in it. As you are reading, note the verses where each discipline is found and what person or group did it; try to discern why they did it and what effect it had on their spiritual lives. Then read the book a second time, including the notes. Now read the book and all of the extra material a third time, but this time do the exercises. If you have noted a discipline that the editors did not provide an exercise for, make up an exercise for that discipline and do it.

- Choose a passage for which an exercise is provided, for example, Genesis 18:3–7 (service), Psalm 123:3 (prayer), Mark 14:3–9 (sacrifice), or Hebrews 10:23 (confession). Read that passage every day for a whole month and do the exercise associated with it. As you are reading the verse or verses, try to put yourself in the scene as a participant or onlooker. If the exercise accompanying the passage becomes stale, think of another and do it.

Suggestions for Three Months

- Access the Web site www.renovare.org and use one of the *Bible Studies for Churches and Small Groups* posted there to guide the study and reflection you do with your church or small group.

- Read a small book of the Bible, doing the exercises, and then memorize it. At the end of the three months, try to write out the entire book from memory or say it in its entirety to a friend or a small group.

Suggestions for a Year or More

- Look up and study the scriptures listed in the Spiritual Disciplines Index. You might want to concentrate on one discipline per month. You could study the scriptures that mention each discipline in the order the books are arranged in the Bible. Or you might read the scriptures in the order given in the chart "A Brief Overview of the With-God Life" (pp. xlvi–xlvii), giving special attention to how each discipline develops as God works to form the People of God. Another suggestion is to concentrate first on a discipline you feel you are strong in and then work on a discipline you feel you are weak in. *Celebrating the Disciplines* (Richard J. Foster with Katherine Helmers) provides supplementary material based on the disciplines and space to keep a journal you might want to use to help you stay on track.

- Read all of the Scriptures cited at the top of "The With-God Life" essay for each section, study them with the aid of commentaries and the notes provided in this Bible, and do at least one exercise per week. We suggest starting with "The People of God in Individual Communion" and working your way through the sections as they are presented.

- Harper San Francisco has published a RENOVARÉ Resource for Spiritual Renewal titled *Spiritual Classics,* which focuses on the disciplines listed in *Celebration of Discipline* from the perspective of classical devotional writers. Read each essay and then read the scripture in this Bible, taking special care to read the notes. If there is an exercise accompanying the notes, do it. If there is no exercise in the Bible, choose one or more of the exercises and reflection questions from *Spiritual Classics.*

- Allow the Christian church year to inform your biblical study and devotional exercises. For example, the church year starts with Advent four weeks prior to Christmas. During this time read and study scriptures that anticipate the coming of the Messiah and do the exercises with those passages. From Christmas Day through January 5, read the accounts of Jesus' birth in the Gospels of Matthew and Luke and do an exercise. Then move on to Epiphany. The Internet has several resources about the church year that will help you decide which scriptures to read. (To find those resources, type "Christian church year" into a search engine like Google and look at the various Web sites.) Another good resource is the *Book of Common Prayer,* containing the "Revised Common Lectionary," which provides suggested Scripture readings for each week of the year and is used by several denominations.

• Concentrate on the life story of one person in the Bible. To help launch your study, use the profiles about biblical characters scattered throughout this Bible (see index on p. 2319). You might want to check out a book from the library that gives other brief biographies of biblical personalities. Try not to focus on those areas we normally associate with biblical exegesis, for example, historical background, culture, genealogy, or famous deeds. Instead, concentrate on how events and surroundings affected the person's spiritual formation. To help you do this, ask questions. For example: How did David's adulterous affair with Bathsheba affect his spiritual life? What did he have to do before he could be back in right relationship with God? What were the long-lasting effects of his affair on his family? How did his adultery affect his long-term relationship with God? What lessons can I learn from the story of David? How do I apply these lessons to my spiritual life? What exercises can I do to help train me so that I will not succumb to sexual or other temptations when they come my way? Then do the exercises.

WHAT IS Renovaré?

Renovaré (from the Latin, meaning "to renew") is an infrachurch movement committed to the renewal of the Church of Jesus Christ in all its multifaceted expressions. Founded by best-selling author Richard J. Foster, Renovaré is Christian in commitment, international in scope, and ecumenical in breadth.

In the *Renovaré Spiritual Formation Bible* we observe how God spiritually formed his people through historical events and the practice of Spiritual Disciplines, that is, The With-God Life. Renovaré continues this emphasis on spiritual formation by placing it within the context of the two-thousand-year history of the Church and six great Christian traditions we find in its life—Contemplative: The Prayer-Filled Life; Holiness: The Virtuous Life; Charismatic: The Spirit-Empowered Life; Social Justice: The Compassionate Life; Evangelical: The Word-Centered Life; and Incarnational: The Sacramental Life. This balanced vision of Christian faith and witness was modeled for us by Jesus Christ and was evident in the lives of countless saints: Antony, Francis of Assisi, Susanna Wesley, Phoebe Palmer, and others. The With-God Life of the People of God continues on today as Christians participate in the life and practices of local churches and look forward to spending eternity in that "all-inclusive community of loving persons with God himself at the very center as its prime Sustainer and most glorious Inhabitant."

In addition to offering a balanced vision of the spiritual life, Renovaré promotes a practical strategy for people seeking renewal by helping facilitate small spiritual formation groups; national, regional, and local conferences; one-day seminars; personal and group retreats; and readings from devotional classics that can sustain a long-term commitment to renewal. Renovaré Resources for Spiritual Renewal, books published by HarperSanFrancisco, seek to integrate historical, scholarly, and inspirational materials into practical, readable formats. These resources can be used in a variety of settings, including small groups, private and organizational retreats, individual devotions, and church-school classes. Written and edited by people committed to the renewal of the Church, all of the materials present a balanced vision of Christian life and faith coupled with a practical strategy for spiritual growth and enrichment.

For more information about Renovaré and its mission, please log on to its Web site (www.renovare.org) or write Renovaré, 8 Inverness Drive East, Suite 102, Englewood, CO 80112-5624, USA.

MAPS

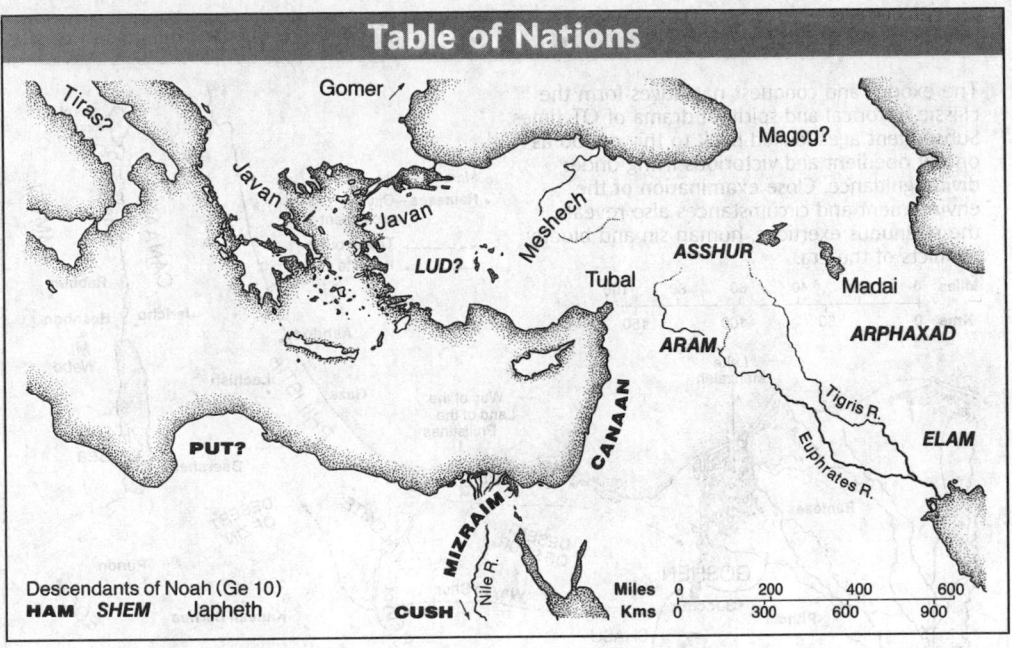

Table of Nations

Tiras?

Gomer

Magog?

Javan

Javan

Meshech

Tubal

ASSHUR

Madai

LUD?

ARAM

ARPHAXAD

CANAAN

Tigris R.

Euphrates R.

ELAM

PUT?

MIZRAIM

Nile R.

Descendants of Noah (Ge 10)
HAM *SHEM* Japheth

CUSH

Miles	0		200		400		600
Kms	0	300		600		900	

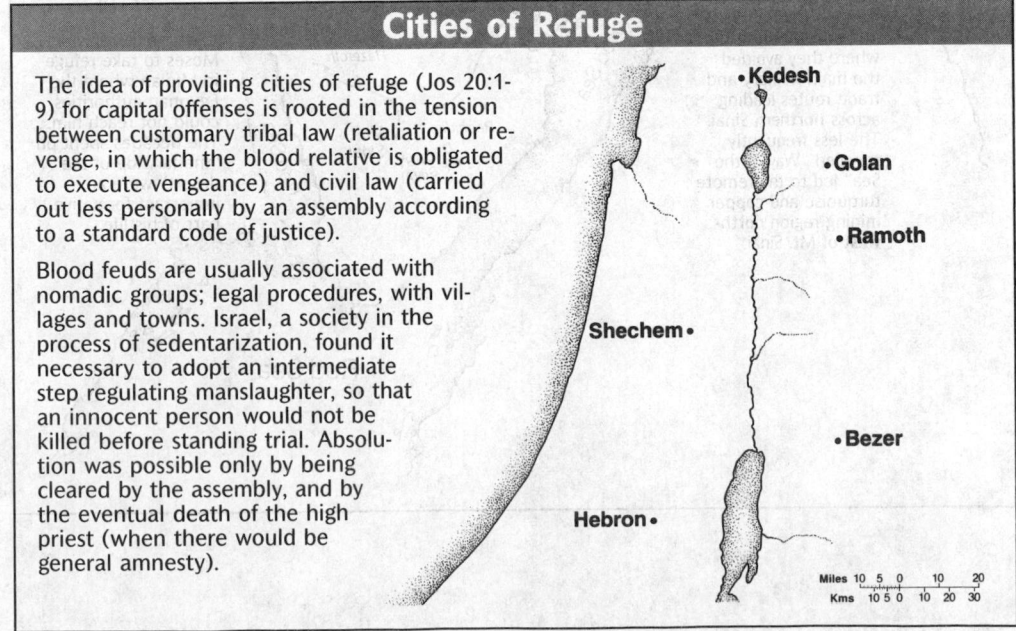

Cities of Refuge

The idea of providing cities of refuge (Jos 20:1-9) for capital offenses is rooted in the tension between customary tribal law (retaliation or revenge, in which the blood relative is obligated to execute vengeance) and civil law (carried out less personally by an assembly according to a standard code of justice).

Blood feuds are usually associated with nomadic groups; legal procedures, with villages and towns. Israel, a society in the process of sedentarization, found it necessary to adopt an intermediate step regulating manslaughter, so that an innocent person would not be killed before standing trial. Absolution was possible only by being cleared by the assembly, and by the eventual death of the high priest (when there would be general amnesty).

• Kedesh

• Golan

• Ramoth

Shechem •

• Bezer

Hebron •

Miles	10	5	0	10	20
Kms	10	5	0	10	20	30

The Exodus

The exodus and conquest narratives form the classic historical and spiritual drama of OT times. Subsequent ages looked back to this period as one of obedient and victorious living under divine guidance. Close examination of the environment and circumstances also reveals the strenuous exertions, human sin and bloody conflicts of the era.

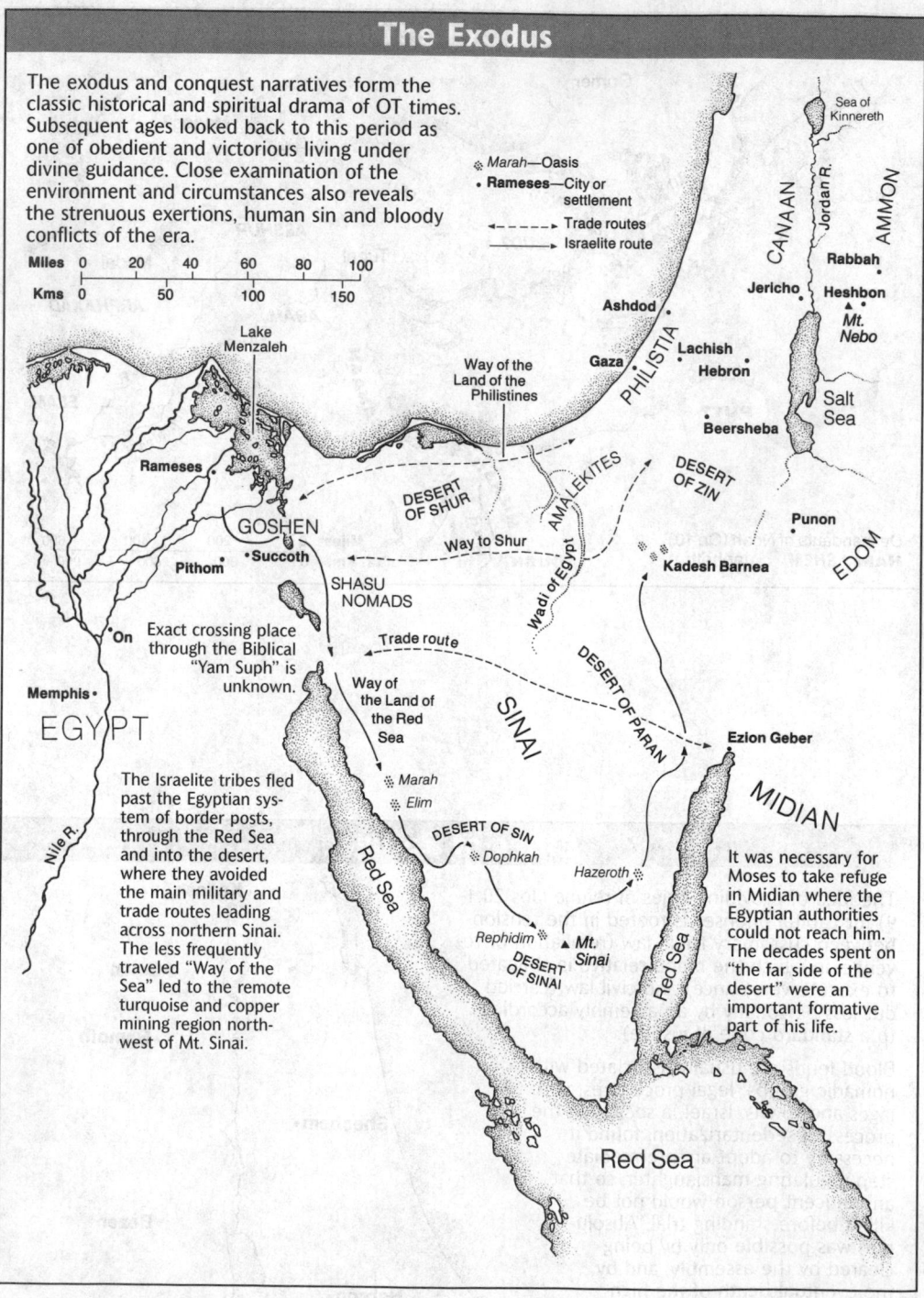

✼ Marah—Oasis
● Rameses—City or settlement
◂- - - - Trade routes
◂- - - - Israelite route

Miles 0   20   40   60   80   100
Kms   0   50   100   150

Lake Menzaleh

Rameses

GOSHEN

● Succoth

Pithom

SHASU NOMADS

● On

Memphis ●

EGYPT

Nile R.

Exact crossing place through the Biblical "Yam Suph" is unknown.

The Israelite tribes fled past the Egyptian system of border posts, through the Red Sea and into the desert, where they avoided the main military and trade routes leading across northern Sinai. The less frequently traveled "Way of the Sea" led to the remote turquoise and copper mining region northwest of Mt. Sinai.

Way of the Land of the Philistines

DESERT OF SHUR

Way to Shur

Trade route

Way of the Land of the Red Sea

✼ Marah
✼ Elim

DESERT OF SIN

✼ Dophkah

Rephidim ✼

▲ Mt. Sinai

DESERT OF SINAI

Hazeroth ✼

Red Sea

SINAI

Wadi of Egypt

AMALEKITES

DESERT OF PARAN

DESERT OF ZIN

✼ ✼
Kadesh Barnea

Punon

EDOM

Ezion Geber

MIDIAN

Red Sea

Red Sea

It was necessary for Moses to take refuge in Midian where the Egyptian authorities could not reach him. The decades spent on "the far side of the desert" were an important formative part of his life.

Ashdod

Gaza

Lachish

Hebron

Beersheba

PHILISTIA

CANAAN

Jordan R.

Sea of Kinnereth

AMMON

Rabbah

Jericho

Heshbon

▲ Mt. Nebo

Salt Sea

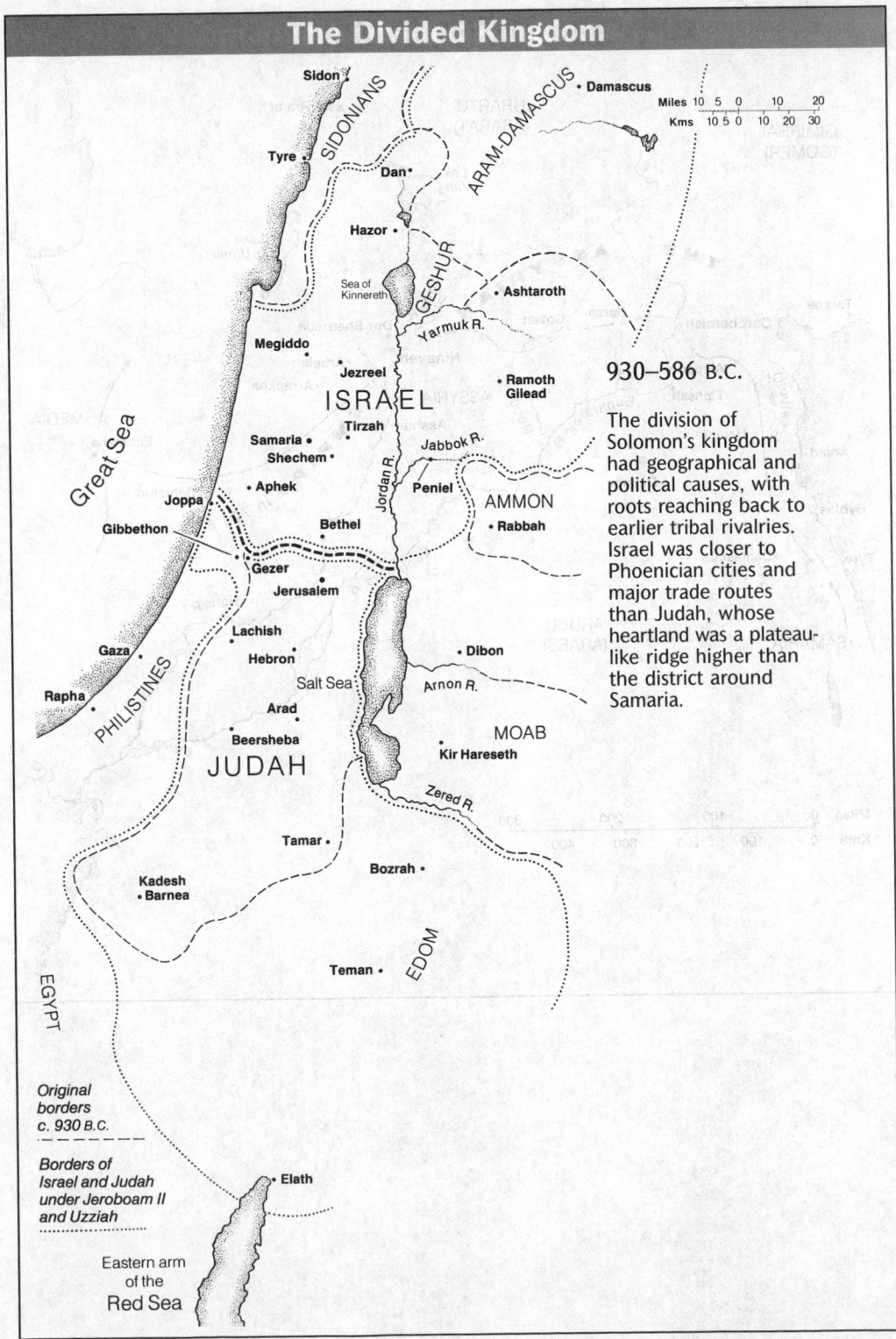

The Divided Kingdom

Sidon

SIDONIANS

Damascus •

ARAM-DAMASCUS

Miles 10 5 0   10   20
Kms 10 5 0 10 20 30

Tyre •

Dan •

GESHUR

Hazor •

Sea of
Kinnereth

• Ashtaroth

Yarmuk R.

Megiddo •

Jezreel •

ISRAEL

• Ramoth
  Gilead

930–586 B.C.

Tirzah •

Samaria •
Shechem •

Jabbok R.

• Aphek

Peniel •

Great Sea

Joppa •

Gibbethon •

Bethel •

Jordan R.

AMMON

• Rabbah

The division of
Solomon's kingdom
had geographical and
political causes, with
roots reaching back to
earlier tribal rivalries.
Israel was closer to
Phoenician cities and
major trade routes
than Judah, whose
heartland was a plateau-
like ridge higher than
the district around
Samaria.

• Gezer

Jerusalem •

Lachish •

Gaza •

Hebron •

• Dibon

Salt Sea

Arnon R.

Rapha •

PHILISTINES

Arad •

Beersheba •

JUDAH

Kir Hareseth •

MOAB

Zered R.

Tamar •

Bozrah •

Kadesh
• Barnea

EGYPT

Teman •

EDOM

*Original
borders
c. 930 B.C.*

*Borders of
Israel and Judah
under Jeroboam II
and Uzziah*

• Elath

Eastern arm
of the
Red Sea

Exile of the Northern Kingdom

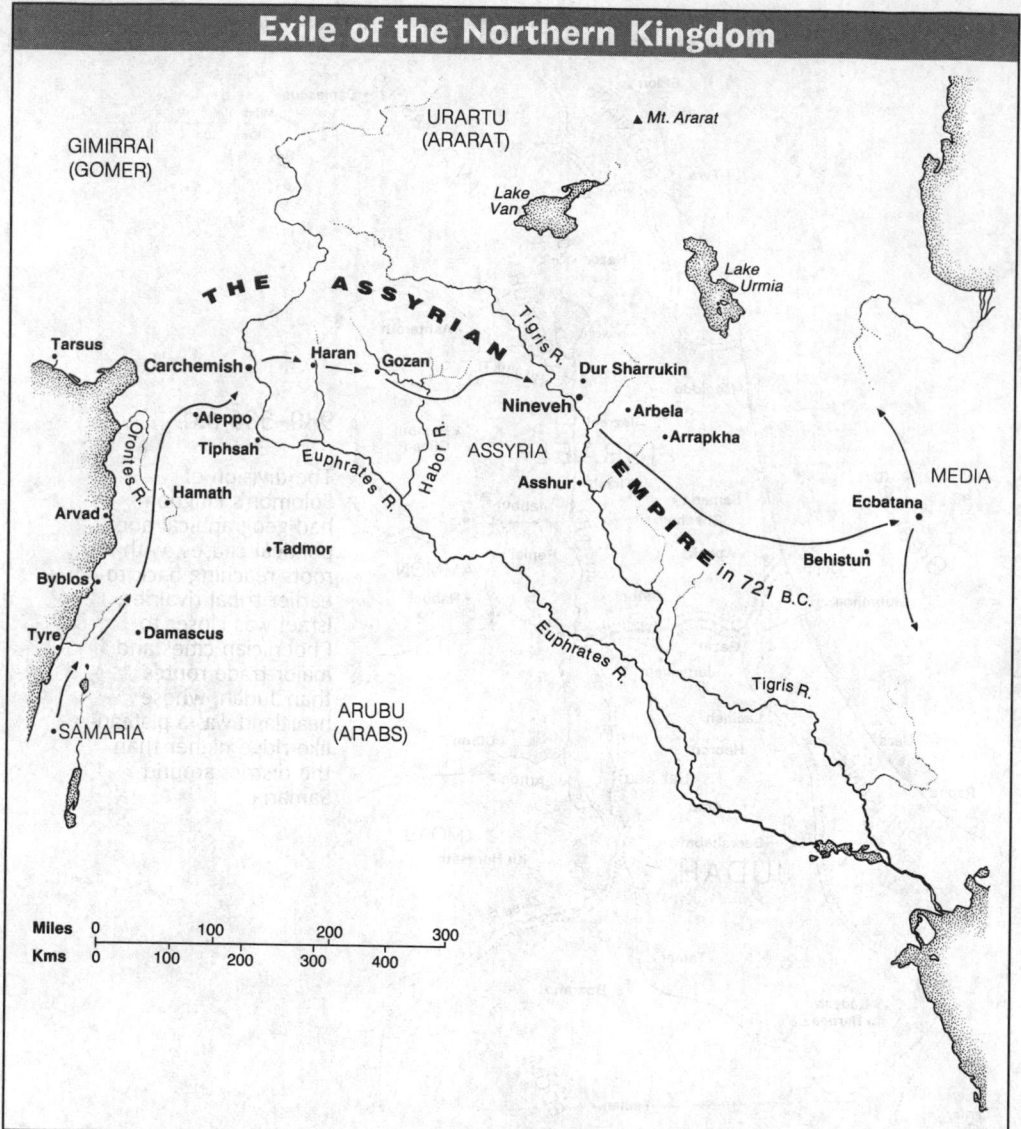

GIMIRRAI
(GOMER)

URARTU
(ARARAT)

▲ Mt. Ararat

Lake
Van

Lake
Urmia

THE   ASSYRIAN

Tarsus

Carchemish   Haran   Gozan   Dur Sharrukin

Tigris R.

Aleppo   Nineveh   Arbela

Tiphsah   Euphrates R.   Arrapkha

ASSYRIA

Hamath   Habor R.   Asshur   EMPIRE in 721 B.C.   MEDIA

Arvad   Orontes R.   Ecbatana

Tadmor   Behistun

Byblos   Euphrates R.

Tyre   Damascus

ARUBU
(ARABS)   Tigris R.

SAMARIA

Miles   0   100   200   300
Kms   0   100   200   300   400

Exile of the Southern Kingdom

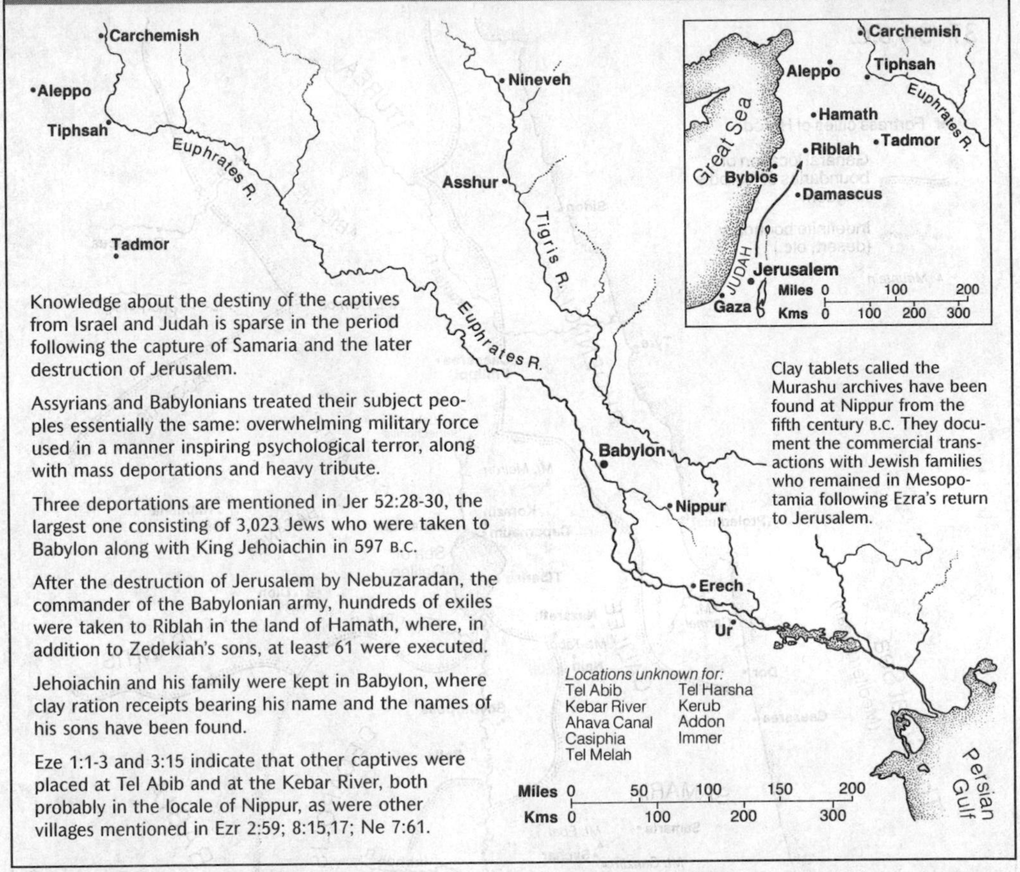

•Carchemish

•Aleppo

Tiphsah

Tadmor

•Nineveh

Asshur•

Euphrates R.

Tigris R.

Euphrates R.

Babylon
•

•Nippur

•Erech

Ur•

Inset map:
•Carchemish
Aleppo
Tiphsah
Euphrates R.
•Hamath
•Riblah
•Tadmor
Byblos•
•Damascus
Great Sea
JUDAH
Jerusalem
Gaza•
Miles 0   100   200
Kms 0 100 200 300

Knowledge about the destiny of the captives from Israel and Judah is sparse in the period following the capture of Samaria and the later destruction of Jerusalem.

Assyrians and Babylonians treated their subject peoples essentially the same: overwhelming military force used in a manner inspiring psychological terror, along with mass deportations and heavy tribute.

Three deportations are mentioned in Jer 52:28-30, the largest one consisting of 3,023 Jews who were taken to Babylon along with King Jehoiachin in 597 B.C.

After the destruction of Jerusalem by Nebuzaradan, the commander of the Babylonian army, hundreds of exiles were taken to Riblah in the land of Hamath, where, in addition to Zedekiah's sons, at least 61 were executed.

Jehoiachin and his family were kept in Babylon, where clay ration receipts bearing his name and the names of his sons have been found.

Eze 1:1-3 and 3:15 indicate that other captives were placed at Tel Abib and at the Kebar River, both probably in the locale of Nippur, as were other villages mentioned in Ezr 2:59; 8:15,17; Ne 7:61.

Clay tablets called the Murashu archives have been found at Nippur from the fifth century B.C. They document the commercial transactions with Jewish families who remained in Mesopotamia following Ezra's return to Jerusalem.

Locations unknown for:
Tel Abib   Tel Harsha
Kebar River   Kerub
Ahava Canal   Addon
Casiphia   Immer
Tel Melah

Miles 0   50   100   150   200
Kms 0   100   200   300

Persian Gulf

Return from Exile

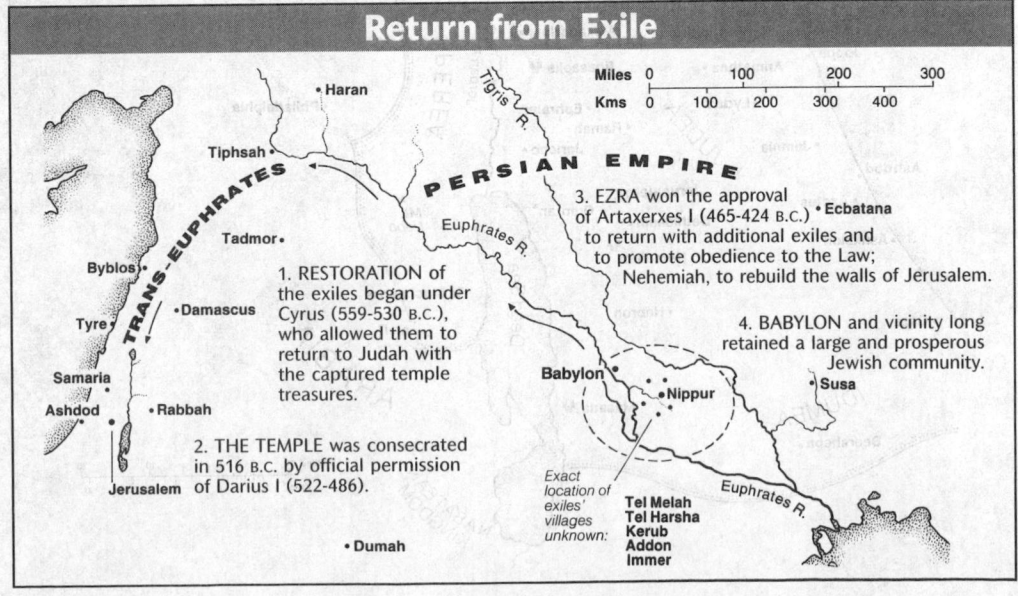

•Haran

Tiphsah•

Tigris R.

Miles 0   100   200   300
Kms 0   100   200   300   400

P E R S I A N   E M P I R E

Euphrates R.

Tadmor•

Byblos•

Tyre•

•Damascus

Samaria•

Ashdod•

•Rabbah

Jerusalem•

3. EZRA won the approval of Artaxerxes I (465-424 B.C.), to return with additional exiles and to promote obedience to the Law; Nehemiah, to rebuild the walls of Jerusalem.

•Ecbatana

1. RESTORATION of the exiles began under Cyrus (559-530 B.C.), who allowed them to return to Judah with the captured temple treasures.

4. BABYLON and vicinity long retained a large and prosperous Jewish community.

Babylon•

•Nippur

•Susa

2. THE TEMPLE was consecrated in 516 B.C. by official permission of Darius I (522-486).

Exact location of exiles' villages unknown:

Tel Melah
Tel Harsha
Kerub
Addon
Immer

Euphrates R.

•Dumah

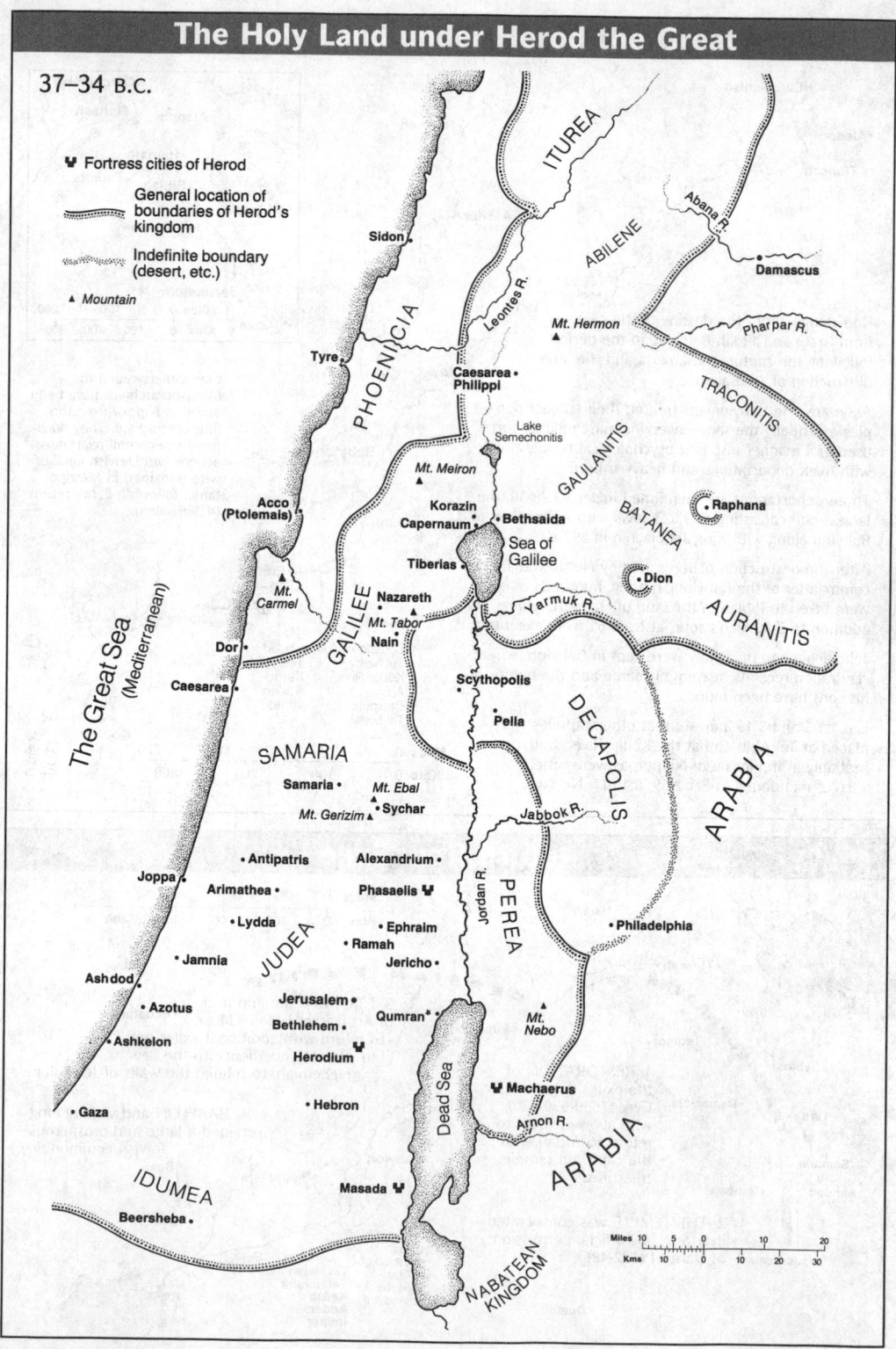

The Holy Land under Herod the Great

37–34 B.C.

♆ Fortress cities of Herod

〰 General location of boundaries of Herod's kingdom

〰 Indefinite boundary (desert, etc.)

▲ Mountain

ITUREA

ABILENE

Abana R.

Damascus

Sidon

PHOENICIA

Leontes R.

Mt. Hermon ▲

Pharpar R.

TRACONITIS

Tyre

Caesarea Philippi

Lake Semechonitis

GAULANITIS

BATANEA

Raphana

Acco (Ptolemais)

Mt. Meiron ▲

Korazin

Capernaum

Bethsaida

Sea of Galilee

Tiberias

Dion

Mt. Carmel ▲

GALILEE

Nazareth

Mt. Tabor ▲

Nain

Yarmuk R.

AURANITIS

Dor

Caesarea

The Great Sea (Mediterranean)

Scythopolis

Pella

DECAPOLIS

ARABIA

SAMARIA

Samaria

Mt. Ebal ▲

Mt. Gerizim ▲ Sychar

Jabbok R.

Antipatris

Alexandrium

Joppa

Arimathea

Phasaelis ♆

Jordan R.

PEREA

Philadelphia

Lydda

Ephraim

JUDEA

Ramah

Jamnia

Jericho

Ashdod

Jerusalem

Azotus

Bethlehem

Qumran*

Mt. Nebo ▲

Ashkelon

Herodium

Dead Sea

Machaerus ♆

Hebron

Arnon R.

Gaza

ARABIA

IDUMEA

Masada ♆

Beersheba

Miles 10 5 0   10   20

Kms   10   0   10   20   30

NABATEAN KINGDOM

Jesus in Judea and Samaria

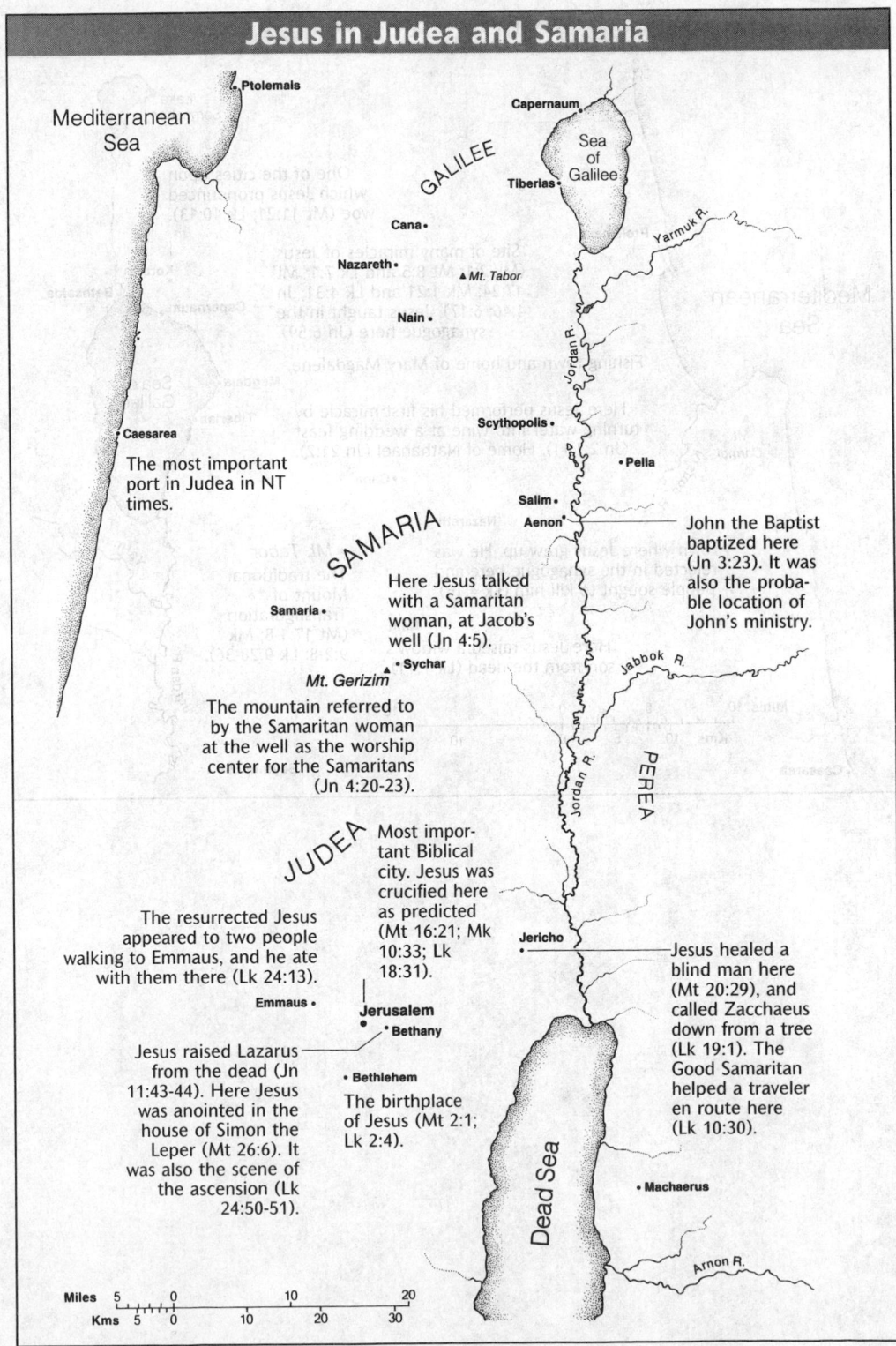

Mediterranean
Sea

Ptolemais

GALILEE

Capernaum

Sea
of
Galilee

Tiberias

Cana

Nazareth

▲ Mt. Tabor

Nain

Jordan R.

Yarmuk R.

Caesarea

The most important port in Judea in NT times.

Scythopolis

Pella

Salim

Aenon

John the Baptist baptized here (Jn 3:23). It was also the proba- ble location of John's ministry.

SAMARIA

Here Jesus talked with a Samaritan woman, at Jacob's well (Jn 4:5).

Samaria

Sychar

Jabbok R.

Mt. Gerizim

The mountain referred to by the Samaritan woman at the well as the worship center for the Samaritans (Jn 4:20-23).

Jordan R.

PEREA

JUDEA

Most impor- tant Biblical city. Jesus was crucified here as predicted (Mt 16:21; Mk 10:33; Lk 18:31).

Jericho

Jesus healed a blind man here (Mt 20:29), and called Zacchaeus down from a tree (Lk 19:1). The Good Samaritan helped a traveler en route here (Lk 10:30).

The resurrected Jesus appeared to two people walking to Emmaus, and he ate with them there (Lk 24:13).

Emmaus

Jerusalem

Bethany

Jesus raised Lazarus from the dead (Jn 11:43-44). Here Jesus was anointed in the house of Simon the Leper (Mt 26:6). It was also the scene of the ascension (Lk 24:50-51).

Bethlehem

The birthplace of Jesus (Mt 2:1; Lk 2:4).

Dead Sea

Machaerus

Arnon R.

Miles 5   0   10   20

Kms   5   0   10   20   30

Jesus in Galilee

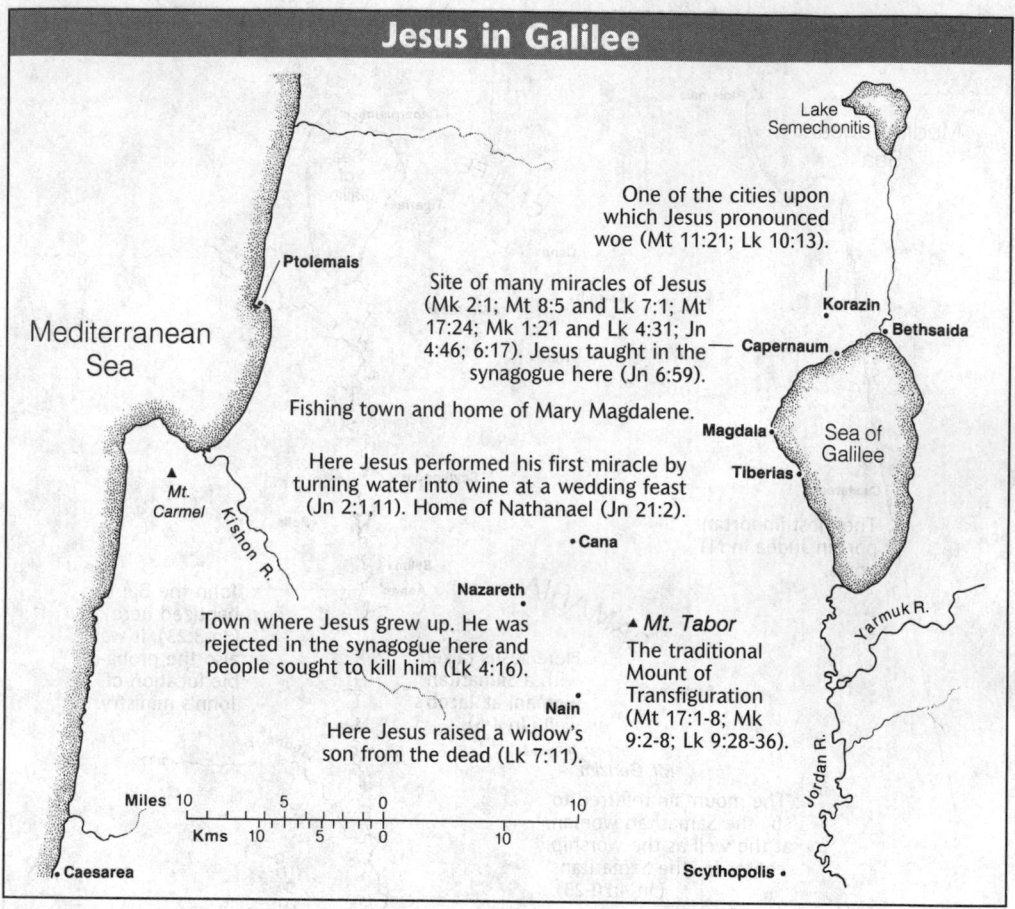

Mediterranean Sea

Lake Semechonitis

Ptolemais

One of the cities upon which Jesus pronounced woe (Mt 11:21; Lk 10:13).

Korazin

Bethsaida

Site of many miracles of Jesus (Mk 2:1; Mt 8:5 and Lk 7:1; Mt 17:24; Mk 1:21 and Lk 4:31; Jn 4:46; 6:17). Jesus taught in the synagogue here (Jn 6:59).

Capernaum

Fishing town and home of Mary Magdalene.

Magdala

Sea of Galilee

Here Jesus performed his first miracle by turning water into wine at a wedding feast (Jn 2:1,11). Home of Nathanael (Jn 21:2).

Tiberias

• Cana

Mt. Carmel

Kishon R.

Nazareth

▲ Mt. Tabor

Town where Jesus grew up. He was rejected in the synagogue here and people sought to kill him (Lk 4:16).

The traditional Mount of Transfiguration (Mt 17:1-8; Mk 9:2-8; Lk 9:28-36).

Yarmuk R.

Nain

Here Jesus raised a widow's son from the dead (Lk 7:11).

Jordan R.

Miles 10   5   0   10

Kms 10   5   0   10

Caesarea

Scythopolis •

Countries of People Mentioned at Pentecost

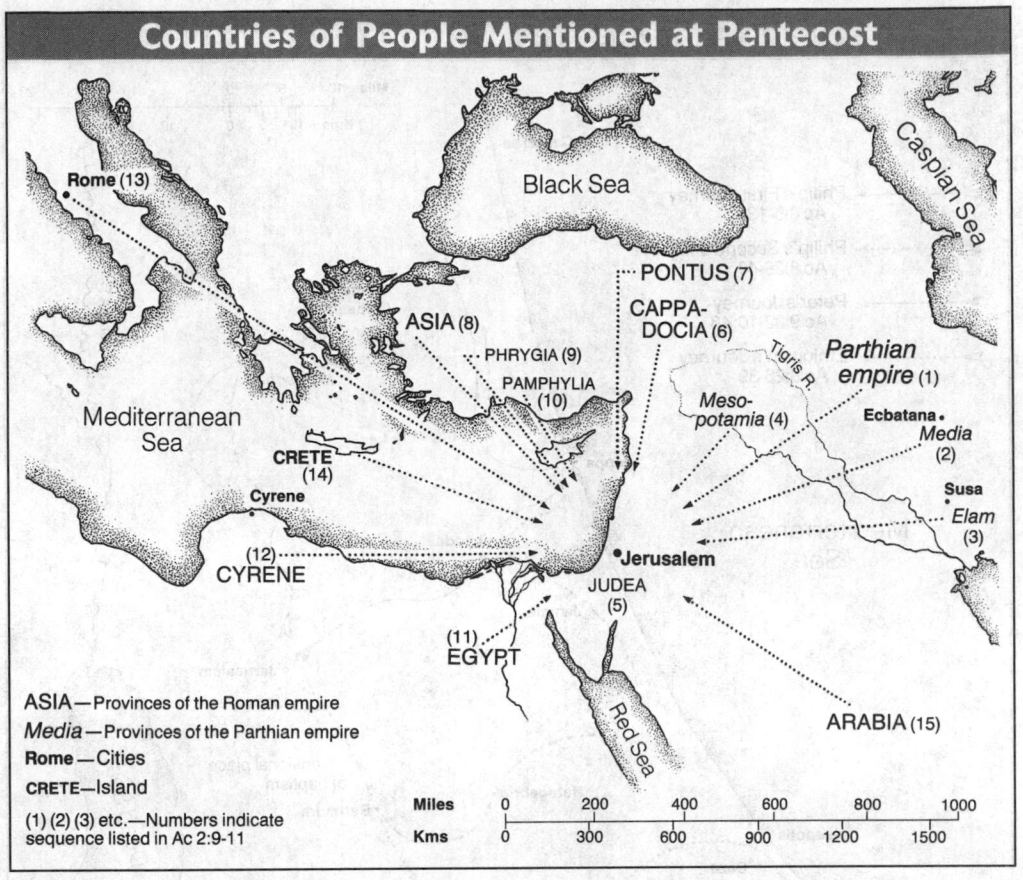

Rome (13)

Black Sea

Caspian Sea

PONTUS (7)

ASIA (8)

CAPPA-
DOCIA (6)

Parthian
empire (1)

PHRYGIA (9)

Tigris R.

PAMPHYLIA
(10)

Meso-
potamia (4)

Ecbatana •
Media
(2)

Mediterranean
Sea

CRETE
(14)

Cyrene

Susa •
Elam
(3)

(12)
CYRENE

• Jerusalem

JUDEA
(5)

(11)
EGYPT

Red Sea

ARABIA (15)

ASIA—Provinces of the Roman empire
Media—Provinces of the Parthian empire
Rome—Cities
CRETE—Island

(1) (2) (3) etc.—Numbers indicate
sequence listed in Ac 2:9-11

	Miles	0	200	400	600	800	1000
	Kms	0	300	600	900	1200	1500

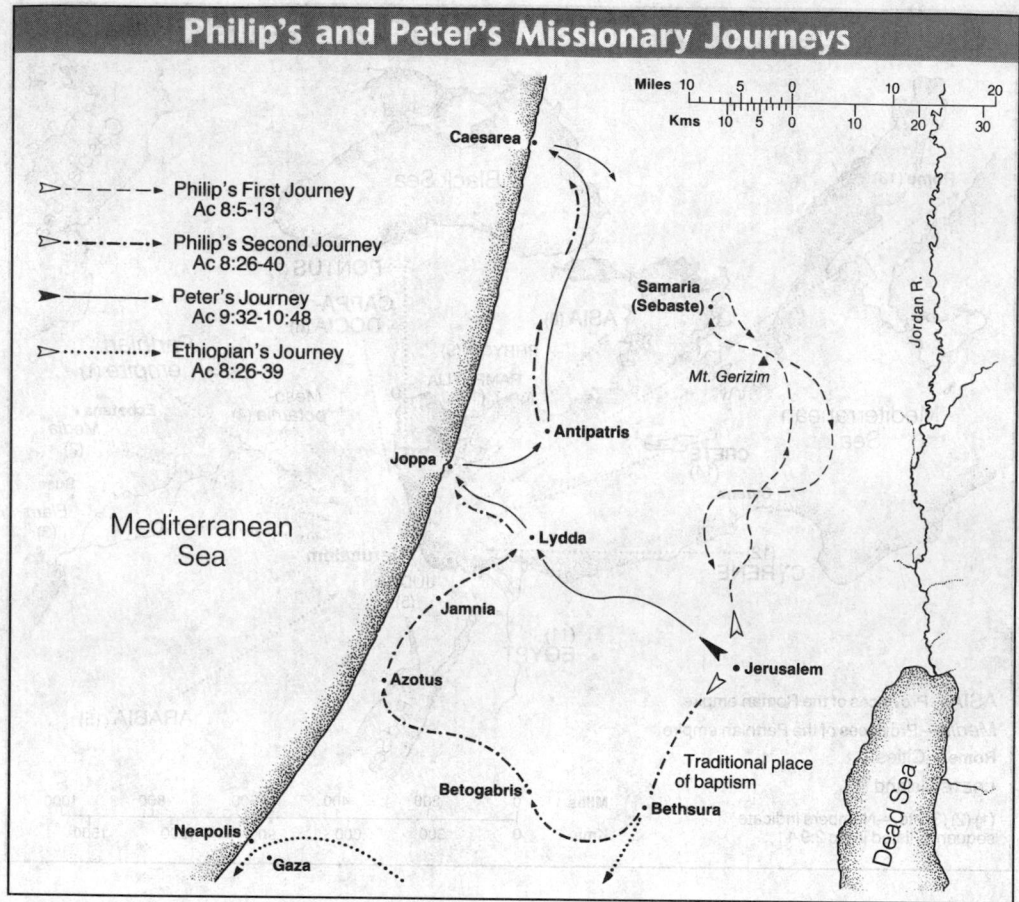

Philip's and Peter's Missionary Journeys

Miles 10   5   0   10   20
Kms   10 5 0   10   20   30

▷ – – – ► Philip's First Journey
           Ac 8:5-13

▷ –·–·–► Philip's Second Journey
           Ac 8:26-40

►——————► Peter's Journey
           Ac 9:32-10:48

▷ ········► Ethiopian's Journey
           Ac 8:26-39

Caesarea

Samaria
(Sebaste)

Mt. Gerizim

Jordan R.

Antipatris

Joppa

Mediterranean
Sea

Lydda

Jamnia

Azotus

• Jerusalem

Traditional place
of baptism

Betogabris

Bethsura

Dead Sea

Neapolis

Gaza

The Spread of the Gospel

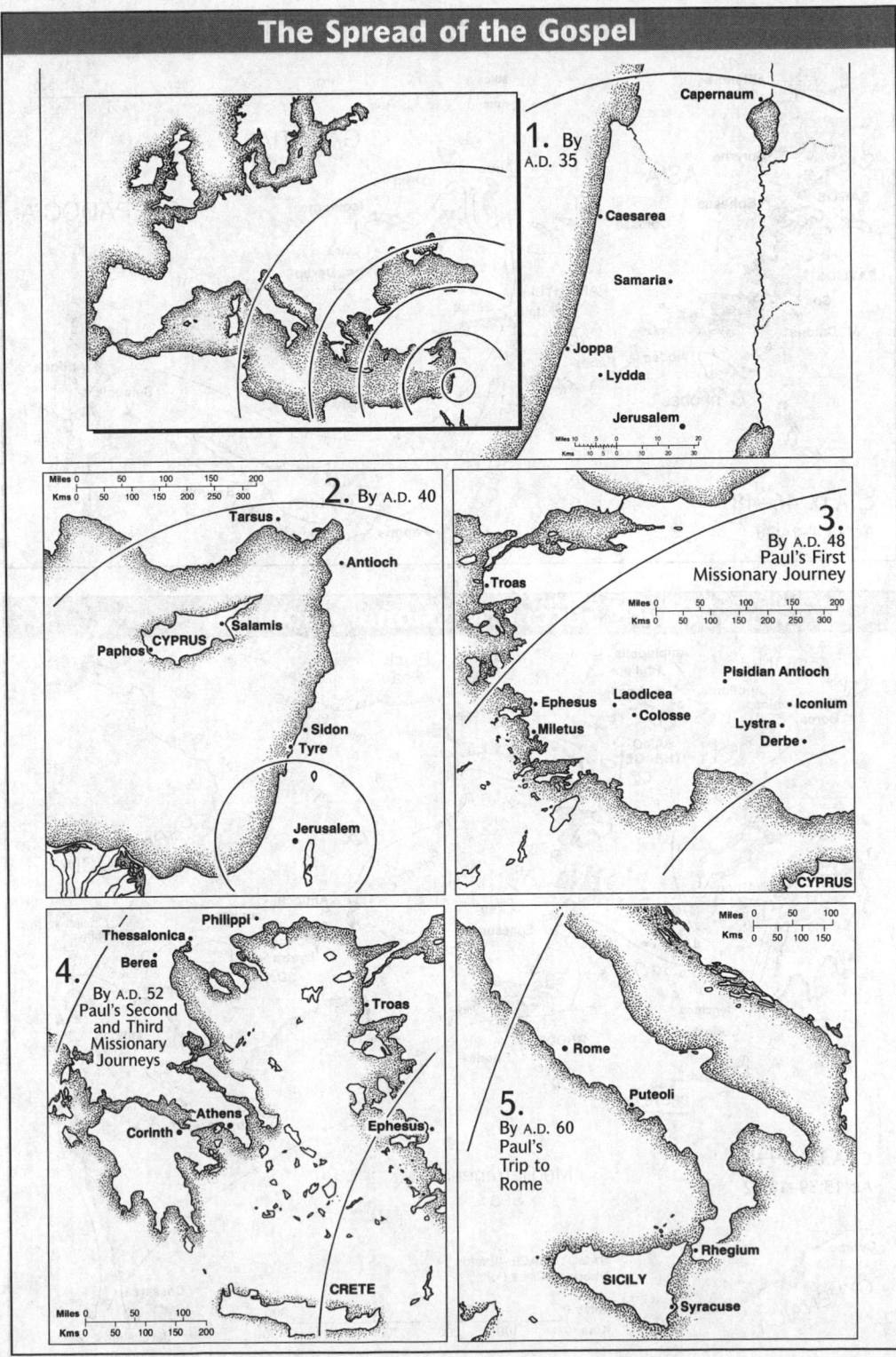

1. By A.D. 35

Capernaum

Caesarea

Samaria

Joppa

Lydda

Jerusalem

2. By A.D. 40

Tarsus

Antioch

CYPRUS

Salamis

Paphos

Sidon

Tyre

Jerusalem

3.
By A.D. 48
Paul's First
Missionary Journey

Troas

Pisidian Antioch

Ephesus

Laodicea

Colosse

Iconium

Miletus

Lystra

Derbe

CYPRUS

4.
By A.D. 52
Paul's Second
and Third
Missionary
Journeys

Philippi

Thessalonica

Berea

Troas

Athens

Corinth

Ephesus

CRETE

5.
By A.D. 60
Paul's
Trip to
Rome

Rome

Puteoli

Rhegium

SICILY

Syracuse

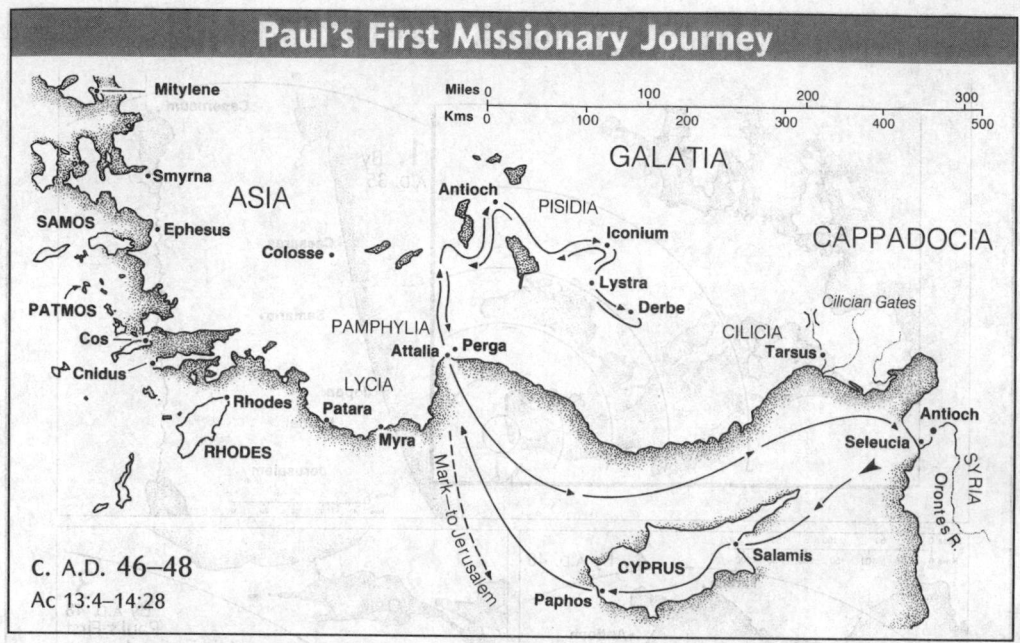

Paul's First Missionary Journey

Mitylene
Smyrna
ASIA
SAMOS
Ephesus
Colosse
PATMOS
Cos
Cnidus
Rhodes
Patara
RHODES
Myra

Miles 0   100   200   300
Kms 0   100   200   300   400   500

GALATIA
Antioch
PISIDIA
Iconium
Lystra
Derbe
CAPPADOCIA
Cilician Gates
CILICIA
Tarsus
Antioch
Seleucia
SYRIA
Orontes R.
PAMPHYLIA
Attalia Perga
LYCIA
Mark—to Jerusalem
CYPRUS
Salamis
Paphos

C. A.D. 46–48
Ac 13:4–14:28

Paul's Second Missionary Journey

MACEDONIA
Amphipolis
Philippi
Apollonia
Neapolis
Thessalonica
Berea
SAMO-
THRACE
Troas
MYSIA
Black
Sea
BITHYNIA & PONTUS
Halys R.
GALATIA
CAPPADOCIA
PHRYGIA
ACHAIA
Athens
ASIA
Antioch
Iconium
Cilician
Gates
Ephesus
Lystra
Derbe
Tarsus
Paul and Silas
Cenchrea
Corinth
RHODES
Rhodes
Antioch
CRETE
Barnabas
and Mark
CYPRUS

C. A.D. 49–52
Ac 15:39–18:22

Cyrene
CYRENAICA

Mediterranean
Sea

SAMOTHRACE—Islands
Rhodes—Cities, Ports

Miles 0   100   200   300
Kms 0   100   200   300   400   500

Caesarea
Jerusalem

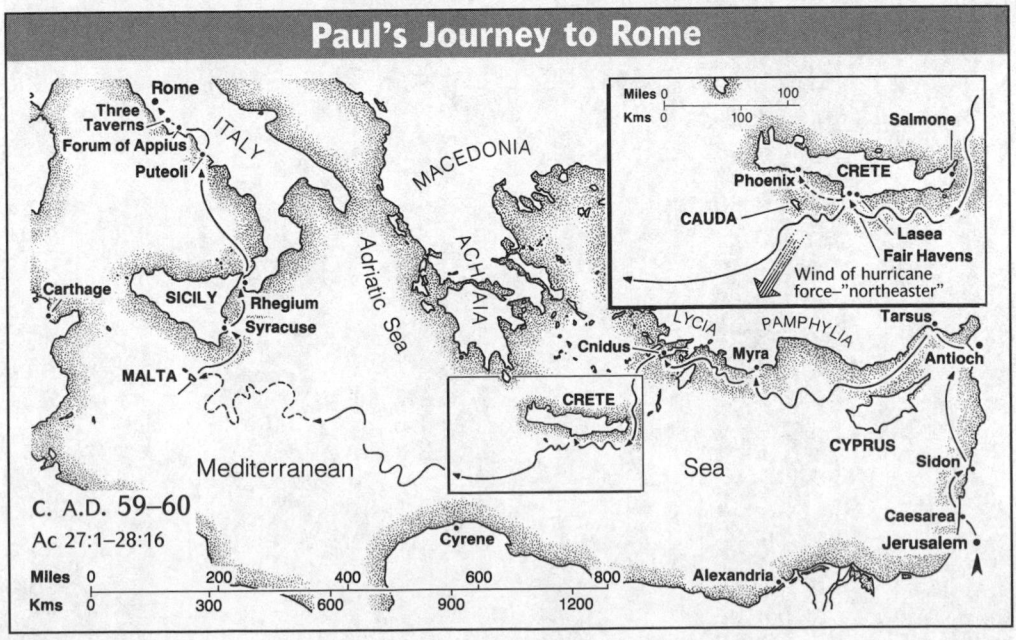

Paul's Third Missionary Journey

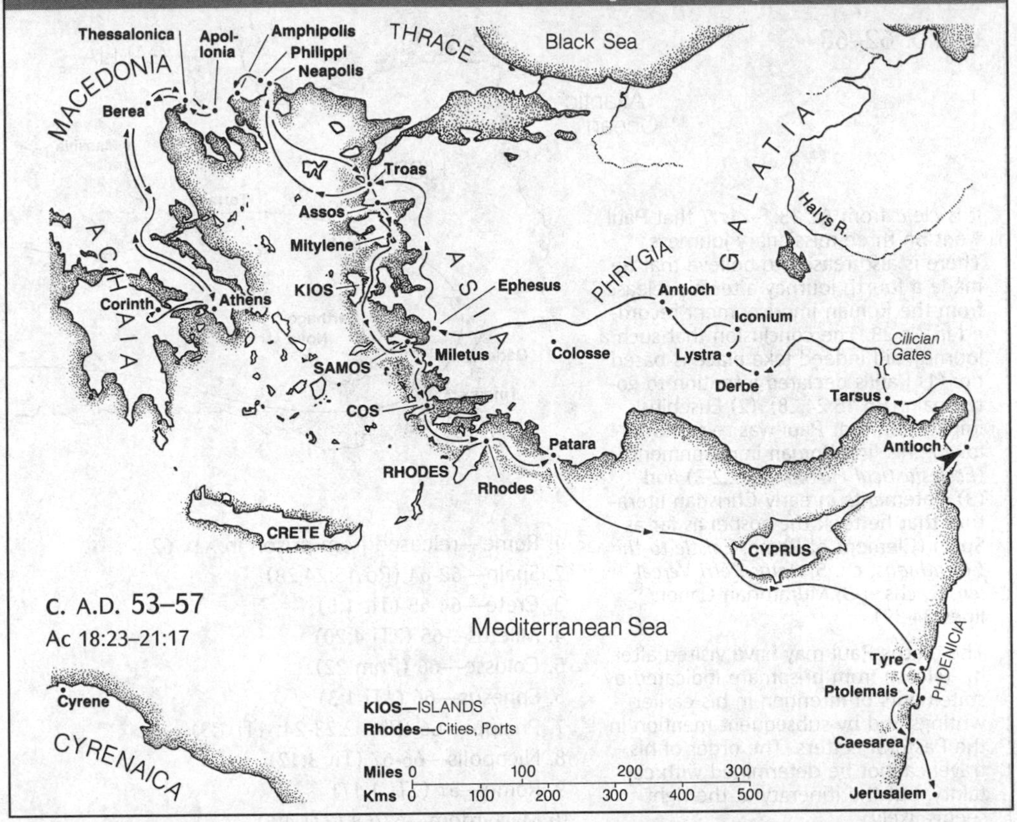

THRACE — Black Sea

Thessalonica — Apollonia — Amphipolis — Philippi — Neapolis

MACEDONIA

Berea

Troas

Assos

Mitylene

KIOS

Corinth — Athens

ACHAIA

Ephesus

ASIA

PHRYGIA — GALATIA

Halys R.

Antioch — Iconium — Lystra — Derbe — Tarsus

Cilician Gates

Antioch

Miletus — Colosse

SAMOS

COS

Patara

RHODES

Rhodes

CRETE

CYPRUS

C. A.D. 53–57

Ac 18:23–21:17

Mediterranean Sea

Tyre

Ptolemais

PHOENICIA

Caesarea

Jerusalem

Cyrene

CYRENAICA

KIOS—ISLANDS
Rhodes—Cities, Ports

Miles 0 — 100 — 200 — 300
Kms 0 — 100 — 200 — 300 — 400 — 500

Paul's Journey to Rome

Rome

Three Taverns

Forum of Appius

Puteoli

ITALY

MACEDONIA

Miles 0 — 100
Kms 0 — 100

Salmone

CRETE

Phoenix

CAUDA

Lasea

Fair Havens

Wind of hurricane force—"northeaster"

Carthage

SICILY

Rheghium

Syracuse

MALTA

Adriatic Sea

ACHAIA

Cnidus

LYCIA — PAMPHYLIA

Myra

CRETE

Tarsus

Antioch

CYPRUS

Sidon

Mediterranean

Sea

C. A.D. 59–60

Ac 27:1–28:16

Cyrene

Alexandria

Caesarea

Jerusalem

Miles 0 — 200 — 400 — 600 — 800
Kms 0 — 300 — 600 — 900 — 1200

Paul's Fourth Missionary Journey

C. A.D. 62–68

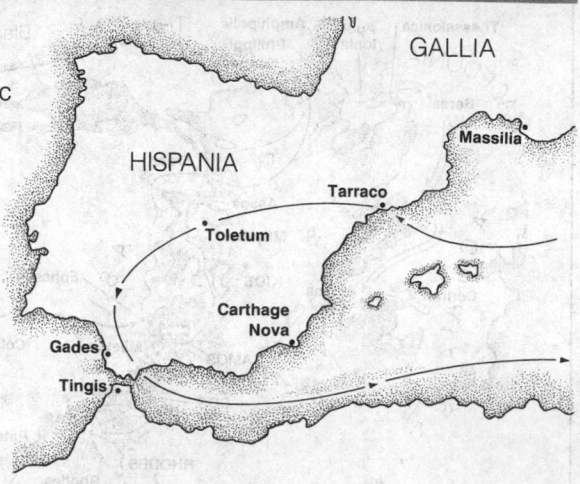

It is clear from Ac 13:1–21:17 that Paul went on three missionary journeys. There is also reason to believe that he made a fourth journey after his release from the Roman imprisonment recorded in Ac 28. The conclusion that such a journey did indeed take place is based on: (1) Paul's declared intention to go to Spain (Ro 15:24,28), (2) Eusebius's implication that Paul was released following his first Roman imprisonment (*Ecclesiastical History*, 2.22.2-3) and (3) statements in early Christian literature that he took the gospel as far as Spain (Clement of Rome, *Epistle to the Corinthians*, ch. 5; *Actus Petri Vercellenses*, chs. 1-3; Muratorian Canon, lines 34-39).

The places Paul may have visited after his release from prison are indicated by statements of intention in his earlier writings and by subsequent mention in the Pastoral Letters. The order of his travel cannot be determined with certainty, but the itinerary at the right seems likely.

1. Rome—released from prison in A.D. 62
2. Spain—62-64 (Ro 15:24,28)
3. Crete—64-65 (Tit 1:5)
4. Miletus—65 (2Ti 4:20)
5. Colosse—66 (Phm 22)
6. Ephesus—66 (1Ti 1:3)
7. Philippi—66 (Php 2:23-24; 1Ti 1:3)
8. Nicopolis—66-67 (Tit 3:12)
9. Rome—67 (2Ti 1:17)
10. Martyrdom—67/68 (2Ti 4:6)

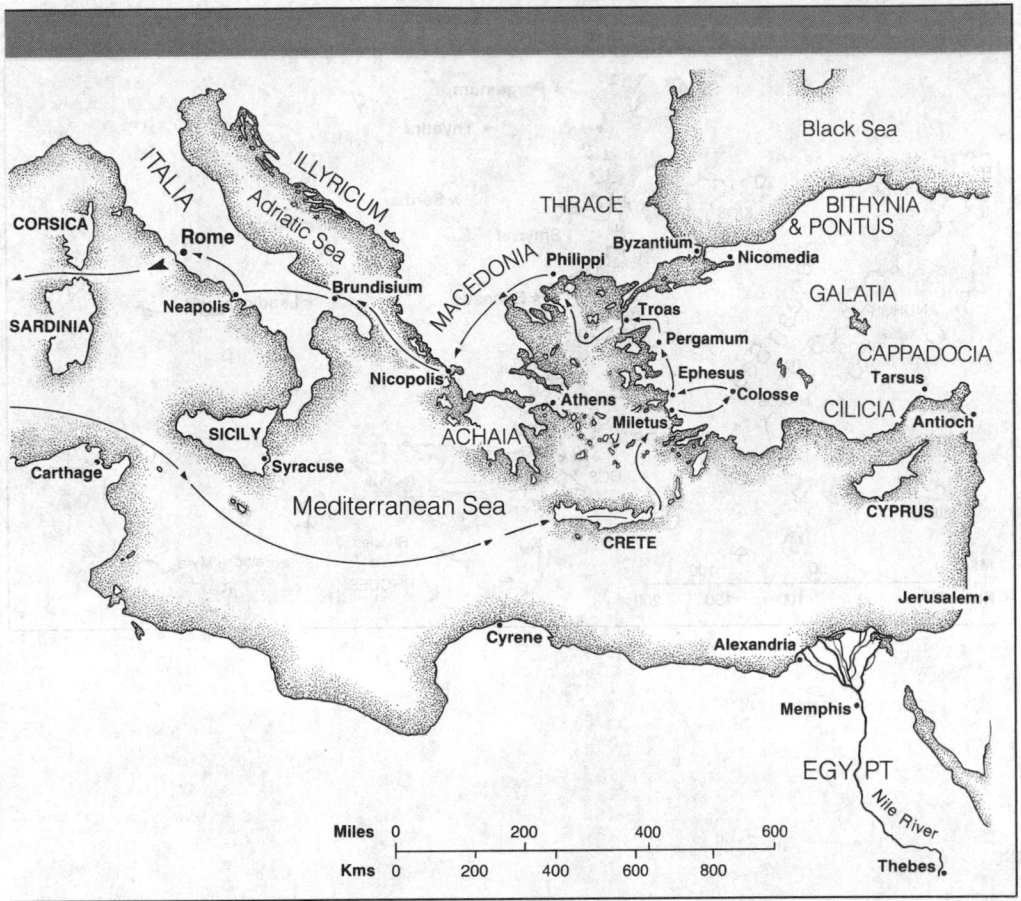

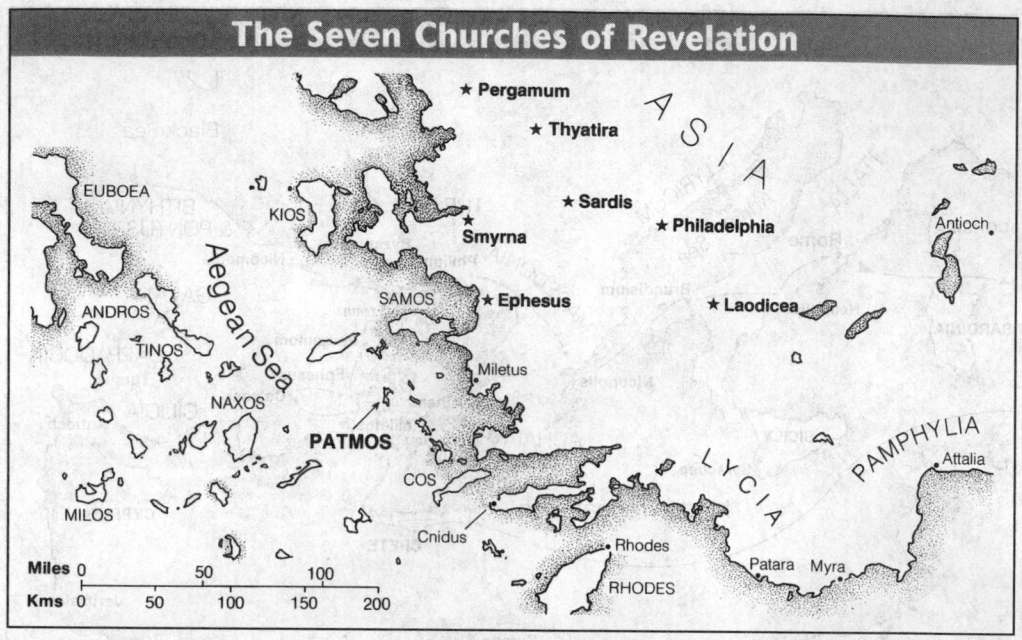

The Seven Churches of Revelation

★ Pergamum

★ Thyatira

ASIA

EUBOEA

KIOS

★ Sardis

★ Philadelphia

Antioch

Smyrna

Aegean Sea

SAMOS

★ Ephesus

★ Laodicea

ANDROS

TINOS

Miletus

NAXOS

PATMOS

LYCIA

PAMPHYLIA

Attalia

COS

MILOS

Cnidus

Rhodes

Patara   Myra

RHODES

Miles 0   50   100

Kms 0   50   100   150   200

BURNEY WINGS PSLM 114 CHAM (THE DIMM
(2785) (2799-2803)
270-271 2385-1
OWNERS) PLAY
BE BOLD SING
REMEMBER YOU WERE
SLAVES IN EGYPT!!
DEUT 15:15

WHAT IS OUR PARADIGM POVERTY (6 MODERN SAM
(IS LEVITS) PARADIGM) OF CLARK DINAH
ADDED RHYTHM CENTER — 273
SIMPLICITY + FRUGALITY

DEFINITION OF WISDOM 25I
ABILITY TO NAVIGATE LIFE WELL
KNOWLEDGE PLUS FAITH
RESPECT OF GOD & OTHERS-HELP
TO LIVE IN BOUNDARIES TO THE
RHYTHMS OF THE CREATION ORDER
TO KNOW LOVE / OBEY OBEY
GOD THROUGH JESUS X + TO
EXALT THEE THEER LORD

' FROM THE LORD? 264
MERCHANT